WHO'S WHO
IN AMERICAN POLITICS
FIFTH EDITION 1975-1976

WHO'S WHO IN AMERICAN POLITICS

FIFTH EDITION 1975-1976

Edited by JAQUES CATTELL PRESS

Consulting Editors

EDMUND L. HENSHAW, Jr.,
 Executive Director, Democratic Congressional Committee

PAUL A. THEIS,
 Former Public Relations Director, Republican Congressional Committee

R. R. Bowker Company
Xerox Education Company
New York and London

Published by R. R. Bowker Co. (A Xerox Education Company)
1180 Avenue of the Americas, New York, N.Y. 10036
Copyright © 1975 by Xerox Corporation

International Standard Book Number: 0-8352-0827-3
International Standard Serial Number: 000-0205
Library of Congress Catalog Card Number: 67-25024

All rights reserved. Reproduction of this work, in whole or
in part, without written permission of the
publisher is prohibited.

Printed and bound in the United States of America

NOTICE: This book has no connection with *Who's Who in America*
or its publisher, Marquis-Who's Who, Inc.

Contents

Foreword	vii
Preface	ix
The President and Members of His Cabinet	x
State Delegations to the 94th Congress	xi
Governors of the States	xviii
State Chairmen	xx
List of Abbreviations	xxii
Biographies	1
Geographic Index	1029

Foreword

Since the fourth edition of *Who's Who in American Politics* was published in 1973, the American political system underwent its most severe case of stress and strain in decades. But it survived. It is alive and well.

As this fifth edition goes to press, we salute the 18,800 men and women whose biographies are included herein for their part in shaping for the better the course and direction of government at all levels during this most difficult period. We welcome them into this 1975-76 edition of *Who's Who in American Politics*.

When this directory was first conceived more than 10 years ago, its objective was to provide an authoritative reference work containing biographical data on the men and women who influence politics and government across America.

To make it as complete and authoritative as possible, a blue ribbon Editorial Advisory Committee of top political officials of the country was established.

And to make it truly a "Who's Who" of American political leaders, special criteria were set up to govern inclusion of persons in the directory. Although the information on biographees was gathered by specially-designed questionnaires, it was checked against reference works and other sources to assure accuracy. Biographees were sent proof copies before publication for an additional check.

The reception of the first and subsequent editions was excellent—from politicians to the press, from political scientists to scholars, from researchers to random readers.

The *Saturday Review* called this "Who's Who" a "new and extremely useful reference tool for everyone connected with politics in the United States." *Publisher's Weekly* cited it as "comprehensive, useful." *Library Journal* said it was a "unique and invaluable source of current information which should be found in every library." *Editor and Publisher* magazine characterized it as "a useful reference book for any newspaper library."

Although we are pleased to have been a part of this biennial publishing venture, changing political conditions preclude us from actively participating as co-editors of this fifth edition, as we have for the past four. We are proud of our association with the publisher, the R.R. Bowker Company, and believe this directory will remain an established and important part of American political life.

For like the air we breathe, politics is a vital part of life in these United States with which we all live daily and which affects and influences each of our lives in uncounted ways. And, hopefully, it always will. *Who's Who in American Politics* provides an insight into and an understanding of this system and the men and women who make it work.

Consulting Editors:
Edmund L. Henshaw, Jr, Executive Director
Democratic Congressional Committee

Paul A. Theis, Former Public Relations Director
Republican Congressional Committee

November, 1975

Preface

The new Fifth Edition of *Who's Who In American Politics* contains biographical sketches of approximately 18,800 men and women who make the American form of government work. Inclusion is based on the active participation of individuals on the national, state and local levels: at the national level, The President of the United States, the Vice President, cabinet and sub-cabinet officers and key presidential appointees, U.S. Senators and Representatives, officials and top staff members of major and minor political parties as well as persons who formerly held such positions and are still active in politics in some form. At the state and local level, Governors, Lieutenant Governors, major state officials and members of state legislatures, mayors and council members of major cities, officials and ranking staff members of major and minor parties, and many others.

As in previous editions, information was gathered from questionnaires requesting such pertinent data as party affiliation, date and place of birth, names of parents, spouse and children, education, present and previous political, government and business positions, military service, publications, memberships, religion, legal (voting) residence and current mailing address.

Every effort has been made to include those eligible. Material submitted by the biographee or gathered from public sources has been edited to our format and a proof sent for approval. When information was not available, and the position warranted inclusion, name, position and current mailing address appears for the benefit of the user. All precautions have been made to avoid errors. However, the publishers do not assume and hereby disclaim any liability to any party for any loss or damage caused by errors or omissions, whether such errors or omissions result from negligence, accident or any cause. In any event, the sole responsibility of the publishers will be the entry of corrected information in a succeeding edition.

A work of this magnitude would not be possible without the help of other organizations and a dedicated staff. Thanks are expressed to the secretaries of state, Democratic and Republican National Committees, governmental departments and state chairmen of both parties who, with a few exceptions, provided names for this edition; also to the staff of Jaques Cattell Press for their enthusiasm and devotion.

Suggestions and comments are invited and should be addressed to the Editors, Who's Who in American Politics, P.O. Box 25001, Tempe, Arizona 85282.

Ann Gammons, Supervising Editor
Anne Rhodes, Administrative Managing Editor
Fred Scott, General Manager
   Jaques Cattell Press

Olga Weber, Managing Editor Directories
Editorial/Publisher Coordination
   R.R. Bowker Company

November, 1975

The President and Members of His Cabinet

Gerald R. Ford
President

Nelson Aldrich Rockefeller
Vice President

Henry Alfred Kissinger
Secretary of State

William E. Simon
Secretary of the Treasury

James Rodney Schlesinger
Secretary of Defense

Edward Hirsch Levi
Attorney General

* Thomas S. Kleppe
Secretary of the Interior

Earl Lauer Butz
Secretary of Agriculture

Rogers C. B. Morton
Secretary of Commerce

John Thomas Dunlop
Secretary of Labor

Forrest David Matthews
Secretary of Health, Education & Welfare

Carla Anderson Hills
Secretary of Housing & Urban Development

William Thaddeus Coleman, Jr.
Secretary of Transportation

* Nominated by President Ford as replacement for Stanley K. Hathaway who resigned on July 25, 1975. Congressional confirmation pending at press time.

State Delegations to the 94th Congress

Number which precedes name of representative designates congressional district.

ALABAMA

Senators
John J. Sparkman (D)
James Browning Allen (D)

Representatives (D-4, R-3)
1. Jack Edwards (R)
2. William Louis Dickinson (R)
3. William Flynt Nichols (D)
4. Tom Bevill (D)
5. Robert Emmet Jones, II (D)
6. John Hall Buchanan, Jr (R)
7. Walter Winkler Flowers, Jr (D)

ALASKA

Senators
Theodore Fulton Stevens (R)
Mike Gravel (D)

Representatives (R-1)
At Large—Donald E. Young (R)

ARIZONA

Senators
Paul Jones Fannin (R)
Barry Morris Goldwater (R)

Representatives (D-1, R-3)
1. John J. Rhodes (R)
2. Morris King Udall (D)
3. Sam Steiger (R)
4. John B. Conlan, Jr (R)

ARKANSAS

Senators
John L. McClellan (D)
Dale L. Bumpers (D)

Representatives (D-3, R-1)
1. William V. Alexander, Jr (D)
2. Wilbur D. Mills (D)
3. John Paul Hammerschmidt (R)
4. R. H. Thornton, Jr (D)

CALIFORNIA

Senators
Alan MacGregor Cranston (D)
John Varick Tunney (D)

CALIFORNIA (con't.)

Representatives (D-28, R-15)
1. Harold T. Johnson (D)
2. Don H. Clausen (R)
3. John Emerson Moss (D)
4. Robert Louis Leggett (D)
5. John Lowell Burton (D)
6. Phillip Burton (D)
7. George Paul Miller (D)
8. Ronald V. Dellums (D)
9. Fortney H. Stark (D)
10. Don Edwards (D)
11. Leo Joseph Ryan (D)
12. Paul Norton McCloskey, Jr (R)
13. Norman Yoshio Mineta (D)
14. John J. McFall (D)
15. B. F. Sisk (D)
16. Burt L. Talcott (R)
17. John Hans Krebs (D)
18. William Matthew Ketchum (R)
19. Robert John Lagomarsino (R)
20. Barry Goldwater, Jr (R)
21. James C. Corman (D)
22. Carlos J. Moorhead (R)
23. Thomas M. Rees (D)
24. Henry Arnold Waxman (D)
25. Edward R. Roybal (D)
26. John Harbin Rousselot (R)
27. Alphonzo Bell (R)
28. Yvonne Brathwaite Burke (D)
29. Augustus F. Hawkins (D)
30. George Elmore Danielson (D)
31. Charles H. Wilson (D)
32. Glenn M. Anderson (D)
33. Delwin Morgan Clawson (R)
34. Mark Warren Hannaford (D)
35. James Frederick Lloyd (D)
36. George Edward Brown, Jr (D)
37. Shirley Neil Pettis (R)
38. Jerry Mumford Patterson (D)
39. Charles E. Wiggins (R)
40. Andrew J. Hinshaw (R)
41. Robert Carlton Wilson (R)
42. Lionel Van Deerlin (D)
43. Clair W. Burgener (R)

xi

COLORADO

Senators
Floyd Kirk Haskell (D)
Gary Hart (D)

Representatives (D-3, R-2)
1. Patricia Schroeder (D)
2. Timothy E. Wirth (D)
3. Frank Edward Evans (D)
4. James P. Johnson (R)
5. William Lester Armstrong (R)

CONNECTICUT

Senators
Abraham A. Ribicoff (D)
Lowell Palmer Weicker, Jr (R)

Representatives (D-4, R-2)
1. William R. Cotter (D)
2. Christopher John Dodd (D)
3. Robert Nicholas Giaimo (D)
4. Stewart Brett McKinney (R)
5. Ronald A. Sarasin (R)
6. Anthony Moffett (D)

DELAWARE

Senators
William Victor Roth, Jr (R)
Joseph Robinette Biden (D)

Representatives (R-1)
At Large—Pierre Samuel du Pont, IV (R)

FLORIDA

Senators
Lawton Mainor Chiles, Jr (D)
Richard Bernard Stone (D)

Representatives (D-10, R-5)
1. Robert L. F. Sikes (D)
2. Don Fuqua (D)
3. Charles E. Bennett (D)
4. William Venroe Chappell, Jr (D)
5. Richard Kelly (R)
6. C. W. Young (R)
7. Sam M. Gibbons (D)
8. James Andrew Haley (D)
9. Louis Frey, Jr (R)
10. Louis A. Bafalis (R)
11. Paul Grant Rogers (D)
12. J. Herbert Burke (R)
13. William Lehman (D)
14. Claude Pepper (D)
15. Dante B. Fascell (D)

GEORGIA

Senators
Herman Eugene Talmadge (D)
Sam Nunn (D)

Representatives (D-10)
1. Ronald Bryan Ginn (D)
2. M. Dawson Mathis (D)
3. Jack Thomas Brinkley (D)

GEORGIA (con't.)

Representatives (D-10) (continued)
4. Elliott Harris Levitas (D)
5. Andrew Young (D)
6. John J. Flynt, Jr (D)
7. Lauren Wylie McDonald, Jr (D)
8. William Sylvester Stuckey, Jr (D)
9. Phillip Mitchell Landrum (D)
10. Robert Grier Stephens, Jr (D)

HAWAII

Senators
Hiram Leong Fong (R)
Daniel Ken Inouye (D)

Representatives (D-2)
1. Spark Masayuki Matsunaga (D)
2. Patsy Takemoto Mink (D)

IDAHO

Senators
Frank Church (D)
James A. McClure (R)

Representatives (R-2)
1. Steven D. Symms (R)
2. George Vernon Hansen (R)

ILLINOIS

Senators
Charles Harting Percy (R)
Adlai Ewing Stevenson, III (D)

Representatives (D-13, R-11)
1. Ralph Harold Metcalfe (D)
2. Morgan Francis Murphy (D)
3. Martin A. Russo (D)
4. Edward J. Derwinski (R)
5. John Fary (D)
6. Henry John Hyde (R)
7. Cardiss W. Collins (D)
8. Dan Rostenkowski (D)
9. Sidney R. Yates (D)
10. Abner J. Mikva (D)
11. Frank Annunzio (D)
12. Philip Miller Crane (R)
13. Robert McClory (R)
14. John Neal Erlenborn (R)
15. Tim L. Hall (D)
16. John B. Anderson (R)
17. George M. O'Brien (R)
18. Robert Henry Michel (R)
19. Tom Railsback (R)
20. Paul Findley (R)
21. Edward R. Madigan (R)
22. George Edward Shipley (D)
23. Melvin Price (D)
24. Paul Simon (D)

INDIANA

Senators
Vance Hartke (D)
Birch Bayh (D)

INDIANA (con't.)

Representatives (D-9, R-2)
1. Ray J. Madden (D)
2. Floyd J. Fithian (D)
3. John Brademas (D)
4. J. Edward Roush (D)
5. Elwood Haynes Hillis (R)
6. David W. Evans (D)
7. John T. Myers (R)
8. Philip H. Hayes (D)
9. Lee Herbert Hamilton (D)
10. Philip R. Sharp (D)
11. Andrew Jacobs, Jr (D)

IOWA

Senators
Richard Clarence Clark (D)
John Chester Culver (D)

Representatives (D-5, R-1)
1. Edward M. Mezvinsky (D)
2. Michael Thomas Blouin (D)
3. Charles E. Grassley (R)
4. Neal Smith (D)
5. Tom Harkin (D)
6. Berkley Warren Bedell (D)

KANSAS

Senators
James Blackwood Pearson (R)
Robert J. Dole (R)

Representatives (D-1, R-4)
1. Keith George Sebelius (R)
2. Martha Keys (D)
3. Larry Winn, Jr (R)
4. Garner E. Shriver (R)
5. Joe Skubitz (R)

KENTUCKY

Senators
Walter Huddleston (D)
Wendell H. Ford (D)

Representatives (D-5, R-2)
1. Carroll Hubbard, Jr (D)
2. William H. Natcher (D)
3. Romano Louis Mazzoli (D)
4. Marion Gene Snyder (R)
5. Tim Lee Carter (R)
6. John Bayne Breckinridge (D)
7. Carl D. Perkins (D)

LOUISIANA

Senators
Russell B. Long (D)
J. Bennett Johnston, Jr (D)

Representatives (D-6, R-2)
1. F. Edward Hebert (D)
2. Corinne Morrison Claiborne Boggs (D)
3. David C. Treen (R)
4. Joe D. Waggonner, Jr (D)
5. Otto Ernest Passman (D)
6. W. Henson Moore, III (R)
7. John B. Breaux (D)
8. Gillis William Long (D)

MAINE

Senators
Edmund Sixtus Muskie (D)
William Dodd Hathaway (D)

Representatives (R-2)
1. David Farnham Emery (R)
2. William S. Cohen (R)

MARYLAND

Senators
Charles McC. Mathias, Jr (R)
J. Glenn Beall, Jr (R)

Representatives (D-5, R-3)
1. Robert Edmund Bauman (R)
2. Clarence Dickinson Long, Jr (D)
3. Paul Spyros Sarbanes (D)
4. Marjorie Sewell Holt (R)
5. Gladys Noon Spellman (D)
6. Goodloe Edgar Byron (D)
7. Parren James Mitchell (D)
8. Gilbert Gude (R)

MASSACHUSETTS

Senators
Edward Moore Kennedy (D)
Edward William Brooke (R)

Representatives (D-10, R-2)
1. Silvio O. Conte (R)
2. Edward P. Boland (D)
3. Joseph Daniel Early (D)
4. Robert Frederick Drinan (D)
5. Paul E. Tsongas (D)
6. Michael Joseph Harrington (D)
7. Torbert H. Macdonald (D)
8. Thomas P. O'Neill, Jr (D)
9. John Joseph Moakley (D)
10. Margaret M. Heckler (R)
11. James A. Burke (D)
12. Gerry Eastman Studds (D)

MICHIGAN

Senators
Philip A. Hart (D)
Robert Paul Griffin (R)

Representatives (D-12, R-7)
1. John Conyers, Jr (D)
2. Marvin L. Esch (R)
3. Garry Eldridge Brown (R)
4. Edward Hutchinson (R)
5. Richard Frank Vander Veen (D)
6. M. Robert Carr (D)
7. Donald W. Riegle, Jr (D)
8. J. Robert Traxler (D)
9. Guy Vander Jagt (R)
10. Elford A. Cederberg (R)
11. Philip E. Ruppe (R)
12. James Grant O'Hara (D)
13. Charles Coles Diggs, Jr (D)

MICHIGAN (con't.)

Representatives (D-12, R-7)
14. Lucien Norbert Nedzi (D)
15. William David Ford (D)
16. John D. Dingell (D)
17. William McNulty Brodhead (D)
18. James Johnston Blanchard (D)
19. William S. Broomfield (R)

MINNESOTA

Senators
Walter Frederick Mondale (DFL)
Hubert Horatio Humphrey (DFL)

Representatives (D-5, R-3)
1. Albert Harold Quie (R)
2. Thomas M. Hagedorn (R)
3. William Eldridge Frenzel (R)
4. Joseph E. Karth (DFL)
5. Donald MacKay Fraser (DFL)
6. Richard Michael Nolan (DFL)
7. Bob Selmer Bergland (DFL)
8. James L. Oberstar (DFL)

MISSISSIPPI

Senators
James Oliver Eastland (D)
John Cornelius Stennis (D)

Representatives (D-3, R-2)
1. Jamie Lloyd Whitten (D)
2. David Reece Bowen (D)
3. Gillespie V. Montgomery (D)
4. William Thad Cochran (R)
5. Chester Trent Lott (R)

MISSOURI

Senators
Stuart Symington (D)
Thomas F. Eagleton (D)

Representatives (D-9, R-1)
1. William Lacy Clay (D)
2. James W. Symington (D)
3. Leonor Kretzer Sullivan (D)
4. William J. Randall (D)
5. Richard Walker Bolling (D)
6. Jerry Litton (D)
7. Gene Taylor (R)
8. Richard Howard Ichord (D)
9. William Leonard Hungate (D)
10. Bill D. Burlison (D)

MONTANA

Senators
Michael J. Mansfield (D)
Lee Metcalf (D)

MONTANA (con't.)

Representatives (D-2)
1. Max Baucus (D)
2. John Melcher (D)

NEBRASKA

Senators
Roman Lee Hruska (R)
Carl T Curtis (R)

Representatives (R-3)
1. Charles Thone (R)
2. John Y. McCollister (R)
3. Virginia Dodd Smith (R)

NEVADA

Senators
Howard Walter Cannon (D)
Paul Laxalt (R)

Representatives (D-1)
At Large—James David Santini (D)

NEW HAMPSHIRE

Senators
Thomas James McIntyre (D)
John D. Durkin (D)

Representatives (D-1, R-1)
1. Norman Edward D'Amours (D)
2. James C. Cleveland (R)

NEW JERSEY

Senators
Clifford Philip Case (R)
Harrison Arlington Williams, Jr (D)

Representatives (D-12, R-3)
1. James Joseph Florio (D)
2. William John Hughes (D)
3. James J. Howard (D)
4. Frank Thompson, Jr (D)
5. Millicent Hammond Fenwick (R)
6. Edwin B. Forsythe (R)
7. Andrew Maguire (D)
8. Robert A. Roe (D)
9. Henry Helstoski (D)
10. Peter Wallace Rodino, Jr (D)
11. Joseph George Minish (D)
12. Matthew John Rinaldo (R)
13. Helen Stevenson Meyner (D)
14. Dominick V. Daniels (D)
15. Edward James Patten (D)

NEW MEXICO

Senators
Joseph M. Montoya (D)
Pete V. Domenici (R)

Representatives (D-1, R-1)
1. Manuel Lujan, Jr (R)
2. Harold Lowell Runnels (D)

NEW YORK

Senators
  Jacob Koppel Javits (R)
  James L. Buckley (Conservative-R)

Representatives (D-27, R-12)
1. Otis Grey Pike (D)
2. Thomas Joseph Downey (D)
3. Jerome A. Ambro (D)
4. Norman F. Lent (R)
5. John W. Wydler (R)
6. Lester Lionel Wolff (D)
7. Joseph Patrick Addabbo (D)
8. Benjamin Stanley Rosenthal (D)
9. James J. Delaney (D)
10. Mario Biaggi (D)
11. James H. Scheuer (D)
12. Shirley Anita Chisholm (D)
13. Stephen J. Solarz (D)
14. Frederick W. Richmond (D)
15. Leo C. Zeferetti (D)
16. Elizabeth Holtzman (D)
17. John Michael Murphy (D)
18. Edward Irving Koch (D)
19. Charles B. Rangel (D)
20. Bella S. Abzug (D)
21. Herman Badillo (D)
22. Jonathan B. Bingham (D)
23. Peter A. Peyser (R)
24. Richard Lawrence Ottinger (D)
25. Hamilton Fish, Jr (R)
26. Benjamin A. Gilman (R)
27. Matthew Francis McHugh (D)
28. Samuel Studdiford Stratton (D)
29. Edward W. Pattison (D)
30. Robert Cameron McEwen (R)
31. Donald J. Mitchell (R)
32. James Michael Hanley (D)
33. William Francis Walsh (R)
34. Frank Horton (R)
35. Barber Benjamin Conable, Jr (R)
36. John J. LaFalce (D)
37. Henry James Nowak (D)
38. Jack Kemp (R)
39. James Fred Hastings (R)

NORTH CAROLINA

Senators
  Jesse Helms (R)
  Robert Burren Morgan (D)

Representatives (D-9, R-2)
1. Walter Beaman Jones (D)
2. L. H. Fountain (D)
3. David Newton Henderson (D)
4. Ike Franklin Andrews (D)
5. Stephen Lybrook Neal (D)
6. Lunsford Richardson Preyer (D)
7. Charles Rose, III (D)
8. W. G. Hefner (D)
9. James Grubbs Martin (R)
10. James Thomas Broyhill (R)
11. Roy A. Taylor (D)

NORTH DAKOTA

Senators
  Milton R. Young (R)
  Quentin N. Burdick (D)

Representatives (R-1)
  At Large—Mark Andrews (R)

OHIO

Senators
  Robert Taft, Jr (R)
  John Herschel Glenn, Jr (D)

Representatives (D-8, R-15)
1. Willis David Gradison, Jr (R)
2. Donald Daniel Clancy (R)
3. Charles William Whalen, Jr (R)
4. Tennyson Guyer (R)
5. Delbert L. Latta (R)
6. William H. Harsha (R)
7. Clarence J. Brown (R)
8. Thomas Norman Kindness (R)
9. Thomas Ludlow Ashley (D)
10. Clarence E. Miller (R)
11. John William Stanton (R)
12. Samuel L. Devine (R)
13. Charles Adams Mosher (R)
14. John F. Seiberling (D)
15. Chalmers Pangburn Wylie (R)
16. Ralph S. Regula (R)
17. John Milan Ashbrook (R)
18. Wayne L. Hays (D)
19. Charles J. Carney (D)
20. James Vincent Stanton (D)
21. Louis Stokes (D)
22. Charles Vanik (D)
23. Ronald M. Mottl (D)

OKLAHOMA

Senators
  Henry L. Bellmon (R)
  Dewey Follett Bartlett (R)

Representatives (D-5, R-1)
1. James Robert Jones (D)
2. Ted M. Risenhoover (D)
3. Carl Bert Albert (D)
4. Tom Steed (D)
5. John Jarman (R)
6. Glenn English (D)

OREGON

Senators
  Mark Odom Hatfield (R)
  Bob Packwood (R)

Representatives (D-4)
1. Les AuCoin (D)
2. Al Ullman (D)
3. Robert Blackford Duncan (D)
4. James Howard Weaver (D)

PENNSYLVANIA

Senators
  Hugh Scott (R)
  Richard Schultz Schweiker (R)

PENNSYLVANIA (con't.)

Representatives (D-14, R-11)
1. William A. Barrett (D)
2. Robert N. C. Nix (D)
3. William Joseph Green (D)
4. Joshua Eilberg (D)
5. Richard T. Schulze (R)
6. Gus Yatron (D)
7. Robert William Edgar (D)
8. Edward G. Biester, Jr (R)
9. E. G. Shuster (R)
10. Joseph Michael McDade (R)
11. Daniel J. Flood (D)
12. John Patrick Murtha (D)
13. R. Lawrence Coughlin, Jr (R)
14. William Singer Moorhead, Jr (D)
15. Fred B. Rooney (D)
16. Edwin D. Eshleman (R)
17. Herman Theodore Schneebeli (R)
18. Henry John Heinz, III (R)
19. William Franklin Goodling (R)
20. Joseph Matthew Gaydos (D)
21. John H. Dent (D)
22. Thomas Ellsworth Morgan (D)
23. Albert W. Johnson (R)
24. Joseph Phillip Vigorito (D)
25. Gary A. Myers (R)

RHODE ISLAND

Senators
John O. Pastore (D)
Claiborne Pell (D)

Representatives (D-2)
1. Fernand Joseph St Germain (D)
2. Edward Peter Beard (D)

SOUTH CAROLINA

Senators
Strom Thurmond (R)
Ernest Frederick Hollings (D)

Representatives (D-5, R-1)
1. Mendel Jackson Davis (D)
2. Floyd Davidson Spence (R)
3. Butler Carson Derrick, Jr (D)
4. James Robert Mann (D)
5. Kenneth L. Holland (D)
6. John Wilson Jenrette, Jr (D)

SOUTH DAKOTA

Senators
George McGovern (D)
James G. Abourezk (D)

Representatives (R-2)
1. Larry Pressler (R)
2. E. James Abdnor (R)

TENNESSEE

Senators
Howard Baker, Jr (R)
William Emerson Brock, III (R)

TENNESSEE (con't.)

Representatives (D-5, R-3)
1. James Henry Quillen (R)
2. John James Duncan (R)
3. Marilyn Laird Lloyd (D)
4. Joe Landon Evins (D)
5. Richard Harmon Fulton (D)
6. Robin Leo Beard, Jr (R)
7. Ed Jones (D)
8. Harold Eugene Ford (D)

TEXAS

Senators
John Goodwin Tower (R)
Lloyd Millard Bentsen, Jr (D)

Representatives (D-21, R-3)
1. Wright Patman (D)
2. Charles Wilson (D)
3. James Mitchell Collins (R)
4. Ray Roberts (D)
5. Alan Watson Steelman (R)
6. Olin E. Teague (D)
7. William Reynolds Archer, Jr (R)
8. Robert Christian Eckhardt (D)
9. Jack Brooks (D)
10. J. J. Pickle (D)
11. William Robert Poage (D)
12. James C. Wright, Jr (D)
13. Jack English Hightower (D)
14. John Young (D)
15. E. de la Garza (D)
16. Richard Crawford White (D)
17. Omar Burleson (D)
18. Barbara C. Jordan (D)
19. George Herman Mahon (D)
20. Henry Barbosa Gonzalez (D)
21. Robert Charles Krueger (D)
22. Robert Randolph Casey (D)
23. Abraham Kazen, Jr (D)
24. Dale Milford (D)

UTAH

Senators
Frank Edward Moss (D)
Edwin Jacob Garn (R)

Representatives (D-2)
1. Koln Gunn McKay (D)
2. Allan Turner Howe (D)

VERMONT

Senators
Robert T. Stafford (R)
Patrick J. Leahy (D)

Representatives (R-1)
At Large—James Merrill Jeffords (R)

VIRGINIA

Senators
Harry Flood Byrd, Jr (Independent)
William L. Scott (R)

VIRGINIA (con't.)

Representatives (D-5, R-5)
1. Thomas N. Downing (D)
2. George William Whitehurst (R)
3. David E. Satterfield, III (D)
4. Robert Williams Daniel, Jr (R)
5. W. C. Daniel (D)
6. Manley Caldwell Butler (R)
7. James Kenneth Robinson (R)
8. Herbert E. Harris, II (D)
9. William Creed Wampler (R)
10. Joseph Lyman Fisher (D)

WASHINGTON

Senators
Warren Grant Magnuson (D)
Henry M. Jackson (D)

Representatives (D-6, R-1)
1. Joel M. Pritchard (R)
2. Lloyd Meeds (D)
3. Don L. Bonker (D)
4. Mike McCormack (D)
5. Thomas Stephen Foley (D)
6. Floyd V. Hicks (D)
7. Brockman Adams (D)

WEST VIRGINIA

Senators
Jennings Randolph (D)
Robert C. Byrd (D)

Representatives (D-4)
1. Robert H. Mollohan (D)
2. Harley Orrin Staggers (D)
3. John M. Slack, Jr (D)
4. Ken Hechler (D)

WISCONSIN

Senators
William Proxmire (D)
Gaylord Anton Nelson (D)

Representatives (D-7, R-2)
1. Les Aspin (D)
2. Robert William Kastenmeier (D)
3. Alvin Baldus (D)
4. Clement John Zablocki (D)
5. Henry S. Reuss (D)
6. William Albert Steiger (R)
7. David R. Obey (D)
8. Robert John Cornell (D)
9. Robert W. Kasten, Jr (R)

WYOMING

Senators
Gale William McGee (D)
Clifford Peter Hansen (R)

Representatives (D-1)
At Large—Teno Roncalio (D)

DISTRICT OF COLUMBIA

Delegate—Walter E. Fauntroy (D)

PUERTO RICO

Resident Commissioner—
Jaime Benitez (Popular Dem, PR)

GUAM

Delegate—Antonio Borja Won Pat (D)

VIRGIN ISLANDS

Delegate—Ronald de Lugo (D)

CLASSIFICATION

SENATE
Democrats............. 61
Republicans........... 37
Conservative-Republican 1
Independent........... 1
Total...............100

HOUSE
Democrats....... 290
Republicans..... 145
Total.......... 435

Governors of the States

	GOVERNORS	LT GOVERNORS
Alabama	George Corley Wallace (D)	Jere Locke Beasley (D)
Alaska	Jay Sterner Hammond (R)	Lowell Thomas, Jr (R)
Arizona	Raul Hector Castro (D)	*
Arkansas	David Hampton Pryor (D)	Joe Purcell (D)
California	Edmund Gerald Brown, Jr (D)	Mervyn M. Dymally (D)
Colorado	Richard D. Lamm (D)	George L. Brown, Jr (D)
Connecticut	Ella Tambussi Grasso (D)	Robert Kenneth Killian (D)
Delaware	Sherman W. Tribbitt (D)	Eugene Donald Bookhammer (R)
Florida	Reubin O'D. Askew (D)	J. H. Williams (D)
Georgia	George D. Busbee (D)	Zell Bryan Miller (D)
Hawaii	George Ryoichi Ariyoshi (D)	Nelson Kiyoshi Doi (D)
Idaho	Cecil D. Andrus (D)	John Victor Evans (D)
Illinois	Dan Walker (D)	Neil F. Hartigan (D)
Indiana	Otis R. Bowen (R)	Robert Dunkerson Orr (R)
Iowa	Robert D. Ray (R)	Arthur Alan Neu (R)
Kansas	Robert Frederick Bennett (R)	Shelby Smith (R)
Kentucky	Julian Morton Carroll (D)	William Litsey Sullivan (D)
Louisiana	Edwin W. Edwards (D)	James E. Fitzmorris, Jr (D)
Maine	James Bernard Longley (Independent)	*
Maryland	Marvin Mandel (D)	Blair Lee, III (D)
Massachusetts	Michael S. Dukakis (D)	Thomas P. O'Neill, III (D)
Michigan	William Grawn Milliken (R)	James J. Damman (R)
Minnesota	Wendell Richard Anderson (DFL)	Rudy George Perpich (DFL)
Mississippi	William L. Waller (D)	William Forrest Winter (D)
Missouri	Christopher Samuel Bond (R)	William C. Phelps (R)
Montana	Thomas Lee Judge (D)	Edward William Christiansen, Jr (D)
Nebraska	John James Exon (D)	Gerald T. Whelan (D)
Nevada	Donal N. O'Callaghan (D)	Robert Edgar Rose (D)
New Hampshire	Meldrim Thomson, Jr (R)	*
New Jersey	Brendan T. Byrne (D)	*
New Mexico	Jerry Apodaca (D)	Robert Earl Ferguson (D)
New York	Hugh L. Carey (D)	Mary Anne Krupsak (D)
North Carolina	James Eubert Holshouser, Jr (R)	James Baxter Hunt, Jr (D)
North Dakota	Arthur A. Link (D)	Wayne Godfrey Sanstead (D)
Ohio	James Allen Rhodes (R)	Richard F. Celeste (D)
Oklahoma	David Lyle Boren (D)	George Patterson Nigh (D)
Oregon	Robert W. Straub (D)	*
Pennsylvania	Milton J. Shapp (D)	Ernest P. King (D)
Rhode Island	Philip William Noel (D)	J. Joseph Garrahy (D)
South Carolina	James Burrows Edwards (R)	William Brantley Harvey, Jr (D)

*Office of Lt Governor nonexistent

	GOVERNORS	LT GOVERNORS
South Dakota	Richard Francis Kneip (D)	Harvey Wollman (D)
Tennessee	L. Ray Blanton (D)	John Wilder (D)
Texas	Dolph Briscoe (D)	William Pettus Hobby (D)
Utah	Calvin Lewellyn Rampton (D)	*
Vermont	Thomas P. Salmon (D)	Brian Douglas Burns (D)
Virginia	Mills Edwin Godwin, Jr (R)	John Nichols Dalton (R)
Washington	Daniel Jackson Evans (R)	John Andrew Cherberg (D)
West Virginia	Arch A. Moore, Jr (R)	*
Wisconsin	Patrick Joseph Lucey (D)	Martin James Schreiber (D)
Wyoming	Ed Herschler (D)	*
American Samoa	Earl B. Ruth (R)	Frank Barnett
Guam	Ricardo J. **Bordallo (D)**	Rudolpho G. Sablan (D)
Puerto Rico	Rafael Hernandez-Colon, (Popular Dem, PR)	*
Virgin Islands	Cyril E. King (Independent)	Juan Luis

*Office of Lt Governor nonexistent

Classification

Governors		Lt Governors	
Democrat	38	Democrat	35
Republican	14	Republican	8
Independent	2	Total	43
Total	54		

State Chairmen

	DEMOCRAT	REPUBLICAN
Alabama	Robert Smith Vance	Edgar Welden
Alaska	Mellie E. Terwilliger	John Bruce Coghill
Arizona	Charles Warren Pine	Harry Rosenzweig
Arkansas	Mack McLarty	A. Lynn Lowe
California	Charles Taylor Manatt	Paul Raymond Haerle
Colorado	D. Monte Pascoe	Carl Michael Williams
Connecticut	William A. O'Neill	Frederick K. Biebel, Jr
Delaware	Ernest E. Killen	Herman Cubbage Brown
District of Columbia	William Lucy	Edmund E. Pendleton, Jr
Florida	Ann Marie Cramer	William M. Taylor
Georgia	Marjorie Clark Thurman	Mack Francis Mattingly
Hawaii	Minoru Hirabara	George Henrickson
Idaho	Deckie M. Rice	Robert G. Linville, Jr
Illinois	John P. Touhy	Don W. Adams
Indiana	Bill Trisler	Thomas Stuart Milligan
Iowa	Tom Whitney	John Cecil McDonald
Kansas	Henry Longley Lueck	John S. Ranson
Kentucky	Marie R. Turner	Charles Russell Coy
Louisiana	Arthur Chopin Watson	James H. Boyce
Maine	David W. Bustin	John R. Linnell
Maryland	Roy Neville Staten	David Ross Forward
Massachusetts	Charles Francis Flaherty, Jr	John Winthrop Sears
Michigan	Morley A. Winograd	William Francis McLaughlin
Minnesota	Henry Fred Fischer	Robert John Brown
Mississippi	Aaron Edd Henry	Clarke Thomas Reed
Missouri	James Earl Spain	Lowell McCuskey
Montana	John Wesley Bartlett	Kenneth R. Neill
Nebraska	Richard White	Anne Batchelder
Nevada	Paul H. Lamboley	Frank J. Fahrenkopf, Jr
New Hampshire	Laurence Ingram Radway	Gerald P. Carmen
New Jersey	James Dugan	Webster Bray Todd
New Mexico	Ben B. Alexander	Jack Stahl
New York	Patrick Joseph Cunningham	Richard Merrill Rosenbaum
North Carolina	James Russell Sugg	Thomas Stephen Bennett
North Dakota	Richard Glen Ista	Allan Chandler Young
Ohio	Paul Tipps	Kent B. McGough
Oklahoma	Bob Funston	Paula Unruh
Oregon	James Richard Klonoski	David M. Green
Pennsylvania	Dennis E. Thiemann	Richard C. Frame
Rhode Island	Charles T. Reilly	H. James Field, Jr
South Carolina	Donald Lionel Fowler	Jesse Lecel Cooksey
South Dakota	Charles Bellman	John Olson
Tennessee	James Ralph Sasser	Dortch Oldham

	DEMOCRAT	REPUBLICAN
Texas	Calvin Ray Guest	John Fisken Warren
Utah	John Hall Klas	T. William Cockayne
Vermont	Robert Branon	Walter Lawrence Kennedy
Virginia	John Joseph Fitzpatrick	George Nottingham McMath
Washington	Neale V. Chaney	Ross E. Davis
West Virginia	J. C. Dillon	Thomas Eugene Potter
Wisconsin	Herbert Kohl	George Parker
Wyoming	Donald Ray Anselmi	Thomas F. Stroock
Canal Zone	Charles Senour Stough	
Guam	Francisco Carbullido	Frank F. Blas
Puerto Rico	Richard C. Durham	Jose Vicente Usera
Virgin Islands	Alexander Farrelly	Raymond J. Smith

List of Abbreviations

AAONMS—Ancient Arabic Order of the Nobles of the Mystic Shrine
AASR—Ancient Accepted Scottish Rite
abstr—abstracts
acad—academic, academy
acct—account, accountant, accounting
Add—Address
adj—adjunct, adjutant
adjust—adjustment
Adm—Admiral
admin—administration, administrative
adminr—administrator
adv—adviser, advisory, advocate
advan—advanced, advancement
advert—advertisement, advertising
AEAONMS—Ancient Egyptian Arabic Order Nobles of the Mystic Shrine
AEF—American Expeditionary Force
aeronaut—aeronautic(s), aeronautical
AF&AM—Ancient Free and Accepted Mason
AFB—Air Force Base
affil—affiliate, affiliation
AFL—American Federation of Labor
agr—agricultural, agriculture
agt—agent
Ala—Alabama
alt—alternate
Alta—Alberta
Am—America, American
AMCBW—American Meat Cutters & Butchers Workmen of North America
anal—analysis, analytic, analytical
anat—anatomic, anatomical, anatomy
Ann—Annal(s)
anthrop—anthropological, anthropology
antiq—antiquary, antiquities, antiquity
antiqn—antiquarian
APO—Army Post Office
app—appoint, appointed
appl—applied
appln—application
Apr—April
apt—apartment(s)
arbit—arbitration
Arch—Archives
archaeol—archaeological, archaeology
archit—architectural, architecture
Ariz—Arizona
Ark—Arkansas
artil—artillery
A/S—Apprentice Seaman
Asn—Association
assoc—associate(s), associated
asst—assistant
astron—astronomical, astronomy
astronaut—astronautical, astronautics
astronr—astronomer
astrophys—astrophysical, astrophysics
attend—attendant, attending
Aug—August

auth—author
Ave—Avenue

b—born
bact—bacterial, bacteriologic, bacteriological, bacteriology
BC—British Columbia
bd—board(s)
behav—behavior, behavioral
bibliog—bibliographic, bibliographical, bibliography
biochem—biochemical, biochemistry
biol—biological, biology
biomet—biometric(s), biometrical, biometry
biophys—biophysical, biophysics
bldg—building
Blvd—Boulevard
BMP—Bricklayers, Masons and Plasterers International Union of America
Bn—Battalion
bot—botanical, botany
br—branch
BRC of US&C—Brotherhood of Railway Carmen of US & Canada
Brig. Gen—Brigadier General
Brit—Britain, British
Bros—Brothers
Bull—Bulletin
bur—bureau
bus—business
B.W.I.—British West Indies

c—children
CofC—Chamber of Commerce
Calif—California
Can—Canada, Canadian
cand—candidate
Capt—Captain
cardiol—cardiology
Cath—Catholic
cent—central
cert—certificate, certification, certified
chap—chapter
chem—chemical(s), chemistry
chmn—chairman
CIO—Congress of Industrial Organizations
clin—clinic(s), clinical
Cmndg—Commanding
Co—Companies, Company, County
co-auth—co-author
co-chmn—co-chairman
co-ed—co-editor
Col—College(s), Colonel
collab—collaboration, collaborative, collaborator
Colo—Colorado
com—commerce
Comdr—Commander
commun—communicable, communication(s)
comn—Commission(s)
comnr—Commissioner

comp—comparative
comput—computation, computer(s), computing
comt—committee(s)
conf—conference
cong—congress(es), congressional
Conn—Connecticut
conserv—conservancy, conservation
consol—consolidated, consolidation
const—constitution, constitutional
consult—consultant, consulting
contrib—contributing, contribution
contribr—contributor
conv—convention
coop—cooperation, cooperative
coord—coordinating, coordination
coordr—coordinator
CORE—Congress of Racial Equality
corp—corporate, corporation
coun—council
counr—councilor, counselor
CPA—Certified Public Accountant
Cpl—Corporal
CPO—Chief Petty Officer
ct—court
ctr—center
cult—cultural, culture
CWA—Communications Workers of America
CWV—Catholic War Veterans
CZ—Canal Zone
Czech—Czechoslovakia

d—daughter
D—Democrat
DAR—Daughters of the American Revolution
DAV—Disabled American Veterans
DC—District of Columbia
Dec—December
Del—Delaware, delegate, delegation
deleg—delegate, delegation
deleg-at-lg—delegate-at-large
Dem—Democrat(s), Democratic
dent—dental, dentistry
dep—deputy
dept—department
develop—development, developmental
DFL—Democrat-Farmer-Labor
dipl—diploma, diplomate
dir—director(s), directory
dist—district
div—division, divorced
doc—document, documentation
Dom—Dominion
Dr—Doctor, drive

E—East
ecol—ecological, ecology
econ—economic(s), economical, economy
economet—econometric(s)
ed—edition, editor, editorial
educ—education, educational

Elec—Election, electric, electrical, electricity
elem—elementary
emer—emeritus
employ—employment
encycl—encyclopedia
eng—engineering
Eng—England, English
engr—engineer(s)
Ens—Ensign
environ—environment(s), environmental
equip—equipment
espec—especially
estab—established, establishment
ETO—European Theater of Operations
eval—evaluation
Evangel—Evangelical
eve—evening
exam—examination(s)
examr—examiners(s)
exec—executive(s)
exhib—exhibition(s)
exp—experiment, experimental
exped—expedition(s)
explor—exploration(s), exploratory
expos—exposition
exten—extension

F&AM—Free and Accepted Mason
facil—facilities, facility
Feb—February
fed—federal
fedn—federation
fel—fellow(s), fellowship(s)
FL—Farmer-Labor
Fla—Florida
found—foundation
FPO—Fleet Post Office
Ft—Fort

Ga—Georgia
gen—general
geog—geographic, geographical, geography
geogr—geographer
geol—geologic, geological, geology
geophys—geophysical, geophysics
Ger—Germany
GHQ—General Headquarters
GOP—Grand Old Party
gov—governing, governor(s)
govt—government, governmental
grad—graduate
Gt Brit—Great Britain
Gtr—Greater
guid—guidance

HA—Hospital Apprentice
hist—historical, history
hon—honorable, honorary
hort—horticultural, horticulture
hosp—hospital(s), hospitalization
hq—headquarters
Hwy—Highway

IAMAW—International Association of Machinists and Aerospace Workers
IBEW—International Brotherhood of Electrical Workers
IBT—International Brotherhood of Teamsters, Chauffeurs, Warehousemen and Helpers of America
ILGWU—International Ladies Garment Workers Union
Ill—Illinois
Imp—Imperial
improv—improvement

Inc—Incorporated
Ind—Indiana
indust—industrial, industries, industry
Inf—Infantry
info—information
ins—insurance
inst—institute(s), institution(s)
instnl—institutional
instr—instruction, instructor(s)
int—international
intel—intelligence
introd—introduction
invest—investigation(s)
investr—investigator
Ital—Italian
ITU—International Typographical Union
IUE—International Union of Electrical, Radio and Machine Workers

J—journal
Jan—January
JOUAM—Junior Order of United American Mechanics
jour—journal, journalism
jr—junior
jurisp—jurisprudence
juv—juvenile(s)

KofC—Knights of Columbus
KofM—Knights of Malta
KofP—Knights of Pythias
Kans—Kansas
KCCH—Knight Commander of Court of Honor
KT—Knight Templar
Ky—Kentucky

La—Louisiana
lab—laboratories, laboratory
lang—language(s)
lect—lecture
lectr—lecturer
legis—legislation, legislative, legislature
lib—liberal
libr—library
libn—librarian
ling—linguistic(s)
lit—literary, literature
Lt—Lieutenant
Lt(jg)—Lieutenant junior grade
Lt(sg)—Lieutenant senior grade
Ltd—Limited
LULAC—League of United Latin American Citizens
LWIU—Leather Workers International Union of America

m—married
mag—magazine
Maj—Major
Man—Manitoba
Mar—March
Mass—Massachusetts
math—mathematic(s), mathematical
Md—Maryland
mech—mechanic(s), mechanical
med—medical, medicinal, medicine
Mediter—Mediterranean
mem—member, memoirs, memorial
ment—mental, mentally
meteorol—meteorological, meteorology
metrop—metropolitan
Mex—Mexican, Mexico
mfg—manufacturing
mfr—manufacture(s), manufacturer(s)
mgr—manager

mgt—management
Mich—Michigan
mid—middle
Midn—Midshipman
mil—military
Minn—Minnesota
Miss—Mississippi
mkt—market, marketing
Mo—Missouri
mod—modern
monogr—monograph
Mont—Montana
M/Sgt—Master Sergeant
mt—mount
Munic—Municipal, Municipalities
mus—museum
MWA—Modern Woodmen of America

N—North
NAACP—National Association for Advancement of Colored People
NASA—National Aeronautics and Space Administration
nat—national, naturalized
NATO—North Atlantic Treaty Organization
navig—navigation
NB—New Brunswick
NC—North Carolina
NDak—North Dakota
Nebr—Nebraska
Nev—Nevada
New Eng—New England
Nfld—Newfoundland
NH—New Hampshire
NJ—New Jersey
NMex—New Mexico
Norweg—Norwegian
Nov—November
NS—Nova Scotia
NY—New York State
NZ—New Zealand

observ—observatory
OCAWIU—Oil, Chemical and Atomic Workers International Union
occup—occupation, occupational
Oct—October
OEEC—Organization for European Economic Cooperation
off—office, official
Okla—Oklahoma
Ont—Ontario
oper—operation(s), operational, operative
optom—optometric, optometrical, optometry
ord—ordnance
Ore—Oregon
orgn—organization(s), organizational

Pa—Pennsylvania
Pac—Pacific
Pan-Am—Pan-American
path—pathologic, pathological, pathology
PEI—Prince Edward Island
Pfc—Private first class
pharm—pharmacy
philos—philosophic, philosophical, philosophy
photog—photographic, photography
phys—physical
physiol—physiological, physiology
pkwy—parkway
Pl—Place
PO—Petty Officer
polit—political, politics
polytech—polytechnic
pop—population

pos—position
postgrad—postgraduate
PR—Puerto Rico
prep—preparation, preparative, preparatory
pres—president
Presby—Presbyterian
prev—prevention, preventive
prin—principal
prob—problem(s)
proc—proceedings
prod—product(s), production, productive
prof—professor, professorial, professional
prog—program(s), programmed, programming
proj—project(s), projectional, projective
prom—promotion
prov—province, provincial
psychiat—psychiatric, psychiatry
psychol—psychological, psychology
PTA—Parent-Teacher Association
pub—public
publ—publication(s), publisher, publishing
Pvt—Private

Qm—Quartermaster
Qm Gen—Quartermaster General
qual—qualitative, quality
quant—quantitative
Quart—Quarterly
Que—Quebec

R—Republican(s)
RAM—Royal Arch Mason
RCIA—Retail Clerks International Association
Rd—Road
RD—Rural Delivery
rec—record(s), recording
regist—registration
registr—registrar
Regt—Regiment, Regimental
rel—relation(s), relative
relig—religion, religious
Rep—Representative, Republican(s)
Repub—Republic
Res—Reserve(s), residence
Ret—Retired
rev—review, revision(s)
RI—Rhode Island
rm—room
ROA—Reserve Officers Association of U.S.
ROTC—Reserve Officers Training Corps
RR—Railroad, Rural Route
RSM—Royal and Select Master-Masons
Rte—Route
rwy—railway

s—son

S—South
SAfrica—South Africa
SAm—South America, South American
sanit—sanitary, sanitation
SAR—Sons of the American Revolution
Sask—Saskatchewan
SC—South Carolina
sch—school(s)
scholar—scholarship
sci—science(s), scientific
SDak—South Dakota
SEATO—South East Asia Treaty Organization
sec—secondary
sect—section
secy—secretary
sem—seminary
Sen—Senator, Senatorial
Sept—September
serv—service(s), serving
Sgt—Sergeant
SHAEF—Supreme Headquarters Allied Expeditionary Force
soc—social, societies, society
sociol—sociologic, sociological, sociology
spec—special
Sq—Square
sr—senior
S/Sgt—Staff Sergeant
St—Saint, Street
sta—station(s)
statist—statistical, statistics
struct—structural, structure(s)
subcomt—subcommittee
subj—subject
substa—substation
suppl—supplement, supplemental, supplementary
supt—superintendent
supv—supervising, supervision
supvr—supervisor
supvry—supervisory
surg—surgical, surgery
surv—survey, surveying
Switz—Switzerland
symp—symposium(s)
syst—system(s), systematic(s), systematical

TAR—Teen-Age Republicans
tech—technical, technique(s)
technol—technologic, technological, technology
tel—telegraph(y), telephone
Tenn—Tennessee
Terr—Terrace
Tex—Texas
theol—theological, theology
theoret—theoretical
trans—transactions

transl—translation(s)
translr—translator
treas—treasurer, treasury
T/Sgt—Technical Sergeant
tuberc—tuberculosis
TV—television
Twp—Township

UAW—United Auto, Aerospace and Agricultural Implement Workers of America
UDC—United Daughters of the Confederacy
UMW—United Mine Workers of America
UN—United Nations
unemploy—unemployment
UNESCO—United Nations Educational, Scientific and Cultural Organization
UNICEF—United Nations Children's Fund
univ—universities, university
UNRRA—United Nations Relief and Rehabilitation Administration
UPW—United Public Workers of America
US—United States
USW—United Steelworkers of America

Va—Virginia
vchmn—vice chairman
vet—veteran(s), veterinarian, veterinary
VFW—Veterans of Foreign Wars
VI—Virgin Islands
vis—visiting
VISTA—Volunteers in Service to America
voc—vocational
vol—volume(s), voluntary, volunteer(s)
vpres—vice president
Vt—Vermont

W—West
w—with
Wash—Washington
WHO—World Health Organization
WI—West Indies
wid—widow, widowed, widower
Wis—Wisconsin
WOW—Woodmen of the World
WVa—West Virginia
Wyo—Wyoming

YMCA—Young Men's Christian Association
YMHA—Young Men's Hebrew Association
YWCA—Young Women's Christian Association
YWHA—Young Women's Hebrew Association

zool—zoological, zoology

WHO'S WHO
IN AMERICAN POLITICS
FIFTH EDITION 1975-1976

Who's Who in American Politics

A

AAGESON, DAVID ELLING (R)
Mont State Rep
b Havre, Mont, June 22, 48; s Arvin Sampson Aageson & Rosalie Labold A; single. Educ: St Olaf Col, BA; Cambridge Univ, fall 70. Polit & Govt Pos: Mont State Rep, Dist 14, 72- Bus & Prof Pos: Farmer-rancher, Aageson Grain & Cattle, currently. Mem: Elks; Jr CofC. Relig: Lutheran. Mailing Add: Gildford MT 59525

AARONS, BARRY MICHAEL (R)
Chmn, Ariz Young Rep League
b New York, NY, Dec 31, 50; s Stuart H Aarons & Florence Josephson A; m 1970 to Linda Chriss A. Educ: Colo State Univ, 70; Ariz State Univ, BA, 71. Polit & Govt Pos: Chmn, Col Young Rep Ariz, 70-71; attache, Ariz House Rep, 71; pres, Northwest Young Rep Club, 71-72; treas, Ariz Young Rep League, 71-72; nat committeeman, 73-74; chmn, Maricopa Co Young Rep League, 72-73; precinct capt, Precinct Ten, Legis Dist 27, Tempe, 72- Bus & Prof Pos: Dir research, Off of Ariz State Treas, 71-73; exec asst, Ariz Corp Comn, 73-; bd dirs, Reliable Commun Corp, 73- Mem: Lions; Tempe Rep Men's Club; Alumni Asn, Gamma Tau Chap, Zeta Beta Tau; Ariz Acad; Gamma Tau Corp (pres, 73-). Honors & Awards: Fel, Nat Sci Found, 70; Man of Year, Gamma Tau Chap, Zeta Beta Tau, 70. Relig: Jewish. Mailing Add: 4729 W Becker Lane Glendale AZ 85304

ABADIE, ARTHUR F (D)
La State Rep
Mailing Add: 1122 Wooddale Blvd Baton Rouge LA 70806

ABATE, ERNEST NICHOLAS (D)
Conn State Rep
b New Haven, Conn, Aug 10, 43; s Nicholas Anthony Abate & Rose Virgulto A; m 1966 to Barbara Zempel; c Charles Porter & Edward Stockton. Educ: Villanova Univ, BS in polit sci, 65; Univ Notre Dame Sch Law, JD, 68; Delta Pi Mu; Blue Key. Polit & Govt Pos: Mem, Stamford Dem City Comt, Conn, 74-; Conn State Rep, 75- Mil Serv: Entered as Pvt, Marine Corps, 67, released as Capt, 72, after serv in Hq Bn Base, Fleet Marine Force Pac, Staff Judge Adv, Mil Judge, 69-72; Navy Achievement Medal. Mem: Am Bar Asn; Drug Liberation Inc (mem bd dirs); Am Judicature Soc; Conn Bar Asn (chmn law-day comt, 74-75, chmn legis liaison comt & mem spec comt lawyers in community, 74-, chmn state-local liaison comt, 75-); YMCA. Honors & Awards: Outstanding Man of Year, Villanova Univ, 65. Relig: Catholic. Mailing Add: 47 Rock Spring Rd Stamford CT 06906

ABATE, JOSEPH FRANCIS (R)
Nat Committeeman, Ariz Young Rep
b Atlantic City, NJ, Jan 3, 46; s Joseph Abate & Carolyn Fiore A; m 1972 to Rory C Hays. Educ: Princeton Univ, AB, 68; NY Univ Sch Law, JD, 71; Princeton Charter Club. Polit & Govt Pos: Pres, Princeton Univ Senate, 67; vchmn, NJ Col Rep, 67; mem, Nat Student Adv Bd for Nixon, 68; chmn, NJ State Youth for Cahill, 69; chmn, NJ State Youth for Rep, 69-70; chmn, 70-; chmn, NJ State Youth for Gross, 70; mem, NJ State Rep Youth Adv Bd, 71; asst to chmn, NJ Rep State Comt, 71-72; chmn, NJ Young Rep, formerly; co-chmn, Nat Young Voters for The President, 72; asst to chmn, NJ Comt to Reelect The President, 72; alt deleg, Rep Nat Conv, 72; mem exec comt, Rep Nat Comt, 72-; co-chmn, Youth Inaugural Comt, 73; mem, Ariz State Rep Comt, 74-; mem, Maricopa Co Rep Comt, 74-; spec counsel, Attorney Gen, Ariz, 74; vchmn, Dist 18 Rep Comt, 74-; nat committeeman, Ariz Young Rep, 75-; Majority legal counsel, Ariz House Rep, 75- Bus & Prof Pos: Spec asst to dir off legal servs, Off Econ Opportunity, 73. Mem: Ariz State Bar (exec coun, Ariz young lawyers sect); Am & Fed Bar Asns; Small Bus Admin; Int Platform Asn. Relig: Roman Catholic. Mailing Add: 1320 E Bethany Home Rd Phoenix AZ 85014

ABBITT, WATKINS MOORMAN (D)
Chmn, Appomattox Co Dem Comt, Va
b Appomattox, Va, May 21, 08; s George Francis Abbitt & Otway C Moorman A; m 1937 to Corinne Hancock; c Anne Culvin, Watkins Moorman & Corinne Hancock. Educ: Univ Richmond, LLB, 31; Omicron Delta Kappa; Delta Theta Phi. Hon Degrees: LLD, Univ Richmond, 65. Polit & Govt Pos: Commonwealth's Attorney for Appomattox Co, Va, 32-38; deleg, Va State Dem Conv, 32-; chmn, Appomattox Co Dem Comt, 37-; Dem elector, 44; deleg, Va State Const Conv, 45; US Rep, Va, 48-72; chmn, Va State Dem Cent Comt, 64-70; deleg, Dem Nat Conv, 72. Bus & Prof Pos: Lawyer; dir, Farmer's Nat Bank of Appomattox. Mem: Am & Va Trial Lawyers Asns; Am Judicature Soc; Forestry Asn; Coun of State Bar. Relig: Baptist. Mailing Add: Appomattox VA 24522

ABBOTT, ALFREDA HELEN (D)
Mem, Calif Dem State Cent Comt
b Oakland, Calif, Apr 8, 31; d Fred Alphonso Lester & Alberta Penn L; m 1954 to Robert Perry Abbott; c Ross Perry & Brian Craig. Educ: Univ Calif, Berkeley, BS, 53; Delta Sigma Theta. Polit & Govt Pos: Deleg, Dem Nat Conv, 72; field rep, Calif State Sen Nicholas Petris, Oakland, 72-; mem, Calif Dem State Cent Comt, 73-; mem, Alameda Co Status Women Comn, 75- Bus & Prof Pos: Probation officer, Alameda Co Probation Off, 53-56; prin, Montclair Presby Church Sch, Oakland, 69-70; group worker, Sr Citizens Ctr, Social Serv Bur, Oakland, 70-72. Relig: Protestant. Mailing Add: 8047 Shay Dr Oakland CA 94605

ABBOTT, BARBARA S (R)
Secy, Middlesex Co Rep Orgn, NJ
b Mannington, WVa, Nov 30, 30; d Ardas Leo Straight & Nellie Starkey S; m 1961 to George Norman Abbott IV. Educ: Wash Sch Secretaries, grad, 49; Rutgers Univ, AB, 59; Rutgers Women's Club; Student Activities Comt. Polit & Govt Pos: Corresponding secy, Middlesex Co Young Rep NJ, 57-58; dist bd elec clerk, Dist Five, Edison Twp, 58-61; campaign secy, Edison Twp Cand, 59, hq mgr, Edison Twp Elec, 59; campaign secy, Middlesex Co Freeholder Cand, 60; mem, Metuchen Rep Club, 61-; committeewoman, Dist Four, Metuchen, 61-; campaign aid, Rodgers' Cong Campaign, 62, campaign coordr, 64; Rep State Committeewoman, NJ, 65; chmn, Helen DuMont Day, Middlesex Co, 65; mem, State Fedn Rep Women, 65-; mem, New Brunswick Rep Club, 65-; mgr, C John Stroumtsos Campaign for Cong, 66; asst in conducting co wide sem, Co Rep Comt, 66; personal adv & campaign activities coordr, Walter J Duff Mayoralty Cand, Metuchen, 67; alt deleg, Rep Nat Conv, 68; state co-chmn, Nixon Tel Campaign, 68; vpres, Middlesex Co Women's Rep Club, 69; munic vchmn, Rep Party, Metuchen, 69-74, chmn, 74; comnr, Middlesex Co Charter Study Comn, 74-75; secy, Middlesex Co Rep Orgn, 75- Bus & Prof Pos: Secy to vpres, C J Osborn Co, Linden, NJ, 5 years; secy to Dean Mary Bunting, Douglas Col, 1 year; asst mgr catalyst sales, Englehardt Minerals Corp, 3 years; teacher, Woodbridge Twp Bd Educ, 59- Mem: NJ Educ Asn; Am Fedn Teachers; Eastern Star; Rutgers Univ Col Alumni Asn (pres, 75-); Roosevelt Hosp Auxiliary. Honors & Awards: Distinguished Alumnus Award, Rutgers Univ Col; Award for Outstanding Serv, Rep Party Metuchen, 68. Relig: Presbyterian. Mailing Add: 67 Home St Metuchen NJ 08840

ABBOTT, GEORGE WILLIAM (R)
m 1955 to Marie Micheo; c Jeanne Marie & George Walter. Polit & Govt Pos: Gen counsel, House Interior & Insular Affairs Comt, 53-57; asst secy, Dept Interior, 57-58; solicitor, 58-60, asst secy pub land mgt, 60-61; mem, Alaska Rwy Comn, 54-61; chmn, Nev Rep Party, 65-72; deleg, Rep Nat Conv, 68; mem, Rep Nat Comt, 70-72. Mailing Add: PO Box 98 Minden NV 89423

ABBOTT, HETTIE (D)
Chmn, Newton Co Dem Cent Comt, Ind
b Manito, Ill, Jan 2, 20; d Perry Owen Bailey & Aggie B Cox B; m 1953 to William Abbott; c Bernard & Douglas Hiestand, Lois (Mrs Abraham) & Charles Abbott. Educ: Morocco High Sch, Ind, grad, 38. Polit & Govt Pos: Vchmn, Newton Co Dem Cent Comt, Ind, 66-73, chmn, 73-; secy, Second Dist Dem Comt, 68- Bus & Prof Pos: Justice of Peace, Lake Twp, Lake Village, Ind, 62- Mem: Moose Club; Am Legion Auxiliary 375; 8 et 40 Salon 668. Honors & Awards: Community Serv Award, first in state, Lake Village Grange, 61 & 62; Oil Painting, first in state, Lake Village Grange, 63. Mailing Add: Rte 1 Lake Village IN 46349

ABBOTT, JAMES (D)
Idaho State Rep
Mailing Add: Swanlake ID 83281

ABBOTT, LONNIE LOWELL (D)
Okla State Rep
b Ada, Okla, Dec 5, 25; s Noah T Abbott & Willie Francis Smith A; m 1947 to Willa Dean Walker; c Tamara Sue. Educ: ECent State Col, BA, 49; Okla Univ, MA, 52. Polit & Govt Pos: Okla State Rep, Dist 25, 60- Bus & Prof Pos: Prin, Homer Schs, 54-64; dir community action, Pontotoc Co, 65; field serv rep, Okla Educ Syst, 66- Mil Serv: Entered as A/S, Navy, 44, released as Seaman 3/C, 46, after serv in Asian Theater, 45-46; Asian Combat Ribbon; Good Conduct Medal. Mem: Nat & Okla Educ Asns; Mason; Shrine. Relig: Baptist. Mailing Add: Rte 3 Ada OK 74820

ABBOTT, S L (R)
Dep State Chmn, Rep Party, Tex
b Fairview, Okla, July 23, 24; s Aaron Floyd Abbott & Vera Goodwin A; m 1945 to Arline E Beahler; c Alan R. Educ: Tex Western Col; Pac Univ, BS, 52, OD, 53; Univ Tex, MA; Omega Epsilon Phi. Polit & Govt Pos: Asst precinct chmn, Rep Party, 60; nominee for Tex State Sen, 62, 64 & 66; mem, Citizen's Adv Coun, El Paso, 65; chmn, El Paso Co Rep Party, 65-66; mem, Rep Nat Comt Task Force to Study State Const Rev, 66-67; mem, Tex Rep Comt Fed Employ, currently; dep state chmn, Rep Party, Tex, currently; cand for comptroller pub acct, State of Tex, 70; Deleg, Rep Nat Conv, 72. Bus & Prof Pos: Pvt practice of optom, 53-; ed, El Pasoan, 65- Mil Serv: Entered as Pvt, Army Air Force, 44, released as M/Sgt, 52, after serv in Pac Theater, 44; Victory & Good Conduct Medals; Bronze Battle Star; M/Sgt, Air Force Res. Mem: CofC. Honors & Awards: Testified as expert witness on Chamizal Treaty with Mex, US Senate For Rels Comt, 63. Relig: Catholic. Legal Res: 1316 Mathias Dr El Paso TX 79903 Mailing Add: 4806 Montana El Paso TX 78203

ABBOTT, WILLIAM SAUNDERS (R)
b Medford, Mass, June 2, 38; s Charles Theodoric Abbott & Evelyn Gertrude A; m 1961 to Susan Ellen Shaw; c Cathryn Clark, Stephen Shaw & David Holbrook. Educ: Harvard Col, AB magna cum laude, 60, Law Sch, LLB magna cum laude, 66; Phi Beta Kappa; DU Club; Hasty Pudding-Inst 1770. Polit & Govt Pos: Mem, Watertown Town Meeting, Mass, 64-66; mem, Watertown Rep Town Comt, 64-66; White House Fel, Washington, DC, 66-67; spec asst to secy agr, 67-68; dir, US Agr Prog Asia, US Dept Agr, 67-68; Rep cand US House Rep, 68; mem, Arlington Rep Town Comt, Mass, 68-73; chmn bd selectmen, Arlington, 72-73; mem, Plymouth Town Meeting, currently; comnr, Educ Comn of the States, currently. Bus & Prof Pos: Attorney, Ropes & Gray, Boston, Mass, 66; attorney, Cabot, Cabot & Forbes, vpres & gen counsel, Cabot, Cabot & Forbes Co, currently; pres, Found to Improve TV, Boston, Mass, currently. Mil Serv: Entered as Ens, Navy, 60, released as Lt(jg), 63, after serv in USS Barry, Atlantic, Caribbean & Mediter Oceans, 60-63; Lt, Res, 63-70; Spec Letter of Commendation from Area Comdr. Publ: The nonjury trial, Harvard Law Rev, 65 & Mod Practice Commentary, 66; Tax aspects of restoring the status quo, Boston Univ Law Rev, 66; The reversed transaction, J Taxation, 67. Mem: Harvard Law Rev; Mass & Am Bar Asns; White House Fel Asn; Harvard Club Boston. Relig: Unitarian. Mailing Add: Herring Way RD 2 Buzzards Bay MA 02532

ABDNOR, E JAMES (R)
US Rep, SDak
b Kennebec, SDak, Feb 13, 23; s Samuel J Abdnor & Mary Wehby A; single. Educ: Univ Nebr, Lincoln, BA, bus admin; Sigma Chi; Univ Nebr Student Coun. Polit & Govt Pos: Precinct worker, Lyman Co Rep Orgn; chmn, Lyman Co Young Rep, 50-52; chmn, SDak Young Rep League, 53-55; SDak State Sen, 56-68, pres-pro-tem, SDak State Senate, 67-68; Lt Gov, SDak, 69-70; US Rep, Second Dist, 73- Bus & Prof Pos: Farmer-rancher, Kennebec, SDak; high sch teacher & coach. Mem: Elks; Mason; Am Legion; SDak Wheat Producers; SDak Stockgrowers. Honors & Awards: Kennebec Jaycees Outstanding Young Farmer; SDak Jaycees Second Place Outstanding Young Farmer. Relig: Methodist. Legal Res: Kennebec SD 57544 Mailing Add: 1227 Longworth House Off Bldg Washington DC 20515

ABE, KAZUHISA (D)
b Pepeekeo, Hawaii, Jan 18, 14; s Manshiro Abe & Matsuyo Fujiwara A; m 1939 to Haruko Murakami; c Arnold T & Clyde T. Educ: Univ Hawaii, AB, 36; Univ Mich Law Sch, JD, 39. Polit & Govt Pos: Judge, Dist Courts of North & South Kohala, Hawaii, 40-44; supvr, Co of Hawaii, 46-52; Sen, Territory of Hawaii, 52-59; Hawaii State Sen, 59-62, vpres, Hawaii State Senate, 63-64, pres, 65-66; assoc justice, Supreme Court of Hawaii, 67-73. Mem: Hawaii State & Hawaii Co Bar Asns; Hilo Hongwanji Mission. Legal Res: 188 Terrace Dr Hilo HI 96720 Mailing Add: Suite 2634 Pac Trade Ctr 190 S King St Honolulu HI 96813

ABEL, GLENN FREDERICK (R)
Chmn, Licking Co Rep Party, Ohio
b Milwaukee, Wis, June 15, 32; s Elmer Charles Abel & Emma Schaefer A; m 1955 to Alice Ann Schroeder; c Lori Ann. Educ: Univ Ill, BArch, 55; Alpha Phi Omega; Phalanx; Am Inst Architects; Ordance Club; Rifle & Pistol Club. Polit & Govt Pos: Mem, Equalization Bd, Newark, Ohio, 64-65, mem bldg code comt, 65-69; chmn, Licking Co Rep Party, 66-; mem, Ohio Electoral Col, 68-72; mem, Ohio Rep State Cent & Exec Comt, 68-72; chmn, Licking Co Bd of Elec, 70-74. Bus & Prof Pos: Proj mgr, Joseph Baker & Assoc Architects, 57-61, chief of prod, 62- Mil Serv: Entered as 2nd Lt, Army, 55, released as 1st Lt, 57, serv as unit commander, 46th RCAT Detachment; reentered, 61, released as 1st Lt, 62 after serv in 150 Armor Cavalry. Mem: Jr CofC Int; Licking Co Hist Soc (trustee); Licking Co Humane Soc (pres); Univ Ill Alumni Asn; Licking Co Retarded Childrens Coun (bd mem). Honors & Awards: Distinguished Serv Award, 64-67; Outstanding Nat Dir US Jaycees; Cert of Award, James F Lincoln Arc Welding Found; Jr CofC Senatorship. Relig: Lutheran. Mailing Add: 1482 Krebs Dr Newark OH 43055

ABELE, HOMER EUGENE (R)
b Wellston, Ohio, Nov 21, 16; s Oscar Abele & Margaret Burke A; m 1938 to Addie Riggs; c Terrell Ann (Mrs Robert Smith), Peter Burke & Andy. Educ: Ohio State Univ Col Law, grad, 53, JD, 70. Polit & Govt Pos: Ohio State Rep, 49-52; asst to campaign mgr for Sen Robert A Taft, Rep Nat Conv, 52; deleg, Rep Nat Conv, 56; US Rep, Ohio, 62-64; judge, Fourth Dist Court of Appeals, Ohio, 67- Bus & Prof Pos: Mem staff, Anchor-Hocking Glass, Lancaster, Ohio; mem staff, Austin Proder Co, McArthur, Ohio, 41; patrolman, Ohio State Hwy Patrol, Van Wert, 41-43 & 46; legis counsel, Spec Transportation Comt, 53-57. Mil Serv: Army Air Corps, 43-46. Mem: Am Legion (exec officer to Past State Comdr & judge advocate, Dept of Ohio, 70-71); Am Legion Buckeye Boy's State (chmn court sect); McArthur Develop Asn (prog chmn); Southeastern Ohio Regional Coun (Vinton Co trustee). Mailing Add: McArthur OH 45651

ABELL, TYLER (D)
b Washington, DC, Aug 9, 32; s George Abell & Luvie Butler Moore A; m 1955 to Elizabeth Hughes Clements; c Dan Tyler & Lyndon. Educ: Amherst Col, AB, 54; George Washington Univ Law Sch, LLB, 59; Phi Delta Phi; Chi Psi. Polit & Govt Pos: Mem, Organizers Comt, Citizens for Lyndon Johnson for Pres, 60; asst to exec asst to Postmaster Gen, Post Off Dept, 61-62, spec asst to Postmaster Gen, 62-63, assoc gen counsel, 63, asst postmaster gen, 64-67; Chief of Protocol, Dept of State, 68-69. Bus & Prof Pos: Law clerk, Covington & Burling, 58-59, George Washington Law Sch, 59 & DC Circuit Court of Appeals, 59-60; partner, Ginsburg & Feldman, 67-68 & McCormack & Bregman, currently. Mil Serv: Entered as Pvt, Army, 55, released as Pfc, 56. Publ: Various law review articles, George Washington Law Rev, 59. Mem: DC & Va Bar Asns; Big Bros of Am (nat dir); Big Bros of Nat Capital Area; DC Health & Welfare Coun. Relig: Episcopal. Mailing Add: 1830 24th St NW Washington DC 20008

ABELN, LYLE (DFL)
Minn State Rep
Legal Res: 10930 Thomas Ave S Minneapolis MN 55431 Mailing Add: State Capitol Bldg St Paul MN 55155

ABER, L M (LARRY) (R)
Mont State Sen
Mailing Add: 228 Third Ave North Columbus MT 59019

ABERCROMBIE, NEIL (D)
Hawaii State Rep
Mailing Add: House Sgt-at-Arms State Capitol Honolulu HI 96813

ABERNATHY, THOMAS JEROME (D)
VChmn, Tenn State Dem Exec Comt
b Jacksonville, Fla, Jan 4, 33; s John Matthews Abernathy, Sr & Helen Price A; m 1961 to Mary Elizabeth Peters. Educ: US Mil Acad, BS, 54; Univ Tenn Col Law, Knoxville, JD, 63; Phi Alpha Delta. Polit & Govt Pos: Admin asst to State Comptroller, Tenn, 63-64; admin asst to State Purchasing Comnr, 64-66; nat committeeman, Tenn Young Dem, 66-68; chmn, Giles Co Elec Comn, 67-70; vchmn, State Dem Exec Comt, Sixth Cong Dist & 17th State Sen Dist, Tenn, 70- Bus & Prof Pos: Attorney-at-law, Abernathy & Abernathy, 66- Mil Serv: Entered as 2nd Lt, Air Force, 54, released as 1st Lt, after serv in 47th Fighter Interceptor Squadron Air Defense Command, 56-58. Mem: Giles Co Bar Asn (pres, 74-75); Tenn Trial Lawyers Asn; Mason; Am Legion; Elks. Relig: Episcopal. Legal Res: 205 W College St Pulaski TN 38478 Mailing Add: PO Box 382 Pulaski TN 38478

ABERNETHY, THOMAS GERSTLE (D)
b Eupora, Miss, May 16, 03; s Thomas Franklin Abernethy & Minnie Agnes Jinkins A; m 1936 to Alice Margaret Lamb; c Margaret Gail, Thomas G Jr & Alice Kay. Educ: Univ Ala, 20-23; Cumberland Univ, LLB, 24; Spec Student, Univ Miss Law Sch, 24-25; Lambda Chi Alpha; honorary, Alpha Kappa Psi. Polit & Govt Pos: Mayor, Eupora, Miss, 27-29; dist attorney, Third Judicial Dist, Miss, 35-42; US Rep, Miss, 42-73; retired. Bus & Prof Pos: Lawyer & dir, NE Miss Coun. Mem: Miss State & Chickasaw Co Bar Asns; Mason; Shrine; Okolona CofC. Relig: Methodist. Mailing Add: Okolona MS 38860

ABINANTI, THOMAS J (D)
b Brooklyn, NY, Dec 28, 46; s Thomas Abinanti & Felicia Maggiacomo A; m 1969 to Beverly Buffa; c Nicole. Educ: Fordham Col, BA, 68; NY Univ Sch Law, JD, 72; student govt, newspaper, debating team. Polit & Govt Pos: Co committeeman, Dem Party, Bronx, NY, 70-72; deleg, Dem Nat Conv, 72; dist committeeman, Dem Party, Norwalk, Conn, 73-74; legis asst, US House Rep, 74; counsel, NY State Assembly Dem Study Group, 75- Bus & Prof Pos: Attorney, Norwalk, Conn, 72-74. Publ: Co-auth, The environment, Ann Survey Am Law, 71. Mem: Am Bar Asn. Honors & Awards: Legis internship, NY State Senate, 69; Ann Survey of Am Law, NY Univ Law Sch, 70. Mailing Add: Park Guilderland Guilderland Center NY 12085

ABLARD, CHARLES DAVID (R)
Gen Counsel, Dept of Army
b Enid, Okla, Oct 25, 30; s Charles R Ablard & Mary M Pattie A; m 1959 to Doris Maria Perl; c Jennifer Ann, Jonathan David & Catherine Mary. Educ: Univ Okla, BBA, 52, LLB, 54; George Washington Univ, LLM, 59; Phi Alpha Delta, Congress Club. Polit & Govt Pos: Judicial officer, Post Off Dept, 58-60; gen counsel, US Info Agency, 69-72; assoc dep attorney gen, Dept of Justice, 72-74; gen counsel, Dept of Army, 75- Bus & Prof Pos: Partner law firm, Ablard & Harrison, 60-63; vpres, Mag Publ Asn, 63-69. Mil Serv: Entered as 2nd Lt, Air Force, 54, released as 1st Lt, 56, after serv in Air Univ, Maxwell AFB, Ala & 43rd AD, Japan; Col, Air Force Res, 75- Publ: Co-auth, The Post Office & Publishers Pursestrings, George Washington Univ Law Rev, 62; ed, Manual of Federal Administrative Procedure, Bar Asn of DC, 64; auth, The international telecommunications consortium conference, European Broadcasting Union J, 70. Mem: Am Bar Asn (mem spec comt, Lawyers in Govt); Barristers; Army-Navy Country Club. Honors & Awards: Plainsman Award, Enid High Sch, Okla. Relig: Episcopal. Mailing Add: 229 S Pitt Alexandria VA 22314

ABLE, WILLIAM F (R)
Chmn, Columbia Rep Party, SC
b Saluda, SC, July 27, 33; s Otis Able & Bertha Riley A; m 1962 to Carol Ann Heft; c Jeffrey & Stephen. Educ: Univ SC, AB, 59, LLB, 61; Tau Kappa Alpha; Omicron Delta Kappa; Phi Alpha Delta. Polit & Govt Pos: City judge, Cayce, SC, 66-68; rev authority, Dept Health, Educ & Welfare, 69-; chmn, Columbia Rep Party, SC, 69-; asst co attorney, Richland Co, 73-74, co attorney, 74- Bus & Prof Pos: Admin asst, Am Bar Asn, 61-63; exec secy, SC Bar Asn, 63-64. Mil Serv: Entered as Pvt, Army, 53, released as Sgt, after serv in 33rd Inf Regt in Caribbean, 54-56; Nat Defense Ribbon; Am Spirit of Honor & Good Conduct Medals. Mem: SC, Richland Co & Am Bar Asns; Commercial Law League; DAV. Relig: Methodist. Legal Res: 4430 Ivy Hall Dr Columbia SC 29206 Mailing Add: 700 Security Fed Bldg Columbia SC 29201

ABLES, CHARLES ROBERT (R)
Mem, Tenn Rep State Exec Comt
b South Pittsburg, Tenn, Sept 13, 30; s William McKinley Ables & Dr Iva Baldwin A; m 1948 to Rada Belle Edmonds; c Patricia Joan & Barbara Elane. Educ: Univ Tenn, Chattanooga, BS, 62, LLB, 65. Polit & Govt Pos: Chmn, Marion Co Rep Party, Tenn, 68-70; mem, Tenn Rep State Exec Comt, 75- Bus & Prof Pos: Attorney-at-law, South Pittsburg, Tenn, 65- Mil Serv: Nat Guard. Mem: AFL-CIO United Lime & Gypsum Workers; Mason (32 degree); Scottish Rite; Lions; CofC. Relig: Presbyterian. Legal Res: 105 Lee Hunt South Pittsburg TN 37380 Mailing Add: Box 232 Cedar Ave South Pittsburg TN 37380

ABLONDI, ITALO H (D)
b Parma, Italy, Aug 25, 29; s Eugene Ablondi & Ernesta Percudani A; m 1952 to Unalane Carter; c Leigh, Kim & Phillip. Educ: Georgetown Univ Sch Foreign Serv, BSFS; St John's Univ Sch Law, LLB. Polit & Govt Pos: Comnr, US Tariff Comn, 72-74; comnr, US Int Trade Comn, 75- Mem: Bar Asn of New York; Am Bar Asn. Legal Res: NY Mailing Add: US Int Trade Comn Washington DC 20436

ABOUREZK, JAMES G (D)
US Sen, SDak
b Wood, SDak, Feb 24, 31; s Charles Abourezk & Lena Mickel A; m 1952 to Mary Houlton; c Charles, Nikki June & Paul. Educ: SDak Sch of Mines, BS Civil Eng, 61; Univ SDak Law Sch, JD, 66. Polit & Govt Pos: Deleg, Dem Nat Conv, 68; Dem cand for Attorney Gen, SDak, 68; US Rep, SDak, 71-73; deleg, Dem Nat Conv, 72; US Sen, SDak, 73-, mem budget comt, US Senate, currently, chmn separation of powers subcomt, currently, chmn Indian Affairs subcomt, currently, chmn Am Indian policy rev comn, currently. Bus & Prof Pos: Attorney-at-law, James Abourezk Law Off, 66-70. Mil Serv: Entered as Recruit, Navy, 48, released as Fireman, 52, after serv in Pac and Far East Theatres, 49-51. Publ: South Dakota Indian jurisdiction, SDak Law Rev, 66. Mem: Am Trial Lawyers Asn; Am & SDak Bar Asns. Relig: Syrian Orthodox. Legal Res: Rapid City SD 57701 Mailing Add: US Senate Washington DC 20510

ABRAHAM, DONALD A (D)
Pa State Rep
Mailing Add: Capitol Bldg Harrisburg PA 17120

ABRAHAM, GEORGE DOUGLAS (D)
Miss State Rep
b Greenville, Miss, June 19, 37; s George Abraham & Lily Thomas A; m 1972 to Sally Montgomery McGee. Educ: Univ Miss, BA, 59, LLB, 61; Omicron Delta Kappa; Kappa Alpha Order. Polit & Govt Pos: Miss State Rep, 67-; consult, Off Emergency Preparedness, 72-75; mem, Nat Civil Defense Adv Coun, 72-75. Bus & Prof Pos: Partner, Abraham & Gleason, Attorneys, currently; pres, Alco Tel Answering Serv, currently. Mem: Miss & Washington Co Bar Asns; Phi Alpha Delta; Elks; Moose. Relig: Methodist. Legal Res: Ashburn Plantation Greenville MS 38701 Mailing Add: Abraham Bldg Greenville MS 38701

ABRAHAM, JULIETTE ELIZABETH (R)
Mem, Rep State Cent Comt, Mich
b Spring Valley, Ill, Sept 14, 18; d Michael Sear & Mary Habib S; m 1946 to Eddie Joseph Abraham; c Edward Spencer. Educ: Woodward High Sch, Toledo, Ohio, grad, 37. Polit & Govt Pos: TAR adv, Rep Party of Lansing, Mich, 67-69, precinct chmn, 68-69; mem, Ingham Co Rep Party, 69-, membership chmn, 69-, mem exec comt, 70-, Sen Robert Griffin chmn, 72; deleg, Mich State Rep Conv, 69-; chmn, Sixth Dist Rep Comt, currently; mem, State Bd Librs, 71-72; mem, Rep State Cent Comt, 71-; deleg, Rep Nat Conv, 72. Relig: Greek Orthodox. Mailing Add: 1125 Hitching Post Rd East Lansing MI 48823

ABRAHAMS, W DEAN (R)
Idaho State Sen
b Topeka, Kans, Sept 3, 15; s Olaf M Abrahams & Sarah Reeder A; married & separated; c Dee Ann (Mrs David Wiley). Educ: Kans State Col, 35-37; Alpha Gamma Rho. Polit & Govt Pos: Legis chmn, Idaho Rep Party, Dist 11, 70-72; Idaho State Sen, Dist 11, 72- Mil Serv: ROTC, Kans State Col. Mem: Nat Livestock Dealers Asn (pres, 66-68, dir, 68-); Idaho Cattle Feeders Asn (secy, 59-63); Lions (past dir, 27 years perfect attendance). Honors & Awards: Friend of 4H, 71. Relig: Methodist. Legal Res: 1802 Montana St Caldwell ID 83605 Mailing Add: 116 S Seventh Ave Caldwell ID 83605

ABRAM, MORRIS BERTHOLD (D)
b Fitzgerald, Ga, June 19, 18; s Sam Abram & Irene Cohen A; formerly m 1944 to Jane McGuire; c Ruth, Ann, Morris Berthold, Jonathan Adam & Joshua Anthony. Educ: Univ Ga, AB summa cum laude, 38; Univ Chicago, JD, 40; Oxford Univ, Rhodes Scholar, BA, 48, MA, 53; Phi Beta Kappa; Omicron Delta Kappa; Phi Kappa Phi. Polit & Govt Pos: Mem prosecuting comt, Internal Mil Tribunal, Nuremburg, Germany, 46; asst to dir, Comt for Marshall Plan, 48; counsel & pub bd mem, Regional Wage Stabilization Bd for South, 51; gen counsel, Peace Corps, 61; chmn, Nat Exec Bd & mem, Subcomt on Prev of Discrimination & Protection Minorities, UN, 63-65; co-chmn, White House Conf Civil Rights, 65; US Rep, UN Comn on Human Rights, 65-68; mem, Nat Adv Coun Econ Opportunity, 67-; co-chmn, Nat Priorities Comt, Dem Party Nat Adv Coun. Bus & Prof Pos: Partner, Paul, Weiss, Rifkind, Wharton & Garrison, New York, NY, 62-68; pres, Brandeis Univ, 68-70; partner, Paul, Weiss, Rifkind, Wharton & Garrison, currently. Mil Serv: USAAF, 41-45, serv to Maj; Legion of Merit. Publ: Co-auth, How to stop violence in your community, 50. Mem: Am, NY State, New York City & Atlanta, Ga Bar Asns; Am Jewish Comt (nat pres, 64-68). Honors & Awards: Hon fel, Pembroke Col, Oxford Univ; Named Hon Citizen of Atlanta, Ga, 66; Human Rights Award, Int League Rights of Man, 74. Legal Res: 165 E 72nd St New York NY 10021 Mailing Add: 345 Park Ave New York NY 10022

ABRAMS, MICHAEL I (D)
Chmn, Dade Co Dem Party, Fla
b Flushing, NY, Dec 7, 47; s Jack Abrams & Sally Miller A; m 1973 to Nancy Jean Pastirjak. Educ: Univ Miami, cum laude, 69; Omicron Delta Kappa; pres, Pi Kappa Alpha & Student Govt. Polit & Govt Pos: Chmn, Fla Youth for Robert Kennedy, 68; hon chmn, Dade Youth for Humphrey-Muskie, 68; pres, Fla Young Dem, 70-71; admin asst to State Treas Tom O'Malley, 71-72; chmn, Sen McGovern's Campaign, 12th Cong Dist, Fla, 72; state field rep, McGovern Fla Campaign, 72; exec dir, Fla Concerned Dem, 72-; chmn, Dade Co Dem Party, currently; vpres, Young Dem Am, currently; mem exec comt, SFla Health Planning Coun, currently. Honors & Awards: Outstanding Undergrad in Southeast, Pi Kappa Alpha; Outstanding Young Dem Fla, 72. Legal Res: 18701 NW 23rd Ave Miami FL 33055 Mailing Add: Dem Party Hq 10 Biscayne Blvd Miami FL 33131

ABRAMS, NANCY JEAN (D)
Nat Committeewoman, Young Dem Fla
b St Petersburg, Fla, Aug 12, 51; d George Pastirjak & Juliette Mastry P; m 1973 to Michael Abrams. Educ: Univ Munich; St Petersburg Jr Col, 2 years. Polit & Govt Pos: Student & asst coordr, Pinellas Co McGovern for President Campaign, 71-72; vchairperson & founder, Pinellas Co Chap, Concerned Dem Fla, 72-73, state treas, 74-75; state committeewoman, Young Dem Fla, 72-73, nat committeewoman, 74-; mem affirmative action comt, State Dem Party, 74-75, mem cent steering comt, 75-; dist committeewoman, Dade Co Dem Party, 74-, chairperson, Annual Issues Conv, 75; admin asst, State Sen Sherman Winn, 74- Honors & Awards: Excellence in Speech Making, Eng Dep & Citizenship Award, Merritt Island High Sch, 69; Appreciation Award, Pinellas Co Concerned Dem, 73; Pres Award, Young Dem Fla, 74. Legal Res: 18701 NW 23rd Ave Miami FL 33055 Mailing Add: 111 NW 183rd St Miami FL 33169

ABRAMS, ROBERT (D)
Pres, Borough of the Bronx, New York
b Bronx, NY, July 4, 38; s Benjamin Abrams & Dorothy Kaplan A; single. Educ: Columbia Col, AB, 60; NY Univ Sch Law, JD, 63; pres, Alpha Chap, Phi Sigma Delta. Polit & Govt Pos: NY State Assemblyman, 66-69; pres, Borough of the Bronx, New York, currently; deleg, Dem Nat Conv, 72; alt deleg, Dem Nat Mid-Term Conf, 74. Bus & Prof Pos: Attorney, Henry H Abrams, New York, 64-69. Publ: Negligent golfer, NY Univ Intramural Law Rev, 3/63. Mem: NY State & Bronx Co Bar Asns; KofP; B'nai B'rith; Dayan Club of Pelham Parkway (pres). Honors & Awards: Membership Award, Bronx Co Zionist Orgn of Am; Interfaith Award of the Coun of Churches, City of New York, 69; Brotherhood Award of B'nai B'rith, 70; Bronx Community Col Medallion for Serv, 70; Scroll of Honor Plaque, United Jewish Appeal, 70. Relig: Jewish. Mailing Add: 2125 Holland Ave Bronx NY 10462

ABRAMS, ROSALIE SILBER (D)
Md State Sen
b Baltimore, Md; m 1953 to William Abrams; c Elizabeth Joan. Educ: Sinai Hosp Sch Nursing; Columbia Univ; Johns Hopkins Univ, BS, 63, MA, 69. Polit & Govt Pos: Mem exec bd, Md Comprehensive Health Planning Agency; Md Comn on Status of Women; chmn, Md Humane Practices Comn; mem exec comt & chmn legis comt, Baltimore Area Coun on Alcoholism, 70-74; exec bd, Am Jewish Comt & mem, Domestic Affairs Comt; mem, Fifth Dist Reform Dem, Md; adv coun, Community Coord Child Care; bd dirs, Md Hosp Educ & Research Found; Md State Deleg, 67-71, chmn, Health & Welfare Subcomt & Ways & Means Comt, Md House Deleg, 67-71; Md State Sen, 71-, mem, Finance Comt & Joint Comt on Capital Budget, Md State Senate, 71-74, mem budget, taxation comt, 75, mem, Comn to Study Implementation of Equal Rights Amendment, chmn, Financial & Housing Subcomt; exec bd, Md Dem State Cent Comt, 74. Mil Serv: Navy Nurses Corps, World War II. Mem: Sinai Hosp (bd dirs); Safety First Club Md (bd); Md Order Women Legislators (pres, 75); Nat Legis Conf (mem intergovt rels comt, 74-); Coun State Govts (vchmn human resources & urban affairs comt). Honors & Awards: Louise Waterman Wise Community Serv Award, 69; Award of Achievement, Am Acad Comprehensive Health Planning, 71; Traffic Safety Award, 71; News-American Award, 71; Woman of Distinction in Med; Jewish Nat Fund Award for legislative ability, 75. Mailing Add: 6205 Wirt Ave Baltimore MD 21215

ABRAMSON, EDWARD (D)
NY State Assemblyman
Mailing Add: 163-39 130th Ave Jamaica NY 11434

ABRAMSON, MURRAY (D)
Md State Deleg
b Dec 28, 02; s Abraham Abramson & Sadie Friedlander A; m 1939 to Helaine Rose Whitehill; c Alan Carroll. Educ: Grad, Baltimore City Col. Polit & Govt Pos: Examr, Baltimore Rent Comn; bus analyst, Off Price Stabilization; Md State Deleg, Fifth Legis Dist, currently, chmn, Baltimore City Deleg, Md House Deleg, 62-70, mem, Budget & Finance Comt, 67, mem, Ways & Means Comt & Legis Coun & Asst Majority Floor Leader, currently; deleg, Md Const Conv. Bus & Prof Pos: Exec, retail clothing firm, 20 years; pres, local retail union, 10 years; bus agent & contract negotiator, Amalgamated Clothing Workers Retail Div, 3 years. Relig: Jewish. Mailing Add: 3118 Parkington Ave Baltimore MD 21215

ABRIL, TONY RODRIGUEZ (D)
Ariz State Rep
b Phoenix, Ariz; s William N Abril & Trinidad Rodriguez A; div; c Mary Ellen (Mrs Ruiz), Pauline (Mrs Garcia), Grace (Mrs Hiouas) & Tony, Jr. Educ: Wiggins Col, 53; Phoenix Col, Ariz, 66. Polit & Govt Pos: Ariz State Rep, 66, 68-70 & 73- Bus & Prof Pos: Cement contractor. Mil Serv: Pvt, Army, 43-45, serv in US Paratroops, Europe, 44-45; Good Conduct Medal. Mem: Am Legion; Cement Masons 394. Relig: Catholic. Mailing Add: 602 W Jones Phoenix AZ 85041

ABSHIRE, DAVID MANKER (R)
b Chattanooga, Tenn, Apr 11, 26; s James Ernest Abshire & Edith Manker Patten A; m 1957 to Carolyn Lamar Sample; c Lupton, Anna, Mary Lee & Phyllis. Educ: US Mil Acad, BS, 51; Georgetown Univ, PhD, 59; Phi Alpha Theta. Polit & Govt Pos: Dir research, House Rep Policy Comt, 58-60; Asst Secy State Cong Rels, 70-72; Mem, Comn on the Orgn of Govt for the Conduct of Foreign Policy, 73-; chmn, US Bd Int Broadcasting, 74-; mem bd adv, Naval War Col, 75- Bus & Prof Pos: Dir spec proj, Am Enterprise Inst, 61-62; exec dir, Ctr Strategic & Int Studies, Georgetown Univ, 62-70, chmn, 73- Mil Serv: Entered as Cadet, US Mil Acad, 47, released as 1st Lt, 55, after serv as Co Comdr, 14th Inf Regt, 25th Div, Korean War, 52-53; Capt Res; Bronze Star with V & Oak Leaf Cluster; Commendation Ribbon with Medal Pendant. Publ: The South Rejects a Prophet: the Life of Senator D M Key, 1824-1900 & co-ed & auth chap, In: Portuguese Africa; a Handbook, 69, Praeger; National Security: Political, Military & Economic Strategies in the Decade Ahead, Hoover Inst, 63. Mem: Foreign Policy Asn; Am Acad Polit & Soc Sci; Int Inst Strategic Studies; Chevy Chase Club; Army & Navy Club. Relig: Episcopal. Mailing Add: 311 S St Asaph St Alexandria VA 22314

ABZUG, BELLA S (D)
US Rep, NY
b New York, NY, July 24, 20; d Emanuel Savitzky & Esther S; m 1944 to Martin Abzug; c Eve Gail & Isobel. Educ: Hunter Col, AB; Columbia Law Sch; Jewish Theol Sem; ed, Columbia Law Rev. Polit & Govt Pos: Initiator, Women Strike for Peace Movement; mem exec comt, Nat & State New Dem Coalition; US Rep, NY, 71-; deleg, Dem Nat Conv, 72; deleg, Dem Nat Mid-Term Conf, 74. Bus & Prof Pos: Practicing attorney 23 years. Legal Res: 37 Banks St New York NY 10014 Mailing Add: 252 Seventh Ave New York NY 10001

ACCARDO, JOSEPH, JR (D)
La State Rep
Mailing Add: PO Drawer F LaPlace LA 70068

ACEBO, ALEXANDER VALENTINO (R)
Auditor Acct, Vt
b Barre, Vt, Sept 5, 27; s Ferman Acebo & Elvira Lastra A; div; c Wendy Lee, Lynn Ann & Nancy Mollie. Educ: Bryant Col, BSBA, 52; Tau Epsilon. Polit & Govt Pos: Sch comnr, Barre, Vt, 64-70; Auditor Acct, Vt, 70- Mil Serv: Entered as Pvt, Army, 46, released as T/Sgt, 49, after serv in Army Finance Div, Far East, 47-49; Theatre Ribbon. Mem: Nat Asn State Comptrollers, Auditors & Treas; New Eng States Munic Finance Officers Asn; Munic Finance Officers Asn US & Can; Barre Elks; Barre Kiwanis (pres, 72-). Relig: Protestant; Treas, Barre Congregational Church, 63- Mailing Add: PO Box 818 Barre VT 05641

ACKAL, ELIAS, JR (D)
La State Rep
Mailing Add: 818 Center St New Iberia LA 70562

ACKER, ROBERT HAROLD (R)
b Morenci, Mich, Feb 13, 28; s Harold E Acker & Hazel C Miller A; single. Educ: Mich State Univ, grad, 51. Polit & Govt Pos: Chmn, Isabella Co Rep Party, Mich, 72-75. Bus & Prof Pos: Bd mem, Mich Life Underwriters Prof Adv Comt, 68-74, Secy, 74- Mem: Saginaw Valley Chartered Life Underwriters; Cent Mich Asn Life Underwriters; Lions. Relig: Methodist. Mailing Add: 109 W Illinois Mt Pleasant MI 48588

ACKERMAN, B DONALD (D)
Committeeman, NY State Dem Comt
b Syracuse, NY, Feb 28, 36; s Bertrand A Ackerman & Josephine Lockwood A; m 1960 to Katherine Stryker; c Steven & Jane. Educ: Cornell Univ, 54-55; State Univ New York Col, Oneonta, BS, 61, MS, 64. Polit & Govt Pos: Committeeman, Schenectady Co Dem Comt, NY, 63-; chmn, Schenectady Co New Dem Coalition, 68-70; committeeman, NY State Dem Comt, 107th Assembly Dist, 72-; deleg, Dem Nat Mid-Term Conf, 74. Bus & Prof Pos: Teacher, Niskayuna Pub Schs, Schenectady, NY, 61- Mil Serv: Entered as Pvt, Army, 56, released as SP-5, 58, after serv in 25th Inf Div, Schofield Barracks, 57-58. Mem: New York

State United Teachers; Common Cause; New York State Dem Comt (sustaining mem); Niskayuna Teachers Asn. Relig: Unitarian. Mailing Add: 812 DeCamp Ave Schenectady NY 12309

ACKERMAN, SAM (D)
b New York, NY, Dec 23, 34; s Joseph Ackerman (deceased) & Regina Marmorstein A; (deceased); m second time 1970 to Martha Sue Gordon; c Jodie Rebecca, David Alan, Valerie Jay & Joseph Bradford. Educ: Cornell Univ, AB, 56; Univ Chicago, MBA, 66; Watermargin. Polit & Govt Pos: Nat bd mem, Am for Dem Action, Ill, 70-; deleg, Dem Nat Conv, 72; deleg, Dem Nat Mid-Term Conf, 74. Bus & Prof Pos: Personnel dir, Continental Coffee, 60-67, sales manpower mgr, CFS-Continental, Inc, Chicago, 67-, dir sales training & educ, 74- Mem: Ill Training Dirs Asn; Chicago Sales Training Asn; Am Soc for Training & Develop; Nat Soc Sales Training Execs; Independent Voters of Ill (chmn, Near South Chap, 74-). Relig: Jewish. Mailing Add: 5318 S Kimbark Ave Chicago IL 60615

ACKERMANN, BARBARA (D)
City Counr, Cambridge, Mass
b Stockholm, Sweden, Mar 1, 25; d Benjamin Mayham Hulley & Joan Carrington H; m 1945 to Paul Kurt Ackermann; c Richard Paul & Joan Barbara. Educ: Smith Col, BA, 45. Polit & Govt Pos: Mem sch comt, Cambridge, Mass, 62-67, counr, 68-71 & 73-, mayor, 72-73; deleg, Dem Nat Conv, 72. Mailing Add: 41 Gibson St Cambridge MA 02138

ACKLEY, GARDNER (D)
b Indianapolis, Ind, June 30, 15; s Hugh M Ackley & Margaret McKenzie A; m 1937 to Bonnie Lowrey; c David A & Donald G. Educ: Western State Teacher's Col, AB, 36; Univ Mich, MA, 37, PhD, 40; Kappa Delta Phi; Tau Kappa Alpha; Phi Kappa Phi. Hon Degrees: LLD, Western Mich Univ, 64 & Kalamazoo Col, 67. Polit & Govt Pos: Consult, Nat Resources Planning Bd, 40-41; economist, Off Strategic Serv, 43-44; econ adv & asst dir, Off Price Stabilization, 51-52; consult, Dept Army, 61; mem, Coun Econ Adv, Washington, DC, 62-, chmn, 64-68; US Ambassador, Italy, 68-69; chmn comt on econ affairs, Dem Policy Coun, 69-72; mem, Sen McGovern's Adv Comt on Taxation & Econ, 72. Bus & Prof Pos: Consult, Ford Found, Brookings Inst, Nat Bur Econ Research, Mich Dept Finance, Fed Govt Agencies & Cong Comts, various times; instr, Ohio State Univ, 39-40; instr econ, Univ Mich, Ann Arbor, 40-41, asst prof, 46-47, assoc prof, 47-52, prof, 52-68, chmn dept, 54-61, Henry Carter Adams univ prof polit econ, 69-; vis staff mem, Univ Calif, Los Angeles, 49; mem ed bd, Am Econ Rev, 53-56; Fulbright research scholar, Italy, 56-57; dir, Soc Sci Research Coun, 59-62, chmn comt soc sci personnel & mem exec comt, 60-61; Ford Found faculty research fel, 61-62; consult, Baker, Weeks & Co, Inc, NY, 69-; bimonthly columnist on econ, Dun's, 71-; dir, Nat Bur Econ Research, 71-; trustee, Joint Coun Econ Educ, 71- Publ: Auth, Stemming World Inflation, Atlantic Inst, 71; An income policy for the 1970's, Rev Econ Statist, 8/72; Observations on Phase II Price & Wage Controls, Brookings Papers on Econ Activity, 72. Mem: Am Econ Asn (comt on honors & awards, 59-, chmn comt on research & publ, 59-61, vpres, 62); Am Asn Univ Prof; Mich Acad Sci, Arts & Letters; fel Am Acad Arts & Sci; Am Philos Soc. Honors & Awards: Cavaliere de Gran Croce dell'Ordine al Merito della Repubblica Italiana. Mailing Add: 907 Berkshire Rd Ann Arbor MI 48104

ACREE, WILLIAM B, JR (D)
Mem Exec Comt, Tenn Dem State Comt
b Memphis, Tenn, May 2, 44; s William B Acree & Kay McClintock A; m 1969 to Elizabeth Markham; c Kelly Jean. Educ: Univ Tenn, BS, 66, JD, 68; Phi Delta Pi; Alpha Tau Omega. Polit & Govt Pos: Mem exec comt, Tenn Dem State Comt, 74- Bus & Prof Pos: Mem law firm, Elam, Glasgow, Tanner & Acree, 73- Mil Serv: Entered as Pvt, Army, 68, released as Sgt, 70. Mem: Tenn & Am Bar Asns; Rotary; Jaycees; WTex Heart Asn (exec comt, 72-). Relig: Baptist. Legal Res: 525 E High St Union City TN 38261 Mailing Add: Box 250 Union City TN 38261

ADA, JOSEPH FRANKLIN (R)
Sen, Guam Legis
b Agana, Guam, Dec 3, 43; s Jose Torres Ada & Regina Herrero A; m 1967 to Rosanne Jacqueline Santos; c Eric J, Tricia, George & Anthony. Educ: Univ Guam, 63-65; Univ Portland, BA, 68; pres & treas, Int Friendship Club. Polit & Govt Pos: Chmn, Gov Comt on Children & Youth, Guam, 64-65; deleg & chmn, Comt on Bill of Rights, Guam Rep Const Conv, 69-70; chmn, Guam Water Pollution Control Comn, 69-72; dep dir, Dept Pub Works, Govt of Guam, 70-72; Sen, Guam Legis, 73- Bus & Prof Pos: Night mgr, Northberry Motel & Apt, Portland, Ore, 67-68; asst gen mgr, Ada's Inc, Agana, Guam, 68-70. Mem: Marianas Asn of Retarded Children; Guam's Northern Little League (vpres, 71-); SPac Games (asst coordr, 71-); Guam Amateur Sports Asn (pres, 72-). Relig: Catholic. Mailing Add: PO Box 6750 Tamuning GU 96911

ADA, VICENTE DIAZ (R)
Sen, Guam Legis
b Agana, Guam, Jan 24, 32; s Vicente Cepeda Ada (deceased) & Dolores Leon Guerrero Diaz A; m 1953 to Teresita Gutierrez Borja; c Vincent Joseph, Anita Marie, Bernaditta Dolores, Vicente Juan, Vicente Pedro, Vicente Edwardo, Vicente Ricardo & Vicente Antonio. Educ: High sch, Guam. Polit & Govt Pos: Mem, Small Bus Admin Adv Coun, Guam, 70-; Sen, Guam Legis, 71-, minority floor leader, 72- Bus & Prof Pos: Bourland Ins. Mil Serv: Entered as Airman Basic, Air Force, 53, released as S/Sgt, 64, after serv in 28th FMS, Ellsworth AFB, SDak, 54-64; Good Conduct Medal; Nat Defense Medal. Mem: Am Legion; PTA. Relig: Catholic. Legal Res: Afame Heights GU 96910 Mailing Add: PO Box 1214 Agana GU 96910

ADAIR, CHARLES WALLACE, JR
US Ambassador, Uruguay
b Xenia, Ohio, Jan 26, 14; s Charles Wallace Adair & Sarah Torrence Goulard A; m 1947 to Caroline Lee Marshall; c Marshall Porter, Caroline & Sarah. Educ: Univ Wis, AB, 35; Am Inst Banking, 37-38; George Washington Univ, 38-39; Princeton Univ, 47-48; Phi Gamma Delta. Polit & Govt Pos: Entered Foreign Serv, 40; vconsul, Nogales, Mex, 40-41 & Mexico City, 41; detailed to Foreign Serv Sch, US Dept of State, 41; vconsul, Bombay, India, 42-46; India desk officer, 46-47; first secy to Embassy & Consul, Rio de Janeiro, Brazil, 48-51; detailed to Nat War Col, Washington, DC 51-52; Counr of Embassy for Econ Affairs, Brussels; dep dir, US Opers Mission, Brussels; dep dir, NATO Adv Bur European Affairs, 52-54; US Comnr on Tripartite Comn for Restitution on Monetary Gold, 54; chmn, Colombo Plans Official Meeting, Seattle, 58; dep asst secy state for econ affairs, 59-61; dep secy gen, Orgn Econ Coop & Develop, Paris, France, 61-63; minister-counr dep chief Mission Am Embassy, Buenos Aires, Argentina, 63-65; US Ambassador, Panama, 65-69; US Ambassador, Uruguay, 69- Bus & Prof Pos: Credit investr, Chase Nat Bank, New York, 35-36 & 37-38, Panama City, 36-37. Mem: Univ Club, Washington; Royal Bombay Yacht Club, India. Relig: Episcopal. Legal Res: Stuart FL Mailing Add: US Dept of State Foreign Serv Washington DC 20521

ADAIR, E ROSS (R)
b Albion, Ind, Dec 14, 07; s Edwin L Adair & Alice Prickett A; m 1934 to Marian Wood; c Caroline (Mrs David Dimmers) & Stephen Wood. Educ: Hillsdale Col, AB, 28; George Washington Univ Law Sch, LLB, 33; LLD, Ind Inst Technol, 64; Delta Sigma Phi; Phi Alpha Delta. Polit & Govt Pos: Former probate comnr, Allen Co, Ind; mem, Interparliamentary Union, 59, 63-65 & 67-70; US Rep, Fourth Dist, Ind, 50-70, ranking minority mem, Foreign Affairs Comt, US House Rep, sr mem, Vet Affairs Comt, formerly; US Ambassador, Ethiopia, 71-74. Bus & Prof Pos: Mem law firm, Adair, Perry, Beers, McAlister & Mallers, Ft Wayne, Ind. Mil Serv: Entered as 2nd Lt, Army, 41, released as Maj, 45, after serv in 1st Army, ETO; Battle Stars for Normandy, Northern France, Ardennes, Rhine & Cent Europe Campaigns; Lt Col (Ret), Judge Adv Gen Corps, Army Res. Mem: Am, Ind & Allen Co Bar Asns; Mason (33 degree); Shrine. Honors & Awards: Silver Helmet Award, Amvets; Nat Asn State Dirs Vet Affairs Award, 65; Distinguished Serv Award, Ft Wayne Jr CofC, 40, Citizen of Week, 49. Relig: Methodist. Legal Res: Apt 1406 Three Rivers N Ft Wayne IN 46802 Mailing Add: 2200 Ft Wayne Bank Bldg Ft Wayne IN 46802

ADAIR, SIDNEY ARTHUR (R)
b Los Angeles, Calif, Feb 16, 28; s Herbert Spencer Adair & Mildred Geneva Gambrell A; m 1975 to Beverly Edgerton Corley; c Scott Laugharn & Christopher Laugharn Adair & J Kevin, Kent E, Mark H, Michael C & Stephen A Corley. Educ: Univ Southern Calif, 45-48; Babson Col, BS magna cum laude, 51; Univ Pa, MBA, 54; Univ Southern Calif, JD, 60; Trinity Univ; Univ Pittsburgh; Univ Calif, Los Angeles; Blue Key; Phi Alpha Delta; Alpha Kappa Psi; Chi Phi. Polit & Govt Pos: Organizer, mem & officer, various Young Rep Clubs, 50-67; victory squad col, 15th Cong Dist, 58, precinct capt, 60; originator, Rep Town Meetings, 58-59; organizer & adv Future Rep of W Los Angeles & Santa Monica, 59-63; speaker, Shell for Gov, 62; organizer & chmn, Miracle Mile Goldwater Comt, 64; organizer, Parklabrea Unit, United Rep of Calif, 64-67, organizer, mem bd & deleg, Wilshire-Crenshaw Unit, 65-67, parliamentarian, Area 11, 66 & 67, organizer & pres, Henry Hazlitt Unit, 66-68; vchmn, Region III, Ronald Reagan for Gov, 66; mem, Friends of Gov Reagan, 66-69; mem, Rep State Cent Comt, Calif, 67-69 & 71-74, assoc mem, 69-71; chmn strategy comt, Comt to Elect Newman, Martin & Ferraro, 68-69; mem, 56th Rep Assembly Club, 69; vchmn, Sch Bd Team, 71. Bus & Prof Pos: Research consult, Tex Elec Serv Co, Ft Worth, 54-55; liaison asst, US Steel Corp, Pittsburgh, Pa, 55-57; dep pub defender, Los Angeles Co, Calif, 60-61; mem legal staff & free enterprises dept, Coast Fed Savings & Loan Asn, Los Angeles, 61-62 & Speakers' Bur, 61-; part-time prof, Woodbury Univ, 62-65; partner, Gaston, Keltner & Adair, 62-65 & Burr, Smith & Adair, 66-71; sole practitioner, S A Adair, 72- Mil Serv: Entered as Pvt, Air Force, 51, released as 2nd Lt, 53, after serv in Human Resources Research Ctr, 52-53; Air Force Res, 53-59, Capt (Ret). Publ: Where do you stand?, Los Angeles Freedom Club, 56 & 58; 12 Legal duties & rights of parents to their children, Coast Fed Savings & Loan Asn, 62; info & educ articles, Los Angeles Co Young Rep, 62-63. Mem: Voices in Vital Am (chmn bd dirs); Temporomandibular Joint Research Found (bd dir); Leakey Found (fel); Calif Trial Lawyers Asn. Honors & Awards: Recipient of Outstanding Trophy, United Fund of Pittsburgh, Pa; Most Outstanding Trophy, Col of Letters, Arts & Sci, Univ Southern Calif; Outstanding Key, Babson Col; several speaking awards; Univ Southern Calif Law Rev. Relig: Unity; church coun chmn, mem, long range planning comt & greeter, First Congregational Church of Los Angeles. Legal Res: 321 Muirfield Rd Los Angeles CA 90020 Mailing Add: 9401 Wilshire Blvd Suite 1025 Beverly Hills CA 90212

ADAMS, A A (D)
Wash State Rep
Mailing Add: 3418 Shorecliff Dr NE Tacoma WA 98422

ADAMS, ALFRED O (R)
b Paola, Kans, 1897; m; c one. Educ: Univ Mo; Washington Univ, Med Sch, MD, 24. Polit & Govt Pos: Wash State Rep, 53-68; Rep Presidential elector, Wash, 72. Bus & Prof Pos: Retired physician & surgeon. Mil Serv: World War I. Mem: Mason. Mailing Add: W 909 Melinda Lane Spokane WA 99203

ADAMS, BERNARD CHARLES (R)
Mayor, Garden Grove, Calif
b Miami, Ariz, Apr 23, 23; s Joseph W Adams & Pauline Mucel A; m to Margaret Ruth Kohnke; c Stephen Michael, Mark Edward & Ginette Marie. Educ: Calif State Polytech Col, San Luis Obispo, BS Archit Eng, 50. Polit & Govt Pos: Bldg dep dir, City of Garden Grove, Calif, 57-63; city councilman, Garden Grove, 70-72, mayor, 72- Bus & Prof Pos: Calif licensed civil engr; self-employed archit engr, Garden Grove, Calif, 63-73. Mil Serv: Entered as Pvt, Air Force, 43, released as S/Sgt, 45, after serv in 404th Bomb Group, Pac, Tinian Isle, 44-45; Air Medal with Oak Leaf Cluster. Mem: Am Soc Prof Engrs; Lions; Elks. Relig: Catholic. Mailing Add: 12151 Burns Dr Garden Grove CA 92640

ADAMS, BROCKMAN (BROCK) (D)
US Rep, Wash
b Atlanta, Ga, Jan 13, 27; s Charles Leslie Adams & Vera Beemer A; m 1952 to Mary Elizabeth Scott; c Scott, Dean, Katherine & Aleen. Educ: Univ Wash, BA Econ, 49; Harvard Univ, JD, 52; Phi Beta Kappa; Phi Delta Theta. Polit & Govt Pos: US Attorney, Western Dist of Wash State, 61-64; US Rep, Seventh Cong Dist, Wash, 65-; deleg, Dem Nat Conv, 68. Bus & Prof Pos: Partner, Little, LeSourd, Palmer, Scott & Slemmons, 52-60; partner, LeSourd, Patten & Adams, 60-61. Mil Serv: Entered as A/5, Navy 44, released as Electronics Technician's Mate 3/C, 46. Publ: Estate & gift taxation of the marital community, Univ Wash Law Rev, 53; Dealer reserves, Taxes, The Tax Mag, 59. Mem: Seattle, Wash, Am & Fed Bar Asns; Phi Beta Kappa. Honors & Awards: Distinguished Serv Award, Seattle Jr CofC, 60. Relig: Episcopal. Legal Res: 1415 42nd Ave E Seattle WA 98102 Mailing Add: US House of Rep Washington DC 20515

ADAMS, DON W (R)
Chmn, Ill State Rep Cent Comt
b Springfield, Ill, Dec 11, 35; s John Adams & Bertha Yates A; m 1962 to E Jane Fulkerson; c Donald Porter, David Yates, Jane E & Mark Spiro. Educ: Northwestern Univ, 2 years; Southern Ill Univ, 1 year; Theta Xi. Polit & Govt Pos: Rep precinct committeeman, Sangamon Co, Ill, 58-68; chmn, Dist Ten, Sangamon Co, 60-61; mem, Rep Exec Comt, Sangamon Co, 60-; admin asst, City of Springfield, Ill, 63-69; committeeman, Ill State Rep Cent Comt, 20th Cong Dist, 66-70, vchmn, 70-74, chmn, 74-; dir, Lincoln Rep Forum, Springfield, 67-; temporary chmn, Rep State Conv, 68; chmn, Ill Electoral Col, 69, mem, Rep Nat Comt, 74- Bus & Prof Pos: Pres of corp, Lincoln Ctr Shopping Ctr, Springfield, Ill, 62-;

owner, Ann Rutledge Pancake House, 62-; pres, Lincoln Depot, Inc, 63- Mil Serv: Air Nat Guard & Res. Mem: Ill Restaurant Asn; United Serv Orgn (bd dirs); Goodwill Industs, Inc (bd dirs); YMCA; Sangamon Co Hist Soc. Relig: Roman Catholic. Mailing Add: 2329 Noble Springfield IL 62704

ADAMS, DONALD GILBERT (D)
Tex State Sen
b Jasper, Tex, Dec 18, 38; s Thomas Gilbert Adams & Dess Hart A; m 1963 to Linda Cullum. Educ: Baylor Univ, BBA & LLB, 63; Phi Alpha Delta. Polit & Govt Pos: Tex State Rep, 69-73; Tex State Sen, 73- Bus & Prof Pos: Attorney-at-law, Adams & Adams. Mem: First Judicial Dist & Tex Bar Asns; Mason. Relig: Methodist. Mailing Add: 601 Forest Lane Jasper TX 75951

ADAMS, DOUG (D)
Ark State Rep
Mailing Add: Box 49 Strawberry AR 72469

ADAMS, EVA BERTRAND (D)
b Wonder, Nev; d Verner Lauer Adams & Cora Varble A; single. Educ: Univ Nev, BA; Columbia Univ, MA, 37; Wash Col Law, LLB, 48; George Washington Univ, LLM, 50; Wash Col Law, Am Univ, JD, 68; Cap & Scroll; Kappa Alpha Theta; Phi Kappa Phi; Kappa Delta Pi. Hon Degrees: LLD, Univ Portland, 66 & Univ Nev, 67. Polit & Govt Pos: Admin asst to Sen Pat McCarran, 40-54, Sen Ernest Brown, 54- & Sen Alan Bible, 54-61; dir, Bur of Mint, Washington, DC, 61-69. Bus & Prof Pos: Teacher, Las Vegas High Sch; instr Eng & asst dean of women, Univ Nev, 37-40; Am Inst Mining Engrs Henry Krumb lectr, 69; mem bd dirs, Tele-Trip Corp, Medallic Art Co, Med Col Pa, Interlochen Ctr for Arts & Mutual Omaha Fund Mgt Co, currently. Mem: Washoe & St Mary's Hosp Guild; Am, Fed, Nev & DC Bar Asns. Mailing Add: 4201 Cathedral Ave NW Apt 1221W Washington DC 20016

ADAMS, FRANK POLLARD (R)
VChmn, Alameda Co Rep Cent Comt, Calif
b Oakland, Calif, Nov 25, 08; s Edson Adams & Jessie Fox A; m 1950 to Analisa Bosche; c Edson, Nora, Peter Stewart & Analisa. Educ: Stanford Univ, AB, 31; Univ Calif, JD, 34; Phi Delta Phi; Delta Tau Delta. Polit & Govt Pos: Vpres, Calif Rep Assembly, 65-66, pres, 67, dir, 69; pres, Lincoln Club Alameda Co, Calif, 67-; mem exec comt, Calif Rep State Cent Comt, 67-, treas, 71-73; mem & treas, Alameda Co Rep Cent Comt, 67-, sr vchmn, 71-; Northern Calif chmn, Rafferty for US Sen Campaign, 68; deleg, Rep Nat Conv, 68 & 72; trustee, Calif State Univs & Cols, 72- Bus & Prof Pos: Attorney-at-law, San Francisco, 35-; vpres, Vacu-Dry Co, 41-; pres, Minerals Mgt Corp, 41-; dir, Research Equity Fund & Research Capitol Fund, currently; dir, secy & treas, William M Brobeck & Assocs & Transaction Inc, currently. Mem: Am, Calif & San Francisco Bar Asns; Univ Club San Francisco; Commonwealth Club San Francisco. Relig: Protestant. Legal Res: 781 Highland Ave Piedmont CA 94611 Mailing Add: 1922 Russ Bldg 235 Montgomery St San Francisco CA 94104

ADAMS, GEORGE DRAYTON, JR (D)
Ga State Rep
b Atlanta, Ga, Apr 8, 15; s George Drayton Adams, Sr & Josephine Adeline A; m 1939 to Frances Elizabeth Hazelrigs; c Patricia (Mrs Sam H Cann) & Angela (Mrs Harold J Smith). Educ: Fulton High Sch, 28-32. Polit & Govt Pos: Mem bd trustees, Atlanta Pub Libr, Ga, 62-69, pres, 70-71, 4th four year appt, Atlanta Pub Libr Bd, currently; Ga State Rep, Dist 36, 66- Bus & Prof Pos: Sales mgr, Blue Plate Foods, Inc, 39-44; pres, G D Adams Co, Atlanta, Ga, 48-75. Mil Serv: Entered as Pvt, Army, 44, released as Cpl, 46, after serv in 232nd Field Artil Bn, 42nd Inf Div, Rhineland & Cent Europe Campaigns; two Campaign Ribbons. Mem: Shrine; Lions; Civitan; Am Legion; VFW. Relig: Baptist. Legal Res: 532 St Johns Ave SW Atlanta GA 30315 Mailing Add: 1977 Sylvan Rd SW Atlanta GA 30310

ADAMS, HERMAN, JR (D)
Tex State Rep
b Jasper, Tex, July 16, 42; s Herman Adams & Susie Sheffield A; single. Educ: Univ Tex, BS, 65; Kappa Alpha Order. Polit & Govt Pos: Prof staff mem, US Senate Post Off & Civil Serv Comt, 70; chmn, Hardin Co Dem Exec Comt, Tex, 68-72; Tex State Rep, Dist 5, 73- Bus & Prof Pos: Businessman. Mem: Silsbee Country Club; Silsbee CofC. Relig: Methodist. Legal Res: 529 Weathersby Silsbee TX 77656 Mailing Add: Rm 400 State Capitol Austin TX 78767

ADAMS, HOOVER (D)
b Dunn, NC, Mar 6, 20; s Alexander Benton Adams & Lou Flora Morgan A; m 1944 to Mellicent Stalder; c Brent, Maere Kay & Bart Stalder. Educ: Dunn High Sch, Grad; Officer Candidate Sch, US Army, mil aide to Maj Gen William C Lee. Polit & Govt Pos: Campaign press secy, US Sen Willis Smith, NC, 50; secy, Harnett Co Dem Conv, on several occasions; chmn, Dunn Alcohol Control Bd, currently; deleg, Dem Nat Conv, 68 & 72; mem, Harnett Co Forum & Harnett Co Bicentennial Comt, currently. Bus & Prof Pos: Ed, publ, owner & founder, Daily Rec, Dunn, NC, 50-; pres, Rec Publ Co, Inc, currently. Mil Serv: Entered as Pvt, Army Air Force, 42, released as Capt, 45, after serv in 101st Airborne Div, Troop Carrier Command Hq, European Command, London, England. Mem: NC Press Asn; Eastern Carolina Regional Housing Authority (chmn); Rotary; 40 et 8, Am Legion; Mason. Relig: Christian Church; Deacon, Hood Mem Christian Church. Legal Res: Lakeshore Dr Dunn NC 28334 Mailing Add: PO Box 811 Dunn NC 28334

ADAMS, J ALLEN (D)
NC State Rep
b Greensboro, NC, Jan 15, 32; s Joseph Allen Adams & Marion Crawford A; m 1953 to LeNeve Foster Hodges; c Ann Caroline, Jefferson Hodges & Spencer Allen. Educ: Boston Univ, 48-49; Univ NC, Chapel Hill, AB, 52, JD, 54; Sigma Nu; Phi Delta Phi. Polit & Govt Pos: Pres, Wake Co Young Dem, NC, 64; chmn, Wake Co Dem Party, 68-72; pres Wake Co Pub Libr Bd, 70-; Dem nominee for NC State Sen, 14th Dist, 72; NC State Rep, 74- Bus & Prof Pos: Partner, Young, Moore & Henderson, Attorneys, Raleigh, NC, 58-67; Sanford, Cannon, Adams & McCollough, Attorneys, 67- Mil Serv: Entered as S/A, Naval Res, 55, released as Lt, 58, after serv in US Naval Ammo Depot, Hawthorne, Nev, Comdr, currently. Mem: Am Bar Asn; NC Acad Trial Lawyers; Nat Legal Aid & Defender Asn; Am Civil Liberties Union; Raleigh CofC. Honors & Awards: Named to Ten Most Outstanding Young Democrats in NC, 62. Relig: Protestant. Legal Res: 1618 Ambleside Dr Raleigh NC 27605 Mailing Add: PO Box 389 Raleigh NC 27602

ADAMS / 5

ADAMS, JAMES WILLIAM (R)
Chmn, Johnson Co Rep Comt, Ky
b Ashland, Ky, Aug 3, 30; s Ted Adams & Alma Howes A; m 1954 to Marilyn Litteral; c James, II & Margaret. Educ: Mayo Voc Sch, Paintsville, 51. Polit & Govt Pos: Chmn, Johnson Co Rep Comt, Ky, 72- Mem: Masonic Lodges. Relig: Protestant. Legal Res: 604 Frank St Paintsville KY 41240 Mailing Add: Box 502 Paintsville KY 41240

ADAMS, JOHN GIBBONS (R)
b Ashland, Ky, March 23, 12; s Samuel Morton Adams & Helen Gibbons A; m 1946 to Margaret Paxton Williams; c Rebecca. Educ: Univ SDak, LLB, 35; George Washington Univ, LLM; Sigma Alpha Epsilon. Polit & Govt Pos: Agt, SDak Dept Justice, 35; vpres, Young Rep Nat Fedn, 41-46; clerk, Comt on Armed Serv, US Senate, 47-49; asst gen counsel, Legis Div, Dept Defense, 49-51, dep gen counsel, 51-53; gen counsel, Dept Army, 53-55; consult orgn & mgt, Atomic Energy Comn, 56-57, mem staff, 58-61; dir, Bur Enforcement, 61-65; mem, US Civil Aeronaut Bd, 65-71. Bus & Prof Pos: Adj prof law, Georgetown Univ, 66-69; prof lectr tax law, Am Univ, 70; counsel, law firm of Leva, Hawes, Symington, Martin & Oppenheimer, 71- Mil Serv: Entered as 1st Lt, Army, 42, released as Col, 46, after serv in ETO; Col, US Army Res; Bronze Star; NAfrican, Italian, French & German Campaign Ribbons. Mem: SDak & DC Bar Asns; Army-Navy Club; Int Club. Relig: Episcopal. Legal Res: 3415 34th Pl NW Washington DC 20016 Mailing Add: 815 Connecticut Ave NW Washington DC 20006

ADAMS, JOHN W (D)
Ga State Rep
b Rome, Ga, Dec 4, 32; s Willie Joe Adams & Gladys McGhee A; m 1956 to Sue Camp; c Joe, Jim, Laura & David. Educ: Auburn Univ; Univ Ga, 1 year 6 months. Polit & Govt Pos: Pres, Young Dem of Floyd Co, Ga, 67; Floyd Co Dem Asn, 70; Ga State Rep, 71- Bus & Prof Pos: Chief dep sheriff Floyd Co Sheriffs Off, Ga, 61-68; sales mgr, Radio Sta WLAQ, 68- Mil Serv: Entered as A/S, Navy, 51, released as Airman, 55, after serv in Aviation. Mem: Am Legion; CofC; Breakfast Optimist Club; Nat Sheriffs Asn; Coosa Country Club. Relig: Baptist. Mailing Add: 7 E Creekview Dr Rome GA 30161

ADAMS, LEROY THOMAS (D)
Committeeman, Ark State Dem Comt
b Bellville, Ill, May 4, 10; s Thomas Leroy Adams & May Ompson A; m 1938 to Martha Virginia Thompson; c Martha Lee. Educ: High sch grad. Polit & Govt Pos: Ward Two committeeman, Paragould Dem Party, Ark, 72-; committeeman, Ark State Dem Comt, 74- Bus & Prof Pos: Asst legis rep, Mo Pac RR, 70-75. Relig: Methodist. Mailing Add: 110 N Third & 1/2 St Paragould AR 72450

ADAMS, MARVIN (D)
Ga State Sen
Mailing Add: 709 Greenwood Rd Thomaston GA 30286

ADAMS, MENDLE E (D)
Ind State Rep
Mailing Add: 804 W Fourth St Marion IN 46952

ADAMS, NELDA (R)
VChmn, Bonneville Co Rep Cent Comt, Idaho
b Idaho Falls, Idaho, July 13, 29; d Paul C Holm & Zula Wilcox H; m 1950 to Richard Norman Adams; c Paul, Greg, Eric, Lindy Lou, Kelly, Brett & Jody. Educ: Ricks Col, 48-49. Polit & Govt Pos: Vchmn, Bonneville Co Rep Cent Comt, Idaho, 74- Relig: Latter-day Saint. Mailing Add: 2155 Richards St Idaho Falls ID 83401

ADAMS, PHILIP J (D)
Chmn, Avon Dem Town Comt, Conn
b Bangor, Maine; s Benjamin F Adams & Grace Russell A; m 1945 to Dorothy Elinor Claire; c Philip J, Jr, Dean E & Dorothy M. Educ: Maine Maritime Acad, BS, 43. Polit & Govt Pos: Mem, Bronx Co Dem Comt, NY, 58; mem, Avon Dem Town Comt, Conn, 70-72, chmn, 72- Bus & Prof Pos: From agt to asst vpres manpower & admin, Aetna Life & Casualty, 47-71, nat dir brokerage agencies, 71- Mil Serv: Entered as Midn, Naval Res, serv in all grades as licensed deck officer, Merchant Marine, maintains unlimited master mariners license, 45- Mem: Nat Asn Life Underwriters; Soc Chartered Life Underwriters; Gen Agents & Mgr Asn; Nat Dem Club; Farmington Field Club. Relig: Catholic. Mailing Add: 18 Reverknolls Avon CT 06001

ADAMS, SALISBURY (CONSERVATIVE)
Minn State Rep
b Duluth, Minn, 1925; married; c four. Educ: Univ Minn, BS in Metallurgical Eng; Harvard Univ Law Sch. Polit & Govt Pos: Mem bd & treas, Wayzata Sch dist 284, Minn, 58-62; Minn State Rep, 62- Bus & Prof Pos: Lawyer. Mil Serv: Navy, 43-46. Mem: Minn Family & Children's Serv (dir). Mailing Add: 60 Myrtlewood Rd Wayzata MN 55391

ADAMS, SAMUEL LAMAR (D)
Ala State Sen
b Tuscaloosa, Ala, July 24, 47; s Forrest Lamar Adams & Ann Koeppel A; m 1969 to Mary Earle Elmore; c Mary Elizabeth. Educ: Univ Ala, BS, 68; Samford Univ, JD, 71; Phi Alpha Delta; Kappa Sigma. Polit & Govt Pos: Asst Attorney Gen, Ala, 71-72; Ala State Sen, 75- Bus & Prof Pos: Attorney-at-law, Samuel L Adams, Dothan, Ala, 72-74 & Adams & Bates, 75- Mem: Am & Ala Bar Asns; Ala Trial Lawyers Asn; Kiwanis; Masons. Relig: Methodist. Legal Res: 302 Meadowbrook Dr Dothan AL 36301 Mailing Add: 129 S Oats St Dothan AL 36301

ADAMS, SHERMAN (R)
b East Dover, Vt, Jan 8, 99; s Clyde H Adams & Winnie Marian Sherman A; m 1923 to Rachel Leona White; c Marion (Mrs William Freese), Jean (Mrs William M Hallagher), Sarah & Samuel. Educ: Dartmouth Col, BA, 20, MA, 40; Sigma Alpha Epsilon. Hon Degrees: LLD, Univ NH, 50, Dartmouth Col, 53, Bates Col, 54, Bryant Col, 51, St Lawrence Univ, 54, Middlebury Col & Center Col, 57; DCL, New Eng Col, 51. Polit & Govt Pos: NH State Rep, 41-44, Speaker, NH House Rep, 43-44; deleg, Rep Nat Conv, 44 & 52; US Rep, NH, 45-47; Gov, NH, 49-53; chmn, Conf New Eng Gov, 51-52; asst to President, 53-58; mem, Gov Task Force on State Reorgn, 69-70; chmn, Mt Washington Comn, 70- Bus & Prof Pos: Treas, Black River Lumber Co, Vt, 21-22; dir, Pemigewasset RR, Concord, NH, formerly; mgr, timberland & lumber opers, Parker-Young Co, Lincoln, 28-45; pres, Loon Mt Corp, 67- Mil Serv: Marine Corps, 18. Publ: First Hand Report, 61; Merican Forests, 69; articles in Life, Appalachia &

Yankee. Mem: Northeastern Lumber Mfrs Asn (dir); sr mem Soc Am Foresters; SAR; NH Soc; Mason (33 degree). Honors & Awards: First Robert Frost Medal, Plymouth State Col. Relig: Episcopal. Mailing Add: Pollard Rd Lincoln NH 03251

ADAMS, SIDNEY (D)
Ky State Rep
Mailing Add: Littcarr KY 41834

ADAMS, THOMAS B (D)
Chmn, Lincoln Dem City Comt, Mass
b 1910; m to Ramelle Cochrane; c John, Peter, Douglas, Henry & Ramelle. Educ: Harvard Univ; Phi Beta Kappa. Polit & Govt Pos: Dem cand for US Sen, Mass, 66; cand for Dem nomination for US Rep, Fifth Cong Dist, Mass, 68; chmn, Lincoln Dem City Comt, 70-; deleg, Dem Nat Conv, 72. Bus & Prof Pos: Retired hotel exec; former ed writer, Boston Herald, 32-35; exec, Waltham Watch Co, until 41; exec, Sheraton Hotel Corp, 46, treas, 54-; faculty, Harvard Univ; treas, Am Acad Arts & Sci; trustee, Chapelbrook Fedn & Neurosci Research Fedn; life trustee, Lincoln Pub Libr, Mass, 70- Mil Serv: Air Force, 42-45, Capt. Mem: Mass Hist Soc (pres); Colonial Soc of Mass; Bd of Appeals of Lincoln; fel Morgan Libr. Mailing Add: Concord Rd S Lincoln MA 01773

ADAMS, THURMAN, JR (D)
Del State Sen
Mailing Add: Box 367 Bridgeville DE 19933

ADAMS, TOM (D)
b Jacksonville, Fla, Mar 11, 17; s Thomas Burton Adams, Sr & Carolyn Hamilton A; div. Educ: Univ Mich, AB, 40; Univ Fla Sch Law; pres, Sr Hon Soc; Alpha Kappa Psi; pres, Phi Delta Theta & Interfraternity Coun. Hon Degrees: Dr Space Educ, Fla Inst Technol, 62; LHD, Trinity Col, 64. Polit & Govt Pos: Fla State Sen, 29th Dist, 56-60; secy of state, Fla, 61-71; Lt Gov, Fla, 71-75; deleg, Dem Nat Conv, 72. Bus & Prof Pos: Real estate & property mgr, H P Holmes, Inc, Detroit, Mich, 40-42; plant supt, Foremost Dairies, Jacksonville & Daytona Beach, Fla, 42-44; owner, dairy farm, Orange Park, 44-46; lumber dealer & property mgr, Orange Park Properties, 48-60; vchmn bd dirs, Fla Inst Technol, 73- Mem: Nat Waterways Conf; Miss Valley Asn; Southeast Basins Inter-Agency Coun; Nat Rivers & Harbors Cong; Rotary. Honors & Awards: Most Outstanding Dem, Fla Young Dem Club, 63; hon Blue Key mem, Univ Fla, 64; hon mem, Omicron Delta Kappa Leadership Fraternity, 65; Leadership award, Fla Waterways Asn, 66; Order of San Carlos, 67. Relig: Baptist. Mailing Add: The Capitol Tallahassee FL 32304

ADAMS, VICTORINE QUILLE (D)
Mem, Dem Party Md
b Baltimore, Md, Apr 28, 12; d Joseph C Quille & Estelle Carey Tate Q; m 1935 to William L Adams; c Gertrude (Mrs Venable). Educ: Coppin State Teachers Col, 30; Morgan State Col, 40; Phi Delta Kappa; Sigma Gamma Rho. Polit & Govt Pos: Chmn, Colored Women's Dem Club, Md, 46-; deleg, Dem Nat Conv, 64; dir, Register to Vote Campaign & Get Out the Vote Campaign, 64; campaign coordr, Dem Party Md, 64-, mem, 75-; Md State Deleg, 66-67; mem, Baltimore City Coun, Fourth Dist, 67- Bus & Prof Pos: Pub sch teacher, Dept Educ, Baltimore, 30-44; mgr, Charm Centre Inc, 50-63. Mem: Small Bus Asn; Nat Asn Negro Bus & Prof Women; Woman Power Inc; United Women's Dem Clubs Md; Nat Coun Negro Women. Honors & Awards: Woman of the Year, Zeta Phi Beta; Afro-Am Honor Roll. Relig: Catholic. Mailing Add: 3103 Carlisle Ave Baltimore MD 21216

ADAMS, WALTER C (D)
b Newtown, Pa, Aug 22, 36; s Walter C Adams & Hazel Worthington A; m 1962 to Nancy L Baier; c Christopher & Kenneth. Educ: Drew Univ, AB, 58; Rutgers Univ, MS, 62, PhD, 63. Polit & Govt Pos: City Councilman, Kent, Ohio, 72-; deleg, Dem Nat Conv, 72. Bus & Prof Pos: Res scientist, Bur of Res in Neurology & Psychiat, Princeton, NJ, 63-67; asst prof biol sci, Kent State Univ, 67-71, assoc prof, 72- Publ: Co-auth, Prevention of ovarian cyst formation by ethamoxytriphetol (MER-25), In: Proc Soc Exp Biol Med, 63; auth, Sterol synthesis in rats with experimentally induced polycystic ovaries, J Endocrinology, 67; Breed differences in the responses of rabbits to atherogenic diets, Atherosclerosis, 73. Mem: Am Asn Advan Sci; Am Physiol Soc; Am Soc Zoologists; Soc for Study of Reproduction. Relig: Protestant. Mailing Add: 336 High St Kent OH 44240

ADAMS, WESTON (R)
SC State Rep
Mailing Add: 1719 Heyward St Columbia SC 29205

ADAMS, WILLIAM WALTER, JR, (WILL) (D)
Mem, Clay Co Dem Cent Comt, Mo
b Tuscaloosa, Ala, July 8, 29; s William W Adams, Sr & Beulah Reeves A; m 1953 to Eleaner Ruth Ormond; c William W, III & James Kevin. Educ: Univ Kans, BA, 51, MA, 54; Columbia Univ, MA, 60, PhD, 68; Pi Sigma Alpha. Polit & Govt Pos: Mem, Clay Co Dem Cent Comt, Mo, 68-, chmn, 70-72. Bus & Prof Pos: Asst prof hist & polit sci, William Jewell Col, 55-58, assoc prof polit sci, 60-65 & 67-68, prof & chmn dept, 68-; exchange prof int rels, Park Col, 63 & vis prof Russian hist, 64; instr polit sci, Univ Mo-Kansas City, 65; vis prof polit sci, Tulane Univ, summer 67 & 68. Mil Serv: Entered as Pvt, Kans Nat Guard, 48, released as Sgt, 56, after serv in 2nd Bn Platoon, Med Co, 137th Inf Regiment, 35th Div. Publ: Communism, realism, & Christianity, In: Protest & Politics: Christianity & Contemporary Affairs, Attic Press, 68; Capital punishment in Imperial & Soviet Russia, Am J Comp Law, Vol 18, No 370; Capital punishment in Soviet criminal legislation, In: On the Road to Communism (ed, Kanet & Volgyes), Univ Kans Press, 72; plus others. Mem: Am Polit Sci Asn; Am Asn Advan Slavic Stud; Cent Slavic Conf. Honors & Awards: Ford fel, foreign area training, 59-60; Kansas City Regional Coun Higher Educ travel grant, summer 64; Danforth teacher grant, 66-67; sabbatical leave, Munich, Germany, fall 71; Kansas City Regional Coun Higher Educ res grant, summer 73. Relig: Baptist. Mailing Add: 135 N Missouri St Liberty MO 64068

ADCOCK, RONNIE W (D)
Chmn, Hunt Co Dem Exec Comt, Tex
b Greenville, Tex, Jan 12, 54; s James Thomas Adcock, Sr & Jean Taylor A; single. Educ: ETex State Univ, 72-; Sigma Chi. Polit & Govt Pos: Pres, Hunt Co Young Dem, Tex, 72-73 & 75-; chmn, Hunt Co Dem Exec Comt, 74-; mem, State Youth Adv Coun, 74- Bus & Prof Pos: Ins adjuster, Adcock Adj & Real Estate, Greenville, Tex, 73- Relig: Methodist. Legal Res: 3914 Templeton Greenville TX 75401 Mailing Add: PO Box 754 Greenville TX 75401

ADDABBO, JOSEPH PATRICK (D)
US Rep, NY
b Queens, NY, Mar 17, 25; s Dominick Addabbo & Anna A; m to Grace Salamone; c Dominic, Dina & Joseph. Educ: City Col; St John's Law Sch, LLB. Polit & Govt Pos: US Rep, NY, 61-; deleg, Judicial Conv; deleg, Dem Nat Mid-Term Conf, 74. Bus & Prof Pos: Gen Practice Law, Ozone Park, NY. Mem: Queens Co Bar Asn. Mailing Add: 132-43 86th St Ozone Park NY 11417

ADELSHEIM, MARTHA ANN HENDERSON (D)
b Pittsburgh, Pa, June 28, 15; d Stuart Llewellyn Henderson & Gertrude Alcliffe Mevis H; m 1942 to Edward Kalman Adelsheim; c David Brook, Peter Dolf & Michael Wood. Educ: Wellesley Col, BA, 36. Polit & Govt Pos: Asst economist, Bur of Labor Statist, US Dept of Labor, 41-43; chmn, Dollars for Dem Drive & other pos with Dem Party; vchmn, Ore Dem Party, 62-64, chmn, 64-67; mem, Dem Nat Comt, 64-67; proj dir, Parent-Child Serv, Off Child Develop, Dept of Health, Educ & Welfare, 68-72. Bus & Prof Pos: Bd mem, KBOO Found, currently. Mem: YWCA; League of Women Voters; World Affairs Coun; Commun Coun of Portland; Oregon's Great Decisions Progs. Mailing Add: 2755 SW Summit Dr Portland OR 97201

ADELSTEIN, STANFORD MARK (R)
Committeeman, SDak Rep State Cent Comt
b Sioux City, Iowa, Aug 19, 31; s Morris Eskiel Adelstein & Bertha Greenburg A; m 1952 to Ita Korn; c Daniel, James David & Jon Stephen. Educ: Univ Colo, Civil Eng, 53, Bus Admin, 55. Polit & Govt Pos: Alt deleg, Rep Nat Conv, 60 & 64; pres, State Young Rep Party, 63-64; secy-treas, Pennington Co Rep Orgn, formerly; committeeman & mem exec comt, SDak Rep State Comt, currently. Bus & Prof Pos: Treas, Humboldt Realty Co; vpres, Lawrence Realty; pres, Colo-Wyo Improv Co; pres, Northwestern Eng Co, SDak. Mil Serv: Entered as Lt, Army, released from Nat Guard as Capt. Mem: Am Soc Civil Engrs; Mil Engrs; SDak Asn Engrs; Am Legion. Relig: Jewish. Legal Res: 1999 West Blvd Rapid City SD 57701 Mailing Add: PO Box 1392 Rapid City SD 57701

ADKINS, JAMES CALHOUN (D)
Justice, Supreme Court Fla
b Gainesville, Fla, Jan 18, 15; s James Calhoun Adkins, Sr & Elizabeth Edwards A; m 1952 to Ethel Fox; c James C III & Linda R. Educ: Univ Fla, JD, 38; Pi Kappa Alpha; Phi Delta Phi. Polit & Govt Pos: Research aide, Supreme Court Fla, 38-39, Justice, 69-; asst attorney gen, Attorney Gen Off, Fla, 39-41; asst state attorney, Eighth Judicial Circuit of Fla, 57-59, judge, 64-69; judge, Alachua Co Court of Rec, 59-61; mem, Gov Hwy Safety Comn, 71-; mem, Gov Coun on Criminal Justice, 71- Mil Serv: Entered as Pvt, Army, 45, released as Pfc, 45, after training. Publ: Florida real estate law & procedure, 59, Trials, Florida criminal law & practice, 66 & Florida civil & criminal discovery, 71, Harrison Co; plus others. Mem: Am Bar Asn; Am Judicature Soc; Am Legion; 40 et 8; Elks. Honors & Awards: James W Day Award for contribution to legal educ, Univ Fla; Distinguished Serv Award, Fla Munic Judges Asn; Outstanding Leadership Award, Fla Hwy Safety Alcohol Educ Asn; Lecturer Award, Acad Fla Trial Lawyers; Outstanding Alumnus, Col Law, Univ Fla. Relig: Methodist. Mailing Add: PO Box 427 Tallahassee FL 32302

ADKISSON, JOHN DAVID (D)
b Phoenix, Ariz, Apr 25, 52; s Johnny Lee Adkisson & Gloria Ann A; single. Educ: Calif State Univ, San Jose, BA, 73; Quill & Scroll. Polit & Govt Pos: Founder chmn pres, San Jose State Students for McGovern, 71-72; deleg, Dem Nat Conv, 72; chmn, Student Liaison to San Jose City Coun, 73- Bus & Prof Pos: Sr materials consult, IBM, San Jose, 72-; broadcast announcer, KSJS FM-Radio, San Jose, 73- Publ: Don Edwards, congressman, 11/72 & Ten most powerful San Joseans, 1/73, Spartan Daily. Honors & Awards: Grant & Scholar, Bank of Am, 70; Lawrence Murphy Trophy for Excellence in Jour, Murphy Found, 72. Mailing Add: 947 Hummingbird Dr San Jose CA 95125

ADROUNIE, DOROTHY (R)
VChmn, Barry Co Rep Comt, Mich
b Everek, Ankara, Turkey, Sept 11, 94; d Tatios Kalaidjian & Rose Minasian K; m 1912 to Dr Harry Adrounie, wid; c Lt Col V Harry & Zabelle Dorothy (Mrs Olson). Educ: Armenian Nat Sch; Am Girls Sem; Battle Creek Sanitarium, hydrotherapy training. Polit & Govt Pos: Deleg, Rep State & Co Convs, Mich; presidential elector, 60; area chmn, Fourth Dist Rep Party, 60-62; mem exec bd, Rep Womens Fedn, 60-64, chmn ways & means, 62-64; vchmn, Barry Co Rep Comt, 60-; alt deleg Rep Nat Conv, 64. Bus & Prof Pos: Sch teacher, Turkey; chmn, State Conserv Dept, Land & Water Div, 64- Mem: Barry Co Rep Women Club; Hastings Literary Club; Mich Women's Club Fedn (state chmn int affairs, 68-). Honors & Awards: Award for Best Adult Educ Prog, Barry Co Rep Women's Club, 58; Silver Tray, Mich Rep Party, 69. Relig: Presbyterian. Mailing Add: 126 S Broadway Hastings MI 49058

ADUBATO, MICHAEL F (D)
NJ State Assemblyman
Mailing Add: State House Trenton NJ 08625

AERNI, RUSSELL W (R)
Chmn, Platte Co Rep Cent Comt, Nebr
b Columbus, Nebr, Apr 8, 29; s Walter F Aerni & Frieda Benning A; single. Educ: Concordia Teachers Col, BS in Ed, 49. Polit & Govt Pos: Chmn, Platte Co Rep Cent Comt, Nebr, 74- Bus & Prof Pos: Asst mgr, Safeway Stores Inc, Omaha, Nebr, 65-69, off mgr, 69-71; bookkeeper & payroll clerk, W F Aerni & Son, Columbus, 71-74, off mgr, 74- Mem: Columbus Toastmasters Int (pres, 74, secy, 75, area VII gov, Dist 24, 75-76); Kiwanis Int (treas, 73 & 74). Honors & Awards: Twenty-five Years Serv Award, Lutheran Church, Mo Synod, 74; Able Toastmaster, Toastmasters Int, 75. Relig: Lutheran; Mo Synod. Mailing Add: 1701 23rd St Columbus NE 68601

AGEE, TOMMYE MCWILLIAMS (D)
Tenn State Sen
b Bledsoe Co, Tenn, July 7, 25; d Frank B McWilliams & Maibelle Austin M; m 1947 to Jerry F Agee, wid; c Deborah. Educ: Univ Chattanooga, 43-45; George Peabody Col, BS, 53, MA, 54. Polit & Govt Pos: Tenn State Sen, Davidson Co, 74- Bus & Prof Pos: Elem teacher, Metrop Nashville Davidson Co, 54-74. Relig: Methodist. Legal Res: 2625 Windemere Dr Nashville TN 37214 Mailing Add: War Mem Bldg Rm 304 Nashville TN 37219

AGNEW, COLVIN HUNT (R)
Chmn, Yellowstone Co Rep Party, Mont
b Alamogordo, NMex, Sept 4, 23; s Clarence Agnew & Esther Hunt A; m 1952 to Alice

Steinway; c Stuart, Lauryn, Scott William & Kirk Edward. Educ: US Naval Acad, BS, 45; Ind Univ Sch Med, MD, 51; Alpha Omega Alpha; Sigma Alpha Epsilon; Nu Sigma Nu. Polit & Govt Pos: Chmn, Yellowstone Co Rep Party, Mont, 71- Bus & Prof Pos: Pvt pract, Sheridan, Wyo, 55-57; mem med faculty, Univ Tex Med Br, Galveston, Tex, 57-59 & Univ Kans Sch Med, Kansas City, Kans, 59-62; pvt pract, Billings, Mont, 62- Mil Serv: Entered as Midn, Navy, 42; Naval Res, 20 years. Publ: Several articles in national med journals. Mem: Mont Med Asn; Am Med Asn (vpres); Am Col Radiology; Radiological Soc of NAm (state councilor). Relig: Episcopal. Mailing Add: 2708 Palm Dr Billings MT 59102

AGNEW, SPIRO THEODORE **(R)**
b Baltimore, Md, Nov 9, 18; s Theodore Spiro Agnew & Margaret Akers A; m 1942 to Elinor Isabel Judefind; c James Rand, Pamela Lee, Susan Scott & Kimberly; 1 grandchild. Educ: Johns Hopkins Univ, 3 years; Univ Baltimore, LLB, 47. Hon Degrees: LLD, Univ Md, Morgan State Col, Ohio State Univ & Loyola Col (Md). Polit & Govt Pos: From minority mem to chmn, Baltimore Co Bd Appeals, Md, 57-61; co exec, Baltimore Co, 62-66; dir, Nat Asn Counties, 63, former chmn transportation comt; former mem exec comt, Nat Gov Conf & former vchmn, conf comt on state-urban rels; former mem, Rep Gov Asn Campaign Comt & Rep Coord Comt Task Force on Fed, Fiscal & Monetary Affairs; Gov, Md, 67-69; mem, Adv Comn Intergovt Rels, 69; Vice President United States, 69-73. Bus & Prof Pos: Teacher night classes law, Univ Baltimore, 59-66; former claims adjuster, Lumbermens Mutual Casualty Co; former personnel dir, Schreibers Food Stores; attorney-at-law. Mil Serv: Entered as 2nd Lt Army 41, released as Capt, 45, after serv in Tenth Armored Div, France & Germany, 44-45; recalled for 1 year during Korean Conflict; Bronze Star; Four Battle Stars; Combat Inf Badge. Mem: Loch Raven Kiwanis; Loch Raven Inter-Commun Coun; Am Legion; Ahepa; Phi Alpha Delta; VFW. Relig: Episcopal. Mailing Add: Towson MD 21212

AGNICH, FRED JOSEPH **(R)**
Tex State Rep
b Eveleth, Minn, July 19, 13; s John Agnich & Angeleine Germaine A; m 1941 to Ruth Harriet Welton; c William F, Richard J & James R. Educ: Univ Minn, BA in Geol, 37. Polit & Govt Pos: Chmn, Dallas Co for Goldwater, Tex, 64; asst southern regional dir in charge of polit orgn, Washington, DC, 64; finance chmn, Tower Campaign, 66; chmn, Dallas Co Rep Party, 67-69 & 71-75; deleg, Rep Nat Conv, 68; Tex State Rep, 70-; mem, Nat Adv Bd Sport Fisheries & Wildlife, Dept Interior, 70-72; Rep Nat Committeeman, Tex, 72- Bus & Prof Pos: Exec vpres, Geophys Serv, Inc, Dallas, 51-56, pres, 56-59, chmn bd, 59-61; vpres & dir, Tex Instruments, Inc, 59-61; dir, Tex Mid-Continent Oil & Gas Asn, currently; chmn bd, Scama Corp, Dallas, currently. Publ: Lead paper on geophysical exploration for lime stone reefs, 55. Mem: Am Asn Petroleum Geophysicists; Soc Exploration Geophysicists; Dallas Geophys & Geol Soc; Air Force Asn; Soc Independent Prof Earth Scientists. Honors & Awards: Outstanding Achievement Award, Univ Minn Alumni Asn, 72. Relig: Presbyterian. Legal Res: 5206 Kelsey Rd Dallas TX 75229 Mailing Add: Suite 830 7540 LBJ Freeway Dallas TX 75240

AGNICH, RICHARD JOHN **(R)**
b Virginia, Minn, Aug 24, 43; s Fredrick Joseph Agnich & Ruth Harriet Welton A; m 1969 to Victoria Webb Trescher. Educ: Stanford Univ, AB Econ, 65; Univ Tex Sch Law, JD, 69; Delta Upsilon. Polit & Govt Pos: Research asst, Tex Rep Party, 68-69; legis asst, US Sen John G Tower, Tex, 69-70, admin asst, 70- Mem: Am & Tex Bar Asns; Rep Admin Men's Soc. Relig: Protestant. Mailing Add: 5206 Kelsey Rd Dallas TX 75229

AGNOLI, BRUNO **(D)**
Mem, NJ State Dem Comt
b New York, NY, Jan 6, 11; s Anthony Agnoli & Victoria Anna Gatti A; m 1938 to Nellie G Taylor; c Brenda (Mrs Perlstein), Tonia (Mrs Greger), Marena Lia, Diana (Mrs Binns), Elissa (Mrs Monprode), Annetta (Mrs Pepper) & Gina. Educ: Toms River High Sch. Polit & Govt Pos: Co committeeman, Dem Party, NJ, 30 years; policeman, Dover Twp, 32-38; spec investr, committeeman & co chmn, Irregular Voting, 32-42; spec sheriff's dep & constable, Ocean Co, 35-45; cand for sheriff, 50; chmn, Ocean Co Elec Bd, 59-60, comnr of registr, 70-72; pres, Regular Dem Orgn of Ocean Co, Inc, 60-; munic chmn, Ocean Co Dem Party, 64; deleg, Dem Nat Conv, 64-72; former pres, Co Seat Dem Club; campaign mgr for many elec; mem, NJ State Dem Comt, 69-; mem, Ocean Co Dem Exec Comt; cand, Ocean Co Bd Freeholders, 73. Relig: Catholic. Mailing Add: 113 James St Toms River NJ 08753

AGNOLI, MARENA LIA **(D)**
Committeewoman, Ocean Co Dem Comt, NJ
b Pinewald, NJ, Oct 28, 44; d Bruno Agnoli, State Committeeman & Nellie Taylor A; div; c Laura Lee & Thomas Leonard Richardson, Jr. Educ: Toms River High Sch, NJ, grad, 61. Polit & Govt Pos: Secy, Regular Dem Orgn of Ocean Co, Inc, NJ 70-; committeewoman, Ocean Co Dem Comt, 70-, co campaign coordr, 71; fund raising co-chairwoman, Dover Twp Dem Munic Comt, 72; deleg, Dem Nat Conv, 72. Bus & Prof Pos: IBM keypunch & verifier operator, Data Anal, Toms River, NJ, 70; legal secy, R B Veeder, 71-72; secy, Hovance Real Estate, 73- Mem: Nat Orgn of Women; Dover Twp Dem Club; Ocean Co Young Dem Orgn. Relig: Presbyterian. Mailing Add: 109 Fischer Blvd Toms River NJ 08753

AGOSTINI, WANDA E **(R)**
Mem, Rep State Cent Comt, Calif
b Medford, Ore, Mar 16, 27; d Irving L Eddy & Amelia Owen E; m 1951 to Leo M Agostini; c Steven Alan Minor & Ellis Owen. Educ: Sacramento City Col, 46-47. Polit & Govt Pos: Shasta Co co-chmn, Shell for Gov Campaign, 62, Goldwater for President Campaign, 64 & Reagan for Gov Campaign, Calif, 66 & 70; mem, Rep State Cent Comt, Calif, 62-, women's vchmn, Northern Div, 74-; vchmn, Shasta Co Rep Cent Comt, 63-70, prog chmn, 73-; pub mem & vpres, Calif State Bd of Nursing Educ & Nurse Registr, 68-, legis chmn, 70-, mem bd, 73-; treas, Comt to Reelect Sen Fred W Marler, Jr, 70; finance chmn of Shasta Co, Lt Gov Ed Reinecke Comt, 70; chmn, Shasta Co Comt to Re-elect the President, 72; membership secy, northern div, Calif Fedn Rep Women, 72- Bus & Prof Pos: Exec secy, United Crusade of Shasta Co, 54-56; pres, Calif State Bd Registered Nurses, 74- Mem: Nat & Calif Fedns Rep Women; Shasta Co Humane Soc; Charisma Toastmistress Club Int; Calif Young Rep; Calif Cong of Parents & Teachers. Relig: Methodist. Mailing Add: 3309 Wilshire Dr Redding CA 96001

AGUIAR, ANTONE SOUZA, JR **(D)**
Mass State Rep
b Fall River, Mass, Jan 2, 30; s Antonio S Aguiar & Angelina Perry A; m 1960 to Gertrud Waltraud Kienert; c Christopher, Stephanie & Elizabeth. Educ: Yale Univ, BA, 52; Georgetown Law Sch, LLB, 55; Phi Delta Phi; Morris Law Club. Polit & Govt Pos: Mem, Bd of Selectmen, Swansea, Mass, 61-70; Mass State Rep, 64- Bus & Prof Pos: Practice of law, Fall River, Mass, 58-; baseball coach, Bradford Durfee Col of Tech, 59-63. Mil Serv: Entered as Pvt, Army, 55, released as 1st Lt, 58, after serv in ETO; Lt Col, Army Res. Mem: Boston Bar Asn; ROA; Portuguese Am Civic League; CofC; Lions. Relig: Roman Catholic. Legal Res: 22 Hetherington Dr Swansea MA 02777 Mailing Add: State House of Reps State Capital Bldg Boston MA 02133

AHERN, JOHN PAUL **(D)**
b Chicago, Ill, July 27, 41; s Thomas Francis Ahern & Eleanor Kane A; m 1965 to Ruth Marian Waldron; c Dylan Thomas & Courtney Elizabeth. Educ: Univ Notre Dame, BA, 63; Univ Chicago Grad Sch Polit Sci, 64, Law Sch, JD, 69, Grad Bus Sch, currently. Polit & Govt Pos: Mem, Seventh Ward Regular Dem Orgn, 64-66; mem, Independent Precinct Orgn, 68-; mem, Independent Voters of Ill, 70-; deleg, Dem Nat Conv, 72. Bus & Prof Pos: Teacher, Chicago Bd Educ, 66; personnel mgr, Jewel Food Stores, Inc, 67-68; loan officer, First Nat Bank of Chicago, 69-72. Mem: Am for Dem Action. Relig: Roman Catholic. Mailing Add: 9338 S Hamilton Ave Chicago IL 60620

AHLERS, JOHN CLARKE **(R)**
b Baltimore, Md, July 3, 27; s John A Ahlers & Madeleine Clarke A; m 1954 to Katherine C Smith; c Clarke Francis, Michael McCardell & Katherine Marie. Educ: Loyola Col, Md, 44-46; Loyola Univ La, AB, 48. Polit & Govt Pos: Exec secy to US Sen J Glenn Beall, Md, 55-63; admin asst to Mayor T R McKeldin, Baltimore, 63-65; admin asst to US Sen George Murphy, Calif, 65-71; admin asst to US Sen Norris Cotton, NH, 71-75; admin asst to US Rep James Cleveland, NH, 75- Bus & Prof Pos: Reporter, New Orleans Time-Picayune, 49-50 & Baltimore Eve Sun, 50-55. Mil Serv: Entered as A/S, Navy, 45, released as Seaman 1/C, 46. Mem: Nat Press Club. Relig: Catholic. Mailing Add: 14129 Flint Rock Rd Rockville MD 20853

AIELLO, ARTHUR FRANK **(R)**
NMex State Rep
b Chicago, Ill, June 18, 30; s Sarfino (Sam) Aiello & Rose Coconato A; m 1952 to Loretta Faye Jones; c Tony Ray, Terry Lee & Cheri Lynn. Educ: Thorton Twp High, grad, 48. Polit & Govt Pos: NMex State Rep, 75- Bus & Prof Pos: Owner & mgr, House of Art Jewelers, Mfg, Wholesale & Retail, 68-75. Mil Serv: Entered as Pvt, Air Force, 50, released as S/Sgt, 54, after serv in 509th Air Police, Walker AFB, Strategic Air Command. Mem: Elks, Roswell Lodge 969; Sertoma Int; Paralyzed Vets of Am. Honors & Awards: NMex Handicapped Person of the Year, 73; Industry of the Year, 74-75, Roswell Chamber of Develop & Com. Relig: Lutheran. Mailing Add: 1309 Camino Real Roswell NM 88201

AIKEN, GEORGE DAVID **(R)**
b Dummerston, Vt, Aug 20, 92; m to Beatrice M Howard (deceased); m 1967 to Lola P; c Dorothy (Mrs Morse), Marjaorie (Mrs Cleverly), Howard (deceased) & Barbara (Mrs Jones). Polit & Govt Pos: Vt State Rep, 30-34, Speaker, Vt State House of Rep, 33-34; Lt Gov, Vt, 33-37; Gov, 37-41; US Sen, Vt, 41-74. Mailing Add: Putney VT 05346

AIKEN, PATRICIA O'BRIEN **(D)**
Md State Deleg
b Marcus, Iowa, May 27, 22; d Michael John O'Brien & Myrtle Toomey O; m 1943 to Albert Shelton Aiken; c Michael A & Honora C. Educ: Univ Md, College Park, 2 years; Adelphi Col, 1 semester; Creighton Univ, 1 semester; Univ Ala Exten, Montgomery, 1 semester. Polit & Govt Pos: Soil Conserv supvr, Anne Arundel Co, Md, 72-73; Md State Deleg, 75- Mem: League of Women Voters; Women's Polit Caucus (1st Pres); Bd Parole Day Care Ctr; Saefern Community (zoning chmn). Relig: Catholic. Mailing Add: 501 Epping Forest Rd Annapolis MD 21401

AIKEN, RUTH MERLE JONES **(R)**
Chmn, Knox Co Rep Comt, Maine
b Boston, Mass, Feb 19, 21; d Frank Poor Jones & Lily Gould Pippy J; m 1950 to Aubrey William Aiken; c David Cobb, Susan Poor & Peter Horton-Jones. Educ: Chamberlain Sch, grad, 40; Mus Sch Fine Arts. Polit & Govt Pos: Rep State Committeewoman, Maine, 57-; mem, Knox Co Rep Comt, currently, secy, 60-64, vchmn, 64, chmn, 64-; pres, Knox Co Rep Women's Club, 62-63; mem, Comt Voc Rehab, 64-65; Knox Co chmn, Citizens for Nixon & Women for Nixon-Agnew, 68; mem exec comt, Maine Rep State Comt, 68-69, chmn Subcomt on Young Rep, 69-; Knox Co chmn, Women for Erwin, 70; mem Planning Bd, Town of Cushing, currently. Bus & Prof Pos: Mem bd dirs, Hands Inc, 65-; pub rels bd, Pen-Bay Med Ctr, currently. Mem: Cushing Hist Soc (chmn bd trustees & pres); Girl Scout Leaders; Boy Scouts (Cub Den Mother). Relig: Methodist. Legal Res: Driftwood Farm Hathorne Point South Cushing ME Mailing Add: Pleasant Point ME 04563

AIKENS, JOAN D **(R)**
b Lansdowne, Pa, May 1, 28; d Robert Wallace Deacon & Bessie Crook D; m 1950 to Donald R Aikens; c Donald R Jr. Educ: Ursinus Col, BA, 50. Polit & Govt Pos: Pres, Swarthmore Coun of Rep Women, Pa, 62-64; precinct committeewoman, Swarthmore Rep Comt, 62-; Pa chmn, Rep Nat Comt Women's Wash Conf, 66; chmn, Pa Coun of Rep Women's Conv, 67 & 68, third vpres & polit activities chmn, Pa Coun of Rep Women, 69-72, pres, 72-; hospitality chmn, Pa Deleg, Rep Nat Conv, 68, alt deleg-at-lg, 72; vchmn, Delaware Co Citizens for Nixon-Agnew, 68; co-chmn, Delaware Co Comt to Reelect the President, 72; mem, Fed Election Comn, 75- Bus & Prof Pos: Fashion consult & commentator, Park Ave Shop, Swarthmore, Pa, 62-; acct exec, Lew Hodges Commun, Valley Forge, Pa, 74- Mem: Riddle Mem Hosp Assoc Auxiliaries. Relig: Protestant. Legal Res: Swarthmore PA Mailing Add: 1435 Fourth St SW Washington DC 20024

AIKENS, JOHNNIE S **(D)**
Mo State Rep
Mailing Add: 4847 Wabada St Louis MO 63113

AIKIN, A M, JR **(D)**
Tex State Sen
Mailing Add: PO Box 385 Paris TX 75460

AINLEY, GRETA M **(R)**
NH State Rep
b Aug 14, 1900; married; c three. Educ: Univ Pa, 21. Polit & Govt Pos: Deleg, Const Conv, NH, 56-64; NH State Rep, 57-68 & 71-; alt deleg, Rep Nat Conv, 60 & 68; mem, Manchester Civic Prog Comn, 60-64; pres, Rep Club. Mil Serv: Lt, Red Cross Motor Corps, 40-46; Quaker Relief, France, 46. Mem: Manchester Red Cross; Manchester Hist Soc; New Eng

Women; Francaise of Paris; Manchester Women's Club. Relig: Catholic. Mailing Add: 1165 Union St Manchester NH 03104

AINSWORTH, WILBURN EUGENE, JR (D)
b Jackson, Miss, Aug 2, 42; s Wilburn Eugene Ainsworth & Johnnie Barlow A; m 1964 to Joy Lynn Williamson; c Lynn. Educ: Millsaps Col, BS, 64; Jackson Sch Law, LLB, 67; Kappa Alpha. Polit & Govt Pos: Admin asst to US Rep G V Montgomery, Miss, 67-73; spec asst to the President, 73- Relig: Methodist. Legal Res: Florence MS 39073 Mailing Add: 8110 Gale St Annandale VA 22003

AISENBERG, MICHELE K (D)
Mem Exec Comt, NY Dem State Comt
b New York, NY, Feb 26, 24; d Dr Maxwell Harris Kaiden & Jean Bernstein; m to Bernard Paul Aisenberg; c Elizabeth & Robert. Educ: Queens Col, BA, 45. Polit & Govt Pos: Dist leader, NY Dem Party, 66-; state committeeperson, 90th Assembly Dist, NY, 72-; mem exec comt, NY Dem State Comt, 74- Mem: Am Jewish Cong (gov coun & exec bd women's div); Westchester Civil Liberties Union (bd dirs); Exec Bd Independent Dem, New Rochelle. Mailing Add: 215 Trenor Dr New Rochelle NY 10804

AJELLO, CARL RICHARD (D)
Attorney Gen, Conn
b Derby, Conn, Aug 22, 32; s Carl R Ajello, Sr & Kathryn Flanigan A; m 1955 to Jacqueline Culmo; c Michele & Carl III. Educ: Univ Conn, BS, 53; NY Univ Sch Law, LLB, 56; Sigma Chi. Polit & Govt Pos: Justice of peace, Ansonia, Conn, 60-64, corp counsel, 64-; Conn State Rep, 63-74, majority leader, 69-72, minority leader, 73-74; Conn mem, Northeastern Forest Fire Protective Asn, 68-73; deleg, Dem Nat Conv, 72; Attorney Gen, Conn, 75- Bus & Prof Pos: Pvt law practice, 60-65; partner, Olderman, Winnick, Condon, Ajello & Savitt, 65-70; partner, Ajello, Hoyle & Spomteimer, 71-; corporator, Griffin Hosp, Derby, Savings Bank of Ansonia & Julia Day Nursery, Ansonia. Mil Serv: Entered as 1st Lt, Army, 57, released as Capt, 60. Mem: Rotary; Elks; Am Trial Lawyers Asn; Naugatuck Valley Bar Asn (pres, 69-71); Am Judicature Soc. Relig: Roman Catholic. Mailing Add: Pulaski Hwy Ansonia CT 06401

AJIFU, RALPH K (R)
Hawaii State Rep
b Kaneohe, Hawaii, June 26, 26; s Matsuume Ajifu & Umito Yamashiro A; m 1949 to Toyoko Takiguchi; c Laura, Clayton, Sharon, Aileen, Michael & Lois. Educ: Benjamin Parker High Sch, grad. Polit & Govt Pos: Mem, Bd of Agr & Conserv, State of Hawaii, 59, chmn, Land Use Comn, 61; Hawaii State Rep, 67-, sgt at arms, 75- Bus & Prof Pos: Owner-mgr, Kaneohe Pork Ctr, 44- Mem: Hawaii Young Farmers Asn; Farm Bur; Kaneohe Community Coun. Relig: Methodist. Legal Res: 45-109 Awele Place Kaneohe HI 96744 Mailing Add: House of Reps Sgt at Arms State Capitol Honolulu HI 96813

AKERS, STANLEY WILLIAM (R)
Ariz State Rep
b Bayfield, Colo, Dec 12, 22; s Clyde William Akers & Norma Cecil Plunkett A; m 1949 to Sharon Hogue; c Stanley W, Jr, Christine, Cathy Lynn, Frank Douglas (deceased) & Alyce. Educ: Phoenix Col, 41. Polit & Govt Pos: Ariz State Rep, 67-, speaker, Ariz House Rep, 73- Bus & Prof Pos: Vpres, F H Hogue Produce Co, 57- Mil Serv: Entered as Aviation Cadet, Air Force, 42, released as First Lt, 45, after serv in Air Transport Command, China-Burma-India, 43-45; Air Medal. Mem: Western Growers Asn; Cent Ariz Growers Asn; United Fresh Fruit & Vegetable Asn (mem adv bd); Mason (32 degree); El Zaribah Shrine. Relig: United Church of Christ. Legal Res: 1011 W Cactus Wren Phoenix AZ 85021 Mailing Add: Off of the Speaker House of Reps Rm 223 House Wing State Capitol Phoenix AZ 85007

AKESON, HARVEY O (D)
Ore State Rep
b Portland, Ore, Nov 14, 37; m. Polit & Govt Pos: Ore State Rep, Multnomah Co, 69- Relig: Lutheran. Mailing Add: 1627 NE 126th Portland OR 97230

AKIN, EDWARD B (D)
Chmn, Mason Co Dem Party, Ill
b Louisville, Ky, June 30, 11; s Edward Leslie Akin & Addie Rafferty A; div; c Michael Leslie. Educ: High Sch grad. Polit & Govt Pos: Mem, Selective Serv Bd 170, Mason Co, Ill, 49-; supt, Div Vet Serv Ment Health, 50-52; Dem committeeman, Precinct One, Mason City, 58-; adminr, Ill Vet Comn, 60-69; chmn, Mason Co Dem Party, 60- Bus & Prof Pos: Asst adj, Dept of Ill, Am Legion, 52-60. Mil Serv: Entered as Pvt, Army, 43, released as T/Sgt, 46, after serv in Co F 328th Regt, 26th Inf Div, ETO, 44-46; Good Conduct Medal; Three Battle Stars; Bronze Star. Mem: AF&AM; Scottish Rite; Shrine; Eastern Star; VFW; Am Legion. Relig: Methodist. Mailing Add: 304 N Keefer Mason City IL 62664

AKINS, JAMES E
US Ambassador to Saudi Arabia
b Akron, Ohio, Oct 15, 26; s Quay I Akins & Bernice Bixler A; m 1954 to Marjorie Abbott; c Thomas Andrew & Mary Elizabeth. Educ: Univ Akron, BS, 47. Polit & Govt Pos: US Ambassador to Saudi Arabia, 73- Publ: The Oil Crisis: This Time the Wolf is Here, Foreign Affairs, 4/73; International Cooperation Efforts on Energy Supply, Am Acad Polit & Social Sci, summer 73. Relig: Quaker. Legal Res: 3833 Savoy Ave Akron OH Mailing Add: Am Embassy APO New York NY 09697

AKIZAKI, CLARENCE YASUO (D)
Hawaii State Rep
b Honolulu, Hawaii, May 12, 28; s Rev Yoshio Akizaki & Hanayo Muramoto A; m 1954 to Peggy Yaeno Shishido; c Claudia Tomiko & Vincent Takao. Educ: Western Col of Radio. Polit & Govt Pos: Hawaii State Rep, 62- Bus & Prof Pos: Mgr, Akizaki Radio & TV Sales, 47-58; pres, Akizaki Enterprises, Inc, 58- Mil Serv: Entered as Pvt, Army, 51, released as Sgt, 52, after serv in First Cavalry Div, Korea; Inf Combat Badge. Mem: Pawaa-McCully Bus & Prof Asn (dir). Relig: Shinto. Mailing Add: 2124 S King St Honolulu HI 96814

ALAIMO, GAETANO JOSEPH (GUY) (D)
b Naro, Italy, Jan 16, 40, nat US citizen, 60; s Vincenzo Alaimo & Grazia Curto A; m 1965 to Antoinette Louise Ditta; c Vincent Anthony, Cheryl Ann, Stephen Gaetano & Tina Louise. Educ: Villanova Univ, 56-57; Monmouth Col (NJ), BA, 60; Seton Hall Univ Sch Law, JD, 64; Chess Club; Shakespearean Club. Polit & Govt Pos: Dem nominee for NJ State Assemblyman, Ocean Co, 67; councilman, South Toms River, NJ, 68-69; secy bd trustees, OCEAN, Inc, Anti-Poverty Agency, Ocean Co, 68-70, trustee, 71-; pres, South Toms River Dem Club, 68-71; secy bd trustees, Ocean Co Legal Serv, 68-71; chmn, Ocean Co Dem Party, formerly; mayor, South Toms River, 71-; mem, South Toms River Planning Bd, 71-; mem, NJ Conf of Mayors, 71- Bus & Prof Pos: Attorney at law, NJ, 65- Mem: Ocean Co, NJ & Am Bar Asns; Phi Alpha Delta; assoc mem Fraternal Order Police. Relig: Roman Catholic. Legal Res: 33 Amherst Rd South Toms River NJ 08753 Mailing Add: PO Box 673 Toms River NJ 08753

ALARCON, ANGELITA (D)
Officer, Calif Dem State Cent Comt
b Los Angeles, Calif; d Manuel Alarcon & Antonia Armas A; single. Educ: Bowie High Sch, El Paso, Tex, 40-41. Polit & Govt Pos: Co-chmn, Fifth Cong Dist, US Rep Phillip Burton, Calif, 68-; field rep, State Assemblyman John Burton, 20th Assembly Dist, 70-; officer, Calif Dem State Cent Comt, currently; mem, Mex-Am Polit Asn, currently; deleg, Dem Nat Conv, 72; deleg, Dem Nat Mid-Term Conf, 74. Mem: Mission Coalition Orgn (chmn, Civics Comt, currently); Am GI Forum; LULAC; Calif Dem Clubs. Honors & Awards: Cert of Merit, Am GI Forum, 72. Relig: Catholic. Mailing Add: 240 San Carlos St San Francisco CA 94110

ALARIO, JOHN A, JR (D)
La State Rep
Mailing Add: 469 Vine Dr Westwego LA 70094

ALATORRE, RICHARD (D)
Calif State Assemblyman
b Los Angeles, Calif, May 15, 43; s Mary Martinez A; c Derrick Joseph & Darrell Joseph. Educ: Calif State Univ, Los Angeles, BA in Sociol, 65; Univ Southern Calif, MPA, 70. Polit & Govt Pos: Dir, Southwestern Region NAACP Legal Defense & Educ Fund, 68-72; admin asst to Calif State Assemblyman Walter Karabian, 71-72; Calif State Assemblyman, 55th Assembly Dist, 73- Bus & Prof Pos: Instr, Univ Calif, Irvine, 69-71. Mem: ELos Angeles Jr CofC. Honors & Awards: Ford Found Fel, 68; Distinguished Serv Award, ELos Angeles, Jr CofC, 70. Legal Res: 315 W Ave 38 Los Angeles CA 90065 Mailing Add: 5916 N Figueroa St Los Angeles CA 90042

ALBANESE, VINCENT MICHAEL (D)
Mem Exec Comt, NY Dem State Comt
b Ozone Park, NY, Dec 17, 26; s Vincenzo Albanese & Lena Temperino A; m 1961 to Nike Demetrius; c Marisa, James, Kathryn, Christopher & Anthony Joseph. Educ: Wesleyan Univ, 45; Rensselaer Polytech Inst, 45-46; St John's Univ Sch Law (NY), LLB, 49; Columbia Univ, 54-55 & 57-59. Polit & Govt Pos: Mem, Mayor Lindsay's Comt Marshals, 70-72; leader, 23rd Assembly Dist Dem Party, 73-; mem exec comt, NY Dem State Comt, 75- Mil Serv: Entered as Naval Officer Cand, Navy, 44-46; Naval Res, Lt(jg) (Ret). Mem: Queens Co Bar Asn (first vpres, currently, bd mgrs, 68-); Am & NY Bar Asns; Am & NY Asn Trials Lawyers. Honors & Awards: Awards, Queens Speech & Hearing Serv Ctr, Queens Col, 66, York Col, City Univ NY, 68-69, Queens Co March of Dimes, 70 & Jamaica CofC, 71; Freedom Fund Award, Jamaica NAACP, 71. Legal Res: 86-59 Santiago St Holliswood NY 11423 Mailing Add: 89-31 161st St Jamaica NY 11432

ALBANO, VINCENT FRANCIS, JR (R)
b New York, NY, May 5, 14; s Vincent F Albano, Jr & Mary Ann Sullivan A; m 1937 to Cathleen Claire Cummings; c Carole (Mrs DeCandido), Elaine (Mrs Jefferson), Kathleen (Mrs Cuttita), JoAnn (Mrs Cohen), Vincent, III & Melanie. Educ: St Francis Xavier; Pace Col. Polit & Govt Pos: Chmn, NY Co Rep Comt, formerly; deleg, Rep Nat Conv, 72. Bus & Prof Pos: Personal Property Appraiser, NY State Tax, 53-60; vpres, Gotham Bank, 60-63; chmn bd, Century Nat Bank, 63- Mem: Elks; KofC; Asn of Knights & Ladies of Equestrian Order of Holy Sepulchre; Columbus Citizens Comt, Inc. Relig: Catholic. Mailing Add: 50 Sutton Pl S New York NY 10022

ALBERGER, WILLIAM RELPH (D)
b Portland, Ore, Nov 11, 45; s Relph Griffin Alberger & Ferne Ahlstrom A; m 1971 to Patricia Ann LaSalle. Educ: Willamette Univ, BA, 67; Univ Iowa, MBA, 71; Georgetown Univ Law Ctr, JD, 73; Phi Eta Sigma; Omicron Delta Kappa; Sigma Chi; Student body pres, Willamette Univ, 66-67. Polit & Govt Pos: Legis asst to US Rep Al Ullman, Ore, 72-75, admin asst, 75- Bus & Prof Pos: From clerical asst to actuarial trainee, Standard Ins Co, Portland, Ore, summers, 64-68; admin asst to dean grad col, Univ Iowa, 67-69. Mem: Am & DC Bar Asns. Honors & Awards: Province Balfour Award, Sigma Chi, 67. Legal Res: 7326 SE Reed College Pl Portland OR 97202 Mailing Add: 3235 S Utah St Arlington VA 22206

ALBERT, CARL BERT (D)
Speaker, US House of Rep
b McAlester, Okla, May 10, 08; s Ernest Homer Albert & Leona Ann Scott A; m 1942 to Mary Harmon; c Mary Frances & David Ernest. Educ: Univ Okla, AB, 31; Oxford Univ, Eng, Rhodes scholar, BA, 33 & BCL, 34; Kappa Alpha; Phi Beta Kappa. Polit & Govt Pos: Legal clerk, Fed Housing Admin, 35-37; US Rep, Third Dist, Okla, 47-, Majority Whip, US House of Rep, 55-62, Majority Leader, 62-71, Speaker, 71-; chmn platform comt, Dem Nat Conv, 64, deleg & permanent chmn, 68, deleg, 72; deleg, Dem Nat Mid-Term Conf, 74. Bus & Prof Pos: Attorney & acct, Sayre Oil Co, 37-38; mem legal dept, Ohio Oil Co, 39-40; attorney, Arnote & Arnote, 46-47. Mil Serv: Entered as Pvt, Army Air Force & Judge Adv Gen Dept, 41, released as Lt Col, 46, after serv in Pac Theater; Col, Army Res, 46; Bronze Star. Mem: Am & Okla Bar Asns; Mason; Elks; Lions. Honors & Awards: Heart of the Year Award, Am Heart Asn, 71; Old St George's Award, United Methodist Church, 71; Minute Man of Year, ROA, 72. Relig: Methodist. Legal Res: 827 E Osage McAlester OK 74501 Mailing Add: 4101 Cathedral Ave NW Suite 1111 Washington DC 20016

ALBERT, THOMAS P (D)
Maine State Rep
Mailing Add: RFD 1 Limestone ME 04750

ALBERTSON, JOHN PATRICK (R)
Committeeman, Conn Rep State Cent Comt
b Bridgeport, Conn, Apr 22, 30; s William J Albertson & Edna C Giblin A; m 1956 to Joan V Gamble; c Kathleen, Laurie Ann, Maureen & Sean. Educ: New York Univ, BA, 53; Univ Bridgeport, 57-58. Polit & Govt Pos: Mem, Bridgeport Rep Town Comt, Conn, 69-; bd mem, Selective Serv Local Bd 14, Bridgeport, 69-; committeeman, Conn Rep State Cent Comt, 70-; mem, Comn on Charter Revision, Bridgeport, 73; pres, Bd of Park Comnrs, 73-; tree warden, Bridgeport, 73- Bus & Prof Pos: Investr, Retail Credit Co, Bridgeport, Conn, 56-60; sales, Knox Inc, 60-69, sales mgr, 69- Mil Serv: Entered as E-1, Army, 53, released as Spec Agt, 55, after serv in Younghaus Field Off, 441st Counter Intel Corp, Far East Command, 54-55;

Good Conduct Medal, UN Serv Medal; Am Defense Serv Medal; Korean Serv Medal. Mem: Conn Zoological Soc (bd dirs); Barnum Festival Soc; KofC (Scribe, St Francis Cabrini Assembly); Sheriff's Asn Fairfield Co. Honors & Awards: Good Citizenship Award, Radio Sta, WICC, Bridgeport, 73. Relig: Roman Catholic. Legal Res: 42 Broadbridge Rd Bridgeport CT 06610 Mailing Add: PO Box 5012 Bridgeport CT 06610

ALBERTSON, WALLACE THOMSON (D)
Mem, Dem Nat Comt, Calif
b Pittsburgh, Pa, July 23, 24; d Peter Smart Thomson & Margaretta Maloney T; m 1952 to Jack Albertson; c Maura Dhu. Educ: Univ Pittsburgh, BA, 45; Columbia Univ, MS, 46; Univ Calif, Los Angeles, MA, 66, doctoral cand, currently; Kappa Kappa Gamma. Polit & Govt Pos: Mem, Los Angeles Co Dem Cent Comt, Calif, 72-; mem, Calif State Dem Cent Comt, 72-; mem, Dem Nat Comt, Calif, 72-, mem charter comn, 73-; sr vpres, SCalif Dem Coun, 73-; deleg, Dem Nat Mid-Term Conf, 74. Mem: Am Civil Liberties Union. Relig: Spiritualist; Ordained Minister, Universal Christ Church, Chartered for own church, The Transistory. Mailing Add: 8948 Rosewood Ave Los Angeles CA 90048

ALBOSTA, DONALD J (D)
Mich State Sen
Mailing Add: 4400 W Fry Rd St Charles MI 48566

ALBRECHT, RAYMOND J (R)
Minn State Rep
Legal Res: Brownton MN Mailing Add: State Capitol Bldg St Paul MN 55155

ALBRECHT, RICHARD RAYMOND (R)
Gen Counsel, Dept of the Treas
b Storm Lake, Iowa, Aug 29, 32; s Arnold L Albrecht & Catherine Boettcher A; m 1957 to Constance Marie Berg; c John, Carl, Richard & Henry. Educ: Univ Iowa, BA, 58, Law Sch, JD, 61; Order of the Coif; Omicron Delta Kappa; Sigma Nu; Phi Delta Phi. Polit & Govt Pos: Gen counsel, Dept of the Treas, Washington, DC, 74- Bus & Prof Pos: Assoc attorney, Perkins, Coie, Stone, Olsen & Williams, Seattle, Wash, 61-67, partner law firm, 68-74. Mil Serv: Army, 55-58. Mem: Am, Fed, Wash State & Seattle-King Co Bar Asns; Rainier Club Seattle. Honors & Awards: Outstanding Citizen of the Year Award, Seattle-King Co Munic League, 68-69. Relig: Christian. Legal Res: Seattle WA Mailing Add: 5521 Devon Rd Bethesda MD 20014

ALBRIGHT, ALBION D (D)
Chmn, 38th Legis Dist Dem Orgn, Wash
b Winchester, Ill, Jan 14, 1898; s John H Albright & Ida L Cox A; m 1928 to Ann K Anderson; c John L D. Educ: Sheldon High Sch, 16-17. Polit & Govt Pos: Chmn bd, Snohomish Co Fire Protection Dist One, Wash, 56-69; vpres, Southern Co Dem Club, 60-64; chmn, Snohomish Co Dem Cent Comt, 64-68, second vchmn, 68-; alt deleg, Dem Nat Conv, 68; chmn, 38th Legis Dist Dem Orgn, 71- Mil Serv: Entered as Pvt, Army, 17, released as Cpl, 19, after serv in Battery D, 123rd Field Artil, 33rd Div, AEF France, 18-19; Div Ribbon. Mem: Mason; York Rite; Shrine; Vet of World War I; Am Legion (Past Comdr). Relig: Protestant. Mailing Add: 3611 Serene Way Alderwood Manor WA 98036

ALBRIGHT, BOYCE S (R)
Chmn, Winston Co Rep Party, Ala
b Haleyville, Ala, Apr 27, 24; s Virgle Hugh Albright & Tiney Posey A; single. Educ: Univ Ala, 42-43; Samford Univ, BA, 47; George Peabody Col, MA, 52; Omicron Delta Kappa; Kappa Phi Kappa; Pi Kappa Alpha; Alpha Phi Omega. Polit & Govt Pos: Supt schs, Winston Co, Ala, 61-; chmn, Winston Co Rep Party, 70- Bus & Prof Pos: Teacher, Haleyville High Sch, 47-60, coordr trade & indust educ, 60-61. Mil Serv: Entered as Pvt, Army, 43, released as S/Sgt, 45, after serv in 373rd Engr Regt, ETO, 43-45; three Battle Stars. Mem: Nat & Winston Co Educ Asns; Ala Educ Asn (chmn prof rels & teacher welfare comt & pub rels comt, past vpres & pres, dist 1); Ala Asn Sch Adminr; Lions. Relig: Baptist; Deacon & teacher Men's Fel Class, First Baptist Church, Haleyville. Mailing Add: PO Box 149 Haleyville AL 35565

ALBRIGHT, JOSEPH PAUL (D)
WVa State Deleg
b Parkersburg, WVa, Nov 8, 38; s M P (Jinks) Albright & Catherine Rathbone A; m 1958 to Patricia Ann Deem; c Theresa Louise, Loretta Kathleen, Joseph Paul, Jr & John Patrick. Educ: Univ Notre Dame, BBA cum laude, 61, Law Sch, JD, 62. Polit & Govt Pos: Asst prosecuting attorney, Wood Co, WVa, 65-68; city attorney, Parkersburg, 68; mem & clerk charter bd, City of Parkersburg, 69-; WVa State Deleg, 71-73 & 75-; counsel to Pres & Majority Leader, WVa State Sen, 73-75. Bus & Prof Pos: Secy & dir, Albright's of Belpre, Inc, Ohio, 59-; pvt practice law, 62-64 & 68-69; assoc, Friends & Albright, 64-68; partner, Albright & Richmond, 69-74; partner, Albright, Fluharty, Bradley & Townsend, 75- Mem: Wood Co & WVa State Bar Asns; Elks; KofC. Relig: Catholic. Mailing Add: 1203 Jackson Ave Parkersburg WV 26101

ALBRIGHT, RAY C (R)
Tenn State Sen
Mailing Add: United Bank Seventh & Chestnut Chattanooga TN 37402

ALBRIGHT, ROBERT E (D)
Ala State Rep
Mailing Add: 2024 Stanhope Dr NE Huntsville AL 35811

ALBRIGHT, ROGER LYNCH (D)
b Evanston, Ill, Nov 5, 22; s Charles Rogers Albright & Laura Lynch A; m 1968 to Linnea Dell Taylor. Educ: Allegheny Col, BA, 44; Boston Univ Sch Theol, 44-45; Phi Delta Theta. Polit & Govt Pos: Moderator, Mendon, Vt, 62-64; chmn sch bd, Barstow Mem Sch, Chittenden, 64-65; chmn, Vt Comn on Human Rights, 67-69; deleg, Vt Dem State Conv, 72; deleg, Dem Nat Conv, 72. Bus & Prof Pos: Dir advert, Rutland Daily Herald, Vt, 56-65; pastor, United Church, West Rutland, 57-65; exec minister, Vt Coun of Churches, 65-68; ed & publ, Vt Freeman, 69-74; dir news & pub affairs, Radio/TV WEZF, Burlington, 72-74; ed & broadcaster, Garden Way Assocs, Charlotte, 74- Mil Serv: Entered as Recruit, Army, 45, released as S/Sgt, 47, after serv in 82nd Abn Div; 2nd Lt (Ret), Air Force Res, ten years; Army Commendation Ribbon. Relig: United Church of Christ. Legal Res: Hanksville Schoolhouse Huntington VT 05462 Mailing Add: Hanksville Schoolhouse Starksboro VT 05487

ALBRITTON, WILLIAM HAROLD, III (R)
Chmn, Covington Co Rep Exec Comt, Ala
b Andalusia, Ala, Dec 19, 36; s Robert Bynum Albritton & Carrie Veal A; m 1958 to Jane Rollins Howard; c William Harold, IV, Benjamin Howard & Thomas Bynum. Educ: Univ Ala, AB, 59, LLB, 60; Phi Beta Kappa; Omicron Delta Kappa; Phi Delta Phi; Alpha Tau Omega. Polit & Govt Pos: Mem, Ala Rep Exec Comt, 68-; chmn, Covington Co Rep Exec Comt, 70- Mil Serv: Entered as 1st Lt, Army, 60, released as Capt, 62, after serv in Judge Adv Gen Corps Off Staff, Ft Hood, Tex. Mem: Am, Ala & Covington Co Bar Asns; Ala Defense Lawyers Asn (dir, 71-73, vpres, 73-); Nat Asn RR Trial Council; Am Judicature Soc. Relig: Presbyterian; Elder. Legal Res: 730 Albritton Rd Andalusia AL 36420 Mailing Add: 109 Opp Ave Andalusia AL 36420

ALCALDE, HECTOR (D)
b New York, NY, Oct 22, 33; s Armando Alcalde & Amelia Castellano A; m 1956 to Norma Jean Spoto; c Cynthia Diane, Richard Allen & Nelson Bruce. Educ: NY State Tech Inst, 53-54; Univ Tampa, BS, 56; Peabody Col, MS, 60; Theta Chi. Polit & Govt Pos: Admin asst to US Rep Sam M Gibbons, Fla, 62-67; mem, Dem Charter Comn, Dem Nat Comt, 74; deleg, Dem Nat Mid-Term Conf, 74. Bus & Prof Pos: Teacher, Hillsborough Co Bd Pub Instr, 56-62. Relig: Roman Catholic. Legal Res: 105 12 Wickens Rd Vienna VA 22180 Mailing Add: 1346 Connecticut Ave NW Suite 401 Washington DC 20036

ALCORN, HUGH MEADE, JR (R)
b Suffield, Conn, Oct 20, 07; s Hugh Meade Alcorn, Sr & Cora Terry Wells A; m 1955 to Marcia Elizabeth Powell; c Thomas Glenn (deceased) & Janet Eileen (Mrs Van Law). Educ: Dartmouth Col, AB, 30; Yale Law Sch, LLB, 33; Phi Beta Kappa; Corbey Court. Hon Degrees: LLD, Univ Hartford, 74. Polit & Govt Pos: Conn State Rep, 37-42, floor leader, Conn House Rep, 39-40, speaker, 41-42; chmn, Suffield Town Rep Comt, 38-52; mem, Conn Rep State Cent Comt, 48-57; mem, Rep Nat Comt, 53-61, chmn, 57-59, gen counsel, 60-61; Rep floor leader, Const Conv, 65. Bus & Prof Pos: Sr partner, Alcorn, Bakewell & Smith, 33-; vis lectr, Ford Found Course in Polit Sci, Univ Mass, 62. Mem: Conn Bar Asn; Am Col Trial Lawyers (fel); Mason (32 degree); Shrine; Elks. Relig: Congregational. Legal Res: 49 Russell Ave Suffield CT 06078 Mailing Add: One American Row Hartford CT 06103

ALCOTT, KITTY MAY (DFL)
Chmn, Dist 29 Dem-Farmer-Labor Party, Minn
b Pine City, Minn, May 3, 23; d Edward J Prochaska & Hazel Ahern P; m 1944 to Floyd McEwen Alcott; c Tracy Wilson & Randi Arnold. Educ: Univ Minn, Minneapolis, BSPharm, 45; Kappa Delta; Kappa Epsilon. Polit & Govt Pos: Mem, Minn State Dem-Farmer-Labor Cent Comt, 60-; mem, Town Meeting Comn, Hopkins, 65-68; secy, Housing & Redevelop Authority, 65-66; mem, Health & Welfare Comn, 67-; mem, Minn State Bd Pharm, 67-, pres, 69, chmn, Pharmpac, 67-, chmn, Dist 29 Dem-Farmer-Labor Party, 70- Publ: The use of the family record as a test for therapeutic responsibility, Nat Bd Pharm, 1/70. Mem: Minn State Pharmaceut Asn; Nat Asn Retail Druggists. Relig: Unitarian. Mailing Add: 245 12th Ave N Hopkins MN 55343

ALDEN, JOHN TAYLOR (R)
Vt State Sen
b Cambridge, Mass, Jan 6, 36; s John Gail Alden & Evelyn Dynan A; m 1960 to Patricia White; c Elisabeth Anne, John Joseph & Richard Taylor. Educ: Boston Univ, 52-55. Polit & Govt Pos: Pres, Vt Young Rep Fedn, 64-66; vchmn, Young Rep Nat Fedn, 65-67; Vt State Rep, Dist 24, 65-71; Asst Majority Leader, Vt House of Rep, 69-71, chmn, House Gen & Mil Affairs Comt, 69-71; mem, Rep State Exec Comt, 67-69; Vt State Sen, 71- Bus & Prof Pos: Ins broker, Mutual & United of Omaha, 62- Mil Serv: Entered as Pvt, Army, 55, released as SP-2, 58, after serv in 54th Missile Bn, Md, 55-58. Mem: Rotary Int; US Jaycees; Vt Farm Bur; Vt State Grange. Relig: Episcopal. Legal Res: West Woodstock VT 05091 Mailing Add: PO Box 427 Woodstock VT 05091

ALDHIZER, GEORGE STATTON, II (D)
Va State Sen
b Broadway, Rockingham Co, Va, June 15, 07; single. Educ: Univ Va, BS & LLB. Polit & Govt Pos: Va State Deleg, 50-52; Va State Sen, 54- Bus & Prof Pos: Lawyer. Mil Serv: Comdr, Naval Res. Mem: Masons; Lions; Elks; Va & Am Bar Asns. Relig: Presbyterian. Mailing Add: Broadway VA 22815

ALDRICH, GEORGE FRANCIS (DFL)
Treas, 61st Dist Dem-Farmer-Labor Party, Minn
b Minneapolis, Minn, Dec 7, 10; s Dr George Malcolm Aldrich & Ruth Alden A; m 1935 to Marjorie Shimel; c Janice (Mrs Johnson), Hillis George, Stephen Charles & Byron Clement. Educ: Cent High Sch, Minneapolis, grad, 29. Polit & Govt Pos: Treas, 35th Dist Dem-Farmer-Labor Party, Minn, 70-72, 61st Dist, 72- Mil Serv: Entered as Pvt, Minn Nat Guard, 28, released as Sgt, 36, after serv in 151st Field Artil. Mem: Independent Ins Agents of Minneapolis; Minn & Nat Asns Ins Agents; Common Cause. Relig: United Church of Christ; treas, Gtr Minneapolis Union Churches, 70- Mailing Add: 227 E Diamond Lake Rd Minneapolis MN 55419

ALDRICH, SPAULDING ROSS (R)
Chmn, Northbridge Rep Town Comt, Mass
b Whitinsville, Mass, Jan 30, 32; s Clarence Edwin Aldrich & Sylva Ann McGilvray; m 1962 to Jacqueline Constance Ducharme; c Melissa Constance, Rebecca Ann Elizabeth & Leslie Hopkins. Educ: Mitchell Col, 50-51; Univ Miss, 56-57. Polit & Govt Pos: Secy, Northbridge Conserv Comn, Mass, 65-69; coordr, Brooke for US Sen, Northbridge, 66; chmn, Northbridge Rep Town Comt, 67-; coordr & campaign staff, Miller for US Cong, 68; bd dirs, Fourth Cong Dist Rep Comt, 68-; chmn, Northbridge Zoning Bd Appeals, 68-; sch committeeman, Northbridge, 69-; coordr, Sargent-Dwight Gubernatorial Campaign & Newman for Secy of State Campaign, Northbridge, 70. Mil Serv: Entered as Pvt, Air Force, 51, released as Cpl, 54, after serv in Hq, 59th Air Defense Warning, Third Air Force, 52-54. Mem: Mass Asn Sch Committeemen; AF&AM; RAM; Am Legion. Relig: Congregational. Legal Res: 52 School St Linwood MA 01525 Mailing Add: PO Box 84 Whitinsville MA 01588

ALEIXO, THEODORE J, JR (D)
Mass State Rep
b Taunton, Mass, Aug 23, 42; to Theodore J Aleixo & Rose M Rico A; m 1963 to Elinor Ruth Soviecke; c Kara Marie, Theodore Jeffrey, III & Paul Mitchell. Educ: Providence Col, 60-62; Boston Univ, AB in hist & govt, 64; Suffolk Univ Law Sch, JD, 68; Suffolk Univ Student Bar Asn; Am Student Bar Asn. Polit & Govt Pos: Mass State Rep, 69-; mem, Taunton

Dem City Comt, 70- Bus & Prof Pos: Ins Broker, Aleixo Ins Agency, 64-70, instr soc studies & athletic coach, Taunton High Sch, 65-69; practicing attorney, Taunton, Mass, 69-; dir, Weir Cooperative Bank, Taunton, 70-; Incorporator, Taunton Savings Bank & Bristol Co Savings Bank, 70. Mem: Portuguese Am Civic Club, Taunton (chmn scholarship comt); YMCA (dir); Ward Five Athletic Club; Taunton Lodge of Elks; Taunton chap of KofC. Honors & Awards: Distinguished Serv Award as Outstanding Young Man in 1970, Taunton Jaycees, 70. Relig: Roman Catholic. Mailing Add: 10 Evergreen Dr Taunton MA 02780

ALESSANDRINI, CORNELIUS A, JR (D)
Chmn, Dickinson Co Dem Party, Mich
b Aurora, Wis, Oct 31, 31; s Cornelius Alessandrini, Sr & Ann Carollo A; single. Educ: Vulcan High Sch, grad, 49. Polit & Govt Pos: Chmn, Dickinson Co Dem Party, Mich, 75- Bus & Prof Pos: Secy-treas & field rep, Construct & Gen Laborers' Union, Local 1329, AFL-CIO, 66- Mil Serv: Entered as A/S, Navy, 52, released as Seaman, 56, after serv in Korean War. Mem: Elks; Am Legion; Laborers' Int Union. Relig: Catholic. Mailing Add: 800 Vulcan St Iron Mountain MI 49801

ALESSIE, JOHN BRUCE (D)
Conn State Rep
b Bridgeport, Conn, Dec 13, 39; s John Robert Alessie & Sarah Bruce A; m 1963 to Jane Sullivan; c Michael & Kimberly. Educ: Univ Dayton, BA, 62; Univ Bridgeport, 64; New Eng Club; Varsity D Club. Polit & Govt Pos: Pres, Ninth Dist Dem Club, 70-72; Conn State Rep, 122 Dist, 75- Bus & Prof Pos: Partner, United Castings Co, 61-; vpres, United Pattern, 61-; partner, United Polishing, 72-73. Mil Serv: Entered as 2nd Lt, Army, 62, released as 1st Lt, 64, after serv in Adj Gen Br, Third Army Hq, 62-64, Capt, Army Res; Army Commendation Medal. Mem: KofC; St Mark Parish (chmn athletic coun & lay adv bd). Relig: Catholic. Mailing Add: 53 Chanbrook Rd Stratford CT 06497

ALEX, JOHN MAYNARD (R)
Mem, Rep State Cent Comt Calif
b Lawrence, Mass, Mar 27, 29; s Joseph Leonard Alex & Rixie Loretta Maynard A; m 1951 to Elizabeth Louise Matson; c Elizabeth Lee, Rebecca Jo, John Matson & Judith Louise. Educ: Colby Col, BA, 50; Univ Chicago Law Sch, JD, 57; Delta Upsilon; Phi Alpha Delta. Polit & Govt Pos: Dep probation officer, Co of Los Angeles, Calif, 58-60, dep dist attorney, 60-69, judge, Citrus Munic Court, 69-; mem, Rep State Cent Comt Calif, 64- Mil Serv: Entered as Pvt, Army, 50, released as Sgt, 54, after serv in Spec Serv, European Theatre of Occup, 50-54; Good Conduct Medal; Expert Marksman; European Theatre of Occup Medal. Mem: Dist Attorneys Asn; Am, Co of Los Angeles, Pomona Valley & Citrus Bar Asns. Relig: Unitarian. Mailing Add: 402 N Cedar Dr Covina CA 91722

ALEXANDER, BEN B (D)
Chmn, Dem Cent Comt NMex
b Guymon, Okla, Oct 31, 20; s O V Alexander & Emma Mable Bates A; m 1942 to Gerry Ann Dunham; c Lee Ann (Mrs Thomas) & Russell B. Educ: Tex Tech Univ, 42. Polit & Govt Pos: Finance chmn, Jack Daniels for US Sen, NMex, 71-72; mem, State Investment Coun, 73-74; chmn, Dem Cent Comt NMex, 74-; mem, Dem Nat Comt, 74-; precinct chmn, Lea Co Dem Comt, 74; deleg, Dem Nat Mid-Term Conf, 74. Mil Serv: Entered as Pvt, Army, 42, released as 1st Sgt, 44, after serv in 89th & 66th Inf Div, US. Mem: Asn Oil Well Servicing Contractors; NMex Amigos; Col Southwest (bd trustees); NMex Oil & Gas Asn. Honors & Awards: Outstanding Citizen of Hobbs, Hobbs Jaycees, 67; Hobbs Citizen of Year, Hobbs Bd Realtors, 71. Relig: Methodist. Legal Res: 831 E Green Acres Hobbs NM 88240 Mailing Add: Box 1331 Hobbs NM 88240

ALEXANDER, CAROL MUELLER (D)
Mem, Cuyahoga Co Dem Exec Comt, Ohio
b Cleveland, Ohio, June 18, 25; d Hans F Mueller & Laura Portmann M; m 1947 to Thomas R Alexander; c Peter L. Educ: Simmons Col, 43-45; Univ Chicago, MA, 48. Polit & Govt Pos: Alt deleg, Dem Nat Conv, 72; mem, Cuyahoga Co Dem Exec Comt, Ohio, 72- Bus & Prof Pos: Research asst, Fedn Community Planning, 67-68; voc counr, Bur Employ Serv, Cleveland, 68-69; instr, Cuyahoga Community Col, 70- Mem: League Women Voters Cleveland; Womens City Club (comt chmn, 68-); Citizens League Gtr Cleveland; Womens Polit Caucus (bd dirs). Relig: Protestant. Mailing Add: 3645 Stoer Rd Shaker Heights OH 44122

ALEXANDER, CECIL L (D)
Ark State Rep
Mailing Add: PO Box 48 Heber Springs AR 72543

ALEXANDER, CLIFFORD L, JR (D)
b New York, NY, Sept 21, 33; m 1959 to Adele Logan; c two. Educ: Harvard Univ, BA, cum laude, 55; Yale Univ Law Sch, LLB, 58; Phi Delta Phi; Alpha chap, Omega Psi Phi. Hon Degrees: LLD, Malcolm X Col, 72. Polit & Govt Pos: Asst Dist Attorney, New York Co, NY, 59-61; exec dir, Manhattanville Hamilton Grange Neighborhood Conserv Proj, 61-62; exec prog dir, Harlem Youth Opportunities Unlimited, 62-63; foreign affairs officer, Nat Security Coun, Washington, DC, 63-64; dep spec counsel to the President, US, 64-67; chmn, Equal Employ Opportunity Comn, 67-69; mayoral cand, Washington, DC, 74. Bus & Prof Pos: Attorney, New York, NY, 63; partner, Arnold & Porter, Washington, DC, 69-; mem bd trustees, Atlanta Univ; adjunct prof law, Georgetown Law Sch; mem bd dirs, NAACP Legal Defense & Educ Fund & Mex Am Legal Defense & Educ Fund; host & co-producer TV prog, Cliff Alexander—Black on White, 71-74; bd dirs, Pa Power & Light Co, 72-; dir, Dreyfus Third Century Fund, 72-; prof, Howard Univ Law Sch, 74-; news commentator, WMAL-TV, Washington, DC, 75-: secy, Nat Urban Coalition, currently. Mil Serv: Army, 58-59. Honors & Awards: Citation, Wash Bar Asn, 69; Omega Man of Year, 69; Frederick Douglass Award, 70; Nominated One of Gifted Young Builders of Tomorrow's Am, Saturday Rev, 74. Relig: Protestant. Mailing Add: 1229 19th St NW Washington DC 20036

ALEXANDER, DAN C, JR (D)
Mem, Ala State Dem Exec Comt
b Mobile, Ala, Aug 19, 38; s D C Alexander, Sr & Mary Francis Goodman A; m to Nancy Fay Southall; c Dan C, III, Virginia Deanne & Susan Elizabeth. Educ: Univ SAla, BS Acctg; Univ Ala, JD; Phi Alpha Delta. Polit & Govt Pos: Secy, Mobile Co Dem Exec Comt, Ala, 66-74, committeeman, 66; deleg, Dem Nat Conv, 68; mem, Ala State Dem Exec Comt, 70-74; mayor's adv, Mobile Co Youth Coun, 70-74; attorney, Mobile Co Tax Assessor's Off, 72-; deleg, Dem Nat Mid-Term Conf, 74; vpres, Mobile Co Bd Sch Comnrs, 74- Bus & Prof Pos: Pres, Sports Assoc, Inc, 65-; mem bd dirs, Allied Acceptance Corp, 66-; pres, Southeastern Towing Co Inc, 74-; pres, Mid-Gulf Corp. Mem: Ala Bar Asn; Ala Trial Lawyers Asn; Ala & Nat Asns Sch Bd; Jr CofC. Legal Res: Route 4 Box 390 Mobile AL 36601 Mailing Add: PO Box 334 Mobile AL 36601

ALEXANDER, FRED D (D)
NC State Sen
Mailing Add: 2140 Senior Dr Charlotte NC 28215

ALEXANDER, HUGH QUINCY (D)
b Moore Co, NC, Aug 11, 11; s Oscar Sample Alexander & Mary Belle Reynolds A; m 1942 to Myrtle Elizabeth White; c Elizabeth, Hugh Quincy, Jr, Stephen White & William George. Educ: Duke Univ; Univ NC, Chapel Hill. Polit & Govt Pos: NC State Rep, 47-49; prosecuting attorney, Cabarrus Co Recorders Court, 50-52; US Rep, NC, 52-62; Chief Counsel, US Senate Rules Comt, currently. Mil Serv: Entered as Ens, Navy, 42, released as Lt, after serv in Pac; Three Pac Campaign Ribbons. Mem: NC, Cabarrus Co & Am Bar Asns; Mason (33 degree); Shrine (Past Master, Cannon Mem Lodge). Honors & Awards: Distinguished Serv Award, Kannapolis Jr CofC, 48. Relig: Presbyterian; Elder. Legal Res: 207 S Main St Kannapolis NC Mailing Add: 525 Monticello Blvd Alexandria VA 22305

ALEXANDER, JANE MARIETTA (D)
b Wilkes-Barre, Pa, Nov 10, 29; d Isaac C Lehmer & Marietta Fisher L; m 1950 to Paul Nelson Alexander; c Nixon, Marstin, Lorinda & Halvard. Educ: Dickinson Col, AB, 51, Dickinson Sch Law, LLB, 54; Chi Omega; Delta Kappa Gamma. Hon Degrees: LLD, Dickinson Sch Law, 73. Polit & Govt Pos: Mem & pres, Dillsburg Borough Coun, Pa, 55-58; mem, Northern Joint Sch Bd, 59-65; Pa State Rep, 92nd Dist, 65-69; mem-at-lg, Pa Coun on Status Women, 67-70; secy, York Co Dem Comt, 70-71; mem, State Adv Coun Comprehensive Health Planning, State Adv Bd Health Care Costs, Task Force on Health Costs & Financing & bd mem, Southcent Pa Health Planning Coun, Inc, currently; parliamentarian, Pa Fedn Dem Women, currently; dir, Bur Foods & Chem, Pa Dept Agr, 72, dep secy, 72- Bus & Prof Pos: Attorney, York & Dillsburg, Pa, currently. Mem: Am & York Co Bar Asns; Pa Bar Asn (mem const law comt, currently); Phi Delta Delta; Pa Fedn Bus & Prof Women's Clubs, Inc. Relig: Lutheran; former Sunday Sch teacher, St Paul's Lutheran Church, Dillsburg. Legal Res: 148 S Baltimore St Dillsburg PA 17019 Mailing Add: 46 S Duke St York PA 17401

ALEXANDER, JESSIE DURRELL (D)
Chairwoman, Bates Co Dem Cent Comt, Mo
b Miami Co, Kans, Apr 14, 19; d John Hedges Allen & Arista Ketchum A; m 1943 to Leo Francis Alexander. Polit & Govt Pos: Committeewoman, West Boone Twp, Mo, 65-75; vchairwoman, Bates Co Dem Cent Comt, Mo, 72-74, chairwoman, 74- Mem: Amsterdam Garden Club (pres); Mo-Kan Club (secy-treas). Relig: Protestant. Mailing Add: Rte 1 Box 15 Drexel MO 64742

ALEXANDER, LEE (D)
Mayor, Syracuse, NY
b Jersey City, NJ, May 18, 27; s Peter Alexander & Rita Rouatcos A; m 1957 to Elizabeth Strates; c James, Matthew, Rita & Stacy. Educ: Syracuse Univ, BA, 50, LLB, 55. Polit & Govt Pos: Councilman-at-lg, Common Coun, City of Syracuse, NY, 67-69 & 69-70, mayor, 70-; mem adv bd & legis action comt, US Conf Mayors, 71; chmn community develop comt, Nat League Cities, 70-74, mem adv bd. Mil Serv: Entered Army, released as Sgt, after serv in ETO. Mem: Syracuse Univ Everson Mus (trustee). Relig: Greek Orthodox; archon dep, 70. Mailing Add: 314 Summit Ave Syracuse NY 13207

ALEXANDER, WILLIAM HENRY (D)
b Macon, Ga, Dec 10, 30; s William Henry Alexander & Elnora Elizabeth A; m 1965 to Gayle Eileen Jackson; c Jill Marie. Educ: Ft Valley State Col, BS, 51; Univ Mich, JD, 56; Georgetown Univ, LLM, 61; Tau Epsilon Rho; Alpha Phi Alpha. Polit & Govt Pos: Legal asst, Soc Security Admin, 61-63; Ga State Rep, 66-75; judge, City Court of Atlanta, 75- Bus & Prof Pos: Attorney-at-law, Atlanta, Ga, 63- Mil Serv: Entered as Pvt, Army, 51, released as Spec Agent, Counter Intel Corps, 53; Nat Defense Serv Medal. Mem: Am Civil Liberties Union; NAACP; Am Bar Asn; Am Judicature Soc; Am Judges Asn. Relig: Roman Catholic. Mailing Add: 3725 Dover Blvd SW Atlanta GA 30331

ALEXANDER, WILLIAM V, JR (BILL) (D)
US Rep, Ark
b Memphis, Tenn, Jan 16, 34; s William V Alexander & Eulalia Spencer Buck A; m 1957 to Gwendolyn Haven (Gwen); c Alyse Haven. Educ: Univ Ark, 50-51; Southwestern at Memphis, BA, 57; Vanderbilt Univ Sch Law, LLB, 60; Phi Delta Phi; Kappa Sigma. Polit & Govt Pos: Comnr, Ark Waterways Comn; secy, Osceola Port Authority; mem, Osceola Civic Ctr Comt; dir, Northeast Ark Econ Develop Dist; dir, Miss Co Off Educ Opportunity; mem, Miss Co Quorum Court; dir, Osceola Munic Port Comn; dir, Osceola Munic Planning Comn; legal research asst to Fed Judge Marion Boyd; resigned all after elected as US Rep, Ark First Dist, 69- Bus & Prof Pos: Assoc, Montedonico, Boone, Gilliland, Heiskell, & Loch, 61-62; partner, law firm, Swift & Alexander, 63- Mil Serv: Entered the Army, 51, released in 53, after serv in Adj Gen Corps. Mem: Osceola, Miss Co, Ark, Tenn, & Am Bar Asns. Relig: Episcopal. Legal Res: 811 W Hale Ave Osceola AR 72370 Mailing Add: US House of Rep Washington DC 20515

ALEXANDER, WM B (D)
Miss State Sen
b Boyle, Miss, Dec 23, 21; s William Brooks Alexander & Vivien Beaver A; m 1950 to Belle McDonald; c Brooks, Becky, John, Jason & Grace. Educ: Miss Col, undergrad; Univ Miss, LLB, 48, JD, 68; Sigma Nu. Polit & Govt Pos: Miss State Sen, 60- Mil Serv: Air Force, 42-46, served in Pac Theater; New Guinea, Philippines & Korean Campaign ribons. Mem: Miss Heart Asn (dir, 70-); State Comdr, VFW; Exchange Club; Mason; Shrine. Relig: Baptist. Legal Res: 517 Fayette Davis Ave Cleveland MS 38732 Mailing Add: 112 N Pearman Ave Cleveland MS 38732

ALFANO, CHARLES THOMAS (D)
Conn State Sen
b Suffield, Conn, June 21, 20; s Dominic Alfano & Rose DiMartini A; m 1954 to Mary Ann Sinatro; c Diane Elizabeth, Andrea Rose, Charles T, Jr & Susan Marie. Educ: Univ Conn, BA, 43; Univ Mich, LLB, 48. Polit & Govt Pos: Munic judge, Suffield, Conn, 49-51 & 54-58; Conn State Sen, 59-, Pres-Pro-Tem, Conn State Senate, 67-, Minority Leader, 73- alt deleg, Dem Nat Conv, 68 & deleg, 72. Bus & Prof Pos: Attorney, Alfano & Bumster, 48- Mil Serv: Entered as A/S, Navy, 42, released as Lt(jg), 46, after serv in Pac Theater. Mem: Am Trial

Lawyers Asn; KofC; VFW; Hartford Club; Univ Club. Relig: Catholic. Legal Res: 50 Marbern Dr Suffield CT 06078 Mailing Add: 100 Constitution Plaza Hartford CT 06103

ALFORD, BOYCE (D)
Ark State Rep
Mailing Add: 1 Idylwood Pine Bluff AR 71601

ALFORD, DALLAS L, JR (D)
NC State Sen
b Durham, NC; s Dallas Lloyd Alford, Sr & Sally Kate Pope A; m 1945 to Margarette Glenn Griffin; c Dallas L, III, Benjamin G, Margarette G & Catherine Elizabeth. Educ: Duke Univ, 31; Delta Sigma Phi. Polit & Govt Pos: Mem Bd of Aldermen, Rocky Mount, NC, 39-42; Nash Co Bd of Comnrs, 48-58, chmn, 52-58; chmn, Nash Co Bd of Health, 52-58; mem, Comt for Study of Revenue Structure of State, 57-58; NC State Sen, 59-61, 65-67 & 73-; chmn, Comt to Study Welfare Probs for State of NC, 62. Bus & Prof Pos: Owner & operator, Alford Ins & Realty Co. Mil Serv: US Navy, 42-46, Lt Comdr. Mem: Rocky Mount Realtors Asn; Lodge 1038, Elks; 40 & 8; Kiwanis; Benvenue Country Club. Relig: First Methodist Church, mem off bd, Rocky Mount, 38-65. Mailing Add: 100 Wildwood Ave Rocky Mount NC 27801

ALI, NED (R)
Chmn, Thompson Rep Town Comt, Conn
b Thompson, Conn, Sept 14, 42; s Shaban Ali & Refie Spaho A; m 1965 to Joan Bushka; c Karen Lee & Scott. Educ: Eastern Conn State Col, BS, 64; Univ Conn, MS, 67, cert, 70. Polit & Govt Pos: Mem, Thompson Rep Town Comt, Conn, 66-, chmn, 70-; registr of voters, Thompson, 67-; mem, State of Conn Scholar Comn, 72- Bus & Prof Pos: Teacher, Woodstock Pub Schs, Conn, 64-68, prin, 68-70, asst prin, 70-; real estate salesman, Conn, 71- Mem: Elem Sch Prin Asn Conn; Elks; Mason. Relig: Islam. Legal Res: Elliott Hill Rd North Grosvenor Dale CT 06255 Mailing Add: PO Box 224 North Grosvenor Dale CT 06255

ALIOTO, JOSEPH LAWRENCE (D)
Mayor, San Francisco, Calif
b San Francisco, Calif, Feb 12, 16; s Giuseppe Alioto & Domenica Lazio A; m 1941 to Angelina Genaro; c Lawrence E, Joseph M, John I, Angela Mia (Mrs Veronese), Thomas R & Michael J. Educ: St Mary's Col, BA, 37; Cath Univ Am, JD, 40. Polit & Govt Pos: Spec asst to the attorney gen, Anti Trust Div, US Dept Justice, Washington, DC, 41-42; mem, Bd Econ Warfare, Washington, DC, 42-44; pres, Bd Educ, San Francisco, Calif, 48-53; pres, Redevelopment Agency, San Francisco, 55-59; mayor, San Francisco, 68- Bus & Prof Pos: Attorney, 48-; pres, Rice Growers Asn, 59-69, gen counsel & bus consult, 68-; chmn bd, First San Francisco Bank, 65-68; gen counsel & bus consult, Charles Krug Winery, 67- Mem: Am Col of Trial Lawyers; Salesian Boys Club; CofC of San Francisco; Sons of Italy. Honors & Awards: Man of the Year Award, Justinian Soc, 68; Gran' Ufficiale, Order of Merit of the Italian Repub, 69; Ordre des Arts et des Lettres, French Govt, 69; French Legion Honor, 71. Relig: Catholic. Legal Res: 34 Presidio Terr San Francisco CA 94118 Mailing Add: Rm 200 City Hall San Francisco CA 94102

ALKIRE, ALMA ASENATH (R)
b Phoenix, Ariz. Educ: Pomona Col, Claremont, Calif, BA, 37. Polit & Govt Pos: Mem staff, US Rep John Rhodes, Ariz, 53-, admin asst, currently. Bus & Prof Pos: Am Red Cross, 44-49; secy-librn, Maricopa Co Med Soc, Ariz, 49-52. Mem: Jr League of Phoenix. Legal Res: Phoenix AZ Mailing Add: Off of Hon John J Rhodes US House of Rep Washington DC 20515

ALLAMAN, CHARLES LEE (D)
Chmn, Fulton Co Dem Cent Comt, Ill
b Canton, Ill, Feb 1, 16; s Charles Edgar Allaman & Katherine Pearl Rings A; m 1937 to Pauline Eva Wright; c Kenneth Charles. Educ: Canton High Sch, Ill, grad, 34. Polit & Govt Pos: Asst supvr, Canton Twp, Ill, 69-71; hwy comnr, 71-; mem bd supvr, Fulton Co, 69-71; chmn, Fulton Co Dem Cent Comt, 74- Bus & Prof Pos: Pres, Local 1357, UAW, 54-57, chmn retired workers, 65-; state dir farm-labor rels, AFL-CIO, 57-60. Mem: Am Legion; Elks; UAW Retired Workers (chmn, Cent Ill Coun, 67-); Twp Officials Ill. Relig: Protestant. Mailing Add: 760 W Locust St Canton IL 61520

ALLARD, RICHARD JAMES (D)
Vt State Rep
Mailing Add: St Albans VT 05478

ALLEN, ARIS TEE (R)
b San Antonio, Tex, Dec 27, 10; s James Allen & Maryetta Whitby A; m 1946 to Faye W, MD; c Aris T, Jr & Lonnie W. Educ: Howard Univ, MD, 44; Alpha Phi Alpha; Chi Delta Mu. Polit & Govt Pos: Md State Deleg, until 74, minority whip, Md House Deleg, 69-74, alt deleg, Rep Nat Conv, 68, deleg & chmn Md deleg, 72. Bus & Prof Pos: Physician, 45-66; mem bd dirs, Colonial Bank & Trust Co, Annapolis, Md, 69. Mil Serv: Capt & Flight Surgeon, Air Force, 51-53. Mem: Am Med Asn; Anne Arundel Co Med Soc; Am Legion; Medico Chirurlical Soc; NAACP. Honors & Awards: Richard Allen Award for Devotion to Church & State; NAACP State Br Award; Med Chi Award, Alpha Phi Alpha; Award, Md State Legis Resolution. Relig: African Methodist Episcopal: Trustee. Mailing Add: 62 Cathedral St Annapolis MD 21401

ALLEN, BEN (D)
Ark State Sen
Mailing Add: 446 Valley Club Circle Little Rock AR 72207

ALLEN, BERNARD GENE (D)
Chairperson, Ottawa Co Dem Party, Mich
b Byron Center, Mich, Dec 4, 46; s Victor Carl Allen & Pauline Van Haitsma A; m 1967 to Sandra Lee Kuiper; c Paula Jo & Terri Lynn. Educ: Western Mich Univ, BA, 68, MA, 73. Polit & Govt Pos: Treas, Ottawa Co Dem Party, Mich, 73-75, chairperson, 75-; alt deleg, Mich Dem State Cent Comt, 73-75, deleg, 75-; alt deleg, Dem Mid-Term Conf, 74. Bus & Prof Pos: Jr high sch educator, Holland Pub Schs, Mich, 68- Mem: Holland Educ Asn (pres); Mich Educ Asn; Hist Soc Mich; Ottawa Co Bicentennial Comt. Honors & Awards: Leadership in Educ Award, Mich Educ Asn, 74; Dean's List, Western Mich Univ; Cert Merit, Child & Family Serv, Mich, 74. Relig: Protestant. Mailing Add: 323 W 20th Holland MI 49423

ALLEN, BOBBY JERALD (D)
Chmn, Sierra Co Dem Party, NMex
b Mangun, Okla, Nov 8, 42; s James W Allen & Mary Ruth Anthony A; m 1911 to Margaret Ida Louis; c Wendy M. Educ: Hot Springs High Sch. Polit & Govt Pos: City comnr, Truth or Consequences, NMex, 72-; mayor pro tem, 73-; mem gov coun, NMex, 74-; mem, Coun Govt, 74-; chmn, Sierra Co Dem Party, 74- Bus & Prof Pos: Allen & Son Music Co, Truth or Consequences, 68- Mil Serv: E-5, NMex Nat Guard, 60-64. Mem: Jaycees; JET. Honors & Awards: Dem Chmn of the Year; Citation for Serv from Secy State, Dem Chmn & Lt Gov, State of NMex. Relig: Baptist. Mailing Add: 710 Charles St Truth or Consequences NM 87901

ALLEN, BRADLEY E (D)
Chmn, Pope Co Dem Comt, Ill
b Golconda, Ill, Nov 7, 14; s Byrd B Allen & Julia Moyers A; m 1938 to Lorraine Collins; c Bradley B & James L. Educ: Golconda Community High Sch, grad, 33. Polit & Govt Pos: Chmn, Pope Co Dem Comt, Ill, 75- Mem: Golconda Masons; Int Union Operating Engrs. Mailing Add: Rte 1 Golconda IL 62938

ALLEN, CHARLES EDGAR (D)
WVa State Deleg
b Windom, WVa, Feb 16, 16; s George E Allen & Martha Browning A; m 1937 to Pearl Caldwell; c Charles Edgar, Jr, Jackie Lee, Margaret, Carol Sue, Betty Jo & Barbara Allen Mullens. Educ: Pub Schs, Wyoming Co. Polit & Govt Pos: WVa State Deleg, 64-68 & 75-; city comnr, Mullens, WVa, formerly. Bus & Prof Pos: Rwy Conductor. Mem: BRT; Mason; Moose. Relig: Baptist. Mailing Add: 902 Poplar St Mullens WV 25882

ALLEN, CHARLES GICE, JR (R)
Mem Exec Comt, Cabarrus Co Rep Party, NC
b Raleigh, NC, Nov 3, 24; s Charles Gice Allen, Sr & Caro McNeill A; m 1950 to Willie Mae McGuirt; c Suzanne & Julie Mae. Educ: Concord High Sch, NC, grad. Polit & Govt Pos: Mem exec comt, Cabarrus Co Rep.Party, 62-; Tax collector, Cabarrus Co, NC, 63-; alt deleg, Rep Nat conv, 68. Bus & Prof Pos: Prof baseball player, Wash Senators & NY Giants, Farm Systs, 47-54; aircraft plant worker, Douglas Aircraft Co, Charlotte, NC, 55-62; real estate broker, Davidson Drive, Concord, 70- Mil Serv: Entered as Seaman, Navy, 43, released as Pharmacist's Mate 2/C, 45, after serv in Med Corps, Am Theater, 43-45. Mem: NC State Asn; Tax Collectors; Shrine; Scottish Rite; Mason. Relig: Protestant. Mailing Add: Rte 2 Box 266 Midland NC 28107

ALLEN, CHARLES HENRY, JR (D)
b Providence, RI, June 10, 12; s Charles Henry Allen & Lottie Greene A; m 1934 to Barbara Downes; c Charles H, III, Barbara M (Mrs Bechtold), Howard A, Gregory G & Pamela J (Mrs Bennett). Educ: Classical High Sch, Providence, RI, 28-30. Polit & Govt Pos: Dir, Civil Defense, Exeter, RI, 68-; chmn, Exeter Dem Town Comt, 70-75. Bus & Prof Pos: Turf foreman, Agr Exp Sta, Univ RI, 37-68; pres, Allens Seed Store, Exeter, 53- Mem: RI Golf Course Supt Asn. Relig: Baptist. Legal Res: S County Trail Exeter RI 02822 Mailing Add: S County Trail Slocum RI 02877

ALLEN, CRAIG ADAMS (D)
Committeeman, Ohio Dem State Cent Comt
b Ironton, Ohio, June 30, 41; s Enoch Stanley Allen & Margaret Adams A; m 1964 to Carol Linda Brewster; c Laura Brewster & Kathryn Adams. Educ: Denison Univ, BA, 63; Ohio State Univ, JD, 66; Omicron Delta Kappa; Rho Beta Chi; Delta Upsilon; Phi Alpha Delta; Moot Court Governing Bd; Denison Fellows Award. Polit & Govt Pos: Chmn, Ohio Students for Kennedy, 62; chmn, Denison Dem Club, 62-63; Dem precinct committeeman, Lawrence Co, Ohio, 62-70; mem, Lawrence Co Dem Exec Comt, 62-; cand for Ohio State Rep, 66; asst prosecuting attorney, Lawrence Co, 67-69; chmn, Lawrence Co, Ohio, 62-70; mem, Lawrence Co Dem Exec Comt, 62-; cand for Ohio State Rep, 66; asst prosecuting attorney, Lawrence Co, 67-69; chmn, Lawrence Co Dem Finance Comt, 67-; deleg, Ohio Dem State Conv, 68-72; village solicitor, Chesapeake, Ohio, 69-73; village solicitor, Athalia, 70-; committeeman, Ohio Dem State Cent Comt, 70- Bus & Prof Pos: Attorney-at-law, Edwards, Klein, Allen & Kehoe, 66- Mil Serv: SP-5, Ohio Nat Guard, 66-72; Expert Rifle Badge. Mem: Ohio & Lawrence Co Bar Asns; Nat Dist Attorneys Asn; Am Judicature Soc; Elks. Relig: Episcopal; Vestryman. Mailing Add: 616 S Fifth St Ironton OH 45638

ALLEN, DANIEL WARREN (D)
Vt State Rep
Mailing Add: 50 Chestnut Ave Rutland VT 05701

ALLEN, DAVID BLISS (R)
b Moulmein, Burma, Sept 16, 39; s Leonard Bliss Allen & Kathleen Smyth A; m 1970 to Juliet Russell Mumma; c Jennifer Russell & Laura Elizabeth. Educ: LaSalle Exten Univ, LLB, 69; Univ Nebr, Omaha, BGS, 71. Polit & Govt Pos: Admin asst, Ore State Legis, 71; campaign mgr, Don Stathos for State Treas Comt, 71-72; alt deleg, Rep Nat Conv, 72; dist planner, Exec Dept, State of Ore, 72-73; exec dir, Western Environ Trade Asn, 73-74. Bus & Prof Pos: Exec officer, Moral Re-Armament, New York, NY 56-66; asst to pres, Up With People, Inc, Tucson, Ariz, 66; managing ed, Pace Mag, Los Angeles, 66-68; asst dir environ resources, Weyerhaeuser Co, 74- Mil Serv: Entered as Pvt E-1, Army, 66, released as 1st Lt, 69, after serv in Hq, Mil Dist of Wash, then Traffic Mgt Agency, MACV, Vietnam, 67-69; Bronze Star; Vietnam Campaign Medal; Vietnam Serv Medal; Cert of Achievement, Mil Dist of Wash. Publ: How to Create Your Own Sing-Out, 66 & Born to Upturn the World, 67, Pace Publ. Mem: Am Soc Composers, Auth & Publ. Honors & Awards: Ark Traveler, Gov Faubus, Ark, 63; Ky Col, Gov Breathitt, Ky, 66. Relig: Baptist. Mailing Add: 168 S 295th Pl Redondo WA 98054

ALLEN, DONALD GEORGE (R)
Chmn, Sprague Rep Town Comt, Conn
b Norwich, Conn, Jan 4, 37; s Donald Carlton Allen & Cecile LaFreniere A; m 1956 to Lorraine Antonia Fortier; c Donald G, Jr, Cheryl Ann, George William, III & Barbara Jean. Educ: Norwich Free Acad, 4 years. Polit & Govt Pos: Chmn, Sprague Rep Town Comt, Conn, currently; past mem bd selectmen, Sprague Conn. Mil Serv: Entered as Pvt, Marine Corps Res, 54, released as Sgt, 62, after serv in Third Spec Inf Co. Mem: Nat Mgt Asn; Muklak Sportsman Club; Sprague Rod & Gun Club; KofC (4 degree); Int Order Alhambra. Relig: Roman Catholic. Legal Res: Westminster Rd Hanover CT 06330 Mailing Add: RFD 1 Box 140 AA Baltic CT 06330

ALLEN, DOZIER T, JR (D)
Chmn, First Dem Cong Dist, Ind
b Gary, Ind, Jan 10, 31; s Dozier T Allen, Sr & Mattie J Henderson A; m 1968 to Arlene McKinney; c Vincent, Patsy & Kyle Allen & Freya Williams. Educ: Los Angeles Jr Col, 1 year; Ind Univ, 2 years; Valparaiso Univ, 2 years. Polit & Govt Pos: Councilman-at-lg, Gary City Coun, Ind, 68-72; trustee, Calumet Twp, 70-74 & 74-; Ind chmn for Nat Black Caucus of Local Elected Off, 71; chmn, First Dem Cong Dist, 74- Bus & Prof Pos: Vpres, Allen Enterprises, currently; secy, Allen Florist, currently; pres, Allen Transit, Inc & Final Investment Mgt Corp, currently; vpres & secy, Mach, Inc, currently. Mil Serv: Entered as Pvt, Army, 52, released as Sgt, 54, after serv in Korea; Korean Serv Medal; Bronze Star; UN Serv Medal; Nat Defense Serv Medal; Good Conduct Medal. Mem: Nat Asn for Sickle Cell Disease, Inc (first vpres & bd mem); Gary Marona House Drug Abuse, Inc (bd mem); Gary Toastmasters Int; Nat Exchange Club; Northwest Ind Urban League (adv bd mem). Honors & Awards: Outstanding Civic & Community Serv Award, United Viscounts, Inc, 67; Councilman of Year Award, NAACP Youth Coun, 69; Black Merit Acad Award, Ind Justice of Peace Asn, 73; Mary White Ovington Award, Gary Adult Br NAACP, 73; Serv Award, Northwest Ind Sickle Cell Found, Inc, 73. Relig: Baptist. Legal Res: 1729 W Seventh Ave Gary IN 46404 Mailing Add: 35 E Fifth Ave Gary IN 46402

ALLEN, ELTON ELLSWORTH (R)
Chmn, Putnam Co Rep Party, WVa
b Hurricane, WVa, July 17, 13; s Noah R Allen & Grace Henderson A; m 1937 to Nancy Roach; c Don & Ann. Educ: Cincinnati Col Mortuary Sci, Embalmer, 38. Polit & Govt Pos: Campaign mgr, Putnam Co Rep Party, WVa, 48, finance chmn, 55-56, chmn, 66-68 & 72-; mem, Town Coun, Hurricane, WVa, 14 years. Bus & Prof Pos: Owner & mgr, Allen Funeral Home, Hurricane, WVa, currently. Publ: Articles in various Funeral Dirs Jour, 66. Mem: WVa Funeral Dirs Asn; AF&AM; KofP; Lions. Honors & Awards: Ky Col. Relig: Baptist. Legal Res: 2914 Putnam Ave Hurricane WV 25526 Mailing Add: 2837 Main St Hurricane WV 25526

ALLEN, GEORGE EDWARD, JR (D)
Va State Deleg
b Victoria, Va, Apr 4, 14; m to Elizabeth Stone A. Educ: Va Polytech Inst; Univ Richmond Law Sch, LLB. Polit & Govt Pos: Alt deleg, Dem Nat Conv, 52, deleg, 60; Va State Deleg, 54-; past pres, Young Dem Clubs of Va. Bus & Prof Pos: Lawyer. Mem: Am Bar Asn; Am Trial Lawyers Asn; Law Sci Acad & Found; Co Club of Va; Commonwealth Club, Richmond. Relig: Baptist. Legal Res: 4610 Sulgrave Rd Richmond VA 23221 Mailing Add: House of Delegates State Capitol Bldg Richmond VA 23219

ALLEN, HILARY P (DFL)
Chmn, Houston Co Dem-Farmer-Labor Party, Minn
b Newburg Twp, Minn, Jan 17, 11; s Albert E Allen & Agnes Gagen A; m 1937 to Laura Bunge; c Carol (Mrs Stanley Barish), Sharon (Mrs Gordon Huseby), Thomas, Laura Joan (Mrs Joseph Deofel) & Michael. Educ: St Johns High Sch, grad, 27. Polit & Govt Pos: Chmn, Houston Co Dem-Farmer-Labor Party, Minn, 40-50 & 74-; treas, First Dist, 46. Bus & Prof Pos: Owner-operator, Allen Farms, Caledonia, Minn, 27- Mem: KofC Coun 1198 (Grand Knight & trustee); Farmers Union (pres, Caledonia Local). Relig: Catholic. Mailing Add: Rte 1 Caledonia MN 55921

ALLEN, IRA E (R)
NH State Rep
Mailing Add: RFD Littleton NH 03561

ALLEN, JACK LEE (R)
Mem, Nebr Rep State Cent Comt
b Robinson, Kans, Apr 2, 41; s Asa Bryan Allen & Ruth Blanche Haney A; single. Educ: Univ Omaha. Polit & Govt Pos: Mem, Young Rep State Bd, Nebr, 58-59; dep co sheriff & chief co probation officer, Sarpy Co, 65-68; alt deleg-at-lg, Rep Nat Conv, 68; mem, Sarpy Co Rep Cent Comt, 68-; mem, Nebr State Rep Cent Comt, 68-; deleg, Nebr State Rep Conv, 68 & 70; mem, Info Adv Comt to the Secy of Com, Washington, DC, 70- Bus & Prof Pos: Ed, Bellevue Press, 61-65 & 68- Mem: Nebr Press Asn; Optimist Club; DeMolay; CofC; Jaycees. Honors & Awards: Received numerous community and prof honors. Relig: Episcopal. Mailing Add: 2809 Sandra St Omaha NE 68147

ALLEN, JACQUE (R)
Chmn, Wichita Co Rep Party, Tex
b Marmaduke, Ark; d Clarence William Bullard & Verna Bradsher B; m 1943 to Dr David H Allen; c Carol (Mrs Wayne Hughes) & Cathy (Mrs Sam Atkins, II). Educ: Cent State Univ, 39-41; Midwestern Univ, 48-; Delta Delta Delta. Hon Degrees: Degree, Cent State Univ. Polit & Govt Pos: Precinct chmn, Wichita Co Rep Party, Tex, 60-72, vchmn, 72-74, chmn, 74-; campaign chmn, Frank Crowley for Cong, 68, George Bush for Sen, 70 & Bob Price for Congress, 74. Bus & Prof Pos: X-ray technician, Univ Ark, 43; secy, Clarinda Corp, Wichita Falls, Tex, 61. Mem: Knife & Fork Club; Carousel Club; Rep Womens Club. Honors & Awards: Sr-Jr Forum Serv Award, 48-58. Relig: Methodist. Mailing Add: 2206 Clarinda Wichita Falls TX 76308

ALLEN, JAMES BROWNING (D)
US Sen, Ala
b Gadsden, Ala, Dec 28, 12; s George C Allen & Mary Ethel Browning A; m 1940 to Marjorie Jo Stephens, wid 56; m 1964 to Maryon Pittman Mullins; c James B, Jr. Educ: Univ Ala. Polit & Govt Pos: Ala State Rep, 39-45; Ala State Sen, 47-51; Lt Gov, Ala, 51-55 & 63-67; US Sen, Ala, 69- Mil Serv: Entered as Ens, Naval Res, 43, released as Lt(jg), 46. Relig: Church of Christ. Legal Res: 1321 Bellevue Dr Gadsden AL 35901 Mailing Add: New Senate Off Bldg Washington DC 20510

ALLEN, JAMES EDWARD (R)
Secy, Magoffin Co Rep Exec Comt, Ky
b Salyersville, Ky, Apr 2, 30; s Alexander Hamilton Allen & Thelma Flint A; m 1960 to Beulah Taulbee; c Alice Lynn & Nina Gayle. Educ: Eastern Ky Univ, 51-53. Polit & Govt Pos: Clerk, Magoffin Co Circuit Court, Ky, 58; secy, Magoffin Co Rep Exec Comt, 60-; alt deleg, Rep Nat Conv, 72. Mil Serv: Entered as Pvt, Nat Guard, 47, released as Pfc, 48, after serv in Co F, 149th Inf, Ky. Mem: Mason (master, Salyersville Lodge 769, 66). Relig: Baptist. Mailing Add: PO Box 99 Salyersville KY 41465

ALLEN, JESSE WILLARD (R)
b Hamilton, Tex, Feb 17, 17; s Shoobie Allen & Ethel Lavelle A; m 1946 to Vivian Zudora Levy. Polit & Govt Pos: Co chmn, Rep Party, Ariz, 60-63; Ariz State Rep, 65-66; first vchmn, Ariz Rep Comt, 66-75; bd mem, Ariz Dept Econ Planning & Develop, 68-; chmn, Santa Cruz Co Rep Comt, 73-75. Mil Serv: Entered as A/S, Navy, 35, released as Lt(jg), 46; World War II Theater Ribbons; Camp Ribbons. Mem: Nat & Am Community Theatre Asn; Ariz Oil & Gas Asn; Ariz Acad Pub Opinion (bd dirs); Elks; VFW. Relig: Roman Catholic. Legal Res: 132 Paseo Contento Nogales AZ 85621 Mailing Add: PO Box 400 Nogales AZ 85621

ALLEN, JOE H (D)
Tex State Rep
b 1941; m to Billye; c Sydney Lisa & James Neal. Educ: Lee Col, AB; pres, Student Asn & Young Dem; presiding off, State Conv Tex Col Student Coun Asn; dir, Circle K; ed, The Lee Lantern; named Outstanding Graduating Student; Lee Col Hall of Fame. Polit & Govt Pos: Committeeman, Precinct 13, Harris Co Dem Exec Comt, Tex, 64-; co-chmn, Baytown & E Harris Co Johnson-Humphrey Campaign, 64; Tex State Rep, Dist 23, Position 3, 66-, chmn, Comt House Admin, Tex House Rep, 63rd Legis. Bus & Prof Pos: Banking, Houston, Tex. Mil Serv: Army Security Agency, 3 years. Mem: Bayshore Rod, Reel & Gun Club (dir); Houston Sportsman Club; Baytown Jr CofC; Rotary; Sierra Club. Relig: Presbyterian. Legal Res: 5315 Bayway Dr Baytown TX 77520 Mailing Add: PO Box 2910 Austin TX 78767

ALLEN, JOHN JOSEPH, JR (R)
b Oakland, Calif, Nov 27, 99; s John Joseph Allen & Catherine Liston Owen A; m 1926 to Carol Cook (deceased); m 1957 to Sally Clement; c Ramona (Mrs McIntyre), Susanne (Mrs Harvey), Catherine Clement, Sally Ann & Verna Lucile. Educ: Univ Calif, AB, 20, JD, 22; Theta Chi. Polit & Govt Pos: Mem, Oakland Bd Educ, Calif, 23-43; mem, Alameda Co Rep Cent Comt, 24-26 & 34-44; vchmn, Orgn State Comn on Sch Dists, 46; US Rep, Calif, 47-59; undersecy transportation, Dept of Com, 59-61; mem, Zoning Comn, McCall, Idaho, 73- Bus & Prof Pos: Attorney-at-law, 22-69, Retired; dir, Ins Securities Inc, 54-67. Mil Serv: A/S, World War I; reentered Navy, Lt, 43, released as Lt Comdr, 45, after serv in Naval Net Depot; Tiburon & various islands in SPac Area; Lt Comdr, Naval Res (Ret). Mem: Elks; Masons; Kiwanis. Relig: Episcopal. Mailing Add: PO Box 721 McCall ID 83638

ALLEN, JOHN NEVILLE (R)
VChmn, First Dist Rep Party, Wis
b Buffalo, NY, July 3, 22; s George Henry Allen & Alice Randall A; m 1950 to Margery Dixon; c Holly, Roberta & Leigh. Educ: Wooster Prep Sch, Conn, grad, 40; Bay Path Bus Col, Mass, grad, 41. Polit & Govt Pos: Precinct committeeman, Rep Party, Kenosha Co, Wis, 62-64; chmn, Goldwater Comt, 64-65, vchmn, 65-66; chmn, Kenosha Co Rep Party, 66-69; vchmn, First Dist Rep Party, 69- Bus & Prof Pos: Various positions, Anaconda Am Brass Co, 41-59, asst sales mgr, Kenosha Div, 59-70, customer serv mgr, 70-73; mgr, Hussey Metals Div, Copper Range Co, 73- Mil Serv: Entered as Pvt, Marine Corps, 42, released as Sgt, 46, after serv in 1st & 4th Divs, SPac & China Theatres, 44-46; Presidential Unit Citation; Good Conduct Medal; Am Campaign Medal; Victory Medal; China Serv Medal; Navy Occup Serv Medal; Asia, Asiatic-Pac Campaign Medal with Two Bronze Stars. Mem: Mason; Elks; Kenosha Country Club; Kenosha Towne Club. Relig: Episcopal. Mailing Add: 406 78th St Kenosha WI 53140

ALLEN, KENNETH PETER (D)
Dir Region I, Young Dem Clubs of Am
b Lewiston, Maine, July 11, 51; s Reginald Forest Allen & Irene Esther Munn A; single. Educ: Univ Maine, Augusta, ALS, 71. Polit & Govt Pos: Cent Maine coordr, Maine Young Dem, 70-71, exec dir, 71-72, pres, 72; secy, Kennebec Co Dem Comt, 72-; mem, Maine Youth Comn, 72-; dir region I, Young Dem Clubs of Am, New Eng & NY, 73- Bus & Prof Pos: Pub rels consult, Augusta, Maine Area, 73- Relig: Congregational. Legal Res: River Rd Sidney ME 04330 Mailing Add: RD 3 Augusta ME 04330

ALLEN, L CALHOUN, JR (D)
Mayor, Shreveport, La
b Shreveport, La, Feb 8, 20; s L Calhoun Allen; m 1948 to Mary Lenore Miller; c Frances Olivia & L Calhoun, III. Polit & Govt Pos: Comnr pub utilities, Shreveport, La, 62-66 & 66-70, mayor, 70- Bus & Prof Pos: Allen Construction Co, Shreveport, La; Asst dir, Caddo-Bossier Civil Defense; exec bd & bd dirs, La State Fair Asn 72, chmn, La State Fair Stadium Comn, 72; comnr, La Stadium & Expos Dist, 72-; fourth dist vpres & exec bd, La Munic Asn, 71- Mil Serv: Entered Navy, 43, released as Lt, 46, after serv in Atlantic & Pac Theatres, 44-46; Korean Conflict, 50-54; Capt, Naval Res, Nat Naval Res Policy Bd of Secy of Navy, 69-71; serv as commanding officer, Naval & Marine Corps Res Training Ctr & various Naval Res Units; Naval rep to Staff of Adj Gen of State of La, presently. Mem: Navy League US; Am Legion (past comdr Lowe-McFarlane Post, mem naval affairs comt, Nat Security Comn); 40 et 8 (chef de gare of voiture No 137, 64-65, pres Southland Dixie Promenade, 65-66, grand chef de gare of La, 66-67); Kiwanis; F&AM. Honors & Awards: Prin speaker at commissioning of USS Shreveport (LPD-12), Puget Sound Naval Shipyard, Bremerton, Wash. Relig: Presbyterian; Elder. Legal Res: 4156 Maryland Shreveport LA 71106 Mailing Add: PO Box 1109 Shreveport LA 71102

ALLEN, LEM B (D)
Chmn, Guadalupe Co Dem Party, Tex
b Luling, Tex, Mar 4, 41; s Louis Fulshear Allen & Frances Gardien A; m 1963 to Mattie Susan Rogers; c Lem B, Jr & Zachary Fulshear. Educ: Tex Technol, Col, 3 years. Polit & Govt Pos: Chmn, Guadalupe Co Dem Party, Tex, 66-; secy-treas, Tex Dem Co formerly, Chmn, currently; mem, comn on Vice Presidential Selection, Dem Nat Comt, 73-, Dem Nat Committeeman, Tex, 75- Bus & Prof Pos: Farmer, 63- Mem: Tex & Southwestern Cattle Raisers Asns. Relig: Episcopal. Mailing Add: Rte 1 Box 339 Kingsbury TX 78638

ALLEN, MARGARET (D)
Miss State Rep
Mailing Add: Box 344 Amory MS 38821

ALLEN, MARY ELIZABETH (D)
b Lawrence, Kans, July 10, 30; d John Selig & Agnes Jost S; m 1953 to Adrian James Allen; c Roger James & Cynthia. Educ: Univ Kans, BS Educ, 52; Pi Lambda Theta; Omicron Nu. Polit & Govt Pos: Women's vpres, Kans Dem Club, 62-63; vchmn, Second Cong Dist Dem Comt, 60-64; vchmn, Shawnee Co Dem Cent Comt, 60-75; secy, Kans State Dem Comt, 64-65, vchmn, 65-75; deleg, Dem Nat Conv, 68; mem, Dem Nat Comt, Kans, 75. Bus & Prof Pos: Teacher voc homemaking, 52-54. Mem: Native Daughters of Kans; Topeka Bar Asn

Auxiliary; Am Home Econ Asn; Kans Home Econ Asn. Relig: Lutheran. Mailing Add: 5048 Brentwood Dr Topeka KS 66606

ALLEN, MELBA TILL (D)
State Auditor, Ala
b Friendship Community, Ala, Mar 3, 33, d Samuel Ben Till & Gertrude Johnson T; m 1950 to Marvin E Allen; c Judy & Randy. Educ: Georgiana High Sch. Polit & Govt Pos: State Auditor, Ala, 67- Bus & Prof Pos: Secy, Haas Davis Packing Co, 51-52; secy, W T Smith Lumber Co, Chapman, Ala, 53-54; cost acct, Cooper Stevedoring Co, Inc, Mobile, 56-63; acct dept, Algernon Blair Inc, Montgomery, 63-66. Mem: Am Bus Women's Asn; Montgomery Co Dem Women; Bus & Prof Women's Asn; Eastern Star; PTA. Honors & Awards: Nat Hon Soc Woman of the Year, 1968. Relig: Baptist. Legal Res: PO Box 36 Hope Hull AL 36043 Mailing Add: Rm 109 The Capitol Montgomery AL 36104

ALLEN, NELSON ROBERT (D)
Ky State Sen
Mailing Add: 113 Gesling Rd Kenwood KY 41169

ALLEN, NORA ALICE (R)
Rep Nat Committeewoman, Ga
b Leesburg, Ga, Aug 16, 21; d George Dennis Moreland, Sr & Nora Davis M; m 1942 to Carroll Coffey Allen; c Carol (Mrs G Clifford Ranew) & George Dennis. Educ: Womans Col Ga, 38-41. Polit & Govt Pos: State chmn youth recruitment, Ga Fedn Rep Women, 65; pres, Lee Co Rep Women's Club, 65; chmn, Lee Co Rep Party, Ga, 65-69; deleg, Rep Nat Conv, 68; third dist chmn, Rep Party of Ga, 68-75, vchmn, 70-; Rep Nat Committeewoman, Ga, 72- Mem: Doublegate Country Club; Radium Country Club. Relig: Baptist. Mailing Add: 2010 W Broad Ave Apt 129 Albany GA 31707

ALLEN, PETER JOHN (D)
Mem, Calif State Dem Cent Comt
b New York, NY, May 21, 07; s Carl Aiello & Rose Sapienza A; m 1945 to Corinne Jan Andrews; c John Monty & Judi Dominique. Educ: Univ Santa Clara; Columbia Univ Ext. Polit & Govt Pos: Organizer & dir, Ulster Co Dem Clubs, NY, 33-37; mem, Ulster Co Dem Cent Comt, 35-36; supvr, Pub Works Admin, 35-37; deleg, Calif State Dem Conv, 50, 68, 70 & 72; mem, Santa Clara Co Grand Jury, Calif, 63; deleg, Dem Nat Conv, 64 & 68; chmn, Gov Edmund G Brown Finance Comt, Santa Clara Co, 66; chmn, Dem Century Club, 67-69; co-chmn, Hubert Humphrey Finance Comt, Northern Calif, 68; chmn, Congressman Don Edwards Campaign, 68; co-chmn, Ninth Cong Dist Dem Party, 69-; mem, Calif, State Dem Cent Comt, 69-, steering comt, 73-; chmn bus & indust comt, Sen Alfred Alquist for Lt Gov, 70; mem state adv & exec comt, Dep Attorney Gen Charles O'Brien for State Attorney Gen, 70; mem adv comt, US Sen John Tunney, 70; mem Policy & Platform Comn, Calif State Dem Party, 71-72; host chmn, Calif State Reform Conv, San Jose, 71; mem exec comt, Edmund Muskie for President in Calif, 71-72. Bus & Prof Pos: Pres, Peter J Allen Corp; owner, Allen's Furniture; adv bd, Camino Calif Bank, 72- Mil Serv: Army Air Force, 42-44. Mem: Calif Furniture Asn; Santa Clara Univ Alumni Asn; Kiwanis Downtown Club of San Jose; DAV (exec bd & adv bd); CofC. Honors & Awards: Golden Bear, Calif Dem Party, 66. Mailing Add: 1610 Hester Ave San Jose CA 95128

ALLEN, RICHARD JOHN (R)
Mich State Sen
b Ithaca, Mich, Aug 6, 33; s Lester John Allen & Erma Prichard V; m 1963 to Joann Wright; c Lester James & Carri Jo. Educ: Mich State Univ, BS, 55, DVM, 57; Sigma Alpha Epsilon. Polit & Govt Pos: Mich State Rep, 69-72; Mich State Sen, 75- Bus & Prof Pos: Owner & vet, State Rd Animal Hosp, Alma, Mich, 58-; assoc prof, Alma Col, 60-69; vpres & treas, Bon Accord Farms, Ithaca, 62- Mem: Am Asn Advan Sci; Mich Vet Med Asn; Rotary; Farm Bur. Relig: Presbyterian. Mailing Add: 1917 W Cheesman Rd Alma MI 48801

ALLEN, RICHARD M (DICK) (R)
Rep Nat Committeeman, Md
m to Nancy; c three. Educ: Cornell Univ; Duke Univ, grad. Polit & Govt Pos: Mem exec comt, Md State Rep Cent Comt, formerly; advance man for President Nixon, 68; deleg, Rep Nat Conv, 68, deleg-at-lg & mem comt on arrangements, 72; Rep Nat Committeeman, Md, 69- Bus & Prof Pos: Nurseryman. Mailing Add: PO Box 1577 Salisbury MD 21801

ALLEN, RICHARD VINCENT (R)
b Collingswood, NJ, Jan 1, 36; s Charles Carroll Allen, Sr & Magdalen Buchman A; m 1957 to Patricia Ann Mason; c Michael G, Kristin A, Mark C, Karen A, Kathryn A & Kevin D. Educ: Univ Notre Dame, BA, 57, univ fel, 57-58, MA, 58; Univ Munich, Relm Found H B Earhart fel, 58-61. Polit & Govt Pos: Sr foreign policy adv, Nixon-Agnew Campaign Comt, 67-68; sr staff mem, Nat Security Coun, The White House, 69, consult, Nat Security Affairs, 70-71, mem, Presidential Comn on Int Trade & Econ Policy, 70-72, dep exec dir, Coun on Int Econ Policy, 71-72, dep asst to the President for Int Econ Affairs, 71-72. Bus & Prof Pos: Asst prof, Ga Inst Technol, 61-62; sr staff mem, Ctr Strategic & Int Studies, Georgetown Univ, 62-66; sr staff mem, Hoover Inst on War, Revolution & Peace, Stanford Univ, 66-68; vpres, Int Resources, Ltd, Denver, Colo, 70-71; pres, Potomac Int Corp, Washington, DC, 72- Bus & Prof Pos: Co-ed, National Security: Political, Military & Economic Strategies in the Decade Ahead, Praeger, 65; co-auth, Democracy & Communism: Theory & Action, Van Nostrand, 67; ed, Yearbook on International Communist Affairs, Hoover Inst, 68. Mem: Am Polit Sci Asn; Intercollegiate Studies Inst (trustee, 69-); Foreign Policy Research Inst (bd dirs, 70-); Am-Portuguese Soc (bd dirs, 74-); Fed City Club. Honors & Awards: Cong Fel, Am Polit Sci Asn, 62; Distinguished Alumnus Award, St Francis Prep Sch, Spring Grove, Pa, 69. Relig: Roman Catholic. Legal Res: 9 E 60th St Brant Beach NJ 08008 Mailing Add: Potomac International Corp 905 16th St NW Washington DC 20006

ALLEN, ROBERT F (D)
Founding Chmn, Fifth Dist New Dem Coalition, NJ
b New York, NY, Dec 26, 28; s Edwin E Allen & Mary Thompson A; m 1956 to Elaine Bender; c Peter & Judd. Educ: State Univ NY, BS, 49; NY Univ, MA & PhD, 57; Columbia Univ, 57-59. Polit & Govt Pos: Dem cong coun, 12th Dist, NJ, 66 & Fifth Dist, 68; chmn, 12th Dist Dem Coalition, 66-67; founding chmn, Fifth Dist New Dem Coalition, 68- Bus & Prof Pos: Acad dean, Monmouth Col, NJ, 56-57; dir grad study, Newark State Col, 57-59, prof, 59-; pres, Sci Resources, Inc, 64-66; chmn bd, 66- Mil Serv: Entered as Pvt, Marine Corps, 51, released as Sgt, 53. Publ: Delinquency Rehabilitation—The Collegefields Program, US Off Health, Educ & Welfare, 66; Educational Training Systems, Macmillan, 68; From Delinquency to Freedom, SC Publ, 69. Mem: Am Acad Polit & Social Sci; Am Psychol Asn; NY Social Clin Psychologists; Inst for Appl Behav Sci. Honors & Awards: NY Univ Founder's Day Award, State Univ NY; Award for Highest Undergrad Scholastic Rating; Community Leaders of Am Award for Outstanding Community Serv. Mailing Add: Tempe-Wick Rd Morristown NJ 07960

ALLEN, RODERICK T (R)
NH State Rep
Mailing Add: RFD 1 Sanbornville NH 03872

ALLEN, STEPHEN WHITING (D)
Chmn, Monona Co Dem Cent Comt, Iowa
b Sioux City, Iowa, Dec 22, 43; s Sewell Ellyson Allen & Frances Whiting A; m 1962 to Joan Annette Shook; c Thomas Whiting & Anthony Michael. Educ: Univ Iowa, BA, 66, JD, 69; Phi Delta Phi. Polit & Govt Pos: Precinct committeeman, Monona Co Dem Cent Comt, Iowa, 70-; deleg, Dist & State Dem Conv, 70-; co attorney, Monona Co, 71- Bus & Prof Pos: Partner, Allen & Allen, Onawa, Iowa, 69- Mem: Iowa Bar Asn (chmn, Am citizenship comt, 70-); West Monona Jaycees (bd mem, 75-); Onawa CofC (pres, 71-72); Onawa Country Club (bd mem & secy, 72-); March of Dimes (chmn, Monona Co Chap, 70-, chmn, Siouxland Chap, 73-74). Legal Res: 1321 Ninth St Onawa IA 51040 Mailing Add: 718 Iowa Ave Onawa IA 51040

ALLEN, SUSAN ROGERS (D)
Mem, Tex State Dem Exec Comt
b Coleman, Tex, Dec 8, 40; d Frank Rogers & Mattie B Miller R; m 1963 to Lem B Allen; c Lemuel Byron, Jr & Zachary Fulshear. Educ: Tex Tech Univ, BMus, 63; Kappa Alpha Theta. Polit & Govt Pos: Vpres, Guadalupe Co Dem Women's Forum, Tex, 70-71, pres, 71-73, alt deleg, Tex State Dem Conv, 72; deleg, Dem Nat Conv, 72; mem, Tex State Dem Exec Comt, 74- Mem: Luling Watermelon Thump Asn; Floribunda Garden Club. Honors & Awards: Outstanding Young Woman of the Year, Beta Sigma Phi, 72. Relig: Episcopal. Mailing Add: Rte 1 Box 339 Kingsbury TX 78638

ALLEN, WILLARD C (R)
Ky State Rep
Mailing Add: Rte W Box 123 Morgantown KY 42261

ALLEN, WILLIAM G (R)
Vt State Rep
Mailing Add: Vergennes VT 05491

ALLENDER, PATRICIA ANNE (D)
b Salem, Ore, Nov 1, 51; d Charles W Allender & Virginia-Lacy A; single. Educ: Univ Ore, 72-73. Polit & Govt Pos: Mem, Dem Nat Rules Comt, Washington, DC, 72; deleg, Dem Nat Conv, 72; McGovern Media Rels coordr, Marion Co, Ore, 72; committeewoman, Precinct 70, Marion Co, 72- Mailing Add: 4629 Nandale Dr Salem OR 97303

ALLER, DOUGLAS JOSEPH (R)
Chmn, NH Young Rep Fedn
b Syracuse, NY, Mar 5, 48; s Howard Byron Aller & Ruth J Nelipowitz A; m 1971 to Candace Lynn Cook. Educ: Georgetown Univ, BSFS, 70; Franklin Pierce Col Law Ctr, 74- Polit & Govt Pos: Chmn, Georgetown Univ Young Rep, 69-70; Nat committeeman, NH Young Rep, 73-74; state chmn, 74-; vchmn, Exeter Rep Town Comt, 74-; vchmn, Rockingham Co Rep Comt, 75-; mem, NH Rep State Comt, 75- Mil Serv: Entered as 2nd Lt, Air Force, 71, released as 1st Lt, 73, after serv in 68th Strategic Missile Squadron, Strategic Air Command, 71-73; 1st Lt, Air Force Res. Legal Res: Epping Rd Exeter NH 03833 Mailing Add: PO Box 415 Exeter NH 03833

ALLEY, G T (TOM) (D)
Ariz State Rep
Mailing Add: 910 Esperanza St Box 155 Ajo AZ 85321

ALLIN, LYNDON KING (MORT) (R)
Mem, Dane Co Rep Party, Wis
b Dearborn, Mich, Feb 7, 41; s Robin Nail Allin, MD & Ruth Emory A; m 1965 to Mary Ann Jennings; c Stephanie Elizabeth. Educ: Univ Wis, BA, 63; Mace, Iron Cross; Chi Psi. Polit & Govt Pos: Staff asst, US Sen Wiley, Wis, 62; mem, Dane Co Rep Party, 62-; state vchmn, Youth for Goldwater, Wis Goldwater for President Comt, 64; exec dir, Univ Wis Comt to Support People of SVietnam, 65-66; nat dir, Youth for Nixon-Agnew, Nixon for President Comt, 67-68; dir, Young Am Salute, 1969 Inauguration for President Nixon, 68-69; ed, President's Daily News Summary, 69-74; staff asst to President, 69-73, spec asst to the President, 73-74; deleg to USSR & escort for returning Soviets on State Dept Cult Exchange of Journalists, 74-75. Bus & Prof Pos: Social studies instr, Janesville, Sr High Sch, Wis, 66-67. Publ: Co-ed, Vietnam: a Book of Readings, Univ Wis Comt to Support People of SViet Nam, 65; auth, A look at Medicare, 62 & Tribute to MacArthur, 64, Insight & Outlook. Mem: DC Police Boys Club; Am Acad Polit & Social Sci. Relig: Protestant. Legal Res: 802 Huron Hill Madison WI 53711 Mailing Add: 4800 Davenport St NW Washington DC 20016

ALLISON, BETTY VIRGINIA (R)
VChmn, Yuma Co Rep Cent Comt, Colo
b Wray, Colo, Feb 5, 25; d Arnold Carl Unger & Thelma Myers U; m 1943 to Stephen Raymond Allison; c Virginia Lee, Stephen Louis, Carole Elaine & Barry Raymond. Educ: Wray High Sch. Polit & Govt Pos: Rep precinct committeewoman, Colo, 55-57; pres, Yuma Co Rep Club, 58-65; vchmn, Yuma Co Rep Cent Comt, 65- Mem: Eastern Star (past Matron); Women's Soc of Christian Serv; Farm Bur. Relig: United Methodist. Mailing Add: Rte 1 Wray CO 80758

ALLISON, E LAVONIA INGRAM (D)
Mem, NC State Dem Exec Comt
b Oxford, NC; d Charles J Ingram (deceased) & Bernice H Roberts I; m 1954 to Ferdinand Vincent Allison, Jr; c K Michele & Ferdinand Vincent, III. Educ: Hampton Inst, BS NY Univ, MA & EdD summa cum laude; Delta Sigma Theta; Calliope Social Club. Polit & Govt Pos: First vpres, J F Kennedy Young Dem Club of Durham Co, NC, 67-70; first vchmn, Durham Co Dem Exec Comt, 68-70, acting chmn, 71, chmn, 72-75; co-chmn educ comt, Durham Comt on Black Affairs, 69-; vpres, Durham Co Dem Women's Club, 70-72 mem exec comt, 70-; secy, NC Polit Action Comt for Educ, 71-; deleg, Nat Black Polit Conv, Gary, Ind, 72; co-chmn, NC Dem Women's Conv, 72; deleg, Dem Nat Conv, 72; mem, NC State Dem Exec Comt, 72-; mem comn on deleg selection & party structure, Dem Nat Comt, 72-; mem, Jefferson-Jackson Dinner Comt, 73; mem, NC Women's Caucus. Bus & Prof Pos: Teacher

health, phys educ, gen sci & gen math, Cent Consolidated Sch, Bel Air, Md; teacher health & phys educ, Druid Jr High Sch, Baltimore & J A Whitted Jr High Sch, Durham, NC; assoc prof phys educ & recreation, NC Cent Univ. Publ: How to run a successful majors club, Jour HPER, 67; Perceptual motor activities for the mentally retarded, Workshop on Phys Educ & Recreation for Ment Retarded, 69. Mem: NC Asn Health, Phys Educ & Recreation (pres-elect, 74-75); Hillside High Sch PTA (pres, 72-73); NC Asn Educators; Am Asn Health, Phys Educ & Recreation; Nat Coun Negro Women. Honors & Awards: Founders Day Award, NY Univ, 69; Distinguished Leadership Award, NC Heart Asn, 70; Woman of the Year, presented in accord with the Prince Hall Masonry of NC, 73. Relig: Baptist. Mailing Add: 1315 McLaurin Ave Durham NC 27707

ALLISON, JAMES PURNEY (D)
Committeeman, Tex State Dem Exec Comt
b Paris, Tex, Jan 16, 47; s Ardell Allison & Billie Louise Parker A; m 1966 to Sandra Juanema Broyles. Educ: ETex State Univ, BS, 67, MS, 68; Univ Tex Sch Law, Austin, JD, 71; Phi Delta Phi; Alpha Chi; Phi Eta Sigma; ETex State Univ Young Dem. Polit & Govt Pos: Legis intern, Tex State Senate, 68-69, urban affairs research dir, 68-71; state pres, Tex Young Dem, 71-73; committeeman, Tex State Dem Comt, 72- Bus & Prof Pos: Attorney-at-law, Cooper, Tex, 71-; co attorney, Delta Co, 73- Mem: Delta Co CofC (dir, 73-); Cooper Kiwanis Club (vpres, 74-). Relig: Baptist. Legal Res: 41 W Side Sq Cooper TX 75432 Mailing Add: PO Box 32 Cooper TX 75432

ALLISON, MANUEL (BUNK) (D)
Ark State Rep
Mailing Add: 501 S Division Morrilton AR 72110

ALLISON, PAMELA ANN (R)
Nat Committeewoman, Ga Young Rep
b Chattanooga, Tenn, Apr 27, 44; d Ben Matthews Allison & Sally Pickett A; single. Educ: St Mary's Jr Col, grad in Lib Arts, 64; Univ Ala, BS in Educ, 67; Pi Beta Phi; Phi Delta Theta Homecoming Queen; pres, Fitts Dorm; mem, Yearbook Staff, Univ Ala. Polit & Govt Pos: Mem, St Mary's Jr Col & Univ Ala Young Rep Clubs; vol worker, Rodney Cook for Cong, Fletcher Thompson for Cong & for US Senate Campaigns, Hal Suit for Gov; mem door to door canvas team, Nixon for President, 72; prog chmn, Metrop, Atlanta Young Rep Club, 71-72; chmn, Rep Nat Conv, Pre-Regist Comt; hostess, Ga Hospitality Suite at Young Rep Leadership Training Sch, Washington, DC, 72-73; publicity chmn, Ga Young Rep, 72-73, Nat Committeewoman, 73- Bus & Prof Pos: Elem sch teacher, DeKalb Co Bd Educ, 67-73. Relig: Episcopal. Mailing Add: 5620 Glenridge Dr Atlanta GA 30342

ALLISON, REGIS (D)
b Eunice, La, Dec 1, 34; s Emile Allison & Rita Frank A; div; c Regis, Jr. Educ: Grambling Col, BS; Loyola Univ Chicago, 64-66; Alpha Mu Gamma; Omega Psi Phi. Polit & Govt Pos: Mem, Jennings Charter Comn, La, 71-72; treas, Jeff Davis Polit Action, 71-72; alt deleg, Dem Nat Conv, 72. Bus & Prof Pos: Bd mem, Imperial Calcasieu Planning Comn, currently. Mil Serv: Entered as Pvt, Army, 53, released as SP-3, 55, after serv in Spec Category Army Personnel with Air Force, 54-55. Mem: Club 26. Relig: Catholic. Mailing Add: 107 Levi St Jennings LA 70546

ALLISON, SANDRA BROYLES (D)
Mem Exec Comt, Young Dem Club Tex
b Alexandra, Ark, July 10, 48; d John Ben Broyles & Geraldine Hughes B; m 1966 to James Purney Allison. Educ: ETex State Univ, MS, 75; Univ Tex, Austin, BS. Polit & Govt Pos: Conv secy, Young Dem Clubs of Tex, 68, mem state exec comt, 68-, nat committeewoman, 70-74. Bus & Prof Pos: Teacher, Austin Indust Sch Dist, 69-71; mem staff, Yantis Independent Sch Dist, currently. Mem: Jr Heritage Women's Club; Tex State Teachers Asn; Austin Asn Teachers. Relig: Baptist. Mailing Add: PO Box 32 Cooper TX 75432

ALLISON, WALTER (R)
Mem Exec Comt, Colo State Rep Party
b Montrose, Colo, Feb 28, 28; s Walter Daniel Allison & Mabel Voss A; m 1969 to Mary Maxine Myers; c L R Haney, Deborah (Mrs Bill Case) & Sharron. Educ: Univ Colo, BMus; Phi Mu Alpha; Sinfonia. Polit & Govt Pos: Chmn, 58th Rep Dist, Colo, 73-75 & Montrose Co Cent Comt, 73-; mem exec comt, Colo State Rep Party, Third Cong Dist, 74- Bus & Prof Pos: Pres, Allisons' Inc, 65- Mil Serv: Entered as Seaman 1/C, Navy, 44, released as SK 3/C, 45. Mem: AF&AM, Grand Junction Consistory; Elks Lodge 1053, Montrose Commandery 19; Kiwanis. Honors & Awards: Retailer of the Year, Rocky Mountain Area, 63. Relig: Protestant. Legal Res: 1413 Chatam Dr Montrose CO 81401 Mailing Add: PO Box 459 Montrose CO 81401

ALLIVATO, BARBARA ROSE (DFL)
Chairwoman, 37th Legis Dist Dem-Farmer-Labor Party, Minn
b Minneapolis, Minn, Mar 11, 38; d William J Allivato & Marjorie Jonas A; single. Educ: Univ Minn, 3 years. Polit & Govt Pos: Chairwoman, 38th Legis Dist Dem-Farmer-Labor Party, Minn, 68- Bus & Prof Pos: Cashier, Clancy Drugs, Edina, Minn, 56-; clerical work, First Nat Bank Minneapolis, 61- Mem: Am Inst Banking. Relig: Catholic. Mailing Add: 5007 France Ave S Minneapolis MN 55410

ALLMAN, ELAINE G (D)
Co-Chmn, Murray Co Dem Cent Comt, Okla
b Sulphur, Okla, Mar 14, 45; d Frank Gibbard & Veva Rogers G; m 1967 to Maurice R Allman. Educ: Swarthmore Col, 62-64; Univ Okla, BA, 66, JD, 69; Kappa Beta Pi; Phi Alpha Delta; Order of the Coif. Polit & Govt Pos: US magistrate, Eastern Dist Okla, 71-72; deleg, Okla Dem Conv, 72; alt deleg, Dem Nat Conv, 72; pres, Murray Co Dem Women's Club, Okla, 72-; precinct chmn, Precinct Ten, Murray Co, 73-; co-chmn, Murray Co Dem Cent Comt, 73- Bus & Prof Pos: Partner, Gibbard, Allman & Allman, Sulphur, 69- Mem: Am & Okla Bar Asns; Murray Co Bar Asn (pres, 72-); Okla Trial Lawyers Asn. Relig: Disciples of Christ. Legal Res: 724 E Eighth Sulphur OK 73086 Mailing Add: PO Box 436 Sulphur OK 73086

ALLNUTT, ROBERT FREDERICK (D)
b Richmond, Va, June 15, 35; s Robert Carhart Allnutt & Evelyn Brooks A; m 1965 to Jan Latven; c Robert David & Thomas Frederick. Educ: Va Polytech Inst, BS, 57; George Washington Univ, Nat Law Ctr, JD, 60, LLM, 62; Tau Beta Pi; Alpha Pi Mu; Order of the Coif. Polit & Govt Pos: Patent examr, US Patent Off, 57-60; patent attorney, NASA, 60-65, asst gen counsel, 65-67, asst admin legis affairs, 67-70; assoc gen counsel, US Comn on Govt Procurement, 70-72; staff dir, US Senate Comt on Aeronaut & Space Sci, 73- Bus & Prof Pos: Attorney, Commun Satellite Corp, 65. Publ: Auth & co-auth of various law jour articles. Mem: Am, Fed, DC & Va Bar Asns. Honors & Awards: Superior Performance Award, US Patent Off, 59; Apollo Achievement Award, NASA, 69. Relig: Episcopal. Mailing Add: 5400 Edgemoor Lane Bethesda MD 20014

ALLOTT, GORDON LLEWELLYN (R)
b Pueblo, Colo, Jan 2, 07; m 1934 to Welda Hall; c Roger Hall & Gordon L, Jr. Educ: Univ Colo, BA, 27, Law Sch, LLB, 29; Phi Gamma Delta. Hon Degrees: LLD, Colo Col, 64, Colo State Univ, 68 & Univ Colo, 69; DE, Colo Sch Mines, 67. Polit & Govt Pos: Co attorney, Prowers Co, Colo, 34 & 40-46, dist attorney, 46-48; chmn, Young Rep League of Colo, 35-38; chmn, Nat Fedn Young Rep, 41-46; Lt Gov, Colo, 50-54; US Sen, Colo, 54-73, Chmn, Senate Rep Policy Comt, 69-72; US Rep, UN, 17th Gen Assembly, 62; vchmn, US deleg, Inter-Parliamentary Union; deleg, Rep Nat Conv, 68 & 72; mem gen adv comt, US Arms Control & Disarmament Agency, 74- Bus & Prof Pos: Dir & attorney, First Fed Savings & Loan, Lamar, Colo. Mil Serv: Entered as Lt, Army Air Force, 42, released as Maj, 46, after serv in 339th Fighter Squadron, SPac Theater; SPac Theater Medal with Seven Battle Stars; Col, Inactive Res. Mem: Colo Bar Asn; Southeast Colo Livestock Asn; Am Legion; VFW; Rotary. Relig: Episcopal. Legal Res: 3427 S Race St Englewood CO 80110 Mailing Add: 560 Capitol Life Ctr Denver CO 80203

ALLRED, WILLIAM DAVID (DAVE) (D)
Tex State Rep
b Austin, Tex, Nov 27, 33; s James V Allred & Joe Betsy Miller A; m 1960 to Patricia Lee Moyer; c Rebecca Lee, Stephen David & James Moyer. Educ: Tex Christian Univ, BA; Columbia Univ, MS. Polit & Govt Pos: Mem staff, US Sen Ralph Yarborough, Tex & US Rep Ray Roberts, Tex; investr, House Govt Activities Subcomt; Tex State Rep, Wichita Co, 67- Bus & Prof Pos: Reporter, Montgomery, Ala Bur of The Assoc Press & Wash Bur of the Houston Post, the Wichita Falls Times & the Corpus Christi Caller-Times. Mil Serv: 2nd & 1st Lt, Army Res; Maj, Army Res, currently. Relig: Disciples of Christ. Mailing Add: 1608 Hayes St Wichita Falls TX 76309

ALLSBROOK, JULIAN RUSSELL (D)
NC State Sen
b Roanoke Rapids, NC, Feb 17, 03; s William Clemens Allsbrook & Bennie Alice Walker A; m 1926 to Frances Virginia Brown (deceased); c Richard Brown, Mary Frances & Alice Harris. Educ: Univ NC, 20-24; Univ NC Law Sch, 22-24; Phi Alpha Delta; Golden Fleece; Order of the Grail; Tau Kappa Alpha. Polit & Govt Pos: Mem bd trustees, Roanoke Rapids Sch Dist, formerly, mem bd, City Comnr & Munic Road Comn, formerly; Secy of State, NC, formerly; NC State Sen, 35-41 & 47-; NC State Rep, 41-46; presidential elector, NC, 36; chmn, Comn Platform & Resolutions, Dem State Conv, 56-58; deleg, Southern Regional Educ Bd Legis Work Conf, 66; mem, Gov Study Comn Pub Sch Syst NC, 67; chmn, Comn Study Rules Civil Procedure, 67. Bus & Prof Pos: Lawyer; dir, Med Found of NC Inc; NC Comn on Nursing & Patient Care; trustee, NC Symphony, Inc & Chowan Col, Murfreesboro, NC. Mil Serv: Lt, Naval Res, 42-45, Lt Comdr, Res. Mem: Mason; Widows Son Lodge; WOW; Kiwanis. Honors & Awards: Distinguished Serv Citation, NC Pub Health Asn, 65. Relig: Baptist. Legal Res: Drawer 40 Roanoke Rapids NC 27870 Mailing Add: State Senate State Capitol Raleigh NC 27602

ALLSHOUSE, J ROBERT (R)
Colo State Sen
Mailing Add: 1191 Geneva St Aurora CO 80010

ALLSTATT, ANGELINE (D)
Ind State Sen
b Johnson Co, Ind, Feb 15, 05; d Charles C Patterson & Margaret Griffith P; m 1927 to Arthur J Allstatt; c David L. Educ: Bus Col, Johnson Co & Indianapolis. Polit & Govt Pos: Secy & bookkeeper, Supt of Pub Instr, State of Ind, 50-53, 59-63; city clerk of Indianapolis, 64-67; various other polit pos; Ind State Sen, 73- Bus & Prof Pos: Secy, Kipp Bros, Indianapolis, 43-50. Mem: Marion Co Womens Dem Club (pres, 73-); Southside Dem Club (treas, 73-); Newman Guild of Butler Univ Womens Assembly Club of Ind. Relig: Christian Church-Bethany. Mailing Add: 1704 Spruce St Indianapolis IN 46203

ALLYN, RUFUS (D)
Conn State Rep
Mailing Add: Ram Point Mason's Island Mystic CT 06355

ALMEDINA, ANGEL (D)
b New York, NY, July 7, 47; s Angelo Almedina & Josephine Martinez A; m 1970 to Nilda Collazo; c Malik. Educ: Bernard Baruch Col; Columbia Univ. Polit & Govt Pos: Rep, Ward I Dem Party, Washington, DC, 73-; pres, Hispanic Am Dem Club, 73-; alt deleg, Dem Nat Mid-Term Conf, 74. Bus & Prof Pos: Washington, DC rep, Nat Asn PR Civil Rights, 70-; consult, La Causa Comun, 72-73; dir, PR Forum, 73-74; consult, Nat Coun La Raza, currently; consult, United Farm Workers, currently. Mil Serv: Entered as Pvt, Army, 66, released as Sgt, 68, after serv in Mil Assistance Command, Vietnam, 67-68; Army Commendation Medal. Mem: United Black Fund (bd mem); United Way; Am Legion; Nat Asn Concerned Vets. Honors & Awards: City Achievement Award, Mayor Walter Washington, Washington, DC; Cardinal Spellman Award. Relig: Catholic. Mailing Add: 2480 16th St Washington DC 20009

ALMEIDA, ALFRED (D)
Mass State Rep
b Plymouth, Mass, Oct 5, 31; s John Almeida & Rose Pacheco A; div. Educ: Boston Univ, AB, 53. Polit & Govt Pos: Planning bd mem, Town of Plymouth, Mass, 64-71; Mass State Rep, 71- Bus & Prof Pos: Inventory coordr, Am Wool & Co, Plymouth, Mass, 53-56; agent, Metrop Life Ins Plymouth, 56-61, home off field rep, 61-63; partner, Twin Rock Ins Agency, 63- Mem: Mass Independent Agts & Brokers Asn; Mutual Ins Agts Asn New Eng; Plymouth Indust Develop Coop (vpres); Lions Club Int; Lions Club. Relig: Catholic. Legal Res: 194 Standish Ave Plymouth MA 02360 Mailing Add: PO Box 123 North Plymouth Sta Plymouth MA 02360

ALMON, RENEAU PEARSON (D)
Justice, Ala Supreme Court
b Moulton, Ala, July 8, 37; s Nathaniel Almon & Mary Johnson A; m 1974 to Deborah Pearson Preer; c Jonathan, Jason & Nathaniel & Thomas L Preer (stepson). Educ: Univ Ala, BS, 61; Samford Univ Cumberland Sch Law, LLB, 64; Omicron Delta Kappa. Polit & Govt Pos: Judge, 36th Judicial Circuit of Ala, 65; judge, Ala Court of Criminal Appeals, 67; justice,

Ala Supreme Court, 75- Mil Serv: Pvt, Army. Mem: Ala & Am Bar Asns; Ala Law Inst; Am Judicature Soc; Kiwanis. Relig: Methodist. Legal Res: 3524 Lancaster Lane Montgomery AL 36106 Mailing Add: PO Box 218 Montgomery AL 36101

ALMOND, JAMES LINDSAY, JR (D)
b Charlottesville, Va, June 15, 98; s James Lindsay Almond & Eddie Burgess A; m 1925 to Josephine Katherine Minter. Educ: Univ Va Law Sch, LLB, 23; Delta Theta Phi; Alpha Kappa Psi; Omicron Delta Kappa. Hon Degrees: LLD, Col William & Mary. Polit & Govt Pos: Asst Commonwealth's Attorney, Roanoke, Va, 30-33; judge, Hustings Court, Roanoke, 33-45; US Rep, Sixth Cong Dist, Va, 46-48; Attorney Gen, Va, 48-57; Gov, Va, 58-62; judge, US Court of Customs & Patent Appeals, 62- Bus & Prof Pos: Practice of law, Roanoke, Va, 23-30; former high sch prin. Mil Serv: Pvt, Army Inf, 18. Mem: Mason; Scottish Rite (33 degree); Shrine (Past Potentate, Kazim Temple, Roanoke); Kiwanis Int; Eagles. Relig: Lutheran. Mailing Add: 208 Wexleigh Dr Richmond VA 23229

ALPERSTEIN, ARNOLD (D)
Dem Nat Committeeman, Colo
b New York, NY, Sept 28, 25; s Herman Alperstein & Ray Schneiderman A; m 1948 to Pearl Greenblot; c Donald Wayne & Ellen Sue. Educ: Univ Mo, LLB, 50. Polit & Govt Pos: Dep dist attorney, First Judicial Dist, Colo, 56-60; chmn, Jefferson Co Dem Party, 63-67; chmn, Second Cong Dist Dem Party, 67-69; chmn adv comt, Colo Dem Party, 67-69; Dem Nat Committeeman, Colo, 68-; mem exec comt, Dem Nat Comt, 68-; deleg & chmn Colo Deleg, Dem Nat Conv, 72. Mil Serv: Entered as Pvt, Army Air Force, 43, released as Sgt, 46, after serv in 8th Air Force, ETO, 45-46; Air Medal. Publ: Article in Frontier 50 & Progressive, 51. Mem: Am Bar Asn; Colo Bar Asn (bd gov, 68-70 & 72-); First Judicial Dist Bar Asn; Am Civil Liberties Union. Relig: Jewish. Mailing Add: 7000 W 14th Ave Lakewood CO 80215

ALPERSTEIN, ARTHUR STUART (D)
Md State Deleg
b Baltimore, Md, Oct 19, 40; s Morris Alperstein & Edith Kres A; m 1966 to Sonya Rovin; c Andrew Ira & Warren Scott. Educ: Western Md Col, BA, 62; Univ Md Sch Law, JD, 65; Nu Beta Epsilon. Polit & Govt Pos: Asst states attorney, Baltimore, Md, 68-69; mem, Dem State Cent Comt Md, 70-72; Md State Deleg, 72-, mem judiciary comt, Md House Deleg, 72-, vchmn motor vehicle laws subcomt, 74-; committing magistrate, Baltimore Co, 72- Bus & Prof Pos: Attorney, 65- Mil Serv: Entered as 1st Lt, Army, released as Capt, 67, after serv in Mil PoliceC; Army Commendation Medal; Nat Defense Medal. Mem: Am Judicult Soc; Jaycees; Nat Soc State Legislators; Nat Defense Attorneys Asn; Nat Dist Attorneys Asn. Honors & Awards: Distinguished Serv Award, Fraternal Order Police, 73; Outstanding Young Marylander Award, Woodlawn Jaycees, 74; Safety Crusader Award, Safety First Club Md. Relig: Jewish. Mailing Add: 4104 Balmoral Circle Pikesville MD 21208

ALPERSTEIN, PEARL (D)
b Kansas City, Mo, Jan 26, 27; d Alex Greenblot & Tillie Kaplan G (deceased); m 1948 to Arnold Alperstein; c Donald W & Ellen Sue. Educ: Univ Mo, Columbia, BJ, 47; Univ Colo, 6 months. Polit & Govt Pos: Precinct committeewoman, Jefferson Co Dem Party, Colo, 54-64, get out the vote chmn, 60-64, vol chmn, 64, dist capt, 64-68, registr chmn, 69-; secy, Colo State Young Dem, 57; deleg, co, cong & state Dem conv & assemblies, 58-, mem, Colo State Dem Cent Comn, formerly, co-chmn, state finance drive, 59; chmn, State Get Out the Vote, 72; deleg, Dem Nat Conv, 72; mem, Lakewood City Coun, 73-; mem housing task force, Denver Regional Coun of Govt, 73-; chairperson, Lakewood Housing Authority, 74-75; mem, Nat & Colo Dem Women's Polit Caucus. Bus & Prof Pos: Former exec dir, Am Jewish Comt. Publ: Ring aroung the world, Farmers Union, 53. Mem: Ment Health Asn; Am Polit Items Collectors Asn (nat vchmn, 72-74); Colo Polit Items Collectors Asn (chmn, 72-74). Honors & Awards: Dem Party Serv Award, 58; Ment Health Asn Award, 69. Relig: Jewish. Legal Res: 12125 W 20th Ave Lakewood CO 80215 Mailing Add: 9485 W Colfax Lakewood CO 80215

ALQUIST, ALFRED E (D)
Calif State Sen
Mailing Add: 777 N First St San Jose CA 95112

ALSAKER, WANDA LOUISE (R)
Chmn, Missoula Co Rep Cent Comt, Mont
b Missoula, Mont, Sept 29, 23; d Arthur B Cook & Myrtle Swanson C; m 1943 to Harry G Alsaker; c Kathy A (Mrs Thibodeau) & Thomas Arthur. Educ: Mod Bus Col, 42-43. Polit & Govt Pos: Rep precinct committeewoman, Missoula Co, Mont, 66-; first vchmn, Missoula Co Rep Cent Comt, 71-73, chmn, 73-; deleg, Rep Nat Conv, 72; mem, Mont Rep State Cent Comt, 75- Bus & Prof Pos: Cashier & secy, Mont Dak Utilities, Missoula, Mont, 43; clerk-typist, US Dept Agr, 46; med secy, Missoula, 52-59; off mgr, Optical Ctr, Missoula, 59- Mem: Exten Homemakers; Missoula & Mont Fedn of Rep Women. Relig: Presbyterian. Mailing Add: 1308 Jackson Missoula MT 59801

ALSOBROOK, HENRY HERMAN (R)
Mem, First Dist Rep Comt, Ga
b Woodland, Ga, Apr 27, 17; both parents deceased; m 1939 to Wilhelmina Pool; c Wilhelmina & Claudette. Educ: Emory Univ, BS, 38. Polit & Govt Pos: Chmn, Effingham Co Rep Party, Ga, 64-69; mem, Effingham Co Sch Bd, 65-; mem, First Dist Rep Comt, 69- Bus & Prof Pos: VPres, Morgans, Inc, Ga, currently. Mil Serv: Entered as A/S, Navy, 44, released as Lt (jg), 46, after serv in Pac; Lt(jg), Naval Res; Am Theater & Asiatic-Pac Ribbons; Philippine Liberation Medal. Mem: Mason; Scottish Rite. Relig: Christian Church. Mailing Add: Railwood Ave Guyton GA 31312

ALSOP, JOHN DE KOVEN (R)
Rep Nat Committeeman, Conn
b Avon, Conn, Aug 4, 15; s Joseph W Alsop & Corinne Robinson A; m 1947 to Augusta Robinson; c Mary Oliver, Augusta McLane & John de Koven, Jr. Educ: Yale Univ, BA, 37; Beta Gamma Sigma; Zeta Psi; Scroll & Key. Polit & Govt Pos: Mem, Avon Rep Town Comt, Conn, 46-71; Conn State Rep, 47-51; mem, State Bd Educ, 53-62; Rep Cand for Gov, 62; mem, Comt Higher Educ, 65-68; deleg, Rep Nat Conv, 52, 60, 68 & 72; Rep Nat Committeeman, Conn, 68- Bus & Prof Pos: Pres, Covenant Group, 53- Mil Serv: Entered as Pvt, Army, 42, released as Capt, 45, after serv in Off Strategic Serv, ETO & China-Burma-India Theatre, 42-45; Bronze Star with Cluster; Theatre Medals; Distinguished Unit Citation; Croix de Guerre, France; Cloud Banner, China. Mem: Mason; VFW; Am Legion; Lions. Relig: Episcopal. Mailing Add: 70 Talcott Notch Rd Avon CT 06001

ALSTADT, WILLIAM ROBERT (D)
b Thebes, Ill, Oct 7, 16; s Henry Lee Alstadt & Gradie Cole A; m 1962 to Laura May Goodness; c Richard Lee, Mary Lyn (Mrs Walker) & Thomas Henry. Educ: Ark State Col, 33-34; Wash Univ, DDS, 38; Carnegie fel orthodontics, 38-39; MSD, Nihon Univ; Dipl, Am Bd Orthodontics; Omicron Kappa Upsilon. Hon Degrees: DDS, Nihon Univ; DMD, Nippon Dent Col; DSc, Kansas City Univ. Polit & Govt Pos: Mem, Little Rock Civil Serv Comn, 49-, chmn, 55-57, former chmn, Safety Coun; mem, Ark Civil Defense Bd, 50-54; mem, Ark Bd Health, 58-62, pres, 59-60; Jr Dep Sheriff; consult, Ark Welfare Dept, Ark Educ TV Comn, 61-; consult, US Dept Defense, 72- Bus & Prof Pos: Orthodontist, 39-; vis lectr, Univ Tenn Sch Dent, Osaka Dent Col & Tokyo Dent Col; consult, Army & Naval Hosp, 47-55; mem, Denver Orthodontic Sem, 46-53; mem, Ark Bd Dent Examr, 46-50, pres, 49-50; hon lectr, Tokyo Dent Col; hon prof, Nihon Univ Sch Dent. Mil Serv: Lt Col, Army, World War II. Mem: Am & Ark Dent Asns; Hon Mem, Japanese, Philippine & Australian Dent Asns. Honors & Awards: First Dipl Award, Buenos Aires Univ Dent Sch, 68; Hon Col, Miss, Ky & Tenn; Hon Admiral, Nebr; Commodore, Okla; hon & awards from Brazil, SAfrica & EAfrica. Relig: Methodist. Legal Res: 11 Edgehill Little AR 72201 Mailing Add: 121 E Fourth At Scott Little Rock AR 72201

ALTAMIRANO, BEN D (D)
NMex State Sen
Mailing Add: 1123 Santa Rita St Silver City NM 88061

ALTEMUS, BARBARA (D)
Mem, Dem Nat Comt, Pa
Mailing Add: 815 Walter St Bethlehem PA 18017

ALTHAUS, KENNETH L (R)
Kans State Rep
Mailing Add: RR 1 Atchison KS 66002

ALTHERR, WILLIAM LEE (R)
Chmn, White Co Rep Party, Ind
b Lafayette, Ind, Mar 11, 24; s Alfred Martin Altherr & Edna Frances Lee A; single. Educ: Purdue Univ, BS civil eng, 48. Polit & Govt Pos: Co surveyor, White Co, Ind, 54-62, co hwy engr, 64-; precinct committeeman, Union Twp, Precinct One, 60-68; chmn, White Co Rep Party, 68- Bus & Prof Pos: Draftsman, Chicago Bridge & Iron Co, Greenville, Pa, 48-49, construction dept, Chicago, 49-50; bldg contractor, Lafayette, Ind, 51-52; surveyor, Co Surveyors Off, 52-53; real estate agent, Monticello, 63. Mil Serv: Entered as Pvt, 43, released as Pfc, 46, after serv in Engr Bn, 3rd Army, ETO, 45-46. Mem: Ind Soc Prof Land Surveyors; Nat Asn Co Engrs; Am Red Cross (chmn, White Co Chap); Ind Asn Co Engrs (pres, 73-74); Rotary; Am Legion. Relig: Methodist. Mailing Add: RR 6 Monticello IN 47960

ALTMAN, CARL F (D)
NH State Rep
Mailing Add: Canaan NH 03741

ALTMAN, JAMES ESTON (R)
VChmn, Jones Co Rep Party, Ga
b Manatee, Fla, Jan 23, 38; s Eston Altman & Alma Bland A; m 1958 to Lois Elaine Middlebrooks; c April Elaine, Allison Leigh & Adriane Ermine. Educ: Ga Inst Technol, BME. Polit & Govt Pos: Mayor protem, Gray, Ga, 66-70; chmn, Jones Co Rep Party, 66-70, vchmn, 71- Bus & Prof Pos: VPres, Altman Machine Co, Inc, Gray, Ga, 60-; registered prof engr, 66- Mem: Ga Soc Prof Engrs; Jones Co Jaycees; Jones Co Kiwanis Club; Jones Co Develop Comn, Inc (treas); Moose. Relig: Baptist. Legal Res: 501 Fraley St Gray GA 31023 Mailing Add: 432 Virginia Ave Gray GA 31023

ALTMEYER, JAMES EMERSON (R)
WVa State Deleg
b Wheeling, WVa, Dec 5, 38; s John D Altmeyer (deceased) & Evelyn Showers A; m 1963 to Edith Stoney; c James, Jr, Joanne, Cameron & Charlotte. Educ: US Mil Acad, BS, 61. Polit & Govt Pos: WVa State Deleg, 74- Bus & Prof Pos: Partner, Altmeyer Funeral Homes, Wheeling, WVa, 74- dir, First Nat Bank of Wheeling & Oglebay Inst of Wheeling. Mil Serv: Entered as 2nd Lt, Army, 61, released as Maj, 72, after serv in 1st Inf Div, SVietnam, 67-68; Maj, Army Res, 72; Silver Star; Bronze Star with three clusters; Meritorious Serv Medal; Army Commendation Medal for Valor with two clusters; Five Air Medals; Vietnamese Cross of Gallantry. Mem: Serra Club; Civitan; Lions; KofC (3 degree). Relig: Roman Catholic. Mailing Add: 19 Elmwood Pl Wheeling WV 26003

ALTOBELLO, HENRY D (D)
Secy, Dem State Cent Comt, Conn
b Meriden, Conn, Oct 1, 07; s Antonio Altobello & Agnes Petrucelli A; m 1930 to Josephine LaMontagne; c Henrietta (Mrs Suzio), Lourde (Mrs Gronback), Daniel, Patricia & Suzanne. Educ: Gettysburg Col; Georgetown Univ. Polit & Govt Pos: Selectman, Southwick, Mass, 38-45; Conn State Sen, 53-55; mayor, Meriden, 54-60; secy, Dem State Cent Comt, currently; deleg, Dem Nat Conv, 56, 64 & 68; deleg, Conn State Const Conv, 65. Bus & Prof Pos: Pres & Chmn Bd, L Suzio Concrete Co, 49-; Pres, York Hill Trap Rock Co, 49-; Chmn Bd, L Suzio Asphalt Co, 57; pres, L Suzio Sand & Gravel Co, 57- Mem: Conn Road Builders Asn; Conn Bituminous Concrete Asn; Conn Ready Mix Concrete Asn; Elks; Eagles. Relig: Catholic. Mailing Add: 165 Brownstone Ridge Meriden CT 06450

ALVAREZ, EUGENIO ALFREDO (D)
b Bayamon, PR, July 21, 18; s Inocencio Alvarez & Juana Rodriguez A; m 1943 to Ines Leon; c Carlota de Jesus & Eugenio Manuel. Educ: City Col New York Baruch Sch Bus, BBA in Int Trade & Econ, 58; Spanish Club; Int League; Student Coun. Polit & Govt Pos: Legis aide, NY State Assembly, 68 & 69-70; deleg, First Judicial Dist Dem Conv, 68, 69, 70 & 72; councilman aide, New York Coun, 70-71; dep dir licensing, New York Taxi & Limousine Comn, 71-72; deleg, Dem Nat Conv, 72; mem, Latino Caucus, Dem Nat Comt, 72-; NY State Assemblyman, 75th Dist, 73-74; dep comnr, New York HDA, currently. Bus & Prof Pos: Export mgr, F W Woolworth Co, 51-60; vpres, Morhan Exporting Corp, 60-71. Mem: World Trade Club of NY, Inc; Monroe Dem Club; Assoc Coun to Inform Our Neighbors, Inc (chmn); Boricuas Austentes, Inc; Circulo Social Manatieno, Inc. Honors & Awards: Awards, Yauco Deportivo Inc, 65, Assoc Coun to Inform Our Neighbors, Inc, 65 & Circulo Social Manatieno, Inc, 73. Relig: Catholic. Mailing Add: 4451 Monticello Ave Bronx NY 10466

AMARAL, ALVIN THEODORE (R)
Hawaii State Rep
b Puunene, Maui, Hawaii, Dec 1, 27; s Alfred G Amaral & Jessie Montalbo A; m 1951 to Dorothy Calasa; c Alvin T, Russell J & Jeffrey D. Educ: St Anthony High Sch, Wailuku, Maui, Hawaii, grad, 45. Polit & Govt Pos: Deleg, Hawaii State Const Conv, 68; Hawaii State Rep, 72- Bus & Prof Pos: Asst cashier, Alexander & Baldwin, Puuenene, Maui, Hawaii, 47-63; ins counselor, Paul Revere Life Ins Co, Kahului, Maui, 63-; realtor in charge, Mike McCormack Realtors, 69- Mil Serv: Entered as Pvt, Army, 46, released as Tech 5, 47, after serv in Hq & Hq Co, Signal Sect, Pac; World War II Victory Medal. Mem: Nat Asn of Real Estate Bd; Maui Co Bd of Realtors (bd dirs, 73-). Relig: Catholic. Legal Res: 286 Puunene Ave Kahului Maui HI 96732 Mailing Add: PO Box 393 Kahului Maui HI 96732

AMATO, VINCENT ANTHONY (R)
Chmn, Middletown Town Rep Comt, Conn
b Middletown, Conn, June 13, 25; s Rosindo Amato & Josephine Petrozzello A; m 1947 to Phyllis W Ahlberg; c Peter Vincent, Steven Paul & Diane Louise. Educ: Mass Inst Technol, 42-43. Polit & Govt Pos: Mem, City Coun, Middletown, Conn, 69-71; comnr, Parking Authority, 71-; chmn, Middletown Town Rep Comt, 72- Bus & Prof Pos: Vpres & secy, Amato's Inc, Middletown, Conn, 49-; owner, Amato's, New Britain, 59-; vpres, Middletown Indust Develop Corp, 70-; secy, Industry for Middletown, 70-; dir, Laurel Bank & Trust Co, 73- Mil Serv: Entered as Aviation Cadet, Army Air Force, 43, released as 2nd Lt, 45, after serv in Training Units. Mem: Hobby Indust Asn Am; Middletown Savings Bank (corporator); Middlesex Mem Hosp (corporator). Honors & Awards: Outstanding Young Man of 1957, Middletown Jaycees; United Fund Annual Award, Middletown. Relig: Catholic. Mailing Add: Ridgewood Rd Middletown CT 06457

AMATUCCI, JEAN (D)
NY State Assemblywoman
b New York, NY, Nov 23, 38; d Daniel J Amatucci & Carmela Verdicanna A; single. Educ: State Univ NY Col Plattsburgh, BS, 60. Polit & Govt Pos: NY State Assemblyman, 98th Dist, 75- Bus & Prof Pos: Nursing pos, Hamilton Ave Hosp, formerly; sch nurse-teacher, formerly; pvt duty nurse, Hamilton Ave Hosp & Monticello Hosp, formerly; camp nurse, Camp Chipinaw & Ten Mile River Boy Scout Camps, formerly; operator, Candy Cone Soft Ice Cream Drive-In, White Lake, 68-73. Publ: Ed jour, NY State Sch Nurse-Teachers Asn, 71-72. Mem: Fel Am Sch Health Asn; Cath Daughters of Am (Past VGrand Regent); Asn for Retarded Children, Sullivan Co; Bethel Dem Club; NY State Sch Nurse-Teachers Asn. Honors & Awards: Distinguished Serv Award, NY State Sch Nurse-Teachers Asn; Cert of Appreciation, Bethel Lions Club. Mailing Add: PO Box 54 White Lake NY 12786

AMBLER, ROBERT B (D)
Mass State Rep
Mailing Add: 36 Church St Weymouth MA 02188

AMBRO, JEROME A (D)
US Rep, NY
b Brooklyn, NY, June 27, 28; s Jerome G & Angela Ambro; m 1955 to Helen Cornell McCooey; c Cathleen, David & Richard. Educ: NY Univ, BA. Polit & Govt Pos: Mem, Suffolk Co Bd Supvr, 68-69; supvr, Huntington, NY, 68-75; US Rep, NY, 75- Mil Serv: Army, 51-53, Korean Conflict. Mem: Nat Asn Urban Affairs (counties steering comt). Honors & Awards: Torch of Liberty Award, B'nai B'rith, 67; Educ Award, Suffolk Co Orgn for Prom of Educ, 70; Serv Award, NY State Recreation & Parks Asn, 72; Distinguished Serv Award, NY State VFW, 74. Relig: Roman Catholic. Legal Res: 22 Zoranne Dr East Northport NY 11731 Mailing Add: 1313 Longworth House Off Bldg Washington DC 20515

AMBROGIO, WILLIAM PETER (D)
Conn State Rep
b Newark, NJ; s John Ambrogio & Angelina Perri A; m to Ethel Mae Leonard; c Anthony Pat, Alfred Edward, John Perri, Robert William, William P, Jr, Nancy (Mrs Roger Harker), Marion (Mrs Ernest Starkey), Edwin P & James A. Educ: Cent Eve Classes (NJ), draftsman, 24-26; Chicago Tech Col, engr, 35-38. Polit & Govt Pos: Mem, Sixth Ward Assembly, Sixth Ward Dem Comt, 48-, chmn, Sixth Ward Dem Comt, 64-; Conn State Rep, 95th Dist, 73- Bus & Prof Pos: Maintenance foreman, Gen Motors Chevrolet Div, Bloomfield, NJ, 26-28; supt maintenance, Great A&P Tea Co, New Haven Div, 28-38; self-employed, 38-70; now retired. Publ: Auth, Melebus Newsletter, monthly, 61-66. Mem: Elks; Am of Ital Descent; Ital Am Civil Rights League; KofC (4 degree); Cerebral Palsy Asn NH (vpres, 59-). Relig: Catholic. Mailing Add: 120 Cedar St New Haven CT 06519

AMBROSE, DELPHIN D (R)
Chmn, Lynn Rep City Comt, Mass
b Lynn, Mass, Jan 9, 07; s Peter D Ambrose & Laura Valeri A; m to Rita N Gibbons; c Gregory Robert, Laura Joan & Sherry Marie. Educ: Boston Univ Col Lib Arts & Sch Law; Delta Sigma Rho; Lambda Alpha. Polit & Govt Pos: Mem, Bd of Pub Welfare, Mass; vchmn, Indust Develop Comt; mem, Lynn Housing Authority; deleg, Mass Rep State Conv; chmn, Lynn Rep City Comt, Mass, 68- Bus & Prof Pos: Pres, Lynn Bd Realtors & Assoc Brokers Corp; dir, Mass Asn of Real Estate Bd, Lynn Tuberc League & Union Hosp. Mil Serv: Entered as Pvt, Army, 42, released as Sgt Maj, 45. Mem: Mass Ins Brokers Asn; Nat Asn Real Estate Bd; Nat Asn Housing & Redevelop Off; Ital Commun Ctr Gtr Lynn; Boston Univ Alumni Asn. Mailing Add: 56 Long Hill Rd Lynn MA 01902

AMBROSE, JOHN ANTHONY (D)
State Dem Committeeman, NY
b Brooklyn, NY, Sept 9, 24; s Joseph Ambrose & Clementina Scandizzo A; m 1951 to Rose-Marie Sowers; c Joseph T & Patricia M. Educ: Brooklyn Col, BA, 50; St John's Univ, MA, 64; NY State War Regents scholar; Omega Delta Phi. Polit & Govt Pos: Dem Committeeman, Brookhaven Town, Suffolk Co, NY, 62-; alt deleg, NY State Dem Conv, 67; secy, Brookhaven Town Dem Comt, 67-68; exec asst to chmn, Suffolk Co Dem Comt, 67-; deleg, Dem Nat Conv, 68; State Dem Committeeman, First Assembly Dist, NY, 70- Bus & Prof Pos: Prod control analyst, Mergenthaler Linotype Co, Brooklyn, 51-53; prod control analyst, Am Machine & Foundry, 53-54; math teacher, Union Free Sch Dist 24, 54- Mil Serv: Entered as Pvt, Army Air Force, 43, released as Pfc, 46, after serv in 1969th Ord Depot Co, Eighth Air Force, Pac Theatre, Okinawa, 45-46; Asiatic-Pac Serv Medal; Am Serv Medal; World War II Victory Medal. Mem: Patchogue Fedn Teachers; Suffolk Co Math Teachers Asn; KofC. Relig: Roman Catholic. Mailing Add: 71 N Howells Point Rd Bellport NY 11713

AMBROSE, MYLES JOSEPH (R)
b New York, NY, July 21, 26; s Arthur P Ambrose & Anna Campbell A; m 1948 to Elaine Miller; c Myles Joseph, Kathleen Anne (Mrs Thomas Ley), Kevin Arthur, Elise Mary, Nora Jeanne & Christopher Miller. Educ: Manhattan Col, BBA, 48; NY Law Sch, JD, 52; Phi Alpha Delta; Alpha Sigma Beta. Hon Degrees: Dr of Laws, Manhattan Col, 72. Polit & Govt Pos: Admin asst US Attorney, Southern Dist, NY, 54-57; asst to US Secy of Treas, Washington, DC, 57-60; exec dir, Waterfront Comn of NY Harbor, 60-63; chief counsel, NY State Joint Legis Comt for Study of Alcoholic Beverage Control Law, 63-65; comnr, US Bur Customs, 69-72; spec asst attorney gen, Off for Drug Abuse Law Enforcement, Dept Justice, 72-; spec consult to the President, 72-; co-chmn, Nat Strategy Coun on Drug Abuse, 72- Bus & Prof Pos: Instr econ & indust rels, Manhattan Col, NY, 54-57; attorney, pvt law practice, NY, 63-69; mem, Speary & Hill Attorneys, Washington, DC & New York, currently; hon consul, Principality Monaco, Washington, DC, currently. Publ: Co-auth, Federal Strategy for Drug Abuse & Drug Traffic Prevention, 73; auth, A big, dirty war, Justice Mag, 6/72; Disrupting heroin traffic, Am Bar Asn J, 9/72. Mem: Am Bar Asn; Asn of the Bar of New York City; Am Soc Int Law; Int Asn Chiefs Police; Guild Cath Lawyers. Honors & Awards: Presidential Mgt Improv Cert, White House, 70; Award for Exceptional Contrib for Effectiveness, US Treas Dept, 70; Knight Comndr, Order of Merit, Repub of Italy, 72; Outstanding Investr of the Year, Soc of Prof Investr, 72; Spec Achievement Award, Asn Fed Investr, DC, 72. Relig: Catholic. Legal Res: 5506 Uppingham St Chevy Chase MD 20015 Mailing Add: 1750 New York Ave Washington DC 20006

AMBROSE, ROBERT PAUL (R)
NH State Rep
b Laconia, NH, Mar 2, 48; s Paul Theodore Ambrose & Jane Langer A; m 1974 to Marilyn Sabella; c Leigh Sabella. Educ: Univ NH, BA cum laude, 70; Univ NC, MA in Econ, 75; Alpha Kappa Delta; Omicron Delta Epsilon; Phi Mu Delta. Polit & Govt Pos: Deleg, NH Const Conv, 74; NH State Rep, 75- Mailing Add: Box 638 Lang St Meredith NH 03253

AMBROSINO, JOSEPH P, JR (R)
Del State Rep
Mailing Add: 24 N Stuyvesant Dr Wilmington DE 19809

AMEMIYA, RONALD YOSHIHIKO (D)
Attorney Gen, Hawaii
b Wahiawa, Oahu, Hawaii, Feb 14, 40; s Keifuku Amemiya (deceased) & Kimi Mito; m 1964 to Ellen Sumiko Fujimoto; c Keith Yoshitaka & Dwight Yoshinobu. Educ: Univ Hawaii, BBA, 62; Hastings Col of Law, Univ Calif, JD, 67. Polit & Govt Pos: Dep attorney gen, Hawaii, 67-72; dir, Off Consumer Protection, 72-74; comnr, Motor Vehicle Ins Off, Hawaii, 74; attorney gen, Hawaii, 74-; mem, Hawaii Dem Party, 67- Mil Serv: Entered as 2nd Lt, Army, 62, released as 1st Lt, 64, after serv in 25th Inf Div; Capt, Army Res. Mem: Am & Hawaii Bar Asns. Honors & Awards: Outstanding Young Man of Am, 73; Outstanding Young Man, Hawaii Jaycees, 73. Mailing Add: 733 Kapaia St Honolulu HI 96825

AMEN, OTTO (R)
Wash State Rep
Mailing Add: Rte 1 Box 45 Ritzville WA 99169

AMENTA, PAUL (D)
Conn State Sen
Mailing Add: 80 Cedarwood Dr New Britain CT 06052

AMES, BOBBIE HACKNEY (R)
b Washington, NC, July 23, 30; m 1950 to John Brewer Ames; c Elizabeth Acra, John Brewer, II, James Hackney & twins, Laurie & David. Educ: Greensboro Col, 48-49; ECarolina Univ, 49-51. Polit & Govt Pos: Dir women's activities, Dallas Co Rep Party, Ala, 12 years; dir women's Party to People Prog under Mary Ellen Miller; pres, Ala Fedn of Rep Women; deleg, Rep Nat Conv, 68; Rep Nat Committeewoman, Ala, 68-72. Bus & Prof Pos: Former owner & operator, Antique Shop; prin, Perry Christian Sch, 66-70, adminr, currently. Mem: Ala Hist Soc; Blackbelt Antiq Soc; Ala Occup Rehabilitation; (Bd Dirs); Selma & Dallas Co Fedn Church Women. Honors & Awards: Woman of Achievement in 1968, Bus & Prof Club. Relig: Community Church. Legal Res: Amesmont Rte 2 Marion AL 36756 Mailing Add: S Washington St Marion AL 36756

AMES, H ROBIE (D)
NH State Rep
Mailing Add: 220 Roxbury St Keene NH 03431

AMES, JOHN STANLEY, III (R)
Mass State Rep
b Boston, Mass, Oct 18, 36; s John S Ames, Jr & Isabel Biddle Henry A; m 1962 to Mary Louise Alford; c John S, IV & Gavin H. Educ: Harvard Col, AB, 58; Hasty Pudding Club; Procellian Club. Polit & Govt Pos: Mass State Rep, 14th Dist, 71-; alt deleg, Rep Nat Conv, 72. Mil Serv: Entered as Ens, Navy, 59, released as Lt(jg), 62, after serv in Landing Ship Tank, WCoast, 60-62. Relig: Protestant. Mailing Add: 235 Main St North Easton MA 02334

AMICK, CAROL CAMPBELL (D)
Mass State Rep
b Cleveland, Ohio; d Charles L Amick & Janet Campbell A; single. Educ: Iowa State Univ, BS; Alpha Lambda Delta; Sigma Kappa. Polit & Govt Pos: Measurer wood, bark & manure, Bedford, Mass, 69-, mem charter comn, 74, mem publ comt, 74-; mem, Gov's Hanscom Task Force, 74-; mem, Comt Criminal Justice Standards & Goals Proj, 75-; Mass State Rep, 37th Middlesex Dist, 75- Publ: Ed, Bedford Minute-man, Minute-man Publs, Inc, 68-74. Mem: Women in Commun, Inc; League Women Voters; Bedford Woman's Community Club; Bedford Coun Human Rels; Friends of Bedford Pub Libr. Relig: Protestant. Mailing Add: 277 The Great Rd Bedford MA 01730

AMIG, ELIZABETH CLEMENT (R)
Mem, Cumberland Co Rep Exec Comt, Pa
b Upper Darby, Pa, Nov 8, 29; d Fred C Clement & Adele Murphy C; div; c Terese, Bruce Clement & Eric Philip. Educ: Gettysburg Col, BA, 52; Pa State Univ, grad work, 68-72; Delta Gamma. Polit & Govt Pos: Mem, Cumberland Co Rep Exec Comt, Pa, 71-; alt deleg, Rep Nat Conv, 72; State Bd Cong chmn, Pa Coun of Rep Women, 72-; vpres, New Cumberland Coun of Rep Women, 72-; spec asst to Pa State Sen Rep Caucus, 73- Bus & Prof Pos: Ed, W Shore Times, Harrisburg, Pa, 63-68; kindergarten teacher, East Pennsboro Sch Dist, 68-72; ed commentator, TV/Radio-Columbia Broadcasting Syst Spectrum Series, Harrisburg, 72;

TV reporter, currently. Publ: Auth & ed, Resolution; to interest man in his community, 64, Let George do it, 65 & Gentlemen don't make headlines, 67, W Shore Times. Mem: New Cumberland Civic Club; Drexel Hills Civil Asn; West Shore Humane Soc; West Shore Theatrical Players, Inc. Honors & Awards: Third pl, Club Scrapbook, Pa Fedn of Women's Clubs, 61, first pl, Club Yearbook, 62. Relig: United Faith of Christ. Mailing Add: 117 Parkview Rd New Cumberland PA 17070

AMLEY, LORETTA ABEL (D)
b Duluth, Minn; d Charles Abel & Anna Botten A; wid; c Vicki, Christopher & Tracey. Educ: Univ Wis, 38-39; Univ Minn, 39-42; Psi Chi; Alpha Lambda. Polit & Govt Pos: Founder & pres, Wilsonian Dem Club, 52-53; area chmn, Primary, Ron Cameron for Gen Assembly, Dem Slate, 56; pres, La Mirada Dem Club, 62-63; founder & pres, Mark Twain Dem Club, 65-67; dir, 19th Cong Dist, Calif Dem Coun, 67-69; chmn, 19th Cong Dist, McCarthy for President Campaign, 68; deleg, Dem Nat Conv, 68 & 72; mem, Co Dem Comt, 70-71; caucus chmn, 19th Cong Dist, McGovern Campaign, 72; community contact, McGovern Campaign, 72. Bus & Prof Pos: Owner & operator, Trigon Mfg Co, Whittier, Calif, 57-63 & Santa Fe Tufting Co, Santa Fe Springs, Calif, 63-67; vpres, Amlian Corp, Vernon, Calif, 67-70. Mem: Am Civil Liberties Union (dir, Southern Calif Affil, 71-72). Honors & Awards: Key Woman, Dem Party, 60 & 64. Relig: Uniterian. Mailing Add: 15633 E Foster Rd La Mirada CA 90638

AMMERMAN, JOSEPH S (D)
Pa State Sen
Mailing Add: 633 State St Curwensville PA 16833

AMMOND, ALENE S (D)
NJ State Sen
Mailing Add: State House Trenton NJ 08625

AMOS, MABEL S (D)
b Brooklyn, Ala; d James Sanders & Hattie Bethea S. Educ: Ala Col at Montavallo; State Teachers Col at Troy; Peabody Col. Polit & Govt Pos: Stenographer, State Tax Comn, Ala, 31; rec secy to Gov, 39-66; Secy of State, formerly. Bus & Prof Pos: Sch teacher. Mem: Bus & Prof Women's Club (exec secy, comn on status of women, first vpres interasn of the comn). Relig: Baptist. Mailing Add: 3142 Norman Bridge Rd Montgomery AL 36105

AMOS, WILLIAM GEORGE (R)
Chmn, Second Cong Dist Rep Party, Ga
b Columbus, Ga, Feb 5, 35; s William G Amos & Isabel Floyd A; m 1957 to Patricia LaRue Gunn; c Evelyn Leigh & Patricia Lynn. Educ: Auburn Univ, BS in building const, 57; pres, Builders Guild & Omicron Delta Kappa; Pi Kappa Phi. Polit & Govt Pos: Bd dirs, Muscogee Young Rep, Ga; admin asst to US Rep Howard H Callaway, Third Dist, Ga, 64-66; campaign mgr, US Rep Howard Callaway for Ga, 66; vchmn, Third Cong Dist Rep Party, Ga, 66-67; nat committeeman, Nat Fedn of Young Rep, 66-67; chmn, Second Cong Dist Rep Party, Ga, 72-; comnr, Lowndes Co Planning Comn, 72- Bus & Prof Pos: Estimator, Jordan Co, 59-61, asst prof mgr, 61-62, proj mgr, 62-64; innkeeper, Holiday Inn of Callaway Gardens, 68-69; pres, Amos Construction Co, Inc, 69-; pres, Helios Inc, 72-; dir, First Nat Bank, Valdosta, 73- Mil Serv: Entered as 2nd Lt, Marine Corps, 57, released as 1st Lt 59, after serv in Second Bridge Co, Force Troops. Mem: Am Inst Constructors; Assoc Gen Contractors; Home Builders Asn; Rotary Int (pres, Valdosta, 73-74); Valdosta CofC (pres, 74-). Relig: Presbyterian; former chmn bd deacons, First Presby Church, Valdosta. Legal Res: 1205 Hickory Dr Valdosta GA 31601 Mailing Add: PO Box 1184 Valdosta GA 31601

AMOSS, WILLIAM H (D)
Md State Deleg
Mailing Add: 2037 Pleasantville Rd Fallston MD 21047

AMSBERRY, JEANNE LOUQUET (R)
Chaplain, Mont Fedn Rep Women
b Wallace, Idaho, July 17, 21; d Floyd W Louquet & Violet Waggoner L; m 1942 to Berton L Amsberry; c Barrie Lynne (Mrs William F Heinecke). Educ: Univ Mont, 45; PEO; Beta Sigma Phi. Polit & Govt Pos: Engrossing clerk, Mont House of Rep, 51; secy, Mont State Rep Cent Comt, 51-55, mem exec comt, 68-; enrolling clerk, Mont State Senate, 55; secy for Congressman Orvin B Fjare, 55-57; pres, Park Co Rep Womens Clubs, Mont, 58-59; pres, Silver Bow Co Rep Womens Club, 60-61; pres, Flathead Co Rep Womens Club, 64-65; dist dir, Mont Fedn of Rep Women, 61-67, pres, 68-72, chaplain, 72-; deleg, Rep Nat Conv, 68. Bus & Prof Pos: Interior decorator & store design, 41-42; physicians asst & x-ray technician, 43-45; bookkeeper, 63-66. Mem: Shrine; Toastmistress Club of Gallatin Co; Gallatin Co Rep Woman's Club. Honors & Awards: Nat Fedn of Rep Womens Club Award for Membership Achievement; Mont Young Rep Sr Rep Award for Distinguished & Outstanding Serv to Mont & Nat Rep Party. Relig: Presbyterian. Mailing Add: 1317 Eleventh Ave Helena MT 59601

ANASTASIA, LAWRENCE J (D)
Conn State Rep
Mailing Add: 303 Newtown Ave Norwalk CT 06851

ANAYA, MIKE (D)
Chmn, NMex Dem State Cent Comt
b Moriarty, NMex, Feb 27, 29; s Lauriano Anaya & Eufracia Martinez A; m 1954 to Mary M Sandoval; c Michaela, Steven, Lawrence, Juanita, Patricia, Roberta, Victoria & Michael Eugene. Educ: Univ NMex, 47-48; NMex Highlands Univ, 48-49; Newman Club. Polit & Govt Pos: Councilman, Moriarty City Coun, NMex, 54-; vchmn, Torrance Co Dem Cent Comt, formerly, chmn, currently; chmn, NMex Dem State Cent Comt, 71-; mem, Dem Nat Chmn Asn, 72-; mem, Dem Nat Comt, 72- Bus & Prof Pos: Dir, EMW Natural Gas Asn, currently; pres, Moriarty Rotary; pres, NMex Food Dealers Asn, 67-69. Mil Serv: Entered as Pvt, Army, 51, released as Sgt 1/C, 53, after serv in 717th AAA Gun Bn, Germany; Best Battery Supply Award in 7th Army. Mem: Am Legion (Dist Comdr, Dept NMex); Keep NMex Beautiful Inc, (Dir, 69-, vpres, 72); Mt Carmel Parish Coun (pres, 72-73). Honors & Awards: Hon Chap Farmer, Future Farmers of Am, 60; Legionnaire of the Year, Am Legion, 65; Citizen of the Year, Moriarty CofC, 66; Col Aide de Camp, Gov Bruce King, 71; Honor Guard, Secy State, NMex, 71. Relig: Catholic. Mailing Add: PO Drawer M Moriarty NM 87035

ANAYA, TONEY (D)
Attorney Gen, NMex
b Moriarty, NMex, Apr 29, 41; s Lauriano Anaya & Eufracia Martinez A; m 1963 to Elaine Marie Bolin; c Kimberly Michele, Toney, II & Kristina Elaine. Educ: Georgetown Univ, BS Foreign Serv; Am Univ Sch Law, JD. Polit & Govt Pos: Attorney Gen, NMex, 75- Mem: NMex & Am Bar Asns; US Supreme Court. Relig: Catholic. Legal Res: 826 Gonzales Rd Santa Fe NM 87501 Mailing Add: PO Box 2477 Santa Fe NM 87501

ANCKER-JOHNSON, BETSY (R)
Asst Secy Sci & Technol, Dept Com
Legal Res: WA Mailing Add: Dept of Commerce Washington DC 20230

ANDELIN, JOHN PHILIP, JR
b Chicago, Ill, June 8, 34; s John Philip Andelin, Sr & Rita Niemann A; single. Educ: Calif Inst Technol, BS, 55, PhD, 66; Stanford Univ, MS, 56; Tau Beta Pi; Sigma Xi. Polit & Govt Pos: Admin asst to US Rep Mike McCormack, Wash, 71- Bus & Prof Pos: Sr research scientist, Ford Motor Co, 66-69; research assoc, Harvard Univ, 69-71. Mem: Am Phys Soc; Am Astron Soc; Optical Soc Am. Honors & Awards: Nat Sci Found fel, 55-56; Hughes doctoral fel, 56-60. Mailing Add: Box 10 Richland WA 99352

ANDERSEN, ALICE KLOPSTAD (R)
b Spink, SDak, Apr 12, 12; d Samuel Andreas Klopstad & Anna Marie Larson K; m 1937 to Daniel Johannes Andersen; c Dianne (Mrs Paul L Tecklenberg). Educ: George Washington Univ, AB polit sci, 41; Kappa Kappa Gamma. Polit & Govt Pos: Personal secy, US Sen William J Bulow, SDak, 34-43; clerk, Civil Serv Comt, US Senate, 41-43; mem staff, US Rep H Allen Smith, 20th Dist, Calif, 66-, admin asst, 69-72; admin asst, US Rep Carlos J Moorhead, Calif, 73- Bus & Prof Pos: Secy, Prudential Ins Co Am, 30-32; secy, Home Owners' Loan Corp, Sioux Falls, SDak, 32-34. Mem: Am Newspaper Women's Club; Columbian Women; George Washington Univ & Chevy Chase Club, Florence Crittenton Home & Hosp (life mem bd mgrs); George Washington Univ Hosp (women's bd); George Washington Univ Alumni Asn. Honors & Awards: Alumni Achievement Award, George Washington Univ Alumni Asn. Relig: Lutheran. Mailing Add: 4441 Lowell St NW Washington DC 20016

ANDERSEN, CHRIS KENNETH (R)
NH State Rep
b Chicago, Ill, Dec 6, 30; s Carl Martin Andersen & Marie Clasen A; m 1969 to Susan Elaine Goodwin; c Kirsten Elaine & Ross Christian. Educ: Palmer Col of Chiropractic, DC, 59. Polit & Govt Pos: NH State Rep, Merrimack Co Dist 25, 63-70, Dist 15, 72-; mem, NH Bd Chiropractic Examrs, 67-72. Mil Serv: Entered as Seaman Recruit, Navy, 50, released as Torpedoman 2/C, 54, after serv in USS Orion, Sixth Submarine Squadron; Nat Defense & Good Conduct Medals. Mem: J F Grostic Research Asn; Rockley Research Acad Inc; N H Palmer Col Alumni Asn; Parker Chiropractic Research Found; NH Chiropractic Asn. Relig: Protestant. Mailing Add: 91 Shawmut St Concord NH 03301

ANDERSEN, ELMER LEE (R)
b Chicago, Ill, June 17, 09; s Arne Andersen & Jennie O Johnson A; m 1932 to Eleanor Johnson; c Anthony, Julian & Emily. Educ: Muskegon Jr Col, grad, 28; Univ Minn, BBA, 31; Alpha Kappa Psi; Delta Sigma Rho. Hon Degrees: LLD, Macalester Col, 65; LHD, Carleton Col, 72. Polit & Govt Pos: Del, Rep Nat Conv, 48 & 64; Minn State Sen, 49-59; chmn coord comt, Minn Rep Campaign, 52; chmn platform comt, Minn State Rep Conv, 56, chmn, 58; Gov, Minn, 61-63; chmn, Minn Const Study Comn, currently. Bus & Prof Pos: In advert & sales prom, H B Fuller Co, 34-37, sales mgr, 37-41, pres & chmn bd, 41-74, chmn bd, 74-; pres, Bush Found, formerly; mem bd, currently; dir, First Trust Co, St Paul; dir, Minn Mutual Life Ins Co, formerly; mem bd regents, Univ Minn, 67-75, chmn bd, 71-75; dir, George A Hormel & Co, Austin, Minn. Mem: Minn Hist Soc; Child Welfare League Am (exec bd, currently); Boy Scouts of Am (exec comt); YMCA; Community Chest. Honors & Awards: Order of the Lion, Finland, 63; Award of Merit, Izaak Walton League, 67; Silver Beaver & Silver Antelope Awards, Boy Scouts of Am; Conserv Award, Minneapolis Jr CofC, 70; Serv to Motoring Award, Am Automobile Asn, 71. Relig: Lutheran. Mailing Add: 2230 W Hoyt Ave St Paul MN 55108

ANDERSEN, KENNETH H (D)
Utah State Rep
Mailing Add: 1795 Lake St Salt Lake City UT 84105

ANDERSEN, LEONARD CHRISTIAN (R)
Iowa State Sen
b Waukegan, Ill, May 30, 11; s Lauritz F Andersen & M Marie Jacobsen A; m 1937 to Charlotte O Ritland; c Karen (Mrs Schneider), Paul Raymond, Charlene Kaye (Mrs Olsson) & Mark Luther. Educ: Huron Col, BA, 33; Univ SDak, law study, 33 & MA, 37; Delta Theta Phi. Polit & Govt Pos: Iowa State Rep, 61-65 & 67-72, chmn, Cities & Towns Comt, Iowa House Rep, 65-67; Iowa State Sen, Dist 26, 73-, mem, Appropriations, Schs, Human Resources & Ethics Comts & chmn, Rules Comt, Iowa State Senate, 73- Bus & Prof Pos: High Sch teacher, 34; econ teacher, Waldorf Col, 35-39; ins salesman, 39-41; econ teacher, Morningside Col, 42-43; life ins salesman & mgr, 43-58; owner, Ins Agency, 58- Mem: Iowa Asn Independent Ins Agts, Sioux City Chap (bd); Farm Bur; Mason (32 degree); Shrine; Lions. Relig: Lutheran, E L C Synod; served 2 terms as chmn of Morningside Lutheran Church, past bd mem. Legal Res: 712 S Glass St Sioux City IA 51106 Mailing Add: 604 Security Nat Bank Bldg Sioux City IA 51102

ANDERSEN, MERREL L (R)
Committeeman, Nebr State Rep Cent Comt
b Curtis, Nebr, Apr 19, 26; s Clarence Andersen & Mary Merrell; m 1950 to Hilda Bollish; c Stephanie, Merrell, Jr & Tamara. Educ: Kearney State Col, 2 years; Creighton Law Sch, LLB. Polit & Govt Pos: Chmn, Gage Co Rep, 62-66; committeeman, 30th Legis Dist, Nebr State Rep Cent Comt, 62-; mem exec comt, Nebr Rep Party, 66-71, finance comt, 68-70, vchmn, 69-72. Bus & Prof Pos: Asst US Attorney, Anchorage, Alaska, 58-61; co attorney, Gage Co, Nebr, 61-66. Mil Serv: Entered as Pvt, Army, 45, released as T-5, 46, after serv in MRU. Mem: Kiwanis; Mason; Farm Bur. Relig: Methodist. Mailing Add: 2211 Elk St Beatrice NE 68130

ANDERSEN, RUDY A (R)
Idaho State Rep
b Santa Barbara, Calif, Nov 18, 11; m to Lois Katherine Jones; c Dr Rudy, Jr, Lody Lyn (Mrs John Reeves) & Clayton. Educ: Univ Wash, BA, 37; Delta Kappa Epsilon. Polit & Govt Pos: Idaho State Rep, Dist 18, 67-, chmn health & welfare comt & mem keep Idaho Green comt, Gov Comt, currently; mem, Boise City Recreation Bd, currently; vchmn, Childrens Home Soc of Idaho, currently. Mailing Add: 4444 Hillcrest Dr Boise ID 83705

ANDERSON, ANDREW EDWIN (R)
VChmn, Seventh Dist Rep Party, Minn
b Fergus Falls, Minn, Feb 12, 40; s Edwin A Anderson & Gundia Foshaug A; m 1962 to Hazel Sowdon; c Janet Elizabeth & Edwin Andrew. Educ: Moorehead State Col, BA, cum laude, 63; Univ Minn, Minneapolis, 1 year; Concordia Col (Minn), 1 year; Circle K; Col Rep. Polit & Govt Pos: Co chmn, Head for Attorney Gen Campaign, 66, mem steering comt, Head for Gov, 70; treas, Seventh Dist Young Rep League, Minn, 66-69; treas, West Otter Tail Young Rep League, 67-68; chmn, Fergus Falls Rep Party, 67-69; co chmn, Nixon for President, 68; deleg, Otter Tail Co Rep Conv, 68-73; deleg, Seventh Dist Rep Conv, 68-73, floor leader Nixon for President, 68, mem credentials comt, 70; deleg, Minn State Rep Conv, 68-73, seventh dist, floor leader Nixon for President, 68, mem credentials comt, 70; chmn, Otter Tail Co Rep Party, 69-71; mem, Minn State Rep Cent Comt, 69-; treas, Seventh Dist Rep Party, 72-73, vchmn, 73- Bus & Prof Pos: Supvr gen acct, Otter Tail Power Co. Mil Serv: Entered as Pvt, Army Res, 57, released as Sgt, 62, after serv in Co B, 409th Inf. Mem: Minn Asn Pub Acct; Minn Soc Cert Pub Acct; Jaycees; Farm Bur; Young Rep League. Relig: Methodist. Mailing Add: 1010 E Mt Faith Fergus Falls MN 56537

ANDERSON, ARNOLD R (D)
Kans State Rep
Mailing Add: 320 Eighth St Wakeeney KS 67672

ANDERSON, BYRON (R)
Secy of State, Colo
Polit & Govt Pos: Pres, Denver Elec Comn, formerly; Secy of State, Colo, currently. Bus & Prof Pos: Pres, Nat Conf State Liquor Adminr, formerly; mem, Colo Bd of Realtors, formerly; Real Estate Broker, 21 years; Ins agent, 30 years. Mem: Nat Asn Secy of State (treas). Mailing Add: State Capitol Denver CO 80203

ANDERSON, C JOSEPH, (D)
b West Terre Haute, Ind, Aug 4, 39; s Elmer Anderson & Anna L Ellingsworth A; m 1962 to Gloria Joyce Bugni; c C Joseph, Mark A & Lisa A. Educ: Ind State Univ, Terre Haute, AB; Ind Univ Sch Law, Indianapolis, JD; Phi Alpha Delta. Polit & Govt Pos: Dep prosecutor, Vigo Co, Ind, 67-68; town attorney, West Terre Haute, 68-; Ind State Rep, 68-72; judge, Vigo Circuit Court, 70-, deleg, Dem Nat Conv, 72. Bus & Prof Pos: High sch teacher, Govt & Eng, Indianapolis & Terre Haute, 63-67. Mil Serv: Entered as Pvt, Army, 57, released as Sp-4, 60, after serv in Army Security Agency, Okinawa & Washington, DC; Good Conduct Medal. Mem: Ind & Terre Haute Bar Asns; KofC. Honors & Awards: Voted one of the Outstanding Freshman Legislators of 69 session. Relig: Catholic. Mailing Add: 3500 College Ave Terre Haute IN 47801

ANDERSON, C MARIE PINGREY (R)
b St Augustine, Fla, June 2, 19; d Douglas Aesop Pingrey & Alberta Smith P; m 1937 to Berchel Lester Anderson; c James Douglas, Darrell Warren, Duane Lester, Ernest Darwin & Alberta Kay (Mrs Jerry Strand). Educ: Hurley High Sch, SDak, grad, 37; Universal Schs, Inc, Dallas, Tex. Polit & Govt Pos: Rep committeewoman, Hurley, SDak, several years; dep clerk of courts, Turner Co, SDak, 66, dep registr of deeds, 67-68, app registr of deeds 68 & 72, dep co sch supt, 68-69; vpres, Turner Co Rep Party, 68-75; mem, Dist II Southeastern Coun Govt Older Am Comt, currently; mem, Turner Co Coun Aging, currently; mem, Turner Co Exec Comt Exten Clubs, currently. Bus & Prof Pos: Bookkeeper, Hurley Munic Liquor Store, SDak, currently; secy & registr, Hurley City Cemetery. Mem: Hurley Hist Soc (pres); Hurley Community Club; Royal Neighbors Asn. Relig: United Methodist; Rec Secy, 70-72. Legal Res: Hurley SD 57036 Mailing Add: Box 302 Hurley SD 57036

ANDERSON, CARL WILLIAM (DFL)
Secy, Dodge Co Dem-Farmer-Labor Party, Minn
b Kasson, Minn, Apr 7, 04; s Jense Anderson & Ella Leth A; m 1928 to La Vanche Jeanette Loomis; c Jane Forrest (Mrs Watson). Educ: Kasson Pub High Sch, 2 years. Polit & Govt Pos: Dodge Co co-chmn, Hubert H Humphrey for Sen, 48, 52 & 56; Dodge Co co-chmn, Orville Freeman for Gov, 56, 58 & 60; Dodge Co co-chmn, Hubert H Humphrey for Pres, 60 & 68; secy, Dodge Co Dem-Farmer-Labor Party, Minn, 65-; deleg, Dem Nat Conv, 68; city councilman, Kasson, 70-; chmn, Dodge Co for Sen H H Humphrey, 70. Mem: Local 1382, Rochester, Minn. Relig: Methodist. Mailing Add: 304 First Ave NW Kasson MN 55944

ANDERSON, CLARENCE R (R)
Mont State Rep
b Worthington, Minn, Oct 10, 01; s Carl A Anderson & Hilma Elofson A; m 1925 to Alma Thompson; c Blanche (deceased); Marylin (Mrs Kirchhoff) & Ruth (Mrs Kincheloe). Educ: Gustavus Adolphus Col, BA, 23; Columbia Univ, 27; Univ Mont, MA, 39. Polit & Govt Pos: Mem several gov study comns on state lands, sch dists, sch finance & taxation, Mont, 35-66; admin asst, State Dept Pub Instr, 49-55; Mont State Rep, Dist 82, 75- Bus & Prof Pos: Coach & high sch teacher, Lake Benton, Minn, 23-25; high sch prin, Sidney, Mont, 25-27; supt schs, Richey, 27-35; elem schs prin, Helena, 35-41; supt schs, Livingston, 41-42; supt schs, Helena, 55-66. Mil Serv: Entered as Field Dir, Army Res, 42, released as Area Dir NChina, 46; 4 Battle Stars. Publ: Co-auth, Montana Earthquakes of 1935, Helena Independent Publ Co, 36; auth, Know Your Schools, State Publ Co, Helena, 72. Mem: Kiwanis; Mason; Nat & Mont Educ Asns; Am Asn Sch Adminrs. Relig: Methodist. Mailing Add: 333 1/2 E Normal Dillon MT 59725

ANDERSON, CLAUDE W (INDEPENDENT)
Va State Deleg
Mailing Add: Box 7 Buckingham VA 23921

ANDERSON, CLIFFORD R, JR (R)
Cal Plan Chmn, Calif Rep State Cent Comt
b Alexandria, Minn, Feb 6, 28; s Clifford R Anderson & Capatola Chase A; m 1950 to Madeline M Graham; c Clifford R, III, Alicia Marie, George Maxwell & Eric Preston. Educ: Univ Calif, Berkeley, BS, 50; Univ Southern Calif, JD, 53; Phi Delta Phi; Pi Kappa Alpha. Polit & Govt Pos: Admin asst to Assemblyman Don Anderson, Calif, 57-58; city councilman, Monterey Park, 58-60; pres, Los Angeles Young Rep, 60; chmn vol clubs, Los Angeles Co Rep Cent Comt, 61-64, chmn cand selection comt, 64-66; state chmn poll watchers, Goldwater Campaign, 64; chmn cand sch, State Calif Rep Party, 64, 66 & 68; Southern Calif precinct chmn, Reagan for Gov Campaign, 66; mem, Calif Rep State Cent Comt, 66-, state cand develop chmn, 66-67, precinct chmn, 67-69, mem exec comt, 67-, Cal plan chmn, 69-; alt deleg, Rep Nat Conv, 68. Mil Serv: Seaman, Navy, 45-46, serv in USS St Paul, Pac Theatre. Mem: Pasadena Bar Asn; Am Judicature Soc; Am Arbit Asn; Defense Research Inst; Rotary. Honors & Awards: Merit Award, Los Angeles Rep Cent Comt. Relig: Lutheran. Mailing Add: 2046 Oak Knoll San Marino CA 91108

ANDERSON, CLINTON PRESBA (D)
b Centerville, SDak, Oct 23, 95; s Andrew Jay Anderson & Hattie Belle Presba A; m 1921 to Henrietta E McCartney; c Sherburne Presba & Nancy (Mrs Ben L Roberts). Educ: Dakota Wesleyan Univ, 13-15; Univ Mich, 15-16; Delta Theta Phi; Pi Kappa Delta. Polit & Govt Pos: NMex State Treas, 33-34; adminr, NMex Relief Admin, 35; chmn & exec dir, Unemploy Compensation Comn, 36; managing dir, US Coronado Expos Comn, 39-40; US Rep, NMex, 41-45; US Secy Agr, 45-48; US Sen, NMex, 49-73; deleg, Dem Nat Conv, 68. Bus & Prof Pos: Reporter, Mitchell Repub, SDak, 16-17; reporter Albuquerque J, 19-22; chmn bd, Mt State Mutual Casualty Co, until 70. Mem: Rotary Int; Mason; Elks. Relig: Presbyterian. Legal Res: 3621 Camino Alameda SW Albuquerque NM 87105 Mailing Add: PO Box 1291 Albuquerque NM 87103

ANDERSON, D G (ANDY) (R)
Hawaii State Sen
Mailing Add: Senate Sgt-at-Arms State Capitol Honolulu HI 96813

ANDERSON, DALE (D)
b Massac Co, Ill, Nov 9, 16; s Henry Lee Anderson (deceased) & Belle Moyer A; m 1941 to Dorothy Elizabeth Rassa; c Mindy (Mrs Voelker) & David. Educ: Mt Vernon Sch Law, law degree, 63. Polit & Govt Pos: Chmn council, Baltimore Co, Md, 59-62, mem, 62-66, co exec, 66-; Dem Nat Committeeman, Md, 70-72; deleg, Dem Nat Conv, 72. Bus & Prof Pos: Home-builder, Overlea-Fullerton Sect Baltimore Co, Md, 50-62. Mil Serv: Entered as Pvt, Army, 42, released as Capt, 46, after serv in Air Materiel Command, 42-46. Publ: Total citizen involvement, unique school-recreation centers answer leisure needs, The Am Co, 70, nat award winning article. Mem: Nat Asn Co (bd dirs, 68-); Md Asn Co (pres, 70-); Am Legion, Overlea-Perry post 130. Relig: Presbyterian. Legal Res: 100 Belhaven Terr Baltimore MD 21236 Mailing Add: Exec Off Co Off Bldg 111 W Chesapeake Ave Towson MD 21204

ANDERSON, DANIEL PHILIP (D)
Chmn, Sheboygan Co Dem Party, Wis
b Plymouth, Wis, Jan 1, 45; s Philip George Anderson & Telona Helen Thompson A; m 1967 to Emily Corinne Maraccini. Educ: Univ Wis, Madison, BS, 67; Univ Southern Calif, 67-69; Univ Wis Law Sch, Madison, JD cum laude, 73. Polit & Govt Pos: Chmn, Sheboygan Co Dem Party, Wis, 74- Bus & Prof Pos: Attorney, Anderson, Damp & Anderson, SC, Plymouth, Wis, 74- Mil Serv: Entered as 2nd Lt, Air Force, 67, released as Capt, 71, after serv in Strategic Air Command, Pac Air Forces Okinawa & Air Training Command; Air Force Commendation Medal & Air Force Commendation with First Oak Leaf Cluster. Mem: Am & Wis State Bar Asns; Sheboygan Co Bar Asn (co-chmn Law Day, 75); Plymouth Pub Libr (trustee, 74-). Honors & Awards: Am Jurisprudence Award in Admin Law, 73. Mailing Add: 953 Dooley Rd Plymouth WI 53073

ANDERSON, DAVID LAWRENCE (D)
Nat Committeeman, Young Dem Clubs Md
b Baltimore, Md, Oct 29, 48; s Robert Lawrence Anderson & Ruth Hahn A; single. Educ: Towson State Col, BS, cum laude, 70; Univ Md Sch Law, JD, 73; Phi Alpha Theta. Polit & Govt Pos: Statewide chmn, Youth for Gov Mandel, 70; youth coordr, Md Muskie Youth, 72; pres, Young Dem Clubs Md, 71-72, nat committeeman, 72-; pres, Forum Four, 73-74; vdir, Mid Atlantic Region for Young Dem Club Am, 73- Bus & Prof Pos: Instr polit sci, Towson State Col, 71-; intern, Off Secy of State Fred L Wineland, summers, 71-73; legis analyst, Md Annotated Code Rev Comn, 73-; legis analyst, Md Dept Legis Reference, 73. Mem: Gtr Parkville Community Coun (vpres, 73-74); Cent Parkville Community Asn (pres, 73-74); Parkville Centennial Comt (chmn, 73-74). Honors & Awards: Outstanding Md Young Dem, Young Dem Clubs Md, 73. Mailing Add: 8600 Summit Ave Baltimore MD 21234

ANDERSON, DONALD B (R)
Ill State Sen
Mailing Add: 1406 Bluff St Peru IL 61354

ANDERSON, EARL L (DFL)
b Middle River, Minn, Nov 17, 35; s Frank Anderson & Harriet A; m 1955 to Janice Cater; c Greg, Donn, Colleen & Karen. Polit & Govt Pos: Chmn, Marshall Co Dem-Farmer-Labor Party, Minn, formerly. Bus & Prof Pos: Ed-publ, Middle River Rec, Minn, 59-68, Red Lake Falls Rec, 66-68, Stephen Messenger & Fallon Co Times, currently. Mem: Minn & Nat Newspaper Asns; Mason; Shrine; Lions. Relig: Lutheran. Mailing Add: Box 48 Stephen MN 56757

ANDERSON, EDWIN DEWEY, SR (R)
Chmn, Starke Co Rep Cent Comt, Ind
b Knox, Ind, Dec 12, 21; s Clarence James Anderson & Amanda Sheldon A; m 1941 to Alberta Marie Smith; c Edwin Dewey, Jr & Howard Brian. Educ: Knox High Sch; Reppert Sch of Auctioning, Decatur, Ind; Ind Univ Exten Real Estate Appraisal Course. Polit & Govt Pos: Precinct committeeman, Starke Co Rep Cent Comt, Ind, 52-66, chmn, 63- Mil Serv: Entered as Pvt, Army, 45, released as Cpl, 45, after serv in 5th Army; Marksman Sharpshooter. Mem: Nat & Ind Auctioneers Asns; Moose (Gov, Lodge 51); Farm Bur; Aviation Club. Relig: Protestant. Mailing Add: RR 2 Knox IN 46534

ANDERSON, EUGENE (D)
Kans State Rep
b Diffee, Ga, Mar 9, 44; s Velver Anderson & Velma Ford A; m 1966 to Mamie Jewel Sapp; c Timothy Eugene, Tamara Elaine & Melanie Jenise. Educ: High Sch grad; 2 years tech sch. Polit & Govt Pos: Kans State Rep, currently. Mil Serv: Entered as Pvt E-1, Army, 62, released as Pfc E-3, 65, after serv in 101st Airborne Div; Army Res, Pfc E-3, 1 year. Relig: Baptist. Mailing Add: 3434 W Harry Wichita KS 67214

ANDERSON, EUGENIE MOORE (DFL)
b Adair, Iowa, May 26, 09; d Ezekiel Arrowsmith Moore & Flora Belle McMillen M; m 1930 to John P Anderson; c Elizabeth Johanna (Mrs Ghei) & Hans Pierce. Educ: Stephens Col, 26-27; Simpson Col, 27-28; Carleton Col, 29-30; Juilliard Inst Musical Art, 30-32. Polit & Govt Pos: Chmn, First Cong Dist Dem-Farmer-Labor Comt, Minn, 44-48; deleg-at-lg, Dem Nat Conv, 48, deleg, 68; mem, Dem Nat comt, 48-49; US ambassador, Denmark, 49-53; US Rep, Third Session UN ad hoc comt on POW's, 52; chmn, State Comn for Fair Employ Practice, 55-60; mem, Dem Nat Adv Comt on Foreign Policy, 57-61; mem, EEMP, Bulgaria, 62-65; mem US deleg with rank of ambassador, UN, 65-68, US Rep, UN Trusteeship Coun,

65-68; mem, State Comn Minn Future; mem, Minn Humanities Comt; co-chmn, Minn Comt for Secure Peace in Mid East. Mem: Minn UN Asn; League of Women Voters. Relig: Methodist. Mailing Add: Tower View Red Wing MN 55066

ANDERSON, FAYNE E (R)
NH State Rep
b Maine, Aug 17, 04; married; c 2. Polit & Govt Pos: NH State Rep, 47-; deleg, NH State Const Conv, 48-64. Bus & Prof Pos: Bldg contractor; pres, Health Ctr. Mem: Mason (32 degree); Pemigewasset Valley Fish & Game Club; KofP. Relig: Protestant. Mailing Add: Warren NH 03279

ANDERSON, FORREST H (D)
b Helena, Mont, Jan 30, 13; s Oscar A Anderson & Nora O'Keefe A; m 1941 to Margaret Evelyn Samson; c Margaret Louise (Mrs Gary Templin), Arlee Joan & Newell Burke. Educ: Univ Mont; Columbus Univ, LLB, 38; Phi Delta Theta. Polit & Govt Pos: Mont State Rep, 43-45; co attorney, Lewis & Clark Co, 45-47; spec counsel, Indust Accident Fund, Mont, 47-49; Assoc Justice, Mont Supreme Court, 53-57; Attorney Gen, Mont, 57-69; deleg, Dem Nat Conv, 68; Gov, Mont, 69-72. Bus & Prof Pos: Attorney-at-law, 38-52. Mem: Mont & Am Bar Asns; Mason (32 degree); Moose; Scandinavian Lodge of Am. Relig: Methodist. Mailing Add: 1727 Jerome Pl Helena MT 59601

ANDERSON, FRED E (R)
Colo State Sen
Mailing Add: 1931 E First St Loveland CO 80537

ANDERSON, GARY L (R)
Nebr State Sen
b Holdrege, Nebr, Oct 8, 39; s Roy C Anderson & Iola Asp A; m 1965 to Ruth Ann Bell; c Kirsten. Educ: Hastings Col, BA, 65; San Francisco Theol Sem, BD, 68; Univ Munich, 68-69. Polit & Govt Pos: Treas, Kearney Co, Nebr, 71-72; Nebr State Sen, 37th Dist, 73- Mil Serv: Entered as Pvt, Army, 58, released as 1st Lt, 68, after serv in USAMTU, Ft Benning, Ga; Distinguished Rifleman; Distinguished Int Shooter; Commendation Ribbon. Publ: Marksmanship, Simon & Schuster, 72. Mem: Lions; Farmers Union. Relig: Presbyterian. Mailing Add: RR 1 Axtell NE 68924

ANDERSON, GENEVA JUNE (D)
Kans State Rep
b Springfield, Mo, Nov 24, 18; d Sherman Victor Stratton & Clara Opal Dill S; m 1937 to Lars Virgil Anderson; c Allen Virgil & Timothy Jon. Educ: Wichita High Sch, Kans, grad, 37; Am Inst Banking, courses in bookkeeping & acct. Polit & Govt Pos: Kans State Rep, 101st Dist, 75- Bus & Prof Pos: Clerk, Post Off Dept, Wichita, Kans, 41-46; clerk, acct dept, Bur Internal Revenue, 46-51; bank teller, City Nat Bank, 69- Mem: Mulvane Bus & Prof Womens Club (legis chmn & pres, 73-74); Kans Fedn Dem Womens Clubs (publicity chmn); Fifth Dist Fedn Dem Womens Clubs (auditor); Southern Sedgwick Co Dem Womens Club (vpres). Relig: Baptist. Mailing Add: 618 Highland Mulvane KS 67110

ANDERSON, GERALD VON, JR (D)
Chmn, Clay Co Dem Exec Comt, Ga
b Vincennes, Ind, May 30, 38; s G Von Anderson & Merry Cargal A; m 1958 to Alyce Roach; c Gerald V, III, David Lee & Leslie Janelle. Educ: NC State Univ, 56-58; Phi Eta Sigma. Polit & Govt Pos: Co chmn, Jimmy Carter Gubernatorial Campaign, Ga, 66 & 70; chmn, Clay Co Dem Exec Comt, 72-; dist coordr, Zell Miller Lt Gubernatorial Campaign, 74; mem, Ga Dem State Exec Comt, 74-; deleg, Dem Nat Mid-Term Conf, 74; mem, Ga Dem Charter Comn, 74-75; mem, Jefferson-Jackson Day Arrangements Comt, 75. Bus & Prof Pos: VPres, Anderson Construction Co of Ft Gaines, 68- Mem: Clay Co Redevelop Corp (dir, 68-); Lions; US Hwy 27 Asn Ga, Inc (secy-treas, 75-). Relig: Presbyterian. Legal Res: 102 Bluff St Ft Gaines GA 31751 Mailing Add: PO Box 220 Ft Gaines GA 31751

ANDERSON, GLEN H (DFL)
Minn State Rep
b Madison, Minn, Oct 24, 38; s Manfred O Anderson & Helen Holen A; m 1964 to Lorna Erickson; c Karla, Lee, Kristi & Mary. Polit & Govt Pos: Minn State Rep, Dist 15B, 73- Mil Serv: Pvt, Army Nat Guard, 58; Capt, Minn Nat Guard. Relig: Lutheran. Mailing Add: RR Bellingham MN 56212

ANDERSON, GLENN M (D)
US Rep, Calif
b Hawthorne, Calif, Feb 21, 13; s William Anderson; m Lee Dutton; c Melinda (Mrs Ming Tang), Evan & Glenn Michael. Educ: Univ Calif, Los Angeles, BA in Polit Sci & Psychol. Polit & Govt Pos: Mem, Los Angeles Co Dem Comt, Calif, 38-50, chmn, 48-50; mayor & city councilman, Hawthorne, 40-43; mem, Calif Dem State Comt, 42-; Calif State Assemblyman, 43-51; chmn, Calif Dem State Cent Comt, 50-52; Lt Gov, Calif, 59-67; US Rep, Calif, 69-, mem, Comt Pub Works, US House Rep, 69-, mem, Comt Merchant Marine & Fisheries, 71- Bus & Prof Pos: Founder & dir, Hawthorne Savings & Loan Asn, 50-; founder & dir, Hawthorne Financial Corp; pres, Downtown Enterprise Inc, currently. Mil Serv: Army, released as Sgt, 45. Legal Res: Harbor City CA Mailing Add: 1230 Longworth House Off Bldg Washington DC 20515

ANDERSON, GORDON A (DFL)
Chmn, 28th Sen Dist Dem-Farmer-Labor Party, Minn
b Pine City, Minn, May 23, 24; s Arnold C Anderson & Emma Ramberg A; m 1950 to Correne V Johnson; c Terrill G & Renee C. Educ: Univ Minn, night exten courses; Minn Sch Bus, 46-47. Polit & Govt Pos: VChmn, Hennepin Co Young Dem-Farmer-Labor, 51; vchmn, Eighth Ward Dem-Farmer-Labor Club, Minneapolis, 51; vchmn, Richfield Dem-Farmer-Labor Club, 65-66, chmn, 66; deleg, Dem-Farmer-Labor State Conv, 66, 68, 70 & 72 & 74; mem, Minn State Dem-Farmer-Labor Cent Comt, 68-70 & 74; mem, Third Dist Dem-Farmer-Labor Cent Comt, 70-; chmn, 28th Sen Dist, Dem-Farmer-Labor Party, 70-; chmn, 37th Dist Dem-Farmer-Labor Party, currently; mem, Richfield Charter Comn, 74. Bus & Prof Pos: Vpres, Goulet's Inc, Minneapolis, 70- Mil Serv: Entered as Pvt, Army Air Force, 42, released as Pfc, 45, after serv in 867th Chem Warfare Co AO, ETO, 44-45; European-African-Mid East Theatre Serv Ribbon; Good Conduct Medal. Mem: Walker Art Ctr; Mason; VFW; Am Legion; Richfield Jaycees. Honors & Awards: Jaycee Bronze Key Award. Relig: Unitarian-Universalist. Mailing Add: 7501 Elliot Ave Richfield MN 55423

ANDERSON, GWEN ADELE (R)
b Lignite, NDak, June 3, 30; d Adolph Odegaard & Beatrice Shannon O; m 1951 to Harlan John Anderson; c Barbara Shannon & Mark Harlan. Educ: Univ SDak, 48-51; Alpha Phi; Radio Guild; Int Relations Club. Polit & Govt Pos: Precinct committeewoman for Hart, Benton Co Rep Cent Comt, Wash, 58-60, dist chmn for Kennewick, 59-60, vchmn, 60-62, state committeewoman, 62-65; deleg, Wash State Rep Conv, 60, 62, 64, 66, 68 & 72; treas, Fourth Cong Dist Rep Club, 63-65; vchmn, Wash State Rep Cent Comt 65-68; vchmn, Wash State Rep Cent Comt Exec Bd, 65-68, dir, State Precinct Training Prog, 66; adv to exec bd, Wash State Fedn of Rep Women, 65-; chmn, Wash State Women for Nixon, 68; deleg, Rep Nat Conv, 68 & 72, co-chmn of housing & mem exec comt, 72; Rep Nat Committeewoman, Wash, 68-73; mem exec bd, Rep Nat Comt, 71-73; mem, Citizens Adv Comt on Foreign Affairs & Spec Adv Comt on Pub Opinion, US Dept of State, 70; co-chmn & exec dir, Wash State Comt for Reelection of the President, 72; mem, Defense Adv Comt on Women in Serv, US Dept of Defense, 72-; coordr, Wash State Inaugural Comt, 73; mem, Nat Inaugural Adv Comt, 73; spec asst to Dep Asst Secy, Health, Educ & Welfare, 73-74; consult to the Vice President, US, 74, dep asst, 74; dep asst to Counselor to the President, US, 74- Bus & Prof Pos: Mem ed bd, Rep Report, 65-66. Publ: Co-ed, A guide for good political manners, 1965. Mem: Am Asn of Univ Women; Benton Co Rep Women's Club; Tri-City Alpha Phi Alumni Club; Community Concert Asn; Mid-Columbia Symphony Guild. Relig: Lutheran. Mailing Add: 2212 S Vancouver Kennewick WA 99336

ANDERSON, HAROLD (R)
SDak State Sen
Mailing Add: RFD 2 Breresford SD 57004

ANDERSON, HERBERT A (D)
NDak State Rep
b Park River, NDak, Mar 16, 21; s Elmer O Anderson & Julia Flaten A; m 1957 to Rosalie Brahee; c Bonnie (Mrs Peter Joing), Kathleen, Barbara & Nancy, stepson, Stephen Carnal. Educ: Walsh Co Agr & Training Sch, Park River, NDak, grad, 40; NDak State Univ, 46-47; Lutheran Bible Inst, Minneapolis, Minn, 57. Polit & Govt Pos: Chmn, Gov Comt for Migrant Labor, 68-70; mem, Traill Co Sch Reorgn Bd, 68-71; NDak State Rep, 71-72, 75- Mil Serv: Entered as Seaman 3/C, Naval Res, 44, released as SF 3/C, 46, after serv in Naval Ship Repair Unit, Pac Theatre, 45-46. Mem: NDak Farm Bur; NDak Farmers Union; Nat Farmers Orgn; Red River Valley Beet Growers Asn; Fargo Prod Credit Asn. Honors & Awards: Soil Conserv Outstanding Farm Award; Goodyear Farm Award. Relig: Lutheran. Mailing Add: Box 46 Hillsboro ND 58045

ANDERSON, HOWARD PALMER (D)
Va State Sen
b Crystal Hill, Halifax Co, Va, May 25, 15; m to Mildred Webb. Educ: Halifax Co Pub Schs; Col of William & Mary, BA; Univ Richmond Law Sch, LLB; Sigma Pi; Delta Theta Phi; Univ Richmond Law Sch Asn. Polit & Govt Pos: Mem, Halifax Co Sch Bd, formerly; Va State Deleg, 58-71; Va State Sen, 71- Bus & Prof Pos: Lawyer; agt, Fed Bur of Invest, formerly. Mil Serv: Lt(sg), Naval Res. Mem: Mason; Lions; Am Legion; VFW; Va Farm Bur Fedn. Relig: Baptist. Mailing Add: 1080 Mountain Rd Halifax VA 24558

ANDERSON, IRVIN NEAL (DFL)
Minn State Rep
b International Falls, Minn, June 18, 23; s Albert Eugene Anderson & Agnes Bodway A; m 1945 to Phyllis J Peterson; c Gregory M & Cynthia J. Educ: Univ Minn, 47. Polit & Govt Pos: Minn State Rep, 65-, Majority Leader & chmn, Comt Rules & Legis Admin, Minn House Rep, 73- Mil Serv: Entered as Aviation Cadet, Navy, 43, released as Lt(jg), 47; Air Medal; Asiatic Theater Ribbon. Mem: Am Legion; VFW; KofC; Moose. Relig: Catholic. Mailing Add: 909 13th St International Falls MN 56649

ANDERSON, JACK Z (R)
b Oakland, Calif, Mar 22, 04; s George H Anderson & Susan Brown A; wid; m 1968 to Matilda E Lindsay; c Mrs Robert Duhrkoop, Mrs Lonzo Epps & Mrs Kevin McCray. Educ: High sch grad. Polit & Govt Pos: US Rep, Calif, 38-52; spec asst to secy, Dept Agr, 55-56; admin asst to the President of the United States, 56-61. Bus & Prof Pos: Mgr, G H Anderson Co, 25-38; pres, Calif Canning Pear Asn, 53-55; mem bd dirs, Bank of Am, 53-55. Mem: Elks; Sainte Claire Club. Relig: Protestant. Mailing Add: 535 Anzar Rd San Juan Bautista CA 95045

ANDERSON, JERALD C (DFL)
Minn State Sen
Legal Res: Box 503 North Branch MN 55056 Mailing Add: State Capitol Bldg St Paul MN 55155

ANDERSON, JOHN B (R)
US Rep, Ill
b Rockford, Ill, Feb 15, 22; m to KeKe A; c Eleanora, John, Jr, Diane, Karen Beth & Susan Kimberly. Educ: Univ Ill, AB, JD; Harvard Law Sch, LLM. Hon Degrees: Doctorate, Wheaton Col, 70, Shimer Col, 71, Biola Col, 71, North Park Col & Theol Sem, 72, Geneva Col, 72 & Houghton Col, 72. Polit & Govt Pos: Adv on staff of US High Comnr in West Berlin; mem, US State Dept Career Dipl Serv, 52; state's attorney of Winnebago Co, Ill, 56-60; US Rep, Ill, 60-; second ranking Rep mem, Joint Comt on Atomic Energy, mem, Rep Policy Comt & Research Comt, chmn, House Rep Conf, US House Rep, 69-, second ranking Rep mem of Rules Comt; deleg, Rep Nat Conv, 72. Bus & Prof Pos: Lawyer; mem faculty, Northeastern Univ Sch Law, Boston, formerly. Mil Serv: Army, 30 months, European Theatre. Publ: Contrib to We propose: a modern congress and Republican papers, Doubleday Anchor, 68; auth, Between two worlds: a congressman's choice, Zondervan, 70; ed, Congress and conscience, Lippincott, 70. Mem: Am Legion; U Club of Rockford; Winnebago Co Bar Asn; Univ Ill Alumni Asn. Relig: Evangelical Free Church; former trustee. Legal Res: Rockford IL Mailing Add: 2720 35th Pl NW Washington DC 20007

ANDERSON, JOHN EDWARD (D)
b Mondovi, Wis, July 6, 43; s L Ellsworth Anderson & Eunice M Johnson A; m 1966 to Lonna M Johnson; c John Steffey, Joseph Page Dameron & Andrew Christian Cook. Educ: Univ Wis-Eau Claire, BA, 66; Pi Delta Epsilon; Sigma Tau Gamma. Polit & Govt Pos: Coordr campaigns, Wis Assembly & State Sen levels, 64-; mem exec comt, Portage Co Dem Party, Wis, 69-70, vchmn, 70-72; vchmn, Wis Seventh Dist Dem Party, 71-72; chmn, Portage Co Humphrey for President, 72; deleg, Dem Nat Conv, 72. Bus & Prof Pos: Asst state ed, Eau Claire Leader-Telegram, 64-67; pub info officer, Univ Wis-Stevens Point, 67-71, dir news & publ, 71-; secy & dir promotions, Favor-Or, Corp of Stevens Point, 71- Mil Serv: Pvt, 32nd

Red Arrow Div, Wis Army Nat Guard, 66-67. Publ: Compiled thousands of articles for newspapers, radio & TV stations throughout Wisconsin. Mem: Cent Wis Press Club (exec secy, 69-); Odd Fellows (conductor, Stevens Point); KofP Lodge Eau Claire. Honors & Awards: First Recipient of Alumni Award, Buffalo Co 4-H Coun Wis, 71. Relig: Episcopal; Vestryman, Episcopal Church of the Intercession. Mailing Add: 2009 Wyatt Ave Stevens Point WI 54481

ANDERSON, JOHN H, JR (R)
Mont State Rep
Mailing Add: PO Box 101 Alder MT 59710

ANDERSON, JOHN HOPE (R)
PA State Rep
b New Park, Pa, May 2, 12; s D Ross Anderson & Helen Nelson A; m to Lelia Reed; c three. Educ: Mercersburg Acad; Gettysburg Col. Polit & Govt Pos: Pa State Rep, 60-; Rep committeeman; mem exec comt, York Co Rep Orgn. Bus & Prof Pos: Pres, Stewartstown RR; served 14 years as sch dir in Fawn Twp; mem bd, York Bank & Trust Co. Mem: White Rose (AAA) Motor Club (dir). Mailing Add: New Park PA 17352

ANDERSON, JOHN MILTON (D)
b San Francisco, Calif, Sept 19, 36; s Herman Frederick Anderson & Martha Warneke A; m 1961 to Jola Lynne Lehds; c Erika Lina & Edward Milton. Educ: Pomoma Col, BA, 58; Univ Calif, Berkeley, LLB, 61; Nu Alpha Phi. Polit & Govt Pos: Admin asst to chmn, Dem Nat Comt, 64; vpres, San Francisco Dem Forum, Calif, 65-67; chmn, Speakers for Gov Brown, NCalif, 66; mem, Chmn Adv Comt, Calif, 66-; mem, Calif Dem Adv Comt, 67-68; advanceman for Sen Robert Kennedy in Colo, Ore, SDak & Calif, 68; alt deleg, Dem Nat Conv, 68; mem, Calif Comn on Dem Party Reform, currently. Mil Serv: Entered as Airman Basic, Air Force Res, 62, released as Airman 2/C, 68, after serv in 631st Hosp Group, Air Defense Command, 66-68. Publ: Working Class Suburb, Frontier Mag, 62; Geneva (Switzerland) Today, San Francisco Chronicle, 63. Mem: Am, Calif & San Francisco Bar Asns; Music Libr Asn. Legal Res: 93 Cazneau Ave Sausalito CA 94965 Mailing Add: 3300 Crocker Plaza San Francisco CA 94104

ANDERSON, JOHN RICHARD (R)
b Midland, Tex, Mar 9, 29; s John Robert Balleu (deceased) & Brookie Lee; m 1951 to Barbara Clayton; c Sarah, Mary, John Robert & Martha. Educ: Univ Okla, BA, 50; Delta Tau Delta. Polit & Govt Pos: Finance chmn, Rep Party, Tex, 62-66, dist committeeman, 66; chmn, Borden Co Rep Comt, formerly. Bus & Prof Pos: Rancher. Mem: Univ Okla Alumni Club; Am Quarter Horse Asn; Southwestern Cattle Raisers Asn; Soc of Range Mgt. Relig: Episcopal. Mailing Add: Box 13 Gail TX 79738

ANDERSON, JOHN WILLIAM (D)
Conn State Rep
b New York, NY, Aug 30, 34; s William Bent Anderson & Mabel Marcoulier A; m 1958 to Romilda Romano; c Susan, John, II, Karen & Kristen. Educ: Hofstra Univ, BA, 59. Polit & Govt Pos: Police comnr, Newtown, Conn, 73-75; Conn State Rep, 106th Dist, 75- Bus & Prof Pos: Vpres, Litho Serv Corp, North Haven, Conn, currently. Mil Serv: Entered as A/S, Navy, 52, released as 2/C sonarman, after serv in USS Waller 466DDE, Sixth Fleet, 52-55; NATO Nat Defense Medal; Good Conduct Medal. Mem: Lions (pub rels dir, Zone 23A-CT). Mailing Add: 24 Rock Ridge Rd Newtown CT 06470

ANDERSON, JOYCE ELLEN (R)
Pres, Nev Fedn Rep Women
b Long Island, NY, Feb 9, 36; d Dean Henry Detton & Maline Pessetto D; m 1959 to William A Anderson; c Royce William & Jillaine Joyce. Educ: Col San Mateo, AA, 55; Holy Cross Hosp Sch Nursing, RN, 58. Polit & Govt Pos: First pres, Rep Women's Club of Crystal Bay & Incline Village, Nev, 65, membership chmn, 70-71; deleg, Co & State Rep Convs, 66, 68 & 70; Americanism chmn, Nev Fedn Rep Women, 69-70, pres, 70-, vchmn membership, 72-; precinct capt, Incline Village, 68-70; deleg, Rep Nat Conv, 72. Bus & Prof Pos: Asst head nurse, Eden Hosp, Castro Valley, Calif, 59; vpres, Ponderosa Ranch, 68- Mem: North Lake Tahoe Women's Club; Horseless Carriage Club. Relig: Latter-day Saint. Legal Res: 1500 Tunnel Creek Rd Incline Village NV 89450 Mailing Add: PO Box 18 Incline Village NV 89450

ANDERSON, L ROBERT (R)
b Provo, Utah, Mar 19, 29; s Robert Clair Anderson & Rachel Holbrook A; m 1951 to Madge Greaves; c Rachel Gwen, Lynette, Lyle Robert, Peter, Andrew, Samuel, William & Daniel Greaves. Educ: Snow Jr Col, 46-48; Univ Utah, LLB, 54; Order of the Coif. Polit & Govt Pos: Chmn, San Juan Co Rep Cent Comt, Utah, formerly. Bus & Prof Pos: Attorney, 54- Relig: Latter-day Saint. Legal Res: 260 Blue Mountain Dr Monticello UT 84535 Mailing Add: PO Box 1057 Monticello UT 84535

ANDERSON, LYMAN FRANK (R)
Wis State Rep
b Feb 16, 26; s Frank Rasmus Anderson & Mary Sholts A; m 1948 to Patricia Elis Todd; c Todd Frank, Kenneth Arthur, Jerry Maurice & Lynette Susan. Educ: Univ Wisconsin, Madison, BA, 50. Polit & Govt Pos: Supvr, Oregon Town Bd, Wis, 61-75; supvr, Dane Co Bd, Madison, Wis, 72-; Wis State Rep, 75- Bus & Prof Pos: Farmer, Oregon, Wis, 42- Mem: Masonic Lodge; Nat Farmers Orgn; Farm Bur. Mailing Add: 875 Union Rd Oregon WI 53575

ANDERSON, MCKENNY WILLIS (D)
Secy-Treas, Dem State Cent Comt, Md
b Easton, Md, Oct 4, 43; s William Pennel Anderson & Virginia Willis A; single. Educ: Easton High Sch, Md, grad, 61. Polit & Govt Pos: Secy-treas, Dem State Cent Comt, Md, 74- Bus & Prof Pos: Mgr, Anderton Farm, Oxford, Md, 72-; parts mgr, ABC Farm Equip Co, 72- Mil Serv: Entered as Pvt, Nat Guard, 66, released as SP-4, 72, after serv in Co B, 2nd Bn, 175th Inf. Mem: Elks; Am Legion; Cambridge Yacht Club; DelMarVa Poultry Growers Indust. Relig: Episcopal. Mailing Add: Anderton Farm Rte 1 Oxford MD 21654

ANDERSON, MILTON JAY (R)
State Committeeman, Rep Party of Tex
b Eagle Lake, Tex, June 4, 28; s B D Anderson, Sr & Ruth Clipson A; m 1951 to Bobbie Fay Dodd; c Cythina Gay, Sharen Lyn & Milton Jay, Jr. Educ: Eagle Lake High Sch. Polit & Govt Pos: State committeeman, Rep Party of Tex, 65-, dep state chmn, 67-72; deleg, Rep Nat Conv, 68; deleg, Rep State Conv & mem, Pre-Conv Platform Comt, 68; mem, Tex State Task Force on Agr; mem, Tex State Task Force for Revenue & Fiscal. Bus & Prof Pos: Pres, Prairie Rice, Inc & Fireside Mills, Inc; vpres, Anderson Agr Chem, Inc; partner, rice & cattle prod. Mem: Rotary; Farm Bur. Relig: United Methodist; Lay del to annual and gen conf. Mailing Add: Rte 1 Box 62 East Bernard TX 77435

ANDERSON, NANCY FIX (D)
b Dallas, Tex, Aug 23, 41; d George Joseph Fix, Jr & Frances Bartlett F; m 1962 to Clifford Hamilton Anderson; c Michael Timothy & Kathryn Bartlett. Educ: Stanford Univ, BA, 65; Univ Calif, Irvine, MA, 67; Tulane Univ, PhD, 73. Polit & Govt Pos: Deleg, Dem Nat Conv, 72; legis dist coordr, Dem Presidential Campaign, 72. Bus & Prof Pos: Spec lectr, La State Univ, New Orleans, 69; instr, Newman Sch, 71 & Tulane Univ La, 72. Mem: Am Hist Asn; Southern Conf British Studies; Nat Orgn Women; Nat Women's Polit Caucus; Am Civil Liberties Union. Honors & Awards: Eng Speaking Union scholar to Oxford Univ, 70. Mailing Add: 2031 Joseph St New Orleans LA 70115

ANDERSON, NELS A (D)
Alaska State Rep
Mailing Add: Box 234 Dillingham AK 99576

ANDERSON, NORMAN CARL (D)
Speaker, Wis State Assembly
b Hammond, Ind, Mar 11, 28; s Carl Anderson & Alma Hagstrom A; m 1954 to Eleanor Shefferman; c Marie L, Carl D, Ruth C & Eric W. Educ: Univ Wis, BS, 51, LLB, 54. Polit & Govt Pos: Wis State Rep, 57-59, 61-, Speaker, Wis State Assembly, 71-; comnr, Madison Redevelop Authority, 58-65. Mil Serv: Entered as Pvt, Army, 46, released as T-5, 47, after serv in 764th Anti-aircraft Artil Bn, Ft Sherman, CZ. Mem: Am Trial Lawyers Asn; State Bar of Wis; Dane Bar Asn; Dane Co Conserv League; Nature Conservancy. Honors & Awards: Award as Conserv Legislator of the Year, Wis Wildlife Fedn, 69; Distinguished Serv Citation & Centennial Medal, Wis Acad of Sci, Arts & Letters, 70. Relig: Lutheran. Mailing Add: 5325 Marsh Rd Madison WI 53716

ANDERSON, OSCAR L (R)
SDak State Rep
b 1897; married; c 2 sons, 2 daughters. Educ: H Park Col, Des Moines. Polit & Govt Pos: SDak State Sen, 64-66; Kingsbury Co Comnr of ASC; mayor, Erwin, SDak, 2 years; co assessor, 2 years; Hartland Twp assessor; sch treas, 13 years; SDak State Rep, currently. Bus & Prof Pos: Farmer; dir of FLB, 10 years; dir of Rea Kings Elec, 10 years. Relig: Lutheran. Mailing Add: Arlington SD 57212

ANDERSON, PETER DAVID (D)
Chmn, Monterey Co Dem Cent Comt, Calif
b Wadena, Minn, Aug 21, 40; s Alfred Parnell Anderson & Emma Stevens A; m 1963 to Jacqueline Kent; c Peter K, Amy E & Seth E. Educ: Univ Minn, Minneapolis, BA, 65, JD, 67; Alpha Delta Phi. Polit & Govt Pos: Sch bd mem, King City, Calif, 71-; mem, Monterey Co Dem Cent Comt, 72-; chmn, 74- Bus & Prof Pos: Attorney, Hutton, Foley, Anderson & Bolles, Inc, 68- Mem: Am, Calif & Monterey Co Bar Asns; Mason (Past Master); Rotary. Relig: Unitarian. Mailing Add: 433 Park Pl King City CA 93930

ANDERSON, RALPH KING, JR (D)
SC State Rep
b Timmonsville, SC, Nov 13, 36; s Ralph King Anderson, Sr & Macie Weaver A; m 1957 to Loretta Lynch; c Debra Arlene & Ralph King, III. Educ: Clemson Univ, 54-56; Univ SC, LLB, 59. Polit & Govt Pos: Chmn, Bd Regist, SC, 61-62; chmn, Florence Co Dem Party, 66-70; SC State Rep, 73-, mem elec law study comt, SC House Rep, 73-; vchmn, 75-, mem mobile home indust study comt, 73, mem judiciary comt, 73- Bus & Prof Pos: Mem, Yarborough, Parrott & Anderson, 59- Mem: PTA; Pee Dee Area Big Bros Asn; Pee Dee Diabetes Asn (chmn bd dirs, 73-); SC Citizens for Life, Inc (bd dirs, 74-); Mason. Relig: Baptist; mem gen bd, SC Baptist Conv, 71-; chmn bd deacons, Greenwood Baptist Church, Florence, SC, 68-71. Legal Res: 2605 Crestwood Ave Florence SC 29501 Mailing Add: PO Box 468 Florence SC 29501

ANDERSON, RAY J (DFL)
Dir, Minn Dem-Farmer-Labor Exec Comt
b Detroit Lakes, Minn, July 4, 15; s Gust A Anderson & Mary Anderson A; m 1942 to Marian Jeanette McDowell; c Donald G & Douglas R. Educ: Minneapolis Cent High Sch, grad, 32. Polit & Govt Pos: Treas, Becker Co Dem-Farmer-Labor Party, Minn, 66-70; mem cent comt, Minn Dem-Farmer-Labor Party, 70-72; alt deleg, Dem Nat Conv, 72; dir, Minn Dem-Farmer-Labor Exec Comt, 72-; deleg, Dem Nat Mid-Term Conf, 74; mem, Dem Nat Comt, Minn, 75- Bus & Prof Pos: Dir, Minn Asn Coops, 70-72. Mem: Nat Farmers Orgn; Minn Farmers Union. Honors & Awards: Cert of Merit, Jr CofC, 59; Mem, Farm Leader Group to Venezuela, Farmers & World Affairs, Inc, 66; Hon Chap Farmer, Future Farmer Am, 70. Relig: Methodist. Mailing Add: PO Box 1 Detroit Lakes MN 56501

ANDERSON, RAYMOND DOUGLAS (R)
Chmn, Bowie Co Rep Party, Tex
b Lincoln Co, Ky, Nov 3, 27; s Thomas Whitley Anderson & Caroline Otto A; m 1953 to Lois Powell; c Douglas, Barbara & Linda. Educ: Univ Tex, Austin, BBA, 53, LLB, 56; Delta Theta Phi. Polit & Govt Pos: Chmn, Bowie Co Rep Party, Tex, 67-70 & 72-; Rep cand for Dist Judge, 70; alt deleg, Rep Nat Conv, 72. Mil Serv: Entered as Pvt, Army, 53, released as Sgt, 55, after serv in Personnel Sect, Ft Bragg, NC. Mem: Texarkana & Northeast Tex Bar Asns; State Bar Tex; Texarkana Eve Kiwanis Club; Kiwanis Int (past Lt Gov, Div 13, Tex-Okla Dist). Relig: Baptist. Legal Res: Rte 2 Box 773-H Texarkana TX 75501 Mailing Add: PO Box 2044 Texarkana TX 75501

ANDERSON, ROBERT BERNERD (R)
b Burleson, Tex, June 4, 10; s Robert Lee Anderson & Elizabeth Haskew A; m 1935 to Ollie Mae; c James Richard & Gerald Lee. Educ: Weatherford Col, Tex, 27; Univ Tex, LLB, 32; Phi Delta Phi. Hon Degrees: LLD, McMurry Col & Tex Christian Univ; LHD, Midwestern Univ, Tex & other hon degrees. Polit & Govt Pos: Mem, Am Coun on NATO; mem bus adv coun, Dept Com, mem, Tex Legis, 32; Asst Attorney Gen, Tex, 32; State Tax Comnr, Tex, 34, Racing Comnr, Tex, 34; mem, State Tax Bd, Tex, 34; chmn & exec dir, Tex Unemploy Comn, 36; Secy of Navy, 53-54; Dep Secy of Defense, 54-55; Secy of Treas, 57-61; chmn, Atlantic-Pac Interoceanic Canal Study Comn, 64-70. Bus & Prof Pos: Began law practice, Ft Worth, Tex, 32; prof law, Univ Tex, 33; dir, various companies, 55-57; trustee, Eisenhower Exchange Fels; dir, CIT Financial Corp, Pan-Am Airways, Goodyear Tire & Rubber Co & Intercontinental Trailsea Corp; ltd partner, Loeb, Rhoades & Co, 61-73; chmn, Robert B

Anderson & Co Ltd, currently. Mem: Navy League Am; The Chancellors; Mason (33 degree); DeMolay (Supreme Coun). Honors & Awards: Cross of the Order of Boyaca, Colombia, 54; Most Exalted Order of the White Elephant, Thailand, 54; Medal of Freedom, 55; Navy Distinguished Pub Serv Award, 55; Grand Cross Court of Honour, 55. Legal Res: 2 E 67th St New York NY 10021 Mailing Add: 1 Rockefeller Plaza New York NY 10020

ANDERSON, ROBERT E (R)
Okla State Sen
Mailing Add: State Capitol Oklahoma City OK 73105

ANDERSON, ROBERT EDWARD (BOB) (D)
Miss State Rep
b Hazlehurst, Miss, Nov 30, 14; m to Bonnie Drane. Polit & Govt Pos: Miss State Rep, 56- Bus & Prof Pos: Farmer & dairyman, currently. Mem: Lions; Touchdown Club; Farm Bur; Miss Milk Producers Asn. Relig: Baptist. Mailing Add: Rte 3 Box 211 Wesson MS 39191

ANDERSON, ROBERT JOHN (DFL)
Third VChmn, 28th Sen Dist Dem-Farmer-Labor Party, Minn
b Minneapolis, Minn, Jan 27, 46; s Carl Oscar Anderson & Ruth Peterson A; single. Educ: Metrop State Jr Col, AA, 69; Univ Minn, part-time; Metrop State Jr Col Young Dem (pres); Student Senate. Polit & Govt Pos: Third vchmn, 28th Sen Dist Dem-Farmer-Labor Party, Minn, 70- Bus & Prof Pos: Factory rep, Denesen Co, currently. Mil Serv: Entered as E-1, Navy, 64, released as E-5, 70, after serv in USS Renshaw DD499 & Naval Res; Nat Defense Medal; Vietnam Serv Medal; Vietnam Campaign Medal. Mem: Richfield Jaycees (dir). Honors & Awards: Youngest Minn State Senate cand. Relig: Lutheran. Mailing Add: 6500 16th Ave S Richfield MN 55423

ANDERSON, ROBERT LAKE (R)
Mem Exec Comt, Nebr State Rep Exec Comt
b Harlan, Iowa, Jan 21, 40; s Lake N Anderson & Helen Peterson A; m 1961 to Betty Jane Schmitz; c Robert L, Jr, Mark, Lizbeth, Kristian & Nicole. Educ: Creighton Univ; Iowa State Univ; Univ Nebr. Polit & Govt Pos: Chmn, Douglas Co Young Rep, Nebr, 69-71; mem, Douglas Co Rep Cent Comt, 69-71 & 72-; nat committeeman, Nebr Young Rep, 71-73; deleg, Nebr Rep Conv, 72; alt deleg, Rep Nat Conv, 72; coordr, Rep Campaign Sem, 72; mem, Nebr State Rep Cent Comt, 72-; lobbyist, Nebr Legis, 72-; mem exec comt, Nebr State Rep Exec Comt, Second Dist, 73-; co-chmn, Douglas Co Rep Cand Recruitment Comt, 73-; co-chmn, Young Rep Region VII, 73- Bus & Prof Pos: Computer Systs Analyst, Tel Co, 66-70. Publ: Ed, Rural Electric Nebraskan, 70- Mem: Omaha Press Club; Cornhusker Ed Asn; Nebr Press Asn; Nat Elec Coop Ed Asn; Nebr Rural Elec Asn. Honors & Awards: Outstanding Young Man of Year, Sun Newspapers, 69; Best Feature Story, Nat Statewide Rural Elec Publ, 72; Nat Judge, Press Serv for mag, 72. Relig: Roman Catholic. Mailing Add: 7055 Iowa St Omaha NE 68152

ANDERSON, ROBERT ORVILLE (R)
Mem, NMex Rep State Cent Comt
b Chicago, Ill, Apr 13, 17; s Hugo A Anderson & Hilda Nelson A; m 1939 to Barbara Phelps; c Katherine (Mrs Thomas K Denton), Julia (Mrs Morgan Smith), Maria (Mrs Thomas Jay Sarday), Robert Bruce, William Phelps, Barbara Burton & Beverley. Educ: Univ Chicago, BA, 39; Psi Upsilon. Hon Degrees: LHD, Colo Col, 65 & Univ NMex, 66; LLD, NMex State Univ, 68. Polit & Govt Pos: Chmn, Rep Party Crusade for Freedom, NMex, 50-53; mem, NMex Rep State Cent Comt, 50-; chmn, Citizens for Eisenhower Comt, 52; chmn, Chaves Co Rep Party, 54-58; chmn, Vol for Mechem, 64; mem finance comt, Nixon for President, 67-68; Rep Nat Committeeman, 68-72. Bus & Prof Pos: Chmn Bd, Aspen Inst Humanistic Studies, Colo, 60-; owner, Lincoln Co Livestock Co, NMex, 62-; chmn bd, Atlantic Richfield Co, NY, 65-, Lovelace Found, NMex, 67 & Eisenhower Exchange Fels, Pa, 69- Mem: Capitol Club; Century Club; Calif Club. Honors & Awards: Man of the Year, NMex, 66. Relig: Episcopal. Legal Res: 612 N Kentucky St Roswell NM 88201 Mailing Add: PO Box 1000 Roswell NM 88201

ANDERSON, ROBERT T (D)
Iowa State Rep
Mailing Add: 338 S Sixth Ave W Newton IA 50208

ANDERSON, SIGURD (R)
b Arendal, Norway, Jan 22, 04; s Karl August Anderson & Bertha Broten A; m 1937 to Vivian Dall Walz; c Kristin Karen. Educ: Univ SDak, BA, 31, LLB, 37; Phi Beta Kappa; Delta Theta Phi; Pi Kappa Delta. Hon Degrees: LLD, Yankton Col, 53 & Gettysburg Col, 58. Polit & Govt Pos: Mem, SDak Young Rep, 37-43; state attorney, Day Co, 39-41; pres, Lincoln Club, 40-41; asst attorney gen, SDak, 41-43, attorney gen, 47-51, Gov, SDak, 51-55; mem, numerous Rep Orgns, 46-; comnr, Fed Trade Comn, 55-64. Mil Serv: Entered as Lt(jg), Naval Res, 43, released as Lt Comdr, 46; Asiatic-Pac Theater Ribbon; Philippine Liberation Medal; Am Theater Ribbon & others. Publ: Numerous articles on trade regulation & anti-trust law. Mem: SDak Hist Soc; Norwegian-Am Hist Asn; Mason, Shrine, Consistory (33 degree), Chapter Lodge; Am Legion; VFW. Honors & Awards: Freedoms Found Award, 63; Americanism Medal for achievements by foreign born citizen, DAR. Relig: Lutheran. Mailing Add: 313 W Seventh Ave Webster SD 57274

ANDERSON, STEVE (D)
Chmn, Marion Co Dem Cent Comt, Ore
b North Bend, Ore, Aug 17, 14; s William P Anderson & Julia Guerin A; m 1955 to Anne Lise Pedersen; c Steve, Jr & Carol. Educ: Willamette Univ, BA, 37, JD, 42; Phi Delta Theta. Polit & Govt Pos: Exec secy, Ore Young Rep, 42, nat committeeman, 47, state chmn, 48; nat vchmn, Young Rep Nat Fedn, 49-52, resigned to support Adlai Stevenson, 52; chmn, Marion Co Dem Cent Comt, Ore, 70- Bus & Prof Pos: Pvt practice law, 45- Mil Serv: Entered as Ens, Navy, 42, released as Lt(sg), 45, after serv in Pal Nob, Mediter & Pac Theatres, 43-45. Publ: Right of Privacy, Univ Ore Law Rev, 2/42. Mem: Ore State Bar; Am Civil Liberties Union; Am Humanist Soc. Relig: Humanist. Legal Res: 3927 Viewcrest Rd S Salem OR 97302 Mailing Add: 468 State St Rm 205 Salem OR 97301

ANDERSON, TERRILL GORDON (DFL)
Secy, Third Dist Dem-Farmer-Labor Party, Minn
b Minneapolis, Minn, Mar 17, 52; s Gordon Arnold Anderson & Correne Johnson A; single. Educ: Normandale State Jr Col, 70-71. Polit & Govt Pos: Liaison officer, Young Dem-Farmer-Labor Party, Richfield, Minn, 67-69; treas, Third Dist Young Dem-Farmer-Labor Party, 69-70; mem exec comt, Minn Dem-Farmer-Labor Party, 70-72, asst to chmn, 72-73; treas, Third Dist Dem-Farmer-Labor Party, 70-73, secy, 74-; vchmn, Minn Dem-Farmer-Labor Youth Caucus, 71-72; staff asst, Minn Dem-Farmer-Labor State Cent Comt, 71- Relig: Unitarian Universalist. Legal Res: 7501 Elliot Ave S Richfield MN 55423 Mailing Add: 730 E 38th St Minneapolis MN 55407

ANDERSON, THOMAS J (AMERICAN PARTY)
Nat Chmn, American Party
m to Carolyn. Educ: Vanderbilt Univ, BA, 34. Hon Degrees: LLD, Bob Jones Univ, 68. Polit & Govt Pos: Vice-presidential nominee, American Party, 72, nat chmn, currently. Legal Res: Gatlinburg TN Mailing Add: Box 1098 Pigeon Forge TN 37863

ANDERSON, THOMAS JEFFERSON (D)
Mich State Rep
b St Joseph, Mo, Nov 21, 19; s Thomas Jefferson Anderson, Sr & Hazel Shultz A; m 1942 to Margaret Anderson; c Laurel Brigette (Mrs Darryl Moore), Eugene Thomas & Craig Jeffrey. Educ: US Army Elec Eng, 43-45 & Marine Corps Elec Eng, 50-51; Ford Motor Co Eng Schs, 46-48. Polit & Govt Pos: Precinct deleg, Dem Party, Mich, 52-60; supvr, Ecorse Twp, 53-58; mem bd supvr, Wayne Co, 53-61; mayor, Southgate, Mich, 58-61, pres, City Coun, 63-64; Mich State Rep, 65-, co-chmn, Comt Conserv, Mich House Rep, 69-74, chmn, 75-, Asst Majority Floor Leader, 71-, chmn, Joint Comt Admin Rules, 75-; chmn, Comt Sci & Technol, Nat Conf State Legislatures, 71-; chmn, Task Force Solid Waste, Coun State Govt, Washington, DC, 72-73. Bus & Prof Pos: Mech Engr, Ford Motor Co, 46- Mil Serv: Entered as Pvt, Army, 43, released as T/Sgt, 46 after serv in Philippine Islands, 45-46; entered as T/Sgt, Marine Corps Res, 46, released as M/Sgt, 52; Good Conduct & Victory Medals; Asiatic Pac & Am Theater Ribbons; Philippine Liberation Ribbon. Publ: History of Detroit's Downriver Area, Wayne Co Pub Libr, 63. Mem: Am Soc for Qual Control; Kiwanis; Marine Corps League; Am Legion. Honors & Awards: Conservationist of Year, Mich Asn Cert Prof Engrs, 69 & Mich United Conserv Clubs, 70; Sparky Hale Award, Mich Bear Hunters Asn, 71. Relig: Protestant. Legal Res: 13726 Sycamore Southgate MI 48195 Mailing Add: House of Reps The Capitol Lansing MI 48901

ANDERSON, VIRGIL ERVIN (R)
Chmn, Corson Co Rep Party, SDak
b Watauga, SDak, Dec 8, 30; s Erick Anderson & Charlotte Peterson A; m 1955 to Shirley; c Sherry & Clay. Polit & Govt Pos: Mayor, McIntosh, SDak, currently; chmn, Corson Co Rep Party, 68- Bus & Prof Pos: Owner, grocery store & farms, 64- Mil Serv: Entered as Enlisted Man, Air Force, 51, released as Airman 2/C, 54, after serv in Strategic Air Command, Korea. Mem: Am Legion; 40 et 8; McIntosh Community Club; Corson Co Wildlife Betterment Club; OAHE Basin Develop Asn. Relig: Presbyterian. Mailing Add: Box 397 McIntosh SD 57641

ANDERSON, WARREN MATTICE (R)
NY State Sen
b Bainbridge, NY, Oct 16, 15; s Floyd E Anderson & Edna Mattice A; m to Eleanor C Sanford; c Warren David, Lawrence C, Richard S & Thomas B. Educ: Colgate Univ, AB, 37; Albany Law Sch, LLB, 40; Alpha Tau Omega. Polit & Govt Pos: Asst Broome Co Attorney, NY, 40-42; NY State Sen, 53-, chmn, Finance Comt, NY State Senate, 66-, chmn, Legis Comt on Expenditure Rev, currently, Pres Pro Tem & Majority Leader, 73-; deleg & mem platform comt, Rep Nat Conv, 72; regional mem-at-lg, Gov Bd, Coun of State Govt, currently. Bus & Prof Pos: Partner, Hinman, Howard & Kattell, Attorneys. Mil Serv: Entered as Pvt, Army, released as 2nd Lt, after serv in Judge Adv Gen Dept; ETO Ribbon. Mem: Am & NY Bar Asns; Fort Orange Club; Binghamton Club; Am Legion. Relig: Presbyterian. Legal Res: 34 Lathrop Ave Binghamton NY 13905 Mailing Add: Seventh Floor Security Mutual Bldg Binghamton NY 13901

ANDERSON, WENDELL RICHARD (DFL)
Gov, Minn
b St Paul, Minn, Feb 1, 33; s Theodore M Anderson & Gladys Nord A; m 1963 to Mary C McKee; c Amy, Beth & Brett. Educ: Univ of Minn, BA, 54, LLB, 60; Phi Delta Phi. Polit & Govt Pos: Minn State Rep, 59-63; Minn State Sen, 63-69; Gov, Minn, 71-; Mem Exec Comt, Dem Nat Comt, 74- Mil Serv: Army, 56-57, 2nd Lt. Mem: Minn Bar Asn; US Olympians. Honors & Awards: Mem, US Olympic Hockey Team, 56 & US Amateur Teams, 55 & 57. Relig: Protestant. Legal Res: 1006 Summit Ave St Paul MN 55102 Mailing Add: State Capitol St Paul MN 55155

ANDERSON, WILLIAM MCOWAN, III (R)
b Pittsburgh, Pa, Sept 8, 29; s William McOwan Anderson, Jr (deceased) & Margaret Walsh A (deceased); m 1953 to Carol Ann Leach; c William McOwan IV, Patrick John & Susanne Lanahan. Educ: Univ Miami, BBA, 53; Univ Pittsburgh, 57-58; Student Govt Coun; Sigma Phi Epsilon; Nat Mkt Asn. Polit & Govt Pos: Mem, Young Rep, 48-57; mem fund raising campaigns for Rep cand in Nat, state & local elec, 53-69; chmn, Hancock Co Rep Party, Miss, 67-69; financial mgt proj staff, Off Financial Mgt & equal employ opportunity counr, Off Dir Representative to Nat Insts Health Recreations & Welfare Asn, Nat Insts Health, Dept Health, Educ & Welfare, 69- Bus & Prof Pos: Labor rels staff, chem & plastics div, Koppers Co Inc, Monaca, Pa, 55-58; field engr, indust diamond div, Elgin Nat Watch Co, Elgin, Ill, 58-60; asst to site mgr, Martin-Marietta Corp, Denver, Colo, 61-62, asst to site mgr & chmn missile site labor rels, Chico, Calif, 62-64, staff indust engr, SPRINT Activation, Orlando, Fla, 64-65; sr proj staff engr, proj control, Saturn II test stand activations & oper, NAm Rockwell Corp, 65-66, supvr budgets, proposals & planning oper, 66-67, supvr configuration doc opers, 67-68, supvr, Apollo Space Craft Planning & Scheduling, Kennedy Launch Opers, Cape Kennedy, Fla, 68-69. Mil Serv: Pvt, Marine Corps, 46-48, with serv in Second Marine Air Wing, Cherry Point, NC; Good Conduct, Victory & Sharpshooter Medals. Publ: Employee/Employer Relations Company Handbook, House Organ Publ, 58; Supervisory Interpretation to Union/Management Contract Agreements, 57-58; Computer Usage & Application, Co Manual, 68. Mem: Nat Mgt Asn (treas & dir); Nat Personnel Asn; Am Legion; Miss Test Opers Recreation Asn (dir); Co Boosters Club (pres). Honors & Awards: Boss of the Year, Miss Jr CofC, 68; Recipient of Gold Titan Award, for meritorious serv during Titan I Missile Site Activations, Martin-Marietta Corp, 63; US Savings Bond Coord 100% of 800 Personnel; Oper Improv Prog Winner for Implementation of Dollar Cost Savings; Outstanding Operations Participant, S-11-5 MTO, 68. Relig: Roman Catholic. Mailing Add: 7 Marcus Court Rockville MD 20850

ANDERSON, WILLIAM ROBERT (D)
b Bakerville, Tenn, June 17, 21; s David H Anderson & Mary McKelvey A; m 1943 to Yvonne Etzel (Bonny); c Michael David & William Robert, Jr. Educ: US Naval Acad, BS, 42. Polit & Govt Pos: Consult to President for Nat Serv Corps, 63-64; US Rep, Tenn, 65-73. Bus & Prof Pos: Chmn, Digital Mgt Corp, 74- Mil Serv: Entered as Ens, Navy, 42, released

as Capt, 62, after serv in 11 submarine combat patrols, Pac; Bronze Star with Combat V; 2 Commendation Medals with Combat V; Presidential Legion of Merit & Unit Citation. Publ: Nautilus 90 north and first under the North Pole, World Publ Co, 59, The useful atom, 66. Mem: Am Legion; VFW; Explorers Club. Honors & Awards: Commanded USS Nautilus on first under-ice crossing of North Pole, 58. Relig: Protestant. Legal Res: Waverly TN 37185 Mailing Add: 2700 Virginia Ave NW Washington DC 20037

ANDOLSEK, LUDWIG JOHN (D)
b Denver, Colo, Nov 6, 10; s Ludvig Andolsek & France Gouze A; m 1945 to Regina A Burnett; c Kathryn M. Educ: St Cloud State Teachers Col, BEd, 35. Polit & Govt Pos: With Nat Youth Admin, 36-42, area dir, Northern Minn, 40-42; asst to personnel officer in charge of Personnel Rels & Grievance Procedures, Vet Admin Hosp, St Cloud, Minn, 47-50; with Civilian Personnel Off, Ellsworth AFB, Weaver, SDak, 50-51; admin asst to US Rep J A Blatnik, 51-62; chief clerk, Comt Pub Works, US House of Rep, 63; vchmn, US Civil Serv Comn, 63-69, comnr, 69- Mil Serv: Army, 42-46, Col. Air Force Res (Ret). Mem: Am Legion; Eagles. Honors & Awards: Amvets Civil Servant of Year Award, 66; VFW Nat Commanders Gold Medal of Merit Award, 72; Distinguished Alumni Award, St Cloud State Col, 73. Legal Res: 9609 Bulls Run Pkwy Bethesda MD 20034 Mailing Add: 1900 E St NW Washington DC 20415

ANDORA, ANTHONY DOMINICK (D)
b Paterson, NJ, Nov 20, 30; s Anthony A Andora & Theresa Matera A; m 1962 to Colleen Gill; c Melissa, Suzanne, Elizabeth, Anthony D, II & Camille. Educ: Newark Col of Eng, 47-48; NY Univ Sch Educ, BS cum laude, 51; Rutgers Univ Sch Law, JD, 54; Kappa Delta Pi; Kappa Phi Kappa; King's Bench. Polit & Govt Pos: Dep attorney gen, NJ, 59-61; pres, Bergen Co Young Dem, 59-62; asst prosecutor, Bergen Co, 61-64; pres, Young Dem Clubs of NJ, 62-64; alt-at-lg, Dem Nat Conv, 64; munic chmn, East Paterson Dem Comt, 64-65; planning bd attorney, Oakland, NJ & borough attorney, East Paterson, 65 & 71, Closter, 71; deleg, Fourth Conf of Young Polit Leaders, NATO Countries, Oxford, Eng, 65; chmn, Bergen Co Dem Comt, 65-69; co-chmn, NJ Reapportionment Comn, 66-69; chmn econ comt, NJ Dem Policy Coun, 70- Mil Serv: Entered as Pvt E-1, Army, 55, released as 1st Lt, 58, after serv in 10th Inf Div and 8th Inf Div, ETO; Capt, Army Res. Publ: Landlord & Tenant Law of New Jersey, Assoc Lawyers Publ Co, 60. Mem: Am Trial Lawyers Asn; Am Bar Asn; Am Legion; Kiwanis; Paterson Jaycees. Honors & Awards: Outstanding Man of the Year, East Paterson, NJ, 66. Relig: Roman Catholic. Mailing Add: 211 Sagamore Lane Franklin Lakes NJ 07417

ANDRADE, CAROLYN MARIE (D)
b Rochester, NY; d John Frances & Catherine Ann; div. Educ: Rochester Bus Inst, 2 years; Univ Conn, 1 year; George Washington Univ; Catholic Univ. Polit & Govt Pos: US Navy Inspector, Navy & Aircraft Material, Hartford, Conn, 41-42; cryptograph clerk, Cent Intel Agency, Washington, DC, 43-44; secy, Signal Corps, Pentagon, 44-46; secy, Off Price Stabilization, Washington, DC, 48-49; personal secy to US Rep Kenneth J Gray, Ill, 57-58; admin asst to US Rep Robert Levering, Ohio, 58-60; exec secy to US Rep Walter Moeller, Ohio, 61; exec asst to US Sen Stephen M Young, Ohio, 62-63; exec asst to US Rep Seymour Halpern, NY, 63; exec asst to US Rep Claude Pepper, Fla, 64; exec secy to US Rep Clair Callan, 65-66; exec asst, Post Office Comt, US Senate, 67-68; exec asst to US Rep Seymour Halpern, NY, 69-70; admin asst to Chmn C Jackson Grayson, Jr, Price Comn, 71-72; admin asst, Senate Comt on Presidential Activities, 72-74; admin asst, Budget Off, US Senate, 75- Relig: Catholic. Mailing Add: 1334 31st St NW Washington DC 20007

ANDRE, HERMAN W (R)
Mem Exec Comt, Young Rep Nat Fedn
b Watertown, SDak, Apr 9, 38; s Garret Andre (deceased) & Frances Van Der Mey A; m 1960 to Janet Ruth Roelfsema. Educ: Calvin Col, AB, 59; Purdue Univ, Lafayette, PhD, 64; Alpha Chi Sigma; Sigma Xi; Phi Lambda Upsilon, vpres, Nu Chap, 60-61, pres, 61-62. Polit & Govt Pos: Chmn, United Citizens for Nixon-Agnew, Second Cong Dist, Ind, 68; vpres, Tippecanoe Co Young Rep, 70-71, pres, 71-72; chmn, Taxpayers Lobby of Ind, 70-; mem exec comt, Ind Young Rep Fedn, 71-; mem exec comt & nat comts, Young Rep Nat Fedn, 71-; dir, United Conservatives of Ind, 72-; trustee, Vincennes Univ, 73- Bus & Prof Pos: Grad teaching & research asst chem, Purdue Univ, 58-62, Procter & Gamble Free Grant fel, 62-63, instr, 63-64, asst prof & exec officer dept chem, 64-69; asst to the pres, Great Lakes Chem Corp, 69-74, corp secy, 74- Mem: Am Chem Soc; Nat Investor Rels Inst; Am Soc Corp Secy; Rotary; Am Inst Chem. Honors & Awards: Sagamore of the Wabash, Off of the Gov, Ind, 72. Relig: Christian Reformed Church. Legal Res: 2304 Ellen Dr Lafayette IN 47905 Mailing Add: PO Box 2200 West Lafayette IN 47906

ANDRESEN, KARL ADOLF (D)
b Oslo, Norway, Feb 3, 24; s Arne J Andresen & Nanna Annette Helgesen A; m 1956 to Helen June Primrose; c Eric Dale, Robert & William. Educ: Luther Col, BA; Univ Minn, MA & PhD; Univ Hawaii; Oxford Univ. Polit & Govt Pos: Vchmn, Eau Claire Co Dem Party, Wis, 63-64, chmn, 64-65 & 68; deleg, Dem Nat Conv, 64; co-chmn, Lyndon Johnson for President Comt, 64; chmn, Bronson LaFollette for Attorney Gen Comt, Eau Claire Co, 64; mem-at-lg, State Admin Comt, Wis Dem Party, 65-67; vchmn, Wis McCarthy for President Comt, 67-68; campaign chmn, Eau Claire Co Nelson for Senate Comt, 68; mem nat bd, Am for Dem Action, 68-; Eau Claire co-chmn, Lucey for Gov Comt, 70; campaign chmn, Thoresen for Cong Comt, 70 & 71-72. Bus & Prof Pos: Prof, Wis State Univ, Eau Claire, 56- Mem: Am Asn Univ Prof; Am Fedn of Teachers. Mailing Add: 327 Lincoln Ave Eau Claire WI 54701

ANDREWS, FREDERICK CHARLES (R)
Chmn, Lake Co Rep Party, Fla
b Farmington, Maine, Aug 13, 25; s Arthur V Andrews & Letha Chamberlain A; m 1946 to Gloria Jane Larsen; c Philip C, John C, Sara J & David C. Educ: Bowdoin Col, BA; Tufts Univ Med Sch, MD; Zeta Psi, Lambda Chap. Polit & Govt Pos: Chmn, Family Planning Adv Comt, Fla, currently; chmn & mem exec comt, Lake Co Rep Party, Fla, 72- Mil Serv: Entered as Pvt, Army Air Corps, 43, released as Cpl, 46, after serv in 303rd Bomber Squadron, 8th Air Force, European Theatre. Mem: Am Bd Family Practice (dipl, currently); Am Acad Family Physicians (fel, deleg, 68-70); Am Med Asn; Fla Med Asn (past vpres, deleg); Coun on Specialty Med (chmn, currently). Relig: Methodist. Mailing Add: 1725 Overlook Dr Mt Dora FL 32757

ANDREWS, HUNTER BOOKER (D)
Va State Sen
b Hampton, Va, May 28, 21; s Henry Stuart Andrews & Dorothy Booker A; m 1950 to Cynthia Collings; c Hunter Booker, Jr & Bentley Robinson. Educ: Col William & Mary, AB, 42; Univ Va Law Sch, LLB, 48; Kappa Alpha. Polit & Govt Pos: Chmn, Hampton Sch Bd, Va, 58-62; deleg, Dem Nat Conv, 60 & 68; chmn, Hampton Dem Comt, 60-63; Va State Sen, 64- Bus & Prof Pos: Partner, Downing, Andrews & Durden, Attorneys, 57- Mil Serv: Entered as A/S, Navy, 42, released as Lt, 46, after serv in Pac Theatre, 42-46; World War II Campaign Ribbon. Mem: Va State & Am Bar Asns; Am Legion; Rotary. Relig: Episcopal. Mailing Add: 222 E Queen St Hampton VA 23369

ANDREWS, IKE FRANKLIN (D)
US Rep, NC
b Bonlee, NC, Sept 2, 25; s Archie Franklin Andrews & Ina Dunlap A; m 1947 to Jo Anne Johnson; c Alice Cecelia & Nina Patricia. Educ: Univ NC, BS, 50, LLB, 52; Phi Alpha Delta. Polit & Govt Pos: NC State Sen, 59-60; Superior Court Solicitor, Dist 10A, NC, 61-64; NC State Rep, 61-62 & 67-72; US Rep, Fourth Dist, NC, 73-, Mem Educ & Labor Comt, US House Rep, 73- Bus & Prof Pos: Mem bd dirs, First Union Nat Bank of NC, Siler City, 62-72; mem exec comt of bd trustees, Univ NC, Chapel Hill, 69-72; chmn comt to select new chancellor, 70-72. Mil Serv: Entered as Pvt, Army, 43, released as M/Sgt, 45; Bronze Star; Purple Heart; ETO Ribbon; Victory Medal. Relig: Baptist. Legal Res: Rte 2 Pine Forest Siler City NC 27344 Mailing Add: PO Box 267 Siler City NC 27344

ANDREWS, JOHN STRIKER (R)
b Cincinnati, Ohio, Apr 25, 19; s Burton Richardson Andrews & Cora Striker A; m 1964 to Marjorie Ann Carney; c Richard J, Christine C & Sally J. Educ: Univ Toledo, BBA, 40. Polit & Govt Pos: Secy, Toledo Airport Comn & mem, Toledo Recreation Comn, Ohio, 51-55; mem, Lucas Co Rep Exec Comt, 52-73, exec dir, 55-62, chmn, 62-66; alt deleg, Rep Nat Conv, 56 & 60, deleg, 64, 68 & 72, chmn Ohio deleg, 72; chmn, Lucas Co Rep Cent Comt, 58-62; chmn, Ohio State Rep Cent & Exec Comts, 65-73; mem, Rep Nat Comt, 65-73, mem exec comt, 70-73, app by nat Rep chmn as chmn, Rep State Chmn Adv Comt, 70-73; chmn, Midwest State Chmn Asn, 70-73. Bus & Prof Pos: Underwriter, Travelers Ins Co, 40-46; ins mgr, Owens-Corning Fiberglas Corp, 46-50, admin asst to pres, 50-53, dir pub rels, 53-55. Mil Serv: Entered as Pvt, Army Air Corps, 44, released as Cpl, 45, after serv in Aviation Cadet Training Prog, 8th Serv Command, Tex; Good Conduct Medal; Am Theater Ribbon. Mem: Mason; Scottish Rite; Shrine; Am Legion; Univ Toledo Alumni Asn. Honors & Awards: Outstanding Young Man of the Year, Toledo Jaycees, 53; Distinguished Serv Award, Ohio Jaycees, 53. Relig: Congregational. Legal Res: 1915 Princeton Dr Toledo OH 43614 Mailing Add: 50 W Broad St Columbus OH 43215

ANDREWS, LEWIS DAVIS, JR (R)
b Bridgeport, Conn, Mar 17, 46; s Lewis Davis Andrews & Beatrice Hawley A; m 1970 to Christina Kane. Educ: City of London Col, Eng, 66; Am Univ, 67; Drew Univ, BA, 68. Polit & Govt Pos: Exec asst, Congressman Thomas J Meskill, 68-70, campaign coordr, Meskill for Gov, Conn, 70; exec dir, Young Rep Nat Fedn, 70; exec dir, Conn Rep State Cent Comt, 71-72; bd mem, Am Coun Young Polit Leaders, currently; dir commun, Off of Gov, Conn, 72-73; dep comnr, Conn Dept Com, 73-74; spec asst to Secy, US Dept Interior, 74- Relig: Episcopal. Legal Res: CT Mailing Add: 317 N St Asaph St Alexandria VA 22314

ANDREWS, MARK (R)
US Rep, NDak
b May 19, 26; m to Mary Willming; c Mark, III, Sarah & Karen. Educ: NDak State Univ, BS, 49. Polit & Govt Pos: Dir, Garrison Conservancy Dist, formerly; Rep Nat Committeeman, NDak, formerly; US Rep, NDak, 63-, mem, Nat Rep Cong Comt, currently. Bus & Prof Pos: Farmer. Mil Serv: Enlisted, Army, app US Mil Acad, West Point, 44, discharged, 46. Mem: NDak Crop Improv Asn; Am Legion; Mason; Shrine; Eagles. Legal Res: Mapleton ND 58059 Mailing Add: Rayburn House Off Bldg Washington DC 20515

ANDREWS, MARY ELOISE OKESON (D)
VChmn, Franklin Co Dem Party, Kans
b Catale, Okla, July 8, 23; d George Manifold Okeson & Verna Dick O; m 1941 to Robert Leon Andrews; c Janith Lea (Mrs Roger Allen Nearmyer) & George Mark. Educ: Ottawa High Sch, grad, 41. Polit & Govt Pos: Vchmn, Franklin Co Dem Party, Kans, 68-; mem & deleg, Third Cong Dist Dem Comt, 68-; mem & deleg, Kans State Dem Comt, 68-; co chmn, DeCoursey for Cong, 70. Bus & Prof Pos: Real estate broker, Ottawa Real Estate, currently. Mem: Franklin Co Bd of Realtors; Nat Inst Real Estate Brokers; Nat Asn Real Estate Brokers. Relig: Church of Christ. Mailing Add: Rte 2 Ottawa KS 66067

ANDREWS, MICHAEL PAUL (D)
b Altoona, Pa, Dec 17, 48; s George Michael Andrews & Agnes Jandora A; single. Educ: Pa State Univ, BA, 66-70; Univ Toledo, JD, 73. Polit & Govt Pos: Dir, Pa Teen-Age Dem, 67-68 & Youth for Humphrey-Muskie Campaign, 68; fund-raiser, Muskie Elec Comt, Washington, DC, 71; legis asst, US Rep Joseph Vigorito, Pa, 73- Bus & Prof Pos: Law clerk, Purcell & Hansen, Washington, DC, 75- Mem: Cong Staff Club. Honors & Awards: Dean's Cert for Outstanding Serv to Univ Toledo Law Sch; Pub Defender Cert for Serv Rendered to People in Toledo, Ohio. Legal Res: 4218 English Ave Erie PA 16510 Mailing Add: 1819 H St Suite 230 Washington DC 20510

ANDREWS, RICHARD R (D)
Ala State Rep
Mailing Add: PO Box 6061 Birmingham AL 35209

ANDREWS, RUTH T (R)
b Delvan, Minn, June 14, 12; d William M Tweeten & Oline Wilhelmsen T; m 1933 to Thomas M Andrews; c Betty (Mrs Mell Geller), Dorothy (Mrs Don Sharp) & Thomas William. Educ: LaCrosse Lutheran Hosp, RN, 32; Chicago Lying-In Hosp, 33. Polit & Govt Pos: Pres, Algonquin Twp Rep Women's Club, 65-66; chmn, McHenry Co Rep Party, Ill, formerly; mem, Gov Adv Coun, 69- Bus & Prof Pos: Gen duty nurse, Cook Co Hosp, 33-45; part-time surg nurse, Avalon, Calif, 46-48; surg & obstetrical nurse, Sherman Hosp, Elgin, Ill, 49-68; sch nurse, Community Unit Dist 300, 68- Mem: Ill & Dist 300 Educ Asns; Ill Asn Sch Nurses; Algonquin Women's Club; Am Legion Auxiliary. Relig: Congregational. Mailing Add: 1313 N River Dr Algonquin IL 60102

ANDREWS, THOMAS COLEMAN, JR (AMERICAN PARTY)
Nat Chmn, American Party
b Richmond, Va, Feb 15, 25; m to Barbara Jane Ransome. Educ: Dartmouth Col, BA; Wharton Sch, Univ Pa. Polit & Govt Pos: Secy, Richmond City Dem Comt, formerly; Va State Deleg, 60-68; nat chmn, American Party, 69- Bus & Prof Pos: Owner, T Coleman Andrews, Jr Ins Agency. Mil Serv: Air Force, combat navigator, auditor gen. Mem: Am

Legion; CofC; Commonwealth Club. Relig: Episcopal. Mailing Add: 1508 Willow Lawn Dr Richmond VA 23230

ANDREWS, W THOMAS (R)
Pa State Sen
b New Castle, Pa, Nov 8, 41; s W Ralph Andrews & Mary Daugherty A; m 1966 to Leslie Jane Nord; c Arlyn Elizabeth & William Robert. Educ: Col of Wooster, BA, 63; Univ Pittsburgh Law Sch, LLB, 66. Polit & Govt Pos: Mem, Lawrence Co Young Rep, Pa, currently; dist attorney, Lawrence Co, 70-72; Pa State Sen, Butler & Lawrence Co, 72-, chmn law & justice comt, Pa State Senate, 75- Mem: Lawrence Co & Pa Bar Asns; Rotary; Jaycees. Relig: Presbyterian. Legal Res: 18 Summit St New Castle PA 16102 Mailing Add: Senate Post Off Main Capitol Bldg Harrisburg PA 17120

ANDREWS, WILLIAM CLAUD (D)
Fla State Rep
b Tampa, Fla, Jan 24, 34; s Claud Fleming Andrews & Agatha Leeuwenburg A; m 1955 to Cedora Platt; c Claudia Lynn, William Claud, Jr & Suzanne Marie. Educ: Univ Fla, BS & BA, 55, LLB, 58; Sigma Alpha Epsilon. Polit & Govt Pos: Fla State Rep, Alachua, Marion, Putnam & Union Counties, 66- Bus & Prof Pos: Attorney, individual practice, 59-; dir, Bank of Hawthorne, 66- Mil Serv: E-2, Army, 58-59; Capt, Army Res, 65. Mem: Am & Fla Bar Asns; Jaycees; Kiwanis; Moose. Relig: Methodist. Legal Res: 206 SE First St Gainesville FL 32601 Mailing Add: PO Box 1036 Gainesville FL 32601

ANDREWS, WILLIAM SMILEY
b Rockville Centre, NY, Jan 7, 49; s Edwin James Andrews & Anita Smiley A; single. Educ: Lafayette Col, AB; Univ Pa, MA; Soles Hall Dining Club. Polit & Govt Pos: Admin asst, US Rep James M Collins, Tex, 72- Mem: Lafayette Col Nat Exec Comt (chmn undergrad rels comt, 72-); Admin Assts Asn; Cong Staff Club. Honors & Awards: George Wharton Pepper Prize, 71 & Minerva & Emil V Novak Prize Govt & Law, Lafayette Col, 71. Legal Res: 120 S Pitt St Alexandria VA 22314 Mailing Add: 66 Foster Rd Tenafly NJ 07670

ANDRINGA, CORNELIUS GEORGE (R)
b Milwaukee, Wis, Mar 9, 31; s Cornelius Andringa & Bessie McKenzie A; m 1954 to Patricia Therese Collins; c Kathy, Eric, Brian, Barbara, Timothy & Mark. Educ: Univ Wis, Madison, BA, 54, LLD, 58, Sigma Chi. Polit & Govt Pos: Chmn, Young Rep of Waukesha Co, Wis, 59-61; vchmn, Waukesha Br, Waukesha Co Rep Party, 61-63 & 63-66; chmn, Waukesha Co Rep Party, formerly. Bus & Prof Pos: Claims adjuster, Rural Mutual Ins Co, 58-61; asst dist attorney, Waukesha Co, 61-64; partner, Collins, Collins & Andringa, Attorneys, 64-; asst family court comnr, Waukesha Co, 64- Mil Serv: Entered as 2nd Lt, Army, 54, released as 1st Lt, 56, after serv in 6th Armored Training Div, Ft Leonard Wood, Mo, 54-56; Capt, Army Res, 58-64; Good Conduct Medal. Mem: Farm Bur; St Mary's Parish Coun (vchmn). Relig: Catholic. Legal Res: 1317 Harris Dr Waukesha WI 53186 Mailing Add: 300 W Main St Waukesha WI 53186

ANDRINGA, ROBERT CHARLES (R)
b Grand Rapids, Mich, Dec 30, 40; s Charles Franklin Andringa & Helen Bisbee A; m 1963 to Susan Valerie Deem; c Dirk & Mark. Educ: Mich State Univ, BA, 63, MA, 64, PhD, 67; Phi Kappa Phi; Beta Gamma Sigma; Omicron Delta Kappa; Blue Key; Delta Tau Delta. Polit & Govt Pos: Minority legis assoc, Comt on Educ & Labor, US House Rep, 69-71, minority staff dir, 71- Bus & Prof Pos: Asst dir, Honors Col, Mich State Univ, 65-67. Mil Serv: Entered as 1st Lt, Army, 67, released as Capt, 69, after serv in Indust Col Armed Forces; Joint Commendation Medal. Mem: Phi Delta Kappa; Am Asn Higher Educ; Mich State Univ Alumni Asn (exec bd, 71-74). Honors & Awards: Outstanding Male Grad, Mich State Univ, 63. Relig: Christian. Mailing Add: 10279 Gainsborough Rd Potomac MD 20854

ANDROUS, MELVIN D (R)
Chmn, Sutter Co Rep Cent Comt, Calif
b Marigold, Calif, Mar 24, 25; s Adrian Edmond Androus & Letta Hartman A; m 1952 to Glenna Rae Potter; c Cheryl (Mrs Crother), Connie (Mrs Higgins) & Colleen (Mrs Lazzarini). Educ: Yuba Col, AA, 48; Univ San Francisco, JD, 51. Polit & Govt Pos: Mem, Sutter Co Rep Cent Comt, Calif, 68-, chmn, 73-; mem, Rep State Cent Comt, Calif, 73-; chmn, Sutter Co Air Pollution Cent Hearing Bd, 72-; chmn, Sutter Co Comt to Re-elect Assemblyman Eugene Chappie, 74. Bus & Prof Pos: In charge of field opers, Calif Cling Peach Adv Bd, Yuba City, Calif, 52-60; owner, Androus Ins & Realty, 60-69; attorney-at-law, 70- Mil Serv: Entered as Pvt, Air Force, 43, released as Sgt, 45; after serv in 12th & 15th Air Force, Italy; Air Medal. Mem: Calif & Am Bar Asns; Calif Trial Lawyers Asn; Commercial Law League; Rotary. Legal Res: 568 S Barrett Rd Yuba City CA 95991 Mailing Add: 335 Teegarden St Yuba City CA 95991

ANDRUS, CECIL D (D)
Gov, Idaho
b Hood River, Ore, Aug 25, 31; s Hal S Andrus & Dorothy Johnson A; m 1949 to Carol M May; c Tana Lee, Tracy Sue & Kelly Kay. Educ: Ore State Univ, 48-49. Polit & Govt Pos: Idaho State Sen, Sixth Dist, 61-66 & 68-70; Dem cand for Gov, Idaho, 66; Gov, Idaho, 71-; mem exec comt, Nat Gov Conf, 71-72; chmn, Fedn Rocky Mountain States, 71-72; deleg, Dem Nat Conv, 72. Bus & Prof Pos: Asst mgr, Workmen's Compensation Exchange, 63-66; agt, Paul Revere Ins Companies, 67, agency supvr, 68, field supvr, 69-70, gen mgr for Idaho, 70- Mil Serv: Entered as Recruit, Navy, 51, released as AT2, 55, after serv in Patrol Squadron 17, Pac Theatre, 52-55; Korean Serv Medal. Mem: Mason; VFW. Honors & Awards: Man of the Year, VFW, 59. Relig: Lutheran. Legal Res: 1805 N 21st St Boise ID 83702 Mailing Add: Statehouse Boise ID 83707

ANDRUS, DAVID CALVIN (R)
b Seattle, Wash, Aug 25, 53; s Calvin Scofield Andrus & Sharon Adair A; single. Educ: Brigham Young Univ, 71-72 & 75-; BYU Col Rep. Polit & Govt Pos: Treas, Utah Teenage Rep, 69-70, chmn, 70-71; alt deleg, Rep Nat Conv, 72. Honors & Awards: Eagle Scout Award, Boy Scouts, 67; Duty to God Award, Boy Scouts & Latter-day Saint Church, 68. Relig: Latter-day Saint; missionary, Northern Argentina, 72-74. Mailing Add: 817 E Third North Brigham City UT 84302

ANDUJAR, ELIZABETH RICHARDS (BETTY) (R)
Tex State Sen
m 1935 to John Jose Andujar, MD. Polit & Govt Pos: Committeewoman, Sen Dist 12 Rep Party, Tex, currently; Tex State Sen, 73- Honors & Awards: Key Rep, 70, 71. 73 & 75. Newsmaker of the Year, 72; only woman elected to state Senate, 72 & 74. Relig: Presbyterian. Mailing Add: 2951 Benbrook Blvd Ft Worth TX 76109

ANGEL, DANIEL DUANE (R)
Mich State Rep
b Detroit, Mich, Dec 23, 39; s Ernest Almond Angel & Hallie Lancaster A; m 1965 to Patricia Schuster. Educ: Taft Col, 57-58; Wayne State Univ, BS, 61, MA, 62; Purdue Univ, PhD, 65; Delta Sigma Rho; Alpha Sigma Phi. Polit & Govt Pos: Mem, Third Dist Rep Exec Comt, Mich, 68-; spec asst to US Sen Robert P Griffin, 69; chmn, Calhoun Co Rep Exec Comt, 70-; chmn platform comt, Mich State Rep Conv, 71; Mich State Rep, 73- Bus & Prof Pos: Asst prof commun, Univ Del, 65-66 & Albion Col, 66-69, dir continuing educ, 69-; vis lectr, Queens Col, 67. Publ: Romney: A Political Biography, Exposition Press, 67; William G Milliken: A Touch of Steel, Pub Affairs Press, 70; Gaposis: the new social disease, Vital Speeches, 68. Mem: Commun Asn Am; Mich Speech Asn; Mich Intercollegiate Speech League; Exchange Club. Honors & Awards: Ford Found fel, 60-61; David Ross fel, 64-65. Relig: Methodist. Mailing Add: 312 Crary Dr Apt 3N Marshall MI 49068

ANGEL, NICK (D)
Treas, Lake Co, Ind
b East Chicago, Ind, Nov 11, 20; s John Angel & Mary Popa A; m 1946 to Darlene Horvath; c Nikki (Mrs Jack Richardson) & Douglas. Educ: Ind Univ, Bloomington, BS in Bus, 43, plus some grad work. Polit & Govt Pos: Ind State Rep, 64-68; treas, Lake Co, 70-; alt deleg, Dem Nat Conv, 72. Bus & Prof Pos: Pub acct, East Chicago, Ind, 57-64; Pub Acct, Angel, Kayes & Paterson, 64-69. Mil Serv: Entered as Pvt, Army, 43, released as Pvt, 43, after serv in Inf. Mem: Northwest Ind Comprehensive Health Planning Coun, Inc; Gary Income Maintenance Prog; Ind Univ Northwest Ctr for Med Educ (pres, 73-); Kiwanis; Mason. Relig: Presbyterian. Mailing Add: 1411 Kraft Dr Munster IN 46321

ANGELL, CHARLIE (R)
Kans State Sen
Mailing Add: 102 Erie Plains KS 67869

ANGELL, JEAN (D)
Dem Nat Committeewoman, NY
Mailing Add: 201 Elmwood Ave Ithaca NY 14850

ANGLACE, JOHN FRANCIS, JR (R)
Chmn, Shelton Rep Town Comt, Conn
b Ansonia, Conn, Dec 27, 31; s John Anglace & Mary Onofrio A; m 1956 to Theresa Marie Palazza; c Sandra Ann & John Leonard. Educ: Univ Conn, 55-56; Univ Bridgeport, BS Indust Rels, 60; Soc for Advan of Mgt; Key Club. Polit & Govt Pos: Treas, Shelton Rep Town Comt, Conn, 72-74; mem, Bd of Apportionment & Taxation, Shelton, Conn, 72-74; chmn, Shelton Rep Town Comt, Conn, 74- Bus & Prof Pos: Personnel asst, US Elec Motors, Inc, 59-63; personnel mgr, Eastern Machine Screw Corp, 63-66, personnel mgr, Burndy Corp, 66-74; personnel & labor rels mgr, Holgrath Corp, Div Howmedica, 74- Mil Serv: Entered as Pvt, Army Res, 49, released as M/Sgt, 60, after serv in Europe, 53-55; ETO Medal; Good Conduct Medal. Publ: Ed, Attendance Control Manual, Burndy, 72. Mem: Cheshire CofC (dir, 74-); Conn Personnel Asn; Conn Bus & Indust Asn; Derby-Shelton Lions (vpres, 66-); Riverside Fish & Game Club (pres, 69-71). Honors & Awards: Horace B Merwin Award, Univ Bridgeport, 60; President's Award, Soc for Advan of Mgt, 60. Relig: Roman Catholic. Mailing Add: 676 Long Hill Ave Shelton CT 06484

ANGLE, SUSAN SCOTT (D)
b Great Bend, Kans, Apr 22, 51; d Robert Raymond Scott & Mary Lee Stewart S; m 1974 to Dennis R Angle. Educ: Kans State Teachers Col, BA, 73, MS, 74. Polit & Govt Pos: Precinct committeewoman, Ellis Co Dem Party, Kans, 72; deleg, Dem Nat Conv, 72. Bus & Prof Pos: Head resident & asst dir student activities, Albion Col, 74- Mem: Am Asn Univ Women; Nat Asn Women Deans, Adminrs & Counrs; Common Cause. Mailing Add: 200 S Mingo Albion MI 49224

ANNENBERG, WALTER H (R)
b Milwaukee, Wis, Mar 13, 08; s M L Annenberg; m 1951 to Leonore Cohn; c Wallis Weingarten. Educ: Univ Pa; Phi Sigma Delta; Sigma Delta Chi. Polit & Govt Pos: US Ambassador to Gt Brit, 69-74. Bus & Prof Pos: Pres, Triangle Publ Inc, Philadelphia, Pa, 42- Mem: Navy League; Newcomen Soc; Alliance Francaise de Philadelphia; Am Soc Newspaper Ed; Int Press Inst. Honors & Awards: Officer, French Legion of Honor; Comdr, Order of the Lion of Finland; Order of the Crown of Italy and Order of Merit of the Ital Repub. Mailing Add: Wynnewood PA 19096

ANNUNZIO, FRANK (D)
US Rep, Ill
b Chicago, Ill, Jan 12, 15; s Ralph Annunzio & Rose Malizzio A; m 1935 to Angeline Alesia; c Jacqueline (Mrs Frank Latto), Linda (Mrs William O'Donnell) & Susan (Mrs Kevin Tynan). Educ: DePaul Univ, BS & MEd. Polit & Govt Pos: Mem, Chicago Comn on Human Rels, Ill; mem adv bd, Cook Co Health & Surv; mem adv comt Ill Indust Comn on Health & Safety & Unemploy Compensation; chmn, War Ration Bd; dir, Ill Dept of Labor; US Rep, Ill, 64- Bus & Prof Pos: Legis & educ dir, USW; asst supvr, Nat Defense Training Prog, Austin Eve Sch, Chicago; teacher, Chicago Pub Schs including Carl Schurz High Sch. Mem: Villa Scalabrini Develop. Fund (gen chmn); Little Flower Soc (bd trustees); Am Comt on Ital Migration (bd dirs); Cath Youth Orgn; Ital-Am Dem Club (Cook Co Chmn). Legal Res: 6315 N Knox Ave Chicago IL 60646 Mailing Add: 2303 Rayburn House Off Bldg Washington DC 20515

ANSELMI, DONALD RAY (D)
Chmn, Wyo Dem State Cent Comt
b Rock Springs, Wyo, July 17, 28; s John Anselmi & Lillie Malmberg A; m 1953 to Dora Giovanini, div; c Mark, Joseph, Kurt & Gina. Polit & Govt Pos: Deleg, Dem Nat Conv, 60, 64, 68 & 72; mem platform comt, 68; vchmn, Wyo Dem State Cent Comt, 65-70, chmn, 70-; chmn, Rock Springs Sweetwater Airport Authority, Wyo, 68-74; mem comn on deleg selection, Dem Nat Comt, 72-74; deleg, Dem Nat Mid-Term Conf, 74. Bus & Prof Pos: Chmn bd dirs, Sweetwater Mem Hosp, 59-69; dir, Am Hotel Motel Asn, 68-75; trustee, Wyo Blue Cross-Blue Shield, 69-75; pres, Colo, Wyo Hotel & Motel Asn, 75- Mil Serv: Entered as Pvt, Air Force, 50, released as Cpl, 52, after serv in Fourth Air Force. Mem: Asn Internationale de l'Hotelerie; Elks; KofC; Am Legion. Relig: Roman Catholic. Mailing Add: Box 1570 Rock Springs WY 82901

ANSELMI, RUDOLPH THEODORE (D)
b Rock Springs, Wyo, May 1, 04; s Joseph Anselmi & Maria Menghini A; m 1929 to Louise Shuster; c Mary Lou (Mrs John Unguren), Lynn (Mrs Thomas Lockhart) & Jeri (Mrs Clifford

E Kirk). Educ: Univ Wyo, BS, 25; Phi Kappa Phi; Pi Gamma Mu; Sigma Chi. Polit & Govt Pos: Chmn sch bd, Dist 4, Rock Springs, Wyo, 36-65; Wyo State Sen, 37-65, minority floor leader, Wyo State Senate, 43-63; vchmn, Wyo State Dem Cent Comt, 45-65, mem exec comt, 50-65; mem Legis Interim Comt & chmn, Sweetwater Co Fair Bd, 50-60; deleg, Dem Nat Conv, 60, 64 & 68; mem, Wyo State Bd Equalization, 65-75, chmn, 75-; mem, State Tax Comn, 65-75, chmn, 75-; mem, Gov Re-orgn Comt, 67-68; vchmn, Wyo Legis-Exec Comn on Reorgn of State Govt, 69-70. Bus & Prof Pos: Dir, NSide State Bank, Rock Springs, Wyo; secy-treas, Huntley Construction Co; pres, Miners Mercantile Bldg Co; bd mem, Cheyenne Fed Savings & Loan, 72-; exec vpres, Cheyenne Serv Corp, 73-75. Mem: KofC; Cheyenne Exec Club; Univ Wyo Alumni Asn; Cheyenne Serra Club. Honors & Awards: Hon Grad, Univ Wyo Sch Com, 62. Relig: Catholic. Legal Res: Box 908 Rock Springs WY 82901 Mailing Add: Apt 17 2608 House Cheyenne WY 82001

ANSPACH, JOHN HENRY **(D)**
Chmn, Lebanon Co Dem Comt, Pa
b Grantville, Pa, Aug 21, 27; s Clarence Harvey Anspach & Margaret I Soliday A; m 1945 to Laura Mae Witmer; c Jeanne Louise, Edward Lloyd & Joseph Alfred. Educ: Lebanon Valley Col, night student, 63-65. Polit & Govt Pos: Committeeman, East Hanover Twp Dem Party, 55-60; tax collector, 57-61; deleg, Dem Nat Conv, 68; co comnr, Lebanon Co, 68-; chmn, Lebanon Co Dem Comt, 72- Bus & Prof Pos: Owner & mgr, Anspach Autos, 51-; dir, Jonestown Bank & Trust Co, Jonestown, Pa, 64- Mem: Nat Auto Truck Wreckers Asn; Jonestown Lions (pres); F&AM; Lebanon Co Shriner's Club; Gideons. Relig: United Methodist. Mailing Add: 3 N Ninth St Lebanon PA 17042

ANTHONY, PHILIP LAVERN **(D)**
Mayor, Westminster, Calif
b Clinton, Iowa, Sept 22, 35; s Elmer LaVern Anthony & Emma Marguetta Domann A; m 1967 to Carolyn Lee Knorzer Bannister; c Dionne Patrice & Philip Roger Anthony & Derek S Bannister. Educ: Pomona Col, 52-54; Calif State Col, Long Beach, BS, 58; Univ Hawaii, MS, 60; Univ Southern Calif, 60-61; Alpha Gamma Sigma. Polit & Govt Pos: Mayor & mem city coun, Westminster, Calif, 62-; mem, Orange Co Dem Cent Comt, 66-72, chmn, 66-68, vchmn, 68-72; mem, Calif Dem State Cent Comt, 72-74; chmn, Orange Co City's Selection Comt, 75- Bus & Prof Pos: Group scientist & supvr chem lab, Autonetics Div, NAm Rockwell Corp, Anaheim, Calif, 61-72, supvr advan instruments, 72- Publ: Auth, Galvanic Corrosion on silver-plated copper wire, Materials Protection, 3/65; co-auth, Nondestructive testing by mutual coupling magnetic sensing probes, NASA, 1/72; auth, Automating PC/multilayer operations, Electronic Packaging & Prod, 1/73; plus others. Mem: Nat Asn Corrosion Engr; Am Electroplaters Soc; Inst Printed Circuits; Nat Mgt Asn; Lions; Elks. Relig: Methodist. Mailing Add: 15842 Villanova Circle Westminster CA 92683

ANTISDEL, LOUIS WILLARD **(D)**
Chmn, Tioga Co Dem Party, NY
b Bradford Co, Pa, Jan 15, 25; s Miles Delmar Antisdel & Gladys Jones A; m 1958 to Delores Rose Smithka; c Pamela Ann, Timothy Aaron & Cynthia Louise. Educ: Williamsport Tech Inst, 42. Polit & Govt Pos: Committeeman, Tioga Co Dem Party, 64-70, chmn, 70- Mil Serv: Entered as Recruit, Army, 50, released as Cpl, after serv in Anti-Aircraft Bn, 50-52. Mem: Nichols-Tioga Lions; Wappassening Hose Co; Nichols Am Legion Post 1624; Tioga Co Men's Garden Club. Mailing Add: RD 1 Box 132 Nichols NY 13812

ANTON, DON CHRIST **(D)**
Chmn, St Louis Co Dem Cent Comt, Mo
b St Louis, Mo, Mar 26, 33; s Christ J Anton & Anna L Thiel A; m 1959 to Aurora I Viglino; c Donald K & Linda A. Educ: Kans State Univ, 50-51; Wash Univ, BSBA, LLB & JD; Delta Sigma Pi; Phi Delta Phi; Sigma Nu; Newman Club. Polit & Govt Pos: Deleg, Dem Nat Conv, 64 & 72; Spec Asst to Mo Attorney Gen, 67-69; Asst Prosecuting Attorney, Jefferson Co, 67-69; committeeman, Concord Twp, 68-; state coordr, Mo Income Tax Referendum, 69-70; counsel, Mo State Senate, 69-70; campaign mgr, Probate Judge, St Louis Co, 70 & Gov, Mo, 71-72; chmn, St Louis Co Dem Cent Comt, 73- Bus & Prof Pos: Counsel, US Army Corps of Engrs, 57-58; attorney, St Louis, 57-; probate attorney, Mercantile Trust Co, 59-60; counsel, US Small Bus Admin, 63-66; consult, Mo Dept Community Affairs, 66-68; pres, Diversified Consult Inc, 68- Mil Serv: Entered as 2nd Lt, Army 56, released as 1st Lt, 58, after serv in Security Agency, Far East. Publ: Prenatal injury—damage suits, Wash Univ Law, 54; Reorganization of the Democratic Party in Missouri, Concord Dem Club, 69; Meramec City, Mo Dept Community Affairs, 70. Mem: Am Judicature Soc; Tax Inst Am; Kiwanis Int; Optimists Int; Jaycees. Relig: Catholic. Mailing Add: 50 Crestwood Exec Ctr 516 Crestwood MO 63126

ANTON, JAMES **(R)**
b Concord, NH, Mar 22, 14; s Max S Anton & Helen Lesher A; m 1954 to Florence A Morrolf; c William, Linda & James. Educ: Univ Ala, AB, 37; Georgetown Univ, LLB, 52. Polit & Govt Pos: NH State Rep, 46-47; treas, Concord, NH Sch Dist, 46-47; asst jour clerk, US Senate, 47-53; chmn, NH Rep Comt Speaker's Bur, 48-50; spec counsel, US Senate, Preparedness Comt, 52-56; chief off compliance, Civil Aeronaut Bd, 56-60; dir, Bur Enforcement, 60-62; hearing examr, Interstate Com Comn, 62-72, admin law judge, 72- Bus & Prof Pos: Instr, bus col; newspaper reporter, 39-42. Mil Serv: Army, 42-45; Air Medal with Clusters; Five Battle Stars. Mem: Am Legion; VFW; Eagles. Relig: Episcopal. Mailing Add: 335 Maryland Ave NE Washington DC 20002

ANTON, PATRICIA ANN **(D)**
b Oskaloosa, Iowa, Nov 29, 53; d Dr George R Anton & MaryLou Cahalan A; single. Educ: Col St Benedict (Minn), currently; Nat Honor Soc. Polit & Govt Pos: Chmn, Fourth Dist Dem Nominating Comt, Iowa, 72; mem, Mahaska Co Dem Nominating Comt, Iowa, 72; alt deleg, Dem Nat Conv, 72. Honors & Awards: Nominee to Iowa Girls' State, Am Legion Auxiliary, 71; Rotary Exchange to Argentina, Rotary Int, 71. Relig: Roman Catholic. Mailing Add: 124 Solar Dr Oskaloosa IA 52577

ANTONE, STEVE **(R)**
Idaho State Rep
b Burley, Idaho, Nov 17, 21; s Andrew Antone & Margaret Glover A; m 1950 to Helen Margaret McKevitt; c Kathleen (Mrs Alfred Coccinello) & Steven Kent. Educ: Heyburn High Sch, grad. Polit & Govt Pos: Idaho State Rep, 68-, chmn, Revenue & Taxation Comt & mem, Bus Comt, Idaho House Rep, currently. Bus & Prof Pos: Supvr, Soil Conserv Dist. Mil Serv: Entered as Pvt, Air Force, 43, released as T/Sgt, 45, after serv in 463rd Bomb Group, 15th Air Force, Italy, 44-45. Mem: AF&AM; Elks; Mason (Master, 58 & 68). Relig: Methodist. Mailing Add: 1141 Link St Rupert ID 83350

ANTONOVICH, MICHAEL DENNIS **(R)**
Calif State Assemblyman
b Calif; s Mike Antonovich & Francis McColm A; single. Educ: Calif State Univ, Los Angeles, BA, 63, MA, 67; Sigma Nu. Polit & Govt Pos: Mem, Youth for Goldwater State Steering Comt, 64, Calif Rep State Cent Comt, 65- & Los Angeles Co Rep Cent Comt, 67-; regional chmn for Gov Reagan, 70; alt deleg, Rep Nat Conv, 72; Calif State Assemblyman, 43rd Dist, 73- Bus & Prof Pos: Instr govt & hist, Los Angeles City Sch Dist, 66-73. Mil Serv: Entered as Pvt, Army Nat Guard, released as Cpl. Mem: Elks; Phi Delta Kappa. Honors & Awards: Calif Rep Assembly Outstanding Legislator of the Year, 73-74 & 74-75. Relig: Lutheran. Mailing Add: 3415 Lowry Rd Los Angeles CA 90027

ANTROBUS, RANDALL LEON **(R)**
Chmn, Pendleton Co Rep Exec Comt, Ky
b Morgan, Ky, Dec 16, 20; s Paul Antrobus & Fannie Harris A; m 1946 to Elnora Ruth Day; c Randall L, Jr & Robert D. Educ: Morgan High Sch & Lafayette Vocation Sch, Ky. Polit & Govt Pos: Precinct chmn, Ky Rep Party, 60-68; chmn, Pendleton Co Rep Exec Comt, 68- Bus & Prof Pos: Eng supvr, Cincinnati Milling Machine Co, 58-66, group mgr, 66- Mil Serv: Entered as Pvt, Army Signal Corps, 42, released as Sgt, 46, after serv in 3361 Signal Serv Bn, China, Burma & India, 44-46; Asiatic Theater Ribbon with Three Bronze Stars. Mem: Inst Elec & Electronics Engrs; Nat Machine Tool Builders (mem elec standards comt); Nat Fire Protection Asn (mem comt elec standards for machine tools); F&AM; RAM. Relig: Protestant. Mailing Add: RR 3 Berry KY 41003

ANZALONE, FRANK L **(D)**
La State Rep
Mailing Add: PO Box 68 Independence LA 70443

APKING, WILLIAM TAPPAN **(R)**
Chmn, Thayer Co Rep Party, Nebr
b Daykin, Nebr, Aug 31, 33; s George Apking & Ruth Tappan A; m 1958 to Sharon Anderson; c David T & Elizabeth A. Educ: Univ Nebr. Polit & Govt Pos: Treas, Alexandria Sch Bd, Nebr, 60-63; chmn, Alexandria City Coun, 60-; chmn, Jefferson Co Young Rep Club, 64-65; chmn, Thayer Co Rep Party, 64-; mem, Nebr Rep State Cent Comt, 69-75; jr chmn, Nebr Rep Founder's Day, 73; mem, Nebr State Rep Exec Comt, 73-; mem & chmn, Blue Valley Coun Govts, 75-; mem & chmn, Thayer Co Sch Reorgn Comt, 75- Mil Serv: Entered as Seaman, Navy, 53, released as PO 2/C, 57. Mem: Goals for Nebr Comt; Nebr State Banker's Asn; Nat Livestock Feeder's Asn; Farm Bur; Am Legion. Relig: Protestant. Mailing Add: Fifth & Vira Alexandria NE 68303

APODACA, JERRY **(D)**
Gov, NM
b Las Cruces, NMex, Oct 3 34; s Raymond Apodaca & Elisa Alvarez A; m 1956 to Clara Melendres; c Cynthia Kay, Carolyn Rae, Gerald Craig, Jeffrey Don & Judith Marie. Educ: Univ NMex, BS, 57; Phi Delta Theta. Polit & Govt Pos: NMex State Sen, Dona Ana Co, 67-74, Dem caucus chmn, NMex State Senate, 69-; deleg, Dem Nat Conv, 68; Dem State Chmn, 69-70; mem, Nat Dem Policy Counc, 69-; Gov, 74- Relig: Roman Catholic. Legal Res: 2410 Acoma Las Cruces NM 88001 Mailing Add: 1401-A El Paseo Las Cruces NM 88001

APONTE, BORRERO MANUEL J **(POPULAR DEM, PR)**
Mayor, Bayamon, PR
b Bayamon, PR, Nov 18, 41; s Luis Aponte Soto & Mercedes Borrero Pascual S; m 1963 to Gertrudis Felix Bonilla; c Sandra Mercedes, Diana Maria, Luisa & Rosa Maria. Educ: Univ Salamanca, Law Degree, 67; Colonia Hispanoamericana; Alpha Beta Chi. Polit & Govt Pos: Mayor, Bayamon, PR, 73- Bus & Prof Pos: Pvt law practice, Bayamon, PR, 67-72. Mem: Colegio de Abogados; Boy Scouts. Relig: Catholic. Legal Res: Carr 167 Km 195 Bayamon PR 00619 Mailing Add: Box 1588 Bayamon PR 00619

APONTE, HUMBERTO **(D)**
Leader, Part A, 63rd Assembly Dist Dem Party, NY
b Cabo Rojo, PR, Sept 7, 24; s Jose T Aponte & Amelia Cofresi A; m 1947 to Anna Maria Ferrer; c Anna M & Roberto. Educ: Metrop Voc High Sch, New York, 4 years. Polit & Govt Pos: Leader, Part A, 63rd Assembly Dist Dem Party, NY, 67-; mem, New York Coun Against Poverty, formerly; mem bd dirs, NY Urban Coalition, formerly; deleg, Dem Nat Conv, 68; Marshal, New York, 71- Bus & Prof Pos: Off mgr for law firm, Dinkes, Mandel & Dinkes; auctioneer, Brooklyn, 73- Mil Serv: Entered as Pvt, Army, 43, released as PFC, 45, after serv in 298 Engr Bn, ETO; Five Bronze Battle Stars; Purple Heart; Victory Medal; Good Conduct Medals; ETO Service Medal. Mem: VFW; Bolivar-Douglas Dem Club; Coun of Puerto Rican Orgn; Lower Eastside Neighborhoods Asns; Grand St Settlement (bd dirs, 72-). Honors & Awards: Lane Bryant Vol Award, 66-67. Relig: Protestant. Mailing Add: 71 Columbia St New York NY 10002

APONTE COLON, ELOY **(POPULAR DEMOCRAT, PR)**
Rep, PR House Rep
Mailing Add: State Capitol San Juan PR 00901

APOSTOL, JOHN CLEO **(R)**
Mayor, Annapolis, Md
b Annapolis, Md, Nov 28, 38; s Cleo John Apostol & Mary Mandris A; m to Wilda Lewis; c Christopher & Angela. Educ: Univ Md, College Park, BS, 62; Tau Kappa Epsilon. Polit & Govt Pos: Mayor, Annapolis, Md, 73- Mil Serv: Entered as Pvt E-1, Army, 62, released as Pfc, 64, after serv in Pac Theatre & Korea, 63-64. Relig: Greek Orthodox. Mailing Add: 96 Summerfield Dr Annapolis MD 21403

APPEL, MELISS A **(R)**
NH State Rep
Mailing Add: 433 Central Rd Box 43 Rye NH 03870

APPELMAN, MARY GOOLD **(D)**
b London, Eng, Feb 8, 26; d Herbert Stewart Goold & Cora Smith G; m 1960 to Evan Hugh Appelman; c Harold Stewart & Hilary Louise. Educ: Vassar Col, AB, 45; Univ Chicago, 50-51; Univ Calif, Berkeley, 55-59. Polit & Govt Pos: Precinct coordr, Schneider for State Rep, 70; co-coordr, Downers Grove Twp Citizens for Adlai Stevenson for Senate, 70; precinct committeeman, Downers Grove Twp, 70-74; co-coordr, Downers Grove Village Walker for Gov, fall 71; alt deleg, Dem Nat Conv, 72. Mem: Common Cause; League of Women Voters; Am for Dem Action (bd, 70-72); Nat Comt for Sane Nuclear Policy (regional bd, 72-74);

Independent Voters of Ill (bd, 70-72). Mailing Add: 4816 Cornell Ave Downers Grove IL 60515

APPLEMAN, RUBY V (R)
NMex State Rep
Mailing Add: 1045 Santa Ana SE Albuquerque NM 87123

APPLEBY, JAMES E (R)
NH State Rep
Mailing Add: 6 Portland St East Rochester NH 03867

APPLEGATE, A EARL (D)
b Frankfort, Ind, Dec 20, 16; s C Earl Applegate & Ester Pearl Young A; m 1940 to Gertrude Fife; c Donald, Nancy (Mrs Spitzer), Roberta Sue, Sheldon & Janet. Educ: Ind Univ, Bloomington, BS, 38; Ind Univ, Indianapolis, MD, 42; Theta Kappa Psi. Polit & Govt Pos: City Health Officer, Frankfort, Ind, 47-67; deleg, Ind Dem Conv, 20 years; Dem precinct committeeman, 20 years; mem exec coun, Ind State Bd Health, 60-64; co health officer, Clinton Co, 66-68; deleg, Dem Nat Conv, 68; chmn, Clinton Co Dem Party, formerly. Bus & Prof Pos: Mem exec coun, Ind Univ, 56-60; chief of staff, Clinton Co Hosp, 66 & 67. Mem: Am & Ind State Med Asns; Clinton Co Med Soc; Moose; Frankfort Country Club. Relig: Methodist. Legal Res: 750 Harvard Terr Frankfort IN 46041 Mailing Add: 1303 S Jackson St Frankfort IN 46041

APPLEGATE, DOUGLAS (D)
Ohio State Sen
b Steubenville, Ohio, Mar 27, 28; s Earl Douglas Applegate (deceased) & Mary Margaret Longacre A; m 1950 to Betty Jean Engstrom; c Kirk Douglas & David Allen. Educ: Steubenville High Sch, grad, 47; Aetna Ins, 51. Polit & Govt Pos: Ohio State Rep, 33rd Dist, Jefferson Co, 61-68; deleg-at-lg, Dem Nat Conv, 64; pres, Jefferson Co Young Dem Club, 66-67; mem, Ohio Comn, Interstate Coop; mem, Dem Policy Making Comt; deleg, Nat Rivers & Harbors Comg, 69; Ohio State Sen, 69-; mem, Ohio Const Revision Comn; Ohio State Senate Finance Comt, Commerce & Labor Comt & Admin of Educ Comt, currently. Bus & Prof Pos: Salesman, Earl D Applegate, realtor, Steubenville, Ohio, 50-57; real estate broker & realtor, 57- Mem: Steubenville Bd Realtors; Ohio & Nat Asn Real Estate Bd; Elks; Eagles. Honors & Awards: Outstanding Young Man of Am, US Jaycees, 65; nominated for John F Kennedy award for Young Dem of Year, 67. Relig: Presbyterian. Mailing Add: Berkeley Place-Lover's Lane Steubenville OH 43952

APPLETON, KENNETH WRIGHT (R)
Vt State Rep
Mailing Add: Bradford VT 05033

AQUILOTTI, SAMUEL (D)
RI State Rep
b Clifton, NJ, Apr 10, 21; s Augustine Aquilotti & Maria Bonelli A; m 1972 to Hansi Jaeger; c Monika & Claudia. Educ: Cent High Sch, Providence, RI, 4 years. Polit & Govt Pos: RI State Rep, 15th Dist, 69-; mem, Permanent Joint Comt on Environ, 71- Bus & Prof Pos: Salesman, Shepard Stores, Providence, RI, 65- Mil Serv: Entered as Pvt, Army, 42, released as Sgt, 45, after serv in 877th Heavy Maintenance, ETO, 43-45; Five Major Battle Stars; Marksman Rifle. Mem: Lions; Toscan Club; Italo-Am War Vet; VFW; Am Legion. Relig: Catholic. Mailing Add: 191 Bridgham St Providence RI 02909

ARABIS, STANLEY LAWRENCE (R)
Chmn, Young Rep Pa
b Hazleton, Pa, Mar 9, 45; s Stanley John Arabis (deceased) & Anna Schwear A; m 1967 to Nancy Elizabeth Hammergren; c Christopher Robert & Mark Allen. Educ: Gen Motors Inst, BS, 68; Pa State Univ, 69; Temple Univ Sch Law, JD, 74; Phi Delta Theta. Polit & Govt Pos: Committeeman, Bucks Co Rep Party, Pa, 68-; mem exec comt, Rep Party Pa, 74-; chmn, Young Rep Pa, 74- Bus & Prof Pos: Sr mech engr, Gen Motors Corp, Trenton, NJ, 68-74; attorney-at-law, Cox, Brady & Arabis, 74- Mem: Am, Montgomery Co & Pa Bar Asns; Fluid Power Soc; Soc Die Casting Engrs. Mailing Add: 57 Cobalt Cross Rd Levittown PA 19057

ARAGON, BENNIE J (D)
NMex State Rep
Mailing Add: 10310 Rafael SW Albuquerque NM 87105

ARAGON, MANUEL LEROY (D)
NMex State Sen
b Albuquerque, NMex, Mar 22, 47; s Manuel C Aragon & Charlotte Gurule A; m 1967 to Rosina Barbara Sedillo; c Gregory Scott & Angela Barbara. Educ: Univ Albuquerque, 65-67; Univ NMex, BA, 70, Law Sch, 70- Polit & Govt Pos: Alt deleg, Dem Nat Conv, 68; pres, Bernalillo Co Young Dem, 68; pres, Young Dem of NMex, 68-69, regional exec vpres, 70-; NMex State Sen, currently. Bus & Prof Pos: Agt, Jefferson Standard Life Ins, 69 & First Nat Life Ins, 69; investr, Bernalillo Co Dist Attorney's Off, 70- Mem: Optimist. Relig: Catholic. Mailing Add: 1019 Tijeras SW Suite 203 Albuquerque NM 87102

ARASMITH, NEIL H (R)
Kans State Sen
b Jewell, Kans, Feb 23, 30; s James H Arasmith (deceased) & Jessie Fields A; m 1951 to Donna Schindler; c David, Jeffrey, Susan & Timothy. Educ: Univ Kans, BA, 51; Phi Kappa Sigma. Polit & Govt Pos: Treas, Phillips Co Hosp Bd Trustees, Kans, 64-69, chmn, 69-72; Kans State Sen, 36 Dist, 72- Bus & Prof Pos: Exec br mgr, Interstate Securities Co, Phillipsburg, Kans, 51- Mil Serv: 2nd Lt, Air Force, Ret, Res. Mem: Lions (secy); Elks (Past Exalted Ruler, dist dep, state vpres & state Americanism chmn); CofC (dir); Phillipsburg Community Fund (chmn), Phillipsburg Rodeo Asn; Hwy 36 Asn. Relig: Protestant. Mailing Add: 230 State Phillipsburg KS 67661

ARBOUR, GERARD JOSEPH (D)
Vt State Rep
Mailing Add: 15 Green Knolls Lane Rutland VT 05701

ARBUCKLE, R DOUGLASS (R)
b Erie, Pa, Jan 2, 52; s William Irwin Arbuckle, II & Virginia Douglass A; single. Educ: Eisenhower Col, AB, 73. Polit & Govt Pos: Alt deleg, Rep Nat Conv, 72. Mailing Add: 312 Mohawk Dr Erie PA 16505

ARBUTHNOT, R E (R)
Kans State Rep
b Haddam, Kans, Nov 1, 19; s Earl Arbuthnot & Blanche Sheelsey A; m 1942 to Jeaane Clark; c Rodney & Cynthia. Educ: Kans State Univ, BS, 42; Farmhouse Fraternity. Polit & Govt Pos: Kans State Rep, 71- Mil Serv: Entered as Aviation Cadet, Air Force, 42, released as Capt, 45, after serv in 15th Air Force, ETO, 44-45; Distinguished Flying Cross; Air Medal. Mem: Mason; Kans Hereford Asn (pres); Kans Livestock Asn; Kans Farm Bur. Relig: United Methodist. Mailing Add: RR Haddam KS 66944

ARCHAMBAULT, BENNETT (R)
b Oakland, Calif; s Albert Joseph Archambault & May Smales A; m to Margaret Henrietta Morgan; c Suzanne Morgan, Michele Lorraine & Steven Bennett. Educ: Ga Inst Technol; Mass Inst Technol, SB; Tau Beta Pi; Lambda Chi Alpha. Polit & Govt Pos: Mem dinner comt for nine Rep Dinners, 64-72; chmn, Midwest Businessmen for Goldwater, 64; co-chmn exec comt, The Comt of 500 Citizens for Goldwater, Ill, 64; mem comt, United Rep Fund 500 Club, 67; bd gov, United Rep Fund of Ill, 67-; vchmn, All-Ill Comt to Elect Richard B Ogilvie Gov, 68; co-chmn, Nat Nixon Sports Dinner, 68; chmn, Rep Nat Finance Comt, Ill, 69-72; mem Chicago Comt, Rep Cong Boosters Club, 70-71; mem, Gov Adv Coun, 70-72; exec co-chmn, Salute to the President Dinner, 71; alt deleg-at-lg, Nat Rep Nominating Conv, 72; alt deleg, Rep Nat Conv, 72; chmn, Rep Indust Workshop Prog, 72; vchmn finance comt, Gov Ogilvie Dinner, 72; co-chmn, Ill Victory 72 Dinner, 72; chmn, Ill Finance Comt to Reelect the President, 72, chmn, Co Sponsored Group Solicitation Prog for Ill, 72; chmn, Ill Comt to Welcome the President, 72; mem finance comt, Hoellen for Cong, 72; mem, President's Comn on Personnel Interchange, 72-74. Bus & Prof Pos: Pres, Stewart-Warner Corp, 54-, chmn, 59-; dir & mem exec & audit comts, Trans Union Corp; dir, Am Mfrs Mutual Ins Co; dir & pres, Thor Power Tool Co; dir & mem exec comt, Am Motorists Ins Co, Kemperco, Inc, Fed Kemper Ins Co & Lumbermens' Mutual Casualty Co; dir & mem audit comt, Harris Bankcorp, Inc; dir & mem examining & dir trust comts, Harris Trust & Savings Bank. Mem: Nat Asn Mfr (pub affairs comt); Ill Mfr Asn (adv bd); Employers' Asn Gtr Chicago (dir); US CofC (policy comt); Am Defense Preparedness Asn, Chicago Post (dir). Honors & Awards: Medal of Merit, US Govt, 45; His Majesty's Medal for Serv in the Cause of Freedom, Brit Govt, 45. Relig: Episcopal. Legal Res: 3240 Lake Shore Dr Chicago IL 60657 Mailing Add: 1826 W Diversey Pkwy Chicago IL 60614

ARCHAMBAULT, LYLE B (D)
Vt State Rep
b Morrisville, Vt, Feb 10, 05; s Joseph L Archambault & Catherine Towne A; m 1931 to Blanche Mureury; c Douglas P, Jean A & Cherolyn M. Educ: Brigham Acad, grad, 25. Polit & Govt Pos: Zone dep collector, US Dept Internal Revenue, 40-48; Vt State Rep, 66-68 & 75-; deleg, Dem Nat Conv, 68. Bus & Prof Pos: Owner-operator, Archambault Furniture Store, Winooski, Vt, 48-64. Mem: Rotary; KofC. Relig: Catholic. Mailing Add: 88 Hood St Winooski VT 05404

ARCHER, VAN HENRY, JR (R)
Committeeman, Tex State Rep Exec Comt
b San Antonio, Tex, Feb 13, 40; s Van Henry Archer, Sr & Dorothy Richey A; m 1962 to Edna Myrick; c Van Henry, III, William Douglas & Stephen Stanton. Educ: Trinity Univ, BA, 63. Polit & Govt Pos: Chmn, Bexar Co Rep Party, Tex, formerly; deleg, Rep Nat Conv, 72; committeeman, Tex State Rep Exec Comt, 19th Dist, currently. Bus & Prof Pos: Loan analyst, Nat Bank of Com, San Antonio, Tex, 65-68; pres, Villita Parking, 68- Mil Serv: Entered as Pvt, Army, 60, released as SP-4, 60, after serv in 5th Army. Mem: Kiwanis. Relig: Episcopal. Mailing Add: 218 W Lynwood San Antonio TX 78212

ARCHER, WILLIAM REYNOLDS, JR (R)
US Rep, Tex
b Houston, Tex, Mar 22, 28; s William Reynolds Archer & Eleanor Miller A; m 1953 to Patricia Moore; c William Reynolds, III, Richard Moore, Sharon Leigh, Elizabeth Ann & Barbara Elise. Educ: Rice Univ, 45-46; Univ Tex, BBA, 49 & LLB, 51; Phi Delta Phi; Sigma Alpha Epsilon. Polit & Govt Pos: Alderman, City of Hunters Creek Village, Tex, 55-62; Tex State Rep, Dist 22, Pos Five, Harris Co, 67-70; US Rep, Seventh Cong Dist, Tex, 71-, mem, Ways & Means Comt, US House of Rep, 73-; deleg, Rep Nat Conv, 72. Bus & Prof Pos: Pres, Uncle Jonny Mill, Inc, Houston, Tex, 59-61; Pres, W R Archer, Inc, 61-; partner, Law Firm of Harris, Archer, Parks & Graul, 67-. Mil Serv: Entered as Pvt, Air Force, 51, released as 1st Lt, 53, after serv as Instr, Off Cand Sch, Lackland Air Force Base, Tex, 51-53; Res, 53-69, Capt. Mem: State Bar of Tex; Houston Bar Asn; Houston Soc for Prev of Cruelty to Animals (dir); Houston Livestock Show & Rodeo. Honors & Awards: Man of the Year Award, Sigma Alpha Epsilon, 69; St Thomas High Sch Outstanding Alumnus Award, 71; NAB Watchdog of the Treas Award, 72; NFIB Guardian of Small Bus Award, 73; Man of the Year, B'nai B'rith Dist 7, 73. Relig: Roman Catholic. Legal Res: 3127 Avalon Houston TX 77019 Mailing Add: US House of Rep Washington DC 20515

AREEDA, PHILLIP E (R)
b Detroit, Mich, Jan 28, 30; s Elias Herbert Areeda & Selma Cope A; single. Educ: Harvard Col, AB, 51, Harvard Law Sch, LLB, 54; Phi Beta Kappa. Polit & Govt Pos: Asst spec counsel to President, 56-61; exec dir, Cabinet Task Force Oil Import Control, 69-70; counsel to the President, 74-75. Bus & Prof Pos: Prof law, Harvard Univ, 61- Publ: Antitrust analysis, Little, Brown, 2nd ed, 74. Mem: Am Law Inst; Int Law Asn; Metrop Club Washington. Mailing Add: Harvard Law Sch Cambridge MA 02138

ARENDS, LESLIE C (R)
b Melvin, Ill; s George Teis Arends & Talea Weiss A; m to Betty Tychon A; c Leslie Talea. Educ: Oberlin Col. Hon Degrees: LLD, Ill Wesleyan Univ. Polit & Govt Pos: US Rep, 17th Dist, Ill, 34-72, 15th Dist, Ill, 72-74, Minority Whip, US House of Rep, 43-72; US deleg to NATO Parliamentarian Conf, 61-; deleg, Rep Nat Conv, 68 & 72. Bus & Prof Pos: Banker & farmer, 20-; emer trustee, Ill Wesleyan Univ. Mil Serv: Navy, World War I. Mem: Am Legion (Post Comdr, Co Comdr, 17th Dist Comdr); Ford Co Farm Bur; Mason (33 degree). Relig: Methodist. Mailing Add: Melvin IL 60952

ARGUE, JOHN S (R)
VChmn, NH Rep State Comt
b Manchester, NH, Aug 18, 27; s Forrest B Argue & M Evelyn Sullivan A; m 1951 to Mary Elliott Peck; c Catherine (Mrs Charles Fountain), John, Thomas, James, Daniel, David, Peter, Michael, Rosemary, Maureen, Christopher & Timothy. Educ: Univ Notre Dame, BS, 50; Georgetown Univ Sch Med, MD, 54; diplomate, Am Bd of Family Practice; pres, Aesculapian Club. Polit & Govt Pos: Vchmn, NH Rep State Comt, 73-; mem, NH Bd Regist in Med, 74- Bus & Prof Pos: Pres, Pittsfield Med & Surg Prof Assoc, 65- Mil Serv: Entered

as Pvt, Army, 46, released as Pfc, 47, after serv in 25th Inf Div, Japan. Mem: Am Acad Family Pract; NH Med Soc; 100 Club of NH; NH Right to Life Comt (treas, 71-); Brady High (sch bd). Honors & Awards: AMA Physicians Recognition Award; Citizen of the Year, Pittsfield, NH, 72. Relig: Roman Catholic. Mailing Add: Fairview Rd Pittsfield NH 03263

ARICO, ANTHONY V, JR (D)
Chmn, Barrington Dem Town Comt, RI
b Bristol, RI, Feb 14, 36; s Anthony J Arico & Mary Chellel A; m 1958 to Joan Grace Tedeschi; c Janice, Laureen & Anthony. Educ: High Sch Equivalency Cert, 54; Univ NH Exten Div, 2 years. Polit & Govt Pos: Committeeman, Barrington Dem Town Comt, RI, 60-, chmn, 66-; mem, Barrington Indust Comt, 65-; secy, 89th Rep Dist Comt, 70- Bus & Prof Pos: Asst off mgr, Narragansett Lithography Co, Inc, 58-61; registered rep, Diamond, Doorley & Co, Inc, 60-62; cost estimator, Bank Lithograph Co, Inc, 61-67; Cost Estimator, United Printing, Inc, 67- Mil Serv: Entered as Airman, Air Force, 54, released as Airman 1/C, 57, after serv in Strategic Air Command, NAfrica. Mem: KofC (former secy, Bishop Hickey Coun). Relig: Roman Catholic. Mailing Add: 166 Lincoln Ave Barrington RI 02804

ARIYOSHI, GEORGE RYOICHI (D)
Gov, Hawaii
b Honolulu, Hawaii, Mar 12, 26; s Ryozo Ariyoshi & Mitsue Yoshikawa A; m 1955 to Jean Miya Hayashi; c Lynn Miye, Todd Ryozo & Donn Ryoji. Educ: Univ Hawaii; Mich State Col, grad; Univ Mich, Law Sch JD; pres, Hawaiian Club, Univ Mich. Polit & Govt Pos: Rep, Territory of Hawaii, 54-58, chmn, Health & Welfare Comt, Hawaii House Rep, 56-58; Sen, Territory of Hawaii, 58-59, chmn, Health & Welfare Comt, Hawaii Senate, 59; Hawaii State Sen, 59-70, chmn, Ways & Means Comt, Hawaii State Senate, 62-64, Majority Leader, 65-66, Majority Floor Leader, 69-70; deleg, Hawaii State Const Conv, 68; Lt Gov, Hawaii, 70-74; Gov, Hawaii, 74- Bus & Prof Pos: Attorney, pvt practice, 52-70; dir, First Nat Bank of Hawaii, 62-70, Honolulu Gas Co, Ltd, 64-70 & Hawaii Ins Guaranty Co, 66-70. Mil Serv: Pvt, Army, 45-46. Mem: Bar Asn of Hawaii; Am Bar Asn; MIS Vet Club; active in various fund drives & community asns. Honors & Awards: Selected as one of top 10 Legislators in Hawaii by Kiwanis Club, 62. Relig: Protestant. Legal Res: Washington Pl Honolulu HI 96813 Mailing Add: State Capitol Honolulu HI 96813

ARKLIN, HENRY (HANK) (R)
b Albany, Calif, July 17, 28; s Haig Arklin & Queenie Abdalian A; m 1970 to Louise Ventura. Educ: Los Angeles City Col; Glendale City Col. Polit & Govt Pos: Comnr Housing & Community Develop, State of Calif, 67-68; Calif State Assemblyman, 41st Assembly Dist, 69-72; Comnr, State of Calif, 73- Mem: San Fernando Valley Bus & Prof Asn; Int Footprinters Asn; Kiwanis; Pacoima-Arleta Businessman's Asn; CofC. Relig: Armenian Apostolic. Legal Res: Granada Hills CA Mailing Add: 10646 Sepulveda Blvd Mission Hills CA 91340

ARLANDSON, JOHN R (DFL)
Minn State Rep
b Minneapolis, Minn, Apr 30, 44; s Clarence D Arlandson & Lucille E Graybill A; m 1969 to Sherry L Simmons; c Mary Elizabeth. Educ: Univ Minn, BA, 66, Law Sch, JD, 69. Polit & Govt Pos: Legis asst to US Sen Walter F Mondale, 72-73; spec asst to Attorney Gen, Minn, 73-74; Minn State Rep, 75- Bus & Prof Pos: Attorney, VISTA, Duluth, 69-70; attorney on Reginald Heber Smith Community Lawyer Fel assigned to Minneapolis Legal Aid Soc, 70-72; attorney, Lifson, Kelber, Breuning, St Louis Park, 74- Mem: Am & Minn Bar Asns; Archdiocesan Urban Affairs Comn. Relig: Catholic. Mailing Add: 1304 S Tyrol Trail Golden Valley MN 55416

ARMBRUSTER, LOREN S (R)
Mich State Rep
b Sebewaing, Mich, Dec 5, 17; s Oscar A Armbruster & Lorena M Mueller; m 1943 to Edna M Golden; c Curtis J, Dennis A & Vicki M. Educ: Mich State Univ, BA & BS, 41. Polit & Govt Pos: Mem, Almer Twp-Bd Rev, Mich, 64-69, chmn, 63-69; Mich State Rep, 84th Dist, 73- Bus & Prof Pos: Voc-agr instr, Coldwater High Sch, 41-43; co agr exten dir, Mich, 46-51; exec vpres, Farmers & Mfg Beet Sugar Asn, 51-73. Mil Serv: Entered as Cadet, Army Air Force, 43, released as 1st Lt, 45, after serv as Aerial Navig Instr, 43-45; recalled as reservist during Korean Conflict, 51-52. Mem: Am Soc Sugar Beet Technol; Boy Scouts (bd dir); Mich Co Agents Asn. Relig: Lutheran. Mailing Add: Rte 1 Box 18 Caro MI 48723

ARMIJO, ALEX J (D)
State Land Comnr, NMex
b Santa Rosa, NMex, May 1, 16; s J Ignacio Armijo & Manuelita Salazar A; m 1938 to Lucy Baca; c Robert, Camilla, Raquel, Cecilia, Dolores & Anthony. Educ: St Michael's Col, 35-37. Polit & Govt Pos: Off mgr, State Tax Comn, NMex; mgr, State Health Dept; asst state comptroller; chief local govt div & budget div, State Dept Finance & Admin; State Auditor; Legis Auditor; State Land Comnr, 69- Mem: Elks. Relig: Catholic. Mailing Add: 444 Camino De Las Animas Santa Fe NM 87501

ARMIJO, JOSE ENRIQUE (R)
Mem, NMex State Rep Cent Comt
Mailing Add: PO Box 1150 Las Vegas NM 87701

ARMIJO ROSALIO (ROSEY) (D)
North Pasco Area Chmn, Franklin Co Dem Cent Comt, Wash
b Edinburg, Tex, Aug 30, 30; s Manuel Badillo Armijo & Esther Castilleja A; m 1949 to Carmen Salazar; c Rosa Linda, Consuelo (Mrs Enrique Curiel), Darlene & Jorge Francisco; one grandchild. Educ: Edinburg Jr High Sch, Tex, 3 years. Polit & Govt Pos: Deleg, Dem Nat Conv, 68; precinct committeeman, Franklin Co Dem Cent Comt, Wash, 69-, North Pasco Area Chmn, 70-; chmn, Chicano Voter Comt, Fourth Cong Dist, 70; area chmn, Tri-Cities Latin Am Voter Comt, 72. Bus & Prof Pos: Construction laborer, George A Grant Construction, Inc Richland, Wash, 61- Mem: Laborers Local 348; Tri-Cities Latin Am Asn (trustee, 72-73); Capt Gray Elem Sch PTA, Pasco (publicity chmn); Benton-Franklin Community Action Comt; Dem Seeking a Newer World. Relig: Catholic. Mailing Add: 1808 N Jefferson Pasco WA 99301

ARMITAGE, CONSTANCE DEAN (R)
Pres, Nat Fedn of Rep Women
b San Francisco, Calif, May 13, 20; d Robert Armstrong Dean & Constance Lawrence D; m 1941 to Norman Cudworth Armitage, wid; c Leslie L (Mrs Vallhonrat) & R Dean (deceased). Educ: Univ Calif, AB, 39; grad studies, Univ Calif, Los Angeles, Univs Florence & Perugia, Italy & Columbia Univ; Univ Ga, MA, 60. Polit & Govt Pos: VChmn, SC Rep Party, 60-62; second vpres, Nat Fedn of Rep Women, 62-67, first vpres, 67-72, pres, 72-; alt deleg, Rep Nat Conv, 60, deleg, 64, 68 & 72, mem platform comt, 64, 70 & 72; mem, President Nixon's 27-Man Adv Coun European Affairs, 71-74; mem, Rep Nat Comt, 72-75; vchmn, US Comn World Pop, 74-75. Bus & Prof Pos: Assoc prof art hist, Wofford Col, 64- Mem: Southeast Col Art Asn; Am Coun of Learned Soc (fel); SC Arts Comn Purchase Comn Nat Endowment for Humanities. Honors & Awards: Mem, US Team World Fencing Championships, Paris, France, 39. Relig: Episcopal. Legal Res: 268 Connecticut Ave Spartanburg SC 29302 Mailing Add: 310 First St SE Washington DC 20003

ARMS, JENA BETH (R)
Secy, First Cong Dist Rep Comt, Tenn
b Johnson City, Tenn, July 13, 49; d Richard Lloyd Perry & Vivian McAulay P; m 1966 to Arnold Clifton Arms; c Myechelle & Richard. Educ: ETenn State Univ, BS, 72. Polit & Govt Pos: Fourth vpres, Carter Co Rep Women's Club, Elizabethton, Tenn, 70-71, third vpres, 72-73; alt deleg, Rep Nat Conv, 72; secy, First Cong Dist Rep Comt, 73- Mem: Elizabethton Jr Women's Club. Relig: Protestant. Mailing Add: Rte 2 Box 274-C Elizabethton TN 37643

ARMSTRONG, ANNE LEGENDRE (R)
b New Orleans, La Dec 27, 27; d Armant Legendre & Olive Martindale L; m 1950 to Tobin Armstrong; c John Barclay II, Katharine Armant, Sarita Storey & twins, Tobin, Jr & James Legendre. Educ: Vassar Col, BA, 49; Phi Beta Kappa. Polit & Govt Pos: VChmn & chmn Kenedy Co Rep Exec Comt, Tex; mem, State Conv Comt, 60; Rep committeewoman, 20th Dist; mem, State Rep Exec Comt, 61-66; deleg & mem platform comt, Rep Nat Conv, 64, deleg & mem platform comt & contests comt, 68, deleg & secy conv, 72, chmn, State Turn Out Our Vote, 64; mem, State Cand Comt, 64-65; dep state vchmn, Region III, Rep Party Tex, 65-66, state vchmn, 66-68; mem steering comt, Women for Nixon, 68; Rep Nat Committeewoman, Tex, 68-73, mem exec comt, Rep Nat Comt, 69-73, co-chmn, 71-73; mem, Defense Adv Comt on Women in the Serv, 71-74; mem, Cost of Living Coun, 73-74; Counr to the President, 73-74; mem, Wage-Price Coun, 74-75. Bus & Prof Pos: Bd dirs, Stratford Hall, 71- Mem: Kenedy Co Sch Bd (trustee, 68-74); Coastal Bend Tuberc & Respiratory Disease Asn (dir). Relig: Episcopal. Mailing Add: Armstrong Ranch Armstrong TX 78338

ARMSTRONG, CONNIE CHARLES (R)
b Longview, Tex, June 26, 25; s Connie Clifton Armstrong & Nora Cornelius A; m 1950 to Harriet Jane Queener; c Chip, Wyn, Mart, Chad & Brett. Educ: Univ Tex, BBA, 50. Polit & Govt Pos: Precinct chmn, Rep Party, Tex, 69-73; committeeman, Ninth Sen Dist Rep Party, 70-72; mayor, Renner, 71-; mem steering comt, Nixon for President, 72; alt deleg, Rep Nat Conv, 72. Bus & Prof Pos: Chmn bd, Nat Feeds Inc, 60-; pres, Armstrong Investments, 67- & Age Inc, 72- Mil Serv: Entered as Pvt, Marine Corps, 43, released as Sgt, 45, after serv in 1st Joint Assault Signal Co, SPac Theatre, 43-45; Silver Star Medal; Presidential Citation; Expert Pistol & Rifle Medals. Mem: Sales & Mkt Execs, Dallas; Dallas Bd of Realtors; Collin Co Mayors Asn; Gtr Dallas Munic League; Mason. Honors & Awards: Distinguished Serv Award, Young Life, 68. Relig: Protestant. Mailing Add: Box 11 Renner TX 75079

ARMSTRONG, JOHN BARCLAY (R)
Chmn, Kleberg Co Rep Party
b San Antonio, Tex, Dec 23, 19; s Charles Mitchell Armstrong & Lucie Carr A; m 1944 to Henrietta Alice Larkin; c Charles Mitchell, Henrietta Julia, Thomas Tobin & Stewart Larkin. Educ: Univ Tex, BA, 42; Alpha Tau Omega. Polit & Govt Pos: Chmn, Kleberg Co Rep Party, Tex, 63-69 & 73- Bus & Prof Pos: Managing partner, John B Armstrong Ranch, 51-; pres, Santa Gertrudis Breeders Int, 57-59; chmn, Beef Indust Coun of Nat Livestock & Meat Bd, 62-69. Mem: Tex & Southwestern Cattle Raisers Asn; Ala & Fla Cattlemen's Asns; Am Nat Cattlemen's Asn. Relig: Episcopal. Legal Res: Hwy 141 W Kingsville TX 78363 Mailing Add: PO Box 193 Kingsville TX 78363

ARMSTRONG, ORLAND KAY (R)
b Willow Springs, Mo, Oct 2, 93; s Rev William C Armstrong & Agnes Brockus A; m 1922 to Louise McCool (deceased); m 1949 to Marjorie E Moore; c Milton McCool, Orland Kay, Jr, Louise (Mrs Cattan), William Stanley & Charles Lindbergh. Educ: Drury Col, BS in Educ, 16; Cumberland Sch Law, LLB, 22; Univ Mo Sch Jour, BJ, 25, MA, 25; Sigma Delta Chi; Pi Delta Epsilon. Hon Degrees: LLD, 56; JD, 69. Polit & Govt Pos: Exec secy, Mo Century of Progress Comn, 31-32; Mo State Rep, 33-37 & 43-45; mem, Children's Code Comn of Mo, 45-47; chmn, Citizens Comn on Reorgn of Exec Br, by app of Sen Comt on Post Off & Civil Serv, 47-48; US Rep, 51-52; speech writer, Rep Cong Comt, 72. Bus & Prof Pos: Teacher Southwest Baptist Col, 16-17; prof jour, Univ Fla, 25-28; mem ed staff, Reader's Digest, 44- Mil Serv: Entered as Pvt, Army Air Corps, 17, released as 2nd Lt, 19, after serv in Taylor Field, Ala, Chanute Field, Ill & Kelly Field, Tex. Publ: The fifteen decisive battles of the United States, McKay Co, 64; Religion can conquer Communism (w Marjorie Armstrong), Thomas Nelson Sons, 64 & Prospect House, 72; The indomitable Baptists (w Marjorie Armstrong), Doubleday, 67; plus others. Mem: Mo Writers' Guild; Am Legion; Vet World War I; Am War Dads; Mil Order of World Wars. Relig: Baptist. Mailing Add: The Highlands Republic MO 65738

ARMSTRONG, ORVILLE RAYNOLD (DFL)
Chmn, Cass Co Dem-Farmer-Labor Party, Minn
b Montevideo, Minn, Aug 31, 21; s Edwin Armstrong & Laura Johnson A; m 1937 to Lyla Olson; c Betty (Mrs Verlyn Helgerson). Educ: Sch Dist 10, Montevideo, Minn. Polit & Govt Pos: Chmn, Powers Twp Bd, Minn, 66-; chmn, Cass Co Dem-Farmer-Labor Party, 70- Bus & Prof Pos: Owner, Armstrong Hardware, Sioux Falls, SDak, 46-55; Owner, Armstrong Construction, Backus, Minn, 59- Relig: Protestant. Mailing Add: Backus MN 56435

ARMSTRONG, RALPH (BUDDY) (D)
Ala State Rep
Mailing Add: 1900 28th Ave S Birmingham AL 35209

ARMSTRONG, ROBERT LANDIS (D)
Comnr Gen Land Off, Tex
b Austin, Tex, Nov 7, 32; s Robert Cochran Armstrong & Louise Landis A; m 1962 to Shannon Harrison; c Martha L, Shannon & Robert L, Jr. Educ: Univ Tex, BA in Govt, 53, LLB, 59. Polit & Govt Pos: Tex State Rep, 63-71; Comnr, Gen Land Off, Tex, 71- Bus & Prof Pos: Attorney-at-law, 58- Mil Serv: Entered as Ens, Navy, 53, released as Lt(jg), 55, after serv in Atlantic-Mediter. Mem: State Bar of Tex; Am Legion; Boy Scouts (Explorer Chmn). Relig: Episcopal. Mailing Add: Gen Land Off State Capitol Austin TX 78711

ARMSTRONG, SALLY JO (R)
Nat Committeewoman, Mont Young Rep
b Roundup, Mont, Aug 2, 43; d Joseph John Uranish & Luise Shelley Seidemann U; m 1963 to John Dodge Armstrong; c Douglas John & Bradley Steven. Educ: Univ Mont, 63. Polit & Govt Pos: Secy, Roundup Young Rep, Mont, 66-67, pres, 70-71; committeewoman, Mont Rep State Cent Comt, 67-69, mem credentials comt, 69; deleg & mem awards comt, Nat Young Rep Conv, 69; mem bd dirs, Mont Fedn Rep Women, 69-71; exec vchmn, Mont Young Rep, 69-71, Nat Committeewoman, 71-; co chmn, Rehberg for Cong, 70. Mem: Roundup Jr Womens Club; Roundup Womens Bowling Asn; Jayceens. Relig: Lutheran. Legal Res: 905 Fifth St W Roundup MT 59072 Mailing Add: Box 763 Roundup MT 59072

ARMSTRONG, WILLIAM LESTER (R)
US Rep, Colo
b Fremont, Nebr, Mar 16, 37; m to Ellen M Eaton; c Anne & William. Polit & Govt Pos: Colo State Rep, 63-64; Colo State Sen, 65-72; Colo Senate Majority Leader, 69-72; US Rep, Fifth Cong Dist, Colo, 73-, mem appropriations comt, US House Rep, currently. Bus & Prof Pos: Pres, KOSI AM-FM, Aurora, Colo, currently; dir, Peoples Bank & Trust Co, Aurora, currently. Legal Res: Aurora CO Mailing Add: Rm 223 Cannon House Off Bldg Washington DC 20515

ARNALL, ELLIS GIBBS (D)
b Newnan, Ga, Mar 20, 07; s Joe Gibbs Arnall & Bessie Lena Ellis A; m 1935 to Mildred DeLaney Slemons; c Alvan Slemons & Alice Slemons. Educ: Mercer Univ, 24; Univ of the South, AB, 28; Univ of Ga, LLB, 31; Phi Beta Kappa; Phi Delta Phi; Kappa Alpha. Hon Degrees: LLD, Atlanta Law Sch, 42, Piedmont Col, 43 & Bryant Col, 48; DCL, Univ of the South, 47. Polit & Govt Pos: Speaker pro tem, Ga House Rep, 33-37; attorney gen, Ga, 39-43; Gov, Ga, 43-47; nat dir, US Office Price Stabilization, 52. Bus & Prof Pos: Pres, Columbus Nat Life Ins Co, Newnan, 46-; pres, Independent Film Producers Export Corp, Beverly Hills, Calif, 48-; chmn bd, Coastal States Life Ins Co, Atlanta, 56-; sr partner, Arnall, Golden & Gregory, Attorneys; comnr, Ga Warm Springs Mem, Franklin D Roosevelt Mem Comn, 70-. Publ: The Shore Dimly Seen, 46; What the People Want, 47. Mem: Int Inst Arts & Sci (Fel); Am Judicature Soc; Nat Asn Life Ins Co (chmn bd, 55-); Soc Motion Picture Arts & Sci; Atlanta Lawyers Club. Legal Res: 213 Jackson St Newnan GA 30263 Mailing Add: Fulton Fed Bldg Atlanta GA 30303

ARNDT, ELIZABETH MOORE (BETTY) (R)
Mem, Mo Rep State Comt
b Newburyport, Mass, Aug 25, 20; d Frederick Arnold Moore & Miriam Delano M; m 1946 to Joseph Manning Arndt, Jr; c Margaret Anne, Martha Howard, Joseph M, III & Marilyn Delano. Educ: Boston City Hosp Sch Nursing, grad, 41. Polit & Govt Pos: Pres, Centralia Rep Women's Club, Mo, 60; treas, Eighth Dist Rep Women's Club, 62; campaign activities chmn, Mo Fedn Rep Women, 62-63, recording secy, 63-65, second vpres, 65-67, first vpres, 67-69, pres, 69-71; deleg, Rep Nat Conv, 64; committeewoman, Centralia Ward II, Rep Party, 66-74; Mo deleg, Nat Fedn Rep Women Conv, 67, vchmn, 119th Legis Dist, 68; deleg, Eighth Dist Conv & Mo State Rep Conv, 68 & 72; mem, Mo Rep State Comt, 70-; chmn youth involvement, Nat Fedn Rep Women, 72-74. Bus & Prof Pos: Pres, Heart of Mo Girl Scout Coun, 67-71. Mil Serv: Entered as 2nd Lt, Army Nurse Corps, 42, released as 1st Lt, 46, after serv in Camp Crowder Gen Hosp, Mo; European, African, Mid Eastern Theater Medal; Victory Medal; Am Theater Medal. Mem: Sorosis Fedn Women's Club; Girl Scouts; Centralia Ment Health Coun; Am Legion; United Fund (bd, 67-). Honors & Awards: Girl Scout Leader & Vol Trainer of Leaders; Rotary Citizen of Week Award, 75. Relig: Protestant. Mailing Add: 5 Sunrise Circle Centralia MO 65240

ARNELL, DONALD E (R)
Ill State Sen
Mailing Add: 815 Thomas St Chicago Heights IL 60411

ARNETT, DIXON (R)
Calif State Assemblyman
b Trenton, NJ, Feb 12, 38; s George Washington Arnett & Annabel Dixon A; m 1961 to Mary Pavlak; c John Dixon, Susan Rae & Robert Michael. Educ: Stanford Univ, BA, 60; Alpha Tau Omega; Walter Army Soc. Polit & Govt Pos: On spec assignment with the US Fed Bur of Narcotics, 60-61; exec dir, San Francisco Bay Area Rep Alliance, Calif, 62-63, mem bd dir, San Mateo Div, 63-67, vpres, 67-68, pres, 68-69, secy, bd trustees, 69-70; assoc mem, San Mateo Co Rep Cent Comt, 62-67, various precinct orgn & elec day assignments, 62-68, elected mem, Fourth Supervisorial Dist, 66 & 68, committeeman, 66-70; admin asst, Rep Minority Caucus, Calif State Assembly, 63-64; assoc mem, Calif Rep State Cent Comt, 63-68, mem, tech adv bd, Cal-Plan, 64-66, appointed mem, 68 & 69; co-mgr, Ruhland for Assembly Comt, 27th Assembly Dist, 64; mem, Tri-City Chap, Young Rep, 64-66, vpres, 65-66; mem, Live Oak Chap, Calif Rep League, 65-68; mem, Younger for Cong Comt & Britschgi for Assembly Comt, 66; mem subcomt on Redwood Shores, Citizens' Comt on Parks & Recreation, 66-67; mem steering comt, Draper for Cong Comt, 67; mem, Parks & Recreation Comn, Redwood City & chmn, sub-comt on bond issue priorities, 67-68; chmn, Sequoia High Sch Dist Permissive Tax Rate Campaign Comt, 68; chmn, Redwood City Nixon-Agnew Comt & mem, Britschgi for Assembly Comt, 68; city councilman, Redwood City, 68-70, chmn, Marina Comt & Redwood City Sch Dist Comt, mem, Legis Comt & Spec Comt on Safety Workers' Benefits; Calif State Assemblyman, 20th Dist, 70-, Minority Whip, 72-; chmn, S San Mateo Co Comt Reelect President, 72. Bus & Prof Pos: Partner, Eastman/Arnett Assocs, 64-65; staff assoc, Off of Gen Secy, Stanford Univ, 65-66, dir, community rels & assoc dir, univ rels, 66-70. Mil Serv: Entered as Pvt, Army Res, 56, released as Capt, 69, after serv in Calif Army Nat Guard, 62-68; Fed Res Ribbon; Two State Active Duty Awards. Publ: Today's Government Handbook, Curricular Serv Inst, 64. Mem: Alumni Asn, Fed Bur of Narcotics Training Sch; Redwood City CofC; Sequoia Dist YMCA (bd dir & co-chmn, membership comt, 68-69); Jr Statesman of Am Found (bd trustees, 68-, pres bd, 75-76); hon mem, Woodwide Terrace Kiwanis. Relig: Protestant. Mailing Add: 680 Warren St Redwood City CA 94063

ARNEY, REX ODELL (R)
Wyo State Rep
b Ashland, Ky, Jan 11, 40; s Harold Leat Arney (deceased) & Frances Odell Cooper A; m 1961 to Anita Louise Rohn; c Dana Lynn, Jill Suzanne & Michele Louise. Educ: Univ Wyo, BA, 62, MA, 63; Univ Ill, JD, 68; Omicron Delta Kappa; Alpha Tau Omega. Polit & Govt Pos: Wyo State Rep, 73- Bus & Prof Pos: Instr, Black Hawk Col, 63-65; partner, Redle, Yonkee & Arney, Attorneys-at-law, 68- Mem: Univ Wyo Alumni Bd; Lions Club; Community Concert Bd; Jaycees; Sheridan Country Club Bd. Honors & Awards: Jaycees Distinguished Serv Award, 70; Outstanding Freshman Legislator, 73. Relig: Presbyterian; Ruling Elder. Mailing Add: 424 S Main Sheridan WY 82801

ARNICK, JOHN STEPHEN (D)
Md State Deleg
b Baltimore, Md, Nov 27, 33; s John Arnick & Josephine Galliard A; div. Educ: Univ Baltimore, BS, 56, LLB, 62. Polit & Govt Pos: Magistrate-at-lg, Baltimore Co, Md, 64-65; Md State Deleg, 66-, Majority Leader, Md House of Deleg, 72-, chmn, Environ Matters Comt, 72- Mil Serv: Entered as Off Cand, Marine Corps, 55, released as Capt, 58, after serv in Third Marine Div, Far E, 56-58. Mem: Baltimore Co Bar Asn; Moose; Bear Creek Civic Club; Line Dem Club; Sons of Italy. Relig: Catholic. Legal Res: 6810 Dunhill Rd Baltimore MD 21222 Mailing Add: 2 Market Place Baltimore MD 21222

ARNOLD, ADRIAN K (D)
Ky State Rep
Mailing Add: Rte 3 Mt Sterling KY 40353

ARNOLD, ALVA LEE (R)
Mem, Los Angeles Co Rep Cent Comt, Calif
b Woodville, Tex, Oct 27, 19; d Daniel Louis Cobb & Ida Mae Risinger C; m 1943 to Ernest Marion Arnold; c James Bowman, Margaret Mary (Mrs Ronald Allison), Teresa (Mrs Jay Holloway), Ernest Bernard, David Daniel, Ann Marie & Stephen Francis. Educ: ETex Baptist Col, grad bus admin, 42; Calif State Univ, Los Angeles, 3 years; Phi Beta Kappa, secy, Gamma Psi Chap, 39-42; Sigma Iota Chi, pres, Phi Chap, 39-42. Polit & Govt Pos: Chmn, Citizens' Freeway Comt, South Pasadena, Calif, 65-66; co-chmn, Mayor's Freeway Comt, 67-68; pres, South Pasadena Rep Women's Club, Federated, 69-70; mem, Rep State Cent Comt, Calif, 69-74; mem, South Pasadena City Freeway Comn, 69-, chmn, 72-; chmn, Jr Rep, Los Angeles Co Rep Women, Federated, 70-72; 54th Assembly Dist precinct chmn, Los Angeles Co Rep Cent Comt, 73-74, alt mem, 74- Bus & Prof Pos: Real estate sales rep, Dart Resorts, Del Rey, Calif, currently. Publ: Series of freeway fact articles, South Pasadena Rev, Newspaper, 66-68. Mem: Woman's Club of South Pasadena; Calif Roadside Coun; Calif Planning & Conserv League; Bus & Prof Womens Club (chmn polit action comt, South Pasadena chap); South Pasadena High Sch PTA. Relig: Catholic. Mailing Add: 1534 Ramona Ave South Pasadena CA 91030

ARNOLD, CLIFFORD DELOS (D)
Ind State Rep
b Hobart, Ind, July 20, 20; s Lloyd Charles Arnold & Mamie Johnson A; m 1940 to Opal Louise Russell; c James Robert. Educ: Emerson High Sch, Gary, Ind, 2 years; law enforcement seminars; US Fed Narcotic Sch. Polit & Govt Pos: Dem precinct committeeman, Michigan City, Ind, 50-63; sheriff, LaPorte Co, 63-71; Ind State Rep, 71- Bus & Prof Pos: With LaPorte Co Police, Ind, 55-71; pub rels, Allied Agents, Inc, Indianapolis, 71- Mil Serv: Entered as PO 3/C, Navy, 43, released as 3rd grade, 45, after serv aboard ship, Pac, 44-45; various overseas citations. Publ: Indiana Police Officers Criminal Law Manual, privately publ, 59. Mem: Nat & Ind Sheriffs Asns; Moose; Eagles; Am Legion; VFW; Lions. Honors & Awards: Jaycees Civic Award; YMCA Youth Award; FBI Citation for capture of two sets of bank robbers & police officer killers. Legal Res: 203 Finch Trail TC Michigan City IN 46360 Mailing Add: House of Reps Capitol Bldg Indianapolis IN 46204

ARNOLD, JIM (D)
Mo State Rep
b South Bend, Ind, Jan 7, 35; s Earl Arnold & Maude Irvine A; m 1964 to Katherine I Doyle; c Bruce Wayne & Earl Bradley. Educ: Tri-State Col, BS, 57; Univ Mo-Columbia, MBA, 71; Alpha Sigma Phi. Polit & Govt Pos: Mo State Rep, currently. Bus & Prof Pos: Owner, Jim Arnold Agency, Waynesville, currently. Mil Serv: Entered as Pvt, Army, 58, released as SP-4, 60, after serv in Comptroller Sect, Ft Leonard Wood, Mo. Mem: Mason; Scottish Rite Bodies; Shrine; CofC; Optimist. Relig: Baptist. Mailing Add: Rte 1 Waynesville MO 65583

ARNOLD, JOHN BURLEIGH (D)
Mem, Mo State Dem Comt
b Lewistown, Mo, May 12, 31; s Egbert F Arnold & Geneva Madge Harris A; m 1952 to Mary Carolyn Brookhart (deceased); c Victor John, Charles Andrew & Sharis Leigh. Educ: Northeast Mo State Teachers Col, 49-52; Univ Mo Sch Law, LLB, 55; Sigma Tau Gamma. Polit & Govt Pos: Probate & magistrate judge, Schuyler Co, Mo, 57-58; Asst Attorney Gen, Mo, 58-60; admin asst to Gov John M Dalton, Mo, 61-62; chmn Speaker's Bur, Mo State Dem Comt, 62-64, mem, Mo State Dem Comt, Eighth Cong Dist, 62-; deleg-at-lg, Dem Nat Conv, 64, 68 & 72. Bus & Prof Pos: Instr, Northeast Mo State Teachers Col, 57-58; vpres & trust officer, Cent Mo Trust Co, 62- Mil Serv: 1st Lt, Army, 57, serv in Judge Advocate Gen Corps. Mem: Mo Bar Asn; Am Bankers Asn; Mo Asn for Social Welfare; Mo Good Roads Asn; CofC. Relig: Christian Church. Legal Res: 1209 Major Dr Jefferson City MO 65101 Mailing Add: 238 Madison St Jefferson City MO 65101

ARNOLD, JOHN HENRY (R)
Del State Rep
b Mountain City, Tenn, Oct 17, 27; s James Benjamin Arnold & Mary Swift A; m 1952 to Lois Irene McKinney; c Linda M, Sharon K, Donna C, Brenda J, Nancy L & Janet L. Educ: Johnson Co High Sch, Tenn, grad, 48. Polit & Govt Pos: Rep dist committeeman, 62-65; Rep dist chmn, 65-72; Del State Rep, 72- Bus & Prof Pos: RR switchman, 54-65, supvr, 65- Mil Serv: Entered as Pvt, Marine Corps, 48, released as S/Sgt, 52, after serv in 1st Marine Div, Korean War, 50-51; G/Sgt, Res, 53-60; 5 Battle Stars; 3 Presidential Unit Citations; Korean Serv Medal; Letter of Commendation. Mem: Lions; Kiamensi Civic Asn. Relig: Church of Christ. Mailing Add: 2223 Downing Lane Wilmington DE 19804

ARNOLD, JOHN P (R)
NH State Rep
Mailing Add: Old County Rd Fracestown NH 03043

ARNOLD, JOHN ROBERT (R)
Chmn, Oktibbeha Co Rep Party, Miss
b Wattensaw, Ark, May 17, 23; s Murray Hunter Arnold & Ruth Steele A; m 1950 to Mary Ann Ficklin; c Elizabeth, Margaret, Carrie, Hunter & Mary. Educ: Miss State Univ, BS, 44. Polit & Govt Pos: Chmn, Oktibbeha Co Rep Party, Miss, 64-; mem exec comt, Miss Rep Party, currently. Bus & Prof Pos: Owner, John R Arnold Farms, 44-69; pres, Howard Furniture Mfg Co, Inc, 57-69, Dodge City, 65-69, Herschede Hall Clock Co, 67-69 & Dodge City Enterprises, 68-69. Mil Serv: Pvt, Army, 43, serv in Training Unit, Ft McClellan. Mem:

Farm Bur; Rotary; Sessums Community Club. Relig: United Methodist. Mailing Add: Sessums MS 39758

ARNOLD, LAVERNE VIRGINIA (R)
Mem Exec Comt, Mich State Rep Cent Comt
b North Little Rock, Ark, June 7, 29; d Adolphos Lofton & Theodore Lacey L; m 1950 to Stephen Douglass Arnold; c Kimberly. Educ: AM&N Col, 47-49; Wayne State Univ, 70-72. Polit & Govt Pos: Precinct deleg & coordr, 13th Cong Dist, 70-; alt deleg, Rep Nat Conv, 72; conv reorgn chmn, Gov Party Revision & Redevelop Comt, 72-74; mem, Gov Recreation Adv Comt, Lansing, 72-; jury comnr, Detroit Recorders Court, 73-; chmn, Mich for Milliken, 13th Cong Dist, 74; mem exec comt & mem Rule 29 Comt, Mich State Rep Cent Comt, 75- Bus & Prof Pos: Property mgt, Arnold's, 50-; owner & mgr, Arnold's Mkt, 65-; secy, Bus United with Officers & Youth, 71-73; notary pub, Wayne Co, Mich, 71- Mem: Community Dist Coun; Dist Coord Coun (secy, 74-). Relig: Protestant. Legal Res: 2900 Magnolia Detroit MI 48208 Mailing Add: 3607 Lawton Detroit MI 48208

ARNOLD, MARTIN BLAIR (D)
b Batesville, Ark, Mar 2, 53; s William Joshua Arnold & Bobbye McAlister A; single. Educ: Univ Ark, BA, 75; Vanderbilt Univ Law Sch, 75-; Phi Beta Kappa; Blue Key; Sigma Nu. Polit & Govt Pos: Summer intern, US Rep, Wilbur D Mills, Ark, 71 & 73; dir of transportation, Mills for President Comt, 72; deleg, Dem State Conv, 72; alt deleg & mem, credentials comt, Dem Nat Conv, 72. Honors & Awards: Cardinal XX Award, Univ Ark, 72, William Jennings Bryan Award, 75. Relig: Methodist. Mailing Add: 1775 Maple St Batesville AR 72501

ARNOLD, NORBERT (DFL)
Minn State Sen
Legal Res: Rte 1 Box 93 Pengilly MN 55775 Mailing Add: State Capitol Bldg St Paul MN 55155

ARNOLD, ROBERT ALMERINE (D)
b Latham, Kans, Mar 27, 21; s Orville Arnold & Elsie McCullough A; m 1943 to Doris Jane Klassen; c Larry Gene & Robert John. Educ: McPherson Col, 40-42. Polit & Govt Pos: Chmn, Young Dem Club, Kans, 52-58, Marion Co Dem Club, 62-68, Fourth Dist Dem Party, formerly & State Credit Union Dept, 68-; mem, Credit Union Coun, 68- Bus & Prof Pos: Chmn, Cuna Mutual Ins Soc-Policyowners Rep, 64-67, secy, 67-69. Mil Serv: Entered as Pvt, Army, 40, released as Sgt, 43, after serv in Co F 137th Inf, 35th Div. Mem: Mutual Ins Agents; Cues For Credit Unions; Kans Credit Union League; Kiwanis; CofC. Relig: Protestant. Legal Res: 306 S Kennedy Hillsboro KS 67063 Mailing Add: Box 3 Hillsboro KS 67063

ARNOLD, S G (R)
Colo State Rep
Mailing Add: 815 Park Lane Boulder CO 80302

ARONOFF, STANLEY J (R)
Ohio State Sen
b Cincinnati, Ohio, June 8, 32; s Irwin I Aronoff & Cecelia Hyman A; m 1958 to Gretchen Vicky Schwab; c Tracy, Jay & Leslie. Educ: Harvard Col & Law Sch; Harvard Glee Club. Polit & Govt Pos: Ohio State Rep, 60-66; Ohio State Sen, 66-; mem, Coun of State Govt, currently. Bus & Prof Pos: Arbitrator, Am Arbit Asn, 66. Mil Serv: Cpl, Army, 57; Soldier of Cycle. Publ: J Am Air Law & Com. Mem: Am, Ohio & Cincinnati Bar Asns. Relig: Jewish. Mailing Add: 700 Tri-State Bldg Cincinnati OH 45202

ARRANTS, JAMES CLATOR (D)
SC State Rep
b Kershaw Co, SC, Feb 25, 17; s Henry C Arrants & Ava McLeod A; m 1963 to Betty Smoak Carter; c Margaret Brock (by first marriage), Donald Rutledge & Duncan Andrew. Educ: Berry Col, BS, 39; Univ SC, LLB, 47. Polit & Govt Pos: SC State Rep, 41-42, 47-48 & 63-; SC State Sen, 51-54. Bus & Prof Pos: Teacher, Mt Pisgah & Iva High Schs; lawyer, currently. Mil Serv: Navy, 42-46. Mem: Am Legion; VFW; Kiwanis. Relig: Methodist. Bd Stewards & Sunday Sch Teacher, Lyttleton St Methodist Church. Mailing Add: Springdale Dr Camden SC 29020

ARREDONDO, DAVID ZALDIVAR (D)
b Lorain, Ohio, Aug 30, 50; s Apolinar Arredondo & Eva Zaldivar A; single. Educ: Miami Univ, AB in Polit Sci, 72; Nat Univ Mex, 73- Polit & Govt Pos: Deleg, Dem Nat Conv, 72; state dir, La Raza de Ohio por McGovern-Shriver, 72. Publ: Latins should unite for progress, Horvitz Papers, 5/72. Mem: United Farm Workers Cincinnati Comt; United Steelworkers of Am Local 1104; Farm Labor Active Students Comt (founder & chmn, 71-72). Relig: Roman Catholic. Mailing Add: 1959 E 36th St Lorain OH 44055

ARRELL, WILLIAM HENRY (DFL)
b Minneapolis, Minn, Dec 18, 17; s William Henry Arrell & Armine Mingo A; m 1940 to Jeanette Marie Gaulke; c Richard, James & Mary Joanne. Educ: Anoka High Sch, Minn, 3 years. Polit & Govt Pos: Mem govt study comt, Brooklyn Center, Minn, 62-63, chmn charter comn, 64-70 & Dem-Farmer-Labor, 69-; chmn, 32nd Sen Dist Dem-Farmer-Labor Party, formerly; deleg, Minn State Dem-Farmer-Labor Conv, 70- Bus & Prof Pos: Salesman, Am Baking Co, Minneapolis Metrop Area, Minn, 44-; steward, Teamsters Local 289, 55-, exec bd mem, 59-, vpres, 67- Mil Serv: Entered as Pvt, Army, 43, released as Pfc, 44, after serv in 392 FAB Inf Div 42. Mem: Am Legion; KofC; Brooklyn Center Hist Soc. Relig: Catholic. Mailing Add: 7019 Perry Ave Brooklyn Center MN 55429

ARRINGTON, GRADY P (D)
Ark State Rep
Mailing Add: 223 Green St Stephens AR 71764

ARRINGTON, JAMES HUGH (D)
b Ozark, Ark, May 23, 04; s William H Arrington & Laura T Fulks A; m 1930 to Veneta C Berry; c Harriet V (Mrs Griffith), Aneta (Mrs Davis) & Laura Berry (Mrs Nigliazzo). Educ: Ark Polytech Col; Okla State Univ; Sigma Nu; Red Red Rose; Okla State Univ Hall of Fame; Okla State Univ Pres Club; Ark Tech Hall of Distinction. Polit & Govt Pos: Chmn, Okla State Dem Cent Comt, 40-46; Okla State Rep, 42-60; Dem Nat Committeeman, Okla, 56-58; deleg, Dem Nat Conv, 68. Bus & Prof Pos: Supt, Alix Pub Schs, 27-29; athletic coach & teacher, Ripley High Sch, 31-33; partner, Ripley Rev; mgr, ranch; buyer, Lake Carl Blackwell Proj, 33-35; pres, Marco Corp, dir, Stillwater Nat Bank & Trust Co, 72- Mem: Mid-Continent Asn; Am Petrol Inst; Isaac Walton League; Okla City Press Asn; Okla Jack & Jennet Asn. Relig: Latter-day Saint. Legal Res: 1724 Kingsbury Lane Oklahoma City OK 73116 Mailing Add: 813 Cravens Bldg Oklahoma City OK 73102

ARRINGTON, ROBERT ERSKIN (D)
Miss State Rep
b Poplarville, Miss, Sept 29, 20; s Arthur Day Arrington & Bessie Peeler A; m 1953 to Elsie Marie McDowell; c James Robert, Robert E, Jr, Plemon Lee & Dawn Marie. Educ: Cranstons Commercial Sch, 46-48; LaSalle Exten Univ, 48-52. Polit & Govt Pos: Miss State Rep, Dist 39, 72- Mil Serv: Entered as Seaman, Navy, 43, released as PO 2/C, 46, after serv in USS Albany, 50-52; Victory, World War II & Korean War Medals. Mem: Hattiesburg Area CofC; Am Legion, Allen B Carter Post; Miss State & Am Bar Asns; SCent Bar Asn. Relig: Baptist. Legal Res: 208 S 24th Ave Hattiesburg MS 39401 Mailing Add: PO Box 22 Hattiesburg MS 39401

ARTERBURN, NORMAN F
Chief Justice, Ind Supreme Court
b Bicknell, Ind, May 13, 02; s Clay H Arterburn & Anna Hoover A; wid; c Faith (Mrs Nicholson), Linda (Mrs Ridgley) & Joan. Educ: Ind Univ, AB, 23; Univ Chicago Law Sch, JD. Polit & Govt Pos: Prosecuting attorney, 12th Judicial Circuit of Ind, 28-30; mem & pres, Ind State Bd Law Exam, 38-44; mem bd mgrs, Ind State Bar Asn, 40-42; Judge, Supreme Court Ind, 55-71, Chief Justice, 71- Bus & Prof Pos: Vis prof law, Ind State Bar Asn; prof law, Washburn Col Law Sch, 28; attorney, Kessinger, Hill & Arterburn, Hill & Arterburn and Arterburn & Hart, 30-54. Publ: Legal publ in Ill, Mich, Pa & Ind Law J. Mem: Mason (32 degree); Shrine; Columbia Club; Kiwanis; CofC. Honors & Awards: Ky Col. Relig: Methodist. Mailing Add: State House Supreme Court Indianapolis IN 46204

ARTERTON, FREDERICK CHRISTOPHER (D)
b New York, NY, Oct 22, 42; s Frederick Harry Arterton & Eleanor Bell A; m 1966 to Janet MacArthur Bond; c Cameron duBignon. Educ: Trinity Col (Conn), BA, 66; Sch Int Serv, Am Univ, MA, 68; Mass Inst Technol, PhD, 73; Pi Sigma Alpha, Phi Kappa Phi; Alpha Chi Rho. Polit & Govt Pos: Co-chairperson, Mass Youth Caucus, 71-72; platform dir, Nat Youth Caucus, 72; nat bd mem, Am for Dem Action, 72-; deleg, Dem Nat Conv, 72; mem drafting subcomt, Dem Platform Comt, 72; mem nat steering comt, New Dem Coalition, 72-; research dir, Mass Inst Technol Task Force on Middlesex Co, 72-73. Bus & Prof Pos: Instr, Wellesley Col, 73. Relig: Episcopal. Mailing Add: 335 Lake Ave Newton MA 02161

ARTHUR, JAMES M (D)
SC State Rep
Mailing Add: Box 705 Union SC 29379

ARTHURS, JACK R (D)
Pa State Rep
Mailing Add: Capitol Bldg Harrisburg PA 17120

ARTRIP, WILLIAM JAMES, JR (D)
WVa State Deleg
b Clintwood, Va, July 16, 24; s William James Artrip, Sr & Lydia Rebecca Childress A; m 1949 to Phyllis Jean Hoff; c William James III & Kimberly Jean. Educ: Va Polytech Inst, 42-43, 46-47; Med Col Va Sch Dent, DDS, 51; Psi Omega. Polit & Govt Pos: WVa State Deleg, 75- Mil Serv: Air Force, 43-46, serv in 8th Air Force, ETO, 44-45. Mem: Rotary; WVa State Hist Soc; Mason Co Hist Soc (pres); Boy Scouts (dist comnr). Relig: Protestant. Mailing Add: Box 6 Southside WV 25187

ARTS, JAMES L (D)
Chairperson, Rusk Co Dem Party, Wis
b Ladysmith, Wis, Jan 15, 45; s Laurence J Arts & Genevieve Dvorak A; m 1973 to Waltraud A Stanchak. Educ: Univ Wis-Madison, 63-64; Ind Univ, Bloomington, 65-66; Univ Wis-River Falls, grad, 73. Polit & Govt Pos: Registr of deeds, Rusk Co, Wis, 73-; chairperson, Rusk Co Dem Party, 75- Mil Serv: Entered as Airman Basic, Air Force, 65, released as S/Sgt, 69, after serv in Security Serv. Mailing Add: Rte 3 Ladysmith WI 54848

ARTY, MARY ANN (R)
b Philadelphia, Pa, Nov 24, 26; d Henry J Scheid (deceased) & Pearl Van Dike S; m to Thomas B Arty; c James Scheid, Janis Marie & John Thomas. Educ: Med Col Pa, Sch Nursing, dipl, 47; Temple Univ, 49-50; West Chester State Col, BS in Educ, 67; Univ Pa, 68; pres, Para Med Asn, 66-67. Polit & Govt Pos: Vpres & legis chmn, Womans Rep Club of Delaware Co, Pa, 66-68, mem exec bd & parliamentarian, 68-; Rep committeewoman, Second Ward, First Precinct, Springfield Twp, 67-; deleg, White House Conf on Children, 70; secy, Delaware Co Rep Exec Comt, 70-72; deleg & mem rules comt, Rep Nat Conv, 72; secy, Delaware Co Govt Study Comn, 73-; secy, Springfield Rep Party, 74- Bus & Prof Pos: Pediatrics nurse specialist for John C Williams, MD, 47-51; head nurse-supvr, faculty rep, Dept Pediat, Hosp of Med Col, Pa, 52-54, instr pediatric nursing, 54-64; dir health dept, & health officer, Springfield Twp, 65- Mil Serv: Cadet Nurse Corps, Med Col Pa, 44-47. Publ: Co-auth, Sex education & family life bibliography, Para Med Asn, West Chester State Col, Pa Dept Health, 67. Mem: Am Pub Health Asn; Pa Pub Health Asn (secy, 74-); Nat Environ Health Asn, Southeast Pa Chap; Am Nurses Asn; Delaware Co Venereal Disease Educ Comt (exec bd). Honors & Awards: Outstanding Grad Nursing Prog, West Chester State Col, 67; Benjamin Rush Award, Delaware Co Med Soc, 72; Gov Award, 74. Relig: Lutheran. Mailing Add: 527 LeHann Circle Springfield PA 19064

ARVEY, JACOB M (D)
Dem Nat Committeeman, Ill
b Chicago, Ill, Nov 3, 95; s Israel Arvey & Bertha Eisenberg A; m 1916 to Edity Freeman; c Erwin, Howard & Helen Sue (Mrs Bresky). Educ: John Marshall Law Sch. Hon Degrees: LLD, Jewish Theol Sem, 66. Polit & Govt Pos: Alderman, 24th Ward, Chicago, Ill, 23-41, committeeman, 34-41; comnr, Chicago Park Dist, 45-67; chmn, Cook Co Dem Party, 46-50; Dem Nat Committeeman, Ill, 50-; deleg, Dem Nat Conv, 48-72. Bus & Prof Pos: Sr mem, Arvey, Hodes & Mantynband & Predecessor Firms, 26- Mil Serv: Entered as Capt, Army, 41, released as Lt Col, 45, after serv in 33rd Inf Div, Pac Theater; Bronze Star with Cluster; Legion of Merit. Publ: Politics, USA; As We Knew Adlai. Mem: Am & Fed Bar Asns; Am Friends of the Hebrew Univ; Nat Adv Coun Synagogue Coun of Am; Am Legion. Relig: Jewish. Legal Res: 2300 N Lincoln Park W Chicago IL 60614 Mailing Add: 1 N La Salle St Chicago IL 60602

ARVIZU, ARTHUR A (D)
Mem, Kern Co Dem Cent Comt, Calif
b Arvin, Calif, Feb 11, 27; s Arthur Ortiz Arvizu & Rachel Vargas A; m 1950 to Mary Frances Schemmel; c Arthur Rahe, Anthony James, Robert John, John Thomas, William Scott, Mary Rachel & Lorraine Francis. Educ: Bakersfield Col, AA in Bus Admin, 48; Alpha Gamma Sigma. Polit & Govt Pos: Treas, Kern Co Dem Cent Comt, 62-64, chmn, 64-66, mem, 66-; mem exec comt, Calif Dem Cent Comt, 64-66; chmn, Kern Co Dem Campaign Comt, 64, chmn elec comt, 64-66; chmn, Viva Brown Comt, 66; deleg, Dem Nat Conv, 68, alt deleg, 72; chmn, Kern Co Econ Opportunity Corp, 68 & 69. Bus & Prof Pos: Pres, Kern Co Fire Dept Benefit & Welfare Asn, 53; organizing pres, Kern Co Fire Fighters Union 1301, 58, pres, 63-64, vpres, 65-; legis rep, Local 1301, 63-64; chmn, Cent Calif Action Assocs, Inc, 68. Mil Serv: Entered as Seaman 2/C, Navy, 44, released as Signalman 3/C, 46, after serv in Commun Pool, SPac; New Guinea & Philippine Theater Ribbons; Okinawa Campaign Ribbon with Bronze Star; Victory Medal. Relig: Catholic. Mailing Add: 2200 Camino Real Bakersfield CA 93305

ASH, ROY L (R)
b Los Angeles, Calif, Oct 20, 18; s Charles K Ash & Fay Dickinson A; m 1943 to Lila M Hornbek; c Loretta (Mrs T T Ackerson, II), Marilyn (Mrs R Stanley Hodge, Jr), James F, Robert C & Charles E. Educ: Harvard Univ, MBA, 47. Polit & Govt Pos: Chmn, President's Adv Coun on Exec Orgn, 69-71; asst to the President, 73-74; dir, Off Mgt & Budget, 73-75. Bus & Prof Pos: Various pos, Bank of Am, 36-49; asst comptroller & chief financial officer, Hughes Aircraft Co, 49-53; co-founder, dir & pres, Litton Industs, Inc, 53-72. Mil Serv: Entered as Pvt, Air Force, 42, released as Capt, 46. Honors & Awards: Baker Scholar, Harvard Univ Grad Sch Bus Admin, 47, Bus Achievement, Harvard Bus Sch, 68; Horatio Alger Award, Am Schs & Cols Asn, 66; Annual Award for Outstanding Exec Mgt, Univ Calif, Los Angeles Grad Sch Bus Admin, 70-71. Relig: Catholic. Mailing Add: 655 Funchal Rd Los Angeles CA 90024

ASHBACH, ROBERT O (R)
Minn State Sen
Polit & Govt Pos: Minn State Rep, formerly; Minn State Sen, 67-Bus & Prof Pos: Pres, construction co. Mailing Add: 1585 Lake Johanna Blvd St Paul MN 55112

ASHBROOK, EDWARD H (R)
Committeeman, Conn Rep State Cent Comt
b Norwalk, Conn, Dec 7, 10; s Samuel Ashbrook & Nellie Hanley A; m 1930 to Mae Wilson; c Shirley (Mrs Donald Byington), Lois (Mrs Joseph Kelley) & Edward, Jr. Educ: Norwalk High Sch. Polit & Govt Pos: Chmn, Norwalk Town Rep Comt, Conn, formerly; committeeman, Conn Rep State Cent Comt, 25th Sen Dist, currently. Mailing Add: 23 Willow St Norwalk CT 06851

ASHBROOK, JOHN MILAN (R)
US Rep, Ohio
b Johnstown, Ohio, Sept 21, 28; s William A Ashbrook & Marie Swank A; m to Jean Spencer; c Barbara, Laura & Madeline. Educ: Harvard Univ, BS with honors, 52; Ohio State Law Sch, JD, 55; Ashland Col, LLD, 63; Delta Theta Phi; Sigma Delta Chi. Polit & Govt Pos: Precinct committeeman, Johnstown Rep Party, Ohio, 54-; chmn, Licking Co Rep Cent Comt, 56-60; chmn, Young Rep Nat Fedn, 57-59; Ohio State Rep, 57-60; chmn, Ohio League Young Rep, 55; US Rep, 17th Dist, Ohio, 61- Bus & Prof Pos: Publ, Johnstown Independent, 53-; spec counsel to Attorney Gen of Ohio, 55-57; attorney-at-law, 55-; publ, Granville Sentinel & Centerburg Gazette, currently. Mil Serv: Navy, 46-48; mem, Byrd Antarctic Exped, 46-47. Mem: Am Conservative Union; Mason (32 degree); KofP; Kiwanis; Lions. Honors & Awards: Named as one of 15 Outstanding Young Men in Politics in US by Sen Paul Douglas, Esquire Mag, 58. Relig: Baptist. Legal Res: 57 S Main St Johnstown OH 43031 Mailing Add: 1436 Longworth House Off Bldg Washington DC 20515

ASHBY, RODERIC ROLAND (D)
Treas, Mississippi Co Dem Cent Comt, Mo
b Charleston, Mo, Dec 28, 19; s Frank Kelly Ashby & Effie Mae Anderson A; m 1943 to Frances Jeanette Fox; c Leslie Ann & Roderic Roland, Jr. Educ: Univ Mo, BS & JD; Phi Delta Phi. Polit & Govt Pos: Prosecuting attorney, Mississippi Co, Mo, 48-; treas, Mississippi Co Dem Cent Comt, 48- Mil Serv: Entered as A/S, Coast Guard, 42, released as 2nd Lt, 45, after serv in Atlantic & Pac, Am & European Theatres, 42-45. Mem: Am Bar Asn; Mason; Shrine; VFW; Am Legion. Relig: Methodist. Mailing Add: 1210 E Commercial St Charleston MO 63834

ASHCRAFT, NITA WENTNER (R)
VChmn, Rep State Cent Comt of Calif
b Amarillo, Tex, June 25, 21; d Atha Pike, foster mother; m to Wayne W Wentner, wid; m to Hale Ashcraft; c Martha (Mrs Philip Koch) & Joy (Mrs James Pratt). Educ: Loretta Heights Col, 37-38. Polit & Govt Pos: Mem, Co Rep Cent Comt, Calif, 65-; mem exec comt, Rep State Cent Comt of Calif, 66-, vchmn Northern dist, 71-; asst appointment secy, Gov Reagan, 67; mem, Calif State Personnel Bd, 67-; deleg & mem platform comt, Rep Nat Conv, 68 & 72; app pres, Calif State Personnel Bd, 70-; mem, Gov Comt on Personnel, currently. Bus & Prof Pos: Real estate salesman, Calif, 56-; life ins broker, 64- Mem: Calif Real Estate Asn; Nat Underwriters Asn. Relig: Protestant. Mailing Add: 2619 Fox Plaza San Francisco CA 94102

ASHCROFT, JOHN DAVID (R)
State Auditor, Mo
b Chicago, Ill, May 9, 42; s James Robert Ashcroft & Grace Pauline Larson A; m 1967 to Janet Elise Roede; c Martha. Educ: Yale Univ, AB, cum laude, 64; Univ Chicago Law Sch, JD, 67; Phi Delta Phi; Phi Sigma Epsilon. Polit & Govt Pos: State Auditor, Mo, 73- Bus & Prof Pos: Asst prof, Southwest Mo State Univ, 67-71, coordr for judicial affairs, 69-73, assoc prof, 71-73. Publ: Co-auth, College law for business, South-Western Publ Co, 71. Mem: Am & Greene Co Bar Asns; Rotary Club Springfield Southeast (2nd vpres); Greene Co Red Cross, Springfield (exec bd); Sunshine Children's Home (dir). Relig: Assemblies of God. Legal Res: Rte 2 Willard MO 65781 Mailing Add: State Auditor's Off Capitol Bldg Jefferson City MO 65101

ASHE, HARRY B (R)
Vt State Rep
Mailing Add: RFD No 3 Barre VT 05641

ASHE, VICTOR HENDERSON (R)
Tenn State Sen
b Knoxville, Tenn, Jan 1, 45; s Robert L Ashe & Martha Henderson A; single. Educ: The Hotchkiss Sch, Lakeville, Conn, 61-63; Yale Univ, BA, 67; Univ Tenn Law Sch, student, 69- Polit & Govt Pos: Aide to Dan H KuyKendall, 64; intern under US Rep Bill Brock, 65; press aide to US Sen Howard H Baker, Jr, 66 & legis aide, 67; Tenn State Rep, 68-74; Tenn State Sen, 75- Mil Serv: Entered as Pvt, Marines, 67, released as Pfc, 68, after serv in Air Wing, San Diego, Memphis, & Jacksonville; Marine Air Res, 68-, Cpl. Mem: East Tenn Heart Fund Bd; Helen Ross McNabb Ment Health Ctr; bd mem, Knox Co Asn of Retarded Children; Civitan Club of Knoxville; Cherokee Country Club. Relig: Baptist. Mailing Add: Box 1382 Knoxville TN 37901

ASHEN, PETE (R)
Mem, San Francisco Co Rep Cent Comt
b Bakersfield, Calif, Sept 20, 27; s Claude Holbert Ashen & Lotta Mae McElroy A; m 1947 to Catherine Irene Grandin; c Claude Frank & Mary Catherine. Polit & Govt Pos: Pres, Calif Young Rep, 61; vchmn, Nat Fedn of Young Rep, 61-63; mem, San Francisco Co Rep Cent Comt, currently, sgt at arms, 68-70, parliamentarian, 70- Bus & Prof Pos: Sales mgr, Milo Harding Co, 52-60; agt, John Hancock Mutual Life Ins Co, 60-66; dir disaster serv, Golden Gate chap, Am Nat Red Cross, 66- Mil Serv: Entered as Seaman, Navy, 45-48 & 50-52, released as Aviation Tech 1/C, after serv in VP-2, Pac & Far East. Mem: F&AM. Relig: Protestant. Mailing Add: 67 Cityview Way San Francisco CA 94131

ASHER, KATHLEEN MAY (D)
Chairperson, Tuscola Co Dem Comt, Mich
b Vassar, Mich, Aug 19, 32; d Thomas Henry Pierce & Jessie Smith P; m 1957 to Donald William Asher; c David & Diane. Educ: Cent Mich Univ, BS, 56, MA, 66; Delta Zeta. Polit & Govt Pos: Mgr, Vassar Dem Hq, Mich, 72; alt, Mich Dem State Cent Comt, 72-74; mem exec comt, Tuscola Co Dem Comt, 72-, chairperson, 75-; precinct deleg, Vassar, 74. Bus & Prof Pos: Speech & dramatics teacher, Standish High Sch, Vassar, Mich, 57-60 & Vassar High Sch, 60-67; speech commun instr, Charles Stewart Mott Community Col, 67-72 & dir women's progs, 72- Mem: Nat & Mich Educ Asns; Mich Women's Studies Asn (pres elect, 75); YWCA (bd dirs, 75); Delta Kappa Gamma. Relig: Presbyterian. Mailing Add: 122 Jefferson St Vassar MI 48768

ASHER, WILLIAM EDWARD (R)
Mont State Rep
b St Louis, Mo, May 17, 40; s Jewel William Asher & Clara Marlen A; m 1959 to Jacqualine Ann Burns; c William Edward, Jr, John Wesley, Jesse Wayne & Benjamin Wade. Educ: High sch, Whittier, Calif, 54-58. Polit & Govt Pos: Mont State Rep, 75- Bus & Prof Pos: Custom cattle hoof trimmer, Bill Asher & Sons, currently. Mem: Life mem Nat Rifle Asn; Farm Bur. Relig: Protestant. Mailing Add: PO Box 467 Manhattan MT 59741

ASHFORD, CHARLIE R (R)
Tenn State Rep
Mailing Add: 701 44 N Second St Memphis TN 38103

ASHLEY, RANDOLPH ALEXANDER, JR (D)
Attorney Gen, Tenn
b Dyersburg, Tenn, Nov 18, 27; s Randolph Alexander Ashley & Mary Maude Barret A; m 1953 to Betty Sue Volz; c Randolph Alexander, III, Jane Barret & Anne Craig. Educ: Southwestern at Memphis, BA, 50; Univ Tenn Col Law, JD, 52; Phi Delta Phi; Omicron Delta Kappa; Sigma Alpha Epsilon. Polit & Govt Pos: Attorney Gen, Tenn, 74- Bus & Prof Pos: Pvt practice of law, 53-74. Mil Serv: Entered as Pvt, Army Air Force, 46, released as Cpl, 47, after serv in Tech Training Command, Continental US. Mem: Am & Tenn Bar Asns; Am & Tenn Trial Lawyers Asn. Relig: Cumberland Presbyterian. Legal Res: 816 Cooper Dr Dyersburg TN 38024 Mailing Add: Supreme Ct Bldg Nashville TN 37219

ASHLEY, THOMAS LUDLOW (D)
US Rep, Ohio
b Toledo, Ohio, Jan 11, 23; s Meredith Ashley & Alida A; m 1967 to Kathleen Marie Lucey; c William Meredith & Mark Michael. Educ: Yale Univ, BA, 48, Univ Toledo Law Sch; Ohio State Univ, LLB, 51. Polit & Govt Pos: With Toledo Publicity & Efficiency Comn, Ohio, 48; US Rep, Ninth Dist, Ohio, 54-, mem, Merchant Marine & Fisheries Comt, US House Rep, 55-, ranking mem banking & currency comt & budget comt, 74-; deleg, Dem Nat Conv, 68. Bus & Prof Pos: Lawyer, Whitehouse, Ohio, 51-52; co-dir press sect & then asst dir spec projs, Radio Free Europe, 52-54. Mil Serv: Entered Army, 42, released as Cpl, 46, after serv in Pac Theater, 43-45. Mem: Common Cause; VFW; Amvets; Moose; Eagles. Legal Res: 2836 River Rd Maumee OH 43537 Mailing Add: Rayburn Off Bldg Washington DC 20515

ASHMORE, ROBERT THOMAS (D)
b Greenville Co, SC, Feb 22, 04; s John Thomas Ashmore & Lena Smith A; m to Willie Vance Linthicum; c Nancy Vance. Educ: Furman Univ Law Sch, 27. Hon Degrees: LLD, Bob Jones Univ, 68; JD, Furman Univ, 71. Polit & Govt Pos: Solicitor, Greenville Co, SC, 30; solicitor, 13th Judicial Circuit, SC, 36-53; US Rep, SC, 53-69; chmn, SC Appalachian Regional Planning & Develop Comn, currently. Bus & Prof Pos: Lawyer, Greenville, 28- Mil Serv: Army, 42-46, Col, Res. Mem: State Jr CofC (organizer & first pres); US Jr CofC (vpres); JOUAM; Odd Fellows; WOW. Honors & Awards: Key to Spartanburg, SC from Mayor Robert L Stoddard, 68; Life Mem & Senator, Jr Chamber Int, 72. Relig: Baptist. Mailing Add: Manly St Rte 9 Greenville SC 29609

ASHTON, ALICE ELINOR (D)
b San Diego, Calif; d James Ryan & Mary Ellen Tracey R; m 1942 to George F Ashton; c Thomas (deceased), Judith (Mrs Foster), Lawrence, John, Patricia & Mary Ann. Polit & Govt Pos: Membership drive chmn, Redlands Dem Club, Calif, precinct chmn, 66-, vpres, 71-72; deleg, Dem Nat Conv, 68 & 72. Mem: Coordr, Suicide Prev in Redlands. Relig: Catholic. Mailing Add: 1544 Crown St Redlands CA 92373

ASHWORTH, L KEITH (D)
Nev State Assemblyman
b Kimberly, Nev, Sept 4, 24; s John Earl Ashworth & Mary Jane Oxborrow A; m 1945 to Colleen Christensen; c Glen Alan, Kenneth Earl & Brian Keith. Educ: Butler Univ, 45-46; Univ Utah, 46-47. Polit & Govt Pos: Pub adminstr, Clark Co, Nev, 50-54; mem, Las Vegas Youth Adv Coun, 58-64; secy, State Bd of Acct, 60-66; Nev State Assemblyman, Dist 4, currently. Speaker of the Assembly, 73- Bus & Prof Pos: Vpres, Sahara-Nev Corp, currently. Mil Serv: Entered as Aviation Cadet, Air Force, 43, released as Flight Off, 45, after serv in

Pilot Schs, Training Command. Mem: Jaycees; Elks (Past Exalted Ruler); Mason, Shrine; Rotary. Honors & Awards: Outstanding Young Man of Las Vegas & Nev, 1958. Relig: Latter-day Saint. Legal Res: 2805 Ashworth Circle Las Vegas NV 89107 Mailing Add: PO Box 14066 Las Vegas NV 89114

ASHWORTH, LUTHER RAY (D)
Va State Deleg
b Danville, Va, Oct 13, 35; s Clarence Luther Ashworth (deceased) & Nann Eva Mize A; m 1959 to Anne Moyler Munford; c Sallie Quarles, George & Anne. Educ: Univ Richmond; Sigma Alpha Epsilon. Polit & Govt Pos: Mem Wakefield Town Coun, Va, 66-69; Va State Deleg, 70-, mem, Comts Gen Laws, Roads & Internal Navig, Conserv & Natural Resources & Agr, Va House of Deleg. Bus & Prof Pos: Secy, Wakefield Oil Co, Inc, 60-61, pres & treas, 61-; secy, M&L Distributors, Inc, 60-61, pres & treas, 61-; farmer, 61- Mil Serv: Entered as Pvt, Army, 57, released as SP-4, 59, after serv in Western Area Command, Kaiserslautern, Germany, 57-59. Mem: Va Wildlife Asn (bd dirs); Wakefield Sportsmen's & Hunt Club; Mason; KT; RAM. Honors & Awards: Distinguished Serv Award, Jaycees, 62; One of Outstanding Young Men of Am, 65; Meritorious Award, Va Petroleum Industs, 70. Relig: Methodist; chmn, Coun Ministries & teacher, Sunday Sch, Wakefield United Methodist Church. Mailing Add: PO Box 128 Wakefield VA 23888

ASHWORTH, RICHARD ANDREW (R)
Dep Under Secy, Dept Agr
b Atlanta, Ga, Dec 16, 29; s Jesse Andrew Ashworth & Mary Emma Boles A; m 1959 to Mildred Frances Dodson; c Bonnie Suzette, Donna Jill & Penny Kay. Educ: Ga State Univ, dipl in jour, 49; Univ Ga, ABJ, 50; Woodrow Wilson Col Law, LLB, 62; Demosthenian Soc & Gridiron, Univ Ga. Polit & Govt Pos: Press secy to Gov of Ga, Atlanta, 61-65; press asst to Lt Gov of Ga, 63-65; admin asst to US Rep S F Thompson, 67-71; asst to Under Secy, Dept Agr, Washington, DC, 71-74, Dep Under Secy, Dept Agr, 74- Bus & Prof Pos: Attorney-at-law, Wilson, Branch, Barwick & Vandiver, Atlanta, 65-66. Mil Serv: Entered as Pvt, Army, 51, released as Cpl after serv in Hq & Hq Co, 8th Inf Div, Continental US, Ft Jackson, SC, 51-52; Inf Leaders Sch, Ft Jackson. Publ: Auth of numerous articles in Atlanta Const, 49-61. Mem: Am Judicature Soc; State Bar of Ga; Bull Elephants. Honors & Awards: Certs of Merit, Dept of Agr, 72 & 74. Relig: Baptist. Mailing Add: 7602 Jaffrey Rd Oxon Hill MD 20022

ASIAF, PETER GEORGE (D)
Mass State Rep
Mailing Add: State Capitol Boston MA 02133

ASKEW, REUBIN O'D (D)
Gov, Fla
b Muskogee, Okla, Sept 11, 28; m to Donna Lou Harper; c Angela Adair & Kevin O'Donovan. Educ: Fla State Univ, BS, 51; Univ Denver; Univ Fla, LLB, 56. Hon Degrees: Notre Dame Univ, Stetson Univ, Rollins Col & Fla Southern Col. Polit & Govt Pos: Asst co solicitor, Escambia Co, 56-58; Fla State Rep, 58-62; Fla State Sen, 62-70, pres pro tem, Fla State Senate; Gov, Fla, 71- Bus & Prof Pos: Attorney-at-law. Mil Serv: Army Paratroopers, Air Force. Mem: Scottish & York Rite Mason; AAONMS; Rotary; YMCA; Am Legion. Honors & Awards: Profile in Courage Award, John F Kennedy Lodge B'nai B'rith Washington, 72; Nat Wildlife Fedn Spec Award, 72; Conservationist of the Year, Fla Audubon Soc, 73; Nat William Booth Award, Salvation Army, 73; Herbert H Lehman Ethics Medal. Relig: Presbyterian. Mailing Add: Capitol Bldg Tallahassee FL 32304

ASPIN, LES (D)
US Rep, Wis
b Milwaukee, Wis, July 21, 38; s Leslie Aspin & Marie Orth A; m 1969 to Maureen Townsend Shea. Educ: Yale Univ, BA, 60; Oxford Univ, MA, 62; Mass Inst Technol, PhD, 66; Phi Beta Kappa. Polit & Govt Pos: Chmn, First Dist Dem Party, Wis, 69-70; US Rep, First Dist, Wis, 71- Bus & Prof Pos: Staff asst to Walter Heller, Econ Adv, Washington, DC, 63; asst prof econ, Marquette Univ, 69-71. Mil Serv: Entered as Lt, Army, 66, released as Capt, 68, after serv in Off Syst Analysis; Distinguished Serv Award. Mem: Am Legion; Urban Observatory. Relig: Episcopal. Legal Res: 206 15th St Racine WI 53403 Mailing Add: 515 Cannon House Off Bldg Washington DC 20515

ASPINALL, OWEN STEWART (D)
b Grand Junction, Colo, Sept 21, 27; s Wayne N Aspinall & Julia Kuns A; m 1966 to Taotafa Lutu; c Robert Stewart. Educ: Univ Denver, BA in Anthrop, 49; Am Univ, LLB, 55; Beta Theta Pi; Delta Theta Phi. Polit & Govt Pos: Dep dist attorney, Mesa Co, Colo, 57-61; Attorney Gen, Am Samoa, 61-62, Territorial Secy, 62-67, Gov, 67-69; legal counsel, US Comptroller for Territory of Guam & Trust Territories of Pac, Saipan & Marshall Islands, 69-72. Bus & Prof Pos: Pvt law practice, Aspinall & Aspinall, Grand Junction, Colo, currently. Mil Serv: Army, 44-46, with 504th Parachute Inf Regt, 82nd Airborne Div. Mem: Am Bar Asn; Lions Int; Am Legion. Relig: Methodist. Mailing Add: PO Box 1974 Grand Junction CO 81501

ASPINALL, WAYNE NORVIEL (D)
b Middleburg, Ohio, Apr 3, 96; s Mack Aspinall & Jessie Edna Norviel A; m to Julia E Kuns (deceased); m 1970 to Essie Jeffers Best; c Wayne Norviel, Jr, Owen Stewart, Richard Daniel & Ruth JoAnne (Mrs Flora). Educ: Univ Denver, BA, 19; Denver Law Sch, LLB, 25; Beta Theta Pi; Phi Delta Phi; Phi Sigma. Hon Degrees: Doctorate, Univ Alaska, Univ Denver, Colo State Univ, Colo Sch Mines & Mesa Col of Grand Junction. Polit & Govt Pos: App to Mo Basin Surv Comn by President Truman; chmn, Colo State Dem Cent Comt, formerly; chmn, Mesa Co Dem Cent Comt, formerly; secy & chmn, Fourth Cong Dist Dem Cent Comt, formerly; Colo State Rep, 31-34 & 37-38, Dem Whip, Colo House Rep, 33, speaker, 37-38; Colo State Sen, 39-48, Dem Whip, Colo State Senate, 39, majority floor leader, 41, minority floor leader, 43-47; US Rep, Colo, 49-73, chmn interior & insular affairs comt, US House Rep, 59-73; chmn pub land law rev comn, 65-71. Bus & Prof Pos: Pub sch teacher; lawyer; peach orchard indust; dist counsel, Home Owners' Loan Corp, 33-34. Mil Serv: Army, Signal Corps, World War I; Capt, Assigned to Mil Gov Serv, World War II, Legal Expert with US & Eng Forces, participated in Normandy Drive as Am Officer with Brit Second Army. Mem: Am Bar Asn; Am Legion; 40 et 8; Blue Lodge, Mason; Scottish Rite (33 degree). Relig: Methodist. Mailing Add: 150 Aspinall Dr Palisade CO 81526

ASTA, RON (D)
Chmn, Pima Co Bd of Supvr, Ariz
b Sacramento, Calif, Jan 31, 42; s Manuel Joseph Asta & Letitia Del Prete A; div; c Mark & Marissa. Educ: Ore State Univ, BS, 63; Univ Ariz, MS, 65; Phi Delta Theta. Polit & Govt Pos: Chmn, Pima Co Bd Supvr, Ariz, 73-; deleg, Dem Nat Mid-Term Conf, 74. Bus & Prof Pos: Assoc planning dir, Pima Co Planning Dept, 65-72. Mem: Am Inst Planners; Am Soc Civil Engrs; Am Inst Architects; Nat Soc Prof Engrs; Italian Am Club. Relig: Catholic. Mailing Add: 737 N Alvernon Tucson AZ 85711

ATCHISON, CHRISTOPHER GEORGE (R)
b Centerville, Iowa, June 22, 49; s James Lindsay Atchison & Leona Eileen McDonald A; m 1974 to Mary Jo Murphy. Educ: Niles Col of Loyola Univ, Chicago, AB in Polit Sci. Polit & Govt Pos: Research asst, Ill Rep State Cent Comt, 71-73, exec asst to chmn, 73-; precinct committeeman, 73- Legal Res: 1330 W Mossman Springfield IL 62702 Mailing Add: 200 S Second Springfield IL 62701

ATCHISON, JEANNINE COWELL (D)
Mem, Colo Dem State Comt
b Toledo, Ohio, May 13, 29; d Charles Ellis Cowell & Frances Lindbeck C; m 1952 to Philip Atchison; c Timothy & Amy. Educ: Univ Colo, Boulder, AB, 51; Univ Colo, Denver Ctr, grad student, 66-; Pi Gamma Mu; Alpha Phi. Polit & Govt Pos: Mem, Comts to Elect Stevenson, Robert F Kennedy & McCarthy, 57-68; deleg, Colo & Denver Co Dem Conv, 66, 68 & 72; precinct committeewoman, Precinct 13 A, Denver Dem Party, 66-72; mem, Colo Dem State Cent Comt, 69-71; mem, Common Cause, 71; Dem co-capt, Denver Dist 13A, 71-72; Dem capt, Denver Dist 10A, 72-; bd mem, Colo Dem Women's Caucus, 72-; mem, Colo Women's Polit Caucus, 72-; mem, Colo Dem State Comt, currently. Bus & Prof Pos: Sales engr, Pa Indust Instruments Corp, Philadelphia, 52-55. Mem: Denver Art Mus; Friends of Contemporary Art; Ellis Sch PTA; Denver Fair Housing Ctr. Relig: Episcopal. Mailing Add: 1353 S Eudora St Denver CO 80222

ATCHLEY, BEN (R)
Tenn State Rep
Mailing Add: PO Box 436 Knoxville TN 37901

ATCHLEY, FRED C (R)
Tenn State Rep
Mailing Add: Court House Sevierville TN 37862

ATHERTON, ALFRED LEROY, JR
Asst Secy Near Eastern & SAsian Affairs, Dept State
b Pittsburgh, Pa, Nov 22, 21; s Alfred Leroy Atherton & Joan Reed A; m 1946 to Betty Wylie Kittredge; c Lynn Kittredge, Michael Anton & Reed Wylie. Educ: Phillips Exeter Acad, 40; Harvard Univ, BS, 44, MA, 47; Univ Calif, Berkeley, 61-62. Polit & Govt Pos: With Foreign Serv, 47-, vcounsel, Stuttgart, Ger, 47-50, Bonn, Ger, 50-52; second secy, Damascus, Syria, 53-56; counsel, Alippo Syria, 57-59; int rels officer, Bur Near Eastern & SAsian Affairs, Dept State, 59-61, dep dir, 65-66, dep asst secy, 70-74, asst secy, 74-; counsel, Calcutta, India, 62-65; country dir, Arab States North, 66-67; country dir, Israel & Arab Israel Affairs, 67-69. Mil Serv: 1st Lt, AUS, 43-45, ETO Ribbon; Air Medal; Silver Star. Mem: Foreign Serv Asn. Relig: Unitarian. Legal Res: 3400 Ordway St NW Washington DC 20016 Mailing Add: Dept of State Washington DC 20037

ATHERTON, FLORA CAMERON (R)
Mem, Rep Nat Finance Comt
b Waco, Tex; d William Waldo Cameron & Helen Emelyn Miller C; m to Holt Atherton; c Ike Simpson, III & Megan Cameron Kampmann. Educ: Sweet Briar Col. Polit & Govt Pos: Mem, Hq Comt, Tex, 57-58; vchmn, Tex Rep State Exec Comt, 58-60; mem, Rep Nat Comt for Prog & Progress, 59; deleg, Rep Nat Conv, 60 & 64, alternate deleg, 68, secy, Platform Comt, 60, mem, Arrangements Comt for Theme & Entertainment, 64; mem, Rep Nat Comt, 60-65; mem, Rep Nat Finance Comt, 65-; mem, Presidential Mission to Latin Am, 69; US deleg, Inter-Am Comn Women, 69-; mem citizen's stamp adv comt, US Post Off Dept, 69- Bus & Prof Pos: Pres, Kamko Found; mem bd dirs, Certain-Teed Prod Corp, 71- Mem: Sweet Briar Col & Witte Mus (bd of trustees); Trinity Univ (bd of trustees & first chmn pres comt); San Antonio World's Fair; Nat Coun Metrop Opera. Legal Res: 315 Westover Rd San Antonio TX 78209 Mailing Add: 4600 Broadway San Antonio TX 78209

ATHEY, TYRAS S (D)
Md State Deleg
b Burtonsville, Md, Mar 30, 27; s Joseph Tyras Athey & Harriett Dowling A; m 1950 to Dorothy Norine O'Lexey; c Darlene, Bryan & Cathleen. Educ: Pub High Sch, 45. Polit & Govt Pos: Md State Deleg, 67- Bus & Prof Pos: Self-employed restaurant bus, Old Farm Inn, Md, 55- Mil Serv: Entered as HA 2/C, Navy, 43, released as HA 1/C, 45, after serv in USS Constellation, 44-45. Mem: Fraternal Order of Police; VFW; CofC; Elks; Vol Fire Dept. Relig: Protestant. Mailing Add: Box 379F Rte 2 Jessup MD 20794

ATKIN, SIDNEY JOSEPH (R)
Utah State Rep
b St George, Utah, July 26, 34; s Rudger C Atkin & Leona Cox A; m 1957 to Mary Ann Hunt; c Shauna, Natalie, Tracy, Maurice, Cory & Kelly. Educ: Dixie Jr Col, 57-59. Polit & Govt Pos: Chmn, Washington Co Rep Party, Utah, 67-69 & 73-75; Utah State Rep, 69- Bus & Prof Pos: Pres, Sugar Loaf Cafe, Corp, 58- Mil Serv: Entered as Pvt, Nat Guard, 53, released as Sgt 1/C, 58, after serv in Battery B 213 FAT. Mem: Utah State Restaurant Asn; Nat Restaurant Asn; Kiwanis; St George CofC; Dixie Colonels. Honors & Awards: Eagle Scout; Outstanding Bus Student, Dixie Col, 58. Relig: Latter-day Saint. Mailing Add: 46 N 200 East St George UT 84770

ATKINS, CHARLES P (CAB) (D)
Chmn, Boone Co Dem Cent Comt, Mo
b Centralia, Mo, Sept 7, 16; s John E Atkins (deceased) & Mayme Ravenscraft A (deceased); m 1944 to Dorothy Mae Tudor. Educ: US Army Air Force Aviation Cadet Sch, 1 year; Creighton Univ, 1 year; Univ Mo, 1 year. Polit & Govt Pos: Chmn, Centralia Twp Dem Comt, Mo, 66-70; chmn, Boone Co Dem Cent Comt, 70-; mem, Mo State Dem Comt, 72- Bus & Prof Pos: Draftsman, A B Chance Co, Centralia, Mo, 39-49, foreman, 49-50, customer serv mgr, 51-60, mgr inventory, 61-69, mgr warehousing & distribution, 70-; mem, 13th Circuit Judiciary Lay Comt, 71-72; mem, Mo Univ Arthritis Ctr Adv Coun, 71-; mem, Active Vol Coun Pub Health Educ Mo, 73- Mil Serv: Entered as Pvt, Army Air Force, 42, released as Capt, 46, after serv in 20th Air Force, Asiatic-Pac Theatre, 45-46. Mem: Moolah Shrine; Boy Scouts; Rotary Int; Am Legion. Relig: Protestant. Mailing Add: 3 Parkview Dr Centralia MO 65240

ATKINS, CHESTER G **(D)**
Mass State Sen
b Geneva, Switz, Apr 14, 48; s Henry Hornblower Atkins & Karkilie Withington A; single. Educ: Antioch Col, BA in Polit Sci, 70. Polit & Govt Pos: Mass State Rep, 33rd Middlesex Dist, Acton-Concord, 70-72; Mass State Sen, Fifth Middlesex Dist, 73- Publ: Getting elected, Houghton-Mifflin, 73. Legal Res: 21 Seneca Rd Acton MA 01720 Mailing Add: Box 986 Acton MA 01720

ATKINS, HANNAH DIGGS **(D)**
Okla State Rep
b Winston-Salem, NC, Nov 1, 23; d James T Diggs & Mabel Kennedy D; m 1943 to Charles N Atkins, MD; c Edmund, Valerie & Charles, Jr. Educ: St Augustine's Col, BS, 43; Univ Chicago Grad Libr Sch, BLS, 49; Sch Law, Oklahoma City Univ & Univ Okla, 65; Alpha Kappa Alpha. Polit & Govt Pos: Mem, Gov Comn on Status of Women, Okla, 70; mem adv comt on Title III, ESEA, Okla State Bd Educ, 70; Okla State Rep, 69-, mem, Environ Quality Comt, mem, Appropriations & Budget, Pub Health & Welfare & chmn, Ment Health Comts, Okla House Rep, 69-, mem, Comn on Educ & Prof Standards Bd, 71-; deleg, Dem Nat Conv, 72; chmn, Okla Co House Deleg, 75- Bus & Prof Pos: Reporter, Winston-Salem J & Sentinel, 45-48; teacher French, Atkins High Sch, 45-48; research asst biochem, Meharry Med Col, 48-49; reference librarian, Fisk Univ, 49-50; sch librarian, Kimberly Park Elem Sch, 50-51; br librarian, Oklahoma City Pub Libr, 53-56; reference librarian, Okla State Libr, Oklahoma City, 62-63, chief gen reference div & acting law librarian, 63-68, instr libr sci, 67-68; instr law, Oklahoma City Univ, 67. Publ: Various contributions to libr sci jour. Mem: Am Asn Law Libr; Spec Libr Asn (pres, Okla Chap); Nat Freedom to Vote Task Force; Okla Co Ment Health Asn. Honors & Awards: Reference librarian, Libr USA, NY World's Fair, 64; Outstanding Woman of the Year, Okla Soroptomist Int, 65; Outstanding Soror, Midwest Region, Alpha Kappa Alpha, Nat Founders Serv Award, 70; Woman of Year, Theta Sigma Phi, 68; Nat Pub Citizen, Nat Asn Social Work, 75. Relig: Episcopal. Legal Res: 5915 NE 63rd St Oklahoma City OK 73111 Mailing Add: Rte 4 Box 799 Oklahoma City OK 73111

ATKINS, JANE HUDSON **(R)**
Mem, Tenn State Rep Exec Comt
b Shelby Co, Tenn, Jan 8, 37; d John Reed Hudson & Maurice Brigham H; m 1956 to Robert D Atkins; c Robert Hudson, Anne Brigham & Mary Marshall. Educ: Belhaven Col, 53-54; Univ Miss, 54-56; Delta Delta Delta. Polit & Govt Pos: Mem, Gibson Co Rep Exec Comt, Tenn, 64-75; mem, Gibson Co Fedn Rep Women, 69-, chmn, 69-71; chmn, Gibson Co Elec Comn, 70-74; chmn, Gibson Co Rep Party, 72-73; secy-treas, Seventh Dist Rep Exec Comt, 72-; mem, Tenn State Rep Exec Comt, 74- Mem: Capitol Club; Strawberry Festival Asn. Relig: Methodist. Mailing Add: 2300 Chere Carol Rd Humboldt TN 38343

ATKINSON, BEVERLY MOON **(R)**
Committeewoman, Ohio Rep State Cent Comt
b Warren, Ohio, Apr 25, 24; d Henry A Moon & Frances Lehman M; m 1944 to Charles F Atkinson; c Thomas Temple & Amy Allen. Educ: Am Inst of Banking, Youngstown, Ohio, 2 years. Polit & Govt Pos: Rep exec committeeman, Fourth Ward, Warren, Ohio, 60-62; Rep precinct committeeman, Warren 4-C, 60-64; deleg, Ohio Rep State Conv, 66, 68 & 70; committeewoman, Ohio Rep State Cent Comt, 66-; chmn, Women for Nixon-Agnew, 19th Cong Dist, 68; alt deleg, Rep Nat Conv, 68, deleg, 72; Rep precinct committeeman, Warren 3-B, 68-; Rep exec committeeman, Third Ward, Warren, 68-; Trumbull Co Chmn, Roger Cloud for Gov, 70. Mem: Trumbull Co Bar Auxiliary; Martha Kenney Cooper Ohioana Libr Asn (co-chmn); Am Legion Auxiliary; PTA; YWCA. Relig: Baptist; Deaconess, former Sunday Sch teacher. Mailing Add: 530 Oak Knoll NE Warren OH 44483

ATKINSON, HAMP **(D)**
Tex State Rep
Mailing Add: 206 James St New Boston TX 75570

ATKINSON, HARRY EUGENE **(INDEPENDENT)**
Mayor, Newport News, Va
b Newport News, Va, Feb 6, 20; s Joseph Atkinson & Lucille Kempton A; m 1943 to Lora Catherine Thompson; c Karen L & Harry E, Jr. Educ: Marshall Wythe Law Sch, 59-61. Polit & Govt Pos: City councilman, Newport News, Va, 62-66; mayor, Newport News, Va, 74- Mil Serv: Entered as Pvt, 37, Marine Corps, retired as Maj. Mem: FBI Acad Assocs; Warwick Am Legion Post 255; VFW Post 176; AF&AM Lodge 336; Int Asn Chiefs Police. Relig: Presbyterian; Elder. Legal Res: 136 Tazewell Rd Newport News VA 23602 Mailing Add: 555 Denbigh Blvd Newport News VA 23602

ATKINSON, MADELYN RUCKS **(D)**
Secy, Union Co Dem Cent Comt, Ark
b Camden, Ark, Dec 13, 30; d Edmond Daniel Rucks & Mamie Ruth Hodnett R; m 1965 to Robert Charles Atkinson; c Charles Randall. Educ: High sch. Polit & Govt Pos: Dep co clerk, Union Co, Ark, 51-62 & 65-66, co & probate clerk, 67-; secy, Union Co Dem Cent Comt, 60-; deleg, Ark State Dem Conv, 62 & 70. Bus & Prof Pos: Abstracter, Security Abstr Co, 48-51; secy, Urbana Lumber Co, 62-65. Mem: El Dorado Bus & Prof Women's Club. Relig: Church of Christ. Mailing Add: Rte 1 Box 219 El Dorado AR 71730

ATKINSON, MYRON HILTON, JR **(R)**
NDak State Rep
b Bismarck, NDak, Sept 22, 27; s Myron Hilton Atkinson & Julia Weber A; m 1951 to Marjory L Barth; c Timothy, Kathleen, Thomas, Patrick, Elizabeth, John & Paul. Educ: Bismarck Jr Col, AS, 47; Univ NDak, BSC, 49, Law Sch, BSJD, 51; Beta-Gamma Sigma; Alpha Tau Omega; Blue Key. Polit & Govt Pos: Chmn, Burleigh Co Rep Party, NDak, 62-63; NDak State Rep, 32nd Dist, 69- Bus & Prof Pos: Partner, law firm of Cox, Pearce, Engebretson, Atkinson, Gunnes, 54-63; vpres, Meyer Broadcasting Co, 64-68; vpres, Robert James, Inc, 68-69; pvt law practice, currently; pres, Mod Homes, Inc, currently; pres, NDak Guaranty & Title Co, currently; pres, Robert James, Inc, 74- Mil Serv: Entered as 2nd Lt, Army, 52, released as 1st Lt, 54, after serv in Judge Adv Gen Corps. Mem: Am Bar Asn; Am Legion; Elks; KofC; Rotary. Relig: Catholic. Legal Res: 106 Ave BW Bismarck ND 58501 Mailing Add: PO Box 1176 Bismarck ND 58501

ATKINSON, THOMAS GEORGE **(NON-PARTISAN)**
Mayor, Green Bay, Wis
b Green Bay, Wis, Mar 9, 28; s Dr Henry S Atkinson & Evelyn Piron A; m 1950 to Patricia Liebergen; c Thomas, Jr, Patrick, William, Mary, Mike & Anne. Educ: Univ Nev, 49-51. Polit & Govt Pos: Alderman, Green Bay, Wis, 58-62, mayor, 73- Bus & Prof Pos: Owner, Atkinson Warehousing & Trucking, Green Bay, Wis, 46- Mil Serv: Entered Navy, 45, released as Gunners Mate 3/C, 46, after serv in Pac Theatre; Victory Medal; Presidential Citation; Am Theatre Ribbon; Asiatic & Pac Theatre Ribbon; Philippine Liberation Medal; Good Conduct Medal. Mem: VFW; Am Legion; Holy Name Soc (pres); Eagles; Nat Rifle Asn. Relig: Catholic. Legal Res: 1032 Ethel Ave Green Bay WI 54303 Mailing Add: 100 N Jefferson Green Bay WI 54305

ATKINSON, TROY CARROL, III **(R)**
Chmn, Marion Co Rep Party, SC
b Florence, SC, Aug 1, 46; s Troy Carroll Atkinson, Jr & Lucia Wyatt Oliver A; m 1974 to Sussanne Cook; c Troy Carroll IV. Educ: Newberry Col, BA, 69. Polit & Govt Pos: Chmn, Marion Co Rep Party, SC, 74- Bus & Prof Pos: Parts mgr, Atkinson Implement Co, Marion, SC, 69- Mil Serv: Entered as Pfc, Nat Guard, 67, released as SP-5, 73. Mem: Rotary; Swamp Fox Booster Club (dir); Marion CofC. Relig: Baptist. Legal Res: 221 W Bond St Marion SC 29571 Mailing Add: Box 601 Marion SC 29571

ATLAS, MORRIS **(D)**
Chmn, Dem Exec Comt Hidalgo Co, Tex
b Houston, Tex, Dec 25, 26; s Sam Atlas & Bertha Cohen A; m 1947 to Rita Wilner; c Scott Jerome, Debra Lynne, Lauren Teri & Lisa Gayle. Educ: Univ Tex, BBA, 49, LLB, 50; Phi Delta Phi; Alpha Epsilon Pi. Polit & Govt Pos: Mem bd regents, Pan Am Univ, 65-, chmn, 72-73; deleg, Dem Nat Conv, 68 & 72; chmn, Dem Exec Comt Hidalgo Co, Tex, 68- Bus & Prof Pos: Partner, Atlas, Hall, Schwarz, Mills, Gurwitz & Bland, 53-; mem bd dirs, McAllen Gen Hosp, 74- Mil Serv: Entered as A/S, Navy, 44, released as Seaman 1/C, 46, after serv in USS Iowa, Pac, 45-46. Publ: Settlement of marital property rights, Tex Law Rev, 51; reprinted as Marital property rights, Tex Bar J, 51. Mem: Am Bar Asn; Asn Ins Attorneys; Tex Asn Defense Coun; Tex Bar Found; Am Legion. Relig: Jewish. Legal Res: 1600 Iris McAllen TX 78501 Mailing Add: 818 Pecan McAllen TX 78501

ATWOOD, GENEVIEVE **(R)**
Utah State Rep
b May 4, 46; d Eugene Atwood & Margaret Fisher A; single. Educ: Bryn Mawr Col, BA, 68; Wesleyan Univ, MA, 73; pres, Undergrad Asn. Polit & Govt Pos: Deleg, Co Rep Party, 74-; Utah State Rep, Dist 1, 75- Bus & Prof Pos: Various jobs, including bilingual secy, France, Ger & Ireland, 68-69; geologist, Inst Geografico de Honduras, 70-71; Consult to Conn Gen Assembly, 71-72; mem staff, Nat Acad Sci, Washington, DC, 72-74; geologist, Ford, Bacon & Davis, Engrs, Utah, 75- Publ: Co-ed, Man, Materials & Environment, NAS/NAE, MIT Press, 73; Rehabilitation Potential of Western Coal Lands, NAS/NAE, Ballinger, 74; co-auth, Stratigraphy, sedimentology & paleoenvironment of Esquias formation of Honduras, Am Asn Petroleum Geologists, 74. Mem: Geol Asns of Am, Utah & Washington, DC; Coun Foreign Rels; Avenues Improv League (bd dirs). Honors & Awards: Utah Jr Tennis Champion, 62, nationally ranked, 61-65. Relig: Episcopal. Mailing Add: 1283 E South Temple Salt Lake City UT 84102

AUBREY, MARK LEE **(R)**
b Joy, Ill, Dec 26, 01; s Charles Aubrey (deceased) & Ora Neely A; m 1923 to Alice Louisa West; c Robert Mark (deceased). Educ: High sch. Polit & Govt Pos: State hwy policeman, Rock Island Co, Ill, 44-46; tax assessor & constable, Drury Twp, 48-56; head dairyman, EMoline State Hosp, 55-65, stores clerk, 65-67; chmn, Polk Co Rep Party, Tex, formerly. Bus & Prof Pos: Tel operator, Chicago, Burlington & Quincy RR, Duncan, Ill, 21-27, Bushnell, 27-30, New Boston, 30-32, on extra list, 32-36; warehouse foreman, Ill Wholesale Grocery, Rock Island, 36-39; bulk agt, Skelly Oil Co, Milan, 39-46. Mem: Dairy Herd Improv Asn, Ill; Order of RR Telegraphers Union; Munic, State & Co Employees Union; AF&AM. Honors & Awards: Highest Producing Dairy Herd Award, Instnl Dairy Herd, State of Ill; scholarship, Macomb Normal Sch; Outstanding Policeman, Ill. Relig: Protestant. Mailing Add: Rte 2 Box 44-A Livingston TX 77351

AUBUT, ADELARD J **(D)**
NH State Rep
Mailing Add: 79 Allds St Nashua NH 03060

AUCHINCLOSS, JAMES COATS **(R)**
b New York, NY, Jan 19, 85; s Edgar Stirling Auchincloss & Maria Sloan A; m 1960 to Vera Rogers Brown; c Douglas, Gordon. Educ: Yale, BA, 08. Polit & Govt Pos: US Rep, NJ, 78th-88th Cong; mayor, Rumson, NJ, 3 terms; mem coun, Borough of Rumson, 12 years; dep police comnr, New York, formerly. Bus & Prof Pos: Founder, past treas, pres & chmn of bd, NY Better Bus Bur; NY Stock Exchange, 10-35, bd of gov, 18 years; Farmers Loan & Trust Co, New York. Mil Serv: NY Nat Guard, 7th Regt, Capt, Mil Intel. Mailing Add: 700 New Hampshire Ave NW Washington DC 20039

AUCHLY, WILLIAM JOSEPH **(R)**
Chmn, Ninth Cong Dist Rep Comt, Mo
b Montgomery Co, Mo, Apr 26, 28; c Marcus Francis Auchly & Anna Theresa Cunningham A; m 1967 to Mary Dione Dimond; c Christopher Marcus. Educ: Montgomery Co High Sch. Polit & Govt Pos: Chmn, Montgomery Co Rep Comt, Mo, 62-72; chmn, Ninth Cong Dist Rep Comt, 66- Bus & Prof Pos: Secy-treas-dir, Producers Grain Co, Number 31, Montgomery Co, Mo, 58; secy & dir, Montgomery Co Bank, 63. Mem: KofC; Mo Farmers Asn; Farm Bur. Relig: Roman Catholic. Mailing Add: RR 2 Montgomery City MO 63361

AUCOIN, LES **(D)**
US Rep, Ore
b Redmond, Ore, Oct 21, 42; m to Susan; c Stacy Lee & Kelly Ray. Educ: Pac Univ, BA, 69. Polit & Govt Pos: Ore State Rep, Washington Co, 71-75, majority leader, Ore House Rep, 73-75, chmn state & fed affairs comt, 73, chmn rules comt, 73, chmn, Washington Co Drug Abuse Coun, 71-72; mem, State Emergency Bd, 73-75; US Rep, Ore, 75- Bus & Prof Pos: Newsman, Redmond Spokesman, 60 & 64, newsman, Portland Oregonian, 65-66; dir pub info & publ, Pac Univ, 66-73; adminr, Skidmore, Owings & Merrill, 73-74. Mil Serv: Army, 61-64. Honors & Awards: Hon assoc, Inst Politics, JFK Sch Govt, Harvard Univ, 74. Legal Res: 1622 Ash St Forest Grove OR 97116 Mailing Add: US House Rep Washington DC 20515

AUER, DELMAR L **(D)**
Ind State Rep
b Columbia City, Ind, Dec 10, 29; s John E Auer & Frances Flaugher A; m 1965 to Marilyn J Hoover; c Sheila (Mrs Henderson), Richard, Cindy & Lindy. Educ: Int Col, Ft Wayne, Ind, BS, 50; Reppert Sch Auctioneering, Decatur, 71. Polit & Govt Pos: Treas, Whitley Co Dem, Ind, 53-57; councilman & pres, Whitley Co Coun, 71-74; Ind State Rep, 16th Dist, 75- Bus

& Prof Pos: Secy-treas, Whitley Co Bd Realtors, 74- Mem: Nat & Ind Auctioneers Asns; Nat Asn Realtors. Relig: Church of the Nazarene. Mailing Add: RR 9 Columbia City IN 46725

AUGSBURGER, JOHN FREDERICK (R)
Ind State Sen
b Gridley, Ill, June 21, 05; s Daniel Augsburger & Leah Gurtner A; m 1934 to Dorothy Lucille Bird; c Carolyn S (Mrs Curtis) & John Bird. Educ: Milford High Sch, grad, 24; Bluffton Col, 25; Phi Delta Kappa. Polit & Govt Pos: Chmn, Milford Town Coun, Ind, 43-46, mem, 68; trustee, Vanburen Twp, Kosciusko Co, 47-55; chmn, Kosciusko Co Sch Reorgn, 59-63; Ind State Sen, Sixth Dist, 69-72, Dist 13, 73- Bus & Prof Pos: Owner, Augsburger's IGA Mkt, 36-62, pres, Augsburger's Inc Supermkts, 62-69. Mem: Nat Asn State Legislators; Mason (32 degree); Shrine; CofC; Millord Lions (charter mem). Relig: Protestant. Mailing Add: RR 1 Syracuse IN 46567

AUGUST, ROBERT BURTON (R)
b Simsbury, Conn, May 18, 21; s Ferdinand Rudolph August & Mildred Paine A; m 1948 to Gladys Thompson; c Betsy, Roberta, Lourie, Ann & Marnie. Educ: Yankton Col, BA, cum laude, 43; Georgetown Univ Law Sch; Phi Delta Phi. Polit & Govt Pos: Conn State Rep, Avon, 54-60, chmn comt gen law, Conn House Rep, 57; chmn, Avon Rep Town Comt, Conn, 60-72; chmn comt suburban town matters, Conn Rep State Coun, 63-; chmn adv comt, Conn Rep State Cent Comt, 63-72. Bus & Prof Pos: Attorney, August & Turner, Simsbury, Conn, 50-72; exec partner, Joseloff, August & Sudarsky, 73- Mil Serv: Entered as Ens, Navy, 43, released as Lt(jg), 46, after serv in LCFF 504 (Cmndg Officer), Pac. Mem: Am Bar Asn; Avon Lions; Curtiss Cemetery Asn; YMCA (state chmn, Hi-Y & Govt Prog, 60-70); VFW. Honors & Awards: Young Man of Year Award, Farmington Valley Jr CofC, 57. Relig: Congregational; Moderator, Avon Congregational Church. Mailing Add: 281 Old Farms Rd Avon CT 06001

AUGUSTINE, NORMAN RALPH
Under Secy Army
b Denver, Colo, July 27, 35; s Ralph Harvey Augustine & Freda Irene Immenga A; m 1962 to Margareta Engman; c Gregory Eugene & Rene Irene. Educ: Princeton Univ, BS magna cum laude, 57, MS, 59; Columbia Univ, Univ Calif, Los Angeles & Univ Southern Calif, postgrad courses; Phi Beta Kappa; Sigma Xi; Tau Beta Pi. Polit & Govt Pos: Asst dir defense research & eng, Off Secy Defense, Washington, DC, 65-70; consult, Off Secy Defense, 71-73; consult, Exec Off of the President, 71-73; Asst Secy Army, 73-75, Under Secy Army, 75-; mem, Defense Systs Mgt Sch Policy Coun, NASA Research & Tech Adv Coun. Bus & Prof Pos: Research asst, Princeton Univ, 57-58; chief engr, Douglas Aircraft Co, Inc, Santa Monica, Calif, 58-65; vpres advan systs, LTV Aerospace Corp Missiles & Space Div, Dallas, Tex, 70-73; mem adv bd, Dept Aeromech Eng, Princeton Univ, 75- Publ: Contrib to articles in prof jour. Mem: Boy Scouts (mem nat prog assessment comt, 75-); fel Inst Aeronaut & Astronaut; Am Defense Preparedness Asn; Am Helicopter Soc (dir); Kiwanis. Honors & Awards: Meritorious Serv Medal, Secy of Defense, 70. Relig: Presbyterian. Legal Res: 1329 Merrie Ridge Rd McLean VA 22101 Mailing Add: Dept of the Army The Pentagon Washington DC 20310

AUKERMAN, JAMES VANCE (D)
RI State Rep
b Detroit, Mich, May 6, 48; s Robert C Aukerman & Louise Rose A; m 1973 to Karin M Nilsson. Educ: Dartmouth Col, AB, 70; Suffolk Univ Law Sch, JD, 75; Kappa Kappa Kappa. Polit & Govt Pos: RI State Rep, Dist 49, 71-, mem, House Finance Comt, 73-; mem, South Kingstown Dem Town Comt, RI, 72-; mem, Comn on State Interns, 73- Mem: Wakefield Rotary Club; Richmond Grange, Number 6-P of H; Common Cause of RI. Relig: Protestant. Mailing Add: 10 Linden Dr Kingston RI 02881

AULT, DAVID R (R)
Maine State Rep
Mailing Add: Wayne ME 04284

AUMAN, TOFFIE CLYDE (D)
NC State Rep
b Jackson Springs, NC, Mar 11, 09; s Claude Auman & Lillie Graham A; m 1936 to Sally Watts; c Two sons & two daughters. Educ: NC State Col. Polit & Govt Pos: Mem, NC Bd of Juvenile Correction, 50-64; NC State Rep, 66- Bus & Prof Pos: Dir, NC RR, 49-50; past dir & pres, NC State Col Agr Found; past dir, NC Farm Bur Ins Co; dir, Sandhill Prod Credit Asn, 50-64; farmer, currently. Mem: NC Farm Bur; Nat Peach Coun, Am Farm Bur; NC Peach Grower's Soc; Adv to Dean of Agr, NC State Col. Honors & Awards: Gamma Sigma Delta Award, NC State Col for contrib to agr. Relig: Presbyterian; Elder, Comnr to Gen Assembly, 55, vpres, Synod's Men's Coun, 59; pres, Men of the Church Fayetteville Presbytery. Mailing Add: Route 1 West End NC 27344

AUMOEUALOGO, SALANOA S P
Rep, Am Samoa Legis
b Tula, Am Samoa, May 27, 12; s Rapi Sotoa & Sarona Rapi S; m 1934 to Faaalo Faamausili; c Afimuao, Asosa, Soli, Malotu, Tauaueaue, Sonny, Maota & Salofi. Educ: Poyer High Sch, Am Samoa. Polit & Govt Pos: Mem, Am Samoa House Rep, 28-56, speaker, 53-54; Rep, Am Samoa Legis, 57-, pres of senate, 69-70 & 73-; pres, Pac Conf Legis, 72-73. Relig: Christian Congregational. Mailing Add: Pago Pago American Samoa

AURAND, DOUGLAS R (D)
Treas, Winnebago Co, Ill
b Dixon, Ill, July 28, 41; s Raymond Aurand & Carrie L Gilbert A; m 1971 to Julie Ann Moore; c David & Christine. Educ: Rock Valley Jr Col, currently. Polit & Govt Pos: Pres, Winnebago Co Young Dem, Ill, 60-70; precinct committeeman, Winnebago Co Dem Party, 68-; treas, Winnebago Co, 70-; treas, Ill Young Dem, 71-72; deleg, Dem Nat Conv, 72; deleg, Dem Nat Mid-Term Conf, 74. Mil Serv: Entered as E-1, Air Force, 60, released as E-4, 64, after serv in Strategic Air Command, 61-64; Outstanding Airman; Good Conduct Medal; Presidential Unit Citation. Mem: Rockford Kiwanis (bd dirs); Boy Scouts (Scoutmaster); Am Legion; Farm Bur; Retail Clerks Union. Relig: Methodist. Mailing Add: 1634 Camp Ave Rockford IL 61103

AUSMAN, LAVERNE G (R)
Wis State Sen
Mailing Add: RR 2 Elk Mound WI 54739

AUSPITZ, JOSIAH LEE (R)
b Philadelphia, Pa, Feb 5, 41; s Herman Jacob Auspitz & Gabriella Hartstein A; m 1965 to Katherine Holahan; c Rachel & Benjamin. Educ: Harvard Col, 63; Brasenose Col, Oxford Univ, Marshall scholar, 63-64; Phi Beta Kappa. Polit & Govt Pos: Mem nat gov bd, Ripon Soc, 67-, ed, Ripon Forum, 67-68, pres, Soc, 69-71; research dir, President's Adv Coun on Exec Orgn, 69; mem, Mass State Rep Platform Comt, 70; mem, Somerville Rep City Comt, Mass, 70- Bus & Prof Pos: Ed adv, Liberian Star, WAfrican Pilot, 64-65; asst to dir, Nigerian Inst Social & Econ Research, 65; tutor in govt, Lowell House, Harvard Col, 70-73. Publ: Co-auth, The Realities of Vietnam, Pub Affairs Press, 68; auth, Reprivatization & Nixon, Washington Monthly, 11/69; What's wrong with politics?, Harpers, 5/74. Mem: Coun Foreign Rels. Relig: Jewish. Mailing Add: 17 Chapel St Somerville MA 02144

AUSTAD, OSCAR MELVIN (R)
b Steel, NDak, Mar 29, 22; s John J Austad & Aagot Swenson A; m 1950 to Dorothy May Hansberger; c Kristi, Lori, Randall, David, Kerri & Michael. Educ: NDak State Univ, 1 year; Augsburg Col, 1 year 6 months; Univ Minn, 1 year. Polit & Govt Pos: Pres, Augsburg Col Rep Club, 47; treas, Hennepin Co Young Rep League, 48-50; Rep precinct committeeman, Sioux Falls, 54-70; treas, Minnehaha Co Rep Cent Comt, 68-70; SDak State Sen, Minnehaha Co, 71-74, Asst Minority Leader, SDak State Senate, 73-74, deleg, Rep Nat Conv, 72. Bus & Prof Pos: Dir, Sioux Falls Credit Bur, 71- Mil Serv: Entered as Pvt, Army, 42, released as Pvt, 43. Mem: Citizens Fact-Finding Comt for Sioux Falls Bd Educ; Minnehaha Co Vis Nurses Asn; Nat Sporting Goods Asn; US CofC; Sioux Falls CofC; Elks; YMCA. Relig: Lutheran; Vpres, First Lutheran Church, 72- Mailing Add: 2216 Allen Dr Sioux Falls SD 57103

AUSTIN, DALE C (D)
Vt State Rep
Mailing Add: Box 119 Newport VT 05855

AUSTIN, EDWARD DONALD (D)
Nat Committeeman, Ohio Young Dem
b Elyria, Ohio, Nov 27, 51; s Edward Donald Austin & Roseann Boyle A; single. Educ: Elyria Cath High Sch, Ohio, grad, 70. Polit & Govt Pos: Pres, Belmont Co Young Dem, Ohio, 72; nat committeeman, Ohio Young Dem, 74- Bus & Prof Pos: Clerk, John G Ruhlin Co, Akron, Ohio, 70-73, mgt consult, 73-74, field supt, 74- Mem: Capitol Club; Smithsonian Assocs. Relig: Roman Catholic. Mailing Add: B9 1170 Nestor Ave Akron OH 44314

AUSTIN, ELLEN JANE (D)
d John J Megivern & Anna O'Neill M; m 1946 to Alvin E Austin; c Suellen (Mrs Jeffrey Heinrich) & Sheila (Mrs Morgan Lacy). Educ: Sacred Heart Acad; Moorhead State Col. Polit & Govt Pos: Committeeman, Second Precinct Fourth Ward, Grand Forks, NDak, 59-; vpres, Grand Forks Co Dem Women, 60-71; secy, Grand Forks Co Dem Exec Comt, 60-67; deleg, Dem State Conv, 62-74; mem state conv site comt, 70; deleg, Dem Women's State Conv, 63, 65, 67, 69, 71 & 73; secy, NDak State Dem Women, 63-65, dir news & publ, 65-73; mem bd dirs, NDak Dem Women's Club, 63-; deleg & publicity coordr for NDak, Dem Nat Conv, 64; NDak publicity coordr, Dem Women's Conf, DC, 66; dir, Region Four Dem Women, 66-73, dir, Region Three, 73-; mem adv comt, NDak Dem Non-Partisan League Legislators, 66-74; secy, 18th Dist Dem Non-Partisan League Exec Comt, 67-74; Dem nominee for Presidential elector, 68; press secy for US Sen Campaign, 68; secy-treas, Northeast Dem Conf of NDak, 68-; mem, NDak Educ Broadcasting Coun, 69-, secy, 69-71; mem, Dem Non-Partisan League Campaign Comt, 70; chmn, 18th Dist Dem Women, 71-74, mem exec comt, currently. asst media dir, Dem Non-Partisan League State Campaign, 72. Publ: Ed, News, NDak Quart Publ of NDak Women, 63-72; column, The last word, Focus, NDak Off Dem Newspaper; ed, News & Views, 18th Dist Dem Women. Honors & Awards: NDak Dem Woman of the Year, 69. Relig: Roman Catholic. Mailing Add: 525 N 25th St Grand Forks ND 58201

AUSTIN, LLOYD JAMES, JR (D)
Chmn, Trinity Co Dem Cent Comt, Calif
b Alturas, Calif, Jan 26, 32; s Lloyd James Austin & Florence Fisher A; m 1956 to Barbara Gaye Batha; c Karen Adell & Kenneth James. Educ: San Francisco State Col, BA, 54; Pac Sch Relig, Berkeley, BD, 58. Polit & Govt Pos: Chmn, Trinity Co Dem Cent Comt, Calif, 64-66 & 73- Bus & Prof Pos: Pastor, Meridian E&R Church, Wilsonville, Ore, 58-62; pastor, Trinity Congregational Church, Weaverville, Calif, 62- Mem: Trinity Co Ment Health Adv Bd; Trinity Co Sch Dist Orgn Comt; Rotary. Relig: United Church of Christ. Mailing Add: PO Box 328 Weaverville CA 96093

AUSTIN, RICHARD H (D)
Secy of State, Mich
b Ala, May 6, 13; m to Ida; c Hazel. Educ: Detroit Inst Technol, Bus Admin, 37; Wayne State Univ; Beta Alpha Psi; Kappa Alpha Psi; Sigma Pi Phi. Hon Degrees: Doctor of Laws, Detroit Col Bus, 70. Polit & Govt Pos: Deleg, Mich Const Conv, 61-62; mem, Mich State Bd Equalization, 62; mem, Wayne Co Bd Supvr, 62; chmn, 15th Cong Dist Dem Party Orgn, 62-64; co-chmn, Mich Comn on Legis Apportionment, 63-65; mem adv group, US Comnr of Internal Revenue, 65; Auditor, Wayne Co, Mich, 66-70; mem, Wayne Co Bd Auditors, 67-70; mem exec comt & treas, Southeastern Mich Coun of Govt, 67-70; Secy of State, Mich, 70- Bus & Prof Pos: CPA, Mich, 42-67; officer & dir, Southwest Detroit Hosp Corp, League Investment Co & Detroit Mem Park Cemetery Asn. Publ: Several articles on state & local taxation, traffic safety & legis apportionment. Mem: Mich Asn CPA's; Am Inst CPA's; Am Acct Asn; Econ Club of Detroit; Gtr Detroit Bd Com. Honors & Awards: Liberty Bell Award, 70; Russworm Award for Contributions in Race Rels, Nat Publ Asn, 70; Silvernale Award, Mich Driver Educ Asn, 72; Distinguished Achievement Award, Mich Asn CPA's, 72; Wolverine Frontiersman Award for New Horizons, State of Mich, 72. Mailing Add: Sec of State Lansing MI 48918

AUSTIN, RUSSELL ANDERSON, JR (R)
b Seattle, Wash, Mar 4, 30; s Russell Anderson Austin & Amanda Ficks A; m 1953 to Barbara Fortnum; c Russell, III, Katherine Lee, Stephen Fortnum, Tracey Ann & Melissa Ann. Educ: Univ Wash, BA, 53, JD, 64; Wash Law Rev; Order of the Coif; Alpha Delta Phi; Phi Alpha Delta. Polit & Govt Pos: Pres, Grays Harbor Co Young Rep, Wash, 56-60; mem exec bd, Grays Harbor Rep Cent Comt, 56-62; councilman, Aberdeen, Wash, 60-62; asst chmn, King Co Rep Cent Comt, 66-70; mem, Rep State Exec Bd, 66-70; pres, Seventh Cong Dist Rep Club, 66-; deleg, Rep Nat Conv, 68 & 72; pres, Young Men's Rep Club King Co, 70-71; committeeman, Rep State Cent Comt, Wash, 70-73. Mil Serv: Entered as A/S, Navy, 50, released as Storekeeper 3/C, 51, after serv in Fasron 895, Sand Point Naval Air Sta, 50-51, Capt, Naval Res, 75- Publ: Inverse condemnation in Washington, Wash Law Rev, 1/65;

Recreational rights titles to beds on western lakes & streams, Natural Resources J, 1/67. Mem: Am Bar Asn; Am Trial Lawyers Asn; Mason; Scottish Rite; Shrine. Honors & Awards: Rep Man of Year Award, Young Men's Rep Club of King Co, 72. Relig: Protestant. Legal Res: 16220 Maplewild Dr SW Seattle WA 98166 Mailing Add: 2120 Pacific Bldg Seattle WA 98104

AVARA, R CHARLES (D)
Md State Deleg
Mailing Add: 3508 Coolidge Ave Baltimore MD 21229

AVENI, VIRGINIA LEE (D)
Ohio State Rep
b Selma, Ala, Oct 5, 33; d Benjamin Baldwin & Ava Snyder B; m 1957 to Joseph T Aveni; c Pamela Ann, Teresa & Benjamin. Educ: Ariz State Univ, BA in educ, 57. Polit & Govt Pos: Ohio State Rep, 17th Dist, 75- Mem: YWCA; League of Women Voters; Nat Asn Women Legislators. Legal Res: 4911 Middledale Rd Lyndhurst OH 44124 Mailing Add: 5001 Mayfield Rd Rm 115 Cleveland OH 44124

AVENSON, DONALD DEAN (D)
Iowa State Rep
b Minneapolis, Minn, Sept 16, 44; s Donald Conrad Avenson & Wilma Morey A; m 1964 to Diane Duda; c Eric & Clay. Educ: Univ Wis-River Falls, BS, 70; Univ Northern Iowa, grad work. Polit & Govt Pos: Precinct chmn, Washington Co Dem-Farmer-Labor Party, Minn, 66-69; mem, Washington Co Dem-Farmer-Labor Cent Comt, 69-70; Iowa State Rep, 15th Dist, 73- Bus & Prof Pos: Off mgr, Oelwein Tool & Die, Iowa, 70- Mem: Ducks Unlimited, Inc; Amateur & Iowa Trapshooting Asns; Izaak Walton League. Relig: Lutheran. Legal Res: 30 Maplewood Dr Oelwein IA 50662 Mailing Add: State House Des Moines IA 50319

AVERY, DENNIS THEODORE (D)
Ind State Rep
b Evansville, Ind, Sept 28, 46; s Theodore T Avery & Francis Harrison A; m 1969 to Donna Jean Cunningham. Educ: Univ Evansville, BS Marketing, 69. Polit & Govt Pos: Deleg, Ind State Dem Conv, 68 & 74; precinct committeeman, Precinct Ten Dem Party, Ind, 72-74; ward coordr, first ward, Evansville, 73, ward leader, 73-; Ind State Rep, Dist 72, 75- Mil Serv: Entered as Pvt, Army, 69, released as SP-5, 71, after serv in 1st Aviation Brigade, Vietnam, 70-71; Good Conduct Medal; Army Commendation Medal; Vietnam Serv Medal; Vietnam Commendation Medal. Mem: Mens Dem Club; Young Dem; VFW. Mailing Add: 1415 Jeanette Ave Evansville IN 47715

AVERY, ISAAC THOMAS, JR (D)
Chmn, Iredell Co Dem Exec Comt, NC
b Burke Co, NC, Mar 11, 16; s Isaac Thomas Avery & Margaret DuBose A; m 1940 to Caroline Long; c Marie A (Mrs Wiggs), Margaret A (Mrs Everhardt), Isaac T III & Mary I. Educ: Univ NC, Chapel Hill, AB, 38, Law Sch, JD, 40. Polit & Govt Pos: Co attorney, Iredell Co, NC, 64-68 & 70-72; chmn, Iredell Co Dem Exec Comt, 74- Mil Serv: Entered as Cpl, Army, released as Capt, after serv in Corps of Engrs, European Theatre; Col, NC Nat Guard, 38-; Am Theatre, Bronze Star; European Theatre with Battle Stars for World War II, Korean Theatre, 51. Mem: NC Bar Asn; Kiwanis. Relig: Presbyterian. Legal Res: 305 Oakhurst Rd Statesville NC 28677 Mailing Add: Drawer 1226 Statesville NC 28677

AVERY, JOHN BUCHANAN, JR (D)
Mem, Tenn Dem Exec Comt
b Alamo, Tenn, Oct 7, 16; c John Buchanan Avery & Edwin Efland A; m 1940 to Beulah Frances James; c Mrs Dan S Arnold, Jr, Mrs Jerald Wayne White & Ann Buchanan. Educ: Baylor Univ, AB, 38; Vanderbilt Univ, LLB, 39. Polit & Govt Pos: City attorney, Alamo & Friendship, Tenn, 46-; Tenn State Rep, 47-49; Tenn State Sen, 49-51; mem, Tenn Const Conv, 59; mem, Crockett Co Dem Primary Bd Elec, 62-65; mem, Tenn Dem Exec Comt, currently; chmn, Crockett Co Dem Exec Comt, formerly. Bus & Prof Pos: Dir, Alamo Develop Corp, 50- Mil Serv: Entered as Ens, Naval Res, 43, released as Lt(jg), 45, after serv in Amphibious Forces, Am, Atlantic, European, Pac & Philippine Theaters, 43-45; Am, Atlantic, European, Pac & Philippine Theater Campaign Ribbons; Victory Medal; Naval Res Ribbon; Lt Comdr, Naval Res (Ret). Mem: Am Bar Asn; Rotary; Am Legion; VFW; Farm Bur. Relig: Southern Baptist. Legal Res: 404 E Church St Alamo TN 38001 Mailing Add: PO Box 127 Alamo TN 38001

AVERY, WILLIAM HENRY (R)
b Wakefield, Kans, Aug 11, 11; s Herman W Avery & Hattie M Coffman A; m 1940 to Hazel Bowles; c Bill, Barbara Ann, Bradley Eugene & Martha Sue. Educ: Univ Kans, AB, 34; Delta Upsilon. Polit & Govt Pos: Dir sch bd, Wakefield, Kans, 47-55; Kans State Rep, 51-55; mem, Legis Coun of Kans, 53-55; US Rep, Kans, 55-65; Gov, Kans, 65-67. Bus & Prof Pos: Farmer & stockman, 34-; pres, Real Petroleum Co, Wichita, 69- Mem: Kans Farm Bur; Mason; Lions Int; Kans Livestock Asn. Honors & Awards: Received Nat 4-H Award, 67. Relig: Methodist. Mailing Add: 724 Eastern Wichita KS 67207

AVITABILE, GEORGE P (R)
b New Britain, Conn, Apr 15, 23; s Alfonso Louis Avitabile & Concetta Mezzanote A; m 1953 to Dorothy Stengel; c Susan Linda. Educ: Mt St Mary's Col (Md), BS, 49; Trinity Col (Conn), 50-51; Yale Univ, 56. Polit & Govt Pos: Civil defense dir, Torrington, Conn, 60-62, 64-66, justice of peace, 60-70; mem, Comn for the Elderly, 69-; chmn, Torrington Rep Town Comt, formerly. Mil Serv: Entered as Pvt, Army, 43, released as 1st Sgt, 46, after serv in 24th Div, Pac Theatre, 43-46; Presidential Citation; Combat Med Badge; Good Conduct Medal. Mem: Torrington & Nat Educ Asns; Conn Educ Asn (mem prof rights & responsibilities comt); Civitan Club Torrington; KofC. Relig: Roman Catholic. Mailing Add: 288 Pineridge Rd Torrington CT 06790

AVON, RANDY KALANI (R)
Fla State Rep
b Honolulu, Hawaii, Sept 25, 40; s Randolph Scott Avon & Pualani Mossman A; m 1963 to Joan Messmore; c Eve, Emmy Lou, Jaimie, Bob & Randy, III. Educ: Univ Fla, BSBA. Polit & Govt Pos: Chmn, Ft Lauderdale Community Rels Bd, Fla, 66-67; chmn, Beach Erosion Comt, 68-69; Fla State Rep, 72- Bus & Prof Pos: Pres, Creative Pub Rels & Mkt, Maui Develop Corp & Security Investment Corp of Fla, currently. Mem: Fla Pub Rels Asn (vpres); United Cerebral Palsy (pres, Broward Co); Lauderdale by the Sea Kiwanis (vpres); Fla Jaycees; US Jaycees. Honors & Awards: Sen George Smathers Award, Fla Jaycees, 70; One of Five Outstanding Young Men, Ft Lauderdale CofC, 71; James McKeithan Mem Award, US Jaycees, 72; Good Govt Award, Ft Lauderdale Jaycees, 73; One of Three Most Effective Freshmen Legislators, Ft Lauderdale News Poll, 73. Relig: Episcopal. Legal Res: 2100 NE 55th St Ft Lauderdale FL 33308 Mailing Add: 2455 E Sunrise Blvd Ft Lauderdale FL 33304

AXEL, JOHN WERNER (R)
Committeeman, Rep State Cent Comt Iowa
b Muscatine, Iowa, June 10, 41; s Chester Walter Axel & Wilma Marolf A; m 1964 to Joan Carol Urenn; c John Andrew & Bradford Joseph Urenn. Educ: Iowa State Univ, BS, 64; Univ Pa, Joseph Wharton scholar, MGA, 66; Gamma Gamma; Cardinal Key; Beta Theta Pi. Polit & Govt Pos: Orgn chmn, Muscatine Co Rep Cent Comt, Iowa, 66-71; co chmn, 71-75; chmn, Young Rep Club, Muscatine, 68-69; bd dirs, Iowa Young Rep State Cent Comt, 68-69; chmn, Ray for Gov Comt, 70; mem, Seventh Judicial Nominating Comn, 70-75; committeeman, Rep State Cent Comt, Iowa, First Dist, 75- Bus & Prof Pos: Vpres admin, The HON Co, Muscatine, Iowa, 66-; pres, Mutual Selection Fund, 72- Mem: Rotary Int; Nat Off Prods Asn (Young Exec Forum, speakers bur); YMCA (bd dirs, chmn long range planning comt); Friends of the Musser Pub Library (bd mem & founder); Geneva Golf & Country Club (chmn long range planning comt). Honors & Awards: Outstanding Young Man, Danforth Found, 55; Distinguished Serv Award, Muscatine Jaycees, 71; Outstanding Young Alumnus, Iowa State Univ, 75. Relig: Episcopal. Mailing Add: 2007 Circle Dr Muscatine IA 52761

AXELROD, HARRY (R)
Mem, Mass Rep State Cent Comt
b Lawrence, Mass, Apr 6, 16; s David Axelrod & Edith Friedman A; m 1939 to Evelyn Neumark; c John, Jane (Mrs John Jay Hahn) & Nancy. Educ: Syracuse Univ, BA, 38; Phi Beta Kappa; Sigma Alpha Mu. Polit & Govt Pos: Mem, Andover Rep Town Comt Mass, 61-, precinct chmn, 61-64, finance chmn, 65 & 66, chmn, 67-71 & 75-; mem, Mass Rep State Cent Comt, currently. Bus & Prof Pos: Treas, John Philip Enterprises, Andover, Mass, 46-66; owner, Walbuck Crayon Co, 48-; treas, Sheraton Rolling Green Motor Inn, Andover, 59-73, pres & owner, 73-; trustee, Danvers State Hosp; mem adv comt, Gtr Lawrence Regional Voc & Tech High Sch; trustee, Essex-Broadway Savings Bank. Mil Serv: Entered as Ens, Navy, 43, released as Lt(jg), 46, after serv in Third, Fifth & Seventh Fleets, Pac Theatre, 44-46; Am Area Campaign Ribbon; Asiatic-Pac Area Campaign Ribbon with Six Stars; Philippine Liberator Campaign Ribbon with one Star; World War II Victory Ribbon. Mem: Am Hotel & Motel Asn; Mass Hotel & Motel Asn (pres); Region IV Asn Human Develop (pres); Gov Club; Kiwanis. Relig: Jewish. Mailing Add: 27 Alden Rd Andover MA 01810

AXELROD, RICHARD A (D)
b Philadelphia, Pa, Nov 3, 41; s Maurice Axelrod & Thelma Rappaport A; m 1966 to Joanne Delores Mutti; c Rachel & Samuel Mutti. Educ: Boston Univ, BA, 64; Temple Univ Sch Law, JD, 68; Phi Sigma Delta. Polit & Govt Pos: Alt deleg, Dem Nat Conv, 72. Bus & Prof Pos: Attorney, Shuman, Denker & Land, Philadelphia, Pa, 68-71; attorney, Vt Legal Aid, Inc, St Johnsbury, Vt, 71-73; counsel, Hoosic River Basin Citizen's Environ Asn, Inc, 73-74; pvt law practice, St Johnsbury, 74- Mem: Northeast Kingdom Ment Health Asn (dir); Am & Vt Bar Asns; Vt Pilots Asn. Mailing Add: Box 471 Lyndonville VT 05851

AXSELLE, RALPH L, JR (D)
Va State Deleg
Mailing Add: 201 North Blvd Richmond VA 23220

AXTMANN, DAVID M (R)
Chmn, Hyde Co Rep Party, SDak
b Rugby, NDak, May 25, 44; s Nick P Axtmann & Christine Massine A; m 1973 to Guenetta JoAnn Lynch. Educ: Univ NDak, BA, 66; Univ NDak Law Sch, JD, 69; Phi Alpha Delta; Phi Alpha Theta. Polit & Govt Pos: Legis intern, NDak House of Rep, 69; law clerk, NDak Supreme Court, 69-70; lawyer, VISTA, 70-71; states attorney, Hyde Co, SDak, 72-; chmn, Hyde Co Rep Party, SDak, currently. Publ: Conclusiveness of judgments, NDak Law Rev, fall 67. Mem: Am & SDak Bar Asns; Am & SDak Trial Lawyers Asn; Highmore Booster Club (secy); Hyde Co Jaycees. Relig: Catholic. Legal Res: 425 Second SW Highmore SD 57345 Mailing Add: Box 187 Highmore SD 57345

AYALA, RUBEN S (D)
Calif State Sen
b Chino, Calif, Mar 6, 22; s Mauricio R Ayala & Erminia Martinez A; m 1945 to Irene Morales; c Ruben Marcia (Buddy), Maurice Edward & Gary Randall. Educ: Pomona Jr Col, 41-42; Los Angeles Nat Electronic Sch, grad, 48; Univ Calif Exten, 51. Polit & Govt Pos: Mem sch bd, Chino, Calif, 54-62; city councilman, 62-64; mayor, 64-66; supvr, San Bernardino Co, 66-73, chmn, 68-72; deleg, Dem Nat Conv, 68; Calif State Sen, 74- Mil Serv: Entered as Pvt, Marines, 42, released as Sgt, 46, after serv in 1st Marine Div, South Pac Theatre, 42-44. Mem: Am Legion; VFW; Native Sons Golden West; Elks; Kiwanis. Honors & Awards: Man of the Year Awards, Chino CofC, 67 & 69, Mex-Am Polit Asn, 70 & Kiwanis, 71; Hon Mem Award, Med Staff Doctor's Hosp Montclair; Citizen of the Year Award, VFW, 72. Mailing Add: 12941 Rhodes Pl Chino CA 91710

AYALA DEL VALLE, LUIS M (NEW PROGRESSIVE, PR)
Rep, PR House Rep
Mailing Add: State Capitol San Juan PR 00901

AYCOCK, ROBERT JAMES (D)
SC State Rep
b Clarendon Co, SC, July 27, 1893; s Robert J Aycock & America Fair Jones A; m 1916 to Helen B Geddings. Educ: Clemson Col, 10-11. Polit & Govt Pos: SC State Rep, 35-36, 49-, chmn, ways & means comt, 60- Bus & Prof Pos: Merchant, firm of Aycock & Rollings; farmer. Mailing Add: Box 38 Pinewood SC 29125

AYLES, KENARD F (R)
NH State Rep
Mailing Add: 26 Manchester St Pittsfield NH 03263

AYLMER, JOHN FRANCIS (R)
Mass State Sen
b Hyannis, Mass, Jan 27, 34; s John J Aylmer & Vina Norris A; m 1957 to Ann McLean; c John, Peter & Patrick. Educ: Mass Maritime Acad, BS, 57; Bridgewater State Col, MA in Educ, 69. Polit & Govt Pos: Selectman & assessor, Barnstable, Mass, 66-; Mass State Sen, Capt & Plymouth Dist, 71- Bus & Prof Pos: Maritime off, Am Trading & Prod Corp, New York, 59-64. Mil Serv: Entered as Ensign, Navy, 57, released as Lt(jg), 59, after serv in Sixth Fleet, Mediterranean Theatre; Lt Comdr, Naval Res, 71. Mem: Lions; Osterville Vet Club.

Honors & Awards: One of Four Outstanding Young Men, Mass, 70. Relig: Catholic. Mailing Add: Tern Lane Centerville MA 02632

AYLWARD, PAUL L (D)
b Stonington, Ill, Mar 1, 08; s Dennis E Aylward & Via Holben A; m 1929 to Karma Ellen Golden; c Paul L, Jr, Patricia (Mrs Thompson) & Peter G. Educ: Univ Ill, BS, 28; Chicago Kent Col Law, LLB, 30; Phi Alpha Delta; Phi Kappa Theta. Polit & Govt Pos: Co & city attorney, Ellsworth, Kans, 33-59; spec attorney, Dept Justice, 40-53; mem & chmn, Kans Park & Resources Authority, 58-62; mem, Nat Vet Comt for Kennedy, 62; deleg, Dem Nat Conv, 62, 68 & 72; mem Credentials Comt, 72; mem nat adv comt, RAD, Dept Agr, 63-66; nominee, US Sen, Kans, 64; chmn, First Dist Dem Orgn & Ellsworth Co Dem Comt, Kans, formerly; chmn, Kans Joint Coun Recreation, 68- Bus & Prof Pos: Dir & vpres, Citizens State Bank, 40-; dir, Ellsworth Develop Co, 60-; dir & pres, Ellsworth Bldg Co, 64-68. Mil Serv: Entered as Lt(jg), Navy, 43, released as Lt, 45, after serv in CVE 87 & 103 CIC Off, Pac; 3 Campaign Ribbons. Publ: Separate trials on appeals, Bar J of Kans, 11/57; Eminent domain in Kansas, Kans Law Rev, 3/59. Mem: Am Bar Asn; VFW; KofC; CofC; Kans Angus Asn. Relig: Roman Catholic. Legal Res: 306 Forest Dr Ellsworth KS 67439 Mailing Add: PO Box 83 Ellsworth KS 67439

AYRES, WILLIAM HANES (R)
b Eagle Rock, Va, Feb 5, 16; s William H Ayres & Loatie Emma Welch A; m to Mary Helen Coventry; c Mrs H J James Mount, Frank H & Judith E. Educ: Western Reserve Univ (Adelbert Col), BA, 36. Polit & Govt Pos: US Rep, Ohio, 50-71. Bus & Prof Pos: Salesman, 36-44; pres, William H Ayres, Inc, 46- Mil Serv: Pvt, Army, released 45. Mem: Am Legion; Amvets; Eagles; Moose. Relig: Methodist. Mailing Add: 660 N Main Akron OH 44310

AZIM, JAMES N, JR (R)
Wis State Rep
b Richland Center, Wis, Jan 17, 36. Educ: St Thomas Col, St Paul, Minn; Marquette Univ; Wis State Col, Platteville, BS, 57; Univ Wis Law Sch, 65. Polit & Govt Pos: Chmn, Gov Coun Traffic Law Enforcement, Wis, formerly; past secy, Blue River Watershed Asn; village trustee, Muscoda, Wis, 60-63; page, Wis State Assembly, 63rd Session; Wis State Rep, 64- Bus & Prof Pos: Instr hist, Muscoda High Sch, Wis, 57-62; Attorney, currently. Mem: Wis Acad Sci, Arts & Letters; Muscoda CofC; Comt to Preserve Rural TV. Legal Res: Muscoda WI 53573 Mailing Add: State Capitol Madison WI 53702

AZZARA, JUDY STANFILL (D)
Mem, Tenn State Dem Exec Comt
b Clarksville, Tenn, May 14, 49; d Charles Edward Stanfill & Bernice Morrow S; div; c Phillip. Educ: Austin Peay State Univ, scholars, 73-75; BS, 75. Polit & Govt Pos: Magistrate, Montgomery Co Court, Tenn, 72-; secy, Tenn Women's Polit Caucus, 74-; mem state coord coun, Tenn Vol Roundtable, 74-; mem, Tenn State Dem Exec Comt, 74- Mem: Nat Women's Polit Caucus; Nat Orgn Women (charter mem, Clarksville chap); Int Meditation Soc. Honors & Awards: Tenn, Ala & Ga Nat Forensic League Champion Extemporaneous Speaking, 67. Mailing Add: 757 Monroe St Clarksville TN 37040

B

BAARSMA, WILLIAM HENRY (D)
Legis Dist Chairperson, Pierce Co Dem Cent Comt, Wash
b Tacoma, Wash, Apr 18, 42; s Clarence H Baarsma & Constance Smith B; m 1968 to Natalie Jane Myers; c William Floyd & Katharine Constance. Educ: Univ Puget Sound, BA, 64; George Washington Univ, AM, 66, DPA, 72; Pi Gamma Mu; Sigma Nu; Intercollegiate Knights. Polit & Govt Pos: White House intern, Dept Housing & Urban Develop, Washington, DC, 65; staff clerk, Off US Sen Henry Jackson, 66-67; admin asst, Tacoma City Mgr, Wash, 67-68; precinct committeeperson, Pierce Co Dem Cent Comt, Wash, 70- & legis dist chairperson, 72- Bus & Prof Pos: Asst prof, Univ Puget Sound, 68-72, assoc prof pub admin, 72- Mem: Am Asn Univ Prof; Am Soc Pub Admin; Am & Western Polit Sci Asns. Honors & Awards: Scottish Rite Found Fel, 64 & 65; Univ Teaching Fel, George Washington Univ, 66-68. Relig: Episcopal. Mailing Add: 3709 N Madison Tacoma WA 98407

BAARSVIK, RICHARD PER (D)
b Acushnet, Mass, Dec 11, 52; s father deceased & Berit Swenson B; single. Polit & Govt Pos: Cand, Sch Comt (first 18 year old to file nomination papers in Mass), 71; mem youth adv comt, Youth Resources, 71-72; mem, Mass Youth Caucus, 71-; alt deleg, Dem Nat Conv, 72; mem, McGovern New Eng Finance Comt, 72; local McGovern coordr, 72; participant, Mass Caucus, 72; mem, Comt for New Vote, 72-; mem, Citizen Participation Polit, 72- Legal Res: 40 Independent St New Bedford MA 02744 Mailing Add: PO Box M-201 New Bedford MA 02744

BABALAS, PETER KOSTAS (D)
Va State Sen
b Boston, Mass, July 8, 22; s Kostas Babalas & Catherine B; m 1948 to Lillie Macheras; c Marcia A & Karen A. Educ: Harvard Col, BA, 45; Univ Va Law Sch, LLB, 50. Polit & Govt Pos: Va State Sen, Norfolk, 67- Bus & Prof Pos: Attorney-at-law, Norfolk, Va, 51-, Babalas & Ermlich, Ltd, currently. Mil Serv: Entered as Pvt, Army, 43, released as 1st Lt, 46, recalled, 51-52, serv in various commands, ETO & Korean War; ETO Medal with 4 Battle Stars. Mem: Va Trial Lawyers Asn; Elks; Saints & Sinners; Mason Lodges to Shrine; numerous other civic & social orgns. Relig: Greek Orthodox. Legal Res: 164 W Belvedere Rd Norfolk VA 23505 Mailing Add: 210 Atlantic Nat Bank Bldg Norfolk VA 23510

BABCOCK, BETTY L (R)
Mont State Rep
Mailing Add: 720 Madison Helena MT 59601

BABCOCK, ROBERT S (R)
Vt State Rep
Mailing Add: RFD 1 South Burlington VT 05401

BABIARZ, JOHN EDWARD (D)
Secy, Dept Admin Serv, Del
b Wilmington, Del, June 6, 15; s Stanley Babiarz & Mary Feret B; m 1939 to Adele F Barczuk; c John E, Jr & Francis S. Educ: Univ Del, BA, 37; Better Bus Bur Inst, Wash Univ, cert, 72. Polit & Govt Pos: Register in Chancery & clerk of Orphans Court, New Castle Co, Del, 49-53; mem policy comt, Dem City Comt, 50-; chmn, Ninth Ward Dem Comt, 51-57; chief clerk, Del House Rep, 55-56; deleg, Dem Nat Conv, 56, 60, 64 & 68; pres, City Coun, Wilmington, 57-61; mem policy comt, Dem State Comt, 57-; mayor, Wilmington, 61-69; secy dept admin serv, Del, 73- Bus & Prof Pos: Treas & gen mgr, Del Bedding Co, Wilmington, 39-69; pres & chief exec officer, Better Bus Bur Del, 69-73. Mil Serv: Entered as Pvt, Army, 45, released as Cpl, 46, after serv in Hq & Hq Co, Africa-Mid East Theatre, 45-46; Africa Mid East Theatre Ribbon; Good Conduct Medal. Mem: VFW; Kiwanis; Am Legion; Eagles; KofC. Honors & Awards: Good Govt Award, Comt of 39, 68 & 69. Relig: Roman Catholic. Mailing Add: 303 Lea Blvd Wilmington DE 19802

BABIN, WILLIAM ALBERT, JR (D)
RI State Rep
b Providence, RI, Jan 17, 29; s William A Babin & Marie E Gaudet B; m 1951 to Hope F Stearns; c Susan L & Janice A. Educ: La Salle Acad, Providence, RI. Polit & Govt Pos: Mem, Comt to Study Probs of Uninsured Drivers, RI, 62; mem, RI House of Rep Comt of Corp, currently; vchmn, Joint Comt Hwy Safety, currently; mem, Gov Comt on Crime, currently; mem, RI Dem Exec Comt, currently; RI State Rep, 66-, Dep Majority Leader, RI House of Rep, currently. Bus & Prof Pos: Self employed ins agt, currently; pres, Mt Pleasant Credit Union, currently. Mem: Dillon Coun, KofC (4 degree, Past Grand Knight). Relig: Catholic. Mailing Add: 50 Biltmore Ave Providence RI 02908

BABLITCH, WILLIAM A (D)
Wis State Sen
Mailing Add: 1609 Michigan St Stevens Point WI 54481

BACA, LEROY (D)
NMex State Rep
Mailing Add: Box 163 Socorro NM 87801

BACCARI, VINCENT JAMES (D)
RI State Sen
b Providence, RI, Nov 25, 15; s Tommaso Baccari & Marietta Bellandese B; m 1945 to Teresa; c Anna Maria (Mrs Danny DeAngelis), Vincent J, Jr & Pia Baccari. Educ: Providence Col, 1 year; RI Col Educ, EdB, 40; Boston Univ Sch Law, LLB, 49. Polit & Govt Pos: First legal counsel, Providence Redevelop Agency, 56-61; first asst trial counsel, State Freeway Acquisition, 61-63; RI State Sen, Dist 8, Providence, 67- Bus & Prof Pos: Attorney-at-law, 49- Mil Serv: Entered as Pvt, Army, 42, released as Capt, 46, after serv in 36th Inf Div, Mediterranean Theatre, 43-46. Mem: RI Bar Asn; Ital Am War Veterans of US, Inc; Order Sons of Italy in Am. Relig: Catholic. Mailing Add: 80 Vinton St Providence RI 02909

BACHER, EDWARD LEONARD (R)
b Gilbertville, Mass, Nov 14, 89; s John Michael Bacher & Anna Maria Mueller B; m 1920 to Corinda La Rocca. Educ: Williams Col, AB, 11; Phi Beta Kappa. Polit & Govt Pos: Deleg, League of Nations Conf on Customs Formalities, Geneva, 23; exec secy, Rep Nat Finance Comt, 44-61, compiler Rep Fact Book, 47-50, consult, currently; exec dir, Rep Nat Comt, 45-49, asst treas, 49-61, comptroller, 52-67, treas, Nat Recount & Fair Elec Comt, 60-61. Bus & Prof Pos: Foreign trader, Java, Sumatra & Straits Settlements, Standard Oil Co, NY, 11-15; secy foreign trade course, Bus Training Corp, NY, 16-17; ed of foreign trade course by mail, 16-18; mem staff, Pac Commercial Co, 17-18; & Quaker City Corp, Philadelphia, 19-20; asst ed, Our World Trade, quart rev, 20-27, ed, 27-45; lectr, Foreign Trade Sch, Georgetown Univ, 23-27; treas & mem bd of trustees, Phi Gamma Delta Educ Found, formerly; mem, Trade Terms Comt, Int CofC, 27-39, mem Am sect, Subcomt to Review Europe-US Trade, 31, mgr, Am Sect & US Sect Inter-Am Coun Com & Prod, 43-45; asst mgr, Foreign Com Dept, US CofC, 20-27, mgr, 27-45, secy nat defense comt, 33-45, conductor nat foreign trade week, 35-45, secy comt on educ, 38-40, secy nat policy coun, 40-41, mem spec comt int postwar probs, 41-45, mgr war serv div, 41-45, mem comt on int econ policy, 44-45; secy, US sect, Can-US Comt, US & Can CofC, 33-45, secy cattleman's comt, 37. Publ: Export Technique, 16; Doing Export Business, 27; Foreign Trade Promotion, 45. Mem: Am Philatelic Soc; Phi Beta Kappa Assocs; Gargoyle, Williams Col; Univ Club; Cong Country Club, Washington, DC. Relig: Congregational. Mailing Add: 4523 Hawthorne St NW Washington DC 20016

BACHLE, BARBARA JEAN (D)
b Elmira, NY, Jan 7, 52; d Joseph Fred Bachle & Miriam Graybill B; single. Educ: Southside High Sch, grad summa cum laude; Elmira Col, 70-71. Polit & Govt Pos: Campaign mgr, John Schamel for State Senate, NY, 70-; deleg, Dem Nat Conv, 72. Bus & Prof Pos: Off mgr, Elmira Serv Ctr, NY State United Teachers, 71- Mem: NEA; NY State United Teachers. Honors & Awards: Mem, Nat Honor Soc, 69. Relig: Methodist. Mailing Add: 411 Bonaview Ave Elmira NY 14904

BACHMAN, HAROLD L (D)
Md State Deleg
Mailing Add: Rte 1 Box 84B Pasadena MD 21122

BACHMAN, ILSE (D)
VChmn, Morgan Co Dem Comt, Ohio
b Nurnberg, Germany, May 9, 24; m 1942 to Henry Bachman; c David Stanley, Thomas Michael, Barbara June & James Jonathan. Polit & Govt Pos: Co-chmn, Morgan Co Jefferson-Jackson Club, Ohio; mem, Dem State Cent Comt, 62-66; deleg-at-lg, Dem Nat Conv, 64, alt deleg, 68; mem, State Cand Screening Comt, Ohio, 66; mem, State Platform Comt, 66; mem, Ohio State Dem Exec Comt, 68-72; vchmn, Morgan Co Dem Comt, currently; co campaign chmn for Gov & State Treas, 70; mem & past secy, Tenth Cong Dist Dem Action Club; app to Ohio Citizen's Comt on State Legis, 71. Mem: Morgan Co Pub Libr; PTA; Fedn Dem Woman of Ohio; The Study Club. Mailing Add: 426 E Union Ave McConnelsville OH 43756

BACHRACH, ANNE JAMESON (D)
Maine State Rep
b Brooklyn, NY, July 19, 19; d Arthur Stedman Jameson & Mary Carter Bingham J; m 1943 to Louis Bachrach; c Elinor Bingham, Peter Daniel, George Jameson & David Arthur. Educ: Sarah Lawrence Col, 37-39; Lab Sch of Design, 39-40; Am Student Union. Polit & Govt Pos: Mem, Brunswick Town Coun, Maine, 70-75; Maine State Rep, Dist 91, 75-; mem, Brunswick

Dem Town Comt, currently. Mem: League of Women Voters; Maine Women's Polit Caucus. Relig: United Church of Christ. Mailing Add: 17 Meadowbrook Rd Brunswick ME 04011

BACIG, THOMAS DAVID (DFL)
Chmn, Eighth Dist Dem-Farmer-Labor Party, Minn
b St Paul, Minn, Oct 2, 37; s Thomas Bacig, Sr & Gertrude Durand B; m 1960 to Carol Ann Mankowski; c Mary Elizabeth, Edward Joseph & Peter Anthony. Educ: Univ Minn, BA, 60, BS, 62, MA, 64, PhD, 71; John Henry Newman Honor Soc; Newman Club. Polit & Govt Pos: Chmn, McCarthy for President, Duluth, Minn, 68; vchmn, 60th Dist Dem-Farmer-Labor Party, 70-74; chmn 19th Precinct, Duluth, 72-; chmn, Eighth Dist Dem-Farmer-Labor Party, 74- Bus & Prof Pos: Instr, Univ Minn, Minneapolis, 62-67; instr, Univ Minn, Duluth, 67-72, asst prof, 72-, pres, Faculty Asn, currently. Publ: The Language of Literature, Minn Proj Eng Ctr, 65; Composition as a humane discipline, Minn Eng J, 70. Mem: Minn Coun Teachers Eng; Am Asn Univ Prof; Nat Coun Teachers Eng; Phi Delta Kappa; Izaak Walton League Am (pres, Duluth Chap, 73-). Honors & Awards: Horace Morris State Oil Award for Outstanding Teaching. Relig: Catholic. Mailing Add: 511 Woodland Ave Duluth MN 55812

BACKES, RICHARD J (D)
NDak State Rep
b Glenburn, NDak, Oct 27, 25; married; c three. Educ: Pub schs. Polit & Govt Pos: NDak State Rep, 61- Bus & Prof Pos: Farmer. Mil Serv: World War II. Mem: Am Legion; Lions; Elks. Mailing Add: Glenburn ND 58740

BACKMAN, JACK H (D)
Mass State Sen
b Saugus, Mass, Apr 26, 22; s Saul Backman & Edith Cohen B; m to Lillian Sagik; c Steven, Barbara, Marjorie & Judith. Educ: Syracuse Univ, AB, 43; Harvard Law Sch, LLB, 48. Polit & Govt Pos: Mem, Town Meeting, Brookline, Mass, 59-; mem, Brookline Housing Authority & Dem Town Comt, 60-; Mass State Rep, 65-70; chmn, Mass Drug Abuse Comt, 68-; Mass State Sen, 70-, chmn, Soc Welfare Comt, 71-, Mass State Senate & chmn Mass Spec Comn on Corrections, 73-; deleg, Dem Nat Conv, 72. Mil Serv: World War II. Mem: Boston Bar Asn; Mass Trial Lawyers Asn; Harvard Law Sch Asn. Mailing Add: 61 Arlington Rd Brookline MA 02167

BACON, MARGARET MARY (R)
Chairwoman, Fulton Co Rep Party, Ky
b Hickman, Ky; d Ernest Duval Johnson & Loula Cecilia Ramage J; m 1940 to John Shaw Bacon; c Mary Cecilia (Mrs Harris), Margaret Elizabeth (Mrs Ciccolella), Agnes Theresa (Mrs Toler) & John Shaw, Jr. Educ: Hickman High Sch, 2 years; Nazareth Acad, 2 years. Polit & Govt Pos: Post off employee, Hickman, Ky, 30-40; chairwoman, Fulton Co Rep Party, 56-, elec comnr, 57- Mem: Hickman CofC; Sacred Heart Altar Soc; Farm Bur; Fulton Co Auxiliary Health Comt; Ky Hist Soc. Relig: Roman Catholic. Mailing Add: Rte 4 Hickman KY 42050

BACON, REBA BROYLES (D)
Mem, Tenn Dem Exec Comt
b Chuckey, Tenn, May 10, 08; d Sidney Hiram Broyles & Daisy Florence Bailey B; m 1939 to Samuel Rankin Bacon; c Janet (Mrs J W Coots); Nancy (Mrs J E Brown) & Susanne. Educ: Tusculum Col, BA, 37; George Peabody Col, MA, 43; Univ Tenn, Knoxville; Peabody Col; PKD. Polit & Govt Pos: Mem, Tenn Dem Exec Comt, Fourth Cong Dist, 70-74, 13th Sen Dist, 74-; mem, Putnam Co Dem Exec Comt, Tenn, 70- Bus & Prof Pos: Classroom teacher, Greene Co, Tenn, 34-36; sch supvr, Decaturville, 37-39; elem sch prin, Greeneville City Syst, 44-46; supt, Athens City Schs, 46-49; prof elem & art educ, Tenn Tech Univ, Cookeville, 49-72. Publ: Several educ articles in Tennessee Teacher, 49-72. Mem: Tenn Art League; Cumberland Art Soc; life mem Nat Educ Asn; Benlee Art Shows (founder & dir); Tenn Tech Univ Arts Comt. Relig: United Methodist. Mailing Add: 915 Allen Ave Cookeville TN 38501

BADEN, JO ANN (D)
VChmn, Montgomery Co Dem Comt, Kans
b Wickes, Ark, Sept 20, 30; d Butler James Felts & Florence Gretchen Smith F; m 1951 to Kenneth Arnold Baden; c Steven Kenneth & Stanley Joe. Educ: Kans State Col, Pittsburg, 50-51; Independence Community Jr Col, 60-61; Sigma Sigma Sigma. Polit & Govt Pos: Census taker, US Agr Census, 64; vchmn, Montgomery Co Young Dem, Kans, 65-68; vchmn, Montgomery Co Dem Comt, 66-, chmn, 70-72; dir, Independence Dem Hq, 66-70; precinct committeewoman, Independence Twp, Montgomery Co Dem Comt, 66-; mem, Gov Docking's Inaugural Comt, 67; census taker, US Civil Defense Surv, 67; secy, Bramble for Cong, Fifth Dist Hq, 68; distributor of materials, Southeast Kans for Humphrey Comt, 68; Gov rep, Southeast Kans Libr Syst, 69-; deleg, Fifth Dist & State Dem Conv, 72; mem comt, Bill Roy for US Senate, 74; mem, Kans Dem State Comt, 75- Relig: Lutheran. Mailing Add: RR 1 Box 55A Independence KS 67301

BADEN, STEVE KENNETH (D)
b Pittsburg, Kans, Jan 23, 52; s Kenneth A Baden & JoAnn Felts B; single. Educ: Independence Jr Col, Kans, 70-71; Kans State Col Pittsburg, BA, 74, MA, 75; Phi Alpha Theta. Polit & Govt Pos: Mem, Docking for Gov Comt, 66, 68 & 70; chmn, Southeast Kans Citizens for Humphrey-Muskie, 68; deleg, Kans State Young Dem Conv, 69-70 & 71-72; pres, Montgomery Co Young Dem, 69-72; hon mem, Gov Docking Inaugural Comt, 70; pres, Independence Juco Young Dem, 70-71; deleg, Young Dem Nat Conv, 71; chmn, Kans Young Dem Reform Comn on Party Structure & Deleg Selection, 71; mem, Kans Dem Reform Comn on Party Structure & Deleg Selection, 71-72; fifth dist chmn, Nat Young Dem Registr Drive, 71-72; staff mem, Muskie Elec Comt, NH Primary, 71-72; regional Muskie coordr, Sullivan Co, NH, 72; deleg, Dem Nat Conv, 72; Leavenworth & Wyandotte Co coordr, Roy for Cong, 72. Publ: The elections of 1824 & 1825, spring 73 & Kansas & the 1960 Democratic Convention, spring 75, Kans State Col J. Relig: Lutheran. Mailing Add: RR 1 Box 55 A Independence KS 67301

BADER, PALMER WALTER (D)
Financial Secy, Deuel Co Dem Orgn, SDak
b Hartley, Iowa, Jan 29, 03; s George Bader & Emma Ruwe; m 1942 to Mabel Anderson; c Janice. Educ: Common Schs, Iowa & SDak. Polit & Govt Pos: Chmn, Deuel Co Dem Orgn, SDak, 42-70, financial secy, 70- Bus & Prof Pos: Owner & operator, Clear Lake Livestock Sales Agency, 43-63. Relig: Am Lutheran. Mailing Add: Box 41 Clear Lake SD 57226

BADHAM, ROBERT EDWARD (R)
Calif State Assemblyman
b Los Angeles, Calif, June 9, 29; s Byron Jack Badham, Jr & Bess Kissinger B (deceased); m 1970 to Anne Carroll; c Sharon Ann, Robert E, Jr, William Arthur, Phyllis Anne & Jennifer Leigh. Educ: Occidental Col, 48-49; Stanford Univ, AB, 51; Phi Gamma Delta. Polit & Govt Pos: Mem, Orange Co Rep Cent Comt, Calif, 62-; Calif Rep State Cent Comt, 62-; Calif State Assemblyman, 71st Dist, 63-; alt deleg, Rep Nat Conv, 64, 68 & 72. Mil Serv: Entered as Ens, Naval Res, 52, released as Lt(jg), 54, after serv as Opers Off, Korean War, CIC Instr, Fleet Training Ctr, Pearl Harbor, 54; China Serv & Nat Defense Ribbons; Korean Serv Ribbon with 2 Stars; UN Medal; Korean Presidential Unit Citation. Publ: Who's an extremist, Orange Co Sun, 9/65, Orange County's coastal freeway, 10/65, Getting specific about a program of social welfare, 5/66. Mem: Balboa Bay Club; Friends of the Libr, Univ Calif, Irvine; Orange Co Coast Asn; Am Legion; Nat Rifle Asn. Relig: Lutheran. Legal Res: 600 Michael Place Newport Beach CA 92660 Mailing Add: 1649 Westcliff Dr Newport Beach CA 92660

BADILLO, HERMAN (D)
US Rep, NY
b Caguas, PR, Aug 21, 29; married; c one. Educ: City Col New York, BA, magna cum laude, 51; Brooklyn Law Sch, LLB cum laude, 54, JD cum laude, 67, Class Valedictorian; Beta Gamma Sigma; Alpha Beta Psi. Polit & Govt Pos: Dep comnr, New York, 62, comnr for relocation, 63-66; pres, Borough of Bronx, NY, 66-70; deleg, NY State Const Conv, 67; deleg, Dem Nat Conv, 68 & 72, mem credentials comt, 68; cand for Dem Nomination for Mayor of New York, 69; US Rep, 21st Cong Dist, NY, 71-; deleg, Dem Nat Mid-Term Conf, 74. Bus & Prof Pos: With Ferro, Berdon & Co CPA, 51-55; attorney, Permut & Badillo, 55-62; attorney, Stroock & Stroock & Lavan, New York, 70-; trustee, NY Univ, 70- Mem: Nat Conf Christians & Jews. Legal Res: 405 W 259th St Bronx NY 10471 Mailing Add: US House of Rep Washington DC 20515

BADOLATO, DOMINIC J (D)
Conn State Rep
Mailing Add: 164 Pennsylvania Ave New Britain CT 06052

BAEHR, GEORGE B, JR (D)
Conn State Rep
Mailing Add: 57 Jerome Ave Trumbull CT 06611

BAER, BYRON M (D)
NJ State Assemblyman
Mailing Add: State House Trenton NJ 08625

BAER, JO WEBB (D)
Mem, Dem Nat Comt, NY
b Mt Sterling, Ala, Feb 28, 36; d John Henry Webb & Annie Southern W; m 1956 to Peter Baer; c Barbara & Kelly. Educ: Vigor High Sch, grad, 54. Polit & Govt Pos: VChairperson, New York New Dem Coalition, 71-72; deleg, Dem Nat Conv, 72 & Dem Mid-Term Conf, 74; mem, Dem Nat Comt, NY, 75- Bus & Prof Pos: Mem tax assessment bd of rev, Town of Orangetown, NY, 75- Mem: Friends of the Nyacks (fund raising chairperson, 75). Mailing Add: 58 Fourth Ave Nyack NY 10960

BAETH, RUSSELL (D)
Mont State Rep
Mailing Add: PO Box 184 Martin City MT 59926

BAETH, WILLIAM R (BILL) (D)
Mont State Rep
Mailing Add: 805 Minnesota Ave Libby MT 59923

BAEZ SANCHEZ, FRANCISCO (POPULAR DEMOCRAT, PR)
Rep, PR House Rep
Mailing Add: State Capitol San Juan PR 00901

BAFALIS, LOUIS A (SKIP) (R)
US Rep, Fla
b Boston, Mass, Sept 28, 29; s Louis John Bafalis & Vesta Reenstierna B; m 1956 to Mary Elizabeth Lund; c Renee Louise & Gregory Louis. Educ: St Anselm's Col, AB, 52. Polit & Govt Pos: Fla State Rep, 64-66; Fla State Sen, 33rd Dist, 67-71; cand for Gov, Fla, 70; US Rep, Tenth Dist, Fla, 73-, mem ways & means comt, US House Rep, 74- Bus & Prof Pos: Investment banker, Palm Beach, 71- Mil Serv: Entered as Pvt, Army, 52, released as Capt, 55, after serv in Artil. Publ: Drug Abuse—Like It Is, H & W B Drew Co, 69. Mem: Lions (vpres, Palm Beach club); Jaycees; CofC; Islanders; F&AM. Relig: First Christian. Legal Res: Creciente 401 S 7150 Estero Blvd Ft Myers Beach FL 33931 Mailing Add: 408 Cannon House Off Bldg Washington DC 20515

BAFFORD, HALLIE B (D)
Chmn, Macon Co Dem Party, Ill
b Macon, Ill, Apr 29, 21; s Benjamin F Bafford & Ona A Avis B; m 1941 to Dorothy M Aukamp; c Jerry E, Peggy J (Mrs Sprague), Jill D (Mrs Snyder), Robin M & Denna L. Educ: Macon Community High, 35-39; Activity Award & Outstanding Award, Macon Community High. Polit & Govt Pos: Rep precinct committeeman, South Macon Precinct 2, Ill, 50-69; vchmn, Macon Co Dem Party, Ill, 56-58, chmn, 68-; supvr, South Macon Twp, 63- Mil Serv: Entered as Pvt, Army, 44, released as Pfc, 45, after serv in 506 Combat MP Unit, ETO; Good Conduct Medal; Two Battle Stars. Mem: Am Legion; Mason; Consistory; Shrine; Eastern Star. Relig: Presbyterian; Elder. Mailing Add: 342 W Eckhardt Macon IL 62544

BAGERT, BEN (D)
La State Rep
b New Orleans, La, Jan 10, 44; s Bernard John Bagert & Philomene Schilleci B; m 1967 to Suzanne Brown; c Suzanne Mary, Bridget Andree & Jeanne. Educ: Loyola Univ (La), AB, 65, JD, 68; Blue Key; Sigma Alpha Kappa. Polit & Govt Pos: La State Rep, 69-, chmn, Judiciary Comt, La House Rep, 72- Bus & Prof Pos: Partner, Law Firm of Bagert & Bagert, 69- Mem: Am Bar Asn; Am & La State Trial Lawyers Asns; Loyola Alumni; Young Mens Bus Club of Gtr New Orleans. Honors & Awards: New Orleans Crime Stopper Award, 66. Relig: Catholic. Legal Res: 5387 Pratt Dr New Orleans LA 70122 Mailing Add: Suite 900 234 Loyola Bldg New Orleans LA 70112

BAGGERLEY, JOBYNA DEE (R)
Pres, Okla Fedn Rep Women
b Richmond, Calif, Mar 15, 26; d Dee Treadway & Koto Kepley T; m 1963 to Robert Earl Baggerley; c Byron & C D Lawson, stepchild, Barbara (Mrs Darryl Simmons). Educ: Okla State Univ, 61; Cent State Univ, 64. Polit & Govt Pos: Pres, Edmond Rep Women, Okla, 67-68; vpres, Okla Fedn Rep Women, 69-70, pres, 71-; mem, Citizens Adv Comt, 69-; mem, Oklahoma Co Rep Exec Comt, 69-; chmn party rules comt, Okla Rep State Comt, 71; pres, Okla Fedn Rep Comt, 71-; mem, Okla Rep State Exec Comt, 71-; deleg, Rep Nat Conv, 72. Mem: Eastern Star. Relig: Presbyterian; Deaconess, First Presby Church. Mailing Add: 3029 Beverly Dr Edmond OK 73034

BAGGETT, AGNES BEAHN (D)
Secy of State, Ala
b Columbus, Ga, Apr 9, 05; d John Richard Beahn & Leila Belle Thomason B; m 1926 to George Lamar Baggett, wid. Educ: Jones Law Sch, Montgomery, Ala. Polit & Govt Pos: Secy of state, Ala, 51-55 & 63-67 & 75-, state auditor, 55-59, state treas, 59-63 & 67-75. Mem: Eastern Star; Altrusa Club; Am Legion Auxiliary; Girls State; Ala State Fedn of Bus & Prof Women's Club. Honors & Awards: Career Woman; Ten Top Women. Relig: Methodist. Mailing Add: 3202 Montezuma Rd Montgomery AL 36106

BAGGETT, W TATE (R)
Chmn, Dist One Rep Comt, SC
b St Stephen, Feb 4, 11; s W T Baggett (deceased) & Sadie Venning B. Educ: St Stephen Pub Sch. Polit & Govt Pos: St Stephen town coun, 2 terms; deleg, Rep Nat Conv, 72; chmn, Berkeley Co Rep Comt, formerly; chmn, Dist One Rep Comt, SC, currently. Bus & Prof Pos: Partner, Lane Mfg Co; farmer & timber broker. Mem: St Stephen Lions Club; Berkeley Co Farm Bur. Relig: Presbyterian. Mailing Add: Box 307 St Stephen SC 29479

BAGLEY, LAURENCE P (R)
Maine State Rep
Mailing Add: 4 Hillside Ave Winthrop ME 04364

BAGLEY, RICHARD MARSHALL (D)
Va State Deleg
b Hampton, Va, May 14, 27; m to Nancy May Murray; c Nancy Lee, Mary Sharon & Richard M, Jr. Educ: Va Polytech Inst, BS in bus admin; Honor Court; Alpha Kappa Psi; Omicron Delta Kappa. Polit & Govt Pos: Va State Deleg, 65-, mem, Appropriations, Chesapeake & its Tributaries, Corp Ins & Banking & Labor Comts, Va House Deleg, currently; served on Deaf & Blind Study Comn, Marine Resources Study Comn, Unified Ports Study Comn, Ment Patient Comn & Permanent Comn for Econ in Govt Expenditures; app to Gov Budget Adv Comt Mem, Legis Comn to Study Higher Educ & Legis Comn to Study Pub Sch Financing. Bus & Prof Pos: Pres, Bagley Investment Co of Hampton, currently; mem bd dirs, United Va Bank/Citizens & Marine, William Byrd Press & Peninsula Savings & Loan Asn, currently. Mil Serv: World War II, Coast Guard; Air Force Res, Maj, currently. Mem: Propeller Club; Merrimac Shores Civic Asn; ROA; Elks; Am Legion. Relig: Episcopal; former vestryman, St John's Episcopal Church. Mailing Add: PO Box 9 Hampton VA 23669

BAGLEY, WILLIAM D (D)
Chmn, Laramie Co Dem Party, Wyo
b Afton, Wyo, Mar 28, 40; s William B Bagley & Della Newswander B; m 1965 to Margaret Ann Seward; c William Seward & John Marion. Educ: Univ Wyo, BBA, 62, JD, 64; Alpha Kappa Psi; Potter Law Club; Sigma Chi. Polit & Govt Pos: Bus mgr & co-ed, Wyo Dem, 59-62; pres, Univ Wyo Young Dem Club, 60-63; mem, Wyo Dem Cent Comt; regional dir, Young Dem Clubs of Am, 63-64; admin asst to US Rep Teno Roncalio, Wyo, 64-66; dep prosecuting attorney, Laramie Co, Wyo, 67-; chmn, Laramie Co Dem Party, 72- Bus & Prof Pos: Owner & mgr, WIDBA Enterprises, 58- Publ: The ought & is of bad check statutes, Wyo Law J, 63 & Northwest Law J, 64; Warranty as a lawyers tools, Wyo Law J, 64. Mem: Fed & Am Bar Asns; Wyo & Am Trial Lawyers Asn; Burro Club. Relig: Latter-Day Saint. Legal Res: 400 W Sixth Ave Cheyenne WY 82001 Mailing Add: PO Box 467 Cheyenne WY 82001

BAGLEY, WILLIAM THOMPSON (R)
b San Francisco, Calif, June 29, 28; s Nino J Baglietto & Rita V Thompson B; m 1965 to Diane L Oldham; c William T, Jr, Lynn L, Walter W, Shana & Tracy. Educ: Univ Calif, Berkeley, BA, with honors & Valedictorian, 49; Univ Calif Law Sch, LLB, 52; Phi Beta Kappa, permanent class pres; Bd Ed, Calif Law Rev. Polit & Govt Pos: Gen counsel & dir, Calif Young Rep, 56; chmn, Marin Co Young Rep, 57; chmn, budget & finance comt, Calif Young Rep, 57; vpres, First Marin Co Rep Assembly, 57; regional dir, Calif Rep Assembly, 58; chmn, Marin Campaign Comts, Weinberger & Powers, 58; vpres, Calif Rep Assembly, 59; mem, Marin Co & State Rep Cent Comt, 60-69; Calif State Assemblyman, Seventh Dist, 60-74, former chmn, Finance & Ins Comt, Judiciary Comt, Revenue & Taxation Comt & Welfare Comt, Calif State Assembly, chmn, Revenue & Taxation Comt; chmn, Spec Comt Open Pub Records & mem, Select Comt Admin Justice; Calif Adv Comt, US Comn on Civil Rights; co-chmn, Marin Co Nixon for Gov, 62; statewide legis liaison, Nixon Staff, 62; mem, Rep Legis Task Froce for Nixon, Rockefeller Presidential Deleg, 64; hon co-chmn, Marin Co Goldwater for Pres Comt, 64; statewide speakers bur, Murphy for Sen Comt, 64; co-chmn, Marin Co Christopher for Gov Comt, 66; Northern Calif staff & speakers bur, Reagan for Gov, 66; statewide campaign comt, Finch for Lt Gov & Flournoy for Controller, 66; chmn, Calif media rels comt, Nixon-Agnew Campaign, 68; chmn media rels comt, Murphy for US Sen Campaign, 70; deleg, Rep Nat Conv, 72; Rep nominee, Calif State Controller, 74. Bus & Prof Pos: Chmn, Commodity Futures Trading Comn, Washington, DC. Mem: San Rafael Elks; Native Sons; Commonwealth Club Calif; Marin Rod & Gun Club; Rafael CofC. Relig: Presbyterian. Legal Res: 1 Fawn Court San Anselmo CA 94960 Mailing Add: 1120 Connecticut Ave NW Washington DC 20036

BAGNAL, HARRY STROMAN (R)
Mem Exec Comt, Forsyth Co Rep Party, NC
b Winston-Salem, NC, May 5, 28; s Luther Nettles Bagnal & Susie Lofton B; m 1959 to Anne Elizabeth Broyles; c Harry S, Jr, David C, Alice Anne, Mary Lofton & Samuel Joseph. Educ: The Citadel, AB, 49; Univ NC, grad sch, 1 year. Polit & Govt Pos: NC State Sen, 66-74, minority leader, NC State Senate, 69-73; mem exec comt, Forsyth Co Rep Party, NC, 66-; mem, NC State Rep Cent Comt, 69-; chmn, NC Rep Party Platform Comt, 70-72. Bus & Prof Pos: Secy-treas, Bagnal Lumber Co, 65-71, owner, Harry Bagnal Lumber Co, 71-; pres, Dimension Enterprises, Inc, 73- Mil Serv: Entered as 2nd Lt, Army, 50, released as 1st Lt, 52, after serv in 3rd Army, ETO, 51-52. Mem: Nat Hardwood Lumber Asn; Hardwood Dimensions Mgrs Asn; Scottish Rite; Forsyth Country Day Sch (bd, 69-); Campbell Col (pres bd, 72-). Relig: Baptist. Mailing Add: 2861 Wesleyan Lane Winston-Salem NC 27106

BAGNARIOL, JOHN A (D)
Wash State Rep
b Renton, Wash, Jan 23, 32; s John M Bagnariol & Violet Umbinetti B; m 1951 to Edna M Kane; c Michael, Jody, David, Sharon, Teresa, Lori, Gina & Angela. Educ: Franklin High Sch, grad, 49. Polit & Govt Pos: Wash State Rep, 66- Mem: Wash Ins Asn; Nat Asn of Life Underwriters; Kiwanis. Relig: Catholic. Mailing Add: Box 836 Renton WA 98055

BAGWELL, EUGENE PARIS (D)
Chmn, St Johns Co Dem Exec Comt, Fla
b St Augustine, Fla, Oct 21, 22; s Charles Curtis Bagwell, DDS & May Paris B; single. Educ: Armstrong Jr Col, 46-47; NGa Col, BSBA, 50; Columbia Univ Sch Bus, 49; Sch Bus Asn. Polit & Govt Pos: Committeeman, St Johns Co Dem Exec Comt, Fla, 67-, chmn, 69- Bus & Prof Pos: Mem acct staff, Fla ECoast Rwy Co, 42-73, asst treas, 73- Mil Serv: Entered as Pvt, Army, 42, released as 1st Lt, after serv in AAA Gun Bn, 42-45 & 51-52; Lt Col, Army Res, currently; 1 Battle Star. Mem: ROA. Relig: Catholic. Mailing Add: 38 Water St St Augustine FL 32084

BAGWELL, HARRISON GAREY (R)
Mem, Rep State Cent Comt of La
b Georgetown, La, Dec 6, 13; s Arthur D Bagwell & Birdie Harrison B; m 1936 to June Sue Ross; c H Garey, Jr, Carole (Mrs John R Shows, Jr), Janet (Mrs Donald R Patt), June (Mrs Robert C Oliver), Barry, Bonnie & Martha Sue. Educ: La State Univ, BA, 40, LLB, 42, JD, 68. Polit & Govt Pos: Pres & founder Sixth Cong Dist Rep Club, 50-60; co-legal counsel La deleg, Rep Nat Conv, 52; deleg or alt deleg, Rep Nat Conv, 52, 56 & 60; mem govt study and recommendation comt, Rep State Cent Comt of La, 52-60, mem, 60-; pres & founder Rep Orgn La, 56-60; mem & secy exec comt, East Baton Rouge Parish Rep Party, 56-, chmn, formerly; chmn, Cong, Sen & Dist Rep Comt, 60- Bus & Prof Pos: Ed, Trumpet Publ Co, Inc, 54-58. Mem: East Baton Rouge Bar Asn. Relig: Protestant. Mailing Add: 5811 Menlo Dr Baton Rouge LA 70808

BAHAKEL, CY N (D)
NC State Sen
b Birmingham, Ala, Apr 12, 21; s father deceased & Mary B; m 1951 to Beverly Boyd. Educ: Univ Ala, AB & LLB, 47; Theta Chi. Polit & Govt Pos: NC State Sen, 73- Bus & Prof Pos: Pres & owner, Cy N Bahakel TV & Radio Stas located throughout the S, Southeast & Midwest, Hq Sta WCCB-TV, Charlotte, NC, 47- Mil Serv: 2nd Lt, Anti-Aircraft Artil. Mem: Mecklenburg Boy Scout Coun, Charlotte Jr Achievement, Charlotte Symphony Orchestra Asn & Charlotte CofC; Mecklenburg Heart Fund Drive. Relig: Baptist; Deacon, Pritchard Mem Baptist Church, currently. Legal Res: 12201 Providence Rd Matthews NC 28105 Mailing Add: PO Box 2449 Charlotte NC 28234

BAHILL, S LARRY (D)
Ariz State Rep
b Washington, Pa, Dec 10, 43; s Stephen Bahill & Tracey Wanda Wrubleski B; m 1973 to Carol Anne Skelley. Educ: Northern Ariz Univ, BS, 69; Univ Ariz, MEd, 70, Law Sch, 70-71; Phi Alpha Theta; Newman Cath Student Ctr; Young Dem; chmn, Elec Comt, 69-70. Polit & Govt Pos: Dem precinct committeeman, 68-; committeeman, Ariz State Dem Party, 70-; Ariz State Rep, 73- Bus & Prof Pos: Substitute teacher, Tucson Dist One, Ariz, 69-71 & 72-; Pima Co Health Educator, 71-72; instr govt, Pima Community Col, 73- Mil Serv: Entered as E-1, Naval Res, 60, released as E-5, 71, after serv in Naval Security Group, 60-66 & Guam, 66-68; Lt(jg), Naval Res, 71-; Meritorious Unit Commendation; Two Naval Res Meritorious Serv Awards; Armed Forces Res Award. Mem: KofC; Am Legion. Honors & Awards: Eagle Scouting Award with Silver Palm, Boy Scouts Am, 61; State winner Pillsbury Cooking Contest, 61. Relig: Catholic. Mailing Add: 3010 E 30th St Tucson AZ 85713

BAHOU, VICTOR SAMUEL (D)
b Watertown, NY, Jan 18, 21; s Samuel Bahou & Najiy Abdo B; m 1944 to Charmotte Mae Ajay; c Carole & Barbara. Educ: Bard Col, BA, 51; Syracuse Univ, PhD, 60. Polit & Govt Pos: Chmn, Cortland Co Dem Comt, NY, formerly. Bus & Prof Pos: Prof polit sci, State Univ NY Col Cortland, 55- Mem: Am & NY State Polit Sci Asns; Eastern Sociol Soc; Nat Munic League; Am Sociol Asn. Mailing Add: 54 Church St Cortland NY 13045

BAILAR, BENJAMIN F
US Postmaster Gen
b Champaign, Ill, Apr 21, 34; m to Anne Tveit; c Christina & Benjamin, Jr. Educ: Univ Colo, BA in Geol, 55; Harvard Univ, MBA, 59. Polit & Govt Pos: Sr asst, Postmaster Gen for support, US Postal Serv, 72, chief financial officer for serv, 72, sr asst postmaster gen admin & mem exec comt, 73, dep postmaster gen & mem bd of gov, 74-75, US Postmaster Gen, 75- Bus & Prof Pos: Coordr & planning staff, Continental Oil Co, Houston, Tex, 59-62; financial analyst, Am Can Co, New York, NY, 62-64, chmn, appropriations comt, 64-67, vpres mkt, 67, pres, Am Can Int, 68. Mil Serv: Entered Navy, 55, released as Lt(jg), 57, after serv in Naval Air Sta, St Louis. Legal Res: Bethesda MD 20034 Mailing Add: US Postal Serv Washington DC 20260

BAILEY, CHARLES LOUIS (R)
b Toledo, Ohio, Dec 14, 53; s Paul Edgar Bailey (deceased) & June Bernice Fisher B; single. Educ: Ohio Wesleyan Univ, BA, 75. Polit & Govt Pos: Citizen Comt mem, Weldishofer for State Rep, Ohio, 66; vol, Siegel for Mayor, Toledo, 69; state vchmn, Ohio League of TAR Clubs; 69-70, state chmn, 70-71; pres, Sylvania TAR Club, 69-71; mem exec campaign comt, Royer for State Sen, 70; pres, Lucas Co TAR Club, 70-71; mem, Lucas Co Rep Exec Comt, 71; TAR coordr, Ohio League of Col Rep Clubs, 71-72, exec dir, 73-74; col voter chmn, Ohio Comt to Reelect the President, 72; alt deleg, Rep Nat Conv, 72; vpres, Ohio Wesleyan Col Rep Club, 72-73, pres, 73-74; precinct committeeman, Lucas Co Rep Cent Comt, 72- Bus & Prof Pos: Mgt analyst, Ohio Gov Sch, 71; employee, Churchills Co, Inc, 72-73. Mil Serv: Entered as 2nd Lt, Marine Corps, 75- Honors & Awards: Outstanding Ohio Wesleyan Univ Freshman, Toledo Area Ohio Wesleyan Univ Alumni Club, 71. Mailing Add: 9445 Brint Rd Sylvania OH 43560

BAILEY, CHARLES PERKINS (R)
Committeeman, NJ Rep State Comt
b Elizabeth, NJ, Nov 4, 09; s Ralph Waldo Bailey & Nellie King West B; m 1940 to Cordelia Mary Curtis; c Barbara (Mrs Hollister) & Deborah West. Educ: Middlebury Col, BS, 32; Columbia Univ, MA, 34; Pi Delta Epsilon; Delta Upsilon. Polit & Govt Pos: Mem staff, Congressman Donald H McLean, 35-36; mem, Union Co Rep Comt, NJ, 36-40, chmn, 58-63; councilman, Westfield, 41-46, mayor, 47-54; mem, Westfield Planning Bd, 47-, chmn, 70-74; freeholder, Union Co, 55-57; deleg-at-lg, Rep Nat Conv, 60; co treas, Union Co, 61-65; deleg,

NJ Const Conv, 66; committeeman, NJ Rep State Comt, 67-; adv comt, Small Bus Admin, NJ, 69-; mem, NJ Hist Sites Coun & Trust, 72- Bus & Prof Pos: Pres, Spray Drying Serv, Inc, Garwood, NJ, 39-; mem bd mgr, Childrens Specialized Hosp, Westfield, 50-; dir, Lincoln Fed Savings & Loan Asn, 63-, dir, First Nat Bank, Roselle, 64-70; dir, First Nat Bank Cent Jersey, Bound Brook, 71- Mem: Rotary; SAR; Echo Lake Country Club; Col Mens Club; Chippewa Yacht Club. Relig: Presbyterian. Mailing Add: 729 St Marks Ave Westfield NJ 07090

BAILEY, CONSUELO NORTHROP (R)
b Fairfield, Vt, Oct 10, 99; d Peter Bent Brigham Northrop & Katherine Fletcher N; m 1940 to Henry Albon Bailey, wid. Educ: Univ Vt, PhB, 21; Boston Univ Law Sch, LLB, 25; Phi Beta Kappa; Sigma Gamma; Kappa Beta Pi; Phi Sigma Pi. Hon Degrees: LLD, Univ Vt, 52, Cedar Crest Col, 56 & Am Int Col, 57. Polit & Govt Pos: State attorney, Chittenden Co, Vt, 27-31; White House Mem, Comt Refugees; mem, US Civil War Centennial Comn; mem at lg, Civil Defense Women Adv Comt; deleg, Rep Nat Conv, 36 & 44, mem final draft comt, 44, secy, 68; Rep Nat Committeewoman, 36-73, vchmn, 52-56, first women chmn, Comt of Call, 60, secy, 64-72; Vt State Rep, 50-52, speaker, Vt House Rep; mem adv bd, US Post Off, 53; Lt Gov, Vt, 54-57; mem, state, co & town Rep comt; Presidential Elector, 56 & 72; mem, Vt Hist Sites Comn, 60-73; mem, Gov Comn Status of Women, 70; Nixon's Am deleg to Geneva, Switz, 70 & Paris, France, 72. Bus & Prof Pos: High sch teacher Latin & hist, Shelburne, Vt, 21-22; former dir, Iroquois Light & Power Co; mem bd, Womens Med Col, Philadelphia, Pa; mem, Peter Bent Brigham Corp; attorney, Burlington, 26-66; mem bd dirs, Tuttle Law Print Co, 57-; owner & operator, Vt Farm, Fairfield. Publ: Primary & Election Laws of Vermont 1928. Mem: Zonta Int; Vt Bar Asn; Vt Asn Blind; Univ Vt Alumni Coun; Vt Order of Women Legislators. Honors & Awards: Off observer for Vt at Las Vegas detonation of atomic bomb, 54; visited Free Ger Repub as Guest of that country with Women in Pub Life, 56; Distinguished Serv Award, Boston Univ, 70, Univ Vt, 71 & Nat Fedn Rep Women, 72. Relig: Episcopal. Mailing Add: 1317 Spear St South Burlington VT 05401

BAILEY, DAVID EMMETT (R)
Chmn, Clinton Co Rep Cent Comt, Ohio
b Wilmington, Ohio, Oct 3, 42; s Emmett Harold Bailey & Marion Wilson B; m 1965 to Constance Calvert; c Katherine Kerns & Laura Shannon. Educ: Ohio State Univ, BS, 64; Phi Kappa Psi. Polit & Govt Pos: Legis aide, Ohio House Rep, 61-64; chmn, Clinton Co Citizens for Nixon-Agnew, 68 & 72; chmn, Clinton Co Cloud for Gov Comt, 70; chmn, Clinton Co Rep Cent Comt, 74- Mailing Add: PO Box 410 Wilmington OH 45177

BAILEY, DENNIS CLARKE (R)
Chmn, Fifth Dist Rep Cent Comt, Iowa
b Des Moines, Iowa, Oct 9, 38; s Clarke E Bailey & Florence Ames B; single. Educ: Southwestern Community Col, Creston, Iowa, AA; Northwest Mo State Col, 1 year. Polit & Govt Pos: Chmn, Union Co Young Rep, Iowa, 63-68; precinct committeeman, Union Co Rep Cent Comt, 64-, chmn, 69-; chmn, Fifth Dist Rep Cent Comt, 72-; mem, Rep State Cent Comt of Iowa, 72- Bus & Prof Pos: Asst mgr, Am Acceptance Corp, 61-63; supvr indust banking, Iowa, currently. Mem: Am Indust Bankers' Asn; Rotary; Eagles; Mason; RAM. Relig: Methodist. Legal Res: 504 N Cedar Creston IA 50801 Mailing Add: Box 453 Creston IA 50801

BAILEY, EDWARD RISTON (R)
Tenn State Rep
b Reagan, Tenn, May 19, 19; s Dorsie Green Bailey & Betty Cricket Stewart B; m 1939 to Mableen Overman; c Betty Carol. Educ: Freed-Hardeman Col, 36-37 & 38-39. Polit & Govt Pos: Mem city coun, Lexington, Tenn, 49-53 & 55-67, mayor, 53-55; Tenn State Rep, 66-; dir, Off Econ Opportunity 68-72; chmn, Tenn Rep State Exec Comt, 69-71. Bus & Prof Pos: Teacher, Henderson Co Dept Educ, Tenn, 39-41; clerk, US Govt, Panama Canal Zone, 41-42; foreman, Procter & Gamble Co, Milan, 43; self employed, Retail Food Sales, 44-50, Mfg & Wholesale Hardwood Lumber, 50- Mem: Shrine; Elks; Moose. Relig: Baptist. Legal Res: N Broad St Lexington TN 38351 Mailing Add: PO Box 296 Lexington TN 38351

BAILEY, FLOYD J (R)
Chmn, Ind Rep State Finance Comt
b Factoryville, Pa, May 13, 04; s S J Bailey; m 1930 to Mary Eggleston Nininger; c Donald J, Carole & Lynn. Educ: Bucknell Univ, BS in Elec Eng, 26, MS in Elec Eng, 27; Columbia Univ, Summer 28; Lambda Chi Alpha. Polit & Govt Pos: Chmn, Fifth Dist Rep Citizens Finance Comt, Ind, 62-72; chmn, Ind Rep State Finance Comt, 72- Bus & Prof Pos: Asst prof math, William & Mary Col, 27-30; co surveyor, James City Co, Va, 28-30; research engr, Goodyear Zeppelin Corp of Akron, Ohio, 30-32; instr, Univ Akron Night Sch, 31; shipping clerk, purchasing agent & cost acct, S J Bailey, Inc, Nicholson, Pa, 32-37, vpres & mgr, Peru, Ind Br, 38-48; vpres, S J Bailey & Sons & mgr, Peru, Ind Br, 48-49; pres, Bailey Mfr Corp, Peru, 49-68; pres, Bailey of Peru, 53-; pres, Floyd J Bailey Lumber Co, 53-; residential real estate developer, currently. Mem: Sigma Delta Psi; Chi Beta Phi; Ind Mfr Asn; Peru Mfr Asn; Peru Rotary. Relig: Presbyterian. Mailing Add: PO Box 63 Peru IN 46970

BAILEY, FRANK I (D)
Ga State Sen
Mailing Add: 6524 Hayes Dr Riverdale GA 30274

BAILEY, HARLEY EVAN (D)
Committeeman, Wood Co Dem Party, WVa
b Cedarville, WVa, July 16, 15; s Herbert Jefferson Bailey & Ervie Stoneking B; m 1935 to Helen Catherine Kirkpatrick; c Carolyn Sue & Lynn Louise. Educ: Ohio Univ, BA in philos, 45; Bible Baptist Sem, B Bibliology, 48, Dr Bibliology, 49; Burton Col, Dr Divinity, 52; Ohio Univ Alumni Asn. Polit & Govt Pos: Dep sheriff, Wood Co, WVa, 57-58; welfare worker, WVa, 63-65; deleg, Rep Nat Conv, 64 & 68; committeeman, Wood Co Dem Party, WVa, 64-; city housing inspector, Parkersburg, 65- Bus & Prof Pos: High sch teacher, Belpre Sch Syst, Ohio, 57-58; minister, Jefferson Baptist Temple, 57-; rep, Waddell & Reed, Inc, 59-; high sch teacher, Calhoun Bd Educ, WVa, 63-64. Mil Serv: Chaplain (Capt), Civil Air Patrol, WVa Wing, 53- Mem: Nat Educ Asn; Mason (32 degree); Eastern Star; WOW. Honors & Awards: One of 300 in US selected for honor of tape recording in John F Kennedy Mem Mus, Boston, Mass. Relig: Baptist. Mailing Add: PO Box 3103 Parkersburg WV 26101

BAILEY, JEAN (D)
Mem, Dem Nat Comt, WVa
Mailing Add: PO Box J Pineville WV 24874

BAILEY, JOHN W, JR (R)
b Southport, Ind, Apr 16, 21; s John W Bailey & Katherine Rypma B; m 1946 to Alice C Schafer; c Allan & Bruce. Educ: Ind Univ, BS in bus, 43; Blue Key; Alpha Kappa Psi; Bd of Aeons. Polit & Govt Pos: Johnson Co chmn, Ind Almanac & Govt Guide, 63-66; finance chmn, Johnson Co Rep Party, Ind, 63-70; finance chmn, Goldwater Campaign, Seventh Cong Dist, 64; alt deleg, Rep Nat Conv, 64, deleg, 68; mem exec comt, Ind Rep Citizens Finance Comt; finance chmn, Sixth Cong Dist Rep Party, 66-70, chmn, formerly; state chmn, Rep Sustaining Victory Prog, 70- Bus & Prof Pos: Ins agt, Bailey & Hill Ins Serv, 46- Mil Serv: Entered as Pvt, Army, 43, released as Capt, 46, after serv in Hq, Ninth Army, ETO, 44-46. Mem: Cent Ind Health Planning Coun; Greenwood Auditorium Comt (chmn); Ind Univ Alumni Asn; Greenwood CofC; El Dorado Country Club. Relig: Methodist. Mailing Add: 605 Valley Lane Ct Greenwood IN 46142

BAILEY, KAY (R)
Tex State Rep
b La Marque, Tex, July 22, 43; d Allan A Bailey, Jr & Kathryn Sharp B; single. Educ: Univ Tex, Austin, LLB, 67; Kappa Beta Pi; Pi Beta Phi. Polit & Govt Pos: Tex State Rep, 72-, vchmn subcomt sources revenue, Tex House Rep, 73, mem revenue & taxation & rules comts, 75-, vchmn, intergovernmental affairs, 75- Bus & Prof Pos: Polit correspondent, KPRC-TV, Houston, Tex, formerly; attorney, Reynolds, White, Allen & Cook, Houston, currently; press secy to co-chmn, Nat Rep Party, Washington, DC, formerly. Mem: Tex Bar Asn (chmn comt advan bar); Tex Rape Prevention Proj (bd dirs); Tex Bill of Rights Found (bd dirs); Harris Co Hist Surv Comt; Citizens Comt Mass Transit Authority (vchmn). Honors & Awards: Houston Bar Asn Award for Best TV Reporter in Jurisp Field; First Woman Elected to Bd Dirs, Houston Jr Bar Asn; Nat Order Women Legislators. Legal Res: 3435 Westheimer Houston TX 77027 Mailing Add: Capitol Sta 2910 Austin TX 78767

BAILEY, MONTE D (D)
b Moroni, Utah, Mar 26, 17; s Gilbert Bailey & Chloe Cook B; m 1939 to Marjorie Irene Jackson; c Linda (Mrs Bill Beynon), Nancy (Mrs Ronald Oyler), Clela (Mrs Robert Dorton) & Karen (Mrs Mike Mooney). Educ: Utah State Univ, BS, 40; Univ Utah, 1 year; Sigma Nu. Polit & Govt Pos: Utah State Sen, 71-72; comnr, Weber Co, 73- Bus & Prof Pos: Pres, Defense Supply Asn, 69- Mil Serv: Entered as Pvt, Army, 45, released as Cpl, 46, after serv in Spec Serv, 3rd & 9th Serv Commands. Mem: Utah, Nat & Ogden Educ Asns; Elks; Am Legion. Relig: Latter-day Saint. Mailing Add: 1592 Ninth St Ogden UT 84404

BAILEY, R WENDELL (D)
Mo State Rep
Mailing Add: 312 E Fourth Willow Springs MO 65793

BAILEY, ROBERT C (D)
Wash State Sen
b Raymond, Wash, 1918; m 1953 to Lena Heller; c one son. Polit & Govt Pos: Wash State Sen, 19th Dist, currently; western admin asst to Julia Butler Hansen, US Rep, Wash, currently. Mil Serv: Navy, World War II. Mem: Eagles; VFW; Am Legion; Mason; Kiwanis; Boy Scout Coun. Mailing Add: 602 W First St South Bend WA 98586

BAILEY, T WAYNE (D)
Dem Nat Committeeman, Fla
Mailing Add: 600 N Salisbury Ave DeLand FL 32720

BAILY, NATHAN A (D)
b New York, NY, July 19, 20; s Saul Baily & Eleanor B; m 1946 to Judith Bernstein; c Alan Eric & Lawrence Joel. Educ: City Col New York, BS in Soc Sci, 40; Columbia Univ, MA, 41; PhD, 46; Phi Beta Kappa; Hist & Econ Clubs. Polit & Govt Pos: Economist, Off of Price Admin, 46-47; comnr, Postal Rate Comn, 70-74, chief economist, 74- Bus & Prof Pos: Fel & tutor, Dept Econ & Hist, City Col New York, 40-46; ed-analyst, Research Inst of Am, 44-45; from asst prof to prof mgt, Am Univ, 47-, founding dean, Sch Bus Admin, 55-70. Publ: Ed, Marketing Profitably Under the Robinson-Patman Act, Pub Affairs, 64 & Marketing Handbooks I & II, Inst Indust Launderers, 72, 73; Guide for establishing a company marketing program, 74; plus others. Mem: US CofC, Am Econ Asn; Am Asn Univ Prof; Am Soc Asn Execs; Washington Soc Investment Anal. Honors & Awards: Distinguished Salesman's Award, Washington Sales Execs Club; Distinguished Serv Award, Soc Relig Orgn Mgt. Legal Res: 5516 Greystone St Chevy Chase MD 20015 Mailing Add: Postal Rate Comn 2000 L St Washington DC 20268

BAIN, CARL EDGAR (R)
Chmn, Richmond Rep City Comt, Va
b Roanoke Co, Va, Jan 23, 27; s Milton Albert Bain & Martha Kate Barton B; m 1951 to Irene Estelle White; c Patricia Ann, Sarah Collie (deceased) & Catherine Irene. Educ: Med Col Va, BS, Pharm, 51; Alpha Sigma Chi; Phi Delta Chi. Polit & Govt Pos: Mem, Richmond Rep City Comt, Va, 66-, chmn, 68-; Rep cand, Va House Rep, Richmond-Henrico, 67 & 69; Va State Deleg, Richmond-Henrico Co, mem, Steering Comt Rep Caucus, Gen Assembly Va, 73-74; app by Gov to Study Comn, 70; mem, ABC Study Comn, 72-74 & Prof & Occup Registration Study Comn, 72-74. Bus & Prof Pos: Pres, Police & Firefighters Assistance, Found of Va, 68; mem bd dirs, Retail Merchants Asn, Richmond, Va, 69- Mil Serv: Entered as Seaman, Navy, 45, released as PhM 3/C, 47. Mem: Va Asn of the Professions (treas, 68-70, pres, 70-); Rotary Int; Willow Oaks Country Club; Bull & Bear Club; Am Legion. Honors & Awards: Nat Award for Contribution to Interprof Rels, Nat Asn Retail Druggists, 72; Distinguished Retailer Award, Retail Merchants Asn Gtr Richmond, 74. Relig: Baptist. Mailing Add: 109 Maple Ave Richmond VA 23226

BAIN, CHARLES ROBERT (R)
Chmn, Berkeley Co Rep Exec Comt, WVa
b Bunker Hill, WVa, Sept 12, 26; s Robert Allen Bain & Anna Cecelia Ivers B; m 1949 to Edna Pauline Sencindiver; c Robin Charlene. Educ: Bunker Hill High Sch, WVa, grad, 47. Polit & Govt Pos: Chmn, Berkeley Co Rep Exec Comt, WVa, 68-, committeeman, Mill Creek Dist, 68-; mem, Berkeley Co Rep Club, 68-; mem Morgan Co Rep Club, 68-; mem Berkeley Co Young Rep Club, 68-; mem Berkeley Co Women's Rep Club, 68-; mem nat voters adv bd, Am Security Coun, 69-; gen track inspector, WVa Racing Comn, 70-; presidential elector, 72. Bus & Prof Pos: Draftsman & salesman, Martinsburg Granite Works, WVa, 55-60, asst mgr, 60- Mil Serv: Entered as Pvt, Army, 44, released as T-5, 46, after serv in 1777th Engrs Construction Bn, Pac Theatre, 45-46; Good Conduct Medal; Pac Campaign Ribbon; numerous unit awards. Mem: Am Rifle Asn; Mason; RAM; KT; Jr Order United Am Mech (state coun WVa). Honors & Awards: Highest State Awards, Jr Order United Am Mech, 65, 67 & 70; Cert of Recognition as Presidential Elector, Richard Nixon & Gov Arch Moore,

Jr, 72. Relig: United Methodist; Treas, chmn nominating & finance comts & mem bd, Darksville United Methodist Church, WVa. Mailing Add: PO Box 38 Bunker Hill WV 25413

BAIN, MARY ANDERSON (D)
b DeKalb, Ill, Sept 19, 11; d Dr Stoddard L Anderson & Ellen Larson A; m 1937 to Herbert Blackman Bain; c Mary Ellen. Educ: Northern Ill Univ, BA, 33. Polit & Govt Pos: State & regional dir, Nat Youth Admin, Ill, 35-43; asst state dir, War Manpower Comn, 43-45; state dir, US Employ Serv, 45-46; regional exec asst, Off Price Admin, 46-47; admin asst, US Rep Sidney Yates, Ill, 65- Bus & Prof Pos: Elem & high sch teacher, Riverside, Ill & Hammond, Ind, 33-35; owner advert agency, Chicago, Ill, 47-55; develop dir, Francis Parker Sch, 56-63; pres, High Sch Dist 225 Sch Bd, Glenview & Northbrook, 65-71. Mem: Womens Polit Caucus; Women's Nat Dem Club; Admin Assts Asn; River Bend Country Club. Relig: Protestant. Legal Res: 6017 Woodley Rd McLean VA 22101 Mailing Add: 2234 Rayburn Off Bldg Washington DC 20515

BAINBRIDGE, PHILLIP E (D)
Ind State Rep
b East Chicago, Ind, Jan 21, 42; s Eugene Bainbridge & Stella Krakowiak B; m 1966 to Caroline Heath Norris; c Mark Cameron, Phillip Eugene & Katharine Louise. Educ: Ind Univ Sch Bus, Bloomington, BS, 64, Sch Law, JD, 68; Alpha Tau Omega. Polit & Govt Pos: Asst to attorney gen, Ind, 66; Ind State Rep, 67-, mem, Civil Code Study Comn, Ind House Rep, 68-71, Interim Joint Comt Taxation, 69-71, State Budget Comt, 70-71 & minority leader, 73-; mem, Gov Comn Med Educ, 70-71. Bus & Prof Pos: Instr labor law & bus law, Purdue Univ, 70-71. Mem: Nat Soc State Legislators; Ind Bar Asn; Hammond Bar Asn; CofC; Ind Foster Parents Asn (dir). Legal Res: 2107 Ridgewood Highland IN 46322 Mailing Add: 2927 Jewett Ave Highland IN 46322

BAIRD, JEFF SCOTT (D)
b Long Beach, Calif, Sept 13, 55; s Bruce Baird & Suzanne Scotchler B; single. Educ: Calif State Univ Fullerton, currently. Polit & Govt Pos: Deleg, Dem Nat Mid-Term Conf, 74; field rep, Calif State Assembly, 74- Mem: YMCA (mem, gov bd); Orange Co Young Dem (treas). Mailing Add: 9322 Melba Dr Garden Grove CA 92641

BAIRD, RAYMOND RENFRO (D)
Tenn State Sen
b Jellico, Tenn, July 6, 14; s Orlando L Baird & Alice Gallaway B; m 1938 to Martha Louise Cagle; c Ray R, Jr & Nancy Louise. Educ: Hiwassee Col; ETenn State Univ; Ed, col newspapers. Polit & Govt Pos: Mem, Dem Exec Comt, Tenn, 46-; Tenn State Rep, 54-60; Tenn State Sen, 60- Bus & Prof Pos: Ed-publisher, The Rockwood Times, 41-; treas, Tenn Press Asn, 56-60, pres, 61-62, dir, 62- Mil Serv: Entered as Pvt, Army, 44, released as Sgt, 46, after serv in 61st Signal Bn, SPac & Japan; Good Conduct Medal; SPac Campaign & Japan Occupation Ribbons; Two Battle Stars; Expert Rifleman's Badge. Mem: Am Legion; VFW; DAV; Civitan; 40 et 8; KofP. Honors & Awards: Named Most Outstanding Legislator for 57 & 65. Relig: Baptist; Sunday Sch Teacher. Legal Res: 132 N Kingston Ave Rockwood TN 37854 Mailing Add: PO Box 297 Rockwood TN 37854

BAIRD, WILLIAM D (D)
Tenn State Sen
Mailing Add: 132 N Kingston Ave Rockwood TN 37854

BAKALY, CHARLES G, JR (R)
Mem Exec Comt, Rep State Cent Comt Calif
b Long Beach, Calif, Nov 15, 27; s Charles G Bakaly & Doris Carpenter B; m 1952 to Patricia Murphey; c Charles G, III, John W & Thomas B. Educ: Stanford Univ, AB, 49; Univ Southern Calif Sch Law, JD, 52; Delta Tau Delta. Polit & Govt Pos: Mem exec comt, Rep State Cent Comt Calif, 71-; deleg, Rep Nat Conv, 72. Bus & Prof Pos: Attorney, O'Melveny & Myers, 56- Mil Serv: Entered as Pvt, Army, 52, released as 1st Lt, 56. Publ: An employer's rights in a NLRB representation election, Los Angeles Bar Bull, 2/63; And after AVCO, Labor Law J, 2/69; Decisions affecting the networks and unions, In: Broadcasting and Bargaining, 70. Mem: Am & Los Angeles Co Bar Asns; Calif Club. Legal Res: 521 Michigan Blvd Pasadena CA 91107 Mailing Add: 611 W Sixth St Los Angeles CA 90017

BAKER, ALMINA ROGERS (D)
Chmn, Hamilton Co Dem Party, NY
b Arietta, NY, Aug 11, 23; d Michael Henry Rogers & Alida Avery R; m 1947 to William Eli Baker; c William Bartle & Barry Lee. Educ: Syracuse Univ, BS, 45; Alpha Omicron Pi. Polit & Govt Pos: Dep co treas, Hamilton Co, NY, 47-; clerk & dep elec comnr, Hamilton Co, 48-; chmn, Hamilton Co Dem Party, currently. Bus & Prof Pos: Asst cashier, Hamilton Co Nat Bank, 45-47. Relig: Catholic. Mailing Add: Lake Pleasant NY 12108

BAKER, ANDREW ZACHARIAH (D)
Tex State Rep
b Bienville Parish, La, Oct 22, 19; s Benjamin Franklin Baker & Delilah Taylor B; m 1945 to Jean Margaret Attwood; c John Robert, Bonnie Jean (Mrs Kenneth Palmer, Jr), Susan Patricia (Mrs Peter Olsen) & David Andrew Howard. Educ: STex Jr Col, AA, 49, STex Col Law, LLB, JD, 53. Polit & Govt Pos: Bd mem & secy, Island Rural High Sch Dist, 58-61 & Galveston Independent Sch Dist, 62-68; committeeman, 17th Dem Sen Dist, 68-70; Tex State Rep, 72- Mil Serv: Entered as Pvt, Army, 39, released as 1st Lt, 45, after serv in 81st Mortar Bn, Europe, 43-45; Silver Star; Two Presidential Citations; Two Purple Hearts; European Theatre Ribbon; Four Battle Stars. Mem: Elks; Lions; VFW; Am Legion; DAV. Relig: Unitarian. Mailing Add: 403 Nat Hotel Bldg Galveston TX 77550

BAKER, ANNE ELIZABETH (D)
b Washington, DC, Oct 20, 51; d Frank Baker, Jr & Miriam-Louise Betz B; single. Educ: Stephens Col, 69-70; Univ Md, Baltimore, 70-; feature ed, Retriever (newspaper). Polit & Govt Pos: Pres, Univ Md-New Dem Coalition, 70-72; alt deleg, Dem Nat Conv, 72; student coordr, McGovern/Shriver for President in Md, 72; secy, Columbia Dem Club, 72-; deleg, Md State New Dem Coalition, 72- Bus & Prof Pos: Photographer, Catonsville Community Col, 71-72. Honors & Awards: Commendation for Student Serv, Univ Md, 72. Relig: Disciples of Christ. Mailing Add: 3113 The Oaks Rd Ellicott City MD 21043

BAKER, ANNETTE (D)
b New York, NY, Nov 30, 23; m to Judge Robert Warren Baker, wid; c Robert Warren, II. Educ: Hunter Col; Principia Col; Univ Southern Calif. Polit & Govt Pos: Deleg, Dem Nat Conv, 64 & 68; Dem Nat Committeewoman, Fla, 64-68. Bus & Prof Pos: Pres-treas, Precision Tool Co, Inc, currently; pres-treas, Precision Mfg Co, Inc, currently; dir, Clearwater Marine Sci Ctr, currently. Mem: Dem Women's Club of Fla; Am Legion Auxiliary; League of Women Voters; Nat Soc of Arts & Letters; Nat Fedn of Women's Clubs. Relig: Christian Science. Mailing Add: 310 Harbor Passage Clearwater FL 33515

BAKER, CHARLES DUANE (R)
b Newburyport, Mass, June 21, 28; s Charles Duane Baker & Eleanor Little B; m 1955 to Alice Elizabeth Ghormley; c Charles D, Jonathan C & Alexander K. Educ: Harvard Col, AB, 51; Harvard Grad Sch Bus Admin, MBA, 55; PiEta Club; Hasty-Pudding Inst of 1770. Polit & Govt Pos: Dep Under Secy, Dept of Transportation, 69-70, Asst Secy for Policy & Int Affairs, 70-71. Bus & Prof Pos: Buyer, Westinghouse Elec Corp, NY, 55-57, purchasing sect supvr, NJ, 57-61; vpres, United Research, Inc, Cambridge, Mass, 61-65; vpres, Harbridge House, Boston, 65-69, pres & chmn, currently. Mil Serv: ARM3, Navy, 46-48, with serv in NAS Coco Solo; reentered as AL3, 51, released as Lt(jg), 53, after serv in VP 10 & VC 4. Publ: Balance of Payments & Merchant Marine, 67 & Intermodal Transport Through the NW Corridor, 68, Harbridge House. Mem: Brae Burn Country Club; Needham Pool & Racquet Club; East India Club; Harvard Clubs Boston & Washington; Nat Aviation Club. Relig: Congregational. Mailing Add: 21 Cleveland Rd Needham MA 02192

BAKER, CHARLES WAYNE (D)
Mem, Pulaski Co Dem Exec Comt, Ark
b Booneville, Mo, Nov 29, 40; s Urban Charles Baker & Viola Imhoff B; m 1961 to Nancy Jewel Lowe; c Julie Renee, Betsy Lynn, Troy Wayne, Susan Lowe & John Keeling. Educ: Univ Mo-Columbia, BA, 62, JD, 65; Phi Kappa Theta. Polit & Govt Pos: Mem, Pulaski Co Dem Exec Comt, Ark, 70-; alt deleg, Dem Nat Conv, 72; Referee in Bankruptcy, Eastern & Western Dist, Ark, 73- Bus & Prof Pos: Assoc, Rogers, Field & Gentry Law Firm, Kansas City, Mo, 65-68; partner, Moses, McClellan, Arnold, Owen & McDermott Law Firm, Little Rock, Ark, 68-72; secy, Baker & Probst, Attorneys, 73- Publ: Planning the tax consequences of partnership agreements, funded with life insurance, to provide for disposition of a deceased partner's interest, Mo Law Rev, winter 65. Mem: Am Bar Asn; Asn Am Trial Lawyers; Phi Delta Phi; Kiwanis; Jaycees. Relig: Catholic. Mailing Add: 49 Sherrill Heights Little Rock AR 72202

BAKER, DONALD MATTHEW (D)
b Beckley, WVa, June 7, 25; s John Charles Baker, Jr & Teresa Cecilia Binns B; m 1959 to Joan Mary O'Hora; c Teresa, Matthew, Timothy, Jennifer, John, Emily & Colin. Educ: Univ Mich, AB, sociol, 50, AM, econ, 52, LLB, 56. Polit & Govt Pos: Orgn & methods examr, Detroit Tank Arsenal, Centerline, Mich, 52-53; admin asst, US Rep James G O'Hara, 59-63; counsel, Subcomt Labor & Comt on Labor & Pub Welfare, US Senate, 63-64; gen counsel, Off Econ Opportunity, 64-69; assoc counsel, Labor Comt on Educ & Labor, US House Rep, 69-71, chief clerk & assoc counsel, Comt Educ & Labor, 71- Bus & Prof Pos: Assoc, Kramer, Morris, Stark, Rowland & Regan, Detroit, Mich, 56-59. Mil Serv: Entered as Cadet, Army Air Force, 43, released as Cpl, 46. Mem: Mich State Bar Asn. Honors & Awards: Exceptional Serv Award, Off Econ Opportunity, 69. Relig: Roman Catholic. Mailing Add: 9708 Digging Rd Gaithersburg MD 20760

BAKER, DOUGLAS J (R)
Vt State Rep
b Whitehall, NY, Sept 15, 38; s Smith M Baker & Lillian Johnson B; m 1958 to Mary Louise Kendall; c Deborah, Douglas M, Laurie & Robert. Educ: Castleton State Col, 57-60. Polit & Govt Pos: Mem, New Haven Planning Comt, 72-; mem, Addison Co Regional Planning Comt, 74-; Vt State Rep, 75- Bus & Prof Pos: Co-owner, Cole's Motel & Restaurant, 72- Mem: Vt State CofC; Vt Travel Adv Bd; Vt Hotel-Motel-Restaurant Asn; Addison Co Farm Bur; Addison Co CofC. Honors & Awards: Outstanding Young Man of Year, 74. Relig: Methodist. Legal Res: Rte 7 New Haven VT Mailing Add: PO Box 525 Middlebury VT 05753

BAKER, E LAMAR (R)
b Chattanooga, Tenn, Dec 29, 15; s Rush Emmons Baker & Sarah Beall B; m 1945 to Sue Batey; c Edward L, Jr & Sarah Susan. Educ: David Lipscomb Col, 36-38; Harding Col, BS in bus admin, 40. Polit & Govt Pos: Rep precinct chmn, 14th Ward, Hamilton Co, Tenn, 62-63; coordr, Hamilton Co Precincts in Chattanooga, 63-64; campaign mgr, Kuykendall for US Senate, 64; chmn, Hamilton Co Exec Comt, 65-66; Tenn State Rep, Dist 2, Hamilton Co, 67-68; Tenn State Sen, 69-70, chmn, Senate Rep Caucus & Hamilton Co Deleg, Tenn State Senate, 69-70; US Rep, Dist Three, Tenn, 70-74; deleg, Rep Nat Conv, 72; consult, US Dept Transportation, 75- Bus & Prof Pos: Pres, Commercial Janitors, Inc, Chattanooga, 62- Mil Serv: Entered as Pvt, Army Air Force, 42, released as Maj, 46, after serv in 560th Bomb Squadron H, 388th Bomb Group H, ETO, 43-45; ETO Ribbon with 3 Oak Leaf Clusters; Good Conduct Medal. Mem: CofC; Am Legion; VFW; Citizens Good Govt League; Civitan; Chattanooga Safety Coun. Relig: Church of Christ; Elder. Mailing Add: 76 S Crest Rd Chattanooga TN 37404

BAKER, GEORGE H, SR (D)
NH State Rep
Mailing Add: Box 116 Hudson NH 03051

BAKER, GORDON D, JR (D)
SC State Rep
Mailing Add: Box 909 Florence SC 29501

BAKER, HAMP (D)
Comnr, Okla Corp Comn
b Stephens Co, Okla, May 3, 33; s David Jeff Baker & Ida Friles B; m 1971 to JoAnn Creel; c Lana Jo Baker Adams, Cynthia Ann (Mrs Mark Morris), Craig Maurice & Erika. Educ: Southeastern Okla State Univ, 61; Univ Okla, 64-65. Polit & Govt Pos: Comnr, Okla Corp Comn, 75- Bus & Prof Pos: Rancher, Ratliff City, Okla, 52-; owner, Baker Construction & Well Servicing Co, Ratliff City, 54-75. Mem: Cattlemen's Asn; Nat Sch Bd Admin; Lions; Gideons. Relig: Assembly of God. Legal Res: Ratliff City OK 73081 Mailing Add: 2900 Lamp Post Lane Oklahoma City OK 73120

BAKER, HAROLD A (R)
Vt State Rep
Mailing Add: 1 Belle-Fred Dr Randolph VT 05060

BAKER, HAYDEN BURNICE (R)
Tenn State Sen
b Pennington Gap, Va, Aug 21, 23; s Thomas Franklin Baker & Emma Pearl Rogers B; m 1943 to Marie Cecelia Holland; c Hayden Bryan, David Lee, James Paul & Gary Lynn. Educ:

Morris Harvey Col, Univ Tenn & Int Correspondence Sch. Polit & Govt Pos: Justice of the peace, Sullivan Co, Tenn, 66-69; Tenn State Sen, 2nd Sen Dist, 68-, secy, Rep Caucus, Tenn State Senate, mem, Finance, Ways & Means, Gen Welfare, Environ, Tourism, Transportation & Safety & Legis Coun Comts, currently. Bus & Prof Pos: Designer, Tenn Eastman Co, 48-; dir, Baptist Childrens Home, 54- Mil Serv: Entered as A/S, Navy, 44, released as Seaman 2/C, 45. Mem: Instrument Soc Am; Nat Asn Power Engrs; Optimist Int (Lt Gov & State membership chmn, Tenn Dist); Farm Bur; Ruritan Int. Relig: Baptist. Mailing Add: 256 Fletcher Ave Kingsport TN 37665

BAKER, HERMAN MERLIN (R)
Chmn, Darke Co Rep Exec Comt, Ohio
b Arcanum, Ohio, Jan 19, 17; s Glen C Baker & Ruth Myers B; m 1939 to Lucille Fenstermaker; c Jerrlyn (Mrs Kent Myers) & Merlin. Educ: Int Bus Col, Ft Wayne, Ind, 36-39. Polit & Govt Pos: Mem, Co Bd Elec, 66-; committeeman, Rep State Cent & Exec Comt of Ohio, 50-; alt deleg, Ohio State Conv, 66, deleg, 68; mem exec comt, Darke Co Rep Exec Comt, 67-, & chmn, 68- Bus & Prof Pos: Mem, Franklin-Monroe High Sch Bd Educ, 59-67, & chmn, 66; twp clerk, 61- Mem: Farm Bur; Rotary. Relig: Protestant. Mailing Add: RR 2 Arcanum OH 45304

BAKER, HOWARD, JR (R)
US Sen, Tenn
b Huntsville, Tenn, 1925; m to Joy Dirksen. Educ: Univ of the South, Sewanee; Tulane Univ; Univ Tenn, LLB, 49. Polit & Govt Pos: US Sen, Tenn, 67-, mem select comt on presidential activities, US Senate, 73-, mem foreign rels comt, 75-; deleg, Rep Nat Conv, 68. Bus & Prof Pos: Attorney. Mil Serv: USNR, World War II; discharged as Lt(jg). Legal Res: TN Mailing Add: 2107 New Senate Bldg Washington DC 20510

BAKER, JACK W (D)
Chmn, Grimes Co Dem Party, Tex
b Navasota, Tex, Nov 30, 29; s Henry Cady Baker & Myrtle Evans B; m 1954 to Jacquelyn E Venable; c Cynthia E, Susan E, John Henry, Ruth Ann & Rosemary. Educ: Tex A&M Col, BS, 51. Polit & Govt Pos: Chmn, Grimes Co Dem Party, Tex, 75- Mil Serv: Entered as 2nd Lt, Army, 51, released as 1st Lt, 53, after serv in QM Corps. Relig: Baptist. Legal Res: RFD 2 Box 17W Navasota TX 77868 Mailing Add: PO Box 909 Navasota TX 77868

BAKER, JACQUELINE RAE (R)
Nat Committeewoman, RI Young Rep
b Grove City, Pa, Nov 4, 52; d Ray Howard Baker & Shirley Leach B; single. Educ: RI Col, BA, 74; Univ RI, 74- Polit & Govt Pos: Page, RI State Senate, 73-74; chmn, RI Young Rep Leadership Conf, 73; nat committeewoman, RI Young Rep, 74- Bus & Prof Pos: Teacher Eng, Barrington High Sch, 74- Publ: Ed, Gourmet of the Party (cookbook), 74. Mem: Barrington Rep Town Comt; Barrington Rep Womens Club; Nat Fedn Rep Women. Honors & Awards: Citizen Scholar Award, 70. Relig: Protestant. Mailing Add: 107 Massasoit Ave Barrington RI 02806

BAKER, JAMES A (D)
Ala State Rep
Mailing Add: 400 29th St Phenix City AL 36867

BAKER, JAMES ESTES
b Suffolk, Va, Jan 21, 35; s Percy Hayes Baker, Sr & Helen Estes B; single. Educ: Haverford Col, BA, 56; Fletcher Sch Law & Diplomacy, MA, 57, MALD, 60; Univ Calif, Berkeley, 70-71. Polit & Govt Pos: Foreign serv officer, US Embassy, Bamako, Mali, 60-61; Niamgy, Niger, 61-62 & Tokyo, Japan, 63-67 & 71-72; foreign serv officer, Dept of State, Washington, DC, 68-70; foreign serv officer, US Embassy, Pretoria, SAfrica, 73-74; adv econ & social affairs, US Mission to UN, 74- Mil Serv: Entered as E-1, Army, 57, released as E-4, after serv in 7th LAV, Ger, 58-59. Legal Res: 166 E 34th St New York NY 10016 Mailing Add: US Mission to UN 799 UN Plaza New York NY 10017

BAKER, JAMES GLEN (D)
Majority Whip, Mo House of Rep
b St Louis, Mo, June 25, 38; s Glen S Baker & Sylvia Davis B; single. Educ: Univ Mo, BA, 60, Harvard Law Sch, LLB, 66; Phi Gamma Delta. Polit & Govt Pos: Mo State Rep, 71-, Majority Whip, Mo House of Rep, 72- Bus & Prof Pos: Attorney, Boston, Mass, 66-69 & Kansas City, Mo, 69- Mil Serv: Entered as 2nd Lt, Army, 61, released as 1st Lt, 62. Mem: Am & Mo Bars; Citizens Environ Coun. Relig: Protestant. Mailing Add: 104 E 41st Kansas City MO 64111

BAKER, JOAN MARIE (R)
b Milwaukee, Wis, Sept 2, 29; d Leslie W Rehm & Adeline Musbach R; m 1952 to Max O Baker; c Christine Ann, Jeffry Rowe, Patrice Marie & Bret Roy. Educ: Univ Wis, Madison, BS, 51; Washburn Univ, currently; Alpha Delta Theta. Polit & Govt Pos: Treas, Jefferson Co Rep Women, 63-64; pres, 65-66; mem campaign activities comt, Kans Fedn Rep Women, 63-64; treas, 65-66, second vpres, 67, first vpres, 68-69, pres, 70-71; secy, Third Dist Young Rep, 63-64; secy, Valley Falls, Kans Low-Cost Housing Authority, 68-70; secy Valley Falls Temporary Planning Comn, 69; mem, 338 Unified Sch Dist Bd, 69-70, vpres, 70-71; mem, Jefferson Co Solid Waste Disposal Comt, 71-; co-chmn, Kans Reelect the President Comt, 72; mem, Nat Adv Comn Drugs, 72-73; Dep Asst Secy of State, Kans, 72-74. Bus & Prof Pos: Relief technologist, Jefferson Co Hosp, 65-; policy examr, Comnr Ins, Kans, currently. Mem: Am & Kans Soc Med Technologists; Am Soc Clin Pathologists; St Mary's Altar Soc. Relig: Roman Catholic. Legal Res: RFD 3 Valley Falls KS 66088 Mailing Add: PO Box 89 Valley Falls KS 66088

BAKER, JOE M (R)
b Asheville, NC, Feb 10, 27; s Joe M Baker & Julia Williams B; m 1950 to Bernice Maupin, div; c Joe M, III, Rebecca L, Cynthia L & Robert L. Educ: US Merchant Marine Acad, BS, 47; Georgetown Univ Sch Foreign Serv, 48-49; Univ Tenn Col Bus, BS in Bus, 50; Lambda Chi Alpha; Delta Sigma Pi; Alpha Eta Rho; Canterbury Club. Polit & Govt Pos: Deleg, Rep State Conv, 60-64; Rep nominee for US Rep, Fifth Dist, Md, 62; mem, Rep State Cent Comt, 62-66, chmn, State Rep Party, 62-66; deleg, Rep Nat Conv, 64. Bus & Prof Pos: Third officer, Lykes Bros Steamship Co, 47-48; salesman, Eckington Bldg Supply Co, Washington, DC, 50-55; managing dir & exec vpres, Int Asn of Wall & Ceiling Contractors, 55- Mil Serv: Lt, Naval Res, 49, Pac Theatre. Mem: Am Soc Asn Exec; Nat Rep Club Capitol Hill (mem, Bd Gov); Washington Soc Asn Exec (bd dirs & secy-treas); Alumni Asn of US Merchant Marine Acad (past nat vpres). Relig: Episcopal. Legal Res: PO Box 69 Annapolis MD 21404 Mailing Add: 1775 Church St NW Washington DC 20036

BAKER, JOHN EDWARD (R)
Chmn, Orange Rep Town Comt, Conn
b East Norwalk, Conn, May 25, 17; s William Henry Baker & Clara Wallin B; m 1946 to Eleanor Brown; c Christie (Mrs Robert Smith) & John A. Educ: New Haven Col, 2 years; Southern Conn State Col. Polit & Govt Pos: Mem, Orange Rep Town Comt, Conn, 60-, chmn, 67-; Conserv Comnr, Orange, Conn, 64-67; chmn, Conn State Shellfish Comn, currently; dir aquaculture div, Conn State Dept Agr, 72- Bus & Prof Pos: Plant foreman, Southern New Eng Tel Co, 55-60, splicing foreman, 60-67, plant staff training, 67-68, maintenance foreman, 67-71. Mil Serv: Entered as BM2/C, Navy, 42, released as CBM, 45, after serv in Mine Sweeping, SAtlantic Area, 43-45. Mem: Indust Mgt Club New Haven (pres, 68-69); Mason; Am Legion. Relig: Episcopal. Mailing Add: 296 Fairlea Rd Orange CT 06477

BAKER, JOHN MARTIN (D)
Ala State Rep
b Albertville, Ala, Oct 6, 44; s Raymond Excell Baker & Ella Jane Gann B; m 1964 to Regena Holdbrooks; c Gina Leigh & Ginger. Educ: Univ Ala, BA, 66, JD, 67; Sigma Delta Kappa. Polit & Govt Pos: Ala State Rep, DeKalb & Cherokee Co, 70- Mem: DeKalb Co Bar Asn; Rainsville CofC; NAm Judges Asn; Rainsville Jaycees; Ala Farm Bur. Relig: Baptist. Legal Res: PO Box 316 Ft Payne AL 35967 Mailing Add: PO Box 186 Rainsville AL 35986

BAKER, KEITH (D)
Iowa State Rep
Mailing Add: Linn Grove IA 51033

BAKER, LLOYD J (L J) (D)
Mo State Rep
b Jacksonville, Mo, Sept 6, 31; s Mr & Mrs Ed Baker; m 1952 to Bonnie Janet Sarbaum; c Michael Jay. Educ: Moberly Jr Col, grad, 58; Univ Mo, 2 years. Polit & Govt Pos: Mo State Rep, Dist 97, 64-, chmn comt atomic energy & indust develop, mem appropriations & govt orgn comts, comts roads & highways & dairying & livestock & chmn, Atomic Energy Comn, Mo House of Rep; mem, Task Force for the 70's & subcomt instr, Northeast Mo State Univ; deleg, White House Conf Aging. Bus & Prof Pos: Nat Detective Agency, Washington, DC, mgr Baltimore Off, formerly; Wabash RR (Eng Dept), 2 years; co surveyor, Randolph Co, 61-65; field engr for Moberly Medium Security Prison, 65. Mil Serv: Marine Corps, 51-56; two meritorious promotions, spec guard at NATO Anniversary Meeting & at Camp David. Mem: Kiwanis; Farm Bur; Grange; CofC; Nat Asn State Legislators; 5000 Dem Club Boone Co. Honors & Awards: Univ Mo Exten Honor Roll. Relig: Baptist; Sunday Sch teacher, pres, Carpenter St Baptist Church Brotherhood. Mailing Add: RFD 3 Box 150 Moberly MO 65270

BAKER, MARGARET PRESLEY (D)
Mem, Ga State Dem Exec Comt
b Homer, Ga, Jan 26, 27; d Levi Weldon Presley & Reba Wells P; m 1943 to Eugene Walter Baker, II; c Cheryl Euginia (Mrs George Burnett), Cathy Margaret & Eugene Walter, III. Educ: Univ Ga, BA, 48. Polit & Govt Pos: Mem, Clayton Co Bd Educ, Ga, 66-; mem, Ga State Dem Exec Comt, 71- Mem: Clayton Co Classroom Teachers Asn; Forest Park Bus & Prof Women; Heart Asn; League Women Voters Clayton Co; PTA. Mailing Add: 885 White Oak Dr Forest Park GA 30050

BAKER, MARIE AGNES (R)
b Boston, Mass, Sept 9, 27; d Robert Aloysius Devlin & Adrianna E DeYoung D; m 1946 to Warren Brydon Baker; c Meredith (Mrs MacAskill), Patricia (Mrs Trottier) & Janice. Educ: Boston Sch Bus, 45. Polit & Govt Pos: Chmn, Goffstown Rep Town Comt, NH, 62-64; NH state chmn, United Citizens for Nixon-Agnew, 68-69; vchmn, Hillsboro Co Rep Comt, 68-74; alt deleg, Rep Nat Conv, 72; vchmn, NH Const Conv, 74- Bus & Prof Pos: Dir, Pitcher Asn, Inc, Derry, NH, 71. Mem: Moore Gen Hosp Assocs; Goffstown Mothers Club; Goffstown Hist Soc; Manchester Bus & Prof Women. Relig: Catholic. Mailing Add: 25 S Mast Rd Goffstown NH 03045

BAKER, NANCY (D)
Mem, Dem Nat Comt, Ark
Mailing Add: 49 Sherrill Heights Little Rock AR 72202

BAKER, NICHOLAS (D)
Ky State Sen
b Hazard, Ky, Apr 10, 37; s Mark Baker & Roberta Brashear B; single. Educ: Georgetown Col, BA, 59; Univ Louisville Sch Law, JD, 66; Kappa Alpha. Polit & Govt Pos: Ky State Sen, 70- Mil Serv: Army. Relig: Baptist. Legal Res: 800 S Fourth St Apt 310 Louisville KY 40202 Mailing Add: 310 W Liberty St Rm 208 Louisville KY 40202

BAKER, PATRICIA ELLIS (D)
Committeewoman, Orleans Co Dem Party, NY
b Gaines, NY, Nov 7, 38; d Charles Otis Ellis & Ruth Winslow E; m 1960 to Roy John Baker. Educ: State Univ NY Col Brockport, BS, 61, MS, 67; Univ Rochester, 63; State Univ NY Buffalo, EdD, 75; Kappa Delta Psi. Polit & Govt Pos: Treas, Orleans Co Dem Party, 69-72, committeewoman, 69-, mem exec bd, 69-, corresponding secy, 72-74; deleg, Dem Nat Conv, 72. Bus & Prof Pos: Elem teacher, Jamestown Pub Schs, NY, 61-62; teacher Am hist, Albion Cent Schs, 62-69; asst prof, State Univ NY Col Brockport, 69- Mem: Nat Educ Asn; NY State Teachers Asn; Nat & NY State Coun for the Social Studies. Mailing Add: 625 E State St Albion NY 14411

BAKER, RALPH A (R)
Chmn, Cherry Co Rep Party, Nebr
b Gordon, Nebr, Oct 2, 95; s Lee R Baker & Adelina Celestenia B; m 1919 to Mary Cole; c Cole D & Geneva J (Mrs Johnson). Educ: SDak Sch Mines, BA. Polit & Govt Pos: Chmn drouth comt, Cherry Co, Nebr, 30-36 & welfare comt, 31-42; co comnr, 32-49; finance mem, Nebr Rep Party, 40-50; regional dir, USO & Civilian Defense, 42-46; mem adv bd, Nebr Bd of Control, 46-49; mem, Nebr State Hwy Comn, 55-57; chmn, Cherry Co Rep Party, Nebr, 56-; deleg, Rep Nat Conv, 60 & 64; chmn, US Govt Savings Bonds, Cherry Co, 66. Bus & Prof Pos: Owner & mgr, Baker Ranch, 20-; pres, Sandhills Cattle Asn, 54-56; mem exec comt, Nebr Stock Growers Asn, 58-62; dir, Life Investors of Nebr, 62-; pres, Sandhills Investment Syndicate, 66. Mil Serv: AEF, Coast Artil Corps, 17-18. Mem: Sesostries AAONMS, Lincoln; Am Livestock Asn; Am Hereford Asn; VFW; Am Legion. Relig: Methodist. Mailing Add: 507 N Main Valentine NE 69201

BAKER, RAYMOND EUGENE (MIKE) (D)
b St Louis, Mo, Sept 24, 47; s Raymond E Baker & Helen Runge B; single. Educ: Westminster Col (Mo), BS, 69; Phi Delta Epsilon; Sigma Chi; Alpha Phi Omega. Polit & Govt Pos: Co campaign mgr, Sen Ike Skelton, Mo, 69; co campaign mgr, Lt Gov William Morris, 72; deleg, Dem Nat Conv, 72. Bus & Prof Pos: Pres, CofC, 72-73; dir, Brookfield Develop Corp; dir, Brookfield Banking Co; pres, Pepsi-Cola Bottling Co of Brookfield Inc. Mem: Mo Soft Drink Asn (legis comt); Nat Soft Drink Asn; Elks; Rotary; Mason. Relig: Presbyterian. Mailing Add: Box 98 125 Maple St Brookfield MO 64628

BAKER, RICHARD HUGH (D)
La State Rep
Mailing Add: 132 Highland Garden Rd Baton Rouge LA 70811

BAKER, RICHARD SCOTT (R)
b Salt Lake City, Utah, Feb 8, 53; s George K Baker & Jessie Hill B; single. Educ: Univ Utah, 71-; Tau Kappa Epsilon (pres, 73-). Polit & Govt Pos: Chmn & organizer, Teenage Rep, Bountiful High, Utah, 71; alt deleg, Rep Nat Conv, 72; voting dist chmn, Davis Co Rep Party, 72-74. Bus & Prof Pos: Asst mgr, Continental Bank, 73- Honors & Awards: Degree of excellence, Nat Forensics Soc. Mailing Add: 1891 S Bonneview Dr Bountiful UT 84010

BAKER, ROBERT WILLIAM (D)
b Brookline, Mass, July 30, 24; s Chauncey William Baker (deceased) & Marion Power B; m 1951 to Rita Agnes Knox; c Cheryl Alison, Jeffrey Clark & Susan Knox. Educ: Hobart Col, AB, 47; Clark Univ, PhD, 53; Am Bd Prof Psychol, dipl. Polit & Govt Pos: Staff clin psychologist, Vet Admin Hosp, Northampton, Mass, 53-54; field selection officer, Peace Corps, part-time, 64-67; alt deleg, Dem Nat Conv, 68 & 72. Bus & Prof Pos: Asst prof psychol, Clark Univ, 54-57, assoc prof, 57-66, prof, 66-, dir psychol clin, 54-55 & 56-65, dean students, 65-68, asst provost student affairs, 69-70, dir psychol serv ctr, 71-, chmn faculty, 72-73. Mil Serv: Entered as Aviation Cadet, Navy, 43, released as Seaman 2/C, 44, after serv in US. Publ: Incidence of psychological disturbance in college students, J Am Col Health Asn, 65; Susceptibility to distraction in academically underachieving & achieving male college students, J, Consult Psychol, 65; Students, parents & the college: responsibilities & prerogatives in grade-reporting, Lib Educ, 53, 325-335, 67. Mem: Am & Mass Psychol Asns (fel); Am Asn Univ Prof (co-chmn comt acad freedom & tenure, Mass Conf, 72-); Am Civil Liberties Union. Mailing Add: 398 May St Worcester MA 01602

BAKER, ROGER LORIN (R)
Mayor, Springfield, Ohio
b Knox Co, Ohio, Nov 29, 34; s John Walker Baker & Marie Dalrymple B; m 1959 to Sonia Ann James; c John Marshall, Nancy Ann & Jason Matthew. Educ: Ohio Wesleyan Univ, BA, 56; Ohio State Univ, MA, 63; Chi Phi. Polit & Govt Pos: City comnr, Springfield, Ohio, 72-, mayor, 74- Bus & Prof Pos: Dir adult educ, Springfield Pub Schs, Ohio, 67-70; prin, Franklin Jr High Sch, Springfield, 70- Mil Serv: Entered as 2nd Lt, Air Force, 56, released as Capt, 65; Capt, Air Force Res. Mem: Ohio Asn Sec Sch Prin. Relig: United Methodist. Mailing Add: 25 Englewood Rd Springfield OH 45504

BAKER, T J (D)
NC State Rep
Mailing Add: 306 E Cliff St Wallace NC 28466

BAKER, WALTER A (R)
Ky State Sen
b Columbia, Ky, Feb 20, 37; s Herschel Tate Baker & Mattie Barger B; m 1965 to Jane Stark Helm; c Thomas Herschel & Ann Tate. Educ: Harvard, AB, magna cum laude, 58, Law Sch, LLB, 61; Phi Beta Kappa. Polit & Govt Pos: Pres, Harvard Law Sch Young Rep, 60-61; election comnr, Barren Co, Ky, 66; Ky State Rep, 23rd House Dist, 68-71; Ky State Sen, Ninth Dist, 72-; mem exec comt, Ky Crime Comn, 72-; Dir, Barren River Mental Health-Mental Retardation Dist, 72- Bus & Prof Pos: Attorney, Brown, Ardery, Todd & Dudley, 61-63; partner, Wilson, Baker, Herbert & Garmon, 63-67; single practitioner, 67- Mil Serv: Maj, Air Force, Ky Air Nat Guard, 61-; Air Force Commendation Medal. Mem: Am & Ky Bar Asns; Barren Co Bar Asn (pres, 70-71); Glasgow Rotary Club (past vpres & dir). Relig: Presbyterian. Mailing Add: 917 S Green Glasgow KY 42141

BAKER, WAYNE A (D)
Conn State Sen
Mailing Add: PO Box 505 8 Wooster Heights Danbury CT 06810

BAKER, WILLIAM ALLEN, JR (D)
b Springfield, Mo, Dec 19, 46; s William Allen Baker, Sr & Barbra L Crayton B; m 1970 to Joetta Ann Scullion; c Eric Allen & Brian Richard. Educ: Univ Wis-Platteville, BS in Polit Sci, 73; Vet Club; Polit Sci Club. Polit & Govt Pos: Vchmn, Young Dem, Univ Wis-Platteville, 70-71; chmn, Student's for Ray Short Comt, 70-71; vchmn, Grant Co Dem Party, Wis, 71-72; chmn, Iowa Co Dem Party, formerly. Bus & Prof Pos: Mem, Nat Farmer's Orgn, currently, & dairy rep, 70- Mil Serv: Entered as Pvt, Marine Corps, 65, released as Cpl, 68, after serv in MAG 13, Vietnam, Chu Lia, 67-68. Mem: Am Legion; VFW. Relig: Roman Catholic. Mailing Add: Box 212 Cobb WI 53526

BAKER, WILLIAM C (D)
b Terre Haute, Ind, July 18, 25; s Esau Baker (deceased) & Ella Cranfielo B; m 1955 to Mae Helen Morgan; c William C Jr, Michael T, Stephen L & David L. Educ: Ind State Univ, BS, 48; Ind Univ Sch Dent, DDS, 52, Sch Med, oral surg residency, 65; Omega Psi Phi; Chi Delta Mu. Polit & Govt Pos: Vprecinct committeeman, Marion Co Dem Comt, Ind, 68-, chmn, Platform Comt & Screening Comt, 71-; deleg, Dem Nat Conv, 72; deleg, Ind State Dem Conv, 72; cand, Marion Co Coroner, 72. Bus & Prof Pos: Pvt practice of gen dent, 52-62 & oral surgery, 65-; staff mem, St Vincents Hosp, Methodist Hosp, Community Hosp & Marion Co Gen Hosp, currently; Mil Serv: Entered as Seaman 2/C, Navy, 43, released as Hosp Corpsman. Mem: Aesculopian Med Soc; Am Dent Asn; Nat Dent Asn (vpres); Am Soc Oral Surgeons; NAACP. Relig: Protestant. Legal Res: 137 Berkley Rd Indianapolis IN 46208 Mailing Add: 17 W 22nd St Indianapolis IN 46202

BAKER, WILLIAM D (R)
Mem Exec Comt, Ariz Rep State Comt
b St Louis, Mo, June 17, 32; s Harold Griffith Baker & Bernice Kraft B; m 1955 to Kay Stokes; c Mark William, Kathryn Xymena, Beth Christie & Frederick Martin. Educ: Colgate Univ, AB, 54; Boalt Hall Sch Law, Univ Calif, Berkeley, JD, 60; Sigma Chi. Polit & Govt Pos: Dep Co attorney, Pinal Co, Ariz, 61-63; spec legal counsel, Ariz Rep State Comt, 64, legal counsel, 65-69, mem exec comt, 72-; hon asst sgt at arms, Rep Nat Conv, 68; mem, Gov Adv Coun, 69-; chmn, Maricopa Co Rep Comt, 69-71; mem exec guid comt, 69-72; mem, Ariz Environ Planning Comn, 74-75. Bus & Prof Pos: Attorney, McBryde, Brumage, Vincent & Baker, Florence, Ariz, 61-63 & Rawlins, Ellis, Burrus & Kiewit, Phoenix, 63-; juv court referee, Maricopa Co Superior Court, 66- Mil Serv: Entered as 2nd Lt, Air Force, 54, released as 1st Lt, 57, after serv in 5th Bomb Wing, Strategic Air Command, 55-57. Mem: Phi Delta Phi; Am Bar Asn; F&AM; York Rite; Shrine. Relig: Episcopal. Legal Res: 5309 N 34th St Phoenix AZ 85018 Mailing Add: 2300 Valley Bank Ctr Phoenix AZ 85073

BAKER, WILLIAM HOWARD (D)
Committeeman, Second Hampden Dist Dem Comt, Mass
b Holyoke, Mass, July 22, 13; s William F Baker & Mary McGrath B; m 1946 to Cecile Hamel; c Patricia Gvenette, David Baker & Gail (Mrs Dygon). Educ: Sacred Heart High Sch, Holyoke, Mass, 3 years. Polit & Govt Pos: Ward chmn, Chicopee City Dem Comt, Mass, 54, vchmn, 59 & chmn, 60 & 71-72; committeeman, Mass Dem State Comt, 60-72, vchmn, 61, committeeman, Second Hampden Dist, 69- Mem: Holyoke Printing & Pressmans Union (recording secy, Local 45). Relig: Catholic. Mailing Add: 11 Charbonneau Terr Chicopee MA 01013

BAKEWELL, CLAUDE I (R)
b St Louis, Mo, Aug 9, 12; s Paul Bakewell, Jr & Mary Fullerton B; m 1936 to Helene Brown; c Helene B. Educ: Georgetown Univ, AB, 32; St Louis Univ Sch Law, LLB, 35; Alpha Sigma Nu; Delta Theta Phi. Polit & Govt Pos: Mem, Bd of Aldermen, St Louis, Mo, 41-45, US Rep, Mo, 47-48 & 51-52; postmaster, St Louis, 58- Mil Serv: Entered as Lt(jg), Navy, 44, released as Lt(jg), 46, after serv in Armed Guard, Asiatic-Pac Theater. Relig: Roman Catholic. Legal Res: 7148 Maryland Ave St Louis MO 63130 Mailing Add: 1720 Market St St Louis MO 63155

BAKKE, KARL EDWARD (R)
Gen Counsel, Dept Com
b New Haven, Conn, July 3, 30; s Edward Wight Bakke & Mary Sterling B; m to Anne-Rosseau Holbein; c Heather (Mrs Stephen Olejnick), Ruelaine (Mrs William Stainback), Shelley & Karl. Educ: Yale Univ, BA, 51; Georgetown Law Sch, JD, 57; Phi Gamma Delta; ed, Georgetown Law J, 56-57. Polit & Govt Pos: Asst secy bd gov, Fed Reserve Syst, 64-68; dep chief counsel, Off Foreign Direct Investments, US Dept Com, 69-70, chief counsel, 70-71, dep gen counsel, dept, 71-73, gen counsel, 73- Bus & Prof Pos: Traffic supvr, Chesapeake & Potomac Tel Co, Washington, DC, 51-57; pvt law practice, 57-60. Mem: Am Bar Asn; Nat Lawyers Club; Phi Delta Phi. Relig: Episcopal. Mailing Add: 6305 Beachway Dr Falls Church VA 22044

BALCH, RICHARD HORROCKS (D)
b Brooklyn, NY, Mar 2, 01; s Burton M Balch & Mary Horrocks B; m 1928 to Elizabeth Prescott; c Cynthia (Mrs Barns), Barbara (Mrs Colt), James P & Richard H, Jr. Educ: Williams Col, BA, 21; Delta Sigma Rho; Phi Delta Theta. Hon Degrees: LLD, Hartwick Col, 55. Polit & Govt Pos: Chmn, Utica City Dem Comt, 48-50 & NY State Dem Comt, 52-55; comnr, NY State Pub Serv Comn, 55-60. Bus & Prof Pos: Pres, Horrocks Ibbotson Co, 42-67. Relig: Presbyterian. Mailing Add: 1202 Parkway Utica NY 13501

BALDRIGE, MALCOLM (R)
Mem, Rep Nat Finance Comt
b Omaha, Nebr, Oct 4, 22; s Howard Malcolm Baldrige & Regina Connell B; m 1951 to Margaret Trowbridge Murray; c Megan Brewster & Mary Trowbridge. Educ: Yale Univ, BA, 44. Polit & Govt Pos: Mem, Waterbury Mayor's Citizens Adv Comt, Conn, chmn, formerly; deleg, Rep Nat Conv, 64, 68 & 72; mem, Conn Gov Comt on Status of Women, formerly; deleg, Conn Const Conv, 65; mem, Conn State Rep Budget Comt, 66-; mem, Conn State Rep Finance Comt, 66-, chmn, 69-72; mem adv comt on labor, Conn State Rep Cent Comt, 67-; co-chmn, Conn United Citizens for Nixon-Agnew, 68; mem, Conn Citizens Comn on State Legis, 68-; mem, Conn State Rep Platform Comt, 68-; mem, Nat Rep Finance Comt, 69- Bus & Prof Pos: Chmn, Yale Nat Bus Gifts Comt, currently; mem, Yale Univ Develop Bd; trustee, Swiss Re-Ins Co; pres, Scovill Mfg Co, Waterbury, 63-69, chmn bd, 69-, dir, currently; dir, AMF Inc, White Plains, NY, Conn Mutual Life Ins Co, The Eastern Co, Am Chain & Cable Co, New York & Torin Corp, Torrington, Conn; dir adv bd, Rodeo Info Found, Denver, Colo, 69-; dir, Rodeo Cowboys Asn, Inc; dir, Gtr Waterbury CofC, chmn, formerly; mem, Bus Coun & Coun Foreign Rels, currently; trustee, US Coun Int CofC; trustee, Waterbury Non-Profit Develop Corp. Mil Serv: Entered as Pvt, Army, 43, released as Capt, 46, after serv in Field Artil, 27th Inf Div, Pac Theatre. Mem: Waterbury Red Cross (Dir, Chmn, Red Cross Drive, 68); Easter Seal Soc (Incorporator); Waterbury Hosp (Trustee). Relig: Congregational. Legal Res: Tomlinson Rd RFD 2 Woodbury CT 06798 Mailing Add: Scovill Mfg Co Scovill Sq Waterbury CT 06720

BALDUCCI, RICHARD J (D)
Conn State Rep
Mailing Add: 63 Styles Ave Newington CT 06111

BALDUS, ALVIN (D)
US Rep, Wis
b Boone, Iowa, Apr 27, 26; s Leo F Baldus & Mildred Corbin B; m 1959 to A Lorayne Reiten; c Deborah, Bruce, Rebecca & John. Educ: Austin Jr Col, Minn, AA. Polit & Govt Pos: Wis State Rep, Dunn Co, 67-74, asst majority leader, Wis State Assembly, 73-74; US Rep, 75- Bus & Prof Pos: Dist rep, Allis Chalmers Mfg Co, 53-64; zone mgr, Investors Diversified Serv, 64- Mil Serv: Merchant Marine, 44-46; Entered as Pvt, Army, 51, released as Sgt, 53, after serv in 2nd Div, Korea, 52-53; Bronze Star; Infantryman's Combat Badge. Mem: DAV. Relig: Catholic. Legal Res: 1901 S Broadway Menomonie WI 54751 Mailing Add: 6721 Pine Creek Ct McLean VA 22101

BALDWIN, DAVID RAWSON (D)
b New Haven, Conn, Nov 2, 23; s Albert A Baldwin & Hilda Rawson B; m 1948 to Dorothy E Sonstrom; c Dwight R, Brian M & James A. Educ: Univ Conn, BS in Govt, 47; Wayne Univ, MPA, 49; Theta Xi. Polit & Govt Pos: Chief assessor, Fayette Co, Pa, 52-56; consult to Gov-Elect, Pa Dem State Comt, 54; budget secy & dep secy admin, Commonwealth of Pa, 59-63; exec asst state treas, 63-65; housing chmn, Pa Deleg to Dem Nat Conv, 63; adv to Dem mem, Pa Gen Assembly, 63-65; asst secy of com, US Dept Com, 65-69. Bus & Prof Pos: Research asst, Conn Pub Expenditure Coun, 48-50; co exec secy, Pa Econ League, 50-52, research assoc, 56-59; vpres, Wayne State Univ, 69-72; assoc vpres financial affairs, Temple Univ, 72- Mil Serv: Entered as A/S, Naval Res, 43, released as Lt(jg), 46, after serv with

convoy duty Pac Theatre. Mem: Am Soc for Pub Admin; Gov Res Asn. Relig: Presbyterian. Mailing Add: 339 Evergreen Rd Jenkintown PA 19046

BALDWIN, DON (D)
Okla State Sen
Mailing Add: State Capitol Oklahoma City OK 73105

BALDWIN, DOUGLAS PARKS (R)
b Lander, Wyo, Oct 22, 36; s Melvin Baldwin & Shirley Jeffers B; m 1960 to Janet LaVerne Curtis; c Clifford Steven. Educ: Am Univ, 66. Polit & Govt Pos: Pres, Park Co Young Rep, Wyo, 62; press secy to US Sen M L Simpson, Wyo, 63-66 & US Sen C P Hansen, Wyo, 67; spec asst to US Rep W H Harrison, Wyo, 67-68; news ed, United Citizens for Nixon-Agnew, 68; admin asst to US Rep John Wold, Wyo, 69-70; conf affairs specialist, Off Econ Opportunity, 71-72; chief info, Bur Outdoor Recreation, US Dept Interior, 72- Bus & Prof Pos: News dir, radio stas, Wyo, 58-62. Mil Serv: Entered as Pvt, Marine Corps, 55, released as Sgt, 59, after serv in 1st, 2nd & 3rd Divs, Okinawa, 56-58. Publ: Cody called him Frank, Denver Post, 61; Political preference prevails in Congressional liaison, Washington Sunday Star, 1/68; William Henry Harrison, bits & pieces, 7/68. Mem: US Senate Press Secy Asn; Toastmasters Int (Pres, Capitol Hill Club, 73-); Eng Speaking Union; Nat Press Club. Honors & Awards: Recipient of Hungarian Freedom Fighters Asn Freedom Award, 65. Relig: Methodist. Mailing Add: 4109 Canyonview Dr Upper Marlboro MD 20870

BALDWIN, LILLIAN HOELL (D)
Chmn, Kent Dem Town Comt, Conn
b Philadelphia, Pa, Sept 2, 13; d Georg S Hoell & Lilly Clason H; m 1948 to C Benham Baldwin; c Antonia Greenwood. Educ: Pierce Bus Col. Polit & Govt Pos: Spec asst, Off Strategic Servs, 42-46; field serv dir, Progressive Party Hq, New York, 46-49; chmn, Kent Dem Town Comt, Conn, 74- Bus & Prof Pos: Asst secy, Comt for Foreign Relief, Am Friends Serv Comt, Philadelphia, Pa, 36-42; secy-treas, Outdoor Traders, Inc, Greenwich, Conn; retired. Mailing Add: Rte 1 Box 164A Kent CT 06757

BALES, ROBERT H (R)
Ind State Rep
Educ: Ind Univ; Alpha Kappa Psi; Sigma Iota Epsilon; Phi Delta Kappa. Polit & Govt Pos: Ind State Rep, currently. Bus & Prof Pos: Pub rels rep, Eli Lilly & Co. Mil Serv: Air Force, Korean War. Mem: Masonic Lodge, Royal Arch Masons; Scottish Rite; Shrine; Ind Univ Alumni Asn; Soc of Friends. Mailing Add: PO Box 34 Danville IN 46122

BALL, CLAIRE MELVIN, JR (R)
Ohio State Rep
b Athens, Ohio, Oct 4, 41; s Claire Melvin Ball, Sr & Glenna Yates B; m 1970 to Judith Lynn Hutchinson; c Tammie Lee, Bradley Scott & Ryan Todd. Educ: Ohio Univ, BBA, 63, MBA, 64; Ohio State Univ Col Law, JD, 66; Delta Phi Delta; Sigma Chi. Polit & Govt Pos: Legis asst, US Rep Clarence E Miller, Tenth Cong Dist, Ohio, 66-68; Athens Co Prosecuting Attorney, Ohio, 68-72; Ohio State Rep, 91st Dist, 73- Bus & Prof Pos: Attorney & partner, Jones & Ball Law Firm, Athens, Ohio, 68- Mem: Nat Dist Attorneys Asn; Red Cross; Kiwanis; Jaycees. Honors & Awards: Excellent Serv in the Advan of Criminal Justice, Ohio Supreme Court, 72; Admitted to practice before all Ohio courts, the US Court of Mil Appeals & the US Court of Claims. Relig: Protestant. Mailing Add: 19 W Washington St Athens OH 45701

BALL, DONALD RAY (R)
b Henderson Co, Ky, July 27, 36; s James Chester Ball & Marjorie Bryant B; m 1955 to Mira Lou Snider; c Donald Ray, Jr, Michael Bryant & Lisa Hays. Educ: Univ Ky. Polit & Govt Pos: Pres, Univ Ky Young Rep Club, 54; alt deleg, Rep Nat Conv, 64; dir, Blue Grass Lincoln Club, Ky, 64-; Ky State Rep, 64-72; chmn Rep Caucus & Rep Policy Comt, Ky House Rep, 66-72; Minority Leader, 68-69; cand procurement chmn, Ky Young Rep Fedn, 65-; chmn, Nat Rep Legislator's Conf, 69; mem Rep Coord Comt, Rep Nat Comt, 69. Bus & Prof Pos: Pres, Ball Homes, Inc, 59-; managing dir, Ky News Media, Inc, 64-; dir, Cent Investors Life Ins Co, 64- Mem: Lexington Homebuilders Asn (Pres); Ky Homebuilders Asn & Nat Asn Homebuilders (Dir); Citizens Asn for Planning Open Space Comt (Chmn); CofC. Honors & Awards: Outstanding Young Man Award of Lexington-Fayette Co, Jaycees, 68. Relig: Baptist. Mailing Add: Rte 8 Old Frankfort Pike Lexington KY 40504

BALL, GEORGE WILDMAN (D)
b Des Moines, Iowa, Dec 21, 09; s Amos Ball & Edna Wildman B; m 1932 to Ruth Murdoch; c John Colin & Douglas Bleakly. Educ: Northwestern Univ, BA, 30, JD, 33. Polit & Govt Pos: Gen Counsel's Off, US Treas Dept, 33-35; assoc gen counsel, Lend-Lease Admin, then Foreign Econ Admin, 42-44; dir, US Strategic Bombing Surv, London, 44-45; gen counsel, French Supply Coun, Wash, 45-46; Under Secy of State for Econ Affairs, 61; Under Secy of State, 61-66; US Permanent Rep to UN, 68. Bus & Prof Pos: Partner, Cleary, Gottlieb, Steen & Hamilton, 46-61; counsel, 66-68 & 69-; chmn, Lehman Bros Int, 66-68; sr partner investment banking, Lehman Bros, 69- Publ: The Discipline of Power, Atlantic-Little Brown, 68. Mem: Columbia Univ (Trustee, Am Assembly). Honors & Awards: Legion of Honor, France; Medal of Freedom, US; Grand Cross, Order of the Crown, Belgium. Legal Res: 860 UN Plaza New York NY 10017 Mailing Add: c/o Lehman Bros One William St New York NY 10004

BALL, ROBERT B, SR (D)
Va State Deleg
Mailing Add: PO Box 9487 Richmond VA 23228

BALL, ROGER ALFORD (D)
Chmn, Claiborne Co Dem Party, Tenn
b Tazewell, Tenn, June 14, 44; s Thomas Franklin Ball & Hester Riley B; single. Educ: Lincoln Mem Univ, BS, 66; Univ Tenn, MS, 69; Delta Pi Epsilon. Polit & Govt Pos: Vchmn, Claiborne Co Dem Party, Tenn, 68-72, chmn, 72- Bus & Prof Pos: Dir voc educ, Claiborne Co Schs, 70- Mem: Am Voc Asn; Tenn Educ Asn; Claiborne Co CofC (bd dirs, 74-); Clinch-Powell River Valley Asn (bd dirs, 68-, secy, 70-). Legal Res: Cedar Fork Rd Tazewell TN 37879 Mailing Add: Box 237 Tazewell TN 37879

BALLAM, LOUIS SHERMAN (R)
NH State Rep
b Walpole, NH, Aug 26, 04; s George Ballam & Lizzio Angier; wid. Educ: Walpole Schs. Polit & Govt Pos: Selectman, Walpole, NH, 48-; NH State Rep, 55-73, Cheshire Co, 75-; Dir, Off Econ Opportunity, NH, formerly; comnr, Cheshire Co, 71-; mem, Walpole Planning Bd. Bus & Prof Pos: Farmer, 20-; pres, Bellows Falk Coop Creamery, formerly. Mem: Cheshire Co Fair Asn; Mason (past master); Elks; Walpole Lions (past pres); Cheshire Co Farm Bur. Relig: Protestant. Mailing Add: Walpole NH 03608

BALLARD, ALDEN G (R)
Vt State Rep
Mailing Add: RFD 2 St Albans VT 05478

BALLARD, JOHN STUART (R)
Mayor, Akron, Ohio
b Akron, Ohio, Sept 30, 22; s Irby S Ballard & Sarah McCormick B; m 1949 to Ruth Frances Holden; c Susan, Karen, John, II, Mark, Ward & John H. Educ: Univ Akron, AB, 43; Univ Mich, LLB, 48. Polit & Govt Pos: Spec agt, Fed Bur Invest, 49-52; mem, Summit Co Rep Exec Comt, Ohio, 56-; prosecuting attorney, Summit Co, Ohio, 57-64; cand, US Senate, Ohio, 62; mayor, Akron, 66-; alt deleg, Rep Nat Conv, 72. Bus & Prof Pos: Attorney-at-law, Akron, 52-56 & 64-65. Mil Serv: Inf, Army, 43-46. Mem: Am, Ohio & Akron Bar Asns; Am Judicature Soc. Honors & Awards: Recipient, Distinguished Serv Award, Akron Jr CofC, 57. Relig: Episcopal. Legal Res: 107 Kenilworth Dr Akron OH 44313 Mailing Add: Munic Bldg High St Akron OH 44308

BALLARD, WILLIAM DONALDSON (D)
Ga State Sen
b Covington, Ga, Mar 15, 27; s Robert Hershell Ballard & Eva Dorminey B; m 1951 to Mary McCullough; c Rebecca Anne, William Donaldson, Frankie Jannelle, Mary Kathryn, Thomas Waters & Susan Kay. Educ: Univ Ga, 45-50, AB, LLB, 50; Kappa Sigma. Polit & Govt Pos: City attorney, Oxford, Ga, 54-, Mansfield, 55, Newborn, 55- & Porterdale, currently; Ga State Rep, 57-70; Ga State Sen, Dist 45, 70 Mil Serv: Entered as Seaman, Naval Res, 44, released as Seaman 1/C, 46, after serv in USS LST 1076, Pac, 44-46; Pac Theatre Medal; Invasion of Japan Medal. Mem: Lions; Am Legion; Rotary; VFW; Elks. Legal Res: 405 Haygood St Oxford GA 31701 Mailing Add: 1122 Monticello St Covington GA 30209

BALLENGER, WILLIAM HOWARD (D)
SC State Sen
Mailing Add: Walhalla SC 29691

BALLEW, ROBERT KING (D)
Mem, Ga State Dem Exec Comt
b Copperhill, Tenn, Mar 1, 26; s Robert Fulton Ballew & Helen King B; m 1949 to Nanette Talley; c Sara Kay & Robert K, II. Educ: North Ga Col; Univ Tenn, LLB; Phi Delta Phi. Polit & Govt Pos: City attorney, Blue Ridge, Ga, 53-; mem, Ga State Dem Exec Comt, 62-; Ga State Sen, 50th Dist, 65-66; mayor, Blue Ridge, 68- Bus & Prof Pos: Attorney-at-law, 53- Mil Serv: Entered as Pvt, Army Air Force, 44, released as Cpl, 46, after serv in ETO. Mem: Tenn & Ga Bars; Am Bar Asn; Mason; Shrine; VFW. Relig: Methodist. Legal Res: E Second St Blue Ridge GA 30513 Mailing Add: PO Box 636 Blue Ridge GA 30513

BALLOU, JOHN WALDO (R)
Mem, Bangor City Coun, Maine
b Bangor, Maine, Sept 29, 25; s William Rice Ballou & Gladys Lowell B; single. Educ: Univ Maine, BA, 49; Yale Univ, LLB, 52; Phi Beta Kappa; Phi Kappa Phi; Phi Gamma Delta. Polit & Govt Pos: Trustee & former chmn, Bangor Water Dist, Maine, 63-67; alt deleg, Rep Nat Conv, 64; mem, Maine Adv Comt on Ment Health, 64-, chmn, 67-; mem, Maine State Mus Comn, 64-, vchmn, 72-; mem, Penobscot Co Rep Comt, 66-68; mem, Bangor City Coun, 67-, chmn, 70. Bus & Prof Pos: Partner, Mitchell & Ballou, 53-75, partner, Mitchell, Ballou & Keith, 75- Mil Serv: Entered as Pvt, Army, 43, released as Sgt, 46, after serv in 87th Inf Div, ETO; European-African-Mid Eastern Theater Campaign Ribbon with Three Battle Stars; Am Theater Campaign Ribbon. Mem: Am Bar Asn (comt on workmen's compensation & employers liability ins law); Maine State Bar Asn (chmn, Grievance Comt, 68-); United Community Serv of Penobscot Valley (vpres); Univ Maine Gen Alumni Coun; Bangor YMCA (bd dirs). Relig: Unitarian. Mailing Add: 52 Montgomery St Bangor ME 04401

BALLOUZ, JOSEPH M (D)
WVa State Deleg
Mailing Add: State Capitol Charleston WV 25305

BALLREICH, STEVE LYNN (R)
Alt Mem, Rep State Cent Comt Calif
b Gallup, NMex, May 5, 50; s Barney Ballreich (deceased) & Ruth Imogene Arbin B; single. Educ: East Los Angeles Col, 69-72; Pasadena City Col, 73; Calif State Univ, Los Angeles, currently; Columbia Sch Broadcasting, currently. Polit & Govt Pos: Alhambra chmn, Goldwater for President, 64 & Nixon for President, 72; pres, East Los Angeles Col Young Rep, 68-70; mem bd dirs, Alhambra Rep Club, 68-; vpres, Calif State Univ Los Angeles Col Rep, 70-71; youth dir, United Rep Calif, Unit 124, 71; field rep, Am for Agnew, 72; youth dir, Monterey Park Rep Club, 73-; alt mem, Rep State Cent Comt Calif, 73-; alt mem, 48th Assembly Dist Rep Cent Comt, 73-; sgt-at-arms, Los Angeles Co Coun Rep, 73-; cand, Alhambra City Coun, 74. Bus & Prof Pos: Field asst, John L Daniel & Assocs, Los Angeles, 68-71; campaign mgr, Jack Bacon & Assocs, 72; sr partner & campaign consult, Campaigns Unlimited, Beverly Hills, 72- Mem: Beverly Hills CofC; Calif Mutual Bus Exchange; Jaycees; Voices in Vital Am; YMCA (prog dir, 73). Honors & Awards: Distinguished Serv Award, Los Angeles Co Rep Cent Comt, 66, 68 & 71. Relig: Methodist. Mailing Add: Apt D 904 N First St Alhambra CA 91801

BALMASEDA, FRANCISCO ANTONIO (D)
b Camaguey, Camaguey, Cuba, Aug 8, 35; s Francisco Fidencio Balmaseda & Zoila Fe Napoles B; m 1955 to Eileen Bahnsen. Educ: San Antonio Col, 58-60; Trinity Univ, BA, 61, MA, 66; Case Western Reserve Univ, Nat Defense Educ Act fel, 67- Polit & Govt Pos: Deleg, Dem Nat Conv, 72. Bus & Prof Pos: Teacher hist, Thomas Jefferson High Sch, San Antonio, Tex, 61-66; Harlandale High Sch, fall 66 & Our Lady of the Lake Col, spring 67; instr hist, Cleveland State Univ, 69-70; instr hist, San Antonio Col, 70- Mil Serv: Entered as Pvt, Army, 55, released as SP-2, 57, after serv in Hq & Hq Co, Signal Long Lines Bn, US 8th Army Rear (Japan), 55-57; Good Conduct Ribbon. Mem: Am Hist Asn; Latin Am Studies Asn; Tex Jr Col Teacher's Asn. Relig: Lutheran. Mailing Add: Apt 4C 2178 NE Loop 410 San Antonio TX 78217

BALSBAUGH, MICHAEL MARK (D)
Ind State Rep
b Peru, Ind, Apr 11, 42; s Marvin Leo Balsbaugh & Patty Louise Mullin B; m 1970 to Marcia

Lynn Davis; c Kimberly, Nanette, Lisa, Missy & Brian. Educ: Taylor Univ, 69; Marion Col (Ind), 69- Polit & Govt Pos: Ind State Rep, Dist 25, currently. Bus & Prof Pos: With Marion Police Dept, 65-70. Mem: JFK Club of Grant Co; Young Dem; Elks; Fraternal Order of Police; YMCA. Legal Res: 1304 Euclid Ave Marion IN 46952 Mailing Add: State Capitol Bldg Indianapolis IN 46204

BALTHAZAR, WILFRED E (D)
Mass State Rep
Mailing Add: State Capitol Boston MA 02133

BALTON, NANCY (D)
Mem, Ark Dem State Exec Comt
Polit & Govt Pos: Mem, Dem Nat Comt, Ark, formerly. Mailing Add: Grider Plantation Osceola AR 72370

BALTZ, WALTER F (R)
Chmn, Third Cong Dist Rep Party, Wis
b Sparta, Wis, Apr 21, 38; s Dr Walter F Baltz & Carolyn R Dunsing B; m 1962 to Ann Marie Nelson; c Anna Maria, Walter F, IV & Andrea M. Educ: Univ Wis-Madison, BS, 64. Polit & Govt Pos: Precinct finance chmn, West Salem Rep Party, Wis, 70, precinct chmn, 70-73, statutory precinct committeeman, 72-74; chmn, La Crosse Co Rep Party, 71-73; statutory chmn, La Crosse Co Rep Cent Comt, 72-74; chmn, Third Cong Dist Rep Party, 73-; mem, Village Coun, 75- Bus & Prof Pos: Credit mgr, Leath & Co, La Crosse, Beloit & Madison, Wis, 64-67; asst credit mgr, Gr Heileman Brewing Co, Inc, La Crosse, 67-70, credit mgr, 70- Mil Serv: Entered as Pvt E-1, Army, 60, released as SP5-E-5, 63, after serv in 1st Cavalry Div, Korea, 62-63. Mem: Mason (Master, Salem Lodge 125, 71); West Salem Rotary (pres, 74-); Am Legion; Nat Rifle Asn; Am Church Union. Relig: Episcopal. Legal Res: 540 Tilson St West Salem WI 54669 Mailing Add: PO Box 846 La Crosse WI 54601

BALZANO, MICHAEL P, JR (R)
Dir, ACTION
b 1927; m to Doris L Ridolfi; c three. Educ: Bryant Col. Polit & Govt Pos: Past mem, Bristol Police Dept & Police Reserves, RI; RI State Rep, 67-72; dir, ACTION, 73- Bus & Prof Pos: Founder of Bristol Colts; asst dist mgr, John Hancock Life Ins Co, East Providence. Mil Serv: Navy, World War II. Mem: Elmwood Terr Improv Asn; March of Dimes Comt; CofC; 50th Jubilee Comt Mt Carmel Church. Legal Res: RI Mailing Add: Action 806 Connecticut Ave Washington DC 20525

BAMBERGER, THOMAS A (D)
Okla State Rep
b Massillon, Ohio, May 28, 26; s Titus Bamberger & Hester Kegerries B; m to Nancy; c Diana, James, Thomas, Kathryn & John. Educ: Ohio State Univ, BA, 48; Okla City Univ, LLB, 53; Phi Delta Theta. Polit & Govt Pos: Okla State Rep, currently, chmn, Comt on Environ Qual, Okla House of Rep, currently. Bus & Prof Pos: Partner, Bamberger & Baer, Attorneys. Mil Serv: Entered as Seaman, Navy, 43, released as PO, 46, after serv in Pac Theater. Mailing Add: 132 1/2 SW 25th St Oklahoma City OK 73109

BANE, DAVID MORGAN
b Uniontown, Pa, Sept 12, 15; to Patricia Miller; c Patricia. Educ: Duke Univ, AB magna cum laude, 38; Univ Pa, LLB, 41; Phi Beta Kappa; Pi Gamma Mu; Alpha Kappa Psi. Polit & Govt Pos: Career officer, US Dept of State Foreign Serv, 47-; vconsul & second secy, Tokyo, 47-49 & Seoul, Korea, 49-50; consul, Bordeaux, 50-52; first secy, Paris, 53-56; Nat War Col, 57-58; dep dir, Off of NE Asian Affairs, 58-59, dir, 59-61; consul gen, Lahore, Pakistan, 61-64; US Ambassador to Gabon, 65-69; polit adv to comdr-in-chief, US Strike Command, MacDill AFB, Fla, 69-71; consul gen, Bombay, India, 71- Mil Serv: Col, Army, 41-46, overseas; Soldiers Medal; Bronze Star; Commendation Award. Mem: Pa Bar Asn. Honors & Awards: Meritorious Civilian Serv Medal, Secy Defense, 71; Grand Officer, Equatorial Star, Gabon. Legal Res: 211 Cordova Blvd NE St Petersburg FL 33704 Mailing Add: Bombay Dept of State Washington DC 20521

BANE, TOM (D)
Calif State Assemblyman
Mailing Add: 5430 Van Nuys Blvd Van Nuys CA 91401

BANEN, ABRAHAM THEODORE (DFL)
Chmn, Koochichina Co Dem-Farmer-Labor Party, Minn
b Eveleth, Minn, Sept 30, 09; s Peter Banen & Marian B; m 1949 to Blanche Bachinski; c Wendy Ann, Thomas & Terrance. Educ: Aibbing Jr Col, 27-29; Univ Wis, BA, 31; Univ Minn, DDS, 34; Phi Sigma Delta. Polit & Govt Pos: Deleg, Dem Nat Conv, 68; chmn, Koochichina Co Dem-Farmer-Labor Party, Minn, currently; mayor, International Falls, Minn, 70- Mil Serv: Entered as 1st Lt, Army, 42, released as Capt, 45, after serv in 8th Inf Div, ETO, 43-45; Two Bronze Stars; Purple Heart; Combat Med Badge; Five campaign ribbons. Mem: Lions; Jr CofC; Mason. Legal Res: 100 Park Ave International Falls MN 56649 Mailing Add: 216 Third Ave International Falls MN 56649

BANER, RICHARD MARTIN (R)
State Chmn, Ill Young Rep Orgn
b Chicago, Ill, Nov 27, 36; s Charles Martin Baner & Ella Detweiler Baner Byrnes; m 1955 to Janet Mae Eastman; c Stephen Martin, Gary Martin, Sandra Mae, Craig Martin & Andrew Martin. Educ: Eureka Col, 54-55; Bradley Univ, BS, 60; John Marshall Law Sch, 65; Lambda Chi Alpha. Polit & Govt Pos: Precinct committeeman, Cruger Twp, Woodford Co, Ill, 68-; 18th Cong Dist Gov, Ill Young Rep Orgn, 69-71; state chmn, 71-; tech adv, Ill State Dept Gen Serv, 70-72; mem steering comt, Reelect of the President, Young Voters, Ill, 72; alt deleg, Rep Nat Conv, 72; Spec Asst Attorney Gen, Ill, 72-; secy, Woodford Co Rep Cent Comt, 72-; asst gen counsel, Young Rep Nat Fedn, 75- Bus & Prof Pos: Assoc, Heyl, Royster, Voelker & Allen Law Firm, Peoria, Ill, 65-70; partner, Kelly & Baner Law Firm, Peoria, 70-72. Publ: Code of medical-legal regulations, Peoria Co Bar Asn, 72. Mem: Peoria & Woodford Co Bar Asns (chmn med-legal comt, 65-); Ill State Bar Asn (ins coun officer, 65-); Ill Defense Coun; Am Bar Asn (pub contract law coun, 69-); Nat Lawyers Club. Relig: Christian. Mailing Add: RR 1 Box 247 Eureka IL 61503

BANG, OTTO T, JR (R)
Minn State Sen
b Madelia, Minn, 1931; m; c four. Educ: Mayville, ND Sch; Univ of Minn, BA. Polit & Govt Pos: Chmn, Edina Rep Comt, Minn, 60-62; Minn State Rep, 62-72; Minn State Sen, 72- Bus & Prof Pos: Vpres, Twin City Ins Agency; dir, Fotomark, Inc. Mem: AF&AM; Scottish Rite; Shrine; Downtown Exchange Club of Minneapolis; Edina CofC. Honors & Awards: Man of Year Award, Edina Sun's, 72. Relig: Lutheran. Mailing Add: 5200 Duggan Plaza Edina MN 55435

BANGERTER, NORMAN H (R)
Utah State Rep
Mailing Add: 4059 Montaia Dr Salt Lake City UT 84119

BANISTER, BETTE M (R)
Secy, Rep Party, Ga
b Athens, Ga, Nov 30, 35; d Dr Walter F McLendon & Marguerite Ward M; c Brian James, Laura Elaine & Marguerite Elizabeth. Educ: Stephens Col, AA, 54; Univ Ga, BSHE, 56; Phi Upsilon Omicron; Chi Omega. Polit & Govt Pos: Secy, Clarke Co Rep Comt, Ga, 66-73; vchmn, 73-; tenth dist dir, Ga Fedn Rep Women, 67-69, vpres, 71-; alt deleg, Rep Nat Conv, 68, deleg, 72; mem, Ga Rep State Cent Comt, 68-; vpres, Clarke Co Fedn Rep Women, 68-; vchairwoman, Tenth Cong Dist Rep Party, 68-73; Ga chmn, Nat Fedn of Rep Women's Educ Adv Comt, currently; pres, Clarke Co Rep Women's Club, 70-72; secy, Rep Party, Ga, 70- Bus & Prof Pos: Salesman, Chappell Realty, Inc, Athens, Ga, 71- Mem: Archaeol Inst Am; Athens Jr Assembly; League Women Voters; Athens Gen Hosp Auxiliary; Heritage Garden Club. Honors & Awards: Woman of the Year in Vol Community Serv, Athens, Ga, 69. Relig: Episcopal. Mailing Add: 525 West View Dr Athens GA 30601

BANK, BERT (D)
Ala State Sen
Mailing Add: 7 Burnt Pine Northport AL 35476

BANKS, CHARLES ALFRED (D)
Mem, Ark Dem State Comt
b Memphis, Tenn, Mar 8, 47; s Albert Alexander Banks & Lucille Pittman B; div. Educ: Univ Ark, BSBA, 69, JD, 72; Blue Key; Phi Alpha Delta; Lambda Chi Alpha. Polit & Govt Pos: Asst Attorney Gen, Ark, 72-73; pub defender, Mississippi Co, 73-75, dep prosecuting attorney, 75-; mem, Ark Dem State Comt, 75- Bus & Prof Pos: Attorney-at-law, Blytheville, Ark, 73-75. Mil Serv: Entered as E-1, Army, 69, released as SP-5, 75, after serv in 306th Ord Bn; SP-5, Army Res, 75. Mem: Rotary (pres); Blytheville Jaycees; Am Bar Asn; Farm Bur; YMCA (bd dirs). Relig: Methodist. Legal Res: 1709 Country Club Rd Blytheville AR 72315 Mailing Add: PO Box 374 Blytheville AR 72315

BANKS, DORIS NININGER (D)
Dem Nat Committeewoman, Colo
b McPherson, Kans, Oct 3, 21; d Harvey Harlow Nininger & Addie Delp N; m 1954 to John Clement Banks; c Nancy, James & stepchildren, Carolyn Ivey & John Robert. Educ: Grinnell Col, BA, 43; Phi Beta Kappa; Mortar Board. Polit & Govt Pos: Precinct committeewoman, Dem Party, Denver, Colo, 52-64; capt-at-lg, Denver Co Dem Party, 60-63, secy, 63-65, vchmn, 65-68; Denver Elec Comnr, 67; comnr, Comn on Community Rels, 67-71, chmn, 69; Dem Nat Committeewoman, Colo, 68-, mem bylaws comt, Dem Nat Comt, 75-; deleg, Dem Nat Conv, 72; mem, Dem Charter Comn & Exec Comt, 72-74; chmn Colo deleg, Dem Nat Mid-Term Conf, 74. Bus & Prof Pos: Reporter, Denver Post, 45-49; Info writer, City & Co of Denver, 52-54. Relig: United Church of Christ. Mailing Add: 1220 Olive St Denver CO 80220

BANKS, J B (JET) (D)
Mo State Rep
Mailing Add: 1442 A North Grand St Louis MO 63106

BANKS, PATRICIA MEISE (D)
Chmn, Wicomico Co Dem Cent Comt, Md
b Salisbury, Md, Mar 11, 29; d Royden Streett Meise, Sr & Marie McFee M; m 1949 to Roger Alan Banks, Sr; c Roger Alan, Jr, Rodney Louis, Bruce Patrick & Joan Marie. Educ: Wicomico High Sch, Salisbury. Polit & Govt Pos: Mem, Wicomico Co Dem Cent Comt, Md, 62-, chmn, 72- Mem: United Dem Womens' Club of Md. Relig: Catholic. Mailing Add: 604 Waverly St Salisbury MD 21801

BANKS, PATRICK (D)
Ga State Rep
Mailing Add: 909 Newport Rd Macon GA 31204

BANKS, PETER LOUIS (D)
Ga State Sen
b Barnesville, Ga, Aug 12, 38; s James Louis Banks & Katherine Gordy B; m 1961 to Janne Butler; c Bonnie Elizabeth, Beverly Grace & Lucretia Jannellen. Educ: Gordon Mil Col, 56-58; Univ Ga, AB, 60, Sch of Law, LLB, 63; Kappa Alpha Order, Phi Delta Phi. Polit & Govt Pos: Ga State Sen, Dist 17, 75- Bus & Prof Pos: Attorney, Banks, Smith & Lambdin, Barnesville, Ga, currently. Mil Serv: Army Res, 55-63. Mem: State Bar Ga; Am Bar Asn. Honors & Awards: One of Five Outstanding Young Men in Ga, Ga Jaycees, 74. Relig: Presbyterian. Legal Res: 164 Murphy Ave Barnesville GA 30204 Mailing Add: 314 Thomaston St Barnesville GA 30204

BANKS, ROGER WARE (D)
b Albuquerque, NMex, Aug 27, 36; s Robert Thurston Banks, Sr & Charlesetta Favors B; m 1966 to Caroline Wellington Giles; c Logan Giles. Educ: Univ NMex, BA, 68, MA, 70; Univ Minn, 71-75; Phi Kappa Phi; Alpha Phi Omega. Polit & Govt Pos: Assoc chairperson, 57th Sen Dist, Dem-Farmer-Labor Party, Minn, 72-74; mem, Fifth Cong Dist Dem-Farmer-Labor Exec Comt, 72-74; mem, Minn State Dem-Farmer-Labor Cent Comt, 72-74; deleg, Dem Nat Mid-Term Conf, 74; mem, Minn Comprehensive Manpower Planning Comn, 74- Bus & Prof Pos: Vol & community developer, US Peace Corps, Punjab, India, 63-65; manpower training & develop prog dir, Off Econ Opportunity Community Action Prog, Albuquerque, NMex, 66-68; consult community action progs, Off Econ Opportunity Region V, Volt Tech Corp, Austin, Tex, 68-70; instr polit sci, Dept Polit Sci Univ Minn, 73-74 & Afro-Am Studies Dept, 74- Mil Serv: Entered as Pvt, Army, 55, released as Pfc, 58, after serv in 77th Spec Forces Group. Publ: Auth, Between the tracks & the freeway: the Negro in Albuquerque, In: Minorities and Politics, Univ NMex Press, 69. Mem: Am & Midwest Polit Sci Asns; Am for Dem Action; Common Cause. Honors & Awards: Nat Aeronaut & Space Admin Pub Sci, Policy & Admin fel, 69; Am Polit Sci Asn, Black Fellow, 70; Award, NMex Fed Exec Asn & Univ NMex; NMex Intergovt Serv Award, 70; Nat Inst Ment Health Policy Evaluation fel, 72-75. Mailing Add: 863 23rd Ave SE Minneapolis MN 55414

BANKSTON, JESSE H (D)
Secy, Dem State Cent Comt La
b Mt Hermon, La, Oct 7, 07; s Leon V Bankston & Allie Magee B; m 1938 to Ruth Paine; c Shirley (Mrs Thomas Newsham), Dale L, Larry S & Jesse H, Jr. Educ: La State Univ, Baton Rouge, AB, 33, MA, 36; NC Univ, Chapel Hill, PhD, 38; Mu Sigma Rho; Pi Sigma Alpha. Polit & Govt Pos: Admin asst, La Civil Serv, 40-44; exec asst, La Dept Inst, 44-47; dir, 47-48; dir, La State Hosp Bd, 48-52; dir, La State Dept Hosp, 56-59; mem & past pres, La State Bd Educ, 68-; mem & secy, Dem State Cent Comt, La, 67-, mem, La Coord Coun for Higher Educ, 73-74; mem, La Educ TV Authority, 74. Mem: Mason; Shrine; Acad Hosp Counrs; Int Inst Hosp Consult (vchmn); Am Hosp Asn; La Hosp Asn. Relig: Baptist. Legal Res: 9526 Southmoor Dr Baton Rouge LA 70815 Mailing Add: 5700 Florida Blvd Suite 318 Baton Rouge LA 70806

BANNAI, PAUL T (R)
Calif State Assemblyman
b Delta, Colo, July 4, 20; s Fakui Bannai & Shino Muto B; m 1946 to Hideko Matsuno; c Kathryn, Don & Lorraine. Educ: Am Inst Banking & Univ Calif, Los Angeles Exten. Polit & Govt Pos: Mem & chmn, City Planning Comn, Gardena, Calif, 69-71, city councilman, 72-73; Calif State Assemblyman, 73- Bus & Prof Pos: Pres, Bannai Realty & Ins, Gardena, currently. Mil Serv: Entered as Cadre, Army, 442nd Inf Regt Combat Team, rep the US Forces at Japanese surrender ceremonies in Bali, Java & Timor, 1st Sgt, 2nd Inf Div, also serv as mil intel specialist. Mem: Lions; Boy Scouts; VFW; Calif Real Estate Asn; Japanese Am Citizens League. Honors & Awards: Order of Merit, Boy Scouts. Relig: Methodist. Legal Res: 1331 W 146th St Gardena CA 90247 Mailing Add: Suite 5150 State Capitol Bldg Sacramento CA 95814

BANNER, JAMES J (D)
Nev State Assemblyman
Mailing Add: 2223 Poplar Ave Las Vegas NV 89101

BANNON, EDMOND JOSEPH (D)
Treas, Ind Dem State Cent Comt
b Kansas City, Kans, Mar 9, 12; s Edmond James Bannon & Rose Goebel B; m 1941 to Patricia Nan Peters; c Peter Fredric. Educ: Kansas City Sch Law, 31-35. Polit & Govt Pos: Mem, Bd Pub Harbors & Terminals, State Ind, 55-56; mem bd trustees, Purdue Univ, 56-59; Region 5 Dir, Asn Gov Bd State Univ & Allied Insts, 58-59; mem, US Trade Develop Mission to SAfrica, 62; financial adv, Ind Dem State Cent Comt, 62, treas, 70-; mem, World's Fair Comt for Ind Days, 64; treas, Branigin for Gov Comt, 64; deleg, Dem Nat Conv, 64, 68 & 72; mem nat adv comt, US Comnr Gen for US Participation in World Exhib, EXPO 67, Montreal, Can, 67; mem, Ind Trade Mission to Orient, 68; mem, State Policy Comn Post High Sch Educ, 68; mem comn Med Educ, State Ind, 69; dir, Old Hickory Dem Club, 69. Bus & Prof Pos: Mem staff various depts, Liberty Nat Bank & Fidelity Nat Bank & Trust Co; Bond Dept, Union & Nat Bank, Kansas City, Mo, 26-35; asst nat bank examr, Comptroller of the Currency, 35-41, nat bank examr, 41-47; first vpres, Purdue Nat Bank Lafayette, 47-49, pres, 49-56, chmn bd & pres, 57- Mil Serv: Entered as Pvt, Army, 43, released as 1st Lt, 46, after serv in staff work, Cent Pac Base Command & Mid Pac, 45-46. Mem: Am Bankers Asn; US & Ind State CofC; Am Inst Mgt (pres coun); Ind Soc Chicago. Relig: Roman Catholic. Legal Res: 30 Maryhill Rd Lafayette IN 47905 Mailing Add: Purdue Nat Bank of Lafayette PO Box 380 Lafayette IN 47902

BANOWSKY, WILLIAM S (R)
Rep Nat Committeeman, Calif
b Abilene, Tex, Mar 4, 36; m to Gay C. Educ: Univ Southern Calif, PhD. Polit & Govt Pos: Chmn, Los Angeles Co Comt to Reelect the President; deleg, Rep Nat Conv, 72; Rep Nat Committeeman, Calif, 72-, Mem, Rep Exec Comt, 74- Bus & Prof Pos: Pres, Pepperdine Univ, currently. Mem: Tech Comt on Spiritual Well-Being; White House Conf on Aging; Nat Adv Coun for Educ Professions Develop. Relig: Church of Christ. Mailing Add: 24255 Pacific Coast Hwy Malibu CA 90265

BARABBA, VINCENT P (R)
Dir, Bur of the Census, Dept of Com
b Chicago, Ill, Sept 6, 34; s John Barabba & Elvira Tucci B; m 1966 to Sheryl Gae Brock; c Heather Anne & Jason Vincent. Educ: Woodbury Univ, BBA, 54; Calif State Univ, Northridge, BS, 62; Univ Calif, Los Angeles, MBA, 64. Polit & Govt Pos: Dir, Bur of the Census, Dept of Com, 73- Bus & Prof Pos: Pres, Commun Assocs, 64-66; pres, Datamatics, Inc, 66-69; chmn bd, Decision Making Info, 69-73; dir, Cent Bank of Glendale, Calif, 72. Mil Serv: Entered as Basic Airman, Air Force, 54, released as Airman 1/C, after serv in Air Defense Command, 54-58. Publ: Auth, Clutter in the Eye of the Beholder, Res Publica-Claremont Men's Col, 74. Mem: Am Mkt Asn; Sales & Mkt Execs of Los Angeles; Am Statist Asn; Beta Gamma Sigma. Honors & Awards: Am Mkt Asn Outstanding Mkt Student; Alumni Asn Outstanding Sr Award. Legal Res: 245 Inverness Lane Tantallon MD 20022 Mailing Add: Bur of the Census Dept of Com Washington DC 20233

BARABY, MARION E (R)
Committeewoman, Maine Rep State Comt
b North Jay, Maine, Nov 19, 00; d Arthur R Kyes & Ella Davenport K; wid; c Elaine (Mrs Littlefield). Educ: Gray's Bus Col, 19-20; exten work, Brown Univ & RI Col Educ. Polit & Govt Pos: VChmn, Auburn Rep City Comt, 69-; committeewoman, Maine Rep State Comt, 69-; pres, Androscoggin Co Women's Rep Club; mem, Maine & Nat Fedn Rep Women. Bus & Prof Pos: Teacher commercial courses, high sch, RI, 20-26; off mgr woolen mill, 26-37; realtor, 36-; mem, Maine Real Estate Comn, 64-69; exec vpres, Maine Asn Realtors, currently. Mem: Nat Asn Real Estate Bd; Maine Asn Real Estate Bd (exec secy, 71-); Auburn Bd Realtors (pres, secy); Nat License Law Officers; Eastern Star. Relig: Protestant. Mailing Add: 16 Dana Ave Auburn ME 04210

BARANELLO, DOMINIC JOSEPH (D)
Mem, Dem Nat Comt, NY
b Brooklyn, NY, Sept 25, 22; s Angelo Baranello & Josephine Belmonte B; m 1955; c Dominic, Jr, Stephen & Christiana. Educ: Brooklyn Law Sch, LLB, 50; Brooklyn Col, 2 years. Polit & Govt Pos: Chmn, Brookhaven Dem Orgn, NY, 56-60; alt deleg, Dem Nat Conv, 60, deleg, 68; dep co attorney, Suffolk Co, NY, 60-62; chmn, Suffolk Co Dem Orgn, 66-72; mem exec comt, NY State Dem Comt, 66-; presidential elector, State of NY, 68; mem, Dem Nat Comt, 72- Bus & Prof Pos: Attorney, 52- Mil Serv: Entered as Pvt, Air Force, 43, released as Pfc, 46. Mem: Suffolk Co Bar Asn; Columbian Lawyers Asn; Elks (Charter Mem Lodge 2138); Am Legion; Medford Fire Dept. Relig: Catholic. Mailing Add: PO Box 132 Holbrook NY 11741

BARBA, JOSEPH FRANCIS, JR (D)
Chmn, Cheshire Dem Town Comt, Conn
b New Haven, Conn, Feb 6, 36; s Joseph F Barba, Sr & Anne Raccuia B; m 1959 to Agnes Marie Carrozzella; c Susan M, Matthew J & Jennifer C. Educ: Yale Univ, BE, 58. Polit & Govt Pos: Mem, Bd of Selectmen, Cheshire, Conn, 70-72; mem, Cheshire Town Coun, 72-74; chmn, Cheshire Dem Town Comt, 74- Bus & Prof Pos: Vpres, Joseph F Barba & Son, Inc, 59-74, trustee, Joseph Barba Co, 74- Mil Serv: Entered as Pvt, E-2, Army, 58, released as SP-4, 64, after serv in active duty & Res. Mem: Nat Soc Prof Engrs; Am Arbit Asn Panel; Wilsonial Prof Men's Club; KofC. Honors & Awards: Distinguished Serv Award, Cheshire Jaycees, 69. Relig: Roman Catholic. Mailing Add: 475 Radmere Rd Cheshire CT 06410

BARBA, JULIUS WILLIAM (R)
Finance Chmn, NJ Rep Finance Comt
b Kearny, NJ, May 22, 23; s John Barba & Rose Lettieri B; m 1970 to Susan Vartanian. Educ: Princeton Univ, AB, 47; Univ Pa Law Sch, LLB, 50; Princeton Cannon Club. Polit & Govt Pos: Asst counsel, President, White House, Washington, DC, 54-57; finance chmn, NJ Rep Finance Comt, 74- Bus & Prof Pos: Lawyer, Shanley & Fisher, 57- Mil Serv: Entered as Ens, Navy, 44, released as Lt(jg), 46, after serv in gunnery off, USS Lewis (DE 535). Mem: Essex Co & Am Bar Asns. Relig: Roman Catholic. Legal Res: Long Hill Rd New Vernon NJ 07976 Mailing Add: 570 Broad St Newark NJ 07102

BARBARO, FRANK J (D)
NY State Assemblyman
Mailing Add: 7705 Bay Pkwy Brooklyn NY 11214

BARBEE, ALLEN CROMWELL (D)
NC State Rep
b Spring Hope, NC, Dec 18, 10; s John Lucian Barbee & Deborah Vester B; m 1942 to Mabel McClellan Dixon; c Rebecca Barnes & Allen Cromwell, II. Educ: Univ NC, 31-32. Polit & Govt Pos: Comnr, Spring Hope, NC, 47-49, mayor, 50-58; NC State Rep, 60- Bus & Prof Pos: Ed-publisher, Spring Hope Enterprise; sales exec & mfrs rep, 38-70; owner, Barbee Agency, 50-70; co-founder & treas, Sload & Barbee Inc, currently. Mil Serv: Entered as Pvt, Army, 42, released as Capt, Air Force, 46, after serv in Ferrying Div, Air Transport Command, ETO, 43-45; ETO & Normandy Invasion Ribbons. Mem: Am Legion; Elks; Shrine; Sphinx Club; Benvenue & Peachtree Hills Country Clubs. Relig: Methodist. Mailing Add: Spring Hope NC 27882

BARBEE, BASIL CALHOUN (D)
Chmn, Nacogdoches Co Dem Comt, Tex
b Lovelady, Tex, Feb 19, 18; s Horace Mode Barbee & Adella Estes B; div. Educ: Stephen F Austin State Univ, BA, Math, 38, BA, Physics, 53, BA, Music, 58. Polit & Govt Pos: Chmn, Nacogdoches Co Dem Comt, Tex, 74- Mailing Add: 4612 SFA Sta Nacogdoches TX 75961

BARBEE, LLOYD AUGUSTUS (D)
Wis State Rep
b Memphis, Tenn, Aug 17, 25; s Ernest Aaron Barbee & Adlina Gillian B; div; c Finn, Daphne & Rustam. Educ: LeMoyne Col, BA in Soc Sci, 49; Univ Wis, Madison, Law Cert, 55 & JD, 56. Polit & Govt Pos: Nat vchmn, student div, Am for Dem Action, 48-49, nat field secy, 51; secy, Pub Welfare Comt, Wis Legis Coun, 56-66, mem, 73-74; law examr, Unemploy Compensation Dept, Indust Comn of Wis, 57-62; mem, Mayor's Comn on Human Rights, 57-62, chmn, 59-61; legal consult, Gov Comn of Human Rights, 59; mem, Gov Comn for UN, 63; Wis State Rep, Sixth Dist, 65-, chmn, Enrolled Bills Comt, 65-66, 71-72, chmn, Judiciary Comt, 73-74 & mem, Justice & Law Enforcement Comt; deleg, Milwaukee Co Dem Coun, 67; deleg, Sixth Ward Unit, Milwaukee Co Dem Party, 63-64, chmn unit, 67-69; deleg, Dem Nat Conv, 68 & 72. Bus & Prof Pos: Attorney, Barbee & Jacobson, Madison, Wis, 56-67; Milwaukee, 62-; vchmn, Educ Film Assocs, 62; bd dirs, Wis Film Assocs, Inc, 63; bd mem, E B Phillips Day Care Ctr, 64-68; team teacher summer law practice course, Univ Wis Law Sch, 68 & 69. Mil Serv: Entered as A/S, 43, Navy, released as SM 2/C, 46. Mem: NAACP; Nat Black Assembly; Wis Black Lawyers Asn; Freedom Through Equality, Inc (pres, 69-); United Black Enterprises; United Black Artists. Honors & Awards: Medgar Evers Award, Milwaukee Br, NAACP, 69; New Image Concept Citations, 70; Milwaukee Courier Award, 70; Milwaukee Co Welfare Rights Orgn Award, 72; Black Press of Wis Award, 72; Zero Population Growth Award, 73. Mailing Add: 321 E Meinecke Ave Milwaukee WI 53212

BARBER, ARTHUR WHITING (D)
b Meriden, Conn, July 4, 26; s Arthur Leslie Barber & Winifred Viola Whiting B; m 1949 to Margaret Shorey; c Jeffrey Whiting, Christopher David, Jonathan Scott, Kimberly Susan & Cynthia Abigail. Educ: Harvard Univ, BA, 50. Polit & Govt Pos: Dep Asst Secy of Defense, Dept of Defense, 62-67. Bus & Prof Pos: With Air Force Cambridge Research Ctr, 50-61 & Mitre Corp, 61-62; pres, Inst Polit & Planning, 67-70; pres, First Commun Co, 70- Mil Serv: Entered Navy, 44, released as Signalman 3/C, 46, after serv in Armed Guard, Pac. Honors & Awards: Outstanding Civilian Award, Dept of Defense, 67- Relig: Unitarian. Mailing Add: 7600 Hemlock St Bethesda MD 20034

BARBER, DEBORAH ANN (D)
Nat Committeewoman, Col Young Dem Clubs of Am
b St Louis, Mo, Apr 9, 52; d Louis Eugene Barber & Virginia Wiggins B; single. Educ: Univ Mo-Columbia, 70-; Nat Honor Soc; Dean's List. Polit & Govt Pos: Alt deleg, Dem Nat Conv, 72; pub rels student coordr, Citizens for McGovern, St Louis Hq, 72; chmn Dem youth voter registr, Students for McGovern, Univ Mo-Columbia, 72; Mo out-state youth & student coordr, Mo Citizens for McGovern, 72; mem, Mo Youth Commun Comt, Dem Party of Mo, 72-; pub rels dir, Univ Mo Young Dem, 72-74; admin vpres, Col Young Dem, Univ Mo, 73, vchmn, 73-74; Nat Committeewoman, Col Young Dem Clubs of Am, 73-; mem, 27th Ward Dem Club, 74- Mem: Women's Polit Caucus. Relig: Baptist. Mailing Add: 614-R Fremont Ave St Louis MO 63147

BARBER, JAMES DAVID (D)
Pa State Rep
b Columbia, SC, Aug 16, 21; s Howard Barber & Sallie Whitaker B; m to Rebecca; c Diane. Educ: Allen Univ. Polit & Govt Pos: Pa State Rep, 190th Dist, Wards 6 & 27, 69-, chmn, Black Caucus, Pa House of Rep, currently. Mem: Mason; NAACP; WPhiladelphia Crusade & United Civic Asns; YMCA. Honors & Awards: Awards, NAACP, Asn for Retarded Children & Am Cancer Soc. Legal Res: 802 N 40th St Philadelphia PA 19104 Mailing Add: Rm 617 Main Capitol Bldg House of Reps Harrisburg PA 17120

BARBER, RICHARD J (D)
Educ: Wayne State Univ, AB, 53, JD, 55; Univ Mich, MA in Econ, 58; Yale Univ, LLM, 59; ed-in-chief, Wayne Law Rev, 54-55. Polit & Govt Pos: Asst to dir, Mich Tax Study, 58; economist, staff of the Joint Cong Econ Comt, 61-62; consult, House Select Small Bus Comt, 63; spec counsel, Senate Subcomt on Antitrust & Monopoly, 65-67; Dep Asst Secy for Policy & Int Affairs, Dept of Transportation, until 70; consult, Senate Com Comt, 72-73. Bus & Prof Pos: Asst prof law, Rutgers Univ, 59-61; assoc prof, Southern Methodist Univ, 61-64; ed, J of Air Law & Com, 63-64; vis prof, Yale Univ, 64-65. Mil Serv: Army, 55-57. Publ: Technological change in American transportation: the role of government action, Va Law Rev, 64; The politics of research, 66; The American Corporation, Dutton, 70; plus other articles in prof & gen periodicals. Mem: Am Econ Asn; Mich & DC Bar Asns. Legal Res: MI Mailing Add: 1000 Connecticut Ave Washington DC 20036

BARBER, ROBERT J (R)
b Detroit, Mich, Aug 26, 06; m 1931 to Gladys Wilkie; c Susan Ann (Mrs Uridge) & Robert F. Educ: Detroit Col of Law, LLB & JD. Polit & Govt Pos: Holder of every pos within the Rep Party of Kalamazoo Co, Mich, commencing with 1947; field of the court, prosecutor, probate judge, spec attorney gen & assoc munic judge; mem of comn, State of Mich Dept of Health, currently; mem bd dirs, Kalamazoo Capitol Off Econ Opportunity Orgn, currently; chmn, Kalamazoo Co Rep Party, formerly. Bus & Prof Pos: Spec agent, Fed Bur Invest, formerly; attorney-at-law. Mil Serv: World War II. Mem: Boy Scouts; KofC; Mich Bar Asn; NAm Judges Asn; Mich Munic Judges Asn. Relig: Catholic. Legal Res: 8430 Tumbleweed Portage MI 49081 Mailing Add: 317 Michigan Bldg Kalamazoo MI 49001

BARBERG, WILLIAM WARREN (R)
b Minneapolis, Minn, Oct 12, 28; s Wayne R Barberg & Lillian Lantto B; m 1959 to Doreen A Sieg; c Lynn Marie, William Warren & Ann Denise. Educ: Stout State Univ, BS, 51; Epsilon Pi Tau; Sigma Tau Gamma; Alpha Phi Omega. Polit & Govt Pos: Col chmn, Stout State Univ Young Rep, 50-52; chmn, Dunn Co Young Rep, Wis, 53-56; chmn, Eau Claire Co Young Rep, 56-58; dist chmn, Tenth Dist Young Rep, 57; vpres, Wis Young Rep, 58; mem exec comt, Eau Claire Co Rep Club, 60-, chmn, 68-; mem adv comt & ins laws rev comt, Wis Legis Coun, 66-69, 71-; alt deleg, Rep Nat Conv, 72. Bus & Prof Pos: Trustee, Nat Asn Life Underwriters, 70-, chmn fed law & legis comt, 72-; mem, Inst Agents Adv Coun, Wis Ins Comnr, 70- Mem: Eau Claire Co Taxpayers Asn; Eau Claire Lions Club; First Wis Toastmasters Club; Wis Asn Life Underwriters; Stout State Univ Found (Pres). Honors & Awards: Outstanding Alumnus, Sigma Tau Gamma; Distinguished Serv Award, Wis Asn Life Underwriters; Man of the Year, Wis Asn Life Underwriters, 70. Relig: Lutheran; pres Bd Deacons & chmn, congregation, formerly. Mailing Add: 3606 Pine Pl Eau Claire WI 54701

BARBIERI, ARTHUR THOMAS (D)
Chmn, Conn Dem State Cent Comt
b New Haven, Conn, Jan 20, 16; s Thomas Vincent Barbieri & Nancy D'Amato B; m 1943 to Marion Cavallaro; c Nancy Marie & Arthur Thomas, Jr. Educ: Yale Univ, 3 years; Alpha Phi Delta. Polit & Govt Pos: Clerk, New Haven, Conn, 52-53; chmn, New Haven Town Dem Comt, 53-; dir pub works, 54-59; committeeman, Conn Dem State Cent Comt, 70-, chmn, Dist 11, currently. Bus & Prof Pos: Pres, Real Estate Co, Arthur T Barbieri, Inc, 57-, Ins Co, 64-, Travel Agency, 68- & Life Ins Co, 69- Mil Serv: Entered as Pvt, Army, 42, released as Lt, 44, after serv in 100th Div Field Artil. Mem: Elks; Melebus Club; Asn Advan Ethical Hypnosis; Int Brotherhood of Magician; DAV; Am Legion Post 48. Honors & Awards: Hon Chief Order of Redmen. Relig: Catholic. Mailing Add: 5 Horsley Ave New Haven CT 06512

BARBOA, EDDIE RODGER (D)
NMex State Sen
b Albuquerque, NMex, Feb 19, 31; s Floyd Barboa & Adalina B; m 1970 to Dorothy Elizabeth Clark; c Deborah (Mrs Caromona), Michell (Mrs Hoffman), Floyd, Eddie, Jr, & Rodney; stepchildren, Bruce, Brian & Brenda (deceased) Flemins. Educ: Midwest Col, Pueblo, Colo, 1 year; Univ NMex, Night Sch. Polit & Govt Pos: Ward chmn, Albuquerque Dem Party, NMex, 63-64, chmn, Dem Action Comt, 64-65; NMex State Rep, 65-66; NMex State Sen, 71- Bus & Prof Pos: Pres, San-Bar Construction Co, Inc, 54- Mem: Coronado Minorities Contractor Asn (pres). Relig: Protestant. Mailing Add: 4025 Isleta Blvd SW Albuquerque NM 87105

BARBOUR, GEORGE H (D)
NJ State Assemblyman
Mailing Add: State House Trenton NJ 08625

BARBOUR, HALEY REEVES (R)
Exec Dir, Miss Rep Party
b Yazoo City, Miss, Oct 22, 47; s Jeptha Fowlkes Barbour, Jr & LeFlore Johnson B (both deceased); m 1971 to Marsha Dickson; c Robert Sterling. Educ: Univ Miss, JD, 73; Omicron Delta Kappa; Phi Delta Phi; Sigma Alpha Epsilon. Polit & Govt Pos: Field rep, Miss Rep Party, 68, dep exec dir, 72-73, exec dir, 73-; regional technician, Bur of Census, 69-70; exec dir, Southern Asn of Rep State Chmn, currently. Mem: Miss Bar Asn; Yazoo Jaycees. Relig: Presbyterian. Legal Res: Wildwood Terr Extended Yazoo City MS 39194 Mailing Add: PO Box 1178 Jackson MS 39205

BARBOUR, ROBERT TAYLOR (R)
b Rock Point, Md, Nov 22, 11; s Robert Guy Barbour & Charlotte May Twiford B; m 1941 to Phyllis Buckley; c Rosemary, Lorena, Lucy & Victoria A. Educ: George Washington Univ, AB, 38; Univ Md, LLB, 41. Polit & Govt Pos: State's attorney, Charles Co, Md, 51-54; chmn, Charles Co Rep Cent Comt, 62-74. Bus & Prof Pos: Practicing attorney, La Plata, Md, 47-, present firm name, Barbour & Zverina, Attorneys; hold unlimited license as Master of Ocean Steamships. Mil Serv: Entered as Pvt, Army, 41, released as Warrant Officer, 45, after serv in 12th Coast Artil Mine Planter Battery, Am Theater; Am Theater Army Serv Ribbon; Atlantic, Pac & Mediter Merchant Marine Serv Ribbons. Mem: Md & Charles Co Bar Asns; Am Trial Lawyers Asn; Charles Co Hist Soc; Soc for Restoration of Port Tobacco. Relig: Episcopal. Mailing Add: Port Tobacco MD 20677

BARBOUR, WALWORTH
b Mass, June 4, 08. Educ: Harvard Univ, AB, 30. Hon Degrees: PhD, Tel Aviv Univ, 71, Hebrew Univ Jerusalem, 72; LLD, Dropsie Univ, 73; DHL, Hebrew Union Col, 74. Polit & Govt Pos: Career ambassador, US Dept of State Foreign Serv, 31-73, Naples, 31-32, Athens, 33-36, Baghdad, 36-39 & 42 & Safia, 39-41, second secy for Greece & Yugoslavia in Egypt, 43-44, second secy, Athens, 44-45, asst chief & chief, Div of Southeastern European Affairs, 45-49, counr, Moscow, 49-51, Dep Asst Secy for European Affairs, 54-55, Dep Chief of Mission, London, 55-56, minister & counr, 56-58, minister, 58-61, US Ambassador to Israel, 61-73; Retired. Honors & Awards: Distinguished Honor Award, Dept of State, 70; Hon Fel, Weizmann Inst, 70. Mailing Add: 14 Grapevine Rd Gloucester MA 01930

BARCLAY, H DOUGLAS (R)
NY State Sen
b July 5, 32; s Hugh Barclay & Dorothy B; m 1959 to Sara Seiter; c Kathryn, David, Dorothy, Susan & William. Educ: Yale Univ, BA, 4 years; Syracuse Univ Col Law, DJ, 3 years. Polit & Govt Pos: NY State Sen, 43rd Dist, 65-; deleg, Rep Nat Conv, 68. Bus & Prof Pos: Attorney-at-law. Mil Serv: Entered as 2nd Lt, Army, released as 1st Lt. Mailing Add: 7377 Bentley Rd Pulaski NY 13142

BARDANOUVE, FRANCIS (D)
Mont State Rep
b Harlem, Mont, Dec 10, 17; s John Pete Bardanouve & Alice Miller B; m 1967 to Venus Tretsven Potts. Polit & Govt Pos: Mont State Rep, 59-, chmn, Appropriations Comt, Mont State House of Rep, mem, Legis Coun, 63-, vchmn, formerly; secy-treas, Ft Belknap Housing Authority, 63-, chmn, currently; deleg, Dem Nat Conv, 72. Bus & Prof Pos: Pres & dir, Equity Coop Asn, 53-; owner, ranching & farming interests. Mem: Farmers Union. Relig: Protestant. Mailing Add: Harlem MT 59526

BAREFIELD, STONE DEAVOURS (D)
Miss State Rep
b Laurel, Miss, July 28, 27; s Samuel S Barefield, Sr & Dinah Deavours B; m 1951 to Bonnie Merle Taylor; c Stone D, Jr, Allen Taylor, Julia Ann & Michael Clayton. Educ: Univ Southern Miss, BS, 52; Univ Miss Sch Law, LLB, 54; Kappa Alpha. Polit & Govt Pos: Miss State Rep, 60-; chmn, Gen Legis Investigating Comt, 70, mem, Legis Comt on Performance Eval & Expenditure Rev, currently. Mil Serv: Merchant Marines, 45-46, Atlantic & Mediter Area; entered as Pvt, Marines, 46, released as Pfc, 48, after serv in Marine Air Wing, Cherrypoint, NC; reentered 50, released as Cpl, 51, after serv in Third Bn, Sixth Marines, Camp LeJeune, NC. Mem: Miss State Bar Asn; F&AM; Lions; Am Legion; Southern Growth Policies Bd. Relig: Methodist. Legal Res: 100 Beverly Hills Rd Hattiesburg MS 39401 Mailing Add: 121 W Front St Hattiesburg MS 39401

BARENGO, ROBERT R (D)
Nev State Assemblyman
b Reno, Nev, Aug 28, 41; s Rosmino Barengo & Mary Maloney A; single. Educ: Calif State Univ, Hayward, BS, 66; Univ Santa Clara, JD, 69. Polit & Govt Pos: Mem, Washoe Co Dem Cent Comt, Nev; Nev State Assemblyman, 73-, chmn, Assembly Judiciary Comt. Bus & Prof Pos: Law clerk, Judge T O Craven, 69-70; dep dist attorney, Washoe Co, 70-73; partner, Legarza, Lee & Barengo, Attorneys-at-law, 73. Mil Serv: Entered as Pvt, Army Res, 61, released, 66. Mem: Am & Nev Bar Asns; Am Trial Lawyers; Am Judicature Soc; Nat Dist Attorneys Asn. Relig: Roman Catholic. Legal Res: 1431 N Virginia St Reno NV 89503 Mailing Add: PO Box 2557 Reno NV 89505

BARER, STANLEY HARRIS (D)
b Walla Walla, Wash, Aug 22, 39; s David Barer & Dorothy Copeland B; m 1962 to Shirley Ovadia; div; c Leigh. Educ: Univ Wash, BA, 61, JD, 63; Order of the Coif; mem bd ed, Wash Law Rev; Phi Delta Phi; Zeta Beta Tau. Polit & Govt Pos: Staff counsel, Com Comt, US Senate, 63-64, maritime counsel, 67-68, transportation counsel, 68-69, gen counsel, 69; asst US dist attorney, Seattle, Wash, 65-66; admin asst to US Sen Warren G Magnuson, Wash, 70- Mem: Fed & Wash State Bar Asns. Legal Res: Rte 3 Country Club Dr Walla Walla WA 99362 Mailing Add: 127 Old Senate Off Bldg Washington DC 20510

BARES, ALLEN R (D)
La State Rep
Mailing Add: 212 N Robinhood Lane Lafayette LA 70501

BARGER, SARA LOUISE (R)
Committeewoman, Ohio State Rep Cent Comt
b Zelienople, Pa, Aug 31, 17; d Clarence Wesley Ifft & Sadie Crea I; m 1942 to Wilber Arlington Barger; c Judy (Mrs Robert A Koopman), Glen Alan & Jean. Educ: Geneva Col, BS bus admin, 40; John Carroll Univ, summer 64. Polit & Govt Pos: Committeewoman, Ohio State Rep Cent Comt, 11th Dist, 70- Relig: Protestant. Mailing Add: 43 W Satin St Jefferson OH 44047

BARGERON, EMORY E (D)
Ga State Rep
Mailing Add: PO Box 447 Louisville GA 30434

BARHAM, MACK ELWIN
Assoc Justice, Supreme Court La
b Bastrop, La, June 18, 24; s Henry Barham & Lockie Harper B; m 1946 to Ann Holt LeVois; c Bret Lane & Megan (Mrs Thomas Richard). Educ: La State Univ Law Sch, JD, 46; Order of the Coif; Blue Key; Phi Alpha Delta; Lambda Chi Alpha; Omicron Delta Kappa; Phi Delta Phi. Polit & Govt Pos: Judge, Bastrop City Court, La, 46-61, Fourth Judicial Dist Court, 61-68 & Court of Appeal, 68; assoc justice, Supreme Court La, 68- Publ: A renaissance of the civilian tradition in Louisiana, La Law Rev, 73; The law of redhibition in France and Louisiana, Tulane Law Rev, 75. Mem: Coun La State Law Inst; Am Bar Asn; Am Judicature Soc; Nat Appellate Judges Conf. Honors & Awards: Freedoms Found of Valley Forge Award, 69. Mailing Add: 5837 Bellaire Dr New Orleans LA 70124

BARINGER, MAURICE E (R)
Treas, Iowa
b Arkansas City, Kans, Dec 4, 21; s George Baringer & Ada B; m 1948 to Dorothy Schlensig; c Sandra, James, Debra & David. Educ: Univ of Kans, BS in Bus, 43; Iowa State Univ, BS, 48, MS, 49. Polit & Govt Pos: Iowa State Rep, 61-68, speaker, Iowa House of Rep, 67-68; treas, Iowa, 69- Bus & Prof Pos: Teacher animal husbandry, Iowa Univ; dir & past pres, Nat Feed Ingredients Asn; dir nutrition, Occo Feeds, Oelwein, Iowa, 56-67. Mil Serv: World War II, 45 months, including two years as antiaircraft artil officer, SW Pac. Mem: Elks; Lions; Farm Bur; Am Legion; Farm House. Relig: Presbyterian; Elder, Sunday Sch Teacher. Mailing Add: 1408 Pleasant Dr West Des Moines IA 50265

BARKA, ERNEST P (R)
NH State Rep
Mailing Add: Box 72 35 W Broadway Derry NH 03038

BARKAN, ALEXANDER ELIAS
b Bayonne, NJ, Aug 9, 09; s Jacob Barkan & Rachel Perelmen B; m 1942 to Helen Stickno; c Lois & Carol. Educ: Univ Chicago, PhB, 33. Polit & Govt Pos: Asst dir, Comt on Polit Educ, AFL-CIO, Washington, DC, 55-57, dep dir, 57-63, dir, 63- Bus & Prof Pos: Textile Workers Union Am, 37-55. Mil Serv: Naval Res, 42-45. Legal Res: 6515 E Halbert Rd Bethesda MD 20034 Mailing Add: 815 16th St NW Washington DC 20006

BARKER, BOB L (D)
NC State Sen
Mailing Add: Rte 6 Box 224A Raleigh NC 27603

BARKER, CHRISTOPHER SYLVANUS, JR (D)
NC State Rep
b Trenton, NC, Sept 7, 11; s Christopher S Barker, MD & Ruth Jane Henderson B; m 1949 to Jean Kouwenhoven; c C S, III, Marie-Anne & Gary Cornelius. Educ: US Naval Acad, BS, 33. Polit & Govt Pos: NC State Rep, 69-, chmn ment health comt, NC House Rep; chmn, NC Drug Authority, currently. Bus & Prof Pos: Broker, McDaniel Lewis & Co, Greensboro, NC, currently. Mil Serv: Entered as Midn, Navy, 28, released as Rear Adm, 59, after commanding USS Courage, Edmonds, Bristol, Stanton & Caloosahatchee; Bronze Star; Legion of Merit; Am, European, African & Pac Theatre Medals; World War II Victory Medal. Mem: Mason; Elks; Shrine; Navy League; ROA. Relig: United Methodist. Mailing Add: 3911 Trent Pines Dr New Bern NC 28560

BARKER, ED (D)
Ga State Sen
Mailing Add: PO Drawer KK Warner Robins GA 31093

BARKER, JAMES PETER (D)
Leader, 37th Assembly Dist Dem Party, NY
b Woodside, NY, Jan 15, 35; s James Barker & Elizabeth Mary McEneaney B; m 1966 to Eileen Maire Kelly; c Elizabeth Mary, Eileen Maire & James Peter. Educ: Villanova Univ, BS, 58; Glee Club; Bus Whirl Staff; Villanovian; Sch Yearbk Staff; Intramural Sports; Metrop Club. Polit & Govt Pos: Leader, 37th Assembly Dist Dem Party, NY, 72-; deleg, Dem Nat Mid-Term Conf, 74. Bus & Prof Pos: Sales mgr, Scripto, Inc, Rego Park, NY, 73- Mil Serv: Entered as E-1, Army, 58, released as SP-4/C, 60, after serv in Staff Judge Adv Off, Ft Knox, Ky; Good Conduct Medal. Mem: 37th Assembly Dist Regular Dem Club; KofC; Sales Execs Club New York; Villanova Univ Alumni Asn; Am Irish Hist Soc. Honors & Awards: Irishman of Year Award, Emerald Soc Court Attaches, 74. Relig: Roman Catholic. Mailing Add: 50-15 47th St Woodside NY 11377

BARKER, JOHN M (R)
Idaho State Sen
Mailing Add: Rte 4 Box 305 Buhl ID 83316

BARKER, ROBERT (R)
b Locust Branch, Ky, Jan 17, 01; s Elias Barker & Fannie Durbin B; m 1926 to Helen Cloyd. Polit & Govt Pos: Chmn, Estill Co Rep Exec Comt, Ky, formerly. Bus & Prof Pos: Ed, Irvine Times, 21-68; ed, Irvine Times-Herald, 68- Mem: Irvine-Ravenna Kiwanis (Treas); Irvine Lodge 137 F&AM (Past Master); Irvine Chap 42, RAM (Past High Priest); Irvine Coun 92 RSM (Past Illustrious Master); Irvine Eastern Star (Past Patron). Legal Res: 602 Elm St Ravenna KY 40472 Mailing Add: 139 Broadway Irvine KY 40336

BARKS, MARION EMMETT (R)
Chmn, Bollinger Co Rep Cent Comt, Mo
b Greenville, Mo, July 8, 28; s Floyd Hershel Barks & Nellie Hill B; m 1961 to Shirley Lou Hoxworth. Educ: Southeast Mo State Col, summer 47. Polit & Govt Pos: Committeeman, Rep Party, Wayne Co, Mo, 8 years; chmn, Bollinger Co Rep Cent Comt, 68- Bus & Prof Pos: Teacher, Upper Turkey Creek Sch, Wayne Co, Mo, 48; foreman, Voc Footwear, Lutesville, 50-63; foreman, Sport Specialty Shoemakers, Chaffee, 64-65; plant mgr & supt, Marble Hill Hat Co, Lutesville, 65-; self-employed electrician; farmer. Relig: Baptist. Mailing Add: PO Box 344 Marble Hill MO 63764

BARKSDALE, HUDSON LEE, SR (D)
SC State Rep
b Barksdale, SC, Jan 28, 07; s John Wesley Barksdale & Mary C Clark B; m to Katie K Knuckles; c Jeanne (Mrs Eddie J Keith) & Hudson L, Jr. Educ: SC State Col, AB, 36; Columbia Univ, MA, 52; Alpha Phi Alpha. Polit & Govt Pos: SC State Rep, 75- Publ: Auth, What the NEA-PR&R Commission Does, Teacher Topics Spartanburg Classroom Teachers, 63; Merit play, Palmetta Educ J, 64; A Development of Modus Operandum for Racial Acceptance, ESAP Prog, 72. Mem: Nat Educ Asn (life mem); NAACP; Am Teachers Asn (bd trustees, 68-75); Spartanburg Bicentennial Comt. Honors & Awards: Boy Scout Silver Beaver, 60; Invited by President John F Kennedy to White House Conf on Educ, 63; Distinguished Serv Award; H Council Trenholm Trophy, Nat Educ Asn, 67; Distinguished Serv Medal, Am Teachers Asn, 67. Relig: Methodist. Legal Res: 331 N Dean St Spartanburg SC 29302 Mailing Add: PO Box 6115 Spartanburg SC 29302

BARLOW, HAVEN J (R)
Utah State Sen
b Clearfield, Utah, Jan 4, 22; s Jesse D Barlow & Isdora Beck B; m 1944 to Bonnie Rae Ellison; c Jesselee E, Heidi E, Haven B, Jr, Duncan E, Stewart E & Rachael E. Educ: Utah State Univ, BA, 44; Univ Utah Law Sch, 47-48; Harvard Grad Sch Bus; Pi Kappa Alpha. Polit & Govt Pos: Vpres, Utah Young Rep, 50; Utah State Rep, 53-57; mem, Gov Adv Comt, Handicapped Children, 60-66; Utah State Sen, 57-, Pres, Utah State Senate, 67-72, chmn, Legis Coun, 66-68 & 71-72, vchmn, 68 & chmn, Joint Legis Oper Comt, 68; mem exec comt, Western Conf Coun State Govt, 67-69 & 71-72, chmn, govt oper comt, 68-70; mem exec comt, Nat Conf Lt Gov, 71-72. Mil Serv: Entered as Seaman, Navy, 43, released as Lt(jg), 46, after serv in Supply Corps, Atlantic, SPac & Philippines; Philippines Liberation Medal; Pac & Atlantic Theater Campaign Ribbons. Mem: Am Soc of Appraisers; Utah State Realty Asn; Utah Asn of Ins Agents; Nat Soc of State Legislators; Rotary. Relig: Latter-day Saint. Mailing Add: 377 N Main Layton UT 84041

BARNARD, AURORA CARO (R)
Mem, Rep State Cent Comt, Calif
b Burke, Idaho, Oct 15, 08; d Frank Caro & Chiara Restelli C; m 1935 to Russell Barnard, wid; c Annette Caro (Mrs Frank Wetherbee) & Roger Keith. Educ: Univ Calif, 2 years. Polit & Govt Pos: Auditor, Eureka Rep Women, Calif, 55-63, parliamentarian, 64-68; secy, Eureka Rep Assembly, 56-58, first vpres, 58-60; Humboldt Co Women's campaign mgr for cand, First Cong Dist, 58; regional vpres, Northern Div, Calif Fedn Rep Women, 59-64; mem, Rep State Cent Comt, Calif, 62-64 & 68-; sgt-at-arms state bd, Calif Fedn Rep Women, 64-66, budget & finance chmn, 69-70, vpres, 70-; state chmn, Secy for Nixon-Agnew, 68; co-chmn, Comt to Reelect the President, San Mateo Co, Calif, 72. Mem: San Francisco Credit Womens Breakfast Club; Eureka Bus & Prof Womens Club (chmn for legis & parliamentarian, currently); Redwood Empire Bus & Prof Women's Club; Eastern Star; White Shrine. Honors & Awards: Named woman of the year for civic participation, 68. Legal Res: 370 W Olive St Sunnyvale CA 94088 Mailing Add: PO Box 752 Sunnyvale CA 94088

BARNARD, CLARE AMUNDSON (R)
Committeewoman, Pasco Co Rep Exec Comt, Fla
b Minneapolis, Minn, Dec 31, 27; d Leon Cornelius Amundson & Charlotte Metcalf A; m 1948 to Henry Clay Barnard; c Henry Clay, III, Matthew Lee & David Michael. Educ: Stephens Col, AA, 48; Delta Chi Delta, pres, 48. Polit & Govt Pos: Committeewoman, Pasco Co Rep Exec Comt, Fla, 63-; mem, Pasco Co Sch Bd, 69-71; alt deleg, Rep Nat Conv, 72; committeewoman, Rep Party Fla, 72- Bus & Prof Pos: Salesman, Bert Chase Realty, Tampa, Fla, 71- Mem: Bicentennial Comn Fla (co chmn); Jr League Tampa; Easter Seal Guild; Pasco Women's Rep Club. Relig: Episcopal. Mailing Add: Rte 1 Box 750 Lutz FL 33549

BARNARD, H B (D)
NMex State Rep
Mailing Add: 104 E 21st St Clovis NM 88101

BARNARD, KEITH W (R)
Chmn, Ventura Co Rep Cent Comt, Calif
b Ventura, Calif, Oct 30, 26; s Morris Hall Barnard & Ruth Dennis B; m 1950 to Ruth Virden Shutt; c Stephen James & Teresa Ann. Educ: Univ Calif, Berkeley, 47-48; Univ Calif, Los Angeles, BS, 50; Pi Kappa Alpha. Polit & Govt Pos: Mem exec comt, 24th State Sen Dist Rep Comt, Calif, 63-69; mem, 13th Cong Dist Rep Comt, 65-69; mem, Rep State Cent Comt, 67; chmn, Ventura Co Rep Cent Comt, 69- Bus & Prof Pos: Chmn, Ventura Co Gen Hosp Adv Comt, 60-69; vchmn, Fillmore Irrigation Co & San Cayetano Water Co, 63-69; vchmn, Ventura Co Agr Stabilization Comt, 64-69; bd mem, Briggs Lemon Asn Santa Paula, 69-, pres, 73-; chmn, Santa Paula Orange Asn, 69-; bd mem, Ojai Tapo Orange Asn, Somis, 73- Mil Serv: Aviation Cadet, Army Air Corps, 44-45. Mem: Ventura Co Taxpayers Asn (Pres); Ventura Co Mounted Sheriffs Posse; Navy League; Fillmore Am Legion; Ventura Co Farm Bur. Mailing Add: 747 Central Ave Fillmore CA 93015

BARNES, DON B (D)
Justice, Okla Supreme Court
b Tulsa, Okla, Dec 25, 29; s N Smith Barnes & Anna Jackson B; m to Jean Merrill; c Brent, Ronnie & Beth. Educ: Univ Okla, LLB, 49; Phi Kappa Psi; Phi Alpha Delta. Polit & Govt Pos: Justice, Okla Supreme Court, 72- Relig: Christian. Legal Res: 1340 E 12th Okmulgee OK 74447 Mailing Add: State Capitol Oklahoma City OK 73105

BARNES, DWIGHT H (D)
b Cambridge, Mass, Apr 16, 20; s Dwight F Barnes & Mary Baker B; m 1941 to Marian Tobey; c Dwight Tobey, Benjamin Lewis & Madge Laurie. Educ: Fresno State Col, BA, 45; Alpha Phi Gamma; Theta Chi. Polit & Govt Pos: Admin asst to US Rep Harold T Johnson, 59- Bus & Prof Pos: Sports ed, Turlock Daily J, Calif, 45-46; ed, Merced Express, 47-48; polit ed, Modesto Bee, 48-59. Mil Serv: Entered as Midn, Navy, 41, released as Lt Comdr, 45, after serv in USS Pensacola & USS Springfield, Pac, 41-45; Capt, Naval Res, 63. Publ: Seapower & Its Meaning, Franklin Watt, 66. Mem: US Naval Inst; US Naval Res Asn; Cong Secy Club; Burros Club. Relig: Protestant. Legal Res: Twain Harte CA 95383 Mailing Add: 2347 Rayburn House Off Bldg Washington DC 20515

BARNES, EUGENE M (D)
Ill State Sen
Mailing Add: 442 W 97th Pl Chicago IL 60628

BARNES, GEORGE FRANCIS (R)
Va State Sen
b Pocahontas, Va, May 25, 19; m 1946 to Grace Hopkins Gillespie; c 6. Educ: Va Polytech Inst, BS, 41. Polit & Govt Pos: Va State Sen, 66-; mem, Gov Budget Adv Comn, 71- Bus & Prof Pos: Farmer, coal operator. Mil Serv: Navy. Mem: Tri-Co Independent Coal Operators Asn; Nat Independent Coal Operators Asn; Farm Bur. Relig: Presbyterian. Mailing Add: Box 506 Tazewell VA 24651

BARNES, HENSON PERRYMOORE (D)
NC State Rep
b Bladen Co, NC, Nov 18, 34; s Lalon Lem Barnes & Maple Cumme B; m 1961 to Kitty Allen; c Rebecca & Amy. Educ: Wilmington Col, AA, 57; Univ NC, AB, 59, LLD, 61; Phi Alpha Delta. Polit & Govt Pos: Chmn, Wayne Co Dem Party, NC, formerly; NC State Rep, 74- Bus & Prof Pos: Attorney, Barnes & Braswell, Goldsboro, NC, 61- Mil Serv: Entered as Pvt, Army, 53, released as E-5, 56, after serv in 11th Airborne Command; Nat Defense Medal; Good Conduct Medal. Mem: Am & NC Bar Asns; Jaycees. Honors & Awards: Outstanding Young Man of Goldsboro Award; Good Govt Man of Year. Relig: Baptist; deacon, First Baptist Church. Mailing Add: 707 Park Ave Goldsboro NC 27530

BARNES, HUGH WILLIAM (R)
b North Wilkesboro, NC, Apr 24, 48; s Thomas Glenn Barnes & Selma Oxford B; div; c Autumne Leigh. Educ: Appalachian State Univ, BS in Polit Sci, 70. Polit & Govt Pos: Secy, NC Fedn of Col Rep, 68-69, state chmn, 69-70; western field coordr, Rouse for Rep State Chmn Comt, NC, 71; dir research, NC Rep Party, 71-72; deleg, NC Rep State Conv, 71 & 72; first voter chmn, NC Fedn of Young Rep, 72; deleg, Rep Nat Conv, 72; dir of spec voter groups, Holshouser for Gov Comt, 72-73; spec asst to Gov for Appointments, 73- Bus & Prof Pos: Teacher, Lenoir City Schs, NC, 70-71. Mem: Jaycees. Relig: Baptist. Mailing Add: PO Box A-25001 Raleigh NC 27611

BARNES, JANE M (R)
Ill State Rep
b Ill, Jan 4, 26; m to Warren S Barnes; c Bruce, Denise, Sam, Scott & Jeffrey. Educ: St Xavier Col & John Marshall Law Sch. Polit & Govt Pos: Treas, Worth Twp Young Rep, 62-64; pres, Worth Twp Rep Women's Orgn, 64-66; mem exec comt, Ill State Fedn Rep Women, 66-74; committeewoman, Worth Twp, 66-74; vpres, Suburban Committeewoman, 68-70; alt deleg, Rep Nat Conv, 72; mem exec comt, Women's Nat Rep Club Chicago & Rep Women Power,

Ill Style, 72-74; Ill State Rep, Eighth Dist, 74- Bus & Prof Pos: Real estate broker, 58; asst chief dep sheriff, Cook Co, Ill, 66-70; admin asst, Ill Dept Ins, 71-73; exec secy, Worth Twp Youth Comn, 73. Mem: Oak Lawn Community Chest (dir); Village of Oak Lawn Bi-Centennial & Spec Events Comn; Chi-Burbanite Bus & Prof Women's Club; Christ Community Hosp Women's Auxiliary; Beverly Lawn Women's Club (past pres). Legal Res: 9825 S Tripp Ave Oak Lawn IL 60453 Mailing Add: 5251 W 95th St Oak Lawn IL 60453

BARNES, RICHARD ERROL **(D)**
SDak State Rep
b Harvey, Ill, May 16, 41; s Chalma Victor Barnes & Eileen Leeson B; m 1963 to Judith Ellen Cook; c Jonathan Andrew & Jill Anne. Educ: Drake Univ, BA & MA; Univ Chicago, BD; Alpha Kappa Delta; Nat D Club. Polit & Govt Pos: SDak State Rep, 73-, mem transportation comt, SDak House Rep, currently, mem joint appropriations comt, 73-; deleg, Dem Nat Mid-Term Conf, 74. Bus & Prof Pos: Assoc minister, First Christian Church, Wichita Falls, Tex, 67-68; prof sociol, Sioux Falls Col, 69-73 & Augustana Col (SDak), 73-74; publ, Sioux Falls Sun, 74- Publ: Ed, Hospital administration, privately publ, 9/71; auth, Community power structure in Sioux Falls, SDak J Social Sci, 6/72. Mem: Sioux Falls CofC (mem retail comt). Honors & Awards: Univ Chicago Disciples Divinity House Book Award from Christian Bd Publ, 64. Relig: Christian Church; ordained clergyman, 66. Mailing Add: 1710 S Menlo Sioux Falls SD 57105

BARNES, RICHARD O **(R)**
Wash State Rep
Mailing Add: 18118 Sixth Ave SW Seattle WA 98166

BARNES, ROY E **(D)**
Ga State Sen
Mailing Add: 639 Maran Lane Mableton GA 30059

BARNES, RUTH FRANCES **(D)**
VChmn, Sixth Cong Dist Dem Party, Mo
b Ray Co, Mo, Sept 7, 03; d Frances Marion O'Dell & Ollie Mae Turner O; m 1926 to James Richard Barnes; c Donald Keith. Educ: Liberty Pub Schs, Mo. Polit & Govt Pos: Dep clerk collectors off, Clay Co, Mo, 22-25; committeewoman & vchmn, 21st Ward, North Kansas City, Mo, 52-54; committeewoman & secy, Clay Co Dem Cent Comt, 56-58; deleg, Dem Nat Conv, 60; treas, Mo Fedn Women's Dem Club, Sixth Cong Dist, 66-68, second vpres, 68-70, first vpres, 70-73, pres 73-; secy-treas, Cent Clay Co Dem Club, 68-71; committeeman, Mo State Dem Cent Comt, 68-, vchmn, formerly; vchmn, Sixth Cong Dist Dem Party, 70-, adv coun, currently. Bus & Prof Pos: Asst pharmacist, Karnes Drug Co, North Kansas City, Mo, 42-52; asst mgr, Karnes Pharmacy, 52-55; asst mgr, North Oak Pharmacy, 55-65; retired, 65. Mem: Am Bus Women's Club; Bus & Prof Club; Am Red Cross (staff aide, region four); Liberty Civic Coun; Dem Clubs. Honors & Awards: Outstanding Dem Woman, Clay Co, Mo, 64-65. Relig: Protestant. Mailing Add: 302 N Water St Liberty MO 64068

BARNES, VERDA WHITE **(D)**
b Willard, Utah, Feb 23, 07; d John McArthur White & Mary Ann Hubbard W; div; c Valorie J (Mrs George H R Taylor). Educ: Albion State Normal Sch, 26; Brigham Young Univ, 27-28; Univ Denver, 30; George Washington Univ, 37-38. Polit & Govt Pos: VPres, Young Dem Clubs, 35-36; exec secy, Idaho Liquor Control Comn, 36; admin asst to asst secy, Dept of Interior, 37-40; vpres, Young Dem Clubs Am, 38-39; regional rep, Nat Youth Admin, 40-42; asst to pub rels dir, War Manpower Comn, 42-44; dir women's activities & regional dir, Polit Action Comt, 44-48; staff mem, Sen Glen Taylor, Sen Thomas Hennings & Congressman Harrison A Williams, Jr, 54-57; mem nat adv comt on polit orgn, Dem Nat Comt, 55-58; admin asst to US Sen Frank Church, Idaho, 64- Mem: League Women Voters; Women's Nat Dem Club; Asn Admin Asst; Idaho Vote Rockers. Legal Res: 398 I St Idaho Falls ID 83401 Mailing Add: 3003 Van Ness St Washington DC 20008

BARNETT, FRANK
Lt Gov, Am Samoa
Mailing Add: Govt House Pago Pago American Samoa

BARNETT, JAMES ARDEN **(R)**
b Jackson, Miss, Aug 4, 24; s Arden Barnett & Vera Turner B; m 1945 to Lucy Owen; c Ruth Elizabeth, James Arden, Jr & Vera Susan. Educ: Univ Miss, BBA, 48, LLB, 49; Univ Miss Hall of Fame; Omicron Delta Kappa; pres of student body, Univ Miss, 47. Polit & Govt Pos: Mem, Fourth Dist Hinds Co Sch Bd, Miss, 54-63; city attorney, Clinton, 58-62; Miss State Rep, Hinds Co, 64-68; Miss State Sen, 27th Dist, 68-71; mem exec comt, Miss Rep Party, 68-71 & Hinds Co Rep Party, 69-71; mem Rep exec comt, City of Clinton, 69-71; Miss chmn for Nat Conf of Rep State Legislators, 69-71; chancery judge, Fifth Chancery Dist, Miss, 71- Bus & Prof Pos: Lawyer & assoc, Barnett, Montgomery, McClintock & Cunningham, 49-65; lawyer & partner, Barnett & Barnett, 65-71. Mil Serv: Entered as Air Cadet, Naval Air Res, 42, active duty, 43-45, organized res, 45-71, Cmndg Officer VF822, 63-66, Comdr(Ret), 70; Distinguished Flying Cross; Air Medal; Asiatic-Pac Ribbon with Three Battle Stars; Philippine Liberation Ribbon with Two Battle Stars; Am Theatre Ribbon; Victory Medal; Naval Res & Armed Forces Res Ribbons. Mem: Miss & Hinds Co Bar Asns; Am Legion; VFW; Lions. Relig: Baptist; chmn of deacons, First Baptist Church of Clinton. Legal Res: 710 E Leake St Clinton MS 39056 Mailing Add: PO Box 686 Jackson MS 39205

BARNETT, JOSEPH H **(R)**
SDak State Rep
b Sioux Falls, SDak, Nov 3, 31; s William H Barnett & Julia Ruth Gurtel B; m 1954 to Kathleen D Bolger; c Joseph P, Sheila Ann, William M, John D, Rita Marie, Paul T, Teresa Jane & James Richard. Educ: Augustana Col, Sioux Falls, SDak, 50-51; Col St Thomas, BA, magna cum laude, 53; Univ SDak Law Sch, LLB, 57; Phi Delta Pi. Polit & Govt Pos: Law clerk to US Dist Judge George T Mickelson, Dist of SDak, 57-58; SDak State Rep, Brown Co, 67-, Speaker Pro Tem, SDak House of Rep, 71-73, Minority Leader, 73- Bus & Prof Pos: Mem, SDak Bd Bar Examr, 63-70, chmn, 68-70. Mil Serv: Entered as Pvt, Army, 53, released as Cpl, 55, after serv in 74th Armored Signal Co, Third Army Div, Ft Knox. Mem: Brown Co Bar Asn; Kiwanis Club; KofC; Elks; Y's Men's Club. Relig: Catholic. Legal Res: 1422 N First St Aberdeen SD 57401 Mailing Add: 500 Capitol Bldg Aberdeen SD 57401

BARNETT, JUDITH ANNE **(D)**
Mem Exec Comt, Fifth Dist Dem Party, Okla
b Alva, Okla, Oct 8, 38; d Robert Clinton Bright & Justine Fash B; m 1963 to Dallas Cody Barnett; c David Rodney Duckworth, Dallas Cody, Jr & Anne Justine. Educ: Univ Okla, 56-58; Northwestern State Col, BSEd, 63; Alpha Chi Omega. Polit & Govt Pos: Alt deleg, Dem Nat Conv, 72; mem exec comt, Fifth Dist Dem Party, Okla, 72-, finance chmn, 73-; ward one co-chmn, Oklahoma Co Dem Party, 73- Mem: Another Mother for Peace; NAACP. Mailing Add: 3126 NW 18th Oklahoma City OK 73107

BARNETT, ROSS ROBERT **(D)**
b Carthage, Miss, Jan 22, 98; s John William Barnett & Virginia Ann Chadwick B; m 1928 to Mary Pearl Crawford; c Ouida (Mrs Atkins), Ross Robert, Jr & Virginia (Mrs Branum). Educ: Miss Col, BS, 22; Univ Miss, LLB, 26; hon mem, Kappa Alpha. Polit & Govt Pos: Gov, Miss, 60-64. Bus & Prof Pos: Comnr, Miss Bar; attorney, Barnett, Montgomery, McClintock & Cunningham, Jackson, currently. Mil Serv: Pvt, Army, 18-19; award for serv as attorney for Selective Serv Bd, Jackson, Miss. Mem: Miss Bar Asn (pres, 43-44); Jackson Hinds Co Bar Asn (pres); Nat Exchange Club; Jackson Exchange Club; Miss Farm Asn. Relig: Baptist; Deacon, First Baptist Church, Jackson. Mailing Add: Barnett Bldg 200 S President Jackson MS 39201

BARNETT, WALLACE M, JR **(R)**
Nebr State Sen
b Lincoln, Nebr, Feb 7, 31; s Wallace M Barnett, Sr & Rose Marie Vanous B; m 1953 to Beverly Joanne Teague; c Joni Marie, Scott Wallace & Bobbie Rae. Educ: Univ Iowa, exten course, 49; Univ Nebr, fire invest & inspection, 1 year & Univ Okla, 1 year; Delta Tau Delta. Polit & Govt Pos: Nebr State Sen, 71- Bus & Prof Pos: Asst State Fire Marshall, Nebr, 70- Mil Serv: Entered as Pfc, Nebr Nat Air Guard, 48, released as Pfc, 50, after serv in 232nd Wing, Nat Air Guard. Mem: Nebr Peace Off Asn; Sertoma Club. Relig: Methodist. Mailing Add: 6201 Francis Lincoln NE 68505

BARNHOUSE, THOMAS DYE **(D)**
Mem, Ohio Dem Finance Comt
b Belle Valley, Ohio, Oct 26, 09; s William Day Barnhouse & Jessie Pearl Archer B; m 1932 to Florence Mabel (Sally) King; c Gloria Kay. Educ: Ohio Univ, BSEE, 33; Command & Gen Staff Col; The Artil Sch; Chi Sigma Chi. Polit & Govt Pos: Dep co engr, Noble Co, Ohio, 33-35; engr, Ohio Dept Hwy, 35-45, admin asst to dir, 46-47, dep dir hwy, 59-62; comnr, Boxing & Wrestling Comn, Columbus, Ohio, 65-70; mem, Ohio Dem Finance Comt, 66-; deleg, Dem Nat Conv, 68; mem, Bd Regist for Prof Engrs & Surveyors, Columbus, Ohio, 72- Bus & Prof Pos: Registered prof engr & registered surveyor, Ohio, WVa & SC; vpres, Newark Concrete, Ohio, 56-59; pres, Barnhouse Assocs, Inc, Columbus, currently. Mil Serv: Entered as 1st Lt, Army, 40, released as Maj, 46, after serv in 37th Inf Div, SPac, 41-43; Col, Field Artil, Ohio Nat Guard, 56; Col(Ret), Army, 69. Mem: Ohio & Nat Soc Prof Engrs; Engrs Club of Columbus, Ohio; Mason (32 degree); Shrine. Relig: Christian. Mailing Add: 2472 Dover Rd Columbus OH 43209

BARNUM, C ROBERT **(R)**
Mem, First Cong Dist Rep Comt, Calif
b Eureka, Calif, Nov 26, 27; s Charles Robert Barnum & Helen Wells B; m 1949 to Patricia Boyle; c Patricia A, Charles R, III, William F, Cathleen H & Janet L. Educ: US Merchant Marine Acad, 45-47; Humboldt State Col, 47; Univ Calif, 48; Alpha Delta Phi. Polit & Govt Pos: Chmn, Young Rep of Humboldt Co, Calif, 57; chmn, Humboldt Co Reagan for Gov Comt, 66-70; mem, Calif Rep State Cent Comt, 68-; mem, First Cong Dist Rep Comt, Calif, currently. Bus & Prof Pos: Pres, Barnum Investment Co, 55- Mil Serv: Cadet-Midn, US Merchant Marine Acad, 45-47. Relig: Protestant. Legal Res: 4441 Fairway Dr Eureka CA 95501 Mailing Add: 207 Fifth St Eureka CA 95501

BARNUM, JOHN WALLACE **(R)**
Dep Secy, Dept Transportation
b New York, NY, Aug 25, 28; s Walter Barnum & Frances Long B; m 1958 to Nancy Russell Grinnell; c Alexander Stone, Sarah Kip & Cameron Long. Educ: Yale Univ, BA, 49, LLB, 57. Polit & Govt Pos: Gen counsel, Dept Transportation, 71-73, Undersecy, 73-74, Dep Secy, 74-; mem, Coun of Admin Conf of US, 73-; adv mem, Coun on Wage & Price Stability, 74- Bus & Prof Pos: Analyst, First Banking Corp, Tangier, Morocco, 50; rep, Bache & Co, London & Paris, 51-52; assoc, Cravath, Swaine & Moore, New York, 57-62; mem, 63-71; chmn bd, Int Play Group, 62-; lectr, Practicing Law Inst; US deleg, Inter-Am Comn Arbitration Comn, 69-71; mem bd dirs & mem exec comt, New York Ctr Mus & Drama, 69- Mil Serv: Lt, Army, 52-54. Mem: Am Arbit Asn (bd dirs, exec comt, 68-); Fed & Am Bar Asns; Am Judicature Soc; Int Legal Aid Asn. Legal Res: NY Mailing Add: Dept of Transportation 400 Seventh St SW Washington DC 20590

BARNYAK, MARY A **(R)**
Mem, Rep State Cent Comt Calif
b Franklin, Kans, Sept 21, 23; d August Kranker & Julia Kramer K; m to Frank E Barnyak. Educ: Valley Jr Col, Van Nuys, Calif, Spanish course, 65. Polit & Govt Pos: Mem, Rep State Cent Comt Calif, 69-; neighborhood chmn & precinct capt, Comt to Reelect the President, 72. Bus & Prof Pos: Secy, Ft Wayne Army Ord Depot, Detroit, Mich, 41-44, US Air Corps, Lockheed, Calif, 44-49, Reconstruction Finance Corp, Jones & Whitlock and Dwyer-Curlett & Co, Los Angeles; self-employed, 55-67; mem, Las Patroncitas Guild, Valley Presby Hosp, Van Nuys, Calif, 72- Mem: Burbank Anglers Club (secy); SCORE; Laurel Oaks Federated Rep Asn; Campo de Cahuenga, Womans Non-Federated Rep Club (secy, 71-). Relig: Catholic. Mailing Add: 4204 Elmer Ave Studio City CA 91602

BAROODY, WILLIAM J, JR **(R)**
Asst to the President
b Manchester, NH, Nov 5, 37; s William J Baroody & Nabeeha Ashooh B; m 1960 to Mary M Cullen; c William J, III, Mary Nabeeha, David Michael, Jo Ellen, Christopher William, Andrew Thomas, Thomas Michael, Philip Francis & Paul Charles. Educ: Holy Cross Col, BA, Eng, 59; Georgetown Univ, 61-63. Polit & Govt Pos: Staff asst, US Rep Melvin R Laird, Wis, 61-64, legis & Press asst, 65-69; mem staff, House Appropriations Comt, 62-64, research dir, House Rep Conf, 68-69; asst exec dir, Comt on Resolutions, Rep Nat Conv, 64; Asst to the Secy of Defense, Dept of Defense, 69-73; Spec Asst to the President, 73-74, Asst to the President, 74- Mil Serv: Entered as Ens, Naval Res, 59, released as Lt(jg), 61, after serv in USS Chilton, Atlantic Fleet, Phibron Two, 59-61. Honors & Awards: Distinguished Pub Serv Award, Dept of Defense. Relig: Melkite Catholic. Mailing Add: 7910 Bolling Dr Alexandria VA 22308

BARR, BRUCE REID **(R)**
Mem Prof Staff, Senate Rep Policy Comt
b Flint, Mich, Feb 2, 35; s Charles Arthur Barr & Jean Hynds B; m 1959 to Patricia Kiermas; c Jennifer Ann, Christopher Reid & Jean Marie. Educ: Am Univ, BA, 60; London Sch Econ, Eng, 67-68; Am Econ Asn. Polit & Govt Pos: Pub rels staff, Rep Cong Campaign Comt, 60;

mem prof staff, Senate Rep Policy Comt, 62- Bus & Prof Pos: Reporter, Dunn & Bradstreet, Inc, 56-59; asst ed, Human Events Newsletter, 61. Mil Serv: Pvt, Army, 55-56, serv in 16th Inf Regt, 1st Div. Mem: Am Polit Sci Asn; Scottish Econ Soc. Honors & Awards: US Cong Staff Fel, 67-68. Relig: Roman Catholic. Mailing Add: 7024 Tilden Lane Rockville MD 20852

BARR, JOSEPH M (D)
b Pittsburgh, Pa, May 28, 06; s James Patrick Barr & Blanche Elizabeth Moran B; m 1949 to Alice White; c Alice Elizabeth & Joseph M, Jr. Educ: Univ Pittsburgh, BS in Bus Admin, 28; Omicron Delta Kappa; Phi Kappa Theta. Polit & Govt Pos: Dem Nat Committeeman, Pa, formerly; mem, Pa State Dem Comt, 36-38, chmn, 54-59; state pres, Young Dem Clubs, Pa, 38-39; deleg, various Dem Nat Conv, deleg, 68 & 72; Pa State Sen, 40-60; Mayor, Pittsburgh, Pa, 59-69. Mem: US Conf of Mayors (pres); Off of Econ Opportunity (adv comt); President's Comn on Civil Defense; Duquesne Univ (adv bd); Am Red Cross. Relig: Catholic. Mailing Add: 6839 Juniata Pl Pittsburgh PA 15208

BARRAGAN, POLLY BACA (D)
Mem-at-lg, Dem Nat Comt
Mailing Add: 8747 Santa Fe Dr Denver CO 80221

BARRE, LAURA KOHLMAN (D)
Mem, Ga Dem Exec Comt
b Atlanta, Ga, Sept 13, 31; d Richard William Kohlman & May Dunagan K; m 1952 to Kenneth Marc Barre; c Anne Carter, Kenneth Marc & Laura Granville. Educ: Univ Ga, AB in Sociol, 52; Alpha Lambda Delta; Alpha Omicron Pi. Polit & Govt Pos: Mem, DeKalb Co Women's Adv Comt, 68-72; poll mgr, Peachtree Precinct, Ga, 70-75; mem, Ga Dem State Exec Comt, 41st Dist, 75- Bus & Prof Pos: Newspaper reporter, Atlanta Const, 52-56; correspondent & feature writer, Atlanta J, 67-72; reporter, Neighbor Newspapers, Inc, 73- Honors & Awards: Outstanding Woman Student in Sociol, Univ Ga, 52. Relig: Episcopal. Mailing Add: 1691 N Springs Dr Dunwoody GA 30338

BARRE, SALLIE MARVIL (R)
Exec Aide to Pres, Nat Fedn of Rep Women
b Spartanburg, SC, Sept 27, 46; d Claude Bertram Barre & Shirley Black B; single. Educ: St Anne's Col, Oxford Univ, Eng, summer 67; Mary Baldwin Col, BA, 68; Phi Alpha Theta. Polit & Govt Pos: Gubernatorial campaign hq mgr, Spartanburg Co Rep Party, SC, 70; exec aide to pres, Nat Fedn of Rep Women, 71- Bus & Prof Pos: Asst dir info serv, Mary Baldwin Col, 68-69; conf coordr, Women in Indust, sponsored by Gen Elec, Am Tel & Tel, Am Can, Int Paper, NAM, Women's Bur at Mary Baldwin Col, 70-71. Mem: Jr League of Washington, DC. Relig: Presbyterian. Legal Res: Fantree Farm Rte One Campobello SC 29322 Mailing Add: 310 First St SE Washington DC 20003

BARRELL, CHARLES ALDEN (D)
Mem, Wood Co Dem Cent & Exec Comts, Ohio
b Buckingham, Va, Mar 21, 09; s Charles Martin Barrell & Fannie Hall B; single. Educ: Hampden Sydney Col, BA, 31; Univ Va, MA, 32; Ohio State Univ, PhD, 38; Pi Sigma Alpha; Sigma Nu. Polit & Govt Pos: Alt deleg, Dem Nat Conv, 64; councilman-at-lg, Bowling Green, 66-; mem, Wood Co Dem Cent & Exec Comts, Ohio, currently. Bus & Prof Pos: Instr, Washington & Lee Univ, 36-38, Ohio State Univ, 38-39 & Oberlin Col, 39-40; from asst prof to prof, Bowling Green State Univ, 40- Mil Serv: Entered as Pvt, Army, 42, released as 2nd Lt, 46. Publ: Representation: Its Numerical & Functional Forms, Ohio State Univ Press, 39; Democracy, In, An Introduction to American Government, Stackpole, 54; Metropolitan government, Topic, Vol 4, No 8. Mem: Am Polit Sci Asn; Am Asn Univ Prof; Kiwanis. Relig: Presbyterian. Mailing Add: 722 N Grove St Bowling Green OH 43402

BARREN, JEAN VANAKEN (R)
Chmn, Jefferson Co Rep Party, Ohio
b Cleveland, Ohio, July 2, 17; d William J VanAken & Florence Swallow V; m to Henry A Barren, Jr, wid; c Henry A, III, William J, Roger Scott & Martha (Mrs Robert B Besuden). Educ: Univ Wis, 2 years; Case Western Reserve Univ, BS; Pi Beta Phi. Polit & Govt Pos: Chmn, Vol for Ike, Jefferson Co, Ohio, 52-56; mem, Steubenville Planning Comn, 58-, chmn, 64-66 & 68; chmn, Vol for Nixon, Jefferson Co, 60; chmn, Jefferson Co Rep Party, 63-; mem, Jefferson Co Bd Elec, 66-; deleg, Rep Nat Conv, 72. Bus & Prof Pos: Asst dean student affairs, Col Steubenville, 71- Mem: Ohio State Bd Elec Officers (bd trustees); Ohio Asn Women Deans & Counrs; Ohio Fedn Rep Women; Salvation Army; Steubenville Country Club. Relig: Presbyterian; Elder, Westminster Presby Church. Mailing Add: 1948 McCauslen Manor Steubenville OH 43952

BARRETT, CONCEPCION CRUZ (R)
Rep Nat Committeewoman, Guam
b Agana, Guam; m to Jack Barrett; c John, Patrick & Elizabeth. Educ: San Francisco State Col, BA; Univ Calif Col Law, Berkeley; Ateneo de Manila Grad Sch. Polit & Govt Pos: Legis asst, Eighth Guam Legis; Sen, 11th Guam Legis; social serv supvr, Off Aging, Pub Health & Social Serv Govt Guam; community action prog supvr, Econ Opportunity Comn; property & relocation mgr, Guam Housing & Urban Renewal Develop; congresswoman, Guam Legis, Chalan Pago-Ordot Dist; Rep Nat Committeewoman, Guam, 72- Bus & Prof Pos: Teacher, Headstart, Econ Opportunity Comn; businesswoman; teacher, Pub Schs, Guam. Legal Res: Chalan Pago GU Mailing Add: PO Box 683 Agana GU 96910

BARRETT, DAVID L (D)
Fla State Rep
Mailing Add: 360H The Capitol Tallahassee FL 32304

BARRETT, EVAN DONALD (D)
b Red Lodge, Mont, June 17, 45; s John Albert Barrett & Geraldine Nussbaum B; m 1963 to Linda June Prinkki; c Kirsten & Erika. Educ: Mont State Univ, 63-65; St John's Univ (Minn), BA, 67; Univ Mont Grad Sch, 67-68. Polit & Govt Pos: Secy, Mont State Univ Young Dem, 64-65; precinct secy, Minn Dem-Farmer-Labor Party, 66; deleg, Dem-Farmer-Labor Cong Dist Nominating Conv, 66; alt deleg, Minn State Dem-Farmer-Labor Nominating Conv, 66; campus coordr, Congressman Alex Olson, Cong Dist Six, 66; mem, Univ Mont Young Dem Exec Bd, 67-68; precinct committeeman, Missoula Co Dem Cent Comt, 68; coordr, Univ Mont McCarthy for President Comt, 68; research analyst, Mont Comn on Exec Reorgn, 69-70, admin asst, 70-71; mem legis staff for exec reorgn, Gov Off, 71; mem, Mont Dem Reform Comn, 70-71 & 74-75; exec secy, Mont Dem Party, 71-74; Mont arrangements chmn, Dem Nat Conv, 71-72, staff mem Mont deleg, 72; deleg, Mont State Dem Charter Conv, 74; alt deleg, Dem Nat Mid-Term Conf, 74; precinct committeeman, Lewis & Clark Co Dem Cent Comt, 74-75; admin asst to Gov Mont, Thomas L Judge, 74- Mem: Eagles; Mont Farmers Union; Am Fedn Teachers, AFL-CIO. Relig: Roman Catholic. Mailing Add: 409 Geddis Helena MT 59601

BARRETT, FRED O (R)
Mont State Rep
Mailing Add: 259 Maple Lewistown MT 59457

BARRETT, JAMES LUTHER (D)
b Maysville, Okla, Mar 3, 34; s George W Barrett & Cora Webb B; m 1961 to Gloria Jeanne Cragg; c Tanyala K, Hollye Jeanne & James Gregory. Educ: Okla Baptist Univ, BA, 59; Am Univ, JD, 63. Polit & Govt Pos: Legis asst to the late US Sen Robert S Kerr, Okla, 60-63; legis asst to the late US Sen J Howard Edmondson, Okla, 63; alt deleg, Dem Nat Conv, 68, deleg, 72; finance chmn, Fifth Dist Dem Party, Okla, 71-73. Mil Serv: Entered as Airman Basic, Air Force, 54, released as Airman 1/C, 57, after serv in Air Training Command, 54-57; Good Conduct Medal; Airman of the Year, Amarillo AFB, 56. Mem: Okla Bar Asn; Fed Bar Western Dist Okla; Am Civil Liberties Union; Alumni Asn, Okla Baptist Univ (pres & bd dirs); NAACP. Mailing Add: 6800 N Bryant Oklahoma City OK 73111

BARRETT, RALPH ROLAND (D)
Chmn, Licking Co Dem Exec Comt, Ohio
b Newark, Ohio, Aug 19, 30; s Robert A Barrett & Juanita L Baker B; m 1969 to Bettie Cooperrider. Polit & Govt Pos: Treas, Licking Co Dem Cent Comt, Ohio, 56-58, chmn, 62-70; mem, Recreation Comn, City of Newark, 59-60; chmn, Licking Co Dem Exec Comt, 62 -; Dem State Cent Committeeman, 17th Cong Dist, 62-; mem, Licking Co Bd of Elec, 62-64, chmn, 64-70; deleg-at-lg, Dem Nat Conv, 68. Mil Serv: Entered as Pvt, Army, 52, released as Sgt, 53, after serv in 5th AAA Bn, ETO, 7th Army; Good Conduct Medal; Army of Occup Medal; ETO Medal. Mem: Newark CofC; Newark J CofC; Newark Exchange Club; Licking Co Chap, Am Red Cross; Eagles. Relig: Presbyterian. Mailing Add: 758 Howell Dr Newark OH 43055

BARRETT, WILLIAM A (D)
US Rep, Pa
Married; c Three. Educ: St Joseph's Col, Philadelphia, Pa. Polit & Govt Pos: US Rep, Pa, 44-46 & 48- Bus & Prof Pos: Real estate broker. Legal Res: 2324 Reed St Philadelphia PA 19146 Mailing Add: 2304 Rayburn House Off Bldg Washington DC 20515

BARRETT, WILLIAM E (BILL) (R)
Chmn, Nebr Rep State Cent Comt
b Lexington, Nebr, Feb 9, 29; s Harold O Barrett & Helen Stuckey B; m 1952 to Elsie L Carlson; c William C, Elizabeth A, David H & Jane M. Educ: Hastings Col, AB; Univ Nebr, Nebr Realtors Inst, grad; Cert Real Estate Broker, Hawaii. Polit & Govt Pos: Rep precinct committeeman, 10 years; pres, Dawson Co Young Rep, formerly; deleg, Rep Co Conv, 58-; deleg or alt deleg, Nebr Rep State Convs, 58-; mem, Nebr Rep State Exec Comt, 64-66, chmn, 72-; mem, Rep Nat Comt, 72-; state coordr, Mobilization of Rep Enterprise Prog, 65-66; deleg, Rep Nat Conv, 68; work in campaigns for various Rep cand, 60-; trustee & co-founder, Nebr Real Estate Polit Educ Comt. Bus & Prof Pos: Admissions counr, Hastings Col, 52-54, asst dir admissions, 54-56; partner, Barrett Agency, Lexington, 56-59; officer, Barrett-Housel & Assocs, Inc, 69-; dir, Farmers State Bank, 69- Mil Serv: Navy. Mem: Nebr Asn Ins Agents; Nat Asn Ins Agents; Dawson Co Bd Realtors; Nebr Asn Realtors; Nat Asn Realtors. Honors & Awards: One of Three Outstanding Young Men of Nebr, Nebr Jaycees, 62. Relig: Presbyterian; Elder, First Presby Church, Lexington; moderator, Presbytery of Platte, 72-73 & chmn gen coun, 73-; mem staff nominating comt, Synod of Lakes & Prairies, 73- Mailing Add: 505 W 17th St Lexington NE 68850

BARRETT, WILLIAM F (D)
NH State Rep
Mailing Add: 649 Green St Manchester NH 03103

BARRETTE, EMERY GEORGE (R)
b St Paul, Minn, June 30, 30; s Gordon Emery Barrette & Clara Emma Kromschroeder B; m 1949 to Audrey Marie Svendsen; c Grant Emery, Michelle Marie & Scott Brentley. Educ: Hamline Univ, BA, 54; Drew Univ, BD, 57. Polit & Govt Pos: Minn State Rep, Dist 44A, 67-69; cand for US Rep, Minn, Fourth Cong Dist, 68; exec dir, Gov Comn on Crime Prev & Control, 68- Bus & Prof Pos: Minister, Minn Conf of Methodist Church, 57-64; juv court chaplain, St Paul Area Coun of Churches, 61-69; chaplain, Ramsey City Juv Court, 61-69; mem bd dirs, Mounds Park Hosp Found, 67-; mem & dir, St Paul Bd Educ, Minn, 70-; dir, Info & Referral Ctr, 71- Mem: St Paul J CofC (vpres, 67-68). Honors & Awards: Liberty Bell Award, Ramsey Co Bar Asn, 66; Serv to Freedom Award, Minn Bar Asn, 66; Named Good Neighbor to the Northwest by WCCO Radio, 66; Harry Brucker Award for Community Serv, 68; Named to Johnson High Sch Grad Hall of Fame, 70. Relig: Methodist, minister. Mailing Add: 718 E Arlington Ave St Paul MN 55106

BARRIENTOS, GONZALO (D)
Tex State Rep
b Galveston, Tex, July 20, 41; s Gonzalo Barrientos, Sr & Christina Mendiola B; m 1960 to Emma Serrato; c Gonzalo Joseph, Angelina, Alicia & Adelita. Educ: Univ Tex, Austin, 60-64. Polit & Govt Pos: Tex State Rep, Travis Co, 75- Bus & Prof Pos: Exec dir, Mex Am Cath Alliance, Austin, Tex, 74-; consult to fed & state prog. Mem: Cent Tex Coun (bd dirs); Tex Coun Alcoholism (bd dirs); Travis Co Transportation Policy Comt. Relig: Roman Catholic. Mailing Add: 2204 Bluebonnet Lane Austin TX 78704

BARRIER, WILLIAM CHRISTOPHER (CHRIS) (D)
Secy-Treas, Pulaski Co Dem Comt, Ark
b Jacksonville, Fla, Nov 2, 42; s Jack A Barrier, Jr & Flora Fay Canant B; m 1964 to Emily Jane Charles; c Catherine Emily & Sarah Eloise. Educ: Hendrix Col, BA, 64; Duke Univ, JD, 67; Blue Key. Polit & Govt Pos: Mem, Pulaski Co Dem Comt, Ark, 68-, secy-treas, 70-; city attorney, Cammack Village, 69-72. Bus & Prof Pos: Assoc, Spitzberg, Mitchell & Hays, Attorneys, 67-70, partner, 71- Mem: Pulaski Co, Ark & Am Bar Asns. Legal Res: 209 Ridgeway Little Rock AR 72205 Mailing Add: 400 Gaines Pl Little Rock AR 72201

BARRINEAU, T BASIL (D)
SC State Rep
Mailing Add: Box 618 Andrews SC 29510

BARRINGER, RUSSELL NEWTON (R)
Treas, NC Rep Party
b Newton, NC, Mar 1, 03; s Hamilton Belton Barringer & Jasey McKenzie B; m 1926 to MaeLee Page; c Amerylis (Mrs Alfred N Costner), Norma (Mrs David A Nichols), Russell N, Jr & David M. Polit & Govt Pos: Mem, NC Rep Exec Comt, 32-; treas, NC Rep Party, 66-; alt deleg, Rep Nat Conv, 68, deleg, 72; app, NC State Banking Comn, 73-; mem, Rep Nat Finance Comt, 74- Bus & Prof Pos: Pres, West Durham Lumber Co, 25-; vpres, Barringer-Whitfield Furniture Co, 45-; pres, Calbar Invest Co, 50-; pres, Dealers Supply Co, 52-; dir, NC Nat Bank, 60- Mem: NC Lumber & Bldg Material Dealers Asn (dir); Kiwanis; Mason; Shrine; Hope Valley Country Club. Honors & Awards: Kiwanian of the Year, 61; NC Lumberman of the Decade, Nat Lumber & Bldg Material Dealers Asn, 63. Relig: Presbyterian. Mailing Add: 3620 Dover Rd Durham NC 27707

BARRINGER, THOMAS LAWSON (D)
Pres, Young Dem Club of NC
b Kannapolis, NC, Nov 8, 40; s Harry Otis Barringer & Mable Perry B; m 1968 to Judith Stokes. Educ: NC State Univ, BS in Indust Eng, 63; Vanderbilt Univ Sch Law, JD, 68; Theta Tau. Polit & Govt Pos: Secy-treas, Precinct 32 Exec Comt, Wake Co Dem Party, NC, 70, chmn, Precinct Five Exec Comt, 72-; third vchmn, Wake Co Dem Exec Comt, 70-71; pres, Young Dem Club of Wake Co, 71; chmn, Wake Co deleg, NC State Dem Conv, 72; Mid East organizer, Young Dem Clubs of NC, 72, pres, 73- Bus & Prof Pos: Law clerk, Judge Frank Parker, NC Court of Appeals, 68-69; assoc, Hollowell & Ragsdale, Raleigh, NC, 69-71; sole practitioner, 71-73; partner, Barringer, Howard & Gruber, 73- Mil Serv: Entered as 2nd Lt, Army, 63, released as 1st Lt, 65, after serv in 116th Intel Corps Group, Washington, DC, 64-65. Mem: Wake Co Young Lawyers Sect (secy-treas, 73-). Honors & Awards: One of Ten Outstanding Young Men, Young Dem Clubs of NC, 72; Hall of Fame, A L Brown High Sch, Kannapolis, 73. Relig: Christian. Mailing Add: 1801 Arlington St Raleigh NC 27608

BARRIOS, HELEN (D)
Mem, Calif State Dem Cent Comt
b Los Angeles, Calif, May 10, 47; d Antonio Barrios & Carmen Millan B; m 1972 to William C Thomas. Educ: East Los Angeles Col, AA, 71; Calif State Univ, Los Angeles, 71-72; Calif State Univ, Long Beach, currently. Polit & Govt Pos: Deleg, Dem Nat Mid-Term Conf, Calif, 74; assoc mem, Calif State Dem Cent Comt, 75-; assoc mem, Orange Co Dem Cent Comt, 75- Bus & Prof Pos: Stewardess, Western Airlines, Los Angeles, Calif, 68- Mem: Nat Women's Polit Caucus; Stewardesses for Women's Rights; Nat Orgn Women; Asn Flight Attendents; Newport Beach Dem Club. Honors & Awards: Dem Key Women, Orange Co Dem Women's Club, 75. Mailing Add: 21921 Harbor Breeze Dr Huntington Beach CA 92646

BARRON, BISHOP N (D)
Ala State Rep
Mailing Add: PO Box 221 Montgomery AL 36101

BARRON, CHARLES LEE (R)
b Twin Falls, Idaho, May 14, 38; s Lloyd Francis Barron & Lenore Ennis B; m 1967 to Gladys Ann Smith; c Lloyd Edgar & Christopher Charles. Educ: Univ Idaho, BS in Geol Eng, 60. Polit & Govt Pos: Co chmn, Idaho Young Rep, 60-67, state chmn & region IX dir, 67-; deleg, Idaho State Rep Conv, 62, 65, 66 & 68; deleg, Rep Nat Conv, 68; vchmn for region IX, Young Rep Nat Fedn, 69-72, mem nat adv bd, 72-; mem, Idaho Adv Coun for Hosp Construction, 70-73; mem bd dirs, Am Conserv Union, Washington, DC, 73-; Idaho State Rep, 73-74. Bus & Prof Pos: Vpres, Sun Valley Ranchers, Inc, Fairfield, 60- & Rocky Mt Grain, Inc, 71- Publ: Monthly column, The Young Rep Report, The Idaho Rep, 67- Mem: Mason (32 degree); Scottish Rite. Relig: Methodist. Mailing Add: Corral ID 83322

BARRON, DEMPSEY JAMES (D)
Fla State Sen
b Andalusia, Ala, Mar 5, 22; s Jessie Carl Dempsey Barron & Minnie Brown B; m 1952 to Louverne Hall; c Stephen C & Stuart J. Educ: Fla State Univ, BS in bus; Univ Fla, LLB. Polit & Govt Pos: Fla State Rep, 56-60; Fla State Sen, 60-, pres, Fla State Senate, 75- Bus & Prof Pos: Attorney, Barron, Redding, Boggs & Hughes, 54-; rancher, D Bar Ranch. Mil Serv: Entered as A/S, Navy, 42, released as GM 1/C, 47, after serv in Pac Theater & ETO. Mem: Panama City & Bay Co CofC (bd dirs); Boys Club of Am (bd dirs). Honors & Awards: Consistently selected by press since 1957 as one of the outstanding mems of legis. Relig: Methodist. Legal Res: 2311 Magnolia Dr Panama City FL 32401 Mailing Add: PO Box 1638 Panama City FL 32401

BARROW, LETHA JEWELL (D)
Chmn, Macon Co Dem Cent Comt, Mo
b LaPlata, Mo, Aug 26, 08; d William S McNeely & Mattie Johnson M; m 1937 to Robert Wilson Barrow; c Jeanne (Mrs Ben Marshall, III). Educ: Droughous Bus Col, 29; Beta Sigma Phi. Polit & Govt Pos: Secy & audit clerk to Mo State Auditor, 33-37; vpres, Young Dem Club Mo, 38; alt deleg, Dem Nat Conv, 40, 48, 52, 56, secy to Mo deleg, 64; committeewoman, Macon Co & Macon City Dem Parties, 50-; pres, Ninth Cong Dist Women's Club; treas, Macon Co Dem Cent Comt, formerly, chmn, currently. Mem: Anti Rust Club; Macon Band Boosters; Macon PTA (vpres); Macon Girl Scouts; Mo Farmers Asn. Relig: Christian Church. Mailing Add: 114 Pace St Macon MO 63552

BARROWS, RAYMOND EDWIN (R)
Chmn, St Clair Co Rep Party, Mo
b Clinton, Mo, Nov 21, 17; s Charley Williams Barrows & Martha Griffin B; m 1943 to Georgia Frances Callison; c Virginia Lee. Educ: Clinton High Sch, 4 years. Polit & Govt Pos: City alderman, Appleton City, Mo, 65; chmn, St Clair Co Rep Party, 68-; chmn, Fourth Cong Dist Rep Party, 70- Bus & Prof Pos: Owner, Barrows Chevrolet Co, 55- Mil Serv: Entered as Pvt, Army, 39, released as S/Sgt, 45, after serv in 231st AFA, ETO, 44-45; Bronze Star. Mem: Optimist; Mason; Scottish Rite; Shrine; VFW. Relig: United Methodist. Mailing Add: 715 N Poplar Appleton City MO 64724

BARRUS, GEORGE A (R)
NH State Rep
Mailing Add: Box 158 Cornish NH 03746

BARRY, DAVID MICHAEL (D)
Conn State Sen
b Manchester, Conn, Nov 7, 30; s John Francis Barry & May D'Arcy B; m 1959 to Judith Ann Leclerc; c Joan, David M, Jr, Michael, Mark & Ryan. Educ: Georgetown Univ, 48-50; Trinity Col, BA, 52; Boston Univ Law Sch, LLB, 55. Polit & Govt Pos: Conn State Rep, 59-61; pres, Manchester Young Dem Club, 60-61; mem, Manchester Dem Town Comt, 60-; mem bd dirs, Manchester, 62-66, dep mayor, 64-66; Conn State Sen, Fourth Dist, 66-71 & 75-; vchmn, Adv Coun to State Dept on Aging, 69-71; counsel to Dem Majority, Conn State Senate, 71; town counsel, Manchester, 71- Bus & Prof Pos: Partner, Bieluch, Barry & Ramenda, 58-68 & Barry & Ramenda, 68-71; sole practitioner, 72- Mil Serv: Army, 55-57, serv in Counter Intel Corps. Mem: Am, Conn & Hartford Co Bar Asns; KofC; Elks. Relig: Roman Catholic. Mailing Add: 473 E Center St Manchester CT 06040

BARRY, HILARY D (DFL)
Mem, Dem-Farmer-Labor State Cent Comt, Minn
s Bernard D Barry & Fern Donely B; m 1952 to Cheryl Teske; c Scott, Mark, Cindy, Carla, Tamara, Teresa, Bruce, Amy, Patrick & Kimberly. Educ: WCent Sch Agr; Univ Minn, Morris, dipl. Polit & Govt Pos: Deleg, State Dem Conv, Minn, 62, 64, 66, 68 & 70; Murray Co chmn, Second Dist Dem Cent Comt, 62-68; deleg, Dem Nat Conv, 68; mem, Dem-Farmer-Labor State Cent Comt, Minn, 72- Bus & Prof Pos: Pres, Barry Construction Co, Lake Wilson, Minn, 56- Mem: KofC; Southwest Minn Contractors Asn (pres). Relig: Catholic. Mailing Add: Lake Wilson MN 56151

BARRY, JOHN D (R)
b Chicago, Ill, Sept 11, 17; s Joseph William Barry & Margaret Beckett B; m 1952 to Jane Powell. Educ: Univ Calif, Los Angeles, 35-38. Polit & Govt Pos: Admin asst to US Rep Hamilton Fish, Jr, NY, 69- Bus & Prof Pos: Ed, Lehman Publ, Catskill, NY, 58-61; pres, John Barry Assocs Inc, NY, 61-69. Mil Serv: Entered as Pvt, Army, 39, released as M/Sgt, 45, after serv in Field Artil, Pac Theatre of Opers, 39-45; Pearl Harbor, Guadalcanal, New Georgia & Good Conduct Medals. Mem: Am Legion; Survivors of Pearl Harbor; Rotary Int; CofC. Legal Res: RD 1 Catskill NY 12414 Mailing Add: 409 Cannon House Off Bldg Washington DC 20515

BARRY, PHILIP M (D)
Mo State Rep
Mailing Add: 5050 Lampglow Ct St Louis Co MO 63129

BARRY, ROBERT R (R)
b Omaha, Nebr, May 15, 15; s Ralph Barry & Ethel Thomas B; m 1945 to Anne Rogers Benjamin; c Cynthia Herndon & Henry Rogers. Educ: Hamilton Col, 33-36; Tuck Sch Bus Admin, Dartmouth Col, 36-37; NY Univ, 38 & 45-46, Law & Grad Finance; Nat Journalistic Fraternity; Alpha Delta Phi. Polit & Govt Pos: Regional chmn, New Eng & Cent States, Willkie Clubs of Am, 40; financial analyst, Under Secy Navy Off, 45; personnel dir & asst to chmn, Dewey for Pres, Rep Nat Campaign Comt, 48; WCoast & Rocky Mountain mgr, Eisenhower Campaign Comt, 51; mem, Eisenhower's personal staff, Denver & Chicago, 52; chmn bus groups, Co Rep Mayoralty Campaign Comt, NY, 49, mem finance comt, 52; chmn finance comt, NY State Citizens for Eisenhower, 54; chmn, Yonkers Citizens for Eisenhower, 56; US Rep, NY, 59-65, mem, Foreign Affairs Comt, Post Off Civil Serv Comt, Govt Oper Comt, US Deleg to NATO 3 times, to UNESCO & to Can Parliamentary Conf, US House of Rep; Rep cand for US Rep, Calif, 66; mem, Nixon-Agnew Nat Campaign Staff, 68; coordr, Sen Murphy's Campaign, San Mateo Co, 70. Bus & Prof Pos: With Kidder Peabody & Co, 37; with Mfg Trust Co, 38-40; contract mgr & statistician, Bendix Aviation Corp, 40-44; asst to Pres, Yale & Towne Mfg Co, New York, 45-50; land develop, mining & farming interest, 50-; pres, Calicopia Corp, 65- Mem: Friendly Sons of St Patrick; Boy Scouts (nat coun & Eagle Scout); US Capitol Hist Asn (founder); Riverside Co Farm Bur; Int Seaman's Union. Honors & Awards: Grand Cross, Eloy Alfaro Found; Man of Year Award, Captive Nations Assembly; Citation for Meritorious Serv, Nat Asn Retired Civil Employees. Relig: Presbyterian. Legal Res: 155 Wildwood Way Woodside CA 94062 Mailing Add: 3001 Normanstone Dr Washington DC 20008

BARRY, TOBIAS (D)
Chmn, Bureau Co Dem Party, Ill
b Chicago, Ill, Apr 12, 24; s Tobias F Barry & Mary Castagnari B; m 1948 to Janet Bruno; c Tobias Mark, Patrick Alan, Michele Beth & Daniel Sean. Educ: Marquette Univ, PhB, 49; Univ Notre Dame, JD, 52. Polit & Govt Pos: Ill State Rep, 60-74, chmn, Bureau Co Dem Party, 63- Bus & Prof Pos: Attorney-at-law. Mil Serv: Navy, World War II, serv, in Pac Theatre. Relig: Roman Catholic. Mailing Add: Ladd IL 61329

BARRY, WARREN E (R)
Va State Deleg
b Boston, Mass, Aug 4, 33; s Charles E Barry & Constance Friery B; m 1956 to Theresa Lynn McKay; c Stanley Glen, James Everett & Scott Michael. Educ: Boston State Col, BS; George Washington Univ, MS. Polit & Govt Pos: Va State Deleg, 70- Bus & Prof Pos: Pres, Springfield Merchants Asn, 65; vpres, Lynch Bros Real Estate Co, 65-66, pres, 67-69; pres, Springfield CofC, 68; pres, Barry Assocs, Realtors, 70- Mil Serv: Entered as 2nd Lt, Marine Corps, 55, released as 1st Lt, 58, after serv in Second Marine Div. Mem: Int Coun Shopping Ctr; Nat Retail Merchants Asn; Jaycees; PTA. Honors & Awards: Local Community Distinguished Serv Award, 69. Relig: Protestant. Mailing Add: 6838 Franconia Rd Springfield VA 22150

BARRY, WILLIAM LOGAN (D)
b Lexington, Tenn, Feb 9, 26; s Henry Daniel Barry & Mary Logan B; m 1966 to Elizabeth Coffman. Educ: Vanderbilt Univ, BA, 48; BL, 50; Phi Beta Kappa. Polit & Govt Pos: Mem, Lexington Bd Aldermen, Tenn, 53-55; Tenn State Rep, 55-67, Majority Leader, Tenn House of Rep, 59-63, Speaker, 63-67; mem, Tenn Legis Coun, 57-67, chmn, 65-67; exec asst to Gov, Tenn, 67-71; Asst Attorney Gen, Tenn, 71- Mil Serv: Entered as Pvt, Army, 50, released as 1st Lt, 53, after serv in Far Eastern Theater. Mem: Tenn Bar Asn; Lions; Elks; KofP; Am Legion. Relig: Baptist. Mailing Add: Natchez Trace Dr Lexington TN 38351

BARTELS, CAROL PICKER (DFL)
Chmn, Crow Wing Co Dem-Farmer-Labor Party, Minn
b Morgan, Minn, Dec 28, 17; d Charles George Picker & Edna Lenore Ellies P; m 1936 to Elmer E Bartels, wid; c William C, Bonita (Mrs Jack Griffith), Charles E, Bette H (Mrs Richard Smitheram) & Brenda A (Mrs Thomas Heglund). Educ: St Joseph's Sch Nursing, St Paul, Minn, 2 years; Med Inst Technol, Minneapolis, 1 year. Polit & Govt Pos: Deleg, Co, Dist & Minn State Dem-Farmer-Labor Conv, 50-70, mem various conv comts; finance chmn & vchmn, McLeod Co Dem-Farmer-Labor Party, Minn, 52-56, chmn, 56-58; deleg, Dem Nat Conv, 56; mem, Minn State Dem-Farmer-Labor Cent Comt, 56-; mem, Brownton Sch Bd, 62-63; secy, Crow Wing Co Dem-Farmer-Labor Party, 64-65, chmn, 66-72 & 75-; dir, Sixth Dist Dem-Farmer-Labor Exec Comt, 70-; dir, Crow Wing Co Welfare Bd, 70- Bus & Prof Pos: Reporter, New Ulm Daily, formerly; mgr & operator, liquor store, gravel bus & farm,

63- Mem: Minn Wild Rice Harvesters Asn; Minn Wild Rice Asn; Morrison, Todd & Crow Wing Co Community Action Coun (dir, 66-). Mailing Add: Ironton MN 56455

BARTER, MERRILL ROBERT (R)
Committeeman, Maine Rep State Comt
b Lubec, Maine, May 6, 29; s Merrill S Barter & Ora Small B; m 1966 to Virginia L Ross; c Merrill Erwin & Jennifer Leigh. Educ: Univ Maine, 47-49; Husson Col, grad, 50; Mu Sigma Chi, Husson Col. Polit & Govt Pos: Town clerk, Boothbay Harbor, Maine, 53-, mem, Bd of Selectmen, 58-67, chmn, 65; chmn, Selective Serv Bd, Lincoln Co, 59-; chmn, Lincoln Co Rep Comt, 64-68; committeeman, Maine Rep State Comt, 68-; chmn, Lincoln Co Comnr, 69- Bus & Prof Pos: Owner, Bob's Photo TV, 53- Mil Serv: Entered as Pvt, Air Force, 51, released as S/Sgt, 52, after serv in 101st Wing. Mem: Maine Electronic Technicians' Asn; Shrine; Mason (32 degree); Lions; Maine Law Enforcement Asn. Relig: Methodist. Legal Res: 15 Atlantic Ave Boothbay Harbor ME 04538 Mailing Add: 19 Townsend Ave Boothbay Harbor ME 04538

BARTH, FRANCIS PHILLIP (D)
NDak State Sen
b Flasher, NDak, Apr 2, 30; s Phillip F Barth & Katherine Leingang B; m 1951 to Burnetta Gerhardt; c Dwight, Geisele, Elwood, MaDonna & Leland. Educ: High sch, 2 years. Polit & Govt Pos: Dem committeeman, 18th Dist, Morton Co, NDak, 51-66; dir, Sch Bd, 53-62, chmn, 7 years; mem, Morton Co Dem Non-partisan League Exec Comt, 60; deleg, Dem State Conv, 62, 64, 66 & 68; secy, Dist 35 NDak Dem Non-Partisan League, 65-66, chmn, 66-; deleg, Dem Nat Conv, 68; NDak State Sen, 71- Bus & Prof Pos: Farmer-rancher, 1400 Acre Ranch, breeding registered Hereford Cattle. Publ: Articles concerning speeches & comments about politics, The Morning Pioneer, Newspaper, Mandan, NDak. Mem: Elks; KofC (Grand Knight, 61-64, State Dep, 64-, deleg, Supreme KofC Conv, 69); Farmers Union; Nat Farmers Orgn; NDak Hereford Asn. Relig: Catholic. Mailing Add: State Capitol Bismarck ND 43215

BARTH, THOMAS EMIL (D)
Chmn, Eau Claire Co Dem Party, Wis
b Milwaukee, Wis, Sept 1, 37; s Emil Barth & Henrietta Steinmann B; single. Educ: Univ Wis-Milwaukee, BS, 59; Univ Wis-Madison, MS, 60, PhD, 68. Polit & Govt Pos: Chmn, Eau Claire Co Dem Party, Wis, 73- Bus & Prof Pos: Assoc prof polit sci, Univ Wis-Eau Claire, 63- Publ: Co-ed, Law & Order in a Democratic Society, Charles Merrill Co, 70; auth, Impact of Supreme Court decisions, J Pub Law, 69. Mailing Add: 419 Jefferson St Eau Claire WI 54701

BARTHELEMY, SIDNEY JOHN (D)
La State Sen
b New Orleans, La, Mar 17, 42; s Lionel Barthelemy & Ruth Fernandez B; m 1968 to Michaele Thibodeaux; c Cherrie Ann & Bridget. Educ: Epiphany Apostolic Jr Col, 60-63; St Joseph Sem, BA, 67; Tulane Univ, MSW, 71. Polit & Govt Pos: La State Sen, 74-, chmn joint subcomt on ment & social health, La State Senate, 74-, mem health, educ & welfare comt, natural resources comt & subcomt on higher educ, 74-; mem, Orleans Parish Dem Exec Comt, currently. Bus & Prof Pos: Admin asst to CEP Dir, 67-69; dir, Parent-Child Ctr, Family Health, Inc, 69-71; tutor-couns coordr labor ed, Urban League of New Orleans, 69-72; dir social serv, Parent Child Develop Ctr, 71-72; dir, Dept Welfare, New Orleans, 72-74; asst dir, Urbinvolve Prog, Xavier Univ, 74- Mem: Community Orgn for Urban Polit (vpres, 73-); Youth Assistance Coun (chmn); Telecommun Adv Comt (chmn, govt use subcomt); Family Service Soc (bd dir). Honors & Awards: Community Serv Award, Desire Community Ctr. Relig: Catholic. Mailing Add: 3903 Virgil Blvd New Orleans LA 70122

BARTHELMES, WES (D)
b Winchester, Mass, May 10, 22; s Albert Wesley Barthelmes & Irma McDevitt B; m to Dorothy Chase; c Lisa & Victoria. Educ: Tufts Col, BA, 47; Middlebury Col, summer 47; L'Institut des Hautes Etudes Internationalies, Geneva, Switz, 47-48; Columbia Univ Grad Sch Jour, MS, 49; Zeta Psi. Polit & Govt Pos: Admin asst to US Rep Edith Green, Ore, 62-65; press secy, US Sen Robert F Kennedy, NY, 65-66; campaign coordr, US Rep Robert Duncan, Ore, 66; admin asst to US Rep Richard Bolling, Mo, 69-70, spec asst to US Sen Frank Church, 70-73; admin asst to US Sen Joe Biden, Del, 73- Bus & Prof Pos: Reporter & asst city ed, Telegram, Worcester, Mass, 49-53 & Washington Post, 53-62. Mil Serv: Entered as Pvt, Army, 43, released as Cpl, 46, after serv in Paratroopers 82nd Airborne Div, ETO, 43-46; Presidential Unit Citation. Publ: George Wallace is alive and well, Washingtonian Mag, 2/69. Mem: Caucus for a New Polit; Alliance for Dem Progress. Honors & Awards: Nat Honor Soc; Washington Newspaper Guild's Guildsman of the Year; Washingtonian Mag Ten Best Admin Asst. Legal Res: Montgomery Co MD Mailing Add: 6317 Dirksen Senate Off Bldg Washington DC 20510

BARTHOLOMEW, LISLE (R)
Vt State Rep
Mailing Add: Rainbow House Benson VT 05731

BARTLETT, CLARENCE EDWARD (R)
NH State Rep
b Concord, NH, Feb 23, 03; s Edward Elbridge Bartlett & Maude Kelley B; m 1921 to Amy Frances Kaime; c Frances (Mrs Marston) & Robert Edward (deceased). Educ: Palmer Col, DC, 22; NY Univ, Traffic Safety Mgt course; Acacia Fraternity. Polit & Govt Pos: Financial Responsibility Admin, NH, 61-66; NH State Rep, 69- Mem: Mason (32 degree). Relig: Protestant. Legal Res: Epsom NH 03234 Mailing Add: Box 7 Epsom NH 03234

BARTLETT, DEWEY FOLLETT (R)
US Sen, Okla
b Marietta, Ohio, Mar 28, 19; s David A Bartlett & Jessie B; m 1945 to Ann C Smith; c Dewey, Jr, Joan & Michael. Educ: Princeton Univ, BSE, 42. Polit & Govt Pos: Okla State Sen, 62-66; Gov, Okla, 67-71; deleg, Rep Nat Conv, 68; mem, Exec Comt Rep Gov, 69; US Sen, Okla, 72-, mem armed serv comt, US Senate, 75- Bus & Prof Pos: Pres, Dewey Supply Co; partner, Keener Oil Co; chmn, Interstate Oil Compact Comn, 70- Mil Serv: Entered as 2nd Lt, Marine Corps, 42, released as Capt, 45, after serv as Combat Divebomber Pilot; Air Medal. Mem: Tulsa CofC; Salvation Army (bd dir); Tulsa Co Chap, Am Red Cross (dir); Independent Petroleum Asn of Am (dir); Okla Independent Producers Asn (dir). Relig: Catholic. Legal Res: Tulsa OK Mailing Add: 140 Old Senate Of Bldg Washington DC 20510

BARTLETT, HAROLD DURWARD (R)
Mem, York Co Rep Comt, Maine
b Thorndike, Maine, July 6, 02; s Ernest Leon Bartlett & Emma Louise Hasty B; m 1926 to Theda Pearl Fernald; c Harold Durward, Jr & Philip Lee. Educ: Univ Maine, 22-23; engr defense training prog, Univ NH, 41-43. Polit & Govt Pos: Mem, Corinna Sch Bd, Maine, 33-40; selectman, South Berwick, 50-52 & 59-61; mem, South Berwick Budget Comt, 55-56; mem, South Berwick Planning Bd, 67-70, trustee, Water Dist, 60-72; chmn, South Berwick Rep Town Comt, 69-72; mem, York Co Rep Comt, 69-; Maine State Rep, 71-73. Bus & Prof Pos: With Kenwood Woolen Mill, Corinna, Maine, 23-38; part owner serv sta, 38-40; elec & electronic mechanic, Portsmouth Naval Shipyard, Kittery, 40-49, electrician, 50-51, electronic planner & estimator, 51-65; elec maintenance, Univ NH, 49-50. Mem: AF&AM; Eastern Star; Rotary. Relig: Methodist; Men's Club, First Paris Federated Church, South Berwick. Mailing Add: 13 Parent St South Berwick ME 03908

BARTLETT, JOE (DORSEY JOSEPH) (R)
Clerk to the Minority, US House Rep
b Clarksburg, WVa, Aug 7, 26; s Flavius Dorsey Bartlett (deceased) & Blanche Hacker B; m 1952 to Virginia Bender; c Linda Louise & Laura Lee. Educ: George Washington Univ & WVa Wesleyan Col. Hon Degrees: LLD, Atlanta Law Sch, Ga, 70 & Salem Col, WVa, 71. Polit & Govt Pos: Page, US House Rep, 41-44, Rep chief of pages, 45-53, reading clerk, 53-70, clerk to the Minority, 70-; chief of pages, Rep Nat Conv, 48, asst to chmn, Comt Arrangements, 52 & 56, chief reading clerk, 60, 64, 68 & 72; mem, Cuyahoga Co Rep Exec Comt, Ohio, 52- Mil Serv: Enlisted as Recruit, Marine Corps, 44; Brig Gen, Marine Corps Res, 75. Publ: Strange legend: curious riddle, an essay in parable form, 68 & Everybody's business—The work of Congress, 75, Cong Rec & other publ; Challenge to service, Jaycees publs & manuals, 70- Mem: Marine Corps Asn; Navy League; ROA; Nat Rep Club of Capitol Hill (Bd Gov & Exec Comt); Ohio State Soc of DC (vpres). Honors & Awards: Spec Resolution, Ga State Senate, 65; George Washington Honor Medal, Freedoms Found Valley Forge, 68; Guest Speaker, 102nd Mem Serv, Gettysburg Nat Cemetery, 69; Distinguished Serv, US Jaycees, 69. Relig: Protestant. Mailing Add: 6128 Long Meadow Rd McLean VA 22101

BARTLETT, JOHN WESLEY (D)
Chmn, Mont State Dem Party
b Harlowton, Mont, Oct 12, 25; s John Bartlett & Eliza Hughe B; m 1944 to Edith Mae Welch; c John Clifton, James Craig & Jan Colleen. Educ: Univ Mont, BS in Pharm, 49; Kappa Psi. Polit & Govt Pos: Dem precinct committeeman, Whitefish, Mont, 50-69, city councilman, 56-60; cong committeeman, Flathead Co Dem Party, 58-62, chmn, 62-69; mem, Area Redevelop Comt, Flathead Co, 58-65; deleg, Dem Nat Conv, 60 & 72; mem, Small Bus Adv Coun, Mont, 60-66; Presidential elector, Mont, 68; mem, State Bd of Health, 69-; chmn, Mont State Dem Party, 71-; mem, Dem Nat Comt, 71-; deleg, Dem Nat Mid-Term Conf, 74. Bus & Prof Pos: Pharmacist & partner, Neville Drug, Whitefish, 49-66; pres, Chalet City Pharm, 66- Mil Serv: Entered as Pvt, Army, 43, released as S/Sgt, 45, after serv in 87th Inf Div, Third Army, ETO; Bronze Star; Combat Infantryman Badge; Purple Heart with Clusters. Mem: Nat Asn Retail Druggists; CofC; Am Legion; Moose; Mason. Honors & Awards: Life memberships, VFW & Whitefish Jaycees. Relig: Methodist. Mailing Add: 144 Montana Ave Whitefish MT 59937

BARTLETT, KENNETH G (R)
b Plymouth, Mich, Mar 13, 06; s Wyman J Barlett & Alta Mae Gill B; m 1930 to Bernice V Kleinhans; c Elizabeth (Mrs John Weinheimer) & John G, MD. Educ: Albion Col, AB, 27, LLD, 55; Syracuse Univ, MA, 31. Polit & Govt Pos: Mem, State of NY, The Moreland Comn on Welfare, 61-63; chmn, comt app by State Comnr of Educ for Statewide Study of Educ TV; NY State Assemblyman, 119th Dist, 67-71; mem, State Comn on Powers of Local Govt, 71-73. Bus & Prof Pos: Vpres pub affairs, Syracuse Univ, 53-71; dir, Onondaga Savings Bank; dir, Metrop Develop Asn; chmn, Regional Hosp Rev Planning Coun Cert NY, 71-; Cent NY Regional Transportation Authority, 72- Honors & Awards: Man of the Year in Educ, Herald-J, 63; received Annual Community Serv Award, Syracuse Rotary, 66. Relig: Presbyterian. Mailing Add: 11 Bradford Dr Syracuse NY 13224

BARTLETT, MAEDEAN C (D)
Vt State Rep
Mailing Add: Richford VT 05457

BARTLETT, MARTIN HANDLEY (R)
Mem, Rep State Cent Comt NMex
b Stillwater, Okla, Dec 21, 07; s Harry Ulyses Bartlett & Eva Maud Whitehead B; div; c Barbara (Mrs Benedict), Diane (Mrs Wellar), Margaret (Mrs McNatt), Deborah (Mrs Ackerman), John & Will. Educ: Oklahoma City Univ, 24-26; Univ Tex, 40; Univ Tex Sch Med, MD, 41; Nu Sigma Nu. Polit & Govt Pos: Mem, Otero Co Rep Cent Comt, NMex, 52-; mem, Rep State Cent Comt NMex, 62-; deleg, Rep Nat Conv, 68. Mil Serv: Entered as 2nd Lt, Army, 42, released as Lt, 46. Mem: Otero Co & NMex State Med Socs; AMA; Am Acad Gen Practice; NMex Sch for the Visually Handicapped (Bd Regents). Relig: Methodist. Legal Res: 414 San Andreas Alamogordo NM 88310 Mailing Add: PO Box 593 Alamogordo NM 88310

BARTLETT, WILLIAM MAYHEW (R)
Mem, DC Rep Party
b New Haven, Conn, Mar 27, 30; s Russell Sturgis Bartlett & Emilie Daggett B; m 1961 to Mary Ellen Barton; c stepdaughters, Sharon, Martha Ann, Mary Ellen, Rodanne & son, Russell Sturgis, II. Educ: Univ Bridgeport, BS, 57; Am Col Life Underwriters, CLU, 67; Theta Sigma; Knights of Thunder. Polit & Govt Pos: Pres, Univ Bridgeport Young Rep, 56-57; first vpres, Prince Georges Co Young Rep, Md, 59-60; mem, Dick Nixon Club, 60; mem, DC Young Rep, 61-65; mem precinct orgn squad, Montgomery Co Rep, 69, adminr, 70-71; chmn, Precinct 33, Washington, DC, 71, chmn, Ward Three, 72-; pub rels chmn, DC Rep Party, 71-, treas, 72-73, mem, currently; pub rels chmn, DC Rep $100-a-plate Dinner, 72. Bus & Prof Pos: Ins agt, Equitable Life Assurance Soc, Washington, DC, 61-65; dir membership prom & health ins activities, Nat Asn of Life Underwriters, 65- Mil Serv: Entered as Seaman Recruit, Navy, 48, released as Hospitalman 3/C, 52, after serv in USS Oriskany, Mediter Theatre, 51. Mem: DC Life Underwriters Asn; Am Soc Asn Exec; Washington Soc Asn Exec; Am Soc Chartered Life Underwriters; Jaycees. Honors & Awards: Spoke Award, US Jr CofC, 64; Distinguished Performance Award, Jaycees, 65. Relig: Episcopal. Mailing Add: 1922 F St NW Washington DC 20006

BARTLEY, DAVID MICHAEL (D)
Speaker, Mass House Rep
b Holyoke, Mass, Feb 9, 35; s James Bartley & Mary Kennedy B; m 1964 to Elizabeth Ann Keough; c David Kennedy, Myles Keough & Susan Elizabeth. Educ: Holyoke Jr Col, 52-54; Univ Mass, Amherst, BA in Govt, 56, MEd, 61. Hon Degrees: PHL, New Eng Sch Law, 72; DHL, New Eng Col Optom, 74. Polit & Govt Pos: Mass State Rep, 63-, speaker, Mass House Rep, 69-; deleg, Dem Nat Conv, 68; chmn, Dem State Conv, 70; Dem Nat Committeeman, Mass, 75- Mil Serv: Army. Mem: KofC; Elks; Boys Club Am; Nat Legis Conf. Honors & Awards: Outstanding Young Leader, Gtr Boston Jr CofC, 71. Relig: Catholic. Mailing Add: 25 Hillcrest Rd Holyoke MA 01041

BARTOLOTTA, LILLIAN M (D)
Committeewoman, Dem State Cent Comt Conn
b Ansonia, Conn, July 10, 30; d Evan Aleskewich & Anna Chupko A; m 1951 to Louis S Bartolotta; c Lynny. Educ: Ansonia High Sch, grad, 48; Sch of Social Work, 60. Polit & Govt Pos: Vchmn, Ansonia Dem Town Comt, Conn, 69-75; committeewoman, Dem State Cent Comt, Conn, 17th Sen Dist, 73- Bus & Prof Pos: Exec dir, Am Red Cross, 48- Mem: Dem Women's Club (organizer, 70); Holy Rosary Women's Club; Valley Comt on Aging (adv comt, 75). Honors & Awards: Cert of Appreciation, Second Missile Bn 55th Artil, 65, Ansonia Lions Club, 70 & Rotary Club, 71. Mailing Add: 48 Root Ave Ansonia CT 06401

BARTON, HAROLD BRYAN (R)
Mem, Ky Rep State Finance Comt
b Madison Co, Ky, Nov 1, 26; s Clyde Tye Barton & Lula Marie Brown B; m 1951 to Nelda Lambert; c Barbara Lynn, Harold Bryan, Jr, Stephen Lambert & Suzanne. Educ: Univ Ky, 44 & 46-48; Univ Louisville Sch Med, MD, 52; postgrad work, Gen Surg Residency, Univ Louisville Hosps, 52-57; dipl, Am Bd Surg. Polit & Govt Pos: City campaign chmn, Rep Party, Ky, 60, 62 & 64; mem bd dirs, Ky Educ Med-Polit Action Comt, 62-66, chmn, 65-; deleg, Rep Nat Conv, 64 & 68, alt deleg, 72; chmn, Fifth Cong Dist Rep Fund Raising Dinner, 65; mem, Ky Rep State Finance Comt, currently; Rep campaign chmn, Whitley Co, 71; mem, Ky Coun on Higher Pub Educ, 71-72; pres, Fifth Dist Rep Lincoln Club, 72-73; chmn, Whitley Co Rep Comt, 72- Bus & Prof Pos: Secy, Corbin Airport Bd, 64-72; mem bd dirs, Am Bus Mens Life Ins Co, 65-66; chief of surg, Southeast Ky Baptist Hosp; nursing home adminr, 73-; vpres, Ky Health Care Facilities, 75- Mil Serv: Entered as A/S, Navy, 44, released as Seaman 1/C, 46, after serv in Commun Intel, Pac Theatre; Unit Citation; Presidential Unit Commendation. Mem: Am Med Asn; Ky Med Asn (legis adv comt & chmn long term care comt); Med Asns; Southeastern & Ky Surg Socs; CofC. Honors & Awards: Corbin Distinguished Citizen Award, 66. Relig: Protestant; Elder & chmn finance comt, First Christian Church. Mailing Add: 1311 Seventh St Rd Corbin KY 40701

BARTON, NELDA ANN LAMBERT (R)
Rep Nat Committeewoman, Ky
b Providence, Ky, May 12, 29; d Eulis Grant Lambert & Rubie Lois West L; m 1951 to Harold Bryan Barton, MD; c William Grant (deceased), Barbara Lynn, Harold Bryan, Jr, Stephen Lambert & Suzanne. Educ: Western Ky Univ, scholar, 47-49; Norton Mem Infirmary Sch Med Technol, grad 50; pres, Beta Omega Chi, 48-49. Polit & Govt Pos: Fifth dist gov, Ky Fedn Rep Women, 63-67; mem, Am & Ky Educ Med Polit Action Comts, 63-; Rep dist campaign chairwoman, 67-; pres, Corbin Rep Woman's Club, 68; Whitley Co Campaign Chairwoman, 68; second vpres, Ky Fedn Rep Woman's Club, 68-70; chairwoman, Whitley Co Rep Party, 68-72; mem, Ky State Rep Cent Comt, 68-; Rep Nat Committeewoman, Ky, 68-; conf chmn for Ky Nat Rep Women's Conf, DC, 69; mem, Adv Coun, Corbin, Ky, 69-70; mem, DO Comt, Rep Nat Comt, 69-72, mem, Rule 29 Comt, 73-75; co-chmn, Urban Renewal & Community Develop Agency, Corbin, 70-73. Bus & Prof Pos: Med technologist, 50-53; mem adv comt assoc degree nursing prog, Cumberland Col, 73- Mem: Ninth Dist Ky Fedn Women's Club (vgov); Women's Auxiliary to Southern Med Asn; Woman's Auxiliary to Ky Med Asn; Woman's Auxiliary to Whitley Co Med Soc; Ossoli Woman's Club. Honors & Awards: Ky Col, 68; PTA Life Mem Award; Ky Rep Woman of the Year, 68-69. Relig: Protestant; Chmn, youth fellowship, Circle Chmn, First Christian Church. Mailing Add: 1311 Seventh Street Rd Corbin KY 40701

BARTON, RICHARD ALAN (D)
b Baltimore, Md, Mar 20, 38; s Alan Striethoff Barton & Nellie Seward B; m 1964 to Judith Ann Strain; c Jennifer Lynne & Michael Alan. Educ: La State Univ, BA, 60; Univ NC, MA, 63; Omicron Delta Kappa; Phi Eta Sigma; Tau Kappa Alpha; Phi Kappa Phi; Pi Sigma Alpha; Phi Alpha Theta; Phi Gamma Delta. Polit & Govt Pos: Mem, Arlington Dem Campaign Comt, Va, 68-75, chmn & mgr, 71; vchmn, Arlington Co Dem Comt, 69-71, chmn, 71-73; chmn Arlington Co deleg, Va State Dem Conv, 71; mem, Arlington Co Planning Comn, 71-, vchmn, 73-75, chmn, 75-; mem, Arlington Co Transportation Comn, 72-; fund raising coordr, Tenth Dist Dem Cong Campaign, 74. Bus & Prof Pos: Staff asst, Postal Rates Subcomt, Post Off & Civil Serv Comt, 65-68, staff dir, Subcomt on Pos Classification, 68-71, Subcomt on Employee Benefits, 71-73 & Subcomt on Postal Serv, 73- Mem: Cong Staff Club; Arlington Comt of 100; Arlington Civic Fedn. Relig: Unitarian; mem bd trustees, Arlington Unitarian Church, 72-, chmn, 74-75. Mailing Add: 5019 36th St N Arlington VA 22207

BARTON, TERRY ALLEN (R)
Mem, Rep State Cent Comt Calif
b Columbus, Ohio, Sept 11, 35; s Albert Jack Barton & Inez Smith B; m 1957 to Barbara Ellen Watts; c Gregory Allen. Educ: Ohio State Univ, BA, 59; Loyola Univ Sch Law, 60-63; Phi Eta Sigma. Polit & Govt Pos: Civil Serv comnr, Seal Beach Civil Serv Bd, Calif, 66-67; planning comnr, Seal Beach Planning Comn, 67-69; mem, Nat Defense Exec Res, 68-69; pres, Seal Beach Rep Assembly, 69-; mem, Rep State Cent Comt Calif, 69- Bus & Prof Pos: Qual control analyst, Gen Motors Corp, Columbus, Ohio, 58-59; supvr contracts & pricing, NAm Rockwell Corp, Downey, Calif, 63- Mil Serv: Entered as 2nd Lt, Air Force, 59, released as 1st Lt, 62, after serv in 18th Dist Off, Spec Invest Hq, 60-63; Capt, Air Force Res, 67. Mem: Nat Contract Mgt Asn; Col Park Homeowner's Asn of Seal Beach (pres); Long Beach Elks Club; Seal Beach CofC; Old Ranch Country Club. Relig: Methodist. Mailing Add: 415 Ocean Ave Seal Beach CA 90740

BARTON, WILLIAM THOMAS (R)
Secy, Salt Lake Co Cent Comt, Utah
b Granger, Utah, Feb 18, 33; s Doran Warr Barton & Beatrice Orullian B; m 1958 to Karen Sue Larson; c Thomas Kim, Allison & Doran Lynn. Educ: Univ Utah, 51-52; Utah Tech Col, 53-54. Polit & Govt Pos: Secy, Salt Lake Co Cent Comt, 73- Bus & Prof Pos: Exec secy, WValley Area CofC, 72-73 & Intermountain Ace Dealers Asn, 73- Mem: Jaycees Int; Lions Int; WValley CofC; (dir, currently). Honors & Awards: JCI Senator Award, Granger Jaycees & Utah Jaycees, 68. Relig: Latter-day Saint. Mailing Add: 3940 W 4100 S Granger UT 84120

BARTRUFF, ROBERT DAVID (D)
Chmn, Dawson Co Dem Comt, Nebr
b Eustis, Nebr, Aug 29, 27; s Otto Christ Bartruff & Sophia Yeutter B; m 1950 to Evelyn Alice Keller; c Carolyn (Mrs Lynden Griese), Jean, Mari Lynn & Janell. Educ: Eustis High Sch, grad, 44. Polit & Govt Pos: Chmn, Dawson Co Dem Comt, Nebr, 74- Bus & Prof Pos: Dir, Fed Land Bank, 67- Mil Serv: Entered as Pvt, Air Force, 46, released as Pvt 1/C, 47, after serv in 8th Air Force. Mem: Lions; Mason (32 degree); Elks; Nebr Wheat Growers. Relig: United Methodist. Mailing Add: RR 1 Eustis NE 69028

BARTSCHI, RULON R (R)
Chmn, Toole Co Rep Party, Mont
b Nounan, Idaho, June 8, 13; s Charles Bartschi & Bertha Wyler B; m 1960 to Theo Fay Martin Kluth; c James R & Julie Ann (Mrs Tueller). Educ: Montpelier High Sch, grad. Polit & Govt Pos: Dist dir, Idaho Young Rep, 40-50; chmn, Custer Co Rep Comt, 45-50; chmn, Toole Co Rep Cent Comt, 60-72 & 75- Bus & Prof Pos: Vpres & mgr, Custer Co Bank, Challis, Idaho, 45-50; auditor, Idaho Dept Finance, 55-56; pres, Bank of Glacier Co, 56-60; exec vpres & mgr, First Nat Bank, Cut Bank, 65-70; retired. Mem: Mason (32 degree); Scottish Rite; Shrine; Elks. Relig: Christian. Mailing Add: Box 670 Shelby MT 59474

BARWICK, PLATO COLLINS, JR (R)
Mem Exec Comt, Lenoir Co Rep Party, NC
b Kinston, NC, June 28, 37; s Plato Collins Barwick & Thelma Banks B; m 1960 to Nancy Coston; c Collins & George Scott. Educ: Wake Forest Univ & Law Sch, BA, 59, LLB, 60; Eta Sigma Phi; Sigma Phi Epsilon. Polit & Govt Pos: Mem, Lenoir Co Young Rep Club, 68 & 69; mem exec comt, Lenoir Co Rep Party, 68-73, chmn, 73-; legal counsel, NC Fedn Young Rep, 69-70, first dist dir, 70-71, chmn, 71-72; area coordr, NC Legis Campaign Comt, 70; asst gen counsel, Young Rep Nat Fedn, 71- Bus & Prof Pos: Assoc, Wallace & Langley, Attorneys, Kinston, NC, 64-66, partner, Wallace, Langley, Barwick & Llewellyn, 66- Mil Serv: Entered as 2nd Lt, Army, released as 2nd Lt, 60, after serv in Mil Police Sch Command, Ft Gordon, Ga, 60-61; NC Nat Guard, 61-67; Capt, Army Res, 67. Mem: Am & NC Bar Asns; Kinston-Lenoir Co CofC (pres); Am Trial Lawyers Asn; Home Builders Asn of Kinston. Honors & Awards: Distinguished Serv Award, Kinston Jaycees, 68 & 70; Grassroots Award, NC Fedn Young Rep, 69, Outstanding Young Rep, 70; Nat Freedom Guard Award, US Jaycees, 72. Relig: Episcopal. Legal Res: 1805 St George Pl Kinston NC 28501 Mailing Add: PO Box 546 Kinston NC 28501

BASHORE, BOYD TRUMAN (INDEPENDENT)
b Washington, DC, June 7, 25; s Wilbur Elsworth Bashore & Mabel Truman B; m 1952 to Judy Campbell; c Brian C, Stephen T, Elizabeth C, Laura L & Charles C. Educ: US Mil Acad, BS, 50. Polit & Govt Pos: Spec asst to US Rep John M Murphy, NY, 73- Mil Serv: Entered as Pvt, Army, 43, released as Col, 71, after serv in various assignments, worldwide; Legion of Merit with Oakleaf Cluster; Bronze Star Medal with V & Two Oakleaf Clusters; Army Commendation Medal. Publ: Various articles on prof or hist mil matters, in prof jour, 43-73. Relig: Protestant. Mailing Add: 6510 Lakeview Dr Falls Church VA 22041

BASILONE, PETER J (D)
Md State Deleg
b Farrell, Pa, May 13, 20; s Joseph Basilone & Josephine Gross B; m 1941 to Theresa K Ladanyi; c Donna (Mrs Roland Willard) & Sandra (Mrs Joseph Spadero). Educ: Dundalk Community Col, 72. Polit & Govt Pos: Asst chief register of wills, Baltimore Co, Md, 69-75; Md State Deleg, 75- Bus & Prof Pos: Owner, Restaurant & Lounge, 46-68. Mil Serv: Entered as Seaman 3/C, Navy, 44, released as Coxswain 45, after serv in USS American Legion, Pac, 44-45. Mem: Mason; Baltimore Co Tavern & Restaurant Asn; Perry Hall Sons of Italy; Kingsville Civic & Dem Club. Mailing Add: 11124 Sheradale Dr Kingsville MD 21087

BASKIN, JEWEL SENN BRELAND (R)
SC State Rep
b Lexington Co, SC; d Eugene Senn & Lessie Lee Jackson S; m to Edward P Breland, wid, July 15, 54; remarried 1958 to Col John S Baskin. Educ: Univ SC; Am Inst of Banking & Financial Pub Rels Sch Northwestern Univ, grad. Polit & Govt Pos: State women's chmn, US Savings Bonds, 60-; SC State Rep, 72- Bus & Prof Pos: Asst cashier & pub rels off, Citizens & Southern Bank of SC, formerly. Mem: Columbia Bus & Prof Women's Club; Credit Women's Breakfast Club; Travel Aid Soc (bd dirs); Columbia CofC; Columbia Area & State League of Women Voters (bd dirs); Altrusa Int. Honors & Awards: First Woman Off, Citizens & Southern Bank of SC. Relig: Episcopal; Mem, Finance Comt & Altar Guild of Women's Orgn, Trinity Episcopal Church, currently. Mailing Add: 6058 Crabtree Rd Columbia SC 29206

BASKIN, WEEMS (R)
SC State Rep
Mailing Add: 2524 Blossom St Columbia SC 29205

BASLER, MARIE LUCILLE (D)
VChmn, Ste Genevieve Co Dem Cent Comt, Mo
b Perryville, Mo, Mar 1, 15; d Henry G Seitz & Marie L McBride S; m 1937 to John J Basler; c John J, Jr, James R, Joseph W, Marie L, Barbara A & Kathleen. Educ: Troy High Sch, Mo, 29-33. Polit & Govt Pos: VChmn, Ste Genevieve Co Dem Cent Comt, Mo, 64- Bus & Prof Pos: Dep recorder of deeds, Ste Genevieve, Mo, 37-42; owner, Old Settlement Title & Abstract Co, 63- Publ: A Tour of Old Ste Genevieve, 75; History of our town, weekly articles, Ste Genevieve Fair Play, 67- Mem: Bus & Prof Womens Club; Ste Genevieve CofC; Found for Restoration of Ste Genevieve. Relig: Catholic. Mailing Add: 50 N Fifth St Ste Genevieve MO 63670

BASMAJIAN, WALTER (D)
Chmn, St Lawrence Co Dem Comt, NY
b Massena, NY, July 22, 22; s John Basmajian (deceased) & Virginia Bochalian B; m 1949 to Marie Billingham; c David W & Gina Marie. Educ: Cent City Bus Inst, 41-42. Polit & Govt Pos: Bldg & zoning inspector, Massena, NY, 56-67; chmn, Massena Dem Comt, 56-; deleg, Dem State Conv, 58-62; deleg, Dem Nat Conv, 64 & 68; former first vchmn, St Lawrence Co Dem Comt, NY, chmn, 68-; deleg, Dem Nat Mid-Term Conf, 74. Bus & Prof Pos: Secy & pres, Massena Bd Trade, 47-48; asst mgr, Seaway Int Bridge Corp, Ltd, 62-65; broker, Basmajian Real Estate, NY, currently; chmn, Massena Neighborhood Ctr, currently; app mem bd educ, Massena Cent Sch Dist, 70- Mil Serv: Entered as Pvt, Army, 43, released as T/5, 46, after serv in 9th Army, 4th Signal Corps, 13th Army Corps, ETO, 44-46; Rhineland-Cent European & African-Mid Eastern Theater Campaign Medals; Good Conduct Medal; Victory Medal; Signal Corps, Army Res, 42-43. Mem: Massena CofC; St Lawrence

Co Community Develop Prog, Inc (dir, 65-); St Lawrence Co Real Estate Bd (pres, 66-); Am Legion; VFW. Honors & Awards: Successful in electing first Dem State Assemblyman in the hist of St Lawrence Co, 70. Relig: Protestant. Legal Res: 10 Sherwood Dr Massena NY 13662 Mailing Add: 183 Main St Massena NY 13662

BASS, HARVEY LEE (D)
Chmn, Bailey Co Dem Party, Tex
b Anson, Tex, Oct 11, 18; s Henry Isom Bass & Mary Evaline Jones B; m 1946 to Willie Marie Bingham; c Carolia Marie & Vina Jeanette. Educ: Meadow High, Meadow, Tex; Correspondence course, Univ Tex. Polit & Govt Pos: Chmn, Bailey Co Dem Party, Tex, 56- Bus & Prof Pos: Co-owner & ed, Aspermont Star, Tex, 46-47; chmn retail activities, CofC, 66, chmn bus activities comt bd, 68-70; West Plains Mus Bd & West Plains Mem Hosp Bd, 68- Publ: Primitive Baptist doctrine: banner of love, 48. Mem: Rotary. Relig: Primitive Baptist. Legal Res: 1903 Ave D Muleshoe TX 79347 Mailing Add: PO Box 488 Muleshoe TX 79347

BASS, HERBERT EDWARD (R)
Chmn, Chowan Co Rep Exec Comt, NC
b Edenton, NC, Feb 19, 20; s Herbert V Bass & Artie White B; m 1944 to Lola Allan; c William E, James H & Robert L. Educ: US Air Force Inst Technol, US Air Force Command & Staff Sch; Debating Soc. Polit & Govt Pos: Chmn, Chowan Co Rep Exec Comt, NC, 64- Bus & Prof Pos: Partner, Bass Bros Sunoco Sta, 62-65. Mil Serv: Entered as Pvt, Army, 40, released as Lt Col(Ret), Air Force, 62, after serv in Asiatic Pac Theater & Korea; Soldiers Medal; Bronze Star; Commendation Ribbon; Am & Asiatic Pac Theater Ribbons; Am Defense & Victory Medals; Korean Serv Medal; UN Serv Ribbon; Japanese Occup Medal; Nat Defense Serv Ribbon; Guided Missile Insignia. Mem: Rotary; VFW; Boy Scouts; CofC. Honors & Awards: Silver Beaver Award, Boy Scouts. Relig: Baptist. Mailing Add: W Queen St Extended PO Box 175 Edenton NC 27932

BASS, PERKINS (R)
b East Walpole, Mass, Oct 6, 12; s Robert Perkins Bass & Edith Bird B; m 1941 to Katharine Jackson, wid; c Alexander, Katharine, William J, Charles F & Roberta. Educ: Dartmouth Col, BA, 34; Harvard Univ, LLB, 38. Polit & Govt Pos: NH State Rep, 39-43 & 47-49; pres, NH State Senate, 49-51; US Rep, NH, formerly; mem, Rep Nat Comt, NH, 64-68; mem, Nat Adv Comt Oceans & Atmosphere, 73- Bus & Prof Pos: Lawyer; dir & mem exec comn, Bird & Son, Inc; trustee, NH Savings Bank, Concord; mem firm, Sheehan Phinney, Bass & Green, 46- Mailing Add: Box 210 Peterborough NH 03458

BASS, ROBERT P, JR (R)
Rep Nat Committeeman, NH
b Peterborough, NH, Sept 23, 23; s Robert P Bass & Edith H Bird B; m 1955 to Patricia May; c Timothy P & Kate P. Educ: Harvard Col, BA, 48, Law Sch, LLB, 51. Polit & Govt Pos: Finance chmn, NH Rep State Comt, 67-68, chmn, 69-71; Rep Nat Committeeman, NH, 70-; deleg, Rep Nat Conv, 72. Bus & Prof Pos: Partner, Cleveland, Waters & Bass, Lawyers, Concord, NH, 60-; dir & mem exec comn, Bird & Son, Inc, East Walpole, Mass, 62- Mil Serv: Entered as Pvt, Army, 42, released as 1st Lt, 46, after serv in 25th Inf Div, Far East Theatre, 45-46. Mem: Coun on Foreign Rels; NH Charitable Fund (distributing dir, 71-); Soc for Protection of NH Forests (dir, 71-). Relig: Protestant. Mailing Add: 16 Centre St Concord NH 03301

BASS, ROSS (D)
b Giles Co, Tenn, Mar 17, 18; s W A Bass (deceased) & Ethel Shook B; div. Educ: Martin Col, Tenn. Polit & Govt Pos: Postmaster, Pulaski, Tenn, 48-54; US Rep, Tenn, 54-64; US Sen, Tenn, 64-67. Bus & Prof Pos: Owner, Ross Bass Assocs, Washington, DC, 67- Mil Serv: Entered as Pvt, Army Air Corps, released as Capt, after serv in 8th Air Force, ETO. Mem: Tenn Asn of Postmasters (pres); CofC; Am Legion; VFW; Elks. Relig: Methodist. Legal Res: 124 Cedar Lane Pulaski TN 38478 Mailing Add: 4000 Massachusetts Ave NW Washington DC 20016

BASSETT, TIMOTHY ARTHUR (D)
Mass State Rep
b Lynn, Mass, Dec 16, 47; s Arthur Bassett & Marguerite Crowley B; married. Educ: St Mary's Boys' High Sch, Lynn, Mass, 65; Mass State Col Salem, BS, 69; Univ NH, Dept Pub Admin, 69-70. Polit & Govt Pos: Deleg, Dem Nat Conv, 72; Mass State Rep, 73- Bus & Prof Pos: Teacher, Lynn Pub Sch Syst, Mass, 70-71; teacher govt, econ & law, St Mary's High Sch, Lynn, 71-72. Mem: Mass Citizens for Participation Polit; Am for Dem Action. Relig: Roman Catholic. Legal Res: 99 Marianna St Lynn MA 01902 Mailing Add: Rm 342 State House Boston MA 02133

BATCHELDER, ANNE (R)
Chmn, Nebr Rep State Cent Comt
Mailing Add: 212 Anderson Bldg Lincoln NE 68508

BATCHELDER, MERTON K (R)
Chmn, Rep Town Comt, Conway, Mass
b Conway, Mass, May 19, 21; s Carlos F Batchelder & Lillian Schneck B; m 1955 to Eleanor A Sears; c William K & Edward D. Educ: Arms Acad, 39. Polit & Govt Pos: Mem finance comt, Conway, Mass, 55-60, selectman, 60-63; deleg, Mass Rep State Conv, 60-66; chmn, Rep Town Comt, Conway, currently, moderator, 65- Bus & Prof Pos: Agt, Union Nat Bank, New Eng & New York and Wholesale Distributor, Dairy Equip, 56-66. Mem: Morning Sun Lodge; Mason; Community Develop Orgn. Relig: Protestant. Mailing Add: New Hall Rd Conway MA 01341

BATCHELDER, WILLIAM GEORGE (R)
Ohio State Rep
b Medina, Ohio, Dec 19, 42; s William George Batchelder, Jr & Eleanor Dice B; m 1966 to Alice Moore. Educ: Ohio Wesleyan Univ, BA, 64; Ohio State Univ Col Law, JD, 67; Omicron Delta Kappa; Phi Alpha Theta; Delta Sigma Rho. Polit & Govt Pos: Admin aide to Lt Gov John W Brown, Ohio, 67; Ohio State Rep, 23rd Dist, 69- Bus & Prof Pos: Assoc attorney, Williams & Batchelder, Medina, 67- Mil Serv: Entered as Pvt, Army, 68, released as Pfc, 68, after serv in Hq, Third Army, Judge Adv Gen Off, 68. Mem: F&AM; Royal Arch Mason; Jaycees; Young Rep; Am Legion. Relig: Episcopal. Mailing Add: 435 E Smith Rd Medina OH 44256

BATCHELOR, DICK J (D)
Fla State Rep
b Fort Bragg, NC, Dec 12, 47; s Garland Woodrow Batchelor & Bessie M Sasser B; single. Educ: Valencia Community Col, AA, 70; Fla Technol Univ, BA, polit sci, 71; Delta Beta Pi. Polit & Govt Pos: Fla State Rep, 74- Bus & Prof Pos: Pub rels & advert. Mil Serv: Entered as E-1, Marine Corps, 66, released as E-4, 68, after serv in H&MS, Vietnam, 67-68; Meritorious Mast. Mem: Jaycees; CofC; Fla Technol Univ Alumni. Honors & Awards: One of top five students, Valencia Community Col. Relig: Baptist. Legal Res: 524 N John St Orlando FL 32808 Mailing Add: PO Box 67 Orlando FL 32802

BATCHELOR, NORMAN FREDERICK (R)
Chmn, Orange Rep Town Comt, Mass
b Orange, Mass, May 8, 22; s Frederick George Batchelor (deceased) & Emily Tortensen B; m 1947 to Carolyn Marie Venette. Educ: St Petersburg, Fla High Sch, grad, 40. Polit & Govt Pos: Selectman, Orange, Mass, 55-58, mem sch comt, 60-65; dep sheriff, Franklin Co, formerly, spec sheriff, currently; chmn, Orange Rep Town Comt, Mass, 61- Bus & Prof Pos: Trustee, Orange Savings Bank, Mass, 60-; dir, Franklin Co Trust Co, Greenfield, Mass, 64-; trustee & mem exec comt, Ahol Mem Hosp, 70- Mil Serv: Entered as Pvt, Air Force, 43, released as Cpl, 45, after serv in 487th Bomb Group, ETO, 44-45; Am Theatre Ribbon, Europe-African-Mid East Ribbon; Good Conduct Medal; World War II Victory Medal. Mem: Am Legion; Kiwanis. Relig: Protestant. Legal Res: 40 Wheeler Ave Orange MA 01364 Mailing Add: PO Box 147 Orange MA 01364

BATDORF, DAVID JONATHAN (D)
Chmn, Berks Co Dem Comt, Pa
b West Reading, Pa, Mar 3, 27; s Jonathan P Batdorf & Elsie L Lechner B; m 1952 to Carol J Spangenburg; c David Jefferson, Jonathan Bright & Rebecca Ann. Educ: Wesleyan Univ, BA, 51; Univ Tenn, LLD, 54; Sigma Chi. Polit & Govt Pos: Pres, Berks Co Young Dem, Pa, 56-58; campaign chmn, Gov David Lawrence, Berks Co, 58; register of wills solicitor, Reading, 58-62; deleg, Dem Nat Conv, 60; committeeman, Wyomissing Borough, 62-; campaign mgr, Gov Milton J Shapp, 66, 70 & 74; campaign mgr, Mayor Victor Yarnell, Reading, 67; city solicitor, Reading, 68-72; mem, Berks Co Dem Exec Bd, 72-74; chief counsel revenue, Pa, 73-; chmn, Berks Co Dem Comt, 74- Bus & Prof Pos: Pvt law practice, 54-; pres, Rosedorf Realty Co, Reading, Pa, 63-; mem bd dirs, Graphic & Commercial Arts, Reading, 63- Mil Serv: Entered as Pvt, Army, 45, released as T/Sgt, after serv in Ger, 45-46. Mem: Endlich Law Club; Am Legion; Grange. Honors & Awards: Man of Year, Reading Jr CofC, 62; Man of Year, Pa Jr CofC, 62; Silver Beaver Award, Boy Scouts, 68, Shikellamy Camp Award, 69; Lamb Award, Lutheran Church Am, 70. Relig: Lutheran. Mailing Add: 1531 Rose Virginia Rd Wyomissing PA 19610

BATE, WILLIAM JOSEPH (D)
NJ State Sen
b Passaic, NJ, Apr 10, 34; s William Warren Bate & Winifred Irene King B; m 1962 to Clara Estrella; c William Edwin & Robert Benedict. Educ: St Peter's Col (NJ), AB cum laude, 55; Georgetown Law Ctr, JD, 58; Rutgers Univ, currently; Order of the Peacock; Gannon Debating Soc; St Thomas More Polit Sci Forum. Polit & Govt Pos: Legis asst to US Rep Charles S Joelson, NJ, 61-66; councilman, City of Clifton, NJ, 66-69; freeholder, Passaic Co, 69-71, dir, 71; NJ State Sen, 72-; deleg, Dem Nat Mid-Term Conf, 74. Mem: NJ State & Passaic Co Bar Asns; Boy Scouts (chmn, Passaic Valley Coun, Clifton-Garfield Dist, 67-); Soc of Friendly Sons of St Patrick (treas, Passaic-Clifton); KofC; St Andrew's Parish Coun (vpres); Elks. Honors & Awards: Outstanding Citizen Award, Clifton Leader, 66 & 71. Relig: Roman Catholic. Legal Res: 45 Summit Rd Clifton NJ 07012 Mailing Add: 970 Clifton Ave Clifton NJ 07013

BATEMAN, HERBERT HARVELL (D)
Va State Sen
b Elizabeth City, NC, Aug 7, 28; s Elbert E Bateman & Edna Buffkin B; m 1954 to Laura Ann Yacobi; c Herbert H, Jr & Laura Margaret. Educ: Col William & Mary, BA, 49; Georgetown Univ Law Ctr, LLB, 56; Omicron Delta Kappa; Pi Kappa Alpha. Polit & Govt Pos: Va State Sen, 68-; mem, Peninsula Ports Authority Va, 68-, Study Comn Va Judicial Syst, 68-, Study Comn Pub Sch Fund Allocation Formula, 68- & chmn, Consumer Credit Study Comn, 70- Bus & Prof Pos: Partner, Jones, Blechman, Woltz & Kelly, Attorneys-at-law, 64- Mil Serv: Entered as Airman, Air Force, 51, released as 1st Lt, 53, after serv in Off Spec Invest. Mem: Am Judicature Soc; Am Legion; Torch Club of Hampton Roads; US Jr CofC; Va Jr CofC. Honors & Awards: Distinguished Serv Award, Hampton Roads Jaycees. Relig: Protestant. Legal Res: 223 Shoe Lane Newport News VA 23609 Mailing Add: PO Box 78 Newport News VA 23607

BATEMAN, RAYMOND HENRY (R)
NJ State Sen
b Somerville, NJ, Oct 29, 27; s Charles Palmer Bateman, Sr & Lydia Coene B; m 1953 to Joan Speer; c Caren Palmer, Raymond, Jr, Christopher Speer & Michael Luther. Educ: Wesleyan Univ, BA, 50; Woodrow Wilson Sch of Pub & Int Affairs, Princeton, grad work, 50-51; Delta Kappa Epsilon. Polit & Govt Pos: NJ State Assemblyman, Somerset Co, 58-68, Asst Majority Leader, NJ State Assembly, 64, Majority Leader, 65-68; mem bd Eagleton Inst Seminar for Young Legislators, 66; deleg Rep Nat Conv, 68 & 72; NJ State Sen, 68-, Majority Leader, NJ State Senate, 69-, Sen Pres, 70-72, Sen Pres Pro-Tem, 73- Bus & Prof Pos: Pres, Bateman & Assocs, Pub Rels & Advert, 58-; former pres, Midland Sch for Brain Injured Children; mem bd, Somerset Trust Co, Somerset Press, Inc & Cent Jersey Press, Inc. Mil Serv: Entered as Pvt, Army, 46, released as S/Sgt, 47, after serv in 8th Army, Japan. Publ: How to Lose an Election, NY Times Mag, 10/62. Relig: Dutch Reformed. Mailing Add: 102 Lamington Rd Somerville NJ 08876

BATES, LARRY (D)
Tenn State Rep
b Childersburg, Ala, Aug 18, 44; s Edward Bates & Inez Agee B; m 1967 to Barbara Ann Bearden; c Charles Edward. Educ: Springfield High Sch, Tenn, 58-62; Univ Tenn, BS, 67; Alpha Gamma Rho; pres student body, Univ Tenn, 2 years. Polit & Govt Pos: Tenn State Rep, Henry, Lake, Obion & Weakley Co, 70- Bus & Prof Pos: Pres, Financial Planners, Inc, Martin, Tenn, 67-; chmn & chief exec off, Reelfoot Bank, Union City Hornbeak, 71-; mem bd dirs, Northwest Tenn Ment Health Ctr, Inc. Mem: Nat Life Underwriters Asn; Int Platform Asn; Easter Seal Ctr for Handicapped (bd dirs, 72-); Mason, Scottish Rite, Alchgma Temple; Univ Tenn Nat Alumni Asn (mem bd gov & nat chmn annual giving). Honors & Awards: Outstanding Male Student Award, Univ Tenn, Martin, 65, twice elected, Mr Volunteer & Most Outstanding Male Student Award. Relig: Baptist. Legal Res: Glenwood Dr Martin TN 38237 Mailing Add: PO Box 308 Union City TN 38261

52 / BATES

BATES, STURGIS GOODWIN, III (D)
Mem Exec Comt, Ga Dem Party
b Ashland, Ky, June 3, 37; s Sturgis Goodwin Bates, Jr & Maynor McWilliams B; m 1963 to Carol Garrison; c Cynthia, Mary Elizabeth, Carol & Meredith. Educ: Emory Univ, 55-60, JD, 67; Shorter Col, BA, 64; Phi Alpha Delta; Alpha Psi Omega; Tau Kappa Alpha; Beta Theta Pi. Polit & Govt Pos: Mem, Dekalb Co Dem Exec Comt, Ga, 69-; mem exec comt, Ga Dem Party, 74-; mem, Dekalb Co Airport Adv Bd, 75- Bus & Prof Pos: Attorney, Fine & Block, 67- Mil Serv: Entered as Aviation Cadet, Air Force, 58, released, 64. Mem: Am Judicature Soc; Am, Ga & Atlanta Bar Asns. Relig: Methodist. Legal Res: 1622 Montcliff Ct Decatur GA 30033 Mailing Add: Suite 1905 100 Colony Sq Atlanta GA 30361

BATHE, JOHN RAYMOND (R)
b Los Angeles, Calif, Jan 8, 45; s Ernest Otto Bathe & Lora Gertrude B; single. Educ: Calif State Univ, Fullerton, BBA, 71; Southwestern Univ (Calif, Sch Law, 71-; Delta Theta Phi. Polit & Govt Pos: Deleg, Rep Nat Conv, 72. Bus & Prof Pos: Founding partner, Legal Libr & Research Serv, 68-73; exec secy-treas, United Student Asn of Am, Inc, 70-71. Mil Serv: Navy. Mem: Am Bar Asn; Calif Attorney Gen Vol Adv Coun; Town Hall of Calif; Asn Environ Prof. Relig: Agnostic. Mailing Add: 195 Blossom Hill Rd 127 San Jose CA 95123

BATISTA MONTANEZ, ARMANDO (NEW PROGRESSIVE, PR)
Rep, PR House of Rep
Mailing Add: State Capitol San Juan PR 00901

BATJER, CAMERON MCVICAR (R)
Justice, Nev Supreme Court
b Smith, Nev, Aug 24, 19; s Robert W Batjer & Mary Belle McVicar B; m 1942 to Lura Gamble; c Lura, Christina & Marybel. Educ: Univ Nev, BA, 41; Univ Utah, JD, 50; Phi Alpha Delta; Lambda Chi Alpha. Polit & Govt Pos: Dist attorney, Ormsby Co, Nev, 54-60; city attorney, Carson City, Nev, 54-60, Justice, Nev Supreme Court, 67- Mil Serv: Entered as Seaman 2/C, Navy, 42, released as Lt(jg), 45, after serv in SPac, 43-44; Naval Res, Lt(Ret). Mem: Am, Utah & Nev Bar Asns; Am Judicature Soc; Elks. Relig: Presbyterian. Mailing Add: 7 Circle Dr Carson City NV 89701

BATT, DAVID L (D)
b Houston, Tex, Oct 22, 34; s William M Batt, Sr & Mary Pearl Fisher B; m 1963 to Joyce Evelyn Dickson; c Michael David & Jeffrey Alan. Educ: La Tech Univ, BS in bus admin, 56; George Washington Univ, 63-65; Kappa Alpha. Polit & Govt Pos: Admin asst to US Rep Joe D Waggonner, La, 62- Mil Serv: Entered as 2nd Lt, Air Force, 56, released as 1st Lt, 59. Relig: Methodist. Legal Res: 1218 Oden St Shreveport LA 71104 Mailing Add: 2310 Candlewood Dr Alexandria VA 22308

BATT, PHILLIP E (R)
Idaho State Sen
Mailing Add: Box 428 Wilder ID 83676

BATTAGLIA, BASIL RICHARD (R)
Chmn, Wilmington Rep City Exec Comt, Del
b Wilmington, Del, Oct 28, 35; s Bruno Battaglia & Carmella Cannatelli B; m 1965 to Elisabeth J King; c Lisa Maria & Michael Basil. Educ: LaSalle Col, AB in polit sci, 59; Mt Vernon Sch Law, LLB, 63. Polit & Govt Pos: Chmn, Rep Eighth Councilmanic Dist, Wilmington, Del; mem, Mayor's Citizens Adv Comt Urban Renewal; vpres, Del Fedn Young Rep; mem bd dirs, Active Young Rep of Wilmington; mem, Rep City Educ Comt; chmn, Rep Fund Raising Dinners; registr in chancery, New Castle Co, 68-; chmn, Wilmington Rep City Exec Comt, 69- Mem: Nat Asn Co Officers; Toys for Tots Comt; Wilmington Jaycees; Univ & Whist Club; St Anthony's Cath Club. Honors & Awards: Outstanding Young Rep, Wilmington, 69; Outstanding Young Rep, Del, 69; Outstanding Young Man of the Year, Wilmington Jaycees, 69. Relig: Roman Catholic. Mailing Add: 2307 Willard St Wilmington DE 19806

BATTAGLIA, EDNA MAE (D)
Committeewoman, NY State Dem Comt
b Toronto, Ont, Jan 24, 21; d Edward John Curtis & Edith Mary Turley C; m 1942 to Anthony Vincent Battaglia; c Barbara (Mrs Stephen Carter), Bruce & Kathleen (Mrs Adrian Schiess, Jr). Educ: Niagara Co Community Col, 64-65. Polit & Govt Pos: Mem, Niagara Falls Scenic Protective Comt, NY, 63-; mem, Niagara Falls Tourist Agency Rev Bd, 63-; committeewoman, Niagara Co Dem Comt, 64-; mem, Niagara Falls Budget Comn, 65; deleg, Dem Nat Conv, 72; mem, Niagara Co Dem Exec Bd, 72-; committeewoman, NY State Dem Comt, 72- Relig: Roman Catholic. Mailing Add: 1707 N Ave Niagara Falls NY 14305

BATTEEN, DENNIS JOHN (R)
Chmn, Faulk Co Rep Party, SDak
b Aberdeen, SDak, Mar 14, 42; s John C Batteen & Dorothy Perry B; m 1965 to Linda Kay Peterson; c Jana Lynne. Educ: Univ SDak, JD; Phi Alpha Theta; Delta Tau Delta. Polit & Govt Pos: States attorney, Faulk Co SDak, 69-; chmn, Faulk Co Rep Party, 70- Mem: SDak & Am Bar Asns; SDak States Attorneys Asn; Mason; Scottish Rite. Relig: Methodist. Mailing Add: Box 237 Faulkton SD 57438

BATTISTA, VITO PIRANESI (R)
Rep State Committeeman, NY
b Bari, Italy, Sept 7, 09; s Vincenzo Battista & Sabina Caputo B; m 1941 to Josephine Palermo; c Sabina (Mrs John Anselmo) & Vincent Charles. Educ: Carnegie Inst Tech, BArch; Mass Inst Tech, MofArch; Ecole de Beaux Arts, Fontainebleau, France; Beaux Arts Inst Columbia Univ; Alpha Phi Delta. Polit & Govt Pos: NY State Assemblyman, 38th Assembly Dist, Kings Co, 68-74; Rep State Committeeman, NY, 70-; chmn, United Taxpayers Party, currently; deleg, Rep Nat Conv, 72. Bus & Prof Pos: Archit designer, NY World's Fair 1939, Inc, 36-37; archit, New York Dept of Pub Works, 37-43, Henry V Murphy, 41-47 & Vito Battista & Assoc, 47-; dir & founder, Inst Design & Construction, 47- Mil Serv: Nat Guard, Engr Corps, 44-46, 1st Lt. Mem: Am Inst Architects; NY Soc architects (dir); NY State Asn Architects (dir); Kiwanis; Unico Nat Hornbostel Prize; Am Inst Architects Prize; MIT Prize. Relig: Roman Catholic. Legal Res: 290 Highland Blvd Brooklyn NY 11207 Mailing Add: 141 Willoughby St Brooklyn NY 11201

BATTLE, JOE (D)
Ga State Rep
Mailing Add: 2308 Ranchland Dr Savannah GA 31404

BATTLE, LUCIUS D (D)
b Georgia, June 1, 18; married. Educ: Univ Fla, BA, 39, LLB, 46. Polit & Govt Pos: Mem staff, War Dept, 42-43; Dept State Positions, 46-51; Spec Asst to Secy of State, 49-53 & 61-62; first secy, Copenhagen, 54-55; first secy, NATO, Paris, 55-62; Asst Secy of State for Educ & Cult Affairs, 62-64; Ambassador to United Arab Repub, 64-67; Asst Secy, Near Eastern & SAsian Affairs, Dept State, 67-68. Bus & Prof Pos: Mgr, student staff, Univ Fla, 40-42; vpres, Colonial Williamsburg, 56-61; vpres corp rels, Commun Satellite Corp, 68-73; sr vpres corp affairs, 74-; pres, Mid East Inst, 73-74. Mil Serv: Lt, Navy, 43-46. Mailing Add: 3200 Garfield NW Washington DC 20008

BATTLE, WILLIAM CULLEN (D)
b Charlottesville, Va, Oct 9, 20; s John Stewart Battle & Mary Jane Lipscomb B; m 1953 to Frances Barry Webb; c William Cullen, Robert Webb & Jane Tavernor. Educ: Univ Va, BA, 41; LLB, 47. Polit & Govt Pos: US Ambassador to Australia, 62-64; mem, State Dept Adv Panel Int Law & Foreign Policy, 66-68; Dem nominee for Gov, Va, 69. Bus & Prof Pos: Predecessor law firm, McGuire, Woods & Battle, Charlottesville & Richmond, Va, mem, 64-71; bd dirs, Va Nat Bank, currently; mem policy bd, US Power Tool Group, Black & Decker Mfg Co; dir, Am Textile Mfrs Inst; trustee, Inst Textile Technol; dir, Texfi Industs, Inc; pres & chief exec officer, Fieldcrest Mills, Inc, Eden, NC, 71- Mil Serv: Naval Res, Lt(sg), 41-45; Silver Star. Mem: Va Bar Asn; NC Textile Mfrs Asn (dir); Conf Bd; Charlottesville-Albermarle Co Community Chest (chmn budget comn); Salvation Army (Va adv bd). Relig: Baptist. Legal Res: PO Box 146 Ivy VA 22945 Mailing Add: Fieldcrest Mills Inc Eden NC 27288

BATTY, BYRON A (R)
Chmn, Warwick Rep City Comt, RI
b Attleboro, Mass, Mar 24, 41; s Arthur E Batty, Jr & Inez Blanchard B; m to Carol Louise Drolette; c Lisa Ann & Robert Byron. Educ: Wentworth Inst, EEE, 61. Polit & Govt Pos: Chmn, Warwick Rep City Comt, RI, 75- Bus & Prof Pos: Inspector, Otis Elevator Co, 61- Mem: Int Union Elevator Constructors; F&AM. Relig: Baptist. Mailing Add: 184 Mill Cove Rd Warwick RI 02889

BAUCUS, MAX (D)
US Rep, Mont
b Helena, Mont, Dec 11, 41; s John Baucus & Jean Sheriff B; single. Educ: Stanford Univ, BA Econ, 64, Law Sch, LLB, 67; SAE. Polit & Govt Pos: Mont State Rep, 72-74; US Rep, Mont, 75-, mem, Mont House Judiciary, Fish & Game & Finance & Claims Comts, vchmn, Finance & Claims Sub-Comt for State Inst, US House Rep, 75- Bus & Prof Pos: Staff attorney, Civil Aeronaut Bd, 67-69 & Securities & Exchange Comn, 69-71; legal asst to chmn, Securities & Exchange Comn, 70-71; attorney-at-law, George & Baucus, Missoula, Mont, 71-75. Mem: Mont & DC Bar Asns. Relig: Christian. Legal Res: 600 Cherry St Missoula MT 59801 Mailing Add: US House Rep Washington DC 20515

BAUER, ALBERT N, JR (D)
Wash State Rep
b Lewistown, Mont, June 6, 28; s Albert Bauer & Florence C Hooper B; m 1953 to Patricia Ellen McQueen; c Jerry Sue, James Allyn & Nancy Ellyn. Educ: Clark Col, 48 & 54-55; Portland State Col, BS, 57; Ore State Col, MEd, 59. Polit & Govt Pos: Dem precinct committeeman, Clark Co, 68-70; Wash State Rep, 17th Legis Dist, 71- Mil Serv: Entered as Seaman Recruit, Navy, 48, released as BM 1/C, 54, after serv in USS LSM 236 & USS Noble 218, Pac & Korea, 52-53; Good Conduct Medal; UN Medal; Korean Serv Medal. Mem: Wash Educ Asn; Vancouver Educ Asn; Am Legion; Wash-Ore Farmers Union; Salmon Creek Community Club. Relig: Methodist. Mailing Add: 13611 NE 20th Ave Vancouver WA 98665

BAUER, ARMAND W (D)
Treas, Sauk Co Dem Party, Wis
b Knowles, Wis, Mar 2, 00; s Frank S Bauer & Anna Schmid B; m 1924 to Audrey VandenBrook, wid; c James M, Jean A, D John, Thomas J & Judith C. Educ: River Falls State Univ, BE, 24; Univ Minn, 27; 3L Club; Agrifallian (pres, 23); Newman Club (pres, 24). Polit & Govt Pos: Co chmn, Stevenson for President Campaign, 52; treas, Sauk Co Dem Party, Wis, 66-69 & 72-, chmn, 68-72; trustee, Sauk City Village Bd, 70-; state deleg, White House Conf on Aging, 71; Sauk Co Supvr, 31st Dist, 71- Bus & Prof Pos: Teacher agr, Hayward High Sch, Wis, 24-26; teacher Wood Co Agr & Normal Sch, Wisconsin Rapids, 26-33; appraiser & mem loan comt, Fed Land Bank, St Paul, 34-35; fieldman & appraiser, Union Trust Co, Madison, Wis, 35-36; territory mgr, Madison Br, Allis Chalmers Mfg Co, 37-65; mem, Wis Realtors, 65-; dir, Sauk City Indust Corp; treas, Sauk-Prairie Indust Develop Corp. Mil Serv: Pvt 1/C, Nat Guard, 19/24. Mem: Black Hawk Coun 1099, KofC; Kiwanis; Sauk City Mens Club; Sauk Co Hist Soc; Four Lakes Boy Scout Coun. Relig: Catholic. Mailing Add: 716 Dallas St Sauk City WI 53583

BAUER, BURNETT CALIX (D)
Ind State Sen
b Underwood, NDak, July 23, 16; s Calix F Bauer & Theresa Reuter B; m 1941 to Helene Cryan; c Elizabeth Ann, Burnett Patrick, Teresa, Margaret, Barbara, Matthew, Bernadette, Mary Frances & Brenda. Educ: Univ Notre Dame, PhB in Com, 38 & MA, 44. Polit & Govt Pos: Ind State Rep, 64-70; Ind State Sen, 72- Bus & Prof Pos: Ed, Red Ball Mag, US Rubber Co, Mishawaka, Ind, 46-49; owner & founder, Lindsay Soft Water Co, South Bend, Ind, 50-; pres & founder, Bauer Distributing Co, 61- Mil Serv: Entered as Pvt, Marine Res, 36, released as 2nd Lt, 39. Publ: Blueprint for Catholic Family Action, Ave Maria Press, Notre Dame, 50. Mem: Lions; KofC; Izaak Walton League; Serra Club; South Bend-Mishawaka CofC. Relig: Catholic. Legal Res: 1010 Hudson Ave South Bend IN 46616 Mailing Add: 1139 Western Ave South Bend IN 46625

BAUER, BURNETT PATRICK (D)
Ind State Rep
b La Porte, Ind, May 25, 44; s Burnett Calix Bauer & Helene Cryan B; single. Educ: St Joseph High Sch, Ind, 62; Univ Notre Dame, BA, 66; Miami Univ Law Sch, 66-68. Polit & Govt Pos: Ind State Rep, formerly; chmn pub health & environ affairs comt, Ind House Rep, 74-, Bus & Prof Pos: Teacher, Muessel Jr High Sch, South Bend, Ind, 68-74; teacher, Madison Jr High Sch, 74- Relig: Roman Catholic. Mailing Add: 1139 Western Ave South Bend IN 46625

BAUER, CARL W (D)
La State Sen
Mailing Add: Hwy 90 E Franklin LA 70538

BAUER, LOIS DARLENE (R)
Secy, Power Co Rep Comt, Idaho
b Long Beach, Calif, Jan 17, 38; d William Thomas Saathoff & Bertha Kasworm S; m 1957 to Richard Lueking Bauer; c Barbara Lois, James Richard & Daniel Eugene. Educ: South High Sch, Salt Lake City, Utah, grad, 56. Polit & Govt Pos: Chmn, Power Co Rep Women, Idaho, 70-; mem & secy, Power Co Airport Bd, 71-; city councilman, American Falls, 72-; secy, Power Co Rep Comt, Idaho, currently. Bus & Prof Pos: Bookkeeper, Bauer Chevrolet, 64-66. Mem: Ninety-Nines, Inc; Beta Sigma Phi; Power Co 4-H Adv Bd; Toastmistress. Honors & Awards: First Lady, American Falls, 74. Relig: Lutheran. Mailing Add: 512 W Park Ave American Falls ID 83211

BAUER, RICHARD L (R)
Secy, Idaho State Rep Party
b Lehi, Utah, May 20, 34; s Benjamen Bauer & Sophia Lucking B; m 1957 to Lois Saathoff; c Barbara, James & Daniel. Educ: Westminster Col, Utah, 4 years. Polit & Govt Pos: Rep precinct committeeman, Power Co, Idaho, 64-67; finance chmn, Power Co Rep Party, 64, chmn, 68-; chmn, Legis Dist 26, Rep Party, 66-68; alt deleg, Rep Nat Conv, 68; vchmn, Idaho State Bd of Aeronaut, formerly, mem & chmn, 72-74; secy, Idaho State Rep Party, 72-, mem exec comt, currently. Bus & Prof Pos: Partner, Gateway Motor Co, Salt Lake City, Utah, 57-63; pres & gen mgr, Bauer Chevrolet Co, Am Falls, Idaho, 63- Mil Serv: Entered as Pvt, Army, 54, released as Sgt, 56, after serv in Corps of Engrs, European Theatre, Ger, 54-56. Mem: AF&AM; Power Co Hist Soc; Power Co Bicentennial Comt; Idaho Hist Soc; Am Legion. Relig: Lutheran. Mailing Add: 512 W Park Ave American Falls ID 83211

BAUGH, JAMES EMORY (D)
Mem, Ga State Dem Exec Comt,
b Milledgeville, Ga, May 19, 20; s Wyatt E Baugh & Lillia Evelyn Womble B; m to Betty George Clark; c Patricia Ann. Educ: Ga Mil Col, dipl, 39; Ga Col Milledgeville, BS in Pre-Med, 41; Uni Ga, AB, 42; Theta Kappa Psi. Polit & Govt Pos: Chmn, Baldwin Co Dem Party, formerly; chmn, Baldwin Co Dem Exec Comt, Ga, formerly; mem, Ga State Dem Exec Comt, 25th State Sen Dist, 71-; mem, Rules Comt to select deleg to Nat Dem Conv, 72. Bus & Prof Pos: Chief staff, Baldwin Co Hosp, 60-61; mem bd trustees, Ga Mil Col, Milledgeville, currently. Mil Serv: Entered as 2nd Lt, Army, 42, released as 1st Lt, 46, after serv in 82nd Airborne Div, World War II, throughout all campaigns of that div from Casablanca to Berlin; Presidential Unit Citation; Five Combat Stars; Two Arrowhead Insignia indicating Beachhead & Airborne Landings; Purple Heart. Mem: State & Dist Med Socs; Baldwin Co Med Soc; Mason; Shrine. Honors & Awards: Recipient of good citizenship award. Relig: Protestant. Mailing Add: Carrington Woods Milledgeville GA 31061

BAUGH, WILBUR E (D)
Ga State Rep
Mailing Add: Box 926 Gordon Rd Milledgeville GA 31061

BAUGHMAN, ROBERT J (D)
b Louisville, Ky, June 18, 37; s Joseph O Baughman & Sally Hoge B; single. Educ: Univ Louisville, BA, 64, JD, 67; Omicron Delta Kappa; Delta Theta Phi; Alpha Phi Omega. Polit & Govt Pos: Staff attorney, Ky Legis Research Comn, 67-70; mem state exec comt, Ky Young Dem, 67-71; legal counsel, Ky Young Dem, 69-70; admin asst to US Rep, Romano L Mazzoli, 71- Mil Serv: Entered as Pvt, Army, 59, released as Sp/4, 62, after serv in 3rd Inf Div, Kitzingen, Ger, 59-62. Publ: Counsel for indigents, Ky Bar J, 69-70. Mem: Ky & Am Bar Asns. Relig: Methodist. Legal Res: 3703 Nanz Ave Louisville KY 40207 Mailing Add: 1435 Fourth St SW Washington DC 20024

BAUM, ELMER CARL (D)
b Culbertson, Nebr, Sept 15, 13; s Emil Baum & Mary Heldt B; m 1932 to Virginia Kuns; c Cynthia (Mrs Gerhardt) & Alan. Educ: Kansas City Col Osteopathy & Surg, DO, 34; Phi Sigma Gamma. Polit & Govt Pos: Dem chmn, Precinct 229, Austin, Tex, 39-69; secy, State Bd Health, 42-69; chmn, State Dem Exec Comt, 68-72. Mem: Tex Asn Osteopathic Physicians & Surgeons; Kiwanis. Honors & Awards: Gen practitioner of the year. Relig: Methodist. Legal Res: 2510 Wooldridge Dr Austin TX 78703 Mailing Add: 908 Nueces Austin TX 78701

BAUM, GLEN FREDERICK (R)
Chmn, Johnson Co Rep Cent Comt, Nebr
b Tecumseh, Nebr, Feb 11, 29; s Fred W Baum & Mary E Leuenberger B; m 1956 to Mary Lou Wood; c William Charles; Thomas Wayne, Sharon Suzanne & John Dana. Educ: Univ Nebr, BSc in Agr, 51, MSc, 57; Alpha Zeta; Voc Agr Club. Polit & Govt Pos: Precinct committeeman, Johnson Co Rep Cent Comt, Nebr, 66-67, chmn, 68- Bus & Prof Pos: Vpres, Bd Educ Serv Unit Four, 69. Mil Serv: Entered as Pvt, Army, 51, released as Cpl, 53, after serv in Signal Corps, Far East Command, 52-53; Korean Serv Medal; UN Serv Medal. Mem: VFW; Farm Bur. Relig: United Church of Christ. Mailing Add: RR 2 Tecumseh NE 68450

BAUM, SHERRY LISS (D)
b Dearborn, Mich; d Anthony Ralph Sansone & Victoria Selwa S; m 1961 to Morton Alex Baum; c Randall Max & Jason Anthony Liss & Christopher Joseph & Geoffrey Leo Baum. Educ: Univ Calif, Irvine, 1 year, cert in social sci, 69. Polit & Govt Pos: Co-chmn, Robert Kennedy for President, West Orange Co, 68; asst chmn, Orange Co Dem Get-Out-The-Vote Dem Ticket, 68; chmn, Cranston for Senate, West Orange Co, 68; publicity chmn, Marina Dem Club, 68-69, pres, 72-; mem, Dem Women of Orange Co, 68-; secy, Calif Dem State Cent Comt, 32nd Cong Dist, 68-72; alt, Orange Co Dem Comt, 69-; mem, by laws comt, Dem of Southern Calif, 69-; mem, Dem Women of Long Beach, 69-; admin asst, Mayor Seal Beach, 70; mem, Orange Co Steering Comt Cory for Controller, 72; Orange Co campaign coordr, Cathy O'Neill Secy State, 72. Bus & Prof Pos: Pub rels dir, Barbara Sterling Sch of Educ Therapy, Garden Grove, Calif, 69; pub rels consult, Community Assoc, Seal Beach, 70. Mem: Int Platform Asn; Dem Women Orange Co; Huntington Beach-Seal Beach League Women Voters (1st vpres, 75-); Seal Beach Hist Soc. Honors & Awards: Los Angeles Times Woman of the Year Nomination, 70. Relig: Science of Mind. Mailing Add: 815 Catalina Ave Seal Beach CA 90740

BAUMAN, ROBERT EDMUND (R)
US Rep, Md
b Bryn Mawr, Pa, Apr 4, 37; s John Carl Bauman & Florence House B; m 1960 to Carol Gene Dawson; c Edward Carroll, Eugenie Marie, Victoria Anne & James Shields. Educ: Capitol Page Sch, Libr Cong, 55; Georgetown Univ Sch Foreign Serv, BS in int affairs, 59, Law Ctr, JD, 64. Polit & Govt Pos: Page, US House Rep, 53-55; page, US Senate spec sessions, 54 staff, House Judiciary Comt, 55-59; pres, Georgetown Univ Young Rep Club, 59-60; asst minority mgr, House Rep Cloakroom, 59-65, mgr, 65-68; nat chmn, Youth for Nixon, 60; mem bd dirs & past nat chmn, Young Am for Freedom, Inc, 60-66; deleg, Rep Nat Conv, 64, alt deleg, 72; secy & mem bd dirs, Am Conservative Union, 64-71, second vpres, currently; mem nat exec comt, Young Rep Nat Fedn, 65-67; exec dir, Md Citizens for Nixon-Agnew Campaign, 68; Md State Sen, 15th Sen Dist, 71-73; US Rep, Md, 73-; mem, Fed Hosp Coun, Dept of Health, Educ & Welfare, currently. Bus & Prof Pos: Attorney-at-law, 68- Publ: Articles published in Nat Rev, Human Events & New Guard. Mem: Am, Md & Talbot Co Bar Asns; Capitol Hill Club, Washington, DC; Talbot Co YMCA. Honors & Awards: Outstanding Young Am Award, 70. Relig: Roman Catholic. Legal Res: Glebe House RD 5 Easton MD 21601 Mailing Add: House Off Bldg Washington DC 20515

BAUMANN, JAMES L (JIM) (D)
Ohio State Rep
b Columbus, Ohio, May 2, 31; s Herman E Baumann & Catherine Haley B; m 1955 to Ann Dougherty; c Matt, Dave, Meg, Lisa, Jim & Steve. Educ: St Charles Col, BA, 53; Ohio State Univ, 66. Polit & Govt Pos: Mem, Columbus City Coun, 65-69; Ohio State Rep, Dist, 60, 70-72 & Dist 32, 72- Bus & Prof Pos: Gen mgr of plumbing partnership, 60- Mil Serv: Army, 54-56. Mem: Columbus CofC; Fraternal Order of Police Assoc; Urban League; Sertoma Club; KofC. Relig: Catholic. Legal Res: 1434 Lonsdale Rd Columbus OH 43227 Mailing Add: 995 Thurman Ave Columbus OH 43206

BAUMGART, MERLE DAVID (D)
b Buffalo, NY, Sept 18, 34; s Dewey F Baumgart & Borghild Quarum B; m 1955 to Beverly J Young; c Martin Dewey & Kirsten Rachel. Educ: Portland State Col, BA, 59; George Washington Univ, MA, 61, study, 61-64. Polit & Govt Pos: Staff mem, Sen Maurine B Neuberger, 61-63; dist leader, Washington, DC Dem Party, 64-68; admin asst to US Rep Peter W Rodino, 66-73. Bus & Prof Pos: Lectr hist, George Washington Univ, 62-64; instr hist, DC Teachers Col, 63-66. Mil Serv: Entered as Pvt, Army, 53, released as Sgt, 56, after serv in Army Mobile Surg Hosp, Seventh Army, ETO, 54-56. Mem: Am Hist Asn; Am Bankers Asn (fed legis rep, 74-); Friendship House, Washington, DC (bd trustees). Relig: Protestant. Mailing Add: 120 Fifth St NE Washington DC 20002

BAUMGARTNER, RENA V (D)
Chmn, Monroe Co Dem Comt, Pa
b Effort, Pa, Dec 26, 34; d Renie Valentine Kresge & Elsie Viola Parks K; m 1959 to William Henry Baumgartner; c Bryan William & Robin Renee. Educ: Polk Twp High Sch, grad, 52. Polit & Govt Pos: Chmn, Monroe Co Dem Comt, Pa, 74- Mem: Amaranth (Royal Matron); Eastern Star; Grange. Relig: Protestant. Mailing Add: RD 1 Kunkletown PA 18058

BAUMGARTNER, STEPHEN ELDON (D)
VChmn, Adams Co Dem Party, Wis
b Adams, Wis, Oct 11, 27; s Steve Baumgartner & Caroline Lamphere B; m 1955 to De Ann Van Tassel; c Bruce, Craige, Janalynn & Darcie. Educ: Adams Friendship High. Polit & Govt Pos: Chmn, Adams Co Dem Party, Wis, 64-70, vchmn, currently; alderman, City of Adams, 64-, mayor, 71- Bus & Prof Pos: Owner, Mobil Filling Station, 57. Mil Serv: Entered as Pvt, Air Force, 46, released as Pfc, 47; Am Theater & Victory Medals. Relig: Protestant. Mailing Add: 151 N Grant St Adams WI 53910

BAUSCH, DEL (D)
Wash State Rep
Mailing Add: 1359 S Second Ave Tumwater WA 98502

BAXLEY, HENRY L (D)
b Markham, Va, Sept 30, 98; s James Leroy Baxley & Emily Hirst B; m 1923 to Mamie Maxfield Yates; c Henry Little, Jr. Educ: Randolph Macon Acad, grad, 17. Polit & Govt Pos: Chmn, Fauquier Co Dem Comt, Va, formerly. Bus & Prof Pos: Farmer, 19-40; Gen Ins Agency, 35-63. Mil Serv: Pvt, Army Air Force, 18-19. Mem: AF&AM; Royal Arch Mason. Relig: Episcopal. Mailing Add: Hume VA 22639

BAXLEY, WILLIAM JOSEPH (D)
Attorney Gen, Ala
b Dothan, Ala, June 27, 41; s Keener Baxley & Lemma Rountree B; single. Educ: Univ Ala, Tuscaloosa, BS, 62, Sch Law, LLB, 64; Alpha Kappa Psi; Phi Alpha Delta; Kappa Sigma. Polit & Govt Pos: Dist attorney, 20th Judicial Circuit Ala, 66-71; Attorney Gen, Ala, 71- Mil Serv: Entered as Airman Basic, Air Force, 65, released as Airman 1/C, 66; Capt, Army Nat Guard Res, 68- Mem: Houston Co & Ala Bar Asns; Kiwanis; Am Legion. Relig: Methodist. Mailing Add: c/o Off of Attorney Gen Montgomery AL 36104

BAXTER, HARRY YOUNGS (D)
Chmn, Des Moines Co Dem Cent Comt, Iowa
b Burlington, Iowa, Sept 29, 30; s Raymond Willard Baxter & Katherine Wickham B; m 1954 to Elaine Bland; c Katherine Janet, Harry Wickham & John Raymond. Educ: Univ Ill, Urbana, BS in Econ & Finance, 52; Theta Chi. Polit & Govt Pos: Chmn, Des Moines Co Dem Cent Comt, Iowa. Bus & Prof Pos: Pres, Schoff & Baxter, Inc, Burlington, Iowa, 68- Mil Serv: Entered as 2nd Lt, Army, 54, released as 1st Lt, 56; Lt Col, Army Res. Mem: Midwest Stock Exchange, Inc; Chicago Bd Trade; Burlington Golf Club; New Crystal Lake Club. Mailing Add: 1016 N Fourth St Burlington IA 52601

BAXTER, J STERLING (R)
Comnr, Pitkin Co, Colo
b Hutchinson, Kans, June 8, 27; s Wilber David Baxter & Helen Sterling B; m 1950 to Peggylee Butler; c Sarah, Rachel, Ruth, Nancy & Margaret. Educ: Univ Kans, BA, MD; Phi Chi. Polit & Govt Pos: Chmn, Pitkin Co Rep Party, Colo, formerly; co-comnr, Pitkin Co, 67- Bus & Prof Pos: Physician, Aspen, Colo, 54- Mil Serv: Entered as A/S, Naval Res, 45, released A/S, 46, recalled as 1st Lt, Army Med Corps, 53, released as 1st Lt, 54. Publ: Open reduction tibial fractures, Rocky Mountain Med J, 57. Mem: Am Med Asn; Am Acad Gen Practice; Mason; Lions. Relig: Methodist. Mailing Add: Box C 307 S Mill Aspen CO 81611

BAXTER, JOHN T (R)
Nat Committeeman, Young Rep Fedn of Va
b Fairmont, Va, Nov 21, 38; s Harry Cameron Baxter & Hallie Herndon B; single. Educ: WVa Univ, BSEE, 59; Sigma Tau Gamma. Polit & Govt Pos: Mem, Third Dist Rep Comt, Va, 64-69; mem, Richmond City Rep Comt, 64-, vchmn, 67; chmn, Young Rep Fedn of Va, 70-71, nat committeeman, 71-; mem exec comt, Va Rep State Cent Comt, 70-71, mem, 70- Bus & Prof Pos: Asst to vpres mkt, Richmond Eng Co, 62-66; mkt res dir, United Va Bankshares, Inc, 66-71; vpres, Faber Mkt Group, 71-72; proprietor, Landmark Research Assocs, 72-

Mem: Am Mkt Asn (pres, 72-); Rotunda Club; St Andrew's Soc; Va Boat Club; Big Bros (dir & mem exec comt, 73-). Relig: Methodist Episcopal. Legal Res: 701-J N Hamilton St Richmond VA 23221 Mailing Add: 201 E Franklin St Richmond VA 23219

BAXTER, PHILIP NORMAN, JR (R)
Mem, Rep State Cent Comt, Calif
b Oakland, Calif, Apr 27, 37; s Philip N Baxter & Marguerithe Dietrich B; m 1967 to Chloe Brent; c Rebecca Anne. Educ: Stanford Univ, BSME, 63; Alpha Phi Omega. Polit & Govt Pos: Mem, El Dorado Co Rep Cent Comt, Calif, 67-69 & 71-, chmn, 69-70; mem, Rep State Cent Comt, Calif, 71- Bus & Prof Pos: Engr, Aerojet Gen Corp, Sacramento, Calif, 68-70; partner & engr, E L S Eng, Placerville, 70- Mem: Aircraft Owners & Pilots Asn; Pleasant Valley Grange. Relig: Agnostic. Mailing Add: 3030 Bucks Bar Rd Placerville CA 95667

BAXTER, SANDY JEAN (R)
Secy, Rep State Cent Comt Nev
b Davenport, Iowa, Mar 1, 39; d Alvin Ralph Baxter & Dorothy Wolters B; div. Educ: Fullerton Jr Col, 64-65. Polit & Govt Pos: Secy, Las Vegas Young Rep Club, 71-72, pres, 72-73; secy, Rep State Cent Comt Nev, 73-; newslett ed, Clark Co Young Rep, 74; state fundraising chmn, Nevadans for Equal Rights Amendment, 74-75. Bus & Prof Pos: Exec secy, Alpha Beta Markets, LaHabra, Calif, 63-70; exec secy, Campaign Hq of Robert List, 70; legal secy, Off Attorney Gen Robert List, Las Vegas, 71- Mem: Las Vegas Young Rep. Relig: Catholic. Legal Res: Apt 24 3136 Eastern Las Vegas NV 89109 Mailing Add: 1 325 S Third Las Vegas NV 89101

BAXTER, SARAH ELIZABETH (R)
Chmn, Jasper Co Rep Party, SC
b Swansea, SC, Oct 25, 31; d Harvey Alexander Williams & Gladys Knotts W; m 1947 to Walter Glenn Baxter; c Sarah Elizabeth (Mrs Sauls) & Walter Glenn, Jr. Educ: Am Sch, Chicago, Ill, grad, 68. Polit & Govt Pos: Chmn, Jasper Co Rep Party, SC, 74-; mem, SC State Comt on Rural Transportation, 75- Mem: Jasper Co Farm Bur (secy, 61-73). Relig: Methodist. Mailing Add: Rte 2 Box 209-A Tillman SC 29943

BAYARD, ALEXIS IRENEE DUPONT (D)
Mem Finance Coun, Nat Dem Comt
b Wilmington, Del, Feb 11, 18; s Thomas F Bayard & Elizabeth duPont B; m 1944 to Jane Brady Hildreth (deceased); c Alexis Irenee duPont, Eugene Hildreth, Richard Henry, Jane Hildreth, John Francis & William Bradford. Educ: Princeton Univ, BA, 40; Univ Va, LLB, 47. Polit & Govt Pos: Pres, Young Dem Del, 48-49; Lt Gov, Del, 49-53; chmn, Dem State Campaign, 54; chmn, Citizens for Kennedy-Johnson, 60; chmn, Citizens for Johnson-Humphrey, 64; chmn, Del Dem State Comt, 66-70; chmn, Del River & Bay Authority, 67-69; mem finance coun, Nat Dem Comt, 70-, Del chmn, currently. Bus & Prof Pos: Attorney-at-law, 48; dir, Farmers Bank of State of Del, 50-; spec counsel, Del Turnpike State Hwy Dept, 62-69; sr partner, Bayard, Brill & Handelman, 65-; dir, Newark Real Estate & Ins Co, 71- Mil Serv: Entered as Pvt, Marine Corps Res, 42, released as 1st Lt, 45, after serv in 28th Regt, Fifth Marine Div, Asiatic Theatre; Purple Heart; Navy & Presidential Unit Citations. Mem: Nat Comn on Uniform Laws; Am Bar Asn; SAR; Am Judicature Soc; Del Soc Mayflower Descendants. Honors & Awards: Young man of the year award, 51. Relig: Episcopal. Legal Res: 1006 Overbrook Rd Westover Hills Wilmington DE 19807 Mailing Add: 300 Market Tower 901 Market St Wilmington DE 19801

BAYH, BIRCH (D)
US Sen, Ind
b Vigo Co, Ind, Jan 22, 28; s Birch Evan Bayh, Sr & Leah Ward Hollingsworth B; m 1952 to Marvella Hern; c Birch Evan, III. Educ: Purdue Univ, BA in Agr, 51; Ind Univ, JD, 60; Ceres; Alpha Zeta; Gimlet; Ind Law J Bd Eds; Order of the Coif; Alpha Tau Omega; light-heavyweight boxing champion; varsity baseball team, Purdue Univ; pres, senior class. Hon Degrees: LLD, Purdue Univ & Anderson Col; LHD, Salem Col, WVa. Polit & Govt Pos: Ind State Rep, 54-62, Speaker, Ind House Rep, 59, Minority Leader, 57 & 61; US Sen, Ind, 63-, chmn, Const Amendments Subcomt, US Senate, 63-, chmn, Subcomt to Investigate Juv Delinquency, 71-, chmn transportation appropriations subcomt, 75-; deleg, Dem Nat Conv, 68. Bus & Prof Pos: Attorney; farmer, 340 acre family farm, Vigo Co, Ind. Mil Serv: Entered as Pvt, Army, 46, released as Pfc, 48, after serv in Occup Forces in Europe. Publ: One Heartbeat Away, Bobbs-Merrill, 66; Remedies available to penal inmates while incarcerated, summer 59 & Suggested improvements in the Indiana legislative process, winter 60, Ind Law J. Mem: Purdue & Ind Univ Alumni Asns; Am & Ind State Bar Asns; Isaac Walton League; Jr CofC. Honors & Awards: Named One of Nations Ten Outstanding Young Men, Nat Jr CofC, 64. Relig: Methodist. Legal Res: Rte 2 Terre Haute IN 46602 Mailing Add: 363 Senate Off Bldg Washington DC 20510

BAYLEY, NED DUANE (R)
b Battle Creek, Mich, Dec 29, 18; s Howard G Bayley & Beulah Sperry B; m 1943 to Lillian Joyce Safstrom; c Gwen Ellen, Will Douglas & Fred Wallace. Educ: Mich State Univ, BS, 40; Univ Minn, 1 year; Univ Wis, PhD, 50; Harvard Univ, 1 year. Polit & Govt Pos: Asst head, Breeding & Mgt Sect, Dairy Cattle Research, Agr Research Serv, Dept of Agr, Beltsville, Md, 55-56, leader, 56-61, asst dir, Animal Husbandry Research Div, 61-67, dep dir, Sci & Educ, Dept of Agr, Washington, DC, 67-68, dir, Sci & Educ, Off of the Secy, 68-72. Bus & Prof Pos: Mem staff, Dairy Husbandry Dept, Univ Wis, 48-53; assoc prof, Dairy Dept, Univ Minn, 53-55. Mil Serv: Entered as Pvt, Army, 42, released as T/Sgt, 46, after serv in ETO, 44-45. Publ: 28 tech publ in field of animal sci & research admin. Mem: Am Dairy Sci Asn; Am Soc of Animal Sci; Am Asn for the Advan of Sci. Honors & Awards: Outstanding Performance Rating, US Dept of Agr, 65; recipient 1970 Nat Civil Serv League Career Serv Award. Relig: Protestant. Mailing Add: 13907 Overton Lane Silver Spring MD 20904

BAYLOR, CHELSEA ANNE (D)
b Princeton, NJ, Sept 4, 48; d Edward R Baylor & Martha Barnes B; single. Educ: Univ Chicago, BA, 70; Phi Sigma Delta; Zeta Beta Tau. Polit & Govt Pos: Zone leader, Friedman for Mayor, Chicago, spring 71; pub rels, Steinberg for Co Legislator, Suffolk Co, NY, 71; asst coordr Suffolk Co, McGovern for President, 72; off mgr, McGovern for President, Smithtown, NY & New Haven, Conn; alt deleg, Dem Nat Conv, 72; campaign mgr, Linton for Legislator, Suffolk Co, 73; Suffolk Co coordr & Nassau-Suffolk Co coordr, Carey for Gov, 74. Bus & Prof Pos: Instr, Am Sch Correspondence, Chicago, 71. Mem: Brookhaven Chap, Nat Dem Coalition. Mailing Add: 2 William Penn Dr Stony Brook NY 11790

BAYONA, HUGO H (D)
b Los Angeles, Calif, June 23, 28; s Jose M Bayona & Enriqueta Herrera B; m 1950 to Alline Aston; c Danielle Victoria. Educ: San Francisco State Col, BS Bus-Sci, 63, grad work bus admin, 63-64; San Jose State Col, grad work bus admin, 65-66; mem, Student Union Planning Comt. Polit & Govt Pos: Alt deleg, Dem Nat Conv, 72. Bus & Prof Pos: Lab tech nuclear physics, Univ Calif Radiation Lab, Berkeley, 3 years; lab tech radio-chem, Tracerlab, Inc, Richmond, 2 years; employ security officer, Calif Dept Human Resources Develop, 64-66; area serv ctr dir, Econ Opportunity Comn, Santa Clara Co, asst prog developer & econ develop specialist, 66-69; job developer, Found Research & Community Develop, Inc, on-the-job training coord & exec dir, 69-70 & 71-73; dep dir, Econ & Social Opportunities, Inc, San Jose, 70; manpower develop consult, currently. Mil Serv: Entered as S/A, Navy, 46, released as Training Devices Tech-2, 51, after serv in Atsugi Naval Air Sta, 9 months, 51; Capt Civil Air Patrol, Air Force, 72-; Good Conduct Medal; Am Theatre Ribbon; World War II Victory Medal; Korean Serv Medal; Navy Occup Serv Medal with Asia Clasp. Mem: Alliance Calif Arts Coun; Am GI Forum US; San Jose Coun Arts (adv bd, 74-); San Jose Mex Am CofC (adv comt, 75-); Golden Gate Univ (adv coun to arts admin prog, 75-). Relig: Catholic. Mailing Add: 91 Cappy Ct San Jose CA 95111

BAYS, G BERNICE (R)
Chairwoman, Randolph Co Rep Comt, Mo
b Linn Creek, Mo, Aug 30, 26; d Robin Huddleston & Gertha Shipman H; m 1946 to Robert Newell Bays; c Kirk Van & Brent Robert. Educ: Moberly Jr Col, 73-74; Beta Sigma Phi. Polit & Govt Pos: State license off, Springfield, Mo, 44-45; dep clerk, Greene Co, 45-50, dep collector, 50-51; chairwoman, Randolph Co Rep Comt, 75- Bus & Prof Pos: Vchmn & bd dirs, Randolph Co Ambulance Dist, currently. Mem: Sun-N-Fun (bd mem & treas); Randolph Co Rep Women (corresponding secy). Relig: Baptist; secy childrens dept, First Baptist Church. Legal Res: 1120 Glenwood Moberly MO 65270 Mailing Add: 1120 Glenwood PO Box 489 Moberly MO 65270

BEACH, EDWARD LATIMER (R)
Secy, US Senate Rep Policy Comt
b New York, NY, Apr 20, 18; s Edward Latimer Beach & Alice Fouche B; m 1944 to Ingrid Bergstrom Schenck; c Edward L, Jr, Hubert Schenck & Ingrid Alice. Educ: US Naval Acad, BS, 39; Nat War Col, 62-63; George Washington Univ, MA, 63. Hon Degrees: ScD, Am Int Univ, 61; LLD, Univ Bridgeport, 63. Polit & Govt Pos: Secy & staff dir, US Senate Rep Policy Comt, 69- Bus & Prof Pos: Prof, US Naval War Col, Newport, RI, 67-69. Mil Serv: Entered as Midn, Navy, 35, Capt(Ret), 66; submarine officer & comdr, Pac Theatre, 42-45, commanded USS Triton during 1st submerged world circumnavigation, 60. Publ: Around the World Submerged, 62, The Wreck of the Memphis, 66, & Dust on the Sea, 72, Holt, Rinehart & Winston; plus numerous articles. Mem: US Naval Acad Alumni Asn; Navy League; Nat Geog Soc; Naval Inst; Cosmos Club. Relig: Protestant. Legal Res: 29 Gravel St Mystic CT 06355 Mailing Add: 1622 29th St NW Washington DC 20007

BEACH, PAUL COLE, SR (R)
b Vincennes, Ind, Aug 2, 07; s William Van Nuys Beach & Eva Helene Houghton B; m 1965 to Geraldine Brill. Educ: Vincennes Univ, 27-29; Ind Univ, Bloomington, 29-31; Delta Tau Delta. Polit & Govt Pos: Asst staff dir, Joint Comt on Printing, US Cong, 47- Bus & Prof Pos: Reporter, copy ed, sports writer, rewrite & syndicated feature ed, Washington Times, DC, 35-40; circulation br mgr, Washington Post, 40-41; reporter & copy ed, Alexandria Gazette, Va, 41-42; reporter, Washington Eve Star, 42-47. Mem: Nat Press Club; Cong Staff Club; Capitol Hill Club; Senate Staff Club. Relig: Christian Scientist. Legal Res: McLean VA 22101 Mailing Add: 1500 Highwood Dr Arlington VA 22207

BEACH, STEPHEN LEEDS, III (D)
Miss State Sen
b Chicago, Ill, July 3, 42; s Stephen Leeds Beach & Aldona Chipas B; single. Educ: Univ Miss, BA & JD; Phi Kappa Phi; Omicron Delta Kappa; Pi Sigma Alpha; Eta Sigma Phi; Sigma Nu; Alpha Phi Omega. Polit & Govt Pos: Miss State Rep, 68-72; Dem chmn, Precinct 37, Jackson, 68-; Miss State Sen, Hinds Co, 72-; mem, Miss Capitol Comn. Bus & Prof Pos: Attorney, Beach, Beach, Luckett & Hanbury. Mem: Jaycees; Mason; York Rite; Scottish Rite; Shrine. Honors & Awards: Cong of Freedom Liberty Award, 70 & 72; Outstanding Young Man of Jackson, Miss, 71. Relig: Methodist. Mailing Add: PO Box 663 Jackson MS 39205

BEACH, WILBUR LEWIS (R)
b Arlington, Ohio, May 9, 17; s John A Beach & Wilhemina Kramer B; m 1940 to Kathryn A Gibson; c Sue Elaine. Educ: Ohio State Univ, BSc, 39; Nat Agr Honor Soc; Lutheran Students Asn. Polit & Govt Pos: Village clerk, Chatfield, Ohio, 52-69; secy, Crawford Co Rep Cent Comt, 58-66, chmn, 66-68; precinct committeeman, Chatfield Rep Party, 58-72; mem, Crawford Co Chil Welfare Bd, 62-69; vol fire chief, Chatfield, 62-69; chmn, Crawford Co Rep Exec Comt, 68-72; co comnr, Crawford Co, 69- Bus & Prof Pos: Pres, Chatfield Hardware Co, Inc, 61-; chmn, Retarded Children, Inc, Crawford Co, 64-67. Mil Serv: Entered as Pvt, Air Force, 44, released as Cpl, 46, after serv in Commun, ETO, 45-46; Good Conduct Medal; ETO Ribbon. Mem: Ohio Hardware Asn; Am Legion; United Commercial Travelers; Crawford Co Conserv League; Am Lutheran Church. Relig: Lutheran. Mailing Add: Box 1 Chatfield OH 44825

BEADLESTON, ALFRED N (R)
Pres, NJ State Sen
b Rumson, NJ, Feb 20, 12; m 1947 to Isabel P Morrell. Educ: Yale Univ, BA, 34. Hon Degrees: LLD, Monmouth Col, 71. Polit & Govt Pos: Area adminr, NJ Off Civilian Defense; councilman, Shrewsbury, NJ, 39-40, Mayor, 41-52; pres Shrewsbury Rep Club, 41-50; treas, Affiliated Rep Club of Monmouth Co, 48-49, first vpres, 50-51; NJ State Assemblyman, 51-67, minority leader, NJ State Assembly, 58-59 & speaker, 64; NJ State Sen, 68-, Asst Majority Leader, NJ State Senate, 70-71, pres, 73-; Acting Gov NJ upon absence of Gov, 73- Bus & Prof Pos: Pres & dir, Beadleston & Woerz, Real Estate Operating Co, New York, formerly, retired. Relig: Episcopal. Legal Res: PO Box 425 Rumson NJ 07760 Mailing Add: 54 Broad St Red Bank NJ 07701

BEAGLE, GAIL JOYCE (D)
b Beaumont, Tex, Nov 25, 35; d Victor Leroy Beagle, Sr & Hazel Jane Block B; single. Educ: Tex Woman's Univ, BS, 58; Univ Tex Grad Sch, summer 59; George Washington Univ Grad Sch, 73-; Theta Sigma Phi; day ed, soc ed & church ed, Daily Lasso; pres, Tex Woman's Univ Methodist Student Movement. Polit & Govt Pos: Jefferson Co campaign mgr, Gonzalez for Gov, Tex, 58; staff asst to US Sen Ralph W Yarborough, Tex, 59; staff asst & press secy to Tex State Sen Gonzalez, 59, staff dir & press secy, 61; dist committeewoman, Tex Young Dem Club, 59-60; secy, Travis Co Precinct, 60; press secy, Gonzalez for US Rep Campaign, Tex, 61; off mgr & press secy, to US Rep Henry B Gonzalez, Tex, 61-63, admin asst & press secy, 63- Bus & Prof Pos: Staff asst, Tex Coun Churches, 58; ed, Methodist Student Movement News, 59-61; admin asst, Tex Methodist Student Movement, 60-61. Mem: Women in

Commun, Inc (pres nat capital punishment chap, 72-74); Bexar Co Dem Women; Tex Soc to Abolish Capital Punishment; Austin Comn on Human Rels; Fedn Orgn Prof Women (ed newsletter, 73-, mem nat bd, 74). Relig: Methodist. Legal Res: 2943 Ashby Pl San Antonio TX 78228 Mailing Add: 2312 Rayburn House Off Bldg Washington DC 20515

BEAHRS, JOHN VICTOR (R)
Councilman, Palo Alto, Calif
b Eufaula, Ala, Oct 19, 12; s Elmer Charles Beahrs & Elsa Kathrine Smith B; m 1938 to Virginia Whitty Oakley; c John Oakley, Richard Hewlett & William Whitty. Educ: Univ Calif, Berkeley, BS, 35; Am Inst Property & Liability Underwriters, CPCU. Polit & Govt Pos: Pres-dir, Palo Alto Stanford Hosp Ctr, Calif, 56-60; pres & dir, Bay Area Hosp Coun, 58-64; councilman, Palo Alto, 63-; dir, Bay Area Health Facil Planning Asn, 64-65; mem, War Risk Adv Comt, US Maritime Comn, US Dept Com, 68- Bus & Prof Pos: Pac Dept marine mgr, Home Ins Co, NY, 46-61; asst vpres, Marsh & McLennan, Inc, 61-65; ins-gen claims mgr, Matson Navigation Co, 65- Mil Serv: Entered as Ens, Navy, 41, released as Lt Comdr, 46, after serv in Amphibious Forces, Pac; Letter of Commendation, Adm R K Turner. Mem: Univ Club, Palo Alto, Calif. Relig: Episcopal. Mailing Add: 1830 Guinda St Palo Alto CA 94303

BEAL, GREGORY JOHN (R)
Mem, Nebr Rep State Cent Comt
b Brule, Nebr, June 8, 42; s Hubert C Beal & Mabel R Whipps B; m 1970 to Janelle Lee Brooks; c Gretchen Raschelle, Gregory John, Jr & Gwen Jennifer. Educ: Doane Col, BA, 63; Wash Col Law, Am Univ, JD, 67; Sigma Phi Theta; Phi Delta Phi; pres, Student Body, Doane Col. Polit & Govt Pos: Chmn, Keith Co Rep Comt, Nebr, 70-; mem, Nebr Rep State Cent Comt, 70-; state's attorney, Keith Co, 71- Mem: Nebr State Bar Asn (exec comt, young lawyers sect); Nebr Asn Trial Lawyers; Am Judicature Soc; Ogallala Optimist Club; Jaycees. Honors & Awards: Mooer's Club Champion, Oral Argument Competition, Wash Col Law, 66 & Outstanding Night Sr, 67. Relig: Methodist. Legal Res: 1015 E 11th St Ogallala NE 69153 Mailing Add: PO Drawer 90 Ogallala NE 69153

BEAL, ROBERT LAWRENCE (R)
b Boston, Mass, Sept 10, 41; s Alexander Simpson Beal & Leona Rothstein B; single. Educ: Harvard Col, BA cum laude, 63, Harvard Univ Sch Bus Admin, MBA, 65; DU Club; Hasty Pudding; Harvard Varsity Club. Polit & Govt Pos: Co-founder, Advance Mag, 60, treas, 60-62; co-founder, Ripon Soc, 62, treas, 68-72. Bus & Prof Pos: Vpres, The Beacon Co, Boston, 65-; lectr real estate, Northeastern Univ, 69- Mem: Gtr Boston Real Estate Bd; Boston Bldg Owners & Mgr Asn; Boston Zool Soc (treas, 72-); Belmont Country Club; Harvard Clubs of Boston. Relig: Jewish. Legal Res: 21 Brimmer St Boston MA 02108 Mailing Add: One Center Plaza Boston MA 02108

BEAL, THADDEUS R (R)
b New York, NY, Mar 22, 17; m to Katharine Putnam; c Katharine, Thaddeus, Alice & George. Educ: Yale Col, grad, 39; Harvard Law Sch, grad, 47. Polit & Govt Pos: Under Secy of the Army, 69-72. Bus & Prof Pos: Assoc, Herrick, Smith, Donald, Farley & Ketchum, Attorneys, Boston, Mass, 47-56, partner, 56-57; vpres, Harvard Trust Co, Cambridge, 57-62, pres, 62- Mil Serv: Entered Navy, 41, released as Lt Comdr, 45. Mem: Cambridge Savings (trustee); Boston Personal Property Trust (trustee); Radcliffe Col (trustee); Middlesex Mutual Ins Co (dir); Cambridge Redevelop Authority. Mailing Add: 108 Brattle St Cambridge MA 02138

BEALL, DARYL E (D)
b Fort Dodge, Iowa, Dec 11, 46; s Wayne Woodrow Beall & Marjorie Pence B; m 1968 to Jo Ann Hasty; c Lora Sue & Scott Michael. Educ: Iowa Cent Community Col, AA, 67; Univ Northern Iowa, 67-68; Buena Vista Col, BA, 69; Drake Univ, 70-; Student Senate pres, 66-67; Alpha Phi Gamma; Phi Alpha Theta. Polit & Govt Pos: Staff mem, Congressman Stanley L Greigg, 66; publicity chmn, Calhoun Co Dem Cent Comt, Iowa, 66-67; co chmn Iowans for Franzenburg for Gov, 68; dist coordr, Youth for Humphrey, 68; campaign chmn, Sorenson for Rep, 68; deleg, Co, Dist & State Dem Conv, 68-74; chmn, Iowa Young Dem State Conv, 70; participant, US Dept State Foreign Policy Conf, 70; committeeman, Young Dem Clubs Am, 70-72; Justice of the Peace, Dallas Co, Iowa, 70-73; mem elec reform comn, Iowa State Dem Cent Comt, 71-72; chmn Urbandale chap, Iowa Polit Action Comt for Educ, 71-72; Dem cand for Secy State, Iowa, 72, mem, Civil Serv Comt, Ft Dodge, 74-, chmn, 75-; mem adv bd, NCent Alcoholism Research Found, 75-; mem, Service Acad Selection Comt, Congressman Berkley Bedell, 75-; steering mem, Home Rule Charter Comn Action Comt, 75- Bus & Prof Pos: Instr polit sci, Urbandale Sr High Sch, 69-74; mgr, Furniture World, Ft Dodge, 74- Mem: Nat Educ Asn; Kiwanis; Am Judicature Soc; Common Cause. Honors & Awards: Polit Intern Award, Iowa Ctr for Educ in Polit, Univ Iowa; Taft fel, Macalester Col; Teachers Medal, Freedoms Found, 74. Mailing Add: 2416 18 Ave N Ft Dodge IA 50501

BEALL, J GLENN, JR (R)
US Sen, Md
b Cumberland, Md, June 19, 27; s Former US Sen J Glenn Beall & Margaret Schwarzenbach B; m 1959 to Nancy Lee Smith; c Victoria Lee. Educ: Yale Univ, BA, 50. Polit & Govt Pos: Chmn, Allegany Co Rep State Cent Comt, Md, 58-62; Md State Deleg, 62-68, Minority Floor Leader, Md House of Deleg, 63-68; US Rep, Md, 69-71; US Sen, Md, 71-, mem budget comt, US Senate, 75- Bus & Prof Pos: Prin, Beall, Garner & Geare, Inc, 50- Mil Serv: Entered as A/S, Navy, 45, released as SHD 3/C, 46; Lt(jg) Res. Mem: Ali Gian Temple Shrine (past Potentate); AF&AM (past Master, Mt Lodge 99). Relig: Episcopal. Legal Res: Beall's Lane Frostburg MD 21532 Mailing Add: 362 Old Senate Off Bldg Washington DC 20510

BEALL, RUSSELL G (D)
WVa State Sen
b Burnt House, WVa, Mar 10, 22; s Roscoe C Beall & Bessie Cox B; m 1948 to Mary Margaret Morris; c Dana & Donna. Educ: WVa Univ, BS. Polit & Govt Pos: WVa State Deleg, 64-66; WVa State Sen, 71-; deleg, Dem Nat Conv, 72. Bus & Prof Pos: Real estate developer; livestock dealer; oil & gas driller & producer. Mil Serv: Capt, Army, 11th Airborne Div, Pac Theatre. Relig: Baptist. Mailing Add: 2102 Maxwell Ave Parkersburg WV 26101

BEALL, WILLIAM HAYES (D)
b Colorado Springs, Colo, Aug 21, 10; s William Henry Beall (deceased) & Josephine Rentz B (deceased); m 1934 to Sarah Jane Dark; c Anne (Mrs Pedro Rosales), David Sprague (deceased) & Douglas Hayes. Educ: Willamette Univ, BA, 32; Yale Univ, MDiv, 35; Univ Ore, 37-38; Sigma Tau; Blue Key. Polit & Govt Pos: Asst chief migratory labor camp prog, Farm Security Admin, US Dept Agr, Washington, DC, 43-44; sr examr, President's Comn on Fair Employment Practices, Washington, DC, 44-45; chief youth activities, Off Mil Govt, US War Dept, Berlin, Ger, 45-47; cand for State Sen, 36th Dist, Ill, 58; cand for US Congress, 14th Dist, 60; deleg, Ill Dem Conv, 58-62; pres, Lombard Dem Club, 59-64; deleg, Ore Dem Conv, 72-74; deleg, Dem Nat Conv, 72; lobbyist, Ore Consumer League, Ore Legis, 71, 73 & 75. Bus & Prof Pos: Dir, Wesley Found, Univ Ore, 36-39; training dir, Cent Coops, Superior, Wis, 48-51; educ serv dir, Coop League US, Chicago, Ill, 51-66; exec dir, Kidney Found Ill, Chicago, 67-70. Publ: Co-auth, Camp Manager's Manual, US Dept Agr, 43; auth, Member Educational Manual for Cooperatives, Coop League, 61; auth, Biography of E R Bowen, In: Great American Cooperators, Interstate Publ, 67. Mem: Asn Coop Educators; Rotary Int; Common Cause; UN Asn US; NAACP. Honors & Awards: Serv Commendation, Peace Corps, 65; Cert Achievement, Kidney Found Ill, 71; Consumer Achievement Award, Ore Consumer League, 73; Distinguished Alumnus Award, Willamette Univ, 74. Relig: Methodist. Mailing Add: 3825 Helen Ave SE Salem OR 97302

BEAM, JACOB DYNELEY
b Princeton, NJ, Mar 24, 08; s Jacob Newton Beam & Mary Prince B; m to Margaret Glassford; c Jacob Alexander. Polit & Govt Pos: Career officer, US Dept of State Foreign Serv, 31-73; vconsul, US Consulate, Geneva, 31-34; secy, US Embassy, Berlin, 34-40; div asst, Dept State, 40-41; secy, US Embassy, London, 41-45; polit officer, Hq US Forces in Ger, 45-47; chief, Div Cent European Affairs, 47-48; consul, Batavia, 49; counr, US Embassy, Djakarta, 49-51; counr, US Embassy, Belgrade, 51-52; acting head, US Embassy, Moscow, 52-53, dep dir policy planning staff, 53; mem bd examr for Foreign Serv, 54-55; dir, Off EEuropean Affairs, 55; dep asst secy state for European affairs, 55-57; US Ambassador to Poland, 57-61; asst dir, Int Rels Bur, US Arms Control & Disarmament Agency, 62-66; US Ambassador, Czech, 66-69; US Ambassador, USSR, 69-73. Mailing Add: 3129 O St NW Washington DC 20007

BEAME, ABRAHAM DAVID (D)
Mayor, New York, NY
b London, Mar 20, 06; s Philip Beame & Esther B; m 1928 to Mary Ingerman Beame; c Bernard & Edmond. Educ: City Col New York, cum laude, BBA, 28; Beta Gamma Sigma. Polit & Govt Pos: Asst budget dir, New York, NY, 46-52, budget dir, 52-62, comptroller, 62-65 & 69-74, mayor, 74-; mem, Mayor's Comt on Mgt Survey, NY State Comn on Const Revision, NY Small Bus Adv Coun, currently. Mem: Nat Conf of Christians & Jews (bd mem, Brooklyn Region); Fedn of Jewish Philanthropies (trustee-at-lg); United Jewish Appeal (chmn, Brooklyn Unit). Honors & Awards: Townsend Harris Medal, City Col New York Alumni Asn. Relig: Jewish. Mailing Add: Gracie Mansion 88th & East End Ave New York NY 10007

BEAN, JOSEPH EDWARD (D)
Chmn, St Mary's Co Dem Party, Md
b St Mary's Co, Md, June 4, 29; s James Lloyd Bean, Sr & Catherine Tennyson B; m 1950 to Betty Jeanne Knupp; c Edward Vernon, Mary Elizabeth & Richard Wayne. Educ: St Michael's High Sch, 4 years. Polit & Govt Pos: Chmn, St Mary's Co Dem Party, Md, 64- Bus & Prof Pos: Rte mgr, Washington Star Newspaper Co, 53- Mem: KofC (Grand Knight, St Michael's Coun, 2 years); Lexington Park Rescue Squad (vol pres, 2 years); Elks. Relig: Catholic. Mailing Add: Chancellors Run Rd Great Mills MD 20634

BEAN, MARY FRANCES (D)
Committeewoman, Tenn State Dem Exec Comt
b Birmingham, Ala, Dec 24, 19; d Scott Paine Kelly (deceased) & Willie Mae Evans K; m 1940 to Joseph Smith Bean; c Joe Scott, Jere W & Daniel A (deceased). Educ: ETenn State Univ, BS, 40; Mid Tenn State Univ, 75- Polit & Govt Pos: Pres, Franklin Co Chap, Tenn Fedn Dem Women, 68-75; co-chmn comt, Women for Kefauver, formerly; women's co-chmn, Dem Elec Nominees, currently; mem consumer panel, Tenn Pub Serv Comn, 74-; committeewoman, Tenn State Dem Exec Comt, 74- Bus & Prof Pos: Instr, Franklin Co High Sch, 54-58; real estate broker, Bean Realty Co, 70- Mem: Tenn Realtors' Asn; Franklin Co Hist Soc; WOW; Franklin Co Country Club; Am Red Cross. Relig: Presbyterian. Mailing Add: Rte 1 Winchester TN 37398

BEARD, CHARLES W (R)
NH State Rep
Mailing Add: 29 Chapin Terr Lakeport Laconia NH 03246

BEARD, DAVID CHESTER (D)
Committeeman, Md Dem State Cent Comt
b Mt Savage, Md, Oct 6, 38; s Bernard Eugene Beard, Sr & Clara Geneva Kemp B; m 1961 to Beverly Jean Cuffley; c Kelley Gayle & Michael Blaine. Educ: Frostburg State Col, BS, 65, APC. Polit & Govt Pos: Committeeman, Md Dem State Cent Comt, 74- Bus & Prof Pos: Supvr boys forestry camps, State Md, 65-69; teacher, Garrett Co Schs, Md, 69- Mil Serv: Md Nat Guard, 56-63. Mem: Am Fedn Teachers; Am Legion; Optimist; Elks. Relig: Catholic. Mailing Add: Rte 1 Box 132A Swanton MD 21561

BEARD, EDWARD PETER (D)
US Rep, RI
b Providence, RI, Jan 20, 40; m 1963 to Marsha Louise Pelosi; c Edward, Jr & Diane. Polit & Govt Pos: RI State Rep, 72; committeeman, RI Dem State Comt, 28th Dist, 73-75; chmn, 28th Dist Dem Comt, 73-75; chmn, Gov Task Force Nursing Home Inspections; US Rep, RI, 75- Bus & Prof Pos: Asst foreman for maintenance painters, RI Sch Design, Providence. Mil Serv: RI Nat Guard, 60-66, SP-5. Mem: Painters Union; Assumption Parish St Vincent DePaul Soc; RI Asn Retarded Children; RI Med Ctr Orgn Family & Friends; Nat Coun Sr Citizens (hon mem). Legal Res: 200 Bay View Ave Cranston RI 02905 Mailing Add: US House Rep Washington DC 20515

BEARD, R D (D)
NC State Rep
Mailing Add: 2918 Skye Dr Fayetteville NC 28303

BEARD, ROBIN LEO, JR (R)
US Rep, Tenn
b Knoxville, Tenn, Aug 21, 39; s Robin Leo Beard, Sr & Dorothy Rochelle Damon B; m 1963 to Catherine Rieniets; c Robin John & Lisa Paige. Educ: Vanderbilt Univ, BA, 61; Sigma Chi. Polit & Govt Pos: Young Rep chmn, Nashville/Davidson Co, Tenn; fieldman, Jarman for Gov, Third, Fourth & Sixth Cong Dists; fieldman, Dunn for Gov, Third, Fourth & Sixth Cong Dists; chmn, Dunn Inaugural Comt, Nashville; Tenn Comnr Personnel, Nashville; US Rep, Sixth Dist, Tenn, 73- Bus & Prof Pos: Asst for develop, Vanderbilt Univ. Mil Serv: Entered as Pvt E-1, Marine Corps, 62, released as 1st Lt, after serv in 2nd AMTRAC Bn; Maj, Marine

Res, 9 years; Two Letters of Commendation. Relig: Methodist. Legal Res: Laurelwood Apts Franklin TN 37064 Mailing Add: 124 Cannon House Off Bldg Washington DC 20515

BEARDEN, JOHN, JR (D)
Ark State Sen
Mailing Add: Box 577 Leachville AR 72438

BEARDSLEY, WALTER RAPER (R)
b Elkhart, Ind, Oct 23, 05; s Andrew Hubble Beardsley & Helen Brown B; m 1929 to Marjory Anna Buchanan; c Robert Buchanan. Educ: Princeton Univ, BS in Polit, with honors, 28; Babson Inst, grad study, 28; London Univ Sch Econ, 29. Polit & Govt Pos: Co chmn, Rep Jr, Ind, 28-30; chmn, Elkhart Co Rep Party, 30-34; deleg, Ind Rep Conv, 30-72; finance chmn, Elkhart Co & Ind State Rep Finance Comts; mem, Elkhart Co Coun, 35-36; Ind State Sen, 36-40; deleg, Rep Nat Conv, 48-, mem, Comt on Arrangements & chmn, Subcomt Transportation, 64; mem, Rules Comt, 68; Rep Nat Committeeman, Ind, 61-68; nat chmn, Rep Cong Boosters Club, 71-74. Bus & Prof Pos: Admin asst to pres, Miles Labs, Inc, Elkhart, Ind, 30-33, vpres, 33-47, pres, 47-61, chmn bd, 61-73; dir, Miles Labs, Inc, 33-; dir, First Nat Bank of Elkhart Co; pres bd trustees, Elkhart Gen Hosp; dir, Capitol Hill Assocs, Inc, Washington, DC, 72-; dir, Truth Publ Co, chmn finance comt, 73- Mil Serv: Entered as 1st Lt, Air Force, 42, released as Lt Col, 45, after serv in Hq Gulf Coast Training Command, San Antonio, Tex, 42, Hq Army Air Force, Washington, DC, 42-43 & XX Bomber Command, China-Burma-India Theater, Kharagpur, India, 44-45; Am Campaign Ribbon; Asiatic-Pac Campaign Ribbon with three Battle Stars; Victory Medal. Mem: Proprietary Asn (hon vpres); Nat Princeton Clubs of NY & Chicago; Sky Club, New York; Union Club, New York. Honors & Awards: Benjamin Franklin fel, Royal Soc Arts, London. Relig: Presbyterian. Legal Res: 2233 Greenleaf Blvd Elkhart IN 46514 Mailing Add: 1127 Myrtle St Elkhart IN 46514

BEARSE, EVA SUE (DFL)
Chairperson, Anoka-Hennepin Co Dem-Farmer-Labor Party, Minn
b Atlanta, Ga, Dec 28, 45; d Sheppard Homans & Eva Buchheit H; m 1965 to Edward Walter Bearse; c Eric Edward & Melanie Beth. Educ: Mich State Univ, BS with honors, 66. Polit & Govt Pos: Off campaign mgr, Allen Co Dem Party, Ft Wayne, Ind, 70-71; precinct chairperson, Dem-Farmer-Labor Party, St Paul, Minn, 72; chairperson, Anoka-Hennepin Co Dem-Farmer-Labor Party, 74- Bus & Prof Pos: Sec teacher math, Minneapolis Pub Schs, 67-70 & 73-75. Mem: Minneapolis Fedn of Teachers. Relig: Episcopal. Mailing Add: 813 40th Lane N Anoka MN 55303

BEASLEY, JERE LOCKE (D)
Lt Gov, Ala
b Tyler, Tex, Dec 12, 35; s Browder Locke Beasley & Florence Camp B; m 1958 to Sara Baker; c Jere Locke, Jr, Julia Ann & Linda Lee. Educ: Auburn Univ, BS, 59; Univ Ala, LLB, 62; Omicron Delta Kappa. Polit & Govt Pos: State campaign mgr, US Sen James B Allen, Ala, 68; Lt Gov, Ala, 71- Bus & Prof Pos: Partner, Beasley, Williams & Robertson, 64-71. Mil Serv: Entered as Pvt E-1, Army Nat Guard, 56, released as Sgt, 65; Capt, Army Res, 65-71. Mem: Am & Ala State Bar Asns; Am Trial Lawyers Asn. Relig: Methodist. Legal Res: 301 N Midway St Clayton AL 36016 Mailing Add: State Capitol Montgomery AL 36104

BEASLEY, KERN GRANT (R)
b Linton, Ind, July 20, 03; s Alfred Milton Beasley & Anna Gertrude Morgan B; m 1961 to Harriet Clark. Educ: Ind Univ, AB, 24; Harvard Univ, 25-26; George Washington Univ, LLB, 26, JD, 28; Acacia; Phi Delta Phi. Polit & Govt Pos: Asst secy, Interstate Com Comt, US Sen, 26-28; prosecuting attorney, 63rd Judicial Circuit Court, Greene Co, Ind, 32-36 & 58-60; deleg, Rep Nat Conv, 68, alt deleg, 72. Bus & Prof Pos: Secy, Miller Construction Co, Ind, 43-; pres, Citizens Nat Bank of Linton, 68. Mil Serv: 1st Lt(Ret), Army Res. Mem: Am & Ind Bar Asns; Mason (32 degree); Shrine; Royal Order of Jesters. Honors & Awards: Meritorious Pub Serv Citation, Navy. Relig: Methodist. Mailing Add: 590 N Main St Linton IN 47441

BEASLEY, LEWIS EDWARD (R)
b Lamar, SC, Feb 9, 29; s Jasper Wesley Beasley & Lois Long B; m 1952 to Terry Kalmus; c Kevin Lewis & Keith Long. Educ: US Mil Acad, BS, 52; Ga Inst Technol, MS, 64. Polit & Govt Pos: Admin asst, US Sen Strom Thurmond, SC, 74- Mil Serv: Entered as 2nd Lt, Army, 52, released as Lt Col, 72, after serv in 1st Cavalry Div, Ft Hood, Tex, 71-72; Silver Star; Distinguished Flying Cross; Bronze Stars; Air Medal; Legion of Merit; Meritorious Serv Medal; Purple Heart. Relig: Methodist. Legal Res: Lamar SC Mailing Add: 4200 Cordell Annandale VA 22003

BEASLEY, MYRA JANE (D)
b Lone Dell, Mo, Apr 30, 04; d George A Williams & Myrtle Hudson W; m 1923 to Richard Emmet Beasley; c Lt Glenn W (deceased). Educ: Clayton High Sch, Clayton, Mo, 1 year. Polit & Govt Pos: Pres, Franklin Co Women's Dem Club, Mo, 3 terms; committeewoman, Central Twp, Franklin Co, 52-; vchmn, Franklin Co Dem Cent Comt, formerly; state committeewoman, Ninth Dist Dem Party, formerly. Bus & Prof Pos: Owner, florist shop, 55-58. Mem: Eastern Star (past matron); Women's Soc Christian Serv. Relig: Methodist. Mailing Add: 720 Virginia St St Clair MO 63077

BEASON, DONALD RAY (R)
Mem, NC Rep Exec Comt
b Mt Airy, NC, Oct 10, 38; s Grover Ray Beason & Irene Spencer B; m 1958 to Janet Thacker; c Mark Christopher & Natalie Joan. Polit & Govt Pos: Pres, Charlotte Young Rep Club, NC, 62-64; precinct chmn, Surry Co, 66-70; mem, Surry Co Rep Exec Comt, 66-70; dist campaign mgr, US Rep Wilmer D Mizell, 68-; mem, NC Rep Exec Comt, 70-; vchmn, Mt Airy City Planning Bd, 70-; alt deleg, Rep Nat Conv, 72; Surry Co chmn, Comt to Reelect the President, 72, Surry Co chmn, Comt for Gov Holshouser, 72. Bus & Prof Pos: Gen mgr, Chevrolet Dealership, 68-72. Mil Serv: Entered as Pvt, Army, 57, released as E-4, 60, after serv in 63rd Artil Group, Hartford, Conn, 57-60. Mem: Nat Soc of Sales Execs; Mason (32 degree); Elks; CofC; Jaycees. Mailing Add: 339 Country Club Rd Mt Airy NC 27030

BEATTIE, CHARLES KENNETH (R)
Chmn, Harford Co Rep Cent Comt, Md
b Whiteford, Md, July 19, 23; s Simon Beattie & Susie Hughes B; single. Educ: Strayers Bus Col, Baltimore, 41-42; Univ Baltimore, 44-46. Polit & Govt Pos: Deleg, Rep Nat Conv, 52, 56, 68 & 72; mem, Serv Acad Comt, First Dist, Md, 73-; chmn, Harford Co Rep Cent Comt, 75-; vchmn, First Cong Comt Md, 75- Mil Serv: Entered as Pvt, Army, 49, released as Pfc, 50, after serv in Cmndd Gen Off, Aberdeen Proving Ground, Md. Mem: Am Cancer Soc (dir); Harford Hist Soc; Northern Cent Lung Asn (dir); Mason. Honors & Awards: Medal, SAR; Archives Honor Roll, Washington, DC. Relig: Presbyterian. Mailing Add: Chestnut St Whiteford MD 21160

BEATTIE, JACK ROBERT (R)
Committeeman, Orange Co Rep Exec Comt, Fla
b Bay City, Mich, Oct 2, 34; s Aaron Joseph Beattie (deceased), stepfather, Owen Randolph Colley & Sadie Young Beattie C; m 1959 to Ernestine Linda Johnson; c John Robert, Jeffrey Lind & Kimberly Young. Educ: Mich State Univ, BA, 56; Univ Mich, DDS, 60; Western Reserve Univ, MS, orthodontics, 63; Sigma Nu; Porpoise Fraternity; Nat Collegiate All Am Swimming Team. Polit & Govt Pos: Committeeman, Orange Co Rep Exec Comt, Fla, 65-, chmn, 68-74; alt deleg, Rep Nat Conv, 68, deleg, 72. Mem: Am Dent Asn (Fla deleg, 68-); Cent Dist & Orange Co Dent Asns; Am Asn Orthodontists (Fla deleg); Kiwanis. Honors & Awards: Nat Competition recipient, Milo Helman Research Award, Am Asn Orthodontists, 64. Relig: First Presbyterian. Legal Res: 561 Via Lugano Winter Park FL Mailing Add: 618 E South St Orlando FL 32801

BEATTIE, ORRIN HAWKINS (R)
Vt State Rep
Mailing Add: Manchester Center VT 05255

BEATTY, JOHN J (D)
Ill State Sen
Polit & Govt Pos: Deleg, Dem Nat Mid-Term Conf, 74; Ill State Sen, 75- Mailing Add: 8343 S Keeler Ave Chicago IL 60652

BEATTY, VANDER L (D)
NY State Sen
Mailing Add: 671 St Johns Pl Brooklyn NY 11216

BEATY, ORREN, JR (D)
b Clayton, NMex, June 13, 19; s Orren Beaty & Edith Mason B; m 1944 to Mary Ethel Turner; c Orren, III, Laura Leigh & Susan Ray. Educ: NMex State Univ, BA, 41; Univ Houston. Polit & Govt Pos: Admin asst to US Rep Stewart L Udall, 56-61; asst to US Secy Interior, 61-68; fed co-chmn, Four Corners Regional Comn, 67-69; Dem nominee for US Rep, Ariz, Third Dist, 70; legis asst to US Rep Mike McCormack, Wash, 71; staff asst to US Rep Morris K Udall, Ariz, 71-72; nat coordr, Rocky Mountain States Muskie Campaign, 71-72; Fla state campaign coordr, McGovern-Shriver Campaign, 72. Bus & Prof Pos: Managing ed, Sun-News, Las Cruces, NMex, 46-47; reporter, polit writer & columnist, The Ariz Republic, 48-55; assoc ed, Cong Quart, 69-70. Mil Serv: 1st Lt, Army, 42-46; Maj, Air Force, 50-52. Legal Res: 5201 W Camelback Rd Phoenix AZ 85018 Mailing Add: 1784 Proffit Rd Vienna VA 22180

BEAUCHAMP, ALFRED J (R)
Vt State Sen
Mailing Add: Box 206 Rutland VT 05701

BEAUCHAMP, ARTHUR PAUL (R)
Chmn, Breckinridge Co Rep Exec Comt, Ky
b McCoy, Ky, Oct 2, 14; s Clarence Beauchamp & Ollie Fentress B; m 1931 to Mary Lee Poole; c Helen (Mrs Mingus), Linda Carol (Mrs Thornhill) & Roy Thomas. Educ: Breckinridge Co High Sch, 29. Polit & Govt Pos: Chmn, Tom Emberton for Gov Campaign, 70; chmn, Breckinridge Co Rep Exec Comt, Ky, 71-; co chmn, Marlow W Cook for Sen Campaign, 74. Bus & Prof Pos: Dist mgr, Columbiana Hybrid Seed Corn Co, 51-58; salesman, Louisville Seed Co, 58-68 & Independent Seed & Wire, Inc, 68-75; Breckinridge Co chmn, Am Red Cross, 61-66. Mem: Am Farm Bur. Honors & Awards: Hon Degree, Breckinridge Co Chap FFA, 60; Plaque in Appreciation for Serv, Am Red Cross, 66; Ky Col, Gov Louie B Nunn, 70; Awarded eight gallon pin for blood given through Am Red Cross, 71. Relig: Protestant; Sunday sch supt, Antioch United Methodist Church, 40-, chmn bd, 60- Mailing Add: RR 1 Box 133 Hardinsburg KY 40143

BEAUCHAMP, DAVID (DFL)
Minn State Rep
Legal Res: 1211 25th Ave S Moorhead MN 56560 Mailing Add: State Capitol Bldg St Paul MN 55155

BEAUCHESNE, WILFRED P (D)
Mass State Rep
b Lawrence, Mass, Sept 3, 23; s Ernest Beauchesne & Alida Laroche B; m 1956 to Constance Jacquelle; c Robert J. Educ: Lawrence High Sch, Mass, 36-39. Polit & Govt Pos: Town counr, Methuen, Mass, 72-75; Mass State Rep, 24th Essex Dist, 75- Bus & Prof Pos: Owner, Tower-Hill Taxi, Franklin Taxi, 48-63 & Tower-Hill Auto Sch, 51- Mem: Elks; Methuen Bd of Trade. Relig: Catholic. Mailing Add: 13 Woodland Circle Methuen MA 01844

BEAUDIN, ROBERT CLAUDE (DFL)
Mayor, Duluth, Minn
b Duluth, Minn, Apr 14, 40; s Emmet Beaudin & Bette Yernberg B; m 1959 to Sharon Marie Hedman; c Sean, Shelley, Sharyl, Shannon & Shane. Educ: Univ Minn, Duluth, BA, 72. Polit & Govt Pos: Pres, Young Dem-Farmer-Labor, Minn, 61; chmn, Seventh Dist Dem-Farmer-Labor Party, 72-74; city councilman, Duluth, Fourth Dist, 73-75, city coun pres, 74-75, mayor, 75- Bus & Prof Pos: Warehouseman, Minn Woolen, 59-62; sprayer, Universal Fiberglass, 63-64; laborer-foreman-supvr, US Steel, 64-73; econ developer, State of Minn, 73-74. Mem: US Conf Mayors; Duluth CofC; Prog Rev Bd-KBJR TV, Duluth. Relig: Lutheran. Mailing Add: 2628 W Skyline Pkwy Duluth MN 55806

BEAULIEU, ERNEST ROBERT (R)
Mem-at-Lg, RI Rep State Cent Comt
b Pawtucket, RI, Feb 7, 28; s Ernest H Beaulieu & Lillian I Moreau B; m 1950 to Adele G Payette; c Paula, Sylvia, Roxanne, Michele & Ernest. Educ: Our Lady of Providence Sem, 2 years. Polit & Govt Pos: Deleg, Rep Nat Conv, 68; chmn, Burrillville Rep Town Comt, RI, formerly; mem-at-lg, RI Rep State Cent Comt, 69- Bus & Prof Pos: Mgr, Seaboard Finance Co, 58-63; pres, Beau-Lieu Rest Home, Inc, 63-; pres, Golden Oaks Manor, Inc, 68-; owner, Beau-Lieu Manor, Inc, 68- Publ: President speaks, Bay State Bul, 3/69; Administrators & inspections, Patience, 5/69. Mem: Am Nursing Home Asn (gov coun mem); RI State Nursing Home Asn; New Eng Regional Nursing Home Asn (bd mem); Lions (bd); Jaycees. Honors

& Awards: Burrillville Jaycees Outstanding Citizen, 66. Relig: Roman Catholic. Legal Res: 10 Steere St Harrisville RI 02830 Mailing Add: PO Box 311 Harrisville RI 02830

BEAUMONT, WILLIAM EUSTACE, JR (D)
Ark State Rep
b Little Rock, Ark, Apr 3, 33; s William Eustace Beaumont & Mary Elizabeth Hocott B; m 1951 to Elli Karoline Heinrich; c William Eustace, III, Mary Elizabeth, Karoline Ann & Suzanna Marie. Educ: Univ Ark, BSBA, 56; Alpha Tau Omega. Polit & Govt Pos: Mem, Health Ins Benefits Adv Coun, US Dept of Health, Educ & Welfare, 65-67; mem, Ark Hosp Adv Coun, 65-; Ark State Rep, 69- Bus & Prof Pos: Pres, Ark Nursing Home Asn, 63, Am Nursing Home Asn, 65-66; chmn, Joint Coun to Improve Health of the Aging, 64-66. Mem: Fellow, Am Col Nursing Home Adminrs; Mason (32 degree). Relig: Methodist. Legal Res: 5 Pamela Dr Little Rock AR 72207 Mailing Add: 105 E Markham Little Rock AR 72203

BEAUPRE, JACK R (D)
Ill State Rep
b Kankakee, Ill, July 21, 36; s Sylvester John Beaupre & Lorna Mardell Wools B; m 1961 to Faith Elgena Friberg; c Susan & Nancy. Educ: Univ Ill, Urbana, BS in Finance, 58; John Marshall Law Sch, JD, 66; Alpha Kappa Lambda. Polit & Govt Pos: Recorder of Deeds, Kankakee Co, Ill, 60-64, Clerk of the Circuit Court, 64-68; Hearing Off, Ill State Dept Revenue, 68-73; Ill State Rep, 73- Bus & Prof Pos: Practicing attorney, Kankakee, Ill, 68- Mil Serv: Entered as 2nd Lt, Army, 69-70, six months active duty training, surface to Air Missile Sch, Ft Bliss, Tex; Capt, Army Res, 10 years. Mem: Am & Ill State Bar Asns; Am Trial Lawyers Asn. Legal Res: 52 Castle Combe Bourbonnais IL 60915 Mailing Add: Rm 2107 State Off Bldg Springfield IL 62706

BEAVER, JAMES RAYMOND (R)
Chmn, Jasper Co Rep Cent Comt, Ind
b Indianapolis, Ind, May 27, 41; s Dr Ernest Raymond Beaver & Jeanette Frances Chapman B; m 1962 to Carole Jean Courtright; c Shannon & Erin. Educ: Ind Univ Bloomington, AB in Govt, 66, Sch Law, JD, 68; Phi Alpha Delta; Student Bar Asn. Polit & Govt Pos: Probation off, Monroe Co Circuit Court, Ind, 67-68; campaign coordr, Landgrebe for Cong, 68; admin asst, US Rep Earl F Landgrebe, 68; chief page, Ind Rep State Conv, 72; chmn, Jasper Co Rep Cent Comt, 72- Bus & Prof Pos: Attorney, Ind, 68- Mem: Ind State & Jasper Co Bar Asns; Farm Bur; Rotary. Relig: Protestant. Mailing Add: 304 S Home Ave Rensselaer IN 47978

BEAVER, ROBERT F (R)
b Columbus, Ohio, July 5, 07; s William C Beaver & Elizabeth Ferguson B; m 1933 to Dorothy Evelyn Brent; c Gary E & Vicki E. Educ: Univ Calif Los Angeles, BA, 32; Univ Southern Calif, Gen Sec Credential, 33; Delta Sigma Phi. Polit & Govt Pos: VChmn & treas, Orange Co Rep Cent Comt, Calif, 62-66, treas, Lincoln Club Orange Co, 63-; foreman protem, Orange Co Grand Jury, 64; chmn subcomt, Orange Co Rapid Transit Comt, 66; vchmn, Comn for Develop Com & Indust, 67-71; deleg, Rep Nat Conv, 68 & 72; treas, Am Revolution Bicentennial Comn Calif, 68-72; treas, Rep State Cent Comt of Calif, 69-71; trustee, Calif State Univ & Cols, 72- Bus & Prof Pos: Col trainee, opers mgr, West Div, asst controller & asst mgr, West Div, Firestone Tire & Rubber Co, Calif, 33-53; pres, Willard-Brent Co, Inc, Los Angeles, 53-; mem, Fullerton Libr Bldg Comn, 70- Mil Serv: Entered as 1st Lt, Army-Inspector Gen, 42, released as Maj, 46, after serv in Trinidad Sector, Base Command & War Dept Price Adjust Bd, Pentagon. Mem: Los Angeles CofC; Merchants & Mfrs Asn; Elks; Hacienda Golf Club; Equestrian Trails, Inc. Honors & Awards: Lincoln Club Man of the Year, 71. Relig: Protestant. Mailing Add: 1235 Margarita Dr Fullerton CA 92633

BEAVERS, RUTH JONES (D)
Chmn, Worth Co Dem Cent Comt, Mo
b Grant City, Mo, Dec 14, 01; d Abner Marshall Jones & Alice Maupin J; m Judge Ellis Beavers, wid; c Joe & Wade. Educ: North-West Teachers Col, 41. Polit & Govt Pos: Auditor, rec secy & vpres, Dem Women's Federated Club, Sixth Cong Dist, Mo, 59-69; twp committeewoman, Dem Cent Comt; chmn, Worth Co Dem Cent Comt, 62-; deleg, Dem State Conv; mem comt, Farmers for Symington, Campaign for Sen Symington; mem campaign comt for Sen Edward Long. Bus & Prof Pos: Owner, Dry-Goods & Ready to Wear, 55-65; owner & operator, 1420 acre farm, currently. Mem: Bus & Prof Women; Eastern Star; Am Legion Auxiliary. Relig: Disciples of Christ; Deaconess, 31- Legal Res: 501 E Third St Grant City MO 64456 Mailing Add: PO Box 453 Grant City MO 64456

BECHAC, A DENIS (D)
Committeeman, Dem State Cent Comt, La
b New Orleans, La, July 11, 39; s Albert M Bechac & Azelie Verret B; m 1963 to Margherita Schultz; c Denis Paul, Andrew Michael & Gina Conchetta. Educ: Southeastern Univ, BA, 60; La State Univ, 60-61. Polit & Govt Pos: Councilman, Town of Mandeville, La, 64-; committeeman, Dem State Cent Comt La, 72- Bus & Prof Pos: Owner, Bechac's Restaurant, 62-; pres, Bechac's Realty, Inc, 72- Mem: Jaycees; Northlake Rotary (treas, 74 & 75); Mandeville Lions (past treas & dir); Mandeville CofC (past pres & dir). Honors & Awards: Mandeville's Outstanding Young Man, 65. Relig: Catholic. Mailing Add: 2025 Lakeshore Dr Mandeville LA 70448

BECHMAN, CHARLES EDWARD (R)
Treas, Johnson Co Rep Cent Comt, Ind
b Whiteland, Ind, June 19, 22; s Henry J Bechman & Henrietta L Diederich B; m 1942 to Ondoise Helen Thornburg; c C William & James A. Educ: Ind Bus Col, 40-46; Washington & Lee Univ, 44. Polit & Govt Pos: Precinct committeeman, Fourth Precinct, Ind, 56-; city councilman, Franklin, 67-71; vpres, Franklin City Plan Comn, 71-; treas, Johnson Co Rep Cent Comt, 71- Bus & Prof Pos: Exec secy, Johnson Co Realty & Ins Agency, 48-64; vpres, Union Bank & Trust Co, Franklin, Ind, 64- Mil Serv: Entered as Pvt, Air Force, 42, released as Sgt after serv in Convalescent Training Dept, 43-46; Sharpshooter & Good Conduct Medals. Mem: Ins Inst Am; Independent Ins Agents Ind; Masonic Lodge; Scottish Rite; Shrine. Relig: Protestant. Mailing Add: 70 Fairground St Franklin IN 46131

BECHT, PAUL FREDERICK (R)
NMex State Sen
b Marshfield, Wis, Sept 14, 37; Frederick Andrew Becht & Beatrice Isabelle Murphy B; m 1970 to Shirley Irving; c William Andrew, Stephen Irving & Lucinda. Educ: Marquette Univ, 55-56; Univ Wis, 57-58; Wis State Univ, BS, 61; Univ Ill, MA, 63; Sigma Phi Epsilon. Polit & Govt Pos: State purchasing agt, State of NMex, 68-70; deleg, Young Rep Nat Conv, 70; NMex State Sen, 73- Bus & Prof Pos: Systems analyst, Sandia Labs, 62- Mem: Nat Purchasing Mgt Asn; Elks; Am Asn of Retarded Children. Relig: Catholic. Mailing Add: 8804 Delamar Ave NE Albuquerque NM 87111

BECK, AUDREY PHILLIPS (D)
Conn State Sen
b Brooklyn, NY, Aug 6, 31; d Gilbert Wesley Phillips, Sr & Mary Reilly P; m 1951 to Curt Frederick Beck; c Ronald Pierson & Meredith Wayne. Educ: Univ Conn, BA, High Honors, 53, Distinction in Economics, MA, 55; Phi Beta Kappa; Phi Kappa Phi; Artus; Gamma Chi Epsilon; Delta Sigma Rho. Polit & Govt Pos: Mem bd finance, Mansfield, Conn, 65-71; Mansfield-Univ Liaison Comt, 67-68; mem, State Housing Comn, 69-71; Conn State Rep, 54th Dist, 69-75, asst minority leader, Conn House Rep, 73-75; deleg, Dem Nat Conv, 72; chmn, Dem State Platform Comt, 74; Nat Legis Conf Comt on Campaign Financing & Legis Ethics, 74-; Coun State Govts Regional Tax Comt, 75-; Conn State Sen, 75-, chmn finance comt. Bus & Prof Pos: Teacher econ, Univ Conn, 60-67, planning economist, Windham Regional Planning Agency, 67-68. Publ: Mansfield Town Government, 60, Connecticut School System, 62 & Connecticut in Focus, 70, League of Women Voters Conn. Mem: League of Women Voters Conn (bd dir, 61-63); Conn Fedn of Dem Women's Clubs (newsletter ed, 69-71); Conn Women's Polit Caucus (bd dir, 72-75); Alert Women's Coalition (adv bd, 72-); Am Soc Planning Officials (vpres). Relig: Protestant. Mailing Add: 100 Dunham Pond Rd Storrs CT 06268

BECK, CLIFFORD WALLACE (RED) (D)
Wash State Sen
b Bloomington, Ind, Aug 12, 08; s Walter C Beck & Augusta E Brummett B; m 1935 to Hope G Etchings. Educ: Stanford Univ, bus admin. Polit & Govt Pos: Wash State Rep, 26th Dist, 61-64; Wash State Sen, 64- Bus & Prof Pos: Mgr property holdings, Kitsap Co, Wash, at present. Mil Serv: Navy for 10 years. Mem: CofC; Fleet Reserve Asn; Kiwanis; Grange; Eagles. Relig: Baptist. Mailing Add: 2400 Beach Dr Port Orchard WA 98366

BECK, EDWARD T (D)
Utah State Rep
Mailing Add: 5557 South 4270 West Kearns UT 84118

BECK, JAMES M (D)
Ga State Rep
b Eton, Ga, May 5, 17; s Eugene Henry Beck & Edmonia Hopson B; m 1946 to Betty Mathis; c Betty Gene, Sarah Virginia & Mary Jane. Educ: George Washington Univ, 38-40. Polit & Govt Pos: Mayor, City of Valdosta, Ga, 66-70 & 72-74; Ga State Rep, Dist 148, 75- Bus & Prof Pos: Operator, Motel & Restaurant, Valdosta, Ga, 50- Mil Serv: Entered as Pvt, Army, 41, released as Maj, 46, after serv in 91st Inf Div, 5th Army, Mediter Theatre Oper, 43-45; Bronze & Silver Stars. Mem: Am Legion; VFW; Elks; Kiwanis. Relig: Methodist. Mailing Add: 2427 Westwood Dr Valdosta GA 31601

BECK, JOHN KEITT (D)
Chmn, Navarro Co Dem Exec Comt, Tex
b Kerens, Tex, Dec 28, 20; s John Caleb Beck & Clyde Daniel B; m 1959 to Cornelia Anne Watson; c Nancy Clyde & John Keitt, Jr. Polit & Govt Pos: Dem chmn, Precinct 17, Navarro Co, Tex, 50-62; councilman, Kerens, Tex, 58-66; chmn, Navarro Co Dem Exec Comt, 62-; finance chmn, Tex Dem Co Chmn Asn, 72- Bus & Prof Pos: Farmer & rancher, 37-; acct & bookkeeper, E K Howell Motor Co, 53-56; pres, Kerens Develop Fund, Inc, 63- Mem: Relief Lodge Number 236 AF&AM; Tex Forestry Asn; Friends of LBJ Libr; Kerens CofC. Honors & Awards: Man of Year Award, Kerens CofC, 69. Relig: United Presbyterian. Legal Res: 106 N Donaldson Ave Kerens TX 75144 Mailing Add: PO Box 143 Kerens TX 75144

BECK, RAYMOND EDWARD (R)
Md State Deleg
b Baltimore, Md, Mar 5, 39; s Albert Edward Beck, Jr & Mary Margaret Korzun B; m to Patsy Mae Stottlemyer; c Kimberly Ann, Kenneth Albert, John Bradley & Raymond Edward, Jr. Educ: Univ Baltimore, AA, LLB & JD; Heuisler Honor Soc; Sigma Delta Kappa. Polit & Govt Pos: Mem & secy, Md Rep State Cent Comt for Carroll Co, 70-72; Md State Deleg, Carroll Co, 72- Bus & Prof Pos: Claims adjuster, Automobile Mutual Ins Co, 66-68; lawyer, Cable, McDaniel, Bowie & Bond, Westminster, Md, 68- Mil Serv: Entered as Pvt, Marines, 56, released as Cpl, 59, after serv in 3rd Pioneer Bn, 3rd Marine Div; Meritorious Mast; Good Conduct Medal. Mem: Am, Md State & Carroll Co Bar Asns; Md Jaycees; Westminster Jaycees (legal counsel, currently). Relig: Roman Catholic. Legal Res: 20 Mark Dr Westminster MD 21157 Mailing Add: 189 E Main St Westminster MD 21157

BECK, SIDNEY FRANKLIN, JR (R)
Chmn, Adams Co Rep Party, Wis
b Greenville, Miss, Oct 23, 28; s Sidney Franklin Beck & Ona Hendon; m 1955 to Geraldine Gray; c Ember, Michael, Sidney, Timothy & Christopher. Educ: Univ Miss, LLB, 54; Beta Theta Pi. Polit & Govt Pos: Vchmn, Adams Co Rep Party, Wis, 72-74, chmn, 75- Mailing Add: 514 Maine St Friendship WI 53934

BECK, WILLIAM E, JR (R)
b Sioux City, Iowa, Dec 4, 10; both parents deceased; m 1930 to Virginia Ell Vene Kirchner; c Susan (Mrs James Thoreson) & Debbie (Mrs Richard Fehlman). Educ: Univ Iowa, BSC, 36; Sigma Delta Chi. Polit & Govt Pos: Mem, State Judicial Nominating Comn, Iowa, 71-; chmn, Dickinson Co Rep Party, 73-75, retired. Mil Serv: Entered as Lt(jg), Navy, 42, released as Lt, 45, after serv in SPac, Adm Bogan Staff, 44-45. Publ: Publ, Spirit Lake Beacon, currently; dir, Mid Am Publ Co, Inc, currently. Mem: Am Legion; VFW; Shrine; Rotary; CofC. Honors & Awards: Many newspaper awards. Relig: Presbyterian. Mailing Add: 1706 Ihaca Spirit Lake IA 51360

BECKER, ALAN STEVEN (D)
Fla State Rep
b Brooklyn, NY, Feb 9, 46; s Jack Becker & Lorraine Mayper B; m 1972 to Nola Nissenson. Educ: Brooklyn Col, AB, 66; Univ Miami Sch Law, JD, 69. Polit & Govt Pos: Asst Pub Defender, Dade Co, Fla, 69-72; Fla State Rep, 72- Bus & Prof Pos: Becker & Poliakoff, Attorneys-at-law, currently. Mem: Am Arbit Asn; Dade Co Bar Asn; Elks; Optimist; Phi Alpha Delta. Mailing Add: 1835 NE 198th Terrace North Miami Beach FL 33179

BECKER, CHARLES J (D)
Mo State Rep
Mailing Add: PO Box 22 Arnold MO 63010

BECKER, FRANK J (R)
b Brooklyn, NY, Aug 27, 99; m to Anne Claire Ferris; c Frances, Betty Ann (Mrs Jack Myers) & Robert. Polit & Govt Pos: NY State Assemblyman, 45-53; US Rep, 83rd-88th Cong, NY. Bus & Prof Pos: Ins broker, 45-; dir, Lynbrook Fed Savings & Loan Asn. Mil Serv: Army, 18. Mem: VFW; Holy Name Soc; Am Legion; Elks; KofC. Relig: Catholic. Mailing Add: 173 Earle Ave Lynbrook NY 11563

BECKER, HENRY TIMOTHY (D)
Mem, Manchester Dem Town Comt, Conn
b Hartford, Conn, Feb 5, 17; s Henry M Becker & Nellie A Conners B; m 1941 to Marie Elizabeth De La Chevrotiere; c Therese, Elaine & Timothy. Educ: George Washington Univ, 50-51; Duquesne Univ, 51-52. Polit & Govt Pos: Mem, Manchester Pension Bd, Conn, 56-60, chmn, 62-66; Dem chmn, Dist Two, Manchester, 58-62; Conn State Rep, until 68; mem, Manchester Dem Town Comt, currently. Bus & Prof Pos: Dist organizer Int Asn Machinists, 47-49; nat rep union label dept, Amalgamated Clothing Workers of Am, 50-60, regional dir, 60-73; nat organizer, Am Fedn Teacher, 56-58; asst dir, New Eng Off Econ Opportunity Trade Union Leadership Training Prog, Univ Mass, 67-69; AFL-CIO labor staff rep, United Way Gtr Hartford, 73- Mil Serv: Entered as Pvt, Army Air Corps, 43, released as Pfc, 45, after serv in NAm Theatre; Cpl, NY Nat Guard, 165th Inf Regt, 34-38; Good Conduct Medal. Mem: KofC; Am Legion; Lions; Army-Navy Club. Relig: Roman Catholic. Mailing Add: 736 Center St Manchester CT 06040

BECKER, MARTIN STANLEY (D)
Md State Deleg
b Washington, DC, June 3, 26; s David Becker & Esther Oscar B; m 1952 to Etta Nezin; c Leslie Ann & Nancy Lee. Educ: George Washington Univ, 6 months; Emory & Henry Col, 2 years; Univ Va, 1 year 6 months; George Washington Univ Law Sch, LLB, 50; Phi Sigma Delta. Polit & Govt Pos: Md State Deleg, 67-, chmn, Montgomery Co Deleg to Gen Assembly, 71, chmn, Econ Matters Comt, Md House Deleg, 71-; chmn, Gov Comn to Study Mechanics Liens, 70-71. Bus & Prof Pos: Mem of the Bar, DC, 50- & State of Md, 56- Mil Serv: Entered as A/S, Navy, 44, released as Ens, 47, after serv in Seventh Fleet, US Naval Port Facilities, Shanghai, China, 46-47; Naval Res, 47-59, Lt(jg); Am Theater & Victory Medals. Mem: CofC; Jaycees; Wheaton Rescue Squad; Young Dem Club; Eastern Montgomery Dem Club. Relig: Jewish. Mailing Add: 8728 Colesville Rd Silver Spring MD 20910

BECKER, MARY KAY (D)
Wash State Rep
Mailing Add: PO Box 81 S Bellingham Sta Bellingham WA 98225

BECKER, NELSON J (R)
Ind State Rep
Mailing Add: 407 Long Tree Lane Logansport IN 46947

BECKER, RALPH ELIHU (R)
Mem, DC Rep Comt
b New York, NY, Jan 29, 07; s Max Joseph Becker & Rose B; m to Ann Marie Watters; c William W, Donald L, Ralph E, Jr & Pamela Rose. Educ: St John's Univ, NY, LLB, 28. Polit & Govt Pos: Founder, NY State Asn Young Rep Clubs, 32, pres, 40-42; founder, Young Rep Nat Fedn, 35, chmn, 46-49; NY deleg, Rep Nat Conv, 36, 40-44 & 45-68, speaker, 48; mem exec comt, Nat Rep Comt, 48; campaign mgr, Dwight D Eisenhower, 52 & 56; Campaign Mgr, Nixon & Lodge, 60; chmn, Nat Sponsors of Cult & Fine Arts Comt for Nixon-Agnew, 68; mem, Inaugural Comts, 53, 57 & 69; former mem, Nat Rep Finance, Cong & Sen Comts; Rep minority counsel, Senate's Rules Elec Comt, 51; app spec ambassador by President Johnson, Independent Ceremonies at Swaziland, 68; chmn, 1970 Joint Dinner Rep Nat Comt & DC Rep Comt; mem, DC Rep Comt, currently; mem finance comt, DC Rep Party, currently; mem, Comn, on the City, currently. Bus & Prof Pos: App by Presidents Eisenhower & Nixon as trustee & gen counsel, John F Kennedy Ctr, for the Performing Arts, Washington, DC, 58-; dir & gen counsel, Am Thrift Assembly, 62-; dir & gen counsel, Metrop Washington Bd Trade, 64-71; app by Secy Interior as dir, gen counsel & mem adv comt, Wolf Trap Farm Park for Performing Arts, Vienna, Va, 66-, dir & gen counsel, Wolf Trap Found; dir & gen counsel, Reconstruct & Develop Corp, 68-; trustee & gen counsel, Belford Towers Found, Inc, 69-; dir, Nat Bank of Washington, DC. Mil Serv: Entered as Pvt, Army, 42, released as Capt, 45, after serv in 30th Inf Div, ETO, 44-45; Bronze Star; NY State Medal Chevalier Legion of Honor; Croix de Guerre with Palm; Belgian Fourragere. Publ: How to Win a Political Campaign; co-auth, Republican Campaign Manual; co-auth, Implementing the National Reinsurance Program, The District of Columbia Insurance Placement Act, Annals of CPCU, 8/68; plus many others. Mem: Am Law Inst; Judge Adv Gen Asn; Soc Int Law; Am Judicature Soc; Nat Coun of Fed Bar Asn; Chevalier & Off, Southern Cross of Brazil; Order of Homayoun second & third class & Order of Taj, second class, Iran; Knight's Cross, Order of Dannebrog, Denmark; Great Cross for Meritorious Serv to Austrian Repub; Antarctic Serv Medal; Order de la Vasa, Sweden; Donor of Political Americana Collections to various orgns including 80,000 items to Smithsonian Inst, Dartmouth Col, St Albans Sch & LBJ Libr, Tex. Relig: Episcopal. Mailing Add: 2916 32nd St NW Washington DC 20008

BECKER, ROBERT WILLIAM (DFL)
Mem, Minn Dem-Farmer-Labor State Cent Comt
b Minneapolis, Minn, Feb 24, 35; s Charles Becker & Marjorie Camp B; m 1958 to Mary Baab; c Elizabeth Anne & David Charles. Educ: Hamline Univ, BA, 59; Mich State Univ, MA, 62, grad study, 62-; Tozer Fel, 58; Woodrow Wilson Nat Fel, 59; Nat Ctr Educ in Polit Fel, 62; Pi Gamma Mu. Polit & Govt Pos: Spec asst to Gov, Mich, 62; mem, Stearns Co Dem-Farmer-Labor Cent Comt, Minn, 65-72, chmn, 68-72; mem, Stearns Co Dem-Farmer-Labor Exec Comt, 65-72; deleg, Minn Dem-Farmer-Labor State Conv, 65, 66, 68, 70 & 72; chmn, Platform Comt, 66; chmn, Credentials Comt, 68; deleg, Dem Nat Conv & mem Credentials Comt, 68; mem, Minn Dem-Farmer-Labor State Cent Comt, 68-; mem, St Cloud Metrop Planning Comn, 69-72; Dem Presidential Elector, 72; treas & campaign mgr, State Senate Dist 17 Vol Comt, 72- Bus & Prof Pos: Asst instr, Mich State Univ, 61-62 & 63; asst prof polit sci, St Cloud State Col, 63- Mil Serv: Entered as Pvt E-1, Army, 53, released as Cpl, E-4, 55, after serv in 1903 Engr Aviation Bn, Far East Command, Korea, 53-54; Good Conduct Medal; Nat Defense Medal; United Nations Korean Serv Medal. Publ: Correlates of legislative behavior, Midwest J Polit Sci, 62. Mem: Am Polit Sci Asn; Midwest Polit Sci Asn; St Cloud Area Dem-Farmer-Labor Club; St Cloud Area Citizens Adv Group. Relig: Methodist. Mailing Add: 320 Third Ave S St Cloud MN 56301

BECKER, WILLIAM JACOB (D)
Chmn, Faulk Co Dem Comt, SDak
b Wessington, SDak, Sept 18, 41; s Jacob William Becker & Bertha Wilhelm B; m 1961 to Linda Lea Kopecky; c William Jacob, Jr, Michelle Mae, Sherri Lynn, Angela Marie, Julie Ann & Robert Earl. Educ: Univ SDak, 59-60. Polit & Govt Pos: Chmn, Faulk Co Dem Comt, SDak, 74- Bus & Prof Pos: Farmer, 60- Mem: Farmers Union. Relig: Methodist. Mailing Add: Miranda SD 57463

BECKERLE, JOSEPH W (D)
Treas, Third Cong Dist Dem Party, Mo
b St Louis, Mo, June 30, 21; m 1948 to Dorothy E Doedli; c Mary Elizabeth & Ann Marie. Educ: St Louis Parochial Schs. Polit & Govt Pos: Mo State Rep, 48-72; treas, Third Cong Dist Dem Party, currently. Mil Serv: Air Corps, World War II, 42-45. Relig: Catholic. Mailing Add: 6145 S Grand Ave St Louis MO 63111

BECKHAM, ROBERT CULP (R)
Ga State Rep
b Darlington Co, SC, Apr 6, 32; s Paul Thurlow Beckham & Leona Gertrude Culp B; m 1968 to Susan Hooper; c William D & Paul T. Educ: Univ SC. Polit & Govt Pos: Ga State Rep, Dist 82, 72-74, Dist 89, 75- Bus & Prof Pos: Pres, Beckham Petroleum Co, Augusta, Ga, currently. Mil Serv: Army, 55. Mem: Ga Oilmens Asn (dir); Jaycees; Rotary; Elks. Legal Res: 3020 Fox Spring Rd Augusta GA 30904 Mailing Add: PO Box 1533 Augusta GA 30903

BECKSTEAD, LUCY (R)
Mem, Rep State Cent Comt of Colo
b Hazelton, Idaho, Oct 28, 20; d Hyrum Johnson & Rilla Shepherd J; m 1943 to Frank L Beckstead. Educ: Idaho State Univ, 37-40; Univ Colo, BS, in Jour, 69. Polit & Govt Pos: Deleg, Wash State Rep Conv, 54; pres, Valley Women's Rep Club, Spokane, 60-62; dist leader, Fourth Legis Dist, Wash, 61-62; co-chmn, Jefferson Co Goldwater for Pres Comt, 63-64; precinct committeewoman, Precinct 501, Jefferson Co Rep Party, 66-67; deleg, State Rep Conv & Assembly, 66 & 68; deleg, Jefferson Co Rep Conv, 66 & 68; dist capt, Jefferson Co Rep Party, 67; mem, Rep State Cent Comt of Colo, 69-; precinct committeewoman, Precinct 314, Jefferson Co Rep Party, currently; vchmn, Rep Dist 24, 73- Bus & Prof Pos: Secy & off mgr, United Air Lines, Inc, Spokane & Seattle, Wash & Boise, Idaho, 46-56; free-lance writer, 66-; mem teaching staff, Nat Writers Club, 70- Relig: Latter-day Saint. Mailing Add: 3505 Miller Court Wheat Ridge CO 80033

BECKWITH, FLORENCE HESS (R)
VChmn, Fourth Dist Rep Comt, Mich
b Clinton Co, Mich, June 11, 09; d John Jacob Hess & Elizabeth Rumbaugh H; m 1935 to Robert Edgar Beckwith; c Robert Edgar, Peter Hess & Jon Gardner. Educ: Olivet Col, AB, 31; Alpha Lambda Epsilon. Polit & Govt Pos: Chmn, Hillsdale Co Rep Comt, Mich, formerly; deleg, Rep Nat Conv, 72; mem, Mich Rep State Cent Comt, currently; vchmn, Fourth Dist Rep Comt, currently. Mem: Hillsdale Co Rep Women (chmn, 70-); DAR (regent); Hillsdale Golf & Country Club; Hillsdale Women's Club (pres, 72-73); Hillsdale Garden Club. Relig: Episcopal. Mailing Add: Rte 2 Lake Wilson Hillsdale MI 49242

BECKWORTH, LINDLEY (D)
b Kaufman Co, Tex, June 30, 13; s Otis Jefferson Beckworth & Josie Slaughter B; m to Eloise Carter; c Gary, Carter, Mary, Linda & John Barney. Educ: Univ Tex; Baylor Univ; Southern Methodist Univ, ETex State Teachers Col; Sam Houston State Teacher Col. Polit & Govt Pos: Tex State Rep, 36-38; US Rep, Third Dist, Tex, 38-52 & 56-66; judge, US Customs Court, NY, formerly; Tex State Sen, 71-72. Bus & Prof Pos: Sch teacher, 3 years; admitted to Tex Bar, 37. Mem: Mason; Odd Fellows. Relig: Baptist. Mailing Add: 505 N Green St Longview TX 75601

BECNEL, BENOIT PAUL (D)
Chmn, St James Parish Dem Exec Comt, La
b Vacherie, La, Sept 27, 25; s Placide Jean Becnel & Antonia Brack B; m 1946 to Lydia Rita Roussel. Educ: High Sch. Polit & Govt Pos: Chmn, St James Parish Dem Exec Comt, Ward Nine, La, currently. Bus & Prof Pos: Salesman, coffee co, 46-48; salesman, furniture co, 48-50; dist mgr, life ins co, 50- Mil Serv: Entered as A/S, Navy, 43, released as PO 1/C, 46, after serv in Pac Theater, 43-45; 5 Campaign Ribbons; Good Conduct Medal. Mem: VFW; Am Legion; Lions; KofC. Relig: Catholic. Legal Res: 616 N Airline Gramercy LA 70052 Mailing Add: PO Drawer J Gramercy LA 70052

BEDELL, BERKLEY WARREN (D)
US Rep, Iowa
b Spirit Lake, Iowa, Mar 5, 21; s Walter Berkley Bedell & Virginia Price B; m 1943 to Elinor Healy Bedell; c Kenneth, Thomas & Joanne. Educ: Iowa State Univ, 40-42; Phi Delta Theta. Polit & Govt Pos: US Rep, Sixth Dist, Iowa, 75- Bus & Prof Pos: Founder & owner, Berkley & Co, Spirit Lake, Iowa, 37- Mil Serv: Entered as Cadet, Army Air Force, 42, released as 1st Lt, 45, after serv as flying instr SE Training Command. Mem: Kiwanis; Am Legion; Izaak Walton League; Shrine; Iowa Great Lakes Student Loan Asn. Honors & Awards: Nations First Small Businessman of the Year, 64. Relig: Methodist. Legal Res: 501 Tenth St Spirit Lake IA 51360 Mailing Add: 503 Cannon House Off Bldg Washington DC 20515

BEDELL, CATHERINE BARNES (R)
Chmn, US Int Trade Comn
b Yakima, Wash, May 18, 14; d Charles H Barnes & Pauline V B; m 1970 to Donald W Bedell; c Melinda Ellen & James Collins May. Educ: Univ Wash, MEd, 36; Alpha Chi Omega. Polit & Govt Pos: Wash State Rep, 52-58; US Rep, Fourth Dist, Washington, 59-70; presidential appointee & mem bd dirs, Bd Incorporators, Nat RR Passenger Corp, 71; chmn, US Int Trade Comn, 71- Mem: Wash Asn for Retarded Children; Bus & Prof Women; Young Rep Fedn; Altrusa & Soroptimist Clubs (hon mem). Relig: Episcopal. Legal Res: 5515 Englewood Hill Dr Yakima WA 98902 Mailing Add: 4101 Cathedral Ave NW Washington DC 20016

BEDELL, EUGENE JAMES (D)
NJ State Sen
b Elizabeth, NJ, May 13, 28; s Eugene A Bedell & Margaret I McCormick B; m 1953 to Arline M Mayer; c Brian, Teresa, Evan, Lauren & Bridget. Educ: Monmouth Jr Col, AA, 50; Monmouth Col, 57-58; Newark State Col, 71-72. Polit & Govt Pos: Dem committeeman, First Dist, Keansburg, NJ, 54-55; pres, Belford Dem Club, 56-57; Dem committeeman, 13th Dist, Middletown Twp, 56-60; state committeeman, Monmouth Co Young Dem, 58-59; munic chmn, Middletown Twp Dem Exec Comt, 61-62; freeholder, Monmouth Co Bd Chosen Freeholders, 65-67; NJ State Assemblyman, 73- Bus & Prof Pos: Bus mgr, Lathers

Int Union Local 346, AFL-CIO, 57- & pres, Southern Dist Coun of Lathers, 59- Mil Serv: Entered as Pvt, Army, 46, released as Tech 5, 48, after serv in 32nd Med Bn, Ft Sam Houston, Tex, 46-47. Mem: Monmouth Co Ment Health Asn (bd trustees, 70-); Monmouth Co Red Cross (bd dirs, 73-); NJ Real Estate Sales; AFL-CIO (deleg, Lathers Int Union, 58 & NJ Bldg & Const Trades Coun, 58-); Lions. Honors & Awards: Numerous awards & honors from many civic, soc, benevolent, bus, fraternal & educ asn. Relig: Roman Catholic. Legal Res: 400 Main St Keansburg NJ 07734 Mailing Add: 1 Church St Keansburg NJ 07734

BEDFORD, HENRY WARD (R)
Treas, Addison Co Rep Comt, Vt
b Houghton, NY, Oct 6, 06; s Henry Clark Bedford & Nelle Crow B; m 1929 to Mary Louise Bates; c Henry F & Crayton W. Educ: Earlham Col, AB, 27; Westminster Choir Col, MusB, 33; Univ Pittsburgh, MA, 36. Hon Degrees: LLD, Univ Vt, 65. Polit & Govt Pos: Treas, Addison Co Rep Comt, Vt, 59-; Vt State Rep, 59-67 & 69-70, chmn appropriations comt, Vt House Rep, 66-69; chmn, Vt State Cols Bd & acting pres, 61-65; mem, Vt State Libr Bd, 65-; moderator, Town of Cornwall, 65-; mem exec comt, Vt State Rep Comt, 68-71; mem, Vt Legis Coun, 69; mem, New Eng Bd Higher Educ, 69; Vt State Sen, 69-75. Bus & Prof Pos: Chmn music dept, Middlebury Col, 36-53; owner, Milaway Farm, 38-71; secy treas, Middlebury Coop Freeze Lockers, 42-65; treas, Porter Hosp, Middlebury, 58-72 & pres, 66-72; treas, Vt Symphony Orchestra, 63- Mem: Rotary; Ayrshire Breeders Asn (dir, 67-); Eastern State Expos (trustee, 67-); Westminster Choir Col (trustee, 67-); Relig: Episcopal. Mailing Add: RFD 2 Middlebury VT 05753

BEDNAR, JOHN M (D)
NH State Rep
b Bridgeport, Conn, Mar 9, 13; married; c Three. Educ: NY Univ, BS, Acct & Pre-Law. Polit & Govt Pos: NH State Rep, 63-; Town moderator; Supvr of checklist; mem, Town Budget Comt. Bus & Prof Pos: Tool & die maker; acct, credit & collections. Mem: Hudson Taxpayers Asn (exec dir); NH Taxpayers Fedn (dir). Relig: Catholic. Mailing Add: 153 Ferry St Hudson NH 03051

BEDNAREK, STANLEY MICHAEL (R)
Mem, Rep State Comt of Pa
b Philadelphia, Pa, Apr 7, 04; s Michael Bednarek & Helen Strzelecki B; m 1934 to Lucy Bielawski; c Ronald S. Educ: Roman Cath High Sch, grad, 23. Polit & Govt Pos: Magistrate, Philadelphia, Pa, 51; deleg, Rep Nat Conv, 68; mem, Rep State Comt of Pa, currently. Bus & Prof Pos: Dir, Kazimierz Wielki S&L Asn, 46-; realtor & ins broker, 45- Mem: Nat Asn Real Estate Bd; Port Richmond Lions; Polish Am Asn; Richmond Polish Asn; Pilsudski Fraternal Asn. Honors & Awards: Man of the Year award, Am Legion; Businessman, Sportsman, Port Richmond Lions Club. Relig: Catholic. Mailing Add: 2607 E Allegheny Ave Philadelphia PA 19134

BEDROSSIAN, ROBERT HAIG (R)
b Philadelphia, Pa, Aug 31, 24; s Edward Hagop Bedrossian & Sirvart Adourian B; m 1948 to Carolyn Mary Head; c Diane Louise, Robert Charles & Karen Lynn. Educ: Haverford Col, AB, 46; Temple Univ Med Sch, MD, 47; Univ Pa Grad Sch Med, MSc in med, 54; Phi Chi. Polit & Govt Pos: VChmn, Clark Co Rep Cent Comt, Wash, 63-64, asst vchmn, 65-66; mem, Gov Adv Coun Comprehensive Health Planning, 68-; Presidential elector, 72. Bus & Prof Pos: Pvt practice, 52-54 & 57- Mil Serv: Entered as Capt, Army Med Corps, 54, released, 57, after serv in Beaumont Army Hosp, El Paso, Tex. Publ: Twenty-two articles in med jours related to diseases of the eye. Mem: Am Acad Ophthal & Otolaryngol; Pac Coast Otolaryngol & Ophthal Soc; Am Med Asn. Relig: Presbyterian. Mailing Add: 3200 Main St Vancouver WA 98663

BEDSAUL, E CLIFFORD (R)
Chmn, Galax City Rep Party, Va
b Galax, Va, July 22, 21; s Charles Curren Bedsaul & Bessie Walker B; m 1948 to Louise Amburn; c Linda Sheryl & Larry Emmett. Educ: Benjamin Franklin Univ. Polit & Govt Pos: Clerk, Fed Bur Invest, Washington, DC, 40-42; chmn, Galax City Rep Party, Va, currently. Bus & Prof Pos: Asst mgr, Porter Furniture Co, Galax, Va, 47-49; resident agent, State Farm Ins Co, 49-69. Mil Serv: Entered as Pvt, Air Force, 42, released as Sgt, 46, after serv in 20th Air Force, Guam. Mem: VFW (past Comdr); Guidans. Relig: Methodist; Treas, First Methodist Church. Legal Res: 108 Front St Galax VA 24333 Mailing Add: Box 758 Galax VA 24333

BEDSOLE, ANN SMITH (R)
b Selma, Ala, Jan 7, 30; d Malcolm White Smith (deceased) & Sybil Huey S; m 1958 to Massey Palmer Bedsole; c Mary Martin Riser, John Henry Martin & Margaret Loraine Bedsole. Educ: Univ Ala, 48; Univ Denver, 55-56. Polit & Govt Pos: Mem, Rep State Exec Comt of Ala, 66-74; deleg & seconded nomination of Nixon for President, Rep Nat Conv, 72; Rep Presidential Elector, 72; chmn Southeast regional adv comt, Nat Park Serv, currently. Mem: Huntingdon Col (trustee); Mobile Historic Develop Found (trustee); Spring Hill Col (regent); Historic Mobile Tours, Inc; Jr League of Mobile. Honors & Awards: M O Beale Scroll of Merit, Mobile Press Register, 71 & 72; First Lady of Mobile for 1972. Relig: Methodist. Mailing Add: 25 Edgefield Rd Mobile AL 36608

BEEBE, MARGARET SCHERF (D)
b Fairmont, WVa, Apr 1, 08; d Charles Henry Scherf & Miriam Fisher S; m 1965 to Perry Elon Beebe. Educ: Antioch Col, 25-28. Polit & Govt Pos: Mont State Rep until 67; vchmn, Flathead Co Dem Cent Comt, Mont, formerly. Publ: The banker's bones, 68, To cache a millionaire, 72 & If You Want a Murder Well Done, 74, Doubleday & Co Inc; plus 22 others. Relig: Episcopal. Mailing Add: 737 First Ave W Kalispell MT 59901

BEEKMAN, ROBERT EARL (D)
b Los Angeles, Calif, June 9, 45; s John Andrew Beekman & Dorothy May Huff; m 1970 to Kathy Minette Fredriksen. Educ: Calif State Univ Fullerton, BA, 67; Georgetown Univ Law Ctr, JD, 73. Polit & Govt Pos: Legis asst, Rep Robert Leggett, 69-71; staff, Architect of the Capitol, 72-73; staff asst, Rep Richard Hanna, dist off, 73-74; admin asst, US Rep Mark W Hannaford, 75- Relig: Presbyterian. Mailing Add: Apt 1221 W 1515 S Jefferson Davis Hwy Arlington VA 22202

BEEMAN, JOSIAH HORTON (D)
b San Francisco, Calif, Oct 8, 35; s Josiah Horton Beeman & Helen Virginia Hooper B; m to Linda Hall. Educ: City Col San Francisco, 53-54; Reed Col, Portland, Ore; San Francisco State Col, AB, 57; Pi Sigma Alpha; Alpha Phi Omega. Polit & Govt Pos: Claims examr, Soc Security Admin, 57-58; pres, Calif Fedn Young Dem, 63-65, nat committeeman, 65-67; admin asst, US Rep Phillip Burton, Calif, 64-67 & 68-69; chmn bd dirs, Young Dem Clubs of Am, 65-67; mem bd supvr, City & Co of San Francisco, Calif, 67-68; vpres Calif Dem Coun, 67-69; deleg, Dem Nat Conv, 68; dir for Cong Liaison, McGovern for President, 72; staff dir Dem caucus, US House Rep, 75- Bus & Prof Pos: Dir of educ, Northern Calif-Nev Coun of Churches, 61-63; secy for int affairs, United Presby Church in the USA, 69-70, dir Washington off, 70-75. Mem: SAR; Knights of Dunamis. Relig: Presbyterian. Legal Res: 705 E Capitol St SE Washington DC 20003 Mailing Add: 1518 House of Rep Washington DC 20515

BEEMER, ELVIN HOMER (R)
Chmn, Taylor Co Rep Party, Iowa
b Bedford, Iowa, Mar 2, 19; s Homer Johnston Beemer & Grace Johnson B; m 1938 to Margaret Ruth Bordner; c Chris Elvin, Cedric Britt & Chad Bordner. Educ: Gravity High Sch, Iowa, grad; Area Econ Develop & Leadership Seminars. Polit & Govt Pos: Financial chmn, Taylor Co Rep Party, Iowa, 64-70, chmn, 70-; census crew leader, 70. Bus & Prof Pos: Pres, Colonial Manors of Bedford, 65- Mil Serv: Entered as Pvt, Army, 42, released as T/Sgt, 45, after serv in Co D, 409th Inf, 103 Div, Rhineland & Cent Europe, 44-45; Prisoner of War, Germany, 44-45; Am Theater Ribbon; Good Conduct Medal; Europe-Africa-Mid East Serv Medal with two Bronze Stars. Mem: Bedford Develop Club; Taylor Co Indust Develop (chmn); Bedford Community Develop; Midcrest Area Develop; Lions; Am Legion. Relig: United Methodist; Lay leader. Mailing Add: 304 Illinois St Bedford IA 50833

BEER, WALTER R, JR (R)
Mem, Vt Rep State Comt
b Pleasantville, NY, Sept 30, 26; s Walter R Beer & Helene Wardell B; m 1953 to Orba Jones; c Kimberly Jean & Leslie Michelle. Educ: Harvard Univ, BS, 46; NY Univ Grad Sch Bus Admin, 49 & 50; Pi Eta. Polit & Govt Pos: Agr census dir, Rutland & Bennington Co, Vt, 57; chmn, Wallingford Rep Comt, 58-66; campaign field dir, Vt Rep State Comt, 62, mem, currently; Rutland Co Chmn, Snelling for Gov Comt, 66, Prouty for Sen Comt, 70 & Comt to Reelect the President, 72. Bus & Prof Pos: Expert mgr, Carl M Loeb, Rhoades, New York, 53-56; self-employed, Wallingford, Vt, 56-58; mem staff, Howe-Richardson Scale, Rutland, 58-62; salesman, Nat Surv, Chester, 63-64; exec dir, Vt Higher Educ Facilities Comn, 64-68; bus mgr, Green Mountain Col, Poultney, 68- Mil Serv: Entered as A/S, Navy, 44, released as Ens, 47, after serv in USS Harwood, Pac Fleet; recalled as Lt, 51-53, serv in USS DeHaven; various mil awards & decorations. Mem: Rotary; Am Legion; Rutland Region CofC; Nat Asn Col Bus Officers. Relig: Methodist. Mailing Add: 26 Bentley Ave Poultney VT 05764

BEERMANN, ALLEN JAY (R)
Secy of State, Nebr
b Sioux City, Iowa, Jan 14, 40; s Albert Beermann & Amanda Schoenrock B; m to Linda Dierking. Educ: Midland Lutheran Col, BA, 62; Creighton Univ Sch Law, JD, 65; Pi Kappa Delta; Phi Alpha Delta; Kappa Phi (pres); German Club; Creighton Univ Student Bar Asn (pres). Polit & Govt Pos: Pres, South Sioux City High Sch TAR, Nebr, 58; pres, Midland Co Young Rep, 60; mem campaign staff, Beermann for Cong, First Dist, Nebr, 62; legal counsel & admin asst to Secy of State, Nebr, 65-67, Dep Secy of State, Nebr, 67-70, Secy of State, Nebr, 71- Mil Serv: Entered as Pvt, Nebr Nat Guard, 65, released as Specialist 4/C, 68; Capt, Army Nat Guard Judge Adv Gen Corps, assigned to Selective Serv, 68-; Spec Citation of Merit; second in class at basic training; Meritorious Serv Award, Nebr Nat Guard. Publ: Contrib ed, Nebraska state government, 68; auth, Would you trade your name, Nebr Real Estate Comn Comment, 68; Travel Nebraskaland, Newspapers of Nebr, 68. Mem: Am Interprof Inst (ethics comt, 68-); Nebr Bar Asn (legal-aid comt, 67-); Am Judicature Soc; Nebr Press Asn; Nebr Farm Bur Fedn. Honors & Awards: Distinguished Serv Plaque, Omaha Legal Aid Soc; Gov deleg, People-to-People Conf; Admiral, Great Navy of State of Nebr; Outstanding Young Man Award, Lincoln Jaycees. Relig: Lutheran. Legal Res: 4730 A St Lincoln NE 68510 Mailing Add: Dept of State Suite 2300 Capitol Bldg Lincoln NE 68509

BEERMANN, RALPH FREDERICK (R)
b Dakota City, Nebr, Aug 13, 12; s Fred W Beermann & Agnes Ellen Ralph B; m 1938 to Marjorie Louise Smythe. Educ: Morningside Col. Polit & Govt Pos: Chmn, Dakota Co Young Rep, Nebr, 46-48; chmn, Dakota Co Rep Cent Comt, 54-60 & 66-70; US Rep, Third Dist, Nebr, 61-62, First Dist, 63-64; dir, Nebr Pub Power Dist; dir, Siouxland Interstate Planning Coun. Bus & Prof Pos: Partner, Beermann Bros, 46-; stockholder & dir, Beermann, Meadowview, Inc & Beermann Farm, Inc, 49- Mil Serv: Entered as T-3, Army, 42, released as M/Sgt, 45, after serv in 601st Ord Bn, African & ETO. Mem: VFW; Am Legion; Farm Bur; CofC; Am Dehydrators Asn. Relig: Lutheran; Exec bd, Nebr Synod, Lutheran Church Am. Legal Res: 20th & Broadway Dakota City NE 68731 Mailing Add: PO Box 98 Dakota City NE 68731

BEERS, ORVAS E (R)
Chmn, Allen Co Rep Cent Comt, Ind
b Noble Co, Ind, Aug 11, 18; s Orvas Edward Beers & Marjorie Adair B; m 1943 to Margaret Helen Roethlisberger (deceased); c Richard Edward. Educ: Hillsdale Col, AB cum laude, 41; Univ Mich Law Sch, JD, 48; Delta Sigma Phi. Polit & Govt Pos: Dep prosecuting attorney, City of Ft Wayne, Ind, 52-57; city chmn, Ft Wayne Rep Party, 58; co attorney, Allen Co, 61-64; chmn, Allen Co Rep Cent Comt, 61-73 & 75-; chmn, Ind Nixon for President, 68; deleg, Rep Nat Conv, 68 & 72, chmn, Credentials Comt, 68. Mil Serv: Entered as Pvt, Army, 41, released as Capt, 46, after serv in ETO; five battle stars; one arrowhead for invasion. Mem: Allen Co Ind Bar Asn (trustee); VFW; Am Legion; Elks; 100% Club. Relig: Episcopal. Mailing Add: 4325 Highwood Dr Ft Wayne IN 46805

BEERY, JOHN THOMAS (D)
Committeeman, Clinton Co Dem Comt, Mo
b Platt Co, May 31, 84; s William Beery & Mary Elizabeth Redden B; m 1903 to Sally M Rails; c Raymond, Ronald & Thalma (Mrs Bowlin). Polit & Govt Pos: Committeeman, Clinton Co Dem Comt, 55-, chmn, 60-66, mem & treas, currently. Bus & Prof Pos: Farmer, 03-25; supvr, Quaker Oats Co, 25-49; treas, Gower Sch Dist, Mo, 54- Mem: Mason; Gower Lions Club; Clinton Co Red Cross (fund chmn); Gower Fire Asn (pres); WCent Mo Fire Asn (bd mem). Relig: Baptist. Mailing Add: RFD 1 Gower MO 64454

BEFORT, ALOIS GEORGE, JR (AL) (D)
Mem, Kans State Dem Comt
b Hays, Kans, Aug 17, 27; s Alois George Befort, Sr & Cathrine Herl B; m 1948 to Mildred E Tomecal; c Alois George, III, David Anthony, Robert Lesley, Amelia Cathrine, Thomas Duane, John Fitzgerald & James Anthony. Educ: Finley Eng Col, Assoc Mech Engr, 55; Nat Mgt Sch, Indust Mgt Assoc, 58; Am Soc Welding Engrs; Nat Mgt Asn. Polit & Govt Pos: Committeeman, Dem Precinct Six, Kans, 57-; mem, Kans State Dem Comt, 64-; chairperson,

Second Cong Dist, Kans & 36th Rep Dist, 70-; alt deleg, Dem Nat Mid-Term Conf, 74. Bus & Prof Pos: Mfg supvr, Bendix Corp, Kansas City, Mo, 49- Mil Serv: Entered as Pvt, Marines, 44, released as Sgt & Aviation Pilot after serv in 5th Div & 2nd Air Wing, Pac Theatre Opers, 44-46 & 50-51; Good Conduct Medal; Presidential Unit Citation; Korean Presidential Citation; Japanese Occup Ribbon; Five Campaign Stars; Korean Serv Ribbon. Mem: KofC (dist dep, Dist 3); Ment Retardation (bd dirs); Wyandotte Co Dem Club (pres, 73-74). Honors & Awards: Knight of the Year, KofC, 74. Relig: Catholic. Mailing Add: 3423 N 56th Pl Kansas City KS 66104

BEGAM, ROBERT G (D)
Chief Counsel, Ariz State Dem Party
b New York, NY, Apr 5, 28; s George Begam & Hilda Hirt B; m 1949 to Helen Gertrude Clark; c Richard J, Lorinda & Michael. Educ: Yale Col, BA, 49; Columbia Univ Law Sch, 49-50; Yale Univ Law Sch, LLB, 52; Yale Club of New York; Mory's Asn. Polit & Govt Pos: Treas, Ariz State Dem Party, 66-72, chief counsel, 72-; deleg, Dem Nat Conv, 68 & 72, mem, Credentials Comt, 72. Bus & Prof Pos: Assoc, Cravath, Swain & Moore, New York, NY, 52-54; gen counsel, Ariz Securities Comn, 56-57; partner, Langerman, Begam & Lewis, 57- Mil Serv: Entered as 1st Lt, Air Force, 54, released as 1st Lt, 56, after serv in Judge Adv Gen Dept, Air Training Command, 54-56. Mem: Am Trial Lawyers Asn; Western Trial Lawyers Asn; United Farm Workers (gen counsel, Ariz, 70-). Relig: Jewish. Legal Res: 161 E Country Club Dr Phoenix AZ 85014 Mailing Add: 1400 Ariz Title Bldg Phoenix AZ 85003

BEGGS, JAMES MONTGOMERY (R)
b Pittsburgh, Pa, Jan 9, 26; s James Andrew Beggs & Elizabeth Mikulan B; m 1953 to Mary Elizabeth Harrison; c Maureen Elizabeth, Kathleen Louise, Teresa Lynn, James Harrison & Charles Montgomery. Educ: US Naval Acad, BS, 48; Harvard Univ, MBA, 55; Sigma Tau. Hon Degrees: LLD, Washington & Jefferson Univ, 72; Dr Aviation Mgt, Embry-Riddle Aeronaut Univ, 72. Polit & Govt Pos: Assoc adminr adv research & tech, NASA, 68-69; Under Secy of Transportation, 69-72; mem, Cost of Living Coun, Comt on Food Prices, 72- Bus & Prof Pos: Div mgr, underseas div, Westinghouse Elec Corp, Baltimore, Md & Pittsburgh, Pa, 55-61, div mgr syst opers, 61-63, vpres defense & space ctr, surface div, 63-67, dir purchases & traffic, 67-68; exec vpres, Gen Dynamics Corp, 74- Mil Serv: Entered as Midn-Ens, Navy, 44, released as Lt Comdr, 54, after serv in submarines, Atlantic Submarine Force, 50-54; Lt Comdr, Naval Res, 54-66; various theater ribbons. Mem: Am Inst Aeronaut & Astronaut; Am Soc Naval Engrs; Howard Co Charter Comn. Relig: Roman Catholic. Mailing Add: 32 Woodoaks Trail St Louis MO 63124

BEGGS, MARY HARRISON (R)
b East Orange, NJ, June 3, 30; d Charles C Harrison & Hazel Edwards H; m 1953 to James Montgomery Beggs; c Maureen Elizabeth, Kathleen Louise, Teresa Lynn, James Harrison & Charles Montgomery. Educ: Conn Col for Women, BA, 52; Phi Beta Kappa. Polit & Govt Pos: Party worker, Precinct, Dist Level, Rep Party, Howard Co, Md, 58-62; mem, Fifth Cong Dist Rep Comt, 62-66; chmn, Rep State Cent Comt, Howard Co, 62-66; mem, Howard Co Planning Comn, 66-70, chmn, Adminr Wives Vol Prog, Rep Nat Comt, 72. Bus & Prof Pos: Eng teacher, Bloomfield High Sch, NJ, 52-53; asst personnel mgr, Mass Mem Hosp, 54-55. Mem: Conn Col Alumnae Coun; League Women Voters; Mo Hist Soc; John F Kennedy Ctr for Performing Arts (adv comt on arts, 71-); Goodwill Industs Guild. Relig: Presbyterian. Mailing Add: 32 Woodoaks Trail St Louis MO 63124

BEGICH, JOSEPH R (DFL)
Minn State Rep
Mailing Add: 1001 W Second St Eveleth MN 55734

BEGIN, ROGER NORMAND (D)
RI State Rep
b Woonsocket, RI, Nov 19, 52; s Paul A Begin & Rita H Beauchemin B; single. Educ: RI Jr Col, 71- Bus & Prof Pos: RI State Rep, Woonsocket, Dist 65, 73- Relig: Roman Catholic. Mailing Add: 443 Welles St Woonsocket RI 02895

BEGLEY, WILLIAM OVERTON, JR (D)
b Nocona, Tex, Sept 23, 23; s William O Begley & Vada Calvery B; div; c Dianna Kathleen (Mrs Phelps), Ron Roy, Angela Ellen & Annmarie Stacey. Educ: High sch, grad, 42. Polit & Govt Pos: Councilman, Kimball, Nebr, 69-70, mayor, 70-; chmn, Kimball Co Dem Party, Nebr, formerly. Bus & Prof Pos: Secy-treas, Am Asn Drilling Contractors, Denver Chap, 60-63. Mil Serv: Entered as Seaman 2/C, Navy, 42, released, 42, after serv in Seabee. Mem: Mason (Jr Warden); Rotary; Am Legion; Toastmasters; Methodist Men's Club. Relig: United Methodist. Legal Res: 720 Jefferson Kimball NE 69145 Mailing Add: Drawer 757 Kimball NE 69145

BEHN, ROBERT DIETRICH (R)
b Washington, DC, Sept 5, 41; s Victor Dietrich Behn & Nona Esther Heffley B; m 1968 to Judith Rutherfoord Howe; c Mark Dietrich. Educ: Worcester Polytech Inst, BS in physics, 63; Harvard Univ, PhD (decision & control), 68; Tau Beta Pi; assoc, Sigma Xi; Theta Chi. Polit & Govt Pos: Mem, Nat Gov Bd, Ripon Soc, Cambridge, Mass, 66-, research dir, 68-69, pres, Ripon Soc Boston-Cambridge, 73; asst to Gov for Urban Affairs, Mass, 69-70; chmn, Gov Task Force on Intercity Transportation, 70-71; mem, Cambridge Rep City Comt, 71-73; alt deleg, Rep Nat Conv, 72; mem, Mass Rep State Comt, 73. Bus & Prof Pos: Lectr bus admin, Harvard Univ Bus Sch, 72-73; assoc prof & dir grad studies, Duke Univ Inst Policy Sci & Pub Affairs, 73- Publ: Ed, The Lessons of Victory, Dial Press, 69; auth various short articles, columns & reviews in Saturday Rev, Boston Globe, Boston Mag, Christian Science Monitor & Ripon Forum; chmn ed bd, Ripon Forum, 72- Relig: Protestant. Legal Res: Apt 5-1 200 Seven Oaks Rd Durham NC 27704 Mailing Add: Inst for Policy & Publ Affairs Duke Univ 4875 Duke Sta Durham NC 27706

BEHNKE, ROBERT E (D)
Wis State Rep
Mailing Add: 4001 W Calumet Rd Milwaukee WI 53209

BEHR, LAWRENCE VAN DER POEL (R)
Chmn Commun Affairs, NC Fedn Young Rep
b Paterson, NJ, Nov 9, 40; s John Henry Behr & Beatrice Vanderpool B; div; c Lawrence, II & Jennifer Hague. Educ: ECarolina Col, 59-63; ECarolina Playhouse; Radio-TV Soc. Polit & Govt Pos: Pres, Pitt Co TAR's, 57-58; pres, ECarolina Young Rep Club, 60-63; deleg, Young Rep Nat Conv, 63; mem, Pitt Co Rep Exec Comt, 63-66; deleg, Rep Nat Conv, 64; Nat committeeman, NC Fedn Young Rep, 65-66, First dist dir, 59-65 & 71, chmn community affairs, currently. Bus & Prof Pos: Chief engr, ECarolina Col Radio-TV, 57-61; pres, Lawrence Behr Asn, Inc, 61-; partner, The Drumstick, 62-63; vpres eng, Farmville Broadcasting Co, 64-; secy-treas, VWB Inc, 65-; mgr spec projs, Multronics, Inc, 65-68; pres, Protection Systs of NC, 67-69; pres, Telecommun, Inc, 72- Publ: Engineering proficiency—operational & economic aspects, J Soc Broadcast Engrs, 64, Book Reviews, 65-; RF Grounding Techniques on Airborne Platforms, Limited, 66. Mem: Soc Broadcast Engrs Inc; Inst Elec & Electronics Engrs; Audio Eng Soc; NC Asn Broadcasters; Bright Leaf Amateur Radio Club. Honors & Awards: Amateur Radio Operator, K4JRZ, Pilots License. Legal Res: 404A Jarvis St Greenville NC 27834 Mailing Add: PO Box 3313 Greenville NC 27834

BEHR, PETER H (R)
Calif State Sen
b New York, NY, May 24, 15; s Karl Howell Behr & Helen Newsom B; m 1942 to Sally Clarkson; c Lola Haskins, Peter H, Jr & Gertrude H. Educ: Yale Col, BA, 37; Yale Univ Law Sch, LLB, 40. Polit & Govt Pos: Mem, Mill Valley Planning Comn, Calif, 54-56; mem, Mill Valley City Coun, 56-60; supvr, Marin Co, 62-68; Calif State Sen, 4th Dist, 71- Mil Serv: Entered as Ens, Navy, 41, released as Lt Comdr, 56, after serv in various ships, Atlantic & Pac, 41-46; Lt Comdr (Ret), Naval Res. Relig: Episcopal. Legal Res: 101 Barbaree Way Tiburon CA 94920 Mailing Add: State Capitol Sacramento CA 95814

BEHRMAN, CAROL IONE (DFL)
VChairwoman, Yellow Medicine Co Dem-Farmer-Labor Party, Minn
b Yellow Medicine Co, Minn, Dec 22, 30; d Clarence C Anderson & Inez Lecy A; m 1949 to Morris Walter Behrman; c Nanon, Leigh, Noelle & Lane. Educ: Belview Pub Sch, grad, 48. Polit & Govt Pos: Chmn, Yellow Medicine Co Dem-Farmer-Labor Party, Minn, formerly, vchairwoman, currently; mem, Dist Seven Comt for Terry Montgomery, 70. Bus & Prof Pos: Key punch operator, Farmers Union, Redwood Falls, Minn, 48-49; typesetter, Wood Lake News, 71. Mem: Farmers Union; PTA; 4-H Club (leader). Honors & Awards: 4-H Club Leader Recognition Award. Relig: Lutheran. Mailing Add: Wood Lake MN 56297

BEILENSON, ANTHONY C (D)
Calif State Sen
b New York State, 1932; m to Dolores Martin; c two sons, one daughter. Educ: Harvard Col, AB, 54, Harvard Law Sch, LLB, 57. Polit & Govt Pos: Calif State Assemblyman, 63-66; Calif State Sen, 67- Bus & Prof Pos: Attorney. Mailing Add: 1373 Westwood Blvd Los Angeles CA 90024

BEILFUSS, BRUCE F
Assoc Justice, Wis Supreme Court
b Withee, Wis, Jan 8, 15; s Walter William Beilfuss & Elsie Dodte B; m to Helen Hendrickson (deceased); m 1961 to De Ette Knowlton; c Mark. Educ: Univ Wis, BA. Hon Degrees: LLD, Univ Wis. Polit & Govt Pos: Supvr, Clark Co, Wis, 40-41, dist attorney, 41-48, circuit judge, 48-64; assoc justice, Wis Supreme Court, 64- Bus & Prof Pos: Chmn, Bd Circuit Judges, 56; chmn, Gov Comn on Law Enforcement & Crime, 65-66. Mil Serv: Entered as A/S, Navy, 43, released as Lt(jg); SPac Ribbon; Philippine Liberation Medal. Mem: Am Judicature Soc; Am Law Inst; Inst Judicial Admin; Rotary; Mason. Relig: Protestant. Legal Res: 4402 Fox Bluff Rd Middleton WI 53562 Mailing Add: Supreme Court Chambers State Capitol Madison WI 53701

BEIRNE, HELEN DITTMAN (R)
Alaska State Rep
Mailing Add: Box 4-BB Anchorage AK 99503

BEISTLE, JAMES H (R)
Chmn, Polk Co Rep Party, Wis
b Allenton, Wis, Dec 29, 36; s John Jacob Beistle & Marie Van Beek B; single. Educ: Univ Wis-Whitewater, BEd, 62; Univ Wis-Madison, MS, 65; Univ Mont, postgrad study; Sigma Tau Gamma. Polit & Govt Pos: Chmn, Polk Co Rep Party, Wis, 75- Bus & Prof Pos: Acct, Washington Farmco Coop, 55-61; instr bus educ, Winter High Sch, Wis, 62-68; mem exec comt, Wis Educ Asn, 65-72; instr bus educ, Unity High Sch, Milltown, 68-; mem bd trustees, Wis Educ Asn Ins Trust, 70- Publ: Auth, A survey of business education in small high schools in Wisconsin, Bus Educ Quart, 66. Mem: Delta Pi Epsilon; Nat & Wis Educ Asns; Northwest United Educators. Relig: Catholic. Legal Res: Hwy 35 Village of Centuria Centuria WI 54824 Mailing Add: PO Box 234 Centuria WI 54824

BELAIR, LAURENCE N (D)
NH State Rep
Mailing Add: 49 Dyer Ave Salem NH 03079

BELANGER, GERARD H (D)
NH State Rep
Mailing Add: 148 Bismarck St Manchester NH 03102

BELANGER, LAURENT WALTER (R)
Fla State Rep
b Manchester, NH, May 31, 31; s Euriel J Belanger & Jessie C Savoy B; m 1959 to Carol Ann Brown; c Michael A, Mark L, Michelle & Elisa. Educ: St Anselm's Col, 50-52; Loyola Univ Sch Dent, DDS, 56; Psi Omega. Polit & Govt Pos: Committeeman, Fla Young Rep Fedn, 65-66; treas, Pinellas Co Rep Exec Comt, Fla, 66-70; Presidential elector, 70; committeeman, Rep Party of Fla, 70-74, asst secy, 70-74; Fla State Rep, 74- Mil Serv: Entered as 1st Lt, Air Force, 56, released as Capt, 58. Mem: Am Dent Asn; Am & Fla Asns of Endodontists; Upper Pinellas Dent Soc. Mailing Add: 8401 36th Ave N St Petersburg FL 33710

BELCHER, PAGE (R)
b Jefferson, Okla, Apr 21, 99; married; c Page, Jr & Carol (Mrs Clyde V Collins). Educ: Friends Univ, Wichita, Kans; Univ Okla. Hon Degrees: LLD, Okla City Univ. Polit & Govt Pos: Campaign mgr & secy, US Rep Ross Rizley, Okla, formerly; court clerk, Garfield Co, Okla mem, Bd of Educ; chmn, Eighth Cong Dist Rep Party, ten years; exec secy, Rep Party of Okla; US Rep, Okla, 50-72; mem, Nat Rep Cong Comt, US House Rep, formerly; deleg, Rep Nat Conv, 68. Bus & Prof Pos: Attorney-at-law. Mem: Garfield Co & Okla Bar Asns; CofC; Kiwanis; Am Legion. Honors & Awards: Recipient, Silver Beaver Award, Boy Scouts. Relig: Methodist. Mailing Add: 1638 S Carson Tulsa OK 74119

BELCHER, TAYLOR GARRISON
b New York, NY, July 1, 20; s Taylor Belcher & Miriam Frazee B; m 1942 to Edith Anthony; c Anthony Wayne & Taylor, III. Educ: Brown Univ, AB, 41. Polit & Govt Pos: Career officer,

US Dept State, Foreign Serv, 45-, vconsul & diplomatic secy, Mexico City, 46-49, consul, Glasgow, 49-54, consul & consul gen, Nicosia, Cyprus, 57-60, with Can Nat Defense Col, 60-61, dir, Off WCoast Affairs, 61-64, US Ambassador, Cyprus, 64-69, US Ambassador, Lima, Peru, 69-74; pres, Cyprus Relief Fund of Am, New York, currently; pres, Garrison's Landing Asn, New York; consult, Dept of State, currently. Bus & Prof Pos: Mgr, coal co, 41-42. Mil Serv: Entered as Ens, Naval Res, 42, released as Lt, 45, after serv in NAtlantic & SPac Theatres; 13 Battle Stars & various Theatre Ribbons. Mem: Foreign Serv Asn. Honors & Awards: Distinguished Honor Award, Dept of State, 68; Grand Cross, Order of the Sun of Peru, 74. Relig: Protestant. Mailing Add: The Dock House Garrison-on-Hudson NY 10524

BELCOURT, AGENOR (D)
NH State Rep
b Baieville, Que, May 25, 01; s Donat Belcourt & Valerie B; m 1942 to Laurine Cote; c Mignonne L. Polit & Govt Pos: NH State Rep, 45-; Const Conv, 48, 56 & 64; chmn, Hillsborough Co Deleg, 57. Bus & Prof Pos: Johns Manville employee, 40 years, retired. Mil Serv: Entered as Pvt, Army, 42, released as Pvt, 43, after serv in Mil Police. Mem: Cath War Vet; Am Legion; Johns Manville Quarter Century Club; Garde Rochambeau; Loyal Club. Relig: Catholic. Mailing Add: 38 Perham St Nashua NH 03060

BELDEN, RICHARD O (R)
Conn State Rep
b Derby, Conn, Aug 13, 34; s Elbridge F Belden & Margaret Cowles B; m 1956 to Bertha M Kurtyka. Educ: Univ Philippines, 60-61. Polit & Govt Pos: Mem, Rep Town Comt, Shelton, Conn, 64-; mem, Bd Apportionment & Taxation, 67-71; alderman, 72-73; mem bldg comt, 72-73; mem & vchmn, Shelton Sewer Comt, 72-75; mem, Bd Tax Rev, 74; Conn State Rep, 113th Dist, 75- Bus & Prof Pos: Factory worker, Sponge Rubber Prod, 52-55; admin & supvry, Sikorsky Aircraft Div, United A/C, 61- Mil Serv: Entered as E-1, Air Force, 55, released as E-4, 61, after serv in 8th Air Force Strategic Air Command & 13th Air Force PACAF, 59-61; Good Conduct Medal; Air Force Longevity; Air Force Commendation Medal. Mem: Army Aviation Asn; Huntington Hist Soc. Mailing Add: 14 Keron Dr Shelton CT 06484

BELEN, FREDERICK CHRISTOPHER (D)
b Lansing, Mich, Dec 25, 13; s Christopher Frederick Belen & Elizabeth Lehman B; m 1943 to Opal Marie Sheets; c Frederick C, Jr. Educ: Mich State Univ, AB, 37; George Washington Univ, JD, 42; Delta Chi. Hon Degrees: LLD, Mich State Univ, 67. Polit & Govt Pos: Admin asst to US Rep Andrew Transue, Mich, 37-39; admin asst to US Rep George D O'Brien, Mich, 40-41; counsel & chief counsel, Post Off & Civil Serv Comt, 46-61; secy, 13th Cong Dist Dem Orgn, Mich, 48; deleg, Wayne Co Dem Conv, 48, Ingham Co Dem Conv, 60, 62, 64 & 66; asst postmaster gen, Bur Opers, Washington, DC, 61, Dep Postmaster Gen, 64-68. Bus & Prof Pos: Attorney, Washington, DC, currently. Mil Serv: Entered as 1st Lt, Army Res, 41, released as Lt Col, 46, after serv as Dep Chief of Intel & Security Div, Off Chief Transportation; Army Commendation Award. Publ: Auth various Cong comt reports & studies. Mem: Mich State Univ Alumni Asn; Nat Defense Transportation Asn; Multiple Sclerosis Soc (bd of dirs); Nat Dem Club (pres, 73-75). Honors & Awards: Recipient, Benjamin Franklin Award, 63; Mich State Univ Distinguished Alumni Award, 63 & Interfraternity Coun Alumnus Award for outstanding achievement in field of pub serv, 64; Nat Bus Publ Silver Scroll for outstanding contributions to improved mail serv & postal efficiency, 64; distinguished alumni award, George Washington Univ, 68. Relig: Presbyterian. Mailing Add: 2658 N Upshur St Arlington VA 22207

BELIEU, KENNETH EUGENE
b Portland, Ore, Feb 10, 14; s Perry Gordon BeLieu & Ilia Jean Rood B; m 1951 to Margaret Katherine Waldhoff; c Kenneth Eugene & Christopher Michael. Educ: Univ Ore, BA, 37; advan mgt prog, Harvard Univ, grad, 55. Polit & Govt Pos: Mem prof staff, Senate Armed Serv Comt, 55-58; staff dir, Preparedness Invest subcomt & Senate Comt of Aeronaut & Space Sci, 58-61; Asst Secy of Navy, Dept Defense, 61-64, Under Secy of Navy, 65; mem, Defense Sci Bd, 66-69; Dep Asst to the President for Cong Rels, 69-71; Under Secy Army, formerly. Bus & Prof Pos: Bus exec, Portland, Ore, 37-40; exec vpres & pres, Leisure World Found, 65-66, mem bd, 65-; mem bd dirs, Inst Strategic Studies, Georgetown Univ, 65-69; mem adv bd, Ryan Aeronaut Co & Continental Motors, 65-69; mem bd, Babcock Electronics Corp, 66-68; mem adv bd, Radio Corp Am, 68-69. Mil Serv: Army, 40-55, Col. Mailing Add: 1214 Westgrove Blvd Alexandria VA 22307

BELIVEAU, SEVERIN MATTHEW (D)
b Rumford, Maine, Mar 15, 38; s Albert Beliveau & Margaret McCarthy B; single. Educ: Georgetown Univ, AB, 60, Law Ctr, JD, 63. Polit & Govt Pos: Co attorney, Oxford Co, Maine, 65-66; Maine State Rep, 67-68; chmn, Maine Dem Party, 68-73; dir, European-NAm Comt, 69-; Maine State Sen, 69-70; pres, Asn Dem State Chmn, 70-; deleg, Dem Nat Conv, 72; mem exec comt, Dem Nat Comt, 72-73; deleg, Dem Nat Mid-Term Conf, 74. Mil Serv: Entered as Seaman Recruit, Coast Guard, 63, released as Seaman, 64. Mem: Am Coun Young Polit Leaders (dir, 68-); Maine Bar Asn (bd gov); Maine Trial Lawyers Asn; KofC. Relig: Roman Catholic. Mailing Add: 150 Congress St Rumford ME 04276

BELK, IRWIN (D)
b Charlotte, NC, Apr 4, 22; s William Henry Belk & Mary Leonora Irwin B; m 1948 to Carol Grotnes; c William Irwin, Irene Grotnes, Marilyn & Carl Grotnes. Educ: Davidson Col; Univ NC, Chapel Hill, BS Com, 46; Kappa Alpha; Delta Sigma Pi. Polit & Govt Pos: Mem Urban Redevelop Comt, Charlotte, NC, formerly; NC State Rep, 59-62; deleg, Dem Nat Conv, 56, 60, 64, 68 & 72; mem, NC Legis Coun, 63-64; mem, Legis Research Comn, 65-66; NC State Sen, Mecklenburg Co, 63-66, chmn, Hwy Safety Comt, vchmn, Appropriations Comt & mem, Banking, Higher Educ, Ins, Local Govt, Penal Insts, Pub Health & Rules Comts, NC Senate, 65-66; Dem Nat Committeeman, NC, 69-72. Bus & Prof Pos: Pres, Belk Enterprises, Inc, Charlotte, NC; vpres & dir, Belk Group of Stores, exec vpres finance, Belk Stores Serv, Inc, pres, Belk Finance Co, pres, Belk Stores Ins Reciprocal & chmn bd adv, The Belk Found, Charlotte; pres, Brothers Investment Co, Charlotte; pres, Monroe Hardware Co, Monroe; vpres & dir, Randolph Mills, Franklinville PMC, Inc, Raleigh; dir, Pilot Mills, Raleigh; dir, Adams-Millis Corp, High Point, First Union Nat Bank & Highland Park Mfg Co, Charlotte, Park Yarn Mill, Kings Mountain, Pilot Realty Co Raleigh, Stonecutter Mills, Spindale, Union Mills Co, Monroe, Hatteras Yacht Co, High Point, Lumberman's Mutual Casualty Co, Chicago, Ill, Cameron Financial Corp, Charlotte, Henry River Mills Co, Henry River, Johnston Mills, Charlotte, NC & Fidelity Bankers Life Ins Co, Richmond, Va. Mil Serv: Sgt, 491st Bomber Group, 8th Air Force, World War II, 2 years overseas. Mem: NC Merchants Asn; Scottish & York Rite Mason; NC Coun of Churches; NC Presby Hist Soc; plus numerous other civic & prof orgn. Honors & Awards: Selected One of Ten Outstanding Young Men in Charlotte, 54-57. Relig: Presbyterian; Former Deacon, Myers Park Presby Church, Charlotte. Legal Res: 400 Eastover Rd Charlotte NC 28207 Mailing Add: Belk Store Serv Inc PO Box 2727 Charlotte NC 28201

BELKER, LOREN B (D)
VChmn, Nebr Dem Party
b Quincy, Ill, June 23, 26; s Bernard John Belker & Verna Leach B; m 1952 to Darlene K Tracy; c Jeffrey Belker & Kendra K Land. Educ: Univ Nebr, 57-58; St Joseph's Col, Ill, 42-43; Quincy Col, 44. Polit & Govt Pos: Mem bus & com comt, Nebr Dem Party, 67, mem, banking, com & indust comt, 69-, vchmn, 70-; chmn, Lancaster Co Dem Cent Comt, 68-; chmn, State Dem Jefferson-Jackson Day Dinner, 69; state campaign chmn, Exon for Gov Comt, 70 & 74; mem, State Adv Coun on Hosps & Med Facilities, 72- Bus & Prof Pos: Dir, Agency Admin, Bankers Life Nebr, Lincoln, 70-; vpres, Midwest Chap, Ins Acct & Statist Asn, 65-66, pres, 69. Publ: Common sense & supervision, Interpreter, 63; The telephone & conservation, Best Ins News, 65; Some second thoughts on pre-authorized checks, Life Off Mgr Asn Educ Prog, 67. Mem: Fel, Life Mgt Inst; Community Chest (chmn, Budget Comt, Exec Comt & Bd Dirs); PTA; Malone Community Ctr; State Young Dem. Honors & Awards: Cited, Lincoln J & City of Lincoln; Cum Laude, Health Ins Asn Am. Relig: Episcopal; Former Sr Warden, Jr Warden & Vestryman. Mailing Add: 2631 Sewell Lincoln NE 68502

BELL, ALEXANDER B (D)
Md State Deleg
Mailing Add: 9618 Cottrell Terr Silver Spring MD 20903

BELL, ALPHONZO (R)
US Rep, Calif
b Los Angeles, Calif, Sept 19, 14; s Alphonzo Bell & Minnewa B; m to Marion McCargo; c Stephen & Fonza Helms; Matthew Temple, Robert Louis, Anthony Edward, Richard Cantrell, Graham McCargo, Harry Morgan & William Remmington Bell. Educ: Occidental Col, BA. Polit & Govt Pos: Mem, Rep Nat Comt & chmn, Rep State Cent Comt of Calif, 56-58; chmn, Los Angeles Co Rep Cent Comt, 58-60; US Rep, Calif, 60- Bus & Prof Pos: Chmn bd dir, Bell Petroleum Co (prior to elec). Mil Serv: Army Air Corps. Legal Res: 4163 Via Marina 209 Marina Del Ray CA 90291 Mailing Add: US House of Rep 2329 Rayburn Bldg Washington DC 20515

BELL, CHARLES FREDERICK (D)
Mem, Alamance Co Dem Exec Comt, NC
b Burlington, NC, Oct 27, 51; s Raymond Edward Bell, Sr & Reba Johnson B; single. Educ: Elon Col, BA, 72; Univ NC, Chapel Hill, 72-73; NC State Univ, 72-73; Elon Col Young Dem. Polit & Govt Pos: Deleg, Dem Nat Mid-Term Conf, 74; mem, Alamance Co Dem Exec Comt, NC, 74-; chmn, Comt to Retain the NC Presidential Primary, currently; publicity chmn, Alamance Co Young Dem Club, currently. Bus & Prof Pos: Asst mgr, R E Bell Co, Burlington, NC, 73- Mem: Burlington-Alamance CofC (state & nat govts comt); Elon Col Alumni Asn; Elon Col Century Club. Honors & Awards: Elon Col Deans List, 70, 71 & 72. Legal Res: 711 E Davis St Burlington NC 27215 Mailing Add: PO Box 445 Burlington NC 27215

BELL, CHARLES PORTER (D)
Mem, Boone Co Dem Cent Comt, Mo
b Rocheport, Mo, Jan 4, 12; s John Wesley Bell & Ossie Jane Potts B; m 1932 to Helen Marguerite Trimble; c Charles Wesley & Sarah Helen (Mrs Ralph Olinger). Polit & Govt Pos: Dist organizer, Young Dem, Mo, 31-32; dir safety & vehicles oper, US Post Off Dept, Columbia, Mo, 36-69, retired; mem, Boone Co Dem Cent Comt, 70- Bus & Prof Pos: Dir youth activities, Boone Co CofC, 66-71; owner, Spinning Wheel Realty, 70- Publ: Youth & conservation, Nat Soil Conserv Serv Mag, 67. Mem: Conserv Fedn Mo (treas); Nat Forestry Asn; Nat Wildlife Fedn; Optimist; Future Farmers Am (hon state farmer & hon mem, Columbia, Ashland & Memphis chap). Relig: Baptist. Mailing Add: 207 N William Columbia MO 65201

BELL, CLARENCE E (D)
Ark State Sen
b Camden, Ark, Feb 1, 12; s Joseph Dudley Bell, III & Dona Massengale B; m 1936 to Hope Raney; c Joseph Dudley, IV, Beverly Jane & Barbara Ann. Educ: Ouachita Col, AB; Univ Ark, MA. Polit & Govt Pos: Ark State Sen, 57- Bus & Prof Pos: High sch prin & coach, Parkin, Ark, 35-41, supt sch, 41-63; pub rels rep, Ark-La Gas Co, 63- Mem: Rotary; Farm Bur; Ark Educ Asn. Honors & Awards: Selected to All-State Football Team in High Sch & Col. Relig: Baptist. Mailing Add: Box 282 Parkin AR 72373

BELL, DALE ALLEN (R)
Chmn, Lawrence Co Rep Party, SDak
b Deadwood, SDak, Feb 1, 50; s Thomas Donald Bell & Helen Schenk B; m 1974 to Jayne Sager. Educ: Black Hills State Col, BS in Polit Sci, 72; pres, Young Rep, 69-71; vpres, Student Body, 70-72. Polit & Govt Pos: Chmn convocations comt, Black Hills State Col, 70-71; nat committeeman, SDak Young Rep, 73-74; field dir, Thorsness for Senate, 73-74; chmn, Lawrence Co Rep Party, 73- Mailing Add: Tinton Rd Spearfish SD 57783

BELL, DAVID ELLIOTT
b Jamestown, NDak, Jan 20, 19; s Reginald Bell & Florence Boise B; m 1943 to Mary Louise Barry; c Susan (Mrs David Rogers) & Peter. Educ: Pomona Col, Calif, BA, 39; Harvard Univ, MA in Econ, 41, Phi Beta Kappa. Hon Degrees: LLD, Pomona Col, Calif, 61, Harvard Univ, 65, Univ Vt, 65, Notre Dame Univ, 66 & Univ NDak, 67. Polit & Govt Pos: Staff mem, Bur Budget, 42, 45-47 & 48-49, dir, 61-62; spec asst to White House, 47-48 & 49-51; admin asst to President Truman, 51-53; adminr, Agency Int Develop, 62-66. Bus & Prof Pos: Adv gen econ, Govt Pakistan Planning Bd & prof field supvr, Harvard Adv Group, 54-57; lectr econ, Harvard Grad Sch, 57-61, secy, Grad Sch Pub Admin, 59-61; vpres, The Ford Found, 66-69, exec vpres, 69- Mil Serv: Marine Corps, 1st Lt, 42-45. Publ: Auth, Allocating Development Resources, Some Observations Based on Pakistan Experience, 59. Mem: Am Econ Asn; Am Soc Pub Admin. Honors & Awards: Received Rockefeller Pub Serv Award, 53. Legal Res: 444 E 52nd St New York NY 10022 Mailing Add: The Ford Found 320 E 43rd St New York NY 10017

BELL, EDWIN GRAHAM (D)
NC State Rep
b Gastonia, NC, Apr 16, 39; s John Clyde Bell & Thelma Henley B; m 1957 to Gayle Walker; c E Graham, Jr, John Chris, Martin Craig, Ann Margaret & Patrick Henley. Educ: IBM Training Ctr, Atlanta, Ga, Programmer, 61. Polit & Govt Pos: Secy, Gaston Co Young Dem Club, NC, 65, pres, 66; pres, Tenth Cong Dist, Young Dem Club, 67; alt deleg, Dem Nat Conv, 68; Young Dem Nat Committeeman of NC, 68-72; secy, Gaston Co Dem Party, 70-;

mem, NC Dem Exec Comt, 70-; bd mem, Govt Study Comt of Dem Party, 70-; NC State Rep, 73- Bus & Prof Pos: Bd mem, NC Premium Finance Asn, 70-, pres, 71; pres, Cardinal Ins, Majestic Int Financing Corp, E Graham Bell Ins & Real Estate & Gen Ins Brokers of NC. Mil Serv: Entered as Airman 2/C, Air Force, 57, released as Airman 2/C, 60, after serv in Mil Air Transport Serv, Europe, 58-59. Mem: Mason. Relig: Lutheran. Mailing Add: Kendrick Rd Gastonia NC 28052

BELL, ELVIN CHARLES (D)
City Councilman, Fresno, Calif
b Merced, Calif, Mar 1, 37; s Albert Lloyd Bell & Lucille Spears B; m 1960 to Viola Frances Bland. Educ: Ft Benning Int Leadership Sch, Ga; Fresno State Col, BA, 59; Univ Santa Clara, adv study, summers, 62-64; LaSalle Univ, LLB, 70; Sigma Chi. Polit & Govt Pos: Pres, Fresno State & Co Young Dem, Calif, 58; city councilman, Fresno, 65- Bus & Prof Pos: Owner, Elvin C Bell Pub Rels & Advert Agency, Fresno; dir, Fresno Advert Club, 63; pres, Fresno Chap, Pub Rels Soc Am, 65. Mil Serv: Entered as Pvt, Calif Army Nat Guard, 54, currently Maj; Calif State Commendation Award with Pendant; Watts Serv Award; Calif Meritorious Award. Publ: Newspaper Expansion, Ed & Publisher, 58; Civic Participation, Grid Mag, 59; Playthings & Toys, Playthings Mag, 59. Mem: Fresno Kiwanis (dir); Fresno State Col Alumni (dir); Nat Guard Asn (by-laws comt); Am CofC Execs; Fresno Press Club. Honors & Awards: Outstanding Young Man of Year, Fresno Co, 63 & 66. Relig: Congregational. Mailing Add: 2908 E Garland Ave Fresno CA 93726

BELL, GEORGE D (D)
Kans State Sen
Mailing Add: 234 N 16th Kansas City KS 66101

BELL, J RAYMOND (R)
Chmn, Foreign Claims Settlement Comn US
b New Orleans, La; s Harry A Bell & Anna Field B; m 1974 to Jeanne Spitzel; c Carol (Mrs Kartes), Bonnie (Mrs Sauve), Joseph Raymond, Jr & Melodie (Mrs Macklin). Educ: New York Univ, 27; Atlanta Law Sch, LLB, 30; Delta Theta Phi. Polit & Govt Pos: Chmn, Foreign Claims Settlement Comn US, 73- Bus & Prof Pos: Mem staff, Georgian-Am, Atlanta, Ga, 27-30, Detroit Times, Mich, 30-33 & Loew's Washington Theatres, Washington, DC, 33-40; vpres, Capital Airlines, Washington, DC, 42-49; vpres, Columbia Pictures Indust, New York, 49-72. Mil Serv: 2nd Lt, Army Intel C. Mem: Am Bar Asn; Asn Bar New York; Pub Rels Soc Am; Nat Press Club; Metrop Club. Honors & Awards: US Army Patriotic Serv Award, 56; Medal of Merit, US Air Force Asn, 66; Am Legion Good Guy Award, 68; Exceptional Serv Award, US Air Force, 72; Man of Year, Air Force Asn, 73. Legal Res: 3546 S Ocean Blvd Palm Beach FL 33480 Mailing Add: 2113 S St NW Washington DC 20008

BELL, JAMES DUNBAR (D)
b Lebanon, NH, July 1, 11; s Frank Upham Bell & Louise Dunbar B; m to Stephanie Mathews. Educ: Univ NMex, BA, 34; Univ Chicago, PhD, 41. Polit & Govt Pos: Chief statistician, NMex Dept Pub Welfare, 36-37; analyst, Off Coordr Inter-Am Affairs, 41-42; spec asst, US Dept Justice, 43-44; labor attache, Bogota, 44-46; career officer, US Dept State Foreign Serv, 47-, secy, Santiago, 47-50, second secy, Manila, 50-53, supvr, Int Rels Officer, 53-55, dep dir, Off of Philippine & SE Asian Affairs, 55-56, dir, Off SW Pac Affairs, 56-57 & 60-64, dep chief, Djakarta, 57-58, US Ambassador, Malaysia, 64-69; campaign mgr, Dem Cand for Cong, 12th Dist, Calif, 70; vchmn, Santa Cruz Co Cent Dem Comt, 72-74. Bus & Prof Pos: Reporter, Albuquerque J, 33-34; instr, Gary, Ind Col, 39-41; asst prof, Hamilton Col, 46-47; Diplomat-in-residence, Univ Calif, Santa Cruz, 69-70, lectr, 70-, fel of Merrill Col, 70-, dir, Ctr for SPac Studies, 73-74. Mailing Add: 14 Kite Hill Rd Santa Cruz CA 95060

BELL, JAMES FARRELL (R)
Ill State Sen
b Joliet, Ill, Sept 8, 32; s James Charles Bell & Gwendolyn Ruth Farrell B; m 1954 to Maryann Christine Belin; c Kimberly, Catherine, Julia & James. Educ: Univ Ill, Urbana-Champaign, 55; John Marshall Law Sch, 64-65; Am Col Life Underwriters, Bryn Mawr, Pa, 65; US Army Command & Gen Staff Col, 72; Scimitar; Theta Chi. Polit & Govt Pos: Mem exec comt, Will Co Rep Party, 62-64, precinct committeeman, 62-66; asst supvr, Will Co Bd Supvr, 69-72; comnr, Will Co Forest Preservation, 69-72; Ill State Sen, 73- Bus & Prof Pos: Owner, Bell Agency Ins, Joliet, Ill, 59- Mil Serv: Entered as 2nd Lt, Army, 55, released as 1st Lt, 58, after serv in Air Defense Sch, Ft Bliss, Tex, 55-58; Lt Col, Army Res. Mem: Ill Life Underwriters Asn; Ill Independent Ins Agents Asn; Am Col Life Underwriters. Relig: Episcopal. Legal Res: 1216 W Acres Rd Joliet IL 60435 Mailing Add: 826 W Jefferson St Joliet IL 60435

BELL, JOHN A
Sen, VI Legis
Mailing Add: PO Box 737 Christiansted St Croix VI 00820

BELL, JOHN GORDON (R)
b Milwaukee, Wis, May 4, 30; s Francis Leonard Bell & Josephine Virginia Cole B; m 1950 to Betty Jean Petrie; c John Gordon, Jr, Thomas Andrews, Christopher David & Theodore Mark. Educ: Harvard Univ, AB, 52; William Mitchell Col Law, LLB & JD, 61; Phi Beta Gamma. Polit & Govt Pos: Town supvr, Mounds View Twp, Minn, 56-57, town chmn, 57-58; justice of the peace, Mounds View, 59-64; chmn, 49th Legis Dist, 66-69; vchmn, Ramsey Co, 69-71; chmn, Fourth Cong Dist Rep Party, 71-73; deleg, Rep Nat Conv, 72. Mem: Minn State Bar Asn; New Brighton Lions; Elks. Mailing Add: 151 Silver Lake Rd St Paul MN 55112

BELL, LELA HACKNEY (D)
b Wellington, Kans, Nov 25, 10; d Edward T Hackney & Mabel Rogers H; m 1937 to Charles Robinson Bell; c Rebecca & Madelyn (Mrs Douglas C Ewing). Educ: Univ Kans, AB, 32; Theta Sigma Phi; Mortar Bd; Pi Beta Phi. Polit & Govt Pos: Mem, State Coun on Arts, Mo, 69-74; deleg, Dem Nat Conv, 72; mem, Mo Coord Bd Higher Educ, 74- Mem: Am Asn Univ Women; PEO; League Women Voters; Modaway Arts Coun; Friends of Univ Mo Libr (bd dirs, 70-). Honors & Awards: Woman of Year, Soroptomists, 71; Distinguished Serv Award, Jr CofC, 72. Relig: Disciples of Christ. Mailing Add: 326 Grand Ave Maryville MO 64468

BELL, MARJORIE BROWN (MARJ) (R)
Chmn, Lewis & Clark Co Cent Comt, Mont
b St Paul, Minn, July 4, 20; d Page Arthur Brown & Adella Davidson B; m 1945 to John Francis Bell; c John F, Jr & Stephen Alan. Educ: Macalester Col, BA, 42; Thalians. Polit & Govt Pos: Rep precinct committeewoman, Lewis & Clark Co, Mont, 68-; secy, Lewis & Clark Co Cent Comt, 69-70, vchmn, 70-73, chmn, 73-; mem rules comt, Mont State Rep Cent Comt, 71-, regional liaison, 73- Bus & Prof Pos: Bookkeeper, Farmers Union Grain Terminal Asn, St Paul, Minn, 42-45; continuity writer & announcer, KGVO, Missoula, Mont, 47-49. Mem: Cowbelles; Arabian Horse Registry of Am, Inc; Lewis & Clark Co Farm Bur (secy, 75-). Relig: Presbyterian. Mailing Add: 4675 Birdseye Dr Helena MT 59601

BELL, NAPOLEON ARTHUR (D)
Mem, Ohio Dem State Exec Comt
b Dublin, Ga, June 17, 27; s Arthur Lee Bell & Ethel Lee Coleman B; m 1956 to Dorothy Jane Lyman; c Kayethel & Napoleon, II. Educ: Mt Union Col, BA, 51; Western Reserve Univ Law Sch, LLB, 54; Blue Key; Kappa Alpha Psi. Polit & Govt Pos: Dem committeeman, Fifth Ward, Columbus, Ohio, 63; mem, Franklin Co Dem Exec Comt, 65; mem, Dem Party Structure & Del Selection Comt, 69; deleg, Ohio State Const Rev Comn; mem, Ohio Dem State Exec Comt, currently; mem, Bd Tax Appeals, 71- Bus & Prof Pos: Attorney exam, Indust Comn Ohio, 55-58; pres & chmn bd, Beneficial Acceptance Corp; attorney, Bowen, Bell, Francis, White & Saunders, 58- Mil Serv: Entered as Pvt, Army, 46, released as Sgt, 47, after serv in 933rd AAA, Pac Theatre. Mem: Columbus Bar Asn; Columbus Area CofC (bd dirs); NAACP (life mem); Concerned Citizens of Columbus (chmn); United Negro Col Fund (state chmn). Honors & Awards: Award of Merit, Ohio Legal Ctr; Man of the Year, Kappa Alpha Psi, 64; Award of Merit, Mahoning Co Young Club, 64, Ohio Legal Ctr & United Negro Col Fund; Mt Union Col Alumni Chair Award, 67. Legal Res: 1975 Sunbury Rd Columbus OH 43219 Mailing Add: 10 E Town St Columbus OH 43215

BELL, RICHARD D (D)
Ind State Rep
Educ: Chem & eng, Purdue Univ. Polit & Govt Pos: Dem precinct committeeman, Ind, 14 years; mem, Ctr Twp Bd, 58-64; Ind State Rep, currently. Bus & Prof Pos: Quality control inspector, Modine Mfg Co. Mem: Boy Scouts (asst dist comnr); Mason (Past Master); Scottish Rite; UAW-CIO; Grange. Honors & Awards: Silver Beaver Award, Boy Scouts. Relig: Methodist. Mailing Add: 524 Allen St LaPorte IN 46350

BELL, RICHARD E
Asst Secy Agr Int Affairs & Commodity Progs
Mailing Add: Dept of Agr Washington DC 20250

BELL, ROBERT DONALD (D)
Committeeman, Ala State Dem Exec Comt
b Luverne, Ala, Jan 11, 38; s John Kendrick Bell & Lurlie Clements B; single. Educ: Auburn Univ, 56-58. Polit & Govt Pos: Co chmn, North Ala Citizens for McGovern for President, 72; chmn, Fifth Cong Dist, formerly; deleg, Dem Mid-Term Conf, 74; co chmn, North Ala Citizens for Impeachment of Richard Nixon, 74; mem, State Affirmative Action Comt, 74-, committeeman, Madison Co Dem Exec Comt, Ala, 74-; committeeman, Ala State Dem Exec Comt, Dist 18, 74- Bus & Prof Pos: Chem engr, Thiokol Chem Corp, Trenton, NJ, 58-64; sr tech sales rep, A-M Corp, Cleveland, Ohio, 64-66; stock broker, mutual funds, ins, real estate, Huntsville, Ala, 66- Mil Serv: Entered as E-1, Army Nat Guard, 61, released as E-4, after serv in Hq & Hq Co, Berlin Crisis, 61-62; Nat Emergency Serv Medal. Mem: Mensa; World Future Soc. Mailing Add: Apt 14 2323 Bob Wallace Ave SW Huntsville AL 35805

BELL, ROBERT HUDSON (R)
Ga State Sen
b Atlanta, Ga, Feb 1, 29; s Ernest Lawson Bell & Mattie Lou Richardson B; m 1958 to Betty Anne Rouse; c Kathryn Leigh & Allison Gaye. Educ: Univ Ga, Atlanta Div, 46-48; Erskine Col, 48-49; Ga State Col, BBA, 54; Sigma Kappa Chi. Polit & Govt Pos: Pres, DeKalb Co Young Rep Club, Ga, 67-68; mem exec comt, DeKalb Co Rep Party, currently; Ga State Rep, 69-72; Ga State Sen, 72- Bus & Prof Pos: Pres, R H Bell & Co, Atlanta, Ga, 62- Mil Serv: Entered as Recruit, Army, 50, released as Sgt, 52, after serv in Inf, Europe, 51-52. Mem: Henderson Mill Civic Asn (pres); Atlanta Athletic Club; Young Rep Club. Relig: Presbyterian. Mailing Add: Box 29561 Atlanta GA 30345

BELL, SAMUEL P, III (D)
Fla State Rep
Mailing Add: 424 House Off Bldg Tallahassee FL 32304

BELL, TERRELL H
Comnr Educ, Dept Health, Educ & Welfare
Mailing Add: Dept Health Educ & Welfare 400 Maryland Ave SW Washington DC 20202

BELL, THOMAS DEVEREAUX, JR (R)
b Niagara Falls, NY, Nov 2, 48; s Thomas D Bell, Sr & Leonore Chisholm B; m 1975 to Margaret McDaniel. Educ: Univ Tenn; George Washington Univ; Phi Gamma Delta. Polit & Govt Pos: Asst to mgr, Brock 1970 Senate Campaign, 69-70; spec asst to US Sen Brock, 70-71; dep dir, Young Voter for the President, 71-73; vchmn & dir, 1973 Inaugural Ball, 73; admin asst to US Sen Bill Brock, Tenn, 73- Legal Res: 5417 N Angela Rd Memphis TN 38117 Mailing Add: 254 Russell Bldg Washington DC 20510

BELL, THOMAS M (D)
Ohio State Rep
Mailing Add: 3020 E 116th St Cleveland OH 44120

BELL, TOM M (D)
WVa State Deleg
b Fayetteville, WVa, Apr 4, 34; s Thomas Matthew Bell & Hazel Wriston B; m 1959 to June Ann Knight; c Greg & Deborah Ann. Educ: Morris Harvey Col, BA, 60; pres, Independent Students Asn. Polit & Govt Pos: Chmn, Fayette Co Dem Exec Comt, WVa, 68-72; sheriff, Fayette Co, 69-; WVa State Deleg, 75- Bus & Prof Pos: Pres, Tom Bell, Inc, 60-68. Mil Serv: Entered as E-1, Army, 55, released as E-5, 62, after serv in 497th Combat Engr Bn, 55-57; Outstanding Recruit, Ft Knox, Ky. Publ: Know the drug threat, Fayette Tribune, 71. Mem: Nat Sheriffs Asn; WVa Sheriffs Asn (treas & bd gov); WVa Co Off Asn (pres); Lions; Mason. Relig: Presbyterian. Mailing Add: 2001 Somerset Lane Oak Hill WV 25901

BELL, WILLIAM FLETCHER (R)
Comnr of Ins, Kans
b Lawrence, Kans, July 26, 29; s Maurice L Bell & Hazel Chanay B; m 1950 to Mona Jean Slack; c Steven Michael & Nancy Diane. Educ: Univ Kans, BS, 57; Sigma Phi Epsilon. Polit & Govt Pos: Exec I, Ins Dept, Kans, 57-58, policy examr, 58-61, accident & health supvr, 61; asst comnr of ins, 61-71, comnr of ins, 71-; secy, Kans Judges Retirement Bd, 71-; chmn, Comt on Surety Bonds & Ins, 71-; mem, Kans Safety Coun, 71-, chmn, 72-73. Mil Serv: Entered as Airman Basic, Air Force, 51, released as Airman 1/C, 53, after serv in Hq Squadron 2500 Air Base Wing, Continental Air Command; Nat Defense Serv Medal. Mem:

Nat Asn Ins Comnr (vpres, 72-73, pres, 73-74, mem financial condition, exam & reporting comt, mem computer application, ins advert regulation & guidelines & prepaid legal expense subcomts, chmn life, accident & health comt, chmn exam & accident & health subcomts, mem annual meetings reevaluation task force & chmn off relocation task force, all currently); Am Legion; Univ Club; Kiwanis. Honors & Awards: Dean's Honor Roll, Univ Kans, 56 & 57. Relig: Baptist. Mailing Add: 843 W 22nd St Lawrence KS 66044

BELLA, VINCENT J (D)
La State Rep
b Berwick, La, July 29, 27; s Joseph John Bella & Loretta Lampe B; m 1948 to Dorothy Parro; c Marsha (Mrs Richard Zulick), Chad Gerard, Blaise Vincent & Bridget Geri. Educ: Univ Southwestern La, 44-45; Molers Barber Col, 46-47. Polit & Govt Pos: Alderman, Berwick, La, formerly; La State Rep, Dist 50, 72- Bus & Prof Pos: Barber, self-employed, 47-64; real estate salesman, Cutrone Realty, 64-66; mgr life, group & accident ins, C J Cutrone Ins, 67; owner, Bella-Sens Ins Agency, currently. Mil Serv: Pfc, Marine Corps, 45-46. Mem: Berwick Vol Fire Dept (fire chief, 51-); La Fire Chiefs Asn; Sickle Cell Anemia Comt; La Fireman's Asn. Honors & Awards: Appreciation Plaque, Boy Scouts, 51; Citizen of the Month, Morgan City-Berwick Women's Prof Club, 61; Col, Staff of Gov McKeithen, 64; Citation of Merit, Law Enforcement & Fireman Training Prog, 64. Relig: Catholic. Legal Res: 452 Pac St Berwick LA 70342 Mailing Add: PO Box 468 Berwick LA 70342

BELLAMY, CAROL (D)
NY State Sen
b Plainfield, NJ, 1942. Educ: Gettysburg Col, grad with honors, 63; NY Univ Sch Law, JD. Polit & Govt Pos: NY State Sen, 23rd Dist, currently, ranking Dem mem, Transportation Comt, mem, Conservation, Recreation & Environ Comt, mem, Commerce & Econ Develop Comt, mem, Soc Serv Comt, mem, Taxation Comt, NY State Senate, currently. Bus & Prof Pos: Asst comnr, New York Dept of Ment Health & Ment Retardation Serv, formerly; with Peace Corps, Guatemala, Cent Am, two years; assoc in corporate law, Cravath, Swaine & Moore, New York, formerly; lawyer, currently. Mailing Add: 278 Henry St Brooklyn NY 11201

BELLANCA, ALFONSO V (R)
Chmn, Erie Co Rep Comt, NY
b Buffalo, NY, June 27, 12; s Philip Bellanca & Mary Gimbrone B; m 1943 to Marie Barone; c Carol (Mrs Bruce), Maryanne (Mrs La Penna) & Alan. Educ: Univ Buffalo, 3 years; Kappa Psi. Polit & Govt Pos: Mem bd assessors, Buffalo, NY, 52-69; chmn, Erie Co Rep Comt, 68- Bus & Prof Pos: Cert assessor, 65-; NY State Assessors, Inst of Assessing Officers, 67- Publ: Author, several papers on assessments on file at Int Asn Assessing Officers, Chicago, Ill. Mem: Int Asn Assessing Officers; Buffalo Athletic Club; Buffalo Launch Club; Transit Valley Country Club; NY State Assessors Asn. Honors & Awards: Named Outstanding Rep of Erie Co, 67; Hall of Fame Award, Chairman's Club, 68. Relig: Roman Catholic. Mailing Add: 566 Richmond Ave Buffalo NY 14222

BELLINO, ROBERT JOHN (R)
Chmn, Manatee Co Rep Exec Comt, Fla
b Pittsburgh, Pa, June 3, 35; s Paul Bellino & Rose Tranquill B; m 1962 to Sherry June Fuller; c Karen Anne & Dara Elizabeth. Educ: Univ Fla, BS, 62, Col Med, MD, 66; Phi Beta Kappa. Polit & Govt Pos: Rep precinct committeeman, Manatee Co, Fla, 73-75; chmn, Manatee Co Rep Exec Comt, 74- Bus & Prof Pos: Internship, St Mary's Hosp, West Palm Beach, Fla, 67; resident, dept psychiat, Univ Fla Col Med, 70; physician & psychiatrist, Bradenton, Fla, 67- Mil Serv: Seaman, Coast Guard, 64-68. Publ: Co-auth, Problems of the military retiree, J Fla Med Asn, 56: 245-248; auth, Psychosomatic problems of military retirement, Psychosomatics, 9-10/69; Perspectives of military & civilian retirement, Ment Hyg, 10/70. Mem: Am & Fla Med Asns; Fla Psychiat Soc (chmn ethics comt, 74-); Manatee Co Med Soc; Elks. Relig: Catholic. Mailing Add: 1607 21st St W Bradenton FL 33505

BELLIS, KENNETH MOHR (R)
b Newburgh, NY, Oct 8, 40; s Warren H Bellis & Marion King B; single. Educ: Colgate Univ, BA, 62; Washington Col Law, Am Univ, 69-72; Cath Univ, Columbus Sch Law, JD, 75; Phi Soc; Phi Delta Alpha; Alpha Chi Epsilon. Polit & Govt Pos: Asst, Katharine St George, US Cong, 62-64; legis asst, John E Hunt, US Cong, 67-72; admin asst, Benjamin A Gilman, US Cong, 73-74. Bus & Prof Pos: Customer serv planner, Southern Calif Edison Co, Los Angeles, 65-67. Mil Serv: Entered as E-1, Air Nat Guard, Air Force Res, 63, released as S/Sgt E/5, 69, after serv in 459th Supply Squadron. Mem: Am Legion; House of Rep Admin Assts Asn; Capitol Hill Toastmasters; Am Field Serv Alumni Asn, Washington, DC. Relig: Episcopal. Legal Res: 17 Weyants Lane Newburgh NY 12550 Mailing Add: Apt 611 1000 Sixth St SW Washington DC 20024

BELLMAN, CHARLES J (D)
Chmn, SDak State Dem Cent Comt
Legal Res: Wecota SD 57480 Mailing Add: Dem State Hq 201 E Capitol Pierre SD 57501

BELLMON, HENRY L (R)
US Sen, Okla
b Tonkawa, Okla, Sept 3, 21; s George D Bellmon & Edith Eleanor Caskey B; m 1947 to Shirley Osborn; c Patricia, Gail & Ann. Educ: Okla Agr & Mech Col, BS, 42. Polit & Govt Pos: Okla State Rep, 46-48; state chmn, Rep State Comt, 60-62, Gov, Okla, 63-67; US Sen, Okla, 69-, mem budget comt, US Senate, 75- Bus & Prof Pos: Farmer & rancher; mem bd dirs, Williams Bros Pipeline, Tulsa, 67-68; part owner, Rush Metals Co, Billings, 68- Mil Serv: Entered Marines, 42, released as 1st Lt, 46, after serv in 4th Marine Div, Pac Theatre; Legion of Merit; Silver Star. Mem: Okla Health Sci Found; Okla Med Research Found (Rep). Relig: Presbyterian. Legal Res: Rte 1 Red Rock OK 74651 Mailing Add: 125 Russell Bldg Washington DC 20510

BELLO, EDWIN L (POPULAR DEM, PR)
Sen, PR Senate
b Guayama, PR, Jan 18, 32; s Leopoldo V Bello & Maria Adela Gonzalez B; m 1959 to Carmen Elisa Rivera; c Ada Lillian, Edwin L & Angel A. Educ: Univ PR, Rio Piedras, BA, 56; Univ Mo, Kansas City, JD, 59; Phi Alpha Delta. Polit & Govt Pos: Legal adv to Gov, PR, 60-62; pres munic comt, Guayama Popular Dem Party, 69-70; Sen, PR Senate, Guayama Sen Dist, 70-, vpres, Appointments Comt & mem Agr & Judiciary Comns, 70-, pres, Internal Matters Comt, secy, Econ & Soc Develop Comts, deleg to Cent Coun of Popular Dem Party, 71-; pres impugnations comt, Popular Dem Party, PR, 71- Bus & Prof Pos: Treas, Bello's Liquilux, Inc, 59-62, pres, 63-69; owner, Bellolux Furniture Store, 67- Mem: Col of Lawyers of PR; Interam Fedn Lawyers; Am & Int Bar Asns; Lions. Honors & Awards: Dean's List. Relig: Catholic. Mailing Add: Hostos 10 Sur Guayama PR 00654

BELLOMINI, ROBERT E (D)
Pa State Rep
b Erie, Pa, June 1, 25; s Joseph Bellomini & Victoria Oligeri B; m to Virginia Nesi. Educ: Gannon Col Night Sch. Polit & Govt Pos: Mem, Young Dem of Erie Co, Pa; Pa State Rep, 64- Bus & Prof Pos: Owner, tavern-restaurant bus. Mem: Bartender's Union, AFL-CIO; KofC, Coun 278; vpres, Wolves Den 8; Ital Sons & Daughters - Nuova Aurora Soc; Charitable Scholarship Grants Orgn. Relig: Catholic. Mailing Add: Capitol Bldg Harrisburg PA 17120

BELMONTE, FRANK SALVATORE (D)
b Chicago, Ill, Feb 4, 29; s Giovianni Belmonte & Lucia Vercillo B; m 1953 to Marlene Iantorno; c Bernadette, Barbara & Bonita. Educ: Crane Tech High Sch, Chicago, 47. Polit & Govt Pos: Committeeman, Cicero Dem Twp Orgn, Ill, 70-; deleg, Dem Nat Mid-Term Conf, 74. Bus & Prof Pos: Court order abstractor, Chicago Title & Trust Co, Ill, 56-67; legal systs analyst, Circuit Court, Cook Co, 67- Mil Serv: Entered as Pvt E-1, Army, 51, released as Pfc, after serv in Mil Police, Far East Command, 52-53; Korean Serv Medal; Japan Occup Medal; Good Conduct Medal. Mem: Cook Co Young Dem Club; Ill Young Dem Club; Cook Co Dem Orgn; Joint Civic Comts Ital-Am; Ital-Am Charitable Orgn Cicero. Relig: Catholic. Mailing Add: 1828 S Austin Blvd Cicero IL 60650

BELMONTE, ROBERT A (R)
b Framingham, Mass, July 2, 30; s Arcangelo Belmonte & Carmela Millefiore B; m 1954 to Eleanor DeStafano; c Dru Theresa & Marcia Lyn. Educ: Yale Univ, BA, 52; Harvard Law Sch, LLB, 55. Polit & Govt Pos: Mem, Framingham Sch Comt, Mass, 58-; Asst Attorney Gen, Mass, 63-64; Mass State Rep, 64-73, Minority Whip, Mass Legis, 71-73; Rep cand, Attorney Gen, Mass, 69; chmn, Framington Rep Town Comt, formerly; alt deleg, Rep Nat Conv, 72; spec justice, Marlboro Dist Court, Mass, 73- Mem: South Middlesex & Middlesex Co Bar Asns; KofC. Relig: Catholic. Mailing Add: 27 Linda Ave Framingham MA 01701

BELSER, KEITH BAKER (D)
Pres, SC Young Dem Clubs
b Washington, DC, Nov 22, 45; s Irvine F Belser & Gladys Baker B; m 1967 to Berverly Black. Educ: Harvard Univ, BA, 68; London Inst Am Studies, 68-69; Spee Club. Polit & Govt Pos: Asst to chmn, SC Dem Party, 68; pres, SC Young Dem Clubs; 69-; precinct pres, Richland Co, 70-71. Bus & Prof Pos: Pres, Belser Co, Investment Properties, 69- Publ: Publ, Harvard Rev, 67-68. Relig: Episcopal. Legal Res: 5615 Lakeshore Dr Columbia SC 29206 Mailing Add: 3106 Devine St Columbia SC 29205

BELT, WILLIAM SCOTT (R)
Comnr, Morrow Co, Ohio
b Marion, Ohio, May 4, 08; s Jacob Milroy Belt & Mae Postel B; m 1936 to Vivian Ruthella Hipsher; c Michael Lynn. Educ: Marion Bus Col. Polit & Govt Pos: Clerk, Co Comnr, Ohio, 37-41; clerk, Common Pleas Court, 41-65; Ohio State Rep, 65-67; rep of Roger Cloud, Auditor of State, formerly; Comnr, Morrow Co, Ohio, 73- Bus & Prof Pos: Dir, Peoples Bank, 57-, mem exec comt, 61- Mem: Kiwanis (pres coun, 11th Div, 73-74); Grange; Farm Bur; CofC. Relig: United Methodist. Mailing Add: RFD 1 Edison OH 43320

BEMISS, FITZGERALD (R)
b Richmond, Va, Oct 2, 22; m to Margaret Page; c Margaret Wickham & Samuel Merrifield, II. Educ: Univ Va. Polit & Govt Pos: Va State Rep, 55-59; Va State Sen, 60-67; chmn, Va Comn Outdoor Recreation, 66-74; mem exec comt, Gov Coun on the Environ, 70-; chmn, Va Comt Reelection of President, 72. Bus & Prof Pos: Pres & treas, Fitzgerald & Co; exec vpres, secy & treas, Woodstock Home & Land Co, Inc; pres, ARA Va SkyLine Co, Inc; dir, United Va Bank; mem bd dirs, James River Corp, Va, 72; exec vpres, ARA Serv Alaska; consult, Argyle Research Corp. Mil Serv: Navy. Mem: Sheltering Arms Hosp (Dir); Atlantic Rural Exposition (Dir); Va Hist Soc (exec comt); Raven Soc, Univ Va. Relig: Episcopal. Legal Res: 1248 Rothesay Rd Richmond VA 23221 Mailing Add: PO Box 1156 Richmond VA 23209

BENAFIELD, JAMES WELDON (BUDDY) (D)
b Coy, Ark, July 5, 27; s Lee Benafield & Grace Hoggard B; m 1949 to Anita Carr; c Susan Dawne & Shannon Carr. Educ: State Col Ark, BSE, 50. Polit & Govt Pos: Mayor, England, Ark, 67-; secy, Ark State Dem Party, formerly; chmn, Ark Racing Comn, currently; alt deleg, Dem Nat Conv, 72; deleg, Dem Nat Mid-Term Conf, 74. Bus & Prof Pos: Owner, J W Benafield Co, J W Benafield Leasing Co, Benafield Finance Co, Benjor, Inc, Benafield Farms & Benafield Motor Co, England, Ark & Benafield Motel, Nashville, Ark. Mil Serv: Vol, Navy, 45-46. Mem: England CofC; Ark Munic League (legis bd); Cent Ark Coun Health Planning; England Kiwanis Club; Ark Consistory. Relig: Methodist; Mem bd stewards, First Methodist Church of England, 10 years; chmn, finance comt. Legal Res: 403 SE Fifth England AR 72046 Mailing Add: PO Box 130 England AR 72046

BENDA, CAROL JOYCE (R)
b Britton, SDak, July 24, 32; d William Schneider & Hannah Eikamp S; m 1951 to Chan A Benda; c Kathryn M, Alan F & Robyn Renae. Educ: Britton High Sch, grad. Polit & Govt Pos: Vchmn, Marshall Co Rep Party, SDak, formerly; clerk of courts, Marshall Co, 69- Bus & Prof Pos: Legal secy, part time, 20 years; cashier, local theater. Mem: Homemakers Exten Club; Farmers Union. Relig: Presbyterian. Mailing Add: Britton SD 57430

BENDELOW, EDWARD MASON (D)
Colo State Rep
b Detroit, Mich, July 24, 41; s Edward M Bendelow & Catherine Kelly B; single. Educ: Wayne State Univ, BA, 64; Cornell Univ, MILR, 68; Univ Denver, JD, 72 & MPA, 73; Alpha Chi; Mackenzie Honor Soc. Polit & Govt Pos: Vol, US Peace Corps, Liberia, 64-66; intern, Int Labor Affairs, US Dept Labor, 67; Colo State Rep, 73- Bus & Prof Pos: Employee rels, Singer Co, New York, 68-69; attorney, law off of John A Criswell, Denver, 72-73; law off of E M Bendelow, 73- Publ: Co-auth, Legal restrictions on municipal finance in Colorado, Denver Urban Observ, 8/72; auth, Municipal finance in Colorado, Univ Denver Law J, 10/73. Mem: Colo Bar Asn; North Denver Civic Asn; Platte River Valley Redevelop Comt; North Denver Youth Serv Bur; United Way Long Range Planning Comt. Honors & Awards: Activities Award, McKenzie Honor Soc, 64. Relig: Catholic. Mailing Add: 4620 Eliot Denver CO 80221

BENDER, RICK S (D)
Wash State Rep
Mailing Add: 3511 NE 158th Pl Seattle WA 98155

BENDHEIM, LEROY S (D)
Va State Sen
b Alexandria, Va, Feb 12, 06; s Charles Bendheim & Edith Schwarz B; m 1934 to Ethel Colman. Educ: George Washington Univ, AB, 28, JD, 29. Polit & Govt Pos: Staff mem, Nat Recovery Admin Rev Bd, 35-36; city councilman, Alexandria, Va, 48-52, vmayor, 52-55, mayor, 55-61; Va State Sen, currently; deleg, Dem Nat Conv, 68. Bus & Prof Pos: Dir, First Fed Savings & Loan Asn Alexandria; dir, Park & Shop Alexandria Corp; dir, Downtown Garage, Inc; instr commercial law, George Washington Univ, 49 & 50; former pres & chmn bd, Colonial Nat Bank, Alexandria, 63-68; dir, First Va Bank, 68-; sr partner, Law Firm of Bendheim, Ratner & Milligan, Alexandria, Va, currently. Mil Serv: Entered as Pvt, Army, 43, released as Sgt, 45, after serv in Third & First Armies, European Theater; Good Conduct Medal; Victory Medal; four campaign battle stars. Publ: Contrib ed, State of Va Probate Law Digest. Mem: Mason (32 degree); Odd Fellows; Elks; Alexandria Sportsman's Club; Nat Lawyers Club. Relig: Jewish. Legal Res: 309 Mansion Dr Alexandria VA 22302 Mailing Add: 718 Jefferson St PO Box 156 Alexandria VA 22313

BENDIXEN, SERGIO (D)
Dem Nat Committeeman, Fla
b Lima, Peru, Dec 1, 48; s Thor J Bendixen & Carmen R More B; single. Educ: Univ Notre Dame, BSChE, 70. Polit & Govt Pos: Dem Nat Committeeman, Fla, 75- Relig: Catholic. Mailing Add: 1800 Michigan Ave Miami Beach FL 33139

BENEDICT, GEORGE WILLIAM (D)
NDak State Rep
b Berthold, NDak, June 27, 06; s Edward Benedict & Mary Rudser B; m 1935 to Pauline Margaret Hornberger; c Garene (Mrs Roy Bibelheimer), Janene (Mrs Gary Haugen), Etoile (Mrs Fred Keiser) & Karen (Mrs Larry Borud). Educ: Ndak State Univ, 29-30. Polit & Govt Pos: Mem, Berthold City Coun, NDak, 46-50; mayor, Berthold, 50-66; chmn, Third Dist Dem Party, 72-74; NDak State Rep, Third Dist, 74- Bus & Prof Pos: Pres, NDak Frozen Foods & Locker Asn, 48-50; dir, NDak Retail Grocers, 63-73; dir, Ward Co Red Cross, 65-75. Mem: Lions; Berthold Farmers Union. Honors & Awards: Life Membership in Retail Grocers; Mayor Award; Red Cross Recognition Award. Relig: Baptist. Mailing Add: Berthold ND 58718

BENEKE, MILDRED STONG (MILLIE) (R)
Mem, Minn Rep State Cent Comt
b Prairie City, Iowa, May 1, 19; d Reuben Ira Stong & Lillian Garber S; m 1939 to Arnold William Beneke; c Bruce Arnold, Paula Rae (Mrs Finnson), Bradford Kent, Cynthia Jane & Lisa Patrice. Educ: Wash Univ, 42-43; Univ Minn, off campus courses, 45-58; Mankato State Col, off campus courses, 51-52, 53-54, 57, 64, 67; Dean's List & Independent Women's Asn, Wash Univ. Polit & Govt Pos: Arrangements chmn, McLeod Co Rep Conv, Minn, 66; chmn, Ward IV Rep Orgn, Glencoe, 67-69; mem, Credentials & Registr Comt, Second Dist Rep Conv, 69; chmn, McLeod Co Rep Comt, 69-73; mem, Minn Rep State Cent Comt, 69-; mem, Platform Comt, Minn State Rep Conv, 70; chmn proj interaction boutique, Minn Correctional Inst Women, Shakopee, Minn, 71-75, vpres & co-founder, Pi House, St Paul, Halfway House, 73-; alderman Ward IV, Glencoe City Coun, 74-; chmn, McLeod Co Steering Comt Diversion Prog, 74- Bus & Prof Pos: Legal secy, Arnold William Beneke, 45. Mem: Girl Scout Leader; Glencoe Citizens' Adv Comts; Citizens' Action Coun Steering Comt to form local comt on drug abuses. Relig: Lutheran. Mailing Add: Glenview Woods Glencoe MN 55336

BENGSTON, GARY L (R)
Chmn, Fifth Cong Dist Rep Comt, Va
b Rockford, Ill, Feb 17, 38; s Tagee S Bengston & Vada Boyd B; m 1960 to Gail Kopp; c Adell Renee, Karen Marie & Jennifer Lynn. Educ: Southern Ill Univ, BS, 60; Univ Chicago Law Sch, JD, 63. Polit & Govt Pos: Mem, Regional Adv Comn, Small Bus Admin, Va, 68-; chmn, Danville Rep Town Comt, Va, 70-72; deleg, Rep Nat Conv, 72; chmn, Fifth Cong Dist Rep Comt, 72-; mem, Va Coun Criminal Justice, 73- Bus & Prof Pos: Spec agt, Fed Bur Invest, Birmingham, Ala & Richmond, Va, 65-68; attorney, Danville, Va, 68-; pres, Westover Cartage Ltd, 72- Mem: Am & Va State Trial Lawyers Asns; Pi Kappa Delta; Lions, Danville Hosts Club (vpres, 68-75, pres, 75-76); Big Bros of Danville (bd mem, 71-). Relig: Lutheran. Legal Res: 284 W Main St Danville VA 24541 Mailing Add: PO Box 2135 Danville VA 24541

BENGTSON, ESTHER G (D)
Mont State Rep
b Froid, Mont, Oct 30, 27; d Goodwin Bergh & Elizabeth Jorgensen B; m 1948 to Lawrence E Bengtson; c Kristianne (Mrs Wilson), Monica (Mrs Holland) & Jennifer. Educ: Univ Mont, 45-47; Eastern Mont Col, 64-67; Sigma Kappa. Polit & Govt Pos: Mont State Rep, Dist 59, 75- Mem: Shepherd & Mont Educ Asns; Farmers Union. Relig: Lutheran. Mailing Add: Shepherd MT 59079

BENGTSON, L H, JR (D)
Okla State Rep
b Stillwater, Okla, June 8, 26; s Leroy H Bengtson & Mildred Horner B; div. Educ: Tulane Univ, BBS, 46; Okla State Univ, MS, 48; Okla Univ; Cent State Univ; Okla City Univ; Beta Alpha Psi; Alpha Kappa Psi; Kappa Tau Pi; Oak Leaves; Pi Kappa Alpha; Punchers; Men's Glee Club. Polit & Govt Pos: Okla State Rep, 64-, vchmn, research & invest, Okla House Rep, 65, vchmn, Okla Co Deleg, 65-67, vchmn, banks & banking, 67-68, vchmn, subcomt pub schs, 69, chmn, parks & recreation, 69 & vchmn, task force indust develop & parks, 69, Majority Whip, currently. Bus & Prof Pos: Pres & gen mgr, Oklahoma City Wranglers Prof Football Team. Mil Serv: Entered as A/S, Navy, 44, released as Ens, 46; Res, 46-50, Lt(jg); Victory Medal; Am Theatre Ribbon. Mem: Capitol Hill Alumni Asn; Lions; Capitol Hill CofC; Red, Red, Rose (pres); Phi Delta Kappa. Relig: Disciples of Christ. Mailing Add: 1309 SW Binkley Oklahoma City OK 73119

BENGTSON, LARRY EDWIN (D)
Chmn, Geary Co Dem Cent Comt, Kans
b Salina, Kans, Dec 29, 39; s Axel Edwin Bengtson & Berniece Johnson B; m 1964 to Judy Ellen Dickey; c Debra, Amy & Angela. Educ: Kans State Univ, BA, 62; Kans Univ, 62-63; Washburn Univ, JD, 65; Beta Sigma Phi; Collegiate Dem; Chancery Club. Polit & Govt Pos: Chmn, Docking for Gov, Kans, 70-72; chmn, Geary Co Dem Cent Comt, 71-; vchmn, Second Cong Dist Dem Comt, 74-; Asst Attorney Gen, Kans, 74- Bus & Prof Pos: Chmn bd trustees, Faith Lutheran Church, 74-; pres, Seasons End Inc, 74- Mil Serv: Entered as 1st Lt, Army, 65, released as Capt, 69, after serv in Staff Judge Adv Corps; Army Commendation Medal with Oak Leaf Cluster. Mem: Mason; Am Legion; Kans Trial Lawyers Asn; Geary Co Dem Club (pres, 72, bd dirs, 72-); Isis Shrine. Honors & Awards: Pub Speaking Champion, Kans 4-H Found, 57; Carl Raymond Gray Scholarship, Union Pac RR, 57; Dairy Champion, Nat Dairy Prod Corp, 56 & 57. Relig: Lutheran. Legal Res: 1212 McFarland Rd Junction City KS 66441 Mailing Add: PO Box 848 Junction City KS 66441

BENHAM, PAUL BURRUS, JR (D)
Ark State Sen
b Memphis, Tenn, Feb 27, 21; s Paul Burrus Benham, Sr & Mary Dale Robertson B; m 1945 to Evelyn Ann Wilkerson; c Paul B, III, Barbara Ann (Mrs John Upper) & James Thomas. Educ: Vanderbilt Univ, 39-42; Sigma Chi. Polit & Govt Pos: Mem, Lee Co Dem Cent Comt, Ark, 65-73; Ark State Sen, 73- Bus & Prof Pos: Owner, Benham Ins & Real Estate, Marianna, Ark, 46- Mil Serv: Entered as Pvt, Army, 42, released as Maj, after serv in Air Force, Mid East, African & European Theatres, 43-45; Lt Col, Nat Guard; Am Defense Medal; Victory Medal; Presidential Unit Citation with Oak Leaf Cluster, Mid East, African & European Campaign Medals with 11 Bronze Stars; Res Medal with Silver Cluster. Mem: Masons; Scottish Rite; Am Legion; VFW; Miss River Pkwy Planning Comn (Int Pres). Relig: Presbyterian; elder, 67. Legal Res: 1 Mission Ave Marianna AR 72360 Mailing Add: PO Drawer 477 Marianna AR 72360

BENINGA, HAROLD T (R)
Kans State Rep
b Riley Co, Kans, Nov 11, 04; s Jacob E & Mary Jones B; m 1925 to Beulah B Heath; c Duane H & Max E. Educ: High Sch. Polit & Govt Pos: Kans State Rep, 75- Mailing Add: 609 Eisenhower Dr Junction City KS 66441

BENISH, JOSEPH MICHAEL (D)
Committeeman, Nat Young Dem
b Wilkes-Barre, Pa, June 15, 52; s Joseph Benish, Sr & Irene Nemkavitch B; single. Educ: Pa State Univ, Wilkes-Barre Campus, AA in Mass Commun, 72; People Help People Prog; disc jockey, Campus Radio Sta; news dir, Campus Newspaper. Polit & Govt Pos: Gov youth adv, Pa Pub TV Network Comn, 69-; campaign coordr, Luzerne Co Dem Comt, Muskie Campaign & Gen Elec, 72; alt deleg, Dem Nat Conv, 72; pres, Luzerne Co Young Dem, Pa, 72-; radio specialist, Majority Press Off, Pa State Senate, 73-; committeeman, Nat Young Dem, 75- Bus & Prof Pos: News reporter, WILK Radio, Wilkes-Barre, Pa, 70-72; pub rel officer, Media Affil, Inc, Wilkes-Barre, 72-73. Mem: Hon mem, King's Col Young Dem. Honors & Awards: Key to the City, Mayor of Wilkes-Barre, Pa, 69; Outstanding Teenager of Am, Outstanding Teenagers of Am, 70. Relig: Catholic. Legal Res: 27 Huber St Wilkes-Barre PA 18702 Mailing Add: Senate Majority Press Off 337 Main Capitol Harrisburg PA 17120

BENITEZ, JAIME (POPULAR DEM, PR)
Resident Comnr, PR
b Vieques, PR, Oct 29, 08; s Luis Benitez & Candida Rexach B; m 1941 to Luz A Martinez; c Clotilde, Jaime & Margarita Ines. Educ: Georgetown Univ, LLB, 30, LLM, 31; Univ Chicago, MA, 38. Hon Degrees: Degrees From NY Univ, Fairleigh Dickinson Univ, Temple Univ, Univ Miami, Univ WIndies, Inter-Am Univ, PR & Cath Univ PR. Polit & Govt Pos: Mem, PR Const Conv, chmn, Comt Bill of Rights, 51-52; mem, US Nat Comn, UNESCO, 48-54; US deleg, Nat Conv UNESCO, Paris, 50 & Havana, Cuba, 52; Resident Comnr, PR, 73-; deleg, Dem Nat Mid-Term Conf, 74. Bus & Prof Pos: From instr to assoc prof social & polit sci, Univ PR, 31-42, chancellor, 42-66; Pres, Univ Syst PR, 66-71; US deleg, Univ Conv, Utretcht, Holland, 48. Publ: Sobre el Futuro Cultural y Politico de Puerto Rico, 66; 25 Anos de Direccion Universitaria, 67; Crisis en el Mundo y en la Educacion, 68; plus others. Mem: Nat Asn State Univs. Legal Res: PR Mailing Add: Rm 1317 House Off Bldg Washington DC 20515

BENITZ, MAX EDWARD (R)
Wash State Sen
b Wathena, Kans, Oct 9, 16; m 1940 to Marie Fern Wilson; c Norma June (Mrs Fortner), Eileen Marie (Mrs Wagner), Alvin Ray, Max, Jr, & Ronnie. Educ: Wathena High Sch, 4 years. Polit & Govt Pos: Wash State Rep, 69-75; Wash State Sen, 75- Bus & Prof Pos: Pres, Wash State Farm Bur, 60-68; mem, bd of dirs, Am Farm Bur, 64-68. Mem: Farm Bur. Relig: Lutheran. Mailing Add: Box 181 Rte 2 Prosser WA 99350

BENJAMIN, ADAM, JR (D)
Ind State Sen
b Gary, Ind, Aug 6, 35; s Adam Benjamin & Margaret Marjanian B; m 1966 to Patricia Ann Sullivan; c Adam Benjamin, III, Alison Louise & Arianne Benjamin. Educ: US Mil Acad West Point, BS, 58; Valparaiso Univ Law Sch, JD, 66; Phi Alpha Delta. Polit & Govt Pos: Zoning Adminr, Gary, Ind, 64-65; exec secy to Mayor, City of Gary, 65-67; Ind State Rep, 67-70; Ind State Sen, 71-; mem, Ind Judicial Study Comn, 70-; mem, Ind State Budget Comt, 74- Bus & Prof Pos: Teacher math & physics, Gary Sch Syst, 61-62; electronics comput programmer, Continental Casualty, 62-63; attorney-at-law, 66- Mil Serv: Entered as Pvt, Marine Corps, 52, released as Cpl, 54, after serv in Third Div, Far East Command, 53-54; reentered as 2nd Lt, Army, 58, released as 1st Lt, 61, after serv in 101st Airborne Div; UN, Korean Theater & Nat Defense Serv Ribbons; Sr Parachutist Wings; Ranger Tab. Mem: Nat Soc State Legislators; Marine Corps League; Am Legion; Gary, Ind & Am Bar Asns. Honors & Awards: Outstanding Freshman Dem Rep; Jaycee Good Govt Award; Outstanding Young Am Award; Outstanding Am of Assyrian Descent; NW Ind Crime Comn Citizen Award. Relig: Catholic Church of the East. Legal Res: 2106 W Third Pl Hobart IN 46342 Mailing Add: 3637 Grant St Suite 7 Gary IN 46408

BENKOVICH, ROBERT MICHAEL (R)
Nev State Assemblyman
b Norristown, Pa, Mar 4, 48; s Andrew Benkovich & Mary Garay B; m 1967 to Regina Marie Ford; c Terry Ann, Sonja Ann, Alexandria Nicoli & Teilhard Descartes. Educ: Villanova Univ, BA in Social Sci, 70; Univ Nev, Reno, currently. Polit & Govt Pos: Nev State Assemblyman, 74- Bus & Prof Pos: Info analyst, Franklin Inst Research Labs, Philadelphia, Pa, 66-70; teacher, Cardinal Dougherty High, Philadelphia, 70-71; parttime teacher, Manogue High, Reno, Nev, 70-; dealer, Nevada Club, Reno, Nev, 71- Mem: Peavine Sertoma; Rittenhouse Astronomical Soc. Honors & Awards: Senatorial Scholar, Pa, 65. Mailing Add: 955 Antelope Rd Reno NV 89503

BENN, CEDRIC SHIRLEY (R)
Mem, Houlton Town Rep Comt, Maine
b Houlton, Maine, Sept 9, 20; s Edward Shirley Benn & Mary Jordon B; m 1948 to Rita Mcattee; c Lawrence, Dorothy, John, Timothy & Patricia. Educ: Hodgson High Sch, grad & postgrad course. Polit & Govt Pos: Chmn, Houlton Town Rep Comt, Maine, 62-66, mem, currently; mem, Aroostook Co Rep Comt, 64-72, chmn, 70-72. Bus & Prof Pos: Mgr, Benn's Auto Sales, Houlton, Maine, 48-56 & 59-; mgr, Sherwin-Williams Co, 56-59. Mem: Houlton CofC; Mason; Elks (Exalted Ruler, 66, trustee, 67-); Houlton Music Parents; Houlton Little League. Relig: Methodist; Pres, Methodist Men's Club, 54. Legal Res: 81 Pleasant Houlton ME 04730 Mailing Add: Box 365 Houlton ME 04730

BENNER, BARBARA YOUNG (R)
b Allentown, Pa, Aug 18, 24; d Robert A Young & Eleanor Soleliac Y; m 1944 to Nolan P Benner Jr; c Joan & Carol. Educ: Pine Manor Jr Col, 44. Polit & Govt Pos: Vchmn, Lehigh Co Young Rep, Pa, 52-53, dir, 52-60; committeewoman, Rep Party, 52-70; dir, Lehigh Co Coun Rep Women, 53-, prog chmn, 61-62, legis chmn, 63-65; dir, Pa Coun Rep Women, 59-64 & 67-70, second vpres, 64-65, pres, 65-67, mem policy comt, 68-; alt deleg, Rep Nat Conv, 60, 64 & 72; deleg, 68; Pa chmn, Women for Nixon-Agnew, 68; vchmn campaign comt, Nat Fedn Rep Women, 68-74, vchmn new citizens comt, 71-72; mem, Lehigh Co Govt Study Comn, 74-75; bd mem, Lehigh Co Planned Parenthood; bd mem, Wiley House-Lehigh Valley Treatment Ctr, currently. Mem: Girl Scouts; Lehigh Co Community Coun; Allentown Civic Little Theater; Lehigh Country Club; Allentown Women's Club (legis chmn). Relig: Presbyterian. Mailing Add: 225 N Broad St Allentown PA 18104

BENNET, AUGUSTUS WITSCHIEF (R)
b New York, NY, Oct 7, 97; s William Stiles Bennet & Gertrude Witschief B; m 1929 to Maxine Layne; c Linda (Mrs Lynch), William Stiles, II & Susanna (Mrs Christopher Humphreys). Educ: Amherst Col, BA, 18; Columbia Univ Law Sch, LLB, 21; Phi Beta Kappa. Polit & Govt Pos: US Referee in Bankruptcy, Southern Dist NY, 23-44; US Rep, NY, 45-46. Mil Serv: Chief Qm, Naval Res Flying Corps, 18-19. Mem: Orange Co Bar Asn; Orange-Rockland Dist, F&AM (past dist dep Grand Master); Newburgh YMCA; CofC; Rotary. Relig: Presbyterian. Legal Res: Balmville Rd MD 16 Newburgh NY 12550 Mailing Add: Box 792 Newburgh NY 12550

BENNET, DOUGLAS JOSEPH, JR (D)
b Orange, NJ, June 23, 38; s Douglas J Bennet & Phoebe Benedict B; m 1959 to Susanne Klejman; c Michael Farrand, James Douglas & Halina Anne. Educ: Wesleyan Univ, BA, 59; Univ Calif, Berkeley, MA, 60; Harvard Univ, PhD, 68; Phi Beta Kappa. Polit & Govt Pos: Prog analyst, Agency for Int Develop, 63-64; spec asst to Ambassador Bowles, US Dept of State, 64-66; staff asst to Vice President Humphrey, 67-69; admin asst to Sen Thomas Eagleton, Mo, 69-73; admin asst to US Sen Abraham Ribicoff, Conn, 73- Mailing Add: Lyme CT 06371

BENNETT, CHARLES E (D)
US Rep, Fla
b Jacksonville, Fla, Dec 2, 10; m 1953 to Jean Fay; c Bruce, Charles, James & Lucinda. Educ: Univ Fla, BA, JD, 34. Hon Degrees: DH, Univ Tampa, 50; LLD, Jacksonville Univ, 43. Polit & Govt Pos: Fla State Rep, 41-42; US Rep, Fla, 49- Bus & Prof Pos: Attorney-at-law. Mil Serv: Army Inf, 42-47; discharged as Capt, awarded Silver Star, Bronze Star, Combat Inf Badge, Inf Hall of Fame, Ft Benning Officer Cand Sch, 58. Publ: Laudonniere & Fort Caroline, 64 & Settlement of Florida, 68, Univ Fla Press. Mem: Jr CofC; DAV; Am Legion; VFW; Mason. Honors & Awards: Awarded Cert by Freedoms Found for outstanding achievement in bringing about a better understanding of the Am way of life, 51, 56; Good Govt Award, Jacksonville & US Jr CofC, 52. Relig: Disciples of Christ. Mailing Add: Fed Bldg Jacksonville FL 32202

BENNETT, CHARLES E (D)
Utah State Rep
Mailing Add: 2729 Alden St Salt Lake City UT 84106

BENNETT, J B (D)
Okla State Sen
Mailing Add: State Capitol Oklahoma City OK 73105

BENNETT, J RICHARD, JR (R)
Mem, Ala State Rep Exec Comt
b Georgiana, Ala, Oct 12, 22; m 1947 to Margery Casey; c Jean & Bruce. Educ: Univ Ala, BS in Bus Admin. Polit & Govt Pos: Butler Co campaign mgr for Eisenhower, Ala, 52; campaign mgr for Abernethy for Gov, 54; mem, Ala State Rep Exec Comt, 54-, vchmn, 62-66, chmn, 69-75; deleg, Rep Nat Conv, 56, 64 & 72, mem platform comt, 64, mem, Nixon Staff, 68; cand for pres, Pub Serv Comn, 60; cand for Ala State Senate, 62; campaign mgr Grenier for US Senate, 66; dir, Nixon Campaign in NFla, 68; mem contest comt, Rep Nat Comt, 72. Bus & Prof Pos: In lumber & pulpwood bus, Greenville, Ala, 47- Mil Serv: Pilot, Army Air Corps, World War II. Mem: CofC; Greenville Indust Develop Bd (chmn); Rotary. Relig: Presbyterian; Deacon, First Presby Church, Greenville. Legal Res: 725 Ft Dale Rd Greenville AL 36037 Mailing Add: PO Box 188 Greenville AL 36037

BENNETT, JOHN (D)
Mich State Rep
b Ohio, May 15, 12; married; c Linda, Carol & Barbara. Educ: Wayne State Univ; Walsh Inst Accountancy; Texas A&M Col, Army spec prog; correspondence course from Dun & Bradstreet in credit & financial anal. Polit & Govt Pos: Treas, Redford Twp, Mich, 10 years; Mich State Rep, 64-, chmn, House Retirement Comt, 65-66 & 69-70. Bus & Prof Pos: Acct. Mil Serv: Vet. Mem: Wayne Twp Treas Asn; Redford Twp Lions Club (dir); Am Soc for Pub Admin; Munic Finance Off Asn; DAV. Relig: Methodist. Legal Res: Redford Township MI Mailing Add: 10052 Mercedes St Detroit MI 48239

BENNETT, JOHN MIRZA, JR (R)
Mem, Tex State Rep Exec Comt
b San Antonio, Tex, June 26, 08; s John Mirza Bennett & Jamie Armstrong B; m 1946 to Eleanor Freeborn; c Eleanor (Mrs Marlow), Carolyn (Mrs Wood), Davis Graves & John Stephen. Educ: Phillips Acad, Andover, Mass, dipl; Princeton Univ, 2 years; Univ Tex, Austin, BA, 31; Cottage Club; Kappa Alpha. Polit & Govt Pos: Finance chmn, Rep Party, Tex, 65 & 66; alt deleg, Rep Nat Conv, 68; mem, Tex State Rep Exec Comt, 70- Bus & Prof Pos: Chmn bd, Nat Bank Com, San Antonio, Tex, 50- Mil Serv: Entered as 2nd Lt, Air Force, 40, released as Maj-Gen, Res, 58; Silver Star; Legion of Merit; Distinguished Flying Cross with one cluster; Bronze Medal; Air Medal with three oak leaf clusters; Groix de Guerre avec Palm. Publ: Letters from England, pvt publ, 46. Mem: Tex & Southwestern Cattle Raisers Asn (dir). Relig: Episcopal. Legal Res: 417 W Dewey Pl San Antonio TX 78212 Mailing Add: 2111 Nat Bank of Com Bldg San Antonio TX 78205

BENNETT, LAURIE EDWARD (D)
SC State Rep
b Springfield, SC, Apr 11, 19; s William Elijah Bennett & Lovie Mildred Dicks B; m 1942 to Margaret Porter Bailey; c Margaret B (Mrs Stover), Emily B (Mrs Lee) & Jane Elizabeth. Educ: Clemson Univ, 4 years. Polit & Govt Pos: Mayor, Springfield, SC, 61-69; SC State Rep, 69- Bus & Prof Pos: Pres, Springfield Gin Co, SC, 62- & Springfield Grain Co, 66- Mil Serv: Entered as Pvt, Army Air Force, 41, released as M/Sgt, 45, after serv in 468th Bomb Group, 20th Air Force, China, Burma, India & Pac Theatres, 44-45; Bronze Star with Bronze Oak Leaf Cluster; Air Medal; Good Conduct Medal; Distinguished Unit Badge; Am Theatre & Asiatic-Pac Theatre Ribbons. Mem: Mason; Am Legion; SC Farm Bur; Country Club of Orangeburg. Relig: Methodist. Legal Res: 12 Aiken St Springfield SC 29146 Mailing Add: PO Box 156 Springfield SC 29146

BENNETT, LOWELL E (R)
b Martinsville, Ill, Feb 28, 26; s Ernie Olin Bennett & Jessie Marie Husted B; m 1948 to Gwendolyn Jean Hart; c Scott A. Polit & Govt Pos: Committeeman, Clark Co Rep Cent Comt, Ill, 54-72, chmn, 57-72; twp supvr, Martinsville, Ill, 61- Bus & Prof Pos: Dir, Martinsville Agr Fair Asn, 60- Mil Serv: Entered as A/S, Navy, 44, released as Yeoman 2/C, 46, after serv in SPac; Iwo Jima & Okinawa Medals with Invasion Stars. Mem: Ill Poland China Asn; Clark Co Swine Improv Asn; Am Legion; Farm Bur. Relig: Protestant. Mailing Add: RR 3 Martinsville IL 62442

BENNETT, MARION D (D)
Nev State Assemblyman
Mailing Add: 1911 Goldhill Ave Las Vegas NV 89106

BENNETT, MARION T (R)
b Buffalo, Mo, June 6, 14; s Phil A Bennett & Mary Bertha Tinsley B; m 1941 to June Young; c Ann (Mrs Paul Guptill) & William Philip. Educ: Southwest Mo State Col, AB, 35; Washington Univ Sch Law, LLB, 38; Delta Theta Phi. Polit & Govt Pos: Mem, Green Co Rep Cent Comt, Mo, 38-42; US Rep, Mo, 43-49; chief comnr, US Court of Claims, 49-72, Judge, 72- Mil Serv: Capt, Air Force Res, 50; Col, Air Force Res, 65-74; Legion of Merit. Publ: American immigration policies—a history, Pub Affairs Press, 63; The immigration and nationality act, The Annals, Am Acad Polit & Social Sci, 9/66; The Court of Claims—a 50 year perspective, Fed Bar J, Vol 29, 70. Mem: Fed Bar Asn; Exchange Club. Honors & Awards: Outstanding Alumnus Award, Southwest Mo State Col, 64. Relig: Methodist. Mailing Add: 3715 Cardiff Rd Chevy Chase MD 20015

BENNETT, OTIS BEE (D)
Miss State Rep
b French Camp, Miss, June 22, 25; s Otis Bee Hennings & Minnie Dismuke Bennett H; m 1952 to Esther Browing; c Richard A & David B. Educ: Sunflower Jr Col, 2 years; Miss State, Starkville, 4 months; Draughons Bus Col, Jackson, 7 months. Polit & Govt Pos: Miss State Rep, 68- Mil Serv: Entered as Pvt, Air Force, 43, released as Sgt, 46, after serv in 20th Air Force, Pac, 27 missions over Japan, 44-45; Good Conduct & Several Theatre Medals; Air Medal with 3 Oak Leaf Clusters; Distinguished Flying Cross. Mem: Shrine; O L McKay Lodge (Past Master); Sunflower Co Farm Bur; Delta Coun; Am Legion. Relig: Methodist. Mailing Add: Rte 1 Box 100 Sunflower MS 38778

BENNETT, PHILIP ROY, JR (D)
Maine State Rep
b Caribou, Maine, Sept 11, 44; s Philip Roy Bennett, Sr & Helen Bell B; m 1974 to Elizabeth Lebel; c Patrick Roy. Educ: Univ Maine, Fort Kent, BS, 67; Kappa Delta Phi. Polit & Govt Pos: Mem, Aroostook Co Dem Comt, currently; city chmn, Caribou Dem Party, Maine, 74-; Maine State Rep, 75- Bus & Prof Pos: Teacher, Caribou Sch Dept, Maine, 66-; officer, Police Dept, 69-70. Mem: Nat Educ Asn; Maine & Caribou Teachers Asn. Relig: Methodist. Mailing Add: 132 Limestone St Caribou ME 04736

BENNETT, REID L (D)
Pa State Rep
b Feb 7, 29; s William H Bennett & Mary Ruth Thompson B; m to Mary Ellen Templeton; c one. Educ: Hartford, Ohio Pub Schs. Polit & Govt Pos: Pa State Rep, 64- Bus & Prof Pos: Acct exec; Red Cross swimming instr. Mil Serv: Army, 48-51; Five Battle Stars. Mem: Mercer Co Tourist Prom Agency; Lions; Mason; Am Water Skiing Asn. Mailing Add: Capitol Bldg Harrisburg PA 17120

BENNETT, ROBERT FREDERICK (R)
Gov, Kans
b Kansas City, Mo, May 23, 27; s Otto Francis Bennett & Dorothy Bess Dodds B; m 1971 to Olivia Fisher; c Robert F, Jr, Virginia Lee, Cathleen Kay & Patricia Ann. Educ: Univ Kans, AB, 50, LLB, 52; Phi Alpha Delta; Delta Sigma Rho. Polit & Govt Pos: Councilman, Prairie Village, Kans, 55-57, mayor, 57-65; Kans State Sen, 65-74, pres, Kans State Senate, 73-74; Gov, Kans, 75- Bus & Prof Pos: Sr partner, Bennett & Lytle, attorneys-at-law, 59-68, Bennett, Lytle & Wetzler, 68-73 & Bennett, Lytle, Wetzler & Winn, 73-; dir & secy, Kans State Bank, 62-68. Mil Serv: Entered as Pvt, Marine Corps, 45, released as Pfc, 46, after serv in 1st Marine Div & 3rd Marine Amphibious Corps, Pac & China Theatres; recalled to active duty, 50-51 & served in 7th Marine Regt, 1st Marine Div, Korea. Mem: Am Bar Asn; Bar Asn of State of Kans; Kans League of Munic; Univ Kans Alumni Asn; Prairie Village Optimist Club. Relig: Protestant. Legal Res: 5315 W 95th Terr Overland Park KS 66207 Mailing Add: State House Topeka KS 66612

BENNETT, THOMAS STEPHEN (R)
Chmn, NC State Rep Exec Comt
b Morehead City, NC, Jan 26, 34; s Jesse Gilbert Bennett & Vera Merrill B; m 1961 to Virginia Thompson; c Thomas S, Jr, Ruth Thompson & David Brian. Educ: Univ NC, AB, 56, LLB, 58; Phi Alpha Delta. Polit & Govt Pos: NC State Rep, 62-66; chmn, Carteret Co Comn, 68-73; pres, Neuse River Coun Govt, 72-74; pres, Atlantic & NC Rwy, 73-; chmn adv bd, NC Marine Resources Ctr, 74-; chmn, NC State Rep Exec Comt, 73- Mem: Elks; Am & NC Bar Asns. Honors & Awards: Jaycees Distinguished Serv Award, 69. Relig: Baptist. Legal Res: River Dr Morehead City NC 28557 Mailing Add: 1005 Shepard St Morehead City NC 28557

BENNETT, VERNA Z (R)
b Clearfield Co, Pa, July 6, 02; d David H Zartman & Mima Jane Rupert Z; m 1923 to Boyd D Bennett; c Victoria Jane (Mrs Wadas); one grandchild. Educ: Indiana Univ Pa, 20-22, 25, 49 & 55; Stroudsburg State Teachers Col, 24; Pa State Univ, 42. Polit & Govt Pos: Pres, Ind Coun Rep Women, Pa, 54-58, mem, State Conv, State Membership, Legis, Chaplain & Prog Comts; vchmn, Ind Co Rep Comt, 58-62, chmn, 62-71; state dir bd, Pa Coun Rep Women, 59-; dep secy, Commonwealth of Pa, 66- Bus & Prof Pos: Sch teacher, 20-46; elem prin, Pa, 30-46. Mem: Pa State Educ Asn; Nat Educ Asn; Eastern Star; Hist Soc of Indiana; Elks Auxiliary; Daughters of 1812. Relig: Presbyterian. Mailing Add: 230 N Sixth St Indiana PA 15701

BENNETT, WALLACE FOSTER (R)
b Salt Lake City, Utah, Nov 13, 98; m 1922 to Frances Grant B; c Wallace Grant, Rosemary (Mrs Robert C Fletcher), Davis Wells, Frances (Mrs Lawrence S Jeppson) & Robert Foster. Educ: Univ Utah, AB, 19. Polit & Govt Pos: US Sen, Utah, 50-74. Bus & Prof Pos: Bd chmn, Bennett's, Salt Lake City; prin, San Luis State Acad, Manassa, Colo, 19-20; vpres, Nat Paint, Varnish & Lacquer Asn, 35-36; pres, Nat Glass Distributors Asn, 37; pres, Salt Lake Rotary, 40; pres, Salt Lake Community Chest, 44-45; pres, Nat Asn Mfgs, 49. Mil Serv: Army Inf, 2nd Lt, 18. Publ: Auth, Faith & freedom, 50; Why I am a Mormon, 58. Mem: Salt Lake Country Club; Alta Club; Timpanogos Club. Relig: Latter-day Saint. Mailing Add: 1430 S 13th East Salt Lake City UT 84105

BENNETT, WAYNE (R)
Iowa State Rep
b Schaller, Iowa, Nov 7, 27; s Wilbur A Bennett & Blanche M Neal B; m 1949 to Barbara Noll; c Gary & Candice. Educ: Iowa State Univ, 44-45. Polit & Govt Pos: Iowa State Rep, 73- Mem: Ida Co Soil Conserv Dist Comnrs; Ida Co Farm Bur; Ida Co 4-H Orgn. Relig: Methodist. Mailing Add: Rte 1 Galva IA 51020

BENNETT, WILLIAM MORGAN (D)
Mem, Calif Dem State Cent Comt,
b San Francisco, Calif, Feb 20, 18; m 1943 to Jane Evangeline Gray; c William M, Jr, James P, Michael A & Joan P. Educ: Univ Calif, Hastings Col Law, LLB, 46. Polit & Govt Pos: Mem, Calif Dem State Cent Comt, currently. Bus & Prof Pos: US Attorney, 45-48; Dep Attorney Gen, Calif, 49-59; chief counsel, Calif Pub Utilities Comn, 59-62, comnr, 63-68; mem, Calif State Bd Equalization, 70- Mil Serv: Entered as Cadet, Air Force, 41, released as Capt, 45, after serv in Europe; Distinguished Flying Cross with Clusters; Six Air Medals; Presidential Unit Citation. Mem: Calif State Bar Asn; Int Coun Environ Law. Legal Res: 35 Evergreen Dr Kentfield CA 94904 Mailing Add: PO Box 1799 Sacramento CA 95808

BENNISON, LEAH ROSE (D)
Chairperson, Van Buren Co Dem Comt, Mich
b Decatur, Mich, Oct 27, 30; d William Kaplan & Lucille Hoffman K; m 1955 to Gordon Alan Bennison; wid; c Marc Samuel. Educ: Decatur Pub Schs, grad, 48. Polit & Govt Pos: Chairperson, Van Buren Co Dem Comt, Mich, 74-; supporting mem, Dem Nat Comt, currently. Mem: Van Buren Co Hist Soc; Hadassah. Relig: Judaism. Mailing Add: 212 W Delaware St Decatur MI 49045

BENO, JOHN RICHARDSON (D)
Chmn, Pueblo Co Dem Party, Colo
b Council Bluffs, Iowa, Nov 13, 31; s George Schendele Beno & Fern Richardson B; single. Educ: State Univ Iowa, 50-51; Loras Col, BA Philos, 55; St Thomas Sem, 55-59; Creighton Univ; Loyola Univ (Chicago), MRE, 70. Polit & Govt Pos: Chmn, Tri-Co War on Poverty, LaJunta, Colo, 65-66; bd dirs, Colo Migrant Coun, 65-66; chmn, Pueblo Co Dem Party, Colo, 75- Bus & Prof Pos: Assoc pastor, Diocese of Pueblo, 59-66, dir, Relig Educ/Liturgy, 66-70, exec dir, Fedn of Diocesan Liturgical Comn, 70-73, dir, Ministry of Christian Serv, Mission Off & Priests' Coun, 73- Relig: Roman Catholic. Legal Res: 2701 E 12th St Pueblo CO 81001 Mailing Add: 225 Clark Pueblo CO 81003

BENSON, BOB (D)
Ky State Rep
Mailing Add: State House of Rep State Capitol Frankfort KY 40601

BENSON, DANIEL LEROY (D)
Chmn, Fairfield Co Dem Exec Comt, Ohio
b Carroll, Ohio, June 29, 09; s James O Benson & Vernia Alspach B; m 1933 to Mary Martha Black; c Robert Lee & David A. Educ: Canal Winchester High Sch, grad, 29. Polit & Govt Pos: Precinct committeeman, Bloom Twp, Precinct B, Ohio, 37-; Co Exec, Fairfield Co, 38-; chmn, Fairfield Co Dem Exec Comt, 68-; mem bd elec, Fairfield Co, 68- Mem: Fairfield Co Agr Soc (vpres, 73-); Ohio Elec Bd Asn; Ohio Fair Managers Asn; United Commercial Travelers. Relig: United Methodist. Mailing Add: 8004 Winchester Rd NW Carroll OH 43112

BENSON, HARRY EDDIE (R)
b Port Arthur, Tex, Dec 13, 25; s William H Benson & Eddie A Rhea B; m 1949 to Mary Nell Harwell; c Elizabeth Ann & David Harwell. Educ: Lamar Jr Col, AS, 47; Univ Houston, BS, 53. Polit & Govt Pos: Alt deleg, Rep Nat Conv, 64; precinct committeeman, Harris Co Rep Party, 64-65; deleg, Rep State & Co Conv, 64, 66, 68, 70, 72 & 74; chmn, Neighbor to Neighbor Fund Dr, 65-66; dir pub rels, Harris Co Rep Party, 66-69, mem pub rels comt, 69-70. Bus & Prof Pos: Estimator prod man, Gulf Printing Co, 52-59; prod mgr, Marsteller, Rickard, Gebhardt & Reed, 59; typographer, Naylor Type & Mats, 59-60; estimator-prod man, Western Lithograph Co, Tex, 60-61; purchasing mgr & Graphic arts buyer, Tenneco Inc, 61- Publ: Former ed, The Banner, monthly publ, Harris Co Tex Rep Party. Mem: Int Graphic Arts Ed Asn; Mason (32 degree); Scottish Rite; KT; RAM. Relig: Methodist. Mailing Add: 13930 Barryknoll Lane Houston TX 77024

BENSON, RICHARD (D)
WVa State Sen
Mailing Add: State Capitol Charleston WV 25305

BENTLEY, ALVIN M, JR (R)
b Washington, DC, May 27, 41; s Alvin M Bentley & Arville Duecher B; m 1961 to Sue Ann Meiers; c Susan & Marianne. Educ: Staunton Mil Acad, Va, 4 years. Polit & Govt Pos: Chmn, Shiawassee Young Rep, 66-67; finance chmn, Shiawassee Co Rep Party, 67-68, chmn, formerly; alt deleg, Rep Nat Conv, 68; finance chmn, Mich Citizens for Nixon, 68; chmn, Sixth Cong Dist for Nixon, 68. Mil Serv: Entered as Seaman Apprentice, US Coast Guard, 60, released as Seaman, 64. Mem: Owosso CofC (Legis Comt); Owosso Area Human Rel Comt (Charter Mem); Alvin M Bentley Found (Bd Trustees); Farm Bur; Mich Partners of the Alliance. Relig: Episcopal. Legal Res: 701 W Oliver St Owosso MI 48867 Mailing Add: Rm 5 & 6 Matthews Bldg Annex Owosso MI 48867

BENTLEY, HELEN DELICH (R)
Chmn, Fed Maritime Comn
b Ruth, Nev, Nov 28, 23; d Michael Delich & Mary Kovich D; m 1959 to William Roy Bentley. Educ: Univ Nev, 41-42; George Washington Univ, 43; Univ Mo, JB, 44. Hon Degrees: LLD, Univ Md, 70; DHL, Bryant Col, 71, Univ Portland, 72; LLD, Univ Alaska, 73 & Univ Mich, 74. Polit & Govt Pos: Campaign mgr, Late Sen James G Scrugham, White Pine Co, Nev, 42; chmn, Fed Maritime Comn, 69-; chmn, Am Bicentennial Fleet, Inc, 73- Bus & Prof Pos: Reporter, Ely Rec, Nev, 40-42; bur mgr, United Press, Ft Wayne, Ind, 44-45; reporter, Baltimore Sun, Md, 45-53, maritime ed, 53-69; TV producer, world trade & Maritime Shows, 50-64; pub rels adv, Am Asn Port Authorities, 58-62 & 64-67. Publ: Ed, Seaport histories of ports of the Americas, history & development; syndicated column; plus many others. Mem: Newspaper Women's Club; Am Women in Radio & TV; Theta Sigma Phi; Baltimore Pub Rels Coun; Md Hist Soc. Honors & Awards: Only woman to trek the Northwest Passage aboard USS Manhattan, 69; GOP Woman of the Year Award, 72; Am Legion Distinguished Serv Medal, 73; Robert M Thompson Award, Navy League of US, 73; Jerry Land Medal, 74. Relig: Greek Orthodox. Legal Res: 408 Chapelwood Lane Lutherville MD 21903 Mailing Add: Fed Maritime Comn 1100 L St NW Washington DC 20573

BENTLEY, ROBERT (R)
Chmn, Wyoming Co Rep Comt, NY
b Arcade, NY, July 17, 18; s Lynn S Bentley & Sara Haley B; m 1943 to Helen G Lero; c Thomas A. Educ: Syracuse Univ, BA, 41, LLB, 43; Phi Delta Phi. Polit & Govt Pos: Law clerk, US Dist Court Western Div NY, 44-46; village police justice, Arcade, NY, 47-49; counsel, NY State Senate, 47; chmn, Wyoming Co Rep Comt, NY, 62-; deleg, Rep Nat Conv, 72; village attorney, Arcade, 67; town attorney, Arcade, 74. Publ: Co-auth, Judiciary article-NY state constitution, 62, New York State Civil Practice Law & Rules, 62; New York Real Property Actions & Proceeding Law, State of New York, 62. Mem: New York State & Wyoming Co Bar Asns; Arcade Lions Club; Warsaw Moose Club; Mason. Legal Res: 415 W Main St Arcade NY 14009 Mailing Add: 270 Main St Arcade NY 14009

BENTLEY, TIMOTHY EDWARD (TIM) (D)
Pres, Young Dem of Ga
b Atlanta, Ga, July 9, 53; s James Asbery Bentley, Jr & Mary Jane Hays B; m 1973 to Mary Jane Callaway. Educ: Ga State Univ, currently; feature writer, The Signal, formerly. Polit & Govt Pos: Mem, DeKalb Co Community Rels Comt, Ga, 71-72; asst postmaster, Ga House of Rep, 71-74; mem, Atlanta Inaugural Comt, 73-74; mem, Young Dem of DeKalb Co, 73-; secy, Young Dem of Ga, 74-75, pres, 75-; mem exec comt & membership chairperson, DeKalb Co Dem Party, 74-; mem exec comt, Dem Party of Ga, 74-, mem affirmative action comt, 75- Mem: Nat Wildlife Fedn. Legal Res: 1520 Farnell Ct Apt 1523 Decatur GA 30033 Mailing Add: PO Box 1975 Atlanta GA 30301

BENTON, RICHARDSON D (R)
NH State Rep
Mailing Add: RFD 2 Box 44A Chester NH 03036

BENTSEN, LLOYD MILLARD, JR (D)
US Sen, Tex
b Mission, Tex, Feb 11, 21; s Lloyd M Bentsen & Edna Ruth Colbath B; m 1943 to Beryl Ann Longino; c Lloyd M, III, Lan C & Tina Ann (Mrs Eric Maedgen). Educ: Univ Tex Sch Law, LLB; Sigma Nu. Polit & Govt Pos: Judge, Hidalgo Co, Tex, 46; US Rep, Tex, 48-54; US Sen, 71-, mem, Finance, Pub Works & Joint Econ Comts, US Senate, chmn, Pub Works Subcomt on Transportation, Joint Econ Subcomt on Econ Growth & Finance Subcomt on Financial Mkts. Bus & Prof Pos: Pres, Lincoln Consol, formerly; resigned all mgt pos & directorships on entering Senate. Mil Serv: Entered as Pvt, Army, 42, served as Squadron Comdr, Army Air Corps, released as Maj, 45, promoted to Col, Air Force Res; Distinguished Flying Cross; Air Medal with Three Oak Leaf Clusters. Mem: Tex Bar Asn. Relig: Presbyterian; former mem bd trustees, Tex Presby Found. Legal Res: Houston TX Mailing Add: Old Senate Off Bldg Washington DC 20510

BENZ, WILLIAM ROBERT (R)
Chmn, Marin Co Rep Cent Comt, Calif
b Sioux Falls, SDak, Mar 14, 31; s Karl John Benz & Maurine Loonan B; m 1955 to Barbara Boyce; c William Robert, II. Educ: Univ Calif, Berkeley, AB, 53; Hasting Col Law, JD, 65; Order of the Coif; Theta Delta Chi. Polit & Govt Pos: Mem, Marin Co Rep Cent Comt, Calif, 72-, chmn, 75-; dir, Marin Rep Coun, 73-, pres, 74; mem, Rep State Cent Comt Calif, 75-; mem, Asn of Rep Co Chmn of Calif, 75- Bus & Prof Pos: Vpres, Loonan Lumber Co & Benz Funeral Home, Sioux Falls, SDak, 55-66; partner, O'Gara & McGuire, Attorneys-at-law, San Francisco, Calif, 66- Mil Serv: Entered as Ens, Navy, 53, released as Lt(jg), 55. Mem: Calif Bar Asn; Univ Calif, Berkeley Alumni Asn. Relig: Episcopal. Mailing Add: 605 Northern Ave Mill Valley CA 94941

BEOUGHER, ETHEL M (D)
b Healy, Kans, July 31, 20; d William H Anderson & Pauline Haverfield A; m 1939 to Clellan O Beougher; c William O, James E, Shirley (Mrs Walker), Judy (Mrs Zerr), Philip, Steven & Susan. Polit & Govt Pos: Gove Twp committeewoman; vchmn, Gove Co Dem Party, Kans, formerly. Relig: Methodist. Mailing Add: Box 95 Gove KS 67736

BEPPU, TADAO (D)
b Maui, Hawaii, Mar 26, 19; s Teizo Beppu & Tora Handa B; m to Alice Nobu Aoki; c William J & Anita M. Educ: Univ Hawaii, BA; Northwestern Univ. Polit & Govt Pos: Nat Committeeman, Young Dem Clubs, Hawaii, 57; deleg, Dem Nat Conv, 60, 68 & 72, mem, Comt Permanent Orgn, 60; secy, State Dem Cent Comt, 56-60, campaign chmn, 60, vchmn, 60-62; Hawaii State Rep, 58-73, vspeaker, Hawaii House of Rep, 65-67, speaker, 67-73. Bus & Prof Pos: Dir, Honolulu Stadium, 66. Mil Serv: Entered as Pvt, Army, 43, released as T/Sgt, 45, after serv in 442nd Reg Combat Team, ETO; Soldiers Medals; Bronze Star; Purple Heart; Combat Infantryman's Badge; Asiatic-Pac & ETO Ribbons; Am Defense & Victory Medals; Presidential Unit Citation with three Battle Stars. Mem: DAV (life mem); 442nd Vet Club; Nat Legis Leaders Conf, Comn on Intergovernmental Rels; Goodwill Industs of Hawaii (dir); United Serv Organ (regional dir). Relig: Congregational. Legal Res: 3350 Sierra Dr Honolulu HI 96816 Mailing Add: 62 Funchal St Honolulu HI 96813

BERDES, GEORGE RAYMOND (D)
b Milwaukee, Wis, Feb 12, 31; s Frank Raymond Berdes & Johanna Galubinski B; m 1953 to Jane Louise Baldauf; c Celia Marie, Beth Mary, John Patrick & Mary Madelyn. Educ: Marquette Univ Col Jour, BA, 53, MA, 59; Sigma Delta Chi. Polit & Govt Pos: Admin asst to US Rep Clement J Zablocki, Fourth Dist, Wis, 65-71; staff consult, Subcomt Int Security & Sci Affairs, House Foreign Affairs Comt, 71- Bus & Prof Pos: Reporter, Appleton Post-Crescent, Wis, 55-57; ed dir, Marquette Univ Press, 57-63; asst prof, Marquette Univ Col Jour, 57-65. Mil Serv: Entered as Pvt, Army, 53, released as SP-4, 55. Publ: Up from ashes (Study & Impressions of Mod Ger); Friendly adversaries; the press & government (Study of Washington Press Corps on Corps with Ctr for Study of the Am Press) 69. Mem: Am Asn Univ Prof; The Burro Club; Milwaukee Press Club; Wis Hist Soc. Honors & Awards: Study & Travel grant from WGerman Govt, 63 & 67; winner, Milwaukee Press Club, Outstanding Reporting in Int Affairs Award. Relig: Roman Catholic. Mailing Add: 6025 Berkshire Dr Bethesda MD 20014

BERDON, ROBERT I (R)
State Treas, Conn
b New Haven, Conn, Dec 24, 29; s Louis J Berdon & Jean C B; m 1964 to Nancy Tarr; c Peter Adlai. Educ: Univ Conn, BA, Law Sch, JD; Druids; Phi Epsilon Pi. Polit & Govt Pos: Legal counsel, New Haven Rep Town Comt, Conn, formerly; mem, Branford Rep Town Comt, formerly; State Treas, Conn, 71- Bus & Prof Pos: Partner, Berdon, Berdon & Young, currently; bd mem, Conn Attorney's Title Guaranty Fund, currently. Mil Serv: 1st Lt, Army, 51-53, serv in France. Mem: Am Arbit Asn (Arbitrator); Munic Finance Officers Asn; Munic Forum NY; Shrine; AF&AM. Honors & Awards: Distinguished Serv Award, Nat Jewish Fund, 61; Distinguished Serv Award, New Haven Rep Town Comt, 68. Relig: Jewish; mem & former secy, Horeb Lodge, B'nai B'rith, mem New Haven Jewish Community Ctr & Congregation Mishkan Israel. Legal Res: Flax Mill Rd Branford CT 06405 Mailing Add: 30 Trinity St Hartford CT 06115

BEREN, DANIEL E (R)
Pa State Rep
b Philadelphia, Pa, Nov 3, 29; s Arthur Beren & Frances Shapiro B; m 1956 to Joan Cranmer; c Day Cranmer, Sandra Elizabeth & Jane Sylvia. Educ: Baldwin-Wallace Col, BA, 52; Temple Univ Law Sch, LLB, 55; Omicron Delta Kappa; Alpha Phi Gamma. Polit & Govt Pos: Judge of elec, Rep Party, Pa, 61-62, committeeman, 62-67; solicitor, Montgomery Co Inst Dist, Pa, 63-66; chmn, Montgomery Co Young Rep, 65-66; Pa State Rep, 67-, minority chmn transportation comt, mem policy comt, urban affairs comt & transportation comn, Pa House of Rep; originator of the Neighborhood Assistance Act; testified on behalf of the Neighborhood Assistance Act before Rep Nat Conv in 1968 & was successful in having the concept included in the 1968 GOP Nat Platform; chief sponsor of Pa Consumer Protection Laws; co-leader in fight to reform Pa Elec Code; chmn, Montgomery Co Rep Comt, 72- Bus & Prof Pos: Partner, Beren & Clancy, Attorneys, Abington, Pa, 64-70; assoc, Waters, Fleer, Cooper & Gallager Law Firm, Jenkintown, Pa, 71- Mil Serv: Entered as Pvt, Army, 55, released as Cpl, 57, after serv in Northern Area Command, Germany; Good Conduct Medal. Mem: Am Trial Lawyers Asn; Am Judicature Soc; Jr CofC; Boy Scouts; Abington Br, YMCA (bd mgrs). Honors & Awards: Letterman, Capt, col track & cross-country teams. Relig: Jewish. Legal Res: 1765 Sharpless Rd Meadowbrook PA 19046 Mailing Add: Capitol Bldg Harrisburg PA 17120

BERENTSON, DUANE (R)
Wash State Rep
b Anacortes, Wash, Nov 22, 28; s Marion O Berentson & Martha E Helseth B; m 1949 to Joanne C Hawkings; c Kristine Ann, Daniel Duane, David Edward, Karen Elizabeth & Karol Linnea. Educ: Univ Wash, 47, 49 & 52; Pac Lutheran Univ, BS, 51; Sigma Nu. Polit & Govt Pos: Wash State Rep, 40th Dist, 63- Bus & Prof Pos: Mem, Dist One Bd, Nat Asn of Securities Dealers, Inc, 68-71. Mil Serv: Naval Air Res. Mem: Kiwanis. Relig: Lutheran. Legal Res: 1490 Country Club Dr Burlington WA 98233 Mailing Add: PO Box 426 Burlington WA 98233

BEREUTER, DOUGLAS K (R)
Nebr State Sen
b York, Nebr, Oct 6, 39; s Rupert Wesley Bereuter & Evelyn Tonn B; m 1962 to Louise Meyer; c Eric David. Educ: Univ Nebr-Lincoln, BA, 61; Harvard Univ, MCP, 66, MPA, 73; Phi Beta Kappa; Sigma Xi; Pi Sigma Alpha; Gamma Theta Upsilon; Sigma Alpha Epsilon. Polit & Govt Pos: Urban planner, US Dept Housing & Urban Develop, San Francisco, 65-66; asst dir planning, Div Nebr Resources, State of Nebr, Lincoln, 66-67, dir, Div State & Urban Affairs, Dept Econ Develop, 67-69, dir, State Off Planning & Prog, 69-71; Nebr State Sen, 75- Bus & Prof Pos: Assoc prof, Univ Nebr-Lincoln, 71-75 & Kans State Univ, 72-; self-employed consult planning & govt affairs, 71- Mil Serv: Entered as 2nd Lt, Army, 63, released as 1st Lt, 65, after serv in 1st Inf Div, Ft Riley, Kans. Mem: Am Inst Planners; Am Soc Planning Officials; Common Cause. Relig: Lutheran. Legal Res: Box 97 Utica NE 68456 Mailing Add: Rm 2000 State Capitol Lincoln NE 68509

BERG, EARL HAROLD, JR (R)
b St Paul, Minn, Nov 29, 47; s Earl Harold Berg & Doris Virginia Robertson B; div. Educ: Southern Ill Univ, BS in Jour, 70; Alpha Delta Sigma; Phi Gamma Delta. Polit & Govt Pos: Spec asst, US Rep Harold R Collier, Ill, 70-71; admin asst, US Rep Robert H Steele, Conn, 71- Bus & Prof Pos: Pres, Kovell-Am, Inc, 69-72. Relig: Baptist. Mailing Add: 4320 Arthur Ave Brookfield IL 60513

BERG, GEORGE L, JR (R)
b Pittsburgh, Pa, May 17, 28; s George L Berg & Marie Toberg B; m 1958 to Marian Buckner; c Scott & Anne Marie. Educ: Univ Pittsburgh, 47-48; Am Univ. Polit & Govt Pos: Admin asst, US Rep Carleton J King, NY, 49- Mil Serv: Entered as Pvt, Army, 50, released as Cpl, 52, after serv in Mil Dist of Washington, DC, 50-52. Relig: Catholic. Mailing Add: 1216 Swann Creek Rd Tantallon MD 20022

BERG, HARRIS ODELL (R)
NDak State Rep
b Grafton, NDak, Nov 4, 35; s Clifford S Berg & Hazel Brekke B; m 1958 to LaVonne Ardell Peterson; c Scott, Lynn, Brenda & Jodi. Educ: Concordia Col, 2 years; NDak State Univ, 1 year. Polit & Govt Pos: NDak State Rep, Dist 16, 69- Bus & Prof Pos: Prof farmer, Berg Farms, 57- Mil Serv: Entered as SA, Navy, 55, released as RM 3/C, 57, after serv in Ninth & 12th Naval Dist, USS Thomaston, 55-57. Mem: Walsh Co Crop Improv Asn (pres); NDak Young Farmers & Ranchers Asn; Mason; Shrine; VFW. Relig: Protestant. Mailing Add: State Capitol Bismarck ND 43215

BERG, OSCAR W (D)
Mem Exec Comt, Kewaunee Co Dem Party, Wis
b Algoma, Wis, May 30, 91; s Charles P Berg & Louise Mueller B; m 1917 to Ellen Larson; c Doris (Mrs Robert Beetz), Bonnie (Mrs Gene Sturchio), Marion (Mrs Julius Hafeman), Venice (Mrs James Gigstead), Beverly (Mrs Fred DePrey), Marvel (deceased) & Owen W. Educ: Algoma High Sch, grad, 10; Valley City State Normal, NDak, summer 14. Polit & Govt Pos: Mem, Dist Sch Bd, Ahnapee, Wis, 23-42, town clerk, 37-47; secy, La Follette Club, 28-38; dir, Algoma Hosp, 35-41; chmn, Kewaunee Co War Mobilization, 41, mem, War Bd & Ration Bd, Kewaunee Co, 41-45; vchmn & chmn, Co Sch Comt, 48-52; dir, Two Co Libr Bd, 48-52; dir, Algoma Farmers Coop, 48-54; from vchmn to chmn, Kewaunee Co Dem Party, 55-69, mem exec comt, 69-; chmn, Sch Reorgn Comt, 61-62; mem, Fed Housing Admin, 63-66; mem, Unified Sch Bd, Algoma, 64-66; vchmn, Kewaunee Co Dem Unit, currently. Publ: Hist articles, four Kewaunee Co papers, 72; History of Ahmapec Town (seven articles), 3/73. Mem: Nat Farm Loan Asn (dir, 24-48); Two Co Guernsey Breeders Asn; Hist Soc Kewaunee Co (treas). Honors & Awards: Award, Kewaunee Co Dem Party. Relig: Lutheran; Chmn, St Paul Lutheran Church, 49-51, secy, 58-61. Mailing Add: 960 Flora Ave Algoma WI 54201

BERG, THOMAS KENNETH (DFL)
Minn State Rep
b Willmar, Minn, Feb 10, 40; s Kenneth Q Berg & Esther Westlund B; m 1965 to Margit Kathryn Larson; c Erik Richard & Jeffrey Scott. Educ: Univ Minn, BA, 62, Law Sch, LLB, 65; Gray-Friars; Theta Chi. Polit & Govt Pos: Minn State Rep, 71- Bus & Prof Pos: Attorney, Off Gen Counsel, Dept of Navy, Wash DC, 65-67; Carlsen, Greiner & Law, Minneapolis, Minn, 67- Mil Serv: Lt, Naval Res. Mem: Minn Bar Asn. Mailing Add: 2112 Newton Ave S Minneapolis MN 55405

BERGER, DAVID GEORGE (D)
Wis State Sen
b Milwaukee, Wis, Oct 27, 46; s Wilford George Berger & Jean Goodsett B; single. Educ: Univ Wis, BA, 69; Marquette Univ, MA, 71; Pi Sigma Alpha. Polit & Govt Pos: Wis State Rep, 18th Dist, 71-75; Wis State Sen, 75- Bus & Prof Pos: Staff asst, Wis Assembly, 69. Mem: Am Polit Sci Asn; KofC; Laborers Union 113. Relig: Roman Catholic. Mailing Add: 4443 N 82nd St Milwaukee WI 53218

BERGER, HAROLD D (D)
Mem Exec Comt, Nassau Co Dem Comt, NY
b Brooklyn, NY, June 7, 21; s Philip Berger & Sarah Arnoff B; m 1942 to Eleanor Suvalsky; c Robert, Lee, Judith & Suzan. Educ: Brooklyn Col, AB, 42; Polytech Inst Brooklyn, 46-48; St John's Univ, LLB, 65. Polit & Govt Pos: Committeeman, Nassau Co Dem Comt, NY, 53-, leader, Green Acre Zone, 63-, mem exec comt, currently; vpres, Valley Stream Dem Club, 56-58, pres, 58-60; chmn legis comt, Nassau Co Youth Bd, 64-; alt deleg, Dem Nat Conv, 68; committeeman, NY State Dem Comt, 72-; leader, 19th Assembly Dist Dem Party, 72- Bus & Prof Pos: Chief chemist, Stein-Hall & Co, New York, 48-53; pres, Berco Industs Corp, 55-; vpres, Charell Consult Co, 66- Mil Serv: Entered as Aviation Cadet, Air Force, 64, released as Capt, 66, after serv in Ninth Photo Tech Squadron, Guam, 65-66. Mem: Rubber Div, Rubber Group, Am Chem Soc; Soc Plastic Engrs; Civic Asn Green Acres (mem bd). Relig: Hebrew. Mailing Add: 30 Eastwood Lane Valley Stream NY 11581

BERGER, L E (D)
NDak State Rep
Mailing Add: State Capitol Bismarck ND 58501

BERGERON, BELVIN FRANCIS (D)
Chmn, West Baton Rouge Parish Dem Exec Comt, La
b West Baton Rouge Parish, La, Oct 5, 24; s Willie Joseph Bergeron & Hester Mary Allain B; m 1950 to Claire Lefebvre; c Lynette Claire, Debra Anne, David Francis, Amy Geralyn, Yvette Marie, Brian Joseph & Brett Joseph. Educ: La State Univ, BS in Bus Admin; Beta Alpha Psi. Polit & Govt Pos: Mem, West Baton Rouge Parish Dem Exec Comt, La, 56-, chmn, 64-; sheriff, West Baton Rouge Parish, 60- Mil Serv: Entered as A/S, Navy, 43, released as Yeoman 1/C, 45, after serv in Pac Theatre; SPac Campaign Ribbon with One Star. Mem: KofC; WOW; Am Legion; VFW; Nat Sheriffs' Asn. Relig: Catholic. Mailing Add: 250 Seventh St Port Allen LA 70767

BERGERON, LOUIS E (D)
NH State Rep
Mailing Add: 7 Susan Lane Rochester NH 03867

BERGHEIM, MELVIN LEWIS (D)
City Councilman, Alexandria, Va
b Boston, Mass, Aug 3, 26; s Samuel Leo Bergheim (deceased) & Bertha Gorfinkle B (deceased); m 1959 to Donna Rose Feldman; c Beth Susanna, Laura Ann, David Abram & Maria Lisa. Educ: Harvard Univ, AB, 47; Columbia Univ, MA, 49, Grad Sch Jour, MS, 51. Polit & Govt Pos: Mem exec comt, Alexandria City Dem Comt, 65-67; staff, United Dem for Humphrey, 68, mem, Vice President Humphrey's Task Force Cities & Ethnic Groups, 68; chmn, Alexandria Howell Gov Comt, 69 & 73; City Councilman, Alexandria, Va, 70-; secy-treas, Metrop Washington Coun Govts, 71-; mem steering comt, Metrop Washington Waste Mgt Agency, 71-; deleg, Dem Nat Conv, 72, chmn task force on urban plank, Conv Platform Comt, 72; mem, Sen George McGovern's Adv Panel on Urban Affairs, 72; exec comt, Northern Va Planning Dist Comn, 72- Bus & Prof Pos: Reporter, Providence J-Bull, RI, 49-50; reporter, Washington Post, 51-54; writer, Cong Quart, 55; proj dir, Govt Affairs Inst, Washington, DC, 56-67; dir research serv, Nat Adv Comn on Civil Disorders, proj dir, Urban Am, Inc & Potomac Inst, Inc, 68-69; sr assoc, Nat League Cities & US Conf Mayors, 69-; dep exec dir, US Conf City Health Officers, 73- Mil Serv: Entered as A/S, V-12, Navy, 44, released as A/S, NROTC, 46, after serv in Harvard Col, 44-46; Lt(jg), Navy, 52-54, Mediter, 52. Publ: Auth, City Hall & the poor, 8/71, What elected officials always wanted to know about federal income taxes, 3/72 & City Hall goes to the conventions, 10/72, Nation's Cities. Relig: Jewish. Mailing Add: 4905 Maury Lane Alexandria VA 22304

BERGLAND, BOB SELMER (DFL)
US Rep, Minn
b Roseau, Minn, July 22, 28; s Selmer Bennett Bergland & Mabel Evans B; m 1950 to Helen Elaine Grahn; c Dianne, Linda, Stevan, Jon, Allan, Billy & Franklyn. Educ: Univ Minn, 2 years; Sears Roebuck scholarship. Polit & Govt Pos: Secy, Roseau Co Dem-Farmer-Labor Party, Minn, 51-52, chmn, 53-54; chmn, Minn State Agr Stabilization & Conserv Serv Comt, US Dept Agr, 61-62, dir Midwest Area Agr Stabilization & Conserv Serv, 63-68; cand, US

House Rep, 68; US Rep, Minn, 71- Bus & Prof Pos: Field Rep, Minn Farmers Union, 48-50; farmer, 50- Mem: Mason; Lions; Minn Farmers Union; Nat Farmers Orgn. Honors & Awards: Gold Letter A, Univ Minn. Relig: Lutheran. Legal Res: Rte 3 Roseau MN 56751 Mailing Add: 1008 Longworth House Off Bldg Washington DC 20515

BERGLIN, LINDA L (DFL)
Minn State Rep
b Oakland, Calif, Oct 19, 44; d Freeman Waterman & Norma Lund W; single. Educ: Minneapolis Col Art & Design, BFA, 67. Polit & Govt Pos: Minn State Rep, 73- Mailing Add: 2309 Clinton Ave S Minneapolis MN 55404

BERGLUND, SHIRLEY M (DFL)
b Appleton, Minn, Dec 8, 16; d George Samuelson & Georgia Hayes S; m 1946 to John L Berglund; c Mary (Mrs Dale Johnson) & Shelley. Educ: Appleton High Sch, Minn, grad. Polit & Govt Pos: Treas, Kandiyohi Co Dem-Farmer-Labor Party, Minn, 66-68, chmn Willmar Fourth Ward, 66-68, second vchmn, 68-70, first vchmn, 70-72, secy, 72-73; mem adv comt, Bus Dept, Willmar Area Voc-Tech Inst, 69; mem, Kandiyohi Co-City of Willmar Libr Bd, 71-; bd mem, Crow River Regional Libr Bd, 71- Bus & Prof Pos: News ed & acct, Appleton Press, Minn, 34-37; secy, Minn State Unemploy Compensation Dept, 37-39; news ed & acct, Willmar J, 39-46; clerk, Off of City Clerk, Willmar, 48-49; clerk, Kandiyohi Co Selective Serv Off, 50-52; acct & secy, Willmar Gas Co, 52-62; acct & credit mgr, Western Region, Minn Natural Div, Minn Gas Co, 62- Mem: Willmar Bus & Prof Women's Club (state finance chmn, currently); Litchfield Bus & Prof Women's Club; Does; Minn Fedn Bus & Prof Women's Club; VFW Auxiliary. Relig: Episcopal. Mailing Add: PO Box 877 Willmar MN 56201

BERGMAN, IRVIN LESTER (R)
Iowa State Sen
b Harris, Iowa, Jan 5, 11; s John Albert Bergman & Tena Miller B; m 1933 to Vera Lucille Donnenwerth; c John Harvey, Judith Ann (Mrs Carrico) & Mary Kathryn. Educ: Harris Consolidated Sch, Harris, Iowa, 12 years. Polit & Govt Pos: Pres, Harris Consolidated Sch Bd, Iowa, 40-57 & Osceola Co Sch Bd, 57-65; mem, Town Coun, Harris, 57-67; Iowa State Rep, First Dist, 67-73; Iowa State Sen, 73- Bus & Prof Pos: Farmer; mem adv bd, Area Voc Sch at Sheldon at time of orgn; mem, Rural Area Develop Bd, Osceola Co; dir, Osceola Co Farmers Mutual Ins Asn; dir, Osceola Co Fair Bd; secy, Harris Vol Fire Dept; pres secy & treas, Harris Community Club, 60- Mem: Farm Bur; PTA. Relig: Lutheran. Mailing Add: Box 116 Harris IA 51345

BERGMAN, LARRY W (D)
Chmn, Sheridan Co Dem Party, Nebr
b Ft Wayne, Ind, May 12, 46; s Wayne H Bergman & Pauline Stemmler B; m 1969 to Susan K Whitacre; c Dane & Kristina. Educ: Concordia Jr Col, AA, 66; Concordia Sr Col, 66-67; Ball State Univ, BA, 68; Concordia Theol Sem, BD, 72; Lambda Alpha. Polit & Govt Pos: Chmn, Sheridan Co Dem Party, Nebr, 74- Bus & Prof Pos: Pastor, St Paul's & Zion Lutheran Churches, Rushville & Hay Springs, Nebr, 72-75 & Grace Lutheran Church, Wood River, 75- Relig: Lutheran-Mo Synod. Legal Res: RR 1 Wood River NE 68883 Mailing Add: Box 6 Wood River NE 68883

BERKES, MILTON (D)
Chmn, Bucks Co Dem Party, Pa
b Philadelphia, Pa, Sept 29, 24; s Morris Berkes & Rose Latinsky B; m 1946 to Ethel Weintraub; c Marcy, Eileen, Howard & Alan. Educ: Temple Univ, BS in educ, 49, MEd, 53. Polit & Govt Pos: Committeeman, Dem Party, Pa, 54-62; chmn bd supvr, Falls Twp, Pa, 56 & 58-65, supvr, 56-, supt, 63-; founder & former chmn, Regional Coop Coun, 58-60; campaign mgr, Michener for Cong Comt, 62; deleg, Dem Nat Conv, 64, alt deleg, 68 & 72; mem exec comt, Bucks Co Dem Party, 64-66, chmn, 68-; Pa State Rep, until 74; mem, State Policy Comt, Pa State Comt, 68-69; mem, Gov Coun Drugs & Alcoholism, 72- Bus & Prof Pos: Teacher & sch guid counr, Philadelphia Sch Dist, 49-62. Mil Serv: Entered as Pvt, Army, 43, released as T/3, 46, after serv in Signal Corps, Asiatic Pac Theater, 44-46; Philippine Liberation Ribbon with 2 Bronze Stars; Asiatic Pac Theatre Serv Medal with 3 Bronze Stars; Meritorious Unit Award; Am Theater Serv, Victory & Good Conduct Medals. Publ: We can work together, Pa Mag, 62; auth, Pa Drug & Narcotics Code 72. Mem: Regional Conf Elected Officials; Bucks Co Asn of Twp Officials; Am Legion; Jewish War Veterans; YMHA, Levittown (vpres). Relig: Jewish; Dir, Temple Shalom of Levittown. Mailing Add: 56 Palm Lane Levittown PA 19054

BERKING, MAX (D)
Mem Exec Comt, NY State Dem Comt
b New York, NY, July 27, 17; m to Dorothy Noyes, wid; c Charles, Peter, Laurence & Charlotte. Educ: Williams Col, 39; Univ Ariz Bus Sch. Polit & Govt Pos: Asst to chmn, Fair Employ Practice Comt, World War II; campaign dir, Int Rescue Comt; bd, Am Comt on Africa; Dem chmn, Rye, NY; NY State Sen, 65; Dem Nominee for co exec, Westchester Co, 69; chmn, Westchester Co Dem Comt, 71-75; mem exec comt, NY State Dem Comt, currently; staff, NY State Assembly, 75. Bus & Prof Pos: Pres, Max Berking, Inc, indust advert and mkt, New York. Publ: Strengthening the Wisconsin legislature, Rutgers Univ, 70. Mem: Williams Club of New York; Urban League of Westchester (Bd). Relig: Congregational. Mailing Add: Drake-Smith Lane Rye NY 10580

BERKLEY, RICHARD L (R)
Polit & Govt Pos: Chmn, Mo State Rep Cent Comt, formerly. Mailing Add: 819 E 19th St Kansas City MO 64108

BERKOWITZ, DAVID J (D)
Young Dem Committeeman, Kans
b Chicago, Ill, July 8, 41; s Morton Harry Berkowitz & Leah Rubin B; single. Educ: Wichita State Univ, BA, 64; Univ Kans, JD, 69; Order of Coif; Phi Delta Phi. Polit & Govt Pos: Pres, Wichita Young Dem, 61-63; Dem precinct committeeman, Sedgwick Co, 62-68; second vpres, Kans Young Dem, 67-68, jr nat committeeman, 70-; pres, Douglas Co Young Dem, 69-70; Dem precinct committeeman, Douglas Co, 70-; Young Dem Committeeman, currently; Douglas Co Attorney. Bus & Prof Pos: Asst gen counsel, Kans Corp Comn, 68-70. Mem: Douglas Co, Kans Am Bar Asn; B'nai B'rith. Honors & Awards: Prize in procedure & oil & gas, Am Jurisp Asn. Relig: Jewish. Legal Res: 1629 W 22nd Terr Lawrence KS 66044 Mailing Add: 915 Louisiana St Lawrence KS 66044

BERKOWITZ, JACQUELINE ELLEN (D)
Mem, New York Co Dem Comt, NY
b New York, NY, June 12, 44; d Simon Berkowitz & E Diane Halpern; single. Educ: Mt Holyoke Col, AB, 65; St John's Univ Sch Law, NY, 73- Polit & Govt Pos: Vpres & secy, New Dem Club, New York, 70-; mem deleg selection comt, Manhattan Women's Polit Caucus, 71-72; mem, New York Co Dem Comt, 71-; deleg, Dem Nat Conv, 72; mem exec coun, New Dem Coalition of NY State, 73- Bus & Prof Pos: Lab analyst, Pfizer, Inc, Brooklyn, 65-68; chemist, Thomas J Lipton, Inc, Englewood Cliffs, NJ, 68-70; research asst, Cornell Univ Med Col, New York, 70-72. Publ: Co-auth, Formation of epitheaflavic acid and its transformation to thearubigins during tea fermentation, J Photochem, 10/71 & Biochemistry of tea fermentation; products of the oxidation of tea flavonols in a modern tea fermentation system, J Food Sci, 5/72. Mem: Am Chem Soc; Student Bar Asn; Fedn Jewish Philanthropies NY (speakers bur, Queens cabinet, New Leadership Div, 67-); Common Cause. Honors & Awards: Regents Scholarship, NY State, 61. Relig: Jewish. Mailing Add: 214 E 51st St New York NY 10022

BERLIN, THEODORE (D)
Pa State Rep
Mailing Add: Capitol Bldg Harrisburg PA 17120

BERLINER, HENRY A, JR (R)
Mem, DC Rep Comt
b Washington, DC, Feb 9, 34; s Henry A Berliner & Josephine Mitchell B; m 1961 to Bodil Iversen; c Tina, John & George. Educ: Univ Mich, AB, 56; George Washington Univ Law Sch, JD with honors, 64; Phi Eta Sigma; Sigma Chi. Polit & Govt Pos: Mem exec comt, Young Rep Nat Fedn, 61-63; mem, DC Rep Comt, 64-, gen counsel, 68-; Asst US Attorney, DC, 66-67; VIP tour dir, Nixon-Agnew Campaign Comt, 68; asst to chmn, Presidential Inaugural Ball, 69; consult, US Info Agency, 70; alt mem, DC Comn on Judicial Disabilities & Tenure; mem, Regional Export Expansion Coun, 70-; pub mem, Dept of State Threshold Rev Bd, 71-72; deleg & chmn DC deleg, Rep Nat Conv, 72. Bus & Prof Pos: Partner, Berliner & Ward, 67-; chmn bd, Sec Nat Bldg & Loan, Inc, 71- Mil Serv: Entered as Ens, Navy, 56, released as Lt, 59, after serv in Atlantic Fleet Squadron; Lt, Naval Res, 59- Publ: State buy American policies, George Washington Law Rev, 3/64; Amendments to Federal Tort Claims Act, 2/67 & Stop the war in Washington—the Nixon anti-crime program, 5/69, DC Bar J. Mem: Phi Delta Phi; DC Bar Asn (judicial selection comt, 70-); Judicial Conf. Relig: Episcopal. Mailing Add: 2870 Upton St Washington DC 20008

BERMAN, ARTHUR LEONARD (D)
Ill State Rep
b Chicago, Ill, May 4, 35; s Morris Berman & Jean Glast B; m 1960 to Sondra; c Adam Elliott & Marcy Ellen. Educ: Univ Ill, Urbana, BS, 56; Northwestern Univ Sch Law, LLB, 58; Phi Epsilon Pi; Tau Epsilon Rho. Polit & Govt Pos: Spec attorney, Ill Dept Ins, 64-67; spec asst to Ill Attorney Gen, 67-68; Ill State Rep, 69- Bus & Prof Pos: Gen practice of law, 58- Publ: Two articles, Northwestern Univ Law Rev. Mem: 50th Ward Regular Dem Orgn (vpres); North Town Community Coun (dir); Bernard Horwich Jewish Community Ctr (dir); West Rogers Park B'nai B'rith; 50th Ward Young Dem. Relig: Jewish. Legal Res: 2701 W Sherwin Ave Chicago IL 60645 Mailing Add: 69 W Washington St Chicago IL 60602

BERMAN, GERTRUDE (D)
NJ State Assemblywoman
b Newark, NJ, July 3, 24; wid. Educ: Montclair State Col, BA; Rutgers Univ, New Brunswick, MSW. Polit & Govt Pos: City councilwoman, Long Branch, NJ, 69-71, city coun pres, 71; NJ State Assemblywoman, Dist Ten, 74- Bus & Prof Pos: Exec dir, Monmouth Co Ment Health, NJ, 67-70, dir, Community Serv, 72-73; social serv planner, Perth Amboy Model City Agency, 71. Mailing Add: 305 Bond St Asbury Park NJ 07712

BERMAN, HOWARD L (D)
Calif State Assemblyman
b Los Angeles, Calif, Apr 15, 41; s Joseph Berman & Eleanore Schapiro B. Educ: Univ Calif, Los Angeles, BA in Int Rels, Law Sch, LLD. Polit & Govt Pos: Calif State Assemblyman, currently, Assembly Majority Leader, 74-, chmn, Assembly Select Comt on Med Malpractice, vchmn, Joint Comt on Legal Equal for Women & Pub Employee-Employer Rels, chmn educ budget, Assembly Ways & Means Comt, 75- Mem: Am Dem Action (nat bd dirs); Calif Anti-Defamation League (bd dirs); Calif Young Dem; Sierra Club Calif. Honors & Awards: Number One Consumer Legislator, Calif Consumer Fedn; 100% Voting Record, League of Conserv Voters & Calif Am for Dem Action; Top three Calif Legislators, Calif Nat Orgn for Women. Relig: Jewish. Mailing Add: 13719 Ventura Blvd Suite F Sherman Oaks CA 91423

BERMAN, JASON S (D)
b Brooklyn, NY, Feb 3, 38; s Max Berman & Emma Friedman B; m 1962 to Rita Zolten; c Julie, Jill & Meredith. Educ: City Col New York, BA, 59; Northwestern Univ, MA, 61; Univ Pittsburgh, doctoral studies, 62-65. Polit & Govt Pos: Staff asst, US Senate Subcomt on Const Amendments, formerly; legis asst, US Sen Birch Bayh, Ind, formerly, admin asst, currently. Bus & Prof Pos: Teaching fel, Univ Pittsburgh, 61-64, Mellon fel, 64-65. Honors & Awards: Univ Scholar, Northwestern Univ, 61. Mailing Add: 7905 Inverness Ridge Rd Potomac MD 20854

BERMAN, MARGARET W (D)
Treas, Piscataquis Co Dem Comt, Maine
b Hawaii, July 23, 17; d James W Donald & Violet Fursey D; m 1966 to John J Berman; c Ralph R Miller & Pamela D (Mrs Denton). Educ: Univ Wash, AB, 38, fifth year dipl, 41; Hunter Col, MS, 58; Omicron Nu; Alpha Gamma Delta. Polit & Govt Pos: Justice of the peace, Guilford, Maine, 70-; chmn, Parkman Dem Comt, 70-; treas, Piscataquis Co Dem Comt, 72- Bus & Prof Pos: Teacher, various states, 41-; payroll & ledger clerk, Army, Seattle, 42-43 & New York, 50-53; teacher, Piscataquis Community High Sch, Maine, 68-; trustee, Parkman Schs, 71- Mem: Am Home Econ Asn; Nat & Maine Teachers Asns; Zephyrus Club; New Eng Aquarium, Boston (charter mem). Relig: Episcopal. Mailing Add: Rte 1 Guilford ME 04443

BERMAN, MURIEL M (D)
m to Philip I Berman; c Nancy, Nina & Steven. Educ: Univ Pittsburgh; Cedar Crest Col; Muhlenberg Col; Carnegie Tech Univ; Pa State Univ Col Optometry, OD; Aspen Inst Humanistic Studies, Colo, 65, Tokyo, Japan, 66. Hon Degrees: Wilson Col, 69; DFA, Cedar Crest Col, 72. Polit & Govt Pos: Nongovt orgn deleg, UNICEF, UN, Thailand, 64, Ethiopia, 66, mem ad hoc comts on Latin Am & Africa; fact-finding ambassador with advice & consent of US State Dept to Brazil, Argentina, Chile & Peru with subsequent lectures on probs & prospects of people there; lectr, UN activities & anal; participant, Art in the Embassies Prog; Dem Presidential Elector, Pa, 68; deleg, Dem Nat Conv, 72. Bus & Prof Pos: Lectr, series

on art; chmn prog comt, Lehigh Valley Educ TV, producer, Col Speak-In, weekly series; curator & researcher, Berman Circulating Art Exhib; vchmn, Women for Pa Bicentennial, 76. Publ: Art catalogues. Mem: Girl Scouts (Chmn Great Valley Coun); Woman's Club (VPres & Fine Arts Chmn); Hadassah (Nat Bd); Allentown Art Mus Auxiliary (Art Appreciation Dir & Lectr); League of Women Voters. Honors & Awards: Woman of Valor citation from Bonds for Israel; Outstanding Woman Award, Allentown YWCA, 73. Mailing Add: 20 Hundred Nottingham Rd Allentown PA 18103

BERMUDEZ RIVERA, EFRAiN (POPULAR DEMOCRAT, PR)
Rep, PR House Rep
Mailing Add: State Capitol San Juan PR 00901

BERNABUCCI, JOHN ROGER, JR (R)
Finance Chmn, NDak Rep Party
b Jamestown, NDak, Aug 9, 30; s John Roger Bernabucci, Sr & Mary Schwader m 1952 to Geraldine DesJardin; c Mary Therese & Paul Anthony. Educ: Iowa State Univ, 48-49; Univ NDak, BS, 52; Tau Kappa Epsilon. Polit & Govt Pos: Finance chmn, Stutsman Co Rep Party, NDak, 57-60, chmn, 60-66; deleg, Rep Nat Conv, 64; NDak State Rep, 29th Legis Dist, 66-70; finance chmn, NDak Rep Party, 72- Bus & Prof Pos: Pres, Coca-Cola Bottling Co, Jamestown, NDak, 65-, Northern Plains Investment Co, 68- & Coca-Cola Bottling Co of LaCrosse, Wis, 70-; dir, Jamestown Hosp Asn, 71-, Jamestown Urban Renewal Agency, 71- & Nat Soft Drink Asn, Washington, DC, 72-; chmn of bd, Stutsman Co State Bank of Jamestown, 72- Mem: Lions; Elks; Mason; El Zagel Shrine. Relig: Lutheran. Mailing Add: 1712 Elmwood Pl Jamestown ND 58401

BERNAL, JOE J (D)
Mem, Dem Nat Comt, Tex
b 1927. Educ: Trinity Univ, BA; Our Lady of the Lake Col, MEd; Tex Tech; NMex A&M. Polit & Govt Pos: Tex State Rep, 59th Legis; Tex State Sen, formerly; deleg, Dem Nat Conv, 72; mem, Dem Nat Comt, currently; deleg, Dem Nat Mid-Term Conf, 74. Bus & Prof Pos: Former teacher; exec dir, San Antonio Archdiocesan Comn for Mex Am Affairs, currently. Mailing Add: 6410 Laurelhill Dr San Antonio TX 78229

BERNARD, BETTY HILL (R)
First VPres, Ark Fedn Rep Women
b Atlanta, Tex, Feb 11, 32; d Troy David Hill & Mary Sparkman H; m 1953 to Charles Taylor Bernard; c Sallie Hill, Mary Troy, Charles Taylor, Jr, David Wesley & John Harbert. Educ: Baylor Univ, AB; Washington Col; Centenary Col; Athenean Club. Polit & Govt Pos: Committeewoman, Ark State Rep Party, 66-; mem, Crittenden Co Rep Recommendations Comt, 66-; mem, Crittenden Co Rep Comt, 66-, chmn, 70-; first vpres, Ark Rep Fedn Women, 67-; alt deleg Rep Nat Conv, 68; pres, Earle Rep Women's Club, 68-; mem, Crittenden Co Elec Comn. Bus & Prof Pos: Pres, Bernard Manor Laundry-Cleaners; teacher Am hist & govt course, Shorter Col, 69. Mem: Ark Tennis Asn. Honors & Awards: Placed tenth, Jr Vets, Southern Lawn Tennis Asn, 70. Relig: Southern Baptist. Mailing Add: Bernard Farms Earle AR 72331

BERNARD, CHARLES TAYLOR (R)
b Helena, Ark, Sept 10, 27; s Charles LaFayette Bernard & Sallie Eakin B; m 1953 to Betty Ann Hill; c Sallie Hill, Mary Troy, Charles Taylor, Jr, David Wesley & John Harbert. Educ: Baylor Univ, BA, 50; Delta Sigma Pi; Tryon Coterie; Baylor CofC. Hon Degrees: LLB, Shorter Col. Polit & Govt Pos: Mem, Earle City Coun, Ark, 52-58; chmn, Crittenden Co Rep Comt, 66-67; treas, Ark State Rep Party, 67-68; vchmn, 69-70, finance chmn, 69, chmn, 70-73; cand for US Senate, 68; mem, Rep Nat Comt, 71-73; deleg & chmn Ark Deleg, Rep Nat Conv, 72; mem, Ark Electoral Col, 72; app adv bd, Small Bus Admin, 73. Bus & Prof Pos: Farming, ginning, elevator oper; owner & operator, Bernard currently. Mil Serv: Navy, 44-45. Mem: Nat Conf Christians & Jews (Bd Dirs, Ark Region); Ark State Banking Comn (chmn, 71); Southern Cotton Ginners Asn; Boy Scouts (exec comt & chmn finance comt, Region Five); Mason (32 degree). Honors & Awards: Silver Beaver Award and Silver Antelope Award, Boy Scouts. Relig: Baptist. Legal Res: Bernard Farms Earle AR 72331 Mailing Add: 1000 Maine St Earle AR 72331

BERNARD, MARY ELIZABETH (D)
NH State Rep
b Dover, NH; d Arthur Peter O'Gorman & Margaret Donnelly O; m 1935 to Albert O Bernard. Educ: McIntosh Bus Col, Dover, NH, 23; Carney Hosp Sch Nursing, Boston, Mass, RN; Carney Hosp Alumnae. Polit & Govt Pos: Supvr check lists, Dover, NH, 63-; mem, Dover City Dem Comt, 43-75; mem, NH Order Women Legislators, 67-; NH State Rep, 67-71 & 75-; mem, Strafford Co Home & Bldg Comt, 69-73; court clerk, House Bldg Comt, Strafford Co, 69; mem exec comt, Strafford Co Dem Comt, 73-74; clerk, Dover Co Dem Deleg, 69-; mem liquor comt, NH House Rep, 73-; vchmn, Strafford Co Bldg Comt, 75- Bus & Prof Pos: Bookkeeper, A O Bernard, Bldg Contractor, 35-52; real estate agt, 35-; writer, Women's Pages, Boston Globe, 56. Mem: Cath Daughters Am (trustee); State Order Women Legislators (historian, 75-); State Insts Comt; Hibernians Ladies Auxiliary (pres); Dover Point Commun Club (treas). Relig: Catholic. Mailing Add: 121 Portland Ave Dover NH 03820

BERNARD, MILLY O (D)
Utah State Rep
Mailing Add: 4081 W 5500 S Kearns UT 84118

BERNARD, SPENCER THOMAS (D)
Okla State Rep
b Rush Springs, Okla, Feb, 5, 15; s Cicero Edgar Bernard & Gertrude Sperling B; m 1935 to Vivian Opal Dorman; c Kay Ann. Educ: High Sch, Rush Springs, Okla, 33. Polit & Govt Pos: Mem, Wheat Adv Comt to the Secy of Agriculture, DC; Okla State Rep, 61- Mem: Lions; Am Bus Club; Okla Cattlemen Asn; Farmers Union; Red Red Rose. Relig: Church of Christ. Mailing Add: Rte 1 Box 158 Rush Springs OK 73082

BERNASHE, ROGER L (D)
Mass State Sen
Mailing Add: State Capitol Boston MA 02133

BERNBAUM, MAURICE MARSHALL
b Chicago, Ill, Feb 15, 10; m to Elizabeth Hahn; c Edwin M & L Marcia. Educ: Harvard Univ, SB, 31; Univ Chicago, summer, 31; Northwestern Univ, 31-32. Polit & Govt Pos: Acct, Dept Treas, 35; economist, US Tariff Comn, 35-36; vconsul, Foreign Serv, 36; vconsul, Vancouver, BC, 36-37; Foreign Serv Sch, 38; vconsul, Singapore, 38-41; vconsul, third & second secy, Caracas, Venezuela, 42-45; second secy & vconsul, Managua, Nicaragua, 45-48; first secy & consul, Quito, Ecuador, 48-50; Nat War Col, 50-51; officer in charge, NCoast Affairs, 51-53; counr, Caracas, 53-59; dir, Off SAm Affairs, Dept State, 55-59; minister counr of embassy, Buenos Aires, Argentina, 59-60; US Ambassador, Ecuador, 60-65; US Ambassador, Venezuela, 65-69. Bus & Prof Pos: Consultant. Mem: Harvard Club, Washington; Cosmos Club; Kenwood Club; Int Club of Washington; Washington Inst Foreign Affairs. Mailing Add: 5108 Westpath Way Bethesda MD 20016

BERNDT, ROBERT J (R)
Del State Sen
Mailing Add: 312 Beverly Place Wilmington DE 19809

BERNER, ALICE VIOLA (D)
Secy, Mont State Dem Comt
b Wolf Point, Mont, Feb 10, 28; d Cleo Reese Cahill & Hazel Nail C; m 1947 to Harvey F Berner; c Jerry Ross, Bonnie Lea, Colleen Kay & Allan Lane. Polit & Govt Pos: Regional dir, Mont State Dem Women's Club, 60-64, secy, 65-; precinct committeewoman, McCone Co Dem Party, Mont, 60-69; secy, McCone Dem Club, 65-69, pres, 69-; deleg, Dem Nat Conv, 68; committeewoman, Eastern Cong Dist Dem Party, currently; secy, Mont State Dem Comt, currently. Mem: Mont Farmers Union; VFW Auxiliary. Relig: Presbyterian. Mailing Add: Star Rte 231 Box A25 Wolf Point MT 59201

BERNHAGEN, JOHN JOSEPH (R)
Minn State Sen
b Hutchinson, Minn, Mar 19, 34; s Edward C Bernhagen & Emma Malek B; m 1956 to Loretta Martha Narr; c Joel, Luann & Paul. Educ: Univ Minn, St Paul, 52-54. Polit & Govt Pos: Minn State Rep, 69-72; Minn State Sen, 73- Bus & Prof Pos: Dir, McLeod Coop Power Asn, Glencoe, Minn, 63-; secy, Minn Asn Elec Coops, Minneapolis, currently. Mil Serv: Entered as Pvt, Army, 54, released as Pfc, 56, after serv in Qm Corps, Europe, 55-56; Good Conduct Medal. Mem: Farm Bur; Am Field Serv. Honors & Awards: Extemporaneous Speaking Award, Region & Minn Farm Bur, second place nationally. Relig: Lutheran. Mailing Add: Rte 1 Hutchinson MN 55350

BERNHARD, BERL (D)
Gen Counsel, Dem Sen Campaign Comt
b New York, NY, Sept 7, 29; s Morris Bernhard & Celia B; m 1952 to Janice Hartman; c Peter Berl, Robin Churchill & Andrew Morris. Educ: Dartmouth Col, BA, 51; Yale Law Sch, LLB, 54; Phi Beta Kappa. Hon Degrees: LLD, Cent State Col, 63. Polit & Govt Pos: Staff dir, US Comn on Civil Rights, 61-63; consult, Off of Secy of State, 63-68; spec counsel, White House Conf To Fulfill These Rights, 66; gen counsel, Dem Sen Campaign Comt, 67-; mem, Vice President Humphrey's Task Force on Order, 68; spec counsel, Dem Nat Comt, 69-70. Bus & Prof Pos: Adj prof law, Georgetown Univ Law Ctr, 63-65; consult, Ford Found, 64-66; counsel, Lawyer's Comt for Civil Rights Under Law, 66-; mem, Bd Higher Educ & chmn, Finance Comt, 67-68; trustee, Joseph E Davies Scholarship Found, 69-; partner, Hughes Hubbard & Reed, 72-75. Publ: Articles in George Washington Law Rev, NC Law Rev, St Louis Rev & others. Mem: DC Bar Asn; Am Arbit Asn (nat panel arbitrators); Asn Interstate Practitioners; Casque & Gauntlet Clubs, Washington, DC. Honors & Awards: Arthur S Flemming Award for One of Outstanding Young Men in Fed Govt, DC Jr CofC, 60; One of Ten Outstanding Young Men in US, US Jr CofC, 63. Legal Res: 5405 Blackistone Rd Bethesda MD 20016 Mailing Add: 1660 L St NW Washington DC 20036

BERNHARD, MARY E (D)
b Columbus, Ohio, Dec 10, 41; d William Joseph Bernhard, Jr & Anna Catharine Klarenbeck B; single. Educ: Marygrove Col, BA, 63; George Washington Univ, 65. Polit & Govt Pos: Exec secy to US Rep Martha W Griffiths, Mich, 64-75; off mgr & exec secy, US Rep Elliott H Levitas, Mich, 75- Mem: Mich State Soc; Cong Staff Club. Legal Res: 18790 Rock Ave Roseville MI 48066 Mailing Add: 301 G St SW Suite 125 Washington DC 20024

BERNIER, LEE GERARD (R)
Chmn, Sixth Cong Dist Rep Party, Ga
b Pelham, Ga, May 6, 41; s Alphonso Thomas Bernier & Myrtle Corbin B; m 1962 to Barbara Jean Rigsby; c LaJeanna & Craig. Educ: SGa Col, 59-60; Ga State Univ, BBA, 66; student rep, SGa Col Student Govt; Real Estate Soc, Ga State Univ. Polit & Govt Pos: Second vchmn, Clayton Co Rep Party, Ga, 68-69, chmn, 69-70; first vchmn, Sixth Cong Dist Rep Party, 70-71, acting chmn, 71-72, chmn, 72- Bus & Prof Pos: Admin asst traffic, Delta Air Lines, Inc, Atlanta. Honors & Awards: Distinguished Serv Award, Jonesboro Jr Woman's Club, 71. Relig: Baptist. Mailing Add: 3079 Jodeco Dr Jonesboro GA 30236

BERNIER, LEO ROBERT (D)
NH State Rep
b Manchester, NH, Dec 26, 51; s Robert Bernier & Jeanette Provencher B; single. Educ: Univ NH Thompson Sch Appl Sci, Assoc Food Serv Mgt, 73; Phi Mu Delta. Polit & Govt Pos: NH State Rep, 73- Mem: Forty-Three Club. Relig: Catholic. Mailing Add: 373 Kimball St Manchester NH 03102

BERNING, KARL I (R)
Ill State Sen
b Seattle, Wash, June 10, 11; s Frank Berning & Clara Rasmussen B; m 1939 to Alpha Mikkelsen; c Grant, Penny (Mrs Larry Schaefer) & Randall. Educ: Blackburn Col; Lake Forest Col; Northwestern Univ. Polit & Govt Pos: Constable, West Deerfield Twp, Ill, 46-53, twp supvr, 53-62, chmn, Lake Co Bd Supvr, 60-62; treas, Lake Co, 62-66; Ill State Sen, 32nd Dist, 66-, minority spokesman Pensions Comt, Ill State Senate, mem, Local Govt, Financial Insts, Exec Appts Comts & chmn, Co Probs Study, chmn, Spanish Speaking People Study, chmn, Model Sch for Deaf Study & Legis Adv to Northern Ill Planning & Zoning, Pension Laws, Chain OLakes Study & Urban Educ Comns, currently. Mem: Lake Co Mus of Hist (adv bd); Klingberg Sch for Handicapped; Nat Soc of State Legis; Mason; Lions. Honors & Awards: Outstanding Legis, Jewish War Vet. Relig: Protestant. Legal Res: 1006 Rosemary Terr Deerfield IL 60015 Mailing Add: 625 Deerfield Rd Deerfield IL 60015

BERNSTEIN, ABRAHAM (D)
NY State Sen
b New York, NY, May 1, 18; m 1941 to Ruth Schub; c David & Barbara. Educ: City Col, New York, BSS; Brooklyn Law Sch, LLB. Polit & Govt Pos: Mem, Affiliated Young Dem; appeal agt, Local Draft Bd; NY State Sen, 60- Bus & Prof Pos: Lawyer. Mil Serv: World War II, Army Commendation Ribbon. Mem: Pelham Pkwy Jewish Ctr (dir); Columbus-Evander

70 / BERNSTEIN

Youth & Adult Ctr; Dist 11, Bronx House & Zionist Orgn Am; Bernard Mogilesky Lodge B'nai B'rith; United Jewish Appeal. Legal Res: 660 Thwaites Place Bronx NY 10467 Mailing Add: 115 Broadway New York NY 10006

BERNSTEIN, GEORGE KASKEL (R)

b New York, NY, Sept 17, 33; s Herman William Bernstein & Annette Kaskel B; m to Edith Friedman; c James A & Susan. Educ: Cornell Univ, BA, 55, Law Sch, LLB, 57; Phi Epsilon Pi; Phi Delta Phi. Polit & Govt Pos: Asst attorney gen, NY State Dept Law, 57-61; dep supt & gen counsel, NY State Ins Dept, 64-67, first dep supt ins, 67-69; Fed Ins Adminr, Dept of Housing & Urban Develop, 69-74, Interstate Land Sales Adminr, 72-74. Bus & Prof Pos: Attorney-at-law. Mem: NY State Dist Attorneys' Asn; Asn of the Bar of the City of New York; Fed & DC Bar Asns. Relig: Jewish. Legal Res: 5407 Spangler Ave Bethesda MD 20016 Mailing Add: 1730 K St NW Washington DC 20006

BERNSTEIN, JAY S (D)
Mem, Dem State Cent Comt Md

b Washington, DC, Mar 22, 42; s Julius A Bernstein & M Ruth Zinkow B; m 1969 to Carolyn M Hayman; c Bradford Scott & Darren Todd. Educ: Univ Md College Park, BA, 64; Am Univ, Washington Col Law, JD, 67; Zeta Beta Tau. Polit & Govt Pos: Pres, Young Dem Clubs Md, 70-71; mem, Dem State Cent Comt Md, 74- Bus & Prof Pos: Attorney-at-law, Washington, DC & State of Md, 68- Mem: Am, Md State, DC & Montgomery Co Bar Asns; Am Judicature Soc. Relig: Jewish. Legal Res: 9104 Shad Lane Potomac MD 20854 Mailing Add: 3520 Connecticut Ave Washington DC 20008

BERNSTEIN, MYRON RONALD (R)
Mem, East Haddam Rep Town Comt, Conn

b Middletown, Conn, May 25, 32; s Charles Bernstein & Frances B; single. Educ: Univ Conn, BS, 55; Boston Univ Law Sch, LLB, 60; Tau Epsilon Phi. Polit & Govt Pos: Mem, East Haddam Rep Town Comt, 60-, chmn, formerly; deleg, Rep State Convs, 60-; mem, Conn Rep Finance Comt, 66-; presidential elector, Rep Nat Conv, 68. Bus & Prof Pos: Dir, Nat Bank of New Eng, East Haddam, 65- Mil Serv: Entered as 2nd Lt, Army, 55, released as 1st Lt, 57, after serv in Intel, Far East. Mem: Am Bar Asn; CofC; Mason; Lions; B'nai B'rith. Relig: Jewish. Mailing Add: Plains Rd Moodus CT 06469

BERRA, PAUL M (D)
Chmn, St Louis City Dem Cent Comt, Mo

b St Louis, Mo, Feb 2, 25; m 1950 to Elizabeth Catherine Gilroy; c Paul Gerald, Richard Lawrence & Ann Marie. Educ: St Louis Univ Sch Commerce & Finance. Polit & Govt Pos: Mo State Rep, 53-64; Mo State Sen, 64-66, City treas, St Louis, 66-; committeeman, 24th Ward Dem Party; deleg, Dem Nat Conv, 68 & 72; chmn, St Louis City Dem Cent Comt, Mo, currently; deleg, Dem Nat Mid-Term Conf, 74. Bus & Prof Pos: Bookkeeper. Mil Serv: Army, 43-46, ETO. Mem: Am Legion; VFW; Past Commanders Club; Red Men; Prof & Bus Men of the Hill. Honors & Awards: St Louis Globe-Dem Award, Third Most Valuable Legislator, 62; St Louis Globe-Dem Award, Second Most Valuable Legislator, 64; Speaker's Award, Most Outstanding Dem, 63. Relig: Catholic; dir sch bd, St Ambrose Church. Mailing Add: 1933 Lilly St Louis MO 63110

BERRONG, ED (D)
Okla State Sen

b Hinton, Okla, Apr 17, 1915; s Jesse H Berrong & Alma Jane Dodd B; m 1938 to Winnie Ola Post; c Ed, Jr, Mark D & Brad. Educ: Southwestern State Col, 33-37, AB, 37; Univ Okla, 37-38; Okla City Col Law, 43-44. Polit & Govt Pos: Mayor, Weatherford, Okla, 49-58; Okla State Sen, Sixth & 27th Dist, 59- Bus & Prof Pos: Owner, Ins Firm, Weatherford, 48-; pres two corp, Weatherford & Elk City, Okla, 59- & 64-; mem bd several corp; pres two indust found, Weatherford, 66- Mil Serv: Entered as A/S, Naval Res, 44, released Lt(jg), 46, after serv in SW Pac, 45-46. Mem: Okla Bar Asn; Okla Ins Agent's Asn; Am Legion; VFW; CofC. Honors & Awards: Outstanding Ins Agent, Okla, twice; Outstanding Serv Awards from various orgns. Relig: Methodist. Legal Res: 507 N Fifth Weatherford OK 73096 Mailing Add: Box 268 Weatherford OK 73096

BERRY, CHARLES EDWARD (D)
Ga State Rep

b Columbus, Ga, July 16, 08; s Turner Edmonds Berry & Annie Belle Lynch B; m 1934 to Martha Louise Bartlett (deceased), m 1968 to Mildred Hogan Holleman; c Charles Edward, Jr, William Turner & Mary Patricia. Educ: Univ of the South, AB, 29; Delta Tau Delta; Red Ribbon Soc, Univ of the South. Polit & Govt Pos: Mayor pro tem, Columbus, Ga, 54, mayor, 55, city comnr, 54-60, exec bd, emer of City of Columbus for life; mem, State Dem Exec Comt, Ga, Ga State Rep, 65-, vchmn, Gen Banking, Banks & Banking & Civil Defense, Defense & Vet Affairs Legis Comt, Ga House Rep, currently; mem ways & means comt, Lt Col Gov Staff of Ga & Ala, currently; vchmn, Ga Comn for Develop of Chattahoochee River Basin, currently. Bus & Prof Pos: Merchandise mgr, Kirven's, 31-42; partner mgr, Columbus Fixture Mfg Co, 43-63, vpres-treas, 63-67, retired; vpres, Trust Co of Columbus, Ga, 69- Mil Serv: Entered as A/S, Navy, 44, released as Seaman 2/C, 44. Mem: Mason; Elks; Moose; Lions; Am Legion (life mem & past dist comdr). Relig: Episcopal; Former Vestryman & Jr Warden, St Thomas Episcopal Church. Mailing Add: 2516 Harding Dr Columbus GA 31906

BERRY, DAN C (D)
NMex State Rep
Mailing Add: Box 67 Eunice NM 88231

BERRY, E Y (R)

b Larchwood, Iowa, Oct 6, 02; m 1928 to Rose Hartinger; c Robert E & Nila Lee. Educ: Morningside Col; Univ SDak Law Sch, LLB, 27. Polit & Govt Pos: States attorney, co judge, Corson Co, SDak; SDak State Sen, 39-43; mem, Mo River States Comt, 40-43; mem, State Bd of Regents of Educ, 46-50; US Rep, SDak, 50-70; retired. Bus & Prof Pos: Lawyer; newspaper ed & publ; ed, SDak Am Journ J, 38-50. Mem: SDak Press Asn; Lambda Chi Alpha; Delta Theta Phi; Sigma Delta Chi; Mason. Mailing Add: Rte 1 Box 254 Rapid City SD 57701

BERRY, EDWARD DEJARNETTE (D)
Chmn, Madison Co Dem Comt, Va

b Charlottesville, Va, Oct 5, 49; s Thornton Lancaster Berry & Annie Ludevine DeJarnette B; single. Educ: Richmond Col(Va), 69-71, Univ Richmond T C Williams Sch Law, JD, 73; Phi Alpha Theta; Pi Sigma Alpha; Sigma Chi. Polit & Govt Pos: Chmn, Madison Co Dem Comt, Va, 74- Bus & Prof Pos: Attorney, Madison, Va, 73- Mem: Va State & Greene Madison Bar Asns; Va Trial Lawyers Asn; Madison Co Farm Bur; Madison Co Feeder Yearling Asn.

Relig: Presbyterian. Legal Res: RR1 Box 112 Madison VA 22727 Mailing Add: Box 391 Madison VA 22727

BERRY, ELMER F, JR (D)
Maine State Sen
Mailing Add: 15 Linwood Ave Auburn ME 04210

BERRY, FRED OGLE, SR (R)
Tenn State Sen

b Knoxville, Tenn, Nov 6, 12; s Ralph Lawson Berry & Myrtle Henderlight B; m 1943 to Ruth Amealia LeCoultre; c Fred O, Jr, Nancy (Mrs Scott), George Edward, Dr David Andrew & seven grandchildren. Educ: Gupton-Jones Mortuary Col, MS, 35; Field Med Sch, Navy, 44. Polit & Govt Pos: Tenn State Rep, 61-62 & 63-64; Tenn State Sen, 65- Bus & Prof Pos: Vpres & dir, Tenn Life & Serv Ins Co, 51-58; pres, Berry Morticians, Inc, 51- Mil Serv: Entered as PhM 3/C, Navy, 43, released as PhM 1/C, 45, after serv in 16th Naval Air Force Aviation Med Corps, 45; Capt, Army Res. Mem: F&AM (Past Master); Scottish Rite & York Rite (32 degree); Shrine; Eastern Star. Honors & Awards: Hon fire chief, Knoxville; hon capt, Tenn Hwy Patrol; Pfizer Award, US Civil Defense Coun, 63; Tenn Funeral Dir of the Year, 68; Conserv Legislator of Decade, 60-70, Tenn. Relig: Methodist. Mailing Add: 3704 Chapman Hwy Knoxville TN 37920

BERRY, GLENYS W (R)
Maine State Rep
Mailing Add: RFD Madison ME 04950

BERRY, JAMES THEODORE (R)

b Greenville, SC, July 7, 19; s William Mason Berry & Catherine McGonigle B; m 1952 to Anita Carolyn Johnson; c Susan D (Mrs McWhorter), C Rhodes (Mrs White), Kathy Lynn & William Grady. Educ: Newberry Col, AB, 42; Kappa Phi. Polit & Govt Pos: Pres, Blackville Precinct Rep Party, SC, 66-; second vchmn, Barnwell Co Rep Party, 66-67, first vchmn, 68-69, chmn, 70-71; committeeman, Exec Comt, SC State Rep Party, formerly. Bus & Prof Pos: Asst supvr prod control, Judson Plant, Deering-Milliken Textiles, Greenville, SC, 48-49; prod supvr, Gerrish-Milliken Plant, Pendleton, 49-51; eng asst, Savannah River Plant, E I du Pont de Nemours, Inc, 51- Mil Serv: Entered as A/S, Navy, 42, released as Lt(sg), 47, after serv in Amphibious Forces, Pac Fleet, 43-46; Am Defense Ribbon; Asiatic-Pac Defense Ribbon with Four Bronze Stars; Philippine Liberation Ribbon with Two Bronze Stars; Victory Ribbon World War II. Mem: Health Physics Soc; Am Legion; Mason. Honors & Awards: Silver Beaver Award, Cent SC Coun Boy Scouts. Relig: Baptist. Legal Res: Williston Rd Blackville SC 29817 Mailing Add: PO Box 417 Blackville SC 29817

BERRY, JOHN M, JR (D)
Ky State Sen
Mailing Add: New Castle KY 40050

BERRY, LEROY (D)
Mem, Calif Dem State Cent Comt

b Birmingham, Ala, Oct 20, 26; s Lester Berry & Lubertha Foster B; m 1949 to Ruth Brothers. Educ: Univ Calif, Los Angeles, BA; Calif State Col, Los Angeles, MA & Admin Credential; Kappa Alpha Psi. Polit & Govt Pos: Pres, Leimert Dem Club, Calif, 58-61; rep, 63rd Assembly Dist Dem Coun, 60-64; southern credentials chmn, Calif Dem Coun, 64-66, region two vpres, 66-68; mem, Dem Co Cent Comt, 63rd Assembly Dist, 67-70; mem, Calif Dem State Cent Comt, 67- Mil Serv: Entered as Pvt, Army, 41, released as Cpl, 45, after serv in Coast Artil Engrs, Air Force, Western Defense Command, 42-44; Marksman Sharpshooter; Good Conduct Medal. Mem: Univ Calif, Los Angeles Alumni Asn (life mem); New Frontier Dem Club; United Teachers of Los Angeles. Relig: Protestant. Mailing Add: 3801 Welland Ave Los Angeles CA 90008

BERRY, LOREN MURPHY (R)
Mem, Rep Nat Finance Comt

b Wabash, Ind, July 24, 88; s Charles D Berry & Elizabeth Murphy B; m 1909 to Lucile Kneipple (deceased); c Loren Murphy, Jr, Martha Sue (Mrs J P Fraim), John William & Elizabeth Anne (Mrs Robert Gray); m 1938 to Helen Anderson Henry (deceased); c Leland Henry. Educ: Northwestern Univ, 09-10. Hon Degrees: LLD, Rio Grande Col. Polit & Govt Pos: Finance Chmn, Montgomery Co Rep Finance Comt, Ohio, 44-50; state finance chmn, Fla Rep Finance Comt, 56-60; mem, Rep Nat Finance Comt, 68- Bus & Prof Pos: Newspaper reporter, Wabash, Ind, Joliet, Ill & Chicago; sold tel dir advert, Marion, Ind, 10, St Louis, Louisville & Indianapolis; vchmn bd, L M Berry & Co, currently; dir, United Telecommun, Inc, Kansas City, Fla Tel Corp, Ocala, Edison Nat Bank, Ft Myers, Fla, Laughter Corp, Dayton, Hulman Realty Co, Dayton, Super Food Serv, Inc, Dayton & Mutual Broadcasting Corp, NY; trustee, Jr Achievement, Dayton & Rio Grande Col; tel dir advert salesman, Bell & Independent Tel Co, 41 states, currently. Mem: US Ind Tel Pioneers; Bell Tel Pioneers Am; Mason (32 degree); Shrine; Capitol Hill Club, Washington, DC. Relig: Episcopal. Legal Res: 1155 Ridgeway Rd Dayton OH 45419 Mailing Add: 3170 Kettering Blvd Dayton OH 45401

BERRY, LOUISE SPAULDING (R)
Mem, Killingly Rep Town Comt, Conn

b Danielson, Conn, Nov 9, 27; d Jacob Lindhurst Spaulding & Frances Upham S; m 1951 to Richard Chisholm Bliss Berry; c Donald Spaulding, Pamela Chisholm, Robin Lee, Christopher Warren & Judith Hastings. Educ: Adelphi Col, Dipl Nursing, 48; Univ Conn, BA, 52, MA, 61; Univ Conn Sch Law, 75-; Univ Conn Concert Band. Polit & Govt Pos: Mem, Killingly Rep Town Comt, Conn, 63-, chmn, 65-70, vchmn, 70-72; mem, Killingly Bd Educ, 66-; mem, Conn State Rep Cent Comt, 72-; Conn State Sen, 73-74. Bus & Prof Pos: Sch nurse, Killingly Schs, Danielson, 52-55; sch nurse, Brooklyn Sch, 58-, dir guid, 61- Publ: The problem of the dropout, 64. Mem: Am Sch Health Asn; Conn Personnel & Guid Asn; Quinebaug Valley Health & Welfare Coun (vpres); Windham Area Community Action Prog; Conn Asn Bd Educ (secy, Region II, 70-72). Honors & Awards: First Prize for The problem of the dropout, from Westab, Inc. Relig: Congregational. Mailing Add: Mashentuck Rd Danielson CT 06239

BERRY, PHILIP P (D)
Maine State Rep
Mailing Add: RFD 1 Saco Buxton ME 04072

BERRY, RICHARD NATHANIEL (R)
Maine State Sen

b Malden, Mass, Nov 4, 15; s Edward Robie Berry & Maude Henneberry B; m 1938 to

Katherine Bunker; c Andrew B, Richard N, Jr & Thomas A. Educ: Univ Maine, BS, 37; Tau Beta Pi; Beta Theta Pi. Polit & Govt Pos: Mem common coun, City of Malden, Mass, 38-39, fire comnr, 47-48; Maine State Rep, 61-66; Maine State Sen, 105th Legis, 66-, Senate Majority Floor Leader, 70-74. Bus & Prof Pos: Consult engr. Mil Serv: Entered as 1st Lt, Army, 42, released as Maj, 46, after serv in Engrs Corps, Col, Army Res, 66. Mem: Maine Water Utilities Asn; New Eng & Am Water Works Asn; Am Soc Civil Engrs. Relig: Congregational. Mailing Add: 11 Tall Pine Rd Elizabeth ME 04107

BERRY, THORNTON GRANVILLE, JR (D)
Judge, WVa Supreme Court of Appeals
b Sutton, WVa, Dec 13, 04; s Thornton Granville Berry & Mamie Newlon Kawalska B; m 1934 to Rita Crockett Brewster. Educ: Va Mil Inst, AB, 28; Washington & Lee Univ, LLB, 34; Phi Delta Phi; Phi Kappa Psi. Polit & Govt Pos: Comnr in Chancery & comnr of Accts, McDowell Co, WVa, 37-40; prosecuting attorney, 40-42; asst US attorney, South Dist, WVa, 39-40; judge Eighth Judicial Circuit, WVa, 52-58; Judge, WVa Supreme Court of Appeals, 58- Mil Serv: Entered as Lt, Navy, 42, released as Lt Comdr, 46, after serv in North Pac, 44-45; Am & Pac Theater Ribbons; Victory Medal; Navy Res Medal; Armed Forces Medal; Lt Comdr (Ret), Naval Res, 64. Publ: South Eastern Reports, West Publ Co. Mem: WVa Judicial Asn; Am Judicature Asn; Am Law Inst; Am Bar Asn; fel Am Bar Found. Relig: Presbyterian. Mailing Add: 1612 Virginia St E Charleston WV 25311

BERRYHILL, CLARE L (R)
Calif State Sen
b Reedley, Calif, Dec 4, 25; s Claude Chalmers Berryhill & Elizabeth Hughes B; m 1950 to Maryellen Rossel; c Betsy, Thomas, Lynne, Janie & Bill. Educ: Modesto Jr Col, Calif, AA, 47; Univ Calif, Santa Barbara, 47. Polit & Govt Pos: Trustee & pres bd trustees, Ceres Elem Sch, Calif, 57-65; vpres Stanislaus Chap, Calif Rep Assembly, 62-63; trustee, Ceres Unified Sch Dist, 65-66; chmn, Farmers for Nixon & Farmers for Kuchel, Stanislaus Co, formerly; Calif State Assemblyman, 30th Dist, 69-70; asst treas, Calif Rep State Cent Comt, 72-73; Calif State Sen, Third Dist, 73- Bus & Prof Pos: Pres, Grape Improv Asn & Growers Harvesting Comt; dir, Calif Raisin Adv Bd & Farm Home Admin Bd. Mil Serv: Vet, World War II. Mem: Amvets; Ceres Lions; Modesto Elks; Old Fisherman's Club; Sons of Italy. Honors & Awards: Outstanding Young Farmer of the Year, 60. Relig: Protestant. Legal Res: 1912 E Taylor Rd Ceres CA 95307 Mailing Add: State Capitol Sacramento CA 95814

BERRYHILL, LYNN MERCER (D)
Chmn, Hamilton Co Dem Comt, Iowa
b Kamrar, Iowa, Oct 18, 07; s Isaac Gale Berryhill & Sarah Espe B; m 1938 to Henrietta Cook. Educ: Univ Northern Iowa, Cedar Falls, 27-30. Polit & Govt Pos: City coun & mayor, Kamrar, Iowa, formerly; chmn, Hamilton Co Dem Comt, 73- Mailing Add: Kamrar IA 50132

BERSON, NORMAN S (D)
Pa State Rep
b New York, NY, Nov 19, 26; s Joseph A Berson & Theresa Levinsky B; m 1955 to Lenora Ersner; c Peter & Erica. Educ: Temple Univ, AB, 50; Univ Pa Law Sch, LLB, 53. Polit & Govt Pos: Pa State Rep, 67-, chmn, House Judiciary Comt, 75-; alt deleg, Dem Nat Conv, 68. Bus & Prof Pos: Partner, Freedman, Berson & O'Donnell, 66. Mil Serv: Entered as Pvt, Army, 44, released as Sgt, 46, after serv in 116th Combat Engrs, Pac, 44-45; Pac Theater Ribbon; Philippine Liberation Medal. Mem: Philadelphia Bar Asn; Philadelphia Housing Asn; Am Jewish Comt; Philadelphia Fel Comn; Citizens Coun Pub Educ. Relig: Jewish. Mailing Add: Capitol Bldg Harrisburg PA 17120

BERTELSEN, VERNER L (R)
Mont State Rep
Mailing Add: Box 65 Ovando MT 59854

BERTINI, CATHERINE (R)
Dir Youth Activities, NY Rep State Comt
b Syracuse, NY, Mar 30, 50; d Fulvio Bertini & Ann Vino B; single. Educ: State Univ NY, Albany, grad, 71; Chi Sigma Theta. Polit & Govt Pos: Pres, Cortland Co TAR, 66-67; legis aide, State Sen Tarky Lombardi, 67-71; pres, State Univ NY Albany Col Rep, 68-69 & 70-71; secy, NY State Col Rep, 68-70; vol dir, Capital Dist Independent for Rockefeller, 70; secy, Asn NY State Young Rep, 70-71; staff, appointments off to Gov, 71; chmn, NY State Young Voters for the President, 71-72; dir youth activities, NY Rep State Comt, 71-; alt deleg, Rep Nat Conv, 72. Mem: Alumni Asn, State Univ, NY, Albany (class counr, 71-). Honors & Awards: Outstanding Sr, Chi Sigma Theta Sorority, 70-71; Outstanding NY State Young Rep, Asn of New York State Young Rep Clubs, Inc, 71. Relig: Roman Catholic. Legal Res: 814 Franklin St Skaneateles NY 13152 Mailing Add: 315 State St Albany NY 12210

BERTINUSON, TERESALEE (D)
Conn State Rep
Mailing Add: 227 Melrose Rd Melrose CT 06049

BERTNESS, KENNETH LEROY (R)
Chmn, Lake Co Rep Comt, SDak
b Lac Qui Parle Co, Minn, Jan 5, 35; s Gustav Adolph Bertness & Irene Sumner B; m 1955 to Joyce Ann Thoreson; c Kevin, Kirk, Brian & Julie. Educ: High sch, grad, 53. Polit & Govt Pos: Chmn, Lake Co Rep Comt, SDak, 74- Bus & Prof Pos: Mgr, Northwestern Bell, Gregory, SDak, 66-67 & Madison, SDak, 67- Mem: Boy Scouts (mem, Sioux Coun Exec Comt, 72-, Owatonna Dist Chmn, 73-); Pan-Am Hwy Asn-Dakota Chap (pres, 72-); Gtr Madison Area CofC (dir, 69-71, comt chmn, currently); Kiwanis; Toastmasters. Honors & Awards: Outstanding Young Man, Chamberlain, Chamberlain Jaycees, 64; Outstanding Young Man, Madison, Madison Jaycees, 69; JCI Senator 13314, SDak Jaycees, 71. Relig: Lutheran. Mailing Add: 618 N Olive Madison SD 57042

BERTONAZZI, LOUIS PETER (D)
Mass State Rep
b Milford, Mass, Oct 9, 33; s Peter John Bertonazzi & Concetta Rossi B; m 1957 to Barbara Szymanski; c Gregg, Lisa & David. Educ: Tufts Univ, BA, 55; Suffolk Univ, MA in Ed, 60; Boston Col, adv grad study; Sigma Nu. Polit & Govt Pos: Mem bd of selectmen, Milford, Mass, 64-69, chmn bd, 65-68; chmn, Blackstone Valley Econ Opportunity Coun, 65-66; first dep dir, Mass Div of Youth Serv, 66-69; Mass State Rep, 69-, chmn subcomt, Joint Comt to Study Admin of Pub Welfare, Mass Legis, 69-71, vchmn, Joint Standing Comt on Social Welfare, 69-, House chmn, Joint Spec Comt to Study Health Serv, 71- & mem, Joint Spec Comt to Redistrict the Legis, 72-; mem adv bd, Comt for the Advan of Criminal Justice, 71-, Mass Ment Health Planning Proj, 72- & Gov Adv Comt Comprehensive Health Planning, 72- Bus & Prof Pos: Teacher govt & lang, Medway High Sch, 58-60, guid coun, 60-62, dir guid, 62-66. Mil Serv: Entered as Pvt, Army, 56, released as Pfc, 58, after serv in Fourth Regt Combat Team, First Army, 56-58; Expert Rifleman Award. Mem: Norfolk Co Teachers Asn; Mass Teachers Asn; Mass Legislators Asn; Nat Coun on Crime & Delinquency; KofC. Honors & Awards: Jimmy Fund Award, 64; Hon Membership Award, Milford Young Dem, 66; Man of the Year Award, Milford Area Heart Fund Asn, 68; Man of the Year, Mass Ital Am War Vet, 73. Relig: Catholic. Mailing Add: 16 Coolidge Rd Milford MA 01757

BERTRAM, RANDALL B (D)
Chmn, Wayne Co Dem Party, Ky
b Albany, Ky, Dec 31, 12; s Elza Bertram & Maggie Ballenger B; m 1942 to Doris Huffaker; c Randall B, Jr & Judith C. Educ: Centre Col Ky, BS, 36; Northwestern Univ Sch Law, 36; Univ Louisville Sch Law, 36-38; Sigma Chi. Polit & Govt Pos: Chmn, Wayne Co Dem Party, Ky, 67- Bus & Prof Pos: Attorney-at-law, Bertram & Bertram, 38- Mil Serv: Entered as Pvt, Air Force, 42, released as Cpl, 45, after serv in Far East Air Force, Pac Theatre, 43-45. Mem: Am & Ky State Bar Asns; Phi Alpha Delta. Relig: Baptist. Legal Res: 115 Evelyn Ave Monticello KY 42633 Mailing Add: PO Box 132 Monticello KY 42633

BERTRAND, JOSEPH GUSTAUS (D)
b Biloxi, Miss, Oct 27, 31; s Francois Albert Bertrand, Sr & Sadie Louise Robinson B; m 1957 to Joan Clara Tyler; c Joseph G, Jr, Joan, Jason, Justin, Jeffrey & Julian. Educ: Univ Notre Dame, Arts & Letters degree, 54, postgrad study, 54-56; Loyola Univ Chicago Sch Law, 59-60. Polit & Govt Pos: Precinct capt, Seventh Ward, Chicago, 56-, committeeman, currently; city treas, Chicago, 71; deleg, Dem Nat Conv, 72; mem exec comt bank adv comt, Small Bus Admin, currently; mem, Gov Ill Adv Coun on Econ Opportunity, currently; mem, Chicago Coun Foreign Rels, currently. Bus & Prof Pos: Cook Co Dept Pub Aid, Ill, 58-59; community organizer, Chicago Comn on Youth Welfare, 59-61; dir sales, Demert & Dougherty, 61-63; mkt dir, Better Brands, Inc, 63-67; vpres commercial loan div, Standard Bank & Trust Co Bank, 67-70; pres, chief exec officer & chmn, Highland Community Bank, 70-72; chmn & chief exec officer, Gateway Nat Bank of Chicago, 72- Mil Serv: Entered as Pvt, Army, 56, released as Sgt, after serv in 159th & 921st Combat Engrs, Group Adj Off, Ft Leonard Wood, Mo, 56-58. Mem: Econ Club of Chicago; Black Bankers of Chicago; Munic Finance Officers Asn of US & Can; Highland Bus Asn; Chicago Boy Scouts Coun (asst treas, exec comt, Chicago Area Coun & Nat Coun). Honors & Awards: State of Israel Prime Minister's Medal, 72; In Ill Basketball Hall of Fame, 73 & Hall of Fame of the Cath League for Basketball, Chicago; Award for Excellence in Pub & Polit Serv, Tuskegee Alumni Asn, 74; Man of the Year Award, Notre Dame Club of Chicago, 74. Relig: Roman Catholic. Legal Res: 7345 S Oglesby Chicago IL 60649 Mailing Add: Rm 206 City Hall 121 N La Salle St Chicago IL 60602

BERTSCH, MARIAN N (R)
VChmn, 32nd Dist NDak Rep Party
b New England, NDak, Nov 13, 11; d Thomas Christian Nelsen & Johanna Christensen N; m 1935 to Harold Schafer; c Haroldeen Anne (Mrs Robert Heskin), Joanne Bee (Mrs James Kack), Dianne Margaret, Edward Thomas & Pamela Rikki; m 1967 to Albert C Bertsch. Educ: Aberdeen Bus Col, 29. Polit & Govt Pos: Mem, Rep Nat Comt, NDak, formerly; mem arrangements comt, Rep Nat Conv, 64, alt deleg, 68 & 72; vchmn, 32nd Dist NDak Rep Party, 68- Bus & Prof Pos: Mem bd dirs, City Ctr Hotel Asn; mem bd dirs, Women Med Col, Pa. Mem: Shrine Auxiliary (Pres); Crippled Children Hosp; Girl Scouts Coun (Pres); Zonta Int; Eastern Star. Honors & Awards: Thanks Badge, Girl Scouts. Relig: Presbyterian. Mailing Add: 1256 N Parkview Dr Bismarck ND 58501

BERUBE, GEORGETTE B (D)
Maine State Rep
Mailing Add: 195 Webster St Lewiston ME 04240

BERUBE, PHILLIP (D)
NDak State Sen
b Belcourt, NDak, Apr 6, 05; s Arthur Berube & Victorine Mongeon B; m 1929 to Alma Casavant; c Leonel, Vivian (Mrs Hurben Cote), Delima (Mrs James Grossal); Lorette (Mrs William Leanard), Harvey, Julian (Mrs Donald Lentz), Adrien & Jackie. Educ: Maryville Pub Sch, 8 years. Polit & Govt Pos: Mem, Co Sch Reorgn Comt, NDak, 47-69; mem, Capitol Bldg Comn; NDak State Sen, 52- Bus & Prof Pos: Farmer; Gen Store & Post Off, 27-30. Mem: Commercial Club; co pres, Farmers Union, 42-68. Relig: Catholic. Mailing Add: State Capitol Bismarck ND 43215

BESHEAR, STEVEN L (D)
Ky State Rep
Mailing Add: 317 Mariemont Drive Lexington KY 40505

BESSEY, CAROL (D)
b Glenn, Mich, Dec 24, 13; m to Boyd G Bessey; c Boyd T & Carol Joy (Mrs Grudecki). Educ: South Haven High Sch. Polit & Govt Pos: Vchmn, Van Buren Dem Comt, 64-67, chmn, formerly; chmn, Van Buren Co Dem Conv. Bus & Prof Pos: Shipping clerk, Arthur Arens. Mem: Bus & Prof Womens Club; Am Legion; Coterie; DAV. Relig: Methodist. Mailing Add: RR 4 Paw Paw MI 49079

BEST, MILLICENT RUDD (R)
Mem, Weston Rep Town Comt, Conn
b Brooklyn, NY, Oct 21, 25; d Augustin Goelet Rudd & Helen Keathen R; m 1950 to Edward Jackson Best; c Stephen Rudd, Susan Donna & William Brewster. Educ: Garden City High Sch, 43; Washington Sch for Secy, 45. Polit & Govt Pos: Mem, Western Rep Town Comt, Conn, 58-, secy, 58-66, vchmn, 66-68, chmn, 68-70; justice of the peace, Weston, 70- Bus & Prof Pos: Stenographer, Flintkote Co, New York, 44-47; secy to publicity dir, Columbia Rec, 47-48; secy to sales mgr, Int Bus Machines, New York & Garden City, 48-50. Mem: Soc Mayflower Decendants; Cedar Point Yacht Club; Norfield Grange. Honors & Awards: State winner, Nat McCall's Sewing Contest. Relig: Protestant. Mailing Add: 190 Goodhill Rd Weston CT 06880

BETENSON, GLEN (R)
Mem, Utah Rep State Cent Comt
b Circleville, Utah, Nov 18, 99; s Joseph Arthur Betenson & Elizbeth M James B; m 1924 to Nellie Synethlia Whittaker; c Druce, Beven Whittaker, Eugene H Bult & Lajauna (Mrs Riddle). Educ: Col Southern Utah, BS, 24; Blackstone Col Law. Polit & Govt Pos: Rep Party worker, 49 years; co attorney, Piute Co, Utah, 43-; mayor, Circleville, currently; chmn, Piute Co Rep Party, formerly; chmn, Dist Rep Party, formerly; mem, Utah Rep State Cent Comt,

currently. Bus & Prof Pos: Play producer, Gay Nineties Revue, East Lynne, Ten Nights in a Bar Room, Hazel Kirt, On the Bridge at Midnight, The Cabin in the Hills, plus others. Relig: Latter-day Saint. Mailing Add: 390 N First East Circleville UT 84723

BETROS, EMEEL S (R)
NY State Assemblyman
Mailing Add: 67 Grand Ave Poughkeepsie NY 12603

BETTS, JACKSON EDWARD (R)
b Findlay, Ohio, May 26, 04; s John Edward Betts & Elizabeth Fisher B; m 1934 to Martha Neeley; c Nancy Lou (Mrs David C Bowman). Educ: Kenyon Col, AB cum laude, 26; Yale Sch Law, LLB, 29; Delta Tau Delta; Phi Delta Phi. Hon Degrees: MA, Kenyon Col, 53; LLD, Ohio Northern Univ, 59, Heidelberg Col, 62, Findlay Col, 65. Polit & Govt Pos: Prosecuting Attorney, Hancock Co, Ohio, 33-37; Ohio State Rep, 37-47; Speaker of the House of Rep, Ohio, 45 & 46; US Rep, Ohio, 51-73. Mem: Mason (33 degree); Rotary; Elks; KofP; Odd Fellows. Relig: Episcopal. Legal Res: 3309 Briarcliff Dr Findlay OH 45840 Mailing Add: 101 1/2 W Sandusky St Findlay OH 45840

BETTS, JAMES E (R)
Ohio State Rep
b Ashtabula, Ohio, Jan 14, 33; s Ralph W Betts & Philena Nelson B; m 1960 to Jean Eilers; c Julianne & Jacqueline. Educ: Ohio Univ, BS, 54; Cleveland State Univ, Marshall Sch Law, currently; Omicron Delta Kappa; Phi Eta Sigma; Beta Theta Pi. Polit & Govt Pos: Ohio State Rep, 75- Bus & Prof Pos: Staff mgr, Jonathan Alder Agency, New England Life, 54- Mil Serv: Entered as 2nd Lt, Army, 55, released as 1st Lt, 57, after serv in Counterintel Corps. Mem: Nat Asn Life Underwriters; YMCA (bd mgr); Fairview Gen Hosp (assoc bd trustees); Nat Asn Ment Health. Mailing Add: 1331 Orchard Park Dr Rocky River OH 44116

BETZ, FRANK HERBERT, III (R)
Dist Comt Leader, Union Co Rep Comt, NJ
b Plainfield, NJ, May 21, 33; s Frank H Betz, Jr & Elsie Teunon B; m 1955 to Carolyn M Schoder; c Brian Cameron, Brooks Hamilton & Catherine Cameron. Educ: Gettysburg Col, AB, 55; NY Univ Grad Sch Bus Admin, MBA, 63; Phi Sigma Kappa. Polit & Govt Pos: Various local appointive positions; dist comt leader, Union Co Rep Comt, NJ, 61-; state platform chmn, NJ Young Rep, 62-63; alt deleg, Rep Nat Conv, 64; co chmn, Union Co Young Rep, 64-65; chmn, Union Co Nixon Now Comt, 68. Bus & Prof Pos: Asst vpres, Chem Bank, New York; pres, Hydron Marine Labs Inc, New York, 71-72, Force Four Marine Corp, Cranford, NJ, 72- & Aloa Marine Am Inc, 73- Mem: New York Yacht Club; Fanwood-Scotch Plains YMCA; Fanwood-Scotch Plains Jaycees. Relig: Protestant. Mailing Add: 605 E Broad St Westfield NJ 07090

BETZ, FRED MCLEAN (D)
b Liberal, Mo, June 2, 96; s John Betz & Margaret McLean B; m 1917 to Lennie Maud Coffman; c Fred M, Jr. Polit & Govt Pos: Deleg, Dem Nat Conv, 32, 52, 64 & 68; mem & chmn bd dirs, Wichita Farm Credit Admin, 35-38; state supvr, Farm Security Admin, 36-50; chmn, State Bd for Voc Educ, 47-67; chmn, Colo Dem Party, 55-58 & 62-64. Bus & Prof Pos: Pres, Betz Publ Co, 20-; regent, Univ Colo, 65- Mil Serv: Entered as Pvt, Colo Nat Guard, 22, released as Pfc, 25. Mem: Elks; Eagles; Odd Fellows; Rotary. Honors & Awards: Mr Colo Dem, 70; Outstanding Publ 1969, Colo Press Asn; Medal, Univ Colo. Relig: Methodist. Mailing Add: 8 Cedar Hills Lamar CO 81052

BETZ, VERNON ELWOOD (R)
Mo State Rep
b Grundy Co, Mo, Jan 21, 18; s Elmer C Betz & Thora Thorstensen B; m 1940 to Gertrude L Koon. Educ: Abesville High Sch (Stone Co), grad 38, scholarship honors. Polit & Govt Pos: Trustee, Lincoln Twp, Grundy Co, Mo, 57-58; judge, Grundy Co Court, Second Dist, 59-60; Mo State Rep, 61-, Rep caucus chmn, Mo State House Rep, 67-70. Bus & Prof Pos: Farmer. Mem: Trenton Shrine Club; Odd Fellows; AF&AM; Eastern Star; RAM. Relig: Christian Church; Elder. Mailing Add: Rte 1 Trenton MO 64683

BEVERLY, ROBERT GRAHAM (R)
Calif State Assemblyman
b Belmont, Mass, July 1, 25; s William James Beverly & Helen Graham B; m 1946 to Elizabeth Louise Weisel; c William J, Barbara L, Robert G, Jr & Brian C. Educ: Univ Pittsburgh, 43; Univ Calif, Los Angeles, 46-48; Loyola Univ Los Angeles, LLB, 51. Polit & Govt Pos: Mayor & city councilman, Manhattan Beach, Calif, 58-67; Calif State Assemblyman, 46th Dist, 67-, Minority Floor Leader, Calif State Assembly, currently; mem, Rep State Cent Comt, Calif, currently; deleg, Rep Nat Conv, 72. Bus & Prof Pos: Attorney-at-law, 52- Mil Serv: Entered as Pvt, Marines, 43, released as Cpl, 46, after serv in Am Theatre. Mem: Calif State Bar; Am Legion; YMCA. Relig: Protestant. Mailing Add: 1611 S Pacific Coast Hwy Redondo Beach CA 90277

BEVILACQUA, FRANCIS J (D)
Mass State Rep
b Haverhill, Mass, Aug 12, 23; s James Michael Bevilacqua & Maria Simonella B; m 1951 to Agnes Catherine Conte; c Frederick James, James Michael, Linda Ann, Francis Joseph, Jr & Michael Anthony. Polit & Govt Pos: Dem State Committeeman; has worked for a new Cent Dist Courthouse & Northern Essex Community Col; Mass State Rep, 59-, chmn Comt of Counties, Mass House Rep, 65-68, Asst Majority Leader, 71-72, mem, Ways & Means Comt, 73-; vchmn, Mass Dem State Comt, 64-68; mem, Spec Comn on Interstate Coop. Bus & Prof Pos: Pres-treas, Country & Town Real Estate, 67- Mem: Holy Name Soc; St Rita's Holy Name Soc; Mass Legis Asn (bd dirs, 70-); KofC; Elks. Mailing Add: 15 Day St Haverhill MA 01830

BEVILACQUA, JOHN J (D)
RI State Sen
b Providence, RI; s Joseph A Bevilacqua & Josephine Amato B; single. Educ: Providence Col, AB, 70; Suffolk Univ, JD, 73; Phi Alpha Delta; Dillon Club; St Thomas Aquinas Club; Polit Union (co-chmn Dem caucus). Polit & Govt Pos: RI State Sen, Seventh Dist, 75-; mem, Neighborhood Adv Coun Comn, 75- Bus & Prof Pos: Attorney-at-law, Providence, RI, 74- Mem: Sons of Italy; KofC; Holy Name Soc St Bartholomew's Church; Am & RI Bar Asns. Relig: Catholic. Legal Res: 125 Pocasset Ave Providence RI 02909 Mailing Add: 86 Weybosset St Providence RI 02903

BEVILACQUA, JOSEPH A (D)
Speaker, RI House Rep
b Providence, RI, Dec 1, 18; s John Bevilacqua & Angelica Inonnoti B; m 1946 to Josephine Amato; c John Joseph, Angelica H, Joseph A & Mary Ann. Educ: Providence Col, BA, 40; Georgetown Law Sch, LLB, 48. Polit & Govt Pos: Mem, Dem State Comt, RI, 50-54; asst adminr of charitable trusts, Dept of Attorney Gen, 50-54; RI State Rep, currently, Dep Majority Leader, RI State House of Rep, 66-68, Speaker, 69-; deleg, Dem Nat Conv, 68. Bus & Prof Pos: Attorney-at-law. Mil Serv: Entered as Cpl, Army-Inf, 41, released as 1st Lt, 46; Purple Heart. Relig: Catholic. Legal Res: 125 Pocasset Ave Providence RI 02909 Mailing Add: 86 Weybosset St Providence RI 02903

BEVILL, TOM (D)
US Rep, Ala
b Townley, Ala, Mar 27, 21; s Herman Bevill & Fannie Fike B; m 1943 to Lou Betts; c Susan B, Donald H & Patricia Lou. Educ: Univ Ala, BS in Bus Admin, 43, LLB, 48. Polit & Govt Pos: Ala State Rep, 58-66; US Rep, Fourth Cong Dist, Ala, 67-; ex officio mem, Dem Nat Mid-Term Conf, 74. Bus & Prof Pos: Attorney-at-law, 48- Mil Serv: Entered as Pvt, Army, 43, released as Capt, 46; Army Res, 46-66, Lt Col; Rhineland Campaign Ribbon with Battle Star; Army Commendation Ribbon; ETO Ribbon with Bronze Star. Mem: Lions; Walker Col (bd trustees); Mason; Shrine. Relig: Baptist. Mailing Add: 1600 Alabama Ave Jasper AL 35501

BEWARD, MARIA A (D)
Regional Dir, Pa Fedn Dem Women
b San Juan, PR, Dec 15, 36; d Oscar Luciano Galo & Maria A Hernandez G; m 1956 to Edward B Beward; c Edward B, Jr, Louise A, Margaret M & Teresa A. Educ: Univ PR, Rio Piedras, AB, 56; Shippensburg State Col, 67; Pa State Univ, State College, 69; Eta Gamma Delta. Polit & Govt Pos: Regional dir dist nine, Pa Fedn Dem Women, 73-; deleg, Dem Nat Mid-Term Conf, 74; mem steering comt, Nat Latino Caucus Dem Party, 74- Bus & Prof Pos: Teacher, Juniata High Sch, Mifflintown, Pa, currently; vpres, Beward Pharm, Inc, currently. Mem: Pa Church Women United (exec bd, state legis chairwoman, 73-); Pa Coun of Churches (exec comt social serv); Women's Civic Club (vpres, 74-); Legis Exchange (exec bd, 74-). Relig: Roman Catholic. Mailing Add: RD 2 Mifflintown PA 17059

BEWLEY, JOE L (R)
Tenn State Rep
Mailing Add: Monte Vista Greeneville TN 37743

BEYMER, JAMES ELTON (R)
Chmn, Kearny Co Rep Party, Kans
b Santa Fe, Kans, Mar 24, 14; s Clyde E Beymer & Ethel Jones B; m 1936 to Evelyn Dean Thorne; c Deanne (Mrs Frank Husted) & Judith (Mrs Richard Rohlf). Educ: Univ Kans, 2 years; Delta Upsilon. Polit & Govt Pos: Mem city coun, Lakin, Kans, 47 & 48, mem sch bd, 64-66; chmn, Kearny Co Rep Party, 68- Mil Serv: Entered as Seaman 2/C, Navy, 44, released as Yeoman 1/C, 46. Mem: Mason; Elks. Relig: Methodist. Legal Res: 503 N Main Lakin KS 67860 Mailing Add: Box 191 Lakin KS 67860

BEZNOSKA, GORDON ADOLPH (D)
Okla State Sen
b Lawton, Okla, Apr 3, 49; s Adolph Beznoska & Golda Northcutt B; single. Educ: Cameron Col, BS, 72; ROTC Officers Club. Polit & Govt Pos: Okla State Rep, 70-72; Okla State Sen, 72- Bus & Prof Pos: Hosp attend, Southwestern Hosp, Lawton, Okla, 66-70; ins agency. Mem: Lawton Jr CofC; bd dirs, Geronimo Boy Scouts. Honors & Awards: Dean's Honor Roll; President's List. Relig: Baptist. Mailing Add: Rte 1 Geronimo OK 73543

BIAGGI, MARIO (D)
US Rep, NY
b New York, NY, Oct 26, 17; s Salvatore Biaggi (deceased) & Mary Campari B (deceased); m 1941 to Marie Wassil; c Jacqueline, Barbara, Richard & Mario, Jr. Educ: NY Law Sch, LLB, 63. Polit & Govt Pos: Detective Lt, New York Police Dept, 42-65; community rels specialist, NY State Div Housing, 61-63; asst to Secy of State, NY, 63-65; US Rep, NY, 69-, mem, comt on merchant marine & fisheries & comt on educ & labor, US House Rep, currently; chmn Coast Guard & navigation subcomt, currently; mem select comt aging, currently; deleg, Dem Nat Conv, 72. Bus & Prof Pos: Sr partner, Biaggi, Ehrlich, Galiber & Lang, New York, 66-; consult, Meadowbrook Nat Bank, 67; former consult, Cent State Bank. Mem: Bronx Co Bar Asn; Trial Lawyers Asn; Nat Police Officers Asn of Am; KofC; Navy League of the US. Honors & Awards: Recipient, Medal of Honor, New York Police Dept, 60; Medal of Honor, nat comt, Can-Ital Centennial, 61; Star of Solidarity, Govt of Italy, 61. Relig: Catholic. Legal Res: 100 E Mosholu Pkwy Bronx NY 10458 Mailing Add: 211 Cannon House Off Bldg Washington DC 20015

BIANCARDI, JOSEPH G (D)
Mem, Essex Co Dem Exec Comt, NJ
b Newark, NJ, July 7, 06; m to Helen Noble; c Arlene (Mrs Panullo); three grandchildren. Educ: Rutgers Univ, labor exten courses; St Peter's Col. Polit & Govt Pos: Mem adv bd, Robert Bruce House, NJ Reformatory, Bordentown, NJ; mem, Essex Co Welfare Bd, 64-65; chmn, Belleville Comn on Civil Rights, formerly; NJ State Assemblyman, formerly; mem, Essex Co Dem Exec Comt, currently. Bus & Prof Pos: Pres, Teamsters Indust & Allied Workers Local Union 97; mem exec bd joint coun, 73, Int Brotherhood Teamsters; vpres, United Cerebral Palsy Rehabilitation Inst of NJ; trustee, Cerebral Palsy Rehabilitation Inst; adminr, Amalgamated Welfare Funds. Mem: Belleville INICO. Honors & Awards: Awarded plaques in recognition of outstanding work & support in aiding civic welfare & charitable endeavors. Mailing Add: 16 King Pl Belleville NJ 07109

BIANCHI, ICILIO W, JR (D)
NY State Assemblyman
Mailing Add: 36 Bellport Lane Bellport NY 11713

BIBB, CHRIS ELLEN (R)
Assoc Mem, Rep State Cent Comt of Calif
b Lennox, Calif, June 22, 48; d Clurman William Bibb & Elvera Allegra Berryman B; single. Educ: Univ Calif, San Diego, BA with high honors, 70; Trinity Col (Dublin), 68-69; US Int Univ, Calif Western Campus, Sch Law, JD, 73. Polit & Govt Pos: Youth comt vchmn, San Diego Co Rep Cent Comt, Calif, 71-72, chmn, 73, speakers bur chmn, 70, assoc mem, 73-; chmn, Univ Calif, San Diego Young Rep, 69-70; chmn, San Diego Co Young Rep, 70-71; Calif deleg, Survival '71, Nat Hwy Traffic Safety, 71; alt deleg, Rep Nat Conv, 72; vpres, La

Jolla Rep Women's Club, Federated, 72-73; assoc mem, Rep State Cent Comt Calif, 73- Mem: Phi Alpha Delta, Beaumont Chap, Am Bar Asn-Law Student Div. Honors & Awards: Semifinalist, White House Fels, 72. Relig: Methodist. Mailing Add: 1278 Essex St San Diego CA 92103

BIBBY, JOHN E (R)
SDak State Sen
b Brookings, SDak, Nov 21, 20; s I J Bibby & Ruth Erwin B; m 1947 to Jean Starksen; c Steven J, Mary Jo & Nathan C. Educ: SDak State Univ, BS, 42. Polit & Govt Pos: SDak State Rep, 63-74; SDak State Sen, 75- Bus & Prof Pos: Dir, Bibby Kallemegn Dairy, 60- & First Nat Bank; pres, Bibby Co. Mil Serv: Entered as 2nd Lt, Marine Corps, 42, released as Capt, 46, after serv in Pac, 44-46; Bronze Star. Mem: Rotary; Mason; Shrine; Am Legion; Brookings CofC. Relig: Methodist. Legal Res: 822 Eighth Ave Brookings SD 57006 Mailing Add: PO Box 630 Brookings SD 57006

BIBBY, JOHN FRANKLIN (R)
b La Crosse, Wis, Aug 26, 34; s Joseph W Bibby & Mildred M Franklin B; m 1958 to Lucile H Hanson; c John Franklin, Jr & Peter Mark. Educ: Wis State Col, La Crosse, BS, 56; Univ Ill, MA, 57; Univ Wis, Madison, PhD, 63. Polit & Govt Pos: Dir arts & sci div, Rep Nat Comt, 65-66, admin aide to nat chmn, 66; res assoc, House Republican Conf, US House of Rep, 67 & 68, res dir, 69-70; staff specialist, Comt on Resolutions, Rep Nat Conv, 68 & 72; chmn, North Shore Rep Club, Milwaukee, Wis, 71-73. Bus & Prof Pos: Fel in govt, Brookings Inst, Washington, DC, 61-62; asst prof polit sci, Univ Wis-Milwaukee, 62-63 & 66-68, assoc prof, 68-72, prof, 72-; asst prof polit sci, Northern Ill Univ, 63-65. Mil Serv: Entered as Pvt E-1, Army, 57, released as Pvt E-2, 58, after serv in Field Artil, Six Mo Res Prog. Publ: Co-auth, On Capitol Hill: studies in the legislative process, Holt, Rinehart & Winston, 67 & Dryden Press, 72; The politics of national convention finances & arrangements, Citizens' Res Found, 68; Congress' neglected function, In: The Republican Papers, Doubleday, 68; plus others. Mem: Am & Midwest Polit Sci Asns. Relig: United Church of Christ. Mailing Add: 5507 N Kent Ave Whitefish Bay WI 53217

BIBLE, ALAN (D)
b Lovelock, Nev, Nov 20, 09; s Jacob H Bible & Isabel Welsh B; m 1939 to Loucile Jacks; c Paul Alfred, William Alan, David Milton & Mrs Robert Watkins. Educ: Univ Nev, BA, 30; Georgetown Univ Sch Law, LLB, 34; Phi Alpha Delta; Lambda Chi Alpha. Hon Degrees: LLD, Rider Col, Univ Nev, Georgetown Univ. Polit & Govt Pos: Dist attorney, Storey Co, Nev, 35-38; Dep Attorney Gen, Nev, 38-42; Attorney Gen, 42-54; US Sen, Nev, 54-74; deleg, Dem Nat Conv, 72; ex officio, Dem Nat Mid-Term Conf, 74. Mem: Nat Asn Attorneys Gen; Univ Nev Alumni Asn; Nev State Bar Asn; Eagles; Mason. Honors & Awards: Order of Merit, Lambda Chi Alpha. Relig: Methodist. Mailing Add: Zephyr Cove NV 89448

BICKERTON, FRANCES CATHERINE BAUR (D)
b Philadelphia, Pa, Feb 21, 49; d Robert Matthew Baur & Louise Owen B; m 1974 to Michael W Bickerton. Educ: Vassar Col, AB, 71; Pittsburgh Theol Sem, MDiv magna cum laude, 74. Polit & Govt Pos: Alt deleg, Dem Nat Conv, 72. Bus & Prof Pos: Asst, St Mark's Episcopal Church, 73-75, research consult, Christian Social Rels Dept, 74-75. Mem: Episcopal Women's Caucus. Honors & Awards: Purdy Award, Pittsburgh Theol Sem, 73. Relig: Episcopal. Legal Res: 2021 Country Club Dr McKeesport PA 15135 Mailing Add: 7721 Stanton Ave Swissvale PA 15218

BIDDLE, JACK, III (D)
Ala State Rep
Mailing Add: 2256 Pinehurst Dr Gardendale AL 35071

BIDEN, JOSEPH ROBINETTE (D)
US Sen, Del
b Scranton, Pa, Nov 20, 42; s Joseph R Biden, Sr & Jean Finnegan B; m 1966 to Neilia Hunter, wid; c Joseph R, III, R Hunter & Naomi Christina (deceased). Educ: Univ Del, BA, 65; Syracuse Univ Col Law, JD, 68. Hon Degrees: LHD, Am Int Col, Mass, 73. Polit & Govt Pos: Councilman, New Castle Co, Del, 70-72; US Sen, Del, 72-; ex officio, Dem Nat Mid-Term Conf, 74; mem, Dem Nat Comt, 75- Bus & Prof Pos: Sr partner, Biden & Walsh Law Firm, 70- Mem: Leukemia Soc of Del; Big Bros of Del; Century Club; YMCA. Relig: Catholic. Legal Res: 2309 Woods Rd Wilmington DE 19808 Mailing Add: Rm 6317 New Senate Off Bldg Washington DC 20510

BIDWELL, EVERETT V (R)
Wis State Sen
b Houston, Minn, Oct 22, 99. Educ: Univ Minn. Polit & Govt Pos: Mem, Co Bd, 10 years; Wis State Assemblyman, 52-66; mem, Gov Thomson's Adv Comts on Indust Develop, on Probs of Land Acquisition & on Oper of Eminent Domain Law; Wis State Sen, 71- Bus & Prof Pos: Former salesman; ice cream mfr; bank vpres; farmer. Mem: Wis Ice Cream Mfrs Asn; Portage CofC. Mailing Add: 612 W Edgewater St Portage WI 53901

BIE, NORMAN (D)
Mem, Dem Nat Comt, Fla
b Tampa, Fla, Dec 22, 26; s Norman Bie, Sr & Rita Monrose B; m 1951 to Katharine Berriman; c Norman III, Edward Berriman & Nancy Lee. Educ: George Washington Univ, 46-47; Asheville Biltmore Jr Col, NC, AA, 48; Univ Fla, JD, 51; Phi Delta Phi; Kappa Alpha. Polit & Govt Pos: Mem, Young Dem, 57-60; pres, Clearwater Young Dem, Fla, 59-60; deleg & chmn fifth cong dist deleg, Dem Nat Conv, 72; mem, Dem Nat Comt, 72- Bus & Prof Pos: Civil Serv attorney-adv, US Air Force, Europe, 54-57; attorney, pvt practice, Clearwater, Fla, 58- Mil Serv: Aviation Radioman 3/C, Navy, 45-46; Capt, Judge Adv Gen Dept, Air Force, 51-54. Publ: Ed & publ, The Constitutional Democrat, 74. Mem: Fla, Am & Clearwater Bar Asns; KofC; ROA. Relig: Catholic. Legal Res: 804 S Evergreen Ave Clearwater FL 33516 Mailing Add: 301 Pierce St Suite 403 Clearwater FL 33516

BIEBEL, FREDERICK K, JR (R)
Chmn, Conn Rep State Cent Comt
Mailing Add: 236 Lordship Rd Stratford CT 06497

BIEGELMEIER, FRANK (D)
b Yankton, SDak, Sept 9, 01; m 1929 to Maude Frances McKenna; c Jean Ann, Mary Lee & Fran D. Educ: Univ SDak Sch Law, LLB, magna cum laude, 26; Tau Kappa Alpha; Phi Delta Phi. Polit & Govt Pos: States attorney, Yankton Co, SDak, 31-34; city attorney, Yankton, 53-59; mem, SDak Tax Study Comn, 59; Chief Justice, SDak Supreme Court, formerly; retired. Mem: Elks; KofC. Relig: Catholic. Legal Res: Yankton SD 57078 Mailing Add: Capitol Bldg Pierre SD 57501

BIEGERT, MAURINE (D)
b Shickley, Nebr, June 6, 29; d Willard Hiner & Marie Kolar Steyer H; m to John Richard Biegert; c Jeffrey Lynn, Deborah Ann & Beth Marie. Educ: Univ Nebr, 46-47 & 48-49. Polit & Govt Pos: Pres, Fillmore Co Teachers Asn, Nebr, 46-47 & 48-49. Polit & Govt Pos: Pres, Fillmore Co Teachers Asn, Nebr, 47-48; pres, Fillmore Co Exten Bd, 52-54; organizer, Fillmore Co Dem Women's Group, 58; co-chmn, Citizens for Kennedy, Fillmore Co, Nebr, 60; Dem Nat Committeewoman, Nebr, 60-73; deleg, Dem Nat Conv, 64, 68 & 72. Bus & Prof Pos: Rural sch teacher, 47-48; 4-H camp counr, 48; frozen foods demonstrator, Int Harvester Co, 49-50. Mem: Nebr Homemakers Asn; Nebr Crippled Children's Asn (bd dirs); Federated Women's Club; Easter Seal Soc Crippled Children & Adults Nebr. Honors & Awards: Named 4-H Pub Speaking Winner, Nebr & Nat 4-H Girls Rec Winner, 45; Nat 4-H Achievement Winner, 46. Mailing Add: Shickley NE 68436

BIELAWSKI, ANTHONY F (D)
Chmn, Bay Co Dem Party, Mich
b Grand Rapids, Mich, Sept 6, 13; m to Sophie; s Jerome, Lawrence & Mary. Educ: Univ Mich & Univ Mich Law Sch. Polit & Govt Pos: Chmn, Bay Co Dem Party, Mich, 54-72 & 75-; deleg, Dem Nat Conv, 68. Bus & Prof Pos: Attorney-at-law. Mailing Add: 205 Shearer Bldg Bay City MI 48706

BIEMILLER, ANDREW J (D)
Dir, Dept of Legis, AFL-CIO
b Sandusky, Ohio, July 23, 06; s Andrew F Biemiller & Pearl Weber B; m 1929 to Hannah Perot Morris; c Andrew J, Jr & Nancy Barbara (Mrs Chris Boerup). Educ: Cornell Univ, AB, 26; Delta Kappa Epsilon. Polit & Govt Pos: Mem exec comt, Farmer-Labor Progressive Fedn, 35-41; secy, Progressive Party, State Conv, 37, 39 & 41; Wis State Assemblyman, 37-42, majority leader, Wis State Assembly, 37-38, minority leader, 39-42; spec asst to labor vchmn, War Prod Bd, 41-44; US Rep, Wis, 45-46 & 49-50; deleg, Dem Nat Conv, 48; labor consult to Secy Interior, 51-52; legis rep, AFL-CIO, 53-55, dir, Dept of Legis, 56-; mem, Atomic Energy Comn Labor-Mgt Adv Comt, 63- Bus & Prof Pos: Instr hist, Syracuse Univ, 26-28 & Univ Pa, 30-31; instr econ, Bryn Mawr Summer Sch for Workers, 30-31; educ dir, Socialist Party, Milwaukee, 33-36; ed, Wis Leader, 34-36; gen organizer, Wis Fedn Labor, 37-41; polit educ dir, Upholsterers Int Union, 47-48. Mem: Nat Press Club; Kenwood Country Club; Cornell Club. Relig: Quaker. Mailing Add: 6805 Glenbrook Rd Bethesda MD 20014

BIENEN, KAY G (D)
Md State Deleg
b New York, NY, Jan 1, 38; d Paul G Gumbinner & Ruth Gumpert G; m 1960 to Sanford M Bienen; c Laura Jeanne & Janet Susan. Educ: Skidmore Col, BA; Univ Md, College Park. Polit & Govt Pos: Dem chief judge, 68-74; coordr for Dem Nominee, Tenth Dist, 70; vpres, Laurel Dem Club, 71; alt deleg-at-lg, Dem Nat Conv, 72; precinct coordr for Dem Presidential Nominee, Fifth Dist, 72; Md State Deleg, 75- Mem: Ment Health Asn of Prince George's Co (bd dirs, 62-); League of Women Voters of Prince George's Co; Oakland Citizens Asn (exec comt, health chmn, 71-73); Gtr Laurel Hosp Authority (Citizens Adv Comt); Prince George's Co Child Abuse Task Force. Mailing Add: 12411 Radnor Lane Laurel MD 20811

BIENSTOCK, WILLIAM H (D)
b New York, NY, Apr 6, 20; s Harry Bienstock & Ray Homnick B; m 1943 to Pauline Weber; c Mark Leslie & Gail Claire (Mrs David Weinstein). Educ: City Col New York, BSS, 40, MS in Ed, 42; pres, Dean 1940 House Plan; Coun Deleg; staff, Microcosm. Polit & Govt Pos: Committeeman, Bronx Co Dem Party, NY, 68; exec bd, Bronx-Pelham Reform Dem Club, 69 & 70; judicial deleg, First Judicial Dist Conv, 69 & 70; deleg, Dem Nat Conv, 72; exec bd, John F Kennedy Independent Dem Club, 72-74. Bus & Prof Pos: Ins broker, 46-; pub adjuster, 46- Publ: Musical compositions. Mem: Concourse Ctr Israel; First Shpoler Benevolent Soc. Relig: Jewish. Mailing Add: 2175 Ryer Ave Bronx NY 10457

BIESTER, EDWARD G, JR (R)
US Rep, Pa
b Trevose, Pa, Jan 5, 31; m to Elizabeth Lauffer; c Ann Meredith, Edward G, III, James Paul & David Robertson. Educ: Wesleyan Univ, BA, 52; Temple Univ, LLB, 55. Polit & Govt Pos: Mem, Various Finance Comts, Rep Party, Pa; mem, Primary & Gen Election Campaign Comt; asst dist attorney, Bucks Co, 6 years; US Rep, Pa, 67-, mem, Judiciary Comt, US House of Rep, 67-72, mem int rels comt, 73- Bus & Prof Pos: Lawyer, Duane, Morris & Hechscher, Philadelphia, I J & D W VanArtsdalen, Doylestown & Biester & Ludwig, Doylestown, formerly. Mem: Kiwanis; Big Bros of Bucks Co (bd dirs); Am & Pa Bar Asns; Bucks Co Asn for the Blind (hon bd dirs). Relig: Reformed Church. Legal Res: Lower Mountain Rd Furlong PA 18925 Mailing Add: 2351 Rayburn Off Bldg Washington DC 20515

BIEVER, VIOLET S (D)
SDak State Rep
b Oelrichs, SDak, Nov 4, 11; d James E Williams & Martha L Dryden W; m 1934 to Joseph N Biever, wid; c Keith, K Duane & Karolyn J (Mrs Howard Fairbanks). Educ: Chadron State Col, BS, 63. Polit & Govt Pos: SDak State Rep, Dist 25, 75- Bus & Prof Pos: Teacher, Oelrichs, SDak, 31-34, Fall River Co, 54-56 & Hot Springs, SDak, 58-67. Mem: Exten Homemakers Club (secy-historian); Am Asn Univ Women; Farmers Union. Honors & Awards: Honored Homemaker, Little Int of Brookings, 64; Eminent Homemaker, SDak State Univ, 74. Relig: Methodist. Mailing Add: RR Oelrichs SD 57763

BIGBEE, JOHN FRANKLIN, JR (R)
NMex State Rep
b Mountainair, NMex, June 18, 34; s John Franklin Bigbee & Mildred Penry B; m 1955 to Povy La Farge; c Amy, Diane & Franklin Mathews. Educ: Colo State Univ, BS with distinction, 55; Alpha Zeta; Omicron Delta Kappa; Alpha Gamma Rho; Livestock Club; Pres, Assoc Students, Colo State Univ. Polit & Govt Pos: NMex State Rep, Torrance Co, 65-66, 70-, mem, appropriations & finance comt, transportation comt & printing & supplies comt, 70-; mem, NMex State Livestock Bd, 67-, chmn, 68-70; chmn revenue comt, State Const Conv, 69. Bus & Prof Pos: Rancher; mgr, Bigbee Bros Cattle Co, 55- Mem: NMex Farm & Livestock Bur, Torrance Co (second vpres, 64-65, bd dirs, 67-); NMex Cattle Growers (bd dirs, 69-); Torrance Co & Vicinity Livestock Protective Asn. Honors & Awards: Conserv Award, NMex Bankers Asn. Relig: Baha'i Faith. Mailing Add: Box 136 Encino NM 88321

BIGBY, WALTER OLIVER (D)
La State Rep
b Slagle, La, Apr 10, 27; s Harvey Madison Bigby & Ethel Swindle B; m 1962 to Flo Whittington; c Walter O, Jr. Educ: La State Univ, Baton Rouge, LLB, 52; Phi Delta Phi; Delta Kappa Epsilon. Polit & Govt Pos: Alderman, Benton, La, 54-62; La State Rep, Bossier Parish, 68- Bus & Prof Pos: Attorney, Bossier City, La, 52- Mil Serv: Entered as A/S, Navy, 44, released as Yeoman 2nd, 45, after serv in Naval Repair Base, San Diego, Calif. Mem: Bossier Bar Asn; Am Legion; 40 et 8; CofC; Lions. Relig: Presbyterian. Mailing Add: 2300 Arlington Place Bossier City LA 71010

BIGHAM, JOHN R (D)
Tex State Rep
Mailing Add: PO Box 154 Belton TX 76513

BIGWOOD, ROBERT MAURICE (R)
b St Thomas, NDak, Dec 5, 18; s William Henry Bigwood & Alta Lydia Young B; m 1949 to Barbara Ione Barr; c Charles, Janet, Patricia, Robert & John. Educ: Univ Minn, BBA, 47; Beta Gamma Sigma; student chap, Soc for Adv of Mgt. Polit & Govt Pos: Chmn, Young Men of Minn, 57, Lincoln Club, 58-59; chmn, Seventh Dist Rep Platform Comt & Minn Rep State Conv Platform Comt, 60; vchmn, Otter Tail Co Rep Comt, 57-61; deleg & mem credentials comt, Rep Nat Conv, 64, deleg & mem rules comt, 68; vchmn, Seventh Cong Dist Rep Orgn Comt, 61-62, chmn, 63-69; vchmn, Minn Rep State Cent Comt, formerly. Bus & Prof Pos: Asst personnel dir, Otter Tail Power Co, 48-49, personnel dir, 49-60, mgr employee rels, 60-65, vpres mgt serv, 65-75, pres, 75-; vpres & dir, Fergus Falls Savings & Loan Asn, 60- Mil Serv: Entered as Pvt, Army, 42, released as Meteorologist, Weather Squadron, SW Pac, 46. Mem: Jaycees; Kiwanis; CofC; Minn Asn Commerce & Indust (dir); Am Legion. Relig: Methodist. Mailing Add: Hoot Lake Rd RR 1 Fergus Falls MN 56537

BILD, FRANK (R)
Mo State Sen
b Romania, Sept 30, 11; s Anton Bild & Katherine Schiebel B; m 1937 to Flora H Huss; c Brian Alan, Norman Anton, Karen Ann & Kathleen Ann. Educ: Normal Col Am Gymnastic Union, BPE, 34; Ind Univ, BS, 34; St Louis Univ, LLB, 42; Phi Delta Kappa; Phi Epsilon Kappa. Polit & Govt Pos: Mo State Rep, 13th Dist, 63-64, 47th Dist, 67-72; chmn, Mo Second Cong Dist Conv, 64; alt deleg, Rep Nat Conv, 72; Mo State Sen, 15th Dist, 73-74, 75- Mil Serv: Entered as 2nd Lt, Army, 42, released as Capt, 46, after serv in 478th Qm Group, China-India-Burma. Mem: Lions; Gardenville Affton Mem Post 300, Concord Village Business Asn; dir, Lutheran Altenheim. Relig: Lutheran. Mailing Add: 7 Meppen Court St Louis MO 63128

BILL, GREGORY DEAN (D)
b Detroit, Mich, Mar 1, 51; s Peter Bill, Sr & Mary B; single. Educ: Univ Mich, AB with honors, 73; Gold Scholar Key. Polit & Govt Pos: Deleg, Dem Nat Conv, 72; aide to Sen McCollough, Mich, 74-; precinct deleg, 15th Dist Dem Exec Bd, 74- Relig: Greek Orthodox. Legal Res: 8087 Virgil Dearborn Heights MI 48127 Mailing Add: Apt 205 712 Tobin Dr Inkster MI 48141

BILLETT, JOHN WILLIAM (D)
b Columbia, Pa, Apr 26, 38; s Thomas Q Billett & Grace Flawd B; m 1969 to Donna Berry; c Elizabeth P & Matthew T. Educ: Sacramento Col, 59-61; Boston Univ, 61-62; McGeorge Sch Law, 62-65. Polit & Govt Pos: Asst exec secy, Gov Off, Calif, 64-66; legis asst, US House Rep, 66-70, admin asst, 74-75; sr consult, Calif State Assembly, 71-72, chief majority consult, 73-74; vpres, ORSA, Inc, Washington, DC, 75- Mil Serv: Entered as Pvt, Army, 56, released as SP-4, 59, after serv as instr, Army Security Agency Sch. Mem: Asn Admin Assts; Calif State Soc. Relig: Episcopal. Mailing Add: 443 Fourth St NE Washington DC 20002

BILLINGS, HAROLD EDWARD (R)
Vt State Rep
Mailing Add: Creek Rd North Clarendon VT 05759

BILLINGSLEY, JOHN G S (R)
Del State Rep
Mailing Add: 110 Briar Lane Newark DE 19711

BILLINGSLEY, LANCE WILLIAM (D)
Chmn, Prince George's Co Dem Comt, Md
b Buffalo, NY, Apr 18, 40; s James Francis Billingsley & Alice Schnell Billingsley Love; m 1962 to Carolyn Gouza; c Lance W II, Brant & Ashlynn. Educ: Univ Md, BA, 61; Univ Buffalo, JD, 64; Phi Sigma Kappa. Polit & Govt Pos: City attorney, College Park, Md, 66-67; asst attorney gen, Md, 67-68; staff asst to US Sen Daniel B Brewster, 68-69; mem, Prince George's Co Dem Comt, Md, 70-74, chmn, 74- Bus & Prof Pos: Partner, Nylen & Gilmore, 64-75 & Meyers, Billingsley & Chapin, 75- Publ: Co-auth, Types of Business Organizations & Considerations in Organizing Them, Md State Bar Asn, 72; ed, The crime, Barrister Mag, ABA Press, 73. Mem: Marriage Inst of Washington (bd dirs, 75-); Barrister Mag (ed bd, 73-); Personal Growth Ctr (bd dirs, 75-); Terrapin Club. Relig: Christian Church; Mem Bd Deacons, Christian Church Disciples, 74- Mailing Add: 2717 Curry Dr Adelphi MD 20783

BILLINGTON, CLYDE MARK, JR (D)
Conn State Rep
b Hartford, Conn, Aug 29, 34; s Clyde Billington, Sr & Annie Spann B; m 1961 to Malora Wright; c Clyde Mark, III, Christal Dawn & Courtney Lance. Educ: Lincoln Univ, BS; Md State Univ, 1 year; Univ Conn, 1 semester; Alpha Phi Alpha. Polit & Govt Pos: Co-chmn, Seventh Dist Dem Party, Conn, 65-; Conn State Rep, Seventh Dist, 71-; chmn permanent orgn, Dem State Conv, 68 & 74. Bus & Prof Pos: Chem engr, Pratt & Whitney Aircraft, 61-67; owner, Clyde Billington Jr Realty, 67- Mil Serv: Entered as Pvt, Army, 59, released as SP, 61, after serv in US. Mem: Urban League; NAACP; Excelsior Lodge; Oakland Civic Asn. Relig: Protestant. Mailing Add: 919 Albany Ave Hartford CT 06113

BILLION, DAVID HENRY (D)
SDak State Sen
b Sioux Falls, SDak, June 29, 43; s Henry Billion & Evelyn Heinz B; m 1965 to Marlene Ann Rance; c Julie, Margaret & David. Educ: Carroll Col(Mont), BA, 65. Polit & Govt Pos: SDak State Rep, 69-71; SDak State Sen, 75- Bus & Prof Pos: Pres, Billion Motors & Sioux Auto Leasing, 74-; secy-treas, Ryan Motors, 74- Mailing Add: 2016 Pendar Lane Sioux Falls SD 57105

BILYEU, CHARLES EDWARD (CHICK) (D)
Idaho State Sen
b Tonopah, Nev, Mar 9, 17; s Hiram Bilyeu & Valencia Bawden B; m 1956 to Diane Thelma Falter; c Brigette A, Clark P & Valencia Jo. Educ: Univ Redlands, BA in Speech, 40; Pasadena Playhouse Col Theatre, Calif, Master of Theatre Arts, 49; Alpha Psi Omega; Pi Kappa Delta. Polit & Govt Pos: Dem precinct committeeman, 62-64 & 66-; chmn, Bannock Co Dem Cent Comt, Idaho, 62-; Idaho State Sen, 35th Dist, Pocatello, 70- Bus & Prof Pos: Assoc Prof, Speech & Drama, Idaho State Univ, 50-; co-producer, full length theatrical feature motion picture, Don't Cry Wolf; dir & actor, Upper NY Summer Theater; owner & dir, Summer Theater, Pocatello, Idaho. Mil Serv: Entered as Pvt, Army, 41, released as Capt, 46, after serv in 190th Ordnance Bn, ETO & Pac; ETO Ribbon with 2 Battle Stars, Pac Theater Ribbon & 1 Battle Star. Mem: Elks; Am Asn Univ Prof. Honors & Awards: Featured speaker throughout Idaho; Master of Ceremonies for State Convs. Relig: Episcopal. Mailing Add: Rte 1 N Box 48 Pocatello ID 83201

BINA, ROBERT F (D)
Iowa State Rep
b Spillville, Iowa, Sept 27, 39; s Wencel Bina Jr & Cornelia Hagemann B; m to Delores DeWilde. Educ: Univ Northern Iowa, 64; Univ Iowa, MA, 68, MFA, 71; Kappa Delta Pi; Kappa Pi; Alpha Phi Gamma; Sigma Alpha Epsilon; Alpha Chi Epsilon. Polit & Govt Pos: Pres, Scott Co Young Dem, Iowa, 68-70; committeeman, Iowa Young Dem, First Dist, 70-71; Iowa State Rep, Dist 80, 75- Bus & Prof Pos: Instr art, Univ Iowa, 68-71; chmn dept fine arts, Palmer Jr Col, 70-; artist-in-residence, Iowa Wesleyan Col, 72; bd trustees, Davenport Munic Art Gallery, 72- Mil Serv: Entered as Pvt, Army, 57, released as E-5, 60, after serv in 37th Field Artillery Bn, Schwaebisch Hall, Germany, 58-60; Good Conduct Medal. Mem: Friends of Art; New Frontier Club; Friends of Univ Iowa Art Mus. Honors & Awards: Purple Key Leadership Award, Univ Northern Iowa, 63. Mailing Add: Apt 8 1641 W George Washington Blvd Davenport IA 52804

BINDEMAN, JACOB EDWARD (R)
Mem, DC Rep State Cent Comt
b Baltimore, Md, Mar 24, 13; s Isaac Bindeman & Sarah Drobis B; m 1942 to Julia Paul; c David Paul & Stuart L. Educ: Georgetown Univ, LLB, 37, LLM, 39; Phi Sigma Delta. Polit & Govt Pos: Chmn, Pub Welfare Adv Coun of the Dist of Columbia, 57-63; mem, DC Rep State Cent Comt, 67-; chmn, Bd Elec, 69- Bus & Prof Pos: Partner, Bindeman & Burka, Washington, DC, 37-; pres, Landmark Realty, Inc, 67- Mem: Bar Asn DC; Am Bar Asn. Honors & Awards: Man of the Year, Washington Hebrew Congregation; Meritorious Pub Serv Award, DC; Distinguished Serv Award, Georgetown Univ. Relig: Jewish. Mailing Add: 3020 Brandywine St NW Washington DC 20008

BINDER, MATTHEW J (R)
Mem, NJ Rep State Comt
b New York, NY, Jan 14, 17; s Matthew Binder & Madelyn Franke B; m 1941 to Ada A Manicardi; c Matthew, Joanne (Mrs Ssekandi) & Carole (Mrs Zurich). Educ: Columbia Col, BA, 38. Polit & Govt Pos: Mem, Bergen Co Planning Bd, NJ, 70-73; mem, NJ Rep State Comt, 74- Bus & Prof Pos: Vpres, Humer-Binder Co, 46-70, pres, 70- Mil Serv: Entered as Pvt, Army, 41, released as Capt, 46, after serv in MedAdminC, Pac Theatre, 43-45. Mailing Add: 23 Forest Ave Old Tappan NJ 07675

BINDER, ROBERT HENRI (R)
Asst Secy for Policy, Plans & Int Affairs, Dept Transportation
b New York, NY, Aug 19, 32; s Ernest R Binder & Lily Simmons B; m 1962 to Mary Jo Ageton; c Ainslie, Hilary & Meredith. Educ: Princeton Univ, AB cum laude, 53; Harvard Univ Law Sch, LLB, 58; Phi Beta Kappa; Cannon Club. Polit & Govt Pos: Dir, Off Int Transportation Policy & Prog, Dept Transportation, 69-70, dep asst secy for Policy, Plans & Int Affairs, 70-73, acting asst secy for Policy, Plans & Int Affairs, 73-74, asst secy for Policy, Plans & Int Affairs, 74- Bus & Prof Pos: Research analyst & legal aspects consult, Johns Hopkins Univ, 57-67; assoc attorney, Kirlin, Campbell & Keating, 58-67, resident partner, 67-69. Mil Serv: Entered as Pvt, Army, 54, released as SP 3/C, 56, after serv in Psychol Warfare Br, Hawaii, Seoul & Tokyo. Mem: NY State & DC Bar Asns; Harvard Club of Washington; Princeton Club of Washington; Congressional Country Club. Honors & Awards: Secy's Award, 73; Secy's Award for Meritorious Achievement, 75. Relig: Episcopal. Legal Res: 1824 Redwood Terr NW Washington DC 20012 Mailing Add: 400 Seventh St SW Washington DC 20590

BINGER, GLENN H (D)
Mo State Rep
Mailing Add: Rte 3 Box 352 Independence MO 64057

BINGHAM, JEFF M (R)
b Salt Lake City, Utah, Sept 20, 46; s Dr Leonard John Bingham & Helen Williams B; m 1969 to Kathleen Brewerton B; c Christopher Brook. Educ: Univ Hawaii, 69; Univ Utah, BS, 71; Pi Sigma Alpha; Sigma Nu. Polit & Govt Pos: Asst to Mayor of Salt Lake City, Utah, 72-74; mem bd dirs, Salt Lake Co Young Rep, 72-74, chmn, 73-74; mem bd dirs, Young Rep League Utah, 72-74; admin asst to US Sen Wallace F Bennett, 74; admin asst to US Sen Jake Garn, Utah, 75- Bus & Prof Pos: Dir intern progs, Hinckley Inst Polit, Univ Utah, 71-72; sr health planner, Great Salt Lake Health Planning Coun, 72. Honors & Awards: Voice for Democracy Award, Hinckley Inst Polit & Pi Sigma Alpha, Polit Sci Hon Soc, 70; Outstanding Young Man of 1973, Salt Lake City Jaycees, 74. Relig: Latter-day Saint. Legal Res: 2333 Dallin St Salt Lake City UT 84108 Mailing Add: 7321 Eldorado St McLean VA 22101

BINGHAM, JONATHAN B (D)
US Rep, NY
b New Haven, Conn, Apr 24, 14; s Hiram Bingham; m to June Rossbach; c Sherrell (Mrs Bland), June Mitchell (Mrs Esselstyn), Timothy W & Claudia R (Mrs Meyers). Educ: Groton; Yale Univ, AB, 36, LLB, 39; Phi Beta Kappa. Polit & Govt Pos: Spec asst to Asst Secy of State, 45-46; asst dir, Off Int Security Affairs, 51; dep & acting adminr, Tech Coop Admin, 51-53; secy to Gov Averell Harriman, NY, 55-58; US Rep on Econ & Soc Coun of UN with rank of Ambassador & prin adv to Ambassador Adlai E Stevenson in econ & social affairs; mem, US deleg to four UN Gen Assemblies, 61-63; US Rep on UN Trusteeship Coun with rank of Minister, 61, pres of Coun, 62; US Rep, NY, 65-; deleg, Dem Nat Conv, 68. Bus & Prof Pos: Spec correspondent for New York Herald Tribune, 35 & 38 in Europe, USSR & Far East; lawyer. Mil Serv: Enlisted as Pvt, World War II; discharged as Capt of Mil Intel. Mem: Various bar asns; Judiciary Comt of New York Bar Asn. Legal Res: Bronx NY Mailing Add: 2241 Rayburn House Off Bldg Washington DC 20515

BINKLEY, MARGUERITE HALL (R)
Mem, Harris Co Rep Exec Comt, Tex
b Greenville, NC, May 22, 26; d Lannie Pope Hall & Glenna Eleanor Nobles H; m 1945 to Warren Haskins Binkley; c Richard Warren (deceased) & Suzanne. Educ: Va Intermont Jr Col, 43-45. Polit & Govt Pos: VChmn, Brooks Co Rep Party, Tex, 56-57; alt deleg or deleg, Rep State Conv, 62-74; supvr numerous campaign hq, Harris Co, 62-; contrib ed, Rep Banner, Houston, 64 & 65; pres, West Univ Rep Women's Club, 67; alt deleg, Rep Nat Conv, 68; secy, Harris Co Rep Party, 68-70 & 74-; mem, Harris Co Rep Exec Comt, 70-; Parliamentarian, Harris Co Coun Federated Rep Women, 71-73; mem citizens adv comt, Tex Const Revision Comt, 73. Mem: Nat Asn of Parliamentarians; Registered Prof Parliamentarian. Relig: Episcopal. Mailing Add: 6523 Buffalo Speedway Houston TX 77005

BINNETTE, JOSEPH E (D)
Maine State Rep
Mailing Add: 128 S Brunswick St Old Town ME 04468

BINSFELD, CONNIE (R)
Mich State Sen
Mailing Add: Rte 2 Maple City MI 49664

BIRCH, JEAN GORDON (R)
Pres, Mont Fedn Rep Women
b Copley Twp, Ill, Aug 17, 21; d Ivan Reynolds Gordon & Marie Van Buren G; m 1943 to Stephen Allen Birch; c Judith & Robin (Dr William Matthews). Educ: Knox Col, BA, 43; Phi Beta Kappa; Phi Mu. Polit & Govt Pos: Pres, Cascade Co Rep Womens Club, Mont, 60-64; campaign activities chmn, Mont Fedn Rep Women, 65-69, dist dir, 69-71 & state pres, 71-; vchmn, Cascade Co Rep Cent Comt, 64-66, committeewoman, 67-69; mem-at-lg exec comt, Nat Fedn Rep Women, 74- Mem: DAR. Honors & Awards: Donald G Nutter Americanism Award, Cascade Co Young Rep, 66. Relig: Methodist. Mailing Add: 2625 Fourth Ave S Great Falls MT 59405

BIRCHLER, VINCENT A (D)
Ill State Sen
Mailing Add: RFD 1 Box 36 Chester IL 62233

BIRD, AGNES THORNTON (D)
Mem, Tenn State Dem Exec Comt
b Wichita Falls, Tex, Sept 15, 21; d Ernest Grady Thornton & Anne Renfro T; m 1946 to Frank Babington Bird; c Patricia (Mrs Parris). Educ: Tex Woman's Univ, BS, 43; Univ Tenn, Knoxville, MS, 59, PhD, 67, JD, 74; Alpha Chi, Alpha Lambda Delta, Delta Phi Delta. Polit & Govt Pos: Mem, Tenn State Dem Exec Comt, 58-; deleg, Dem Nat Conv, 60; mem Tenn adv comt, US Civil Rights Comn, 62-73; mem, Tenn Comn on Human Rels, 63-67; pres, Tenn Fedn Dem Women, 64-65; parliamentarian, Nat Fedn Dem Women, 73- Bus & Prof Pos: Draftsman, Humble Oil & Refining Co, Wichita Falls, Tex, 43-45; clerk, Aluminum Co of Am, Alcoa, Tenn, 47-49; teacher, Blount Co Sch Syst, Maryville, Tenn, 51-53; instr, Univ Tenn, Knoxville, 63-67; asst prof polit sci, Maryville Col, Maryville, 69-72; pvt pract law, Maryville, 75- Publ: Co-auth, Money as a Campaign Resource, Citizen's Research Found, 66; auth, Reforming the electoral process, AAUW J, 4/74; auth, Women in politics-changing perceptions, J Asn Study Perception, 75. Mem: Am Polit Sci Asn; Am Asn Univ Women (vpres, local br; mem, Nat Legis Comt, 73-); Chilhowee Club (trustee, gen Fedn Womens Clubs, 74-); Southern Polit Sci Asn. Relig: Unitarian. Legal Res: Cold Springs Rd Maryville TN 37801 Mailing Add: Box 647 Maryville TN 37801

BIRD, JORGE (POPULAR DEM, PR)
b Guayama, PR, Aug 23, 10; s Agustin Bird Elias & Angelica Fernandez Cintron E; m 1934 to Victoria L Vilella; c Luisa Angelica (Mrs Roberto Inclan), Victoria Josefina (Mrs Jose Antonio Saenz de Ormijana), Nellie Aurora, Agustin Jorge & Jorge Pablo. Educ: Univ PR; Phi Eta Mu. Polit & Govt Pos: Mem Adv Comt, PR Develop Bank, bd dirs, Popular Dem Party, PR & PR Police Comn; committeeman, Nat Dem Party (on leave); mem, Sch Bd PR Voc Training Courses, Citizens Comt on improv of rels between PR citizenship & govt; adv, Secy of Com, mem, Tourism Adv Comt, Econ Develop Admin, PR, currently. Bus & Prof Pos: Pres & owner, Bird Restaurants, Inc, Jorge Bird Elec Appliances, Inc & PR Airways; dir, Amstell Brewery Corp, PR; dir, Int Investment Corp; founder & first pres, PR Conv Bur; dir, Marriott Corp, currently; pres & owner, Jorge Bird Travel Serv, Inc; Bird Gasoline Sta; Real Estate & Farming. Publ: Relato de un Viaje a Espana y Niza (Spanish booklet); co-sponsor, Man in the City of the Future, Columbia Univ Grad Sch Bus, 68; Apuntes de Mis Viajes por el Mundo, Ed Madrid, Spain, 69. Mem: PR CofC (pres); Inter-Am CofC (dir); Sales Exec Club; Elks; US Navy League; YMCA; Lions. Honors & Awards: Man of the Year, PR CofC; PR Patriot Eugenio Maria de Hostos Award; Good Will Ambassador-at-lg, Lions Int; Award of the Cross of the Gentlemen of Equator of Repub of Gabon (Africa); Comendador of Order of Christopher Columbus of Dominican Repub. Relig: Catholic. Legal Res: Ramirez de Arellano 1-5 Garden Hills Bayamon PR 00619 Mailing Add: PO Box BA Rio Piedras PR 00928

BIRD, MARY LOUISE (R)
VPres, Okla Fedn Rep Women
b Bunker Hill, Kans, July 29, 07; d Eugene Oscar Humes & Alberta Markley H; m 1931 to Lloyd Phillip Bird; c Alberta (Mrs Phillip Royal), Lloyd Phillip, Jr & James Markley. Educ: Univ Kans, AB, 29; Botts Bus Col, Okla, 30. Polit & Govt Pos: Various Rep precinct off; treas, Ponca City Rep Women's Club, Okla, 67-68, mem bd dirs, 67-, pres, 73-74; secy, Kay Co Rep Comt, 67-; secy, Kay Co Rep Exec Bd, 67-; charter mem & mem bd dirs, Eve Chap, Kay Co Rep Women, 70-; alt deleg, Rep Nat Conv, 68, deleg & mem rules comt, 72; treas, Okla Fedn Rep Women, 69-72, vpres, 73 & 75-, pres, 74. Mem: Eastern Star; Am Asn Retired Persons (charter mem, Ponca City Chap). Relig: Methodist. Mailing Add: 214 Virginia Ave Ponca City OK 74601

BIRD, RONALD CHARLES (D)
Tex State Rep
b St Louis, Mo, Dec 10, 36; s Charles Robert Bird & Lillian Sciales B; m 1959 to Barbara Josephine Macauley; c Mark C, Mauri C & Bart C. Educ: La State Univ, Baton Rouge, 55-56; Washington Univ, BSBA, 60; St Mary's Univ Sch Law (Tex), 71-74; Phi Delta Phi; Tau Kappa Epsilon. Polit & Govt Pos: Mem, Bexar Co Dem Exec Comt, Tex, 68-72; Tex State Rep, Bexar Co, Dist 57-D, 73- Bus & Prof Pos: Attorney, currently. Mil Serv: Entered as 2nd Lt, Army, 60, released as Capt, 67; Capt, Res. Mem: CofC. Relig: Catholic. Legal Res: 1011 Kayton Ave San Antonio TX 78210 Mailing Add: PO Box 2910 Austin TX 78767

BIRD, STEPHEN CRABTREE (D)
WVa State Deleg
b Bluefield, WVa, Mar 7, 39; s Stephen Ward Bird & Eliza Crabtree B; div; c Debra Lynn. Bird. Educ: Concord Col, BS, 61; WVa Univ Sch Dent, DDS, 66; Blue Key; Phi Delta. Polit & Govt Pos: WVa State Deleg, 74- Mil Serv: Entered as Pvt, Marine Corp, 57, released as Pfc, 64. Mem: Elks; Mason; Scottish Rite (32 degree); Shrine; Gideons. Relig: Protestant. Mailing Add: 1622 Blizzard Dr Parkersburg WV 26101

BIRDSONG, JIMMY (D)
Okla State Sen
b Little Rock, Ark, Apr 27, 25; s Jesse E Birdsong & Jewell A B; m to Martha K Lefler; c James Michael & Nancy Kay. Educ: Oklahoma City Univ, LLB. Polit & Govt Pos: Okla State Sen, 65-, asst majority floor leader, Okla State Senate, 69-72, majority floor leader, 73-74. Mil Serv: Army; Purple Heart; Three Battle Stars. Mem: Mason (32 degree); Shrine; Okla Bar Asn; SOklahoma City CofC; Am Trial Lawyers Asn; Community Action Prog (bd dirs). Relig: Protestant. Mailing Add: 816 SW 36th St Oklahoma City OK 73109

BIRKELAND, ARTHUR C (R)
Chmn, Day Co Rep Cent Comt, SDak
b Pierpont, SDak, Aug 7, 04; s Christ H Birkeland & Anna Askvold B; m 1949 to Verna Dorothy Thompson. Educ: Northern State Col, SDak, BS, 30; Univ SDak; Univ Wis; Sigma Delta Epsilon; Pi Kappa Delta. Polit & Govt Pos: Chmn, Day Co Rep Cent Comt, SDak, formerly; alt deleg, Rep Nat Conv, 64; Northeast Vpres, SDak Econ Opportunity, 65-66; committeeman, SDak Rep State Comt, currently. Bus & Prof Pos: Pres bd, Coop Elevator, Pierpont, SDak, 64-66. Mem: Mason; Scottish Rite; Shrine; Farm Bur; Twp Union (Twp Supvr). Relig: Lutheran; Secy, Church Board, Lutheran Church, Pierpont, SDak, 56-66. Mailing Add: Pierpont SD 57468

BIRKENHOLZ, CARROLL MERLE (R)
b Newton, Iowa, Oct 22, 23; s Henry C Birkenholz, Sr & Mima C Montgomery B; m 1947 to Agnes Lorene Keating; c Janet (Mrs Comer) & David. Educ: Univ Iowa, 41-42; Moorhead State Teachers Col, 43. Polit & Govt Pos: Chmn, Newton City Bd of Rev, Iowa, 64-69; chmn, Jasper Co Rep Cent Comt, formerly. Bus & Prof Pos: Vpres, United Fed Savings & Loan Asn, Des Moines, Iowa, 58-62. Mil Serv: Entered as Pvt, Air Force, 43, released as Capt, 52, after serv in 307th Bomb Wing, Pac Theatre, World War II & Korea, 44-45 & 51-52, Res, Maj. 52-69; Purple Heart; Distinguished Flying Cross; Air Medal with two Clusters; Presidential Unit Citation. Mem: Newton Bd Realtors (pres, currently); Elks. Relig: Methodist. Mailing Add: 305 E 28th St S Newton IA 50208

BIRKHEAD, KENNETH MILTON (D)
b St Louis, Mo, Nov 15, 14; s Leon Milton Birkhead & Agnes Schiereck B; m 1943 to Barbara Belwood; c David Keehn & Scott Belwood. Educ: Mo Valley Col, AB, 49; Univ Mo, MA, 50. Polit & Govt Pos: Asst to chmn, Dem Nat Comt, 48 & 50-52, finance dir, 57-59; staff dir, Dem Sen Campaign Comt, 52-53; asst to the Majority Whip, US Senate, 53-55; secy, Nat Capital Dem Club, 59-64; confidential asst to the Secy Agr, Dept Agr, 61-66, adminstr, Rural Community Develop Serv, 66-68; nat exec dir, Citizens for Johnson-Humphrey, 68; nat exec dir, Citizens for Humphrey, 68; nat exec dir, Citizens for Humphrey-Muskie, 68; spec asst to US Sen Thomas J McIntyre, 69- Bus & Prof Pos: Asst to dir, Friends of Democracy, 37-48; nat dir, Am Vets Comt, 55-57; consult, Albert & Mary Lasker Found, 59-61. Mil Serv: Entered as Pvt, Air Force, 42, released as 1st Lt, 46, after serv in Air Transport Command. Mem: Am Acad of Polit & Social Sci; Int Town & Country Club, Falls Church, Va. Honors & Awards: Distinguished Serv Award, US Dept of Agr, 64. Relig: Protestant. Mailing Add: 6445 Queen Anne Terr Falls Church VA 22044

BIRNBAUM, LAWRENCE M (R)
Chmn, Traverse Co Rep Party, Minn
b Hankinson, NDak, June 1, 24; s John L Birnbaum & Veronica Novack B; m 1949 to Lorraine M Widhalm; c Ronald, Patricia, Lawrence, Jr, Mary Theresa, Jerome, Joan, Anthony, Stephen, Duane & Kelan. Educ: NDak State Sch Sci. Polit & Govt Pos: Chmn, Traverse Co Rep Party, Minn, 70- Bus & Prof Pos: Auto mechanic, Brackin Chevrolet Co, 49-50; auto mechanic, Moody Chevrolet & Buick Co, 50-53, serv mgr, Storsteen Chevrolet, 53-60; serv mgr, Hansen Oil Co, 60- Mil Serv: Entered as Pvt, Army, 43, released as Pfc, after serv in 720 Mil Police Bn, Japan, 43-44. Mem: Am Legion; KofC. Relig: Catholic. Mailing Add: Browns Valley MN 56219

BIRNSTIHL, ORVILLE E (DFL)
Minn State Rep
b Morrison Co, Minn, Dec 27, 17; s Charles G Birnstihl & Estella Snow B; m 1939 to Alice L Cornell; c Daniel J. Educ: High sch, grad, 35. Polit & Govt Pos: Minn State Rep, 75- Bus & Prof Pos: Owner, Fremont City Bus Lines, Nebr, 46-52; owner, Birnstihl Motors, Fremont, 52-63; owner, B C Charolais Breeders, Faribault, Minn, 62-75. Mil Serv: Entered as Sgt, Army, 45, released 46, after serv in Pac Theatre; Good Conduct Medal; Expert Rifleman Badge. Mem: Lions; VFW; Am Legion; Elks; Eagles. Honors & Awards: 100% Pres Award, Lions. Relig: Lutheran. Legal Res: Rte 5 Western Ave Faribault MN 55021 Mailing Add: Rm 224 State Off Bldg St Paul MN 15515

BIRT, WALTER ARTHUR (R)
Maine State Rep
b New Haven, Conn, Sept 22, 15; s Walter Howard Birt & Mary Jane MacNevin B; m 1946 to Dorothy Fern Larlee; c Walter Howard (deceased) & Douglas Edward. Educ: Garret Schenck High Sch, East Millinocket, Maine. Polit & Govt Pos: Mem, Penobscot Co & East Millinocket Rep Comts, 63-; Maine State Rep, 63-, asst majority leader, Maine House Rep, 73-75; vchmn, Maine Sesquicentennial Comn, formerly; mem, Am Revolution Bicentennial Comt, currently. Bus & Prof Pos: Power sta operator, Great Northern Paper Co, 34- Mil Serv: Entered as Pvt, Air Force, 42, released as Sgt, 46, after serv in Fourth Air Force. Mem: Mason (Past Master); CofC (past pres); IBEW. Honors & Awards: Eagle Scout. Relig: United Church of Christ. Mailing Add: 33 Pine St East Millinocket ME 04430

BISBEE, KENNETH M (R)
NH State Rep
Mailing Add: Hampstead Rd RFD 2 Derry NH 03038

BISCHOFF, DOUGLAS GEORGE (R)
Utah State Sen
b Salt Lake City, Utah, Oct 19, 26; s Carl Bishoff & Gertrude Kirchoff B; m 1954 to Cohleen Jensen; c Tamara & James Douglas. Educ: Columbia Univ, BS & MS, 53; Univ Utah, BA,

58; Phi Kappa Phi. Polit & Govt Pos: Chmn pub rels & mem exec comt, Salt Lake Co Rep Comt, Utah; deleg, Rep Nat Conv, 68; chmn, Salt Lake Co Rep Cent Comt, currently; Utah State Sen, 70- Mil Serv: Entered as A/S, Navy, 43, released as Pharmacists Mate 1/C, 46; Am Theater Ribbon; Asiatic Pac Medal; Victory Medal. Mem: Lions Int. Relig: Latter-day Saint. Mailing Add: 267 S State Salt Lake City UT 84101

BISH, BETTY J (R)
Chmn, Butler Co Rep Party, Pa
b Butler, Pa, Jan 30, 26; d Frank G Cooper & Edith Davis C; m 1943 to Clarence O Bish; c Connie Lee & Dennis F. Educ: Butler Sr High Sch, Pa, until 43. Polit & Govt Pos: Committeewoman, Butler Twp Rep Party, Pa, 66-73; vchmn, Butler Co Rep Party, 71-72, chmn, 72- Bus & Prof Pos: Pres, Chrysler Acct Asn, 68-70. Mem: Franklin Twp Women's Club; Butler Coun Rep Women; Butler Twp Rep Club. Honors & Awards: Boy Scout's Award for Serv, 65; Lifetime Acct Award, Chrysler Corp, Detroit, Mich, 68. Relig: United Presbyterian. Mailing Add: 116 Greenwood Dr Butler PA 16001

BISH, MILAN D (R)
Mem, Nebr State Rep Exec Comt
b Harvard, Nebr, July 1, 29; s Charles Bish & Mabel E Williams B; m 1951 to Allene Rae Miller; c Cindy, Linda & Charles Paul. Educ: Hastings Col, BA, 51; Delta Phi Sigma. Polit & Govt Pos: Mem, Hall Co Rep Cent Comt, Nebr, 69-; mem, Nebr State Rep Exec Comt, 69-, mem finance comt, 69-; chmn, Nebr Rep Cent Comt, 71-73. Bus & Prof Pos: Pres, Bish Machinery Co, 51-; dir, Commercial Nat Bank, 67-; dir, Five Points State Bank, 71- Mem: Rotary Int (dist gov); Mason (32 degree); Shrine; Elks; Eagle. Relig: Presbyterian; Elder. Legal Res: 2012 W Louise Grand Island NE 68801 Mailing Add: PO Box 1365 Grand Island NE 68801

BISHOP, BEVERLY A (D)
NH State Rep
Mailing Add: 8 Beacon St Nashua NH 03060

BISHOP, BRADLEY CHARLES (R)
b Washington, DC, May 1, 47; s Charles Royce Bishop & Marilyn Biddick B; single. Educ: Wis State Univ-Platteville, BS with honors, 69. Polit & Govt Pos: Mem exec comt, Wis State Univ-Platteville Young Rep, 67-69; chmn, Third Cong Dist Young Rep, Wis, 69; secy-treas, Iowa Co Rep Party, 69-71, chmn, formerly; campaign mgr, Citizens for Scallon for Wis Assembly, 70; chmn youth task force, Rep Party of Wis, 71-72; mem, Iowa Co Zoning Bd of Adjust, 71-; five co chmn, Farm Families for Reelec of the President, 72; co-supvr dist 18, Iowa Co Bd Supvr, 72- Bus & Prof Pos: Farmer, 60-; secy & treas, C R Bishop & Sons Inc, 71- Mem: Wis Agri-Bus Coun; Wis Farm Bur. Mailing Add: Rte 1 Cobb WI 53526

BISHOP, CECIL W (RUNT) (R)
b Johnson Co, Ill, June 29, 90; s William C Bishop & Belle Zada Ragsdale B; m 1911 to Elizabeth Hutton; c Jack Hutton, Sr (deceased); two grandchildren; two great grandchildren. Educ: Anna High Sch, Ill; Union Acad, Anna, Ill. Polit & Govt Pos: US Rep, 25th Dist, Ill, 40-54; asst postmaster gen, US, 55-56; supt of Indust Prog for Ill, 57-58; asst to dir, Dept Labor, Ill, 59-60. Bus & Prof Pos: Merchant-tailor, Ladies & Gents, 10-23; city clerk, Carterville, Ill, 16-18; served as mem of local draft bd during World War I; postmaster, Carterville, 23-33; crusade chmn, Williamson Co, 60-66. Mem: Lions Int, Lions Club; Elks; Odd Fellows; Crab Orchard Golf Country Club; Boat & Yacht Club. Honors & Awards: Played semi-pro baseball & football; winner of several golf tournaments, including second place trophy at Southern Ill Sr Golf Tournament, 66 & 70 in 75 year class. Mailing Add: 210 Olive St Carterville IL 62918

BISHOP, DONALD E (R)
Mich State Sen
b Almont, Mich, Feb 27, 33; s G C Bishop & Jane W B; m 1955 to Nancy Michael; c Rebecca, Susan, Judith, Martha & Michael. Educ: Oberlin Col, BA, 55; Detroit Col Law, JD, 66. Polit & Govt Pos: Mich State Rep, 63rd dist, 67-71; Mich State Sen, 16th dist, 71-, chmn, Comt Corp & Econ Develop, Mich State Senate, currently. Bus & Prof Pos: Attorney, Martin & Bishop, Rochester, currently; secy & dir, Litex, Inc, 69-; dir, Nat Bank of Rochester, Mich, 69-; incorporator, Rochester Retirement Home Inc, 70. Mil Serv: Entered as Pvt, Army, 55, released as SP-3, 57, after serv in 532nd Field Artil Observation Bn, ETO, 56-57. Mem: Mich & Oakland Co Bar Asns. Relig: Congregational. Mailing Add: 2332 W Avon Rd Rochester MI 48063

BISHOP, EDNA NOE (D)
b Morristown, Tenn, Jan 11, 12; d William Arthur Noe & Minnie Phillips N; m 1940 to William Harry Bishop; c Jeanne (Mrs Charles Lenox). Educ: Carson-Newman Col, BS, 60; Hypation Sorority. Polit & Govt Pos: Mem, Hamblen Co Dem Women's Club, Tenn, 60-, mem exec comt, 60-; mem, Hamblen Co Comt for McGovern, 72; deleg, Tenn Dem State Conv, 72; deleg, Dem Nat Conv, 72; secy, Dem Primary Bd, 72- Bus & Prof Pos: Teacher, Hamblen Co Schs, 35-45; teacher, Morristown City Sch, 50-75. Mem: Nat & Morristown Educ Asns; Tenn Educ Asn; Eastern Star; Farm Bur. Honors & Awards: Bronze Award Medallion, Nat Dem Conv, 72. Relig: Baptist. Legal Res: Andrew J Hwy Morristown TN 37814 Mailing Add: Talbott TN 37877

BISHOP, HENRY SAMUEL (D)
VChmn, Ga State Dem Party
b Alma, Ga, Sept 19, 42; s Bernard Alton Bishop & Mary Madden B; m 1964 to Nancy Elaine Baker; c Henry Samuel, III & Peggy Lynn. Educ: Univ Ga, BBA, 64; Gridiron; Greek Horsemen; X Club; pres, Sigma Nu. Polit & Govt Pos: Mayor, City of Alma, Ga, 68-; vchmn, Ga State Dem Party, 70-; mem bd dirs, vpres & pres, Ga Munic Asn, 69-; mem, State Planning & Community Affairs Policy Bd, currently; mem, State Bd Natural Resources, currently; mem bd dirs, Ga Planning Asn, currently. Bus & Prof Pos: Mgr, Bishop Funeral Home, 64-69; owner, Bishop Ins Agency, 65-73; owner, Pinelawn Mem Gardens, 66-; owner, Southeast Egg Producers, 68-; pres, First Fed Savings & Loan, 73- Mem: Lions (pres, 70); Shrine; Okefenokee Golf & Country Club; Mason (master). Relig: Baptist; Sunday Sch teacher, First Baptist Church, 63-67, jr choir leader, 66, pres, Brotherhood, 69. Mailing Add: PO Box 2005 Alma GA 31510

BISHOP, JAMES A (D)
b Alma, Ga, Sept 9, 42; s B A Bishop & Mary Madden B; m 1964 to Mary Elizabeth Raulerson; c James A, Jr. Educ: Univ Ga, BA, 64; Walter F George Sch Law, Mercer Univ, LLB, 67; Biftad Hon Scholastic Soc; Greek Horsemen Hon Soc; X Club; Gridiron Secret Soc; Inter-Fraternity Coun (treas, pres); Sigma Nu (secy & vpres); Phi Delta Phi (secy, pres). Polit & Govt Pos: Mem, Ga State Dem Exec Comt, formerly. Bus & Prof Pos: Mem firm, Alaimo Taylor, 69, partner, Alaimo, Taylor & Bishop, currently. Mem: Brunswick Bar Asn; Am Bar Asn; State Bar Ga (eighth dist rep exec coun); Am Cancer Soc (bd dirs); Humane Soc Glynn Co (bd dirs & third vpres). Relig: Presbyterian; Deacon, adv & sponsors, Sr High Youth Fellowship, St Simons Island Presbyterian Church. Mailing Add: 26 Wimberly Rd St Simons Island GA 31522

BISHOP, JIMMY (D)
Tenn State Rep
Mailing Add: 916 Meadow St Brownsville TN 38102

BISHOP, JOHN J, JR (R)
Md State Sen
b Baltimore, Md, Dec 6, 27; s John Joseph Bishop, Sr & Mary Lillian Freshline B; m Doris Lee Anderson; c John J, III, Suzanne Mary, Karen Lee, Patricia Ann, Michael Raymond & Paul Francis. Educ: Univ Baltimore, AA, 49, JD, 52. Polit & Govt Pos: Md State Sen, 66- Mil Serv: Entered as Seaman, Coast Guard, 46, released as Seaman 1/C, 47, after serv in Am Theatre of Operations. Mem: Md State Bar Asn; Baltimore Co Bar Asn; Soc State Legis; assoc Eagleton Inst of Politics. Honors & Awards: Award, Md Asn Retarded Children. Relig: Catholic. Legal Res: 6671 Loch Hill Rd Baltimore MD 21239 Mailing Add: 600 E Joppa Rd Towson MD 21204

BISHOP, LEONARD LEE (R)
Mem, Maine Rep State Comt
b Presque Isle, Maine, Aug 6, 00; s Jake W Bishop & Elizabeth Lamoreau B; m 1922 to Alma Frances Cheney; c Leonard L, Jr, Leatrice (Mrs Gallant) & Carolyn Cheney (Mrs LaChance). Educ: Shaw's Bus Col, 20-21. Polit & Govt Pos: Trial justice, Sagadahoc Co, 48-55; mem, Gov Exec Hwy Safety Comt, 55-67; dep dir, Local Civil Defense, 57-; trustee, Bowdoinham Water Dist, 59-74, chmn, 66-74; dir, Bowdoinham Fed Credit Union, 63-74, pres, 63-64; vchmn, Bowdoinham Town Rep Party, 68-; chmn, Sagadahoc Co Rep Comt, 70-72; mem, Maine Rep State Comt, 72-; gen chmn, Bowdoinham Bicentennial Celebration. Bus & Prof Pos: Agent, asst mgr & mgr, Metrop Life Ins, 21-28; dist mgr, Mutual Life NY, 28-31; state mgr, Fidelity Mutual Ins, Maine, 31-33; ins broker, 33-44; owner, Richmond Ins Agency, 44-; Len Bishop Real Estate Agency, 48-; publ, Richmond Bee, 46-61. Mem: Kennebec Valley Bd Realtors; Maine & Nat Bd Realtors; Masonic Bodies (32 degree); Bowdoinham Beautification Comt. Honors & Awards: Many awards & trips as leading producer & underwriter for ins co. Relig: Universalist; Maine bd Trustees, 38-52, chmn, 6 years. Mailing Add: Rte 24 Bishop Farm Bowdoinham ME 04008

BISHOP, TILMAN (R)
Colo State Sen
Mailing Add: 2697 G Rd Grand Junction CO 81501

BISHOP, TILMON MELVIN (D)
Miss State Rep
Mailing Add: 116 First St Magee MS 39114

BISPO, NAOMI MARIE (R)
Assoc Mem, Rep State Cent Comt Calif
b Seattle, Wash, Nov 23, 02; d Jesse Anderson Allred & Josephine L Moss A; m 1923 to William Lawrence Bispo; c Frances A (Mrs Lewis) & Robert L. Educ: Univ Calif, Los Angeles, 2 years. Polit & Govt Pos: Treas, Southwest Women's Rep Club Federated, 57-59, secy, 59, pres, 60-61; vchmn, Nixon for Pres, Southwest Hq, 60; co-chmn, Nixon for Gov, 31st Cong Hq, 62; mem & treas, 63rd Assembly Dist Rep Party, 62-64 & 64-66, alt mem, 67-69; treas, 31st Cong Dist Rep Party, 62-66; mem, Crenshaw-Ladera Rep Women, Federated, 62-, second vpres, 71-72, pres, 73-; mem rules comt, Los Angeles Co Cent Comt, 64-66; secy Southwest & Centinela Valley Rep Club, 68, treas, 69-70, pres, 71-73; supvr, Neighbors for Nixon-Agnew, Southwest, Inglewood, Hawthorne & South Bay Area, 68; sustaining mem, Nat Hq Rep Party, assoc mem, Rep State Cent Comt of Calif, currently; co-chmn, Reagan for Gov, Region Eight Hq, 70; alt, 63rd Assembly Dist Cent Comt, 67-73; precinct chmn, Inglewood Dist Comt to Reelect the President Hq, 72. Bus & Prof Pos: Dir of dramatics, El Retiro Girls Sch, San Fernando, Calif, 22; clerk, Los Angeles Water & Power, 23; sales rep, Avon Prod, Inc, Pasadena, Calif, 41- Mem: Am Legion Auxiliary; 8 et 40; Int Toastmistress Club; S Ebell Club; Am Cancer Soc Vol. Honors & Awards: Ten Year Award, Los Angeles Am Cancer Soc; Los Angeles Co Rep Cent Comt Cert Commendation, 74; Plaque Appreciation, SW Centinela Valley Rep Club, 74. Relig: Catholic. Mailing Add: 7710 Brighton Ave Los Angeles CA 90047

BISPO, WILLIAM LAWRENCE (R)
b Danville, Calif, Jan 26, 97; s Edward Lawrence Bispo (deceased) & Mary Lewis B (deceased); m 1923 to Naomi Marie Allred; c Frances Ann (Mrs Lewis) & Robert Lewis. Educ: Southern Calif Sch Pub Admin, BSPA, 52. Polit & Govt Pos: Hq chmn for three assembly cand & two cong cand, 62-68; vol polit work, Rep Party, Calif, 63-71; assoc mem, State Rep Cent Comt Calif, 63-68 & 73-74, mem, 69-71, mem platform comt; alt co cent committeeman, 63rd Assembly Dist Rep Party, Calif, 65-68; treas, Primary Campaign Comt Cong Cand, 68; primary hq chmn, State Attorney Gen E Younger, 70; hq asst & chmn dep registr voters, Reagan Campaign, 70; hq asst & chmn dep registr voters, Nixon Campaign, 72; victory squad work senate & assembly elec; mem, Vol Adv Coun. Bus & Prof Pos: Bill payable acct, Zellerbach Paper Co, Los Angeles, 20; from stock rec clerk to acct receivable acct, White Auto Co, 20-27; from clerk-typist to sr clerk of assessments, Civil Serv, City of Los Angeles, 27-64; retired. Mil Serv: Enlisted as Seaman, Naval Res, 18, released as Yeoman 1/C, 22, after serv at Submarine Base, San Pedro, Calif, 12th Naval Dists. Mem: Univ Southern Calif Alumni Asn; Univ Southern Calif Sch Pub Admin Alumni Asn; Am Legion (exec comt, treas, first vcomdr); Los Angeles Civil Ctr Speakers Club; Los Angeles City Employees Asn. Honors & Awards: Retired Los Angeles City Employees Asn Award & Spec Citation, Bd Pub Works, City of Los Angeles, Spec Citation, Retirement Bd; 50 Year Gold Mem Card, Am Legion, two mem campaign awards; Boy Scout Comt Chmn, 10 years; Sons of Legion Chmn, 8 years. Relig: Catholic. Mailing Add: 7710 Brighton Ave Los Angeles CA 90047

BISSELL, KEITH (D)
Tenn State Rep
Mailing Add: 253 Main St E Oak Ridge TN 37830

BISSELL, MARILYN ROMAINE (R)
NC State Rep
b Jamestown, NY; d John Ernest Weaver & Romaine Cherry W; m 1951 to Harold Arthur Bissell; c Karen Romaine, Kathleen Martha & Leslie Kay Marilyn. Educ: Grove City Col, Grove City, Pa, BS in Commerce, 49; Sigma Theta Chi; Theta Alpha Phi. Polit & Govt Pos: Vchmn, Mecklenburg Rep Party, NC; bd mem, Charlotte Mecklenburg Rep Women's Club, Rep Party, vchmn, Precinct 48, formerly; NC State Rep, 72- Bus & Prof Pos: Teacher, Lago Colony Sch, Aruba, Netherlands, WIndies, 51-53; acct, Tarco, Inc, 62-71. Mem: Am Asn Univ Women; League of Women Voters; Charlotte Charity League (mem bd); Charlotte Women's Polit Caucus; Girl Scouts (mem troop 333 Comt). Relig: Presbyterian. Mailing Add: 2216 Providence Rd Charlotte NC 28211

BISSETT, DELIA BELLE (R)
Committeewoman, Ark Rep State Comt
b Atlantic, Iowa, Dec 19, 41; d K E Destler & Dorothy Bonnell D; m 1962 to Joe Bissett, MD; c Robert Knight & William Bonnell. Educ: Univ Ark, Fayetteville, 59-62; Univ Ark, Little Rock, BA, 63; Beta; Kappa Kappa Gamma, Sophomore & Sr Counr, Civic Club, AWS, Singphony. Polit & Govt Pos: Mem, Pulaski Co Rep Comt, 72-; mem exec comt, 72-; committeeman, Ark Rep State Comt, 74-; dir, The Elec Laws Inst, 74- Bus & Prof Pos: Teacher, Little Rock, Ark, 63-67 & Iowa City, Iowa, 67-68. Relig: Methodist. Mailing Add: 2004 Clapboard Hill Rd Little Rock AR 72207

BISTLINE, BEVERLY BARBARA (D)
Idaho State Rep
b Coeur d'Alene, Idaho, Aug 28, 22; d Francis M Bistline & Anne Glindemann B; div. Educ: Univ Idaho Southern Br, jr col cert, 41; Univ Idaho, BA, 43; Univ Utah Sch Law, LLB, 54; Univ Southern Calif, MA in cert tax, 55; Delta Gamma. Polit & Govt Pos: Vchairperson, Legis Dist 33 Dem Party, Idaho, 72-74; precinct four committeewoman, Bannock Co Dem Party, 74-; Idaho State Rep, Dist 33, 74- Bus & Prof Pos: Attorney-at-law, Pocatello, Idaho, 55- Mil Serv: Entered as Seaman, Navy, 44, released as Yeoman 2/C, 47, after serv in Chief of Naval Opers & Naval Air Transport Serv, Washington, DC & Moffett Field, Calif, 45-47; Good Conduct Medal; Overseas Medal. Mem: Am, Idaho State & Sixth Dist Bar Asns; Soroptimist Int; PEO. Relig: United Church of Christ. Legal Res: 351 N Garfield Pocatello ID 83201 Mailing Add: PO Box 8 Pocatello ID 83201

BITTERMAN, MARY G F (D)
VChmn, Dem Party Hawaii
b San Jose, Calif, May 29, 44; d John Dennis Foley & Zoe Joyce Hames F; m 1967 to Morton Edward Bitterman; c Sarah Fleming. Educ: Dominican Col, 62-64; Georgetown Univ Sch Foreign Serv, 64-65; Univ Santa Clara, BA, 66; Bryn Mawr Col, MA, 68, PhD, 71. Polit & Govt Pos: Deleg & arrangements chmn, Dem Nat Mid-Term Conf, 74; vchmn, Dem Party Hawaii, 74- Bus & Prof Pos: Research assoc in Hawaiian hist, Hawaii Environ Simulation Lab, Univ Hawaii, 71-72, proj mgr, 72-74; exec dir & gen mgr, Hawaii Pub TV, 74- Publ: Auth, The early Quaker literature of defense, Church Hist, Vol XXXXII, No 2, 6/73; The problem of communication between technicians & decisionmakers, In: Regional Environmental Management, Ford Found, 3/74. Mem: Hawaiian & Friends Hist Asns; Nat Asn Educ Broadcasters; Honolulu Community Media Coun. Mailing Add: 229 Kaalawai Pl Honolulu HI 96816

BITTLE, EDGAR HAROLD (R)
Iowa State Rep
b Des Moines, Iowa, Feb 26, 42; s Harold Albert Bittle & Ruth Davis B; m 1966 to Barbara Paul; c Bradford Paul, Wendy Elizabeth & Deborah Ann. Educ: Cornell Univ, BA in Govt, 64; Univ Mich, Law Sch, JD, 67; Sigma Phi. Polit & Govt Pos: Orgn chmn, Polk Co Rep Party, Iowa, 68-72, precinct committeeman, 68-73; Iowa State Rep, Dist 66, 73- Bus & Prof Pos: Bus attorney, Des Moines, Iowa. Mem: Acanthus Lodge; Nat Orgn Legal Probs in Educ (state chmn); Nat Coun Sch Attorneys (exec comt); Sertoma Club of Des Moines. Relig: Presbyterian; Elder, Cent Presbyterian Church. Mailing Add: 919 45th St West Des Moines IA 50265

BITTLE, RUSSELL HARRY (R)
Pa State Rep
b Pottsville, Pa, Mar 27, 38; s Russell B Bittle & Margaret A Gaffney B; m 1962 to Mary Jane Bietsch; c Russell B, Jr & Timothy B. Educ: Gettysburg Col, AB, 60; Univ Fla, Col Law, 61-62; Dickinson Sch Law, LLB, 64; Kappa Delta Rho; Phi Alpha Delta; Reed Law Club; Corpus Juris Soc. Polit & Govt Pos: Asst dist attorney, Franklin Co, Pa, 65-68; Pa State Rep, Franklin & Cumberland Co, 68-, Minority Caucus Secy, 75- Bus & Prof Pos: Attorney-at-law, with James A Strite, 65-68; pvt practice, 68- Mem: Mason; Chambersburg Rod & Gun Club; CofC; Franklin Co Farmers Asn; Rotary Int. Relig: Lutheran. Legal Res: 811 Woodlawn Circle Chambersburg PA 17201 Mailing Add: Capitol Bldg Harrisburg PA 17120

BIVENS, EDWARD, JR (R)
Mayor, Inkster, Mich
b Indiana, Pa, Feb 8, 23; s Edward Bivens, Sr & Charlotte McCreary B; m 1950 to Irene Edna Stewart; c Annette (Mrs Willia Johnson), Michael Kevin, Nalani Marie, David Edward, Scott W Rennick & stepson Gregory Stewart. Educ: Santa Ana Jr Col, Calif, 46-47; Univ Pittsburgh; Detroit Inst Technol; Wayne State Univ, AB & MEd, 66; Lampodes; Omega Psi Phi. Polit & Govt Pos: Trustee bd educ, Inkster Pub Sch Dist, Mich, 66-68; precinct deleg, Rep Party, 68-70, vchmn, 70-73; mayor, Inkster, Mich, 70-; deleg, Rep Nat Conv, 72. Bus & Prof Pos: Trustee, Mich Munic League, 70-; bd mem, Northwest Child Guid Clin, 71-; chmn, Community United for Action, Western Wayne Co, 72- Mil Serv: Entered as Pvt, Army, 42, released as M/Sgt, 59, after serv in Battery C 85th Artil Bn, Southwest Pac, 42-46, recalled 55, Sgt 1/C. Publ: Abuses of Child Guidance, 68. Mem: Am Newspaper Guild; VFW; Disabled Am Vet; Elks (Exalted Ruler). Relig: Methodist. Legal Res: Apt 16 Bldg K-262 Cherryhill Manor Apts Inkster MI 48141 Mailing Add: 2121 Inkster Rd Inkster MI 48141

BJORLIE, LIV BERGLIOT (D)
b Tolna, NDak, Dec 30, 32; d Frederick T Lundeby & Anna Samuelson L; m 1952 to Elmer Peder Bjorlie; c Peter, Anna, John, Paul & Laura. Educ: Valley City State Teachers Col, 50-51 & 69. Polit & Govt Pos: Pres, Barnes Co Dem Women, NDak, 58-59; dist dir, NDak Dem Party, 61-69, cong campaign dir, 63 & 66; Dem Nat Committeewoman, NDak, formerly; chmn, Dem Mid West Conf Session, 65, mem exec comt, 67-69; mem, President's Coun on Youth, 67; mem, Nat Site Comt & Credentials Comt, Dem Nat Comt, 67-68, mem, Rules Comt, 69, mem, Nat Comn on Rules & mem, Site Comt, 1972 Dem Nat Conv, currently; deleg, Dem Nat Conv, 68 & 72. Bus & Prof Pos: Teacher, 51-52; off mgr, Valley Realty, NDak, 66; off mgr, Farmers Union Ins, 67. Mem: Int Platform Asn; NDak Judicial Comn; Peace Corps Adv Coun; Nat Farmers Union; Zonta. Relig: Lutheran. Mailing Add: 1380 Central Ave N Valley City ND 58072

BJÖRNSON, VAL (R)
b Minneota, Minn, Aug 29, 06; m; c three daughters, two sons. Educ: Univ of Minn, 30. Polit & Govt Pos: State Treas, Minn, 50-54 & 56-75; Rep nominee for US Sen, 54. Bus & Prof Pos: Radio, newspaper fields; assoc ed, St Paul Pioneer Press & Dispatch, 47-50, 55-56. Mil Serv: Navy, 42-46. Mem: Nat Asn of State Auditors, Comptrollers & Treas. Mailing Add: 2914 46th Ave S Minneapolis MN 55406

BLACHLY, QUENTIN A (R)
Chmn, Porter Co Rep Party, Ind
b Hammond, Ind, Sept 10, 34; s Glenn M Blachly & Viola Albert B; m 1957 to Joanne Rogan; c David, Mary Kathryn, Gregory & Joyce Grant. Educ: Valparaiso Univ, AB, 56; Valparaiso Univ Sch Law, LLB, 59; Phi Alpha Delta; Theta Chi. Polit & Govt Pos: Attorney, Valparaiso Zoning & Planning Comns, Ind, formerly; attorney, Kouts; Ind State Rep, 67-68; chmn, Porter Co Rep Party, 68-; mem, Gov Big P Comt, 72- Mem: Am, Ind State & Porter Co Bar Asns; Rotary. Relig: Protestant. Mailing Add: RR 4 Joliet Rd Valparaiso IN 46383

BLACK, CHARLES RAY, JR (R)
Mem Exec Comt, Young Rep Nat Fedn
b Charlotte, NC, Oct 11, 47; s Charles Ray Black, Sr & Lorraine Garrison B; m 1970 to Rozanne Lander; c Wesley Garrison. Educ: Univ Fla, BA, 69; Am Univ Law Sch, JD, 74. Polit & Govt Pos: Dir chap serv, Young Am for Freedom, Inc, 71-72; dir orgn, Jesse Helms for US Senate, 72; spec asst to US Sen Jesse Helms, 73-; mem exec comt, Young Rep Nat Fedn, currently. Mem: Nat Conservative Polit Action Comt (chmn); Am Conserv Union (bd dirs); Charles Edison Mem Youth Fund (bd dirs). Relig: Presbyterian. Legal Res: 5920 Sandy Fork Rd Raleigh NC 27609 Mailing Add: 3709 Colonial Ave Alexandria VA 22309

BLACK, DAVID STATLER (D)
b Everett, Wash, July 14, 28; s Lloyd Llewelyn Black & Gladys Statler B; m 1952 to Nancy Haskell B; c David Lloyd, Andrew Haskell & Kathleen Louise. Educ: Stanford Univ, BA, 50; Univ Wash, LLB, 54; Phi Delta Phi; Delta Kappa Epsilon. Polit & Govt Pos: Asst Attorney Gen, Wash State, 57-61; counsel, Wash Pub Serv Comn, 57-61; gen counsel, Bur Pub Rds, US Dept Com, DC, 61-63; vchmn, Fed Power Comn, 63-66; adminr, Bonneville Power Admin, 66-67; Under Secy of the Interior, 67-69. Bus & Prof Pos: Lawyer, Preston, Thorgrimson & Horwitz, Seattle, Wash, 54-57; vpres & adminr, Dreyfus Corp, New York 69-70; lawyer, Pierson, Ball & Dowd, Washington, DC, 70- Mem: Wash State Bar Asn. Legal Res: 12109 Piney Glen Lane Potomac MD 20854 Mailing Add: Pierson Ball & Dowd 1000 Ring Bldg Washington DC 20036

BLACK, ERNEST F (R)
Secy, Lucas Co Rep Cent Comt, Ohio
b Whitehouse, Ohio, Apr 17, 15; s William Gerard Black & Nettie Elliott B; m 1934 to Evelyn Viola Vitello; c Carolyn (Mrs Roger Kosch). Educ: Monclova High Sch, Ohio, grad, 33. Polit & Govt Pos: Twp constable, Ohio, 43-57; twp trustee, Monclova Twp, Lucas Co, 57-; secy, Lucas Co Rep Cent Comt, Ohio, 63- Bus & Prof Pos: Stationary engr, Toledo Edison Co, 41. Mem: Mason. Relig: Protestant. Mailing Add: 7465 Maumee-Western Rd Maumee OH 43537

BLACK, HARRY GORDON (R)
b Lexington, Ky, Nov 2, 07; s Henry Gordon Black & Nancy Walters B; m 1934 to Dorothy Carr; c Gordon Carr. Educ: Univ Ky Col Law, LLB, 32; Lambda Chi Alpha. Polit & Govt Pos: City attorney, Hawesville, Ky, 40-49; chmn, Hancock Co Rep Party, formerly; co attorney, Hancock Co, 49-70; alt deleg, Rep Nat Conv, 52; mem for Hancock Co, Green River Crime Coun. Mem: Am & Ky State Bar Asns; Am Judicature Soc; Ky Hist Soc; Univ Ky Alumni Asn. Relig: Methodist; Trustee. Mailing Add: Hawesville KY 42348

BLACK, JOHN WOODLAND (D)
Mem, Calif Dem State Cent Comt
b Spokane, Wash, Sept 22, 25; s Hugh James Black & Margaret Woodland B; m 1959 to Iryne Codon; c John McKenzie, Catherine Louise, Bridget Dianne, James Joseph, Ian Andrew & Timothy Matthugh. Educ: Colo Univ, 44-45; Univ Wash, AB, 47; Columbia Univ, M in Int Affairs, 49; George Washington Univ, JD, 59. Polit & Govt Pos: With State Dept, 49-50; foreign serv officer, 50-55; US Sen, 55-61; spec asst to Secy of Com, 61; dep dir, US Travel Serv, 61-64, dir, 65-68; mem, Calif Dem State Cent Comt, 71-, mem exec comt, 73-75; Dem Cand US Rep, 39th Cong Dist, Calif, 72; vchmn, Orange Co Dem Cent Comt, 73- Bus & Prof Pos: Asst dean col law, Western State Univ, 73- Mil Serv: Naval Res, 45-46. Mem: Am Bar Asn. Mailing Add: 1646 Irvine Ave Newport Beach CA 92660

BLACK, KENNETH LEIGH (R)
b Washington, DC, July 29, 39. Educ: Univ SC, BA; Cath Univ. Polit & Govt Pos: Admin asst to US Rep Barry M Goldwater, Jr, Calif, 75- Mil Serv: Army Res, 62-69. Mem: Bull Elephants (chmn); Cong Staff Club (bd dirs). Legal Res: 110 Calhoun St Johnston SC 29401 Mailing Add: 1421 Longworth House Off Bldg Washington DC 20515

BLACK, KENNETH WALLACE (R)
VChmn, Tazewell Co Rep Cent Comt, Ill
b Peoria, Ill, Dec 10, 12; s Wallace J Black & Margaret Robinson B; m 1938 to Edith Adele Lowry; c Barbara (Mrs Robert Walker Brown); Kenneth L & Bruce W. Educ: Bradley Univ, BS, 34; Univ Chicago, JD, 37; Sigma Chi. Polit & Govt Pos: Rep precinct committeeman, Third Precinct, Washington Twp, Ill, 53-; vchmn, Tazewell Co Rep Cent Comt, 53-; pub adminr, Tazewell Co, 56-60; alt deleg, Rep Nat Conv, 68. Bus & Prof Pos: Dir, First Nat Bank of Washington, Ill; city attorney, Washington, 41-53 & 57-; pres, Washington Twp Libr Bd, 51-; chmn, bd of trustees, Bradley Univ, 71-; pres & dir, Ill Valley Libr Syst, 66-70. Mem: Peoria Co & Tazewell Co Bar Asns; Am Judicature Soc; Ill State Bar Asn; Am Bar Asn. Relig: Lutheran. Legal Res: 501 S Main St Washington IL 61571 Mailing Add: PO Box 157 Washington IL 61571

BLACK, LEONA ROBERSON (D)
b Tex, Jan 14, 24; d Eddie Roberson & Mattie Lewis R; m 1946 to David Lanzy Black; wid; c Willie L (deceased). Educ: Prairie View Col, 34-35; Roosevelt Univ, Assoc Degree in Acct/Bus Mgt; Chicago Univ, 62-63 & 64-65; Roosevelt Univ Alumni Soc; Roosevelt Alumni Asn. Polit & Govt Pos: Exec dir, Independent Wards Coalition; mem, Ill Dem Women's Caucus; mem, Independent Polit Orgn; mem, Ill Black Caucus; secy, admin asst, campaign & off mgr, Alderman A A Rayner & Alderman Anna R Langford; southside coordr, Donald

P Moore & Bernard Carey, 72; deleg, Dem Nat Conv, 72; admin chief, Fraud & Complaint Div, Cook Co States Attorney's Off, 72-; dir, Victim-Witness Assistance Proj, 74- Bus & Prof Pos: Key punch operator, time keeper, scale clerk, cost acct clerk & expeditor, Int Harvester Co, Chicago, 54-61; postal clerk & asst supvr during Christmas, 60-63; asst file clerk, financial budget clerk & head financial clerk, Cook Co Dept Pub Aid; asst off Mgr, Oak Forest Hosp. Mem: Roseland Heights Community Orgn; Roseland Community Orgn (bd dirs); Educ Comt, Chicago State Col; Kensington Police Community Workshop; S Chicago Ave Prog for Youth (organizer & bd dirs). Relig: Christian Methodist Episcopal. Mailing Add: 9800 S Martin Luther King Dr Chicago IL 60628

BLACK, SHIRLEY TEMPLE (R)
US Ambassador, Ghana
b Santa Monica, Calif, Apr 23, 28; d George Francis Temple, Sr & Gertrude Cregier T; m 1950 to Charles Alden Black; c Linda Susan, Charles Alden, Jr & Lori Alden. Educ: Westlake Sch, Los Angeles, grad, 45; Col Notre Dame, fel, 72. Polit & Govt Pos: Mem, numerous Rep financial & campaign comts at all levels from co to nat, Calif & US, 52-; mem, Hosp Adv Coun, Calif, 67; mem, Women's Adv Comt, Nixon-Agnew, 68; mem, Rep State Cent Comt, Calif, 68-; mem, Calif Coun on Criminal Justice, 69; chmn, Youth Week Golden Gate Centennial, San Francisco, 69; US deleg to the UN, 69-72; dep chmn, US deleg, UN Prep Comn, UN Conf Human Environ, 70-72; mem US deleg, UN Conf Human Environ, 72; spec asst to chmn, Coun Environ Quality, 72-74; US Ambassador, Ghana, 74- Mem: Acad of Motion Picture Arts & Sci; Acad of TV Arts & Sci; World Affairs Coun, San Francisco; Asia Found; San Francisco Symphony Asn. Honors & Awards: Kiwanis Int Award, Houston, 67; Dame, Order of the Knights of Malta, Paris, France; Hon Gov, Acad of TV Arts & Sci; John Swett Award, Calif Teachers Asn; Annual Laymans Award, Alameda Educ Asn. Relig: Episcopal. Legal Res: Woodside CA 94062 Mailing Add: Am Embassy PO Box 194 Accra Ghana

BLACK, WAYNE L (D)
Dem Nat Committeeman, Utah
b Cowley, Wyo, June 17, 19; m to Bettina; c Six. Educ: Univ Utah, JD. Polit & Govt Pos: Asst co attorney, Salt Lake Co, Utah, 2 years; asst dist attorney, Third Judicial Dist, 3 years; mem, Comn on Uniform State Laws, Utah, currently; chmn, Salt Lake Co Dem Party, 4 years; deleg, Dem Nat Conv, 64, alt deleg, 68; Dem Nat Committeeman, Utah, currently. Bus & Prof Pos: Attorney-at-law. Mil Serv: Lt, Navy, World War II, with serv as Commun Officer, USS Lunga Point; Participated in Leyte, Lingayan Gulf, Iwo Jima, Okinawa & Yellow Sea Opers; Presidential Unit Citation. Mem: Phi Alpha Delta; Univ Club. Honors & Awards: Appeared before US Supreme Court, Circuit Court of Appeals, Fed & State Courts as trial & appellate attorney. Relig: Latter-day Saint. Legal Res: 3941 Mt Olympus Way Salt Lake City UT 84117 Mailing Add: Suite 400 10 Broadway Bldg Salt Lake City UT 84101

BLACK, WILFORD REX, JR (D)
Utah State Sen
b Salt Lake City, Utah, Jan 31, 20; s Wilford Rex Black, Sr & Elsie Isabelle Manning B; m 1942 to Helen Shirley Frazer; c Susan (Mrs Richard Lee Blackwell), Janet (Mrs Ralph Colby Rytting), Cindy Gay, Joy Lynne, Peggy Ann, Vanna Rae, Helen Gayle & Rex Frazer. Educ: Cyprus High Sch, Magna, Utah, grad, 38. Polit & Govt Pos: Deleg, Dem state & co conv, Utah, 68; Dem voting dist chmn, 70-72; Utah State Sen, 73- Bus & Prof Pos: Locomotive engr, Denver & Rio Grande RR, 41-; pres bd, Rail-Ops Credit Union, 59-; secy Utah state legis bd, United Transportation Union, 69-, legis rep, Local 1038, 69-, vice local chmn, 70- Mil Serv: Entered as Pvt, Army, 42, released as T/4 Sgt, 45, after serv in 729 Rwy Bn, ETO, 43-45; Good Conduct Medal; Four Battle Stars. Mem: DAV. Relig: Latter-day Saint. Mailing Add: 826 N 1300 West Salt Lake City UT 84116

BLACKBURN, BEN B (R)
Gen Counsel, DeKalb Co Rep Exec Comt, Ga
b Atlanta, Ga, Feb 14, 27; m to Mary Pandora; c Michael James, Robert Bentley, Kathryn Ann & David Thomas. Educ: Emory Univ, Atlanta, 44-45; Univ NC, Chapel Hill, AB, 47; Emory Univ Law Sch, LLB, 54. Polit & Govt Pos: Rep precinct worker, 54-64; with State Attorney Gen Off, Ga, 55-56; secy, Fourth Cong Dist Rep Exec Comt; gen counsel, DeKalb Co Rep Exec Comt, 64-; chmn, DeKalb Co Conv, 66; US Rep, Ga, 67-74; deleg, Rep Nat Conv, 72. Bus & Prof Pos: Dept store supvr, W T Grant Co, Richmond, Va, 49; salesman, Union Carbide Nat Carbon Div, 49-50; attorney, 56- Mil Serv: Navy, V-12 Training 44-46, Lt(jg), 50-52. Mem: Am, Ga, Atlanta & Decatur-DeKalb Bar Asns; Lawyers Club. Relig: Episcopal. Mailing Add: 1274 Brookforest Dr NE Atlanta GA 30324

BLACKBURN, CLARENCE, JR (D)
Tenn State Rep
Mailing Add: Pine Hill Blountville TN 37617

BLACKBURN, MCKINLEY LEE (R)
Chmn, Sixth Cong Dist Rep Party, SC
b Augusta, Ga, Apr 3, 32; s Otis W Blackburn & Evelyn Howland B; m 1956 to Barbara Jean Crosby; c Cynthia Ann, McKinley Lee, Jr & Deborah Diane. Educ: The Citadel, BS, 56; Brigadier Club, Inc; Pee Dee Citadel Club. Polit & Govt Pos: Precinct chmn, Florence Co Rep Party, SC, 70-72, co chmn, 72-74; chmn, Sixth Cong Dist Rep Party, 74-; dist chmn for Gov Edwards, 75. Bus & Prof Pos: Engr, Southern Bell Tel & Tel Co, 56-72, develop supvr, 72- Mil Serv: Entered as Seaman, Navy, 50, released as Yeoman 3/C, 52. Mem: VFW Post 3181 (sr vcomdr); AFM; CofC; Lions; United Way. Honors & Awards: SC State Serv Award, Jaycees, 63 & 65; Southern Bell Tel & Tel Co Community Serv Award, 63 & 65; VFW SC Community Serv Award, 68; Scouter's Key, Boy Scouts, 70. Relig: Baptist. Mailing Add: 1919 E Sandhurst Dr Florence SC 29501

BLACKBURN, ROBERT E, JR (D)
Fla State Rep
b Tampa, Fla, Dec 5, 12; s R Ed Blackburn & Mary Edmondson B; m 1940 to Frances Catherine Bishop; c Barbara (Mrs Cook). Educ: Univ Fla, 2 years; Univ Tampa, 6 months. Polit & Govt Pos: Mem, Hillsborough Co Port Authority, 49-52; sheriff, Hillsborough Co, Fla, 53-65; Fla State Rep, 69- Bus & Prof Pos: Merchant, Tampa, Fla, 43-50; real estate broker, 50-52; spec agent, Bankers Life Co, 65- Mem: Fla Sheriffs Asn (hon life mem); Fla Sheriffs Boys Ranch; Future Farmers of Am (hon life mem). Relig: Methodist. Legal Res: 312 Glen Ridge Ave Temple Terrace FL 33617 Mailing Add: PO Box 16624 Temple Terrace FL 33687

BLACKHAM, ANN ROSEMARY (R)
VPres, Nat Fedn of Rep Women
b New York, NY, June 16, 27; d Frederick Alfred DeCain & Letitia Stolfe D; m 1951 to James William Blackham, Jr; c Ann Constance & James William, III. Educ: Ohio Dominican Col, AB, 49; Ohio State Univ, MA, 50; Lincoln Filene Sch Mgr, cert, 51; Nat Poetry Award Soc; Eng Honors Soc; Jr League of Cath Women; Rho Sigma Beta; Fashion Inst; Lit Guild. Polit & Govt Pos: Chmn precinct III, Winchester Rep Town Comt, Mass, 56-65; chmn, Winchester Rep Finance Comt, 59-64; membership chmn, Mass Fedn Rep Women, 60-62, finance chmn, 62-64; pres, Women's Rep Club Winchester, 60-62; vchmn, Winchester Rep Town Comt, 64-65; pres, Mass Fedn Rep Women, 64-69; assoc mem exec comt, Mass Rep State Comt, 64-69, dep chmn, 65-66; mem, Mass State Civil Defense Coun, 65-; New Eng regional dir, Nat Fedn Rep Women, 67-, secy, 68-72, vpres, 72-; alt deleg, Rep Nat Conv, 68 & 72; mem, President's Task Force on Women's Rights & Responsibilities; mem, Bd of Econ Adv to the Gov; mem, Special Comn on the Economy of the Commonwealth; vchmn, Mass Rep Finance Comt, 70-; chmn, Gov Comn Status Women, 70-; mem, Gov Ad Hoc Judicial Selection Comn, 72-73. Bus & Prof Pos: Store mgr, Filene's Dept Store, Winchester, 51-53; sales mgr & corporate dir, James T Trefrey, Inc, Realtor, 66-68; pres & founder, Ann Blackham & Co, Realtors, 68-; bd dirs, Gtr Boston Real Estate Bd, 72-73; corporator & trustee, Charlestown Savings Bank, 74- Mem: Brokers Inst; Nat Asn Real Estate Bd; Mass Asn Real Estate Bd; League Women Voters; Doric Dames (treas founding bd, 70-71, vpres, 71-73). Honors & Awards: Broadcaster's award, Civic Leadership, 62; Mass Order Paul Revere Patriots; Mass Award Meritorious Serv, 74; Mass Fed Women's Club Pub Serv Award, 75. Relig: Catholic. Mailing Add: 33 Canterbury Rd Winchester MA 01890

BLACKMAN, RICK ROBERT (R)
b San Francisco, Calif, Feb 3, 48; s Robert Ralph Blackman & Mary Kelley B; single. Educ: Calif State Univ, San Jose, currently. Polit & Govt Pos: Staff intern, Calif State Assemblyman Crandall's Dist Off, 70; mem, Santa Clara Co Rep Cent Comt, 71-74, youth chmn, 71-72; field staff, Calif Comt to Reelect President Nixon, 72; deleg, Rep Nat Conv, 72; mem, Rep State Cent Comt, Calif, 73-74. Legal Res: Apt 1-A 476 S Seventh St San Jose CA 95112 Mailing Add: PO Box 4865 San Jose CA 95126

BLACKMUN, HARRY ANDREW
Assoc Justice, US Supreme Court
b Nashville, Ill, Nov 12, 08; s Corwin M Blackmun & Theo H Reuter B; m 1941 to Dorothy E Clark; c Nancy Clark, Sally Ann & Susan Manning. Educ: Harvard Univ, BA summa cum laude, 29, LLB, 32; Phi Beta Kappa. Hon Degrees: LLD, DePauw Univ, 71, Hamline Univ, 71, Ohio Wesleyan Univ, 71, Morningside Col, 72, Wilson Col, 72, Dickinson Sch Law, 73 & Ohio Northern Univ, 73. Polit & Govt Pos: US Circuit Judge, Eighth Circuit Court of Appeals, 59-70; assoc justice, US Supreme Court, 70- Bus & Prof Pos: Law clerk, Hon John B Sanborn, US Court of Appeals, 32-33; assoc, jr partner & partner, Dorsey, Colman, Barker, Scott & Barber, & predecessor firms, Minneapolis, Minn, 34-50; gen counsel & mem sect of admin, Mayo Clin, Rochester, 50-59; dir, Rochester Airport Co, 52-60; dir & mem exec comt, Rochester Methodist Hosp, 54-70; dir, Kahler Corp, 58-63; trustee, William Mitchell Col Law, 59-74; trustee, Hamline Univ, 64-70; mem, Adv Comt on Research to Fed Judicial Ctr, 68-70; mem, Adv Comt on the Judge's Function to Am Bar Asn Spec Comt on Minimum Standards for the Admin of Criminal Justice, 69-70. Publ: Miscellaneous articles in legal & med publ. Mem: Mayo Asn, Rochester, Minn; Am & Minn Bar Asns; Olmsted Co Third Judicial Dist Bar Asn; Rotary Club Rochester. Relig: Methodist; Trustee & mem bd publ, Methodist Church, 60-72. Legal Res: Arlington VA Mailing Add: US Supreme Ct Washington DC 20543

BLACKORBY, LILA ROSE (R)
Committeeman, Ill Rep State Cent Comt
b Jerseyville, Ill; d Arthur William Dabbs & Lora Reed D; m 1946 to Harold Richard Blackorby; c Peggy (Mrs Paul Wheaton) & David. Educ: High Sch, grad. Polit & Govt Pos: Committeewoman, Jersey Co Rep Party, Ill, 51-60, dep registr, 51-; deleg, Ill Rep Women's Conv, 52-68; vpres, Jersey Co Rep Women's Club, 56-60 & 66-, membership chmn, 60-69; deleg, Judicial Comn, 59 & 64; precinct committeewoman, Ninth Precinct, Jersey Co Rep State Comt, 60-, secy, 63-69; dep co clerk & recorder of deeds, Jersey Co, 62-; deleg, Rep State Conv, 62, 64 & 66; deleg, Appellate Judicial Conv, 64; chmn, Gov Ogilvie's Campaign, 68; committeeman, Ill Rep State Cent Comt, currently. Relig: Methodist. Mailing Add: 205 Walton Jerseyville IL 62052

BLACKSHEAR, JESSE (D)
Ga State Rep
Mailing Add: PO Box 9182 Savannah GA 31401

BLACKWELL, DAVID M (D)
NC State Rep
Mailing Add: 1206 Maiden Lane Reidsville NC 27320

BLACKWELL, LUCIEN E (D)
Pa State Rep
Mailing Add: Capitol Bldg Harrisburg PA 17120

BLACKWELL, MORTON CLYDE (R)
Mem Exec Comt, Young Rep Nat Fedn
b La Jara, Colo, Nov 16, 39; s William George Blackwell & Rebecca Barbara Blissard B; m 1972 to Helen Jane Reddy. Educ: La State Univ; Phi Eta Sigma; Alpha Chi Sigma; Phi Gamma Delta; Varsity Debate Sq; Young Rep, La State Univ Young Am for Freedom. Polit & Govt Pos: Pres, Baton Rouge Young Rep, 62-63; state col chmn, La Young Rep Fedn, 63-64, chmn, 64-66; mem from East Baton Rouge Parish, La State Rep Cent Comt, 63-72; mem nat steering comt, Youth for Goldwater, 64; deleg, Rep Nat Conv, 64, alt deleg, 68; dir, Sparky Hall for Cong Campaign, Sixth Dist, La, 66; Young Rep Nat Committeeman, La, 66-70; student activities coordr, Louis Nunn Ky Gubernatorial Campaign, 67; exec dir, Col Rep Nat Comt, 68-70; mem exec comt, Young Rep Nat Fedn, 71-; chmn, Comt for Responsible Youth Polit, 71-; mem, Arlington Co Rep Comt, Va, 72- Bus & Prof Pos: Pres, Admin Co, 64-; polit consult, youth orgn, 70-; acct exec, Richard A Viguerie Co, 72- Honors & Awards: Youngest deleg, 1964 Rep Nat Conv. Relig: Episcopal. Mailing Add: 3128 N 17th St Arlington VA 22201

BLACKWELL, ROBERT (D)
Asst Secy Maritime Affairs, Dept Com
Legal Res: VA Mailing Add: Dept of Commerce Washington DC 20230

BLACKWELL, W E (BILL) (D)
Mo State Rep
Mailing Add: Rte 2 Hermann MO 65041

BLACKWELL, WALLACE NORMAN (R)
b Augusta, Ga, Mar 25, 27; s Miller James Blackwell & Maureen McNorril B; m 1952 to Joan Blount; c Wallace N, II (Wally) & Clete Rivers. Educ: US Merchant Marine Acad, BS, 48. Polit & Govt Pos: City chmn, North Augusta Munic Rep Party, SC, 67-70; chmn, Aiken Co Rep Party, formerly. Bus & Prof Pos: Area engr, E I Du Pont de Nemours, 58-70. Mil Serv: Entered as Ens, Navy, 48, released as Lt(jg), 51 after serv in USS Helena (CA 75), US 7th Fleet, Korea, 49-51; Theatre Ribbons; Korean Action; UN Medal. Mem: Instrument Soc Am; Am Legion Post 71; North Augusta Optimist Club. Relig: Baptist. Mailing Add: 1118 Crestview Dr North Augusta SC 29841

BLADES, RAY (R)
Mem, Mo Rep State Comt
b Holliday, Mo, Nov 10, 17; s Ira Jean Blades & Susie Krembs B; m 1941 to Lucille Fisher; c Joy & Kent. Educ: Holliday High Sch, Mo, grad. Polit & Govt Pos: Sgt-at-arms, Rep Nat Conv, 68; chmn, Monroe Co Rep Party, Mo, 68-; mem, Mo Rep State Comt, 68-; mem, Mo State Rep Adv Comt, Ninth Dist, 69- Bus & Prof Pos: Farmer & cattle raiser, NMo. Mem: Progressive Club, Paris, Mo; Moose, Moberly; Mark Twain Country Club, Paris. Honors & Awards: Attended Inauguration of President Nixon, Washington, DC, 69. Relig: Disciples of Christ. Mailing Add: Rte 1 Paris MO 65275

BLAHUTA, RENEE MARIA (R)
Pres, Alaska Fedn Rep Women
b Linz, Austria, June 17, 32; d Hans Kolman & Maria Keck K; m 1953 to Ludvik Alton Blahuta; c Audrey Renee. Educ: High sch, Linz, Austria, grad, 50. Polit & Govt Pos: Pres, Fairbanks Rep Women's Club, 70-72 & Alaska Fedn Rep Women, 74- Bus & Prof Pos: Asst to archivist & curator manuscripts, Univ Alaska, Fairbanks, 70- Mem: Alaska Libr Asn. Relig: Roman Catholic. Mailing Add: 1919 Jack St Fairbanks AK 99701

BLAINE, RICHARD ALLAN (R)
RI State Rep
b Newton, Mass, Mar 26, 28; s Irving E Blaine & Hope Woodmansee B; m 1951 to Charlotte Eldredge; c Susan Elizabeth, Robin Ann & Richard A, Jr. Educ: Univ RI, BS, 49. Polit & Govt Pos: Mem, Scituate Zoning B of Rev, RI, 65-68; mem, Scituate Rep Town Comt, 66-; RI State Rep, 54th Dist, 68- Mil Serv: Pvt, Army, Specialized Training Res Prog, 45-46. Mem: RI Asn Ins Agents; F&AM; Scituate Lions; Scituate Libr (bd dirs); Scituate Rep Club. Relig: Congregational. Legal Res: Rockland Rd North Scituate RI 02857 Mailing Add: Box 155 North Scituate RI 02857

BLAIR, CECIL R (D)
La State Sen
Mailing Add: PO Box M Lecompte LA 71346

BLAIR, FRANK S (R)
Chmn, Weber Co Rep Party, Utah
b Ogden, Utah, July 2, 28; s J Clifford Blair & Charlotte Skeen B; single. Educ: Weber State Col, AS, 48; Brigham Young Univ, BS, 53; EDD; Univ Utah, 55-57; Phoenix; Brigadiers. Polit & Govt Pos: Chmn, Rep Voting Dist, Ogden, Utah, 63-65 & Legis Dist, 65-69; chmn, Weber Co Rep Party, Utah, 73-; chmn cent comt, 73-; mem, Utah State Rep Cent Comt, 73- Bus & Prof Pos: Co-owner, Meadow Brook Dairies, Ogden, Utah, 43-48; adminr, Ogden City Schs, 62-73; instr, Weber State Col, 70-71; developer & owner, Col Mall, 70-; coop educ specialist, State of Utah, Salt Lake City, 73-; instr, Brigham Young Univ, formerly. Mil Serv: Entered as Ens, Naval Res, 53, released as Lt(jg), 55, after serv in Amphibious Forces, Pac; Comdr, Naval Res, currently; Korean, Good Conduct & Int Forces Medals. Publ: Auth, Uncle uncle, Utah Sch Adminr, 71. Mem: Phi Delta Kappa (pres, 71-72); Rotary Int; Weber Co Libr Bd (chmn, 69-); Phi Rho Pi; Ben Lomond Coun Int Reading Asn. Honors & Awards: Master M Men Award, Latter-day Saint Church, 59; Distinguished Admission Adv, Brigham Young Univ, 69 & 71. Relig: Latter-day Saint. Mailing Add: 1063 S 1200 W Ogden UT 84401

BLAIR, JAMES B (D)
Chief Legal Counsel, Dem Party, Ark
b Elkins, Ark, Oct 27, 35; s William Joe Blair & Mildred Woolsey B; m 1957 to Margaret Gibson; c Heather Elaine, Arden Sue & James Rufus. Educ: Univ Ark, BA, 55, JD, 57; Blue Key, Delta Theta Phi Scholar Key; Phi Eta Sigma; Acacia. Polit & Govt Pos: Campaign mgr, Washington Co Young Dem, Ark, 64, pres, 65; legal counsel, Young Dem of Ark Clubs, 65-66; deleg, Dem Nat Conv, 68 & 72; deleg, Ark State Dem Conv, 68, 70 & 72; mem, State Cent & Exec Comts & chief legal counsel, Dem Party, Ark, 68- Bus & Prof Pos: Ed & chief, Ark Law Rev, 56-57; lawyer, Fayetteville, 57; partner, Crouch, Jones & Blair, Springdale, 59, Crouch, Jones, Blair & Cypert, & Crouch, Jones, Cypert & Waters, 69. Mem: Washington Co, Ark & Am Bar Asns; Local Bar Asn; Motor Carrier Lawyers Asn. Relig: Baptist. Legal Res: Rte 9 Fayetteville AR 72701 Mailing Add: 111 Holcomb Springdale AR 72764

BLAIR, JAMES H
Asst Secy Housing & Urban Develop for Fair Housing & Equal Opportunity
Mailing Add: Dept of Housing & Urban Develop Washington DC 20410

BLAIR, RUSSELL (D)
Hawaii State Rep
Mailing Add: House Sgt-at-Arms State Capitol Honolulu HI 96813

BLAIR, SCOTT (R)
Wash State Rep
Mailing Add: 8712 25th Ave NE Seattle WA 98115

BLAIR, W ROBERT (R)
b Clarksburg, WVa, Oct 22, 30; s William Robert Blair & Eleanor Price B; m 1952 to Patricia Louise Gochenour; c Steven, Mark & Susan. Educ: WVa Univ, AB, 52, LLB, 54; Phi Kappa Psi; Phi Delta Phi; Mountain; Sphinx Coun of Fraternity Pres; Fi Bator Capor; comdr, Arnold Air Soc; Mountaineer Week Team; Gtr WVa Weekend Comt. Polit & Govt Pos: Legal consult, Park Forest Planning Comn, Ill, 59-61; Rep precinct committeeman, Monee Twp, Will Co, 59-71; vchmn & mem exec comt, Will Co Rep Cent Comt, 62-71; Ill State Rep, 64-74, chmn, Vet Affairs Personnel & Pension Comt, mem, Ill Hwy Study Comt, 65-71; chmn, 67-71, vchmn, Ill Pub Employee Pension Laws Comt, 67-70, Speaker of the House, 71-74; deleg, Rep Nat Conv, 72; chmn, Transportation Study Comn & Mem Exec Comt, Nat Conf State Legis Leaders, currently. Bus & Prof Pos: Attorney-at-law, 54-; pres, Fairfax Realty Co, 60-; asst to pres, Swift & Co, 61-63. Mil Serv: Entered as 2nd Lt, Air Force, 54, released as 1st Lt, 56, after serv as a Judge Adv in Tech Training; Nat Defense Serv Medal. Mem: Will Co, Ill State & Am Bar Asns; South Suburban, Ill State & Nat Asn Real Estate Bd. Relig: Methodist. Legal Res: 124 Shabbona Dr Park Forest IL 60466 Mailing Add: PO Box 157 Crete IL 60417

BLAISDELL, CLESSON J (D)
NH State Sen
b Keene, NH, Sept 18, 26; married; c Three. Educ: Keene High Sch. Polit & Govt Pos: NH State Rep, until 67; ward checklist supvr; former selectman; mem, State Softball Comn; mem, State Athletic Comt; NH State Sen, 75- Bus & Prof Pos: Sporting goods salesman, Keene. Mil Serv: Navy, 44-46. Mem: Kiwanis; KofC (4 degree); Am Legion; Little League Comn. Relig: Catholic. Mailing Add: 72 Ridgewood Ave Keene NH 03431

BLAKE, JOSEPH BRADLEY (R)
Chmn, Denver Co Rep Party, Colo
b Denver, Colo, Dec 24, 35; s John Leorn Blake & Berniece Clarke B; m 1964 to Elizabeth Rowland; c Anne Clarke & Joseph Bradley, Jr. Educ: Dartmouth Col, BA, 58; Univ Colo, LLB, 61; Kappa Sigma. Polit & Govt Pos: Spec agt, Fed Bur Invest, 61-64; legis asst to Sen Gordon Allott, Colo, 67-70; regional counsel & dep regional adv, US Dept Housing & Urban Develop, Denver, 70-74; chmn, Denver Co Rep Party, 75- Bus & Prof Pos: Vpres & regional mgr, Ticor Mortgage Ins, 74- Mem: Denver Rotary Club (secy, 75-); YMCA (bd dirs, 74-); Colo Bar Asn; St Joseph Hosp (bd dirs, 75-); Denver Law Club. Relig: Presbyterian. Mailing Add: 6225 E 17th Ave Pkwy Denver CO 80220

BLAKE, ROY CLIFFORD, SR (R)
Chmn, Brooklin Town Rep Comt, Maine
b Brooklin, Maine, June 21, 99; s Charles Deering Blake & Annie Frances Batcheler B; m 1926 to Catherine Veronica Ryan; c Roy C, Jr. Educ: Univ Maine; City Col New York. Polit & Govt Pos: Chmn, Brooklin Town Rep Comt, Maine, 57-; committeeman, Maine State Rep Comt, 58-68; chmn, Maine Bd Arbit & Conciliation, 65-67; treas, Hancock Co, 66-; chmn, Second Cong Dist Rep Orgn, 68-69; chmn, Hancock Co Rep Comt, 70-72. Bus & Prof Pos: Bookkeeper, Maine Lighterage Co, New York, 22-24; spec rep, J C Penney Co, 24-52; dep sheriff, Hancock Co, Maine, 57-66. Mem: AF&AM; KT; Consistory; Shrine; Hancock Co Shrine Club. Mailing Add: Carolo Acres Brooklin ME 04616

BLAKE, ROY M (D)
Tex State Rep
Mailing Add: 324 Burrows Nacogdoches TX 75961

BLAKELEY, CLAUDE R, JR (R)
Mo State Rep
Mailing Add: 436 W Brook Neosho MO 64850

BLAKELEY, GARY (D)
Nat Committeeman, NMex Young Dem
b New Orleans, La, Sept 2, 48; s Jess Chancey Blakeley & Dorothy Brown B; single. Educ: Eastern NMex Univ, BS, 70; Univ NMex, one year. Polit & Govt Pos: Permanent page-boy, NMex State Senate, 63-64, student intern, 66-67, bill reader, 29th Session; legis asst to Off Lt Gov, NMex, 64-66; pres, NMex Teen Dem, 64-66; mem exec comt, NMex Young Dem Clubs, 65-, vpres, 68-71, chmn, 68-69; pres, Roosevelt Co Young Dem Clubs, 66-68; mem, NMex Gov Comt on Children & Youth, 66-; student intern & staff aide, Off NMex Secy of State, 68-69; mem, NMex Youth Adv Comn on the Selective Serv, 70-; dir govt affairs, Albuquerque CofC, 72-; nat committeeman, NMex Young Dem, 75- Bus & Prof Pos: Mem bd dirs, McKillip Ins, Inc, 70- Mem: Nat Asn Col Student Govt; Mason; Order of DeMolay; NMex Boy's State Prog; Key Club Am. Honors & Awards: Outstanding DeMolay of NMex, 65; Outstanding Young Citizen of NMex, DAR & Am Legion, 66; NMex Distinguished Serv Award, 71. Relig: Baptist. Mailing Add: 401 Second St Albuquerque NM 87101

BLAKELY, RONNY D (R)
b Nashville, Ark, Apr 21, 40; s Henry Marcus Blakely & Ethel Leone Elder B; m 1959 to Jeanne Neece; c Mark Kevin (Kip). Educ: Univ Ark, Fayetteville, 4 years; Letterman's Club. Polit & Govt Pos: Vchmn, Howard Co Rep Party, Ark, 66-70, chmn, 70-74; comnr, Nashville City Planning Comn. Bus & Prof Pos: Credit mgr & asst mgr, Smith Bros Furniture, 62-63; field underwriter, Mutual of NY, 63-65; owner, Ronny Blakely Ins Agency, 65-66; owner, Hillside Ins & Investment Co, 66-; dir, Nashville Fed Savings & Loan Asn. Mem: Nashville PTA (pres); Nashville CofC (pres); Nashville Rotary (dir). Relig: Baptist. Legal Res: 617 N Fourth St Nashville AR 71852 Mailing Add: PO Box 237 Nashville AR 71852

BLAKEMORE, RICHARD EUGENE (D)
Nev State Sen
b Parsons, Kans, Sept 21, 22; s John Butler Blakemore & Carolyn Fox B; m 1958 to Angela Catherine Majerus; c Brian Fox & John Russell. Educ: Pasadena Jr Col, 2 years. Polit & Govt Pos: Mem, Nev Dem State Cent Comt, 62 & 64; chmn, Nye Co Dem Cent Comt, Nev, 62 & 64, mem, 68-; deleg, Dem Nat Conv, 68; Nev State Sen for Nye, Mineral, White Pine, Lincoln & Esmeralda Counties, 72- Mil Serv: Entered as A/S, Navy, 40, released as Chief PO, 46, after serv in Torpedo Squadron 12, Air Group 12, S & Southwest Pac, 42-44; Personal Citation; Air Medal. Mem: CofC; Lions; Nev Aviation Trades Asn; Elks; Shrine. Relig: Protestant. Mailing Add: Tonopah Airport Box 672 Tonopah NV 89049

BLAKNEY, E R (D)
b Lynn Co, Tex, Oct 1, 19; s Earnest R Blakney & Dora McBee B; m 1940 to Nell Shadden; c Sharon, Richard Max & Gerald M Ince. Polit & Govt Pos: Precinct chmn, Dem Party, Tex, 54-70; chmn, Lynn Co Dem Party, formerly. Mil Serv: Entered as Pvt, Army, 44, released as T-5, 46, after serv in 32nd Div, Pac, 45-46. Relig: Methodist. Mailing Add: New Home TX 79383

BLANCETT, THOMAS JOSEPH (R)
Chmn, Neosho Co Rep Comt, Kans
b Pittsburg, Kans, July 13, 25; s Thomas J Blancett & Josephine Yartz B; m 1950 to Pearl Alford; c Thomas J, III & Rick M. Educ: Pittsburg State Col, 3 years. Polit & Govt Pos: Chmn, Neosho Co Rep Cent Comt, Kans, 66-; precinct committeeman, currently. Mil Serv: Entered as Pvt, Marine Corps, 43, released as Cpl, 46, after serv in 5th Marine Div, Pac Theater, Iwo

Jima, 44-46. Mem: Am Legion (dist comdr); VFW; Elks. Relig: Protestant. Mailing Add: 11 E Eighth Chanute KS 66720

BLANCHARD, JAMES JOHNSTON (D)
US Rep, Mich
b Detroit, Mich, Aug 8, 42; s James Robert Blanchard & Rosalie Johnston Snyder B; m 1966 to Paula Parker; c Jay. Educ: Mich State Univ, BA, 64, MBA, 65; Univ Minn Law Sch, JD, 68; Blue Key; Delta Tau Delta. Polit & Govt Pos: Asst Attorney Gen, Mich, 69-74; admin asst to Attorney Gen, Mich, 70-71; Asst Dep Attorney Gen, 71-72; US Rep, Mich, 75- Mem: Am Bar Asn; Asn Asst Attorneys Gen; Ferndale Jaycees; Mich State Univ Alumni Asn Oakland Co (exec bd). Legal Res: 1 Woodside Pleasant Ridge MI 48069 Mailing Add: 301 W Fourth St Royal Oak MI 48067

BLANCHARD, JAMES LENDSAY (R)
b Thomson, Ga, June 27, 19; s James Wilson Blanchard & Frankie Paschal B; m 1945 to Frances Stewart. Educ: Thomson High Sch, grad. Polit & Govt Pos: Alderman, Sparta, Ga, 53-54; chmn, Hancock Co Rep Party, formerly. Bus & Prof Pos: Self employed, feed & farm supply bus, 45- Mil Serv: Entered as Pvt, Army, 40, released as 2nd Lt, 45, after serv in 862nd AAA (AW) Bn, Aleutian Islands, 43-44. Mem: VFW (comdr, 48); Am Legion; Masonic Blue Lodge; Shrine; Scottish Rite. Relig: Protestant. Legal Res: Rabun St Sparta GA 31087 Mailing Add: PO Box 26 Sparta GA 31087

BLANCHETTE, PATRICIA LOUISE (D)
NH State Rep
b Exeter, NH, Mar 6, 52; d Thomas Jennings, Sr & Jean Jordan J; div. Educ: Univ NH, BA. Polit & Govt Pos: NH State Rep, 74- Mem: Nat Asn Social Workers. Mailing Add: 3 Central St Newmarket NH 03857

BLANCK, RICHARD JOSEPH (R)
Chmn, Cooper Co Rep Cent Comt, Mo
b Boonville, Mo, June 11, 35; s Albert Frank Blanck, Sr & Mildred Whitehurse B; m 1960 to Danielle Louise Snow; c Amanda Louise, Richard Joseph, Jr, Kathryn Louise, Susan Louise & Neil Edward. Educ: Univ Mo-Columbia, BS in bus & pub admin, 57, SJD, 61; Phi Delta Phi. Polit & Govt Pos: Prosecuting attorney, Cooper Co, Mo, 64-72; chmn, Cooper Co Rep Cent Comt, 74-; chmn, Fourth Cong Dist Rep Comt, 74-; mem, Coord Bd for Higher Educ for State of Mo, 75- Bus & Prof Pos: Lawyer-pvt practice, Butler, Mo, 61-62 & Conway & Blanck, Boonville, 62- Mil Serv: Entered as 2nd Lt, Army, 57, released as 1st Lt, 59, after serv in 7th Inf Div Artil, Korea, 58-59. Mem: Boonville CofC (dir, 74-); SS Peter & Paul's Parish Coun (pres, 74-); Boonslick Concerts, Inc (pres, 75); Kiwanis; KofC. Relig: Roman Catholic. Legal Res: 818 Bingham Rd Boonville MO 65233 Mailing Add: 215 Main St Boonville MO 65233

BLANDFORD, DONALD JOSEPH (D)
Ky State Rep
b Detroit, Mich, Apr 4, 38; s Joseph Ellis Blandford & Maude Merrimee B; m 1961 to Mary Jane O'Bryan. Educ: Owensboro Cath High Sch, grad. Polit & Govt Pos: Ky State Rep, 68- Bus & Prof Pos: Raiser, purebred cattle, currently. Mem: Farm Bur; Nat Farmers Orgn; Am Polled Hereford Asn. Relig: Catholic. Mailing Add: RR 2 Philpot KY 42366

BLANDFORD, JOHN RUSSELL (R)
b Buffalo, NY, Feb 20, 18; s Raymond S Blandford & Mary Jennie Pooley Perkins B; m 1944 to Barbara Jane Waterhouse; c Marcia Ann (Mrs Irwin R Hoener). Educ: Hobart Col, BA, 39; Yale Law Sch, LLB, 46; Phi Beta Kappa; Tau Kappa Alpha. Polit & Govt Pos: Counsel, US House of Rep Armed Serv Comt, 42-63, chief counsel, 63-72. Mil Serv: Entered as 2nd Lt, Marine Corps, 41, released as Maj, 46, after serv in First Marine Div, Pac Theater, Guadalcanal & New Britain, Res; Maj Gen, Res; Presidential Unit Citation; Theater Ribbons with Stars; Legion of Merit; Army, Navy & Air Force Distinguished Pub Serv Awards. Mem: NY, Va & DC Bars; US Supreme Court; Sojourners Lodge. Honors & Awards: Rockefeller Pub Serv Award, for Law & Legis, 66. Relig: Methodist. Legal Res: 4520 N 39th St Arlington VA 22207 Mailing Add: 1815 N Ft Myer Dr Arlington VA 22209

BLANEK, FRANK JOSEPH, JR (D)
Committeeman, Ill Dem Cent Comt
b Panama CZ, Jan 7, 35; s Frank Blanek, Sr & Betty Drosdova B; m 1958 to Sally Ann Miller; c Michael, Betty Lynn, Debbie & Donna. Educ: St Procopious Col, BA, Pol Sci; vchmn, Student Govt Assoc. Polit & Govt Pos: Chmn, Dem Orgn Lisle Twp, Ill, 68-; Dem committeeman, Lisle Seventh Precinct, Lisle Twp, currently; mem, Dupage Co Dem Cent Comt, currently; committeeman, Ill Dem Cent Comt, 67- Bus & Prof Pos: Supvr, Int Harvester Co; pres, Benet Realty Co, currently. Mil Serv: Entered as E-2, Army Nat Guard, 56, released as Sgt, 62, after serv in 133rd Signal Bn; Top Honor Student, Ft Leonard Wood, Mo. Mem: Homewoners Orgn; Ill Youth Comn (regional adv bd). Honors & Awards: Chicago Tribune Outstanding Achievement Award, Army Nat Guard, 61. Relig: Catholic. Mailing Add: 1606 Burlington Ave Lisle IL 60532

BLANGERS, NELL ELIZABETH (D)
Dem Nat Committeewoman, Kans
b Kansas City, Mo, June 18, 09; d Roy Cleveland Solomon & Mary Elizabeth Hanson S; m 1947 to Clement John Blangers. Educ: St Joseph's Acad, Fontbonne, St Louis, Mo. Polit & Govt Pos: VChmn, Sixth Dist Kans Dem Fedn Womens Clubs, 58-60; vchmn, Saline Co Dem Cent Comt, 58-60, chmn, formerly. vchmn, Kans Sixth Cong Dist, 58-62; vchmn, First Dist Kans Dem Fedn Womens Clubs, 62-64; vchmn, Kans Dem State Comn, 64-65; Dem Nat Committeewoman, Kans, 65-; deleg, Dem Nat Conv, 68 & 72; mem, Kans State Dem Comt, currently. Bus & Prof Pos: Mem, Saline Co Adv Coun, Kans Health Facilities Information Serv, 64 & 65. Mem: Saline Co Adv Coun, Kans Health Facilities Information Club; Womens Kans Day Club. Relig: Catholic. Mailing Add: 113 S Connecticut Salina KS 67401

BLANK, EDWARD C, II (D)
Tenn State Sen
Mailing Add: Middle Tenn Bank Bldg Columbia TN 38501

BLANK, FRED E, JR (R)
Committeeman, NJ Rep State Comt
b Collingswood, NJ, May 25, 23; s Fred E Blank (deceased) & Mary Cooper B (deceased); m 1949 to Dorothy M Lamach; c Maryellen (Mrs Andrew Levin), Fred E Blank, III, Lorraine D & Betty R. Educ: Darby High Sch; Rutgers Univ Exten, real estate & ins; appraisal sch, Mil Assistance Inst. Polit & Govt Pos: Committeeman, NJ Rep State Comt, 69-; freeholder, Cape May Co, 71. Bus & Prof Pos: Realtor, Coastal Realty, Ocean City, NJ, 60- Mil Serv: Entered as T/5, Army, 42, released as T/5, 46, after serv in 540th Amphibian Trac Bn, Pac, 43-46. Mem: NJ Realtor Asn (vpres, Sixth Dist); Boy Scouts (vpres, Atlantic area coun). Honors & Awards: Scouter of Year, Boy Scouts of Am, Ocean City, NJ. Relig: Baptist. Mailing Add: 856 Park Pl Ocean City NJ 08226

BLANKS, WILLIAM FRANCIS (D)
Mem, Ga Dem Exec Comt
b Macon, Ga, Dec 1, 15; s Otis Lowe Blanks & Mary Norine Roberts B; m 1951 to Louise Searcy; c Dorothy (Mrs Fish) & W F, Jr. Educ: Mercer Univ Law Sch, LLB, 39; Kappa Sigma. Polit & Govt Pos: City attorney, Montezuma, Ga, 57-; chmn, Macon Co Dem Party, formerly; vchmn, Ga Elec Bd, 67-; mem, Ga Dem Exec Comt, 71- Bus & Prof Pos: Pres, Montezuma CofC, 53; bd attorney, Macon Co Bd Educ, 55-; pres, Montezuma Develop Corp, 63-; comn attorney, Mid-Flint Area Planning & Develop Comn, 64- Mil Serv: Entered as Pvt, Army, 42, released as Capt, 46, after serv in Commun Zone, ETO, 44-46; Lt Col (Ret), Judge Adv Gen Corps, Army Res, 69. Mem: State Bar of Ga; Am Bar Asn; Am Judicature Soc; City Attorneys Asn of Ga; Am Legion. Honors & Awards: Silver Beaver Award, Boy Scouts. Relig: Baptist. Legal Res: Rte 2 Montezuma GA 31063 Mailing Add: PO Drawer 311 Montezuma GA 31063

BLANTON, JOY SUE (D)
b Ada, Okla, July 6, 36; d S C Van Curon & Helen Trask V; div; c F Craig, Paula A & C Todd. Educ: Univ Ky, 55-56; Alpha Delta Pi. Polit & Govt Pos: Sixth cong dist chmn, Ky Young Dem, 69, mem exec comt, 69-, nat committeewoman, 70-72; mem exec bd, Ky Dem Women's Clubs. Bus & Prof Pos: Admin asst, Ky Legis Research Comn, 68- Relig: Catholic. Mailing Add: 104 Marlowe Ct Frankfort KY 40601

BLANTON, L RAY (D)
Gov, Tenn
b Hardin Co, Tenn, Apr 10, 30; s Leonard A Blanton & Ova Delaney B; m 1949 to Betty Jane Littlefield; c Debbie, David & Paul. Educ: Univ Tenn, BS, 51. Polit & Govt Pos: Tenn State Rep, 64-66; US Rep, Tenn, 67-73; Gov, Tenn, 74- Bus & Prof Pos: Vpres, Tenn Plant Mix Asphalt Asn, 65-66. Mem: Adamsville Lions; Moose; Shrine; Mason; Boy Scouts (Area Coun). Relig: Methodist. Legal Res: PO Box 96 Adamsville TN 38310 Mailing Add: State Capitol Nashville TN 37219

BLAS, FRANK F (R)
Chmn, Guam Rep Cent Comt
b Agana, Guam, Mar 20, 41; m 1971 to Tina; c Frank F, Jr & Lynette M. Educ: Univ Guam, AA, 62; Univ Portland, BBA, 65. Polit & Govt Pos: Campaign chmn, AA, 62; gen elec, 72; mem, Travel Indust Mgt Coun, 72; spec asst to the Gov, Guam, 72-; chmn bd dirs, Guam Visitors Bur, 72-; chmn, Guam Rep Cent Comt, 73-; mem, Rep Nat Comt, 73- Mem: US Air Force Asn; Guam Jaycees. Relig: Roman Catholic. Mailing Add: PO Box 74 Agana GU 96910

BLASBALG, ARNOLD LEO (R)
Chmn, Coventry Rep Town Comt, RI
b Providence, RI, June 30, 40; s Hyman Blasbalg & Jean Hassenfeld B; m 1969 to Ruth Rubin; c Michelle Lyne, Dana Leanne & Jule Heather. Educ: Brown Univ, AB, 62; Boston Univ Law Sch, JD, 65. Polit & Govt Pos: Chmn, Coventry Rep Town Comt, 70-72 & 75-; mem, Coventry Charter Comt, 72, chmn, charter review comt, 75; pres, Coventry Town Coun, 72-74. Mem: Lions; Elks; Kent Co Bar Asn; CofC. Relig: Hebrew. Mailing Add: 55 Wisteria Dr Coventry RI 02816

BLASSIE, JOHN J (D)
Mo State Rep
Mailing Add: 4400 Oleatha St Louis MO 63116

BLATCHFORD, JOSEPH H (R)
Mem, Rep State Cent Comt Calif
b Milwaukee, Wis, June 7, 34; s George Nason Blatchford & mother, deceased; m 1967 to Winifred Anne Marich; c Andrea Nicole, Nicholas George & Antonia Nason. Educ: Univ Calif, Los Angeles, 56; Univ Calif, Berkeley, LLD, 61; Phi Kappa Psi (pres, 55). Hon Degrees: DHL, Seton Hall Univ & Kenyon Col; DH, Chapman Col, 70. Polit & Govt Pos: Legis asst, US Cong, 57; dir, Peace Corps, 69-71; dir, Action, 71-72; mem, Rep State Cent Comt Calif, currently. Bus & Prof Pos: Founder & exec dir, ACCION Int, 60-64. Mil Serv: 2nd Lt Army, 56. Honors & Awards: Distinguished Serv Award, Univ Calif, Los Angeles, 70. Relig: Protestant. Mailing Add: 545 S Norton Ave Los Angeles CA 90020

BLATNIK, JOHN A (DFL)
b Chisholm, Minn, Aug 17, 11; m 1955 to Gisela Hager; c Thomas H, Stephanie & Valerie. Educ: Winona State Teachers Col, Minn, BE, 35; Univ Chicago; Univ Minn, 41-42, grad work in Pub Admin. Polit & Govt Pos: Minn State Sen, 40-44; US Rep, Minn, 46-74; mem, Dem Nat Comt, 62-72; deleg, Dem Nat Conv, 68; ex officio, Dem Nat Mid-Term Conf, 74. Bus & Prof Pos: Teacher & sch admin, 8 years. Mil Serv: Army Air Corps Intel & Off of Strategic Servs, 42-46, discharged as Paratrooper Capt; Bronze Star Medal with Oak Leaf Cluster; Air Medal. Mailing Add: 417 1/2 Fourth St SW Chisholm MN 55719

BLATT, NANCIE MILLER (D)
Mem, Dem State Cent Comt, Mich
b Detroit, Mich, May 9, 38; d Samuel A Miller & Bernice Smokler M; m 1957 to Martin Jay Blatt; c Lauren, Susan & Stephanie. Educ: Univ Mich, BA, 62, MA, 68. Polit & Govt Pos: Mem exec comt, Second Dist Dem Orgn, Mich, 73-75; deleg, Dem Nat Mid-Term Conf, 74; alt mem, Dem State Cent Comt, 75- Bus & Prof Pos: Substitute teacher, Livonia Pub Schs, Mich, 62-74; sales rep, Stewart Oxygen Serv, Detroit, 74- Mem: Livonia League Women Voters (chairperson educ comt, 71-); Livonia Bus & Prof Women's Club (deleg bicentennial comt, 75-, deleg, Southeast Mich Coun Govts; criminal justice comt, 73-); Livonia Interested Dem. Honors & Awards: Distinguished Serv Award, Mich Coun Parents & Teachers, 72. Relig: Jewish. Mailing Add: 19482 Parker Livonia MI 48152

BLATT, SOLOMON (D)
Speaker, SC House of Rep
b Blackville, SC, Feb 27, 96; s Nathan Blatt & Mollie B; m 1920 to Ethel Green; c Soloman, Jr. Educ: Univ SC, LLB, 17. Hon Degrees: LLD, Univ SC & Lander Col. Polit & Govt Pos: Trustee, Barnwell Sch, 34 years; mem, Gov Blackwood's Staff; SC State Rep, 33-, Speaker, SC House of Rep, 35-47 & 51-; trustee, Univ SC, 36-48. Bus & Prof Pos: Attorney-at-law,

17-; lawyer, Firm of Blatt & Fales. Mil Serv: Sgt, Army, 18-19, with 323rd Inf, 81st Div. Mem: Am Legion; Mason. Mailing Add: Barnwell SC 29812

BLATZ, JEROME V **(CONSERVATIVE)**
Minn State Sen
b Bloomington, Minn, 1923; married; c nine. Educ: Notre Dame Univ, BA; Harvard Univ, LLB. Polit & Govt Pos: Minn State Sen, 62- Bus & Prof Pos: Lawyer. Mailing Add: 11044 Glen Wilding Lane Bloomington MN 55431

BLAUSHILD, BABETTE LOUISE **(D)**
b Cleveland, Ohio, Nov 14, 27; d Louis Rosen & Florence Smith R; div; c Eric Lewis, Steven Andrew & Lisa Kay. Educ: Western Reserve Univ, 59-60. Polit & Govt Pos: Nat dir woman's polit action, Presidential Campaign of Hubert H Humphrey, Washington, DC, 72; alt deleg, Dem Nat Conv, 72. Bus & Prof Pos: Reporter, Channel 61, Cleveland, 69; columnist, Cleveland Press, 69-72; contrib ed, Cleveland Mag, 72-73; pres, Discover Yourself, Inc, 72- Publ: Co-auth, Why College Students Fail, Funk & Wagnalls, 70; auth, Confessions of an unpublished writer, Saturday Rev, 63. Mailing Add: 1 Bratenahl Pl Cleveland OH 44108

BLAYLOCK, CHET **(D)**
Chmn, Mont Dem State Exec Comt
Mailing Add: 502 Third Ave Laurel MT 59044

BLAYLOCK, LEN EVERETTE **(R)**
b Little Rock, Ark, Dec 8, 18; s David Penn Blaylock & Minnie Bradford B; m 1941 to Melba Winona Wright; c David Robert, Len E, Jr, Melvin James, Betty Louise & Dale Alan. Educ: Baylor Univ, 51-52; Ark Polytech Col, BA, 62; Ark State Teachers Col, 63. Polit & Govt Pos: Field representative, Rep Nat Committeeman Ark, 64-67; twp committeeman, Perry Co Rep Comt, 65-67; comnr, Ark Dept Pub Welfare, 67-72; Southwest regional rep, Welfare Reform Planning, 71-72; Rep nominee Gov, 72; committeeman, Ark State Rep Exec Comt, formerly. Bus & Prof Pos: Owner, Nimrod Trading Post, Nimrod, Ark, 59-61; prin, Perry Sch, 61-64. Mil Serv: Entered as Pvt, Air Force, 39, released as Maj, 59, after serv in Strategic Air Command as Navigator-Bombardier & Radar Observer, 52-59, Maj Res; Theatre Campaign Ribbon; Unit Citations; Legion of Merit. Mem: AF&AM; VFW. Honors & Awards: Nolan Blass Award, Ark Conf Social Work, 71. Mailing Add: Rte 1 Perryville AR 72126

BLAZER, SONDRA KAY **(D)**
Secy, Warren Co Dem Exec & Cent Comts, Ohio
b Middletown, Ohio, June 2, 37; d John Charles Gordon & Ora Lillie Stewart G; m 1956 to Ralph J Bays, wid, 69; c Sherry Kay, Cynthia Rae & Robert Jay; m 1972 to Charles M Blazer. Educ: Univ Cincinnati Evening Col, currently; Delta Tau Kappa; Alpha Sigma Lambda, Beta Chap; Phi Kappa Epsilon. Polit & Govt Pos: Secy, Warren Co Dem Womens Club, Ohio, 63-67; Dem Precinct committeeman, Franklin Twp SE, 64-; secy, Warren Co Dem Exec & Cent Comts, 65-; mem, Warren Co Bd Elections. Bus & Prof Pos: Reporter & church ed, Middletown J, Ohio, 55-56; assoc ed, Warren Co Reporter, 66-67, managing ed, 67-72; free lance writer, currently. Mem: Community Day Hosp, Middletown, Ohio (former vol worker); Warren Co Ment Health & Retardation Bd (chmn); Lebanon Correctional Inst (Citizens Adv Comt); Gov Traffic Safety Comt; Warren Co Safety Coun (secy, 72-). Honors & Awards: Placed first in short story contest, sponsored by Beta Sigma Phi, 64; placed 70th of 200 winners in short story contest sponsored by Writers Digest, 66; received second pl in columns div of new media awards given by Ohio Dept of Hwy Safety, 69, placed first, 70. Relig: Methodist; Sr High Church Sch; Teacher, Hunter Community United Methodist Church, formerly, secy, Church Worship Comt, currently. Mailing Add: 3730 Beatrice Dr Franklin OH 45005

BLEASE, EUGENE S **(D)**
SC State Rep
Mailing Add: 207 Greenwood Highway Saluda SC 29138

BLEDSOE, CARL BEVERLY **(R)**
Colo State Rep
b Aroya, Colo, Oct 6, 23; s Carl Bledsoe & Josie Main B; m 1946 to Alice Elizabeth Cotellessa; c Robert Carl, Thomas Beverly & Christopher Joel. Educ: Univ Colo, 41-42; Colo State Univ, BS, 49; Alpha Zeta; Farm House. Polit & Govt Pos: Mem, Kit Carson Sch Bd, Dist R-1, Colo, 59-71; Colo State Rep, 72- Bus & Prof Pos: Self-employed rancher, currently. Mil Serv: Entered as Pvt, Army, 42, released as Sgt, 45, after serv in 5th Air Force Signal Corps, Pac Theatre, 43-45; Theatre Ribbons. Mem: VFW; Colo Farm Bur; Colo & Nat Cattlemen's Asns. Relig: Protestant. Legal Res: C B Bledsoe Ranch Wild Horse CO 80862 Mailing Add: PO Box 516 Hugo CO 80821

BLEICHER, MICHAEL N **(D)**
Mem, Dem Nat Comt, Wis
b Cleveland, Ohio, Oct 2, 35; s David B Bleicher & Rachel Faigin B; m 1957 to Betty M Isack; c Helene Carol, Laurence Aaron & Benjamin Daniel. Educ: Calif Inst Technol, BS, 57; Tulane Univ, MS, 59, PhD, 61; Univ Warsaw, PhD, 61. Polit & Govt Pos: Deleg, Wis State Dem Conv, since 64, chmn, resolutions comt, 68; ward orgn chmn, Dane Co Dem Party, 64-66; chmn, 66-68, mem exec bd, 68-; deleg & mem credentials comt, Dem Nat Conv, 68 & 72; state chmn, New Dem Coalition, 68-69; mem, party reform comt, Wis Dem Party, 69; mem, Dem Nat Comt, Wis, 72-; deleg, Dem Nat Mid-Term Conf, 74. Bus & Prof Pos: Teaching asst math, Tulane Univ, 57-60; exchange fel, Univ Warsaw, 60-61; Nat Sci Found fel, Univ Calif, Berkeley, 61-62; asst prof, Univ Wis Madison, 62-66, assoc prof, 66-69, prof, 69-, chmn math dept, 72-74. Publ: Excursions into Mathematics, Worth, 69; co-auth, Selects mathematics III, Heidelberger Taschenbucher 86, Springer Verlag, 71; auth, A new algorithm for Egyptian fractions, J Number Theory, 72; plus others. Mem: Am Civil Liberties Union; Am Fedn Teachers; Sigma Xi; Am Math Soc; Math Asn Am. Relig: Jewish. Mailing Add: 1930 Regent St Madison WI 53705

BLESSEY, GERALD HENRY **(D)**
Miss State Rep
b Biloxi, Miss, July 8, 42; s Walter J Blessey, III & Geraldine Fountain B; m 1969 to Rose Ann Joachim. Educ: Univ Miss, BS Polit Sci & JD; Harvard Univ, Masters Law; Phi Alpha Delta; Omicron Delta Kappa. Polit & Govt Pos: Miss State Rep, 72- Bus & Prof Pos: Asst prof of law, Univ Miss, 68-69; lawyer, Biloxi, Miss, 70- Mil Serv: Entered as 2nd Lt, Army, 66, released as 1st Lt, 68; after serv in 55th Mil Intel Detachment, First Field Force, Vietnam, 67-68; Bronze Star; Vietnam Serv Medal; Nat Defense Medal. Mem: VFW; Am Legion; Elks; Jaycees; Marine Technol Soc. Honors & Awards: Outstanding Contribution, Miss Acad Sci, 74; Outstanding Freshman Legislator, 72. Relig: Catholic. Legal Res: 111 Fred Haise Blvd Biloxi MS 39530 Mailing Add: PO Drawer L Biloxi MS 39533

BLEVINS, JOHN MORRISON **(R)**
Ind State Rep
b Anderson, Ind, Oct 9, 47; s F Leonard Blevins & Dorothy Morrison B; m 1970 to Jill Annette Jackson. Educ: Anderson Col, AB, 69; Ind Univ, JD, 74. Polit & Govt Pos: Ind State Rep, 72- Mailing Add: 1414 E Eighth St Anderson IN 46012

BLICK, BENNY GEORGE **(R)**
Co-Dir Region Nine, Young Rep Nat Fedn
b Twin Falls, Idaho, Sept 24, 43; s George Leonard Blick & Marie Senften B; m 1966 to Mary Anne Wren; c Geianne Marie & Jeffrey Todd. Educ: Univ Idaho, BS in bus, 65; Alpha Kappa Psi; Sigma Chi. Polit & Govt Pos: Precinct committeeman, Twin Falls Co Rep Party, 70-; chmn, Twin Falls Co Young Rep, 70-72; chmn dist six, Idaho Young Rep League, 71-73, chmn, 73-75; co-dir, Region Nine, Young Rep Nat Fedn, 73- Bus & Prof Pos: Owner-partner, Blick Bros Farms, Castleford, Idaho, 61-; owner, Benny Blick Trucking, 71-; realtor, John Lutz, Realtors, Twin Falls, 74- Mil Serv: Entered as 2nd Lt, Army, 67, released as Capt, 70, after serv in 183rd Reconnaissance Airplane Co, Vietnam, 68-69; Bronze Star; Army Commendation; Air Medal with Twelve Oak Leaf Clusters. Mem: Castleford Men's Club; Elks; Rotary; Am Nat Cattlemen's Asn. Honors & Awards: Hard Charger Award, Young Rep Nat Fedn, 73- Outstanding Young Men of Am, Nat Jaycees, 74. Relig: Episcopal. Mailing Add: Rte 1 Castleford ID 83321

BLILEY, THOMAS J, JR **(INDEPENDENT)**
Mayor, Richmond, Va
b Richmond, Va, Jan 28, 32; s Thomas J Bliley & Carolyn Fagan B; m 1957 to Mary Virginia Kelley; c Mary Vaughan & Thomas J, III. Educ: Georgetown Univ, BA, 52. Polit & Govt Pos: VMayor, Richmond, Va, 68-70, Mayor, 70- Bus & Prof Pos: Pres, Joseph W Bliley Co. Mil Serv: Entered as Ensign, Navy, 52, released as Lt, 55, after serv in Staff Comdr, 6th Fleet, 53-55. Mem: Rotary. Relig: Catholic. Mailing Add: 408 Henri Rd Richmond VA 23226

BLISS, BRUCE JAMES **(R)**
Chmn, North Attleboro Rep Town Comt, Mass
b Providence, RI, May 18, 35; s Carlton H Bliss & Ethel McKechnie B; m 1957 to Phebe Ann; c Karen Lee, Bruce James, Jr, Judith Ann & Susan Jane. Educ: Brown Univ, AB in chem, 57; Lambda Chi Alpha. Polit & Govt Pos: Deleg, Mass State Rep Conv, 64-74; chmn, North Attleboro Rep Town Comt, Mass, 64-; mem, Selective Serv Bd, Mass, 65-, chmn, 74-; mem, North Attleboro Bd Water Comn, 67-74, chmn, 68-74; mem, North Attleboro Elec Comn, 67-, chmn, 68-; rep, North Attleboro Town Meeting, 74- Bus & Prof Pos: Metallurgist, Tex Instruments, 58-66; Gorham Corp, 66-68; sealer weights & measures, Town of North Attleboro, 62-; mfg engr, Engelhard Industs, 68-70; plant mgr & vpres, Metaloy Inc, 70- Publ: Paper in 6th Symposium on Vacuum Techniques. Honors & Awards: Holds five patents in field of metalworking. Relig: Protestant. Mailing Add: 156 Raymond Hall Dr North Attleboro MA 02760

BLISS, DONALD T **(R)**
Mass State Rep
Mailing Add: State Capitol Boston MA 02133

BLISS, MARY PATRICIA **(R)**
VChmn, Floyd Co Rep Cent Comt, Ind
b New Albany, Ind, Dec 16, 42; d Myers Elwood Murphy & LaVerne Pixley M; m 1962 to Richard Earl Bliss; c Mark Myers & Richard Matthew. Polit & Govt Pos: VChmn, New Albany Rep Party, Ind, 71; vchmn, Floyd Co Rep Cent Comt, 72- Bus & Prof Pos: Travel consult, Clarksville, Ind, 72- Mem: Jaycee Wives Club; Psi Iota Xi; Gtr Louisville Consumer Coun; Mem Hosp Auxiliary (bd mem). Relig: Protestant. Mailing Add: 1656 Harriet Ct New Albany IN 47150

BLISS, RAY CHARLES **(R)**
Rep Nat Committeeman, Ohio
b Akron, Ohio, Dec 16, 07; s Emil Bliss & Emilie Wieland B; m 1959 to Ellen Palmer. Educ: Univ Akron, AB, 35; Phi Kappa Tau. Hon Degrees: LHD, Univ Akron, 68. Polit & Govt Pos: Precinct committeeman & mem, Summit Co Rep Exec Comt, Ohio, 32-; deleg, Ohio State Rep Conv, 32-; mem, Summit Co Bd of Elections, 36-, chmn, 45-46 & 49-50; chmn, Summit Co Rep Cent Comt, 42-64; mem, Ohio Rep State Cent & Exec Comt, 44-74, chmn, 49-65; deleg-at-lg, Rep Nat Conv, 52-72, mem, Rules Comt, 52, chmn, Ohio deleg, 56, vchmn, 60, chmn, Site Comt, 60 & 68, adv to exec comt, Arrangements Comt, 64 & 72, chmn, 68; Rep Nat Committeeman, Ohio, 52-, mem bipartisan comt study methods financing quadrennial nat nominating conv, 73-, mem & subcomt chmn rule 29 comt, 73-74, adv to site comt for 76 Rep Nat Conv; mem, Nat Rep Exec Comt, 52-, vchmn, 60-65 & 70-; chmn, Midwest Rep State Chmn Asn, 53-65; chmn, Rep Nat Subcomt on Big City Politics, 61; chmn, Rep State Chmn Adv Comt to Rep Nat Chmn, 62-65; chmn, Rep Nat Comt, 65-69; presiding officer, Rep Nat Coordr Comt, 65-69; presiding officer, Rep Joint Leadership of Cong, 65-69. Bus & Prof Pos: Secy-treas, Wells & Bliss, Inc, 33-37; pres, Tower Agencies, Inc, Akron, Ohio, 47-; mem bd trustees, chmn subcomt develop & mem subcomt finance, Univ Akron, 70-74, mem, Develop Found. Publ: The role of the state chairman, In: Politics USA, Doubleday, 60. Mem: Kiwanis; Akron City Club; Union Club of Cleveland; 1925 F Street Club, Inc, Washington, DC; Mason (32 degree). Honors & Awards: Univ Akron Alumni Honor Award, 65. Relig: Episcopal. Legal Res: 2535 Addyston Rd Akron OH 44313 Mailing Add: 425 First Nat Tower Akron OH 44308

BLISS, ROBERT LANDERS **(R)**
Mem, New Canaan Town Rep Comt, Conn
b Binghamton, NY, Nov 19, 07; s George Calvin Sherwood Bliss & Katherine Barbara Scheider B; m 1942 to Friede Smidt; c John Smidt & Friede Sherwood (Mrs Thomas M Brayton). Educ: Cornell Univ, AB, 30, grad, 31; Sigma Delta Chi; Psi Upsilon; Beth L'Amed; Sphinx Head; Aleph Samach. Polit & Govt Pos: Mem, New Canaan Town Rep Comt, Conn, 48-51 & 72-, chmn, 51-62; state Rep cent committeeman from 26th Sen Dist, 54-56; chmn, Fairfield Co Rep Comt, 62-64; Conn State Sen, 26th Dist, 62-67; spec dep sheriff, Fairfield Co; consult, Weicker for US Senate Comt, 69-70; co-chmn, Rep Bienniel Fund Drive, 72. Bus & Prof Pos: Owner, Vegaline Kennels, purebred show beagles, 45-, judge & exhibit 13 in beagles; pub rels dir, Nat Asn of Ins Agents, 47-49; asst to Publ, PM Newspaper, 40; exec vpres, Pub Rels Soc of Am, Inc, NY, 49-56; pres & pub rels counsel, Robert L Bliss Inc, New York, 56-; mem, Conn Transportation Authority, 74-75; dir, Sierra Blanca Corp, currently. Mil Serv: Entered as 2nd Lt, Army Air Corps, 42, released as Maj, 46, after serv as Chief,

Pub Affairs Sect, Air Serv Command, Wright Field, Ohio. Publ: Co-auth, Handbook of Public Relations, McGraw-Hill, 2nd ed, 71; articles on int pub rels, Communique, 64-66; articles on nat pub rels, numerous Am publ, including Pub Rels J & Pub Rels Quart, 50- Mem: Int Pub Rels Asn; Pub Rels Soc Am; Nat Soc State Legislators (founding charter mem, first life mem & first vpres, 65-); Univ Club. Relig: Baptist. Mailing Add: 162 Park St New Canaan CT 06840

BLOBAUM, ROBERT E (R)
b Fairbury, Nebr, July 31, 28; s Herman C Blobaum & Anna Spilker B; m 1950 to Lois Prange; c Robert, Jr, Cynthia, Joel, David & John. Educ: Fairbury Jr Col, 48; Univ Nebr, BA, bus admin, 50; Alpha Kappa Psi; Beta Sigma Psi. Polit & Govt Pos: Chmn, Washington Co Rep Party, Nebr, formerly. Bus & Prof Pos: Pres, Great Plains Serv, Inc, 55-73. Mil Serv: Entered as Pvt, Army, 51, released as Cpl, 53, after serv in Corps Engr, Washington, DC, Ft Belvoir, 51-53. Mem: Am Legion. Relig: Lutheran. Mailing Add: 608 S 18th Blair NE 68008

BLOCH, STUART FULTON (R)
Chmn Finance Comt, Ohio Co Rep Party, WVa
b Wheeling, WVa, Apr 23, 33; s Thomas Moffatt Bloch & Nancy Fulton B; m 1959 to Stephanie Hawkins; c Karen Fulton, Stuart Stephenson, Caroline Bennett & Thomas M, II. Educ: Phillips Exeter Acad, 48-52; Princeton Univ, AB cum laude, 56. Polit & Govt Pos: Chmn, WVirginians for Goldwater for Pres, 64; alt deleg, Rep Nat Conv, 64, deleg, 68; mem, Finance Comt, Ohio Co Rep Party, WVa, 68-, chmn, currently. Bus & Prof Pos: Sales rep, Whitehall Prod, Inc, 59, advert mgr, 60, advert mgr & vpres, 61-; dir, The Bloch Bros Tobacco Co, Wheeling, 62, pres, 70-; dir, Whitehall Pipe Co, Richmond Hill, NY, 64; vpres, Helme Prod, Inc, 70-; dir & pres, Wheeling Country Day Sch, currently. Mil Serv: Entered as 2nd Lt, Air Force, 57, released as 1st Lt, 59. Mem: Nat Asn Tobacco Distributors (dir young exec div); Assoc Tobacco Mfrs, Inc (dir); Half Dollar Trust & Savings Bank (dir & mem exec comt); Young Pres Orgn; Region III Adv Coun, Nat Alliance of Businessmen. Relig: Protestant. Legal Res: 40 Orchard Rd Wheeling WV 26003 Mailing Add: 4000 Water St Wheeling WV 26003

BLOCK, BARBARA ANNE (R)
Mem, DC Rep Comt
b New York, NY, Jan 16, 48; d Theodore L Block & Stella Stashin B; single. Educ: Georgetown Univ Sch Foreign Serv, BSFS, 69; Young Rep; Women's Serv Orgn; ECampus Women's Orgn. Polit & Govt Pos: Chmn, Capitol Hill Vol Comt, DC Young Rep, formerly, admin vpres & secy, formerly; staff asst, DC Rep Comt, 71, mem, 73-, chmn youth comt, 73, mem nominating comt, 74-; legis aide to US Sen Charles H Percy, Ill, 71-75; legis asst to US Rep Richard Kelly, Fla, 75- Bus & Prof Pos: Staff mem, Nat Fedn Bus & Prof Women's Clubs, Inc, 69-70. Mem: Georgetown Univ Alumni Asn; Ripon Soc. Honors & Awards: Outstanding Serv Award, DC Col Rep Fedn. Relig: Roman Catholic. Mailing Add: 3900 Tunlaw Rd NW Washington DC 20007

BLOCK, ETHEL LASHER (R)
Mem, NY State Rep Exec Comt
b Tivoli, NY, Sept 9, 19; d Harold Lasher & Emma Du Bois L; m 1942 to Dr David Edgar Block; c Ann M, David E, III & Harold M. Educ: St Francis Hosp Sch Nursing, Poughkeepsie, NY, RN, 39. Polit & Govt Pos: First pres, Red Hook Womens Rep Club, 62, 63 & 64; secy, Dutchess Co Rep Comt, 63-64, vchmn, 65-; committeewoman, NY Rep State Comt, 67-; mem, NY State Rep Exec Comt, 70-; deleg, Rep Nat Conv, 72. Bus & Prof Pos: Surg nurse, NDutchess Hosp, Rhinebeck, NY, 39-42; off nurse, Red Hook, 45-57. Mem: DAR; Eastern Star; Nat Fedn Garden Clubs; Fedn Rep Women; PTA. Relig: Episcopal. Mailing Add: 19 North Rd Tivoli NY 12583

BLODGETT, WILLIAM B (D)
Maine State Rep
Mailing Add: Augusta Rd Waldoboro ME 04572

BLOEDEL, FLORA HOWELL (D)
Mem, Berkshire Co Dem Orgn, Mass
b Morristown, NJ, Dec 4, 24; d Malcolm Clifford Howell & Flora Laidlow Jones H; m 1948 to Prentice Bloedel; c Carla, Ellen & Lawrence H. Educ: St Lawrence Univ, AB. Polit & Govt Pos: Mem, Grassrooters, Berkeley, Calif, 52-55; secy, King Co Dem Cent Comt, Seattle, Wash, 68-70; mem, Williamstown Dem Town Comt, Mass, 71-; deleg, Dem Nat Conv, 72; mem, Berkshire Co Dem Orgn, 72- Bus & Prof Pos: Clerk, Bell Tel Labs, New York, 44-45; aide, Rockefeller Found, 46-48; exec secy, Cambridge Sch, Weston, Mass, 48-50; aide, Univ Calif Libr, Berkeley, 50-51; secy, Mus of Art & Art Dept, Williams Col, Mass, 71- Mem: League of Women Voters; Mus of Natural Hist; Am Civil Liberties Union; Sierra Club; Defenders of Wildlife. Legal Res: Bee Hill Rd Williamstown MA 01267 Mailing Add: PO Box 654 Williamstown MA 01267

BLOMEN, HENNING ALBERT (SOCIALIST LABOR PARTY)
Mem Nat Exec Comt, Socialist Labor Party
b New Bedford, Mass, Sept 28, 10; s Gustav A Blomen & Clara E Magnuson B; m 1945, div; m 1969 to Constance Zimmerman; c Frances (Mrs Tripp). Educ: Somerville High Sch, Mass, grad, 28. Polit & Govt Pos: Cand for Gov, Mass, 64, 72 & 74; Cand for Vpres of US, 64; Cand, President of the US, 68; nat organizer & mem Nat Exec Comt, Socialist Labor Party, currently. Bus & Prof Pos: Machine assembler, Dewey & Almy Chem Co, Div of W R Grace, Inc, 38-69. Relig: Brotherhood of Man. Mailing Add: 25 County St Ipswich MA 01938

BLOODWORTH, BENTON BARCLAY (D)
Miss State Rep
Mailing Add: Westview Dr Grenada MS 38901

BLOODWORTH, JAMES NELSON (D)
Assoc Justice, Supreme Court of Ala
b Decatur, Ala, Jan 21, 21; s Benjamin McGowan Bloodworth & Marguerite Nelson B; m to Jean Gregg Shelton; c Catherine, Sandra & Jean Marguerite. Educ: Athens Col, 38-39; Univ Ala, Sch Com, BS, 42, Sch Law, LLB, 47; grad, Appellate Judges Seminar, NY Univ Law Sch, 69; Omicron Delta Kappa; Kappa Alpha Order. Polit & Govt Pos: Judge, Recorder's Court, City of Decatur, Ala, 48-51; co solicitor, Morgan Co, Ala, 51; assoc mem, Bd Pardons & Paroles, Montgomery, 51-52; circuit judge, Eighth Judicial Circuit, 59-68; chmn, Ala Dem Steering Comt, 61-63; assoc justice Supreme Court of Ala, Montgomery, 68- Bus & Prof Pos: Attorney-at-law, Calvin & Bloodworth, Attorneys-at-law, Decatur, Ala, 47-58; faculty adv, Nat Col State Trial Judges, 67, lectr, 67-, faculty adv, grad courses, 71; faculty, Am Acad Judicial Educ, 70- Mil Serv: Entered as Pvt, Army, 43, released as Capt, 46, after serv in 12th Armored Div & First Armored Div, Am & European Theaters, 43-46; Res, 46-64, Lt Col (Ret); Three Combat Battle Stars; Combat Infantryman's Badge; Bronze Star. Publ: Index to Official Proceedings of the Constitutional Convention of 1901 of the State of Alabama, Univ Ala, 48. Mem: Morgan Co, Montgomery Co, Ala & Am Bar Asns; Am Legion. Relig: Presbyterian; Ruling Elder. Legal Res: 3221 Bankhead Ave Montgomery AL 36106 Mailing Add: Supreme Ct Judicial Bldg PO Box 218 Montgomery AL 36101

BLOOM, ELAINE (D)
Fla State Rep
b New York, NY; d Julius Bernstein & Ethel Scherer B; m to Philip Bloom; c Anne & David. Educ: Barnard Col, BA, 57; Pre-Law Soc; Debate Club; Polit Coun. Polit & Govt Pos: Mem, Local Govt Study Comn, Dade Co, 70-71; deleg, White House Conf on Children, 70; chairperson, Comn on Status Women, Dade Co, Fla, 71-72; mem, Fla Regional Manpower Coun, 73-74; mem, Manpower Planning Coun, Dade Co, 71-74; pres adv bd & trustee, Fla Int Univ, 72-; Fla State Rep, 74- Bus & Prof Pos: Analyst, TV Prog Content, Columbia Broadcasting Syst, 57-61; radio prog moderator, WIOD, Miami, Fla, 72-; asst dir, Women's Inst, Fla Int Univ, 73-74. Mem: Nat Coun Jewish Women (sect pres & state legis chairperson, nat bd mem, 72-); Third Century, USA (trustee); Miami Comt Foreign Rels; Gtr Miami Jewish Fedn (chairperson, North Dade Area Bd). Honors & Awards: Pres Leadership Award, Gtr Miami Jewish Fedn, 72; Outstanding Serv Human Rights, Dade Co Nat Orgn for Women, 72; Leadership in Women's Concerns Award, Fla Int Univ, 73; Outstanding Woman in Polit, Fla Fedn Bus & Prof Women, 74; Hannah Solomon Award, Nat Coun Jewish Women, 75. Relig: Jewish. Legal Res: 20435 NE 20th Ct North Miami Beach FL 33179 Mailing Add: 1401 Brickell Ave Miami FL 33131

BLOOM, GEORGE I (R)
Mem, Rep State Comt Pa
b Burgettstown, Pa, Sept 2, 98; s Charles Bloom & Tilly Caplan B; m 1958 to Luella Hawkins Boeschen. Educ: Univ Pittsburgh, BS, 20, LLB, 22; Lambda Phi. Polit & Govt Pos: Mem, Rep State Comt Pa, 39-, chmn, 56-63; secy to Gov Martin, Pa, 43-47; admin asst to US Sen Martin, Pa, 47-56; mem, Rep Nat Comt, 56-63; chmn, Comt Supervising TV, Radio & News Reel Coverage, Rep Nat Conv, 60; mem, Pa Athletic Comn, Pa Pardons Bd, Pa Bd of Finance & Revenue & Adv Comt Elec & Elec Laws; chmn, Pa Employees Retirement Bd, Pa Munic Employees Retirement Bd & Gov Pa Tax Comt; secy, Commonwealth of Pa, 63-65; chmn, Pa Pub Utility Comn, currently. Bus & Prof Pos: Partner, Firm of Bloom, Bloom, Rosenberg & Bloom, Washington, Pa, 22- Mil Serv: Navy, World War I. Mem: Am, Pa & Washington Co Bar Asns; Order of Coif; Nat Asn Regulatory Utility Comnr. Honors & Awards: Cited by Pa Legis Corr Asn for Coop, 46; Named Pitt Letterman of Year, 63. Legal Res: Wilson Apts Washington PA 15301 Mailing Add: North Off Bldg Harrisburg PA 17120

BLOOM, JEREMIAH B (D)
NY State Sen
b New York, NY, May 25, 13; s Samuel Bloom & Celia Anderman B; m 1941 to Dorothy Sotland; c Barton William. Educ: St John's Univ & St John's Law Sch, NY. Polit & Govt Pos: Mem, City Coun, New York, 50-57; NY State Dem committeeman, 58-; NY State Sen, 58- Bus & Prof Pos: Secy & dir, No-Cal Corp, 51-; asst secy & dir, Kirsch Beverages, Inc, 51-; partner, Bloom & Epstein Law Firm. Mil Serv: Entered as A/S, Navy, 43, released as CPO, 45, after serv in Am Theater. Mem: Unity Club of Brooklyn; Am Legion; Jewish War Vets; Mason. Relig: Jewish. Legal Res: 3215 Ave H Brooklyn NY 11210 Mailing Add: 110 E 42nd St New York NY 10017

BLOOM, PRESCOTT E (R)
Ill State Sen
Mailing Add: 424 Hollyridge Circle Peoria IL 61614

BLOOMER, ROBERT A (R)
Vt State Sen
Mailing Add: 122 Church St Rutland VT 05701

BLOSSER, CLARENCE (R)
Exec Chmn, Hocking Co Rep Party, Ohio
b Logan, Ohio, May 16, 01; s William Calvin Blosser (deceased) & Anna Myers B; m 1935 to Mary Christine Keller; c Clarence William & Charles Jacob. Polit & Govt Pos: Finance chmn, Hocking Co Rep Party, Ohio, 58-62; field rep for US Rep Homer Abele, 62-64; finance chmn, Tenth Cong Dist, Ohio, 62-; mem, Ohio State Rep Finance Comt, 62-; exec chmn, Hocking Co Rep Party, 68- Bus & Prof Pos: Owner, Blossers Restaurant, Logan, Ohio, 30-66; dir, Farmers & Merchants Bank, 47-; treas, Clover Enterprise Corp, 66- Mem: Cent Ohio & Ohio State Restaurant Asns; Mason (32 degree); York Rite; Shrine. Relig: Protestant. Mailing Add: 264 Midland Pl Logan OH 43138

BLOSSER, JAMES RICHARD (R)
b Jefferson City, Mo, Oct 29, 51; s Robert D Blosser & Marjorie B; single. Educ: Drury Col, AB, 73. Polit & Govt Pos: Vol, Mo Rep State Comt, 64, employee, 66; vpres, Cole Co TAR, 68-70; deleg, Eighth Dist Rep Conv, 72; deleg, Mo Rep State Conv, 72; alt deleg, Rep Nat Conv, 72; adv mem, Bond for Governor, 72; sustaining mem, Nat Rep Party, 73. Mem: Drury Col Young Rep (vpres, 72-). Relig: Disciples of Christ. Mailing Add: 1329 Moreland Ave Jefferson City MO 65101

BLOUIN, MICHAEL THOMAS (D)
US Rep, Iowa
b Jacksonville, Fla, Nov 7, 45; s Harold J Blouin & Alice Berry B; m 1967 to Suzanne Diers; c Twins, Lisa & Amy. Educ: Loras Col, BA, 66; Delta Sigma; Forensics Squad; vpres, Inter-Club Coun. Polit & Govt Pos: Second dist committeeman, Iowa Young Dem, 65, nat committeeman, 66-68; pres, Loras Col Young Dem, 65-66; task force chmn for Reorganizing Iowa Dem Party, 69; Iowa State Rep, Dist 49, Dubuque Co, 69-72, mem legis coun, Iowa Gen Assembly, 71-72; mem Iowa deleg, Midwest Legis Coun on Environ, 70-; Iowa State Sen, Dist Ten, 73-74; US Rep, Iowa, 75- Bus & Prof Pos: Mgr, Safety Equip Co, Dubuque, Iowa, 66; field underwriter, NY Life Ins, 67; teacher, Nativity Elem Sch, 67-69; adv consult, Salescount, Inc, Dubuque, Iowa, 69- Relig: Catholic. Mailing Add: 1848 Keyway Dr Dubuque IA 52001

BLOUIN, ROBERT RICHARD (R)
Committeeman, Cook Co Rep Cent Comt, Ill
b Chicago, Ill, July 16, 26; s Joseph Blouin & Florence Schuit B; m 1947 to Marie Louise Szymanski; c James Robert & Sharon Marie. Educ: St Willibrord High Sch, grad. Polit & Govt Pos: Campaign mgr, Ill State Sen Ron Swanson, 62-66 & 70; Campaign Mgr, Alderman

Yausic, 67; treas, Ninth Ward Regular Rep Orgn, Ill, 62-68; committeeman, Cook Co Rep Cent Comt, 68-; deleg, Rep Nat Conv, 72. Bus & Prof Pos: Pres, Blouin Builders Inc, 47-63; pres, Con-Tempus Inc, 71. Mil Serv: Entered as A/S, Navy, 44, released as 3/C PO, 46, after serv in Armed Guard, Europe. Mem: Nat Asn Plastic Fabricators; Am Legion; VFW; Lions. Relig: Catholic. Mailing Add: 600 W 119th St Chicago IL 60628

BLOUNT, CLARENCE W (D)
Md State Sen
b NC, Apr 20, 21; s Charles J Blount & Lottie Tillery B; m to Edith Gordine; c Michael C Blount & O Edward & Mark G Chisholm. Educ: Morgan State Col, BA, 50; Georgetown Univ, 54-58; Johns Hopkins Univ, MLA, 65; Alpha Phi Alpha. Polit & Govt Pos: Chmn, Baltimore Community Action Comn, Md, 68-; chmn, Md State Bd Rev of Health & Ment Hygiene, 69-71; Md State Sen, Baltimore City, 71-; deleg, Dem Nat Mid-Term Conf, 74; mem, Dem Nat Comt, currently. Bus & Prof Pos: Teacher soc studies, Baltimore Pub Schs, Md, 50-61, head dept soc studies, 54-59, spec asst, 59-61, asst prin, 61-69; lectr Am govt, Morgan State Col, 54-69; prin, Dunbar Commun High Sch, 69- Mil Serv: Entered as Pvt, Army, 42, released as 1st Lt, 46, after serv in 317th Engr Combat Bn, Mediterranean Theatre, 44-46; 92nd Inf Div Citation. Mem: Nat Educ Asn; Pub Sch Adminr & Supvrs Asn Baltimore; Baltimore Urban League; NAACP; Nat Conf Christians & Jews (regional bd). Honors & Awards: Several citations by local clubs, civic groups & sch. Relig: Methodist. Mailing Add: 3600 Hillsdale Rd Baltimore MD 21207

BLOUNT, JUILUS A (D)
La State Rep
Mailing Add: Walker LA 70785

BLOUNT, WINTON M (R)
b Union Springs, Ala, Feb 1, 21; s Winton M Blount & Clara Belle Chalker B; m 1942 to Mary Katherine Archibald; c Winton M, III, Thomas A, S Roberts, Katherine (Mrs James V Miles, III) & Joseph W. Educ: Univ Ala, 39-41; Sigma Nu. Hon Degrees: LHD, DH, LLD & DCL. Polit & Govt Pos: State chmn, Ala Citizens for Eisenhower-Nixon, 52; Southeastern dir, Vol for Nixon & Lodge, 60; pres, Ala CofC, 63-65; pres, US CofC, 68-69; Postmaster Gen, US Postal Serv, 69-71; Rep Cand, US Sen, 72. Bus & Prof Pos: Founder, Blount Bros Corp, Montgomery, Ala, 46, pres & chmn bd, 46-68; chmn bd, Benjamin F Shaw Co, Wilmington, Del, 67-68; past dir, Gulf Am Fire & Casualty Co, Montgomery, Ala, First Nat Bank of Montgomery, Kershaw Mfg Co, Montgomery, Jackson-Atlantic, Inc, Atlanta, Ga & Cent of Ga Rwy Co, Savannah; chmn exec comt, Blount, Inc, 73-74; dir, Union Camp Corp, 73-; dir, Interfinancial Inc, 73-; trustee, Univ Ala; chmn bd, pres & chief exec officer, Blount Inc, 74- Mil Serv: 1st Lt, Army Air Corps, 42-45. Mem: Omicron Delta Kappa; Southern States Indust Coun, Nashville, Tenn; Am Mgt Asn; Nat Asn of Mfrs; Nat Coun on Crime & Delinquency. Honors & Awards: Man of the Year, Montgomery, 61; Golden Knight of Mgt Award, Ala Coun of Nat Mgt Asn, 62; Court of Honor Award, Montgomery, Ala Exchange Club, 69; Ala Acad Honor; Nat Brotherhood Award, Nat Conf of Christians & Jews, 70. Relig: Presbyterian. Mailing Add: Rte 10 Box 43 Vaughn Rd Montgomery AL 36111

BLUE, BRANTLEY (R)
Comnr, Indian Claims Comn
b Pembroke, NC, Oct 11, 25; s D L Blue (deceased) & Ada Lowry B; m 1950 to Dorothy Milam; c Janet & Patricia. Educ: Pembroke State Col, 43-44 & 46; Cumberland Univ, LLB, 49; Blue Key; Phi Alpha Delta. Polit & Govt Pos: Judge, Kingsport, Tenn, 55-59; mem judicial comt, Sullivan Co Rep Party, Tenn, 64-68; comnr, Indian Claims Comn, Washington, DC, 69- Mil Serv: Entered as Seaman, Navy, 44, released as Seaman 1/C, 46, after serv in a destroyer, Atlantic & Pac Theatres. Mem: Kingsport Bar Asn; Kingsport Exchange Club; Am Legion; VFW; Moose. Honors & Awards: Recipient of Distinguished Alumnus Award, Pembroke State Col, 69; first Indian to be app to Indian Claims Comn. Relig: Christian Church of NAm. Legal Res: 9309 Glenbrook Rd Fairfax VA 22030 Mailing Add: c/o Indian Claims Comn Sixth Floor 1730 K St NW Washington DC 20006

BLUE, CAROLYN HARRISON (D)
b Pinehurst, NC, July 22, 28; d Howard Russell Harrison & Lois Hendren H; m 1948 to Thomas Harold Blue; c Thomas Harold, Jr, Sharon B (Mrs Reid) & Christy Lynne. Educ: Sandhill Commun Col, Southern Pines, NC, 68. Polit & Govt Pos: Pres, Moore Co Young Dem Club, NC, 60-64; nat committeewoman, NC Young Dem Club, 64-66; campaign mgr, Voit Gilmore, cand for Cong, 68-69; vpres, Moore Co Dem Exec Comt, 68-70, chmn, 70-74; alt deleg, Dem Nat Conv, 72. Bus & Prof Pos: Secy, Qual Oil Co of West End, Inc, 55-67; secy, Candor Oil Co, Inc, 70-73. Mem: NC Hist Soc; Foxfire Golf & Country Club; Pinecrest High Sch Adv Comt; Moore Co Cancer Soc (area chmn). Relig: Presbyterian. Mailing Add: Box 117 Eagle Springs NC 27242

BLUE, GEORGE (D)
b Huron, SDak, Feb 12, 27; m to Belva Meyer; c Thomas, Kathleen & James. Educ: Huron Col; Univ SDak Law Sch, LLB. Polit & Govt Pos: Beadle Co States Attorney, SDak; SDak State Sen, until 66; chmn, SDak State Dem Party, 69-73; mem, Dem Nat Comt, 70-72. Bus & Prof Pos: Lawyer. Mem: Legis Research Coun; Izaak Walton League; KofC; Elks; Am Legion. Relig: Catholic. Mailing Add: 126 Third St SW Huron SD 57350

BLUE, GEORGE RIEBEL (D)
b Houston, Tex, Dec 10, 16; s Kaa Frank Blue & Eulalie Leonard B; m 1944 to Elizabeth Lida Beard, div; remarried 1970 to Catherine Colquitt; c Kaa Frank, II, Leslie R, George R, Jr, Sarah & Robert. Educ: Soule Col, New Orleans, 33; Tulane Univ, BA, 37, LLB, 39; Univ Miss, 54. Polit & Govt Pos: Spec agent, Fed Bur Invest, US Dept Justice, DC, 40-45; US Attorney, Eastern Dist La, 52-56; finance chmn, Rep Party La; chmn, Jefferson Parish Rep Exec Comt, 57-61; mem adv comt on rules of criminal procedure, US Supreme Court, 61-71; La State Rep, Jefferson Parish, 64-72; mem, Nixon Task Force on Crime & Law Enforcement, 68-72. Bus & Prof Pos: Partner, Beard, Blue, Schmitt & Treen, 47-; nat vpres, Soc of X-FBI Agents, 61. Mil Serv: Entered as Pfc, Marine Corps Res, 35, released as 2nd Lt, 41. Mem: New Orleans Bar Asn; La & Am Bar Asns; Am Judicature Soc; La Comn on Law Enforcement & Admin of Justice. Relig: Episcopal. Legal Res: 5308 Haring Ct Metairie LA 70002 Mailing Add: 833 Howard Ave New Orleans LA 70113

BLUE, WILLIAM ROY (D)
Mem Exec Comt, Genesee Co Dem Party, Mich
b Flint, Mich, Feb 8, 33; s Albert O Blue & Marion Wotzka B; m 1954 to Marilyn Marie Anderson; c James Albert, Diane Marie, Robert William, Daniel Scott & Thomas Patrick. Educ: Flint Community Jr Col, Mich, Assoc Bus, 56; Flint Col, Univ Mich, BA in Bus, 58. Polit & Govt Pos: Mem, Flint Bd Educ, Mich, 65-68; Dem nominee, US House Rep, Seventh Dist, 68; chmn, Mich Seventh Dist Citizens for Kennedy, 68; mem, Mich Dem Polit Reform Comn, 69-; mem exec comt, Genesee Co Dem Party, 69-; mem, Mich Dem Comt Opposed to Antiballistic Missiles, 69-; cand for Dem nomination for Mich Secy of State, 70; mem, Levin for Gov Comt, 70; precinct deleg, 70- Bus & Prof Pos: Sales rep, Standard Register Co, 58-62, Int Bus Machines Corp, 62-64 & Perry Printing Co, 64- Mil Serv: Entered as Pvt, Army, 54, released as SP-3, 55. Mem: Flint Jr CofC; Dollars for Scholars (vpres); Jr Achievement of Flint (bd dirs). Honors & Awards: Flint's Outstanding Young Man, Flint Jr CofC, 66. Relig: Roman Catholic. Mailing Add: 6908 Orange Lane Flint MI 48505

BLUECHEL, ALAN JOSEPH (R)
Wash State Sen
b Edmonton, Alta, Aug 28, 24; s Joseph Harold Bluechel & Edith Daly B; m 1957 to Aylene Loughnan; c Gordon Blair & Turner Farllon. Educ: Univ BC, BA & BASc, 48; Beta Theta Pi. Polit & Govt Pos: Washington State Rep, First Dist, 67-74; mem, World's Fair Comn, 67-; mem, King Co Flood Control Adv Bd, 68-70; mem, King Co Conserv Comt, 70-; Wash State Sen, 45th Dist, 75-, mem, Transportation & Utilities Comt, Wash State Senate, mem, Natural Resources Comt & minority-chmn, Financial Insts Comt. Bus & Prof Pos: Vpres, Loctwall Corp, Lynnwood, Wash, 48-64, pres, 64-; pres, C-M Inn Co, Crystal Mountain, 65-; mem, Wash State Trade Fair Mission, Japan, 65 & 66. Honors & Awards: Seattle Jr CofC Keyman of the Year Award. Relig: Presbyterian. Legal Res: 12534 68th Ave NE Kirkland WA 98033 Mailing Add: Wash State Senate Legislative Bldg Olympia WA 98504

BLUM, WILLIAM L (D)
b Philadelphia, Pa, Mar 6, 52; s Charles Maurice Blum & Barbara Greenstein B; m 1974 to Cheryl F Coodley. Educ: Mass Inst Technol, SB, 74; Boston Univ Sch Law, 74- Polit & Govt Pos: Worker, Shapp for Gov Campaign, Lower Merion Twp, Pa, 66; chmn high sch vol, McCarthy for President Campaign, 68; asst coordr, Shapp for Gov Campaign, Lower Merion Twp & Montgomery Co, 70; dep registr vital statist, Lower Merion Twp, 71 & 72; asst dir, McGovern for President Campaign Comt, 17th Sen Dist, 71-72; deleg, Dem Nat Conv, 72; mem, Main Line Independent Dem, 73- Relig: Jewish. Mailing Add: 645 Hazelhurst Ave Merion Station PA 19066

BLUMBERG, JANE WEINERT (D)
Mem, Dem Nat Comt
b Seguin, Tex, Sept 24, 17; d Hilmar Herman Weinert & Hilda Blumberg W; m 1940 to Roland Krezdorn Blumberg; c Carla Ann, Hilmar Daniel & Edward Austin. Educ: Univ Tex, BA, 37; Northwestern Univ, MA, 38; Kappa Kappa Gamma. Polit & Govt Pos: Secy, Bd Educ, Seguin Independent Sch Dist, Tex, 57-65; mem, Tex Hosp Adv Comn, 60-64; mem, Dem Nat Comt, 72- Bus & Prof Pos: Dir, Seguin State Bank & Trust Co, 53-, chmn bd, 71- Mem: Phi Beta Kappa; Alpha Lambda Delta; Seguin Shakespeare Club; Daughters of the Repub of Tex. Relig: Lutheran. Mailing Add: Rte 2 Box 236 Seguin TX 78155

BLUME, JOYCE CAMPBELL (D)
Chairwoman, Women's Div, Dem State Cent Comt, Ill
b Keokuk, Iowa, Dec 11, 32; d Peyton Campbell & Nelle Davis C; m 1950 to Robert Edward Blume; c Robert Peyton, William Jeffrey, Helene Campbell & Hollis Christine. Polit & Govt Pos: Chairwoman, Cass Co Dem Cent Comt, Ill, 62-66; pres, Dem Women's Orgn, 64-66; alt deleg, Dem Nat Conv, 64 & 68; chairwoman cent Dist Women's Div, Dem State Cent Comt, 65-72, Chairwoman, Women's Div, Comt, currently; secy, Comn Employ of Handicapped, Ill, 65-68. Bus & Prof Pos: Chief probation officer, Cass Co, Ill, 64-71. Mem: DAR; Women's Club; Pub Libr Asn (bd dirs); Ill Probation & Parole Asn. Relig: Methodist. Mailing Add: 17 Woody Ave Beardstown IL 62618

BLUME, NORBERT L (D)
Ky State Rep
b 1922; m 1944 to Marie Buecker. Educ: Univ Louisville; Univ Ky. Polit & Govt Pos: Ky State Rep, 64-, house speaker, Ky Gen Assembly, 72-, deleg, Dem Nat Conv, 72. Bus & Prof Pos: Labor Rep. Mil Serv: Navy, World War II. Mem: VFW. Relig: Catholic. Mailing Add: 4224 Northwestern Pkwy Louisville KY 40212

BLUMENAUER, EARL (D)
Ore State Rep
Mailing Add: 7317 SE Woodward Portland OR 97206

BLUMENTHAL, ALBERT HOWARD (D)
NY State Assemblyman
b New York, NY, Oct 13, 28; s Bennet M Blumenthal & Matilda B; m 1958 to Joel Marie Winik; c Daniel J, Ann Marie, Peter A & David M. Educ: Col William & Mary, BA, 49; NY Univ Law Sch, LLB, 51, Grad Sch, LLM, 56. Polit & Govt Pos: NY State Assemblyman, 69th Dist, 63-, majority leader, currently. Bus & Prof Pos: Counsel, Phillips, Nizer, Benjamin, Krim & Ballon, 74- Mil Serv: Entered as Pvt, Army, 51, released as Cpl, 53. Mem: Am, NY Co & NY State Bar Asns. Legal Res: 90 Riverside Dr New York NY 10024 Mailing Add: 720 Columbus Ave New York NY 10025

BLUMENTHAL, CHARLES S (D)
Md State Deleg
Mailing Add: 519 Barrymore Dr Oxon Hill MD 20021

BLUMENTHAL, TOBY NEVIS (R)
b Chicago, Ill, May 7, 33; d Max Ivan Nevis & Rose Chayes N; m 1954 to Dr Bernard J Blumenthal; c Julie Yetta, Paul Charles, Amy Lynne, Barry Morris & Ruth Hanna. Educ: Northwestern Univ, Evanston, BM, 54; Univ Houston, MM, 57; Sigma Alpha Iota; Sigma Delta Tau. Polit & Govt Pos: Alt deleg, Rep Dist Conv, Pasadena, Tex, 68, deleg, 70 & 72; deleg, Tex Dem State Conv, 70 & 72, mem resolutions comt, 70, mem platform & resolutions comts, 72; alt deleg, Dem Nat Conv, 72. Bus & Prof Pos: Concert pianist, Soloist with Chicago Symphony, 47, Shreveport Symphony, 56 & Houston Symphony, 58, 60, 62, 69 & 70; played with, Houston Chamber Orchestra Music Guild, Lyric Art String Quartet & Young Audiences, Inc. Mem: Southeast Harris Co & Harris Co Med Auxiliary; Pasadena Federated Music Club; Tuesday Music Club; Pasadena Civic Music Asn. Relig: Jewish. Mailing Add: 2118 Locklaine Dr Pasadena TX 77502

BLUTHARDT, EDWARD EARL (R)
Ill State Rep
b Chicago, Ill, Dec 10, 16; s Charles Edward Bluthardt & Edna May Clause B; m 1941 to Dorothy Gertrude Dickstein; c Edward Earl, Jr, & Bonnie Kay (Mrs James Stella). Educ: Ill Col, AB, 39; John Marshall Law Sch, JD, 50; Delta Theta Phi; Sigma Pi Soc. Polit & Govt

Pos: Village magistrate, Shiller Park, Ill, 55-57, pres, 61-73; Ill State Rep, 66- Bus & Prof Pos: Partner, Jacobson & Bluthardt Law Firm, 50-70. Mil Serv: Entered as Pvt, Army, 42, released as First Lt, 46, after serv in Artil, ETO, 44-46; Good Conduct Medal; ETO Ribbon with Two Battle Stars. Mem: Ill & Chicago Bar Asns; Schiller Park Lions Club; Izaak Walton League; Leyden Twp Regular Rep Orgn. Relig: Episcopal. Mailing Add: 4042 Gremley Terr Schiller Park IL 60176

BLY, BELDEN G, JR (R)
Mass State Rep
Educ: Harvard Univ; Dartmouth Col; Boston Univ; Northeastern Univ, BA, LLB, MEd & JD. Polit & Govt Pos: Mass State Rep, currently; bipartisan selection as legis deleg to attend the White House Conf on Educ; alt deleg, Rep Nat Conv, 68. Bus & Prof Pos: Teacher, 22 years; attorney-at-law. Mem: Essex Co Teachers' Asn. Honors & Awards: A winner of Nat Sci Found Award in Bact at Univ Colo. Mailing Add: 46 Auburn St Saugus MA 01906

BLYTHE, COY DANIEL, SR (R)
Rep Committeeman, Ill Rep State Cent Comt
b Shelbyville, Ill, Jan 8, 18; s Harold M Blythe & Ada Reeder B; m 1941 to Evelyn Marie Arthur; c Coy Daniel, Jr. Educ: Univ Ill, 1 year. Polit & Govt Pos: Rep precinct committeeman, Precinct One, Shelbyville, Ill, currently; secy, Shelby Co Rep Cent Comt, Ill, 6 years; Rep Committeeman, Ill Rep State Cent Comt, currently; spec investr for the Attorney Gen, State of Ill, currently. Bus & Prof Pos: City policeman, Shelbyville, Ill, 3 years; salesman, Kaskaskia Co, 18 years; security officer, Oliver Corp, 6 years. Mil Serv: Entered as Pvt, Air Force, 42, released as Sgt, 46, after serv in US. Mem: Am Legion; Moose. Honors & Awards: Several awards & honors, Moose. Relig: Protestant. Legal Res: 117 E N Seventh St Shelbyville IL 62565 Mailing Add: PO Box 206 Shelbyville IL 62565

BLYTHE, E BRUCE, JR (R)
Ky State Rep
b 1927. Educ: Univ Ky. Polit & Govt Pos: Ky State Rep, currently. Bus & Prof Pos: Advert & pub rels; pres, Blythe Advert; pres, Swing Image Corp. Mil Serv: Maj, Ky Air Nat Guard. Mem: Louisville Jaycees; Univ Ky Alumni Asn. Relig: Presbyterian. Mailing Add: 516 Altagate Rd Louisville KY 40206

BLYTHE, WILLIAM JACKSON, JR (R)
Tex State Rep
b San Antonio, Tex, Aug 15, 35; s Col William J Blythe, Sr & Bess Tyson B; m 1970 to Charlene Cotten. Educ: Univ Va, 54-55; Univ Tex, Austin, BA, 61; Univ Tex Ex-Students Asn & Longhorn Club; Univ Va Alumni Asn. Polit & Govt Pos: Mem cand recruitment comt, vol chmn, legis campaign coordr comt & vol chmn, lit distribution comt, 1968 Nixon campaign, Harris Co Rep Party; life mem & past pres, Rep Victory Club; mem & past dir, Harris Co Young Rep Club; regional dir, Rep Party Tex; election judge, Rep Primary Election; deleg, two Rep Co Conv; past chmn, orgn comt, Travis Co Rep Party; past mem, Travis Co Rep Party Exec Comt; Tex State Rep, 70- Bus & Prof Pos: Pres, William Blythe Real Estate. Mil Serv: Served eight years active & reserve duty, Army; hon discharge with citations. Mem: Houston Jr CofC; Houston Livestock Show & Rodeo; Inst Hispanic Culture Houston; SAR; Sons Confederate Vets. Honors & Awards: Charles A Perlitz Jr Mem Award for leadership training through community develop, Houston Jr CofC, 71-72. Relig: Baptist. Mailing Add: Room 43 2815 Greenridge Houston TX 77027

BOARD, JOSEPH BRECKINRIDGE (D)
Committeeman, Schenectady Co Comt, NY
b Princeton, Ind, Mar 5, 31; s Joseph Board & Rachel Unthank B; m 1955 to Kjersti Danielson; c Ian Robert, Annika Caroline & Amanda Anne. Educ: Ind Univ, Bloomington, AB, 53, JD, 58, PhD, 62; Oxford Univ, BA, 55, MA, 61; Phi Beta Kappa. Polit & Govt Pos: Adv Young Citizens for Johnson, 64; committeeman, Schenectady Co Comt, NY, 67-; vchmn, Glenville Town Comt, 71-; alt deleg, Dem Nat Conv, 72. Bus & Prof Pos: Lectr, Ind Univ, 58-59; asst prof, Elmira Col, 59-61; assoc prof, Cornell Col, 61-65; prof & chmn dept polit sci, Union Col (NY), 65- Publ: The Government & Politics of Sweden, Houghton-Mifflin, 71. Mem: Am Asn Univ Prof; Northeastern Polit Sci Asn (exec coun, 72-); Soc Advan Scand Studies (exec coun, 72-); Am Polit Sci Asn; Freedom Forum Schenectady. Honors & Awards: Rhodes Scholar, 53; Fulbright fel, Fulbright-Hays Prog, 68. Relig: Episcopal. Mailing Add: 15 Sunnyside Rd Scotia NY 12302

BOARDMAN, ROBERT EMMETT (D)
Mem, Dem State Exec Comt, Vt
b Burlington, Vt, May 20, 32; s Ira Munn Boardman & Dorothy McMahon B; m 1955 to Nancy Katherine Chandler; c Carla Marie, Robert Emmett, Jr, Kevin Michael & Joanne McMahon. Educ: Col Holy Cross, BS, 54. Polit & Govt Pos: Mem, Dem State Exec Comt, Vt, 66-; Vt State Sen, Chittender-Grand Isle Dist, 69-75. Bus & Prof Pos: Treas, Hickok & Boardman, Inc, 60-; trustee, Burlington Savings Bank, 68-; Univ Vt, 71- Mil Serv: Entered as Pvt, Army, 54, released as Sp-3/C, 56, after serv in Counter Intel Corp. Mem: CofC. Honors & Awards: Vt & New Eng Jaycee Distinguished Serv Awards, 67; Freshman Sen Award, Vt Legis, 69. Relig: Roman Catholic. Legal Res: 208 Meadowood Dr South Burlington VT 05401 Mailing Add: 346 Shelburne Rd Burlington VT 05401

BOAS, ROGER (D)
b San Francisco, Calif, Aug 21, 21; s Benjamin Boas & Larie Kline B; m 1958 to Nancy Lee Magid; c John Roger, Christopher, Anthony & Lucy. Educ: Stanford Univ, AB, 42. Polit & Govt Pos: Supvr, City & Co of San Francisco, Calif, 61-72, chmn, Planning & Develop Comt; chmn, Calif State Dem Cent Comt, 68-70; Dem cand for Cong Sixth Cong Dist, 72. Bus & Prof Pos: Owner, Boas Pontiac, San Francisco, 45-; producer & moderator, World Press, Nat Educ TV Prog, 60-72. Mil Serv: Officer, Army; serv in 3rd Army, ETO; Silver Star; Bronze Star; Campaign Ribbon & Five Battle Stars. Mem: Outer City YMCA; San Francisco Homemakers' Serv; Northern Calif Region, Nat Conf Christians & Jews; World Affairs Coun of Northern Calif. Mailing Add: 950 Van Ness San Francisco CA 94102

BOATNER, ROY ALTON (D)
Okla State Sen
b Durant, Okla, Nov 9, 41; s Frank Boatner & Minnie Mattingly B (deceased); m 1967 to Winona Arlene Walker. Educ: Southeastern State Col, BS, 64, MEd, 72; Southern Methodist Univ, 65; Sigma Tau Gamma. Polit & Govt Pos: Okla State Rep, 70-74; Okla State Sen, 75- Bus & Prof Pos: Off mgr, Snak-Bar Inc, Dallas, Tex, 64-65; credit rep, Ford Motor Co, 65-66; ins adjustor, Am Rd Ins Co, 66-67; prin, Achille High Sch, Okla, 67-70; partner, Gray & Boatner Real Estate, 67- Mil Serv: Entered as Airman 3/C, Air Force Res, 64, released as Sgt, 70, after serv in 4780th Hosp Unit, Air Defense Command. Mem: Okla Educ Asn; CofC. Relig: Baptist. Mailing Add: Rte 1 Calera OK 74730

BOATWRIGHT, DANIEL E (D)
Calif State Assemblyman
Mailing Add: 1035 Detroit Ave Concord CA 94518

BOATWRIGHT, MARY H (R)
Rep Nat Committeewoman, Conn
b Houston, Tex, Apr 8, 20; m 1946 to Victor T Boatwright; c Dorsey, John William, Mary Taliaferro. Educ: Trinity Col (DC), BA, 41. Polit & Govt Pos: Vchmn, Stonington Rep Town Comt, Conn, 56-; burgess, Stonington Borough, 59-65; Conn State Rep, 61-69; mem, State Platform Comt, 70; Rep Nat Committeewoman, Conn, 72- Bus & Prof Pos: Reporter, San Francisco Chronicle, 44-46. Publ: Ed, Westerly Hosp Aid News. Mem: Mashantucket Land Trust (mem bd); East Conn Symphony (mem bd); Danu Arts Coun (mem bd); The Arts Coun (mem bd); Stonington Libr (secy book comt). Relig: Roman Catholic. Mailing Add: 16 Denison Ave Stonington CT 06378

BOBBITT, WILLIAM HAYWOOD
Chief Justice, NC Supreme Court
b Raleigh, NC, Oct 18, 00; s James Henry Bobbitt & Eliza May Burkhead B; m 1924 to Sarah Buford Dunlap (deceased); c Sarah (Mrs John W Carter), William Haywood (deceased), Buford (Mrs Ekkehart Sachtler) & Harriet (Mrs Dan S Moss). Educ: Univ NC, BA, 21. Hon Degrees: LLD, Davidson Col, 53 & Univ NC, 57. Polit & Govt Pos: Trustee Brevard Col, 33-52; Judge, 14th Judicial Superior Court, NC, 39-54; mem, NC Judicial Coun, 49-54; mem Comn to Study Improv Admin Justice in NC, 47-49; Assoc Justice, NC Supreme Court, 54-69, chief justice, 69- Bus & Prof Pos: Lawyer, Charlotte, NC, 22-38. Mem: Am & NC Bar Asns; Am Judicature Soc; Univ NC Alumni Asn; Civitan Club. Relig: Methodist. Legal Res: PO Box 1841 Raleigh NC 27602 Mailing Add: Justice Bldg Raleigh NC 27602

BOBROFF, HAROLD (D)
Committeeman, Nassau Co Dem Party, NY
b New York, NY, Apr 29, 20; s Max Bobroff & Mary Platofsky B; m 1945 to Marion Hemendinger; c Caren Kay & Fredric Jon. Educ: City Col New York, BBA, 47; NY Law Sch, LLB, 51. Polit & Govt Pos: Committeeman, Nassau Co Dem Party, NY, 52-; zone leader, Woodmere, 55-58; NY State Dem Committeeman & chmn, 15th Assembly Dist, Nassau Co, 58-71; chief dep attorney, Nassau Co, NY, 62-63; chief counsel, Joint Legis Comt Ins Rates & Regulation, 65-, counsel, Joint Legis Comt on Villages, 68- Bus & Prof Pos: Partner, Bobroff & Olonoff, CPA, 49-; partner, Bobroff, Olonoff & Scharf, Attorneys-at-Law, 53-; gen counsel & dir, South Nassau Develop Corp, 66- Mil Serv: Entered as Pvt, Army, 42, released as Capt, 46, after serv in Field Artil, Second Armored Div, ETO, 42-45; ETO, NAfrican & Sicilian Ribbons; Bronze Star with Cluster; Distinguished Unit Citation with Cluster; Belgian Fouraggere. Mem: Nassau Co & NY Co Bar Asns; Masons; B'nai B'rith; Nassau Community Col (trustee, 68-). Relig: Jewish; Pres & trustee, Temple Sinai of Lawrence. Mailing Add: 795 Hampton Rd Woodmere NY 11598

BOCK, BENNIE W, II, (D)
Tex State Rep
b Lockhart, Tex, May 17, 42; s Bennie Walter Bock & Ruth Margaret Sue Blackwell B; m 1965 to Kathy C Holmberg; c Suzanne C & Lucretia C. Educ: Univ Tex, Austin, BBA, 64; St Mary's Univ Sch Law, Tex, JD, 68; Delta Sigma Pi; Delta Theta Phi. Polit & Govt Pos: Statistician, Voter Registr Div, Dem Nat Comt, Washington, DC, 64; dir air transportation, Dem Nat Conv, 64; admin asst, US Rep J J Pickle, Tex, 68; legal counsel & clerk, Tex State Senate Comt on State Affairs, 69 & 71; Asst Attorney Gen, Law Enforcement Div, Tex, 69-70, Bond Div, 70-71; Tex State Rep, 73- Publ: The limestone & lime industry of Texas, Tex Bus Rev, Univ Tex, 5-6/68. Mem: Univ Tex Ex-Student's Asn (life mem); Am Bar Asn; Tex Hist Soc; Lions; Jaycees. Honors & Awards: Student Rep to Am Bar Asn, St Mary's Univ Sch Law, 68; Student Del to Am Bar Asn Conv, 68. Relig: Episcopal. Legal Res: 402 Oakwood New Braunfels TX 78130 Mailing Add: PO Box 591 New Braunfels TX 78130

BOCKBRADER, CLAYTON EDWARD (R)
Chmn, Denton Co Rep Party, Tex
b Ft Lewis, Wash, Mar 18, 45; s Donald Edward Bockbrader & Maxine Henderson B; single. Educ: NTex State Univ, BA in Polit Sci. Polit & Govt Pos: Chmn, Denton Co Rep Party, Tex, 75- Bus & Prof Pos: Owner, Chambers-Bockbrader Serv, currently. Mil Serv: Entered as Pvt E-1, Army, 67, released as SPC-5, 69, after serv in 3rd Armored Div, Ger, 67-69. Relig: Episcopal. Mailing Add: 212 Marietta Denton TX 76201

BOCKEMUEHL, RICHARD GEORGE (R)
Chmn, Pend Orielle Co Rep Cent Comt, Wash
b Newport, Wash, Aug 8, 39; s Frank William Bockemuehl & Jeanne Delores Schibsby B; m 1967 to Linda Joyce Kelley; c Tracy Claire, Mark Wade & Eric Francis. Educ: Univ Wash, BA Gen Bus, 64; Chevrolet Sch Merchandising & Mgt, Warren, Mich, grad, 73; Phi Delta Theta; Sundodgers. Polit & Govt Pos: Committeeman, Pend Oreille Co Rep Cent Comt, Wash, 70-72, chmn, 71- Bus & Prof Pos: Owner-mgr, Sundance Cedar Co, Priest River, Idaho, 68-70; automobile sales, Courtesy Chevrolet-Pontiac, Newport, Wash, 70- Mil Serv: Entered as E-1, Army, 57, released as E-4, 58; E-4, Army Res, 65. Mem: Lions (pres, 71). Honors & Awards: Chevrolet Truck Sales Hall of Fame, 70-74; Chevrolet Legion of Leaders, 70-74. Relig: Protestant. Legal Res: 529 W Third Newport WA 99156 Mailing Add: Box 117 Newport WA 99156

BOCKENKAMP, RON (D)
Mo State Rep
Mailing Add: 413 D St Bonne Terre MO 63628

BOCKHORST, ESTELLE WILFERTH (R)
VChmn, Mo State Rep Cent Comt
b Jefferson City, Mo, Oct 22, 96; d Nichalos Wilferth & Mary Knernschield W; m to Diedrich Soloman Bockhorst, wid. Polit & Govt Pos: Cert copy clerk, State Bd of Health Dept, Mo, 20; elector, Rep Nat Conv, 60, alt deleg, 64, deleg, 68; committeewoman, Cole Co Rep Comt, currently; mem, Mo State Rep Cent Comt, Eighth Cong Dist, currently, vchmn, currently, mem, Budget Comt, 67 & 70; mem, Eighth Cong Dist Rep Comt, currently; deleg, Nat Fedn of Rep Women, Washington, DC, 67; co-chmn, Eighth Cong Dist Nixon-Agnew Campaign Comt, Mo, 68. Bus & Prof Pos: Notary Public, currently. Mem: Rep Fedn Women's Club; church & farm orgn. Honors & Awards: Nominated Community Leader of Am, 68. Relig: Evangelical & Reformed Church. Mailing Add: Star Rte 2 Jefferson City MO 65101

BOCKHORST, JOHN HERB (R)
Committeeman, Greene Co Rep Cent Comt, Mo
b Springfield, Mo, Sept 24, 26; s John Herbert Bockhorst & Melvina Walker B; m 1948 to Marilyn Brown; c Julie & Bart. Educ: Southwest Mo State Col, BA, 49; Sigma Tau Gamma. Polit & Govt Pos: Committeeman, Greene Co Rep Cent Comt, Mo, 63-, chmn, formerly. Mil Serv: Entered as E-2, Navy, 44, released as E-4, 46, after serv in Air Force, US, 44-46. Mem: Life Underwriters Asn; Gen Agents & Mgr Asn; Mason; Shrine; Kiwanis. Relig: Episcopal. Legal Res: 2507 Hillsboro Springfield MO 65804 Mailing Add: 1736 E Sunshine Suite 905 Springfield MO 65804

BOCKMAN, GLEN O (D)
b Birch Tree, Mo, Apr 14, 31; s William O Bockman (deceased) & Della Marie Ball B; m 1955 to Lois Ludene Trammel; c Jeffrey G, Tina L, Lisa K & Brian A. Educ: Birch Tree High Sch. Polit & Govt Pos: Chmn, Shannon Co Welfare Comt, Mo, 69-71; treas, Shannon Co Dem Cent Comt, formerly. Bus & Prof Pos: Mem ins staff, MFA Mutual Ins Co, 53; owner, real estate, 60. Mil Serv: Entered as Pvt, Army, 49, released as Cpl, 51, after serv in Korea. Mem: Birch Tree Develop Corp (pres); Ozark Develop Corp; Delphian Lodge 137; St Louis Consistory (32 degree); Abuu Ben Adhem Temple. Relig: Baptist. Mailing Add: PO Box 6 Birch Tree MO 65438

BODDEN, MARK LELAND (D)
b Brooklyn, NY, July 12, 50; s Albert Bodden & Dorit McKenzie B; single. Educ: Cornell Univ Sch of Indust & Labor Rels, BS, 72; George Washington Univ Law Sch. Polit & Govt Pos: Queens Co Co-Organizer, Comt to Make Richard Ottinger Sen Ottinger, NY, 70; Cornell Coordr, Cong Campaign of William Greenawalt, 25th Cong Dist, NY, 70; mem, Comn on Youth Affairs, New York Dem Comt, 71-72; alt deleg, Dem Nat Conv, 72; asst clerk, Doc Room, US House Rep, 72-; legis asst to US Rep Charles B Rangel, NY, 74- Publ: The question of black faculty members here at ILR, Voice, fall 72. Mem: Am Bar Asn, Law Student Mem; Common Cause. Relig: Episcopal. Mailing Add: 111-30 173rd St Jamaica NY 11433

BODIFORD, RAY (R)
Tenn State Rep
b Pocahontas, Tenn, June 14, 36; s John Edgar Bodiford (deceased) & Martha LouDella Kirk B (deceased); m 1959 to Bernice Nixon; c Rhonda Rene & Richard Scott. Educ: Selmer High Sch, Tenn, grad, 54. Polit & Govt Pos: Co chmn, Howard Baker for Senate & Nixon for President, Tenn, 66; pres, McNairy Co Young Rep Club, 67-68; treas, McNairy Co Rep Party, 70-74; Tenn State Rep, 70th Dist, 72- Bus & Prof Pos: Advert mgr & part owner, Hamilton & Co, Selmer, Tenn, 65-67; owner, Bodiford Ins Agency, Selmer, 67- Mil Serv: Entered as Pvt, Marine Corps, 54, released as S/Sgt, 65; Good Conduct Medal; Korean Serv Medal; Expert Rifleman's Badge; Nat Defense Medal. Mem: Parent Teachers Orgn; Am Legion; VFW; Jaycees; Quarterback Club. Honors & Awards: Outstanding Young Man & Outstanding Jaycee, Selmer Jaycees, 68; Man of Year, WOW, 74. Relig: Church of Christ. Legal Res: Rte 3 Selmer TN 38375 Mailing Add: PO Box 219 Selmer TN 38375

BODINE, RICHARD CLAY (D)
Ind State Rep
Educ: Ind Univ Sch of Bus; Ind Univ Law Sch. Polit & Govt Pos: Ind State Rep, 63-69 & 71-72, 75-, Speaker, Ind House Rep, 65, Minority Leader, 67 & 71-72. Bus & Prof Pos: Attorney-at-law. Mil Serv: Air Force, Korea. Mem: Co, State & Am Bar Asns; Am Legion; Phi Delta Phi. Relig: Protestant. Mailing Add: 208 1st Nat Bank Bldg Mishawaka IN 46544

BODRON, ELLIS BARKETT (D)
Miss State Sen
b Vicksburg, Miss, Oct 25, 23; s Ellis Barkett Bodron & Helen Ellis B; m 1960 to Jane Workman; c Helen Estelle & Lawrence Ellis. Educ: Univ Miss, LLB & BA, 46; Phi Delta Phi; Omicron Delta Kappa; Phi Eta Sigma; Phi Kappa Alpha. Polit & Govt Pos: Miss State Rep, 48-52; Miss State Sen, 52-, chmn, Finance Comt, Miss State Senate. Bus & Prof Pos: Partner, Law Firm of Ramsey, Bodron & Thames, 57- Mem: Nat Conf of State Legis Leaders; Legis Adv Comt; Southern Regional Educ Bd; Lions; CofC. Legal Res: 2209 Cherry St Vicksburg MS 39180 Mailing Add: Rm 708 First Nat Bank Bldg Vicksburg MS 39180

BODWELL, MARGARETTA LOTT (MARGE) (R)
b Xenia, Ohio, Sept 19, 20; d Crampton Bigle Lott & Christel Haines L; m 1947, div; c Roger Allen, Robert Neal & Elizabeth Mae. Educ: Univ Cincinnati, BA, 43; Univ Mich, 45-47; Univ NMex, 64; Phi Sigma. Polit & Govt Pos: Vchairwoman, Oter Co Rep Party, 64-70, chairwoman, 70-72; mem, NMex State Cent Rep Comt, 8 years; deleg, Rep Nat Conv, 72. Bus & Prof Pos: Analytical chemist, Nat Cash Register Co, Dayton, Ohio, 43-44; teacher high sch, Xenia, 44-46; analytical chemist, Dept Interior, Washington, DC, 45; critic teacher, Univ Mich, 47-48; elem teacher, Las Cruces, NMex, 54-56, elem teacher, Alamogordo, 63- Mem: Kappa Kappa Iota; DAR (State VRegent); Children of the Am Revolution (state sr pres, 72-74); Am Asn of Univ Women. Relig: Methodist. Mailing Add: 2201 12th Alamogordo NM 88310

BOE, JASON DOUGLAS (D)
Ore State Sen
b Los Angeles, Calif, Mar 10, 29; s Christian J Boe & Lillian Eggers B; m 1952 to Kathryn Reule; c Eric, Peter & Brian. Educ: Pac Lutheran Univ, BA, 51; Univ Wash, 51-52; Pac Univ, OD, 55. Polit & Govt Pos: City councilman, Reedsport, Ore, 58-64; Ore State Rep, Douglas Co, 64-70, Minority Whip, Ore House of Rep, 67, Minority Leader, 69; alt deleg, Dem Nat Conv, 68; Ore State Sen, 70- Bus & Prof Pos: Optometrist, Reedsport, 56- Publ: Various articles on taxation & educ in The Portland Oregonian & the Ore J. Mem: Ore & Am Optom Asns; Rotary; CofC; Jr CofC. Relig: Lutheran. Mailing Add: 2078 Hawthorne Ave Reedsport OR 97467

BOE, NILS A (R)
b Baltic, SDak, Sept 10, 13; s Rev N Boe & Sissel C Finseth B; single. Educ: Univ Wis, BA, 35, LLB, 37; Phi Alpha Delta. Hon Degrees: LLD, Huron Col (SDak), 72. Polit & Govt Pos: SDak State Rep, 51-59, Speaker of the House, SDak House Rep, 55-59; Lt Gov, SDak, 63-65, Gov, 65-69; dir, Off of Intergovernmental Affairs, Exec Off of the President, Washington, DC, 69-71; Chief Judge, US Customs Court, NY, 71- Bus & Prof Pos: Attorney, May, Boe & Johnson, 46-65. Mil Serv: Entered as Ens, Navy, 42, released as Lt(sg), 45. Mem: Minnehaha Co Farm Bur; Elks; Am Legion; VFW; Odd Fellows. Relig: Lutheran. Legal Res: 504 S Duluth Sioux Falls SD 57104 Mailing Add: US Customs Ct One Fed Plaza New York NY 10007

BOECKMAN, DUNCAN EUGENE (R)
Gen Counsel, Rep State Exec Comt, Tex
b Houston, Tex, Sept 17, 26; s Eugene Frank Boeckman & Nancy Duncan B; m 1955 to Elizabeth Ann Mayer; c Nancy Kathryn, Daniel Duncan & Caroline Albert. Educ: Univ Tex, BBA, Law Sch, LLB; Phi Delta Phi. Polit & Govt Pos: Legal counsel, Dallas Co Rep Party, Tex, 62-64; chmn, Dallas Co Rep Conv, 64; alt deleg, Rep Nat Conv, 64 & 68; gen counsel, Rep State Exec Comt, 64-; chmn justice comt, Tex Coun Fed Employ, 69- Bus & Prof Pos: Partner, Golden, Potts, Boeckman & Wilson, 57- Mil Serv: Entered as Seaman, Navy, 44, released as Seaman 1/C, 46. Mem: Am, Tex & Dallas Bar Asns; Am Judicature Soc; Dallas Country Club. Relig: Methodist. Legal Res: 5380 Nakoma Dr Dallas TX 75209 Mailing Add: 2300 Republic Nat Bank Tower Dallas TX 75201

BOEHLER, CONRAD JOSEPH (D)
Chmn, Harlan Co Dem Party, Nebr
b Orleans, Nebr, Jan 16, 30; s Joseph John Boehler & Lorette Marie Fuller B; m 1953 to June Elaine Karlson; c John Burton, Barbara June, Bryce Conrad, Michael Shawn & Scott Allan. Educ: Kearney State Teachers Col, 1 year. Polit & Govt Pos: Precinct Committeeman, Orleans Twp, Nebr, 63; chmn, Harlan Co Dem Party, 65-; supvr, Harlan Co, Dist Five, 71- Bus & Prof Pos: Farmer, 53- Mil Serv: Entered as Seaman Apprentice, Navy, 51, released as PO3/C, after serv in Atlantic Theatre, 51-53; Presidential Unit Citation. Mem: Am Legion; KofC; CofC; Nat Farmers Orgn; Lions. Relig: Catholic. Mailing Add: Rte 1 Orleans NE 68966

BOEHLERT, SHERWOOD LOUIS (R)
b Utica, NY, Sept 28, 36; s Sherwood J Boehlert & Elizabeth M Champeaux B; m 1958 to Jean Bone; c Mark Christopher, Tracy Ann & Leslie Jane. Educ: Utica Col; Syracuse Univ, BS, 56-61; Tau Mu Epsilon; Pi Delta Epsilon; Alpha Delta Epsilon. Polit & Govt Pos: Exec asst to Rep Alexander Pirnie, NY, 64-72; exec asst to US Rep Donald J Mitchell, NY, 73- Bus & Prof Pos: Staff asst, Wyandotte Chem Corp, 61-63; mgr, Pub Rels, 63-64. Mil Serv: Army, Specialist 3/C, 56-58. Publ: Telling the congressman's story in: The Voice of Government, John Wiley & Sons, 68. Mem: Pub Rels Soc of Am. Relig: Catholic. Legal Res: 129 Elm St Oriskany NY 13424 Mailing Add: 5105 Bradford Dr Annandale VA 22003

BOENIGER, HENRY R (D)
RI State Rep
b Westerly, RI, Jan 11, 47; s Thomas J Boeniger & Minnie Murano B; m 1969 to Karen Lynch; c Stacie & Shelli. Educ: Univ RI Exten, 70-71; Life Underwriters Training Courses, 73. Polit & Govt Pos: Mem, Westerly Dem Town Comt, RI, 72-; RI State Rep, 50th Dist, 75- Bus & Prof Pos: Ins rep, Westerly-Prudential, 74- Mil Serv: Entered as Airman, Air Force, 66, released as Airman 3/C, after serv in 450th Bomb Wing, Minot, NDak; Expert Sharp Shooter. Mem: Nat Asn Life Underwriters; Elks Lodge 678; Westerly Pawcatuck Jaycees; Calabrese Soc. Honors & Awards: Recruit of the Year, 72; Nat Quality Award. Relig: Roman Catholic. Mailing Add: PO Box 364 Danielle Ave Westerly RI 02891

BOERSMA, P DEE (R)
b Mt Pleasant, Mich, Nov 14, 46; d Henry W Boersma & Vivian Anspach B; single. Educ: Cent Mich Univ, BS cum laude, 69; Ohio State Univ, PhD, 74; Beta Beta Beta; Pi Kappa Phi; Kappa Delta Pi; Mortar Bd; Alpha Chi Omega; pres, Student Senate & Assoc Women Students. Polit & Govt Pos: Mem, President's Task Force on Women's Rights & Responsibilities, 69; student rep, Nat Fedn Rep Women, 69; adv, US Deleg to UN Status Women Comn, 74; adv, US Deleg to UN World Pop Conf, 74. Bus & Prof Pos: Univ fel, Ohio State Univ, 69-73, teaching assoc, 70-74; trustee, Cent Mich Univ, 70-74; asst prof, Inst Environ Studies, Univ Wash, currently. Publ: A report on the United Nations Commission on the Status of Women & Mass Media, J Univ Film Asn, 3-4. Mem: Am Asn Advan Sci; Am Geol Soc; Am Ornithologists Union; Sigma Xi. Honors & Awards: David H Morgan Leadership Award, Cent Mich Univ, 67, Chippewa Award, 69. Legal Res: 5609 Second Ave NW Apt 15 Seattle WA 98107 Mailing Add: 112 Sieg FR-40 Univ of Wash Seattle WA 98195

BOESE, ELSIE JEAN (R)
Rep Nat Committeewoman, La
b New Orleans, La, Jan 19, 25; d John Roderick McGivney & Elsie Buist M; m 1946 to Dr H Lamar Boese, MD; c Robert Lamar. Educ: Sophie Newcomb Col, Tulane Univ, BA, 45; Alpha Delta Pi. Polit & Govt Pos: Pres, Eighth Dist Rep Women's Club, 62-63 & 67-68; deleg, Rep Nat Conv, 64 & 68; mem, Rep State Cent Comt La, 64-, vchmn, 64-68; mem, Rapides Parish Rep Comt, 64-; pub rels dir, Eighth Dist Rep Party, 64-; Rep Nat Committeewoman, La, currently. Bus & Prof Pos: Social worker, Am Red Cross, 45-46; teacher, retarded children, 53-55; script writer, educ TV, 53-55. Mem: St Frances Cabrini Hosp, Auxiliary (Orientation Chmn); Poet's Circle (treas); Woman's Auxiliary, Rapides Parish Med Soc; Our Lady of Prompt Succor Altar Soc; Matinee Musical Club. Honors & Awards: La Farm Bur Freedom Award, 64 & 69; Distinguished Serv Award, 12th Dist Dept La VFW, 67. Relig: Roman Catholic. Mailing Add: 831 City Party Blvd Alexandria LA 71301

BOESE, H LAMAR (R)
Rep Finance Chmn, Eighth Cong Dist, La
b Ardmore, Okla, June 28, 24; s W H Boese & Wynoma McGill B; m 1946 to Jean McGivney; c Robert Lamar. Educ: Tulane Univ, BS, 45, MD, 47; Pi Kappa Alpha. Polit & Govt Pos: Rep Finance Chmn, Eighth Cong Dist, La, 64-; alt deleg, Rep Nat Conv, 72; coun mem health manpower shortage bd, Nat Health Serv Corps currently; pres, Rapides Parish Rep Munic Exec Comt, La, currently. Mil Serv: 1st Lt, Army, 50-52; Paratrooper Jump Master Badge. Publ: Sjorgen's syndrome, Ochsner Clinic Reports, 57; Carcinoids of the GI tract, Annals of Internal Med, 56; Gastro-colic fistula, Annals of Surg, 56. Mem: Am Med Asn; Am Col Surgeons; Southeastern Surg Cong; Am Proctologic Soc; Alton Ochsner Surg Soc. Relig: Catholic. Legal Res: 831 City Park Blvd Alexandria LA 71303 Mailing Add: PO Box 5086 Alexandria LA 71301

BOETTNER, JOHN LEWIS, JR (D)
WVa State Deleg
b Frostburg, Md, June 18, 43; s John Lewis Boettner, Sr & Grace Mitter B; m 1968 to Mary Catherine Frerotte. Educ: WVa Univ, AB, 65; Col of Law, WVa Univ, JD, 68; Phi Delta Phi; Beta Theta Pi. Polit & Govt Pos: WVa State Deleg, 75- Bus & Prof Pos: Attorney-at-law, Charleston, WVa, 68- Publ: Auth, Techniques of trying a pollution case, Practical Lawyer, 6/75; co-ed, Public Interest Reports, Appalachian Res & Defense Fund, WVa, 1/72-6/74. Mem: Sierra Club, (pres, Appalachian Group, 74-); Community Coun, United Fund Kanawaha Valley; Wilderness Soc; Am Bar Asn. Relig: Methodist. Legal Res: 847 Edgewood Dr Charleston WV 25302 Mailing Add: 1022 Charleston Nat Plaza Charleston WV 25301

BOFFETTI, RAYMOND JOHN (D)
Mass State Rep
b Taunton, Mass, June 10, 24; s Mario Boffetti (deceased) & Mary Mazzoleni B; m 1950 to G Louise Smith; c James Thomas & Paul Francis. Educ: Monsignor James Coyle High Sch, 38-42. Polit & Govt Pos: Mem, Taunton Sch Comt, Mass, 68-73; Mass State Rep, 73- Mil Serv: Entered as Pvt, Army, 43, released as T/5, 46, after serv in 366th Med Bn, ETO, 44-46; Good Conduct Medal; Combat Med Medal. Mem: Elks; Sons of Italy; VFW; Am Legion; Taunton Boy's Club Asn. Honors & Awards: Boy's Club Am Award, 73. Mailing Add: 10 Johnson St Taunton MA 02780

BOGARDUS, O A (R)
b Warsaw, Ky, Dec 5, 03; s O A Bogardus, Sr & Nancy Ballard B; m 1929 to Sarah Carroll; c Graves C & O A, III. Educ: Hanover Col, 22-23; Ohio State Univ, 23-24; Phi Gamma Delta. Polit & Govt Pos: Chmn, Gallatin Co Rep Comt, Ky, formerly; mayor, Warsaw, 56-68; dep comnr, Ky State Hwy Dept, 68- Bus & Prof Pos: Pres, Gallatin Sand & Gravel Co, Ky, 46-61. Mem: Mason (32 degree); Shrine; Lions. Relig: Protestant. Mailing Add: Box 145 Warsaw KY 41095

BOGART, VINCENT L (D)
b Kirwin, Kans, June 8, 22; s Leroy Lindsay Bogart & Maude Wickwar B; m 1952 to Julia Ruth Henry; c Candace, Lee, Celeste & Cynthia. Educ: Kans State Univ, BS, 53; Washburn Law Sch, LLB, 55, JD, 70; Sigma Nu. Polit & Govt Pos: Committeeman, Dem Precinct Comt, Kans, 56-62; mem, Co Dem Cent Comt, 56-64; mem, Dist Dem Comt, 56-64; mem, Kans State Legis, 57-59; mem, Kans State Dem Coun, 57-61 & 66-69; off parliamentarian, Co Dem Comt, 58-60, chmn, 60; mem, Kans State Dem Comt, 60; comnr, Wichita City Comn, 63-67; mayor, Wichita, 64-65; key-note speaker, Kans State Dem Party Coun, 66; chmn, Kans State Dem Platform Comt, 66-67; legis rep to Gov, Kans, 67-69; trustee, Wichita State Univ, 68; deleg & mem platform comt, Dem Nat Conv, 68; comnr, Wichita Pub Bldg Comn, Kans, 68-69; regent, Kans Bd Regents, 69; spec asst to Attorney Gen, Kans, 72-74. Mil Serv: Entered as Aviation Cadet, Army Air Force, 43, released as 1st Lt, 46, after serv in 11th Air Force, Asiatic-Pac Theatre, 45-46; Asiatic-Pac Theatre Ribbon; Victory Medal. Mem: Wichita, Kans & Am Bar Asns; Kans Trial Lawyers Asn; VFW. Relig: Presbyterian. Legal Res: 227 N Belmont Pl Wichita KS 67208 Mailing Add: 444 N Market Wichita KS 67202

BOGDAN, ALBERT ALEXANDER (D)
b New York, NY, Feb 28, 36; s Alexander Vincent Bogdan & Blanche Capp B; m 1959 to Edwina Helena Schachinger; c Andrea Elizabeth, Albert Edward, Stephan Alexander & Alyssa Bianca. Educ: City Col New York, BEE, 58; Univ Mass, Amherst, MBA, 69. Polit & Govt Pos: Alt deleg, Dem Nat Conv, 68; chmn Berkshire Coun, Mass Comn Against Discrimination, 68-74; chmn comn; mem planning comt, Mass Dem Coun, 69-72; cand, Mayor of Pittsfield, 73; chmn, Dukakis for Gov, Pittsfield, 74; chmn, Berkshire Coop Area Manpower Planning Syst Comt. Bus & Prof Pos: Appln engr, Radio Receptor, Brooklyn, NY, 57-58; syst engr, Sperry Gyroscope, Great Neck, 58-59; prog engr, Lehigh Design Co, Newark, NJ, 59-61, prog mgr, Gen Elec Co Ord Syst, Pittsfield, 61-69; exec dir, Pittsfield Urban Coalition, 69-74; pres, Bridgeport Econ Develop Corp, 74- Mem: Inst Elec & Electronics Engrs; Bridgeport Regional Arts Ctr; NAACP; Bridgeport Urban Coalition; Bridgeport Coun Econ Adv. Relig: Unitarian. Mailing Add: 109 Alpine St Bridgeport CT 06610

BOGDAN, JOSEPH (D)
Conn State Rep
Mailing Add: 22 Roller Terrace Milford CT 06460

BOGDEN, CHARLES (R)
Mem, Marion Co Rep Cent Comt, Ind
b Indianapolis, Ind, Jan 20, s Daniel Bogden & Frieda Bier B; m 1946 to Martha Louise White; c Charles, Jr & Dennis. Educ: Ben Davis High Sch, 4 years. Polit & Govt Pos: Precinct committeeman, Wayne Twp Rep Party, Ind, 52-, campaign mgr, 66 & 70, ward chmn, 66-; pres, Wayne Twp GOP, Inc, 69-; asst to co chmn, Marion Co Rep Cent Comt, 68-, mem, 70- Bus & Prof Pos: Circulation mgr, Indianapolis Times, 39-41; asst to purchasing, Guarantee Auto Stores, Inc, 41- Mil Serv: Entered as Pvt, Army, 42, released as Pfc, 46, after serv in 435th Army Artil, 443rd Inf & 76th Signal Construction, ETO, 43-45; Asiatic-Pac Theatre, 45; Am Theatre Ribbon; Europe-Africa Mid East Theatre Ribbon with five Bronze Stars; Asiatic-Pac Theatre Ribbon; Good Conduct Ribbon; World War II Victory Medal. Mem: Wayne Twp Vol Fire Dept (secy-treas); Ind Vol Fireman Asn (12th Dist Secy); DAV. Honors & Awards: Mr Wayne Twp Rep Plaque. Relig: Protestant. Mailing Add: 636 S Worth St Indianapolis IN 46241

BOGGS, CORINNE MORRISON CLAIBORNE (D)
US Rep, La
b Brunswick Plantation, La, Mar 13, 16; d Roland Claiborne & Corinne Morrison C; m 1938 to Thomas Hale Boggs, wid; c Barbara (Mrs Paul Sigmund, Jr), Thomas Hale, Jr & Corinne (Mrs Steven V Roberts). Educ: Newcomb Col, Tulane Univ, BA, 35. Polit & Govt Pos: Co-Chmn, Oper Crossroads for Adlai Stevenson, 56, Presidential Inaugural Balls, 61 & 65 & Ladybird Spec, for Lyndon Johnson, 64; US Rep, Second Dist, La, 73- Mem: Cong Club; Woman's Nat Dem Club. Relig: Roman Catholic. Legal Res: 623 Bourbon St New Orleans LA 70130 Mailing Add: 1519 Longworth Off Bldg Washington DC 20515

BOGGS, DANNY JULIAN (R)
b Havana, Cuba, Oct 23, 44; s Robert Lilburn Boggs & Yolanda Pereda B; m 1967 to Judith Susan Solow; c Rebecca. Educ: Harvard Univ, AB, 65; Univ Chicago Law Sch, JD, 68. Polit & Govt Pos: Vpres, Harvard Young Rep Club, 64-65; vpres, Univ Chicago Young Rep Club, 66-68; campaign mgr, Second Cong Dist Ill, 68; dep comnr, Ky Dept Econ Security, 69-70; admin asst, Gov Louie B Nunn, Ky, 70-71; legis counsel Rep legislators, Ky Gen Assembly, 72; legal counsel & chief researcher, Nixon-Humph Ky Campaign, 72; alt deleg, Rep Nat Conv, 72; assoc dep to asst secy for admin, US Dept Commerce, 73; asst to Solicitor Gen of US, 73-75; Rep cand for Ky State Rep, 20th Dist, 75. Bus & Prof Pos: Law clerk, Cravath, Swaine & Moore, New York, 67-68; instr, Univ Chicago Law Sch, 68-69; pvt law practice, 75- Publ: Foreign policy: a redefinition in the singular, Harvard Conservative, 65; Viewpoints (column), Newsday, 69-70. Mem: Am, Ky & Bowling Green-Warren Co Bar Asns; Mont Pelerin Soc; Philadelphia Soc. Honors & Awards: Harvard Univ Nat Scholar, 61-65; Nat Merit Scholar, 61-65; Charles Coolidge Debate Prize, Harvard Univ, 64 & 65; Mechem Scholar, Univ Chicago, 65, Moot Court Championship, 68. Legal Res: 1216 Cabell Dr Bowling Green KY 42101 Mailing Add: 334 E Tenth St Bowling Green KY 42101

BOGGS, J CALEB (R)
b Kent Co, Del, May 15, 09; m to Elizabeth Muir; c James Caleb, Jr & Marilu. Educ: Univ Del, AB; Georgetown Univ, LLB. Hon Degrees: LLD, Del State Col & Bethany Col. Polit & Govt Pos: Judge of Family Court, New Castle Co, Del; US Rep-at-lg from Del to 80th, 81st & 82nd Cong; Gov, Del, 52-60; chmn, Nat Gov Conf, 59; pres coun, State Govt, 60; US Sen, Del, 61-72. Bus & Prof Pos: Lawyer, Bayard, Brill & Handelman, Wilmington, Del, currently; dir, Artesian Savings Bank, Del Safety Coun, Blood Bank Del, Inc, Goldey-Beacom Col, Former Mem Cong, Ins Co & Del Motor Club AAA, currently. Mil Serv: Army Res, Col (Ret); Brig Gen, Del Nat Guard, enlisted 26, retired; five campaigns ETO; Legion of Merit; Bronze Star with Cluster; French Croix de Guerre with Palm. Mem: Kiwanis; Am Bar Asn; Am Judicature Soc; Nat Rep Club Capitol Hill; Alpha Phi Omega. Relig: Methodist. Mailing Add: 1203 Grinnel Rd Wilmington DE 19803

BOGGS, JUDITH ROSLYN (D)
Mem, Calif Dem State Cent Comt
b Portland, Ore, Nov 7, 39; d Max Breall & Mary Perel Breall Lauber; B; m 1962 to Dale H Boggs; c Melissa Leigh. Educ: Univ Wash, BA, 61; Phi Sigma Sigma. Polit & Govt Pos: Campaign coordr, McGovern-Shriver Hq, 72, La Canada-La Crescenta; campaign coordr, Jerome Waldie for Gov, 22nd Dist, Calif, 73-74; mem steering comt, ACT, Pasadena, 73-; deleg, Dem Nat Mid-Term Conf, 74; mem, Calif Dem State Cent Comt, 21st Dist, 75- Honors & Awards: Sphinx Award, Phi Sigma Sigma. Relig: Jewish. Mailing Add: 418 Oliveta Pl La Canada CA 91011

BOGGS, ROBERT J (D)
Ohio State Rep
Mailing Add: RR 4 Jefferson OH 44047

BOGINA, AUGUST, JR (R)
Kans State Rep
b Girard, Kans, Sept 13, 27; s August Bogina, Sr & Mary Blazic B (deceased); m 1949 to Velma M Rank; c Kathleen A, August III, Michael E & Mark A. Educ: Kans State Univ, BS Eng; Alpha Tau Omega. Polit & Govt Pos: City engr, Fairway, Kans, 62-64, Lenexa, Kans, 64-67 & Harrisonville, Mo, 67-69; precinct committeeman, Kans Rep Party, 70-74; chmn, Rep City Comt, 72-74; Kans State Rep, 75- Bus & Prof Pos: Owner, Bogina & Assoc, Lenexa, Kans, 62-70; pres, Bogina Architect-Engrs, 70- Mil Serv: Entered as Pvt, Army, 46, released as Cpl, 48. Mem: Nat & Mo Soc Prof Engrs; Kans Eng Soc; Kans Soc Land Surveyors; Mo Asn Registered Land Surveyors. Relig: Catholic. Mailing Add: 13513 W 90th Pl Lenexa KS 66215

BOHIGIAN, ROBERT J (D)
Mass State Rep
Mailing Add: State Capitol Boston MA 02133

BOHLKE, LLOYD ELMER (R)
b Kenesaw, Nebr, June 27, 27; s Elmer Martin Bohlke & Marie Jacobitz B; m 1952 to Zella LaVonne Phillips; c Kathleen A, Michele Susan & Timothy Lloyd. Educ: Hastings Col, BS, 50. Polit & Govt Pos: Clerk, Wanda Twp, Nebr, 58-62; chmn, Adams Co Rep Party, formerly. Bus & Prof Pos: Teacher, Fullerton Pub Schs, 50-52 & Hastings Pub Schs, 53-54. Mem: Farm Bur; Lions. Relig: Protestant. Mailing Add: Kenesaw NE 68956

BOHLS, CLEO EVELYN (R)
Second VPres, Nat Fedn Rep Women
b Little Rock, Ark, Dec 2, 24; d William Roy Evans & Edna Gray E; m 1944 to Louis F Bohls; c Linda (Mrs Don R Ellis) & David. Educ: Bus sch. Polit & Govt Pos: Pres, North Star Rep Women's Club, 65-66; chmn, Oper Early Bird, John Tower Sen Campaign, 66; first vpres, Tex Fedn Rep Women, 68, pres, 69-71; campaign mgr, Bexar Co Comnr, 68; prog chmn, Nat Fedn Rep Women, 72-73, second vpres, currently; campaign mgr, Rep Co Comnr Campaign, 72- Mem: League Women Voters; Bexar Co Hosp Dist (bd mgrs); Local Draft Bd 9; St Mary's Univ Jr Guild; Tex PTA (life mem); Bexar Co Hosp Dist. Honors & Awards: One of Ten Outstanding Women, Bexar Co, 65. Mailing Add: 123 Meadowood San Antonio TX 78216

BOILEAU, GERALD JOHN (NON-PARTISAN)
b Woodruff, Wis, Jan 15, 00; s John R Boileau & Sophia Daigle B; m 1925 to Monica McKean; c Nancy (Mrs Nirschl) & Mary (Mrs Bailey). Educ: Marquette Univ Law Sch, LLB, 23; Alpha Sigma Nu; Delta Theta Phi. Polit & Govt Pos: Dist Attorney, Marathon Co, Wis, 26-31; US Rep, Seventh Dist, 31-39; circuit judge, 16th Judicial Circuit, 42-70; temporary circuit judge, Br One, Milwaukee Co, 70-72. Mil Serv: Entered as Pvt, Army, 18, released as Cpl, 19, after serv in 11th Field Artil, AEF; Muese Argonne Offensive Ribbon. Publ: Plea bargaining, 67 & Plea of insanity in criminal cases, 68, Wis State Bull. Mem: Marathon Co Bar Asn; State Bar of Wis; KofC (4 degree); Elks; Am Legion. Relig: Roman Catholic. Mailing Add: 914 Grand Ave Wausau WI 54401

BOISVERT, EMILE E (D)
NH State Rep
Mailing Add: 259 Clay St Manchester NH 03103

BOISVERT, WILFRID A (D)
NH State Rep
Mailing Add: 14A King St Nashua NH 03060

BOLAND, ARDNEY JAMES, SR (D)
Chmn, Escambia Co Dem Exec Comt, Fla
b Wacissa, Fla, Dec 18, 20; s Patrick Henry Boland & Charlie P Clifton B; m 1950 to Mary Olive Stephens; c Ardney James, Jr, Stephanie Ann, Sara Diane, Patrick Henry & Bruce Heald. Educ: Univ Fla, BSA, 43; Fla State Univ, MAE, 48; YMCA; Wesley Found; Epworth League; CLO. Polit & Govt Pos: Co sch supt, Jefferson Co, Fla, 49-53; chmn, Escambia Co Dem Exec Comt, 74- Bus & Prof Pos: Sch teacher, Escambia Co, Fla, 53-64, sch prin, 64- Publ: Mathematics home work, Fla J Math, 62. Mem: Escambia Educ Asn; Fla United Services Orgn; Nat Educ Asn; Mason; Hadji Temple Shrine. Relig: Methodist. Mailing Add: 1201 E Barcia St Pensacola FL 32503

BOLAND, EDWARD P (D)
US Rep, Mass
b Springfield, Mass, Oct 1, 11. Educ: Boston Col Law Sch. Polit & Govt Pos: Mass State Rep, 35-40; register of deeds, Hampden Co, Mass, 41-52; US Rep, Mass, 53-; ex officio, Dem Nat

Mid-Term Conf, 74. Mil Serv: US Army, Pac Theatre of Opers, Capt, 46. Legal Res: 146 Fed Off Bldg Springfield MA 01101 Mailing Add: 2111 Rayburn House Off Bldg Washington DC 20515

BOLAND, KATHLYNN ANN (D)
b Washington, DC, Nov 12, 53; d Edward Michael Boland & Arden Rose Voegely B; single. Educ: Yale Univ, 73- Polit & Govt Pos: Deleg, Dem Nat Conv, 72. Mem: Sierra Club; Wyo Environ Group. Honors & Awards: Most Outstanding Sr, Natrona Co High Sch; Dist Champion, Nat Forensics League, 72; Voice of Dem, VFW, 72; Nat Betty Crocker Winner, Gen Mills, Inc, 72; US Senate Youth, William Randolph Hearst Found, 72. Legal Res: 3840 Alpine Dr Casper WY 82601 Mailing Add: 1647 Yale Sta New Haven CT 06520

BOLDEN, DECORSEY E (R)
Md State Deleg
Mailing Add: 313 S Second St Oakland MD 21550

BOLDEN, MELVIN REED (D)
b Baltimore, Md, Jan 28, 19; s Jacob Percy Bolden & Mary C Reed B; m 1949 to Gwyndolyn Claire Hale. Educ: Philadelphia Col Art, 37-41. Polit & Govt Pos: Chmn, Loudon Dem Party, NH, 64-69; chmn, Merrimack Co Dem Party, formerly; mem bd dirs, NH Coun Better Schs, 66-, NH Artists Asn, 67- & NH Social Welfare Coun, 67-; comnr, NH Comn Human Rights, 67-; chmn Gov Adv Bd, Off Econ Opportunity, 68- Bus & Prof Pos: Supvr installation mech, Glenn Martin Aircraft Co, Baltimore, 41-44; staff artist, Afro-Am Newspapers, 43-45; staff artist & layout designer, Our World Mag, New York, 45-47; art dir, Detecto Scales Co, Brooklyn, 48-50; free lance illustrator & cover artist, Saturday Rev, 49-55; advert illustrator, Reynolds Aluminum, Revere Copper Brass, Ginn & D C Heath; illustrator & designer, Grolier Soc, McGraw Hill & World Publ Co. Publ: Illustrations published in Boy's Life Mag, Fortune, Bus Week, Wall Street J & New York Times. Mem: New Eng Elec Rwy Hist Soc. Relig: Unitarian. Legal Res: Beck Rd Loudon NH 03301 Mailing Add: RR 8 Concord NH 03301

BOLDT, JIM (D)
Wash State Rep
Mailing Add: 2401 W Canal Dr Kennewick WA 99336

BOLEN, DAVID BENJAMIN
US Ambassador to Botswana, Lesotho, Swaziland
b Heflin, La, Dec 23, 23; s Charles E Bolen & Nina Airy B; m 1949 to Betty L Gayden; c Cynthia N (Mrs Joachim Koester), Myra L & David B, Jr. Educ: Univ Colo, Boulder, BS & MS, 50; Harvard Univ, MPA, 60; Nat War Col, 66-67; Kappa Alpha Psi. Polit & Govt Pos: Vconsul, Am Embassy, Monrovia, Liberia, 50-52, econ officer, Am Embassy, Karachi, Pakistan, 52-54; int economist, Dept of Commerce, 55-57; officer-in-charge, Afghanistan Affairs, Dept of State, 62-64, officer-in-charge, Nigerian Affairs, 64-66; first secy-econ/commercial off, Am Embassy, Bonn, WGer, 67-71, econ counr, 71-72, econ/commercial counr, Am Embassy, Belgrade, Yugoslavia, 72-74; US Ambassador to Botswana, Lesotho, Swaziland, 74- Mil Serv: Entered as Pvt, Air Force, 43, released as Sgt, 46, after serv in 2nd Air Force. Publ: Co-auth, World Economic Policies & Problems, Harper & Row, 65; Economic development in Africa, Foreign Serv J, 64. Mem: Foreign Serv Asn. Honors & Awards: mem, Olympic Team, 48; Norlin Distinguished Alumni Award, Univ Colo, 69; Univ Colo Hall of Honor, 69. Relig: Protestant. Legal Res: 7908 16th St Washington DC 20017 Mailing Add: American Embassy Gaborone Dept of State Washington DC 20520

BOLEY, GEORGE W (D)
Colo State Rep
Mailing Add: 107 - 32 1/2 Lane Pueblo CO 81003

BOLGER, WILLIAM J (D)
b McHenry, Ill, Apr 16, 25; s Thomas A Bolger & Grace Doherty B; m 1949 to Carol Dolores Murray; c Kathleen, Murray, William & Candace. Polit & Govt Pos: Deleg, Dem Nat Conv, 56-72; Dem precinct committeeman & alderman, First Ward, McHenry, Ill, 57- Mil Serv: Entered as Pvt, Marine Corps, 44, released as Cpl, 46, after serv in 1st Marine Div, SPac, Okinawa & China, 44-45; Purple Heart; Letter of Commendation with Ribbon. Mem: McHenry Pub Libr (pres, 60-); McHenry Little League (secy, 54-); VFW; Am Legion; Cath Order of Foresters. Relig: Catholic. Mailing Add: 906 N Allen Ave McHenry IL 60050

BOLIN, WESLEY H (D)
Secy of State, Ariz
b Butler, Mo, July 1, 08; s D S Bolin & Margaret B; m to Marion Knappenberger; c Wesley, Jr, Tom, Bill, Steven & Bruce. Educ: Phoenix Jr Col. Polit & Govt Pos: Constable, WPhoenix Precinct 38, Ariz, 3 terms; justice of peace, 44; Secy of State, Ariz, currently. Mem: Nat Secretaries of State; Elks; Moose; Jr CofC. Honors & Awards: Outstanding work with Boy Scouts. Relig: Protestant. Legal Res: 2920 W Manor Dr Phoenix AZ 85014 Mailing Add: State House Phoenix AZ 85007

BOLLING, RICHARD WALKER (D)
US Rep, Mo
b New York, NY, May 17, 16; s Richard Walker Bolling & Florence Easton B; m 1964 to Jim Grant; c 3. Educ: Univ of the South, BA, 37, MA, 39; Vanderbilt Univ, grad study, 40; Phi Beta Kappa. Hon Degrees: DCL, Univ of the South, 63, Kans City Col Osteopathy & Surg, 67; LLD, Rockhurst Col, 71. Polit & Govt Pos: US Rep, Fifth Dist, Mo, 48-, mem joint econ comt & House rules comt, US House Rep, currently. Bus & Prof Pos: Teacher & coach, Univ of the South; vet adv & dir student activities, Univ of Kans City, Mo. Mil Serv: Entered as Pvt, Army, 41, released as Lt Col, 46. Publ: Auth, House Out of Order, 65 & Power in the House, 68, E P Dutton & Putnam's, 74. Honors & Awards: Received Cong Distinguished Serv Award, Am Polit Sci Asn. Relig: Episcopal. Legal Res: Walnut Towers 722 Walnut St Kansas City MO 64108 Mailing Add: 2465 Rayburn House Off Bldg Washington DC 20515

BOLLING, ROYAL L, JR (D)
Mass State Rep
Mailing Add: State Capitol Boston MA 02133

BOLSTER, PAUL (D)
Ga State Rep
Mailing Add: 1043 Ormewood Ave SE Atlanta GA 30316

BOLTON, ANN D (R)
b Stamford, Conn, Apr 4, 30; d Frank D'Elia & Paula Pepe D; div; c Jamie Lynn & Keith Patrick. Educ: Merrill Bus Sch, Stamford, Conn, 48-50. Polit & Govt Pos: Personal secy, US Rep Albert P Morano, 52-58 & US Rep Hastings Keith, 59; admin asst to US Rep Edward J Derwinski, 60- Bus & Prof Pos: Legal secy, Moore & Epifano, Attorneys-at-Law, 50-52. Mem: Congressional Secy Club (pres, 75-); Admin Assts' Asn. Relig: Catholic. Mailing Add: 6031 N 22nd Rd Arlington VA 22205

BOLTON, ARTHUR KEY (D)
Attorney Gen, Ga
b Griffin, Ga, May 14, 22; s Herbert Alfred Bolton & Eunice Maddox B; m 1946 to Marion Lee Cashen; c Arthur Key, Jr & Marian Lee. Educ: NGa Col, 39-41; Univ Ga Law Sch, LLB, 43; Univ Ala Law Sch; Phi Delta Phi. Polit & Govt Pos: Ga State Rep, 49-65, chmn, Tax Equalization Comt, Ga House of Rep, 59-65, chmn, Spec Judiciary Comt, 61-62, mem, Const Revision Comt, 63-64, vchmn, Rules Comt & Floor Leader, 63-65; co adminr, Spalding Co, 50-65; Judge, Criminal Court, Griffin, 52-65; Attorney Gen, Ga, 65- Bus & Prof Pos: Attorney-at-Law, 47- Mil Serv: Entered as 2nd Lt, Army, 43, released as Capt, 46, after serv in 97th Inf Div, Mo, 43-44, 118th Inf Regt, Eng, 44 & 36th Armored Inf Regt, Third Armored Div, Ger, 44-45; ETO Ribbon with 3 Campaign Stars; Purple Heart; Silver Star; Combat Inf Badge; Am Defense Medal; Victory Medal. Mem: Univ Ga Law Sch Alumni Asn; La Grange Col Parents Asn (pres, 70-); NGa Col Alumni Asn (coun mem); CofC; Kiwanis. Honors & Awards: Man of the Year Award, Griffin, Ga, 62; Pub Serv Award, Ga Munic Asn, 65, Key Citizen Award, 70; Officers Cand Sch Hall Fame, Ft Benning, Ga, 73; NGa Col Alumni Hall Fame, 73. Relig: Baptist. Legal Res: Griffin GA 30223 Mailing Add: State Law Dept 132 State Judicial Bldg Atlanta GA 30334

BOLTON, EDGAR SIMPSON (CONSTITUTION)
Chmn, Constitution Party, La
b Waynesboro, Miss, Sept 22, 05; s James Franklin Bolton & Mary Doby B; m 1945 to Jewell Lamar Roberts. Educ: High Sch. Polit & Govt Pos: Dir of prog, Constitution Party, La, 65-66, chmn, 66- Bus & Prof Pos: Pres, Bolton Industs Inc, 66- Mem: Save Our Schs (founder & coordr, 70). Honors & Awards: Cert of Appreciation, Nat Police Officers Asn Am. Mailing Add: 1006 N Third West Monroe LA 71291

BOLTON, ELDON L, JR (D)
Miss State Rep
Mailing Add: Drawer 100 Gulfport MS 39501

BOLTON, FRANCES P (R)
b Cleveland, Ohio, Mar 29, 85; d Charles William Bingham & Mary Perry Payne B; m to Chester C Bolton, wid; c Charles Bingham, Oliver Payne (deceased), Kenyon Castle & Elizabeth (deceased). Educ: Miss Spence's Sch for Girls, NY; Alpha Iota; Beta Sigma Phi; Delta Kappa Gamma; Phi Delta Gamma; Theta Sigma Phi. Polit & Govt Pos: US Rep, Ohio, formerly. Mem: Mt Vernon Ladies' Asn; League of Rep Women; Soc of Women Geographers; League of Women Voters; Women's Advert Club. Relig: Presbyterian. Mailing Add: Rm 301 May Lee Bldg 2490 Lee Blvd Cleveland Heights OH 44118

BOLTON, JAMES CARROLL (R)
b Chicago, Ill, July 8, 12; s Jarvis Arthur Bolton & Elizabeth Carroll B; m 1942 to Jean Stevens Garlick; c James C, Jr & David Murray. Educ: Univ Ill, BS, 35; Sigma Alpha Epsilon. Polit & Govt Pos: Admin asst to US Rep Glenn R Davis, Wis, 65-75; mem, President's Comt on Employ Physically Handicapped, formerly; mem, President's Conf Occup Safety, formerly; part-time polit consult, 75- Bus & Prof Pos: Br mgr, Motors Acceptance Corp, 38-42; sales mgr, Pyle Chevrolet & Cadillac, 45-52; field dir, Wis Mfrs Asn, 52-65. Mil Serv: Navy, 42-45, Res, 45-55; Comdr (Ret). Mem: Elks; ROA; Am Legion. Mailing Add: 8513 Cyrus Pl Alexandria VA 22308

BOLTZ, RICHARD ALAN (R)
b Scholfield, Wis, Aug 1, 32; s Frank A Boltz & Victoria Kulick B; m 1959 to Ann Carlisle; c Paul, Tom & John. Educ: Univ Wis, BS, 55, LLB, 57; Gamma Eta Gamma. Polit & Govt Pos: Secy, Brown Co Rep Party, Wis, 59-63, chmn 64-67; chmn, Eighth Cong Dist Rep Party, 67-71; alt deleg, Rep Nat Conv, 68; mem, Wis State Comn of Uniform State Laws, 69-73; state vchmn, Wis Lawyers for Nixon Comt, 72; vchmn, Reelect the President Comt, Wis, 72. Publ: Loss or impairment of earning capacity, Wis Bar Bull, 4/70. Mem: State of Wis Bar Asn (mem negligence sect); Brown Co Bar Asn (chmn negligence sect); Wis Acad Trial Lawyers (bd dirs); Am & Wis Trial Lawyers Asns. Honors & Awards: Recipient Distinguished Serv Award, Brown Co, 65. Relig: Protestant. Mailing Add: 2607 Oakwood Ave Green Bay WI 54301

BOND, CHRISTOPHER SAMUEL (R)
Gov, Mo
b St Louis, Mo, Mar 6, 39; s Arthur Doerr Bond & Elizabeth Green B; m 1967 to Carolyn Ann Reid. Educ: Princeton Univ, AB, cum laude, 60; Univ Va Law Sch, LLB, 63; Omicron Delta Kappa; Cottage Club; Order of the Coif. Hon Degrees: LLD, Westminster Col & William Jewell Col, 73. Polit & Govt Pos: Clerk, Fifth US Circuit Court of Appeals, Ga, 63-64; Rep nominee, US Rep, Mo, 68; Asst Attorney Gen, 69-70; State Auditor, 71-73, Gov, Mo, 73-; mem exec comt, Nat Gov Conf, 74-75. Bus & Prof Pos: Attorney, Covington & Burling, Washington, DC, 65-67; attorney, Mexico, Mo, 67- Mem: Bar of Mo; Rep Gov Asn (chmn, 74-); Jaycees; Sch of Ozarks (bd trustees). Honors & Awards: Most Outstanding Graduating Student, Univ Va Law Sch, 63; One of Ten Outstanding Young Men Award, US Jaycees, 74. Relig: Presbyterian. Legal Res: 14 S Jefferson Rd Mexico MO 65265 Mailing Add: Exec Mansion Jefferson City MO 65101

BOND, JULIAN (D)
Ga State Sen
b Nashville, Tenn, Jan 14, 40; s Dr Horace Mann Bond & Julia Washington B; m 1961 to Alice L Clopton; c Horace Mann, II, Phyllis Jane, Michael Julian, Jeffrey Alvin & Julia Louise. Educ: Morehouse Col, Atlanta, Ga, BA, 71. Hon Degrees: LLD, Lincoln Univ (Pa), Bard Col, Univ Syracuse, Dalhousie Univ, Wesleyan Univ, Univ Conn & Eastern Mich Univ. Polit & Govt Pos: Ga State Rep, 67-74; Ga State Sen, 75-; mem state exec comt, Ga Dem Party, currently. Bus & Prof Pos: Mem bd, Student Voice, Inc & Southern Educ & Research Assocs, currently. Publ: Poetry in 5 anthologies, 2 languages besides English. Mem: Southern Conf Educ Fund, Inc (mem bd); Robert Kennedy Mem Fund (mem bd); Martin Luther King, Jr Mem Ctr (mem bd); Highlander Research & Educ Ctr (mem bd). Mailing Add: 361 West View Dr SW Atlanta GA 30310

BOND, LEE GEORGE (R)
Mem, Nev State Rep Cent & Exec Comts
b Warrenton, Va, Nov 6, 26; s E Logan Bond & Myrtle Dougherty B; m 1962 to Joanne West; c Alexandra. Educ: Emory Univ, 2 years; Sacramento State Col, 1 year; Univ Nev, Reno; Sigma Alpha Epsilon. Polit & Govt Pos: Ward Leader, Reno Rep Party, Nev, 68-69; chmn, Washoe Co Rep Cent Comt, formerly; mem, Nev State Rep Cent & Exec Comts, currently; deleg, Rep Nat Conv, 72; campaign mgr, US Sen Paul Laxalt, 74. Bus & Prof Pos: Co-owner, Reno Fuel, 61-63; sales engr, Fuller-O'Brien Corp, 63- Mil Serv: Entered as Cadet, Air Force, 46, released as 1st Lt, 51, after serv in 2nd Air Force. Mem: Oil Heat Inst; Smithsonian Inst; Boy Scouts; Elks; Mason. Relig: Episcopal. Mailing Add: 4010 Canyon Dr Reno NV 89502

BOND, RICHARD LEE (R)
b Kansas City, Kans, Sept 18, 35; s Clarence Ivy Bond & Florine Hardison B; m 1958 to Suzanne Sedgwick; c Mark Richard & Amy Lynne. Educ: Univ Kans, AB, 57, Sch Law, LLB, 60; Tau Kappa Epsilon (pres). Polit & Govt Pos: City Attorney, Overland Park, Kans, 60-62; dist asst, US Rep Robert F Ellsworth, Kans, 61-62, admin asst, 62-66; admin asst to US Rep Larry Winn, Kans, 67- Bus & Prof Pos: Law assoc, Pflumm & Mitchelson, 60-62. Mem: Kans & Johnson Co Bar Asns; Pi Sigma Alpha (pres); Phi Delta Phi; Rotary. Relig: Presbyterian. Mailing Add: 4901 W 97th Terr Overland Park KS 66104

BOND, RICHARD MILTON (R)
Wash State Rep
b Spokane, Wash, Apr 23, 24; s Joseph McKinley Bond & Ethel Campbell B; m 1946 to Patty Hendrickson; c David Preston, Marc Douglas & Andrew Joseph. Educ: Univ Calif, Berkeley, BS, 46; Calif Inst Technol, 42-43; Univ Southern Calif, Commercial Pilot License, 45; Phi Gamma Delta; pres, Assoc Univ Calif, Berkeley, 44-45. Polit & Govt Pos: Wash State Rep, 75- Bus & Prof Pos: Vpres sales, Calor Gas Co, 51-57; pres, Solar Gas Co, 55-, Solar Gas Ltd, 60 & Solar Petroleum Corp, 74. Mil Serv: Entered as Pfc, Marine Corps, 42, released as Lt, 45. Mem: Spokane Engrs Asn (pres); Spokane Chap, Air Force Asn (pres); Nat LP-Gas Asn (nat & state dir); Rotary; Nat Rifle Asn. Honors & Awards: Eagle Scout, 38. Relig: Christian. Legal Res: S 4226 Crestline Spokane WA 99203 Mailing Add: N 411 Havana St Spokane WA 99202

BONDI, GENE L (D)
Chmn, Sheridan Co Dem Party, Wyo
b Acme, Wyo, May 20, 13; s Bert Bondi & Mary Realon B; m 1941 to Elizabeth Poynter; c Bert Roger & Harry Gene. Educ: Sheridan Co High Sch, grad. Polit & Govt Pos: Dem precinct committeeman, Dist Three, Ward Three, Sheridan Co, Wyo, 56-; state committeeman, Wyo Dem Party, Sheridan Co, 60-; mem finance comt & exec comt, Dem State Cent Comt, 62-; alt deleg, Dem Nat Conv, 68 & 72; chmn, Sheridan Co Dem Party, Wyo, currently. Bus & Prof Pos: Assoc bd mem, Western Reserve Life Ins Co. Mem: Wyo State Am Cancer Soc (bd dirs); Sheridan Kiwanis; Salvation Army (adv bd); Elks. Relig: Catholic. Legal Res: 320 Sherman Ave Sheridan WY 82801 Mailing Add: PO Box 383 Sheridan WY 82801

BONDSHU, ROBERT EUGENE (R)
Mem, Rep State Cent Comt Calif
b Chico, Calif, May 28, 29; s Harold H Bondshu & Anita B; m 1956 to Rachel Ann Dunnington; c William Harold, Coby Ann, Frank Albert & Krista Sue. Educ: Col of the Pac, AA, 50; Omega Phi Alpha. Polit & Govt Pos: Secy-treas, Mariposa Co Rep Cent Comt, 58-62, chmn, 62-75; mem, Rep State Cent Comt Calif, 62- Mil Serv: Entered as Pvt, Air Force, 50, released as 1st Lt, 56, after serv in Air Training Command & Cadet Pilot Training Prog, Strategic Air Command, duty in Alaska, Japan & Korea. Mem: Independent Ins Agents Asn; Lions; VFW; Air Force Asn; Vol Fire Dept, Mariposa. Relig: Methodist. Mailing Add: Box 808 Mariposa CA 95338

BONEBRAKE, RICHARD DUANE (D)
Ore State Rep
b Roseburg, Ore, Jan 14, 31; s William Fredick Bonebrake & Willimena Royer B; m 1952 to Jeannine Bernice Bentley; c Pixie Jean, Dixie Lee, David Duane, Mitzi Sue & Tammy Lynn. Educ: Linfield Col, BA, 61; Univ Ore, MA, 66; Theta Chi. Polit & Govt Pos: Ore State Rep, 75- Bus & Prof Pos: Teacher, Fremont Jr High Sch, Roseburg, Ore, 61-63, vprin, 63- Mil Serv: Entered as Airman, Air Force, 53, released as S/Sgt, 57, after serv in 97th Air Defense Command, 54-57; Good Conduct Medal. Mem: Ore Asn Sec Sch Adminr; Nat & Ore Educ Asns. Honors & Awards: YMCA Appreciation Award, 68; Education Citizen of the Year, Roseburg Educ Asn, 72; Gateway Timber Found Appreciation Award, 75. Relig: Baptist. Mailing Add: Rte 3 Box 150 Roseburg OR 97470

BONER, WILLIAM HILL (D)
Tenn State Rep
b Nashville, Tenn, Feb 14, 45; s Doris Boner (deceased) & Martha Mai Barbour B; m 1972 to Barbara Andrews; c Richard Andrew & Sheree Leigh Abernathy & Christine Marie Boner. Educ: Mid Tenn State Univ, BS, 67; George Peabody Col, MA, 69; Kappa Delta Pi; Sigma Club; Varsity Basketball & Tennis Teams; Circle K Club; Phys Educ Club, Booster Club. Polit & Govt Pos: Tenn State Rep, Third Dist, 70-72, 52nd Dist, 74- Mem: Optimist; ENashville YMCA (bd mgr, 71-); Nashville Area CofC (govt rels comt, 72-); Nashville Chap, Pub Rels Soc Am; Nashville Press Club. Honors & Awards: Distinguished Serv Award, Franklin Road Jaycees, 71; Outstanding Young Citizen Awards, Music City Jaycees, 75. Relig: Methodist. Mailing Add: 2509 Brittany Dr Nashville TN 37206

BONES, WALTER (R)
SDak State Rep
b Minneapolis, Minn, Jan 20, 27; s Walter I Bones & Fayetta Conners B; m 1950 to Deweenta Gray; c Walter, III, Cathy (Mrs Lyle Van Hove), Steve, Judy, Jim, John & Susan. Educ: Iowa State Univ, BS; Block & Bridle Club; Delta Tau Delta. Polit & Govt Pos: SDak State Rep, 75- Bus & Prof Pos: Bd dirs, Am Nat Cattlemens Asn, 69-70; bd adv, McKennan Hosp, Sioux Falls, SDak, 72- Mil Serv: Entered as Seaman, Navy, 45, released as ETM 3/C, 46, after serv in Pac Theatre. Mem: Shrine; SDak Stockgrowers Asn; Elks; Rotary; Farm Bur. Honors & Awards: Outstanding Young Farmer, 61; Nat Block & Bridle Club Award, 68; Pres Award, SDak Stock Growers Asn, 69. Relig: Baptist; mem bd trustees, First Baptist Church, 73- Legal Res: RR 1 Hartford SD 57033 Mailing Add: RR 1 Parker SD 57053

BONETTI, ADDO E (D)
Conn State Rep
Mailing Add: 513 Park Ave Torrington CT 06790

BONETTO, JOSEPH F (D)
Pa State Rep
b Allegheny Co, Pa, Apr 20, 21; s Frank Bonetto & Maria Franco B; m to Helene Kropelak; c four. Educ: Turtle Creek High Sch. Polit & Govt Pos: Pa State Rep, 64-; chmn bd, Plum Borough Munic Authority; Dem chmn, Plum Borough, 17 years. Bus & Prof Pos: Equip supvr. Mil Serv: Army, T/Sgt, topographical engr; SPac Theater. Mem: UMW. Mailing Add: Capitol Bldg Harrisburg PA 17120

BONGARTZ, FERDINAND A (R)
Mem, Vt Rep State Comt
b Orange, NJ, Nov 5, 23; s Ferdinand A Bongartz & Laura Pressler B; m 1948 to Joan Bowen; c Dulce, Lauren, Seth, Jennifer & Melissa. Educ: Pa State Univ, 43-44; Susquehanna Univ, BS, 47; Phi Mu Delta. Polit & Govt Pos: Mem, Manchester Town Rep Comt, Vt, 58-; selectman, Town of Manchester, 63-69, chmn bd, 65 & 68; mem, Vt Rep State Comt, 65-; chmn, Bennington Co Rep Party, Vt, formerly; mem, Manchester Sch Bd, 69-; chmn, Manchester Town Planning Comn, 68-; supvr, Unorganized Town of Glastenbury, 68-; vchmn, Bennington Co Regional Planning & Develop Comt, 70-; mem, Dist Environ Control Comn Eight, 72- Bus & Prof Pos: Owner & Operator, Manchester Woodcraft, Manchester Ctr, Vt, 50- Mil Serv: Entered as A/S (V-12), Navy, 42, released as Lt(jg), 46, after serv in USS Foss, Destroyer Escort 59, Atlantic Destroyer Fleet, 44-46. Mem: Boy Scouts. Honors & Awards: Silver Beaver Award, Ethan Allen Coun, Boy Scouts. Relig: Congregational. Legal Res: Manchester VT 05255 Mailing Add: Manchester Center VT 05255

BONICELLI, DERITO (D)
Chmn, Huerfano Co Dem Party, Colo
b Ideal, Colo, Dec 21, 18; s Morandi Bonicelli & Cotilda B; m 1940 to Caryl Kathrine Ralya; c Harold E, Caryl Ann, Debra, Derito James, Celine & Janine. Educ: St Marys Sch, grad, 37. Polit & Govt Pos: Councilman, Walsenburg, Colo, 57-63; chmn, Walsenburg Dem Party, 63-70; chmn, Huerfano Co Dem Party, 68-; mayor, Walsenburg, 69-; vchmn, 26th Sen Dist Dem Party, 70- Bus & Prof Pos: Owner, Firestone Store, 45, Misty Haven Resort Cabins, Cuchara, Colo, 65 & B-K Drive-In, 69. Mil Serv: Entered as Buck Pvt, Army, 41, released as Sgt Maj, 45, after serv in 214th Antiaircraft Artil Gun Bn, ETO, 42-45; Good Conduct & Bronze Star Medals. Mem: Elks; Lions; VFW; Am Legion. Relig: Catholic. Mailing Add: 323 E Seventh St Walsenburg CO 81089

BONIOR, DAVID E (D)
Mich State Rep
b Detroit, Mich, June 6, 45; s Edward Bonior & Irene B (deceased); m 1967 to Sybil Louise Rader; c Andrew & Julie. Educ: Univ Iowa, BA, 67; Univ Detroit, 67-68; Chapman Col, MA, 72; Sigma Alpha Epsilon. Polit & Govt Pos: State probation off, Macomb Co Probate Court, Mich, 67-68; Mich State Rep, 75th Dist, 73-; mem, Macomb Co Dem Exec Comt, currently. Mil Serv: Entered as Airman, Air Force, 68, released as S/Sgt E-5, 72, after serv in 479th Tactical Fighter Squadron, Tactical Air Command. Mem: YMCA. Relig: Catholic. Mailing Add: 103 Riverside Dr Mt Clemens MI 48043

BONKER, DON L (D)
US Rep, Wash
b Denver, Colo, Mar 7, 37; m 1971 to Carolyn Jo Ekern. Educ: Clark Col, AA, 62; Lewis & Clark Col, BA, 64; Am Univ, 64-66. Polit & Govt Pos: Res asst to US Sen Maurine B Neuberger, Ore, 64-66; auditor, Clark Co, Wash, 66-72; Dem cand, Secy of State, 72; US Rep, Wash, 75- Mil Serv: US Coast Guard, 55-59. Mem: Clark Col Alumni Asn (bd dirs); United Good Neighbors (bd dirs); Clark Co Health & Welfare Planning Coun (bd dirs). Legal Res: 3536 Wilderness Dr SE Olympia WA 98503 Mailing Add: US House Rep Washington DC 20515

BONNETT, THOMAS WINSLOW (D)
Vt State Rep
b Hanover, NH, Nov 21, 52; s Robert Wilcox Bonnett & I Joyce Smith B; single. Educ: Bennington Col, degree, 75; Mayday Collective; Meridan Social Club; col govt pres, 74. Polit & Govt Pos: Chmn, Orange Co Dem Comt, Vt, 73-75; Vt State Rep, 74- Bus & Prof Pos: Busboy & waiter, 67-70; road construction laborer, 71; mason tender, 72; researcher & author, State Govt, Vt, 73-74. Publ: Handbook of Vermont State Government, Vt State Govt, 73. Mem: Am Dem Action; For Land's Sake; Am Civil Liberties Union. Honors & Awards: All-League Basketball Team, 69-70. Mailing Add: East Thetford VT 05043

BONNEY, EDWARD MAYSON (D)
b Buckfield, Maine, Apr 5, 33; s Mayson Turner Bonney & Beatrice Dean B; m 1957 to Betty Joyce Smith; c Kerry David, Edward Mayson, Jr & Brian Everett. Educ: Emerson Col; Austin Col. Polit & Govt Pos: Chmn, Freeport Dem Town Comt, Maine, 63-66; mem & chmn, Freeport Sch Comt, 64-67; chmn, Cumberland Co Dem Comt, 66-67; exec dir, Maine Dem State Comt, 67-73; mem & chmn, Freeport Govt Study Comt, 70-71; mem & chmn, Freeport Charter Comn, 71-72; mem & chmn, Appointments Comt, 72-74; mem, Ord & Finance Comts, 72-74; Freeport councilman, Dist One, 72-75. Bus & Prof Pos: Asst air traffic controller, Fed Aviation Agency, New York, 57-59; dept mgr, W T Grant Co, Portland, Maine, 59-67. Mil Serv: Entered as Airman, Air Force, 52, released as Airman 1/C, 56, after serv in 3555th Troop Combat Crew Training Wing, Air Training Command, 54-56; Nat Defense Serv Medal; Good Conduct Medal. Mem: Maine State Bar Asn (exec dir). Relig: Protestant. Mailing Add: 4 Nathan Nye St Freeport ME 04032

BONSELL, WILLIAM RICHARD (R)
Minority Doorkeeper, US House of Rep
b Huntington, Pa, Oct 1, 18; s Carl Scott Bonsell & Ruth Prindle B; m 1962 to Katie Rosenthal; c William Dailey, Susan Lynn, Thomas Alexander, Mark Joseph & James G. Educ: Juniata Col, BS, 41; Thompson Bus Col. Polit & Govt Pos: Asst bill clerk, US House of Rep, 47-49; exec asst auditor gen, Pa, 50-51; prof staff mem, Senate Comt on Appropriations, 51-52; Sgt-at-Arms, US House of Rep, 52-54, Minority doorkeeper, 54- Mil Serv: Entered as Pvt, Army, 51, released as S/Sgt, 45; Presidential Unit Citation. Mem: Am Legion; Mason. Legal Res: Huntington PA 18622 Mailing Add: 4213 Kingsmill Lane Annandale VA 22003

BONTEMPO, SALVATORE A (D)
b Newark, NJ, Aug 14, 09; s Joseph M Bontempo & Angelina Andreacco B; m 1948 to Gloria Manzardo; c Thomas J & Paul N. Educ: Univ Notre Dame, BA, 32; Seton Hall Univ Law Sch, JD, 40. Polit & Govt Pos: Dir of purchases, Newark, NJ; supply div, US Air Force; city comnr, Newark, NJ; dir Vet Serv, comnr of Conserv & Econ Develop, mem, Atomic Energy Comn, chmn Interstate Coop Comn & mem Housing Admin, State of NJ; adminr, Bur

Security & Consult Affairs, US State Dept; Sr US Deleg UN, Geneva; chmn, NJ Dem Party, 69-73; mem, Dem Nat Comt, 72-73; chmn, NJ Hwy Authority & NJ Area Redevelop Authority, currently; mem, NJ Interstate Sanit Comn & Mass Transit Study Comn, currently. Bus & Prof Pos: Chmn bd, Braidburn Corp. Mil Serv: Entered as Lt, USAF, 42, released as Col, 46, after serv in Air Materiel Command & all theatres of oper; Legion of Merit; other time evaluated decorations. Relig: Roman Catholic. Mailing Add: Brooklake Rd Florham Park NJ 07932

BONVEGNA, JOSEPH S (D)
Md State Sen
Mailing Add: 3511 Gough St Baltimore MD 21224

BOOK, RONALD LEE (D)
b Pleasington, Calif, Dec 3, 51; s Harold Book & Delores Betty Koret B; single. Educ: Univ Fla, AA; Fla Int Univ; Student Sen & Justice, Traffic Court, Univ Fla. Polit & Govt Pos: Campaign mgr, Elton Gissendanner for mayor, senate & cong, Fla, 65-72; mem, North Miami Youth Rels Bd; student affairs vpres, Fla State Young Dem; exec dir, North Dade Youth for Progress, 68-73; mem bd dirs, Dade Co Young Dem, 70-; aide asst & campaign dir, US Rep William Lehman, Fla, 72-73; campaign mgr, Harwitz for Mayor, 73; admin asst to Fla State Rep Alan Becker, Dist 103, 73- Bus & Prof Pos: Adminr, Publix Mkt, 68-73; Assoc, Stuart P Rose & Assocs, Pub Rels, 72- Publ: Research into Phosphates in Waterways, Privately Publ, 71; Phosphates in Dade County waterways, Fla Naturalist, 71. Mem: Dade Co Concerned Dem; North Miami Striders-Run for Fun (organizer, 73); Gold Coast Dem Club; North Bay Polit Club; Lions Int. Honors & Awards: State Sci Fair Winner & Co Winner, 71; Silver Knight Award, Miami Herald, 71; Award for Distinguished Serv, North Miami Jr CofC, 71; Award for serv & recognition, City of North Miami, 72; nominee for Outstanding Citizen in Dade Co, B'nai B'rith, 73. Relig: Jewish. Mailing Add: 12905 Cherry Rd North Miami FL 33161

BOOKER, EDWARD HAMILTON (D)
La State Rep
b Lake Charles, La, Dec 22, 38; s H H Booker, Jr & Margaret Elisabeth Donohue B; m 1969 to Luce Marie Robert Lutgen. Educ: Loyola Univ, New Orleans, La, BA; Tulane Univ, JD; Alpha Delta Gamma; Phi Delta Phi. Polit & Govt Pos: La State Rep, 68- Mem: La State & Criminal Courts Bar Asns; Jr CofC; Young Democrats. Relig: Roman Catholic. Mailing Add: 2833 General Pershing St New Orleans LA 70115

BOOKHAMMER, EUGENE DONALD (R)
Lt Gov, Del
b Lewes, Del, June 14, 18; s William H Bookhammer & Winifred H Jenkins B; m 1942 to Katherine Williams; c Joy & Jean. Educ: Lewes High Sch, 36; Am Tech Soc, 38. Polit & Govt Pos: Deleg, Rep Nat Conv, 52, 56 & 60; Del State Sen, 62-68; chmn, Sussex Co Rep Party, Del, 64-66; Lt Gov, Del, 69- Bus & Prof Pos: Owner, Bookhammer Lumber Mills, 40; owner, Joy Beach Develop Co, 50-; pres, Rehoboth Bay Dredging Co, currently. Mil Serv: Entered as Pvt, Army, 43, released as M/Sgt, 46, after serv in 1st, 3rd & 9th Army, ETO, 44-46; Purple Heart; Five Campaign Ribbons. Mem: Am Banking Inst; Am Legion; CofC; VFW; Boy Scouts. Relig: Protestant. Legal Res: RD Lewes DE 19958 Mailing Add: Legislative Hall Dover DE 19901

BOOKOUT, JERRY (D)
Ark State Sen
Mailing Add: 1730 Crestview Jonesboro AR 72401

BOONE, ALEXANDER GORDON, JR (D)
b Baltimore, Md, Aug 21, 33; s A Gordon Boone & Edith Marion Flint B; m 1956 to Sylvia Jane Hayes; c A Gordon, III, Anne Gordon Herbert & John Rawlings Marshall. Educ: Univ Md, 56-60; Univ Baltimore, LLB, 63; Phi Kappa Sigma. Polit & Govt Pos: Pres, Univ Baltimore Young Dem, 62-63; exec secy, Nat Legis Leaders Conf, 63; pres, Baltimore Young Dem, Md, 66-67; nat committeeman, Md Young Dem, 66-67; mem, Md Dem State Cent Comt, formerly; deleg, Dem Nat Conv, 68; deleg, Dem Nat Mid-Term Conf, 74. Mil Serv: Entered as Airman 1/C, Air Force, 53, released as S/Sgt, 56, after serv in Air Defense Command, Far East. Mem: Md & Am Bar Asns; Am Judicature Soc; Jr CofC; Elks. Relig: Roman Catholic. Legal Res: Oak Hill House Bellona Ave Baltimore MD 21212 Mailing Add: 11 W Pennsylvania Ave Towson MD 21204

BOONE, LATHAM, III (D)
Tex State Rep
Mailing Add: PO Box 271 Navasota TX 77868

BOOSE, JERRY DALE (R)
Chmn, Ill Young Rep Orgn
b Elgin, Ill, June 21, 42; s M Dale Boose & G LaVerne Brown B; m 1974 to Carol M Jahn. Educ: Univ Ill, BS, 64, JD, 67; Phi Delta Phi; Kappa Alpha Si; Sigma Phi Epsilon. Polit & Govt Pos: Asst attorney gen, Ill, 69-74; legis aide, State Rep R Bruce Waddell, 70-74; chmn, Ill Young Rep Orgn, 73-; dir, Regional Transportation Authority, Chicago, 74- Bus & Prof Pos: Assoc, Jordan, Akemann & Miles, Elgin, Ill, 67-70; partner, Shearer, O'Brien, Blood, Agrella & Boose, St Charles, 70- Mem: Ill State & Kane Co Bar Asns; Elgin Jaycees; Boy Scouts of Am (vpres, Two Rivers Coun, 70-). Honors & Awards: Distinguished Citizens Award, Elgin Jaycees, 74. Relig: Methodist. Legal Res: 2490 W Highland Elgin IL 60120 Mailing Add: 303 E Main St St Charles IL 60174

BOOTH, ARDEN (R)
Kans State Sen
b Fairview, Kans, Dec 4, 11; s James H Booth & Sophia Dorothy Mellenbruch B; m to Dorothy Lyons; c Jannine (Mrs Clark), Clyne Foust, Hank & Elizabeth. Educ: Kans State Univ, 30-31; Baker Univ, BS, 40; Univ Kans, 40-41; Farm House. Polit & Govt Pos: Kans State Sen, Dist 2, 70- Bus & Prof Pos: Owner & mgr, Radio KLWN, Lawrence, Kans, 50- Mil Serv: Entered as Pvt, Army, 42, released as T-5, 45, after serv in Spec Serv, Hawaii. Mailing Add: Radio KLWN Lawrence KS 66044

BOOTH, BERT (R)
Md State Deleg
b Baltimore, Md, Aug 24, 25; d Owen Rudisill Stagmer & Emma Ports S; m 1943 to David Edwin Booth; c David E, Jr, James David, II & Richard Colton; Owen Rudisill Stagmer, III. Educ: Univ Md Sch Pharm, 42-43. Polit & Govt Pos: Md State Deleg, 75- Mem: League Women Voters; Orgn Women Legislators; Nat Orgn Women; Womens Polit Caucus. Relig: Humanist. Mailing Add: 11231 Greenspring Ave Lutherville MD 21093

BOOTH, JAMES C, JR (D)
Mem Finance Comt, Sixth Cong Dist Dem Party, Ga
b Hahira, Ga, July 7, 37; s J Cecil Booth, Sr (deceased) & Helen Mathis B (deceased); m 1967 to Margo Schwab. Educ: Emory Univ, BA, 59; Omicron Delta Kappa; Pi Sigma Alpha; Pi Delta Epsilon; Sigma Alpha Epsilon. Polit & Govt Pos: Pres, Emory Univ Young Dem, 59; mem, Fayette Co Indust Develop Bd, Ga, 66-67; mem, Fayette Co Dem Exec Comt, 67-70; Lt Col & aide-de-camp, Gov of Ga Staff, 67-70; mem finance comt, Sixth Cong Dist Dem Party, 71-; mem, Ga State Dem Exec Comt, formerly. Bus & Prof Pos: Managing ed, Walton Tribune, Monroe, Ga, 61-64; ed, Jackson Herald, Jefferson, 64-65; ed, Fayette Co News, Fayetteville, 65-69; univ ed, Emory Univ, 70; managing ed, J-Free Press, Jonesboro, 70- Mil Serv: Ga Air Nat Guard, 59-65; Spec Commendation, Air Training Command. Publ: Life, a vicious cycle, poem, Archon Mag, 68. Mem: Atlanta Press Club; Suburban Newspapers of Atlanta, Inc; Atlanta Chap, Sigma Delta Chi; Rotary Club of Peachtree City; Ga Asn Future Homemakers Am. Honors & Awards: Outstanding Young Man, Fayette Co, Ga, 68; several state & nat awards for excellence in jour. Relig: Lutheran. Legal Res: 112 Hill Top Dr Peachtree City GA 30214 Mailing Add: Box 368 Jonesboro GA 30236

BOOTH, MARY BENSON (R)
b Bryn Mawr, Pa, June 19, 40; d Richard Benson & Mary Pew B; m 1965 to Frederick Roberts; c Frederick Benson. Educ: Univ Colo, Boulder, grad, 62; Cosmopolitan Club. Polit & Govt Pos: Deleg, Colo State Rep Conv, 64, alt deleg, 68 & 70; secy-treas, Eagle Co Rep Cent Comt, formerly. Mem: Farm Bur. Relig: Episcopal. Legal Res: Star Rte PO Box 215 Gypsum CO 81637 Mailing Add: Gypsum Creek Ranch Gypsum CO 81637

BOOTHE, MRS VAL (D)
Polit & Govt Pos: Mem, Dem Nat Comt, Utah, formerly. Mailing Add: 644 E Beecher Ave Brigham City UT 83402

BOOZER, F VERNON (R)
Md State Deleg
Mailing Add: 614 Bosley Ave Towson MD 21204

BORAH, DAN V (R)
b Olney, Ill, Oct 8, 22; s O C Borah & Margaret Vernor B; m 1944 to Betty Glover; c Dan, Jr, James E, Kathryn E, Julie Y, Sally J & Chris R. Educ: Univ Ill, 2 years. Polit & Govt Pos: Precinct committeeman, Rep Party, Ill; chmn, Richland Co Rep Comt, formerly. Bus & Prof Pos: Pres, Borah & Bolunder, Inc, 56-; dir, Olney Trust & Banking Co, 60-; vpres, Olney Homes, Inc, 61- Mem: Rotary; Elks. Relig: Methodist. Legal Res: 1301 Whittle Ave Olney IL 62450 Mailing Add: RR Olney IL 62450

BORCHERS, ALBERT WEBBER (R)
Ill State Rep
b Decatur, Ill, July 1, 06; s Charles Martin Borchers & Alice Bowman B; m Margaret Stevens (deceased); c Margret (Mrs Dean Cuttill) & Elizabeth (Mrs Herbert Hawkins). Educ: Univ Ill, BA, 31; Sigma Delta Kappa; Alpha Phi Omega; Cavalry Club. Polit & Govt Pos: Asst Supvr, Macon Co Bd Supvrs, Ill, 12 years; Ill State Rep, 69- Bus & Prof Pos: Pres, Bath Inc, Decatur, 35-59, chmn bd, 59- Mil Serv: Entered as Pvt, Army, 25, released as Cavalry Sgt, 46, after serv in 80th Inf Div Cavalry Troop, ETO, 44-45; Four Battle Stars; Two Purple Hearts; Bronze Star, Liberation of France, Croix de Guerre with Palm; Commendation, Good Conduct, European Theatre, Victory, Pearl Harbor, Occup of Germany & Reserve Serv Medals; European & Am Theater Ribbons. Mem: VFW; Decatur & Macon Co Hist Comt. Relig: Protestant. Mailing Add: 695 S Crea Decatur IL 62522

BORDALLO, MADELEINE MARY (D)
Dem Nat Committeewoman, Guam
b Graceville, Minn, May 31, 33; d Christian Peter Zeien & Mary Evelyn Roth Z; m 1953 to Ricardo Jerome Bordallo; c Deborah Josephine. Educ: St Mary's Col, South Bend, Ind, 52; St Katherine's Col, AA in Music, 53. Hon Degrees: BCommunServ, Univ Guam, 68. Polit & Govt Pos: Dem Nat Committeewoman, Guam, 65-; pres, Women's Dem Party & mem exec bd, Dem Party, 65-; mem exec bd, Dem Campaign Comt, 66; deleg, Dem Nat Conv, 68 & 72; mem, Nat Charter Comn, Nat Dem Party, 73- Bus & Prof Pos: Local news ed, traffic mgr & prog dir sales dept, KUAM Radio-TV, 54-59, women's dir, 59-63. Publ: Fashion & travel articles for local newspapers. Mem: Marianas Asn Retarded Children (pres, 63-64 & 73-); Brodie Mem Sch Exceptional Children; Guam Mem Hosp Vol Asn; Guam Women's Club; Fedn Asian Women's Asns (pres, 67-). Relig: Catholic. Mailing Add: PO Box 1458 Agana GU 96910

BORDALLO, RICARDO JEROME (D)
Gov, Guam
b Agana, Guam, Dec 11, 27; s Baltazar Bordallo & Josephine Pangelinan B; m 1953 to Madeleine Mary Zeien; c Deborah. Educ: Univ San Francisco, 47-50. Polit & Govt Pos: Sen, Guam Legis, 56-70; Minority Leader, 64-66; chmn, Fifty-Star Flag Raising Ceremony, Guam, 60; deleg, Nat Legis Conf, Ill, 60 & NJ, 64; charter chmn, Dem Party Guam, 60-63; chmn, 71-; chmn, Tuberc Drive Gov Ball, 61; deleg, Fifth SPac Conf, Am Samoa, 62; deleg, Second Inaugural Salute, President Kennedy & Nat Conf Dem State Chmn, Washington, DC, 63; deleg, Dem Nat Conv, 64 & 68; deleg, Legis Leaders Conf, PR, 65; nominee for Gov, Guam, 70; Gov, Guam, 74- Bus & Prof Pos: Dealership, Toyota Motor Co, Guam, 56-; chmn bd dir, Family Finance Co, Inc, 59-; dealership, Guam Chrysler Motor Sales, 66-; incorporator & chmn bd, Am Enterprises & publisher daily newspaper, Pac J, 66-68. Mil Serv: Army, 53, Pvt. Mem: Marianas Lions Club; Marianas Asn for Retarded Children; Young Men's League of Guam; Navy League of Guam; Guam CofC. Relig: Catholic. Mailing Add: PO Box 1458 Agana GU 96910

BORDAS, PHYLLIS JEAN (R)
Chairperson, Clearfield Co Rep Party, Pa
b Wallaceton, Pa, June 1, 34; d Harry Edward Hamer & Beatrice Bertha Smeal H; div; c Scott Vincent, Terri Lynn, Dawna Marie & Beth Ann. Educ: Pa State Univ, 53-54. Polit & Govt Pos: Councilwoman, Wallaceton, Pa, 64-65; coun pres, 65-68; pres planning comn, Clearfield Co, 67-73; pres, Clearfield Co Rep Women, 68-70; committeewoman & mem exec comt, Clearfield Co Rep Party, 67-73, chairperson, 73- Relig: United Methodist. Legal Res: 405 1/2 E Market St Clearfield PA 16830 Mailing Add: Box 606 Clearfield PA 16830

BORDEN, LAUREEN ESTELLE **(DFL)**
VChmn, Crow Wing Co Dem-Farmer-Labor Party, Minn
b Bemidji, Minn, May 5, 43; d Loren L Winch & Arlene Booth W; m 1962 to John Clarence Borden; c Michael Roy. Educ: Bemidji State Col. Polit & Govt Pos: Mem vol comts for Sen Mondale, Sen Humphrey, State Sen Winston Borden & State Rep Don Samuelson; deleg, Minn State Dem-Farmer-Labor Conv, 65-; vchmn, Crow Wing Co Dem-Farmer-Labor Party, 64-; vchmn, Co Exten Bd, 67- Bus & Prof Pos: Tax consult, H&R Block, Inc, 69- Mem: Cross Lake Local Farmers Union (secy); Sixth Dist Garden Clubs (vchmn); Center Homemakers (chmn). Honors & Awards: Leadership Award, Farmers Union. Relig: Presbyterian. Mailing Add: Box 49 Merrifield MN 56465

BORDEN, WINSTON WENDELL **(DFL)**
Minn State Sen
b Brainerd, Minn, Sept 1, 43; s Ralph Waldo Borden & Hazel Converse B; m 1970 to Betty Rae McRoberts. Educ: St Cloud State Col, BA, 65; Univ Minn, MA & JD, 68; Student Body Pres; pres, debate team. Polit & Govt Pos: Chmn, Minn Young Dem-Farmer-Labor Party, 64; State Dem-Farmer-Labor Internship, 64; mem, Minn State Dem-Farmer-Labor Cent Comt, 65-70, 74-; deleg-at-lg, Dem Nat Conv, 68; charter mem, Nat Citizens for Humphrey Comt, 68; mem, Minn Humphrey Campaign Comt, 68; mem tech rev bd, Gov Coun Aging, 68-70; Minn State Sen, 71-, Asst Senate Majority Whip, Minn State Senate, 73- Bus & Prof Pos: Counr, Univ Minn, 66-68; consult, Upper Midwest Res & Develop Coun, Minn, 67-68; attorney, 68-; instr polit sci, Wis State Univ, Superior, 68-70; partner, Borden, Wise & Steinbauer, Attorneys-at-law, currently; mem bd dirs, St Cloud State Col, 71-; mem bd dirs, PORT, 72-; mem bd dirs, Camp Confidence for Ment Retarded, 72-; pres, Brainerd Area United Fund, 72- Mem: Am Civil Liberties Union; St Cloud State Col Alumni Asn (bd dirs); Exchange Club; YMCA; Jaycees. Honors & Awards: Brainerd Distinguished Serv Award, Brainerd Jaycees, 72. Relig: Catholic. Mailing Add: 514 Grove Brainerd MN 56401

BORDIERE, MARCUS H **(D)**
Conn State Rep
Mailing Add: 433 Monroe St New Britain CT 06052

BORELLI, FRANK PETER, JR **(R)**
Mem, Rep State Cent Comt Calif
b Hollister, Calif, July 27, 35; s Frank Borelli & Clara La Macchia B; m 1962 to Josephine Filice; c Carla, Gia, Frank P, III & Stephen. Educ: Univ Santa Clara, BS, 56, LLD, 60. Polit & Govt Pos: Mem, San Benito Co Rep Cent Comt, Calif, 68-; mem, Rep State Cent Comt Calif, 69- Bus & Prof Pos: Attorney-at-law, O'Brien & Borelli, Hollister, Calif, 61- Mil Serv: Entered as Pvt E-2, Army, 58, released as Pvt E-2, 59, Army Res, 59-68. Mem: Calif & San Benito Co Bar Asns; San Benito Co CofC (pres, 69-); Elks; Farm Bur. Relig: Catholic. Mailing Add: 1878 Prune St Hollister CA 95023

BOREN, DAVID LYLE **(D)**
Gov, Okla
b Washington, DC, Apr 21, 41; s Lyle H Boren & Christine McKown B; m 1968 to Janna Lou Little; c Carrie Christine & David Daniel. Educ: Yale Univ, BA, 63; Oxford Univ, MA, 65; Univ Okla Col Law, JD, 68; Phi Beta Kappa; Am Asn Rhodes Scholars; Phi Delta Phi; Delta Sigma Rho; Distinguished Mil Grad ROTC, 63; mem staff, Okla Law Rev. Polit & Govt Pos: Asst to liaison dir, Off of Civil & Defense Mobilization, Washington, DC, 59-62; propaganda analyst, US Info Agency, 62-63; prog chmn, Yale Young Dem, 62-63; coordr, Yale Conserv Asn, 62-63 & speaker, Yale Polit Union, 62-63; mem, Speakers Bur, US Embassy, London, Eng, 63-65; Okla State Rep, Seminole Co, 66-74; deleg, Dem Nat Conv, 68; Gov, Okla, 75- Bus & Prof Pos: Counr for Freshman, Univ Okla, 65-66; attorney-at-law, pvt practice, Seminole & Wewoka, Okla, 68-; asst prof polit sci, Okla Baptist Univ, 69, prof polit sci & chmn div soc sci, 69- Mil Serv: Co Comdr, Okla Army Nat Guard, 1st Lt, currently; Army Medal. Mem: Yale Club of Okla; Seminole CofC; Jaycees; Seminole Sportsmans Club; ROA. Honors & Awards: Bledsoe Prize as Outstanding Okla Univ Law Grad, 68; One of Three Outstanding Young Oklahomans, Okla State Jr CofC, 69. Relig: Methodist; Assoc Dist Lay Leader. Legal Res: 917 Wilson St Seminole OK 74868 Mailing Add: State Capitol 2302 Lincoln Blvd Oklahoma City OK 73105

BOREN, LYLE H **(D)**
b Waxahachie, Tex, May 11, 09; s Mark Latimer Boren & Nanie Mae Weatherall B; m 1936 to Christine McKown; c David Lyle & Susan Hope. Educ: East Cent Col, BA, 28; Okla State Univ, MA, 36; Pi Kappa Delta; Eugene Field Soc of Authors & Writers. Polit & Govt Pos: Pres, Okla Dem Fraternity, 35-36; US Rep, Okla, 37-47; asst ins comnr, State Ins Comn, 70-73. Bus & Prof Pos: Pres, Okla Cattle Co, 46-55; pres, Seminole Petroleum Co, 48-57; Washington rep, Asn of Western Rwy, 53-70; pres, Bodrain Co, 65- Mil Serv: Entered as Ens, Navy, 36, released as Lt Comdr, 55, after serv in Eighth Naval Dist. Publ: Who is Who in Oklahoma, Harlow Publ, 35; Fables in Labels, Nat Capitol Press, 40; History of the Santa Fe Trail, Eastern Cent J, 35. Mem: Okla Cattlemen's Asn (founder); Elks; Odd Fellows; Rotary; Am Legion. Relig: Church of Christ. Mailing Add: 2924 Chapel Hill Rd Oklahoma City OK 73120

BORING, DENZEL D **(D)**
b Warsaw, Mo, Jan 4, 26; s Jesse Oscar Boring & Zelda Wisdom B; m 1947 to Mabel Frances Fergerson; c Rebecca Lynn & Roberta Lea. Educ: Warsaw High Sch, grad, 45. Polit & Govt Pos: Chmn, Benton Co Dem Party, Mo, formerly. Bus & Prof Pos: Owner & operator, Davis Paint Assoc Store, Warsaw, 54-69; agt, Am Family Ins Co, Madison, Wis, 55- Mil Serv: Entered as Pvt, Army, 44, released as Sgt, 46, after serv in 3rd Div, 15th Inf, ETO, 45-46; Purple Heart; Good Conduct; Two Battle Stars. Mem: Mason; Eastern Star (patron, Osage Valley Chap 502, 56). Relig: Southern Baptist. Mailing Add: Box 95 Warsaw MO 65355

BORK, ROBERT H **(R)**
Solicitor Gen, Dept Justice
Legal Res: CT Mailing Add: Dept of Justice Washington DC 20530

BORNHEIMER, JAMES W **(D)**
NJ State Assemblyman
Mailing Add: State House Trenton NJ 08625

BORRELLO, A CHARLES **(D)**
La State Rep
Mailing Add: 4767 Eunice Dr New Orleans LA 70127

BORST, LAWRENCE MARION **(R)**
Ind State Sen
b Champaign Co, Ohio, July 16, 27; s Lawrence M Borst & Mary Waldeck B; m 1947 to Eldoris; c Philip, Elizabeth & David. Educ: Ohio State Univ, DJourn, 50. Polit & Govt Pos: Ind State Rep, 67-68; deleg, Rep Nat Conv, 68; Ind State Sen, 69-; chmn, Ind Budget Comt, 73- Mailing Add: 1725 Remington Dr Indianapolis IN 46227

BORT, JOSEPH PARKER **(R)**
Supvr, Alameda Co Bd of Supvr, Calif
b Avalon, Calif, July 23, 15; s Milo C Bort & Mary Parker B; m 1942 to Jacklyn Taylor; c Samuel P, Daniel C & Peggy Jo. Educ: Univ Calif, Berkeley, BS; Boalt Hall of Law, Univ Calif, LLB; Tau Beta Pi. Polit & Govt Pos: Councilman, City of Berkeley, Calif, 63-67; supvr, Alameda Co Bd of Supvr, 67-, chmn, 73-74; chmn, Metrop Transportation Comn, 71-73. Bus & Prof Pos: Life ins salesman, 46-60; attorney, 60- Mil Serv: Entered as Ens, Navy, 43, released as Lt, 46, after eng duty, Brooklyn Navy Yard. Mem: Calif State Bar; Alameda Co Bar Asn; Estate Planning Coun; Am Soc Chartered Life Underwriters; Co Supvr Asn Calif (pres, 75-). Relig: Christian Science. Legal Res: 615 San Luis Rd Berkeley CA 94707 Mailing Add: Rm 703 Central Bldg Oakland CA 94612

BORTELL, GLEN E **(R)**
Iowa State Rep
Mailing Add: RR 1 St Charles IA 50240

BOSCH, ALBERT H **(R)**
b New York, NY, Oct 30, 08; s Henry Bosch & Margaretha Hamburger B; m 1936 to Theresa Hoenig; c Marilyn M & Alice A. Educ: St John's Univ, LLB, 33. Polit & Govt Pos: Former mem, Woodhaven Rep Asn, NY & Richmond Hill Rep Club; committeeman, Queens Co Rep Party, 49-52; US Rep, Fifth Dist, 83-86 Cong; co judge, Queens Co, 61-62; State Justice, 11th Judicial Dist, NY Supreme Court, 62- Bus & Prof Pos: Lawyer, firm, Archer, Bosch & Engeler, 45-60; trustee, Hamburg Savings Bank. Mem: Am & Queens Co Bar Asns; Steuben Soc Am; Mason; Elks. Mailing Add: 182-30 Wexford Terr Jamaica NY 11432

BOSCH, ROBERT D **(R)**
b Muscatine, Iowa, May 22, 22; s Glenn Bosch & Freda Schmiekel B; m 1947 to Miriam Kopf; c Amy & Kathryn. Educ: Muscatine High Sch, 4 years. Polit & Govt Pos: Alderman, Muscatine, Iowa, 58-60, mayor, 60-65; chmn, Muscatine Co Rep Party, formerly. Bus & Prof Pos: Draftsman, Grain Processing Corp, 47-56; owner, Bosch Pest Control Co, 49-; pres, Rid-A-Bird, Inc, 59-; pres, Am Chem Co, 62-; vpres, Discount Sales Co, Inc, 62- Mil Serv: Entered as Pvt, Army, 44, released as Pvt, 46, after serv in 103rd Div, 44-46. Mem: Am Soc Appraisers; Iowa Real Estate Brokers; Moose; Shrine; Mason. Relig: Protestant. Legal Res: 517 Roscoe Ave Muscatine IA 52761 Mailing Add: PO Box 22 Muscatine IA 52761

BOSCHWITZ, RUDY **(R)**
Rep Nat Committeeman, Minn
b Berlin, Ger, Nov 7, 30; s Ely Boschwitz & Lucy Dawidowicz B; m 1956 to Ellen Lowenstein; c Jerry, Ken, Dan & Tom. Educ: Johns Hopkins Univ, 47-49; NY Univ, BS, LLB. Polit & Govt Pos: Rep Nat Committeeman, Minn, 71-; deleg, Rep Nat Conv, 72. Bus & Prof Pos: Pres, Plywood Minn, Inc, 63- Mil Serv: Entered as Pvt, Army, released as Pfc after 2 years serv. Relig: Jewish. Legal Res: 17250-D 19th Ave N Plymouth MN 55391 Mailing Add: 5401 E River Rd Fridley MN 55421

BOSCO, JOSEPH A **(INDEPENDENT)**
b Boston, Mass, Mar 25, 38; s Joseph Bosco & Emma Pacillo B; m 1969 to Carol W Beebe; c Carla Anne & David Lyndon. Educ: Harvard Col, AB cum laude, 60, LLB, 65; House Comt, Phillips Brooks House; Pre-law Soc; Lincoln's Inn Soc; Howe Club. Polit & Govt Pos: Law clerk to US Attorney, Mass, summer 64; law clerk to Chief Justice & Assoc Justices, Mass Superior Court, 65-67; legal counsel to gov, Mass, 67-68; mem transition team, Dept of Transportation, 68-69, Spec Asst to the Secy, 69-73; app, Nat Hwy Safety Adv Comt, currently. Mil Serv: Entered as Ens, Navy, 60, released as Lt(jg), 62, after serv in USS Hancock, Far East; Lt Comdr, Naval Res; Commanding Officer's Commendation, USS Hancock, 61; Naval Res Intel Div Award, 65, 66 & 68. Mem: Fed Bar Asn (chmn urban mass transportation comt); Boston, Mass & Am Bar Asns; Harvard Club. Honors & Awards: Honors Paper, Harvard Law Sch, 65; Dept Transportation Award, 72. Legal Res: 3121 Newark St NW Washington DC 20008 Mailing Add: 1700 K St NW Washington DC 20006

BOSMA, CHARLES EDWARD **(R)**
Ind State Sen
b Beech Grove, Ind, Apr 8, 22; s Mitchell C Bosma & Emma Rodert B; m 1945 to Margaret Pauline Hagge; c Janice Irene, Rhonda Jeanne & Brian Charles. Educ: Purdue Univ, 40-43, BS, 70; Beta Sigma Psi. Polit & Govt Pos: Rep precinct committeeman, Marion Co, Ind, 61-66, Rep ward chmn, 62-66; city chmn, Beech Grove Rep Campaign, 65; Ind State Rep, 62-64 & 66-68; Ind State Sen, 68-; mem, Ind Comn for Handicapped, currently. Bus & Prof Pos: Gen mgr & pres, Bosma Dairy, Inc, 46- Mil Serv: Entered as Pvt, Army, 43, released as Capt, 46, after serv in Field Artil, ETO, 45; Am Theater Ribbon & European Theater Ribbon with 2 Battle Stars. Mem: Nat Soc State Legislators; Community Serv Agency for Deaf (dir); Am Legion; Kiwanis; Beech Grove Businessmen's Asn. Relig: Lutheran, Missouri Synod. Mailing Add: 95 S 17th Ave Beech Grove IN 46107

BOSONE, REVA BECK **(D)**
d Christian Mateus Beck & Zilpha Chipman B; div; c Zilpha (Mrs Crouch). Educ: Univ Calif, Berkeley, BA, 19; Univ Utah, JD, 30. Polit & Govt Pos: Utah State Rep, Majority Floor Leader & chmn sifting comt, Utah House Rep, 33-35; judge, Salt Lake City Munic Court, 36-48; Utah State Dir, Educ on Alcoholism, 47-48; US Rep, Utah, 49-52, legal counsel, labor subcomt, US House of Rep, 57-61; judicial officer, US Post Off Dept, 61-68. Bus & Prof Pos: Former high sch teacher, Ogden, Utah. Mem: Utah & Fed Bar Asns; Wash Forum; Nat Order Women Legislators; State of Utah Women Legislators. Honors & Awards: Utah Hall of Fame, 43; Award for Distinguished Serv, Univ Calif, Berkeley, 70; Susa Young Gates Award, 73. Legal Res: 2792 Sonnet Dr Salt Lake City UT 84106 Mailing Add: 2808 University Dr Lawrence KS 66044

BOSSE, BERT ROLAND **(D)**
Chmn, Lebanon Dem Party, Conn
b St Agatha, Maine, Dec 20, 39; s Donat Bosse & Winnie Lizotte B; m 1961 to Rachel Lavartue; c Dean, Valerie & Andrew. Educ: Ft Kent State Col, BS, 66; St Joseph Col, MA, 70. Polit & Govt Pos: Secy, Lebanon Dem Town Comt, Conn, 68-70, chmn, 70-; treas, 19th Dist Dem Asn, 72- Bus & Prof Pos: Elem Teacher, Van Buren Sch Syst, Maine, 59-62; elem

teacher, Lebanon Sch Syst, Conn, 62-65, jr high sch teacher, 65-69, sr high sch teacher, 69- Mem: Lebanon, Conn & Nat Educ Asns; KofC; Elks. Relig: Catholic. Legal Res: Rte 289 Lebanon CT 06249 Mailing Add: PO Box 61 Lebanon CT 06249

BOSSE, VIRGINIA MAE (R)
Chairwoman, Fourth Dist Rep Party, Ky
b Pleasuridge, Ky, Jan 5, 27; d Rev Paul Roberts Barnett & Ethel L Hornback B; m 1943 to Joseph William Bosse; c Jo Ann (Mrs Raymond Shofner), Joseph Lawrence, Linda Louise (Mrs John Harrod), Robert Gerald & John Raymond. Educ: Southern High Sch, Ky, grad, 49. Polit & Govt Pos: Co-capt, C-42 Dist Rep Party, Jefferson Co, Ky, 65, committeewoman, 70, co-chairwoman, 72-73; capt, C-84 Dist Rep Party, 69; mem, Jefferson Co Zoning Bd Adjust, 69-73; Ky representative, Rep Nat Leadership Conf, 72; deleg, Rep Nat Conv, 72; third vchmn, City-Co Rep Exec Comt, 72-73; alt deleg, Ky Fedn Rep Women, 73; co-chairwoman, B Dist Rep Party, 73-; chairwoman, Fourth Dist Rep Party, 72- Bus & Prof Pos: Real estate broker, 59-73. Mil Serv: 1st Lt, Civil Air Patrol, 45-47, serv in Squadron 3, Boman Field, Louisville, Ky; Youngest female adj in Civil Air Patrol. Mem: South Jefferson Rep Club (pres, 69-70, dir, 71-73); Buttons & Bows Womans Club (vpres, 69-); Trumpeteers Rep Womans Club (co membership chmn, 69-73); Women's Rep Club Louisville & Jefferson Co; PTA (various offices). Honors & Awards: Ky Col, Gov Louie B Nunn, 69; Dinner in honor, South Jefferson Rep Club, 70; Appreciation Cert, Louisvile & Jefferson Co Rep Orgn, 72; Mem Comt Plaque, Rep Nat Conv, 72. Relig: Baptist. Mailing Add: 3614 S Park Rd Louisville KY 40219

BOSSERT, WILLARD MAX (R)
VChmn, Clinton Co Rep Party, Pa
b Mill Hall, Pa, July 9, 06; s John Smith Bossert & Minnie Holmes B; m 1931 to Edythe Hoy; c Jane (Mrs Schwab), Thomas Hoy, Willard Max, Jr, Bethany Ann & Barbara Susan. Educ: Lock Haven State Col, BS in Educ, 32; Columbia Univ, MA in Health & Phys Educ, 40; Univ Pa, advan study; Phi Kappa Sigma. Polit & Govt Pos: Mayor, Mill Hall, Pa, 40-47; chmn, Clinton Co Comnr, 48-60; sch dir, Bald Eagle Nittany High Sch, 58-59; Pa State Rep, 76th Dist, 61-72; vchmn, Clinton Co Rep Party, 75- Bus & Prof Pos: Dean of men, Lock Haven State Col, 35-40, head football coach, 35-46, dir of athletics & prof of health & phys educ, 39-46; owner & operator, Hardware Store, 46-61 & Dairy Farm, 50- Mem: Pa State Asn Co Comnr; Lock Haven State Col Alumni Asn (pres); Elks; Eagles, FofMA. Relig: Presbyterian; elder. Mailing Add: Old Beech Creek Rd Beech Creek PA 16822

BOSSHARD, RYLLA JANE (R)
Mem, La Crosse Co Rep Exec Comt, Wis
b Clatskanie, Ore, May 3, 23; d Loyd Stanley Hattan & Gertrude Anne Phillips H; m 1944 to John Bosshard; c John, III, Sabina, William Hattan & Kurt Robert. Educ: Stanford Univ, BA, 44; Theta Sigma Phi; Delta Delta Delta. Polit & Govt Pos: Deleg, Wis Rep State Conv, 48-; area vpres, La Crosse Co Rep Women, 52-62, pres, 62-64; vchmn, Third Dist Rep Party, 63-; mem, Wis State Rep Exec Comt, 63-72, chmn, Hqs, 67-72; mem, Higher Educ Aids Bd, 65-, chmn, student financial aids comt, 68-; mem, Constitutional Rev Comt, 67-; mem steering comt, Rep Party Wis, 67-; alt deleg, Rep Nat Conv, 68; mem exec comt, Wis Women's Polit Caucus, 72-; mem, La Crosse Co Rep Exec Comt, 72-; mem, La Crosse Co Wis Women's Polit Caucus, 72- Bus & Prof Pos: Dir, First Nat Bank, Bangor, 64-; dir, La Farge State Bank, 69-; dir, Farmer's State Bank, Hillsboro, Wis, currently; mem ed adv bd, Encounters Mag, currently. Mem: Am Asn Univ Women; PEO; Stanford Alumni Asn; Delta Delta Delta Alumni; Am Legion Auxiliary. Relig: Baptist. Mailing Add: Box 247 Bangor WI 54614

BOSSIE, ROBERT F (D)
NH State Sen
Mailing Add: 188 Oneida St Manchester NH 03102

BOSTER, DAVIS EUGENE
US Ambassador to Bangladesh
b Rio Grande, Ohio, Sept 14, 20; s Ernest Gordon Boster & Nelle Davis B; m 1942 to Mary Elizabeth Shilts; c Davis E, Jr, Janis Curtis, James Shilts, Thomas Daniel & Barbara Anne. Educ: Mt Union Col, AB, 42. Polit & Govt Pos: Staff asst to Secy of State, Washington, DC, 58-59, officer in charge of USSR Bilateral Affairs, 59-61, sr seminar in foreign policy, 61-62; polit officer, US Embassy, Mexico City, 62-63; spec asst to Asst Secy for Inter-Am Affairs, Dept of State, 64-65, spec asst to Under Secy for Econ Affairs, 65; polit counr, US Embassy, Moscow, USSR, 65-67; dep chief of mission, US Embassy, Kathmandu, Nepal, 67-70; dep chief of mission, US Embassy, Warsaw, Poland, 70-73; head of US deleg to European-Security Conf, Geneva, Switz, 73-74; US Ambassador to Bangladesh, 74- Mil Serv: Entered as A/S, Navy, 42, released as Lt(sg), 47, after serv in various sea & shore commands, US, Atlantic & Pac Theatres; Comdr, Naval Res. Mailing Add: US Embassy Dacca c/o Dept of State Washington DC 20520

BOSTON, EUGENE ALFRED (R)
Mem, Rep State Cent Comt, Calif
b Fresno, Calif, Oct 15, 28; s Kevork Nerses Boston & Agnes Thompson B; m 1955 to Eva Stella Bielecka; c Diane, Kenneth & Margo. Educ: Univ Calif, Los Angeles, BA; McGill Univ, MD; Nu Sigma Nu. Polit & Govt Pos: Co-chmn, Goldwater for President Comt, Fullerton, Calif, 64; mem, Rep State Cent Comt, Calif, 68- Mil Serv: Entered as 2nd Lt, Air Force, 51, released as 1st Lt, 53, after serv as Personnel Officer, US. Mem: Am & Orange Co Med Asns; Am Acad of Gen Practice (pres, 67); Kiwanis Int. Honors & Awards: Cert, Am Bd of Family Practice, 71. Relig: Protestant. Mailing Add: 8370 Waverly Circle Buena Park CA 90620

BOSTROM, CHARLENE EMERSON (R)
Secy, Bethel Rep Town Comt, Vt
b Haverhill, Mass, Aug 25, 29; d Paul Stover Emerson & Eleanor Terry Graham E; m 1956 to Kenneth Robert Böstrom; c James Alexander & Karen Nöyd. Educ: Centenary Jr Col, Hackettstown, NJ, AA, 49; Cornell Univ Sch Nursing, 49-51; Sigma Epsilon Phi. Polit & Govt Pos: Mem, Vt Rep State Platform Comt, 68; deleg, Vt Rep State Conv, 72; alt deleg, Rep Nat Conv, 72; secy, Bethel Rep Town Comt, Vt, 72-; chmn bicentennial comt, Bethel, currently. Mem: Bethel PTA; Bethel Women's Club (ways & means comt, 71-73). Mailing Add: PO Box 47 Bethel VT 05032

BOSWELL, HILDAGARDEIS (D)
b Daisytown, Pa, Jan 12, 34; d Homer Lee Boswell & Lenora Bell B; m to Lawrence Smith, div. Educ: Univ Pittsburgh, 54-57; Barnard Col, Columbia Univ, 58; NY State Sch Indust & Labor Rels, Cornell Univ, summer, 58-59; Inst for Polit Educ, Morgan State Col, BA, 61; Univ Md Sch Law, 62-63; Alpha Kappa Alpha. Polit & Govt Pos: Soc worker, City of Baltimore, Md, 63-66; human rels specialist, Md Comt Human Rels, 66-; mem, Baltimore Model Cities Prog, 68-; bd examr, Comn of Personnel, 69-; Md State Deleg, 70-74; deleg, Dem Nat Conv, 72; mem finance comt, Dem Nat Comt, 75. Bus & Prof Pos: Lectr; mem urban adv coun, WBAL-TV, 74. Mem: Nat Order Women Legislators; Dem Nat Comt; League of Women Voters; NAACP; Baltimore Urban League. Honors & Awards: Key to City of St Louis; Citation for outstanding work in field of human rels; Distinguished Citizens Award, Mich State Legis, 72; Merit Award, Nat Black Women's Polit Leadership Caucus, 73; Md Coord Coun Award, Nat Orgn Women, 73. Relig: Protestant. Mailing Add: 1208 Druid Hill Ave Baltimore MD 21217

BOTTIGER, R TED (D)
Wash State Sen
b Tacoma, Wash, 1932; m to Darlene E; c Three. Educ: Univ Puget Sound, BA; Univ Wash Law Sch, LLB. Polit & Govt Pos: Wash State Rep, formerly; Wash State Sen, 73- Bus & Prof Pos: Attorney-at-law. Legal Res: 15711 62nd Ave E Puyallup WA 98371 Mailing Add: 8849 Pacific Ave Tacoma WA 98444

BOTTORFF, LEWIS MADISON (D)
Mem, Nebr State Dem Cent Comt
b Gretna, Nebr, Sept 13, 11; s Arthur Madison Bottorff & Georgia Campbell B; m 1936 to M Pauline Rogers; c Judith P (Mrs Moore) & William Arthur. Educ: Univ Nebr, BS in agr, 35, MA, 37; Alpha Zeta; Gamma Sigma Delta; Palladian Literary. Polit & Govt Pos: Mem, Nebr Dem State Cent Comt, 58-62, 70-; vchmn, Sarpy Co Dem Cent Comt, 59-61, chmn, 62-68; vchmn, Sarpy Co Zoning Comn, 61-; chmn, Sarpy Co Planning Comn, 70- Bus & Prof Pos: Pres of bd, South Omaha Prod Credit Asn, 39-41; Pres of Bd, Pioneer Tel Coop, Phillomath, Ore, 49-51. Mil Serv: Entered as 1st Lt, Army, 41, released as Maj, 46, after serv in ETO 70th Inf Div, 274th Inf Div & European Theater Mil Govt, 45-46; Combat Inf Medal; Bronze Star. Mem: Sarpy Co Farm Bur; Mason; Scottish Rite; Tangier Shrine; Farmer's Union. Relig: Methodist. Mailing Add: Rte 1 Papillion NE 68046

BOTTUM, JOSEPH HENRY (R)
b Faulkton, SDak, Aug 7, 03; s Joseph Henry Bottum & Sylvia Grace Smith B; m 1929 to Nellie Bergita Bang; c Mary Jo. Educ: Yankton Col, 20; Univ Mich, LLB, 23; Univ SDak, 27; Lambda Chi Alpha. Polit & Govt Pos: States attorney, Faulk Co, SDak, 33-36; chmn, SDak Young Rep League, 34-42; dir taxation, SDak, 37-43; chmn, SDak Rep Cent Comt, 46-48; Lt Gov, SDak, 60-62; US Sen, SDak, 62-63; judge, Seventh Judicial Circuit, 69- Bus & Prof Pos: Attorney-at-law, St Paul, 28-30; Jacobs & Bottum, Faulkton, 30-36; partner, Bottum & Beal, Rapid City, 55- Mem: Elks; Mason (33 degree dep of the Supreme Coun, SDak); Scottish Rite (Chap Commandry, Red Cross of Constantine); Shriner (past Potentates); Odd Fellows. Relig: Congregational. Legal Res: 910 St Charles St Rapid City SD 57701 Mailing Add: Pennington County Court House Rapid City SD 57701

BOU, BLAS L (POPULAR DEMOCRAT, PR)
Rep, PR House Rep
Mailing Add: State Capitol San Juan PR 00901

BOUCHARD, DAVID J (D)
NH State Rep
Mailing Add: 33 Buffumsville Rd Somersworth NH 03878

BOUCHARD, L PHILIP (D)
Vt State Rep
Mailing Add: Franklin VT 05457

BOUCHARD, ROBERT ALEXANDER (D)
b Clayton, NY, Oct 18, 19; s Albert A Bouchard & Elizabeth M Yott B; m 1946 to Frances T Ryan; c Albert T, Joseph J, Robert Wm, Mary M, James P, Gerald F & Patrick L. Educ: St Mary's High Sch, Clayton, NY dipl, 37; Maritime Radio Sch, Boston, Mass, 1 year, Ship Radio License. Polit & Govt Pos: Chmn, Clayton Dem Town Comt, 66; treas, Jefferson Co Dem Comt, NY, 67, vchmn, 68-70, chmn, formerly. Mil Serv: Radio off, Merchant Marine, 42-45. Mem: KofC (Coun 350, Clayton, Fourth degree Watertown KofC, NY); Nat Asn Broadcast Employees & Technicians, AFL-CIO-CLC (pres, Local 24). Relig: Catholic. Mailing Add: 249 Winslow St Watertown NY 13601

BOUCHER, HENRY A (RED) (D)
Lt Gov, Alaska
b Nashua, NH, Feb 27, 21; m to Alfheidur Heida; c four daughters, one son. Polit & Govt Pos: Mem, Fairbanks City Coun, Alaska, 61-64, mayor, Fairbanks, 66-70; Lt Gov, Alaska, 71- Bus & Prof Pos: Owner, PanAlaska Sports, 59-; founder, Alaska Goldpanners Baseball Team; dist sales mgr & vpres sales, Northern Region, Alaska Airlines; exec dir, Fairbanks Indust Develop Corp, 68-70. Mil Serv: Entered Navy, 37, retired as Chief Aerographers Mate, 57, after serv in USS Enterprise, 4 years. Mem: Fairbanks Youth Recreation Prog (founder). Honors & Awards: President's Award for Physical Fitness, 62. Legal Res: 814 Old Belt Juneau AK 99801 Mailing Add: Pouch AA Juneau AK 99801

BOUCHER, HENRY MASON (D)
Chmn, Adair Co Dem Cent Comt, Mo
b Cairo, Mo, Apr 13, 07; s Robert Mason Boucher & Olive Holbrook B; m 1928 to Madeline Allen B; c Jane Allen (Mrs Gary L Hartman). Educ: Cent Methodist, 25-27; Northeast Mo State Univ, BS, 31; Univ Mo-Columbia, MA, 36; Blue Key; Sigma Tau Gamma. Polit & Govt Pos: Chmn, Adair Co Dem Cent Comt, Mo, 72-; mem, Gov Legis Coun, 73-; mem, Gov Adv Coun, 75- Bus & Prof Pos: Supt schs, Memphis, Mo, 34-40; owner & mgr wholesale auto parts, Memphis, 45-58; supt schs, Kahoka, 58-63; dean student affairs, Northeast Mo State Univ, 63-72, emer dean, 72- Mil Serv: Entered as Lt(sg), Navy, 42, released as Comdr, 45, after serv in Am & Pac Theatres; Naval Res, 45-58. Mem: VFW; Shrine; Mason; Kiwanis; Phi Delta Kappa. Honors & Awards: Hon Col, Gov Dalton's Staff, 60. Relig: Methodist. Mailing Add: 17 Overbrook Dr Kirksville MO 63501

BOUCHER, JAMES A (D)
Wyo State Rep
Mailing Add: 1203 Park Ave Laramie WY 82070

BOUCHER, LAURENT J (R)
NH State Rep
Mailing Add: 1261 Hooksett Rd Hooksett NH 03106

BOUCHER, WILLIAM PAUL (R)
NH State Rep
b Manchester, NH, Apr 4, 30; s George E Boucher (deceased) & Violet Rivard B; m 1952 to Eleanor McKinnon; c William Patrick & Martin Paul. Educ: High sch equivalency, US Armed Forces Inst. Polit & Govt Pos: NH State Rep, 71-; chmn, Londonderry Sch Bd, 71- Bus & Prof Pos: Gunsmith, 56-70. Mil Serv: Entered as Recruit, Army, 49, released as Pfc, 51, after serv in 65th Engrs; Far East Command, Okinawa, 50-51. Relig: Catholic. Legal Res: Litchfield Rd Londonderry NH 03053 Mailing Add: Box 243 Londonderry NH 03053

BOUCK, JOHN F (R)
Chmn, Cayuga Co Rep Party, NY
b Auburn, NY, Apr 18, 41; s Frederick B Bouck & Mary Berry B; m 1963 to Linda Delaney; c Terri Lynn, David John & Jennifer Ann. Educ: Auburn Community Col, 59-61. Polit & Govt Pos: Chmn, Cayuga Co Rep Party, NY, 69- Mem: Auburn Jaycees (vpres, 68, pres, 69); Civil Air Patrol; Air Force Asn; Kiwanis; Sennett Vol Fire Dept. Honors & Awards: Runner-up, Outstanding Young Man of the Year, Jaycees, 69 & 70, Outstanding Young Man of Year in Auburn, 72-73. Relig: Episcopal. Mailing Add: 34 S Hunter Ave Auburn NY 13021

BOUDREAU, ANNE M (D)
Maine State Rep
Mailing Add: 81 Lincoln St Portland ME 04103

BOULDEN, KENNETH WEBSTER (D)
Del State Rep
b Perryville, Md, Dec 7, 18; s William Theodore Bouldon & Martha Amelia Gallion B; m 1938 to Olive Roberta Walker; c Kenneth W, Jr & Billie Ann Todd. Educ: High sch, Perryville, Md. Polit & Govt Pos: Del State Rep, 69-, chmn, Highways & Transportation Comt & Del Comn Interstate Coop, mem, Admin Serv Comt, Pub Safety Comt & Atlantic States Marine Fisheries Comn, Del House Rep, currently. Mailing Add: Swanwyck Estates 114 Somers Ave New Castle DE 19720

BOULEY, RICHARD L (D)
Chmn, Grafton Co Dem Comt, NH
b Concord, NH, Nov 8, 38; s George J Bouley & Dora A Morgan B; m 1965 to Linda J Pallait; c James. Educ: Plymouth State Col, BE, 60. Polit & Govt Pos: Chmn, Littleton Town Dem Comt, NH, 66-74; mem, NH Dem State Comt, 68-; chmn, Grafton Co Dem Comt, 64- Bus & Prof Pos: Instr, Littleton High Sch, NH, 60-, athletic dir, 64- Mem: Nat & NH Educ Asns; Int Asn Approved Basketball Officials. Relig: Catholic. Legal Res: Helter Skelter Rd Littleton NH 03561 Mailing Add: Box 546 Littleton NH 03561

BOULTON, GRACE (R)
Rep Nat Committeewoman, Okla
b Ardmore, Okla, Oct 4, 26; d W T Ward & Grace Johnson W; m 1948 to Don Carroll Boulton; c Ann Elaine & Scot William. Educ: Vassar Col, 44-46; Univ Okla, BA, 48; Sigma Iota Pi; Alpha Chi Omega. Polit & Govt Pos: Alt deleg, Rep Nat Conv, 64 & 72, deleg, 68; mem & pres, Millwood Bd Educ, 67-70; vchmn, Fifth Cong Dist Rep Party, Okla, 67-71, vchmn, Okla Rep Cent Comt, 71-72; Rep Nat Committeewoman, Okla, 72- Bus & Prof Pos: Chemist, Phillips Petroleum Co, 48-49. Mem: Kiwanis Ladies. Relig: Disciples of Christ. Mailing Add: 1701 NE 63rd St Oklahoma City OK 73111

BOURASSA, DONALD CRAIG (R)
Exec Dir, Maine Rep State Comt
b Portland, Maine, Oct 17, 50; s Donald Jean Bourassa & Priscilla Ann Bryant B; single. Educ: Dartmouth Col, AB, 73; Phi Beta Kappa; Psi Upsilon. Polit & Govt Pos: Field coordr, Harrison Richardson Rep Campaign, 74; field coordr, US Rep William S Cohen, 75-; exec dir, Maine Rep State Comt, 75- Mem: Appalachian Mountain Club; Natural Resources Coun Maine; Abenaki Ski & Outing Club. Mailing Add: 7 Spruce St Augusta ME 04330

BOURQUE, GEORGE J (D)
Mass State Rep
Mailing Add: State Capitol Boston MA 02133

BOUSSON, EDWARD J, JR (R)
Tenn State Rep
Mailing Add: 1163 Berclair Rd Memphis TN 38122

BOUTELLE, PAUL BENJAMIN (SOCIALIST WORKERS PARTY)
b New York, NY, Oct 13, 34; s Anton Charles Boutelle & Anna May Benjamin B; div; c Daryl. Educ: Jr High Sch 120, 3 years. Polit & Govt Pos: Mem, Young Socialist Alliance, 60-61, Fair-Play-for-Cuba Comt, 61-63, Comt to aid the Monroe Defendants, 62-63, Freedom Now Party & Malcolm X's Orgn of Afro-Am Unity, 64 & Socialist Workers Party, 65-; cand, Manhattan Boro pres, 65, attorney-gen of NY, 66, Vice President of US, 68, mayor, New York, 69 & US Rep, 18th Cong Dist, NY, 70; founding chmn, Afro-Am Against the War in Vietnam, 65; secy, Black United Action Front of Harlem, 66-67; an organizer, Black contingent in the mobilization against the Vietnam war at the UN; off coordr & asst to Rev James Bevel, leader of the Spring Mobilization Comt to end the war, 67; chmn, Comt of Black Am for Truth about the Mid East, 70; lectr & commun dept, Africa Info Serv, New York, 72- Bus & Prof Pos: Salesman, Mar-Rahman Real Estate Brokers, 58; educ rep, Field Enterprises Educ Corp, 59-61; dir, Pan-African Book Distributors & sales rep, The Negro Book Club, 61-63; sales rep, Encycl Britannica, 63, 64, 66 & 69; formerly, part-time taxi driver; columnist, The Militant, 67; currently, salesman, Pathfinder Press & nat lectr on politics, the Mid Eastern Africa, racial problems. Publ: Ed & auth introd, Case for a Black party, 67, Black uprisings, 68 & Murder in Memphis, 68, Pathfinder Press. Relig: Atheist. Legal Res: 990 Bronx Park S Bronx NY 10460 Mailing Add: Fifth Floor 410 West St New York NY 10014

BOVERINI, WALTER JOHN (D)
Mass State Sen
b Lynn, Mass, June 5, 25; s Attilio Boverini & Luisa Francia B; m 1968 to Christine M Kirvan; c Luisa. Educ: Boston Col, BS, 50; MS, 52. Polit & Govt Pos: Mass State Rep, Ninth Essex Dist, 71-73; Mass State Sen, First Essex Dist, 73-, mem, Comt on Govt Regulations & Comt on Post Audits & Oversight, Mass State Sen, 73-, chmn, Joint Comt on Educ, 73-; mem, Mass Comn on Arts & Humanities & Comn on Interstate Coop, 73- Bus & Prof Pos: Head football coach, St Mary's High Sch, Lynn, Mass, 50-54; head football coach, Lynn Eng High Sch, 55-65, dir phys educ, 55-70. Mil Serv: Entered Air Force, 43, released as S/Sgt, 46, after serv in 8th Air Force, ETO, 43-46; Air Medal with four Oak Leaf Clusters; Distinguished Flying Cross. Mem: Mass Asn Phys Educ Dirs; Mass Asn Legis; KofC; Amvets; Sons of Italy. Relig: Catholic. Mailing Add: 18 Western Ave Lynn MA 01904

BOWE, JOHN EDWARD (ED) (R)
Mem, Rep State Cent Comt, Calif
b Los Angeles, Calif, July 3, 18; s John Edward Bowe & Inez DeCandia B; m 1951 to Ruby Louise Thiesen. Educ: Stockton High Sch, Calif, grad, 36; State Univ NY Sch of Criminal Justice, grad parole inst prog of Nat Coun on Crime & Delinquency, 72. Polit & Govt Pos: Vpres, Tulare Co Rep Assembly, 64, pres, 65; campaign chmn, Tulare & Kings Co for Sen George Murphy, 64 & Dinuba City for Calif Assemblyman Gordon Duffy, 64 & 66; mem, Tulare Co Rep Cent Comt, 64-67; mem, Rep State Cent Comt of Calif, 65-; vpres, Tulare Co Rep Cent Comt, 66; campaign chmn, Tulare Co for Gov Ronald Reagan, 66; chief, Calif State Div of Housing & Community Develop, 67-71; mem, Calif Youth Authority Bd, 71-74. Bus & Prof Pos: Optician, Riggs Optical Co, Stockton, Calif, 36-38; asst off mgr, Nat Biscuit Co, Sacramento, 38-41; dist mgr, Half Moon Fruit & Produce Co, Dinuba, 46-56; owner, Dinuba Hardware Co, 56-67. Mil Serv: Entered as Pvt, Army, 41, released as Capt, 46, after serv in D Squadron, 112th Army Air Force, Continental US. Mem: Am Legion; Lions Int; Commonwealth Club of San Francisco; Dinuba CofC; Dinuba Merchants Asn. Relig: Roman Catholic. Mailing Add: 1500 Seventh St Sacramento CA 95814

BOWEN, DAVID REECE (D)
US Rep, Miss
b Houston, Miss, Oct 21, 32; s David Reece Bowen & Lera Pinnix B; single. Educ: Univ Mo, 50-52; Harvard Univ, AB, 54; Oxford Univ, MA; Univ Chicago, 65-66; Kappa Alpha Order. Polit & Govt Pos: Prog analyst, Off Econ Opportunity, Washington, DC, 66-67; coordr Fed-State prog, Off Gov, Miss, 68-72; US Rep, Miss, 73- Bus & Prof Pos: Asst prof polit sci & hist, Miss Col, 58-59; asst prof polit sci, Millsaps Col, 59-64; staff assoc, US CofC, Washington, DC, 67-68. Mil Serv: Entered as E-1, Army, 57, released as E-2, 58, after serv in 3rd Army, Ft Jackson, SC. Mem: EMiss Coun; Delta Coun; Miss Farm Bur Fedn. Relig: Protestant. Legal Res: Box 137 Rte 1 Cleveland MS 38732 Mailing Add: 116 Cannon House Off Bldg Washington DC 20515

BOWEN, DUANE GLENN (DFL)
Secy, Douglas Co Dem-Farmer-Labor Party, Minn
b Black River Falls, Wis, Mar 27, 35; s Glenn Edwin Bowen & Frances Dunningan B; m 1970 to Darlene Jaqua. Educ: Univ Minn, Minneapolis, BS, 65. Polit & Govt Pos: Secy, Douglas Co Dem-Farmer-Labor Party, Minn, 70- Bus & Prof Pos: Off worker, Repub Creosoting Co, St Louis Park, Minn, 61-62; instr bus educ, Independent Sch Dist 206, Alexandria, 66- Mil Serv: Entered as Airman 3/C, Air Force, 56, released as Airman 2/C, 66, after serv in Hq Squadron, Air Defense Command, 56-60. Mem: Minn Educ Asn; Am Voc Asn; VFW; Elks. Relig: Catholic. Mailing Add: 905 Irving Alexandria MN 56308

BOWEN, OTIS R (R)
Gov, Ind
b Rochester, Ind, Feb 26, 18; s Vernie Bowen & Pearl Wright B; m 1939 to Elizabeth Steinmann; c Rick, Judy, Tim & Rob. Educ: Ind Univ, AB in Chem, 39; Ind Univ Med Sch, MD, 42; Alpha Omega Alpha; Phi Beta Pi; Delta Chi. Hon Degrees: LLD, Valparaiso Univ, Butler Univ & Anderson Col, 73. Polit & Govt Pos: Coroner, Marshall Co, Ind, 52-56; Ind State Rep, Marshall Co, 57-72; Minority Leader, Ind House of Rep, 65-66, Speaker, 67-68 & 69-72 chmn, Pub Health Comt, 61-62 & 63-64, chmn, Comn to Study Aid to Dependent Children in Ind, 63-64; cand for nomination for Gov, State Rep Conv, 68; deleg, Rep Nat Conv, 72; Gov, Ind, 73-; mem steering comt, Educ Comn of the States, 73-; mem Standing Comt on crime reduction & pub safety, Nat Gov Conf, 73- Bus & Prof Pos: Intern, Mem Hosp, South Bend, Ind; pvt practice med, Bremen, Ind, 46-72; former mem staff, Bremen Community, Parkview, St Joseph's of South Bend, St Joseph's of Mishawaka & Mem Hosp. Mil Serv: Entered as 1st Lt, Army, 43, released as Capt, 46, after serv in Med Corps, Pac Theater & Okinawa Campaign. Publ: Several articles in med jour. Mem: Ind State Med Asn (legis comt, 58-, 13th Dist coun, 65-69); Am Med Asn; Ind Ment Health Asn; CofC; Am Legion. Honors & Awards: Merit Award, Ind Pub Health Asn, 71; Alumnus of the Year, Ind Univ Sch Med, 71; Dr Benjamin Rush Award for outstanding pub serv, Am Med Asn, 73. Relig: Lutheran; past vpres, Congregation, past chmn bd finance and past mem, Lutheran Church Sch Bd, St Paul's Lutheran Church, Bremen, Ind. Mailing Add: 206 State Capitol Indianapolis IN 46204

BOWEN, ROBERT O'DELL (D)
Utah State Sen
b Spanish Fork, Utah, Oct 16, 27; s James Miller Bowen & Belua Amelia Gallup B; m 1946 to Lucile Livingston; c Kent, Marsha & Blake. Educ: Univ Utah, 45; Brigham Young Univ, BA, 50; Stanford Univ, Gen Elec fel econ, summer 60; Utah State Univ, Nat Defense Educ Act Insts, summers 63 & 67; Univ Kans, Experienced Teacher Fel Prog, 68, MA, 69; Goldbrickers. Polit & Govt Pos: State & co deleg, Dem Party, Utah, 64-71; secy, Citizen's Party, Spanish Fork, 65-71; Utah State Rep, 71-72, Asst Majority Whip, Utah House Rep, 71-72, vchmn, Govt Opers Interim Comt, 72; Utah State Sen, 73-, mem, Educ, Pub Safety, State Affairs & Exec Appropriations Comts, Utah State Senate, 73- Bus & Prof Pos: Qm, VFW, Spanish Fork, 66-67, Comdr, 67-68. Mil Serv: Entered as Pvt, Army, 46, released as 2nd Lt, 47, after serv in Inf Replacement Training Ctr, Ft Bragg & Ft Dix, 46-47, recalled 50-52, serv in Eighth US Army, Korea 2nd Div 9th Inf, 51-52; Capt, Army Res; Bronze Star; Army Commendation Ribbon; Combat Inf Badge; Four Campaign Stars. Mem: Nat, Utah & Nebr Educ Asns. Relig: Latter-day Saint. Mailing Add: 560 N Second West Spanish Fork UT 84660

BOWEN, THOMAS OTIS (D)
SC State Sen
Mailing Add: Sumter SC 29150

BOWEN, WILLIAM A (D)
RI State Sen
Mailing Add: 73 Prescott Ave East Providence RI 02915

BOWEN, WILLIAM F (D)
Ohio State Sen
b Cincinnati, Ohio, Jan 30, 29; s William F Bowen & Henrietta R Washington B; m 1956 to Dolores Lee Freeman; c William F, III, Kevin Braxton & Terrence Samuel. Educ: Xavier Univ, 52-55. Polit & Govt Pos: VChmn, Hamilton Co Dem Party Young Dem, Ohio, currently, mem, Ohio Party Struct & Deleg Select Comt & chmn, Subcomt on Grassroot Participation, currently; mem, Ohio Dem Party Exec Comt, Ohio Dem Const & Rules Comt

& Gov Task Force on Admissions, Commitment Procedure & Patients' Rights, currently; app, Gov Task Force on Corrections, currently; mem, President's White House Conf on Youth; Ohio State Rep, 69th Dist, 66-68, Dem Minority Whip, 108th Gen Assembly, Ohio House of Rep; alternate deleg, Dem Nat Conv, 68; Ohio State Sen, Ninth Sen Dist, 70-, mem, Judiciary, Ways & Means, Environ Affairs & Commerce & Labor Comts, Ohio State Senate, currently; deleg, Nat Black Polit Conv, 72. Bus & Prof Pos: Self-employed. Mem: Hamilton Co Black Caucus (charter mem, chmn); Black Elected Dem of Ohio (nat conf & exec vpres); F&AM; Wayfarers Club Cincinnati; NAACP. Honors & Awards: Various community serv awards; hon mention, John F Kennedy Pub Serv Award, Ohio League of Young Dem; Outstanding Freshman Rep, Ment Health Asn; Resolution by 107th Gen Assembly for outstanding leadership during riot disorders in Cincinnati. Relig: Baptist. Mailing Add: 3662 Reading Rd Cincinnati OH 45229

BOWER, GLEN LANDIS (R)
b Highland, Ill, Jan 16, 49; s Ray Landis Bower & Evelyn Ragland B; single. Educ: Southern Ill Univ, Carbondale, BA, 71; Chicago-Kent Col Law, JD with honors, 74; Phi Alpha Delta. Polit & Govt Pos: Chmn, Midwest Fedn Col Rep Clubs, 71-72; alt deleg, Rep Nat Conv, 72; secy, Col Rep Nat Comt, 72-73. Bus & Prof Pos: Mem adv coun, US Small Bus Admin, 71- Mil Serv: 1st Lt, Air Force Res, currently. Mem: Am Bar Asn; Asn Trial Lawyers Am; Kiwanis; SAR; Ill State Hist Soc. Relig: United Methodist. Mailing Add: PO Box 51 Beecher City IL 62414

BOWER, JOHN DAVID (R)
Kans State Rep
b McLouth, Kans, Dec 17, 11; s David Earl Bower & Mabel Kimmel B; m 1936 to (Maude) Agnes Black; c Ronald David & Ruth Ann. Educ: McPherson Col, AB, 38. Polit & Govt Pos: Dir, McLouth Rural High Sch, Kans, 49-55; Kans State Rep, 53-; dir, Watershed Dist, 56-59. Mem: Farm Bureau; Kiwanis. Relig: Baptist. Mailing Add: Rte 1 McLouth KS 66054

BOWERS, ARTHUR ROBERT (D)
Ohio State Rep
b Steubenville, Ohio, Feb 16, 19; s Robert W Bowers & Helen Foreman B; m 1943 to Betty Jane Wright; c Robert, Karen (Mrs David Gargano), Rebecca (Mrs Gary Anderson), Melissa & Kathryn. Educ: Steubenville Cath Cent Col, Ohio, grad; Serv Schs. Polit & Govt Pos: City councilman, Steubenville, Ohio, 3 terms; Ohio State Rep, 33rd Dist, 69-72, 98th Dist, 72- Bus & Prof Pos: Owner, Bower's Tile & Marble Contracting Co, currently. Mil Serv: Entered as Pvt, Army, 42, released as Platoon Sgt, 45, after serv in 101st & 17th Airborne Div with Parachute Regt, ETO, 44-45; Two Purple Hearts; Bronze Star; Four Campaign Stars. Mem: Elks; Eagles; Am Legion; DAV; Polish Athletic Club. Relig: Catholic. Mailing Add: Eft's Lane Steubenville OH 43952

BOWERS, EDGAR R (BUDDY) (R)
Mem, Tenn State Rep Exec Comt
b Rockwood, Tenn, Oct 19, 37; s Raymond S Bowers & Edna Ruth Berrong B; m 1961 to Alma Kay Shoun; c David Berrong. Educ: Ga Inst Technol, 55-60; Ga State Univ, 61-63; Emory Univ Sch Law, BA, 65, JD with distinction, 66; Phi Alpha Delta; Bryan Hon Soc. Polit & Govt Pos: Collegiate chmn & mem, Ga Young Rep State Exec Comt, 61-63; chmn & mem, Fourth Dist, Tenn Young Rep State Exec Comt, 69-72; chmn, Roane Co Rep Exec Comt, Tenn, 70-74; mem, Harriman Bd Educ, 70-, chmn, 72-73; mem, Roane Co Bd Voc Educ, 73-; mem, Tenn State Rep Exec Comt, 74- Bus & Prof Pos: Assoc, J Polk Cooley, Attorneys-at-law, Rockwood, Tenn, 66-68; partner, Newcomb & Bowers, Attorneys-at-law, Harriman, 68-70; attorney, law dept, Union Carbide Corp, Nuclear Div, Oak Ridge, 70- Mil Serv: Entered as Pvt, Ga Army Nat Guard, released as SP 5/C, after serv in Co D, 878th Engr Bn & Co D, 648th Maintenance Bn, 48th Armored Div, 59-65. Mem: Daniel Arthur Rehabilitation Ctr, Oak Ridge, Tenn (mem bd dirs); Kingston Rotary (bd dirs, 75-); Roane Co Hist Soc (mem bd gov, 67-, pres, 73-74); Roane Co Unit, Am Cancer Soc. Honors & Awards: Lawyer's Title Award, Lawyer's Title Ins Corp/Emory Univ Law Sch, 66; Outstanding Young Man of the Year, Harriman Jaycees, 70; Outstanding Young Rep of the Year, Tenn Young Rep Fedn, 72. Relig: Baptist. Mailing Add: Rte 5 Box 21 Harriman TN 37748

BOWERS, JACK L (R)
Asst Secy Installations & Logistics, Dept Navy
Legal Res: VA Mailing Add: Dept of the Navy Washington DC 20350

BOWERS, KATHRYN INEZ (D)
b Memphis, Tenn, May 2, 43; d James E Haralson & Harriett Thomas H; m 1961 to Maurice Bowers; c Desaree & Montrice. Educ: Griggs Bus Col, Memphis, Tenn, 63; Memphis State Univ, 68-70. Polit & Govt Pos: Comnr, Shelby Co Elec Comn, Tenn, currently; aide, Gov, 75- Bus & Prof Pos: Gift buyer, Kar-Hill Beauty Supplies, 64-67; employ counr, Allied Employ Agency, 67-68; dir publ, LeMoyne-Owen Col, 70- Mem: Dem Women Shelby Co; Longview Heights Civic Club; Memphis & Shelby Co Manpower Coun; Memphis OIC (bd mem & secy); Southeast Area Coun Bd Educ. Honors & Awards: Mother of the Year, Longview Elem Sch, 71. Relig: Catholic. Mailing Add: 843 E Gage Memphis TN 38106

BOWIE, LEON (R)
Maine State Rep
Mailing Add: Rte 1A Gardiner ME 04345

BOWLER, ANN (R)
Mem, Rep State Cent Comt, Calif
b Batesville, Ark, Apr 7, 18; m 1946 to John D Bowler, Jr. Educ: Univ Detroit, BA. Polit & Govt Pos: Mem, Rep State Cent Comt, Calif, 56-, Southern regional vchairwoman, currently; mem, Los Angeles Co Rep Cent Comt, 56-; dist supvr, Bur of Census, 60; deleg, Rep Nat Conv, 64 & 68; Rep Presidential elector, 64; mem exec comt, Rep Nat Comt, formerly; first vpres, prog chmn & conv chmn, s div, Calif Fedn Rep Women, currently. Mem: Red Cross. Mailing Add: 177 Rivo Alto Canal Long Beach CA 90803

BOWLER, BARBARA B (R)
NH State Rep
Mailing Add: Box 85 Lochmere NH 03252

BOWLER, ORSON LLOYD (R)
Finance Chmn, Franklin Co Rep Party, Idaho
b Salt Lake City, Utah, Dec 17, 31; s Orson Cuttler Bowler & Sarah Lloyd B; m 1960 to Janice Wilde; c Suzanne, Janalyn, Orson Paul, Matthew Wilde & David Clyde. Educ: Univ Utah, BS, 59, EdD, 66; Univ Idaho, MNS, 63; research asst, 62-63, research fel, 64-65. Polit & Govt Pos: Chmn, Teton Co Rep Cent Comt, Idaho, 68-69; finance chmn, Franklin Co Rep Party, Idaho, 70- Bus & Prof Pos: Teacher math & sci, Soda Springs High Sch, Idaho, 59-62; supt, Teton Co Sch Dist 401, Driggs, 64-69; supt, Eastside Sch Dist 201, Preston, 69- Mil Serv: Entered as Pvt, Army, 53, released as SP-3, 56, after serv in Detachment 3, 6400 SU USA Regt, Portland, Ore. Publ: A History of Federal Activities in Education, In: School Organization and Administration for Utah Teachers, Univ Utah, 64. Mem: Am Asn Sch Adminr; Phi Delta Kappa; Lions. Relig: Latter-day Saint. Mailing Add: 58 South Third East Preston ID 83263

BOWLES, CARL (R)
Ky State Rep
Mailing Add: Rte 3 Tompkinsville KY 42167

BOWLES, CHESTER (D)
b Springfield, Mass, Apr 5, 01; s Charles Bowles & Nellie Harris B; m 1934 to Dorothy Stebbins; c Barbara B (Mrs Coolidge), Chester, Jr, Cynthia, Sarah & Samuel. Educ: Yale Univ, BS, 24. Hon Degrees: LLD, Am Univ, 46, Howard Univ, 56, Oberlin Col, 57, Bard Col, 57, Univ RI, 59, Univ Mich, 61, Yale Univ, 68 & Davidson Col, 72. Polit & Govt Pos: Conn Elector for Franklin D Roosevelt, 40; deleg, Dem Nat Conv, 40, 48, 56 & 60, chmn, Dem Nat Platform, 60; dir, Off Price Admin, 42-45; dir, Econ Stabilization Comn, 45-46; Am deleg, UNESCO Conf, Paris, 46, mem nat comt, 46-47; asst to dir gen, UN, 47-48; Gov, Conn, 49-51; US Ambassador, India, 51-53 & 63-69; US Rep, Second Dist, Conn, 58-59; Under Secy of State, 61-62; spec asst to President Kennedy on Asia, Africa & Latin Am Affairs, 62-63. Bus & Prof Pos: Reporter, Springfield Rep, 24-25; mem staff, George Batten Co, 25-29; established Benton & Bowles, Inc, New York, 29, chmn bd, 36-41; Shaw lectr, Bryn Mawr Col, 53-54; Berkeley lectr, Univ Calif, 56; Godkin lectr, Harvard, 56; Chubb lectr, Yale Univ, 57. Publ: The conscience of a liberal 62; The makings of a just society, 63; Promises to keep—my years in public life, Harper & Row, 71; plus others. Mem: Rockefeller Found (trustee); Inst African-Am Rels (trustee); Asia Soc; Conn State Grange; Essex Yacht Club. Relig: Unitarian. Mailing Add: Hayden's Point Essex CT 06426

BOWLES, LAWRENCE LEONARD (R)
b North Tarrytown, NY, Oct 14, 40; s Leonard Turner Bowles & Catherine Mulligan B; single. Educ: Univ NC, Chapel Hill, BA with honors, 62; Harvard Law Sch, LLB, 65; Rotary Found fel, Law Col, Univ Calcutta, India, 66-67. Polit & Govt Pos: Admin asst to US Rep Charles R Jonas, NC, 68-72; legis asst to US Rep James G Martin, NC, 73- Bus & Prof Pos: Personal trust adminr, Chase Manhattan Bank, New York, 65-66; commercial loan analyst, First Union Nat Bank, Charlotte, NC, 67. Mem: Harvard Law Sch Asn, Washington, DC; Capitol Hill Club, Washington, DC. Relig: Episcopal. Legal Res: 3330-B S Wakefield St Arlington VA 22206 Mailing Add: 115 House Off Bldg Washington DC 20515

BOWMAN, ALICE J (D)
Committeewoman, Umatilla Co Dem Cent Comt, Ore
b Bowman, NDak, Oct 5, 21; d John Dahl & Esther Norgren D; m 1941 to Kenneth C Bowman; c Kenneth Clark, John Earl, James Daniel & Trudy Esther. Educ: Signey High Sch. Polit & Govt Pos: Committeewoman, Umatilla Co Dem Cent Comt, Ore, 58-, chmn, 69-73; pres, West End Dem Club, 62-67; chmn, Elect Bob Duncan, Umatilla Co, 68, Cong Al Ullman, 70; Fed Civil Defense Surv, 68. Mem: Horizen Club; 4-H Leader; Echo High Sch Band Mothers; VFW Auxiliary 4943 (pres, 2 years); PTA; Echo Booster Club. Honors & Awards: Wakan Award, Campfire Girls. Relig: Methodist; Sunday sch teacher. Mailing Add: North Hill Rte 1 Echo OR 97826

BOWMAN, FLETCHER C, JR (D)
Mem, Luna Co Dem Cent Comt, NMex
b 1936; m 1958 to Mary Scrimshire; c Kathryn Irene. Educ: McMurry Col, BS; NMex Western Univ, MA, 66. Polit & Govt Pos: NMex State Rep, until 66; mem, Deming Bd Educ, 68-, vpres, currently; mem, Luna Co Dem Cent Comt, currently. Bus & Prof Pos: Field underwriter, NY Life Ins, currently. Mil Serv: Army, Third Armored Div, NATO Forces, 55-57. Mem: CofC; Luna Co Hist Soc; Am Legion Boys State. Relig: Methodist, Methodist Men. Mailing Add: PO Box 1067 Deming NM 88030

BOWMAN, GEORGE MCKINLEY (R)
Mem Exec Comt, 18th Dist Rep Party, NDak
b Osakis, Minn, Dec 23, 25; s William McKinley Bowman & Eve Sieler B; m to Darlene Toby; c G Toby & Victoria. Educ: Univ Minn, BS in Agr Eng, 50; Plumb Bob; Tau Kappa Epsilon; Alpha Phi Omega; Award of the Gopher. Polit & Govt Pos: Mem exec comt, Conservative Club of NDak, 64-66; Rep precinct committeeman, Grand Forks Twp, NDak, 66-; chmn, Grand Forks Co Rep Party, 66-67; mem exec comt, 18th Dist Rep Party, 73- Bus & Prof Pos: Engr, Tart-Ide Corp, Minneapolis, Minn, 50; sales engr, Kaiser Aluminum & Chem Sales, Inc, Chicago, Ill, 52-53; dist sales mgr, FMC Corp, Osakis, Minn, 53-58; engr, Lockwood Grader Corp, Grand Forks, NDak, 59-62; mgr, NAm Pump Corp, Grand Forks, 63- Mil Serv: Entered as Recruit, Army, 50, released as Pfc, 62, after serv in Engr Research & Develop Labs, Ft Belvoir, Va, 50-52. Mem: Am Soc Agr Engrs; Elks; Am Legion; CofC. Relig: Catholic. Mailing Add: 5026 Belmont Rd Grand Forks ND 58201

BOWMAN, JAMES A (D)
Ga State Rep
Mailing Add: Box 169 Jeffersonville GA 31044

BOWMAN, JOHN T (D)
Mich State Sen
b Monterey, Tenn, July 19, 21; m 1940 to Mary Elizabeth Broderick; c Darryl Joyce. Educ: Wayne State Univ; Univ Detroit. Polit & Govt Pos: Justice of the Peace, Roseville, Mich, 39-43; Mich State Rep, 54-60; Mich State Sen, 62-; deleg, Dem Nat Conv, 68. Bus & Prof Pos: Pub rels. Mil Serv: Navy, World War II. Mem: Amvets; Am Legion; F&AM; Shrine. Relig: Baptist. Mailing Add: 26816 Oakland Roseville MI 48066

BOWMAN, MYRTEL C (R)
Committeeman, Mont State Rep Party
b Sprague, Wash, May 12, 10; s Casper J Bowman & Leta Robertson B; m 1931 to Eva E Lewis; c Merton Allen, Donna C (Mrs Smith), Sharon K (Mrs Dorr) & Gary Wain. Educ: Univ Mont, 1 year; Sigma Alpha Epsilon. Polit & Govt Pos: Rep precinct committeeman, Lake Co, Mont, 58-; campaign mgr, Dick Smiley for Congressman, Western Dist, 66 & 68; chmn, Lake Co Rep Cent Comt, 66-71, chmn finance comt, 66-; mem platform comt on credentials, Mont State Rep Party, 68, platform comt on agr, 68 & 70, comt on nominating

officer, 69, committeeman, 69-, co-chmn, Finance Comt, 71-; mem indust & labor comt, Mont State Rep Conv, Helena, Mont, 72. Bus & Prof Pos: Machinery salesman, retired; now cattle rancher. Mem: Western Mont Angus Asn (pres, 72-); Western Mont Masons Welfare Asn (pres, 47-48); Ronan Lodge 131 (secy, 58-62 & 69-, treas, 63-68); charter mem, Missoula Scottish Rite (past Venerable Master, Lodge of Perfection, past comdr, Coun Kadosh); Pondera Scottish Rite (past pres & past treas). Honors & Awards: Serv & Key Award, Demolay, 48; Grand Cross of Color, Rainbow, 48; Serv Award, Salish Shrine Club, 68; Outstanding Serv Award, Ronan Lodge 131, 63; Award for serv to church, community & masonary, Royal Order of Scotland, 71. Relig: Methodist; past chmn church bd; presented hist of Methodist Church at Brady, 60. Mailing Add: Rte 1 Box 33 Ronan MT 59864

BOWMAN, THELMA SHANKS (R)
VChmn, Tenn Rep State Exec Comt
b Limestone, Tenn, Apr 30, 23; d E Ruble Shanks & Letha Williams S; m 1948 to Dr Hoyle E Bowman; c E Carolyn, Hoyle E, Jr, Suzanne, Barbara & John E. Educ: Johnson City Bus Col, Tenn, 42; George Washington Univ, 45-57; ETenn State Univ, 68; Beta Sigma Phi. Polit & Govt Pos: Mem, Tenn Rep State Exec Comt, 62-, vchmn, 70-; chmn, Carter Co Rep Women for Goldwater, 64; vpres, Nat Fedn of Rep Women of Carter Co, 64-; co chmn, Nixon for President, 68; dist chmn, Dunn for Gov, 70, Brock for Senate, 70 & Quillen for Cong, 70. Bus & Prof Pos: Liaison secy, Off of Dependency Benefits, Washington, DC, 44-45; secy, Vet Admin, Mountain Home & Johnson City, Tenn, 46-48; secy to pres, Emory & Henry Col, 48-50. Mem: Womens Med Auxiliary; Boys Club of Am (bd dirs, 66-); March of Dimes; PTA; Harold McCormick Better Govt Comt. Honors & Awards: Outstanding Woman of Year, VFW Post 2166, 66-67; Outstanding Accomplishments, Boys Club of Am, 67-68. Relig: Protestant; Teacher, Presbyterian Church, 69-71. Mailing Add: 209 S Lynn Ave Elizabethton TN 37643

BOWMAN, WILLARD L (D)
Alaska State Rep
Mailing Add: 1112 E 69th Ave Anchorage AK 99502

BOWRING, EVA
b Nevada, Mo, Jan 9, 92; d John F Kelly & M Belle Hinkes; m 1911 to T F Forester, wid; remarried 1928 to Arthur Bowring, wid; c Frank H, James Harold & Jo Donald. Polit & Govt Pos: US Sen, Nebr, 54; mem Fed Parole Bd, 56-64. Bus & Prof Pos: Cattle rancher, operator Bar 99 Ranch, Merriman, Nebr, 28-; registered Hereford breeder. Mailing Add: Bar 99 Ranch Merriman NE 69218

BOWSHER, CHARLES ARTHUR (D)
b Elkhart, Ind, May 30, 31; s Matthew A Bowsher & Ella M West B; m 1963 to Mary C Mahoney; c Kathryn M & Stephen C. Educ: Univ Ill, Urbana, BS, 53; Univ Chicago, MBA, 56; Pi Kappa Alpha. Polit & Govt Pos: Asst Secy of the Navy for Financial Mgt, 67-71. Bus & Prof Pos: Mem corporate audit staff, Chrysler Corp, Highland Park, Mich, 53; partner, Arthur Andersen & Co, Chicago, Ill, 56-67, Washington, DC, 71- Mil Serv: Army, 54-55. Mem: DC Inst CPA; Am Inst CPA; Univ Club, Chicago; Burning Tree Club; Fed City Club, Washington, DC. Honors & Awards: Distinguished Pub Serv Award, Navy, 69. Relig: Protestant. Mailing Add: 4503 Boxwood Rd Washington DC 20016

BOWYER, EDNA L (R)
Secy-Treas, Warren Co Rep Exec Comt, Ohio
b King Mills, Ohio, Apr 30, 17; d Perry Leroy Bowyer & Clara Belle Arnold B; single. Educ: The Miller Sch of Bus, 36-37. Polit & Govt Pos: Pres, Warren Co Rep Women's Club, Ohio, 63; clerk of bd of co comnr, Warren Co, Ohio, 63-64; Recorder, Warren Co, 64-; Secy-Treas, Warren Co Rep Exec Comt, 64-; Secy-Treas, Warren Co Rep Cent Comt, 64-71, Secy, 71- Mem: Ohio Recorders Asn (treas, 68, secy, 69, third vpres, 70, second vpres, 71, pres, 72); Nat Asn Co Recorders & Clerks (comt for fed grant for standardization of practices & procedures & bd dirs, 71); Warren Co Hist Soc (trustee, 64-67 & 72, vpres, 69, pres, 70 & 71); Franklin Area Hist Soc; Int Asn Clerks, Recorders, Elec Off & Treas (historian, 71). Mailing Add: 61 Walnut St Kings Mills OH 45034

BOX, E O (R)
b Goliad Co, Tex, May 13, 93; s Louis Joshua Box & Lillian Arabella Thornton B; m 1913 to Mary E Haynes; c E O & John Harold. Educ: Univ Tex, BA, 27; Southern Methodist Univ, MA, 28 & MS, 32. Polit & Govt Pos: Deleg, Rep Nat Conv, 72. Bus & Prof Pos: Prof physics, ETex State Univ, 30-53 & ECent State Col, 53-60. Relig: Presbyterian. Mailing Add: 100 S Morrison Dr Ada OK 74820

BOYCE, DANIEL ROUSE (DAN) (D)
Miss State Sen
Mailing Add: PO Box 386 Pelahatchie MS 39145

BOYCE, JAMES H (R)
Chmn, Rep State Cent Comt La
b Carrollton, Mo, 1922; m 1943 to Jane; c James H, John C & Jerry T. Educ: La State Univ, 40-42. Polit & Govt Pos: State chmn, Vol for Nixon, 60; Rep State Finance Chmn, 64; Goldwater Finance Chmn, 64; alt deleg, Rep Nat Conv, 64; mem, Rep State Cent Comt La, 70-, chmn, 72-; campaign chmn, David C Treen for Gov, 71-72. Bus & Prof Pos: Pres, Boyce-Curran Machinery, Inc, 46-47; owner, Caterpillar Tractor Co Dealership, 47; pres, Boyce-Harvey Machinery, Inc, 47-60; pres, Boyce Machinery Corp, 60-; mem bd dirs, City Nat Bank, Baton Rouge. Mem: Baton Rouge Better Bus Bur; East Baton Rouge Airport Comn; Nat Alliance of Businessmen (metro chmn, 69-72); YMCA; Pub Affairs Res Coun. Relig: Episcopal. Mailing Add: 7655 Boyce Dr Baton Rouge LA 70809

BOYCE, MERLE HUNTER (R)
Mem Exec Comt, Los Angeles Co Rep Cent Comt, Calif
b Wilmington, Calif; s Ben Owen Boyce & Elma Crosby B; m to Joanne; c Lisa, Shaunna, Randall, Holly, James & Maureen. Educ: Compton Col, AA; Pepperdine Col; Univ Southern Calif; Calif Col Med, MD. Polit & Govt Pos: Organizer & first pres, Harbor Young Rep, Calif, 51; mem, SBay Young Rep, formerly; Rep Cand for US Rep, 62; mem, Steering Comt & Speakers Bur, Rafferty campaign, 62; chmn, Dodger Stadium Rallies for Goldwater, 63 & 64; former chmn Speakers Bur, Los Angeles Co Rep Cent Comt, chmn, Membership Comt, 66, mem exec comt, currently; mem, Calif Rep State Cent Comt, 62-66 & 69-70, chmn, Hospitality Comt, 65-66; chmn, Coun of Rep Vol, 63-66; mem, United Rep Finance Comt, Los Angeles Co, 63-70, mem exec comt; chmn, Los Angeles Co Ninth Inning Rally, 64; deleg, Rep Nat Conv, 64; chmn, Bill Miller for VPres Campaign, 64; gen chmn, Calif State Rep Conv, 65; mem, SBay Comt for Reagan for Gov, 66; panel mem, Big City Conf, Rep Nat Comt, 66, sustaining mem; mem, Rep Assocs; state campaign dir, Jud Leetham for Attorney Gen of Calif, 66; chmn, 46th Assembly Dist Rep Cent Comt, 67-70; mem, Local Area Planning Comt for Calif Rehabilitation Planning Proj Comt, 68 & 69; pub mem, Calif Coun on Intergovt Rels, 68-70. Bus & Prof Pos: Lab instr chem, Pepperdine Col; intern lectr & faculty mem, Pac Hosp, Calif Col of Med; staff mem, Pac Hosp, Long Beach & Physicians & Surgeons Hosp, Compton; chmn, Pub Rels Comt, Bay Harbor Hosp, former chief of staff. Mil Serv: Serv as Ball Turret Gunner, B-17, 8th Air Force, 42-46; 1st Lt, Air Force Res; Air Medal with Three Clusters. Mem: Am & Calif Med Asns; Bay Harbor Div Med Soc; Redondo Beach CofC; Calif Col of Med. Honors & Awards: Recipient Merit Award, Los Angeles Co Rep Cent Comt, 63; Leadership Award, ITS Fraternity, 62; YMCA Serv Award, Los Angeles; Nat Found March of Dimes Award; nominated Citizen of Year, Redondo Beach, 58. Relig: Presbyterian; Sunday Sch Teacher. Legal Res: 28220 Ella Rd Palos Verdes Estates CA 90274 Mailing Add: 1615 Pacific Coast Hwy Redondo Beach CA 90277

BOYD, BAXTER JACKSON (D)
Mem, Tenn State Dem Exec Comt
b Cheatham Co, Tenn, July 15, 01; s Gabe Boyd & Corinna Elliott B; m 1924 to Stella Mae Harper; c Helen (Mrs Bruce Button) & Jean (Mrs Hall). Educ: LaSalle Exten Univ, Chicago, Ill, LLB, 29. Polit & Govt Pos: Comnr revenue, State Tenn, 58-59, clerk supreme court, 59-63, mem bd probation & parole, 63-69; mem, Tenn State Dem Exec Comt, 66-; deleg, Dem Nat Conv, 68. Bus & Prof Pos: Lawyer, Ashland City, Tenn, 29- Mem: Am, Tenn & Davidson Co Bar Asns; Cheatham Co CofC (past pres); Lions (past pres, Ashland; past dist gov, Mid Tenn). Relig: Church of Christ. Legal Res: 209 S Main St Ashland City TN 37015 Mailing Add: PO Box 156 Ashland City TN 37015

BOYD, CHARLES W (D)
Fla State Rep
Mailing Add: 432 House Off Bldg Tallahassee FL 32304

BOYD, ELOISE AGUSTA METZGER (R)
Chmn, Sumter Co Rep Party, Ala
b San Bernardino, Calif, June 28, 22; d Edward Delos Metzger & Ella Papenhausen M; m 1945 to Clarence Addison Boyd; c Clarence Pierce & Smith Delos. Educ: Univ Redlands, BA cum laude, 44; Radcliffe Col, 1 year; Mortar Bd; Beta Lambda Mu. Polit & Govt Pos: Chmn, Sumter Co Rep Party, Ala, 59- Bus & Prof Pos: Teacher, Jr High Sch, Bakersfield, Calif, fall 45; instr Eng, Livingston Col, Ala, 48. Mem: Am Asn Univ Women; Women of the Church Presbyterial Pres; hon life mem, Tuscaloosa Presbytery. Relig: Presbyterian. Mailing Add: Box 102 Emelle AL 35459

BOYD, JACK (R)
NH State Rep
Mailing Add: 28 Borad St Hollis NH 03049

BOYD, JESSE PIERSON (R)
Chmn, Cecil Co Rep Cent Comt, Md
b Elkton, Md, Sept 5, 34; s Elwood Lindsay Boyd & Emily Pierson B; m 1952 to Adrienne Louise Zieber; c Jesse, Jr & Karen Louise. Educ: Elkton High Sch, 52. Polit & Govt Pos: Town comnr, Elkton, Md, 70-; chmn, Cecil Co Rep Cent Comt, Md, 70- Bus & Prof Pos: Mem staff, Meter Dept, Conowingo Power Co, Md, 55- Mem: Kiwanis; Md Munic League (vpres, Dist 9, 74-75); Mason; Shriner. Relig: Protestant. Mailing Add: 508 Hollingsworth Ave Elkton MD 21921

BOYD, JOSEPH ARTHUR, JR (D)
Justice, Fla Supreme Court
b Hoschton, Ga, Nov 16, 16; s Joseph Arthur Boyd & Esther Puckett B; m 1938 to Ann Stripling; c Joanne (Mrs Robert Goldman), Betty Jean (Mrs David Jala), Joseph, James & Jane. Educ: Piedmont Col, 36-38; Univ Miami Law Sch, JD, 48; Pi Kappa Psi; Phi Alpha Delta. Hon Degrees: LLD, Piedmont Col, 63. Polit & Govt Pos: City attorney, Hialeah, Fla, 51-58; co comnr, Dade Co, 58-68, vice mayor, 67; chmn, Dade Co Comn, 63; dir, State Asn of Co Comnr, 64-68; justice, Fla Supreme Court, 69-; juror, Freedom Foundation Awards, twice. Mil Serv: Entered as Pvt, Marines, 43, released as Sgt, 46, after serv in 1st, 2nd, 3rd, 5th & 6th Marine Corps Div, SPac Theatre; Good Conduct Medal; Pac Theatre, Am Theatre, World War II Victory Medal; Japanese Occup Medal with one campaign star. Mem: Am Bar Asn; Hialeah-Miami Springs CofC; Iron Arrow Honor Soc, Univ Miami; Miami Scottish Rite; Am Legion (past state Comdr, 53). Honors & Awards: Top Hat Award, Bus & Prof Women's Clubs of US for advancing the status of women, 67. Relig: Baptist. Mailing Add: 2210 Monaghan Dr Tallahassee FL 32302

BOYD, MCDILL (R)
Rep Nat Committeeman, Kans
b Phillipsburg, Kans, 1907; s Frank W Boyd & Mamie Alexander B; m 1930 to Marie Kriekenbaum; c Patricia (Mrs W L Hiss) & Marcia (Mrs Tom Krauss). Educ: Kans State Univ, 25-27; Phi Delta Theta. Polit & Govt Pos: Publicity dir, Rep State Comt, Kans, 38, 40, 46 & 50; coordr, Eisenhower Campaign, Kans, 52; mem, Kans Bd Regents, 53-56, chmn, 56; admin asst, Gov Edward F Arn, 54; dir, Robert J Dole Cong Campaign, 62, chmn, First Dist Rep Party, 62-66; Rep Nat Committeeman, 66-; Nixon Coord Kans, 68; deleg, Rep Nat Conv, 68 & 72; chmn, Mid-West Conf, Rep Nat Comt, Des Moines, 69 & Indianapolis, 71. Bus & Prof Pos: Partner, Boyd Family, Ed & Publ, 30-; Dir, First Nat Bank, Phillipsburg, Kans, 45-; dir, Kans Nebr Natural Gas Co, Hastings, Nebr, 67-; trustee, William Allen White Found; dir, Kans State Univ Endowment Asn; trustee, Dane G Hansen Trust & Dane G Hansen Found, 64- Mem: Kans Citizens Coun Educ; Kans Ment Health Asn; Nat Asn Ment Health (bd dirs, 66-); Kans Fund Dir Ment Health; Kans Press Asn. Honors & Awards: Participant, UN Econ & Soc Coun, Geneva, 70; William Allen White Found Award, 71. Relig: Presbyterian. Mailing Add: 451 Third St Phillipsburg KS 67661

BOYD, OBIE DALE (R)
b Pilot Point, Tex, July 28, 25; s Tilmon Henson Boyd & Julia Elizabeth Standley B; m 1954 to Ruby Alice Simmons. Educ: Tex Christian Univ, 46-50. Polit & Govt Pos: Precinct chmn, Rep Party, Ft Worth, Tex, 64-; deleg, Tex Rep State Conv, 66, 68, 70 & 72, mem, Nominations Comt, 70, mem, Rules Comt, 72; standing comt chmn, Tex State Rep Exec Comt, 66-; alt deleg, Rep Nat Conv, 68. Bus & Prof Pos: Salesman, Tex Elec Serv Co, Ft Worth, Tex, 52-69; sales engr, Westinghouse Elec Supply Co, 69-70; sales rep, Mid-Cities Elec Wholesale Co, 70-; sales estimator, Anderson Fixture Co, 72- Mil Serv: Entered as A/S, Navy, 43, released as PO 2/C, 46, after serv in Postal Serv, SPac, 43, 46, recalled, 50-51 as S/Sgt, Marine Corps, serv in Air Intel, Second Air Wing; Presidential Unit Citation. Mem: Illum Eng Soc. Relig: Baptist. Mailing Add: 7248 Ellis Rd Ft Worth TX 76112

BOYD, RANDALL SCOTT (D)
b Pierre, SDak, June 27, 52; s Williard Wallace Boyd & Helen Fravel B; single. Educ: Riggs High Sch, grad, 71. Polit & Govt Pos: Chmn, Students for Robert F Kennedy, SDak, 67-68; pres, Hughes & Stanley Co Young Dem, 68-71; deleg, SDak State Dem Conv, 72; chmn, Haakon Co Dem Party, formerly; area rep for US Sen George McGovern, 73-; first asst chief clerk, SDak House Rep, 73- Bus & Prof Pos: Rancher, 71- Mem: KofC. Relig: Roman Catholic. Mailing Add: PO Box 128 Ottumwa SD 57565

BOYD, ROBERT STEWART (R)
b Ardmore, Okla, May 24, 35; s Tom Stewart Boyd & Virginia Latcham B; m 1968 to Sara Jeffrey; c Kimberly, Karen Lee & Hadley. Educ: Univ Kans, BSc, 58; St Louis Univ Sch Law, 60-61; Harvard Bus Sch, MBA, 63; Sigma Tau, Tau Beta Pi; Sigma Alpha Epsilon. Polit & Govt Pos: Exec asst, Gov Henry Bellmon, Okla, 65-67; minority staff dir, Comt on the Budget, US Senate, 75- Bus & Prof Pos: Financial analyst, Skelly Oil Co, Tulsa, Okla, 63-64; exec dir, Okla World's Fair Comn, New York, 64-65; asst to the Pres, Midwest Research Inst, Kansas City, Mo, 67-68; vpres corp finance, H O Peet & Co, Kansas City, 68-72; dir corp finance, investment banking, B C Christopher & Co, Kansas City, 72-75. Mil Serv: Entered as 2nd Lt, US Air Force, 58, released as Capt, 61, after serv in Mil Air Transport Command. Publ: Co-auth, Report of Mayor's Comn on Civil Disorder, Kansas City Riot Study, Sept 68. Mem: Various investment banking & investment analysts groups (nat & local). Mailing Add: 209 Midvale St Falls Church VA 22046

BOYD, ROZELLE (D)
Mem, Dem Nat Comt, Ind
b Indianapolis, Ind, Apr 24, 34; s William C Boyd, Sr & Ardelia Leavell B; single. Educ: Ind Cent Col, 52-53; Butler Univ, BA, 57; Northwestern Univ, 59; Ind Univ, MA, 66; Alpha Phi Alpha. Polit & Govt Pos: Councilman, Marion Co Dem Party, Ind, 65-70; councilman, Indianapolis City Coun, 70-, minority leader, 71-; deleg, Dem Nat Conv, 72; secy, Marion Co Dem Cent Comt, 72-; mem, Dem Nat Comt, 72- Bus & Prof Pos: Teacher, Indianapolis Pub Schs, 57-68; lectr, Ind Univ, 67-, asst dean, 68- Mem: Ind State Black Caucus (treas, 71-73); Indianapolis Black Caucus (chmn, 71-73). Honors & Awards: Honors & Awards: Man of the Year, Iota Lambda of Alpha Phi Alpha, 66; Teaching Award, Freedoms Found. Relig: United Presbyterian. Mailing Add: 2527 E 35th St Indianapolis IN 46218

BOYD, WAYNE EDWIN (R)
Nat Committeeman, Nebr Fedn Young Rep
b Lebanon, Nebr, Aug 6, 39; s Thomas Dalton Boyd & Rava Winters B; m 1963 to Diane Kathleen Davis; c Scott Thomas & Laurie Lynn. Educ: Iowa State Univ, 57-59; Morningside Col, 59-61; Univ SDak, JD, magna cum laude, 64; Delta Tau Delta. Polit & Govt Pos: Treas, Dakota Co Young Rep, Nebr, 66, chmn, 67; chmn const comt, Nebr Fedn Young Rep, 68, first dist dir, 69, mem resolutions comt, 71, secy, 71, nat committeeman, currently; city attorney, South Sioux City, 68-71; spec asst attorney gen, Nebr Game & Parks Comn, 70; spec prosecutor, Dixon Co, 70; mem, Dakota Co Rep Cent Comt, 70; deleg, Nebr Rep State Conv, 70; chmn, Dakota Co Rep Party, 70-73. Bus & Prof Pos: Partner, Smith, Smith & Boyd, Attorneys, 44- Publ: Three papers published. Mem: Mason; Rotary; Elks; Farm Bur; South Sioux City CofC. Relig: Lutheran. Mailing Add: 2601 Dakota Ave South Sioux City NE 68876

BOYER, DENNIS LEE (D)
b Allentown, Pa, July 13, 49; s Erwin Andrew Boyer & Grace Choyce B; m 1971 to Barbara Catherine Murphy. Educ: Univ Md, College Park, 69-70; Pa State Univ, Reading, 71-73; Vet Asn of Berks Campus. Polit & Govt Pos: Deleg, Dem Nat Conv, 72; coordr, Pa Vet for McGovern, 72. Bus & Prof Pos: Counr, Prog to Advance Vet Educ, Pa Dept Educ, 73-; coordr, Pa Vietnam Vet Against the War Defense Comt, 73- Mil Serv: Entered as Airman Basic, Air Force, 67, released as S/Sgt, 71, after serv in Combined Intel Ctr, Mil Assistance Command, Vietnam, Southeast Asia, 70-71; Vietnam Campaign Ribbons; Mil Airlift Command Achievement Award; Air Force Commendation Medal. Publ: Co-ed, An annotated bibliography of environmental studies of Israel, USAF ETAC TN 70-4, 70 & A selected annotated bibliography of environmental studies of Iraq, Jordan, Lebanon, & Syria, USAF ETAC TN 70-5, 70, USAF Environ Tech Appln Ctr. Mem: VFW; Berks Dem Coun. Relig: United Church of Christ. Legal Res: RD 1 Mertztown PA 19539 Mailing Add: PO Box 4114 VVAW Mt Penn PA 19606

BOYER, ELROY G (D)
Md State Sen
b Baltimore, Md, May 5, 20; m to Laura Hogans. Educ: Univ Md; Washington Col, AB, 42; Univ Md Sch Law, LLB, 45. Polit & Govt Pos: Md State Deleg, 59-70; past pres, Md Young Dem & Kent Co Young Dem; Md State Sen, 70- Bus & Prof Pos: Attorney, Rock Hall & Betterton, Md. Mem: Am Bar Asn; Md State Bar Asn; Kent Co Bar Asn. Relig: Methodist. Mailing Add: 107 Court St Chestertown MD 21621

BOYER, JAMES GAMBRELL (D)
Mem, State Dem Cent Comt La
b Fort Benning, Ga, Dec 22, 28; s Emile James Boyer & Louise Gambrell B; m 1963 to Helen Margaret House; c William Richard & Catherine Gambrell. Educ: La State Univ, BA, 49, JD, 51; Lambda Chi Alpha; Phi Delta Phi. Polit & Govt Pos: City attorney, Lake Charles, La, 58-60; mem, State Dem Cent Comt, 64-; chmn, Calcasieu Parish Dem Exec Comt, 68-; deleg, Dem Nat Conv, 68. Bus & Prof Pos: Mem bd dirs, Gulf Nat Bank, Lake Charles, La, 68-; mem bd dirs, Lake Charles Mem Hosp, currently. Mil Serv: Entered as Pvt, Air Force, 51, released as 2nd Lt, 53; Maj, Res, currently. Mem: Southwest La, La & Am Bar Asns; State Bar Tex; Young Mens Bus Club; Am Legion. Relig: Episcopal. Legal Res: 330 Drew Park Dr Lake Charles LA 70601 Mailing Add: PO Box 1527 Lake Charles LA 70601

BOYER, STANLEY CLARK (R)
Ind State Rep
b Acton, Ind, Sept 28, 27; s Roscoe Boyer & Angeline Lawson B; m 1948 to Nevelyn Fae Horner; c Teresa (Mrs James Holderman), Stanley M & Lana K. Educ: Franklin Twp High Sch, Wanamaker, Ind, 4 years. Polit & Govt Pos: Ind State Rep, 71-; precinct committeeman & twp chmn, Marion Co Rep Party, currently; fleet maintenance mgr, City of Indianapolis, currently. Bus & Prof Pos: Toolmaker & machinist; owner & operator, Serv Garage. Mil Serv: Entered as Pvt, Marine Corps, 45, released as Cpl, 47, after serv in Fleet Marine Force, Pac Theatre, 46-47; Good Conduct Medal; Victory Medal; Expert Rifle & Carbine Award. Mem: F&AM; Scottish Rite; Murat Shrine; Franklin Twp Rep Club; Indianapolis Press Club. Relig: Protestant. Mailing Add: 4153 S Butler Indianapolis IN 46203

BOYHAN, CYNTHIA ANNE (D)
State Committeewoman, Wyo Dem Party
b Elbert Co, Ga, June 23, 34; d John Wayne McCalla & Flo Haynes M; m 1958 to John H Boyhan; c Wayne Michael, Leslie Anne & Stephen Kelly. Educ: Col William & Mary, BA, 56; Alpha Chi Omega. Polit & Govt Pos: Justice of the Peace, Dubois, Wyo, 62-70 & 72; state committeewoman, Wyo Dem Party, Fremont Co, 68-72; alt deleg, Dem Nat Conv, 72; app, Wyo Bd CPA, currently. Bus & Prof Pos: Reporter, Wyo Eagle, Cheyenne, 56; social worker, Laramie Co Welfare Dept, 57 & Fremont Co Welfare Dept, 57-59; teacher, Dubois Sch, 67-69; mem & clerk, Fremont Co Sch Dist 2, currently; staff writer, Wyo State J, currently. Relig: Quaker. Mailing Add: Box 571 Dubois WY 82513

BOYKIN, ULYSSES W (R)
Chmn, First Cong Dist Rep Orgn, Mich
b Knoxville, Tenn, Oct 17, 14; s Ulysses S Boykin, Sr & Curtis Bell Heard B; m 1965 to Nancy Merritt; c Ulysses W, III. Educ: Wayne State Univ, 36-38 & 62. Polit & Govt Pos: Clerk, City Elec Comn, Detroit, 36-37, inspector, State Rwy Comn, 37-38; exec secy, Nonpartisan Voters League, 38; comnr, Detroit Metrop Area Planning Comn, 45-55; mem bd dirs, Wayne Co Rep Precinct Orgn, 50-; pres, Rep Voters League, 50-55; mem adv bd, First Cong Dist Rep Precinct Orgn, 50-; deleg, resident chmn, First Cong Dist Rep Orgn, 64-66, mem exec bd & pub rels dir, 71-, chmn, currently; vchmn, Wayne Co Rep Educ Orgn; pub rels dir, Wolverine Rep State Orgn; exec secy, Metrop Voters League, currently; chmn, Detroit Metrop Black Div, Comt Relection of the President, 71-73; mgr, Nixon-Griffin Hqs for Blacks in Detroit, Mich, 72-73. Bus & Prof Pos: City ed, Mich Chronicle, 36-37; ed & publ, Detroit Tribune, 45-51; Mich ed, Pittsburgh Courier, 62-63; ed & publ, Press Facts, 61-66; pub rels counr & ed, Mich Herald, currently; dir pub affairs & pub rels, Radio Sta WGPR, 69-; pres, Urban Commun Consult, Inc, 70-; ed, Urban Facts, 70-; pres, U W Boykin & Assocs, 71- Mil Serv: Mem, Off Price Admin Appeal Bd, Mich, World War II. Publ: Handbook on the Detroit Negro, Minority Study Assocs, 43. Mem: Mich State Coun Block Clubs (pres, 69-); Educ Orgn for Freedom Studies; Am Asn Minority Consult; Nat Asn Urbanologists; Asn Black Broadcasting (exec secy, 70-). Honors & Awards: Serv award, Comt Reelection of the President, 73. Relig: Baptist. Legal Res: 1675 W Boston Blvd Detroit MI 48206 Mailing Add: 330 Trowbridge Detroit MI 48202

BOYLAN, JOHN HENRY (R)
Vt State Sen
Mailing Add: Island Pond VT 05846

BOYLAN, PAUL F (D)
Mont State Sen
Mailing Add: Star Route Bozeman MT 59715

BOYLE, JAMES P (D)
b Peabody, Mass, Nov 25, 04; s Michael A Boyle & Catherine F Rahilly B; m 1930 to Gladys G LeCain; c Mary L (Mrs William F Doody) & Ann F (Mrs Richard L Flynn). Educ: Peabody High Sch, grad, 25; St John's Preparatory Col, 27. Polit & Govt Pos: Mem, Mass Dem State Comt, Third Essex Dist, 52-64, Second Essex Dist, 64-68, vchmn, 52-56, treas, 56, secy, 64-68; mem, Mass Emergency Finance Bd, 60-67; Presidential Elector, 64; alt deleg, Dem Nat Conv, 64, deleg-at-lg, 68, deleg-at-lg, Dem Nat Mid-Term Conf, 74; trustee, Peabody Inst Libr, 74- Bus & Prof Pos: Notary Pub, real estate broker; acct, Dept State Auditor, 67-74. Mem: Ancient Order of Hibernians; KofC; Elks; Eire Soc Boston; Charitable Irish Soc (Holy Name). Honors & Awards: Pub Official of the Month, Boston City Hall News & State House Reporter, 64. Relig: Roman Catholic. Legal Res: 234 Washington St Peabody MA 01960 Mailing Add: PO Box 562 Peabody MA 01960

BOYLE, JUNE (D)
Dem Nat Committeewoman, Wyo
b Greeley, Colo, Sept 30, 17; d Walter J Ott & Millicent W O; m to James M Boyle; c Kathleen (Mrs Champlain) & Michael J. Educ: Univ Colo, BFA; Delta Phi Delta; Alpha Phi. Polit & Govt Pos: Chmn, Albany Co Dem Party, Wyo; Wyo State Rep, formerly; Dem Nat Committeewoman, Wyo, currently; deleg, Dem Nat Conv, 68 & 72; mem, Wyo Comn Status of Women, 66-; Wyo State Sen, 72- Mem: SE Wyo Ment Health Ctr; Laramie United Fund; Laramie Woman's Club; Univ Wyo Faculty Women's Club; League of Women Voters. Relig: Catholic. Mailing Add: 706 S 14th St Laramie WY 82070

BOYLE, KENNETH RAYMOND (D)
Ill State Rep
b Springfield, Ill, Nov 27, 37; s Clarence Boyle & Mary Yacup B; m 1960 to Janet Mildred Thalmann; c Michelle Diane. Educ: Univ Ill, AB, 59, LLB, 62; Phi Beta Kappa; Pi Sigma Alpha; Univ Ill Scholarship Key. Polit & Govt Pos: Legal adv, Dept Pub Safety, State of Ill, 65-66, asst attorney gen, 66-68; Ill State Rep, 49th Dist, 71-72, 49th Dist, 73-; deleg, Dem Nat Mid-Term Conf, 74. Mil Serv: Entered as Pvt, Army, released as E-5, 68. Mem: Ill State Bar Asn; Macoupin Co Bar Asn; Am Judicature Soc; Macoupin Co Farm Bur; Elks; CofC; KofC. Relig: Catholic. Mailing Add: RR 2 Carlinville IL 62626

BOYLE, LOUIS LAWRENCE (D)
Chmn, Williamsburg Dem Comt, Va
b Richmond, Va, July 31, 49; s Rev Lewis Venerable Boyle & Alice Brand B; m 1971 to Kathleen Thompson. Educ: Col William & Mary, BA, 71, MA, 73; Lyon G Tyler Hist Soc. Polit & Govt Pos: Chmn, Williamsburg Dem Comt, Va, 73- Bus & Prof Pos: Sixth grade social studies teacher, Newport News Pub Schs, 71-75. Mem: Nat, Va & Newport News Educ Asns. Relig: Presbyterian. Mailing Add: 1407-A N Mt Vernon Ave Williamsburg VA 23185

BOYLE, NORMAN WILLIAM (R)
Chmn, Jasper Co Rep Comt, Iowa
b Appleton, Wis, Apr 20, 30; s Henry Anthony Boyle & Viola Sack B; m 1953 to Esther Sevenich; c Nancy, Craig, Susan, Mary, Thomas & Ellen. Educ: Wis State Univ, Oshkosh, 48-50; Univ Wis-Madison, BS, 52; Sigma Delta Chi; Iowa Alpha Sigma. Polit & Govt Pos: Chmn, Jasper Co Rep Comt, Iowa, 74- Bus & Prof Pos: City ed, Geneseo Rep, Geneseo, Ill, 52-53; publ ed, Maytag Co, Newton, Iowa, 56-64, mgr commun, 64-67, asst pub rels dir, 67- Mil Serv: Entered as Pvt, Army, 53, released as Cpl, after serv in US Pub Info Off, Alaska Gen Depot, Ft Richardson, Alaska, 53-55. Mem: Pub Rels Soc Am; Kiwanis; Newton Country Club; CofC. Honors & Awards: Distinguished Serv Award, Newton Community, 64. Relig: Catholic. Legal Res: 913 S 11th Ave W Newton IA 50208 Mailing Add: 403 W Fourth St N Newton IA 50208

96 / BOYNTON

BOYNTON, MARJORIE CHASE (R)
Asst Secy, Rep State Cent Comt Calif
b Grand Forks, NDak, Feb 3, 25; d Victor Newton Chase & Lucy Beatt C; m 1949 to Searles R Boynton, DDS; c Paige, Kevin & Tammy. Educ: Univ NDak, PhB, 46; Phi Beta Kappa; Sigma Upsilon Nu; Matrix; Delta Gamma. Polit & Govt Pos: Pres, Ukiah Rep Women, Calif, 60-62; women's vchmn, Rep Cent Comt, 62-64; mem, Rep State Cent Comt, Calif, 62-, asst secy, 69-; chmn women's div, First Cong Dist Rep Party, 62-64; secy, Rep Calif Co Chmn Assoc, 66-; chmn, Mendocino Co Rep Cent Comt, currently; chmn, First Cong Dist Rep Orgn, 71-; alt deleg, Rep Nat Conv, 68, deleg, 72. Mem: Am Cancer Soc; Am Asn Univ Women; PTA; PEO; Am Contract Bridge League. Relig: Protestant. Mailing Add: 711 Willow Ave Ukiah CA 95482

BOZICK, PETER A (D)
Md State Sen
Mailing Add: 5606 Lansing Dr Camp Spring MD 20031

BOZZUTO, RICHARD CARL (R)
Conn State Sen
b Waterbury, Conn, Mar 16, 30; s John Bozzuto; m 1953 to Angela Elizabeth Gerarde; c Richard Carl, Jr, Christine Marie, Marcia Louise & Elizabeth Ann. Educ: Am Int Col, BS in personnel admin, 52; Charter Life Underwriter, Am Col Life Underwriters, 69; Zeta Chi. Polit & Govt Pos: Chmn, Watertown Town Coun, Conn, 67-69; chmn, Watertown Town Rep Party, 70-73; Conn State Sen, 72- Bus & Prof Pos: Rep vol, Salt Lake City, Utah, 20-54; bd dirs, Salt Lake City Rep Women's Club, 55-59, pres, 60-61; secy to first vpres, Utah Fedn Rep Women's Clubs, 61-65, pres, 66-67; immediate past pres, 68-72, pres, formerly; hospitality vchmn, Nat Fedn Rep Women, 68- Bus & Prof Pos: Secy, J B Walker, Inc, 30-57, secy-treas, 57-; co-owner, Walker Sand & Gravel Co, 48- Mem: Salt Lake City Bus & Prof Women's Club; Utah State Fedn Bus & Prof Women's Clubs; Women's Legis Coun Utah; Coun of Women, Salt Lake City. Honors & Awards: Nat GOP Fund Drive Award, 62. Relig: Latter-day Saint. Mailing Add: 1455 S Fourth E Salt Lake City UT 84115

BOZZUTO, VICTOR J (D)
b Waterbury, Conn, Sept 1, 21; s John Bozzuto & Louise Laudate B; m 1944 to Rae L Anderson; c William, Robert, Vicky & Anthony. Educ: High Sch. Polit & Govt Pos: Chmn, Lincoln Co Dem Cent Comt, Idaho, 63-67; mayor, Shoshone, Idaho, 66-; dir, Idaho Munic League, 66-; State Dem Committeeman, formerly. Bus & Prof Pos: Owner, Shoshone Furniture Co, 61- Mil Serv: Entered as A/S, Navy, 42, released as Seaman 1/C, 45, after serv in Pac. Mem: Am Legion Post 11, Shoshone (first vcomdr); Lions; CofC; Shoshone PTA. Relig: Roman Catholic. Mailing Add: 318 West B Shoshone ID 83352

BRABY, GUDVOR WIKANE (R)
b Jondal, Norway, Sept 16, 99; d Sivert Sjursen Wikane & Dorthea Maria Mickelson W; wid; c Elaine (Mrs Manhart), Lois (Mrs Odysseus), Joyce (Mrs Reed) & Bryan Dean (deceased). Educ: Salt Lake Bus Col, grad; Univ Utah. Polit & Govt Pos: Rep vol, Salt Lake City, Utah, 20-54; bd dirs, Salt Lake City Rep Women's Club, 55-59, pres, 60-61; secy to first vpres, Utah Fedn Rep Women's Clubs, 61-65, pres, 66-67; immediate past pres, 68-72, pres, formerly; hospitality vchmn, Nat Fedn Rep Women, 68- Bus & Prof Pos: Secy, J B Walker, Inc, 30-57, secy-treas, 57-; co-owner, Walker Sand & Gravel Co, 48- Mem: Salt Lake City Bus & Prof Women's Club; Utah State Fedn Bus & Prof Women's Clubs; Women's Legis Coun Utah; Coun of Women, Salt Lake City. Honors & Awards: Nat GOP Fund Drive Award, 62. Relig: Latter-day Saint. Mailing Add: 1455 S Fourth E Salt Lake City UT 84115

BRACHTENBACH, ROBERT F (R)
Justice, Wash Supreme Court
b Sidney, Nebr; m to Nancy; c five. Educ: Univ Wash, BS, LLB. Polit & Govt Pos: Wash State Rep, 63-67, Minority Whip, mem, Judicial Coun, Wash State House of Rep, 63-65, mem, Legis Coun, 65-67; deleg, Rep Nat Conv, 68; justice, Wash Supreme Court, 72- Bus & Prof Pos: Lawyer, Felthous, Brachtenbach & Peters, 55-72. Mem: Am Bar Asn. Honors & Awards: One of Ten Outstanding Young Men in Wash, 63. Mailing Add: Legis Bldg Olympia WA 98502

BRACKETT, NOY E (R)
Idaho State Rep
Mailing Add: Box 403 Twin Falls ID 83301

BRADEMAS, JOHN (D)
US Rep, Ind
b Mishawaka, Ind, Mar 2, 27; single. Educ: Harvard Univ, BA magna cum laude, 49; Oxford Univ, PhD, 54, Rhodes Scholar for Ind; Phi Beta Kappa. Hon Degrees: LLD, Univ Notre Dame, St Mary's Col, Ind, Middlebury Col & Columbia Col; LHD, Brandeis Univ; hon fel, Brasenose Col, Oxford Univ, 73. Polit & Govt Pos: Admin asst to US Rep Thomas Ludlow Ashley, Ohio, 55; legis asst to US Sen Pat McNamara, Mich, 55; exec asst to Adlai E Stevenson, 55-56; US Rep, Third Dist, Ind, 58-, Majority Floor Whip, US House of Rep, 71-73, Chief Dep Majority Whip, 73-; deleg, Dem Nat Conv, 68 & 72. Pos: Asst prof polit sci, St Mary's Col. Mil Serv: Navy, 45-46. Mem: F&AM; Ahepa; Am Legion; Fel, Am Acad of Arts & Sci; Nat Hist Publ Comn. Relig: Methodist. Legal Res: 750 Leland Ave South Bend IN 46616 Mailing Add: 2134 Rayburn Bldg Washington DC 20515

BRADEN, JAMES DALE (R)
Kans State Rep
b Kans, Aug 2, 34; s James Wesley Braden & Olive M Reed B; m 1952 to Naomi J Carlson; c Gregory, Michael, Ladd & Amy Susanne. Educ: Wakefield High Sch, grad, 52; Am Col Life Underwriters, CLU, 70. Polit & Govt Pos: Bd mem, Clay Co Sch Bd, Kans, 65-; Kans State Rep, 63rd Dist, 75-, mem, Educ, Assessment & Taxation Comt & Agr & Livestock Comt, Kans House of Rep, 75- Bus & Prof Pos: Life ins agt, Wakefield, Kans, 64- Mem: Kans Asn Life Underwriters (pres, 74-75); Am Soc Chartered Life Underwriters; Elks; Wakefield Lodge 396; Million Dollar Round Table (life & qualifying mem). Honors & Awards: Master Life Underwriter, Indianapolis Life Ins Co, 69. Relig: Methodist. Legal Res: 606 Grove Wakefield KS 67487 Mailing Add: Box 305 Wakefield KS 67487

BRADEN, MARGARET MIZE (R)
b Emporia, Kans, d Robert H Mize, DD & Margaret Moore M; m 1937 to Forrest Clifford Braden; c Barbara Louise, Robert Mize & Forrest Arthur. Educ: Univ Kans, BA; Pi Beta Phi. Polit & Govt Pos: Pres, Yuma Co Rep Women, Ariz, 56-57; precinct committeewoman, 58-; secy, Yuma Co Rep Cent Comt, 58-59; mem, Ariz Adv Comt to US Comn Civil Rights, 68, deleg, US Comn Civil Rights Conf, 71; vchairwoman, Ariz Rep State Cent, 60-61; Rep Nat Committeewoman, Ariz, 62-72; chmn, Thirteen Western States Rep Conf, 68-69; mem exec comt, Rep Nat Comt, 62-72; mem US Deleg, Conf on Inter-Am Comn of Women, Bogota, Colombia, 63; bd mem, Coun Govts, currently. Mem: San Pablo Home for Youth, Phoenix (bd dirs); Yuma Co (welfare bd); Human Rels Comn, Yuma; Yuma City-Co Libr (bd). Relig: Episcopal. Mailing Add: 700 Second Ave Yuma AZ 85364

BRADFORD, ELWOOD WALTER (D)
Ariz State Rep
b Yuma, Ariz, Feb 11, 09; s Walter Edward Bradford & Lizzie Dyer B; m 1937 to Ruth Victoria Maye; c Michael E & Julie (Mrs Battenfield). Educ: Univ Ariz, BSBA, 33; Kappa Sigma. Polit & Govt Pos: Mem, Ariz State Bd Regents, 57-71; Ariz State Rep, 71- Bus & Prof Pos: Sales rep, New York Life Ins, formerly. Mil Serv: Entered as Lt(jg), Navy, released as Lt Comdr, 46, after serv in 12th & 14th Naval Dist. Mem: Elks; KofC. Mailing Add: PO Box 4456 Yuma AZ 85364

BRADFORD, ROBERT EDWARD (R)
b Roanoke, Va, June 27, 31; s Miller Hughes Bradford & Helen Boyd Gardner B; m 1970 to Nancy R Rondelli; c Laura Ann. Educ: Washington & Lee Univ; Sigma Delta Chi; Scabbard & Blade; Lambda Chi Alpha (pres, 53-54). Polit & Govt Pos: Admin asst, US Rep Richard Poff, Va, 58-68; regional dir, Nat Young Rep Fedn, 63-65; chmn, Bull Elephants, 65-68; exec dir, Ill Rep Party, 68-70; admin asst, US Sen William Brock, Tenn, 71- Bus & Prof Pos: News dir, WRAD, Radford, Va, 54-56; news ed, WMAL-TV, Washington, DC, 57-58. Mil Serv: Entered as 2nd Lt, Army, 57, released as 1st Lt, 57; Capt, Army Res, 57-62. Mem: Am Fedn TV & Radio Artists; Nat Defense Transportation Asn; Jaycees; PTA; Westgate Civic Asn. Honors & Awards: 17 Awards for radio newscasting, Assoc Press, 54-58; Bull Elephant of the Year, 67 & 68; Dwight Eisenhower Award, Ill Young Rep, 69; Outstanding Serv Award to Ill Rep Party, 69; hon fel, Inst Polit, Harvard Univ, 71. Relig: Methodist. Mailing Add: 423 Mill St Vienna VA 22180

BRADFORD, ROBERT FISKE (R)
b Boston, Mass, 1902. Educ: Harvard, AB, 23, LLB, 26, LLD, 48. Polit & Govt Pos: Gov, Mass, 47-48. Bus & Prof Pos: Partner, Palmer & Dodge; dir, Cambridge Trust Co, ITB Mgt Corp & Trust Mgt Corp; trustee, Boston Five Cents Savings Bank & Simmons Col. Mailing Add: One Beacon St Boston MA 02108

BRADFORD, WILLIAM HOLLIS, JR (D)
Mem, Montgomery Co Dem Cent Comt, Md
b St Petersburg, Fla, Feb 11, 37; s Dr William Hollis Bradford & Treva Waymire B; m 1970 to Karol Ann Greeson; c Stacey Ann & Leslie Leigh Bradford & Kelly Ann & Eric Johnson. Educ: Duke Univ, AB, 59, JD, 62; George Washington Univ, LLM, 64; Phi Beta Kappa; Order of the Coif; Delta Tau Delta. Polit & Govt Pos: Precinct chmn & vchmn, Montgomery Co Dem Party, Md, 67-74; pres, Montgomery Co Young Dem, 68-69; vpres, Md Young Dem, 67-68; mem charter rev comn, Rockville, 73-75; mem, Montgomery Co Dem Cent Comt, 74- Bus & Prof Pos: Attorney, Hamel, Park, McCabe & Saunders, 62-67, partner, 67- Publ: Co-auth, Commission on Maryland General Assembly Reform Report, 67; ed, Section of Taxation Annual Report, Am Bar Asn, 72 & 73. Mem: Am & Md Bar Asns; Bar Asn of DC; Washington Figure Skating Club (bd gov, 74-). Mailing Add: 1202 Azalea Dr Rockville MD 20850

BRADLEY, AGNES ALBERTA (ANGEL) (R)
Committeewoman, Dade Co Rep Exec Comt, Fla
b Boston, Mass, Apr 3, 21; d John I Barnes & LyVonie I Bamford B; m 1942 to Charles Vernon Bradley; c Pamela Bamford. Educ: Quincy High Sch, grad, 39; Katharine Gibbs Sch, Boston, grad & cert, 41; New York Flyers Club Sch, pvt pilot, 50. Polit & Govt Pos: Sponsor, Dade Co Young Rep, 67-; sustaining mem, Rep Nat Cong Comt; sustaining mem, Rep Nat Finance Comt; sustaining mem, Rep Nat Comt, 66-; sustaining mem, Fla Rep Party, 66-, spec asst finance chmn, 71-72; mem nat coun, Women's Nat Rep Club; mem, Nat Fedn Rep Women, 66-; mem, Fla Fedn Rep Women, 66-; deleg, Rep Nat Conv, 68, deleg, co-chmn host comt & mem platform comt, 72; charter court observers prog, juvenile court syst, Crime Comn, 69-70, mem women's div, speakers bur, 70; mem, Dade Co Comn Status Women, 70-; mem steering comt, Dade Co Coun One Thousand; mem finance comt, Dade Co Rep Exec Comt, 72-, dist committeewoman, 72-; club chmn, Women for Nixon-Agnew Comt, 68; area chmn, Nixon-Agnew Research Comt, 68; state coord, Citizens Vol for the Comt for the Reelec of the President, 72, asst to the state chmn, 72; deleg, Rep Nat Leadership Conf, 72; liaison, Univ Miami Comn Status of Women, 73; mem Comprehensive Health Planning Coun SFla, 73. Bus & Prof Pos: Exec secy to pres, Merchants Coop Bank, Boston, 41-46; off mgr, R E Bradley & Sons, Inc, NY, 46-50; real estate saleswoman, Miami, 53-; secy-treas, Diversified Rep Inc, 55-71; pres/Owners, Power Equip Sales Corp, 62- Mem: Katharine Gibbs Sch Alumnae Asn Dade Co (pres); Aircraft Owners & Pilots Asn; Variety Club; Miami Springs Rep Club; Elephant Forum (secy, 72-); Riviera Rep Women's Club. Honors & Awards: Vol Awards for Serv from Variety Club; Outstanding Rep in Dade Co, 72. Relig: Episcopal. Mailing Add: 12855 Hickory Rd Keystone Islands North Miami FL 33161

BRADLEY, DAVID HAMMOND (R)
NH State Sen
b Keene, NH, May 8, 36; s Homer S Bradley & Alice I Proctor B; m 1960 to Ann DeRoma; c David H, Jr, Jeffrey C & Christopher R. Educ: Dartmouth Col, AB, 58; Harvard Law Sch, JD, 65; Phi Gamma Delta. Polit & Govt Pos: Mem, Hanover Sch Bd, NH, 66-69, chmn, 67-68; mem, Dresden Interstate Sch Bd, 66-69, chmn, 68-69; exec councilor, NH Sch Bd Asn, 68-; NH State Rep, 71-73; NH State Sen, 73- Bus & Prof Pos: Lawyer & partner, Stebbins & Bradley, Hanover, NH, 65- Mil Serv: Entered as Ens, Navy, 58, released as Lt(jg), 61, after serv in Destroyers, Atlantic Ocean, 58-61; Lt, Naval Res. Publ: Toward simplified rules of order, NH Bar J, 69. Mem: Grafton Co, NH & Am Bar Asns; Rotary. Relig: Protestant. Mailing Add: Fox Field Lane Hanover NH 03755

BRADLEY, DAVID J (D)
NH State Rep
Mailing Add: 34 Occom Ridge Hanover NH 03755

BRADLEY, DOROTHY MAYNARD (D)
Mont State Rep
b Madison, Wis, Feb 24, 47; d Charles Crane Bradley & Maynard Riggs B; m to Rick Applegate. Educ: Colo Col, BA, 69; Phi Beta Kappa. Polit & Govt Pos: Mont State Rep, Gallatin Co, 71-; deleg, Dem Nat Conv, 72. Mailing Add: PO Box 931 Bozeman MT 59715

BRADLEY, GERALD ALLEN (D)
Ill State Rep
b Chicago, Ill, Oct 15, 27; s Gerald F Bradley & Marie Ryan B; m 1951 to Mary Margaret Condon; c David A, Michael E, Kathryn M & Margaret M. Educ: Ill Wesleyan Univ, PhB,

50; Phi Gamma Delta. Polit & Govt Pos: Pres, McLean Co Young Dem, Ill, 54-58; treas, McLean Co Cent Comt, 62-66, precinct committeeman, 68-69; Ill State Rep, 69- Bus & Prof Pos: Owner, Bloomington Tent & Awning Co, 56- Mil Serv: Entered as Pvt, Army, 50, released as Sgt 1/C, 52, after serv in Sixth Armored Div. Mem: KofC; Am Legion; Elks; Order of Titans. Relig: Catholic. Mailing Add: 1506 E Washington Bloomington IL 61701

BRADLEY, GORDON ROY (R)
Wis State Rep
b Utica, Wis, July 9, 21; s Roy Carl Bradley & Mayme Thrall B; m 1946 to Bettylou Hazel Fisher; c LuAnn Marie. Educ: Univ Wis, Madison, 1 year. Polit & Govt Pos: Sch clerk, Oshkosh, Wis, 46-62, town clerk, 62-67, town supvr, 67-; Wis State Rep, 69- Relig: Protestant. Mailing Add: 2644 Elo Rd Oshkosh WI 54901

BRADLEY, JANET MARY (D)
Mem, Southeast Dist Dem Comt, Alaska
b Baltimore, Md, May 9, 35; d Francis Joseph Litz & Ella Doris Manning L; m 1958 to Richard Alan Bradley; c Anne, Mary Katheryn, Alana & Richard Alan, Jr. Educ: Dunbarton Col Holy Cross, BA magna cum laude, 57; Univ Dijon, 57-58; Univ Wash, 70-73. Polit & Govt Pos: Auke Bay Precinct rep, Juneau Dem Precinct Comt, Alaska, 67-72; alt deleg, Dem Nat Conv, 72; campaign coordr, McGovern for President, Southeast Alaska Dist Three & Four, 72; secy, Southeast Alaska Dist Dem Conv, 72; mem, Southeast Dist Dem Comt, 72-; asst dir, Alaska State Comn Human Rights, 74-; mem, Juneau Bicentennial Comt; chairperson, Juneau Equal Rights Asn, currently. Bus & Prof Pos: Instr in French, Univ Alaska & Juneau-Douglas Community Col, 69-72. Mem: Am Asn of Teachers of French; Kappa Gamma Pi; League of Women Voters; Common Cause. Honors & Awards: Fulbright Scholarship, US Gov, 57. Relig: Catholic. Mailing Add: Box 594 Fritz Cove Rd Juneau AK 99801

BRADLEY, JOHN ALBERTSON (R)
Mem, NJ Rep State Comt
b Pleasantville, NJ, Apr 1, 08; s Joseph Harry Bradley & Elizabeth Albertson B; m 1938 to Mildred Marie Hoole; c Elizabeth (Mrs Mullis), John A, II & Charles C. Educ: Drexel Univ, scholarship, 30; BS, 32; Rutgers Univ, MEd, 65; Columbia Univ, Cert, 68; Blue Key; Theta Chi. Polit & Govt Pos: Chief of field training, NGB, US Army, Washington, DC, 50-52; chief of admin, Army Nat Guard Bur, 52-53; sr adv, Rep Korea Army, UN Command, Korea, 53-55; plans & operations officer, Mil Dist, Washington, DC, 55-59 mem, Middlesex Co Rep Comt, NJ, 67-; mem, NJ Rep State Comt, 69- Bus & Prof Pos: Spec investr & mgr, Retail Credit Co, Philadelphia, 33-37; gen mgr, Credit Rating Serv, Plainfield, NJ, 38-40; teacher hist, Franklin High Sch, Somerset, 63-; prof mil sci, Rutgers State Univ, 59-63. Mil Serv: Inf Officer, Army Res, 32-40; inf & gen staff officer, Army, 41-63, released as Col, 63 after serv in 78th, 79th, 3rd, 6th, & 9th div, Repl, Sch, & Far East Command, UN, KMAG, MDW & OCSA, 32-63; Legion of Merit, Army Commendation Medal with Oak Leaf Cluster, Korean Distinguished Serv Medal with Gold Star, various campaign & serv awards. Publ: Administrative Instructions-Field Training, Nat Guard, 51; US Govt State Funeral Plans, Washington, DC, 57; The Reserve Officer Training Corps, Rutgers Univ, 62. Mem: Nat Educ Asn; charter mem, Asn US Army; First Savings & Loan Asn (dir); Milltown CofC; Cent Jersey Am Red Cross (exec bd). Honors & Awards: Jennings Hood Award, Drexel Univ, 32; Rotarian of the Year, 62; Rep of the Year, Milltown, 65. Relig: Methodist. Mailing Add: 316 N Main St Milltown NJ 08850

BRADLEY, JOHN DANIEL, III (R)
SC State Rep
b Atlanta, Ga, May 26, 46; s John Daniel Bradley, Jr & Dorothy Jones B; m 1970 to Beverly Cox; c John Daniel, IV & David Charles. Educ: The Citadel, BA, 68; Univ SC Sch Law, JD, 71; Phi Alpha Delta. Polit & Govt Pos: Mem exec comt, Charleston Co Rep Party, SC, 72-74, first vchmn, 74-; SC State Rep, 75- Mil Serv: 1st Lt, Army Res, 71-, Signal Corps. Mem: Washington Light Inf; Sons of Confederate Vets; Charleston Evening Optimist Club; SC Bar Asn; Asn of Citadel Men. Relig: Southern Baptist. Legal Res: 308 Swift Ave Charleston SC Mailing Add: PO Box 157 Mt Pleasant SC 29464

BRADLEY, JOSEPH P, JR (D)
Pa State Rep
Mailing Add: Capitol Bldg Harrisburg PA 17120

BRADLEY, MICHAEL JOSEPH (D)
b Philadelphia, Pa, May 24, 97; s Dennis J Bradley & Hannah McCarthy B; m 1919 to Emily Angiuli; wid; c Raymond J, Marian T, Catharine B (Mrs Arter) & Edward J. Educ: High Sch. Polit & Govt Pos: Dep ins comnr, Commonwealth of Pa, 35-37; US Rep, Pa, 37-47; chmn, Dem Co Exec Comt, Philadelphia, 45-48; collector of customs, Port of Philadelphia, US Treas Dept, 48-53; dep managing dir, City of Philadelphia, 53-55; chmn, Bd of Rev of Taxes & Bd of Viewers, Philadelphia, 55- Bus & Prof Pos: Investment, security & brokerage bus, Philadelphia, 20-35. Mil Serv: Entered Navy, 17, released as chief radio electrician, 20, after serv in Europe, 17-20. Mem: Independence Nat Park Adv Comn; KofC; Am Legion. Relig: Roman Catholic. Mailing Add: 9737 Redd Rambler Dr Philadelphia PA 19115

BRADLEY, RICHARD L (R)
NH State Rep
Mailing Add: Thornton Gore Rd Woodstock NH 03293

BRADLEY, ROBERT EARL (BOB) (D)
Alaska State Rep
b Santa Monica, Calif, Nov 26, 44; s Robert Henry Bradley & Mildred Hogan B; m 1966 to Marcia Elaine Petro; c Robert Marc. Educ: Sheldon Jackson Col, Alaska, 64-65 & 67; Alaska Methodist Univ, 65-66, BA, 68; Univ Alaska 66; Circle K. Polit & Govt Pos: Founder, Young People for Gruening, 68; mem, Mountain View Dem Club, 73; Alaska State Rep, 75- Bus & Prof Pos: Instr, Kodiak Borough & Anchorage Borough, 68-69 & 70-71; exec dir, Southeast Alaska Community Action Prog, Inc, 71-73; dep dir develop, Community Enterprise Develop Corp, 73- Mil Serv: Entered as E-2, Alaska Army Nat Guard, 68- Mem: Alaska Educ Asn; Mountain View Lions Club. Relig: Latter-day Saint. Mailing Add: 601 Bragaw St Anchorage AK 99504

BRADLEY, ROBERT JAMES (R)
Chmn, Ballard Co Rep Party, Ky
b Burlington, Vt, Feb 24, 02; both parents deceased; m 1929 to Ruby Miller Barlow; c Melissa. Educ: Norwich Univ, BS, 23; Phi Kappa Delta. Polit & Govt Pos: Chmn, Ballard Co Rep Party, Ky, 72- Bus & Prof Pos: Chief engr, Am Fireworks, Mass; chief plant engr, Olin, New Haven, Conn; works mgr, Security Hardware, Brooklyn, NY; asst to pres, Polymers Inc, Vt, 64-69; pres, Bradley Assoc, Consultants & Engrs, 69- Mem: Ballard Co Country Club (dir). Honors & Awards: Ky Col, Barlow CofC. Relig: Protestant. Legal Res: Greenlawn Ave at Sixth Barlow KY 42024 Mailing Add: Box 155 Barlow KY 42024

BRADLEY, THOMAS (D)
Mayor, Los Angeles, Calif
b Calvert, Tex, Dec 29, 17; s Lee Thomas Bradley & Crenner Hawkins B; m 1941 to Ethel Mae Arnold; c Lorraine & Phyllis. Educ: Southwest Univ Law Sch, LLB, 56; Univ Calif, Los Angeles; Kappa Alpha Psi, former Grand Polemarch; Student Bd, Univ Religious Conf. Polit & Govt Pos: Mem, Los Angeles Police Dept, Calif, 40-62; mem, Calif State Dem Cent Comt; city councilman, 10th Dist, Los Angeles, 63-73, cand for mayor, Los Angeles, 69 & 73, mayor, 73-; chmn, State, Co & Fed Affairs Comt; chmn, Pub Works Priority Comt; chmn, Comt Proposed Legis; mem bd dirs, Joint Comn Ment Health Children; former mem, Peace Corps Adv Coun; mem, Coun Intergovt Rels; deleg, Dem Nat Mid-Term Conf, 74. Bus & Prof Pos: Attorney-at-law, 62- Mem: Los Angeles Urban League; NAACP; Southern Calif Conf on Community Rels; Los Angeles Co Conf of Negro Elected Off; UN Asn of Los Angeles (bd dirs). Honors & Awards: Letterman, Track Team, Univ Calif, Los Angeles; All City & Southern Calif Champion, 440 Yards, Polytech High Sch, Los Angeles. Relig: African Methodist Episcopal; Trustee. Legal Res: 3807 Welland Ave Los Angeles CA 90008 Mailing Add: 240 City Hall Los Angeles CA 90012

BRADLEY, W E (BRAD) (R)
Alaska State Sen
Mailing Add: PO Drawer 8670 Anchorage AK 99508

BRADLEY, WILLIAM D (BILL) (D)
Okla State Rep
b Fife, Tex, Jan 13, 13; s Henry Duncan Bradley & Winnie Belle Walker B; m 1941 to Margaret Price; c Henry Price & Patricia Evelyn (Mrs Scott). Educ: Daniel Baker Col, BA. Polit & Govt Pos: Okla State Rep, 53- Mil Serv: Entered as Pvt, Air Force, 42, released as 1st Lt, 45. Mem: Am Legion; Mason; Shrine; Farm Bur; Farmers Union. Relig: Presbyterian. Mailing Add: 1120 N Pine Waurika OK 73573

BRADNER, MICHAEL DRAKE (D)
Speaker, Alaska House Rep
b Washington, DC, Mar 1, 37; s George H Bradner & Alice Abbott B; single; c Michelle, Bonnie & twins Hiede & Heather. Educ: Univ Alaska, BA, 64, grad work, 68. Polit & Govt Pos: Field rep, Off Gov, 65-66; Alaska State Rep, 66-, chmn, House Rules Comt & mem, Finance Comt & Alaska Legis Coun, Alaska House of Rep, House Speaker, currently. Bus & Prof Pos: River pilot, Yutana Barge Lines, 57-62; night ed, Fairbanks News-Miner, 62-65; ed, Jessen's Daily, 67-68; writer, currently. Honors & Awards: Young Man of the Year Award, Jaycees, 68. Mailing Add: Box 2183 Fairbanks AK 99701

BRADSHAW, JOHN ROGERS (R)
b Sudbury, Mass, Apr 17, 30; s Forrest Dean Bradshaw & Katherine Rogers B; m 1967 to Bess Nichols; c John R, Jr, Betsy A & Peter D. Educ: Northeastern Univ; Clark Univ; Boston Univ. Polit & Govt Pos: NH State Rep, 65-66; NH State Sen, 67-73, majority leader, NH State Senate, 69-70, pres, 71-73; alt deleg, Rep Nat Conv, 72. Bus & Prof Pos: Sales engr, R H White Sales Co, Auburn, Mass, 52-54; sales engr, Hilco Supply Co, Sudbury, 54-57; partner, Bramil Pump & Supply Co, Keene, NH, 57-59, owner & gen mgr, 59- Mil Serv: Pfc, Marine Corps, 51-52. Mem: NH Water Works Asn; Maine Water Utilities Asn; New Eng Water Well Drillers Asn; Mason; Shrine. Honors & Awards: Conserv Legislator of the Year, 70. Relig: Congregational. Mailing Add: Nelson NH 03457

BRADSHAW, MARK (D)
Okla State Sen
Mailing Add: State Capitol Oklahoma City OK 73105

BRADSHAW, PAUL LUDWIG (R)
Mo State Sen
b Jefferson City, Mo, July 17, 30; s Jean Paul Bradshaw (deceased) & Catherine Ann Brandt B; div; c Jean Paul, II. Educ: Univ Mo, AB, 52, LLB, 54; Mystical Seven; Beta Theta Pi; Phi Delta Phi; Delta Sigma Rho. Polit & Govt Pos: State coordr, Rep Nat Campaign, Mo, 60; chmn, Greene Co Rep Party, 65-70; pres, Mo Asn of Rep, 68; chmn Nixon-Agnew Campaign Comt, Seventh Cong Dist, 68; Mo State Sen, 71- Bus & Prof Pos: Partner, Neale, Newman, Bradshaw & Freeman Law Firm, Springfield, Mo, 56-; sr vpres & gen counsel, Ozark Air Lines, Inc, St Louis, 68- Mil Serv: Entered as 2nd Lt, Air Force, 54, released as 1st Lt, 56, after serv in 3800 Air Base Wing, Maxwell Air Force Base, Ala, 54-56; Maj, Air Force Res, currently. Mem: Greene Co Bar Asn; Mason (32 degree); Shrine; Elks; CofC. Relig: Congregational. Legal Res: 833 E Elm Springfield MO 65804 Mailing Add: 705 Woodruff Bldg Springfield MO 65806

BRADY, EDWIN FRANCIS (R)
Chmn, Benton Co Rep Comt, Mo
b Warsaw, Mo, May 26, 15; s F M Brady & May Sands B; m 1937 to Juanita Porter; c Robert Francis. Educ: William Jewell Col, 32-34; Univ Mo, 34-37; Univ of Tex, Law Sch, summer 37; Kappa Alpha Order. Polit & Govt Pos: Prosecuting attorney, Benton Co, Mo, 49-54; chmn, Benton Co Rep Comt, 68 Mil Serv: Entered as Ens, US Naval Res, 44, released as Lt, 46, after serv in Amphibious Forces, Pac Ocean, invasion of Okinawa & second invasion of Philippines, 45-46; ribbons & one battle star. Mem: 29th Judicial Circuit Bar Asn (pres, 43-); Warsaw CofC (pres, 47-); 30th Judicial Circuit Bar Asn (pres, 65-); Benton Co Hist Soc; Lions. Relig: Southern Baptist. Legal Res: 716 W Jackson St Warsaw MO 65355 Mailing Add: Box 277 Warsaw MO 65355

BRADY, ELWARD T (D)
La State Rep
Mailing Add: Box 65-D Bayou Dularge Rte Houma LA 70360

BRADY, HAROLD EDWARD (D)
Chmn, Plymouth Co Dem Party, Iowa
b Marion, Ohio, Oct 6, 27; s Leonard Edward Brady & Jemima Ann Ault B; m 1948 to Mildred Elizabeth McGovern; c Barbara Ann (Mrs David Stanley) & Carol Jeanne. Educ: Marion Col, BA, 50; Evangel Theol Sem, BDiv, 56; Univ Wis-Madison, MS, 62; Univ SDak, EdD, 75. Polit & Govt Pos: Alt deleg, Dem Nat Conv, 72; chmn, Plymouth Co Dem Party, Iowa, 74- Mil Serv: Entered as A/S, Navy, 45, released as PO 3/C, 46. Mem: Am & Upper

Midwest Asns of Collegiate Registr & Admissions Officers; Rotary. Relig: United Methodist. Mailing Add: 1108 Cent Ave SE Le Mars IA 51031

BRADY, JAMES JOSEPH (D)
Mem, Dem State Cent Comt, La
b St Louis, Mo, Feb 29, 44; s Robert M Brady & Arlene Coleman B; m 1967 to Karen Nix; c James Sean & Kathleen Melissa. Educ: Southeastern La Univ, BA, 66; La State Univ Law Sch, JD, 69; pres, Student Body, Southeastern La Univ & La State Univ Law Sch. Polit & Govt Pos: Mem, Dem State Cent Comt, La, 70-; deleg, Dem Nat Mid-Term Conf, 74. Mem: La State Bar Asn (mem, House of Deleg, 74); La Trial Lawyers Asn; Alexandria Jaycees; LCQ Lamar Soc. Honors & Awards: Outstanding Sr, La State Univ Law Sch, 69. Relig: Baptist. Mailing Add: 6504 Joyce St Alexandria LA 71301

BRADY, RODNEY HOWARD (R)
b Sandy, Utah, Jan 31, 33; s Kenneth A Brady & Jessie Madsen B; m 1960 to Carolyn Ann (Mitzi) Hansen; c Howard Riley, Bruce Ryan & Brooks Alan. Educ: Univ Utah, BS & MBA, 57; Harvard Univ, DBA, 66; Phi Kappa Phi; Tau Kappa Alpha; Beta Gamma Sigma; Harvard Club. Polit & Govt Pos: Asst secy admin & mgt, Dept Health, Educ & Welfare, 70-72, adv & consult, 72- Bus & Prof Pos: Missionary, Church of Jesus Christ Latter-day Saints, 53-55; teaching assoc, Harvard Bus Sch, 57-59; vpres, Mgt Systs Corp, Cambridge, Mass, 62-65; vpres & mem exec comt, Aircraft Div, Hughes Tool Co, Culver City, Calif, 66-70; exec vpres, chmn exec comt & mem bd dirs, Bergen Brunswig Corp, 72-; chmn bd dirs, Health Appln Syst, 72-; chmn bd dirs, Uni-Managers Int; chmn, Nat Adv Comt, Univ Utah; mem, Nat Adv Coun to Brigham Young Univ & Harvard Univ; mem, Nat Comt Boy Scouts Am. Mil Serv: Entered as 2nd Lt, Air Force, 59, released as 1st Lt, 62, after serv in Auditor Gen Unit, US. Publ: Survey of management planning & control systems, 62; The impact of computers on top management decision making in the aerospace & defense industry, 66; Management by objectives in the public sector, Harvard Bus Rev, 73; plus others. Relig: Latter-day Saint; Chmn, President's Subcabinet Exec Off Group, 72. Mailing Add: Bergen Brunswig Corp 1900 Ave of the Stars Los Angeles CA 90067

BRAECKLEIN, BILL (D)
Tex State Sen
Mailing Add: 2273 First Nat Bank Bldg Dallas TX 75202

BRAGDON, ORSON H (R)
NH State Rep
b Wells, Maine, Aug 27, 02; m 1925 to Helen Newton; c 3 boys, 3 girls. Educ: Amherst High Sch. Polit & Govt Pos: Auditor, Town of Amherst, NH, 30 years; treas, Hillsborough Co Soil Conserv Dist; pres, NH Soil Conserv Dist Supvr Asn, formerly; pres, Hillsborough Co Farm Bur, formerly; NH State Rep, 57- Bus & Prof Pos: Dairy farmer. Mem: Amherst Men's Club. Relig: Congregational. Mailing Add: Amherst NH 03031

BRAGG, JOHN THOMAS (D)
Tenn State Rep
b Woodbury, Tenn, May 19, 18; s Minor Elam Bragg & Luree B; m 1945 to Annie Lee McElroy; c John T, Jr & David McElroy. Educ: Middle Tenn State Univ, BS; Univ Tenn, grad study in hist; Kappa Alpha. Polit & Govt Pos: Foreman, Rutherford Co Grand Jury, Tenn, 58-66; chmn, Rutherford Co Elec Comn, 60-63; Tenn State Rep, 65-68 & 71-, chmn, Finance, & Ways & Means Comts, Tenn House Rep, 72-; Dem Cand, US Rep, Tenn, 68; mem govt opers comt, Nat Legis Conf; chmn fiscal affairs & govt opers comt, Southern Legis Conf; mem-at-lg gov bd, Coun State Govts. Bus & Prof Pos: Publ, Rutherford Courier, Tenn, 46-58; pres, Courier Printing Co, 58- Mil Serv: Entered as Pvt, Air Force, 42, released as S/Sgt, 46. Mem: Am Legion; Farm Bur; Printing Indust of Am; Stones River Country Club; Sportsman's Club. Relig: Baptist. Legal Res: 1530 Mercury Blvd Murfreesboro TN 37130 Mailing Add: 320 South Church St Murfreesboro TN 37130

BRAILEY, TROY F (D)
Md State Deleg
Mailing Add: 2405 Baker St Baltimore MD 21216

BRAITHWAITE, MELANIE JANE (D)
b Delaware Co, Ohio, July 29, 41; d James Edward Cavendish & Patricia Worrell; m 1962 to Robert Oleh Braithwaite; c Robert Spencer, James Auburn & Charles Alistair. Educ: Ohio State Univ, BA in Hist, 73; Phi Alpha Theta. Polit & Govt Pos: Secy, Ohio State Univ Students & Faculty, Humphrey for President Comt; alt deleg-at-lg, Dem Nat Conv, 72; alt deleg, Dem State Conv, 74; deleg, Franklin Co Conv, 73 & 75. Bus & Prof Pos: Exec secy & pub rels coordr, several bus & univ pos, 62-72; admin spec in pub rels, Auditor of State of Ohio, 72-75. Publ: Managing ed, Ohio Archivist, Soc Ohio Archivists, 71-72; Annual Report of State of Ohio, Auditor of State of Ohio, 72, 73 & 74. Mem: Am Hist Asn; Franklin Co Young Dem; Am Asn Univ Women. Relig: Roman Catholic. Mailing Add: 22 Electric Ave Westerville OH 43081

BRAMBLETT, SANDRA GAIL (D)
b Atlanta, Ga, Sept 10, 49; d Homer Ralph Bramblett & Artholene Smith B; single. Educ: Univ Dijon, summer 70; Univ Ga, AB, cum laude, 71; Kappa Delta Epsilon; Kappa Delta Pi; Alpha Lambda Delta; Phi Beta Kappa. Polit & Govt Pos: Cong intern, US House of Rep, summer 71; legis intern, Ga House of Rep, spring 72; alt deleg, Dem Nat Conv, 72; asst press secy, US Sen Sam Nunn, Ga, 73- Bus & Prof Pos: Polit secy, Ga State Rep Gerald T Horton, The Research Group, 72-73. Honors & Awards: Honor's Day Participant, Univ Ga, 68-71, Top 10% Sr Class Award, 71. Relig: Baptist. Mailing Add: Rte 3 Cumming GA 30130

BRAMSON, GEORGE (D)
Chmn, Sacramento Co Dem Cent Comt, Calif
b Passaic, NJ, May 30, 28; s Reuben Bramson & Kazemira Kankowska B; m 1954 to Judith Ann Rubin; c Carolyn, Phyllis Ann & Peter Andrew. Educ: Lafayette Col, BS in metallurgical eng, 51. Polit & Govt Pos: Chmn, Sacramento Co Dem Cent Comt, Calif, 68- Bus & Prof Pos: Aerospace Prog mgr, Aerojet Solid Propulsion Co, Sacramento, Calif, 58- Mil Serv: Entered as 2nd Lt, Army Ord Corps, 55, released as 1st Lt, 58, after serv in Picatinny Arsenal, Dover, NJ. Mailing Add: 7809 Greenridge Way Fair Oaks CA 95628

BRAMSTEDT, ALVIN OSCAR (R)
b Cosmopolish, Wash, May 9, 17; s Oscar Bramstedt & Ruth Lindgren B; m 1940 to Rosa Lea Bailey; c Susan (Mrs Mellin), Janet (Mrs Felton), Alvin, Jr & Shelley Carol. Educ: Grays Harbor Jr Col, 36-37; Univ Wash, 38-39. Polit & Govt Pos: Chmn, Nixon-Agnew Campaign, Alaska, 68; chmn, Rep Party Alaska, 71-73. Bus & Prof Pos: Announcer, KXRO, Aberdeen, Wash, 34-39; announcer, KFAR, Fairbanks, Alaska, 40-43, mgr, 43-47, gen mgr, Midnight Sun Broadcasters, 47-59, pres, 59- Mem: Alaska Nippon Kai (chmn, 67-); March Dimes for Alaska (chmn, 63-); Alaska Broadcasters Asn; Alaska CofC (vpres, 68-). Honors & Awards: Alaska Man of the Year, 69. Relig: Protestant. Mailing Add: 2612 Brooke Dr Anchorage AK 99503

BRANCATO, JASPER M (D)
Mo State Sen
b Kansas City, Mo, Nov 26, 07; m 1942 to Zaira Follina; c Jo Ann (Mrs Cannova). Educ: Kansas City Sch Law. Polit & Govt Pos: Dem ward leader, Jackson Co, Mo; Mo State Sen, 56- Bus & Prof Pos: Real estate investor; vpres, Zaira Realty Corp. Mil Serv: Army, Qm Corps, World War II, 2 years. Mem: KofC (4 degree); Kansas City CofC; Mo Peace Officers Asn; Am Legion. Relig: Catholic. Mailing Add: 619 W 12th Kansas City MO 64106

BRANCH, MARSHA BAKER (D)
Mem Exec Comt, Ga Dem Party
b Baxley, Ga, Mar 13, 37; d Henry Grady Baker & Hulda Summerall B; m 1956 to Alvin Edward (Eddie) Branch; c Debra Charmaine, Michael Edward (Buddy), Marsha Maleia & Grady Stephen. Educ: Albany Jr Col, 69. Polit & Govt Pos: Mem bd dirs, League Women Voters, Albany, Ga, 68; mem, Comprehensive Health Planning Coun, 71-75; mem, Citizens Adv Comt, Albany, 72; mem & secy, Genesis Adv Coun, Baxley, 74; mem exec comt, Ga Dem Party, 75- Bus & Prof Pos: Real estate & farm mgr, Baxley, Ga, 74- Mem: DAR. Relig: Baptist. Mailing Add: Rte 3 Box 209 Baxley GA 31513

BRANCHINI, FRANK CAESAR (D)
b New Haven, Conn, Sept 9, 51; s Caesar Branchini & Anna Romanow B; single. Educ: Lake Forest Col, 69- Polit & Govt Pos: Youth coordr, Ottinger for Cong, NY, 68; adv, Students for Polit Action & Reform in Cortlandt, 70; coordr, Lake Forest Col Chap, Movement for a New Cong, Ill, 70; coordr, Lake Forest Col Students & Faculty for McGovern, 72; hq mgr, McGovern for President, 72; deleg, Dem Nat Conv, 72. Publ: Telephone tax resistance, Peace & Social Concerns Comt, Lake Forest Friends Meeting, 1/72; War tax resistance, Peale Kit, People's Ctr for Peace & Justice, 9/72. Mem: Dem Asn of Cortlandt; United Farm Workers Support Comt. Relig: Society of Friends. Mailing Add: 2 Cook Lane Croton-on-Hudson NY 10520

BRAND, EDWARD CABELL (D)
Mem, Salem Dem City Comt, Va
b Salem, Va, Apr 11, 23; s William Fitzgerald Brand & Ruth Cabell B; 2nd m 1964 to Shirley Hurt; c Sylvia Cabell, Miriam Holmes, Edward Cabell, Jr, Marshall Cabell, Ruth Elison Pence (Liza), Richard Franklin Pence, John Wilson Pence & Caroline Anthony. Educ: Va Mil Inst, BSEE, 44. Polit & Govt Pos: With Mil Govt & Dept of State, Europe, 2 years; mem, Salem Dem City Comt, Va, currently; alt deleg, Dem Nat Conv, 68. Bus & Prof Pos: Mem staff, Ortho-Vent Shoe Co, now Stuart McGuire Shoe Co, 49-, pres, 62-; chmn of bd, Brand-Edmonds Advert; part-time instr bus admin & sales mgt, Roanoke Col. Mil Serv: Army, 70th Inf Div, Europe, 4 years, Capt. Mem: Pres Asn of Am Mgt Asn; Young Pres Orgn; Int Platform Asn; Nat Indust Conf Bd; Newcomen Soc NAm. Honors & Awards: Outstanding Citizen Award, Dist 10, Va Coun of Soc Welfare, 67; Urban Serv Award, Off of Econ Opportunity, 67. Relig: Presbyterian. Legal Res: 701 W Main St Salem VA 34153 Mailing Add: PO Box 551 Salem VA 24153

BRANDENBURG, JOHN PETER (R)
Ohio State Rep
b Columbus, Ohio, Nov 11, 44; s W Paul Brandenburg & Virginia Moorman B; m 1967 to Colleen Ann Fitzpatrick. Educ: St Joseph's Col (Ind), BA, 66; Univ Cincinnati, Col Law, JD, 69; Loyola Univ, Rome, Italy, 64-65; Phi Alpha Delta. Polit & Govt Pos: Ohio State Rep, 73- Bus & Prof Pos: Attorney partner, Brandenburg, Slutsky & Issenmann, 69- Mem: Am & Cincinnati Bar Asns; Kiwanis. Relig: Catholic. Mailing Add: 2777 Montana Ave Cincinnati OH 45211

BRANDL, JOHN EDWARD (D)
b St Cloud, Minn, Aug 19, 37; s Edward Joseph Brandl & Mercedes Hiemenz B; m 1960 to Rochelle Ann Jankovich; c Christopher John, Mary Katherine & Amy Frances. Educ: St John's Univ, BA, 59; Harvard Univ, MA, 62 & PhD, 63. Polit & Govt Pos: Syst analyst, Off of the Secy Defense, 63-65, consult, 65-68; consult, Dept Comm, Off Econ Opportunity & Civil Serv Comn, 65-68; consult, Dept Health, Educ & Welfare, 65-68 & 69-, dep asst secy for educ planning, 68-69; mem, Gov Coun Econ Adv, Minn, currently. Bus & Prof Pos: Lectr econ, Boston Col, 61-62; research assoc Univ Minn, summer 62, dir, Sch Pub Affairs, 69-; teaching fel, Harvard Univ, 62-63; asst prof econ, St John's Univ, Minn, 65-67; dir educ prog, asst prof & research assoc, Univ Wis, 67-68; vis lectr, Univ Philippines, summer 68; vis prof, Univ Sydney, summer 73. Mil Serv: Entered Army, 63, released as 1st Lt, 65; Joint Serv Commendation Medal. Publ: Damage limiting: a rationale for the allocation of resources by the US & the USSR, classified mongr in Off Dir Defense Research, 64; Education program analysis at HEW, Joint Econ comt, Compendium, 69; On the treatment of incommensurables in cost-benefit analysis, Land Econ, 11/69. Mem: Am & Cath Econ Asns; Econometric Soc; Delta Epsilon Sigma; Tri-Cap, Inc. Honors & Awards: Named one of Outstanding Young Men of Am, US Jr CofC, 67. Relig: Catholic. Mailing Add: Sch of Pub Affairs Univ of Minn Minneapolis MN 55455

BRANDON, JAMES WILLIAM (D)
Mem Exec Comt, Ark Dem State Comt
b Poplar Bluff, Mo, July 19, 32; s James Alexander Brandon & Gerine Marshall B; m 1957 to Phyllis Louise Dillaha; c James Alexander, II & Philip Dillaha. Educ: Vanderbilt Univ, 50-52; Univ Ark, BSBA, 56; Blue Key; Alpha Kappa Psi; grand master, Kappa Sigma Xi Chap. Polit & Govt Pos: Nat chmn, Youth for Kefauver, 52; alt deleg, Dem Nat Conv, 56; pres, Pulaski Co Young Dem, Ark, 58 & 67; Ark State Rep Pulaski Co, 61-65; Ark State Sen, 15th Dist, Pulaski Co, 65-67; deleg, Ark Seventh Const Conv, 69; mem, Ark Dem State Comt, 70-, mem exec comt, 70-; deleg, Ark Dem State Conv, 72; arrangements chmn for Ark deleg, Dem Nat Conv, 72. Bus & Prof Pos: Student working in summer jobs for Sen Kefauver, Tenn & Gov McMath, Ark; acct exec, Ted Lamb & Assocs, Inc, 56-61; owner-operator, Brandon Advert Agency, 62- Mil Serv: Entered as 2nd Lt, Army Inf, 57, released as 1st Lt, Ret Res, after 6 months active duty at Ft Benning & Riley. Publ: Auth, Campaign of 1952, Ark Advocate, 9/72. Mem: Pulaski Co Ment Health Asn; Ark Advert Fedn; Ark Asn Ment Health; Leawood Heights Property Owners Asn; President's Club. Honors & Awards: Distinguished Alumnus Award, Little Rock Kappa Sigma Alumni Asn, 65. Relig: Episcopal; Former vestryman & Sunday sch teacher at Trinity Episcopal Cathedral Parish. Legal Res:

14 Wingfield Circle Little Rock AR 72205 Mailing Add: The Brandon Agency 301 Peoples Pl 301 Louisiana St Little Rock AR 72201

BRANDON, PHYLLIS DILLAHA (D)
Committeeman, Pulaski Co Dem Comt, Ark
b Little Rock, Ark, July 31, 35; d Calvin Arthur Dillaha & Vera Burt D; m 1957 to James William Brandon; c James Alexander, II & Philip Dillaha. Educ: Univ Ark, BA, 57; Mortar Bd; Kappa Kappa Gamma. Polit & Govt Pos: State chmn, Housewives for Humphrey/Muskie, Ark, 68; deleg, Dem Nat Conv, 68 & 72; committeeman, Pulaski Co Dem Comt, 68-; comnr, Pulaski Co Elec Comn, 70-; deleg, Ark State Dem Conv, 72; deleg, Pulaski Co Dem Conv, 72; pres, city-wide PTA Coun, 73- Bus & Prof Pos: Camera woman & reporter, KTHV TV Sta, 56; reporter, Ark Dem, 57; assoc ed, Home & Garden Sect, Ark Gazette, 58-59. Publ: Many articles concerning Little Rock, when fed troops were sent there to open schs in 57; plus others. Mem: Leawood Garden Club; Pulaski Co Asn Ment Health; Brady PTA. Relig: Episcopal; pres, Cathedral Churchwomen, Trinity Episcopal Parish, 73- Mailing Add: 14 Wingfield Circle Little Rock AR 72205

BRANDOW, GEORGE WILLIAM (R)
b Elmore, Ohio, Sept 28, 14; s Albert A Brandow & Emma S Croll B; m 1935 to Emeline Bahnsen; c Robert Henry & Jean Louise. Polit & Govt Pos: Secy, US Rep, Ohio, 48 & 49; chmn, Ottawa Co Rep Cent & Exec Comt, formerly; mem, Ottawa Co Elec Bd, 58-62; deleg, Rep Nat Conv, 60. Bus & Prof Pos: Owner, George W Brandow Agency, 45-; pres, Bank of Elmore Co, 62-; vpres, Walbridge-Lake Ins Agency, 63- Mil Serv: Entered as Pvt, Army, 43, released as S/Sgt, 45, after serv in 5th Serv Command; Pvt, 148th Inf Ohio Nat Guard, 32-35. Mem: Ottawa Co Ins Agents Asn; F&AM; Scottish Rite; Grotto; Shrine. Relig: United Church of Christ. Mailing Add: 143 E Rice St Elmore OH 43416

BRANDT, DIANE (D)
Iowa State Rep
Mailing Add: 3705 Hillside Dr Cedar Falls IA 50613

BRANDT, DONALD EDWARD (R)
Chmn, Ramsey Co Rep Party, Minn
b Wells, Minn, Nov 12, 25; s Ervin Brandt & Caroline Luddeke B; m 1950 to Reva Jean Bannister; c Carolyn Jean & Terry Louise. Educ: Gustavus Adolphus Col; Harvard Univ; Univ Minn, BA, 48; Chi Phi. Polit & Govt Pos: Local & legis campaign chmn, 62-70; chmn, Ramsey Co Rep Party, Minn, 70- Bus & Prof Pos: Exec secy, Minneapolis Aquatennial, 58-60; pres, Northwestern Indust Ed, 66; pub rels coordr, Minn Mining & Mfg Co, 68- Mil Serv: Entered as A/S, Navy, 43, released as Lt(jg), 46, after serv in USS Hope & Renville, Pac, 45-46. Mem: Mason. Relig: Lutheran. Mailing Add: 958 Woodlynn St Paul MN 55113

BRANDT, JOHN B (D)
Ill State Sen
Mailing Add: 2719 W Logan Blvd Chicago IL 60647

BRANDT, KENNETH (R)
Pa State Rep
b Lancaster Co, Pa, Nov 17, 38; s Amos Franklin Brandt & Anna Ebersole B; m 1958 to Jean Marie; c Kenneth Edward, Kirby Eugene, Kelly Louise, Karen Ann & Kevin Ellis. Educ: Elizabethtown Area High Sch. Polit & Govt Pos: Mem sch bd, Elizabethtown Area Sch Dist, 69-; Pa State Rep, 98th Legis Dist, 73- Bus & Prof Pos: Owner, A F Brandt's Sons, Elizabethtown, Pa, 60- Mem: Elizabethtown Jaycees (secy, first vpres, pres & chmn bd, 60-); Pa Jaycees; US Jaycees. Honors & Awards: JCI Senatorship, Elizabethtown Jaycees, 71. Relig: Protestant. Legal Res: Village of Falmouth Bainbridge PA 17502 Mailing Add: Pennsylvania House of Reps House PO Harrisburg PA 17120

BRANDT, NEILL MATTESON (R)
Mem, Sturbridge Rep Town Comt, Mass
b Orange, NJ, May 12, 15; s Neill O Brandt & Dorothy Matteson B; m 1941 to Dorothy Elizabeth Engelmann; c Mary Kathleen & Elizabeth Krista. Educ: St Lawrence Univ, BS, 37; grad study, Univ Rochester, Univ Pittsburgh & Worcester Polytech Inst. Polit & Govt Pos: Mem, Sturbridge Rep Town Comt, Mass, 64-; moderator, Town of Sturbridge, 70- Bus & Prof Pos: Sci instr, Richfield Springs, NY, 37-42; chemist, Bausch & Lomb, 42-46; fel, Mellon Inst, 47-53, sr fel, 53-59; sr staff physicist, Am Optical Co, 59-64, chief physicist, 64- Mem: Am Chem Soc; Am Ceramic Soc; British Soc Glass Tech. Relig: Catholic. Mailing Add: Cedar St Sturbridge MA 01566

BRANDT, WILLIAM B (R)
Mem, Nebr Rep State Cent Comt
b Unadilla, Nebr, Dec 4, 24; m 1947 to Rose Marie Stoner; c Robert W, Karen Sue, Joan Marie, Jane Elizabeth. Educ: Nebr State Teachers Col; Univ Idaho; Univ Nebr, BS, 49, JD, 52. Polit & Govt Pos: Nebr State Sen, 61-64; chmn, Otoe Co Rep Party, formerly; mem, Nebr Rep State Cent Comt, currently; mem, Nebr Rep State Finance Comt, currently. Bus & Prof Pos: Attorney & dir, Unadilla First Nat Bank & The Am Bank, Burr, Nebr. Mil Serv: Army Res. Mem: Nat Packers & Stockyards Adv Comt; Am Legion; VFW. Mailing Add: Unadilla NE 68454

BRANIGIN, ROGER DOUGLAS (D)
b Franklin, Ind, July 26, 02; s Elba L Branigin & Zula Francis B; m 1929 to Josephine Mardis; c Roger D, Jr & Robert M. Educ: Franklin Col, AB, 23; Harvard Univ, LLB, 26; Phi Delta Phi; Theta Alpha Phi; Alpha Phi Omega; Phi Delta Theta. Hon Degrees: LLD, Franklin Col, 56, Butler Univ, 65, Ind Univ, 69, Vincennes Univ, 70, & Ind State Univ, 72. Polit & Govt Pos: Gen counsel, Fed Land Bank, Louisville, Ky, 30-38; Gen Counsel, Farm Credit Admin of Louisville & Related Banks, 33-38; chmn, Tippecanoe Dem Co Cent Comn, Ind, 38-56; permanent chmn, Dem State Conv, 48; chmn, Conserv Comn, Ind, 48-50; Gov, Ind, 65-69; deleg, Dem Nat Conv, 68. Bus & Prof Pos: Dir, Lafayette Life Ins Co, Lafayette Nat Bank & Gen Tel Co of Ind, 58-; dir, Nat Home Corp, 66-; partner, Stuart, Branigin, Ricks & Schilling, Lafayette, 69- Mil Serv: Entered as Capt, Judge Adv Gen Dept, Army, 42, released as Lt Col, 46, after serv as chief, legal div, Transportation Corps, Washington, DC, 44-46; Legion of Merit; Army Commendation Medal. Mem: Am Col of Trial Lawyers; Am Law Inst; Am Col Probate Coun; Am Judicature Soc; Ind State Bar Asn; other civic & prof orgns. Relig: Baptist; Am Baptist Conv. Legal Res: 611 S Seventh St Lafayette IN 47901 Mailing Add: Eighth Floor Life Bldg Lafayette IN 47902

BRANN, KEITH EDWARD (R)
Secy, Preble Co Rep Cent & Exec Comts, Ohio
b Richmond, Ind, Dec 31, 38; s Virgil Milo Brann & Elsie Louise Grooms B; m 1960 to Judy Carolyn Maggard; c Martin Allen, Michael Lee & D'Arcy Linette. Educ: Ball State Univ, 1 year. Polit & Govt Pos: Secy, Preble Co Rep Cent & Exec Comts, Ohio, 67- Mem: Eaton Jaycees; Eaton Area CofC (treas, 71-); Preble Co Young Rep; Am Cancer Soc; Eaton Community Chest (treas). Mailing Add: 425 N Barron St Eaton OH 45320

BRANNAN, CHARLES F (D)
b Denver, Colo, Aug 23, 03; s John B & Ella Louise Street B; m 1932 to Eda V Seltzer. Educ: Univ Denver, LLB, 29, LLD, 48; DSc, Colo Agr & Mech Col, 48; Sigma Alpha Epsilon. Polit & Govt Pos: Asst regional attorney, resettlement admin, US Dept Agr, Denver, 35-37, regional attorney, solicitor's off, Denver, 37-41, regional dir, Farm Security Admin, 41-44, assoc adminr, 44, Asst Secy Agr, 44-48, Secy Agr, 48-53. Bus & Prof Pos: Attorney, 29-35; gen counsel, Nat Farmers Union, Denver, 53-; mem bd dirs, Cent Bank & Trust Co, Colo; mem bd dirs, World Health Found, Tex; mem, Bd of Water Comnr, Denver. Mem: Athletic Club, Denver; Int Club of Wash, Inc, Washington, DC. Mailing Add: 3131 E Alameda Denver CO 80209

BRANNEN, JAMES HENRY, III (R)
Mem, Rep Town Comt Colchester, Conn
b Queens, NY, Dec 25, 40; s James H Brannen & Barbara Halsey B; m 1965 to Wendy Elaine Simmons; c Keree Nicole & Myia. Educ: Northrop Inst Technol, BSAAE, 64; Wash Col Law, 64-66; Alpha Eta Rho; Am Inst Aeronaut & Astronaut. Polit & Govt Pos: Mem, Vice President Task Force on Youth Motivation, Washington, DC, 66-67; deleg, Rep State Conv, 72, Rep State Dist Conv, 72; Conn State Rep, 48th Assembly Dist, 73-74; mem, Rep Town Comt of Colchester, currently; Rep cand for US Senate, Conn, 74; mem, Spec Comt to Study Rep Party, Conn. Bus & Prof Pos: Pilot, United Airlines, 67- Mem: Air Line Pilots Asn; Jaycees (vpres, 72-73). Honors & Awards: Merit, Task Force on Youth Motivation, 67; Jaycee of Month, Conn Jaycees, 72. Mailing Add: Palmer Rd RFD 2 Colchester CT 06415

BRANON, ROBERT J (D)
Chmn, Vt Dem State Party
Polit & Govt Pos: Vt State Sen, 75- Mailing Add: Fairfield VT 05455

BRANSCOMB, ANNE WELLS (D)
b Statesboro, Ga, Nov 22, 28; d Guy Herbert Wells & Ruby Hammond W; m 1951 to Lewis McAdory Branscomb; c Harvie Hammond & Katharine Capers. Educ: Univ NC, Chapel Hill, BA, 49; London Sch Econ, 50-51; Radcliffe Col, MA, 51; George Washington Univ, JD, 62; Rotary Found fel, 50; Order of the Coif; Phi Beta Kappa; Pi Gamma Mu; Valkyries; Alpha Psi Omega; Pi Beta Phi. Polit & Govt Pos: Secy, Western Suburban Dem Club, Montgomery Co, Md, 56-57; Dem precinct committeewoman, Boulder Co, 64; pres, Dem Women of Boulder, 64-65; secy, Boulder Co Dem Cent Comt, 65-67; deleg, co, cong & state Dem conv, 66; historian, Colo Dem Assembly, 66; vchmn, Colo Dem State Cent Comt, 67-69; Colo coordr for citizens groups, Humphrey-Muskie Presidential Campaign, 68; deleg, Dem Nat Conv, 68; hearing officer, Credentials Comt, 72; chmn, Colo State Dem Comn to Study Elective Processes, 69; comnr, Boulder Housing Authority, 69-70; exec asst to nat campaign dir, McGovern-Shriver Campaign, 72. Bus & Prof Pos: Intel officer, Cent Intel Agency, Washington, DC, 51; research assoc, Pierson, Ball & Dowd, Attorneys, Washington, DC, 62; law clerk, US Dist Court, Colo, 62-63; assoc, Williams & Zook, Attorneys, Boulder, Colo, 63-66; pvt practice, 66-69; attorney, Arnold & Porter, Washington, DC, 69-72; commun counr, Teleprompter Corp, 73; vpres, Kalba-Bowen Assoc Inc, 74- Publ: A crisis of identity: Public broadcasting and the law, Pub Telecommun Rev, 2/75; The cable fable, will it come true?, J Commun, winter 75. Mem: Am, NY & DC Bar Asns; Am Polit Sci Asn; Fed Commun Bar; Women's Nat Dem Club. Relig: Protestant. Mailing Add: Five Hidden Oak Lane Armonk NY 10504

BRANSON, DALE R (D)
Idaho State Rep
b Craigmont, Idaho, June 21, 24; s D Lester Branson & Helen Houchens B; m 1946 to Arleen Johnson; c George N, James L, Susan K, Patsy A, Robert D & David W. Educ: Santa Monica Bus Col, 43. Polit & Govt Pos: Mayor, Nezperce, Idaho, 60-62; chmn, Lewis Co Dem Cent Comt, formerly; Idaho State Rep, 73- Bus & Prof Pos: Asst mgr, Dokken Implement Co, Nezperce, 48- Mem: Lewis Co Wheatgrowers Asn; Lions; Elks. Relig: Lutheran. Mailing Add: 502 Walnut Nezperce ID 83543

BRANSON, IVAN THORPE (R)
Chmn, Nevada Co Cent Rep Comt, Calif
b Mariposa, Calif, Nov 9, 01; s Alvin Thorpe Branson & Mary Eliza Simmons B; m 1962 to Signe Linnea Zettergren; c Kathryn (Mrs Ferrera), Bill R, Walter Thorpe & James Ivan. Educ: High sch, Stockton, Calif, 14-19. Polit & Govt Pos: Mem, Draft Bd 88, San Francisco, Calif, 41-46; Nat Exchange Club rep consult, Dept of State, Orgn UN, 45; chmn, Nevada Co Cent Rep Comt, Calif, 70- Bus & Prof Pos: Morse Telegrapher, various corp, 19-31; pres, Commercial Telegraphers Union, Pac Coast Broker Div, 29-31; founder & pres, Morning Glory Caterers, San Francisco, Calif, 31-65; owner, Cow Ranch, Morning Glory Ranch, 65- Mem: Islam Temple, AAONMS (potentate, 57); CofC; Tahoe Cattlemens Asn (dir, 65-75); Ready-Springs Sch (mem, elem sch bd, 75-); Golden Chain Coun of the Mother Lode, Inc, (immediate past pres, Auburn, Calif). Honors & Awards: Presidential Citation from H S Truman for draft bd work. Relig: Protestant. Legal Res: Indian Springs Rd Rough & Ready CA 95975 Mailing Add: Box 246-X Star Rte Rough & Ready CA 95975

BRANSTAD, TERRY EDWARD (R)
Iowa State Rep
b Leland, Iowa, Nov 17, 46; s Edward Arnold Branstad & Rita Garland B; m 1972 to Christine Ann Johnson. Educ: Univ Iowa, BA, 69; Drake Univ Law Sch, 71-72. Polit & Govt Pos: Iowa State Rep, 73- Mil Serv: Entered as Pvt E-1, Army, 69, released as Sgt E-5, 71, after serv in 503rd Mil Police Bn, 70-71; Army Commendation Medal; Soldier of the Quarter, First Quarter, 1971. Mem: Am Legion; Winnebago Co Farm Bur. Relig: Catholic. Legal Res: RR Lake Mills IA 50450 Mailing Add: State House of Reps Des Moines IA 50319

BRANSTOOL, CHARLES EUGENE (D)
Ohio State Rep
b Mt Vernon, Ohio, Dec 13, 36; s Charles H Branstool & Bonnie Motter B; m 1958 to Mary Jo Torrens; c Mary Martha, Marshall, John, David & Chuck. Educ: Ohio State Univ, BS in Agr, 58; Alpha Gamma Sigma. Polit & Govt Pos: Pres, North Fork Bd Educ, Utica, Ohio, 68-74; Ohio State Rep, Dist One, 75- Bus & Prof Pos: Partner, Branstool Bros Gen Farming,

Utica, Ohio, 62- Mil Serv: Entered as A/S, Navy, 59, released as Lt, Naval Res, after serv in Explosive Ordnance Disposal Unit, Naval Ammunition Depot, Portsmouth, Va, 59-62. Mem: Licking Farm Bur; Am Legion; Sertoma; Jaycees. Honors & Awards: Outstanding Utica Area Jaycee, Jaycees, 68; Ohio Outstanding Young Farmer, 70; Hon Chap Farmer, Utica Future Farmer of Am. Relig: Presbyterian. Mailing Add: Star Rte Utica OH 43080

BRANTLEY, HASKEW HAWTHORNE, JR (R)
Ga State Sen
b Birmingham, Ala, Sept 28, 22; s Haskew Hawthorne Brantley & Maggie Lee Hicks B; m 1948 to Miriam Laughlin; c Jaquelyn Marie, Margaret Lynn, Susan Elizabeth & Michael David. Educ: Ga Inst Technol, BS, 48; Sigma Alpha Epsilon. Polit & Govt Pos: Ga State Rep, 14th Dist, 66-74; Ga State Sen, 74- Bus & Prof Pos: Pres, Am Tire Co, 58-66; vpres, Brantley-Katz Co Inc, 66- Mil Serv: Entered as Cadet, Navy, 42, released as Lt, 46, after serv as Naval Aviator. Mem: Ga Asn of Retarded Children (dir); Atlanta & Decalb Real Estate Bds; Atlanta & Cherokee Country Clubs. Relig: Episcopal. Mailing Add: 6114 Riverside Dr NW Atlanta GA 30328

BRANTLEY, LEW (D)
Fla State Sen
Mailing Add: 326 Senate Off Bldg Tallahassee FL 32304

BRANTON, RAYMOND (D)
Mem, Ark Dem State Comt
b Corsicana, Tex, Oct 5, 24; s Lonnie Wilson Branton & Rachael Wood B; m 1949 to Lois Walker; c Raymond, Jr, Mary Laurel & Amelia Kay. Educ: Univ Ark, Fayetteville, BArch; Theta Tau. Polit & Govt Pos: Mem, Pulaski Co Dem Comt, Ark, 69-75; mem, Ark Dem State Comt, 74- Bus & Prof Pos: Architect, Little Rock, Ark, 58- Mil Serv: Entered as Pvt, Marine Corps, 44, released as Sgt, 46, after serv in 4th Aircraft Wing, Pac Theatre, 45-46. Mem: Am Inst Architects; Nat Exchange Club. Relig: Episcopal. Mailing Add: 30 Pine Tree Loop North Little Rock AR 72116

BRANYON, EDGAR WATTERSON (D)
Chmn, Marion Co Dem Party, Ala
b Kennedy, Ala, Sept 28, 90; s John S Branyon & Alpha Smith B; m 1919 to Nell Emily Walker; c Dr E W, Jr & Mary Nell. Educ: Florence Univ, 2 years; Peabody Col, BS, 16, MA, 19; Cornell Univ, grad work, 24. Polit & Govt Pos: Supt educ, Marion Co, Ala, 40-50; chmn, Marion Co Dem Party, currently. Bus & Prof Pos: Teacher, Rural Schs, Fayette Co, Ala, Walker Co High Sch, Jasper, Cent High Sch, Jackson, Miss, 13-16 & Alabertville High Sch, Ala, 20-27; prin, Hamilton High Sch, Ala, 27-35. Mil Serv: Pfc, Chem Warfare Serv, Astoria, NY, 18-19. Publ: People Are Funny, 50; History of Marion County Alabama, 60; History of My Life, 65. Mem: Mason; Civitan Club. Relig: Baptist; treas, Hamilton Baptist Church, 27-60, lifetime Deacon, 20- Mailing Add: Box 307 Hamilton AL 35570

BRASCO, FRANK J (D)
b Brooklyn, NY, Oct 15, 32; m 1959 to Linda Gralla; c Lauren, Arthur, Meredith & Jennifer. Educ: Brooklyn Col, BA, 54; Brooklyn Law Sch, LLB, 57; Brooklyn Col & Law Sch Alumni Asns. Polit & Govt Pos: Mem, Kings Co Dem Exec Comt, NY, exec mem, Kings Co Young Dem & asst dist attorney, Kings Co, formerly; US Rep, NY, 67-74; deleg, Dem Nat Mid-Term Conf, 74. Bus & Prof Pos: Attorney-at-law. Mil Serv: Army, Inf, 58, Army Res; 4th Judge Adv Gen Detachment Unit, NY, Capt; USA Res Officers' Asn. Mem: Old Mill Civic Asn (bd of dir); Kings Co Criminal Bar Asn; Police Athletic League; Brownsville Boys' Club; Abe Stark Philanthropies, Inc (bd mem). Relig: Roman Catholic. Mailing Add: 650 Autumn Ave Brooklyn NY 11208

BRASSEY, VERNON K (R)
Idaho State Sen
Mailing Add: 3200 Treasure Dr Boise ID 83703

BRASWELL, THOMAS EDWARD, JR (D)
b Elm City, NC, Feb 24, 21; s Thomas Edward Braswell & Sadie Moore McCauley B; div; c John McCauley; Harry Armstrong, Thomas Edward, III & Andrew Sutherland. Educ: Duke Univ, AB, 42; Harvard Bus Sch, 42-43; Harvard Law Sch, LLB, 48. Polit & Govt Pos: Attorney, Dept Justice, 48-51; prof staff mem, Comt on Armed Servs, US Senate, 53-69, chief counsel & staff dir, 69- Mil Serv: Entered as Enlisted, Air Force, 42, released as Capt, 46, recalled to active duty, Korean War, 51, released as Maj, 53; Col, Air Force Res; World War II Victory Medal, Am Theater Award; Asiatic Pac Theater Award. Mem: City of Alexandria Planning Comn (chmn, 69-); Alexandria Bd Architectural Review); Alexandria Libr Co; NC & DC Bar. Relig: Protestant; St Paul's Episcopal Church, Alexandria. Mailing Add: 1200 S Washington St Apt 223E Alexandria VA 22314

BRATAAS, NANCY OSBORN (R)
Minn State Sen
b Minneapolis, Minn, Jan 19, 28; d John Draper Osborn & Flora Warner O; m 1948 to Mark Gerard Brataas; c Mark Gaylord & Anne Draper. Educ: Univ Minn, 2 years, Alpha Phi. Polit & Govt Pos: Pres, Olmsted Co Rep Workshop, Minn, 57-59; city chairwoman, Olmsted Co Rep Party, 58-59, co chairwoman, 59-61; deleg, Rep Nat Conv, 60, 64 & 68; vchairwoman, Minn Rep Party, 61-63, chairwoman, 63-69; chairwoman, Minn Rep Finance Comt, 69-73; Minn State Sen, 75-, mem educ comt, labor & com comt & select comt on nursing homes, Minn State Senate, 75- Bus & Prof Pos: Data processing consult, Kans Gubernatorial Primary, 70; polit consult, Irwin Mgt Co, Columbus, Ind, 71; dir nat tel campaign, Comt Reelection of President, Washington, DC, 72; owner, Nancy Brataas Assocs, 73; state planning & mgt consult, Mich Gov Milliken's Voter Contact Prog, 74; data processing & mgt consult, Northeast Chap March Dimes, Cleveland, Ohio, 74. Am Asn Univ Women; League Women Voters; Zonta Int. Honors & Awards: Testimonial Dinner, 69. Relig: Episcopal. Legal Res: 839 10 1/2 St SW Rochester MN 55901 Mailing Add: 113 State Off Bldg St Paul MN 55155

BRATTON, RICHARD WALDO (R)
Chmn, Weston Co Rep Cent Comt, Wyo
b Basin, Wyo, Feb 28, 33; s Ralph Waldo Bratton & Madeliene Baker B; m 1959 to Alice Walk Peckham; c Richard John, Randall James & Beth Imogene. Educ: Mont State Univ, BS, 60; M-Club; Varsity Basketball. Polit & Govt Pos: Finance chmn, Custer Co Rep Cent Comt, SDak, 66, chmn, 68-72; city councilman, Custer City, 66-67, mayor, 68-72, pres, SDak Munic League, 70-72; chmn, Weston Co Rep Cent Comt, Wyo, 72- Bus & Prof Pos: Vpres, Custer Develop Corp, 67-69; mem bd, SDak Elec Mediation Bd, 70-71; mem bd dirs, Wyo Bus Polit Comt, 72- Mil Serv: Entered as Pvt, Marines, released as Sgt, 59, after serv in Ninth Marine Regt, Third Marine Div, Japan & Okinawa, 56-59; Good Conduct Medal; Bn Honorman; Marine Recruit Depot, San Diego. Mem: Bus-Indust Polit Action Comt; SDak Elec Coun Custer Rotary Club; Black Hills Area Coun, Boy Scouts; Custer CofC; Newcastle Lions Club, Wyo (bd dirs, 72-). Honors & Awards: Presidential Award of Honor, Newcastle Jaycees, Newcastle, Wyo; Citation for Loyalty awarded by Custer VFW, 69; Pub Servant of the Year awarded by Custer Jaycees, 70. Relig: Episcopal. Mailing Add: 220 Highland Newcastle WY 82701

BRATTON, ROBERT WELLS (R)
Finance Chmn, Rep Party, Wash
b Chehalis, Wash, Feb 26, 31; s Robert Bratton & Alma Wells B; m 1954 to Aileen Marie Connolly; c Michael Scott, Christine Ann & Robert Daniel. Educ: Whitman Col, BA, 53. Polit & Govt Pos: Rep area chmn, 48th Legis Dist, King Co, Wash, 60-61, precinct committeeman, 60-65, finance chmn, 62-63, dist chmn, 64 & 65; neighbor to neighbor chmn, King Co, 64; dist chmn, 41st Legis Dist, King Co, 65-66, precinct committeeman, 65-70; chmn, King Co Dan Evans for Gov Comt, 68; mem steering comt, John Spellman for Co Exec, 69; finance chmn, Rep Party, Wash, 70- Bus & Prof Pos: Salesman, Int Bus Machines Corp, Seattle, 56-68, dist mkt rep, 69- Mil Serv: Entered as Pvt, Army, 53, released as Sgt, 56, after serv in Finance Corps, 6th Army, 54-56. Mem: Wash State Heart Asn; Whitman Col Alumni Asn; Wash Athletic Club; Mercer Island Country Club. Honors & Awards: First winner of Int Bus Machine Corp Community Activity Award for 11 western states, 69; Distinguished Wash Citizen Award, 69. Relig: Protestant. Mailing Add: 6207 82nd SE Mercer Island WA 98040

BRAULT, ADELARD LIONEL (D)
Va State Sen
b Winsted, Conn, Apr 6, 09; m to Clarice Louise Covington. Educ: Columbus Univ Sch Law, LLB. Polit & Govt Pos: Mem, Fairfax Bd Co Supvr, 62-63; Va State Sen, 66- Bus & Prof Pos: Lawyer. Mil Serv: Lt Comdr, Navy. Mem: Fairfax Co Bar Asn; Am & Va State Bar Asns. Relig: Catholic. Mailing Add: PO Box 248 Fairfax VA 22030

BRAUN, ART (D)
Minn State Rep
Mailing Add: State Capitol Bldg St Paul MN 55155

BRAUN, CARL P (D)
Idaho State Rep
Mailing Add: RR 1 Orofino ID 83544

BRAUN, VIRGINIA MARY (R)
Mem, Rep State Cent Comt of Calif
b Detroit, Mich, Dec 5, 17; d Judson Bradway (deceased) & Florence Elizabeth Michell D; m 1940 to Henry August Braun; c Henry Michael, Barbara Michell (Mrs Telford Alander Walker), Judson & Cynthia Gilbert. Educ: Briarcliff Jr Col, 1 year; Garland Jr Col; Alumna Garland Col; pres, freshman class, Briarcliff Jr Col & Garland Jr Col. Polit & Govt Pos: Precinct capt, Rep Hq, Pasadena & Los Angeles, Calif, 50-69; mem bd, San Marino Rep Women's Club Federated, 61-66, prog chmn, three years; deleg, State & Nat Conv Rep Federated Women, 64-68; mem, Los Angeles Co Rep Finance Comt, 64-69; mem Women's Div, Freedoms Found Valley Forge, Los Angeles, 64-69; founder & pres, Pasadena Rep Women's Club Federated, 67-69, adv bd, 69-, protocol chmn, 71-73, resolutions chmn, 73; registr of voters, 67-; alt deleg, Rep Nat Conv, 68 & 72; mem, Calif Rep State Cent Comt, currently; asst secy, Calif Br of Patriotic Educ, Inc, currently; protocol chmn, Calif State Bd of Federated Women, currently; citizens chmn, Los Angeles Co Fedn of Rep Women, Inc, 70, resolutions chmn, 71-73; mem Gov Reagan's Comn, Teachers' Prep & Licensing, 71-74; mem Los Angeles Co Rep Bd Southern Div, Calif Rep Women Federated, 72 & 73. Bus & Prof Pos: Dance teacher, Arthur Murray Studio, Detroit, Mich, 39. Mem: Pasadena Jr League; Pasadena Guild Childrens Hosp; Nine O'Clock Players; Civic League of Pasadena; Costume Coun Los Angeles Art Mus. Relig: Congregational. Mailing Add: 1585 Orlando Rd Pasadena CA 91106

BRAUN, WALTER W (R)
b Virginia, Nebr, Feb 18, 30; s Frederick W Braun & Viola Snyder B; m 1951 to Louise Woltemath; c Judith Ann, Kathryn Jean & Shauna Lee. Educ: Commercial Exten Sch Com, 2 years. Polit & Govt Pos: Secy, Beatrice Park Bd, Nebr, 65-; chmn, Gage Co Rep Cent Comt, formerly. Bus & Prof Pos: Nat bank examr, comptroller of currency, US Treas Dept, 55-58; vpres, Beatrice Nat Bank, Nebr, 68- Mil Serv: Entered as Pvt, Air Force, 50, as S/Sgt, 54, after serv in 566th Air Defence Group, 50-54. Mem: Jaycees (past pres); Sertoma Club (dir); CofC (first vpres). Honors & Awards: Beatrice Outstanding Young Man Award, 63; Nebr Distinguished Serv Award, 64, Jr Chamber Int Senatorship. Relig: Lutheran. Mailing Add: 400 Morton Dr Beatrice NE 68310

BRAY, CLAUDE A, JR (D)
Ga State Rep
b West Point, Ga, July 14, 32; s Claude A Bray & Fay Smith B; m 1955 to Carolyn Ann Irwin; c Charles Bradley, Claudia Allison & Carolyn Ann. Educ: Univ Ga, LLB, 54; Gridiron; Phi Eta Sigma; Biftad; pres, Law Students Adv Coun; chief justice, Honor Court, Law Sch; pres, Student Bar; Sigma Nu. Polit & Govt Pos: Co attorney, Meriwether Co, Ga, 65-66; Ga State Rep, 31st Dist, 66-72, 66th Dist, 72-, vchmn state of repub comt, Ga House Rep, 70-, mem judiciary & ways & means comts, currently. Bus & Prof Pos: Mem bd dirs, Hometown Loan Corp, Manchester, 66- & Meriwether Fed Savings & Loan Asn, 68- Mil Serv: Entered as 1st Lt, Air Force, 54, released as Capt, 56, after serv in Hq, Judge Adv Gen, 14th Air Force, 54-56; Capt, Air Force Res. Mem: Ga State Judicial Circuit Bar Asn; Manchester Jaycees; Franklin D Roosevelt Little White House Mem Comn; Manchester CofC (bd dirs); Kiwanis. Relig: Baptist. Legal Res: 111 Mayes Way Manchester GA 31816 Mailing Add: 105 Broad St Manchester GA 31816

BRAY, JAMES HOUSTON (JAMIE) (D)
Co Comnr, Harris Co, Tex
b Louisville, Miss, Nov 29, 26; s McKinley Charles Bray & Irnie Mae Miller B; m 1948 to Joveda Murphy; c Deborah Jo (Mrs Hutson), James Houston Jr & Monroe LaMonte. Educ: High Sch. Polit & Govt Pos: Tex State Rep, 24th Legis Dist, Pos Six, formerly; Co Comnr, Precinct Two, Harris Co, 71- Bus & Prof Pos: Pres & chmn bd, Ascot, Inc, 55- Mil Serv: Entered as Seaman, Merchant Marine, 43, released as Lt(jg), 51, after serv in various theatres, 43-51. Mem: Nat Burglar & Fire Alarm Asn; Rotary; Mason; Shrine; Pasadena Rodeo Asn (dir). Relig: Methodist; Bd Stewards, First Methodist Church. Legal Res: 1313 Skylark Pasadena TX 77502 Mailing Add: PO Box 6247 Pasadena TX 77506

BRAY, RICHARD D (R)
Ind State Rep
Mailing Add: 389 E Washington St Martinsville IN 46151

BRAY, WILLIAM GILMER (R)
b Mooresville, Ind, June 17, 03; s Gilmer Bray & Dorcas Mitchell B; m 1930 to Esther Debra; c Richard D. Educ: Ind Univ, LLB, 27; Tau Kappa Alpha; Acacia. Hon Degrees: LLD, Vincennes Univ. Polit & Govt Pos: Prosecuting attorney, Morgan Co, 27-31; temporary chmn, Rep State Conv; precinct committeeman, Rep Party, Ind; US Rep, Ind, 51-74, ranking minority mem, Armed Serv Comt, US House of Rep, formerly. Bus & Prof Pos: Attorney-at-law, pvt practice. Mil Serv: Entered as Capt, Army, 41, released as Col, 46, after serv in 193rd & 767th Tank Bn, Fourth Armored Group, Mil Govt, Korea, Asiatic-Pac Theater; Col, Army Res, 46-63; Silver Star. Publ: Russian frontiers; from Muscovy to Khrushchev, Bobbs-Merrill Co, Inc, 63. Mem: Armor Asn (dir); Am Legion; VFW; Amvets; Mason (33 degree). Relig: Quaker. Mailing Add: 489 N Jefferson St Martinsville IN 46151

BRAYMAN, HAROLD HALLIDAY (R)
b Washington, DC July 11, 35; s Harold Brayman & Martha Wood B; c Sarah Elizabeth Gardiner & Harold Halliday, Jr. Educ: Princeton Univ, AB, 57; London Sch Econ, 57-58; Columbia Univ Sch of Jour, MSJ, 59. Polit & Govt Pos: Legis asst, US Sen, J Caleb Boggs, Del, 69-70; mem prof staff, Pub Works Comt, US Senate, 70- Bus & Prof Pos: Staff writer, Detroit News, 59-61; Staff Writer, Nat Observer, 61-69. Publ: Living with Inflation, Dow Jones & Co, 67. Mem: Sigma Delta Chi; Nat Press Club. Relig: Presbyterian. Mailing Add: Apt 4 1719 35th St NW Washington DC 20007

BREATHITT, EDWARD THOMPSON, JR (D)
b Hopkinsville, Ky, Nov 26, 24; s Edward Thompson Breathitt & Mary Jo Wallace B; m 1948 to Frances Holleman; c Mary Fran, Linda, Susan & Edward, III. Educ: Univ Ky, LLB & BA in com; pres, Lamp & Cross; sr men's honorary; Omicron Delta Kappa. Hon Degrees: LLD, Univ Ky, Marshall Col & Ky Wesleyan Col. Polit & Govt Pos: Mem state campaign staff, former VPres Alben W Barkley's successful campaign for reelection to US Senate; chmn, State Speakers Bur, Adlai Stevenson's Presidential Campaign, 52; pres, Young Dem Clubs of Ky, 52; mem, State Pub Serv Comn; State Personnel Comnr; Ky State Rep, 3 terms; Gov, Ky, 63-67; Dem Nat Committeeman, 67-72, mem comn on rules, Dem Nat Comt, 69-72; deleg, Dem Nat Conv, 72. Bus & Prof Pos: VPres, pub affairs, Southern Rwy Syst, Washington, DC, currently. Mil Serv: Entered Army Air Force, 43, released as Aviation Cadet, 45. Mem: Jaycees; Kiwanis; Elks; Hopkinsville CofC (dir). Honors & Awards: Lincoln Key Award, 66; seconded nomination of Lyndon B Johnson for President of US. Relig: Methodist. Mailing Add: PO Box 24 Hopkinsville KY 42240

BREAUX, JOHN B (D)
US Rep, La
b Crowley, La, Mar 1, 44; s Ezra H Breaux, Jr & Katherine Berlinger B; m 1964 to Lois Gail Daigle; c John, Jr, William Lloyd & Elizabeth Andre. Educ: Univ Southwestern La, BA in Polit Sci, 65; La State Univ, JD, 67; Lambda Chi Alpha; Student Bar Asn; tennis team; Moot Court finalist, 66. Polit & Govt Pos: Legis asst, US Rep Edwin W Edwards, 68-69, dist asst, 69-72; US Rep, Seventh Dist, La, 72- Bus & Prof Pos: Partner, Brown, McKernan, Ingram & Breaux, 67-68. Mem: Int Rice Festival Asn (bd dirs); Jaycees; CofC; Pi Lambda Beta; Phi Alpha Delta. Honors & Awards: Am Legion Award. Legal Res: Crowley LA 70526 Mailing Add: US House of Rep Washington DC 20510

BREAUX, JOHN RICHARD (D)
La State Rep
b Breaux Bridge, La, Dec 16, 38; s Joseph Wade Breaux & Marie Louise Thevenet B; m 1957 to Judith Ann Sherville; c Desiree Frances, Denise Ann, John Richard, Jr & Brett Allen. Educ: Univ Southwest La, 2 years. Polit & Govt Pos: Vpres, Eighth Ward Rep Dist, Dem Party, La, 61; council-at-lg, Jeanerette, La, 63-67; La State Rep, 68-; mem, Dem State Cent Comt, La, currently. Bus & Prof Pos: Sales mgr, Evangeline Food & Pepper Prod, Inc, 66-67; sales mgr, Jeanerette Motor Co, 67-69; banker, Sugarland State Bank, 69. Mil Serv: Entered as Yeoman 3/C, Naval Res, 56, released, 64. Mem: Rotary; Jaycees; KofC. Honors & Awards: Outstanding Young Men in Am, 67. Relig: Roman Catholic. Legal Res: 310 Doll St Jeanerette LA 70544 Mailing Add: PO Box 229 Jeanerette LA 70544

BRECHT, WARREN F (R)
Asst Secy for Admin, US Dept Treas
b Detroit, Mich, May 21, 32; s August F Brecht & Margaret Roos B; m 1954 to Joyce Southard; c Amy E, Stephen F, David C. & Peter J. Educ: De Pauw Univ, BA, 54; Univ Mich Law Sch, 55; Harvard Univ Bus Sch, MBA, 59; Phi Beta Kappa; Sigma Chi. Polit & Govt Pos: Dep Asst Secy Mgt & Budget, US Dept Interior, 71-72; Asst Secy for Admin, US Dept Treas, 72- Bus & Prof Pos: Vpres & treas, Mgt Systs Corp, Cambridge, Mass, 61-65; systs analyst, W R Grace & Co, Cambridge, 59-60; partner in charge admin, Peat, Marwick, Livingston & Co, Boston, 65-69, prin in charge prof practice, mgt consult dept, Peat, Marwick, Mitchell & Co New York, 69-71. Mil Serv: Entered as 2nd Lt, Air Force, 55, released as 1st Lt, 57, after serv in Air Materiel Command; Air Force Commendation Ribbon from Comdr, Air Materiel Command, 57. Mem: Fed Govt Acct Asn. Honors & Awards: Outstanding Young Man Award, Lexington Jaycees, Mass, 68. Mailing Add: 9 Orchard Way N Rockville MD 20854

BRECKINRIDGE, JOHN BAYNE (D)
US Rep, Ky
b Washington, DC, Nov 29, 13; s Dr Scott Dudley Breckinridge & Gertrude Ashby Bayne B; m 1954 to Helen Congleton; c Knight (Mrs Dietrich) & John Bayne. Educ: Univ Ky, AB, 37, LLB, 39; Kappa Alpha. Polit & Govt Pos: Spec attorney, Anti-Trust Div, US Dept Justice, 40-41; Chief Indust & Projs Licensing Div, Bd Econ Warfare, 41-42; Ky State Rep, 56-59; deleg, White House Conf Children & Youth, 60; mem rules comt, Dem Nat Conv, 60; mem, Ky Constitution Rev Comt, 60-62; Attorney Gen, Ky, 60-64 & 68-72; mem, Ky Comn Children & Youth, 60-64 & 68-72; mem, Southern Interstate Nuclear Bd, 62, past chmn & vchmn; chmn, Ky Adv Comt Nuclear Energy, 60-66; past chmn, Ky Sci & Tech Coun; dir, Ky Atomic Energy & Space Auth, 66-67; chmn, Ky Water Pollution Control Comn, 68, mem, 68-; mem, Ky Health & Geriatric Auth, Ky Turnpike Auth, Ky Pub Sch Auth, Ky State Property & Bldg Comn, Ky State Arch & Records Comn, Ky Employees Retirement Syst & Ky Teachers Retirement Syst, 68-72; US Rep, Ky, 72-; deleg, Dem Nat Mid-Term Conf, 74. Bus & Prof Pos: Attorney, 46- Mil Serv: Entered as 1st Lt, Army, 41, released as Col, 46, after serv in Joint-US United Kingdom Commanding Officer Mil Liaison Hqs, Albania; Asst Chief Int Div, USAFIME Hqs; Joint US-United Kingdom Chief Econ & Supply Officer, Mil Liaison Hq, Balkan, 46; Secy of Army Commendation medal for Performance of Duties in Connection with Int Security Affairs. Publ: Articles for Ky Law J, 63-64 & spec issue, 63. Mem: Franklin Co Bar Asn; Am Judicature Soc; Ky Hist Soc; Civil War Round Table; Ky Law Enforcement Coun. Honors & Awards: Wyman Award, Nat Asn Attorneys Gen. Relig: Presbyterian. Legal Res: 1100 Fincastle Rd Lexington KY 40502 Mailing Add: 1507 Longworth House Off Bldg Washington DC 20515

BREECE, GEORGE W (D)
NC State Rep
b Fayetteville, NC, July 20, 45; s J Wilbur Breece & Barbara Pearsall B; single. Educ: Montreat-Anderson Jr Col; Atlantic Christian Col, BA, 71; Delta Sigma Phi. Polit & Govt Pos: Campaign coordr, Rose for Cong, 70; nat youth dir, Humphrey for President, 72; mem, NC & Nat Young Dem, currently; NC State Rep, currently. Bus & Prof Pos: Assoc with Rogers & Breece Funeral Home, formerly. Mil Serv: Entered as Pvt, Army, 67, released as Sgt E-5, 70, after serv in Mortuary Br, 3rd Army; Outstanding Trainee, Army Training Ctr, Ft Bragg, 67. Mem: Fayetteville Jr CofC; KofP; Nat Conf State Legislators. Honors & Awards: One of Outstanding Young Dem of NC, 72; Outstanding Young Dem of Cumberland Co, 74. Relig: Methodist. Legal Res: PO Box 1975 Fayetteville NC 28302 Mailing Add: House of Rep Raleigh NC 27611

BREED, WILLIAM JACK (R)
b Poplarville, Miss, June 27, 21; s William Jack Breed & Mary Elma Smith B; m 1945 to Ellen Rose Batson; c Nell Inda & Mary Ellen. Educ: US Maritime Serv Officer Training Sch, Engr License Steam-Diesel, 43. Polit & Govt Pos: Chmn, Miss Cand Comt, 62-68; deleg, Rep Nat Conv, 68; Chmn, Hinds Co Rep Exec Comt, formerly. Bus & Prof Pos: Vpres, Capitol Hardware Co, Inc, Jackson, Miss, 54-; owner, Breed Sales Co, 58-; owner, Dunrovin Cattle & Timber Farm, Leesburg, 61-; dir, Dixie Nat Life Ins Co, Jackson, 68- Mil Serv: Entered as Midn, Naval Res, 42, transferred to Maritime Serv, released as 2nd Eng Officer, 45, after serv in Troop Carrier & Ammunition Ships, European, Mediterranean, Near East & Far East, 42-45; European, Mediterranean, Near East & Far East Campaign Ribbons. Mem: Nat & Am Wholesale Lumber Asns; Aircraft Owners & Pilots Asn; Mason; Country Club Jackson. Honors & Awards: Gold Key Fund Raising Award, Miss Rep Party; Maywood Nat Sales Winner, 5 years. Relig: Baptist. Legal Res: 4085 Old Canton Rd Jackson MS 39216 Mailing Add: PO Box 4827 Jackson MS 39216

BREGMAN, JACOB I (D)
Treas, Montgomery Co Dem Cent Comt, Md
b Hartford, Conn, Sept 12, 23; Aaron Bregman & Jennie Katzoff B; m 1948 to Mona Madan; c Janet Paula, Marcia Lynn & Barbara Jean. Educ: Providence Col, BS, 43; Polytech Inst Brooklyn, MS, 48, PhD, 51; Sigma Xi; Phi Lambda Upsilon. Polit & Govt Pos: Trustee, Village of Park Forest, Ill, 63-67; chmn, Ill Air Pollution Control Bd, 63-67; dir, Regional Asn of Municipalities of South Cook & Will Co, Ill, 65-67; comnr, Ohio River Valley Sanitation Comn, 67-68; dep asst secy, US Dept Interior, 67-69; mem, Dem State Cent Comt Md, currently; treas, Montgomery Co Dem Cent Comt, 74- Bus & Prof Pos: Head phys chem labs, Nalco Chem Co, 50-59; dir chem sci, IIT Research Inst, 59-67; pres, Wapora, Inc, 69- Mil Serv: Entered as Pvt, Army, 43, released as T/Sgt, 46, after serv in 3rd Army, ETO, 44-46; 2 Battle Stars. Publ: Auth, Corrosion Inhibitors, MacMillan, 61; co-ed, Surface Effects in Detection, 63 & co-auth, The Pollution Paradox, 66, Spartan. Mem: Am Chem Soc; Am Inst Chem Engrs; Am Fisheries Soc. Relig: Hebrew. Mailing Add: 5630 Old Chester Rd Bethesda MD 20014

BREHM, WILLIAM KEITH
Asst Secy Defense Manpower & Reserve Affairs
b Dearborn, Mich, Mar 29, 29; s Walter Elmer Brehm & Lucille Hankinson B; m 1952 to Delores Soderquist; c Eric & Lisa. Educ: Univ Mich, BS, 50, MS, 52; Phi Eta Sigma. Polit & Govt Pos: Dep Asst Secy Defense, Off Asst Secy Defense, 67-68; Asst Secy of the Army, 68-70; Asst Secy Defense Manpower & Reserve Affairs, 73- Bus & Prof Pos: Research assoc, Eng Research Inst, Univ Mich, 50-52; design specialist, Eng Dept, Convair, San Diego, Calif, 52-57, chief of opers anal, Convair Astronautics, 58-59, exec staff asst to vpres planning, Convair Div, Gen Dynamics Corp, 60-62; corporate dir develop planning, NAm Aviation, Inc, El Segundo, Calif, 62-64; vpres, Dart Industs, Inc, 70-73. Mem: Opers Research Soc Am. Honors & Awards: Secy of Defense Meritorious Civilian Serv Medal; Dept of the Army Distinguished Civilian Serv Award. Relig: Protestant. Mailing Add: 4061 Ridgeview Circle Arlington VA 22207

BREITEL, CHARLES DAVID (R)
Chief Judge, NY Court of Appeals
b New York, NY, Dec 12, 08; s Herman L Breitel & Regina D Zuckerberg B; m 1927 to Jeanne S Hollander; c Eleanor B (Mrs Burton Z Alter) & Vivian. Educ: Univ Mich, AB, 29; Columbia Univ, LLB, 32. Hon Degrees: LLD, Long Island Univ, 52 & Yeshiva Univ, 74. Polit & Govt Pos: Dep asst dist attorney, New York Co, 35-39; asst dist attorney, 39-41, mem chief indictment bur, Dist Attorney's Off, 41; counsel to Gov, NY, 43-50, mem several state comns, 44-50; Justice, NY Supreme Court, 50-52; justice, appellate div, first dept, 52-66; mem, Fed Comn on Int Rules & Judicial Procedure, 59-64, mem, Nat Crime Comn, 65-67; assoc judge, NY Court of Appeals, 67-73, Chief Judge, 73- Publ: Co-auth, Counsel on appeal, McGraw-Hill, 68; auth, Courts & lawmaking, In; Legal Institutions Today & Tomorrow, Columbia, 59; The lawmakers, Cardozo Lecture, Asn of the Bar of the City of New York, 65. Mem: Am Bar Asn; Am Acad Arts & Sci (fel); Am Bar Found (fel); Am Law Inst (mem coun); Inst of Judicial Admin; Am Jewish Comt. Honors & Awards: Columbia Univ Fedn Alumni Medal, 59, Columbia Univ Law Sch Alumni Asn Medal for Excellence, 75. Relig: Jewish. Legal Res: 146 Central Park W New York NY 10023 Mailing Add: 74 Trinity Pl New York NY 10006

BREKKE, LOLA M (R)
Mem, Rep State Cent Comt of Calif
b Scobey, Mont, May 1, 31; d Roger Von Kuster & Ragnhild Veis V; m 1956 to George O Brekke, Jr; c Charlotte Sue & Lisa Ann. Educ: Minot State Col, standard teaching credential, 52; Sigma Sigma Sigma. Polit & Govt Pos: Precinct chmn, Federated Rep Women's Club of Sacramento, 65, first vpres, 66, pres, 67, legis chmn & parliamentarian, 69; assoc mem, Rep State Cent Comt of Calif, 67-68, mem, 69-; hq chmn, Sacramento Co Comt to Reelect Gov Reagan, 70; recording secy, Northern Div, Calif Fedn of Rep Women, 72-73, legis chmn, Statewide, 73-; alt deleg, Rep Nat Conv, 72; hq chmn, Sacramento Co Comt to Reelect the President, 72. Bus & Prof Pos: Elem sch teacher, Conrad, Mont, 52-53; elem sch teacher, Billings, Mont, 53-55 & Grand Forks, NDak, 55-56. Mem: Nat, Mont & NDak Educ Asns; PTA; Girl Scouts. Relig: Lutheran. Mailing Add: 7016 Trabert Ct Carmichael CA 95608

BREMNER, D ROGER (D)
Nev State Assemblyman
b Las Vegas, Nev, Dec 8, 37; s George Bremner & Jeanne James B; m 1965 to Annette Dismukes; c Eric David & Elizabeth Ann. Educ: Univ Nev, Reno, BS in Bus Admin, 60, Univ Nev, Las Vegas, 70-; Alpha Tau Omega; Blue Key. Polit & Govt Pos: Vpres, Nev State Young Dem, 69-70; Nev State Assemblyman, 73- Bus & Prof Pos: Agt, State Farm Ins, Las Vegas, Nev, 63- Mil Serv: Entered as 2nd Lt, Army, 60, released as 1st Lt, 62, after serv in Defense Clothing & Textile Supply Ctr. Mem: Southern Nev Mus (dir, 72-). Relig: Protestant. Mailing Add: 821 Fairway Dr Las Vegas NV 89107

BRENDA, GUST GOTTLIEB, JR (D)
WVa State Deleg
b Rush Run, Ohio, Sept 4, 20; s Gust G Brenda, Sr & Ella Ellis B; m 1940 to Marrietta May Lewis; c Ronald Keith & Bruce Kevin. Educ: Weir High Sch, 39. Polit & Govt Pos: WVa State Deleg, 68- Bus & Prof Pos: Planner & work coordr, Weirton Steel Co, 30 years. Mil Serv: Entered as Seaman, Navy, 44, released as 3/C PO, 46. Mem: Am Rifle Asn; Am Ord Asn; Am Legion; Hancock Co Sportsman Asn; Moose. Relig: Protestant. Mailing Add: 322 Culler Rd Weirton WV 26062

BRENNAN, AMY (D)
Nat Committeewoman, Conn Young Dem
b Springfield, Mass, Nov 23, 47; d Christopher James Brennan & Ann Marie Welch B; single. Educ: Cent Conn State Col, BS, 69; Theta Sigma Delta. Polit & Govt Pos: Alt deleg, Conn Dem State Conv, 72; asst voter registr, Conn Dem Campaign, 72; presidential ballot, 72, advance woman, 72; Nat Committeewoman, Conn Young Dem, 72-; mem, Southington Dem Town Comt, 72-; deleg, Dem Nat Mid-Term Conf, 74. Bus & Prof Pos: Elem teacher, Oxford, Conn, 69-70; substitute teacher, Southington, 71. Relig: Catholic. Mailing Add: 651 West St Southington CT 06489

BRENNAN, DOROTHY TERESA (D)
Committeewoman, Dem Party, Pa
b Philadelphia, Pa, Apr 30, 16; d Murray S Oliver & Sarah Cannon O; m 1933 to Melvin George Brennan, Sr; c Melvin George, Jr, Sarah E (Mrs McCullough) & Arlene F (Mrs West); four grandchildren. Polit & Govt Pos: Committeewoman, Dem Party, Pa, 50-, ward leader, Third Dem Ward, Philadelphia, 65-68 & 70-; clerk, Marriage Bur, 64-68; deleg, Dem Nat Conv, 68; chief probate clerk, Register of Wills, 68-72, second dep to registrar, 72-; vpres party liaison, Dem Women's Forum, 72- Mem: Community Action Dem Women's Forum (vpres); Concern Women Group (chmn); Philadelphia Comt for Aid to Biafran Children (co-chmn); Community Nursing Serv Bd (dir); YMCA. Relig: Methodist Episcopal. Mailing Add: 5917 Osage Ave Philadelphia PA 19143

BRENNAN, EDWARD (R)
Rep Nat Committeeman, Hawaii
b New York, NY, Sept 3, 15; m 1955 to Germaine; c Ricky & Marty. Educ: Manner Sch Dramatic Arts, NY. Polit & Govt Pos: Campaign chmn, gubernatorial, cong & mayoralty races for Rep cand; mem, State of Hawaii Econ Develop Comn, 62-65; chmn, Honolulu Planning Comn, 66-70; Rep Nat Committeeman, Hawaii, 72- Bus & Prof Pos: Pac regional mgr, Gold Bond Stamp Co, Honolulu, currently. Mem: Waikiki Adv Comt (vchmn); Hawaii World Trade Asn; Honolulu Japanese CofC; Sales & Mkt Exec Honolulu; Univ Hawaii Found; Hawaii Coun, Nat Coun Crime & Delinquency; Bishop Mus Asn; Jr Achievement of Hawaii. Relig: Temple Emanu-El. Mailing Add: 966 Waiholo St Honolulu HI 96821

BRENNAN, JOSEPH EDWARD (D)
Attorney Gen, Maine
b Portland, Maine, Nov 2, 34; s John Brennan & Catherine B; m 1968 to Mary Katherine Gonya; c Joseph E & Tara Elizabeth. Educ: Boston Col, BS, 58; Univ Maine Sch Law, LLB, 63. Polit & Govt Pos: Maine State Rep, 65-71, asst minority leader, 67-71; co attorney, Portland, Maine, 71-72; Maine State Sen & Minority Leader, 73-74; Attorney Gen, Maine, 75- Bus & Prof Pos: Mem, Bd of Visitors, Baxter State Sch for Deaf, 73-74; chmn, Maine Trial Court Revision Comt, 74-75. Mil Serv: Army, 53-55. Relig: Roman Catholic. Legal Res: 92 Craigie St Portland ME 04102 Mailing Add: Dept of Attorney Gen State House Augusta ME 04330

BRENNAN, PETER J (D)
b New York, NY, May 24, 18; s John J Brennan & Agnes Moore B; m to Josephine Brickley; c Peter J, Jr, Joan (Mrs Frank Tetro) & Peggy (Mrs Stephen Tritto). Educ: City Col New York. Polit & Govt Pos: Secy of Labor, 73-75. Bus & Prof Pos: Pres, New York City Bldg & Construction Trades Coun, AFL-CIO, 57-73 & 75-; pres, NY State Bldg & Construction Trades Coun, 58-73; vpres, NY State AFL-CIO; mem, NY State Job Develop Authority, NY State Labor Dept Safety Adv Comt, Nat Adv Comt Educ Disadvantaged Children, NY State Workmen's Compensation Adv Comt, Adv Bd Prevailing Wages Pub Works in NY State & NY State Urban Develop Corp. Mil Serv: Navy, serv in Submarine Forces, World War II. Honors & Awards: Awards from Police Athletic League, United Serv Appeal, Gtr NY Fund, VFW, John F Kennedy Libr & Cong Medal Honor Soc. Mailing Add: Bldg & Construction Trades Coun 441 Lexington Ave New York NY 10017

BRENNAN, ROBERT MICHAEL (D)
RI State Rep
b Providence, RI, Oct 12, 46; s William Henry Brennan & Anne E Gearin B; single. Educ: Providence Col, BS, 68; New Eng Sch Law, JD, 71; Delta Theta Phi; Tribune; Kozuch Senate, 70-71. Polit & Govt Pos: RI State Rep, Dist 36, 75-, mem labor comt, RI House Rep, 75- Bus & Prof Pos: Supvr, New England Tel Co, 69-; attorney, Lovett & Linder Ltd, 71- Mil Serv: 1st Lt, Army Res, 68. Mem: RI & Am Bar Asns; Am Trial Lawyers Asn. Relig: Roman Catholic. Mailing Add: 141 Timberline Rd Warwick RI 02886

BRENNAN, THOMAS EMMETT (D)
Justice, Supreme Court of Mich
b Detroit, Mich, May 27, 29; s Joseph Terrance Brennan & Jeannette Sullivan B; m 1951 to Pauline Mary Weinberger; c Thomas Emmett, Jr, John Seamus, Margaret Ann, William Joseph, Mary Beth & Ellen Mary. Educ: Univ Detroit Law Sch, LLB, 52; Delta Theta Phi; Upsilon Delta Sigma. Polit & Govt Pos: Judge, Common Pleas Court, Detroit, Mich, 61-63; judge, Circuit Court, Wayne Co, 63-67; Assoc Judge, Supreme Court of Mich, 67-69, Chief Justice, 69-70, Justice, 70- Bus & Prof Pos: Attorney-at-law, Detroit, Mich, 53-61; partner, Waldron, Brennan & Maher, 57-61; bd trustees, Marygrove Col, 69-70; adj prof polit sci, Univ Detroit, 69-71; pres, Thomas M Cooley Law Sch, 72- Publ: Videotape—the Michigan experience, Hastings Law J, 11/72. Mem: Am Bar Asn; State Bar of Mich; Mich Comn on Law Enforcement & Criminal Justice; Nat Conf of Chief Justices; Nat Col of Appellate Judges. Relig: Roman Catholic. Legal Res: 1137 Alton St East Lansing MI 48823 Mailing Add: Supreme Court of Mich Lansing MI 48933

BRENNAN, WILLIAM J, JR
Assoc Justice, US Supreme Court
b Newark, NJ, Apr 25, 06; s William J Brennan & Agnes McDermott B; m 1928 to Marjorie Leonard; c William Joseph, Hugh Leonard & Nancy. Educ: Univ Pa, BS, 28; Harvard Univ, LLB, 31. Polit & Govt Pos: Superior Court Judge, 49-50; appellate div Judge, NJ, 50-52; Justice, NJ Supreme Court, 52-56; Assoc Justice, US Supreme Court, 56- Bus & Prof Pos: Attorney, Pitney, Hardin, Ward & Brennan. Mil Serv: Gen Staff Corps, Army, 42-45; Legion of Merit. Legal Res: NJ Mailing Add: US Supreme Court Washington DC 20543

BRENTS, ALVIN LEE (D)
Secy, Wyandot Co Dem Cent & Exec Comts, Ohio
b Stark, La, Aug 1, 10; s William A Brents & Lissie McCubrins B; m 1930 to Helen G Bink; c Joan (Mrs Morral), Sharon K (Mrs Clark), Gary E & Marcia L. Educ: Smithville Sch, Sycamore, Ohio, Eighth grade grad. Polit & Govt Pos: Committeeman & secy, Wyandot Co Dem Cent & Exec Comts, Ohio, 40- Bus & Prof Pos: Salesman, I H Co Machinery, 33-42; grocer, 42- Mem: Elks; Sportsmans Club (pres, 20 years). Relig: Protestant. Mailing Add: 111 Main St Harpster OH 43323

BRESETTE, MICHAEL CHARLES (D)
Vt State Rep
b Montpelier, Vt, June 9, 45; s Elwin Lawson Bresette & Marie Amedy B; m 1970 to Linda Leavens. Educ: Johnson State Col, BS, 68; Alpha Tau Omega. Polit & Govt Pos: Vt State Rep, 75-; mem, Educ Comn of the States, currently, mem, Gov Comn on Children & Youth, currently. Bus & Prof Pos: Teaching prin, Brighton Elem Sch, Vt, 68- Mem: Island Pond Med Ctr (pres); Orleans-Northern Essex Home Health Agency (bd dirs); Lions (secy-treas); Brighton Home & Sch Asn (pres). Legal Res: East Charleston Rd Island Pond VT 05846 Mailing Add: Box 461 Island Pond VT 05846

BRETT, JOSEPH E (D)
Mass State Rep
b Washington, DC, 1907. Educ: Dean Acad, Franklin. Polit & Govt Pos: Mem, Quincy City Coun & Quincy Conserv Comn, formerly; Mass State Rep, currently; deleg, Dem Nat Conv, 68. Mem: Elks; Eagles; KofC; Moose; United Commercial Travelers. Relig: Catholic. Mailing Add: 254 Fenno St Quincy MA 02170

BREUNINGER, LEWIS TALMAGE (R)
Mem, Rep Nat Finance Comt
b Washington, DC, July 23, 94; s Lewis E Breuninger & Sadie Love B; wid; c Lewis T, Jr. Educ: Johns Hopkins Univ, AB, George Washington Univ, LLB. Hon Degrees: LLD, Southeastern Univ. Polit & Govt Pos: Mem, Rep Nat Finance Comt, 48-, vchmn, 56-69; Rep Nat Committeeman for Washington, DC, 60-68. Bus & Prof Pos: Pres, L E Breuninger & Sons, Inc, 28- Mil Serv: Entered as Ens, Navy, 17, released as Lt(jg), 21. Mem: Capitol Hill Club; Army-Navy Club; Metrop Club; Nat Press Club; Kiwanis. Relig: Methodist. Legal Res: 2701 Foxhall Rd NW Washington DC 20007 Mailing Add: 1825 F St NW Washington DC 20006

BREWER, ALBERT PRESTON (D)
b Bethel Springs, Tenn, Oct 26, 28; s Daniel Austin Brewer & Clara Yarber B; m 1951 to Martha Helen Farmer; c Rebecca Ann & Beverly Alison. Educ: Univ Ala, BA & LLB. Hon Degrees: LHD, Jacksonville State Univ; LLD, Samford Univ. Polit & Govt Pos: Mem, Decatur City Planning Comn, 56-63; Ala State Rep, 55-67, Speaker, Ala House of Rep, 63-67; Lt Gov, Ala, 67-68, Gov, 68-70. Bus & Prof Pos: Lawyer. Mem: Phi Alpha Delta; Delta Sigma Phi; Am Bar Asn; Mason; Am Legion. Honors & Awards: One of Four Outstanding Young Men of Ala, Ala Jr CofC. Relig: Baptist. Mailing Add: Box 975 Decatur AL 35601

BREWER, AUBREY HORACE (D)
Miss State Rep
Mailing Add: Box 172 Corinth MS 38834

BREWER, GUY R (D)
NY State Assemblyman
Mailing Add: 107-35 170th St Jamaica NY 11433

BREWER, HARPER, JR (D)
Tenn State Rep
b Memphis, Tenn, Dec 22, 37; s Harper Brewer, Sr & Daisy Lambert B; m 1966 to Peggy Ann Cox; c Kimberly Michelle. Educ: Fisk Univ, AB in Chem, 58, MA in Sci Educ, 64; Alpha Phi Alpha. Polit & Govt Pos: Tenn State Rep, 72-, asst majority leader, Tenn House Rep, 74- Bus & Prof Pos: Vpres, Brewer Delivery Serv, 72-; admin asst, Memphis City Sch, 74-; pres, Memphis Area Teachers Credit Union, 74- Mem: Nat, Tenn & Memphis Educ Asns; Urban Policies Inst; Mason. Relig: Baptist. Mailing Add: 990 N Idlewild Memphis TN 38107

BREWER, JAMES H (D)
Ark State Rep
Mailing Add: Rte 3 Blanton Dr Trumann AR 72472

BREWER, JOHN ROBERT (D)
b Telfair Co, Ga, June 11, 34; s Floyd Arnold Brewer, Sr & Mary Hardwick B; m 1960 to Faye Deloach; c Celia Jo Ann. Educ: Brewton-Parker Col, Ga, AA; Mercer Univ, BA; Ga Southern Col, MA; Southern Baptist Theol Sem, BD; hon mem, Phi Theta Kappa. Polit & Govt Pos: Deleg, Dem Nat Conv, 72. Bus & Prof Pos: Prof Eng, Brewton-Parker Col, Ga, 63- Publ: The walls came tumbling down, Western Recorder, 61. Mem: Montgomery Co Lions (chaplain, 63-73); F&AM (Aural Lodge); RAM (Sinai Chap); KT (Olivet Commandery); Ga Heart Asn (dir, 66-). Honors & Awards: Outstanding Young Men Award, Outstanding Young Men of Am, Inc, 69; Bronze Medallion for Meritorious Serv, Am Heart Asn, 71. Relig: Baptist. Mailing Add: Box 27 Ailey GA 30410

BREWER, MYRENE RICH (R)
Rep Nat Committeewoman, Utah
b Ogden, Utah, Dec 17, 06; m 1928 to Joseph West Brewer; c Sharlene (Mrs Jay W Glasmann), Joseph West, Jr, Edward Rich, Alexander L, Rodney Rich & Mary (Mrs Christopher Ford). Educ: Univ Mich, BA, 27; Univ Calif, Berkeley; Univ Utah; Utah State

Univ. Polit & Govt Pos: Precinct & dist voting chmn, 32-38 & 60-64; vpres, Utah State Federated Women's Rep Clubs, 68-72; pres, Weber Co Women's Rep Club, 69-71; Rep Nat Committeewoman, Utah, 72- Bus & Prof Pos: Elem sch teacher, 27-28; chmn bd, J W Brewer Tire Co, Ogden, Utah, currently. Mem: McKay-Dee Hosp (vol, 56-, vpres, Hosp Found Bd, 70- Relig: Latter-day Saint. Mailing Add: 2460 Taylor Ave Ogden UT 84401

BREWER, SAM, JR (R)
Ky State Rep
Mailing Add: Rte 3 Irvine KY 40336

BREWER, WILLIAM DODD
US Ambassador to Sudan
b Middletown, Conn, Apr 4, 22; s Arnold Brewer & Cornelia Dodd B; m 1949 to Alice Van Ess; c John V E, Daniel A & Priscilla J. Educ: Williams Col, BA cum laude, 44; Fletcher Sch, MA, 47; Theta Delta Chi. Polit & Govt Pos: Career officer, Foreign Serv, 47-, dept chief of mission, Kabul, Afghanistan, 62-65, policy planning coun, Dept State, 65-66, country dir, Arabian Peninsula, 66-70, US Ambassador to Mauritius, 70-73; US Ambassador to Sudan, 73- Mil Serv: Am Field Serv, Italy & India, 44-45; Campaign Ribbons. Publ: Patterns of Gesture among Levantine Arabs, Am Anthropologist, 4-6/51; US Area Interests in Persian Gulf, Princeton Univ Conf, 10/68; Yesterday & Tomorrow in Persian Gulf, Mid East J, spring 69. Mem: Foreign Serv Asn; Mid East Inst. Honors & Awards: Arthur S Flemming Award, 60. Relig: Christian. Legal Res: N Salem Rd Ridgefield CT 06877 Mailing Add: Dept of State Washington DC 20521

BREWSTER, EDWARD RICHARD (D)
Kans State Rep
b Alexandria, La, Sept 30, 43; s John Edward Brewster (deceased) & Helen Caskey Brewster Childress; m 1966 to Joan Gibson; c John Grayson. Educ: Okla Baptist Univ, BA, 65; Univ Kans, 66-68; Washburn Univ Sch Law, JD, 73. Polit & Govt Pos: Mem bd, Rural Water Dist Six, Shawnee Co, Kans, 74-; Kans State Rep, 75- Bus & Prof Pos: Asst news dir, WREN Radio, Topeka, Kans, 65-68; news dir, KTSB-TV, Topeka, 68-70; asst mgr, Kans Motor Car Dealers Asn, 70-71; exec dir & legal counsel, Kans Mobile Housing Inst, 71-; attorney, 73- Mem: Kans Trial Lawyers Asn (mem bd gov, 74-); Downtown Topeka Rotary. Relig: Southern Baptist. Legal Res: 5334 SW Wanamaker Rd Topeka KS 66610 Mailing Add: 1515 Topeka Ave Topeka KS 66612

BREWSTER, KAREN JOY (R)
Nat Committeewoman, Mich Fedn of Young Rep
b Dixon, Ill, Sept 4, 39; d Robert Cameron Brewster & Dorothy Helmick B; single. Educ: Stephens Col, 59; Mich State Univ, BA, 61, MA, 66; Gamma Phi Beta. Polit & Govt Pos: Nat committeewoman, Mich Fedn of Young Rep, 70-; chmn, Mich Nixonettes Young Voters for the President, 72; mem nat gov bd, Ripon Soc Inc, 74-; pres, Mich Ripon Soc, 75-; chmn, Local Selective Serv Bd, 75- Bus & Prof Pos: Teacher of emotionally disturbed, Wyandotte Spec Proj Class, 61-63 & Grosse Pointe Pub Sch, 63-65, crisis teacher & first asst prin, Grosse Pointe Pub Sch, 67- Mem: Mich & Nat Educ Asns; Mich Asn for Teachers of Emotionally Impaired; Founders Soc Detroit Inst Art; Vol Probation Officer, Grosse Pointe. Honors & Awards: Outstanding Young Rep, Mich Fedn of Young Rep, 73. Relig: Protestant. Mailing Add: 2315 Allard Grosse Pointe Woods MI 48236

BREYFOGLE, JOHN WILLIAM, JR (R)
b Olathe, Kans, Aug 12, 06; s John William Breyfogle & Kate O Taylor B; m 1973 to Sara Jayne Scott; c John W III, Robert T & Ann E. Educ: Univ Kans, LLB; Phi Gamma Delta; Phi Delta Phi. Polit & Govt Pos: Rep cent committeeman, Johnson Co, Kans, 46-58; mem, Johnson Co Rep Cent Comt, formerly, chmn, 48-58; mem, Johnson Co Rep Exec Comt, formerly; deleg, Rep Nat Conv, 48 & 68. Bus & Prof Pos: Dist chmn, Jr Am Bar Conf, Kans, 48; pres, Olathe Community Hosp Found, Inc, 62-64. Mil Serv: Entered as Lt(jg), Navy, 43, released as Lt, 45, after serv in Pac Theatre, 44-45. Mem: Am Col or Probate Counsel; AF&AM; VFW; Am Legion; Johnson Co Farm Bur. Relig: Methodist. Mailing Add: 7079 E McDonald Dr Scottsdale AZ 85253

BRIAN, EARL WINFREY (R)
Mem, Rep State Cent Comt Calif
b Raleigh, NC, Feb 26, 42; s Earl Winfrey Brian & Blanche Barringer B; m 1964 to Jane Lang; c Earl W, III. Educ: Duke Univ, MD, 66; Phi Eta Sigma; Pi Kappa Alpha. Polit & Govt Pos: Exec secy, Calif State Social Welfare Bd, 67-68; dir, Calif State Dept Health Care Serv, 70-72; mem, US Health Serv Indust Comt, 71-72; mem, Calif Coun on Criminal Justice, 72-; mem, Calif Bd of Corrections, 72-; mem, Calif Job Corp Exec Bd, 72-; comnr, Western Interstate Comn for Higher Educ, 72-; secy, Health & Welfare Agency, State of Calif, 72-; mem, Calif Coun on Intergovt Rels, 73-; mem, Rep State Cent Comt Calif, 73- Bus & Prof Pos: Intern, dept surg house staff, Watts Med Ctr, Durham, NC, 65-66; intern/admin asst, dept surg house staff, Stanford Univ Med Ctr, Palo Alto, Calif, 66-67; flight surgeon, US Army, 68-70. Mil Serv: Entered as 1st Lt, Army, 68, released as Maj, 70, after serv in 1st Cavalry Div (AM), Repub of S Vietnam, 68-69; Silver Star; Bronze Star; Air Medal for Valor; Air Medal for Aerial Combat Duty. Publ: The cycliphase investment technique, Xecoa Tech Publ, 68; Hospital utilization—a California experience, 4/72 & Foundation for medical care control of hospital utilization; CHAP—A PSRO prototype, 4/73, New Eng J Med. Mem: Sacramento Med Soc; Am Pub Health Asn; Commonwealth Club of San Francisco; Sacramento Rotary; Sutter Lawn Tennis Club. Honors & Awards: One of Five Outstanding Young Men, Calif Jaycees, 73; SCI World Sphere Award, Adv Bd, Calif Mus Found, 73; One of Ten Outstanding Young Men, US Jaycees, 74; Nat Distinguished Serv Award, Pi Kappa Alpha, 74. Relig: Methodist. Mailing Add: 2025 Zonal Ave Los Angeles CA 90033

BRICKER, DALE EUGENE (R)
Mem, Rep State Cent & Exec Comt, Ohio
b Dover, Ohio, Jan 29, 25; s Franklin Benjamin Bricker & Beatrice Mae Rodd B; m 1949 to Elinor Irene Downs; c Barry Owen. Educ: Furman Univ, 44. Polit & Govt Pos: Clerk, Mansfield City Coun, Ohio, 58-63; secy, Richland Co Exec Comt, 58-; pres, Richland Co Young Rep Club, 59; secy, Richland Co Rep Cent Comt, 61-62; off mgr-div elec, Richland Co, 64-; pres, Richland Co Rep Club, 68-; mem, Ohio State Rep Cent & Exec Comts, 72-; co-chmn, 17th Cong Dist Caucus Comt, 72-, chmn legis elec comt, 73- Bus & Prof Pos: Cataloging & standardization technician, Shelby Air Force Depot, 49-58. Mil Serv: Entered as Pvt, Army Med Training Detachment, 43, released as Cpl, 46, after serv in 410th Qm Depot Co Cent Asiatic-Pac Theatre, 44-46; Am Theatre Ribbon; Asiatic-Pac Theatre Ribbon with One Bronze Star; US Victory Medal; Good Conduct Medal; Cent Pac Area Unit Citation. Mem: Shelby Fed Employees Credit Union; life mem Mansfield Stamp & Coin Club; Ohio Asn Elec Off (legis comt, 66-); Fraternal Order Police Assocs; F&AM. Honors & Awards: Young Rep of the Year, Richland Co Young Rep Club, 59; Toastmaster of the Year, Mansfield Toastmasters Club, 62; Spec Ed Excellance Award for T M Tiding Bul, 66 & 67. Relig: Christian Church of NAm. Legal Res: 274 Wood St Mansfield OH 44903 Mailing Add: 7 S Diamond St Mansfield OH 44902

BRICKER, JOHN WILLIAM (R)
b Madison Co, Ohio, Sept 6, 93; s Lemuel S Bricker & Laura King B; m 1920 to Harret Day; c John Day. Educ: Ohio State Univ, AB, 16, LLB, 20; Delta Chi; Order of the Coif. Hon Degrees: LLD, Ohio State Univ, 40. Polit & Govt Pos: Pres, Buckeye Rep Club, Ohio, 23-24; asst attorney gen, Ohio, 23-27, attorney gen, 32-36; mem, Utilities Comn Ohio, 27-32; Gov, Ohio, 38-45; Rep cand, Vice President of the US, 44; US Sen, Ohio, 47-59; mem, Exec Comt, Rep Party, formerly; deleg, Rep Nat Conv, 72. Bus & Prof Pos: Trustee, Ohio State Univ, 47-68; mem bd, Repub Steel Corp, 59-, Buckeye Savings & Loan Co, 60- & Buckeye Steel Castings Co, 61- Mil Serv: 1st Lt, Army, 18. Mem: Am Bar Asn; Univ Club; Athletic Club; Rotary; Ohio State Faculty Torch Club. Relig: Congregational. Mailing Add: 2407 Tremont Rd Columbus OH 43215

BRICKLEY, JAMES H (R)
b Flint, Mich, Nov 15, 28; s J Harry Brickley & Marie E Fischer B; m 1950 to Marianne E Doyle; c Janice Marie, James T, William J, Brian J, Kathleen Mary & Kelle Ann. Educ: Univ Detroit, PhB, 51, LLB, 54; NY Univ, LLM, 58; Delta Theta Phi; Ed, Univ Detroit Law J, 53-54. Polit & Govt Pos: Spec agent, Fed Bur Invest, 54-58; comnr, Detroit Metrop Area Regional Planning Comn, 62; councilman, Common Coun, City of Detroit, 62-65, pres pro-tem, 66-67; mem, Gov Comt on Local Govt, 65; chief asst prosecutor, Wayne Co, Mich, 67-68; US Attorney, Eastern Dist, Mich, 68-69; Lt Gov, Mich, 71. Bus & Prof Pos: Lectr in Govt, Univ Detroit, 59- Mem: Am & Mich State Bar Asns; Soc of Former Spec Agents of the Fed Bur of Invest. Relig: Catholic. Mailing Add: 9136 Bridge Hwy Dimondale MI 48821

BRIDGES, DUANE N (R)
Chmn, Norton Co Rep Party, Kans
b Colorado Springs, Colo, May 21, 14; s Mark Bridges & Nell Harmonson B; m 1940 to Claudia Manning. Educ: Univ Kans, BS, 37; Kappa Sigma. Polit & Govt Pos: Chmn, Norton Co Rep Party, Kans, 65- Bus & Prof Pos: Purchasing agent, Folger Coffee Co, 37-42; owner & operator, Bridges Ins Agency, 46- Mil Serv: Entered as 1st Lt, Army, 42, released as Maj, 46, after serv in 84th Inf Div, ETO, 44-46; Col, Kans Army Nat Guard Res, 54-; Bronze Star; ETO ribbon with three battle stars; Occup Medal; Reservist Medal; Am Victory Medal Combat Inf Badge. Mem: Rotary; Asn US Army; Am Legion; CofC; Kans Nat Guard Asn. Relig: Protestant. Legal Res: 610 W Woodsfield Norton KS 67654 Mailing Add: 110 W Main Norton KS 67654

BRIDGES, HENRY LEE (D)
State Auditor, NC
b Franklin Co, NC, June 10, 07; s John Joseph Bridges & Ida Loraine Carroll B; m 1936 to Clarice Hines; c Joseph Henry & George Hines. Educ: Mars Hill Jr Col, NC, AB, 29; Wake Forest Univ, BA, 31; Wake Forest Law Sch, 33. Polit & Govt Pos: State auditor, NC, 47- Bus & Prof Pos: Mem bd trustees, Wake Forest Univ, 42-52, 55-58, 60-63 & 65-; exec dir, Nat Asn State Auditors, Comptrollers & Treas, 58-69; mem bd trustees, Southeastern Baptist Theol Sem, 67- Mil Serv: Entered as Pvt, Nat Guard, 34, released as Army Maj, 45. Mem: KT; AF&AM; RAM (Choraz, Chap 13); AAONMS; Societas Rosecrucians in Civitatibus Foedaratis. Relig: Baptist; chmn, Bd of Deacons. Mailing Add: 2618 Grant Ave Raleigh NC 27608

BRIDGES, JOHN FISHER (R)
b Concord, NH, Feb 11, 33; s H Styles Bridges & Sally Clement B; m 1974 to Barbara Elizabeth Grueter; c Cynthia (Mrs Howard Hansen, Jr). Educ: Wentworth Inst, grad, 53. Polit & Govt Pos: NH State Rep, 70-72; counr, NH Gov Coun, 72-74; deleg, Rep Nat Conv, 72. Mil Serv: Entered as Pvt, Army, 54, released as Cpl, 56, after serv in 30th Tank Bn. Mem: New Eng Col (bd trustee, 69-); NH Truck Owners (bd dirs, 68-74); NH Small Bus Adv Bd (mem chmn, 68-70). Honors & Awards: Outstanding Freshman Legislator, News Media & Rutgers Univ, 71. Mailing Add: Pulpit Rd Bedford NH 03102

BRIDGES, WEBSTER E, JR (R)
b Concord, NH, Dec 21, 33; s Webster E Bridges & Hazel Brown B (deceased); m 1956 to Helen Dunn; c Webster E, III & James Edward. Educ: Univ NH, BS in bus, 55. Polit & Govt Pos: Dir, Souhegan Young Rep, NH, 64; deleg, Rep State Conv, 64, 66, 68 & 72; chmn, Brookline Rep Comt, 64-; NH State Rep, 67-73, Asst Majority Leader, NH State House of Rep, 69-70; alt deleg-at-lg, Rep Nat Conv, 68 & 72; Hillsborough Co chmn, Nixon for President Campaign, 68; spec asst to Gov, 73- Bus & Prof Pos: Rep, The Sperry & Hutchinson Co, 63-68; New Eng sales mgr, Hoffman Motors Corp/BMW, 68- Mil Serv: Cpl, Army Res, 54-56, serv in Hon Guard, 1st Regt Combat Team, US Mil Acad, West Point; Good Conduct Medal; Sharpshooter Award; Expert Rifleman Award. Mem: Local Heart Fund; NH Jaycees; Souhegan Valley Jaycees; Merrimack Valley Region Asn. Honors & Awards: Holder, Nat Competition Drivers License, Sports Car Club of Am; Sperry & Hutchinson Co Citizenship Award, 67. Relig: Episcopal. Mailing Add: Milford St Brookline NH 03033

BRIDWELL, RENA OLIVE (R)
Chairwoman, Muskingum Co Rep Club, Ohio
b Zanesville, Ohio, June 9, 11; d Joseph Omer Wilson & Martha Jane Mathews W; m 1930 to Howard Jay Bridwell; c Linda (Mrs James Lucas) & Melissa (Mrs John Eckstein). Educ: Zanesville High Sch; Meredith Bus Col, dipl, 28. Polit & Govt Pos: Auditor, Muskingum Co Welfare Dept, 57; clerk, Muskingum Co Comnrs, 58-; pres, Muskingum Co Women's Rep Club, 60-66; chairwoman, Muskingum Co Rep Club, Ohio, 66-; mem bd trustees, Zanesville Art Ctr, 73- Bus & Prof Pos: Secy, Alva R Rea, pres, Eclipse Laundry Co, 30-41. Mem: Nat Secretaries Asn (Zanesville Chap). Relig: Lutheran. Mailing Add: 2455 Vinsel Dr Zanesville OH 43701

BRIER, JACK H (R)
Nat Committeeman, Kans Young Rep Fedn
b Kansas City, Mo, June 25, 46; s Marshall William Brier & Marie Pearl Munden B; single. Educ: Univ Kans, 64-67; Washburn Univ, Topeka, BBA, 70. Polit & Govt Pos: Dep Asst Secy of State, Kans, 69-70, Asst Secy of State, 70-; Nat Committeeman, Kans Young Rep Fedn, 71- Mem: Am Soc Pub Adminr. Relig: Protestant. Legal Res: 8239 Woodward Overland Park KS 66204 Mailing Add: 2145 Virginia Topeka KS 66605

BRIGGS, FRANK A (D)
NH State Rep
Mailing Add: Depot Rd East Kingston NH 03827

BRIGGS, FRANK P (D)
b Armstrong, Mo, Feb 25, 94; s Thomas H Briggs & Susan Almira Pyle B; m 1916 to Catherine Allen Shull; c Thomas Frank, Eugene Allen, Darlene Ruth, Betty Barbara & Dorothy Catherine. Educ: Cent Col, Fayette, Mo, 11-14; Univ Mo, BJ, 15; Sigma Delta Chi. Hon Degrees: DSc, Cent Col, 61. Polit & Govt Pos: Mayor, Macon, Mo, 30-33; Mo State Sen, 33-45, pres, Mo State Senate, 41-45; US Sen, Mo, app to fill unexpired term of Harry S Truman, 45; mem, Mo Conserv Comn, 47-; asst Secy of Interior for Fish & Wildlife, 61-68; mem, Int Comn for NAtlantic Fisheries, 61- Bus & Prof Pos: Ed, Fayette Dem-Leader, Mo, 15; city ed, Moberly Monitor-Index, 16-17; ed, Trenton Times, 17-18, city ed, 19; night ed, Shawnee Morning News, Okla, 19-23; ed & owner, Macon Chronicle-Herald, Mo, 24- Mem: Mason; Elks; Rotary; Nat Press Club, Washington. Honors & Awards: Distinguished Pub Serv Award, Sch of Jour Univ Mo, 58. Mailing Add: Box 15 Macon MO 63552

BRIGGS, JOHN VERN (R)
Calif State Assemblyman
b Alpena, SDak, Mar 8, 30; s Leslie R Briggs & Jessie Rae Snedaker B; m 1951 to Carmen Nicasio; c Kathleen, Daniel & Ronald. Educ: Fullerton Jr Col, AA in Bus Admin, 54; Long Beach State Col, BS in Bus Admin, 56. Polit & Govt Pos: Pres, Walter Knott Young Rep, 60; Calif State Assemblyman, 67-, mem comt agr, Calif Gen Assembly, 71- Bus & Prof Pos: Owner, Continental Ins Brokers, 65- Mil Serv: Entered as Pvt, Air Force, 48, released as S/Sgt, 52, after serv in Mil Air Transport Serv, Korea, 50; Presidential Unit Citation. Mem: Buena Park CofC; Buena Park Jr CofC; Rotary; Elks; VFW. Relig: Catholic. Mailing Add: 1400 N Harbor Blvd Fullerton CA 92632

BRIGGS, ROBERT ALVIN, JR (R)
Bonus Mem, Rep State Cent Comt, Colo
b Greeley, Colo, Dec 24, 37; s Robert Alvin Briggs & Leta Edison B; m 1957 to Shirley Christine Abbott; c Robert Reuben & Christy Lynn. Educ: Colo State Univ, BS, 59, MS, 61. Polit & Govt Pos: Deleg, Co & State Rep Assemblies, Colo, 68 & 70; dist capt, Adams Co Rep Party, 68-69; mem agr adv comt, Colo Dept Agr, 69; deleg, Colo Assembly, 70; bonus mem, Rep State Cent Comt, 69-; mem, Colo Environ Comn, 70-72; Adams Co co-chmn for Nixon, 72; precinct committeeman, Rep Party, Colo, 72-; mem, Adams Co Rep Cent Comt, 72- Bus & Prof Pos: Pres, Briggs Greenhouse, Inc, 61-; pres, Briggs Carnation Farm, 61- Mem: Colo Flower Growers Asn; Westminster Jaycees; Westminster Lodge; Rotary (bd dirs, Westminster Club, 71-73); Nat Presby Mariners (First Mate, 72-74). Honors & Awards: Man of the Year, Westminster, 63 & 68; One of Three State Chaplains Honored by US Jaycees, 67; Distinguished Serv Award, Colo Flower Growers Asn, 70. Relig: Presbyterian. Mailing Add: 6851 N Pecos Denver CO 80221

BRIGHT, JOE L (D)
NC State Rep
Mailing Add: RFD 2 Vanceboro NC 28586

BRIGHTMAN, SAMUEL CHARLES (D)
b Lancaster, Mo, June 22, 11; s Samuel Charles Brightman & Alberta Steele B; m 1947 to Lucy Kirk Cleaver; c Samuel Charles, Jr, Elizabeth Cleaver, George Forsha & David Sherwood. Educ: Washington Univ, AB, 32; Univ Mo, BJ, 33; Sigma Delta Chi; Alpha Tau Omega. Polit & Govt Pos: Dept asst adminr, Surplus Property Admin, 45; spec asst to Housing Expediter, 46; asst dir publicity, Dem Nat Comt, 47-52; dir publicity, 52-57; dep chmn pub affairs, 57-65; managing ed, Dem Digest, 53-56, ed, 56-61. Bus & Prof Pos: Reporter, St Louis Star-Times, 33-35; copy ed, Cincinnati Post, 35, chief copy ed, 35-40; news ed, Radio Sta KSD, St Louis, 37; Wash correspondent, Louisville Courier-Journal, 40-42, spec writer & copy ed, 47; writer for The Nation, TV Guide & New York Times; consult, ABC & CBS; ed, Adult & Continuing Educ Today. Mil Serv: Entered as Pvt, Army, 42, released as Capt, 45; after serv in publicity & psychol warfare in Europe; in charge news coverage for First Army, Omaha Beach, Normandy Invasion; participated in Liberation of Paris, Exec Officer, Pub Rels Detachment for Allied Forces in occupation of Berlin. Mem: Nat Press Club; Nat Capital Dem Club; Kenwood Country Club. Relig: Episcopal. Mailing Add: 6308 Crathie Lane Bethesda MD 20016

BRILES, JAMES E (R)
Iowa State Sen
b Prescott, Iowa, Mar 31, 26; m to Lorene Tindall; c Three sons & two daughters. Educ: Prescott High Sch. Polit & Govt Pos: Iowa State Rep, 4 terms; Iowa State Sen, 64- Bus & Prof Pos: Assoc with father in auction bus. Mil Serv: Asiatic-Pac Theater, 44-46. Mem: Am Legion; VFW. Relig: Methodist. Mailing Add: 806 Seventh St Corning IA 50841

BRILEY, CLIFTON BEVERLY (D)
b Nashville, Tenn, Jan 11, 14; s Clifton Weaver Briley & Willie Whithorne Vaughan B; m 1934 to Dorothy Gordon; c Clifton Beverly, Jr & Martha Diane (Mrs Easterling). Educ: Vanderbilt Univ; Cumberland Univ, LLB; Pi Kappa Alpha. Hon Degrees: LLD, Cumberland Univ. Polit & Govt Pos: Secy, Tenn State Dem Exec Comt, 48-50; judge, Davidson Co, 50-63; mayor, Metrop Nashville & Davidson Co, Tenn, 63-75; deleg, Dem Nat Conv, 68; mem, President's Adv Comn on Intergovt Rels; mem, Nat Comn Productivity, 71- Bus & Prof Pos: Partner in Law Firm of Atkinson & Briley. Mil Serv: Entered as A/S, Navy, 43, released as Navigational Qm 1/C, 45; Pac & Am Theater Ribbons & Seven Bronze Stars; Presidential Unit Citation; Commanding Officer Citation. Publ: Author of articles & contrib to books on local govt & reformed govt structure. Mem: Nat Asn Counties; US Conf Mayors; Nat League Cities; Tenn Co Serv Asn; Tenn Munic League. Relig: Baptist. Mailing Add: 1406 Winding Way Nashville TN 37216

BRILEY, JOHN MARSHALL (R)
Mem, Ohio Rep Finance Comt
b Monmouth, Ill, Jan 10, 05; s Lewis Henry Briley & Mary Frances Ryan B; m 1931 to Dorothy Louise DeWolf; c Suzanne (Mrs Rene H M Gimbrere), Millicent (Mrs David Bowerman), John Marshall, Jr & Michael Marshall. Educ: Monmouth Col, Ill, AB, 27; Harvard Univ, LLB, 30; Tau Kappa Alpha; Alpha Tau Omega. Polit & Govt Pos: Mem exec comt, Lucas Co Rep Comt, Ohio, 58-74; deleg-at-lg, Rep Nat Conv, 60 & 64; chmn, Ohio Rep Finance Comt, 61-62, life mem, 62-; Rep cand for US Sen, Ohio, 62; mem, Rep Nat Finance Comt, 63-70; chmn, Citizens for Goldwater-Miller, Ohio, 64; mem, Fed Prison Bd, chmn, Ohio Bd Regents, 64-75; treas, Citizens for Nixon-Agnew, Ohio, 68; chmn, Presidential Task Force on Prisoner Rehabilitation, 69. Bus & Prof Pos: Partner, Shearman & Sterling, 30-51; chmn, Hotel Pierre, New York, pres, Owens-Corning Fiberglas Int, 55-60; sr vpres, Owens-Corning Fiberglas Co, 52-71. Mem: NY State Bar Asn; Asn of the Bar of New York; Am Soc Int Law; life mem Moose; KofM (Master Knight). Relig: Roman Catholic. Mailing Add: 26 Dogwood Lane Stamford CT 06903

BRILL, NEWTON CLYDE (R)
Chmn, Howell Co Rep Comt, Mo
b Mt Grove, Mo, Mar 10, 36; s Newton Clyde Brill & Marie Young B; m 1958 to Margaret Carolyn Saunders; c Julia Elizabeth, Margaret Ann & Joel Newton. Educ: Univ Mo, AB in Polit Sci, 58, LLB, 64; Phi Eta Sigma; Order of the Coif; Phi Delta Phi. Polit & Govt Pos: Chmn, Howell Co Rep Comt, Mo, 64- Bus & Prof Pos: Partner, Law Off of Moore Brill, 64- Mil Serv: Entered as 2nd Lt, Marine Corps, 58, released as 1st Lt, 61, after serv in 3rd Bn 11th Marines, 1st Marine Div, Camp Pendleton, Calif; Capt, Marine Corp Reserves, 63. Publ: Voir Dire Examination of Jurors, Law Rev, Univ Mo Law Sch, 64. Mem: Howell Co & Mo Bar Asns; Kiwanis. Relig: Southern Baptist. Mailing Add: Box 527 West Plains MO 65775

BRILLIANT, MOLLIE WEXLER (D)
VChmn, Dade Co Dem Exec Comt, Fla
b Chelsea, Mass, Dec 22, 14; d Jacob Wexler & Bertha Rathman W; m 1948 to Judge Meyer Mack Brilliant; c Cynthia Beth & Joni Fern. Educ: Emerson Col, 1 year; Boston Univ, 2 years; Harvard Univ, one course. Polit & Govt Pos: Committee mem, Dade Co Dem Exec Comt, Fla, 58-62, area chmn, 62-66, vchmn, 66-; pres, Dem Women's Club Dade Co, 64-66, pres & co-chmn coun, 66; 12th Cong Dist vpres, Dem Women's Clubs Fla, 66-, second vpres, currently; deleg, Dem Nat Conv, 68, vchmn, Women's Activities, 72; actg chmn, Dem Exec Comt, 70; chmn, Miami City Dem Comt, 71-; first vpres, Women's Comt of 100; chmn women's comt, Manpower Planning Agency & Dade Co Comn Status of Women, currently; Southeastern chmn, Gov Comn Status of Women, currently. Bus & Prof Pos: First vpres coun continuing educ, Miami Dade Community Col, currently. Publ: Jewish women in American history, under Mollie Williams, Am Jewish Forum, 43. Mem: Flagler Granada Jewish Community Ctr; Gtr Miami Jewish Community Ctr Bd; Nat Coun Jewish Women; Leukemia Soc; Combined Jewish Appeal. Honors & Awards: Citation of Merit, Leukemia Soc; Cert of Appreciation, Dem Exec Comt, Dade Co; Golden Donkey Award, Dem Exec Comt; Women Doer Award, Dem Party; Outstanding Dem Award, Young Dem Dade Co. Relig: Hebrew. Mailing Add: 5835 SW 50 Terr Miami FL 33155

BRIMMER, ANDREW FELTON
b Newelton, La, Sept 13, 26; s Andrew Brimmer & Vellar Davis B; m 1953 to Doris Millicent Scott; c Esther Diane. Educ: Univ Wash, BA, 50, MA, 51; Univ Bombay, India, Fulbright Fel, 51-52; Harvard Univ, PhD, 57. Hon Degrees: LLD, Marquette Univ, 68, Nebr Wesleyan Univ, 68, Long Island Univ, 69, Oberlin Col, 69, Tufts Univ, 70, Colgate Univ, 70 & Atlanta Univ, 70. Polit & Govt Pos: Economist, Fed Reserve Bank, New York, 55-58; mem, Fed Reserve Cent Banking Mission to Sudan, 57; dep asst secy, Dept of Com, 63-65, Asst Secy of Com, 65-66; mem bd of gov, Fed Reserve Syst, 66- Bus & Prof Pos: Asst prof, Mich State Univ, 58-61, Wharton Sch Finance & Com & Univ Pa, 61-63. Mil Serv: Army, 45-46. Publ: Life Insurance Companies in Capital Marketing, 62; Survey of Mutual Funds Investors, 63. Mem: Fel Am Acad Arts & Sci; Am Econ Asn; Coun Foreign Rels; Asn for Study of Negro Life & Hist (pres, 70-); Am Finance Asn. Honors & Awards: Named Govt Man of the Year, Nat Bus League, 63; Arthur S Flemming Award (one of ten outstanding young men in govt serv), Capitol Press Club, 66. Legal Res: PA Mailing Add: Fed Reserve Bd 20th St & Constitution Ave NW Washington DC 20551

BRIMMER, CLARENCE ADDISON (R)
b Rawlins, Wyo, July 11, 22; s Clarence A Brimmer & Geraldine Zingsheim B; m 1953 to Emily Docken; c Geraldine, Phillip, Andrew & Elizabeth. Educ: Univ Mich, BA, 44, Law Sch, JD, 47; Sigma Delta Chi; Sigma Phi Epsilon; Phi Delta Phi. Polit & Govt Pos: Munic Judge, Rawlins, Wyo, 48-54; chmn, Carbon Co Rep Party, 48-56; Rep State Committeeman, 61-62; mem, Gov Water Study Comt, 65-66; chmn, Wyo Rep Party, 67-71; mem, Rep Nat Comt, 67-71; Attorney Gen, Wyo, 71-74; US Attorney, 75- Bus & Prof Pos: Dir, Rocky Mountain Mineral Law Found. Mil Serv: Entered as Pvt, Air Force, 45, released as Sgt, 46. Mem: Rawlins Lions Club; AF&AM (Past Master); Elks (Past Exalted Ruler); Rawlins Jr CofC; CofC. Relig: Episcopal; sr warden vestry, St Thomas Episcopal Church. Legal Res: 1420 W Sixth Ave Cheyenne WY 82001 Mailing Add: PO Box 668 Cheyenne WY 82001

BRINDLEY, JOSEPH DURWOOD (D)
Ala State Rep
b Royal, Ala, Aug 23, 39; s Van Buren Brindley & Betty Bellenger B; m 1961 to Syble Delean Hazelrig; c Patrick Andrew & Elizabeth Anne. Educ: Jacksonville State Univ, BS, 64; Univ Ala, MA, 66; Phi Delta Kappa. Polit & Govt Pos: Ala State Rep, 74-; mem, Ala State Dem Exec Comt, currently. Bus & Prof Pos: Dir community serv, Snead State Jr Col, 71- Mil Serv: Marine Corps Res, 57-63. Mem: Ala & Nat Educ Asns; Nat Coun Community Serv; Jacksonville Univ Nat Alumni Asn (pres); Community Develop Soc. Relig: Baptist. Mailing Add: Rte 8 Boaz AL 35957

BRINEGAR, CLAUDE S (R)
b Rockport, Calif, Dec 16, 26; m to Elva Jackson; c Claudia, Meredith & Thomas. Educ: Stanford Univ, BA econ, with great distinction, 50, MS math statist, 51, PhD econ research, 54; Phi Beta Kappa; Sigma Xi. Polit & Govt Pos: Secy of Transportation, 73-75. Bus & Prof Pos: With Union Oil Co Calif, 53-65, vpres econ & corp planning, 65-73, sr vpres, mem bd dirs & mem exec comt, 68-73 & 75-; pres, Union 76 Div, 71-73; pres, Pure Oil, until 73; instr exten div, Univ Calif, Los Angeles, 55-60, Whittier Co, 56 & Calif Inst Technol, 57. Mil Serv: Army Air Corps, serv in Japan & Korea. Publ: A statistical analysis of speculative price behavior, Stanford Univ, 70; contrib articles on econ, statist & mgt to prof jour. Mem: Young Pres Orgn; Am Statist Asn; Mid-Am Club, Chicago; Calif Club, Los Angeles. Mailing Add: Union Oil Co Calif 461 S Boylston Los Angeles CA 90017

BRINEY, JAMES WILSON, JR (R)
Mem, Oakland Co Rep Exec Comt, Mich
b Pontiac, Mich, July 10, 47; s James Wilson Briney, Sr & Barbara Sanford B; single. Educ: Univ Detroit, Cert Polit Sci, 68; Olivet Col, Mich, BA, Philos, 69; Christian Theol Sem, Indianapolis, grad studies, student coun, 65-69, pres two terms; col admin coun, 67-69; Pontiac Alumni Award, Outstanding student, 68; founding father, Int Hegelian Soc, SC, 68; Winebrenner Theol Sem, 73 & 74. Polit & Govt Pos: Alt deleg, Mich Rep State Conv, 68, deleg, 70; cand, Mich State Rep, 62nd Dist, 68 & Rep nominee, 72; asst to Richard G Lugar, Mayor of Indianapolis, & Pres Nat League of Cities, 69-70; co-founder, Mandate, 70; cand, Mich State Sen, 17th Dist, 70; Pontiac City Comn Appointee to Sr Citizens Housing Comn, 70; trustee bd dirs, Pontiaction, Inc; admin asst, Mich State Sen Donald E Bishop, 71-;

deleg-at-lg, Oakland Co Rep Exec Comt, Mich, 71-73, mem, 73- Bus & Prof Pos: Instr, Mich Migrant Prog, Frankfort, 69; asst instr polit sci, Mich State Univ, 73-75, teaching const revision, currently. Publ: Columnist, The Clarkston News & The Pontiac Times. Mem: Oakland Co Asn Retarded Children (asst dir, 72-). Honors & Awards: Youngest cand, Mich House of Rep. Mailing Add: 62 E Iroquois Rd Pontiac MI 48053

BRINK, RANDALL WILSON (R)
Chmn, Dist Two Rep Comt, Idaho
b Lewiston, Idaho, Feb 22, 55; single. Educ: NIdaho Col, AA; Phi Ro Pi; Oriad Creative Writers Guild. Polit & Govt Pos: Precinct committeeman, Kootenai Co Rep Cent Comt, Idaho, 73-; chmn, Dist Two Rep Comt, 74- Bus & Prof Pos: Pres, Brink Aviation Enterprises, 73- Mem: Coeur D'Alene Community Theatre (bd dirs). Relig: Presbyterian. Legal Res: Rte 1 Box 1 Rathdrum ID 83858 Mailing Add: Rte 3 Box 40 Rathdrum ID 83858

BRINKHAUS, ARMAND JOSEPH (D)
La State Rep
b Sunset, La, Nov 7, 35; s Dr Armand L Brinkhaus & Julia Thoms B; m 1957 to Margaret Bellemin; c Armand, Michelle, Celeste, Julia, Andre, Renee & Marguerite. Educ: Springhill Col, 54; Univ Southwestern La, 54-56; Loyola Law Sch, La, LLB, 60, JD, 68; pres, Delta Theta Phi; bus mgr, Loyola Law Rev. Polit & Govt Pos: La State Rep, St Landry Parish, 68- Bus & Prof Pos: Pvt practice, Judge Kalieste J Saloom, Jr, Lafayette, 61-62; pvt practice, John L Olivier, Sunset, 62- Mem: Am Bar Asn; Am Judicature Soc; Am Trial Lawyers Asn; La Sweet Potato Asn; La Asn Young Men's Bus Clubs (pres, 62-). Honors & Awards: Distinguished Serv Award, La Third Circuit Court Appeal, 61. Relig: Roman Catholic. Mailing Add: PO Drawer E Sunset LA 70584

BRINKLEY, JACK THOMAS (D)
US Rep, Ga
b Faceville, Ga, Dec 22, 30; s Lonnie E Brinkley & Pauline Spearman B; m 1955 to Alma Lois Kite; c Jack Thomas, Jr & Fred Alen II. Educ: Young Harris Col, 47-49; Univ Ga, LLB, 59; Phi Alpha Delta; Blue Key. Polit & Govt Pos: Ga State Rep, 112th Dist, 65-67; US Rep, Ga, 67-; deleg, Dem Nat Conv, 72. Bus & Prof Pos: Attorney, Young, Hollis & Moseley, 59-61; attorney, Coffin & Brinkley, 61-66. Mil Serv: Entered as Pvt, Air Force, 51, released as 1st Lt, 56. Mem: Columbus, Ga & Am Bar Asns; Mason. Relig: Baptist. Legal Res: 4108 Appalachian Way Columbus GA 31907 Mailing Add: 2412 Rayburn House Off Bldg Washington DC 20515

BRINKLEY, WILLIAM T (D)
Ky State Rep
Mailing Add: 311 W Lake St Madisonville KY 42431

BRINKMAN, BERNARD J (DFL)
Minn State Rep
b Farming, Minn, 1926; married; c Five. Educ: Albany High Sch. Polit & Govt Pos: Minn State Rep, 64-; chmn, Local Sch Bd, formerly. Bus & Prof Pos: Owner & operator, Brinky's, Richmond, Minn; farmer. Mil Serv: Navy, 44-46. Mem: Civic & Com Club; Lions; Am Legion. Relig: Catholic. Mailing Add: Richmond MN 56368

BRINLEY, RAY LLOYD (R)
b Fletcher, Mo, Sept 1, 06; s Edward Henry Brinley & Clara Scaggs B; m 1943 to Eva Verona Dickinson McKinnon. Educ: High Sch Grad. Polit & Govt Pos: Chmn, Jefferson Co Rep Party, Mo, formerly. Bus & Prof Pos: Farmer. Mem: Mason; RAM (High Priest, Copestone Chap 33, 59); Bonne Terre Coun 43; DeSoto Commandery 56 (Comdr, 72); Farm Bur Fedn (pres, Jefferson Co, 70-73 & serv as resolution chmn, legis chmn & nat affairs chmn). Honors & Awards: Citation for Outstanding Agr Performance, De Kalb Agr Asn, 49; Citation for Leadership & Guid, Bd Curators, Univ Mo, 64; Named to Bd of Sponsors for Support of Nat Security Educ, Inst for Am Strategy, 72. Relig: Protestant. Mailing Add: Box 213A Rte 1 Dittmer MO 63023

BRINTON, DONALD EUGENE (D)
Colo State Rep
b Fairfield, Iowa, Feb 16, 27; s Thomas Eugene Brinton & Maude Lucile Pickard B; m 1951 to Marilyn Jean McLachlan; c Kathy (Mrs Bill Parker), Mark, Debbie (Mrs Elmer Maestas), Ellen, Barry & Sarah. Educ: Univ Northern Iowa, BA, 50; Univ Iowa, MA, 51; Pi Gamma Mu. Polit & Govt Pos: Colo State Rep, 65-66 & 75- Bus & Prof Pos: Teacher, Del Norte, Colo, 51-52 & Sch Dist 11, Colorado Springs, Colo, 52- Mil Serv: Entered as Pvt, Air Force, 45, released as Cpl, 46, after serv in Pac Theatre, 46. Mem: Colo Educ Asn. Relig: Methodist. Mailing Add: 212 Bassett Dr Colorado Springs CO 80910

BRISCOE, BILL (D)
Okla State Sen
Mailing Add: State Capitol Oklahoma City OK 73105

BRISCOE, DOLPH (D)
Gov, Tex
Mailing Add: State Capitol Austin TX 78711

BRISCOE, JEAN (D)
Dem Nat Committeewoman, Mo
Mailing Add: PO Box 499 New London MO 63459

BRISCOE, JOHN HANSON (D)
Md State Deleg
b Leonardtown, Md, Apr 10, 34; s John Henry Thomas Briscoe & Hilda Maddox B; m 1956 to Sylvia Weiss; c Lisa Jane, Janice Lynn, Dana Elizabeth & John Hanson, Jr. Educ: Mt St Mary's Col, AB, 56; Univ Baltimore, LLB, 60. Polit & Govt Pos: Md State Deleg, 62-, chmn econ affairs comt, Legis Coun, Md Legis, 70-; chmn ways & means comt, Md House Deleg, 71-73; vchmn environ quality comt, Southern Conf State Govt, 70-; chmn, Southern Legis Conf, Coun State Govt, 71-72. Mem: St Mary's Co & Md State Bar Asns; Lions; KofC. Relig: Catholic. Legal Res: Box 317 Hollywood MD 20636 Mailing Add: 17 Shangri-La Dr Lexington Park MD 20635

BRISTLEY, CALVIN WESLEY, JR (R)
Chmn, Sandusky Co Rep Cent Comt, Ohio
b Fremont, Ohio, Apr 28, 26; s Calvin Wesley Bristley, Sr & Helen Elizabeth Fuzesy B; m 1950 to Patricia Rose Huntzinger; c Rebecca Kay, Eric David & Rachael Ann. Educ: Ohio Univ, 46-48; Univ Cincinnati, LLB, 51; Phi Alpha Delta. Polit & Govt Pos: City solicitor, Fremont, Ohio, 56-; mem, Sandusky Co Rep Cent Comt, 56-, vchmn, 62-67, chmn, 67- Bus & Prof Pos: Secy-treas, Sandusky Co Law Libr Asn, Ohio, 59-75; dir, Sandusky Co YMCA, 69, vpres, 71-72, pres, 72- Mil Serv: Pvt, Air Force, 44-45. Publ: Validity of municipal ordinances prescribing penalties greater than state laws, Univ Cincinnati Law Rev, 5/51. Mem: Am & Ohio State Bar Asns; Kiwanis. Relig: Lutheran. Legal Res: 412 S Jefferson St Fremont OH 43420 Mailing Add: 323 S High St Fremont OH 43420

BRISTOW, WALTER JAMES, JR (D)
SC State Sen
b Columbia, SC, Oct 14, 24; s Dr Walter J Bristow & Caroline Belser Melton B; m 1952 to Katherine Stewart Mullins; c Katherine M & Walter J, III. Educ: Va Mil Inst, 41-43; Univ NC, AB, 47; Univ SC Law Sch, LLB cum laude, 49; Harvard Law Sch, LLM, 50; Pi Gamma Mu. Polit & Govt Pos: Asst counsel, US Sen Subcomt on Privileges & Elec, 56; SC State Rep, 57-58; SC State Sen, 59- Bus & Prof Pos: Assoc, Marchant, Bristow & Bates, Attorneys. Mil Serv: Army, 43-46, 292nd Field Observ Bn; Col, SC Nat Guard. Mem: Elks (Past Exalted Ruler, Lodge 1190); Am Legion; VFW; Mil Order World Wars; Alpha Tau Omega. Relig: Presbyterian; deacon, First Presby Church. Mailing Add: State House Columbia SC 29211

BRITT, HENRY MIDDLETON (R)
Permanent Mem, Ark Rep State Comt
b Olmstead, Ill, June 9, 19; s Henry Middleton Britt, Jr & Sarah Theodosia Roach B; m 1942 to Barbara Jean Holmes; c Nancy Marsh, Sarah Barbara & Melissa. Educ: Univ Ill, Urbana, AB in Polit Sci, 41, Col Law, JD, 47; Phi Alpha Delta; Delta Phi; Phalanx. Polit & Govt Pos: Pres, Young Rep Club, Univ Ill, formerly asst US Attorney, Western Dist, Ark, 53-58; cand for Gov, Ark, 60; gen counsel, Rep Party, Ark, 62-64; Rep mem, Garland Co Bd Elec Comnrs, 62-66; chmn, Garland Co Rep Cent Comt, 62-66; Circuit Judge, 18th Judicial Dist, 66-; permanent mem, Ark Rep State Comt; alt deleg, Rep Nat Conv, 68; mem Exec Bd, Ark Comn on Crime & Law Enforcement, 68-71; mem Cent Planning Coun, Ark Crime Comn, 72- Bus & Prof Pos: Pvt practice of law, Hot Springs, Ark; mem, Exec Comt, State Judicial Coun, 72- & State-Fed Judicial Coun, 72-75. Mil Serv: Entered Army, 41-46, serv in Persian Gulf Command, 42-44; Capt (Ret), Judge Adv Gen Corps, Army Res. Mem: Ill State Bar Asn; Am Judicature Soc; Am & Ark Bar Asns; Hot Springs Jr CofC. Honors & Awards: Nat Col State Trial Judges fel; partic, Midwest Training Conf on Organized Crime & Law Enforcement, Univ Notre Dame, 72; Sertoma Serv to Mankind Award. Relig: Presbyterian; Elder, Deacon & Trustee. Mailing Add: 126 Trivista Hot Springs AR 71901

BRITT, LUTHER JOHNSON, JR (D)
NC State Sen
b Lumberton, NC, Aug 10, 32; s Luther J Britt & Beta Elkins B; m 1955 to Sarah Williams; c Sally B, L Johnson, III, H Brooks & Lee Elkins. Educ: Wake Forest Univ, BS, Law Sch, JD; Phi Delta Phi; Alpha Sigma Phi. Polit & Govt Pos: City attorney, Lumberton, NC, 66-, chmn, Robeson Co Dem Party, 67-70; NC State Sen, 20th Senate Dist, 71-73, 12th Senate Dist, 73- Bus & Prof Pos: Partner, L J Britt & Son, Attorneys, 55- Mil Serv: Entered as Pvt, Army, 56, released as SP, 58, after serv in 8th Inf Div, Ger. Mem: Am, NC & Robeson Co Bar Asns; NC Jaycees (pres). Honors & Awards: One of Outstanding State Jaycee Pres, 67. Legal Res: 603 W 25th Lumberton NC 28358 Mailing Add: Box 1015 Lumberton NC 28358

BRIZZI, FRANCIS J (D)
b New York, NY, Oct 24, 21; s Frank Albert Brizzi & Margaret Diffley B; m 1945 to Rita Lee Downey; c Dona Jeanne (Mrs Thomas Dolan), Laura Lee (Mrs Justin Henderson) & Francis John, Jr. Educ: Am Univ, 44-45. Polit & Govt Pos: Fingerprint technician, Fed Bur Invest, 41-45; spec asst, US Sen Estes Kefauver, Tenn, 45-63; admin asst to US Sen Herbert S Walters, Tenn, 63-65; coordr, Citizens for Johnson-Humphrey, 64-65; asst to regional dir, Post Off Dept, 65-68; staff dir, Comt on Vet Affairs, US Senate, 71- Bus & Prof Pos: Exec dir, Govt Consult Serv, 68-71. Mil Serv: Entered as Pvt, Air Force, 42, released as Pfc, 43. Mem: Life mem, DAV. Relig: Catholic. Mailing Add: 8606 Rockdale Lane Springfield VA 22153

BROAD, ELI (D)
b New York, NY, June 6, 33; s Leon Broad & Rebecca Jacobson B; m 1954 to Edythe Lois Lawson; c Jeffry Alan & Gary Steven. Educ: Mich State Univ, BA, cum laude, 54; Beta Alpha Psi. Polit & Govt Pos: State chmn for US Sen Alan Cranston, Calif, 68; deleg, Dem Nat Conv, 68; mem, Nat Indust Pollution Control Coun, 71-; nat vchmn, Dem for Nixon Campaign, 72. Bus & Prof Pos: Asst prof acct, Detroit Inst Technol, 55-56; chmn & pres, Kaufman & Broad Bldg Co, 57-68; chmn, Kaufman & Broad, Inc, 68-; mem vis comt, Univ Calif, Los Angeles Grad Sch Mgt; mem, Bus Comt for the Arts; mem, Exec Comt of Int Forum for Los Angeles World Affairs Coun; dir, Haifa Univ; mem adv bd, Inst Int Educ; dir, CMI Corp, Madison, Wis, currently. Mem: Nat Asn Housing Producers; Coun Housing Producers (dir); Mich State Univ Develop Bd (dir); City of Hope (trustee); Pitzer Col, Claremont (trustee). Honors & Awards: Man of the Year, City of Hope, 65; Prof Builder of the Year, Prof Builder Mag, 67; Distinguished Alumni Award, Mich State Grad Sch Bus Admin, 68. Relig: Jewish. Legal Res: 1 Oakmont Dr Los Angeles CA 90049 Mailing Add: 10801 Nat Blvd Los Angeles CA 90064

BROADBENT, PETER EDWIN, JR (R)
Nat Committeeman, Young Rep Fedn Va
b Richmond, Va, May 16, 51; s Peter Edwin Broadbent & Nancy Norris B; single. Educ: Duke Univ, BA, 73; Univ Va Sch Law, 74-; Psi Upsilon; Phi Delta Phi; Alpha Phi Omega. Polit & Govt Pos: Vchmn, NC Col Rep Fedn, 71-72; dir scheduling, Sen Jesse Helms Staff, 72; chmn, NC Young Am for Freedom, 72-73; nat committeeman, Young Rep Fedn Va, 73-; mem, Richmond City Rep Comt, 74- Mem: Am Bar Asn (law student div); Intercollegiate Studies Inst; Law Christian Fellowship. Relig: Episcopal. Legal Res: 21 Ampthill Rd Richmond VA 23226 Mailing Add: 2659 Barracks Rd Apt 4 Charlottesville VA 22901

BROADWATER, TOMMIE, JR (D)
Md State Sen
b Washington, DC, June 9, 42; s Tommie Broadwater, Sr & Lula Cunningham B; m 1959 to Lillian Patricia Prince; c Tommie, III, Tanya Barita, Jacqueline Patrice & Anita. Educ: Southeastern Univ. Polit & Govt Pos: Councilman, Glenarden, Md; mem, Dem State Cent Comt, Md; Md State Sen, 75- Bus & Prof Pos: Ins agt, Progressive Life Ins Co & United Ins Co Am; bail bondsman, Prince Georges, St Mary's & Charles Co, 67- Mem: NAACP (life mem); Prince Georges CofC; DC CofC; Bondsmen's Asn; Ploughman & Fishermen Dem Club (charter mem). Relig: Baptist. Mailing Add: 3309 Hayes St Glenarden MD 20801

BROCK, MARGARET MARTIN (R)
Mem Exec Comt, Rep Nat Finance Comt
b Los Angeles, Calif; d James R Martin & Pauline Cornwell M; m 1933 to George C Brock, wid. Educ: Mt Vernon Sem, 25. Polit & Govt Pos: Trustee, Rep Assocs, Los Angeles; chmn, women's div United Rep Finance Comt, Los Angeles Co; mem, Rep Nat Finance Comt, 52-, mem exec comt, 69-; deleg, Rep Nat Conv, 52-; mem, President's Comt on Aging, 56-60. Mem: Founding mem Jr League of Los Angeles; Federated Rep Women's Clubs; Rep Assocs of Los Angeles; Capitol Hill Club, Washington, DC; Women's Nat Rep Club, NY. Relig: Protestant. Mailing Add: 1404 Century Towers W 2220 Ave of the Stars Los Angeles CA 90067

BROCK, ROBERT LEE (D)
b Pawnee Rock, Kans, Dec 27, 24; s Eddie Ray Brock & Vivian Crawford B; m 1952 to Mary Louise Heim; c Robert L, Jr, Edward H, Alan D, Steven R & Darin C. Educ: Univ Kans, AB, 50, Sch Law, LLB, 51; Phi Beta Kappa; Phi Delta Phi; Tau Kappa Epsilon. Polit & Govt Pos: Pres, Young Dem Clubs of Kans, 59-60; chmn, Second Dist Dem Party, Kans, 66-73; deleg, Dem Nat Mid-Term Conf, 74; chmn, Kans Dem State Cent Comt, 74-75. Bus & Prof Pos: Pres, Inn Opers, Inc, 61- & Topeka Inn Mgt, Inc, 69- Mil Serv: Aviation Elec Technician Mate 3/C, Naval Air Corps, Am Theatre, 43-46. Mem: Int Asn Holiday Inns (bd mem, 62-, pres, 64-65); Elks; Univ Kans Bus Sch Bd Adv; Univ Kans Alumni Asn Bd Dirs; Chancellor's Assocs, Univ Kans. Honors & Awards: Billy Hutson Kans Innkeeper of Year Award, Kans Hotel & Motel Asn, 65; Top TEKE Alumnus of Year, Tau Kappa Epsilon, 73; Kansan of the Year, Native Sons & Daughters of Kans, 73. Relig: Congregational. Legal Res: 1533 Stratford Rd Topeka KS 66604 Mailing Add: 2209 W 29th St Topeka KS 66611

BROCK, WILLIAM EMERSON, III (BILL) (R)
US Sen, Tenn
b Chattanooga, Tenn, Nov 23, 30; s William Emerson Brock, Jr & Myra Kruesi B; m 1957 to Laura Handly; c William E, IV, Oscar Handly, Laura Hutcheson & John Kruesi. Educ: Washington & Lee Univ, BS in Com, 53; Sigma Alpha Epsilon. Polit & Govt Pos: Nat committeeman, Tenn Young Rep, 61-; US Rep, Third Dist, Tenn, 62-70; deleg, Rep Nat Conv, 68 & 72; US Sen, Tenn, 70-, mem, Finance Comt, Banking Housing Urban Affairs Comt & Govt Orgn Comt, US Senate, currently. Bus & Prof Pos: Prod asst, Brock Candy Co, 56-63, vpres mkt, 63- Mil Serv: Entered as Ens, Navy, 53, released as Lt(jg), 56, after serv in 7th Fleet, Far East, 54-56; Korean War & UN Serv Ribbons; Lt, Naval Res, 61- Mem: CofC; Jr CofC; Am Legion; Chowder & Marching Soc; Area Literacy Movement. Honors & Awards: Outstanding Young Man of the Year, Tenn Jaycees, 65; Distinguished Serv Award, Chattanooga Jaycees, 66; Award for Outstanding Serv to TAR, 67; Award for Outstanding Serv to Cong Adv Coun of Young Rep Nat Fedn; Distinguished Legislator, Young Am Inaugural Comt, 69. Relig: Presbyterian; former Sunday sch teacher. Legal Res: Dogwood Dr Lookout Mountain TN 37350 Mailing Add: US Senate Washington DC 20510

BROCKBAN, W HUGHES (R)
Utah State Rep
Mailing Add: 777 E South Temple Salt Lake City UT 84102

BROCKER, NAIDA LOUISE (R)
b Laramie, Wyo, Apr 15, 44; d William Andrew Simson & Naida Cox S (deceased); m 1962 to Gordon Ernest Brocker; c Kelli Lea & John Gordon. Educ: La Salle Col Exten. Polit & Govt Pos: Alt deleg, Colo State Rep Conv, 67 & 68; secy, Jackson Co Rep Party, Colo, formerly. Mem: Colo Fedn Womens Clubs; Colo State & North Park Cowbelles; North Park Roping Club; Snowbird Theta Rho Girls Club. Honors & Awards: Rocky Mt Snowmobile Powder Puff Champion, 67 & 68; queen of various rodeos. Relig: Presbyterian. Mailing Add: PO Box 644 Walden CO 80480

BROCKETT, GLENN F (R)
Iowa State Rep
Mailing Add: 502 Orchard Dr Marshalltown IA 50158

BROCKFELD, RUSSELL G (R)
Mo State Rep
Mailing Add: 310 Wightman St Warrenton MO 63383

BROCKMAN, MARY LAURA (R)
Committeewoman, Co Rep State Comt, Fla
b Abington, Pa, Apr 24, 51; d Albert Norton Brockman & Barbara Bachman B; single. Educ: Fla State Univ, 69-70; Fla Jr Col at Jacksonville, 71-72; Univ NFla, 72- Polit & Govt Pos: Treas, Duval Co TAR, 64-66, vpres 66-67, pres, 67-68; secy, Fla Fedn TAR, 67-68, Fla State Univ Young Am for Freedom, 69-70, Fla State Univ Young Rep, 69-70 & Fla Fedn Col Young Rep, 70-71; deleg, Nat Young Am for Freedom Nat Conv, Houston, 71; chmn, Fla Jr Col Young Rep, 71-72; chmn, Duval Co Young Am for Freedom, 71-72; deleg, Rep Nat Conv, 72; secy, Duval Co Young Rep, 72-73; committeewoman, Rep State Comt, Duval Co, 74- Honors & Awards: Miss Fla Fedn TAR, Fla TARS, 68; Achievement Award for Membership, Fla Fedn Young Rep, 70; One of Top Five Young Rep, Fla, 74; Young Rep Nat Fedn Silver Hardcharger Award, 75. Relig: Presbyterian. Mailing Add: 2617 Algonquin Ave Jacksonville FL 32210

BRODE, MARVIN JAY (D)
Mem, Shelby Co Dem Exec Comt, Tenn
b Memphis, Tenn, Aug 26, 31; s Howard Moe Brode & Erneice Jacob B; m 1965 to Freda Jean Cohn; c William Howard, Robert Mark & Laura Mary. Educ: Vanderbilt Univ, BA, 53; Vanderbilt Law Sch, LLB, 54; Tau Kappa Alpha; Phi Alpha Delta; Zeta Beta Tau. Polit & Govt Pos: Acting spec city judge, Memphis, Tenn, 57-64; asst city attorney, 65-66; Tenn State Rep, 63-67; hon mem, Gov Staff, 66-; mem, Shelby Co Dem Exec Comt, 66- Bus & Prof Pos: Attorney, Brode & Smith, 65-66; attorney, Brode & Sugg, 66- Mem: President's Comt on Traffic Safety; Shelby Co Bar Asn; Tenn Comn on the Performing Arts; Mayor's Community Action Comt; Memphis, Shelby Co Safety Coun. Honors & Awards: Auth of Tenn Seat Belt Law & worker in the field of motor traffic safety. Relig: Jewish. Legal Res: 4841 Walnut Grove Rd Memphis TN 38117 Mailing Add: Suite 3116 100 N Main Bldg Memphis TN 38103

BRODERICK, FAY LEONE (D)
b Gardiner, Maine, June 3, 33; d Paul C Willett & Ruth E Markham W; m 1957 to Richard Howard Broderick; c Michael K, Richard H & Paul J. Polit & Govt Pos: Mem, Maine Dem State Comt, 63-64; Dem Nat Committeewoman, Maine, 64-72; deleg & chmn Permanent Orgn Comt, Dem Nat Conv, 68; deleg to seven State Dem Conv. Bus & Prof Pos: Mem, Lincoln Employee Bd Appeals, 71-72 & 73- Mem: Lincoln Dem Womans Club (pres, 73-74); Lincoln Hosp Auxiliary. Relig: Episcopal. Mailing Add: Transalpine Rd Lincoln ME 04457

BRODERICK, RICHARD HOWARD (D)
Mem, Maine State Dem Comt
b Portland, Maine, Mar 26, 25; s John H Broderick & Dorothy Giles B; m 1957 to Fay Leone Willett; c Michael, Richard & Paul. Educ: Univ Maine; Portland Univ Law Sch. Polit & Govt Pos: Maine State Rep, 57-58; chmn, Gov Exec Coun, Maine, 65-66; deleg, Dem Nat Conv, 68; mem, Maine State Dem Comt, 71- Bus & Prof Pos: Attorney-at-law, 50- Mil Serv: Navy, 42-46, after serv in Underwater Demolition Unit 23, Europe & Pac. Mailing Add: Lincoln ME 04457

BRODEUR, ROBERT J (D)
NH State Rep
Mailing Add: 38 Washington St Claremont NH 03743

BRODHEAD, WILLIAM MCNULTY (D)
US Rep, Mich
b Cleveland, Ohio, Sept 12, 41; s William McNulty Brodhead & Agnes Franz B; m 1965 to Kathleen Garlock; c Michael Kennedy & Paul Andrew. Educ: Wayne State Univ, AB, 65; Univ Mich Law Sch, JD, 67; Psi Chi. Polit & Govt Pos: Precinct deleg, 70; mem exec bd, 17th Dist Dem Party, 69-; mem, Wayne Co Dem Comt, 71-; Mich State Rep, 71-74; membership chmn & mem finance comt, Mich Dem Party, 73-74; US Rep, 17th Dist, Mich, 75- Bus & Prof Pos: Pvt law practice, 68, attorney, City Detroit, 69-71. Mem: Detroit, Mich & Am Bar Asns. Legal Res: 16199 Warwick Detroit MI 48219 Mailing Add: House of Rep Washington DC 20515

BRODSKY, RICHARD EUGENE (D)
b Providence, RI, Nov 15, 46; s Irving Brodsky & Naomi Richman B; m 1972 to Margaret A Stone. Educ: Brown Univ, AB, 68; Harvard Univ Law Sch, JD, 71; Phi Beta Kappa. Polit & Govt Pos: Legal asst to Fed Community Comn comnr Nicholas Johnson, Washington, DC, 71-72; deleg & mem credentials comt, Dem Nat Conv, 72; dep coordr, State of Va & coordr, Bridgeport, Conn, McGovern-Shriver Campaign, 72; legis asst to US Rep Frank E Evans, Colo, 73; trial attorney, Securities & Exchange Comn, 73- Publ: Co-auth, The interstate commerce omission, Grossman Publ, 70 & Free sports on TV: is the end near?, Sport Mag, 8/72. Mem: DC Bar. Relig: Jewish. Mailing Add: 4701 Willard Ave Chevy Chase MD 20015

BRODY, BRENDA (D)
Mem, Conn Dem State Cent Comt
Polit & Govt Pos: Mem, Conn Dem State Cent Comt, 26th Sen Dist, 74- Mailing Add: 79 Clinton Ave Westport CT 06880

BROKAW, GARY H (D)
Kans State Rep
Mailing Add: 508 Waverley Coffeyville KS 67337

BROMFIELD, BETSY BYRON (R)
b Boston, Mass, June 30, 14; d Walter Harwood Byron & Helen Marie Annis B; div; c Sally (Mrs Robert Bruce Whitney) & Ann Cameron. Educ: Miss Porter's Sch, Farmington, Conn; Leland Sch Drama, Boston, Mass, 1 year. Polit & Govt Pos: Precinct area chmn, Nixon Campaign, Pac Palisades, 60; assoc mem, Rep State Cent Comt, 62-64; precinct chmn, Goldwater-Miller Campaign, Santa Barbara, 64; registr precinct chmn, Santa Barbara Co Rep Cent Comt, 65, co-chmn precinct, 65-66; precinct coordr, Friends of Gov Reagan, Santa Barbara Co, 66; mem, Rep State Cent Comt, 64-72, chmn, Speakers Bur, 66-72; mem, exec bd, 68-72; deleg, Rep Nat Conv, 68, hon deleg 72 & secy, Calif Favorite Son Deleg, 68; mem, Calif Rep Victory Squad Comt, 70; state hq off mgr, Flournoy for Gov, Calif, 74- Bus & Prof Pos: Actress, summer stock, Kennebunk, Maine, 33-34; comparison shopper, R H Macy & Co, New York, 37-38; Bd dirs, Get Oil Out Inc, Santa Barbara, Calif, 73- Mem: Jr League, Boston, Mass & Syracuse, NY; Vincent Club, Boston. Relig: Protestant. Mailing Add: 1930 Tollis Ave Santa Barbara CA 93108

BROMLEY, DAN (D)
Kans State Sen
Mailing Add: RR2 Box 74A Atchison KS 66002

BROMWELL, JAMES EDWARD (R)
b Cedar Rapids, Iowa, Mar 26, 20; s Max T Bromwell & Olive McDuff B; m 1946 to Dorothy Bennett; c Maxwell Thomas, Helen Kirk (Mrs Dent), Catherine McDuff & James Edward, Jr. Educ: Univ Iowa, BA, 42, LLB, 50; Harvard Univ, MBA, 47; Phi Delta Phi; Omicron Delta Kappa. Polit & Govt Pos: Asst co attorney, Linn Co, Iowa, 56-59; US Rep, Second Dist, Iowa, 61-65. Bus & Prof Pos: Owner & operator, farm, Center Point, Iowa, currently. Mil Serv: Entered as Pvt, Army, 42, released as Capt, 45, after serv in Europe. Mem: Am Legion; Elks; Mason; Kiwanis; Linn Co Farm Bur. Mailing Add: 1920 Ridgeway Dr SE Cedar Rapids IA 52403

BRONEMANN, JERALD RAYMOND (R)
b Monticello, Iowa, May 19, 40; s Roland Samuel Bronemann & Velma Tobiason B; m 1968 to Barbara Rogers; c Rand Roland Joseph. Educ: Univ Iowa Col of Bus Admin, BBA, 62, Col of Law, BL, 65; Sigma Pi. Polit & Govt Pos: Chmn finance, Jones Co Rep Party, Iowa, 68-69, chmn, formerly. Bus & Prof Pos: Self-employed attorney, Monticello, Iowa, 65- Mem: Iowa State, Am & Jones Co Bar Asns; Farm Bur. Relig: Lutheran. Legal Res: 402 Pinehaven Dr Monticello IA 52310 Mailing Add: Box 301 Monticello IA 52310

BRONSON, MINNIE L (D)
VChmn, Clinton Co Dem Party, Ind
b Kirklin, Ind, July 26, 15; d John W Bronson & Lina Wagenblass B; single. Educ: Kirklin High Sch, grad, 33. Polit & Govt Pos: Clerk-treas, Town of Kirklin, Ind, 52-67; dep co clerk, Clinton Co, 56-63, co clerk, 63; Dem precinct committeewoman, Precinct One, Kirklin Twp, Clinton Co, 40's & 64-; vchmn, Clinton Co Dem Party, 70-, writer, ed & publ, Clinton Co Crower, Dem monthly newslett, currently. Bus & Prof Pos: Off mgr, Canning Factory, Kirklin, Ind, 41-52; off clerk, State Hwy, Frankfort, 52-53; off mgr, Optical Industs, Indianapolis, 53-55; secy, Morrison & Robbins Law Off, Frankfort, 64- Mem: Eastern Star (treas, 45-72); Clinton Co Dem Women's Club (adv, 71-); Ind Women's Dem Club. Relig: Presbyterian. Mailing Add: N Ohio St Kirklin IN 46050

BRONSTON, JACK E **(D-LIBERAL)**
NY State Sen
b Plainfield, NJ, Jan 10, 22; m to Adele; c Deena Rhoda & David. Educ: Harvard Univ, AB magna cum laude, 42; Harvard Law Sch, LLB, 48; NY Univ Sch Law, LLM, 48; Phi Beta Kappa. Polit & Govt Pos: NY State Sen, currently. Bus & Prof Pos: Partner, Rosenman, Colin, Kay, Petschek, Freund & Emil, New York, 73- Mil Serv: 1st Lt, Marine Corps, 42-46. Mailing Add: 184-37 Hovenden Rd Queens NY 11432

BROOKE, ALBERT BUSHONG, JR **(R)**
b Paducah, Ky, June 23, 21; s Albert Bushong Brooke, Sr (deceased) & Ruth Crawford B; m 1947 to Virginia Joyce Rogers; c Albert B, III, Susan Rogers, Roger W & Virginia Joyce. Educ: Univ Ky, AB in journalism, 47; Phi Beta Kappa; Epsilon Chapter. Polit & Govt Pos: Spec & admin asst to US Sen Thruston B Morton, Ky, 58-68; mem, Fed Power Comn, 68-75. Bus & Prof Pos: Reporter, Grand Rapids Press, Mich, summer 40; bookkeeper, Elk Horn Coal Corp, Wayland, Ky, 41-42; reporter & asst city ed, The Herald, Lexington, Ky, 46-57; acct exec pub rels, Van Sant, Dugdale & Co, Baltimore, Md, 57-58. Mil Serv: Entered as Pvt, Army Air Force, 42, released as 1st Lt, 46, after serv in 9th Tactical Air Command, 9th Air Force, ETO; ETO Ribbon with 6 Battle Stars. Mailing Add: 8619 Highgate Rd Alexandria VA 22308

BROOKE, D G **(D)**
Utah State Rep
Mailing Add: 761 Roosevelt Ave Salt Lake City UT 84105

BROOKE, EDWARD WILLIAM **(R)**
US Sen, Mass
b Washington, DC, Oct 26, 19; s Edward William Brooke & Helen Seldon B; m 1947 to Remigia Ferrari-Scacco; c Remi (Mrs Coyle) & Edwina Helene. Educ: Howard Univ, BS, 41; Boston Univ Law Sch, LLB, 48, LLM, 50. Hon Degrees: JD, Portia Law Sch, 63; DPA, Northeastern Univ, 64 & Suffolk Univ, 69; LLD, Am Int Col, 65, Emerson Col, 65, George Washington Univ, 67, Howard Univ, 67, Boston Univ, 68, Johns Hopkins Univ, 68, Hampton Inst, 68, Morehouse Col, 68, Cath Univ Am, 68, Bowdoin Col, 69, NAdams State Col, 69, Skidmore Col, 69, Boston State Col, 71, Univ Mass, 71, Univ NH, 71, Xavier Univ La, 71 & Amherst Col, 72; DSc, Lowell Technol Inst, 67 & Worcester Polytech Inst, 65; LHD, Framington State Col, 70; ed, Boston Univ Law Rev, 46-48. Polit & Govt Pos: Rep nominee, Secy State, Mass, 60; chmn, Boston Finance Comn, 61-62; Attorney Gen, Mass, 63-66; deleg, Rep Nat Conv, 64 & 68; US Sen, Mass, 67-, mem banking, housing & urban affairs comt, comt appropriations, select comt stand & conduct, spec comt aging & joint comt defense prod, US House Rep, currently. Bus & Prof Pos: Lawyer. Mil Serv: Entered as 2nd Lt, Army, 42, released as Capt, 45, after serv in 366th Inf Regt, ETO & with Partisans, Italy; Bronze Star; Combat Infantryman's Badge. Publ: The Challenge of Change, Little-Brown, 66. Mem: Mass & Boston Bar Asns; fel Am Bar Asn; fel Am Acad Arts & Sci; Opera Co Boston (chmn bd). Honors & Awards: Charles Evans Hughes Award, Nat Conf Christians & Jews, 67; Distinguished Serv Award, Amvets; Spingarn Medal, NAACP, 67. Relig: Episcopal. Legal Res: 535 Beacon St Newton Centre MA 02159 Mailing Add: 421 Old Senate Off Bldg Washington DC 20510

BROOKER, ROSALIND POLL **(R)**
Mem, New Bedford City Coun, Mass
b Fall River, Mass, Sept 28, 28; d Israel Poll & Anna Ezring P; c Shelley Gail, Bradford Guy & Donna Lee. Educ: Boston Univ, JD, 52; assoc ed, Boston Univ Law Rev; Lambda Delta Pi. Polit & Govt Pos: Mem, New Bedford City Coun, Mass, 69-71, 71-73 & 73-; alt deleg, Rep Nat Conv, 72; Bristol Co coordr, Reelect Sen Edward W Brooke, 72; Rep state committeewoman, Third Bristol Dist, 73- Bus & Prof Pos: Attorney, New Bedford, Mass, 52-; Indust Accident Comnr, Commonwealth Mass, 73- Mem: New Bedford, Bristol Co & Mass Bar Asns; Mass Asn Women Lawyers; numerous civic, charitable & relig orgns. Honors & Awards: Presentation, Whalers Drum & Bugle Corps, 72; Pub Servant, W H Carney Lodge 200, Int Elks, 73. Relig: Hebrew. Mailing Add: 419 Union St New Bedford MA 02740

BROOKHART, SAMUEL HENRY **(R)**
Chmn, Lawrence Co Rep Cent Comt, Ill
b Sumner, Ill, May 2, 14; s William Lee Brookhart & Carrie Alice Legg B; m 1939 to Martha Cunningham; c Carol Ann (Mrs Arthur A Eubank, Jr). Educ: Eastern Ill Univ, BS in Ed, 70. Polit & Govt Pos: Twp supvr, Christy Twp, Ill, 54-58; Rep precinct committeeman, Christy Twp, Precinct 1, 58-; chmn, Lawrence Co Rep Cent Comt, 67- Bus & Prof Pos: Teacher, Clark Co Sch Syst, 35-37; teacher, Lawrence Co Sch Syst, 37-43 & 46-47, prin & teacher, Petrolia Sch, 47-69; prin, Petty Sch, 69- Mil Serv: Entered as Pvt, Army, 43, released as 1st Lt, 46, after serv in 45th Div, 157th Inf Regt, ETO, 44-45; Bronze Star. Mem: Lawrence Co Teachers Orgn; Ill & Nat Educ Asns. Relig: United Church of Christ; Deacon. Mailing Add: RR 3 Sumner IL 62466

BROOKING, JOHN R S **(R)**
b Louisville, Ky, Nov 27, 31; s Harry K Brooking & Margaret Sampson B; m 1954 to Charlotte Jarvis; c John Sampson, Susan King & Anne Margaret. Educ: Centre Col Ky, BA, 53; Cincinnati Law Sch, LLB, 60; Alpha Phi Omega; Beta Theta Pi. Polit & Govt Pos: City attorney, Parkhills, Ky, 66-; chmn, Kenton Co Rep Exec Comt, Ky, formerly. Bus & Prof Pos: Partner, Adams & Brooking, attorneys; regent, Northern Ky State Col, 68-72. Mil Serv: Entered as Ens, Navy, 53, released as Lt, 57, after serv in USS Bear, Korea; China Serv Medal. Mem: Am, Ohio, Ky & Kenton Co Bar Asns; CofC (dir). Relig: Episcopal. Mailing Add: 1132 Audubon Rd Park Hills KY 41011

BROOKMAN, EILEEN B **(D)**
Nev State Assemblyman
b Denver, Colo, Oct 25, 21; m to George G Brookman; c Michael L & Deborah L. Educ: Los Angeles City Col. Polit & Govt Pos: Nev State Assemblyman, 67-; mem, Gov Comt Status Women; app to serve on comt selected by Gov Laxalt; app by Secy Interior Walter Hickel to study allocation of water from Truckee-Carson Basin; mem, Clark Co Dem Cent Comt. Mem: Human Rels Comn; Nat Comt Support Pub Schs; Nev Indian Comn, NCCJ; Nat Coun Crime & Delinquency (co-chmn Nev State Comt); B'nai B'rith. Honors & Awards: Woman of Year, Clark Co, 69; Outstanding Woman of Year, B'nai B'rith; Outstanding Serv Recognition, Indians of Nev; Ky Col, 68. Mailing Add: 1900 Cochran St Las Vegas NV 89105

BROOKS, ARTHUR VAN NORDAN **(D)**
Ohio State Rep
b New York, NY, May 8, 36; s Fred A Brooks & Marion S B (deceased); m 1959 to Lesley Simpson Wells; c Lauren Elizabeth, Caryn Alison, Anne Kristen & Thomas Eliot. Educ: Cornell Univ, BS, 58; Univ Mich Law Sch, LLB, 63; Sigma Alpha Epsilon; Aleph Samach; Quill & Dagger. Polit & Govt Pos: Ohio State Rep, 14th Dist, 75- Bus & Prof Pos: Attorney, Baker, Hostetler & Patterson, 63- Mil Serv: Entered as Ens, Navy, 58, released as Lt(jg), 61, after serv in USS Galveston (CLG-3). Mem: Ohio Bar Asn (bd gov of real property sect, chmn, land use planning comt); Am & Cleveland Bar Asns. Honors & Awards: Outstanding Young Man of the Year, Cleveland Jaycees, 70. Mailing Add: 2385 Kenilworth Rd Cleveland Heights OH 44106

BROOKS, CHET EDWARD **(D)**
Tex State Sen
b Prescott, Ariz, Aug 18, 35; s C E Brooks, Sr & Julia Deats Biddle B; m 1959 to Fay Lamar; c Laura Lea & Tracie Lynn. Educ: San Jacinto Col & San Angelo Col, AA; Univ Tex, BA; Sigma Delta Chi. Polit & Govt Pos: Mem steering comt, Nat Dem Campaign, Harris Co, Tex, 60, 64, 68 & 72; Tex State Rep, 62-66; Tex State Sen, 66- Bus & Prof Pos: Owner, Brooks Agency, 58-; real estate ed, Houston Post, Tex, 59-63. Mil Serv: Navy, 54-56; Army Res, 56-62. Mem: Eagles; Harris Co Grand Jury Asn. Honors & Awards: Numerous serv awards from educ asns & civic groups. Relig: Methodist. Legal Res: 1603 Blackburn Dr Pasadena TX 77502 Mailing Add: PO Box 1302 Pasadena TX 77501

BROOKS, DORIS L **(R)**
Chmn, Broome Co Rep Comt, NY
b Towando, Pa, Mar 20, 12; d Ira I Steele & Ada L Green S; m 1936 to James A Brooks; c Richard A. Educ: Lowell Bus Sch, 32; Broome Tech Community Col. Polit & Govt Pos: Pres, Endicott Woman's Rep Club, 50-52; chmn, Union Town Rep Comt, 54-56; vchmn, Broome Co Rep Comt, 60-72, chmn, 72-; dep clerk, Broome Co, 63-66; Broome Co Rep Elec Comnr, 66- Bus & Prof Pos: Broker, Doris Brooks Real Estate, 60- Mem: Zonta Club Binghamton (finance chmn, 72-); Elec Comnr Asn NY State; Woman's Soc United Methodist Church; Rebekah; Grange. Honors & Awards: Bronze Plaque for Distinguished Serv to Rep Party, 61. Relig: Methodist. Mailing Add: 110 Birdsall St Endicott NY 13760

BROOKS, GEORGE HENRY **(D)**
Mem, Weld Co Dem Cent Comt, Colo
b Pittsburgh, Pa, Nov 28, 17; s James Clemer Brooks & Elizabeth Leith B; m 1942 to Georgia Mildred Milligan; c Bryan Leith, Janet Helen, Margie Ruth & Roger Hunt. Educ: Sterling Col, BA, 41; Univ Kans, MEd, 52; Univ Northern Colo, EdD, 69. Polit & Govt Pos: Precinct committeeman, Weld Co Dem Party, Colo, 62-; mem, Weld Co Dem Cent Comt, Colo, 63-; chmn, Fourth Cong Dist, Colo, 65-69; mem, Colo Dem State Exec Comt, formerly; deleg, State Dem Assembly & Conv, 66 & 68; deleg, Nat Dem Conv, 68. Bus & Prof Pos: Asst mgr, Campus Ctr, Univ Exten, Univ Kans, 52-55; dist scout exec, Long's Peak Coun, Boy Scouts, 55-59, asst scout exec, 59-61; asst to dean, Grad Sch, Univ Northern Colo, 66-, dir, Off Int Educ, 73- Mil Serv: Entered as Ens, Navy, 42, released as Lt, 45, after serv in Motor Torpedo Boat Squadron 6 & Subchaser Training Ctr, SPac & Miami, Fla, 42-45; Res, Lt Comdr; Am Theatre Ribbon; SPac-Asian Theatre Ribbon with Star; Good Conduct Medal; Expert Pistol Shot; Expert Rifleman. Mem: Phi Delta Kappa; Kiwanis. Relig: Presbyterian; Ruling Elder, 46- Mailing Add: 1726 19th Ave Greeley CO 80631

BROOKS, JACK **(D)**
US Rep, Tex
b Crowley, La, Dec 18, 22; m 1960 to Charlotte Collins; c Jack Edward, Katherine Inez & Kimberly Grace. Educ: Lamar Jr Col; Univ Tex, BJ, 43, JD, 49. Polit & Govt Pos: Mem, Tex Legis, 46-50; US Rep, Tex, 52- Bus & Prof Pos: Lawyer. Mil Serv: Marine Corps. Legal Res: Beaumont TX Mailing Add: 2449 Rayburn Off Bldg Washington DC 20515

BROOKS, JOHN H **(R)**
Idaho State Rep
Mailing Add: Rte 2 Gooding ID 83330

BROOKS, MARILYN ELIZABETH **(R)**
Committeewoman, Maine Rep State Comt
b Dexter, Maine, Oct 19, 31; d John Dudley Mosley & Marjorie Farr M; m 1952 to Ralph Joseph Brooks; c Deborah Eileen. Educ: Dexter High Sch, Maine, grad, 50. Polit & Govt Pos: Finance chmn, Newport Rep Town Comt, 64-70, treas, 64-; committeewoman, Maine State Rep Comt, 68-; mem exec comt, Penobscot Co Rep Comt, 68-; dist mgr census, US Census Bur, 70. Bus & Prof Pos: Secy, State of Maine, 50; secy, W S Emerson Co, 52; secy, Maine Food Plan, 60; real estate broker, Brooks & Brooks Agency, 64- Mem: Am Legion Auxiliary; Eastern Star; Penobscot Rep Womans Club; Sebasticook Valley Hosp Auxiliary; Newport Womans Club. Relig: Protestant. Legal Res: RFD 2 Newport ME 04953 Mailing Add: Box 366 Newport ME 04953

BROOKS, MARY ELIZABETH **(R)**
Dir, Bur of the Mint, Dept of the Treas
b Colby, Kans; d Sen John Thomas & Florence Jessie Johnson; m first to Arthur J Peavey, Jr & second to C Wayland Brooks; wid; c John Thomas & Elizabeth Ann (Mrs Eccles). Educ: Mills Col; Univ Idaho, BA; Kappa Kappa Gamma. Polit & Govt Pos: Exec secy to US Sen John Thomas, 42-45; mem, Rep Nat Comt, 57-63, vchmn, 60-63, asst chmn, 65-69; official hostess, Rep Nat Conv, 60; Idaho State Sen, 21st Dist, 64-69; dir, Bur of the Mint, Dept of Treas, 69- Bus & Prof Pos: Owner & mgr, Flat Top Livestock Co, Muldoon, Idaho; banker's asst, First Security Corp. Mem: Ill Ment Health Bd; Children's Home & Aid, Chicago; Lighthouse for the Blind; Immigrant Serv League; Defense Adv Comt on Women in Serv. Honors & Awards: Woman of Year, NY Women's Nat Rep Club, 69; Idaho Woman of Year, 70; Univ of Idaho Hall of Fame, 72; Exceptional Serv Award, Dept of Treas; I Left My Heart in San Francisco Award, San Francisco Conv & Visitors Bur, 73. Relig: Presbyterian. Legal Res: Carey ID 83320 Mailing Add: Dept of the Treas 15th St & Pennsylvania Ave NW Washington DC 20220

BROOKS, OLIVE **(D)**
b Mobile, Ala; d Stewart Brooks (deceased) & Emma Conner B (deceased); single. Educ: Shorter Col, Randolph Macon Woman's Col, Univ Ariz, Columbia Univ & New Sch of Social Research, Undergrad Work; Phi Mu. Polit & Govt Pos: Dep clerk, US Dist Court, Mobile, Ala, 18-19; chief, Pub Rels Unit, US Army Dist Engrs, Panama Canal Dept, Ancon, CZ, 41-46; writer-ed The Panama Canal Co & CZ Govt, Balboa Heights, 62, 63 & 64; vchmn, CZ Regional Dem Party, Ancon, 68; deleg, vchmn, CZ deleg & CZ rep, Platform Comt, Dem Nat Conv, 68, deleg, 72; Dem Nat Committeewoman, 70-72. Bus & Prof Pos: Socioecon writing, Mobile, Ala & New York; asst ed, Shell Progress mag, Shell Oil Co, New York, 35-40; correspondent for various US newspapers & news mag, also US & Brit wire serv, 44-73; reporter & copyreader, The Nation, Panama City, Rep of Panama, 47-49; copyreader,

reporter & desk ed, The Panama Am, 49-69. Publ: Panama Quadrant (poetry book), Bookman Assocs, New York, 60-61; various articles in bus, econ & related subjects. Mem: Overseas Press Club of Am, New York; Nat Asn of Retired Fed Employees, Washington, DC. Mailing Add: Leesburg Gardens Washington St Leesburg VA 22075

BROOKS, PATRICIA KERSTEN (D)
Chmn, Dem Town Comt of New Canaan, Conn
b Chicago, Ill, Dec 17, 26; d Robert C Kersten & Mable Frances Harrington K; m 1950 to Lester J Brooks, Jr; c Lester James, III, Jonathan Lawrence & Christopher Robinson. Educ: Vassar Col, BA, 47; Univ Minn, Minneapolis, MA, 48; Univ London, 49. Polit & Govt Pos: Chmn, Dem Town Comt of New Canaan, Conn, 72- Bus & Prof Pos: Copy & scriptwriter, Mutual Broadcasting Syst, 49-51, columnist & writer, Philippine Mag, 51-53; free lance writer, Reader's Digest, New York Times, Holiday, Venture, McCall's, Ladies Home J, House & Garden, Better Homes & Gardens, Christian Sci Monitor, Boston Globe, Art in Am & Saturday Rev, 53- Publ: Co-auth, The Presidents' Cook Book, 68, auth, The Philippines: Wonderland of Many Cultures, 68 & Meals While you Wait, 70, Funk & Wagnalls. Mem: Soc Mag Writers; Soc Am Travel Writers; Vassar Col Alumnae Asn; NAACP; Nat Urban League. Honors & Awards: Best travel article on the Philippines, Philippine Tourist & Travel Asn, 66; Critics Circle Award, Venture Mag, 68. Mailing Add: 43 Marshall Ridge Rd New Canaan CT 06840

BROOKS, PETER STUYVESANT (D)
VChmn, Orange Co Dem Exec Comt, NY
b Newburgh, NY, June 23, 42; s Frank Brooks & Anne Armstrong Rice B; div. Educ: Colgate Univ, 59-61; NY Univ, BA, 63; Columbia Univ. Polit & Govt Pos: Deleg, Dem Nat Conv, 72; mem, Orange Co Dem Exec Comt, NY, formerly, vchmn, currently; city assessor, Newburgh, currently. Bus & Prof Pos: Instr, Dutchess Community Col, 66-67; instr, Mt St Mary Col, 69-70; instr, Southhampton Col, 71-73; real estate broker, Unireal Inc, Newburgh, NY, currently. Mil Serv: Entered as Pvt E-1, Army, 68, released as Cpl E-3, 69. Mem: Am & Eastern Sociol Asns; Am Asn Univ Prof. Relig: Episcopal. Mailing Add: Danskammer Farm Box 1172 Newburgh NY 12550

BROOKS, RONNIE LEE (DFL)
VChmn, Fourth Dist Dem-Farmer-Labor Party, Minn
b Irvington, NJ, Aug 21, 44; d E Nelson Durchlag & Dorothy Kreielsheimer D; m 1966 to Roger Alan Brooks; c Kirsten Ailsa. Educ: Goucher Col, 62-64; Columbia Univ, summer 64; Univ Mich, Ann Arbor, BA, 65; Mich State Univ, MA, 67. Polit & Govt Pos: Coordr, Fourth Cong Dist, Minn, McGovern for President, 71-72, state campaign dir, Minn, 72, field staff, Ohio & NJ, 72; alt deleg, Dem Nat Conv, 72; vchmn, Fourth Dist Dem-Farmer-Labor Party, Minn, 72-; dir, Senate majority research, Minn State Senate, 73- Bus & Prof Pos: Research asst, Off of Nat Security Studies, Bendix Systs Div, Ann Arbor, 66; asst instr polit sci, Mich State Univ, 67-68; instr social sci, Lansing Community Col, 68-69; coordr curriculum eval, James Madison Col, Mich State Univ, 69; asst coordr common mkt, Minn State Col Syst, St Paul, 71-72. Mem: Am Civil Liberties Union; Sierra Club; Am for Dem Action; Pi Sigma Alpha; Phi Kappa Phi. Honors & Awards: Dean's Scholar, Goucher Col, 63-64; Internship Grant, Computer Inst for Social Sci Research, Mich State Univ, 67-68. Mailing Add: 1685 Princeton Ave St Paul MN 55105

BROOKS, THOMAS LEE (D)
Miss State Rep
Mailing Add: Box 892 Tupelo MS 38801

BROOKS, THOMAS NORMAN (TOMMY) (D)
Miss State Sen
Mailing Add: RFD 1 Box 57 Carthage MS 39051

BROOKS, TOM (R)
Chmn, Kitsap Co Rep Party, Wash
b Addy, Wash, July 23, 33; s Robert Porter Brooks & Vivia Belfrage B; m 1954 to Rovena Mae Engelhardt; c Merle David, Claudia Lynn, Christina Gay & Jason Thomas. Educ: Jenkins High Sch, grad, 51. Polit & Govt Pos: Chmn, Kitsap Co Rep Party, Wash, 75- Mil Serv: Entered as Airman Recruit, Navy, 52, released as PHA-3, 55, after serv in VF92, Pac Theatre, 54-55; China Serv Ribbon; Nat Defense Medal. Mem: Jr Chamber Int (life mem); Elks; Eagles. Relig: Protestant. Legal Res: Rte 1 Box 1 Silverdale WA 98383 Mailing Add: PO Box 758 Silverdale WA 98383

BROOM, VERNON H (D)
Justice, Miss Supreme Court
b Columbia, Miss, Jan 16, 24; s J C Broom & Bertha Herrin B; m to Cleme Johnson; c Judy (Mrs Herring) & Susan (Mrs Herron). Educ: Univ Miss, BBA & LLB, 48. Polit & Govt Pos: Dist attorney, Columbia, Miss, 52-64, circuit judge, 71-72; justice, Miss Supreme Court, 72- Mil Serv: Pvt, Army, 44-45, serv in 1st Inf Div, ETO; Purple Heart; Combat Infantryman's Badge; Bronze Star. Mem: Miss State Bar; Lions; Am Legion; VFW; DAV. Mailing Add: PO Box 50 Columbia MS 39429

BROOME, DEAN CARL (D)
Chmn, Pierce Co Dem Exec Comt, Ga
b DeKalb Co, Ga, July 5, 18; s Carl Jackson Broome & Exie Lurline Cunard B; m 1947 to Janie Kate Hice; c Dean Carl, Jr, Amelia Janet & Alice Lurline. Educ: Ga Eve Col, Atlanta, Ga, BS in Com, 42; Col Speakers Club. Polit & Govt Pos: Spec writer, Ord Dept, Qm Corps, 42; mem, Selective Serv Bd, Pierce Co, Ga, 52-54; dir, Civil Defense, Pierce Co, 56-58; chmn, Pierce Co Dem Exec Comt, 58- Bus & Prof Pos: Reporter, The Atlanta Constitution, Atlanta, Ga, 41-42. Mil Serv: Entered as Pvt, Army, 42, released as Technician 3/C after serv on Stars & Stripes, Mid East, 45; Mid East Ribbon. Mem: Rotary. Relig: Baptist. Mailing Add: 123 Marion St Blackshear GA 31516

BROOMFIELD, CHARLES S (D)
b Clay Co, Mo, June 11, 37; m 1962 to Charlene Leist (deceased); c Andrea Lynn & Leah Dawn. Educ: William Jewell Col, AB & teachers' cert. Polit & Govt Pos: Mo State Rep, 64-72, asst majority floor leader, Mo House Rep, 68-72; deleg, Dem Mid-Term Conf, 74; assoc judge, Clay Co Court, 74- Bus & Prof Pos: Taught Am govt & Am hist, North Kansas City High Sch, formerly; corp pub affairs officer, Hallmark Cards, Inc, 72- Mem: Sigma Nu; North Kansas City Jaycees; Am Cancer Soc (pres, SW Unit); AF&AM; North Kansas City CofC. Honors & Awards: Received St Louis Globe-Dem Newspaper Meritorious Serv Award, 70. Relig: Methodist. Mailing Add: 3635 N Main Kansas City MO 64116

BROOMFIELD, WILLIAM S (R)
US Rep, Mich
b Royal Oak, Mich, Apr 28, 22; s Dr S C Broomfield (deceased) & Fern B (deceased); m 1951 to Jane Thompson; c Susan, Nancy & Barbara Ann. Educ: Mich State Univ. Hon Degrees: LLD, Dongguk Univ, Seoul, Korea, 68. Polit & Govt Pos: Mich State Rep, 48, 50 & 52, speaker pro tem, Mich House of Rep, 53; Mich State Sen, 54; US Rep, Mich, 56-, mem int rels comt, US House Rep, currently; US deleg, NATO Parliamentarians' Conf, Paris, 60; cong deleg, US Nat Comn for the US Educ, Sci & Cult Orgn, Boston, 61-62; US deleg, Can-US Interparliamentary Conf, 61-64, 67-69 & 71-72; US deleg, US-UK Parliamentary Conf, Bermuda, 62; US Ambassador, 22nd UN Gen Assembly, 67; US deleg, US-UK Interparliamentary Conf, 69. Relig: Presbyterian. Legal Res: 5750 Whethersfield Lane Apt 4C Birmingham MI 48010 Mailing Add: 2435 Rayburn House Off Bldg Washington DC 20515

BROTHERS, ROBERT GENE (D)
Chmn, Mason Co Ky Dem Exec Comt
b Carlisle, Ky, July 9, 40; s Maurice G Brothers & Wilma Perry B; m 1966 to Judith Huber; c Shawn & Cynthia. Educ: Eastern Ky Univ, MA, 62; Ky Sch Mortuary Sci, 63; Young Dem Club. Polit & Govt Pos: Co coroner, Mason Co, Ky, 61-68; mayor, Washington, Ky, 72-; chmn, Mason Co Ky Dem Exec Comt, 73- Bus & Prof Pos: Field rep, Ky Legis Research Comn, 72-74; partner, Brothers Funeral Home, Maysville, Ky, 74- Mil Serv: Entered as Pvt, Army, 63, released as Drill Sgt, E-6, after serv in Basic Training Brigade, Ft Knox, Ky, 63-64; Good Conduct Medal. Mem: DeKalb Lodge Odd Fellows; Old Washington, Inc; Buffalo Trace Area Develop Dist. Relig: Methodist. Legal Res: Main St Washington KY 41096 Mailing Add: Rte 2 Box 174 Maysville KY 41056

BROTHERTON, W T, JR (D)
Pres, WVa State Senate
b Charleston, WVa, Apr 17, 26; s W T Brotherton (deceased) & Kathryn Slack B; m 1950 to Ann Jourdan Caskey; c Elizabeth Ann, William T, III & Laura Jane. Educ: Washington & Lee Univ, AB & LLB. Polit & Govt Pos: Investr, Kanawha Co Prosecuting Attorney's Off, WVa, 50-53; WVa State Deleg, 52-64; WVa State Sen, 64-, chmn judiciary comt, WVa State Senate, Majority Leader, 71-72, pres, 73-; alt deleg, Dem Nat Conv, 68. Bus & Prof Pos: Attorney-at-law, currently. Mil Serv: Navy, 44-46. Mem: Mason; Kappa Alpha; Phi Alpha Delta; Am Bar Asn; Action for Appalachian Youth. Honors & Awards: WVirginian of the Year, Gazette-Mail, 70. Relig: Episcopal; mem vestry, St Matthews Episcopal Church, 59-62, 68-70 & 71-73. Mailing Add: 1020 Kanawha Valley Bldg Charleston WV 25301

BROTHERTON, WILBUR V (R)
Mich State Rep
Mailing Add: 23622 Beacon Dr Farmington MI 48024

BROTZMAN, DONALD G (R)
Asst Secy Manpower & Reserve Affairs, Dept Army
b Logan Co, Colo, June 28, 22; s Harry Brotzman & Priscilla Ruth Kittle B; m 1944 to Louise Love Reed; c Kathleen L & Donald G (Chip). Educ: Univ Colo, BBS & LLB, 49; Beta Theta Phi; Phi Delta Phi. Polit & Govt Pos: Colo State Rep, 50-52; Colo State Sen, 52-56; mem, Colo Crime Comn, 52-56; comnr, Uniform State Laws from Colo, 54-; Rep cand, Gov of Colo, 56; US Attorney, Dist Colo, 59-61; US Rep, Colo, 63-64 & 67-74, mem, Ways & Means Comt & House Task Force Transportation, US House Rep, formerly; deleg, Rep Nat Conv, 68; mem, Nat Rep Cong Comt, 70; observer, Disarmament Conf; Asst Secy Manpower & Reserve Affairs, Dept Army, 75- Bus & Prof Pos: Attorney-at-law, Boulder, Colo, 49- Mil Serv: Army, 1st Lt, Inf, Pac Theatre, 42-46. Mem: Elks; Rotary; Mason; Am & Fed Bar Asns. Honors & Awards: Chosen by Colo Press as Outstanding Freshman Mem of House, 51; Outstanding Freshman Sen, 53; received Distinguished Serv Award from Colo Jr CofC, 54. Relig: Methodist; Trustee. Mailing Add: 735 Highland Ave Boulder CO 80302

BROUGHTON, VIRGINIA LEE (D)
Committeewoman, Mont Dem State Cent Comt
b Shelby, Mont, Apr 8, 24; d Ernest Ralph Holderby & Emily M Yurko H; m 1947 to LeRoy Alexander Broughton, Sr; c Suzanne E (Mrs Charles H Eckermann) & LeRoy A, Jr. Educ: Col Great Falls, 47-49; Beta Sigma Phi. Polit & Govt Pos: Secy, Lewis & Clark Dem Womens Club, Helena, Mont, 70-72; deleg, Dem Nat Conv, 72; regional dir, State Dem Women's Club, 72-75, vpres, 75-; secy to Speaker House Rep, Mont, 73-; committeewoman, Mont Dem State Cent Comt, 72- Bus & Prof Pos: Ed, Montana Democrat, 70- Mem: Brotherhood Rwy & Steamship Clerks, AFL-CIO. Relig: Roman Catholic. Mailing Add: 928 11th Ave Helena MT 59601

BROUILLARD, RICHARD P (R)
NH State Rep
Mailing Add: 300 Holman St Laconia NH 03246

BROUILLET, FRANK B (D)
Supt of Pub Instr, Wash
b Puyallup, Wash, May 18, 28; s Vern F Brouillet & Doris Darr B; m 1956 to Marge Ellen Sarsten; c Marc & Blair. Educ: Col Puget Sound, BA, BE, MA, 47-51; Univ Mont, 52; Univ Wash, EdD, 66; Phi Gamma Mu; Phi Delta Kappa; Sigma Chi. Polit & Govt Pos: Wash State Rep, 56-72, chmn, Joint House-Senate Interim Comt on Educ, Wash State Legis, 65-72, comnr, Interstate Compact for Educ, 66-72; Supt of Pub Instr, Wash, 72- Bus & Prof Pos: Dir overseas progs, Am Heritage Asn, 64-65; asst coordr col rels, Univ Wash, 65-68; asst to the pres, Highline Community Col, Midway, Wash, 68- Mil Serv: Entered as Pvt, Army, 53, released as Spec Agent, 55, after serv in Counter Intel Corps, Alaska. Publ: Coordinator of higher education, Col of Educ Rec, Univ Wash, 64; International education, Wash Educ, 65. Mem: Wash Educ Asn; Mason (32nd degree); Grange; Elks. Relig: Presbyterian. Mailing Add: 619 Seventh Ave SW Puyallup WA 98371

BROUILLETTE, FRANCIS DELORE (D)
b Iron Mountain, Mich, Dec 3, 31; s William Brouillette & Julia Groh B; m 1956 to Pauline Andreini; c Mary, Joseph, Ann & Lisa. Educ: Marquette Univ; Delta Theta Phi. Polit & Govt Pos: City attorney, Iron Mountain, Mich, 58-60; prosecuting attorney, Dickinson Co, 60-; chmn, Dickinson Co Dem Party, 61-72, Dem campaign chmn, 68; deleg, Dem Nat Conv, 68; treas, 11th Cong Dist, 69-; Dem cand for US Rep, Mich, 74. Mil Serv: Entered as Pvt, Army, 55, released as Pfc, 57, after serv in radio opers, France. Mem: Dickinson Co Bar Asn; Upper Peninsula Prosecuting Attorneys Asn; Elks; United Commercial Travelers; Pine Grove Country Club (bd dirs). Relig: Catholic. Mailing Add: 507 Quinnesec St Iron Mountain MI 49801

BROUN, PAUL C (D)
Ga State Sen
b Shellman, Ga, Mar 1, 16; s Leroy Augustus Broun & Annie Edwards B; m 1938 to Gertrude Margaret Beasley; c Paul Collins, Jr, Conway Castleman & Michael Shannon. Educ: Univ Ga, BS, 37. Polit & Govt Pos: Ga State Sen, 63- Bus & Prof Pos: Merchant. Mil Serv: Lt Col, Army Inf, World War II. Mem: Moose; VFW; DAV; Am Legion; pres, Athens CofC, 58. Relig: Episcopal. Mailing Add: 287 W Broad St Athens GA 30601

BROUSSARD, JAMES HUGH (R)
Chmn, Hays Co Rep Party, Tex
b Houston, Tex, May 6, 41; s Charles Hugh Broussard & Ethel Rollins; m 1962 to Margaret West Day; c David Hugh. Educ: Harvard Col, AB, 63; Duke Univ, MA, 65, PhD, 68. Polit & Govt Pos: Vchmn, High Sch Young Rep, Tex, 58-59; treas, Harvard Young Rep Club, 62-63; chmn, Rep Precinct, Durham, NC, 65-67; vchmn, Hays Co Rep Party, Tex, 72-74, chmn, 74-75. Bus & Prof Pos: Asst prof hist, Clarkson Col, 70-71 & Southwest State Univ, 71- Mil Serv: Entered as 1st Lt, Army, 68, released as Capt, 70, after serv in Adj Gen Sch, 68-70; Capt, Army Res, 70- Publ: Some determinants of know-nothing electoral strength in the south, 1856, La Hist, 66; Regional pride and Republican politics, S Atlantic Quart, 74. Mem: Lions; Jaycees; Am Hist Asn; Orgn Am Hist; Southern Hist Asn. Relig: Episcopal. Legal Res: 608 Franklin Dr San Marcos TX 78666 Mailing Add: PO Box 982 San Marcos TX 78666

BROUSSARD, MARCUS ANSON, JR (D)
Chmn, Vermilion Parish Dem Exec Comt, La
b Abbeville, La, Feb 14, 29; s Marcus Anson Broussard & Muriel Alice Brady B; m 1951 to Barbara Ann Schlesinger; c Marcus, III, James George, Edward Brady, Catherine Clare, Patricia Ann & Virginia Lynn. Educ: Univ Southwestern La, BA, 52; Loyola Univ (La), LLB, 55; Blue Key; Alpha Sigma Nu; St Thomas More Law Club. Polit & Govt Pos: Judge, City Court of Abbeville, La, 58-; chmn, Vermilion Parish Dem Exec Comt, 65- Mem: Am & La Bar Asns; Am Judicature Soc; Kiwanis. Relig: Catholic. Legal Res: Rte 1 Box 241 Abbeville LA 70510 Mailing Add: PO Box 7 Abbeville LA 70510

BROVERMAN, ROBERT LEE (D)
Chmn, Shelby Co Dem Cent Comt, Ill
b Pana, Ill, July 1, 31; s Harry Broverman & Elizabeth Bradach B; single. Educ: Millikin Univ, 49-51; Southern Ill Univ, BA, 53; Univ Ill, Urbana, JD, 57; Tau Kappa Epsilon; Phi Alpha Delta. Polit & Govt Pos: Precinct committeeman, Shelby Co Dem Cent Comt, Ill, 58-, secy-treas, 68-72, chmn, 72-; Asst Ill Attorney Gen, Shelby Co, 61-64, State's Attorney, 64-68 & 72-; master in chancery, Shelby Co. Mem: Ill & Am Bar Asns; Am Judicature Soc; Moose; CofC (dir, Shelbyville Chap). Relig: Presbyterian. Mailing Add: 123 W Main St Shelbyville IL 62565

BROWN, ALBERT D, JR (AL) (D)
Tex State Rep
Mailing Add: 5633 Parkcrest San Antonio TX 78239

BROWN, AMY CAMILE (D)
b Nashville, Tenn, May 27, 54; d Coleman Edward Brown & Bernice West B; single. Educ: Vanderbilt Univ; Oxford Univ, currently; Women's vpres, Arts & Sci; Alpha Lambda Delta; Lotus Eaters; Athenians; Mortar Bd; Univ Human Rels Comn. Polit & Govt Pos: Deleg, Dem Nat Conv, 72. Mem: Pull-Tight Players (bd mem, 72-73). Relig: Roman Catholic. Legal Res: 957 Glass St Franklin TN 37064 Mailing Add: Box 4959 Sta B Vanderbilt Univ Nashville TN 37235

BROWN, ARTHUR C (R)
Wash State Rep
Mailing Add: 16020 Densmore Ave N Seattle WA 98133

BROWN, B MAHLON (D)
Majority Floor Leader, Nev State Sen
b Shreveport, La, Jan 21, 14; s Bert Mahlon Brown & Pearl Sells B; m 1938 to Lucille Cummings; c B Mahlon, III & Stephen Cummings. Educ: Univ Calif, Los Angeles, 31-34; George Washington Univ, LLB, 37; Sigma Alpha Epsilon. Polit & Govt Pos: Justice of Peace, Las Vegas Twp, Nev, 41 & 42; Nev State Sen, 50-, Minority Floor Leader, Nev State Sen, 55-65, Majority Floor Leader, 65-, Pres Pro Tem, 67-68; Nev coordr, Johnson-Humphrey Campaign, 64; Presidential appointee, Adv Comn Intergovt Rels, 69-; mem exec comts, Nat Legis Conf, 71 & 73 & Nat Conf State Legis Leaders, 72 & 73. Bus & Prof Pos: Attorney, Brown & Deaner, 47. Mil Serv: Entered as Ens, Navy, 43, released as Lt, 46, after serv in SPac, 44-45. Mem: Am Judicature Soc; Am Bar Asn; Rotary; Elks; Variety Club. Relig: Presbyterian. Legal Res: 60 Country Club Lane Las Vegas NV 89109 Mailing Add: Nevada Bldg Suite 307 109 S Third Las Vegas NV 89101

BROWN, BASIL W (D)
Mich State Sen
b Vandalia, Mich, Mar 20, 27; m 1950 to Ermajeanne Seeger; c Lisa Denise. Educ: Western Mich Univ, AB; Univ Mich, LLB. Polit & Govt Pos: Mich State Sen, 56-72 & 75- Bus & Prof Pos: Attorney. Mil Serv: Navy; 3 decorations. Relig: Episcopal. Mailing Add: 43 Connecticut Highland Park MI 48203

BROWN, BENJAMIN D (D)
Ga State Rep
b Montezuma, Ga, Nov 14, 39; s Gen Lee Brown, Sr & Nettie Mitchell B (deceased); m to Lydia Marie Tucker; c Benjamin Kennedy & Barry Mitchell. Educ: Clark Col, AB; Howard Univ, JD, 64; nat vpres, Am Law Students Asn, 63-64; Phi Beta Sigma; Sigma Delta Tau. Polit & Govt Pos: Mem exec comt, Fulton Co Dem Club; vpres, Fulton Co Young Dem Club; mem, Ga Young Dem Deleg, Dem Nat Conv, 64, deleg, 72; mgr, Horace T Ward Campaign for Ga State Senate; mem, All Citizens Registr Comt; Ga State Rep, 135th Dist, 65-, chmn legis Black caucus, currently; mem rules comn, Dem Nat Comt; mem, Ga State Dem Exec Comt, 71-, info vchmn, currently; mem charter comn, Nat Dem Party, 73. Bus & Prof Pos: Boys counr, Butler YMCA, 56-60; recreation staff coordr, New York Welfare Dept, 61; guest lectr, Dartmouth Col & Harvard Univ, 63; law clerk, Hollowell, Ward, Moore & Alexander, 64; instr bus admin, Clark Col; co-founder & vpres, Wright, Jackson, Brown, Williams & Stephens, Inc, 69- Publ: Will the Negro gain equality?, Atlanta Inquirer, 66; Black politics & the South, Dem Nat Comt, 70. Mem: NAACP (exec secy, Atlanta Br); Atlanta Clark Col Alumni Club (vpres); Butler YMCA; Big Bros of Am; Grady Homes Boys Club & Girls Club (bd mem). Honors & Awards: Young Man of Year, Atlanta Y's Men Club, 65; cited by Clark Col Faculty for Outstanding Leadership to Col & Atlanta Community, 61; Prominent Leader in Atlanta Student Movement, 60-61; Whitney Young Mem Fel to Mass Inst Technol, 71-72. Relig: Christian Methodist Episcopal. Mailing Add: 33 Howard St SE Atlanta GA 30317

BROWN, BOB M (D)
Mem Exec Comt, Idaho State Dem Cent Comt
b Hereford, Tex, Feb 24, 37; s Erle Marie Foster B (father deceased); m 1965 to Judith Hyatt; c Eliot, Catherine & Rebecca. Educ: Tex Tech Univ, BA, Polit Sci, 60; Hastings Law Sch, 66-69, student body pres, 67. Polit & Govt Pos: Dir, Cong Dist Dem Hq, Tex, 60 & 64-65; conv dir, Idaho State Dem Cent Comt, 73-74, mem exec comt, 74- Bus & Prof Pos: Job placement dir, Voc Dept, North Idaho Col, 71- Mil Serv: Entered as 2nd Lt, Air Force, 60, released as 1st Lt, 63, after serv in 337th Group, Air Defense Command; Air Force Commendation Medal; Distinguished Unit Citation. Mem: Northwest Community Col Placement Asn; PTA Coun (pres, 74-75); Idaho Voc Guid Asn (secy-treas, 74-75). Honors & Awards: Community Ambassador to Chile, City of Lubbock, Tex, 59. Relig: Unitarian. Mailing Add: 1421 St Maries Ave Coeur d'Alene ID 83814

BROWN, BUSTER JACK (D)
Assoc Chmn, Nebr Dem Party
b Palmer, Nebr, Feb 2, 44; s Jack Alfred Brown & Maxine Lamberson B; single. Educ: Univ Nebr-Lincoln, BA, 67, MA, 73. Polit & Govt Pos: Committeeman, Nebr Dem Party, 72-, assoc chmn, 74-; deleg, Dem Nat Mid-Term Conf, 74. Mil Serv: Entered as Pvt, Army, 67, released as 1st Lt, 70, after serv in Signal Support Detachment, First Signal Brigade, Vietnam, 69-70; Nat Defense Serv Medal; Vietnam Serv Medal; Vietnam Commendation Medal; Bronze Star; Parachute Badge. Mem: Latin Am Res Asn. Legal Res: RR 2 Palmer NE 68864 Mailing Add: 709 N 33 St Apt 7 Omaha NE 68131

BROWN, CARMELA MARGARET (D)
Treas, Iowa State Dem Cent Comt
b Des Moines, Iowa, July 7, 38; d Joseph Thomas Romeo & Gazzo R; m 1957 to John R Brown, Jr; c Katherine Augusta & John III. Educ: St Joseph Academy, High Sch, grad, 56. Polit & Govt Pos: Treas, Iowa State Young Dem, 65-66; precinct committeewoman, Co Dem Party, 68-; chairwoman, Sen Dist Dem Comt, 75-; committeewoman, Fourth Dist Dem Cent Comt, 75-; treas, Iowa State Dem Cent Comt, 75- Bus & Prof Pos: Serv rep, Northwestern Bell Tel Co, 57-62; teller, Brenton Banks, Inc, 62-65; treas, Iowa Aviation, Inc, 65-72; secy, Iowa State Gen Assembly, 65-, secy to speaker pro tem, 75-; receptionist-bookkeeper, Iowa-Des Moines Nat Bank, 74- Mem: Iowa Chap of 99; Iowa Right to Life Orgn; Iowa Womens Polit Caucus. Relig: Catholic. Mailing Add: 8810 Urbandale Ave Des Moines IA 50322

BROWN, CHARLES HARRISON (D)
b Coweta, Okla, Oct 22, 20; s Sherman Brown & Frankie C Harrison B; m 1942 to Jean M Vinyard; c Ann M & Robert H. Educ: Drury Col, 37-38; George Washington Univ, 39; Lambda Chi Alpha; Seven Sages. Polit & Govt Pos: US Rep, Mo, formerly. Bus & Prof Pos: Asst prog dir, Radio Sta KWTO, Springfield, Mo, 37-38; radio publicity dir, Mo Conserv Comn, 40; alumni secy, Drury Col, 41-42; acct exec, Gardner Advert Co, 43-45; pres, Brown Radio-TV Prod, Inc, Springfield, 45-; partner, Brown Bros Advert Agency, Nashville, St Louis & Springfield, 45-; pres, Charles H Brown, Inc, Pub Rels Counrs, 61- Mem: Elks; Nashville Lions. Relig: Presbyterian. Legal Res: 541 Dale Dr Incline Village NV 89450 Mailing Add: Suite 400 1250 Connecticut Ave NW Washington DC 20036

BROWN, CHARLES M (D)
La State Sen
Mailing Add: Box 869 Tallulah LA 71282

BROWN, CLARENCE EBBERT (D)
b Fruita, Colo, Aug 10, 07; s John Fredrik Brown & Anna Barbra Ebbert B; m 1938 to Ida May Ashworth; c Clarice Jean (Mrs Kruschwitz), Carolyn Mae (Mrs Regier), Annetta Jane (Mrs Cowart) & Ruth Eileen. Educ: McPherson Col, 29-31; Ft Hays Kans State Col, BS in Agr, 38. Polit & Govt Pos: Asst state weed supvr, Gove Co & State Bd Agr, Kans, 40-43; conserv technician, Gove Co Agr Stabilization & Conserv Comt, 46-47; dist supvr, Gove Co Soil Conserv Dist, 49-56; dir, State Assoc Soil Conserv Dist Supvrs, 50-54; mem, State Soil Conserv Comt, 53-56; mem, Gov Watershed Rev Bd, 54-56; chmn, Gove Co Dem Cent Comt, formerly; chmn, Gove Co Exten Coun; mem, Gove Co Ment Health Comt, 70- Mem: Kans Nurseryman's Asn; Western Kans Develop Asn; Rotary; High Plains Paint Horse Asn; Kans Farmers Union. Relig: Church of the Brethren; Mem Dist Cabinet, Kans, Nebr & Colo Dist; Rep, State CROP Bd, Mem, Friendship Acre Comt. Mailing Add: Box 155 Quinter KS 67752

BROWN, CLARENCE J (R)
US Rep, Ohio
b Columbus, Ohio, June 18, 27; s Clarence J Brown (deceased) & Ethel McKinney B (deceased); m 1955 to Joyce Eldridge; c Elizabeth Ellen (deceased), Clarence J, III, Catherine Helen McKinney & Roy Eldridge. Educ: Duke Univ, BA in econ, 47; Harvard Grad Sch Bus Admin, MBA, 49; Omicron Delta Kappa; pres, Phi Kappa Sigma. Polit & Govt Pos: Mem, Champaign Co Rep Exec Comt, Ohio, 60-; US Rep, Ohio, 65-, mem, Govt Opers, Interstate & Foreign Com & Joint Econ Comts, US House of Rep, currently; deleg, Rep Nat Conv, 72; mem, Adv Coun Intergovt Rels, 73- Bus & Prof Pos: Ed, Blanchester Star Rep, 49-53; ed & publisher, Franklin Chronicle, 53-57; ed, Urbana Daily Citizen, 57-65, publisher, 59-67; pres, Brown Publ Co, 65- Mil Serv: Entered as A/S, Naval Res, 44-46, commissioned as Ens, 47, serv in Korean War, 50-52, released as Lt(jg); Am Defense Medal; Korean Serv Medal with two Battle Stars. Publ: Articles relating to newpaper bus & govt. Mem: Sigma Delta Chi; Nat Newspaper Asn; Rotary; Farm Bur; CofC. Relig: Presbyterian; Trustee, Nat Presby Church, 67-73. Legal Res: 430 Scioto St Urbana OH 43078 Mailing Add: 2242 Rayburn House Off Bldg Washington DC 20515

BROWN, CLARK SAMUEL (D)
VChmn, Forsyth Co Dem Exec Comt, NC
b Roanoke, Va, June 9, 11; s John Perry Brown & Rosa Clark B; m 1938 to Macie Brown; c Clark S, Jr & John Thomas. Educ: New York City Col, 4 years; Omega Psi Phi. Polit & Govt Pos: Deleg, Dem Nat Conv, 64 & 68; vchmn, Forsyth Co Dem Exec Comt, NC, currently. Bus & Prof Pos: Pres, Clark Brown & Sons Inc, Winston-Salem, NC, 30-69. Mem: NC & Nat Funeral Dirs Asns; Mason; Elks; KofP. Relig: Baptist. Legal Res: 1025 N Cameron Ave Winston-Salem NC 27101 Mailing Add: 727 N Patterson Ave Winston-Salem NC 27101

BROWN, CLAUDE WILSON **(D)**
Committeeman, Tex State Dem Exec Comt
b Talpa, Tex, Dec 7, 04; s Thomas Pikney Brown & Hattie Lee Hughes B; m 1926 to Christine Grace McGowen; c Claudyne (deceased); four grandchildren. Hon Degrees: LHD, McMurray Col. Polit & Govt Pos: Deleg, Tex Indust Comn, 60-72; mem, Emergency Planning Comn; committeeman, Tex State Dem Exec Comt, 63- Bus & Prof Pos: Partner, Brown & Thorp Oil Co & Terry Investment Co; owner real estate, McCamey, Fort Worth, Beaumont; dir, West Tex Utilities Co, Abilene, 66-75 & Security State Bank, McCamey, Tex. Mem: McMurray Col (trustee). Honors & Awards: Special Tex Ranger, 71. Relig: Methodist; mem & dir, Tex Methodist Found. Legal Res: Country Club Lane McCamey TX 79752 Mailing Add: PO Box 1029 McCamey TX 79752

BROWN, DARRYL NEWTON **(R)**
Chmn, Androscoggin Co Rep Comt, Maine
b Richmond, Maine, Dec 28, 44; s Alfred Clyde Brown & Nona Fogg B; m 1968 to Elaine Kelley; c Warren & Toby. Educ: Univ Maine, BS, 66, MS, 69; Northwestern Univ, 70; Sigma Xi; Alpha Gamma Rho. Polit & Govt Pos: Chmn, Town Planning Bd, 73- & Town Rep Comt, Livermore Falls, Maine, 74-; chmn, Androscoggin Co Rep Comt, 74- Bus & Prof Pos: Research asst, Univ Maine, 66-69; instr of soils, Delaware Valley Col, Pa, 69-71; asst prin, Livermore Falls High Sch, Maine, 71-72; consult soil scientist, 72- Mem: Am Soc Agronomy; Soil Sci Soc Am; Soil Conserv Soc Am; Asn Consult Soil Scientist; Boy Scouts Am (cubmaster). Mailing Add: PO Box Q Livermore Falls ME 04254

BROWN, DAVID EMERSON **(R)**
VChmn, Ill Rep State Cent Comt
b Toledo, Ohio, Jan 3, 26; s David Era Brown & Crystal Emerson B; m 1950 to Marjorie Frey; c David E, Jr, Judith Anne & Thomas Kiess. Educ: Univ Ill, Urbana, BS in Accounting, 49; Loyola Univ, JD, 53; Ma Wan Da; Beta Theta Pi. Polit & Govt Pos: Area chmn, New Trier Rep Orgn, 60-64, pres, 60-70, committeeman, 70-; founder, Rep Teens of Ill, 62; vchmn, mem exec comt & tenth dist committeeman, Ill Rep State Cent Comt, 64-; bd of gov, United Rep Fund of Ill, 64-; chmn, Nixon Ticker Tape Parade, Chicago, 68; chmn, Nixon's Mt Prospect Rally, 68; co-chmn, Finance Comt to Elect Richard B Ogilvie, 68. Bus & Prof Pos: Acct, Kemper Ins, New Orleans, La, 49-53, off mgr, 53-55, asst counsel, Chicago, Ill, 55-61, asst gen counsel, 61-67, assoc gen counsel, 67- Mil Serv: Entered as A/S, Navy-Air Force, 44, released as Seaman 2/C, 46, after serv in V-5 & V-12. Mem: Am Bar Asn; Civic Fedn (bd dirs) Pub Affairs Coun; Glen View Club; Chicago Tennis Patrons, Inc. Relig: Methodist. Legal Res: 1209 Greenwood Ave Wilmette IL 60091 Mailing Add: Kemper Insurance Long Grove IL 60049

BROWN, DAVID MILLARD **(R)**
Chmn, Pennington Co Rep Comt, Minn
b Fergus Falls, Minn, Oct 11, 18; s David Lloyd Brown & Elsie Wright B; m 1941 to Helen Elise Fisher; c David Lloyd, Helen Eve (Mrs Donald H Faes) & Tamara Alexis. Educ: NDak Agr Col, BS, 41; Univ Minn, Minneapolis, MA, 51; Univ NDak, EdD, 57. Polit & Govt Pos: Secy, Todd Co Rep Comt, Minn, 52-53; pres, Marshall-Pennington Young Rep League, 58-60; Justice of the Peace, Goodridge, Minn, 58-75; adminr, Pennington Co, 63; chmn, Pennington Co Rep Comt, 68-; mayor, Goodridge, Minn, 75- Bus & Prof Pos: Teacher, Wildrose, NDak, 41-42; supt, Karlsruhe, NDak, 42; elem prin, Maple Plain, Minn, 46-48; supt schs, Hewitt, 48-53; secy, Fergus Casket Works, Ind, 50-; supt schs, Goodridge, Minn, 53- Mil Serv: Entered as 2nd Lt, Army Air Force, 42, released as 1st Lt, after serv in Assam Air Depot, China-Burma-India, Upper Assam, 45-46; Res, 46-69, Lt Col; Theater Medals. Mem: Nat, Minn & Goodridge Educ Asns; Minn State High Sch League; Farmers Union. Relig: Lutheran; chmn, Higher Educ Comt Northern Dist Minn of Am Lutheran Church, 70-71, pres, Men of the Church, Goodridge Lutheran Parish, 71-72, pres, Faith Lutheran Church, 73- Mailing Add: Goodridge MN 56725

BROWN, DAVID SAMUEL **(R)**
b Athens, Ohio, Feb 6, 47; s Samuel Kennard Brown & Betty France B; m 1969 to Nancy Gaston. Educ: Ohio Univ, BA, 69; Phi Kappa Sigma. Polit & Govt Pos: Pres, Athens Co Young Rep, Ohio, 65-66; exec bd dir, Ohio Univ Young Rep, 66-67; admin asst to US Rep Clarence Miller, Ohio, 69- Mem: Bull Elephants; Cong Staff Club; Admin Asst Asn. Legal Res: Pine St Plains OH 45780 Mailing Add: 3286 Applegate Ct Annandale VA 22003

BROWN, DAVID W **(D)**
b Evanston, Ill, Aug 16, 37; s Lloyd W Brown & Nancy Coleman B; m 1964 to Alice Bean; c Peter Bean. Educ: Princeton Univ, BA, 59; Univ Col, Univ London, 59-60; Harvard Law Sch, LLB, 63. Polit & Govt Pos: Counsel to US Rep Edward I Koch, NY, 69- Bus & Prof Pos: Assoc lawyer, Patterson, Belknap & Webb, New York, 66-68. Mil Serv: Entered as 1st Lt, Army Res, 63, released as Capt, 65, after serv in 562nd Artil, 6th Missile Bn, West Ger. Mem: Asn of the Bar of the City of New York; NY & Am Bar Asns; Princeton Club of New York; Community Serv Soc. Relig: Protestant. Mailing Add: 29 Bethune St New York NY 10014

BROWN, DAVID WILLIAM **(D)**
Chmn, Palo Alto Co Dem Party, Iowa
b Emmetsburg, Iowa, Sept 23, 49; s John Joseph Brown & Joyce Devlin B; m 1971 to Janet T Molloy; c David John & Michael Joseph. Educ: Univ Iowa, BA, 72; Phi Kappa Psi. Polit & Govt Pos: Chmn, Palo Alto Co Dem Party, Iowa, 74- Bus & Prof Pos: Spec agt, Prudential Ins Co Am, 72-; real estate, 72- Mem: Emmetsburg Lions Club (pres, 75-). Legal Res: 106 Madison Emmetsburg IA 50536 Mailing Add: PO Box 509 Emmetsburg IA 50536

BROWN, EDGAR ALLAN **(D)**
Chmn, Barnwell Co Dem Exec Comt, SC
b Aiken Co, SC, July 11, 88; s Augustus Abraham Brown & Elizabeth Howard B; m 1913 to Annie Love Sitgreaves B; c Emily (Mrs R M Jeffries, Jr). Educ: Clemson Col, LLD; Med Col SC, LHD, 64. Polit & Govt Pos: Court stenographer, Second Circuit, SC, 08-18; Col on Gov Cooper's staff; chmn, Barnwell Co Dem Exec Comt, 14-; mem, SC State Dem Exec Comt, 14-, chmn, 22-26 & 52-53; SC State Rep & pres pro tem, SC House of Rep, 21-26; Dem Nat Exec Committeeman; deleg-at-lg, Dem Nat Conv, 24, 32 & 40-; Cand for US Sen, 26 & 38; SC State Sen, 29-73. Bus & Prof Pos: Lawyer & businessman. Mem: Coun of State Govts. Mailing Add: Box 248 Barnwell SC 29812

BROWN, EDMUND GERALD **(D)**
b San Francisco, Calif, Apr 21, 05; s Edmund Joseph Brown & Ida Schuckman B; m 1930 to Bernice Layne; c Barbara (Mrs Charles Edward Casey), Cynthia (Mrs Joseph Kelly), Edmund Gerald, Jr & Kathleen (Mrs George Rice). Educ: San Francisco Col Law, LLB, 27; sr class pres. Hon Degrees: LLD, Univ San Francisco, 59, Univ Santa Clara & Univ San Diego, 61; DCL, Calif Col Med, 64; LHD, Univ Judaism, 65. Polit & Govt Pos: Dist Attorney, San Francisco, 43-50; Attorney Gen, Calif, 50-58; Gov, Calif, 58-66. Bus & Prof Pos: Partner, Ball, Hunt, Hart & Brown, Beverly Hills, Calif, currently. Mem: Calif State Bar; Am & San Francisco Bar Asns; fel Am Col Trial Lawyers; Native Sons of Golden West. Relig: Catholic. Mailing Add: Ball Hunt Hart & Brown 450 N Roxbury Dr Beverly Hills CA 90210

BROWN, EDMUND GERALD, JR **(D)**
Gov, Calif
b San Francisco, Calif, Apr 7, 38; s Edmund Gerald Brown & Bernice Layne B; single. Educ: Univ Santa Clara, 55-60; Univ Calif, Berkeley, BA, 61; Yale Univ Law Sch, JD, 64. Polit & Govt Pos: Law clerk, Justice Matthew O Tobriner, Calif Supreme Court, 64-65; mem, Los Angeles Co Crime Comn, 69-70; trustee, Los Angeles Community Cols, 69-70; Secy of State, Calif, 71-75; Gov, Calif, 75- Mem: Calif State Bar. Mailing Add: State Capitol Sacramento CA 95814

BROWN, EDWARD D **(D)**
Utah State Rep
Mailing Add: 853 Emeril Ave Salt Lake City UT 84116

BROWN, EDWARD G **(D)**
Ky State Rep
b 1920. Educ: Western State Col. Polit & Govt Pos: State dir recreation, Ky, 59-60; Ky State Rep, 64- Bus & Prof Pos: Land & home developer. Mil Serv: Air Force, World War II. Mem: Am Legion; Optimist Club. Relig: Baptist. Mailing Add: 301 N Sunrise St Bowling Green KY 42101

BROWN, EMILY CECILE **(D)**
b Nashville, Tenn, May 27, 54; d Coleman Edward Brown & Bernice West B; single. Educ: Vanderbilt Univ, presently. Polit & Govt Pos: Vpres, Williamson Co Young Dem, Tenn, 70-72; alt deleg, Dem Nat Conv, 72. Mem: Vol Women's Roundtable; Nat Women's Polit Caucus; Nashville Polit Caucus; Williamson Co Dem. Relig: Catholic. Legal Res: 957 Glass St Franklin TN 37064 Mailing Add: Box 2576 Sta B Vanderbilt Univ Nashville TN 37235

BROWN, ERNEST EUGENE **(R)**
b Clarksville, Tenn, Oct 19, 34; s William Brady Brown & Lucy Elinor Moorefield B; m 1963 to Barbara Rose Kauth; c Evan Richard. Educ: Paducah Jr Col, 54; Murray State Col, 55-56; Univ Ky, BS in Civil Eng, 59; Sigma Chi. Polit & Govt Pos: Treas, McCracken Co Young Rep Club, Ky, 65-67, chmn, 68-69, dir, 69-; Lone Oak 1 Precinct capt, John S Cooper Campaign, 66; chmn, McCracken Co Rep Gubernatorial Campaign, 67; chmn, McCracken Co Rep Exec Comt, formerly. Mil Serv: Entered as Ens, Coast & Geodetic Surv, 59, released as Lt(jg), 61, after serv in US. Mem: Am Soc Civil Engrs; Nat Soc Prof Engrs; Ky Soc Prof Engrs (vpres, Ky Lake chap, 68-69, pres, 69-); Lutheran Layman's League; Ky Young Rep Fedn. Relig: Lutheran. Mailing Add: 4007 Court Ave Paducah KY 42001

BROWN, FRED JAMES **(D)**
Chmn, Henry Co Dem Cent Comt, Ill
b Victoria, Ill, Feb 5, 13; s James Lewis Brown & Emma Josephine Johnson B; c Gail Lynn & Fred J, Jr. Educ: Ill Wesleyan Univ, 32-34; Chicago Kent Col Law, LLB, 37; Pi Kappa Delta; Chicago Kent Round Table; Soc Chicago Kent Honor Men. Polit & Govt Pos: City comnr, Kewanee, Ill, 43-45, mayor, 45-50, city attorney, 55-75; asst attorney gen, State of Ill, 60-68; chmn, Henry Co Dem Cent Comt, 60-; city attorney, Geneseo, 62-65; mem, Ill Dem Cent Comt, currently. Bus & Prof Pos: Gen practice law, 37-; dir, Kewanee Nat Bank, Ill, 55-70; attorney, Kewanee Community Unit Sch Dist 230, 59-; dir, Blake's Bootery, 60-70; attorney, Kewanee Airport Authority, 64-74. Mil Serv: Entered as Pvt, Army, 43, released as Sgt, 45, after serv in Judge Adv Gen Dept; recalled to active serv, 50 as Capt, Camp Carson, Colo, released 52; Meritorious Conduct Medal; ETO Ribbon; Victory Medal; five Battle Stars. Mem: Henry Co & Ill Bar Asns; Elks; Rotary (past pres); VFW (past comdr). Relig: Methodist. Legal Res: RR 1 Kewanee IL 61443 Mailing Add: 110 1/2 W Second St Kewanee IL 61443

BROWN, FREDERICK TRACY **(R)**
Chmn, Maine Young Rep
b Bar Harbor, Maine, Apr 11, 48; s Frederick F Brown & Rebecca Taylor B; single. Educ: Ricker Col, BA, 70; Tau Epsilon Phi, vchancellor, social bd chmn. Polit & Govt Pos: Field coordr, Maine Rep State Comt, 72-73, mem, 74-; mem, Mount Desert Rep Town Comt, Maine, 72-; mem, Hancock Co Rep Comt, 72-; fieldman, Richardson for Gov, 73 & 74; acct exec, Curtis for US Sen, Mo, 74; chmn, Maine Young Rep, 74- Bus & Prof Pos: Research asst, Edward A Grafe & Assocs Inc, 74- Relig: Roman Catholic. Mailing Add: Summit Rd Northeast Harbor ME 04662

BROWN, G HANK **(R)**
Colo State Sen
b Denver, Colo, Feb 12, 40; s Harry W Brown & Anna Marie Hanks B; m 1967 to Nana Beth Morrison; c Harry W, Jennifer Christy & Lori Ann. Educ: Univ Colo, Boulder, BS, 61, grad study, 61-62, JD, 69; Beta Alpha Psi; Phi Alpha Delta; Blue Key; Heart & Dagger; Sumalia; Delta Tau Delta. Polit & Govt Pos: Spec groups chmn, Brotzman for Cong Comt, 66; field dir, Dominick for Senate Comt, 67-68; 1200 club chmn & secy, Weld Co Rep Cent Comt, 71-73; Colo State Sen, 73- Bus & Prof Pos: Asst to pres, Monfort of Colo, Inc, 69-72, vpres, 72- Mil Serv: Entered as Seaman, Navy, 62, released as Lt, 66, after serv in VR-22 & DaNang, Vietnam, 65-66; Lt, Naval Res, 66-69; Air Medal with 2 gold stars; Naval Unit Citation; Vietnam Serv Medal; Expeditionary Forces Medal; Nat Defense Medal. Publ: Weekly column, Town & Country, currently. Mem: Colo Bar Asn; Elks; Rotary; Toastmasters; Colo Cattlemen's Asn. Honors & Awards: Student body pres, Univ Colo, 60-61 & Outstanding Leadership Award, 61; Greeley Jaycees Distinguished Serv Award, 72; Colo Jaycees Outstanding Young Man of 1973. Relig: Episcopal. Mailing Add: 1741 35th Ave Ct Greeley CO 80631

BROWN, GARRY ELDRIDGE **(R)**
US Rep, Mich
b Kalamazoo, Mich, Aug 12, 23; s E Lakin Brown & Blanche Jackson B; c Frances Esther, Mollie Earl, Amelia Logan & Abigail Victoria. Educ: Kalamazoo Col, AB, 51; George Washington Univ Law Sch, LLB, 54. Hon Degrees: DH, Lawrence Inst Technol, 64. Polit & Govt Pos: US Comnr, US Dist Court fo the Western Dist of Mich, 57-62; deleg, Mich Const Conv, 62; Mich State Sen, 21st Dist, 62-67; US Rep, Mich, 67- Bus & Prof Pos: Partner, law firm of Ford, Kreikard, Brown & Staton, 54-67. Mil Serv: Entered as Pvt, Army, 46, released

as 2nd Lt, 47, after serv in 24th Inf Div. Mem: Am, Mich State & Kalamazoo Co Bar Asns; Am Legion; Elks. Honors & Awards: Lettered in football, baseball & basketball at Kalamazoo Col, 48-51. Relig: Presbyterian. Mailing Add: 321 W Eliza Schoolcraft MI 49087

BROWN, GEORGE EDWARD, JR (D)
US Rep, Calif
b Holtville, Calif, Mar 6, 20; s George Edward Brown & Bird Alma Kilgore B; m to Rowena Somerindyke. Educ: Univ Calif at Los Angeles, BA, 46. Polit & Govt Pos: Mayor & councilman, Monterey Park, Calif, 54-58; Calif State Assemblyman, 59-62; US Rep, Calif, 63-70 & 73-; deleg, Dem Nat Mid-Term Conf, 74. Bus & Prof Pos: Eng personnel, Dept of Water & Power, Los Angeles, Calif, 47-57; exec secy, Engrs & Architects Asn, 57-58. Mil Serv: Entered as Pvt, Army, 44, released as 2nd Lt, 46. Mem: Am for Dem Action; Urban League; IBEW; Kiwanis; Am Legion. Relig: Methodist. Legal Res: Colton CA 92324 Mailing Add: House of Rep 2342 Rayburn Bldg Washington DC 20515

BROWN, GEORGE HAY (R)
b Denver, Colo, Feb 4, 10; s Orville G Brown & Clara Topping B; m 1932 to Catherine Smith (deceased); c Ann Catherine. Educ: Oberlin Col, AB, 29; Harvard Univ, MBA, 31; Univ Chicago, PhD, 45; Delta Sigma Pi. Polit & Govt Pos: Consult, War Prod Bd, 43; secy adv comt, US Dept Com, 65-69, dir, Bur of the Census, 69-73; consult, Gen Accounting Off, 74- Bus & Prof Pos: Divisional sales mgr, Mallinckrodt Chem Works, St Louis, Mo, 31-36; instr-prof mkt, Univ Chicago, 37-54, dir develop, Biol Phys & Social Sci Div, Sch Social Serv & Sch Bus, 48-50, dir bus probs bur, 50-54; mgr-dir mkt research off, Ford Motor Co, Dearborn, Mich, 54-69; secy, The Conf Bd, Inc, New York, 73- Publ: International Economic Position of New Zealand, Univ Chicago Press, 46; Readings in Marketing from Fortune, Holt, 53; Brand loyalty: fact or fiction, Advert Age, 51. Mem: Am Econ Asn; Am Mkt Asn; Beta Gamma Sigma; River Club, New York, NY; Cosmos Club, Washington, DC. Relig: Presbyterian. Mailing Add: 870 UN Plaza New York NY 10017

BROWN, GEORGE L (D)
Lt Gov, Colo
Polit & Govt Pos: Mem, Dem Nat Comt, currently. Mailing Add: 4849 E 32nd St Denver CO 43215

BROWN, GIBBS W (D)
Pres, Calif Fedn of Young Dem
b Sacramento, Calif, Jan 8, 54; s Gibbs Heartzill Brown & Doris Katherin Jurasin B; single. Educ: Univ San Francisco, 72- Polit & Govt Pos: Youth coordr, Tunney for Senate Campaign, San Francisco, Calif, 70 & Alioto for Mayor Campaign, 71; state-wide youth coordr, Alioto for Gov Campaign, 73-74; pres, Calif Fedn of Young Dem, 74-; mem nat comt, Young Dem of Am, 74-; mem exec comt, Calif Dem Party, 74-, mem affirmative action comt, 75- Bus & Prof Pos: Dir, San Francisco Frontlash, 75- Mil Serv: Army, 70; Expert Rifle Award. Relig: Roman Catholic. Legal Res: 1830 44th Ave San Francisco CA 94122 Mailing Add: 3068 16th St San Francisco CA 94103

BROWN, GREGORY BRUGH (D)
Pres, Ark Young Dem
b Little Rock, Ark, Sept 22, 47; s Henry Martin Brown & June Gingles B; single. Educ: Little Rock Univ, BBA, 69; Univ Ark Sch Law, Little Rock, 73-; Phi Alpha Delta; Acacia. Polit & Govt Pos: Committeeman, Exec Comt, Ark Young Dem, 72-74, pres, 74-; treas, Saline Co Young Dem, 72-74; committeeman, Saline Co Dem Comt, 72-; committeeman, Ark Dem State Comt, 74-; treas, Fed Affairs Comt, Ark Dem Party, 74- Bus & Prof Pos: Exec vpres & dir, Gingles Dept Stores, Benton, Ark, 69-; vpres, Brown Realty, 69- Mem: Trace Creek Country Club. Relig: Methodist. Mailing Add: 501 N Market Benton AR 72015

BROWN, HAROLD D, JR (D)
Chmn, Ulster Co Dem Party, NY
b Ellenville, NY, Apr 30, 32; s Harold & Mrs Brown; m 1953 to Shirley M Stratton; c Denise, Kathleen & Janine. Educ: Ellenville High Sch, NY, grad, 51. Polit & Govt Pos: Committeeman, Wawarsing Dem Town Comt, NY, 52-, chmn, 71-73; chmn, Ulster Co Dem Party, 73- Mem: Am Fedn State, Co & Munic Employees. Mailing Add: Box 44 KA Grahamsville NY 12740

BROWN, HERMAN CUBBAGE (R)
Chmn, Del Rep State Comt
b Milford, Del, Mar 15, 25; s Herman Brown & Grace Cubbage B; m 1946 to Nancy Norris; c Herman C, Jr, Dennis Eugene & Linda Joan. Educ: Univ NC, Chapel Hill, BA in Econ, 48; George Washington Sch Law, LLB, 50; Phi Beta Kappa. Polit & Govt Pos: Dep Attorney Gen, Del, 54; mem exec comt, Kent Co Rep Party, Del, 67-, chmn, 67-69; mem, Del Rep State Comt, 67-69, chmn, 73-; deleg, Rep Nat Conv, 68. Bus & Prof Pos: Sr partner, Brown, Shiels & Borros, Dover, Del, 50-; dir, Del State Fair, 53-; gen counsel, First Nat Bank of Harrington, 63-; pres & dir, Paradise Alley Farms, Inc, Felton, 69-; pres & dir, Harrington Raceway, Inc, 69-75. Mil Serv: Entered as Aviation Cadet, Army Air Force, 43, released as 1st Lt, 45, after serv in 15th Air Force, ETO, Italy, 44-45; Air Medal; various campaign ribbons. Mem: Am & Del Bar Asns; Am Legion; Del Vet World War II; Am Judicature Soc. Relig: Methodist. Legal Res: RD 1 Box 231 Dover DE 19901 Mailing Add: PO Drawer F Dover DE 19901

BROWN, IRIS EILEEN (R)
VChmn, Chesapeake Rep City Comt, Va
b Suffolk, Va, Oct 5, 28; d Jesse Julian White (deceased) & Elma Elizabeth Kindley W; m second time, 1960 to Benjamin Brown; c Deborah Leah (Mrs Horace Michael Darnell), Samuel Julian & Jennifer Sue. Educ: South Norfolk High Sch. Polit & Govt Pos: Chmn, South Norfolk Borough of Chesapeake, Va, 71-; alt deleg, Rep Nat Conv 72; one of the fourth dist leaders for the Elect of Robert Daniel to Cong & William Scott to Senate, 72; mem, Reelect the President Comt, 72; electoral officer, 72-; pres, Cent Chesapeake Rep Women's Club, 72-; vchmn, Chesapeake Rep City Comt, 72- Bus & Prof Pos: Bookkeeper & off mgr, Planters Chem Div of Thompson/Haywood, 67. Mem: Portlock Community Ctr Operating Comt (secy, 70-). Honors & Awards: Participant, Coop Work Training Prog, 66-67. Relig: Protestant; Asst secy, Rosemont Christian Church, 71-73. Mailing Add: 437 Rutgers Ave Chesapeake VA 23324

BROWN, J MARSHALL (D)
b 1924; m to Ellen McInnis; c 1. Polit & Govt Pos: La State Rep, 52-60; campaign mgr & chmn, Finance Comt for Elec of Gov John J McKeithen; La campaign mgr for President Johnson, 64; mem & pres, La State Bd of Educ, 62-; Dem Nat Committeeman, La, until 72; deleg, Dem Nat Conv, 68 & 72. Bus & Prof Pos: Pres, Marshall Brown Ins Agency, Inc. Mem: President's Club; Nat Capital Dem Club; Plimsoll Club of New Orleans. Mailing Add: 1901 Lafayette Gretna LA 70053

BROWN, J WALTER (D)
Miss State Rep
b Natchez, Miss, Feb 9, 39; s John Walter Brown & Rose Martello B; m 1963 to Joan Elizabeth Hicks; c Walter Jeffrey, Patrick Kevin & Melissa Lynn. Educ: Univ Miss, BA, 63; Univ Miss Law Sch, JD, 65; Claiborne Soc; Phi Delta Phi. Polit & Govt Pos: Legis asst, Congressman John Bell Williams, 62; Miss State Rep, 68-72 & 75-; mem law enforcement comn, State of Miss, 69- Bus & Prof Pos: Instr polit sci, Univ Southern Miss, 65-69; attorney-at-law, 65- Mil Serv: Entered as Seaman Recruit, Navy, 57, released as Yeoman 3/C, 59, after serv in Staff, Comdr Serv Squadron 4, Res, 59-62. Publ: On University of Mississippi, Student, 62. Mem: Am & Miss Bar Asns; Am Judicature Soc; KofC; Adams Co Ment Health Asn (bd dirs). Relig: Catholic. Legal Res: 221 Linton Ave Natchez MS 39120 Mailing Add: 114 S Wall St Box 1047 Natchez MS 39120

BROWN, JAMES ELMER (R)
US Spec Ambassador to Nepal
b Falconer, NY, Sept 22, 27; s Joseph Sanford Brown & Charity B; m 1957 to Gloria Gayle Gay; c C Richard, C David, Jennifer Gayle, Christopher James & Kimberly Ann. Educ: Univ Maine, 49-50; Ricker Jr Col, Houlton, Maine, 51-52; Univ Maine Law Sch, JD, 54; Kappa Delta Phi. Polit & Govt Pos: Mem, Durham Rep Cent Comt, Maine, 50-52; mem, Androscoggin Co Young Rep, 51, officer, 52-53; deleg, Rep State Conv, Maine, 52; precinct chmn, Rep Party, Tremonton, Utah, 62; chmn, Melich for Gov, Northern Utah, 64; finance chmn, Burton for Cong, Utah, 64-68; chmn, Box Elder Co Rep Party, 65-70; mem, Rep State Cent Comt, Utah, 66-; chmn, Burton Cong Club, 68-69; treas, Utah Rep Party, 70-75; mem bd vis, Air Force Acad & mem exec panel, Naval Opers, app by President Ford, 75; Spec Ambassador to Nepal, 75- Bus & Prof Pos: Spec agt, Fed Bur Invest, Washington, DC, 54-59; staff asst, Thiokol Corp, Brigham City, Utah, 59-61, legal asst to vpres, 61-62, mgr, customer rels, 62-63, mgr, customer/pub rels, 63-74, aerospace group exec, 74-; dir, Continental Tel Co; dir & co-owner, Bear River State Bank; dir, Snowbird Ski Corp. Mil Serv: Entered as A/S, Navy, 45, released as PO 46, after serv in Amphibious Forces, US & Cuba. Publ: Utah hunting, Gun World, 67; plus numerous publ in trade mag. Mem: Pub Rels Soc Am; Soc of Former Spec Agts, Fed Bur Invest; Utah Peace Officers Asn; Elks; Mason. Honors & Awards: Three letters of commendation from Fed Bur Invest Dir J Edgar Hoover; Am Legion Outstanding Student Award, Lisbon Falls High Sch, Maine, 48. Relig: Latter-day Saint. Mailing Add: 221 East Fifth North Tremonton UT 84337

BROWN, JAMES HARVEY (D)
La State Sen
m to Dale; c Cami & Gentry. Educ: Univ NC; Cambridge Univ; Tulane Univ Sch Law; pres, Sch Law, 66; Phi Delta Theta. Polit & Govt Pos: La rep, Nat Rivers & Harbors Cong, Washington, DC, formerly; Dist 21 mem, La Const Conv, 72; La State Sen, Caldwell, Catahoula, Concordia, Franklin, LaSalle & Tensas Parishes, 72-, mem joint legis comt for hwy financing, vchmn senate hwy & transportation comt, La State Senate, currently. Bus & Prof Pos: Attorney & partner, Dale, Richardson & Dale, Ferriday & Vidalia, La, currently. Mem: Am Bar Asn; Am Judicature Soc; La Jaycees; La Am Legion (Fifth Dist Judge Advocate & VComdr, Comdr, Post 148, Ferriday); Vidalia Lions. Relig: Presbyterian. Mailing Add: Box 797 Ferriday LA 71334

BROWN, JAMES HYATT (D)
Fla State Rep
b Orlando, Fla, July 12, 37; s J Adrian Brown & Madoline Worley B; m 1965 to Cynthia Rodriguez; c J Powell, H Kellim & P Barrett. Educ: Univ Fla, BSBA, 59; Phi Eta Sigma; Fla Blue Key; Phi Delta Theta. Polit & Govt Pos: Fla State Rep, Dist 31, 72-, chmn growth & energy comt, Fla House of Rep, 74- Bus & Prof Pos: Pres, Brown & Brown, Inc, 61- Mem: Shrine; F&AM; Scottish Rite (32 degree); Daytona Beach Kiwanis Club; Daytona Beach CofC. Honors & Awards: Hall of Fame, Univ Fla, 58. Relig: Baptist. Mailing Add: 213 Riverside Dr Ormond Beach FL 32074

BROWN, JAMES MONROE (D)
b Pulaski, Tenn, June 17, 28; s John Tyler Brown & Theola McCollum B; m 1957 to Anne Elizabeth McKissack. Educ: Bridgeforth High Sch, Pulaski, Tenn, 46-48; Armed Forces Schs, 51-52. Polit & Govt Pos: Pres, Giles & Lawrence Co Voters Coun, Tenn, 63-69; mem exec comt, Giles Co Dem Orgn, 68; deleg, Dem State Conv, 68; deleg, Dem Nat Conv, 68, alt deleg, 72; co-chmn, Tenn Voters Coun, 68-; co-chmn, Giles Co Dem Exec Comt, formerly; mem, Pub Rec Comn of Giles Co, 72-, justice of the peace & magistrate, Giles Co, 72-; mem, Sch Comt of Giles Co Quart Court, 73-74; mem, Giles Co Rabies Comn, 73-74. Bus & Prof Pos: Debit mgr, Union Protective Life Ins Co, 56-60; asst mgr, Queen Ann Funeral Home, 60- Mil Serv: Entered as TN 3/C, Navy, 44, released as TN 1/C, 46, recalled, 51-55, serv in USS McIntyre, Tide Water & Gerring, in Atlantic, Pac, Mediter & Caribbean Theatres, 44-46 & 51-55; Good Conduct, Pac Theatre & UN Medals. Publ: A stranger in my town powerless and black, Coun News, 4/69. Mem: Elks; Am Legion; NAACP. Honors & Awards: Man of the year, 68. Relig: Methodist. Legal Res: 726 Childers St Pulaski TN 38478 Mailing Add: 410 N First St Pulaski TN 38478

BROWN, JAMES NELSON (JIM) (R)
b Mason, Mich, Dec 9, 26; s Nelson DeCamp Brown & Maxine Marie Ludwick B; m 1951 to Joan Loris Hull; c Timothy Wells, Amy Joan, Jennifer Lynn & Melissa Katherine. Educ: Mich State Univ, BA, 51; Blue Key; Sigma Delta Chi; Alpha Gamma Rho. Polit & Govt Pos: Chmn, Ingham Co Rep Comt, Mich, 67-68 & 72-74; deleg, Rep Nat Conv, 68; Mich State Rep, 68-72. Bus & Prof Pos: Ed & publ, Ingham Co News, 51-68; vpres, Panax Corp, East Lansing, 68- Mil Serv: Entered as Pvt, Marine Corps, 44, released as Cpl, 47, after serv in 2nd Marines, ETO, 45-46. Mem: Mich Press Asn; Am Legion; VFW; Marine Corps League; Kiwanis. Relig: Protestant. Legal Res: 2070 Riverwood Dr Okemos MI 48864 Mailing Add: 222 W Ash St Mason MI 48854

BROWN, JEAN ISABELLE (R)
VChmn, Lake Co Rep Comt, Mich
b Sanilac Co, Mich, Aug 3, 26; d Otis Shephard & Edith Clark S; m 1946 to William L Simonson, wid; m 1964 to Darrell Clayton Brown; c Rodney Wayne, Richard Dean & Janice Mae Simonson. Educ: Eastern Mich Univ, BS, 60, MA, 62; Cent Mich Univ, EdS, 69; Kappa Delta Pi. Polit & Govt Pos: Co-chmn, Lake Co Rep Comt, Mich, formerly, vchmn, currently; chmn, Lenore Romney for US Senate, Lake Co, 70; chmn, US Rep VanderJagt Club for Lake Co, 70-73; chmn, US Sen Robert Griffin for Lake Co, 72- Bus & Prof Pos: Elem & spec educ

teacher & consult, Lapeer, Genesee & Mason Co Schs, Mich, 44-49, 57-61 & 64-68; exec dir, Saginaw Asn Retarded Children, 61-63, therapeutic teacher, ment retarded & emotionally disturbed, Lapeer State Home & Training Sch, 63-64; sch psychologist, Mason & Lake Co, 68-; part-time instr, West Shore Community Col, 69-; cert psychol examr, State of Mich, 70- Mem: Nat & Mich Educ Asns; Coun Except Children; fel Am Asn Ment Deficiency; Nat Asn Sch Psychologists. Relig: United Methodist. Legal Res: Box 231 Baldwin MI 49304 Mailing Add: 308 E Loomis St PO Box 574 Ludington MI 49431

BROWN, JEFFREY MICHAEL **(LIBERTARIAN)**
Col Rep, Rep Party of Wis
b Milwaukee, Wis, Aug 29, 46; s Paul David Brown & Ruth Hartzheim B; div. Educ: Univ Wis-Superior, BS, 74; Phi Beta Lambda; Club Politique; Col Rep. Polit & Govt Pos: Mem exec comt, Douglas Co Rep Party, Wis, 71-74; exec dir, Wis Col Rep, 73-74, state chmn, 74; mem exec comt, Rep Party of Wis, 74, dist field rep, 74, col rep, currently. Bus & Prof Pos: Indust supvr, Am Can Co, Detroit, Mich, 73 & Colart Corp, Milwaukee, Wis, 75- Mil Serv: Entered as Pvt, Army, 64, released as SP-6, 70, after serv in Satellite Commun Agency, Army Materiel Command, 69-70; Vietnam Serv Medal with 4 Bronze Campaign Stars; Vietnam Campaign Medal; Presidential Unit Citation; Meritorious Unit Commendation. Mem: Smithsonian Inst; Patton Mus Soc. Mailing Add: 2616 N Frederick Ave Milwaukee WI 53211

BROWN, JESSE FRANCES **(D)**
b Carlton, Ga, Dec 27, 91; s Wyley Pink Brown & Sarah Kathrine Power B; m 1911 to Pearl Mae Moon; c Reba (Mrs Bobo), John Allison & Peggy (Mrs Hutchen). Educ: Carlton High Sch, Ga. Polit & Govt Pos: Substitute mail carrier & temporary carrier, 19-57; ex-officio justice of peace, 203rd Dist, Madison Co, Ga; chmn, Madison Co Dem Exec Comt, Ga, formerly; Lt Col aide-de-camp, Gov Ga Staff, 67-70. Bus & Prof Pos: Pres & dir, Free State Coop Fire Ins Co of Madison Co, Ga. Mem: F&AM; Mason. Honors & Awards: Cert of recognition, Agr Adjust Act, 68. Relig: Baptist, Treas, Carlton Baptist Church, 21-64. Mailing Add: Rte 2 Carlton GA 30627

BROWN, JOHN WALTER, JR **(D)**
Miss State Rep
Mailing Add: Box 1047 Natchez MS 39120

BROWN, JOHN WILLIAM **(R)**
b Athens, Ohio, Dec 28, 13; s James A Brown & Daisy Foster B; m 1943 to Violet A Helman; c Rosalie (Mrs Angelus). Educ: Pi Kappa Alpha; Anchor & Chain Soc; NROTC. Polit & Govt Pos: Mayor, Medina, Ohio, 50-53; Lt Gov, Ohio, 53-57 & 63-74; Gov, Ohio, 57; Ohio State Rep, 59-60; Ohio State Sen, 61-62; deleg, Rep Nat Conv, 68 & 72; State Lake Lands Adminr, currently. Bus & Prof Pos: Pres, Investors Heritage Life Ins Co of Ohio, Columbus; former owner, John W Brown, Inc, Ins & Real Estate, Medina; former prin broker, Gerspacher-Lincoln & Assocs, Real Estate & Gerspacher-Block, Real Estate & Ins. Mil Serv: Entered as 2/C PO, Coast Guard, 42, released as 1/C PO, 45, after serv in ETO; Comdr, Coast Guard Res; Good Conduct Medal; Am Theater Ribbon; ETO Ribbon with Two Stars; Expert Pistol Medal; Victory Medal; Reserve Medal. Mem: F&AM; RAM; RSM; KT; Scottish Rite. Relig: Methodist. Mailing Add: 401 Baxter St Medina OH 44256

BROWN, JOSEPHINE M **(R)**
Mem, Rep State Cent Comt Calif
b Thayer, Mo, Oct 16, 09; d Samuel Lee Sagaser & Mary Emma Faulkner S; m 1935 to Floyd Greer Brown. Educ: Univ Ariz, AB, 30; Univ Southern Calif; Univ Calif, Berkeley, 52; Sacramento State Col, 54. Polit & Govt Pos: Mem, Rep State Cent Comt Calif, 69- Bus & Prof Pos: Teacher, Tucson City Schs, Ariz, 31-35, Miss Preston's Sch for Girls, 35-36 & Pinal Co Sch, Florence, Ariz, 38-43; teacher & supvr, North Sacramento Sch Dist, 44-67, dir spec serv, 68- Mem: Delta Kappa Gamma; Calif Adminr of Spec Educ; Calif Asn of Supvr of Child Welfare; Calif Teachers' Asn; Soroptimist Club. Relig: Presbyterian. Mailing Add: 3400 Brockway Ct Sacramento CA 95818

BROWN, JUDITH CLAIRE **(R)**
Chmn, Nye Co Rep Cent Comt, Nev
b Eureka, Calif, Sept 12, 38; d Haakon Horntvedt & Hilda Clarke H; m 1960 to N L Pete Brown; c Jessica Claire & Jason Charlton. Educ: San Jose State Col, 56-57; Humboldt State Univ. Polit & Govt Pos: Chmn, Nye Co Rep Cent Comt, 74- Bus & Prof Pos: Owner, Valley Sand & Gravel, 72- Mailing Add: PO Box 118 Pahrump NV 89041

BROWN, KATHARINE KENNEDY **(R)**
Life Mem, Montgomery Co Rep Comt, Ohio
b Dayton, Ohio; d Grafton Claggett Kennedy & Louise Achey K; m to Kleon Thaw Brown (deceased). Educ: Dana Hall, student, 06-08. Polit & Govt Pos: Life mem, Montgomery Co Rep Comt, Ohio; alt deleg-at-lg, Rep Nat Conv, 28; mem, Rep State Comt, 28-; Rep Nat Committeewoman, Ohio, 32-68, dir, Western Women's Div, 36, vchmn, Rep Nat Comt, 44-52; deleg-at-lg, Rep Nat Conv, 32 & 44-68, alt deleg, 72; pres, Ohio Fedn Rep Women's Orgn, 40-70; mem bd trustees, Wilberforce Univ, 56; mem bd dirs, Nat Fedn Rep Women; adv coun, Women's Nat Rep Club, NY; mem, League Rep Women, DC. Publ: What You Want to Know About the Great Game of Politics; Rudiments of Political Organization. Mem: Jr League of Dayton (founder & twice pres); DAR (regent, Jonathan Dayton Chap, 70-72); Dayton Circle (chmn); Colonial Dames; Taft Mem Found (vpres, pres, bd trustees). Honors & Awards: Silver Gala Honoree, Silver Anniversary, Nat Fedn Rep Women, 63. Relig: Presbyterian. Legal Res: Duncarrick Keowee & Webster Sts Dayton OH 45401 Mailing Add: PO Box 324 Dayton OH 45401

BROWN, KEITH LAPHAM **(R)**
Rep Nat Committeeman, Colo
b Sterling, Ill, June 18, 25; s Lloyd H Brown & Marguerite Briggs B; m 1949 to Carol Liebmann; c Susan Griffith, Michael Briggs, Linda Lapham & Benjamine Liebmann. Educ: Univ Tex, LLB, 49; Phi Delta Phi; Sigma Alpha Epsilon. Polit & Govt Pos: Finance chmn, Rep Party Colo, 70-73; mem exec comt & regional chmn, Rep Nat Finance Comt, 70-75; regional finance chmn, Comt to Reelect the President, 72; finance chmn to US Sen Peter Dominick, 74; Rep Nat Committeeman, Colo, 75- Bus & Prof Pos: Lawyer, Tex, 49-55 & Okla, 55-59; pres, Brown Investment Corp, Denver, Colo, 60- Mil Serv: Entered as Seaman, Navy, 43, released as Ens, 46, after serv in Palawan Island, Philippines. Mem: Nat Western Livestock Asn; Colo Bar Asn; Boys Club (exec bd); Univ Denver Social Sci Found; Denver Country Club. Legal Res: 370 Humboldt Denver CO 80218 Mailing Add: 1600 Broadway Denver CO 80202

BROWN, KEITH SPALDING **(R)**
Chmn, Pima Co Rep Finance Comt, Ariz
b Hinsdale, Ill, June 15, 13; s William Bruce Brown & Sara Morgan Gardner B; m 1937 to Katherine Noyes McKennan; c Keith Spalding, Julie (Mrs Parker D Perry), Katherine M, Stephen G. Educ: Phillips Acad, cum laude; Yale Univ, BA, 35; Alpha Delta Phi. Polit & Govt Pos: Mem, Continental Pub Sch Bd, 47-65, pres, 59-65; Ariz State Rep, 55-58; vchmn, Ariz Rep Comt, 59-60, chmn, 63-65, mem exec comt, 72-; mem, Rep Nat Comt, 63-65, mem exec comt, 64-65; deleg & vchmn Ariz deleg, Rep Nat Conv, 64, deleg, 68; mem, US Annual Assay Comn, 71; chmn, Southern Ariz Comn to Reelect the President, 72; chmn, Pima Co Rep Finance Comt, 73-74; mem, Rep Nat Finance Comt, 73- Bus & Prof Pos: With Procter & Gamble Co, 35-37; prod supvr, Lyon Metal Prod Co, Aurora, Ill, 37-39; staff mem, Booz, Fry & Allen & Hamilton Mgt Consult, Chicago, 39-42; owner-operator, Santa Rita Ranch, Tucson, 46-70; vpres & dir, Southwestern Research & Gen Investment Co, 65; chmn bd, Am Atomics Corp, 65-; dir, Southern Ariz Bank, currently. Mailing Add: 3200 N Swan Rd Tucson AZ 85712

BROWN, LILLIAN CUNNINGHAM **(D)**
Mem, Calif Dem State Cent Comt
b Piedmont, SC, Mar 7, 15; d Joseph L Cunningham & Nellie Burdion C; m 1934 to William Lee Brown; c Donald Lee, Lila M (Mrs Fred Sanders) & Gerald Julius. Educ: Pasadena, 12 years. Polit & Govt Pos: Secy, FDR Club, Pasadena, Calif, 64-65, vpres, 68-69; mem, Calif Dem State Cent Comt, 68- Mem: League of Women Voters; NAACP. Relig: Baptist. Mailing Add: 300 W Washington Blvd Pasadena CA 91103

BROWN, MARILYN B (ANN) **(R)**
Committeewoman, Maine Rep State Comt
b Skowhegan, Maine, July 29, 31; d Donald E Boulette & Aura Vigue B; m 1949 to Robert Elton Brown; c Shannon. Educ: Univ Maine, BA, 53; Phi Mu. Polit & Govt Pos: Mem, Harmony Rep Town Comt, Maine, 54-; mem, Somerset Co Rep Comt, 68-; committeewoman, Maine Rep State Comt, 68-; mem, Second Dist Rep Comt, 70- Bus & Prof Pos: Teacher Eng & speech, Dexter High Sch, Maine, 53-55; teacher Eng, Piscataquis Community High Sch, Guilford, 55-58; teacher Eng & French, Harmony High Sch, 60-63; speech therapist, Skowhegan Pub Schs, 63- Mem: Nat Educ Asn; Maine Teachers Asn; Maine Speech & Hearing Asn; Patriarchs Club (dir). Relig: Catholic. Mailing Add: RFD 1 Harmony ME 04942

BROWN, MARION FULLER **(R)**
Mem, York Rep Town Comt, Maine
b Kansas City, Mo, May 14, 17; d Charles T Thompson (deceased) & Marion Moreau T (deceased); m to Henry M Fuller, wid; m 1967 to Brooks Brown, Jr; c Alexandra (Mrs O Kelly Anderson, Jr), Martha (Mrs Geoffrey Clark), Henry Weld & Emily Anne. Educ: Bradford Jr Col, 36; Smith Col, BS, 38. Polit & Govt Pos: Mem, York Rep Town Comt, Maine, 52-; mem, York Co Rep Comt, 58-66; mem, Maine Rep State Comt, 60-66, secy, 62-66; consumer mem, Maine Milk Comn, 60-66; mem, Women's Div, McIntire for Sen, 64; deleg, Rep Nat Conv, 64; Rep Nat Committeewoman, 66-72; mem, York Planning Bd, 66-; Maine State Rep, 67-72; app to Hwy Beautification Comn by President Nixon, 71-; mem, Maine Legis Compensation Comn, 73-74; trustee, York Hosp, 74-; app to Gov Longley's Comn on Maine's Future, 75- Bus & Prof Pos: Dir, Strawberry Banke Inc, 71- Mem: York Women's League; Women's Hosp Comt; Pine Tree Soc for Crippled Children & Adults (dir). Relig: Protestant. Mailing Add: Ram's Head Farm York ME 03909

BROWN, MARTIN PARKS **(D)**
Ga State Sen
b Hart, Ga, Nov 29, 14; s Heber C Brown & Hattie Parks B; m 1938 to Joyce Winn; c Jerry Parks, Sandra Joyce & Martin Boyce. Educ: Hartwell High Sch, 32. Polit & Govt Pos: Ga State Rep, 61-66; Ga State Sen, 68- Bus & Prof Pos: Merchant; cotton farmer; fertilizer dealer. Mil Serv: Army, 43-46; Battle Star, Cent European Campaign. Relig: Baptist. Mailing Add: Eberton Hwy Hartwell GA 30643

BROWN, MIRIAM BLACKBURN **(R)**
Chmn, Spencer Co Rep Party, Ky
b Marion, Ky, June 25, 00; d Walter Asiel Blackburn & Cora Hurley B; m 1938 to Knox Brown, Jr, wid; c Joe Blackburn & Mary Jane (Mrs Glenn C Marcum). Educ: Georgetown Col, 18-20; Wash Univ, AB, 22; Univ Chicago, MA, 31; Lambda Omicron Mu; Alpha Chi Omega. Polit & Govt Pos: Dep US clerk, Paducah, Ky, 22-36; chmn, Spencer Co Rep Party, 40- Bus & Prof Pos: Teacher & head hist dept, Paducah, Ky, 24-38. Publ: Political & Economic Conditions of Kentucky 1890-1900, Univ Chicago, 31. Mem: Ky Educ Asn; PTA; Kings Daughters; Ky Heritage Comn; Ky Hist Soc. Relig: Baptist. Mailing Add: RR 3 Vaucluse Farm Taylorsville KY 40071

BROWN, MONA KATHERINE **(R)**
b Blue Ridge, Mo, Oct 7, 17; d Omer Elgin Marshall & Frankie Leland Wright M; m 1945 to Jack Edward Brown; c Mona Marie. Educ: Northwest Mo State Col. Polit & Govt Pos: Pres, Daviess Co Federated Rep Women, Mo, 61-69; chmn, Daviess Co Rep Party, 62-69 & 72-74; Sixth Dist Mem, Mo Rep State Comt, 64-69. Mem: Eastern Star; Farm Bur; Mo Farmers Asn; Women's Soc of Christian Serv; VFW Women's Auxiliary. Relig: United Methodist. Mailing Add: Rte 3 Box 126 Jamesport MO 64648

BROWN, OMAR **(R)**
Chmn, Rep Territorial Comt of VI
b St Thomas, VI, Aug 4, 09; widower; c Omar, Jr. Educ: Parochial schs & pub schs of St Thomas. Polit & Govt Pos: VI Territorial Rep, 38-52; chmn, Rep Territorial Comt of VI, currently; deleg, Rep Nat Conv, 68; mem, Rep Nat Comt, currently. Bus & Prof Pos: Hotel owner. Mem: Rotary Club; St Thomas Rep Club. Relig: Catholic. Mailing Add: PO Box 521 Charlotte Amalie St Thomas VI 00801

BROWN, OTHA NATHANIEL, JR **(D)**
Mem, Dist Dem Comt, Conn
b DeQueen, Ark, July 19, 31; s Otha Nathaniel Brown, Sr & Elizabeth B; div. Educ: Cent State Col, Ohio, BS cum laude, Univ Conn, MA & cert in syst technol, 70; Univ Bridgeport, prof dipl in admin; NY Univ, cert in counseling; Springfield Col (Mass), cert in counseling, summer 65; Queens Col (NY), cert in counseling, summer 69; Boston Univ, cert in counseling, summer 71; Alpha Kappa Mu; Phi Alpha Theta; Kappa Delta Pi; life mem Alpha Phi Alpha. Polit & Govt Pos: Mem, Dist Dem Comt, Conn, 62-; city councilman, Norwalk, 63-69; mem bd dirs, Anti-Poverty Bd, Conn, 65-; Conn State Rep, 67-74, majority leader common coun, Conn House Rep, 68-69; chmn, Pub Welfare Corrections, Humane Insts,

71-72; pres, State Fedn of Black Dem Clubs, 73-; alt deleg, Dem Mid Term Conf, 74. Bus & Prof Pos: Teacher, Stratford, Conn, 57-60; teacher, Stamford, Conn, 60; guidance counr, Bd Educ, Stamford, 62-; mem bd trustees, Univ Conn, 75- Mil Serv: Entered as 2nd Lt, Army, 52, released as 1st Lt, 54, after serv as Psychol Warfare Officer. Publ: A case for alpha outreach, The Sphinx, Alpha Phi Alpha, 5/66; Minority groups & politics of the power structure, Conn Govt, Univ Conn, winter 70; School counselors: a new role & image for the 70's, Conn Teacher Mag, 3/72. Mem: Am Personnel & Guid Asn; Spec Interest Group Syst Research (comt, 70-); 4-Town Drug Network (bd dirs, 71-); Community Ment Health Bd (bd dirs, 71-); Elks. Honors & Awards: Norwalk Young Man of the Year Award, 67; Conn Outstanding Young Man of the Year Award, 67; Alpha Man of the Year Award, 69; NAACP Leadership Award, 70. Relig: Methodist. Mailing Add: 208 Flax Hill Rd Apt 6 Norwalk CT 06854

BROWN, PAUL EDWARD (R)
b Raymond, NH, Apr 27, 35; s Theodore Haywood Brown & Bessie Quimby B; div; c Thomas Edward & Vanessa Ann. Educ: Raymond High Sch, grad. Polit & Govt Pos: Mem, NH State Rep Comt, 64-67; chmn, Gtr Derry Young Rep, 66; deleg, Rep State Conv, 66, 68 & 70; mem, Town & Co Rep Comts, 66-67; NH State Rep, 67-68; Rockingham Co coordr, Nixon for President, 67-68; advance man, Nixon Staff, 68; treas, NH Fed of Young Rep, 69, vchmn, formerly; former asst clerk, NH House of Rep; campaign staff mem of Gov Walter Peterson, 70; comnr, NH Comn of Eminent Domain, 71- Bus & Prof Pos: Owner, Paul Brown Int, currently. Mil Serv: Entered as Basic Airman, Air Force, 55, released as A/1C, 59. Relig: Protestant. Mailing Add: Freetown Rd Raymond NH 03077

BROWN, PAUL NEIL (D)
Colo State Rep
b Denver, Colo, June 17, 42; s Clifford Neil Brown & Katherine Virginia Shaver B; m 1965 to Susan Jane Seely; c Natalie Sue. Educ: Mesa Co Jr Col, 67; Univ Colo, Boulder, BA, 70. Polit & Govt Pos: Colo State Rep, 75- Mil Serv: Entered as E-1, Air Force, 61, released as E-4, 64, after serv in 49th Tac Fighter Squadron, Europe, 63-64; Good Conduct Medal. Mem: Realtors; Sertoma Int; Toastmasters Int. Mailing Add: 2042 Bunting Ave Grand Junction CO 81501

BROWN, PAUL WESLEY (R)
Justice, Ohio Supreme Court
b Cleveland, Ohio, Jan 14, 15; s William Brown & Mary E Foster B; m 1942 to Helen Louise Page; c Susan, Julie, Barbara, Mary, Jeffrey, Molly & Daniel. Educ: Ohio State Univ, AB, 37, LLB, 39; Phi Kappa Alpha; Phi Delta Phi. Polit & Govt Pos: Deleg, Rep Nat Conv, 48; judge, Court of Appeals of Ohio, 60-64; Justice Ohio Supreme Court, 64-69 & 75-; Attorney Gen, Ohio, 69-74. Mil Serv: Entered as 2nd Lt, Field Artil, 41, released as Maj, 46, after serv in First Armored Div, ETO; Silver Star; Purple Heart; ETO Medal; Two Battle Stars. Legal Res: Youngstown OH Mailing Add: 2396 Wimbledon Rd Columbus OH 43221

BROWN, PRENTISS MARSH (D)
b St Ignace, Mich, June 18, 89; s James J Brown & Minnie Gagnon B; m 1916 to Marion E Walker; c James J, Prentiss M, Paul W, Mariana (Mrs Rudolph), Ruth (Mrs Evanshevski), Barbard (Mrs Laing) & Patricia (Mrs Watson). Educ: Albion Col, AB, 11; Univ Ill; Phi Beta Kappa; Delta Sigma Rho; Delta Tau Delta. Polit & Govt Pos: US Rep, Mich, 33-37; US Sen, 37-43; adminr, Off Price Admin, 43-44; mem adv bd, Reconstruction Finance Corp, Detroit & Mich, 43-44; State Bd Law Examr & various city & co attorneyships, formerly; mem, Mich Hist Comn, 48-65; chmn, Mackinac Bridge Authority, 52- Bus & Prof Pos: Pres, First Nat Bank, St Ignace, 33-65; chmn bd, Detroit Edison Co, 44-; dir, Nat Bank of Detroit, 48-66; dir, Parke Davis & Co, 55-63. Mem: Mason (33rd degree). Relig: Methodist. Mailing Add: 11 Prospect St Ignace MI 49781

BROWN, RALPH (D)
WVa State Deleg
Mailing Add: State Capitol Charleston WV 25305

BROWN, RALPH R (R)
Exec Dir, Rep State Cent Comt Iowa
b Mt Pleasant, Iowa, Dec 13, 44; s Rex R Brown & Meta F Moyle B; single. Educ: Drake Univ, BA, 67, JD, 69; Phi Eta Sigma; Omicron Delta Kappa; Phi Alpha Delta. Polit & Govt Pos: Campaign fieldman, US Rep Fred Schwengel, 66 & 68; research asst, US Sen Jack Miller, 67; asst co attorney, Scott Co, Iowa, 72; secy, Iowa State Senate, 73-75; exec dir, Rep State Cent Comt Iowa, 75- Bus & Prof Pos: Attorney, Dircks, Berger & Saylor, Davenport, Iowa, 69-73. Mem: Drake Univ (bd trustees, 70-); State Comn Status of Women, 69-75. Relig: Protestant. Legal Res: 3612 Ingersoll Ave Des Moines IA 50312 Mailing Add: 1540 High St Des Moines IA 50309

BROWN, RANDY (R)
Committeewoman, Rep Party Tex
b Harleton, Tex, July 24, 22; d Harry Reynolds Taylor & Mattie Sue Etheridge T; div; c Lauren Shelley, Melissa Anne & Kristin Leigh. Educ: Mary Hardin Baylor Col, Helen Zene Wortman scholar, 41-42, BA, 42; Univ Okla, 46-50; Theta Sigma Phi; Sigma Tau Delta; Royal Academia Soc. Polit & Govt Pos: Deleg, Tex State Rep Convs, 62, 64, 66, 68, 70, 72 & 74; pub rels chmn, Harris Co Rep Party, 64-65, precinct chmn, 66-70, chmn cand comt, 74-; committeewoman, Rep Party Tex, 72-, chmn pub rels comt, 75- Bus & Prof Pos: Teacher, George West, Tex, 42-43 & Harleton, 43-44; ed, Harris Co Rep Banner, 63-65; girl friday, acct exec & media dir, Ray Cooley & Assocs, Inc, Houston, 65-70; owner & acct exec, Randy Brown & Assoc, 70-; news editor, Houston Tribune, 73- Mil Serv: Entered as A/S, WAVES, 44, released as Sp-2/C, 46, after serv in Naval Air Sta, Pac, 45-46. Publ: Heritage (poem), NY Times, 44; Randy at random (column), Rep Banner, 63-65 & Houston Tribune, 73- Relig: Christian. Mailing Add: 3028 Univ Blvd Houston TX 77005

BROWN, RAY O (D)
Ky State Rep
Mailing Add: Sandy Hook KY 41171

BROWN, RICHARD ARTHUR (D)
b New York, NY; s Benjamin Brown & Ruth Halper B; m 1950; c Jennifer Jo. Educ: City Col New York, BBA, 40. Polit & Govt Pos: State orgn dir, NY Vol for Stevenson, 52; campaign mgr, Akers for Cong, 54; pub rels dir, NY State Stevenson for Pres, 55-56; exec dir, NY Comt for Dem Voters, 59-65; admin asst to US Rep James H Scheuer, NY, 65-71; campaign mgr, Scheuer for Mayor, 69; campaign mgr, Scheur for Cong, 72; campaign mgr, Kislak for Cong, 72; campaign consult, Jordan for Mayor of Jersey City, 71; polit consult, Washington, DC, 71-; campaign consult, Carey for Gov, 73-74. Mil Serv: Entered as Pvt, Army, 41, released as T/5, 45. Mem: Anti Defamation League B'nai B'rith; Bonds for Israel; Bronx Found for Sr Citizens (pres, 70-). Relig: Jewish. Legal Res: New York NY Mailing Add: 2030 Allen Pl NW Washington DC 20009

BROWN, RICHARD LANE, III (D)
NC State Rep
b Albemarle, NC, Oct 3, 40; s Richard L Brown, Jr & Charlotte Palmer B; m 1966 to Janet Wales. Educ: Univ NC, BS, 63, LLB, 65; NY Univ, LLM, 66; Phi Alpha Delta; Sigma Nu; dir, Univ NC Alumni Asn. Polit & Govt Pos: Pres, Univ NC Young Dem Club, 63-64; secy, NC Young Dem, 64-65; NC State Rep, 32nd House Dist, 71- Bus & Prof Pos: Attorney & partner, Brown, Brown & Brown, 67- Mem: Am Bar Asn; NC Courts Comt; Rotary. Relig: Lutheran. Legal Res: Rte 3 Randle's Ferry Rd Norwood NC 28128 Mailing Add: Box 400 Albemarle NC 28001

BROWN, RICHARD ROSS (R)
Supvr, San Diego Co, Calif
b Tracy, Minn, Jan 28, 33; s Henry Norvan Brown & Helen McCorquodale B; m 1951 to Harriet Elaine Hunnewell; c Richard Douglas, David Ross & Donald James. Educ: Sweetwater High Sch, Calif, 4 years. Polit & Govt Pos: Pres, CofC, El Cajon, Calif, 64-65; mem, Rep State Cent Comt Calif, 64-; assoc mem, San Diego Rep Cent Comt, 64-; city councilman, El Cajon, 66-, mayor, 67-68; mem, Revenue & Taxation Comt, League of Cities, 66-69, mem transportation comt, 69-; mem, Gov Task Force on Transportation, 67; chmn exec comt, Rep Assoc San Diego Co, 67-68; alt deleg, Rep Nat Conv, 68; chmn, San Diego Region Comprehensive Planning Orgn, 68-; legis chmn, League Calif Cities, San Diego Div, 68-; chmn regional comt, Calif Coun Criminal Justice, 69; chmn, Calif State Bd of Transportation, 72-73; supvr, San Diego Co, 73- Bus & Prof Pos: Pres & gen mgr, Dilaine Corp, DBA, Brown Tool Eng Co, El Cajon, 56-; vchmn, San Diego Co Indust Asn, 59-60; pres & gen mgr, Dilaine Indust Inc, 61-; mem bd dirs, San Diego Employers Asn, 66-69. Mem: Nat Asn Mfgs; San Diego Employers Asn; El Cajon, Calif & San Diego CofC; Rotary. Honors & Awards: El Cajon Citizen of Year, 72. Relig: Protestant. Mailing Add: 480 Horizon Hills Dr El Cajon CA 92020

BROWN, ROBERT HENRY (D)
b Nashville, Tenn, Aug 2, 26; s Warren H Brown & Libby Forgy B; m 1963 to Deloris M Roby. Educ: Univ Ind, 2 years. Polit & Govt Pos: Deleg, Ind Dem State Conv, 68 & 70; deleg, Dem Nat Conv, 68 & 72; chmn, Labor Comt to Reelect Sen Hartke, Ind, 70. Bus & Prof Pos: Int rep, Machinist Union, 10 years. Mil Serv: Entered as Seaman, Navy, released as Boatswain Mate, after serv in SPac Theatre, 42-45. Mem: IAMAW, AFL-CIO; VFW; Am Legion; Elks. Relig: Protestant. Mailing Add: 708 Kennedy Dr Ft Branch IN 47648

BROWN, ROBERT J (R)
Chmn, Minn State Rep Cent Comt
Mailing Add: 4940 Viking Dr Minneapolis MN 55435

BROWN, ROBERT JOHN (R)
Minn State Sen
b Stillwater, Minn, June 15, 35; s Lindsay R Brown & Bertha Fiorito B; m 1959 to Janet Rae Johnson; c Anthony, Daniel, Linda, Michael & Andrew. Educ: Col of St Thomas, 53-54; Winona State Col, BS, 57; Univ Minn, MA, 58 & PhD, 64; Kappa Delta Pi. Polit & Govt Pos: Mem, Dakota Co Rep Exec Comt, Minn, 60-62; co chmn, Dakota Co Young Rep League & mem, State Bd Dirs, Minn Young Rep League, 62; city chmn, Stillwater Rep Party, 63-64; mem, Washington Co Rep Exec Comt, 63-; Minn State Sen, 51st Dist, 67-; chmn, Fourth Cong Dist Rep Party, 69-; chmn, Minn State Rep Party, 73-; mem, Rep Nat Comt, 73- Bus & Prof Pos: Teacher & counr, Farmington High Sch, Minn, 58-60; guid dir, Simley High Sch, South St Paul, 60-63; instr, Univ Minn, 63-64; assoc prof, Col St Thomas, 64- Mem: Minn Asn Sec Sch Prin; Jaycees; CofC (chmn recreation comt, St Croix); Minn Educ Coun. Relig: Catholic. Mailing Add: Col of St Thomas 2115 Summit Ave St Paul MN 55105

BROWN, ROBERT JOSEPH (R)
Mont State Rep
b Missoula, Mont, Dec 11, 47; s Clifford Andrew Brown & Jeanne Knox B; single. Educ: Mont State Univ, BA, 70; Pi Kappa Delta; Lambda Chi Alpha; pres, Assoc Students, 69-70. Polit & Govt Pos: Mont State Rep, 71- Mem: Kalispell Jaycees; Bozeman Elks. Relig: Presbyterian. Mailing Add: Rte 1 Whitefish MT 59937

BROWN, ROLLAND D (R)
b Crooksville, Ohio, Oct 12, 11; s Herbert H Brown & Chloe Williams B; m 1935 to Rhea Dawson; c Sally L (Mrs Birkimer) & Beth D (Mrs Heinz). Educ: Ohio Univ, Engr, 32; Phi Kappa Tau. Polit & Govt Pos: Mem, Ohio State Rep Cent Comt, 37-52; mem, Conserv Comn, 39-48; chmn, Grant Co Rep Party, Ark, 67-74; mem, Ark Reclamation Comn, 70- Bus & Prof Pos: Engr, Manhatton Coal Co, Ohio, 32-40; self-employed, Sonny Hill Aggregates Corp, 40-42 & 45-58; self-employed, Sheridan White Rock Inc, 58- Mil Serv: Entered as Pvt, Army, 42, released as M/Sgt, 45, after serv in 18th Cavalry Reconnaissance Squadron, ETO, 43-45; Good Conduct Medal; European-African, Mid East Campaign Ribbon with three Bronze Stars; one Overseas Bar. Mem: Mason; CofC; Rotary; Rep Time Club. Relig: Protestant. Mailing Add: 580 Jones St Sheridan AR 72150

BROWN, SARAH S (R)
Secy, Tippecanoe Co Rep Comt, Ind
b Union Twp, Ind, Jan 16, 32; d Harry H Stewart & Nell G Hiett S; m 1954 to Robert E Brown; c James D, Barbara Jo & Rodger S. Educ: High Sch. Polit & Govt Pos: Investr of poor relief, Fairfield Twp, Ind, 51-70; mgr, West Lafayette Auto License Br, 70; mem, Tippecanoe Co Bd Voter Regist, 71-75; clerk, Tippecanoe Circuit & Superior Courts, 75-; secy, Tippecanoe Co Rep Comt, Ind, 66- Mem: Lafayette Bus & Prof Womens Club; Ind State Fedn Rep Women (chmn special activities); Tippecanoe Co Rep Womens Club (parliamentarian); Am Legion Auxiliary. Relig: Quaker. Mailing Add: 6403 Sleeper Rd Lafayette IN 47905

BROWN, SHERROD CAMPBELL (D)
Ohio State Rep
b Mansfield, Ohio, Nov 9, 52; s Charles Brown & Emily Campbell B; single. Educ: Yale Univ, BA. Polit & Govt Pos: Ohio State Rep, 61st Dist, Richland Co, 75- Mem: Ohio Farm Bur; Common Cause; Ohio Citizens' Coun; Jaycees. Honors & Awards: Youngest person ever elected to Ohio Legis. Relig: Lutheran. Mailing Add: 514 Marion Ave Mansfield OH 44903

BROWN, TED WILLIAM (R)
Secy of State, Ohio
b Springfield, Ohio, Apr 19, 06; s George A Brown (deceased) & Mabel Rhonemus B (deceased); m 1926 to Florence Mitchell; c Marilyn Ann (Mrs Bruning), Barbara Lou (Mrs Larkins) & Sherrie Lucille (Mrs Rogers). Educ: Wittenberg Col; past pres, Kappa Phi. Polit & Govt Pos: Recorder, Clark Co, Ohio, 32-36; admin post, Ohio Bur Motor Vehicles, 40-44; Secy of State, Ohio, 51-; deleg, Rep Nat Conv, 68 & 72. Bus & Prof Pos: Formerly owner of heating & ventilating business. Publ: Compiler & publ of Ohio Elec Statistics, Fed, State & Co Officers Roster, Ohio Population Report, Ohio Elec Laws, Our Flags, Ohio's Capitals, Ohio's Elec Story, plus others. Mem: Nat Asn of Secys of State; Ohio Asn of Co Rec; Springfield, Ohio, Jr CofC; Masonic Lodge; Grotto. Honors & Awards: Three nat awards for educ booklets & pamphlets used in educ prog as Secy of State; received Nat Am Heritage Award (non-partisan group) three times; Freedom Found at Valley Forge Award, 70. Relig: Methodist. Legal Res: 6036 Dublin Rd Dublin OH 43017 Mailing Add: 14th Floor State Off Tower 30 E Broad St Columbus OH 43215

BROWN, THOMAS E (D)
b Lampasas, Tex, Sept 18, 00; s Thomas P Brown & Hattie Hughes B; m 1923 to Anna Cleo Bowers; c Thomas E, Jr. Educ: High sch grad, 19. Polit & Govt Pos: Dem Precinct Committeeman, 50-52; vchmn, Eddy Co Dem Cent Comt, NMex, 52-54; chmn, Dem Cent Comt, 54-56; Dem Nat Committeeman, NMex, 56-72; treas, Western States Dem Conf, 62-63, chmn exec comt, 65; deleg, Dem Nat Conv, 68. Bus & Prof Pos: Dir, NMex Boys Ranch; dir, Baptist Found NMex; mem bd trustees, Col of Artesia; pres, Brown Pipe & Supply of Artesia, Inc. Mem: Southeastern NMex Agr Research Asn (dir); Artesia CofC (dir); Rotary Club; Mason (32nd degree). Relig: Baptist; Deacon. Mailing Add: PO Box 68 Artesia NM 88210

BROWN, THOMAS ELZIE, JR (D)
NMex State Rep
b Coleman, Tex, Oct 24, 29; s Thomas Elzie Brown & Anna Cleo Bowers B; m 1949 to Mary Frances Gandy; c Mary Ann, Paula Jean & Thomas Elzie, III (Tracy). Educ: Baylor Univ, BBA, 51. Polit & Govt Pos: City councilman, Artesia, NMex, 56-62, chmn planning comn, 62-63; NMex State Rep, 67-; deleg, Dem Nat Conv, 72. Bus & Prof Pos: Exec vpres, Brown Pipe & Supply Co, 51; partner, BYB Enterprises, currently. Mem: Lions; Elks. Relig: Baptist. Legal Res: 2407 Cerro Rd Artesia NM 88210 Mailing Add: PO Box 68 Artesia NM 88210

BROWN, THOMAS HENRY (D)
Mich State Rep
b Loogootee, Ind, July 29, 17; s John Sylvester Brown & Emma Mae Draime B; m 1945 to Helen Catherine Hunter; c Paul Thomas, Robert Timothy, Judith Ann (Mrs Bullock), Joanna Catherine, Bonnie Leah & Mary Beth. Educ: Loogootee High Sch, 4 years. Polit & Govt Pos: Nankin Twp trustee, Wayne Co, Mich, 61-63, treas, 63-65, supvr, 65-66; chmn, League of Westland Dem Voters, 63-65, mem exec bd, 70; exec bd mem, 15th Dist Dem Orgn, 63-70; mem, Wayne Co Bd Supvrs, Wayne Co, Mich, 65-69; Mayor, Westland, 66-69; deleg, Dem Nat Conv, 68; Mich State Rep, 37th Dist, 71- Bus & Prof Pos: Food prod salesman; hosp attend; hardware salesman; operator, Mobilgas Serv Sta; sales & customer rels, Shell Oil Distributor. Mil Serv: Entered as Pvt, Army, 40, released as S/Sgt, 45, after serv in 5th Army, Europe, Africa & Italy, 42-45; European Theatre ribbon with 5 battle stars. Mem: VFW; Amvets; Lions; Moose; Wayne Ford Civic League. Relig: Catholic. Mailing Add: 1917 Eagle Ct Westland MI 48185

BROWN, THOMAS WALTER (D)
NY State Assemblyman
b Evanston, Ill, Oct 13, 30; s Walter Thomas Brown & Dorothy Kuhn B; m 1958 to Kathleen Bergan; c Cailin Christine, Kerry Kathleen, Megan Maureen, Thomas Bergan & Michael Kearney. Educ: Fordham Univ, BS, 53; Univ Chicago Law Sch, 1 year; Union Univ Albany Law Sch, JD, 58. Polit & Govt Pos: Co legislator, Albany Co, NY, 68-71; NY State Assemblyman, 102nd Dist, 71-; mem select comt on correctional insts & progs, 71- Bus & Prof Pos: Attorney, Dugan, Lyons, Murphy, Peatak & Brown, Albany, NY, 58- Mil Serv: Entered as Pvt, Army, 55, released as SP-3, 56, after serv in Inf, US. Publ: Running the Boston Marathon, Am Diabetic Asn Forecast, 70; auth, The silent epidemic, Blue Cross-Blue Shield Health Report, 2/73. Mem: Am Bar Asn; Am Judicature Soc; Am Asn RR Trial Counsel; Elks. Relig: Roman Catholic. Mailing Add: 5 Holmes Dale Albany NY 12208

BROWN, TORREY CARL (D)
Md State Deleg
b Chicago, Ill, Feb 28, 37; s Clifton Brown & Mildred Anderson B; m 1957 to Donnajean Marx; c Jay Therron & Rafe Tennyson. Educ: Wheaton Col (Ill), AB, 57; Johns Hopkins Univ Sch Med, scholar, 58, USPHS grant, 58-59, Josiah Macy, Jr Found scholar, 59, MD, 61; Alpha Omega Alpha. Polit & Govt Pos: Md State Deleg, 70- Bus & Prof Pos: From instr to assoc prof med, Sch Med, Johns Hopkins Univ, 66-, asst prof med care & hosp, Sch Hyg & Pub Health, 69-, chief emergency med serv, Hosp, 66-71, dep dir off health care prog, 69-72, dir alcoholism prog, 69-72, assoc dir drug abuse ctr, 70-71, dir, 71-; dir univ health serv, 71-; prin investr, Man Alive Drug Abuse Prog, Baltimore, 70-; mem coun circulation sect renal disease, Am Heart Asn. Publ: Co-auth, Acute response of plasma renin & aldosterone secretion to diuretic administration, Am J Physiol, 66; Relation in plasma renin to sodium balance & arterial pressure in experimental renal hypertension, Circulation Research, 66; auth, The laboratory examination of urine, Lab Vol, Tice's Encycl Med, 68. Mem: Johns Hopkins Med Soc; Southern Salt, Water & Kidney Club; Am Fedn Clin Research; Am Soc Nephrology; Am Col Physicians (fel, 69-). Relig: Baptist. Legal Res: 3941 Canterbury Rd Baltimore MD 21218 Mailing Add: Johns Hopkins Hosp Baltimore MD 21205

BROWN, VIRGINIA MAE (D)
Comnr, Interstate Com Comn
b Pliny, WVa, Nov 13, 23; d Felix Melville Brown (deceased) & Hester Ann Crandall B; m 1955 to James Vernon Brown; c Victoria Anne & Pamela Kay. Educ: WVa Univ, AB; WVa Col Law, JD, 47. Polit & Govt Pos: Asst Attorney Gen, State of WVa, 52-61, Counsel to Gov, 61, Ins Comnr, 61-62; mem, Pub Serv Comn, 62-64; comnr, Interstate Com Comn, 64-, chmn, 69. Mem: Am & WVa State Bar Asns. Relig: Methodist. Legal Res: Pliny WV 25158 Mailing Add: Interstate Com Comn Bldg 12th St & Constitution Ave Washington DC 20423

BROWN, WALTER FREDERICK (D)
Ore State Sen
b Los Angeles, Calif, July 28, 26; s Walter Andrew Brown & Emily Anna Weber B; m 1950 to Barbara Mae Porter Stahmann; c Jeffrey David, Kendall Paul & David Walter. Educ: Univ Southern Calif, AB cum laude, 49, Law Ctr, JD, 52; Harvard Univ Law Sch, fall 57; Boston Univ Sch Grad Studies, MA in Govt, 61; Judge Adv Gen Sch, 64-65; Univ Ore Sch Librarianship, summers 72, 73 & 75; Phi Eta Sigma; Blackstonian; Blue Key; Phi Kappa Phi; Phi Beta Kappa; Delta Theta Phi; Kappa Sigma. Polit & Govt Pos: Committeeman, First Cong Dist Dem Comt, Ore, 72-74; precinct 158 committeeman, Clackamas Co Dem Party, 72-; mem, Multnomah Co Pub Safety Retirement Bd, 72-; Ore State Sen, Dist 13, 75-, vchmn judiciary comt, mem human resources comt & environ & energy comt, Ore State Senate, 75- Bus & Prof Pos: Assoc prof & librn, Northwestern Sch Law, Lewis & Clark Col, 70- Mil Serv: Entered as Seaman 1/C, Navy, 44, released as Comdr, Judge Adv Gen Corps, 70, after serv as legal officer, Naval Sta, Subic Bay, Luzon, Philippines, 61-64; Am Theatre; Asiatic-Pac Theatre; Navy Occup; China Serv; World War II Victory; Nat Defense Serv Medal with one Bronze Star; Naval Res Medal; Armed Forces Exped Medal (Vietnam). Publ: Auth, Criminal jurisdiction over visiting naval forces under international law, Washington & Lee Law Rev, spring 67; Miranda errors—always prejudicial or sometimes harmless?, Judge Adv Gen J, 9-11/69. Mem: Am & Fed Bar Asns; VFW; Ore Consumer League; Sierra Club (mem legal comt). Relig: Unitarian Universalist. Legal Res: 2104 SW Wembley Park Rd Lake Oswego OR 97034 Mailing Add: Northwestern Sch Law Lewis & Clark Col Portland OR 97219

BROWN, WARD B (R)
NH State Sen
Mailing Add: Box 404 East Hampstead NH 03826

BROWN, WILLIAM BURBRIDGE (D)
Justice, Ohio Supreme Court
b Chillicothe, Ohio, Sept 10, 12; s Henry Renick Brown & Mabel Downs B; m 1943 to Jayne Stone; c Henry Renick, II & Susan (Mrs Dennis Eshbaugh). Educ: Williams Col, Mass, AB, 34; Harvard Univ, LLB, 37; Delta Kappa Epsilon; Lincoln's Inn. Polit & Govt Pos: Price attorney, Consumers Durable Goods Br, Off Price Admin, Washington, DC, 42-43, chief price attorney, Honolulu Dist Off, 43-44, chief attorney in charge of enforcement div, 44-45; judge, Court of Tax Appeals, Territory of Hawaii, 46-47, treas, ex-officio-bank examr, ins comnr, fire marshal & securities comnr, Territory of Hawaii, 47-51; substitute judge, Hawaii Supreme Court, 51-55; judge, Second Circuit Court, 51-55; judge, Chillicothe Munic Court, Ohio, 57-61; judge, Court of Appeals, Fourth Dist, Ohio, 60-67, presiding judge, 65-67; justice, Ohio Supreme Court, 73- Bus & Prof Pos: Law clerk, Ritter & Daugherty, Toledo, Ohio, 37-39; attorney, Simpson & Brown, Chillicothe, 39-42; instr bus law, Univ Hawaii, 45-46; attorney, Honolulu, 45-47; attorney, Chillicothe, Ohio, 67-72. Publ: Brown's Rural Directory, 40. Mem: Ohio State, Hawaii & Am Bar Asns; Am Judicature Soc; Am Judges Asn. Relig: Episcopal. Mailing Add: 80 W Fifth St Chillicothe OH 45601

BROWN, WILLIAM D (D)
La State Sen
Mailing Add: 2212 Pargoud Monroe LA 71201

BROWN, WILLIAM HILL, III (R)
Chmn, Equal Employ Opportunity Comn
b Philadelphia, Pa, Jan 19, 28; s William Hill Brown, Jr & Ethel L Washington B; m 1953 to Sonya M Brown; c Michele Denise. Educ: Temple Univ, BS, 52; Univ Pa Law Sch, JD, 55; Alpha Phi Alpha. Polit & Govt Pos: Chief of frauds, Dist Attorney's Off, Philadelphia, Pa, 68, Dep Dist Attorney, 68; comnr, Equal Employ Opportunity comn, 68-69, chmn, 69- Bus & Prof Pos: Assoc, Norris, Schmidt, Green, Harris & Higginbotham, 56-62; partner, Norris, Green, Harris & Brown, 62-64; partner, Norris, Brown & Hall, 64-68; mem regional bd dirs, First Pa Banking & Trust Co, 68-73. Mil Serv: Entered as Pvt, Army Air Force, 46, released as Cpl, 48, after serv in 12th Air Ammunition Squadron, Far East, 47-48; World War II Victory Medal. Publ: Auth, Sex discrimination, it isn't funny, it is illegal & the battle has just begun, Good Govt, winter 71; The light at the top of the stairs: the Equal Employment Opportunity Act of 1972, Personnel Admin, 6/72; Equal employment & the employment of minors & women, In: Handbook of Modern Personnel Administration, 72. Mem: Philadelphia, Am, Fed, & Pa Bar Asns; Am Trial Lawyers Asn; Am Arbit Asn. Honors & Awards: Award of Recognition, Alpha Phi Alpha, 69. Relig: Episcopal. Legal Res: 4728 Osage Ave Philadelphia PA 19143 Mailing Add: 4701 Willard Ave Apt 1635 Chevy Chase MD 20015

BROWN, WILLIAM HOLMES
Parliamentarian, US House of Rep
b Huntington, WVa, Sept 3, 29; m 1971 to Jean Elizabeth Smith; c Sara Holmes. Educ: Swarthmore Col, BS, 51; Univ Chicago, JD, 54. Polit & Govt Pos: Parliamentarian, US House of Rep, currently. Mil Serv: Entered as Ens, Naval Res, 54, released as Lt(jg), 57; Lt Comdr, Res. Legal Res: Oakland Green Rte 2 Leesburg VA 22075 Mailing Add: Speaker's Rms US Capitol Washington DC 20515

BROWN, WILLIAM JOSEPH (D)
Attorney Gen, Ohio
b Youngstown, Ohio, July 12, 40; s Joseph Brown & Margaret O'Neil B; single. Educ: Duquesne Univ, BA; Ohio Northern Univ Col Law, JD; Delta Theta Phi; Phi Kappa Theta; Delta Theta Phi. Polit & Govt Pos: Chmn, Humphrey for President Comt, Columbiana Co, Ohio, 68; Attorney Gen, Ohio, 71- Bus & Prof Pos: Attorney, Off Econ Opportunity, Youngstown, Ohio. Mil Serv: Entered as E-1, Army, 63, released as E-4, 69, after serv in 444 Personal Serv Unit. Mem: Am, Ohio State, Mahoning Co & Columbiana Co Bar Asns; Am Legion. Relig: Catholic. Legal Res: 833 Mission Hills Lane Worthington OH 43085 Mailing Add: State House Annex Columbus OH 43215

BROWN, WILLIE B (D)
NJ State Assemblyman
Mailing Add: State House Trenton NJ 08625

BROWN, WILLIE L, JR (D)
Calif State Assemblyman
b Mineola, Tex, Mar 20, 34; s Willie Lewis Brown, Sr & Minnie Collins B; m 1957 to Blanche Vitero; c Susan Elizabeth, Robin Elaine & Michael Elliott. Educ: San Francisco State Col, AB, 55; Univ Calif Hastings Col Law, JD, 58; Phi Alpha Delta; Alpha Phi Alpha. Polit & Govt Pos: Committeeman, Co Dem Comt, Calif, 60-62; Calif State Assemblyman, 65-; mem, Calif Dem State Cent Comt, currently; deleg, Dem Nat Conv, 68, deleg & chmn Calif deleg, 72; deleg, Dem Nat Mid-Term Conf, 74. Mil Serv: SP-3, Nat Guard. Honors & Awards: Fel, Crown Col, Univ Calif, Santa Cruz. Relig: Protestant. Legal Res: 1524 Masonic Ave San Francisco CA 94117 Mailing Add: 666 Octavia San Francisco CA 94102

BROWN, WINTHROP GILMAN
b Maine, July 12, 07; m to Peggy Bell; c three. Educ: Yale Univ, BA, 29, LLB, 32. Polit & Govt Pos: Attorney, Lend Lease Admin, 41; exec officer, Harriman Mission & Mission for Econ Affairs, London, 41-45; dir, Off of Int Trade Policy, 45-48; counr, London, 52-55; dir, Int Coop Admin Mission, United Kingdom, 55-57; minister-counr, India & Nepal, 57-60; US Ambassador, Laos, 60-62; dep commandant, Nat War Col, 62-64; US Ambassador, Korea, 64-67; spec asst to Secy State for liaison with gov of the states, 67-68, Dep Asst Secy of State for EAsian & Pac Affairs, 68-72; retired. Bus & Prof Pos: Law clerk, 32-38; lawyer, 38-41. Honors & Awards: Superior Serv Award, State Dept, 52, Distinguished Honor Award, 73; Distinguished Fed Civilian Serv Award by President Kennedy, 63. Mailing Add: 2435 Tracy Pl NW Washington DC 20008

BROWNE, ELIZABETH WINGREENE (D)
Ore State Sen
b Minneapolis, Minn, Apr 4, 26; d William Alexander Wingreene & Margaret Blackwood W; m 1949 to Colbert Hughes Browne; c Claudia, Scott, Paula Jane & Christopher. Educ: Univ Minn, BA, 48; Univ Chicago, MA, 51; Univ Ore, LLB, 66. Polit & Govt Pos: Dir, Sch Dist 76, Ore, 61; dep dist attorney, Lane Co, 67-68; referee, Lane Co Circuit Court, 68-69; Ore State Rep, 69-70; munic judge pro tem, Oakridge, Ore, 70; Ore State Sen, 71- Bus & Prof Pos: Instr, Dade Co, Fla, 51-58; attorney-at-law, Ore, currently. Publ: Gault—Its impact in Oregon, Willamette Law Rev, 67; ed, Juvenile Judges Digest & Handbook on Juvenile Law, Ore State Bar. Mem: Am Bar Asn; Judicature Juv Judges Asn; Bus & Prof Womens Asn. Relig: Protestant. Mailing Add: Laurel Butte Dr Oakridge OR 97463

BROWNE, JEROME FIELDING (D)
Mem Exec Comt, Dunn Co Dem Party
b Metropolis, Ill, Jan 10, 21; s William Louis Browne & Mary Nellius B; m 1955 to Virginia Valetta Richartz; c William Theodore. Educ: High Sch. Polit & Govt Pos: Sgt-at-Arms, First Ward Dem-Farmer-Labor Club, Minneapolis, 50-51, vchmn, 52; secy, Dunn Co Dem Party, 59-62, chmn, 63-65 & 72-73; Dem Statutory chmn, Dunn Co, Wis, 64-; chmn, Dunn Co Humphrey-Muskie Campaign, 68; bd mem, Town of Menomonie, 68-69; Conservationists for Proxmire, 70; chmn, Dunn Co Humphrey for President Comt, 72. Bus & Prof Pos: Dock & warehouse foreman, S J Groves & Sons, Antigua, BWI, 41-42; from order clerk to foreman, Kraft Foods Co, 44-58; parts sales mgr, Richartz Implement, 58-; mem adv comt, Eau Claire Tech Sch, 68- Mem: Dunn Co Fish & Game Asn; Nat Wildlife Fedn; Moose; Nature Conservancy. Relig: Congregational. Mailing Add: Rte 6 House Hill Menomonie WI 54751

BROWNE, ROBERT SPAN (D)
b Chicago, Ill, Aug 17, 24; s William H Browne, Jr & Julia Barksdale B; m to Nguyen Thi Huoi; c Hoa Nguyen, Mai Julia, Ngo Alexi & Marshall Xuan. Educ: Univ Ill, BA, 44; Univ Chicago, MBA, 47; City Univ New York, 64-69; Phi Eta Sigma; Alpha Phi Alpha. Polit & Govt Pos: Deleg, Dem Nat Conv, 68; deleg, Nat Black Polit Conv, 72. Bus & Prof Pos: Instr, Dillard Univ, 47-49; secy, Watchtower Life Ins Co Houston, 49-50; indust field secy, Chicago Urban League, 50-53; economist, Int Coop Admin (stationed in Cambodia & Vietnam), 55-61; asst prof econ, Fairleigh Dickinson Univ, 64-69; exec dir, Black Econ Research Ctr, 69- Mil Serv: Entered as Pvt, Army, 44, released as Sgt, 46. Publ: Race Relations in International Affairs, Pub Affairs Press, 61; co-ed, The Social Scene, Winthrop, 72; The case for two Americas, NY Times Mag, 8/68. Mem: Am Comn on Africa (bd dirs); Harlem Commonwealth Coun (bd dirs); Pa Community Serv (bd dirs); Emergency Land Fund; 21st Century Found & DJB Found. Mailing Add: 214 Tryon Ave Teaneck NJ 07666

BROWNE, ROY EDWARD (R)
Chmn, Summit Co Rep Cent Comt, Ohio
b Barberton, Ohio, Oct 16, 04; s Herbert C Browne & Nellie Neitz B; m 1933 to Harriet Elizabeth Brooker; c Walter R, Royce & Carolyn (Mrs Gay). Educ: Cleveland Marshall Law Sch, LLB, 29; Univ Akron, BA, 37; Pi Kappa Delta; Lambda Chi Alpha. Polit & Govt Pos: Asst attorney gen, Ohio, 36-42; law dir, Akron, 42-53; chmn, Summit Co Rep Exec Comt, 53-63; chmn, Summit Co Rep Cent Comt, 53-; mem, Bd of Elec, Summit Co, 53-; deleg, Rep Nat Conv, 68; mem, Ohio Rep State Cent Comt, currently. Mem: Mason (32nd degree); Shrine; Lions. Relig: Methodist. Mailing Add: 1910 First Nat Tower Akron OH 44308

BROWNE, RUTH T (D)
Secy, Kans Dem State Cent Comt
b Norton, Kans, Mar 11, 30; d John W Hickert & Mary Fink H; m 1952 to John C Browne; c Michael, John C, II, Mary, Theresa, James & Daniel. Educ: Loretto Heights Col, AB in hist, 51. Polit & Govt Pos: Precinct committeewoman, Dem Party, 56-; chmn, Clay Co Dem Party, 64-68; secy, Kans Dem State Cent Comt, 65-; vpres, Kans Cult Arts Comn, 67-; deleg, Dem Nat Conv, 68 & 72; mem, NCent Kans Health Planning Coun, 68-; charter mem, Church Parish Coun, 70-; pres bd, Clay Center Libr, 70-; mem exec bd, NCent Kans Libr Systs, Manhattan, Kans, 70-; vchmn, Clay Co Dem Comt, formerly, chmn, currently. Mem: Nat Farmers Union; Clay Center Country Club; Landon Lect Series of Kans State Univ (patron); Clay Center Libr Club. Relig: Catholic. Mailing Add: 1603 Fifth St Clay Center KS 67432

BROWNE, SECOR DELAHAY (R)
Mem, Charlestown Rep Town Comt, RI
b Chicago, Ill, July 22, 16; s Aldis Jerome Browne & Elizabeth Cunningham B; m 1970 to Constance Ely Haden; c Patrick R & Giles C; stepchildren, Dana, Sabra, Russell, C Keller, Kinard & Chesley Haden. Educ: Harvard Univ, AB, 38; Signet Soc; Hasty Pudding; Inst of 1777. Polit & Govt Pos: Mem, Lincoln Rep Town Comt, Mass, 62-68; Asst Secy for Research & Technol, Dept of Transportation, 69; chmn, Civil Aeronaut Bd, 69-72; mem, Charlestown Rep Town Comt, RI, 75- Bus & Prof Pos: Engr draftsman, Kroeschell Eng Co, Chicago, Ill, 38-39; engr salesman, Barber-Colman Co, Rockford, 39-42, mgr aircraft prod, 46-51; Clifford Mfg Co, Waltham, Mass, 51-55; pres & chmn bd, Browne & Shaw Co, 55-69, Browne & Shaw Research Corp, 63-68; assoc prof, Mass Inst Technol, 58-69; transportation consult, Edwards Browne Assocs, London, Eng, 67-69; vis prof, Mass Inst Technol, 73-; pres, Secor D Browne Assoc, Inc, Washington, DC, 73- Mil Serv: Entered as Aviation Cadet, Army Air Corps, 42, released as Maj, 46, 46, after serv in 50th Troop Carrier Squadron, 314th Group, First Allied Airborne Army, Europe-African-Mid East Theatre, 44-46; Eight Battle Stars; Two Presidential Unit Citations; Bronze Star. Publ: The national interest in supersonic transport, 1/65 & National transportation: a study in conflicts, 3/66, Tech Rev; The quiet airport: it could mean a decaying city, too, Boston Herald Traveler, 11/29/68. Mem: Soc of Automotive Engrs; fel Royal Aeronaut Soc; assoc fel Am Inst Aeronaut & Astronaut; Nat Aviation Club, Washington, DC; Aero Club of Washington. Mailing Add: PO Box 217 Charlestown RI 20813

BROWNE, WILLIAM V (D)
Exec Dir, Dem State Comt, NJ
b New York, NY, Nov 3, 21; s William S Browne & Della Curry B; m 1949 to Kathleen Hannon; c Colleen & Patricia. Educ: Univ Calif, Berkeley, 2 years; Fordham Univ, 1 year. Polit & Govt Pos: Dem leader, Hazlet Twp, NJ, 59; chmn, Citizens for Kennedy, Monmouth Co, 60; chmn, Citizens for Hughes, 61; asst to state treas, NJ, 62-63; asst to state chmn, Dem Party, 63-64; exec dir, Dem State Comt, 64-; alt deleg, Dem Nat Conv, 68; chmn, Dem for Cahill, Newark, NJ, 69; asst to chmn, Rep State Comt, 70; admin asst to US Rep E Forsythe, 70-73. Mil Serv: Entered as Pvt, Army, 42, released as Warrant Officer, 46, after serv in CID. Mem: Am Legion; KofC; Holy Name Soc. Relig: Catholic. Mailing Add: 13 Bucknell Dr Hazlet NJ 07730

BROWNELL, HERBERT (R)
b Peru, Nebr, Feb 20, 04; s Herbert B & May A Miller B; m 1934 to Doris A McCarter; c Joan, Ann, Thomas McCarter & James Barker. Educ: Univ Nebr, BA, 24; Yale Univ, LLB, 27. Polit & Govt Pos: NY State Assemblyman, 32-37; chmn, Rep Nat Comt, 44-46; US Attorney Gen, 53-57; personal rep of President on Study of Colorado River, 73- Bus & Prof Pos: Attorney, Root, Clark, Buckner & Ballatine, 27-29; attorney, Lord, Day & Lord, New York, 29-53 & 57- Mem: Am, NY State & New York Bar Asns; New York Century Asn; Downtown Asn. Relig: Methodist. Mailing Add: 25 Broadway New York NY 10004

BROWNELL, THOMAS F (D)
Mass State Rep
b Boston, Mass; s John H Brownell & Willena MacQuarrie B; m to Margaret T Donovan; c Karyn. Educ: Suffolk Univ, BS, 63, Law Sch, JD, 66; Boston Univ Grad Law Sch Taxation. Polit & Govt Pos: Asst Attorney Gen, Mass, 70-71; Mass State Rep, 73- Bus & Prof Pos: Legis counsel & attorney, Mass Taxpayers Found, 67-70. Mil Serv: Entered as Pvt, Army, 58, released as Pvt E-2, 63, after serv in 101st Inf, 58-63. Mem: Am, Norfolk Co & Quincy Bar Asns. Mailing Add: 15 Moreland Rd Quincy MA 02169

BROWNING, CHAUNCEY H, JR (D)
Attorney Gen, WVa
b Charleston, WVa, Nov 21, 34; s Chauncey H Browning (deceased) & Evelyn Mahone B; m 1969 to Patricia Ann Lewis; c Chauncey H, III, Charles Preston & Steven Thomas. Educ: WVa Univ, AB, 56, LLB, 58. Polit & Govt Pos: Law clerk, US Dist Court for Southern Dist, WVa, 58; attorney-in-charge, Legal Aid Soc, Kanawha & Putnam Co, 59-60; Comnr Pub Insts, WVa, 62-68; Attorney Gen, WVa, 69- Bus & Prof Pos: Attorney-at-law, Charleston, WVa, 58-62; mem exec comt, Nat Asn Attorneys Gen, 72-73. Publ: Former ed, WVa Law Quart. Mem: WVa Comn on Aging; WVa Ment Retardation Comn (vpres); Am, WVa & Kanawha Co Bar Asns. Relig: Methodist. Legal Res: 709 Canterbury Dr Charleston WV 25314 Mailing Add: State Capitol Charleston WV 25305

BROWNING, GEORGE MORTIMER (D)
b McHenry, Md, Dec 19, 14; s Jessie Frank Browning & May Williams B; m 1935 to Mary Margaret Kelly; c Mary Jane & Nathan Criss. Educ: Elec & Bus Courses & High Sch. Polit & Govt Pos: Forest supt, Md State Dept Forestry, 34-41; state trooper, Md State Police, 41-43; mem & chmn, Md Dem State Cent Comt, formerly. Bus & Prof Pos: Chief maintenance, Pa Elec Co, 43- Mem: AF&AM; Consistory (32nd degree); Ali Ghan Temple; Ali Ghan Relief Asn; Moose. Relig: Episcopal. Mailing Add: Rte 1 Box 358-A Oakland MD 21550

BROWNING, JAMES ARTHUR, JR (D)
b Kansas City, Mo, Nov 20, 30; s James Arthur Browning & Mary Elizabeth Van Arsdall B; single. Educ: Univ Calif at Los Angeles, AB in polit sci, 52, Law Sch, LLB, 57; Theta Delta Chi; Phi Delta Phi. Polit & Govt Pos: Pres, Oxnard Dem Club, Calif, 60; mem exec comt, Calif Dem State Cent Comt, 62-64; chmn, Ventura Co Dem Cent Comt, 62-64; deleg, Dem Nat Conv, 64; consult, Calif State Senate Comt on Elec & Reapportionment, 75- Bus & Prof Pos: Assoc, F Gile Tiffany, Jr, attorney-at-law, 57-61; partner, Tiffany, Hunt, Browning & Brown, Oxnard, 61-73. Mil Serv: Entered as 2nd Lt, Air Force, 52, released as 1st Lt, 54, after serv as Adj, 529th Air Defense Group; Nat Defense Serv Medal. Mem: Ventura Co, Calif & Am Bar Asns; Legal Air Asn of Ventura Co. Mailing Add: Apt 12 2524 T St Sacramento CA 95816

BROWNING, SARAH LOUISE (R)
b Bourne, Mass, Jan 23, 52; d Robert Weston Browning & Marjorie Pike B; single. Educ: New Eng Col, Henniker, NH, BA in Polit Sci, 73. Polit & Govt Pos: Summer intern, US Rep Louis C Wyman, NH, 71, youth coordr & staff asst, 72; staff asst, Young Voters for the President, NH, 71-72; youth adv, Comt for the Reelec of the President, 72; deleg, Rep Nat Conv, 72; deleg, NH Rep State Conv, 72; staff asst to Majority Leader, NH House Rep, 73-, staff asst to Speaker, 75; grants mgt & admin rep, NH State Coun Aging, 73. Relig: Protestant. Mailing Add: 25 Helen St Manchester NH 03104

BROWNMAN, HAROLD L
Asst Secy of Install & Logistics, Dept Army
Mailing Add: Off Secy of Army Dept of the Army Washington DC 20310

BROWNSTEIN, ESTHER SAVELLE (D)
b New York, NY, Nov 21, 14; d Joseph Savelle & Celia Roskin S; m 1938 to Philip Nathan Brownstein; c Michael Jay. Educ: Maryland Univ, 55-60. Polit & Govt Pos: Exec asst, US Rep Carl D Perkins, Ky, 72- Mailing Add: 560 N St SW N-102 Washington DC 20024

BROYHILL, JAMES EDGAR (R)
Rep Nat Committeeman, NC
b Wilkes Co, NC, Apr 5, 92; s Isaac Broyhill & Margaret Parsons B; m 1921 to Satie L Hunt; c Allene (Mrs W Stevens), Paul H, James T & Bettie (Mrs Willard Gortner). Polit & Govt Pos: Rep Nat Committeeman, NC, 48-; deleg, Rep Nat Conv, 8 times. Bus & Prof Pos: Exec head, Broyhill Furniture Factories, Lenoir Chair Co, Lenoir Furniture Corp, Lenoir Veneer Co, Nat Veneer Co, Harper Furniture Co, Lenoir Furniture Forwarding Co, Canover Furniture Co, Broyhill Plastics, Inc, Broyhill Panel Plant, Rutherford Furniture Co, Pacemaker Furniture Co, Broyhill Consolidated Warehouse Corp & Otis L Broyhill Furniture Co; dir, Wachovia Bank & Trust Co, C&N-NRwy; mem adv bd, Am Mutual Liability Ins Co; mem bd of gov, Am Furniture Mart. Mil Serv: Army. Mem: Mason; KofP; Charlotte City, Lenoir & Forest Country Clubs. Relig: Baptist. Legal Res: Wilkesboro Rd Lenoir NC 28645 Mailing Add: Box 775 Lenoir NC 28645

BROYHILL, JAMES THOMAS **(R)**
US Rep, NC
b Lenoir, NC, Aug 19, 27; s James Edgar Broyhill & Satie Hunt B; m 1951 to Louise Horton Robbins; c Marilyn, Eddie & Philip. Educ: Univ NC, BS in Com, 50; Phi Delta Theta. Polit & Govt Pos: US Rep, NC, 63- Bus & Prof Pos: Exec, Broyhill Furniture Indust of Lenoir, NC, 46-63. Mem: Mason; Shrine. Relig: Baptist. Legal Res: Lenoir NC Mailing Add: Rayburn House Off Bldg Washington DC 20515

BROYHILL, JOEL T **(R)**
b Hopewell, Va, Nov 4, 19; m to Jane Marshall Bragg; c Nancy Pierce, JaneAnne & Jeanne Marie. Educ: George Washington Univ. Polit & Govt Pos: US Rep, Va, 52-74. Bus & Prof Pos: Real estate, bldg exec. Mil Serv: Army, World War II. Mem: Arlington Co, Va CofC; Arlington Co Planning Comn; Arlington Optimist Club; Am Legion; VFW. Relig: Lutheran; Trustee, Resurrection Lutheran Church. Mailing Add: 4845 Old Dominion Dr Arlington VA 22207

BROZEK, MICHAEL FRANCIS **(D)**
State Pres, Dem Youth Caucus of Wis
b Chicago, Ill, Mar 18, 52; s Chester J Brozek & Evelyn Pociask B; single. Educ: Univ Wis-Eau Claire, BA, 74; Tau Kappa Epsilon; Iota Sigma Chap. Polit & Govt Pos: Chairperson, Price Co Young Dem, Wis, 69-71; chairperson, Lake Superior Dist Young Dem, 70-72; vchmn, Tenth Cong Dist Dem Party, 71-72; vchmn, Seventh Cong Dist Dem Party, 73-75; state vpres, Young Dem Clubs of Wis, 71-73; alt deleg, Dem Nat Conv, 72; coordr, Obey & Thoresen for Cong, 72; campaign mgr, Zeman for Wis State Rep, 72; Nat Committeeman, Young Dem Clubs of Am, 72-75; vchairperson, Price Co Dem Party, 72-73; state pres, Dem Youth Caucus of Wis, 73- Bus & Prof Pos: Partner, House of Print, 73- Mem: Cath Youth Orgn. Honors & Awards: Phillips CofC Presidents Award, Young Dem Clubs of Wis, 71; Outstanding State Officer, Bayfield Co Young Dem, 72; Outstanding State Officer, Van Buren Young Dem, 72. Relig: Roman Catholic. Mailing Add: Rte 1 Box 1 Phillips WI 54535

BRUBAKER, ROBERT LEE **(R)**
b Greenfield, Ohio, July 14, 17; s Kinsey Jerry Brubaker & Louise Leutkemeier B; m 1942 to Betty Brock; c John A, Electa J, Robert Loring, Mary Melissa & Susannah. Educ: Vanderbilt Univ, AB, 37; Vanderbilt Law Sch, LLB, 39; Omicron Delta Kappa; Chi Phi. Polit & Govt Pos: Judge, Washington Court House, Munic Court, Ohio, 52-55; judge, Fayette Co Probate & Juv Court, 52-61; chmn, Fayette Co Rep Exec Comt, formerly. Mil Serv: Entered as Chief Specialist, Naval Res, 42, released as Lt, 45, after serv in Destroyer Div 25, Cent Pac, 44-45. Mem: Fayette Co & Ohio State Bar Asns; Washington Court House CofC; Fayette Co Community Chest; Scioto-Paint Valley Guid Ctr. Relig: Episcopal. Mailing Add: 232 N Main St Washington Court House OH 43160

BRUCE, BEVERLY JOAN **(D)**
VChmn, SDak Dem Party
b Mitchell, SDak, May 11, 27; d Jack C Thurman & Lorraine Tormey T; m 1949 to John Murray Bruce; c David, Robert, John P (Pete), Steven & Susan. Educ: Notre Dame Jr Col, grad, 47; Beta Sigma Phi. Polit & Govt Pos: Precinct capt, Davison Co, SDak, 66-, co vchmn, 68-; mem, SDak State Planning Comn, 70; vchmn, SDak Dem Party, 70-; mem, Dem Nat Comt, 72- Bus & Prof Pos: Mem, Comts of Pub Rels & Conv, CofC, 4 years; partner, Bruce Sign Co, Mitchell, SDak. Mem: VFW Auxiliary; Am Legion Auxiliary; Elks; Holy Spirit Altar Soc; Holy Family Altar Soc. Relig: Catholic. Mailing Add: W Hwy 16 RR 2 Mitchell SD 57301

BRUCE, DANNY MONROE **(D)**
SC State Rep
b Spartanburg Co, SC, Apr 13, 50; s Carl David Bruce & Grace Ramsey B; single. Educ: Spartanburg Methodist Col, AA, 70; Western Carolina Univ, BS, 72; Univ SC, 74. Polit & Govt Pos: SC State Rep, Dist 38, 75- Bus & Prof Pos: Teacher hist, Paul M Dorman High Sch, SC, 72-74; owner, Exxon Serv Ctr, Campobello, currently. Mem: Lions Int; Farm Bur. Relig: Baptist. Mailing Add: Box 242 Campobello SC 29322

BRUCE, JAMES EDMOND **(D)**
Ky State Rep
b 1927. Educ: Univ Tenn, BS. Polit & Govt Pos: Vpres, Christian Co Farm Bur, Ky, formerly; Ky State Rep, 64- Bus & Prof Pos: Farmer. Mem: Elks. Relig: Methodist. Mailing Add: Rte 1 Hopkinsville KY 42240

BRUCE, KATHARINE FENN **(R)**
Mem, Mass Rep State Comt
b Cambridge, Mass, Nov 8, 25; d Thomas Legare Fenn & Margaret Fleck F; m 1947 to William Lane Bruce; c Jeffrey Fenn, Thomas Lane, Beverly Lorena & Meredith Lucile. Educ: Westbrook Col, Portland, Maine, 43-45; Lamson Sch Music, Boston, Mass, 45-47. Polit & Govt Pos: Pres, Newton Women's Rep Club, Mass, 62-64; mem, Mass Rep State Comt, 64-, vchmn, 72-75, acting chmn, 75; vchmn, Newton Rep City Comt, 66-69. Mem: United Fund, Newton; Am Red Cross; All Newton Music Sch; YMCA (first woman bd mem, 71-75); Newton Mayor's Youth Comn (only woman mem, 70-75). Relig: Congregational. Mailing Add: 934 Beacon St Newton Centre MA 02159

BRUCE, MARION **(D)**
Chmn, Randall Co Dem Exec Comt, Tex
b Randall Co, Tex, Mar 26, 12; s Robert William Bruce & Ellen Sophia Osgood B; m to Louise Evans; c Robert, Barbara (Mrs Ray Cullin), Sharon (Mrs Mac Jones) & Helen (Mrs E J Moorman). Educ: Univ Tex. Polit & Govt Pos: Chmn, Randall Co Dem Exec Comt, Tex, currently; mem, Randall Co Bd Educ & Tax Equalization Bd; co deleg, Tex Dem State Conv, 20 years; alt deleg, Dem Nat Conv, twice. Bus & Prof Pos: Rancher & Shorthorn breeder. Mem: Kiwanis (Dist Lt Gov, Downtown); Mason; Potter Randall Citizens Comt (chmn, Group Work & Recreation coun); Oper Drug Alert. Relig: Baptist. Mailing Add: Rte 2 PO Box 11 Amarillo TX 79105

BRUCE, PAUL LOVE **(D)**
Chmn, Hamblen Co Dem Exec Comt, Tenn
b Morristown, Tenn, July 9, 33; s John Bernard Bruce & Minnie Anderson B; m 1961 to Gayle Hartman; c Paula Ann, John Richard & Ronald Powell. Educ: Carson Newman Col, BS, 59; Columbian Lit Soc. Polit & Govt Pos: Chmn, Hamblen Co Dem Exec Comt, Tenn, 69-; mem, Tenn State Dem Exec Comt, 74-; vchmn, First Cong Dist Chairpersons, Tenn, 74- Bus & Prof Pos: Bookkeeper & credit mgr, Bradley's, Inc, 59; acct & auditor, Taylor & Russell, 59- Mil Serv: Entered as Pvt, Air Force, 51, released as S/Sgt, 55, after serv in Security Serv, Alaskan Air Command, 52-54; Good Conduct Medal. Mem: Morristown Lions; Moose; Am Legion; Morristown CofC. Relig: Baptist. Mailing Add: RR 3 Morristown TN 37814

BRUCKERHOFF, VERNON E **(R)**
Mo State Rep
b St Mary's, Mo, July 31, 44; s William Bruckerhoff; single. Educ: Southeast Mo State Col, BS, 66; Student Senate City-Col Rels Comt; Alpha Phi Omega. Polit & Govt Pos: Chmn, Southeast Mo State Col Rep Club, formerly; chmn, Mo Col Rep Clubs, 2 years; participant, Rep Leadership Training Sch, Washington, DC; committeeman, Perry Co Rep Party, Mo; Mo State Rep, 70-, mem comts agr, educ & roads & hwys, Mo House Rep, 70-, mem comt environ, 72-73, Rep caucus comt on educ, 72 & 1973 inaugural comt, 73; chmn, Kit Bond for Gov Comt, 71-72; mem, Mo Goals Comn & Mo Comt Environ. Bus & Prof Pos: Teacher & farmer. Mem: Southeast Mo Coun Social Studies (treas); Area Retarded Children's Asn (treas); Southeast Mo Dist Boy Scout Coun; Mo Conserv Fedn; Mo Farm Bur. Relig: Catholic. Mailing Add: RFD 1 St Mary's MO 63673

BRUECK, KARL ARTHUR **(D)**
Chmn, Miami Co Dem Comt, Kans
b Paola, Kans, July 24, 10; s William B Brueck & Katherine Amelia McGrath B; m 1964 to Thelma M Hart. Educ: Univ Kans, AB, 32; Sigma Nu. Polit & Govt Pos: Vpres, Kans Young Dem & pres, Third Dist Young Dem, 39-40; chmn, Miami Co Dem Comt, 50-; pres, Kans Dem Club, 53-54; Kans State Rep, 55-61; permanent chmn, Second Cong Dist Dem Conv, 56; deleg, Dem Nat Conv, 56, 60 & 64, alt deleg, 68; hwy comnr, Fourth Kans Div, 67-75. Bus & Prof Pos: Ed, The Western Spirit Newspaper, Paola, 30-42; rep, Equitable Life Assurance Soc, 46- Mil Serv: Entered as S 1/C, Naval Res, 42, released as SK 1/C, 45, after serv in SW Pac. Mem: Kans Dem Ex-Serv Men's Club; CofC; Elks; VFW; Am Legion. Honors & Awards: Nat Qual Award, Nat Asn Life Underwriters, 54-75; Nat Leaders Corps, Equitable Life Assurance Soc, 69-75. Relig: Roman Catholic. Legal Res: 4 Brookside Dr Paola KS 60071 Mailing Add: 133 S Pearl Paola KS 66071

BRUEN, DAVID D **(D)**
Treas, Putnam Co, NY
b Brewster, NY, Aug 14, 29; s M Raymond Bruen & Mildred Duncan B; m 1951 to Marilyn King; c Diana Mary, Margaret Ann, David Matthew, Bonnie Theresa, Kathleen Gay, James Duncan, Mary, Marilyn Ann & Susan. Educ: Fordham Univ Sch Bus, BS, 51. Polit & Govt Pos: Co treas, Putnam Co, NY, 61-; chmn, Putnam Co Dem Party, 70-73 & 75-; mem, NY State Dem Comt, 97th Dist, 70- Bus & Prof Pos: Owner, Vail-Bruen Ins Agency, Brewster, NY, 61-; independent real estate broker, 65- Mem: NY State Independent Ins Agts Asn; NY State Treas & Finance Officers Asn; Elks; KofC; Ancient Order Hibernians. Relig: Roman Catholic. Mailing Add: Birch Hill Rd Brewster NY 10509

BRUGGENSCHMIDT, JOSEPH G **(D)**
Ind State Sen
Educ: Purdue Univ. Polit & Govt Pos: Mem, Perry Co Long Range Planning Comn, Ind; dist forester, Ind Dept Conserv, 3 years; Ind State Rep, 63-72; Ind State Sen, 75- Bus & Prof Pos: Consult forester. Mil Serv: Marine Corps, Korea. Mem: VFW; KofC; Jaycees. Relig: Catholic. Mailing Add: 520 1/2 Maine St Jasper IN 47546

BRUMBAUGH, D EMMERT **(R)**
b Henrietta, Pa, Oct 8, 94; s Moses R Brumbaugh & Sara Florence Stewart B; m to Carolyn Acker; c four. Educ: Martinsburg Summer Normal Sch; Int Correspondence Sch; Hood Col, citation on 75th Convocation. Hon Degrees: Dr in Commercial Sci, Franklin & Marshall Col. Polit & Govt Pos: Chmn, Blair Co Draft Bd, World War II; US Rep, Pa, 43-47; State Secy Banking, Pa, 47-51; deleg, Rep Nat Conv, 51, 55 & 60; Pa State Sen, 62-67. Bus & Prof Pos: Chmn bd, Cent Pa Nat Bank of Claysburg; partner, Brumbaugh Ins Agency, Queen Lumber Co; dir, Pa State Mutual Fire Ins Co. Mil Serv: World War I, 58th Brigade Hq, AEF. Mem: Claysburg Rotary Club; Claysburg Am Legion Home Asn (trustee, Altoona Hosp); Blair Co Automobile Asn (dir); Union League, Philadelphia; Blairmont Country Club. Relig: United Church of Christ. Mailing Add: Claysburg PA 16625

BRUMMET, DONALD EUGENE **(D)**
Ill State Rep
b Dahlgren, Ill, June 3, 14; s John McKindree Brummet & Olga Gibbs B; m 1936 to Nina Evelyn Ingram; c Don Carroll, Tonya Ann & Mary Dell. Educ: Southern Ill Univ, 32-35; charter mem & organizer local fraternity. Polit & Govt Pos: Mem, Vandalia City Coun, Ill, 51-58; Ill State Rep, 71- Bus & Prof Pos: Mgr, Coca-Cola Bottling Co, Vandalia, Ill, 39-46; mgr, Vandalia Airport, 46-49; owner, Superior Fertilizer Co, 49- Mil Serv: Merchant Marine, 43-44. Mem: Mason; Eastern Star; Shrine; CofC; Nat Farmers Orgn. Relig: Baptist. Mailing Add: 412 N Locust Vandalia IL 62471

BRUMMETT, CLAUDIA MAE **(D)**
Mem, Dem Nat Comt, Tex
b Amarillo, Tex, Feb 28, 27; d Claude J Brummett & Mae Kight B; single. Educ: Amarillo Col, AS, 46; Univ Colo, 48; Gamma Theta Chi; Iota Sigma Alpha; Beta Sigma Phi. Polit & Govt Pos: Chmn precinct three, Potter Co Dem Exec Comt, Tex, 56-62, secy, 58-69, chmn precinct one, 62-69; vchmn women's activities, Potter Co Dem Party, 60; co-chmn, Area Dem Hq, 62 & 64; gen chmn, Gov Day, 63; state Dem committeewoman, 31st Sen Dist, Tex, 63-70; vchmn, 31st Sen Dist Dem Exec Comt, 63-70; deleg & mem Rules Comt, Dem Nat Conv, 64, deleg & mem Credentials Comt, 68; chmn poll tax & regist subcomt, Tex State Dem Exec Comt, 64-70, chmn publicity subcomt, 68; founder & exec chmn, League of Dem Women, 64-; deleg & mem credentials comt, Tex State Dem Conv, 68, secy, 72; mem, Dem Nat Credentials Comt, 72; state co-chmn, Women for Dolph Briscoe for Gov, 72; mem comn on deleg selection, Dem Nat Comt, 72-; deleg, Gov Conf on Voc & Tech Educ, Tex, 73; second vpres, SCent Region, Nat Fedn Dem Women, currently; deleg, Dem Nat Mid-Term Conf, 74; mem, Dem Nat Comt, Tex, 75- Bus & Prof Pos: Stenographer, Panhandle & Santa Fe Rwy, 48-55, claim investr, 55-59; chief diversion & tracer clerk, Santa Fe Rwy, Western Lines, 59-69; rancher & bus mgr, JAL Ranch, Alvarado, Tex, 68-; partner, JAL Co & Cowden-Brummett Livestock Co, 68-; secy, J&M Steel Corp, Ft Worth, 71-; vpres, Western Tool & Mfg Co, Inc, Alvarado, 75- Mem: Armstrong Co Hist Soc; Tex Designer Craftsman; Tex Artist-Craftsman Guild; Tex & Southwestern Cattle Raisers Asns. Honors & Awards: Exhibiting & demonstrating craftsman, Salado Art Show, San Antonio Artists' Jamboree, Pan Am Mus, Sq House Mus, Tex Tech Art Mus & Carlin Gallery. Relig: Baptist. Mailing Add: JAL Ranch Box 308 Alvarado TX 76009

BRUNETTE, WALTER STEPHEN (R)
Vt State Rep
b Lawrence, Mass, Jan 1, 1909; s Alfred Joseph Brunette & Caroline St Cyr B; m 1936 to Marjorie Elizabeth Dixon; c Carolyn Bilodeau & David Walter. Educ: Assumption Col, BA, 31. Polit & Govt Pos: Mem sch bd, Lunenburg, Vt, 42-51; Vt State Rep, Dist Essex 1, 75- Bus & Prof Pos: Supt, Cellucord Corp, Gilman, Vt, 35-58; inventory controller, Gilman Paper Co, 58-66; purchasing agt, Ga-Pac Corp, Gilman, 66-72. Mem: Am Asn Purchasing Agts; Elks; Cath Order Foresters. Relig: Catholic. Mailing Add: Commercial Ave Gilman VT 05904

BRUNING, ELSIE IRENE (D)
b Anderson, Ind, July 18, 11; d Charles Edward Stone & Sally Monroe Porter S; m 1927 to Bland Byrket; m 1937 to Leslie E Bruning; c James Edward Byrket & Leslie B & Jeffrey F Bruning. Educ: Anderson & Richmond, Ind Pub Schs. Polit & Govt Pos: Secy, Crawford Co Dem Cent Comt, Mo, formerly. Mem: Cuba Rebekah Lodge 739 (past noble grand); Royal Neighbors Am (oracle); Cuba Mem Am Legion Auxiliary 522 (pres, currently); Rivershade Home Econ Club; Two Score Plus Club. Relig: Methodist. Legal Res: 107 S Lawrence Cuba MO 65453 Mailing Add: PO Box 396 Cuba MO 65453

BRUNNER, FRANK, JR (R)
Chmn, Iron Co Rep Party, Wis
b Chicago, Ill, Aug 14, 06; s Frank Brunner, Sr & Mary Siewatz B; m 1926 to Hazel May Girsch; c Margaret, Jeanett (Mrs Jerry White), Rev Richard; Frank R, Eleanor (Mrs Jim Nyholm), June Schenzel; Rev Rosswell B, Robert B & Kathy (Mrs John Kadrlik). Polit & Govt Pos: Chmn, Iron Co Rep Party, Wis, 75- Bus & Prof Pos: Forest ranger, Wis Dept Natural Resources, 30-68. Mem: F&AM (32 degree); Shrine; Eastern Star; Kiwanis; Nat Rifle Asn. Honors & Awards: State of Wis Gov Serv Award; State of Wis Merit Award. Relig: Methodist. Mailing Add: Echo Lake Rd Mercer WI 54547

BRUNNER, JOHN L (D)
Pa State Rep
b Langeloth, Pa, Aug 18, 29; s John J Brunner & Violet Riley B; m 1954 to Frances E Byrne; c Mary Margaret, Michael Damian & Monica Jane. Educ: Duquesne Univ, AB, 53; Georgetown Univ Law Sch, LLB, 56. Polit & Govt Pos: Pa State Rep, 65- Mil Serv: Entered as Pvt, Army, released as S/Sgt. Relig: Roman Catholic. Mailing Add: Capitol Bldg Harrisburg PA 17120

BRUNNER, MERLIN A (R)
Chmn, Waupaca Co Rep Party, Wis
b Leopolis, Wis, July 19, 24; s Albert N Brunner & Elithe J Chapin B; m 1951 to Joan T Brunner; c Barbara (Mrs Wolf), Mark, Paul, Peter & Beth. Educ: Wis State Univ, Stevens Point, BS, 48; Univ Wis, 50. Polit & Govt Pos: Chmn, Waupaca Co Rep Party, Wis, 75- Bus & Prof Pos: Teacher, New London, Wis, 48-51; sales mgr, Edison Wood Prod, 51-63; divisional pres, Simmons Juv Prod, 63- Mil Serv: Entered as Pvt, Army, 43, released as S/Sgt, 45, after serv in Co E 328th Inf, ETO, 44-45; Maj (Ret), Army Res; Bronze Star; Purple Heart. Mem: Rotary; New London Hosp Bd. Legal Res: 712 W Washington St New London WI 54961 Mailing Add: 613 E Beacon Ave New London WI 54961

BRUNNER, MICHAEL E (R)
b Cleveland, Ohio, Jan 26, 43; s Edmund C Brunner; single. Educ: Bowling Green State Univ, BS, 65, MBA, 67; George Washington Univ, 74- Polit & Govt Pos: Asst dir admin serv, Educ Comn of States, 72-73; legis asst, US Rep Orval Hansen, 73-75, US Rep Garry Brown, Mich, 75- Bus & Prof Pos: In-charge auditor, Ernst & Ernst, CPA's, 70-72. Mil Serv: Entered as 2nd Lt, Army, 68, released as Capt, 70, after serv as Commanding Officer, Army Student Co, Fitzsimons Gen Hosp; 712th Prev Med Unit, Korat, Thailand; Army Commendation Medal. Mem: POETS (pres); Bull Elephants; Toastmasters. Mailing Add: 4343 Lee Hwy 502 Arlington VA 22207

BRUNOW, JOHN B (D)
Iowa State Rep
Mailing Add: 110 West Wall Box 486 Centerville IA 52544

BRUNSDALE, CLARENCE NORMAN (R)
b Sherbrooke, NDak, July 9, 91; s Knute H Brunsdale & Anna Margaret Nordgaard B; m 1924 to Carrie Lajord; c Margaret Marie (Mrs Larson) & Helen Lucille (Mrs Williams). Educ: Luther Col, BA. Hon Degrees: LLD, Luther Col, 51. Polit & Govt Pos: NDak State Sen, 27-34 & 41-51, floor leader, NDak State Senate, 45-49; Gov, NDak, 51-57, US Sen, by appointment, 59-60. Bus & Prof Pos: Mgr, Brunsdale Farms, 14-31; dir, First Nat Bank, Portland, NDak, 20-33; Goose River Bank, Mayville, 20-66; dir & pres, First & Farmers Bank, Portland, 33-40. Mem: Local Civic Club & similar organizations. Relig: Lutheran. Mailing Add: 235 Second Ave NW Mayville ND 58257

BRUNSTAD, DONNA LEAH (D)
b Kittery, Maine, June 21, 38; d Philip E Fritz & Grace Spear Farr F; m 1960 to George Eric Brunstad; c Eric, Mark & Darin. Educ: Univ Maine, Orono, 56-58; Univ NH, 58-59; Western Conn State Col, BA, 73; Phi Mu. Polit & Govt Pos: Vpres, League of Women Voters, Exter, NH, 69-71; deleg, Nat & Conn Dem State Conv, 72; mem, Redding Dem Town Comt, Conn, 72; mem exec bd & treas, Conn McGovern for President Comt, 72. Mem: Am Mkt Asn; Nat Orgn for Women; Nat & Conn Women's Polit Caucus. Mailing Add: One Sullivan Dr West Redding CT 06896

BRUNTHAVER, CARROLL G (R)
b Fremont, Ohio, Mar 27, 32; s Carroll G Brunthaver, Sr & Betty Hessick B; c Susan & Jeffrey. Educ: Ohio State Univ, BS, 54, PhD, 60; Alpha Zeta; Gamma Sigma Delta. Polit & Govt Pos: Govt pos, Agr Stabilization & Conserv Serv, US Dept Agr, 69-72, Asst Secy for Agr for Commodity Progs & Int Affairs, 72-74. Bus & Prof Pos: Instr agr econ, Mich State Univ, 60-61; research dir, Grain & Feed Dealers Nat Asn, Washington, DC, 61-66; assoc dir of research, Comco, Memphis, Tenn, 66-69. Mil Serv: Entered as 2nd Lt, Air Force, 56, released as 1st Lt, 57. Mem: Am Agr Econ Asn. Honors & Awards: Distinguished Alumni Award, Ohio State Univ Col Agr, 73. Relig: Protestant. Mailing Add: 9416 Macklin Ct Alexandria VA 22309

BRUNTON, PAUL D (R)
Okla State Rep
b Negritos, Peru, Aug 19, 44; s Charles Clarke Brunton & Mary McGuire B; single. Educ: Univ Okla, BA, 66; Univ Tulsa, JD, 71; Sigma Chi. Polit & Govt Pos: Okla State Rep, 74- Bus & Prof Pos: Self-employed attorney, Tulsa, Okla, 71- Mil Serv: Entered as 2nd Lt, Army Spec Forces, 66, released as 1st Lt, 68, after serv in B-36 Spec Forces, SVietnam, 67-68. Mem: Okla Bar Asn; Am Trial Lawyers Asn. Relig: Roman Catholic. Legal Res: 3105 E 26th Pl Tulsa OK 74114 Mailing Add: 100 Center Plaza Tulsa OK 74119

BRUTON, GEORGE A (D)
NH State Rep
b Manchester, NH, Jan 25, 97; married; c three. Educ: Columbia Law Sch. Polit & Govt Pos: Contact rep, finance officer & loan guaranty officer, US Vet Admin, 38 years; NH State Rep, 61- Mil Serv: Vet, World War I. Mem: Am Legion; KofC. Relig: Catholic. Mailing Add: 632 Belmont St Manchester NH 03104

BRUTON, H DAVID (D)
b Candor, NC, Dec 31, 34; s Earl D Bruton & Evelyn Burt B; m 1957 to Frieda Bryant; c David, Evelyn & Ann. Educ: Univ NC, AB, 57; Univ NC Sch Med, MD, 61; Delta Psi. Polit & Govt Pos: Vchmn bd educ, Moore Co, NC, 68-74; deleg, Dem Nat Mid-Term Conf, 74. Bus & Prof Pos: Pvt practice pediatrics, Southern Pines, NC, 66-; chmn legislative comt, State Med Soc, 71- Mil Serv: Capt, Air Force, Med Corps, 64-66. Mem: Am Med Asn; Am Pediatric Soc; State Med & Pediatric Soc; Kiwanis. Honors & Awards: The Most Outstanding Intern Award, Univ NC Sch Med, 62; Outstanding Young Man of Year Award, Southern Pines Jaycees, 68. Relig: Methodist. Mailing Add: 520 Highland Rd Southern Pines NC 28387

BRYAN, ELTON EUGENE (D)
WVa State Deleg
b Philippi, WVa, Apr 3, 35; s Bedford H Bryan & Mae Cottrell B; m 1958 to Barbara Sue Cole; c Kimberly Sue & Timothy Eugene. Educ: Alderson Broaddus Col, 58; Marshall Univ & WVa Univ, exten courses. Polit & Govt Pos: Mem, exec comt, WVa State Dem Party, currently; WVa State Deleg, Dist 29, 74- Bus & Prof Pos: Vpres, Bruce Mining Corp; pres, BBC Enterprises & Bryan Bros Mem. Mil Serv: Entered as Pvt, Army, 54-57, after serv in 101st Airborne Armored Div, ETO. Mem: Philippi Area CofC; Saudemi; VFW; Lions Club; Barbour Co Park & Recreation Authority. Relig: Methodist. Mailing Add: 4 Hilltop St Philippi WV 26416

BRYAN, L L (DOC) (D)
Ark State Rep
Mailing Add: 305 South Van Couver Russellville AR 72801

BRYAN, MARVIN ALLEN (D)
b Wayland Springs, Tenn, Nov 1, 04; s Robert Lee Bryan & Lona Phillips B; m 1930 to Grace Morrow. Educ: St Joseph Sch, 21. Polit & Govt Pos: Tenn State Sen, 41-45; supvr, Tenn State Bd Elec, 48-52; supt banks, Tenn, 58-73; deleg, Dem Nat Mid Term Conf, 74- Mil Serv: A/S, Navy, 23-27; CSK, 43-46, serv in USS Walde, SPac Theatre. Mem: Shrine; VFW; Am Legion; Lions; Odd Fellows. Relig: Methodist. Mailing Add: PO Box 176 St Joseph TN 38481

BRYAN, RICHARD H (D)
Nev State Sen
b Washington, DC, July 16, 37. s Oscar W Bryan & Lillie Pleasants B; m 1962 to Bonnie Fairchild; c Richard H, Jr, Leslie L & Blair A. Educ: Univ Nev, AB, 59; Univ Calif, Hastings Col Law, LLB, 63; Phi Alpha Theta; Alpha Tau Omega. Polit & Govt Pos: Dep dist attorney, Clark Co, Nev, 64-66, pub defender, 66-68; counsel to juv court, 68-69; Nev State Assemblyman, Clark Co, 68-72; Nev State Sen, 72- Mil Serv: 2nd Lt, Army, 59-60; Capt, Army Res. Mem: Am Bar Asn; Am Trial Lawyers Asn; Am Judicature Soc; Elks; Mason. Honors & Awards: Distinguished Serv Award, Vegas Valley Jaycees; selected as One of Two Legislators to Attend Nat Legis Conf. Relig: Episcopal. Legal Res: 3680 Mountcrest Las Vegas NV 89109 Mailing Add: Bank of Nevada Suite 510 225 E Bridger Las Vegas NV 89101

BRYAN, STANLEY GATEWOOD (D)
Va State Deleg
b Norfolk, Va, Feb 15, 30; s Clarence Gatewood Bryan & Elnora Hadley B; m 1959 to Marvourneen Elizabeth Albertson; c Jo Ann & Stanley G, Jr. Educ: Col William & Mary, 47-53, BA & BCL; Sigma Nu. Polit & Govt Pos: Va State Deleg, 66- Bus & Prof Pos: Attorney-at-law, Law Firm of Bryan & Griffin. Mil Serv: Entered Army, 53, released as Pfc, 55, after serv in 716th MP Bn, Korean War; Good Conduct Medal. Mem: Am Bar Asn; Moose; Va Farm Bur. Relig: Methodist. Mailing Add: 801 George Washington Hwy S Chesapeake VA 23323

BRYAN, WALKER M (D)
NMex State Rep
b 1910. Educ: Tex A&M Univ. Polit & Govt Pos: City Water Comnr, Carlsbad, NMex; Mayor, Carlsbad; NMex State Rep, 59- Bus & Prof Pos: Motel operator. Mem: Lions; Mason (all bodies); CofC. Relig: Methodist. Mailing Add: Box 580 Carlsbad NM 88220

BRYANT, BRITAIN HAMILTON (D)
Sen, VI Legis
b Louisville, Ky, Mar 21, 40; s William H Bryant & Virginia Wells Throgmorton B; m 1965 to Peyton Gresham; c Anne (Nina) Hamilton & Stewart Wells. Educ: Univ Louisville, BSL, 62, Sch Law, LLB, 64; Beta Theta Phi; Phi Alpha Delta. Polit & Govt Pos: Sen, VI Tenth & Eleventh Legis Dist of St Croix, 72-; pres, Eleventh Legis, 75. Bus & Prof Pos: Attorney & partner, Bryant, Costello, Burke & Scott, Attorneys-at-law, Christiansted, St Croix, VI, 65- Mem: VI Bar Asn (bd gov, secy, 67-70, vpres, 72); World Peace Through Law Orgn; VI Judicial Counsel; Judicial Conf US Court Appeals for Third Circuit (permanent mem); Am Revolution Bicentennial Comn (mem bd dirs); VI Law Enforcement Admin Adv Comn (mem gov bd). Relig: Presbyterian. Legal Res: 3 Estate Bety's Jewel Christiansted St Croix VI 00820 Mailing Add: 7 King St Christiansted St Croix VI 00820

BRYANT, CARL P (D)
Chmn, Pleasants Co Dem Party, WVa
b Davis, WVa, June 30, 41; m 1963 to Jocele Lynch; c Kristin Jocele. Educ: WVa Univ, BS, 63, Law Sch, JD, 68; Theta Chi; Phi Alpha Delta; Scabbard & Blade. Polit & Govt Pos: Prosecuting attorney, Pleasants Co, 69-; city attorney, St Marys, 74-; chmn, Pleasants Co Dem Party, 72- Mil Serv: Entered as 2nd Lt, Army, 63, released as 1st Lt, 65, after serv in 11th Air Assault Div, Ft Benning, Ga; Army Commendation Medal. Mem: WVa State Bar (bd gov & mem exec comt); WVa Law Asn; Am Bar Asn; Prosecuting Attorney's Asn; Third Judicial Circuit Bar Asn. Relig: Roman Catholic. Mailing Add: Oakwood Terr St Marys WV 26170

BRYANT, CECIL FARRIS (D)
b Ocala, Fla, July 26, 14; s Charles Cecil Bryant & Lela Margaret Farris B; m 1940 to Julia Burnett; c Julie Lovett, Cecilia Ann & Allison Adair. Educ: Univ Fla, BS, 35; Harvard Law Sch, JD, 38; Phi Delta Phi; Alpha Kappa Psi; Kappa Delta Pi; Alpha Phi Omega; Blue Key; Gold Key; Alpha Tau Omega. Hon Degrees: Fla Southern Col, Rollins Col, Fla State Univ & Fla Atlantic Univ. Polit & Govt Pos: Fla State Rep, 42 & 46-55, Speaker, Fla House Rep, 53; chmn Fla deleg, Dem Nat Conv, 52 & 60, deleg, 64 & 68; Gov, Fla, 60-65; dir, Off of Emergency Planning, Exec Off of President, 66-67; mem, Nat Security Coun, 66-67; chmn, Adv Comn on Intergovt Rels, 66-69. Bus & Prof Pos: Partner, Bryant, Dickens, Rumph, Franson & Miller, Attorneys, chmn bd, Voyager Life Ins Co, 65-; pres, Nat Life of Fla Corp, 68-; Channel 12 TV, Jacksonville, 72- Mil Serv: Entered as Ens, Navy, 42, released as Lt, 46, after serv in Anti-Submarine Warfare, Atlantic, Pacific, Mediter & Caribbean; Lt, Naval Res. Publ: Co-auth, Government and Politics in Florida. Mem: Am & Fla Bar Asns; VFW; Rotary; Elks. Honors & Awards: Gold Key Distinguished Serv Award, Fla Jr CofC, 48 & 50. Relig: Methodist. Legal Res: 1870 Challen Ave Jacksonville FL 32205 Mailing Add: Box 2918 Jacksonville FL 32203

BRYANT, CLOVIS (D)
Ark State Sen
Mailing Add: 615 North 12th St Van Buren AR 72956

BRYANT, CURTIS CONWAY (D)
Co-Chmn, Pike Co Dem Party, Miss
b Tylertown, Miss, Jan 15, 17; s Monroe Bryant & Anna Luter B; m 1941 to Emogene Gooden; c Gladys Jean (Mrs Billye Jackson) & Curtis Conway, Jr. Educ: South McComb High Sch, 40-41. Polit & Govt Pos: Chmn, Miss Dem Party, 68-70; mem bd, South West Inc SMO Bd, 68-70; deleg, Dem Nat Conv, 68, alt deleg, 72; deleg, Miss Dem State Conv, 68 & 70; chmn, Miss Dem Party Employ Comt, 68-70; co-chmn, Pike Co Dem Party, 68- Mem: Mason (Master); Celaks (chmn, Legis Comt); NAACP. Relig: Baptist. Mailing Add: Box 333 B McComb MS 39648

BRYANT, JOHN WILEY (D)
Tex State Rep
b Lake Jackson, Tex, Feb 22, 47; s Robert L Bryant; m to Janet Watts; c Amy Louise. Educ: Southern Methodist Univ, BA, 69, Law Sch, LLB. Polit & Govt Pos: Tex State Rep, 74- Bus & Prof Pos: Attorney, Dallas, Tex, currently. Mem: Pleasant Grove CofC; Southeast Dallas Kiwanis. Relig: Methodist. Legal Res: 6506 Wofford Dallas TX 75227 Mailing Add: 8225 Bruton Rd Dallas TX 75217

BRYANT, KELLY (D)
Secy of State, Ark
b Hope, Ark, Aug 28, 08; s C C Bryant (deceased) & Annie Nelson B; m to Elizabeth Sutton; c Elizabeth Ann. Educ: Univ Ark, 30, BS, 34; Lambda Chi Alpha. Polit & Govt Pos: State printing clerk, State of Ark, until 63, Secy of State, 63- Bus & Prof Pos: Ed & publ, The Hope J. Mem: Ark Sheriff's Asn (exec secy); Nat Asn Secretaries State; Rotary Club; Little Rock Club. Relig: Methodist; Bd of Stewards 25 years. Legal Res: 1405 S Main St Hope AR 71801 Mailing Add: 210 Summit House Apts 400 N University St Little Rock AR 72205

BRYANT, WILLIAM R, JR (R)
Mich State Rep
Mailing Add: 331 Mt Vernon Grosse Pointe Farms MI 48236

BRYANT, WINSTON (D)
Ark State Rep
Mailing Add: 726 E Page St Malvern AR 72104

BUBNA, MARY ANN R (R)
Committeewoman, Rep State Cent & Exec Comt, Ohio
b Laganadi, Italy, Jan 9, 09; d Frank Nunnari & Domenica Versace N; wid; c Joseph A & Frank A Romeo & Catherine D (Mrs Yadlovsky). Educ: Spencerian Bus Col, 2 years. Polit & Govt Pos: Precinct committeeman, Cuyahoga Co Rep Cent & Exec Comts, 44-, mem, 44-, secy, 58-60, wardleader, 58-, asst vchmn exec comt, 74-; mem, Cuyahoga Co Notary Pub Comn, 51-; app, City Civic Comt, until 67; committeewoman, State Rep Cent & Exec Comts, Ohio, 68-, secy prog & lit comt, 69-; deleg, State Rep Conv, 70, mem conv comt, 72; deleg-at-lg, Ohio Fedn Rep Women Nat Conv, 71; alt deleg, Rep Nat Conv, 72. Bus & Prof Pos: Self employed tax acct & pub acct, 40-; notary pub, 50- Mem: Acct Bd, Ohio; Ins Bd Ohio; Cleveland Ins Bd Ohio; Cleveland Basebelles; Ohio Fedn Rep Women. Honors & Awards: Scroll & Hon award, Lt Gov Brown; Hon Lt Gov Ohio; Vol Award, Cath Nat Vet Group; Scroll & Cert, Ripon Club; Cert of Appreciation-Recognition, Boy Scouts. Relig: Catholic. Legal Res: 3512 Carlyle Ave Cleveland OH 44109 Mailing Add: 3190 Fulton Rd Cleveland OH 44109

BUCHANAN, JOHN C (D)
Va State Sen
Mailing Add: PO Box 1006 Wise VA 24230

BUCHANAN, JOHN HALL, JR (R)
US Rep, Ala
b Paris, Tenn, Mar 19, 28; s John Hall Buchanan & Ruby Lowrey B; m to Elizabeth Moore; c Elizabeth & Lynn. Educ: Samford Univ, 49; Univ Va; Southern Theol Sem, Louisville; Pi Kappa Alpha; Student Senate. Hon Degrees: LLD, Samford Univ. Polit & Govt Pos: US Rep, Sixth Dist, Ala, 64-, mem int rels comt, educ & labor comts, US House Rep, mem US deleg to UN, 28th Gen Assembly, 73 & Sixth Spec Session, 74, secy, Nat Rep Cong Comt, currently; dir finance, Ala Rep Party; chmn, Jefferson Co Rep Party. Bus & Prof Pos: Minister, Baptist Church, Ala, Tenn & Va until 62; supply pastor, Baptist Church, Birmingham area, Ala, 62-64. Mil Serv: Navy. Mem: Mason (Master); Am Legion; Five Points YMCA; Shrine; Scottish Rite. Honors & Awards: Congressman of the Year, Am United for Separation of Church and State, 65; Univ Va Sesquicentennial Award for Pub Serv, 69; Cited by Nat Alliance of Postal & Fed Employees. Relig: Baptist. Legal Res: 2909 Highland Ave Birmingham AL 35205 Mailing Add: 2159 Rayburn House Off Bldg Washington DC 20515

BUCHANAN, MARY ESTILL (R)
Secy of State, Colo
b San Francisco, Calif, Nov 15, 34; d Carl A Henlein & Elizabeth Yager H; m to Dodds I Buchanan; c David, Stephen, Helen, Eugene, Catharine & Bruce. Educ: Wellesley Col, BA, 56; Harvard Univ; MA in Bus Admin, 62. Polit & Govt Pos: Secy of State, Colo, 74- Publ: Women in Management, Personnel Admin, 68. Mailing Add: State Capitol Denver CO 80203

BUCHANAN, PATRICK JOSEPH (R)
b Washington, DC, Nov 2, 38; s William Baldwin Buchanan & Catherine Crum B; m 1971 to Shelley Ann Scarney. Educ: Georgetown Univ, AB cum laude, 61; Columbia Univ Grad Sch Jour, MS, 62. Polit & Govt Pos: Spec asst to the President, 69-73, spec consult, 73-74. Bus & Prof Pos: Ed writer, St Louis Globe-Dem, Mo, 62-64, asst editorial ed, 64-66; exec asst to Richard M Nixon, New York, 66-69; syndicated columnist, St Louis Globe-Dem & NY Times Spec Features, 75- Publ: The New Majority, Girard Bank, 3/73. Relig: Catholic. Mailing Add: 5052 Loughboro Rd NW Washington DC 20016

BUCHEN, PHILIP WILLIAM (R)
Counsel to the President
b Sheboygan, Wis; s Gustav W Buchen & Eleanor Jung B; m 1947 to Beatrice Loomis Gold; c Victoria (Mrs J C B Aler) & Roderick L. Educ: Univ Mich, AB, JD. Hon Degrees: LLD, Grand Valley State Col, 74. Polit & Govt Pos: Exec dir, Domestic Coun Comt on Right of Privacy, 74-75; Counsel to the President, Washington, DC, 74- Bus & Prof Pos: Partner, Ford & Buchen, 41-42, Butterfield, Keeney & Amberg, 43-47 & Amberg, Law & Buchen, 48-55; vpres bus affairs, Grand Valley State Col, 61-67; partner, Law, Buchen, Weathers, Richardson & Dutcher, 67-74. Mem: Kent Country Club; University Club Grand Rapids; University Club Washington; Mich Bar Asn. Legal Res: 703 Cambridge Blvd SE Grand Rapids MI 49506 Mailing Add: White House Off 1600 Pennsylvania Ave Washington DC 20500

BUCHENHOLZ, JANE JACOBS (D)
b New York, NY, Oct 28, 18; d Joseph Jacobs & Sofia Frucht J; div; c Nancy & Susan. Educ: Hunter Col, AB, 42; New Sch Social Research, 47-49; Phi Beta Kappa; Phi Sigma. Polit & Govt Pos: Dir Nat Roosevelt Day Dinner, Am for Dem Action, 61-66, nat secy, 65-67, mem nat bd, 63-; research consult for voter regis, Nat Coun Negro Women, 64; secy-treas, foreign policy coun, NY Dem Party, 66-; nat adv coun, Nat Conf for New Politics, 66-67; nat bd, Comt for Sane Nuclear Policy, 66-68; exec dir, Broadway for Peace, 68; campaign mgr, Mel Dubin for Cong, Brooklyn, 68; alt deleg, Dem Nat Conv, 68; deleg, New Dem Coalition NY, currently; mem nat coun, Nat Emergency Civil Liberties Comt, currently; mem exec comt, Ansonia Independent Dem, 68; Dem dist leader, 67th Assembly Dist, Part C, NY, 71- Bus & Prof Pos: Math teacher, control chemist & plant pathologist, 42-46; remedial reading teacher, Reading Clin, NY Univ, 46-49; spec teacher emotionally disturbed children, 48-49; pianist & accompanist for mod dance classes, 55-61; exec dir, Call for Action, Radio Sta WMCA, 62-64; spec consult for syst & inventory control, Crown Fabrics Div, Bangor Punta Indust, 66-68; dir develop, New Sch Social Research, 68-72 & New Lincoln Sch, 71-72; gen distributor, Golden Prod, 72- Honors & Awards: Chap Chmn Award, Am for Dem Action, 63. Relig: Jewish. Mailing Add: 205 West End Ave New York NY 10023

BUCHMANN, ALAN PAUL (R)
Nat Committeeman, Ohio League Young Rep Clubs
b Yonkers, NY, Sept 5, 34; s Paul John Buchmann & Jessie Perkins B; m 1959 to Lizabeth Ann Moody. Educ: Yale Univ, BA, 56; Univ Munich, 56-57; Yale Law Sch, LLB, 60; Phi Beta Kappa. Polit & Govt Pos: Dir campaign div, Ohio League Young Rep Clubs, 66-67, vchmn, 67-68, conv chmn, 68, gen counsel, 68-69, chmn credential comt, conv, 69, exec secy, 70-71, chmn, 71-72, nat committeeman, 72-; pres, Rep Club, 66-67; first vpres, Gtr Cleveland Young Rep Club, 66-67, pres, 68, exec comt, 66-69; secy, Ripon Club Cleveland, 68-69, vpres, 70-72; deleg, White House Conf on Children, 70; mem, Selective Serv Syst Bd 22, 71; mem exec comt, Shaker Heights Rep Club, 71-; mem, Cuyahoga Co Rep Exec Comt, currently. Bus & Prof Pos: Attorney, Squire, Sanders & Dempsey, 60- Publ: Auth, Electric transmission lines and the environment, Cleveland State Law Rev, 5/72. Mem: Cleveland, Cuyahoga, Ohio State & Am Bar Asns; Nat Soc RR Trial Counsel. Honors & Awards: Robert A Taft Distinguished Serv Award as Ohio's Outstanding Young Rep, 69; Outstanding Young Rep State Chmn, 71. Relig: Episcopal. Legal Res: 17210 Parkland Shaker Heights OH 44122 Mailing Add: 1800 Union Com Bldg Cleveland OH 44115

BUCK, ARTHUR L (D)
Wyo State Rep
b Wichita, Kans, 1906; m to Irene Sue. Educ: Carleton Col, BA; Colo State Col, MA; Univ Wyo; Northwestern Univ. Polit & Govt Pos: Wyo State Rep & Minority Whip, Wyo House Rep, formerly; Wyo State Rep, 75- Bus & Prof Pos: Teacher. Mil Serv: Army, World War II; Army Commendation Ribbon. Mem: Elks; Odd Fellows; Pi Delta Epsilon; Phi Delta Kappa; Am Vets Comt. Relig: Congregational. Mailing Add: 3018 Thomes Cheyenne WY 82001

BUCK, FRANK F (D)
Tenn State Rep
b Trousdale Co, Tenn, Sept 26, 43; s John Oliver Buck & Georgia Baird B; m 1962 to Lena Ann Graves; c Kathy Ann & Melinda. Educ: Tenn Technol Univ, BS; Univ Tenn, JD; Phi Alpha Delta; Phi Kappa Delta. Polit & Govt Pos: Tenn State Rep, 72- Bus & Prof Pos: Attorney, Foutch & Buck, 68- Mem: Tenn Bar Asn; Smithville Jaycees; Tenn Farm Bur. Relig: Protestant. Mailing Add: Rte 1 Dowelltown TN 37059

BUCK, THOMAS BRYANT, III (D)
Ga State Rep
b Columbus, Ga, Mar 2, 38; s Thomas Bryant Buck, Jr & Violet Burrus Litchfield B; single. Educ: Emory Univ, BA, 59, LLB, 62; Alpha Phi Omega; Kappa Alpha Order. Polit & Govt Pos: Ga State Rep, 67- Mil Serv: Army Res, 63-69, Pfc; Outstanding Basic Trainee. Mem: Am Bar Asn; State Bar of Ga; Phi Delta Phi; Kiwanis; Green Island Country Club. Relig: Baptist. Legal Res: 2033 Wynnton Rd Columbus GA 31906 Mailing Add: PO Box 196 Columbus GA 31902

BUCKALOO, ROBBIE BROADWAY (R)
Chmn, Karnes Co Rep Party, Tex
b North Zulch, Tex, Oct 3, 12; d Charles Lee Broadway & Minerva Harris B; m 1933 to Mack Thurston Buckaloo, Jr; c Jan. Educ: Mary Harden-Baylor Col, BA, 31; Royal Academia. Polit & Govt Pos: Chmn, Karnes Co Rep Party, Tex, 70- Bus & Prof Pos: High sch Eng teacher, Three Rivers High Sch, Three Rivers, Tex, 32-34; bank dir, First State Bank, Three Rivers, 50-60; vpres, Buckaloo, Inc, Kenedy, 50- Relig: United Methodist. Legal Res: 802 Seventh St Kenedy TX 78119 Mailing Add: Box 570 Kenedy TX 78119

BUCKLEY, ANNA PATRICIA (D)
Mass State Sen
b Brockton, Mass, Mar 21, 24; d Michael Hernan & Ann Fitzmaurice H; m 1946 to Daniel J Buckley; c Kevin Michael, Daniel J, Jr, Paul, Patrice & Nancy J (Mrs Gregory F Buckley). Educ: Williams Sch Bus, grad 43; Stonehill Col (Mass), spec courses; Bridgewater State Col, spec courses. Polit & Govt Pos: Admin asst to Lt Gov Francis X Bellotti, Mass, 62-64; admin asst to Auditor Thaddeus Buczko, Mass, 65-72, secy, Mass State Dem Comt, 68-; coun-at-lg, Brockton City Coun, 72-73; Mass State Sen, 73-, chmn comt election laws & legis res coun, Mass State Senate, 73, mem comt counties & comt post audit & oversight, 73- Mil Serv: Entered Army, 43, released, 45, after serv in Women's Air Corps. Mem: Plymouth Co Dem League; Am Legion; AFL-CIO; Mass Electoral Col. Relig: Catholic. Legal Res: 16 Rutland Sq Brockton MA 02401 Mailing Add: Rm 219 State House Boston MA 02233

BUCKLEY, CECELIA ANNE (D)
Second VPres, Mont State Dem Womens Club
b Great Falls, Mont, Aug 11, 40; d Lawrence William Fasbender & Peggy Blossom F; m 1964 to Thomas E Buckley; c Brian Thomas & Diane Renee. Educ: Col Great Falls, 60; Gamma Sigma Sigma. Polit & Govt Pos: Pres, Wheatland Co Dem Women, 66-68; regional dir, Mont State Dem Womens Club, 70-72, second vpres, 72-; alt committeewoman, Wheatland Co Dem Cent Comt, 70- Bus & Prof Pos: Third grade teacher, Harlowton, Mont, 60-62 & Big Timber, 62-64; bookkeeper & tax consult, Harlowton, 70-75. Mem: Bus & Prof Womens Club (pres); Comprehensive Health Planning Bd (secy). Honors & Awards: Outstanding Leader in Volunteer Effort on Behalf of Sr Citizens, Gov Thomas L Judge, 74. Relig: Catholic. Legal Res: 114 C Ave SE Harlowton MT 59036 Mailing Add: Box 192 Harlowton MT 59036

BUCKLEY, JAMES L (CONSERVATIVE-R)
US Sen, NY
b New York, NY, Mar 9, 23; s William Frank Buckley & Aloise Steiner B; m 1953 to Ann Frances Cooley; c Peter Pierce, James Wiggins, Priscilla Langford, William Frank, David Lane & Andrew Thurston. Educ: Yale Univ, BA, 43, LLB, 49. Polit & Govt Pos: Campaign mgr, William F Buckley for Mayor, New York, 65; cand for US Sen, NY, 68; US Sen, NY, 71-, mem budget & com comts, US Senate, 75- Bus & Prof Pos: Assoc, Wiggin & Dana; vpres & dir, Catawba Corp, 53-70. Mil Serv: Entered as A/S, Naval Res, 43, released as Lt(jg), 46, after serv in WPac. Legal Res: NY Mailing Add: Old Senate Off Bldg Washington DC 20510

BUCKLEY, JAMES TIMOTHY (D)
b Sedalia, Mo, Jan 16, 39; s John Thomas Buckley & Thelma Stevens B; m 1965 to Mary Jo Jackson; c James Patrick, John Robert, Robert Jackson & Brendan Connor. Educ: St Benedict's Col, AB, 60; Univ Mo, LLB, 63; Phi Delta Phi. Polit & Govt Pos: Treas, Collegiate Young Dem of Kans, 58; pres, St Benedict's Col Young Dem, 60; chmn, Pettis Co Dem Comt, Mo, formerly; deleg, Dem Nat Conv, 72. Bus & Prof Pos: Asst prosecuting attorney, Pettis Co, Mo, 63-65; spec asst to attorney gen, Mo, 66. Mil Serv: Mo Div, Nat Guard, 63-69. Mem: Mo, Am & Pettis Co Bar Asns; Mo Asn Trial Attorneys (mem bd dirs, 66-); Am Trial Lawyers Asn. Relig: Catholic. Mailing Add: 1002 Sylvio Dr Sedalia MO 65301

BUCKLEY, JOHN JOSEPH (R)
Mayor, Lawrence, Mass
b Boston, Mass, Aug 12, 29; s John Joseph Buckley & Sara Conway B; m 1960 to Marie T Costello; c John & Paul. Educ: Boston Col, BS & BA, 52; St John's Sem, 57-59; pres, Sr Class; pres, Debating Soc. Polit & Govt Pos: Chief aide, Elliot L Richardson, 64; spec asst to US Sen Leverett Saltonstall, 65; sheriff, Middlesex Co, Mass, 70-; deleg, Dem Nat Mid-Term Conf, 74; mayor, Lawrence, Mass, 74- Bus & Prof Pos: Pres, John J Buckley Furniture Co, Falmouth, Mass; New Eng area salesman, Doubleday & Co, New York; state dir, Mass Coun Crime & Correction, 2 years; exec dir, New England Citizen Crime Comn, 68. Publ: How to start a youth resource council, Mass Coun Crime & Correction, 69; On the criminal justice system, 9/71 & Hand gun control, 4/72, Boston Globe. Mem: Criminal Law Revision Comt (treas); Mass Police Chiefs Asn; Mass Bar Asn (subcomt prison reform); World Affairs Coun (bd mem); Gtr Lowell Coun, Mass (bd dirs). Relig: Roman Catholic. Mailing Add: 10 Mt Vernon St Lawrence MA 01843

BUCKLEY, JOHN REED (D)
b Kansas City, Mo, Sept 9, 21; s Albert Patrick Buckley & Rebecca Grace Skinner B; m 1940 to Meriam Ruth Mollins; c John Reed Jr, Stephen M & Wayne P. Polit & Govt Pos: Mem staff of US Rep Fascell, Fla, 55-, admin asst, currently. Mem: Miami Springs Jaycees; Fla State Soc; Burro Club; Capitol Hill First Friday Club; Fla Admin Assts. Honors & Awards: Bill Rolleston Award for Outstanding State VPres, Fla Jaycees; Roy Haines Award for Outstanding State Soc Pres. Relig: Catholic. Legal Res: 557 De Soto Dr Miami Springs FL Mailing Add: 2160 Rayburn Bldg Washington DC 20515

BUCKLEY, SHARON ALBERT (D)
b Plainfield, NJ, Jan 21, 45; d Charles Gerald Albert & Estelle Gibbs A; m 1967 to Raymond Forder Buckley, Jr; c Kenneth Slane. Educ: Kalamazoo Col, 63-66; Wash Univ, AB, 67; Alpha Sigma Delta. Polit & Govt Pos: Co-capt, McGovern Bonhomme Orgn, Mo, 72; campaign mgr, Buckley for Mo State Rep, 93rd Dist, 72; alt deleg, Dem Nat Conv, 72; corresponding secy, Bonhomme Twp Dem Club, Mo, formerly, mem exec bd & chmn polit action comt, 73-; mem, Madison Co Dem Club & Edwardsville Ad Hoc Comt. Bus & Prof Pos: Caseworker child welfare, Mo Div Welfare, 68-70. Mem: New Dem Coalition Metrop St Louis. Relig: Presbyterian. Mailing Add: 810 North St Mt Vernon IL 62864

BUCKLEY, WILLIAM FRANK, JR (R)
b New York, NY, Nov 24, 25; s William Frank Buckley & Aloise Steiner B; m 1950 to Patricia Taylor; c Christopher T. Educ: Univ Mex, 43; Yale Univ, BA with honors, 50; Torch Honor Soc; Elizabethan Club; Fence Club; Skull & Bones; Class Day Orator; chmn, Yale Daily News. Hon Degrees: LHD, Seton Hall Univ, 66, Niagara Univ, 67 & Mt St Mary's Col, 69; LLD, St Peter's Col, Syracuse Univ & Ursinus Col, 69, Lehigh Univ, 70 & Lafayette Col, 72; DScO, Curry Col, 70; LittD, St Vincent Col, 71, Fairleigh Dickinson Univ, 73 & Alfred Univ, 74. Polit & Govt Pos: Cand for Mayor of New York, 65; app by the President to the US Info Agency Adv Comn, 69-72. Bus & Prof Pos: Asst instr Spanish, Yale Univ, 47-51; assoc ed, Am Mercury, 52; founder & ed-in-chief, Nat Rev, 55-; syndicated columnist, On the Right, 62-; host weekly TV Show, Firing Line, 66-; chmn of the bd, Starr Broadcasting Group, Inc, 66-; lectr munic govt, New Sch Social Research, 67-68; covered nat polit conv, Am Broadcasting Co TV Network, 68. Mil Serv: Entered as Pvt, Army, 44, released as 2nd Lt, 46, after serv in Inf. Publ: Auth, The Governor Listeth, 70 & Inveighing We Will Go, 72, Putnam; ed, American Conservative Thought in the 20th Century, Bobbs-Merrill, 70; plus others. Mem: NY Yacht Club; Nat Press Club; Mont Pelerin Soc; Coun on Foreign Rels; Century Club. Honors & Awards: George Sokolsky Award, Am Jewish League Against Communism, 66; Distinguished Jour Achievement Award, Univ Southern Calif, 68; Emmy Award for Outstanding TV Prog Achievement, 69; Liberty Bell Award, New Haven Co Bar Asn, 69; Man of Year Award, Young Americans for Freedom, 70. Relig: Catholic. Legal Res: CT Mailing Add: Nat Rev 150 E 35th St New York NY 10016

BUCKMAN, HAROLD V (R)
NH State Rep
Mailing Add: Box 143 Ashland NH 03217

BUCKNER, DEL L (D)
Utah State Rep
Mailing Add: 3869 S 4000 W Granger UT 84120

BUCKOWITZ, GEORGIA MARIE (D)
b St Louis, Mo, Sept 11, 18; d George Alfonse Lappin & Margaret Irene O'Malley; m 1938 to Louis William Buckowitz; c Georgia Patricia (Mrs Rankin). Educ: Mo Bus Col; St Mary's Col, 32-36. Polit & Govt Pos: Secy, Tenth Ward Dem Club, St Louis, Mo, 38-60; dep collector revenue, St Louis, 65-73, dir parks, recreation & forestry, 73-; deleg, Dem Nat Conv, 72. Bus & Prof Pos: Secy & technician, O Sherman Jones, MD, 36-39; owner, Georgia's Gift & Card Shop, St Louis, Mo, 50-61, chmn, 60-66, pres, 66-73. Mem: Alexian Bros Hosp Auxiliary; McDonnell Planetarium (chmn); Forest Park Assocs (pres); St Louis Women's CofC; DeMenil Found (bd mem). Honors & Awards: Award of Appreciation, Gov Warren E Hearnes, Mo, 69; Americanism Award, Am Legion, 73; St Louis Beautification Comn Award, 74; Woman of Year Award, Midwest Temple Daughters Elks; Community Serv Award, Women's CofC, 74. Legal Res: 3515 Oregon Ave St Louis MO 63118 Mailing Add: 5600 Clayton Rd St Louis MO 63110

BUCKRIDGE, MARILYN L (D)
VPres, Wash Fedn Dem Women
b Colorado Springs, Colo, Sept 5, 32; d Robert E Lewis & Virginia Manning L; c Lisa, Eric, Sara, Kurt & Amy. Educ: Col of Idaho. Polit & Govt Pos: Mem, Wash Dem State Exec Comt, 62-64; deleg, Dem Nat Conv, 64; mem, Wash Dem State Rules Comt, 64; chmn, Snohomish Co Pub Asst Adv Bd, 64-66; mem exec comt, Referendum 15, 66; exec secy, Wash State Humphrey Campaign, 68; vpres, Wash Fedn Dem Women, 68-, chmn platform comt, 70; chmn, 38th Legis Dist Dem Party, 68-; mem, Wash State Dem Credentials Comt, 70. Mem: Everett League of Women Voters. Relig: Episcopal. Mailing Add: Box 174-C Rte 1 Vaughn WA 98394

BUCKSON, DAVID PENROSE (R)
b Townsend, Del, July 25, 20; s Leon J Buckson & Margaret Hutchison B; m 1963 to Patricia Maloney; c Brian, David H, Eric, Kent & Marlee. Educ: Univ Del, BA, 41; Dickinson Sch Law, LLB, 48; Sigma Nu. Polit & Govt Pos: Chmn, Kent Co Rep Exec Comt, Del, 56; judge, Court of Common Pleas, Dover, 56-57; Lt Gov, Del, 57-60, Gov, 60-61, Attorney Gen, 63-71; alt deleg, Rep Nat Conv, 68. Mil Serv: Entered as 2nd Lt, Army, 41, released as Maj, 46, after serv in 198th Coast Artil Regt, Southwest Pac, 42-45. Mem: Del & Am Bar Asns; Am Judicature Soc; Rotary; Del Vets. Relig: Methodist. Mailing Add: 55 W Main St Middleton DE 19709

BUCKWAY, DALLAS HENRY (D)
Utah State Rep
b Ogden, Utah, Nov 2, 37; s Henry Buckway & Verba Sessions B; m 1961 to Carol A Thompson; c Dallas, Jr, Cory & Michael. Educ: Weber State Col; Int Rels Club. Polit & Govt Pos: Secy, Utah Young Dem, Utah, 62-63; mem, Weber Co Tax Study Comt, 66; Utah State Rep, currently; chmn, Weber Co Dem Comt, currently. Bus & Prof Pos: Owner, U & I Carpet Ctr, 64- Relig: Latter-day Saint. Mailing Add: 5470 S 800 E Ogden UT 84403

BUCZKO, THADDEUS (D)
Auditor, Commonwealth of Mass
b Salem, Mass, Feb 23, 26; s Ignacy Buczko & Veronica Brzozowska B; single. Educ: Norwich Univ, BA with honors, 49; Boston Univ Sch of Law, LLB, 51; US Army Command & Gen Staff Col, grad, 72. Polit & Govt Pos: Former postmaster, Salem, Mass; mem, Salem City Coun, 56-59; second Essex sen dist campaign coordr, Edward M Kennedy for US Sen; Mass State Rep, 59-64; chmn comt on rules, Dem State Conv, Springfield, 63; auditor, Mass, 64-; deleg, Dem Nat Conv, 68. Bus & Prof Pos: Attorney-at-law, 51- Mil Serv: Entered as A/S, Navy, 44, released as Fireman 1/C, 46, after serv in Asiatic-Pac Theater; re-entered as 2nd Lt, Army, 52, serv as Unit Tank Comdr & asst staff Judge Adv, Third Armored Div, Korean War; at present, Col, Army Res, 357th CA Area Hq B, Boston Army Base, Mass; Asiatic-Pac Theater Campaign Star. Mem: Nat Asn of State Auditors, Comptrollers & Treasurers; Am Acct Asn; Am, Boston & Fed Bar Asns. Relig: Roman Catholic. Legal Res: 47 Butler St Salem MA 01970 Mailing Add: 276 Essex St Salem MA 01970

BUDAGHER, LINDA R (R)
Young Rep Nat Committeewoman, NMex
b Albuquerque, NMex, June 28, 48; d John Budagher & Frances Ramirez-Rodriguez B; single. Educ: NMex Highlands Univ, BA; Newman Club; Col Young Rep. Polit & Govt Pos: Voter registr, Albuquerque, NMex, 71-; Young Rep Nat Committeewoman, NMex, 71-, mem, US Youth Coun, 72-; mem, Bernalillo Co Rep Cent Comt, 71- & Exec Comt, 72-; mem, NMex Rep State Cent Comt, 71- & Exec Comt, 73-; Rep ward chmn, Bernalillo Co, 71-; mem, Adv Comt for Reelec of the President, 72; deleg, Rep Nat Conv, 72; North Valley-Bernalillo Co coordr for Reelec of the President, 72. Bus & Prof Pos: Personnel mgr, Budagher Construction, Albuquerque, 70- Mem: Am Asn Univ Women; St Joseph's Hosp Auxiliary; Albuquerque Tutorial Serv. Relig: Catholic. Mailing Add: 5804 Pauline Rd NW Albuquerque NM 87107

BUDD, JOSEPH LINCOLN (R)
b Salt Lake City, Utah, May 31, 11; s John C Budd & Lucille McGinnis B; m 1936 to Ruth Francis Peterson; c Betty Louis (Mrs Frank C Fear), Mary Kaye (Mrs Stanley Flitner) & Nancy Ruth. Educ: Univ Wyo, 29-30; Utah State Univ, 32-34. Polit & Govt Pos: Pres, Wyo Reclamation Asn, 43-45; mem, Interstate Streams Comn, 50-; Wyo State Rep, 51-63, minority floor leader, Wyo House Rep, 59, speaker, 61; chmn, Big Piney Sch Trustees, 60-64; Rep Nat Committeeman, Wyo, 64-68; comnr, Wyo Game & Fish Comn, 67-70. Bus & Prof Pos: Mgr & partner, Budd Hereford Ranch, Big Piney, Wyo, 34-; pres, Budd Ranches Inc, 67-; dir, Pac West Ins Co, 68-, Pac-Atlantic Life Ins Co & Wyo Safety Found. Mem: Wyo Stock Growers Asn (second vpres, 69-); Am Cattlemen's Asn; Am Hereford Asn (first vpres, 70, pres, 71-72); Shrine; Elks. Relig: Presbyterian. Mailing Add: PO Box 340 Big Piney WY 83113

BUDDY, GEORGE JOSEPH (D)
b Philadelphia, Pa, Mar 21, 47; s George Joseph Buddy (deceased) & Beatrice Chase B; single. Educ: Sophia Univ, 66-67; Delaware Co Community Col, AA, 72; Univ Ore, Sigma Delta Chi scholar, 72 & 73, BS, 74. Polit & Govt Pos: Vchmn, McGovern for President Comt, Pa, 72; deleg, Dem Nat Conv, 72; info writer, Pa House Rep, 74- Mil Serv: Entered as E-1, Army, 66, released as E-4, 69, after serv in Army Security Agency, Japan, 66-68. Legal Res: 3 Crum Creek Rd Castle Rock Newtown Square PA 19073 Mailing Add: 265 Cumberland St Harrisburg PA 17102

BUDGE, HAMER HAROLD (R)
b Pocatello, Idaho, Nov 21, 10; s Alfred Budge & Ella Hoge B; m 1941 to Jeanne Keithly; c Kathleen. Educ: Col Idaho, 28-30; Stanford Univ, BA, 33; Univ Idaho, LLB, 36; Sigma Alpha Epsilon. Polit & Govt Pos: Idaho State Rep, 39, 41 & 49, Majority Floor Leader, Idaho House of Rep; US Rep, Idaho, formerly; mem, Securities & Exchange Comn, 64-69, chmn, 69-71. Bus & Prof Pos: Attorney-at-law, Boise, Idaho, 26-42 & 46-51. Mil Serv: Lt Comdr, Naval Res, 42-45. Mem: Am & Idaho Bar Asns; Elks; Idaho CofC; Salvation Army. Relig: Latter-day Saint. Mailing Add: 1000 Roanoke Bldg Minneapolis MN 55402

BUDGE, REED WILLIAM (R)
Idaho State Sen
b Logan, Utah, Jan 7, 21; s Thomas B Budge & Duella Alvord B; m 1943 to Gweneth Steffensen; c twins, Reed Douglas & Linda Duella (Mrs Crozier), Randall Christian, Brian William & Suzanne. Educ: Utah State Univ, BS, 46; Sigma Nu; Intercollegiate Knights; Alpha Epsilon Delta. Polit & Govt Pos: Co comnr, Caribou Co, Idaho, 63-67; Idaho State Sen, Dist 32, 67- Bus & Prof Pos: Co-mgr, Fish Haven Resort, Bear Lake Co, Idaho, 46-51; pres & mgr, Budge Land & Livestock Co, 50-61; rancher, Soda Springs, Idaho, 61. Mil Serv: Entered as Pvt, Army, 43, released as T/Sgt, 45, after serv in 2nd Armored Div, 66th Regt, European & Mid Eastern Theatres, 44-45; ATO Serv Ribbon; European-Africa-Mid Eastern Serv Ribbon; Good Conduct Medal; Purple Heart Medal; Silver Star Medal; Belgian Fourragere. Mem: Bear River Compact Comn; Pac Northwest Basin Comn; Kiwanis; Idaho Cattlemans Asn. Relig: Latter-day Saint. Mailing Add: 231 S First East Soda Springs ID 83276

BUECHNER, JOHN WILLIAM (JACK) (R)
Mo State Rep
b St Louis, Mo, June 4, 40; s John Edward Buechner & Gertrude Emily Richardson B; m 1965 to Marietta Rose Coon; c Patrick John & Terence Jerome. Educ: St Benedict's Col (Kans), AB, 62; St Louis Univ, JD, 65. Polit & Govt Pos: Pres, St Benedict's Young Rep, Mo, 60-62; asst co counr, St Louis Co Div Law, 66-68; mem, Gravois Twp Rep Club, 68-70 & 71-73; mem, BonHomme Twp Rep Club, 70-73; area coordr, Danforth for Attorney Gen, 71-72; vchmn, Mo State Legis Campaign, 72-; Mo State Rep, 94th Dist, 73- Bus & Prof Pos: Partner, Miller & Buechner, Attorneys, St Louis, 68-73. Mem: Phi Delta Phi; Am Bar Asn; Lawyers Asn; Kirkwood Jaycees; Sierra Club. Honors & Awards: Potts Mem Award, Kirkwood Jr Football League, 69; Civic Recognition, Clayton Optimists, 69. Relig: Roman Catholic. Mailing Add: 14 Ponca Trail Kirkwood MO 63122

BUEHL, WILLIAM ANTHONY (TONY) (R)
Ariz State Rep
b Brooklyn, NY, Dec 20, 34; s William Adolph Buehl & Doris Johnson B; m 1957 to Bobby June Mangels; c William Sanford. Educ: Univ Ariz, 56-60; Civitan. Polit & Govt Pos: Ariz State Rep, 65-, chmn ways & means comt, Ariz House Rep, 69-70, chmn designate, ways & means comt, 71-72. Bus & Prof Pos: Salesman, Mangels Realty, Tucson, Ariz, 57-66; owner, Tony Buehl Agency, Ins, 63-69; pres, Henderson Realty, 66-69. Mil Serv: Entered as Pvt, Marine Corps, 53, released as Cpl, 56, after serv in Marine Corps Track Team, Japan, 54 & Korea, 55; Good Conduct Medal; Nat Defense Medal; UN Medal; Korean Medal. Mem: Tucson Bd Realtors; Eagleton Inst Polit; Ariz Acad. Relig: Protestant. Mailing Add: Tony Buehl Ins Agency 4580 E Broadway Tucson AZ 85701

BUEHLER, HERBERT J (D)
NJ State Sen
Mailing Add: State House Trenton NJ 08625

BUEHLER, PAUL RICHARD (D)
b Medford, Wis, Nov 24, 93; s William Buehler & Elizabeth Gertz B; m 1922 to Helen Albertina Resech (deceased); remarried 1969 to Cecilia F Walton Williams; c Armin Paul, Ervin Roland, Phyllis Helen (Mrs Keith Hutson), Lorraine Elizabeth (Mrs Richard Peters) & John Williams. Educ: Bus Col Night Sch. Polit & Govt Pos: Assessor, Wis, 26-27; supvr, Medford, 52-54; secy & treas, Taylor Co Dem Party, 62-64, chmn, 64-69, first vchmn, 69-73; supvr, Taylor Co Bd, Wis, 70-, mem law & order & forest & zoning comts & chmn older Americans comt, currently. Mil Serv: Entered as Pvt, Army, 18; Purple Heart, Campaign Ribbons. Mem: Vet World War I (Comdr, 67-73); DAV (Comdr, 58-73); Am Legion; VFW; Local Farmers Union (vpres). Honors & Awards: Citation for Meritorious Serv as Post Comdr, Am Legion. Relig: Lutheran. Mailing Add: Rte 2 Medford WI 54451

BUELL, ROBERT C (R)
Mass State Rep
Mailing Add: State Capitol Boston MA 02133

BUENEMAN, JANET ANN (R)
Chmn, Warren Co Rep Cent Comt, Mo
b Mexico, Mo, July 10, 42; d Melvin V Hanssen & Mildren Cathine Phillips H; m 1961 to Thomas James Bueneman; c Ann, Abby & Thomas James, II. Educ: Lindenwood Col, 60-61; Young Rep, LCIC, League of Women Voters. Polit & Govt Pos: Co chmn, Nixon for President, 68 & 72; committeewoman, Ward II, 68-70; committeewoman, Hickory Grove Twp, 70-; chmn, Warren Co Rep Cent Comt, Mo, 70- Bus & Prof Pos: Owner, Rolling Hill Farm, Wright City, Mo, 63-73. Mem: Am, Mo & East-Cent Angus Asns; Warren Co Hist Soc (treas, 70-72); Mo Rep Women's Club (exec bd, 70-73). Relig: United Church of Christ. Mailing Add: Rolling Hill Farm Rte 2 Wright City MO 63390

BUETTNER, JOYCE MARGUERITTE (D)
Committeeman, Monroe Co Dem Comt, NY
b Austin, Minn, Nov 17, 37; d Gale George Ellis & Belle Chandonnet E; m 1958 to Albert Valentine B; c Brian, Carol & David. Educ: Univ Minn, Minneapolis, BA cum laude, 58. Polit & Govt Pos: Second ward rep, Greece Dem Comt, NY, 70-71, ward leader, 71-; committeeman, Monroe Co Dem Comt, 70-; deleg, Dem Nat Conv, 72. Mem: Greece Residents Organized to Act (treas, 68-69 & exec comt, 69-71). Relig: Roman Catholic. Mailing Add: 99 Jamestown Terr Rochester NY 14615

BUFFINGTON, NANCY CATHERINE (R)
Wash State Sen
b Logan, Utah, Mar 24, 39; d Fred Roberts & Lucy Harris R; div; c Tom, Tim, Sheryl & Sharlene. Educ: Seattle Community Col; Univ Wash. Polit & Govt Pos: Wash State Sen, 75-, mem state govt comt, social & health serv comt & judiciary comt, Wash State Sen, 75-; mem, Social & Health Serv Regional Comt, Region Ten, 75-; mem, Wash State Coun on Elderly & Aging, 75- Bus & Prof Pos: Swim & fitness instr, West Seattle YMCA, 67-69; prof model, various stores & co, 68-72; fitness coordr, Seattle Jewish Community Ctr, 69-73; prog dir, Cardiopulmonary Research Inst, Seattle, 70-74. Publ: Auth, Women in cardiac rehabilitation, Wash State Med J, 72. Mem: Coun Planning & Affiliates; West Seattle YMCA (bd mem); Juv Court; Munic League; Am Asn Med Technicians. Honors & Awards: Outstanding Serv Award, YMCA, 69; Outstanding Serv Award, Cardiopulmonary Research Inst, 75. Relig: Catholic. Legal Res: 5919 47th St SW Seattle WA 98126 Mailing Add: 108 Insts Bldg Olympia WA 98504

BUFFONE, CHARLES JOSEPH (D)
Mass State Rep
b Worcester, Mass, May 19, 19; s Joseph Buffone & Antoinette Belsito B; m 1941 to Marion C Santora; c Linda (Mrs James Ruda). Educ: Portia Law Sch, 1 year; St John's Univ (NY), 1 year. Polit & Govt Pos: Mass State Rep, 60-68 & 71. Bus & Prof Pos: Pub rels, Buffone Enterprise, 53- Mil Serv: Navy, 43-47, PO 2/C; World War II Medal; Good Conduct Medal; Pac Theatre Ribbon; Commendation of Duty. Mem: Ital & Am Bus & Prof Club; UNICO Orgn; Sons of Italy; Am Legion Post 201; Lady of Loreto Men's Club. Honors & Awards: Grocer's Mfg Award; Scout Awards; Neighborhood Award. Relig: Catholic. Mailing Add: 61 Harold St Worcester MA 01604

BUFFUM, WILLIAM BURNSIDE
Asst Secy State Int Orgn Affairs
b Binghamton, NY, Sept 10, 21; s Frederick Francis Buffum & Lucy Davis B; m 1944 to Alma Emma Bauman; c Karen (Mrs Joseph Clarkson), Diane (Mrs James Klieforth) & Andrea. Educ: Oneonta State Teachers Col, BEd, 43; Univ Pittsburgh, MLitt, 49; Oxford Univ, 46; Harvard Univ, 52-53; Sigma Chi Sigma. Polit & Govt Pos: Vconsult, Dept State, Stuttgart, Ger, 46-49; polit officer, Conn, 53-58; dir polit affairs, Bur Int Orgn Affairs, 59-67; Dep Asst Secy State, 65-67; Dep US Rep to UN, 67-70; US Ambassador to Lebanon, 70-74; Asst Secy State Int Orgn Affairs, 75- Bus & Prof Pos: Instr, Univ Pittsburgh, 46-49. Mil Serv: Army, 43-46. Mailing Add: Dept of State Washington DC 20520

BUFORD, JOSEPH LEONE (D)
Chmn, Scotland Co Dem Cent Comt, Mo
b Alder Gulch, Mont, Sept 26, 13; s Joseph Luck Buford & May Hinch B; single. Educ: Northeast Mo State Univ, BS cum laude, 50; Blue Key; Thalian Guild; Kappa Delta Pi; Col Players. Polit & Govt Pos: Mem, Harrison Twp Dem Comt, Mo, 40-75; chmn, Scotland Co Dem Cent Comt, 58- Bus & Prof Pos: Prin, Gorin High Sch, Mo, 45-65; head dept Eng, Scotland Co R-I, Memphis, Mo, 67-75; retired, 75. Mil Serv: Entered as Pvt, Army, 42, released as Sgt Maj, 45, after serv in Combat Engrs, African-European Theatre. Publ: Auth, Man from Galilee, Hist Publ Co, 41; Ella Ewing-Giantess, Nemo Publ Co, 58. Mem: Am Legion; Mo State Teachers Asn; Mo Hist Soc. Relig: Baptist. Mailing Add: Gorin MO 63543

BUGATTO, B JOHN (R)
Mem, San Francisco Co Rep Cent Comt, Calif
b San Francisco, Calif, July 20, 34; s Mario Bugatto & Lietta De Martini B; m 1961 to Maria De Martini; c Barry, Annette & Robert. Educ: St Mary's Col of Calif, AB, 57; Univ San Francisco Sch Law, LLB, 61; Phi Delta Phi. Polit & Govt Pos: Mem, Bay Area Transportation Study Comn, Calif, 68-69; alt deleg, Rep Nat Conv, 68; mem, San Francisco Co Rep Cent Comt, Calif, 70-; mem, NCent Coast Regional Comn, 74-75. Mil Serv: Entered as Airman Basic, Air Force, 58, released as Airman, 2/C, 63, after serv in 631st Res Unit, Continental Air Command, 58-63. Mem: Calif & San Francisco Bar Asns; Columbus Civic Club; Lions; Ital Fedn of Calif. Relig: Roman Catholic. Legal Res: 3632 Lyon St San Francisco CA 94123 Mailing Add: 470 Columbus Ave San Francisco CA 94133

BUGGS, JOHN ALLEN (D)
b Brunswick, Ga, Nov 20, 15; s John Wesley Buggs & Leonora Clark B; m 1943 to Mary Gale Brown; c Zara Gale (Mrs William Taylor) & Diane Dorinda (Mrs Robbie Dix). Educ: Dillard Univ, BA, 39; Fisk Univ, MA, 41; Loyola Univ Los Angeles, 54; Alpha Phi Alpha. Hon Degrees: LHD, Chapman Col, 72. Polit & Govt Pos: Exec dir, Los Angeles Co Comn on Human Rels, Calif, 54-67; dep dir, Model Cities Admin, US Dept Housing & Urban Develop, 67-69; dep staff dir, US Comn on Civil Rights, 71-72, staff dir, 72- Bus & Prof Pos: Teacher, Athens, Ala, 41-42; dir, Fessenden Acad, Martin, Fla, 42-51; social case worker, Los Angeles, 51-52, dep probation officer, 52-54; vpres, Nat Urban Coalition, 69-71. Publ: Functional Education at Fessenden Academy, Common Ground, 49. Mem: Nat Asn Human Rights Workers; Am Arbit Asn (bd dirs, 73-); Vol in Tech Assistance (bd dirs, 72-); Boy Scouts (nat coun, 71-); NAACP. Honors & Awards: Man of the Year, Omega Psi Phi, 61; Bishop's Award of Merit, Episcopal Diocese of Los Angeles, 64; Cert of Merit, Howard Univ Alumni Asn of Southern Calif, 67; Cert of Merit, Los Angeles Br, Asn for Study of Negro Life & Hist, 67; Citation, Crenshaw Neighbors, Los Angeles, 69. Relig: Episcopal. Legal Res: 2805 Village Lane Wheaton MD 20906 Mailing Add: 1121 Vermont Ave NW Washington DC 20425

BUGLIONE, NICHOLAS JOSEPH (D)
Mass State Rep
b Lawrence, Mass, Sept 12, 32; s Nicola Buglione; m 1954 to Joan Shirley Habeeb; c Suzanne Marie & Lisa Ellen. Educ: Air Force Commun Sch, cert; Salem State Col, 5 years; Lee Inst, cert real estate, 72. Polit & Govt Pos: Mem town meetings, Methuen, Mass, 61-72, sch committeeman, 65-73; Mass State Rep, Methuen, 69- Bus & Prof Pos: Off supvr, Avco Corp, Wilmington, Mass, 61-69. Mil Serv: Entered as Airman Basic, Air Force, 52, released as S/Sgt, 56, after serv in Commun, Korean Conflict, 53-54; Good Conduct Medal; UN Medal; Korean Medal; 1 Battle Star; Nat Defense Medal. Mem: Mass Legislators Asn; Methuen Bd Trade; Children Protective Serv; KofC; Boosters Club. Honors & Awards: Avco Corp Cost Reduction Award; Outstanding Serv Awards, Ital Am War Vet & East End Civic Asn. Relig: Catholic. Mailing Add: 32 Quincy St Methuen MA 01844

BUHL, LLOYD FRANK (R)
Chmn, Eighth Cong Dist Rep Party, Mich
b New Haven, Mich, Jan 9, 18; s William C Buhl & Bessie L Meier B; m 1940 to Rosamond Davidson; c William C, Robert L, Marcia E & Karl E. Educ: High Sch. Polit & Govt Pos: Assessor, Deckerville, Mich, 39-46, trustee, 63-69; justice of the peace, Marion Twp, 46-69; mem, Sanilac Co Rep Comt, 50-51; asst state chmn & organizer, Eisenhower Campaign,

Mich, 52; mem ed & legis coun, Rep Farm Coun, 52; mem, Sanilac Co Rep Comt, 56-60; chmn, Sanilac Co Rep Party, 67-68; chmn, Eighth Cong Dist Rep Party, 69-; pres, Village of Deckerville, 69-; mem, Probate Judge's Retirement Bd, Mich, 71. Bus & Prof Pos: Publisher, Deckerville Recorder & Carsonville J, 35-69; mem, Cath Family Serv, 65 & Cath Charities Bd, 71; chmn, Sanilac Co United Fund, 71. Mem: Odd Fellows; DOKK; KofP (Past Grand Chancellor); charter mem Deckerville Lions Club. Relig: Presbyterian; Elder, former chmn bd trustees. Legal Res: 3665 N Main St Deckerville MI 48427 Mailing Add: 2534 Black River St Deckerville MI 48427

BUHLER, DAVID LIDDLE (R)
Chmn, Utah TAR
b Salt Lake City, Utah, July 13, 57; s Robert Earl Buhler & Phyllis Liddle B; single. Educ: Univ Utah, 75- Polit & Govt Pos: Chmn, Utah TAR, 74-; mem exec bd, Rep Party Utah, 74-; summer fel, Rep Nat Comt, 75. Bus & Prof Pos: Distribution asst, Newspaper Agency Corp, 74- Mem: Explorers (asst to pres, Jim Bridger Dist, 74-); Nat Explorer Post Pres Asn. Relig: Latter-day Saint. Mailing Add: 1076 S Fifth East Salt Lake City UT 84105

BUHR, GLENN (D)
Committeeman, Iowa Dem State Cent Comt
b Bremer Co, Iowa, Apr 29, 30; s Elmer Buhr & Lucinda Schroeder B; m 1955 to Florence D Wederquist; c Barbara, Lori Lynn & David. Educ: Univ Northern Iowa, BA, 52; Univ Maine, 59; Middlebury Col, MA, 66; Pi Gamma Mu; Alpha Mu Gamma. Polit & Govt Pos: Precinct committeeman, Polk Co Dem Cent Comt, Iowa, 70-; chairperson, Iowa Dem Conf, 71-; deleg, Dem Nat Conv, 72; chairperson reform comt, Iowa Dem Party, 73-74; committeeman, Iowa Dem State Cent Comt, 74- Bus & Prof Pos: Instr German, Roosevelt High Sch, Des Moines, Iowa, 58-62; asst prof German, Simpson Col, Indianola, Iowa, 61- Mil Serv: Entered as Pvt, Army, 52, released as SP-3, after serv in ETO, 54-55. Mem: Am & Iowa Civil Liberties Union; NAACP; Am Asn German Teachers; Urban Concern Comn of Des Moines Presbytery. Honors & Awards: Human Rels Award, Des Moines Human Rights Comn, 69; Fulbright Summer Study grant to Ger, 74. Relig: Presbyterian. Mailing Add: 4127 30th St Des Moines IA 50310

BUISSON, CYDNEY ANN (R)
b Detroit, Mich, June 21, 49; d Robert R Buisson & Patricia Fuller B; single. Educ: Mem Hosp Sch Radiological Tech, CRT, 74. Polit & Govt Pos: Alt deleg, Rep Nat Conv, 72; Presidential elector, 72. Mailing Add: 232 San Carlos Way Novato CA 94947

BULCAO, DOUGLAS WILLIAM (D)
b New Orleans, La, Mar 8, 42; s William A Bulcao & Olive Woodham B; m to Carolyn Frances Farr; c Christian Farr & Scott Woodham. Educ: Univ of the South, BA Polit Sci, 64; Loyola Univ Sch Law, 66; George Washington Univ, grad work int affairs, 69-70; Phi Gamma Delta; Black Ribbon Soc; Order of Gownsmen. Polit & Govt Pos: Legis asst to US Rep John R Rarick, La, 67-71; legis asst to US Rep Joe D Waggonner, Jr, La, 71- Relig: Episcopal. Legal Res: 404 Fremaux Ave Slidell LA 70458 Mailing Add: 6221 N 23rd St Arlington VA 22205

BULEN, LAWRENCE KEITH (R)
b Pendleton, Ind, Dec 31, 26; s Lawrence Elston Bulen & Ople Odell Benefiel B; div; m 1970 to N Carole Guillot; c Lisa K, Leslie Kathleen & Kassee. Educ: Ind Univ, AB, 49, JD, 52; Phi Delta Phi; Sigma Nu; Skull & Crescent; Falcon; Sphinx. Hon Degrees: DHL, Vincennes Univ, 72. Polit & Govt Pos: Dist chmn, Young Rep, Ind, 54; committeeman, Rep Party, 54-64; deleg, Rep State Conv, 54-72; Ind State Rep, 60-64; chmn, Marion Co Rep Cent Comt, 66-72; chmn, 11th Dist Rep Comt, 66-74; mem, Ind Rep State Cent Comt, 66-74; deleg, Rep Nat Conv, 68 & 72; Rep Nat Committeeman, Ind, 68-74; mem exec comt, Rep Nat Comt, 69-74; chmn, Ind Nixon Inaugural Comt, 69 & 73; mem steering comt, Mid-West Rep Conf, 69; US deleg, UN Econ & Social Coun, 49th Session, Switz, 70 & 55th Session, Geneva, 73; US Observer, UN Natural Resources Conf, Nairobi, Kenya, 72. Bus & Prof Pos: Attorney, Bulen & Castor. Mil Serv: Entered as Pvt, Air Force, 45, released as Sgt of Guard, 46; Lt, Air Force Res, 49-50; Occupation of Japan Medal; Asia & SPac Ribbons. Mem: Indianapolis Lawyers Asn; Mason; Am & Ind Bar Asns; Scottish Rite. Relig: Disciples of Christ. Legal Res: 8323 Rahke Rd Indianapolis IN 46217 Mailing Add: 143 E Ohio St Rm 300 Indianapolis IN 46204

BULGER, WILLIAM M (D)
Mass State Sen
Mailing Add: State Capitol Boston MA 02133

BULGERIN, LORETTA (R)
Chmn, Eastland Co Rep Party, Tex
b Houston, Tex, Aug 3, 30; d Donald Morrison Davis & Lillian Harvey D; m 1953 to Harold James Bulgerin; c Stephen Mitchell, Donald Lawrence, Curtis Wayne, Keith Edward & Claudia Diane. Educ: Southwestern Univ, BS in Biol, 52; Alpha Chi; Cardinal Key; Delta Zeta. Polit & Govt Pos: Vchmn, Eastland Co Rep Party, Tex, 66-68, chmn, 68-; pres, Eastland Co Rep Women's Club, 70-74. Mem: Am Soc Clin Pathologists; Woman's Auxiliary to Am Med Asn; Civic League & Garden Club (pres, 72-73); Eastland High Band Boosters (candy chmn, 74 & 75); United Methodist Women. Relig: Methodist. Mailing Add: 1800 W Plummer Eastland TX 76448

BULL, CORALEE KITCHINGS (D)
b SC; d Boyce Dexter Kitchings & Mary Getzen K; m to Rear Adm John Carraway Bull, wid; c John C, Jr, MD. Educ: Winthrop Col; Univ Wash; George Washington Univ. Polit & Govt Pos: Admin asst to US Rep Mendel L Rivers, SC, 57-71; admin asst to US Rep Mendel J Davis, 71-72, asst to US Rep Mendel J Davis, Beaufort Dist Off, SC, 73- Bus & Prof Pos: Bd dirs, First Carolina Bank, Beaufort, SC. Relig: Episcopal. Legal Res: 1207 Bay St Beaufort SC 29902 Mailing Add: Box 1066 Beaufort SC 29902

BULLARD, GLADYS (D)
Dem Nat Committeewoman, NC
Mailing Add: 5601 Lambshire Raleigh NC 27612

BULLARD, PERRY (D)
Mich State Rep
b Cleveland, Ohio, Sept 2, 42; s Charles Winston Bullard & Trudie Kissner B; single. Educ: Harvard Univ, AB, 64; Univ Mich Law Sch, JD, 70. Polit & Govt Pos: Mich State Rep, 73- Mil Serv: Entered as Ens, Navy, 64, released as Lt(jg), 68, after serv in Fleet Air Reconnaissance Sq 1, 7th Fleet, 65-68; 13 Air Medals; Letter of Commendation. Publ: Co-auth, Restrictions on student voting: an unconstitutional anachronism?, Univ Mich J Law Reform, 12/70. Mem: Am & Mich Bar Asns; Nat Lawyers Guild; Vietnam Vet Against the War. Legal Res: 535 Elm St Ann Arbor MI 48197 Mailing Add: Mich House of Rep Lansing MI 48901

BULLEN, CHARLES W (R)
Utah State Rep
Mailing Add: 1624 Sunset Dr Logan UT 84321

BULLEN, REED (R)
Utah State Sen
Mailing Add: 172 E First North Logan UT 84321

BULLETT, AUDREY KATHRYN (D)
Chairperson, Lake Co Dem Comt, Mich
b Chicago, Ill, Feb 12, 37; d Louis Hill & Eva B Reed H; m 1965 to Clark Ricardo Bullett, Jr; c Iris J Hill. Educ: Ferris State Col, 63-64; Univ Mich, Ann Arbor, 65-66. Polit & Govt Pos: Corresponding secy, Lake Co Dem Comt, Mich, 60-62, vchmn, 72-75, chairperson, 75-; precinct deleg, Fifth Dist Dem Party, 66-67; deleg, Mich Dem State Conv, 75; mem, Mich Dem State Cent Comt, 75- Bus & Prof Pos: Librn, Idlewild Pub Libr, Mich, 60-63; clerk-typist, Lake Co Treas Off, 63-65; dep co clerk, Lake Co, 69-72; dist court clerk, 78th Dist Court, 73-; adminr, Lake Co Pub Employ Prog, 71- Mem: Yates Twp Fire Dept (fire personnel, 69-); Lake Co Planning Comn; Idlewild CofC; VFW. Relig: Baptist. Legal Res: Rte 1 Box 52 Baldwin MI 49304 Mailing Add: PO Box 373 Baldwin MI 49304

BULLOCK, ELMER DAVID (R)
Chmn, Rep Town Comt, Milton, Vt
b Georgia, Vt, July 10, 08; s Roy Eben Bullock & Maggie Linehan B; m 1935 to Charlotte Mabel Hurlbut; c Carolyn (Mrs Earl Fisher), Sanford & Timothy; three grandchildren. Educ: Vt State Agr Sch, 30. Polit & Govt Pos: Sch dir, 6 years; clerk of sch bd, 3 years; town lister, 7 years; town grand juror, 6 years; fence viewer, 16 years; Justice of the Peace, 48-; chmn, Rep Town Comt, 7 years; Vt State Rep, 63-68; town auditor, 71-, chmn bd, Civil Authority, 73-74. Bus & Prof Pos: Retired dairy farmer. Mem: Georgia, Vt, Bicentennial Comt (chmn); Banner Grange 356 (Past Master); Sexton Milton Boro Cemetery Asn. Mailing Add: RD 3 Milton VT 05468

BULLOCK, GEORGE DANIEL (R)
b San Francisco, Calif, Dec 19, 42; s J H Bullock & Jane Cottrell B; m 1969 to Mary Brown. Educ: Portland State Col, AB, 64; Stanford Univ, MA, 65. Polit & Govt Pos: Mgt intern, Ore Workman's Compensation Comn, summer 62; admin asst to US Sen Ted Stevens, 71; sr policy adv, Off of Econ Opportunity, Exec Off of the President, 71-73, acting dir, Policy Anal Staff, 72-73, cong rels specialist, 73, planning & rev adv, 73-74, acting assoc dir, Off Prog Rev, 74; spec asst to Gov Daniel J Evans for fed-state rels, Wash, 74- Bus & Prof Pos: Instr hist, Portland State Univ, summers 66 & 69 & Southern Methodist Univ, 69-70; asst prof hist, Univ Alaska, 70-71; radio-TV polit commentator, KTVF-KFRB, Fairbanks, Alaska, 70 & 72. Mem: Orgn Am Historians; Soc for Historians of Am Foreign Rels; Alaska State Soc (2nd vpres, 71-72, 1st vpres, 72-73, pres, 73-74); Wash State Soc. Relig: Protestant. Legal Res: Olympia WA Mailing Add: 334 Eighth St SE Washington DC 20003

BULLOCK, JOHN WILLIAM (D)
Mass State Sen
b Arlington, Mass; s Patrick Bullock & Josephine Johnston B; m 1953 to Jacqueline Theresa LaRue; c Barbara, Nancy, Caroline & Ellen. Educ: Arlington High Sch, grad. Polit & Govt Pos: Mem & chmn, Bd Selectmen, Arlington, Mass, 62-74; mem, Arlington Dem Town Com, 62-74; Mass State Sen, 72- Mil Serv: Entered Army, 47; released as Pfc, 48. Mem: Mass Citizens Life, Inc. Honors & Awards: Award, Mass Asn Retarded Children, 64, Medford Am Legion Post 45, 74 & Mass Asn Paraplegics, 74. Relig: Catholic. Legal Res: 196 Jason St Arlington MA 02174 Mailing Add: State House Rm 507 Boston MA 02133

BUMGARDNER, BERT EDWARD (D)
Chmn, Wolfe Co Dem Party, Ky
b Lee Co, Ky, Aug 7, 18; s George Washington Bumgardner & Alice Evans B; m 1945 to Monell Iona Tyra; c Darrell Edward & Sheila Jean. Educ: Lees Jr Col, 35-37; Ky Wesleyan Col; Univ Ky, 52-56. Polit & Govt Pos: Clerk, Wolfe Co Court, Ky, 58-; chmn, Wolfe Co Dem Party, 73- Bus & Prof Pos: Sch Teacher, Wolfe Co Bd Educ, Ky, 38-42 & 45-58. Mil Serv: Entered as Pvt, Air Force, 42, released as T/Sgt, 45, after serv in ETO, 44-45. Relig: Methodist. Mailing Add: Campton KY 41301

BUMGARDNER, DAVID WEBSTER, JR (D)
NC State Rep
b Belmont, NC, Nov 2, 21; s David Webster Bumgardner & Winnifred Ballard B; m 1948 to Sara Margaret Jones; c Sharon Inez (Mrs Hill) & Sandra Jo. Educ: Belmont Abbey Col, 38-40; Gupton-Jones Col Mortuary Sci, 41-42. Polit & Govt Pos: NC State Rep, 67- Mem: Nat Funeral Dirs Asns; Conf Funeral Serv Examining Bd US; Am Legion; VFW; Belmont Masonic Lodge. Relig: Baptist. Legal Res: 209 Peachtree St Belmont NC 28012 Mailing Add: PO Box 904 Belmont NC 28012

BUMGARNER, CARROLL E (D)
WVa State Deleg
Mailing Add: State Capitol Charleston WV 25305

BUMPERS, DALE L (D)
US Sen, Ark
b Charleston, Ark, Aug 12, 25; s William Rufus Bumpers & Lattie Jones B; m to Betty Flanagan; c Dale Brent, William Mark & Margaret Brooke. Educ: Univ Ark, Fayetteville, 48; Northwestern Law Sch, 51. Polit & Govt Pos: City attorney, Charleston, Ark, 52-70; mem, Co Bd Educ, 52-70; mem, Charleston Sch Bd, 57-70; spec justice, Ark Supreme Court; Gov, Ark, 71-75; deleg, Dem Nat Conv, 72; mem, Dem Nat Comt, 72-; US Sen, Ark, 75- Bus & Prof Pos: Pres, Charleston CofC & Charleston Indust Develop Corp. Mil Serv: Entered as Pvt, Marines, 43, released as Sgt, 46 after serv in Pac. Mem: United Fund, Boy Scout & Cancer Fund Drives; CofC. Relig: Methodist. Legal Res: PO Box 98 Charleston AR 72933 Mailing Add: Senate Off Bldg Washington DC 20510

BUNCH, RALPH E (D)
b Portland, Ore, Apr 11, 27; s Ralph E Bunch & Ruth C Cooper B; m 1965 to Mutsuko Motoyama; c Lenalee (Mrs Brooks), James Jefferson & Genji Motoyama. Educ: Lewis & Clark Col, BS, 51; Univ Ore, MA, 61 & PhD, 68. Polit & Govt Pos: Precinct committeeman

div leader & chmn, Dollars for Dem, Multnomah Co, Ore, 58-60; alt deleg, Dem Nat Conv, 72; Dem nominee, US Rep, First Dist, Ore, 72. Bus & Prof Pos: Elem & high sch teacher, Ore Pub Schs, 51-60; eighth grade teacher, US Army Dependent Sch, Tokyo, Japan, 57-58; prin, Brownfield High Sch, Alta, Can, 62-63; chmn social sci div, Wenatchee Valley Col, Wash, 64-66; asst prof, Polit Sci Dept, NTex State Univ, 68-70; assoc prof, Polit Sci Dept, Portland State Univ, 70- Mil Serv: Entered as Seaman 2/C Combat Aircrewman, Navy, 45, released as Seaman 1/C, 46 after serv in Boot Camp & Sch. Publ: Orientational profiles: a method for micro-macro analysis of political attitudes, Western Polit Sci Quart, 12/71; ed, Denton Voice, 69- Mem: Am & Western Polit Sci Asns; Japanese Am Citizens League; Am Civil Liberties Union; Common Cause (chmn orgn comt, Ore Chap, 72). Relig: Unitarian. Mailing Add: 6111 SW Taylors Ferry Rd Portland OR 97219

BUNDY, SAM D **(D)**
NC State Rep
Mailing Add: 110 Grimmersburg St Farmville NC 27828

BUNDY, WILLIAM P **(D)**
b Washington, DC, Sept 24, 17; m to Mary Acheson; c Michael, Caroline & Christopher. Educ: Yale Col, BA, 39; Harvard Univ, MA, 40, LLB, 47. Polit & Govt Pos: Mem Bd Nat Estimates, Cent Intel Agency, 51-61; staff dir, Pres Comn on Nat Goals, 60-61; Dep Asst Secy of Defense for Int Security Affairs, 61-63, Asst Secy of Defense for Int Security Affairs, 63-64; Asst Secy of State for EAsian and Pac Affairs, 64-69. Bus & Prof Pos: Attorney-at-law, 47-51; vis prof & sr research assoc, Mass Inst Technol, 69-71; ed, Foreign Affairs, 72- Mil Serv: Army, 41-46, Maj. Mailing Add: 1087 Great Rd Princeton NJ 08540

BUNKER, A G **(R)**
NDak State Rep
b Equality, Ill, Apr 16, 27; s Warren Sam Bunker & Helen Duty B; m 1961 to Norene Leverson. Educ: Univ Wyo, 47-49; NDak State Univ, BS, 52; Blue Key; Scabbard & Blade; Alpha Tau Omega. Polit & Govt Pos: NDak State Rep, 67- Bus & Prof Pos: Vpres, Security Int Ins Co, 62- Mil Serv: Entered as Pvt, Army, 45, released as Sgt, 47, after serv in 6th Armored Div, recalled 52 as 1st Lt. Mem: Nat Asn Life Underwriters; Elks; Am Legion; NDak State Univ Alumni Bd. Honors & Awards: Outstanding Alumni Award, NDak State Univ Bus Econ Club. Relig: Lutheran. Mailing Add: State Capitol Bismarck ND 58501

BUNKER, BETTY BARGER **(D)**
Mem, Ark State Dem Comt
b Sikeston, Mo, Dec 29, 21; d Ewell Harrison Barger & Tot Gresham B; m 1941 to Nelson Waldo Bunker, III; c Sarah (Mrs Farr), William Whithorne & Jed Barger. Educ: Sikeston Pub Sch, grad, 40. Polit & Govt Pos: Mem, Co Dem Comt, Ark, 50; mem, Ark State Dem Comt, 70- Bus & Prof Pos: Owner, Finishing Touch Gift Shop, 69-; secy & treas, Bunker Farms, Inc. Mem: PTA; Lake Village Civic Club. Honors & Awards: Woman of the Year, Lake Village, Ark. Relig: Methodist. Legal Res: S Lakeshore Rd Lake Village AR 71653 Mailing Add: PO Box 507 Lake Village AR 71653

BUNKER, ELLSWORTH
US Ambassador-At-Lg
b Yonkers, NY, May 11, 94; s George R Bunker & Jean Polhemus Cobb B; m to Harriet Butler (deceased); m 1967 to Carol Laise; c Ellen B (Mrs Fernando Gentil), John Birkbeck & Samuel Emmet; twelve grandchildren. Educ: Yale Univ, BA, 16. Hon Degrees: LLD, Yale Univ, 59, Mt Holyoke Col, 62 & Windham Col, 63. Polit & Govt Pos: US Ambassador, Argentina, 51, Italy, 52-53, India, 56-61 & Nepal, 56-59; pres, Am Red Cross, 53-56; deleg, UN Gen Assembly, 56; mediator, UN, Indonesian-Netherlands dispute, 62 & Saudi Arabia-Egypt dispute, 63; consult to Secy of State, 63; US Ambassador, Orgn Am States, 64-66; US Ambassador-at-lg, Dept of State, 66 & 73-; US Ambassador, Viet Nam, 67-73. Bus & Prof Pos: Dir, Nat Sugar Refining Co, 27-40, pres, 40-49, chmn bd, 49- Mem: Asia Found; Asia Soc & Exp in Int Living; New Sch Social Research; Vt Coun on World Affairs; Coun Foreign Rels. Honors & Awards: Grand Cross Knight of the Repub of Italy, 54; Presidential Medal of Freedom with Spec Distinction, 63 & 68; Nat Order First Class, SViet Nam, 73. Relig: Episcopal. Legal Res: RFD 2 Putney VT 05346 Mailing Add: Dept of State Washington DC 20520

BUNKER, NORENE RAE **(R)**
Treas, 21st Dist Rep Comt, NDak
b Mobridge, SDak, July 11, 31; d Tilford M Leverson & Ethel Florence Moe L; m 1961 to Ardis Gray Bunker. Educ: Interstate Bus Col, Fargo, NDak, 49-50. Polit & Govt Pos: Treas, 21st Dist Rep Comt, NDak, 70-; alt deleg, Rep Nat Conv, 72; pres, NDak Fedn Rep Women, 75- Bus & Prof Pos: PBX & steno, credit mgr, Store Without A Name, Fargo, NDak, 50-55; bookkeeper, Monarch Lumber Co, Great Falls, Mont, 55-60; bookkeeper, Nash Finch (Piggly Wiggly-Northland), Fargo, NDak, 60-61; off mgr, Hagstrom Bros, St Paul, Minn, 61-62. Mem: Am Red Cross (bd, Minn-Kota Chap, 69-); NDak Frazer Hall; First Lutheran Church Women. Relig: Lutheran. Mailing Add: 721 Southwood Dr Fargo ND 58102

BUNN, GEORGE **(D)**
b St Paul, Minn, May 26, 25; s Charles Bunn & Harriet Foster B; m 1949 to Fralia Suter Hancock, div; c Peggy Joan, Peter Wilson & Matthew George; m 1975 to Anne Crosby Coolidge. Educ: Univ Wis, BS in Elec Eng, 46; Columbia Univ, LLB, 50; Tau Beta Pi; Eta Kappa Nu; Phi Eta Sigma; Order of the Coif. Polit & Govt Pos: Attorney, Gen Counsel's Off, Atomic Energy Comn, 50-51; mem staff preparedness subcomt, US Senate, 57; counsel to President's Adv on Disarmament, 61-62; gen counsel, US Arms Control & Disarmament Agency, 61-69; US deleg, 18 Nation Disarmament Conf, 62-68; UN Disarmament Comn, 65; alt US Rep with rank of Ambassador, Geneva Disarmament Conf, 68. Bus & Prof Pos: From assoc to partner, Arnold, Fortas & Porter, 51-61; prof law, Univ Wis-Madison, 69-, dean, Law Sch, 72-75; mem Linowitz Comn, Am Coun on Educ Spec Comt on Campus Tension, 69-70. Mil Serv: Entered as A/S, Naval Res, 43, released as Ens, 46, after serv in USS Logan, Pac, 45-46. Publ: Nuclear nonproliferation treaty, 68 & Banning gas and germ warfare, 69, Wis Law Rev; Missile limitation: by treaty or otherwise, Columbia Law Rev, 70. Mem: Am & Wis Bar Asns; Arms Control Asn. Legal Res: 1834 Camelot Dr Madison WI 53705 Mailing Add: Law Sch Univ of Wis Madison WI 53706

BUNN, STAN **(R)**
Ore State Rep
Mailing Add: Rte 2 Box 267 Dayton OR 97114

BUNNELL, OMAR B **(D)**
Utah State Rep
Mailing Add: 640 North Third E Price UT 84501

BUNTE, DORIS **(D)**
Mass State Rep
Mailing Add: State Capitol Boston MA 02133

BUNTEN, WILLIAM WALLACE **(R)**
Kans State Rep
b Topeka, Kans, Apr 5, 30; s Robert Muir Bunten & Mary Rock B; m 1961 to JoAnn Francis Heyka; c William W, Jr, Sandra & Ann. Educ: Univ Kans. Polit & Govt Pos: Kans State Rep, 32nd Dist, 62-64, 34th Dist, 64-66 & 47th Dist, 66- Mil Serv: Entered as Pvt, Marine Corps, 52, released as Capt, 54, after serv in 1st Marine Div, Far East Theater; Far Eastern Theater, Korean Theater & UN Serv Ribbons. Mem: CofC; 20-30 Int; Elks; Farm Bur. Relig: Methodist. Mailing Add: 1200 Merchants Nat Bank Bldg Topeka KS 66611

BUNTING, EUGENE **(R)**
b Selbyville, Del, Mar 6, 28; s Clayton A Bunting & Frances E Burrows B; m 1946 to Mary E Gray; c Helen B (Mrs Robert E Stevens), Clayton E, Rachel A & Mary J. Educ: Selbyville High Sch; Greenbriar Mil Sch; Goldey Beacom Sch Bus. Polit & Govt Pos: Chmn, Sussex Co Rep Party, Del, 66-68 & 72-74; Secy of State, Del, 69-73; chmn, Del Rep State Comt, formerly; mem, Rep Nat Comt, formerly; deleg, Rep Nat Conv, 72. Bus & Prof Pos: Mem bd trustees, Baltimore Trust Co, Selbyville, Del. Mem: Fruit Tree Growers Asn; Eastern Regional Nurserymen's Asn; Mason; Shrine; Rotary. Relig: Methodist; Chmn bd trustees, Salem Methodist Church. Mailing Add: Buntings Nurseries Inc Selbyville DE 19975

BUNTING, PEGGY **(R)**
Idaho State Rep
Mailing Add: 944 Lewis St Boise ID 83702

BUNYAN, S WYANNE **(D)**
Dem Nat Committeewoman, Calif
b St Petersburg, Fla, May 6, 45; d Dr Gerald Wyant Bunyan & Martha Young Mikesell; m 1970 to Frank Dave Rothschild. Educ: Wash State Univ, 63-64; Baylor Univ, 64-65; Ohio State Univ, 65; Eastern NMex Univ, 66; Calif State Univ, BA, 67; Georgetown Univ, JD, 71. Polit & Govt Pos: Deleg, Dem Nat Conv, 72; comnr, Dem Deleg Selection Comn, 72-; comnr, Juv Justice Comn, 72-; Dem Nat Committeewoman, Calif, 72-76; mem, Calif Dem Party State Cent Comt, 72-76; vice chair adv comn to Joint Comt on Restructuring the Judiciary. Bus & Prof Pos: Law clerk, Colton & Murphy, Washington, DC, 69-70; legal intern corp finance, Securities & Exchange Comn, summer 70; law clerk, Wilkinson, Cragun & Barker, 70-71; mem faculty, Univ Calif, Hastings Col Law, 71-, asst dean, 72-; dir, Coun on Legal Educ Opportunity Summer Inst, 73. Mem: Kappa Beta Pi; Am, Calif & San Francisco Bar Asns; Barristers Club; Commonwealth Club. Legal Res: 415 Panoramic Hwy Mill Valley CA 94941 Mailing Add: 198 McAllister St San Francisco CA 94102

BUNYAN, WILLIAM PRICE, III **(R)**
Chmn, Meade Co Rep Cent Comt, Kans
b Los Angeles, Calif, Aug 21, 38; s William Price Bunyan, II & Loraine Gregory B; m 1969 to Susan Fisher. Educ: Col Emporia, 57-59; Kans Univ, BA, 61, post grad study, 61-62; St Mary of the Plains Col, Sec & Elem Cert, 69-71; Pi Sigma Alpha; Delta Chi. Polit & Govt Pos: Chmn, Meade Co Young Rep, Kans, 62-67; precinct committeeman, Fowler Twp, 62-; committeeman, 36th Sen Dist Young Rep, 63-65; Meade Co Deleg, Dist & State Young Rep Conv, 63-71; chmn, Citizens for Goldwater, 64; Meade Co Deleg, Presidential Dist & State Nominating Conv, 64-72, treas, Meade Co Rep Cent Comt, 64-68, vchmn, 68, chmn, 68-; vchmn, Kans Young Rep, 65-67; chmn, First Cong Dist Young Rep, 67-69; Kans Deleg, Nat Young Rep Conv, 67 & 69; chmn, Sebelius for Cong, Meade Co & area chmn, Frizzell for Attorney Gen, 68; dir, Region Seven Young Rep, Kans, Nebr, Mo, Iowa & Okla, 69-71; mem, Young Rep Nat Exec Comt, 69-71; area chmn, Van Sickle for Attorney Gen, 70; chmn, Meade Co Van Sickle for Attorney Gen, 74. Bus & Prof Pos: Farmer rancher, Bill & Greg Bunyan's Lazy W Bar Ranch, Fowler, 62-; teacher, Dodge City Sch Syst, Kans, 71- Mil Serv: Entered as Pvt, Army Res, 56, released as SP-4, 64, after serv in 489th AAA Bn. Mem: Fowler Jaycees (pres, 70-); Meade Co Farm Bur; Meade Co Hist Soc (treas, 72-); Nat & Kans Hist Soc. Honors & Awards: Key Man Award, Fowler Jaycees, 67. Mailing Add: Fowler KS 67844

BURACZYNSKI, ANTHONY C **(D)**
Vt State Rep
b North Walpole, NH, Sept 23, 08; married; c one daughter. Educ: Hinsdale High Sch, NH. Polit & Govt Pos: City councilman, Torrington, Conn, 42-50; mem, Motor Vehicle Racing Comn, 63-64; mem, Vt Civil Authorities, 63-; Vt State Rep, 63- Bus & Prof Pos: Proprietor of cabins. Mem: KofC; Elks; Eagles; Rotary; Polish Nat Alliance. Relig: Catholic. Mailing Add: RFD 1 152 Putney Rd Brattleboro VT 05301

BURBACH, JULIUS W
Nebr State Sen
b Hartington, Nebr, Apr 5, 12; m 1937 to Bernice Jensen. Educ: Holy Trinity High Sch. Polit & Govt Pos: Mem sch bd, Nebr; Nebr State Sen, 57- Bus & Prof Pos: Grain & feed dealer, livestock feeder. Mem: Crofton CofC; Knox Co Agr Asn (dir); Livestock Feeders Asn (dir); KofC; Elks. Relig: Catholic. Mailing Add: Crofton NE 68730

BURBIDGE, KEITH A **(D)**
Ore State Sen
Mailing Add: 4271 Ivory Way NE Salem OR 97303

BURCH, CLYDE MONROE **(D)**
b Callao, Mo, July 4, 26; s Durwood Burch & Isabel Dunseith B; m 1953 to Marilyn Leathers; c Mona, Karen, John, James & Rebecca. Educ: Northeast Mo State Col, BSE, 50; Univ Minn, 51; Univ Mo, Kansas City, JD, 54. Polit & Govt Pos: City attorney, Fulton, Mo, 55-59; asst attorney gen, Jefferson City, 61-64; mem, Mo Gov Comn Local Govt, 67-; deleg, Dem Nat Conv, 68; mem, State Platform Comt, Mo Dem Party, 72. Bus & Prof Pos: Instr, Westminster Col, 59-60; prof govt, Northeast Mo State Col, 64- Mil Serv: Entered as A/S, Naval Res, 45, released as PO, 46. Publ: Missouri presidential elections, 1900-1968, Miss State Teachers Asn, 68. Mem: Am Polit Sci Asn; Mo Bar Asn; Mo Hist Soc; Mo State Teachers Asn; Mason. Honors & Awards: Outstanding Publ Serv Award, Am Fedn Police, 72; Award of Merit, Mo Water Pollution Bd. Relig: Baptist. Mailing Add: RR Bethel MO 63434

BURCH, DEAN (R)
b Enid, Okla, Dec 20, 27; s Bert Alexander Burch & Leola Atkisson B; m 1961 to Patricia Meeks; c Shelly, Dean & Dianne. Educ: Univ of Ariz, LLB, 53; Phi Delta Theta; Blue Key. Polit & Govt Pos: Asst Attorney Gen, Ariz, 53-54; admin asst to Sen Barry Goldwater, 55-59; dep dir, Goldwater for President Comt, 63-64; chmn, Rep Nat Comt, 64-65; chmn, Goldwater for Senate Comt, 68; mem, Bd Regents, Ariz, 69; chmn, Fed Commun Comn, 69-74; Counr to the President, 74-75. Bus & Prof Pos: Attorney, Dunseath, Stubbs & Burch, Tucson, 59-69; partner, Pierson, Ball & Dowd, 75- Mil Serv: Col, Army Res. Legal Res: 5000 Westpath Terr Washington DC 20016 Mailing Add: 1000 Ring Bldg Washington DC 20036

BURCH, FRANCIS BOUCHER (D)
Attorney General, Md
b Baltimore, Md, Nov 26, 18; s Louis Claude Burch & Constance M B; m 1947 to Mary Patricia Howe; c Francis B, Jr, Catherine H (Mrs Jenkins); Richard C, Constance B, Edwin H, Robert S & Mary Patricia. Educ: Loyola Col, Baltimore, PhB summa cum laude, 41; Yale Law Sch, LLB, 43; Phi Delta Phi. Polit & Govt Pos: Mem, Mayor's Comt Conflict of Interest, Baltimore, Md, 60, pres, Civil Serv Comn, 60-61, chmn, Mayor's Comt Mass Transit, 61, chmn, Mayor's Comt Scholar Prog, 61, city solicitor, 61-63, mem, Bd Estimates, 61-63, mem, Pension Study Comt, 62; mem, Standard Policy Bd, State of Md, 60-61, ins comnr, 65-66, Attorney General, 66-; deleg, Dem Nat Conv, 68. Bus & Prof Pos: Dir various corp; counsel, vpres & chmn exec comt, Baltimore Jr Asn Com, 50-54; secy, vpres & pres, Jr Bar Asn Baltimore City, 52-54; dir, Legal Aid Bur, 54. Mil Serv: Entered as Seaman 1/C, Coast Guard, 44, released, 45, after serv in Vol Port Security Force, Baltimore. Publ: On calling a constitutional convention, Daily Rec, Baltimore, 50. Mem: Southern Conf Attorneys General; Nat Asn Attorneys General (pres, 70-71); Eastern Seaboard Conf Attorneys General; Coun State Govts (exec comt, 72-); Am Bar Asn. Honors & Awards: Pub Servant Award, Dept Md, CWV, 67; Humanitarian Award, Nu Beta Epsilon Nat Law Fraternity, 68; Man of the Year Award, Nat Jewish Hosp, Denver, 69; St Thomas More Soc Man of all Seasons Award, 69; Loyola Col Alumnus of the Year Award, 70. Relig: Catholic. Legal Res: 207 Chancery Rd Baltimore MD 21218 Mailing Add: One S Calvert Bldg Rm 1400 Baltimore MD 21202

BURCH, PALMER LYLE (R)
State Treas, Colo
b Ordway, Colo, Mar 27, 07; s Robert H Burch & Nancy Robinette B; m 1946 to Elvera M Hultquist; c Susan. Educ: Cent Bus Col, Denver, Colo, 24. Polit & Govt Pos: Colo State Rep, 47-48, 51-58 & 61-70, majority leader, Colo Gen Assembly, 69-70; mem, Denver Bd Educ, 59-67, pres, 63-67; State Treas, Colo, 71- Bus & Prof Pos: Treas, Bennett Properties Co, Denver, Colo, 35-68. Mem: Life mem Bldg Owners & Mgrs Int Asn; life mem Colo Cattlemen's Asn. Relig: Lutheran. Legal Res: 395 Fairfax St Denver CO 80220 Mailing Add: State Capitol Denver CO 80203

BURCH, THOMAS J (D)
Ky State Rep
Mailing Add: 4850 Brenda Dr Louisville KY 40219

BURCH, WILLIAM ALVA (R)
b Butler, Mo, Oct 19, 25; s Jerry Burch & Mary Edith Searfus B; m 1950 to Barbara Joan Ehart; c William Douglas, Larry Dean & Brett Duane. Educ: Butler High Sch, dipl, 43. Polit & Govt Pos: Mem, Twp Bd, Mt Pleasant, Mo, 54; treas-collector, Bates Co, 56-64; Mt Pleasant Twp committeeman, 64-; chmn, Bates Co Rep Party & Rep Cent Comt, formerly; alt deleg, Rep Nat Conv, 72. Mil Serv: Entered as Seaman 2/C, Navy, 45, released as Seaman 1/C, 46, after serv in Navy Air Corps; Naval Res, 46-51. Mem: Odd Fellows; Lions; Am Legion; IBT; PTA. Relig: Reorganized Latter-day Saint. Mailing Add: Rte 4 Box 39 Butler MO 64730

BURCHETT, DEWEY ELDRIDGE, JR (D)
Chmn, Bossier Parish Dem Exec Comt, La
b Shreveport, La, Nov 18, 39; s Dewey Eldridge Burchett & Patti Ogilvie B; m 1967 to Patricia Gayle Bolender; c Dewey Eldridge III & Edward Bolender. Educ: La State Univ & Agr & Mech Col, BA in govt, 62, Law Sch, JD, 70; Phi Alpha Delta; Arnold Air Soc; Scabbard & Blade; Polit Sci Asn. Polit & Govt Pos: Chmn, Bossier Parish Dem Exec Comt, La, 72- Bus & Prof Pos: Partner in law firm, Thomas, Prestridge & Burchett, 73-; secy & attorney, Bossier Levee Dist, 75-; attorney, Bossier City Fire & Police Civil Serv Bd, 75- Mil Serv: Entered as 2nd Lt, Air Force, 62, released as Capt, 67, after serv in 1st Air Commando Wing, Tactical Air Command; Commendation Medal. Mem: Bossier Dem Asn (chmn, 73-); Exchange Club; Jaycees; Am, La & Local Bar Asns. Honors & Awards: Outstanding Local Pres, La Jaycees, 74. Relig: Presbyterian. Mailing Add: 2417 Melrose Ave Bossier City LA 71011

BURCHETT, KNOX RYAN (R)
Mem, Va Rep State Cent Comt
b Albany, Ky, Oct 24, 33; s Joe R Burchett & Sallie Booher B; m 1960 to Mikell Ann Preston; c Michelle & Sarah. Educ: Univ Ky, BS in Civil Eng, 54, MS in Civil Eng, 58. Polit & Govt Pos: Vchmn, Virginia Beach Rep Comt, 70-72; deleg, Rep Nat Conv, 72; mem, Va Rep State Cent Comt, 72- Bus & Prof Pos: Sales engr, Price Bros Co Inc, 58; vpres, Aggregate Serv Inc, 59-62; mgr, Lite Cast Prod Co, Inc, 62-63; mgr, Am Precast Concrete Inc, 63-65; mgr precast & wood prod, Lone Star Industs Inc, 65- Mil Serv: Entered as 2nd Lt, Air Force, 54, released as 1st Lt, 56, after serv in 7030th Support Group, 12th Air Force, Ger, 54-56. Publ: Repair of architectural cast in place structural concrete, Concrete Construction, 4/72 & Am Concrete Inst, 12/73. Mem: Va Soc Prof Eng; Va Prestressed Concrete Asn (pres, 73-); Va Comn for Regulation of Professions & Occupations; Am Soc Testing & Material; Thoroughgood Civic League (vpres, 72-73, pres, 73-). Relig: Methodist. Mailing Add: 1412 Dunstan Lane Virginia Beach VA 23455

BURDICK, QUENTIN N (D)
US Sen, NDak
b Munich, NDak, June 19, 08; s Usher L Burdick & Emma Robertson B; m to Jocelyn Birch; c Jonathan, Jan (Mrs Glenn Hill), Jennifer, Jessica, Leslie, Birch & Gage. Educ: Univ Minn, BA & LLB. Polit & Govt Pos: US Rep, NDak, 58-60, US Sen, 60-; ex officio, Dem Nat Mid-Term Conf, 74. Legal Res: 1110 S Ninth St Fargo ND 58103 Mailing Add: 305 C St NE Apt B106 Washington DC 20002

BURDITT, GEORGE MILLER (R)
b Chicago, Ill, Sept 21, 22; s George Miller Burditt & Flora Hardie B; m 1945 to Barbara Helen Stenger; c Betsey Anne, George M, III, Deborah Jane & Barbara Lee. Educ: Harvard Col, AB, 44, Law Sch, LLB, 48; Pi Eta. Polit & Govt Pos: Chmn, Young Rep Orgn Cook Co, Ill, 52-53; vpres, Young Rep Orgn Ill, 53-54; chmn, Western Springs Plan Comn, 53-55; exec vpres, Regular Rep Orgn Lyons Twp, 54-55; state vchmn, Ill Citizens for Eisenhower-Nixon, 56; state chmn, Vol for Witwer, 60; Ill State Rep, 65-72, asst majority leader, Ill House Rep, 71-72; Rep cand for US Sen, 74. Bus & Prof Pos: Attorney, Swift & Co, 48-54; partner, Chadwell, Keck, Kayser, Ruggles & McLaren, 54-68; partner, Burditt & Calkins, 69- Mil Serv: Entered as Cadet, Army Air Force, 43, released as 2nd Lt, 45, after serv in Southeast Training Command as Twin Engine Pilot Instr & Air Transport Command as Four Engine Ferry Pilot. Publ: The current status of weights & measures problems, Soap & Chem Specialties, 4/64; Weights & measures, foods & drugs, & uniformity, Asn of Food & Drug Officials of the US Quart Bull, 10/64; Need for new uses of the regulatory power to establish food standards, Food Drug Cosmetic J, 3/65. Mem: Am, Ill, Chicago & WSuburban Bar Asns; Kiwanis. Relig: Congregational. Mailing Add: 540 S Park Rd La Grange IL 60525

BURETA, LYNN MARIE (D)
Chairperson, Eighth Assembly Dist Dem Party, Wis
b Milwaukee, Wis, Apr 17, 51; d Ralph John Bureta & Helen B; single. Educ: Univ Wis-Milwaukee, BA, 74. Polit & Govt Pos: Mem Staff, McGovern for President, Wis, 72; deleg, Dem Nat Conv, 72; deleg, Wis Dem State Conv, 72-74; chairperson, Eighth Assembly Dist Dem Party, 73-; mem staff, Nelson for Senate, 74; deleg, Milwaukee Co Dem Coun. Relig: Catholic. Mailing Add: 3477 S 35th St Milwaukee WI 53215

BURFORD, DOROTHY WRIGHT (R)
Chmn, Ripley Co Rep Cent Comt, Mo
b Doniphan, Mo, Oct 2, 03; d Thomas Lyon Wright & Clara B Robinson W; m to Peyton Jerome Burford; c Virginia Jerry (Mrs William S McAninch). Educ: Galloway Col, 22-23; Stephens Col, AA, 24. Polit & Govt Pos: Mem, Mo State Rep Comt, 42-70; deleg, Rep Nat Conv, 56 & alt deleg, 68; chmn, Ripley Co Rep Cent Comt, 56-; vchmn, Tenth Dist Rep Comt, 74- Bus & Prof Pos: Mgr gravel div, T L Wright Lumber Co, 26-40. Relig: Methodist. Mailing Add: 101 Summit St Doniphan MO 63935

BURFORD, ROBERT F (R)
Colo State Rep
b Grand Junction, Colo, Feb 5, 23; s Ellery E Burford & Cleone Fitzpatrick B; m 1951 to Judith M Allen; c Joseph Ellery, Robert Kelley, Richard F & Joyce. Educ: Colo Sch Mines, EM, 44; Theta Tau. Polit & Govt Pos: Chmn, Eagle Co Rep Comt, Colo, formerly; Colo State Rep, 75- Mil Serv: Entered as Pvt, Marines, 44, released as Cpl, 46, after serv in 1st Marine Div, Pac Theatre; Pac Theatre Ribbon & two Stars. Mem: Mason; Farm Bur. Mailing Add: 113 Mira Monte Rd Grand Junction CO 81632

BURG, JAMES ALLEN (JIM) (D)
SDak State Rep
b Mitchell, SDak, Apr 22, 41; s Albert Leo Burg & Pearl Linafelter B; m 1967 to Bernice Marie Kaiser; c Jeff, Cory, Julie & Casey. Educ: SDak State Univ, BS, 63; Alpha Zeta; Block & Bridle Club; Agr Club; 4-H Club; Newman Club. Polit & Govt Pos: Chmn, Jerauld Co Dem Party, SDak, 73-75; SDak State Rep, 75- Bus & Prof Pos: Fieldman, Fed Land Bank of Omaha, 65-68; owner-mgr, Firesteel Ranch Corp, 68- Mil Serv: Entered as Pvt E-1, Army Nat Guard, 63, Capt, currently. Mem: Farmers Union; Co Dr Clin Comt; Farm Bur; Jaycees; Co Land Use Planning Comt (chmn, currently). Honors & Awards: Outstanding Young Relig Leader, Local Jaycees, 74; Outstanding Freshman Legislator, SDak State Legis, 75. Relig: Roman Catholic. Mailing Add: RR 1 Wessington Springs SD 57382

BURG, MARY LOU (D)
Dep Chmn, Dem Nat Comt
b Slinger, Wis, Feb 10, 31; d Leo R Burg & Henrietta Loew B (deceased); single. Educ: Rockford Col Women, 1 year; Univ Nev, 2 years; Univ Wis, Madison, BS, 52; Delta Delta Delta. Polit & Govt Pos: Chmn, Women's Comt, Wash Co Dem Party, Wis, 60-64, chmn, Wash Co Dem Party, 66-68; precinct committeewoman, Fourth Ward, West Bend, 64-70; mem-at-lg, Dem Admin Comt, 67-68; Dem Nat Committeewoman, 68-, vchmn, Dem Nat Comt, 70-72, dep chmn, 73- Bus & Prof Pos: Dir of continuity & pub affairs, WEMP Radio, Milwaukee, 58-64, sales rep, Sta WYLO, Milwaukee, 64-67, gen mgr, 67-70. Mem: Milwaukee Advert Club. Relig: Methodist. Legal Res: 407 S Sixth Ave West Bend WI 53095 Mailing Add: 1625 Massachusetts Ave NW Washington DC 20036

BURGENER, CLAIR W (R)
US Rep, Calif
b Vernal, Utah, Dec 5, 21; s Walter H Burgener & Nora Taylor B; m 1941 to Marvia Hobusch; c Rod, Greg & John. Educ: San Diego State Col, AB, 50; Blue Key; Sigma Chi. Polit & Govt Pos: Councilman, San Diego, Calif, 53-57, vmayor, 55-56; chmn, San Diego Co Nixon for Pres Campaign, 59; consult spec educ, US Dept Health, Educ & Welfare, 59-64; Calif State Assemblyman, 76th Dist, 63-67; Calif State Sen, 38th Dist, 67-73; US Rep, 42nd Dist, Calif, 73- Bus & Prof Pos: Pres & owner, Clair W Burgener Co, Realtors, 47- Mil Serv: Entered as Cadet, 43, Army Air Corps, released as 2nd Lt, 46; reentered, 52-53, serv in Korean Conflict, SPac; Air Medal. Mem: Am Legion; VFW; Nat Asn Retarded Children; President's Comt on Ment Retardation (vchmn); Nat Adv Comt on Handicapped Children. Relig: Latter-day Saint. Legal Res: PO Box 1191 Rancho Santa Fe CA 92067 Mailing Add: Suite 107 7860 Mission Center Ct San Diego CA 92108

BURGESS, BARBARA ANN (D)
Second VChmn, San Bernardino Co Dem Cent Comt, Calif
b Hurst, Ill, Nov 2, 22; d Arthur Michael Knowles & Lorena McKenzie K; m 1956 to Delbert Jack Burgess; c Carol Lee (Mrs Terry Barnard), Linda C (Mrs Ralph Forry), Russell D & William J. Educ: Riverside Jr Col, AA, 42; Pasadena City Col, 64. Polit & Govt Pos: Publicity chmn, Yucaipa Dem Club, Calif, 64-69 & 72-75 secy, Jim Evans for Assembly, 73rd Assembly Dist, 68; deleg, Calif Dem State Cent Comt, 68-70; chmn, San Bernardino Co Women for Tunney, 70; chmn, Proj '70, 73rd Assembly Dist, 70; chmn, San Bernardino Co Dem Registr, 70; secy, San Bernardino Co Dem Cent Comt, 71-75, second vchmn, 75-, chmn finance & fund-raising, 72-74, chmn pub rels comt, 75-76; juror, San Bernardino Co Grand Jury, 73-; registration coordr, Third Supvr Dist, 74-75; app to Comn on Status of Women, San Bernardino Co, 75- Bus & Prof Pos: Asst cashier, Hills Bros Coffee, Inc, Los Angeles, 45-57; off mgr, Hall Trucking, Montebello, 62-64; off mgr & secy, Bodle, Fogel, Julber & Reinhardt, Attorneys-at-Law, San Bernardino, 67-68; research dir, Commun Ctr, 69-73. Mil Serv: Released as A/M 3/C after serv in Naval Air Corps, 42-45. Publ: A professional guide to mobile-home feasibility studies, Coord Commun, Inc, 70. Mem: Yucaipa Bus & Prof Women (pres, 74-75); Eagle Rock Chap, Royal Order of Amaranth; Mothers' Club;

DeMolay; Yucaipa Am Legion. Relig: Methodist. Mailing Add: 35170 Elm Lane Yucaipa CA 92399

BURGESS, DENNY D (R)
Kans State Rep
Mailing Add: PO Box 292 Wamego KS 66547

BURGESS, GERALD RAY (D)
Ala State Rep
b Duke, Ala, Dec 13, 36; s Josh Robert Burgess & Willie Pauline Sampler B; m 1955 to Lavada Ann Carroll; c Bridget Elaine, Lawanna Raye, Lisa Ann & Gerald Ray, Jr. Educ: Jacksonville State Univ, BS in Sec Educ, 58; Football, J Club. Polit & Govt Pos: Ala State Rep, Dist 58, currently. Bus & Prof Pos: Teacher & football & baseball coach, Headland High Sch, East Point, Ga, 58-59; territory mgr, Wholesale Div, B F Goodrich Tire Co, 59-65; partner, City Tire Co, 65-; owner & salesman, Burgess Trailer Park, currently; mem bd dirs, Heritage Farms Inc, Tucker, Ga. Mil Serv: Pvt, Nat Guard, 57-62; Naval Res, 62-66, Naval Air Res, 66- Mem: Mason; Shrine. Relig: Baptist. Mailing Add: 501 E 49th St Anniston AL 36201

BURGESS, HUGH (D)
Md State Deleg
b Ellicott City, Md, Sept 15, 29; s Lionel Burgess & Lenna L Baker B; m 1949 to Doris Aileen Royer; c Sandra Lee, Deborah Ann, Stephan Hugh, Reid Edwin & Holly Ellen. Educ: Western Md Col, AB, 49; Univ Baltimore, LLB, 63. Polit & Govt Pos: Md State Deleg, 67- Mem: Am Bar Asn; Kiwanis; Mason; Odd Fellows; Grange. Relig: Methodist. Legal Res: 3999 College Ave Ellicott City MD 21043 Mailing Add: Box 126 Ellicott City MD 21043

BURGESS, ISABEL ANDREWS (R)
b Cleveland, Ohio; d William H Andrews & Alice Ball A; m 1939 to Richard S Burgess; div; c Richard Ball, Thomas H & Mrs Allen Cordsen. Educ: Mills Col; Western Reserve Univ. Polit & Govt Pos: Ariz State Rep, 53-54, 56-58 & 60-66; Ariz State Sen, 67-69; mem, Nat Transportation Safety Bd, 69- Relig: Episcopal. Legal Res: Phoenix AZ Mailing Add: Nat Transportation Safety Bd 800 Independence Ave SW Washington DC 20594

BURGESS, JOHN STUART (R)
b New York, NY, May 10, 20; s Frederick Vaughn Burgess & Olive Hornbrook Moore B; m 1947 to Ronda Helen Prouty; c Frederick Moore & Helen Prouty. Educ: Univ Vt, BA, 50; Northeastern Univ Sch of Law, LLB, 49; JD, 72; Sigma Delta Psi; Sigma Phi. Polit & Govt Pos: Chmn, Brattleboro Rep Town Comt, Vt, 49-51 & 53-63; chmn, Windham Co Rep Comt, 50-51; legal counsel, Off Price Stabilization, 51; town attorney, Brattleboro, 53-; spec counsel, Vt Hwy Dept, 55-58; moderator, Brattleboro Union High Sch Dist, 58-; Vt State Rep Dist, 4 & 5, 66-71, speaker, Vt House of Rep, 69-71, chmn const rev comn, 68-71, mem civil defense comn & legis coun, 69-71; Lt Gov, Vt, 71-75; chmn, Vt Bicentennial Comn, 73- Mil Serv: Entered as Pvt, Army Field Artil, 41, released as Capt, 46, after serv in 7th Fighter Command, Pac Theatre, 45-52; recalled as 1st Lt, Air Force, 51-53; with serv in 90th Bomb Squadron, Korean Theatre; Air Force Res, Lt Col, 62-; Distinguished Flying Cross; Air Medal; Foreign Decorations. Mem: Nat Asn Munic Attorneys (state chmn); Nat Asn Claimants Compensation Attorneys; Am Legion (mem, Nat Americanism Adv Comn); VFW. Relig: Episcopal. Legal Res: 50 Western Ave Brattleboro VT 05301 Mailing Add: 12 Park Pl Brattleboro VT 05301

BURGESS, WARREN RANDOLPH (R)
b Newport, RI, May 7, 89; s Isaac Bronson Burgess & Ellen Wilbur B; m 1917 to May Ayres; remarried 1955 to Helen Hamilton Woods; c Leonard Randolph & Julian Ayres. Educ: Brown Univ, AB, 12; fel & LLD, 37; Columbia Univ, PhD, 20; Delta Upsilon; Phi Beta Kappa. Hon Degrees: LLD, Univ Rochester, 48, Bowdoin Col, 59 & Univ Calif, 62. Polit & Govt Pos: Chmn, NY State War Finance Comt, 43-44; Dep to Secy Treas, 53-54; Undersecy of Treas, 55-57; US Permanent Rep to NATO, 57-61, chmn, Atlantic Treaty Asn, 61-63, vchmn, 63-; vchmn, Atlantic Coun of US, 73- Bus & Prof Pos: Assoc, Fed Reserve Bank of New York, 20, dep gov, 30-36, vpres, 36-38; vchmn, Nat City Bank of New York, 38-48, chmn exec comt, 48-52; pres, NY State Bankers Asn, 40-41; chmn, Econ Policy Comn, Am Bankers Asn, 40-44, pres, 44-45, chmn, Pub Debt Policy Comt, 46-47; chmn bd, City Bank Farmers Trust Co; dir, Discount Corp, Int Banking Corp & UPRR Royal-Liverpool Group Ins Co in US; pres, Per Jacobsson Found & Reserve City Bankers Asn, 52; trustee, Robert Col, Teachers Col & Columbia Univ; regent prof, Univ Calif, Berkeley, 62. Publ: The Reserve Banks & the Money Market, 27, rev ed, 36 & 46; ed, Interpretations of Federal Reserve Policy, 30; co-auth, Europe & America—The Next Ten Years, 70; contrib of many articles to prof jour. Mem: Am Econ Asn; Am Philos Soc. Honors & Awards: Comdr, French Legion of Honor. Relig: Protestant. Legal Res: Queenstown MD 21658 Mailing Add: Atlantic Coun of the US 1616 H St NW Washington DC 20006

BURGIN, CHARLES EDWARD (D)
Chmn, McDowell Co Dem Party, NC
b Marion, NC, Dec 16, 38; s Arnold Charles Burgin & Hattie L McCormick B; m 1967 to Ellen Salsbury; c Ellen & Lucy. Educ: Univ NC, Chapel Hill, BA; Duke Univ, LLB. Polit & Govt Pos: Co solicitor, McDowell Co, NC, 66-68; chmn, McDowell Co Dem Party, 72- Bus & Prof Pos: Attorney-at-law, Dameron & Burgin, Marion, NC, 69- Mem: NC & Fed Bar Asns; NC State Bar. Relig: Methodist. Legal Res: 101 Viewpoint Dr Marion NC 28752 Mailing Add: PO Box 549 Marion NC 28752

BURGIN, WILLIAM GARNER, JR (D)
Miss State Sen
b Rock Hill, SC, Aug 3, 24; m 1968 to Catherine W Williams; c Helen, William, III, Susan & Robert Melville. Educ: Univ Miss, BA & LLB, 47. Polit & Govt Pos: Miss State Sen, 52-; mem, Miss Comn Budget & Acct, 64-; mem, Miss Medicaid Comn, 69- Bus & Prof Pos: Attorney. Mem: Mason; Elks; Lions. Relig: Baptist. Mailing Add: 518 Second Ave N Columbus MS 39701

BURGIO, JANE (R)
NJ State Assemblyman
Mailing Add: State House Trenton NJ 08625

BURGLAND, JANE HARVEY (R)
b Burbank, Calif, Jan 2, 31; d Leonard A Harvey & Irene Bailey H; m 1953 to Milo G Burgland; c Lynn M, Rene Ann, Sheree Lea & Gary William. Educ: Stephens Col, AA, 51; Univ Ariz, BA, 54; Alpha Xi Delta. Polit & Govt Pos: Pub rels, Ulster Co Legis & Cand, NY, 65-68; precinct chmn, Arlington Precinct 112, Tarrant Co Exec Comt, Tex, 69-; deleg, Rep Nat Conv, 72; campaign mgr, Tex State Legis Cand, 72; Rep cand, Tex State Sch Bd, 74. Mem: Arlington Rep Womens Club; Tex Sen Dist 12 Rep Club; Pub Affairs Luncheon Club of Dallas. Honors & Awards: One of Top Ten Rep Women in Tex, 73. Relig: Methodist. Mailing Add: 3700 Shady Valley Dr Arlington TX 76013

BURGUM, KATHERINE K (R)
b Minneapolis, Kans, Feb 26, 15; m 1944 to Joseph Burgum, wid; c Bradley, Barbara & Douglas. Educ: NDak State Univ, BS, 37; Columbia Univ, MA, 39; Phi Upsilon Omicron; Gamma Phi Beta. Polit & Govt Pos: Past pres, 11th Dist Rep Womans Club, Cass Co, NDak; past secy, 11th Dist Rep Party; mem, Arthur Sch Bd, 66-; alt deleg, Rep Nat Conv, 68, deleg, 72; Rep Nat Committeeman, NDak, 68-72; mem nat motor vehicle safety adv coun, Dept of Transportation, 70-; mem, NDak Gov Comt Traffic Safety, currently. Bus & Prof Pos: Teacher, Sayville Jr High & High Sch, NY, 37-39; asst prof, Wayne State Univ, 39-47; NDak rep, McCalls Mag Cong for Better Living, 57; dir, Farmers Elevator Co, Arthur, 71-; dean, Col of Home Econ, NDak State Univ, 72- Publ: Aircargo Potential for Fresh Fruits & Vegetables, 46 & Aircargo Potential for Sea Food, 47 (w Rietz Larsen), Wayne State Univ. Mem: Am & NDak Home Econ Asns; Northwest Farm Mgrs; NDak Farm Bur; Phi Upsilon Omicron. Honors & Awards: Aviation Writers Prize for Outstanding Contribution to Commercial Aviation Through Aircargo Studies, 49; Outstanding Woman Educator Award, NDak State Univ Mortar Bd, 73. Relig: Methodist; past secy, Arthur Methodist Church Bd. Legal Res: Arthur ND 58006 Mailing Add: Col of Home Econ NDak State Univ Fargo ND 58102

BURKE, BILLY BROWN (D)
WVa State Deleg
b Stouts Mills, WVa, Mar 14, 28; s Roy Hammond Burke & Freda Brown B (deceased); m 1952 to Marjorie Carol Hardman; c Roberta Diane & Carolyn Sue. Educ: Glenville State Col, 45-48. Polit & Govt Pos: WVa State Deleg, 66-, chmn comt finance, WVa House Deleg, 71-; mem, Gilmer Co Planning Comn, 71- Bus & Prof Pos: Pres, M & B Coal Co, 48-49; operating engr, Pipeline Indust, 49-58, construction supvr, 58-62; pres, B & F Trucking Co, 55-58; owner & mgr, Hardman Hardware Co, 62-; pres, Gilmer Co Indust Develop Asn, 63-; pres, Gilmer Realty Co, Inc, 64; pres, Gilmer Co Med Ctr, Inc, 70- Mem: AF&AM; Rotary; Gilmer Co Vol Fire Dept; PTA; Farm Bur. Honors & Awards: Friend of 4-H, 72; Award of Merit, WVa Voc Rehabilitation, 74. Relig: Baptist; deacon & Sunday sch supt. Legal Res: 22 Sumac Ct Glenville WV 26351 Mailing Add: PO Box 367 Glenville WV 26351

BURKE, EDWARD L (D)
Mass State Sen
Mailing Add: State Capitol Boston MA 02133

BURKE, FRANK WELSH (D)
b Louisville, Ky, June 1, 20; s Joseph M Burke & Ann Welsh B; m 1943 to Evalyne Hackett; c Lynn (Mrs Dennis Clare), JoAnn (Mrs George Schuhmann), Lucy & Frank, Jr. Educ: Univ Southern Calif, 38-39; Xavier Univ, PhB, 42; Univ Louisville, LLB, 48; Alpha Sigma Nu; Phi Kappa Psi. Polit & Govt Pos: Asst city attorney, Louisville, Ky, 50-51, dir pub safety, 52, exec asst to mayor, 52-53; Ky State Rep, 57; US Rep, Ky, 58-62; deleg, Dem Nat Conv, 68 & 72; Mayor, Louisville, Ky, 69-75. Bus & Prof Pos: Attorney-at-law, 48- Mil Serv: Entered as Pvt, Army, 42, released as 1st Lt, 46, after serv in various truck co, ETO, 44-45; Europe, Africa & Mid East Campaign Ribbons with 3 Battle Stars. Mem: Phi Alpha Delta; Ky Bar Asn; Am Legion; VFW; KofC. Relig: Catholic. Mailing Add: 1234 Eastern Pkwy Louisville KY 40204

BURKE, GEORGE GERALD (D)
b Brooklyn, NY, Aug 3, 32; s John F Burke & Ruth Joyce B; m 1959 to Sandra Bachofen; c Jeanne Marie, Susan Lee, Joanne & George G, III. Educ: Univ Mass, AB, 56; Boston Col Law Sch, LLB, 59; Adelphia; Owls; Lambda Chi Alpha. Polit & Govt Pos: City councillor, Quincy, Mass, 60-67, pres, City Coun, 66-67; Mass State Rep, First Norfolk Dist, 65-67; dist attorney, Norfolk Co, 67-; deleg, Dem Nat Conv, 68; deleg, Dem Nat Mid-Term Conf, 74. Bus & Prof Pos: Attorney, Barry & Burke, 59- Mil Serv: Capt, Armor Unit, Army Res, 51-64. Mem: Am Bar Asn; Am Trial Lawyers Asn; Dist Attorney's Asn; Am Legion; Elks. Honors & Awards: Former Rookie of Boston Celtics; selected All Am, All East & All New Eng in Basketball. Relig: Catholic. Mailing Add: 174 Warren Ave Quincy MA 02170

BURKE, GERARD PATRICK (INDEPENDENT)
Exec Secy, President's Foreign Intel Adv Bd
b Darby, Pa, Apr 3, 30; s Patrick J Burke & Mary E Breslin B; m 1955 to Ann Marie; c Gerard P, Jr, Maura Anne & Christine Marie. Educ: Col of the Holy Cross, AB, 52; Georgetown Univ Law Ctr, JD, 58; Inst Comp Law, Univ Paris, 60-61; Phi Delta Phi. Polit & Govt Pos: Staff & mgt pos, Nat Security Agency, 57-70, exec asst to dir, 65-69; exec secy, President's Foreign Intel Adv Bd, 70- Mil Serv: Entered as Ens, Navy, 52, released as Lt, after serv in US Atlantic Fleet & US Naval Security Group, 52-57; Naval Res, Lt Comdr. Mem: DC & Fed Bar Asns; Int Asn of Chiefs of Police. Honors & Awards: Meritorious Award for Pub Admin, William A Jump Found, 67. Relig: Roman Catholic. Mailing Add: 1117 Spotswood Dr Silver Spring MD 20904

BURKE, HENRY PATRICK (D)
b Scranton, Pa, May 12, 42; s Thomas Joseph Burke & Dorothy McCloskey B; single. Educ: Univ Scranton, BS, 64; Villanova Univ, JD, 67. Polit & Govt Pos: Deleg, mem platform comt & chmn task force on jobs, prices & taxes plank, Dem Nat Conv, 72; mem, Lackawanna Co Dem Exec Comt, Pa, 72; spec asst, attorney gen, Pa, 72- Mem: Am & Pa Bar Asns; Pa Trial Lawyers Asn; KofC (advocate, Scranton Coun 280, 71-); Am Heart Asn (asst treas, Keystone Chap, 72-). Relig: Roman Catholic. Mailing Add: 1041 N Webster Ave Scranton PA 18510

BURKE, J HERBERT (R)
US Rep, Fla
b Chicago, Ill, Jan 14, 13; s Joseph P Burke (deceased) & Catherine Lobert B; m to Evelyn Krumtinger; c Michele Kathleen & Kelly Ann. Educ: Chicago Cent YMCA Col, AA, 36; Northwestern Univ; Chicago Kent Col Law, JD, 40. Hon Degrees: LHD, Drake Col, 67 & Ft Lauderdale Univ, 70. Polit & Govt Pos: Co comnr, Broward Co, Fla, 52-66; mem, Fla State Rep Comt, 54-59; app by President Eisenhower to Southeast Adv Bd Small Bus, 56-60; deleg, Rep Nat Conv, 68 & 72, mem platform comt, 68; US Rep, Fla, 66-, mem comt on foreign affairs & subcomts on European affairs, Asiatic & Pac affairs & foreign econ policy, US House Rep, currently; mem exec comt, Nat Rep Cong Comt, currently; deleg, Foreign Econ Policy Conf, 73-; treas US deleg, Inter-Parliamentary Union, 73- Bus & Prof Pos: Law practice, Chicago, Ill, 40-49 & Fla, 49-; partner, Law Firm of Abrams, Anton, Robbins, Resnick & Burke, Hollywood, currently. Mil Serv: Entered as Pvt, Army, 42, released as Capt, 45, after serv in 90th Inf Div; Purle Heart; Bronze Star Medal; ETO Medal with 5 Battle Stars; Am

Theater Ribbon. Mem: Hollywood Am Legion Post 92 (past comdr); Amvets; Eagles; 40 et 8; VFW. Honors & Awards: Distinguished Serv Award, Am Const Action, 67-71; Watchdog of Treas Award, Nat Asn Businessmen, 67-72; Serv to Israel Award, 69; Meritorious Citation, Amvets, 69; Citation for Meritorious Serv, Nat Asn Retired Civil Employees, 71. Relig: Catholic. Legal Res: 1218 Hollywood Blvd Hollywood FL 33020 Mailing Add: 1125 Longworth House Off Bldg Washington DC 20515

BURKE, JAMES A (D)
US Rep, Mass
b Boston, Mass, Mar 30, 10; m 1968 to Aileen A McDonald. Educ: Suffolk Univ. Polit & Govt Pos: Registr Vital Statist, Boston, Mass; Mass Gen Court, 10 years; vchmn, Mass Dem State Comt, 4 years; US Rep, Mass, 58-, mem ways & means comt, chmn subcomt on social security, ranking mem unemployment compensation subcomt & mem joint internal revenue taxation comt, US House of Rep, currently; deleg, Dem Nat Conv, 68. Mil Serv: Army, Spec Agt, Counterintel, 77th Inf Div; 4 Battle Stars. Legal Res: Milton MA 02186 Mailing Add: 241 Cannon House Off Bldg Washington DC 20515

BURKE, JEROME A (D)
Mem, Ohio Co Dem Exec Comt, WVa
bWheeling, WVa, Nov 25, 37; s Richard Vincent Burke & Elizabeth Greene B; m 1966 to Janet Ruth Miller; c Jerome A, Jr. Educ: West Liberty State Col, 1 year. Polit & Govt Pos: Mem, Small Bus Admin Adv Bd, WVa, 62; alt deleg, Dem Nat Conv, 64, deleg, 68; chief dep clerk, Ohio Co Court, 65; vpres, Ohio Co Young Dem, 66; chmn, Wheeling Human Rights Comn, WVa, 67; mem, Ohio Co Dem Exec Comt, 68- Bus & Prof Pos: Co-mgr, Foodland Co. Mem: KofC (fourth degree); Jr CofC. Jaycee of the Month & Key Man of the Year, Wheeling Jaycees, US Jaycees Key Club. Relig: Roman Catholic. Mailing Add: 164 E Cove Ave Wheeling WV 26003

BURKE, JOHN A (D)
NH State Rep
Mailing Add: 42 W Baker St Manchester NH 03103

BURKE, KEVIN MICHAEL (D)
Mass State Rep
b Somerville, Mass, Dec 7, 46; s Michael Joseph Burke & Mary Finn B; m 1970 to Patricia Ann Lynch. Educ: Univ Conn, BA, 68; Boston Col, JD, 71; Sigma Alpha Epsilon. Polit & Govt Pos: Asst corp counsel, Boston, Mass, 72-75; mem, Dem City Comt, Beverly, currently; Mass State Rep, 75-, mem comt state admin, Mass House Rep, 75- Mem: Mass Bar Asn; Beverly Ward Two Civic Asn. Relig: Catholic. Legal Res: 39 Thorndike St Beverly MA 01915 Mailing Add: Rm 38 State House Boston MA 02133

BURKE, MARTIN BYRAM (D)
Conn State Rep
b Hartford, Conn, May 5, 40; s E Fenton Burke & Frances Greene B; m 1963 to Ellen C Schopfer; c Matthew B, Jonathan C & Andrew C. Educ: Colgate Univ, AB, 63; Union Univ Albany Law Sch, JD, 66; Sigma Chi. Polit & Govt Pos: Comnr, Charter Rev Comn, Vernon, Conn, 69-70; mem, Vernon Dem Town Comt, 69-; town attorney, Ellington, 73-; Conn State Rep, 56th Dist, 75- Bus & Prof Pos: Partner, Flaherty, Burke & Marder, Vernon, Conn, 68-; lectr, Rensselaer Polytech Inst, 69-70 & Wethersfield Sch Law, 73-74. Mem: Am, Conn, NY State & Tolland Co Bar Asns; Elks. Relig: Catholic. Legal Res: 38 Reed St Rockville CT 06066 Mailing Add: 351 Merline Rd Vernon CT 06066

BURKE, MICHAEL A (D)
Mo State Rep
b St Louis, Mo, Dec 2, 44; s Andrew Edgar Burke & Helen Walsh B; single. Educ: Forest Park Community Col, 69-71; Univ Mo-St Louis, 72. Polit & Govt Pos: Mo State Rep, 73- Mil Serv: Entered as Airman Basic, Air Force, 66, released as Sgt, 69, after serv in Mil Airlift Command; Air Force Commendation Medal. Relig: Roman Catholic. Mailing Add: 2338 Gaebler Overland MO 63114

BURKE, NANCY AELISHIA (R)
VChmn, Young Rep Nat Fedn
b Des Moines, Iowa, Dec 2, 33; d Harold Vincent Burke & Aelishia Smith B; single. Educ: Univ NMex, BA, 56; Univ Albuquerque, 69; Alpha Delta Pi. Polit & Govt Pos: Deleg, Young Rep Nat Fedn, 61, 63, 65, 67, 69 & 71, co-dir, Region XI, 61-63, dir, Region XI, 67-69, chmn issue develop comt, 69-71, vchmn, 71-; precinct secy, Bernalillo Co Rep Party, NMex, 64-68, mem, Bernalillo Co Cent Comt, 64-69; nat committeewoman, NMex Young Rep, 64-69; deleg, Atlantic Alliance of Young Polit Leaders, Luxemburg, 68; alt deleg, Rep Nat Conv, 68; Western Conf chmn, NMex Rep Party, 69-70; mem, Rep State Cent Comt, NMex, 69- Bus & Prof Pos: Teacher, Highland High Sch, Albuquerque Pub Schs, NMex, 56-59, chmn dept Eng, 70- Mem: Asn Supv & Curriculum Develop; Nat & NMex Coun Teachers of Eng; Albuquerque Classroom Teachers; NMex Educ Asn. Relig: Presbyterian. Mailing Add: 5624 Princess Jeanne NE Albuquerque NM 87110

BURKE, PAUL E, JR (BUD) (R)
Kans State Sen
b Kansas City, Mo, Jan 4, 34; s Paul E Burke & Virginia Moling B; m 1955 to Patricia Ann Pierson; c Anne Elizabeth, Kelly Patricia, Alice Catherine & Jennifer Marie. Educ: Univ Kans, BS, 56; Sigma Alpha Epsilon. Polit & Govt Pos: Rep precinct committeeman, Prairie Village, Kans, 61-66; chmn, Prairie Village Rep Cent Comt; councilman, Prairie Village, 62-65; comnr, Kans Turnpike Authority, 65-69, chmn, 69; Kans State Rep, Dist 28, 73-74; Kans State Sen, 75-, adv comn to Secy of Corrections, Kans. Bus & Prof Pos: Exec vpres, Webbco, Kansas City, Mo, Wichita & Topeka, Kans, 59-; pres, Gen Controls Div, Nat Distributor Adv Coun Int Tel & Tel, 75-; pres, Metrop Develop Co, currently. Mil Serv: Entered as 2nd Lt, Air Force, 56, released as 1st Lt, 58, after serv as pilot & radar controller, US; Comdr, Naval Air Res, 12 years. Relig: Episcopal. Mailing Add: 8229 Cherokee Circle Leawood KS 66202

BURKE, ROBERT H (R)
Calif State Assemblyman
b Des Moines, Iowa, July 16, 22; s Henry Burke & Mabel Anderson B; m 1954 to Claire Spencer; c Bradley, Spencer & Carrie. Educ: Iowa State Col; Univ Calif, Berkeley, BS in Eng, 49. Polit & Govt Pos: Trustee, Huntington Beach City Sch Dist, Calif, 63-66; Calif State Assemblyman, 70th Dist, 67-, mem elec & reapportionment, munic & co govt & state employ, retirement & mil affairs comts, Calif State Assembly; mem, Rep State Cent Comt Calif, currently. Mil Serv: Entered as Pvt, Air Force, 42, released as 1st Lt, 46, after serv in Pac Theatre. Mem: Am Petroleum Inst; Am Inst Mech Engrs; Kiwanis; Toastmasters; Huntington Beach CofC. Honors & Awards: Named Outstanding Man of Year, Huntington Beach Chap, United Rep of Calif; Received One of Five Outstanding Legislator Awards, Calif Rep Assembly, 67. Relig: Protestant. Legal Res: 8362 Malloy Dr Huntington Beach CA 92646 Mailing Add: Suite G 17732 Beach Blvd Huntington Beach CA 92647

BURKE, ROBERT JAMES (D)
Treas, WVa Dem Exec Comt
b Wheeling, WVa, Sept 3, 34; s Richard Vincent Burke & Elizabeth Greene B; m 1958 to Dolores Louise Moski; c Timothy James, Sheila Marie, Patrica Jean, Daniel Martin, Paula Anne & Roberta Frances. Educ: West Liberty State Col, night sch, 7 years. Polit & Govt Pos: Vchmn, Ohio Co Dem Exec Comt, WVa, 64, chmn, 68; dir, WVa Young Dem Clubs, 64; assoc campaign mgr, WVa Campaign, 66; exec secy, WVa Young Dem, 66; chmn, Citizens for Sprouse for Gov, 67-68; deleg-at-lg, Dem Nat Conv, 68; treas, WVa Dem Exec Comt, 68- Bus & Prof Pos: Vpres, Warwood Tool Co, 63-65, pres, 65-; vpres, Waller Chem, 67-; secy, Warwood Manor, 67-, mem bd dirs, West Liberty Col Found, 73- Mil Serv: Entered as Pvt, Army, 54, released as SP-3, 56, after serv in Adj Gen Corp; Good Conduct Medal. Mem: Am Hardware Mfg Asn; KofC; Elks; Eagles; Am Legion. Honors & Awards: Outstanding Small Businessman, Nat CofC, 69. Relig: Roman Catholic. Mailing Add: 36 Orchard Rd Wheeling WV 26003

BURKE, ROBERT WILLIAM (D)
b Davenport, Iowa, Feb 6, 32; s Tom Burke & Albena McConohy B; m 1952 to Frances Green; c Barbara, Dick, Marilyn, Karen & Shonale. Educ: St Joseph Sch, DeWitt, Iowa. Polit & Govt Pos: Precinct committeeman, Clinton Co Dem Party, 56-70, chmn, Clinton Co Dem Cent Comt, formerly; cong dist deleg, 70; deleg, Dem Nat Conv, 72. Bus & Prof Pos: Farmer, 55- Mil Serv: Entered as Pvt, Army, 52, released as Cpl, 54, after serv in 747 Heavy Equip Co; Nat Defense Serv Medal. Mem: Nat Farmers Union; KofC; Am Legion; Co Pork Producers. Relig: Catholic. Mailing Add: RFD 1 DeWitt IA 52742

BURKE, WALTER T (D)
Mass State Rep
Mailing Add: State Capitol Boston MA 02133

BURKE, YVONNE BRATHWAITE (D)
US Rep, Calif
b Los Angeles, Calif, Oct 5, 32; d James T Watson & Lola Moore W; div; m 1972 to William Burke. Educ: Univ Calif, Los Angeles, AB, 52; Univ Southern Calif, LLB, 56; Harvard Univ, Inst Polit, fel, 72; Pi Sigma Alpha; Alpha Kappa Alpha. Polit & Govt Pos: Dep Corp Comnr, Calif, 58-60; Calif State Assemblyman, 63rd Dist, 67-73; deleg, Dem Nat Conv, 68, alt deleg, 72; mem, Coun on Criminal Justice, Calif, 69; US Rep, 37th Cong Dist, Calif, 73- Mem: Women Lawyers; Nat Asn Negro Bus & Prof Women; Langston Law Club; Legion Lex; Leimert Park Dem Club. Honors & Awards: KNX Newsradio 1972 Woman of the Year. Relig: Methodist. Mailing Add: 1 Manchester Blvd Inglewood CA 90301

BURKEE, WALLACE E (NON-PARTISAN)
Mayor, Kenosha, Wis
b Kenosha, Wis, May 19, 26; s Norman F Burkee & Viola Chamberlain B; m 1950 to Jean Mattson; c Christine A (Mrs Hobbs), James & Allison. Polit & Govt Pos: Alderman, Kenosha, Wis, 58-62, Mayor, 67-; pres, Alliance of Cities, 69-74. Bus & Prof Pos: Owner, Burkee Agency, Real Estate-Ins, 59-67. Mil Serv: Entered as Pvt, Army Air Force, 43, released as Sgt, 46, after serv in 449th Bomb Group. Mem: Shrine; Elks; Am Legion. Relig: Lutheran. Mailing Add: 7544 26th Ave Kenosha WI 53140

BURKHARDT, DOROTHY JEAN (R)
Mem, Va Rep State Cent Comt
b Hebron, Ky, Sept 27, 11; d John Chester Hall Hood & Callie Clore H; m 1955 to George Burkhardt, III; c Carol (Mrs John H Rose) & Raymond K Poole & George Burkhardt, IV. Educ: Miller Sch Business, Cincinnati, Ohio, grad, 29. Polit & Govt Pos: Mem, Alexandria City Rep Comt, Va, 62-, vchmn, 62-65 & 68-; cand, Va House Deleg, 63; cand, Alexandria City Coun, 64 & 66; mem Mamie Eisenhower Libr Proj comt, Nat Fedn Rep Women, 63-64, deleg dist & state conv; co-chmn, Vol Participation Comt for the Inaugural; mem, Women for Nixon Comt; charter mem & first pres, Potomac Coun Rep Women, Alexandria, Va; chmn house-to-house canvas comt, Rep Party, Va, 64, asst coordr, MORE Comt, 65; vpres, Va Fedn Rep Women, 64-66, pres, 66-68; mem adv comt, Elem & Sec Educ Act, Alexandria Pub Schs, 65-66; mem, Va Rep State Cent Comt, 66-; chmn credentials comt, Nat Fedn Rep Women Conv, Washington, DC, 67; alt deleg, Rep Nat Conv, 68; dir, President's Comt on Consumer Interests, 69-; mem, Comn on Status of Women, Commonwealth of Va, 70- Bus & Prof Pos: Mem women's adv bd, Fidelity Savings & Loan Asn, Alexandria, Va; stenographer & secy, Treas Dept, Cincinnati, Ohio & Washington, DC; mfrs rep, East Coast Post Exchange; owner sales showroom, 55-65; secy-treas, Va Home Loan Corp, Alexandria, 61-; Treas, Stag Shops Inc, Arlington, Alexandria & Manassas, Va, 65-; real estate salesman, Robertson & Heck Inc, Arlington & Alexandria, 66-69. Mem: Cub Scouts; Beverly Hills Women's Club, Alexandria (charter mem); CofC; Old Dominion Bus & Prof Women's Club; Toastmistress Club. Honors & Awards: Elected Va Rep Woman of the Year, Va Fedn Rep Women, 69. Relig: Presbyterian. Mailing Add: 3400 Russell Rd Alexandria VA 22305

BURKHART, STEPHEN (R)
Chmn, Livingston Co Rep Exec Comt, Ky
b Wallins, Ky, Aug 26, 31; s S B Burkhart & Serena Long B; m 1954 to Jean Paul; c Gregory, Carol & Bruce. Educ: Berea Col, BA, 51; Univ WVa, 51; Univ Louisville, MD, 55; Am Bd Family Practice, dipl, 72; Alpha Kappa Kappa. Polit & Govt Pos: Chmn, Livingston Co Rep Exec Comt, Ky, 68- Bus & Prof Pos: Mem, Livingston Co Bd Health, Ky, 64-; pres, Crittenden Co Hosp Med Staff, 66-; vchmn & bd mem, Western Ky Regional Ment Health Bd, 67-69, chmn, 69-70; mem adv, Local Draft Bd 113, 67-; pres, Salem Nursing Home, Inc, 67- Mil Serv: Entered as 1st Lt, Air Force, 56, released as Capt, 58, after serv in Strategic Air Command, Ga, 56-58. Mem: Am & Ky Med Asns; Livingston Co Med Asn (pres, 62-); Am & Ky Acad Family Practice; Regional Adv Comt Voc Educ. Relig: Baptist. Mailing Add: Salem KY 42078

BURKLEY, PAUL EDWIN (R)
Ind State Rep
b Logansport, Ind, Dec 15, 19; s Dr Howard W Burkley & Charlotte Grace B; m 1949 to Freda Rose Wells; c Paul Edwin, Jr, Linda Kay, Donna Jean & Angela Sue. Educ: Seymour High Sch, 37. Polit & Govt Pos: Ward chmn, Marion Co Rep Comt, Ind, 64-72; mem, flood control bd, Indianapolis, 68-70 & bd pub works, 70-72; mem, Wayne Twp Adv Bd, 67-71; Ind State

Rep, 73- Bus & Prof Pos: Financial analyst, Gen Motors, Indianapolis, 50- Mem: Am Conservative Action; Lions; Wayne Twp Rep Club. Relig: Christian Church. Mailing Add: 2102 Gerrard Speedway IN 46224

BURKMAN, CAROL LYNN (R)
Pres, Neosho Co Fedn Rep Women, Kans
b Ada, Kans, Feb 21, 30; d Lee Spence VanMeter & Doris Lambertson V; m 1951 to Reuben J Burkman, MD, div; c Ronald Lee, Jeanine Hyacinth & Garry Linn. Educ: Kans Wesleyan Univ, 48-50; Univ Kans, 51; Kans State Univ, BS, 52; Beta Sigma Chi. Polit & Govt Pos: Treas, Neosho Co Rep Cent Comt, Kans, 64-70; co-chmn, Kans Young Rep Fedn, 65-67, mem exec bd, 67-; deleg, Nat Young Rep Conv, 67; sustaining mem, Rep Party, Washington, DC, 68; deleg, Rep Nat Conv, 68; distinguished mem, Rep Fivescore Club, Kans, 68; treas, Fifth Dist Rep Party, 68-; attended 17th annual Rep Women's Conf, Washington, DC, 69; crew leader, Bur Census, 70; sustaining mem, Nat Rep Party, 70; third vdir, Fifth Dist Fedn Rep Women of Kans, 70-72, first vdir, 72-; publicity chmn, Neosho Co Fedn Rep Women, 70-72, pres, 72- Bus & Prof Pos: Typist, Univ Kans Med Ctr, 52; teacher, Kansas City, 52-53 & 54-55; typist-secy, Cent Packing Co, Kansas City, 53-54; teacher home econ, Neosho Co Community Jr Col, 73- Mem: Am Asn Univ Women; PEO; PTA; Woman's Day Club; Am Cancer Soc (mem co educ comt). Honors & Awards: Invited to President Nixon's Inauguration & Inaugural Ball, 68 & invited to 1973 Inauguration. Relig: Presbyterian. Legal Res: 1608 S Malcolm Chanute KS 66720 Mailing Add: 3036 Conrow Dr Manhattan KS 66506

BURKS, TOMMY (D)
Tenn State Rep
b Cookeville, Tenn, May 22, 40; s Walter Fred Burks & Christine Gilliam B; m 1960 to Charlotte Rose Gentry; c Kimberly Lynn, Kelly Leigh & Kerry Lou. Educ: Tenn Polytech Inst, BS, 62; Alpha Gamma Sigma; Block & Bridle; Aggie Club. Polit & Govt Pos: Tenn State Rep, Putnam & Jackson Co, 71-72, Putnam & Cumberland Co, 73- Mem: Lions; Farm Bur; Putnam Co & Tenn Livestock Asns. Honors & Awards: Outstanding Young Farmer of Year, Jaycees; Am Farmer Degree. Relig: Church of Christ. Mailing Add: Rte 3 Monterey TN 38574

BURLEIN, LESTER F (R)
Chmn, Wayne Co Rep Comt, Pa
b Honesdale, Pa, Feb 1, 07; s Frederick George Burlein & Carrie Theobald B; m 1928 to Una Catherine Foster; c Joan M (Mrs Michelotti), Joyce A (Mrs Osborne) & John P. Educ: Pa State Col. Polit & Govt Pos: Chmn, Wayne Co Rep Comt, Pa & Northeast Chmn Asn, Rep Party, 53-; asst chmn, Rep State Comt, 62; primary campaign co-chmn, Scranton for Gov, 62; Dep Secy of Hwy, Pa, 63. Bus & Prof Pos: Proj engr, Pa Hwy Dept, 32-36; plant engr, Lummus Co, 55-61; consult engr, L F Burlein Engrs, 61-63; chmn, Pa Turnpike Comn, 63- Mem: Soc Prof Engrs; Am Soc Mech Engrs; Am Soc Hwy Engrs; Am Ord Asn; Mason. Relig: Lutheran. Mailing Add: 758 Ridge St Honesdale PA 18431

BURLESON, DAN L (D)
WVa State Deleg
b Lang, WVa, Jan 23, 47; s Orville C Burleson & Pauline Reid B; m 1968 to Carolyn Sue Main; c Andrew & Michelle. Educ: Southern WVa Community Col, 74- Polit & Govt Pos: Pres local union 9690, United Mine Workers Am, 71-72, exec bd mem, 72-, Int Rules Comt, 73- & temporary bd dirs, Fed Credit Union, 73; WVa State Deleg, 75- Mil Serv: Entered as Pvt, Marine Corps, 66, released as Sgt, after serv in Hq Bn, Washington, DC; Good Conduct Medal. Mem: Moose; Lions; Am Legion Post 106; Southgate CB Club; Jaycees. Relig: Baptist. Legal Res: 1328 Popular St Mullens WV 25882 Mailing Add: Box 53 Mullens WV 25882

BURLESON, DAVID J (D)
Ark State Rep
b Auburn, Ala, Dec 31, 19; s David J Burleson & Alice Wesson R; m 1945 to Lillian Oliver; c Ann (Mrs Owen), Clare (Mrs Simmonds), Jane (Mrs Turner) & David O. Educ: Univ Ark, BSBA, 47, LLB, 50; Sigma Chi. Polit & Govt Pos: Ark State Rep, 59-67 & 75- Bus & Prof Pos: Attorney, Fayetteville, Ark, 50- Mil Serv: Entered as Aviation Cadet, Army Air Force, 42, released as Capt, 45, after serv in 10th Air Force, China-Burma-India, 43-45; Lt Col, Air Force Res, currently. Mem: Ark Bar Asn; Mason (32 degree); Ark Farm Bur; Am Legion; VFW. Relig: Methodist. Legal Res: 1028 Sunset Dr Fayetteville AR 72701 Mailing Add: PO Box 507 Fayetteville AR 72701

BURLESON, OMAR (D)
US Rep, Tex
b Mar 19, 06; s J M Burleson & Betty B; m 1929 to Ruth DeWeese. Educ: Abilene Christian Col, 24-26; Hardin-Simmons Univ, 26-27; Cumberland Univ Law Sch, 27-29; Univ Tex, LLB; Vanderbilt Univ. Hon Degrees: LLD, Hardin-Simmons Univ, 67. Polit & Govt Pos: Spec agt, Fed Bur Invest, formerly; co judge, Jones Co, Tex & co attorney, formerly; US Rep, Tex, 47-; deleg, Dem Nat Conv, 68; deleg, Dem Nat Mid-Term Conf, 74. Bus & Prof Pos: Attorney-at-law. Mil Serv: Navy, 3 years. Legal Res: Anson TX 79501 Mailing Add: US House of Rep Washington DC 20515

BURLESON, ROBERT ODELL (D)
Tenn State Rep
Mailing Add: Roan Mountain TN 37687

BURLESON, WILLIAM BRICE (D)
b Yellville, Ark, Oct 11, 38; s William Brice Burleson, Sr & Oza Lancaster B; m 1964 to Phyllis Ann Rea; c Scotty Dean & Robin Dee. Educ: Yellville-Summit High Sch, grad, 55. Polit & Govt Pos: Secy, Marion Co Dem Cent Comt, Ark, formerly; fire chief, Yellville Fire Dept, 68- Bus & Prof Pos: Ins agt, Tank Rea Ins Agency, 60- Mil Serv: Entered as Pvt, Army, 60, released as SP-5, 66, after serv in 346th Ord Co. Mem: Yellville Jaycees. Relig: Protestant. Mailing Add: PO Box 457 Yellville AR 72687

BURLISON, BILL D (D)
US Rep, Mo
b Wardell, Mo; s J I Burlison & Lillie Marler B; m to Barbara Ann Humphreys; c James David, Andrew Jefferson & Laura Anne. Educ: Southeast Mo State Col, BA & BS in Educ; Univ Mo, LLB & MEd; Phi Alpha Theta; Phi Delta Phi; Pi Kappa Delta; Sigma Chi; Alpha Phi Omega. Polit & Govt Pos: Spec asst to Attorney Gen, Mo, formerly; prosecuting attorney, Cape Girardeau Co, formerly; US Rep, Mo, 69- Mil Serv: Marine Corps, 3 years. Mem: AF&AM. Relig: Baptist. Legal Res: 740 Watkins Cape Girardeau MO 63701 Mailing Add: 1338 Longworth House Off Bldg Washington DC 20515

BURNETT, BENIFIELD (R)
Chmn, Carlotte Co Rep Party, Va
b Prince Edward Co, Va, Oct 8, 30; s Farris Berkley Burnett & Effie V Hall B; m 1951 to Ruth Bethel Fairbanks; c Robert Lewis, Shirley Rae, Teresa Ann & Sherry Lee. Polit & Govt Pos: Campaign mgr, Charlotte Co Rep Elec Comt, Va, 64; chmn, Goldwater Comt, 64; vchmn, Fifth Dist Rep Party, formerly; chmn, Charlotte Co Rep Party, 64-67 & currently. Bus & Prof Pos: Pres, Keysville Heating, Inc, 60- Mil Serv: Navy, 48-52. Mem: Keysville AF&AM Lodge 154; Charlotte Co Red Cross (dir). Relig: Methodist. Mailing Add: RFD 1 Box 378 Keysville VA 23947

BURNETT, BOB J (R)
Wyo State Rep
Mailing Add: 1067 Bonita Rd Laramie WY 82070

BURNETT, GAIL TINER (R)
Secy, Lake Co Rep Party, Colo
b Hartshorne, Okla, Apr 22, 20; d George Tiner & Sadie Poor T; m 1956 to John Wesley Burnett, Jr; c John Wesley, III. Educ: Colo Mountain Col, 69. Polit & Govt Pos: Rep committeewoman, Precinct Four, Colo, 68-; secy, Lake Co Rep Party, 69-; treas, Lake Co Rep Women, formerly; second vchmn, Lake Co Rep Cent Comt, currently. Mem: Rebekah (chmn UN pilgrimage for youth, sponsored by Odd Fellows & Rebekahs, chief matriarch, Ladies Encampment Auxiliary); Odd Fellow Cemetery Asn. Relig: Christian Church of NAm. Legal Res: 424 E Tenth Leadville CO 80461 Mailing Add: Box 582 Leadville CO 80461

BURNETT, JACK ALEXANDER (D)
Tenn State Rep
b Saundersville, Tenn, Mar 17, 32; s Dave M Burnett & Pauline Gregory B; m 1958 to Mary Carpenter; c Barrie Alice & Melissa Karen. Educ: Mid Tenn State Univ, 3 years. Polit & Govt Pos: Chmn, Sumner Co Dem Party, Tenn, 71-75; Tenn State Rep, 44th Dist, 75- Mil Serv: Entered as Pvt, Army, 49, released as Maj, 69, after serv in 772 MP Bn, Korea, 51-52; Lt Col, Tenn Nat Guard; UN Medal; Korea Medal with Two Bronze Stars; Nat Defense Medal; Good Conduct Medal. Mem: VFW; Am Legion. Relig: Episcopal. Mailing Add: 271 Sherry Circle Gallatin TN 37066

BURNETT, SAM THOMAS (D)
Tenn State Rep
b Nashville, Tenn, Aug 1, 42; s Sam T Burnett & Elizabeth Clarke B; m 1967 to Wanda Gail; c Michael Todd & Phillip Duane. Educ: Cumberland Univ, AA; Tenn Wesleyan Col, BS; Univ Tenn Col Law, JD; Phi Alpha Delta; Sigma Phi Epsilon. Polit & Govt Pos: Attorney, Jamestown, Tenn, 67-; Tenn State Rep, 71- Mem: Tenn & Am Bar Asns; Am Trial Lawyers Asn; Rotary. Relig: Church of Christ. Mailing Add: Box 609 Jamestown TN 38556

BURNEY, DWIGHT WILLARD (R)
b Hartington, Nebr, Jan 7, 92; m 1914 to Edna Wales (deceased); m 1965 to Grayce E Hahn; c Donald, Dwight, Jr, Willard & Keith. Educ: Univ SDak, 2 years. Polit & Govt Pos: Nebr State Sen, 45-57, Spec Sessions, 46, 52 & 54; Lt Gov, Nebr, 57-65, Gov, 60-61. Bus & Prof Pos: High sch teacher & supt, formerly; farming & livestock bus, currently. Publ: Nebraska's farmer governor, Hasting Tribune, 67. Mem: Scottish Rite; Mason, KCCH (32nd degree); Eastern Star; Nebr Ment Health Bd. Honors & Awards: Agr Award for Distinguished Serv, 66; Key Man in Agr, 62; 50 Year Shipper Award, 66; Adm, Nebr Navy. Relig: Congregational. Mailing Add: Polk NE 68654

BURNHAM, BARBARA WELLS (D)
Mem, Hull Dem Town Comt, Mass
b Quincy, Mass, Dec 14, 46; d Roger Appleton Burnham & Phyllis Kline B; single. Educ: Boston Univ, BA, 68; Univ Md, College Park, 70-71; Temple Univ, summer 71; Syracuse Univ, 73-; Alpha Phi. Polit & Govt Pos: Peace Corps vol, Venezuela, 68-70; area coordr, Gerry Studds for Cong, 12th Dist, Mass, 72; alt deleg, Dem Nat Conv, 72; town coordr, McGovern Primary Campaign, Hull, Mass, 72; mem, Hull Dem Town Comt, Mass, 72-; social planner, Syracuse Model Cities, NY, 72- Bus & Prof Pos: Teacher, Hull Pub Schs, 71. Mem: Nat Orgn Women; Citizens for Participation Polit; Women's Polit Caucus. Mailing Add: 63 Highland Ave Hull MA 02145

BURNHAM, ERNEST C, JR (R)
Conn State Rep
Mailing Add: PO Box 172 Clinton CT 06413

BURNS, ANDREW JOSEPH, (D)
Md State Deleg
b Baltimore, Md, July 25, 27; s Andrew Joseph Burns, Sr & Anne Belle Tunstall B; m 1953 to Shirley Nina Taylor; c Andrew J, III, Michael T, Raymond B, Richard T, Patrick T & Christopher T. Educ: Loyola Col, Baltimore, Md, BS, 50; Univ Md Law Sch, LLB, 60; Dean's List, Loyola Col; Zeta Eta Theta; Gamma Eta Gamma. Polit & Govt Pos: Md State Deleg, 67- Bus & Prof Pos: Attorney-at-law, Baltimore, Md, 60- Mil Serv: Seaman, Navy, 45-46; reentered as Ens, 50, released as Lt(jg), 54, after serv in USS Putnam; Lt, Naval Res, 47-50 & 54-; NAtlantic & Am Defense Ribbons; World War II Victory Medal; Korean & China Serv Medals; UN & Naval Res Medals; Japan & Ger Occup Medals. Mem: Am Bar Asn; Asns of Defense Trial Counsel; KofC (4 degree); Grand Advocate, Order of Alhambra; Friendly Sons of St Patrick. Relig: Catholic. Legal Res: 6033 Bellona Ave Baltimore MD 21212 Mailing Add: 1027 Munsey Bldg Calvert & Fayette St Baltimore MD 21202

BURNS, ARTHUR FRANK (R)
Chmn Bd Gov, Fed Reserve Syst
b Stanislau, Austria, Apr 27, 04; s Nathan Burns & Sarah B Juran B; m 1930 to Helen Bernstein; c David & Joseph. Educ: Columbia Univ, AB, 25, AM, 25, PhD, 34; Phi Beta Kappa. Hon Degrees: LLD, Lehigh Univ, Brown Univ, Dartmouth Col, Oberlin Col, Wesleyan Univ, Swarthmore Col, Long Island Univ, Univ Chicago, Rikkyo Univ, Fordham Univ, Columbia Univ, 70, NY Univ, 70 & Univ Calif, 70; LHD, Rutgers Univ & Pepperdine Col, 70; ScD, Univ Pa & Univ Rochester; DEcon, Chungang Univ, Korea, 70; DPhil, Hebrew Univ, Jerusalem, 70; dipl, Cath Univ Am, 73. Polit & Govt Pos: Chmn, Presidential Coun Econ Adv, 53-56; mem, US Adv Coun on Social Security Financing, 57-58; mem, NY Temporary State Comn on Econ Expansion, 59-60; mem, Presidential Adv Comn on

Labor-Mgt Policy, 61-66; mem, Gov Comt on Minimum Wage, NY, 64; Counr to the President of the US, 69-70; Chmn Bd Gov, Fed Reserve Syst, 70- Bus & Prof Pos: Prof econ, Columbia Univ, 41-69; pres, Nat Bur Econ Research, New York, 57-67. Publ: Measuring Business Cycles (w W C Mitchell), 46; Frontiers of Economic Knowledge, 54; The Business Cycle in a Changing World, 69. Mem: Am Econ Asn; Am Acad Arts & Sci; Am Statist Asn; Acad Polit Sci; Am Philos Soc. Relig: Jewish. Legal Res: Watergate East 2510 Virginia Ave NW Washington DC 20037 Mailing Add: c/o Bd of Gov Fed Reserve Syst Washington DC 20551

BURNS, BRIAN DOUGLAS (D)
Lt Gov, Vt
b Burlington, Vt, Nov 17, 39; s Walter F Burns & Eugenia Lanctot B; m 1959 to Linda Jeanne Brouillard; c Rebecca Anne, Brian Patrick, Jennifer Lynn, Cynthia Jeanne & Brendan Alton. Educ: Univ Vt. Polit & Govt Pos: State pres, Young Dem Clubs, 66-68; Vt State Rep, 67-74; vchmn, Burlington Dem Party, Vt, 68, chmn, 69; mem legis coun, State of Vt, 69-; Lt Gov, Vt, 75- Bus & Prof Pos: Pres, Richmond Realty, Vt, 4 years. Mil Serv: Entered as Pvt, Army-Vt Nat Guard, 59, released as Pfc, 59, after serv in Judge Adv Gen Corps. Mem: Truax Assocs of Richmond. Relig: Catholic. Mailing Add: 67 Caroline St Burlington VT 05401

BURNS, DONALD HOWARD (D)
Maine State Rep
b Skowhegan, Maine, Mar 18, 28; s Harry W Burns & Maude Clevland Burns Creamer; m 1970 to Patricia Hall; c Norleen & Lorriana. Educ: High Sch grad. Polit & Govt Pos: Chmn, Somerset Co Dem, 72-74; chmn, Anson Town Comt, 73-; Maine State Rep, 75- Bus & Prof Pos: Criminal investr, Somerset Co Sheriff Dept, 69-74. Mil Serv: Entered as Pvt, Air Force, 46, released as MSgt, 68; Retired; Commendation Medal with one Oak Leaf Cluster; Good Conduct Ribbon & several other serv ribbons. Mem: Mason; Lions; VFW; Am Legion. Relig: Methodist. Mailing Add: Embden Pond Rd North Anson ME 04958

BURNS, EDWARD FRANCIS, JR (R)
Pa State Rep
b Branchdale, Pa, Jan 28, 31; s Edward Francis Burns & Regina Larkin B; m 1955 to Joan Friel; c Edward, Joseph & Robert. Educ: LaSalle Col, BA, 52; Temple Univ, MEd, 57, grad study, 57-62; Villanova Univ, 62-63; Prafectus Club. Polit & Govt Pos: Recreation dir, Bensalem Twp, 60-69, sch dir, 71-; Pa State Rep, 73- Bus & Prof Pos: Elem teacher, Philadelphia Bd Educ, 54-58; sec teacher, Pennsbury Sch Dist, 58-59, Neshaminy Sch Dist, 59-72. Mil Serv: Entered as Seaman, Navy, 50, released as 3/C PO after serv in DE 585-USS D A Joy, Atlantic, 52-54; Chief Warrant Officer, Navy Res, 65-72, Naval Air Sta & Aviation Schs Command; Nat Defense Serv Ribbon & Star; UN Korean Conflict & 2 Stars; Naval Reserve Medal; Armed Forces Reserve Medal. Publ: Co-auth series prog hist texts (w Dr Donald Chipman), US Navy, 71. Mem: US Naval Reserve Asn; Am Legion. Relig: Roman Catholic. Mailing Add: Capitol Bldg Harrisburg PA 17120

BURNS, FORREST G (D)
Colo State Rep
Mailing Add: 311 Willow Valley Rd Lamar CO 81052

BURNS, GARTH F (D)
Nat Committeeman, Young Dem Clubs of Kans
b Jacksonville, Ill, May 2, 49; s Ralph F Burns & Renee Smith B; m 1975 to Deborah Ann Stansbrough. Educ: Hutchinson Community Jr Col, AA, 69; Univ Kans, 69-71 & 73-75; Young Dem of Kans; Concerned Students for Higher Educ; Student Mobilization. Polit & Govt Pos: Pres, Hutchinson Community Jr Col Young Dem, 68-69; campaign staff mem, Bevkowitz for Douglas Co Attorney, Kans, 72; treas, Douglas Co Dem Cent Comt, 72-; nat committeeman, Young Dem Clubs of Kans, 73-; voter regist dir, Douglas Co, 74. Bus & Prof Pos: Labor pool, Packaging Corp Am; dishwasher & food handler, Univ Kans Dorms; truck driver, Standard Mercantile Co Inc; hod carrier, Mel Quisanbevry Masonary Co; laborer, Comet Corp. Mem: East Lawrence Improv Asn; Am Soc Mech Engrs Student Chap at Univ Kans; Inst Elec & Electronics Engrs Student Chap at Univ Kans. Mailing Add: 1319 New Jersey Lawrence KS 66044

BURNS, HAROLD WILBUR (R)
NH State Rep
b Whitefield, NH, Dec 4, 26; s Clayton W Burns & Lillian A Savage B; m 1948 to Eleanor A Tedesco; c John M, Sandra L (Mrs Kimball) & Scott C. Educ: Whitefield High Sch, grad. Polit & Govt Pos: Mem, Whitefield Sch Bd, NH, 62-; NH State Rep, currently, vchmn banks & ins comt, NH House of Rep; mem exec bd, Coun Ins Legislators. Bus & Prof Pos: Partner, Burns Ins Agency, Whitefield, NH, 51- Mil Serv: Entered as Pvt, Army, 45, released as Sgt, 46, after serv in 1st Army, 45-46. Mem: Nat Asn Mutual Ins Agents; Am Legion; Mason; Grange; Coos Co Law Enforcement. Relig: Methodist. Mailing Add: Burns Lake Whitefield NH 03598

BURNS, JAMES MACGREGOR (D)
b Melrose, Mass, Aug 3, 18; s Robert Arthur Burns & Mildred Bunce B; m to Joan Simpson; c David, Stewart, Deborah & Mecki. Educ: William Col, BA, 39; Harvard Univ, MA & PhD, 47. Polit & Govt Pos: Exec dir, Nonferrous Metals Comn, Nat War Labor Bd, Denver, Colo, 42-43; deleg, Dem Nat Mid Term Conf, 74. Bus & Prof Pos: Prof polit sci, Williams Col, 41- Mil Serv: Entered as Pvt, Army, 43, released as M/Sgt, 46, after serv in several inf div in Pac & Western Pac; Bronze Star. Publ: Roosevelt: The Soldier of Freedom, Harcourt Brace, 70; Presidential Government, Prentice-Hall, 65; Uncommon Sense, Harper & Row, 72. Mem: Am Polit Sci Asn (pres, 75-76); Am Hist Soc; Am Philos Soc. Honors & Awards: Pulitzer Prize; Nat Book Award; Francis Parkman Prize. Mailing Add: High Mowing Bee Hill Rd Williamstown MA 01267

BURNS, JOHN HOWARD
b Pauls Valley, Okla, Dec 12, 13; s Arthur Parsons Burns & Susan Elizabeth Matthews B; single. Educ: Denison Univ, 31-32; Univ Okla, BA, 35. Polit & Govt Pos: Secy to Mem of Cong, 40-41; vconsul, Juarez, Mex, 41-43; vconsul, Belem, Para, Brazil, 43-44; third secy, Am Embassy, Rio de Janeiro, Brazil 44-47; first secy, Haiti, 49-52; foreign serv inspector, 52-54; mem staff, Nat War Col, 54-55; consul gen, Frankfurt, 55-57; exec dir, Bur European Affairs, 57-58; spec asst, Dep Under Secy of State for Admin, 58-60; counr, Bonn, 60-61; US Ambassador, Cent African Repub, 61-63; spec asst, Supreme Allied Comdr, Europe, 63-65; US Ambassador, Tanzania, 65-69; Dir Gen, Foreign Serv, Dept of State, 69-73. Mailing Add: Pauls Valley OK 73075

BURNS, JOHN J (D)
b Binghamton, NY, July 12, 21; s William P Burns & Marie Hennessey B; m 1948 to A Teresa McMahon; c Patrick, Sheila, John, Joseph, Thomas, Marie, Jean, Ann, Daniel, Vincent, Teresa & Robert. Polit & Govt Pos: Exec asst to mayor, Binghamton, NY, 53-57, mayor, 58-65; chmn, NY Dem State Comt, 65-73; deleg, Dem Nat Conv, 68. Mil Serv: Entered serv in Coast Guard, 42, released as Radarman 1/C, 45, after serv in Atlantic Theater. Mem: Police Benevolent Asn; Int Asn Fire Fighters; Am Fedn State Co & Munic Employees; Am Legion; KofC. Relig: Roman Catholic. Mailing Add: 97 Main St Binghamton NY 13905

BURNS, MARY FRANCES (D)
Mem, Mo State Dem Comt
b Gallatin, Mo, July 30, 09; d Virgil Edward Knight & Julia Nichols K; m 1931 to Russell Burns; c Conrad Ray & Julia Kaye (Mrs Stanley Norris); three grandchildren. Educ: Chillicothe Bus Col, grad secy & bookkeeper, 29. Polit & Govt Pos: Vchmn, Daviess Co Dem Cent Comt, Mo, 62-64 & 70-74, chmn, 64-70; mem, Mo State Dem Comt, 66- Mem: Rebekah; Past Noble Grand Club; Mo State Dem Club; New Frontier Dem Women's Club. Honors & Awards: Awarded Ten Year Gold Pin as 4-H Leader. Relig: Methodist. Mailing Add: Rte 3 Gallatin MO 64640

BURNS, MICHAEL EMMETT (R)
b Texas City, Tex; s William Arthur Burns, II & Betty Siros B; m 1966 to Diana Sessions. Educ: Harvard Col, AB, 65; Univ Tex Law Sch, LLB, 68, Grad Sch Bus, 69; George Washington Univ Sch Bus, 70-73; Hasty Pudding Club. Polit & Govt Pos: Admin intern, US Rep Joe Skubitz, Kans, 65; staff attorney, Rep Party of Tex, 68-69; legis asst, US Sen John Tower, Tex, 69-71, Minority Counsel, Comt on Banking, Housing & Urban Affairs, US Senate, 71-73; exec asst, Comptroller of the Currency, 73- Mem: Am, Tex & DC Bar Asns; Phi Delta Phi. Legal Res: Austin TX Mailing Add: 421 1/2 Sixth St SE Washington DC 20003

BURNS, ROBERT H (R)
b Philip, SDak, Sept 15, 28; s Harry D Burns & Elizabeth Harvey B; m 1949 to Doris E Sorensen; c James, Deborah & Cynthia. Educ: Philip High Sch, SDak, 4 years. Polit & Govt Pos: Vchmn, SDak Young Rep League, 54-56, nat committeeman, 56-58; chmn, Lyman Co Rep Cent Comt, 57-62; vchmn, Young Rep Nat Fedn, 58-60; SDak State Rep, 60-64; mem, Lyman Co Sch Bd, 67-68; SDak State Sen, 68-72; chmn, SDak Rep State Cent Comt, 71-73. Bus & Prof Pos: Mgr, Tri State Milling Co, Vivian, SDak, 50-69; owner & mgr, Vivian Tel Co, 57-69; owner & mgr, Burns Feed Lots, 61-69; dir, Big Bank Bldg Corp, Pierre, SDak, 69. Mem: Mason; Elks; Wheat Growers; Isaak Walton League. Honors & Awards: Named Jaycee Outstanding Young Am. Relig: Lutheran. Mailing Add: Vivian SD 57576

BURNS, ROBERT J (D)
SDak State Rep
Mailing Add: 1122 S Second Ave Sioux Falls SD 57105

BURNS, ROBERT JOHN (D)
Supvr, Johnson Co, Iowa
b Oxford, Iowa, Aug 22, 22; s John William Burns & Regina Cash B; m 1944 to Ada Margaret Wilson; c Michael, Sheila, Anthony, Stephen, Linda, Margery & Maureen. Educ: Univ Iowa; Univ Kans. Polit & Govt Pos: Dem committeeman, Johnson Co Dem Party, Iowa, 56-64; Iowa State Sen, 21st Dist, 65-69; Supvr, Johnson Co, 71- Bus & Prof Pos: Gen agt, Lincoln Mutual Life Ins. Mil Serv: Entered as Pvt, Army, 43 released as Sgt, 45, after serv in Rainbow Div; Purple Heart; Combat Inf Badge; Battle of Rhineland Ribbon & 2 Battle Stars. Mem: Am Legion; Kiwanis. Relig: Catholic. Mailing Add: 15 Bedford St Iowa City IA 52240

BURNS, WILLIAM L (R)
NY State Assemblyman
Mailing Add: 23 Whitney Dr Amityville NY 11701

BURNS, WILLIAM LLOYD (R)
Finance Dir, Gogebic Co Rep Comt, Mich
b Central Lake, Mich, May 20, 94; s Elias Burns & Mary Ann Wilson B; m 1919 to H Mable Williams; c Robert William (deceased), Dorr Harold, Jeanne Louise (Mrs Bennett), Mary Margaret (Mrs Tinder) & Roberta Gayle (deceased). Educ: Central Lake High Sch, grad. Polit & Govt Pos: Finance dir, Gogebic Co Rep Comt, Mich, 45-; mem, State Cent Comt at various times; deleg or alt deleg, Rep Nat Conv, 24 years. Bus & Prof Pos: Dir, Gogebic Nat Bank, Ironwood, 12 years, Lake Superior Dist Power Co, 25 years & Upper Peninsula Develop Bur, 30 years; pres, Burns Chevrolet-Cadillac, Inc, 27-55; pres, Cent Credit Corp, 31-; pres, Upper Peninsula Develop Bur, 41-43. Mem: Kiwanis; Mason; Shrine; Elks; Planning Comn. Honors & Awards: Man of the Year, Ironwood CofC, 59, Citizen of the Year, 72. Relig: Methodist. Mailing Add: 215 E Arch St Ironwood MI 49938

BURNSIDE, MAURICE GWINN (D)
b Columbia, SC, Aug 23, 02; s James Walter Burnside & Olivia America McCants B; m 1937 to Evelyn Jackson Pell; c Marilyn McCants. Educ: The Citadel, 19-22; Furman Univ, BS, 26; Univ Tex, MA, 28; Duke Univ, PhD, 38; Lambda Chi Alpha; Pi Gamma Mu. Polit & Govt Pos: Mem, Parole & Probation Exam Bd, WVa, 39-41; head, Workers Educ, 43-45; head, Citizens Recreation Prog, Huntington, 43-45; regional coordr, Inter-Am Affairs, WVa, Eastern & Southern Ohio & Eastern Ky Cult & Bus Rels; US Rep, WVa, 49-53 & 55-57; br chief, Nat Security Agency, 52; deleg & mem platform comt, Dem Nat Conv, 60; former asst to Secy Defense; legis liaison for Defense Dept, US House Rep, 61-68. Bus & Prof Pos: Instr, Greenville High Sch, SC, 31-32; purchaser, Duke Libr, 33-35; grad research in off, Gov, SC, 35-36; instr, Auburn Univ, 36-37; prof polit sci, Marshall Univ, 37-48, head dept, 41-45; legis rep, Nat Educ Asn, 59-61; mgrs rep, 53; pres, Tri-State Tobacco Warehouse Co, 56-70. Publ: Pardon, Parole & Indeterminate Sentence with Special Reference to South Carolina, 38; co-auth, Union Check List of Newspapers of US & Canada, Govt of WVa, 49. Mem: Am Polit Sci Asn; Am Pub Admin Asn; Am Cols & Univs (founder, Int Rels Clubs); Am Asn Univ Prof; Soc Polit Sci Asn. Relig: Presbyterian; elder. Mailing Add: 2009 Hermitage Rd Wilson NC 27893

BURNSIDE, ROBERT H (D)
SC State Rep
Mailing Add: Box 1516 Columbia SC 29202

BURRALL, FREDERIC H (R)
Fla State Rep
b Green Bay, Wis, Sept 19, 35; s Frederic M Burrall & Arvilla Hoberg B; m 1962 to Bette

Stewart; c Christina & Julianna. Educ: Univ Wis-Green Bay, 57-58; Fla State Univ, 58-59; Univ Fla, BS in Jour, 61. Polit & Govt Pos: Fla State Rep, 74- Bus & Prof Pos: Publicity dir, Fla Dept of Com, 67-70; ed, Punta Gorda Herald News, Fla, 70-74. Mil Serv: Entered as Airman Basic, Air Force, 53, released as Airman 3/C, 57, after serv in Air Police, Europe & Far East, 54-57. Mem: Elks; Am Legion. Mailing Add: 206 NW Salem Ave Port Charlotte FL 32304

BURRELL, CONSUELO KITZES (D)
NMex State Sen
Mailing Add: Box 418 Santa Fe NM 87501

BURRESS, RICHARD THOMAS (R)
b Omaha, Nebr, Dec 22, 22; s B J Burress & Lea Dickinson B; m 1951 to Jan Eaton; c Bonny & Lee. Educ: Univ Omaha, AB, 44; Univ Iowa Law Sch, JD, 48; NY Univ Grad Law Sch, ML, 53. Polit & Govt Pos: Spec agt, Fed Bur Invest, 48-53; dep asst gen counsel, Nat Labor Rels Bd, 56-58; minority counsel, House Educ & Labor Comt, 61-63; counsel, House Rep Conf, 65-69; dir, House Rep Policy Comt, 65-69; Dep Asst to the President, 69-71; chmn, Renegotiation Bd, 71-74; White House liaison & asst to Vice President, 74; assoc dir, Hoover Inst, 74- Bus & Prof Pos: Attorney, Lockheed Aircraft Corp, 58-61. Mil Serv: 1st Lt, Marine Corps, 43-46. Mem: Am & Calif Bar Asns; Soc Former Spec Agts, FBI. Mailing Add: 5521 Mohican Rd Washington DC 20016

BURRIS, RICHARD S (R)
Mem Exec Comt, Brown Co Rep Party, Wis
b Madison, Wis, May 17, 29; s Kenneth C Burris & Nora Thurber B; m 1954 to Bernice E Mackin; c Nancy Ann, Kathleen Marie, Sharon Mary, Mary Jo & Richard S. Educ: Univ Wis, Madison, BS, Theta Delta Chi. Polit & Govt Pos: Chmn, Comt to Reelect John W Byrnes, Cong, 64 & 66; secy, Brown Co Rep Party, Wis, 67-69, mem exec comt & chmn precinct orgn, 69-71, chmn, 71-75, mem exec comt, 75- Bus & Prof Pos: Supt diversified prod div, Green Bay Packaging, 58-75, sales rep, 75-; co-chmn nat affairs legis comt, Green Bay CofC, 72-73; chmn state affairs-legis comt, Green Bay Area CofC, 73-74. Mil Serv: Entered as 2nd Lt, Army, 54, released as 1st Lt, 56, after serv in 536 MP Co, ETO, Ger, 55-56; Capt, Army Res, 4 years; Occup Medal. Mem: YMCA; Tech Asn Pulp & Paper Indust. Relig: Catholic. Mailing Add: 2673 S Van Buren Green Bay WI 54301

BURROUGHS, CLIFFORD E (R)
Iowa State Sen
b Butler Co, Iowa, Jan 28, 17; s Alfred Burroughs & Effie Bohner B; m 1940 to Mary Virginia Pooley; c Vicki (Mrs Bixler), Craig, Paul, Kent, Linda (Mrs Mataragas), Bruce, Neil & Brian. Educ: Greene High Sch, 35. Polit & Govt Pos: Mayor, Greene, Iowa, 48-50; chmn finance, Butler Co Rep Party, 62-66, chmn, 69-74; Iowa State Sen, 74- Bus & Prof Pos: Vpres & dir, Investment Planning, 68-72; treas & dir, Allison Indust, 71-73, dir, 73-74. Mil Serv: Pvt, Army, 45, serv in Engrs & as Separation Counr. Mem: Farm Bur; Am Legion; Trans-Miss Philatelic Soc; Iowans for Right to Work (dir). Mailing Add: 510 Fifth St Greene IA 50636

BURROUS, KERMIT O (R)
Ind State Rep
b Peru, Ind, 1931. Educ: Ball State Univ; Ind Univ. Polit & Govt Pos: Ind State Rep, 60-64, 67-72 & 75- Bus & Prof Pos: Farmer; salesman, Duane Horst Ford Sales. Mem: Kiwanis (bd dirs). Relig: Methodist; Kokomo dist leader, Mexico Methodist Church. Mailing Add: Rte 3 Peru IN 46970

BURROW, CHARLES C, III (D)
Mem, Ark Dem State Comt
b Wynne, Ark, Nov 15, 45; s Charles C Burrow, II & Mildred Burnette B; m 1967 to Mary Christine Johnston; c Jessica Johnston & Charles C, IV. Educ: Marion Inst, 63-64; Univ Ark, BSBA, 68; Sigma Alpha Epsilon. Polit & Govt Pos: Bd mem, First Dist Off Econ Opportunity, 73-74 & State Hosp Bd, 74-75; mem, Ark Dem State Comt, 74- Bus & Prof Pos: Owner, Burrow Farm, McCrory, Ark. Mem: Rotary (bd, 74); Farm Bur (pres, 74); Young Dem. Relig: Methodist. Legal Res: 1107 Marion Wynne AR 72396 Mailing Add: Box 268 McCrory AR 72101

BURROW, GORDON W (R)
NY State Assemblyman
Mailing Add: 65 Harvard Ave Yonkers NY 10710

BURROWS, ADOLPH J (D)
NH State Rep
Mailing Add: 3 Parson Ave RFD 1 Box 199 Claremont NH 03743

BURROWS, GEORGE BILL (D)
Nebr State Sen
b Adams, Nebr, Oct 21, 30; s Chase Burrows & Blanche N Graves B; m 1954 to Norma J Conneally; c Greg W, Jay A, Mark S & Laureen A. Educ: Nebr Wesleyan Univ, 1 year; Univ Nebr, BSci; Theta Chi. Polit & Govt Pos: Nebr State Sen, 75- Mil Serv: Entered as 2nd Lt, Army, 53, released as 1st Lt, after serv in Korea, 54-55. Mailing Add: Rte 1 Adams NE 68301

BURROWS, MARY MCCAULEY (R)
Ore State Rep
b Palco, Kans; d Carl McCauley & Lucille Cottington M; m 1952 to Charles Burrows; c Charles Patrick, Thomas Michael, Candice Shawn & Shane Micah. Educ: Northwest Christian Col, 50-52. Polit & Govt Pos: Secy, Western Shasta Co Rep Assembly, Ore, 62-65; treas, Young Rep Fedn Ore, 66-67, co-chmn, 67-68; Rep precinct committeewoman, Lane Co, currently; chmn, Lane Co Young Rep, 67; vchmn, Lane Co Rep Cent Comt, 68-70; campaign chmn, Elect Bob Packwood Sen, Lane Co, 68 & Reelect Gov Tom McCall, 70; secy, Ore Rep State Cent Comt, 71-72; Ore State Rep, Dist 41, 73- Mem: Western Lane Co Rep Women (publicity chmn). Relig: Christian; deaconess, First Christian Church, Eugene, Ore. Mailing Add: 1305 Firwood Way Eugene OR 97401

BURROWS, PAT (D)
Colo State Rep
Mailing Add: 300 Iris St Broomfield CO 80020

BURRUSS, ROBERT S, JR (R)
Minority Leader, Va State Senate
b Lynchburg, Va, Nov 9, 14; m 1947 to Margaret Hanna Brooks; c Rebecca M, James R, Hanna B & Mary Scott. Educ: Va Polytech Inst, BS. Polit & Govt Pos: Va State Sen, 64-, Minority Leader, Va State Senate, currently. Bus & Prof Pos: Dir, Peoples Nat Bank & Trust Co, formerly; mem adv bd, First & Merchants Nat Bank; owner & operator, Ralco Stores, Inc; owner, R S Burruss Lumber Co, 53-; lumber mfr & farmer. Mil Serv: Army Corps Engrs, 5 years, released as Lt Col, after serv in ETO. Mem: Izaak Walton League; Boonsboro Co Club; Willis River Hunt Club; Shrine; Elks. Relig: Methodist. Legal Res: 3240 Landon St Lynchburg VA 24503 Mailing Add: PO Box 270 Lynchburg VA 24505

BURSLEY, GILBERT E (R)
Assoc Pres Pro-Tem, Mich State Senate
b Ann Arbor, Mich, Feb 28, 13; s Philip Everette Bursley & Flora Peters B; m 1949 to Vivette Mumtaz; c Philip Everette, II. Educ: Univ Mich, BA, 34; Harvard Bus Sch, MBA, 36; George Washington Univ, 53-54, postgrad work in int rels. Polit & Govt Pos: Mil attache, Istanbul, 46-49; with Joint US Mil Adv Mission, Athens, 49-52, Army Psychol Warfare Hq, Wash, 53 & UN Truce Supvr Orgn, Palestine; sr mil adv, Israel-Jordan & Israel-Egypt Mixed Armistice Comns, 54; Am consul & pub affairs officer in chg US Info Agency Prog, Belgian Congo, French Equatorial Africa, Ruanda Urundi, Cameroons & Angola, 55-57; consult, World Wide Broadcasting Found, 57; chmn, Ann Arbor Rep City Comt, Mich, 59-60; Mich State Rep, 60-62; Mich State Sen, 64-, asst pres pro tem, Mich State Senate, 66, assoc pres pro tem, currently, Asst Majority Leader, 71-75, chmn educ comt, formerly, chmn, int com comt, urban mass transportation comt, abortion law reform comt, econ develop comt, corp comt & agr comt, currently; chmn, Mich Comn on Intergovt Rels; mem, US Trade & Investment Mission to Cameroons & Ivory Coast, 68; Mich UN Day chmn, 68-75; mem, Mich Bicentennial Comn, 72-; mem exec & steering comts, Educ Comn of the States, 73-; vchmn educ task force, Nat Conf State Legis, 74- Bus & Prof Pos: Asst dir, Develop Coun, Univ Mich, 57-65; assoc, Conductron Corp, 65-66. Mil Serv: Army, World War II, 3 Campaign Stars; Lt Col, Korean War. Mem: Elks; Rotary; VFW; Am Legion; SAR. Relig: Episcopal. Mailing Add: 2065 Geddes Ave Ann Arbor MI 48104

BURSON, WILLIAM H (BILL) (D)
State Treas, Ga
b Thomaston, Ga, July 31, 28; s J Brooks Burson & Mildred Pitts B; m 1951 to LaVerne Womble; c Forrest Brooks, Nancy Leigh, Mildred Louise & William Womble (deceased). Educ: Univ Ga, BA in jour, magna cum laude, 48; Phi Beta Kappa; Phi Kappa Phi; Omicron Delta Kappa; Blue Key; Biftad; X Club; Sphinx; Sigma Chi; Phi Eta Sigma; Lambda Chi Alpha. Polit & Govt Pos: Press secy, Herman E Talmadge, Gov, Ga, 53-54 & US Sen, 57-62; exec secy, Attorney Gen Eugene Cook, Ga, 55-56; asst to Comptroller Gen James L Bentley, Jr, Ga, 63; prin speechwriter, Gov Carl E Sanders, Ga, 63; dir, Ga State Bd Probation, 63-65; asst to regional dir, Post Off Dept, 65-67; dir, Ga State Dept Family & Children Serv, 67-70; State Treas, Ga, 71- Bus & Prof Pos: News ed, Thomaston Times, 43-45; dir news bur, Univ Ga, 46-48; polit writer, Ga, bur mgr, Birmingham, Ala & Jackson, Miss & war correspondent, Korea, United Press, 48-53; dir info, Assoc Industs Ga, 55. Mil Serv: Cpl, Miss Nat Guard & Army Res, 52-60. Honors & Awards: Speaker of Year, Emory Univ, 67; Rural Serv Award, Off Econ Opportunity, 68; Man of Year, Flagg Mem Baptist Church, Milledgeville, 68; Cert of Appreciation, Dept Agr, 68; Citizenship Award, Druid Hills Civitan Club, Atlanta, 69. Relig: Baptist. Legal Res: 501 Jackson Ave Thomaston GA 30286 Mailing Add: Apt 1 3004 Buford Hwy NE Atlanta GA 30329

BURSTEIN, ALBERT (D)
NJ State Assemblyman
b Jersey City, NJ, Nov 22, 22; s Julius Burstein & Hannah Siegel B; m 1950 to Ruth Appelblatt; c Jeffrey C, Diane B & Laura S. Educ: Columbia Col, AB, 47. Columbia Univ Sch Law, LLB, 49. Polit & Govt Pos: NJ State Assemblyman, 71-, chmn educ comt, NJ State Assembly, 73-, vchmn joint comt on pub schs, 73- Mil Serv: Entered as Pvt, Army, 43, released as Sgt, 45, after serv in 44th Inf Div, ETO; Combat Inf Badge; Battle Stars. Mem: Am & NJ Bar Asns; Jewish Hosp & Rehabilitation Ctr (trustee). Relig: Jewish. Mailing Add: 140 Thatcher Rd Tenafly NJ 07670

BURSTEIN, KAREN (D)
NY State Sen
b Brooklyn, NY, July 20, 42; d Herbert Burstein & Beatrice Sobel B; m 1972 to Eric Lane. Educ: Bryn Mawr Col, BA, 64; Fisk Univ, 64-65; New Sch Social Research, 65; Fordham Univ Sch Law, JD, 70. Polit & Govt Pos: NY State Sen, Ninth Sen Dist Nassau/Queens, 73- Bus & Prof Pos: Teacher, precol prog, Fisk Univ, Tenn, 65; film ed, Colorvision Int, NY, 66; staff attorney, Nassau City Law Serv, NY, 70-72; spec prof law, Hofstra Univ, currently. Mem: Wilderness Soc; NAACP; Nat Women's Polit Caucus; Am Jewish Cong; Am Civil Liberties Union. Honors & Awards: Robert F Kennedy Mem, Nat Info Bur, 72; Community Serv Award, Jewish Life; Nassau Woman of Year, NY Inst Technol, 73. Relig: Jewish. Legal Res: 1015 Cedar Lane Woodmere NY 11598 Mailing Add: NY Senate Albany NY 12224

BURT, ADDISON MOORE (R)
b Sharon, Ga, Feb 14, 19; s Paul Duffy Burt & Dinah Moore B; m 1938 to Louise Dunnaway; c Lavenia (Mrs Goolsby) & Carol. Educ: Crawfordville High Sch, Ga, 4 years. Polit & Govt Pos: Councilman, City of Washington, Ga, 60-70 & 73-; chmn, Wilkes Co Rep Party, formerly; mem adv coun, Small Bus Admin, 71- Bus & Prof Pos: Dir, Farmers & Merchants Bank, 73- Mil Serv: Entered as Pvt, Army, 44, released as S/Sgt, 46. Mem: F&AM; KofC; Shrine; Rotary Int; Wilkes Co CofC. Honors & Awards: Plaque for Outstanding Community Serv, Washington-Wilkes CofC; Small Businessman of Year, State of Ga, 72; Boss of Year Plaque, Jaycees, 73. Relig: Methodist. Legal Res: 33 Lexington Ave Washington GA 30673 Mailing Add: PO Box 220 Washington GA 30673

BURTON, DANIEL FREDERICK (DFL)
Chmn, Second Cong Dist, Minn Dem-Farmer-Labor Party
b Chicago, Ill, Oct 3, 15; s Clyde Daniel Burton & Hazel Henthorne B; m 1950 to Verona Devine; c John Daniel. Educ: Univ Chicago, MS, 40, PhD. 47; Phi Delta Theta. Polit & Govt Pos: Chmn, Sixth Mankato Precinct, Minn Dem-Farmer-Labor Party, 62; chmn, Blue Earth Co Dem-Farmer-Labor Party, Minn, 62-68; chmn, Second Cong Dist Johnson for President Comt, 64; chmn, Second Dist, Minn Dem-Farmer-Labor Cand Comt, 64 & 66; vchmn, Minn Water Resources Rev Comt, 66; mem, Const Reform Comn, Minn Dem-Farmer-Labor Party, 68-70, vchmn const comt, Minn State Conv, 70; chmn, Blue Earth Co Vols for Humphrey, 70; mem, Minn State Bd Educ, 71-, pres, 73-74; chmn, 29th Sen Dist Minn Dem-Farmer-Labor Party, 72-75; chmn, Second Cong Dist, 75- Bus & Prof Pos: Instr botany, Miss State Col, 46-48; asst prof biol, Mankato State Col, 48-50, assoc prof, 50-60, prof, 60-; vis prof, Baldwin-Wallace Col, 69-70. Mil Serv: Entered as Pvt, Army, 42, released as 1st Lt, Med Admin Corps, 46, after serv in 6th Army, Pac; Pac & Am Theatre Ribbons; Philippine Liberation, Japanese Occup & Good Conduct Medals. Publ: Anatomy of the cotton leaf &

effects induced by 2, 4-dichlorophenoxyacetic acid; Bot Gazette 111, 325-331, 50; The absorption of minerals by plant leaves, In: Research Problems in Biology, Investigations for Students, Doubleday, 63. Mem: Am Asn Advan Sci; Am Inst Biol Sci; Bot Soc Am; Econ Soc Am; Am Fern Soc. Relig: Episcopal. Mailing Add: 512 Hickory St Mankato MN 56001

BURTON, GEORGE AUBREY, JR **(R)**
Secy, Rep State Cent Comt La
b Texarkana, Ark, June 21, 25; s George Aubrey Burton & Theo Simmons B; m 1947 to Joan Cunningham; c George Aubrey, III & Sandra. Educ: Centenary Col, La, BS, 51, Study of La Law, 53-57; pres, Delta Tau Omicron. Polit & Govt Pos: Mem, Caddo Parish Rep Comt, La, 54-60, chmn, 60-; mem citizens adv comt, Caddo Parish Sch Bd, 55-56, mem rapid learner comt, 57-59; mem citizen's adv bd, Shreveport Housing Rehabilitation, 56-57; alt deleg, Rep Nat Conv, 60; mem, Rep State Cent Comt La, 60-, secy, 72-; chmn, Lyons for Cong, 61; mem citizens adv comt, Caddo Parish Police Jury, 67-68; comnr of finance, City of Shreveport, 71-; chmn, Rep Fourth Cong Dist Comt, 70-72. Mil Serv: Entered as A/S, Navy, 43, released as Seaman 1/C, 46, after serv in 107 NCB, Sea Bees, Pac, 44-46. Mem: Am Inst CPA; La Soc CPA; Shreveport Jaycees; Sertoma Club; Jr ROTC Parents Club. Relig: Methodist. Mailing Add: 770 Delaware Shreveport LA 71106

BURTON, JOE **(R)**
Ga State Rep
Mailing Add: 2598 Woodwardia Rd NE Atlanta GA 30345

BURTON, JOHN LOWELL **(D)**
US Rep, Calif
b Cincinnati, Ohio, Dec 15, 32; s Thomas P Burton, MD & Mildred L Leonard B; m 1963 to Michele Hall, div; m 1975 to Sharon Bain; c Kimiko. Educ: San Francisco State Col, BA, 54; Hastings Col Law, 1 year; Univ San Francisco Col Law, LLB, 60. Polit & Govt Pos: Mem, San Francisco Co Dem Comt, Calif, 60-62; Dep Attorney Gen, Calif, 61; pres, San Francisco Young Dem, 62; Calif State Assemblyman, 20th Dist, 65-74, chmn joint comt on econ conversion, Calif State Assembly, 69-71, chmn rules comt, 71-74; pres, Calif Dem Coun, 69-70; co-chmn, Calif Deleg Dem Nat Conv, 72; chmn, Calif Dem State Cent Comt, 73-74; mem, Dem Nat Comt, 73-74; US Rep, Calif, 75- Bus & Prof Pos: Mem law firm, Burton, Blumenthal & Burton, 61- Mil Serv: Army, 54-56, serv in Austria. Mem: San Francisco Co, Am & Calif State Bar Asns; Bartenders Union; Union State Employees. Honors & Awards: Man of the Year, Women Legis Action, 65; Am Jurisp Award, Univ San Francisco; All Far West Conf Basketball Team; Calif Soc Autistic Children Award, 74. Legal Res: 674 Wisconsin St San Francisco CA 94103 Mailing Add: 1513 Longworth Off Bldg Washington DC 20515

BURTON, JULIA ANN **(D)**
b St Louis, Mo, Mar 13, 22; d Elmer D Gordon & Fay DeMont G; m 1945 to Bryce McNamee Burton; c Ann Gilbert Burton Wootten, Linda Kay (Mrs Michael Hatch), Nanci (Mrs Lawerence Cummings), Kathleen, Christine Sue & Rebecca Jane. Educ: Ind Univ, Bloomington, 1 year. Polit & Govt Pos: Deleg, Dem Nat Conv, 68 & 72; vchmn, Fulton Co Dem Party, Ind, 68-72, chmn, formerly; vchmn, Fifth Dist Dem Party, 68-72; vchmn, Ind State Dem Party, 68-72; mem, Dem Nat Comt, formerly; pres, Ind Rep Women's Fedn, 73-75. Bus & Prof Pos: Vpres, Dem News, 70. Mem: Fulton Co Nat Found (chmn, 50-). Relig: Baptist. Mailing Add: RR 2 Rochester IN 46975

BURTON, LAURENCE JUNIOR **(R)**
b Ogden, Utah, Oct 30, 26; s Laurence S Burton & Marguerite Roghaar B; m 1947 to Janice Shupe; c Carol, Susan, Sally & Laurence Shupe. Educ: Weber Col, AA, 48; Univ Utah, BS in Polit Sci, 51; Utah State Univ, MS in Polit Sci, 56; postgrad work, Georgetown Univ & George Washington Univ, 57-58. Polit & Govt Pos: Asst to US Rep Henry A Dixon, 57-58; state vchmn, Young Rep, 59; admin asst to Gov George D Clyde, Utah, 60-62; US Rep, Utah, 63-70; deleg, Rep Nat Conv, 68; dir cong rels, Fed Aviation Agency, 71-73. Bus & Prof Pos: Asst prof polit sci, Weber Col, 58-60. Mil Serv: Navy Air Corps, 45-46. Mem: Am Soc Pub Admin; Kiwanis; Am Legion. Relig: Latter-day Saint. Legal Res: UT Mailing Add: 9354 Reed Circle Captains Cove MD 20022

BURTON, MARION B **(R)**
b Little Rock, Ark, Nov 23, 30; s Melven Boyd Burton, Sr & Helen Tedstrom B; c Allyson Leigh, Jennifer Lynne, George Tyler & Amelia Jynkens. Educ: Pa State Univ, BS, 52; Univ Mich Law Sch, JD, 58; Sigma Pi Sigma; Scabbard & Blade; Quarterdeck Soc; Phi Alpha Delta; Phi Gamma Delta. Polit & Govt Pos: Clerk to Chief Justice of Ark Supreme Court, 59-61; campaign mgr, Ricketts for Gov, Ark, 62. asst to state chmn, Rep State Comt, 62-63; legal counsel to Rep Nat Committeeman, 63-; chmn, Pulaski Co Rep Comt, 64-66; campaign dir, Rockefeller for Gov, 66 & 70; exec secy, Ark State Gov, 67-69, legal adv, 69-70; deleg, Ark Const Conv, 69. Bus & Prof Pos: Jr engr, Temco Aircraft Corp, 56; attorney, Russell & Hurley, 61-62; gen counsel, W Rockefeller & Assocs, 70- Mil Serv: Entered as Midn, Navy, 48, released as Lt(jg), 56; Comdr, Naval Res, 60-72, Capt, 72-; Navy Unit Citation; UN Ribbon; Korean Campaign Ribbon with 2 Campaign Stars; Nat Defense Medal. Mem: Am Bar Asn; Little Rock Metrop YMCA (chmn); ROA. Relig: Methodist. Legal Res: 10 Robinwood Little Rock AR 72207 Mailing Add: 1720 Tower Bldg Little Rock AR 72201

BURTON, MELVIN MATTHEW, JR **(R)**
b Salisbury, NC, Feb 14, 29; s Melvin M Burton & Ivory Walker B; m 1955 to Jacqueline Scott. Educ: Howard Univ, AB, 50, LLB, 53; Georgetown Univ, 56-58; Phi Beta Sigma. Polit & Govt Pos: Precincts co-chmn, DC Exec Comt for Rockefeller, 68; mem & ward coordr, DC Rep Cent Comt, 68-, chmn housing comt, 69-; mem, Speaker's Comt Inaugural & Law & Legis Comt Inaugural, 69; chmn precincts comt, DC Rep Party, 70; campaign chmn, Dr William Chin Lee, DC Deleg to Cong, 72; mem, DC Regional Adv Coun, Small Bus Admin, currently. Bus & Prof Pos: Partner, McDaniel, Burton & Daniels, Lawyers, 56-; mem, DC Bicentennial Assembly, 72- Mil Serv: Entered as 2nd Lt, Air Force, 54, released as 1st Lt, 56, after serv in Judge Adv Legal Off; Nat Defense Serv Medal; Good Conduct Medal. Mem: Nat Bar Asn; Howard Univ Law Alumni Asn; Am Civil Liberties Union; Am Arbit Asn; Ripon Soc. Relig: Baptist. Mailing Add: 700 Seventh St SW Washington DC 20024

BURTON, PHILLIP **(D)**
US Rep, Calif
b Cincinnati, Ohio, June 1, 26; married; c one daughter. Educ: Univ of Southern Calif, AB, 47; Golden Gate Law Sch, LLB, 52. Polit & Govt Pos: Nat officer, Young Dem, formerly; Calif State Assemblyman, 56-64; deleg to Atlantic Treaty Asn Conf, France, 59; US Rep, Calif, 64-; deleg, Dem Nat Conv, 68 & 72; founder, Calif Dem Coun; secy, 88th Cong Dem Club; chmn, Dem Study Group; deleg, Dem Nat Mid-Term Conf, 74. Bus & Prof Pos: Attorney. Mil Serv: Korean Vet. Mem: George Washington High Alumni Asn; Blue Key. Legal Res: San Francisco CA Mailing Add: 2454 Rayburn House Off Bldg Washington DC 20515

BURTON, THOMAS LAWSON **(R)**
VChmn, Tenth Cong Dist Rep Comt, Ga
b Bowman, Ga, Aug 5, 22; s Joseph Homer Burton, Sr & Tolver Grimes B; m 1946 to Mary Jo Johnson; c Mary Thomas, Margaret Joan & Linda Laine. Polit & Govt Pos: Chmn, Elbert Co Rep Comt, 64-73; chmn dist adv coun, Small Bus Admin, currently; area vchmn, Tenth Cong Dist Rep Comt, 72-73, first vchmn, 73- Bus & Prof Pos: Owner & mgr, Branding Iron Restaurant, Elberton, Ga, 46-70; supvr mortgage loan dept, Goss Real Estate, 71-; exec vpres, Tranquility Investment, Inc, Elberton, currently. Mil Serv: Entered as Pvt, Army Air Corps, 42, released as T/Sgt, 45, after serv, in 15th Air Force, ETO, 44-45; Air Medal with Silver Cluster; Air-Combat Medal, Balkans & Ger; Rome-Arno Campaign Ribbon; Southern & Northern France Campaign Ribbons. Mem: Ga Asn Realtors; Elks Lodge 1100; VFW Post 5456; Am Legion Post 14. Legal Res: 83 Carey St Elberton GA 30635 Mailing Add: PO Box 213 Elberton GA 30635

BURTON, VERONA DEVINE **(DFL)**
Treas, Blue Earth Co Dem-Farmer-Labor Party, Minn
b Reading, Pa, Nov 23, 22; d John Edward Devine & Verona Dillman D; m 1950 to Daniel Frederick Burton; c John Daniel. Educ: Hunter Col, AB, 44; State Univ Iowa, MS, 46, PhD, 48, Sigma Xi; Sigma Delta Epsilon; Delta Kappa Gamma; Sigma Zeta. Polit & Govt Pos: Deleg, Minn State Dem-Farmer-Labor Party, 64, 66 & 72; precinct chairwoman, Dem-Farmer-Labor Party, 62-68, pres, 70-; mem, Mankato Bd Health, 69-, chmn, 71-; first vchairwoman, Blue Earth Co Dem-Farmer-Labor Party, 70-72, treas, 72-; mem women's adv comt, Minn Human Rights Comn, 73-, chairperson, 75- Bus & Prof Pos: Prof, Mankato State Col, 48- Publ: Note on the culture of lychnis embryos, Proc Iowa Acad Sci, 48; Embryogeny of lychnis alba, Am J Bot, 50; The absorption of minerals by plant leaves, Research Prob in Biol, Anchor, 63. Mem: Int Soc Plant Morphol; Am Asn Advan Sci; Bot Soc Am; Am Fern Soc; Am Asn Univ Prof. Honors & Awards: Elsie Seringhaus scholar by Hunter Col, Woods Hole Biol Sta; grad & res assistantships, Univ Iowa. Relig: Episcopal. Mailing Add: 512 Hickory St Mankato MN 56001

BUSBEE, GEORGE D **(D)**
Gov, Ga
b Vienna, Ga, Aug 7, 27; s Perry Green Busbee & Nell Dekle B; m 1949 to Mary Elizabeth Talbot; c Beth Talbot, Jan Guest, George Dekle, Jr & Jeff Talbot. Educ: Duke Univ; Univ Ga, BBA, 49, LLB, 52; Phi Delta Theta. Polit & Govt Pos: Ga State Rep, 57-74, Majority Leader, Ga House of Rep, formerly; Gov, Ga, 74- Bus & Prof Pos: Attorney. Mil Serv: Navy, World War II. Relig: Baptist. Legal Res: 1205 Third Ave Albany GA 31075 Mailing Add: Off of the Governor Atlanta GA 30334

BUSBEE, MAURY JUDSON **(D)**
SC State Rep
b Aiken Co, SC, Apr 22, 47; s Jimmy C Busbee & Mae Furtick B; single. Educ: Anderson Col, AA, 68; Lander Col, BA, 72. Polit & Govt Pos: SC State Rep, 74- Bus & Prof Pos: Mgr, Busbee Hardware Co. Mil Serv: Entered as E-2, Army, 68, released as E-4, 70, after serv in 101st ABN, S Vietnam; Two Bronze Stars, Purple Heart. Mem: VFW; Jaycees. Relig: Baptist. Mailing Add: 44 S Main Wagener SC 29164

BUSCH, J MICHAEL (JOHN) **(R)**
Mich State Rep
b Saginaw, Mich, Mar 26, 46; s Frank J Busch; m 1973 to Barbara C Wolfe. Educ: Ferris State Col, BS, 68; Detroit Col of Law, 68-70; Phi Kappa Delta; Sigma Phi Epsilon. Polit & Govt Pos: Advanceman, Sen Robert Griffin, 72-73; mem, Saginaw Co Rep Exec Comt, 72-, co & state deleg, 72-74; publicity chmn, Saginaw Co Rep Comt; Mich State Rep, Dist 100, 75- Bus & Prof Pos: Probate court officer, Saginaw Co. Mem: Saginaw Twp Jaycees; Saginaw Exchange Club; State Asn for Retarded Children; Nat Asn for Retarded Children. Honors & Awards: Won nat debate honors, 68; Man of the Year Award for outstanding serv to sch & community, 68. Legal Res: 2735 Wellesley Saginaw MI 48603 Mailing Add: State Capitol Lansing MI 48901

BUSCH, VIRGINIA MARIE **(D)**
Secy, Fourth Cong Dist Dem Party, Colo
b Greeley, Colo, June 28, 21; d Robert N G Hibler & Della Hood H; m 1965 to Melvin Frank Busch; c Bettye (Mrs Robert F Paden) & Billy Scott Harrod. Educ: Greeley High Sch, Colo, GED, 64; Aims Col Adult Div, Ft Lupton, Colo, 68-69. Polit & Govt Pos: Ft Lupton precinct committeewoman, Weld Co Dem Party, Colo, 52-58; justice of the peace, Ft Lupton, 58-63; vchmn, Weld Co Dem Cent Comt, 59-66, vchmn & ex-officio mem exec comt, 69-; secy, Fourth Cong Dist Dem Party, 64-; ex-officio mem, Dem State Exec Comt, 69- Bus & Prof Pos: Clerk, Assessor's Off, Greeley, Colo, 63-65. Mem: Jane Jefferson Dem Club; League of Women Voters; Eve Belles Toastmistress Club; Am Legion Auxiliary (girls state comt); Ft Lupton Garden Club (chmn, Blue Star Mem Hwy Comt). Honors & Awards: Awarded grant from Sears, Roebuck & Co for Blue Star Roadside Park, 69. Relig: Lutheran. Legal Res: 930 McKinley Ave Ft Lupton CO 80621 Mailing Add: PO Box 141 Ft Lupton CO 80621

BUSER, BURTON L **(D)**
b Seneca, Kans, Aug 31, 34; s George J Buser & Elizabeth Karnowski B; m 1956 to Patricia A Rethman; c Steven & Stacy. Educ: Washburn Univ, Topeka. Polit & Govt Pos: Mem exec bd, Shawnee Dem Cent Comt, Kans, 68-72, cand chmn, 72; vchmn, Gov Robert Docking Inaugural Ball 71, 70-71, gen chmn, 73; exec bd, Shawnee Co Dem Action Comt, 70-; deleg, Dem Nat Conv, 72; vchmn, Robert Docking Campaign, 72. Bus & Prof Pos: From commun rep, engr, spec rep, commun sales mgr to sales & serv mgr, Southwestern Bell Tel Co, 51-; bd dir, 7-Step Found, 72- Mil Serv: Entered as Pvt, Army, 53, released as Cpl, 55, after serv in Inf; European Theatre Ribbon; Good Conduct Medal. Mem: KofC (Grand Knight, 69 & 70). Honors & Awards: Distinguished Salesman Award, Sales & Mgt Exec, 68; VIP, WREN Radio Sta, 69. Relig: Catholic. Mailing Add: 1192 Seabrook Topeka KS 66604

BUSH, BAKER HOSKINS **(D)**
Treas, Phillips Co Dem Comt, Ark
b Helena, Ark, Aug 1, 36; s James Robert Bush & Margaret Hoskins B; m 1936 to Nicole Holmes; c Nicole Hoskins. Educ: Memphis State Univ, BS, 58, Kappa Sigma. Polit & Govt Pos: Alderman, Fifth Ward, Helena, Ark, 66-; treas, Phillips Co Dem Comt, 69-; mem, Ark First Cong Dist Comt, 70- Bus & Prof Pos: Secy-treas, Delta Plantation, Inc, 66; dir, Helena Compress Co, 66; comnr, Laconia Levee Dist, 66; pres, BPB, Inc, 69; chmn, Phillips Co

Indust Comt, 70. Mem: Ark Munic League; Ark Farm Bur; Memphis State Univ Alumni Asn. Relig: Roman Catholic. Legal Res: Neil Rd Helena AR 72342 Mailing Add: 325 York St Helena AR 72342

BUSH, BILLIE VOSS (D)
Mem Exec Comt, Miss Dem State Cent Comt
b El Paso, Ark, June 24, 14; s John Marvin Bush & Cordelia Voss B; m 1943 to Helen Reames; c Sally C & Paris Keats. Educ: Hendrix Col, AA, 34; Ark State Teachers Col, AB, 35; Tulane Col Law, 48. Polit & Govt Pos: Deleg, Dem Nat Conv, 72; deleg, Dem Nat Mid-Term Conf, 74; mem exec comt, Miss Dem State Cent Comt, 75- Mil Serv: Navy, 35-47, Lt(jg), serv in 6th Marine Div on OSS China, Pac-China; Lt Comdr (Ret) Naval Res; Presidential Unit Commendation. Mem: Miss Hist Soc; Am Civil Liberties Union. Relig: Unitarian. Mailing Add: 842 Oakleigh Ave Gulfport MS 39501

BUSH, DOROTHY VREDENBURGH (D)
Secy, Dem Nat Comt
b Baldwyn, Miss, Dec 8, 16; d Will Lee McElroy & Lany Holland M; m 1962 to John W Bush. Educ: Miss State Col for Women, BS, 37; Beta Sigma Phi. Polit & Govt Pos: Asst secy, Young Dem of Am, 41, vpres, 43-48, acting pres, 44; nat committeewoman, Ala Young Dem, 41-50; secy, Dem Nat Conv, 44-; secy, Dem Nat Comt, 44- Bus & Prof Pos: Dir, Coastal Caribbean Oils & Minerals, Ltd & Pancoastal, Inc; mem bd of adv, Int Univ of Commun. Mem: Ark Traveler; Nat Fedn Bus & Prof Women. Relig: Baptist. Mailing Add: C 1409 Lakeshore Dr Columbus OH 43204

BUSH, GEORGE (R)
b Milton, Mass, June 12, 24; m 1945 to Barbara Pierce; c George W, John E, Neil M, Marvin P & Dorothy W. Educ: Yale Univ, BA in econ, 48; Phi Beta Kappa; Delta Kappa Epsilon. Polit & Govt Pos: Vchmn, GOP Task Force Job Opportunity; chmn, Harris Co Rep Party, Tex; deleg, Rep Nat Conv, 64 & 68; US Rep, Tex, 66-70, mem ways & means comt, US House of Rep; US Ambassador, UN, 71-73; chmn, Rep Nat Comt, 73-74; chief, US Liaison Off, Peoples Repub of China, 74- Bus & Prof Pos: Vpres, Zapata Petroleum Co, 52-59; pres & chmn, Zapata Off-Shore Co, 54-66. Mil Serv: Entered as Ens, Naval Res, 42, released as Lt(jg), after serv as Navy Pilot; Distinguished Flying Cross; Three Air Medals. Relig: Episcopal. Legal Res: TX Mailing Add: Dept of State Washington DC 20520

BUSH, GOLDEN HARTZELL (R)
Committeewoman, Edgar Co Rep Party, Ill
b Paris, Ill, Dec 5, 08; d Charles Perry Todd & Eliza Jane Griffin T; m 1927 to Ora Clayton Bush; c Shirley Ann (Mrs Ogden), Phillip Ray & Harold Jay. Educ: Larkin Elem Sch. Polit & Govt Pos: Secy to Edgar Twp Assessor, 47-; mem, Ill Fedn Rep Women, 60-; mem, Edgar Co Rep Women's Club, 60-; committeewoman, Edgar Co Rep Party, 60-, chmn, 65-73, chmn annual Rep barbecue. Mem: Edgar Co Home Exten; Farm Bur; Women for Better Foods for Better Living. Relig: Baptist. Mailing Add: RR3 Chrisman IL 61924

BUSH, GORDON DALLON (D)
City Comnr, City of East St Louis, Ill
b East St Louis, Ill, Nov 16, 42; s Claude Arthur Bush & Lillian Pearson B; m 1971 to Brenda Lavondria Lampley. Educ: Southern Ill Univ, Edwardsville, BA, 70, MS, 71; St Louis Univ, PhD student polit sci, currently; Kappa Alpha Psi. Polit & Govt Pos: Assoc planner, East St Louis Model City Agency, Ill, 59-71; comnr pub property & bldgs, City of East St Louis, 71-; deleg, Dem Nat Conv, 72. Bus & Prof Pos: Steel x-ray inspector, Gen Steel Indust, Granite City, Ill, 63-65. Mil Serv: Entered as Pvt E-1, Army, 66, released as 1st Lt, 69, after serv in 249th Engr Bn ETO, 67-69; 1st Lt, Army Res, 3 years; Nat Defense Medal; Letter of Commendation; Cert of Appreciation from Lt Col Maxwell & Lt Col Couisins, Past Comdrs of 249th Engr Bn; Group Comdrs Maintenance Award. Publ: Study of insurance availability in East St Louis, St Louis Post Dispatch, 69. Mem: Am Inst Planners; Madison & St Clair Co Urban League; East St Louis Jaycees; Gtr East St Louis CofC; Aswan Imp Coun Temple 115. Honors & Awards: Cert of Merit, United Supreme Coun, 68; Model City Agency Award, Community Develop Comt, East St Louis, Ill, 72; Distinguished Serv Award, 72; Cert of Appreciation, City of Lincoln Heights, Ohio, 72; Outstanding Young Citizen, East St Louis Pro-Heights Social Civic Club, 73. Relig: Baptist. Mailing Add: 1103 LaPleins Dr East St Louis IL 62203

BUSH, JOHN WILLIAM (D)
b Columbus, Ohio, Sept 17, 09; s William Hayden Bush & Esther Brushart B; m 1962 to Dorothy McElroy; c Jan Hayden (Mrs Jennings) & Emily Ann (Mrs Bennett). Educ: Va Polytechnic Inst, BS; vpres, Cotillion Club; bus mgr, The Bugle, 31. Polit & Govt Pos: Mem city coun, Portsmouth, Ohio, 42, 43 & 44; state purchasing supt, Gov Lausche's Cabinet, 49-57; dir of com, Gov Di Salle's Cabinet, 59-61; comnr, Interstate Com Comn, 61-72; Spec Transportation Adv to Senate Com Comt, 72-; dir, Ohio Vietnam Vets Bonus Comn, 74- Bus & Prof Pos: Pres, Ohio Syst, Inc, 46-; pres, Franklin Serv Corp, 57- Mem: Nat Asn State Purchasing Off. Relig: Episcopal. Mailing Add: 1409 Lake Shore Dr Columbus OH 43204

BUSHEMI, MARION J (D)
Ind State Rep
m 1959 to Ethel Maude Morris. Educ: Gary Bus Col, elec eng course, 2 years; grad, Dale Carnegie Course Human Rels; Hazlett Leadership Course. Polit & Govt Pos: Ind State Rep, 59-60 & 63-, mem labor & natural resources comts & ranking minority mem, Affairs of Lake Co Comt, Ind House Rep, currently; app by President Kennedy as chmn, comn on new jobs & new growth in community, 61; chmn, Comn on Utilization of Available Lake Co Labor, 63; app mem, Little Calumet River Adv Coun, 70- Bus & Prof Pos: Operator restaurant bus, formerly; steel worker, US Steel, 34 years, first aid & safety inspector, 9 years, retired. Mil Serv: Ind Nat Guard, Cpl, World War II. Mem: Dale Carnegie Alumni Asn; Nat Soc State Legislators; CIO Local 1014; Moose; Izaak Walton League. Honors & Awards: Plaque for Outstanding Voting Record on Environ Issues, Glen Park Chap, Isaak Walton League, 72. Relig: Roman Catholic. Mailing Add: 4101 Fillmore St Gary IN 46408

BUSHFIELD, VERA CAHALAN (R)
b Miller, SDak, Aug 9, 89; d Maurice Francis Cahalan & Mary Ellen Conners C; m to Harlan John Bushfield, wid; c Mary Janith, John Pearson & Harlan John, Jr. Educ: Univ Minn; Dakota Wesleyan Univ; Stout Inst Wis. Polit & Govt Pos: US Sen, SDak, 47-48. Mem: Eastern Star; Bus & Prof Women's Club; PEO; Woman's Club; Garden Club. Relig: Presbyterian. Mailing Add: 209 Third Ave E Miller SD 57362

BUSHNELL, MARY B (R)
b Garner, Iowa, Oct 9, 32; d Edwin Frederick Bock & Lenabelle McGinnes B; m 1953 to Frederic Ransom Bushnell, Jr; c Frederic R, III, John Bock, Cade Jay & Edwin G (Ned). Educ: Iowa State Univ, 50-53; Delta Delta Delta. Polit & Govt Pos: Mem bd, Ogle Co Women's Rep Club, Ill, 58-70, pres, 68-70; precinct committeeman, Marion Twp, Ogle Co Rep Cent Comt, 62-; alt deleg, Rep Nat Conv, 72. Mem: Ogle Co Hist Soc; Iowa Hist Soc; Coop Exten; Stillman Valley Woman's Club; Gen Fedn of Women's Clubs. Relig: Presbyterian. Mailing Add: Walnut Creek Farms Box 34 Stillman Valley IL 61084

BUSINGER, JOHN ARNOLD (D)
Mass State Rep
b Cleveland, Ohio, Feb 5, 45; s Kenneth Arnold Businger & Mary Bertha Hack B; single. Educ: Boston Col, AB, cum laude, 67, Law Sch, 67-69. Polit & Govt Pos: State treas, Col Dem Clubs of Mass, 66-67; admin & legis asst, late State Rep H James Shea, Jr, 70; mem, Brookline Town Meeting, 70-; Mass State Rep, 13th Norfolk Dist, 71-; deleg, Dem Nat Conv, 72. Mil Serv: Seaman, Navy, 69. Publ: Working for Jim Shea, In: The People vs Presidential War, Dunellen Press, 70. Relig: Catholic. Mailing Add: 33 St Paul St Brookline MA 02146

BUSSIE, FRAN MARTINEZ (D)
b New Orleans, La, May 6, 35; d John Ozuna Martinez & Althea Williams M; m 1972 to Victor Bussie; c Michael Q Nolan, Jr. Educ: McMain High Sch. Polit & Govt Pos: Alt deleg, Dem Nat Mid-Term Conf, 74; mem, Gov's Comt Employ Handicapped, La Comn Status Women, La State Med Care Adv Coun & La Drug Abuse Adv Coun, currently. Bus & Prof Pos: Secy, Pub & Consumer Rels Dept, Gulf Union Corp, 56; stand-by mgr, Mgr Training Sch, Avon Co, 66-69; exec dir, Baton Rouge Asn Ment Health, 69-73; community serv officer, La AFL-CIO, 73- Mem: League Women Voters; La Conf Social Welfare; La Asn Retarded Children; Off & Prof Employees Local 383; YWCA. Honors & Awards: Pub Off Award, La Asn Retarded Children; Superior Serv in Ment Health, Ment Health Asn Gtr Baton Rouge; Ment Health Serv Award, Delta Sigma Theta. Relig: Methodist. Legal Res: 3235 McConnell Dr Baton Rouge LA 70809 Mailing Add: PO Box 3477 429 Govt St Baton Rouge LA 70821

BUSSIE, VICTOR (D)
Mem-At-Lg, Dem Nat Comt
b Montrose, La, Jan 27, 19; s Christopher Bussie & Fannie Lacaze B; m 1972 to Fran Martinez; c Deanna Jeanne (Mrs Love) & Carolyn Lee (Mrs Huff) & stepson, Michael Q Nolan, Jr. Educ: Fair Park High Sch, grad, 40; Beta Gamma Sigma; Omicron Delta Epsilon. Hon Degrees: LLD, Nicholls State Univ, 71. Polit & Govt Pos: Mem-at-lg, Dem Nat Comt, 73-; mem, Nat Defense-Exec Reserve, La, currently; mem, Nat Pub Adv Comt Regional Econ Develop, currently; mem, La Comn Govt Ethics, currently; mem, La Health, Social & Rehab Servs Policy Bd, currently; deleg, Dem Nat Mid-Term Conf, 74. Bus & Prof Pos: Pres, Shreveport Fire Fighters Local 514, La, 44-56; pres, Shreveport Cent Trades & Labor Coun, 48-57; vpres, La State Fedn Labor-AFL, 49-57; pres, La AFL-CIO, 56- Mil Serv: Entered as Seaman, Navy, 43, released as CPO, 46; Lt, La Nat Guard, 50-53. Mem: Defense Orientation Conf Asn; Nat Asn Ment Health (bd dirs, 66-); Am Nat Red Cross (SE area adv coun); Am Pub Welfare Asn. Honors & Awards: Outstanding Serv Award, Nat Asn Ment Health, 67; Pub Serv Award, US Post Off Adv Bd, 69; Distinguished Serv Award, Am Nat Red Cross, 69; Distinguished Consumer Safety Award, Consumer Safety Glazing Movement, 73; Outstanding Contribution, La Asn Community Action Agencies. Relig: Methodist. Legal Res: 3235 McConnell Dr Baton Rouge LA 70809 Mailing Add: PO Box 3477 Baton Rouge LA 70821

BUSSMAN, RALPH E (D)
Kans State Rep
Mailing Add: RR L Mound Valley KS 67354

BUSTERUD, JOHN A (R)
b Coos Bay, Ore, Mar 7, 21; m 1953 to Anne Witwer B; c John W, James P & Mary Holt. Educ: Univ Ore, BS; Yale Univ Law Sch, LLB; Phi Beta Kappa. Polit & Govt Pos: State pres, Calif Young Rep, 55-56; Calif State Assemblyman, 56-62; Rep nominee, State Treas, 62; mem, Calif Const Rev Comn, 65-; dep asst secy environ qual, Dept of Defense, 71-72; mem, President's Coun on Environ Qual, 72-; US sr environ adv, Econ Comn for Europe, currently. Bus & Prof Pos: Attorney-at-law. Mil Serv: Army, 43-46; Army Res, Lt Col (Ret). Mem: Am Bar Asn; Am Acad Polit Sci; Bohemian Club; Chi Psi; Phi Delta Phi. Legal Res: 102 Mountain View Ave San Rafael CA 94901 Mailing Add: 3229 Reservoir Rd NW Washington DC 20007

BUSTIN, DAVID W (D)
Maine State Rep
Mailing Add: 185 Mount Vernon Ave Augusta ME 04330

BUTCHMAN, ALAN A (D)
b Framingham, Mass, Aug 4, 38; m to Gillian Lamb; c Alycia & Amanda. Educ: Bowdoin Col, AB, 60; Boston Col Law Sch, LLB, 65; Georgetown Law Sch, LLM, 68. Polit & Govt Pos: Attorney, US Dept Labor, 65-70; admin asst, US Rep Brock Adams, Wash, 70- Mil Serv: Entered as 2nd Lt, Army, 60, released as 1st Lt, 62. Mem: Mass & DC Bars. Mailing Add: 528 Cedar St NW Washington DC 20012

BUTENKO, CONSTANTINE (R)
Chmn, 47th Legis Dist Rep Party, Wash
b Harbin, Manchuria, June 16, 18; s Mitrofan Efimouich Butenko & Carolina Radzinonowich B; m 1941 to Tamara Vladimirouna Melikov; c Elizabeth (Mrs John Peterson), Constantine, Maria (Mrs Wolfgang Anderson), Joel Michael & Christopher Ronald. Educ: Univ Wash, 40-42. Polit & Govt Pos: Precinct committeeman, 47th Legis Dist Rep Party, Wash, 68-75, regional chmn, 69-70, chmn, 70-; deleg, Rep Nat Conv, 72; deleg, Rep Leadership Conf, Washington, DC, 75. Bus & Prof Pos: Supvr, Boeing Airplane Co, 51-54, sr supvr, 54-56, gen supvr, 56- Mem: Mfg Eng & Mgt Asn; East Hill Community Orgn (pres, 68-). Mailing Add: 14234 SE 216 St Kent WA 98031

BUTERA, ROBERT JAMES (R)
Majority Leader, Pa House Rep
b Norristown, Pa, Jan 21, 35; s Harry Butera & Anne Constable B; m to Constance J Hanson; c Robert J, Jr & Nina Hanson. Educ: Univ Pa, Wharton Sch Com & Finance, BS in Econ, 56; Dickinson Sch Law, LLB, 59; Beta Theta Phi. Polit & Govt Pos: Pa State Rep, 63-, Majority Whip, Pa House Rep, 67-69, Minority Whip, 69-73, Majority Leader, 73- Bus & Prof Pos: Partner, Butera & Detwiler Law Firm, 60-; ed, Montgomery Co Law Reporter, 61-66. Mil Serv: Pa Nat Guard, 69, Pfc. Mem: Montgomery Co & Pa Bar Asns. Relig: Roman

Catholic. Legal Res: 1926 Brandon Rd Norristown PA 19401 Mailing Add: Capitol Bldg Harrisburg PA 17102

BUTH, MARTIN D (R)
Mich State Rep
b Comstock Park, Mich, Oct 18, 17; m 1943 to George Ann Shaw; c Martin D, III & George S. Educ: Mich State Univ, grad. Polit & Govt Pos: Trustee, Plainfield Twp, Mich, formerly; Mich State Rep, 59- Bus & Prof Pos: Dairy farmer. Mem: Mich Purebred Dairy Cattle Asn; Mich Farm Bur; Rotary. Relig: Episcopal. Mailing Add: 6244 Lincolnshire Ct SE Grand Rapids MI 49500

BUTLER, ARTHUR D (D)
Committeeman, Amherst Dem Town Party, NY
b Detroit, Mich, Oct 13, 23; s Dwight Butler & Mae Byers B; m 1945 to Kathleen Lehman; c Terese, Pamela & Sandra. Educ: Manchester Col, BA, 44; Univ Minn, MA, 46; Univ Wis, PhD, 51. Polit & Govt Pos: Mem bd trustees, Cleveland Hill Sch Dist, 61-65; committeeman, Amherst Dem Town Party, NY, 68-; deleg, Dem Nat Conv, 72. Bus & Prof Pos: From lectr to prof, State Univ NY Buffalo, 48-, univ ombudsman, 69-70, assoc provost, Faculty Social Sci & Admin, 72-75, provost, 75- Publ: Co-ed, Readings in Economics (2 vols), Smith, Keynes & Marshall, 58 & 59; auth, Labor Economics & Institutions, Macmillan, 60; co-auth, Labor market behavior in a full employment economy, Indust & Labor Rels Rev, 70. Mem: Am Econ Asn; Indust Rels Research Asn; Econometric Soc; Am Asn Univ Prof; Am Civil Liberties Union. Relig: Unitarian. Mailing Add: 151 Washington Hwy Buffalo NY 14226

BUTLER, CHARLES FREDERICK (R)
b Quincy, Mass, July 10, 33; s Percy T Butler & Ethel Sutermeister B; m 1959 to Alice Ryan; c Charles F, Jr, Colin M, Christopher R & Alison F. Educ: Boston Univ, AA & AB, 59; George Washington Univ Law Sch, JD with honors, 64; Sigma Phi Epsilon. Polit & Govt Pos: Air transport examr, Civil Aeronaut Bd, 59-63; admin-legis asst, US Rep Hastings Keith, Mass, 63-65; US Rep, Int Civil Aviation Orgn, 69-71; Dir Bur Int Affairs, Civil Aeronaut Bd, 71-74. Bus & Prof Pos: Washington rep for int proc & asst vpres, Eastern Airlines, 65-69; spec adv, Air Transport Asn Am, 74; pres, Butler Assoc Inc, currently. Mil Serv: Entered as E-1, Army, 53, released as E-4, 55, serv in 1264th Army, Camp Kilmer, NJ. Publ: Auth, The Path to International Legislation Against Hijacking, Oceana Publ, 71; International Cooperation on Outer Space, US Senate Comt Sci & Astronaut. Mem: Nat Lawyers Club; Int & Nat Aviation Clubs. Honors & Awards: Cert of Honor Award, Civil Aeronaut Bd. Relig: Protestant. Mailing Add: 7706 Radnor Rd Bethesda MD 22034

BUTLER, GARY LEE (D)
Ind State Rep
b Lawrenceburg, Ind, Feb 25, 34; s Lee Jonas Butler & H Alberta Sweeney B; m 1964 to Phyllis Brown; m 1971 to Deanna S Fisher. Educ: Franklin Col, 1 year. Polit & Govt Pos: Pres, Ninth Cong Dist Young Dem, 66-70; nat committeeman, Young Dem Clubs of Am, Ind, 67-69; deleg, Ind State Dem Conv, 68 & 70; precinct committeeman, Dearborn Co Dem Cent Comt, 68-; Ind State Rep, 70- Bus & Prof Pos: Owner, Butler Lumber Co, Lawrenceburg, Ind & secy, Lehigh Acres, Inc, currently. Mem: Am Numismatic Asn; Nat Muzzle Loading Rifle Asn; Fraternal Order of Police; Can Numismatic Asn; Ind Sportsmen's Coun. Honors & Awards: Ind Young Dem Outstanding Serv Award, 70. Relig: Baptist. Mailing Add: RR 2 Box 384 Lawrenceburg IN 47025

BUTLER, JOSEPH HARDWICK (R)
b Macon, Ga, Aug 20, 35; s Walter Clark Butler, Sr & Edna Ruth Hardwick B; single. Educ: Ga Inst Technol, Atlanta, BCE, 57, MSCE, 63; Chi Epsilon; Sigma Xi; Lambda Chi Alpha. Polit & Govt Pos: Deleg, Rep Nat Conv, 72; chmn, Bibb Co Rep Party, Ga, 73-75. Bus & Prof Pos: Sr engr, Ga Kraft Co, 63- Mil Serv: Maj, Army Res, 71- Mem: Boy Scouts (exec bd, Cent Ga Coun); Nat Soc Prof Engrs; Am Conservative Union. Honors & Awards: Silver Beaver Award, Boy Scouts, 70. Relig: Methodist. Mailing Add: 2591 Allen Rd Macon GA 31206

BUTLER, KATHRYN ELLEN (R)
b Olney, Md, July 19, 54; d Orton Camichael Butler & Betty Johnson B; single. Educ: William Woods Col, 72-73; Chi Omega. Polit & Govt Pos: Alt deleg, Rep Nat Conv, 72; col chmn, Young Voters for the President, William Woods Col, 72. Relig: Methodist. Mailing Add: 2547 Howard Rd Germantown TN 38138

BUTLER, KENNETH (D)
Okla State Sen
Mailing Add: State Capitol Oklahoma City OK 73105

BUTLER, MANLEY CALDWELL (R)
US Rep, Va
b Roanoke, Va, June 2, 25; m to June Nolde B. Educ: Univ Richmond, AB, 48; Univ Va Law Sch, 50; Phi Beta Kappa. Polit & Govt Pos: Chmn, Roanoke City Rep Party, Va, 60-61; Va State Deleg, 62-71, Minority Leader, Va House of Deleg, 66-71; US Rep, Sixth Dist, Va, 72- Mil Serv: Ens, Naval Res. Mem: Va State Bar; Am Bar Asn; Tau Kappa Alpha; Omicron Delta Kappa; Phi Gamma Delta. Relig: Episcopal; vestryman, St John's Episcopal Church. Legal Res: 845 Orchard Rd SW Roanoke VA 24014 Mailing Add: House Off Bldg Washington DC 20515

BUTLER, MARTYN DON (R)
Chmn, Clear Creek Co Rep Cent Comt, Colo
b Centralia, Kans, Dec 11, 39; s Dr Martyn E Butler & Donna K Cole B; m 1964 to Penelope A Biggs; c Martyn O & Mollie K. Educ: Kans State Col Pittsburgh, BS, 67; Phi Delta Theta. Polit & Govt Pos: Dist capt, Dist One, Denver, Colo, 72-73; chmn, Clear Creek Co Rep Cent Comt, 73-; mem, Colo State Plumbing Bd, 74- Bus & Prof Pos: Owner, Butler Graphics, 72- Mil Serv: Entered as E-1, US Marine Corps, 60, released as E-3, 64, after serv in Pub Info Off. Mem: Lions. Relig: Episcopal Church. Mailing Add: Rte 7 Box 126N Evergreen CO 80439

BUTLER, NEIL ARTHUR (D)
Mayor, Gainesville, Fla
b Orange Heights, Fla, Dec 3, 27; s Neil Butler & Bertha Kennedy B; m 1962 to Dorothy Young; c Neil A, Jr, Annette (Mrs W Mann), Archie Frank, Danny Keith & Andre Lia. Educ: Morris Brown Col, 49-52; Univ Fla, BS, 67, MS, 71; Sigma Theta Tau; Omega Psi Phi. Polit & Govt Pos: City comnr, Gainesville, Fla, 69-, Mayor, 71-72 & 74- Bus & Prof Pos: Staff nurse, Alachua Gen Hosp & Univ Fla Hosp, Gainesville, 65-67; staff nurse, Vet Admin Hosp, Gainesville, 67-68; head nurse pediat unit, Univ Fla, 68-69, grad research asst, 70-71, instr community health, Col Med, 71-; vpres, Emmer Develop Corp, Gainesville, 69-70. Mil Serv: Entered as Seaman, Navy, 44, released as Storekeeper 3/C, 46, after serv in Asiatic-Pac Theatre, 45-46; World War II Victory Medal; Asiatic-Pac Medal; Am Serv Medal. Mem: Am Nurses Asn; Am Acad Polit & Social Scientists; Int Platform Asn. Honors & Awards: Gainesville Civitan Club Outstanding Citizen of Year Award, 69; Dist 10 Fla Nurses Asn Community Serv Award, 69; Alpha Kappa Alpha Award for Contribution to Black Heritage, 71; Gainesville Club Coun Award Meritorious Serv as Mayor, 71. Relig: African-Methodist-Episcopal. Mailing Add: 1214 SE 17th Dr Gainesville FL 32601

BUTLER, RICHARD C, JR (R)
VChmn, Pulaski Co Rep Comt, Ark
b Little Rock, Ark, Sept 21, 37; s Richard C Butler & Gertrude Remmel B; single. Educ: Washington & Lee Univ, BA, 59; Univ Mo, Columbia, summer 61; Univ Ark, LLB, 62; Southern Methodist Univ Southwestern Grad Sch Banking, dipl, 72. Polit & Govt Pos: Page, Rep Nat Conv, 52, asst sgt-at-arms, 56 & 60, alt deleg, 68 & 72; pres, Washington & Lee Univ Young Rep Club, 58-59; pres, Univ Ark Young Rep Club, 60-61; Young Rep Nat Committeeman, Ark, 61-62; mem, Pulaski Co Rep Comt, 62-, vchmn, currently; exec dir, Ark Rep State Comt, 64, chmn rules comt, 68, mem from Pulaski Co, 66-68, mem exec comt, 72-; elec comnr, Pulaski Co, 68-70; regional chmn, Big Rock Rep Region, 72- Bus & Prof Pos: Assoc, House, Holmes & Jewell Law Firm, 63-68; trust officer, Commercial Nat Bank, Little Rock, 68- Mil Serv: Entered as Pvt, Army Res, 62, released as SP-6, 68, after serv in 431st Civil Affairs Co. Mem: Delta Theta Phi; Am Bar Asn; Am Judicature Soc; Country Club of Little Rock; Big Brothers of Pulaski Co, Inc. Relig: Christian. Legal Res: 417 E Tenth St Little Rock AR 72202 Mailing Add: PO Box 624 Little Rock AR 72203

BUTLER, ROBERT NEIL (D)
b New York, NY, Jan 21, 27; s Fred Butler & Easter Carole B; m 1950 To Diane McLaughlin; c Anne Christine, Carole Melissa & Cynthia Lee. Educ: Columbia Col, BA, 49; Columbia Univ Col Physicians & Surgeons, MD, 53; Nacoms Hon Soc; Phi Gamma Delta. Polit & Govt Pos: Research physician, Nat Insts Health, 55-62; sr surgeon, US Pub Health Serv, 55-62; deleg, Dem Nat Conv, 68; active mem, DC Dem Party; DC Dem for Peace & Progress; Nat Pres Campaign, 68; chmn, DC Adv Comt on Aging, Govt of DC, 69-; consult, US Senate Spec Comt on Aging, 71- Bus & Prof Pos: Mem faculty, George Washington Med Sch, 59-; research psychiatrist & gerontologist, Washington Sch Psychiat, 62-; mem faculty, Washington Psychoanalytic Inst, 62-; consult, St Elizabeths Hosp, 63-, Nat Inst Ment Health, 67- & Dept Pub Welfare, 68-; assoc clin prof, Howard Univ, 72- Mil Serv: Entered as Seaman, Merchant Marine, 45, released as Ens, 47, after serv in Atlantic, Mediter & Pac Theatres; Lt Comdr, US Pub Health Serv, 62-; Atlantic, Mediter & Pac Ribbons. Publ: Human Aging, US Pub Health Serv, 63; Aging & Mental Health, C V Mosby Co, 73; Why Survive? Being Old in America, Harper & Row, 75; plus others. Mem: Group for Advan of Psychiat; Am Psychiat Asn; Gerontological Soc; Am Geriatrics Soc; Nat Coun on Aging (bd, 69-). Relig: Episcopal. Mailing Add: 3815 Huntington St NW Washington DC 20015

BUTLER, WARREN HAROLD (R)
Dep Asst Secy for Community Planning & Develop, Dept Housing & Urban Develop
b Paterson, NJ, Sept 23, 36; s Harold M Butler & Alice Jahn B; m 1964 to Kristin Alma Westberg; c Alison Paige, Karen Suzanne & Jennifer Ruth. Educ: Northwestern Univ, BA with honors in hist, 58; Yale Univ Law Sch, LLB, 61; Univ Calif, Los Angeles, 61-62. Polit & Govt Pos: Legis asst to US Rep William B Widnall, NJ, 62-69; spec asst to Secy George Romney, Dept Housing & Urban Develop, 69, spec asst to the Asst Secy for Model Cities, 69-71, exec asst to the Asst Secy for Community Develop, 71-72, Dep Asst Secy for Community Develop, 72-74, Dep Asst Secy for Community Planning & Develop, 74- Publ: Administering Congress: The role of the staff, Pub Admin Rev, 3/66; A new approach to low & moderate income home ownership, Rutgers Law Rev, fall 67; Citizen participation in model cities, Denver Law Rev, 71. Mem: Am Polit Sci Asn; Fed Bar Asn; DC Bar. Honors & Awards: Am Polit Sci Asn Cong Staff Fel. Relig: Lutheran. Mailing Add: 7005 Arandale Rd Bethesda MD 20034

BUTLER, WENDELL P (D)
b Sulphur Well, Ky, Dec 18, 12; s Henry Butler & Pearl Pace B; m 1947 to Edna Ford; c Wendell Ford & twins, Rendell & Kendell. Educ: Western Ky State Col, BA, 36; Univ Ky, MA, 50; Phi Delta Kappa; Kappa Delta Pi. Polit & Govt Pos: Ky State Sen, 47-51; State Supt Pub Instr, Ky, 52-55, 60-63 & 68-71; State Comnr Agr, Ky, 64-67 & 72-75; deleg, Dem Nat Conv, 68. Bus & Prof Pos: Teacher pub schs, Metcalfe Co, Ky, 31-36; supt schs, 38-42; pres & mgr, Sch Serv Co, Frankfort, 56-59. Mil Serv: Lt, Navy, 42-46. Mem: Nat Educ Asn; Farm Bur; Am Legion; VFW; Mason. Honors & Awards: Distinguished Serv Award, Coun of Chief Sch Officers, 72. Relig: Methodist. Mailing Add: 121 Crittendon Rd Frankfort KY 40601

BUTLER, WILLIAM CHESTER (D)
Miss State Sen
Mailing Add: PO Box 86 Eupora MS 39744

BUTLER, WILLIAM DANIEL (D)
b San Francisco, Calif, May 18, 45; s William Joseph Butler & Kathryn Lamanet B; single. Educ: Univ Wyo, BA, 67; Univ Ark, Fayetteville, MA, 70; Univ Idaho, 70-; Phi Alpha Theta. Polit & Govt Pos: Deleg, Idaho State Dem Conv, 72 & 74; secy, Latah Co Dem Cent Comt, 72-74, precinct committeeman, 74-; alt deleg, Dem Nat Mid-Term Conf, 74. Bus & Prof Pos: Teacher, Ft Richardson, Alaska, 67-69; coordr, New Student Orientation, Univ Idaho, 72-73, instr geog, 73-, area coordr, Res Halls, 73-75. Mem: Nat Asn RR Passengers; Phi Alpha Theta; Phi Theta Chap (pres, 72-73). Relig: Catholic. Mailing Add: PO Box 3373 University Sta Moscow ID 83843

BUTROVICH, JOHN (R)
Alaska State Sen
b Fairbanks, Alaska, 1910; married; c One. Polit & Govt Pos: Alaska Territorial Sen, 44-58; Alaska State Sen, 62- Bus & Prof Pos: Owner ins agency. Mem: Pioneers of Alaska; Elks. Mailing Add: 1039 Fifth Ave Fairbanks AK 99703

BUTSCHER, BRENDA JOYCE (R)
Chmn, Garrett Co Rep Cent Comt, Md
b Needmore, Pa, June 7, 40; d Virgil Lynch & Florence McKee L; m 1965 to Thomas Bennett Butscher; c James Arthur & Lisa Jo. Educ: Southern Fulton High Sch, Warfordsburg, Pa, grad, 58. Polit & Govt Pos: Vpres, Southern Rep Women, 71-72, pres, 72-75; alt deleg, Rep Nat Conv, 72; sgt-at-arms, Md Rep Fedn Women, 73-75; chmn, Garrett Co Rep Cent Comt, 74- Mem: Oakland Homemakers (prog chmn, 75-); Center Street PTA; St Paul's United

Methodist Church Bd; United Methodist Women. Relig: Methodist; Sunday sch teacher. Legal Res: Herrington Manor Rd Oakland MD 21550 Mailing Add: Rte 1 Box 223Z Oakland MD 21550

BUTTERFIELD, ALEXANDER PORTER (INDEPENDENT)
b Pensacola, Fla, Apr 6, 26; s Horace Bushnell Butterfield & Susan Armistead Alexander B; m 1949 to Charlotte Mary Maguire; c Leslie Carter (deceased), Alexander Porter, Jr, Susan Carter & Elisabeth Gordon. Educ: Univ Calif, Los Angeles, 46-48; Univ Md, European Div & College Park, BS in Int Affairs, 56; Nat War Col, 66-67; George Washington Univ, MS in Int Affairs, 67; Sigma Nu. Polit & Govt Pos: Dep Asst to the President, 69-73; Secy to the Cabinet, 69-73; mem, Nat Armed Forces Mus Adv Bd, Smithsonian Inst, 70-; adminr, Fed Aviation Admin, 73-75; consult, Dept Transportation, currently. Mil Serv: Entered as Aviation Cadet, Air Force, 48, released as Col (Ret), 69, after serv as fighter pilot & mem Skyblazers, US jet aerobatic team, Europe, 49-53, aide to comdr, Fourth Allied Tactical Air Force, NATO, 54-55, opers officer, interceptor squadron, 55-56; acad instr, US Air Force Acad, 57-59, sr aide to comdr-in-chief, US Pac Air Forces, 59-62, comdr reconnaissance forces, SE Asia, 62-64, policy planner, Hq, 64-65, mil asst to Spec Asst to Secy Defense, 65-66, sr US mil rep & CINCPAC rep, Australia, 67-69; Legion of Merit; Distinguished Flying Cross; Bronze Star; Air Medal with 4 Oak Leaf Clusters; Joint Serv Commendation Medal; Air Force Commendation Medal; Army Commendation Medal; serv ribbons for Ger, Laos, Vietnam & Antarctica; rated as Command Pilot & Parachutist. Mem: Acad Polit Sci. Relig: Episcopal. Mailing Add: 7416 Admiral Dr Alexandria VA 22307

BUTTERFIELD, ALTON (TONY) (D)
Wyo State Rep
b Salt Lake City, Utah, June 20, 10; m to Lucile; c four. Educ: Jordan High Sch, Salt Lake City. Polit & Govt Pos: Wyo State Rep, 65-, mem transportation & hwys comt, labor & fed rels comt & rules & procedure comt. Bus & Prof Pos: Locomotive engr for Union Pac. Mem: Rawlins Baseball Asn (bd mem); Union Pac Oldtimers Club; Odd Fellows; Quarterback Club; Carbon Co Conserv Club. Relig: Latter-day Saint; Sunday sch supt, 14 years. Mailing Add: 1113 Alder St Rawlins WY 82301

BUTTERS, SHIRLEY SUE (D)
b Pike Co, Mo, Aug 11, 34; d William J Moore, Jr & Velma S Simpson M; m 1952 to David L Butters; c David M, Cary L & Richard L. Educ: Bowling Green High Sch, grad, 52. Polit & Govt Pos: Secy, Pike Co Young Dem, Mo, 53, vpres, 54 & pres, 65-68; corresponding secy, Mo Young Dem, 67, admin vpres, 68; deleg, Dem Nat Conv, 68 & 72; coordr, Mo State Dem Comt, 68 & 69; Dem Nat Committeewoman, Mo, 68-73. Bus & Prof Pos: Dep collector revenue, State License Off, 65- Mem: Eastern Star (Past Matron, Bowling Green Chap); VFW Auxiliary. Relig: Baptist. Mailing Add: 311 N Main Cross Bowling Green MO 63334

BUTTON, DANIEL E (R)
b Dunkirk, NY, Nov 1, 17; s Roy Button & Alice Root B; m 1945 to Revecca B Pool; c Nancy, Sarah, Daniel, Jr, Jefferson & Mary Caroline; m 1969 to Rena P Posner. Educ: Univ Del, AB, 38; Columbia Univ, MS, 39; Phi Kappa Phi. Polit & Govt Pos: US Rep, NY, 67-70. Bus & Prof Pos: Reporter, Wilmington News, Del, 39-43; reporter, Assoc Press, New York, 43-46; dir pub rels, Univ Del, 47-51; asst to pres, State Univ NY, 52-58; exec ed, Albany Times-Union, 60-66; exec dir, Arthritis Found, 71-, pres, 72- Publ: Lindsay: A Man for Tomorrow, Random House, 65. Mailing Add: 1212 Ave of the Americas New York NY 10036

BUTTS, CHARLES LEWIS (D)
Ohio State Sen
b Hartford, Conn, Feb 16, 42; s W Marlin Butts & Jeanne Elizabeth Beattie B; m 1963 to Alice Gould; c John Marlin, Paul Michael, Joanna Jeanne & Helen Matilda. Educ: Oberlin Col, BA, 67. Polit & Govt Pos: Campaign dir, Stokes for Mayor, 65 & 67; mem & secy, Civil Serv Comn, Cleveland, Ohio, 67-69; deleg, Dem Nat Conv, 72; Ohio State Sen, 75- Bus & Prof Pos: Pres, First Class Housing, 69-72; pres, Franklin Publ Co, 72- Relig: Christian. Mailing Add: 4514 Franklin Blvd Cleveland OH 44102

BUTTS, FLAVEL J (R)
Mo State Rep
Mailing Add: 119 Lake Rd Box 581 Candenton MO 65020

BUTZ, EARL LAUER (R)
Secy, US Dept Agr
b Noble Co, Ind, July 3, 09; s Herman Lee Butz & Ada Tillie Lower B; m 1937 to Mary Emma Powell; c Dr William Powell & Thomas Earl. Educ: Purdue Univ, BSA, 32, PhD, 37; Sigma Xi; Sigma Delta Chi; Tau Kappa Alpha; Alpha Zeta; Alpha Gamma Rho. Hon Degrees: LLD, Purdue Univ, Lafayette, 73; DPA, Tri-State Col, 73. Polit & Govt Pos: Research economist, Fed Land Bank, 35-36; agt, Bur Agr Econ, US Dept Agr, 37, collab, 42-44, Asst Secy, 54-57, Secy, 71-; chmn int orgn, Food & Agr Orgn of UN, Rome, Italy, 55-56; committeeman, Ind State Rep Comt, 58-62; chmn bd dirs, Commodity Credit Corp; counr to the President for Nat Resources. Bus & Prof Pos: Research economist, Brookings Inst, 44; instr agr econ, Purdue Univ, 37-46, head dept, 46-53, dean, Sch Agr, 57-68, dir, Agr Exten Serv & Exp Sta, 57-58, dean, Continuing Educ, 68-71, vpres, Purdue Research Found, 68-71; mem adv comt, Export-Import Bank, 59-61; lectr agr econ, Univ Wis, Rutgers Univ & Univ Chicago; dir, Investment Seminar Farm Found, Chicago & Found Am Agr, Washington, DC. Publ: The Production Credit System for Farmers, Brookings Inst, 44; Price Fixing for Foodstuffs, Am Enterprise Asn, 50; plus research bulletins & many mag & jour articles. Mem: Nat Planning Asn (Can-Am Comt, Chicago & Montreal); Nutrition Found; Am Agr Econ Asn; Am Farm Bur Fedn; Capitol Hill Club. Honors & Awards: Commun & Leadership Award for Outstanding Communicator of the Year, Toastmasters Int, 72; Commendation, 106th Annual Session of Deleg Body, Nat Grange, 72; Award for Distinguished & Meritorious Serv, Am Farm Bur Fedn, 72. Relig: Protestant. Legal Res: 312 Jefferson Dr West Lafayette IN 47906 Mailing Add: US Dept of Agr Washington DC 20250

BUXBAUM, LAURENCE RICHARD (D)
Mass State Rep
b New York, NY, Mar 9, 42; s Arthur Michael Buxbaum & Sylvia Keller B; m 1963 to Gloria Lynn Mishuris; c Deborah Lisa & Evan Reece. Educ: Williams Col, BA, 63; Harvard Law Sch, LLB, 66; Phi Beta Kappa; Zeta Psi. Polit & Govt Pos: Asst Attorney Gen, Chief Consumer Protection Div, Mass, 69-71; mem & vchmn finance comt, Sharon, Mass, 70-72; Mass State Rep, 12th Norfolk Dist, 73- Bus & Prof Pos: Attorney, Boston, Mass, 66-69 & Sharon, Mass, 71-72. Mem: Mass & Boston Bar Asns. Relig: Jewish. Mailing Add: 5 Peacock Hill Sharon MA 02067

BUXTON, CLAYTON EVANS (R)
b Salem, Mass, Mar 21, 14; s Ralph Clayton Buxton & Verna Delahunt B; m 1939 to Ruth A Delaronde; c Ruthann (Mrs Joseph DeGilio), John Clayton & Laura Jane; three grandchildren. Educ: Salem High Sch, grad, 32, postgrad course, 33-34; several univ exten courses. Polit & Govt Pos: Campaign rep & chmn, John Volpe Campaign, Danvers, Mass, 60-68; participant in all local, co, state & nat elec for Rep cand, 60-; publicity chmn, Danvers Rep Town Comt, Mass, 60-, vchmn, 65-69, chmn, 69-72; deleg, Mass Rep State Conv, 66-74. Bus & Prof Pos: Advert, cartooning & art work, Buxton Advert, 40-; locomotive engr, Boston & Maine RR Corp, Boston, 41-; broker, Clayton & Buxton Real Estate, Danvers, 60- Publ: Weekly cartoon panel, North Shore Weeklies, 68-69; many free lance cartoons & articles in area newspapers. Mem: Brotherhood Locomotive Engrs; Rockport Art Asn; AF&AM (engrosser, 65-); Anchor Club (vpres); RAM. Relig: Congregational. Mailing Add: 7 Bowdoin St Danvers MA 01923

BUZAID, NORMAN A (D)
Chmn, Danbury Town Dem Comt, Conn
b Danbury, Conn, Mar 26, 23; s Chicary N Buzaid & Josephine Gabriele B; m 1955 to Helen W; c Ann Marie, Peter N, John H, James G & Christopher J. Educ: Fordham Col, BSS, 47, LLB, 50. Polit & Govt Pos: City councilman, Danbury, Conn, 54-66; Conn State Sen, 58-60; chmn, Danbury Town Dem Comt, 68-; deleg, Dem Nat Mid-Term Conf, 74. Bus & Prof Pos: Attorney, Danbury, Conn, 50- Mil Serv: Entered as Pvt, Army Air Force, 42, released as Sgt, 45, after serv in China-Burma-India Theatre, 43-45. Mem: Am, Conn & Danbury Bar Asns. Relig: Roman Catholic. Mailing Add: 68 Deen Hill Ave Danbury CT 06810

BUZHARDT, J FRED, JR (R)
b Greenwood, SC, Feb 21, 24; s J Fred Buzhardt, Sr & Edna Hardin B; m 1946 to Imogene Sanders; c Linda, J Fred, III, George & Jill. Educ: West Point, BS, 46; Univ SC, LLB magna cum laude, 52. Polit & Govt Pos: Admin asst to US Sen Strom Thurmond, SC, 58; alt deleg, Rep Nat Conv, 68; gen counsel, Dept Defense, 70-74; Spec Counsel to the President, 73-74. Bus & Prof Pos: Pvt practice law, 52-57 & 66-68. Mil Serv: Air Force, 46-50. Mailing Add: 40 S Port Royal Dr Hilton Head Island SC 29928

BUZZI, LLOYD DAVID (R)
Kans State Rep
b Arkansas City, Kans, Mar 4, 41; s Kenneth T Buzzi & Ada Boyer B; m 1959 to Judith Martin; c Diedra & Randall. Educ: Univ Kans, BA, 63; Sigma Alpha Epsilon; K-Club. Polit & Govt Pos: Kans State Rep, 73- Bus & Prof Pos: Ins agt, 66-69; owner, Buzzi & Assocs, 69- Mem: Jaycees; Farm Bur; CofC; Elks; Lawrence Asn Life Underwriters. Honors & Awards: Lawrence Boys Club Serv Award, 74-75; Distinguished Serv Award-Outstanding Young Man, Jaycees, 75. Legal Res: Rte 4 Lawrence KS 66044 Mailing Add: PO Box 3247 Lawrence KS 66044

BYBEE, JOHN MONROE (R)
b Idaho Falls, Idaho, May 19, 49; s George Monroe Bybee (deceased) & Barbara Jean Waters B; m 1975 to Carma Lu Child. Educ: Univ Utah, BA, 73, Col Law, cand for JD; Delta Phi Kappa. Polit & Govt Pos: Deleg, Salt Lake Co Rep Conv, 72; deleg, Rep Nat Conv, 72, mem rules comt, 72; chmn, Young Voters for the President, Univ Utah, 72; voting dist chmn, Salt Lake Co Rep Party, 72-; deleg, Utah State Rep Conv, 74. Relig: Latter-day Saint. Mailing Add: 862 Browning Ave Salt Lake City UT 84105

BYCK, MARY HELEN (D)
b Louisville, Ky, June 28, 07; d Cyrus Adler & Alice Goldsmith A; m to Dann C Byck, Sr (deceased); c Lucy (Mrs Shapero), Elizabeth (Mrs Goodman) & Dann C, Jr. Educ: Vassar Col, 28. Hon Degrees: LHD, Catherine Spalding Col. Polit & Govt Pos: Chmn, Jefferson Co Dem Gubernatorial Campaign, 63; served as campaign chmn for several mayoralty campaigns; Dem Nat Committeewoman, Ky, until 72; deleg, Dem Nat Conv, 68 & 72. Bus & Prof Pos: Pres, Byck Bros & Co, 60-64, chmn bd, 64- Mailing Add: 332 Penruth Ave Louisville KY 40207

BYE, GARRY O (D)
NDak State Rep
b Devils Lake, NDak, Oct 31, 42; s Olav Bye & Ruth Nestegard B; m 1966 to Lorna B Veiman; c Andrea & Christopher. Educ: Lake Region Jr Col, Assoc BA, 62; NDak State Univ, BS, 65. Polit & Govt Pos: Dep state treas, NDak, 66-69; NDak State Rep, 74- Bus & Prof Pos: Area develop coordr, Cent Power Elec Coop, Minot, NDak, 69-70, asst to gen mgr, 70- Mil Serv: Entered as Pvt, Army Nat Guard, 64, released as SP-5, 71; Expert Rifleman. Mem: Minot CofC; NDak Water Users Asn; Nat Rural Elec Coop Asn. Relig: Lutheran. Mailing Add: 913 21st St NW Minot ND 58701

BYERLY, RICHARD L (D)
Iowa State Rep
Mailing Add: 7555 Northwest 16th Ankeny IA 50021

BYERS, BERNARD (D)
Ore State Rep
Mailing Add: 3221 S Main Rd Lebanon OR 97355

BYERS, CHARLOTTE Z (R)
Maine State Rep
Mailing Add: Box 223 Newcastle ME 04553

BYERS, FRANCIS ROBERT (R)
Wis State Rep
b Marion, Wis, Mar 30, 20; s Elmer S Byers & Luella DeVaud B; m 1948 to Florence Marquette; c Cristy, Tracy & Jamie. Educ: Univ Wis, PhB, 43; Acacia. Polit & Govt Pos: Supvr, Waupaca Co Bd, Wis, 50-60; chmn, Waupaca Co Rep Party, 56-60; comnr, Northeastern Wis Regional Planning Comn, 67-69; Wis State Rep, Waupaca Co, 69-, mem nat research & environ qual comt, Wis House Rep, 70- Bus & Prof Pos: Ed, Marion Advertiser, Wis, 46-67; ed, Manawa Advocate, 56-59; partner, Cinderella Beauty Salon, 62-; ed, Tigerton Chronicle, 65-67; dir, Marion State Bank, 66- Mil Serv: Entered as A/S V-7, Navy, 43, released as Lt, 46, after serv in Amphibious Forces, Pac Theatre, 43-46; Unit Citation; Purple Heart; Philippine Liberation, Pac Theatre & Victory Ribbons. Mem: Mason; Rotary; Am Legion; Conserv Club. Relig: Methodist. Mailing Add: 357 Garfield Ave Marion WI 54940

BYERS, HAROLD D (D)
Ill State Sen
Mailing Add: 2218 Park Hill Highland IL 62249

BYERS, WILLIAM H (R)
Mem, Los Angeles Co Rep Cent Comt, Calif
b Pasadena, Calif, May 11, 27; s Paul W Byers & Kathryn G Duff B; m 1975 to Joann R Crutchfield; c Paul W & Carol Ann. Educ: Claremont Men's Col, 4 years. Polit & Govt Pos: Mem, Los Angeles Co Rep Cent Comt, Calif, 60-; co-chmn, Comt to Reelect Congressman Glenard P Lipscomb, US Rep, 24th Dist, Calif, 62 & 64, campaign mgr, 66, field rep, 67-70; mem, Calif Rep State Cent Comt, 62-, mem exec comt, 75-; campaign mgr, Comt to Relect Congressman John Rousselot, US Rep, 24th Dist, Calif, 70, field rep, 70-72; field rep, US Rep Jerry L Pettis, 33rd Dist, Calif, 72; campaign mgr, Comt to Reelect Charles Conrad, Comt to Elect John Conlon & Comt to Elect Tim Dolan, 72. Bus & Prof Pos: Pres, William H Byers Agency Inc, 53-; partner, Byers Assocs, Campaign Consults, 72- Mil Serv: Entered as A/S, Navy, 45, released as Yeoman 3/C, 46, after serv in 31st Naval Construction Bn, SPac Theater, 45-46. Relig: Protestant. Legal Res: 852 Highpoint Dr Claremont CA 91711 Mailing Add: PO Box 351 Claremont CA 91711

BYINGTON, HOMER MORRISON, JR
b Naples, Italy, May 31, 08; s Homer Morrison Byington & Jeanette Lindsley Gregory B; m 1932 to Jane Craven McHarg; c Homer Morrison. Educ: Yale Univ, AB, 30. Polit & Govt Pos: Foreign Serv officer & secy, Diplomatic Serv, 30; with Dept of State, Washington, DC, 30-32; press officer, US Deleg to UN Conf on Int Orgn, San Francisco, 45; dep polit adv, Supreme Allied Comdr, Allied Force Hq, Mediter Theater Oper, 46-47; first secy of embassy, Am Embassy, Rome, 45-47, counr, 47, minister plenipotentiary, 48; dir, Off Western European Affairs, Dept of State, 50; counr embassy, Madrid, 54-57; US Rep 14th Session Econ Comn for Asia & Far East, 58; Ambassador, Malaya, 57-61; spec asst to Dep Under Secy of State for Admin, Dept of State, 61-62; Am Consul Gen, Naples, Italy, 62-72. Mem: Metrop Club; Chevy Chase Club. Honors & Awards: Medal of Freedom, 46. Legal Res: CT Mailing Add: Box 18 FPO New York NY 09521

BYKER, GARY (R)
Mich State Sen
b Alvord, Iowa, Nov 27, 20; s Date Byker & Johanna Van Leeuwen B; m 1944 to Henrietta Blankespoor; c Joanne Kay (Mrs Deckinga), Gaylen James, David G, Harlan Jay, Carl Henry & Gretchen Geri. Educ: Calvin Col, AB, 54; Mich State Univ, grad work. Polit & Govt Pos: Bd supvr, Ottawa Co, Mich, 65-67; Mich State Sen, 68- Bus & Prof Pos: Real estate broker, Byker Realty, 56-68. Mil Serv: Entered as Pvt, Army Nat Guard, 40, released as Sgt, 45, after serv in 34th Div, 133rd Inf, African & European Theatres, 42-44; Purple Heart with 2 Clusters; Silver Star. Mem: CofC; Hudsonville Christian Sch Soc; VFW; Farm Bur; Calvin Alumni Asn. Relig: Protestant. Mailing Add: 5732 School Ave Hudsonville MI 49426

BYLES, ROBERT VALMORE (D)
Chmn, Sabine Parish Dem Exec Comt, La
b Robeline, La, Dec 7, 37; s Robert Simion Byles & Ann Murray B; m 1962 to Sandra Summerlin; c Robert V, Jr, Rebecca Kay & Raymond Gale. Educ: Northwestern State Col (La), 55-56; La Technol Inst, 56-57; Lambda Chi Alpha. Polit & Govt Pos: Fire chief, Many Vol Fire Dept, La, 64-68; search pilot, Sabine Parish Civil Defense, La, 64-; scuba diver, Sheriff Dept Rescue Squad, 64-; chmn, Sabine Parish Dem Exec Comt, 68-; staff, Many Local Draft Bd, 53 & 72- Bus & Prof Pos: Partner, Byles Bros Welding & Tractor Co, 60-72; owner, R V Byles Indust, 72- Mil Serv: Entered as AA, Navy, 59, released as AA, 60, after serv in sch. Mem: Sabine Parish CofC; Many Jaycees; Sabine Shrine; Sabine Hist & Cult Soc; Lions. Honors & Awards: Jaycee of Year, Many Jaycees, 66; Outstanding Fire Chief, Many Vol Fire Dept, 67; Hon State Fire Marshall, La State Fire Marshall, 67; Hon Mem Senate, La Senate, 70; La Outstanding Young Man, La Jaycees, 70. Relig: Baptist. Mailing Add: 1750 Robby St Many LA 71449

BYNUM, BEN (D)
Tex State Rep
Mailing Add: 2033 S Lipscomb Amarillo TX 79109

BYNUM, PRESTON C (R)
Ark State Rep
b Pryor, Okla, June 8, 39; s Homer Franklin Bynum & Roma May Hays B; m 1962 to Linda Sue Allen; c Leasa Sue, Angela Dawn & Charlotte Candice. Educ: Univ Ark, 57-60. Polit & Govt Pos: Mem city coun, Siloam Springs, Ark, 62-68; Ark State Rep, Benton Co, 69- Bus & Prof Pos: Partner, Bynum Motor Co, Siloam Springs, Ark, 60-; bd dirs, Liberty Savings & Loan Asn, 67- Mil Serv: Entered as Pvt, Ark Nat Guard, 55, released as SP-4/C, 64, after serv in B Battery, 936 Field Artil Bn, 142nd Group. Mem: Siloam Springs CofC (bd dirs); Sales & Mkt Club of Northwest Ark (bd dirs). Honors & Awards: Outstanding Young Man of 67, Siloam Springs, Ark. Relig: Baptist. Legal Res: 1003 S Maxwell Siloam Springs AR 72761 Mailing Add: Rte 2 Siloam Springs AR 72761

BYRAM, STANLEY HAROLD (R)
Secy, Ind Rep Finance Comt
b North Vernon, Ind, Jan 11, 06; s Henry Nelson Byram & Iona Fleming B; m 1969 to Sarah Black; c Beverly (Mrs William Anderson) & Barbara (Mrs Leo Jordan). Educ: DePauw Univ, AB, 28; Beta Theta Pi. Hon Degrees: DLitt, Lincoln Mem Univ, 64; LHD, Lincoln Col, 66. Polit & Govt Pos: Chmn, Rep Citizens Finance Comt of the Seventh Dist, Ind, 58-61; vchmn & mem exec comt, Rep Citizens Finance Comt of Ind, 58-65; mem, Nat Rep Finance Comt, 59-65; deleg, Rep Nat Conv, 60; chmn, Ind Finance Campaign, 60; chmn, Ind Rep Finance Comt, 60-63 & secy, 74-; treas, Ind State Rep Cent Comt, 61-65; mem, Ind State Off Bldg Comn, 71- Bus & Prof Pos: Pres Grassyfork, Inc, 45-70, retired chmn, 70. Mem: Am Fisheries Soc; NY Algernon Sidney Sullivan Asn; Coun of the Sagamores of the Wabash; Ind Soc of Chicago. Legal Res: 310 E Harrison St Martinsville IN 46151 Mailing Add: PO Box 464 Martinsville IN 46151

BYRD, GARY E, JR (D)
SC State Rep
Mailing Add: Rte 1 Box 616 Hartsville SC 29550

BYRD, HAL CLIFFORD (R)
Rep Nat Committeeman, SC
b Bunn Level, NC, Aug 25, 18; s James Caleb Byrd & MeLinda Hobbs B; m 1943 to Martha Lisabeth Harris; c Hal C, Jr, Martha (Mrs David Carlton Bird) & Melinda Anne. Educ: Campbell Col, 36; NC State Univ, BS, 40; Command & Gen Staff Sch, Ft Leavenworth, Kans, dipl, 44; Phi Psi; Phi Kappa Tau. Polit & Govt Pos: Precinct pres, Rep Ward One, Box Five, 64-65; state committeeman, Spartanburg Co Rep Party, 64-66; vchmn, Spartanburg Co Develop Comn, 65-; finance chmn, SC Rep Party, 66-; deleg-at-lg, Rep Nat Conv, 68; chmn, Inaugural Comt, State of SC, 69; Rep Nat Committeeman, SC, 72-; chmn, Spartanburg Planning & Develop Comn, 73- Bus & Prof Pos: Partner & owner, Byrd & Vermont Real Estate & Ins Co, 47-48; indust engr, Deering Milliken Serv Corp, 48-49, vpres & purchasing agt, 49- Mil Serv: Entered as 2nd Lt, Army, 40, released as Maj, 45, after serv in 31st Training Bn, Camp Croft, SC, First Regt, Camp Reynolds, Pa & Army Serv Forces Personnel Replacement Depot, 41-45; Army Commendation Ribbon; Expert Badge. Mem: Nat Asn Purchasing Mgt; Carolinas-Va Asn Purchasing Mgt; Piedmont Club; Country Club of Spartanburg; SC State CofC. Honors & Awards: Several awards for civic & polit activities. Relig: Presbyterian. Mailing Add: 1009 Glendalyn Circle Spartanburg SC 29302

BYRD, HARRY FLOOD, JR (INDEPENDENT)
US Sen, Va
b Winchester, Va, Dec 20, 14; s Harry Flood Byrd & Anne Douglas Beverley B; m 1941 to Gretchen Bigelow Thomson; c Harry Flood, III, Thomas Thomson & Beverley Bigelow (Mrs George P Greenhalgh, III). Educ: Va Mil Inst; Univ Va. Polit & Govt Pos: Va State Sen, 47-65; US Sen, Va, 65- Bus & Prof Pos: Pres & ed, Winchester Eve Star, Va, 35-; pres & ed, Harrisonburg Daily News-Rec, Va, 37- Mil Serv: Lt Comdr, Naval Res. Mem: Am Legion; VFW; Rotary; Elks; Moose. Relig: Episcopal. Legal Res: Winchester VA 22601 Mailing Add: 417 Senate Off Bldg Washington DC 20510

BYRD, ROBERT C (D)
Majority Whip, US Senate
b North Wilkesboro, NC, Jan 15, 18; s Cornelius Sale Byrd & Ada Kirby B; m 1937 to Erma James; c Mona Carole & Marjorie Ellen. Educ: Beckley Col, Concord Col, Morris Harvey Col, 50-51; Marshall Col, 51-52; Am Univ, JD, 63. Polit & Govt Pos: WVa State Deleg, 46-50; WVa State Sen, 50-52; US Rep, WVa, 52-58; US Sen, WVa, 58-, Majority Whip, US Senate, 71-; deleg-at-lg, Dem Nat Conv, 60. Relig: Baptist. Legal Res: Sophia WV 25929 Mailing Add: 105 Russell Senate Off Bldg Washington DC 20510

BYRD, ROBERT LEE (D)
Del State Rep
b Easton, Md, May 18, 49; s Paul Otis Byrd & Helen Frances Cannon B; m 1970 to Bernadette Marie Callahan. Educ: Troy State Univ, 67-70; Delta Chi. Polit & Govt Pos: Del State Rep, Dist 15, 75-, chmn, Labor & Com Comt, Del House Rep, 75- Bus & Prof Pos: Sales rep, Travelers Ins Co, Wilmington, Del, 72-74, gen mgr, Colonial Ins Co, 74- Mil Serv: Entered as E-1, Army Nat Guard, 70; E-4, Del Army Guard Res. Mem: Christiana Hundred Dem Club. Mailing Add: 10 Beech Ave Elsmere Wilmington DE 19805

BYRD, ROBERT THOMAS, III (D)
Tenn State Sen
b Augusta, Ga, July 23, 42; s Robert T Byrd, Jr & Mary Emma Snelling B; m 1968 to Mildred Grace Kyle; c Ellen Kyle. Educ: Augusta Col, 60-62; Ga Southern Col, AB, 65; Cumberland Sch Law, Samford Univ, JD, 70; Alpha Phi Omega; Sigma Delta Kappa. Polit & Govt Pos: Tenn State Sen, Ninth Dist, 74- Mem: Elks; Tenn Trial Lawyers Asn; Bradley-Cleveland CofC; Am & Tenn Bar Asns. Honors & Awards: Spoke of Quarter, Jaycees, 73. Relig: Protestant. Legal Res: 4704 Cree Lane Cleveland TN 37311 Mailing Add: PO Box 705 Cleveland TN 37311

BYRD, WADDELL (D)
Committeeman, SC Dem Party
b Marion, SC, Aug 26, 30; s Furman B Byrd & Isabella Dew B; m 1949 to Mary Sawyer; c Waddell Dale, Jr & Ken Elliott. Educ: Woodrow Wilson Sch Law; Sigma Delta Kappa. Polit & Govt Pos: Precinct chmn, Dem Party, SC; chmn, Marion Co Dem Party, exec committeeman, 64-; magistrate, Marion Co, 64-; deleg, Dem State Conv, 6 years; deleg, Dem Nat Conv, 68; state pres, SC Magistrate Asn, 68-69; state exec committeeman, SC Dem Party, 69-; SC State Rep, 70-72. Bus & Prof Pos: Attorney-at-law, Marion, SC, 58- Mem: Am Bar Asn; SC State Bar; SC Trial Lawyers Asn (dir); Jaycees (pres); WOW (counsel comdr). Honors & Awards: Young Man of the Year, 55; Magistrate of the Year, 70. Relig: Methodist. Legal Res: 1201 N Main St Marion SC 29571 Mailing Add: PO Box 65 Marion SC 29571

BYRNE, BRENDAN T (D)
Gov, NJ
b New York, NY, Dec 28, 08; s Thomas J Byrne & Clara Janson B; m 1937 to Rena H Faecher; c Mary P, Michael K & Judith A. Educ: Fordham Univ, AB magna cum laude, 30, MA, 36. Polit & Govt Pos: Dir nationwide campaign, Contribute to Your Polit Party, 58-65; partic, nonpartisan prog to modernize archaic elec laws, 57-65; participant & registr, Inform Yourself & Vote Prog, 57-65; mem, President's Comn on Registrn & Voter Participation, 62-65; Gov, NJ, 75- Bus & Prof Pos: Chmn social studies dept, John Adams High Sch, New York, 31-42; ed, Facts Mag, Read Mag & New Books Digest, 46; research dir & copywriter, Grady Advert Agency, 47; dir progs, Am Heritage Found, 47-50, assoc dir, 56, exec dir, 56 & 57-65; pub affairs consult, Fed Elec Corp, 65-; trustee, Richmond Hills Savings Bank, 69-; pub rels dir, Nat Citizens Community for Better Sch, 50; vpres, Valley Forge Found, 51-52; exec vpres, Goldby & Byrne, Inc, philanthropic consult, New York, 54-55; vchmn, NY Comn Hist Observances, 60-63; mem, New York Bd Educ, 61-64; dir, Nat Conf Citizenship, 62- Mil Serv: Lt Comdr, Naval Res, 42-45; Navy Letter of Commendation. Publ: Three Weeks to a Better Memory, 51; Let's Modernize Our Horse-and-Buggy Election Law, 61; How to Help or Hurt Your Country, 63. Mem: Am Polit Sci Asn; Authors League Am; Am Acad Polit Sci; Pub Rels Soc; Am Mgt Asn. Honors & Awards: Freedoms Found George Washington Honor Medal for Pub Speaking, 63; Gold Good Citizenship Medal, SAR, 48. Mailing Add: 621 Industrial Ave Paramus NJ 07652

BYRNE, EMMET FRANCIS (R)
b Chicago, Ill, Dec 6, 97; s James Patrick Byrne & Mary Alice Murphy B; m 1929 to Mary Margaret Farrell; c Sally (Mrs James Martin), Molly (Mrs Thomas Sikorski), Barbara (Mrs Richard Brown), Patrice (Mrs Robert Williams), Emmet F, Jr, Judith (Mrs Neville Lancaster), Mrs Robert Kern & Thomas F. Educ: Loyola Univ, 16-17; DePaul Univ Law Sch, LLB, 20. Polit & Govt Pos: Asst corp counsel, Chicago, Ill, 21-23; asst states attorney, Cook Co, 23-28; chmn bd 86, Selective Serv, World War II; hearing officer, Ill Commerce Comt, 47-48; US Rep, 56; past mem, Rep Exec Comt, Chicago, Ill; mem, Chicago Regional Export Expansion Coun, currently. Bus & Prof Pos: Attorney, currently. Mil Serv: Pvt, Army, 18-19, serv in Ord, Camp Hancock, Ga. Mem: Chicago Bar Asn (comt on cand & comt on criminal law); Phi Alpha Delta; Evanston Rep Orgn; Chicago Alumni Asn; Am Legion. Relig:

Catholic. Legal Res: 828 Judson Ave Evanston IL 60202 Mailing Add: 33 N LaSalle St Chicago IL 60602

BYRNE, JAMES ALOYSIUS (D)
b Philadelphia, Pa, June 22, 06; m 1939 to M Virginia Mullin. Educ: St Joseph's Col. Polit & Govt Pos: Chief disbursing officer for State Treas, Pa; US Marshal for Eastern Dist of Pa; Pa State Rep, 50-52; US Rep, Pa, 52-72. Bus & Prof Pos: Funeral dir. Mailing Add: 2315 E Cumberland St Philadelphia PA 19125

BYRNE, JANE (D)
Mem, Dem Nat Comt, Ill
Mailing Add: 121 N LaSalle St Chicago IL 60602

BYRNE, PEGGY MARY (DFL)
Minn State Rep
b Minneapolis, Minn, Dec 17, 49; d Joseph Emmett Byrne & Anna Mary Scheller B; single. Educ: Univ Minn, BA, 71, grad work, 71- Polit & Govt Pos: Minn State Rep, 75- Honors & Awards: Swedish-Kennedy Scholar Found grant. Relig: Roman Catholic. Legal Res: 524 Van Buren St Paul MN 55103 Mailing Add: Rm 214 State Off Bldg St Paul MN 55155

BYRNES, JOHN CARROLL (D)
Md State Sen
b Baltimore, Md, Sept 1, 39; s Joseph R Byrnes & Ann Sullivan B; m 1970 to Helen McCausland; c Helen Pierson & Ann D'Arcy. Educ: Loyola Col, BS Polit Sci, 61; Univ Md Sch Law, JD, 66; Pres, Loyola Zeta Eta Theta & Loyola Col Club; vpres, Loyola Alumni Asn; class pres, Univ Md Law Sch; pres, Student Bar Asn; founder, Univ Md Legis Research Comn. Polit & Govt Pos: Deleg, Const Conv, 67; chmn issues & legis comt, Young Dem Clubs Md, 68; vpres, Third Dist Young Dem Club, 68; mem, Third Dist Citizens for Good Govt, currently; Md State Sen, 44th Legis Dist, 71-, vchmn, Finance Comt, Md State Senate, 75-, mem rules comt, open space comt & investigations comt, 75-; deleg, Dem Nat Mid-Term Conf, 74; chmn, Md Comn on Intergovt Rels, 75- Mil Serv: Army. Mem: Am, Md & Baltimore City Bar Asns; Herring Run Club Inc (chmn). Honors & Awards: Univ Md Law Sch Distinguished Serv Award & Law Day Award, Student Bar Asn; Silver Key Citation, Am Law Student Asn; KofC Commendation; Patriots Award, Joint Vets Comt; Outstanding Young Man of the Year, Baltimore Jaycees, 74. Mailing Add: 5221 Loch Raven Blvd Baltimore MD 21239

BYRNES, JOHN WILLIAM (R)
b Green Bay, Wis, June 12, 13; s Charles W Byrnes & Harriet Schumacher B; m 1947 to Barbara Preston; c John Robert, Michael, Bonnie Jean, Charles, Barbara & Elizabeth. Educ: Univ Wis, BA, 36; Univ Wis Law Sch, LLB, 38. Hon Degrees: LLD, Lawrence Univ, 62. Polit & Govt Pos: Dep comnr of banking, State of Wis, 38-40; Wis State Sen, 41-44, majority floor leader, 43-44, chmn judiciary comt, 43-44; US Rep, Wis, 45-72, ranking minority mem ways & means comt, US House of Rep, 63-72, chmn House Rep policy comt, 59-65; deleg, Rep Nat Conv, 56, 60, 64 & 68, chmn Wis deleg, 64. Bus & Prof Pos: Gen law practice, 39-44; partner, Law Firm of Foley, Lardner, Hollabaugh & Jacobs, 73- Mem: DC Bar; Wis Bar Asn. Honors & Awards: George Washington Award, Am Good Govt Soc, 62; Distinguished Pub Serv Award, The Tax Found, 63. Relig: Roman Catholic. Legal Res: 1215 25th St S Arlington VA 22202 Mailing Add: 815 Connecticut Ave NW Washington DC 20006

BYRNES, WILLIAM B (D)
Md State Deleg
Mailing Add: PO Box 77 Eckhart Mines MD 21528

BYROADE, HENRY A
US Ambassador to Pakistan
b Allen Co, Ind, July 24, 13; m to Jitka Henson; c Gene, Alan, John & Linda. Educ: US Mil Acad, BS, 37; Cornell Univ, MS in Eng, 41. Polit & Govt Pos: Dep dir of the Off of Ger & Austrian Affairs, Dept of State, 49; dir, Bur Ger Affairs & asst secy of state for Near East, SAsian & African affairs, 49-52; US Ambassador to Egypt, 55-56; US Ambassador to Union of SAfrica, 56-59; US Ambassador to Afghanistan, 59-62; chmn disarmament adv staff, Arms Control & Disarmament Agency, 62; US Ambassador to Burma, 63-68; State Dept Adv to Indust Col Armed Forces, Washington, DC, 68-69; US Ambassador to Philippines, 69-73; US Ambassador to Pakistan, 73- Mil Serv: World War II, command of Serv Supply, Eastern India, command of Serv Supply, Eastern China, responsibility for air base construction in China, responsibility for coord policy affecting opers in India, China & Southeast Asia; Distinguished Serv Medal; Legion of Merit with 2 Oak Leaf Clusters; Air Medal; Spec Breast Order of the Yun Hua. Legal Res: Woodburn IN Mailing Add: US Embassy Islamabad Pakistan

BYRON, GOODLOE EDGAR (D)
US Rep, Md
b Williamsport, Md, June 22, 29; s William Devereux Byron & Katharine Edgar B; m 1952 to Beverly Barton Butcher; c Goodloe Edgar, Jr, Barton Kimball & Mary McComas. Educ: Univ Va, AB, 51; George Washington Univ, JD, 53; Gamma Theta Upsilon; Kappa Alpha Order. Polit & Govt Pos: Co attorney, Frederick Co, Md, 59-62; pres, Young Dem Clubs of Md, 61-62; Md State Deleg, 63-67; Md State Sen, 67-70; US Rep, Md, 71- Bus & Prof Pos: Mem bd visitors, Md Sch for Deaf, 65- Mil Serv: Entered as 1st Lt, Army, 55, released as Capt, 57, after serv in Judge Adv Gen Corps. Publ: The production and admissibility of government records in federal tort claims cases, Md Law Rev, spring 60. Mem: Eagles; Red Men; Optimist; Ali Ghan Shrine; Mason. Honors & Awards: Distinguished Serv Award, Jr CofC, 65. Relig: Episcopal; vestry, All Saints Episcopal Church. Mailing Add: 306 Grove Blvd Frederick MD 21701

BYRON, KATHARINE EDGAR (D)
b Detroit, Mich, Oct 25, 02; d Brig Gen Clinton Goodloe Edgar & Mary McComas E; m to William Devereaux Byron, wid; c William D, Jr, James Edgar, Goodloe Edgar, David Wilson, II (deceased) & Louis McComas. Educ: Liggett Sch, Detroit, Mich; Holton-Arms Sch, Wash; Westover Sch, Middlebury, Conn. Polit & Govt Pos: US Rep, Sixth Dist, Md, formerly; councilwoman, Williamsport, 38-40. Bus & Prof Pos: Chmn flood disaster, Red Cross, Williamsport, Md, 36; mem bd, W H Edgar & Son, Sugar Brokers, Detroit, Mich & W D Byron & Sons, Tanners, Williamsport, Md, formerly. Mem: Woman's Nat Dem Club; Cong Club; Army & Navy Club; Arts Club Washington, DC; Soc Register Asn. Relig: Episcopal. Legal Res: MD Mailing Add: 3202 Scott Pl NW Washington DC 20007

BYSTROM, IRENE NEVILLE (D)
Chmn, Lincoln Co Dem Party, Nebr
b Lincoln, Nebr, July 1, 18; d Keith Neville (former Gov of Nebr) & Mary Virginia Neill M; m 1942 to Roy Victor Bystrom; c Patricia Margaret (Mrs Richard G Stansbury, Jr), Keith Neville & William Victor. Educ: Stephens Col, AA, 37; Univ Nebr, BS in Educ, 39; Sawyers Sch of Bus, 41; Pi Lambda Theta; Kappa Kappa Gamma. Polit & Govt Pos: Co-chmn, Women for Kennedy, Nebr, 60; secy, Nebr Jane Jefferson Club, 60-61; Nebr State Dem Cent Committeewoman, 45th Dist, 60-66, 68 & 70-73; mem, State Prom Comt, 61; Lincoln Co chmn, Morrison for Gov, 62-64; mem, Higher Educ Facilities Act Comn, 64-66, & 70-; vchairwoman, Nebr Dem Party, 64-68; leader, Nebr Deleg to Women's Conf, Washington, 66; state coordr, Robert F Kennedy primary campaign, Nebr, 68; chmn, Women's Activities in Nebr Dem Party, 68-69; mem, Hist Research Comt, 71-; publicity chmn, Lincoln Co Dem Women, 73-; chmn, Lincoln Co Dem Party, 74-; mem, Nebr 1202 Comn, 74- Bus & Prof Pos: Third grade teacher, Ashland Sch, Nebr, 39-40; block worker, Am Heart Fund, 69-75; bd mem, North Platte Jr Col Found, 74- Publ: Columnist, Party girls, Nebr Dem, monthly, 69-70. Honors & Awards: Nebr Ladies Skeet Champion, 57, 59 & 61; Pac Northwest Ladies Skeet Champion, 64; Lincoln Co Outstanding Dem Woman Award, 70. Relig: Episcopal. Mailing Add: 316 E Circle Dr North Platte NE 69101

C

CABALLERO, RAYMOND CESAR (D)
Chmn, El Paso Co Dem Comt, Tex
b El Paso, Tex, Feb 6, 42; s Romualdo M Caballero & Elmira Hernandez C; m 1965 to Dorothy McGill; c Theresa, Jennifer, Deborah & Raymond McGill. Educ: Univ Tex, El Paso, BBA, 63; Univ Tex, Austin, LLB, 67; George Washington Univ, LLM, 72; Phi Delta Phi. Polit & Govt Pos: Asst US Attorney, El Paso, Tex, 67-69; attorney, Tax Div, US Dept Justice, Washington, DC, 69-73; chmn, El Paso Co Dem Comt, Tex, 74- Mem: Am & El Paso Bar Asns. Relig: Roman Catholic. Legal Res: 4520 Cumberland Circle El Paso TX 79903 Mailing Add: 1610 State Nat Plaza El Paso TX 79901

CABANISS, THOMAS EDWARD (R)
b Farmville, Va, Oct 16, 49; s Frank Edward Cabaniss & Myrtle Stembridge C; m 1972 to Ann Chrystene Taylor. Educ: NC State Univ, BS, 72; Univ Va Law Sch, 72-; Phi Kappa Phi; Tau Beta Pi; Alpha Pi Mu. Polit & Govt Pos: Youth coordr, St Clair for Cong, 70; deleg & mem platform comt, Va Rep State Conv, 71, deleg & mem nominating comt, 72; alt deleg, Rep Nat Conv, 72. Bus & Prof Pos: Coop student, Burlington Industs, Clarksville, Va, 69-70. Mem: Am Inst Indust Engrs; Am Bar Asn, Law Student Div. Relig: Baptist. Mailing Add: 710 Overlook Rd Chase City VA 23924

CABELL, EARLE (D)
b Dallas, Tex, Oct 27, 06; s Ben E Cabell & Sadie Pearre C; m 1932 to Elizabeth Holder; c Elizabeth Lee (Mrs Pulley) & Earle, Jr. Educ: Tex A&M, 25; Southern Methodist Univ, 26. Polit & Govt Pos: Mem, Gov Econ Adv Comn, Tex, 52-57; adv bd, Small Bus Admin, 53-60; mayor, Dallas, Tex, 61-64; US Rep, Fifth Dist, Tex, 65-72. Bus & Prof Pos: Coorganized, Cabell's, Inc, 32, served as secy-treas, exec vpres, pres & chmn bd; former dir & mem exec comt, Grand Ave Bank & Trust Co, Dallas, Tex; pres, Tex Mfrs Asn, 55; Dairy Prod Inst of Tex, 56; Dallas Crime Comn, 56-57; Dallas Sales Exec Club, 57. Mem: Legion of Honor; DeMolay; Elks; Dallas Country Club; Dallas City Club. Honors & Awards: Son & grandson of former mayors of Dallas. Relig: Episcopal. Mailing Add: 3701 Turtle Creek Blvd Dallas TX 75219

CABELL, JOHN ALLEN (D)
Chmn, Harrison Co Dem Cent Comt, Ind
b Kiowa, Okla, Oct 25, 09; s George Samuel Cabell & Elizabeth Mildred Winn C; m 1936 to Norma Ruth Windell; c James Windell, Richard Allen, Bruce David & Rebecca Ellen. Educ: High sch grad, 28. Polit & Govt Pos: Twp trustee, Harrison Twp, Ind, 47-54; treas, Harrison Co Dem Cent Comt, 48-59, chmn, 59-; clerk, Circuit Court, Harrison Co, 57-64; bridge administr, Ind State Toll Bridge Comt, 65-69. Bus & Prof Pos: Farm owner & operator, Corydon, Ind, 35- Mem: KofP; Farmers Union; Nat Farmers Orgn; Farm Bur Ind. Relig: Lutheran. Mailing Add: Rte 5 Box 79 Corydon IN 47112

CABLE, JOHN LEVI (R)
b Lima, Ohio, Apr 15, 84; s Davis Joseph Cable & Mary Harnley C; m 1910 to Rhea Watson; c Alice Mary (Mrs Samuel P Hayes) & Davis Watson. Educ: Kenyon Col, LLB, 06; George Washington Law Sch, JD, 09; Delta Tau Delta. Hon Degrees: MCL, Kenyon Col. Polit & Govt Pos: Prosecuting attorney, Allen Co, Ohio, 16-20; US Rep, Fourth Dist, Ohio, 21-25 & 29-33, auth act granting independent citizenship to Am women, 22, co-auth, Restrictive Immigration Act with Nat Aliens Quota Syst, 24, auth, Fed Corrupt Practices Act of 1925 & sponsor of act to present medals to officers & men of the Byrd 'Little America' Antarctic Exploration & drafted report with bill, 30; cand, Gov, Ohio; spec asst to Attorney Gen & Reconstruction Finance Corp, Ohio, 33-37; Rep presidential elector, 36; govt appeal agent, Selective Serv Bd, Lima, 48-60. Bus & Prof Pos: Dir & officer, Client Corps, currently. Publ: American Citizenship Rights of Women, US Senate Subcmt on Immigration, 72nd Cong; Loss of Citizenship; Denaturalization; The Alien in Wartime, Nat Law Bd Co, 43; Decisive Decisions of United States Citizenship, Michie Co, 68. Mem: Am Bar Asn; Lima Kiwanis Club; YMCA; Mason (32 degree); Elks. Honors & Awards: John L Cable Manuscript Collection Established by Syracuse Univ, 65. Relig: Episcopal. Legal Res: 1315 Lakewood Ave Lima OH 45801 Mailing Add: 117 N Washington Dr Sarasota FL 33577

CABRERA, ANGELINA (D)
b Brooklyn, NY; m to Robert Cabrera. Educ: Carnegie Inst Technol, courses in Span, French, Ital & polit sci, 51-54; New Sch Social Research, courses in polit sci, 65-66. Polit & Govt Pos: Mem, Robert F Kennedy for US Sen Campaign, NY, US Ambassador Goldberg for Gov, Carter Burden for City Coun, Herman Badillo for Mayor, Herman Badillo for Cong & Hugh L Carey for Gov Campaigns, 64; staff asst & exec secy to US Sen Robert F Kennedy, 65-68; mem, Robert F Kennedy for President Campaign, 68 & McGovern for President Campaign, 72; mem, Dem Nat Comt, comnr, Mikulski Deleg Selection Comn & Compliance Rev Comn; comnr on Credentials Comt, 72, initiator, Latino Div; deleg-at-lg, Dem Nat Conv, 72; mem & vchmn, NY State Dem Comt; deleg, Dem Nat Mid-Term Conf, 74. Bus & Prof Pos: Secy,

Marine Div, US Army at Ft Hamilton, Brooklyn, NY, secy to vpres, Richard Lapeira, New York, secy, Sales Dept, E R Squibb & Sons, Brooklyn & translr, Foreign Sales Dept, N J Heinz Co, Pittsburgh, Pa, 45-55; exec secy to dir tourism, Econ Develop Admin, Commonwealth of PR, Off in New York, 55-65; assoc dir, Capital Formation, Inc, 68-69, vpres & mem exec comt, 69-72; dir community affairs & pub rels, Nat PR Forum, Inc, New York, 72- Mem: Citizens Union (vpres, mem nominating comt & local cand comt); Aspira of New York (mem bd); Robert F Kennedy Mem Found (Friend); Alliance of Latin Arts (chmn); Community News Serv (mem bd). Mailing Add: 150 Columbia Heights Brooklyn NY 11201

CABRERA ALEJANDRO, ERNESTO (POPULAR DEMOCRATS, PR)
Rep, PR House Rep
Mailing Add: State Capitol San Juan PR 00901

CACCIATORE, SAMMY (D)
b Tampa, Fla, Aug 2, 42; s Sam Cacciatore & Margarita Garcia C; m 1963 to Carolyn Michels; c Elaine Michel & Sammy Michel. Educ: Orlando Jr Col, AA, 62; Stetson Univ, BA & JD, 66; Delta Theta Phi. Polit & Govt Pos: Asst Pub Defender, Ninth Judicial Circuit, State of Fla, 66-67; alt deleg, Dem Nat Conv, 72. Bus & Prof Pos: Assoc law offices, Billings, Frederick & Rumberger, Orlando, Fla, 66-67; James H Nance, Melbourne, 67-70, partner, Nance & Cacciatore, 70- Mem: Fla Bar; Brevard Co Bar Assn; Assn Am Trial Lawyers; Acad Fla Trial Lawyers; Brevard Co Law Libr Trustees. Relig: Roman Catholic. Mailing Add: 525 N Harbor City Blvd Melbourne FL 32935

CACERES MORELL, VICTOR M (POPULAR DEMOCRATS, PR)
Rep, PR House Rep
Mailing Add: State Capitol San Juan PR 00901

CADE, JOHN A (R)
Md State Sen
Mailing Add: 348 S Putney Way Severna Park MD 21146

CADE, JOHN H, JR (R)
Rep Nat Committeeman, La
Mailing Add: Box 1830 Alexandria LA 71301

CADIGAN, PATRICK J (D)
b Springfield, Ill, Nov 1, 36; s Joseph A Cadigan & Eva Kress C; m 1967 to Patricia Lock; c Joseph L & Andrew R. Educ: Wash Univ, AB, 58; Univ Ill, LLB, 61; Sigma Alpha Epsilon; Phi Delta Phi. Polit & Govt Pos: Parliamentarian & legal adv to Lt Gov, Ill State Sen, 65 & 67; circuit court magistrate, Seventh Judicial Circuit, Ill, 65-67; deleg, Dem Nat Conv, 68; asst to Gov Ill, 68-69; staff asst to Sen Minority Leader, Ill State Sen, 67-68 & 69- Bus & Prof Pos: Assoc, Roberts & Kepner, Springfield, 61-65; assoc, Gillespie, Burke & Gillespie, 67- Mil Serv: Entered as Airman, Air Nat Guard, 61, released as Airman 1/C, 66, after serv in 180th Tactical Fighter Squadron, 61-62. Mem: Am Bar Assn; Ill Supreme Court; US Seventh Circuit Court Appeals; Sangamo Club; Island Bay Yacht Club. Relig: Roman Catholic. Mailing Add: 2317 Wiggins Springfield IL 62704

CADWALLADER, JAMES KERRICK (R)
Mem, Rep State Cent Comt of NMex
b Alamogordo, NMex, Apr 10, 27; s Edgar E Cadwallader & Allene Blacker C; m 1955 to Jane Briner; c Allene Beth, Jan Elaine, Laurel Anne, Gwynn Adele & James Bruce. Educ: Colo State Univ, BA; Univ NMex, grad work, 2 years. Polit & Govt Pos: VChmn, Otero Co Rep Party, NMex, 65-66, chmn, formerly; mem, Rep State Cent Comt of NMex, 66- Bus & Prof Pos: Owner, Cadwallader Orchards. Mil Serv: Entered as A/S, Navy, 45, released as SN, 46, re-entered as SN, 51, released, 52; Am & Asiatic-Pac Theater Ribbons; Korean Conflict Medal. Relig: Lutheran-Mo Synod. Mailing Add: High Rolls Mountain Park NM 88325

CAEMMERER, JOHN D (R)
NY State Sen
b Brooklyn, NY, Jan 19, 28; s Albert John Caemmerer & Helen Rooney C; m 1958 to Joan Holt; c Jeanne, John, Matthew, Kathleen & Christine. Educ: Univ Notre Dame, BS, 49; St John's Univ, LLB, 57; Monogram Club. Polit & Govt Pos: Pres, Williston Park Rep Club, NY, 58-60; village attorney, Williston Park, 59; dep co attorney, Nassau Co, 60-62; committeeman, North Hempstead Rep Party, 60-, chmn, 66-72; dep town attorney, North Hempstead, 62-66; NY State Sen, Seventh Dist, 66-, chmn villages comt, NY State Legis, 66-68, vchmn, Senate Judiciary Comt, 67-68, chmn Senate Subcomt on Right of Privacy, 68-71, chmn, Senate Comt Transportation, 69-, chmn, NY Select Legis Comt Transportation, 71-, secy, Senate Majority Conf, 73-; deleg, Rep Nat Conv, 68 & 72; chmn, Task Force on Com & Transportation, Nat Legis Conf, Washington, DC, 73- Bus & Prof Pos: Real estate & ins broker, 54-58; attorney, Pratt, Caemmerer & Cleary, 57- Mem: Am Bar Assn; Nassau Co Cath Lawyer's Guild; Maritime Law Assn; KofC; Kiwanis. Honors & Awards: Merit Award, Village of Williston Park. Relig: Roman Catholic. Mailing Add: 11 Post Ave East Williston NY 11596

CAFFERTY, PASTORA SAN JUAN (D)
b Cienfuegos, Las Villas, Cuba, July 29, 40; d Jose Antonio San Juan & Hortensia Hourruitiner S; m 1971, wid. Educ: St Bernard Col, BA, 62; George Washington Univ, MA, 66, PhD, 71. Polit & Govt Pos: White House fel, Dept of Transportation, Washington, DC, 69-70; spec asst to Secy of Housing & Urban Develop, 70-71; mem, Dem Nat Charter Comn, 73-74; mem, Ill State Dem Exec Comt, 73-74; dir, Chicago Urban Transit Dist, 73-74; deleg, Dem Nat Mid-Term Conf, 74; dir, Regional Transportation Authority, Ill, 74- Bus & Prof Pos: Asst prof, Sch Social Serv Admin, Univ Chicago, currently. Publ: Co-ed, The Diverse Society: Implications for Social Policy, (in press); auth, Spanish-speaking Americans: economic assimilation or cultural identity, In: Pieces of a Dream, Ctr Migration Studies, New York, Inc, 72; Puerto Rican return migration: its implications for bilingual education, Ethnicity, 3/75. Legal Res: 260 E Chestnut Apt 912 Chicago IL 60611 Mailing Add: Univ Chicago Sch Soc Serv Admin 969 E 60th St Chicago IL 60637

CAFFERY, PATRICK THOMSON (D)
b Franklin, La, July 6, 32; s R Earl Caffery & Letitia Decuir C; m 1954 to Anne Bercegeay; c Patrick, Jr, Kevin & Michael. Educ: Univ Southwestern La, BA, 55; La State Univ Law Sch, JD, 56; pres student body, Univ Southwestern La; Blue Key. Polit & Govt Pos: Asst dist attorney, 16th Judicial dist, La, 58-62; La State Rep, 64-68; US Rep, Third Dist, La, 68-72. Bus & Prof Pos: Assoc & managing ed, La Law Rev, 55-56; attorney-at-law. Mem: Am Bar Assn; Atchafalaya Basin Causeway Comn; Rotary; Evangeline Area Boy Scout Coun; Iberia Crippled Children's Assn (dir). Honors & Awards: Distinguished Serv Award, New Iberia Jaycees, 59; House of Deleg, La Bar Assn, 62. Relig: Catholic. Mailing Add: New Iberia LA 70560

CAFFREY, JAMES T (D)
Iowa State Rep
Mailing Add: 2312 SW 12th St Des Moines IA 50315

CAFIERO, JAMES S (R)
NJ State Sen
b North Wildwood, NJ, Sept 21, 28; m to Patricia E Campbell; c Jamey, Drew & Stephen. Educ: Princeton Univ, AB, 50; Univ Pa Law Sch, LLB, 53. Polit & Govt Pos: Asst prosecutor, Cape May Co, NJ, 2 years; mem & past pres, Cape May Co Young Rep Club; mem, North Wildwood Men's Rep Club; solicitor, City of North Wildwood & Boroughs of West Wildwood & Woodbine, currently; NJ State Assemblyman, Dist 1, 68-71; NJ State Sen, 72-, Rep Majority Whip, 73- Bus & Prof Pos: Attorney-at-law, Wildwood, NJ, 54-; mem bd dir, Marine Nat Bank, currently. Mil Serv: Lt, Naval Res (Ret). Mem: Wildwood Jr CofC; Am Bar Assn; Cape May Co Community Concerts Assn; Kiwanis; Navy League. Relig: Roman Catholic. Legal Res: 410 Ocean Ave North Wildwood NJ 08260 Mailing Add: 3303 New Jersey Ave Wildwood NJ 08260

CAFIERO, RENEE VERA (D)
Committeewoman, Kings Co Dem Comt, NY
b New York, NY, Oct 3, 43; d Henry M Pachter & Hedwig Rösler P; m 1962 to Arthur D Cafiero; div. Educ: Queens Col (NY), BA in Music, 66. Polit & Govt Pos: Alt deleg, Dem Nat Conv, 72; committeewoman, Kings Co Dem Comt, NY, 72-; corresponding secy, WBrooklyn Independent Dem, 73- Bus & Prof Pos: Research asst, Samuel Ambaras, Inc, Antiquarian Bookseller, New York, 66-69; ed asst, Pet Libr Ltd, 69-70; sr copy ed, Harper & Row, Publs, Jr Books, 70- Mem: Gay Activists Alliance of Brooklyn (secy, 72-); Assn Harper & Row Employees; Am Civil Liberties Union; Nat Comt for Sane Nuclear Policy; Common Cause; Mattachine Soc, Inc of NY (vpres, secy & mem exec bd various times, 64-). Relig: Deist. Mailing Add: 164 Hicks St Brooklyn NY 11201

CAGLE, ROY FRANCIS (R)
Chmn, Jasper Co Rep Comt, Mo
b Detroit, Mich, Aug 8, 38; s Roy C Cagle & Frances Godina C; m 1960 to Karen Lee Taylor; c Christopher L, Kelly K & Cortnee L. Educ: Kans State Col Pittsburg, BSEd, 61. Polit & Govt Pos: Chmn, Jasper Co Rep Comt, Mo, 73- Bus & Prof Pos: Prin, Roy Cable & Assocs, Joplin, Mo. Mil Serv: Entered as 2nd Lt, Army, 61, released as 1st Lt, 63, after serv in 3rd Inf Div, Ger. Mem: Scottish Rite; Shrine; Kans State Col Pittsburg Alumni Assn (bd dirs); Distinguished Athletes Assn; Nat Assn Intercollegiate Athletics. Relig: Methodist. Legal Res: 2801 Kansas Ave Joplin MO 64801 Mailing Add: Box 1224 Joplin MO 64801

CAHILL, WILLIAM T (R)
Gov, NJ
b Philadelphia, Pa, June 25, 12; m to Elizabeth B Myrtetus; c Eight. Educ: St Joseph's Col, AB, 33; Rutgers Law Sch, LLB, 37. Hon Degrees: BCL, Seton Hall Univ, St Joseph's Col & Rutgers Univ. Polit & Govt Pos: Prosecutor, City of Camden; first asst prosecutor, Co of Camden; Dep Attorney Gen of NJ; spec agent, Fed Bur of Invest; mem, NJ State Legis; US Rep, NJ, 58-70; Gov, NJ, 71-; deleg, Rep Nat Conv, 72. Bus & Prof Pos: Attorney. Relig: Catholic. Legal Res: Morven Princeton NJ 08540 Mailing Add: State House Trenton NJ 08625

CAHILLANE, SEAN FRANCIS (D)
Mass State Rep
b Springfield, Mass, Feb 9, 51; s Maurice John Cahillane & Eileen Bridget Carney C; single. Educ: Stone Hill Col, BA, 73. Polit & Govt Pos: Mass State Rep, 75- Mailing Add: 141 Phoenix Terr Springfield MA 01104

CAHOON, HOWARD C, JR (R)
Mass State Rep
Mailing Add: State Capitol Boston MA 02133

CAIN, FRANCIS JOSEPH (D)
b Burlington, Vt; s Leo Andrew Cain & Elizabeth Carpenter C; m 1947 to Mary Jane Allen; c Michael, William, Carolyn, Thomas, Martha, Patricia, Karen Elizabeth, Susan, Barbara, & Brian. Educ: St Michael's Col, AB, 43; Am Inst Property & Liability Underwriters, CPCU, 51. Polit & Govt Pos: Park comnr, Burlington, Vt, 58-62, alderman, Ward I, 62-65, mayor, 65-; deleg, Dem Nat Conv, 68; candidate, US House Rep, 74- Mil Serv: Entered as Midn, Naval Res, 43, released as Lt(jg), 46, after serv in European, Mediter & Pac Theatres, 44-46. Mem: Soc Chartered Property Casualty Underwriters; KofC (4 degree); Am Legion. Relig: Catholic. Mailing Add: 22 Bilodeau Court Burlington VT 05401

CAIN, FRED F (D)
Mass State Rep
b Arlington, Mass, Nov 5, 09; s James F Cain & Ethel Taylor C; m 1928 to Ann T Walsh; c Ethel F (Mrs Butters), Fred D, Robert J, James K, Ann J (Mrs Burke), George M & Catherine (Mrs Todd). Educ: Woburn High Sch, Mass, grad, 26. Polit & Govt Pos: Mass State Rep, 25th Dist, 65-, clerk, Comt on Counties, Mass House Rep, 65-66, chmn comt local affairs, mem comt banks & banking & vchmn comt pub welfare, 67-68, chmn comt elec laws, 69-70, mem ways & means comt, 71-; mem, Interstate Coop Comn, 65-; mem, Munic Probs Comn, 67-; mem, Gov Hwy Safety Comn, 67- Bus & Prof Pos: Treas, Fred F Cain, Inc, 36- & NAm Acceptance Co, 40-; pres & chmn bd, Commercial Bank & Trust Co, 68- Mem: Nat Soc State Legislators (dir, 67-); Tewksbury Wilmington Elks (charter trustee); Wilmington Rotary (charter pres); Boston Madison Sq Garden Club; Wilmington KofC. Honors & Awards: Quality Award for Community Serv, Saturday Eve Post, 64; Sr Citizens Pub Serv Award, Sr Citizens Am, 66; Dale Carnegie Award for Community Leadership, 69; Award for Outstanding Community Serv, Time Mag, 70; Man of Year, Middlesex Co Dem Club, 71. Relig: Catholic. Legal Res: 19 Clark St Wilmington MA 01887 Mailing Add: 580 Main St Wilmington MA 01887

CAIN, GERARD A (D)
Del State Rep
Mailing Add: 2 Stallion Dr Newark DE 19713

CAIN, JAMES DAVID (D)
La State Rep
b Pitkin, La, Oct 13, 38; s Alton J Cain, Sr & Mary Etta Thornton; m 1961 to Goldie Bonds; c Melissa Ann & James David, Jr. Educ: McNeese State Univ, BA, MEd, 62. Polit & Govt Pos: La State Rep, Dist 32, 72- Bus & Prof Pos: Sch teacher & head coach, E Beauregard High Sch, 64-72. Mil Serv: Entered as E-1, Army, 58, released as Pfc E-3, 60, after serv in 52nd MP Co. Mem: Beauregard Parish Cattlemen's Asn; Am Brahman Breeder's Asn; La Coaches Asn; McNeese Alumni Asn; Beauregard CofC. Honors & Awards: Outstanding Coach in Dist, six times; Coach of the Year in State La, twice. Relig: Baptist. Mailing Add: PO Box 427 Dry Creek LA 70637

CAIN, RUTH RODNEY (DFL)
Assoc Chairperson, Minn Dem-Farmer-Labor Party
b Austin, Minn, May 17, 35; d Charles Frank Chambers & Ruth Woolery C; m 1957 to Richard Ralph Cain; c Jennifer, Anna & Joseph. Educ: Univ Minn, 53-56. Polit & Govt Pos: Chairwoman, Dist 50B Dem-Farmer-Labor Party, 68-70; campaign staff, St Paul Mayoral Campaigns, 70-72; off mgr, Fourth Cong Dist Dem-Farmer-Labor Party, St Paul, 71-72; assoc chairperson, Minn Dem-Farmer-Labor Party, 72-; mem, Dem Nat Comt, currently. Bus & Prof Pos: Serv rep, NW Bell, Minneapolis, 56-57; Serv Rep, SW Bell, Kansas City, Mo, 57-58; waitress, Savannah, Mo, 58; caseworker, Buchanan Co, Mo, 58-59. Legal Res: 5750 Portland White Bear Lake MN 55110 Mailing Add: 730 E 38th St Minneapolis MN 55407

CAIN, VIRGINIA HARTIGAN (D)
Northern Nev Coordr, Dem State Cent Comt
b Brooklyn, NY, May 1, 22; d James Gerard Hartigan & Virginia Hainza Williams H; m 1944 to Edmund Joseph Cain; c Edmund J, III, Mary Ellen (Mrs Samuel Patrick McMullen), James Michael; two grandchildren. Educ: NY Univ, BA, 43; Univ Del, MEd, 63; Univ Nev, Reno, 69-73; Newman Club, Pan-Am Soc; Speech Club; Drama Soc. Polit & Govt Pos: Vchmn, Bus & Prof Men & Women for John F Kennedy, 60; mem, Gov Comt on Status of Women, Nev, 68-; mem, Gov Adv Bd, Girls Training Sch, 70-74; Northern Nev coordr, Dem State Cent Comt, 70-; Northern Nev coordr for George McGovern; deleg, Dem Nat Conv, 72 & Dem Nat Mid-Term Conf, 74; Northern Nev chmn, Dem Telethon, 74. Bus & Prof Pos: Personnel counr, Research & Develop Labs, US Govt, 43-46; research asst, Group Dynamics, Univ Del, 56-57; high sch teacher, Nev, 68-73; spec proj coordr, Nat Coun Juv Court Judges, 74- Mem: United Way (exec bd, 69); Bus & Prof Women (legis chmn, 74-75); Planned Parenthood (exec bd); Northern Nev Ment Health Asn (adv bd); Dem Women's Club (vpres, 73-74). Honors & Awards: Best Legis Prog, Reno Bus & Prof Women. Relig: Christian. Legal Res: 3710 Clover Way Reno NV 89502 Mailing Add: Box 8000 Univ Nev Reno NV 89507

CAJERO, CARMEN (D)
Ariz State Rep
Mailing Add: 104 West Dist Tucson AZ 85714

CALABRESE, ANTHONY O (D)
Ohio State Sen
b Forli Del Sannio, Campobasso, Italy, July 20, 11; s Raffaele Calabrese & Filomena Giammari C; m 1931 to Mary Margaret Buzzelli; c Anthony O, Jr & Leonard Michael. Educ: Western Reserve Univ, 58-60. Hon Degrees: LLD, Bethany Col. Polit & Govt Pos: Nominee, Cleveland City Coun, Ohio, 50; ward leader, 19th Ward Dem Party, 50; precinct committeeman, Dem Party, 52-56; Ohio State Rep, 52-56; Ohio State Sen, 63-; Minority Leader, Ohio State Senate, 71-72, 73-; deleg, Dem Nat Conv, 68. Bus & Prof Pos: Pres, Real Estate Appraisal & Bus Consults, 50-; pres, Calabrese & Assocs, 50-; mkt consult, Massillon Savings & Loan Co, 64- Mem: Appraisers Asn, Ohio; KofC; Sons of Italy; Boys Town of Italy; Columbus Day Civic Club. Honors & Awards: Man of Year Award, 62; Cross of Order of Merit, Repub of Italy, 59. Relig: Roman Catholic. Mailing Add: 12618 Fairhill Rd Cleveland OH 44120

CALABRESE, SYLVIA M (D)
Recording Secy, 14th Cong Dist Dem Orgn, Mich
b Detroit, Mich, Dec 31, 34; d Orland J Calabrese & Ralphine Barretta C; single. Educ: East Commerce High Sch, diploma, 53. Polit & Govt Pos: Recording secy, 14th Dist Young Dem, Mich, 65-67; recording secy, Fighting Fourteenth Dem Club, 66-67; exec bd, Am Dem Action, Metrop Detroit Chap, 67-68; precinct deleg, Dem Party, Mich, 66-72; recording secy, 14th Cong Dist Dem Orgn, 67-; mem, Citizens for Kennedy, 68; alt deleg, Dem Nat Conv, 68, deleg, 72; deleg, Dem Nat Mid-Term Conf, 74. Bus & Prof Pos: Supvr, Mich Blue Cross, 58-61, procedure analyst, 61-68, specialist, 68-71, supvr, 71- Relig: Roman Catholic. Mailing Add: 14667 Collingham Detroit MI 48205

CALANDRA, JOHN D (R)
NY State Sen
Mailing Add: 88 Beech Tree Lane Bronx NY 01803

CALDEN, GERTRUDE BECKWITH (R)
Mem, Rep State Cent Comt Calif
b Santa Paula, Calif, Apr 18, 09; d Ralph Leslie Beckwith & Bernice Hart Hall B; m 1961 to Guy Cecil Calden, Jr, wid; c Thad Carlyle MacMillan. Educ: Woodbury Col, grad in Bus; Santa Barbara City Col; Univ Calif, Berkeley; Univ Calif, Los Angeles; Univ Calif, Santa Barbara; Univ Affiliates. Polit & Govt Pos: Admin asst to Santa Barbara Co campaign chmn, Nixon-Lodge campaign, Calif, 60; assisted recruitment & strategy, Nixon for Gov, Santa Barbara Co, 62; organizer & charter pres, Montecito Rep Women's Club, Federated. 63-65; vpres, Santa Barbara Rep Assembly, 64-65; organizer, Coldspring, Mission Area, Riviera, Alamar, GALS & Santa Maria Rep Women's Clubs, Federated, 65-68; mem, 13th Cong Dist Rep Comt, 65-; co chmn, Robert Finch for Lt Gov, 66; pres, Santa Barbara Co Fedn of Rep Women's Clubs, 66-70; mem bd of dirs, Calif Federated Rep Women, Southern Div, 66-69; assoc mem, Rep State Cent Comt of Calif, 67-68, mem, 69-, mem, Speakers Bur, 67-69, mem platform comt, 69-70; deleg, Nat Conv, Nat Fedn of Rep Women, 67 & 69; deleg, Rep Women's Nat Spring Conf, 68 & 69; co fedn coordr, Women for Nixon-Agnew, 68; mem, State Adv Comt on Continuing Educ for Calif Community Cols, 69-70; nat chmn, Community Serv Comt, Nat Fedn of Rep Women, 69-71; chmn, Santa Barbara Co Women for Sen Murphy, 70; mem & secy, Santa Barbara Co Rep Cent Comt, until 73; deleg, Nat Rep Leadership Conf, 72; Santa Barbara Co chmn, Reelect the President Campaign, 72; mem community adv comt, State Employment Development Dept, 75- Bus & Prof Pos: Co-founder & pres of community coun, Santa Barbara City Col, Calif, 57-63; mem bd of dirs, Santa Barbara Personnel Asn, 57-58; chmn teacher recognition div, Santa Barbara Co Selective Teacher Recruitment Coun, 60; pres adult educ adv comt, Santa Barbara Community Col, 67-69; mem bd of dirs, Santa Barbara Work Training Prog Inc, 69-, treas, 73-74; bd dirs, Recording for the Blind, Santa Barbara, 74-; mem, Nat Adv Coun Adult Educ, 74- Publ: Contributed various poems, Gossamer Wings, 39. Mem: Zonta Int; Calif Hist Soc; Nat Soc of Parliamentarians; Calif Parliamentary Soc; Int Platform Asn. Relig: Protestant. Mailing Add: 745 Calle de los Amigos Santa Barbara CA 93105

CALDWELL, E A (RED) (D)
Okla State Sen
Mailing Add: State Capitol Oklahoma City OK 73105

CALDWELL, IRENE CATHERINE (R)
State Committeewoman, Mass Rep State Comt
b Medford, Mass, Apr 30, 21; d Pacifico Antonelli & Emilia Quarato A; m 1959 to Owen Manson Caldwell. Educ: Somerville High Sch, Mass. Polit & Govt Pos: Mem, Mass Women Fedn Rep Club, 52; pres, Women's Columbus Rep Club, Mass, 60; mem, Boston City Comt, 60; vchmn, Rep Ward Comt, Jamaica Plain, 68; alt deleg, Rep Nat Conv, 68; state committeewoman, Mass Rep State Comt, 68- Relig: Catholic. Mailing Add: 50 Lochstead Ave Jamaica Plain MA 02130

CALDWELL, J EDWARD (D)
Chmn, Fairfield Co Dem Party
b Bridgeport, Conn, June 13, 27; married. Educ: Fairfield Univ, BA cum laude; Univ Conn Law Sch, LLB. Polit & Govt Pos: Conn State Sen, 59-74; chmn, Fairfield Co Dem Party, 71-; state comptroller, Conn, currently. Bus & Prof Pos: Attorney. Mailing Add: 773 Huntington Turnpike Bridgeport CT 06610

CALDWELL, JAMES CARLTON (R)
b Decatur, Ala, Sept 24, 25; s James Carlton Caldwell, Sr (deceased) & Jewel Farrar C; m 1946 to Mary Griswold; c James Wesley, Carlton Dewitt, Mark Rankin & Bruce Griswold. Educ: Univ Chattanooga, BBA, 50. Polit & Govt Pos: Tenn State Rep, 59-68; spec counsel to Gov for Legislation, currently. Bus & Prof Pos: Pres, Caldwell & Assoc Inc, 54-; secy, Nat Motor Club, Inc, 59- Mil Serv: Entered as Pvt, Army Air Corps, 43, released as Cpl, 46, after serv in 160th Liaison Sq Commando, South Pac, 44-45; Battle Ribbons. Mem: Insurors; Orange Grove Ctr Retarded Children (bd mem); Chartered Property & Casualty Underwriters Soc (secy); Jr CofC; CofC; Signal Mt Golf & Country Club. Honors & Awards: Young Man of the Year, Tenn, 56. Relig: Baptist; Deacon. Mailing Add: 1116 Crownpoint Rd West Signal Mountain TN 37377

CALDWELL, JAMES EVERT (D)
b Denver, Colo, Feb 25, 42; s Joseph Clark Caldwell, Sr & Evelyn Mae Proffitt C; m 1964 to Joyce Elaine Hoeme; c James E, Jr & Stephanie Elaine. Educ: Kans State Teachers Col, BS, 64; Univ Mo-Kansas City Sch Dent, DDS, 71; Xi Psi Phi. Polit & Govt Pos: Chmn, Osborne Co Dem Party, Kans, formerly; First Dist rep, Kans State Dem Comt, formerly. Bus & Prof Pos: Pres, Univ Mo-Kansas City Dent Study Club for Continuing Educ, 71-; mem staff, Osborne Co Mem Hosp, 71- Mil Serv: Entered as Airman Basic, Air Force Res, 60, released as Airman 1/C, 63, after serv in Strategic Air Command, US. Mem: Am Acad Oral Surg; Am Acad Gen Practitioners; Midwest Functional Jaw Orthopedics; Northwest Dist Dent Soc; Mason. Relig: Lutheran Mailing Add: 202 S Fourth Osborne KS 67473

CALDWELL, JAMES LAWRENCE (JIMMY) (D)
Miss State Sen
Mailing Add: 324 Beverly Circle Crystal Springs MS 39059

CALDWELL, JIM (R)
Ark State Sen
b Dardanelle, Ark, Oct 29, 36; m 1955 to LaFerne; c Vicki, Sherri, Patti & Kelli. Educ: Harding Col; Univ Tulsa, 58. Polit & Govt Pos: Ark State Sen, 68-, mem, Rds & Hwys, Educ & Finance & Banking Comts, Ark State Senate, currently; app mem, Educ Comn States; chmn, Ark Rep Party, 73-75; mem, Rep Nat Comt, 73-75. Bus & Prof Pos: Owner, real estate interest & moving & storage business. Mem: Rogers CofC (bd dirs); Kiwanis Club; York Col (bd dir); Nat Soc State Legislators; Northwest Ark Econ Develop Dist (exec bd). Mailing Add: 1002 S Sixth St Rogers AR 72756

CALDWELL, JOHN JAY, JR (R)
Chmn, Marengo Co Rep Party, Ala
b Demopolis, Ala, July 12, 23; s John Jay Caldwell & Alice Ars C; m 1947 to Mary Lane Lee; c Cathy & John Jay. Educ: Auburn Univ, BS, 47; Alpha Omega Pi; Phi Delta Theta. Polit & Govt Pos: Chmn, Marengo Co Rep Party, Ala, 68- Bus & Prof Pos: Log & timber buyer, Miller & Co, Inc, York, Ala, 48-63, log & timber buyer, Demopolis, Ala, 63- Mil Serv: Entered as A/S, Navy, 43, released as Ens, 46 after serv in assembly & repair plant, Seattle, Wash, 45-46. Mem: Lions Int. Relig: Methodist. Legal Res: US Hwy 80 E Demopolis AL 36732 Mailing Add: PO Box 148 Demopolis AL 36732

CALDWELL, JOHNNIE L (D)
Comptroller Gen, Ga
b Taylor Co, Ga, Aug 10, 22; m 1942 to Martha Smisson; c Patricia Ann, Barbara Sue & Johnnie L, Jr. Educ: Woodrow Wilson Law Col. Polit & Govt Pos: Ga State Rep, 55-71; Comptroller Gen, Ga, 71- Bus & Prof Pos: Attorney, Thomaston & Zebulon. Mil Serv: US Army, World War II. Mailing Add: State Capitol Atlanta GA 30331

CALDWELL, LEWIS A H (D)
Ill State Rep
b Chicago, Ill, Oct 12, 05; s Lewis A H Caldwell, Sr (deceased) & Mary Prince C (deceased); m 1947 to Ruth Stimpson; c Barbara & Phyllis Y. Educ: Northwest Univ, BS, 33, MS, 40; Alpha Phi Alpha. Polit & Govt Pos: Case worker, Cook Co Bur Pub Aid, Ill, 33-41; probation officer, Cook Co Family Court, 41-48; Ill State Rep, 29th Dist, 67- Bus & Prof Pos: Mgr, Baldwin Ice Cream Co, 52-61; sales rep, Hawthorn-Mellody Farms Dairy, 61-67. Publ: The Policy King, New Vistas Publ Co, 46; Chicago—City of Opportunity & Progress, Cosmopolitan CofC, 61. Mem: Cosmopolitan CofC (vpres, exec dir, 68-). Relig: Methodist. Mailing Add: 7321 S Shore Dr Chicago IL 60649

CALDWELL, MILLARD FILLMORE, JR (D)
b Knoxville, Tenn, Feb 6, 97; s Millard Fillmore Caldwell & Martha Jane Clapp C; m 1925 to Mary Rebecca Harwood; c Sally Perkins (Mrs McCord) & Susan Beverly (Mrs Dodd). Educ: Carson & Newman Col, 13-14; Univ Miss, 17-18; Univ Va, 19-22; Alpha Kappa Psi; Blue Key; Kappa Sigma; Phi Alpha Delta. Hon Degrees: LLD, Rollins Col, Univ Fla, Fla Southern Univ & Fla State Univ. Polit & Govt Pos: Co attorney, Santa Rosa Co & City

attorney, Milton, Fla, 25-32; mem, Fla State Legis, 28-32; US Rep, Fla, 33-41; Gov, Fla, 45-49; chmn bd control, Southern Regional Educ, 48-51; chmn, Fla Comn Const Govt, 57-65; Justice, Supreme Court of Fla, 62-66, Chief Justice, 66-69. Mil Serv: Entered as Pvt, Army, 18, released as 2nd Lt, 19. Mem: Newcomen Soc; Huguenot Soc; SAR. Relig: Protestant. Legal Res: 3502 Old Bainbridge Rd Tallahassee FL 32303 Mailing Add: Forum Bldg Tallahassee FL 32302

CALDWELL, NEIL (D)
Tex State Rep
b Gulf, Tex, Nov 13, 29; s Allen Caldwell & Mattye Hester C; m 1956 to Mary Lou Dorchester; c Bruce Shelton, Matthew Ray, Leigh Ann & Declan Neil. Educ: Univ Tex, BA, 54, LLB, 57; Phi Alpha Delta; Silver Spurs Serv Orgn. Polit & Govt Pos: Tex State Rep, Dist 23, 60- Bus & Prof Pos: Prof law, STex Col Law, 58-59. Mil Serv: Entered as Pvt, Army, 51, released as Pfc, 53, after serv in 3rd Army, US. Mem: Am Legion; Tex Bar Asn; Brazoria Co Bar Asn. Honors & Awards: Photography winner, Houston Div, Nat Newspaper Snapshot Award. Relig: Baptist. Legal Res: 1810 Meadowview Dr Alvin TX 77511 Mailing Add: Angleton Savings Annex Angleton TX 77515

CALDWELL, NORMAN CARL (R)
Chmn, Oscoda Co Rep Party, Mich
b Mio, Mich, Nov 25, 34; s Evert Allen Caldwell & Irene Dorothy Speck C; m 1952 to Donna Lu Vance; c Michael Eugene, Catherine Sue, Linda Lu & Marla Jane. Educ: Mio Agr High Sch, 52. Polit & Govt Pos: Trustee, Bd Educ, 66-67, vpres, 67-68, pres, 68-70; trustee, Mentor Twp, 66-; co surveyor, Oscoda Co, Mich, 68-; chmn, Oscoda Co Rep Party, currently. Bus & Prof Pos: Pres, Caldwell Land Surv, Inc, 71- Mem: Mich Soc Registered Land Surveyors (dir, 72-); Am Cong Surv & Mapping; Oscoda Co Med Aid Fund; Mio CofC; Ausable River Hist Soc. Relig: Protestant. Legal Res: 301 E 13th St Mio MI 48647 Mailing Add: Box 445 Mio MI 48647

CALHOON, ED LATTA (R)
b Beaver, Okla, Dec 9, 22; s Walter Lee Calhoon & Wina Rae Latta C; m 1949 to Felice Hazel Warburton; c Scott & Lane Felice. Educ: Northwestern State Col, BS, 47; Univ Okla Sch Med, MD, 51. Polit & Govt Pos: Chmn, Beaver Co Rep Party, Okla, formerly; mem bd regents, Okla Col Lib Arts, 65; mem, Health Serv Research & Develop Dept, Dept Health, Educ & Welfare, 70-; mem, Nat Adv Health Coun, 70- Bus & Prof Pos: Dir, Okla State Cancer Soc, 58-; trustee, Okla State Med Asn, 63-, mem, coun prof educ, 64-, pres elect, 69, pres, 70-71; mem, State Ment Health Planning Bd, 65; adv, Okla Regional Med Progs. Mil Serv: Pvt, Army, 42-43. Mem: Okla Med Polit Action Comt; Okla Univ Med Sch Alumni (pres); Mason. Relig: Methodist. Mailing Add: Box 70 Beaver OK 73932

CALHOUN, ANNE C (R)
Ga State Rep
Mailing Add: 2337 Kings Way Augusta GA 30904

CALHOUN, HARLAN MAYBERRY (D)
Judge, Supreme Court of Appeals of WVa
b Franklin, WVa, Oct 25, 03; s H Mayberry Calhoun & Virginia Mullenax C; wid; m 1954 to Florene Simpson Baker; c Ann Fredlock (Mrs G T Williams) & Joseph Harlan. Educ: Potomac Jr State Col, 21-23; WVa Univ, LLB, 26; Phi Delta Phi; Kappa Sigma. Polit & Govt Pos: Prosecuting attorney, Hardy Co, WVa, 33-36; judge, 22nd Judicial Circuit, WVa, 37-58; judge, Supreme Court of Appeals of WVa, 58-, pres court, 62 & 67. Bus & Prof Pos: Conduct practice court, Col Law, WVa Univ, 49-; chmn, Judicial Coun WVa, 60- Mem: WVa Judicial Asn; Am Bar Asn; Am Judicature Soc; Nat Coun Appellate Judges; Mason. Relig: Methodist. Legal Res: 1549 E Virginia St Charleston WV 25311 Mailing Add: Supreme Court of Appeals State Capitol Charleston WV 25305

CALHOUN, JOHN A (D)
b Berkeley, Calif, Oct 29, 18; s George Miller Calhoun & Ellinor McKay Miller C; single. Educ: Univ Calif, BA, 39; Harvard, MA, 40. Polit & Govt Pos: VConsul, Tijuana, Mex, 41-42; third secy & vconsul, Tehran, Iran, 42-44; for serv officer & consul, Berlin, Ger, 46-49; dep dir, Off German Polit Affairs, Dept State, 50; first secy, Am Embassy & consul, Seoul, Korea, 53-55; adv, US Deleg to Geneva Conf on Korea & Indo-China, 54; Air War Col, Maxwell AFB, 55-56; first secy, Am Embassy, Paris & mem, US Deleg to NATO, 56-57; from dep dir to dir, Exec Secretariat, Dept of State, 57-60; counsr, Am Embassy, Athens, Greece, 60-61; US Ambassador to the Repub of Chad, 61-63; Am minister, Berlin, Germany, 63-67; minister-counsr polit affairs, Saigon, Vietnam, 67-68; US Ambassador to Tunisia, 69-72; retired. Bus & Prof Pos: Mem bd trustees & dirs, World Affairs Coun, Int Hospitality Ctr, San Francisco Planning & Urban Renewal Asn, San Francisco Conserv Music & Alliance Francaise, San Francisco, currently. Mil Serv: Ens, Supply Corps, Naval Res, overseas duty, 44-46. Mem: Am Foreign Serv Asn; Delta Tau Delta; Commonwealth Club, San Francisco. Mailing Add: 720 Lovell Ave Mill Valley CA 94941

CALHOUN, NATHAN MEREDITH (D)
b Vidalia, La, Feb 10, 26; s Robert D Calhoun & Anna Perrault C; m 1951 to Jean Falkenheiner; c Katharine & Mary Ann. Educ: La State Univ, LLB, 50; Delta Kappa Epsilon; Phi Delta Phi. Polit & Govt Pos: Chmn, Concordia Parish Dem Exec Comt, La, formerly. Bus & Prof Pos: Partner, Dale, Richardson & Dale, 50-60; partner, Falkenheiner & Calhoun, 60- Mil Serv: Enlisted, Navy, 43, released as TM 3/C, 46. Mem: KofC; Holy Name Soc; Am Legion; La State & Am Bar Asns. Relig: Catholic. Legal Res: 415 Georgia St Vidalia LA 71373 Mailing Add: PO Box 308 Vidalia LA 71373

CALI, JOHN F (D)
NJ State Assemblyman
Mailing Add: State House Trenton NJ 08625

CALIFANO, JOSEPH A, JR (D)
b Brooklyn, NY, May 15, 31; s Joseph Anthony Califano & Katherine Gill C; m 1955 to Gertrude Zawacki; c Mark Gerard, Joseph Anthony, III & Claudia Frances. Educ: Holy Cross Col, AB, 52; Harvard Univ, LLB, 55. Polit & Govt Pos: Spec asst to gen counsel, Dept of Defense, 61-62; spec asst to Secy of Army, 62-63; gen counsel, Dept of Army, 63-64; spec asst to Secy & Dep Secy of Defense, 64-65; spec asst to President of US, 65-69; gen counsel, Dem Nat Comt, 70-72; mem, Coun Foreign Rels; mem, Dem Nat Charter Comn, currently. Bus & Prof Pos: Lawyer, Dewey, Ballantine, Bushby, Palmer & Wood, New York, 58-61; partner, Arnold & Porter, Washington, DC, 69-71; partner, Williams, Connolly & Califano, 71-; mem bd overseers, Sch Law Vis Comt, Harvard Univ, currently; mem, Bd Child Welfare League, Annual Corporate Bd of Children's Hosp, Washington, DC; bd dirs, Fed City Club; bd trustees, Mater Dei Sch. Mil Serv: Lt(sg) Naval Res, 55-58. Publ: The Student Revolution: A Global Confrontation, 69 & A Presidential Nation, 75, W W Norton. Mem: Am Judicature Soc; Am, Fed & DC Bar Asns; Asn of Bar City of New York. Honors & Awards: Recipient Distinguished Civilian Serv Award, Dept of Army, 64; Distinguished Serv Medal, Dept of Defense; One of Ten Outstanding Young Men, Jr CofC; Very Distinguished Pub Serv Award, Fed City Club, 71. Legal Res: 3551 Springland Lane Washington DC 20008 Mailing Add: 1000 Hill Bldg Washington DC 20006

CALKINS, JOHN THIERS (R)
b Elmira, NY, May 14, 25; s John Thiers Calkins, Sr & Laura Westervelt C; m 1952 to Patricia Painton; c Sharon Lucille & Carolyn Leigh. Educ: Syracuse Univ, AB, 49; Univ London, summer courses, 51; Georgetown Univ Law Ctr, JD, 57; Am Polit Sci Asn Cong Staff Fel, Grad Inst Int Studies, Geneva, Switz, 65; Psi Upsilon; Phi Kappa Alpha. Polit & Govt Pos: Admin asst to US Rep J C Davies, 39th Dist, NY, 49-51; admin asst to US Rep Sterling Cole, 37th Dist, NY, 53-57; exec asst to US Rep Howard Robison, 33rd Dist, NY, 58-70; answer desk, Rep Nat Comt, 60; chmn, Comt Spec Assts to Chmn, Rep Cong Campaign Comt, 62-68; exec dir, Nat Rep Cong Comt, 70-75; exec asst & dep to Counr to President, White House, 75- Bus & Prof Pos: Lectr, Univ NH, Conn Col & Elmira Col; acct exec, Mellor Advert Agency, 52; dir, Elmira Data Processing Corp, NY, 64- Mil Serv: Entered as Pvt, Army, 43, released as S/Sgt, 46, after serv in Army Disbursing Off, Manila, Philippines & New Guinea, 43-46; SW Pac Theater Ribbon with 2 Battle Stars; Maj, Res, 60-69. Mem: Am Legion; SAR; Order of Lafayette; Capitol Hill Club; Elmira City Club. Relig: Episcopal. Legal Res: 448 Breesport Rd Horseheads NY 14845 Mailing Add: 2329 California St NW Washington DC 20008

CALL, GEORGE F (INDEPENDENT)
Maine State Rep
Mailing Add: 118 Pine St Lewiston ME 04240

CALLAHAN, FRANCIS P (R)
NH State Rep
Mailing Add: South Village Box 55 Westmorland NH 03467

CALLAHAN, H L (SONNY) (D)
Ala State Rep
Mailing Add: PO Box 1208 Mobile AL 36601

CALLAHAN, JAMES CHRISTOPHER (R)
b Rutherfordton, NC, Dec 17, 51; s James Arthur Callahan & Janie Gray C; single. Educ: Univ NC, Chapel Hill, Morehead scholar. BA, 74; Wake Forest Univ Sch Law, currently; Phi Delta Phi; Pi Kappa Alpha. Polit & Govt Pos: Deleg, Rep Nat Conv, 72, mem nat rules comt, 72. Honors & Awards: Outstanding Teenager of NC, Outstanding Americans Found, 70. Relig: Methodist. Legal Res: 38 Chimney Rock Rd Rutherfordton NC 28139 Mailing Add: 371-A Glendare Dr Winston-Salem NC 27104

CALLAHAN, ROBERT C (R)
NH State Rep
Mailing Add: Spofford NH 03462

CALLAHAN, VINCENT FRANCIS, JR (R)
Va State Deleg
b Washington, DC, Oct 30, 31; s Vincent F Callahan & Anita Hawkins C; m 1960 to Dorothy Budge; c Vincent F, III, Elizabeth L, Anita M, Cynthia & Robert B. Educ: Georgetown Univ, BS in FS, 57; Am Univ Grad Sch, DC, 58-59; Kappa Alpha Phi. Polit & Govt Pos: Alt deleg, Rep Nat Conv, 64; chmn, Goldwater for President Comt, Northern Va, 64; pres, Old Dominion Rep Club, McLean, Va, 64-65; cand, Lt Gov, Va, 65- chmn, US Senate Campaign, Va, 66; vchmn, Fairfax Co Rep Comt, 66-68; chmn, Va Rep Finance Comt, 66-68; mem, Rep State Cent Comt, 66-; Va State Deleg, 67-, chmn, House-Senate Joint Republican Caucus, Va State Legis, currently; sgt at arms, Rep Nat Conv, 68; chmn Nixon for President comt, North Va, 68; co-chmn, US Senate Campaign, Va, 70; co-chmn, Northern Va Comt to Reelect President, 72. Bus & Prof Pos: Pres, Callahan Publ, Washington, DC, 58- Mil Serv: Entered as Pvt, Marine Corps, 50, released as Cpl, 52, after serv in Third Marine Div; Lt, Coast Guard Res, 59-63. Mem: Nat Press Club; Aviation/Space Writers Asn; US Naval Inst; Kiwanis. Relig: Roman Catholic. Legal Res: 6220 Nelway Dr McLean VA 22101 Mailing Add: 6631 Old Dominion Dr McLean VA 22101

CALLAN, HERBERT QUENTIN (D)
Vt State Rep
Mailing Add: Rte 1 Sheldon VT 05483

CALLAS, MICHAEL G (D)
Treas, Washington Co Dem Cent Comt, Md
b Hagerstown, Md, Apr 14, 21; s George Callas & Pella Stratos C; m to Betty Jane Kohler. Educ: Johns Hopkins Univ, BS, 43, MS, 48; Omicron Delta Kappa; Kappa Epsilon. Polit & Govt Pos: Treas, Washington Co Dem Cent Comt, Md, 70- Bus & Prof Pos: Dir, Antietam Bank & First Fed, Hagerstown, Md, 72-; chmn, Market House Study, Hagerstown & Downtown Improv Comn, 73-74; pres, Assoc Builders & Contractors, Inc, 73-75. Mil Serv: Entered as Pvt, Army, 43, released as Capt, 47, after serv in 29th Engrs, Pac Theatre. Mem: Boy Scouts (dir, Mason Dixon Coun, 65-); Boys' Club Hagerstown (dir alumni, 66-); Md State CofC (regional dir, 68-). Relig: Greek Episcopal. Legal Res: 1610 Fountain Head Rd Hagerstown MD 21740 Mailing Add: PO Box 888 Hagerstown MD 21740

CALLAWAY, HOWARD HOLLIS (R)
b LaGrange, Ga, Apr 2, 27; s Cason Jewell Callaway & Virginia Hand C; m to Elizabeth Walton; c Elizabeth Walton, Virginia Hand, Howard Hollis, Jr, Ralph Walton & Edward Cason. Educ: Ga Inst Technol, 45; US Mil Acad, 45-49. Polit & Govt Pos: Mem bd regents, Univ Syst of Ga, 53-64; US Rep, Third Dist, Ga, 65-66; Rep nominee for Gov of Ga, 66; deleg, Rep Nat Conv, 64 & 68; Rep Nat Committeeman, Ga, 68-73, vchmn, Rep Nat Comt, 68-73; civilian aide to Secy of Army, formerly, Secy of the Army, 73-75; chmn, 1976 President's Elec Campaign, 75- Bus & Prof Pos: Pres, Callaway Gardens, Pine Mt, Ga, 53-72; pres, Interfinancial, Inc, Atlanta, 72-73. Mil Serv: Entered as 2nd Lt, Army, 49, released as 1st Lt, 52, after serv in 17th Inf Far East Command, Korea, 50; Combat Infantryman Badge; Korean Serv Medal Three Bronze Stars; Republic of Korea Badge; Presidential Unit Citation Badge; UN Serv Medal. Mem: Nat 4-H Serv Comt; Freedoms Found at Valley Forge, Pa. Relig: Episcopal. Legal Res: Pine Mountain GA 31822 Mailing Add: 1515 S Jefferson Davis Hwy Arlington VA 22202

CALLICOTT, WILLIAM EDWARD (D)
Miss State Rep
b West Point, Miss, June 16, 24; m 1952 to Margaret Sorrells; c William E, Jr & Alan T. Polit & Govt Pos: Miss State Rep, 60- Bus & Prof Pos: Ins agt. Mil Serv: Nat Guard. Mem: Am Legion; VFW; 40 et 8; Rotary. Relig: Presbyterian. Mailing Add: 212 Wildleaf Dr Senatobia MS 38668

CALLOWAY, DEVERNE LEE (D)
Mo State Rep
b Memphis, Tenn, June 17, 16; m 1946 to Ernest A Calloway. Educ: LeMoyne Col; Atlanta Univ; Northwestern Univ; Pioneer Bus Inst; Quaker Sch; AB in Eng. Polit & Govt Pos: Mo State Rep, 62-; deleg, Dem Nat Mid-Term Conf, 74. Bus & Prof Pos: Teacher; secretarial & clerical work for Fair Employ Practices Coun, Jewish Welfare Fund, Health Dept of Chicago; staff asst, United Serv Orgn Club, Ft Huachuca, Ariz; Am Red Cross, Calcutta, India. Mem: YWCA; Nat Coun Negro Women; Order of Women Legislators; Am Dem Action; NAACP. Relig: Congregational. Mailing Add: 4309 Enright St Louis MO 63108

CALLOWAY, JAMES RICHARD (D)
b Hot Springs, NC, Nov 2, 28; s Norman Astor Calloway & Kate Hall C; m 1949 to Helen Gebhart; c James R, Jr & Susan Jane. Educ: George Washington Univ, AB, 59, LLB, 63. Polit & Govt Pos: Spec asst to US Sen Allen Frear, Del, 49-61; prof staff mem, comt, on govt opers, US Senate, 61-65, chief counsel & staff dir, 65-73, chief coun & staff dir, counsel, Comt on Appropriations, US Senate, 73- Mil Serv: Entered as Pvt, Army, 52, released as Sgt, 54, after serv in Chem Corps, Korea. Mem: DC & Am Bar Asns. Relig: Presbyterian. Legal Res: New Castle DE Mailing Add: 3111 Savoy Dr Fairfax VA 22030

CALOGERO, NICHOLAS J (R)
NY State Assemblyman
Mailing Add: 10 Proctor Blvd Utica NY 13501

CALOGERO, PASCAL FRANK, JR (D)
Assoc Justice, La Supreme Court
b New Orleans, La, Nov 9, 31; s Pascal F Calogero, Sr & Louise Moore C; m 1955 to Geraldine James; c Deborah Ann, David, Pascal, III, Elizabeth, Thomas, Michael, Stephen & Gerald. Educ: Loyola Univ, La, Col Arts & Sci, 49-51; Loyola Univ Sch Law, JD, 54; Blue Key; Alpha Sigma Nu; Alpha Delta Gamma; St Thomas More Law Club. Polit & Govt Pos: Mem, La Dem State Cent Comt, 63-71, mem subcomt on party reform in deleg, selection, 71; deleg, Dem Nat Conv, 68; Assoc Justice, La Supreme Court, 73- Bus & Prof Pos: Partner, law firm, Landrieu, Calogero & Kronlage, 58-69; partner, Calogero & Kronlage, 69-73; gen counsel, Stadium & Expos Dist, 70-73. Mil Serv: Entered as 2nd Lt, Army, 54, released as Capt, 57, after serv in Judge Adv Gen Corps. Mem: Am, La State, & New Orleans Bar Asns; Gtr New Orleans Trial Lawyers Asn. Honors & Awards: Dean's Award; Number One Graduate, Loyola Univ Sch Law, 54. Relig: Roman Catholic. Legal Res: 3524 Gentilly Blvd New Orleans LA 70122 Mailing Add: Rm 211 Supreme Ct Bldg 301 Loyola Ave New Orleans LA 70112

CALTON, BETTY JOAN (D)
Secy, Wright Co Dem Comt, Mo
b Sullivan, Mo, Oct 12, 34; d John Cecil Doyle & Mae Vaughn D; m 1950 to Jones Wallace Calton; c Patricia Joan, Kathleen (Mrs Warren Windhorst); Elizabeth & Michael. Educ: Greene Co Pub Schs, Springfield, Mo. Polit & Govt Pos: Committeewoman, Union Twp, Mo, 62-; mem bd gov, White House Conf on Children & Youth, 68; secy, Wright Co Dem Comt, Mo, 68- Mailing Add: Valley View Farms Grovespring MO 65662

CALVERT, LAWRENCE CONRAD (R)
Chmn, Cullman Co Rep Exec Comt, Ala
b Cullman, Ala, Nov 18, 44; s Conrad J Calvert & Hertilene Garner C; m 1969 to Doris O'dean Rhodes. Educ: Univ Ala, BA, 66. Polit & Govt Pos: Chmn, Cullman Co Rep Exec Comt, Ala, 70- Bus & Prof Pos: Teacher, Good Hope High Sch, Cullman, Ala, 66-, asst prin, 70- Mem: Cullman, Ala & Nat Educ Asns; Nat Farm Orgn. Relig: Church of Christ. Mailing Add: Rte 6 Cullman AL 35055

CALVERT, WILLIAM BAILEY (D)
b Woodlawn, Md, Sept 5, 37; s Wilson Levering Calvert & Erma Bailey C; m 1972 to Janet Susan Asher. Educ: Univ Baltimore, AA, 58, LLB, 60; Sigma Delta Kappa. Polit & Govt Pos: Co attorney, Cecil Co Md, 62-; chmn, Cecil Co Dem Comt, 66-70; deleg, Dem Nat Conv, 68; vchmn Eastern Shore Region, Dem State Cent Comt, Md, formerly. Mil Serv: Entered as Pvt, Marine Corps Res, 60, released as Sgt, 66. Mem: Md & Cecil Co Bar Asns; Am Judicature Soc; Am Legion; Kiwanis. Relig: Episcopal. Legal Res: RD 1 Box 426 A Perryville MD 21903 Mailing Add: 131 E Main St Elkton MD 21921

CALVO, HORACE LAWRENCE (D)
Ill State Rep
b Chicago, Ill, Jan 4, 27; s Horace L Calvo, Sr & Mary C Drew C; m 1947 to Josephine E Beth; c Larry Alan, Mary Elizabeth, David William & Linda Beth. Educ: Univ Ill, Champaign, 44-45; Lincoln Col Law, 50-51; St Louis Univ, LLB, 54. Polit & Govt Pos: Asst Attorney Gen, Ill, 60-68; Ill State Rep, 55th Dist, 69- Bus & Prof Pos: Clerk-off auditor & internal revenue agt, US Treasury Dept, 47-55; title examr, Title Ins Corp, St Louis, Mo, 55-56; attorney-at-law, Granite City, Ill, 56- Mil Serv: Entered as Pvt, Army Air Force, 44, released as Counter Intel Agt, 47, after serv in 702nd Counter Intel Corps, ETO, 46-47. Mem: Am Bar Asn; Am Trial Lawyers Asn; Ill Legis Invest Comn; KofC; Am Legion. Relig: Roman Catholic. Mailing Add: 24 Oaklawn Granite City IL 62040

CALVO, VICTOR (D)
Calif State Assemblyman
Mailing Add: 270 Grant Ave Palo Alto CA 94306

CAMACHO, CARLOS GARCIA (R)
b Agana, Guam, Nov 16, 24; s Felix Martinez Camacho & Antonia Cruz Garcia; m 1955 to Lourdes Duenas Perez; c Carlos Anthony, Felix James, Thomas John, Mary Margaret, Ricardo Jose, Francis Gerard & Victor Charles. Educ: Aquinas Col, 46-49; Marquette Univ, DDS, 54; Delta Sigma Delta. Polit & Govt Pos: Sen, Guam Legis, 64-66; Gov, Guam, formerly; deleg, Rep Nat Conv, 72. Bus & Prof Pos: Dentist, Govt of Guam, 54-55; dentist, Cath Med Ctr, 55-56 & 58-69. Mil Serv: Entered as Capt, Army, 56, released as Capt, 58, after serv in Dent Corps, Camp Zama, Japan, 56-58. Mem: Am Med Asn; KofC (4 degree). Relig: Roman Catholic. Mailing Add: Father Duenas Dr Tamuning GU 96910

CAMACHO, LOURDES PEREZ (R)
Pres, Guam Fedn Rep Women
b Agana, Guam, Sept 23, 28; d Jesus Perez & Margarita Duenas P; m 1955 to Carlos Garcia Camacho; c Carlos Anthony, Felix James, Thomas John, Mary Margaret, Ricardo Jose, Francis Gerard & Victor Charles. Educ: Sienna Heights Col, 50-51; Mercy Col Detroit, BS in biol, 54. Polit & Govt Pos: Med technologist, Guam Mem Hosp, Govt Guam, 54-55, cytotechnologist, Pub Health Dept, 62-69; pres, Guam Fedn Rep Women, 69-; First Lady of Guam, 69- Bus & Prof Pos: Med technologist, Cath Med Ctr, Agana, Guam, 55-56. Mem: Guam Exec Wives Club (pres); Am Cancer Soc (pres, Guam Unit, bd dirs, Hawaii Div); Christian Mothers Soc, Tamuning, Guam (vpres); Guam Women's Club (hon pres); Guam Bus & Prof Women's Club (hon pres). Relig: Roman Catholic. Legal Res: Father Duenas Dr Tamuning GU 96910 Mailing Add: Govt House Agana GU 96910

CAMERA, JOSEPH LEONARD (D)
Ohio State Rep
b Franklin, Mo, Aug 14, 14; s Joseph Anthony Camera & Nellie Lowe C; m 1939 to Laverne Diewald; c Thomas, Jan, Sandra Shuler, Michael, Mary Lawrence, Leonard, Guy & Shawn. Educ: High sch, 4 years. Polit & Govt Pos: Councilman, Lorain City Coun, Ohio, 62-69; Ohio State Rep, 53rd Dist, 69-, chmn agr, com & labor comt, Ohio House Rep, currently. Bus & Prof Pos: Field supvr, Am Shipbldg, 42-47; field supvr, Spohn Corp, 50-69. Mem: Elks; KofC; Pipefitters Local Union; Nat Soc State Legislators; CofC. Relig: Catholic. Mailing Add: 1147 Tenth St Lorain OH 44052

CAMERON, JAMES DUKE (R)
Chief Justice, Ariz Supreme Court
b Richmond, Calif, Mar 25, 25; s Charles Lee Cameron & Ruth Mabry C; m 1954 to Suzanne Jane Pratt; c Alison Valerie, Craig Charles & Jennifer Elaine. Educ: Univ Calif, Berkeley, AB, 50; Univ Ariz Col Law, LLB, 54; Univ Southern Calif; Phi Alpha Delta; Lambda Chi Alpha. Polit & Govt Pos: Page, Ariz deleg, Rep Nat Conv, 48, alt deleg, 52; pres, Pima Co Young Rep Club, 53-54; pres, Yuma Co Young Rep Club, 54-55; mem bd trustees, Yuma City-Co Libr, 59-68; judge, Yuma Co Superior Court, 60; treas, Ariz Rep Party, 60-62; mem, Ariz State Bd Pub Welfare, 63-64, chmn, 64; judge, Ariz Court Appeals, Div 1, 65-71, chief judge, 3 years; chief justice, Ariz Supreme Court, 71- Bus & Prof Pos: Mem bd dirs, Surety Savings & Loan Asn, 65-70; faculty mem, Appellate Court Seminar, NY Univ, 68-70. Mil Serv: Entered as Pvt, Army, 44, released as Pfc, 46, after serv in Inf. Publ: Arizona Appellate Forms & Procedures, Hooper Publ Co, 68. Mem: Am Bar Asn; Inst Judicial Admin; Shrine; Mason; Elks. Honors & Awards: Legion of Honor, DeMolay. Relig: Christian Science. Legal Res: PO Box 1 Yuma AZ 85364 Mailing Add: State Capitol Bldg Phoenix AZ 85007

CAMERON, RONALD BROOKS (D)
b Kansas City, Mo, Aug 16, 27; m to Constance C; c Victoria Brooks, Richard Malcolm. Educ: Western Reserve Univ; Univ of Calif. Polit & Govt Pos: Calif Legis, 58-62; US Rep, Calif, 62-67; Dem nominee controller, 70. Bus & Prof Pos: CPA, 54. Mil Serv: Marine Corps, 45. Mailing Add: 14602 Montevideo Dr Whittier CA 90605

CAMERON, WARD FRANCIS (D)
Supvr, Butte Co, Calif
b Flint, Mich, Mar 17, 21; s Ward A Cameron & Francis Brady C; m 1944 to Joyce A Howard; c Howard F, Dane A & Brady Lee. Educ: Flint Jr Col, Mich, 1 year. Polit & Govt Pos: Co publicity chmn, Brown for Gov, Calif, 58 & 66; mem, Gov Brown's Adv Comt on Pub Info, 62-66; co publicity chmn, Johnson for President, 64, (Bizz) Johnson for US Rep, Calif, each elec year; co chmn, Cranston for US Sen, Calif, 68; chmn, Butte Co Dem Cent Comt, 68-72; co-chmn, Unruh for Gov, 70; NCalif coordr, Tunney for US Sen, 70; supvr, Butte Co, 72- Bus & Prof Pos: Supermkt mgr, Millers Mkts, 47-51; radio salesman, K-Pay Radio, Chico, Calif, 52-, sales mgr, 4 years. Mil Serv: Entered as Pvt, Army, 42, released as Sgt, 45, after serv in 1st US Inf Div, European from NAfrica, Sicily to France & Czech; Eight Battle Stars; Three Assault Landings; Seven Overseas Time Stripes; Bronze Star Medal; Unit Citations; Div Decorations. Mem: Chico Exchange Club; Northern Travelers Club, Chico; Chico Dem Club; Paradise Dem Club; Region Civil Defense (mem staff). Relig: Protestant. Mailing Add: 1837 Merrill Rd Paradise CA 95969

CAMFIELD, JUANITA F (D)
Committeewoman, Tex State Dem Exec Comt
b Thurber, Tex, Feb 25, 17; d Singleton Camfield & Hattie Ball C; single. Educ: San Angelo Col, 50; Real Estate Inst, grad, 64. Polit & Govt Pos: Committeewoman, Tex State Dem Exec Comt, 25th Sen Dist, 72- Mem: San Angelo Bd Realtors; San Angelo Bus & Prof Women's Club; Tex Fedn Bus & Prof Women's Clubs; San Angelo Women's Polit Caucus; San Angelo CofC. Honors & Awards: Tex Fedn Bus & Prof Women's Clubs Awards, 61-64. Relig: Unitarian-Universalist. Mailing Add: 2415 W Harris San Angelo TX 76901

CAMIEL, PETER (D)
Mem-At-Lg, Dem Nat Comt
Mailing Add: 1421 Walnut St Philadelphia PA 19102

CAMMACK, BENJAMIN FRANKLIN, JR (D)
Miss State Rep
b Rockport, Miss, June 16, 08; married. Polit & Govt Pos: Miss State Rep, formerly & 75- Bus & Prof Pos: Farmer; cattleman; merchant. Mem: Copiah Co Farm Bur; Hazlehurst Touchdown Club. Relig: Methodist. Mailing Add: Rte 1 Hazlehurst MS 39083

CAMP, DANA MARTHA (D)
b Sharon, Pa, July 18, 52; d Herbert Lawrence Camp & Betty Delores Brewington C; single. Educ: Univ Southern Calif, 70- Polit & Govt Pos: Vol, Kennedy for President, Los Angeles, 59-60; Baxter Ward for Mayor & for Roberti, Tunney & other campaigns, 66-72; vol precinct capt, Kennedy for President, Los Angeles, 68; student worker, Kennedy Action Core, Los Angeles, 68-69; adv bd, McGovern for President, Pasadena, 72; deleg, Dem Nat Conv, 72; vol, Brown for Gov Campaign, 73-74; co-chairperson, Univ Southern Calif Students for Brown, 73-74. Mem: Pub Rels Students Soc Am; Nat Orgn Women; Am Civil Liberties Union; Proj Help. Relig: Catholic. Mailing Add: 2511 N Lincoln Ave Altadena CA 91001

CAMP, GEORGE (R)
Okla State Sen
b Drumright, Okla, Aug 15, 26; s Ira Camp & Susie Dittmeyer C; m 1949 to Lora Lee Atchison; c Mark Arnold & Cheryl Ann. Educ: Univ Okla, LLB, 50; Phi Delta Phi. Polit & Govt Pos: Precinct chmn, Major Co Rep Party, Okla, 50-51, chmn, 52-54; co attorney, Major Co, 51-53; deleg, Rep State Conv, 52, 63 & 65; deleg & mem rules comt, Rep Dist Conv,

52; deleg, Rep Co Conv, 52, 63 & 65; Asst US Attorney, West Dist Okla, 54-61; precinct chmn, Okla Co Rep Party, 62-64; Okla State Rep, Oklahoma Co, 64-72; mem, Okla State Rep Comt, 65-66; mem, Spec State Rules Rev Comt, 65-66; Okla State Sen, 72- Bus & Prof Pos: Dir & officer, Mortgage Investors Exchange, Inc, 62-66; chmn bd & pres, Serendipity, Inc, 66. Mil Serv: Entered as Pvt, Army, 45, released as Cpl, 46, after serv in 81st Inf; South Philippines, Victory, Am Pac Theater, Philippine Liberation & Good Conduct Medals; Army Res, 46-48. Mem: Am Bar Asn (gen practice comt); Univ Okla Col Law Asn; Lions; Sportsman's Club; Oklahoma City CofC. Relig: Methodist. Mailing Add: 2411 NW 46th Oklahoma City OK 73112

CAMP, HERBERT V, JR (R)
Conn State Rep
b Hartford, Conn, Mar 31, 35; s Herbert V Camp & Blanche M Lawton C; m 1963 to Alice J Brath; c Kristin A, Lawton M, Whitney L & Andrienne V. Educ: Wesleyan Univ, 53-57; Columbia Law Sch, 57-60; Sigma Chi; Alpha Delta Phi. Polit & Govt Pos: Chmn, Ridgefield Charter Comn, Conn, 68; Conn State Rep, 111th Assembly Dist, 69-, House chmn joint comt on finance, 73- Bus & Prof Pos: Law clerk, Los Angeles, Calif, 61. Mem: Am, Conn & NY Bar Asns; Kiwanis; Jaycees. Honors & Awards: Distinguished Serv Award, Ridgefield Jaycees, 68. Relig: Methodist. Legal Res: Craigmoor Rd Ridgefield CT 06877 Mailing Add: PO Box 686 Ridgefield CT 06877

CAMP, JOHN NEWBOLD (HAPPY) (R)
b Enid, Okla, May 11, 08; s John Roland Camp & Minnie Catherine Newbold C; m 1930 to Vera Juanita Overman; c John, III, Kay (Mrs Dan D Dillingham), Pat (Mrs Roy Gilbert Rainey) & Steven Richard. Educ: Phillips Univ, 3 years. Polit & Govt Pos: Okla State Rep, 43-63; chmn, State Bd Pub Affairs, 67-68; US Rep, Sixth Dist, Okla, 69-74; deleg, Rep Nat Conv, 72. Bus & Prof Pos: Chmn bd, Waukomis State Bank, Waukomis, Okla. Mil Serv: Pvt, Nat Guard, 46 months. Mem: Lions; Mason (32 degree); Shrine; Jesters; Future Farmers Am. Honors & Awards: Silver Beaver, Boy Scouts. Relig: Disciples of Christ. Mailing Add: 100 N Main Waukomis OK 73773

CAMP, KENNETH RAY (D)
Ark State Rep
b Osceola, Ark, Apr 11, 38; s John Earl Camp & Gertrude Lee C; m 1961 to Wanda Lee Kirklin; c Kendell, Kemuel & Janeene. Educ: Ark State Univ, BSA, 63, MSE, 66; Future Farmers Am; Agr Club; Pershing Rifles. Polit & Govt Pos: Ark State Rep, Dist 68, 71-, freshman caucus leader, Ark House Rep, 71-, mem legis audit comt, 73- Bus & Prof Pos: Instr voc agr, Knobel High Sch, Ark, 63-65; prin, Black Rock Pub Schs, 66-68; supt schs, Brookland Pub Sch, 68- Mem: Alpha Tau Alpha; Farm Bur; Lions; Neighborhood Comn; Boy Scouts. Relig: Church of Christ. Legal Res: 208 Bush Jonesboro AR 72401 Mailing Add: PO Box 1661 Jonesboro AR 72401

CAMPBELL, A HARTWELL (D)
NC State Rep
b Buies Creek, NC, Oct 8, 16; s Dr Leslie Hartwell Campbell & Viola Haire C; m 1942 to Verda Harris; c Thomas Hartwell, Vann & Neal. Educ: Campbell Col, AA, 34; Wake Forest Univ, BS, 36; Univ NC Grad Sch, 37-38; Yale Univ, BD, 41; Gamma Sigma Epsilon. Polit & Govt Pos: Mem city bd educ, Greenville, NC, 57-63; mem, Greenville Plan Bd, 62-64; mem city coun, Greenville, 63-64; chmn, Wilson Co Econ Develop Comn, 64-69; NC State Rep, 15th Dist, 69- Bus & Prof Pos: Minister, Immanuel Baptist Church, Greenville, NC, 41-46; builder & mgr, TV Sta WNCT, 50-63; organizer & pres, Sentinel Life Ins Co, 56-59; pres, owner & gen mgr, Campbell Broadcasting, Inc, WGTM, Wilson, 64-69. Mem: Wilson-Rocky Mountain SME Club; Rotary; CofC; Wilson Co Young Dem Club. Honors & Awards: Tar Heel of the Week, Raleigh News & Observer. Relig: Baptist; deacon, First Baptist Church; Sunday Sch teacher. Mailing Add: 1709 Wilshire Blvd Wilson NC 27893

CAMPBELL, ALBERT D (D)
Kans State Rep
Mailing Add: 919 W Fourth Larned KS 67550

CAMPBELL, AMBROSE LEO (D)
RI State Sen
b Pawtucket, RI, Dec 20, 08; s Joseph Edward Campbell & Anne Farrell C; m 1936 to Alice M Branigan; c Ann Judith (Mrs Desrosiers), Daniel L, M Kathleen (Mrs Furtado) & Henry V. Educ: Pawtucket High Sch, 25-29. Polit & Govt Pos: Mem city coun, Pawtucket, RI, 52-62; RI State Sen, 62- Bus & Prof Pos: Sales mgr, Campbell Auto Supply, 48- Mem: RI Asn Retarded Children; Blackstone Valley Chap for Retarded Children; Moose; KofC; Horsemen's Benevolent & Protective Asn. Relig: Catholic. Mailing Add: 513 Walcott St Pawtucket RI 02861

CAMPBELL, ANNE D (D)
Mem, Dem Nat Comt, NJ
Mailing Add: 206 W State St Trenton NJ 08608

CAMPBELL, ANONA JEANNE (R)
Mem, Rep State Cent Comt of Calif
b Calexico, Calif, Oct 6, 30; d John William Propes & Norma Anona Cooley P; m 1950 to Norman Campbell; c Russell William & Richard Alan. Educ: Fullerton Jr Col, 48-49; Univ Calif, Santa Barbara, 50. Polit & Govt Pos: Dist precinct chmn, 70th Assembly Dist, Calif, 64-67; mem, Rep State Cent Comt of Calif, 69- Bus & Prof Pos: Vpres & treas, Magic Carpet Travel Agency, Inc, 68-70; secy-treas, Magic Caper Travel Agency, 70-; owner-mgr, Travelmakers, 72- Mem: Federated Rep Women of Huntington Beach; Native Daughters of Golden West; Calif Rep Assembly. Relig: Protestant. Mailing Add: 10011 Crailet Dr Huntington Beach CA 92646

CAMPBELL, ARCHIBALD ALGERNON (D)
Va State Deleg
b Wytheville, Va, July 23, 21; m to Eloise Richberg. Educ: VMI, BA; Univ Va, LLB. Polit & Govt Pos: Va State Deleg, 66-, chmn finance comt, 74- Bus & Prof Pos: Attorney. Mil Serv: Marine Corps. Mem: Rotary; Southwest Va Horsemen's Asn; Wytheville Vol Fire Dept; Wythe Community Concert. Relig: Presbyterian. Mailing Add: First Nat Exchange Bank Bldg Wytheville VA 24382

CAMPBELL, CARROLL ASHMORE, JR (R)
b Greenville, SC, July 24, 40; s Carroll Ashmore Campbell & Anne Williams C; m 1959 to Iris Rhodes; c Carroll Ashmore, III & Richard Michael, II. Educ: McCallie Sch, Tenn; Univ SC. Polit & Govt Pos: Campaign dir, Fourth Cong Dist, SC, 68; campaign mgr for mayor's race, Greenville, 69; SC State Rep, 70-74, Asst Minority Leader, SC House Rep, 73-74; mem state adv comt, SC Rep Party, 71; alt deleg, Rep Nat Conv, 72; Rep cand for Lt Gov, SC; exec asst, Gov James B Edwards, currently. Bus & Prof Pos: Pres, Handy-Park Parking Serv; vpres, Rex Enterprises, Tallahassee; owner, Walnut Grove Farms; real estate broker. Mem: Nat Parking Asn; Arabian Horse Registry of Am; Downtown Greenville Asn; Greenville CofC; Greenville Horse Show Asn. Honors & Awards: Distinguished Serv Award, Wade Hampton Taylors Jaycees, 71; Woodmen of the World Citizenship Award, 73; Knights of Columbus Award, 73. Relig: Episcopal. Legal Res: Rte 1 Fairview Rd Fountain Inn SC 29644 Mailing Add: 206 E Coffee St Greenville SC 29601

CAMPBELL, CHARLES D (D)
Conn State Rep
Mailing Add: 31D Robert Treat Dr Milford CT 06460

CAMPBELL, CHARLES M (CHUCK) (R)
Ill State Rep
b Danville, Ill, Oct 11, 21; m 1943 to Marjorie Barton; c Con & Randy. Educ: Univ Ill, BS in Bus Admin, 43; Sigma Chi. Polit & Govt Pos: Ill State Rep, 63-65 & 67-, permanent mem adv comt, Ill Pub Aid Comn, Ill House Rep, vchmn water resources comt, 67-68, chmn, munic comt, 69-70, vchmn human resources, 73-; mem exec comt, Co Rep. Mil Serv: Lt(jg), Navy, 42-46, serv in Seventh Fleet, Pac Theatre, 43-46; Silver Star. Mem: Am Bus Club; Am Legion; Elks; YMCA; CofC. Relig: Presbyterian. Mailing Add: 102 N Logan Ave Danville IL 61832

CAMPBELL, CLARENCE GRADY, JR (R)
VChmn, Laurens Co Rep Party, Ga
b Royston, Ga, Dec 27, 26; s Clarence Grady Campbell, Sr & Vara Malone C; m 1954 to Bonnie Lou Gardiner; c Paul David & Chris Elaine. Educ: Emory Univ, BA, 49, Sch Med, MD, 54; Alpha Kappa Kappa. Polit & Govt Pos: Vchmn, Laurens Co Rep Party, Ga, 64-66 & 72-, chmn, 66-70; chmn, First Cong Dist Rep Comt, 66-68. Mil Serv: Entered as Pvt, Army, 46, released as Sgt 4, 48; after serving in 161st Med Sta Hosp, Japan, 47-48. Mem: Laurens Co Med Soc; Med Asn Ga (Comt Quackery, 72-); Am Med Asn; Ga Radiol Soc; Am Col Radiol. Honors & Awards: Dipl, Am Bd Radiol, 58. Relig: Baptist. Mailing Add: PO Box 809 Dublin GA 31021

CAMPBELL, CLIFFORD V (R)
Kans State Rep
b Beloit, Kans, Aug 20, 21; s Terrance A Campbell & Elisa Studer C; m 1943 to Faye Huffman; c Jeannine, James R & Terry W. Educ: High Sch. Polit & Govt Pos: Kans State Rep, 75- Mil Serv: Entered as Pvt, Air Force, 42, released as Sgt, 46. Relig: Methodist. Mailing Add: Star Rte Beloit KS 67420

CAMPBELL, CRAIG BARTLETT (D)
Ind State Rep
b Anderson, Ind, July 22, 38; s Jack B Campbell & Lois Howerton C; m 1961 to Joan Christine Koebke; c Scott Bartlett & Christine Elizabeth. Educ: DePauw Univ, AB, 60; Ind Univ Sch Law, Bloomington, LLB, 64; Phi Delta Phi; Beta Theta Pi. Polit & Govt Pos: Dep prosecuting attorney, Madison Co, Ind, 64-70; Ind State Rep, 71-, Asst Minority Floor Leader, Ind House Rep, 73-74, speaker pro tem, 75- Bus & Prof Pos: Partner, Campbell, Campbell & Mattingly, Anderson, Ind, 66- Mil Serv: Entered as Pvt, Army, 60, released as SP-4, 61, after serv in 1st Div, Ft Riley, Kans. Mem: Anderson Col Ctr for Pub Serv (sr fel); Indiana Univ Law Sch Alumni Asn (dir); Nat Soc of State Legislators; Indiana Code Revision Comn; Edgewood Country Club. Relig: Presbyterian. Mailing Add: 915 Spring Valley Dr Anderson IN 46011

CAMPBELL, DELLA B (R)
b Winamac, Ind, Jan 16, 14; d Joseph Carlisle Wagerman & Elsie Doyle W; m 1937 to Charles S Campbell, MD; c Timothy, Mary Ellen, Catherine & Daniel. Educ: Ind Univ, GN, 36; Sigma Theta Tau; Phi Mu. Polit & Govt Pos: Alt vchmn, Marion Co Rep Cent Comt, 54-56, vchmn, 56-60; educ chmn, State Rep Cent Comt of Ore, 60-62, vchmn, 63-67, secy, formerly. Bus & Prof Pos: Staff nurse, Indianapolis Pub Health Nursing Asn, 36-38. Mem: Womens Auxiliary, Ore State Med Soc; Assistance League of Salem. Relig: Presbyterian. Mailing Add: 3391 Country Club Dr S Salem OR 97302

CAMPBELL, DONALD A (R)
Chmn, Montgomery Co Rep Party, NY
b Amsterdam, NY, Aug 2, 22; m; c three. Educ: Columbia Univ, honor scholar; Albany Law Sch, 48; cum laude; Columbia Univ Varsity C Club. Polit & Govt Pos: NY State Assemblyman, 51-68, clerk, NY State Assembly, 68-73; chmn, Montgomery Co Rep Party, 59-; deleg, Rep Nat Conv, 68. Bus & Prof Pos: Treas, Amsterdam, Chuctarunda & Northern RR Co; adv bd Amsterdam Br, Marine Midland Nat Bank of Troy; attorney-at-law, 48-; dir & vpres, Community Serv Broadcasting Corp, 69- Mil Serv: Army, World War II, Lt, 3 years. Mem: Justinian Nat Hon Legal Scholarship Soc; F&AM; AAONMS; CofC; Am Legion. Honors & Awards: Amsterdam Jr CofC Young Man of Year, 57; NY State Amvet of the Year, 62; PBA Legis Award, 64. Relig: Episcopal; Vestryman, Coun. Mailing Add: 120 Market Amsterdam NY 12010

CAMPBELL, FRANK (D)
Ala State Rep
Mailing Add: PO Box 992 Livingston AL 35470

CAMPBELL, GENE (D)
Fla State Rep
Mailing Add: 434 House Off Bldg Tallahassee FL 32304

CAMPBELL, GEORGE W (R)
Finance Chmn, Beaver Co Rep Comt, Pa
b Connellsville, Pa, Dec 4, 22; s Clyde Sparks Campbell & Catherine Strawn C; m 1950 to Lois Katherine Ruff; c Jill Katherine, Beth Ann & Lynn Ellen. Educ: Westminster Col, Pa, BBA, 44; Univ Pittsburgh, DDS, 50; Univ Tex, Residency in oral surg, 53-55; Alpha Sigma Phi; Psi Omega. Polit & Govt Pos: Sch dir, Rep Party, 62-; deleg, Rep Nat Conv, 64 & 68; mem, Beaver Co Rep Comt, Pa, 66-, finance chmn, 68-; pres, Black Hawk Sch Bd, 70-73. Bus & Prof Pos: Mem bd trustees, Univ Pittsburgh, 68- Mil Serv: Entered as A/S, Navy, 43, released as Lt(jg), 46, after serv in Amphibious Forces, Pac Area; Pac Campaign Ribbon. Mem: Am Dent Asn; Am Soc Oral Surgeons; Mason; Shrine; Beaver Co Cancer Soc, (bd dirs,

58-). Relig: Presbyterian. Legal Res: 2 Davidson Dr Beaver Falls PA 15010 Mailing Add: 290 W Park Rochester PA 15074

CAMPBELL, JACK M (D)
b Hutchinson, Kans, Sept 10, 16; s John M Campbell & Blanche E Chain C; m 1945 to Ruthanne DeBus; c Patty, Terry, Mike & Kathy. Educ: Washburn Col, AB magna cum laude, 38, LLB, 40. Hon Degrees: Doctorate, Col Santa Fe, 65, NMex State Univ, 65, NMex Inst Mining & Technol, 66; Tau Delta Pi. Polit & Govt Pos: Mem, State Bd Finance, NMex, 55-59; NMex State Rep, 56-62, Speaker House of Rep, 61-62, chmn Legis Coun, 62; Gov, NMex, until 67. Bus & Prof Pos: Agent, Fed Bur Invest, 41-42; exec secy, NMex Oil & Gas Asn, 46-47; Attorney, Atwood, Malone & Campbell & Campbell, Russell, Albuquerque & Roswell, 48-63; chmn, Inst for State Prog in 70's, Chapel Hill, NC, 67-69; attorney, Stephenson, Campbell & Olmsted, Santa Fe, 67-70; dir, Inst Soc Res & Develop, Univ NMex, 69-70; counsel, Olmsted & Cohen, 70-72; pres, Fedn of Rocky Mt States, currently; counsel, Campbell & Bingaman, Santa Fe, 73-. Mil Serv: Entered as Pvt, Marine Corps, 42, released as 1st Lt, 45, after serv in SPac; Capt, Marine Corps Res. Mem: Rotary; Am Legion; VFW. Honors & Awards: Elected hon mem-at-lg, Delta Sigma Rho-Tau Kappa Alpha Forensic Soc, 65. Relig: Roman Catholic. Mailing Add: 34 Sena Plaza Santa Fe NM 87507

CAMPBELL, JAMES PHILANDER, JR (R)
Under Secy, US Dept Agr
b Athens, Ga, Apr 9, 17; s James Philander Campbell, Sr & Lorraine Montez Proctor C; m 1943 to Elizabeth Ann McCreery; c Elizabeth Ann (Mrs Phil Prichard), Vivian Lorraine, J Phil, III, John Alan, Jennifer Claire & Janice. Educ: George Washington Univ, 34; studied agr in Denmark, 38-39; Univ Ga, BSA, 40; Phi Kappa Phi; Kappa Alpha. Polit & Govt Pos: Ga State Rep, 49-54; comnr, Ga Dept Agr, 55-69; Under Secy, US Dept Agr, 69-, mem nat adv comts to Secy Agr for Hog Cholera Eradication & for Wholesome Meat & Food Inspection, 69. Bus & Prof Pos: Trustee, Univ Ga Found, currently. Mil Serv: Entered as Cadet, Air Force, 42, released as 1st Lt, 45, after serv in Air Force Training Command, Tex. Mem: Am Legion; Farm Bur; Rotary; Athens Country Club. Relig: Baptist. Legal Res: Watkinsville GA 30677 Mailing Add: Dept of Agr Mall 12th & 14th St SW Washington DC 20250

CAMPBELL, JOHN TUCKER (D)
Mayor, Columbia, SC
b Calhoun Falls, SC, Dec 12, 12; s John Brown Gordon Campbell & Mary Tucker C; m 1936 to Gerta Davis; c James Gordon. Educ: Columbia Pub Schs, SC; spec classes, Union SC. Polit & Govt Pos: Mem, Columbia City Coun, SC, 54-58 & 66-70, Mayor, Columbia, 70- Mil Serv: Entered as Pvt, Army Air Force, 43, released as 2nd Lt, 46, after serv in Air Transport Command, Europe & Southwest Pac, 44-46; European & Southwest Pac Ribbons. Mem: Exec Asn Gtr Columbia, SC; SC Pharmaceutical Asn; Nat League of Cities; Mason; Shrine. Honors & Awards: Distinguished pres & gov, Optimist Int. Relig: Methodist. Mailing Add: 4037 Kilbourne Rd Columbia SC 29205

CAMPBELL, JOSEPH (R)
b New York, NY, Mar 25, 00; s Thomas Campbell & Anne Conneil C; m to Dorothy Bostwick; c Frederick, Douglas, Robert, Alan, Colin, Mrs John V B Dean, Mrs Henry A Rudkin, Jr & W T Sampson Smith, Jr. Educ: Columbia Univ, AB, 24; Alpha Delta Phi. Hon Degrees: LLD, Columbia & Colgate Univs. Polit & Govt Pos: Mem, Atomic Energy Comn, 53-54; Comptroller Gen, US, 54-65. Bus & Prof Pos: Assoc, Lingley, Baird & Dixon, Accts, 24-27; asst comptroller, Valspar Corp, 27-29, comptroller, 29-32; partner, R T Lingley & Co, 32-33 & Joseph Campbell & Co, Accts, 33-41; asst treas, Columbia Univ, 49-55, treas & vpres, 49-55; emer trustee, Trinity Col. Mem: Am Inst Accts; Conn State Soc CPA; Union League & Madison Sq Garden Clubs, New York; Seawanhaka Corinthian Yacht Club, Long Island; Chevy Chase Club. Relig: Episcopal. Mailing Add: 3111 Woodland Dr NW Washington DC 20008

CAMPBELL, KERMIT LEON (R)
b Chickalah, Ark, Dec 29, 10; s John Thomas Campbell & Alta Brown C; m 1939 to Gladys Orene Fountain; c Shirley Pat (Mrs Shelby Fryar), Alta Lou (Mrs Ted Mullenix), John W & Roy Leon. Educ: Chickalah High Sch, Ark, 11 years. Polit & Govt Pos: Secy, Montgomery Co Elec Bd, Ark, 70-; chmn, Montgomery Co Rep Party, 70-74. Bus & Prof Pos: Fire control aid, US Forest Serv, 48-54, lookout dispatcher, 55-66, recreation asst rdr, 67-68, air detection observer, 69-70; part owner & asst operator, Gen Store, 59-60. Mem: Montgomery Co CofC. Honors & Awards: Achievement Award; Suggestion Award; Trophy for Youth Work from Gov Winthrop Rockefeller Relig: Primitive Baptist. Mailing Add: Box 626 Oden AR 71961

CAMPBELL, LEONARD WAYNE (D)
b El Centro, Calif, Feb 5, 25; s Leonard Frederick Campbell & Winnie Crawford C; m 1946 to Beth Patsy Harmon; c Robert Wayne, Nancy Marie (Mrs Bob Ward) & Richard Alan. Educ: Univ Ark, Fayetteville, Off Cand Sch, Army Air Force, 43-44. Polit & Govt Pos: Chmn, Yavapai Co Dem Cent Comt, Ariz, formerly. Bus & Prof Pos: Owner, Hopi House Trading Post, 61-63; sgt in charge of northern div, Ariz Corp Comn, 64-69; owner, Farmers Ins Group Agency, 70- Mem: Rotary; Elks; Kiwanis; Odd Fellows (Noble Grand, 70-). Relig: Protestant. Legal Res: 1046 Whipple St Prescott AZ 86301 Mailing Add: PO Box 1033 Prescott AZ 86301

CAMPBELL, LESLIE DUNLOP, JR (D)
Va State Sen
b Doswell, Va, Jan 26, 25; s Leslie Dunlop Campbell & Norine Dickson C; m 1959 to Eleanor Miller Dickson; c Sarah Payne, Mary Scott, Leslie Dunlop, III & Virginia Wells. Educ: Randolph-Macon Col, 42 & 46-48; Univ Richmond Law Sch, LLB, 51; Phi Alpha Delta. Polit & Govt Pos: Substitute judge, Hanover Co Court, Va, 54-55; Commonwealth's attorney, Hanover Co, 56-63; Va State Sen, 26th Dist, 63-71, Fourth Dist, 71- Bus & Prof Pos: Pvt law practice, 51-; assoc, Campbell & Ellis, Attorneys, 55-70, Campbell & Campbell, 70- Mil Serv: Entered as A/S, Navy, 44, released as RM 3/C, 46. Mem: Va Bar Asn; Montpelier Ruritan Club; Hanover Jr CofC; Am Legion Post 206; Jamestown Soc. Relig: Episcopal. Legal Res: Lochland Rte 2 Doswell VA 23047 Mailing Add: 133 Hanover Ave Ashland VA 23005

CAMPBELL, MARILYN R (R)
NH State Rep
Mailing Add: 79 Brady Ave Salem NH 03079

CAMPBELL, PAULINA YAGER (R)
Secy, Rep Party, Va
b Page Co, Va, Oct 5, 27; d Paul Robert Yager & Mattie Jones Y; m 1946 to Loren Emerson Campbell. Educ: Harrisonburg Bus Col, 50. Polit & Govt Pos: Secy, Rep Party, Va, 68-; mem, Page Co Rep Comt, 70-; deleg, Rep Nat Conv, 72; chmn const & by-laws comt, Page Co Rep Womens Club, 74- Bus & Prof Pos: Admin secy off plant mgr, Merck & Co, Inc, Elkton, Va, 50- Relig: Christian. Mailing Add: 601 Maryland Ave Shenandoah VA 22849

CAMPBELL, TERRY LELAND (R)
Okla State Rep
b Peoria, Ill, June 13, 41; s Clarence Ralph Campbell & Virginia Cochrane C; m 1971 to Barbara Ann Hite. Educ: Colo Sch Mines, BS, 64; Krannert Grad Sch Bus, Purdue Univ, MS in Indust Admin, 68; Theta Tau; Sigma Phi Epsilon; Press Club. Polit & Govt Pos: Rep nominee, US Rep, Fifth Dist, Okla, 70; Okla State Rep, Dist 100, 73- Bus & Prof Pos: Mgt trainee, Climax Molybdenum, 64-65; econ analyst, Kerr-McGee Corp, 68-70; exec asst to pres, Moss-Am Co, 70; corporate planning consult, Oklahoma City, Okla, 71-72; corporate controller, West Aspen Co, 72-73. Mil Serv: Entered as 2nd Lt, Army, 65, released as 1st Lt, 67, after serv in 140th Combat Support Co, Vietnam, 66-67. Mem: Am Inst Mining & Petroleum Engrs; Okla Coalition for Clean Air; Bethany & Warr Acres, Okla CofC; Children's Convalescent Ctr (dir). Honors & Awards: President's Award, Oklahoma City Jaycees, 70. Relig: Christian Church. Mailing Add: 6710 NW 59th Terr Bethany OK 73008

CAMPBELL, THELMA LUNGER (D)
Bd Mem, Pa Fedn Dem Women
b Bloomsburg, Pa, May 4, 16; d Carroll Lunger & Lynwilla Parker L; m 1948 to Ralph Christian Campbell; c Sherry (Mrs Bruce Morrison); Howard Allen & Robert Charles Fuehrer. Educ: Bloomsburg High Sch, 34. Polit & Govt Pos: Committeewoman, Bloomsburg Dem Town Comt, Pa, 54-; vchmn, Columbia Co Dem Party, 60-74; revenue agt corp tax, Dept Revenue, Harrisburg, 71-; deleg, Dem Nat Conv, 72; bd mem, Pa Fedn Dem Women, 72- Mem: Local 1977 (secy union, 74); Eastern Star; Columbia Co Dem Women; Women of the Moose; Am Legion Auxiliary. Honors & Awards: Outstanding Work in Politics for the Women of the State of Pa, 73; Cert of Appreciation for Notable Assistance in the Crusade to Conquer Cancer, 62. Relig: Presbyterian. Mailing Add: 129 W Ninth St Bloomsburg PA 17815

CAMPBELL, THOMAS HUMPHREYS, III (D)
Miss State Rep
b Yazoo City, Miss, July 26, 32; s Thomas Humphreys Campbell, Jr & Frances Hasselle C; m 1962 to Phyllis Veronica Sellier; c Thomas H, IV & John K. Educ: Univ Miss, BA, 54, LLB, 58; Phi Alpha Delta; Sigma Alpha Epsilon. Polit & Govt Pos: Miss State Rep, Yazoo Co, 60-64, Yazoo Co, Dist 19, 68-72, Yazoo-Sharkey Co, Dist 29, 72- Bus & Prof Pos: Partner, Campbell & Campbell, Attorneys, Yazoo City, 58- Mil Serv: Entered as 2nd Lt, Air Force, 54, released as 1st Lt, 56, after serv in 3rd Strategic Support Squadron, 2nd Air Force, Strategic Air Command; Capt, Air Force Res, 56-57. Mem: Miss Bar Asn; Yazoo Co Bar Asn; Elks; Lions; Yazoo Co CofC. Relig: Episcopal. Mailing Add: 229 Custer St Yazoo City MS 39194

CAMPBELL, TRUMAN F (R)
Chmn, Fresno Co Rep Cent Comt, Calif
b Fresno, Calif, March 26, 28; s James Watson Campbell & Ida Truman C; m 1948 to Janice M; c Kathleen, Laurie & Robin. Educ: Univ Calif, Berkeley, AB in Polit Sci, Hastings, LLB & JD; Theta Delta Chi; Phi Alpha Delta. Polit & Govt Pos: Mem, Fresno Co Rep Cent Comt, Calif, 52-, treas 67-69, vchmn, 69-71, chmn, 71-; mem, Rep State Cent Comt, Calif, 69-, mem exec comt, 73-, finance comt, 73-, secy, 75-; mem, United Rep Calif; mem, Calif Rep Assembly. Bus & Prof Pos: Attorney-at-law, Campbell & McFeeters, 52- Publ: Contrib to Calif State Bar Asn & local periodicals. Mem: Fresno Co, Calif & Am Bar Asns; Calif & Am Trial Lawyers Asns; Univ Calif, Hastings Alumni Asn. Relig: Christian. Mailing Add: 730 L St Fresno CA 93721

CAMPBELL, W M (D)
SC State Rep
Mailing Add: 1610 Crestwood Columbia SC 29205

CAMPBELL, WILLIAM (R)
Calif State Assemblyman
Mailing Add: 7624 Painter Ave Whittier CA 90601

CAMPBELL, WILLIAM COWDEN (R)
b West Middlesex, Pa, Mar 27, 16; s Thomas Bruce Campbell & Ethel Davis C; m 1937 to Dorothy Marshall; c Wm Bruce, James, Thomas & Richard. Polit & Govt Pos: Sch dir, 50-; mem, Mercer Co Rep Comt, Pa, 50-54, chmn, formerly; deleg, Rep Nat Conv, 68. Bus & Prof Pos: Pres, Shenango Steel Bldgs, Inc. Mem: Future Farmers of Am (hon farmer); Mason; Grange. Relig: Presbyterian. Legal Res: RD 2 Pulaski PA 16143 Mailing Add: West Middlesex PA 16159

CAMPOBASSO, ELEANOR M (D)
Mass State Rep
b Lawrence, Mass, Aug 10, 22; d Thomas Lannon & Marie Qualters L; m 1945 to Daniel J Campobasso; c Carole Ann & Daniel J, Jr. Educ: St Mary's Acad, grad. Polit & Govt Pos: Mem, Arlington Town Meeting, Mass, 54-70; mem, Arlington Dem Town Comt, 60-68; Mass State Rep, 65-; committee- woman, Mass Dem State Comt, 68-; deleg, Mass State Dem Conv, 70. Mem: Marine Corps League; Am Legion Auxiliary; VFW Auxiliary. Honors & Awards: Distinguished Serv Award, Marine Corps League. Relig: Catholic. Mailing Add: 15 University Rd Arlington MA 02174

CANADA, ANDREW JOSEPH, JR (R)
Va State Sen
b Lynchburg, Va, May 8, 39; father & mother deceased; m to Vicki Buhr; c Elizabeth Kass, A J, III, Kelli B & Mary K. Educ: Hampden-Sydney Col, BA, 62; T C Williams Sch Law, Univ Richmond, LLB, 65; Phi Delta Phi; Sigma Chi. Polit & Govt Pos: Aide, Secy Health, Educ & Welfare, 64; Va State Sen, City of Virginia Beach, 71-; mem bd dirs, Am Coun Young Polit Leaders; chmn, Young Voters for President Nixon, 72; mem, Va Rep State Cent Comt, 72. Bus & Prof Pos: Asst Commonwealth Attorney, City of Virginia Beach, Va, 65-67; partner, Ansell, Butler & Canada, Attorneys-at-Law, 67- Mem: Va Trial Lawyers Asn; Virginia Beach Jaycees (secy & legal counsel); Princess Anne Lions Club (pres); Va Coun on

Alcoholism & Drug Dependence, Inc (bd dirs); Virginia Beach Boys' Club (bd dirs). Relig: Episcopal. Mailing Add: 4336 Virginia Beach Blvd Virginia Beach VA 23452

CANADA, BUD (D)
Ark State Sen
Mailing Add: 400 W Willowbrook Hot Springs AR 71901

CANADAY, ALYCE D
b New York, NY, d Florence Doherty & Ann Happ D; m; c Henry T. Educ: Julia Richman High Sch; Grace Inst Bus Sch. Polit & Govt Pos: Staff asst to US Sen Styles Bridges, NH, 51-61; staff asst to US Sen Kenneth B Keating, NY, 61-63; staff asst to US Rep Richard C White, Tex, 65-68; admin asst to US Rep Peter N Kyros, Maine, 68- Bus & Prof Pos: Personnel staff mem, Shell Oil Co. Mil Serv: Recruiter, Women's Army Corps, 43-45. Mem: Salvation Army Auxiliary; Capitol Hill First Friday Club. Mailing Add: Apt 525 4201 S 31st St Arlington VA 22206

CANADAY, TRAVIS (D)
b Enville, Tenn, Feb 10, 18; s William Victor Canaday & Lucy Lee C; m 1938 to Margie Bullman. Educ: Morris Chapel, Tenn, 4 years. Polit & Govt Pos: Mem, Chester Co Court, Tenn, 55-, probate officer, Juv Judge & Co Judge, 68-70, clerk & master, Chancery Court, 70-; chmn, Chester Co Dem Exec Comt, formerly; deleg, Const Conv, 64-69. Relig: Methodist. Mailing Add: Enville TN 38332

CANALES, TERRY (D)
Tex State Rep
Mailing Add: PO Box 1646 Alice TX 78332

CANCEL RIOS, JUAN J (POPULAR DEMOCRATS, PR)
Sen, PR Senate
Mailing Add: State Capitol San Juan PR 00901

CANDON, PATRICK JAMES (D)
Vt State Rep
b Pittsford, Vt, Mar 12, 08; s James Patrick Candon & Margaret Carrigan C; m 1944 to Evelyn Bashaw. Educ: Rutland Bus Col, Vt, grad, 26. Polit & Govt Pos: Vt State Rep, Dist Two, 72- Bus & Prof Pos: Postmaster, Pittsford, Vt, 33-69. Mem: Nat Asn of Postmasters; Lions Int; Nat Asn of Retired Fed Employees. Relig: Catholic. Mailing Add: Plains Rd Pittsford VT 05763

CANDON, THOMAS HENRY (D)
Vt State Rep
Mailing Add: 5 Royce St Box 23 Rutland VT 05701

CANFIELD, JACK (D)
WVa State Deleg
b Pittsburgh, Pa, June 2, 41; s James W Canfield & Clydetta Canfield Walker; m 1961 to June Louise Smith; c John Michael, Christopher Alan & Susan Elaine. Educ: Potomac State Col, AA, 61; WVa Univ, BSJ, 63; Sigma Delta Chi; Phi Sigma Nu. Polit & Govt Pos: Comt asst, US House Rep, 63-64; press secy, Gov Hulett C Smith, WVa, 65-69; deleg, Dem Nat Conv, 68; exec dir, WVa Dem State Exec Comt, 69-71; press secy, John D Rockefeller IV, WVa, 71-72; chmn, State Platform Comt, 72; WVa State Deleg, 75- Bus & Prof Pos: News anchorman, WSAZ-TV, Charleston, WVa, 69; partner, Canfield, Miller & Assocs, 73- Mem: Catholic Charities (bd mem, 75-). Honors & Awards: Outstanding Male Grad Jour, WVa Univ, 63. Relig: Roman Catholic; choir dir, St Agnes Church, 72- Mailing Add: 5411 Staunton Ave SE Charleston WV 25304

CANFIELD, JOHN LEMUAL (D)
Chmn, 15th Cong Dist Dem Party, Mich
b Senath, Mo, Sept 14, 17; s Oda Thomas Canfield & Ethel Hollis C; m 1939 to Claudene Caldwell; c Ruth Ann & Glenda Sue. Educ: High Sch. Polit & Govt Pos: Precinct deleg, Dem Party, Mich, 46-; exec bd mem, 16th Dist Dem Party, 50-64; chmn, Dearborn Twp Dem Club, 55-57; park comnr, Dearborn, 55-57, trustee, 57-59, supvr, 59-63; mem bd supvrs, Wayne Co, 59-; alt deleg, Dem Nat Conv, 60, deleg, 64 & 68; mayor, Dearborn Heights, formerly; chmn, 15th Cong Dist Dem Party, 64-; alt deleg, Dem Nat Mid-Term Conf, 74. Mil Serv: Entered as A/S, Navy, 43, released as PO 3/C, 45. Mem: Rotary; Elks; Moose; Mason; UAW. Relig: Protestant. Mailing Add: 7026 N Inkster Rd Apt 105 O Dearborn Heights MI 48127

CANION, JUDITH COLLEEN (R)
b Alice, Tex, Aug 7 52; d Ollie Lee Canion & Lorna Jean Kaiser C; single. Educ: La State Univ, Baton Rouge, 70-; mem, Dormitory Coun, 71-; soc chmn, Kappa Delta Epsilon, 73-74; chmn flag football, Women's Intramurals, 73-74. Polit & Govt Pos: State TAR secy, La, 68-69, chmn, 69-70; secy, Univ Young Rep, La, 71-; exec vchmn, State Col Young Rep, 72- Mem: YMCA; Women's Recreation Asn. Honors & Awards: State Outstanding TAR Girl, Col Young Rep La, 70; Key to City of New Orleans, Mayor, 71. Relig: Lutheran. Legal Res: 3526 Lang St New Orleans LA 70114 Mailing Add: Box 20855 La State Univ Baton Rouge LA 70803

CANION, NANCY ELIZABETH (R)
Chmn, Galveston Co Rep Comt, Tex
b East Liverpool, Ohio, July 27, 40; d Mearl Freeman Davis & Elizabeth A Wyper D; m 1962 to James Marvin Canion. Educ: Univ Tex, Austin, BS, 62; Univ Houston, teaching cert, 64. Polit & Govt Pos: Precinct chmn, Galveston Co Rep Comt, Tex, 73-, co chmn, 74-; chmn, 17th Sen Dist, Rep Comt, 74-; pres, Clear Creek Rep Womens Club, 74- Mem: Pecan Forest Civic Club (vpres, 73-74); Am Asn Univ Women. Relig: Presbyterian. Mailing Add: 1016 Shadow Circle League City TX 77573

CANN, CATHERINE E (KAY) (D)
NDak State Rep
b International Falls, Minn, Mar 7, 12; d Steven James McHugo & Grace Latta M; m 1936 to Stanley F Cann; c Steven James & John Daniel. Educ: Valley City State Col; NDak State Univ; Moorhead State Col, BA, 64. Polit & Govt Pos: Deleg, Dem Nat Conv, 72; NDak State Rep, 75- Bus & Prof Pos: Art reviewer & columnist, Fargo Forum, 65-71; art reviewer & hostess, The Gallery, KFME-Educ TV, 68-69; art reviewer & columnist, Midweek, 71-, vpres, 72-; art reviewer & columnist, 72-73. Mailing Add: State Capitol Bismarck ND 43215

CANNON / 141

CANNEY, DONALD JAMES
Mayor, Cedar Rapids, Iowa
b Iowa City, Iowa, Oct 8, 30; s John J Canney & Alice E Mickle C; m 1955 to Gloria F Oberer; c Kevin, Timothy & Michael. Educ: Oceanside-Carlsbad Col, 53; Riverside Jr Col, 54; Iowa State Univ, 54-57; State Univ Iowa, BS in Civil Eng, 59; Phi Eta Sigma. Polit & Govt Pos: Comnr pub improv, City of Cedar Rapids, 66-69, mayor, 69- Bus & Prof Pos: Engr, City of Riverside, Calif, 54; spec proj engr, City of Cedar Rapids, 54-62. Mil Serv: Entered as Pvt, Marines, 51, released as S/Sgt, 54, after serv in 1st Div, Major Command, Korea, 52-53; Presidential Unit Citation; Spec Meritorial Promotion; Korean Serv Medal with Three Combat Stars; Nat Defense Medal; UN Medal; Good Conduct Medal. Mem: Am Pub Works Asn; Nat Soc Prof Engrs; Nat Asn Co Engrs; Iowa Highway Research Bd; Cedar Rapids Engrs Club. Honors & Awards: Cert of Appreciation, 9th Naval Dist. Relig: Catholic. Legal Res: 436 Fleetwood Rd NW Cedar Rapids IA 52405 Mailing Add: City Hall Cedar Rapids IA 52401

CANNEY, ETHEL M (R)
NH State Rep
b Milton, NH, Feb 3, 03; d Guy LeRoy Hayes & Myrta Emma Clements H; m 1921 to Ralph Wilson Canney; c Philip Carl, Lois Elaine (Mrs DiPrizio), Ralph Wilson Jr, Paul Joseph, Priscilla Joyce (Mrs Dutile), Carolyn Ethel & Carroll E. Educ: Nute High Sch, 19; Keene Normal Sch, summer 20. Polit & Govt Pos: NH State Rep, 75- Mem: State Rep Woman's Club (pres); Rochester & Farmington Woman's Club; Grange; NH Order Women Legislators. Relig: Protestant. Legal Res: Farmington NH 03835 Mailing Add: Rte 2 Meaderboro Rd Rochester NH 03867

CANNON, DAVID COKER (R)
b Raleigh, NC, Sept 27, 37; s Doyle Leroy Cannon & Katherine Coker C; m 1964 to Ilvi Joe; c Katherine & Benjamin. Educ: Clemson Univ, BSME, 59; Case Inst Technol, MSME, 65; Block C. Polit & Govt Pos: Chmn, Darlington Co Young Rep, SC, 66-67; chmn, Darlington Co Rep Party, formerly. Bus & Prof Pos: Sr develop engr, Sonoco Prod Co, 67-70, proj leader, 71- Mil Serv: Entered as 2nd Lt, Army, 60, released as 1st Lt, 68. Mem: Instrument Soc of Am; Kiwanis Club of Hartsville. Mailing Add: PO Box 11 Hartsville SC 29550

CANNON, HOWARD WALTER (D)
US Sen, Nev
b St George, Utah; s Walter Cannon & Leah Sullivan C; m to Dorothy Pace; c Nancy Lee & Alan Howard. Educ: Ariz State Teachers Col, BE, 33; Univ Ariz, LLB, 37. Hon Degrees: LLD, Ariz State Col, 62. Polit & Govt Pos: US Sen, Nev, 58-; ex officio deleg, Dem Nat Mid-Term Conf, 74. Mil Serv: Maj Gen, Air Force Res. Legal Res: Las Vegas NV Mailing Add: 5312 Portsmouth Rd Spring Hill MD 20016

CANNON, HUGH (D)
Mem, NC Dem State Exec Comt
b Albemarle, NC, Oct 11, 31; s Hubert N Cannon & Nettie Harris C; m 1956 to Jessie Mercer; c John Stuart, Marshall & Martha. Educ: Davidson Col, AB, 53; Oxford Univ, BA, 55, MA, 60; Harvard Law Sch, LLB, 58; Phi Beta Kappa; Omicron Delta Kappa; Am Asn of Rhodes Scholars; Phi Gamma Delta. Polit & Govt Pos: Asst to Gov, NC, 61; dir admin, NC, 61-65; mem, NC Dem State Exec Comt, 72- Bus & Prof Pos: Partner law firm, Sanford, Cannon, Adams & McCullough, 65- Mil Serv: Capt, NC Nat Guard, 62-68. Mem: Am, NC, & Wake Co Bar Asns; NC State Bar; Nat Educ Asn (parliamentarian). Relig: Methodist. Legal Res: 3333 Allegheney Dr Raleigh NC 27609 Mailing Add: PO Box 389 Raleigh NC 27602

CANNON, JOE WESLEY (R)
Committeeman, Ill Rep State Cent Comt
b Bowen, Ill, June 2, 23; s Harry Claud Cannon & Lillian Mae Brown C; m 1946 to Josephine Gerdes; c Jill Susanne, Joe David, Jeffrey Lynn, Jonathan Lee & James Gregory. Educ: Ill Col, AB, 47; Univ Ill, BS, 49, MD, 51; Gamma Nu; Alpha Kappa Kappa. Polit & Govt Pos: Mem, sch bd, 57-63; alt deleg, Rep Nat Conv, 64; Committeeman, Ill State Rep Cent Comt, 66-; pres, Lacon Park Dist, 70-72. Bus & Prof Pos: Deleg, State Meeting of Ill Acad Gen Practice, 60-65. Mil Serv: Entered as Pvt, Army Air Force, 43, released as 1st Lt, 45, after serv in 357th Fighter Group, Eighth Air Force, ETO, 44-45; Eight Air Medals; ETO Ribbon. Mem: Am Med Asn; Ill Med Soc; Am Acad of Gen Practice; Mason; Lacon Country Club (pres, 72-73). Relig: Methodist. Mailing Add: 900 Harmony Lane Lacon IL 61540

CANNON, ROSS W (D)
Mem, Dem State Comt, Mont
b Butte, Mont, May 1, 29; s Paul Cannon & Caroline Duffes C; m 1957 to Natalie Norby; c Stephanie S & Davis S. Educ: Univ Mont, BA & LLB; George Washington Univ, LLM; Sigma Chi; Phi Delta Phi. Polit & Govt Pos: Mem, Lewis & Clark Co Dem Cent Comt; asst attorney gen & dep co attorney, 65-69; mem, Dem State Comt, currently; mem, State Planning & Develop Comn, currently. Bus & Prof Pos: Attorney adv, Interstate Com Comn, Washington, DC, 57-59; Attorney-at-law, Helena, Mont, 59-; mem bd dirs, Helena Model Cities & First Security Bank of Helena, currently. Mil Serv: Entered as 2nd Lt, Air Force, 55, released as 1st Lt, after serv in 380th Air Refueling Sq, Strategic Air Command, 55; Am Defense Medal; Maj, Air Force Res. Mem: YMCA; Mont Bar Asn; Mont Club; First Dist Bar Asn; Am Trial Lawyers Asn. Relig: Presbyterian. Mailing Add: 2130 Highland St Helena MT 59601

CANNON, THOMAS QUENTIN (R)
Utah State Rep
b Salt Lake City, Utah, Apr 29, 06; s Jesse Fox Cannon & Margaret Ann McKeever C; m 1934 to Katherine Bowman; c Thomas Quentin, Jr, Richard Bowman, Kathleen (Mrs Roger B Pinnock) & Jesse Fielding. Educ: Univ Utah, AB, 31; George Washington Univ, LLB, 35; Georgetown Univ, JD, 38; LLM magna cum laude, 70; Delta Phi; Delta Theta Phi. Polit & Govt Pos: Attorney, Reconstruction Finance Corp, 39; law clerk to chief justice, Utah Supreme Court, 41; dep enforcement attorney & Asst US Attorney, Off Price Admin, 47; reference attorney, US House Rep, 47, 49 & 63; Dep Attorney Gen, Utah, 63-67; dep co attorney, Salt Lake Co, 67-69; Utah State Rep, 69- Bus & Prof Pos: Pvt law practice, Cannon & Duffin, 47-; pres & bd mem, Salt Lake City Bd Educ & Salt Lake Co Recreation Bd, 51-60; pres & bd mem, Salt Lake Area Vocation Sch, 51-60; gen counsel, Days of 47, 53-60; vpres, Utah Judicial Qualifications Comt; Nat Hwy Safety Comt, 75- Mil Serv: 2nd Lt, QmC; Lt Col, Utah State Guard. Mem: Am Bar Asn; Am Trial Lawyers Asn; SAR; Rotary Int; Bonneville Knife & Fork Club. Relig: Latter-day Saint; European gen counsel, 61-62. Legal Res: 5340 Cottonwood Lane Salt Lake City UT 84117 Mailing Add: 510 Ten Broadway Bldg Salt Lake City UT 84101

CANTRELL, JOE MARION (D)
Colo State Rep
b Athens, Tex, Aug 29, 29; s James O Cantrell & Beatrice Shaver C; m 1950 to Lela B Edwards; c Sharon & Valerie. Educ: Southwestern State Col, BS, 57; Univ Okla, Norman, MSS, 58; Alpha Phi Sigma; Chi Alpha; Okla Student Teachers Asn; Univ Okla Engr Club. Polit & Govt Pos: Colo State Rep, Dist 19, 75- Bus & Prof Pos: Pub sch teacher, Widefield Sch Dist 3, 58-; mem bd dirs, Security Water Dist, 64-, Security Sanitation Dist, 64- & Mem Hosp, 71-; mem adv comt, Beth El Nursing Sch, 73- Mil Serv: Entered as Pvt, Army, 53, released as Cpl, 55, after serv in Chem Corp, 53-55; Sr Asst Sanitarian, US Pub Health Serv, 59-; Good Conduct Medal. Mem: Nat & Colo Educ Asns; Colo Hosp Asn; Colo Biol Teachers. Honors & Awards: Spec Mem Award, Memorial Hosp, 74; Spec Legis Award, Colo Credit Union League, 75. Relig: Assembly of God (Pentecostal). Mailing Add: 521 Hickory Dr Security CO 80911

CANTRELL, ORBY LEE (D)
Va State Deleg
b Pound, Va, Nov 10, 06; m to Janie Mullins. Educ: Radford Col. Polit & Govt Pos: Mayor, Pound, Va; Va State Deleg, 52- Bus & Prof Pos: Merchant; bank dir; pres, Breaks Interstate Park Asn, formerly. Mem: Mason; Lions; Wise Co CofC. Mailing Add: Box 188 Pound VA 24279

CANTU, VIDAL, JR (R)
Chmn, Webb Co Rep Party, Tex
b Laredo, Tex, Aug 18, 38; s Vidal V Cantu & Esperanza Lozano C; m 1964 to Alicia Vela; c Vidal Alonso, Arnoldo Hiram & Leticia. Educ: Tex A&M Univ, BBA, 64; Alpha Chi. Polit & Govt Pos: Vchmn, Webb Co Rep Party, Tex, 70-72, chmn, 72 & 74- Mil Serv: Entered as DK2 E5, Navy, 58, released as DK2 E5, after serv in USS Valley Forge. Mem: Nat Home Furnishing Asn; Retail Furniture Asn SW (vpres, 72); President's Adv Coun on Minorities; Optimist; Cosmopolitan. Relig: Catholic. Mailing Add: Sam Moore Bldg 212 Laredo TX 78040

CANULLA, GUIDO J (D)
RI State Sen
Mailing Add: 67 Bourne Ave Tiverton RI 02878

CANZONETTI, ANDREW JOSEPH (D)
Committeeman, Conn State Dem Party
b New Britain, Conn, Sept 1, 20; s Aurelio Canzonetti & Grace Ranaldi C; m 1946 to Ruth Zuroms; c David, Richard, Andrew & Susan. Educ: Ohio Univ, AB, 42; Univ Chicago, MD, 44; Phi Beta Kappa; Alpha Omega Alpha; Phi Eta Sigma. Polit & Govt Pos: Chmn sch bd, New Britain, Conn, 56-60; chmn, New Britain Dem Town Comt, 68-72; presidential elector, 68; committeeman, Conn State Dem Party, 72-; mem, Affirmative Action Comt, Conn, 75. Bus & Prof Pos: Pvt practice gen surg, 50-72; corp med dir, Scovill Industs, Waterbury, Conn, 72- Mil Serv: Entered as Lt, Navy, 45, released as Lt, 46, after serv in MedC, SPac. Publ: Articles on gen surg, Surg J & J AMA. Mem: Am Med Asn (alt deleg); Hartford Co Health Care Plan (pres); Hartford Co Physicians for Social Responsibility Orgn (pres); Conn Med Soc (assoc counr). Honors & Awards: Educ Award, Am Fedn Teachers, 60; Red Feather Award, Community Chest, 61; Good Govt Award, Jaycees, 64. Mailing Add: 111 Virginia Ave New Britain CT 06052

CAPALBY, JOSEPH RICHARD, SR (D)
VChmn Platform Comt, Ariz State Dem Party
b Chicago, Ill, Mar 11, 20; s Frederico Capalby & Josephine De Paolo C; m 1939 to Mary Ellen McDow; c Audrey (Mrs Tom Hafley); Wilma Jean (Mrs Guy Salisbury); Joseph R, II, Fred Michael, II & Patty Jo. Educ: John L Marsh Sch, Chicago, Ill; LaSalle Exten Univ. Polit & Govt Pos: Vchmn publicity & finance chmn, Mohave Co Dem Cent Comt, 64-66, chmn, 66-70, deleg, Dem Nat Conv, 68, hon vpres from Ariz, 68; past mem, Small Bus Admin, until 68; vchmn, Ariz State Dem Cent Comt, 68-70, sr vchmn, formerly; mem, McGovern Comt, 68-; dir, Ariz Consumer's Coun, 68-; vchairman platform comt, Ariz State Dem Party, 68- Mem: Golden Paradise Landowners (chmn, 63-70); charter mem Moose. Relig: Catholic. Mailing Add: 1010 Parkview Ave Kingman AZ 86401

CAPANEGRO, MICHAEL J (D)
b Queens Co, NY. Educ: NY Univ, BS; Cornell Law Sch, LLB, 55, JD, 70. Polit & Govt Pos: NY State Assemblyman, 60-66; asst counsel to minority leader, NY State Senate, 66-74, counsel, 72-74; mem, NY State Dem Party, formerly; mem, Dem Nat Comt, formerly. Bus & Prof Pos: Attorney-at-law. Mil Serv: Army Air Force; Lt, Coast Guard Res. Mem: Am Judicature Soc; Am Bar Asn; NY State Asn of Plaintiff Trial Lawyers; Columbia Lawyers; Am Legion. Legal Res: 32-38 168th St Flushing NY 11358 Mailing Add: 136-17 41st Ave Flushing NY 11355

CAPECELATRO, RALPH ETTORE (R)
Mem, Conn Rep State Cent Comt
b Orange, Conn, Oct 26, 21; s Gennaro Ettore Capecelatro & Frances Cuzzocreo C; m 1944 to Elaine Scialla; c Jane (Mrs Bove), Mark J & Thomas R. Educ: Norwich Univ, BA, 42; Maroon Key; Iota Pi Kappa. Polit & Govt Pos: Chmn, Bd of Tax Review, Orange, Conn, 58-63, second selectman, 63-69, first selectman, 69-; chmn, Regional Coun, Elec Officers, 73-75; mem, Conn Rep State Cent Comt, 72- Bus & Prof Pos: Partner, Hillside Farms Co, 45-; pres, Hillside Motor Lines Inc, 63-67. Mil Serv: Entered as 2nd Lt, Army, 42, Capt, 45, after serv in 115th Cavalry, Western Defense Command. Mem: Am Legion Post 127; Dept Community Affairs (adv coun); Criminal Justice Supvry Bd; Nat League of Cities (safety comt); Conn Farm Bur. Relig: Catholic. Mailing Add: 148 Englewood Dr Orange CT 06477

CAPEN, RICHARD GOODWIN, JR (R)
b Hartford, Conn, July 16, 34; s Richard Goodwin Capen & Virginia Ann Knowles C; m 1962 to Joan Lees Lambert; c Christopher Goodwin, Kelly Lambert & Catherine Knowles. Educ: Columbia Univ, AB, 56. Polit & Govt Pos: Dep Asst Secy of Defense, 69-70, asst to Secy of Defense for Legis Affairs, 70-71; alt deleg, Rep Nat Conv, 72. Bus & Prof Pos: Asst to dir, Structural Clay Prod Inst, Washington, DC, 59-60; mem staff, Presidential Campaign, 60; San Diego Co mgr, William Aldrich Co, San Diego, Calif, 61; dir pub affairs, Copley Newspapers, La Jolla, 61-69, vpres & dir, 71-74, sr vpres, dir & mem exec comt, 74-; dir, Purolator Serv, Inc, Lake Success, NY, 72- Mil Serv: Entered as Ens, Navy, 56, released as Lt(jg), 59, after serv in USS Ernest G Small, Seventh Fleet. Publ: Various articles. Mem: Friends of Research; Pub Rels Soc of Am; Nat Asn Mfrs; Nat Asn Pub Affairs Officers; Mil Order of World Wars. Honors & Awards: Six Freedoms Found Awards, Pub Address Category; San Diego Outstanding Young Man of the Year, 67; Calif Outstanding Young Man of the Year, 69. Relig: Presbyterian. Mailing Add: 6104 Avenida Cresta La Jolla CA 92037

CAPINERI, JOSEPH A (D)
RI State Rep
b Pawtucket, RI, May 2, 29; m to Ethel M Pierce. Educ: Providence Col, BA, 51; Boston Univ Law Sch, LLB, 54. Polit & Govt Pos: RI State Rep, 57- Bus & Prof Pos: Attorney-at-law; bd dirs, Equitable Credit Union. Mem: Elks; Moose; RI Hist Soc; Sons of Italy; Am Bar Asn. Mailing Add: 24 Alexander McGregor Rd Pawtucket RI 02861

CAPLAN, MILTON IRVING (D)
Mem, Hamden Dem Town Comt, Conn
b New Haven, Conn, Aug 12, 33; s Morris Caplan & Diana Weissman; m 1956 to Patricia Irene Stein; c Deborah Lee, Mark Andrew & David Oren. Educ: Yale Univ, BA, 55; Univ Conn Law Sch, JD, 58. Polit & Govt Pos: Mem, Hamden RTM, Conn, 63-65; mem, Hamden Dem Town Comt, 66-; Conn State Rep, 67-71. Bus & Prof Pos: Partner, Merriam, Virshup & Caplan, Attorneys, 63- Mem: Conn & Am Bar Asns; Yale Club of New Haven; Yale Alumni Fund; Grad Club. Relig: Jewish. Mailing Add: 354 Belden Rd Hamden CT 06514

CAPOZZOLI, JEANNE JOHNSON (D)
Committeewoman, NY State Dem Party
b Webster, SDak, June 24, 40; d Raymond Johnson & Edith Feller J; m 1963 to Nicholas Capozzoli; c Lisa & Nicholas. Educ: Univ Colo, Boulder, BS, 63; Kappa Delta Pi; Pi Beta Phi. Polit & Govt Pos: Secy, US Sen George McGovern, SDak, Washington, DC, 58-60; Dem committeewoman, Clarkstown, NY, 69-; co-chairwoman, McGovern for President Comt, Clarkstown, 72; deleg-at-lg, Dem Nat Conv, 72; committeewoman, NY State Dem Party, 72-; mem state comt for elec of delegs to Dem Nat Mid-Term Conf, 74 & to Dem Nat Conv, 76. Bus & Prof Pos: Teacher social studies, Calhoun High Sch, Merrick, 63-65 & Clarkstown High Sch, New City, 65-68. Mem: PEO; Hudson River Sloop Restoration, Inc. Relig: Episcopal. Mailing Add: 20 Meadow Lark Dr West Nyack NY 10994

CAPOZZOLI, LOUIS J (D)
b Italy, Mar 6, 01; s Gabriele Capozzoli & Christina Ciongola C; m 1927 to Adele M Valli; c Louis J, Jr, Christine (Mrs Raso) & Gloria (Mrs Barbieri). Educ: Fordham Univ, LLB, 22. Polit & Govt Pos: Asst dist attorney, NY Co, 30-37; NY State Assemblyman, 39-40; US Rep, NY, 41-44; justice, City Court, New York, 47-50; judge, Court of Gen Sessions, 51-57; justice, Supreme Court, NY, 57-66; assoc justice, Appellate Div NY, 67-72. Mem: Asn of NY Supreme Court Justices; NY Co Lawyers Asn; Columbian Lawyers Asn; Fordham Law Alumni; Grand St Boys Asn. Relig: Catholic. Legal Res: 2 Fifth Ave New York NY 10011 Mailing Add: 27 Madison Ave New York NY 10010

CAPPARELLI, RALPH C (D)
Ill State Rep
b Chicago, Ill, Apr 12, 24; s Ralph Capparelli & Mary Drammis C; m 1952 to Cordelia; c Ralph & Valerie. Educ: Northern Ill Univ, BS in Educ; Sigma Nu. Polit & Govt Pos: First vpres, 41st Ward Dem Orgn, 65-; Ill State Rep, 71- Bus & Prof Pos: Supvr recreation, Chicago Park Dist, 53-67; adv, Columbia Bank, Chicago, 67-; secy-treas, Jefferson Travell, 68- Mil Serv: Entered as A/S, Navy, 43, released as S/1C, 46, after serv in Acorn 39, Pac Theatre, 44-46; Battle Star. Mem: Nat & Ill Recreation Socs; Lions; KofC (4 degree); Eagles; Am Legion. Relig: Catholic. Mailing Add: 7312 N Oriole Chicago IL 60648

CAPPS, CHARLES WILSON, JR (D)
Miss State Rep
Mailing Add: Box 308 Cleveland MS 38732

CAPPS, ELAINE FOLK (D)
Nat Committeewoman, Young Dem NC
b Hanover, Pa, Nov 18, 45; d Donald Tracey Folk & Pauline Armstrong F; m 1968 to John T Capps, III. Educ: Univ Md, College Park, BS, 68; Tau Beta Sigma; Alpha Gamma Delta. Polit & Govt Pos: First vpres, Dem Women Lenoir Co, NC, 72-74, secy, Lenoir Co Dem Party, 72-74; vchairperson, First Dist, Young Dem NC, 72-73, deleg selection comt, 75, nat committeewoman, 75-; mem exec coun, NC Dem Party, 75- Bus & Prof Pos: Instr, Lenoir Community Col, 69-73; freelance home economist, Dunn, NC, 74- Mem: Harnett Co Dem Women; Bishop Method Clothing Construction Coun; Harnett Co Bicentennial Comt (art chmn, 75-). Honors & Awards: Top Ten, NC Young Dem, 73. Relig: United Methodist. Mailing Add: 1007 W Cumberland St Dunn NC 28334

CAPPS, GILMER N (D)
Okla State Sen
Mailing Add: State Capitol Oklahoma City OK 73105

CAPPS, JOHN PAUL (D)
Ark State Rep
b Steprock, Ark, Apr 17, 34; s Edwin H Capps & Vivian Pinegar C; m 1955 to Elizabeth Ann Vaughan; c Paula Ann, Kimberley Kay & John Paul, Jr. Educ: High Sch & Beebe Jr Col. Polit & Govt Pos: Ark State Rep, White Co, 65- Bus & Prof Pos: Announcer, KWCB, Searcy, Ark, 55-57, asst mgr, 58-65, sta mgr, 65-; announcer, KTHV, Little Rock, Ark, 57-58; vpres & gen mgr, KWCK, Searcy, 71- Mil Serv: Army Res, 53-61. Mem: Lions; Searcy Jaycees; White Co Asn Ment Health (bd); Searcy CofC. Honors & Awards: Distinguished Serv Award, Searcy Jaycees, 68. Relig: Church of Christ. Mailing Add: 914 N James Searcy AR 72143

CAPPS, R WALTER (D)
Mem, Russell Co Dem Exec Comt, Ala
b Opelika, Ala, Aug 24, 12; s Robert Tolleigh Capps & Mary Frances Huguley C; m 1931 to Etta Griffin; c Hilda (Mrs D Lamar Windsor) & Jean (Mrs Robert E Schooler). Educ: Beauregard High Sch, 29. Polit & Govt Pos: Mem, Russell Co Dem Exec Comt, Ala, 34-, chmn, formerly. Bus & Prof Pos: Farmer & cattleman, Russell Co, 30- Mem: WOW; Farm Bur; Ala & Russell Co Cattlemen's Asn. Honors & Awards: Hon Lt Col, Ala State Militia. Relig: Baptist. Mailing Add: Rte 1 Box 226 Opelika AL 36801

CAPUTO, BRUCE (R)
NY State Assemblyman
b New York, NY, Aug 7, 43; s Anthony J Caputo & Doris Burke C; single. Educ: Harvard Col, BA, 65, Bus Sch, MBA, 67; Georgetown Law Sch, JD, 71; Porcellian Club; Varsity Club. Polit & Govt Pos: NY State Assemblyman, 73- Bus & Prof Pos: Dir & vpres, ICF, Inc, 69- Mil Serv: Entered as 2nd Lt, Army, 67, released as GS 13, 69, after serv in Off Secy Defense,

67-69. Mem: PTA; Ital City Club; Hudson River Mus; Yonkers Hist Soc; Big Bros-Big Sisters (bd dirs). Mailing Add: 250 Pondfield Rd West Yonkers NY 10708

CAPUTO, NICHOLAS (D)
Mem, Dem Nat Comt, NJ
Mailing Add: Hall of Records 469 High St Newark NJ 07102

CAPUZI, LOUIS F (R)
Ill State Rep
b Chicago, Ill, Nov 6, 20; m to Geneva R Flatt; c Three. Educ: Northwestern Inst Foot Surg & Chiropody, DSC, 42. Polit & Govt Pos: Ill State Rep, currently. Mil Serv: Europe, 2nd Armored Div, 27 months; Bronze Star; Purple Heart. Mem: Am Legion; VFW; Amvets (Capt, William J Clark, I Will Post). Mailing Add: 710 N Rockwell Chicago IL 60612

CARACCIOLA, JOSEPH JOHN (R)
Vt State Rep
b Whitehall, NY, Sept 13, 15; s Bruno Caracciola & Francis C; m 1942 to Anna Smith. Educ: Whitehall High Sch, NY, 4 years. Polit & Govt Pos: Mem, Rep Co Comt; Vt State Rep, 63- Bus & Prof Pos: Owner, Caracciola Real Estate. Mil Serv: Entered as Seaman 2/C, Navy, 43, released as Yeoman 2/C, 46, after serv in Am & Pac Theatres. Mem: Am Legion; Elks; Farm Bur; Vt Police Asn; Nat Realtors Asn. Relig: Catholic. Legal Res: Hunt St Bennington VT 05201 Mailing Add: Box 486 Bennington VT 05201

CARANCI, ANTHONY BENJAMIN, JR (R)
Chmn, North Providence Rep Town Comt, RI
b North Providence, RI, Aug 17, 30; s Antonio Benjamin Caranci & Carmella Ciprano C; m 1957 to Matilda Angeloni; c Patricia Ann & Maria Susan. Educ: Univ Mass, Turf Managers School; Univ RI. Polit & Govt Pos: Mem, North Providence Rep Town Comt, RI, 52-, chmn, 59-; comnr, Providence Worster RR, 58-62; mem, Rep State Cent Comt of RI, 59-; mem state appeal bd, Automobile Body Repair Shop Hearing Bd, 62-; mem, Town Coun, North Providence, 71- Bus & Prof Pos: Chmn, Univ Mass Winter Sch Seminar, 68 & 69. Mil Serv: Entered as Pvt, Army, 51, released as Cpl, 53, after serv in 76th Construct Engrs, Far East Command, Korea, 51-53. Publ: Golfdome, & The Golf Course Reporter, Nat Mag; Turf Clippings, New Eng Mag. Mem: New Eng Golf Course Supt Asn; Amvets; Mass-Turf Grass Coun (pres, 73-); RI Golf Course Supt Asn; Golf Course Supt Asn Am. Relig: Catholic. Mailing Add: 22 Hill View Dr North Providence RI 02904

CARANICAS, PERRY CHARLES (D)
Nat Bd Mem, Am Dem Action
b Greece, Aug 28, 35; s Charilaos Caranicas & Joanne Zissakis C; m 1958 to Doris Arlene Folkedal; c Charles & Andrew. Educ: Univ Minn, BSCE, 58, MSCE, 60, grad work, 62-64; Delta Upsilon. Polit & Govt Pos: Nat bd mem, Am Dem Action, 73- Bus & Prof Pos: Asst to pres, GRACO, Inc, Minneapolis, MN, 64-67; dir materials, Cornelius Co, Minneapolis, 67-70; vpres, Bayer & McElrath, Mgt consult, 70- Mem: Am Soc Quality Control; Dem-Farmer-Labor Feminist Caucus, Minn. Mailing Add: 4832 Elliot Ave S Minneapolis MN 55417

CARAWAY, WILLIAM JAMES (BILL) (D)
Tex State Rep
b Greenville, Tex, Apr 22, 45; s Glenn F Caraway (deceased) & Edna Busby C; m 1974 to Kippy Payne. Educ: ETex State Univ, BS, 66, MS, 69; Young Dem. Polit & Govt Pos: Tex State Rep, Dist 100, 74- Bus & Prof Pos: Instr govt, ETex State Univ; instr hist & govt, San Jacinto Col. Mil Serv: La Porte Air Nat Guard, 68-74. Mem: Acad Polit Sci; Orgn Am Hist; Tex Hist Soc; Tex Jr Col Teachers Asn; Acad Human Resources. Relig: Presbyterian. Legal Res: 16202 Buccaneer Lane Houston TX 77058 Mailing Add: PO Box 2910 Austin TX 78767

CARBAJAL, RICHARD A (D)
NMex State Rep
Mailing Add: 1001 Camino del Llano Belen NM 87002

CARBONE, EUGENE R (D)
b St Paul, Minn, Mar 2, 08; s Paul Carbone & Marian LePiane C; m 1934 to Raphaela Felice; c Marian (Mrs Cruz) & Paul Emil. Educ: Oak Park & River Forest Twp High Sch, 4 years. Polit & Govt Pos: Chmn, Calif Dem State Cent Comt, 60-64; dir, 33rd Agr Dist, 64-66; dir, San Benito Water & Flood Control Dist; deleg, Dem Nat Conv, 68. Bus & Prof Pos: Pres, Hollister Canning Co, 54. Mem: Elks; KofC. Relig: Catholic. Legal Res: 1255 San Benito St Hollister CA 95023 Mailing Add: PO Box 100 Hollister CA 95023

CARBONNEAU, ROLAND JOSEPH (D)
Maine State Sen
b Lewiston, Maine, Mar 14, 20; s Henry A Carbonneau & Anna Bureau C; m 1947 to Jeanne Marie Bureau; c Claud R, Robert J, Nina C & Colette S. Educ: Roberts Bus Acad, grad, 36; US Armed Forces Inst, 42-45. Polit & Govt Pos: Comnr, Lewiston, Maine, Pub Works Comn, Maine; comnr Health & Welfare Comn, Lewiston; Maine State Sen, 75- Bus & Prof Pos: Dir & past pres, Lewiston Develop Corp & Maine State Grocers Asn, 15 years; dir & vpres-treas, LTA United Grocers Inc, 15 years; owner, mgr & butcher, Carbonneau's Supermarket, 47-72. Mil Serv: Entered as Pvt, Army Res, 42, released as Maj (Ret), after serv in Qm Corp, US & European Theatres, 42-68; Mil Campaign Battle Stars; ETO. Mem: Mil Order World Wars; ROA (life mem); Civic & Indust Develop Groups. Honors & Awards: Grocer of the Year Award, Maine State Grocers Asn, 62. Relig: Catholic. Mailing Add: 51 Pleasant St Lewiston ME 04240

CARBULLIDO, FRANCISCO (R)
Chmn, Guam Rep Party
Mailing Add: PO Box 2797 Agana GU 96910

CARCIERI, ANTHONY J (D)
RI State Rep
Mailing Add: 118 Majestic Ave Warwick RI 02888

CARD, ANDREW HILL, JR (R)
Mass State Rep
b Brockton, Mass, May 10, 47; s Andrew Hill Card & Joyce Whitaker C; m 1967 to Kathleene Marie Bryan; c Tabetha & Rachel. Educ: US Merchant Marine Acad, Kings Point, 66-67; Univ SC, BS in Eng, 71; Am Soc Civil Engrs; Cadet Coun. Polit & Govt Pos: Chmn planning bd & secy, Permanent Sch Bldg Comn, Holbrook, Mass, 71-; chmn, Holbrook Rep Town Comt, 73-; Mass State Rep, Eighth Norfolk Dist, 75- Bus & Prof Pos: Struct design engr, Maurice A Reidy Inc, Boston, Mass, 71-73 & David M Berg, Inc, Needham, 73- Mil Serv: Midn, Navy, 65-67. Mem: Mass Continuing Congregational Fel (asst moderator, 74-); Holbrook Jaycees; Norfolk Co Rep Club (vpres, 73-). Relig: Congregational; deacon, Winthrop Congregational Church, 71-74, trustee, 74- Mailing Add: 221 N Franklin St Holbrook MA 02343

CARDIN, BENJAMIN LOUIS (D)
Md State Deleg
b Baltimore, Md, Oct 5, 43; s Meyer M Cardin & Dora Green C; m 1964 to Myrna Edelman; c Michael & Deborah. Educ: Univ Pittsburgh, BA, 64; Univ Md, JD, 67; Order of the Coif; Omicron Delta Epsilon; Druids; pres, Pi Lambda Phi; vpres, Nu Beta Epsilon. Polit & Govt Pos: Md State Deleg, 67-, vchmn ways & means comt, Md House Deleg, 71-74, chmn, 74-mem, Gov Comn for Minimum State Housing Standards, 67-; mem, Gov Comn for Prof Negotiations, 70-; vchmn, Gov Comn Sch Financing, 72- Mem: Am Bar Asn; AF&AM; Young Dem of Md; UN Asn; Pi Lambda Phi Alumni Asn; Safety First Club Md (bd mem). Honors & Awards: William Stroble Thomas Award for graduating first at law sch; Safety Crusader Award. Relig: Jewish. Mailing Add: 2509 Shelleydale Dr Baltimore MD 21209

CARDIN, CARL WILLIAM (R)
b St Louis, Mo, Mar 28, 25; s William Mervin Cardin (deceased) & Alberta Johnson C; m 1948 to Marianne Margaret Miller; c Kristin Deeanne, Julie Anne, William Page & Thomas George. Educ: Knox Col, 42 & 46; Univ Tulsa, BA, 49; Tau Kappa Epsilon. Polit & Govt Pos: Pres, Univ Tulsa Young Rep, 48; admin asst to US Rep Errett Scrivner, Kans, 55-58; Rep precinct chmn, Md, 58-59; departmental asst to US Rep E W Hiestand, Calif, 59; info officer & spec asst to the comnr, Fed Housing Admin, Washington, DC, 60; mem, Md Rep State Cent Comt, 63-65; admin asst to US Rep John Paul Hammerschmidt, Ark, 67-72; admin asst to US Sen Robert P Griffin, Mich, 73- Bus & Prof Pos: Newsman, Radio Sta KOMA, Oklahoma City, Okla & KCMO, Kansas City, Mo, 49-55; mem, prof staff (polit specialist), US CofC, 61; news ed, Nat Broadcasting Co Three-Star Extra, 62-65, desk supvr, Nat Broadcasting Co News, Washington, DC, 65-67. Mil Serv: Entered as Pvt, Army, 43, released as Sgt, 45, after serv in 612th Field Artil, Mule Pack, China-Burma-India, 44-45; Maj, Army Res; four Battle Stars. Publ: They Grade the Congress, US CofC, 62; Communications Satellites, Army Info Digest, 4/66. Mem: Nat Asn Radio & TV News Dirs; Nat Press Club; US House & Senate Radio-TV Gallery; Writers Guild of Am; Cong Secy Club. Relig: Episcopal. Mailing Add: 7821 Old Chester Rd Bethesda MD 20034

CARDWELL, BRUCE ELLIOTT (D)
Treas, Ind Fifth Dist Young Dem, Ind
b Tipton, Ind, Aug 1, 39; s John Marlow Cardwell & Harriett Ethyl Jeffers C; m 1960 to Judith Ann Johnson; c Marleta Ann, Marsha Arlene, Mark Elliott & Marchele Mae. Educ: Ind Bus Col, 57-59; Ind Univ, Kokomo, 62-68, Ft Wayne, BS Sec Educ, 69; Butler Univ, 70-73. Polit & Govt Pos: Treas, Ind Fifth Dist Young Dem, 70-; precinct committeeman, Liberty Twp, 70-; chmn, Tipton Co Dem Party, formerly; Tipton Co deleg, Ind Dem State Conv, 70 & 72. Bus & Prof Pos: Clerk, Chrysler Corp, Kokomo, 59-61; laborer, Continental Steel Corp, 61; clerk, Argonaut Div, Gen Motors Corp, Kokomo, 61-62, factory worker, Delco Radio Div, 62-69; teacher Am Hist, Taylor Community Schs, Ctr, Ind, 69; supvr inspection, Ind State Dept Pub Instr, 71- Mil Serv: Entered as Pvt, Army Res, 61, released as Sgt E-5, 67, after serv in 2nd Bn, 423rd Regt, 70th Div. Mem: Ind State Teachers Asn; Tipton Co Young Dem Club; Ind Farm Bur Asn. Relig: Church of the Brethren. Mailing Add: Rte 1 Sharpsville IN 46068

CAREY, DAVID JAMES (D)
Mem, Colo Dem State Cent Comt
b Denver, Colo, July 25, 42; s James L Dean & Shirley L Schelling D; single. Educ: George Washington Univ, BA, 65; Univ Denver Col Law, JD, 68; Phi Alpha Delta. Polit & Govt Pos: Pres, George Washington Univ Young Dem, 62-63; deleg, Denver Co & State Dem conv, Colo, 64, 66 & 68; Dem precinct committeeman, 65-; mem, Denver Co Dem Cent Comt, 65-; mem bd dirs, Denver Young Dem, 67-68, vpres, 68-69; pres, John F Kennedy Dem Club, 68-70; mem, Colo Dem State Cent Comt, 69-; pres, Colo Young Dem, 69-71. Bus & Prof Pos: Attorney-at-law, Eberhardt, Safran & Payne, Denver, 69- Mem: Am Bar Asn; Am Civil Liberties Union; Colo Trial Lawyers Asn; Southwest Denver Serv Orgn; Toastmasters, Int. Relig: Roman Catholic. Mailing Add: 1243 Gaylord St No 406 Denver CO 80206

CAREY, FRANCES DODGE (R)
Mem, Maine Rep State Comt
b South Paris, Maine, Aug 16, 20; d Frank Albert Dodge & Phyllis Taylor D; m 1951 to Albert S Carey; c Sandra (Mrs Richard MacGown) & Judith (Mrs Leonard Belleau). Educ: South Paris High Sch, grad, 38; Bliss Bus Col, grad, 40; Lambda Chi. Polit & Govt Pos: Secy, Sheriff F F Francis, Oxford Co Sheriff's Dept, 42-51; secy, Civil Defense & Pub Serv, Oxford Co, 65-; secy, Paris Town Rep Comt, 65-70; co treas, Oxford Co, 67-68; clerk, State Hwy Comt, 103rd Legis, Maine, 67-68; mem, Maine Rep State Comt, 68-; secy, Oxford Co Rep Comt, 70-; ballot clerk, Paris. Mem: South Paris Grange; South Paris Mothers Club; South Paris Planning Bd; Rebecca Lodge; Androscoggin Valley Regional Planning Comn. Honors & Awards: Alumna of the Year Award, 64. Relig: Baptist. Mailing Add: RFD 1 South Paris ME 04281

CAREY, HUGH L (D)
Gov, NY
b Brooklyn, NY, Apr 11, 19; s Dennis J Carey & Margaret Collins C; m 1947 to Helen Owen; c Alexandria, Christopher, Susan, Peter (deceased), Hugh, Jr (deceased), Michael, Donald, Marianne, Nancy, Helen, Bryan, Paul, Kevin & Thomas. Educ: St John's Col; St John's Law Sch, JD, 51; Phi Delta Phi. Hon Degrees: Hon degrees from Canisius Col, Yeshiva Univ, Long Island Univ, Villanova Univ, St John's Law Sch & Polytech Inst NY. Polit & Govt Pos: US Rep, NY, 60-75, Gov, 75-; deleg, Dem Nat Mid-Term Conf, 74. Bus & Prof Pos: Lawyer. Mil Serv: NY Nat Guard, Lt Col, serv in 101st Cavalry, Inf, Officer Cand Sch & France, Belgium, Holland & Germany; Bronze Star; Croix de Guerre with Silver Star, Combat Inf Award. Mem: Boy Scouts Finance Camp; Am Legion; VFW; CWV; KofC. Relig: Catholic. Legal Res: 9 Prospect Park W Brooklyn NY 11215 Mailing Add: State Capitol Albany NY 12224

CAREY, PATRICIA JEAN I (R)
Secy Exec Comt, Oakland Co Rep Orgn, Mich
b Mersea Twp, Ont, Can, May 2, 29; d Albert Edwin Peterson & Madeline Brown P; m 1949 to James Francis Carey; c James Edward, Monica Jean, Maureen Bridget, Cheryl Lynn, Mark Edwin & Kathryn Mary (deceased). Educ: Bus Inst, Detroit, Mich, 2 years, Alpha Iota. Polit

& Govt Pos: Precinct deleg, Rep Party, Troy, Mich, 60-66; held off of pres, secy, coun deleg, prog chmn & parliamentarian, Birmingham-Troy Rep Women's Club, 60-71; now Troy Rep Women's Club, 71-; deleg, Mich Rep State Conv, 60-; dir, Troy Rep Party, 63-65; comt mem, Oakland Co Rep Party, 63-; ex officio mem, Oakland Co Rep Exec Comt, 65-69, mem, 66-67; coun deleg, Coun Rep Women's Club, 63-64, ex officio mem, 65-69; secy, 18th Cong Dist Rep Comt, 64-65; mem budget & finance comt, Mich State Rep Cent Comt, 65-67, secy exec comt, 67-69; alt deleg, Rep Nat Conv, 68; secy exec & co comts, Oakland Co Rep Orgn, 68- Bus & Prof Pos: Off mgr, H M Harper Co, Detroit, 48-50; secy emergency rm, Providence Hosp, Southfield, 67-68; exec secy & off mgr, Am Variable Annuity, Oak Park, 68-69; admin asst & secy to secy-treas, MultiVest Funding Corp, 69-70; abstractor & exec secy, Aluminum Co of Am (ALCOA), 70-72; dir, admin asst to exec vpres & asst secy bd trustees, Detroit Osteopathic Hosp Corp, 72- Mem: Beta Sigma Phi; PTA; Women's Econ Club Detroit; Girl Scouts; St Thomas More Altar Soc. Relig: Roman Catholic. Mailing Add: 1514 Brentwood Dr Troy MI 48084

CAREY, RALPH P (R)
b Old Forge, Pa, Apr 1, 25; s Thomas Carey & Lena Perfilio C; m 1966 to Teresa Petrocelli; c Thomas Ralph & Ralph P, II. Educ: Bucknell Univ & Wilkes Col, 46-48, BA, 48; Dickinson Sch Law, Carlisle, Pa, JD, 51; Corpus Juris Soc; Student Coun. Polit & Govt Pos: Town chmn, Old Forge, Pa, 58-62, town solicitor, 63-69; secy, Lackawanna Co Rep Comt, 62-72, chmn, formerly; hearing examr, Pa Liquor Control Bd, 62-70; deleg, Rep Nat Conv, 68; solicitor, South Abington Twp, Pa, 70-; solicitor, Lackawanna Co Inst Dist, 72-73; solicitor, Lackawanna River Basin Sewer Authority, 73- Bus & Prof Pos: Partner, Casey, Carey & Mazzoni, Attorneys, 62- Mil Serv: Entered as Pvt, Army, 43, released as 1st Sgt, 46, after serv in 118th Inf Div, ETO, 44-46; Lt, Res, 47-50; Good Conduct Medal; ETO Ribbon with Northern France Battle Star. Mem: Elks (Past Exalted Ruler); Moose; Lions (past pres); Scranton CofC; Am Legion. Relig: Roman Catholic. Legal Res: 600 Shady Lane Rd South Abington Township PA 18508 Mailing Add: RD 1 Scranton PA 18508

CAREY, RICHARD JAMES (D)
Maine State Rep
b Waterville, Maine, Jan 7, 29; s Augustus Joseph Carey & Alma Vashon C; m 1952 to Helen Muriel Fortin; c Michael, Steven, Gregory, Denise, Martha & Peter. Educ: Univ Maine, 2 years. Polit & Govt Pos: Councilman, Waterville, Maine, 62-64, alderman, 65-68, mayor, 69-; Maine State Rep, 67- Bus & Prof Pos: Chief survey parties, James W Sewall Co, Old Town, Maine, 55-60; self-employed registered land surveyor, Waterville, 60- Mil Serv: Entered as Pvt, Air Force, 48, released as Cpl, 52, after serv as Troop Carrier, 49-52; Presidential Unit Citation. Mem: Am Cong Surv & Mapping; KofC; Am Legion; Community Leaders Am. Relig: Roman Catholic. Legal Res: 27 Sterling St Waterville ME 04901 Mailing Add: Mayor's Off City Hall Waterville ME 04901

CAREY, WILLIAM ARTHUR (D)
Mass State Rep
b Boston, Mass, Jan 28, 20; s William Carey & Anne Ward C; m 1943 to Mary Carroll; c William A, Jr, Robert R, Michael J, James F, Richard J, Maryanne & Kathleen. Educ: Suffolk Univ Law Sch, 38-39. Polit & Govt Pos: Mem, Easthampton, Mass Town Meeting, 65-75; Mass State Rep, Second Dist, 75- Bus & Prof Pos: Claim rep, Hartford Ins Group, 40-74. Mil Serv: Entered as Aviation Cadet, Marine Corps, 42, released as 1st Lt, after serv in VMR 153 MAG 25, SPac; Marine Corps Reserve, Capt (Ret); Air Medal with Gold Star; SPac Theatre Campaign; Two Battle Stars. Mem: Am Legion; VFW; KofC; Delmarva Claim Mgrs Asn. Relig: Catholic. Mailing Add: 92 Holyoke St Easthampton MA 01027

CARGILE, RICHARD FRANKLIN (R)
Treas, Eighth Dist Rep Party, Ga
b Ocilla, Ga, Nov 15, 32; s (father deceased) Thelma M C; m 1969 to Blondean Bullington. Educ: SGa Col, 49-50; Mercer Univ, 50-51; Ga State Col, BBA, 58. Polit & Govt Pos: Chmn, Irwin Co Rep Party, Ga, 67-70 & 72-74, treas, 70-72; treas, Eighth Dist Rep Party, Ga, 68- Bus & Prof Pos: News dir, Ben Hill Broadcasting Co, Fitzgerald, Ga, 60-68; opers mgr, Sizland Broadcasting Co, Inc, Ocilla, Ga, 68- Mil Serv: Entered as Pvt, Army Security Agency, 52, released as S/Sgt, 55, after serv in 327 Commun Reconnaissance Co, Japan, 53-55; Korean Serv Medal; Far E Theater Medal; Good Conduct Medal. Mem: Nat Asn Broadcasters; Int Broadcasters Soc; Rotary; Am Legion Post 100; Irwin Co Farm Bur. Honors & Awards: Serv-above-self award, Ocilla Rotary Club; excellent award, Ga Assoc Press Broadcasters Asn, 67; Commun Leader of Am award, 69; hon mem, Ga Future Homemakers Asn, 69. Relig: Baptist. Legal Res: 650 Cargile Rd Ocilla GA 31774 Mailing Add: PO Box 321 Ocilla GA 31774

CARGO, DAVID FRANCIS (R)
Chmn, Clackamas Co Rep Comt, Ore
b Dowagiac, Mich, Jan 13, 29; s Francis Clair Cargo & Mary Harton C; m 1960 to Ida Jo Anaya; c Veronica Ann, David Joseph, Patrick Michael, Maria Elena Christina & Eamon Francis. Educ: Univ Mich, AB in Lit, 51, MA in Pub Admin, 53 & LLB, 57; Delta Sigma Pi. Polit & Govt Pos: NMex State Rep, 63-66; Gov, NMex, 67-70; deleg, Rep Nat Conv, 68; chmn, Clackamas Co Rep Comt, Ore, 75- Bus & Prof Pos: Attorney-at-law, Portland, Ore, 71- Mil Serv: Entered as Pvt, Army, 53, released as Cpl, 55, after serv in Finance Corps. Mem: City Club; Ore Hist Soc; World Affairs Coun; Isaac Walton League (exec bd) Honors & Awards: Nominated One of the Ten Outstanding Young Men in Am, NMex Jr CofC, 64; Man of the Year, Albuquerque Jaycees, 64. Relig: Roman Catholic. Mailing Add: 750 Briercliff Lane Lake Oswego OR 97034

CARL, COLIN JOSEPH (D)
Mem, Tex State Dem Exec Comt
b Houston, Tex, Nov 18, 43; s Urbane Smith Carl & Claudia Phyllis Richardson C; m 1973 to Carol Ann Lukin. Educ: Harvard Col, BA magna cum laude, 65; Univ Tex, JD, 70; Dean's List. Polit & Govt Pos: Asst campaign mgr, John Hill for Attorney Gen, Tex, 72; asst co coordr, McGovern-Shriver State Hq, 72; mem, Tex State Dem Exec Comt, 72- Bus & Prof Pos: Legis intern, Tex Legis Internship Prog & staff asst, House Rules Comt, Tex House Rep, 66-67; prog dir, Tex Legis Internship, 67-69; law clerk, US Dist Court, Tex, 70-72; attorney, Elec Div, Tex Secy of State, 72; Asst Attorney Gen, Tex, 73- Mem: Am Bar Asn; State Bar Tex; Univ Tex Ex-Students Asn; Harvard Club Houston (mem exec comt); West Austin Dem. Honors & Awards: Valedictorian & membership in cum laude soc, Kinkaid High Sch, 61; J H Jones Scholar, Houston Endowment, Inc, 61. Relig: Jewish. Legal Res: Apt 302 505 W Seventh Austin TX 78701 Mailing Add: PO Box 12254 Austin TX 78711

CARLENO, HARRY EUGENE (D)
Mem Exec Comt, Arapahoe Co Dem Cent Comt, Colo
b Denver, Colo, Mar 3, 28; s Benjamin Edward Carleno & Elizabeth B DeRose C; m 1957 to Ann Marie Kraft; c Gregory Scott, Paul Christopher, Jennifer Ann & Machelle Lynn. Educ: Univ Denver, BS in Bus Admin, 51, LLB, 55 & JD, 70; Phi Delta Phi; Brewer Inn. Polit & Govt Pos: Dep dist attorney, First Judicial Dist, Colo, 58-60; precinct committeeman, Dem party, 58-62, dist capt, 62-66; mem, Arapahoe Co Dem Cent Comt, 58-65, chmn, 65-68, mem exec comt, 62-; dep dist attorney, 18th Judicial Dist, 60-68; chmn, Career Serv Bd, Englewood, 61-64; mem exec comt, Colo State Dem Cent Comt, 65-68; Munic Judge, City of Wheatridge, Colo, 72- Bus & Prof Pos: Gen practice of law, Englewood, Colo, 56-; pres, Accident Report Serv, Inc, 60-62; mem nat panel arbitrators, Am Arbit Asn, 70- Mil Serv: Entered as Pvt, Army Air Force, 46, released as 1st Lt, 53, after serv in Am Theater; Am Defense, Air Force Res & Victory Medals; Am Theater & Am Defense Ribbons; Col, Res Staff Judge Adv, Aerospace Defense Command, 63. Mem: Colo, Denver & Arapahoe Co Bar Asns; CofC; Arapahoe Co Ment Health Asn. Relig: Roman Catholic. Mailing Add: 5471 S Sherman St Littleton CO 80120

CARLETON, MARILYN JEAN (R)
VChmn, Logan Co Rep Cent Comt, Colo
b Oak Park, Ill, July 29, 26; d Elmer H Wirth & Margaret Binder W; m 1949 to Neil Lamont Carleton; c Christy A, Cynthia S, Robert B & Thomas M. Educ: Univ Colo, BA, 48, grad study, 48-49; Alpha Omicron Pi; Young Rep. Polit & Govt Pos: Secy, Young Rep, Colo, 45-47; vpres, Logan Co Rep Women, 61-62, pres, 62-63; secy, 63-64; vchmn, Logan Co Rep Cent Comt, 66- Relig: Protestant. Mailing Add: 302 Taylor Sterling CO 80751

CARLEY, ROBERT JOSEPH (D)
RI State Rep
b West Warwick, RI, May 16, 30; s Edward Linus Carley & Agnes Barrett C; m 1952 to Nellie Petrarca; c James C, Roberta L, Darleen R, Robert T, Thomas R & Edward H. Educ: Bryant Col, BS in Acct & Finance, 50, BS in Educ, 53. Polit & Govt Pos: Tax assessor, West Warwick, RI, 60-64; RI State Rep, currently. Bus & Prof Pos: Partner, acct off firm, Carley & Petrarca, 54-; officer, ins off firm, 63- Mem: Nat Soc Pub Acct; Elks; Sons of Italy Lodge; Holy Ghost Brotherhood; KofC. Honors & Awards: West Warwick Man of the Year, West Warwick Jaycees, 64. Relig: Catholic. Mailing Add: 7 Lanphear St West Warwick RI 02893

CARLILE, MARGARET LOUISE (D)
Nat Committeewoman, Okla Young Dem
b Sallisaw, Okla, July 21, 51; d Foreman Carlile & Juanita Reed Slaughter C; single. Educ: Northeastern State Col, 70; Okla State Univ, BA, 73; Phi Alpha Theta. Polit & Govt Pos: Youth coordr, Edmondson for US Senate, 72; Nat Committeewoman, Okla Young Dem, 72-; pub rels staff, McSpadden for Gov, 74- Mem: Asn of Women Students (second vpres, 71-72); Women's Rights Comn (chairperson, 71-72). Honors & Awards: Outstanding Young Dem, Fedn of Dem Women, 72. Relig: Methodist. Mailing Add: 803 College Rd Warner OK 74469

CARLIN, JOHN WILLIAM (D)
Kans State Rep
b Salina, Kans, Aug 3, 40; s John William Carlin & Hazel Johnson C; m 1962 to Ramona Lenore Hawkinson; c David & Lisa. Educ: Kans State Univ, BS, 62; Phi Kappa Phi; Blue Key; Farm House. Polit & Govt Pos: Kans State Rep, 73rd Dist, 71- Mem: Kans Holstein Asn (bd dirs, 70-); Holstein Asn Am (accredited Holstein judge, 67-); Lions. Relig: Lutheran. Mailing Add: Smolan KS 67479

CARLING, RICHARD JUNIUS (R)
Utah State Sen
b Salt Lake City, Utah, Dec 6, 37; s Jacob Junius Carling & Reba Olsen C; m 1961 to Diane Saxey; c Angela, Cynthia, Teresa & Douglas Richard. Educ: Univ Utah, BS in Polit Sci, 62, JD, 65; Phi Delta Phi. Polit & Govt Pos: Held various voting dist off & deleg pos, Utah, 61-73; legis dist vchmn, Rep Party, 62-63; mem, Salt Lake Co Rep Cent Comt, 62-65, secy, 68; dir, Salt Lake Co Young Rep, 67-68; Utah State Rep, 67-73; mem, Utah State Rep Cent Comt, 71-; Utah State Sen, 74-, mem labor, bus & econ develop comt, appropriations & higher educ comts, Utah State Senate, currently; bd dirs, Community Serv Coun, Salt Lake Area, 75. Bus & Prof Pos: Compiler water rights sect, Utah State Engrs Off, 60-62; owner-mgr, Security Credit Asn, 62-65; attorney-partner, Mock, Shearer & Carling, 65- Mem: Am Bar Asn; Salt Lake Community Action Prog (trustee); Salt Lake Proj Head Start (mem policy adv comt); Explorer Post adv, Boy Scouts; Salt Lake Co Asn Retarded Children (dir). Relig: Latter-day Saint. Legal Res: 1075 Alton Way Salt Lake City UT 84108 Mailing Add: 1000 Continental Bank Bldg Salt Lake City UT 84101

CARLINO, PHIL THOMAS (D)
Chmn, Nev Dem State Cent Comt
b Buffalo, NY, Apr 22, 26; s Phil Thomas Carlino & Angeline DiNardo; m 1946 to Florence Margaret Mahan; c Beverly Ann & Glenn Joseph. Educ: Univ Buffalo, 50-53. Polit & Govt Pos: Dem precinct capt, Las Vegas, Nev, 69-70; chmn, Nev Dem State Cent Comt, 70-; first vpres, Dem Party of Nev, 70-71, state chmn, 71- Bus & Prof Pos: Owner, Buffalo Radio Presentations, NY, 53-56; pres, Cointique Corp, 56-63; prof numismatist, Buffalo, NY & Las Vegas, Nev, 56-; pres, Fremont Coin Co, 63- Mil Serv: Entered as A/S, Navy, 43, released as PO 2/C, 46, after serv in 7th Fleet, SPac, 43-46, recalled, two years serv in Naval Training, Bainbridge, Md; Good Conduct Medal; Philippine Liberation Medal; SPac Ribbon with two Bronze Stars; Am Defense Serv Medal; World War II; Korean Conflict. Mem: Life mem Am Numismatic Soc; Prof Numismatic Guild; Am Legion; VFW; Nat Rifleman's Asn. Relig: Methodist. Mailing Add: 1829 Howard Las Vegas NV 89104

CARLISLE, GEORGE LANGFORD (D)
Committeeman, Dem Exec Comt Fla
b Jacksonville, Fla, Jan 19, 24; s Franklin Paul Carlisle, Sr & Edith West C; m 1944 to Thelma Grace Martin; c Gary George, Terry Jack & Merry Linda (Mrs Rhoden). Educ: Clay High Sch, grad, 43. Polit & Govt Pos: Supvr of Elec, Clay Co, Fla, 49-52, circuit court clerk & comptroller, Clay Co, Fla, 57-, court clerk, 73-; committeeman, Clay Co Dem Precinct 11, 67-; committeeman, Dem Exec Comt, 70- Mil Serv: Entered as Seaman, Navy, 44, released as Seaman 1/C, 46, after serv in Armed Guard, ETO; European & Good Conduct Medals. Mem: State Asn Court Clerks (past pres); Nat Asn for Court Admin; VFW; Am Quarterhorse Asn; Moose. Relig: Methodist. Legal Res: Gary Rd Green Cove Springs FL 32043 Mailing Add: PO Box 698 Green Cove Springs FL 32043

CARLISLE, GRACE MARTIN (D)
Committeewoman, Fla State Dem Exec Comt
b Mt Pleasant, Fla, Apr 6, 27; d Daniel Stephen Martin & Lela Victoria Shaw M; m 1944 to George Langford Carlisle; c Gary George, Terry Jack & Merry Linda (Mrs Rhoden). Educ: Clay High Sch, 45. Polit & Govt Pos: Dep clerk circuit court, Clay Co, Fla, 57-; committeewoman, Clay Co Dem Exec Comt, Precinct 11, Penney Farms, 64-; committeewoman, Fla State Dem Exec Comt, Clay Co, 74- Mem: Am & Fla Quarter Horse Asns; Elk Does; VFW Auxiliary; Village Improvement Asn. Relig: Methodist. Legal Res: Gary Rd Green Cove Springs FL 32043 Mailing Add: PO Box 698 Green Cove Springs FL 32043

CARLISLE, JOHN REID (D)
Ga State Rep
b Griffin, Ga, Mar 8, 42; s Ernest Franklin Carlisle, Jr & Henrietta Brewer C; m 1965 to Carole Flynn Conniff; c Carole Flynn & Christine Catherine. Educ: Univ Ga, BA, Sch Law, LLB; Phi Delta Phi; Phi Delta Theta; Sphinx Club; Int Fraternity Coun, vpres. Polit & Govt Pos: Ga State Rep, 72-, asst admin floor leader, Ga House Rep, 75- Bus & Prof Pos: Attorney-at-law, Griffin, Ga, 66- Mem: Griffin & Ga Bar Asns; Rotary. Honors & Awards: Young Man of Year, Spalding Co, Ga. Relig: Baptist. Mailing Add: PO Box 551 Griffin GA 30223

CARLISLE, LILBURN WAYNE (D)
Secy, Saline Co Dem Cent Comt, Ark
b Benton, Ark, Mar 16, 36; s Lilburn Carlisle & Dollie Thomas C; m 1958 to Sandra Walls. Educ: Ouachita Baptist Col, BA, 58. Polit & Govt Pos: Secy, Saline Co Dem Cent Comt, Ark, 70- Mil Serv: 2nd Lt, Army, 58. Mem: Nat & Ark Real Estate Asns; Ark Ins Asn; Lions. Relig: Baptist. Mailing Add: 300 E Conway Benton AR 72015

CARLISLE, RAOUL (D)
Secy-Treas, St Francis Co Dem Cent Comt, Ark
b Petersburg, Ind, Dec 23, 97; s James Carlisle & Clara Jackson C; m 1921 to Martha Louise Norfleet Cargill; c Martha Esme (Mrs Rufus Woody, Jr), Betty Claire (Mrs George Morledge, Jr) & Marshall Norfleet, 15 grandchildren, 1 great grandchild. Educ: Univ Calif, Berkeley, 3 years. Polit & Govt Pos: Secy-treas, St Francis Co Dem Cent Comt, Ark, currently; deleg, Dem Nat Mid-Term Conf, 74. Bus & Prof Pos: Sports ed, Daily Times Herald, Forrest City, Ark. Mil Serv: Entered as Pvt, Marine Corps, 18, released, 19, reentered, 42, released as S/Sgt, 45, after serv as pub rels chief, Hq, Eighth Naval Dist, New Orleans; various awards & medals. Mem: Charter mem Nat Turf Writers Asn; US Basketball Writers Asn; Football Writers of Am Asn; Nat Wildlife Fedn; Ark Wildlife Fedn. Honors & Awards: Honored at Churchill Downs, Louisville, Ky for covering 50 consecutive Ky Derbys, 68; several awards for outstanding coverage of sports events; Ky Colonel; hon mayor, Louisville, New Orleans, Memphis, Washington, Baltimore & New York. Relig: Episcopal. Mailing Add: PO Box 421 Forrest City AR 72335

CARLISLE, VERVENE (VEE) (D)
Utah State Rep
b Salt Lake City, Utah; d Garnett Walpole Carlisle & Lulu Ericksen C; div. Educ: Granite High Sch, grad. Polit & Govt Pos: Utah State Rep, Dist Four, 71-72 & 75- Bus & Prof Pos: Asst vpres, Women's Div Consumer Serv, Tracy-Collins Bank & Trust, 70- Mem: Salt Lake CofC; Proj Reality (bd dirs); Zonta Club; Bus & Prof Womens Club; Utah Heritage Found. Mailing Add: 8 Hillside Ave Salt Lake City UT 84103

CARLSON, ALF A (R)
Vt State Rep
Mailing Add: 60 Chatterton Park Proctor VT 05765

CARLSON, ARNE H (R)
Minn State Rep
b New York, NY, Sept 24, 34; s Helge Carlson & Kerstin Magnusson C; m 1965 to Barbara Duffy; c Arne H, Jr & Anne Gilles. Educ: Williams Col, BA, 57; Univ Minn Grad Sch, 57-58; Chi Psi. Polit & Govt Pos: Majority leader, City Coun, Minneapolis, 65-67; mem, Welfare Bd & Park Bd, 65-67; Minn State Rep, 71-, house minority whip, currently. Bus & Prof Pos: Dir, Alfred Adler Inst Minn, formerly; Real Estate Broker, currently. Mil Serv: Entered as Pvt, Army, 59, released as Pvt, 60, after serv in Ft Leonard Wood, Mo; Soldier of the Cycle. Relig: Protestant. Mailing Add: 4301 Fremont Ave Minneapolis MN 55409

CARLSON, CLIFFARD D (R)
Rep Nat Committeeman, Ill
b Aurora, Ill, Dec 30, 15; s John I Carlson & Alma C (both deceased); m 1941 to Betty Lisette McLallen, wid; c John McLallen, & Carol Ann. Educ: NCent Col, 33-34; Univ NMex, BA, 37. Polit & Govt Pos: Deleg, Rep Nat Conv, 60, 64 & 68; mem, Ill Rep State Cent Comt, 15th Cong Dist, 65-, vchmn & finance chmn, currently; state-wide finance chmn & dinner chmn, Scott for Treas, 62; state-wide finance chmn, Scott for Gov Campaign, 64; chmn, Kane Co Rep Finance Comt; mem & vpres, bd gov & mem exec comt, United Rep Fund of Ill; mem, Ill Rep Finance Coord Comt; co-chmn, All-Ill Comt to elect Richard Ogilvie, 68; vchmn & coordr, Percy for Sen Comt, 66; mem fund raising comt for Richard M Nixon, 68; US Rep, 15th Dist, Ill, 72-73, cong adv 17th Session UNESCO Gen Conf, Paris, France, 72; Rep Nat Committeeman, Ill, 73-; chmn, Comn Develop Fox River, formerly. Bus & Prof Pos: Pres, Carlson Tool & Machine Co, Carlson Trading Corp, Geneva, Ill & Fisher Brush Machinery Corp, Baltimore, Md; dir, State Bank Geneva & Chronicle Publ Co. Mil Serv: Lt(jg), Naval Res, Pac Theatre, World War II. Mem: Ill State CofC; Ill Mfrs Asn; Nat Asn Mfrs; Elks; Pi Kappa Alpha. Relig: Episcopal. Mailing Add: 921 S Batavia Ave Geneva IL 60134

CARLSON, DONNA JEAN (R)
Ariz State Rep
b Emmett, Idaho, Feb 19, 38; d William J Burchfield & Florence Lappin B; m 1962 to Eric Jerome Carlson; c Daniel J, Richard R & John M Wayne; Kevin E & Douglas D Carlson. Educ: Univ Idaho, 61. Polit & Govt Pos: State committeeman, Rep Party, Ariz, 68-; pres, Coord Coun Rep Women, 71-73; Ariz State Rep, Dist 29, 75-, vchmn, House Judiciary Comt, Ariz House Rep, mem, Com Comt, Govt Opers Comt & Counties & Munic Comt, 75- Relig: Protestant. Mailing Add: 447 W Hillview Circle Mesa AZ 85201

CARLSON, EDGAR A (R)
Chmn, Tioga Co Rep Comt, Pa
b Harwick, Pa, Sept 2, 29; s Edwin G Carlson & Effie Haglund C; m 1949 to Margaret J Jenkins; c James E, Ann Lee (Mrs Ronald Strong) & Janis Lynn. Educ: Lycoming Col, polit sci course, 67. Polit & Govt Pos: Committeeman, Tioga Co Rep Comt, Pa, 58-70, chmn. 72-; co treas, Tioga Co, 66- Mem: Bloss Masonic Lodge 350; Williamsport Consistory; Covington Grange; Irem Temple; Hillside Rod & Gun Club. Relig: Lutheran. Mailing Add: 144 Morris St Blossburg PA 16912

CARLSON, ELIZABETH KATHRYN (D)
Chmn, Washington Co Dem Party, Nebr
b Blair, Nebr, Dec 26, 14; d Louis Grimm & Elizabeth Quinlan G; m 1953 to Robert J Carlson. Educ: Blair High Sch, Nebr, grad, 32. Polit & Govt Pos: Secy, Blair Planning Comn, Nebr, 70-73; chmn, Washington Co Dem Party, 70-; secy, Gov Comn on the State of Women, 71- Bus & Prof Pos: Contract exam, Corps of Engrs, retired in 68. Mem: Eagles Auxiliary (past pres & secy, Blair Auxiliary 3215, 65-73, trustee, Nebr State Auxiliary, 70-73). Relig: Catholic. Mailing Add: 1759 Wilbur Dr Blair NE 68008

CARLSON, ELMER GUSTAV (D)
b Massena, Iowa, Apr 24, 09; s Carl Fredrick Carlson & Christina F C; div; c Nancy & Jennifer. Polit & Govt Pos: Dem Nat Committeeman, Ill, 52; deleg, Dem Nat Conv & Nat Platform Committeeman, 64; Dem Precinct Committeeman, Iowa, 66- Mem: Lions Int; CofC; Nat Farmers Union; Zig-i-zag; Shrine; 100 Bushel Corn Club. Honors & Awards: Worlds Champion Corn Husker, Nat Corn Husking Contests, 35. Relig: Presbyterian. Mailing Add: 115 Circle Dr Audubon IA 50025

CARLSON, FRANK (R)
b Concordia, Kans, Jan 23, 93; s Charles E Carlson & Anna Johnson C; m 1919 to Alice Fredrickson; c Eunice Marie (Mrs Ed Rolfs). Educ: Concordia Normal & Bus Col; Kans State Col. Hon Degrees: LLD, Bob Jones Univ, 51, Springfield Col, 53, William Jewell Col, 55, St Benedict's Col, 61, Kans State Univ, 62, Baker Univ, Southwestern Univ & Ottawa Univ. Polit & Govt Pos: Kans State Rep, 29-33; chmn, State Rep Comt, Kans, 32-34; US Rep, Kans, 6 terms; mem state & fed affairs comn, Hoover Comn Reorgn; Gov, Kans, 46-50; chmn, Interstate Oil Compact Comn, 49; chmn, Nat Gov Conf, 49; chmn, Coun State Govt, 50; vchmn, Pres Nat Safety Conf, 50; US deleg UN; US Sen, Kans, 50-69. Bus & Prof Pos: Farmer, stockman. Mil Serv: World War I. Mem: Mason 33 degree); Int Coun Christian Leadership; Menninger Found; Inst Logopedics. Honors & Awards: Agr Hall of Fame, 64. Relig: Baptist. Mailing Add: Concordia KS 66901

CARLSON, HOWARD (DFL)
Chmn, Meeker Co Dem-Farmer-Labor Comt, Minn
b Meeker Co, Minn, Mar 5, 14; s Frank Carlson & Emly Okeson C; m to Sylvia Lawson; c H Jerome, Jannan & Jonette (Mrs Dale Engan). Educ: Gustavus Adolphus Col, BA, 34. Polit & Govt Pos: Chmn, Meeker Co Agr Stabilization & Conserv Serv, Dept Agr, 56-68; mem, Minn State Agr Stabilization & Conserv Serv, Dept Agr, 68-69; chmn, Meeker Co Dem-Farmer-Labor Comt, 70-; mem, Gov Energy Task Force, 72-74. Bus & Prof Pos: Chmn sch bd, Independent Dist 464, Minn, 6 years; mgr, Coop Creamery, 5 years. Mem: Golden Fleece 89 (past master); Zurah Temple; Minn Farmers Union. Relig: Lutheran. Mailing Add: Rt 1 Grove City MN 56243

CARLSON, JACK WILSON
Asst Secy Energy & Minerals, Dept of Interior
b Salt Lake City, Utah, Nov 20, 33; s Oscar William Carlson & Gretta Wilson C; m 1954 to Renee Pyott; c Catherine, Christine, Steven, Diane, John, David & Paul. Educ: Univ Utah, BS, 55, MBA, 57; Harvard Univ, MPA & PhD, 63. Polit & Govt Pos: Sr Staff economist, Coun Econ Adv, 66-68; asst dir for prog eval, US Off Mgt & Budget, 69-71, asst to dir for planning & econ affairs, 72-74; Asst Secy Energy & Minerals, Dept of Interior, 74- Bus & Prof Pos: Instr, Univ Utah, 55-57. Mil Serv: Entered as 2nd Lt, Air Force, 57, released as Maj, 66, after serv in Air Defense Command, Air Training Command, 57-59, assoc prof, Air Force Acad, 59-64, asst for spec studies, Off of Secy of Air Force, 65-66; Two Commendation Medals. Mailing Add: 18 Masters Court Potomac MD 20854

CARLSON, JOHN PHILIP (R)
b Shickley, Nebr, Apr 16, 15; s Rev Christopher Theodore Carlson & Klara Blomquist C; m 1950 to Maryjo Suverkrup. Educ: Luther Col, Nebr, 31-33; Wayne State Col, AB, 35; Georgetown Univ, JD, 51; Columbia Univ, MA, 67; Pi Gamma Mu; Phi Alpha Delta; Sigma Tau Delta. Polit & Govt Pos: Vet rels adv, Off Price Admin, 46-47; training specialist, Dept of Navy, 47-56; minority counsel, Comt on Govt Opers, US House Rep, 56- Bus & Prof Pos: Teacher & athletic coach, Nebr Pub High Schs, 35-42. Mil Serv: Entered as Aviation Cadet, Army Air Force, 42, released as Capt, 45, after serv in 460th Bomb Group, 15th Air Force, Italy, 44 & Personnel Distribution Command, US, 44-45; Lt Col (Ret), Air Force Res; Distinguished Flying Cross; Air Medal with Oak Leaf Cluster. Mem: Nat Lawyers Club; Am & Fed Bar Asns; Am Econ Asn; Capital Hill Club. Honors & Awards: Am Polit Sci Asn Cong Staff fel, Columbia Univ 64-65 & 66-67. Relig: Lutheran. Mailing Add: 2206 Belle Haven Rd Alexandria VA 22307

CARLSON, LEVI E (R)
Chmn, 27th Dist Rep Comt, NDak
b Nome, NDak, Jan 16, 19; s Henry Carlson & Annie Strand C; m 1948 to Elsie Victoria Wrede; c Esther (Mrs Glen Rockwell), Eunice, DeLoris, Naomi & Carol. Polit & Govt Pos: Chmn, 27th Dist Rep Comt, NDak, 74- Mailing Add: Nome ND 58062

CARLSON, LOREN MERLE (R)
b Mitchell, SDak, Nov 2, 23; s Clarence Arvid Carlson & Edna M Rosenquist C; m 1950 to Verona Gladys Hole; c Catherine Ann, Bradley Reed & Nancy Jewel. Educ: Yankton Col, BA, 48; Univ Wis, Madison, MA, 52; George Washington Univ, LLB, 61; Pi Kappa Delta. Polit & Govt Pos: Dir legis res, SDak Legis Coun, 53-59; admin asst to US Sen F Case, 59-63; state budget officer, State of SDak, 63-68; admin asst to US Rep L Pressler, SDak, 75- Bus & Prof Pos: Asst dir govt res, Univ SDak, 49-51, dir hwy laws study, 63, dean continuing educ, 68-75. Mil Serv: Entered as A/C, Navy, 45, released as Seaman 1/C, 46, Victory Medal; Am Theatre Ribbon. Publ: Bibliography of South Dakota Government, Govt Res Br, 51; South Dakota chapter on intergovernmental relations, Knestbaum Report, 57; South Dakota chapter on governmental reorganization, Midwest J Pub Admin, 72. Mem: Lions (pres, 74-75); Nat Univ Exten Asn (chairperson, Region IV, 73-74); SDak Comt on the Humanities (chairperson, 74-75); Am Soc Pub Admin; Pi Sigma Alpha. Honors & Awards: Cert of Merit, SDak Am Legion, 74. Relig: Lutheran. Legal Res: 229 Catalina Vermillion SD 57069 Mailing Add: Rm 1238 Longworth House Off Bldg Washington DC 20515

CARLSON, LYNDON R (DFL)
Minn State Rep
Mailing Add: State Capitol Bldg St Paul MN 55155

CARLSON, ROY (DFL)
Minn State Rep
Mailing Add: State Capitol Bldg St Paul MN 55155

CARLSON, STEPHEN THOMAS
b Minneapolis, Minn, Oct 15, 45; s Charles K Carlson & Mary Jane Smith C; separated; c Joshua. Educ: Univ Vt, BA, 67; Univ Minn, 67-68. Polit & Govt Pos: Legis asst to US Rep James Jeffords, Vt, 75- Bus & Prof Pos: Chief, Capitol Bur, Burlington Free Press, Vt, 70-74. Legal Res: Gunner Brook Rd Plainfield VT 05667 Mailing Add: 501 Cannon House Off Bldg Washington DC 20515

CARLTON, C C (D)
Ark State Rep
Mailing Add: PO Box 809 Nashville AR 71852

CARLTON, VASSAR B
Chief Justice, Fla Supreme Court
b Island Grove, Fla, Nov 13, 12; s Benjamin Franklin Carlton & Zeffie Ergle C; m 1959 to Grace Ramer, wid; c Mary Carol (Mrs Crisafulli), Martha (Mrs Fulmer), Barbara & Pamela. Educ: Univ Fla, 31-33; Stetson Univ, LLB, 37; Phi Alpha Delta. Polit & Govt Pos: Judge, Brevard Co, Fla, 41-54; Circuit judge, Ninth Judicial & 18th Judicial Circuit, 54-69; Justice, Fla Supreme Court, 69-73, Chief Justice, 73- Mem: Mason (32 degree); Shrine; Kiwanis; Elks (Past Exalted Ruler); Jaycees. Honors & Awards: Good Govt Award, twice. Relig: Baptist. Legal Res: 1103 Gardenia St Tallahassee FL 32303 Mailing Add: Supreme Court Bldg Tallahassee FL 32304

CARLUCCIO, DANIEL JOHN (D)
b Hoboken, NJ, Feb 10, 41; s Paul V Carluccio & Evelyn Hoster C; m 1965 to Judith Ellen Filker; c Michele & Matthew. Educ: St Peter's Col (NJ), BS, 62; NY Univ Law Sch, LLB, 65. Polit & Govt Pos: Committeeman, Ocean Co Dem Comt, NJ, 67-70; registr chmn, 69 & 72; campaign mgr, Gasser for Cong, 68; munic chmn, Dover Twp Dem Party, 69-70; committeeman, NJ State Young Dem, Ocean Co, 69-71; campaign mgr, Gasser-McLaughlin, 71; deleg, Dem Nat Conv, 72. Bus & Prof Pos: Partner, Citta, Gasser, Carluccio & Holzapfel, 68- Mil Serv: Entered as Pvt, Army Reserve, 67, released as E-4, 72, after serv in 404th CA Co. Mem: Ocean Co Bar Asn (trustee, 70-73, treas, 71-72, secy, 72-73); Am Judicature Soc; NJ Trial Lawyers Asn. Mailing Add: 31 Blue Jay Dr Toms River NJ 08753

CARMEN, GERALD P (R)
Chmn, NH Rep State Comt
Mailing Add: 308 Crestview Circle Manchester NH 03104

CARMICHAEL, GILBERT ELLZEY (R)
Mem Exec Comt, Miss Rep Party
b Columbia, Miss, June 27, 27; s Calvin Ellzey Carmichael & Clyde Smith C; m 1954 to Carolyn Dean White; c Gilbert Scott. Educ: Tex A&M Univ, BS, 50. Polit & Govt Pos: Chmn, Lauderdale Co Rep Party, Miss, formerly; deleg, Rep Nat Conv, 68 & 72; mem, Gov Emergency Coun, Miss, 69-70; mem, Miss Adv Comt to Cabinet Comt on Educ, 70; mem, Lauderdale Co Rep Exec Comt; mem finance comt, Miss State Rep Party, mem exec comt, currently; Rep Party cand for US Sen against J O Eastland, Miss, 72; app mem, Nat Hwy Safety Adv Comt, 73-74, chmn, 74- Bus & Prof Pos: Pres, Carmichael Volkswagen, Inc, 61-, Gil Carmichael, Inc, 65 & The Carriage House, 70. Mil Serv: Entered as Recruit, Coast Guard, 45, released as Seaman 1/C, 46, after serv in NAtlantic; reentered as Ens, 51, released as Lt(jg), 53; Lt(jg), Coast Guard Res; Silver Life Saving Medal; Am Theater Ribbon; Victory Medal. Mem: Miss Automobile Dealers Asn (pres, 70); Meridian Indust Found (pres, 69-71); Meridian Art Asn; St Joseph Hosp (trustee); Miss Hosp (chmn bd). Honors & Awards: Time Mag Award; Qual Dealer Award, State of Miss; Mississippian of Year Award, Miss Broadcaster's Asn, 72; Sertoma Serv to Mankind Award, 74; King of Jr Auxiliary, Meridian, 75. Relig: Episcopal. Mailing Add: 2009 39th St Meridian MS 39301

CARMICHAEL, OLIVER CROMWELL, JR (R)
Chmn, Rep Nat Finance Comt
b Birmingham, Ala, Mar 10, 20; s Oliver Cromwell Carmichael & Ruth Crabtree C; m 1946 to Ernestine Morris; c Carmen C (Mrs Murphy), Oliver Cromwell, III, Ernestine, II (Mrs Nickle) & Stanley Clark. Educ: Vanderbilt Univ, AB, 40; Duke Univ Law Sch, LLB, 42; Columbia Univ, MA, 51, PhD, 52; Phi Beta Kappa, Omicron Delta Kappa & Beta Theta Pi; Order of the Coif. Hon Degrees: DCL, Franklin Col, LLD, Univ Notre Dame, Wabash Col & Centre Col. Polit & Govt Pos: Deleg, Rep Nat Conv, 64, 68 & 72; chmn, Ind Rep Citizens Finance Comt, 66-69; mem, Rep Nat Finance Comt, 72, treas, 74-, chmn, 75- Bus & Prof Pos: Exec dir, Vanderbilt Univ Develop Found, 55-56; pres, Converse Col, 56-60; chmn, Assoc First Capital Corp, First Bank & Trust Co, 60- & Marshall Co Bank & Trust Co, 65- Mil Serv: Lt(sg), Naval Res. Publ: New York Establishes a State University. Mem: Morris Park Country Club, South Bend; Pickwick Club, Niles, Mich; Ocean Club; Country Club of Fla. Relig: Presbyterian. Legal Res: 110 N Esther St South Bend IN 46617 Mailing Add: 1700 Mishawaka Ave South Bend IN 46604

CARMICHAEL, RICHARD DONALD (R)
Chmn, De Kalb Co Rep Exec Comt, Ala
b Bessemer, Ala, Oct 19, 35; s Joseph Newton Carmichael & Lucy Plunkett C; m to Beverly Jean Williams; c Richard Donald, Jr & Cynthia Jean. Educ: Samford Univ, BS in pharm, 58. Polit & Govt Pos: Chmn, Bessemer Young Rep, Ala, 64-68; mem, Jefferson Co Rep Exec Comt, 64-66; regional coordr, Jefferson Co Rep Party, 65-66; mem, Ala Rep State Exec Comt, 65-66; town councilman, Rainsville, 69; chmn, De Kalb Co Rep Exec Comt, 69-; mayor, Rainsville, 69- Mem: Ala & Am Pharmaceutical Asns; Plainview High Sch PTA; Civitan Club; Ruritan Club. Honors & Awards: New Jaycee Award, 68. Relig: Methodist; chmn bd, Robertson Chapel Methodist Church; dir, Methodist Youth Fel. Mailing Add: 1640 Moss Rock Rd Birmingham AL 35226

CARMIGGELT, COEN JAN WILLEM (R)
Chmn, Lake Co Rep Cent Comt, Calif
b Morotai, Indonesia, Dec 28, 47; s Hans Christoffer Carmiggelt & Hennie Elisabeth Panjer C; single. Educ: Mt San Antonio Col, Pomona, Calif, AA, 66; Humboldt State Col, BA, 68; secondary teaching cert, 70. Polit & Govt Pos: Chmn, Lake Co Rep Cent Comt, Calif, 73-; deleg, Rep State Cent Comt Calif, 73- Bus & Prof Pos: Lab mgr, Clear Lake Algal Research Unit, Lakeport, Calif, 70- Mem: Lakeport Yacht Club. Relig: Atheist. Mailing Add: 226 Grace Lane Lakeport CA 95453

CARMODY, CHARLES EDWARD (R)
Chmn, 12th Cong Dist Rep Party, Mich
b Norwalk, Ohio, Jan 22, 31; s James Gilbert Carmody & Martha Kail C; m 1953 to Doris Louise; c William James, Todd Gregory & Christopher Scott. Educ: Kent State Univ, BA, 53; Ohio State Univ, JD, 55; Delta Theta Phi; Sigma Alpha Epsilon. Polit & Govt Pos: City attorney, Warren, Mich, 60-65; chmn, 12th Cong Dist Rep Party, 75- Bus & Prof Pos: Attorney, Perica, Breithart & Carmody, Warren, Mich, 65- Mem: Village of Warren, Macomb Co & Mich Bar Asns. Legal Res: 158 S Wilson Mt Clemens MI 48043 Mailing Add: 28225 Mound Rd Warren MI 48090

CARMONA, RALPH CHRIS (D)
b East Los Angeles, Calif, Jan 5, 51; s Dario Palacio Carmona & Maria Luz Montanez C; single. Educ: Univ Southern Calif, Los Angeles, BA, 73; Univ Calif, Santa Barbara, currently; Forum for Student Awareness, 72; Movimento Estudiantine Chicano de Aztlan. Polit & Govt Pos: Deleg, Dem Nat Conv, 72; precinct interviewer, Nat Broadcasting Co News, Mayor Runoff, Calif, 72; campaign coordr, McGovern for President Comt, 40th Assembly Dist, Los Angeles, 72; cong intern, Cong Intern Prog, Washington, DC, 72; research asst, Polit Sci Dept, Univ Southern Calif, Los Angeles, 72-73; job develop spec, Model Cities, United Commun Efforts, Inc, 73. Mem: Chicano Dem Caucus; UN Asn of USA; Nat Dem Latino Caucus; Chicano Moratorium Comt. Honors & Awards: Am Legion Sch Award, Navy Post 278, 69; Scholarship, Univ Southern Calif Scholarship Comt, 69; Educ Opportunity Grant, 69; Ford Found Doctoral Fel, 73. Relig: Catholic. Mailing Add: 5868 E Hubbard St Los Angeles CA 90022

CARNAHAN, ERNEST BRYAN, JR (D)
b Garwood, Mo, Mar 12, 26; s Ernest Bryan Carnahan, Sr & Lillie Boyer C; m 1949 to Wanda Edwina Roark; c Ronald Ernest & Donald Edwin. Educ: Ellsinore High Sch, 12 years. Polit & Govt Pos: Chmn, Carter Co Dem Cent Comt, Mo, formerly; Treas, Tenth Cong Dist, 70. Bus & Prof Pos: With Mo State Dept Agr, 66- Mil Serv: Entered as Seaman 2/C, Navy, 44, released as Ship Fitter 3/C, 46, after serv in Pac Theatre, 44-46. Mem: AF&AM (32nd degree Mason); Eastern Star; Agr Stabilization & Conserv; VFW. Relig: Baptist. Mailing Add: Rte 1 Ellsinore MO 63937

CARNAHAN, WANDA EDWINA (D)
VChmn, Carter Co Dem Cent Comt, Mo
b Ellsinore, Mo, July 26, 29; d William Thomas Roark & Ora Berry R; m 1949 to Ernest Bryan Carnahan; c Ronald & Donald. Educ: Ellsinore High Sch. Polit & Govt Pos: Vchmn, Carter Co Dem Cent Comt, Mo, 62-66, secy, formerly, vchmn, currently; secy, Eighth Dist Resolutions Comt, 64; mem, Mo State Dem Comt, 67-68; secy, Carter Co Dem Club, 67-; mem, State Platform Comt, 68; deleg, Mo State Dem Conv, 68; deleg, Mo Dem Women's Federated State Conv, 69 & 70; pres, Carter Co Women's Dem Club, 67-; auditor, Tenth Dist Women's Federated Club, 69-; fifth vpres, Tenth Dist Women's Dem Fedn, 72- Bus & Prof Pos: Pres, ILGWU, 68-, pres exec bd, 68-, mem dist labor coun, 68-, mem Mo-Ark Labor Coun, 68-, mem, shop comt, 68-, COPE chmn, 68-, mem, Mo-Ark Dist Coun, 68-, chairlady, Local 410, 69-, chairlady, Mo-Ark Bd, 72- Mem: Eastern Star (Past matron & past dist dept grand matron); Am Legion Auxiliary, PTA. Honors & Awards: Letters of thanks for polit help from US Sen H H Humphrey, Gov Warren E Hearnes, Mo, Lt Gov William Morris, Sen Edward Long, US Sen Stuart Symington, US Reps Bill D Burlison, and Richard H Ichord, Mo. Relig: General Baptist. Mailing Add: Ellsinore MO 63937

CARNEAL, GEORGE UPSHUR, JR (R)
b New York, NY, May 31, 35; s George Upshur Carneal & Florence Nutt C; m 1958 to Susan Muzzey; c George, III, Scott Hamilton, Erik St John & Kristen Dahlander. Educ: Princeton Univ, AB, 57; Univ Va Sch Law, LLB, 61. Polit & Govt Pos: Law clerk to Hon E Barrett Prettyman, Judge of the US Court of Appeals, DC, 61-62; staff asst, Off of President-Elect Richard M Nixon, 68-69; Spec Asst to Secy John A Volpe, Dept of Transportation, 68-70; gen counsel, Fed Aviation Admin, 70-72. Bus & Prof Pos: Partner, Hogan & Hartson, Washington, DC, 62-68 & 73- Mil Serv: Entered as Pvt, Army, 58, released as Sgt, 63, after serv in Army Inf Res. Publ: The unified bar controversy, 9/67 and The unified bar—a constructive proposal, 11/67, DC Bar Asn J. Mem: DC Bar Asn; Metrop Club; Order of the Coif; Raven Soc; Chevy Chase Club. Relig: Protestant. Mailing Add: 1148 Daleview Dr McLean VA 22101

CARNELL, MARION P (D)
SC State Rep
Mailing Add: Box 119 Ware Shoals SC 29692

CARNES, CHARLES L (D)
Ga State Rep
Mailing Add: 6650 Powers Ferry Rd NW Atlanta GA 30339

CARNES, DAVID BERNARD (D)
b Gadsden, Ala, Nov 13, 43; s Roy B Carnes (deceased) & Ilava Campbell C; single. Educ: Tulane Univ, BA & JD; Columbia Univ, 6 months; mem, Tulane Univ Scholars & Fellows Prog; pres, Pi Kappa Alpha. Polit & Govt Pos: Mem, Etowah Co Bd Educ, Ala, 68-70; mem, Etowah Co Dem Exec Comt, 70-; Ala State Rep, 70-74. Mem: Am, Etowah Co & Ala Bar Asns; Exchange Club; Mason. Relig: Episcopal. Legal Res: 1206 Goodyear Ave Gadsden AL 35903 Mailing Add: 823 Forrest Ave Gadsden AL 35901

CARNES, MRS JACK (D)
Dem Nat Committeewoman, Ark
Polit & Govt Pos: Dem Nat Committeewoman, Ark, 44-; deleg, Dem Nat Conv, 44- Bus & Prof Pos: Prof worker, oil indust & pvt investments. Mem: Crippled Childrens Found; Bus & Prof Women's Club; Camden & Little Rock Country Clubs. Mailing Add: 308 Washington NW Camden AR 71701

CARNES, JAMES EDWARD (R)
Chmn, Belmont Co Rep Cent & Exec Comts, Ohio
b Wheeling, WVa, Feb 19, 42; s Edward A Carnes & Avis E Hoop C; m 1962 to Nancy Ann Taylor; c Jeffrey & Karen. Educ: Bethany Col, 1 year; Col of Com, Wheeling, WVa, 1 year. Polit & Govt Pos: Pres, Rep Club, 70; mem, Belmont Co Rep Cent Comt, Ohio, 70-; chmn, Belmont Co Rep Cent & Exec Comts, 70-; mem bd elec, 70; deleg, Rep Nat Conv, 72. Bus

& Prof Pos: Bookkeeper, C V & W Coal Co, 62-69; off mgr, Cravat Coal Co, Holloway, Ohio, 69-; owner, Carnes Mobile Homes & Appliance, Barnesville, Ohio, currently. Mem: Flushing Rotary; Belmont Co Hist Soc. Honors & Awards: Prince of Peace Contests, dist finals, jr & sr years of high sch; hon Lt Gov State of Ohio. Relig: Christian Church. Mailing Add: 612 N Broadway Barnesville OH 43713

CARNEY, CHARLES J (D)
US Rep, Ohio
b Youngstown, Ohio, Apr 17, 13; s Michael G Carney & Florence Grogan Grimm; m 1938 to Mary Lucille Manning; c Mary Ellen (Mrs John Leshinsky) & Ann (Mrs James Murphy). Educ: Youngstown State Univ, 3 years. Hon Degrees: HHD, Cent State Univ (Ohio), 59; LLD, Col Osteop Med & Surg. Polit & Govt Pos: Ohio State Sen, 50-70, Minority Leader, Ohio State Senate, 69-70; US Rep, Ohio 71- Bus & Prof Pos: Mem, United Rubber Workers Union, 34, vpres & pres, Local 102, pres, Dist Coun 1, 40-43, staff rep & dist dir, 42-50; staff rep, United Steelworkers Am, 50-68. Relig: Roman Catholic. Legal Res: Youngstown OH 44511 Mailing Add: 1123 Longworth House Off Bldg Washington DC 20515

CARNEY, JOHN JOSEPH (D)
Mem, Cuyahoga Co Dem Exec Comt, Ohio
b Cleveland, Ohio, June 16, 10; s John J Carney & Celia McCafferty C; m 1941 to Virginia M Dreisig; c John J, Jr, James A, Jeanne M & Joseph D. Educ: Western Reserve Law Sch, LLB, 43; Baldwin Wallace Col; John Carroll Univ; dean, Delta Theta Phi, 43. Hon Degrees: LLD, Wilberforce Univ, 58. Polit & Govt Pos: Ohio State Rep, 37-47, Dem Leader, Ohio House of Rep, 37-41; chmn, Ohio Soldiers & Sailor Comn, 46; vchmn, Cuyahoga Co Dem Exec Comt, 51, mem, 56-; auditor, Cuyahoga Co, 51-63, mem bd of elec, 66-, chmn, currently; Dem Nat Committeeman, 52; alt deleg, Dem Nat Conv, 64, deleg, 68; vchmn, Cuyahoga Co Dem Orgn, formerly; chmn, Bd Elec, Cleveland, 72-; pres, Ohio Elec Off, 72-73; judge, Cuyahoga Co Court Common Pleas, currently. Bus & Prof Pos: Dir, Charity Hosp, Ohio, 63-; vchmn, 64-65. Mil Serv: Capt, 45; Four ETO Campaign Ribbons. Publ: Appraisal Techniques, Self, 57; Income Approach to Value, The Appraisal J, 65. Mem: Amvets (former Nat Judge Advocate); Cuyahoga Co Bar Asn; Ohio State Auditors Asn; Int Asn Assessing Officers; Ohio Auditors Asn. Honors & Awards: Produced First film on Real Estate. Relig: Roman Catholic. Legal Res: 18777 Lookout Circle Fairview Park OH 44126 Mailing Add: 220 St Clair NW Cleveland OH 44113

CARNEY, THOMAS E (D)
Ohio State Sen
Mailing Add: 935 North Ward Ave Girard OH 44420

CARNEY, THOMAS JOSEPH (D)
Ohio State Rep
b Youngstown, Ohio, Feb 17, 34; s Thomas Joseph Carney & Loretta Ann Holzbach C; m 1956 to Mary Rita McNicholas; c Thomas Joseph, III, Gregory & Mary. Educ: Youngstown State Univ, BS, 56. Polit & Govt Pos: Pres, Mahoning Valley Regional Mass Transit Authority, Ohio, 69-71; mem, Mahoning-Trumbull Coun Govt, 69-71; chmn, Boardman Twp Trustees, 70-72; Ohio State Rep, 73- Bus & Prof Pos: Mgr moving & storage div, J V McNicholas Transfer Co, 62-73. Mil Serv: 2nd Lt, Army Res, 57, serv as Guided Missile Co Comdr; Capt, Res, 9 years. Relig: Roman Catholic. Mailing Add: 60 Melrose Ave Youngstown OH 44512

CAROTHERS, JOSIAH S ROBINS, JR (D)
Ala State Rep
b Winfield, Marion Co, Ala, Sept 15, 38; s Josiah Showell Robins Carothers, Sr & Katherine Harris Carothers; m 1958 to Barbara Noel Burns; c Josiah Showell Robins, III & Merritt Burns. Educ: Auburn Univ, BS, 60; Alpha Gamma Rho. Polit & Govt Pos: Indigent Care Bd, Houston Co, Ala, 72-; mem, Bd Zoning Adjustment, Dothan, Ala, 72-74; Ala State Rep, 74-, mem rules comt, Ala State House Rep, 74-, mem, health comt & com & transportation comts, 74- Bus & Prof Pos: Vpres, Burks Trading Co, Inc, Dothan, Ala, 63-; teacher-vocational agr, Ashford High Sch, Ashford, Ala, 65- Mil Serv: Entered as Pvt, Ala Nat Guard, 54, released as SP-4, 60. Mem: Asn US Army; Am Voc Asn; Houston Co Cattlemen's Asn (dir, 70-); Elks; Mason. Honors & Awards: Ala 4-H Alumni Award, Ala Exten Serv, 68; Houston Co Leadership Award, State CofC, Ala Extension Serv, Liberty Nat Life Ins Co, 68; Hon State Farmer, Future Farmer's Am, 70; Serv Award as Long-time Chmn of Tri-States Beef Cattle Show, Dothan-Houston Co CofC, 73. Relig: Methodist. Mailing Add: Rte 8 Box 33 Dothan AL 36301

CAROTHERS, NEIL, III (R)
Mem, Rep Nat Finance Comt
b Fayetteville, Ark, Oct 11, 19; s Neil Carothers (deceased) & Eileen Hamilton C (deceased); m 1955 to Mary Crocker deLimur; c Neil & Andre Sperry. Educ: Blair Acad, 35-37; Princeton Univ, BS in Elec Eng, 41; Rhodes Scholar, Oxford Univ, BA, 50, MA, 55; Cap & Gown Club; Myrmidon Soc. Polit & Govt Pos: Consult, Research & Develop Bd, US Dept Defense, 51; asst sci adv, US Dept State, 51-53, pub mem, Inspection Corps, 70; spec asst to the dir, Nat Sci Found, 53-61, consult to the dir, 62-63; dep to mem, Nat Aeronaut & Space Coun; rep, Nat Security Coun Planning Bd & Opers Coord Bd; mem, DC Rep Comt, 68-; mem, Rep Nat Finance Comt, 68-; finance chmn, DC Rep Party, 68-70; chmn, Rep Finance Comt, DC, 70- Bus & Prof Pos: Asst to dir, guided missiles prog, Johns Hopkins Appl Physics Lab, Md, 46-48; bd dirs, Provident Securities Co, San Francisco, currently; consult, currently. Mil Serv: Entered as Ens, Naval Res, 41, released as Lt Comdr, 45, after serv as Experimental Test Pilot & Engr, Patuxent River Naval Air Test Univ, 43-45. Mem: Nat Coun Foreign Policy Asn (chmn, Washington DC Area, trustee, New York, NY, 69-); Wash Inst Foreign Affairs; Am Asn Advan Sci; Capitol Hill Club; Fed City Club. Relig: Episcopal. Legal Res: 2500 Q St Washington DC 20007 Mailing Add: 1701 Pennsylvania Ave Washington DC 20006

CARPENTER, DENNIS E (R)
Calif State Sen
b Minneapolis, Minn, Sept 3, 28; s Frank Henry Carpenter & Helen Luedtke C; m 1968 to Madine; c Kenneth R, Bruce H, Frank H, II & Scott R & stepdaughter, Suzanne. Educ: Univ Calif, Los Angeles, BA, 52, LLB, 58; Alpha Tau Omega; Phi Delta Phi. Polit & Govt Pos: Spec agt, Fed Bur Invest, 54-58; chmn, Orange Co Rep Cent Comt, Calif, 62-67, exec comt, 68-; chmn, Calif Plan Comt, Rep State Cent Comt, 62-69, mem exec comt, 62-, vchmn, Rep State Cent Comt, 67-69, chmn, 69-7Q; deleg, Rep Nat Conv, 68; Calif State Sen, 34th Dist, 70- Bus & Prof Pos: Attorney, 58-; lawyer, Fulop, Rolston, Burns & McKittrick, Newport Beach, Calif, 73-; chmn, Orange Co Airport Comn, Santa Ana, 67-69. Mil Serv: Entered as Pvt, Army, 46, released as 1st Lt, 48. Mem: Am, Calif, Orange Co & Harbor Area Bar Asns. Relig: Presbyterian. Legal Res: 2433 Vista Nobleza Newport Beach CA 92660 Mailing Add: PO Box CC Irvine CA 92664

CARPENTER, ELSA MANNHEIMER (R)
b St Paul, Minn, Nov 23, 26; d Carl Mannheimer & Isabelle Chapel M; m 1950 to Walter Schenck Carpenter; c Ann, Scott, Matthew & Judd. Educ: Univ of Minn, Minneapolis, 44-47; Sigma Alpha Sigma; YWCA. Polit & Govt Pos: Rep aldermanic campaign worker, for Harmon Ogdahl, 59, John Johnson, 63 & Dick Erdall, 67; blockworker, 59-71; precinct chairwoman, 60-64; mem, Fifth Dist Cong Campaign Comt John Johnson, 64; mem, Minn State Rep Platform Comt, 64; mem, 37th Legis Dist Campaign Comt, 66; Rep ward chairwoman, 67-69; mem, Minn State Rep Cent Comt, 67-73; Park Bd campaign mgr, Aldermanic Campaign Comt, 69; vchairwoman, Fifth Dist Rep Party, 69-71, chairwoman, 71-73; mem, Elec Laws Task Force, 70; Fifth Dist chairwoman, Head for Gov, 70; chairwoman, Erdall for Alderman Vol Comt, 71-73; mem, Park Bd Campaign Comt, 71; chairwoman, Fifth Dist Search Comt, 71; mem, Minn State Rep Exec Comt, 71-73; deleg, Rep Nat Conv, 72; staff asst, State Ethics Comn, 74-; mem bd publ, Univ Minn, currently. Mem: League of Women Voters; Citizens League (bd dirs). Relig: Unitarian. Mailing Add: 4724 Emerson Ave S Minneapolis MN 55409

CARPENTER, LIZ (D)
Mem-At-Lg, Dem Nat Comt
Mailing Add: 4701 Woodway Lane NW Washington DC 20016

CARPENTER, MICHAEL EUGENE (D)
Maine State Rep
b Houlton, Maine, Sept 3, 47; s Arthur Bernard Carpenter & Electa Astel C; single. Educ: Univ Maine, Orono, BA, Psychol, 69; Sigma Phi Epsilon. Polit & Govt Pos: Maine State Rep, 75-, mem state govt comt & co & local govt comt, Maine House Rep, 75- Mil Serv: Entered as 2nd Lt, Army, 65, released as Capt, 73, after serv in 101 Abn Div, Vietnam, 70-71; Combat Inf Badge; two Bronze Stars; two Air Medals; Vietnamese Cross of Gallantry; Army Commendation Medal. Mem: VFW. Relig: Catholic. Legal Res: 1 South St Houlton ME 04730 Mailing Add: PO Box 413 Houlton ME 04730

CARPENTER, PAUL B (D)
Calif State Assemblyman
Mailing Add: 12062 Valley View Garden Grove CA 92645

CARPENTER, TERRY M (R)
Nebr State Sen
b Cedar Rapids, Iowa, Mar 28, 1900; m 1931 to Hazeldeane Carruthers; c 2. Polit & Govt Pos: Nebr State Sen, 53- Mailing Add: PO Box 170 Scottsbluff NE 69631

CARPER, FRANCES IZEZ (D)
Chmn, Colo 17th Dist Dem Party
b Goodland, Kans, July 26, 10; d Francis James O'Brien & Inez Strom O; m 1941 to George James Carper, Co Judge; c Virginia Carol (Mrs Roberts) & Billie Frances (Mrs Busby). Educ: High Sch, Phillipsburg, Kans. Polit & Govt Pos: Vchmn, Kit Carson Co Dem Cent Comt, Colo, 57-61, chmn, 61-72; mem exec comt, 72-74, vchmn, 75-; vchmn, Colo Fourth Judicial Dist Dem Party, 61-; vchmn, Colo Third US Cong Dist, Dem Party, 63-69; chmn, Colo 17th Sen Dist Dem Party, 63-; deleg, Dem Nat Conv, 64 & 68, mem permanent orgn comt, 64; chmn, Fifth Dist Dem Party, 70-73. Mem: Burlington Zonta Club. Relig: Catholic. Mailing Add: 372 14th St Burlington CO 80807

CARR, BILLIE FISHER (D)
Chmn Exec Comt, Coahoma Co Dem Party, Miss
b Memphis, Tenn, Jan 20, 32; d William Hunt Fisher & Daisy Tucker F; m 1950 to Oscar Clark Carr, Jr; c Oscar Clark, III, Blanche Busby, Palmer Scott, John Thomas Fisher & E'Lane Tucker. Educ: Bennett Jr Col, Millbrook, NY, 49; Southwestern at Memphis, 71; Postgrad Ctr Ment Health, New York, Cert Clin Coun, 75. Polit & Govt Pos: Women's chmn, Humphrey campaign, Dem Dist Two, Miss, 68; deleg, Dem Nat Conv, 72; coord relig commun, McGovern-Shriver, NY State, 72; chmn, Dem Party of Coahoma Co, Miss, 72-; chmn, Dem Exec Comt Coahoma Co, 72-; mem, Miss State Dem Exec Comt, 72-75. Bus & Prof Pos: Counr, Parish Coun Ctrs, Inc, New York, 74- Mem: Delta Ministry; Asn Christian Training & Serv, (bd mem, 74-); Comt Southern Churchmen; Nat Women's Caucus. Honors & Awards: Distinguished Serv, Coahoma Opportunities Inc, 71. Relig: Episcopal; Reader, Gen Bd Examining Chaplains, 73-74. Legal Res: Rte 2 Box 156 Clarksdale MS 38614 Mailing Add: 1158 Fifth Ave New York NY 10029

CARR, BILLIE J (D)
Mem, Dem Nat Comt, Tex
b Houston, Tex, June 1, 28; d Williams Brooks McClain & Irene Martin M; div; c David Brooks, Billy Brooks & Michael Lloyd Carr; Marshel Bokie & Debra Etue. Educ: Univ Houston, 46-48, 71. Polit & Govt Pos: Precinct comt mem, Houston, Tex, 54-72; polit organizer, Harris Co Dem, 54-; mem state comt, Dem Party Tex, 64-66 & 72-; co-chmn, McGovern-Shriver Campaign, 72; mem, Dem Nat Comt, 72-; co-chairperson, Nat New Dem Coalition, 75- Publ: How To Do It!, or Organizing a Precinct Can Be Fun (hand book), 69. Mem: Nat Polit Women's Caucus; Am Civil Liberties Union; Common Cause; Am for Dem Action. Honors & Awards: Life-time mem, Nat Forensic League. Legal Res: 5307 Beechnut Houston TX 77035 Mailing Add: 2418 Travis Suite 3 Houston TX 77006

CARR, DAVID A (D)
Committeeman, Westchester Co Dem Party, NY
b New York, NY, Aug 9, 46; s Charles Carr & Geraldine Siegler Co; m 1968 to Susan Rothstein C; c Michael Scott. Educ: Adelphi Univ, BA, 69; Antioch Sch Law, 74- Polit & Govt Pos: Committeeman, Westchester Co Dem Party, NY, 70-; committeeman, Yonkers Dem City Comt, 70-; coordr, Wall St for McGovern, 72; alt deleg, Dem Nat Conv, 72; coordr, Westchester Comt for McGovern, 72; mem exec comt, United Dem for McGovern, 72; vchmn, Concerned Dem of Yonkers, 72-; mem exec comt, Concerned Dem of Westchester, 73-; deleg, Dem Nat Mid-Term Conf, 74. Mem: Am Polit Sci Asn; Yonkers Citizens Union; Am Civil Liberties Union (coordr). Relig: Jewish. Legal Res: 1 Vincent Rd Bronxville NY 10708 Mailing Add: 1401 S Edgewood St Arlington VA 22204

CARR, DELMAN R (R)
Chmn, Isle of Wight Co Rep Party, Va
b Crewe, Va, Aug 31, 18; s Chester Lloyd Carr & Dollie V Rhodes C; m 1938 to Sally Glenn Scott; c Delman Lew & Chester Glenn. Educ: Carrsville High Sch, 35-36. Polit & Govt Pos:

Mem, Isle of Wight Co Agr Stabilization & Conserv Serv, US Dept Agr, 50-55; mem, Va State Agr Stabilization & Conserv Serv, 56-; chmn, Isle of Wight Co Rep Party, Va, 68- Mem: Va Forest Inc; Soil Conserv Soc US; Va Farm Bur; Nat Farmers Orgn; Windsor Ruritan Club. Relig: Baptist; Deacon, Cososse Baptist Church. Mailing Add: RFD 1 Carrsville VA 23315

CARR, GLADYS B (R)
b Las Animas, Colo; d Oliver M Banta & Meta M Elliott B; wid. Educ: Santa Barbara State Col. Polit & Govt Pos: Councilwoman, First Ward, Santa Barbara, Calif, currently. Bus & Prof Pos: Escrow officer, First Nat Bank, ten years & Bank of Am, Nat Trust & Savings Asn, five years; mgr, Off Escrow Dept, First Am Title Co, 58-62; vpres, Estado Escrow Co, 62-64. Mem: League of Women Voters; Cancer Asn; Toastmistress Club; Rep Women; hon life mem Calif Escrow Asn; comt mem many civic orgns. Honors & Awards: Winner of many tennis trophies. Relig: Methodist. Mailing Add: 1112 Quinientos Santa Barbara CA 93103

CARR, JAMES DREW (R)
Mem, Aroostook Co Rep Comt, Maine
b Houlton, Maine, July 17, 35; s Wilder Drew Carr & Verna Elizabeth Hall C; single. Educ: Ricker Col, 53-54; Bowdoin Col, 54-55; Babson Inst, BS, 60; Boston Univ Law Sch, LLB, 64; Blue Key Nat Honor Soc; Beta Theta Pi. Polit & Govt Pos: Chmn, Houlton Rep Town Comt, Maine, 65-67; Judge of Probate, Aroostook Co, 66-; alt deleg, Rep Nat Conv, 68; mem, Aroostook Co Rep Comt, 68- Bus & Prof Pos: Attorney, James D Carr Law Off, 65- Mil Serv: Entered as Pvt E-2, Army, 55, released as Pvt 1/C, 56, after serv in Artil, Fourth Army, Ft Bliss, Tex. Mem: Maine State & Aroostook Co Bar Asns; Masonic Blue Lodge; Elks; Rotary. Relig: Episcopal. Legal Res: 67 High St Houlton ME 04730 Mailing Add: Box 301 Houlton ME 04730

CARR, JAMES K (D)
b Redding, Calif, Jan 15, 14; s Francis Carr & Mary Kennedy C; m 1939 to Katherine Kergan; c Mary K (Mrs William Chapman), Ann (Mrs Gene Dallosto), Susan (Mrs Michael Taylor) & Margaret (Mrs Dino Boito); 4 grandchildren. Educ: Univ Santa Clara, BS, 34. Hon Degrees: DrEng, Univ Santa Clara, 68. Polit & Govt Pos: Consult, Works Progress Admin, Geol Surv Dept Interior, Shasta Co Surveyor's Off & City Engr Off, Redding, Calif, 34-36; Geol Survey Dept Interior, Shasta Co Surveyor's Off, City Engr Off, Redding, Calif, 34-36; Bur Reclamation, Dept Interior, 36-51; asst gen mgr, Sacramento Munic Utility Dist, 53-61; chmn, Calif Water Comn, 59-61; bd regents, Univ Santa Clara, 59-65; Undersecy, Dept of Interior, Washington, DC, 61-64; gen mgr pub utilities, City-Co of San Francisco, 64-70, dir airports, San Francisco Int Airport, 70-; dir airports, Sacramento, currently. Mem: Fel Am Soc Civil Engrs; Sacramento CofC; Rotary; KofC. Honors & Awards: Civil Govt Award, 64, Am Soc Civil Engrs. Relig: Catholic. Mailing Add: 3320 Marconi Ave Sacramento CA 95821

CARR, JOE C (D)
Secy of State, Tenn
b Cookeville, Tenn, June 20, 07; m 1934 to Mary Oliver Hart; c Carolyn (Mrs Welch) & Joe C, Jr. Educ: Nashville Pub Schs. Polit & Govt Pos: Page, Tenn State Senate, 23; page, Tenn House Rep, 25, bill clerk, 29 & 31, asst chief clerk, 33-35, reading clerk, 37, chief clerk, 39 & 53; secy, Orgn Young Dem Clubs of Tenn, 32, pres, 34; pres, Young Dem Clubs Am, 41; Secy of State, Tenn, 41-44, 45-72 & 75-; deleg, Dem Nat Conv, 68. Bus & Prof Pos: Trustee, Belmont Col & Baptist Hosp. Mil Serv: 44-45. Mem: Nat Asn Secy of State; Scottish Rite Mason (33 degree); York Rite Mason; Royal Order of Jesters; Elks. Relig: Baptist; deacon. Mailing Add: 3508 Hampton Ave Nashville TN 37215

CARR, M ROBERT (D)
US Rep, Mich
b Janesville, Wis, Mar 27, 43; s Milton R Carr (deceased) & Edna Blood C; single. Educ: Univ Wis, BS, 65, Law Sch, JD, 68; Mich State Univ, East Lansing, Ford Found grant polit sci, 68. Polit & Govt Pos: Staff asst, US Sen Gaylord Nelson, 67; staff mem, Mich Senate Minority Leader's Off, 68-69; admin asst to State Attorney Gen, 69-70, asst, 70-72; counsel to Spec Joint Comt on Legal Educ, Mich Legis, 72; Dem cand for US Rep, Sixth Dist, Mich, 72; US Rep, Mich, 74- Mem: Am Civil Liberties Union; Mich & Wis State Bar Asns; Am Bar Asn; Common Cause. Legal Res: 308 Michigan Ave Apt 8 East Lansing MI 48823 Mailing Add: House of Rep Washington DC 20515

CARR, OSCAR CLARK JR (D)
b Memphis, Tenn, Aug 4, 23; s Oscar Clark Carr & Blanche Rembert Busby C; m 1950 to Billie Fisher; c Oscar Clark, III, Blanche Busby, Palmer Scott, John T Fisher & E'Lane Tucker. Educ: Cornell Univ, 41-42; US Naval Acad, BS with distinction, 45; Psi Upsilon. Hon Degrees: Dr Canon Law, Berkeley Divinity Sch, 72. Polit & Govt Pos: Chmn, Mississippians for Robert Kennedy, 68; Coahoma Co chmn, Humphrey Campaign, 68; deleg, Dem Nat Conv, 68; mem, Dem State Exec Comt, Miss, 68-71; McGovern finance chmn, Miss, 72. Bus & Prof Pos: Pres, Carr Planting Co, Inc, Clarksdale, Miss, 48-; pres, Delta Coun, Stoneville, 61-62; dir, Cotton Coun Int, Memphis, Tenn, 64-67; chmn, First Nat Bank, Clarksdale, Miss, 64-69; dir, Samelson Cigar Co, Memphis; vpres for develop, Episcopal Church, New York, 71- Mil Serv: Entered as Midn, Navy, 42, released as Lt(jg), 47, after serv as asst gunnery officer in USS Wisconsin, Pac, 45-47. Mem: Nat Cotton Coun; Newcomen Soc; Am Acad Polit & Social Sci; Naval Acad Alumni Asn; Berkeley Divinity Sch, New Haven, Conn (bd trustees, 70-, vchmn bd, 72-). Relig: Episcopal. Legal Res: Rte 2 Box 161 Clarksdale MI 38614 Mailing Add: 1158 Fifth Ave New York NY 10029

CARR, ROBERT M (D)
Iowa State Sen
b Bernard, Iowa, May 9, 37; s M L Carr & Mae C; m 1960 to Rose T Connolly; c Tim, Mark & Kimberly. Educ: Loras Col, 54-55. Polit & Govt Pos: Precinct worker, Dubuque Co Dem Party, 60-64; precinct committeeman, Dubuque Co Dem Cent Comt, 65-72; co-chmn, Second Dist Platform Comt, 72; chmn, Dubuque Co Platform Comt, 72; Iowa State Rep, Dist 20, 73-74; Iowa State Sen, 74- Bus & Prof Pos: Securities rep, Waddell & Reed, Inc, 67-70, div mgr, 70- Mem: Nat Asn Securities Dealers; Dubuque Eve Optimist. Honors & Awards: Outstanding Pres & Friend of Boy Award, Dubuque Eve Optimist, 69. Relig: Catholic. Mailing Add: 2030 Deborah Dr Dubuque IA 52001

CARR, THOMAS CASWELL (D)
Ga State Rep
b Rhine, Ga, July 4, 12; s E F Carr & Kathleen Ryals C; m 1941 to Margaret Jordan; c Margaret Jordan & Kathleen Dorothy. Educ: Mid Ga Col; Univ Ga; Ga Southern Col, BS, 38; Mass Inst Technol, grad work, 42-43. Polit & Govt Pos: Mayor, Sandersville, Ga, 52-59; Ga State Rep, 63-66 & 71- Bus & Prof Pos: Fertilizer mfr, seed farmer. Mil Serv: Army Air Corps, 1st Lt, 42-45. Mem: Mason; Shrine; Rotary; CofC. Relig: Methodist. Mailing Add: N Smith St Sandersville GA 31082

CARR, WILLIAM PITTS (D)
VChmn, Dem Party Ga
b Thomasville, Ga, June 21, 47; s John C Carr & Ophie Hall C; div. Educ: Univ Ga, BBA, 69; Duke Univ Sch Law, JD, 71; Phi Eta Sigma; Phi Kappa Phi; Omicron Delta Kappa; Phi Delta Phi; Kappa Sigma. Polit & Govt Pos: Campaign mgr, Ford Spinks Pub Serv Comn, 72; campaign mgr, George Busbee Gubernatorial Race, 73-74, mem state coord comt, 74; mem, Ga Dem State Exec Comt, 73-, vchmn, Ga Dem Party, 74-, chmn, Fifth Cong Dist, 74-, mem affirmative action comt, 75- Bus & Prof Pos: Assoc, Neely, Freeman & Hawkins, Attorneys, Ga, 72-73; sr partner, Carr, Wadsworth, Abney & Tabb, 73- Publ: The juvenile court vs due process, Ga State Bar J, 11/71. Mem: Am, Ga & Atlanta Bar Asns; Am Trial Lawyers Asn; Ga Defense Lawyers Asn. Relig: Episcopal. Legal Res: 330 Angonne Dr NW Atlanta GA 30305 Mailing Add: 1019 Hunt Bldg Atlanta GA 30305

CARRAGHER, ROBERT J (D)
Conn State Rep
Mailing Add: 56 Newton St Hartford CT 06106

CARRELL, BOBBY (D)
Ga State Rep
Mailing Add: RFD 2 Monroe GA 30655

CARRIER, ESTELLE STACY (R)
Secy, Rep Nat Comt
b Grimes Co, Tex, Sept 3, 13; d David Dixon Mabry & Rosa Miller M; m 1933 to Jack Leonard Stacy, wid; m 1974 to John B Carrier; c Richard A. Polit & Govt Pos: Pres, Converse Co Rep Women's Club, Wyo, 59-61; pres, Wyo Fedn Rep Women, 60-62; vchmn, Wyo Rep State Comt, 60-66; precinct committeewoman, Southeast Precinct, Douglas, 64-; Rep Nat Committeewoman, Wyo, 66-, mem exec comt, Rep Nat Comt, 69-, secy, 72-; mem site selection comt, Rep Nat Conv, 68, mem arrangements comt, chmn comt permanent orgn & deleg, 68; mem, Defense Adv Comt for Women in the Serv, 70-, app by Secy Defense Laird chmn, 71, took office, 72-73; informal adv, Spec Adv on Pub Opinion, US State Dept, 70-; mem nat adv comt on safety in agr, app by Secy of Agr Earl Butz, 75. Bus & Prof Pos: Vpres, Stacy Drilling Co, 47-63, pres, 63-; secy & vpres, Teno United, 58-63, pres, 63- Publ: Women in Politics, Wyo on Rev, 62. Mem: Wyo Drilling Asn; Converse Co Libr Bd Trustees (pres, 65-); Wyo Taxpayers Asn; Wyo Safety Coun (mem bd dirs, 67-); CofC. Relig: Episcopal. Legal Res: 3 Hilltop Rd Douglas WY 82633 Mailing Add: PO Box 96 Douglas WY 82633

CARRIER, MARIA L (D)
Mem, Dem Nat Comt, NH
b Washington, DC, Aug 21, 20; d Vito Stefano Lozupone & Maria Colacicco L; m 1942 to Paul Vernon Carrier; c Stephan Paul & James G. Educ: Univ NH, BA, 67, MA, 70; Phi Sigma Alpha; Pi Gamma Mu. Polit & Govt Pos: Deleg, Dem Nat Conv, 68; mem, Dem Nat Platform Comt, 68; NH State Rep, 69-71; state coordr, Muskie for President Campaign, 71-72; mem, Dem Nat Comt, NH, 72- Bus & Prof Pos: Instr, Merrimack Valley Br, Univ NH, currently; mem, Manchester Indust Coun, 74- Mem: Am Civil Liberties Union; United Commun Serv Gtr Manchester; League Women Voters; Am Asn Univ Women; NH Coun Better Schs. Relig: Protestant. Mailing Add: 2125 Elm St Manchester NH 03104

CARRIGG, JOSEPH L (R)
b Susquehanna, Pa, Feb 23, 01; s Thomas J Carrigg & Ellen Houlihan C; m 1946 to Catherine E O'Neill. Educ: Niagara Univ; Albany Law Sch; Dickinson Law Sch; Devils Own; Woolsach; Phi Sigma Kappa. Polit & Govt Pos: Dist attorney, Susquehanna, Pa, 36-48, mayor, 50-51; US Rep, Tenth Dist, Pa, 51-59; dir of practice, US Treas Dept, 60-61; mgr, State Workmen's Ins Fund, Dept Labor & Indust, Pa, 63-71. Bus & Prof Pos: Attorney-at-law, 26- Mem: Fed Bar Asn; Moose; KofC; Serra Int; Lions Int. Relig: Roman Catholic. Mailing Add: 1704 Wyoming Ave Scranton PA 18509

CARRILLO, EMILIO (D)
Ariz State Rep
Mailing Add: 1961 Calle Mecedora Tucson AZ 85705

CARRINGTON, JAMES MALCOLM (JIM) (D)
Mo State Rep
b St Louis, Mo, Apr 17, 04; s Fred Carrington & Rose Taylor C; m 1951 to Lillian Lysette Herd; c James M, Jr, Betty Rose (Mrs Carter) & Edward Carter (deceased). Educ: Howard Univ, grad, 25; Kappa Alpha Psi. Polit & Govt Pos: Mo State Rep, 67th Dist, 73- Bus & Prof Pos: Salesman, City Prod Corp, St Louis, 40-63; photographer, St Louis Globe-Dem Newspaper, 63-71. Publ: Meet my friends, 61-63 & Thru the camera's eye, 63-64, New Citizen; Mine eyes have seen (weekly), St Louis Peoples Guide Newspaper & St Louis Am Newspaper, 72- Mem: St Louis Comprehensive Health Ctr; Boy Scouts; First Ward Regular Dem Orgn; Howard Univ Alumni Asn; Mayor's Youth Coun of Gtr St Louis. Honors & Awards: Prizes & Citations, Annual Christmas Lighting Contest, 55-70; Good Neighbor Award, St Louis Argus, 62; Police Community Rels Award, Seventh Dist, St Louis Police Dept, 62; Amateur Photographers Awards, St Louis Globe-Dem Newspaper, 63; Power of Print Award, Time Mag, 72. Relig: Baptist. Mailing Add: 5860 Highland Ave St Louis MO 63112

CARRINGTON, RUTH GIBSON (D)
VChmn, Mont State Dem Cent Comt
b Burr Oak, Kans, Dec 6, 24; d Lucious Dean Gibson & Mina Oglevie G; div. Educ: Univ Mont, MA, 67. Polit & Govt Pos: Mem rules comt, Dem Nat Comt, 72-73; vchmn, Mont State Dem Cent Comt, 73- Bus & Prof Pos: Teacher, Mt Diablo Sch Dist, Mont, 51-54; teacher, Navy Dependents Schs, 56-63; instr Eng, Miles Community Col, 67-69; teacher, Hysham High Sch, 73-75. Mem: Mont Educ Asn (pres, Treasure Co Unit, 73-75); Treasure Co Bicentennial Comn (chmn, 74-75). Mailing Add: Box 294 Hysham MT 59038

CARROLL, BEATRICE JESSOP (BEA) (D)
b Millville, Utah, Feb 23, 03; d Ephraim Jessop & Sylvia Chance Yeates J; m 1947 to Casper G Carroll. Educ: Utah State Univ, BS, 29, MS, 48; Columbia Univ, summer 30; Univ Southern Calif, summers 32, 38, 40 & 43; Univ Hawaii, summer 34; Univ Utah, 49; Theta Alpha Phi. Polit & Govt Pos: Deleg, many Utah and Davis Co, Dem Conv; chmn, Dist Nine, Kaysville, Utah, 60-66; Vchmn, Utah State Dem Conv, 70, mem resolutions comt, 71 & mem platform comt, 72; Davis Co Cand for State Legis, 70; vchmn, Davis Co Dem Party, 70-71, chmn,

formerly; deleg, Dem Nat Conv, 72. Bus & Prof Pos: Elem sch teacher, Utah & Idaho, 21-26, high sch teacher, 27-34; social case worker, State of Calif, Los Angeles, 37-38; teacher, Los Angeles City Schs, 38-41; educ health counr, Douglas Aircraft, Santa Monica, Calif, 42-43; personnel counr, NAm Aircraft, Inglewood, 43-45; asst field dir, Am Red Cross, 45-46; dean girls & dir guid, David High Sch, Kaysville, Utah, 46-68. Publ: How to get along with women, Ladies Home J, 1/50, Women, Home Chat Mag, London, Eng, 3/51 & High school guidance, J Nat Asn Women Deans & Counr, 6/58. Mem: Nat Asn Women Deans & Counr; Nat Rocky Mt Regional Contact; Utah Asn Women Deans & Counr; Utah Sch Counr Asn; Am Asn Univ Women (state legis chmn, 69-). Honors & Awards: Listed as Woman with Most Unusual War Occupation, Off War Info, 42; bronze plaque for meritorious serv to Davis Co, Soroptimist Fedn Am, 64; citation for exceptional serv, Nat Asn Women Deans & Counr, 68; exchange educ to SAfrica for Am Field Serv, 68; only woman to head a major polit party in Utah. Relig: Latter-day Saint. Mailing Add: 338 E First South Kaysville UT 84037

CARROLL, GEORGE ARTHUR (D)
Maine State Rep
b Limerick, Maine, Mar 3, 19; s William Thomas Carroll & Mary Ann Fox C; m 1942 to Rita Rose Morin; c Nancy Lee (Mrs John H Weeks), Arthur George & Anthony Robert. Educ: Limerick High Sch, grad; US Army Tel Carrier Sch, NAfrica; Ins & Real Estate Courses. Polit & Govt Pos: Maine State Rep, 65-69, 75-; mem, New Eng Bd Higher Educ, 67; chmn, York Co Muskie for Pres in 72 Comt; chmn, York Co Dem Comt, 67-69; mem, Maine Dem Comt, 70-; vchmn, Maine Munic Appeals Bd, 70- Bus & Prof Pos: Owner & mgr, Alderwood Farm, 48-; owner, George A Carroll Ins & Real Estate Agency, 65-; chmn, Limerick Bd of Appeals, 69. Mil Serv: Entered as Pvt, Army, 41, released as 1st Lt, 48, after serv in Fifth Army, 57th Signal Bd, European Theatre, 43-44; NAfrica & European Campaign Ribbons. Mem: New Eng Milk Producers Asn; Holstein Friesian Asn of Am; DAV (serv officer, White-Tibbetts Post SS); Am Legion; VFW. Honors & Awards: Amended Sinclair Law to Encourage Formation of More Sch Dists; Named Maine Turnpike Gold Star Mem Hwy. Relig: Catholic. Mailing Add: Elm St Limerick ME 04048

CARROLL, GEORGE FRANCIS (D)
b Corona, NY, June 7, 23; s William H Carroll, Sr & Capitolia Greene C; m 1968 to Catherine L Miles; c Joann M & George E. Educ: Flushing High Sch, 4 years. Polit & Govt Pos: Sgt-at-arms, NY Dem State Comt, formerly, admin asst to chmn, formerly, vchmn, formerly; deleg, Dem Nat Conv, 68; dir of research, NY State Assembly Minority, currently. Mil Serv: Entered as Pvt, Army, 41, released as Sgt, 45, after serv in Corp of Engrs; ETO, 43-45. Relig: Roman Catholic. Mailing Add: Apt C2 111-17 Northern Blvd Corona NY 11368

CARROLL, GRACE (D)
Chmn, Ariz Dem Exec Comt
Mailing Add: 2134 N Edison Terr Tucson AZ 85716

CARROLL, HOWARD THOMAS (D)
Chmn, Albany Co Dem Cent Comt, Wyo
b Laramie, Wyo, May 20, 17; s Thomas Francis Carroll & Gertrude Noxon C; m 1947 to Jean Satra; c Teri & Lori. Educ: Univ Wyo, BS, 40; Sigma Alpha Epsilon. Polit & Govt Pos: Chmn, Albany Co Dem Cent Comt, Wyo, 67- Mil Serv: Entered as 2nd Lt, Army, 40, released as Maj, 46, after serv in Inf, Asiatic-Pac Theater, 40-46. Mem: Am Soc Rural Appraisers; Elks; VFW; Am Legion. Relig: Catholic. Mailing Add: 2103 Spring Creek Dr Laramie WY 82070

CARROLL, HOWARD WILLIAM (D)
Ill State Sen
b Chicago, Ill, July 28, 42; s Barney M Carroll (deceased) & Lyla Price C; m 1973 to Eda Stagman. Educ: Roosevelt Univ, BSBA, 64; DePaul Univ Col Law, JD, 67; Nu Beta Epsilon. Polit & Govt Pos: Pres, 50th Ward Young Dem, Chicago, 67-70; mem host comt, Dem Nat Conv, 68; mem youth adv bd, Dem Nat Comt, 68-; deleg to exec bd, Atlantic Alliance Young Polit Leaders, 70-71; state treas, Young Dem, 70, alt nat committeeman, 71; Ill State Rep, 13th Dist, 71-73; gen counsel, Young Dem Clubs Am, 71; first vpres, Young Dem Clubs Am, 71-; Ill State Sen, 15th Dist, 73-, vchmn, Senate Revenue Comt, mem, Senate Judiciary Comt & Finance & Credit Comt; chmn, Legis Adv Comt, NEastern Ill Planning Comn; vchmn, Judicial Adv Coun for Ill; mem, Exec Appointment & Admin Comt; mem, State's Attorney's Study Comn; mem, Property Tax Study Comn; mem exec comt, Cook Co Young Dem; mem, Dem State Platform Comt & Subcomt on Human Rights. Bus & Prof Pos: Staff counsel, Chicago Transit Authority, 67-71; attorney, Chicago, Ill, 71-; mem bd gov, State of Israel Bond Orgn Gtr Chicago, 72-; exec bd, Zionist Orgn Chicago, 72-; planning comt, Metrop Jewish Community, 72- Mem: Am Bar Asn; Decalogue Soc Lawyers; Northtown Ment Health Coun; River Park Athletic Asn; B'nai B'rith; Mason. Honors & Awards: Israel Bond Man of Year, Budlong Wood B'nai B'rith, 71. Relig: Jewish. Mailing Add: 134 N LaSalle St Chicago IL 60602

CARROLL, JOHN S (R)
Hawaii State Rep
Mailing Add: House Sgt-at-arms State Capitol Honolulu HI 96813

CARROLL, JOHN SPENCER (D)
b Boulder, Colo, June 10, 28; s Earl T Carroll & Sylvia Petrie C; m 1969 to Rebecca Louise Bradley; c Marjorie Dianne, Barbara Lynn, Debra Hunt, John Edward, Douglas Edward Bradley & Morgan Lenore. Educ: Univ Colo, AB, 50; Univ Denver, LLB, 52; Univ Philippines, 52-53; Phi Alpha Delta. Polit & Govt Pos: Precinct committeeman, Colo, 50-51; mem, Colo Dem State Cent Comt, 50-51 & 65-74; asst prog officer, US Agency Int Develop, 61-62; admin asst to Gov, Colo, 62-63; hearing officer, Colo Real Estate Comn, 63-65; Colo State Rep, 69-74. Bus & Prof Pos: Attorney, Carroll, Bradley & Ciancio, PC, 69- Mil Serv: Entered as Pvt, Army, 46, released as Pfc, 48, after serv in 5th Inf Div. Mem: Colo Bar Asn; State Bar of Calif; Am & Colo Trial Lawyers Asns; UN Asn. Legal Res: 7725 Newton St Westminster CO 80030 Mailing Add: 61 W 84th Ave Denver CO 80030

CARROLL, JULIAN MORTON (D)
Gov, Ky
b Paducah, Ky, Apr 16, 31; s Elvie Beeler Carroll & Eva Heady C; m 1951 to Charlann Harting; c Kenneth Morton, Iva Patrice & Bradley Harting. Educ: Univ Ky, AB, 54, LLB, 56; Phi Delta Phi. Polit & Govt Pos: Ky State Rep, Third Dist, 62-70, Speaker, House of Rep, 68-70; deleg, Dem Nat Conv, 68 & 72; trustee, Paducah Jr Col, 69-; Lt Gov, Ky, 71-74, Gov, 75- Mil Serv: Entered as 2nd Lt, Air Force, 56, released as 1st Lt, 59; Capt, Air Force Res, 62- Mem: Am & Ky Bar Asns; Optimist Club; Nat Asn of Home Builders; Nat Comt for Support Pub Schs. Relig: Cumberland Presbyterian. Legal Res: Rte 1 West Paducah KY 42086 Mailing Add: State Capitol Frankfort KY 40601

CARROLL, PATRICK D (D)
Ind State Sen
b Lexington, Ky, Feb 17, 41; s William A Carroll & Gertrude Eudy C; m 1960 to Carole Rhodehamel; c Elizabeth Lynn. Educ: Ind Univ, AB, 63, Sch Law, LLB, 66; Delta Upsilon. Polit & Govt Pos: Ind State Sen, 73- Bus & Prof Pos: Lawyer, Bloomington, Ind, 68- Legal Res: 1203 E Second St Bloomington IN 47401 Mailing Add: 110 1/2 N Walnut Bloomington IN 47401

CARROLL, THOMAS CHARLES (D)
Mem, Ky Dem State Cent Comt
b Louisville, Ky, Sept 1, 21; s Tarlton Combs Carroll & Irene Crutcher C; m 1959 to Julianne Kirk. Educ: Harvard Col, BA, 42; Univ Ky Col of Law, LLB, 48; Phi Delta Phi; Hasty Pudding Club; Institute of 1770. Polit & Govt Pos: Nat committeeman, Young Dem Clubs Ky, 52-56, pres, 60-62; orgn chmn, Dem State Campaign, 62 & 64, campaign coordr, 63; legal counsel, Ky State Dem Cent Exec Comt, formerly, mem, currently; mem, Ky Dem State Cent Comt, currently; chmn, Jefferson Co Dem Exec Comt, 64-68, mem, 64-72; chmn, Ky Comt on Dem Party Structure; finance chmn, Jefferson Co Dem Campaign, 69; deleg, Dem Nat Conv, 60, 64, 68 & 72; mem, Dem Nat Credentials Comts, 68 & 72; mem, Dem Nat Charter Comn, mem exec comt, currently; permanent parliamentarian, Dem Nat Comt, currently; treas, Ky Dem Campaign Comt, 72. Bus & Prof Pos: Attorney-at-law. Mil Serv: Entered as Pvt, Army, 42, released as Capt, 46, after serv in Sixth Army Group, ETO; Five Battle Stars. Mem: Am Trial Lawyers Asn; Ky State Bar Asn; Am & Louisville Bar Asns; Jefferson Club; Pendennis Club; Owl Creek Country Club. Honors & Awards: Outstanding Lawyer Award, Ky State Bar Asn, 57; Deleg, NATO Conf in Europe, 61. Relig: Protestant. Legal Res: 1603 Evergreen Rd Anchorage KY 40223 Mailing Add: 1112 Kentucky Home Life Bldg Louisville KY 40202

CARROZZELLA, JOHN A (D)
b New Haven, Conn, Aug 19, 30; s John C Carrozzella, MD & Lucille Gagliardi C; m 1955 to F Jeanette Tortorici; c John C, Christopher, William J & Lawrence P. Educ: Yale Univ, BA, 52; Univ Conn Law Sch, LLB, 55. Polit & Govt Pos: Asst prosecutor, Wallingford, Conn, 55-58; Conn State Rep, 59-73; deleg, Dem Nat Conv, 72; mem adv comt, State Task Force on Organized Crime, 73-; deleg, Dem Nat Mid-Term Conf, 74. Mil Serv: Entered as Pvt, Army, 56, released as SP-2, 58, after serv in QM Corps, Philadelphia, Pa. Mem: Conn Bar Asn; Nat Asn Defense Trial Lawyers; Elks. Relig: Catholic. Legal Res: 178 Long Hill Rd Wallingford CT 06492 Mailing Add: PO Box 823 Wallingford CT 06492

CARRUTH, GEORGE SIMMONS (DOC) (D)
Miss State Rep
b Summit, Miss, Nov 6, 06; married. Polit & Govt Pos: Miss State Rep, 52- Bus & Prof Pos: Employee, ICRR, vpres employ serv club, currently. Mem: Mason; Shrine; Eastern Star. Relig: Methodist. Mailing Add: RFD 2 Box 34 Summit MS 39666

CARSE, HENRY H (R)
Vt State Rep
Mailing Add: Hinesburg VT 05461

CARSON, DIDI (D)
Mem, Dem Nat Comt, Nev
Mailing Add: 2700 Pinto Lane Las Vegas NV 89107

CARSON, ROBERT TREBOR (R)
Hon Life Chmn, Rep Party of Hawaii
b Butte, Mont, Dec 17, 16; s Robert Stephen Carson & Ethel Jones C; single. Educ: Univ Mont; Univ Calif, 28-29; Stanford Univ, 31-32. Polit & Govt Pos: Has held every off in Rep Party of Hawaii, chmn, 44-52, hon life chmn, currently; campaigner in 36 states for Thomas E Dewey, 47; mem, Territorial Grand Jury, 49; dir, Fed Housing Admin, Hawaii & Guam, 54-57; mem land comt, Hawaii House of Rep, 59; mem land comt, Hawaii Senate, 59-60; campaigner, Western States, Nixon for Pres, 60; campaigner Calif, Nixon for Gov, 62; admin asst to US Sen Hiram L Fong, 60- Bus & Prof Pos: Newspaperman, Hearst Papers & Honolulu Advertiser, sports announcer & news commentator, NBC & Hawaii Sta KGU, & foreign & war correspondent, 38-49; investment banker, pres, Honolulu Stock Exchange & exec secy, Honolulu Auto Dealers Asn, 49-54; asst to Henry J Kaiser, gen mgr of Kaiser TV & Radio Network, 57-58; pres, Distributors of Hawaii, 58-61; chmn bd, Pan Pac House, 59-61. Mem: Waialae Country Club; Mason (32 degree); Shrine (past potentate, Aloha Temple, Hawaii); US Senate Staff Club; Cong Secretaries. Honors & Awards: Played first baseman, Pac Coast League, Sacramento, Calif; Only person to hold presidency for 2 terms in US Asn Admin Assts; Only person to have held Presidency of both US Senate Staff Club & US Asn Admin Assts. Legal Res: PO Box 1872 Honolulu HI 96805 Mailing Add: 1313 New Senate Off Bldg Washington DC 20510

CARSON, WALLACE P, JR (R)
Minority Floor Leader, Ore State Senate
b Salem, Ore, June 10, 34; s Wallace P Carson & Edith Bragg C; m 1956 to Gloria Stolk; c Wallace Scott, Carol Elizabeth & Steven Bruce. Educ: Stanford Univ, BA, 56; Willamette Univ Law Sch, JD, 62; Phi Delta Theta; Delta Theta Phi. Polit & Govt Pos: Mem, Ore Rep State Cent Comt, 65-67; Ore State Rep, 67-71, Majority Leader, Ore House Rep, 69-71; Ore State Sen, 71-, Minority Floor Leader, Ore State Senate, 71- Bus & Prof Pos: Attorney, Carson & Carson, Salem, 62- Mil Serv: Entered as 2nd Lt, Air Force, 56, released as 1st Lt, 59, after serv in Korea & Far East as Jet Pilot; Capt, Air Force Res, 59-70; Lt Col, Ore Air Nat Guard, 70- Publ: Writ of Mandamus, Legal Educ Series, Ore State Bar, 64; Speed at some distance from the scene—twilight zone of admissible evidence, Willamette Law J, 61. Mem: Marion Co Bar Asn; Ore State Bar Asn; Am Bar Asn. Honors & Awards: Comdr Trophy, Air Force Flight Sch, 56; Distinguished Serv Award, Salem Jaycees, 68; one of Five Ore Outstanding Young Man of Year, 68. Relig: Episcopal. Mailing Add: 1309 Hillendale Dr SE Salem OR 97302

CARSTEN, ARLENE DESMET (D)
Mem, San Diego Co Dem Cent Comt, Calif
b Paterson, NJ, Dec 5, 37; d Albert F Desmet & Ann Greutert D; m 1956 to Alfred John Carsten; c Christopher Dale & Jonathan Glenn. Educ: Alfred Univ, 55-56; Univ Calif Exten Courses. Polit & Govt Pos: Vpres, San Dieguito Dem Club, 65-67 & 70, treas, 69; 80th Assembly Dist Rep, Calif Dem Coun, 67-69; mem, San Diego McCarthy for President Campaign Comt, 68; mem, Calif Dem State Cent Comt, 68-; mem exec comt, Unruh for Gov, San Diego North Co Coord, 70; co-chmn, 42nd Cong Dist Dem Party, 70-; app Legis Liaison Comt, Calif, Dem Nat Platform Comt, 72; dir, Muskie for President Campaign, San Diego, 72; mem, San Diego Co Dem Cent Comt, Calif, 73-, treas, 73-74. Bus & Prof Pos: Exec dir,

Inst for Burn Med, 72- Mem: Am Civil Liberties Union; Family Serv Asn; Am Burn Asn; Women's Int League Peace & Freedom; San Diego Co Ment Health Adv Bd. Honors & Awards: Key Woman Award, Dem Party, 68 & 72; San Diego Ment Health Asn First Annual Community Award, 74; San Diego Soc Clin Psychologists Award, 75. Relig: Ethical Culture. Mailing Add: 1415 Via Alta Del Mar CA 92014

CARSTEN, CALVIN F
Nebr State Sen
Mailing Add: Avoca NE 68307

CARSWELL, GEORGE HARROLD (R)
b Irwinton, Ga, Dec 22, 19; s George Henry Carswell & Claire Ethel Wood C; m 1944 to Virginia Simmons; c Virginia Ramsay Langston, Sarah Nan Cherry, George Harrold, Jr & Scott Simmons. Educ: Duke Univ, AB, 41; Univ Ga, Lumpkin Sch of Law, 41-42; Mercer Univ, Walter F George Sch of Law, LLB, 48; Sigma Nu. Polit & Govt Pos: US attorney, Northern Dist Fla, Tallahassee, Fla, 53-58; Dist Judge, Chief Judge, US Dist Court, 58-69; Circuit Judge, Court of Appeals, Fifth Circuit, Tallahassee, Fla, 69-70. Bus & Prof Pos: Owner & organizer, Wilkinson Co Telephone Co, Irwinton, Ga, 47-48; assoc attorney, Ausley, Collins & Truett, Tallahassee, Fla, 49-51, partner, Carswell, Cotten & Shivers, Law Firm, 51-53; attorney-at-law, 70- Mil Serv: Entered as A/S, Midshipmans Sch, Naval Res, 42, released as Lt, USNR, 45, after serv in Third & Fifth Fleets, Atlantic & Pac, USS Baltimore CA-68, 43-45; Ribbons for Atlantic & Pac Theatre active duty at sea. Publ: Opinions as US District Judge, Northern District, Florida, Fed Supplement, 58-69; Opinions for Fifth Circuit, US Court of Appeal sitting by designation, as dist judge, 61-69 & as circuit judge, 69-70. Mem: Coun of the Admin Conf of the US; Fed Bar Asn; Am Judicature Soc; Sons of Am Revolution; Nat Exchange Club. Honors & Awards: Distinguished Alumnus award, Mercer Univ; Most Outstanding Past Member Award, Fla Bar, Young Lawyers; Distinguished Citizen Award, Stetson Univ, Sch of Law. Relig: Episcopal. Legal Res: 833 Lake Ridge Dr Tallahassee FL 32303 Mailing Add: PO Box 546 Tallahassee FL 32302

CARSWELL, MINNIE F (R)
NH State Rep
Mailing Add: Longa Rd Merrimack NH 03054

CARTER, ABE PARKER (R)
Chmn, Monroe County Rep Exec Comt, Ky
b Tompkinsville, Ky, Dec 11, 07; s James Clark Carter, Sr & Idru Tucker; m 1931 to Evelyn Evans, wid; c James Evans, MD, Rebecca (Mrs Nevius) & Jack Parker. Educ: Western Ky State Teachers Col, 28-31; Cumberland Univ Col of Law, LLB, 32; Jefferson Sch of Law, LLB, 33. Polit & Govt Pos: Treas, Monroe Co, Ky, 32-35, sheriff, 36-42, judge, 42-46, co attorney, 46-; chmn, Monroe Co Rep Exec Comt, 60- Mem: Mason; F&AM; Ky State & Am Bar Asns. Relig: Baptist. Mailing Add: 602 Idru St Tompkinsville KY 42167

CARTER, ALLEN RUFFIN (D)
SC State Sen
Mailing Add: 418 South Blvd Charleston SC 29406

CARTER, C KAY (D)
La State Sen
Mailing Add: 6280 Buncombe Rd Shreveport LA 71109

CARTER, CHARLES HILL, JR (D)
Chmn, Charles Dem City Comt, Va
b Charles City, Va, Aug 16, 19; s Charles Hill Carter & Emily Harrison C; m 1960 to Helle Margarethe Klingemann; c Charles Hill, Robert Randolph & Harriet Emily. Educ: Va Polytech Inst, BS, 43. Polit & Govt Pos: Chmn, Charles City Bd Supv, Va, 52-; chmn, Charles Dem City Comt, 58- Mil Serv: Army, 43, serv in OCS Anti Aircraft. Relig: Episcopal. Mailing Add: Shirley Plantation Charles City VA 23030

CARTER, DAVID R (D)
b Mondovi, Wis, Jan 16, 38; s Frank E Carter & Tracy M Talle C; m 1956 to Mary Jane Schmit; c Jacqueline Lee, Catherine Ann, David R, Jr, Stephen Frank & Jennifer Mary. Educ: Univ Wis, Exten; Morraine Park Tech Inst. Polit & Govt Pos: Treas, Waukesha Co Dem Party, Wis; chmn, Menomonee Falls Dem Party & Fond du Lac Co Dem Party; deleg, Wis State Dem Conv, 64-73; alt deleg, Dem Nat Conv, 72; temporary chmn, Fond du Lac Co McGovern for President Comt, 72. Mil Serv: Entered as Basic Airman, Air Force, 56, released as Airman 1/C, 60. Mem: Jaycees; Eagles; Moose; CofC. Relig: Presbyterian. Mailing Add: Box 41 Ripon WI 54971

CARTER, DONALD VICTOR (D)
Maine State Rep
b Waterville, Maine, Nov 1, 27; s Fred Carter & Mabel Montminy C; m 1953 to Wilma Siegmann; c Linda, Doreen, Donald V, Jr & Lee. Educ: Univ Md, Overseas Br; Univ Maine; Colby Col, BA in Hist. Polit & Govt Pos: Admin asst, Dept Army in Europe, 48-53; first selectman & chmn bd selectmen, Assessors & Overseer of the Poor, 63-64; chmn, Winslow High Sch Bldg Comt, 64; chmn, Winslow Dem Town Comt, 64-68; Maine State Sen, Kennebec Co, 65-66; councilman, Winslow, 69-; Maine State Rep, 69- Bus & Prof Pos: Spec agt, Prudential, 57-66; proprietor, Donald V Carter Ins Agency, 66- Mil Serv: Entered as Pvt, Army, 45, released as S/Sgt, 48, after serv in ETO. Mem: Winslow Sportsman's Asn (secy, 64-); VFW McCrillis-Rousseau Post 8835; Messalonskee Fish & Game Club; DAV. Relig: Roman Catholic. Mailing Add: 7 Baker St Winslow ME 04901

CARTER, ERNEST RAWLS (R)
Chmn, Bertie Co Rep Comt, NC
b Ahoskie, NC, Sept 1, 27; s Ernest Randolph Carter & Lucie Tayloe C; m 1956 to Rebecca Edwards; c Jennifer Kay & Ernest, Jr. Educ: Louisburg Jr Col; Univ NC; Phi Theta Kappa. Polit & Govt Pos: Mem, Powellsville Govt Town Comt, 58-66; Chmn, Bertie Co Rep Comt, NC, 66- Bus & Prof Pos: Owner & Partner, E R Carter & Son, 50-66. Mil Serv: Entered as Pvt, Army, 45, released as Cpl, 47, after serv in Inf; Good Conduct & Victory Medals. Mem: Vol Fire Chief; Lions. Relig: Methodist. Mailing Add: Box 33 Powellsville NC 27967

CARTER, EVA MEADOR (R)
Chmn, Cameron Co Rep Comt, Tex
b Hattiesburg, Miss, Sept 19, 21; d Edward Harmon Meador & Bess Ruth Fullen M; m 1943 to Samuel Cutter Carter, MD; c Samuel Cutter III, Isabelle Louise (Mrs Rotter) & Elizabeth. Educ: Univ Southern Miss, 39-41; Univ Tenn, 42-43; Memphis State Univ, 51-52; Alpha Sigma Alpha. Polit & Govt Pos: Rep precinct chmn, Eisenhower Campaign for President, Memphis, Tenn, 52-58; mem, Texas & Nat Rep Womens Fedns, 52-; mem, Goldwater for President Campaign, Harlingen, Tex, 64; campaign mgr for local city comnrs, mayor & sch bd trustees, Harlingen, Tex, 64-75; chmn Cameron Co, John Tower for Senate Campaign, 66 & 72; campaign worker, George Bush for Sen, Cameron Co, 70-; chmn, Cameron Co Rep Comt, Tex, 74- Publ: Auth, Mountain climbing Comanche style, Flying Physicians Mag, 11/74. Mem: United Fund Drive; Cameron-Willacy Co Med Auxiliary; Mayors Flood Control Bd; League Women Voters; Rio Grande Valley Int Music Festival (treas, 60-). Honors & Awards: Rep Tops in Tex Award, 71; Cert Appreciation, Harlingen Pub Schs, 72; Cert of Award, United Fund of Harlingen, 74. Relig: Episcopal. Mailing Add: 1201 Ferguson Dr Harlingen TX 78550

CARTER, HARRY W (D)
Ark State Rep
Mailing Add: 8913 Morris Manor Apt 4 Little Rock AR 72204

CARTER, HUGH A (D)
Ga State Sen
Mailing Add: PO Box 97 Plains GA 31780

CARTER, J C (R)
Chmn, Harlan Co Rep Party, Ky
b Bowling Green, Ky, July 26, 23; s Charles M Carter, Sr & Lassie Steen C; m 1947 to Evelyn Mitchell; c Jennifer M (Mrs Emery), Joan & Jeffrey. Educ: Univ Tenn; Reppert Auction Sch, grad. Polit & Govt Pos: Ky State Sen, Ninth Dist, formerly; chmn, Harlan Co Rep Party, Ky, 75- Bus & Prof Pos: Owner, Carter Realty Auction Co; realtor; auctioneer; owner of motels, auto dealerships, hardware stores & ins bus. Mil Serv: World War II, 3 years in Field Artil. Mem: Rotary. Relig: Methodist; chmn comt built new church, 60. Mailing Add: Carter Realty Auction 2202 S Court St Scottsville KY 42164

CARTER, JACK WILKES (D)
Ga State Rep
Mailing Add: PO Box 381 Adel GA 31620

CARTER, JAMES EARL, JR (D)
b Archery, Ga, Oct 1, 24; s James Earl Carter & Lillian Gordy C; m 1946 to Rosalynn Smith; c John William, James Earl, III, Donnel Jeffrey & Amy Lynn. Educ: Ga Southwest Col, 41-42; Ga Inst Technol, 42-43; US Naval Acad, BS, 46; Morris Brown Col, 72. Polit & Govt Pos: Ga State Sen, 62-66; Gov, Ga, 71-74. Bus & Prof Pos: Peanut farmer & warehouseman, Plains, Ga, 53- Mil Serv: Entered Navy, 47, released as Lt, 53, after serv on submarines & battleships. Relig: Baptist. Legal Res: Plains GA 31780 Mailing Add: PO Box 1976 Atlanta GA 30301

CARTER, JARED GLENN
Dep Under Secy, Dept of the Interior
b Wingate, Tex, Feb 25, 35; s Troy M Carter & Mildred Ruby Miles C; m 1955 to Bonnie Mae McIntyre; c Troy Miles, Brian Charles & Cheryl Lynn. Educ: Univ Calif, Los Angeles, BA, 56; Stanford Univ, LLB, 62; Order of the Coif. Polit & Govt Pos: Law clerk, US Supreme Court Justice William O Douglas, 62-63; asst legal adv econ affairs, Dept of State, 67-71; dep dir, Off Ocean Affairs, Dept Defense, 71-74; Dep Under Secy, Dept of the Interior, 74- Bus & Prof Pos: Asst prof law, Stanford Univ, 63-65; assoc, Cooley, Crowley, Gaither, Castro, Godward & Huddleston, San Francisco, 65-67. Mil Serv: Marine Corps Res, 56-59. Mailing Add: Dept of the Interior Washington DC 20240

CARTER, JOHN WILLIAM (D)
b Portsmouth, Va, July 3, 47; s James Earl Carter, Jr & Rosalynn Smith C; m 1971 to Judy Langford. Educ: Ga Inst Technol, BS, 72; Univ Ga, JD, 75. Polit & Govt Pos: Deleg, Dem Nat Mid-Term Conf, 74. Mil Serv: Entered as E-3, Navy, 68, released as E-5, 70, after serv in USS Grapple, Pac. Mailing Add: Box 207 Calhoun GA 30701

CARTER, JOSEPH HENRY, SR (JOE) (D)
b Enid, Okla, July 18, 32; s Dwight Henry Carter & Alice Wilson C; m 1957 to Beverly R Blood; c Joseph H, Jr, Russell Morris & Valerie Alice. Educ: Univ Tulsa, BA Econ, 57, BA Jour, 59. Polit & Govt Pos: Assoc ed & polit writer, Okla J, 65-68; staff asst to President Lyndon B Johnson, 68; research asst & staff dir, Comt Orgn Study & Rev, US Rep Julia B Hansen, 68-70 & 74-75; exec asst & press secy, Gov Okla, 70-73; dir commun, Dem Nat Comt, 73; admin asst to US Rep Ted Risenhoover, Okla, 75- Mil Serv: Enlisted in Army 52, released as Cpl, 54; Good Conduct Medal; Nat Serv Medal. Mem: AF&AM; Nat Dem Club; Admin Asst Asn; Sigma Delta Chi; Chmn Club Dem Party Okla. Honors & Awards: Nominated for Pulitzer Prize as co-author for reporting on state prison, Okla J, 66. Legal Res: Rt 11 Box 72 Moore OK 73060 Mailing Add: 1407 Longworth House Off Bldg Washington DC 20515

CARTER, MALCOLM M (R)
NH State Rep
b Concord, Mass, Sept 27, 18; married; c Four. Educ: Milford & Stearn's Prep. Polit & Govt Pos: Selectman, Milford, NH, 6 years, chmn bd, 2 years; NH State Rep, 63- Bus & Prof Pos: Proprietor & operator, Carter's Mobil Serv Sta; sales rep, Quaker Oats Co, formerly; dir, Amherst Bank & Trust, NH, currently. Mem: F&AM. Relig: Unitarian. Mailing Add: Jennison Rd Milford NH 03055

CARTER, MARIAN ELIZABETH (R)
Secy, Colo Rep State Cent Comt
b Greatbend, Kans, June 14, 35; d Clarence John Glantz & Ella Bartel G; m 1957 to J Braxton Carter; c J Braxton, II, David Brian & Carol Elizabeth. Educ: Univ Colo, BA, 57; Colo State Univ, 57-58; Kappa Delta. Polit & Govt Pos: Vchmn, El Paso Co Young Rep, Colo, 66; Rep precinct committeewoman, El Paso Co, 66-73; secy, Young Rep League of Colo, 67; secy, Rep state representative dist 19, 67 & 69, nat committeewoman, 69-70; mem, Colo Rep State Cent Comt, El Paso Co, 69-, secy, 73-; chmn, Colo Young Rep, 71-; deleg, Rep Nat Conv, 72. Bus & Prof Pos: With Pub Rels Dept, Ill Inst Technol, 57-58; pub trustee, El Paso Co, Colo, 69-73. Mem: Eastern Star; Rep Women's Roundtable; Young Rep; Assistance League of Colorado Springs; Altrusa. Honors & Awards: One of Outstanding Young Women of Am, 70; Outstanding Young Rep Woman, El Paso Co, Colo, 70. Relig: Protestant. Mailing Add: 2521 N Chelton Rd Colorado Springs CO 80909

CARTER, PAUL THOMAS (R)
Deleg, Rep State Cent Comt, Calif
b Gladstone, Mich, Feb 7, 22; s Fred J Carter & Elizabeth Richards C; m to Majel Louise Wheeler; c Candace J, Christine (Mrs Hagin), David & Douglas Beach. Educ: Mich State Univ Sch Bus, BBA; Univ Southern Calif Col Com, grad with honor; NAm Ins Schs, grad; Home Off Sch for exec spec agent training, Philadelphia, Pa, grad ranking first, nationwide; Blue Key, Nat Scholastic Hon. Polit & Govt Pos: Deleg, Rep State Cent Comt, Calif, 69- Bus & Prof Pos: Rate clerk, underwriter & spec agent, Ins Co of NAm, Los Angeles; mgr, San Diego Serv Off, NAm Group & Northwest Serv Off, NAm, Portland, Ore; partner, Cosgrove & Dunn Ins Agency & Cosgrove, Dunn, Carter & Higgins, San Diego, Calif; pres, Coroom & Black/Carter & Higgins, 70 & San Diego Ins Corp & Borrego Valley Ins Inc, currently. Mil Serv: Artil Off, Army, World War II & Korean conflict, with serv in Ital Campaign, Tenth Mt Div & US Counterintel Corps, Ft Holabird, Md; Bronze Star for Meritorious Serv. Mem: Pac Homes Corp, Los Angeles; Comn on World Serv & Finance; Lions Int; Calif Brokers Asn; All Am Stadium, Inc. Relig: Methodist; past chmn off bd, Methodist Church, La Mesa. Mailing Add: 5181 Mt Helix Dr La Mesa CA 92041

CARTER, REX LYLE (D)
SC State Rep
b Honea Path, SC, June 20, 25; s D B Carter & Eunice Y Carter C; m 1955 to Lucy Florida Gulledge; c Lucy Coulter & Kimberly Lyle. Educ: Erskine Col, AB, 50; Univ SC, LLB, 52; Exchequer, Phi Delta Phi; Omicron Delta Kappa; pres, Law Sch Student Body. Polit & Govt Pos: SC State Rep, 53-, Speaker, SC State House Rep, 57- Bus & Prof Pos: Lawyer, Carter & Hill. Mil Serv: Coast Guard, 43-46, serv in Atlantic & Pac Theatre. Mem: Int Rels Club (pres); Philomathean Lit Soc (pres). Mailing Add: Box 10304 Fed Station Greenville SC 29603

CARTER, ROBERT CORNELIUS (R)
Chmn, Roseau Co Rep Comt, Minn
b Chicago, Ill, June 4, 17; s John Gordon Carter & Christina Abrahamson C; m 1937 to Georgia Irene Richardson; c John Merwin. Educ: Univ Ill, Champaign, BS, 45; Gonzaga Univ Col Law, LLB, 48; Phi Alpha Delta. Hon Degrees: JD, Gonzaga Univ Col Law, 68. Polit & Govt Pos: Chmn, Roseau Co Rep Party, Minn, 71- Bus & Prof Pos: Partner, Yon & Carter, Attorneys-at-Law, Roseau, 69-72; sr partner, Carter & Carter, Attorneys-at-Law, Roseau, 72- Mil Serv: Entered as Pvt, Army Air Force, 41, released as 1st Lt Pilot, after serv in Army 8th Air Force, ETO, 44-45; Seven Air Medals; Presidential Unit Citation; Four Combat Theatre Ribbons. Mem: Minn State Bar Asn; Am Trial Lawyers Asn; Am Judicature Soc; Wildlife Soc; Minn Citizens Natural Resources Comt (secy, 64-65). Relig: Baptist. Mailing Add: Beaver Farms Wannaska MN 56761

CARTER, ROBERT S (R)
Rep Nat Committeeman, DC
b Rochester, NY, Sept 7, 25. Educ: Gannon Col, AB, 49; Columbia Univ, 51. Polit & Govt Pos: Exec asst to chmn, Rep Nat Comt, 52-57; chief sgt at arms, Rep Nat Conv, 64; secy, DC Rep Comt, 70-72 & 75-; Rep Nat Committeeman, DC, 72- Bus & Prof Pos: With, Continental Airlines, 60-66; owner, Robert Carter Assocs, Pub Rels Consult, 66- Mem: President's Adv Comt on the Arts (secy, 69-). Relig: Roman Catholic. Mailing Add: 601 I St SW Washington DC 20024

CARTER, TIM LEE (R)
US Rep, Ky
b Tompkinsville, Ky, Sept 2, 10; s James Clark & Idru Tucker C; m 1931 to Kathleen Bradshaw; c William Starr. Educ: West Ky Univ, AB, 34; Univ Tenn Sch Med, MD, 37; Alpha Omega Alpha. Polit & Govt Pos: Chmn, Monroe Co Rep Exec Comt, 52-64; US Rep, Ky, 65-, chmn, Republican Task Force on Health, US House Rep, 71-; alt deleg, Rep Nat Conv, 68 & deleg, 72; mem, President's Comn on Marihuana & Drug Abuse, 71- Bus & Prof Pos: Chief of Staff, War Mem Hosp, 53-57. Mil Serv: Entered as 1st Lt, Army, released as Capt, 45, after serv in 38th Inf Div, Southwest Pac Theater; Combat Medic Badge; Bronze Star Medal. Mem: Ky Med Asn; Ky Acad Gen Practice; Am Med Asn; Am Acad Gen Practice; Farm Bur. Relig: Baptist. Legal Res: 701 N Main St Tompkinsville KY 42167 Mailing Add: 2441 Rayburn Off Bldg Washington DC 20515

CARTER, TOMMY (D)
Ala State Rep
Mailing Add: Rte 2 Elkmont AL 35620

CARTER, WALTER LOYD (R)
Chmn, De Kalb Co Rep Party, Tenn
b Smithville, Tenn, May 25, 28; s Charlie Floyd Carter & Verrah Trapp C; m 1944 to Bertha Frances Robinson; c Walteen & Joe Donald. Educ: De Kalb Co Schs, 12 years. Polit & Govt Pos: Chmn, De Kalb Co Rep Party, Tenn, 64-; co campaign mgr, Charlie Howell, Dan Kuykendall, Senate Race, Howard Baker, Senate Race, & Goldwater & Miller, 64; co coordr, US Sen Howard Baker, Jr, 66; co campaign mgr, President Nixon, 68 & US Sen Bill Brock, 70; coordr fourth dist for Gov Dunn, 70; presidential elector, 72; finance chmn, President Nixon & US Sen Baker Campaign, Tenn, 72. Bus & Prof Pos: Owner & mgr, Walter L Carter Truck Lines, 59- Mem: Aircraft Owners & Pilots Asn; State Rep Capitol Club; Farm Bur; Belle-Mont Club; Lions (vchmn, 72-). Honors & Awards: Gov Merit Award, 72. Relig: Baptist. Mailing Add: Carter St Smithville TN 37166

CARTER, WILLIAM C, JR (R)
Tenn State Rep
b Chattanooga, Tenn, Nov 12, 26; s William C Carter & Marjorie Slaughter C; m 1967 to Carol Sharpe; c William C, III. Educ: Univ Tenn, 45; Tenn Wesleyan Col, 47-48; Univ Chattanooga, BBA, 49. Polit & Govt Pos: Pres, Tenn Young Rep Fedn, 56-57; campaign mgr, Bill Brock Cong Campaign, 64; spec field rep, Congressman Brock's Staff, 65; dir orgn, Tenn State Rep Party, exec dir exec comt, 66-67; Tenn State Rep, 67-68 & 73-, secy, Fiscal Rev Comt, 67-68, house whip, 75- Bus & Prof Pos: Dir budgets, Chattem Drug & Chem Corp, 57-65; field rep, Bus Digest & Forecast, 65-69; self-employed, Real Estate & Ins, 69- Mil Serv: Entered as Seaman 1/C, Navy Air Corps, 44, released as ARM 1/C, 46, after serv in World War II. Mem: Nat Off Mgt Asn (dir, 66-); Indust Personnel Club; Commercial Personnel Club; Tenn Law Enforcement Asn; Nat Wildlife Fedn. Relig: Methodist. Legal Res: Rte 3 Soddy TN 37379 Mailing Add: 1815 Bailey Ave Chattanooga TN 37404

CARTER, WILLIAM LACY (R)
Tenn State Rep
b Memphis, Tenn, Dec 2, 25; s William Lacy Carter & Aline Dettwiller C; m 1945 to Juanita Thomas Gossett; c Autumn Gayle, Lynda Dayle, William Thomas & Blair Wayne. Educ: La Tech Univ, 2 years; Columbia Univ, grad midshipmans sch. Polit & Govt Pos: Co Elec Comnr, 68-70; Tenn State Rep, 70-; campaign coordr, Bill Brock for US Sen, 70. Mil Serv: Entered as A/S, Navy, 43, released as Lt, 57, after serv in SPac & Korea. Mem: Jaycees; VFW; Am Legion. Honors & Awards: Chattanooga Jaycee of the Year, 60-61. Relig: Lutheran. Legal Res: 612 Marr Dr Signal Mountain TN 37377 Mailing Add: 1305 Broad St Chattanooga TN 37402

CARTLIDGE, THOMAS MORRIS (D)
Tex State Rep
b Dallas, Tex, June 22, 42; s Morris Hill Cartlidge & Imogene Evans C; single. Educ: Stephen F Austin State Univ, BA, 65; Midwestern Univ, MA, 72; Phi Kappa Delta. Polit & Govt Pos: Tex State Rep, 75- Bus & Prof Pos: Teacher, Wichita Falls Independent Sch Dist, Tex, 70-72; sales rep, Tex Boot Co, Lebanon, Tenn, 74. Mil Serv: Entered as 2nd Lt, Marine Corps, 65, released as Capt, 70, after serv in 1st Marine Div, Vietnam, 66-68, Inf Co Comdr, 68; Capt, Res, 71; Naval Commendation Medal with Combat V; Vietnamese Cross of Gallantry with Palm Leaves; Combat Action Ribbon; Presidential Unit Citation with Bronze Star; Nat Defense Serv Medal; Vietnamese Serv Medal with 4 Stars; Vietnamese Campaign Medal. Publ: Auth, Recent State Constitutional Revision, Tex Const Rev Comn, 73. Mem: Kiwanis; Am Legion; VFW. Relig: Methodist. Legal Res: Box 447 Henrietta TX 76365 Mailing Add: Box 2910 Austin TX 78767

CARTWRIGHT, ARTHUR (D)
Mich State Sen
b Madison, Ala, s William Cartwright & Catherine Scales C; div; c Arthur, Jr, Melvin, Everett H, Wade R, Thelma Octavier, Mary Catherine & Bryan L. Educ: Indust High Sch, Birmingham, Ala. Polit & Govt Pos: Constable, Wayne Co, Mich, 33-43; Bailiff of Common Pleas Court, 43-60; Mich State Rep, 63-64; Mich State Sen, Fifth Dist, 66-, chmn hwys & transportation comt, mem Mich legis coun, chmn coun subcomt on equip, mem health, social serv & retirement & munic & elec comt, Mich State Senate. Bus & Prof Pos: Real estate dealer, currently. Mem: NAACP; SW Dem Club. Relig: Protestant, mem steward's bd, Bethel African Methodist Episcopal Church. Legal Res: 2901 Oakman Blvd Detroit MI 48238 Mailing Add: 7541 Linwood Detroit MI 48206

CARTWRIGHT, DONALD MACK (D)
Tex State Rep
b Houston, Tex, Mar 2, 40; s O V Cartwright & Cecile Watson C; m 1966 to Janice Kay Moore; c Hugh Gentry & Brandie Leigh. Polit & Govt Pos: Tex State Rep, 75- Bus & Prof Pos: Pres, D & M Assocs, San Antonio, Tex, 73- Mil Serv: Marine Corps, 57-65; serv in 1st Bn, 1st Marine Div, 63-65. Mem: Rotary Int; WBexar CofC (bd dirs, 74). Relig: Methodist. Mailing Add: 8727 Angel Valley San Antonio TX 78227

CARTWRIGHT, WILBURN (D)
b Georgetown, Tenn, Jan 12, 92; s J R Cartwright & Emma Baker C; m 1920 to Carrie Staggs (deceased); m 1970 to Coree Adams; c Doralyn Emma (Mrs Leo Gordon) & Wilburta May (Mrs Arnold). Educ: Univ Okla, LLB, 21; Southeastern State Teachers Col, Durant, Okla, grad, 23; Acacia. Polit & Govt Pos: Okla State Rep, 15-19; Okla State Sen, 19-23; US Rep, 3rd Dist, Okla, 27-43; Secy of State, Okla, 47-51, state auditor, 51-55; vchmn, Okla Corp Comn, 55- Bus & Prof Pos: Prin & supt of schs, 21-27. Mil Serv: Serv as Maj, Army, 43-44, Mil Govt NAfrica, Mediterranean Area, Italy, 43-44; NAfrica, Mediterranean & Italy Serv Ribbons; citation for injury. Mem: Odd Fellows (Past Grand Master); Mason; Lions; Am Legion; VFW. Relig: Baptist. Mailing Add: 316 NW 42nd Oklahoma City OK 73118

CARTY, JOSEPH WYNDELL (D)
Miss State Rep
Mailing Add: Box 794 West Point MS 39773

CARTY, MELVILLE A (D)
b Phillipsburg, NJ, Dec 23, 01; s Melville H Carty & Annie Sigafoos C; m 1939 to Thelma C Sloan; c Geraldine Ann & Melville A, Jr. Educ: Pub Sch. Polit & Govt Pos: Councilman, Borough of Alpha, Warren Co, NJ & chmn, Planning Bd, 62-66; comnr, Delaware River Joint Toll Bridge Comn, 64-; alt deleg, Dem Nat Conv, 72. Bus & Prof Pos: Partner, Phillipsburg Bridge & Equipment Co, 30-66; pres, M A Carty & Son Supply Co, Inc, 62-66. Mem: Mason, Miami Consistory, Mahi Temple Shrine; West Jersey Shrine Club; Lehigh Valley Club; Tall Cedars of Lebanon. Legal Res: 5 Fairview Heights Phillipsburg NJ 08865 Mailing Add: 309 S Main St Phillipsburg NJ 08865

CARUBBI, ANGELO JOSEPH, JR (D)
b Galveston, Tex, Jan 1, 32; s Angelo Joseph Carubbi & Madeline Marie La Barbera C; div; c Kathy, Richy, Tommy, Kelly & Amy. Educ: Univ Notre Dame, PhB Comm; Univ Tex, Austin, LLB; Phi Alpha Delta; Phi Kappa Theta. Polit & Govt Pos: Asst, Attorney Gen of Tex, 66, exec asst to Attorney Gen of Tex, Austin, 67-68; deleg, Dem Nat Conv, 72. Bus & Prof Pos: Assoc, Gordon, Gordon & Buzzard, Pampa, Tex, 58-60; sr partner, Carubbi, Warner & Jeter, 60-66; assoc, Dyche, Wheat, Thornton & Wright, Houston, 69-70; partner, Dyche, Wright, Sullivan, Bailey & King, Houston, 71- Mil Serv: Entered as Pvt, Army, 52, released as Sgt, 54, after serv in First Armored Div, Ft Hood, Tex, 52-54. Mem: Am & Houston Bar Asns; Pampa KofC; Notre Dame Club of Houston; Ex-Students Asn of Univ Tex. Honors & Awards: W Texan of the Month, W Tex CofC, 65; nominated for Five Outstanding Young Texans, Pampa Jaycees, 67. Relig: Roman Catholic. Legal Res: 1310 Kipling Houston TX 77006 Mailing Add: 1600 Mellie Esperson Bldg Houston TX 77002

CARVALHO, AMERICO (MAC) (R)
Ariz State Rep
Mailing Add: 7827 East Thunderbird Scottsdale AZ 85254

CARVEL, ELBERT NOSTRAND (D)
b Shelter Island, NY, Feb 9, 10; s Arnold W Carvel & Elizabeth Nostrand C; m 1932 to Ann Valliant; c Mrs Charles L Palmer, Edwin Valliant, Ann Hall & Mrs Michael R Giles. Educ: Univ Baltimore, JD, 31; Sigma Delta Kappa; Alpha Zeta. Hon Degrees: LLD, Del State Col, 64. Polit & Govt Pos: Trustee, Univ Del, 45-, vchmn, bd trustees, 72; pres, Del Pardon Bd, 45-49; chmn, Del State Dem Comt, 46-47 & 54-57; Lt Gov, Del, 45-49, Gov, 49-53 & 61-65; deleg, Dem Nat Conv, 48-64; jointly nominated Adlai E Stevenson for President on the Dem Ticket, 52; chmn, Del Const Rev Comt, 68-69; trustee, Univ Baltimore, 68-74; mem, Del Bicentennial Comn, 68-70; chmn, Del Dem Renewal Comn, 70-71; co-chmn Delawareans for Orderly Develop, 71-; mem, Del Bicentennial Medal Comt, 72-73. Bus & Prof Pos: Treas Valliant Fertilizer Co, 36-45, pres, 45-72, chmn bd, 72; vpres, Milford Fertilizer Co, 37-61,

chmn bd, 61-; dir, Sussex Trust Co, 41-49; dir, Peoples Bank & Trust Co, 57-, chmn bd, 75-; vpres, Laurel Grain Co, 65-; chmn, Fischer Enterprises, Inc, 70-75. Mem: Mason (33 degree); Del Consistory; Lions; Grange; Sussex Co Soc of Archaeol & Hist. Honors & Awards: Designated Comdr, Order Orange, Nassau by Queen Juliana of the Netherlands, 51; The Vrooman Award, 65; Gold Medal for Good Citizenship, SAR, 67; Sussex Co Serv Club Award for Serv to Agr, 69; Silver Beaver Award, Boy Scouts of Am, 70. Relig: Episcopal; former Vestryman & former Sr Warden, St Philips Episcopal Church, chmn, Delmarva Ecumenical Agency, 71-73. Legal Res: 107 Clayton Ave Laurel DE 19956 Mailing Add: Box 111 Laurel DE 19956

CARVER, JOHN A, JR **(D)**
b Preston, Idaho, Apr 24, 18; s John A Carver & LaVerne Olson C; m 1942 to Ruth Patricia O'Connor; c John A, III, Craig Roger & Candace Elaine. Educ: Brigham Young Univ, AB; Georgetown Univ, LLB; Boise Col; George Washington Univ; Univ Idaho; Univ Mont. Hon Degrees: LLD, Univ Guam, 66. Polit & Govt Pos: Various civil serv positions, 40-47, including regional dir civilian personnel div, Off of Secy of War, New York, 42-43; Asst Attorney Gen, Idaho, 47-48; admin asst to US Sen Frank Church, 57-61; Asst Secy, Dept of Interior, 61-64, Under Secy, 64-66; comnr, Fed Power Comn, 66-72. Bus & Prof Pos: Attorney, Carver, McClenahan & Greenfield, Boise, Idaho, 48-57; prof law, Univ Denver Col Law, 72- Mil Serv: Entered as Pvt, Army, 43, released as 1st Lt, Air Force, 46, after serv in Strategic Bombing Surv, Eng & Japan; ETO, Asiatic & Am Theatre Ribbons. Honors & Awards: John Carroll Medal of Merit, Georgetown Univ, 72. Mailing Add: 5639 Montview Blvd Denver CO 80207

CARVER, RICHARD E **(R)**
Mayor, Peoria, Ill
b Peoria, Ill; married; c Kathryn, Stephen, Cynthia & Susan. Educ: Bradley Univ, BS in Bus Admin. Polit & Govt Pos: Adv bd mem, Bradley Univ Urban Affairs Inst; bd mem, United Rep Fund of Ill; bd mem, Dist 150 Voc Adv Bd; alderman, Peoria, Ill, 69-73, mayor, 73- Bus & Prof Pos: Dir, Provident Fed Savings & Loan Asn of Peoria, Ill Lumberdealers Asn & Peoria YMCA; chmn & labor negotiator, Peoria Lumberdealers Asn. Mil Serv: Maj, Air Force Res. Honors & Awards: Outstanding Young Man of the Year, Peoria, Ill, 69; Retailer of the Year, five times nat runner-up. Mailing Add: City Hall Bldg 419 Fulton St Peoria IL 61602

CARVER, WILLIAM BRYAN, JR **(D)**
VPres, Floyd Co Dem Asn, Ga
b Rome, Ga, Feb 20, 30; s William Bryan Carver, Sr & Ethel Bates C; m 1948 to Ina Delle Landers; c Karen, June, Marcus & Douglas. Educ: Shorter Col, 52-53; Univ Ga Exten Ctr, 66-68. Polit & Govt Pos: Vpres, Floyd Co Dem Asn, Ga, 71-; mem, Ga State Dem Exec Comt, formerly. Bus & Prof Pos: Bookkeeper, Southern Bearings & Parts Co, 47-52; supply room clerk, Burlington Mills, Inc, 52-53; supvr cost estimating & anal, Gen Elec Co, 53- Mem: Rome Gen Elec Supvy Club, Inc; Gen Elec Athletic Asn. Relig: Baptist. Mailing Add: 9 Castlewood Dr Rome GA 30161

CARWILE, HOWARD H **(INDEPENDENT)**
Va State Deleg
Mailing Add: Suite 407 Heritage Bldg 10th & Main Sts Richmond VA 23219

CARY, ASHTON HALL **(R)**
VChmn, Troup Co Rep Party, Ga
b LaGrange, Ga, Dec 13, 23; s Ashton Hall Cary, Sr & Edna Freeman C; m 1949 to Betty Baugh; c Edna Helen, Ashton Hall, III, John Huntley, Elizabeth Hanson & Bradley Henry. Educ: Ga Sch Technol, BS in ChE; Alpha Tau Omega. Polit & Govt Pos: Deleg, Precinct, Co Dist & State Convs, Ga, 64, 68 & 70; mem exec comt, Sixth Dist Rep Party, 64-66; mem exec comt, Troup Co Rep Orgn, 64-, treas, 64-66; finance chmn for G Paul Jones for Cong, Troup Co, 66; deleg, Rep Nat Conv, 68; asst treas, Troup Co Rep Party, Ga, 70-72, vchmn, 72-; comnr, Troup Co, 70-; chmn, Sixth Dist Asn of Co Comnrs of Ga, 70- Bus & Prof Pos: Mem bd dirs, Am Red Cross, 50, Dunson Sales, 50, United Appeal, 54, La Grange CofC, 54 & La Grange Welfare Asn, 68; trustee & treas, City Co Hosp, 60; asst mgr, Dunson Mills, formerly; partner, A B & B Travel Serv, 71- Mil Serv: Entered as Pvt, Army, 42, released as Pfc, 46, after serv in Cavalry, ETO, 45; two Battle Stars, Rhineland & Cent Europe. Publ: Several textile articles in Textile World & Textile Indust. Mem: Elks; Am Legion; Moose; Highland Country Club. Relig: Presbyterian. Legal Res: 1114 Cameron Mill Rd La Grange GA 30240 Mailing Add: PO Box 1076 La Grange GA 30240

CARY, RUTH MARGARET **(R)**
Committeewoman, NJ Rep State Comt
b Mountain View, NJ, May 3, 17; d Charles Edward Nelson & Martha Gertrude Compton N; m 1947 to Harry DeWitt Cary, wid; c Michael DeWitt & Kevin Robert. Educ: Paterson Cent High Sch, dipl, 36. Polit & Govt Pos: Mem dist election bd, Mansfield Twp, 64-68; pres, Mansfield Twp Rep Club, 64-73; secy, Warren Co Rep Comt, 64-74; mem, Warren Co Rep Exec Comt, 64-; mem staff, Warren Co Sheriff's Off, 67-68; legis aide, State Senator Wayne Dumont, Jr, 68-; committeewoman, NJ Rep State Comt, 69-; Warren Co rep & mem bd gov, NJ Fedn Rep Women, 69-74; Rep mem, Warren Co Bd Elections, 71-, comnr registr, 72-75; deleg, Rep Nat Conv, 72; mem, Mansfield Twp Planning Bd, 74- Bus & Prof Pos: Mem off staff, inventory control, Curtiss-Wright Corp, West Caldwell, NJ, 40-45 & I Stern & Co, New York, NY, 45-48. Mem: PTA; Washington Womens Club, NJ; Phillipsburg Rep Area Coun; Mansfield Twp Rep Club; Green Valley Riding Club. Relig: Methodist. Mailing Add: Cary Rd RD 1 Box 296 Oxford NJ 07863

CASASSA, HERBERT ALFRED **(R)**
NH State Rep
b Fitchburg, Mass, Mar 9, 97; married; c One son. Educ: Fitchburg High Sch. Polit & Govt Pos: NH State Rep, 61-; chmn, Hampton Munic Budget Comn, formerly; alt deleg, Rep Nat Conv, 72. Bus & Prof Pos: Pres, Colt News Store, Inc. Mem: CofC (dir); Hampton Kiwanis; Elks. Relig: Catholic. Mailing Add: Box 307 Hampton NH 03842

CASDIN, JOSEPH CHARLES **(D)**
City Councillor, Worcester, Mass
b Fiskdale, Mass, Mar 8, 14; s Simon Cohen Casdin & Ida Ostroff C; m 1937 to Miriam Joan Whitman; c Jeffrey W, Ruth Ann (Mrs Friedberg) & Deborah Sue. Educ: Boston Univ, two years; Tau Delta Phi. Polit & Govt Pos: City Councillor, Worcester, Mass, 56-, mayor & chmn sch comt, 59-60, 62 & 67-68; deleg, Dem Nat Conv, 64 & 68. Bus & Prof Pos: Dir, Home Fed Savings & Loan Asn, 59-; owner, Casdin Gallery, Worcester, 64-; partner, Profit, Tech & Ericius Funds, 68-; broker, Hornblower & Weeks, Hemphill-Noyes, 69- Mem: CofC (dir, Worcester Area, 58-63); Mason (32 degree); KofP; Probus Club; Kiwanis. Relig: Reform Judaist. Mailing Add: 12 Lenox St Worcester MA 01602

CASE, CLIFFORD PHILIP **(R)**
US Sen, NJ
b Franklin Park, NJ, Apr 16, 04; s Clifford Philip Case & Jeannette Benedict C; m 1928 to Ruth Miriam Smith; c Mary Jane (Mrs William M Weaver), Ann (Mrs John C Holt) & Clifford Philip, III. Educ: Rutgers Univ, AB, 25; Columbia Univ, LLB, 28; Phi Beta Kappa; Phi Delta Phi; Delta Upsilon. Hon Degrees: LLD, Rutgers Univ, 55, Middlebury Col, 56, Rollins Col, 57, Rider Col, 59, Bloomfield Col, 62, Columbia Univ, 67, Princeton Univ, 67 & Upsala Col, 69; DPS, Seton Hall Univ, 71. Polit & Govt Pos: Mem, Rahway Common Coun, NJ, 38-42; NJ State Assemblyman, 43-44; US Rep, Sixth Dist, NJ, 45-53; US Deleg, 21st UN Gen Assembly; US Sen, NJ, 54-, mem, Senate Foreign Rels & Appropriations Comts & mem, Technol Assessment Bd, currently; deleg, Rep Nat Conv, 56, 64 & 68; mem, UN Comt on Peaceful Uses of Seabed, 71. Bus & Prof Pos: Assoc, Simpson Thacher & Bartlett, NY, 28-39, mem, 39-53; pres, Fund for Repub, 53-54. Mem: Essex Club; Fed City Club; Capitol Hill Club; Century Asn; Coun Foreign Rels. Honors & Awards: Award, City of Hope, Nat Med Ctr, 67; Justice Louis D Brandeis Award, NJ Region, Zionist Orgn of Am, 69; cited by, DAV, NJ, 71; Citizen's Award, Acad Med NJ, 72; Profile in Courage Award, Am Fedn Govt Employees, 72. Relig: Presbyterian. Legal Res: 191 W Milton Ave Rahway NJ 07065 Mailing Add: 315 Senate Off Bldg Washington DC 20510

CASE, GEORGE MILTON **(D)**
Miss State Rep
b Canton, Miss, July 5, 34; s Willie Case & Mamie Smith C; single. Educ: Univ Miss, BBA, 55, Sch Law, LLB, 56; Omicron Delta Kappa; Phi Delta Phi. Polit & Govt Pos: Miss State Rep, 60- Bus & Prof Pos: Attorney. Mil Serv: Entered as 1st Lt, Army, 57, released as 1st Lt, 59, after serv in Judge Adv Gen Dept. Mem: KofP; Mason; Shrine; Lions Int; Elks. Relig: Baptist. Mailing Add: Green Acres Subdivision Canton MS 39046

CASEMENT, JOAN MURPHY **(D)**
b Providence, RI, Aug 31, 35; d Neale D Murphy & Mary Behan M; div; c Caitlin. Educ: RI Col, BEd, 57; Dramatic League; staff, Anchor Newspaper. Polit & Govt Pos: Deleg, Dem Nat Conv, 72; deleg, Dem Nat Mid-Term Conf, 74; chairwoman, RI Women's Polit Caucus, 75- Bus & Prof Pos: Teacher, Providence, RI, 60-66; teacher, New York, NY, 66-67; resource room teacher for children with learning disabilities, Barrington, RI, 67-75. Mem: Barrington Teachers Asn (first vpres, 73-74, negotiation chairperson, 73-75); RI Educ Asn (mem legis comn); Nat New Dem Coalition (mem exec bd, 75). Mailing Add: 71 Keene St Providence RI 02906

CASEY, DAN **(D)**
b Dumbarton, Scotland, Mar 22, 38; s John Michael Casey & Elizabeth C; m 1968 to Mary Virginia Skotch; c Laura Anne & John Edward. Educ: Marquette Univ, BSME, 68; Triangle Fraternity. Polit & Govt Pos: Precinct committeeman, Precinct 77, York Twp, 72-; deleg, Dem Mid Term Conf, 74; chmn comt to elec Dem, Du Page Co, 74-75; chmn, York Twp Dem Orgn, 75- Mem: Lombard Dem Club; Du Page Co Dem Cent Comt. Relig: Catholic. Mailing Add: 326 N Martha St Lombard IL 60148

CASEY, DENNIS D **(R)**
Mont State Rep
Mailing Add: 420 Johnson St Wolf Point MT 59201

CASEY, JOSEPH EDWARD **(R)**
Chmn, West Haven Rep Town Comt, Conn
b New Haven, Conn, Oct 7, 13; s John E Casey & Mary E Cain C; m 1942 to Marjorie Stone; c Joseph E, Jr & Walter S. Educ: Wharton Sch Finance, Univ Pa; Conn Col Com. Polit & Govt Pos: Chmn, West Haven Rep Town Comt, Conn, currently; former exec secy to Mayor, West Haven; legis bulletin clerk, Conn Gen Assembly, 61-66; former mem, US Selective Serv Adv Comt; dir pub rels, City of West Haven, 68-72; spec asst to Comptroller, State of Conn, 72- Mem: Elks. Relig: Catholic. Mailing Add: 145 Church St West Haven CT 06516

CASEY, JOSEPH S **(D)**
La State Rep
b New Orleans, La, Sept 29, 13; s Joseph A Casey & Dora Stubbs C; m 1942 to Lillian K McGraw; c Joseph T, Phyllis O & Roy A. Educ: Loyola Univ, New Orleans, LLB, 37, AB, 38. Polit & Govt Pos: La State Rep, 52-56 & 60- Mil Serv: Entered as Pvt, Army, 41, released as Cpl, 42. Relig: Catholic. Legal Res: 871 Lopaz St New Orleans LA 70124 Mailing Add: Suite 201 2621 Canal St New Orleans LA 70119

CASEY, JOSEPH T **(R)**
Chmn, Clayton Co Rep Party, Ga
b Rocky Mount, NC, May 1, 43; s Lemuel Wyatt Casey & Maude Swanson C; m 1964 to Sonja Marie Jennings; c Robert, Kevin, Jo Marie, Heather & Jeremy. Educ: Bob Jones Univ, 61-62; Clayton Jr Col, 70-73. Polit & Govt Pos: Chmn, Clayton Co Rep Party, Ga, 75- Bus & Prof Pos: Schedular, Delta Airlines, 67- Relig: Latter-day Saint. Mailing Add: 2615 Rosedale Dr Morrow GA 30260

CASEY, ROBERT J **(R)**
b Youngstown, Ohio. Educ: Kent State Univ, BA; Youngstown Univ & Ohio State Univ, LLB; Blue Key; Delta Upsilon. Polit & Govt Pos: Deleg, Rep Nat Conv, 72; chmn, Comt for Survival of a Free Cong, Washington, DC, currently. Bus & Prof Pos: Pub rels dir, Westinghouse Air Brake Co, Pittsburgh, formerly; chmn bd, Morristown Bank, Ohio, formerly; pres, Casey, Newton & Co, Washington, DC, currently; exec dir, Nat Asn Rail Passengers, Washington, DC, currently; dir, Trefeis Corp, Youngstown, currently. Mil Serv: Entered Air Force, World War II, Ger, released as Comdr, Navy Res; Distinguished Flying Cross; Air Medal with Four Oak Leaf Clusters. Publ: Transformation of an old line bank into a modern marketing system, Bank Mkt Asn, 59; The Keystone Corridor, Rail Publ Inc, 70; Analysis of voting patterns in a suburban community, Nat Rev, 67. Mem: Pub Rels Soc Am; Sigma Delta Chi; Press Club Pittsburgh (dir); Capitol Hill Club of Wash. Honors & Awards: Golden Quill Awards, sponsored by nine Pittsburgh orgn, 62, 68 & 69. Mailing Add: 206 Valley Court Dr Pittsburgh PA 15237

CASEY, ROBERT P **(D)**
Auditor Gen, Pa
b Jackson Heights, NY, Jan 9, 32; s Alphonsus L Casey & Marie Cummings C; m to Ellen Harding; c Eight. Educ: Holy Cross Col; George Washington Univ Law Sch, AB, LLB, JD;

pres sr class, Holy Cross Col; athletic scholarship, Holy Cross Col; trustee scholarship, George Washington Univ; Order of the Coif. Polit & Govt Pos: Pa State Sen, 62-67; alt deleg-at-lg, Dem Nat Conv, 64, deleg, 68; Auditor Gen, Pa, 69- Bus & Prof Pos: Attorney. Publ: Auth, Counter Claims Against the United States, George Washington Law Rev, 1/57. Mem: Cancer Drive; Lackawanna United Fund Dr. Honors & Awards: Admitted to practice before, Lackawanna Co Courts, Supreme & Superior Courts of Pa; DC & Fed Courts; Middle Dist of Pa Court. Legal Res: 2002 N Washington Ave Scranton PA 18509 Mailing Add: Finance Bldg Harrisburg PA 17120

CASEY, ROBERT RANDOLPH (BOB) (D)
US Rep, Tex
b Joplin, Mo, July 27, 15; s Sam Russel Casey & Mabel Caywood C; m 1935 to Hazel Marian Brann; c Hazel Mary (Mrs Ronald Harron), Bob, Jr, Catherine, Bonnie (Mrs Paul Quinton), Michael, Shawn, Bridget (Mrs Howard Poizner), Eileen, Timothy & Kevin. Educ: Univ Houston, 34-36; STex Col Law, 36-40. Polit & Govt Pos: City attorney, Alvin, Tex, 42-43, mem sch bd, 43; asst dist attorney, Harris Co, 43-47, Tex State Rep, 49-50, Judge, 51-58; US Rep, 22nd Dist, 59- Bus & Prof Pos: Clerk, Skelly Oil Co, 34-35, Barnsdall Oil Co, 35 & Shell Oil Co, 35-41; attorney-at-law, 41-43 & 47-51. Mem: Tex Bar Asn. Relig: Protestant. Legal Res: 2256 Dryden Rd Houston TX 77025 Mailing Add: 2256 Rayburn Bldg Washington DC 20515

CASEY, THOMAS A (D)
La State Sen
Mailing Add: 435 Audubon Blvd New Orleans LA 70125

CASEY, WALTER PEVEAR, JR (R)
b Glendora, Calif, Aug 4, 18; s Walter Pevear Casey, Sr & Irene LaFetra C; m 1946 to Margaret Lehr Perkins; c Steven Shannon, Michael Andrew & Ann LaFetra. Educ: Univ Calif, Berkeley, BA, 42; Sigma Nu. Polit & Govt Pos: Campaign chmn, Cong Cand, Nev, 54, Gov, 58, Sen Cand, 56 & 68; mem bd dirs, Las Vegas CofC, 60-65, pres, 64-65; mem, Colo River Comn, Nev, 67-71; mem, Bd Dirs Las Vegas Conv Authority, 69-71; chmn, Clark Co Rep Cent Comt, 71-72; state chmn, Nev Rep Party, 72-75. Bus & Prof Pos: Pres, Pac Water Conditioning Asn, 62-63. Mil Serv: Ens, Navy, 42-45, serv in Pan Am Airways. Mem: Shrine; Nat Asn Mfrs; Mason; Elks; Kiwanis. Honors & Awards: Irish Descendant Outstanding Community Contribution, Friendly Sons of St Patrick, 65. Relig: Protestant. Mailing Add: PO Box 14810 Las Vegas NV 89114

CASEY, WILLIAM J (R)
Chmn, Export-Import Bank US
Polit & Govt Pos: Under Secy State Security Assistance, formerly. Legal Res: NY Mailing Add: 811 Vermont Ave NW Washington DC 20571

CASHEN, HENRY CHRISTOPHER, II (R)
b Detroit, Mich, June 25, 39; s Raymond Cashen & Catherine C; m 1967 to Leslie Renchard; c Raymond, II. Educ: Brown Univ, AB, with Honors, 61; Univ Mich Law Sch, LLB, 63; Sphinx Club; Psi Upsilon. Polit & Govt Pos: Dep counsel to the President, 69-70; dep asst to President, 70-73. Bus & Prof Pos: Attorney-at-law, Dickinson, Wright McKean & Cudlip, 64-69; Colson & Shapiro, 73- Mem: State Bar Mich; Am Bar Asn; Supreme Court US; Country Club Detroit; Univ Club Detroit. Relig: Roman Catholic. Mailing Add: 1735 New York Ave NW Washington DC 20006

CASHMAN, PETER LENIHAN (R)
Lt Gov, Conn
b Cleveland, Ohio, May 22, 36; s Eugene Ramiro Cashman & Pauline Lenihan C; m 1966 to Susan Green; c Robert Stafford Green & Johanna Gillett. Educ: Yale Univ, BA, 59; Fence Club. Polit & Govt Pos: Dir, Rep State Fair, Conn Rep State Cent Comt, summer 66; mem, Conn State Rep Finance Comt, 68-69; treas, William G Moore for State Sen, 20th Dist, 68; Conn State Sen, 20th Dist, 71-73, Pres Pro Tempore, Conn State Senate, 73; alt deleg, Rep Nat Conv, 72; Lt Gov, Conn, 73- Bus & Prof Pos: Teacher hist, Canterbury Sch, New Milford Conn, 59-61; dir develop & admin asst to headmaster, 61-66; vpres, Inquiry Eval, Inc, Guilford, 66-69, on leave, currently. Mem: Canterbury Sch Alumni Asn (pres); Canterbury Sch (bd trustees). Relig: Catholic. Mailing Add: State Capitol Hartford CT 06115

CASKEY, WILBURN (D)
b West Liberty, Ky, Jan 5, 21; s Ivory Blankenship Caskey; m 1950 to Dorothy Ann Coonrod; c Jeff & Pike. Educ: Centre Col, BA; Sigma Alpha Epsilon; C Club. Polit & Govt Pos: Past mem, Ky Develop Coun & Ky Adv Comts on Planning & Zoning & on Metrop Govt; mem, Water Pollution Control Comt; mayor pro tem, Ashland, 51-53, mayor, 55-59, mem city comt, 51-55; pres, Ky Munic League, 67-68; chmn, Boyd Co Dem Exec Comt, formerly; mem, Citizens Comt on State Legislatures, currently. Mil Serv: Entered as Pvt, Marine Corps, 42, released as 1st Lt, 46, after serv in Pac Theater; Pac Theater Ribbon. Mem: Tuberc Asn & Home for the Aged (dir); Elks; Am Legion. Honors & Awards: Jaycees Outstanding Young Man of Ashland, 53. Relig: Methodist. Mailing Add: 2811 Cumberland Ave Ashland KY 41101

CASO, RALPH GEORGE (R)
Nassau Co Exec, NY
b New York, NY, Nov 26, 17; s George Ralph Caso & Josephine DeNicola C; m 1955 to Grace Milone; c Ralph George, Jr & Jolisa. Educ: Hofstra Univ, 2 years; NY Univ, BS; NY Univ Law Sch, JD; Alpha Tau Omega; Phi Alpha Delta. Polit & Govt Pos: Pres, Rep Recruits, 51-52; councilman, Hempstead, 53-61, supvr, 61-65, presiding supvr, 65-70; vchmn, Bd of Supvr, Nassau Co, 65-70, Nassau Co Exec, 71-; deleg, Rep Nat Conv, 68. Bus & Prof Pos: Attorney, 49- Mil Serv: Entered as Pvt, Army, 42, released as M/Sgt, 45, after serv in Y Force, China, 43-45; Three Combat Stars; Bronze Star Medal for Meritorious Serv. Mem: Nassau Co Bar Asn; Nassau Lawyers Asn; NY State Co Execs Asn; Nat Asn Co Officers; Metrop Regional Coun. Honors & Awards: Torch of Liberty Award, B'nai B'rith; Annual Achievement Award, Long Island Columbia Asn; Grass Roots Award, Nassau Co Press Asn; Man of Year Award, Asn for Help of Retarded Children; St Francis Col Charter Award. Relig: Catholic. Mailing Add: County Exec Bldg 1 West St Mineola NY 11501

CASON, GARY CARLTON (R)
Chmn, Muscogee Co Rep Party, Ga
b Columbus, Ga, Mar 2, 43; s Carlton B Cason & Nadine S C; m to Kathryn Greene; c Gary C, Jr, Dana Lynn, Stephen Dale & Tiffany. Educ: Columbus Col; Auburn Univ, BA, 69; Nat Econ Honor Soc. Polit & Govt Pos: Vchmn, Muscogee Co Rep Party, Ga, 74-75, chmn, 75- Bus & Prof Pos: Parts mgr, Hardaway Ford Inc, 60-69; asst vpres, Nat Bank & Trust Co, 69-72; vpres & treas & owner, Dale Ace Hardware, 72- Mem: Columbus Jaycees; Columbus CofC; Boy Scouts (asst scoutmaster, Troop 6). Honors & Awards: Key Man, Columbus Jaycees, 73. Relig: Episcopal; mem vestry, Trinity Episcopal Church. Mailing Add: 3128 College Dr Columbus GA 31907

CASON, WILLIAM J (D)
Mo State Sen
b Higginsville, Mo, Oct 1, 24; married; c Brian Austin, William Wilson, Patrick Jennings & Candiss Anne. Educ: Univ Mo, BS, LLB, with honors; Sigma Nu. Polit & Govt Pos: Mo State Sen, 60-; prosecuting attorney, Henry Co, 6 years. Bus & Prof Pos: Lawyer, 51-; acct; grocery clerk. Mil Serv: Army Air Corps, World War II, bomber pilot 3 years. Mem: Jr CofC; CofC. Honors & Awards: Distinguished Serv Award, Mo Acad Gen Practice; Citation of Merit, Mo Hosp Asn; St Louis Globe-Democrat Award. Relig: Christian. Mailing Add: 215 E Franklin Clinton MO 64735

CASS, MILLARD, (D)
Adminr, Off of Wage Stabilization
b Norfolk, Va, Nov 8, 16; s Sigismund Cass & Ridia Schreier C; m 1943 to Ruth Claire Marx; c Sandra Jean (Mrs Jeffrey A Burt), Ronald Andrew & Pamela Celeste. Educ: Univ Va, BS, 38, LLB, 40; Phi Beta Kappa; Omicron Delta Kappa; Order of Coif; Raven Soc. Polit & Govt Pos: Attorney, Securities & Exchange Comn, 41; attorney, Nat Labor Rels Bd, 41-45, legal asst to gen counsel, 45-46; asst to Asst Secy of Labor, 46-47, asst to Under Secy of Labor, 47-50, spec asst to Secy of Labor, 50-55, Dep Under Secy of Labor, 55-71; Mobilization Planning Coordr, 62-71; exec officer, Manpower Admin, 63-64; Liaison Officer with State Governors, 69-71; admin dir, Construction Indust Stabilization Comt, 71-; admin dir, Pay Bd, 71-73; adminr, Off of Wage Stabilization, 73- Bus & Prof Pos: Attorney-at-law, Portsmouth, Va, 40-41. Mem: Va State & Am Bar Asns; Montgomery Co Coun of PTA's, Md; Md Cong Parents & Teachers; Montgomery Co Scholarship Fund. Honors & Awards: Distinguished Serv Award, US Dept of Labor, 60; Distinguished Career Serv Award, 71; Rockefeller Pub Serv Award, 66; Montgomery Co Educ Asn Hornbook Award, 68; Nat Civil Serv League Career Serv Award, 69. Relig: Jewish; bd mgr, Washington Hebrew Congregation, 59-, pres, 70-72; bd dirs which estab Int Synagogue at John F Kennedy Airport, New York, NY, 59-64. Mailing Add: 2103 Plyers Mill Rd Silver Spring MD 20902

CASSELLA, STEFAN DANTE (D)
b Hackensack, NJ, Sept 7, 51; s Norman William Cassella & Rose Mary Zeppieri C; single. Educ: Cornell Univ, BS, 73; Georgetown Univ Law Ctr, currently. Polit & Govt Pos: Alt deleg, Dem Nat Conv, 72. Bus & Prof Pos: Comput programmer & analyst, Opers Research, Inc, Silver Spring, Md, currently. Mem: New York Civil Liberties Union; Common Cause; AMCBW. Relig: Catholic. Legal Res: 477 Riverside Ave Rutherford NJ 07070 Mailing Add: 420 Seventh St SE Washington DC 20003

CASSELMAN, WILLIAM E, II (R)
Counsel to the President
b Washington, Pa, July 8, 41; s William E Casselman & Lucy Bobbs C; m 1967 to Caroline Murfitt; c Katharine & Lee. Educ: Claremont Men's Col, BA Govt, 63; Univ Madrid, 63-64; George Washington Univ, JD, 68; Delta Theta Phi; Pi Sigma Alpha. Polit & Govt Pos: Legis asst, US Rep Robert McClory, 65-69; staff asst, White House, 69; dep spec asst to the President, 69-71; gen counsel, Gen Serv Admin, 69-73; legal counsel to the Vice President, 73-74; counsel to the President, 74- Publ: Co-ed, Reforming the fiscal & budgetary machinery of the congress, In: We Propose: A Modern Congress, McGraw-Hill, 66; co-auth, Automatic data processing as a major information tool of the congress, In: Information Support, Program Budgeting & the Congress, Spartan, 68; auth, The Kennedy assassination & the Freedom of information act—the administrative & judicial experience, Philadelphia Lawyer, 5/74. Mem: Am Bar Asn (sect admin law, sect pub contracts law); Fed Bar Asn (nat coun). Honors & Awards: Alumni Achievement Award, George Washington Univ, 75, Distinguished Serv Commendation, Fed Bar Asn, 74. Relig: Protestant. Legal Res: 400 S Fairfax St Alexandria VA 22314 Mailing Add: White House Washington DC 20500

CASSERLY, JAMES R (DFL)
Minn State Rep
Mailing Add: 1100 Vincent Ave N Minneapolis MN 55411

CASSIANO, FRANK ANTHONY (D)
b Philadelphia, Pa, July 5, 21; s Louis R Cassiano & Josephine Gruerio C; m 1948 to Mary Robinson; c Josephine Ruth & Frank A, Jr. Educ: Villanova Univ, BS, 44. Polit & Govt Pos: Vchmn, Precinct Two, Morehead City, NC, 60-62; mem, Carteret Co Bd Elec, 62-70; chmn, Carteret Co Dem Party, formerly. Bus & Prof Pos: Rep, Jefferson Standard Life Ins, 53-; mil liaison, Carteret Co, 55-70; bd dirs, CofC, 62-65. Mil Serv: Entered as Pvt, Marine Corps, 40, retired as Capt, 53, after serv from Guadalcanal to Korea, 42-53; Theatre Ribbons; Letter of Recommendation; Presidential Unit Citation. Mem: Life Underwriters Asn; Rotary; Elks (all chairs, 67-72, exalted ruler, 71-72); Port City Investment Club. Relig: Roman Catholic. Legal Res: 2913 Evans St Morehead City NC 28557 Mailing Add: PO Box 276 Morehead City NC 28557

CASSIBRY, NAPOLEON LE POINT, II (D)
Miss State Sen
b Gulfport, Miss, Aug 3, 18; s Oscar Fillis Cassibry (deceased) & Mary Kathryn Campbell C; m 1952 to Byrd Austell; c Byrd Austell, Jr. Educ: Miss State Univ Exten, grad indust acct, 42; LaSalle Univ Exten, grad law, 68. Polit & Govt Pos: Deleg, Dem Nat Conv, 60; Col on gov staff, Gov Ross R Barnett, Miss, 60-63 & Gov Paul Johnson, Jr, 64-67; mem, Agr & Indust Bd, State Miss, 60-63; secy, Harrison Co Develop Comn, 63-66; Miss State Sen, 68- Bus & Prof Pos: Mem bd dirs, Miss Mfg Asn, 58-64, chmn legis action comt, 60-63; attorney-at-law, 68- Mil Serv: Entered as Asst Purser-Pharmacist Mate, Merchant Marine, 45, released as Purser-Pharmacist Mate, 47, after serv in Atlantic, Caribbean & Mediterranean Theatres, 45-47. Mem: Am Judicature Soc; Am Bar Asn; Elks; Navy League; SAR. Relig: Presbyterian. Legal Res: 910 Wanda Pl Gulfport MS 39501 Mailing Add: PO Box 1686 Gulfport MS 39501

CASSIDY, CLIFTON WILSON, JR (D)
b San Antonio, Tex, Oct 30, 27; s Clifton Wilson Cassidy & Winifred Lynn C; m 1952 to Sally Otis; c Elynn, Clifton Wilson, III, Kelly Anne & Michael. Educ: Univ Tex, Austin, BBA, 50; Delta Sigma Phi; Phi Kappa Sigma. Polit & Govt Pos: Chmn, Dallas Co Dem Exec Comt, Tex, 64; deleg, Dem Nat Conv, 64 & 68, mem security adv comt, 72; chmn, Pub Safety Comn, Tex, 66-; mem, Tex Comt of 100, 70; mem develop bd, Univ Tex, Dallas, currently; ex officio mem, Dem Nat Mid-Term Conf, 74. Bus & Prof Pos: Pres, Richardson Savings & Loan; pres, Cassidy Feed Mills, Inc; chmn exec comt First Bank & Trust; dir, Tex Bank & Trust; dir,

Dallas Title & Guaranty. Mil Serv: Entered as A/S, Navy, released as Lt; Lt, Res. Mem: Coun Social Agencies; Dallas Summer Musicals; Dallas Assembly; Rotary; Brook Hollow Golf Club. Honors & Awards: Distinguished Alumni Award, Univ Tex, 66. Relig: Methodist. Mailing Add: 10211 Hollow Way Dallas TX 75229

CASSIDY, JOHN EDWARD (D)
b Omaha, Nebr, July 6, 52; s John William Cassidy & Dolores Alex C; single. Educ: Univ Nebr, Lincoln, 70- Polit & Govt Pos: Deleg, Dem Nat Conv, 72. Mem: Int Retail Clerk Asn. Relig: Catholic. Mailing Add: 3075 S 34th Omaha NE 68105

CASSIDY, ROBERT VALENTINE (D)
Mem Exec Comt, Blair Co Dem Party, Pa
b Newry, Pa, Feb 14, 30; s Edward C Cassidy & Florine M Harker C; single. Educ: Lock Haven State Col, BSEd, 51; Cath Univ Am, MA, 53; Univ Dayton, 54; Ohio State Univ, 59-67; Case Western Reserve Univ, 60-68; Xavier Univ, 63; John Carroll Univ, 68; Univ Toledo, 70; Pa State Univ, University Park, 74. Polit & Govt Pos: Chmn, Knox Co Dem Party, Ohio, 71-72; deleg, Dem Nat Mid-Term Conf, 74; councilman, Newry Borough, Pa, 74-; committeeman & mem exec comt, Blair Co Dem Party, 74- Bus & Prof Pos: Counr, Mt Vernon City Schs, Ohio, 69-72, Portage Area Sch Dist, Pa, 72 & Adm Peary Area Voc-Tech Sch, Ebensburg, 73- Mem: Newry Lions (vpres, 74-75, pres, 75-); Grange (exec comt, Blair Co Patrons of Husbandry, 74-, doorkeeper, Scotch Valley, 74-); Blair Co Ancient Order of Hibernians (vpres, 75-); Blair Co League of Women Voters. Relig: Roman Catholic. Mailing Add: 211 South St Newry PA 16665

CASSTEVENS, BILL (D)
b Winston-Salem, NC, May 9, 28; married; c two. Educ: Lynchburg Col, BSBA. Polit & Govt Pos: Deleg, Dem Nat Mid-Term Conf, 74. Bus & Prof Pos: Secy-treas, Ohio State CAP Coun, UAW, currently, dir, Region 2, currently; mem exec bd, UAW Int; mem bd trustees, Med Mutual & Med Mutual Life Ins, Cleveland, currently. Mem: Metrop JOBS Coun; Ohio Gov's Comt Occup Safety & Health; Cleveland State Univ (bd trustees); Gtr Cleveland United Torch Serv; Ohio Gov's Coun Judicial Selection. Mailing Add: Rm 301 601 Rockwell Ave Cleveland OH 44114

CASTALDO, MARGARET HOUKE (D)
NH State Rep
b Des Moines, Iowa, July 27, 48; d Thomas Henry Houke & Mary Alice Davis H; m 1971 to Neil F Castaldo. Educ: George Peabody Col, BA, 70; George Washington Univ, MFA, 74. Polit & Govt Pos: NH State Rep, 75- Bus & Prof Pos: Teacher, Community Sch, Concord, NH, 71-72; art teacher, Rundlett Jr High, Concord, 72-74. Mem: Gtr Concord Child & Family Servs (clerk exec bd, 72-). Mailing Add: 292 Pleasant St Concord NH 03301

CASTELLINI, WILLIAM MCGREGOR (R)
Chmn, St Landry Parish Rep Exec Comt, La
b Cincinnati, Ohio, June 29, 28; s William A A Castellini & Ruth E McGregor C; m 1960 to Helen Louise Olivier. Educ: Univ Cincinnati, BBA, 49; Univ Southwestern La, 60-61; Alpha Kappa Psi; Scabbard & Blade; Phi Delta Theta. Polit & Govt Pos: Pres, St Landry Parish Rep Club, La, 64; alt deleg-at-lg, Rep Nat Conv, 64; mem-at-lg, St Landry Parish Rep Exec Comt, 64-72, chmn, 72-; committeeman, Fourth Ward Rep Comt, Opelousas, currently. Bus & Prof Pos: Owner, W M Castellini Co, 54-; pres, Calona Farms Inc, 63-72; pres, Cascala Inc, 73- Mil Serv: Entered as 2nd Lt, Army, 49, released as 1st Lt, 53; Ohio Nat Guard, 147th Inf Regt & Army Res, Lafayette, La, until 58; Third Korean War Winter Campaign Ribbon; Nat Defense Medal; United Nations Medal, Korean Presidential Citation. Mem: 37th Div Vets Asn; Opelousas Little Theatre (mem bd, past pres & secy); La Yambilee (mem bd, past pres, vpres & treas); La Sweet Potato Asn (bd dirs, 73-); St Landry Parish Sweet Potato Asn. Honors & Awards: Mr Yam, 69. Relig: Roman Catholic. Mailing Add: 330 Highland Dr Opelousas LA 70570

CASTILLO, ALVINO E (D)
NMex State Rep
Mailing Add: Drawer 68 Raton NM 87740

CASTILLO, JOSEPH A (D)
Chmn, Pima Co Bd Supvr
b Los Angeles, Calif, Dec 26, 33; s Joseph E Castillo & Feliciana Gallegos C; m 1952 to Dorothy V Rios; c Steven, Dorthina, Karl & Eric. Educ: Eagleton Inst of Polit, Rutgers Univ, summer 68. Polit & Govt Pos: Councilman, South Tucson, Ariz, 61-66; precinct committeeman, 62-66; Ariz State Sen, Dist 10, 67-72; chmn, South Tucson Housing Authority, 69-; dir, Tucson Community Coun, formerly; chmn, Pima Co Bd Supvr, Dist Five, 73- Bus & Prof Pos: Pres & owner, Pima Blueprint Co, Inc, Tucson; dir, Girls Club of Tucson. Mem: Soc Reproduction Engrs; Blueprinters Asn of Ariz; St Mary's Hosp; Lions Int; US CofC. Relig: Catholic. Mailing Add: 1520 N Camino Miraflores Tucson AZ 85705

CASTLE, MICHAEL NEWBOLD (R)
Del State Sen
b Wilmington, Del, July 2, 39; s James Manderson Castle, Jr & Louisa Bache C; single. Educ: Hamilton Col, AB, 61; Georgetown Univ Law Sch, LLB, 64; Alpha Delta Phi. Polit & Govt Pos: Mem bd dirs, Wilmington Young Rep, New Castle Co Young Rep, Del Young Rep, 64-; first vpres, Wilmington Young Rep, 64-; dep attorney gen, State Attorney Gen Off, 65-66; Del State Rep, Sixth Dist, 67-69; Del State Sen, 69- Bus & Prof Pos: Attorney, Connolly, Bove & Lodge, 64- Mem: DC, Del & Am Bar Asns. Relig: Roman Catholic. Mailing Add: Connolly Bove & Lodge Farmers Bank Bldg Wilmington DE 19801

CASTLE, ROBERT MARVIN (D)
Mem, Calif State Dem Cent Comt
b Lubbock, Tex, Oct 21, 20; s Robert Ira Castle & Clara Lillie Hammond C; m 1952 to Alice Louise Kern; c Jacqueline Patricia & Stephen Christopher. Educ: Tex Tech Col, BA, 47, MA, 51; Sigma Delta Pi; Phi Delta Kappa. Polit & Govt Pos: Mem, Calif State Dem Cent Comt, 58-; pres, Bakersfield Dem Club, 59; secy, Kern Co Dem Cent Comt, 60-62; co-chmn, 18th Cong Dist Cent Comt, 62-64; Vpres, 15th Dist Agr Asn, 62-66; deleg, Dem Nat Conv, 64 & 68; mem, Electoral Col, 64; comnr, Kern Co Housing Authority, 74- Bus & Prof Pos: Proj coordr, Kern Co High Sch Dist, 58-; asst prof, Fresno State Col Exten, 62-66. Mem: Calif Teachers Asn; Nat Educ Asn; Calif Asn of Adult Educ; Mason; Elks. Relig: Presbyterian. Mailing Add: 3311 Christmas Tree Lane Bakersfield CA 93306

CASTLEBERRY, KELLY L (D)
b South Charleston, WVa, Jan 17, 26; s William Thomas Castleberry & Thelma Stover C; m 1945 to Lorena Russe; c Kelly L, II, David & Martin. Educ: Pub schs of Kanawha Co. Polit & Govt Pos: WVa State Deleg, 60-66; mem, Kanawha Co Dem Exec Comt, formerly; deleg, Dem Nat Conv, 68; deleg, Dem Nat Mid-Term Conf, 74. Bus & Prof Pos: Realtor. Mil Serv: Army, 45-47. Mem: Mason (32 degree); Nat Asn Real Estate Bds; WVa Asn Realtors; Shrine; Royal Order of Jesters. Relig: Methodist. Mailing Add: 717 Jefferson St South Charleston WV 25309

CASTLES, WESLEY (NON-PARTISAN)
Assoc Justice, Mont Supreme Court
b Superior, Mont, Sept 26, 18; s William Castles & Catherine Irwin C; m 1939 to Ruth Olive Blake; c Susan Lynn (Mrs Billings), Judith Kay (Mrs Golberg) & Deborah Jane. Educ: Univ Mont, BS in forestry, 39, JD, 49. Polit & Govt Pos: Co attorney, Missoula Co, Mont, 52-53; chmn & exec secy, Unemploy Compensation Comn, Mont, 53-55; exec secy to Gov, 55-56; assoc justice, Mont Supreme Court, 57- Bus & Prof Pos: Chmn, Criminal Law Comn, Mont, at present. Mil Serv: Entered as Pvt, Army Air Corps, 44, released as Cpl, 45. Relig: Protestant. Mailing Add: York Rte Helena MT 59601

CASTRO, ALBERT C (D)
Mem-at-Lg, State Dem Party Wis
b Milwaukee, Wis, Jan 26, 28; s Albert Castro & Aurora Cardenas C; m 1954 to Patricia Louise Rutzen; c Jeffrey, Lisa Marie & David. Educ: Boys Tech High Sch, 42-45; Local 24 Grad Apprentice Sheet Metal Worker, 48-53. Polit & Govt Pos: Chmn, Greenfield, Greendale, Hales Corners Dem Unit, Wis, 69-71; mem, Milwaukee Co Dem Party Exec Bd, 69-73; mem-at-lg, State Dem Party Wis, 71-, state admin comt mem, 71-; chmn, McGovern Campaign Fourth Dist Wis, 72; deleg, Dem Nat Conv, 72; mem, Latin Caucus Dem Party, 72. Mil Serv: Entered as Pvt, Army, 45, released as Pfc, 47, after serving in 283-AAA AW Bn SP, Fourth Army, Ft Bliss, Tex. Mem: Local 24 Sheet Metal Workers AFL-CIO. Relig: Catholic; Mem, Holy Name Soc, St Johns Evangelist Church. Mailing Add: 4471 S 83rd St Greenfield WI 53220

CASTRO, RAMON (D)
Mem, Calif Dem State Cent Comt
b Monolith, Calif, Nov 8, 26; s Jose Castro & Arnulea Esparza C; m 1967 to Marian Dolores Bonner. Educ: Univ Calif, Berkeley, AB, 53; Univ San Francisco Sch of Law, LLB, 59; Univ Calif Honor Soc; Nat Soc Scabbard & Blade. Polit & Govt Pos: Dep city attorney, San Diego, Calif, 61-63; mem, Sen Robert Kennedy's Campaign Comt, San Diego Co, 68; co-chmn, Humphrey for President, San Diego Co, 68; mem, Calif Dem State Cent Comt, 68- Bus & Prof Pos: Attorney, San Diego, Calif, 63-65, Sheela, Lightner, Hughes & Castro, 66-; asst prof law, Univ San Diego, 66- Mil Serv: Entered as 2nd Lt, Army, Inf, 53, released as 1st Lt, 55, after serv in 69th & 9th Inf Div, continental US, 54-55, Res, 55-60. Mem: State Bar of Calif; San Diego Co Bar; Am Bar Asn; Am Judicature Soc; Am Trial Lawyers Asn. Relig: Catholic. Mailing Add: 4291 Arista Dr San Diego CA 92103

CASTRO, RAUL HECTOR (D)
Gov, Ariz
b Cananea, Sonora, Mex, June 12, 16; s Francisco D Castro & Rosario Acosta C; m 1947 to Patricia Norris; c Mary Pat & Beth E. Educ: Northern Ariz Univ, BA, 39, LLD; Univ Ariz, LLB, 49; Phi Alpha Delta; Phi Sigma Delta. Polit & Govt Pos: Dep Dist Attorney, Tucson, Ariz, 50-54, dist attorney, 54-58, juvenile court judge, 59-61, superior court judge, 62-64; US Ambassador to El Salvador, 64-68; US Ambassador to Bolivia, 68-70, deleg, Dem Nat Conv, 72; Gov, Ariz, 75- Bus & Prof Pos: Instr Spanish, Univ Ariz, 46-49; sr partner, Castro & Wolfe, Law Firm, Tucson, 49-51. Mil Serv: Entered as Pvt, Ariz Nat Guard, 37, released as 1st Sgt, 39, after serv in Inf, US. Publ: Several opinions while supreme court judge. Mem: Pima Co Bar Asn; Am Judiciary Soc; Nat Coun Juvenile Court Judges; Am Soc Int Law; Am Foreign Serv Asn. Honors & Awards: Outstanding Naturalized Citizen Award, Pima Bar Asn, 63; Americanism award, DAR, 64; Distinguished Pub Serv Award, Univ Ariz, 66; Matias Delgado Decoration, Govt El Salvador. Relig: Catholic. Legal Res: 3701 E River Rd Tucson AZ 85718 Mailing Add: State Capitol Phoenix AZ 85007

CASTRO, RICHARD THOMAS (D)
Colo State Rep
b Denver, Colo, Sept 29, 46; s Archie Castro & Josephine McGrath C; m 1972 to Virginia Lucero; c Chris, Phil, Ron, Brenda & Richard, Jr. Educ: Trinidad State Jr Col, AA, 68; Metro State Col, BA in Sociol, 70; Denver Univ, MSW in Community Orgn, 72. Bus & Prof Pos: Counr, Curtis Park Ctr, 68-69; counr, Denver Youth Serv, 69-70; ment health counr, Longmont, Colo, 70-71; dir, Westside Coalition, Neighborhood Planning Bd, 71-75; co-ed, Westside Recorder, Monthly, 72-74. Mem: YMCA; Colo Heart Asn; Plan Metro Denver; Common Cause; Westside Action Coun. Honors & Awards: Student of Year, Minority Students, Denver Univ, 72; Plaque of Appreciation given by residents in community; hon mem Colo Correction Asn. Relig: Catholic. Legal Res: 159 W Ellsworth Denver CO 80223 Mailing Add: State Capitol Bldg Denver CO 80203

CASTRO, THOMAS HENRY (D)
Mem, Calif Dem State Cent Comt
b Huntington Park, Calif, July 30, 54; s Henry Thomas Castro & Thelma Contreras C; single. Educ: Univ Madrid, 75; Harvard Col, 75- Polit & Govt Pos: Campaign aide, Humphrey for President, Calif, 72; legis intern, Mass Gen Assembly, 72-73; nat youth dir, Dem Nat Comt, 73; statewide field coordr, Alan Cranston for US Senate, 74; legis aide, US Sen Alan Cranston, 75-; mem, Calif Dem State Cent Comt, 75- Bus & Prof Pos: Pres, Proj Develop Educ Resources, Inc, Cambridge, Mass, 73-74; dir commun, Jobs for Progress, Inc, Los Angeles, Calif, 74-75. Mem: World Affairs Coun; Am Coun Young Polit Leaders; Harvard Club Southern Calif; Nat Cong Hispanic Citizens; Soaring Soc Am. Honors & Awards: Spec guest, XVII Int Inst Iberoam Lit Cong, 75. Relig: Roman Catholic. Mailing Add: 2904 Live Oak Huntington Park CA 90255

CASTRO, WILLIAM A (D)
RI State Sen
Mailing Add: 110 Brown St East Providence RI 02914

CASWELL, JEANNE MARIE (D)
Mem Exec Comt, Washington Co Dem Party, Ore
b Bemidji, Minn, Aug 11, 52; d Richard Lowell Caswell & Shirley Mae Barclay C; m 1975 to Patrick James Furrer. Educ: Portland State Univ, BS, 75; Univ Ore, 74-75. Polit & Govt Pos: Dem Precinct committeewoman, 71-; mem exec comt, Washington Co Dem Party, Ore,

71-; deleg, Ore State Dem Conv, 72; deleg, Dem Nat Conv, 72. Bus & Prof Pos: Alternatives dir, Metrop Pub Defender, 70- Publ: Co-auth, Oregon Judges Sentencing Handbook, 74. Mem: Ore Corrections Asn; Common Cause; Nat Womens Polit Action Comt; Co Drug Adv Bd; Co Womens Corrections Bd. Mailing Add: 10250 SW McDonald St Tigard OR 97223

CATALDO, ANGELO R (D)
Mass State Rep
Mailing Add: State Capitol Boston MA 02133

CATANIA, SUSAN (R)
Ill State Rep
b Chicago, Ill, Dec 10, 41; d John J Kmetty & Helen Giffrow K; m 1963 to Anthony Edward Catania; c Susan, Rachel, Sara, Melissa & Amy. Educ: St Xavier Col, Ill, BA in Chem; Northwestern Univ, grad work in chem; Sigma Phi Sigma. Polit & Govt Pos: Ill State Rep, 73-; chairwoman, Ill Comn on the Status of Women, 74- Bus & Prof Pos: Info dir, W C McCrone Assocs, 63-70; self-employed free lance tech ed, 70- Publ: Ed, Gas Chromatography, Marcel Dekker, 72; co-auth, Failure analysis of integrated circuits, State Microscopical Soc of Ill Centennial Proc. Mem: Soc for Tech Commun; Am Chem Soc; Nat Orgn Women. Honors & Awards: Scholar, Univ Colo, 62; Relig: Roman Catholic. Legal Res: 2801 S Michigan Ave Chicago IL 60616 Mailing Add: State House Springfield IL 62706

CATE, BYRON LEE (D)
Okla State Sen
b Norman, Okla, Jan 18, 42; s Roscoe Simmons Cate, Jr & Frances Ethel Mitchell C; m 1963 to Sylvia Sharon Martin; c Christie Lee, Byron Lee, Jr & Chad Mitchell. Educ: Univ Okla Col Law, JD, 72; Phi Gamma Delta. Polit & Govt Pos: Justice of the Peace, First Dist, Norman, Okla, 64-66; Okla State Rep, 44th Dist, Cleveland Co, 66-74; Okla State Sen, 75- Mem: Okla Bar Asn; Jaycees; Okla Coun on Environ (mem exec comt); CofC. Honors & Awards: Nominated for Three Outstanding Young Oklahomans, Norman Jaycees, 69. Relig: Presbyterian. Mailing Add: 2712 Aspen Circle Norman OK 73069

CATE, GEORGE H (D)
NH State Rep
Mailing Add: 101 Landaff Rd Landaff NH 03585

CATE, JOHN O (R)
NH State Rep
Mailing Add: RFD 8 Concord NH 03301

CATE, MILTON A (R)
NH State Rep
Mailing Add: 40 Charles St Penacook NH 03301

CATE, REX (D)
Committeeman, Ark State Dem Party
b Boydsville, Ark, June 5, 29; s Roy L Cate & Fannie Benson C; div; c Rex Neil. Educ: Ark State Col, 47-48. Polit & Govt Pos: Chmn, Alexander for Cong, Clay Co, Ark, 68, Dale Bumpers for Gov, 70 co coordr, 72; committeeman, Ark State Dem Comt, 70-; mem, Clay Co Dem Comt, 73-; co coordr, Bumpers for US Senate, 74. Bus & Prof Pos: Star route mail carrier, 49-51; mgr, McDougal Gin Co, 55-63, Pfeiffer Gin Co Inc, 63- Mil Serv: Entered as Pvt, Army, 51, released as Cpl, 52, after serv in 57th Field Artil, Eighth Div, Korea; Korean Serv Medal with Two Bronze Serv Stars; UN Serv Medal. Mem: Southern Ginners Asn (bd of dirs); Mason (32 degree); Am Legion (comdr); CofC; Ark Jaycees. Relig: Methodist. Mailing Add: Box 114 Piggott AR 72454

CATES, CHARLES BRADLEY (BRAD) (R)
NMex State Rep
b Mt Vernon, Ill, Apr 20, 50; s Marshal Byrne Cates & Jean Starwalt C; single. Educ: NMex State Univ, BBA, 72; Univ NMex, JD, 75; Blue Key; Sigma Chi; pres & exec vpres, Assoc Students, NMex State Univ. Polit & Govt Pos: Mem, NMex Rep State Exec Comt, 71-72; vpres, NMex Young Rep, 72; chmn youth adv comt, US Dept Transportation, 72-74; NMex State Rep, Dist 27, 75-, mem, Judiciary & Pub Affairs Comt, NMex House Rep, 75-; mem, NMex Rep State Cent Comt, 75- Bus & Prof Pos: Aide, White House Domestic Coun, summers 73 & 74; real estate salesman, 72- Mem: March of Dimes (bd dirs, Albuquerque, 74-); Young Rep. Relig: Presbyterian. Mailing Add: 4509 Dona Marguerita NE Albuquerque NM 87111

CATES, ERIC O, JR (D)
Ala State Rep
Mailing Add: Rte 2 Box 222 Greenville AL 36037

CATES, PHILLIP RAY (D)
Tex State Rep
b Pampa, Tex, Jan 6, 47; s Herman Ray Cates & Laverne Robertson C; m 1970 to Nancy Kay Holt. Educ: Western Tex State Univ, BS, 69; Lambda Chi Alpha; Alpha Phi Omega. Polit & Govt Pos: Tex State Rep, Dist 66, 71- Bus & Prof Pos: Staff, Cabot Corp, Pampa, Tex, currently. Mem: Pampa CofC; Gray-Roberts Co Farm Bur; Gray-Roberts Co Farmers Union. Relig: Baptist. Legal Res: 709 Mora Pampa TX 79065 Mailing Add: Box 2910 Capitol Station Austin TX 78767

CATHER, CHARLES WILLIAM (D)
Kans State Rep
b Oklahoma City, Okla, Mar 16, 44; s Charles Ivan Cather & Mary Morgan C; m 1964 to Linda Kay Prohoroff; c Michelle, Melissa, Charles & Stacy. Educ: Univ Okla, BA, 66; Oklahoma City Univ, JD, 69; Phi Delta Phi. Polit & Govt Pos: Kans State Rep, 71- Bus & Prof Pos: Salesman, Southwestern Bell Tel Co, 64-66; contract negotiator, Air Force Logistics Command, 66-70; lawyer, Davis, Bruce, David & Cather, Attorneys, 70-73 & Blase, Holloway, Blase & Cather, 73-75; William Cather Attorney, 75- Mem: Kans, Okla & Wichita Bar Asns; Mason. Relig: Unitarian. Mailing Add: 2935 S Seneca Wichita KS 67217

CATHEY, ROBERT REYNOLDS, SR (R)
Chmn, Maury Co Rep Party, Tenn
b Marshall Co, Tenn, Apr 16, 32; s Robert Lee Cathey & Grace Reynolds C; m 1953 to Laura Barnes; c Barbara Lynn, Nancy Ann, Christie Leigh & Robert, Jr. Educ: Mid Tenn State Univ, BSecon, 54; Track & Sabre Club. Polit & Govt Pos: Chmn, Maury Co Rep Party, Tenn, 74- Mil Serv: Entered as 2nd Lt, Army, 55, released as 1st Lt, 58, after serv in 8th Army,

Korea, 56-57. Mem: Nat Asn Independent Ins Agents; Maury Co CofC (pres, 73-74); Maury Co Insurors; Kiwanis (pres, 73-74); Maury Co United Givers Fund (pres, 75-). Honors & Awards: Long Rifle Award, Boy Scouts Am, 72. Relig: Methodist. Legal Res: 205 Haven Circle Columbia TN 38401 Mailing Add: Box 311 Columbia TN 38401

CATLETT, LEON BIDEZ (D)
b Dardanelle, Ark, Mar 26, 09; s Samuel Graham Catlett & Alix Bidez C; m 1936 to Sally Cooper. Educ: Univ Ark, LLB, 32; Kappa Alpha; Phi Alpha Delta. Polit & Govt Pos: Secy, Ark Dem State Comt, 60-63, chmn, 63-68. Bus & Prof Pos: Vchmn bd trustees, Univ Ark, 60-70. Mil Serv: Pvt, Army, 42-43. Mem: Am Legion; Country Club of Little Rock; Little Rock Club; Capitol Club; Ark Consistory. Relig: Presbyterian; elder. Mailing Add: 727 Pyramid Bldg Little Rock AR 72201

CATO, L E (D)
Mem, Ga State Dem Exec Comt
b Warm Springs, Ga, Oct 25, 35; s Edward Cato & Gertrude Criswell C; m 1962 to Rita Henderson; c Von & Vic. Educ: Univ Houston, 53-55; Ga State Univ, 58-59; Mercer Univ, Atlanta, BSPharm, 62; Sigma Nu. Polit & Govt Pos: Chmn, Spalding Co Busbee Gov Campaign, 75; mem, Ga State Dem Exec Comt, 75-; mem drafting comt, Ga Dem Charter Comn, currently. Bus & Prof Pos: Chief pharmacist, St Joseph Hosp, Atlanta, Ga, 61-62; pres, Cato Corp, Griffin, 62- & Mid-Ga Cattlemen's Asn, 74- Publ: Auth, Articles in Mid-Ga Beef Cattlemens Asn Bull Sheet, Ga Cattlemens Asn & Atlanta J. Mem: Am Cattlemens Asn; Am Pharmaceutical Asn; Ga Cattlemens Asn (bd dirs); Elks; Moose. Honors & Awards: Lunsford-Richardson Pharm Award, 60; Leadership Award, Nat Col Coun for the UN, 57. Relig: Baptist. Legal Res: Rte 1 Box 29 Williamson GA 30292 Mailing Add: 315 S Eighth St Griffin GA 30223

CATT, VIRGINIA ANN (D)
Dem Nat Committeewoman, Nev
b Chicago, Ill, Feb 18, 31; d Joseph A Piekut & Anna Formella P; m 1957 to Charles E Catt; c Donald Norman, Julie Ann & Trudy Marie. Educ: John Marshall Law Sch, 3 years. Polit & Govt Pos: Secy, Las Vegas Young Dem, Nev, 55-57, pres, 63-64; clerk of Justice Court, Las Vegas Twp, 55-57; secy, Nev State Dem Cent Comt, 56-58, mem, 58-68, treas, 64-66; alt deleg, Dem Nat Conv, 56; precinct capt & mem, Clark Co Dem Cent Comt, 56-71, chairwoman, 60-62; Nat Committeewoman, Young Dem of Nev, 57-59, 61-63, 67-69, state pres, 64-67; mem coord comt & chmn banquet & luncheon, Young Dem Clubs of Am Nat Conv, 63 & 69; campaign secy, Howard W Cannon Sen Campaign, 64; state vchmn, Citizens for Kennedy, 67-68; Dem Nat Committeewoman, Nev, 72-; deleg, Dem Nat Mid-Term Conf, 74. Mem: Paradise Bus & Prof Women's Club; Las Vegas Legal Secys; Las Vegas Press Club; Clark Co Parents & Teachers Orgn. Relig: Catholic. Mailing Add: 343 Desert Inn Rd E Las Vegas NV 89109

CATTERSON, JAMES M, JR (R)
b Long Island, NY, July 5, 30; s James M Catterson & Dorothy Downs C; m 1955 to Lola Fae Hartwig; c Lynn Fae & James Michael. Educ: Niagara Univ, AB, cum laude, 52; St John's Univ Sch Law, LLB, 58; Delta Epsilon Sigma; Phi Delta Phi. Polit & Govt Pos: Asst Attorney Gen, State of New York, 58-59; Asst US Attorney, Eastern Dist NY, 59-61; Asst Dist Attorney, Chief Rackets Bur, Suffolk Co, 63-67; Rep cand, US House Rep, First Cong Dist, 66 & 68; counsel to Majority Leader, NY State Assembly, 69-74, counsel to Minority, 75- Bus & Prof Pos: Partner, Catterson & Nolan, Attorneys, 68-; counsel, NY Chap, Prof Air Traffic Controllers Orgn, 69- Mil Serv: Entered as 2nd Lt, Army, 52, released as 1st Lt, 55, after serv in 19th Inf Regt, 24th US Div, Korea, 53-54; Army Res, 54-66, Maj; Korean Serv Medal; UN Serv Medal; Am Defense Ribbon; ROK Presidential Citation. Mem: Maryhaven Sch for Retarded Children (adv bd); Suffolk Co & Fed Bar Asns; NY State Dist Attorney's Asn. Relig: Roman Catholic. Legal Res: Druid Hill Rd Belle Terre Port Jefferson NY 11777 Mailing Add: 314 Main St Port Jefferson NY 11777

CATZ, PHYLLIS FOX (D)
Committeeperson, 151st Dem Area Comt, Pa
b Pittsburgh, Pa, June 24, 42; d Sam Fox & Ruth D Pollas F; m 1964 to Sanford J Catz; c Sheryl & Ellen. Educ: Chatham Col, BA, 64; Univ Pittsburgh; Carnegie-Mellon Univ; Temple Univ; Beaver Col, Lehigh Univ; Marywood Col; Mortar Bd. Polit & Govt Pos: Committeeperson, 151st Dem Area Comt, Pa, 71-; deleg, Dem Nat Conv, 72; bd mem, Montgomery Co Bd Welfare, 72- Bus & Prof Pos: Soc worker, Pa Dept Pub Welfare, summers 63 & 64; instr, Pittsburgh Pub Schs, 64-65 & Springfield High Sch, Montgomery Co, 65-67 & 72- Mem: Nat Educ Asn; Nat Women's Polit Caucus (local convener); Am Asn Univ Women; Lower Gwynedd Educ Study Group; Concerned Citizens for Educ. Mailing Add: 309 Llewellyn Rd Ambler PA 19002

CAUBLE, FLORENCE HORKAN (R)
Mem Exec Comt, Ga Rep Party
b Moultrie, Ga, July 4, 29; d George Arthur Horkan & Martha Olliff H; m 1950 to Dr John A Cauble; c Sally, Susan & David. Educ: Wesleyan Col, AB, 50. Polit & Govt Pos: Pres, Cherokee Co Fedn Rep Women, Ga, 60-65; dir women's activities, Ninth Cong Dist, Prince Cong Campaign, 64; Ninth Cong Dist Dir, Ga Fedn Rep Women, 64-65, treas, 65-68; vchmn, Cherokee Co Rep Party, 64-66; chmn, Co Conv Comt, Ga Rep Party, 66, mem, Ninth Dist Comt & State Comt, 66-68, mem, Exec Comt, 68-; Rep Nat Committeewoman, 68-72. Bus & Prof Pos: Teacher, DeKalb Co, Ga, 50-51. Honors & Awards: Callaway Award, Outstanding Rep Woman, Ga, 66. Relig: Methodist. Legal Res: Sunset Dr Canton GA 30114 Mailing Add: Rte 6 Box 51 Canton GA 30114

CAUBLE, JOHN A (R)
Mem, Ga State Rep Comt
b Lupton City, Tenn, Jan 1, 28; s George Clifford Cauble & Charlotte Honeycutt C; m 1950 to Florence Horkan; c Sally, Susan & David Horkan. Educ: Emory Jr Col, Oxford, Ga, 44-46; Emory Univ, BA, 49; Emory Univ Sch Med, MD, 54; Phi Delta Theta. Polit & Govt Pos: Chmn, Cherokee Co Rep Party, Ga, 64-68 & 71-72; chmn, Ninth Cong Dist Rep Party, 66-70; mem, Ga State Rep Exec Comt, 66-70; deleg Rep Nat Conv, 68, mem, Ga State Rep Comt, currently. Bus & Prof Pos: Physician, Canton, Ga, 56- Mil Serv: Entered as Pvt, Army, 46, released as Sgt, 47. Mem: Am Med Asn; Acad Gen Practitioners; Med Asn Ga; Ga Med Polit Action Comt; Cherokee-Pickens Med Soc. Relig: Methodist. Legal Res: Rte 6 Box 51 Canton GA 30114 Mailing Add: 200 Marietta St Canton GA 30114

CAUDELL, JAMES A (R)
NMex State Rep
Mailing Add: 1704 Tomasita NE Albuquerque NM 87112

CAUDILLO, SONIA RAMIREZ (D)
b San Jose, Calif, July 29, 36; d Salome T Caudillo & Marcelina Ramirez C; div. Educ: San Jose City Col, 56-57; Foothill Col, Calif, 71-73. Polit & Govt Pos: Secy, Mex-Am Polit Asn, 70-71, northern regional secy, 72-73; deleg, Tenth Cong Dist Dem Party, 70-72; deleg, Santa Clara Co Dem Cent Comt, 70-; deleg, Calif Dem State Cent Comt, 70-; deleg, 17th Cong Dist Dem Party, 73-; alt deleg, Dem Nat Conv, 72. Mem: Family Coun Ctr (bd dirs, 72-). Honors & Awards: Honor, Dem Party, 72. Legal Res: 1489 Monroe St Santa Clara CA Mailing Add: Apt 31 660 Tyrella Mountain View CA 94040

CAUDLE, JOSEPH EDWARD (D)
WVa State Deleg
b Camp Lejune, NC, June 3, 45; s Robert Earl Caudle & Jeanne Lyerla C; m 1970 to Paula Jean Butcher. Educ: US Air Force Acad, Nat Hon Soc scholar, 63, BS Physics, 67; Univ Hamburg Physical Inst, Fulbright scholar, MS, 68; Georgetown Univ, grad work, 69; Georgetown Univ Law Ctr, 74-; US Air Force Acad Asn Grad. Polit & Govt Pos: WVa State Deleg, 75- Bus & Prof Pos: Physicist, Presearch Inc & Vitro Labs, 71-74. Mil Serv: Entered as 2nd Lt, Air Force, 67, released as Capt, after serv in AFTAC, Washington, DC, 68-71; Capt, Air Force Reserve, 75. Publ: Co-auth, A review of strategic offensive & defensive draft Presidential memoranda-1961-1968, 69 & auth, Nuclear pumped laser concept, 73, US Air Force J; auth, Countermeasures Options Against Deepwater Mines, Presearch Inc, 72. Mem: Jaycees, Kiwanis; Explorer Scouts (adv). Honors & Awards: Jaycee Spoke Award. Mailing Add: 100 S Raleigh St Martinsburg WV 25401

CAUFIELD, JUDITH ANN (D)
b Madison, Ind, Aug 3, 43; d Walter N Leach & Effie S Horine L; m 1965 to Louis A Caufield; c Lisa Ann, Lori Ann, Leslie Ann & Louis Albert, Jr. Educ: Eastern Ky Univ, BS, 65; Univ Wash, 70-; Student Nat Educ Asn; Newman Club; Young Dem; Col Choir & Band. Polit & Govt Pos: Acting chmn credentials comt, King Co Dem Conv, Wash, 72; mem credentials comt, Wash Dem State Conv, 72; alt deleg, Dem Nat Conv, 72. Bus & Prof Pos: Teacher, New Albany, Ind, 65-66, Jeffersonville, 66 & Renton, Wash, 67-; counsr-tutor, Culturally Disadvantaged Prog, Renton Sch Dist, 69-70. Mem: Nat, Wash & Renton Educ Asns; Citizens for the Specific Lang Disability Child; St Stephen Martyr Comt for Cath Educ. Relig: Roman Catholic. Legal Res: 17016 128th Ave SE Renton WA 98055 Mailing Add: PO Box 524 Renton WA 98055

CAUTHORN, JOSEPHINE F (D)
Ariz State Rep
Mailing Add: 1830 E Spring St Tucson AZ 85719

CAVANAUGH, JOHN J, III
Nebr State Sen
Mailing Add: 1919 S 35th Ave Omaha NE 68105

CAVNAR, SAMUEL MELMON (R)
Mem, Nev State Rep Comt
b Denver, Colo, Nov 10, 25; m 1948 to Lenora Woodgate; c Dona (Mrs Joseph Hambly) & Judy (Mrs Terry Wallen). Polit & Govt Pos: Spec consult, Individual US Sen & Congressmen, 52-; mem, Allott for US Sen Comt, Colo, 54 & 60; mem, Celebrities for Goldwater Comt, 66; mem, Celebrities for Reagan for Gov, 66-70; nat gen chmn, Oper Houseclean, 66, 68 & 72-74; nat cand chmn, Citizens Comt to Elect Rep Legislators, 66, 68, 70 & 72-74; mem, Calif State & Los Angeles Co Rep Cent Comts, formerly; nat gen chmn, Proj Prayer; exec dir, Proj Alert; cand, US Rep, 30th Cong Dist, Calif, 68 & 70; mem, Celebrities for Nixon Comt, 68-72; publ, Nat Rep Statesman, Washington, DC, 69-; nat chmn, Nat Labor Reform Comt, 69-; sustaining mem, Rep Nat Comt; western states chmn & nat co-chmn, Am Taxpayers Army; area II chmn, Gov Welfare Reform Comt, 70; mem, Dominick for US Senate Comt; mem, Spec Citizens for Towell for Cong Comt, 72; cand for US Sen, Nev, 74; gen chmn, Comt Law & Order in Am, 75; mem, Nev State Rep Comt, currently; mem, Clark Co Rep Comt, currently. Bus & Prof Pos: Dist mgr, US CofC, eight western states, 53-58; owner, Cavnar & Assocs, Mgt Consult, Washington, DC, Las Vegas, Denver & Reseda, Calif, 58-; nat chmn & bd dirs, Civic Asn of Am, 60-; vpres, Lenz Assoc Advert, Inc, Van Nuys, 60-; dist mgr west states, Nu-Orm Plans, Inc; consult to architect & contractor, First US Missile Site, Wyo; prin organizer, Westway Corp & Subsidiaries, Southern Calif Develop Co; chmn, bd dirs, Boy Sponsors, Inc, Denver; pres, Continental Am Video Network Asn Registry, Inc, 67-; pres, United Sales Am, Las Vegas & Denver, 69-; sr mgt consult, Broadcast Mgt Consult Serv, Hollywood, Las Vegas, Denver & Washington, DC, 70-; pres, dir & mem exec comt, Am Ctr for Educ, currently; publ, Nat Independent, Washington, DC, 70-, Nat Labor Reform Leader, 70- & Nat Conserv Statesman, 75-; author & lectr. Mil Serv: Combat Vet, Navy, 42-45, Amphibious Forces, Pac & Atlantic Theatres; Air Force Res, Korean War; Comdr, 20th Air Div US Coast Guard Auxiliary Search & Rescue Forces for four Western states, 59-60. Publ: Auth, Run Big Sam Run, 76. Mem: Return Pueblo Comt (Chmn); Am Legion (past Comdr & mem, Nat Conv Distinguished Guest Comt); DAV; VFW; Air Power Mem Stadium Found & Air Power Show. Honors & Awards: Spec awards from Rotary, Toastmaster & Lions; aide-de-camp to Gov Ky; Good Citizenship Award, SAR; Ky Col. Legal Res: Apt 212 3196 Maryland Pkwy Paradise Valley NV 89109 Mailing Add: 300 1430 K St NW Washington DC 20005

CAWLEY, CLIFFORD J (D)
RI State Rep
Mailing Add: 2556 Pawtucket Ave East Providence RI 02914

CAWLEY, ROBERT LUCIAN (D)
Committeeman, Fifth Suffolk Dem Dist, Mass
b Boston, Mass, July 30, 34; s Michael Joseph Cawley & Delia A Conway C; m 1962 to Patricia A O'Sullivan; c Christopher, Suzanne, Robert & Laura. Educ: Boston Col, BSBA, 60; Northeastern Univ, MA, 73. Polit & Govt Pos: Mass State Rep, 63-68; committeeman, Fifth Suffolk Dem Dist, 68-; Mass State Sen, 69-72, dir, Senate Personnel, 73- Bus & Prof Pos: Sales prom mgr, Signet Club Play, 61-63. Mil Serv: Entered as Pvt, Marine Corps, 52, released as Cpl, 55, after serv in First Marine Div, Korea, 53; Presidential Unit Citation with two battle stars; Purple Heart; Good Conduct Medal; Korean Presidential Unit Citation. Mem: Mass Legis Asn; VFW; Am Legion; Order of Purple Heart; KofC. Honors & Awards: One of Ten Outstanding Young Men of Gtr Boston, 69. Relig: Catholic. Mailing Add: 53 Chesbrough Rd West Roxbury MA 02132

CAWOOD, F CHRIS (D)
Tenn State Rep
Mailing Add: 1413 Market Chattanooga TN 37411

CAWTHORN, MERLE SLOAN (D)
b Grand Cane, La, Feb 8, 19; d William Oscar Sloan & Birdie Griffin S; m 1938 to Joe Terrell Cawthorn, wid; c Melody Merle. Educ: Grand Cane High Sch, La, grad, 35. Polit & Govt Pos: Clerk, Agr Exten Serv, La, 37-38; mem, La State Dem Cent Comt, formerly; alt deleg, Dem Nat Conv, 68; Outreach coordinator, De Soto Area Action Asn, local Off Econ Opportunity, La, 69-70; exec dir, Housing Authority, Mansfield, La, 70- Bus & Prof Pos: Owner, Melody Realty Co, Mansfield, La, 60-69. Mem: De Soto Dept Club; Mansfield Elem PTA; Mansfield Garden Club; Mansfield High Sch Band Boosters Club. Honors & Awards: Lady Citizen Award, De Soto Dept Club, Mansfield, 65. Relig: Baptist; Pres, Dorcus Sunday Sch Class, First Baptist Church. Legal Res: Highland Dr Mansfield LA 71062 Mailing Add: PO Box 671 Mansfield LA 71052

CAWTHORNE, DENNIS OTTO (R)
Mich State Rep
b Manistee, Mich, Apr 29, 40; s Clifford Haney Cawthorne & Marie Schimke C; single. Educ: Albion Col, AB, 62; Harvard Univ Law Sch, JD, 65; Phi Beta Kappa; Omicron Delta Kappa; Sigma Chi. Polit & Govt Pos: Deleg, Nat Legis Conf, 67, 70 & 72; Mich State Rep, 67-, Rep Leader Mich House of Rep, 75- Bus & Prof Pos: Cong asst, Rep Robert P Griffin, Washington, DC, 57-58; mgr, Mackinac Island CofC, 62-65; instr, Muskegon Community Col, 65-66. Mem: State Bar Mich; Eagles; Jaycees. Honors & Awards: One of Five Outstanding Young Men of Mich, Mich Jaycees, 71. Relig: Roman Catholic. Legal Res: 510 Browning Ave Manistee MI 49660 Mailing Add: House of Rep Capitol Bldg Lansing MI 48901

CAYETANO, BENJAMIN JEROME (D)
Hawaii State Rep
b Honolulu, Hawaii, Nov 14, 39; s Bonifacio Marcos Cayetano & Eleanor Infante C; m 1958 to Lorraine Gueco; c Brandon, Janeen & Samantha. Educ: Univ Calif, Los Angeles, BA, 68; Loyola Univ Sch Law, JD, 71. Polit & Govt Pos: Comnr, Hawaii Housing Authority, 72-74; Hawaii State Rep, 74- Bus & Prof Pos: Attorney-at-law, self-employed, 71-75. Mem: Oahu Metrop Planning Orgn. Mailing Add: 1835 Palamoi St Pearl City HI 96782

CAYFORD, WESTON LLOYD (WES) (R)
b Spokane, Wash, June 6, 25; s Howard Henry Cayford & Edith Parr C (by adoption); m 1955 to Colleen Norma Orr; c Merry Edith Gines, Diana Smith, Stephanie Hardin, Dennis Deen, Laura & Allyson Cayford. Educ: Emmett High Sch, Idaho, grad, 44. Polit & Govt Pos: Finance chmn, Gem Co Rep Cent Comt, Idaho, 70, chmn, formerly. Mem: Gem Co CofC; Gem Co Horse Racing Asn. Relig: Baptist. Legal Res: Rte 3 Emmett ID 83617 Mailing Add: PO Box 402 Emmett ID 83617

CECCARELLI, DAVID PAUL (D)
Wash State Rep
b Seattle, Wash, June 1, 33; s Henry Paul Ceccarelli & Helen Lundberg C; m 1953 to Lois Ann Mortensen; c Paul David, John Michael, Daniel Richard & Joseph Andrew. Educ: Seattle Univ, BCS in Com & Finance, 55; Pan Xina. Polit & Govt Pos: Wash State Rep, 34th Dist, 67- Bus & Prof Pos: Advert, Gen Elec Co, 53-58; dist mgr, Libby McNeill & Libby, 58-; sales, Quadrant Corp, 70- Mem: Univ Toastmasters; West Seattle Coun Youth Affairs (bd mem). Relig: Catholic. Mailing Add: 1330 Harbor Ave SW Seattle WA 98116

CECIL, ELMER JAMES (DFL)
Vchmn, Beltrami Co Dem-Farmer-Labor Party, Minn
b Williston, NDak, June 7, 22; s Elmer E Cecil & Lois Agnes Bennett C; m 1953 to Lorraine Freadhoff; c Catherine, James & Thomas. Educ: Univ NDak, PhB, 49; Univ Wis, Madison, MS, Polit Sci, 58; Univ Minn, Minneapolis, 61-65; Jr Class Pres, Student Coun; Theta Chi. Polit & Govt Pos: Co coordr, Bergland for Cong Campaign, 68; vchmn, Beltrami Co Dem-Farmer-Labor Party, Minn, 68-; coordr, Rep Bob Falk, Sen Gene Mammenga, Gov Anderson, Bob Bergland & Sen Humphrey, 70; coordr, Treas Mammenga for Sen Comt, Dist 64A, 70; adv, Bemidji State Col Dem-Farmer-Labor Group, 70-71; co-chmn, Beltrami Co Comt, Anderson for Gov Campaign, 71. Bus & Prof Pos: Teacher, pub high schs, NDak & Minn, 52-61; asst prof polit sci, Bemidji State Col, 65-; mem, City Charter comn, Bemidji, Minn, 70. Mil Serv: Entered as Pfc, Army, 41, released as T/S, 45, after serv in 164th Inf Regt, Americal Div, SPac Theatre, 42-45; Combat Inf Badge, three campaigns, Philippines Liberation; Presidential Unit Citation, Navy; Bronze Star. Publ: Findings of Bemidji Upward Bound Pollsters Similar to National Results, Idea Exchange, 4/68; co-auth, Micro-City: Attitude Study of Three Cities, Quart Digest Urban & Regional Research, summer 69. Mem: Minn State Col Inter-Faculty Orgn; Am Legion; Elks. Relig: Roman Catholic. Mailing Add: 1211 Bixby Ave Bemidji MN 56601

CECILE, ROBERT EARL (D)
b Syracuse, NY, Nov 25, 30; s Earl Francis Cecile & Marie Damico C; m 1951 to Norma Jean McBurney; c Robert E, Jr, David J, Karen M, Daniel D, Kathy A, Joseph L, & James H. Educ: Syracuse Univ; Univ Dayton; Miami Univ; Univ Southern Miss, BS, 61; Univ Okla, MA, 63, PhD, 65; Nat Defense Educ Act grad fel, 3 years; Pi Sigma Alpha; Pi Gamma Mu. Polit & Govt Pos: Dem cand, US House of Rep, Seventh Cong Dist, Ohio, 68; mem, Ohio Comt to Revise Struct of Nat Conv & Party Selection, 69; pres, Clark Co Young Dem Club, 69; mem, Clark Co Dem Exec Comt, formerly; mem, Ohio State Dem Exec Comn, 69-70; cand, Dem nomination for secy of state, Ohio, 70; mem, Ohio Dem Platform comn, summer, 70; field coordr, Howard Metzenbaum for US Senate, 70; exec asst to Gov John J Gilligan, Ohio, 71-73; chmn, Educ Comn of the States, 71-; chmn, Am Revolution Bicentennial Adv Comn, 72-75; comnr, Ohio Youth Comn, 73-75; mem campaign staff, John Glenn for US Sen, 74. Bus & Prof Pos: Teaching asst polit sci, Univ Okla, 64-65; asst prof polit sci, Winona State Col, 65-66; naval intel agent, Off Naval Intel, Washington, DC, 65; asst prof polit sci, Wright State Univ, 66-69, acting chmn dept, 67-68; assoc prof, Cent State Univ, Wilberforce, Ohio, 69-71; mem, Mad River Green Local Bd of Educ, Clark Co, Ohio, 70-; assoc dean, Syracuse Univ, 75- Mil Serv: Entered as Pvt, Air Force, 50, released as T/Sgt, 62, after serv in Strategic Air Command, US, Europe & MidE, 52-54; Lt Comdr, Naval Res, 64-74; Aircrew-member Badge; Nat Defense Medal; Expert Pistol; Army of Occup, Germany Ribbon; Good Conduct Medal. Publ: Frame of Reference for Study of American Foreign Policy, J Minn Acad Sci, 68; Teaching American Foreign Policy in Secondary Schools, Soc Stud, 68. Mem: Am Polit Sci Asn; Midwest Polit Sci Asn; ALF-CIO (pres, Wright State Univ Fedn of Teachers, deleg, Dayton-Miami Valley Labor Coun); NAACP; Lions Int. Relig: Catholic. Mailing Add: 121 Ruskin Ave Syracuse NY 13207

CEDERBERG, ELFORD A (R)
US Rep, Mich
b Bay City, Mich, Mar 6, 18; married; c two. Educ: Bay City Jr Col. Polit & Govt Pos: Mayor, Bay City, Mich, 49-51; US Rep, 52-; deleg, Rep Nat Conv, 68. Bus & Prof Pos: Mgr, Nelson

Mfg Co. Mil Serv: 41-45, Capt, participant in Normandy Invasion, France & Ger; 5 Battle Stars; Bronze Star. Mem: Lions (past pres); Elks; Odd Fellows; Mason (33 degree); Am Legion. Relig: Evangelical. Legal Res: Midland MI 48640 Mailing Add: 7100 Sussex Pl Alexandria VA 22307

CEFKIN, J LEO (D)
Chmn, Fourth Cong Dist Dem Party, Colo
b Rochester, NY, Mar 16, 16; s Mischa Cefkin & Bluma Jacobson C; m 1949 to Rose Mackanick; c Judith B, Barbara L, Jonathan S & Melissa S. Educ: Los Angeles City Col, AA, 39; Univ Southern Calif, BA, 48; Columbia Univ, MA, 49, PhD, 54; Pi Sigma Alpha. Polit & Govt Pos: Precinct committeeman, Larimer Co Dem Party, Colo, 58-72; deleg, Colo Dem State Conv, 60-72; mem exec comt, Larimer Co Dem Party, 60-, chmn, 61-63, co exec, 69-; chmn, Colo Prof for Johnson-Humphrey, 64; chmn, Colo Prof for Humphrey-Muskie, 68; deleg, Dem Nat Conv, 68; chmn, Fourth Cong Dist Dem Party, Colo, 72- Bus & Prof Pos: Mem nat coun, Am Prof for Peace in Mid East, currently; mem ed bd, Africa Today & mem ed adv bd, Social Sci J, currently. Mil Serv: Entered as Pvt, Army, 43, released as Pfc, 45, after serv in 409th Inf Div, ETO, 44-45; Combat Infantryman's Badge. Publ: Background of Current World Problems, David McKay, 67; Politics '72, issues, Quart J Africanist Opinion, spring 72; Southern Africa & the 1972 election campaign, Africa Today, summer 72; plus others. Mem: Am Polit Sci Asn; Western Asn Africanists (pres-elect, 74-); Int Studies Asn (steering comt); fel African Studies Asn; Western Soc Sci Asn. Honors & Awards: Harris T Guard Distinguished Prof & Top Prof, Colo State Univ; Nat Merit Award, Nat Jewish Welfare Bd. Relig: Jewish. Legal Res: 1932 Sheely Dr Ft Collins CO 80521 Mailing Add: Dept of Polit Sci Colo State Univ Ft Collins CO 80521

CELEBREZZE, ANTHONY J (D)
b Anzi, Italy, Sept 4, 10; s Rocco Celebrezze & Dorothy Marcoguiseppe C; m 1938 to Anne Marco; c Anthony J, Jean Ann & Susan Marie. Educ: John Carroll Univ; Ohio Northern Univ, LLB, 36. Hon Degrees: DD, Wilberforce Univ, 55; LLD, Fenn Col, 62, Boston Col, 63, LaSalle Col, 63 & Ohio Northern Univ, 63; PhD, RI Col, 64; DPubServ, Bowling Green State Univ, 64; DHL, Miami Univ, 65. Polit & Govt Pos: Ohio State Sen, 51-53; mayor, Cleveland, Ohio, 53-62; secy, Dept Health, Educ & Welfare, 62-65; mem, President's Adv Comn on Intergovt Rels, 59-; mem, Sixth Circuit Court of Appeals, 65- Mil Serv: Seaman, Navy. Mem: Am Munic Asn. Honors & Awards: Nat Fiorello LaGuardia Award, 61; Gullick Award, Camp Fire Girls, Inc, 62; Peter Canisius Medal, Canisius Col, 63; Gold Medallion City of Rome, 63; Eleanor Roosevelt Humanities Award. Relig: Catholic. Mailing Add: 17825 Lake Rd Lakewood OH 44107

CELEBREZZE, ANTHONY J, JR (D)
Ohio State Sen
Mailing Add: 16401 Marquis Ave Cleveland OH 44111

CELEBREZZE, FRANK D (D)
Justice, Ohio Supreme Court
b Cleveland, Ohio, Nov 13, 28; s Frank Celebrezze & Mary Delsander C; m 1949 to Mary Ann Armstrong; c Judith, Frank, Laura, David, Brian, Stephen, Jeffrey, Keith & Matthew. Educ: Ohio State Univ, 48; Baldwin-Wallace Col, BS, 52; Cleveland-Marshall Law Sch, JD, 56; Delta Theta Phi. Polit & Govt Pos: Ohio State Sen, 56-58; spec counsel, Ohio Attorney Gen, 60-62; judge, Common Pleas Court, Cuyahoga Co, 64-72; justice, Ohio Supreme Court, 72- Bus & Prof Pos: Lawyer-gen trial practice, Cleveland, Ohio, 57-65. Mil Serv: Entered as Pvt, Army, 46, released as Pfc, after serv in 11th Airborne Div, Pac Theatre, 46-47. Mem: Exchange Club; Cleveland, Co, Ohio State & Am Bar Asns. Honors & Awards: Excellent Judicial Serv Award, Ohio Supreme Court, 72; Outstanding Alumnus Award, Cleveland-Marshall Law Sch, 73; Community Serv Award, AFL-CIO, 73-; Outstanding Vet Award, Cuyahoga Co Joint Vet Comn, 74. Relig: Roman Catholic. Mailing Add: 8619 Whippoorwill Lane Parma OH 44130

CELEBREZZE, JAMES P (D)
Mem, Ohio State Dem Exec Comt
b Cleveland, Ohio, Feb 6, 38; s Frank D Celebrezze & Mary Delsander C; m 1967 to Daria R Yurkiw; c James Patrick, Jr & Leslie Ann Rose. Educ: Ohio State Univ, BS, 60; Cleveland Marshall Col Law, Cleveland State Univ, JD, 67. Polit & Govt Pos: Mem, Ohio State Dem Exec Comt, currently; Ohio State Rep, Fourth Dist, 65-74; chmn, Cuyahoga Co Legis Deleg, currently. Bus & Prof Pos: Teacher, Cleveland Sch Dist, 62-68; attorney-at-law, 67- Mil Serv: Entered as Pvt, Army, 60, released as SP-4, 62, after serv in 2/28 Artil, ETO, 61-62; Lt, Naval Res, 70- Mem: Am Bar Asn; Ital Sons & Daughters of Am; Ukrainian Prof Soc; Brook Park Jaycees; Delta Theta Phi. Relig: Roman Catholic. Legal Res: 14612 Sheldon Blvd Brook Park OH 44142 Mailing Add: 1001 Terminal Tower Cleveland OH 44113

CELESTE, RICHARD F (D)
Lt Gov, Ohio
Mailing Add: State House Columbus OH 43215

CELLA, CARL EDWARD (R)
Mem, Conn Rep State Cent Comt
b New Haven, Conn, Apr 2, 41; s Louis Cella & Helen Beale C; m 1964 to Mauriann Lynn Parmelee; c Carl E, Jr, David Scott & Lynn Jean. Educ: Georgetown Univ, AB, 63; Univ Conn Sch Law, JD, 66. Polit & Govt Pos: Third cong dist liaison, Conn Rep State Cent Comt, 73-75, mem, 74-, secy, Judicial Council, 73-75. Bus & Prof Pos: Partner, Loughlin, Kraemer, Noonan & Cella, Attorneys-at-law, 71- Publ: Co-auth, Products liability in Connecticut, Conn Law J, 66. Mem: KofC (Pinto Coun 5); NHaven Jaycees; Am, Conn & New Haven Bar Asns. Mailing Add: 90 Highland Park Rd North Haven CT 06473

CELLER, EMANUEL (D)
b Brooklyn, NY, May 6, 88; s Henry H Celler & Josephine Muller C; m 1914 to Stella B Baar, wid; c Judith C & Jane B (Mrs Sydney B Wertheimer). Educ: Columbia Col, AB, 10; Columbia Univ Law Sch, LLB, 12. Hon Degrees: LLD, Yeshiva Univ & Brooklyn Col. Polit & Govt Pos: US Rep, NY, 22-72, ranking majority leader, Judiciary Comt, US House Rep, formerly; mem, Platform & Resolutions Comts, Dem Nat Conv, 44-60; deleg, Dem State Conv, NY; trustee, Jewish Nat Fund. Bus & Prof Pos: Lawyer; dir, Fischbach & Moore & Oppenheimer Fund; organized Brooklyn Nat Bank; mem, Weisman, Celler, Spett, Modlin & Wertheimer, New York, currently. Publ: You Never Leave Brooklyn. Mem: Am, Co & Brooklyn Bar Asns; Am Jewish Comt; Am Jewish Cong. Honors & Awards: Award & Medallion of Commendatore of the Order Merit of Repub of Italy; Alexander Hamilton Award, Columbia Univ Alumni Asn. Legal Res: 9 Prospect Park West Brooklyn NY 11215 Mailing Add: 425 Park Ave New York NY 10022

CENARRUSA, PETER THOMAS (R)
Secy of State, Idaho
b Carey, Idaho, Dec 16, 17; s Joseph Cenarrusa & Ramona Gardoqui C; m 1947 to Freda B Coates; c Joe Earl. Educ: Univ Idaho, BS in Agr, 40; Tau Kappa Epsilon. Polit & Govt Pos: Idaho State Rep, 51-67, speaker, Idaho House of Rep, 63-67; mem, Idaho Bd Land Comnrs & Idaho Bd of Examr; parliamentarian, Idaho Rep State Conv, 62, chmn, 64; chmn, Idaho Legis Coun, 63; chmn Idaho Govt Reorgn Comt; Idaho deleg mgr for bd mgrs, Coun State Govt, 63-; Secy of State, Idaho, 67-; chief elec officer, State of Idaho, 71; mem, Idaho Comn on Human Rights & State Purchasing Adv Bd. Bus & Prof Pos: High sch teacher, Cambridge, Carey & Glens Ferry, Idaho, 40-41 & 46; teacher voc agr, Vet Admin, Blaine Co, 46-51; owner, Cenarrusa Livestock & Farming, 48- Mil Serv: Entered Marine Corps, 42, released as 1st Lt, 46, after serv as Naval Aviator, VMF 421, El Toro, Calif, VMSB 932, Cherry Point, NC & instr in naval aviation, Corpus Christi, Tex; Maj (Ret), Marine Corps Res, 46-59; Am Theatre, Victory & World War II Medals. Mem: Blaine Co Livestock Mkt Asn; Blaine Co Woolgrowers Asn; Carey CofC; Univ Idaho Alumni Asn; Idaho Flying Legislators. Honors & Awards: Named Hon Farmer, Future Farmers of Am, 55. Relig: Catholic. Legal Res: Carey ID 83320 Mailing Add: 2400 Cherry Lane Boise ID 83701

CENOTTO, LAWRENCE ARTHUR, IV (LARRY) (R)
Mem, Rep State Cent Comt Calif
b St Louis, Mo, Oct 20, 31; s Lawrence A Cenotto, III & Mary Smith C; m 1952 to Barbara Mary Grogan; c Lawrence A, V, Lisa Dawn, Loring Ames, Locke Ashley & Laird Andrew. Educ: Compton Col, AA, 51; Calif State Col Long Beach; Univ Calif, Berkeley; Univ Calif, Los Angeles, 1 year; Beta Phi. Polit & Govt Pos: Founder, Amador, Calaveras, El Dorado & Inyo Co Young Rep, Calif, 67; chmn, Amador Co Young Rep, 67; mem, Amador Co Rep Cent Comt, 67-, chmn, formerly; field admin asst to Calif State Assemblyman Gene Chappie, 67-; region VI vpres, Calif Young Rep, 68, resolutions chmn, 69; mem, Rep State Cent Comt Calif, 69- Bus & Prof Pos: Sports dir, KTMS, Santa Barbara, Calif, 60-63; news ed, KBEE, Modesto, 63-64; reporter & photographer, Sacramento Bee, 64-67; sportscaster, KAHI, Auburn, 72. Mil Serv: Entered as Pvt, Army Mil Police, 52, released as Cpl, 54, after serv in 91st Mil Police Bn, Korea, 53-54; Miscellaneous minor ribbons & unit decorations. Mem: Nat Sportscasters Asn; Amador Co Hist Soc; Jackson Quarterback Club; Ital Benevolent Soc; Kit Carson Mt Men. Mailing Add: 211 W Sierra View Dr Jackson CA 95642

CERASOLI, ROBERT ANGELO (D)
Mass State Rep
b Quincy, Mass, July 12, 47; s Angelo Barnardino Cerasoli & Maria Ann Pasquale C; div. Educ: Am Univ, BA, 69; Northeastern Univ, MA, 72; Am Inst Banking, 70. Polit & Govt Pos: Mgt trainee, Norfolk Co Trust Co, Quincy, Mass, 69-70; planning asst, Quincy City Hall, 71-72; legis asst, Mass State Senate, 72-74; Mass State Rep, 75- Mem: Eagles (chaplain, John Adams Aerie 1180); Sons of Italy Lodge 1295; Italian Int Sports Club (bd dirs). Relig: Roman Catholic. Legal Res: 21 Whiton Ave Quincy MA 02169 Mailing Add: Rm 342 State House Rep Boston MA 02133

CERMAK, ALBINA ROSE (R)
Committeewoman, Rep State Cent Comt Ohio
b Cleveland, Ohio; d Frank J Cermak & Rose Marek C; single. Educ: Cleveland Col, Western Reserve Univ. Polit & Govt Pos: Vchmn & secy, Cuyahoga Co Rep Cent & Exec Comts, Ohio, 39-53; chairwoman, Rep Women's Orgn Cuyahoga Co, 39-53; deleg, Rep Nat Conv, 40, 44, 52 & 64, mem resolutions comt, 44 & 52; bd mem, Ohio Fedn Women's Rep Clubs, 40-53 & 62-; mem, Rep Cent & Exec Comts, 20th Cong Dist, 40-53 & 62-; secy, Rep State Cent & Exec Comts Ohio; mem, Cuyahoga Co Bd Elec, 46-53; US Collector Customs, Ohio Dist, 53-61; cand for mayor, Cleveland, 61; secy, Ohio Real Estate Comn, 63; bailiff, Cuyahoga Co Common Pleas Court, 64-65; State examr, State Auditor's Off, 65-67, admin specialist, 67-71; committeewoman, Rep State Cent Comt Ohio, 23rd Cong Dist, 66-; vchmn, Cuyahoga Co Rep Exec Comt, currently. Mem: Ohio Asn Elec Officer; League Women Voters; Women's City Club Cleveland (bd mem); Int Women's Year Comt (adv bd); Bus & Prof Women's Club. Honors & Awards: Selected 1 of 10 Outstanding Cleveland Career Women; Life Mem Award, DePaul Maternity & Infant Home, 69. Relig: Roman Catholic; bd mem, Cuyahoga Regional Coun & Cleveland Diocesan Coun, Nat Coun Cath Women. Mailing Add: 3719 Rocky River Dr Cleveland OH 44111

CERVANTES, ALFONSO J (D)
b St Louis, Mo, Aug 27, 20; married; c six. Educ: St Louis Univ. Polit & Govt Pos: Alderman, St Louis, Mo, 49-59, pres, Bd of Aldermen, 59-63, mayor, formerly. Bus & Prof Pos: Pres, Cervantes & Assocs, gen ins. Honors & Awards: Recipient, citations for work in field of human rights; nat recognition for address calling upon indust to fit long-time unemployed into jobs; Outstanding Man of Year, CofC, Metrop St Louis, 55. Mailing Add: c/o City Hall 1206 Market St Louis MO 63103

CERVANTES, ALFRED F (D)
Committeeman, Santa Clara Co Dem Cent Comt, Calif
b Del Rio, Tex, Dec 8, 33; s Epigmenia Fuentes C & father deceased; m 1958 to Oralia Rios; c Donna Dorothy, Antionette Marie & Arlene Francis. Educ: Univ Tex, Austin, 59-60; Tex Western Col, 60-64. Polit & Govt Pos: Pres, Kenney-Juarez Dem Club, 67-68; deleg, Dem Nat Conv, 68; committeeman, Santa Clara Co Dem Cent Comt, 68-; mem, Selective Serv Syst. Mil Serv: Entered as Pvt, Army, 51, released as Sgt, 54, after serving in 97 AAA Gun Bn; Good Conduct Medal; Nat Defense Serv Medal; Korean Serv Medal with Three Bronze Stars; Syngman Rhee Citation. Mem: Painters Local Union; Notre Dame Dad's Club; Mex Am Community Orgn; St Mary's Dad's Club. Relig: Catholic. Mailing Add: 2630 Gassmann Dr San Jose CA 95121

CERVENKA, WILLIAM JOSEPH (R)
Chmn, Runnels Co Rep Party, Tex
b Rowena, Tex, Feb 5, 31; s E J Cervenka & Otillia Gengross C; m 1953 to Theresa Ann Guilbeau; c Frank, Annette & Christopher. Educ: Tex A&M Univ, BS; Phi Kappa Phi; Alpha Zeta. Polit & Govt Pos: Secy-treas, Runnels Co Rep Party, Tex, 63-66, chmn, 66- Mil Serv: Entered as 2nd Lt, Air Force, 52, released as 1st Lt, 54, after serv in Japan; Maj, Air Force Res; Korean Serv Medal; UN Serv Medal; Nat Defense Serv Medal. Relig: Catholic Mailing Add: Rte 1 Ballinger TX 76821

CESSAR, RICHARD J (R)
Pa State Rep
b Etna, Pa, Dec 1, 28; s Joseph Cessar & Helen Savor C; m 1950 to Dolores P Whitehill; c Richard Reed, Christine Lynn, Candace Ann, Robert Scott & Scott David. Educ: Rio Grande Col, 1 year. Polit & Govt Pos: Chmn, Etna Rep Party, Pa, 68-; admin asst, Majority Leader

Lee A Donaldson, 67-70; Pa State Rep, 30th Dist, 71- Bus & Prof Pos: Police off, Boro of Etna, Pa, 50-67. Mem: Etna Vol Fire Dept 2; Allegheny Co Firemen's Asn; Western Pa Firemans Asn; Fraternal Order of Police Lodge 91; Elks (Past Exalted Ruler). Relig: Catholic. Legal Res: 149 Grant Ave Pittsburgh PA 15223 Mailing Add: Capitol Bldg Harrisburg PA 17120

CESTARI, CONSTANCE G (R)
Chmn, North Branford Rep Town Comt, Conn
b New Haven, Conn, Nov 7, 31; d Dominic Griego & Laura Cappiello G; m 1953 to Arnold John Cestari; c Mark Robert & Arnold John, Jr. Educ: Southern Conn State Col, 70-72. Polit & Govt Pos: Mem, North Branford Rep Town Comt, Conn, 70-, vchmn, 71-74, chmn, 74-; Justice of the Peace, North Branford, 72- Bus & Prof Pos: Treas, Third Cong Dist Rep Womans Asn, 73-; transcriber, Conn State Senate, 73- Mem: Conn Rep Key Club; North Branford Rep Womens Club (organizer); Conn & Nat Fedn Rep Womens Club. Relig: Roman Catholic. Mailing Add: 230 W Pond Rd Ext North Branford CT 06471

CETRONE, V E (GENE) (D)
Mont State Sen
Mailing Add: 2315 Broadwater Ave Billings MT 59102

CHABERT, LEONARD J (D)
La State Rep
Mailing Add: Rte 3 Box 135 Houma LA 70360

CHACON, ALICIA (D)
Mem, Dem Nat Comt, Tex
Mailing Add: 8741 Old Country Rd El Paso TX 79909

CHACON, MATIAS L (D)
NMex State Sen
Educ: Ind Univ, BS; Univ NMex, LLB. Polit & Govt Pos: NMex State Rep, 57-64, Majority Floor Leader; NMex State Sen, 64-66 & 75-; state pres, NMex Young Dem. Bus & Prof Pos: Lawyer. Mil Serv: World War II. Mem: Am Legion; VFW; KofC; Elks. Relig: Catholic. Mailing Add: 239 Onate St NW Espanola NM 87532

CHACON, PETER ROBERT (D)
Calif State Assemblyman
b Phoenix, Ariz, June 10, 25; s Petronilo Chacon & Severa Velarde C; m 1953 to Jean Louisa Picone; c Christopher, Paul, Ralph & Jeffrey. Educ: Calif State Univ, San Diego, AB, 53, MA, 62; Phi Delta Kappa. Polit & Govt Pos: Calif State Assemblyman, 79th Dist, 70- Bus & Prof Pos: Vprin, Sherman Elem Sch, San Diego, Calif, 68-69; coordr compensatory educ, Elem Div, San Diego City Schs, 69-70. Mil Serv: Entered as Pvt, Army Air Force, 43, released as S/Sgt, 45, after serv in 15th Air Force, ETO & Mediter Theatre, 44-45; Air Medal with 5 Oak Leaf Clusters. Publ: Ed, The Teacher, San Diego Co Teachers Asn publ, 60-62. Mem: Calif Teachers Asn; NAACP; GI Forum; VFW; Nat Conf Christians & Jews. Relig: Catholic. Legal Res: 38 Catspaw Cape Coronado CA 92118 Mailing Add: State Capitol Rm 5175 Sacramento CA 95814

CHAFEE, JOHN HUBBARD (R)
b Providence, RI, Oct 22, 22; s John Sharpe Chafee & Janet Hunter C; m 1950 to Virginia Coates; c Zechariah, Lincoln, John, Georgia & Quentin. Educ: Yale Univ, BA, 47; Harvard Univ, LLB, 50; Delta Kappa Epsilon. Polit & Govt Pos: RI State Rep, 57-63, Minority Leader, RI House of Rep, 59-63; Gov, RI, 63-69; deleg, Rep Nat Conv, 64 & 68; chmn, Compact for Educ, 65; mem, Nat Rep Coord Comt & Exec Comt, Rep Gov Asn; Chmn, Nat Rep Gov Asn, 68; Secy of the Navy, 69-72. Bus & Prof Pos: Lawyer & partner, Edwards & Angell, Providence, RI, currently. Mil Serv: Enlisted Marine Corps, serv in 1st Div, 42-46, Guadalcanal, Okinawa & China; 50-52, 1st Div, Korean War, discharged as Capt. Mem: Am Legion. Relig: Episcopal. Mailing Add: Ives Rd East Greenwich RI 02818

CHAFFEE, FLORENCE ESTHER (R)
b Beaver, Pa, Apr 27, 04; d Benjamin Heideger & Nellie T Camp H; m 1925 to Lyle LaVerne Chaffee. Educ: Duff's Iron City Bus Col, grad, 23. Polit & Govt Pos: Pres, vpres & bull chmn, St Petersburg Women's Rep Club, 48-61; dir, Pinellas Co Rep Exec Comt, 48-70, secy, 66; alt deleg, Rep Nat Conv, 60, deleg, 64 & 72; treas, Fla Fedn Rep Women, 61-63; vpres, Pinellas Co Women's Rep Club, 65-67, pres, 67-69, corresponding secy, 70, vpres, 72-74. Mem: Fla Fedn Women's Clubs; St Petersburg Woman's Club (corresp secy, 75-); Toastmistress Club; Church Drama Guild. Honors & Awards: Princess, in recognition of vol work, Heart Ball, 73. Relig: Christian Church; Christian Women's Fel, Mirror Lake Christian Church; Year Book Circle Leader; prog & worship chmn, 73-75. Mailing Add: 808 16th Ave N St Petersburg FL 33704

CHAFIN, GERALD L (D)
WVa State Deleg
Mailing Add: State Capitol Charleston WV 25305

CHAFIN, MARY ELIZABETH (D)
Mem, NC State Dem Exec Comt
b Atlanta, Ga, Feb 2, 42; d Howard Lamar Chafin & Elizabeth Power C; single. Educ: Greensboro Col, BA, 64; Univ NC, Chapel Hill, MPA, 72; Zeta Tau Alpha, hon initiate. Polit & Govt Pos: Deleg, Dem Nat Conv, 72; campaign chmn, Liz Hair for Co Comnr, NC, 72 & 74; vchmn precinct comt, Mecklenburg Co Dem Party, 72-74, chmn precinct comt, 74-75; vpres, Charlotte Women's Polit Caucus, 73, pres, 74; mem, Charlotte Munic Info Rev Bd, 74-; mem, NC State Dem Exec Comt, 74- Bus & Prof Pos: Assoc dean of students, Univ NC, Charlotte, 73- Mem: Am Soc Pub Admin (vpres, Cent Piedmont Chap, 72, pres, 73); Charlotte Area Fund (prog develop specialist, 65-67, dir prog planning, 68-70, asst dir, 70-72); League of Women Voters (mem bd, 71); Vol Action Ctr (bd dirs, 74-); Common Cause. Relig: Methodist. Mailing Add: 1912 Lombardy Circle Charlotte NC 28203

CHALOUX, MAURICE EUGENE (D)
Vt State Rep
b St Johnsbury, Vt, Sept 29, 51; s Gerard Eugene Chaloux & Gemma Donna C; single. Educ: St Johnsbury Acad, High Sch, 69. Polit & Govt Pos: Town lister, St Johnsbury, Vt, 73-75, Vt State Rep, 75- Bus & Prof Pos: Vpres, Begin & Chaloux Realty Inc, Vt, 74- Mil Serv: Entered as Pvt E-1, Army, 69, released as SP-5, 72, after serv in Army Security Agency, TUSLOG Det 4, Sinop, Turkey, 70-71; Soldier of the Month. Mem: St Johnsbury Jaycees (pres, 74-75). Relig: Roman Catholic. Mailing Add: 149 Railroad St St Johnsbury VT 05819

CHAMBER, ERNEST
Nebr State Sen
Mailing Add: 3223 N 27th Ave Omaha NE 68111

CHAMBERLAIN, CHARLES E (R)
b Locke Township, Mich, July 22, 17; m 1943 to Charlotte Mary Craney; c Charlotte Ellen, Christine Clark & Charles Jr. Educ: Univ Va, BS, LLB, 49. Polit & Govt Pos: Internal Revenue Agent, US Treas Dept, 46-47; city attorney, East Lansing, Mich, formerly; legal counsel, Mich Sen Judiciary Comt, 53-54; prosecuting attorney, Ingham Co, 55-56; US Rep, Mich, 56-74. Bus & Prof Pos: Attorney-at-law. Mil Serv: World War II, 4 years; Commanding Officer of Vessels, Pac & Atlantic; Coast Guard Res. Mem: Mich State Bar; Am Bar Asn. Legal Res: East Lansing MI 48823 Mailing Add: 245 Fed Bldg Lansing MI 48901

CHAMBERLAIN, JEAN NASH (R)
Chmn, 18th Dist Rep Comt, Mich
b Chicago, Ill, Oct 14, 34; d Wm Edmund Nash & Virginia LaFon N; m 1953 to James Staffield Chamberlain; c James William, William Staffield, Caren Thomas & Martha Jean. Educ: Univ SC, 50-52. Polit & Govt Pos: Precinct capt, Royal Oak, Mich, 60-70; chmn, Local Sch & City Cand, 66-74; pres, Royal Oak Rep Womens Club, 68-70; vchmn, Oakland Co Rep Party, 70-73; staff, Huber for Congress, 18th Dist, 72-74; chmn, 18th Dist Rep Comt, 73- Bus & Prof Pos: Mem Develop chmn, Royal Oak & Madison Heights CofC, 75- Mem: Mich Fedn Rep Women; Royal Oak CofC; PTA; Red Run Golf Club; Girl Scouts (leader troop 825). Mailing Add: 1213 Vinsetta Blvd Royal Oak MI 48067

CHAMBERLAIN, THOMAS WILSON, SR (R)
Md State Deleg
b Oak Park, Ill, June 12, 23; s Donald Edward Chamberlain & Agnes Elizabeth Kennedy C; m 1948 to Helen Elizabeth Wacker; c Thomas W, Jr, William J & M Elizabeth. Educ: Springfield Jr Col, 42-43; George Washington Univ, 41-42; Univ Ill, Urbana, BS, 50; Tau Nu Tau; Phalanx; Kappa Sigma. Polit & Govt Pos: Md State Deleg, 75- Bus & Prof Pos: Sales admin, Kaiser Aluminum, Chicago, Ill, 50-58, New York, NY, 58-61, Erie, Pa, 61-63 & Baltimore, Md, 63- Mil Serv: Entered as Pvt, Army Air Force, 43, released as Sgt, 46, after serv in 11th Air Force, Alaskan/Aleutians Campaign, 43-45. Mem: Lutherville-Timonium Recreation Coun (exec vpres, 73-); Scout Troop 832 (treas, 69-); Baltimore Co Fed Rep Club; Pine Valley-Valley Wood Community Asn; Alpha Gamma Club of Kappa Sigma. Honors & Awards: Eagle Scout, 39; Scout Gov of Ill, 39. Relig: Presbyterian. Legal Res: 307 Galway Rd Timonium MD 21093 Mailing Add: Legis Off Rm 309 Md House Deleg Annapolis MD 21404

CHAMBERLIN, GUY W, JR
Asst Secy Admin, Dept Com
Mailing Add: Dept Com Washington DC 20230

CHAMBERS, ALEX A (R)
b Lorman, Miss, Dec 10, 34; s McKinley Chambers & Henrietta Hooks C; m 1960 to Rilla George Morrison; c Twan-Alexis Alfreda. Educ: Stillman Col, BA, 60; Duke Univ, MDiv, 68; Phi Beta Sigma; pres, Chancellors Club. Hon Degrees: DD, Kittrell Col, Kittrell, NC, 68; LittD, Nat Theol Sem, Kansas City, Mo, 71; LLD, Natchez Col, Natchez, Miss, 71; LHD, Stillman Col, 72. Polit & Govt Pos: Exec committeeman, Greenville Co Rep Party, 71-74; deleg, SC Rep State Conv, 72; deleg, Rep Nat Conv, 72; gov appointee, SC Comt on Modernization of Judicial System, 72; mem bd, Greenville Co Sch Bd, 72-74. Bus & Prof Pos: Assoc minister, Hayes Tabernacle Christian Methodist Episcopal Church, Los Angeles; minister to youth, Vermont Ave Presby Church; minister, St Joseph Christian Methodist Episcopal Church, Chapel Hill, NC; auditor, J C Penney Co, Los Angeles; dir, programming & leadership develop, Bd Christian Educ, Christian Methodist Episcopal Church, Memphis, Tenn; minister, Israel Metrop Christian Methodist Episcopal Church, Greenville, SC; exec vpres & gen mgr, Van Hoose Mortuary, Tuscaloosa, Ala; vis prof, Kittrell Col, 66-67; prof relig, Furman Univ, 72-; chmn bd, Gamzkm Corp, 72-; sr minister, Williams Inst Christian Methodist Episcopal Church, New York, currently. Mil Serv: Entered as Pvt, Army, 56, released as SP-4, 58, after serv in Med Unit, US, 56-58; Good Conduct Medal. Publ: The Negro in the United States, J Negro Hist, 61. Mem: Gtr Greenville Ministerial Alliance; Greenville Literacy Asn; Rotary; Greenville Co Comt on Sickle Cell Anemia; Greenville Co United Fund (bd dirs, 72-). Honors & Awards: Alumni of the Year, Stillman Col, 68, Distinguished Alumni Award, 70; Richard Allen Award, African Methodist Episcopal Church, 70. Relig: Christian Methodist Episcopal Church; Mem Gen Bd, 70-74 & ed, Eastern Index. Mailing Add: 2225 Seventh Ave New York NY 10027

CHAMBERS, LOUIS (D)
Mem, Tenn Dem Exec Comt
b Lebanon, Tenn, March 22, 90; s James Louis Chambers & Lula Wharton C; m 1946 to Lucile Wharton. Educ: David Lipscomb Col; Cumberland Univ; Vanderbilt Univ. Polit & Govt Pos: Mem, Tenn State Dem Exec Comt, 42-52 & 70-, secy, 50-52; deleg, Dem Nat Conv, 52; chmn, Wilson Co Dem Exec Comt, 56-66; deleg, State Const Conv, 59 & 65. Bus & Prof Pos: Lawyer, 13-; Justice of the Peace, Wilson Co, Tenn, 56-72. Mil Serv: Army, World War I; Muese-Argonne Sector Ribbon. Mem: Mason; Shrine; Am Legion. Mailing Add: 133 Public Sq Lebanon TN 37087

CHAMBERS, MARY PEYTON (D)
NH State Rep
b Poca, WVa, Aug 31, 31; d Henry H Peyton & Hilda Cary P; m 1957 to Wilbert F Chambers; c Henry, James & Jane. Educ: WVa Wesleyan Col, AB; George Peabody Col, MSpecEd; Alpha Xi Delta. Polit & Govt Pos: NH State Rep, Dist 13, 72-, Asst Minority Leader, NH House Rep, 72-74, Dep Minority Leader, 75- Bus & Prof Pos: Elem teacher, Putnam Co, WVa, 52-54; teacher spec educ, Kanawha Co, 55-56; dir spec educ, Childrens Ctr, Burlington, Vt, 56-58. Mem: League Women Voters; Women's Polit Caucus; NH Dem Women (polit action chmn). Relig: Protestant. Mailing Add: Box 284 Etna NH 03750

CHAMBERS, PATRICK B (D)
b Ft Dodge, Iowa, Oct 2, 44; s John B Chambers & Alice Kennedy C; m 1968 to Sandra Kay Martin; c Ryan Patrick, Jennifer Erin & Nathan Brandon. Educ: Univ SDak, BA, 67; Univ Iowa, JD, 71; Phi Delta Theta. Polit & Govt Pos: Chmn, Hamilton Co Dem Cent Comt, Iowa, 72-73. Bus & Prof Pos: Law clerk, Hon Warren J Rees, Justice, Supreme Court Iowa, 71-72; attorney, Lund & Chambers, 72- Mem: Am, Judicial Dist 2B & Iowa State Bar Asns; Hamilton Co Bar Asn. Relig: Catholic. Mailing Add: 927 Boone Webster City IA 50595

CHAMBERS, RAY BENJAMIN (R)
b Long Beach, Calif, Apr 7, 40; s James R Chambers & Eileen Cox Chambers; m 1966 to Mary Alice Kepler. Educ: Univ Redlands, BA magna cum laude, 62; Rutgers Univ, MA, 63; Omicron Delta Kappa; Alpha Gamma Nu. Polit & Govt Pos: Asst to US Rep Del Clawson, Calif, 63-65; exec asst to US Rep Robert F Ellsworth, 65-66; campaign consult, Ruppe for Cong, 66; admin asst to US Rep Philip E Ruppe, Mich, 67-71; dep asst secy community & field serv, Dept Health, Educ & Welfare, 71-73; Dir Cong Affairs, Dept of Transportation, 73-75. Bus & Prof Pos: Pres, Chambers & Co, 75- Mil Serv: Enlisted in Coast Guard Res, 63, stand by res, 69. Relig: Methodist. Mailing Add: 1431 Woodacre Dr McLean VA 22101

CHAMBERS, ROBERT EUGENE (D)
Mem, Wichita Co Dem Orgn, Tex
b Corpus Christi, Tex, Mar 5, 10; s R S Chambers & Minta Chandler C; m 1934 to Lollie Dee King; c Celeste (Mrs Bohnn), Neva (Mrs Dawson) & R E, Jr. Educ: Rice Univ, BS, 33; Houston Law Sch, 34-35; STex Sch Law, 35-36; Univ Tex, LLB, 36. Polit & Govt Pos: Asst to Lyndon B Johnson, Dem Nat Conv, 56, deleg, 60, 64 & 68; mem, State Dem Exec Comt, Tex, formerly; mem, Wichita Co Dem Orgn, currently. Bus & Prof Pos: Attorney, pvt practice, Houston, 37-42; attorney, J S Abercrombie, 42-48; attorney & gen mgr, Armour Properties, Wichita Falls, 48- Mil Serv: Retained by War Man Power Comn to construct & operate 100-octane plants, World War II. Mem: Wichita Co, Tex State & Am Bar Asns; Tex Bar Found; Nat Petroleum Coun. Honors & Awards: Outstanding Leadership, WTex CofC, 66. Relig: Church of Christ. Legal Res: 2413 Clayton Wichita Falls TX 76308 Mailing Add: 1107 Oil & Gas Bldg Wichita Falls TX 76301

CHAMBERS, ROSAMOND A (R)
b Boston, Mass, Feb 24, 26; d Robert Brayton Almy & M Rosamond Adie A; m to John Hackett Chambers, wid; c Mary Brayton. Educ: Beaver Country Day Sch, high sch grad, 43. Polit & Govt Pos: Mem, Bd Selectman, Stowe, Vt, 62-65 & 70-, chmn bd, 75-; justice of the peace, Stowe, 66-70. Bus & Prof Pos: Owner, Mt Mansfield Kennels, Stowe, Vt, 48-; owner-mgr, Ten Acres Lodge, Stowe, 51-72; partner, Custom Catering, Stowe, 70-; salesman, Pall D Spera Real Estate, Stowe, 74- Mailing Add: Hoodoo House RFD 1 Stowe VT 05672

CHAMBERS, WILLIAM CLYDE (R)
b Fort Gaines, Ga, Sept 13, 99; s I P Chambers & Nell Speight C; m 1921 to Frankie Eoline Grimsley; c William Clyde, Jr. Polit & Govt Pos: Chmn, Clay Co Rep Party, Ga, formerly. Mem: Mason; Shrine. Relig: Methodist. Legal Res: 204 Jackson St Fort Gaines GA 31751 Mailing Add: PO Box 95 Fort Gaines GA 31751

CHAMBLEE, JONES M (D)
SC State Rep
Mailing Add: Rte 7 Box 145 Anderson SC 29521

CHAMBLESS, THOMAS SIDNEY (D)
Mem, Dougherty Co Dem Exec Comt, Ga
b Albany, Ga, Jan 6, 43; s Marion Sidney Chambless & Hazel Thomas C; m 1968 to Nancy Ann Wheelhouse. Educ: Emory Univ, AB, 65; Univ Ga Sch Law, JD, 68; Phi Delta Theta. Polit & Govt Pos: Co-chmn, Southwest Ga Area Goals for Ga Prog, 71-; mem, Ga State Dem Exec Comt, 71-74; mem, Dougherty Co Bd Elec, 73-; mem, Dougherty Co Dem Exec Comt, 73- Mil Serv: Ga Army Nat Guard, 68-74. Mem: Am & Albany Bar Asns; State Bar Ga (second dist rep, state exec coun, younger lawyers sect, 72-); Albany Sertoma Club (pres, 74-); Dougherty Co Heart Asn (bd dirs, 72-). Relig: Episcopal. Legal Res: 1720 Lynwood Lane Albany GA 31707 Mailing Add: PO Box 23 Albany GA 31702

CHAMBLISS, DONALD R (D)
Miss State Rep
b Purvis, Miss, Feb 10, 32; married. Polit & Govt Pos: Miss State Rep, 60-64 & 75- Bus & Prof Pos: Real estate broker. Mem: Mason; Lions; Farm Bur; Miss Bd Realtors; Nat Asn Bd Realtors. Relig: Baptist. Mailing Add: 1295 Stateline Rd Southhaven MS 38637

CHAN, AGNES ISABEL (R)
Secy, San Francisco Co Rep Cent Comt, Calif
b San Francisco, Calif, Oct 3, 17; d Luke Shang Chan & May Cheung C; div; c Maureen Annette (Mrs Gee) & Melville Arnold. Educ: San Francisco State Col, AB, 53, MA, 57; Univ Calif; Univ Southern Calif; Univ San Francisco. Polit & Govt Pos: Campaign coordr, Earl Louie for Assembly, 20th Assembly Dist, Calif, 64; chmn, 20th Assembly Dist Rep Orgn, 65-66; mem, San Francisco Co Rep Cent Comt, 20th Assembly Dist, 66-, chmn, 20th Assembly Dist, 73-74, secy, 74-; women's coordr, Spencer Williams for Attorney Gen Calif, 66; Chinese Women's chmn, Ronald Reagan For Gov, 66; hq coordr, Thomas Kuchel for US Senate, 68; hg coordr, Richard M Nixon for President, 68; mem, Rep State Cent Comt Calif, 69-; campaign coordr, George Murphy for US Senate, 70; mem, Steering Comt, Reelec of Gov Ronald Reagan, 70; mem, Adv Comt, Educ of Bilingual Children, Dept of Health, Educ & Welfare, 70-; mem, Educ Comt, Nat Rep Heritage Groups Coun, 71-; alt deleg, Rep Nat Conv, 72; Chinese women's chmn, Calif Comt to Reelect President Nixon, 72; mem, Finance Comt, Bay Area Comt to Reelect Nixon, 72; high-risers chmn, San Francisco Comt to Reelect President Nixon, 72; elector, Electoral Col for Calif, 72; Bay Area Chinese chmn, Flournoy for Gov, 74. Bus & Prof Pos: Teacher, San Francisco Unified Sch Dist, 53-; bd dirs, Chinese Resource Develop Ctr, 73- Mem: San Francisco Classroom Teachers Asn; San Francisco Opera Guild; Calif Hist Soc; Rep Alliance San Francisco; Calif Chinese-Am Rep Asn (bd dirs, 71-). Honors & Awards: Distinguished Serv Award, San Francisco Rep Co Cent Comt, 66, Victory Squad Award, 69; Elephant Award, San Francisco Co Rep Cent Comt, 74. Relig: Congregational. Mailing Add: 980 Sacramento St San Francisco CA 94108

CHANCE, GENIE (D)
Alaska State Sen
b Dallas, Tex; d Albert Sidney Broadfoot & Jessie Butler B; m 1971 to William Knight Boardman; c Winston C, Jr, Albert Broadfoot & Jan. Educ: ETex State Teachers Col, 43; Southern Methodist Univ, 43-44; Paris Jr Col, 44; NTex State Univ, BS, 46; Baylor Univ Grad Sch, 47. Polit & Govt Pos: Alaska State Rep, 69-74; Alaska State Sen, 75- Bus & Prof Pos: Mem, Defense Adv Comt Women in the Serv, 67-, chmn pub rels comt, 68, vchmn, 69- Publ: Year of decision & action, US Geol Surv Prof Paper, 67. Mem: Alaska State Press Club; Alaska Press Women; Nat Fedn Press Women; Bus & Prof Women; Alaska Children's Serv, Inc (bd dirs); NAACP. Honors & Awards: McCall's Top Golden Mike Award for Outstanding Women Pub Serv Broadcaster, 65; Four First Place Awards & Golden Nugget Award, 67, Alaska Press Women; 11 First Place Awards, Alaska State Press Club, 64-68; First Place Award, Nat Fedn Press Women, 67; Lady of Year Award, Camp Fire Girls, 69. Relig: Protestant. Legal Res: 1101 H St Anchorage AK 99501 Mailing Add: PO Box 2392 Anchorage AK 99501

CHANCE, GEORGE (D)
Ga State Rep
Mailing Add: PO Box 373 Springfield GA 31329

CHANCE, JEAN CARVER (D)
Committeewoman, Fla Dem State Exec Comt
b Gainesville, Fla, Sept 4, 38; d William G Carver (deceased) & Mary Hull C; m 1964 to Chester B Chance; c Mark & Jennifer. Educ: Univ Fla, BS in Jour, 60, MA in Jour, 69; Theta Sigma Phi; Alpha Chi Omega. Polit & Govt Pos: Precinct committeewoman, Alachua Co Dem Exec Comt, Fla, 68-; committeewoman, Fla Dem State Exec Comt, 75- Bus & Prof Pos: Newspaper reporter, Miami Herald, Sarasota Herald-Tribune, Gainesville Sun & Tampa Tribune, 60-67; asst prof jour, Univ Fla, 70- Mem: League of Women Voters; Soc Prof Journalists; Sigma Delta Chi; Asn for Educ in Jour; Univ Fla Admin Coun. Relig: Protestant. Mailing Add: 6915 NW 65th Ave Gainesville FL 32601

CHANCEY, C RAY (D)
Chmn, Jackson Co Dem Cent Comt, Ill
b Murphysboro, Ill, Dec 4, 14; s Walter A Chancey & Hattie M C; m 1940 to Mary Jeannette Richardson; c Robert Bruce. Educ: Southern Ill Univ, 34-36. Polit & Govt Pos: Precinct committeeman, Jackson Co Dem Cent Comt, Ill 52-, vchmn, 62-67, chmn, 67-; vchmn, 21st Cong Dist Dem Comt, 68-; chmn, 58th Legis Dist Dem Comt, 70-; admin asst to Ill Secy of State, 73- Bus & Prof Pos: Restaurant owner, RayMar Cafe, Murphysboro, Ill, 40-54; retired, 54-61; real estate & ins, C Ray Chancey Agency, 61- Mem: Elks; CofC. Relig: United Methodist. Mailing Add: 1911 Spruce St Murphysboro IL 62966

CHANDLER, A LEE (D)
SC State Rep
Mailing Add: Drawer 519 Darlington SC 29532

CHANDLER, ALBERT BENJAMIN (D)
b Corydon, Ky, July 14, 98; s Joseph Chandler & Callie Sanders C; m 1925 to Mildred Watkins; c Marcella (Mrs Thomas D Miller), Mildred (Mrs James J Miller), Joseph Daniel & Albert Benjamin, Jr. Educ: Transylvania Col, AB, 21; Harvard, 21-22; Univ Ky, LLB, 24; Pi Kappa Alpha. Hon Degrees: LLD, Transylvania Col, 36 & Univ Ky, 37. Polit & Govt Pos: Master comnr, Circuit Court, Woodford Co, Ky, 28; Ky State Sen, 29-31; Lt Gov, Ky, 31-35; Gov Ky, 35-39 & 55-59; US Sen, Ky, 39-48; chmn, Woodford Co Dem Exec Comt, formerly; Dem Nat Committeeman, Ky, formerly. Bus & Prof Pos: Receiver officer, Inter-Southern Life Ins Co, Louisville, Ky, 32; organizer, Ky Home Life Ins Co, Louisville, 32; high comnr of baseball, 45-51; comnr, Continental Football League, 65; pres, Int Baseball Cong, Wichita; dir, Coastal States Life Ins Co, Ga; vpres & dir, First Flight Golf, Chattanooga, Tenn, currently. Mil Serv: Serv as Capt, Army, 18, Res, Judge Adv Gen Dept, one of five Sen designated by US Senate to visit world battlefronts, 43. Mem: Ty Cobb Found (trustee); Univ Ky (chmn bd trustees); Transylvania Col Bd Trustees & Fund Raising Comt (chmn); Am Legion; 40 et 8. Honors & Awards: Named Kentuckian of Year, Ky Press Asn; one of first ten named to Ky Sports Hall of Fame, 57; received Cross of Mil Serv, United Daughters of Confederacy, 59. Relig: Episcopal; received Bishop's Medal, 59. Mailing Add: 191 Elm St Versailles KY 40383

CHANDLER, BONITA T (D)
Secy, Webster Co Dem Exec Comt, Ky
b Poole, Ky, July 24, 43; d Arnold Tapp & Lila Melton T; m 1961 to Tommy W Chandler; c Lucia Ann & Tommye Karen. Educ: Univ Ky, BS, 64. Polit & Govt Pos: Secy, Webster Co Dem Exec Comt, Ky, 68-; deleg, Ky State & Nat Dem Conv, 72. Bus & Prof Pos: Bus teacher, Webster Co High Sch, Dixon, 64-65; legal secy, Tommy Chandler Law Off, Providence, 65-68; bookkeeping serv & income tax consult, 68- Mem: Pakendall Woman's Club (secy, 67-); Garden Club (parliamentarian, 68-); Luncheon Club; Missionary Soc. Honors & Awards: Young Woman of the Year, Providence Bus & Prof Womens Club, 66. Relig: General Baptist. Mailing Add: Benjamin Terr Providence KY 42450

CHANDLER, ELEANOR (D)
Committeeman, Nassau Co Dem Party, NY
b New York, NY, June 3, 28; d Jack Reiff & Sadie Peskowitz R; m 1951 to Robert Chandler; c Douglas Jay & Lawrence Mark. Educ: City Col New York, BS, 49, MA, 50. Polit & Govt Pos: Mem exec bd, Rockville Centre Comt Human Rights, NY, 67-69; mem steering comt, Allard Lowenstein for Cong, 68 & 70; committeeman, Nassau Co Dem Party, 69-; corresponding secy, Dem Club of Rockville Centre, 70-72, vpres, 72; exec bd, New Dem Coalition Rockville Centre, 70-; deleg, Dem Nat Conv, 72; dist coordr, McGovern Presidential Campaign, 72. Bus & Prof Pos: Social studies teacher, New York City Pub Schs, 49-55. Mem: League of Women Voters; Comt for Better Educ. Relig: Hebrew. Mailing Add: 592 Hempstead Ave Rockville Centre NY 11570

CHANDLER, JAMES MELTON (R)
Chmn, Bee Co Rep Party, Tex
b Bee Co, Tex, Mar 14, 21; s James Smith Chandler & Ella Billingsley C; m 1946 to Idella Nelson; c James M, Jr, Nelson E, Kenneth D, Della Jean, Byron L & Mary K. Educ: Tex A&I Univ, 39-40. Polit & Govt Pos: Chmn, Precinct Eight, Tex, 66-70; chmn, Bee Co Rep Party, 70- Bus & Prof Pos: Stock farmer, 46-; ins agent, Southern Farm Bur, 70- Mil Serv: Entered as Pvt, Marines, 41, released as Cpl, 45, after serv in Ninth AAA & Fleet Marines, Southwest Pac, 41-45; Good Conduct Medal; Pac Theatre Ribbon. Mem: Boy Scouts (troop committeeman); Lions. Relig: Methodist. Mailing Add: PO Box 98 Normanna TX 78142

CHANDLER, JOHN P H, JR (R)
NH State Rep
b Boston, Mass, Aug 6, 11; s John Parker Hale Chandler & Madeleine Julia Vogel C. Educ: Harvard Col, BS, 34. Polit & Govt Pos: Selectman, Warner, NH, 3 years, trustee, 20 years, mem budget comt, 20 years; mem, Chandler Reservation Comt, 20 years; NH State Rep, 43-45, 51 & 73-; NH State Sen, 47 & 67-69; mem, Gov Coun, 53, 55 & 57; deleg, Rep Nat Conv, 56, 60, 68 & 72; mem, Const Conv, 74. Mem: SAR (state chmn, Franklin Pierce Brigade, vchmn, NH Conservative Union & Liberty Amendment Comt). Mailing Add: Chandler Hwy Warner NH 03278

CHANDLER, LARRY DEAN (R)
Single. Educ: Univ Iowa, BA, jour, 70; Rutgers Univ, MA, polit sci, 71; Phi Beta Kappa; Kappa Tau Alpha. Polit & Govt Pos: Exec dir, Wyo Rep Party, 71-72; admin asst to minority leader, Ohio State Rep Charles F Kurfess, 73- Bus & Prof Pos: Newspaper reporter, Cedar Falls Rec, 70. Honors & Awards: Eagleton fel. Relig: Methodist. Mailing Add: 2475 Shore E Columbus OH 43227

CHANDLER, NANCY ANN (D)
Dem Nat Committeewoman, Maine
b Stoneham, Mass, Aug 30, 33; d George Albert Ramsdell & Evangeline Gray Lister R; m 1954 to Bruce W Chandler; c Brooks W, Kimberly G & Kristin J. Educ: Bates Col, AB & RN, 57. Polit & Govt Pos: Secy, Ward II Dem Orgn, Waterville, Maine, 61; secy, China Dem Town Comt, 63; chmn, orgn comt, Kennebec Co Dem Comt, 65-67; committeewoman, Maine State Dem Comt, 68-; co-chmn, Maine Get-Out-the-Vote Drive, 70; chmn, Maine Dem Women's Conf, 71; deleg, Dem Nat Conv, 72; state field coordr, Maine McGovern Campaign, 72; Dem Nat Committeewoman, Maine, 72-, mem charter comn, Dem Nat Comt, 73-, mem 1976 site selection comt; mem, Maine Gov Adv Comt Ment Health, 72- Bus & Prof Pos: Nurse, Winchester Hosp, Mass, 56-57; instr maternal & child health nursing, Washington Hosp Ctr, DC, 57-59; coordr rehabilitation nursing, Thayer Hosp, Waterville, Maine, 60-62. Mem: 500 Club; 400 Club; Southport Yacht Club; Maine Audubon Soc; China Hist Soc. Relig: Unitarian. Mailing Add: Strawberry Meadows South China ME 04358

CHANDLER, RICHARD (D)
Ky State Rep
Mailing Add: 1471 Bluegrass Ave Louisville KY 40215

CHANDLER, RODNEY DENNIS (R)
Wash State Rep
b LaGrande, Ore, July 13, 42; s Robert J Chandler & Edna Hagey C; m 1963 to Joyce Elaine Laremore; c John Gifford & Amanda Joy. Educ: Eastern Ore Col, 61-62; Ore State Univ, BS, 68; Sigma Delta Chi. Polit & Govt Pos: Wash State Rep, 75- Bus & Prof Pos: News correspondent, KOMO TV News, Seattle, Wash, 68-73; asst vpres mkt, Wash Mutual Savings Bank, 73- Mil Serv: Entered as Pvt, Nat Guard, 59, released as SP-4, 64. Mem: Rotary; Mortgage Bankers Asn; YMCA. Honors & Awards: Sigma Delta Chi Award for Excellence in Broadcast Journalism, 72. Relig: United Methodist. Mailing Add: 13003 NE 143rd Kirkland WA 98033

CHANEY, BERT (D)
Kans State Sen
Mailing Add: 915 E 13th Hutchinson KS 67501

CHANEY, BUENA (R)
Chmn, Seventh Dist Rep Party, Ind
b Coxville, Ind, Nov 16, 21; parents deceased; m 1949 to Betty Jo Williams; c Tamara & Lisa. Educ: Wabash Col, AB, 43; Ind Univ Law Sch, JD, 48; Sigma Delta Kappa. Polit & Govt Pos: Chmn, Vigo Co Rep Party, Ind, 60-69; chmn, Sixth Dist Rep Party, 62-66; chmn, Seventh Dist Rep Party, 66-; chmn, Ind Rep State Cent Comt, 67-72; deleg, Rep Nat Conv, 68. Bus & Prof Pos: Attorney-at-law, 48- Mil Serv: Entered as Pvt, Army, 43, released as T-4, 46, after serv in 21st Evacuation Hosp, SPac; Capt, Army Res, 52. Mem: Am, Ind & Terre Haute Bar Asns; Am & Ind Trial Lawyers Asn. Relig: Protestant. Mailing Add: RR 51 Box 615 Terre Haute IN 47805

CHANEY, ISABELLE CAROLINE (R)
Mem, Harrison Co Rep Cent & Exec Comt, Ohio
b Cadiz, Ohio; d William Grant Kent & Margaret Gaines K; m to G F Stevens; wid; m 1954 to Lawrence Hayden Chaney; c Naomi (Mrs Root) & stepchildren Wayne A (deceased), Virginia L (Mrs McMaster) & Donald O Stevens. Educ: Exten courses, Geneva State Col; pvt lessons, commercial course, pub speaking & law. Polit & Govt Pos: Dep clerk, Harrison Co Probate & Juv Court, Ohio, 29-54; secy, Harrison Co Prosecuting Attorney, 57-65; chairwoman, Harrison Co Rep Party, 13 years; alt deleg, Rep Nat Conv, 60 & 68; chairwoman & pres, Harrison Co Rep Women's Club, formerly; mem, State Rep Cent & Exec Comt, formerly; state chmn pub affairs, formerly; mem, Harrison Co Rep Cent & Exec Comt, currently; Presidential Elector, 18th Dist, 72, attended Inauguration guest of Cong Inaugural Comt; mem, Harrison Co Bd Elections; co govt aide, Buckeye Girl's State, 73- Bus & Prof Pos: Legal Secy, Pettay & Mosser, Attorneys, 55-57; researcher & news correspondent, 65-70, news correspondent, currently. Mem: Ohio Dept Daughters of Union Vet Civil War (treas); Am Legion Auxiliary; Cadiz Women's Civic Club; Ohio Fedn Women. Relig: Methodist; Lay speaker, various bds & comns, past pres, Woman's Soc Christian Serv. Legal Res: County Rd 5 Cadiz OH 43907 Mailing Add: PO Box 244 Cadiz OH 43907

CHANEY, LONIE (D)
Nev State Assemblyman
Mailing Add: 504 Kasper Ave Las Vegas NV 89104

CHANEY, MARY C (R)
Chmn, Siskiyou Co Rep Cent Comt, Calif
b Neola, Utah, Dec 11, 17; d William Henry Crozier & Mary Amanda Elliott C; m 1948 to Harold Oaks Chaney; c Lani (Mrs Coy Welborn), Dwight Leon Guillotte, Alan Edward & Harold Oaks, Jr. Educ: Thom D Dee Hosp, Ogden, Utah, RN. Polit & Govt Pos: Pres, Weed Rep Women Fedn, 60-; vchmn, Siskiyou Co Rep Cent Comt, 62-67, chmn, 67-; mem, State Rep Cent Comt Calif, 71- Mem: Calif Farm Bur. Relig: Protestant. Mailing Add: Rte 1 Box 1058 Weed CA 96094

CHANEY, NEALE V (D)
Chmn, Wash State Dem Comt
b Lewiston, Idaho, Mar 22, 21; s Benjamin Franklin Chaney & Mary Katherine Isaman C; m 1942 to Mary Louise Mehan; c Mary Cathleen, Margie Colleen (Mrs Todd), Melissa Candace (Mrs Thompson) & Christopher B. Educ: Univ Wash, 3 years. Polit & Govt Pos: Dist chmn, 48th Legis Dist, 60-62; exec bd mem, King Co Dem Cent Comt, 60-68; exec bd mem, Wash State Dem Comt, 62-68, exec dir, 69, chmn, 70-; mem, Dem Nat Comt, 70-; deleg, Dem Nat Conv, 72. Bus & Prof Pos: Partner, Farwest Advert Agency, Seattle, 46-56; publ, Eastsider, Weekly Newspaper, 56-61; mgr, King Co Airport, 64-68. Mil Serv: Entered as Pvt, Army, 42, released as 1st Lt, 46, after serv in Field Artil. Relig: Episcopal. Legal Res: 16131 SE 15th Bellevue WA 98008 Mailing Add: Arctic Bldg Seattle WA 98104

CHAPIN, DIANA DERBY (D)
b St Joseph, Mich, Nov 15, 42; d David Norman Derby & Gladys Henke D; m 1968 to James Burke Chapin; c James Derby & David Sheffield. Educ: Univ Mich, BA, cum laude with honors in Eng, 64; Cornell Univ, MA, 66, PhD, 71. Polit & Govt Pos: Deleg, Dem Nat Conv, 72; Dem leader, 35th Assembly Dist, Part B, NY, 72-; mem, Dem Nat Mid-Term Conf, 74; dist adminr, Congressman Benjamin S Rosenthal, 74- Bus & Prof Pos: Instr Eng, Queens Col (NY), 69-71, asst prof, 71-74. Publ: IO & the Negative Apotheosis of Vanni Fucci, Dante Studies, 71. Mem: Mediaeval Acad Am; Mod Lang Asn; Nat Women's Polit Caucus; 1776 Dem (exec comt, 74-); New Dem Coalition. Honors & Awards: Nat Merit Finalist, 60; Laurel Harper Seeley Scholar, Univ Mich Alumnae, 62-63; Woodrow Wilson Found Fel, 64, Woodrow Wilson Dissertation Fel, 68. Relig: Congregational. Mailing Add: 35-46 79th St Jackson Heights NY 11372

CHAPIN, DWIGHT LEE (R)
b Wichita, Kans, Dec 2, 40; s Nortan Spencer Chapin & Betty Helena C; m 1963 to Susan Howland; c Tracy H & Kimberly S. Educ: Univ Southern Calif, BA, 63; Sigma Chi. Polit & Govt Pos: Field rep, Gubernatorial Cand Richard Nixon, 62; advan man, Richard Nixon, 64 & 66; personal aide to Presidential Cand Nixon, 67-69; spec asst to the President, 69-70; dep asst to the President, 70-73. Bus & Prof Pos: Vpres, W Clement Stone Enterprises, currently. Relig: Presbyterian. Mailing Add: 620 Ridge Rd Winnetka IL 60093

CHAPIN, HOWARD B (D)
NC State Rep
Mailing Add: Rte 5 Box 419 Washington NC 27889

CHAPIN, JOHN CARSTEN (R)
b Detroit, Mich, Oct 1, 20; s Roy Dikeman Chapin & Inez Tiedeman C; m 1964 to Helen Willard; c Suzanne (Mrs Christopher Wilkins), John Jr, Deacon Samuel, David Dwight & Alyson Sayre. Educ: Yale Univ, BA, 42; George Washington Univ, MA, 67; Zeta Psi. Polit & Govt Pos: Commun dir, 14th Dist Rep Party, Mich, 58-62; chmn, Citizens for Romney, DC, 67-68; mem exec comt, Rockefeller for Pres, 68; vchmn finance comt, DC Rep Comt, 68; spec asst to Secy, Dept Housing & Urban Develop, 69-73. Bus & Prof Pos: Acct exec, MacManus, John & Adams, Detroit, Mich, 46-50; commun dir, Diocese of Mich, 50-62; commun warden, Nat Cathedral, DC, 62-69; consult, DC Redevelop Land Agency, 73; teacher, Landon Sch, 73- Mil Serv: Entered as Pfc, Marine Corps, 42, released as Capt, 45, after serv in 4th Marine Div, Pac, 43-44; Two Purple Hearts. Mem: Philatelic Found (trustee); Chevy Chase Club. Relig: Episcopal. Mailing Add: Londonderry VT 05148

CHAPLEAU, LOUIS CAREY (D)
b Greenfield, Mass, Nov 15, 07; s Louis A Chapleau & Mary Carey C; m 1933 to Mary Hubbard; c Adrienne (Mrs Wolf), Marilyn (Mrs Barashkoff), Edward A & Louis Carey. Educ: Univ Notre Dame, JD, 30. Polit & Govt Pos: Chmn, St Joseph Co Dem Orgn, Ind, 42-44; co attorney, St Joseph Co, 44-46; deleg, Ind Dem Conv, 53-; proxy deleg, Dem Nat Conv, 60, deleg, 64, 68 & 72; deleg, Dem Nat Mid-Term Conf, 74. Bus & Prof Pos: Former attorney, South Bend Community Sch Corp. Mem: St Joseph Co, Ind State & Am Bar Asns; Bar Asn Seventh Circuit; Nat Asn Univ & Col Attorneys. Relig: Catholic. Mailing Add: 605 N Coquillard Dr South Bend IN 46617

CHAPLIN, RONALD L (R)
NMex State Rep
Mailing Add: 4820 Hilton NE Albuquerque NM 87110

CHAPMAN, ALICE HACKETT (R)
Mem, Calaveras Co Rep Cent Comt, Calif
b Hillsboro, Md, Sept 22, 02; d Thomas Cox Hackett & Mary Louise Holt H; wid. Educ: Los Angeles Bus Col, grad, 18; univ exten courses. Polit & Govt Pos: Secy to city attorney, Los Angeles, Calif, 30-49; mem, Calaveras Co Rep Cent Comt, 58-, chmn, 67-68. Mem: Soroptimist Club; Bus & Prof Womens Club Calaveras Co; Ebbetts Pass Wonderland Asn; Nathan B Forrest chap, UDC. Honors & Awards: Serv Award, City of Los Angeles; Outstanding Performance Award, State Rep Cent Comt, 67-68. Relig: Episcopal. Mailing Add: PO Box 76 Hathaway Pines CA 95233

CHAPMAN, BRUCE K (R)
Secy of State, Wash
b Evanston, Ill, Dec 1, 40; s Landon L Chapman & Darroll Berge C; single. Educ: Harvard Col, BA, with honors, 62. Polit & Govt Pos: Mem city coun, Seattle, Wash, 71-75; Secy of State, 75- Bus & Prof Pos: Publ, Advance Mag, 60-64; ed writer, NY Herald Tribune, 65-66; pub affairs consult, Urban Affairs, Seattle, 66-71. Mil Serv: Air Force Res, 64-70. Publ: Co-auth, The Party That Lost Its Head, 66; auth, The Wrong Man In Uniform, 67; co-auth, Report to the President on Youth, 69. Mem: US Comn on Civil Rights for Wash State; Allied Arts Seattle; Nat Trust for Historic Preservation; Inst for Comp & Foreign Studies, Univ Wash; Wash State Am Revolution Bi-Centennial Comt. Relig: Episcopal. Mailing Add: Legis Bldg Olympia WA 98504

CHAPMAN, CHARLES HICKERSON, JR (R)
b Dothan, Ala, Apr 17, 20; s Charles Hickerson Chapman & Florie Malone C; m 1943 to Martha Farmer; c Charles Hickerson, III, Davis F & Florrie Lou. Educ: Washington & Lee Univ, BS, 41. Polit & Govt Pos: Mem, Rep Nat Comt, Ala, 64-72; deleg, Rep Nat Conv, 68. Bus & Prof Pos: Pres, Chapman Construction Co, Dothan, 46-; chmn bd, Malone Industs, Inc; dir, First Nat Bank, Dothan; dir, Dothan Oil Mill Co. Mil Serv: Naval Res, 42-45, Lt. Mem: Houston Country Heart Fund; Dothan CofC (dir). Mailing Add: PO Drawer 220 Dothan AL 36302

CHAPMAN, EUGENIA SHELDON (D)
Ill State Rep
b Fairhope, Ala, Jan 10, 23; d Chauncey Bailey Sheldon & Rose Donner S; m 1948 to Gerald M Chapman; c George, Andrew, John & Katherine. Educ: Chicago State Univ, BEd, 44. Polit & Govt Pos: Mem bd educ, Dist 214, Cook Co, Ill, 61-64, secy, 62-64; Ill State Rep, 64- Bus & Prof Pos: Pub sch teacher, Cicero, Ill, 44-47, Chicago, 47-51. Mem: League Women Voters; PTA; Dem Women's Groups. Honors & Awards: Best Freshman & Best Legislator Awards, Independent Voters of Ill. Relig: Protestant. Mailing Add: 16 S Princeton Ct Arlington Heights IL 60005

CHAPMAN, HARRY A, JR (D)
SC State Sen
b Greenville, SC, Feb 9, 36; s Harry A Chapman & Mildred Marett C; m 1956 to Mona Ruth

Freeman C; c Karen Camille. Educ: Univ SC, BA, 58, LLB, 60; pres, Lambda Chi Alpha, 56; Phi Delta Phi; Blue Key. Polit & Govt Pos: SC State Rep, 63-66; SC State Sen, 67- Bus & Prof Pos: Lawyer, Foster, Johnston, Ashmore & Chapman. Mem: Am & SC Bar Asns; Civitan Club; SC Crippled Children Soc (exec comt); Greenville Co Crippled Children Soc. Relig: Baptist. Mailing Add: State House Columbia SC 29211

CHAPMAN, OSCAR LITTLETON (D)

b Omega, Va, Oct 22, 96; s James Jackson Chapman & Rosa Archer Blount C; m 1940 to Ann Kendrick; c James. Educ: Univ Denver, BA, 22-24; Univ NMex, 27-28; Westminster Law Sch, Denver, LLB, 29; Colo State Col Educ, Augustana Col, Howard Univ, LLD, 49; Univ Denver, 51; Western State Col Colo, 61; Phi Alpha Delta. Polit & Govt Pos: Asst chief probation officer, Juv Court, Denver, Colo, 22-24, chief probation officer, 24-27; campaign mgr, Edward P Costigan for US Senate, 30 & Alva B Adams for US Senate, 32; Asst Secy of Interior, 33-45, Undersecy of Interior, 46-49, Secy of Interior, 49-53; campaign co-chmn with Gov Leslie Miller, Wyo for President Roosevelt in 11 Western states, 40; advance man for President Truman in nat campaign, summer & fall, 48; co-chmn with India Edwards, Citizens for Lyndon B Johnson, 60. Bus & Prof Pos: Attorney-at-law, Chapman, Duff & Lenzini, 53- Mil Serv: Navy, 18-20. Relig: Methodist. Mailing Add: 4975 Hillbrook Lane NW Washington DC 20016

CHAPO, CAROLYN LEE (R)

New Voter Chmn, Rep State Cent Comt Ore

b Sacramento, Calif, Nov 15, 53; d Louis Chapo & Bonnie Lee Griggs C; single. Educ: American River Col, AA, 73; Ore State Univ, BS, 75; Alpha Gamma Sigma; Delta Delta Delta. Polit & Govt Pos: Rec secy, Sacramento Co Young Rep, Calif, 72-73; pres, Ore Col Rep, 73-75; committeewoman, Benton Co Cent Comt, 74-75; state coordr Ore Col Rep, Rep State Cent Comt Ore, 74-75, new voter chmn, 75- Bus & Prof Pos: Bookkeeper, Dr Jensen & Dr Bittner, Calif, 69-70; fashion coordr, hi-bd supvr & sales clerk, J C Penneys, Sacramento, 70-73. Mem: Ore & Am Home Econ Asns; Eastern Star; Good Samaritan Hosp Vol. Honors & Awards: Sara Ida Shaw Award, Delta Delta Delta, winter 75, Janet Schultz Award, May, 75. Relig: Protestant. Legal Res: Apt 15 620 NW 21st Corvallis OR 97330 Mailing Add: 2530 Ione St Sacramento CA 95821

CHAPPELL, WILLIAM VENROE, JR (BILL) (D)

US Rep, Fla

b Kendrick, Fla, Feb 3, 22; s William Venroe Chappell & Laura G Kemp C; m 1944 to Marguerite Gutshall; c Judith Jane (Mrs Edward Taylor), Deborah Kay (Mrs Thomas Bond), William V, III & Christopher Clyde. Educ: Univ Fla, BA, 47, LLB, 49, JD, 67; Phi Alpha Delta; Tau Kappa Alpha. Polit & Govt Pos: Co prosecuting attorney, Marion Co, Fla, 50-54; Fla State Rep, 54-64 & 67-68, speaker, Fla House Rep, 61-63; US Rep, Fla, 69-; deleg, Dem Nat Mid-Term Conf, 74. Bus & Prof Pos: Owner, J & J Elec Co, currently; bd mem, Bank of Belleview. Mil Serv: Entered as Aviation Cadet, Navy, 42, released as Lt(jg), 47, after serv in Training Command, 44-46; Capt Res, 46-72. Mem: Fla, Inter-Am & Am Bar Asns; Int Lawyers Asn; Am Trial Lawyers Asn. Honors & Awards: Allen Morris Award for the Most Valuable Mem of 1967 Fla House of Rep & the Most Effective in Debate. Relig: Methodist. Legal Res: 1910 SE 12th St Ocala FL 32670 Mailing Add: 1124 Longworth House Off Bldg Washington DC 20515

CHAPPIE, EUGENE A (R)

Calif State Assemblyman

b Sacramento, Calif, Mar 28, 20; s Albert Chappie & Irma Sperinde C; m 1941 to Paula Di Benedetto; c Susan, Eugene, II, John, Tina & Linda. Educ: Sacramento High Sch, Sacramento; Nat Sch, Los Angeles. Polit & Govt Pos: Supvr, El Dorado Co, Calif, 50-65; Calif State Assemblyman, until 67, 69-; deleg, Rep Nat Conv, 68, alt deleg, 72. Bus & Prof Pos: Rancher. Mil Serv: Entered as Pvt, Air Force, 42, released as Capt, after serv in Amphibious Tractor Bn, Pac, 46; Am Defense, Asiatic Pac & Good Conduct Medals; Bronze Star. Mem: Rotary; Am Legion; Pilot Hill Grange; Native Sons; Farm Bur. Relig: Catholic. Mailing Add: 438 Colusa Hwy Yuba City CA 95991

CHARBONNET, LOUIS, III (D)

La State Rep

b New Orleans, La; s Louis Charbonnet, Jr & Myrtle Labat C; m to Simone Monette; c Kim. Educ: Commonwealth Col of Sci, BS. Polit & Govt Pos: La State Rep, Dist 96, currently, mem judiciary comt, munic & parochial affairs comt & labor & indust comt, La House Rep, currently, floor leader, Orleans Parish deleg, 75- Bus & Prof Pos: Mem bd dirs, Treme Child Develop Ctr, 72-, La State Mus Bd, 72- & Total Community Action Agency, 73-; pres, Cresent City Funeral Dir, 74- Mil Serv: SP-4, Army, 61. Mem: Autocrat Social & Pleasure Club; Vikings Carnival Krewe; Treme Community Improv Asn. Relig: Catholic. Legal Res: 1607 St Phillip St New Orleans LA 70116 Mailing Add: 1615 St Phillip St New Orleans LA 70116

CHARETTE, ROBERT L (D)

Wash State Rep

b Aberdeen, Wash, 1923; m to Betty; c Three. Educ: Grays Harbor Jr Col; Univ Wash Law Sch; Phi Kappa Psi; Phi Delta Phi. Polit & Govt Pos: Wash State Rep, 66-, Majority Leader, Wash House Rep, currently. Bus & Prof Pos: Lawyer, Charette & Brown. Mil Serv: Army; Purple Heart. Mem: Am Bar Asn; Eagles; Elks; VFW; Am Legion. Mailing Add: Box 63 Aberdeen WA 98520

CHARFAUROS, EDWARD (D)

Sen, Guam Legis

Mailing Add: Guam Legislature Box 373 Agana GU 96910

CHARITY, RUTH LACOUNTESS HARVEY (D)

Dem Nat Committeewoman, Va

b Danville, Va; d Dr Charles Cliffon Harvey (deceased) & Annie Lovelace H; m 1968 to Ronald Karl Charity; c Khris Wayne. Educ: Howard Univ, AB, 45, JD, 49; Howard Chapter; NAACP; French Club; Sociology Club; Literary Guild; Student Counr. Polit & Govt Pos: Indust rel analyst, Wage Stabilization Bd, Washington, DC; exec to dir, President Johnson's Comt on Consumer Affairs; consumer specialist, Off Econ Opportunity; deleg, Dem Nat Conv, 72; Dem Nat Committeewoman, Va, 72-; mem, Dem Exec Comt, 74- Bus & Prof Pos: Pres, Southeastern Lawyers Asn; pres & mem exec comt, Old Dom Bar Asn; regional rep, Nat Asn Women Lawyers; & regional rep, Int Fedn of Women Lawyers; mem, bd dirs, Nat Bar Asn. Mem: Danville Bar Asn; Va Trial Lawyers Asn; Va State Bar; Alpha Kappa Alpha Inc (past Nat Supreme Parliamentarian Alumna). Honors & Awards: First Black Woman elected to Danville City Coun, 70; First Woman elected to presidency of Va Coun on Human Rels, 70; First Black Woman from the South elected to Nat Dem Comt, 72; Marguerite L Adams Polit Action Award, Alpha Kappa Alpha, 73; NAACP Award for Contribution in the Field of Civil Rights & Outstanding Leadership in Civil Rights. Relig: Baptist. Legal Res: 514 S Main St Danville VA 24541 Mailing Add: 453 S Main St Danville VA 24541

CHARKOUDIAN, ARPPIE (R)

VChmn, Mansfield Rep Town Comt, Conn

b Springfield, Mass, Dec 13, 25; d Nishan N Charkoudian & Azniv Sanjian C; single. Educ: Am Inst of Banking, Cert, 46; Tanglewood, Lenox, Mass, summer 47; Springfield Col, 57-58. Polit & Govt Pos: Ward comt mem, Springfield Rep City Comt, Mass, 57-59; state committeewoman, Mass Rep Party, 58 & 59; chmn, Mansfield Rep Town Comt, Conn, 68-72, vchmn, 72-; vchmn, Mansfield Charter Comn, 69; Justice of the Peace, Mansfield, 71- Bus & Prof Pos: Teller, Springfield Nat Bank, Mass, 43-47; exec secy, Springfield Symphony Orchestra Asn, 47-56; Eastern area rep, Columbia Artist Mgt, New York, 56-57; girls prog dir, Springfield YMCA, 57-59; assoc mgr, Jorgensen Auditorium, Univ Conn, 59- Mem: Zonta Int; Asn of Col & Univ Concert Mgrs; Univ of Conn League; Hampden Co Musicians' Asn; Am Fedn Musicians. Relig: Armenian Apostolic. Legal Res: N Eagleville Rd Storrs CT 06268 Mailing Add: 2 Lakeside Apt Storrs CT 06268

CHARLES, ERLAND W (R)

Chmn Sixth Dist, Minn Rep State Cent Comt

b Montevideo, Minn, Dec 2, 26; s Ernest H Charles & Clara Erlandson C; m 1949 to Joyce Loehr; c Wayne & Carter. Polit & Govt Pos: Rep precinct chmn, Stevens Co, Minn, 58; chmn, Stevens Co Rep Finance Comt, 59; chmn, Stevens Co Rep Comt, 59-62; chmn, Seventh Cong Dist Rep Comt, 61-62; chmn sixth dist, Minn Rep State Cent Comt, 61-; deleg, Rep Nat Conv, 64 & 68; chmn, Stevens Co Nixon Campaign Comt, 68 & 72; chmn, Seventh Cong Dist Farmers for Nixon Campaign, 72; mem, State Rep Planning Comt, 74-75. Bus & Prof Pos: Farmer, Minn, 47-; mem bd dirs, DirAction Inc, Minneapolis, 65- Mil Serv: Entered as Cadet, Army Air Force, 44, released as Pfc, 46, after serv in 10th Air Force. Mem: Am Farm Bur; Mason; Am Legion; Jaycees; Aircraft Owners & Pilots Asn; Flyers Inc. Relig: Lutheran. Mailing Add: Hancock MN 56244

CHARLTON, WM STUART (R)

Chmn, Delaware Co Rep Party, Iowa

b Manchester, Iowa, Nov 19, 28; s Shannon B Charlton & Etna Barr C; m 1952 to Lois D McCord; c Deborah, Pamela, Barbara, Bruce & Rebecca. Educ: Univ Iowa, BA, 50, JD, 52; Phi Kappa Psi; Phi Delta Phi. Polit & Govt Pos: Delaware Co Attorney, Iowa, 55-64; state secy, Young Rep of Iowa, 56-60, state chmn, 60-64; gen counsel, Young Rep Nat Fedn, 63-65; deleg, Rep Nat Conv, 64; chmn, Delaware Co Rep Party, Iowa, 64- Bus & Prof Pos: Farm mgr, 54-; attorney, Gilkey, Gould & Charlton, 54-58, Charlton, Charlton & Willey, 58- Mil Serv: 1st Lt, Air Force, 52-54. Publ: Joint tenancy in bank accounts, Iowa Law Rev, 51. Mem: Am Bar Asn; Rotary; Jr CofC; Mason; KofP. Honors & Awards: Local Dist Serv Award, Jr CofC, 58. Relig: Presbyterian. Legal Res: 800 Ridgewood Dr Manchester IA 52057 Mailing Add: 401 E Main St Manchester IA 52057

CHARNLEY, DONN (D)

Wash State Rep

b Detroit, Mich, Apr 3, 28; s Mitchell V Charnley & Margery Lindsay C; m to Lucile Janousek; c Scott W, E Ann, Brent R, Janet S & Craig M. Educ: Seattle Univ, 46-48; Univ Wash, BS, 51, MS, 63; Univ Minn, 62-63. Polit & Govt Pos: Wash State Rep, currently, chmn subcomt pub transportation & planning, Wash House Rep, 73- Bus & Prof Pos: Teacher, Ryther Child Ctr, 51-53; teacher, Ballard & West Seattle High Schs & Asa Mercer Jr High Sch, 53-60; counr, West Seattle High Sch, 60-66; prof geol, Shoreline Community Col, 65-; lectr geol, Univ Wash, 65- Mem: Nat Asn Geol Teachers; Northwest Geol Asn. Honors & Awards: Educ psychol grant, Nat Defense Educ Act, 62. Legal Res: 19344 11th Ave NW Seattle WA 98177 Mailing Add: Rm 338 House Off Bldg Olympia WA 98501

CHARTIER, GLENN DELL (D)

Chmn, Cloud Co Dem Party, Kans

b Clyde, Kans, Mar 31, 93; s Charles Dunning Chartier & Cora Trussel C; m 1920 to Dora Istas. Educ: Kans State Univ, 11. Polit & Govt Pos: Vpres, Farm Bur, Concordia, Kans, 38; dir rural electrification, Belleville, 40-45; chmn, US Dep Agr Br, Concordia, 40-51; chmn, War Bd, 41-50; chmn, Defense Bd, 45-50; agent & adjuster, Fed Crop Ins, State of Kans, 50-53; chmn, Cloud Co Dem Party, 63-; mem, Cent Kans Libr Bd & Exec Bd, 70- Mem: Elks; Eagles; Moose; Kiwanis; Mason. Honors & Awards: Balanced Farming & Family Living Award, 50; Soil Conserv Cert of Award, 51. Relig: Episcopal. Mailing Add: Rte 2 Box 59 Clyde KS 66938

CHASE, ANTHONY GOODWIN (R)

Dep Adminr, Small Bus Admin

b San Francisco, Calif, Feb 15, 38; s Goodwin Chase & Gudrun Mack C; m 1960 to Karen Lynne Zeissler; c Betsy Marie, Whitney Marie, Goodwin Samuel & Anthony Joseph. Educ: Univ Wash, BA, 60; Georgetown Univ Law Ctr, JD, 67; Phi Delta Phi; Georgetown Law J; Beta Theta Pi; Univ Wash Oval Club; mem, Bd of Control & pres, Inter-Fraternity Coun, Univ Wash, 60; Pi Omicron Sigma (pres, 60). Polit & Govt Pos: Nat bank examr, US Treas, 62-65; Asst US Comptroller Currency, DC, 65-67; asst to Gov for Fed State Rels, Olympia, Wash, 67-68; cand, US House Rep, Wash, 68; legal counsel, State Wash, 68-69; spec asst to US Secy of Com, 69-70; gen counsel, Small Bus Admin, 70-71, dep adminr, 71-; mem under secy group, US Domestic Coun, 71-; Fed Adv Coun on Regional Econ Develop, 71-; Securities Adv Comn Indust Issuers, 72-73. Bus & Prof Pos: Consult, Am Security & Trust Co, DC, 67; law practice; adj prof corp law, Georgetown Univ Law Sch, 71-; Wharton Sloan grant & guest lectr, Univ Pa, 73; attorney-at-law, Brownstein, Zeidman, Schomer & Chase, Washington, DC, 73- Mil Serv: Entered as 2nd Lt, Marine Corps, 60, released as 1st Lt, 62, after serv in First Bn, First Marines; Res Capt. Publ: Venture capital & the federal government, Bus Lawyer, fall 70; The emerging financial conglomerate: the liberalization of the Bank Holding Company Act, 1970, Georgetown Law J, Vol 60, No 5; This little agency went to market (w Eric Weinmann), Banking Law J, Vol 89, No 3; plus others. Mem: DC & Washington Bar Asns; Am Bar Asn (corp, banking & bus law sect, admin law sect); Fed Bar Asn (gen counsel's comt); Admin Conf of the US. Honors & Awards: Outstanding Young Man Award, Wash State Jaycees, 68; Outstanding Young Man of Am Award, 69; Am Jurisp Award, 67; SBA Silver Medal for Meritorious Serv & Spec Achievement Award, 70, SBA Gold Medal for Distinguished Serv. Relig: Episcopal. Legal Res: 732 N Stadium Way Tacoma WA 98403 Mailing Add: No 4 Carvel Circle Washington DC 20016

CHASE, CYRIL CHARLES (D)
Idaho State Sen
b Athol, Idaho, Oct 26, 17; s Fred B Chase & Sylvia Jane Norman C; m 1937 to Verdie Jane Shepherd; c Charles Ray, Dixie Lee & Sylvia Jane (deceased). Educ: High Sch; correspondence courses in elec eng. Polit & Govt Pos: City councilman, St Maries, 48-52; Idaho State Sen, 61-67 & 70-, asst to Dem Minority Leader, Idaho State Senate, currently, mem Senate state affairs, judiciary & rules, labor, in lieu land, ways & means, educ, transportation & defense comts, currently, caucus chmn, Dem Party, 71-72; chmn, Area Redevelop Admin, Area Redevelop Comt, Benewah Co & Lower Shoshone Co, 63-65. Bus & Prof Pos: Plant supt, Pot Latch Forests, Inc, 41-46; partner, Benewah Meat & Locker Co, St Maries, Idaho, 46-54; partner, Chase Shepherd Lumber Co, Calder, Idaho, 48-54; pres, Chase Chevrolet Pontiac, Inc, St Maries, Idaho, 54- Mem: Elks; Eagles; Kiwanis; Jr CofC (pres); Mason (32 degree). Relig: Methodist. Mailing Add: 201 11th St St Maries ID 83861

CHASE, DEWAYNE ARTHUR NEWTON (R)
Mem, Kans State Exec Rep Comt
b Omaha, Nebr, May 4, 02; s D A N Chase & Harriet Annette Ayer C; m 1926 to Mary Emaline Ramsey; c D A N, III. Educ: Washburn Univ, AB, 24; Kappa Sigma. Polit & Govt Pos: Mayor, Fredonia, Kans, 43-52; chmn, Fifth Dist Rep Comt, Kans, 62-; chmn, Wilson Co Rep Comt, Kans, 62-; mem, Kans State Exec Rep Comt, 62-; deleg, Rep Nat Conv, 68. Bus & Prof Pos: Store mgr, Montgomery Ward & Co, 28-30; owner, Burke Printing Co, Fredonia, Kans, 30- Mem: Elks; AF&AM; Mason (32nd degree). Honors & Awards: Tennis letterman in col, 24. Relig: Methodist. Mailing Add: 415 N 11th Fredonia KS 66736

CHASE, ELIZABETH ANN (D)
Secy, West Brookfield Town Dem Comt, Mass
b Plymouth, Mass, Sept 1, 39; d Cecil Hilton Crowell, Sr & Florence Agnes MacCartney C; m 1959 to Richard Olsen Chase; c Dawn Carroll & Marc Vernon. Educ: Mass Col Art, 57-60. Polit & Govt Pos: Coordr, South Worcester Co, McCarthy for President, 68; coordr, McGovern for President, 72; deleg-at-lg, Dem Nat Conv, 72; mem, Dem Adv Coun, Worcester-Franklin-Hampden-Hampshire Dist, 72-75; mem exec bd, Citizens for Partic in Polit Action, Boston, 72-; secy, West Brookfield Town Dem Comt, 72- Bus & Prof Pos: Writer-art reviewer, Craft Horizons Mag, NY, 68; instr adult art educ, Southbridge & North Brookfield, 68-70; farm worker, Sturbridge, 71; artist, currently; vpres & bd trustees, Family Planning Found, Inc, 74-75; mem citizenship educ task force, Mass Dept Educ, 73-75. Publ: Meet the Massachusetts Democratic delegation!, The Quabbin, West Brookfield, 7/4/72; A surrealistic adventure, 7/11/72 & A minority report, 7/13/72, Eve News, Southbridge. Mem: Cent Mass Family Planning Coun (bd dirs, 72-); West Brookfield Conserv Comn; Bandstand Music Comt, West Brookfield; South Cent Coun Children (chmn proposal rev comt, 75-). Legal Res: Longhill Rd West Brookfield MA 01585 Mailing Add: PO Box 342 West Brookfield MA 01585

CHASE, GARY C (R)
Chmn, Idaho Young Rep League
b Coeur d'Alene, Idaho, Oct 16, 49; s Harry D Chase & Eunice Sisson C; single. Educ: Univ Idaho Col Bus, BS, 72; Alpha Kappa Psi. Polit & Govt Pos: Chmn, Idaho Col Rep League, 70-72; dir, Pac Northwest Col Rep, 71-72; chmn, Idaho Rep Youth Caucus, 73-74; vchmn, Legis Dist Six, Idaho Rep State Cent Comt, 74-; chmn, Idaho Young Rep League, 75- Bus & Prof Pos: Asst mgr, W T Grants, Lewiston, Idaho, 72-75. Relig: Presbyterian. Mailing Add: 2813 11th Ave Lewiston ID 83501

CHASE, JOHN WILLIAM (R)
Chmn, Lawrence Co Rep Cent Comt, Ind
b Medora, Ind, Mar 7, 26; s Maurice Chase & Catherine Hamilton C; m 1950 to Evelyn M Nelson; c Cheryl Lynn & Lisa Ann. Educ: Ind Univ, 1 year. Polit & Govt Pos: Deleg, Ind State Rep Conv, 52-58; chmn, Lawrence Co Young Rep, 53; driver examr, Bur of Motor Vehicles, 57-60, clerk, Lawrence Circuit Court, 61-68; chmn, Lawrence Co Rep Cent Comt, 66-; mgr, Bedford License Br, 69- Mil Serv: Entered as Seaman, Navy, 44, released as Coxswain, 46, after serv in USS Pitt, Pac, 44-46; Victory Medal; Am Area Campaign Medal; Asiatic Pac Area Campaign Medal with one star. Mem: F&AM; RSM; RAM; K T; Ind Consistory S P R S 32. Honors & Awards: Awarded Sagamore of the Wabash. Relig: Methodist. Mailing Add: Rte 1 Bedford IN 47421

CHASE, NANCY BASTIEN (R)
Chmn, Second Cong Dist Rep Party, Mich
b Chicago, Ill, May 8, 16; d Alvin E Bastien & Lena Kelly B; m 1944 to Charles Borden Chase; c Charles Borden, III, Barbara Bastien & Peter Bastien. Educ: Art Inst Chicago, 36-37. Polit & Govt Pos: Vchmn, Ann Arbor City Rep Comt, Mich, 64-66; chmn, Washtenaw Co Elly Peterson for US Sen Campaign, 66; hq chmn, Washtenaw Co Rep Comt, 66 & 67; mem, Mich State Rep Cent Comt, 67-68, chmn, 67-68, mem, State Finance Exec Comt, 67-68; mem, Second Cong Dist Rep Comt, 67-, chmn, 71-; chmn, Washtenaw Co Rep Comt, formerly; mem, State Bd of Canvassers, 73-; vchmn, Mich Rep State Comt, currently. Mil Serv: Am Red Cross Clubmobile, Europe, 44-46. Mem: Community Camp Placement Comt; United Fund & Community Serv Ann Arbor; Thrift Shop Asn; Ann Arbor Women's City Club; Rep Women's Club. Relig: Congregational. Mailing Add: 1 Regent Dr Ann Arbor MI 48104

CHASE, NANCY WINBON (D)
NC State Rep
b Fremont, NC, Oct 12, 03; d Robert Edward Winbon & Kate Davis W; m 1922 to John B Chase (deceased); c John B, Jr & Thomas E (deceased); 4 grandchildren. Educ: Fremont High Sch, 21. Polit & Govt Pos: Mem sch bd, Eureka, NC, 59-60; mem, Charles B Aycock Sch Bd, 60-62; co-chmn, Wayne Co Dem Campaign, 60; vchmn, Eureka Dem Precinct, 60-61; mem, State Welfare Study Comn, 61-62; mem, Gov State Traffic Safety Coun & State Tobacco Adv Comn; NC State Rep, 63-, mem legis comn to study emotional child, NC House Rep, subcomt legis research comt to study & make recommendations on awarding degrees in trade schs & mem comn to study barriers of educ, currently; mem, Wayne Co Exten Adv Comn, 64; deleg, Dem Nat Conv, 68; mem, Gov Study Comt Archit Barriers & mem bd, NC Land Use Planning Cong, currently. Bus & Prof Pos: Housewife. Mem: NC Adv Comt to Peace Corps; NC Ment Health Found (bd mem); NC Farm Bur Fedn; Comt on Educ & Employ Women; Bus & Prof Women's Club (chmn legis comt). Honors & Awards: South's Most Outstanding Woman of Year, Progressive Farmer, 64; Citation & Plaque for Serv to Rural People, NC Farm Bur Women, 67; Spec Award for Leadership & Outstanding Serv, NC Ment Health Asn, 68; Distinguished Serv Award, Arthritis Found, 69. Relig: Methodist; teacher, adult Sunday sch, Eureka Methodist Church, 47-64, treas, 59-64, bd stewards, 59-64, lay speaker. Mailing Add: Box 226 Eureka NC 27830

CHASE, RAYMOND F (D)
NH State Rep
Mailing Add: 30 Sheep Davis Rd Concord NH 03301

CHASE, RUSSELL CUSHING (R)
NH State Rep
b Boston, Mass, Feb 5, 07; s William Cooledge Chase & Mabel Cushing C; m to Katherine Elizabeth Owen; c Barbara (Mrs Wetherbee) & David Owen. Educ: Northeastern Univ, BSCE, 29. Polit & Govt Pos: NH State Rep, 69- Bus & Prof Pos: Various eng jobs, Mass, 29-42; from NE mgr asphalt dept to mgr mgt training, Shell Oil Co, 42-67. Mem: Boston Soc Civil Engrs; Rotary; Mason. Relig: Unitarian. Mailing Add: Middleton Rd Wolfeboro NH 03894

CHASE, THEODORE, JR (D)
Committeeman, Somerset Co Dem Comt, NJ
b Boston, Mass, Aug 20, 38; s Theodore Chase & Dorothea Newman C; m 1965 to Victory Van Dyck; c Vanessa. Educ: Harvard Col, AB, 60; Univ Calif, Berkeley, PhD, 66. Polit & Govt Pos: Alt deleg, Dem Nat Conv, 72; committeeman, Somerset Co Dem Comt, NJ, 72-; ward chmn, Franklin Twp, currently. Bus & Prof Pos: Research assoc, Dept Biol, Brookhaven Nat Lab, 66-69; asst prof biochem, Rutgers Univ, New Brunswick, 69-73, assoc prof biochem, 73- Publ: Co-auth, articles in, Biochemistry, 8:1012; auth, Flavor enzymes, In: Food-related enzymes, Am Chem Soc, 74; co-auth, Determination of protein immobilized on solid support by tryptophan content, Anal Biochem, 57:421. Mem: Am Soc Microbiol; Am Chem Soc; Am Ornithologists Union; Brit Ornithologists Union; Wilson Ornithological Soc. Mailing Add: Old Georgetown Rd RD 1 Princeton NJ 08540

CHASNOFF, JOEL (D)
Md State Deleg
b Uncasville, Conn, July 18, 36; s Hillel Chasnoff & Sadie Frank C; m 1957 to Sue Prosen; c Debra Hill & Lori Beth. Educ: Univ Conn, AB, 57; Georgetown Univ Law Sch, JD, 64; Pi Sigma Alpha; Phi Sigma Delta. Polit & Govt Pos: Md State Deleg, 75- Bus & Prof Pos: Attorney, Off of Solicitor, Dept of Labor, Washington, DC, 65-69; attorney-at-law, Silver Spring, Md, 69- Mil Serv: Entered as 2nd Lt, Army, 58, released as 1st Lt, 61, after serv in Nat Security Agency, Fort Meade. Mem: Fed, Am & DC Bar Asns; Montgomery Co & Md Bar; Tamarack Triangle (pres). Legal Res: 1321 Mimosa Lane Colesville MD 20904 Mailing Add: 8728 Colesville Rd Silver Spring MD 20910

CHASTAIN, CHARLES WILLIAM, III (D)
Chmn, St Francois Co Dem Cent Comt, Mo
b Plattsburg, Mo, Oct 17, 30; s Charles William Chastain & Faith Payne C; m 1954 to Caroline Parker Saunders; c Charles William, Jane Martindale, John Langdon, Catherine Payne, Caroline Parker & Edward Saunders. Educ: Harvard Univ, AB, 48; Columbia Univ Col Physicians & Surgeons, MD, 52; Nu Sigma Nu. Polit & Govt Pos: Pres, Harvard Liberal Union, 49-50; pres, St Francois Co Dem Club, Mo, 67; committeeman, St Francois Twp Dem Party, 71-; chmn, St Francois Co Dem Cent Comt, 72- Bus & Prof Pos: Partner, Med Arts Clin, 60-; chief of staff, Madison Mem Hosp, 64-65; secy med staff, Farmington Community Hosp, 71-73; pres, Farmington Lancaster Corp, 72- Mil Serv: Entered as Capt, Army, 57, released in 59, after serv in Med Corps, 5th Army Hq, Chicago. Publ: Co-auth, Report on Accessability to Health Services, 71 & Handbook on Health Activities Service Profile, 72, Mo Gov Adv Coun on Comprehensive Health Planning. Mem: Am Med Asn; Mo State Med Asn (comn mem, 69-); Mineral Area Med Asn (pres, 66, deleg to state, 66-); Am Acad Family Physicians (nat deleg, 72-); Mo Acad Family Physicians (bd trustees, 71-). Honors & Awards: Nat scholar, Harvard Univ, 48. Relig: Roman Catholic. Legal Res: Highway F Farmington MO 63640 Mailing Add: c/o Med Arts Clin Farmington MO 63640

CHASTEEN, JOE L (R)
Wyo State Rep
Mailing Add: 820 South Tenth Laramie WY 82070

CHATALAS, WILLIAM (BILL) (D)
Wash State Rep
b Constantinople, Turkey, 1907; m to Goldie; c Three sons. Educ: Univ Wash Exten Sch. Polit & Govt Pos: Wash State Rep, currently. Bus & Prof Pos: Sales & pub rels mgr. Mem: Ahepa; Eagles; Rainer Bus Men's Club; Mt Baker Improv Club; CofC. Mailing Add: 4803 42nd Ave S Seattle WA 98118

CHATBURN, J VARD (R)
Idaho State Rep
b Albion, Idaho, Aug 7, 08; s John B Chatburn & Zella Handy C; m 1929 to Eva Lemmon; c Jeannine (Mrs LaVere Bennett), John Vard, Jr & James Oliver. Educ: Albion State Normal Sch, 25-27. Polit & Govt Pos: Trustee, Albion Sch Bd, Idaho; hwy comnr, Albion; Idaho State Rep, 57- Mem: Mason; Elks; Grange; Farm Bur. Honors & Awards: Idaho Grassman, 64; Idaho Legis Conservationist, 65. Mailing Add: Box 97 Albion ID 83311

CHATELAIN, LEON, JR (R)
Committeeman, DC Rep Comt
b Washington, DC, Mar 8, 02; s Leon Chatelain & Bertha Ashbacher C; m 1944 to Mary Wysong; c Jo Ann, Edward Russell & Leon, III. Educ: George Washington Univ, BArch, 27; Alpha Chi Rho; Scarabs; Theta Delta Chi. Polit & Govt Pos: Committeeman, DC Rep Comt, 64-, chmn, formerly. Bus & Prof Pos: Owner, Leon Chatelain, Jr, Architect, 30-39; partner, Chatelain, Gauger & Nolan, 59- Mem: Am Inst Architects; fel Construction Specification Inst; sr mem Nat Soc Real Estate Appraisers; Mason (past master); Shriner. Honors & Awards: President's Comt Employ Handicapped distinguished serv award; Cosmopolitan Club's distinguished serv medal; Wash Bd Trade Man of the Years. Relig: Methodist. Mailing Add: 1632 K St NW Washington DC 20006

CHATHAM, RAY B (RAY) (D)
Miss State Sen
Mailing Add: PO Box 1390 Hattiesburg MS 39401

CHATTIN, CHESTER COLES (D)
Assoc Justice, Supreme Court of Tenn
b Winchester, Tenn, Nov 2, 07; s Edward Walter Chattin & Ellen Shadow C; m 1935 to Mary Eleanor Kiningham; c Mary Kay. Educ: Univ of the South, BS; Cumberland Law Sch, LLB; Phi Gamma Delta. Polit & Govt Pos: Asst dist attorney gen, Tenn, 35-37 & 39-47; Tenn State Rep, 40-44; dist attorney gen, 18th Judicial Circuit of Tenn, 47-58, circuit judge, 58-62;

Judge, Court of Appeals of Tenn, 62-65; Assoc Justice, Supreme Court of Tenn, 65- Bus & Prof Pos: Dir, Farmers Nat Bank, Winchester, Tenn, 47- Mil Serv: Entered as Draftee, Navy, 45, released as Hosp Apprentice 1/C, 45, after serv in Hosp Corps. Mem: Int Platform Asn; Boy Scouts (Mid Tenn Coun); Tenn Law Enforcement Officers Asn; Mason; Shrine. Relig: Episcopal. Mailing Add: Winchester TN 37398

CHAVES, JOSEPH J (D)
RI State Sen
Mailing Add: 193 Honeyman Ave Middletown RI 02840

CHAVEZ, MELCHOR (D)
Tex State Rep
b La Feria, Tex, Oct 27, 34; s Dionicio Chavez & Matilde Camacho C; m 1963 to Gloria Martinez; c Gloria Annette. Educ: Tex Southmost Col, 57-59; Univ Tex, 59-60; Univ Tex Sch Law, 63; Delta Theta Phi. Polit & Govt Pos: Tex State Rep, Dist 51, 75- Bus & Prof Pos: Vpres, Harlingen Sch Trustees, 70-; partner, Chavez & Barnard, Attorneys, Harlingen, Tex. Mil Serv: Entered as Pvt, Army, 53, released as SP-4, 56, after serv in Guided Missile Unit, 4th Army. Mem: Harlingen Jaycees; Kiwanis; Am & Tex State Bar Asns; Cameron Co Bar Asn (secy, vpres, 74-75). Honors & Awards: Outstanding State Dir, Tex Jaycees, 67; Outstanding Young Man of Harlingen, 67. Relig: Catholic. Mailing Add: 1906 Pease Harlingen TX 78550

CHAVEZ, RICHARD (D)
Mem, Dem Nat Comt, Calif
Legal Res: CA Mailing Add: 331 W 84th St New York NY 10024

CHAVEZ, WILLIE M (R)
NMex State Sen
Mailing Add: 1012 Santa Anita Dr Belen NM 87002

CHEATHAM, JOHN BRYAN (D)
Chmn, Miller Co Dem Cent Comt, Ark
b Village, Ark, Sept 19, 96; s William Andrew Cheatham & Martha McCall C; m 1923 to Gladys Jones; c Nancy (Mrs Whitecotton) & Gladys Sue. Educ: Ark Agr & Mech Col, 14-16; Cumberland Univ Law Sch, 30; Garland Lit Soc. Polit & Govt Pos: Chmn, Miller Co Dem Cent Comt, Ark, 67-; chmn, Miller Co Elec Comn, 70- Bus & Prof Pos: Supvr, Mobil Unit Sect, Postal Transportation Serv, US Post Off Dept, 18-65; retired. Mem: Miller Co & Ark Bar Asns; Nat Postal Transport Asn; Nat Asn Retired Fed Employees. Mailing Add: 2317 Locust St Texarkana AR 75501

CHEEK, EARL HERMAN, SR (D)
Mem, Ga State Dem Exec Comt
b Hart Co, Ga, Dec 28, 16; s George Thomas Cheek & Fannie Sanders C; m 1937 to Frances Marion Hunter; c Earl H, Jr, Carol A (Mrs Barckley) & Mary France (Mrs Larimer). Educ: Univ Ga, BA, 37, MA, 51; Phi Kappa Phi; Kappa Delta Pi; Agr Club; Saddle & Sirloin; 4-H Club; Future Farmers Am. Polit & Govt Pos: Admin aide to US Sen Nunn, Ga, 74; mem, Ga State Dem Exec Comt, 74- Bus & Prof Pos: Voc agr teacher, Baker Co, Ga, 37-39, Early Co, Ga, 39-55 & Houston Co, Ga, 55-74. Mil Serv: Entered as Aviation Cadet, Air Force, 42, released as 2nd Lt, 45, after serv in B-29 Army Air Force-235th BU-CCTS VH, 44-45, Lt Col Air Force Res (Ret), 72. Mem: ROA; Air Force Asn; Farm Bur; Lions; Am Legion. Honors & Awards: Outstanding Future Farmer Am, State Ga Chap, 5 times; Outstanding Young Farmer, 72; Outstanding Agr Teacher of Ga, 66; Outstanding Agr Teacher of the South, 68; Ga Voc Teacher of Year, 74. Relig: Baptist. Legal Res: Houston Lake Rd Perry GA 31069 Mailing Add: Box 114 Perry GA 31069

CHEEK, WILL T (D)
Secy, Tenn State Dem Exec Comt
b Nashville, Tenn, Oct 4, 43; s Will T Cheek & Bessie Louise Courtwright C; m 1970 to Jeannie Stanley; c Bill & Catherine. Educ: Mid Tenn State Univ, BS, 65; Univ Ala, MA, 66; Pi Gamma Mu. Polit & Govt Pos: Dir research, Gov Staff Div for Indust Develop, Tenn, 66-70; secy, Young Dem Clubs Tenn, 66-70; mem, Tenn State Dem Exec Comt, Fifth Cong Dist, 70-, secy, 73- Bus & Prof Pos: Publ, Tenn Report, 70-72; pres, Will T Cheek, Consult, 72- Mem: Nashville Press Club (bd dirs, 74-); Nashville City Club; City of Hope (mem, Gtr Nashville Exec Coun); Tenn Green Asn (chmn bd, 72-); Nashville Area Jr CofC. Mailing Add: 712 Enquirer Ave Nashville TN 37205

CHEEVER, GENE G (R)
b Brookings, SDak, Dec 30, 28; s Herbert E Cheever & Margaret Williams C; m 1952 to JoAnn Coughlin; c Patrick, Timmothy, Dan & Todd. Educ: SDak State Univ, BS, 51; Univ Ill, MS, 52; Blue Key; Delta Tau Delta. Polit & Govt Pos: Chmn, Butte Co Rep Party, SDak, formerly; State Cent Committeeman, Butte Co, formerly. Bus & Prof Pos: Football coach & dir of phys educ, Dakota Wesleyan Univ, 52-53; football coach & athletic dir, Watertown High Sch, 54-55; sales mgr, Black Hills Clay Prod Co, 56-62, mgr, 63-; pres, Belle Fourche CofC, 70-71. Relig: Catholic. Mailing Add: Box 428 Belle Fourche SD 57717

CHEEVER, HERBERT EDWARD, JR (D)
b Brookings, SDak, Aug 26, 38; s Herbert Edward Cheever, Sr & Margaret Williams C; m 1959 to Sydna Riedesel; c Jason, Michael & Gene. Educ: SDak State Univ, BS, 60; Univ Iowa, MA, 63, PhD, 66. Polit & Govt Pos: Co-chmn, Brookings Co McGovern for Sen Comt, 68; consult, Sen Select Comt Nutrition & Human Needs, summer 69; deleg, SDak State Dem Conv, 70 & 72; chmn, Brookings Co Dem Party, 70-74; dir comput opers, SDak Dem Party, 70-, treas, 73-74; consult reapportionment, Dem Caucuses, SDak State Legis, 71; mem, Gov Comt Children & Youth, 71-72; SDak Dem Party Comn to Implement Reforms in Deleg Selection Process, 71-72; dist chmn, Sen McGovern Presidential Campaign, spring 72; campaign mgr, Gov R F Kneip Reelec Campaign, 72 & 74. Bus & Prof Pos: Asst prof, Kans State Col, 63-65, Wis State Univ, LaCrosse, 66-68 & SDak State Univ, 68- Mem: Am Asn Univ Prof; SDak Social Sci Asn. Mailing Add: 405 20th Ave Brookings SD 57006

CHEL, FRED W (D)
Calif State Assemblyman
b Rotterdam, Netherlands, Nov 30, 29; m 1952 to Elizabeth June Malak; c Frederick William & Lisette. Educ: Pepperdine Univ, BA in polit sci, 52; Univ Calif Los Angeles Law Sch, JD, 55. Polit & Govt Pos: US Govt appeals agent, Selective Serv Syst, formerly, chmn, Appeal Bd 5, formerly; Calif State Assemblyman, 58th Dist, 74- Bus & Prof Pos: Dir, Long Beach Legal Aid Found, formerly. Mem: Am, Calif State, Los Angeles Co & Long Beach Bar Asns; Los Altos YMCA. Legal Res: 6308 Eliot St Long Beach CA 90803 Mailing Add: 2750 Bellflower Blvd Suite 208 Long Beach CA 90815

CHELF, FRANK, SR (D)
b Elizabethtown, Ky, Sept 22, 10; s Judge Weed S Chelf & Hallie Wrather C; m to Louise Rash; c Caroline, Bonnie & Frank, Jr. Educ: St Mary's Col; Centre Col; Cumberland Univ, LLB; Phi Delta Theta. Polit & Govt Pos: US Rep, Ky, 45-67; prosecuting attorney, Marion Co, 12 years. Bus & Prof Pos: Attorney. Mil Serv: Maj, Army Air Force, World War II. Mem: Am Legion; VFW; KT; Eastern Star. Relig: Presbyterian. Mailing Add: Lebanon KY 40033

CHENEY, KIMBERLY B (R)
Attorney Gen, Vt
b Manchester, Conn, Nov 25, 35; s Kimberly Cheney & Margreta Swenson C; m 1960 to Barbara Suter; c Alison & Margreta. Educ: Yale Univ, BA, 57, LLB, 64. Polit & Govt Pos: Asst Attorney Gen, Vt, 67-68, Attorney Gen, 73-; state's attorney, Washington Co, 69-72. Bus & Prof Pos: Attorney, Gumbart, Corbin, Tyler & Cooper, New Haven, Conn, 64-67. Mil Serv: Entered as Ens, Navy, 58, released as Lt, 60. Publ: Safeguarding legal rights of children, Children, 69. Mem: Conn & Vt Bar Asns; Nat Dist Attorneys Asn. Relig: Episcopal. Mailing Add: 7 Greenock Ave Montpelier VT 05602

CHENNAULT, ANNA CHAN (R)
Mem, DC Rep Comt
b Peiping, China, June 23, 25; d Y W Chan & Bessie Jeong C; m to Gen Claire Lee Chennault, wid; c Claire Anna & Cynthia Louise. Educ: Ling Nan Univ, China, BA. Hon Degrees: LittD, Chung-ang Univ, Seoul, Korea, 67; LLD, Lincoln Univ, 70. Polit & Govt Pos: Appointee, Presidents Adv Comt on the Arts, John F Kennedy Ctr for the Performing Arts, US Nat Comn for the UN Educ, Sci & Cult Orgn & Secy of Transportation John A Volpe's Comt for US Int Transportation Expos; spec asst to chmn of US CofC of Pac & Southeast Asia; Bd Trustees, Ctr for Study of the Presidency; co-chairwoman, Nat Rep Heritage Group Coun; chmn, Asian-Am Rep Nat Comt; adv, Nat League of Families of Am Prisoners & Missing in Southeast Asia; adv, mem, Nations's Capitol Chap, Air Force Asn; chmn, Awards, 14th Air Force Asn Exec Comt, Am Acad of Achievement, Dallas, Tex; adv, Radio of Free Asia Bd Visitors, Civil Air Patrol; co-chmn, Women for Nixon-Agnew Nat Adv Comt, 68; chmn, Rep Women's Nat Finance Comt, 68; vchmn, Rep Nationalities Div, 68, adv, Rep Nat Finance Comt, spec adv to chmn, Inaugural Comt, 69, vchmn in charge of pub rels, Gov Reception Comt, 69; deleg, Rep Nat Conv, 72; co-chmn, Salute to Heritage, Inaugural Comt, 72; mem bd dirs, DC Nat Bank, 72; chmn, US Citizens in Asia for Nixon, 72; spec asst to exec dir, Inaugural Comt, 72-73; mem, Women's Adv Comt on Aviation, Dept Transportation, 73-; mem, DC Rep Comt, currently; app, Am Revolution Bicentennial Adv Comt, 75- Bus & Prof Pos: Feature writer, Hsin Ming Daily News, Shanghai; ed & pub rels officer, Civil Air Transport Bull, Taipei, Taiwan, 47-57; chief of Chinese Sect, Machine Transl Research, Georgetown Univ, 58-63; US correspondent, Hsin Shen Daily News, 58-; broadcaster, Voice of Am, Washington, DC, 63-66; spec correspondent to Washington, DC, Cent News Agency, 65-; writer, lecturer, aviation consult & vpres int affairs, The Flying Tiger Line, Inc, Washington, DC, 68- Publ: A Thousand Springs, 62 & Chennault & the Flying Tigers, Paul S Erikson, Inc; Dictionary of New Simplified Chinese Characters, Georgetown Univ Press, Washington, DC, 63. Mem: Nat Press Club; DC Rep Comt; League of Rep Women DC; Friends of Chung-ang Univ; Nat League of Am Pen Women. Honors & Awards: Woman of Distinction Award, Tex Technol Col, Lubbock, 66; Freedom Award, Order of Lafayette, 66 & Free China Asn, 66; Golden Plate Award for Champion of Democracy & Freedom, Am Acad of Achievement, 67; Lady of Mercy Award, Mt Carmel Mercy Hosp & Med Ctr, Southfield, Mich, 72. Relig: Catholic. Legal Res: Watergate E 2510 Virginia Ave NW Washington DC 20037 Mailing Add: Suite 1020 Investment Bldg 1511 K St NW Washington DC 20005

CHENOWETH, J EDGAR (R)
b Trinidad, Colo, Aug 17, 97; s Thomas Beaseman Chenoweth & Esther Rebeca Shamberger C; m 1919 to Ruth Ollevia Crews; c William B, Wanda Elizabeth, John Edgar, James Richard & Ruth Anne. Educ: Univ Colo. Polit & Govt Pos: Asst dist attorney, Third Judicial Dist, Colo, 29-33; judge, Las Animas Co, 33-41; chmn, Rep State Comt, 37-40; US Rep, Third Cong Dist, Colo, 41-49 & 51-65. Mem: Am & Colo Bar Asns; Mason; Elks; Eagles. Relig: Baptist. Legal Res: 1315 Alta St Trinidad CO 81082 Mailing Add: Box 48 Trinidad CO 81082

CHENOWETH, JOHN CRAIG (D)
Minn State Sen
b St Paul, Minn, May 20, 43; s William Vernon Chenoweth, Sr & Florine Ann Johnson C; m 1969 to Mary Sharon Naughton. Educ: St John's Univ, Minn, BS in Govt, 65; John Carroll Univ, 65; St Paul Sem, 65-66; William Mitchell Col Law, 67-68; student body pres, St John's Univ. Polit & Govt Pos: Cong campaign dir, Second Dist, Minn, 66; mem, Dem-Farmer-Labor State Cent Comt, Minn, 68-; Minn State Rep, 68-70; Minn State Sen, 70-, chmn metrop & urban affairs comt, Minn State Senate, 73- Bus & Prof Pos: Stockbroker, Paine, Webber, Jackson & Curtis, 70- Mil Serv: Minn Nat Guard. Relig: Roman Catholic. Mailing Add: 1378 Searle St St Paul MN 55101

CHERBERG, JOHN ANDREW (D)
Lt Gov, Wash
b Pensacola, Fla, Oct 17, 10; s Fortunato Cherberg & Annie Rand C; m 1935 to Elizabeth Anne Walker; c Dr James Walker, Kay (Mrs Ray Cohrs) & Barbara (Mrs Dean Tonkin). Educ: Univ Wash, BBA in econ, mkt & advert, 33, Col of Educ, Life Teaching Dipl, 34; Sigma Nu; Oval Club; Fir Tree. Polit & Govt Pos: Lt Gov, Wash, 57-, chmn, Nat Conf of Lt Gov, 68-69, Data Processing Authority, mem, State Capitol Comt, State Finance Comt, Oil & Gas Conserv Comt & State Patrol Retirement Bd; mem, World Fair Comn, 70 & 74. Bus & Prof Pos: Teacher & football coach, Cleveland High Sch, Seattle, Wash, 34-38; teacher & football coach, Queen Anne High Sch, Seattle, 38-46; football coach, Univ Wash, 46-56. Mem: Seattle Local, Am Fedn of TV & Radio Artists; Nat Asn of Football Coaches; Nat Acad of TV Arts & Sci; US Army Asn; Nat Educ Asn. Honors & Awards: Hon US Navy Seabee; Hon Ky Col; Honor Achievement Award by Bikur Cholim; VFW Achievement Award; Hon Chief, Yakima Indian Nat. Relig: Catholic. Legal Res: 505 Howe St Seattle WA 98109 Mailing Add: Legislative Bldg Olympia WA 98504

CHERKASKY, WILLIAM BENJAMIN (D)
b Madison, Wis, Aug 11, 24; s Benjamin Cherkasky & Anna C; m 1950 to Shirley Schroeder; c Mara, Clare & Lisa. Educ: Northwestern Univ; Univ Wis, BBA, 49; Beta Alpha Psi. Polit & Govt Pos: Former legis dir for US Sen Gaylord Nelson, Wis, admin asst, currently; many & varied polit positions, Wis, 49-; area supvr, Econ Develop Admin, US Dept of Com, 66. Bus & Prof Pos: Pres, Valley Realty Co, Appleton, Wis, 56-60; pres, Quaker Dairy Co,

Appleton, 60-66. Mil Serv: Entered as Pvt, Army, 43, released as Pfc, after serv in 89th Inf Div, ETO; Bronze Star; ETO Ribbon with Three Battle Stars. Honors & Awards: Cert of Commendation & Award, Dept of Com, 66. Relig: Unitarian. Legal Res: WI Mailing Add: 7312 Rebecca Dr Hollin Hills Alexandria VA 22307

CHERRY, ANNIE LEE **(D)**
b Graceville, Fla, Sept 4, 23; d Fred Hamilton Stokes & Mattie Dixon S; m 1942 to Samuel Alex Cherry; c Gloria (Mrs Sorrells), Camille (Mrs Sherer) & Samuel A, Jr. Educ: Campbell's Bus Col, grad, 43. Polit & Govt Pos: Mem, State Bd Educ, Ala, 71-; deleg, Dem Nat Conv, 72; deleg, Dem Nat Mid-Term Conf, 74. Bus & Prof Pos: Vpres, Allied Furniture Sales Co, 55- Mem: League Women Voters; Womens Div CofC; PTA; Delta Kappa Gamma; Future Homemakers Am. Honors & Awards: Dothan's Woman of Year, Bus & Prof Women's Club, 59. Relig: Methodist; mem, United Methodist Women. Mailing Add: 1328 S St Andrews St Dothan AL 36301

CHERRY, FRANK ELLIOTT **(R)**
Chmn, Sioux Co Rep Party, Nebr
b Douglas Co, Nebr, Aug 10, 13; s Earl Roe Cherry & Grace Ellen Warren C; m 1942 to Lucille Caroline Wegehoeft; c William David & Grace Anne. Educ: Univ Nebr, BS, 36; Pershing Rifles; Phi Gamma Delta. Polit & Govt Pos: Chmn, Sioux Co Rep Party, Nebr, 64- Bus & Prof Pos: Dir, First Nat Bank, Morrill, Nebr, 46-; dir, local Rural Electrification Admin Coop, 52-68. Mil Serv: Entered as Pvt, Army, 42, released as T/Sgt, 46, after serv in Air Force Finance, 42-46. Mem: Nebr Stock Growers Asn; Nebr Beef Coun; Am Nat Cattlemen's Asn (beef prom comt, 67-); AF&AM (past Master, Sioux Lodge); Am Legion. Relig: Methodist. Mailing Add: Box 452 Harrison NE 69346

CHERRY, GWENDOLYN SAWYER **(D)**
Fla State Rep
b Miami, Fla, Aug 27, 23; d William Benjamin Sawyer, Sr & Alberta Louise Presley; m 1960 to James Learon Cherry; c Mary Elizabeth & William Sawyer Barnett. Educ: Fla A&M Univ, BS, 46, JD cum laude, 65; NY Univ, MA, 50; Nat Sci Found fels, Univ Calif, Los Angeles, 58, Morgan State Col, 59 & Fisk Univ, summers 60 & 61. Polit & Govt Pos: Fla State Rep, Dist 96, 70-72, Dist 106, 72-; chairwoman minority affairs, Dem Nat Conv, 72; chairperson, Nat Women's Polit Caucus, 72-73; founder & treas, Nat Asn Black Women, 72- Bus & Prof Pos: Asst prof law, Fla A&M Univ, 67-68; law practice, Abramson & Butter, 67-68; asst dir, Legal Serv Prog, Inc, Domestic Rels Univ, 68-; hearing officer, Dade Co Sch Bd, 69; area dir, Brownsville Ctr, EOPI, 69; US Coast Guard Attorney, 70; attorney, 73-; mem exec bd, Southern Regional Coun, 74- Publ: Co-auth, Portraits In Color, 61; auth, various professional publ to sci & educ journals. Mem: Nat Asn Women Lawyers; bd mem, YWCA; Am Asn Univ Women; Fla Women's Lawyer's Asn; Am Bar Asn; Order Women Legis. Honors & Awards: Dade Co First Negro Woman Attorney Plaque, Sigma Gamma Rho, 65; Dean of Dem Women in the Florida Legislature, 74-; Concern, Interest & Involvement with the Leadership of Tomorrow Plaque, Cherry Cadre & Corps, Inc, 74; Outstanding Woman in Politics Award, Dade Co Bus & Prof Women Club, 74; Distinguished & unselfish service in the area of Human Relations Plaque, Concerned Citizens, 74. Legal Res: 2545 NW 46th St Miami FL 33142 Mailing Add: 636 NW Second Ave Miami FL 33136

CHERRY, HOWARD L **(D)**
Ore State Rep
Mailing Add: 1602 N Willamette Blvd Portland OR 97417

CHERUBINI, LILLIAN M WILLIAMS **(R)**
Committeewoman, NJ State Rep Party
b Philadelphia, Pa, Oct 6, 16; d Earl Williams & Rebecca Cromley W; m 1936 to Perry Cherubini; c Earl, Judy (Mrs Dallago) & Nancy Ann (Mrs Merritt). Educ: Bridgeton High Sch, dipl. Polit & Govt Pos: First vpres, Cumberland Co Rep Party, NJ, 69-70; committeewoman, NJ State Rep Party, 70- Mem: NJ Fedn Rep Women (rep, Cumberland Co, 73-); Cumberland Co Rep Orgn; Cumberland Co Women's Rep Club. Relig: Catholic. Mailing Add: 40 Hitchner Ave Bridgeton NJ 08302

CHESNEY, CHESTER ANTON **(D)**
b Chicago, Ill, Mar 9, 16; s Anthony Chesney & Anna Stupak C; m 1943 to Betty Jane Uetrecht; c Elizabeth Ann. Educ: DePaul Univ, BS, 39; Northwestern Univ Grad Sch, 47. Polit & Govt Pos: US Rep, 11th Cong Dist, Ill, 48-50; fed-state liaison officer, Fed Civil Defense Admin, 50-51; committeeman, Elk Grove Twp Dem Orgn, 62-; alt deleg, Dem Nat Conv, 68. Bus & Prof Pos: Asst vpres, Advance Mortgage Corp, 53-60; vpres & dir, Avondale Savings & Loan Asn, 60- Mil Serv: Entered as Pvt, Air Force, 41, released as Maj, 46; Am Defense, Am Theater, Asiatic-Pac Theater & ETO Ribbons; Victory Medal. Mem: Northwest Real Estate Bd; Northwest Builders Asn; Soc of Real Estate Appraisers; VFW; Moose. Honors & Awards: Was Little All American, 38, played for Cincinnati Bengals, 39 & Chicago Bears, 39-40; played with world champions in 40. Relig: Catholic. Mailing Add: 801 E Golfview Dr Mt Prospect IL 60056

CHESTER, JOSEPH ARNATHEN, SR **(D)**
Md State Deleg
b Wilson, NC, Mar 4, 14; s Arthur Chester & Fannie Fasion C; m 1934 to Pearl V Brothers; c Fannie Elzina (Mrs Wilbur Alston, Jr), Pearl B (Mrs Walter B McCants), Joseph A, Jr, James A, Andia (Mrs H Watkins), William T & Irvin E. Educ: Wilson High Sch, NC; Art Soc Club; Bus Men's Soc Club; Pals Soc Club. Polit & Govt Pos: Dist committeeman, Dem Club Baltimore, 34-47; chmn, Fed Neighborhood Improv Asn, 58-69; pres, New Area Dem Club East Baltimore, 64-69; Md State Deleg, Second Dist, 67-, mem appropriations comt & subcomt health & educ, Md House Deleg, currently; mem bd, Mt Royal Dem Club; mem, City County Dem & ESide Dem Clubs; mem, Nat Negro Legis Comt; vchmn human resources, Intergovt Task Force, Nat Legislators Conf, currently. Bus & Prof Pos: Chmn, Hue Chem Sales & Hue Janitorial Supply Co. Mil Serv: Entered as Steward Mate, Navy, 44, released as PO, 45. Mem: Northeastern Dem Club (exec bd). Relig: Baptist. Mailing Add: 3027 E Federal St Baltimore MD 21213

CHEW, CHARLES, JR **(D)**
Ill State Sen
b Greenville, Miss, Oct 9, 22; s Charles Chew, Sr & Celia Jenkins C; m 1961 to Carolyn Lawson; c Lorenzo. Educ: Tuskegee Inst, BS in Bus, 42. Polit & Govt Pos: Councilman, Chicago, Ill, 63-67; Ill State Sen, 66- Bus & Prof Pos: Vpres, Jackson Mutual Life Ins Co, 58; vpres, South Parkway Safe Deposit Corp, currently. Mil Serv: Entered as Seaman 1/C, Navy, 43, released as PO, 46, after serv in SPac; Philippine Liberation & Good Conduct Medals; 2 Battle Stars. Mem: VFW; Am Friendship Club; NAACP. Relig: Baptist. Mailing Add: 37 W 78th St Chicago IL 60620

CHICKERING, ROBERT L **(D)**
b Ionia Co, Mich, June 7, 17; s Ernest E Chickering & Daisy Doty C; wid; remarried 1957 to Iva Stevens; c Sharon (Mrs Newby), Patricia (Mrs Sorge) & Margaret (Mrs Andrews). Educ: Belding High Sch, Mich, grad, 36. Polit & Govt Pos: Chmn, Dem Party Columbia Co, Wis, formerly. Bus & Prof Pos: Farmer, Ionia Co, Mich, 35-39; partner, E E Chickering & Sons, Ionia Co, 39-45; treas, Chickering Vegetable Equipment Co, Belding, 45-50; treas & mgr, Endeavor Farm, Wis, 50-59; owner, Portage Gardens, Wis, 59- Mem: Mason (Past Master, 52-73); Optimist Club. Relig: United Methodist. Mailing Add: 2607 Hamilton St Portage WI 53901

CHIKASUYE, CLESSON Y **(D)**
Mem Coun, City & Co of Honolulu
b Honolulu, Hawaii, July 10, 19; s Izumi Chikasuye & Oen Tsuda C; m 1944 to Lorraine M Schmoker; c Clesson William & Kenneth A. Educ: Univ Hawaii, BA, 40; Stanford Univ Law Sch, 41-42; Univ Colo Law Sch, LLB, 44; Tau Kappa Epsilon & Phi Kappa Phi. Polit & Govt Pos: Secy, vpres & pres, Dem Precinct Club, Honolulu, Hawaii, 48-54; mem, State Labor & Indust Rels Appeal Bd, 51-53; mem, Cent Comt, Dem State Party, 55-56; mem coun, City & Co of Honolulu, 57-; deleg, Dem Nat Conv, 68. Mem: Am & Hawaii Bar Asns; Nat Asn of Counties; Queen's Med Ctr; Honolulu Japanese CofC. Relig: Lutheran. Legal Res: 1350 Ala Moana Blvd Honolulu HI 96814 Mailing Add: 510 Bishop Ins Bldg 33 S King St Honolulu HI 96813

CHILDERS, C **(D)**
Fla State Sen
Mailing Add: 232 Senate Off Bldg Tallahassee FL 32304

CHILDERS, ERASMUS ROY **(R)**
Chmn, Wilcox Co Rep Exec Comt, Ala
b Selma, Ala, Mar 17, 25; s Erasmus Roy Childers & Margaret Miller C; m 1956 to Bebe Skinner; c Nancy & Marcus. Educ: Auburn Univ, BS, 48; Chi Epsilon; Tau Beta Pi; Kappa Alpha. Polit & Govt Pos: Chmn, Wilcox Co Rep Exec Comt, Ala, 66-; mem, Rep State Exec Comt, Ala, 68- Bus & Prof Pos: Owner, Midway Plantation, Catherine, Ala, 49- Mil Serv: Entered as Pvt, Air Force, 43, released as Flight Officer, 45, after serv in Troop Carrier Command; Res, 45-66, Capt; Pilot Rating. Mem: Ala Cattlemen's Asn; Ala Farm Bur; Camden Exchange Club; Am Legion. Relig: Reformed Presbyterian; Deacon in Camden Assoc Reformed Presby Church. Mailing Add: Rte 1 Catherine AL 36728

CHILDERS, EUGENE M **(D)**
Ga State Rep
b Rome, Ga, Oct 17, 38; s Claude Edward Childers & Vassie Genever Cagle C; m 1959 to Martha A Bynum; c Mark Eugene & Margaret Ann. Educ: Model High Sch, 56. Polit & Govt Pos: Ga State Rep, Dist 15, 75- Mil Serv: Marine Corp Res, 55-61. Mem: CWA Local 3219 (pres); Floyd Co Ment Retarded Asn (bd dirs); Floyd Co Wild Life (bd dirs); United Fund (bd dirs). Relig: Baptist. Mailing Add: 15 Kirkwood Rome GA 30161

CHILDERS, JACK **(D)**
NC State Sen
Mailing Add: 1 Childers Ct Lexington NC 27292

CHILDERS, ROBERT LEE **(D)**
WVa State Deleg
Mailing Add: State Capitol Charleston WV 25305

CHILDERS, WYON DALE **(D)**
Fla State Sen
b Fla, Nov 25, 33; s Neil R Childers & Myrtle R Smith C; m 1953 to Ruth A Johnson; c Gail, Jeanna, Karen & Marvel. Educ: Fla State Univ, BS, 55. Polit & Govt Pos: Fla State Sen, Dist 2, 70-72, Dist 1, 72- Bus & Prof Pos: Teacher, Santa Rosa Co Schs, 56; vpres & gen mgr, A&E Stores, Pensacola, Fla, 57. Mem: Farm Bur; Lions; Am Pharmaceut Asn; Fla Coun Crime & Delinquency; Pensacola CofC. Relig: Baptist. Legal Res: 5900 Chicago Ave Pensacola FL 32506 Mailing Add: 5901 Memphis Ave Pensacola FL 32506

CHILDS, JAMES HENRY **(D)**
Mem, Dem State Cent Comt Calif
b St Louis, Mo, Sept 9, 38; s Elmo James Childs & Allie Mae Anthony C; m 1958 to Johnnie B Fite; c James L, Avery O C, Della R, Brenda, Christopher & Stephanie Ann. Educ: Bakersfield Jr Col, AA, 69; Calif State Col, Bakersfield, BA, 71, postgrad work, 71- Polit & Govt Pos: Chmn polit comt, Local 700 Serv Employees Int Union, 73-74, deleg, Cent Labor Coun, 74-75; deleg, Dem Mid Term Conf, 74; deleg, State Dem Comt 16th Sen Dist, 75; mem, Dem State Cent Comt Calif, currently. Bus & Prof Pos: Pres LVN comt, Kern Co Employ Asn, 68-75; dir, Kern Co Econ Opportunity Corp, Off of Econ Opportunity, 70; mem regional health comt, Univ Calif, Los Angeles West Med Campus Dist Three, 71; mem allied health comt, Calif State Col, Bakersfield, 71-72. Mil Serv: Entered as Recruit, Navy, 57, released as Seaman, 59, after serv in Commun & Eniwetok Atomic Test. Mem: Asa Philip Randolph Inst, Kern, Inyo & Mono Co (pres, 73-); Kern Co Econ Opportunity Corp (mem adv bd, 75-); COPE of Kern, Inyo & Mono Co (deleg, 74-). Mailing Add: 412 S Haley St Bakersfield CA 93307

CHILDS, JOHN LAWRENCE **(LIBERAL)**
VChmn, Liberal Party, Ill
b Eau Claire, Wis, Jan 11, 89; s John Nelson Childs & Helen Janette Smith C; m 1915 to Grace Mary Fowler. Educ: Univ Wis, BA, 11; Columbia Univ, MA, 24, PhD, 31; Sigma Delta Chi; Phi Alpha Tau; Kappa Delta Pi; Delta Sigma Rho. Hon Degrees: LHD, Southern Ill Univ, 68. Polit & Govt Pos: Founder & first state chmn, Ill Liberal Party, vchmn, currently. Bus & Prof Pos: Grad secy, Univ Wis, 11-12; intercollegiate dept, YMCA, 12-16; foreign secy int comn, YMCA, Peking, China, 16-27; prof philos of educ, Teachers Col, Columbia Univ, 37-54, emer prof educ, 54-; vis prof, Univ Mich, 57-58, Univ Ill, 58-59, Southern Ill Univ, 60-61, 62-63 & adj prof, 64-; educator & lectr, Univ Wis, 65. Publ: Education & Morals, 50; American Pragmatism & Education; co-auth, Education in the Age of Science, 59. Mem: Fel Am Educ Asn; Am Fedn Teachers; fel Am Asn Arts & Sci; Nat Comn Educ Reconstruction; Nat Comn Acad Freedom. Honors & Awards: Order of the Abundant Harvest, Chinese Nat Govt, 21; Nicholas Murray Butler Silver Medal, 51; Wm H Kilpatrick Award, 56; Educ Award, Wayne State Univ, 58; League for Indust Democracy Award, 59; John Dewey Soc

Award, 65; Nat Acad Educ Award, 66; Distinguished Serv Medal, Teachers Col, Columbia Univ, 68. Mailing Add: 4141 N Rockton Ave Rockford IL 61103

CHILDS, PEGGY (D)
Ga State Rep
b Tallulah Falls, Ga, Nov 17, 37; d Samuel Trebble Maxwell & Bertha Harvey M; m 1957 to Mobley Free Childs; c Mobley F, Jr (Moby) & Christy El Lena. Educ: Univ Ga, BA in jour, 58, MEd in counseling, 61. Polit & Govt Pos: Mem, Dem Reorgn Comt, 74; Ga State Rep, 51st Dist, (Decatur, Atlanta-DeKalb), 75-, mem judiciary, state insts & properties & retirement comts, mem spec comt on crime & drugs, asst majority whip, Ga House Rep, currently; secy, DeKalb Delegation, currently. Bus & Prof Pos: Chmn bd, Tallulah Prod Inc, 68-70 & Trinity Child Develop Ctr, 74-75; sponsored, Wallenda Walk Across Tallulah Gorge, 70. Publ: Ed, Vocational Technical Education in Georgia, State Dept of Educ, 69. Mem: State CofC (mem goal comt, 75). Honors & Awards: Key Coach Award as outstanding debate coach in Southeast, Emory Univ Barkley Forum; life membership, Ga Cong Parents & Teachers by 13th Dist PTA Coun. Relig: Methodist; mem social concerns comn, Decatur First United Methodist Church. Mailing Add: 520 Westchester Dr Decatur GA 30030

CHILDS, T ALLEN, JR (D)
Chmn, Richmond Co Dem Exec Comt, Ga
b Fayetteville, Tenn, Oct 3, 20; s Thomas Allen Childs, Sr & Era Gunter C; m 1949 to Gladys Mildred Tompkins; c Vicki Eileen & Allen Hampton. Educ: John Marshall Univ, Atlanta, Ga, LLB, 48. Polit & Govt Pos: Comnr, Augusta Housing Authority, Ga, 72-; chmn, Richmond Co Dem Exec Comt, 74- Bus & Prof Pos: Partner, Allgood & Childs, Attorneys, Augusta, Ga, 54-; vpres & dir, Atlantic Prem Corp, Augusta, 74- Mil Serv: Entered as A/S, Navy, 43, released as PO 3/C, 46, after serv in European & Pac Theatres. Mem: Am, Ga State, SC State & Augusta Bar Asns; Augusta Area Trial Lawyers Asn; Ga Defense Lawyers Asn. Relig: Southern Baptist. Legal Res: 3112 Lake Forest Dr W Augusta GA 30904 Mailing Add: PO Box 1523 Augusta GA 30903

CHILES, JOHN RUSSELL (R)
Tenn State Rep
b Jonesboro, Tenn, June 19, 08; s John Russell Chiles, Sr & Ollie Venore Hale C; m 1940 to Sarah Elizabeth Parham; c Mary Margaret Chiles Burtis, Sarah Hale Chiles Shelburne & John Parham. Educ: Carson-Newman Col, BS, 32. Polit & Govt Pos: Treas, Sullivan Co Rep Orgns, Tenn; Tenn State Rep, Second Dist, 74- Bus & Prof Pos: Foreman, Tenn Eastman Co, Kingsport, 33-52, asst dept supt, 52-66, dept supt, 66-73, retired. Mem: Kiwanis Club of Kingsport; Farm Bur of Tenn. Relig: Baptist. Mailing Add: 3012 Cliffside Rd Kingsport TN 37664

CHILES, LAWTON MAINOR, JR (D)
US Sen, Fla
b Lakeland, Fla, Apr 30, 30; m 1951 to Rhea Grafton; c Tandy, Lawton M, III, Edward G & Rhea Gay. Educ: Univ Fla, BSBA, 52, LLB, 55; Alpha Tau Omega; Phi Delta Phi; Fla Blue Key; Univ Fla Hall of Fame. Hon Degrees: Fla Southern Col & Jacksonville Univ. Polit & Govt Pos: Fla State Rep, 58-66; Fla State Sen, 66-70; US Sen, 71-; deleg, Dem Nat Mid-Term Conf, 74; mem, Dem Nat Comt, currently. Mil Serv: Army Artil, Korean Conflict. Mem: Fla Bar Asn; Kiwanis; Lakeland Quarterback Club; March of Dimes; CofC. Honors & Awards: Commendation Award, Fla Agr Coun; Meritorious Pub Serv Award, Legis Poll; United Fund Award of Spec Merit; Outstanding Young Man, Jaycees. Relig: Presbyterian. Legal Res: 940 Lake Hollingsworth Dr Lakeland FL 33803 Mailing Add: 2107 Dirksen Senate Off Bldg Washington DC 20510

CHILSEN, WALTER JOHN (R)
Wis State Sen
b Merrill, Wis, Nov 18, 23; s Walter Burt Chilsen & Margaret Sullivan C; m 1952 to Roseann Edl; c Jon, Anna, Kristine, Elizabeth, Paul, Matthew & twins, Peter & Patricia. Educ: Lawrence Col, BS, 49. Polit & Govt Pos: Wis State Sen, 29th Dist, 66-, mem select comt on Univ Wis, Wis State Senate, 67-68, mem pub welfare comt, 67-68 & 69-70, mem educ comt, 67-68, vchmn, 71, secy Rep caucus, 67-68, chmn, 69-70 & 71, vchmn labor, taxation, ins & banking comt & chmn Kerner adv comt, 69-70, co-chmn adv comt on uniform consumer credit code, 69-70 & 71, chmn adv comt on med educ, 69-70 & 71, mem Wis natural beauty coun, 69-70, 71 & 73-, chmn agr comt, 71, chmn agr & rural develop comt, vchmn exec comt, Wis State Rural Develop Coun, mem health, educ & welfare comt, educ commun bd, Wis environ educ coun, agr comt of midwest conf of coun of state govt & nat legis conf, intergovt rels comt, 73-, asst minority leader, 74; Rep cand for US Cong, Spec Elec, 69. Bus & Prof Pos: Associated with WSAU-TV, Wausau, Wis, TV newscaster, 10 years, TV advert acct exec. Mil Serv: Entered as Pvt, Army Air Corps, 43, released as 1st Lt, 45, after serv as Bombardier, 7th Air Force, Pac Theatre; Purple Heart. Mem: St Mary's Home & Sch Asn; St Mary's Holy Name; Am Legion; KofC; Marathon Co Workshop for Handicapped. Honors & Awards: Designated Eagleton Inst Polit Scholar, 67-68. Relig: Roman Catholic. Legal Res: 1821 Town Line Rd Wausau WI 54401 Mailing Add: Rm 315 South State Capitol Madison WI 53702

CHIMBOLE, LARRY (D)
Calif State Assemblyman
Mailing Add: 807 W Ave J Lancaster CA 93435

CHING, DONALD D H (D)
Hawaii State Sen
b Honolulu, Hawaii, Jan 13, 26; s Dai Sun Ching & Sun Hoo Wong C; m 1951 to Kazuko Shikuma; c Donna Rae, Deborah Ann, Sandra Kay, Jeffrey & Melvin. Educ: Univ Hawaii, BA, 50; George Washington Univ Law Sch, LLB, 53. Polit & Govt Pos: Hawaii Territorial Rep, 58-59; Hawaii State Rep, 59-66; Hawaii State Sen, 67- Bus & Prof Pos: Vpres & asst secy, Bank of Hawaii, 66- Mil Serv: Entered as Pvt, Army, 45, released as Tech 4/C, 47, after serv in Hawaiian Med Depot, Hawaii. Mem: Am & Hawaii Bar Asns. Relig: United Church of Christ. Mailing Add: 2005 Aamanu St Pearl City HI 96782

CHIN-LEE, WILLIAM (R)
Mem, DC Rep Cent Comt
b Washington, DC, Apr 22, 23; s Ying Hong Chin & Lee Ngon Win C; m 1948 to Nancy A Wong; c William Bruce, Peter E, Sandra L, Cynthia D & Warren D. Educ: Am Univ, AA, 44; George Washington Univ, MD, 47; Wash Hosp Ctr, internship & residency, 53; George Washington Univ Med Soc. Polit & Govt Pos: Precinct chmn, 63-66; alt deleg, Rep Nat Conv, 64 & 72; mem, DC Rep Exec Comt, 64-69, DC Rep Cent Comt, 63-; chmn educ comt, Nat Rep Heritage Groups Coun, 71- Bus & Prof Pos: Jr attend physician, Washington Hosp Ctr, DC, 53-; pres, Chin Inc, 58-; dir & pres, Lee Fed Credit Union, 66; dir, Tai-Tung Restaurant, 67. Mil Serv: Entered as Pvt, Army, 44, released, 46, entered Air Force, 51, released as Capt, 53; Good Conduct Medal; Am Theater Ribbon; Victory Medal. Mem: Hippocrates-Galen Med Soc, Washington, DC; Mid-Atlantic Chinese Med & Health Asn (dir, 71-); DC & Am Socs of Internal Med; DC Med Soc. Relig: Methodist; former mem bd, Union Methodist Church, DC; past trustee & mem bd, Chinese Commun Church. Mailing Add: 3223 Chesapeake St NW Washington DC 20008

CHINNICI, JOSEPH W (R)
NJ State Assemblyman
Mailing Add: State House Trenton NJ 08625

CHISHOLM, SHIRLEY ANITA (D)
US Rep, NY
b Brooklyn, NY, Nov 30, 24; d Charles St Hill & Ruby Seale H; m 1949 to Conrad Chisholm. Educ: Brooklyn Col, BA in Sociol, 46; Columbia Univ, MA in Childhood Educ, 52. Hon Degrees: LLD, Talladega Col, 69, Wilmington Col (Ohio), 70, La Salle Col, William Patterson Col, Univ Maine, Portland & Capital Univ, 71, Pratt Inst, 72 & Kenyon Col, 73; LHD, NC Col Durham, 69, Hampton Inst, 70 & Coppin State Col, 71. Polit & Govt Pos: NY State Assemblywoman, 55th Dist, 64-68; US Rep, 12th Dist, NY, 68-; Dem Nat Committeewoman, NY, formerly; deleg, Dem Nat Comt, 72; deleg, Dem Nat Mid-Term Conf, 74. Bus & Prof Pos: Nursery sch teacher, Mt Calvary Child Care Ctr, New York, 46-52; pvt nursery sch dir, Friend in Need Nursery, Brooklyn, 52-53; dir, Hamilton-Madison Child Care Ctr, New York, educ consult, Div of Day Care, New York, 59-64. Publ: Unbossed & Unbought, Houghton Mifflin, 70; The Good Fight, Harper & Row, 73; Rather be Black than Female, McCall's, 9/70. Mem: League of Women Voters; Dem Women Workshop; NAACP (Brooklyn Br); Brooklyn Home for Aged People (bd dirs); Nat Asn Col Women. Honors & Awards: Human Rels Award, Cent Nassau Club of Bus & Prof Women, 65; Citation for Outstanding Serv in the field of early childhood educ & welfare, Sisterhood of Concord Baptist Church, Brooklyn, 65; Outstanding Serv in Good Govt Plaque Christian Women's Retreat, 65; Cert of Honor award for outstanding achievement in serv to youth, Jr High Sch 271, Brooklyn, 65; Woman of Achievement Award at Waldorf Astoria, Key Women Inc, 65. Relig: Methodist. Mailing Add: 1355 President St Brooklyn NY 11213

CHMIELEWSKI, FLORIAN (DFL)
Minn State Sen
Mailing Add: Sturgeon Lake MN 55783

CHO, MARIA CHUNGSOOK (R)
Mem, Rep State Cent Comt Calif
b Changnyun, Kyongsang-Pukdo, Korea, Nov 17, 31; d Sam Sool Kim & Tae Sun Woo K; m 1957 to Benjamin Cho; c Ann Byongsook & Julia Hyonsook. Educ: Seoul Nat Univ, 47-51. Polit & Govt Pos: Assoc mem, Rep State Cent Comt, Calif, 64-66, mem, 69-, mem platform comt, 67-68; vchmn nationality comt, Orange Co Rep Women Federated, 65-67; vchmn, Reagan for Gov comt, 66; membership chmn, Buena Park Rep Women Federated, 67, vpres, 68; chmn, Woman for Nixon in Buena Park, 68; state comt chmn, Calif to reelect Ivy Baker Priest State Treas, 70. Bus & Prof Pos: Dir, I M B Electronics Inc, Santa Fe Springs, Calif, 68-; chmn, Sister City Comt, Buena Park, 71-; mem, Arts & Cult Comn, 71- Mem: Korean Cath Asn Southern Calif. Relig: Roman Catholic. Mailing Add: 8470 Philodendron Way Buena Park CA 90620

CHOATE, CLYDE L (D)
Ill State Rep
b West Frankfort, Ill, June 28, 20; m 1947 to Mabel Madonna Ross; c Elizabeth Ellen & Madonna Kim. Educ: Anna-Jonesboro High Sch. Polit & Govt Pos: Ill State Rep, currently, Minority Whip, 69th, 70th, 75th & 76th Gen Assemblies, Ill State House Rep, Majority Whip, 71st & 72nd Gen Assemblies, Majority Leader, 74th Gen Assembly, Minority Leader, 77th & 78th Gen Assemblies; deleg, Dem Nat Conv, 68, chmn Ill deleg, 72; state cent committeeman, Dem Party, Ill, 69-70. Mil Serv: Army, Pvt, World War II; served 31 months overseas in European Theatre; S/Sgt; cited for bravery in action; Purple Heart; French Fourragere; Bronze & Silver Stars; Presidential Citation; Cong Medal Honor. Mem: Am Legion; VFW; Mil Order Purple Heart; Cong Medal of Honor Soc; Elks. Mailing Add: RR 1 Anna IL 62906

CHONG, ANSON (D)
Hawaii State Sen
b Honolulu, Hawaii, Aug 8, 38; s Lt Col (Ret) Kim Fan Chong & Lily Pao-Hu Cheng Chong Winters; single. Educ: Colgate Univ, BA with honors, 61; Columbia Univ, MA, 63; Yale Univ, Nat Urban fel, summer 71. Polit & Govt Pos: Peace Corps Vol, Eastern Nigeria & lectr, Univ Nigeria, 64-66; prog economist & foreign serv officer, State Dept, Agency Int Develop, Khartoum, Lagos & Bangkok, 66-69; res analyst, State Dept Planning & Econ Develop, Hawaii, 69-70; planner, City & Co, Honolulu, 70-71; spec asst to DC City Coun Chmn Gilbert Hahn, Jr & US Sen Daniel Inouye, Hawaii, 71-72; Hawaii State Rep, 72-74; Hawaii State Sen, 74- Bus & Prof Pos: Portfolio analyst, Merrill Lynch, Pierce, Fenner & Smith, Inc, NY, 63-64. Mil Serv: Served six months active duty, Army Signal Corps, Pvt, 25th Inf Div, Schofield, Hawaii, 56; Expert Rifleman. Publ: Economic development of Hawaii & growth of tourism before 1945, Erickson Enterprises, NY, 63. Mem: UN (bd dir, & vpres Hawaii chap, 71-); Young Dem Honolulu; Young Dem Hawaii; Honolulu Jaycees; Soc Int Develop. Honors & Awards: Outstanding State Legislators Conf, Eagleton Inst Polit, Rutgers Univ, 74; Outstanding State Legislator Award, Honolulu Sertoma Club, 75. Relig: Congregational. Mailing Add: PO Box 813 Honolulu HI 96808

CHONKO, LORRAINE N (D)
Maine State Rep
Mailing Add: New Lewiston Rd Pejepscot Topsham ME 04067

CHREST, JAMES H (D)
Ore State Rep
Mailing Add: 9112 North Kimball Ave Portland OR 97203

CHRISTENSEN, CHESTER S (D)
Nev State Assemblyman
Mailing Add: 974 Pyramid Way Sparks NV 89431

CHRISTENSEN, EARL R (R)
Wyo State Sen
b Sheridan, Wyo, Dec 20, 19; married; c Four. Educ: Univ Wyo. Polit & Govt Pos: Wyo State

Sen & Pres, Senate, currently. Bus & Prof Pos: Rancher. Mem: Stock Growers Asn; Farm Bur; Mason; Shrine; Eastern Star. Relig: Methodist. Mailing Add: Box 580 Newcastle WY 82701

CHRISTENSEN, EDWIN B (R)
NH State Rep
Mailing Add: 89 South St Concord NH 03301

CHRISTENSEN, HARVEY MOELLER (D)
Mem, SDak State Dem Cent Comt
b Omaha, Nebr, Nov 5, 18; s Christian Moeller Christensen & Anna Jessen C; m 1946 to Lavolla Beth Anderson; c Joyce Ann, Lyle Allen, Bruce Moeller & Dean Patrick. Educ: Nettleton Commercial Col, Sioux Falls, SDak, 2 years. Polit & Govt Pos: SDak State Rep, Dist 22, 70-72; mem, SDak State Dem Cent Comt, 75- Bus & Prof Pos: Bookkeeper, Jerauld Co Farmers Union, Wessington Springs, SDak, 38-42, dept mgr, 46-51, gen mgr, 51- Mil Serv: Entered as Pvt, Air Force, 42, released as M/Sgt, 46, after serv in 68th Air Serv Group, China-Burma-India, 43-45. Mem: Mason; Eastern Star; Kiwanis; Am Legion; CofC. Honors & Awards: Hon chap farmer, FFA Club. Relig: United Church of Christ. Mailing Add: 601 E Main St Wessington Springs SD 57382

CHRISTENSEN, J LLOYD (D)
Chmn, Franklin Co Dem Cent Comt, Idaho
b Mink Creek, Idaho, July 7, 18; s Lars Henry Christensen & Serena Hammersmark C; m 1940 to Reana Whitehead; c Lo Ree (Mrs Robert Gang), Iva Lou (Mrs John Morgan), Rhonda (Mrs A J Shomas), Sonya (Mrs Melvin Ray), Paulette, Jay Lloyd, Lee Grand, Mary Ann & John Mark. Educ: Utah State Univ, 37-38. Polit & Govt Pos: Chmn, Franklin Co Dem Cent Comt, Idaho, 60-; alt deleg, Dem Nat Conv, 68; mem, Idaho Dem State Comt, currently. Relig: Latter-day Saint. Mailing Add: Rte 2 Box 205 Preston ID 83263

CHRISTENSEN, L D (LEE) (D)
NDak State Sen
Mailing Add: State Capitol Bismarck ND 58501

CHRISTENSEN, RALPH M (R)
NDak State Rep
b Schafer, NDak, Dec 21, 11; s J P Christensen & Rekka Restad C; m 1933 to Arlene Boe; c Richard, Sonja (Mrs Tucker) & James. Educ: Univ NDak; Dakota Bus Col, grad, 31. Polit & Govt Pos: Chmn, Dist Rep Party, NDak & mem, NDak Rep State Exec Comt, 17 years; pres, NDak Pub Welfare Bd, 57-; deleg, NDak Const Conv, 70; alt deleg, Rep Nat Conv, 72; NDak State Rep, 73- Bus & Prof Pos: Pres & mgr, Christensen Corp, 44- Mem: All York Rite Masonic Bodies; Shrine; Elks; Sons of Norway; Lions. Relig: Lutheran. Mailing Add: 303 Third St E Watford City ND 58854

CHRISTENSEN, WALTER (D)
b Mercer, NDak, Apr 21, 10; married; c Seven. Educ: Pub Sch. Polit & Govt Pos: Pres, Mercer Sch Bd, NDak, formerly; NDak State Rep, 61-66; State Treas, NDak, 67-68; deleg, Dem Nat Mid-Term Conf, 74. Bus & Prof Pos: Farmer. Relig: Lutheran. Mailing Add: Mercer ND 58559

CHRISTENSON, HAL (R)
NDak State Sen
Mailing Add: State Capitol Bismarck ND 58501

CHRISTGAU, VICTOR (R)
b Austin, Minn, Sept 20, 94; s Fred Christgau & Adeline Vanselow C; m 1931 to Muriel Doyle. Educ: Univ Minn Col of Agr, BS, 24, grad student, 23-25; Gamma Sigma Delta. Polit & Govt Pos: Minn State Sen, 27-29; US Rep, Minn, 29-33; from asst dir to dir prod div & asst adminr, Agr Adjustment Admin, 33-35; adminr, Minn Works Prog Admin, 35-38; dir & commr, Minn Employ Security Agency, 38-54; dir, Bur Old Age & Survivors Ins, 54-63, exec asst & asst to commr, Social Security Admin, 63-67. Mil Serv: Entered as Pfc, Army, 18, released as Sgt 1/C, 19, after serv in Eng Corps. Mem: Am Pub Welfare Asn; Am Soc Pub Admin; Former Members of Cong, Inc, Washington, DC; Am Legion; VFW. Honors & Awards: Outstanding Achievement Award, Univ Minn, 55; Distinguished Serv Award, US Dept Health, Educ & Welfare, 66. Relig: Lutheran. Mailing Add: Rte 5 Austin MN 55912

CHRISTIAN, CLARENCE CARR, JR (D)
WVa State Deleg
b Princeton, WVa, Nov 24, 27; s Clarence Carr Christian & Lola Mae Cooke C; m 1938 to Hallie Mae Shupe; c Lawrence Lee, Geoffrey Wayne. Educ: Concord Col. Polit & Govt Pos: WVa State Deleg, 56- Bus & Prof Pos: Locomotive engr. Mem: Brotherhood Locomotive Engrs; Kiwanis; Elks; Mercer Anglers Club. Relig: Presbyterian; Deacon. Mailing Add: Box 282 Princeton WV 24740

CHRISTIAN, GEORGE (D)
b Austin, Tex, Jan 1, 27; s George Eastland Christian & Ruby Scott C; m 1950 to Elizabeth Brown (deceased 1957); m 1959 to Jo Anne Martin; c Elizabeth, Susan, George Scott, Bruce, John & Brian. Educ: Univ Tex, BJ, 49. Polit & Govt Pos: Austin Bur chief, Int News Serv, 56; press secy & exec asst to Gov Price Daniel, Tex, 57-63, state campaign mgr, 62; pres secy & admin asst to Gov John Connally, 63-66; admin asst to President of US, 66-; press secy to President of US, 66-69, polit pub rels, currently. Bus & Prof Pos: Correspondent, Int News Serv, Austin, 49-56. Mil Serv: Entered Marine Corps, 44, serv in Pac Theater, Occupation of Japan, 45-46, 6th Marines, 2nd Div. Publ: The President Steps Down, Macmillan, 70. Relig: Episcopal. Mailing Add: 1600 Am Bank Tower Austin TX 78701

CHRISTIAN, JOHN MANDEVILLE (D)
b Tuscaloosa, Ala, Nov 10, 41; s George William Christian & Grace Mandeville C; m 1966 to Mildred McCain; c John Mandeville Jr, Andrew McCain & Grace Callaway. Educ: Univ Ala, 4 years; Phi Gamma Delta. Polit & Govt Pos: Exec asst to US Rep Walter Flowers, Ala, 69- Mil Serv: Entered as Pvt, Army Nat Guard, 61, released as Sgt, 69, after serv in Co A, 1st Bn, 200th Inf. Mem: Tuscaloosa Jaycees; Outdoor Advert Asn Am; Cong Secy Club Washington, DC. Relig: Methodist. Legal Res: 512 Main Ave Northport AL 35476 Mailing Add: 401 Cannon House Off Bldg Washington DC 20515

CHRISTIAN, MAUD TRUBY (D)
Mem, WVa Dem State Exec Comt
b Christian, WVa, July 2, 06; d George Thomas Christian & Martha Ann Duff C; single. Educ: Morris Harvey Acad; Morris Harvey Col; Marshall Univ. Polit & Govt Pos: Off reporter, WVa House of Deleg, 31-33; secy, Gov of WVa, 33-36; off reporter, Criminal & Circuit Courts of McDowell Co, 37-71; mem, WVa Dem State Exec Comt, 40-; deleg, Dem Nat Conv, 64, mem platform comt & deleg, permanent secy, WVa Deleg & mem credentials comt, 72. Mem: Nat Shorthand Reporters Asn; WVa Shorthand Reporters Asn; Cert Shorthand Reporter. Honors & Awards: Dem Woman-of-the-Year for WVa, 63. Relig: Methodist. Mailing Add: PO Box 172 Man WV 25635

CHRISTIANSEN, EDWARD WILLIAM, JR (BILL) (D)
Lt Gov, Mont
b Fargo, NDak, Feb 24, 14; s Dr Edward William Christiansen & Mabel Claire Cork C; m 1947 to Hattie James; c Linda Susan (Mrs Doane) & Deborah Ann. Educ: NDak State Col, 31-33. Polit & Govt Pos: Mont State Rep, Eighth Dist, 65-72; mem bd dirs, Mont Develop Corp, 70-; chmn, Mont Energy Adv Coun; pres, Mont State Senate; mem, Mont Environ Qual Coun; Lt Gov, Mont, 73- Bus & Prof Pos: Vpres, Hardin Auto Co, Mont, 47-; pres, Hardin Broadcasting Inc, 63- Mem: Hardin Youth Coun; Campfire Girl's Asn; Boy Scouts; Elks; Ft Custer Golf Club. Honors & Awards: Distinguished Serv Award from Hardin Jaycees, 70; Outstanding Serv to Sr Citizens Award, Cascade Co, 71; Outstanding Citizen Award, Big Horn Co CofC, 73. Relig: Catholic. Mailing Add: State Capitol Helena MT 59601

CHRISTIANSEN, RAYMOND C (D)
Polit & Govt Pos: Chmn, Alaska Dem Party, formerly; Alaska State Sen, 71-73. Mailing Add: PO Box 35 Bethel AK 99559

CHRISTIANSON, ROGER ALLEN (DFL)
Mem, Minn State Dem-Farmer-Labor Cent Comt
b Albert Lea, Minn, May 29, 43; s Howard Clare Christianson & Elvina E Trytten C; m 1962 to Sharon Rae Blizard; c Vicki Lynn, Timothy Allen & Tonya Noël. Educ: Univ Minn, Minneapolis, BA, 65; William Mitchell Col Law, St Paul, JD, 70; Theta Chi; vpres bd gov, William Mitchell Col Law, 69-70; ed, William Mitchell Opinion, 69-70. Polit & Govt Pos: Polit intern, Dist 48 Dem-Farmer-Labor Party, Minn, 64; deleg, Ramsey Co Dem-Farmer-Labor Cent Comt, 66 & Dem-Farmer-Labor State Conv, 70; chmn, Dist 47 Dem-Farmer-Labor Party, formerly; third vchmn, Fourth Cong Dist Dem-Farmer-Labor Party, 70-72, chmn, formerly, publicity dir, 70, youth coordr, 71-; coordr bd race, Ramsey Co Dem-Farmer-Labor Party, 70; mem, Minn State Dem-Farmer-Labor Cent Comt, 71-; mem, State Exec Comt, 72-; Spec Asst Attorney Gen, State of Minn, 73- Bus & Prof Pos: Claims rep, Travelers Ins Co, 65-71; lawyer, 71- Mem: Minn & Ramsey Co Bar Asns; William Mitchell Alumni Asn (pres, bd dirs, 72-); St Paul CofC (mem legis comt, 72-). Mailing Add: 1510 Summit Ave St Paul MN 55105

CHRISTIE, JOHN M (R)
b Aug 14, 10; m to Dorothy A Farrell. Educ: George Washington Univ, 35; Am Inst of Banking, 37; Rutgers Univ Grad Sch of Banking, 40. Polit & Govt Pos: Asst treas, Inaugural Comt, 53, spec asst to chmn, 57 & 69; treas Rep Nat Comt, 69-74. Bus & Prof Pos: Dir, Govt Employees Ins & Life Ins Co, Govt Employees Financial Corp, Criterion Ins Co & Washington Gas Light Co, currently; chmn bd, Cent Charge Serv, Inc & Riggs Nat Bank of Washington, DC, currently; trustee, Mortgage Investors of Washington & Human Resources Research Orgn, currently; mem, Nat 4-H Found Adv Coun, currently. Mem: DC Bankers Asn; Salvation Army Adv Bd (chmn finance & budget comt, 68-); Boy's Club of Metrop Police; Fed City Coun (trustee); Transportation Asn of Am (mem, Investor Panel). Legal Res: 9519 W Stanhope Rd Rock Creek Hills Kensington MD 20795 Mailing Add: 310 First St SE Washington DC 20003

CHRISTMAN, LARRY HERMAN (D)
Ohio State Rep
b Galion, Ohio, June 1, 40; s Herman Henry Christman & Alesta Heinlein C; m 1964 to Linda Louise Ritchie; c Ted & Nancy. Educ: Bluffton Col, BA, 62; Ohio State Univ, MA, 63; Miami Univ, 68; Wright State Univ, 72. Polit & Govt Pos: Mem charter comn, Englewood, Ohio, 69-70, Englewood City Coun, 71-72; Ohio State Rep, 73- Bus & Prof Pos: Pres, Northmont Dist Educ Asn, 70-71. Relig: Methodist. Mailing Add: 7112 Kinsey Rd Englewood OH 45322

CHRISTOWE, MARGARET WOOTERS (R)
Vt State Rep
b Philadelphia, Pa; d Joseph Wooters & Margaret Murphy W; m to Stoyan Christowe. Educ: Educated in Pa & Southern Calif. Polit & Govt Pos: Mem, Vt Rep State Comt, 68-; mem, Drug-Alcohol Rehabilitation Comn, Vt, 71-; Vt State Rep, 75- Publ: Auth of articles & stories in nat mag & newpapers, including, Travel Mag, Christian Sci Monitor, DAC News & Scholastic Mag. Mem: Children's Asn United for Spec Educ; Vt Church Women United (mem exec bd, 69-). Legal Res: Old Rte 100 West Dover VT 05356 Mailing Add: State House Montpelier VT 05602

CHRISTY, DONALD (R)
Kans State Sen
b Scott City, Kans, Nov 23, 09; s Marion Estes Christy & Effie May Ater C; m 1933 to Helen Georgia Shedd; c Donald Owen, Arthur Estes & Alice Aileen. Educ: Kans State Univ & Tex A&M Univ, MS. Polit & Govt Pos: Mem, Area Property Tax Study, Kans, 54; served on US Dept Agr Adv Comt on Equip & Struct, 6 years, Kans State Bd Agr, 12 years, Kans State Fair Bd, 12 years, Scott Co Fair Bd, Kans, 24 years, Kans Water Resources Bd, 13 years, Kans Watershed, 4 years & helped in formation of Soil Conserv Bd, Scott Co, Kans; Kans State Sen, 39th Dist, 69- Bus & Prof Pos: Teacher irrigation drainage & soil conserv, Tex A&M Univ, 9 years; farmer & banker, Scott Co, Kans, currently. Publ: Terracing, 40. Mem: Lions; Farm Bur; CofC. Honors & Awards: Soil Conserv Award, Kans Bankers; Chmn Award, Kans Asn Soil Conserv Dist Supvr; Outstanding Individual Year, Mid Cent Chap, Am Soc Agr Eng. Relig: Christian Church of NAm; elder, First Christian Church & Sunday sch teacher. Legal Res: 1005 Washington Scott City KS 67871 Mailing Add: Box 103 501 Main Scott City KS 67871

CHRISTY, JAMES THOMAS (R)
b Cincinnati, Ohio, Nov 2, 47; s Thomas P Christy & Mary Vatsures C; m 1975 to Grace S Thunborg. Educ: Univ Cincinnati, BBA, 69; Col Law, JD, 72; Delta Sigma Pi. Polit & Govt Pos: Legis asst to US Rep Walter E Powell, 73-74; admin asst to US Rep Thomas N Kindness, Ohio, 75- Mil Serv: 2nd Lt, Army, 72, 1st Lt Army Res. Publ: The Federal Election Campaign Act: the existing law & proposals for reform, Cincinnati Bar J, Autumn 74. Mem: Am, Ohio & Cincinnati Bar Asns; Admin Asst Asn; Univ Cincinnati Alumni Asn. Legal Res: 6481

Navaho Trail Cincinnati OH 45243 Mailing Add: 1440 Longworth Bldg Washington DC 20515

CHRISTY, WILLIAM (D)
Ind State Sen
Polit & Govt Pos: Ind State Sen, 55-72 & 75-, chmn Dem Caucus, Ind State Senate, 63. Bus & Prof Pos: Steelworker, Youngstown Sheet & Tube Co; pres, Lake Fed Savings & Loan Asn, Hammond, Ind. Mem: Steel Workers Local Union; Lake Co Indust Union Coun. Relig: Christian Church. Mailing Add: 7106 Grand Ave Hammond IN 46323

CHRONISTER, ROCHELLE RUTH (R)
Chmn, Wilson Co Rep Cent Comt, Kans
b Neodesha, Kans, Aug 27, 39; d Charles Edward Beach & Arlene Laveta Hare B; m 1961 to Bert Chronister; c Pamela & Philip. Educ: Univ Kans, BA, 61; Mortar Bd. Polit & Govt Pos: Mem, Rankin Mem Libr Bd, 67-69; mem, Wilson Co Dole for Senate Comt, 68; precinct committeewoman, Wilson Co, 68-; mem & vchmn, Wilson Co Young Rep, 68-, chmn, 68-69; nat committeewoman, Kans Young Rep Fedn, 69-71; mem, Unified Sch Dist 461 Bd, 69-; vchmn, Wilson Co Rep Cent Comt, 70-72, chmn, 72-; mem, Two Co Spec Educ Coop Bd, 71-73; mem, Kans Adv Coun, Title III, Elem & Sec Educ Act, 71-, chmn-elect, 73-74. Bus & Prof Pos: Research virologist, Univ Kans Med Ctr, Kansas City, 61-64. Mem: Girl Scouts (leader, 69-); North Lawn PTA (pres, 69-70). Honors & Awards: Outstanding Young Rep Woman, Kans Fed Young Rep, 70. Relig: Methodist. Mailing Add: Rte 2 Neodesha KS 66757

CHUBB, ELIZABETH LOUISE (R)
VChmn, Cattaraugus Co Rep Exec Comt, NY
b Randolph, NY, Oct 23, 22; d Leslie Aldrich Smith & Pansy Walters S; m 1939 to Adolph Ernest Chubb; c Joseph, Patricia (Mrs Robert Zollinger), Carol Marie (Mrs George Bousman) & Margaret Ann. Educ: Randolph Cent Sch, NY, 5 years. Polit & Govt Pos: VTreas, Cattaraugus Co Rep Comt, NY, 62-64, committeeman, 62-; secy, Randolph Rep Club, 62-73; vchmn, Cattaraugus Co Rep Exec Comt, 66- Mem: Randolph Homemakers; Grange; Cattaraugus Co Coop Exten Serv. Relig: Catholic. Mailing Add: Bowen Rd Randolph NY 14772

CHUMBRIS, PETER NICHOLAS (R)
b Washington, DC, Jan 14, 14; s Nicholas Andrew Chumbris & Nicholetta Andrews C; m 1948 to La Joy Shelton; c Nicholas A, John Peter & William Dirksen. Educ: Univ Md, BA, 35; Georgetown Univ Law Ctr, LLB, 38, LLM, 39; Omicron Delta Kappa; Latch Key Soc. Polit & Govt Pos: Asst attorney gen, NMex, 49-51, spec asst attorney gen, 51-53; assoc gen counsel, US Sen Subcomt Juv Delinquency, 54-57; chief counsel, US Sen Antitrust Subcomt, Judiciary, 57- Bus & Prof Pos: Attorney-at-law in assoc with Judge Walter M Bastian, Washington, DC, 39-48; attorney-at-law, Albuquerque, NMex, 51-54. Publ: Case notes, et al, Georgetown Law J, 37; The Causes & Cures of Juvenile Delinquency, 15-minute radio prog, 52-53. Mem: Delta Theta Pi; DC, NMex, Fed & Am Bar Asns. Honors & Awards: Jaycees Gold Key Award, 47; Outstanding Young Washingtonian Award; Outstanding Greek Orthodox of West; Ahepa Distinguished Serv Award for youth & religious serv. Relig: Greek Orthodox. Mailing Add: 4200 Cathedral Ave Washington DC 20016

CHUMURA, RUDY (D)
Mass State Rep
Mailing Add: State Capitol Boston MA 02133

CHUMURA, STEVE T (D)
Mass State Rep
Mailing Add: State Capitol Boston MA 02133

CHURCH, FRANK (D)
US Sen, Idaho
b Boise, Idaho, July 25, 24; m to Bethine Clark; c Forrest & Chase. Educ: Stanford Univ, AB & LLB; Phi Beta Kappa. Polit & Govt Pos: State chmn, Young Dem of Idaho, 52-54; US Sen, Idaho, 56-, chmn, Senate Spec Comt Aging, co-chmn, Senate Spec Comt Termination of Nat Emergency, chmn, Senate Foreign Rels Subcomt Multinational Corp, Senate Interior Subcomt Water & Power Resources, currently; keynoter, Dem Nat Conv, 60, deleg, 72; US Deleg, 21st Gen Assembly of UN; chmn, US Deleg to US-Can Interparliamentary Conf, 69, 70 & 71. Bus & Prof Pos: Attorney-at-law. Mil Serv: Enlisted as Pvt, Army, World War II, commissioned 44; Mil Intel in China, Burma, India. Honors & Awards: Named Nat Jaycee Outstanding Young Man, 57. Legal Res: Boise ID Mailing Add: Rm 245 Russell Senate Off Bldg Washington DC 20510

CHURCH, JAMES OLIVER (R)
b Bridgeport, Conn, Dec 24, 21; s James O Church & Mabel Cliffe C; m 1948 to Kathryn MacNaughton; c Sally K. Educ: Springfield Col, BS, 43. Polit & Govt Pos: Rep, Trumbull Town Meeting, Conn, 59-61; mem, Trumbull Rep Town Comt, 61-66, chmn, formerly. Bus & Prof Pos: Spec agent, Northwestern Mutual Life Ins Co, Conn, 50- Mil Serv: Entered as Pvt, Army, 42, released as Capt, 46, after serv in 84th Div, ETO, 42-46, Res, 46-65, Maj (Ret); Bronze Star. Publ: History of 418 Regiment USAR, Privately Publ, 65. Mem: Northwest Mutual Life Ins Co Agents Asn; YMCA. Relig: Protestant. Mailing Add: 20 Placid St Trumbull CT 06611

CHURCH, JOHN TRAMMELL (D)
b Raleigh, NC, Sept 22, 17; s Charles Randolph Church & Lela Johnson C; m 1943 to Emma Thomas Rose; c John Trammell, Jr & Elizabeth Howard (Mrs William M Bacon, III). Educ: Catawba Col, 36-37; Univ NC, BS, 42. Polit & Govt Pos: Former chmn, Vance Co Dem Exec Comt, NC; former mem, Henderson City Coun; NC State Rep, 66-70; NC State Sen, 70-72; past chmn, NC Dem Exec Comt; deleg, Dem Nat Conv, 72. Bus & Prof Pos: Chmn bd, Rose's Stores, Inc, currently. Mil Serv: Capt, Marine Corps Res, 42-45, serv in SPac, 44-45; Three Distinguished Flying Crosses & Ten Air Medals. Mem: NC Merchants Asn; Am Retail Fedn; Univ NC Bus Found; Kappa Alpha; Rotary. Honors & Awards: Past Tar Heel of the Week; Businessman in the News, NC Citizens Asn; O B Michael Distinguished Alumnus Award, Catawba Col, 73. Relig: Methodist. Mailing Add: 420 Woodland Rd Henderson NC 27536

CHURCH, MARGUERITE STITT (R)
b New York, NY, Sept 13, 92; d William James Stitt & Adelaide Forsythe S; m 1918 to Ralph E Church; wid; c Ralph Edwin, Jr, William Stitt & Marjory Williams (Mrs Wood). Educ: Wellesley Col, AB, 14; Columbia Univ, AM in polit sci, 17; Phi Beta Kappa; Delta Kappa Gamma. Hon Degrees: LLD, Russell Sage Col, 58, Lake Forest Col, 60 & Northwestern Univ, 62; DHL, Nat Col Educ, 63. Polit & Govt Pos: US Rep, 13th Dist, Ill, 51-63; House of Rep deleg, inauguration of President, Mex, 58; deleg, White House Conf on Children & Youth, 60; US Deleg, UN Gen Assembly, 61; deleg, Rep Nat Conv, 64; mem, Presidential Task Force on the Aging, 70; mem planning bd, White House Conf on Aging, 70; mem adv comt, Admin on Aging, Dept Health, Educ & Welfare, 71-73. Bus & Prof Pos: Consult psychologist, State Charities Aid Asn, New York City; teacher, Wellesley Col, 1 year. Mem: Ill Children's Home & Aid Soc; Cong Club & Nat Alumnae Asn Wellesley Col; Bus & Prof Women's Clubs; Phi Beta Kappa Assocs; Zonta Int. Honors & Awards: VIP Award, Ill Club for Cath Women, 60; Founders' Day Award, Loyola Univ, 62; Merit Award, Civic Affairs Assocs, Inc, 60. Relig: Methodist. Mailing Add: 300 Church St Evanston IL 60201

CHURCHILL, EUGENE L (R)
Maine State Rep
Mailing Add: Orland ME 04472

CHURCHILL, WILLIAM LLOYD (R)
Mem, Durham Rep Town Comt, Conn
b New York, NY, Nov 22, 29; s Henry Lloyd Churchill & Helen Stevens C; m 1957 to Jane Lindemuth; c Andrew, Ian, Bruce & Matthew. Educ: Wesleyan Univ, 47-49; Stanford Univ, BA, 51, grad study, 52; Delta Tau Delta. Polit & Govt Pos: Mem, Durham Indust Develop Comn, Conn, 67-68; chmn, Durham Planning & Zoning Comn, 67-72; mem, Durham Rep Town Comt, 67-; Conn State Rep, 100th Assembly Dist, 73-74. Bus & Prof Pos: Advert intern, Palo Alto Times, Calif, 52-53; ed asst, Lane Publ Co, Menlo Park, 53-54 & 56-57; dir gen info serv, Stanford Research Inst, Menlo Park, 58-60; dir eng serv, Hiller Aircraft Corp, Palo Alto, 60-64; dir pub info & publ, Wesleyan Univ, 65-74; secy, Col & asst to pres, Conn Col, 75- Mil Serv: Entered as Pvt, Army, 54, released as SP-3, 56, after serv in 4th Inf Div, Ger, 55-56; Good Conduct Medal; Ger Occup Medal. Mem: Am Col Pub Rels Asn (chmn, New Eng Dist, 73-74); Educ Writers of Am. Relig: Congregational. Mailing Add: Haddam Quarter Rd Durham CT 06422

CIAMPI, FRANCIS W (D)
Conn State Rep
Mailing Add: 30 W Main St Waterbury CT 06702

CIANCI, VINCENT ALBERT (R)
Mayor, Providence, RI
b Providence, RI, Apr 3, 41; s Dr Vincent A Cianci & Esther Capobianco C; m 1973 to Sheila Bently; c Nicole. Educ: Fairfield Univ, BS in govt, 62; Villanova Univ Grad Sch, MA in polit sci, 65; Marquette Univ Sch Law, JD, 66; Phi Delta Phi. Polit & Govt Pos: Spec asst to Attorney Gen, RI, 69, prosecutor of organized crime & anti-corruption strike force, Dept Attorney Gen, 73; mayor, Providence, 75- Bus & Prof Pos: Attorney, RI Supreme Court, 67; admitted to practice before US Court of Mil Appeals, 67; instr govt, Bryant Col, 69. Mil Serv: Entered as Pvt, Army, 66, released as 1st Lt, 69, after serv in Mil Police Corps. Mem: Am Judicature Soc; Nat Dist Attorney's Asn; Italo-Am Club of RI; Sons of Italy; KofC. Relig: Roman Catholic. Legal Res: 145 Blackstone Blvd Providence RI 02906 Mailing Add: City Hall Providence RI 02903

CIARAMITARO, NICK (D)
Mem Exec Bd, Macomb Co Dem Comt, Mich
b Detroit, Mich, Dec 17, 51; s Sam Ciaramitaro & Catherine Sorrentino C; single. Educ: Univ Detroit, AB; Wayne State Univ Law Sch, 74-; Phi Alpha Theta; Alpha Sigma Nu. Polit & Govt Pos: Chmn, Macomb Co Young Dem, Mich, 72, vchmn, 72-73, officer-at-lg, 73-74; dir regist, Macomb Voters Regist Comt, 72; alt deleg, Dem State Cent Comt, 72-74; vchairperson, Mich Young Dem, 72-; exec bd, 12th Cong Dist Dem Comt, 72-; chmn, 12th Cong Dist Young Dem, currently; assoc field staff rep, Mich Dem Party, 73-; deleg, Dem Nat Mid-Term Conf, 74; mem exec bd, Macomb Co Dem Comt, 74- Mem: Roseville Bi-Centennial Comt (treas). Relig: Roman Catholic. Mailing Add: 25784 Normandy Roseville MI 48066

CIARLONE, ANTHONY MICHAEL (D)
Conn State Sen
b New Haven, Conn, May 8, 29; s Gaetano Ciarlone & Carmela Ciarlone C; m 1953 to Jean Patricia Irons; c Cynthia, Linda, Jeanmarie & Cathy. Educ: Quinnipiac Col, AS, 49. Polit & Govt Pos: Mem bd alderman, New Haven, Conn, 65-68; Conn State Rep, 67-70; Conn State Sen, 71- Bus & Prof Pos: Corp exec. Mem: Wooster Sq Community Asn; Wooster Sq Renewal Community; Alpha Club; St Michaels Holy Name Soc; New Haven Catholic Sch Bd Educ. Relig: Catholic. Mailing Add: 232 St John St New Haven CT 06511

CICCARELLO, LOUIS S (D)
Conn State Sen
b Middletown, Conn, Oct 26, 38; m 1965 to Marilyn Hankins; c Jeffrey, Matthew & Lynne. Educ: Wesleyan Univ; Stanford Univ; Delta Sigma. Polit & Govt Pos: Mem, Norwalk Bd of Estimate, Conn, 67-73; chmn, Bd of Estimate & Taxation, 71-73; Conn State Sen, 25th Dist, 75- Bus & Prof Pos: Attorney, Firm of Lovejoy, Cuneo & Curtis, currently. Mem: Norwalk Exchange Club; Norwalk-Wilton, Conn & Am Bar Asns. Legal Res: Sasqua Rd East Norwalk CT 06855 Mailing Add: PO Box 720 Norwalk CT 06850

CICENIA, ALICE (D)
Mem, Dem Nat Comt, SC
Mailing Add: 141 Carolina Ave Summerville SC 29483

CICHOCKI, JAMES Z (D)
Chmn, Livingston Co Dem Party, Mich
b Detroit, Mich, Oct 7, 17; s Thomas Cichocki & Wanda Jankowski C; m 1975 to Sylvia Cichocki Tkacz; c Tom, Jerry, Larry & Suzan. Educ: Wayne State Univ, 36-37. Polit & Govt Pos: Mem tax allocation bd, Livingston Co, Mich, 75-; chmn, Livingston Co Dem Party, 75- Mem: UAW. Mailing Add: 7498 Oreknob Fenton MI 48430

CICIONE, ANTHONY J (D)
Del State Sen
Mailing Add: Manchester Apts 701 Colonial Ave Elsmere Wilmington DE 19805

CIMINI, ANTHONY J (R)
Pa State Rep
b DuBois, Pa, Feb 12, 22; s Alexander Cimini & Catherine Benny C; m 1943 to Doris E Johnson; c Judith (Mrs Noviello), Lisa M & Anthony J, Jr. Educ: Lycoming Col, BA, 54; Bucknell Univ, MA, 64. Polit & Govt Pos: Treas, Lycoming Co Young Rep, Pa, 54-56;

committeeman, Lycoming Co Rep Party, 54-60; Pa State Rep, 75- Bus & Prof Pos: Grocery & meat mkt merchant, Williamsport, Pa, 47-69 & educator, 54-74. Mil Serv: Entered as Pvt, Army Air Force, 42, released as Sgt, 45, after serv in 8th Air Force, European Theatre, 43-45; Presidential Unit Citation; European Theatre Medal; Victory Medal; Good Conduct Medal; Am Theatre Medal; 4 Battle Stars. Mem: Kiwanis; Am Legion; VFW; Vol Fireman; Lycoming Co 4-H Club (dir, 75). Honors & Awards: Am Cancer Soc Award, 74. Relig: Roman Catholic. Legal Res: 361 E Mountain Ave South Williamsport PA 17701 Mailing Add: PO Box 163 Main Capitol Bldg Harrisburg PA 17120

CIMINO, DAVID JOHN (D)
Chmn, Woodstock Dem Town Comt, Conn
b Enfield, Conn, Sept 15, 47; s Dominic C Cimino & Mary E C; single. Educ: Providence Col, AB, 69. Polit & Govt Pos: Chmn, Woodstock Dem Town Comt, Conn, 74- Bus & Prof Pos: Instr hist, Woodstock Acad, Conn, 70- Mem: Woodstock Acad Educ Asn (pres, 72-); Windham Co Dem Asn. Honors & Awards: Outstanding Citizen, Enfield, Conn, 66. Mailing Add: PO Box 204 South Woodstock CT 06267

CINCOTTA, GEORGE A (D)
NY State Assemblyman
b Brooklyn, NY, Dec 5, 14; s George A Cincotta & Lillian Cirina C; m 1938 to Theresa D'Antonio; c Lillian (Mrs Fiore) & George, Jr. Educ: St Johns Col. Polit & Govt Pos: Mem, New York City Coun, formerly; mem coord coun, 71st precinct, New York Police Dept; NY State Assemblyman, 59-, mem joint legis comt on state's com, econ develop, tourism & motor boats, ranking mem Assembly comt on com, indust & econ develop & mem Assembly comt on govt employees, NY Gen Assembly, currently. Bus & Prof Pos: Bus exec. Mem: Andrew Jackson Club (pres); KofC; YMCA; Lions. Mailing Add: 96 Maple St Brooklyn NY 11225

CINELLI, ADELE P (D)
NMex State Rep
Mailing Add: Box 338 Albuquerque NM 87103

CINTRON, HECTOR
Sen, VI Legis
Mailing Add: PO Box 757 Frederiksted St Croix VI 00840

CIOCI, LOUIS MICHAEL (D)
RI State Rep
b Providence, RI, Aug 30, 40; s John R Cioci & Marie I Gammino C; m 1970 to Jeanne V Stamp; c Valerie, Michaela & Jessica. Educ: Boston Col, AB, 63; Suffolk Univ Law Sch, LLB, 67. Polit & Govt Pos: Asst legal counsel, Dept Social & Rehabilitative Serv, RI, 69; mem, 56th Dist Rep Comt, 73-74; RI State Rep, Dist 56, 75- Mem: Am & RI Bar Asns; Am Judicature Soc; Madonna Della DiFesa Soc. Mailing Add: 143 Pine Hill Ave Johnston RI 02919

CIPRIANI, HARRIET EMILY (D)
Dir Women's Activities, Dem Nat Comt
b New York, NY; d Floyd Stickels & Emily Gaetke S; m 1945 to Alfred Berne Cipriani. Educ: Flushing High Sch, NY, grad; Art Students League, New York. Polit & Govt Pos: Secy, DC Dem Cent Comt, 60-64, vchmn, 64-67; deleg, Dem Nat Conv, 60, 64 & 68, secy to DC, deleg, 60 & sgt-at-arms, 64; alt Dem nat committeewoman, DC, 64-67, committeewoman, 67-68; nat coordr, Women for Humphrey, 68; dep dir women's activities, Dem Nat Comt, 68-69, dep vchmn, 69-72, dir women's activities, 71- Mem: League of Women Voters US; Woman's Nat Dem Club; DC Dem Woman's Club; Urban League. Relig: Nonsectarian. Mailing Add: 1761 Harvard St NW Washington DC 20009

CISNEROS, ROGER (D)
Colo State Sen
Mailing Add: 1456 S Xavier St Denver CO 80219

CIZEK, DOLORES ADELE (D)
b St Louis, Mo, Jan 6, 30; d Ernest Everett Miller (deceased) & Margaret Steyh M (deceased); m 1951 to James John Cizek; c Deborah & Robert. Educ: Univ Chicago, BA, 51. Polit & Govt Pos: Deleg, Dem Nat Conv, 72. Bus & Prof Pos: Corp officer, Squire Shop of Hinsdale, Ltd, 52-; polit columnist, six weekly newspapers, DuPage Co, Ill, 71- Mem: Ill Press Asn; League Women Voters; Common Cause; Comt Ill Govt; Ill Planning & Conserv League. Relig: Unitarian. Mailing Add: 8025 S County Line Rd Hinsdale IL 60521

CLAFLIN, RUSSELL G (R)
NH State Rep
b Philadelphia, Pa, Oct 27, 14; wid; c One son. Educ: Harvard Univ. Polit & Govt Pos: Deleg, NH Const Conv, 56-64; NH State Rep, 57- Bus & Prof Pos: Retired land surveyor. Mil Serv: Field Artil, Army, ETO, World War II. Relig: Congregational. Mailing Add: Box 577 Wolfeboro NH 03894

CLAGGETT, BAY (DFL)
Secy, Chippewa Co Dem-Farmer-Labor Party, Minn
b Montevideo, Minn, Nov 27, 09; s George A Claggett & Alma Bay C; wid; m 1971 to Catherine Lilly; c Heather (Mrs Dustrud) & Pamela (Mrs Gray). Educ: Univ Minn, Minneapolis, LLB, 34; Alpha Tau Omega. Polit & Govt Pos: Chippewa Co attorney, Minn, 66-; secy, Chippewa Co Dem-Farmer-Labor Party, 70- Mem: Minn, Dist & Chippewa Co Bar Asns; Nat Dist Attorneys Asn; Montevideo CofC. Relig: Unitarian. Mailing Add: 503 Merriam Ave Montevideo MN 56265

CLAMAN, BARBARA BRITTON (R)
Chmn, Union Co Rep Comt, NJ
b Rahway, NJ, Jan 10, 24; d Richard DeMille Britton & Gladys Van Why B (deceased); m 1950 to Arnold Y Claman; c Constance, Catherine & Victoria. Educ: Columbia Univ Barnard Col, BA, 49. Polit & Govt Pos: Chmn, Westfield Rep Town Comt, NJ, 61-65 & 67-69; chmn, Union Co Rep Comt, 74- Bus & Prof Pos: Econ analyst, NY Port Authority, 49-51; dist mgr, US Census Oper, 70. Mil Serv: Entered as Seaman, Navy, 44, released as Radioman 2/C, 46, after serv in Comairlant, Norfolk, Va. Mem: Col Women's Club of Westfield; Community Players, Inc. Relig: Protestant. Mailing Add: 6 Rutgers Ct Westfield NJ 07090

CLAMPITT, BRUCE WILLARD (R)
Chmn, Hardin Co Rep Party, Iowa
b New Providence, Iowa, Aug 31, 09; s Ralph R Clampitt & Lela Norman C; m 1938 to Jennye E Evans; c Robert B & Joyce E. Educ: Iowa State Univ, BS; Life Underwriter's Training Coun, LUTC. Polit & Govt Pos: Twp, precinct chmn, Rep Party, Iowa, 6 years; chmn, Hardin Co Rep Party, 66- Bus & Prof Pos: Voc agr teacher, Sloan Pub Sch, 38-42; co exten dir, Plymouth Co, Iowa, 42-45; ins fieldman, Farm Bur Ins, 45-50; ins agent, Columbus Mutual Ins Co, 50-55; ins agent, Mutual of NY, 55-; pres, S Hardin Rural Tel Coop. Mem: Local, State & Nat Life Underwriters Asns; Iowa Cancer Soc; Mason. Relig: Society of Friends. Mailing Add: RFD New Providence IA 50206

CLANCHETTE, ALTON E (D)
Maine State Sen
Mailing Add: 9 Libby St Pittsfield ME 04967

CLANCY, DONALD DANIEL (R)
US Rep, Ohio
b Cincinnati, Ohio, July 24, 21; m 1949 to Betty Jane Mangeot; c Kathleen Ann (Mrs Donald W Hedrick), Patricia & Danny. Educ: Xavier Univ, Ohio, prelaw; Univ Cincinnati, LLB, 48. Polit & Govt Pos: City councilman, Cincinnati, Ohio, 50-60, mayor, 57-60; US Rep, Second Dist, Ohio, 61-; deleg, Rep Nat Conv, 72. Bus & Prof Pos: Pvt law practice. Relig: Roman Catholic. Legal Res: 7403 Greenfarms Dr Cincinnati OH 45224 Mailing Add: 2313 Rayburn Bldg Washington DC 20515

CLANCY, JEAN THERESA (D)
Committeewoman, NY State Dem Orgn
b Ellenville, NY, Aug 4, 28; d Harry L Clancy & Agnes L Wilkilow C; single. Educ: Ellenville High Sch, grad. Polit & Govt Pos: Pres, 12th Ward Dem Club, NY, 58-60; Dem committeewoman, Fifth Dist, 12th Ward, Schenectady, 58-; deleg, NY State Dem Conv, 66; chmn, Preforum Luncheon for Gubernatorial Cand, 66; mem, Schenectady Co Dem Publicity & Pub Rels Comt, 66-67; mem, Schenectady Co Dem Planning Bd, 66-69; co-chmn, Dem Women's Anniversary Luncheon, 67; chmn prog & planning comt, Women's Dem Club, 67-68; mem, Schenectady League Women Voters, 67-71; rep, NY State Annual Polit Conv, 67-; chmn, Dem Woman of the Year Award, 68; deleg, Dem Nat Conv, 68; mem, NY State Womens Legis Forum, 64-; committeewoman, NY State Dem Orgn, 105th Assembly Dist, 68- Bus & Prof Pos: Supvry equip clerk, NY Tel Co, 62-65, asst dial serv supvr, 65- Mem: Schenectady Mus; Schenectady Co Hist Soc; Cath Daughters of Am (Court St Catherine); Schenectady Co Fedn Womens Clubs; Friends of Schenectady Co Pub Libr. Relig: Catholic. Mailing Add: 911 McClellan St Schenectady NY 12309

CLANCY, LYNN J (D)
NDak State Rep
b Valley City, NDak, Aug 14, 39; s John E Clancy & Frances Starke C (deceased); m 1966 to Janice Gail Fredricks; c Frances & Patrick. Educ: Valley City State Col, BS, 61; Viking Pilot; Music Educators Nat Conf; Nat Educ Asn; EBC; Newman Club. Polit & Govt Pos: Chmn, Dist 24 Dem Non-Partisan Party, NDak, 73-74; NDak State Rep, Dist 24, 74- Bus & Prof Pos: Teacher, Bowdon, NDak; Adana, Turkey; Upper Heyford, England, 61-65; asst secy-treas, NDak Farmers Union, 65- Mil Serv: Entered as Airman Basic, Air Nat Guard, 56, released as Airman 1/C, 62, after serv in 194th Fighter Squadron, 56-62. Mem: Eagles. Honors & Awards: Distinguished Serv Award, Jaycees. Relig: Roman Catholic. Mailing Add: Rte 3 Valley City ND 58072

CLAPLANHOO, EDWARD E (D)
Dem Nat Committeeman, Wash
b Neah Bay, Wash, Aug 8, 28; s Arthur E Claplanhoo & Ruth E Allabush C; m 1969 to Thelma J Thumma Tolliver; c Karen (Mrs Jack Werkau) & Vernon Tolliver. Educ: State Col Wash, BS in Forestry, 56. Polit & Govt Pos: Mem, Makah Indian Tribal Coun, 66-68, chmn, 69-71; pres, Northwest Affiliated Tribes of Indians, 71; alt deleg, Dem Nat Conv, 72; Dem Nat Committeeman, Wash, 72- Bus & Prof Pos: Prof forester, 57-68; pub rels, 68-73. Mil Serv: Entered as Recruit, Army, 50, released as Sgt 1/C, 52, after serv in Specialized Unit, 81st Eng Boat Co, Europe, 52. Mem: Soc Am Foresters; Am Legion; Clallam Co Dem Club. Relig: Assembly of God. Mailing Add: PO Box 496 Neah Bay WA 98357

CLAPP, PAUL WOOD (R)
Mayor, High Point, NC
b High Point, NC, Apr 23, 16; s Stanford Darlington Clapp & Laura Black C; m 1937 to Maebelle Williams; c Nancy Mae (Mrs Davis). Educ: LaSalle Exten Univ, Acct, 36; Univ NC, Chapel Hill, Tax Law, 41. Polit & Govt Pos: City councilman, High Point, NC, 63-65 & 69-73, mayor, 73- Bus & Prof Pos: Collector revenue, City of High Point, NC, 42-45; mgr, Nat Upholstery Co, High Point, 45-48; pres, Nat Springs Corp, Tupelo, Miss, 48-66, chmn bd, 66-73. Mem: AF&AM (Past Master); Kiwanis; Red Men (Past Great Sachem NC); String & Splinter Club. Relig: First Reformed Church; elder. Mailing Add: 331 Woodrow Ave High Point NC 27262

CLARDY, GEORGE L (R)
Chmn, Lees Co Rep Party, Ga
b Fayette, Ala, Dec 10, 27; s Berry Burlington Clardy & Cora Etta Corbett C; m 1947 to Helen Joyce Rasberry; c George Alan & Stanley Wayne. Educ: High Sch grad. Polit & Govt Pos: Chmn, Lee Co Rep Party, Ga, 64-65, 68 & 70-; mem, Ga State Rep Cent Comt, 64-; finance chmn & mem, Second Cong Dist Rep Exec Comt, 72- Bus & Prof Pos: Serv mgr, Leeland Farms & Equipment, 60. Mil Serv: Entered as A/S, Navy, 45, released as EM 3/C, 50, after serv in SPac; Victory Medal; Good Conduct Medal; Pac Theatre Ribbon. Mem: Am Legion; Commun Club; Brotherhood. Relig: Baptist; Deacon, First Baptist Church, 8 years. Mailing Add: Rte 3 Box 44 Leesburg GA 31763

CLARDY, VIRGINIA MAE (DFL)
First VChmn, First Cong Dist Dem-Farmer-Labor Party, Minn
b Wellington, Mo, Dec 16, 23; d James Henry Price & Mattie Frances Walton P; m 1943 to James Elburn Clardy; c Winston Clinton, James Elburn, Rebecca Lanice, David Cornelius, Mary Frances & Cathy Ranee. Educ: Gen Hosp Sch Nursing, Kansas City, Mo, RN, 43; Univ Minn Sch Pub Health, 45-47. Polit & Govt Pos: Precinct chmn, Dem-Farmer-Labor Party, Burnsville, Minn, 65-; organizer & charter mem, Burnsville Dem-Farmer-Labor Club, 65; deleg, Minn State Dem-Farmer-Labor Conv, 66, 68 & 70; first vchmn, First Cong Dist Dem-Farmer-Labor Party, 68-; mem, Burnsville Human Rels Bd, 69-; chmn, Dakota Co Vol for Warren Spannaus for Attorney Gen, 70. Bus & Prof Pos: Pub health nurse, Kansas City, Mo, 44-45; orthopedic staff nurse, Methodist Hosp, St Louis Park, 66- Mem: Minn State & Nat Nurses Asn; Gen Hosp Sch Nursing Alumnae Asn; Burnsville League of Women Voters; Dakota Co Ment Health Asn. Relig: Methodist; Mem, Womens Soc Christian Serv, Grace

United Methodist Church, Burnsville. Mailing Add: 1116 High Circle Dr Burnsville MN 55378

CLARENBACH, DAVID E (D)
Wis State Rep
b St Louis, Mo, Sept 26, 53; s Henry G Clarenbach & Kathryn F C; single. Educ: Univ Wis-Madison, 71-74. Polit & Govt Pos: Co bd supvr, Dane Co, Wis, 72-74; City coun alderperson, Madison, 74; Wis State Rep, 75- Legal Res: 130 E Gorham Madison WI 53703 Mailing Add: 112 N State Capitol Madison WI 53702

CLARK, BETTY JEAN (D)
Ga State Rep
b Atlanta, Ga, Mar 13, 44; d Reuben Ransom, Sr & Myrtle Linder R; m 1971 to Theodore Clark. Educ: David T Howard High Sch, grad, 62; Atlanta Area Tech Clerical & Secretarial Sch, 66-68. Polit & Govt Pos: Ga State Rep, 55th Dist, 73- Bus & Prof Pos: Secy-ins clerk, personnel dept, Scripto, Inc, 64-72. Mem: Concerned Citizens of DeKalb (rep, 71-). Relig: Baptist. Mailing Add: 2139 Flat Shoals Rd SE Apt 3 Atlanta GA 30316

CLARK, BILL (D)
Tex State Rep
b Tyler, Tex, Mar 2, 46; s A D Clark, Jr & Virginia Skeen C; single. Educ: Univ Tex, 64-70; Baylor Univ Law Sch, 71-75; Phi Gamma Delta. Polit & Govt Pos: Tex State Rep, 75- Bus & Prof Pos: Attorney, Clark & Calhoun law firm, 74-75. Mil Serv: Entered as E-1, Tex Army Nat Guard, 69, released as 2nd Lt, 75, after serv in 12-A Reservists. Mem: State Bar Tex; Am & Smith Co Bar Asns. Relig: Methodist. Mailing Add: PO Box 3561 Tyler TX 75701

CLARK, CLABIE (D)
Chmn, Jefferson Davis Parish Dem Comt, La
b Kaplan, La, Apr 8, 20; s Ovey Clark & Elodie Simon C; m 1939 to Louella Vallot; c Kenneth Dale, Daniel Lee, Jeanette Faye & Cheryl Lynn. Polit & Govt Pos: Chmn, Jefferson Davis Parish Dem Comt, La, 60 & 75-; mem, State Dem Cent Comt La, 64- Bus & Prof Pos: Owner, tire & appliance store, 48; farmer, 64. Relig: Catholic. Legal Res: 722 First St Jennings LA 70546 Mailing Add: PO Box 698 Jennings LA 70546

CLARK, CYNTHIA M (R)
NH State Rep
Mailing Add: 20 Langdon St Plymouth NH 03254

CLARK, DAVID (D)
Chmn, Bladen Co Dem Comt, NC
b Lincolnton, NC, July 4, 22; s Thorne Clark & Mabel Gossett C; m 1951 to Kathryn Goode; c David, Allison Thorne, Walter & Caroline. Educ: Washington & Lee Univ, 41-43; Univ NC, LLB, 50; Phi Delta Theta. Polit & Govt Pos: NC State Rep, 51-53 & 55-57; pres, Lincoln Co Young Dem Club, 54; chmn, NC Reorgn Comn, 55-57; NC State Sen, 63; mem, Gov Comt on State Govt Reorgn, currently; chmn, Bladen Co Dem Comt, NC, 74- Bus & Prof Pos: Pres, Lynnwood Court, Inc, Town & Country, Inc, Great Piedmont Corp & Florasota Gardens, Inc, currently. Mil Serv: Entered as Pvt, Air Force, 43, released as 1st Lt, 45, after serv in 5th Air Force, Pac Theater; Air Medal. Mem: NC, Am & Lincoln Co Bar Asns; Rotary; VFW. Relig: Presbyterian. Legal Res: Rte 1 Iron Station NC 28080 Mailing Add: Elizabethtown NC 28337

CLARK, DEMPSEY C (R)
b Eudora, Ark, June 2, 08; s Dennis Clark & Sarah Hall C; m 1927 to Eliziebeth Drew; c Willie Mae (Mrs Charley Jackson), Joe Walter, Dempsey, Jr, James Edward, Roosevelt & Virginia. Educ: Ark Baptist Col, 66-67. Polit & Govt Pos: Co coordr, Chicot, Drew & Desha Counties, Ark, 66; chmn exec bd, Eudora Citizen Improv Club, 67-; chmn, Chicot Co Apt Inc, 70-; chmn, Chicot Co Rep Comt, 70-74; mem, Chicot Co elec comt, currently. Bus & Prof Pos: Hon mem, Chicot Co Mem Hosp, 69-70; mem, Sanitation Develop Comt, 70- Mem: RAM (seventh degree, Holly Ridge Lodge). Relig: Baptist; Minister. Mailing Add: Hwy 65 Eudora AR 71640

CLARK, DICK (D)
Fla State Rep
Mailing Add: 6725 SW 133 Terrace Miami FL 33156

CLARK, DONALD E (D)
Chmn Bd Comnrs, Multnomah Co, Ore
b Silverton, Ore, Apr 25, 33; s Harold Edward Clark & Vera Mary C; m 1971 to Shirley Paulus; c Donna Kim, Donald E, Jr & Rick Paulus. Educ: Vanport Col, 2 years; San Francisco State Col, AB, 56; Portland State Univ, 1 year; Theta Nu. Polit & Govt Pos: Sheriff, Multnomah Co, Ore, 63-67, co comnr, 69-, chmn bd comnrs, currently; adv, President's Comn on Law Enforcement & Justice, Washington, DC, 66; mem, Task Force on Order & Justice, 68; deleg, Dem Nat Conv, 68; mem, Criminal Law Rev Comt, Ore State Legis, 68-69; chmn, City-Co Health Comt, Portland, 71- Bus & Prof Pos: Consult & dir, Police Design Assoc, Portland, Ore, 67-68; assoc dir Law Enforcement Progs, Portland State Univ, 67-68; mem, Multnomah Co Welfare Comn, 68-; bd dirs, Comprehensive Health Planning Asn, Portland, 70-; mem exec bd, Columbia Region Asn Govt, 71- Publ: A Forward Step: Educational Backgrounds for Police, C C Thomas, 66; auth, Jail management section In: Municipal Police Administration, Int City Mgt Asn, 6th ed; numerous articles in Police Mag, Police Chief, Law & Order & others. Mem: Life mem Nat Sheriff's Asn; Ore State Sheriff's Asn; Int Asn of Chiefs of Police; Int Asn of Police Prof; Mil Police Asn. Honors & Awards: Reverence for Law Award for Ore. Relig: Unitarian. Legal Res: Portland OR 97221 Mailing Add: Rm 605 Multnomah County Courthouse Portland OR 97204

CLARK, DOROTHY C (R)
Mem, Utah Rep State Cent Comt
b Moab, Utah, Oct 8, 24; d John Whitbred Corbin & Ila Palmer C; m 1945 to Dr Stanley N Clark; c Stanley Corbin, David Crawford and Kevin Newell. Educ: Univ Utah Sch of Nursing, RN, 46; Brigham Young Univ, BS, 62. Polit & Govt Pos: Deleg, Utah State & Utah Co Rep Convs, 64-; state women's coordr, US Senate Race, Utah, 64 & 70; voting dist vchmn, Rep Party, 65-69; mem, Utah Rep State Finance Comt, 65-; mem, Utah Co Rep Cent Comt, 65-; mem, Utah Rep State Cent Comt, 65-, vchmn, 71-74; mem, Utah Rep State Exec Comt, 69-74; deleg, Rep Nat Conv, 72; presidential elector, Electoral Col, 72; Rep primary cand, US Cong, First Dist, Utah, 74. Bus & Prof Pos: Registered nurse, Utah State Nurses Asn, 46-; vchmn adv coun, Timpanogos Community Ment Health Ctr, 74- Mil Serv: Entered as Student, Cadet Nurse Corps, 44, released, 46, upon grad. Mem: Utah State Nurses Asn (legis chmn, 72-74, legis consult, 74-); Am Nurses Asn (bd trustees); Utah State Med Asn (auxiliary rep, Polit Action Comt, 65-74); Nat Coalition for Action in Polit; Utah Arthritis Found (bd dirs, 68-). Relig: Latter-day Saint. Mailing Add: 1075 E Elm Ave Provo UT 84601

CLARK, ELWIN NAIL (D)
b Joliet, Ill, Mar 4, 26; s James Howard Clark & Ethelyn Nail C; m 1951 to Mary Frances McGinnis; c Jill Ann, Cynthia Lynn, Mark Allen & Tracy Lee. Educ: Roosevelt Col, BA in Econ, 50; Polit Econ Club. Polit & Govt Pos: Chmn, Citizens for Paul Douglas, Will Co, Ill, 48, 54, 60 & 66; chmn, Citizens for Kennedy, 14th Cong Dist, 60; exec vpres, Will Co Dem Victory Club, 60-64; chmn, Oper Support, 14th & 15th Cong Dist, 61-65; security chief, Citizens for McCarthy, Dem Nat Conv, 68, deleg, 72. Bus & Prof Pos: Economist, US Govt, 51-52; real estate broker, 53- Mil Serv: Entered as Aviation Cadet, Navy, 44, released 46, after serv in US. Mailing Add: 901 Dawes Ave Joliet IL 60435

CLARK, EZRA THOMPSON (R)
Utah State Sen
b Farmington, Utah, Dec 3, 14; s Nathan George Clark & Cleo Call C; m to Geraldine M; c Ezra T, Jr, Anne (Mrs George C Pingree), James E, Janet (Mrs W Robert Wright), Ilene & Mark H. Educ: Brigham Young Univ, BS, 37; Alpha Kappa Psi. Polit & Govt Pos: City councilman, Bountiful, Utah, 45-46; mem, Davis Co Sch Bd, Utah, 52-56; mem, Utah State Sch Bd, Salt Lake City, 59-60; bd mem & pres, Bountiful Water Sub-Conservancy Dist, 55-65; bd mem, chmn bd & pres, Weber Basin Conservancy Dist, 65-; Utah State Sen, 67- Bus & Prof Pos: Vpres, Bountiful State Bank, 53-62; pres, Growers Mkt Co, Salt Lake City, 53-; bd mem & pres, Davis Co Bank, Farmington, 62- Mem: Rotary. Relig: Latter-day Saint. Mailing Add: 1106 East 400 North Bountiful UT 84010

CLARK, FRANK M (D)
b Bessemer, Pa, Dec 24, 15; m 1941 to Patricia Loy; c Frank, Jr & Kelly. Educ: Pittsburgh Sch of Aeronaut. Polit & Govt Pos: Chief of police, Bessemer, Pa, 45; US Rep, 25th Dist, Pa, formerly; deleg, NATO Pariliamentary Conf, 56, inspection tour of NATO Bases, 60 & 63, NATO Conf, Paris, 64 & 66 and Brussels, 67, 68, 69 & 70 & NATO Parliamentary Conf, New York, 65; deleg to visit Ger Govt, 57, Int Christian Leadership Peace Conf, The Hague, 58, Nat Roads Conf, SAm, 59, Int Hwy Conf, 61, Int Roads Conf, Sydney, Australia, 58 & SAm, 65 & Coast Guard Loran Sta in Mediter, 68 & 69; deleg, Dem Nat Conv, 68 & 72; deleg, Dem Nat Mid-Term Conf, 74. Mil Serv: Flight Officer & Glider Pilot, Army Air Force, World War II; Lt Col, Air Force Res. Mem: Am Legion (past comdr); VFW (past comdr); 40 et 8; Odd Fellow (Past Grand Master); Consistory. Relig: Presbyterian. Mailing Add: Bessemer PA 16112

CLARK, FRED G
Asst Secy Admin & Mgt, Dept Labor
Mailing Add: Dept of Labor Washington DC 20210

CLARK, FRED STEPHEN (D)
b Savannah, Ga, July 10, 36; s H Sol Clark & Matilda Shapiro C; m 1970 to Nancie Meddin; c Jonathan Abby. Educ: Cornell Univ, AB, 58; Univ Ga Sch Law, LLB, 61; Phi Sigma Delta; Phi Alpha Delta. Polit & Govt Pos: Asst US attorney, South Dist Ga, 64-66; asst city attorney, Savannah, Ga, 68-70, police court judge pro tem, 68-70; chmn, First Sen Dist Dem Party Conv, 70; mem, Ga State Dem Exec Comt, formerly; asst town attorney & recorder pro-tem, Thunderbolt, Ga, 71- Bus & Prof Pos: Partner, Brannen & Clark, Savannah, Ga, 64-73; partner, Lee & Clark, 73- Mil Serv: Entered as Airman Basic, Ga Air Nat Guard, 61, released as Yeoman 2/C, 67, after serv in Coast Guard Res. Publ: Defense of indigents in Georgia, Ga Bar J, 64; Annual survey of Georgia law agency 1965-1968, Mercer Univ Law Rev, Vol 26; Interest in usuary, Encycl Ga, Harrison Co, 71. Mem: Savannah, Fed & Am Bar Asns; State Bar Ga; Scribes. Honors & Awards: Outstanding Young Man of Savannah, 68; One of Five Outstanding Young Men of Ga, 68. Relig: Jewish. Legal Res: 4726 Cumberland Dr Savannah GA 31405 Mailing Add: 300 Bull St Suite 711 Savannah GA 31401

CLARK, GEORGE N (D)
Ala State Rep
Mailing Add: Box 6 Eutaw AL 35462

CLARK, GILBERT EDWARD
b Thompson Ridge, NY, Jan 15, 17; s Theodore Gilbert Clark & Kathryn Cornelius Morgan Jones C; m 1943 to Lyla Elaine Sween; c Bonnie Lee, Theodore Edward & George Kirsten. Educ: Syracuse Univ, BA, 38, MA, 40. Polit & Govt Pos: Career officer, Dept State, 46-, info officer & vconsul, Am consulate gen, Bombay, India, 46-49, consul, 49-51, pub affairs staff, Bur Near East, SAsian & African Affairs, 51-53, second secy, consul, first secy Am Legation, Tangier, Morocco, 53-56, exec off of President, Bur of Budget, 56-57, Dept State, 57-58, Nat War Col, 58-59, Am consul gen, Amsterdam, Netherlands, 59-61, counr of embassy, dep chief of mission, Am Embassy, Pretoria, Transvaal, Repub SAfrica, 61-65, dir Off WAfrica Affairs, 65-66, country dir, Southern Africa Affairs, 66-68, US Ambassador, Mali, 68-70, US Ambassador, Senegal & Gambia, 70-73; sr foreign serv inspector, Dept of State, 74, foreign affairs consult, Cong Research Serv, 75- Bus & Prof Pos: Reporter, Middletown (NY) Times Herald, 37; grad asst instr, Syracuse Univ, 38-39, asst prof, 46; prod mgr, Whitney Graham Publ Co, Buffalo, 40-41. Mil Serv: Lt Col, Army Signal Corps, China-Burma-India, 41-45; Bronze Star. Mem: Am Foreign Serv Asn; Sigma Delta Chi; Alpha Phi Omega. Honors & Awards: Grand Officer, Order of the Lion, Senegal, 73. Relig: Episcopal. Mailing Add: 4421 Hawthorne St NW Washington DC 20016

CLARK, GRACIE MAE (R)
Chmn, Appanoose Co Rep Party, Iowa
b Mystic, Iowa, Nov 3, 20; d John Frost & Jennie Hamilton F; m 1937 to Ted D Clark; c Billy D & Sally (Mrs Gerald Banks). Educ: Mystic Pub Schs, Iowa, 11 years. Polit & Govt Pos: Secy to Iowa State Rep & State Sen Ted D Clark, 49-55; former secy & vchmn, Appanoose Co Rep Party, Iowa, chmn, 68-; pres, Rep Women, 70-71; alt deleg, Rep Nat Conv, 72. Bus & Prof Pos: Bookkeeper, Ted Clark's Thermogas, 49- Mem: Eastern Star; Rebekah Lodge; White Shrine; Mystic Develop Comt; Bus & Prof Club. Relig: Methodist. Mailing Add: Box 123 Mystic IA 52574

CLARK, HUBERT WOODY (D)
Ark State Rep
b Forrest City, Ark, Aug 1, 34; s Hubert Lee Clark & Vera Sulcer C; m 1951 to Eunita Reed; c Mikeal & Scheryl. Educ: Forrest City High Sch, grad. Polit & Govt Pos: Ark State Rep, 69- Mem: Mason (32 degree); Lions; Forrest City Jr CofC; Boy's Club. Relig: Baptist. Mailing Add: 2311 E Broadway Forrest City AR 72335

CLARK, JAMES, JR (D)
Md State Sen
b Ellicott City, Md, Dec 19, 18; married. Educ: Iowa State Col, BS, 41. Polit & Govt Pos: Md State Deleg, 59-63; Md State Sen, 63-; Howard Co Soil Conserv Dist Supvr, currently. Bus & Prof Pos: Farmer. Mil Serv: Air Force, 41-45. Mem: Rotary; VFW. Mailing Add: Altholton Village Ctr Simpsonville MD 21150

CLARK, JAMES A (D)
Tex State Rep
b Lovelady, Tex; m to Rosalie Sawyer; c James, Pat & Rose Mary. Educ: Univ Houston, BS; A&M Serv Sch, 1 year. Polit & Govt Pos: Tex State Rep, Dist 99, 71- Mil Serv: Navy. Mem: Int Longshoremens Local 1273 (vpres). Relig: Baptist. Legal Res: 2212 Hickory Lane Pasadena TX 77502 Mailing Add: Suite 100 1706 Strawberry Pasadena TX 77502

CLARK, JANET (DFL)
Minn State Rep
Mailing Add: 3025 Cedar Ave S Minneapolis MN 55407

CLARK, JOHN CONRAD (D)
Dir, Export-Import Bank of US
b New York, NY, Feb 19, 13; s John C Clark & Marie A Sparnecht C; m 1949 to Lillian Fischer; c Roger Scott. Educ: NY Univ Sch Bus Admin, 2 years; Univ NC, exten div. Polit & Govt Pos: Dir, Export-Import Bank of US, 69- Bus & Prof Pos: Pres, John C Clark & Co, Inc, New York, 47-67; asst mgr bond dept, Chase Manhattan Bank, 47-51; mgr & vpres bond dept, Wachovia Bank & Trust Co, Winston-Salem, NC, 51-67, sr vpres pub finance, 67-69. Mil Serv: Entered as 2nd Lt, Army, 41, released as Maj, 45, after serv in Anti-Aircraft Artil, CZ & ETO; Lt Col inactive, Army; ETO Citation for Ardennes, Rhineland & Cent Europe Campaigns. Publ: The bankers handbook, and popular government, Univ NC & Am Banker, Int Issue, 11/69. Mem: Rotary; Munic Forum of NY; Investment Bankers Asn; Munic Finance Forum; Munic Treas Asn of US. Honors & Awards: Cert of Award as Mem Finance Comt, Gov of NC Study Comn on Pub Sch Syst, 68. Relig: Presbyterian. Legal Res: 4141 River St Arlington VA 22207 Mailing Add: 811 Vermont Ave Washington DC 20571

CLARK, JOHN FRANKLIN, III (D)
b Florence, SC, July 25, 44; s John Franklin Clark, Jr & Ellen Bryant; m 1966 to Helen Horton; c John Franklin IV. Educ: Davidson Col, AB, 66; Univ Paris, 68; Haile Selassie I Univ, 69-70; Syracuse Univ, PhD, 74; Pi Kappa Alpha. Polit & Govt Pos: Legis asst, US Rep John W Jenrette, Jr, SC, 75- Bus & Prof Pos: Instr polit sci, Benedict Col, Columbia, SC, 72 & Univ SC, 73; asst prof, polit sci, Univ Fla, 73-75. Mil Serv: Entered as 1st Lt, Army, 70, released as Capt, 72, after serv in US Army Adj Gen Sch, Ft Benjamin Harrison, Ind, 70-72; Nat Defense Serv Medal & Army Commendation Medal. Publ: Co-auth, National attributes associated with dimensions of support for the United Nations, Int Orgn, 71. Mem: Am Polit Sci Asn; Int Studies Asn; African Studies Asn. Honors & Awards: Nat Defense Educ Act Fel, 66-67, 67-68 & 68-69; Shell Int Studies Research Fel, 69-70. Legal Res: 1002 Longstreet St Kingstree SC 29556 Mailing Add: 426 Cannon House Off Bldg Washington DC 20515

CLARK, JOHN HOWARD (R)
Iowa State Rep
b Keokuk, Iowa, Nov 24, 46; s Howard Arthur Clark & Margaret Ruhl C; single. Educ: Drury Col, BA, 69; Kappa Alpha. Polit & Govt Pos: Iowa State Rep, 71-73 & 75- Bus & Prof Pos: Ins agt, Ed S Lofton & Sons. Mem: Iowa Asn Independent Ins Agts; Kiwanis. Relig: Congregational. Mailing Add: 916 N 11th Keokuk IA 52632

CLARK, JOHN R (D)
Fla State Rep
b Hancock, Md, June 9, 24; s John N Clark & Della Alderton C; m 1963 to Geneva Rolfe; c John R, Jr (deceased), Douglas, Robert, Sandra, James, Edward & Randall. Educ: Transylvania Col, BA, 47; Univ Ky, MA, 49; Pi Kappa Alpha. Polit & Govt Pos: Fla State Rep, Polk, Highlands & Osceola Co, 66- Bus & Prof Pos: Educator, 49- Mil Serv: Entered as Pvt, Army, 45, released as T-4, 46, after serv in Transportation Corps, ETO, 45-46. Mem: Am Legion. Relig: Protestant. Mailing Add: 515 Queens Loop Lakeland FL 33803

CLARK, LAWRENCE STEVEN (D)
Committeeman, Alexandria Dem City Comt, Va
b Philadelphia, Pa, Jan 28, 47; s Jonathan Lewis Clark, Jr & Ruth S; separated; c Keith. Educ: Ohio Northern Univ, BSEE, 70. Polit & Govt Pos: Committeeman, Alexandria Dem City Comt, Va, 73-, chairperson city affairs comt, 74-; chmn, City Housing Availability Bd, 73-75; deleg, Dem Nat Mid-Term Conf, 74; comnr, Human Rights, Alexandria, 75- Bus & Prof Pos: Engr & proj engr, Technical Servs Corp, 71-74; proj engr, Unified Industs, Inc, 74-75, proj mgr, 75- Mil Serv: Army, six years, active & reserve; Good Conduct Medal. Publ: Auth, Federal specification for microwave ovens, Govt Printing Off, 7/72. Mem: Am Asn Advan Sci; Inst Elec & Elec Engrs; Am Civil Liberties Union; Consumers Union; Young Dem Club. Mailing Add: 530 N Columbus St Alexandria VA 22314

CLARK, LELA TIMBES (R)
Chmn, Tishomingo Co Rep Party, Miss
b Prentiss, Miss, Jan 22, 04; d Columbus Allen Timbes & Lura Nixon T; m 1927 to Julius Edwin Clark, wid; c Patsy (Mrs Pace) & Janette (Mrs Pike). Educ: Miss State Col, BS in Elem Educ, 51. Polit & Govt Pos: Vchmn, Local Rep Party Orgn, 70-75; chmn, Tishomingo Co Rep Party, Miss, 75- Bus & Prof Pos: Teacher, Burnt Mills & Wright Sch, Tishomingo Co, 20-22, Tishomingo Elem & Paden, 23-29, Paden Elem, 41-49 & Iuka Elem Sch, 49-69; saleswoman, Compton's Encycl, Tishomingo Co, 53-73; pub health worker, Tishomingo Co Health Dept, summers 58, 64, 65 & 66; supply elem teacher, Iuka Elem & Burnsville Sch, 75- Publ: Auth articles, In: Tishomingo Co News, J H Biggs, Iuka, Miss, 75. Mem: Co, State & Nat Teachers Asn; Retired Teachers Asn; Order of Eastern Star (Worthy Matron, 47-48, organist, 70-75); Am Legion Auxiliary (pres, Iuka, Miss). Honors & Awards: Diamond Pen for 25 years serv, 4-H Club. Relig: Missionary Baptist. Mailing Add: 604 S Fulton St Iuka MS 38852

CLARK, LOUIS M (D)
Ga State Rep
Mailing Add: Rte 2 Danielsville GA 30633

CLARK, LYN HENDERSON (D)
Mem, Dem Nat Comt, Md
b New York, NY; d Leon Henderson & Myrlic Hamm H; m to William Giddings Clark; c Elizabeth Henderson & William Giddings, Jr. Educ: George Washington Univ, BA. Polit & Govt Pos: Off dir, Citizens for Kennedy, 60; vchmn, Joseph D Tydings Senate Campaign, Md, 62, co-chmn, Joseph D Tydings County Senate Campaign, 70; deleg & secy, Dem Nat Conv, 68; secy, Montgomery Co Dem Cent Comt, formerly; chmn, Md Dem Party Const & Bylaws Comt, 72, co-chmn, Md Dem Party, 73-; mem, Dem Nat Comt, Md, 73-; comnr, Md Dept Transportation, 73-; deleg, Dem Nat Mid-Term Conf, 74. Mem: George Washington Univ Alumni Asn (pres); Am Heart Asn (mem fundraising bd, 74-); Nat Asn State Chmn (exec comt, 75-); Montgomery Co Heart Asn (mem bd); Md Heart Asn (mem bd). Relig: Episcopal. Mailing Add: 9810 Summit Ave Kensington MD 20795

CLARK, MARION O'DONALD (R)
Chmn, Suwannee Co Rep Exec Comt, Fla
b Dowling Park, Fla, May 11, 40; s H Frank Clark & Abbie Willis C; m 1967 to Shirley Ethel Barrs; c Rhonda Lynn & Kevin O'Donald. Educ: Lafayette High Sch; Am Inst Banking. Polit & Govt Pos: Mem bd trustees, Suwannee Co Hosp, Fla, 70-74, chmn bd, 73-74; chmn, Suwannee Co Rep Exec Comt, 75- Bus & Prof Pos: Secy adv bd, Suwannee-Hamilton Voc Tech Sch, 71- Mil Serv: Entered as Pvt, Army, 63, released as Pfc, 65, after serv in Admin Co; Good Conduct Medal. Mem: F&AM; Suwannee Co CofC (dir, 69-75). Relig: Methodist. Legal Res: Newburn Rd Live Oak FL 32060 Mailing Add: PO Box 183 Live Oak FL 32060

CLARK, MEREDITH P (R)
Rep Nat Committeewoman, VI
b Oconto Falls, Wis, Jan 14, 27; m 1950 to Philip Clark; c James William & Meriweather Kaye. Educ: Lawrence Univ, BA, 48; NY Sch of Social Work, 49. Polit & Govt Pos: Territorial secy, Rep Party, 64-68; br treas, St Croix, 65-67; mem, Rep Territorial Comt, VI, 64-; exec vchmn, VI Nixon for President Comt & mem, VI Inauguration Comt for Nixon-Agnew; Rep Nat Committeewoman, VI, 68-; VI publicity chmn, 17th Annual Rep Women's Conf, 69; mem task force, VI Comprehensive Health Planning Coun, 69-71; adv inaugural comt, Gov VI, 71; mem arrangements & chmn VI housing, Rep Nat Conv, 72; mem, St Croix Bd Appeals for Med Assistance, 72- Bus & Prof Pos: Dept head of stock, Saks Fifth Ave, 48-49; psychiat social work, 49-50; secy, US Govt, 51-53, VI Tel Co, 56 & law off, 56-57; vpres, The Pentheny, Ltd, 73- Mem: Red Cross; Nat Fedn Bus & Prof Women's Clubs (chmn, Christiansted Legis Comt, 71-72); St Croix Forum; St Croix Island Ctr; Tennis Club of St Croix. Relig: Methodist. Legal Res: Estate The Sight Christiansted St Croix VI 00820 Mailing Add: Box 788 Christiansted St Croix VI 00820

CLARK, NANCY RANDALL (D)
Maine State Rep
Mailing Add: RFD 2 Lambert Rd Freeport ME 04032

CLARK, PEARL MAE (D)
VChmn, Pulaski Co Dem Comt, Mo
b St Louis, Mo, Apr 2, 00; d William Albert Logan & Bertha Luecke L; wid; c Norma Louise (Mrs Judkins). Educ: Waynesville Grade & High Schs, 05-17. Polit & Govt Pos: Committeewoman & vchmn, Pulaski Co Dem Comt, Mo, 65- Mem: Pulaski Co Hosp Auxiliary; Harmony Home Exten Club; Womens Dem Club; United Methodist Womens Soc Christian Serv; Eastern Star (past matron); Relig: Methodist. Mailing Add: 402 W Hwy 66 Waynesville MO 65583

CLARK, PHILIP CANNADY (R)
b Hutchinson, Kans, June 4, 26; s Walter Lawrence Clark & Mabel Cannady C; m 1950 to Meredith Kaye Plier; c James William & Meriweather Kaye. Educ: Univ Wis-Madison, 43 & 46-47; Lawrence Col, BS, 48; Northwestern Univ, BS, 46; Univ Colo, 54-55; Tau Beta Pi; Chi Epsilon; Phi Mu Alpha; Delta Tau Delta; Sextant. Polit & Govt Pos: Mem, Territorial Comt, Rep Party, VI, 66-70, first vchmn, 66-68; deleg, Rep Nat Conv, 68 & alt delg, 72; mem, VI Bd Elec, St Croix, 68-70; deleg, Second Const Conv VI, 71-72; sen & vpres, VI Legis, 71-73; mem, VI Law Enforcement Comn, 71-73; mem, VI Adv Planning Bd, 72-, chmn, 73- Bus & Prof Pos: Asst mgr, Little Harbor Club, Mich, summers, 45-48; asst mgr, Thunder Mt Resort, Colo, summer 55; land surveyor, Charles L Hillbron & Assoc, Inc, Christiansted, St Croix, VI, 56-57; vpres & gen mgr, Young-Clark Ins, Ltd, 57-71, pres & gen mgr, 71-; treas VI Title & Trust Co, 57-66, pres, 67-69, vpres, 69-; licensed ins agent, 57-; treas, Pentheny, Ltd, 61- Mil Serv: Entered as A/S, Naval Res, 44-46 & 48-54, released as Lt, 54, after serv as Beachmaster, Underwater Demolition, Amphibious Forces, Atlantic Fleet, 48-54, Res, 43-69, Lt; Retired. Mem: Ins Agents Asn VI; charter mem Rotary Club St Croix; St Croix CofC; Island Ctr of St Croix; Tennis Club of St Croix. Relig: Presbyterian. Legal Res: Estate the Sight Christiansted St Croix VI 00820 Mailing Add: PO Box 788 Christiansted St Croix VI 00820

CLARK, RAMSEY (D)
b Dallas, Tex, Dec 18, 27; m to Georgia Welch; c Ronda Kathleen & Tom C. Educ: Univ Tex, BA, 49; Univ Chicago, MA & JD, 50. Polit & Govt Pos: Asst attorney gen, Dept Justice, 61-65, dep attorney gen, 65-67, acting attorney gen, 66-67, attorney gen, 67-69; cand, US Sen, 74. Mil Serv: Marine Corps, 45-46. Mailing Add: 37 W 12th St New York NY 10011

CLARK, RICHARD CLARENCE (D)
US Sen, Iowa
b Paris, Iowa, Sept 14, 29; s Clarence Clark & Bernice Anderson C; m 1954 to Jean Shirley Gross; c Julie Ann & Thomas Richard. Educ: Upper Iowa Univ, BA, 53; Univ Md, Wiesbaden, Ger, 50-52; Univ Frankfurt, Ger, 51-52; Univ Iowa, MA, 56; secy, Phi Alpha Theta; Pi Kappa Delta. Polit & Govt Pos: Campaign worker, Hershel Loveless for Gov, 56 & 58 & Harold E Hughes for Gov, 62; mem campaign staff, E B Smith for US Sen, 62; chmn, Gov Legis Comt, 63; mem, Dem Platform Comt, 62 & 64; pres, Fayette Community Sch Bd, 62-65; chmn, Off Emergency Planning in Iowa & Iowa Civil Defense Admin, 63-65; mem, Gov Comn on State & Local Govt, 64-; admin asst to US Rep John C Culver, 65-72; campaign mgr, Culver for Cong, 64-70; US Sen, Iowa, 73- Bus & Prof Pos: Eng teacher, Wadena High Sch, Iowa, 53-54; research asst, Univ Iowa, 55-56, instr hist, 56-59; asst prof hist, Upper Iowa Univ, 59-64. Publ: Witches Beware, Northwestern Univ Press, 53; Some Personal Observations on the Russian Economy, Mo Valley Research & Develop Coun, 63; Political Implications Mobility in the Public Service, Am Soc of Pub Admin, 66. Mil Serv: Entered as Pvt, Army, 50, released as Cpl, 52, after serv in 78th Field Artil, Intel, Ger, 51-52. Mem: Am Hist Asn (Conf on European Hist); Am Asn Advancement of Slavic Studies; Am Asn Univ Prof; UN Asn of the US; Mem of Cong for Peace Through Law. Honors & Awards: Named Nat Oratorical Champion & Nat Discussion Champion, 53. Legal Res: 1825 Eighth Ave Marion IA 52302 Mailing Add: 404 Russell Off Bldg Washington DC 20510

CLARK, RICHARD ORVILLE (D)
Miss State Rep
Mailing Add: 601 Highway 25 South Iuka MS 38852

CLARK, RICHARD OWEN (D)
Mem, Alameda Co Dem Cent Comt, Calif
b Kansas City, Mo, Jan 29, 31; s Sterling Howard Clark & Elizabeth C; m 1969 to Gloria Clare Molina. Educ: St Mary's Col, Moraga, Calif, BA, 55; Univ Calif, 55; Univ San Francisco, 59-60; Debate Soc; Western All-Stars (Football), 54; St Mary's Football Championship Team, 54. Polit & Govt Pos: Chmn, Albany Dem Party, Calif, 62 & 64; alt deleg, Dem Nat Conv, 64 & 68; mem tax equalization bd, Alameda Co, 65, chmn, Local Agency Formation Comn, 69, chmn, Interagency Coun Waterfront Planning, 69-70; mayor, Albany, Calif, 66-70, city councilman, 64-66 & 70-; mem, Alameda Co Dem Cent Comt, 66-; mem comt bldg laws, League Calif Cities, 67; co-chmn, Alameda Co for Robert Kennedy Campaign, 68; mem, Calif State Dem Cent Comt, Seventh Cong Dist, 68-; mem, Dem State Cent Comt, 69; vchmn & chmn, Alameda Co Mayors Conf, 69; mem exec comt, Asn Bay Area Govt, 69-; dir, Bay Area Rapid Transit Dist, 69-; deleg, Seventh Cong Dist Dem Coun, 69. Bus & Prof Pos: Claims adjuster, Travelers Ins Co, San Francisco, 62-66; agent, NY Life Ins Co, 66-68; agent, Farmers Ins Group, Oakland, 69-; real estate, commercial & retail leasing, Grubb & Ellis Co, 69- Mil Serv: Entered as 2nd Lt, Marines, 55, released 59; Maj, Marines Res; commanding officer, HMN-769 Helicopter Squadron, Alameda NAS, 69-71. Mem: Albany CofC; Marine Corps ROA; Am Legion. Honors & Awards: Outstanding Men of Am Award, Jr CofC, 66; Outstanding Community Serv Award, Lions, 67. Relig: Roman Catholic. Mailing Add: Farmers Life Ins 4130 Broadway Oakland CA 94611

CLARK, RICHARD R (D)
Tenn State Rep
Mailing Add: 5113 Nolensville Rd Nashville TN 37211

CLARK, ROBERT BREWSTER (R)
b Brewster, Mass, Aug 6, 27; s Edgar C Clark & Alice Nutting C; div; m 1972 to Betsy Greenwood Gambrill; c Christopher N & Frederica Thayer. Educ: Harvard Col, AB, 49; George Washington Univ Law Sch, JD, 65. Polit & Govt Pos: Staff mem, Joint Defense Staff, Dept of Defense, 50-52; with US Foreign Serv, Dept of State, 53-60, polit officer, US Embassy, Beirut, Lebanon, 54-56 & US Consulate-Gen, Genoa, Italy, 58-60; mem prof staff, Rep Policy Comt, US Senate, 61, Rep counsel, Comt on Appropriations, 62- Mil Serv: Entered as A/S, Navy, 45, released as Seaman 2/C, 46, after serv in 16th Atlantic Group Fleet, Atlantic Theatre. Mem: Mass & DC Bars; Univ Club, Washington, DC. Relig: Protestant. Legal Res: Prince Lane Brewster MA 02631 Mailing Add: University Club 1135 16th St NW Washington DC 20036

CLARK, ROBERT GEORGE (INDEPENDENT)
Miss State Rep
b Ebenezer, Miss; s Robert Flecher Clark & Julian Williams C; m 1970 to Essie B Austin; c Robert George, II. Educ: Jackson State Col, BS, 53; Fla A&M Univ, 60; Mich State Univ, MA, 59, doctoral work, 62; Western Mich Univ, 65. Hon Degrees: LLD, Mary Holmes Col, West Point, Miss, 58 & Prentiss Inst, 72. Polit & Govt Pos: Chmn, Holmes Co Regular Dem & Loyal Dem Parties; chmn, Nat Black Assembly of Miss; vchmn, Nat Black Assembly for Southern Region, US; mem polit coun, Nat Black Assembly; chmn, Alcohol Abuse Comt, Div Comprehensive Health & the State Comt on Nurse-Midwives; pres, Black Elec Off Miss, 67-; Miss State Rep, 67-, chmn alcohol abuse comt, Miss House Rep, currently; deleg, Dem Nat Conv, 68 & 72; chmn & organizer, Comt of Combined Orgn for Disasters, 69-; chmn, Mississippians United for Progress, 70-; deleg, Dem Nat Mid-Term Conf, 74. Bus & Prof Pos: Pres, Miss Dept Health, Phys Educ & Recreation, 65-; chmn, Miss Educ Resources Ctr, 70; owner, House of Clark Furniture Store. Publ: Political power prelude to change, Afro-Am, 68. Mem: Holmes Co Teachers Asn (pres, 69-). Honors & Awards: Man of the Year Award in Community Serv, 68; Alumnus of Year, Jackson State Col, 68; Man of Year in State Affairs, 69; Outstanding Serv & Inspiration to Humanity Award. Relig: Baptist. Legal Res: Gen Delivery Ebenezer MS 39064 Mailing Add: PO Box 184 Lexington MS 39095

CLARK, ROBERT L
Nebr State Sen
Mailing Add: 2622 El Rancho Rd Sidney NE 69162

CLARK, SANDRA LYNN (R)
Tenn State Rep
b Knoxville, Tenn, Apr 26, 48; d Herman L Clark & Willadean Steele C; single. Educ: Univ Tenn, Knoxville, currently. Polit & Govt Pos: Deleg, Tenn Rep State Const Conv, 71 & 72; Tenn State Rep, 73- Bus & Prof Pos: Ed & publ, Halls Shopper, currently. Mailing Add: 4520 Doris Circle Knoxville TN 37918

CLARK, SHIRLEY M (R)
NH State Rep
b Waterbury, Conn, May 13, 23; married. Educ: Pa State Col; Univ NH, BA, MA; Phi Kappa Phi; Phi Beta Kappa; Pi Gamma Mu; Pi Sigma Alpha. Polit & Govt Pos: NH State Rep, 61-72 & 75- Mem: Lee Planning Bd; Am Acad Polit & Social Sci; Lee Stompers (pres); NH Women's Golf Asn. Relig: Episcopal. Mailing Add: RFD 1 Newmarket NH 03857

CLARK, THOMAS C (D)
Conn State Rep
Mailing Add: 10 Jeffrey Dr Farmington CT 06032

CLARK, TOM C (D)
b Dallas, Tex, Sept 23, 99; s William H Clark & Jennie Falls C; m 1924 to Mary Ramsey; c William Ramsey, Mildred (Mrs Thomas R Gronlund) & Thomas Campbell, Jr (deceased). Educ: Va Mil Inst, 17-18; Univ of Tex, AB, 21, LLB, 22; Phi Alpha Delta; Delta Tau Delta; Order of the Coif. Hon Degrees: LLD, Bethany Col, 45, John Marshall Col, 45, Centre Col, Tex Tech Col, Mo Valley Col, 48, Dickinson Sch Law, 59, Northwestern Univ, 60, Vincennes Univ, 60, St Louis Univ & Univ Mont, 61, Univ Maine, 62, Boston Univ, Ohio Wesleyan Univ, St John's Univ, Univ San Diego, Suffolk Univ, George Washington Univ, NY Univ Law Sch, Syracuse Univ, La Salle Col & Univ Fla. Polit & Govt Pos: Civil dist attorney, Dallas Co, Tex, 27; asst attorney gen in charge antitrust div, Dept Justice, 43, in charge criminal div, 43-45, attorney gen, 45-49; assoc justice, US Supreme Court, 49-67; dir, Fed Judicial Ctr, 68-69. Bus & Prof Pos: Assoc, Clark & Clark, Dallas, 22-27. Mil Serv: 153rd Inf, Army, World War I. Mem: State Bar Tex; Am, Dallas & Fed Bar Asns; hon fel Am Col Trial Lawyers. Honors & Awards: Silver Buffalo Award, 60 & Silver Beaver Award, 62, Boy Scouts; Gold Medal, Am Bar Asn, 62-; First Annual Award, Am Judicature Soc, 62; President Key, Loyola Univ Distinguished Alumnus Awards, Ex-Students Asn, Univ Tex, 62 & Univ Tex Law Sch, 64. Relig: Presbyterian. Legal Res: Dallas TX Mailing Add: Supreme Court Bldg Washington DC 20543

CLARK, W MURRAY (D)
NH State Rep
Mailing Add: Box 1 Lincoln NH 03251

CLARKE, BERKLEY ZACHEUS, JR (R)
Chmn, Dinwiddie Co Rep Comt, Va
b Sutherland, Va, May 28, 30; s Berkley Zacheus Clarke & Alice Hovey C; m 1953 to Letha Fern Congdon; c Janet Lynn, Dana Sue, Judith Gail & Gwyn Ellen. Educ: Va Polytech Inst, BS, 51; Okla State Univ, 52. Polit & Govt Pos: Chmn, Dinwiddie Co Rep Comt, Va, 70- Bus & Prof Pos: Farmer, Sutherland, Va, 53- Mil Serv: Entered as Airman Basic, Air Force, 51, released as Airman 2/C, 53. Mem: Ruritan Nat; Va Farm Bur; AF&AM. Relig: Methodist. Mailing Add: Rte 1 Box 25 Sutherland VA 23885

CLARKE, CLIFTON WINTHROP (R)
Chmn, Chelsea Rep City Comt, Mass
b Chelsea, Mass, Feb 19, 10; s James Douglas Clarke & Mae Wells C; m 1936 to Jennie Delores Tarlowski; c Clifton Winthrop, Jr. Educ: Chelsea Sr High Sch, 4 years. Polit & Govt Pos: Deleg, Mass Rep State Conv, 31-; committeeman, Chelsea Sch Comt, 32; originator, Suffolk Co Rep Club, 39; chmn, Chelsea Rep City Comt, Mass, 40-44, 48-52 & 68-; deleg, Rep Nat Conv, 52 & 56; mem, Mass Rep State Finance Comt, 53; mem, Excise Bd, 61 & 65; chmn, Alcoholic Beverage Comn, 68-; app to Chelsea Housing Authority by Gov Sargent, 69- Bus & Prof Pos: Gen contractor, Chelsea & Boston, Mass, 36-62; mem bd dirs, Chestnut Credit Union, Chelsea, 40-44; gen construction inspector-sr, Metrop Dist Comn, 62- Mem: AF&AM. Relig: Protestant. Mailing Add: 167 Central Ave Chelsea MA 02150

CLARKE, GEORGE W (R)
Wash State Sen
Mailing Add: 3835 W Mercer Way Mercer Island WA 98040

CLARKE, GEORGE W (R)
Hawaii State Rep
Mailing Add: House Sgt-at-arms State Capitol Honolulu HI 96813

CLARKE, JACK WELLS (D)
Mem, State Dem Cent Comt, La
b Abingdon, Va, June 26, 14; s James Sydnor Clarke & Ottie Wells C; m 1938 to Dorothy Irelan. Educ: Williams Col, AB, 35; NY Univ Sch Bus Admin, 35-37; Phi Delta Theta. Polit & Govt Pos: Vchmn, Caddo Dem Asn, La, 66-67, chmn, 67-68; deleg, Dem Nat Conv, 68; chmn, La Fourth Cong Dist Dem Campaign Comt, 68; La Dem Party Elector, 68; mem, State Dem Cent Comt, 39th Dist, 68-; mem & vchmn, Caddo Parish Dem Exec Comt, 68-; state vpres, Dem Alliance of La, currently. Bus & Prof Pos: Bond analyst & statistician, DuBosque & Co, New York, 35-37; from asst mass budget-statist dept to mgr, Lion Oil Co, El Dorado, Ark, 38-42, asst to pres, 46-51; dir pub & financial rels, Tex Eastern Transmission Corp, 51-55; exec vpres, Freestate Indust Develop Co, Shreveport, La, 55-56, pres & dir, 56-68; pres & dir, NShreveport Develop Co, 56-68; self-employed, 68- Mil Serv: Entered as Ens, Naval Res, 42, released as Lt, 45, after serv in all theatres, 42-45; Lt, Naval Res, Retired; Am Theatre & Victory Medals; Pac-Asiatic Ribbon with two Battle Stars; African-European Ribbon with one Battle Star; Philippine Liberation Ribbon with two Battle Stars. Mem: Am Indust Develop Coun; Am Ord Asn; Int Coun Assessing Officers; Int Coun Shopping Ctrs, Inc; Urban Land Inst. Honors & Awards: Cert appreciation, Am Petroleum Inst. Relig: Episcopal; former vestryman, St Mary's Episcopal Church, Shreveport. Legal Res: 708 Azalea Dr Shreveport LA 71106 Mailing Add: PO Box 6 Shreveport LA 71161

CLARKE, JAMES THOMPSON (R)
Asst Secy Mgt, Dept Interior
b Petoskey, Mich, May 18, 37; s James H Clarke & Imogene Thompson C; m 1968 to Patricia W Kemp; c James Timothy & Jonathan Robert. Educ: Col Wooster, BA, 59; Univ Mich, MBA, 61. Polit & Govt Pos: Asst Secy Mgt, Dept Interior, 73- Bus & Prof Pos: Partner, Coopers & Lybrand, Detroit, Mich, 70-73. Mil Serv: Entered as Ens, Navy, 62, released as Lt, 65, after serv in Naval Supply Ctr, Calif. Publ: Co-auth, A triple play with EDP, Lybrand J, 68; Automated budgeting and forecasting, Asn Systs Mgt, 73. Mem: Am Inst CPA; Mich Asn CPA. Relig: Presbyterian. Mailing Add: 1394 Canterbury Way Rockville MD 20854

CLARKE, NEIL (R)
SDak State Rep
b Winner, SDak, Aug 28, 37; s Cornelius Clarke & Katharine Carter Clarke Cassidy; m 1958 to Patricia Louise Winter; c Beth Lynne, Curtis Neil & Jill Anne. Educ: SDak State Univ, BS, 59; Arnold Air Soc. Polit & Govt Pos: Comnr, Stanley Co, SDak, 67-68; SDak State Rep, 75- Mil Serv: Entered as 2nd Lt, Air Force, 59, released as Capt, 63, after serv in Strategic Air Command, 60-63; Capt, SDak Air Nat Guard, 63-67. Mem: Elks; Air Force Asn; Stockgrowers; YMCA (bd dirs, 75-). Honors & Awards: Area Outstanding Young Farmer, 68. Relig: Episcopal. Legal Res: Ft Pierre SD 57532 Mailing Add: 1220 E Cabot Pierre SD 57501

CLARKE, P JOSEPH (D)
Ky State Rep
b Danville, Ky, Mar 12, 33; s Phillip Joseph Clarke, Sr & Marie Newton C; m to Anne Dooling; c P J, III, John, Geoffrey & David. Educ: Univ Notre Dame, BS in CE, 55; Georgetown Univ Law Ctr, JD, 60. Polit & Govt Pos: Ky State Rep, 70-, chmn, House & Joint Interim Appropriations & Revenue Comt, Ky Gen Assembly, 72-; chmn, Ethics & Campaign Finance Comt, Nat Conf State Legislators, 73-; chmn, Environ Qual Comt, South Conf Coun State Govts, 72-74, mem gov bd, 74-; mem exec comt, Nat Legis Conf, 73-74. Bus & Prof Pos: Attorney-at-law, Danville, Ky, 60- Relig: Roman Catholic. Legal Res: 420 Boone Trail Danville KY 40422 Mailing Add: Box 297 Danville KY 40422

CLARKE, RUSSELL LELAND (R)
Mem, Rep State Cent Comt Calif
b Selma, Calif, Mar 28, 23; s Rozell Frank Clarke & Karen Nelson C; m 1962 to Jeanne Dausse; c Judith (Mrs Gregory Allan Farmer), Stanley Nelson & Janine Dale. Educ: City Col of San Francisco, AA, 43. Polit & Govt Pos: Mem, Mendocino Co Rep Cent Comt, 58-, chmn, 60-65; mem, Calif Rep State Cent Comt, 58-, mem exec comt, 60-64, secy-treas co

chmn asn, 61-65; regional vpres, Young Rep of Calif, 59, nat committeeman, 60, exec vpres, 61; state co-chmn, Young Californians for Nixon for Pres, 60; alt deleg, Rep Nat Conv, 60; mem, First Cong Dist Rep Comt, 60-, orgn chmn, 60; NCoast Region chmn, Nixon for Gov Comt, 62. Bus & Prof Pos: Exec Bd Calif, Asn of Employers, Inc, 66- Mil Serv: Entered as Pvt, Army, 43, released as M/Sgt, 46, after serv in 97th Inf Div European & Asiatic Theaters; Army Res, 46-68, Maj; Am, European, Asiatic Theater, Good Conduct, Japanese Occupation, World War II Victory Medals. Mem: Am Mil Engrs; F&AM; RAM; Elks; Am Legion. Relig: Episcopal. Legal Res: 181 Fairview Ct Ukiah CA 95482 Mailing Add: 245 E Standley Ukiah CA 95482

CLARKE, TERREL E (R)
Ill State Sen
b Mar 11, 20; m to Catherine; c Three. Educ: Univ Colo, BS; Harvard Grad Sch Bus Admin, MBA. Polit & Govt Pos: Committeeman, Lyons Twp Rep Comt, 54-71; Ill State Rep, 56-66; Ill State Sen, 66-, Rep Asst Leader, Ill State Senate, 70-72. Bus & Prof Pos: Teacher, Univ Kans, 2 years; ins broker. Mil Serv: Army, 43-46, ETO. Relig: Episcopal. Mailing Add: 4070 Central Ave Western Springs IL 60558

CLARKSON, C JACK (R)
Chmn, Rush Co Rep Party, Ind
b Rushville, Ind, Dec 18, 30; s Harold L Clarkson & Dorothy V C; c Jean, Jon & Ann. Educ: Butler Univ, BA, 57; Ind Univ Law Sch, JD, 58; Order of Coif; Phi Delta Phi. Polit & Govt Pos: Prosecuting attorney, Rush Co, Ind, 59-66; chmn, Rush Co Rep Party, Ind, 64- Mailing Add: 127 W Second St Rushville IN 46173

CLARKSON, E MILTON (D)
Chmn, Refugio Co Dem Exec Comt, Tex
b Refugio, Tex, Dec 2, 20; s Robert P Clarkson & Iris Catherine Baumgartner C; m 1942 to Wilma Belle Summers; c William Edward (Bill). Educ: Mercy Acad, Refugio, Tex, grad, 38. Polit & Govt Pos: Chmn, Refugio Co Dem Exec Comt, Tex, 67- Bus & Prof Pos: Newspaper reporter, Refugio Timely Remarks, 37-39; time keeper & clerk, Heard & Heard, Inc, 39-45, truck dispatcher & br mgr, 46- Mil Serv: Entered as Pvt, Army, 42, released as Pfc, 45, after serv in 333rd Ord Depot Co, 9th Army, ETO, 43-45; ETO Combat Ribbon. Mem: KofC (third degree); Am Red Cross (disaster chmn, Refugio Chap, 66-). Relig: Roman Catholic. Legal Res: 505 W Heard St Refugio TX 78377 Mailing Add: PO Box 429 Refugio TX 78377

CLAUSEN, DON H (R)
US Rep, Calif
b Ferndale, Calif, Apr 27, 23; m to Ollie Piper C; c Beverly & Dawn Marie. Educ: San Jose State Col, V5 Prog, USN; Calif Polytech; Weber Col, Ogden, Utah; St Mary's Col. Polit & Govt Pos: US Rep, Calif, 63-; past mem, Bd of Supvr, Del Norte Co; alt deleg, Rep Nat Conv, 72. Bus & Prof Pos: Clausen Assoc Ins Agency, Crescent City, Calif; Clausen Flying Serv, Crescent City, Calif; Air Ambulance Serv. Mil Serv: Navy Carrier Pilot, Asiatic-Pac. Mem: Del Norte CofC; Unit Redwood Empire Asn. Legal Res: Earl Dr Crescent City CA 95531 Mailing Add: US House of Rep 2433 Rayburn Bldg Washington DC 20515

CLAUSSEN, PETER HENRY, III (D)
Chmn, Dodge Co Dem Party, Nebr
b Takoma Park, Md, Oct 11, 48; s Peter Henry Claussen, Jr & Marion Roberts C; single. Educ: Midland Lutheran Col, BA, 71; Univ Nebr, MEd, 75; Sigma Rho. Polit & Govt Pos: Chmn, Dodge Co Dem Party, Nebr, 74- Mem: Jaycees; Fremont Educ Asn. Legal Res: 1828 E Frederiksen Fremont NE 68025 Mailing Add: 1836 Pebble Fremont NE 68025

CLAVEAU, THOMAS J (D)
NH State Sen
Mailing Add: 117 Highland St Hudson NH 03051

CLAWSON, DELWIN MORGAN (DEL) (R)
US Rep, Calif
b Thatcher, Ariz, Jan 11, 14; m 1934 to Marjorie Anderson C; c Larry (deceased) & James. Educ: Gila Col, Thatcher, Ariz. Polit & Govt Pos: With US Employ Serv & Fed Pub Housing Authority, 41-47; mem, Park & Recreation Comn, Compton, Calif, 50-53; mem, Compton City Coun, 53-57; dir, Los Angeles Co Sanit Dists, One, Two & Eight, 57-63; mayor, Compton, 57-63; US Rep, 63- Bus & Prof Pos: Salesman & bookkeeper, 34-41; mgr, Mutual Housing Asn of Compton, 47-63. Mem: Kiwanis Int; Exec Dinner Club; CofC; Boy Scouts; Community Chest. Honors & Awards: Citizen of the Year Award, Compton CofC, 60; Boy Scout Silver Beaver Award, 60; Watchdog of Treas Award, Nat Assoc Businessmen, 63-; Nat Fedn Independent Bus Man of Year, 72 & 73. Relig: Latter-day Saint. Legal Res: Downey CA Mailing Add: 4201 Massachusetts Ave Washington DC 20016

CLAWSON, DOROTHY ESTEP (R)
Pres, Tenn Fedn Rep Women
b Cumberland Gap, Tenn, Aug 1, 26; d James Dallard Estep & Nell Howard E; m 1950 to John Franklin; c James Rogers, John Estep & Suzanne Lee. Educ: Mary Baldwin Col, BA, 48; Carson-Newman Col, 51; Univ Tenn, Knoxville, 55. Polit & Govt Pos: Co & Second Dist Campaign Chmn for Sen Howard Baker, 68 & 72, Sen Bill Brock, 70, Congressmen Quillen & Duncan, every 2 years, Gov Dunn, 70 & President Nixon, 72; Pres, Tenn Fedn Rep Women. Bus & Prof Pos: Sch teacher, Morristown City Schs, 54- Mem: Am Asn Univ Women (legis chmn); Alpha Delta Kappa; Morristown Educ Asn; Ladies Reading Circle; ETenn Heart Asn (bd dirs, 69-75). Honors & Awards: First Lady of Morristown, Tenn, 67; Volunteer Award, Tenn Heart Asn, 70; First Runner-up, Tenn Rep Woman of Year, 69; First Woman in state to be app Foreman of Grand Jury. Relig: Baptist. Mailing Add: Buffalo Trail Morristown TN 37814

CLAWSON, JAMES HOWARD (R)
Chmn, Columbia Co Rep Cent Comt, Ore
b Redgranite, Wis, July 19, 20; s Holly Elmer Clawson & Lida Brooks Graves C; m 1942 to Nancy Lamberson; c Burrell Edward, Richard James, Carl William & Wendy Sue. Educ: Univ of Ore, 2 years; Northwestern Col of Law, 3 years. Polit & Govt Pos: Port comnr, Port of St Helens, Ore, 52-60; Rep precinct committeeman, 58-; chmn, Columbia Co Rep Cent Comt, 64- Bus & Prof Pos: Credit mgr, Portland Gen Elec Co, 42-47; pres & mgr, Credit Bur of Columbia Co, Inc, 48- Mil Serv: Entered as A/S, Coast Guard, 42, released as Aviation Machinist 3/C, 45, after serv in Elizabeth City, NC. Mem: Am Legion; Elks; Kiwanis; CofC; Assoc Credit Burs of Am. Legal Res: 17 Crescent Dr St Helens OR 97051 Mailing Add: Box 247 St Helens OR 97051

CLAWSON, JOHN THOMAS (DFL)
Minn State Rep
b St Paul, Minn, Aug 7, 45; s Eugene Woodrow Clawson & Lila Lavon Christensen C; m 1968 to Susan Ann Luetje. Educ: Augsburg Col, BA, 67; Northwestern Lutheran Theol Sem, MDiv, 71. Polit & Govt Pos: Minn State Rep, 75- Bus & Prof Pos: Pastor, First Lutheran Church, Harris, Minn & Calvary Lutheran Church, Stanchfield, 71-74; pastoral consult, Hazelden Found, Center City, 71-74, chaplain, 74- Mem: Chisago Co Coun Exceptional Individuals (bd dirs); Minn Asn Children with Learning Disabilities; Minn Asn Chem Dependancy; Chisago Co Jaycees. Relig: Lutheran. Mailing Add: Box 336 Center City MN 55012

CLAY, LUCIUS DUBIGNON (R)
b Marietta, Ga, Apr 23, 97; s Alexander Stephen Clay & Frances White C; m 1918 to Marjorie McKeown; c Lucius D, Jr & Frank B. Educ: US Mil Acad, BS, 18. Polit & Govt Pos: US Ambassador, personal rep of President, Berlin, Ger, 61-62; former chmn, Rep Nat Finance Comt. Bus & Prof Pos: Dir, Lehman Corp, 49-72 & Chase Int Investment Corp, 63-72; sr managing dir, Lehman Bros Inc, 63-73; chmn, Fed Nat Mortgage Asn, 70-73; trustee, Presby Hosp, NY. Mil Serv: Instr, Officers' Training Camp, 18-19; Engr Sch Appl, 19-20; asst prof mil sci & tactics, Ala Polytech Inst, 20-21; construction qm & post engr, Ft Belvoir, Va, 21-24; instr civil eng, US Mil Acad, 24-27; field mapping, 11th Engrs CZ, 27-30; asst to dist engr, Pittsburgh, in charge construction lock & dam two, Allegheny River, 30-33; asst to chief of engrs, River & Harbor Sect, 33-37; consult on develop water resources to Nat Power Corp, Philippine Commonwealth, 37-38; in charge construction Denison Dam, 38-40; asst to adminr, Civil Aeronaut Admin on Airport Prog, 40-41; dir material, Army Serv Forces, 42-44; comdr, Normandy Base, 44; dep dir war mobilization & reconversion, 45; dep mil gov, 45-47; comdr-in-chief, European Command & Mil Gov, US Zone, Ger, 47-49. Publ: Decision in Germany, 50. Mem: Army & Navy Club; Univ Club; Links Club; Pinnacle Club; Blind Brook Club. Mailing Add: 633 Third Ave New York NY 10017

CLAY, RUDOLPH (D)
Ind State Sen
b Gary, Ind, July 16, 35; s Lucy Hunter Elliott C; m 1957 to Christine Swan; c Rudolph, Jr. Educ: Ind Univ, 55-56; Minority Businessmen Steering Comt. Polit & Govt Pos: Ind State Sen, 72- Mil Serv: Entered as Pvt, Army, 59, released as SP-4, 61, after serv in Chaplain Corps. Honors & Awards: Outstanding Young Man of Am, Jaycees, 71. Relig: Methodist. Legal Res: 4201 W Tenth Ave Gary IN 46402 Mailing Add: 562 Broadway Gary IN 46402

CLAY, WILLIAM LACY (D)
US Rep, Mo
b St Louis, Mo, Apr 30, 31; s Irving C Clay & Luella Hyatt C; m 1953 to Carol Ann Johnson; c Vicki Flynn, William Lacy, Jr & Michelle Katherine. Educ: St Louis Univ, BS in Hist & Polit Sci, 53. Polit & Govt Pos: Dem Alderman, 26th Ward, St Louis, Mo, 59-64, Dem committeeman, 64-; US Rep, First Dist, 69-; deleg, Dem Nat Conv, 72; deleg, Dem Nat Mid-Term Conf, 74. Bus & Prof Pos: Real estate broker, St Louis, Mo, 55-59; mgr, Indust Life Ins Co, 59-61; educ coordr, Steamfitters Local No 562, 66-67. Mil Serv: Entered as Pvt, Army, 53, released as Cpl, 55. Publ: Anatomy of an economic murder, St Louis Bd of Alderman, 63. Mem: NAACP; CORE; Narcotics Anonymous; Jr CofC; Friends of Scouts. Honors & Awards: Distinguished Citizens award, Alpha Kappa Alpha, 69; Argus Award, St Louis Argus Newspaper, 69. Relig: Catholic. Legal Res: 5146A Minerva St Louis MO 63113 Mailing Add: 1209 Longworth House Off Bldg Washington DC 20515

CLAYBURGH, BENNIE JAMES (R)
Rep Nat Committeeman, NDak
b Scobey, Mont, Jan 31, 24; s Mark John Clayburgh & Anna Horvick C; m 1948 to Mina Tennison (deceased); m 1970 to Beverly Fredrickson Manternach; c James, Robert, John & Richard. Educ: Univ NDak, BA, 46, BS, 47; Temple Univ Sch Med, MD, 49; Mayo Found, Rochester, Minn, MS in Orthopaedic Surg, 56; Blue Key; Beta Theta Pi. Polit & Govt Pos: Mem, NDak State Rep Exec Comt; vchmn, NDak Rep State Comt, 62-64, chmn, 64-65; chmn, Grand Forks Dist Rep Exec Comt, 62-; deleg & mem platform comt, Rep Nat Conv, 64 & 72, alt deleg, 68; Rep Nat Committeeman, NDak, 68-, mem exec comt, 71-72 & 75- Bus & Prof Pos: Orthopaedic surgeon, Orthopaedic Clin, Grand Forks, NDak, 56- Mil Serv: Entered as 1st Lt, Air Force Med Corps, 51, released as Capt, 53, after serv in 28th Strategic Bomber Wing. Mem: Am Med Asn; Am Acad Orthopaedic Surg; Am Bd Orthopaedic Surg; Clin Orthopaedic Soc. Relig: Lutheran. Legal Res: 1626 Belmont Rd Grand Forks ND 58201 Mailing Add: 201 S Fourth St Grand Forks ND 58201

CLAYTON, BILLY WAYNE (D)
Tex State Rep
b Olney, Tex, Sept 11, 28; s William Thomas Clayton & Myrtle F Chitwood C; m 1950 to Delma Jean Dennis; c Brenda (Mrs Hatfield) & Thomas Wayne. Educ: Tex A&M Col, BS in Agr Econ. Polit & Govt Pos: Tex State Rep, 62-, Speaker of the House, 75- Bus & Prof Pos: Pres, Springlake Enterprises, Inc, 64-; dir-at-lg, Water, Inc, Lubbock, Tex, 69- Mem: Interstate Conf on Water Probs (nat exec comt); Mason; Lions. Honors & Awards: Award for Outstanding Serv in Water Conserv, Ft Worth Press; First Award of WTex Water Inst for Meritorious Contributions to Develop & Conserv WTex Water Resources; Commendation, Tex Water Rights Comn. Relig: Baptist. Mailing Add: Box 38 Springlake TX 79082

CLEARY, PATRICK JAMES (R)
43rd Dist Representative Committeeman, Ill Rep Party
b Momence, Ill, Jan 20, 29; s James Augustine Cleary & Nellie DeWitt C; m 1955 to Alice Marie Duval; c Mary Elizabeth, James Augustine & Michael John. Educ: Cent YMCA Col, 46; Univ Chicago, Chicago Loop Br, 47. Polit & Govt Pos: Legis asst, Ill Sen, 51-59; pub adminr, Kankakee Co, 54-57; city clerk, Kankakee, 55-57; secy, Kankakee Zoning Bd & Police Comn, 55-57; mem, Kankakee Pension Bd, 57-61; co clerk & clerk of the co & probate courts, Kankakee Co, 58-62; 43rd Dist representative committeeman, Ill Rep Party, 66-; Northern Ill dir, All-Ill Comt for Ogilvie for Gov, 68 & Citizens Comt to Reelect Gov Richard B Ogilvie, 72; committeeman & mem exec comt, Kankakee Co Rep Party, 66-; chmn bd rev, State of Ill Dept of Labor, 69-73; mem, Gov Adv Bd, State of Ill, 69-73; staff asst, US Rep George O'Brien, Ill, 74. Bus & Prof Pos: Mem ed staff, Kankakee J, 45-52; spec staff correspondent, Chicago Sun-Times & Chicago Daily News, 47-52; reporter, Gary Post Tribune, 52, pub rels exec, Plumbing Contractors Asn of Chicago & Vicinity, 56-58; co-publisher & vpres, Farmers Weekly Rev, Inc, 62- Mem: Chicago Press Club; Ill Press Asn; Chicago Press Vet Asn; Nat Press Club, Washington, DC; Will Co, Ill Newspaper Publ Asn. Relig: Roman Catholic. Mailing Add: 1905 E Oak St Kankakee IL 60901

CLEAVELAND, BRADFORD IRA (R)
b Lakeville, Conn, Jan 19, 16; s Paul Bradford Cleaveland & Gladys Traver C; m 1941 to Lise Graser; c Paul B, II, Nancy J, Katherine L, Lisa A & John E. Educ: Yale Univ, 34-38. Polit & Govt Pos: Chmn, Caldwell Co Rep Party, Tex, 60-66 & 72-74. Bus & Prof Pos: Pres, Ellmag Oil Corp, 41-48; owner, Cleaveland Well Serv, 48- Relig: Episcopal. Legal Res: 715 S Pecan Ave Luling TX 78648 Mailing Add: PO Box 308 Luling TX 78648

CLEM, CHESTER (R)
Fla State Rep
Mailing Add: 2799 Whipoorwill Lane Vero Beach FL 32960

CLEMENT, ALFRED WILLIAM (BILL), JR (D)
Committeeman, Wash Dem State Party
b Bellingham, Wash, Sept 18, 26; s Alfred William Clement, Sr & Josephine Johnston C; m 1954 to Dorothy Jane Hubert; c Scott & Kevin. Educ: Western Wash State Col, 43-45; Stanford Univ, AB, 47, AM, 49; Pi Sigma Alpha. Polit & Govt Pos: Chmn, Whatcom Co Dem Cent Comt, Wash, 70-72; committeeman, Wash Dem State Party, currently; spec asst to Cong Lloyd Meeds, 72; app mem, Whatcom Co Planning Comn, 74- Bus & Prof Pos: Retail grocer, 53-; child welfare worker, State of Wash, 53-54; prog coordr, Western Wash State Col, 72- Mil Serv: Entered as Pfc, Army, 50, released as Cpl, 52, after serv in 11th Engr Combat Bn, IX Corps, Korea, 51-52. Mem: Am Polit Sci Asn; Masons (Bellingham Bay Lodge 44); Scottish Rite. Relig: Protestant. Mailing Add: 639 Lake Whatcom Blvd Bellingham WA 98225

CLEMENT, ARTHUR JOHN HOWARD, III (D)
Chmn, Durham Co Dem Exec Comt, NC
b Cleveland, NC, Mar 23, 34; m to Dolores Williams; c Three. Educ: Howard Univ, BA, 55, LLB, 60; Scabbard & Blade. Polit & Govt Pos: Mem, State Dem Exec Comt, NC, 68-, vchmn, 71-72; secy, Durham Co Dem Exec Comt, 68-72, chmn, 74-; pres, Durham Co Young Dem Club, 69-71; mem rev coun, Dem Party in NC, 70-72; chmn, NC Black Polit Caucus, formerly. Bus & Prof Pos: Spec agt, Charleston Dist, NC Mutual Life Ins Co, SC, 56-57, legal asst, 61-62, claims supvr, Durham, NC, 62-; clerk, Levy & Krauss, Newark, NJ, 60-61; assoc, Moore & Martin, Charleston, SC, 65- Mil Serv: Army, 55-56, 2nd Lt. Mem: Nat Bar Asn; Nat Conf Black Lawyers (NC state coordr); PTA (officer, 70-); NAACP; Durham Human Rels Comn (educ comt). Honors & Awards: Kings Club, Inc Civic Award, 73. Relig: Episcopal; former secy of vestry & vestryman, St Titus Episcopal Church; licensed lay reader. Mailing Add: 2505 Weaver St Durham NC 27707

CLEMENT, D B (R)
SDak State Rep
Mailing Add: Armour SD 57313

CLEMENTE, ART (D)
Wash State Rep
Mailing Add: 4422 228th SE Bothell WA 98011

CLEMENTE, JOHN F (D)
Mem, Cumberland Co Dem Comt, Maine
b Portland, Maine, Apr 10, 45; s Emilio Anthony Clemente & Mary C Cipriano C; single. Educ: Gorham State Col, Univ Maine, BS, 68; Student Senate; Young Dem Club; Newspaper Staff. Polit & Govt Pos: Deleg, Maine Dem State Conv, 66, 68 & 70; mem, Cumberland Co Dem Comt, 66-; mem, Portland City Dem Comt, 66-; Maine State Rep, 71-73; deleg, Dem Nat Conv, 72. Bus & Prof Pos: Teacher, Portland Sch Syst, Maine, 68-70. Mem: Portland & Maine Teachers' Asn; Nat Educ Asn. Relig: Roman Catholic. Mailing Add: 45 Eastern Promenade Portland ME 04101

CLEMENTS, CHARLES MCCALL, III (R)
Mem, Ga Rep State Cent Comt
b Columbus, Muscogee Co, Ga, Nov 27, 41; s Charles McCall Clements, Jr & Embelle Thurmond C; single. Educ: Emory Univ, 60-61; Emory at Oxford, 61-62; Univ Ga, AB, 65; steward, Univ Ga chap, Pi Kappa Phi, 63-65. Polit & Govt Pos: Membership dir, Univ Ga Young Rep Club, 64-65; secy, Marion Co Rep Party, Ga, 65-68, chmn, formerly; deleg, Rep Dist Conv, 66 & 68; co-chmn, Area III, Third Cong Dist Ga, Rep Exec Comt, 66-68, treas, 68-70; deleg & mem resolutions comt, Ga State Rep Conv, 68, sgt-at-arms, 70; city councilman, Buena Vista, 65-68, chmn, Citizens Adv Comt on Housing Needs, 68-, mayor pro tem, 70-; mem, Ga Rep State Cent Comt, 72- Bus & Prof Pos: Partner, Clements Hardware & Furniture Co, Buena Vista, 65-; vchmn, Marion Co Re-Develop Corp, 68- Mem: Lions Int. Honors & Awards: Guest at Inauguration of President Richard M Nixon and related events, 69; Bronze Medallion for Meritorious Service in Fight Against Heart Disease, Am & Ga Heart Asns. Relig: Baptist; Deacon, First Baptist Church, Buena Vista. Mailing Add: Box 56 Baker St Buena Vista GA 31803

CLEMENTS, JOHN V (R)
Chmn, Baraga Co Rep Comt, Mich
b Baraga, Mich, Jan 14, 13; s J Edward Clements & Bernardine Vaughan C; m 1947 to Elizabeth Rees Furbeck; c Ann Mitchell, Jane Elizabeth, John Vaughan, Jr, Margaret Rees & Miriam Louise. Educ: St Mary's Col, Minn, 30-32; Cardinal Club; vpres of class. Polit & Govt Pos: Secy bd educ, L'Anse Schs, Mich, 46-49; chmn, Baraga Co Rep Comt, 54-56 & 64-; mem bd rev, Baraga Twp, 56-65; nominee for Mich State Auditor, 58 & 60; alt deleg, Rep Nat Conv, 64; mem, Baraga Twp Sch Adv Comt, 64-66; chmn, Ojibwa Housing Comn, 65-; secy, 11th Cong Dist Rep Comt, 64- Bus & Prof Pos: State agent, Royal Globe Ins Group, 53-66; pres, Baraga Co Agency, Inc, 53- Mil Serv: Entered as Pvt, Army Air Corps, 41, released as S/Sgt, 45, after serv in Seventh Ferrying Group of Air Transport Command; Good Conduct Medal; ETO, Pac, China-Burma-India & Am Theater Ribbons. Publ: Package auto insurance, Rough Notes Mag, 64. Mem: Upper Peninsula, Mich & Nat Asns of Ins Agents; Am Legion; VFW; KofC. Relig: Catholic. Legal Res: Box 200 Rte 1 Buckland Dr Baraga MI 49908 Mailing Add: 1 N Front St L'Anse MI 49946

CLEMENTS, MAURICE L (R)
Idaho State Rep
Mailing Add: Rte 4 Nampa ID 83651

CLEMENTS, RITA CROCKER (R)
Rep Nat Committeewoman, Tex
b Newton, Kans, Oct 30, 31; d H Mason Crocker & Florabel West C; m 1952 to Richard Daniel Bass; m 1975 to William P Clements, Jr; c Richard Daniel, Jr, Barbara Joan, Bonnie Louise & James Edward. Educ: Wellesley Col, 49-50; Univ Tex, BA cum laude, 53; Pi Beta Phi. Polit & Govt Pos: Dallas Co Rep Party, Tex, 58-61, canvass chmn, 60-63; campaign activities chmn & bd mem, Nat Fedn Rep Women, 63-67; door-to-door canvass chmn, Rep Nat Comt, 64, mem, Rep Nat Finance Comt, 71-72, Rep Nat Committeewoman, Tex, 73-; alt deleg, Rep Nat Conv, 64 & 72, deleg, 68; orgn chmn, Tex Rep Party, 66-72; get-out-the-vote chmn, Tex Comt to Reelect the President, 72; mem, Nat Adv Coun Econ Opportunity, 72-75; Nat Vol Serv Adv Coun, 74-, chmn prog develop comt, 74- Bus & Prof Pos: Mem bd dirs, Lange Co, 71-72. Mem: Jr League of Dallas, Inc; Hockaday Sch (chmn scholar comt, 71-, chmn Student Affairs & Residence Comt); United Way Dallas (vchmn admissions comt); Spec Care Sch (chmn bd, 72-). Relig: Episcopal. Mailing Add: 4670 Christopher Pl Dallas TX 75204

CLEMENTS, RUTH WELCH (D)
VChmn, Conway Co Dem Cent Comt, Ark
b Conway, Ark, Nov 14, 17; d John Walter Welch & Nancy Jane Waters W; div; c Rebecca Jane (Mrs Raymond Bryant) & Frank Benjamin, Jr. Educ: Ark State Teachers Col, BSE, 38; Alpha Sigma Tau. Polit & Govt Pos: Secy, Lt Gov of Ark, 51-67; vchmn, Conway Co Dem Cent Comt, 55-67, chmn, 67-68, vchmn, 68-; mem, Ark Dem State Comt, currently. Bus & Prof Pos: Legal secy, Gordon & Gordon, Attorneys, Morrilton, 48- Mem: Bus & Prof Women's Club. Relig: Baptist. Mailing Add: 805 N Morrill Morrilton AR 72110

CLEMENTS, WILLIAM P, JR (R)
Dep Secy Defense
Legal Res: TX Mailing Add: Dept of Defense Pentagon Washington DC 20301

CLEMM, LESTER V (D)
Idaho State Rep
Mailing Add: Rte 1 Box 105 Troy ID 83371

CLEMON, U W (D)
Ala State Sen
Mailing Add: 1628 Castleberry Way Birmingham AL 35214

CLENDANIEL, HOWARD A (D)
Del State Rep
Mailing Add: 670 N Bedford St Georgetown DE 19947

CLENDENING, JUNE YVONNE (D)
b Pittsburgh, Pa, Apr 27, 33; d Edwin Alfred Glenn & Margaret Hartley G; m 1950 to James Leonard Clendening; c Valerie Ann & Nancy Yvonne. Educ: Md Park High Sch, grad, 51; Strayers Bus Col, 51. Polit & Govt Pos: Admin asst to US Rep Thomas Ludlow Ashley, Ohio, 75- Relig: Presbyterian. Mailing Add: 4203 Forestville Rd Forestville MD 20028

CLEVELAND, ADOLPHUS (D)
Mem Finance Comt, Dem Party Tex
b Lubbock, Tex, Oct 26, 42; s W D Cleveland, Sr & Etha C; m to Shirley Ann; c Linda & Lachelle. Educ: Wayland Baptist Col, BA Polit Sci, 66; Tex Technol Univ Sch Law, 70-71. Polit & Govt Pos: Precinct capt, Lubbock Co Dem Party, Tex, 72-; deleg, Tex State Dem Conv, 72-74; deleg, Dem Nat Mid-Term Conf, 74; cand city councilman, Lubbock, 74 & Parks & Recreation Bd, 74; mem steering comt, Tex Dem of Lubbock, 74-; mem, South Plains Dem Party, 74-; mem finance comt, Dem Party Tex, 75- Bus & Prof Pos: Pastor, New Jerusalem Baptist Church, Tex, 66 & Triangle Baptist Church, 66-67; teacher, Utah Elem Sch, 68; asst juv probation officer, Lubbock Co Juv Probation Off, 68-70; mem, Lubbock Interdenominational Ministerial Alliance, 68, pres, 73-; secy & co founder Progressive Minority Groups, 69-70; pres, United Black Coalition of Lubbock, 69-70; attendant, Lubbock State Sch, 70; outreach worker, Lubbock Co Community Action Bd, 73-74. Mem: NAACP; Tex Corrections Asn. Honors & Awards: Outstanding Male Freshman, Wayland Baptist Col, 61; Outstanding Community Serv Award, Lubbock Alumnae Chap, Delta Sigma Theta, 75. Relig: Baptist. Legal Res: 2625 E Auburn Lubbock TX 79403 Mailing Add: Box 1791 Lubbock TX 79408

CLEVELAND, CHARLES (D)
Okla State Sen
Mailing Add: State Capitol Oklahoma City OK 73105

CLEVELAND, DOROTHY HASKELL (R)
b Seattle, Wash, Jan 31, 15; d Claude Carroll Haskell & Lillian E Johnson H; m 1940 to John Keith Cleveland, Sr; c John Keith, Jr, Bruce Haskell & Brian Carroll. Educ: Univ Wash, 60; Cornish Sch of Music, 6 years. Polit & Govt Pos: Juv protection chmn, Seattle, Wash, 55; Rep precinct committeewoman, Langley, 69-; pres, South Whidbey Rep Women' Club, 69-72; chmn, Island Co Rep Cent Comt, formerly. Bus & Prof Pos: Asst buyer, Women's Wear, Frederick & Nelson, Seattle, Wash, 65-67; exec secy to vpres, 67-68, mgr, Better Women's Ready to Wear, 58-65. Mem: Wash Cong of Parent-Teacher; Eastern Star; Swedish Club; Everett Yacht Club; Langley Planning Comn. Honors & Awards: Several vocal positions for music; Seattle High Sch City Award; Mayor's Award, Juv Protection; Langley Planning Coun Award. Relig: Protestant. Legal Res: 906 Edgecliff Dr Rte 1 Box 285-B Langley WA 98260 Mailing Add: 906 Edgecliff Dr Langley WA 98260

CLEVELAND, HARLAN (D)
b New York, NY, Jan 19, 18; s Stanley Matthews Cleveland & Marian Phelps Van Buren; m 1941 to Lois W Burton; c Carol Zoe (Mrs Palmer), Anne Moore (Mrs Kalicki) & Alan Thorburn. Educ: Phillips Acad, Andover, Mass, 34; Princeton Univ, AB, 38; Rhodes Scholar, Oxford Univ, 38-39. Hon Degrees: LLD, Rollins, Franklin & Marshall & Middlebury Cols, Kent State, Ariz State, Boston, Brandeis & Korea Univs; LHD, Alfred Univ, Kenyon Col & Univ Pittsburgh; DCL, Am Univ. Polit & Govt Pos: Writer, Farm Security Admin, 40-42; off bd econ warfare, Foreign Econ Admin, 42-44; exec dir econ sect, Allied Cont Comn, Rome, 44-45, acting vpres, 45-46; dep chief of mission, UNRRA, Rome, 46-47; dir China off, Shanghai, 47-48; dir China aid prog, Econ Coop Admin, Washington, DC, 48-49; dep asst adminr, 49-51; asst dir for Europe, Mutual Security Agency, 52-53; Asst Secy State for Int Orgn Affairs, 61-65; US Ambassador, NATO, 65-69. Bus & Prof Pos: Exec ed & publ, The Reporter, 53-56; dean Maxwell Grad Sch Citizenship & Pub Affairs, Syracuse Univ, 56-61; pres, Univ Hawaii, 69-74; dir, Aspen Inst Prog Int Affairs. Publ: The Obligations of Power, 66, NATO: the Transatlantic Bargain, 70 & The Future Executive, 72, Harper & Row. Mem: Am Polit Sci Asn; Am Soc Pub Admin (pres, 70-71); Waikiki Yacht Club; Century Club, New York; Int Club, Washington, DC. Honors & Awards: US Medal of Freedom, 46; Woodrow Wilson Award, Princeton Univ, 63; Claude Moore Fuess Award, Phillips Acad; Grand Knight

174 / CLEVELAND

Off, Order of the Crown of Italy; Gold Star, Order of the Brilliant Star of China. Relig: Episcopal. Legal Res: 5 Honey Brook Dr Princeton NJ 08540 Mailing Add: Aspen Inst for Humanistic Studies PO Box 2820 Princeton NJ 08540

CLEVELAND, HILARY PATERSON (R)
b Orange, NJ, Dec 7, 27; d David Archibald Paterson & Marjorie Sclater P; m 1950 to James Colgate Cleveland; c Cotton, James, David, Lincoln & Susan. Educ: Vassar Col, BA, 48; Grad Inst Int Rels, Geneva, Switz, MA, 50. Polit & Govt Pos: Deleg, Rep Nat Conv, 72. Bus & Prof Pos: Assoc prof, Colby-Sawyer Col, 55-75. Relig: Episcopal. Mailing Add: Main St New London NH 03257

CLEVELAND, JAMES C (R)
US Rep, NH
b June 13, 20; s Dr & Mrs Mather Cleveland; m 1950 to Hilary Paterson; c Cotton Mather, James Colby, David Paterson, Lincoln Mather & Susan Slater. Educ: Colgate Univ, magna cum laude; Yale Law Sch, 48; Phi Beta Kappa. Polit & Govt Pos: NH State Sen, 50-62; US Rep, NH, 62- Bus & Prof Pos: Partner, Cleveland & Bass, 60-62; lawyer, (on leave), Cleveland, Waters & Bass, 62-; organizer, incorporator, officer & dir, New London Trust Co. Mil Serv: World War II, Field Artil, 40th Inf Div, Pac Theatre; Bronze Star for Valor; discharged as Capt, 45; recalled active overseas duty, Korean War. Legal Res: New London NH 03257 Mailing Add: 2246 Rayburn House Off Bldg Washington DC 20515

CLIFFORD, CLARK MCADAMS (D)
b Ft Scott, Kans, Dec 25, 06; s Frank Andrew Clifford & Georgia McAdams C; m 1931 to Margery Pepperell Kimball; c Margery Pepperell (Mrs Wm H Lanagan, Jr), Joyce Carter (Mrs Granville A Burland) & Randall (Mrs Ed I Wright). Educ: Wash Univ, St Louis, LLB, 28; Kappa Alpha. Polit & Govt Pos: Naval Aide to US President, 46, spec counsel, 46-50; US Secy of Defense, 68-69. Bus & Prof Pos: Assoc, Holland, Lashly & Donell, 28-33, St Louis, Mo; partner, Holland, Lashly & Lashly, 33-37, Lashly, Lashly, Miller & Clifford, 38; dir, Phillips Petroleum Co; sr partner, Clifford & Miller, Wash, 50-68, Clifford, Warnke, Glass, McIlwain & Finney, 69-; dir, Knight-Ridder Newspapers Inc. Mil Serv: Lt(jg), Navy, 44, promoted to Capt, 46; awarded Naval Commendation Ribbon. Mem: Fed, Am, Mo, DC & St Louis Bar Asns. Honors & Awards: Medal of Freedom presented by the President. Legal Res: 9421 Rockville Pike Bethesda MD 20015 Mailing Add: 815 Connecticut Ave Washington DC 20006

CLIFFORD, ROBERT WILLIAM (D)
Maine State Sen
b Lewiston, Maine, May 2, 37; s William H Clifford, Sr & Alice S C; m 1964 to Clementina Radillo; c Laurence & Matthew. Educ: Bowdoin Col, BA, 59; Boston Col, LLB, 62; Sigma Nu. Polit & Govt Pos: City coun, Lewiston, Maine, 68-71; Mayor, Lewiston, 71-73; bd trustees, Maine Criminal Justice Acad, State of Maine, 72-73; State Sen, 13th Dist, Maine, 73- Bus & Prof Pos: Partner, Clifford & Clifford, Attorneys, 65- Mil Serv: Entered as 2nd Lt, Army, 62, released as Capt, 64, after serv in 2nd Qm Group, 7th Army, VII Corps, 63-64; Army Commendation Medal. Publ: John D Clifford, Jr, 1887-1956, Bowdoin Col, 59. Mem: Maine Star Bar Asn; Maine Trial Lawyers Asn; Am Judicature Soc; Auburn-Lewiston Kiwanis Club; Lewiston-Auburn Jaycees. Relig: Roman Catholic. Mailing Add: 14 Nelke Pl Lewiston ME 04240

CLIFTON, A D (D)
Ga State Rep
Mailing Add: Rte 2 Metter GA 30439

CLIFTON, MARGIE (D)
Mem Exec Comt, Dem Party Ga
b Ware Co, Ga, Apr 11, 36; d John Wesley Herndon, Sr & Edna Crosby H; m 1954 to Harry Anderson Clifton; c Thomas Anderson, Harry Anderson, Jr, John Martin & Christie Robin. Educ: Waresboro High Sch, grad, 53. Polit & Govt Pos: Mem exec comt, Dem Party Ga, 74-, chmn, Seventh Dist Charter Comn, 74-75, mem state drafting comt. Mem: Waycross Woman's Club (pres, 74-); Waycross & Ware Co Ment Health Asn (rec secy, 74-75); Waycross Art Asn; Ware Co Exchangette Club (bd dirs, 75-); Garden Club. Honors & Awards: Woman of Year, Waycross Woman's Club, 75. Relig: Baptist. Mailing Add: 713 Summit St Waycross GA 31501

CLINARD, MARY KNIGHT (D)
Chairwoman, Williamson Co Dem Exec Comt, Tenn
b Nashville, Tenn, Oct 4, 25; d Charles Leonard Knight & Odessa Bruce K; m 1956 to Joseph Marion Clinard, Jr; c Joseph M, III & Dessa Dianne. Educ: George Peabody Teachers Col, 43-44; Pi Gamma Chi. Polit & Govt Pos: City comnr & planning comnr, Fairview, Tenn, 67-71, vmayor, 67-69, mayor, 69-71, trustee, Blue Grass Regional Libr Syst, Columbia, Tenn, 74-; chairwoman, Williamson Co Dem Exec Comt, 74- Publ: News of Fairview, column, Review-Appeal, 72-74. Mem: Williamson Co Citizens Adv Comt; WAVES, Inc (bd mem, 72-); Williamson Co Bi-Centenniel Comt. Relig: Methodist. Legal Res: Hunting Camp Rd Fairview TN 37062 Mailing Add: Rte 2 Box 75 Fairview TN 37062

CLINE, C F (D)
Mo State Rep
b Sikeston, Mo, July 8, 39; s Curtis H Cline & Marie Price C; m 1972 to E Kay Ireland; c Susan. Educ: San Francisco State Univ, 64-65; Southeast Mo State Univ, 71-72. Polit & Govt Pos: Mo State Rep, 73-, vchmn comt on educ, Mo House Rep, 75- Bus & Prof Pos: Pres, Delta Mgt Co, 72-; pres, Clines Island Investment Co, 74- Mil Serv: Entered as Airman Basic, Air Force, 57, released as Staff Sgt, after serv in 7th Air Force, Pac Air Forces, Vietnam, 66-67; Air Force Commendation Medal. Mem: AF&AM (jr warden, Sikeston Lodge 310); Order of Eastern Star (past patron, Essex Chap 237); Delta Scottish Rite Club (pres); SEMO Shrine Club. Honors & Awards: Hon Legion Honor, Order DeMolay, 73. Relig: Baptist. Legal Res: 601 Elm St Sikeston MO 63801 Mailing Add: PO Box 1023 Sikeston MO 63801

CLINE, HAROLD BRANTLEY, JR (R)
Adv, NC Fedn Col Rep
b Charlotte, NC, Apr 26, 51; s Harold Brantley Cline & Jerry McMillan C; single. Educ: NC State Univ, BA, 73; ECarolina Univ, MA, 75; Univ Miss; Phi Kappa Phi; Pi Sigma Alpha. Polit & Govt Pos: Treas, NC Fedn Col Rep, 72-73, sgt-at-arms, 73-74, adv, 74- Relig: Presbyterian. Mailing Add: 840 Churchill Dr Gastonia NC 28052

CLINE, ROBERT CORDE (R)
Calif State Assemblyman
b San Francisco, Calif, May 6, 33; s John W Cline, MD & Edith Bertha Corde C; m 1955 to Betty Clare Robison; c Bruce & Caren. Educ: Univ Calif, Berkeley, AB, 55, MBA, 60. Polit & Govt Pos: Assoc mem, Rep State Comt Calif, 62-64, mem, 64-; mem, Los Angeles Co Rep Cent Comt, 62-65; Rep nominee, US House Rep, 22nd Cong Dist, 64 & 66; Southern Calif campaign dir, Max Rafferty for US Senate, 68; campaign mgr, Councilman Donald D Lorenzen, Los Angeles City Coun, 69; vpres, Los Angeles Jr Col Dist Bd Trustee, 69-70, pres, 70-71; Calif State Assemblyman, 64th Dist, 70- Bus & Prof Pos: Financial analyst, Litton Industs, Beverly Hills, Calif, 60-64; partner, Cline, Holzberg & Co, 64- Mil Serv: Entered as Pvt, Army, 46, released as SP-4 (Res), 62, after serv in 513th Antiaircraft Missile Bn, Seattle Defense, Ft Lawton, Wash, 56-58. Mem: Canoga Park CofC; Kiwanis; Van Nuys Jaycees; San Fernando Valley Bus & Prof Asn (dir & treas). Relig: Episcopal. Mailing Add: 19240 Nordhoff Northridge CA 91324

CLINGAN, LEE (D)
Ind State Rep
Educ: Purdue Univ. Polit & Govt Pos: Ind State Sen, 61-66; mem, Fountain Co Draft Bd, 16 years; Ind State Rep, 75- Bus & Prof Pos: Ins agt; livestock auctioneer. Mil Serv: 1st Lt; Bronze Star; Purple Heart; Combat Infantryman's Badge. Mem: Am Legion; VFW; Mason; DAV; Elks. Mailing Add: 121 Elm Dr Covington IN 47932

CLINTON, ELLAREE AVANT (D)
VChmn, Polk Co Dem Cent Comt, Iowa
b Des Moines, Iowa, Jan 5, 22; d Thomas Burke Avant & Mattie Bradshaw A; m 1947 to William James Clinton; c Michael Allan & David Andrew. Educ: Iowa State Univ, BS in Child Develop, 64; Drake Univ, MS in Educ, 69, additional study, 70-72; Delta Sigma Theta. Polit & Govt Pos: Precinct committeewoman, Polk Co Dem Cent Comt, Iowa, 64-, vchmn, 72-; secy, John F Kennedy Dem Club, 66; deleg-at-lg, Dem Nat Conv, 68; mem exec bd, Iowa State Dem Cent Comt, 68; precinct committeewoman, dist chmn & mem exec bd, Iowa Dem Conf, 69- Bus & Prof Pos: Child develop caseworker, Iowa Children's & Family Serv, 64-; child develop consult for teachers, Tiny Tot Day Care Serv, 68-, mem bd dirs, 69-; teacher, Des Moines Pub Schs, 69- Mem: Nat & Iowa Asns for Educ of Young Children; Nat & Iowa Educ Asns; life mem Iowa State Univ Alumni Asn. Honors & Awards: Prof Teaching Cert, Iowa State Dept Pub Instr, 73. Relig: Methodist. Mailing Add: 1190 Tenth St Des Moines IA 50314

CLIPSON, JAMES HUGH, JR (R)
Chmn, Colorado Co Rep Party, Tex
b Lissie, Tex, Aug 21, 38; s James Hugh Clipson & Ana Mae Causey C; m 1960 to Jane Katherine Andersen; c Julie Ruth, Jane Louise, Jerri Lynn & James Wilber. Polit & Govt Pos: Mem, Bush Campaign Comt, Colorado Co, Tex, 64; Rep chmn, Precinct 17, Eagle Lake, Tex, 64-; chmn, Colorado Co Rep Party, Tex, 66- Bus & Prof Pos: Operator, Rice Farming & Ranching, 58- Mil Serv: Entered as Airman, Air Force Res, 58, released as Airman 3/C, 64, after serv in Alamo & Tater, 446 Troop Carrier Wing, Houston, 56-64, Inactive Res, 64-66. Mem: Elks; Tex Jaycees; Tex Farm Bur; Lions. Relig: Presbyterian. Legal Res: 626 Willow Eagle Lake TX 77434 Mailing Add: Box 832 Eagle Lake TX 77434

CLODFELTER, MARK (D)
Mich State Sen
Mailing Add: 710 McKinley St Flint MI 48507

CLOOS, DUANE GEORGE (D)
Chmn, Ford Co Dem Party, Ill
b Cabery, Ill, Dec 16, 26; s George Cloos & Stella Nicholson C; m 1950 to Norma Corinne Corriveau; c Dawn (Mrs Roger Boma); Angela Rae & Michael Duane (deceased). Educ: Kankakee High Sch, dipl. Bus & Prof Pos: Owner & operator, Cloos Body Shop, 51 Mil Serv: Entered as Seaman, Navy, 44, released as Gunners Mate 3/C, 46, after serv in Southeast Asia, 45-46. Mem: Am Legion; Mason. Relig: Methodist. Mailing Add: 129 E Vine St Piper City IL 60959

CLOSE, ALBERT STEPHEN (R)
Mem, Rep Cent & Exec Comt Ohio
b Sandusky, Ohio, May 10, 05; s Albert C Close & Walla Young C; single. Educ: Univ Pa, grad, 26; Western Reserve Law Sch, LLB, 30; Alpha Tau Omega. Polit & Govt Pos: Secy, Erie Co Rep Cent & Exec Comt, Ohio, 40-; mem, Ohio Rep Cent & Exec Comt, 62-; mem, Erie Co Bd Elec, 68- Bus & Prof Pos: Partner & mem, A C Close Agency, gen ins; partner & mem, Close & Close, Attorneys-at-law. Mem: Erie Co & Ohio Ins Agents Asns; Erie Co, Ohio & State of Ohio Bar Asns. Relig: United Presbyterian. Legal Res: 336 E Adams St Sandusky OH 44870 Mailing Add: PO Box 555 Sandusky OH 44870

CLOSE, ELMER HARRY (R)
NH State Rep
b Toledo, Ohio, July 16, 37; s Joseph Kempf Close & Luette Spitzer C; m 1966 to Margot Pierce; c Josephine P & Amanda S. Educ: Harvard Col, AB cum laude, 58; Harvard Univ Law Sch, LLB, 61. Polit & Govt Pos: NH State Rep, Keene, Ward Four, 73-; mem judiciary comt, NH House Rep, 73-74, vchmn labor comt, 75- Bus & Prof Pos: Lawyer, Shearman & Sterling, New York, 62-66 & Keene, NH, 66-70; pres & gen mgr, WKNE Corp, 70-; pres, Greylock Broadcasting, Pittsfield, Mass, 70- Mil Serv: Entered as Pvt, Marine Corps, 62, released as Cpl, 66. Mem: NH & Fed Commun Bar Asns; Rotary. Relig: Protestant. Legal Res: 103 School St Keene NH 03431 Mailing Add: Box 466 Keene NH 03431

CLOSE, G R (BOB) (R)
Tex State Rep
Mailing Add: 1101 S Drake Perryton TX 79070

CLOSE, GEOFFREY ROBINSON (R)
Chmn, Harford Co Rep Cent Comt, Md
b Bel Air, Md, Nov 11, 47; s Albert Patterson Close & Lucile Robinson C; m 1973 to Jeanne Proto. Educ: Univ Md, College Park, 65-66; Harford Community Col, 66-68; Univ Ariz, BA, 71; Presidents Honor Club, Univ Ariz. Polit & Govt Pos: Chmn, Harford Co Rep Cent Comt, Md, 74-; town comnr-vchmn, Bel Air, Md, 75- Bus & Prof Pos: Real estate salesman, Rice & Walter Real Estate Inc, Bel Air, Md, 72-; ins underwriter, Harford Mutual Ins Co, 74- Mem: Citizens Interested in Polit Expression; Harford Co Bd Realtors; Md Munic League. Relig: Catholic. Mailing Add: 707 Hickory Ave Bel Air MD 21014

CLOSE, MELVIN DILKES, JR (D)
Nev State Sen
b Provo, Utah, Apr 24, 34; s M D Close & Hope Coleman C; m 1956 to Saundra Wood; c Melvin D, III, Stephanie & Michael. Educ: Brigham Young Univ, BS, 56; Univ Calif, JD, 61. Polit & Govt Pos: Nev State Assemblyman, 65-71, speaker, Nev Assembly, 67-69, Minority Floor Leader, 69-71; Nev State Sen, 71- Mil Serv: Army, 56-58. Mem: Elks; Kiwanis. Mailing Add: 3838 Delaware Lane Las Vegas NV 89109

CLOSZ, HAROLD F, JR (R)
Chmn, Muskegon Co Rep Finance Comt, Mich
b Muskegon, Mich, Aug 16, 23; s Dr Harold F Closz & Elizabeth Cox C; m 1944 to Mary Jean Phipps; c Michael Charles, Harold F, III, Catherine McCormick, John Chapin & Thomas Murray. Educ: DePauw Univ, BA, 47; Delta Tau Delta. Polit & Govt Pos: Chmn, Muskegon Co Young Rep, Mich, 48-50; vchmn, Muskegon Co Rep Comt, 48-50, chmn, 62-68; mem, Rep State Cent Comt, 50-52; alderman, North Muskegon, 58-62; deleg, Rep Nat Conv, 68; chmn, Muskegon Co Rep Finance Comt, 68- Bus & Prof Pos: Mgr, Bridgeways Inc, 48-51; mgr terminal, Roadway Express Inc, 51-66. Mil Serv: Entered as Pvt, Army Air Force, 43, released as 1st Lt, 45, after serv in 448th Bomber Squadron, Second Div, Eighth Air Force, European Theater, 44-45; Air Medal with Five Oak Leaf Clusters; European Theater Ribbon and Four Battle Stars. Mem: Kiwanis; Transportation Club; West State Press Club; North Muskegon Community Club. Relig: Roman Catholic. Mailing Add: 825 Miller Dr North Muskegon MI 49445

CLOUD, DREW (D)
b Nov 27, 23; m 1946 to Bobbie Jean Brown; c Linda Dru (Mrs Paul Omstead). Polit & Govt Pos: Chmn, NMex Dem Party, 70-72. Mailing Add: 1130 Madeira Dr SE Apt 410 Albuquerque NM 87108

CLOWARD, MCRAY (D)
Mem, Utah Dem State Cent Comt
b Monroe, Utah, May 2, 24; s Elwin H Cloward & Lorene Warenski C; m 1946 to Marius Larson; c M Gregory, Charisse & Krista. Educ: Southern Utah State Col, Cedar City, AS, 49; Utah State Univ, BS, 50, grad work, 55-; Univ of Bridgeport, MS, 54; Peabody Col, EdD, 60; Beloit Col, 63-; Phi Kappa Phi; Kappa Delta Pi; Phi Delta Kappa; Sigma Alpha Epsilon. Polit & Govt Pos: Dist & precinct officer, Cedar City Dem Party, Utah, 62; deleg, Utah State & Co Dem Conv, 62-73; mem, Iron Co Dem Cent Comt, 63 & 72-73; mem, Utah Dem State Cent Comt, 64-; chmn, Iron Co Dem Party, 64-72; cand from Iron & Kane Counties for Utah State Rep, 72. Bus & Prof Pos: Prof, Col Southern Utah, 50-; vpres & bd mem, Meadow Lake Estates, 65-; pres & chmn of bd, Brian Head Ski Corp, 66- Mil Serv: Entered as Pvt, Army, 43, released as S/Sgt, 46, after serv in 137th Evacuation Hosp, ETO, 44-46; European Theatre Ribbon; Unit Citations; Good Conduct Medal. Publ: Small colleges can build adequate dormitories, Col & Univ Bus, 49; My discovery of the South, Peabody Reflector, 56; Higher education and community service, Utah Educ Asn Mag, 68. Mem: Nat & Utah Educ Asns; Mt Plains & Utah Adult Educ Asns; Am Personnel & Guid Asn. Honors & Awards: Cand for Outstanding Citizen. Relig: Latter-day Saint. Mailing Add: 328 S 500 W Cedar City UT 84720

CLOWER, RONALD LEE (D)
Tex State Sen
b Stamps, Ark, Oct 1, 40; s Argus Eugene Clower, Jr & Lillian Vickers C; m 1962 to Sarah Virginia Gatewood; c Sarah Mellany & Elizabeth Vickers. Educ: Southern Methodist Univ, BBA, 63, LLB, 66; Phi Delta Phi; Delta Kappa Epsilon. Polit & Govt Pos: Law clerk, US Dist Judge Sarah Hughes, 66-67; legis & admin aide to US Sen Ralph W Yarborough, 67-68; mem staff, Hubert Humphrey Campaign, 68; pres, Tex Young Dem Clubs, 70-71; Tex State Sen, Dist Nine, 73- Bus & Prof Pos: Partner, Clower & Stanford, 69- Mem: Am & Tex Bar Asns; Camp Fire Girls (bd dirs, Dallas Region); Sierra Club; March of Dimes (dir). Relig: Episcopal. Legal Res: 1608 Ruth Dr Garland TX 75042 Mailing Add: Texas Senate Austin TX 78711

CLOWES, DEAN KAY (D)
b Brackenridge, Pa, Jan 16, 23; s Philip J Clowes & Florence Marvin C; m 1951 to Gladys Crowley; c Joan Ellen, Kathleen P & Philip D. Educ: Va Polytech Inst, ASTP, 43-44; The Citadel, BS, 49. Polit & Govt Pos: Labor adv, Mutual Security Agency, 50-51; foreign serv officer, US Dept State, 52-53, pub mem selection bd, 63, pub mem inspector gen, 64; mem, Dem Nat Charter Comn, currently. Bus & Prof Pos: Rep & asst dir, United Steelworkers Am, 48-60, int affairs rep, 61-64, dir polit action dept, 68-; prof indust rels, Ford Found, India, 60-61; dep dir, AFL-CIO African-Am Labor Ctr, 64-68. Mem: United Steelworkers Am; Int Metalworkers' Fedn (mem exec bd). Mailing Add: 504 Blick Dr Silver Spring MD 20594

CLUNIS, WAGER FREDERICK (D)
Mem, Eighth Cong Dist Dem Exec Comt, Mich
b Elkton, Mich, Aug 27, 02; s Frederick E Clunis & Lavina M Wager C; m 1929 to Alice M Seddon; c Gail E, Wager F Jr, & Douglas J. Educ: Cent Mich Univ, AB, cum laude, 32; Univ Mich, MA, 34. Polit & Govt Pos: Trustee, Elkton-Pigeon-Bay Port Sch Bd Educ, Mich, 44-; mem, Huron Co Dem Comt, 61-; mem, Eighth Cong Dist Dem Exec Comt, 65-; Dem cand cong, Eighth Cong Dist, 66; deleg, Dem Nat Conv, 68. Bus & Prof Pos: Univ & pub sch teacher, 25 years; mem bd dirs, Elton Coop Farm Produce Co, 44-59; mem bd dirs, Elton Petroleum Coop, 44-59. Mem: Mich Asn Sch Bd; Nat Asn Sch Bd; Nat & Mich Educ Asns; Rotary Int; Mason. Honors & Awards: Hon chap farmer, Future Farmers Am; High Sch Alumni Award for being greatest contributor to community. Relig: Methodist. Mailing Add: 4204 Pigeon Rd Elkton MI 48731

CLYBURN, WILLIAM R (D)
SC State Rep
Mailing Add: Box 631 Kershaw SC 29067

CLYDE, ROBERT F (R)
Utah State Rep
Mailing Add: RFD Heber UT 84032

CLYNES, JAMES JOSEPH (D)
Conn State Rep
b Hartford, Conn, Sept 24, 23; s James Henry Clynes & Josephine McAloon C; m 1949 to Rhoda Mary Leonard; c Nancy Ann & James William. Educ: New Britain High Sch, 4 years. Polit & Govt Pos: Conn State Rep, 67- Mil Serv: Entered as A/S, Navy, 42, released as Water Tender 2/C, 46, recalled 50-52. Mem: Am Legion; Kiwanis. Relig: Catholic. Mailing Add: 31 Birchcrest Dr Southington CT 06489

CMICH, STANLEY A (R)
Mayor, Canton, Ohio
b Glencampbell, Pa. Educ: Ohio State Univ. Polit & Govt Pos: Liquor agent in charge for 18 co, Ohio Dept of Liquor Control, 49-51; safety dir, Canton, Ohio, 52-57, mayor, 63-; deleg, Rep Nat Conv, 72. Bus & Prof Pos: Gen prod mgr, A G Stafford Co, Canton, Ohio, 58-62; mem bd dirs, Stark Co Construction. Mil Serv: With AUS, World War II. Mem: Am Judicature Soc; Elks; Eagles; Moose; KofC (4 degree). Honors & Awards: Canton Negro Sports Asn Award for Outstanding Serv as Mayor; Gtr Canton CofC Award for Outstanding Performance; Equal Opportunity Award, Canton Urban League; Am Legion Citation for Meritorious Serv; Americanism Award, Polonia Found Ohio, Inc. Relig: Roman Catholic. Legal Res: 138 20th St NE Canton OH 44714 Mailing Add: 218 Cleveland Ave SW Canton OH 44702

COATSWORTH, JOSEPH S (D)
Conn State Rep
b Long Beach, Calif, Dec 16, 42; s Joseph Coatsworth & Janet Bell C; m 1964 to Kathleen Ruth Balinski. Educ: Univ Wis, Madison, BA, 67; grad work, Trinity Col, Conn, 69-70. Polit & Govt Pos: Mem, Cromwell Dem Town Comt, Conn, 70-; Conn State Rep, 76th Dist, 71-73, 32nd Dist, 73-; chmn, Cromwell Charter Comn, 72-73. Bus & Prof Pos: Teacher, Middletown, Conn, 67-69; dir, Conn Housing Investment Fund, Hartford, 71-72; with Hartford Nat Bank & Trust Co, Inc, currently. Mem: Nat Soc State Legislators (bd gov, 72-); Middlesex Col Regional Adv Coun, 72- Relig: Methodist. Mailing Add: 49 Coles Rd Cromwell CT 06416

COBB, AMELIE MARY (R)
Committeewoman, Rep Party Tex
b Houston, Tex, July 1, 41; d James Edward Suberbielle & Julia Moffett S; m 1965 to Howell Cobb; c Catherine Louise, Howell, III, Thomas Hart, Mary Ann, Caroline Therese & John Lamar. Educ: Univ St Thomas (Tex), 59-60; Univ Houston, 60-61; Lamar Univ, 61-62; Zeta Tau Alpha. Polit & Govt Pos: Committeewoman, Rep Party Tex, Dist Four, 74- Mem: Jr League Beaumont (asst treas, 75-76); Beaumont Symphony Women's League (pres, 74-75); Zeta Tau Alpha Alumnae; Jefferson Co Coun on Alcoholism (bd dirs, 74-75). Honors & Awards: Outstanding Vol, State Dept Pub Welfare, 74. Relig: Roman Catholic. Mailing Add: 1385 Thomas Rd Beaumont TX 77706

COBB, ANDREW WHITNEY (R)
b Elsie, Mich, Feb 12, 11; s Lyman Jason Cobb & Estella Grenlund C; m 1936 to Elizabeth Jean Mansfield; c Lawrence, Lee, Shirley Larsen, Martha Coates & Alan. Educ: Mich State Univ, BS, 34; Alpha Zeta; Pi Kappa Phi; Varsity Club. Polit & Govt Pos: Justice of the Peace, Duplain Two, Mich, 45-50; Mich State Rep, Clinton Co, 50-54; Mich State Rep, Eaton Dist, 55-64; comnr, Clinton Co, 69-71; admin asst to Mich State Treas, 71- Bus & Prof Pos: Dairy farmer, 36- Mem: Farm Bur; Centennial Farm Asn; Mich Milk Producer's Asn; Mich Artificial Breeders; Dairy Herd Improv Asn. Honors & Awards: Mich 4-H Alumni Award; Fed Land Bank 50th Anniversary Medal; Mich Milk Producer's Asn Distinguished Serv Award. Relig: Methodist. Mailing Add: 9702 Island Rd Elsie MI 48831

COBB, J C (D)
Dem Nat Committeeman, Okla
b Iowa Park, Tex; m to Rheba; c Larry. Educ: NTex State Univ; Capitol Col of Pharmacy, BS in Pharmacy. Polit & Govt Pos: Mayor, Tishomingo, Okla, 50-54; secy, State Bd of Pharmacy, 51-62; precinct, co & dist chmn, Dem Party, 62-68; chmn rules comt, two Okla Dem State Conv; deleg, Dem Nat Conv, 64, 68 & 72; Dem Nat Committeeman, Okla, 68-; deleg, Dem Nat Mid-Term Conf, 74. Bus & Prof Pos: Pharmacist; retail drug bus. Mem: Rotary; Nat Asn of Retail Druggists; Shrine. Relig: Presbyterian; Elder, Presby Church. Mailing Add: 215 W Main Tishomingo OK 73460

COBB, JOHN BYNUM, II (D)
Mem, Shelby Co Dem Exec Comt, Tenn
b Memphis, Tenn, Oct 24, 32; s John Bynum Cobb & Edna Sennett C; m 1962 to Mary Lee Billingsly; c Lynn Ann & John Bynum, III. Educ: Memphis State Univ, BS, 55; Vanderbilt Univ, LLB & JD, 60; Kappa Sigma; Phi Delta Phi. Polit & Govt Pos: Mem, Shelby Co Dem Exec Comt, Tenn, 60-, chmn, formerly; alt delg, Dem Nat Conv, 68. Bus & Prof Pos: Attorney-at-law. Mil Serv: Air Force, 55, Strategic Air Command, Alaska; Capt, Res. Mem: Memphis & Am Trial Lawyers Asns; Tenn Club; Tenn Trial Lawyers (Bd Gov); Memphis Bar Asn. Relig: Baptist. Mailing Add: 83 W Walnut Grove Ct Memphis TN 38117

COBB, LAURENCE ARTHUR (R)
NC State Rep
b Teaneck, NJ, May 20, 33; s Gardiner Cobb & Georgette Robedee C; m 1960 to Edna Faye Pugh; c Laura Georgette & Glenn Laurence. Educ: Rutgers Univ, 51-52; Univ NC, Chapel Hill, BS in BA, 55, Sch Law, JD with honors, 58; Washburn Univ Sch Law, 55-57; Chi Psi (dir, Alpha Sigma); Phi Alpha Delta. Polit & Govt Pos: Precinct supvr, Mecklenburg Co Rep Party, NC, 66-69, registr chmn, 69-70; NC State Rep, 70- Bus & Prof Pos: Legal res asst, Inst Govt, Chapel Hill, NC, 58-59; attorney, Fairley, Hamrick, Monteith & Cobb, Charlotte, 62- Mil Serv: Entered as 1st Lt, Air Force, 59, released as 1st Lt, 62, after serv as Judge Adv Gen Corps, Fla, 59-62; Maj, Air Force Res, 62- Mem: Am Bar Asn; Commercial Law League Am (fel); Lions (dir, Charlotte Southern Club); Mecklenburg Cancer Soc (dir); Kidney Found Mecklenburg Co (dir). Relig: Episcopal. Mailing Add: 3022 Sharon Rd Charlotte NC 28211

COBB, MICHAEL WILLIAM (R)
Chmn, Santa Clara Co Rep Cent Comt, Calif
b Los Angeles, Calif, Mar 5, 36; s William Armstrong Cobb & Caroline Frankel C; m 1962 to Barbara Ann Male; c Michael Eric & Linda Anne. Educ: Univ Santa Clara, MBA, 74; Univ Calif, Berkeley, BSME, 58, MS Eng Sci, 63; Tau Kappa Epsilon. Polit & Govt Pos: State chmn, Calif Young Rep, 69-70; chmn & co-chmn, Numerous Co Campaigns for Nixon, Murphy, Reagan & others, 69-72; regional dir, Flournoy for Gov, 74; chmn, Santa Clara Co Rep Cent Comt, 73-; mem exec comt, Rep State Cent Comt, 74- Bus & Prof Pos: Project mgr, Itek Corp-OSD, Palo Alto, Calif, 66-70; advan develop engr, GTE-Sylvania Sociosystems Lab, Mt View, Calif, 70-71; asst dir mkt, ESL Inc, Sunnyvale, 71-75; mgr mkt develop, Gen Elec Co Fast Breeder Reactor Dept, Sunnyvale, 75- Honors & Awards: Resolution No 163 Calif State Assembly, 70, presented by Assemblyman Earle Crandall at the Rep State Cent Comt. Mailing Add: 3863 Dixon Pl Palo Alto CA 94306

COBB, STEPHEN ARCHIBALD (D)
Tenn State Rep
b Moline, Ill, Jan 27, 44; s Archibald William Cobb & Lucile Dyer Bates C; m 1971 to Nancy Hendrix. Educ: Harvard Univ, AB cum laude, 66; Vanderbilt Univ, MA, 68, PhD, 71, Law

Sch, currently. Polit & Govt Pos: State coordr, Tenn Vol for McCarthy, 68; pres, Davidson Co Young Dem, 70; deleg, Tenn State Dem Conv, 70, alt deleg, 72; Nat Committeeman, Tenn Young Dem Clubs, formerly; campaign mgr, Davidson Co McGovern-Shriver Presidential Campaign, 72; cand for Dem nomination, Tenn State Legis, 72; Tenn State Rep, 74- Bus & Prof Pos: Asst prof sociol, Tenn State Univ, 70-72; head dept criminal justice, 73-74; mem, Tenn Criminal Justice Manpower Develop Comt, 72- Publ: Auth, Defense spending and foreign policy in the House of Representatives, J Conflict Resolution, 9/69; The United State Senate and the impact of defense spending concentrations, In: Testing the Theory of the Military-Industrial Complex, ed, Rosen, 73; The impact of defense spending on senatorial voting behavior: a study of foreign policy feedback, In: Sage International Yearbook of Foreign Policy Studies, ed, McGowan, 73. Mem: Am Sociol Asn; Southern Sociol Soc; Am Asn Univ Prof. Honors & Awards: Nat Merit Scholar, Nat Defense Educ Act Fel and other undergrad and grad fels. Relig: Methodist. Mailing Add: 1929 Castleman Dr Nashville TN 37215

COBB, STEPHEN HENRY (STEVE) (D)
Hawaii State Rep
b Honolulu, Hawaii, Dec 5, 42; s William Ballinger Cobb & Olivine Steffens C; m 1972 to Inmi Song. Educ: Univ Hawaii; Calif State Col Los Angeles, BA in Jour & Philos, 66; Sigma Delta Chi. Polit & Govt Pos: Field worker 42 states, John F Kennedy for President, 60; field worker, Daniel K Inouye, US Senate Campaign, 62; canvasser, Gale McGee US Senate Campaign, 64; field worker, Robert Kennedy Campaign, Calif, 68; Dem State Senate Nominee, Hawaii, 70; bd dirs, Hawaii Young Dem, 71-72; Hawaii State Rep, Eighth & Ninth Dists, 72- Bus & Prof Pos: Mkt & loans, Bank of Hawaii, 70-72. Mil Serv: Entered as Pvt, Army, 66, released as Capt, 70, after serv in Ft Knox & Vietnam Americal Div, 11th Brigade, 68-69; Army Res, Capt, 4 years; Silver Star; Bronze Star; Air Medal; Army Commendation Medal; Purple Heart; 3 Vietnam Serv Awards. Mem: Hawaii Little League Baseball (state treas, 71-75); DAV. Honors & Awards: Vet of Year, Kiwanis, Honolulu, 70. Relig: Roman Catholic. Legal Res: 615 Hunalewa St Honolulu HI 96816 Mailing Add: State Capitol Honolulu HI 96813

COBBE, MARGARET HAMMETT (D)
b Gaffney, SC, Aug 3, 20; d Davis Eugene Hammett (deceased) & Ava Era Barrett H; m 1943 to Jerome Francis Cobbe (deceased); c Jerome Francis, Jr, Sheila (Mrs Tobin); Michael Timothy & Luane Carol. Educ: Strayer's Bus Col, Washington, DC, secy course, 38. Polit & Govt Pos: Secy, Gulfport Area Dem Club, Fla, 61-62; secy, Pinellas Co Dem Exec Comt, 62-65, vchmn, 65-69; legis chmn, St Petersburg Women's Dem Club, 67-68, first vpres, 68-70, pres, 71; alt deleg, Dem Nat Conv, 68, chmn women's activities, Fla Host Comt, 72; eighth cong dist chmn, Women for Humphrey, 68; eighth cong dist vpres, Dem Women's Club of Fla, 68-71; St Petersburg Hq mgr, Askew for Gov Campaign, 70; pres, Dem Women's Club Fla, 71-73; mem, Gov Adv Comt, 71-74; mem adv comt, Dem Exec Comt, Fla, 71-73; mem, Fla Campaign Comt, 72; comnr & state Equal Rights Amendment coordr, Gov Comn on Status of Women, currently; mem affirmative action comt, Fla Dem Exec Comt, currently. Bus & Prof Pos: Secy, Bur Old Age & Survivors Ins, Washington, DC, 40-43; pvt secy to pres, Glenn E McCormick Co, Inc, St Petersburg, Fla, 55-59. Mil Serv: Entered as Pvt, Women's Army Corps, Army Air Force, 43, released as Sgt, 45, after serv in Air Transport Command, ETO, 44-45; Good Conduct Medal. Mem: League of Women Voters, St Petersburg, Fla; Suncoast Consumers' League, Inc (co-founder, vpres, currently). Honors & Awards: Top Fund-raiser Cert, Pinellas Co Dem Exec Comt, 64; Perfect Attendance Cert, 65; Outstanding Dem Woman of Fla, 69. Relig: Baptist; former Supt, young people's dept, Pasadena Baptist Church; former teacher, Adult Women's Sunday Sch Class. Mailing Add: 901 62nd St Gulfport FL 33707

COBBS, LYLE RICHARD (R)
Idaho State Sen
b Boise, Idaho, July 22, 30; s Hartzell Cobbs (deceased) & Edith Miller C; m 1954 to Donna Lee White; c Nancy Marie, Diane Elizabeth, Kathryn Ann & Lyla Renee. Educ: Northwest Christian Col, 49-51. Polit & Govt Pos: Idaho State Rep, Ada Co, 64-73; Idaho State Sen, currently. Mil Serv: Entered as Pvt, Army, 51, released as Cpl, 53, after serv in Army Res, Inf, Korea, 52; several mil awards & decorations. Mem: Kiwanis Int; Mason. Relig: Christian Church. Mailing Add: 7211 Court Ave Boise ID 83705

COBLEIGH, NEAL WAYNE (R)
NH State Rep
b Lebanon, NH, June 9, 01; s Marshall Day Cobleigh & Alice Aldrich C; m 1928 to Dorothy Esson; c Marshall William, Richard Esson & Dorothy Jacqueline (Mrs Richard Lavigne). Educ: Univ NH, 20-22; Phi Mu Delta. Polit & Govt Pos: Various ward off, Ward 1, Nashua, NH, 24-40; alderman, City of Nashua, 35-37; NH State Rep, currently. Bus & Prof Pos: Owner & founder, Nashua Credit Bur, 22-27, Merchants Protective Bur, Hartford, 27-30 & Merchants Credit Bur, Boston, 30-32; abstractor, 32-53 & with NH Dept Pub Works, 53-69; Retired. Relig: Congregational. Mailing Add: 36 Edgewood Ave Nashua NH 03060

COBURN, ROSCOE NEWTON (R)
NH State Rep
b Milford, NH, Jan 10, 98; s Stephen Carroll Coburn & Ida Belle Goodwin C; m 1921 to Blanche Lorraine Anderson; c Sandra (Mrs Newbold). Educ: Milford High Sch, NH, grad, 16. Polit & Govt Pos: Chmn, NH Selective Serv Bd 17, Milford, NH, 48-68; selectman, Milford, 50-52; NH State Rep, 65- Mil Serv: Pvt, Army, 18-19, serv in Co C 1st US Engrs, ETO. Mem: Rotary; Mason; VFW; Vet World War I; Am Legion. Honors & Awards: Am Legion Citation. Relig: United Church Christ. Mailing Add: 78 Elm St Milford NH 03055

COBURN, TOM C (D)
Ala State Rep
Mailing Add: 1107 E Third St Tuscumbia AL 35674

COCA NAVAS, RAFAEL (POPULAR DEMOCRATS, PR)
Rep, PR House Rep
Mailing Add: State Capitol San Juan PR 00901

COCHRAN, DALE M (D)
Iowa State Rep
b Ft Dodge, Iowa, Nov 20, 28; s Melvin Cochran & Gladys C; m 1952 to Jeanene Hirsch; c Deborah, Cynthia & Tamara. Educ: Iowa State Univ, BS, 50; Pi Kappa Phi. Polit & Govt Pos: Iowa State Rep, 65-, Minority Floor Leader, 71-; staff mem US Rep Merwin Coad, formerly; dir, Co Exten, formerly. Bus & Prof Pos: Owner & operator 400 acre farm; pub rels dir, Hartland, Inc; past farm ed, Ft Dodge Messenger. Mem: Iowa Soybean Asn (bd, 69-); Iowa Soybean Promotion Bd (bd, 72-); various farm orgn. Relig: Methodist. Legal Res: Rte 1 Box 109 Eagle Grove IA 50533 Mailing Add: State Capitol E Tenth & Grand Ave Des Moines IA 50319

COCHRAN, FRANKLIN DELANO (D)
Chmn, Lake Co Dem Party, Tenn
b Tiptonville, Tenn, Oct 20, 37; s Clarence Ulas Cochran & Essie Berry C; m 1958 to Patsy Jo Whitfield; c Kent. Educ: David Lipscomb Col; Univ Tenn; Univ Tenn Col Law; Alpha Tau Omega; Phi Alpha Delta. Polit & Govt Pos: Tenn State Rep, 62-71; Lake Co attorney, 63-; city attorney, 65-; chmn, Lake Co Dem Party, 71- Mem: Am Bar Asn; Tenn Trial Lawyers Asn; Mason; Kiwanis; Farm Bur. Relig: Church of Christ. Mailing Add: 301 Church Tiptonville TN 38079

COCHRAN, WILLIAM C (D)
Ind State Rep
Mailing Add: 4300 Green Valley New Albany IN 47150

COCHRAN, WILLIAM THAD (R)
US Rep, Miss
b Pontotoc, Miss, Dec 7, 37; s William Holmes Cochran & Emma Grace Berry C; m 1964 to Rose Clayton; c Thaddeus Clayton & Katherine Holmes. Educ: Univ Miss, BA, 59, JD cum laude, 65; Trinity Col, Dublin, 63-64; Omicron Delta Kappa; Phi Kappa Phi; Phi Delta Phi; Pi Kappa Alpha. Polit & Govt Pos: US Rep, Miss, 73- Bus & Prof Pos: Partner, Watkins & Eager, Attorneys-at-law, Jackson, Miss, 65-72. Mil Serv: Entered as Ens, Navy, 59, released as Lt(jg), 61, after serv as legal officer in USS Macon; Lt, Navy Res, 61-63, instr, Naval Officer Cand Sch, Newport, RI. Mem: Am Bar Asn; Miss State Bar Asn (pres, Young Lawyers Sect, 72-73). Honors & Awards: Fel, Rotary Found, 63-64; Outstanding Young Man of Year, Jackson Jr CofC, 71; One of Three Outstanding Young Men of the Year in Miss, Miss Jr CofC, 71. Relig: Baptist. Legal Res: Rte 5 Jackson MS 39212 Mailing Add: 6102 Woodmont Rd Alexandria VA 22307

COCHRANE, JOHN CAMPBELL (R)
NY State Assemblyman
b Bay Shore, NY, Nov 16, 29; s John Campbell Cochrane & Helen Spach C; m 1952 to Elizabeth Cook; c Susan B, Elizabeth A, John C & James R. Educ: US Naval Acad, BS Eng, 51. Polit & Govt Pos: Alt deleg, Rep Nat Conv, 68; chmn, Islip Rep Town Comt, NY, 68-70; NY State Rep Committeeman, Third Assembly Dist, 70-72; NY State Assemblyman, Sixth Dist, 73- Bus & Prof Pos: Pres, Cochrane & Craven Agency Inc, 56-; dir, First Nat Bank of Bay Shore, 57-; trustee, United Fund of Long Island, 63- Mil Serv: Entered as Midn, Navy, 47, released as Lt(jg), 55, after serv in USS Melvin & USS Antietam; Capt, Naval Res, currently; Armed Forces Res Medal; Nat Defense Award; European Occup Ribbon. Mem: Bay Shore Lions; Bay Shore Yacht Club (rear commodore). Relig: Episcopal. Mailing Add: 80 Concourse E Brightwaters NY 11718

COCHRANE, PAT (D)
Wash State Rep
b Melville, Mont, July 28, 16; d John Walker Hart & Eleanor Armstrong H; m 1940 to Gordon S Cochrane; c Helen & James; two grandsons. Educ: Mont State Col, sci major; Boston Univ, MS in Biol & Psychol; teachers cert in Mont & Mass; Pi Beta Phi. Polit & Govt Pos: Active in Dem Party in Wash, since 52; Dem precinct committeeperson, Benton Co, Wash; campaign mgr for Fred Yoder for Cong; alt deleg, Dem Nat Conv, 56 & 64; state chairperson, Adlai E Stevenson Let's Talk Sense Fund, 56; legis chairperson, Wash State Dem Women's Fedn, 2 years; publicity chairperson, 4 years; mem finance comt, Wash State Dem Cent Comt, 5 years, state committeewoman, Benton Co, 6 years; state chairperson, Dollars for Dem, 5 years; co-chairperson, Benton Co Johnson for President, 64; deleg, White House Conf Int Coop & US Comn for UNESCO Conf, 65; cand for Wash State Legis, 72; legis chairperson, Benton Co Dem Cent Comt, currently; deleg, Wash State Conf Children & Youth & White House Conf Children & Youth; deleg, Dem Nat Mid-Term Conf, 74; app to Wash State Comt on Law & Justice & Wash State Rural Legal Aid Comt, 75; Wash State Rep, 75- Bus & Prof Pos: Teacher chem, Jr Col; salesperson, Western Auto Store, Lynn, Mass; owner, Columbia Book Store, Richland, Wash, 5 years; owner, Upstairs Book Store, currently. Mem: Am Asn Univ Women; Bus & Prof Women's Club; Common Cause; UN Asn (bd gov, currently). Mailing Add: 1636 Howell Ave Richland WA 99352

COCHRANE, WILLIAM MCWHORTER (D)
b Newton, NC, Mar 6, 17; s William Daniel Cochrane & Veazey Fillingim C; m 1945 to Thornton Shirley Graves; c William Daniel & Thomas McWhorter. Educ: Univ NC, AB, 39, LLB, 41; Yale Univ, LLM, 51; Order of the Golden Fleece. Polit & Govt Pos: Exec secy to the late US Sen W Kerr Scott, 54-58; admin asst to US Sen B Everett Jordan, NC, 58-73; exec dir, Joint Cong Comt on 1969 Presidential Inaugural Ceremonies, 68; exec dir, Joint Cong Comt Presidential Inaugural Ceremonies, 72-73; staff dir, US Senate Comt Rules & Admin, 72- Bus & Prof Pos: Asst dir, Inst of Govt, Univ NC, 40-42 & 45-52, admin dir inst, assoc research prof pub law & govt & managing ed, Popular Govt, 52-54. Mil Serv: Entered as A/S, Naval Res, 42, released as Lt, 45, after serv in Atlantic, 43-44 & Mediter, 44-45; Lt Comdr, Naval Res, 45-66; Ready Res Medal; Am Theater Ribbon; European-African Ribbon with Star; Victory Medal; Naval Res Serv Medal. Mem: NC State Bar; NC Bar Asn; CofC; Nat Capital Dem Club. Relig: Methodist. Legal Res: PO Box 3 Chapel Hill NC 27514 Mailing Add: 305 Senate Off Bldg Washington DC 20510

COCKAYNE, T WILLIAM (BILL) (R)
Chmn, Utah Rep Party
b Sheffield, Eng, July 14, 06; m 1934 to Mary; c Joan (Mrs F De Metrovich), Thomas William, Jr, Nancy Bowers, David M & Janet M. Polit & Govt Pos: Alt deleg, Rep Nat Conv, 72; Utah State Rep, currently, mem, Pub Health & Welfare, Elec, Revenue & Taxation & Pub Safety Comts, Utah House Rep, currently; mem, Subcomts Bus Regulation & Labor & Family Serv, currently; chmn, Utah Rep Party, 72- Bus & Prof Pos: Sr vpres, secy-treas, mem exec comt & bd dirs, Utah-Idaho Sugar Co, formerly, mem bd dirs, currently; vpres, dir & secy-treas, Layton Sugar Co & Gunnison Sugar, Inc, formerly; dir, Walker Bank & Trust Co, currently. Mem: Utah Mfrs Asn; Utah Taxpayers Asn; Salt Lake City Airport Adv Comt; United Fund; Help Utah Grow. Relig: Latter-day Saint. Mailing Add: 2485 Skyline Dr Salt Lake City UT 84108

COCKERILL, LEON HERBERT, JR (R)
b Omaha, Nebr, Aug 25, 27; s Leon Herbert Cockerill, Sr & Eva Martin C; m 1949 to Helen Arlene Pederson; c Pam Nadine, Lon Adair, Randi Allyn, Brian Bruce & Leon Herbert, III. Educ: Mapleton, NDak, Dist Seven, 11 years. Polit & Govt Pos: Chmn, Dist 22 Rep Party,

NDak, formerly. Bus & Prof Pos: Farming, 50-69. Mem: AF&AM; Farm Bur. Relig: Presbyterian. Mailing Add: Mapleton ND 58059

CODINHA, PAUL PHILLIP (R)
Mem, Gloucester Rep City Comt, Mass
b Gloucester, Mass, June 7, 39; s Joequien E Codinha & Esther Cortina C; m 1970 to Dorothea Helen Makarowitz; c Phaedra Ann. Educ: NY Inst of Finance; North Shore Community Col, AS in Bus Admin, 73. Polit & Govt Pos: Mem, Gloucester Rep City Comt, Mass, 63-, chmn, 65-66; chmn ways & means comt, Cape Ann Young Rep Club, 63-64, pres, 64-65; chmn, Sen Jack Quinlan for Lt Gov Comt, Essex Co, 70. Bus & Prof Pos: Financial acct, Raytheon, Bedford. Mil Serv: Entered as Pvt, Army, 57, released as Sp/4, 60; recalled to active duty during Berlin Crisis for nine months; Good Conduct Medal. Mem: KofC (3 degree); Elks. Relig: Roman Catholic. Mailing Add: 6 Beacon Blvd South Peabody MA 01960

CODR, FRANCIS W (R)
Region VII Dir, Nat Young Rep Fedn
b Butler Co, Nebr, Sept 1, 43; s A J Codr & Eleanor Kantor C; m 1969 to Teresa Daunita Kaczmarek; c Francis D W, II & Tara Nichole. Educ: Univ Nebr, 63-64. Polit & Govt Pos: Chmn, United Citizens for Nixon, 67-68; chmn, Douglas Co Young Rep, 68-69; state pub rels dir, Nebr Young Rep, 69-70, dist II dir, 70-71; pub rels dir, Douglas Co Rep, 71-; region VII dir, Nat Young Rep Fedn, 71- Bus & Prof Pos: Vpres mkt, Continental Gen Ins Co, currently. Mil Serv: Entered as Seaman E-1, Navy, 61, released as E-4, 63, after serv in USS Lexington, CVA-16, SPac & Training Unit, 61-63; Good Conduct Medal. Mem: Am Col Life Underwriters; Nebr Asn Health Underwriters (bd dirs, 67-72); Nebr Asn Life Underwriters; Omaha Businessmen's Asn (bd dirs, 72-). Relig: Catholic. Mailing Add: 105 S 53rd St Omaha NE 68123

CODY, THOMAS G (R)
Asst Secy Admin, Dept Housing & Urban Develop
b Holyoke, Mass, Feb 18, 29; s John F Cody & Mary Scanlon C; m 1956 to Kathleen Maguire; c Kathleen Anne & Joseph K. Educ: Col of the Holy Cross, AB, 50; Boston Col Grad Sch Arts & Sci, 50-52; Harvard Bus Sch, MBA, 57. Polit & Govt Pos: Exec dir, Equal Employ Opportunity Comn, Washington, DC, 72-74; asst secy admin, Dept Housing & Urban Develop, 74- Bus & Prof Pos: Mkt staff, Keystone Camera Co Inc, Boston, Mass, 56-58; product mgr, Am Enka Corp, Concord, 58-61; sales mgr, Atlas Controls Inc, Natick, 61-62; vpres, Fry Consults, Chicago, Ill, Los Angeles, Calif & Washington, DC, 62-72. Mil Serv: Entered as Pvt, Marine Corps, 53, released as 1st Lt, 55, after serv in Korea, 54-55. Mem: Harvard Club New York. Mailing Add: 78 E Queen Anne Circle Annapolis MD 21403

COE, DONALD MELVIN (D)
Committeeman, Wash Dem Comt
b Orting, Wash, Aug 18, 08; s Charles A Coe & Maud Bouldron C; m 1947 to Edith Margaret Kreitlow; c Charles Lee & Anthony Wayne. Educ: Wash State Univ, BS highest honors, 37; Univ Wis, 37-39; PhD, 43; Sigma Xi; Phi Kappa Phi; Phi Sigma. Polit & Govt Pos: Mem, Local Draft Bd, St Paul, Minn, 62-67; chmn, Clallam Co Dem Cent Comt, Wash, 73-75; area rep, Cong Bon Bonker's Staff, currently. Bus & Prof Pos: Asst prof, Iowa State Univ, 45-47; plant pathologist, Calif Dept Agr, 47-51 & US Dept Agr, Alaska, 51-54; assoc prof, Univ Fla, 54-58; dir div plant indust, Minn Dept Agr, 58-67; plant scientist, US Dept Agr, 67-71; retired. Honors & Awards: Alpha Zeta Scholar Award, 34. Relig: Unitarian. Legal Res: 507 E Spruce Sequim WA 98382 Mailing Add: PO Box 661 Sequim WA 98382

COE, MARGARET WYMAN (R)
b Washington, DC, July 8, 19; d William Howard Wyman & Mary Louise Barlup W; m 1943 to George Hughes Coe; c Jeanne (Mrs Lake). Educ: Averett Col, 34-36; Wash Sch for Secretaries. Polit & Govt Pos: Vchmn, Madison Rep Town Comt, Conn, 66-68, chmn, 68-70, ex officio mem; Justice of the Peace, Madison, 75- Bus & Prof Pos: Secy, Liberty Nat Bank, Washington, DC, Mutual Broadcasting Co & Haloid Co. Mem: Eastern Star; Yale-New Haven Hosp Auxiliary; Am Red Cross; Madison Women's Rep Club; DAR. Relig: Congregational. Mailing Add: 48 Stonewall Lane Madison CT 06443

COE, ROBERT H, JR (D)
Chmn, Yuba Co Dem Cent Comt, Calif
b Sacramento, Calif, Aug 23, 50; s Robert Hunter Coe & Virginia Mae Brooks C; single. Educ: Yuba Col, AA, 70; Univ Calif, Davis, BA, 72; Yuba Col Scholar Key, 70. Polit & Govt Pos: Vchmn, Yuba Co Dem Cent Comt, Calif, 74-75, chmn, 75-; mem exec comt, Calif Dem Cent Comt, 75- Bus & Prof Pos: Mgr, Buttes Ins Agency, Live Oak, Calif, 75- Publ: Camp Far West, an early military installation, 73, Claude Chana, from rags to riches, 73, Wheatland News; co-auth, History of Wheatland, 1874-1974, Wheatland Hist Soc, 74. Mem: Wheatland Hist Soc (secy, 74-75); Nat Asn Ins Agents. Relig: First Christian Church, Disciples of Christ. Legal Res: 414 C St Wheatland CA 95692 Mailing Add: PO Box 698 Wheatland CA 95692

COELHO, ANTHONY L (D)
b Dos Palos, Calif, June 15, 42; s Otto Ignacio Coelho & Alice Elizabeth Branco C; m 1967 to Phyllis Eileen Butler; c Nicole Elizabeth. Educ: Loyola Univ, Los Angeles, BA Polit Sci, 64; Phi Sigma Kappa. Polit & Govt Pos: Admin asst to US Rep B F Sisk, Calif, 70- Relig: Catholic. Legal Res: Carlucci Rd Dos Palos CA 93620 Mailing Add: c/o B F Sisk MC 2217 Rayburn Bldg Washington DC 20515

COELHO, PETER J (D)
RI State Rep
b East Providence, RI, May 10, 21; s Joseph Bernardino Coelho & Eugenia Lopes C; m 1944 to Julia De Pina; c Jean A (Mrs Talva), Carol C (Mrs Lopes), Julie A (Mrs Moniz), Sheila J (Mrs Gervais) & Susan Lee. Educ: Inst Appl Sci, Chicago, cert, 45; Univ RI Exten, cert 62. Polit & Govt Pos: Secy, Ward Two Dem City Comt, 61-62; RI State Rep Dist 84, 66- Bus & Prof Pos: Owner-operator, Coelho Painting Co, 47-65; spec agt, NY Life Ins Co, 65-68; exec dir, Homes for Hope Found, 68-; exec dir, RI Housing Investment Fund, 72- Mil Serv: Entered as Pvt, Army Air Force, 42, released as Sgt, 46, after serv at Tuskegee Army Air Field, 42-46. Mem: Cape Verdean Progressive Ctr; Diocesan Human Rels Comn; Pius X Assembly; KofC (4 degree). Relig: Catholic. Mailing Add: 155 Leonard Ave East Providence RI 02914

COEN, ALVIN M (D)
Mayor, Huntington Beach, Calif
b Binghamton, NY, June 1, 37; s Irwin Eli Coen & Molly Ambramowitz C; m 1961 to Felicia Marie Sharpe; c Josh Adam, Jeffrey Dana & Mark Steven. Educ: Harpur Col, BA, 59; Univ Ariz, JD. Polit & Govt Pos: Councilman, Huntington Beach, 66-, mayor, 68-69, 72-73 & 74-75. Bus & Prof Pos: Attorney-at-law, 64- Mil Serv: Air Force Res. Mem: Calif State Bar; Orange Co Bar Asn; Huntington Beach Jaycees. Honors & Awards: Huntington Beach Jaycees Distinguished Serv Award, 66; cert of merit for distinguished serv to law & community, 69; Citizen of the Year, Huntington Beach, 73. Mailing Add: 18582 Beach Blvd Huntington Beach CA 92648

COERR, WYMBERLEY DERENNE (INDEPENDENT)
b New York, NY, Oct 2, 13; m to Eleanor Hicks; c two. Educ: Yale Univ, BA, 36. Polit & Govt Pos: Career officer, US Dept of State Foreign Serv, 39-43, 47-, vconsult, Montreal, 40-41, Honduras, 41-43 & Mex, 43-44, second secy, Suva, Fiji Islands, 47-48, Batavia, 48-50 & Indonesia, 50-51; officer in charge of Indonesian Affairs, 51-54; counr, Honduras, 54-55, Guatemala, 55-56, Nat War Col, 56-57 & LaPaz, 57-59, dir, Off WCoast Affairs, 59-60, Acting Asst Secy of State for Inter-Am Affairs, 60-61, US Ambassador, Uruguay, 62-65; US Ambassador, Ecuador, 65-67; dir res & anal for Latin Am, 69-, dep dir for coord, 69-72; adv, Off Environ Affairs, US Dept State, 72- Bus & Prof Pos: Mgr educ dir, Consumer Coop Corps, 43-47. Legal Res: McLean VA Mailing Add: Rm 7822 US Dept of State Washington DC 20520

COFFEE, JOHN MAIN (D)
b Tacoma, Wash, Jan 23, 97; s William Buckingham Coffee & Anne Rae Main C; m 1923 to Lillian Mary Slye; c John Main, Jr. Educ: Univ Wash, AB, 18, LLB, 20; Yale Univ, JD, 21; Sigma Upsilon; Xi Pi; Alpha Sigma Phi. Polit & Govt Pos: Mem, Tacoma Civil Serv Comn, Wash, 26; chmn, Co-City Unemploy Relief Comt, Tacoma, 30-32; secy, State Recovery Bd Nat Recovery Admin, 33-35; US Rep, Wash, 37-47, chmn, Liberal Bloc, US House Rep, 39-45. Bus & Prof Pos: Lawyer, at present. Publ: Why not a West Point for diplomats?, Coronet Magazine, 44; A study of Alcoa, This Week Mag, 45. Mem: Elks; Eagles; Grange; Yale Club, Washington, DC & Seattle. Relig: Unitarian. Legal Res: 4104 Sixth Ave Tacoma WA 98406 Mailing Add: 811 Washington Bldg Tacoma WA 98402

COFFEY, JOHN F (D)
Mass State Rep
Mailing Add: State Capitol Boston MA 02133

COFFEY, JOHN P, JR (D)
b Portland, Maine, Mar 14, 43; s John P Coffey & Mary F McGinley C; div; c Kathleen Marie, Theresa Lee, Barbara Jean & John Patrick. Educ: Pub Info & Commun Relat Sch, New Rochelle, NY, grad, 64. Polit & Govt Pos: Campaign aide, Curtis for Cong Comt, Gen Elec, 64; Curtis for Gov Comt, Gen & Primary Elec, 66; area coordr Nebr & SDak, Kennedy for Pres Comt, Primary Elec, 68; advan coordr, Curtis for Gov Comt, Gen Elec, 70; vchmn, Sagadahoc Co Dem Comt, 70-72; field coordr, McGovern for President Comt, Calif, 72; campaign mgr, WTex for McGovern/Shriver, 72; spec asst to comnr, Dept of Com, 72- Mil Serv: Entered as Pvt E-1, Army, 62, released as Sgt E-5, 66, after serv in Air Defense Command. Mem: KofC; Maine Press Asn. Relig: Catholic. Legal Res: 15 Higgins St Augusta ME 04330 Mailing Add: State House Augusta ME 04330

COFFEY, MAX E (D)
Ill State Sen
Mailing Add: RR 4 Charleston IL 61920

COFFEY, VIRGINIA MAE (D)
Chmn, Harlan Co Dem Party, Nebr
b Orleans, Nebr, Apr 11, 29; d Alvin Custer Steadman & Ora Alice Kennedy S; m 1946 to Robert Ray Coffey; c Judith Anne (Mrs Foster), Janet Rae (Mrs Kittle), Robert James, Brent Alvin & Bruce Jay. Educ: Orleans Pub Sch, grad. Polit & Govt Pos: Vchmn, Harlan Co Dem Party, Nebr, 66-70, chmn, 70-; deleg, Nebr Dem State Conv, 68-70 & 72; 38th Legis dist mem, Nebr State Dem Cent Comt, 72- Mem: Eastern Star; Am Legion Auxiliary; Epsilon Sigma Alpha Int. Relig: Presbyterian. Mailing Add: Box 190 Orleans NE 68966

COFFMAN, MILTON M, JR (D)
Wyo State Rep
b Casper, Wyo, Mar 5, 32; s Milton G Coffman & Charlotte Gantz C; m 1958 to Patricia Hurley; c James Milton & John Patrick. Educ: Univ Wyo, BA; Univ Denver, MPA; Phi Delta Theta. Polit & Govt Pos: City councilman, Casper, Wyo, 65-69, mayor, 68-69, chmn, Community Planning Comn, 69-75; Wyo State Rep, 75- Bus & Prof Pos: Sales mgr, Casper Coca Cola Co, Wyo, 59-62; officer, Title Guaranty Co, Casper, 62-68, secy-treas, 68-75; pres, Natrona Co Abstr Co, 68-75. Mil Serv: Entered as Pvt, Army, 54-56, after serv in Polar Bear Command, Territory of Alaska, 55-56; Good Conduct Medal. Mem: Rotary; CofC; Casper Civic Symphony; Boy Scouts Am (dist finance chmn); Wyo Asn Munic. Honors & Awards: Outstanding Young Man of Year, Jr CofC, 67. Relig: Episcopal. Legal Res: 1725 Bellaire Dr Casper WY 82601 Mailing Add: 537 W Center St Casper WY 82601

COGAN, JOHN FRANCIS, JR (D)
State Committeeman, Mass Dem Party
b Boston, Mass, June 13, 26; s John Francis Cogan & Mary Galligan C; m to Mary Therese Hart; c Peter G, Pamela E, Jonathan C & Gregory M. Educ: Harvard Col, AB cum laude, 49; Harvard Law Sch, LLB, 52. Polit & Govt Pos: Mem, Lexington Dem Town Comt, Mass, 62-, chmn, 67-68; mem, Lexington By-Law Comt, 65-66; representative mem, Lexington Town Meeting Mem, 65-73; trustee, Lexington Trustee of Pub Trusts, 66-67; mem, Lexington Capital Expenditures Comt, 67-; state committeeman, Mass Dem Party, 68- Bus & Prof Pos: Partner, Hale & Dorr, Boston, Mass, 52-; pres & dir, Fund Research & Mgt, Inc, Boston, Pioneer Fund Inc, Pioneering Mgt Corp, Pioneer II & Pioneer Plans Corp; chmn exec comt & dir, Pioneer Western Corp, Fla, 68-; sr vpres & dir, Western Reserve Life Assurance Co, Ohio, 68-; dir, Walker Home for Children, 70; dir, Spaulding & Slye Corp, 71-; trustee, Boston Univ Med Ctr, 72- Mil Serv: Entered as A/S, Navy, 44, released as PO, 46, after serv in CBMU 509, Pac Theatre, 44-46. Mem: Univ Hosp (pres & trustee); Boston, Am & Inter-Am Bar Asns; Boston Estate & Bus Planning Coun. Legal Res: 29 Patterson Rd Lexington MA 02173 Mailing Add: 28 State St Boston MA 02109

COGHILL, JOHN BRUCE (R)
Chmn, Rep Party of Alaska
b Fairbanks, Alaska, Sept 24, 25; s William Alexander Coghill & Winefred Fortune C; m 1948 to Frances Mae Gilbert; c Patricia M (Mrs Brown), John B, Jr, James A, Jerald F, Paula M & Jeffry G. Educ: Franklin K Lane High Sch, grad, 48. Polit & Govt Pos: Precinct chmn, Nenana Precinct, Alaska, 48-52; mem, House of Rep, Territorial Legis, 52-54 & 57-59; deleg, Alaska State Const Conv, 55-56; Alaska State Sen, 59-65; mayor, City of Nenana, 61-; admin

aid, Gov Hickels Staff, 67-68; dist chmn, Rep State Party, 71-72; deleg & chmn deleg, Rep Nat Conv, 72; state chmn, Rep Party of Alaska, 72-; mem, Rep Nat Comt, 72- Bus & Prof Pos: Partner, Coghill's Inc, Nenana, Alaska, 48-; owner, Tortella Lodge & Apts, 51-, J B Coghill Co Oil Co, 58- & Nenana Fuel Co, 60- Mil Serv: Entered as Pvt, Army, 44, released as S/Sgt, 46, after serv in Alaska Command, Pacific Theatre, 44-46; Pacific Theatre Ribbon. Mem: Int Consumer Credit Asn; VFW; Alaska Jaycees; State Sch Bd Asn; F&AM. Relig: Episcopal. Mailing Add: PO 268 Nenana AK 99760

COGMAN, DON VERNON **(R)**
b Ponca City, Okla, Aug 11, 47; s Harold Cogman & Mary McDaniel C; m 1968 to Diana Gay Brown. Educ: Univ Okla, BS, 69; Omicron Delta Kappa; Gamma Gamma; Beta Theta Pi. Polit & Govt Pos: Research dir, Okla Rep State Comt, 68-69, asst chmn, 69-72; admin asst to US Sen Dewey Bartlett, Okla, 73- Mil Serv: Sgt, Air Force Res, 4 years. Relig: Presbyterian. Legal Res: 536 NW 41st Oklahoma City OK 73118 Mailing Add: 140 Russell Senate Off Bldg Washington DC 20510

COHALAN, PETER FOX **(R)**
b Sayville, NY, Jan 10, 38; s John P Cohalan, Jr & Marian Fox C; m 1966 to Mary Louise Kjeldsen; c Pierce & Mary Aisling O'Leary. Educ: Manhattan Col, BA, 60; Fordham Univ Law Sch, JD, 63. Polit & Govt Pos: Law clerk, Suffolk Co Court, Riverhead, NY, 64; asst town attorney, Islip, 66-67, town supvr, 72-; alt deleg, Rep Nat Conv, 72; mem, NY State Rep Comt. Bus & Prof Pos: Law partner, Levy, Bishop & Cohalan, Esqs, 68- Mem: NY & Suffolk Co Bar Asns; Sayville Rotary Club; Skills Unlimited; Suffolk Co Salvation Army. Relig: Roman Catholic. Legal Res: 203 Academy St Bayport NY 11705 Mailing Add: 655 Main St Town Hall Islip NY 11751

COHEE, DARWIN DICK **(R)**
b Whittier, Calif, Feb 7, 26; s William Vincent Cohee & Vesta D King C; m 1945 to Nell Arlene Sever; c Renee (Mrs Smith) & Evelyn (Mrs Harrison). Educ: Brawley Union High Sch, Calif, grad; Maritime Speciality Sch, Avalon, Calif. Polit & Govt Pos: Mem, Calif Rep State Cent Comt, 68-, mem, exec bd, 73-; mem, Imperial Co Rep Cent Comt, 68-, finance chmn, 68-71, vchmn, 69-70, mem exec bd, 69-, chmn, formerly. Bus & Prof Pos: Rancher; bd mem, Bonanza Chem Co, Brawley, Calif, 69- Mil Serv: US Maritime Sch, Merchant Marines, 44-46; Pac & Atlantic Serv Ribbons. Mem: Calif Chmn Asn (mem, 71-); Co Chmn Asn (south-cent area chmn, 73-); Elks; Calif Farm Bur (bd mem, Imperial Co Chap, 68-); Calif Beet Growers Asn. Relig: Presbyterian; bd trustees, First Presbyterian Church, Brawley, Calif & bd sessions, 73- Mailing Add: 633 S Rio Vista Brawley CA 92227

COHELAN, JEFFERY **(D)**
b San Francisco, Calif, June 24, 14; m 1939 to Evelyn Elizabeth Ellis; c Pamela Joy (Mrs David Benson), Catherine Anna, Terrence Daniel & Lt(jg) Timothy Douglas, USNR. Educ: Univ of Calif, AB; Grad Sch of Econ, Univ of Calif; Fulbright research scholar, Leeds & Oxford Univs, 53-54. Polit & Govt Pos: Secy-treas, Milk Drivers & Dairy Employees Local 302, 42; mem, Berkeley Welfare Comn, 49-53; city coun, Berkeley, 55; former mem, Armed Serv & DC Comts; US Rep, Calif, 58-70. Bus & Prof Pos: Consult, Univ of Calif, Inst of Indust Rels. Mem: Commonwealth Club of Calif. Legal Res: Berkeley CA Mailing Add: 5609 Broad Branch Rd NW Washington DC 20015

COHEN, BERNARD S **(D)**
Committeeman, Alexandria Dem City Comt, Va
b Brooklyn, NY, Jan 17, 34; s Benjamin Cohen & Fannie Davis C; m 1958 to Rae Rose; c Bennett Alan & Karen Linda. Educ: City Col NY, BBA, 56; Georgetown Univ, JD, 60; Phi Alpha Delta. Polit & Govt Pos: Economist, US Dept Labor, 56-61; committeeman, Alexandria Dem City Comt, 63-, vchmn, 64-67, chmn, 67-68. Bus & Prof Pos: Lawyer; dir, Va Citizens Consumer Coun, 68-69; prof lectr law, George Washington Univ Law Sch, currently. Publ: Co-auth, Environmental Rights & Remedies, Lawyers Coop Publ Co, 72. Mem: Am Trial Lawyers Asn; Alexandria & Am Bar Asns; Northern Va Trial Lawyers Asn; Int Platform Asn. Relig: Jewish. Mailing Add: 4001 Ft Worth Ave Alexandria VA 22304

COHEN, DAVID **(D)**
City Councilman, Philadelphia, Pa
b Philadelphia, Pa, Nov 13, 14; s Frank Cohen & Rachel Krangel C; m 1946 to Florence Herzog; c Mark B, Denis P, Sherrie J & Judy L. Educ: Univ Pa, BS, 34, LLB, 37; Order of the Coif. Polit & Govt Pos: Dem committeeman, Philadelphia, Pa, 54-, treas, ward exec comt, 56-66, ward leader, 17th ward, 66-, mem, Dem city comt, 66-; city councilman, Eighth Dist, 68-, chmn, City Coun Health & Welfare Comt, 68-71; deleg, Dem Nat Conv, 68; mem, State Comt New Dem Coalition, Pa, 69- Bus & Prof Pos: Law practice, 38- Mil Serv: Entered as Pvt, Army, 43, released as S/Sgt, 46, after serv in Med & Eng Corps, Pac Theatre, British & Dutch New Guinea, 44-46; Pac Theatre awards. Mem: Philadelphia, Pa & Am Bar Asns; Philadelphia Patent Law Asn; Urban League. Honors & Awards: Various community awards. Relig: Jewish. Legal Res: 5635 N 16th St Philadelphia PA 19141 Mailing Add: Suite 1420 1420 Walnut St Philadelphia PA 19102

COHEN, DAVID NORMAN **(D)**
Chmn, Ontario Co Dem Party, NY
b. Troy, NY, Aug 16, 38; s John I Cohen & Betty Weinstein C; m 1965 to Susan Steinborn; c Leslie, Johanna & Josh. Educ: State Univ NY Binghamton, BA, 59; Brooklyn Law Sch, LLB, 62, JD, 67. Polit & Govt Pos: City attorney, Geneva, NY, 66-68 & 72-; chmn, Ontario Co Dem Party, 74- Mil Serv: Entered as Pvt, Nat Guard, released as E-5, 62-68. Mem: Geneva Lions; Am Heart Asn (pres, Finger Lakes Chap, 72-73); Geneva Savings Bank (trustee); Geneva Gen Hosp (trustee). Relig: Jewish. Mailing Add: 19 Maplewood Dr Geneva NY 14456

COHEN, EDWIN SAMUEL **(R)**
b Richmond, Va, Sept 27, 14; s LeRoy S Cohen & Miriam Rosenheim C; m 1944 to Helen Herz; c Edwin Carlin, Roger & Susan Wendy. Educ: Univ Richmond, BA, 33; Univ Va, LLB, 36; Omicron Delta Kappa; Phi Beta Kappa; Pi Delta Epsilon; Order of the Coif; Raven Soc Univ Va; Phi Epsilon Pi. Polit & Govt Pos: Mem & counsel, Adv Group on Subchapter C (Corporate Transactions), Comt on Ways & Means, US House of Rep, 56-58; consult, Va Income Tax Study Comn, 66-68; mem, Adv Group to Comnr of Internal Revenue, 67-68; Asst Secy for Tax Policy, Treas Dept, 69-72, Under Secy of Treas, 72-73. Bus & Prof Pos: Assoc, Sullivan & Cromwell, New York, 36-49; partner, Root, Barrett, Cohen, Knapp & Smith, 49-65; prof law, Univ Va, 65-68, Joseph M Hartfield prof law, 68-69 & 73-; counsel, Barrett, Knapp, Smith & Schapiro, New York, 65-69; Covington & Burling, currently. Publ: Co-auth, A technical revision of the federal income tax treatment of corporate distributions to shareholders, Columbia Law Rev, 52; auth, Taxing the state of mind, Tax Exec, 60; Substantive federal tax reform, Va Law Rev, 64. Mem: Am Law Inst; Am Judicature Soc; Am, NY State & Va State Bar Asns. Honors & Awards: Nat Achievement Award; Alexander Hamilton Award, US Treas Dept. Relig: Jewish. Legal Res: 104 Stuart Pl Ednam Forest Charlottesville VA 22901 Mailing Add: Covington & Burling 888-16th St NW Washington DC 20006

COHEN, GERALD M **(D)**
Mass State Rep
Mailing Add: State Capitol Boston MA 02133

COHEN, LAWRENCE DAVID **(DFL)**
Mayor, St Paul, Minn
b St Paul, Minn, Apr 17, 33; s Sol Cohen & Rose Bromberg C; m 1959 to Anita Gail Wolfe; c Sam, Charles, Amy & Scott. Educ: Univ Minn, BA, 55, JD, 57; Phi Delta Phi; Sigma Alpha Mu. Polit & Govt Pos: Chmn, Young Dem-Farmer-Labor Party, Fourth Cong Dist, Minn, 54-55, Dem-Farmer-Labor Party, Fourth Cong Dist, 64-66, St Paul Housing & Bldg Code Appeals Bd, 68-70 & Rev Bd, Minn Security Hosp, 70-72; mem, Ramsey Co Bd of Comnrs, 70- & St Paul-Ramsey Co Criminal Justice Adv Comt, 70-; chmn, St Paul-Ramsey Co Detention & Corrections Authority, 72-; vchmn, St Paul-Minneapolis Metrop Airports Comn, 72-; mem, Ramsey Co Welfare Bd, 72-; mayor, St Paul, 72- Bus & Prof Pos: Attorney, Harold Ruttenberg Law Firm, St Paul, Minn, 57-63 & Ruttenberg, Orren, Griswold & Cohen Law Firm, 63-71. Mem: Ramsey Co & Minn State Bar Asns; Big Bros of Gtr St Paul, Inc (bd dirs, 68); Am Pub Works Asn. Relig: Jewish. Legal Res: 1812 Wordsworth Ave St Paul MN 55116 Mailing Add: 15 W Kellogg Blvd St Paul MN 55102

COHEN, MARK B **(D)**
Pa State Rep
b New York, NY, June 4, 49; s David Cohen & Florence Herzog C; single. Educ: Univ Pa, BA, 70. Polit & Govt Pos: Cong Intern, US House of Rep, 67; sen intern, US Senate, 68; Pa State Rep, 74- Mem: Olney-Lindley Lions; Big Four Fathers Asn; Olney Community Coun; Ogontz Area Neighbors Asn; Oak Lane Community Action Asn. Relig: Jewish. Legal Res: 5635 N 16th St Philadelphia PA 19141 Mailing Add: 1420 Walnut St Suite 1420 Philadelphia PA 19102

COHEN, MARVIN S **(D)**
Parliamentarian, Ariz Dem Party
b Akron, Ohio, Oct 16, 31; s Norman J Cohen & Faye Abramovitz C; m 1953 to Frances E Smith; c Samuel D, Jeffrey L & Rachel A. Educ: Univ Ariz, BA & LLB; Phi Beta Kappa; Blue Key; Phi Kappa Phi; Chain Gang; Delta Sigma Rho. Polit & Govt Pos: Pres, Young Dem of Ariz, 60; chmn, Pima Co Dem Cent Comt, 60, parliamentarian, 70-; spec asst to the solicitor, Dept of Interior, 61-63; pres, Dem for Better Govt, 64; precinct committeeman; parliamentarian, Ariz Dem Party, 70- Bus & Prof Pos: Chief civil dep co attorney, Pima Co, Ariz, 58-60; first city attorney, Tucson, 61; attorney, Boyle, Bilby, Thompson & Shoenhair, 63- Mil Serv: Entered as 2nd Lt, Air Force, 53, released as 1st Lt, 55. Mem: Am Trial Lawyers Asn; B'nai B'rith; Ariz & Pima Co Bar Asns; Am Bd Trial Advocates. Relig: Jewish. Mailing Add: 4645 E San Carlos Pl Tucson AZ 85716

COHEN, MORRIS N **(D)**
Conn State Rep
Mailing Add: 24 Terry Plains Rd Bloomfield CT 06002

COHEN, NATHAN **(D)**
Chmn, Wash Co Dem Comt, Maine
b Bangor, Maine, Feb 13, 13; s Jacob Cohen & Alice C; m 1946 to Miriam Berman. Educ: Univ of Maine, BA. Polit & Govt Pos: Mem, Dem City Comt, Maine, formerly; mem, Eastport City Coun, 58, chmn, 59-60; Dem State Committeeman, Wash Co, 62-65; deleg, Dem Nat Conv, 64, alt deleg, 72; mem, Gov Exec Coun, Maine, 65-72; mem, Wash Co Dem Comt, Maine, chmn, currently; chmn, Eastport Dem City Comt, currently. Bus & Prof Pos: Pres, Wash Co Econ Develop Corp, 66- Mil Serv: Entered as Pvt, Air Force, 43, released as Pfc, 46. Mem: Eastport CofC; Salvation Army, Eastport; Am Legion; CofC; Eastport Mem Hosp (trustee). Relig: Jewish. Mailing Add: 39 Boynton St Eastport ME 04631

COHEN, SY **(D)**
b Brooklyn, NY, Oct 28, 18; s Isidor Cohen & Pauline Kahnner C; m to Geraldine Wayman; c David & Paul. Educ: NY Univ, 37-50; Brooklyn Col, 40-41; Univ Wis, 42. Polit & Govt Pos: Exec bd, NY State Socialist Party, 46-47; vchmn, Comt on Human Rels, Town of New Windsor, 70-73; deleg, Dem Nat Conv, 72; deleg, Dem Nat Mid-Term Conf, 74. Bus & Prof Pos: Mgr, Textile Workers Union of Am Joint Bd, 45-; mgr, NY State CIO Standing Comt on Polit Action, 46-50, secy-treas, CIO, 47-50; secy-treas, AFL-CIO, Hudson Valley Area, 50-, mem, NY State AFL-CIO Standing Comt on Polit Educ, 50-, Nat coordr, 26th & 27th Cong Dist AFL-CIO, 62-; standing mem, Jewish Labor Comt, 70- Mil Serv: Entered as Pvt, Army Air Force, 43, released as Sgt, 44, after serv in Air Force. Mem: Cornell Sch of Mgt & Labor Educ & Rels; Hudson Valley Econ Coun; Northern Metrop Hosp Coun; Independent Fedn of Textile Employees; Textile Union Workers. Honors & Awards: Man of the Year Award, AFL-CIO, 59. Relig: Hebrew. Mailing Add: 522 Union Ave New Windsor NY 12550

COHEN, TED E **(D)**
b New York, NY, Aug 13, 22; s Irving Cohen & Gertrude Canton C; div; c Constance, James & Ellen. Educ: Bucknell Univ, 40-41; US Naval Acad, 41-43; Fla Int Univ, BA, 75; Sigma Alpha Mu. Polit & Govt Pos: Chmn, Dade Co Dem Exec Comt, Fla, 71-72; state committeeman, Fla State Dem Exec Comt, 71-74; Fla State Rep, 72-74. Bus & Prof Pos: Pres, Ted Cohen Assocs, Pub Rels, 60- Mil Serv: Entered as Midn, Navy, 41, released, 43, after serv in US Naval Acad, Annapolis. Publ: Florida fashion directory, Ted Cohen, 69-71. Mem: Elks (Exalted Ruler, 71-72); Shrine (Ambassador, 66-); Jewish War Vet (nat dep legis off, 72-74); Miami Beach Jr CofC; Miami Beach Civitan Club. Honors & Awards: Distinguished Serv Award, US Jr CofC, 52; Cooper-Taylor Mem Award, Fla Jr CofC, 61; Merit Award, Fla Fashion Coun, 65-67; United Teachers Legis Award, 74; Dem Legis Award, 74. Relig: Jewish. Legal Res: 4101 Pine Tree Dr Miami Beach FL 33140 Mailing Add: 1 Lincoln Rd Miami Beach FL 33139

COHEN, WILBUR JOSEPH **(D)**
b Milwaukee, Wis, June 10, 13; s Aaron Cohen & Bessie Rubenstein C; m 1938 to Eloise Bittel; c Christopher, Bruce & Stuart. Educ: Univ Wis, PhB, 34; Artus; Phi Kappa Phi; Athenia. Hon Degrees: LHD, Adelphi Col, 62, Univ Wis, 66, Brandeis Univ, 68, Kenyon Col, Univ Louisville & Univ Detroit, 69, Cleveland State Univ & Ohio State Univ, 70 & Fla State

Univ, 71. Polit & Govt Pos: Asst to exec dir, President Roosevelt's Cabinet Comt Econ Security, 34-35; tech adv to comnr for social security, Dept Health, Educ & Welfare, 35-52, dir div research & statist, Social Security Admin, 53-56, asst secy for legis, 61-65, Under Secy, 65-68, Secy, 68-69; chmn, President Kennedy's Task Force on Health & Social Security, 60-61. Bus & Prof Pos: Prof pub welfare admin, Sch Social Work, Univ Mich, 56-61 & 69-; vis prof, Univ Calif, Los Angeles, 57; lectr, Cath Univ, 61-62; pres, Nat Conf Social Welfare, 69-70; prof educ & dean sch educ, Univ Mich, 69-, co-chmn, Inst of Gerontology, 69- Publ: Retirement Policies in Social Security, Univ Calif, 57; co-auth, Social Security: Programs, Problems and Policies, Irwin, 60; co-auth, Income and Welfare, McGraw, 62; plus others. Mem: Nat Asn Social Workers; Am Pub Welfare Asn (pres, 75-76); Am Econ Asn; Indust Rels Res Asn; Nat Dem Club. Honors & Awards: Asn Phys & Ment Rehabilitation Award, 65; Nat Asn Ment Retarded Children Award, 66; Am Pub Health Bronfman Prize & Rockefeller Pub Serv Award, 67; Murray-Green Award and Vols of America Award, 68; Hull House Jane Addams Medal, 75. Relig: Jewish. Legal Res: 620 Oxford St Ann Arbor MI 48104 Mailing Add: Sch of Educ Univ of Mich Ann Arbor MI 48104

COHEN, WILLIAM S (R)
US Rep, Maine
b Bangor, Maine, Aug 28, 40; s Reuben Cohen; m 1962 to Diane Dunn; c Kevin & Christopher. Educ: Bowdoin Col, BA cum laude, 62; Boston Univ Law Sch, LLB, 65; James Bowdoin Scholar; Undergrad Research Fel; Alumni Fund Scholar, Sewall Latin Prize; Emery Latin Prize, twice; Paul Nixon Award for Leadership; mem, Lt Mag & Dramatics Club; co-capt, Varsity Basketball; mem, All State; New Eng Hall of Fame Team. Polit & Govt Pos: Mem, Zoning Bd Appeals, Bangor, 67-69; mem staff, Gov State Credit Research Comt, 68; mem, Bangor City Coun, 69-72, chmn finance comt, 70-71; mem, Bangor Sch Comt, 70-71; mayor, Bangor, 72; trustee, Unity Col, Maine; mem bd of overseers, Bowdoin Col, 73; US Rep, Maine, 73- Bus & Prof Pos: Asst ed-in-chief, J Am Trial Lawyers Asn, 65-66, co-ed & auth, Volumes 32 & 33; partner, Paine, Cohen, Lynch, Weatherbee & Kobritz, Law Firm, 66-72; instr, Husson Col, Maine, 66; asst co attorney, Penobscot Co, 68-70; instr, Univ Maine, 68-72; ed, Maine Trial Lawyers Asn, co-chmn no fault-ins comt & judicial selection comt, formerly vpres, 70-72. Publ: Lawyers and judges, the nature of the judicial process (book rev), Boston Univ Law Rev. Honors & Awards: Fel, John F Kennedy Inst Polit, 72; Distinguished Serv Award, Jaycees, 73, Outstanding Young Man, 73. Relig: Unitarian-Universalist Church. Legal Res: Bangor ME 04401 Mailing Add: 1223 Longworth House Off Bldg Washington DC 20515

COHORN, LEON JAMES (D)
Chmn, Dawson Co Dem Comt, Tex
b Sinton, Tex, Feb 6, 37; s Marshall Franklin Cohorn & Annie Lou Cline C; m 1959 to Eva Mildred Paul; c Lisa Camille & Mark Alan. Educ: Hardin-Simmons Univ, BA, 60. Polit & Govt Pos: Chmn, Dawson Co Dem Comt, Tex, 69- Bus & Prof Pos: Agent, Southern Farm Bur Ins Co, Waco, Tex, 63-67 & Nat Farmers Union Ins Co, Denver, Colo, 67- Mil Serv: Entered as 2nd Lt, Army, 60, released as 1st Lt, 62, after serv in Second Armored Div, 60-62. Mem: Nat Asn Securities Dealers; Kiwanis; Nat Farmers Union. Relig: Baptist. Legal Res: 209 Highland Dr Lamesa TX 79331 Mailing Add: Rte D Lamesa TX 79331

COIL, HENRY WILSON, JR (R)
b Riverside, Calif, Dec 27, 32. Educ: Univ Calif, Berkeley; West State Univ Col Law; Alexander Hamilton Inst; Theta Tau; Lambda Chi Alpha; Phi Phi; water polo team. Polit & Govt Pos: Mem, Riverside Young Rep, Calif, 50-64; spec dep, Riverside Co Sheriff's Dept, 62-; city councilman, Riverside, Calif, 63-67; mayor pro tem, 64-65, mem, youth & community comt & city hall comt; mem, Econ Opportunity Bd Riverside Co, 64-67; mem, Calif Rep Assembly, 65-; pres, League of Calif Cities, 67- Bus & Prof Pos: Civil engr, Calif Elec Power Co, 57-58, summers 49-55; civil engr, C V Brown Gen Contractors & Civil Engrs, 58-59; plant engr, Hydro Conduit Corp, 59-64; consult engr, Marcus W Meairs Co, 65-; plant engr, Alcan Aluminum Corp, 67-70; mgr opers & eng, Fruit Growers Supply Co, 70- Mil Serv: Engr, Navy, 55-61, Philippines; Mil Commendation. Mem: Am Concrete Inst; Am Pub Works Asn; Los Angeles Engrs Club; Assoc Gen Contractors Asn; Am Soc Civil Engrs. Honors & Awards: Eagle Scout Award, Boy Scouts, 48, Award of Merit, Silver Beaver, 67; One of Outstanding Young Men of Am, US Jaycees, 64, One of Ten Outstanding Young Men of Calif, Jaycees, 65. Mailing Add: 3505 Beechwood Pl Riverside CA 92506

COKER, ERNEST ANDREW, JR (D)
Mem, Tex State Dem Exec Comt
b Houston, Tex, Oct 12, 33; s Ernest Andrew Coker & Evelyn Gilmore C; m 1958 to Joyce Anne Willis; c Cynthia Carol & Cameron Clay. Educ: Baylor Univ, BA & LLB. Polit & Govt Pos: Mem, Tex State Dem Exec Comt, Fifth Sen Dist, 72- Mil Serv: Entered as 2nd Lt, Air Force, 56, released as 1st Lt, 58, after serv in Judge Adv Gen Dept, Strategic Air Command. Relig: Baptist. Mailing Add: 107 Ridgewood Rd Conroe TX 77301

COLBERG, RICHARD A (D)
Mont State Sen
Mailing Add: State Senate State Capitol Helena MT 59601

COLBERT RAMIREZ, SEVERO E E (POPULAR DEMOCRATS, PR)
Rep, PR House Rep
Mailing Add: State Capitol San Juan PR 00901

COLBURG, DOLORES (D)
Supt Pub Instr, Mont
b Big Timber, Mont, Apr 3, 32; d Victor Jerome Erickson & Doris Webb E; div. Educ: Eastern Mont Col, 61-62; Univ Colo, 62-63; Univ Mont, BA with honors, 64; Col Young Dem. Polit & Govt Pos: Secy, Yellowstone Co Dem Cent Comt, Mont, 56-57; vpres, Col Young Dem, Univ Mont, 63-64; Supt Pub Instr, Mont, 69- Mem: Am Asn Univ Women; Coun Chief State Officers; Nat Educ Asn; Am Asn Sch Adminr; Univ Mont Alumni Asn. Relig: Protestant. Legal Res: 301 W Lawrence Helena MT 59601 Mailing Add: PO Box 992 Helena MT 59601

COLBY, WILLIAM EGAN
Dir, Cent Intel Agency
b St Paul, Minn, Jan 4, 20; s Elbridge Colby & Margaret Egan C; m 1945 to Barbara Heinzen; c Jonathan, Catherine (deceased), Carl, Paul & Christine. Educ: Princeton Univ, BA, 40; Columbia Univ, LLB, 47; Phi Beta Kappa. Polit & Govt Pos: With Nat Labor Rels Bd, 49-50; attache, Am Embassy, Stockholm, Sweden, 51-53 & Rome, Italy, 53-58, first secy, Am Embassy, Saigon, Vietnam, 59-62; chief, Far East Div, Cent Intel Agency, 62-67, exec dir, 72-73, dep dir opers, 73, dir, 73-; Ambassador Dir, Civil Opers & Rural Develop Support, Saigon, 68-71. Mil Serv: Maj, Army, 41-45; Silver Star; Bronze Star; St Olaf's Medal; Croix de Guerre. Mem: Cosmos; Spec Forces Club; Linge Klubben Club; France Combattant Club. Relig: Roman Catholic. Legal Res: 5317 Briley Pl Washington DC 20016 Mailing Add: Cent Intel Agency Washington DC 20505

COLCLOUGH, ANDREW EVERETT (R)
Chmn, Young Rep Fedn Va
b Ottawa, Ont, Apr 20, 43; s Otho T Colclough & Virginia Brown C; m 1966 to Virginia Louise Barberousse; c Steven Randolph. Educ: Duke Univ, AB, 65; Washington & Lee Univ, LLB, 68; Phi Alpha Delta. Polit & Govt Pos: Treas, Young Rep Fedn Va, 70-71, chmn, 71-; mem, Va State Rep Exec Comt, 71-73; mem, Va State Rep Cent Comt, 71-73; chmn, Young Virginians for Scott for US Senate, 72. Bus & Prof Pos: Attorney, Adams, Porter, Radigan & Mays, 68- Mem: Am & Arlington Bar Asns; Va State Bar; Northern Va Lawyers Asn (secy, currently); Arlington Jaycees. Honors & Awards: Jaycee of the Year, Lexington Jaycees, 68; Young Rep of the Year, Young Rep Fedn of Va, 72. Relig: Baptist. Mailing Add: 3115 S Sixth St Arlington VA 22204

COLCORD, HARRY HENRY (D)
b Wausau, Wis, Aug 10, 51; s Robert Earl Colcord, Sr & Josephine Rieck C; m 1972 to Patrice Mary Raugh. Educ: Univ Wis-Stevens Point, BS, 73; Phi Alpha Theta; Polit Sci Asn. Polit & Govt Pos: Chmn Seventh Dist Youth, Staff Advance Man, Humphrey for President, 72; alt deleg, Dem Nat Conv, 72. Bus & Prof Pos: Student asst, Univ Wis, 71-72. Honors & Awards: Highest Acad Honors, Dean, Col of Letters & Sci, 70-72. Relig: Catholic. Mailing Add: 909 1/2 S Sixth Ave Wausau WI 54401

COLDREN, JOHN (R)
Ind State Rep
b Portland, Ind, Jan 6, 44; s Colwell Coldren & Nilah May C; m 1965 to Diane Wiley; c Jade, Eric & Julie. Educ: Manchester Col, BS, 66; Ind Univ Sch Law, Bloomington, JD, 69; Phi Alpha Delta. Polit & Govt Pos: Ind State Rep, 75- Bus & Prof Pos: Attorney, Keith Fraser Law Off, Portland, Ind, 69-71 & Coldren & Frantz, 71- Mem: Jay Co, Ind State & Am Bar Asns; Portland Found (secy, 75-76); Portland Lions. Honors & Awards: Outstanding Young Man of Year, Portland Jaycees, 72. Relig: Methodist. Legal Res: 520 E High Portland IN 47371 Mailing Add: Box 1013 Portland IN 47371

COLDWELL, COLBERT (D)
b El Paso, Tex, Apr 30, 21; s Ballard Coldwell & Eleanor Eubank C; m 1945 to Ida Wesson; c Carlisle Navidomskis & Ballard Eubank. Educ: Tex A&M Univ, BS, 43. Polit & Govt Pos: Mem sch bd, Clint, Tex, 54-62; precinct chmn, Clint, 56-58; US Comnr, El Paso, 65-66; judge, El Paso Co, Tex, 67-70; chmn, El Paso Co Dem Party, formerly. Bus & Prof Pos: Cottonseed oil mill mgr, Navasota, Tex, 46-50; farmer, El Paso Co, 50-; attorney, El Paso, 61- Mil Serv: Entered as Pvt, Army, 43, released as 1st Lt, 46, after serv in 32nd Cavalry Reconnaissance Squadron, Am Theatre. Mem: Am & El Paso Co Bar Asns; State Bar Tex; El Paso Kiwanis Club. Relig: Catholic Anglican Communion. Legal Res: 992 Old Hueco Tanks Rd El Paso TX 79927 Mailing Add: 1400 Bassett Tower El Paso TX 79901

COLE, BERT L (D)
State Comnr Pub Lands, Wash
b Arlington, Wash, May 12, 10; m 1937 to Norma Chittick. Educ: Western Wash Col Educ; Univ Wash, BA in Sociol, 35. Polit & Govt Pos: State comnr pub lands, Wash, 57-; mem sch bd, Quillayute Valley Sch Dist; comnr, Clallam Co; city councilman, Montesano; mem pub lands comt, Interstate Oil Compact Comn; state coordr, NCascades Study; mem, Interagency Comt for Outdoor Recreation; mem, State Adv Comt Rural Area Develop; state coordr between fed govt & univs, McIntire-Stennis Coop. Forestry Research Prog; mem adv coun, Pub Land Law Rev Comn. Bus & Prof Pos: Owner, logging bus, Forks, Wash; asst mgr, Nat Bank of Com, Montesano Br; jr high sch prin, Montesano; grade sch prin, Adna. Mil Serv: Entered as Pvt, Army, 42, released as Capt, 47, after serv in Signal Corps. Mem: CofC; Am Legion; Eagles; Elks; Mason. Mailing Add: Dept Natural Resources Olympia WA 98504

COLE, BETH ELLEN (D)
b Baltimore, Md, Nov 24, 37; d Albert J Shochat & Rose Blechman S; m 1960 to Donald Alan Cole; c Cynthia, Deborah & Julia. Educ: Mary Washington Col, Univ Va, BA, 59. Polit & Govt Pos: Chmn citizens' comt, Tydings Campaign, 70; pub rels dir, McGovern Primary Campaign, 71-72; off mgr & staff, McGovern Campaign, 72; deleg, Dem Nat Conv, 72; hq mgr & exec secy staff, Reelec Campaign Mandel-Lee, 74. Mem: Woman's Suburban Dem Club (legis chmn, 71); Regency Estates Citizens' Asn; Georgetown Hill PTA. Relig: Jewish. Mailing Add: 11706 Castlewood Ct Potomac MD 20854

COLE, CHARLES MORTON (R)
Treas, 17th Cong Dist Rep Comt, Ohio
b Topeka, Kans, Nov 16, 26; s Ferd Cole & Mary C; m 1947 to Shirley Ann Hauger; C Kevin Eugene & Thomas Courtney. Educ: Ohio State Univ, 45-46. Polit & Govt Pos: Past treas & past pres, Knox Co Young Rep Club, Ohio; chmn, Knox Co Rep Cent & Exec Comts, 60-70 & 72-74, secy, 70-72; treas, 17th Cong Dist Rep Comt, 60-; asst doorkeeper, Rep Nat Conv, 64, deleg, 68; mem, Knox Co Bd Elec, 70-; comnr, Knox Co, 72- Bus & Prof Pos: Asst mgr, Sears Roebuck & Co, 50-71. Mem: Mason; Scottish Rite; Shrine; CofC. Relig: Congregational. Mailing Add: 711 E High St Mt Vernon OH 43050

COLE, DAVID A (R)
b Bath, NY, Mar 19, 37; s Sterling Cole & Elizabeth Thomas C; m 1968 to Brandreth McAlpin McKinley. Educ: George Washington Univ, AA, 62; Univ Wyo, BSL, 64. Polit & Govt Pos: Staff Asst to Congressman Howard Robison, 65; consult, Nat Rep Cong Comt, 66, asst to exec dir & dir admin, 69-74; assoc dir, 75-; field rep, Iowa Rep State Cent Comt, 66-67; spec asst to US Rep Wiley Mayne, 67-69. Mem: Capitol Hill Club; Elks. Relig: Episcopal. Mailing Add: 2612 Fort Scott Dr Arlington VA 22202

COLE, JACK H (D)
Ga State Rep
b Dalton, Ga, July 4, 35; s Jim P Cole & Sadie Caylor C; m 1957 to Mary C Ingle; c Tammy & Katrina. Educ: Dalton High Sch, Ga, grad, 51. Polit & Govt Pos: Ga State Rep, 67- Bus & Prof Pos: Dir, Cole Concrete Prod, Inc, 62-; vpres, Cook & Ingle Equip Co, 64-; pres, Cook & Ingle Co, Inc, 64-; dir, First Nat Bank, Dalton, Ga, 69-; pres, Cook & Ingle Plastics, Inc, 72- Mil Serv: Entered as Airman, Air Nat Guard, 58, released as S/Sgt, 63, after serv in 129th Aircraft Control & Warning Squadron. Mem: Elks; Dalton Country Club. Legal Res: 1802 Elaine Way Dalton GA 30720 Mailing Add: PO Box 626 Dalton GA 30720

COLE, JAMES WILLIAM (D)
b Preston, Ga, Oct 24, 96; s James Henry Cole & Sarah Elizabeth Ball C; m 1925 to Jesie Pritchard. Educ: Univ Ga. Polit & Govt Pos: Past mayor, Parrott, Ga, 3 terms, councilman, 60-; chmn, Terrell Co Dem Comt, formerly. Bus & Prof Pos: Farmer, Terrell Co, Ga, 41- Mil Serv: Entered as Pvt, Army, 18, released as Sgt 1/C, 19, after serv in Chief Finance Off, Paris, France. Mem: Am Farm Bur; Am Legion; 40 et 8; VFW. Relig: Methodist. Mailing Add: PO Box 196 Parrott GA 31777

COLE, JORDAN D (D)
Vt State Rep
Mailing Add: RD 2 Box 2 Putney VT 05346

COLE, JOSEPH E (D)
Finance Chmn, Dem Nat Comt
Polit & Govt Pos: Vchmn, Dem Nat Comt, until 74, finance chmn, 75-; Dem Nat Committeeman Ohio, 75- Legal Res: OH Mailing Add: Dem Nat Comt 2600 Virginia Ave NW Washington DC 20037

COLE, KENNETH J (D)
Pa State Rep
b Gettysburg, Pa, Feb 13, 36; s Richard M Cole & Cathrine Codori C; m 1966 to Marilyn Spear; c Virginia, Laura, Ted & twins, Kenneth Casey & Kathrine. Educ: Gettysburg Col, 58-60. Polit & Govt Pos: Committeeman, Adams Co Dem Comt, Pa, 63-, pres, 64-66, chmn, 68-; committeeman, Pa State Dem Party, 66-68; Pa State Rep, 75- Mil Serv: Entered as A/S, Navy, 54, released as PO 3/C, 58. Mem: Elks; Moose; Am Legion; VFW; CWV. Relig: Roman Catholic. Mailing Add: RD 1 Gettysburg PA 17325

COLE, LINCOLN P, JR (R)
Mass State Rep
Mailing Add: State Capitol Boston MA 02133

COLE, LOUIS V (LOUIE) (R)
Chmn, 53rd Dist Rep Cent Comt, Calif
b Paris, Tex, July 26, 01; s Vance Murray Cole, Sr & Martha E Wood C; div; c Louis, Jr. Educ: Univ Calif, Los Angeles, 21-24; Biggers Bus Col, Los Angeles, Cert, 24; Phi Beta Sigma. Polit & Govt Pos: Chmn, 53rd Dist Rep Cent Comt, Calif, 40-; mem, Area Minority Adv Comt, 48-52; chmn, Spec Comt to Elect Dwight D Eisenhower & Richard M Nixon, 52; comnr, Los Angeles Co Human Rels, 54-62; nominee for Calif State Assemblyman, 53rd Dist, 62 & 68; mem, Rep State Cent Comt of Calif, 69-70; Rep Victory Squad & Airlift, 71; mem, Exec comt, Los Angeles Co Rep Cent Comt. Publ: Publ, Los Angeles Comet, 49-50. Mem: Univ Calif, Los Angeles Alumni Asn; Mason (32 degree); NAACP; Los Angeles Urban League; Gtr Cent CofC. Honors & Awards: Co of Los Angeles Award of Honor; State of Calif Great Seal; Phi Beta Sigma George Washington Carver Award; Valiant Knights Benevolent Soc Achievement Award; 35 Year Serv Award, Hamilton Methodist Church. Relig: Methodist. Mailing Add: 1363 E Washington Blvd Los Angeles CA 90021

COLE, RALPH A (R)
Colo State Sen
b Plattsmouth, Nebr, Mar 25, 15; married. Polit & Govt Pos: Colo State Rep, formerly; Colo State Sen, 73- Bus & Prof Pos: Lawyer. Mailing Add: 10 Wedgeway Littleton CO 80120

COLE, THOMAS E (R)
b Bath, NY, Mar 28, 33; s W Sterling Cole & Elizabeth Thomas C; m 1959 to Joan Beth Matthews; c Craig M Cuthbert, Linda, Thomas E, Jr, Betsy D & Andrew J. Educ: Colgate Univ, AB, 54; Sigma Nu. Polit & Govt Pos: Spec asst to US Rep Howard W Robison, NY, 65-66; admin asst to US Rep Louis C Wyman, NH, 67-69; admin asst to US Sen Norris Cotton, NH, 69-70; exec asst, US Sen James L Buckley, NY, 71-74, admin asst, 74- Bus & Prof Pos: Plant mgr, Seneca Foods Corp, Dundee, NY, 61-63; prod coordr, Honeywell Inc, St Petersburg, Fla, 63-64. Mil Serv: Entered as Off Cand, S/A, Navy, 54, released as Lt(jg), 57, after serv in USS Newport News, Atlantic Fleet & Sixth Fleet, Mediterranean; Nat Defense Medal; European Occup Medal. Mem: Bull Elephants; Cong Secy Club; Asn Admin Assts & Secy; Senate Staff Club. Relig: Protestant. Legal Res: 532 W Lake Rd Hammondsport NY 14840 Mailing Add: 11710 Devilwood Dr Rockville MD 20854

COLE, TOM C (D)
Committeeman, Ariz State Dem Comt
b Yuma, Ariz, Sept 13, 37; s D C Cole & Faye Benton C; m 1960 to Helen Joyce Edwards; c Brent Thomas, Scott Benton & Helen Toby. Educ: Brigham Young Univ, BS, 60; Univ Ariz Col of Law, LLB, 63; Phi Gamma Delta; Phi Delta Phi. Polit & Govt Pos: Chmn, Yuma Co Dem Cent Comt, Ariz, 68-70, committeeman, 72-; vchmn, Ariz State Dem Comt, formerly, committeeman, 72- Bus & Prof Pos: Partner law firm, Westover, Keddie & Choules, Yuma, 66- Mem: Am, Ariz State & Yuma Co Bar Asns; Elks. Relig: Episcopal. Legal Res: 2400 Fourth Pl Yuma AZ 85364 Mailing Add: PO Box 551 Yuma AZ 85364

COLE, WILLIAM EDWIN, JR (D)
b Chestertown, Md, Mar 25, 53; s William Edwin Cole, Sr & Ellen Thomas C; single. Educ: Queen Anne's Co High Sch, grad, 72. Polit & Govt Pos: Deleg, Dem Nat Conv, 72; campaign coordr, Hargraves for Cong, 72; legis asst to Deleg John R Hargraves, Md, 72- Bus & Prof Pos: Jr vpres, Bloomingdale Construction Co, Inc, Queenstown Vol Fire Co; MD State Fireman's Asn; Queen Anne Co Chap Red Cross (dir). Honors & Awards: Cert, Outstanding Fireman, Queenstown Vol Fire Co, 72. Relig: Methodist. Legal Res: Centreville MD 21617 Mailing Add: Box 15 Queenstown MD 21658

COLE, WILLIAM JENNINGS BRYAN (R)
Treas, Rep State Cent & Exec Comt Ohio
b South Webster, Ohio, Apr 26, 97; s John Wesley Cole & Amelia Charlotte Potts C; m to Margaret Ethel Hughes; c Rosemary (Mrs Williamson), Alice Joan (Mrs Hess) (deceased), Ronald Caven & William Howard (deceased). Educ: Rio Grande Col, 16-17. Polit & Govt Pos: Past pres, Scioto Co Men's Rep Club; mayor, South Webster, Ohio, 31-39; exam, Dept Taxation, Ohio, 39-42; dir, Scioto Co Bd Elecs, 42-; deleg, Rep State Conv, 56-74; treas, Rep State Cent & Exec Comt Ohio, 62-; treas, Rep Nat Conv, 64 & 72. Mil Serv: Pvt, Army, 18. Mem: Ohio Asn Elec Officials (chmn legis comt & treas); Lions (pres, South Webster Lions Club). Relig: Methodist. Mailing Add: Tyrell St South Webster OH 45682

COLEMAN, C JOSEPH (D)
Iowa State Sen
b Clare, Iowa, Mar 14, 23; m 1954 to Polly Pflanz; c Joe, Jr, Kevin & Kerry. Educ: Iowa State Univ; Bradley Univ. Polit & Govt Pos: Iowa State Sen, 56-, Minority Whip, Iowa State Senate, 56- Bus & Prof Pos: Farmer; technician, US Dept Agr, formerly; bank dir. Mem: Am Soybean Asn (dir); Am Soybean Inst (vpres). Legal Res: Clare IA 50524 Mailing Add: State Capitol E Tenth & Grand Ave Des Moines IA 50319

COLEMAN, E THOMAS (R)
Mo State Rep
Mailing Add: 2919 NE Russell Rd Kansas City MO 64117

COLEMAN, FLOYD BUTLER (R)
Ind State Rep
b Palmyra, Ind, Dec 24, 17; s George Washington Coleman & Kathryn Klinker C; m 1940 to Eva Lenore Owens; c David Owen, Janet Sue, Diann Elaine (Mrs Penland), Anita Nell, Brenda Lynn, Loretta Gail, Stanley Roger & Rachel Marie. Educ: Ind Univ, Bloomington, BS, 40; Ind Univ, Indianapolis, MD, 45; Nu Sigma Nu. Polit & Govt Pos: Coroner, DeKalb Co, Ind, 48-64; Ind State Rep, DeKalb & Steuben Counties, 13th Dist, 69- Mil Serv: Entered as Pvt, Army, 42, released as Capt, 48, after serv in Ind Univ Med Sch, 42-45 & Percy Jones Army Hosp, Battle Creek, Mich, 46-48. Mem: Am Med Soc; DeKalb Co Med Soc (pres, 64-); Am Acad Gen Practitioners; Ind Flying Physicians; Lions. Relig: Church of Christ. Mailing Add: 425 S Wayne Waterloo IN 46793

COLEMAN, J MARSHALL (R)
Va State Deleg
Mailing Add: PO Box 1206 Staunton VA 24001

COLEMAN, JAMES SAMUEL, JR
b Mobile, Ala, June 8, 06; s James Samuel Coleman (deceased); & Mary Belle Peteet C (deceased); m to Eleanor Ruth Montgomery (deceased); c James Samuel, III; m to Mary Ruth Morgan Hobbs. Educ: US Naval Acad; Univ Ala Law Sch. Polit & Govt Pos: Rural mail carrier, Ala; Ala State Sen, 32nd Dist, 46-50 & 54-56; Assoc Justice, Supreme Court, Ala, 57-75. Bus & Prof Pos: Concrete inspector, 27-28; teacher, Marion Inst & Southern Mil Acad; pvt practice of law, 34-56. Mil Serv: Navy, 42-45. Mem: VFW; Am Legion; Sons Confederate Vet; Lions. Honors & Awards: Outstanding Mem & Best Parliamentarian, Ala State Senate, 55. Relig: Presbyterian; Ruling Elder. Mailing Add: 2803 Woodley Rd Montgomery AL 36111

COLEMAN, JOHN PATRICK (D)
b Minneapolis, Minn, Sept 11, 31; s James W Coleman & Marjorie J Fox C; m 1954 to Patricia A Reding; c Maureen & Kathleen. Educ: St Thomas Col, BA, 53; Univ Minn, 56-58; Arnold Air Soc. Polit & Govt Pos: Press liaison man for US Rep Joe Karth, Fourth Dist, Minn, 61-64; mem, Minn Dem State Cent Comt, 61-65; deleg, Dem Nat Conv, 64; info dir, Off of Emergency Preparedness, Exec Off of the President, Washington, DC, 64-72. Bus & Prof Pos: Dem columnist, Coleman's Corner & feature writer, St Paul-Minneapolis Suburban Newspapers, Minn, 60-64. Mil Serv: Entered as 2nd Lt, Air Force, 53, released as 1st Lt, 55, after serv in 848th Air Control & Weather Squadron, Hokkaido, Japan, 54-55; Capt, Air Force Res, 60-; Korean Serv, UN & Nat Defense Medals. Publ: Red Rover, Red Rover. Mem: VFW; Nat Press Club; KofC; Lions. Relig: Catholic. Mailing Add: 3655 Trinity Dr Alexandria VA 22304

COLEMAN, MARION WILFORD (D)
Chmn, Clay Co Dem Cent Comt, Ill
b Iola, Ill, Nov 11, 17; s Elmer Coleman & Sadie Williams C; m 1947 to Mildred Feldhake; c Thomas, Charles, William, Richard & James. Educ: Eastern Ill Col, Charleston, Ill, 1 year. Polit & Govt Pos: Chmn, Clay Co Dem Cent Comt, Ill, 68- Mil Serv: Entered as Pvt, Army, 42, released as S/Sgt, 45, after serv in 311th Inf, 78th Div, ETO, 44-45; Good Conduct Medal. Mem: Am Legion; Nat Farmers Orgn; Farmers Union; Odd Fellows. Relig: Baptist. Mailing Add: RR 4 Box 79 Louisville IL 62858

COLEMAN, MARY STALLINGS (NON-PARTISAN)
Assoc Justice, Mich Supreme Court
b Tex; d Leslie C Stallings & Agnes Huther S; m 1939 to Creighton R Coleman; c Leslie (Mrs Donald Jackson Hagan) & Carol (Mrs Ival Lee Salyer). Educ: Univ Md, BA, 35; George Washington Univ, JD, 39; Mortar Board; Alpha Lambda Delta; Alpha Psi Omega; Phi Kappa Phi (distinguished mem); Phi Delta Delta; Alpha Omicron Pi (Outstanding Mich Alumna Award). Hon Degrees: DH, Nazareth Col (Mich), 73; LLD, Alma Col, Olivet Col, 73, Eastern Mich Univ, 74 & Western Mich Univ, 74. Polit & Govt Pos: Probate & juvenile court judge, Calhoun Co, Mich, 61-73; Assoc Justice, Mich Supreme Court, 73-; mem, Int Women's Year Comn, 74. Bus & Prof Pos: Lawyer, Washington, DC, 40-46; partner, Wunsch & Coleman, Battle Creek, Mich, 50-61; trustee, Albion Col, 70- Publ: Journal & Periodicals. Mem: Am Bar Found (fel); Mich State Bar; Am Judicature Soc; Nat Asn Juvenile Court Judges; Nat Probate Judges Asn. Honors & Awards: Serv to Children Awards, Calhoun Co Asn Sch Bd, 64, Fraternal Order of Police, 67 & Young Adult Coun NAACP, 69; Distinguished Alumni, Univ Md, 73; Relig Heritage Am Award, Bus & Prof Leader-Law, 74. Relig: Episcopal. Legal Res: 355 E Hamilton Lane Battle Creek MI 49015 Mailing Add: Mich Supreme Court Law Bldg Box 88 Lansing MI 48933

COLEMAN, NANCY JOHNSON (D)
b Springfield, Tenn, Jan 30, 35; d Will Irvin Johnson & Irene Sawyers J; m 1956 to Richard Carlton Coleman; c Charles Edward, II, Cynthia Anne & Tammy Carol. Educ: Austin Peay Univ, 56-57; Draughons Bus Col, 54-56; Patricia Stevens Col, 61-62. Polit & Govt Pos: Secy, Robertson Co Dem Exec Comt, Tenn, 74-; deleg, Dem Nat Mid-Term Comt, 74; deleg, Tenn State Conv, 74-75; mem, Gov Comt, Robertson Co, 75-; supporting mem, Dem Nat Comt, currently. Bus & Prof Pos: Homemaker & farmer, Springfield, Tenn, 56- Mem: DAR; Am Legion (pres, Post 48); United Methodist Women (pres); Am Women in Ger (vpres, 68-70); Protestant Women of Ger (pres, 70). Relig: Methodist. Mailing Add: Rte 5 Springfield TN 37172

COLEMAN, NICHOLAS D (DFL)
Minn State Sen
b St Paul, Minn, 1925; m to Bridget Finnegan; c Nicholas, Patrick, Brendan, Meghan & Christopher. Educ: Col of St Thomas, BA; Univ Minn. Polit & Govt Pos: Minn State Sen, 62-; exec dir, Johnson-Humphrey Vol Comt, 64. Bus & Prof Pos: Owner, Coleman Advert

Agency. Mil Serv: Vet. Mem: St Paul Area CofC; St Paul Sales & Mkt Execs; Ran-View VFW. Mailing Add: 79 Western Ave N St Paul MN 55102

COLEMAN, RONALD D (D)
Tex State Rep
b El Paso, Tex, Nov 29, 41; s Ralph M Coleman & Louise Hooper C; m to Jacquelyn Mowbray; c Kimberly Michelle. Educ: Univ Tex, El Paso, BA, 63; Univ Tex Law Sch, Austin, JD, 67; Lambda Chi Alpha; Orange Key. Polit & Govt Pos: First asst co attorney, El Paso Co, Tex, 69-72; Tex State Rep, 73- Mil Serv: Entered as Lt, Army, 67, released as Capt, 69, after serv in Armored Unit, Third Army, 67-69; Army Commendation Medal. Mem: El Paso Bar Asn (membership comt, 71-, chmn lawyers referral comt, 72-); Tex State Bar Asn; US Fifth Circuit. Relig: Presbyterian. Mailing Add: 1101 E Robinson El Paso TX 79902

COLEMAN, TERRY L (D)
Ga State Rep
Mailing Add: 1201 Fourth Ave Eastman GA 31023

COLEMAN, THOMAS D (R)
Ind State Rep
Mailing Add: 227 Park Ave New Castle IN 47362

COLEMAN, THOMAS WILLIAM (R)
Chmn, Latimer Co Rep Party, Okla
b Shady Point, Okla, Sept 22, 23; s Aden Arthur Coleman & Amelia Boyken C; m 1942 to Marie Mashburn; c Amelia Ann & Tommye Lynn. Educ: High Sch. Polit & Govt Pos: Chmn, Latimer Co Rep Party, Okla, 65-; deleg, Rep Nat Conv, 68. Bus & Prof Pos: Owner, New & Used Automobile agent, 52-69. Mil Serv: Army, 43, Pvt. Mem: CofC; Am Legion. Relig: Baptist. Legal Res: Rte 2 Talihina OK 74571 Mailing Add: Box 607 Talihina OK 74571

COLEMAN, WILLIAM L (D)
b Marysville, Ohio, Feb 6, 14; s John Henry Coleman & Marie Zacharias C; m 1940 to Rose Anna Green; c William Henry, Thomas Hewitt, Charlotte Marie, Stephen G, Rose Anna & Michael S. Educ: Ohio Northern Univ, polit sci; Ohio State Univ Col of Law, JD, 39; mem staff, Northern Rev & pres, Sophomore Class, Ohio Northern Univ; Gamma Eta Gamma; Col Law Rep, Ohio State Student Senate; mem staff, OSU Lantern. Polit & Govt Pos: Mem, Young Dem State Exec Comt, Ohio, 12 years; permanent chmn, State Dem Convs, 40-54; prosecuting attorney, Union Co, 41-49; served as permanent chmn of Young Dem Nat Conv, 47; mem, Union Co Bd of Elec, 54-66 & 68-; deleg, Dem Nat Conv, 56-, chmn deleg, 60, secy deleg, 64; chmn, Dem State Exec Comt, Ohio, 56-66 & 68-74; Dem cand for Lt Gov, 66; mem, Comn on Selection of Vice President Cand, Dem Nat Comt, 73- Mem: Union Co Bar Asn; Blue Cross Cent Ohio (bd trustees); Ohio State Nat Law Coun (bd trustees); Newcomen Soc NAm; Kiwanis. Relig: Lutheran; Pres, Church Coun, Trinity Lutheran Church. Mailing Add: RFD 1 Milford Center OH 43045

COLEMAN, WILLIAM MATTHEW (D)
Comnr, Mercer Co, Pa
b Sharon, Pa, Mar 30, 22; s Patrick Henry Coleman & Mary Purcell C; m 1951 to Evelyn De Sales Driscoll; c Mary Gertrude & Elizabeth Ann. Educ: Minor Judiciary Procedure Cert, 56, 57 & 58; Shenango Valley Commercial Inst, 60-61; La Salle Acct Sch, cert, 67. Polit & Govt Pos: Committeeman, Fourth Ward Dem Comt, Sharon, Pa, 50-, alderman, 56-69; chmn, Sharon Dem Comt, 62-66; chmn, Mercer Co Dem Comt, 66 & 67; comnr, Mercer Co, Pa, 68- Mil Serv: Entered as Pfc, Army, 42, released as 1st Sgt, 46, after serv in ETO, 43-46. Mem: Elks; Am Legion; Fraternal Order of Police; KofC. Relig: Catholic. Mailing Add: 272 Cedar Ave Sharon PA 16146

COLEMAN, WILLIAM THADDEUS, JR (R)
Secy of Transportation
b Philadelphia, Pa, July 7, 20; m 1945 to Lovida Hardin; c William T, III, Lovida Hardin, Jr & Hardin L. Educ: Univ Pa, summa cum laude, 41; Harvard Law Sch, magna cum laude, 46. Polit & Govt Pos: Law secy to Judge Herbert F Goodrich, US Court Appeals, Third Circuit, 47; US Supreme Court law clerk, Staff of Late Justice Felix Frankfurter, 48; consult, US Arms Control & Disarmament Agency, 63-75; sr consult & asst counsel, President's Comt on Assassination of President Kennedy, 64; mem, US Deleg to 24th Session of UN Gen Assembly, 69; mem, Nat Comn Productivity, 71-72; Secy of Transportation, 75- Bus & Prof Pos: Sr partner, Law Firm of Dilworth, Paxson, Kalish, Levy & Coleman, Philadelphia; spec counsel to Southeastern Pa Transportation Authority; dir, Pan Am World Airways, Inc, Penn Mutual Life Ins Co, First Pa Corp, Philadelphia Elec Co & Western Saving Fund Soc; mem bd gov, Am Stock Exchange; trustee, Rand Corp; trustee, Brookings Inst. Mem: Am Col Trial Lawyers; Coun on Foreign Rels; Am Law Inst; Am Bar Asn; Am Arbit Asn. Honors & Awards: One of the auth of legal brief that persuaded Supreme Court to outlaw segregation in pub schs, 54; app by former Gov Scranton, Pa, to assist in removing racial restrictions at Girard Col, Philadelphia, 65. Mailing Add: Off of the Secy Dept Transportation Washington DC 20590

COLES, ALBERT LEONARD (D)
Mem, Conn Dem State Cent Comt
b Bridgeport, Conn, Nov 8, 09; s Joseph Coles & Margaret Lennon C; m 1946 to Eileen M Pelath; c Kevin A, Matthew A, Brigid M (Mrs Thornton), Albert L, Jr & Mary Norah. Educ: Yale Univ, BA, 31, Yale Law Sch, LLB, 33; Phi Beta Kappa; Phi Alpha Delta. Polit & Govt Pos: Conn State Sen, 39-41 & 45-47, majority leader, Conn State Senate, 41; judge, City Court Bridgeport, 49-51; chmn, Bridgeport Dem Town Comt, 52-55; Attorney Gen, Conn, 59-63; judge, Superior Court Conn, 63-65; mem, Conn Dem State Cent Comt, 74- Bus & Prof Pos: Dir, People's Savings Bank, 66-, United Illuminating Co, 68- & Southern New Eng Tel Co, 69-; trustee, Park City Hosp, 69-; pres, United Way of Eastern Fairfield Co, 74-75. Relig: Roman Catholic. Legal Res: 140 Sailors Lane Bridgeport CT 06605 Mailing Add: 855 Main St Bridgeport CT 06604

COLES, FRANK VAN DE VEN (R)
b Ottumwa, Iowa, Nov 26, 02; s William Franklin Coles & Anna Marie Van de Ven C; m 1961 to Helen Margaret Lewis; c Linda (Mrs Raymond W Miller). Educ: Iowa Wesleyan Col, BA, 25; Univ Iowa, DDS, 29; Pi Kappa Delta; Omicron Kappa Upsilon. Hon Degrees: DSc, Iowa Wesleyan Col, 67. Polit & Govt Pos: Deleg, Rep State Conv, 58-, mem rules comt, 64; chmn, Henry Co Rep Party, Iowa, formerly; deleg, Rep Nat Conv, 68. Bus & Prof Pos: Dentist, Mt Pleasant, Iowa, 29-; Sr Dent Surgeon, US Pub Health Serv, 50-67. Mil Serv: Entered as Sr Dent Surgeon, Pub Health Serv, 58, released, 67 after serv in Pub Health Serv Res. Publ: Dental Education, Iowa Dent J, 59, 62 & 68. Mem: Am Pub Health Asn; Am Dent Asn; Res Off Asn US Pub Health Serv; Asn US Mil Surgeons; Mason. Honors & Awards: Received Rep Party Serv Award; Legion of Honor, Kiwanis. Relig: Methodist. Mailing Add: 606 E Monroe St Mt Pleasant IA 52641

COLHAPP, BARBARA JONES (DFL)
First VChairwoman, Carver Co Dem-Farmer-Labor Party, Minn
b Mahnomen, Minn Feb 13, 35; d A Elton Jones & Ida Tastad J; m 1959 to Ted C Colhapp; c Andrea & Aaron. Educ: Concordia Col (Minn), BA, 57; Univ Nebr, MA, 58; Phi Kappa Delta. Polit & Govt Pos: Secy, Carver Co Dem-Farmer-Labor Party, Minn, 64-68, chairwoman, 68-70, first vchairwoman, 70-; Carver Co deleg, State Dem-Farmer-Labor Conv, 66 & 68; deleg, Minn State Dem-Farmer-Labor Party Cent Comt, 72- Bus & Prof Pos: Pub sch teacher, 59-63. Mem: Carver Co Sch for Retarded; Carver Co Cancer Orgn; League of Women Voters. Relig: Protestant. Mailing Add: 1294 Valley View Rd Chaska MN 55318

COLLARO, ANDREW (D)
Mass State Rep
Mailing Add: State Capitol Boston MA 02133

COLLAZA, NECTOR (POPULAR DEMOCRATS, PR)
Rep, PR House Rep
Mailing Add: State Capitol San Juan PR 00901

COLLET, ANNE HENDERSHOTT (R)
Chairwoman, Licking Co Rep Party, Ohio
b Wellston, Ohio, July 22, 32; d Donald Cecil Hendershott & Elsie Perry H; m 1959 to George Edward Collet; c Catherine, Christine & Martha. Educ: Bowling Green State Univ, 50-51; Ohio State Univ, BS in Home Econ, 55, grad study, 65, 71 & 72. Polit & Govt Pos: Vchairwoman, Licking Co Rep Party, Ohio, 69-71, chairwoman, 71-; mem credentials comt, Ohio Rep Women, 74-75. Mem: Licking Co Home Econ Asn; Licking Co Licensed Beverage Asn (secy, 75-76); Lions Auxiliary (vpres, 75-76); Licking Co Rep Women. Relig: Catholic. Mailing Add: Rte 1 Harbor Hills Hebron OH 43025

COLLETTA, MIKE (R)
Alaska State Sen
Mailing Add: PO Box 3188 Anchorage AK 99501

COLLEY, LYNN ALLAN (R)
Chmn, Scott Co Rep Cent Comt, Mo
b Sanford, Maine, Oct 31, 45; s Leonard V Colley & Phyllis A Treadwell C; single. Educ: Southeast Mo State Univ, 63-67. Polit & Govt Pos: Committeeman, Scott Co Rep Cent Comt, Mo, 66-, chmn, 68-; chmn, 157th Legis Dist Rep Comt, 66-68. Bus & Prof Pos: Educ chmn, Sikeston Asn Life Underwriters, 72- Mem: AF&AM; Dexter Coin Club (pres); Elks; Sikeston Coun on the Arts (treas); Sikeston Little Theatre, Inc (pres). Honors & Awards: Tom L Chidester Mem Award, Sikeston Little Theatre, 65; Am Legion History Award, 63; Leading Sales Staff Award, Metropolitan Life Ins Co, 73. Relig: Southern Baptist. Legal Res: 305 Edmondson Sikeston MO 63801 Mailing Add: PO Box 74 Sikeston MO 63801

COLLIER, ALBERT (TOM) (D)
Ark State Rep
Mailing Add: 2713 Ivy Newport AR 72112

COLLIER, BETTY FAY (D)
Mem Exec Comt, Oakland Co Dem Party, Mich
b Morgan Co, Ala, May 12, 35; d Luther Guy Wilson & Dessemer Brown W; m 1952 to Nathan DeVoid Collier; c Linda, Tammy & Janice. Educ: Pontiac Bus Sch, Mich, 66; Oakland Community Col, 68-72. Polit & Govt Pos: Mich State treas, Am Independent Party, 67-68; secy, Wallace Campaign, Oakland Co, Mich, 67-68, off mgr, 68; deleg, Dem Nat Conv, 72; secy, 19th Dist Dem Party, 72-; mem exec comt, Oakland Co Dem Party, 72- Mailing Add: 3656 Dill Rd Drayton Plains MI 48020

COLLIER, CHARLES RUSSELL (R)
Chmn, San Mateo Co Rep Cent Comt, Calif
b St Louis, Mo, Apr 10, 23; s Charles Whitfield Collier & Pauline Russell C; m 1947 to Carol Lineer; c Constance, Kathleen & Suzanne. Educ: Stanford Univ, AB with honors, 47, MBA, 48; Delta Sig. Polit & Govt Pos: Vchmn, Rep Alliance, Calif, 66-68, chmn, 68-70; finance chmn, San Mateo Co Rep Cent Comt, 69-73, chmn, 75-; mem, Rep State Cent Comt Calif, 69-75. Bus & Prof Pos: Exec vpres, Pac Plan of Calif, 59-70; owner, Russell Collier Real Estate Investments, 70-73. Mil Serv: Entered as Pvt, Army, 43, released as 1st Lt, 46, after serv in 69th Div, ETO, 44-46; Bronze Star for Valor with Oak Leaf Cluster; Purple Heart. Mem: Better Bus Bur; Peninsula Advert Club; Foothills Club. Relig: Catholic. Mailing Add: 800 Welch Rd Palo Alto CA 94304

COLLIER, CLINT C (D)
Chmn, Neshoba Co Loyalist Dem Party, Miss
b Philadelphia, Miss, Aug 24, 10; s John Collier & Lena Stribling C; m 1940 to Alaid Johnson; c Ann, Steve & Helen. Educ: Jackson Col, 40-41; Howard Univ, 41-47. Polit & Govt Pos: Deleg, Dem Nat Conv, 68; chmn, Nesholia Co Loyalist Dem Party, Miss, currently; Bus & Prof Pos: Teacher of math, 52-65; minister, United Methodist Church, 59-69. Mil Serv: Entered as Seaman 2/C, Navy, 42, released as Seaman 1/C, 45. Mem: Nat Educ Asn; Miss Teachers Asn. Relig: Christian. Mailing Add: Rte 7 Box 187 Philadelphia MS 39350

COLLIER, HAROLD R (R)
b Lansing, Mich, Dec 12, 15; s Joseph Howard Collier & Anna Koener C; m 1938 to Carol Jean Bangert; c Calvin Joseph, Harold Paul & Lynne Ann (Mrs Kulp). Educ: J Sterling Morton Jr Col, 33-34; Lake Forest Col, 34-37; Quill & Scroll Soc; DiGamma Alpha Epsilon. Polit & Govt Pos: Chmn, Cook Co Rep Cent Comt, Ill Berwyn twp committeeman; secy-treas, Cook Co Supvr Asn, 3 years; alderman, Berwyn City Coun, 51; pres, Berwyn Pub Health Bd; pres, Young Rep Club; secy, Third Legis Dist Rep Comt; chmn, First Sen Dist Rep Comt; mem, Rep Policy Comt; US Rep, Ill, 56-75. Bus & Prof Pos: Ed, Berwyn Beacon, 37-38; ed dept, Life Publ, 38-42; personnel mgr, Match Corp Am, 39-51; advert & sales promotion mgr, McAlear Mfg Co, 51-56. Mem: Riverside Dr Improvement Asn; Lake Forest Col Alumni Asn; Nat Coun Drug Abuse (Adv Bd); Int Platform Asn; Am Soc Indust Security. Relig: Methodist. Legal Res: 1950 Hopewood Dr Falls Church VA 22043 Mailing Add: 2202 L'Enfant Plaza Washington DC 20008

COLLIER, JAMES BRUCE **(R)**
Chmn, Lawrence Co Rep Cent Comt, Ohio
b Ironton, Ohio, Sept 25, 20; s James W Collier & Faye Clark C; m 1943 to Bette Elaine Fawcett; c James, Jr & Gretchen J (Mrs Randall). Educ: Miami Univ, 38-41; State Univ Iowa, LLB, 49; Delta Kappa Epsilon; Phi Beta Phi. Polit & Govt Pos: Mem, Lawrence Co Rep Cent Comt, Ohio, 50-, chmn, 67-; mem, Ironton Sch Bd, 63-67. Mil Serv: Entered as Flying Cadet, Army Air Corps, 41, released as Capt, 46, after serv in 504th Bomb Group, 20th Air Force; Air Medal; Purple Heart. Mem: Lawrence Co, Ohio & Am Bar Asns; Elks; Rotary. Relig: Episcopal. Legal Res: 1111 Mastin Ave Ironton OH 45638 Mailing Add: 411 Center St Ironton OH 45638

COLLIER, JOHN L E **(R)**
Calif State Assemblyman
Educ: Occidental Col, AB; Army Intel Sch, Harrisburg, Pa; Prisoner of War Intel Sch, London, Eng. Polit & Govt Pos: Calif State Assemblyman, currently, chmn Rep caucus assembly, chmn Los Angeles deleg, chmn comt educ, vchmn comt water, formerly, mem ways & means comt, educ comt & transportation comt, currently. Mil Serv: Combat Intel Officer, Army, World War II; in invasion, Sicily, Italy, France & Holland. Mem: F&AM; Am Legion; VFW; Amvets; Kiwanis Int. Honors & Awards: Auth first law to regulate lobbyists, sch financing formula which carries name, reduction of classroom size for first, second & third grades, act providing for construction of sewage reclamation plant & coauth, Calif Water Plan. Legal Res: 832 Cooper Ave Los Angeles CA 90042 Mailing Add: Rm 3098 State Capitol Sacramento CA 95814

COLLIER, RANDOLPH **(D)**
Calif State Sen
b Etna, Calif; m 1971 to Barbara Ferris; c John, Suzanne, Camille & Natalie. Educ: Univ Calif. Polit & Govt Pos: Police judge, Yreka, Calif, 25-28; Calif State Sen, 38-; mem, Calif Dem State Cent Comt, 68- Bus & Prof Pos: Pres, Siskiyou Co Title Co. Mem: Odd Fellows; Eagles; Eastern Star; Mason; Shrine. Relig: Episcopal. Mailing Add: Rm 5052 State Capitol Sacramento CA 95814

COLLIER, WOODROW WILSON **(D)**
Chmn, Weakley Co Dem Exec Comt, Tenn
b Martin, Tenn, Nov 20, 15; s John Bevley Collier & Fannie Craig C; m 1933 to Modean Jacobs; c Shirley Ross & Betty Gail. Educ: Stella Ruth High Sch, Tenn, 2 years. Polit & Govt Pos: Mem, Weakley Co Dem Exec Comt, Tenn, 57-, chmn, 68-; co chmn, Farmers for Kennedy & Johnson, 60; co chmn farmers for Johnson & Humphrey, 64; mem & chmn, Co Agr Comt, 62-68; deleg chmn, Dem State Conv, 68; chmn, Co Primary Elec Comn, 69- Bus & Prof Pos: Livestock farmer, 30-; woodcraft art craftsman, 50-; dir, sta WCMT Laymen Prog, 68. Mem: Tenn Livestock Asn; Co CofC Agr Comt; Farm Bur; Co Farm Bur. Honors & Awards: 4-H Leadership & Training Award; cert achievement, Univ Tenn Col Agr. Relig: Methodist; lay speaker. Mailing Add: Rte 4 Martin TN 38237

COLLIGAN, ALLEN LEROY **(DFL)**
Mem Exec Comt, Mahnomen Co Dem-Farmer-Labor Party, Minn
b Bagley, Minn, Oct 20, 41; s Thomas F Colligan & Adeliene Rotsien C; m to Rosemarie Riewer; c Susan & Karen. Educ: Bemidji State Col, BS. Polit & Govt Pos: Chmn, Clearwater Co Young Dem-Farmer-Labor Party, Minn, 60-61; mem, Mahnomen Co Dem-Farmer-Labor Party, 68-, co deleg, 69-, Mem exec comt, currently; deleg, State Conv, 72. Bus & Prof Pos: Teacher, Mahnomen High Sch, 8 years; businessman, 2 years; beauty shop owner, 4 years; drive-in restaurant owner, 70- Mem: State Employees Union; Jaycees (state dir); Nat Educ Asn. Relig: Lutheran; Treas, Mo Synod, 2 years. Mailing Add: Mahnomen MN 56557

COLLINS, BARBARA-ROSE **(D)**
Mich State Rep
b Detroit, Mich, Apr 13, 39; d Lamar N Richardson, Sr & Versa Jones R; wid; c Cynthia Lynn & Christopher Loren. Educ: Wayne State Univ, 57- Polit & Govt Pos: Mem, Detroit Pub Schs Bd, Region 1, Mich, 71-73; comnr, Human Rights Comn, Detroit, 74-75; Mich State Rep, 75- Mem: Int Afro-Am Mus (trustee); Jeffries Day Care & Cult Ctr (bd gov); Black Teachers Caucus. Relig: Black Christian Nationalist. Legal Res: 2256 Leland Detroit MI 48207 Mailing Add: State Capitol Bldg Lansing MI 48901

COLLINS, CARDISS W **(D)**
US Rep, Ill
b St Louis, Mo, Sept 24, 31; m George W Collins, wid 1972; c Kevin. Educ: Northwestern Univ, degree in Prof Acct, 67. Polit & Govt Pos: Committeewoman, Chicago's 24th Ward Regular Dem Orgn, currently; US Rep, Ill, Seventh Dist, 73-, mem, Comt Govt Opers, Subcomt Legal & Monetary Affairs & Subcomt Govt Activities, US House Rep, 73- Bus & Prof Pos: Stenographer, Ill Dept Labor, formerly; secy, acct & revenue auditor, Ill Dept Revenue, formerly. Mem: Lawndale Youth Comn (vpres); NAACP; Gtr Lawndale Conserv Comn. Relig: Baptist. Legal Res: Chicago IL Mailing Add: US House of Rep Washington DC 20515

COLLINS, CATHERINE MARY **(R)**
b Green Bay, Wis, Aug 16, 50; d Francis Thurman Collins & Mary Helen Gotto; single. Educ: Univ Ill, Urbana, BS, 72; Theta Sigma Phi. Polit & Govt Pos: Pres, Univ Ill Col Rep, 71-72; cand for deleg to Rep Nat Conv, Ill 21st Cong Dist, 72; alt deleg-at-lg, Rep Nat Conv, 72; mem, Alexandria Young Rep, Va, currently & Cook Co Young Reps, Ill, currently; intern, Commun Div, Rep Nat Comt, summer 71. Bus & Prof Pos: Spec asst to the exec dir of state field opers, Ill Comt for Reelec of the President, 72; staff asst, Cost of Living Coun, Off of the Gen Counsel, 72-73; conv mgr, Conrad Hilton Hotel, Chicago, Ill, 73- Mem: Women in Commun, Chicago chap. Relig: Roman Catholic. Mailing Add: 426 W Briar Pl Chicago IL 60657

COLLINS, CONSTANCE SULLIVAN **(R)**
Counr, Conn Fedn Rep Women's Clubs
b Holyoke, Mass, Jan 29, 24; d George Wilmer Sullivan & Elizabeth O'Neil S; m 1949 to James Francis Collins; c James Barry, Elizabeth Frances, Patricia Alice & Mary Ellen. Educ: Holyoke Sch Nursing, 42; Boston Univ, Sargent Col, BS in Phys Therapy & Phys Educ, 50; Univ Hartford, MA in Educ, 69; Veterans Club; Phys Therapy Club; Basketball Team; Horseback Riding Club. Polit & Govt Pos: Co-chmn ward, Rep Town Comt, Conn, 52-61; mem exec bd, Hartford Co Rep Women's Asn, 55-, chmn mem comt, 59-61, pres, 61-63, counr, treas & chmn nominating comt, 63-65, chmn legis comt, 64-66; mem, Nat Fedn Rep Women, 55-; alt deleg, Rep State Conv, 58; mem exec bd, Women's Rep Club Hartford, 58-61; mem exec bd, Conn Coun Rep Women, 60-64, mem rev by-laws comt, 62, mem nominating comt; alt deleg, Rep Nat Conv, 64 & 68; pres, Conn Fedn Rep Women's Clubs, 68-69, counr, 69- Bus & Prof Pos: Teacher, Hartford, Conn, 66- Mil Serv: Entered as Seaman, WAVES, 44, released as PO 1/C, 46, after serv as Cartographer, Suitland, Md. Mem: Sargent Col Alumnae; Boston Univ Alumni; Phys Therapy Asn; Sargent Club, Hartford; City Club of Hartford. Relig: Roman Catholic. Mailing Add: 44 Harvest Lane West Hartford CT 06117

COLLINS, DANIEL **(D)**
Mem, Dem Nat Comt, NY
Mailing Add: 819 Carroll St Brooklyn NY 11215

COLLINS, EMMETT MARVIN **(R)**
b Corpus Christi, Tex, Apr 11, 34; s Bruce Livingston Collins & Lucile Tankersley C; single. Educ: Southern Methodist Univ, BBA, 54, JD, 59; Blue Key; Phi Alpha Delta; Alpha Kappa Psi; Alpha Tau Omega. Polit & Govt Pos: Asst to US Rep Bruce Alger, Tex, formerly; exec dir, Dallas Co Rep Hq, 60-62; exec dir, Rep Party, Tex, 63-67; campaign mgr, Linwood Holton, Rep Cand for Gov, Va, 69; Campaign Mgr, Paul Eggers, Rep Cand for Gov, Tex, 68; Campaign Mgr, George Bush, Rep Cand for US Senate, 70; regional dir, Comt for Reelec of the President, 72; admin asst to US Rep Alan Steelman, Tex, 73- Bus & Prof Pos: Partner, Collins-Knaggs & Assocs, 67-71; pres, River City Inn, Inc, Austin, 71-73. Mil Serv: Entered as 2nd Lt, Air Force, 55, released as 1st Lt, 57; Capt, Air Force Res. Relig: Methodist. Legal Res: 2710 Douglas Dallas TX 75219 Mailing Add: 907 Sixth St SW Number 115 Washington DC 20024

COLLINS, FRANCIS JAMES **(R)**
Mem, Brookfield Rep Town Comt, Conn
b Danbury, Conn, Nov 20, 33; s Thomas Collins (deceased) & Sarah Lowe C; m 1956 to Dora M Rencsko; c Kevin J, Keith A, Kathleen A, Kristy & Kyle. Educ: Miami Univ, Oxford, Ohio, BS, 55; Univ Conn Sch Law, LLB, 62. Polit & Govt Pos: Mem, Brookfield Rep Town Comt, 64-; Conn State Rep, 165th Dist, 67-74, Minority Leader, Conn House Rep, 71-72; speaker, 73-74; chmn, Rep State Conv, 72. Bus & Prof Pos: Partner & attorney, Cutsumpas, Collins & Hannafin, Danbury, Conn; dir, Conn Attorneys Title Co, 72- Mil Serv: Entered as Pvt, Army, 56, released as Spec 4/C, 58, after serv in QmC, Ft Lee, Va. Mem: Univ Conn Law Sch Alumni Asn; Am Bar Asn; Brookfield Exchange Club; Brookfield Community Chest; Brookfield CofC. Relig: Roman Catholic. Mailing Add: Beech Tree Rd Brookfield CT 06805

COLLINS, GEORGE WELTON **(D)**
Chmn, Yazoo Co Dem Party, Miss
b Yazoo Co, Miss, Jan 5, 31; s Willie Collins & Viola Vaughn C; m 1954 to Laura B Thomas. Educ: Jackson State Col, BS, 62. Polit & Govt Pos: Chmn, Beat One, Dover Precinct, Miss, 68-; chmn, Yazoo Co Dem Party, Miss, 68-; deleg, Dem Nat Conv, 72; deleg, Dem Nat Mid-Term Conf, 74. Mil Serv: Entered as Pvt, Army, 51, released as Pfc, 53, after serv in 44th Inf Div; Nat Defense Medal; Good Conduct Medal. Mem: F&AM; NAACP (pres); Yazoo Co Dem Party, Miss; Yazoo Community Action Bd; Miss Voter Registr & Educ League. Relig: Protestant. Mailing Add: Rte 3 Box 256 Yazoo City MS 39194

COLLINS, JAMES MITCHELL **(R)**
US Rep, Tex
b Hallsville, Tex, Apr 29, 16; s Carr Pritchett Collins & Ruth Woodall C; m 1942 to Dorothy Colville Dann; c Michael James, Nancy Miles & Dorothy (Mrs Weaver). Educ: Southern Methodist Univ, BSc, 37; Northwestern Univ, MBA, 38; Harvard Sch Bus, MBA, 43; pres of Harvard Student Body; Cycen Fjodr; Phi Delta Theta; Blue Key; Alpha Kappa Psi. Polit & Govt Pos: US Rep, Tex, 68-; deleg, Rep Nat Conv, 72. Bus & Prof Pos: Vpres, Fidelity Union Life Ins Co, Dallas, Tex, 46-54, pres, 54-65. Mil Serv: Entered as Pvt, Army, 43, released as Capt, 46, after serv in 1197 Engrs; ETO, 1 year; Medal of Metz; Four Battle Stars. Mem: Am Legion; VFW. Honors & Awards: Outstanding Mustang Award, Southern Methodist Univ. Relig: Baptist. Legal Res: 10311 Gaywood Rd Dallas TX 75229 Mailing Add: 2419 Rayburn House Off Bldg Washington DC 20515

COLLINS, LEROY **(D)**
b Tallahassee, Fla, Mar 10, 09; s Marvin H Collins & Mattie Brandon C; m 1932 to Mary Call Darby; c LeRoy, Jane, Mary Call & Darby. Educ: Cumberland Univ, LLB, 31. Polit & Govt Pos: Fla State Rep, 34-40; Fla State Sen, 40-54; chmn, Southern Regional Educ Bd, 55-57; mem, Nat Adv Coun Peace Corps; chmn, Nat Pub Adv Comt on Area Develop, US Dept of Com, Gov, Fla, 55-60; chmn of Nat Gov Conf & Southern Gov Conf, formerly; chmn, Comt on Goals for Higher Educ in the South, 61-62; dir, Community Rels Serv, Dept of Com, 64-65, Under Secy of Com, 65-66; Dem cand, US Sen, Fla, 68. Bus & Prof Pos: Pres, Nat Asn of Broadcasters, 61-64. Mil Serv: Navy, Lt. Mem: Nat Conf of Christians & Jews (Honor Corps); Am Bar Asn; Int Radio & TV Soc; Nat Munic League; US Int CofC. Relig: Episcopal. Legal Res: The Grove Adams & First Ave Tallahassee FL 32303 Mailing Add: Ervin Varn Jacobs & Odom PO Box 1170 Tallahassee FL 32302

COLLINS, MARCUS **(D)**
Ga State Rep
Mailing Add: Rte 1 Pelham GA 31779

COLLINS, MARTHA LAYNE **(D)**
Dem Nat Committeewoman, Ky
Mailing Add: Nicholasville Pike Versailles KY 40386

COLLINS, MARVIN BOBBY **(D)**
SC State Rep
b Tarpon Springs, Fla, Mar 17, 29; s Marvin Bartow Collins & Idella Hughes C; m 1948 to Marie Mock; c Mark Ryan & Marcia Ann. Educ: Climax High Sch, Ga, 47. Polit & Govt Pos: SC State Rep, 75- Bus & Prof Pos: Chmn, Quik Way Food Stores, Inc, Anderson, SC, 66-, Quik Way of Carolina, Inc, 67-, Travelers Petrol Inc, 71- & Sports Way Stores Inc, 74-; partner, Lease Way Enterprises, 72- Mil Serv: Entered as Pfc, Army, 52, released as S/Sgt, 54, after serv in 82nd Airborne Div. Mem: Southern Bank & Trust Co (dir); Comt 100; Food Retailers Asn SC (dir); Salvation Army (dir); Nat Asn Convenience Stores. Relig: Baptist. Legal Res: 221 Timberlake Rd Anderson SC 29621 Mailing Add: PO Box 564 Anderson SC 29621

COLLINS, MICHAEL A **(D)**
NH State Rep
Mailing Add: 8 Taylor St Salem NH 03079

COLLINS, OAKLEY C (R)
Ohio State Sen
b Lawrence Co, Ohio, 1916. Educ: Ohio Univ, BS, 38. Polit & Govt Pos: Ohio State Sen, 52-72, 75-; Ohio State Rep, formerly; mem, Ohio Rep State Exec Comt, 68- Bus & Prof Pos: High sch adminr, 19 years. Legal Res: 1005 Kemp Lane Ironton OH 45638 Mailing Add: State Capitol Columbus OH 43215

COLLINS, P C, JR (D)
NC State Rep
Mailing Add: Rte 1 Box 96 Laurel Springs NC 28644

COLLINS, PHILIP W (R)
Ill State Sen
Mailing Add: 525 Jeffery Ave Calumet City IL 60409

COLLINS, RICHARD T (R)
State Auditor, Del
b Wilmington, Del, Mar 4, 46; s William R Collins & Barbara Torbert C; single. Educ: Goldey Beacom Sch Bus, 65-67; Univ Del, BA, 72, grad work, 72-73. Polit & Govt Pos: State Auditor, Del, 75- Bus & Prof Pos: Vpres pub rels, Miller Orgns, 73; partner, The Agency, Inc Pub Rels, 73-75. Mil Serv: Entered as Pvt, Army, 67, released as Sgt, 69, after serv in 1st Mil Intel Attachment, 1st Inf Div, SVietnam, 68-69; Nat Defense Medal; Vietnam Campaign Ribbon; Vietnam Expedition Forces Ribbon; Bronze Star; Vietnamese Distinguished Unit Ribbon; Vietnamese Cross of Gallantry. Mem: VFW; Am Legion. Relig: Episcopal. Mailing Add: 1100 Lore Ave Wilmington DE 19809

COLLINS, SAMUEL WILSON, JR (R)
Maine State Sen
b Caribou, Maine, Sept 17, 23; s Samuel Wilson Collins & Elizabeth Black C; m 1952 to Dorothy Small; c Edward, Elizabeth & Diane. Educ: Univ Maine, BA; Harvard Law Sch, JD; Phi Beta Kappa; Phi Kappa Phi; Delta Tau Delta. Polit & Govt Pos: Trustee, Rockland Sch Dist, 49-61; Maine State Sen, 75- Bus & Prof Pos: Lawyer, Rockland, Maine, 47- Mem: Maine State Bar Asn (bd gov). Relig: Unitarian Universalist. Mailing Add: Rockland ME 04841

COLLINS, WILLIAM A (D)
Conn State Rep
Mailing Add: 7 Berkeley St Norwalk CT 06850

COLLISHAW, LYMAN E (R)
NH State Rep
b Exeter, NH, May 10, 99; married; c Two. Educ: Exeter schs. Polit & Govt Pos: NH State Rep, 59- Mil Serv: Vet, World War I. Mem: Imp ORM; Am Legion; World War I Vets; Bow Lake Camp Owners Asn; NH Seacoast Regional Develop Asn. Relig: Episcopal. Mailing Add: 63 Hayes Park Exeter NH 03833

COLLUM, THAD L (R)
Mem, Rep State Finance Comt, NY
b Corsicana, Tex, July 24, 98; s Simon C Collum & Pauline P Kelly C; m 1926 to Eleanor Anne Boshart; c Edward Boshart & Thad Phillips. Educ: Cornell Univ, CE, 21; Sigma Phi Epsilon; Quill & Dagger. Hon Degrees: LLD, Lemoyne Col, 67. Polit & Govt Pos: Mem, Rep State Finance Comt, NY, 52-; mem, NY State Bd Regents, 54-67, vchancellor, 62-67; deleg, Rep Nat Conv, 64 & 68; Deleg, NY State Constitutional Conv, 67, chmn, Onondaga Co Rep Party, 47-68. Bus & Prof Pos: Instr & civil engr, Cornell Univ, 20-23; struct engr, pvt practice, 23-28; treas, Henderson-Johnson Co, 28-68; treas, Collum Acoustical Co, 34-68. Mil Serv: Entered as Seaman, Navy, 18. Relig: Protestant. Mailing Add: Marvelle Rd Fayetteville NY 13066

COLMER, WILLIAM MEYERS (D)
b Moss Point, Miss, Feb 11, 90; s Henry Colmer & Anna S Meyers C; m 1917 to Ruth Miner; c William Meyers, James Henry, Thomas Warren. Educ: Millsaps Col, Jackson, Miss, 10-14; Pi Kappa Alpha. Polit & Govt Pos: Co attorney, Jackson Co, Miss, 21-27; dist attorney, Second Dist, 28-33; US Rep, Miss, 32-73, sponsor & chmn spec comt, Post-War Econ Policy & Planning, 78th-79th Cong, mem, Nat Forest Reservation Comn & chmn, House Rules Comt, 90th & 92nd Cong, formerly; comnr, Miss State Park Comn, 73- Bus & Prof Pos: Sch teacher, 14 years; attorney-at-law. Mil Serv: Entered as Pvt, Army, 18, released as Regt Sgt Maj, 19. Mem: Am Legion; 40 et 8; Mason (33 degree); WOW; Rotary. Honors & Awards: Omicron Delta Kappa Leadership Award, Univ Miss; George Washington Am Good Govt Award, 57; Watch Dog of the Treas Award, Nat Asn Businessmen, 65-66, 67-68 & 69-72; Served in US Cong longer than any person in the State of Miss. Relig: Methodist. Mailing Add: 2017 Beach Blvd Pascagoula MS 39567

COLO, H THOMAS (D)
Mass State Rep
Mailing Add: State Capitol Boston MA 02133

COLON, VICTOR A (POPULAR DEMOCRAT, PR)
Rep, PR House of Rep
Mailing Add: State Capitol San Juan PR 00901

COLONNA, ROCCO J (D)
Ohio State Rep
Mailing Add: 14431 Parkman Blvd Brook Park OH 44142

COLSON, DOROTHY FOSS (R)
NH State Rep
b New Haven, Conn, May 17, 21; d Winfred L Foss & Dorothy Chaplain F; m 1953 to Edward A Colson; c Robin, Kim & Heather. Educ: Mt Holyoke Col, BA, 43; Boston Univ, MSW, 48. Polit & Govt Pos: NH State Rep, 75- Bus & Prof Pos: Chief social worker, NH Child Guid Clins, 49-53; social work consult, Dover-Keene-Manchester Clins, 53-57; mem, Nashua Community Coun, 57-59; social worker, Headstart, Nashua, 63-65; social work consult, Vis Nurse Asn, Nashua, 68- Mil Serv: Entered as Ens, Naval Res, 43, released as Lt(jg). Mem: Nat Asn Social Workers; Mid Merrimack Health Planning Bd; Matthew Thornton Health Planning Bd. Honors & Awards: Gate City Chap, Nat Asn Physically Handicapped Serv Award. Relig: Unitarian. Mailing Add: 8 Merrill Lane Hollis NH 03049

COLTEN, A THOMAS (R)
Mem, Rep State Cent Comt, La
b Detroit, Mich, Oct 21, 22; s Arthur L Colten & Judith G C; m 1947 to Jane H Kimmel; c Connie, Craig E & Lee A. Educ: Tex A&M, 44-45; Washington & Lee, 46; DePauw Univ, BA, 47; Sigma Delta Chi; Pi Sigma Alpha; Delta Upsilon. Polit & Govt Pos: Vchmn, Washington Parish Rep Comt, La, 48-55; chmn, Webster Parish Rep Comt, formerly; mem, Rep State Cent Comt La, 57-; mayor, Minden, La, 67-; mem Rep Polit Action Coun, 69-; deleg, La Const Conv, 73. Bus & Prof Pos: Bus mgr, Bogalusa, La Daily News, 47-55; publ-owner, Minden Press-Herald, 55-65; mem bd dirs, Minden Bank & Trust Co, 73. Mil Serv: Entered as Pvt, Army, 42, released as Sgt, 46, after serv in Spec Services & Infantry. Mem: La Press Asn; La CofC Mgrs Asn; Int City Mgt Asn; Nat Ed Asn; La Munic Asn. Honors & Awards: Minden La Boss of the Year, 63; La Publ of the Year, 65; Minden La Man of the Year, 67. Relig: Presbyterian. Legal Res: 1202 Drake Dr Minden LA 71055 Mailing Add: PO Box 580 Minden LA 71055

COLTON, JOHN PATRICK (D)
Mem, Tenn State Dem Exec Comt
b Memphis, Tenn, Feb 4, 38; s John P Colton & Cleo Carter C; m 1964 to Cheryl Lancaster; c Colleen Ann & Carrie Ann. Educ: Univ Tenn, 56-57; Memphis State Univ, BS, 61, LLB, 64. Polit & Govt Pos: Deleg, Tenn State Const Conv, 71; mem, Tenn State Dem Exec Comt, 74- Bus & Prof Pos: Sr partner, Colton & Blancett, Attorneys-at-law, 74- Publ: Co-auth, In the courts, Memphis & Shelby Co Bar Asn, 70. Mem: Am, Tenn & Memphis & Shelby Co Bar Asns; Am Trial Lawyers Asn; Am Judicature Soc. Relig: Roman Catholic. Legal Res: 246 Rose Rd Memphis TN 38117 Mailing Add: 100 N Main Bldg Suite 1205 Memphis TN 38103

COLTON, WILLIAM ANTHONY (D)
b Brooklyn, NY, Mar 6, 46; s William Colton, Sr & Frances De Lucia C; single. Educ: St John's Univ (NY), BA, 68; Brooklyn Col, MS, 71. Polit & Govt Pos: Chmn membership, Bensonhurst Independent Dem Club, 68-70, co-chmn, Club, 70-72, chmn, 72-; deleg, Dem Nat Conv, 72. Bus & Prof Pos: Teacher, New York, 69- Mem: United Fedn Teachers, New York; Grassroots Comt for Better Educ in New York (exec bd, 72-); Lewis Latimer Sch-Community Adv Bd (del-at-lg, 72-); KofC, Columbus Chap; Holy Rosary Head Star Adv Bd. Honors & Awards: Annual Award for Peace & Democracy, Bensonhurst Independent Dem, 72. Relig: Catholic. Mailing Add: 1463 E Third St Brooklyn NY 11230

COLVARD, LANDON, SR (D)
b Bledsoe Co, Tenn, July 29, 21; s William (Bill) Lafayette Colvard & Addie Mae Childres C; m 1943 to Hortense Amelia Graham; c Landon (Laney), Jr, Thad Ronald (Ronny), Daniel Graham (Danny) & Rebecca Ann (Beckie). Educ: Life Underwriters Sch & various other sales sch, 40-65. Polit & Govt Pos: Court clerk, Bledsoe Co, Tenn, 46-50; dep clerk-master, under Hortense Colvard, Tenn, 46-73; mem, Bledsoe Co Dem Exec Comt, 46-73; mem, Tenn Court Clerks, 50-72; deleg, Tenn Const Conv, 53-55 & 71-; Tenn State Sen, 9th Dist, 55-57; grand jury foreman, Bledsoe Co, 73-, comnr of elec & secy, 73-; chmn, Bledsoe Co Dem Party, formerly. Bus & Prof Pos: Life underwriter, Liberty Nat Life Ins Co, 59-73; real estate rentals, currently. Mil Serv: Entered as Pvt, Army, 43, released as Cpl. Mem: Chattanooga Asn of Life Underwriters; Tenn Asn of Co Elec Comnr; Scottish Rite of Freemasonry; Lions; Alhambra Temple Shrine. Honors & Awards: Poet Laureate, Tenn Const Conv, 71; Quarterly Honor Agent, Liberty Nat & Torch Club, 72; Nat Sales Achievement Award, Nat Asn of Life Underwriters, 72. Relig: Church of Christ. Mailing Add: Box 453 Pikeville TN 37367

COLVIN, EDWIN A (R)
Vt State Rep
Mailing Add: Holliday Dr Shaftsbury VT 05262

COLVIN, MARK THOMAS (R)
b Watertown, NY, Sept 20, 53; s John F Colvin & Ruth Berry C; single. Educ: Jefferson Community Col, AA, 73; Oswego State Col, BA, 75. Polit & Govt Pos: Alt deleg, Rep Nat Conv, 72. Mem: Copenhagen Civic Club. Relig: Congregational. Mailing Add: Washington St Copenhagen NY 13626

COLVIN, WILLIAM ALVIN (D)
Chmn, Beaver Co Dem Comt, Okla
b Balko, Okla, Oct 5, 09; s Charles Edward Colvin & Birdie Alice Horsman C; m 1938 to Lorene L Slater; c Willis Dwayne, Curtis Dale, Eloyse Kathleen (Mrs Savely) & Alice Raynelle (Mrs Jefferis). Polit & Govt Pos: Chmn, Beaver Co Dem Comt, Okla, 64- Bus & Prof Pos: Balko Sch Bd; bd dirs, Ins Co; Organizing Comt for REA Coop; pres, Panhandle Tel Coop, 50- Mem: Okla Wheat Growers; Beaver CofC; charter mem Balko Lions Club; Okla Cattleman's Asn; Okla Young Dem. Mailing Add: Balko OK 73931

COLWELL, CARLTON (D)
Ga State Rep
Mailing Add: PO Box 6 Blairsville GA 30612

COLYER, CHARLES CONSTANT (R)
b Altoona, Pa, Nov 14, 21; s Charles C Colyer & Helen Bingham C; m 1941 to Virginia Mae Conrad, wid; c Robert A, Charles C, III, Charlene & Diann. Educ: Carnegie Inst Technol, BS, 47; Tau Lambda Epsilon. Polit & Govt Pos: Mem town bd, Griffith, Ind, 56-60; chmn, Lake Co Rep Cent Comt, formerly. Bus & Prof Pos: Asst dir of research, Am Oil, 63-73, coordr of emissions research, 73- Mil Serv: Entered as Cadet, Air Force, 43, released as 2nd Lt, 45. Publ: Numerous articles on fuels & lubricants research, Soc of Automotive Engrs, Am Soc of Lubrication Engrs, Nat Petroleum Refiners Asn. Mem: Soc of Automotive Engrs (F & L tech comn chmn, 71-); Am Soc for Testing Materials (bd dirs, 72-). Honors & Awards: Lincoln Award, Lake Co Rep Cent Comt, Ind, 72. Relig: Methodist. Mailing Add: 12220 Kingfisher Rd Crown Point IN 46307

COMANS, RAYMOND (D)
Miss State Rep
Mailing Add: Box 272 Decatur MS 39327

COMBS, ALWILDA GERTRUDE BROWN (D)
b Mulberry, Ind, Jan 21, 92; d John Gibson Brown & Martha Jane Bryant B; m 1912 to William Bown Combs; c Lillian Mae (Mrs Charles W Hendricks); William Brown; Martha Gertrude (Mrs William Albert Richards); John Gordon & James Robert; twelve grandchildren & five great-grandchildren. Educ: Valparaiso Univ, 09. Polit & Govt Pos: Pres, Co Dem Woman's Club, Ind, 50; vchmn, East Clinton Co Dem Party, formerly. Mem:

Eastern Star; Union Vet Auxiliary; Farm Bur; Home Demonstration Club; Sr Citizens Club. Relig: United Methodist. Mailing Add: 1159 E Clinton Frankfort IN 46041

COMBS, BERT THOMAS (D)
b Manchester, Ky, Aug 13, 11; s Stephen Gibson Combs & Martha Jones C; m 1969 to Helen Clark Simons; c Lois Ann & Thomas George. Educ: Cumberland Col, 29-31; Univ of Ky, LLB, 37; Order of the Coif; Phi Delta Phi. Polit & Govt Pos: City attorney, Preston, Ky, 50; commonwealth attorney, 31st Judicial Dist, Ky, 50-51; Judge, Court of Appeals, 51-55; Gov, Ky, 59-64; Judge, US Court Appeals, Sixth Circuit, 67-72. Bus & Prof Pos: Attorney-at-law, 38-41, 46-51, 64-; attorney, Tarrant, Combs, & Bullitt, currently. Mil Serv: Capt, Army, serv in Judge Adv Gen Dept, 41-46; Bronze Star. Mem: Am Bar Asn; Jr Bar Asn Ky; Mason (32 degree). Relig: Baptist. Mailing Add: 2600 Citizens Plaza Louisville KY 40202

COMBS, ROBERT LEE, JR (D)
Third VChmn, NC Dem State Party
b Moorseville, NC, Jan 12, 52; s Rev Robert L Combs & Elsie Hunter C; single. Educ: Appalachian State Univ, BA, 75, grad work, 75-; Law Asn; Polit Sci Asn; Col Dem Club (pres, 71-73); Students Concerned About Mountain Planning. Polit & Govt Pos: Third vchmn, Sweetwater precinct, Catawba Co Dem Party, NC, 70-74; vchmn, Tenth Cong Dist Young Dem, 72-73; mem exec comt, Young Dem NC, 72-73; pres, Wataulga Co Young Dem Comt, 74-75; third vchmn, NC Dem State Party, 75- Honors & Awards: Outstanding Col Dem, NC Young Dem, 73; Appalachian State Univ Co-Curriculum Award, Appalachian State Univ Student Develop. Relig: Presbyterian. Legal Res: 500 21st St SE Hickory NC 28601 Mailing Add: 720A E Howard St Boone NC 28607

COMER, WILLIAM JOSEPH (D)
Colo State Sen
b Cumberland, Md, May 20, 35; s Francis John Comer & May Hinkle C; m 1958 to Daphne Joan Deming; c Babette, Colleen, Danielle, Casey & Shannon. Educ: La Salle Col, BA, 57; Univ Northern Colo, MA, 70. Polit & Govt Pos: Colo State Sen, 75- Bus & Prof Pos: Teacher, El Paso Co, 57- Mil Serv: Entered as 2nd Lt, Army, 57, released as 1st Lt, 59. Mem: Colorado Springs Teachers Asn; Colo & Nat Educ Asns; Nat Coun Social Studies. Mailing Add: 14 E Monument Colorado Springs CO 80903

COMFORT, THOMAS EDWIN (D)
b Streator, Ill, Apr 15, 21; s Patrick James Comfort & Jane Dickinson C; m 1945 to Evelyn Lorraine Trotter; c Thomas E, Jr, Judith Ann, Patrick J, Kathleen Ann & Michael J. Educ: Northwestern Univ, Evanston, AB, 43; Univ Ill, Urbana, MA, 51, PhD, 54; Phi Beta Kappa; Phi Eta Sigma; Eta Sigma Phi. Polit & Govt Pos: Alt deleg, Dem Nat Conv, 72. Bus & Prof Pos: Instr foreign lang, St Ambrose Col, 47-49; instr French, Univ Ill, Urbana, 49-54; asst prof, Tex A&M Univ, 54-58, assoc prof, 60-61 & 63-65; dir Eng lang prog, US Info Serv, Morocco, 58-60; dir, Turkish Air Force Lang Sch, Izmir, 61-63; prof French, Ill State Univ, 65-, head dept, 65-74. Mil Serv: Entered as Apprentice Seaman, Navy, 41, released as Lt(jg), 46, after serv in Landing Ship, Tank, 687 & 828, Pac Theater Oper, 43-46; Lt(Ret), Naval Res, 23 years; PTO with Five Battle Stars; Am Theater; Philippine Liberation Medal; Victory Medal. Mem: Mod Lang Asn; Am Asn Teachers of French; Am Coun Teaching of Foreign Lang. Relig: Roman Catholic. Mailing Add: Box 275 Towanda IL 61776

COMMONS, DORMAN LELAND (D)
Mem, Dem Nat Comt, Calif
b Denair, Calif, Mar 5, 18; s Walter F Commons & Minnie C; m 1941 to Gerry Barnett; c David Brian, Leslie (Mrs Carabas), Stanley Barnett & Spencer Charles. Educ: Stanford Univ, AB in Econ, 40; Modesto Jr Col, 2 years; Univ Calif, Exten Div, CPA, 47. Polit & Govt Pos: Mem, State Bd Educ, Calif, 62-70, pres, 70-71; deleg, Dem Nat Conv, 68; mem, Nat Export Expansion Coun, 68-69; mem exec comt, Nat Comt for Support Pub Schs, 68-72; state chmn, Wilson C Riles Campaign for State Supt of Pub Instr, 70 & 74; Southern Calif chmn, George McGovern for President Campaign, 72; mem, Dem Nat Comt, Calif, 72- Bus & Prof Pos: Sr acct, John F Forbes & Co, Los Angeles, 43-47; sr vpres & dir, Douglas Oil Co, Los Angeles, 47-64; sr vpres finance, Occidental Petroleum Corp, 64-72; financial consult, 72-; dir, Natomas Co, 73, spec asst to pres & mem exec comt, 74, pres & chief exec officer, 74- Mil Serv: Army, 43, Pvt. Mem: Const Rights Found (pres, 70-74). Relig: Protestant. Mailing Add: 155 Jackson St Apt 2503 San Francisco CA 94111

COMPTON, RANULF (R)
b Poe, Ind, Sept 16, 78; s William Charles Compton & Alice Emily True C; m 1907 to Florence Jane Mabee; c William Ranulf, Douglass Mabee & Alice (Mrs Giffen). Educ: Harvard Univ, 04. Polit & Govt Pos: Mil secy, Gov of NY, 18-20; asst secy, NY, 20-21; US Rep, Third Dist, Conn, 42-45; Staff Major to Gov of Conn, 46. Bus & Prof Pos: Pres, SJersey Broadcasting Co, Camden, NJ, 45- Mil Serv: Capt, 103rd NY Inf, 12, 369th US Inf, 18, released as Maj, 19, after serv in Tank Corps, US & France, Acting Brig Gen, Third Brigade, Argonne, 18; Distinguished Serv Cross, NY; Legion of Honor, France; Purple Heart; US Border, St Mihiel, Argonne & Amiens Campaign Ribbons. Mem: Mason, Blue & Commandery; Am Legion; VFW; Order of La Fayette; CofC. Relig: Episcopal. Legal Res: 42 Middle Beach Rd Madison CT 06443 Mailing Add: Box 507 Madison CT 06443

COMPTON, RICHARD WESLEY (R)
Chmn, Montgomery Co Rep Comt, Ala
b Montgomery, Ala, Sept 4, 25; s Robert Emmett Compton & Eloise Parsons C; m 1949 to Margaret Seay; c Dale, Ann & Eloise. Educ: Auburn Univ, BS, 48; Sigma Nu; Alpha Phi Omega. Polit & Govt Pos: Mem, Ala State Rep Exec Comt, 62-; mem, Second Cong Dist Rep Exec Comt, 62-; chmn, Montgomery Co Rep Comt, 62-; deleg, Rep Nat Conv, 68; chmn, Ala Rep Forum, 68-69. Bus & Prof Pos: Estimator & construction supvr, Bear Bros, Inc, 49-64; owner, Richard Compton, Gen Contractor, 64- Mil Serv: Entered as Pvt, Air Force, 43, released as 2nd Lt, 45, after serv in Am Theatre, 43-45, Lt Col, Res, 45-69. Mem: Assoc Gen Contractors Am; Capital City Kiwanis Club; Kiwanis; Montgomery CofC. Relig: Presbyterian. Legal Res: 1228 Magnolia Curve Montgomery AL 36106 Mailing Add: PO Box 1706 Montgomery AL 36103

COMSTOCK, KIRKE WHITE (D)
b Jackson, Mich, June 6, 30; s Kirke White Comstock & Marie Harris C; m 1953 to Dorothy Florence Brand; c William Louis, Karen Clark & Kristin Brand. Educ: Univ Mich, BS in Aeronaut Eng, 54; Zeta Psi. Polit & Govt Pos: City Councilman, Palo Alto, until 71, mayor, 71-74, mgr, Interiors Eng, 71- Bus & Prof Pos: Passenger & cargo equip mgr, United Air Lines, San Francisco, 71- Publ: Cost estimation for supersonic transports, J Soc Automotive Engrs, 64. Mem: United Air Lines Mgt Club; Sierra Club (mem, Comt for Green Foothills); Calif Tomorrow; Audubon Soc. Relig: Unitarian. Mailing Add: 595 Tennyson Ave Palo Alto CA 94301

CONABLE, BARBER BENJAMIN, JR (R)
US Rep, NY
b Warsaw, NY, Nov 2, 22; s Barber Benjamin Conable & Agnes G Gouinlock C; m 1952 to Charlotte Elizabeth Williams; c Anne E, Jane A, Emily C & Samuel W. Educ: Cornell Univ, AB, 42, Law Sch, LLB, 48; Order of the Coif. Polit & Govt Pos: NY State Sen, 53rd Dist, 63-65; US Rep, 37th Dist, NY, 65-73, 35th Dist, 73-, chmn research comt, US House Rep, 71-73, chmn policy comt, 74-, mem ways & means & budget comts, currently. Mil Serv: Entered as Pfc, Marine Corps, released as Lt after World War II, Maj after Korean War; Col (Ret), Marine Corps Res; Iwo Jima & Japanese Occup Medals. Relig: Protestant. Legal Res: Box 155 Alexander NY 14005 Mailing Add: 2228 Rayburn House Off Bldg Washington DC 20515

CONAGHAN, DOROTHY DELL (R)
Okla State Rep
b Oklahoma City, Okla, Sept 24, 30; d John Joseph Miller (Joe) & Wilhelmina Boyer M; m 1951 to Brian Francis Conaghan, wid; c Joseph Lee, Charles Alan & Roger Lloyd. Educ: Univ Okla, 49-51. Polit & Govt Pos: Secy, Okla State Young Rep, 57; Rep chmn, Precinct One, Tonkawa, Okla, 60-62; vchmn, Kay Co Rep Party, 61-65; mem, Kay Co Rep Exec Comt, 61-; chmn, Tonkawa Rep Party, 62; mem, Bellmon Belle orgn for Henry Bellmon, 62; campaign mgr for State Rep Brian F Conaghan, 62-72; pres, Tonkawa Rep Women's Club, 63; mem inaugural comt, Gov Henry Bellmon, 63; mem, Okla Rep State Exec Comt, 67-; vchmn, Sixth Cong Dist Rep Party, 67-71; mem, Bellmon Belle State Exec Comt, 68; deleg, Rep Nat Conv, 68; Okla State Rep, Dist 38, 73- Mem: Ohoyohoma Club; Eastern Star (Past Matron, Worthy Matron, 59); Delphi Study Club; Am Legion Auxiliary; PTA. Relig: Christian Church of NAm; Children's Div Chmn, Sixth Grade Sunday Sch Teacher, 68. Legal Res: 904 E Grand Tonkawa OK 74653 Mailing Add: PO Box 402 Tonkawa OK 74653

CONAHAN, WALTER CHARLES (R)
b Leola, SDak, Apr 20, 27; s Perry Anthony Conahan & Nina Martinson C; m 1957 to Marjorie Ann Dean; c Christine Mary. Educ: SDak State Univ, 52. Polit & Govt Pos: Staff asst, US Rep Harold O Lovre, SDak, 55-56 & US Rep R Walter Riehlman, NY, 57-58; press secy, US Sen Karl E Mundt, SDak, 58-72; spec asst to fed co-chmn, Old West Regional Comn, 72-73; legis affairs officer, Nat Transportation Safety Bd, 73-74; admin asst to US Rep James Abdnor, SDak, 75- Bus & Prof Pos: Assoc ed, Clear Lake Courier, SDak, 52-55; mgr, Perry's Cafe, Leola, 55. Mil Serv: Entered as Pvt, Army, 45, released as Technician Fourth Grade, 47, after serv in Army Finance, 172nd Unit, Pac, 45-46. Mem: Sigma Delta Chi; Am Legion; House Admin Asst Asn; Senate Press Secy Asn. Honors & Awards: Citation for achievement as outstanding male graduate in journalism at SDak State Univ, 52; First Place Blue Pencil Award for News Story, Fed Ed Asn, 70. Legal Res: Leola SD 57456 Mailing Add: 5105 Linwood Dr Oxon Hill MD 20021

CONCANNON, DONALD O (R)
b Garden City, Kans, Oct 28, 27; s Hugh Christopher Concannon & Margaret McKinley C; c 1952 to Patricia June Davis; c Chris Owen, Debra Lynn & Craig Alan. Educ: Garden City Jr Col, AA, 48; Washburn Univ Topeka, BA, 52, Law Sch, JD, 52; Kappa Sigma. Polit & Govt Pos: Chmn, Kans Young Rep Fedn, 59-61; chmn, Kans Presidential Electors, 60; chmn, Kans State Rep Party, 68-70. Bus & Prof Pos: Secy-treas, Spikes, Inc, 58-74; pres, Fortune Ins Co, Inc, 72-74, chmn, 74. Mil Serv: Entered as A/S, Navy 45, released as GM3/C, 46, after serv in SPac. Mem: Am & Kans Bar Asns; CofC; Mason. Honors & Awards: Man of the Year, Hugoton CofC. Relig: Protestant. Mailing Add: 129 N Jackson Hugoton KS 67951

CONDIE, ANGUS R (R)
Idaho State Rep
b Preston, Idaho, Oct 19, 07; s Gideon Condie & Carrie Clausen C; m 1935 to Marian Glenn; c Reed, Boyd, Philip, Keith, Clyde & Clair. Educ: Utah State Univ, MEd, 67. Polit & Govt Pos: Co comnr, Franklin Co, Idaho, 47-55; Idaho State Rep, 68- Bus & Prof Pos: Secy, Preston Whitney Irrigation Co, 37-; prin, Jr High Sch Dist 201, 46- Mem: Rotary; Preston CofC. Relig: Latter-day Saint. Mailing Add: Rte 3 Preston ID 83263

CONDON, JOHN F (R)
City Councilman, San Mateo, Calif
b San Bernardino, Calif, Apr 2, 10; s Harold F Condon & Minnie Julia Brennan C; m 1937 to Elizabeth Harvey; c Barbara (Mrs Larry Sonsini) & Joan (Mrs Michael Paul). Educ: Command & Gen Staff Col, Ft Leavenworth, Kans, grad, 41; Armed Forces Staff Col, Norfolk, Va, grad, 50; Indust Col of Armed Forces, Washington, DC, grad, 54. Polit & Govt Pos: Chmn & comnr, Bd Harbor Comnrs, San Mateo Co, Calif, 61-72; city councilman, San Mateo, 69-, mayor, 71-72 & 74-75. Bus & Prof Pos: Dist mgr, San Mateo Co Harbor Dist, 73. Mil Serv: Entered as Pvt, Nat Guard, 28, released as Cpl, 30; entered as Capt, Army, 41, retired as Col, 60; various theaters; Bronze Star; Iranian Order of Efdekar (first & second class). Mem: Am Legion; Am Juridical Soc; ROA (treas, San Mateo Co Conv & Visitors Bur). Honors & Awards: Senate Resolution Award, Calif, Assembly Resolution Award; City Coun Resolution Award, San Mateo. Mailing Add: 170 W Poplar Ave San Mateo CA 94402

CONDON, LESTER P (INDEPENDENT)
m 1946 to Vera Crossley; c Thomas J, John K, Leslie Patricia, Marietta & Lisa Ann. Educ: Providence Col, BS, 43. Polit & Govt Pos: Asst Secy Admin, Dept Housing & Urban Develop, formerly; dir & chmn bd, Nat Ctr Housing Mgt, 72- Bus & Prof Pos: Dir & exec vpres, Fed Nat Mortgage Asn, 72- Mem: Soc Former Spec Agents Fed Bur Invest; Asn Fed Investr; Phi Delta Phi; Inst Internal Auditors; Am Legion. Honors & Awards: Distinguished Serv Awards, Housing & Home Finance Agency, 57 & US Dept Housing & Urban Develop, 72. Relig: Catholic. Legal Res: 1306 Janney's Lane Alexandria VA 22302 Mailing Add: 1133-Fifteenth St NW Washington DC 20005

CONELLY, CARL ROBERT (R)
b Hawthorne, Nev, Sept 30, 12; s Thomas Middleton Conelly & Mabel Ann Finley C; m 1931 to Jacqueline Jane Eckley; c Juliann & Robynn. Educ: Univ Nev, Reno; Univ Calif, Berkeley. Polit & Govt Pos: Trustee, San Lorenzo Valley Unified Sch Dist, Calif, 47-58; mem statewide comt, Eisenhower-Nixon Campaign, 52-56; chmn, Santa Cruz Co Rep Assembly; chmn, Santa Cruz Co Rep Cent Comt, formerly; dir & pres, Calif Asn Co Rep Cent Comt Chmn, 60-65; mem exec comt, Rep State Cent Comt Calif, 64-70; dir bd, affiliates, Univ Calif, Santa Cruz, 64-; pres, Santa Cruz Co Asn Grand Jurors, 64-; hon life mem, Santa Cruz Co Rep Assembly, 65-; state dir, Calif Rep Assembly, 66- Bus & Prof Pos: Real estate & ins broker, Carl Conelly Realty, 44-; trustee, Cabrillo Col, 58- Mem: San Lorenzo Valley Asn Ins Agents;

CofC; Calif Real Estate Bd; Cabrillo Music Guild (dir); Commonwealth Club San Francisco. Honors & Awards: Received Santa Cruz Man of Year Award, 58; lectured on Russia following trip in 59. Legal Res: Rte 2 Box 36 Ben Lomand CA 95005 Mailing Add: PO Box 827 Boulder Creek CA 95006

CONEY, JACK ARTHUR (R)
b Dayton, Ohio, July 17, 18; s Joseph P Coney & Ethel Margolis C; m 1948 to Mercedes Campos; c Jeffrey. Educ: Northwestern Univ, BS, 40, JD, 43; Phi Epsilon Pi; Tau Epsilon Rho. Polit & Govt Pos: Asst corp counsel, Peoria, Ill, 45; mem, US Bd Rent Control, 47; representative, 43rd Dist Rep Comt, 48-64; alt deleg, Rep Nat Conv, 56, 60, 64 & 72. Mem: Peoria Bar Asn; Nat Trial Lawyers Asn; Creve Coeur Club; Standard Club of Chicago; Am Bus Club. Relig: Jewish. Legal Res: 4810 Knoxville Peoria IL 61614 Mailing Add: First Nat Bank Bldg Peoria IL 61602

CONGDON, DAVID RALPH (R)
b Rutland, Vt, Jan 15, 37; s Ralph W Congdon & Natalie Allbee C; single. Educ: Univ Vt, BA, 60, Col Med, MD, 64. Polit & Govt Pos: Mem, Wallingford Rep Town Comt, Vt, 60-70; mem, Rutland Co Rep Comt, 71; mem, US Northeastern Rep Conf, Washington, DC, 71; chmn, Castleton Rep Town Comt, Vt, formerly; mem, Nat Rep Leadership Conf, Washington, DC, 72; co-chmn, Vt Finance Comt to Reelect the President, 72; co-chmn, Rutland Co Campaign to Elect Fred Hackett for Gov, Vt, 72; deleg, Rep Nat Conv, 72; chmn, Vt First Lincoln Day Dinner, 72-73. Bus & Prof Pos: Co-founder & pres, Castleton Med Ctr, Inc, 67- Mil Serv: Capt, Med Corps, Air Force, 64-67, serv in 551st Air Force Hosp, Otis AFB, Mass. Mem: Rutland Co Cancer Soc; Am Forestry Asn; Wallingford High Sch Alumni Asn (pres, 68-); Rutland Co & Vt State Med Socs. Honors & Awards: People to People-Good Will Ambassador to Soviet Union, Poland, Czech, E & W Germany, Finland & Belgium, 70. Relig: Congregational. Mailing Add: Castleton Med Ctr Inc Castleton VT 05735

CONKLIN, CHARLES ROSS (D)
b Delta, Colo, June 23, 20; s George Ross Conklin & Adaline Weeks C; m 1942 to Marjorie Jane David; c Marty (Mrs Thomas Eugene Durlin) & Leslie. Educ: Harvard Col, BA, 48; Harvard Law Sch, LLB, 51; Phi Beta Kappa. Polit & Govt Pos: Colo State Rep, 55-60 & 65-66, Speaker, Colo House of Rep, 57-60; dep dist attorney, Seventh Judicial Dist, Colo, 57-58; asst dir, Pub Land Law Rev Comn, Washington, DC, 67-71; staff specialist, Policy Develop Div, Water Resources Coun, 71; spec counsel on pub lands & environ matters, Comt on Interior & Insular Affairs, US House Rep, 71-74; staff dir, 74- Bus & Prof Pos: Partner, Conklin, Carroll & Willett, Law Firm, 60-66. Mil Serv: Entered as Yeoman 3/c, Navy, 42, released as Chief Yeoman, 45. Relig: Episcopal. Mailing Add: 540 N St SW Washington DC 20024

CONKLIN, GEORGE WILLIAM (D)
b Rome, Italy, Nov 14, 08; s William H Conklin & Iola Schmidlapp C; m 1944 to Anne P Thomas; c Holly Anne (Mrs Fitzgerald) & Iola S (Mrs Benedict). Educ: Dartmouth Col, BA, 31; Princeton Univ, 31-32; Univ Pa, BArch, 34; Sigma Chi. Polit & Govt Pos: Selectman, Woodbridge, Conn, 63-67; chmn, Dem Town Comt, Woodbridge, 63-69; mem adv comt, Conn Zoning Statutes, 66; chmn, Third Cong Dist McCarthy for Pres Campaign, 67-68; deleg, Dem Nat Conv & mem permanent orgn comt, 68; mem nat affairs comt, Caucus Conn Dem, 69; mem steering comt, Alliance for 70, New Haven, 70-; chmn, Polit Action Comt, Conn, 70- Bus & Prof Pos: Co-chmn architect's comt, New Haven Festival Arts, 62; chmn pub rels comt, Am Inst Architects, 62-64. Mil Serv: Entered as Lt(jg), Navy, 42, released as Lt Comdr, 46, after serv in Naval Oper Base Oran, NAfrica, 42-44; Lt Comdr(Ret), Naval Res, 46; NAfrica, ETO Campaign Ribbons. Publ: Politics & Fine Arts, Podium, 64; Master Plan, Chicopee, Mass, 66; New Boroughs Program, Urban Design, 67. Mem: Conn Soc Architects; Am Inst Architects; Jamaica Soc Architects; Conn Urban Renewal Asn; Conn Fedn Planning & Zoning Agencies. Relig: First Church of Christ. Mailing Add: Hickory Rd Woodbridge CT 06525

CONKLIN, RICHARD JAMES (D)
Chmn, Meagher Co Dem Cent Comt, Mont
b Williston, NDak, Feb 2, 30; s Hobert F Conklin & Marie Vavrosky C; m 1955 to Michiko Ann Shinozaki; c Teresa Marie, Nancy Ann, Matthew Kenneth & Colleen Felicia. Educ: Carroll Col, AB, 52; Eda Jima Specialist's Sch, Japan, court reporter; Mont State Univ Law Sch, JD, 59; Calif State Univ, Fresno, 72; Phi Alpha Delta; Tammany Soc; Tu Kappa Alpha. Polit & Govt Pos: Smoke jumper foreman, Forest Serv, US Dept Agr, 49-58; ward chmn, Mont Dem State Orgn, 55-58; committeeman, Mont Dem State Cent Comt, 59-67; City Attorney, White Sulphur Springs, 67-; chmn, Meagher Co Dem Cent Comt, 68-; Co Attorney, Meagher Co, 68-75. Bus & Prof Pos: Contract miner, Anaconda Copper Mining Co, Butte, Mont, 55-57; self-employed attorney-at-law, 59- Mil Serv: Entered as Pvt, Army Nat Guard, 50, released as Sgt, 53, after serv in 163rd Inf Combat Team, recalled as Pvt E-2, Army, 53-56, Korea; Good Conduct Medal; Am Defense Serv Medal; Korean Serv Medal. Publ: Auth of series of articles, Mont Sports Outdoors, Ace Publ Co, 60-65; Lenticular lessons, Western Heir, 70; Yerdon treasure, Western Treas, 70. Mem: Am & Mont Bar Asns; Co Attorney's Asn; Probate Counsel; Elks. Honors & Awards: Numerous speaking awards from various cols & CofC, 52-72. Relig: Roman Catholic. Legal Res: 415 E Monroe White Sulphur Springs MT 59645 Mailing Add: Box 749 White Sulphur Springs MT 59645

CONKLIN, WILLIAM T (R)
NY State Sen
b Brooklyn, NY; m to Jessie F Hanrahan; c Joyce (Mrs Jack Jarrard), William & Patricia (Mrs W Davis). Polit & Govt Pos: Mem tenure comt, NY State Senate, 50 & 53; NY State Sen, 56-, chmn Senate comt banks, NY State Senate, currently, chmn joint legis comn ment & physical handicap, 63-69, chmn joint legis comt to revise banking law, currently; deleg, Rep Nat Conv, 72. Bus & Prof Pos: Mem bd dirs, Bay Ridge Savings & Loan Asn. Mem: Uptown CofC of New York (dir); Guild for Exceptional Children (pres); NY Chap Hemophilia Found (sponsor); Asn for Help of Retarded Children (dir); Bay Ridge Day Nursery (dir). Honors & Awards: Cited by Ambassador J G McDonald for Charitable Affairs Leadership. Mailing Add: 7905 Colonial Rd Brooklyn NY 11209

CONLAN, JOHN B, JR (R)
US Rep, Ariz
b Oak Park, Ill, Sept 17, 30; s John B Conlan & Ruth Anderson C; m 1968 to Irene Danielson; c Christopher Douglas & Kevin Matthew. Educ: Northwestern Univ, BS, 51; Harvard Law Sch, LLB, 54; Fulbright scholar, Univ Cologne, Ger, 54-55; Hague Acad Int Law, Netherlands, 58; Delta Upsilon. Polit & Govt Pos: Mem, Ariz Rep State Comt, 62-; Ariz State Sen, Maricopa Co, 65-72; mem, Gov Crime Comn & Coun Orgn State Govt, 67-70; US Rep, Fourth Dist, Ariz, 73- Bus & Prof Pos: Attorney-at-law; partner, Hughes, Hughes & Conlan. Mil Serv: Entered as 1st Lt, Army, 56, released as Capt, 61, after serv in 24th Inf Div, ETO. Mem: Ariz & Ill Bar Asns. Honors & Awards: George Washington Honor Medal, Freedoms Found at Valley Forge, 57; Outstanding Young Man in Ariz Award, Jaycees, 64. Relig: Christian. Legal Res: Scottsdale AZ Mailing Add: 130 Cannon House Off Bldg Washington DC 20515

CONLAN, ROBERT J (D)
b New York, NY, Mar 9, 45; s John Conlan & Helen McDougal C; single. Educ: Fordham Univ, BA, 68. Polit & Govt Pos: Dir, Nat Comt to Elect Charles Evers, Gov Miss, 70-71; asst, Mayor New York, 71-73; admin asst, US Rep Frederick W Richmond, NY, 75- Bus & Prof Pos: Instr, Bache & Co Inc, 67-69. Mil Serv: Entered as Pvt, Army, 65, released as Sgt, 67, after serv in 3rd Army; Nat Defense Ribbon. Legal Res: 351 Pacific St Brooklyn NY 11217 Mailing Add: 124 Sixth St NE Washington DC 20002

CONLEY, GERARD P (D)
Maine State Sen
Mailing Add: 29 Taylor St Portland ME 04102

CONLEY, HARRY V (D)
Committeeman, Ohio Dem Cent Comt
b Scioto Co, Ohio, Aug 23, 27; s Thomas J Conley & Lola Rigsby C; m 1953 to Marilyn Brimner C; c Jeani & Lee Ann. Educ: Ohio State Univ, DVM, 56; Alpha Psi. Polit & Govt Pos: Committeeman, Ohio Dem Cent Comt, 64-; mem, Logan Co Dem Exec Comt, 64-; chmn, Logan Co Dem Cent Comt, 66-72; pres, City Coun, Belle Center, currently. Mil Serv: Entered as Pvt, Army, 46, released as Pfc, 49, after serv in Med Corps, 48-49. Mem: Second Ohio Dist, Ohio & Am Vet Med Asns; CofC; Mason. Relig: Methodist. Legal Res: Belle Center OH 43310 Mailing Add: Box 687 Belle Center OH 43310

CONLEY, RAYMOND K, JR (R)
NH State Rep
Mailing Add: Box 102 Center Sandwich NH 03227

CONLIN, EDWARD JOSEPH (R)
Vt State Rep
b Windsor, Vt, Aug 22, 97; m to Frances O'Neill. Educ: Windsor High Sch, 15. Polit & Govt Pos: Vt State Rep, 59-; town & village auditor, formerly; mem, Rutland Rwy Comn, formerly. Bus & Prof Pos: Asst mgr, Metrop Life Ins Co, formerly; retired. Mil Serv: Cpl, Air Corps, World War I. Mem: Am Legion; KofC; Bd of Hist Sites (chmn). Relig: Catholic. Mailing Add: 6 Dewey Ave Windsor VT 05089

CONLIN, FRANK (D)
NDak State Sen
Mailing Add: State Capitol Bismarck ND 58501

CONLIN, MICHAEL H (R)
Mich State Rep
b Detroit, Mich, July 11, 43; s Henry T Conlin & Dorothy Marie Love C; single. Educ: Univ Mich, Ann Arbor & Eastern Mich Univ, BA, Econ; Alpha Kappa Psi; Delta Upsilon. Polit & Govt Pos: Asst for cong rels, Dept Housing & Urban Develop, Washington, DC, 69; asst to John A Volpe, Secy Transportation, 70; Mich State Rep, 23rd Dist, 75-, mem, Corp & Finance Comt, Econ Develop Comt, Civil Rights Comt & Urban Affairs Comt, Mich House Rep, 75- Bus & Prof Pos: Managing ed, Huron Valley Adv, Ann Arbor, Mich, 68-69; asst to chmn, Nat RR Passenger Corp, AMTRAK, 71; exec, Mich Nat Bank, Lansing, 73-74. Mem: Jackson Co Bi-Centennial Comn; YMCA; DAV; Univ Clubs of Lansing, Mich & Washington, DC; Capitol Hill Club Washington, DC. Relig: Roman Catholic. Legal Res: 1211 Tanbark Lane W Jackson MI 49203 Mailing Add: State Capitol Lansing MI 48901

CONLIN, ROXANNE BARTON (D)
b Huron, SDak, June 30, 44; d Marion William Barton & Alice Madden B; m 1964 to James Clyde Conlin; c Jacalyn Rae & James Barton. Educ: Drake Univ, Readers Digest scholar, BA, 64; Drake Univ Col Law, Fisher Found scholar, 64-66, JD, 66; Phi Beta Kappa, Alpha Lambda Delta, Kappa Beta Pi. Hon Degrees: LLD, Univ Dubuque, 75. Polit & Govt Pos: Vchmn, Iowa Young Dem, 64-66, nat committeewoman, 65-67; dep indust comnr, Iowa, 67-68; asst attorney gen, Dept Justice, Iowa, 69-; mem, Iowa Comn on Status of Women, 72-; vchmn deleg, Dem Nat Mid-Term Conf, 74; mem nat steering comt, Nat Womens Polit Caucus, 74-75. Bus & Prof Pos: Lawyer, Des Moines, Iowa, 66-67. Publ: ERA vs Equal Protection, Where are we now?, Drake Law Rev, 75. Mem: Am & Iowa Bar Asns; River Hill Day Care Ctr (bd dirs); Polk Co Rape/Sexual Assault Care Ctr (bd dirs); Nat Orgn Women. Honors & Awards: Outstanding Young Woman of Iowa, 74; Award for Outstanding Serv to Civil Liberties, 74; Chi Omega Social Serv Award, 64. Legal Res: 1623 SW Evans Des Moines IA 50315 Mailing Add: State Capitol Des Moines IA 50319

CONMEY, LARRY J (D)
Chmn, Jones Co Dem Party, Iowa
b Anamosa, Iowa, Apr 22, 40; s Lawrence J Conmey & Pearl Allen C; single. Educ: Loras Col, BA, 62; St Louis Univ, LLB, 65. Polit & Govt Pos: City attorney, Anamosa, Iowa, 66-73, judicial magistrate, 73-; chmn, Jones Co Dem Party, Iowa, 69- Bus & Prof Pos: Attorney-at-law, 65- Mem: Am, Iowa & Jones Co Bar Asns. Relig: Catholic. Legal Res: 716 Gainauillo St Anamosa IA 52205 Mailing Add: Box 327 Anamosa IA 52205

CONN, WALTER JENNINGS (R)
Conn State Rep
b Kent, Conn, Jan 7, 22; s Walter Denny Conn & Sarah Louise Jennings C; m 1946 to Helena Cecila Hulton; c Walter Timothy, Suzanne & Sarah Ellen. Educ: New Milford High Sch, grad, 39. Polit & Govt Pos: Mem, New Milford Rep Town Comt, Conn, 55-, treas, 57-63; mem, New Milford Salary Study Comt, 57-58; mem, New Milford Sewer Comn, 59-63; Conn State Rep, 73- Bus & Prof Pos: Owner & pres, Conn's Dairy, Inc, New Milford, 55-; mem adv bd, Conn Nat Bank, New Milford Off, 71-; corporator, New Milford Savings Bank, 72- Mem: Lions; Odd Fellows; Conn Asn Food Sanitarians; CofC; United Fund (dir). Relig: Episcopal. Mailing Add: 225 Danbury Rd New Milford CT 06776

CONNALLY, ELIZABETH WARREN (R)
Nat Committeewoman, Tenn Young Rep Fedn
b Nashville, Tenn, Nov 26, 47; d Joseph Moore Warren, III & Louise Haury W (both deceased); m 1971 to John Edwin Connally; c Joseph Warren. Educ: Lindenwood Col Women, BA in Hist & Polit Sci, 69; Vanderbilt Univ, work toward MA in Eng Hist. Polit

& Govt Pos: Staff asst to US Sen Bill Brock, Tenn, 72; nat committeewoman, Tenn Young Rep Fedn, 73-; asst to finance dir, Tenn Rep Party, 75- Mem: Tenn Fine Arts Ctr Cheekwood (Swan Ball art comt); Nashville Symphony Guild (music educ prog, chmn art for Ital Street Fair); O'More Sch Design Guild; Friends of Children's Hosp at Vanderbilt. Honors & Awards: Woman of the Year, Tenn Young Rep Fedn, 75. Relig: Episcopal. Mailing Add: 4141 Woodlawn Ave Apt 5 Nashville TN 37205

CONNALLY, JOHN BOWDEN **(R)**
b Floresville, Tex, Feb 27, 17; s John B Connally & Lela Wright C; m 1940 to Idanell Brill; c John B, III, Sharon (Mrs Ammann) & Mark. Educ: Univ Tex Sch Law, LLB, 41. Polit & Govt Pos: Secy, US Rep Lyndon B Johnson, 39; admin asst to Sen Lyndon B Johnson, 49; Secy of Navy, 61; Gov, Tex, 63-69; vchmn Tex deleg, Dem Nat Conv, 56 & 60, chmn, 64 & 68, deleg, 68; Secy of Treas, 71-72; spec adv to the President, 73. Bus & Prof Pos: Gen mgr, Radio Sta KVET, Austin, Tex, 46-49; attorney, Powell, Wirtz & Rahaut, Austin, 49-52; attorney, Richardson & Bass, Ft Worth, 52-61; partner, Vinson, Elkins, Searls & Connally, Houston, 69-71; partner, Vinson, Elkins, Searls, Connally & Smith, 72-; dir, Falconbridge Nickel Mines Ltd Can, 73-; trustee, Andrew W Mellon Found, 73-; mem adv comt reform, Int Monetary Syst, 73- Mil Serv: Entered Navy, 41, released as Lt Comdr, 46, after serv in Atlantic & Pac, 46; Legion of Merit; Bronze Star. Mem: Conf Bd New York; Santa Gertrudis Breeders Int (dir, 73-) Houston CofC (vchmn, 75-); Pin Oaks Horse Show Asn (dir, 73-); Univ Tex Ex-Students Asn. Honors & Awards: Distinguished Alumnus Award, 61. Relig: Methodist. Mailing Add: 2100 First City Nat Bank Bldg Houston TX 77002

CONNAUGHTON, THERESA GONZALES **(D)**
b Santa Fe, NMex, Mar 7, 49; d Florentino Gonzales & Eufemia Vigil C; m 1969 to Martin Connaughton; c Damien. Educ: Col of Santa Fe, 67-70; NMex State Univ, BA, 71; Univ Ill, Urbana, 72-; Pi Gamma Mu; Students for McGovern-Shriver. Polit & Govt Pos: Deleg, NMex Dem State Conv, 72; alt deleg, Dem Nat Conv, 72. Honors & Awards: Tuition scholarship, Col Santa Fe, 67. Relig: Roman Catholic. Legal Res: 1654 Cole Village Las Cruces NM 88001 Mailing Add: 2022 A Orchard St Urbana IL 61801

CONNELL, JACK **(D)**
Ga State Rep
Mailing Add: PO Box 308 Augusta GA 30903

CONNELL, JEROME F, SR **(D)**
Md State Sen
Mailing Add: 400 Stately Dr Pasadena MD 21122

CONNELL, TED C **(D)**
b Hamlin, Tex, Dec 5, 24; s Albert A Connell, Sr & Edna Bell Lawrence C; div; c Mark Stanley & Carol Juanette. Educ: Army War Col, BS in Mil Sci, 49. Polit & Govt Pos: Deleg & sgt-at-arms, Tex State Dem Conv, 48-, chmn, Bell Co Deleg, 60; chmn, Vet Affairs Comn Tex, 58-61; deleg, Dem Nat Conv, 60, 64 & 68, asst sgt-at-arms, 64 & 68; mayor, Killeen, Tex, 62-66; mem, Am-Philippine Comn, 63-68; mem, Vet Land Bd, Tex, 63-69; deleg, Philippine-Am Assembly, 66; tech asst to US panel, Philippine-US Presidential Vet Comn, 66; field dir, Vet Adv Comn, US Vet Admin, 67-68; mem, Am Battle Monuments Comn, 68-; mem, Presidential fact-finding missions to Vietnam & Guam; civilian consult, Presidential visits to Uruguay & Cent Am. Bus & Prof Pos: Partner, Chevrolet Co, 46; pres, Connell Chevrolet Co, Inc, 55-; mem planning coun, Chevrolet Motors Div, Gen Motors Corp; owner, Modern Dry Cleaners & Laundry, Connell Ins Agency & T C & E Real Estate Co; dir, First Nat Bank, Killeen; chmn bd dirs, Rio Airways, Inc; dir & vpres, First State Bank, formerly. Mil Serv: Entered as Pvt, Army, 43, released as M/Sgt, 45, after serv in Field Artil, Tank Destroyer Bn, 98th Inf, SPac Theatre, 43-45; Lt Col, Army Res as exec officer, Policy & Plans Div, Off of the Chief of Info, currently; Four Battle Stars; Meritorious Pub Serv Award, Dept of the Navy; Ordre Militaire du Combattant de L'Europe, French Govt. Mem: Nat & Tex Automobile Dealers Asn; VFW; Boy Scouts (mem-at-lg, nat exec coun); Gtr Killeen CofC (pres, 69-). Honors & Awards: Man of the Year, ETex Serv Medal, VFW, 65; Carl L Estes Award as Outstanding Citizen of Tex in 1966, Am Legion, 66. Relig: Baptist. Mailing Add: PO Box 666 Killeen TX 76541

CONNELL, WILLIAM A, JR **(D)**
Mass State Rep
Mailing Add: State Capitol Boston MA 02133

CONNELLY, BRIAN ROBERT **(R)**
Chmn Campaign Comt, Mich Rep State Cent Comt
b Evanston, Ill, Aug 17, 35; s William Henry Connelly & Jane Kaye C; m 1958 to Janet Lou Harris; c Patrick William, Michael Leslie & Kelley Margaret. Educ: Mich State Univ, 53-58; Pi Kappa Phi. Polit & Govt Pos: Chmn campaign pub rels comt, Ann Arbor Rep Comt, Mich, 65, 66 & 67; chmn pub rels comt, Washtenaw Co Rep Comt, 66, vchmn, 69, finance chmn, 72-; councilman, City of Ann Arbor, 67-69; mem, Washtenaw Co Nixon for President Comt, 68; chmn, Ann Arbor City Rep Comt, 69-; chmn campaign comt, Mich State Rep Cent Comt, 69-; chmn, Jack Shuler for Univ Mich Regent Campaign Comt, 70; campaign coordr, Reelect Justice John Dethmers to Mich Supreme Court Comt, 70; campaign coordr, Mary Coleman & James Thorburn for Mich State Supreme Court, 72. Bus & Prof Pos: Prog dir, WKHM Radio, Jackson, Mich, 59-61; vpres, Connelly Co, 61-66, pres, Brian Connelly Advert, Inc, 66- Mil Serv: Entered as Pvt, Army, 58, released as Sp-4, 64, after serv 6 months active duty, 5 years 6 months active res. Mem: Civitan Int. Relig: Episcopal. Mailing Add: 500 Parklake Ave Ann Arbor MI 48103

CONNELLY, EDWARD W **(R)**
Mass State Rep
Mailing Add: State Capitol Boston MA 02133

CONNELLY, ELIZABETH ANN **(D)**
NY State Assemblyman
b Brooklyn, NY, June 19, 28; d John Walter Keresey & Alice Marie Mallon K; m 1952 to Robert Vincent Connelly; c Alice, Robert Vincent, Jr, Margaret & Therese. Educ: Walton High Sch, Bronx, NY, grad, 46. Polit & Govt Pos: Secy, N Shore Dem Club, Staten Island, NY, 67-73; NY State Assemblyman, 74- Mem: Bus & Prof Women's Orgn; Mayor's Comt on Status of Women, New York; Bd Trustees Staten Island Hosp, Serv Auxiliary Staten Island Hosp. Honors & Awards: Vol of Year, Staten Island Hosp, 72 & 73. Relig: Roman Catholic. Legal Res: 94 Benedict Ave Staten Island NY 10314 Mailing Add: Legis Off Bldg Albany NY 12224

CONNER, DOYLE E **(D)**
State Comnr of Agr, Fla
b Starke, Fla, Dec 17, 28; s J Leon Conner & Ruby Norman C; m 1953 to Johnnie (Kitten) Bennett; c Doyle, Jr, John Bryant & Kimberly Ann. Educ: Univ of Fla, BS, 52. Polit & Govt Pos: Fla State Rep, Bradford Co, 50-59; State Comnr of Agr, Fla, 61- Bus & Prof Pos: Ins bus, Starke & Miami, Fla, 52; farmer. Mem: CofC; Farm Bur; Fla Cattlemen's Asn; Mason; Shrine. Honors & Awards: One of Nation's Outstanding Youths, Outdoor Writers of Am, 47; One of Five Outstanding Young Men in Fla, Fla Jaycees, 50; Served as youngest Speaker of Fla House of Rep, 57; One of Ten Outstanding Young Men in Nation, US Jaycees, 61. Relig: Baptist. Legal Res: 2902 Woodside Dr Tallahassee FL 32303 Mailing Add: Capitol Bldg Tallahassee FL 32304

CONNER, PAUL H **(D)**
Wash State Rep
b Port Angeles, 1925; m to Thelma; c Four. Educ: Port Angeles Bus Col; Western Wash Col; Univ Wash. Polit & Govt Pos: Wash State Rep, currently; Wash State Sen, 57. Bus & Prof Pos: Licensed real estate broker. Mem: Eagles; Grange; Lions; Elks; Toastmasters. Mailing Add: Rte 4 Box 355 Sequim WA 98382

CONNER, WARREN JOHN **(R)**
b Aspen, Colo, July 25, 20; s Milton G Conner & Margaret Ann Harrington C; single. Polit & Govt Pos: Secy, Pitkin Co Rep Cent Comt, Colo, formerly; committeeman, Precinct 2, Rep Party of Colo, 50- Bus & Prof Pos: Pitkin Co Assessor, 47-58, chief appraiser, Pitkin Co Assessor's Off, 58- Publ: Assessment of Ski Areas, 1/68 & Speculative Land, 6/69, CATAlog. Mem: Am Soc of Appraisers; Colo Assessor's Asn; Elks. Relig: Catholic. Legal Res: 534 E Hopkins Ave Aspen CO 81611 Mailing Add: PO Drawer 159 Aspen CO 81611

CONNERS, MAYNARD GILBERT **(R)**
Maine State Rep
b Cherryfield, Maine, June 15, 18; s Gilbert Hill Conners & Mildred Willey Conners; m 1971 to Blanche Prince; c Sally & David Songer. Educ: High sch grad; ICS course in contracting & building. Polit & Govt Pos: Maine State Rep, Augusta, 75- Mil Serv: Entered as Seaman 2/C, Navy, 42, released as Boatswains Mate 1/C, 45, after serv in European & Pac Theatres; Bronze Star-Iwo Jima. Mem: Mason; VFW; Am Legion. Relig: Baptist. Mailing Add: Box 131 Franklin ME 04634

CONNERS, MICHAEL F **(D)**
b Albany, NY, Mar 12, 49; s Richard J Conners & Margaret Egan C; m 1972 to Helen Lynn Nichols. Educ: Siena Col (NY), BS, 71; Pi Iota Tau; Capital City Club (vpres); Officials Club (pres). Polit & Govt Pos: Worker, Albany Co Dem Party, First Dist Tenth Ward, 71-73, Sixth Dist Fourth Ward, 73-; deleg, Dem Nat Conv, 72; Albany chmn, Am Freedom Train Comt, 75; mem, Albany Bicentennial Comn, 75- Bus & Prof Pos: Laborer, Local 190, Albany, NY, 67-70, sewer repair foreman, 71-73; independent ins agt, Michael F Conners & Son, 73-; asst scrap metal buyer, Ontario Scrap Metal, Inc, 74- Mem: Independent Mutual Ins Agts (educ comt, 74-75); Ancient Order of Hiberians (bicentennial rep & comt chmn, 75); CofC (liaison to bicentennial comt, 75); Int Brotherhood Laborers. Honors & Awards: Student Activity Award, Siena Col Student Senate, 71; Alumni Fund Drive Award, Siena Col Alumni Asn, 73. Relig: Roman Catholic. Mailing Add: 3 Kerry Lane Albany NY 12211

CONNOLLY, JOHN STEVENS **(DFL)**
b St Paul, Minn, Feb 16, 32; s John Lawrence Connolly & Marie Stevens C; m 1958 to Carol McLellan; c John, Kathleen, Ann, William, Shelgh, Ignatius & Brigit. Educ: St Thomas Col, 51-54; Georgetown Law Ctr, 54-57. Polit & Govt Pos: Pub defender, Ramsey Co, Minn, 59-61; chmn, Minn Orgn, McCarthy for Pres, 68; deleg, Dem Nat Conv, 68; chmn, Fourth Dist Dem-Farmer-Labor Party, Minn, formerly; mem, Minn Dem-Farmer-Labor State Exec Comt. Bus & Prof Pos: Attorney-at-law, pvt practice, St Paul, Minn, 57- Mem: Am Bar Asn (chmn, Comt Legal Aid & Judicial Defendants for Minn); Am for Dem Action (bd dirs, Minn Br). Relig: Catholic. Legal Res: 1382 Summit Ave St Paul MN 55105 Mailing Add: 100 McColl Bldg St Paul MN 55101

CONNOLLY, LAURENCE E, JR **(D)**
Maine State Rep
Mailing Add: 91 State St Portland ME 04101

CONNOLLY, MICHAEL JOSEPH **(D)**
Mass State Rep
b Boston, Mass, Apr 20, 47; s Michael Joseph Connolly, Jr & Florence McCarthy C; m 1971 to Lynda Murphy; c John. Educ: Col of the Holy Cross, AB, 69; New Eng Sch Law, 76; Young Dem; Boston Club. Polit & Govt Pos: Legis aide, Boston City Coun, 69-70; mem, West Roxbury Local Adv Coun, Mass, 70-72; mem, Dem Ward Comt, West Roxbury, 72-; Mass State Rep, 73-, chmn comt on air pollution in Boston, Mass House Rep, currently. Bus & Prof Pos: Teacher, Boston Latin Sch, 69 & 71-72. Mil Serv: Entered as Pfc, Army Nat Guard, 69, serv in Mil Police. Mem: Mass Coun Older Am; Health Planning Coun for Gtr Boston; Citizens for Participation Polit; KofC; Soc in Dedham Apprehension Horse Thieves. Relig: Roman Catholic. Mailing Add: 122 Montclair Ave Roslindale MA 02131

CONNOLLY, PHYLLIS FERN · **(R)**
Regional Dir, NDak Fedn Rep Women
b Beulah, NDak, Feb 11, 29; d Willie Keller & Clara Heihn K; m 1953 to James Louis Connolly; c Sheila (Mrs Paul Quickstad) & James Michael. Educ: Bismarck Jr & Sr High Schs, NDak, 41-43. Polit & Govt Pos: Pres, Dist 33 Rep Women's Fedn, NDak, 59-; NDak vchmn, Goldwater Nomination Comt, 64; mem nat comt, Presidential Campaign, 64; alt deleg, Rep Nat Conv, 64, deleg, 72; area orgn chmn, Election Campaign, 66; charter pres, Mercer Co Rep Women's Fedn; coordr, West Dist, TARS, 68; regional dir, NDak Fedn Rep Women, 70-; vchairwoman, NDak Rep State Comt, formerly. Mem: Cowbelles; Farm Bur; Am Red Cross; PTA; State Cancer Bd. Relig: Protestant. Legal Res: Golden Valley ND 58641 Mailing Add: Connolly Ranch Dunn Center ND 58626

CONNOLLY, VIRGINIA STRAUGHAN **(R)**
Conn State Rep
b Manchester, Conn, June 25, 14; d Wayland Kemper Straughan & Ruth Wright S; m 1935 to James Cyril Connolly; c Pamela (Mrs David L Bartlett, IV) & James Patrick. Educ: Hartford Hosp Sch Nursing, RN, 34; St Joseph Col, BS, 51; Nat Communicable Diseases Ctr, US Dept Health, cert, 69. Polit & Govt Pos: Secy, Simsbury Housing Authority, Conn, 67-71; chmn & munic agt, Simsbury Comn on Aging, 71-; Conn State Rep, 71-, chmn pub health & safety comt, Conn Gen Assembly, 73- Bus & Prof Pos: Staff mem, Hartford Vis Nurses

Asn, 34-35; surgical staff, Hartford Hosp, 46-48; admin, Simsbury Vis Nurses Asn, 50-65; epidemiologist, St Francis Hosp, 68-; dir, Simsbury Bank & Trust Co, 71- Publ: Hospital epidemiology, Conn Nurses Asn J, 69; A program for infection control, Supvr Nurse, 71. Mem: St Barnabas Guild for Nurses; Order Women Legislators; Simsbury Hist Soc. Relig: Episcopal. Mailing Add: 91 Old Farms Rd Simsbury CT 06092

CONNOR, JOHN THOMAS (D)
b Syracuse, NY, Nov 3, 14; s Michael J Connor & Mary V Sullivan C; m 1940 to Mary O'Boyle; c John Thomas, Geoffrey & Lisa Forrestal. Educ: Syracuse Univ, AB, magna cum laude, 36; Harvard Univ, JD, 39; Phi Beta Kappa; Phi Kappa Psi; Phi Kappa Phi; Phi Kappa Alpha. Polit & Govt Pos: Gen counsel, Off Sci Research & Develop, Washington, DC, 42-44; counr, Off Naval Research & spec asst to Secy of Navy, 43-47; Secy of Commerce, 65-67. Bus & Prof Pos: Lawyer, Cravath de Gersdorff, Swaine & Wood, New York, NY, 39-42; gen attorney, Merck & Co, Rahway, NJ, 47, secy & counsel, 47-50, vpres, 50-55, pres & dir, 55-65; incorporator, Commun Satellite Corp; dir, Gen Motors Corp; dir, Gen Foods Corp; pres & dir, Allied Chem Corp, 67-69; chmn & dir, 69-; dir, Chase Manhattan Bank, 68- Mil Serv: Entered as 2nd Lt, Marine Corps, 44, released as 1st Lt, 45. Mem: Bus Coun; Coun Foreign Rels; Syracuse Univ (trustee); Tuskegee Inst (trustee). Relig: Roman Catholic. Mailing Add: Blue Mill Rd RD 2 Morristown NJ 07960

CONNOR, ROBERT JOSEPH (D)
NY State Assemblyman
b Union City, NJ, Nov 3, 27; s John Joseph Connor & Anna Murphy C; m 1954 to Marcia Katherine Nightingale; c Leslie S, R David, Steven P, Jeffrey A, Michael D, Siobhan E, Lawrence, Tania & Matthew. Educ: Mt St Mary's Col, BS in Chem, 51. Polit & Govt Pos: Legislator, Rockland Co Legis, NY, 70-75; NY State Assemblyman, 75- Mil Serv: Entered as Pvt, Army, 46, released as Sgt, 47, after serv in 2nd Inf Div. Legal Res: 29 Prides Crossing New City NY 10956 Mailing Add: 60 Maple Ave New City NY 10956

CONNOR, ROBERT T (D)
Borough Pres, Staten Island, NY
b Washington, DC, 1919; m 1947 to Carol Pouch; c Susan & Robert, Jr. Educ: Boston Col; US Naval Acad; City Univ New York, BA, 74. Hon Degrees: LLD, St John's Univ, 72. Polit & Govt Pos: Opers officer, Cent Intel Agency, 46-49; staff officer, Foreign Serv, Dept State, 49-51, vconsul, US Foreign Inst, Mexico City; councilman-at-lg, Staten Island, NY, 63-65, Borough Pres, 65-; mem, Bd of Estimate, New York, currently. Bus & Prof Pos: Exec, Pouch Terminals, 51-63. Mil Serv: Entered as A/S, Navy, 36, released as Lt Comdr, 45; Capt, Naval Res, 45- Mem: KofC; Naval Acad Alumni Asn; Am Legion; VFW; NY Coun Navy League. Honors & Awards: Outstanding Serv Award, Salvation Army; Distinguished Citizens Award, B'nai B'rith; Wagner Col Distinguished Citizenship Award; Outstanding Citizen Award, Am Legion. Relig: Catholic. Legal Res: 88 Coventry Rd Staten Island NY 10304 Mailing Add: Borough Hall St George Staten Island NY 10301

CONNOR, ROBERT THOMAS (R)
Del State Rep
b Philadelphia, Pa, Jan 2, 38; s Albert L Connor & Nancy Owens C; single. Educ: West Chester State Col, BA, 61; Villanova Univ, MA, 64; Univ Del. Polit & Govt Pos: Del State Rep, 71-; alt deleg, Rep Nat Conv, 72. Bus & Prof Pos: Dir child guid, New Castle, Del, 65- Mem: Nat Educ Asn; Del State Educ Asn; New Castle Rotary Club. Honors & Awards: Outstanding Young Educator, Del Jaycees Award, 68. Relig: Roman Catholic. Mailing Add: 18 Crippen Dr New Castle DE 19720

CONNORS, HOLLIS GAY (R)
Treas, State of Mont
b Minn, Feb 21, 12; d Daniel Victor Dotson & Evelyn Felenzer D; m 1960 to Thomas Eugene Connors. Educ: Northwestern Sch Law, LLB, 49. Polit & Govt Pos: Treas, State of Mont, 73- Bus & Prof Pos: Pvt practice of law, Helena, Mont, 52-73. Mem: Mont Bar Asn; First Judicial Dist Bar Asn; Am Judicature Soc. Relig: Christian. Legal Res: 205 N Harrison Townsend MT 59644 Mailing Add: State Capitol Helena MT 59601

CONNORS, JOHN H (D)
Iowa State Rep
Mailing Add: 1316 East 22nd Des Moines IA 50317

CONNORS, JOHN HENRY (D)
Chmn, Saratoga Co Dem Party, NY
b Mechanicville, NY, Jan 28, 29; s Joseph Connors & Anna Hickey C; m 1954 to Kathleen Hebert; c John Gregory, Kevin Edward, Patricia Ann, Thomas Edward, Maureen Anna & Shannon Alice. Educ: Russell Sage Col, 50-52. Polit & Govt Pos: Mayor, Mechanicville, NY, 61-69; chmn, Saratoga Co Dem Party, 74-; pres, NY State Conf Mayors, Albany, 67-69. Bus & Prof Pos: Ins & real estate broker, Capital Dist, 54-; pres, Connors-Ridge Homes Inc, Capital Dist, 62- Mil Serv: Entered as Pvt, Army, 50, released as Sgt 1/C, 52, after serv in Corp Engr. Mem: Saratoga Co Bd Realtors (pres); Elks; KofC; Mechanicville Country Club. Relig: Roman Catholic. Legal Res: 122 N Second St Mechanicville NY 12118 Mailing Add: PO Box 69 Park Plaza Mechanicville NY 12118

CONOLY, MARTHA VIRGINIA (D)
Chmn, Culberson Co Dem Comt, Tex
b ElDorado, Ark, Dec 16, 35; d Goyne Talmage Hinson & Flora Bertha Emerson H; m 1954 to John Edward Conoly; c Timothy Edward, Judith Ann, Mary Virginia & Donna Marie. Educ: Southern Methodist Univ correspondence course in Real Estate Law, 69. Polit & Govt Pos: Chmn, Culberson Co Dem Comt, Tex, 72- Bus & Prof Pos: Corp officer & bookkeeper, Wildhorse Valley Farms, Inc, 53-; owner-realtor, Conoly Realty Co, 68-; corp officer & bookkeeper, Van Horn Chem & Supply, Inc; Tex Mem: Van Horn Zoning Comn; Tex Elec Asn (charter mem); CofC (dir); Culberson Co Hosp Auxiliary (charter mem, 70, chmn finance comt, 73-, secy, 73, treas, 74-75); VFW Auxiliary (charter mem, 75). Honors & Awards: Charter Mem Pin, Auxiliary to the Culberson Co Hosp, 71, 300 Hour Bar, 74. Relig: Catholic. Legal Res: 206 W Sixth Van Horn TX 79855 Mailing Add: PO Box 747 Van Horn TX 79855

CONOVER, MAX (D)
Mont State Sen
Mailing Add: PO Box 46 Broadview MT 59015

CONRAD, LARRY A (D)
Secy of State, Ind
m 1957 to Mary Lou Hoover; c Jeb Allyn, Amy Lou, Andrew Birch & Jody McDade. Educ: Ball State Univ, AB, 57; Ind Univ Sch Law, LLB, 61. Polit & Govt Pos: Secy of State, Ind, 70-; chief counsel, US Senate Subcomt Const Amendments, 64-69. Mem: Am Bar Asn; March of Dimes (state chmn, 73-75); Northwest Ind Sickle Cell Found (mem adv bd); Pub Action through Correctional Effort (bd dirs); Ind Am Revolution Bicentennial Comn (chmn festivals comt). Legal Res: 7153 N Meridian St Indianapolis IN 46260 Mailing Add: 201 State House Indianapolis IN 46204

CONRAD, PRISCILLA PAULETTE (D)
b Scottsbluff, Nebr, Aug 10, 32; d Carl John Greisen & Jacqueline Gullett G; m 1963 to Louis Neal Conrad; c Cynthia J, Randy J & Louis N. Educ: Loretto Heights Col, 1 year; Pa State Univ, 2 years. Polit & Govt Pos: Dem committeewoman, Precinct 1602, Denver, Colo, 63-67; vcapt, 16th Dist Dem Party, 67-68; liaison for Dem Party & White Buffalo Coun of Am Indians, 67-68; vchmn, Denver Co Dem Party, 68-73; mem, Comt on Party Struct-Deleg Selection & Human Rights Comn, Colo Dem Party, 69; co-founder, Colo Dem Women's Caucus & Denver Co Women's Caucus, 72, membership chmn, Denver Co Women's Caucus, currently. Bus & Prof Pos: Mgr, basic stock, Gimbels Retail Stores, Philadelphia, Pa, 57-60; mgr, ready-to-wear, Joslins Retail Store, Aurora, Colo, 60-62; buyer, coats, May D&F Retail Store, Denver, 62-63; state coordr, Cystic Fibrosis Res Found, 71-73; admin para legal, Dist Attorney's Off, Second Judicial Dist, Denver, currently. Mem: Nat Orgn Women; Nat Neighbors; Jane Jefferson Dem Club Colo; John F Kennedy Dem Club; Gtr Parkhill, Inc. Honors & Awards: Merit Award for Contribution to Educ TV. Relig: Lutheran. Mailing Add: 2870 Magnolia Denver CO 80207

CONRADT, ERVIN W (R)
Wis State Rep
b Bovina, Wis, Oct 4, 16; m 1938 to Grace Voight. Educ: Spring Brook Elem Sch, Outagamie Co, Wis. Polit & Govt Pos: Supvr, Town Bd, Wis, 51-52, chmn, 53-67; mem bd, Outagamie Co, 53-; Rep precinct committeeman, 56; mem, Rep Statutory Comt, 57-58; chmn, Outagamie Co Hwy Comt, 66; Wis State Rep, 64-, mem comt excise & fees, 67, chmn comt printing, vchmn comt hwy & transportation comt, Wis State Legis, 69. Bus & Prof Pos: Farmer; ins agt, 57-59. Mem: Church Coun (pres). Mailing Add: Rte 2 Shiocton WI 54170

CONROY, EDWARD THOMAS (D)
Md State Sen
b New York, NY, Jan 31, 29; s William Conroy & Mary Clifford C; m 1951 to Mary Ann O'Connor; c Edward John & Kevin. Educ: Fordham Univ, BS, 51; Georgetown Law Ctr, JD, 56, LLM, 57; Delta Theta Phi. Polit & Govt Pos: State vchmn, Vet for Kennedy, Md, 60; Md State Deleg, 62-66, chmn, Prince George's Co Deleg, 62-65; Md State Sen, 24th Dist, Prince George's Co, chmn const & pub law comt, Md State Senate, 75-; chmn, Gov Comt to Promote Employ for Handicapped, Prince George's Co, 69-; mem, President's Comt Employ Handicapped, currently; chmn consumer protection comt, Southern Coun State Govts, currently. Bus & Prof Pos: Practicing attorney, Edward T Conroy & Assocs, 57- Mil Serv: Entered as 2nd Lt, Army, 52, released as 1st Lt, 54, after serv in Inf; Silver Star Medal; 2 Purple Hearts; Spec Commendation by Gen Mark W Clark. Publ: Articles published on legal subjects pertaining to torts, med-legal practice, etc. Mem: Am Trial Lawyers Asn; Int Platform Asn; Lions; Am Legion; KofC (4 degree). Honors & Awards: Fordham Univ Encaenia Award; Outstanding Md Official, Md Munic League, 67 & 71; Outstanding Disabled Am Vet in US, 68; Nat Comdr, Disabled Am Vet, 71-72. Relig: Catholic. Mailing Add: 12432 Shawmont Lane Bowie MD 20715

CONROY, RICHARD L (R)
Chmn, Jefferson Co Rep Cent Comt, Ore
b Madras, Ore, Mar 5, 33; s John E Conroy & Mary Ann Riley C; m 1961 to Irene J Reif; c Mary Elaine, Sheila Ann, John Daniel & Erin Marie. Educ: Univ Ore; Kappa Sigma. Polit & Govt Pos: Chmn, Jefferson Co Rep Cent Comt, Ore, currently, precinct committeeman, 59-64. Mil Serv: Entered as Pvt, Army, 56, released as SP-4, 58, after serv in 17th Signal Bn, Karlsruhe, Ger. Mem: Ore Auto Dealers Asn (bd dirs, 72-77); Madras-Jefferson Co CofC (pres, 73 & 74); Scottish Rite; Madras Lions Club (secy, 73); Elks. Relig: Episcopal; Mem, Bishops Comt, St Marks Episcopal Church, 64-67 & 74-75, pres, Bishops Comt, 72-73. Mailing Add: Box 48 Bean Dr Madras OR 97741

CONROY, THOMAS R (D)
Mont State Rep
b Harlowton, Mont, Nov 12, 34; s Clement M Conroy & Edna Marie Buckland C; m to Colleen L Barnes; c Harlan, Denise, Berwyn, Michelle, Lyndon & Molly. Educ: Rocky Mountain Col, 54. Polit & Govt Pos: Mont State Rep, 75- Bus & Prof Pos: Rancher. Mem: Elks; KofC. Relig: Catholic. Mailing Add: 607 W Third St Hardin MT 59034

CONSIDINE, JOHN J (D)
Fla State Rep
Legal Res: 721 W Tiffany Dr 1 West Palm Beach FL 33407 Mailing Add: 434 House Off Bldg Tallahassee FL 32304

CONSTANTINO, PATRICK RONALD (D)
b Puunene, Hawaii, May 6, 43; s Francisco Constantino (deceased) & Felisa Cabacungan C; m 1961 to Corazon Bio; c Cary Carl, Darlene Frances, Pamely Christine & Jamie Lynn. Educ: Maui Community Col, 61-62; Univ Calif, Los Angeles, 62-64. Polit & Govt Pos: Vpres, Young Dem Hawaii, 66-67, dir, 70-71; pres, Coun Polit Assocs, 67-; deleg, Dem Nat Conv, 68; deleg & mem credentials comt, Hawaii Dem Conv, 68, deleg & mem Maui select credentials comt, 70; secy, 27th Dem Precinct Maui, 68-69 & 70-71; mgt asst to mayor, Co Maui, Hawaii, 69-; mem, Hawaii Dem Party; mem, Co Traffic Safety Coun, Employ of Handicapped, Comt on Drag Racing & Jury Comn. Publ: Mayor Announces Cabinet, 11/68, Youngest Member of the Cabinet, 1/69 & First Filipino to be Appointed to a Cabinet Position, 1/69, Maui Newspaper Co. Mem: Pukalani Filipino Community Asn; Maui Jr CofC; J Walter Cameron Ctr (rev panel); Big Brothers, Inc; Int Platform Asn. Relig: Catholic. Mailing Add: 388 Kilani Pl Pukalani HI 96788

CONTA, DENNIS J (D)
Wis State Rep
Mailing Add: 3489 N Hackett Ave Milwaukee WI 53211

CONTE, JOHN J (D)
Mass State Rep
Mailing Add: State Capitol Boston MA 02133

CONTE, SILVIO O (R)
US Rep, Mass
b Pittsfield, Mass, Nov 9, 21; s Ottavio Conte & Lucia Lora C; m 1947 to Corinne Louise Duval; c Michelle, Sylvia, John F X & Gayle. Educ: Boston Col; Boston Col Law Sch, JD, 49; hon mem, Phi Delta Phi & Pi Sigma Alpha. Hon Degrees: LLD, Williams Col & Hampshire Col, 70, North Adams State Col, 72 & Univ Mass, Amherst, 73. Polit & Govt Pos: Mass State Sen, 51-58; US Rep, First Dist, Mass, 59-; deleg & mem platform comt, Rep Nat Conv, 60, 64, 68 & 72, chmn subcomt bldg greater prosperity, 72; vchmn, Rep Cong Campaign Comt, Washington, DC. Bus & Prof Pos: Law practice, 50-65. Mil Serv: Entered as Seaman 1/C, Navy, 42, released as Mechanic 3/C, 44. Honors & Awards: Admitted to practice before the Supreme Court of the US; named Outstanding Young Man of Year, Mass Jr CofC, 54; football at Boston Col. Relig: Catholic. Relig: Catholic. Legal Res: Blythewood Dr Onota Lake Pittsfield MA 01201 Mailing Add: 239 Cannon House Off Bldg Washington DC 20515

CONTILLO, PAUL J (D)
NJ State Assemblyman
Mailing Add: State House Trenton NJ 08625

CONVERSE, KENNETH E (D)
Okla State Sen
Mailing Add: State Capitol Oklahoma City OK 73105

CONWAY, JAMES FRANCIS (D)
Mo State Sen
b St Louis, Mo, June 27, 32; s Charles Francis Conway & Amelia Buchholz C; m 1955 to Joan Carol; c Michael John, Stephen James, Diane Marie, Matthew Joseph & Daniel Francis. Educ: Gen Motors Inst; St Louis Univ, BS, 55 & MBA, 64. Polit & Govt Pos: Mo State Rep, 65th Dist, 67-74; Mo State Sen, 75- Bus & Prof Pos: Pres, ACI Plastics, Inc, 67- Mil Serv: Entered as Pvt, Army, 55, released as Spec 3/C, 57, after serv in 13th Inf Regt, 8th Inf Div, Ger, 57; Hon Student, Radio Mech Sch, Ft Carson, Colo, 56. Mem: Engrs Club of St Louis; St Vincent de Paul Soc; St Louis CofC. Relig: Catholic. Mailing Add: 3811 Flora Pl St Louis MO 63110

CONWAY, JAMES STEPHEN (D)
Mass State Rep
b Malden, Mass, July 4, 30; s Michael Stephen Conway & Beatrice McGonagle C; m 1951 to Ann Rowena Boudreau; c Cheryl Ann & Stephen Marc. Educ: Malden High Sch, grad. Polit & Govt Pos: Mem sch comt, Malden, Mass, 64-65; city councillor, Malden, 66-69; Mass State Rep, 69- Bus & Prof Pos: Bank clerk, First Nat Bank of Malden, Mass, 53-58; ins agt, John Hancock Mutual Ins Co, 58- Mil Serv: Entered as Pvt, Army, 48, released as Pfc, 49, after serv in 37th Field Artil Bn, Ft Lewis, Wash; 26th Inf Div, Nat Guard, 49-60. Mem: KofC; Hibernians; Moose; Eagles; Holy Name Soc. Relig: Catholic. Mailing Add: 67 Gilbert St Malden MA 02148

CONWAY, JOHN (R)
Finance Chmn, Eighth Dist Rep Party, Wis
b Appleton, Wis, Sept 10, 24; s John Conway & Jane Evans C; m 1966 to Carole M Steiner; c John, Jr, Lydia Jane, Vickie & Catherine. Educ: Northwestern Univ, BS, 49; Delta Upsilon. Polit & Govt Pos: Chmn, Outagamie Co Rep Party, Wis, 61-63; chmn, Eighth Dist Rep Party, 63-67, finance chmn, 69-; Wis Housing Chmn & Sgt at arms, Rep Nat Conv, 64, deleg, 68; mem, Aeronaut Coun, State of Wis, 68-, chmn, 72- Bus & Prof Pos: Pres, Conway Hotel Co, 52-; sr vpres, Air Wis, 66-; pres, Lakeshore Inn, Inc, 68- Mil Serv: Entered as Pvt, Army Air Forces, 44, released as 2nd Lt, 46, after serv in 513th Troop Carrier Group, China-Burma-India Theatre, 45-46; Bronze Star. Mem: Cornell Soc of Hotel Men; Rotary; Am Legion; Appleton Area CofC. Relig: Protestant. Mailing Add: 1530 Reid Dr Appleton WI 54911

CONWAY, JOHN E (R)
NMex State Sen
Mailing Add: 2352 Apache Lane Alamogordo NM 88310

CONWAY, JOHN O'CONNOR (D)
Chmn, Oswego Co Dem Comt, NY
b Oswego, NY, July 24, 11; s Daniel H Conway & Ellen O'Connor C; m 1962 to Mary Fitzgibbons; c Ellen. Educ: Harvard Col; Georgetown Univ Law Sch, LLB, 38. Polit & Govt Pos: Chmn, Oswego Co Dem Comt, NY, 58-; mayor, Oswego, 68- Bus & Prof Pos: Attorney-at-law, 46- Mil Serv: Entered Army, 42, released as 1st Lt, 46, after serv in 13th Cavalry, Tank Co Comdr, Light Tanks, ETO, 20 months; Bronze Star. Legal Res: 136 E Sixth St Oswego NY 13126 Mailing Add: 11 W Bridge St Oswego NY 13126

CONWAY, WILLIAM RAYFORD (D)
Fla State Rep
b Green Cove Springs, Fla, July 25, 11; s James Franklin Conway & Idella Jane Minton C; m 1950 to Dianne Anger; c William R, Jr, Robert Fisher, James Marvin, Julia Ann & John Charles. Educ: Univ Fla, BSBA, 36; Pi Kappa Phi. Polit & Govt Pos: Fla State Rep, Dist, 35, 66- Bus & Prof Pos: Pres, Fla Liquified Gas Asn, 50. Mil Serv: Entered as Lt(jg), Navy, 42, released as Lt Comdr, 45, after serv in PT Boats, SW Pac Theatre; Commanding Officer, Naval Res Training Div, re-50; Bronze Star; numerous battle stars. Mem: Univ Fla Nat Alumni Asn; Shrine; Mason; VFW; Kiwanis. Relig: Episcopal. Mailing Add: 116 Banyan Dr Ormond Beach FL 32074

CONWELL, EVELYN LONA (R)
Chmn, Northwestern Dist Rep Party, Alaska
b Kotzebue, Alaska, Oct 31, 30; d Louis Reich Sr & Mamie Holland R; m 1952 to George H Conwell, Jr; c May, Marie Loraine, Helen Diane, Georgianna, Camille Dorothy, Louise Sarah, Lenora Rose, Allan Brian & Lucinda Bernice. Educ: High sch correspondence course, grad, 46. Polit & Govt Pos: Nurse's aide, Bur Indian Affairs Hosp, Kotzebue, Alaska, 46-52; magistrate, Kotzebue, 59-60; city clerk, 59-66, food stamp supvr, 68-; cand, Alaska House Rep, Dist 17, 66; secy, Bur Indian Affairs Soc Serv, 67-68; chmn, Northwestern Dist Rep Party, 67-; mem, State Comt Nutrit, Kotzebue, 69; mem, Native Land Selection Comt, 73-74; mem, Nat Adv Coun Nurse Training, 73-; exec dir, Nana Regional Housing Authority, 75. Mem: March of Dimes (chmn); Am Cancer Soc (chmn); Alaska Crippled Children Asn; PTA (vpres & secy); Cath Ladies Altar Soc (pres, secy & treas). Relig: Catholic. Mailing Add: Box 125 Kotzebue AK 99751

CONYERS, JOHN, JR (D)
US Rep, Mich
b Detroit, Mich, May 16, 29; s John Conyers & Lucille C; single. Educ: Wayne State Univ, BA, 57; Wayne State Univ Law Sch, LLB, 58. Hon Degrees: LLD, Wilberforce Univ, 69. Polit & Govt Pos: Secy, 15th Cong Dist Dem Orgn; legis asst, Congressman John D Dingell, 58-61; referee, Mich Workmens Compensation Dept, 61-63; US Rep, 64-; mem House Comt Govt Opers, US House Rep, 71-, chmn Subcomt on Crime, House Judiciary Comt, 73; organized fact finding missions, Ala, 65, Miss, 66 & 67; deleg, Dem Nat Conv, 68 & 72. Bus & Prof Pos: Sr partner, Conyers, Bell & Townsend, Law Firm, 59-61; mem bd trustees, Martin Luther King Mem Ctr & Southern Elec Fund, 70-; vchmn, Am for Dem Action, 71- Mil Serv: Entered as Pvt, Army, 50, released as 2nd Lt, 54, after serv in Korea, 1 year; combat & merit citations. Publ: Co-auth, To change the course of history, In: Many Shades of Black, (ed, Wormley & Fenderson), Morrow, 69; auth, Politics & the Black revolution, Ebony, 8/69. Mem: Coun Foreign Rels; Multi-Cult Inst; Mem Cong for Peace Through Law; Med Comt Human Rights; Joint Action Community Serv (bd dirs, 68-). Honors & Awards: Rosa Parks Award for civil rights activities, Southern Christian Leadership Cong, 67. Relig: Baptist. Legal Res: 19970 Canterbury Rd Detroit MI 48221 Mailing Add: 2444 Rayburn House Off Bldg Washington DC 20515

CONZEMIUS, GEORGE ROBERT (DFL)
Minn State Sen
b Hastings, Minn, July 23, 36; s George Henry Conzemius & Margaret Driscoll C; m 1962 to Karen Jeanne Thorson; c Martha Jane, Anne Marie, Kristin Margaret & Sarah Jeanne. Educ: Univ Minn, BS, 59; Univ Oslo, Norway, 59; Delta Theta Sigma; Univ Minn Football Team; Agr Educ Club. Polit & Govt Pos: Deleg, Goodhue Co Dem-Farmer-Labor Party, Minn, 64-65, secy, 65-66; alderman, Cannon Falls City Coun, 65-66; chmn, Co Dem-Farmer-Labor Conv, 66; deleg, Minn State Dem-Farmer-Labor Conv, 66; Minn State Sen, Sixth Dist, 67- Bus & Prof Pos: Farmer, 55-; voc agr & sci teacher, Cannon Falls High Sch, 60-67. Mil Serv: Entered as Pvt, Army Res, 59, released as Airman 2/C, Air Force Res, 65. Mem: Nat Educ Asn; Future Farmers of Am; Farmer's Union; Delta Theta Sigma Alumni Corp. Relig: Catholic. Mailing Add: 800 W Hoffman Cannon Falls MN 55009

COODY, W G (BILL) (D)
Tex State Rep
Mailing Add: PO Box 572 Weatherford TX 76086

COOK, CECIL W (D)
NMex State Rep
b Rotan, Tex, July 18, 30; s Sam Cook & Addie B Carter C; m 1953 to Maxine Nuckols; s Sammy, Sandra & Jimmy. Educ: Eastern NMex Univ, grad, 56. Polit & Govt Pos: NMex State Rep, currently. Bus & Prof Pos: Dir, Roosevelt Co CofC, 63-65; secy-treas, Bd Educ, Portales, NMex, 65-; dir, NMex Asn Ins Agts, 66-68. Mil Serv: Entered as Seaman, Navy, 50, released as Radioman 3/C, 54, after serv in Task Force 77, Korea. Mem: Lions; Mason. Relig: Baptist. Legal Res: Valley Manor Estates Portales NM 88130 Mailing Add: PO Box 904 Portales NM 88130

COOK, CHARLES DAVID (R)
NY State Assemblyman
b Deposit, NY, Feb 26, 35; s Edward William Cook & Lillian Hicks C; m 1957 to Dorothy Behrens; c Linda Susanne, John Charles & Jeffrey David. Educ: Hartwick Col, BA, 56; Tau Kappa Epsilon. Polit & Govt Pos: Treas, Delaware Co, NY, 66-71; comnr, Social Serv, 71-72; NY State Assemblyman, 105th Dist, 73- Bus & Prof Pos: Ed, Bainbridge News, NY, 57-58 & Deposit Courier, 60-66. Mil Serv: Entered as Pvt E-1, Army, 58, released as SP-4, after serv in 37th Armor Unit, Ger, 59-60. Relig: Methodist. Mailing Add: 19 Prospect St Delhi NY 13753

COOK, CHARLES W
Dep Under Secy Air Force Space Syst
Mailing Add: Dept of Air Force Washington DC 20330

COOK, CLAYTON HENRY (D)
Chmn, Oldham Co Dem Exec Comt, Tex
b Moundridge, Kans, Apr 21, 12; s Herbert Cook & Bertha Wilkening C; m 1941 to Margery Maxine Manning; c Larry Clayton, Ronald Leigh, Michael Craig & Melanie Beth. Educ: Moundridge High Sch grad, 29. Polit & Govt Pos: Co chmn, Johnson for Sen Campaign, Tex, 48, 54 & 60, Stevenson & Kefauver Campaign, 56, Kennedy & Johnson Campaign, 60, Connally for Gov Campaign, 64 & Johnson & Humphrey Campaign, 64; mem, Tex Econ Comn, 50-54; chmn, Oldham Co Dem Exec Comt, 56-; mem, Gov Comt on Aging, 70-; adv, Tex Const Rev Comn. Mem: AF&AM (Past Master, Vega Masonic Lodge 899); Int Platform Asn; Vega Kiwanis Club; Amarillo Little Theater (bd dirs). Honors & Awards: Past Lt Gov Div 6 & past dist chmn, Past Lt Govs, Tex-Okla Dist, Kiwanis Int; Accredited One Act Play, Tex Univ Interscholastic League. Relig: Methodist. Mailing Add: Box 57 Vega TX 79092

COOK, DON W (R)
NY State Assemblyman
b Rochester, NY, July 8, 19; m 1944 to Dorothy Yanke; c Thomas, Kathleen & Susan. Polit & Govt Pos: Justice of the Peace, Henrietta, NY, 52-56; town supvr, 56-67; mem, Monroe Co Bd Supvrs, 56-67; NY State Assemblyman, 135th Dist, 67-; mem, Rochester Transportation Bd; chmn, Monroe Co Rep Comt, 72- Bus & Prof Pos: Salesman, William H Archer Corp & Clyde Milling Corp; proprietor, Henrietta Poultry Farm, 47-56. Mil Serv: Entered as Pvt, Marine Corps, 42, released as Sgt. Mem: Am Legion; Lions; VFW; Shrine; Mason. Relig: Presbyterian. Mailing Add: PO Box 37 Henrietta NY 14467

COOK, DONALD EUGENE (D)
Comnr, Beadle Co, SDak
b Ford City, Mo, July 2, 20; s Lloyd Cook & Cora Myrick C; m 1946 to Maxie Louise White; c Sidney Thomas & Connie Sue (Mrs Charles Rowen). Educ: King City High Sch, 33-36. Polit & Govt Pos: City councilman, King City, Mo, formerly; comnr, Beadle Co, SDak, 70-; alt deleg, Dem Nat Mid-Term Conf, 74. Bus & Prof Pos: Farmer-rancher, Mo & SDak, 46-75; owner-mgr, Cook's Feed & Seed Store, King City, 47-62; owner-mgr, Cook Seed Co, Huron, SDak, 62-75. Mil Serv: Entered as Pvt, Army, 42, released as 1st Sgt, 45, after serv in Med Corps, ETO, 3rd Army, 44-45; Bronze Star & Five European Combat Medals. Mem: Huron CofC; Shrine; Masonic Lodge; Am Legion; Sertoma. Relig: Presbyterian. Legal Res: 1829 Dexter Ct Huron SD 57350 Mailing Add: Box 823 Huron SD 57350

COOK, DONALD L (R)
Vt State Rep
Mailing Add: Fair Haven VT 05743

COOK, DORIS JEAN (D)
b Coraopolis, Pa, June 16, 34; d George Fredrick McAuley & Helen Shulin M; m 1955 to Jerome Joseph Cook; c Karen Jean, Kathleen Marie, Susan Ann & John George. Educ: Eastern High Sch, grad, 52. Polit & Govt Pos: Deleg, Dem Nat Conv, 72; Dem precinct deleg & Dem state deleg, Mich, 72-; mem, 18th Cong Dist Exec Bd, 73-; mem, Macomb Co Dem Exec Comt, 74- Bus & Prof Pos: Salesperson, Minn Fabrics, Inc, 70- Mem: PTA; United Dem of Warren, Mich (vpres, 75-). Relig: Catholic. Mailing Add: 31171 Fairfield Warren MI 48093

COOK, EUGENE OTIS (D)
RI State Rep
b Stoneham, Mass, Dec 14, 20; s Fred Otis Cook & Margaret Rivers C; m 1942 to Doris Mary Carey; c Michael F, Ronald E & Richard A. Educ: Cent High Sch, Providence, RI, grad, 38. Polit & Govt Pos: Mem town coun, Burrillville, RI, 68-70, town moderator, 70-74, RI State Rep, 74- Bus & Prof Pos: Cook Machy Assoc, 68- Mil Serv: Entered as A/S, Navy, 44, released as Seaman 1/C, 46, after serv in Asiatic Theatre, 45-46. Mem: Lions (bd dirs, 68-); Northwest Community Nurses (bd dirs, 70-); Bi-Centennial Comt. Relig: Catholic. Legal Res: Cooper Hill Rd Mapleville RI 02839 Mailing Add: Box 187 Mapleville RI 02839

COOK, FRANKLIN CHARLES (R)
b Los Angeles, Calif, Feb 13, 44; s Howard Frank Cook & Victoria Holdstock C; m 1973 to Eileen Lynn Casey; c Kevin Scott Cagle & Erin Elizabeth. Educ: Occidental Col, BA, 67; Phi Gamma Delta. Polit & Govt Pos: Legis asst, Sen Mark O Hatfield, Ore, 69-; mem, Rep State Cent Comt Calif, 74- Bus & Prof Pos: Dir & owner, Challenge-Cook Bros, Industry, Calif, 71-, Community Bank, Huntington Park, 72- & Stonewood Shopping Ctr, Downey, 74-; chmn bd, Inst Neighborhood Studies, Washington, DC, 74-; mem bd, ANERA, Washington, DC, 74- Mil Serv: Entered as E-1, Army Nat Guard, 68, released as E-3, 73. Mem: Am Friends Serv Comt; Mid East Comt; Southwest Region Peace Educ Div. Relig: Quaker. Legal Res: 1100 Kewen Dr San Marino CA 90108 Mailing Add: 15421 E Gale Ave Industry CA 91744

COOK, GEORGE EDWARD (D)
Ind State Rep
b Decatur, Ind, Apr 24, 27; s George Clyde Cook & Dorothy Labelle McCloskey C; m 1950 to Lois Anne Barrett; c Gary Lee, Pamela Anne, Douglas Edward & Jerry Alan. Educ: Grovertown High Sch, 45. Polit & Govt Pos: Marshall Co Councilman, Ind, 62-74; treas, Marshall Co Cent Dem Comt, 68-72; treas, Michiana Area Coun of Govts, 70-74; Ind State Rep, Dist 18, 74- Bus & Prof Pos: Co-owner, Cook Bros Furniture, Plymouth, Ind, 49-; partner, C&S Enterprises, Plymouth, 68- Mil Serv: Entered as Apprentice Seaman, Navy, 45, released as Coxswain, 46, after serv in CMBU 630, Pac Theatre, 45-46; Pac Theatre Serv Award; Good Conduct Medal. Mem: VFW; Am Legion; Northern Ind Econ Develop Asn; Eagles; Moose. Relig: Protestant. Mailing Add: 622 Rex St Plymouth IN 46563

COOK, GEORGIA MAE (D)
Chmn, Hand Co Dem Party, SDak
b Wessington, SDak, Feb 22, 29; d Bernard Nelson Rombough (deceased) & Lucy Stobbs R; m 1946 to Jacques Morris Cook; c Terry Alan, Michael Morris & Jackie Ann (Mrs Jerry Poindexter). Educ: Miller High Sch, SDak, 43-45. Polit & Govt Pos: Precinct committeewoman, Hand Co Dem Party, SDak, 50-68, vchmn, 68-74, chmn, 74-; youth chmn, SDak State Grange, 59-65; dist vchmn, Dem Party SDak, 74. Bus & Prof Pos: Co-owner, Cook Hereford Cattle Ranch, 46-; Star Rte mail contractor, US Govt, 66-; comnr, State Real Estate Comn, SDak, 73- Mem: Nat & SDak State Grange; Jobs Daughters Coun; SDak State Farm Safety Coun (vchmn, 60-74); SDak Star Rte Mail Contractors Asn (secy-treas, 68-75). Relig: Presbyterian. Mailing Add: Rte Box 5 Ree Heights SD 57371

COOK, HOWARD C (R)
b Toledo, Ohio, Feb 20, 18; s Henry D Cook & Caroline Ackerman C; m 1943 to Elizabeth Marie Ruch; c Susan E & Howard C, Jr. Educ: Wittenberg Univ, AB, 39; Harvard Univ Law Sch, LLB, 42, JD, 69; Phi Gamma Delta. Polit & Govt Pos: Deleg, Rep Nat Conv, 48, alt deleg, 68 & 72; mem, Civil Serv Comn, Toledo, Ohio, 48-51; vmayor, Toledo, 52-53; Toledo Councilman, 52-53 & 59-66; vchmn, Lucas Co Charter Comn, 58-59; cand for US Rep, Ohio, 60 & Ohio House of Rep, 64; Ohio State Sen, 66-74, chmn com & labor comts, Ohio State Senate, until 74. Bus & Prof Pos: Pres, Riverside Hosp, 62-; attorney-at-law, currently. Mil Serv: Aviator, Navy, World War II, 42-45; Naval Air Ferry Command Squadron VRF2. Mem: Am Bar Asn; Toledo CofC; Gtr Toledo Ment Health Asn (bd dirs); Amvets; RONS. Relig: Lutheran; past pres, Lutheran Men's League, Toledo; past vpres, Brotherhood of Am Lutheran Church. Mailing Add: 3818 Beechway Blvd Toledo OH 43614

COOK, JACK RANDALL, SR (R)
Chmn, Andrews Co Rep Party, Tex
b Caddo, Tex, May 27, 24; s Joe McMeen Cook & Minnie Jackson C; m 1950 to Yvonne Gober; c Jack Randall, Jr & Robert Owen. Educ: Weatherford Jr Col, 42-43; Tarleton State Col, 46-48. Polit & Govt Pos: Campaign mgr, State Rep, Andrews Co, Tex, 62; precinct chmn, Precinct Three, Andrews Co, 62-63; deleg, Tex Rep Conv, 62-70; chmn, Andrews Co Rep Party, 63-; deleg, Rep Nat Conv, 72. Bus & Prof Pos: Subsurface pressure analyst, Shell Oil Co, McCamey, Tex, 49-50, pumper, Denver City & Seminole, 50-53, area subsurface pressure analyst, Hobbs, NMex, 54-60, Andrews, Tex, 60-65, well analyst, Andrews, 65- Mil Serv: Entered as A/S, Navy, 43, released as Radioman 3/C, 46, after serv in Armed Guard Pac, Honolulu, New Guinea, Pac Islands, Okinawa & Calcutta. Mem: Andrews Boys Club of Am; Toast Masters Club; CofC. Relig: Church of Christ; Lay Teacher, Permian Church of Christ. Mailing Add: 1318 Alpine Dr Andrews TX 79714

COOK, JAMES HARVEY (D)
Miss State Rep
Mailing Add: Box 235 Weir MS 39772

COOK, JOHN LEWIS (R)
Chmn, Charlton Rep Town Comt, Mass
b Natick, Mass, Oct 22, 18; s Arthur Rupert Cook & Margaret Dudley Lewis C; m 1953 to Gretchen Clough; c Jonathan Clough, Margaret Dudley, Heidi & Polly. Educ: Northeastern Univ, BSBA, 41. Polit & Govt Pos: Mem, Charlton Rep Finance Comt, Mass, 51-62; mem, Charlton Sch Comt, 62-; Charlton Rep Town Comt, 68-69 & 70-, chmn, currently; Rep cand, Mass State Sen, 68; mem, Dudley Charlton, Southbridge Regional Sch Planning Bd, 68-69. Bus & Prof Pos: Owner & operator, Dairy Farm, Charlton; mem, Dudley Charlton Regional Sch Comt, currently. Mil Serv: Entered as Pvt, Army Air Force, 42, released as T/Sgt, 45, after serv in Hq Squadron, 13th Army Air Force, Southwest Pac, 43-45; Northern Solomon, Bismark Archipelago & Philippine Liberation Ribbons; Good Conduct Medal. Mem: Worcester Co Farm Bur Asn; New Eng Milk Prod Asn; Nat Farmers Orgn. Relig: Protestant. Mailing Add: Stafford St Charlton MA 01507

COOK, KENNETH R (D)
RI State Rep
b Woonsocket, RI, Apr 18, 29. Educ: Cumberland schs. Polit & Govt Pos: RI State Rep, 64- Bus & Prof Pos: Shipping clerk. Mil Serv: Army, 51-53; serv in Ger. Mem: Textile Workers of Am (vpres local 1539); Amvets; Ital Working Men's Club. Mailing Add: 313 Estes St Woonsocket RI 02895

COOK, KENNETH RICHARD (D)
b Midwest, Wyo, Aug 27, 33; s Glenn Warren Cook & Virginia L Glenn C; m 1955 to Arlene Rae Croco; c Tracey Susan & Valerie Ann. Educ: Univ Wyo, BS, 55; Inter-Fraternity Coun; Pi Delta Kappa; Phi Epsilon Phi; Fourth Estate Club; Sigma Nu. Polit & Govt Pos: Admin asst to US Sen Gale McGee, Wyo, 59-73 & 75- Bus & Prof Pos: Staff writer, UPI, Denver, Colo, 57-58; news ed, Powell Tribune, Wyo, 58-59. Mil Serv: Entered as Recruit, Navy, 55, released as Journalist 3/C, 57, after serv in Submarine Forces, Atlantic Fleet, 55-57. Mem: Asn Admin Asst. Relig: Methodist. Legal Res: Powell WY 82435 Mailing Add: 4307 Selkirk Dr Fairfax VA 22030

COOK, MARJORIE JEANNE (MARGE) (D)
Secy, Knox Co Dem Comt, Maine
b St George, Maine, Dec 28, 21; d Forrest Alexander Wall & Pearle Ames W; m 1937 to Hartford Manvas Cook; c Jeanne (Mrs Hayden M Soule, Jr), Brian Alexander, Barry Walker, Patrick David & Jay Quentin. Educ: St George High Sch, grad, 36, commercial course, 69-70; Georges Valley Adult Educ, shorthand & bookkeeping; Bowdoin Col Assessors' Sch, cert 71 & 72. Polit & Govt Pos: Secy, St George Dump Comt, 63-64; cand, Maine State Rep, 66; chmn, Knox Co Marine Fisheries Exten Comt, 66-67; mem, Maine Dem State Comt, 66-70; secy, St George Dem Town Comt, 66-, selectman, St George, 69-; mem, Gov Keep Maine Scenic Comt, 66-; justice of peace, 66-; secy, Maine Marine Fisheries Comt, 68-69; mem, Maine Dem Platform Comt, 68-70; assoc supvr, Knox-Lincoln Soil & Water Conserv, 71-; mem, Gov Adv Coun Status Women, 71-; mem, Legis Comt Interim Study Maine Marine Fisheries, 72-73; secy, Knox Co Dem Comt, Maine, currently. Publ: Auth, Town reports, Maine Times, 3/72; NC Wyeth letters (rev), Down East, 3/72; Scott woodlands, KLSWCD Newsletter, 11/72; plus others. Mem: Nat Resources Coun; Maine Arborist Asn; St George PTA; Georges Valley High Am Field Serv; Rebekah. Honors & Awards: Homemaking prizes ribbons & contest prizes; New Eng Rep, CBS Cinderella Show. Relig: Protestant. Mailing Add: Wallston Rd Tenants Harbor ME 04860

COOK, MARLOW WEBSTER (R)
b July 27, 26; s Floyd T Cook & Mary Lee Webster C; m 1947 to Nancy E Remmers; c Christine, Caroline, Nancy, Mary Louise & Marlow Webster, Jr. Educ: Univ Louisville, Col Arts & Sci, 46-48; Univ Louisville Sch Law, LLB, 50. Polit & Govt Pos: Ky State Rep, 57-61; co judge, Jefferson Co, Ky, 61-68; alt deleg, Rep Nat Conv, 68, deleg-at-lg, 72; US Sen, Ky, 68-75; co-chmn, 1973 US Senate Youth Prog, US Senate, formerly. Bus & Prof Pos: Attorney-at-law, Hottell & Stephenson, Louisville, 52-61. Mil Serv: Entered Submarine Serv, Atlantic & Pac Theaters, 45-46. Publ: The challenge of urbanization, Am Co Govt Mag, 9/68; New hope for corrections: the creation of a national institute, Ky Law J, 72. Mem: Ky State & Louisville Bar Asns; US Coast Guard Acad (bd overseers); Pikeville Col (bd trustees); Bank of Louisville (bd dirs). Honors & Awards: Ky Broadcasters Asn Man of Year, 70; Asn of Gen Contractors of Ky Man of the Year, 71; Nat Fedn of Independent Businessmen Ky Man of the Year, 72; One of two Senators app by Pres of Senate to rep US at 15th Commonwealth Parliamentary Conf, Trinidad, 69; deleg, 11th Mex-US Interparliamentary Conf & 14th Can-US Interparliamentary Conf. Relig: Catholic. Mailing Add: 600 Federal Pl Louisville KY 40202

COOK, MARTHA ROBINSON (R)
Mem, Rep Nat Finance Comt
b Winchester, Va, Aug 8, 34; d Harry Delmer Robinson & Louise Hall R; m 1962 to William F Cook, Jr; c Westwood Beverley Byrd & Anne Robinson Byrd. Educ: Bennett Jr Col, AA, 54. Polit & Govt Pos: Chmn, Chapel Dist, Va, 67-71; vchmn, Seventh Dist Rep Party, 68-; co-chmn, Ladies for Lin, 69; campaign chmn & women rep, Va Fed Rep Women Comt, 69; chmn, Women for Robinson, Seventh Dist, 70-72; mem, Va State Rep Finance Comt, 70-73, chmn women's div, 71-73; mem, Rep Nat Finance Comt, 71-; chmn, Clarke Co Rep Comt, 73- Bus & Prof Pos: Bd mem, Powhalan Sch, 64-67; bd mem, Va Sch for the Deaf & Blind, 70- Mem: Millwood Country Club; 1925 F Street Club. Relig: Episcopal. Mailing Add: Roselawn RFD Box 16 Boyce VA 22620

COOK, NANCY (D)
Del State Sen
Mailing Add: Kenton DE 19955

COOK, PATSY HAINES (D)
b Dawson, Ga, Oct 6, 37; d Kimbrough Wheeles Haines & Vivian Pipkin H; m 1953 to Heyward Hilliar Cook, Jr; c Cathy (Mrs Short), Heyward, III, Sam & John; one grandchild. Educ: Terrell High Sch, Dawson, Ga, dipl, 55; Albany Area Voc Sch, dipl bus, 67. Polit & Govt Pos: Co-chmn, Carter for Gov Campaign, Lee Co, Ga, 70; admiral, Gov Ga Staff, 71-; mem, Ga State Dem Exec Comt, formerly. Bus & Prof Pos: Secy, sci research, DeKalb Agr Research, Inc, 68-69. Mem: Am Red Cross (co-chmn, Lee Co); Lee Co PTA Asn (pres, 67-); Lee Co Home Demonstration Club. Honors & Awards: First place, State Tennis Championship, 54. Relig: Methodist. Legal Res: Walnut St Leesburg GA 31763 Mailing Add: PO Box 384 Leesburg GA 31763

COOK, RICHARD K (R)
b White Plains, NY, Nov 14, 31; s Albert James Cook, mother deceased; m 1959 to Marjorie Ann Shellabarger; c Geoffrey Scott, Patrick Kelsey, Sarah Elizabeth & Catherine Eby. Educ: George Washington Univ, AB; Tau Kappa Epsilon; Alpha Kappa Psi; Gate & Key. Polit & Govt Pos: Mem bd dirs, DC Young Rep, 59-60; mem local Rep campaigns & Nixon Campaign Staff, 60; admin asst, US Rep Edwin B Dooley, NY, 61-62; legis asst, US Rep Oliver P Bolton, Ohio, 62-64; minority staff mem, House Comt Banking & Currency, 64-69; spec asst to President, 69- Bus & Prof Pos: Research asst, Am Trucking Asn, Washington,

DC, 58-61. Mil Serv: Air Force, 50-54. Relig: Episcopal. Legal Res: 501 Canterbury Lane Alexandria VA 22314 Mailing Add: White House 1600 Pennsylvania Ave Washington DC 20500

COOK, RUTH E (D)
NC State Rep
Mailing Add: 3413 Churchill Rd Raleigh NC 27607

COOK, VERNON (D)
Ore State Sen
Mailing Add: 519 N E Fourth Gresham OR 97030

COOK, VERNON F (D)
Ohio State Rep
Mailing Add: 2607 Owaisa Rd Cuyahoga Falls OH 44221

COOK, WILLIAM A (R)
b Patrick, SC, Nov 23, 25; s Rev John Edward Cook (deceased) & Mary Emily Cox C (deceased); m 1963 to Wanda A Edwards; c William A, Jr & John Kendrick. Educ: Univ SC, AB, 47, LLB, 49; Harvard Law Sch, LLM, 50; mem, Wig & Robe; pres, Omicron Delta Kappa. Polit & Govt Pos: Attorney, legis coun Gen Assembly, SC, 50-53; legis asst to US Rep John J Riley, 53-62; admin asst to US Rep Albert Watson, 63-70; admin asst to US Rep Floyd Spence, SC, 71- Mil Serv: Entered as Pvt, Army, 44, released as T/Sgt, 46, after serv in Co K, 242nd Inf, 42nd Inf Rainbow Div, ETO, 45-46; Bronze Star; Combat Inf Badge; Rhineland & Cent Europe Campaign Ribbons; Lt Col, Army Res, Judge Adv Gen Corps. Mem: Am Legion; VFW. Relig: Methodist. Legal Res: 213 Academy Way Columbia SC 29206 Mailing Add: 120 House Off Bldg Washington DC 20515

COOKE, CHARLES MAYNARD, JR (R)
Dep Asst Secy for Legis on Educ, Dept Health, Educ & Welfare
b Honolulu, Hawaii, Oct 19, 31; s Charles Maynard Cooke & Mary Cooper C; m 1967 to Diane Smith; c Mary E & Stephanie M; stepchildren: Kirsten, Scott M & Mona Lindquist. Educ: US Naval Acad, BS, 53; Univ Wash, MA, 60. Polit & Govt Pos: Avionics officer, 43rd Bomb Wing, Tucson, Ariz, 54-58; assoc prof hist, US Air Force Acad, Colo, 60-65; plans officer, Hq, US Mil Asst Command, Vietnam, 66-67; asst for Vietnam, Off of Asst Secy of Defense, 67-69; spec adv for Vietnam to the Under Secy of State, 69-70; dir off spec concerns, Dept of Health, Educ & Welfare, 70-73, Dep Asst Secy for Legis on Educ, 73- Mil Serv: Entered as 2nd Lt, Air Force, 53, resigned as Maj, 69; Legion of Merit; Bronze Star; Air Force Commendation Medal; Air Force Commendation Ribbon; Repub of Vietnam Staff Serv Medal, 1/C. Mem: US Naval Inst. Relig: Episcopal. Mailing Add: 825 Arcturus-on-the-Potomac Alexandria VA 22308

COOKE, EDWARD FRANCIS (D)
Treas, Allegheny Co, Pa
b Boston, Mass, Jan 14, 23; s Peter Joseph Cooke & Nora Regan C; m 1947 to Dorothy Mary Cleary; c Patricia Anne, Nancy Jean & Mary Elizabeth. Educ: Middlebury Col, AB, 47; Brown Univ, MA, 49; Northwestern Univ, PhD, 53; Blue Key; Pi Sigma Alpha; Delta Upsilon. Polit & Govt Pos: Mem, Pub Serv Inst Bd, Commonwealth of Pa, 60-70; chmn, Oakmont Dem Comt, Pa, 63-72; state co-chmn, Oper Support, 64; mayor, Oakmont, 66-69; treas, Allegheny Co, 68-; exec dir, Comt to Reelect Sen Clark, 68; deleg, Dem Nat Conv, 68. Bus & Prof Pos: From instr to asst prof polit sci, Knox Col, Ill, 48-55; dir, Citizenship Clearing House for West Pa, 55-62; from asst prof to assoc prof polit sci, Univ Pittsburgh, 55-64, prof, 64-, dir ctr for polit, 63-73; bd trustees, La Roche Col, 69-72; state chmn, Munic Finance Off Asn US, 70-; pres, Pa Co Treas Asn, 72- Mil Serv: Entered as Seaman, Navy, 43, released as Lt(jg), 46, after serv in LCI (M) 356, Pac; Silver Star Medal; Navy Unit Citation. Publ: Pennsylvania politics, Holt, 65; Detailed analysis of the US Constitution, Littlefield, 65; Big City politics, In: Practical politics in the US, Allyn & Bacon, 69. Mem: Pa Polit Sci Asn; Am Asn Pub Admin; Pa Hist Asn; Civic Club Allegheny Co (bd dirs, 71-74); VFW. Relig: Catholic. Mailing Add: 810 Ninth St Oakmont PA 15139

COOKE, JOHN WARREN (D)
Va State Deleg
b Mathews, Va, Feb 28, 15; m to Anne Brown Rawn. Educ: Va Mil Inst. Polit & Govt Pos: Va State Deleg, 42-; chmn, Mathews Co Dem Party, 71- Bus & Prof Pos: Newspaper publ, pres, Tidewater Newspapers, Inc; dir, Tidewater Tel Co. Relig: Episcopal. Mailing Add: Mathews VA 23109

COOKE, MARGARET ROBB (R)
b San Diego, Calif, Aug 27, 44; d Carroll Joseph Cooke & Phyllis Robb C; single. Educ: Mich State Univ, BA, 66. Polit & Govt Pos: Research asst, Mich Rep State Cent Comt, summer 65, hon mem, 65-67 & 70-75; vchmn, Mich Fedn Col Rep, 65-66; mem, Seventh Dist Rep Comt, 70; co-chmn, Mich Fedn Young Rep, 70-72, treas, 74-75; asst secy, Young Rep Nat Fedn, 71-73, mem exec comt, 73-75; Mich deleg aide, Rep Nat Conv, 72; mem, Mich Women's Comn, 75- Bus & Prof Pos: Training mgr, J L Hudson Co, Detroit, 66-70; personnel mgr, Flint Br, 70-72; personnel dir, B Siegel Co, Detroit, 72-73; field dir, Mkt Opinion Res, Inc, Detroit, 73- Mem: Am Mkt Asn; Mkt Research Asn; Women's Econ Club Detroit; Detroit CofC United Found. Relig: Episcopal. Mailing Add: 2315 Allard Grosse Pointe Woods MI 48236

COOKE, MARY SWANEY (D)
Chmn, Donley Co Dem Party, Tex
b Clarendon, Tex, July 23, 98; d William Henry Cooke & Halcyon Moore C; single. Educ: Clarendon Jr Col, AA, 18; Univ Tex, BA, 24; Alpha Delta Pi. Polit & Govt Pos: Chmn, Donley Co Dem Exec Comt, formerly; chmn, Donley Co League of Dem Women, formerly; chmn, Donley Co Women's Activities, 60-62; chmn, Donley Co Dem Party, currently; mem, Panhandle adv comt, Tex Const Rev Comn, 65; committeewoman, Tex State Dem Exec Comt, 30th Sen Dist, 65-66. Bus & Prof Pos: Instr, Panhandle Independent Sch, 18, Clarendon Independent Schs, 19-20; instr, Mary S Cooke Sch Dancing, 24-64. Mem: Clarendon Duplicate Contract Bridge Club (dir); affiliated with Am Contract Bridge League; Tex State CofC. Relig: Episcopal. Mailing Add: PO Box 717 Clarendon TX 79226

COOKE, MICHAEL DALE (D)
Miss State Rep
Mailing Add: 303 1/2 W Main St Tupelo MS 38801

COOKE, MURIEL KATHERINE (R)
NH State Rep
b Ellis, Kans, Nov 23, 04; d Clarence E Cooke & Mary A Helmick C; single. Educ: Kans Wesleyan Univ, BA, 28; Wichita State Univ, MA, 50; Delta Kappa Chi. Polit & Govt Pos: Ward clerk, Ward Four, Keene, NH, 72-; treas, Cheshire Co Rep Comt, Ward Four, Keene, NH, 72-; NH State Rep, 73- Bus & Prof Pos: High sch teacher, Union Sch Dist, Keene, NH, 30-52; AV dir, 53-68. Publ: Do we dare, NH Educator, spring, 58. Mem: League Women Voters; NH Hist Soc; Nat Retired Teachers Asn (asst state dir); Cheshire Hosp Aid Soc. Relig: Congregational; mem, State World Mission Bd. Mailing Add: 44 Court St Keene NH 03431

COOKE, WILLIAM LEON (D)
Chmn, Bertie Co Dem Exec Comt, NC
b Aulander, NC, May 19, 25; s W A Cooke & Nina P C; m 1953 to Betty Butler; c Elizabeth L. Educ: Univ NC, AB & LLB, 50; Phi Alpha Delta. Polit & Govt Pos: Secy, Bertie Libr Bd, NC, 53; attorney, Bertie Bd of Educ, 53-73; chmn, Bertie Co Dem Exec comt, NC, currently. Bus & Prof Pos: Partner, Pritchett, Cooke & Burch, 50- Mil Serv: Entered as Aviation Cadet, Navy, 43, released as Ens, 46, after serv in Pac; Lt(Ret), Naval Res, 65; Victory Medal; Asiatic-Pac Theatre Ribbon. Mem: Am & NC Bar Asns; Rotary; VFW. Relig: Baptist. Mailing Add: W Gray St Windsor NC 27983

COOKSEY, JESSE LECEL (R)
Chmn, SC Rep Party
b Spartanburg, SC, May 23, 32; s Isaac Lecel Cooksey & Corrine Goldsmith C; m 1956 to Jean Eastep; c Edwin, Ann, Jesse D & Julia. Educ: Wofford Col, AB, 54; Alpha Sigma Phi. Polit & Govt Pos: City councilman, Spartanburg, SC, 65-73; chmn, Spartanburg Co Rep Party, 70-74 & SC Rep Party, 74- Bus & Prof Pos: Life ins sales, Financial Planning Asn, 58- Mil Serv: Entered as 2nd Lt, Army, 54, released as 1st Lt, 58, after serv in 3rd Inf Div. Mem: Rotary; VFW; Mason; Spartanburg CofC (dir). Relig: Methodist. Mailing Add: 1055 Riverview Dr Spartanburg SC 29301

COOLAHAN, JOHN CARROLL (D)
Md State Sen
b Baltimore, Md, Oct 29, 32; s John Edward Coolahan & Blanche H Zimmerman C; m 1956 to Joanna Helen Sakievich; c Michael John, William Donald, Kathleen Marie, James Patrick & Joseph Dennis (deceased). Educ: Western Md Col, AB in Econ, 58; Univ Baltimore, LLB, 66. Polit & Govt Pos: Md State Deleg, formerly; Dem Dist Exec, 62-66; state exec dir, Md Home Improv Comt, 62-; Md State Sen, 75- Mil Serv: Entered as Pvt, Marine Corps, 51, released as Sgt, 54; Purple Heart; Good Conduct Medal; Korean Area Ribbon. Mem: KofC; Order of the Alhambra; Arbutus Social Club; Arbutus Commun Asn; Patapsco Dem Club. Relig: Roman Catholic. Mailing Add: 4625 Magnolia Ave Baltimore MD 21227

COOLEY, GEORGE EDWARD (D)
City Councilman, Seattle, Wash
b Clinton, Ill, Dec 15, 27; s George S Cooley & Ada Murray; div; c Mark & Andy. Educ: Univ Ill, BS, 50; George Washington Univ, grad, 52; Univ Wash, grad, 58. Polit & Govt Pos: City councilman, Seattle, Wash, 70-, chmn, Finance, Budget & Labor Comts, Seattle City Coun, 72-; chmn, Sewer Comt, Munic of Metrop Seattle, 72-; chmn, Munic Employees Retirement Bd, 72- Mil Serv: Entered as Pvt, Army, 46, released as Med Corpsman, 47, after 8th Army, Army of Occup, Japan, 46-47. Publ: Mounted patrol proposed for Seattle police, The Wash Policeman, 11/72. Mem: Munic Finance Officers Asn; Kiwanis. Relig: Unitarian. Legal Res: Apt 33 2001 Westlake Ave Seattle WA 98109 Mailing Add: 1112 Seattle Munic Bldg Seattle WA 98104

COOLIDGE, CLYDE ROCHELEAU (R)
b Manchester, NH, Dec 8, 38; s Theodore A Coolidge (deceased) & Gladys Harris C (deceased); m 1962 to Patricia Ann Gagne; c Catherine Anne, David Matthew, Mary Elizabeth & Stephen Harris. Educ: Univ NH, BA, 60; Boston Col Law Sch, JD, 63; Phi Beta Kappa; Phi Kappa Phi; Pi Gamma Mu; Tau Kappa Alpha; Pi Sigma Alpha; Sigma Beta. Polit & Govt Pos: Deleg, Rep Nat Conv, 68 & 72; mayor, Somersworth, NH, 68-72; assoc justice, Somersworth Dist Court, 73; mem, Comn on Uniform State Laws, 74- Bus & Prof Pos: Lectr taxation, Whittemore Sch Bus, Univ NH, 66-75; attorney & partner, Coolidge, Cullinare & Cullinare, Somersworth, NH, 69-75; trustee, Merchants Savings Bank, Dover, NH, 70- Mil Serv: Entered as 1st Lt, Air Force, 63, released as Capt, 66, after serv in Air Transport Command & Strategic Air Command, Moody & Pease Air Force Bases, NH, 63-66. Mem: Am, NH & Strafford Co Bar Asns; Am Legion. Honors & Awards: Outstanding Young Man of the Year Award, NH Jaycees, 68. Relig: Unitarian. Mailing Add: 54 Mt Vernon St Somersworth NH 03878

COOLMAN, KAREN (D)
Fla State Rep
b Norfolk, Va, Aug 26, 47; m 1968 to Charles Douglas Coolman; c Clay & Corey. Educ: Mich State Univ, BA in Art Hist, 68; Phi Beta Kappa; Pi Beta Phi. Polit & Govt Pos: Mem law enforcement subcomt, Broward Co Charter Comn, 74, Broward Co Community Serv Coun, 74; mem ad hoc audit rev comt, Broward Co Community Rels Comn, 74 & Citizens Comt to Establish Broward Co Comn Status Women, 74-75; mem, Platform Subcomt, Broward Co Dem Exec Comt, Dem Women's Club Broward Co, Concerned Dem Broward Co, Young Dem Broward Co & Fla & Broward Co Women's Polit Caucus; Fla State Rep, 75- Bus & Prof Pos: Asst buyer, Jordan Marsh Dept Store, 68; commercial artist, Colonial Williamsburg, Inc, 69; instr, Broward Community Col, 74; dir, Women's Awareness Inc, 74; founder & first pres, Broward Co Women Against Rape, Inc, 74; bd dirs, Specialized Urban Ministries Ft Lauderdale & chairperson, Task Force Women's Ministries, 74-75. Mem: Nat Orgn Women (Fla State coordr, 73-74, ed, Fla State Newsletter, 73-74, nat bd dirs, 74-75). Honors & Awards: First woman elected to Fla Legis from Broward Co, 74. Legal Res: 1911 Bayview Dr Ft Lauderdale FL 33305 Mailing Add: 2378 W Oakland Park Blvd Suite 6 Ft Lauderdale FL 33311

COOMBE, PATRICIA J (R)
b Washington, DC, Feb 26, 30; d George Neville Jeffries & Lois Katherine Pettit J; div; c Stephen Jeffries. Polit & Govt Pos: Staff asst, US Rep William E Minshall, Ohio, 60-75. Mailing Add: 8715 First Ave Apt 722-C Silver Spring MD 20910

COOMBS, WILLIAM ELMER (R)
b Keosauqua, Iowa, Jan 17, 11; s Elmer C Coombs & Myra Moon C; m 1934 to Katheryn Rose Logan; c Katheryn Wickham & Ann Siracusa. Educ: Univ Calif, Los Angeles, BA in Econ, 33; Loyola Univ, Los Angeles, JD, 54; Lambda Chi Alpha. Polit & Govt Pos: Mem

planning comn, Rialto, Calif, 61-62, city councilman, 62-66; mem adv bd, San Bernardino Co Young Rep, 66-68; mem adv bd, Calif Young Am Freedom, 67-; Calif State Sen, 20th Dist, 67-73; alt deleg, Rep Nat Conv, 72. Bus & Prof Pos: CPA, Los Angeles, 47-51; controller, Twaits-Wittenberg Co, 52-54; overseas bus mgr, Morrison-Knudsen Int, 54-56; asst prof, Calif State Col Chico, 56-58; treas & house counsel, Matich Corp, 58-61; sr partner, Coombs & Friel, attorneys, 62-74. Publ: Construction accounting & financial management, McGraw-Hill, 58, numerous articles for Mech Contractor Mag, 65-70 & alt column & article for Contractor, Buttenheim, 70-; plus others. Mem: Calif Soc CPA; Am Inst CPA; Am Bar Asn; Am Judicature Soc; Rotary Int. Relig: Protestant. Legal Res: 5810 Date Ave Rialto CA 92376 Mailing Add: Box 146 Rialto CA 92376

COONEY, JAMES B (D)
NH State Rep
Mailing Add: 588 Hillside Ave Berlin NH 03570

COONEY, LEIGHTON H, JR (D)
Maine State Rep
b Temple, Tex, Aug 28, 44; m 1969 to Holly Ann Burton. Educ: Lake Forest Col, BA, 67; Univ Maine, grad prog, currently. Polit & Govt Pos: Mem, Sabattus Town Dem Comt, Maine, 70-; mem, Androscoggin Co Dem Comt, 70-, vchmn legis deleg from Co, 73-; Maine State Rep, 71-, mem joint select spec comt govt reorgn, 71-72, chmn, comt state govt, 71-, mem comt agr, 73-, mem, Comt on Performance Audit; deleg, Nat Conf Criminal Justice, 73; mem, New England Bd Higher Educ Subcomt; mem, Gov Select Comt on Personnel. Mem: Nat Educ Asn; Maine Teachers Asn; Sabattus Lake Asn (pres); Am Civil Liberties Union; Nat Wildlife Fedn. Relig: Christian. Mailing Add: Box 246 Sabattus ME 04280

COONEY, NANCY ANN (D)
b Cohasset, Mass, Dec 29, 42; d Wilfred O'Mara Cooney & Eleanor Trowt C; single. Educ: Mt Holyoke Col, BA, 65; Boston Col, MA, 72. Polit & Govt Pos: Mass state comt rep, Citizens for Participation Polit, 69-71, secy, Boston Chap, 69-72, vchmn environ comt, 71-72; deleg, Dem Nat Conv, 72. Relig: Congregational. Mailing Add: 37 S Russell St Boston MA 02114

COONS, HAROLD MEREDITH (R)
b New Market, Ind, July 31, 11; s Merle F Coons & Clara Van Cleave C; m 1938 to Margaret Louise Richman; c Stephen M & Philip M. Educ: Wabash Col, AB, 32; Ind Univ Law Sch, Bloomington, JD, 36; Sr Counsel & Panhellenic Coun, Wabash Col; Beta Theta Pi; Phi Delta Phi. Polit & Govt Pos: Chmn, Crawfordsville Young Rep, Ind, 32; various precinct, local & co offices, Crawfordsville, Indianapolis & New Albany, Ind, 32-68; chmn, Floyd Co Rep Cent Comt, formerly; alt deleg, Rep Nat Conv, 72. Bus & Prof Pos: Lawyer, Crawfordsville, Ind, 36-37; claims attorney, Aetna Casualty & Surety Co, Indianapolis, 37-43; partner & claims attorney, Pruyn & Coons Ins Adjust, 46-59; pres & claims attorney, Coons & Horton, Inc, New Albany, 60-68; lawyer, 68- Mil Serv: Entered as Pvt, Army, 43, released as Cpl, 46, after serv in 870 Field Artil Bn, 66th Div, 7th Mil Police Criminal Invest Detachment, ETO, 44-46; Maj(Ret), Army Res; Good Conduct, ETO & Victory Medals. Mem: Floyd Co & Ind Bar Asns; Nat Asn Independent Ins Adjusters; Ind Independent Ins Adjusters Asn; Am Legion. Honors & Awards: Sagamore of the Wabash, 69. Relig: Presbyterian; Elder, St John's United Presby Church, New Albany; trustee, New Albany Presbytery. Mailing Add: 1312 Riddle Rd New Albany IN 47150

COONS, MARION M (R)
Chmn, Lucas Co Rep Cent Comt, Iowa
b Macedonia, Iowa, Apr 11, 15; s Lindsey D Coons & Luella McDowell C; m 1940 to Margaret Lorrene McReynolds; c Kenton Richard & Kenneth Lee. Educ: State Univ Iowa, BSc, 38. Polit & Govt Pos: Councilman, Lamoni, Iowa, 44-46; councilman, Chariton, Iowa, 52-56; mem sch bd, Chariton Community Sch Dist, 62-70; chmn, Lucas Co Rep Cent Comt, 60- Bus & Prof Pos: Treas, Hy-Vee Food Stores, Inc, 43-, vpres, 71-; chmn bd, Nat Bank Trust Co, 63- Mem: Nat Asn Credit Mgt; Nat Asn Acct; Shrine; Mason; Rotary. Relig: Methodist. Legal Res: 607 Ashland Ave Chariton IA 50049 Mailing Add: 1801 Osceola Ave Chariton IA 50049

COOPER, ANNA (R)
Treas, Ind Rep State Cent Comt
b Madison, Ind, Mar 16, 43; d Eugene Louis Cooper & Pauline Saltzgabber C; single. Educ: Ind Univ; Lincoln Jr Col; Transylvania Univ. Polit & Govt Pos: Treas, Ind Rep State Cent Comt, 74- Bus & Prof Pos: Child welfare employee, Jefferson Co Welfare Dept, Ind, 63-64; elem teacher, Madison Consol Schs, 66; secy, Madison Bank & Trust, 67- Mem: Tri Kappa; Bank Admin Inst. Relig: Methodist. Mailing Add: 235 Cedarwood Dr Madison IN 47250

COOPER, BILL (D)
Ga State Rep
Mailing Add: 3286 Powder Springs Rd Marietta GA 30060

COOPER, CARLOS M (R)
Kans State Rep
Mailing Add: Lake Forest Bonner Springs KS 67214

COOPER, CHARLES ARTHUR
Asst Secy Int Affairs, Dept of the Treas
b Chicago, Ill, Dec 23, 33; s S Robert Cooper & Betty Greenabaum C; m 1966 to Janis Starr Stone; c Elizabeth Starr, Melora Christina & Jared Alexander. Educ: Swarthmore Col, BA, 55; Mass Inst Technol, PhD(econ), 60; Russian Studies Prog, Harvard Univ, 57-59. Polit & Govt Pos: With Coun Econ Adv, Washington, DC, 61-63; econ adv to Robert W Komer, Spec Asst to the President for Civilian Progs, Vietnam, 66-67; assoc dir, Agency Int Develop & econ counr, Am Embassy, Saigon, Vietnam, 67-68, minister-counr econ affairs, 70-73; dep asst to President for int econ affairs, Nat Security Coun, 73-74; asst secy int affairs, Dept of the Treas, 74- Bus & Prof Pos: Mem staff, Rand Corp, Santa Monica, Calif, 63-66 & 68-70. Mil Serv: Air Force, 59-60. Publ: Ed, Economic Development in the Middle East, 71. Mem: Am Econ Asn; Phi Beta Kappa. Honors & Awards: Superior Honor Award, Agency Int Develop, 68. Mailing Add: Dept of Treas Washington DC 20220

COOPER, CHARLES M (D)
b Sweetwater, Tex, Sept 19, 26; s William Homer Cooper & Maydell Street C; m 1949 to Serena Carlin Fisher; c William T, Charles F, Delilah (Mrs Garner) & Jack Daniel. Educ: Southwestern Univ (Tex), 47-49; Stephen F Austin State Col, BS, 49; Kappa Sigma, Southwestern Univ; Forresters, Stephen F Austin State Col. Polit & Govt Pos: Press aide, Fred R Harris for Senate, 62-64; pub rels, Okla State Dept Hwy, 64; pub rels, Okla Good Rd & St Asn, 64-66; press aide, Preston J Moore, Dem for Gov, Okla, 66; admin asst/press aide, US Rep Clem Rogers McSpadden, Second Dist, Okla, 73-75. Bus & Prof Pos: Continuity writer, Radio Sta KEVA, Shamrock, Tex, 49-50; advert salesman, Daily News, Anadarko, Okla, 50 & 52-53; ed, Tribune, Temple, 53-60, Am, Antlers, 60-62 & Daily Times, Pryor, 67-72. Mil Serv: Entered as Seaman Apprentice, Naval Res, 43, released as RMN2, 46, after serv in various commun, Pac Theatre, 44-46; recalled as RMN2, Naval Res, 1 year 6 months, US Naval Commun Ctr, Treasure Island, San Francisco, Alameda Naval Air Sta. Publ: History of the big pasture, Okla Hist Chronicles of Okla, 66. Mem: Mason; Elks; Am Legion (Comndr, Tyler Hunt Post, Temple, Okla, 56 & Sullivan Lewis Post 182, Pryor, 71-); VFW; Lions. Honors & Awards: Sweepstakes Trophy, Okla Press Asn/Okla State Fair, 54-55 & 68; Boss of Year, Pryor Jaycees, 70; awards for gen excellence of Temple Tribune & Pryor Daily Times. Relig: Presbyterian. Legal Res: Box 308 Pryor OK 74361 Mailing Add: T-3 3861 St Barnabas Rd Marlow Heights MD 20023

COOPER, DANIEL S (D)
Mich State Sen
b Los Angeles, Calif, Mar 10, 30; s Israel Cooper & Edith Korin C; m 1957 to Hilda Winshall; c Eve, Elizabeth & Joanne. Educ: Detroit Cent High Sch, 4 years; Wayne State Univ, BA, 54 & JD, 57. Polit & Govt Pos: Mich State Rep, 65-70; Mich State Sen, 71- Bus & Prof Pos: Attorney, 57-70. Mil Serv: Entered as Recruit, Army, 48, released as Pvt, 49, after serv in 41st Armed Inf Bn; Reentered as 2nd Lt, 53, discharged, 54, after serv in Transportation Corp, Oakland Army Base. Publ: Law revision articles, Wayne State Univ Law Rev; Probation. Mem: Am Bar Asn; Oak Park Youth Guid Bd; B'nai B'rith. Relig: Jewish. Mailing Add: 13150 Dartmouth Oak Park MI 48237

COOPER, ELDON W (D)
Colo State Sen
Mailing Add: 1720 Mable Ave Denver CO 80229

COOPER, FRED FERRIS (D)
Supvr, Alameda Co, Calif
b San Francisco, Calif, May 12, 28; s Fred F Cooper & Elizabeth Zandt C; m 1968 to Virginia Langan; c Jeffrey, Bryan & Katy. Educ: Hastings Col of Law, Univ Calif, JD, 52. Polit & Govt Pos: Deleg, Alameda Co Cent Labor Coun, 49-52; rep, 18th Assembly Dist Dem Coun, Calif, 55-57; chmn, Berkeley Caucus, 57; Alameda Co chmn, Mosk for Attorney Gen, 58 & 62, Edmund G Brown for Gov Calif, 66 & Humphrey for President, 68; mem, Berkeley Urban Renewal Comt, 60; mem, Berkeley Apt Design Comt, 62-64; chmn, Dewey for City Coun Campaign, 63; chmn, Cohelan for Cong Campaign, 66; mem, City-Univ Liaison Comt, Calif, 65-; deleg, Dem Nat Conv, 64 & 68; mem, Alameda Co Bd Supvr, Dist Three, 71-, supvr, Co, 71-; mem exec comt, Asn Bay Area Govt, 71-; mem, San Francisco Bay Conserv & Develop Comn, 73- Bus & Prof Pos: Pres, Biotronics, Inc, 60-67; trustee, Herrick Mem Hosp, Berkeley, 62-67; pres, East Bay Rehabilitation Ctr, 62-68. Mil Serv: Entered as Pvt, Army, 52, released as Cpl, 54, after serv in Hq Area Command, Ger, 53-54; Nat Serv Medal; Korean Medal. Mem: Calif & Alameda Co Bar Asns; Am Judicature Soc; Oakland Law Forum; Am Arbit Asn (panel arbitrator, 60-). Relig: Protestant. Mailing Add: 1104 Bismark Lane Alameda CA 94501

COOPER, GLORIA CLAIRE (D)
Mem, Calif Dem State Cent Comt
b Jamaica, NY, Feb 22, 22; d Nathan Lebenson & Ruth Baumgarten L; m 1942 to Albert W Cooper; c Ronald Allen & Blair Lee. Educ: Ventura Jr Col, 6 months. Polit & Govt Pos: Mem, Ventura Co Dem Cent Comt, Calif, 54-56, 69-; secy women's div, Southern Calif Dem Orgn, 66-68; mem, Calif Dem State Cent Comt, 67- Bus & Prof Pos: Owner, Sewelson & Cooper Rug & Carpets, 51-69. Relig: Jewish. Mailing Add: 3175 Outrigger Ave Ventura CA 93003

COOPER, GUY L (D)
b Humboldt, Nebr, Feb 9, 07; s Guy L Cooper, Sr & Josiphene Bruun C; m 1928 to Evelyn Mae Kerr; c Prudence Ann (Mrs Heimdec) & Dr Guy L, III. Educ: Univ Nebr, AB, 28; Gamma Sigma Delta; Alpha Theta Chi; Chi Phi. Polit & Govt Pos: Deleg, Dem Nat Conv, 72; mem platform comt, Dem Nat Comt, Washington, DC, 72; dir, Univ Nebr Found, currently; precinct committeeman & mem, Century Club, currently; second vpres, Nebr Pub Power Dist, currently. Bus & Prof Pos: Bd chmn, O A Cooper Co, Humboldt, Nebr, 58-; dir, Edison-Dehy-Edison, Nebr, 62; vchmn bd, Hammond Mills, Oklahoma City, currently; first vpres, Lydia Bruun Woods Mem Libr; mem pres adv coun, Peru State Col. Mil Serv: Sr, ROTC. Publ: Numerous articles in Feedstuffs & other feed trade publ. Mem: Am Feed Mfrs Asn; Mid-W Feed Mfrs Asn; Elks; KofC (4 degree); Falls City Country Club. Honors & Awards: Cooper Neuculair Station named in honor. Relig: Catholic. Legal Res: Rte 1 Humboldt NE 68376 Mailing Add: c/o O A Cooper Co PO Box 7 Humboldt NE 68376

COOPER, HOMER CHASSELL (D)
Mem, Ga State Dem Exec Comt
b Baltimore, Md, Oct 28, 23; s Homer Eber Cooper & Clara Chassell C; m 1951 to Patricia Montgomery Irvin; c Alice Holmes, Ben Irvin & Marian Wooddell. Educ: Oberlin Col, AB, 49; Univ Mich, Ann Arbor, MA, 53, PhD, 57. Polit & Govt Pos: Mem, Clarke Co Dem Exec Comt, Ga, 70-; pres, Clarke Co Dem Club, 72-73; comnr, Clarke Co, 73-; app mem, Ga Dem Party Charter Comn, 74-; mem, Ga State Dem Exec Comt, 74- Bus & Prof Pos: Asst study dir, Survey Research Ctr, Univ Mich, 53-55; instr, Univ Mont, 56-59; asst prof, Tuck Sch Bus Admin, Dartmouth Col, 59-61; asst prof, Grad Sch Bus, Univ Pittsburgh, 61-64; dir, Social Sci Research Inst, Univ Ga, 64-70; assoc prof sociol, Univ Ga, 70- Mil Serv: Entered as Pvt, Army, 44, released as S/Sgt, 46, after serv in 95th Field Hosp, China-Burma-India Theater. Publ: Co-auth, Group Differences in Attitudes & Votes, Inst Social Research, 56; co-ed, Future of Georgia, Ga Dept Educ, 70; auth, Evaluation of poverty programs, Va Polytech Inst, 68. Mem: Am Sociol Asn; Ga Sociol Asn (pres, 69-70); Am Polit Sci Asn; Am Asn for Pub Opinion Research; China-Burma-India Vet Asn. Mailing Add: 145 Pendleton Dr Athens GA 30601

COOPER, J DANNY (R)
Mem, Rep State Exec Comt Ala
b Clanton, Ala, Apr 1, 48; s Wiley Grady Cooper & Mary Lucille Lowery C; m 1970 to Patricia Diane Carter. Educ: Univ Montevallo, BA, 70, MEd, 73; Alpha Tau Omega. Polit & Govt Pos: Grad, Four Young Rep Nat Leadership Conf, Wash, 67-70; staff mem, Nixon for President, Rep Nat Conv, 68; admin vchmn, Young Rep Fedn Ala, 69-71; alt deleg, Rep Nat Conv, 72; coordr, Friends of Richard Nixon Speakers Bur, 72; mem, Rep State Exec Comt, Ala, 72-; area coordr, Ala Rep Party, currently. Bus & Prof Pos: Dir vet affairs, Univ

Montevallo, currently. Mem: Am Cancer Soc (crusade chmn, Shelby Co, 72); Ala Vet Affairs Asn (exec comt); Vol Bur Gtr Birmingham (bd dirs); Montevallo Bicentennial Comn (chmn); Montevallo Jaycees (treas). Honors & Awards: Outstanding Serv Award, Ala Eta Omega Chap, Alpha Tau Omega, 70. Relig: Baptist; deacon, Univ Baptist Church, currently. Legal Res: Monte Villa Montevallo AL 35115 Mailing Add: PO Box 2657 Univ of Montevallo Montevallo AL 35115

COOPER, JAMES LEROY (R)
Ariz State Rep
b Mesa, Ariz, Dec 4, 15; s Orson Prince Cooper & Sybil Cora Newell C; m to Mildred Adelia Post; c James Gary, Gayle (Mrs Richard H Bramwell); Morris Post, Conny (Mrs Laurence N Johnson), William Newell & Jan. Polit & Govt Pos: Ariz State Rep, 69- Mem: Farm Bur; United Dairymen of Ariz; Maricopa Co Dairy Herd Improv Asn; Ariz Milk, Inc. Honors & Awards: Hon State Farmer, Ariz Future Farmers of Am. Relig: Latter-day Saint. Mailing Add: 951 S Lazona Dr Mesa AZ 85204

COOPER, JEROME GARY (D)
Ala State Rep
b Lafayette, La, Oct 2, 36; s Algernon Johnson Cooper (deceased) & Gladys Mouton C; m to Gloria Giles; c Patrick, Joli (Mrs Sharon. Educ: Univ Notre Dame, BS in Finance, 58. Polit & Govt Pos: Ala State Rep, Dist 103, 75-, mem rules comt & vchmn ins comt, Ala House Rep, currently. Bus & Prof Pos: Vpres, Christian Benevolent Ins Co, 69- Mil Serv: Entered as 2nd Lt, Marine Corps, 58, released as Maj, 69, after serv in a variety of units; Lt Col, Marine Corps Res, currently; Three Purple Hearts; Bronze Star; Vietnamese Cross of Gallantry. Mem: YMCA; Red Cross; United Fund. Honors & Awards: Omega's Citizen of the Year, 74. Mailing Add: PO Box 25 Mobile AL 36601

COOPER, JOHN B (D)
Utah State Rep
Mailing Add: 620 N Center Lehi UT 84043

COOPER, JOHN SHERMAN (R)
US Ambassador, EGer
b Somerset, Pulaski Co, Ky, Aug 23, 01; s John Sherman Cooper & Helen Gertrude Tartar C; m 1955 to Lorraine Rowan Shevlin. Educ: Centre Col, 18-19; Yale Col, AB, 23; Harvard Law Sch, 23-25; Beta Theta Pi. Hon Degrees: LLD, Centre Col, Univ Ky, Georgetown Col, Berea Col, Eastern Ky State Col, Yale Univ & Univ Pittsburgh; LHD, Lincoln Mem Univ; DCL, Nasson Col, Maine. Polit & Govt Pos: Ky State Rep, 28-30; co judge, Pulaski Co, 30-38, circuit judge, 45-46; US Sen, Ky, 46-48, 52-54 & 56-72; US Deleg, Gen Assembly UN, 49, 50, 51 & 68; adv to Secy of State, Dean Acheson, NATO Coun Ministers, London & Brussels, 50; US Ambassador, India & Nepal, 55-56; Cong adv to US Deleg, UNESCO Conf, Paris, 58; mem, President's Comn on the Assassination of President John F Kennedy, 64; senate adv to US Deleg, Treaty Signing Conf Establishing the Asian Develop Bank, Manila, 65; rapporteur for mil comt, NATO Parliamentarians Conf, 66-67; US Ambassador, EGer, 74- Bus & Prof Pos: Mem law firm, Gardner, Morrison & Rogers, Washington, DC, 49-51. Mil Serv: Enlisted as Pvt, Army, 42, released as Capt, 46, after serv in Third Army, Normandy, France, Luxembourg, Ger & headed reorgn Ger Judicial Syst of Bavaria; Bronze Star Medal. Mem: Am & KY Bar Asns; Centre Col (bd trustees); Am Legion; VFW. Honors & Awards: Rep Recipient of Award for Distinguished Serv in the Senate for the 88th Cong, Am Polit Sci Asn, 65. Relig: Baptist. Legal Res: 503 N Main St Somerset KY 42501 Mailing Add: US Ambassador to EGer Dept of State 2201 C St NW Washington DC 20521

COOPER, JOHN W (D)
Idaho State Rep
Mailing Add: 823 Mullan Ave Coeur d'Alene ID 83814

COOPER, M J (D)
SC State Rep
Mailing Add: Rte 1 Box 22 Piedmont SC 29671

COOPER, ROLAND (D)
Chmn, Wilcox Co Dem Party, Ala
b Robertsdale, Ala, Aug 13, 13; s Mr & Mrs W R Cooper; m to Stella Handly; c 3. Polit & Govt Pos: Worker with Ala State Hwy Dept, 35-39; mayor, Camden, Ala, 48-54; deleg, Dem Nat Conv, 52; Ala State Sen, 54-72; chmn, Wilcox Co Dem Party, 72- Bus & Prof Pos: Serv sta operator, 37-47; Chrysler-Plymouth dealership, 45-; operator, cattle farm, 50- Mem: Mason; Shrine; Camden Exchange Club. Relig: Baptist. Mailing Add: Camden AL 36726

COOPER, THEODORE
Asst Secy Health, Dept Health, Educ & Welfare
Legal Res: MD Mailing Add: Dept of Health Educ & Welfare Washington DC 20201

COOPER, WILLIAM HURLBERT (R)
Finance Chmn, DC Rep Comt
b Philadelphia, Pa, Oct 19, 24; s Charles M Cooper (deceased) & Lois Hurlbert C; m 1951 to Joanne Coffin; c Charles Morgan B, William Hurlbert, Jr & Arthur S. Educ: Colgate Univ, Hamilton, NY, 42-43; Western Reserve Univ, Cleveland, BA, 46; George Washington Univ, MD, 49; Delta Kappa Epsilon; Nu Sigma Nu. Polit & Govt Pos: Founder & chmn, DC Polit Action Comt, 62-; mem, DC Rep Cent Comt, 63 & 68-; alt deleg, Rep Nat Conv, 68, vchmn & deleg, 72; Am exec comt, Rep Nat & DC Comts, 1970 Dinner; nat bd, Am Rep Polit Action Comt; asst treas, DC Rep Comt, formerly, finance chmn, currently. Bus & Prof Pos: Obstetrician-gynecologist, Washington, DC, 52-; research projs done for Wallace Labs, Syntex Labs & Hoffmann-LaRoche. Publ: A Husband's Guide to Menopause, Simon & Shuster, 69; The pill & figure changes, Va Med Monthly, 68. Mem: Am Med Asn; DC, Kober & Arlington Co Med Socs; Pan Am Med Soc. Relig: Episcopal. Mailing Add: 825 New Hampshire Ave NW Washington DC 20037

COOPERMAN, ARTHUR J (D)
NY State Assemblyman
b New York, NY, Dec 22, 33; s Herman Cooperman & Rose Hirschfeld C; m 1959 to Norma Bezrod; c Seth. Educ: NY Univ Col, BA, 55; NY Univ Sch Law, LLB, 60. Polit & Govt Pos: Co committeeman, 24th Assembly Dist, Queens Co, NY, 66-; NY State Assemblyman, 69-; deleg, Dem Judicial Conv, Queens Co, 68. Bus & Prof Pos: Practicing attorney, 61-66; asst counsel grievance comt, Asn of Bar of City of New York, 67-68; pvt law practice, currently. Mil Serv: Entered as 2nd Lt, Army, 55, released as 1st Lt, 57, after serv in 34th Signal Bn, 7th Corps, Europe, 56-57. Mem: Asn of Bar of City of New York; Queens Co Bar Asn. Relig: Jewish. Legal Res: 80-22 169th St Jamaica NY 11432 Mailing Add: 89-31 161st St Jamaica NY 11432

COPE, RON
Nebr State Sen
Mailing Add: 20 Hillcrest Dr Kearney NE 68847

COPELAND, DAVID Y, III (R)
Tenn State Rep
b Tampa, Fla, Jan 10, 31; s David Y Copeland & Lora Kramp C; m 1950 to Mary Ethel Leamon; c David Michael & Valerie Anne. Educ: McKenzie Bus Col, 49. Polit & Govt Pos: Tenn State Rep, 68-, mem finance, ways & means, educ, fiscal rev & policy comts, Tenn House Rep, vchmn House Rep caucus. Bus & Prof Pos: Owner, Ace Shade & Awning Co, Chattanooga, Tenn, 53-59; vpres, Copelands, Inc, 59- Mil Serv: Entered as Pvt, Army, 51, released as Sgt, 53, after serv in 71st AAA Gun Bn. Mem: Chattanooga Water Ski Club; Ment Health Asn. Relig: Baptist. Mailing Add: 8950 Fuller Rd Chattanooga TN 37421

COPELAND, FRED E (GENE) (D)
Mo State Rep
b Cooter, Mo, June 12, 32; m 1952 to Patricia Ann Weber; c Fred, Lisa Ann, Leslie Ann. Educ: Ark State Col, Jonesboro, Ark. Polit & Govt Pos: Mo State Rep, 60- Bus & Prof Pos: Real estate, ins & farming; owner, Fred E Copeland Agency. Mil Serv: Navy, 52-56. Mailing Add: 1399 Mill St New Madrid MO 63869

COPELAND, J WILLIAMS (D)
Assoc Justice, NC State Supreme Court
b Woodland, NC, June 16, 14; s Luther Clifton Copeland & Nora Benthall C; m 1941 to Nancy Sawyer; c Emily C (Mrs Bagby), James W, Jr & Buxton S. Educ: Guilford Col, AB, 34; Univ NC, Chapel Hill, JD with honors. Polit & Govt Pos: NC State Sen, 51-61; judge, NC Superior Court, 61-75; assoc justice, NC State Supreme Court, 75- Mil Serv: Entered as Ens, Navy, 42, released as Lt(sg), 46, after serv in N&SPac, 43-45. Publ: Asst ed, NC Law Rev, 36-37. Mem: Mason; Shrine. Relig: Methodist. Legal Res: 407 E High Murfreesboro NC 27855 Mailing Add: PO Box 157 Murfreesboro NC 27855

COPELAND, LEON TROY (D)
WVa State Deleg
b McLoud, Okla, June 9, 42; s Troy Copeland & Lydia Hammermeister C; m 1973 to Sandra Kay Honaker; c Shawn Alan. Educ: Univ Mich Col Lit, Sci & Arts, BA in Polit Sci, 64; Ind Univ Col Law, JD, 67. Polit & Govt Pos: WVa State Deleg, 74-, chmn comt on const rev, WVa House Deleg, 75-; mem, Citizens Welfare Adv Coun, Area 17, WVa, 74- Bus & Prof Pos: Worker, VISTA, Off Econ Opportunity, 67-68; reporter, Beckley Post Herald, WVa, 68-69; lawyer, Charleston, 69- Mem: WVa State Bar; WVa Bar Asn; Community Coun Charleston; Elks; Eagles. Relig: Protestant. Mailing Add: 721 Churchill Dr Charleston WV 25314

COPENHAVER, EVERETT TAYLOR (R)
State Auditor, Wyo
b Kinross, Iowa, Apr 22, 98; s Milton Copenhaver & Sarah LeFever C; m 1930 to Ethel Gertrude Whitman (deceased); m 1971 to Mildred Jesmer; c Evalyn Grace (Mrs Peoples), Ross D & Constance I (Mrs Peetz). Educ: Univ Nebr, 17-19. Polit & Govt Pos: Chmn, Converse Co Rep Cent Comt, Wyo, 34-36; mem, Wyo State Legis, 39-42; dep secy of state, Wyo, 43-44; asst state examr, 45-46, state auditor, 47-54 & 67-, secy of state, 54-58, state treas, 63-67; treas, Wyo Rep State Cent Comt, 43-49. Bus & Prof Pos: Acct. Mem: Odd Fellows; Rebekah; Mason; Eastern Star; Shrine. Relig: Methodist. Legal Res: 404 W Second Ave Cheyenne WY 82001 Mailing Add: Rm 116 State Capitol Cheyenne WY 82001

COPENHAVER, MARION LAMSON (D)
NH State Rep
b Andover, Vt, Sept 26, 25; d Joseph Fenwick Lamson & Christine Forbes L; m 1946 to John Harrison Copenhaver, Jr; c John H, III, Margaret, Christine C (Mrs Miller), Eric & Lisa. Educ: Univ Vt, 44-46; Delta Delta Delta. Polit & Govt Pos: NH State Rep, 73- Mem: Dartmouth-Hitchcock Ment Health Ctr (mem citizen's adv coun); Dem Women of NH. Relig: Unitarian. Mailing Add: 42 Rayton Rd Hanover NH 03755

COPENHAVER, ROSS D (R)
Wyo State Rep
Mailing Add: 565 College Dr Powell WY 82435

COPITHORNE, DAVID MICHAEL (D)
b Boston, Mass, May 31, 38; s Edward A Copithorne & Mary M Small C; m 1961 to Martha Witherell; c D Bradford & Mark Larimer. Educ: Colby Col, BA, 60; Columbia Univ Sch Law, LLB. Polit & Govt Pos: Chmn, Belknap Co Dem Comt, NH, 68-70, treas, formerly. Bus & Prof Pos: Clerk, NAACP Legal Defense Fund, 63-64; lawyer, Snierson, Chandler & Copithorne, 65- Mem: NH & Belknap Co Bar Asns. Relig: Protestant. Legal Res: Belknap Mountain Rd Gilford NH Mailing Add: RFD 5 Laconia NH 03246

COPPINGER, FRANCIS X (D)
Mass State Rep
Mailing Add: State Capitol Boston MA 02133

COPPS, LYMAN WILLIAM (R)
Chmn, Winnebago Co Rep Party, Wis
b Marshfield, Wis, Oct 2, 22; s Dr Lyman A Copps & Stella Murat C; m 1946 to Charlotte Risch; c Jane, Marcia & Paul. Educ: Univ Wis, 40-42; Lawrence Univ, BS, 47; Psi Upsilon. Polit & Govt Pos: Precinct chmn, Neenah Rep Party, Wis, 55-60, chmn, 60-62; vchmn, Winnebago Co Rep Party, 62-65, chmn, 65- Bus & Prof Pos: Vpres & dir, Nat Inst of Locker & Freezer Provisioners, 54-56; chmn publicity, Nat Tissue Asn, 60-62; dir, Nat Acct Mkt Asn, 72- Mil Serv: Entered as Pvt, Marine Corps Res, released as Lt(jg), Naval Res, after serv in Navy, Pac. Mem: Elks; Optimists. Relig: Presbyterian. Mailing Add: 303 11th St Neenah WI 54956

COPPS, MICHAEL JOSEPH (D)
b Milwaukee, Wis, Apr 23, 40; s Edmund James Copps, Jr & Ruth Klemm C; m 1970 to Elizabeth Catherine Miller; c Robert Edmund & Mary Elizabeth. Educ: Wofford Col, BA, 63; Univ NC, Chapel Hill, PhD, 67; Phi Beta Kappa. Polit & Govt Pos: Admin asst to US Sen Ernest F Hollings, SC, 75- Bus & Prof Pos: Asst prof Am hist, Loyola Univ (La), 67-70.

Mem: Pi Gamma Mu (local chap pres, 63). Mailing Add: 7948 Central Park Circle Alexandria VA 22309

CORAY, CARLA WINN (R)
Rep Nat Committeewoman, Hawaii
b Smithfield, Utah, Aug 25, 25; d William Frank Winn & Lavon Cragun W; m 1946 to Max S Coray; c Craig Winn & Lisa Nalani. Educ: Utah State Univ, BS; Brigham Young Univ, grad work; Univ Hawaii, 66-67; Theta Alpha Phi; Lambda Rho; Alpha Sigma Nu; 12 Outstanding Sr Class Mems Fraternity; Spurs; ed, Univ Yearbook. Polit & Govt Pos: Pres, Star Valley League of Rep Women, Wyo, 56-57; pres, Kona League of Rep Women, 61-64; W Hawaii Rep, Rep State Women's Adv Coun, 63-64; deleg, Rep Nat Conv, 64 & 72; campaign chmn, W Hawaii Rep, 64; Hawaii State Campaign Chmn, Fedn of Rep Women; first vpres, Hawaii State Fedn of Rep Women, 67-68; newsletter ed, Oahu League of Rep Women, 67-68; secy, Hawaii State Rep Party, 67-68, chmn, 69 & 71-75, vchmn, 69-71; Rep Nat Committeewoman, Hawaii, currently. Bus & Prof Pos: Drama co-chmn, Am Asn Univ Women, 68. Mem: Southwest Dist Wyo Educ Asn; Southwest Dist Speech Asn; Wyo Speech Asn; Rocky Mountain Theater Conf; Afton Women's Club, Wyo. Relig: Latter-day Saint. Mailing Add: 83 Lunalilo Home Rd Honolulu HI 96821

CORAZZINI, LEO R (D)
Mass State Rep
Mailing Add: State Capitol Boston MA 02133

CORBER, ROBERT JACK (R)
b Topeka, Kans, June 29, 26; s Alva Forrest Corber & Katherine Salzer C; m 1949 to Joan Irene Tennal; c Janet, Suzanne, Wesley Sean & Robert Jack, II. Educ: Univ Kans, BS in Aero Eng, 46; Washburn Univ, LLB cum laude, 50; Univ Mich, Law Grad Study, 50-51; Sigma Alpha Epsilon; Phi Alpha Delta. Polit & Govt Pos: Chmn, Arlington Co Rep Comt, Va, 60-62; chmn, Tenth Cong Dist Rep Comt, 62-64; mem, Rep Nat Comt, 64; alt deleg, Rep Nat Conv, 64; chmn, Va Rep State Cent Comt, 64-68. Bus & Prof Pos: Partner & mem exec comt, Steptoe & Johnson, 51- Mil Serv: Entered as A/S, Navy, 44, released as Lt(jg), 47. Publ: Co-auth, Federal Administrative Practice Manual, Jr Bar Sect, DC; Civil aeronautics board, Admin Law Rev, Am Bar Asn, 64; Interstate charter rights for carriers of passengers, ICC Practitioners J, 2/67. Mem: Am & DC Bar Asns; Am Judicature Soc; Am Legion; Optimist. Relig: Methodist. Mailing Add: 3701 N Harrison St Arlington VA 22207

CORBET, LEO FRANK, JR (R)
Ariz State Sen
b Lordsburg, NMex, Nov 16, 36; s Leo Frank Corbet, Sr & Lucille Young C; m 1959 to Barbara Sue Mills; c Kelly Sue, Jill Catherine & Katy Elizabeth. Educ: Univ Ariz, BS in BPA, 59, LLB, 63; Sigma Chi; Phi Delta Phi. Polit & Govt Pos: Ariz State Sen, 71-, chmn senate judiciary comt, 73- Mil Serv: Air Nat Guard, discharged 65. Mem: State Bar of Ariz; Maricopa Co Bar; Am Trial Lawyers Asn; Ariz Club. Relig: Presbyterian. Mailing Add: 1452 E McLelland Blvd Phoenix AZ 85014

CORBETT, ALICE CATHERINE (D)
Dem Nat Committeewoman, Ore
b Seattle, Wash, July 17, 29; d Marshall Richard Reckard & Carolyn Bauer R; m 1948 to James J Corbett. Educ: Univ Ore, BS, 48; Marylhurst Col grad work, 50. Polit & Govt Pos: Pres, Multnomah Co Young Dem, Ore, 54-56; Nat Committeewoman, Young Dem Ore, 54-58; vchmn, Multnomah Co Dem Cent Comt, 56-58; credentials chmn, State Dem Party, 56-58; Ore State Sen, 59-67; Dem Nat Committeewoman, 60-; deleg, Dem Nat Conv, 68 & 72; pres, Jane Jeff Dem Women, Ore, 70-; co comnr, Multnomah Co, 75- Bus & Prof Pos: Educator, Sch Dist 1, Portland, Ore; Investments, Corbett Enterprises, Ore, 60-; pres, Corbett Investments, 65- Publ: Retarded children, Ore Dem, 54. Mem: Am Asn Univ Women (vpres, Womens Investment group, formerly); Multnomah Athletic Club; Nat Comt for Mills Col; Willamette Soc (vpres, 65-); South East Dem Women (prog chmn, 70). Honors & Awards: Voted one of ten most outstanding women graduates from Univ Ore, 59. Relig: Episcopal. Mailing Add: 2222 NE Schuyler Portland OR 97212

CORBETT, JERRY G (D)
Chmn, Calhoun Co Dem Comt
b Hardin, Ill, Jan 19, 17; s Barth Corbett & Margaret Fisher C; m 1955 to Joan Dufner; c Kelly Ann & J Dufner. Educ: St Louis Univ; Univ Ill. Polit & Govt Pos: Precinct committeeman, Hardin, Ill, 60-; mem, Export Adv Bd Ill, 62-64; chmn, Calhoun Co Dem Comt, 62-; chmn, Co Chairmen's Orgn, 20th Dist, 64-67; mem, Ill Hwy Transportation Comn, currently; cand for reapportionment of Ill, 65; mem, Hwy Planning Study Comn & Hwy Safety Comt, 66; mem, Local Govt Selection Comn, 67-69; Ill State Rep, 50th Dist, 68-72; co chmn, Ill Dem State Cent Comt, formerly. Bus & Prof Pos: Owner, West Auto, GE Appliance Store, nationwide grocery store & Int Harvester Dealership, Hardin, Ill, formerly; owner, Corbett Farms, 54; adminr, Corbett Ford, 56-; pres, Dufner-Corbett Chevrolet-Oldsmobile-Buick, Hermann, Mo, 60-; owner, Corbett Ford Dealer, Hardin, Ill, currently; grain & livestock farmer, currently; real estate, currently. Mil Serv: Entered as Pvt, Army, 42, released as 1st Lt, 46, after serv in Hq Unit Lord Louis Mountbatten, SE Asia Command, 43-46. Mem: Mo Auto Dealers Asn; Nat & Ill Auto Dealers Asns; Am Legion; VFW; Feeders Asn Ill; Lions (dir). Honors & Awards: Played minor league baseball. Relig: Catholic. Mailing Add: French & County Rd Hardin IL 62047

CORBETT, MICHAEL TIMOTHY (D)
b St Paul, Minn, Feb 12, 45; s Eugene Louis Corbett, Sr & Anne Kane C; m 1971 to Mary Jo Quigley. Polit & Govt Pos: Admin asst to US Rep William A Barrett, Pa, 70- Relig: Roman Catholic. Legal Res: 1445 S 28th St Philadelphia PA 19146 Mailing Add: 907 Sixth St SW Washington DC 20024

CORBID, JOHN (DFL)
Minn State Rep
Legal Res: RR 2 Oklee MN 56742 Mailing Add: State Capitol Bldg St Paul MN 55155

CORBIN, DONALD LOUIS (D)
Ark State Rep
b Hot Springs, Ark, Mar 29, 38; s Louis Emerson Corbin & Louise Sheffield C; m 1961 to Loretta Icenhower; c Donald Byron. Educ: Univ Ark, Fayetteville, JD, 66; Sigma Alpha Epsilon. Polit & Govt Pos: City attorney, Lewisville, Ark, 68-; Ark State Rep, 71- Bus & Prof Pos: Attorney-at-law, Stamps, Ark, currently. Mem: Southwest Ark Bar Asn (vpres, 73-74; pres, 74-75); bd dirs, Haven Home for Ment Retarded, Human Develop Ctr & Ment Health-Ment Retardation Ctr, Texarkana, Ark; bd dirs, Ark Epilepsy Soc. Relig: Church of Christ. Legal Res: 408 Patton Dr Lewisville AR 71845 Mailing Add: PO Box C Lewisville AR 71845

CORBIN, GARY GEORGE (D)
Mich State Sen
b Bedford, Ind, Dec 13, 41; s George Corbin & Mamie Saltz C; m 1962 to Sheila Buck; c Susan & Sally. Educ: Anderson Col, BA, 63, MDiv, 67. Polit & Govt Pos: Comnr, Genesee Co, Dist 12, Mich, 70-74; Mich State Sen, Dist 25, 75- Bus & Prof Pos: Supvr, Bedford Park Syst, Ind, 59; with mgt div, Alaska Dept Fish & Game, 61; worker, Delco Remy Div, Gen Motors, 62-67; minister, Community Church of God, Clio, Mich, 67-74. Mem: Community Coord Child Care Asn; Flint Area Urban League; Mich Dept Educ Coun on Postsec Educ. Relig: Protestant. Legal Res: 11500 Colonial Woods Dr Clio MI 48420 Mailing Add: PO Box 240 Capitol Bldg Lansing MI 48902

CORBIN, LELAND WAYNE (R)
Mem, Calif Rep State Cent Comt
b Brook, Ind, Sept 11, 14; s Zephaniah Franklin Corbin & Sylvania Kemper C; m 1937 to Catherine Elizabeth Billet; c David Wayne, Nancy (Mrs Ransford B Berry) & Elinor. Educ: Ind Cent Col, AB, 36; Univ NMex, MA, 50; Univ South Calif, 2 summers; Univ Calif Exten, San Diego, 2 summers; San Diego State Col, 6 summers; Univ Ind, Bloomington, 1 year. Polit & Govt Pos: Mem, Calif Rep Assembly, 64-; mem, Calif Rep State Cent Comt, 65-; sustaining mem, San Diego Co Rep Cent Comt, 67- & Rep Nat Comt, 68- Bus & Prof Pos: Mem, Calif State Coun of Educ, Burlingame, Calif, 67- Mil Serv: Entered as Ens, Navy Res, 44, released as Lt(jg), 46, after serv in Air Support Control Units, Pac Area, 44-46; Lt, Naval Res (Ret). Mem: Legis coun, South sect, Calif Teachers Asn, 60-; Nat Educ Asn; San Diego Teachers Asn (bd dir, 63-68, vpres, 68-69 & pres, 69-). Relig: Protestant. Mailing Add: 4470 Adair St San Diego CA 92107

CORCORAN, HOWARD V (R)
Mem, Rep Nat Finance Comt, Washington, DC
b Wheeling, WVa, Sept 16, 06; s Harry P Corcoran & Mary S Gilligan C; m 1934 to Margaret M Sears; c Mary (Mrs Richard Pauley), Harriet (Mrs George Spillers) (deceased), Margaret (Mrs Charles Wendy), Howard V, Jr & John N. Educ: WVa Univ, AB in Pre-Law, 29; Linsly Tech Inst, Mech Eng, 43; Univ Pa Wharton Sch Finance, Investment Banking Inst, 3 years; Alpha Sigma Phi; Newman Club. Polit & Govt Pos: Chmn Ohio Co Rep Finance Comt, WVa, 56-59; vchmn, WVa Rep State Exec Comt, 58-61, chmn, 61-64; chmn, Recruit for 60 Campaign, 60, WVa Rep State Campaign, 60-62 & WVa Rep Finance Comt, 64-67 & 68-69; mem, WVa Rep State Exec Comt, First Sen Dist, 65-; chmn, Nixon for President Comt & Nixon Agnew Comt, 68; alt deleg, Rep Nat Conv, 60-68, deleg, 72; mem, Rep Nat Finance Comt, Washington, DC, 68- Bus & Prof Pos: Asst gen mgr, Wheeling Steel Corp, 35-52; past pres, Wheeling Hosp; chmn-treas, Corcoran Church Goods Co, WVa, 52-69; vpres & mem exec comt, WVa Hosp Serv; gen partner & allied mem, A E Masten & Co, 64-70, vpres & allied mem, 74- Mil Serv: ROTC, 33-41. Mem: Rotary; KofC; Knights of St George; Serra Int; Pittsburgh Club. Honors & Awards: Recipient of Papal Decoration, Knights of St Gregory. Relig: Roman Catholic. Legal Res: 5 Georgtown Apt 1229 Wheeling Rd Wheeling WV 26003 Mailing Add: 1269 National Rd Wheeling WV 26003

CORCORAN, THOMAS JOSEPH (D)
Dem Nat Committeeman, Kans
b Dubuque, Iowa, Nov 12, 22; s Clem T Corcoran & Pauline May Banfield C; m 1945 to Evelyn Mary Solomon; c Kathleen (Mrs Hefner), Thomas J, Jr, Patricia (Mrs Vincent) & Michael. Educ: Rockhurst Col, Mo; Shrivenham Univ, Eng; Alpha Delta Gamma. Polit & Govt Pos: Finance chmn, past state chmn & treas, Kans State Dem Comt; co-chmn, Kans Kennedy Campaign Comt, 60; finance chmn, Kans Johnson & Humphrey Campaign Comt, 64; past pres, Young Dem Kans; Dem Nat Committeeman, Kans, 65-; deleg, Dem Nat Mid-Term Conf, 74. Bus & Prof Pos: Mem, bd dirs, Country Club Bank, Kansas City, Mo, 65-69; mem bd dirs, Aristo Foods, Inc, 66-72; br mgr, West Chem Prod Inc, Kansas City, Mo, 71- Mil Serv: Entered as Pvt, Air Force, 42, released as Pfc, 45; ETO Ribbon with three Bronze Stars; Good Conduct Medal. Mem: VFW; KofC. Relig: Catholic. Mailing Add: 7171 Fountaindale Topeka KS 66610

CORDERMAN, JOHN PRINTZ (D)
Md State Sen
b Hagerstown, Md, May 14, 42; s John E Corderman & Gertrude Printz C; m 1966 to Ann Bender; c Elizabeth Ann & Robert Daniel. Educ: Hagerstown Jr Col, AA, 63; Univ Md, College Park, BA, 65; Univ Md Sch Law, JD, 68; Phi Alpha Delta; Phi Delta Theta. Polit & Govt Pos: Dep State Attorney, Washington Co, Md, 71-74; Md State Sen, 75- Bus & Prof Pos: Attorney, Wagaman, Wagaman & Meyers, P A, Hagerstown, Md, 69- Mem: Am, Md & Washington Co Bar Asns; Hagerstown Jaycees; Antietam Exchange. Honors & Awards: Washington Co Outstanding Young Man, Hagerstown Jaycees, 74. Relig: Lutheran. Legal Res: 33 Mealey Pkwy Hagerstown MD 21740 Mailing Add: 82 W Washington St Hagerstown MD 21740

CORDOVA, JORGE LUIS (NEW PROGRESSIVE, PR)
b Manati, PR, Apr 20, 07; m to Dora Rodriguez; c Jorge Luis, Jr, Elvira (Mrs Gonzalez), Irene (Mrs Subira) and Fernando. Educ: Cath Univ Am, BA, 28; Harvard Univ, LLB, 31. Polit & Govt Pos: From judge, Superior Court of PR to assoc justice, Supreme Court of PR, 40-46; resident comnr, US House Rep, PR, 69-72. Bus & Prof Pos: Attorney-at-law, San Juan, PR, 31-40, 46-68 & 73. Mem: PR & US Bar Asns. Relig: Roman Catholic. Mailing Add: Box 4631 San Juan PR 00905

CORDREY, RICHARD STEPHEN (D)
Del State Sen
b Milford, Del, Sept 8, 33; s John A Cordrey & Rachel Smith C; m 1953 to Mary Jane Bowen; c Richard J & Stephen B. Educ: Goldey-Beacom Sch Bus, ABA, 53. Polit & Govt Pos: Treas, Millsboro Town Coun, 68-69, vpres, 70-71; Del State Rep, 38th Dist, 71-73; Del State Sen, 20th Dist, 73- Bus & Prof Pos: Partner, John A Cordrey & Co, Millsboro, Del, 56- Mil Serv: Entered as Pvt, Army, 54, released as Pfc, 56, after serv in Signal Corps. Mem: Lions. Relig: Episcopal. Mailing Add: Box 486 Millsboro DE 19966

COREY, LEROY DALE (R)
b Carroll, Iowa, July 4, 42; s Virgil E Corey & Elsie Gaide C; m 1966 to Susan Louise Walrod; c Pamela Sue. Educ: Iowa State Univ, 4 years; Delta Sigma Rho. Polit & Govt Pos: Publicity chmn, Iowa Col Young Rep, 64-65; dir, Iowa TAR, 66-68; chmn, Iowa Young Rep, formerly; Region Seven vchmn, Nat Young Rep, 71-73; chmn, Conservative Coalition of Iowa, currently. Bus & Prof Pos: Advert coordr, Latta's Inc Waterloo, Iowa, 65-71; pres, Iowa Gen

Housing Co, Cedar Falls, 71- Mem: Nat Fedn Independent Bus; US Indust Coun; Waterloo-Cedar Falls Bd Realtors; Iowa & Nat Asn Realtors. Relig: Lutheran. Mailing Add: 3011 Shady Lane Cedar Falls IA 50613

COREY, WILLIAM W (D)
NH State Rep
Mailing Add: 126 Union St Manchester NH 03103

CORLEW, JOHN G (D)
Miss State Sen
Mailing Add: Box 787 Pascagoula MS 39567

CORLEY, CECIL LUCAS, JR (R)
b Murfreesboro, Tenn, Aug 20, 26; s Cecil Lucas Corley, Sr & Clarice Dill C; m 1952 to Suzanne Harris; c Celia Renee. Educ: Isaac Litton High Sch, Nashville, Tenn, grad, 45. Polit & Govt Pos: Chmn, Sumner Co Rep Party, Tenn, formerly; chmn, Sumner Co Brock for Senate, 70; chmn, Comt for Better Govt, 71; deleg, Rep Nat Conv, 72; Tenn State Rep, 44th Dist, 72-74. Mil Serv: Entered as Pvt, Air Force, 45, released, 45, after serv in Squadron X, Keesler Field, Miss. Mem: Mason; Shrine; Lions; Am Legion. Honors & Awards: Outstanding Serv, Nat Found, 59; Distinguished Serv Award, March of Dimes, 59. Relig: Church of Christ. Legal Res: 542 W Main St Gallatin TN 37066 Mailing Add: Lock Four Rd Gallatin TN 37066

CORMAN, JAMES C (D)
US Rep, Calif
b Galena, Kans, Oct 20, 20; m 1946 to Virginia Little (deceased); c Mary Anne & James C, Jr; m 1974 to Patti Lear Lopez-Pereira; c Christine, Eric & Marisa Lopez-Pereira. Educ: Grad Univ Calif, Los Angeles, 42 & Univ Southern Calif Law Sch, 48. Polit & Govt Pos: Mem, City Coun Los Angeles, 57-60; US Rep, Calif, 60-, mem, Ways & Means Comt & Small Bus Comt, currently; named by President Johnson to Nat Adv Comn on Civil Disorders, 67-68. Bus & Prof Pos: Attorney-at-law, 49-57. Mil Serv: Entered as Pvt, Marine Corps, 42, serv in 3rd Marine Div, World War II at Bougainville, Guam, Iwo Jima, released 46; reentered, 50 & released, 52; Col, Marine Corps Res at present. Mem: Am, Calif, Los Angeles & San Fernando Valley Bar Asns; Lions. Relig: Methodist. Legal Res: Reseda CA Mailing Add: 2252 Rayburn House Off Bldg Washington DC 20515

CORMANEY, THEODORE MICHAEL (R)
b Buena Vista, Iowa, July 2, 37; s Melvin Cormaney & Margaret Drackley C; m 1964 to Patricia Rae Katzenmeyer. Educ: Univ Wis, 63. Polit & Govt Pos: Exec secy, Wis Fedn Young Rep, 63-65; exec secy, Rep Assembly Campaign Comt, 65-67; analyst, Wis State Assembly, 65-67, Rep caucus pub rels dir, 67-; exec dir, Young Rep Nat Fedn, DC, 67-69; asst chief page, Rep Nat Conv, 68; nat dir, One Million Young Am for Nixon-Agnew, Washington, DC, 68; exec dir, Young Am Salute, Presidential Inauguration Celebration, 69; exec asst to Congressman William A Steiger, 69-72. Mil Serv: Entered as E-1, Air Force, 57, released as E-3, 60, after serv in Air Intel Serv, Alaskan Command. Relig: Episcopal. Mailing Add: 3701 Massachusetts Ave NW Washington DC 20016

CORN, CHARLES MCCUTCHEN (D)
b Hamilton Co, Tenn, Nov 4, 37; s W T Corn & Frances Hardwick C; m to Susan Callaway. Educ: Duke Univ, BA, 59; Vanderbilt Univ, JD, 62; Theta Chi. Polit & Govt Pos: Chmn, Bradley Co Dem Party, Tenn, 70-72; deleg, Dem Nat Conv, 72. Mil Serv: Entered as Pvt, Army, 62, released as Pfc, 63. Mem: Tenn, Ga & Am Bar Asns. Relig: Unitarian. Legal Res: My Ringer Rd Cleveland TN 37311 Mailing Add: PO Box 1164 Cleveland TN 37311

CORNABY, KAY S (R)
Chmn, Second Dist Rep Party, Utah
b Provo, Utah, Jan 14, 36; s Sterling A Cornaby & Hilda Stoker C; m 1965 to Linda Rasmussen; c Alyse, Derek, Tara & Heather. Educ: Brigham Young Univ, BA, 60; Univ Heidelberg, 61-63; Harvard Law Sch, JD, 66; Phi Eta Sigma; Blue Key. Polit & Govt Pos: Chmn, 17th Dist Rep Party, Utah, 70-73; chmn, Second Dist Rep Party, 73- Bus & Prof Pos: Attorney-at-law, New York, 66-69; attorney-at-law, Salt Lake City, Utah, 69- Mem: Am, New York & Utah Bar Asns; Harvard Club of Utah (treas). Legal Res: 3794 Hermes Dr Salt Lake City UT 84117 Mailing Add: 1406 Deseret Bldg Salt Lake City UT 84111

CORNELIUS, MICHAEL RAE (D)
NH State Rep
b Bemidji, Minn, July 27, 53; s Carl James Cornelius & Louise MacAndless C; single. Educ: Dartmouth Col, AB, 75. Polit & Govt Pos: Mem, Hanover Dem Town Comt, NH, 73-; NH State Rep, 75-, mem, Comt Exec Depts & Admin & Dem Budgetary Task Force, NH House Rep, 75- Bus & Prof Pos: Mem bd dirs, US Youth Coun, Washington, DC, 71-, exec vpres, 74- Mem: Nat Am Indian Youth Comt Arrow, Inc (chmn); NH Young Dem. Mailing Add: 44 Lebanon St Hanover NH 03755

CORNELL, GEORGE (TIP) (D)
Chmn, Tazewell Co Dem Comt, Ill
b Livingston Co, Ill, Mar 20, 10; s George E Cornell, Sr & Bertha Vetter C; m 1939 to Pauline Jenkins; c Karen L (Mrs William Schmidcall), George E, Jr, Raymond R & Laura B. Polit & Govt Pos: Assessor, Fondulac Twp, 66-; chmn, Tazewell Co Dem Comt, Ill, currently. Bus & Prof Pos: Various jobs, construction work; semi-retired. Mem: Lathers Local 36 (chmn, 20 years). Relig: Catholic. Legal Res: 228 Everett St East Peoria IL 61611 Mailing Add: PO Box 2233 Peoria IL 61611

CORNELL, ROBERT JOHN (D)
US Rep, Wis
b Gladstone, Mich, Dec 16, 19; s Ralph Florman Cornell & Veronica Sullivan C; single. Educ: St Norbert Col, BA, 41; Cath Univ Am, MA, 47, PhD, 57; Pi Gamma Mu. Polit & Govt Pos: Chmn, Eighth Dist Wis Dem Party, 69-74; US Rep, Wis, 75- Bus & Prof Pos: Teacher, Southeast Cath High Sch, Philadelphia, Pa, 41-47; prof, St Norbert Col, De Pere, Wis, 47-74. Publ: The Anthracite Coal Strike of 1902, Atheneum Publ, 71. Mem: Am Hist Asn; Labor Hist; Acad Polit Sci; Orgn Am Hist; Am Cath Hist Asn. Legal Res: 103 Grant St De Pere WI 54115 Mailing Add: US House of Rep Washington DC 20515

CORNETT, JOHN CHRIS (D)
Ky State Sen
b Lawrence, Ind, Aug 6, 10; s Christopher C Cornett & Minnie Croft Jones C; m to Goldie Slone; c Elizabeth Ann (Mrs Reed) & Earl McCoy. Educ: Morehead State Univ, AB, 35; Univ Ky Law Sch, 38-40; Cumberland Law Col, JD; Phi Delta Phi; Phi Alpha Delta. Polit & Govt Pos: Ky State Rep, 30-40; co judge, Knott Co, Ky, 42-46; Commonwealth attorney, Ky, 46-50; circuit judge, Ky, 50-70; Ky State Sen, 72- Bus & Prof Pos: Rural sch teacher, Knott Co Bd Educ, Hindman, Ky, 29-41; chmn exec comt of bd trustees, Alice Lloyd Col, currently. Relig: Methodist. Legal Res: Cornett Valley Mallie KY 41836 Mailing Add: Hindman Hotel Hindman KY 41822

CORNING, ERASTUS, II (D)
Mayor, Albany, NY
b Albany, NY, Oct 7, 09; s Edwin Corning & Louise Maxwell C; m 1932 to Elizabeth N Platt; c Erastus, III & Elizabeth (Mrs Dudley). Educ: Yale Col, AB, 32; Phi Beta Kappa; Chi Psi. Polit & Govt Pos: NY State Assemblyman, 36; NY State Sen, 37-41; mayor, Albany, NY, 42-; deleg, NY State Const Conv, 67; deleg, Dem Nat Conv, 44-72. Bus & Prof Pos: Pres, Albany Assocs, Inc, 32-; dir, Nat Commercial Bank, 46-; pres, Union River Lumber Co, 66- Mil Serv: Entered as Pvt, Army, 44, released as Pfc, 45, after serv in 2nd Inf Div, Europe, 44-45; Combat Inf Badge. Mem: Am Legion; VFW. Relig: Episcopal. Mailing Add: 116 S Lake Ave Albany NY 11208

CORNWALL, ROBERT DAVID (R)
Mem Exec Bd, Klamath Co Rep Cent Comt, Ore
b Syracuse, NY, Apr 5, 26; s Alfred E Cornwall, Sr & Sally Sink C; m 1953 to Beverly Grace Voogt; c Robert David & James Patrick. Educ: Pub Schs, Syracuse & Skaneateles, NY. Polit & Govt Pos: Pres, 19th Dist Rep Assembly, Calif, 60-61; mem, San Francisco Co Rep Cent Comt, 60-61; mem bd dirs, Calif Rep Assembly, 61; co campaign chmn, Sen Thomas Kuchel, 62; mem, Calif State Rep Cent Comt, 65-67, mem exec comt, 67; chmn, Siskiyou Co Rep Cent Comt, 65-67; chmn, Calif First Assembly Dist Comt, 66-67; area chmn, Calif Rep Co chmn Asn, 67; co-chmn Klamath Co, Ore Secy of State Campaign, 68; deleg, Ore Rep State Conv, 68; finance chmn, Klamath Co Rep Cent Comt, 68-70; vchmn, Reelect Gov Tom McCall Comt, Klamath Co, 70; mem exec bd, Klamath Co Rep Cent Comt, Ore, 72-; coordr, Klamath Co Reelect the President Comt, 72. Bus & Prof Pos: Vpres, Ideas Unlimited, 58-63; sales mgr, Marco Adv, 63-71, vpres sales, 71- Mil Serv: Entered as Seaman 3/C, Navy, 44, released as Seaman 1/C, 46, after serv at Receiving Sta, Philippine Islands; Victory Medal; Am Theater, Asiatic-Pac & ETO Medals; Philippine Liberation Ribbon. Mem: Mt Shasta Lions Club; Klamath Falls Lions Club; Elks; Klamath Co CofC; Am Field Serv (pres, Klamath Falls, 71-). Honors & Awards: Polit lectr to cols, schs & other orgns. Relig: Episcopal. Mailing Add: 929 Pacific Terr Klamath Falls OR 97601

CORPSTEIN, PETE (R)
Ariz State Rep
Mailing Add: 4342 E Highlands Dr Paradise Valley AZ 85253

CORREA, LUIS MANUEL (POPULAR DEM)
b San Juan, PR, June 23, 54; s Manuel Correa Calzada & Clarissa Marquez C; single. Educ: Georgetown Univ, 72-73; Harvard Univ, 73-74; Catholic Univ, 74- Polit & Govt Pos: Asst, Popular Dem Party Campaign Hqs, 71-72; asst, Inauguration of the Gov, 72; deleg, Dem Nat Mid-Term Conf, 74. Relig: Catholic. Mailing Add: Reseda 1917 Sta Maria Rio Piedras PR 00927

CORREA, NAOMI LOKALIA (D)
b Honolulu, Hawaii, June 23, 27; d William Lanier Reeves & Henrietta Minor R; m 1943 to Edward Lindsey Correa; c Edward, Jr, Fay, Henrietta (Mrs Clyde Texiera), Charlotte (Mrs Dan Coltan), Rose Mary (Mrs Tom Durate, Jr), Elizabeth, Kingston, Nowlin, Keolani, Laanui, Weston, Leialoha, Cody & Malia. Educ: Sacred Hearts Acad High Sch, Honolulu. Polit & Govt Pos: Precinct pres & dist organizer, Hawaii Dem Party, 46-73; mem, Consumer Protection Adv Bd; mem, Hawaii Dem State Cent Comt; deleg, Honolulu Co Dem Conv, Hawaii Dem State Conv & Dem Nat Conv, 72. Mem: Holy Trinity Altar Soc. Relig: Roman Catholic. Mailing Add: 332 Kuliouou Rd Honolulu HI 96821

CORRIGAN, J J P (R)
Justice, Supreme Court of Ohio
b Cleveland, Ohio, July 27, 01; s Patrick J Corrigan & Norah Walsh C; m to Nancy McGuinness. Educ: John Carroll Univ, AB, 22; Georgetown Univ, JD, 25. Polit & Govt Pos: City Prosecutor, Cleveland, Ohio, 32-36; judge, Court of Common Pleas, Cuyahoga Co, Ohio, 56-62; judge, Court of Appeals of Ohio, 62-69; Justice, Supreme Court of Ohio, 69- Bus & Prof Pos: Attorney-at-law, 26-36; attorney, Davis & Young, Law Firm, Cleveland, Ohio, 35-56. Mil Serv: Entered as Pvt, Army, 42, released as 2nd Lt, 45 after serv in V Corps, ETO, 43-45; Five Battle Stars; One Invasion Arrowhead; Bronze Star Medal; Battlefield Commission. Mem: Cleveland, Cuyahoga Co, Ohio State & Am Bar Asns; Am Judicature Soc. Relig: Roman Catholic. Legal Res: 11524 Edgewater Dr Cleveland OH 44102 Mailing Add: Judiciary Annex Columbus OH 43215

CORRIGAN, JOANN MARY (D)
Committeewoman, Second Dist Dem Party, Pa
b Pittsburgh, Pa, July 7, 39; d Vincent P Corrigan & Joann M Deely C; single. Educ: Duquesne Univ, BA, 69. Polit & Govt Pos: Committeewoman, Second Dist Dem Party, 70-; campaign worker, Flaherty for Mayor, 70; campaign worker, McGovern for McGovern for President, 72; campaign staff, Walgren for Cong, 72; vpres, Allegheny Co Young Dem, 72; alt deleg, Dem Nat Conv, 72. Relig: Roman Catholic. Legal Res: 333 Akron Ave Pittsburgh PA 15216 Mailing Add: 820 Carriage Rd Pittsburgh PA 15220

CORRIGAN, PATRICIA OUIMETTE (D)
VChmn, Berlin Dem Town Comt, Conn
b Hartford, Conn, Sept 7, 30; d Clifford Ouimette & Elsie Backman O; m 1948 to James Patrick Corrigan, Sr; c Barbara (Mrs Rudnick), Kevin, Mark, Kimberly, James, Jr & Suellen. Educ: Hartford Pub High Sch. Polit & Govt Pos: Pres, Berlin Young Dem, Conn, 57-58; vchmn, Berlin Dem Town Comt, Conn, 62-; committeewoman, Conn Dem State Cent Comt, Ninth Dist, 74-; secy, Berlin Charter Comn, 71-73; chmn, Zoning Bd Appeals, 72- Mailing Add: 106 Worthington Point Rd Berlin CT 06037

CORSE, WAHNETA (D)
Chairperson, Lafayette Co Dem Cent Comt, Mo
b Waverly, Mo, Sept 22, 14; d William L Zeysing & Martha Shafer Z; wid; c Kay (Mrs Gerald Emery) & Sandra (Mrs Herbert Soendker). Educ: Cent Mo State Col, 3 years; Sigma Sigma Sigma. Polit & Govt Pos: Committeewoman, Lafayette Co Dem Cent Comt, Mo, 68-, vchmn, 70-74, chairperson, 74- Bus & Prof Pos: Exec vpres, Wellington Bank, Mo, 50-; treas,

Wellington-Napoleon Schs R-9, 65-70; treas, Wellington-Napoleon Rd Dist, 65- Mem: Bus & Prof Womens Club. Relig: Methodist. Mailing Add: Tanyard Dr Wellington MO 64097

CORSER, JOHN BLISS, JR (R)
NH State Rep
b Scranton, Pa, June 25, 06; s John Bliss Corser & Fanny Gildersleeve Laverty C; m 1934 to Maude Mitchell Daniel. Educ: Princeton Univ, BS, 27, MFA in Archit, 30; Cloister Inn. Polit & Govt Pos: NH State Rep, 75- Bus & Prof Pos: Assoc, Holden, McLaughlin & Assocs, Architects, 31-53; partner, Holden, Egan, Wilson & Corser, Architects, 53; partner, Holden, Yang, Raemsch & Corser, Architects, 72. Mil Serv: Entered as 1st Lt, Army, 41, released as Maj, 46, after serv in 86th Inf Div, 331st Field Artillery Bn, Am, Europe & Pac, 43-46; Lt Col (Ret), Army Res, 54. Mem: Emer mem Am Inst Architects. Mailing Add: North Rd Hancock NH 03449

CORSKIE, JOHN CAMPBELL (R)
Vt State Rep
Mailing Add: 21 Pinewood Rd Montpelier VT 05603

CORSO, PHILIP LOUIS (R)
Chmn, Chicopee Rep City Comt, Mass
b Chicopee, Mass, Nov 16, 42; s Philip L Corso (deceased) & Rose A Giblo C; m 1961 to Carol Lee Chinnock, div; remarried 1973 to Claudia McHugh; c Corrine & Christine. Educ: Westfield State Col, BSE, 64; Univ Mass, MA, 70. Polit & Govt Pos: Pres, Chicopee Young Rep, Mass, 63-64; co chmn, Citizens for Nixon-Agnew, 68; chmn, Chicopee Rep City Comt, 68- Bus & Prof Pos: Social studies teacher, Chicopee High Sch, Mass, 64- Mem: Chicopee & Mass Teachers Asns. Relig: Catholic. Mailing Add: 30 Sunnymeade Ave Chicopee MA 01020

CORSON, NEAL CRAIG (R)
Maine State Sen
b Waterville, Maine, Aug 24, 47; s Anson George Corson & Eileen Thomas C; single. Educ: Bowdoin Col, AB, 70; Alpha Rho Upsilon. Polit & Govt Pos: Maine State Rep, 69-71; Maine State Sen, Dist 17, 75- Mil Serv: Entered as 2nd Lt, Army, 70, released as 1st Lt, after serv in 145th Aviation Bn, 72-74, Aviator Badge. Mem: Kiwanis; Am Legion. Mailing Add: 9 Houghton St Madison ME 04950

CORSON, PHILIP LANGDON (R)
b Plymouth Meeting, Pa, Oct 31, 98; s Walter Harris Corson & Katherine Irene Langdon C; m 1930 to Helen Payson. Educ: Haverford Col, BA, 19. Hon Degrees: LLD, Ursinus Col, 59. Polit & Govt Pos: Vchmn, Rep Finance Comt, Pa, 58-63; treas, Rep State Comt Pa, 60-72. Bus & Prof Pos: Pres, G & W H Corson, Inc, Plymouth Meeting, Pa, 33-53, chmn of bd, 53-72, dir, Hughes Foulkrod Co, Pa Mfrs Asn Ins Co & Continental Bank, 69-72; mem bd trustees, Germantown Acad & Ursinus Col. Mil Serv: Pvt, Army, 18-19. Mem: Merion Cricket Club; Mid-Ocean Club; Pinehurst Country Club; Plymouth Country Club; Racquet Club of Philadelphia. Honors & Awards: Philadelphia Amateur Golf Champion, 25-29. Relig: Society of Friends. Mailing Add: Plymouth Meeting PA 19462

CORTES, CARLOS F (R)
Assoc VChmn, Kans Rep State Comt
b San Francisco, Calif, July 1, 07; s Carlos Eliseo Cortes & Reine Blum C; m 1933 to Florence Frieda Hoffman; c Carlos E & Gary H. Educ: Univ Calif, Berkeley, BA, 29; Alpha Chi Rho. Polit & Govt Pos: Adv mem, Johnson Co Rep Cent Comt, Kans, 70-73; assoc vchmn, Kans Rep State Comt, 70-; alt deleg, Rep Nat Conv, 72; mem, Johnson Co State Rep Exec Comt, 72- Bus & Prof Pos: Exec vpres, Hoffman Cortes Contracting Co, 61-73; vpres, Hoffman Investment Co, Kansas City, Mo, 62-73; pres, Plaza Towers Investment Co, Kansas City, 73- Mem: Western Hist Asn; Am Humanics Found (trustee, 60-, asst secy, 68-); Real Estate Bd of Kansas City; CofC, Kansas City, Mo; CofC of Gtr Kansas City. Honors & Awards: Silver Beaver, Boy Scouts City Area Coun, 58 & Silver Antelope, NCent Region, 72. Mailing Add: 6717 Belinder Rd Mission Hills KS 62208

CORTEZ, LUIS ABRAN (D)
City Councilman, Colorado Springs, Colo
b Trinidad, Colo, June 14, 35; s Luis Abran Cortez & Maclovia Madrid C; m 1960 to France C Perea; c Eugene M, David D, Evelyn D & Julian F. Educ: Trinidad State Jr Col, Colo, AA, 61; Adams State Col, BA, 63, MA, 69. Polit & Govt Pos: Deleg, Rep Nat Conv, 72; city councilman, Colorado Springs, Colo, 72- Bus & Prof Pos: Elem teacher, Adams Co, Colo, 63-65; elem teacher, Colorado Springs Pub Schs, Colo, 65-69; assoc dir, Urban League Colorado Springs, 69-70; counr, El Paso Community Col, Colorado Springs, 70- Mil Serv: Entered as Recruit, Air Force, 54, released as A/1C, 57, after serv in Tex, Wyo, Korea & Colorado Springs. Mem: Latin Am Educ Found, Inc; Am GI Forum; Kiwanis; Quarterback Club. Relig: Roman Catholic. Mailing Add: 902 Ellston Ct Colorado Springs CO 80907

CORUJO COLLAZO, JUAN (POPULAR DEMOCRAT, PR)
Rep, PR House of Rep
Mailing Add: State Capitol San Juan PR 00901

CORY, JAMES KENNETH (D)
State Controller, Calif
b Kansas City, Mo, Sept 29, 37; s Clifford Cory & Mary Jane White C; m 1958 to Lucile Ann DesJardins; c Philip, Janet & David. Educ: Orange Coast Col, 2 years; Univ Southern Calif, 3 years; Univ Calif, 1 year; Delta Sigma Phi. Polit & Govt Pos: Consult to educ comt, Calif State Assembly, 61-63; chief admin officer, Calif Legis, 64-65; Calif State Assemblyman, 69th Dist, 66-74, chmn joint comt pub domain, Calif State Assembly, until 74, chmn Dem caucus, 70-; deleg, Dem Nat Conv, 68 & 72; State Controller, Calif, 75- Mem: Artificial Kidney Found (mem bd dirs); Westminster Elks; Westminster Merit Syst Comn. Relig: Protestant. Legal Res: 9051 Vons Dr Garden Grove CA 92641 Mailing Add: State Capitol Sacramento CA 95814

COSBY, CURTIS R (D)
Mem, Dem Party of Ga
b Atlanta, Ga, Oct 10, 14; s Roland Cosby & Roberta Hampton. Educ: Morehouse Col, AB, 42; Blayton Sch Bus & Acct, grad, 56. Polit & Govt Pos: Mem, Dem Party, Ga, 74-; mem, Fulton Co Dem Exec Comt, 74- Mil Serv: Entered as Pvt, Army, 43, released as Sgt, 45, after serv in QM Corp, European Theatre. Mem: Esquires Social & Civic Club; Braves 400; Atlanta Hawks Booster Club. Relig: Episcopal. Mailing Add: 8 Anderson Ave SW Atlanta GA 30314

COSS, FRANK (POPULAR DEMOCRAT, PR)
Rep, PR House of Rep
Mailing Add: State Capitol San Juan PR 00901

COSSAR, GEORGE PAYNE (D)
Miss State Rep
b Webb, Miss, Aug 26, 07; s John Harper Cossar & Lottie Pattison Thompson C; m 1933 to Elizabeth Finney; c George Payne, Jr, John Thompson & Bill Finney. Educ: Univ Miss, LLB, 31; Omicron Delta Kappa; Phi Alpha Delta; Sigma Nu. Polit & Govt Pos: Miss State Rep, 44-48 & 52-, mem mgt comt, Miss House Rep, vchmn, 72-; mem nat exec comt, Nat Conf State Legis Leaders, 62-; mem adv bd, Southern Conf Coun of State Govts, 66-69. Bus & Prof Pos: Lawyer. Mem: Farm Bur; Delta Coun; Mason (32 degree); Scottish Rite; Shrine. Honors & Awards: Named to Hall of Fame, Univ Miss, 31. Relig: Methodist; teacher, Men's Bible Class, 25 years. Legal Res: 109 Vine St Charleston MS 38921 Mailing Add: Cossar Bldg Charleston MS 38921

COSTA, WILLIAM THOMAS, JR (D)
Committeeman, Vt Dem State Comt
b St Johnsbury, Vt, June 9, 32; s William Thomas Costa, Sr & Almina Botazzi C; m 1964 to Gay Buttura; c Kelli Gay, Kara Almina & Kiersten Alyssa. Educ: Norwich Univ, 51-53; Univ Notre Dame, BS cum laude, 56; Sigma Alpha Epsilon. Polit & Govt Pos: Vchmn, Caledonia Co Dem Comt, Vt, 61-63; town trustee, St Johnsbury, 64-67, mem zoning bd, 64-68; chmn, St Johnsbury Dem Comt, 65-72; committeeman, Vt Dem State Comt, 65-; mem, Gov Davis Bi-Partisan Blue Ribbon Study Comt on Social Welfare in Vt, 69; notary pub, 69-; mem, St Johnsbury Downtown Planning Comn, 70-; mem, Vt State Hwy Bd, 73- Bus & Prof Pos: Partner, Green Mountain Super Market, St Johnsbury, 59-; pres, Costa Realty Co, Inc, St Johnsbury, 63-; dir, Citizens Savings Bank & Trust Co, 72-; pres, Recreation, Inc, 72- Mil Serv: Entered as 2nd Lt, Army, 56, released as 1st Lt, 58, after serv in Qm Corps, Metz, France, ETO, 57-58, Capt, Res, 58- Mem: Vt Retail Asn (dir, 68-); Vt Retail Grocers Asn; Vt Bowling Asn; KofC; Rotary Int. Honors & Awards: Distinguished Serv Award, St Johnsbury Jr CofC. Relig: Roman Catholic; dir, St John's Pastoral Comn, 69- Mailing Add: One Woods Dr St Johnsbury VT 05819

COSTACAMPS, RAMON (D)
b Mayaguez, PR, Nov 6, 30; s Onofre Costacamps & Felicita Oliveras C; m 1956 to Carmen M Sanabria; c Carmen Felicita; Jose Alberto & Jose Roberto. Educ: Univ PR, BS, 55; Phi Eta Mu. Polit & Govt Pos: Mem regional expert & expansion coun, US Dept Com; chmn bd, PR Commun Authority, 73-74; deleg, Dem Nat Mid-Term Conf, 74; treas, Co Popular Dem Party, 74. Bus & Prof Pos: Vpres, A Sanabria, Inc, 68-; vpres, Water Works Suppliers, Inc, 69-; prin, Ramon Costacamps & Assocs, 72- Mil Serv: Entered as Pfc, Army, 50, released as Cpl, 51, after serv in 3rd Div, Korea; Lt, Army Res, 60; Combat Infantry Badge; Good Conduct Medal; Four Battle Stars. Mem: Water Pollution Control Fedn; PR Col Eng; Am Water Works Asn (pres, PR Sect, 75-); PR Soc Eng; Lions. Honors & Awards: Order of Merit, Phi Eta Mu, 71. Relig: Catholic. Mailing Add: 21 H St Villa Caparra Guaynabo PR 00657

COSTANTINI, EDMOND (D)
b Wilkes-Barre, Pa, Dec 26, 32; s Edmund S Costantini & Armida Maturi C; m 1956 to Agnes Hansen; c Lisa. Educ: NY Univ, BA, 54; Univ Conn, MA, 56; Univ Calif, PhD, 66; Phi Beta Kappa, Pi Sigma Alpha. Polit & Govt Pos: Asst to the Northern Calif campaign mgr, John Kennedy Campaign, 60; asst campaign mgr, Northern Calif, Salinger-for-Sen Primary Campaign, 64; co campaign coordr, Gov Edmund Brown Campaign, 66; staff secy for educ, Gov Calif, 66; pres, Davis Dem Club, 67-68; mem, Co Grand Jury, 67-68; mem, Calif Dem Adv Coun, 67-69; co campaign chmn, Robert Kennedy Campaign, 68; deleg, Dem Nat Conv, 68; co campaign chmn, Jess Unruh Gubernatorial Campaign, 70; chmn comt on party orgn, Calif Dem Party Reform Comn, 70-71; mem exec comt, Calif Muskie Campaign, 72; co co-chairperson, Edmund Brown, Jr Gubernatorial Campaign, 74. Bus & Prof Pos: Research analyst pub affairs, NBC-TV, NY, 61-62; research analyst, Inst Gov Studies, Univ Calif, Berkeley, 62 & 64, teaching fel social sci, 62-63; prof polit sci, Univ Calif, Davis, 64-, chmn dept of polit sci, 71- Mil Serv: Entered as Pvt, Army, 57, released as Sp-4, 63. Publ: Co-auth, Politics and Parties in California, Macmillan, 70, Competing elites within a political party, Western Polit Quart, 69 & Women as politicians, J of Social Issues, 72. Mem: Am & Western Polit Sci Asns; Am Civil Liberties Union. Honors & Awards: Falk Fel; Nat Sci Found grant. Mailing Add: Dept of Polit Sci Univ of Calif Davis CA 95616

COSTANZA, MARGARET (D)
Mem, Dem Nat Comt, NY
b LeRoy, NY, Nov 28, 32; s Philip Joseph Costanza & Concetta Granata C; single. Educ: East High Sch, 46-50. Polit & Govt Pos: Exec dir, Robert F Kennedy Sen Campaign, Rochester, NY, 64; vchmn, Monroe Co Dem Comt, 66-; chmn, NY State Dem Women's Conf, NY State Dem Comt, 68; mem adv coun, Small Bus Admin, 68-; alt deleg, Dem Nat Conv, 72; mem, Dem Nat Comt, 72-; Dem cand for Cong, 35th Dist, 74; council-mem-at-lg & vmayor, Rochester, NY, 74- Bus & Prof Pos: Admin asst & exec secy to John J Petrossi, Rochester, NY, 54-; mem adv comt, Community Savings Bank, Rochester, NY, 69- Mem: Am Cancer Soc, Rochester, NY; Rochester CofC (Women's Coun); Rotary Horse Show Comt. Relig: Roman Catholic. Mailing Add: 19 C Seneca Manor Dr Rochester NY 14621

COSTANZO, NICHOLAS (R)
VChmn, Orange Co Rep Comt, NY
b Middletown, NJ, Feb 8, 17; s Sam Costanzo & Candito Meola C; m 1946 to Grace Ingrassia; c Paul & Nicholas, Jr. Educ: Drake Univ, 37-39. Polit & Govt Pos: Mem, Middletown Men's Rep Club, NY; sustaining mem, Rep Nat Comt; mem, NY State Gov Club; chmn, First Ward Rep Comt, 61-63; chmn, Middletown Rep Comt, 63-67; vchmn, Orange Co Rep Comt, 67-69; supt, US Assay Off, New York, 69- Mil Serv: Entered as Pvt, Army, 42, released as S/Sgt, 46, after serv in Field Artil, ETO, 44-46. Relig: Catholic. Mailing Add: 132 Wickham Ave Middletown NY 10940

COSTELLO, J DANIEL (D)
b Atlantic City, NJ, Jan 1, 39; s Robert J Costello & Margaret O'Brien C; m 1962 to Patricia Murdock; c Timothy & Matthew. Educ: St Mary's Col (Md), AB, 60; Cath Univ Am, 60-63. Polit & Govt Pos: Mem, Montgomery Co Dem Cent Comt, Md, 70-73; admin asst to US Rep James M Hanley, NY, 74- Relig: Roman Catholic. Mailing Add: 12321 LaPlata St Silver Spring MD 20904

COSTELLO, JAMES (D)
RI State Sen
b Providence, RI, Feb 25, 17; m to Elena Arute; c Mary Ann & Deborah. Educ: Chrysler

Corp-Master Technician Sch & Ford Inst, NY; Brown Univ, exten courses in state govt & admin. Polit & Govt Pos: Mem, Lincoln Town Coun, RI, 6 years; RI State Sen, 63- Bus & Prof Pos: Automobile dealer; pres & treas, Warwick Ford Co & Jaelco Realty Co; vpres & treas, RI Credit Accident Health Life Ins Co. Mem: Cumberland-Lincoln Fraternal Order Police; RI Dealer's Asn (vpres); Blackstone Valley Hist Soc; Warwick Airport Lions Club; Lincoln KofC (4 degree). Mailing Add: Harris Ave Lincoln RI 02865

COSTELLO, PHILIP NEILL, JR **(R)**
Mem, Madison Rep Town Comt, Conn
b Grand Island, Nebr, Sept 23, 30; s Philip N Costello & Lucile Reimers C; m 1954 to Joy Carter Dixon; c Philip, Jr & Sharon Elizabeth. Educ: Yale Univ, BA; Harvard Law Sch, LLB; Lincolns Inn Soc. Polit & Govt Pos: Town attorney, Madison, Conn, 59-; mem, Madison Rep Town Comt, 62-; mem, Conn Rep State Cent Comt, 66-70; Conn State Rep, 71-73; Conn State Sen, 73-74. Bus & Prof Pos: Law partner, Daggett, Colby & Hooker, New Haven, Conn, 60- Mem: Am Bar Asn; Elks; Jaycees. Honors & Awards: Distinguished Serv Award, Madison Jaycees, 60. Relig: Roman Catholic. Legal Res: 205 Church St New Haven CT 06503 Mailing Add: PO Box 16 Madison CT 06443

COSTELLO, TIMOTHY WILLIAM **(LIBERAL)**
b Brooklyn, NY; s Thomas Costello & Mary Kine C; m 1941 to Genevieve Sullivan; c Genevieve (Mrs William Cusik); Joseph, Mary-Kay, Peter, John & Barbara. Educ: Fordham Univ, BS, 37, MA, 39 & PhD(psychol), 40. Polit & Govt Pos: Chmn, NY State Liberal Party, 62-65; Dep Mayor-City Adminr, New York, 66-72. Bus & Prof Pos: Prof psychol & mgt, Grad Sch Bus Admin, NY Univ, 46-66. Mil Serv: 1st Lt, Army, 43-46. Publ: Abnormal Psychology (w Dr S Zalkind), Prentice-Hall, 62. Mem: Am Psychol Asn; life mem NAACP; Pride of Judea Children's Serv (bd mem); New York Hosp Corp (trustee); Cath Interracial Coun (mem bd). Relig: Roman Catholic. Mailing Add: 415 Central Park W New York NY 10023

COSTIN, CECIL GUERRY, JR **(D)**
b Port St Joe, Fla, Oct 15, 23; s Cecil Guerry Costin, Sr & Lola Pridgeon C; m 1957 to Margaret Mixson; c Charles Anthony & Margaret Renee. Educ: Univ Fla, LLB, 48; Delta Theta Phi; Pi Kappa Phi. Polit & Govt Pos: City attorney, Port St Joe, Fla, 48-67; Fla State Rep, Gulf Co, 53-63; attorney, Gulf Co Sch Bd, 60-; chmn, Gulf Co Dem Exec Comt, formerly; prosecuting attorney, Gulf Co, 68- Bus & Prof Pos: Vpres & dir, Citizens Fed Savings & Loan Asn, Port St Joe, Fla, 58-; pres, St Joe Natural Gas Co, Inc, 62- Mil Serv: Entered as Air Cadet, Navy, 43, released as Ens DL, 46. Mem: 14th Judicial Circuit Bar Asn; Mason; Morocco Temple Shrine; Kiwanis. Relig: Baptist. Legal Res: 2005 Constitution Dr Port St Joe FL 32456 Mailing Add: 221 Reid Ave Port St Joe FL 32456

COTE, ALBERT E **(D)**
Maine State Rep
Mailing Add: 138 Bartlett St Lewiston ME 04240

COTE, HAROLD ARTHUR **(D)**
Chmn, Enfield Dem Town Comt, Conn
b Enfield, Conn; s Arthur Rudolph Cote & Ethyl Dunne C; m 1949 to Anne A Sullivan; c Harold A, Jr, William, Susan & John. Educ: Western New Eng Col, BBA, 53. Polit & Govt Pos: Dem regist voters, 58-67; councilman, Enfield Coun, Third Dist, Conn, 67-72; chmn, Enfield Dem Town Comt, Conn, 72- Mil Serv: Entered as A/S, Navy, 41, released as QM 1/C, 45, after serv on Destroyer European & Pac Theaters. Mailing Add: 343 Elm St Enfield CT 06082

COTE, JOSEPH LEO **(D)**
NH State Rep
b Concord, NH, Sept 13, 14; s Joseph A Cote & Dina Marcotte C; m Theresa N Michaud; c Joseph L, Jr, Linda (Mrs Paul Bongiovanni), Candace (Mrs Malcolm MacDonald), Donna (Mrs Larry Banks), Holly (Mrs Richard Arey) & Kendall J. Educ: Cent High Sch, grad, 34; Springfield Trade Sch; NH Tech Sch; Riddle McKay Flying Sch, Tenn. Polit & Govt Pos: NH State Rep, 69-; selectman, Manchester, Ward Four, 73- Bus & Prof Pos: Commercial pilot, flight instr & licensed airplane mechanic. Mil Serv: Army Res, 42-43; Naval Res, 43-44. Mem: OX5 Club of Am. Relig: Catholic. Mailing Add: 659 Hall St Manchester NH 03104

COTE, KENDALL J **(D)**
NH State Rep
Mailing Add: 284 Fremont St Manchester NH 03103

COTE, MARGARET SULLIVAN **(D)**
NH State Rep
b Nashua, NH, Mar 13, 98; d Alfred E Cote & Margaret Sullivan C; single. Educ: NH Univ, BA, 22; Boston Univ, MA, 50; Phi Kappa Phi; Alpha Chi Omega. Polit & Govt Pos: Mem, Nashua Bd Educ, NH, 64-; NH State Rep, 69- Bus & Prof Pos: Teacher, Nashua High Sch, NH, 30-63, chmn mod lang dept, 59-63; dir, NH Coun for Better Schs, 63-69; instr French, Daniel Webster Jr Col, 68-69. Mem: Am Asn Teachers French; Nashua Teachers' Union; Am Fedn Teachers; Nashua Community Concert Asn (trustee); Nashua Col Club. Relig: Roman Catholic. Mailing Add: 273 Main St Nashua NH 03060

COTNER, HOWARD PAUL **(D)**
Okla State Rep
b Wichita Falls, Tex, Aug 10, 25; s Hugh Henry Cotner & Wilma C Bodenhamer; c Paul Stephen, Kathy Lynn & Deborah Kay. Educ: Altus Jr Col, Okla, 1 year; Univ Okla, BA in Jour, 48; Alpha Delta Sigma; Sigma Phi Epsilon. Polit & Govt Pos: Okla State Rep, Dist 52, 71- Bus & Prof Pos: Owner & mgr, Jackson Co Abstract Co, currently. Mem: Okla Land Title Asn; Kiwanis; Mason (32 degree); Scottish Rite; Shrine. Honors & Awards: Outstanding Young Man of Year, Okla Jr CofC, 58. Relig: Methodist; lay speaker. Mailing Add: PO Box 756 Altus OK 73521

COTNER, MERCEDES R **(D)**
VChmn, Cuyahoga Co Dem Party, Ohio
b Cleveland, Ohio, Mar 3, 05; d John S Trapp & Caroline Auer T; m 1927 to George Winfield Cotner; c Timothy & Gerald. Educ: St Mary High Sch, Cleveland, grad. Polit & Govt Pos: Precinct committeeman, 21st Ward Dem Club, Ohio, 36-, ward leader, 41-; secy, Fed Dem Women Ohio, 48-52, mem, currently; councilman, Ward 21, 54-64; city clerk, Cleveland, 64-; vchmn, Cuyahoga Co Dem Party, 60-; cand for Mayor, Cleveland, 73. Bus & Prof Pos: Off mgr, Harrington Electric Co, Cleveland, 18-30. Publ: Ed, City Record, Official J City Coun, 64- & Annual Report, City Coun, 64- Mem: Cosmopolitan Dem Women; Cuyahoga Co Dem Women; Int Inst Municipal Clerks. Honors & Awards: Bus Woman of the Year, Western Reserve Chap Prof Bus Women, 73; Dem Woman of the Year, Cuyahoga Co Dem Women, 74. Relig: Roman Catholic. Legal Res: 3301 W 100 St Cleveland OH 44111 Mailing Add: City Hall Cleveland OH 44114

COTTAM, HOWARD R **(D)**
b St George, Utah, July 27, 10; s Heber Cottam & Edith Brooks C; m 1934 to Katherine Stokes; c Lillian Meredith (Mrs John M Williams, Jr). Educ: Brigham Young Univ, BS, 32; Univ Wis-Madison, PhM, 38, PhD, 41; Nat War Col, dipl, 53; Blue Key. Polit & Govt Pos: Chief, Prog Appraisal Div, War Food Admin, 42-44; agr economist, Paris, 44-46; agr attache, Rome, 46-47, first secy & consul, 47-50, counr of embassy & chief food & agr div, Econ Coop Admin Spec Mission to Italy, 50-52; assigned to Nat War Col, Washington, DC, 52-53; counr & dep dir, US Oper Mission, Int Coop Admin, The Hague, 53-56; US Minister & Dir Oper, Mission, Rio de Janeiro, 56-60; dep asst secy of state, Near Eastern & SAsian Affairs, 60-63; US Ambassador, Kuwait, 63-69; NAm Rep Food & Agr Orgn UN, 69-74; int consult, 75- Bus & Prof Pos: Research asst, fel, teaching asst & asst to dean of men, Univ Wis, 35-39; research asst, Ohio State Univ, 39-40; asst prof, Pa State Col, 40-42; vis prof, Am Univ, 74- Publ: Articles in J Am Statist Asn, Social Forces, Rural Sociol & Foreign Agr. Mem: Am Asn Advan Sci; Soc Int Develop; Am Polit Sci Soc; Agr Econ Asn; Am Dietetic Asn. Mailing Add: 2245 46th St NW Washington DC 20007

COTTEN, SAMUEL R **(D)**
Alaska State Rep
b Juneau, Alaska; s Samuel L Cotten & Kathryn Russell C; single. Educ: Univ Alaska, Anchorage, 69-72, Fairbanks, 71. Polit & Govt Pos: Alaska State Rep, 75- Bus & Prof Pos: Tech rep, Xerox Corp, Anchorage, Alaska, 72- Mil Serv: Entered as E-1, Navy, 65, released as E-5, 69, after serv in USS Schoefield Deg 3, Western Pac, 66-69; Vietnam Service Medal; Nat Defense Medal. Legal Res: Mausel Rd Eagle River AK 99577 Mailing Add: Box 296 Eagle River AK 99577

COTTER, WILLIAM R **(D)**
US Rep, Conn
b Hartford, Conn, July 18, 26; s William W Cotter & Mary E O'Loughlin C. Educ: Trinity Col, BA, 49. Polit & Govt Pos: Treas, Hartford Dem Town Comt, Conn, 53-60; councilman, Hartford, Conn, 54-55; exec aide to Gov A A Ribicoff, 55-57; dep ins comnr, 57-64, comnr, 64-; treas, Conn State Dem Cent Comt, 62-; deleg, Dem Nat Conv, 64; US Rep, First Cong Dist, Conn, 71-, mem ways & means comt, US House Rep, 74- Mem: KofC; Elks (Exalted Ruler); Wethersfield Country Club. Relig: Roman Catholic. Mailing Add: 247 Fairfield Ave Hartford CT 06114

COTTLE, L GLEN **(D)**
Utah State Rep
b Plain City, Utah, Feb 9, 15; s Laurence N Cottle & Rosella Lund C; m 1938 to Margaret Hansen; c Roger G, Craig H & Margaret Ann. Educ: Weber State Col, 1 year; Utah State Univ, BS in Educ, 55; Lambda Chi Alpha. Polit & Govt Pos: Chmn voting dist, Weber Co Sixth Voting Dist, 64-; chmn, Seventh Legis Dist Dem Orgn, 70; Utah State Rep, Dist 35, 71-73 & 75- Bus & Prof Pos: Dairy Herd Improv Asn tester, US Dept Agr, Logan, Utah, 40-42; dairy & food inspector, Utah State Dept Agr, Salt Lake City, 42-44; fieldman, Sego Milk Co, Richmond, 44-46; supvr, Nat Pub Serv Ins Co, Seattle, 46-52; teller, Commercial Security Bank, Ogden, Utah, 52-54; elem teacher, Ogden City Schs, 55- Mem: Nat Educ Asn; Utah Credit Union League (bd dirs); Ogden Lions Club; Ogden Teachers Credit Union (pres). Relig: Latter-day Saint. Mailing Add: 3012 N 300 E Ogden UT 84404

COTTON, MARY ELIZABETH **(D)**
NH State Rep
b Springfield, Ohio, Nov 7, 45; d Justin LeRoy Fagan & Alwilda Catherine Paden F; m 1969 to John Newell Cotton. Educ: Mercy Cent Sch Nursing, grad, 64; postgrad training in pharmacol, Community Hosp, grad, 67. Polit & Govt Pos: Portsmouth, NH coordr, Muskie for President Campaign, Raiche for Gov Campaign & Crowley for Gov Campaign, 72; mem, Reelect McIntyre for Sen Campaign, 72; deleg, NH State Dem Conv, 72; NH State Rep, 73-, mem comt educ & comt state insts, NH House Rep, 73-; mem Portsmouth City Deleg & Rockingham Co Deleg, 73-; mem, Portsmouth Dem City Comt, 73- Bus & Prof Pos: Staff nurse, Mercy Hosp, Springfield, Ohio, 64-68; office nurse, Springfield, 68-69; off nurse, New York, summer 68. Mem: Nat & NH Orgn Women Legis; Cystic Fibrosis Found; Seacoast Area Figure Skating Club. Relig: Protestant. Mailing Add: 22 Pine Ave W Portsmouth NH 03801

COTTON, NORRIS **(R)**
b Warren, NH, May 11, 00; s Harry Lang Cotton & Elizabeth Moses C; m 1927 to Ruth Isaacs. Educ: Wesleyan Univ; George Washington Univ Law Sch. Polit & Govt Pos: Former clerk, NH State Sen; dist attorney, Grafton Co, 33-39; justice, Munic Court of Lebanon, NH, 39-44; NH State Rep, 44-46; US Rep, NH, 47-54; US Sen, NH, 54-74. Bus & Prof Pos: Lawyer, firm of Cotton, Tesreau & Stebbins, Lebanon, NH. Mem: Am, NH & Grafton Co Bar Asns; Lebanon CofC; Odd Fellows. Mailing Add: 15 Kimball St Lebanon NH 03766

COTTON, W DAVIS **(D)**
Chmn, Richland Parish Dem Exec Comt, La
b Jonesville, La, Feb 9, 04; s George Spencer Cotton & Elizabeth Davis C; m 1927 to Anna Mae Allen; c Carole, Jean Ann & Stephen Wayne. Educ: La State Univ Law Sch, LLB, 27, JD, 69. Polit & Govt Pos: La State Sen, 40-44; chmn, Richland Parish Dem Exec Comt, 60-; mem, La Const Rev Comn, 70- Bus & Prof Pos: Pres, First Nat Bank, Rayville, La, 52- Mil Serv: Entered as 1st Lt, Army, 42, released as Lt Col, 46, after serv in 17th Maj Port, ETO; Bronze Star; ETO Ribbon with Two Battle Stars. Mem: La Law Inst (mem coun, 59-); fel Am Bar Found; La State Bar Asn; Mason (32 degree); La State Univ Alumni Fedn. Relig: Methodist. Legal Res: 219 Julia St Rayville LA 71269 Mailing Add: PO Box 857 Rayville LA 71269

COTTRELL, ARTHUR MAXSON, JR **(R)**
b Westerly, RI, May 8, 06; s Arthur Maxson Cottrell & Virginia Hunkins C; m 1929 to Violet Harkness Hoegland Tangeman; c John Trowbridge & Arthur Maxson, III. Educ: Georgetown Univ Sch of Foreign Serv, 27-28. Polit & Govt Pos: Councilman, Westerly, RI, 38-39, pres town coun, 40-45; RI State Sen, Westerly, 41-48; RI State Rep, 58-60; chmn, Hopkinton Rep Town Comt, formerly; RI State Sen, Hopkinton, 60-68. Bus & Prof Pos: Secy, C B Cottrell & Sons Co, 31-53. Mil Serv: Entered as Pfc, 101st Cavalry, NY Nat Guard, released as BM 2/C, after serv with Coast Guard Temporary Res, 43-45. Mem: YMCA; CofC; NY Yacht Club; AAONMS; Elks. Relig: Episcopal. Legal Res: Broad St Ashaway RI 02804 Mailing Add: Box 37 Westerly RI 02891

COTTRELL, JOAN SWEETLAND (R)
Mem, Rep State Cent Comt Calif
b Orient, SDak, July 3, 21; d Frederick Lorenzo Dow Sweetland & Rose-Margaret Anglin S; m 1946 to Joseph Elijah Stancil; m 1972 to J A Cottrell; c Lisa (Mrs Ronald Rohrer), Joseph E, Jr & Edward Sean. Educ: Presentation Sch Nursing, Aberdeen, SDak, RN, 42; Sacramento State Col, BA in Psychol, 70; Calif State Univ, Sacramento, MSC, 72. Polit & Govt Pos: Secy, Federated Rep Women, El Dorado Co, Calif, 62-63, pres, 63-64; mem, Rep State Cent Comt Calif, 65-; mem adv bd, El Dorado Ment Health Prog, Calif, 68- Mil Serv: Entered as 2nd Lt, Army Nurse Corps, 42, released as 1st Lt, 46, after serv in 16th Evacuation Hosp Unit, Mediter Theatre, 5th Army, 43-45; 2 Battle Stars, Naples-Foggia & Rome-Arno Campaigns; 2 Bronze Serv Stars, North Appenines Campaign & Po Valley Campaign; Battle Participation Awards. Mem: Calif State Nurses' Asn. Relig: Roman Catholic. Mailing Add: 1849 Fairchild Dr Carmichael CA 95608

COUGHLIN, JOHN DENNIS (R)
Treas, Ward Co Rep Party, NDak
b Scobey, Mont, Feb 5, 18; s Richard James Coughlin & Gertrude McMallan C; m 1942 to Virginia Maureen Hyde; c Mary Virginia, Jean Ann & John Dennis. Educ: Univ Notre Dame, 40. Polit & Govt Pos: Treas, Ward Co Rep Party, NDak, 58-; mem, NDak State Bd Pardons, 59-; NDak State Sen, 67-74. Bus & Prof Pos: Pres, Williston Basin Gas Co, Minot, NDak, 54-; dir & pres, Westland Oil Co, 60-; dir, Union Nat Bank. Mem: KofC; Elks; Rotary; Minot Country Club; Minot CofC (pres, 59-). Relig: Catholic. Legal Res: Rte 1 Minot ND 58701 Mailing Add: PO Box 1273 Minot ND 58701

COUGHLIN, R LAWRENCE, JR (R)
US Rep, Pa
b Wilkes Barre, Pa, Apr 11, 29; s R Lawrence Coughlin & Evelyn Wich C; m 1958 to Elizabeth Poole Sellers Worrell; c Elizabeth S, Lynne W, Sara S & R Lawrence, III. Educ: Yale Univ, BA, 50; Harvard Sch Bus Admin, MBA, 54; Temple Law Sch, LLB, 58; St Anthony Soc. Polit & Govt Pos: Pa State Rep, 65-66; Pa State Sen, 67-68; US Rep, 13th Dist, Pa, 69- Bus & Prof Pos: Plant foreman, Heintz Mfg Co, Philadelphia, Pa, 54-56, asst to mfg vpres, Heintz Div, Kelsey, Hayes Co, 56-58; attorney-at-law, Saul, Ewing, Remick & Saul, 60-66, partner, 67-69. Mil Serv: Entered as 2nd Lt, Marine Corps, 50, released as Capt, 52. Mem: Am, Pa & Philadelphia Bar Asns; Villanova Univ Develop Coun; Rosemont-Villanova Civic Asn. Honors & Awards: Outstanding Young Man, Main Line Jr CofC, Ardmore, Pa, 65. Relig: Episcopal. Legal Res: 829 Mt Moro Rd Villanova PA 19085 Mailing Add: 306 Cannon Bldg Washington DC 20515

COULSON, ROBERT (R)
b Grayslake, Ill, May 10, 12; c three. Educ: Dartmouth Col, AB; Univ Chicago, JD. Polit & Govt Pos: Ill State Rep, formerly; mayor, Waukegan, 49-57; former asst state's attorney, Lake Co; Ill State Sen, 62-73; deleg, Rep Nat Conv, 72. Mil Serv: 41-46, counter-intel, OSS agent in China-Burma; Lt Col, US Inf Res. Mem: Am Legion; Shrine; Lake Co Bar Asn. Mailing Add: 1031 Pacific Ave Waukegan IL 60085

COULTER, KIRKLEY SCHLEY (R)
b Nashville, Tenn, July 26, 14; s John Lee Coulter & Phoebe Frost C; m 1945 to Irene Marie Brun Prazmowski; stepchildren, Barbara M (Mrs Rich). Educ: Am Univ, BA, 35, MA, 63; Univ Wis, 36; Columbia Univ, 40-41; Omicron Delta Kappa; Pi Gamma Mu; Alpha Tau Omega. Polit & Govt Pos: Mem staff, US Sen Hugh Butler, Nebr, 41-42 & 46-47, admin & legis asst, 47-53; chief clerk & staff dir, US Senate Comt on Interior & Insular Affairs, 53-54; chmn, Arlington Co Rep Exec Comt, 54; asst to undersecy interior, 54-55; asst dir, Off Territories, Dept Interior, 55, dep dir, 55-57; legis adv, 57-60; dir div intl commercial rels, US Tariff Comn, Washington, DC, 60-62; minority economist, antitrust & monopoly subcomt, US Senate Judiciary Comt, 63- Mil Serv: Entered as enlistee, Army, 42, released as 1st Lt, 46. Mem: Joint founder Arlingtonians for a Better Co; Am Econ Asn; Polish Am Hist Asn. Relig: Episcopal. Mailing Add: 6300 Lakeview Dr Falls Church VA 22041

COULTER, RAYMOND CURTIS (R)
b Philadelphia, Pa, Apr 8, 18; s Clifton Alison Coulter (deceased) & Elizabeth Mae Hankey C (deceased); m 1942 to Ruth Melvina Waldo; c Linda Alison (Mrs Andrew Mayo) & Robert Waldo. Educ: Univ Ore, BS, 40 & LLB, 47; Phi Alpha Delta. Polit & Govt Pos: Ore State Rep, 49-51; gen counsel, League of Ore Cities, 52-56; regional solicitor, Dept of the Interior, Portland, Ore, 57-62, asst solicitor for power, Washington, DC, 62-66, assoc solicitor, Div of Water Resources & Procurement, 66-69, dep solicitor, Dept, 69-73; solicitor, Atlanta, Ga, currently. Bus & Prof Pos: Attorney-at-law, Grants Pass, Ore, 47-52, attorney-at-law, Eugene, Ore, 56-57. Mil Serv: Entered as Pvt, Army, 42, released as Capt, 46, after serv in IV Corps Hq in Italy, Mediter Theatre, 44-45. Mem: Ore State Bar; Fed Bar of Ore; Ore State Soc of Washington, DC. Relig: Presbyterian. Mailing Add: Suite 405 148 Cain St Atlanta GA 30303

COULTER, STEVEN ARTHUR (D)
Nev State Assemblyman
b Los Angeles, Calif, Aug 4, 47; s Carroll Woodrow Coulter & Teresa Rollo C; single. Educ: Univ Nev, Reno, BA, 69. Polit & Govt Pos: Treas, Washoe Co Young Dem, 73-75; northern chmn, Young Dem of Nev, 73-75; mem, Washoe Co Dem Cent Comt, 74-; mem Nev State Dem Cent Comt, 74-; Nev State Assemblyman, 75- Bus & Prof Pos: Newsman, KCRL Radio-TV, Reno, 66-69 & 73-75; newsman, United Press Int Audio, Washington, DC, 70-72. Mil Serv: Entered as Pvt E-1, Army, 69, released as SP-5, 71, after serv in Walter Reed Army Med Ctr, Washington, DC, 70-71. Mem: Nev Veteran's Caucus (vchmn, 74-75). Mailing Add: PO Box 13877 Reno NV 89507

COULTER, WILLIAM ALFRED (R)
Chmn, Palmer Rep Town Comt, Mass
b Palmer, Mass, June 3, 23; s Alfred Coulter & Jane Henry C; m 1948 to Constance Elaine Moore; c Carol Elaine, Susan Mae & James Alfred. Educ: Northeastern Univ, 1 year; Lynchburg Col, 1 year. Polit & Govt Pos: Assessor, Palmer, Mass, 16 years, chief assessor, 5 years; mem, Palmer Rep Town Comt, 15 years, chmn, currently. Bus & Prof Pos: Folding paper box salesman, Fed Paper Bd, 21 years, plant mgr, Palmer Div, 24 years; trustee, Wing Mem Hosp, 8 years; corporator, Palmer Savings Bank, 5 years. Mil Serv: Entered as Pvt, Army Air Force, 43, released as Flight Officer, 45, after serv in 8th Air Force. Mem: Blue Lodge Mason; Melha Temple Shriner (Scottish Rite); Lions; CofC. Relig: Protestant. Mailing Add: 77 Squier St Palmer MA 01069

COUNCE, ELMER WYLIE (R)
Mem, Weakley Co Rep Exec Comt, Tenn
b Lake, Miss, Nov 17, 21; s James Ephraim Counce & Emma Duncan C; m 1946 to Marilucile Dodd; c Benjamin Travis. Educ: Union Univ, Tenn, 41-42; Univ Tenn, Martin, 46-47, Univ Tenn, Knoxville, BS, 48, MS, 56; Alpha Zeta; Grad Club; Independent Students Orgn. Polit & Govt Pos: Mem, Weakley Co Rep Steering Comt, Tenn, 58-; mem, Weakley Co Exec Comt, 61-; mem, Ninth Dist Exec Comt, 68-; mem comt, Educators for Nixon, 68-; alt deleg, Rep Nat Conv, 72; deleg, Tenn State Conv, 72-; adv, Tenn Col Young Rep, 75. Bus & Prof Pos: Teacher voc agr, Hardin Co Cent High Sch, Tenn, 48-49; supvr farm training, Weakley Co, 49-51; instr agron, Univ Tenn, Martin, 51-56, asst prof & dir alumni & placement, 53-63, assoc prof & faculty sen, 70- Mil Serv: Entered as Apprentice Seaman, Coast Guard, 42, released as PO 3/C, 45, after serv in Pac & Atlantic. Publ: Co-auth, Sugarbeet Varieties and Feasibility Studies, Univ Tenn Agr Exp Sta, 64, Lime and fertilizer experiments on soy beans, Bull 391, 5/65 & Tritacale compared with other small grains in Tennessee, Tenn Farm & Home Sci, 7-9/72. Mem: Soil Conserv Soc Am; Am Soc Agron; Am Tree Farmers Asn; Asn Southern Agr Workers; Future Farmers Am Alumni. Honors & Awards: Hon Serv, Univ Tenn Alumni, 63; Commanders Citation, Am Legion, 65; citation, Soil Conserv Soc Am, 68. Relig: Methodist. Mailing Add: Elm St Extension Martin TN 38237

COUNCILL, J PAUL, JR (D)
Va State Deleg
Mailing Add: PO Box 119 Franklin VA 23851

COUNIHAN, GENEVRA R (D)
Mass State Rep
Mailing Add: State Capitol Boston MA 02133

COUNTIE, DAVID R (R)
Mo State Rep
Mailing Add: 303 Northmoor Dr Ballwin MO 63011

COURNOYER, WILFRED W (D)
NH State Rep
b Ashburnham, Mass, Oct 4, 11; married; c Three. Educ: Conant High Sch. Polit & Govt Pos: NH State Rep, 61-72 & 75- Bus & Prof Pos: Operates variety store. Mil Serv: Prof soldier, 36-56; retired, Chief Warrant Officer 2. Mem: KofC (3 degree); ROA; Holy Name Soc; Am Legion; VFW. Relig: Catholic. Mailing Add: 20 Union St Jaffrey NH 03452

COURSE, KENNETH W (D)
Ill State Sen
b Chicago, Ill; single. Educ: DePaul Univ; CPA coaching, LaSalle Exten Univ. Polit & Govt Pos: Ill State Rep, formerly, Ill State Sen, 71- Bus & Prof Pos: Wholesale, retail fuel oil. Mil Serv: World War II, 101st Airborne Div. Mem: Moose; Lions; Am Legion; VFW; KofC. Mailing Add: 3413 W Armitage Ave Chicago IL 60647

COURTNEY, JAMES H (D)
Chmn, Clay Co Dem Cent Comt
b Clay Co, Ind, Aug 7, 21; s Henry M Courtney & Irene Montgomery C; m 1955 to Betty J Phillips; stepson, Harold Ray. Educ: US Army Signal Sch, Camp Crowder, Mo, 42, US Army Br Intel Sch, Ft Harrison, Ind, 46; Terre Haute Commercial Col, 66. Polit & Govt Pos: Dem precinct committeeman, Brazil, Ind, 56-70; secy, Clay Co Dem Cent Comt, 69-70, chmn, 70-; constable, Brazil Twp, 69- Mil Serv: Entered as Pvt, Army, 42, released as S/Sgt, 54, after serv in 24th Inf Div, Pac Theatre, 44-46, Korea, 50-54; Good Conduct Medal; Am Campaign Medal; Asiatic Pac Medal; Battle Star; Victory Medal; Occup with Japan Clasp; Nat Defense Medal; Korea Serv with one Battle Star, one Silver Star; Presidential Unit Citation; UN Medal; Expert, Sharpshooter Medal. Mem: Ind Constables Asn (secy-treas, 70-); VFW; DAV; Nat Rifle Asn; Ind Rifle & Pistol Asn. Honors & Awards: Cert of Appreciation, State of Ind Fight Against Communist Aggression Throughout the World, 55; Recognition of Outstanding Contribution Made, Dem Party of Ind, 68; Cert of Merit in recognition of distinguished achievement in Dem Party, 73; elected Chief of the Shawnee Nation in URB (Hawk Clan), Spring Coun, Tecumseh Confederacy, Xenia, Ohio, 75. Relig: Roman Catholic. Mailing Add: 727 S Morgan Rte 4 Brazil IN 47834

COURTNEY, RICHARD TRAVERS, JR (D)
Mem, Worcester Dem City Comt, Mass
b Worcester, Mass, Aug 12, 23; s Richard Travers Courtney & Marguerite L Dubois C; m 1948 to Densye M Tasse; c Denise (Mrs Lovendale), Richard T, III, Michael C, Suzette M, Marie Patrice, Mark E, Colleen M, Timothy J, Christopher E, Francis L, Sean J, Peter & Kerry. Educ: Univ Buffalo, 43; Boston Col Sch Bus Admin, 46-48; Sch Law, JD, 50. Polit & Govt Pos: Mem, Worcester Dem City Comt, Mass, 64-; alt deleg, Dem Nat Conv, 68. Bus & Prof Pos: Judge advocate, US Air Force, Carsell AFB, Ft Worth, Tex, 51-53; lawyer, Worcester, Mass, 53-; pub defender, Worcester, 60-63. Mil Serv: Entered as Pvt, Army Air Force, 43, released as 1st Lt, 45, after serv in 15th Air Force 750 Bombardment Group, ETO, 44-45; Air Medal with Two Clusters; European Battle Ribbon with Four Stars. Mem: Worcester Co Bar Asn; Am Judicial Soc; KofC; Leading Families of Am; Worcester Area Asn Retarded Children. Relig: Catholic. Legal Res: 20 Fourth St Worcester MA 01608 Mailing Add: 595 Park Ave Worcester MA 01603

COURY, EDWARD P (D)
Mass State Rep
Mailing Add: State Capitol Boston MA 02133

COUSINS, JAMES HAROLD (D)
b Fullerton, Calif, Sept 21, 42; s Charles Harold Cousins & Lucille Martin C; m to Kathryn Lafler. Educ: Univ Calif, Los Angeles, BA, 64, MA, 67; Alpha Gamma Omega. Polit & Govt Pos: Legis asst, US Rep Richard T Hanna, 71-73; admin asst, 73-74; admin asst, US Rep Jerry M Patterson, Calif, 75- Bus & Prof Pos: Social studies teacher, Anaheim High Sch Dist, Calif, 65-69; vis lectr, Chapman Col, Orange, 67-70. Legal Res: 11301 Euclid Sp 14 Garden Grove CA 92642 Mailing Add: 3017 Dent Pl NW Washington DC 20007

COUTERMARSH, ERNEST R (D)
NH State Rep
Mailing Add: 22 Meadowbrook Dr Nashua NH 03050

COUTURE, ALFRED V **(D)**
Vt State Rep
Mailing Add: 29 Murray St Burlington VT 05401

COVELLO, DALLICE FERN **(D)**
b New York, NY, Sept 12, 45; d Emmett P Covello & Dallice Hill C; single. Educ: Bronx Community Col, AAS; Richmond Col (NY), currently. Polit & Govt Pos: Alt deleg, Dem Nat Conv, 72; coordr, Nat Gay Community for McGovern. Publ: Co-auth, Sisterhood Songs, 5/20/71 & auth, Gays Sing, 6/72, Purple Pluto Press; ed, Purple Rage Mag, 3/72. Mem: Gay Women's Liberation Front (chmn, 70-72); Gay Polit Caucus (spokeswoman, 72); Nat Coalition of Gay Orgn (spokeswoman, 72-). Mailing Add: 118 E 11th St New York NY 10003

COVERDELL, PAUL D **(R)**
Ga State Sen
Mailing Add: Suite 607 1447 Peachtree St NE Atlanta GA 30309

COVEY, JOHN KNOX **(R)**
b Coudersport, Pa, Aug 25, 06; s James Garfield Covey & Kathryn Knox C; m 1930 to Helen Hunt; c James Hunt & Susan Candace. Educ: Cornell Univ, 28; Lehigh Univ, CE, 29; Pa State Univ, 36; Jefferson Med Col, MD, 40; dipl, Am Bd Ophthalmology, 50; Alpha Kappa Kappa. Polit & Govt Pos: Pres, Bellefonte Borough Bd of Health, Pa, 44-50, pres, Sch Bd, 47-65; pres, Bellefonte Area Joint Sch Bd, 53-65, chmn Joint Sch Authority, 65-; past pres, Centre Co Sch Bd, 60-65; alt deleg, Rep Nat Conv, 64; mem, Pa State Platform Comt, 70; mem, Pa State Rep Comt, 70-74. Bus & Prof Pos: Chief of surg, Centre Community Hosp, 69-71. Publ: Ocular tumors in a rural practice, Pa Med J, 5/46; Medical advice for counselors, Chap on Ophthalmology, Outline for Pa State Classes, 60; Myths and facts about eye care, Todays Health, 6/62. Mem: Am Asn Advan Sci; Pan-Am Asn Ophthalmology; Am Med Asn; Am Acad Ophthalmology & Otolaryngology; Asn for Research in Vision & Ophthalmology. Relig: Presbyterian. Mailing Add: 130 E Linn St Bellefonte PA 16823

COVEY, SUSAN CANDACE **(R)**
b Bellefonte, Pa, Nov 28, 49; d John Knox Covey & Helen Hunt C; single. Educ: Pa State Univ, University Park, BS, 70; Gamma Pi Epsilon. Polit & Govt Pos: Dist coordr, Pa State Teen Age Rep, 68; precinct vchmn, N Ward, Bellefonte, Pa, 70-72; mem, Centre Co Rep Exec Bd, 70-74; adv, State Col Teen Age Rep Club, 71-72; pres, Bellefonte Area Coun Rep Women, 71-74; alt deleg, Rep Nat Conv, 72; Bellefonte area vchmn, Centre Co Rep Party, 72-74. Bus & Prof Pos: Ophthalmic asst, Bellefonte, 70-74. Mem: Bellefonte Bus & Prof Women's Club (finance comt, 72-74); Am Asn Univ Women; DAR (good citizen chmn, Bellefonte Chap, 70-74); Int Platform Asn. Honors & Awards: Leadership Award, Am Legion, 63; Commendation, Nat Merit Scholar Comt, 67. Relig: Presbyterian. Mailing Add: 130 E Linn St Bellefonte PA 16823

COVIELLO, CHARLES JOSEPH, JR **(D)**
Pres, Conn Young Dem
b Bridgeport, Conn, July 10, 48; s Charles Joseph Coviello, Sr & Rose Panettieri C; m 1970 to Anne Cecile Suchenski. Educ: Fairfield Univ, BA in Polit Sci, 70, MA in Educ, 75; Bridgeport Area Club; St Ives Pre-Legal Guild. Polit & Govt Pos: Campaign aide & youth coordr, Lyddy for State Senate, Conn, 68; campaign aide & coordr, Daly for US Cong, 70; legis aide, Conn State Senate, 70-71; pres, Bridgeport Young Dem, 72-74; Bridgeport campaign coordr, McGovern for President, 72; recording secy, Non-Partisan Regional Vote Comt, 72-74; campaign coordr, Mullane for Mayor, Bridgeport, 73; get out the vote chmn, Bridgeport Comt Primary, 74; campaign coordr, Clark for Sheriff, Fairfield Co, 74; pres, Conn Young Dem, 74-, lobbyist, Conn Gen Assembly, 75- Bus & Prof Pos: Teacher, St Thomas Sch, Fairfield, Conn, 70-73; teacher, St Ann's Sch, Bridgeport, 73-74; dir alumni rels, Fairfield Univ, 74- Publ: Co-auth, Toward a two party system, Fairfield Univ J, 70. Mem: Kiwanis Int; Am Alumni Coun; KofC; Bridgeport Ment Health Asn. Relig: Catholic. Mailing Add: 30 Fern St Bridgeport CT 06606

COVINGTON, DEAN **(D)**
Mem Exec Comt, Seventh Cong Dist Dem Party, Ga
b Rome, Ga, Mar 14, 16; s Leon Covington & Bobbie Verner C; m 1939 to Elsie Peace; c Dean, Jr, William Lee, Robert Culpepper, Richard Peace, Barbara Graham & David Barron. Educ: Univ Ga, AB in polit sci, Law Sch, LLB; Sigma Alpha Epsilon; Phi Delta Phi; Blue Key; Scabbard & Blade; Jr Cabinet; Sigma Delta Kappa. Polit & Govt Pos: Asst solicitor, City Court, Floyd City, Ga, 40-41; mem, bd registr, Floyd Co, 40-41; Ga State Rep, 47-52; mem, Gov Staff, Ga, 49-; former deleg, Ga Dem Conv; deleg, Dem Nat Conv, 64; mem exec comt, Seventh Cong Dist Dem Party, Ga, currently; co attorney, 69. Bus & Prof Pos: Officer & mem bd dirs, Nat Home Develop Co & Quality Home Builders; secy & mem bd dirs, Radio Sta WSOM. Mil Serv: Entered as Lt, Army, 42, released as Lt Col, 45, after serv in 20th Armored Div, ETO; Hon Res, 65; Bronze Star; ETO Campaign Ribbon. Mem: Am & Ga Bar Asns; Am Jurisprudence Soc; Farm Bur; Kiwanis; Am Legion; VFW. Honors & Awards: Nat Golf Champion, Kiwanis Int, 50 & 51, Distinguished Lt Gov for Kiwanis, 73. Relig: Methodist; Chmn, Bd of Stewards, First Methodist Church, 64-65, chmn, bd trustees, currently. Legal Res: 230 Lakeshore Dr Rome GA 30161 Mailing Add: Metro Bldg Third Ave Rome GA 30161

COWAN, BOYD LYNN **(R)**
Chmn, Hopkins Co Rep Exec Comt, Ky
b Sullivan, Ky, Aug 22, 97; s Louis Franklin Cowan & Hepsy Mahaley Armstrong C; m 1933 to Autense Whitfield. Educ: Asbury Col, 1 year; Western Ky Univ, BS; Basketball team, Western Ky Univ, 4 years; Kit Kat Club. Polit & Govt Pos: Warrant writer & asst field clerk, Brooks Tobacco Loose Leaf Floor, US Govt, 55; election comnr, 58-67; Rep organizer, 62-; Rep cand, US Rep, Ky, 63; chmn, Hopkins Co Rep Exec Comt, 68- Bus & Prof Pos: Owner & mgr, coal mine, 35-55; technician, Ky Artificial Breeders, 55-63 & Hopkins Co Agr Stabilization & Conserv Serv, 20 years. Mil Serv: Entered as Pvt, Air Force, 17, released as Sgt, 19, after serv in 850th Provisional Aero Squadron Wing. Mem: South Hopkins Ky Farm Bur (chmn). Honors & Awards: Hon life mem & pin, Future Farmers Am; pins & medals for 20 years serv as 4-H leader, Farm Bur Youth. Relig: Christian. Mailing Add: RR 2 White Plains KY 42464

COWAN, JAMES RANKIN **(R)**
Asst Secy Defense for Health & Environ
b Washington, DC, Oct 21, 19; s James Henry Cowan & Frances Hall C; m 1960 to Juanita Geraldine Branch; c James R, Jr, MD, Jay Charles & Jill. Educ: Howard Univ, BS, 39; Fisk Univ, MA, 40; Meharry Med Col, MD, 44. Hon Degrees: DS, Bloomfield Col, 71. Polit & Govt Pos: Comnr, NJ State Dept Health, 70-74; chmn health ins benefits adv coun, Social Security Admin, 72-74; Asst Secy Defense for Health & Environ, 74- Bus & Prof Pos: Pvt practice med & surg, East Orange, NJ, 53-70. Mil Serv: Entered as Capt, Army, 50, released as Maj, 53, after serv in Med Corps as Chief Surg, 28th Sta Hosp, Regensburg, Ger, 51-53. Mem: Am Col Prev Med; Uniformed Serv Univ of Health Sci (bd regents); NJ Col Med (bd trustees); Howard Savings Inst, Newark, NJ (bd dirs); North NJ Radio Co (bd dirs). Honors & Awards: Fel, Acad Med of NJ, 70; Award of Honor, Alpha Gamma Lambda Chap, Alpha Phi Alpha, 71; Award of Recognition, Mt Carmel Guild of NJ, 74; fel, Acad Med of Washington, DC, 74; Brotherhood Award, Nat Conf Christians & Jews, NJ Region, 75. Legal Res: 2 Warner Rd Maplewood NJ 07040 Mailing Add: 1945 Kirby Rd Falls Church VA 22043

COWAN, PAUL EARL **(D)**
Chmn, Jackson Co Dem Exec Comt, NC
b Sylva, NC, Apr 4, 46; s Paul E Cowan, Sr (deceased) & Anne McConnell C; m 1966 to Lynda Beck; c Paul E, III (Chip). Educ: Southwestern Tech Inst, Sylva, Bus Admin, 66; Western Carolina Univ, 67-70. Polit & Govt Pos: Mem, Jackson Co Young Dem Club, 70-; Webster Precinct Judge, 72; second vchmn, Jackson Co Dem Exec Comt, 72-74; cand, Part-Time Co Comnr, 74; chmn, Jackson Co Dem Exec Comt, 74- Bus & Prof Pos: Agt, Nationwide Ins Co, 70- Mem: Jackson Co Jaycees (local dir); Jackson Co Young Dem Club; Boy Scouts of Am; Jackson Co Recreation Comn. Honors & Awards: Order of the Arrow, Boy Scouts of Am, Outstanding Scoutmaster of the Year, 68; Jaycee of the Month, 7 times, 70-73; Keyman, Jaycees, 71; Outstanding Young Man of the Year, 71. Relig: Methodist. Legal Res: Rte 3 Sylva NC 28779 Mailing Add: Box 425 Sylva NC 28779

COWAN, TED M **(R)**
Okla State Rep
b Stillwater, Okla, May 27, 40; s Robert Bruce Cowan & Mildred Todd C; m to Patricia Wettack; c Drew, Elizabeth & Matt. Educ: Coffeyville Jr Col, AA, 60; Kans State Teachers Col, AB, 63. Polit & Govt Pos: Okla State Rep, Tulsa, Dist 79, 75- Bus & Prof Pos: Research chemist, Sun Oil Co, Tulsa, 63-72; consult chemist, Richard Bigda & Assocs, Tulsa, 72- Mailing Add: 3562 S Sandusky Tulsa OK 74135

COWDEN, JULIANAN **(D)**
Secy, Tex State Dem Exec Comt
b Midland, Tex; d Robert Edwin Cowden & Jett Baker C; single. Educ: Hockaday Jr Col, grad, 41; Univ Tex, BA, 44; Zeta Tau Alpha. Polit & Govt Pos: Committeewoman, Tex State Dem Exec Comt, 12th Sen Dist & vchmn, Resolutions Subcomt, 60-68; pres, Johnson Co Dem Woman's Club, 60-; alt deleg, Dem Nat Conv, 64, deleg & mem rules & order of bus comt, 68, deleg, 72; chmn, Deleg Comt Dem Conv, 68; deleg, State Dem Conv & mem comt party nomination, 68; mem, Speaker's Comt of 100, 70-71; Dem precinct chmn, 70-72; mem, Nat Dem Credentials Comt, 72; secy, Tex State Dem Exec Comt, 72-; mem, Nat Fedn Dem Women. Bus & Prof Pos: Instr & exhibitor, Ft Worth Art Ctr, Tex, 64-66; demonstrating craftsman, Salado Craft Show, 67-71; partner, JAL Corp, 67-; demonstrating craftsman, San Antonio Artist's Jamboree, 67-71; mem bd & secy, Alvarado State Bank, 69; treas, J & M Steel Corp, Ft Worth, 71-; mem, Gov Conf Tech & Voc Educ, 72; partner, Cowden-Brummett Livestock Co; vpres, Western Tool & Mfg Co, Alvarado, currently. Mem: Univ Tex Ex-Students' Asn; life mem Hockaday Alumnae Asn; Alvarado Independent Sch Bd (pres); Delta Kappa Gamma; Hockaday Sch (bd trustees). Honors & Awards: Exhibit of Jewelry in Southwestern Int Craft Mus, Santa Fe, NMex, 67-69; One Man Show, Square House Mus, Panhandle, Tex, 71. Relig: Episcopal. Legal Res: JAL Ranch Alvarado TX 76009 Mailing Add: PO Box 305-308 Alvarado TX 76009

COWDEN, THOMAS K **(R)**
b Hickory, Pa, Jun 14, 08; m; c Dr John W & Jean W. Educ: Ohio State Univ, BS, 30 & MS, 31; Cornell Univ, PhD, 37. Hon Degrees: Purdue Univ, 37. Polit & Govt Pos: Serv on many govt & nat comts for econ develop & agr policy; Asst Secy for Rural Develop & Conserv, US Dept Agr, 69-72, counr to Secy Agr, 72- Bus & Prof Pos: Prof agr econ, Pa State Univ, 31-37; prof agr econ, Purdue Univ, 37-43; dir research, Am Farm Bur Fedn, 43-49; head of dept agr econ, Mich State Univ, 49-54, dean col agr & natural resources, 54-69. Mem: Am Farm Econ Asn. Legal Res: VA Mailing Add: Dept of Agr 14th St & Independence Ave SW Washington DC 20250

COWELL, ALICE V **(D)**
b Memphis, Mo, Sept 22, 26; d Milo E Franklin & Frances A Hudnall F; m 1963 to Marion Hillis Cowell. Educ: Memphis High Sch, Mo, dipl. Polit & Govt Pos: Vchmn, Scotland Co Dem Comt, Mo, formerly. Bus & Prof Pos: Bookkeeper, Auto Dealer, Ind, 42-56, Mo, 56-59. Mem: Ladies Auxiliary; Farm Bur. Relig: Protestant. Mailing Add: RR 2 Memphis MO 63555

COWELL, RONALD RAYMOND **(D)**
Pa State Rep
b Phillipsburg, Pa, Dec 14, 46; s Stephen T Cowell & Lucille D Pryzyblek C; m 1968 to Virginia Segin; c Robert & Richard. Educ: Univ Pittsburgh, BA, 70. Polit & Govt Pos: Pres, Young Dem Club of Allegheny Co, 71-73; admin asst to Pa State Sen, 71-74; Pa State Rep, 34th Dist, 75- Bus & Prof Pos: Dir off-campus housing, Univ Pittsburgh, 71-74. Mem: Churchill Area Ecol Comt (Wilkins Twp rep); Group Against Smog & Pollution (mem bd dirs); Italian-Am Citizens Club of Wilkins Twp. Relig: Roman Catholic. Mailing Add: 121 Gilmore Dr Pittsburgh PA 15235

COWEN, JAMES LAURENCE **(INDEPENDENT)**
Chmn, US RR Retirement Bd
b Boston, Mass, Apr 27, 25; s Benjamin Michael Cowen (deceased) & Mary Cohen C (deceased); m 1956 to Muriel Lois Cohen Peretsman; c Judith Ann & Susan Lisa. Educ: Harvard Univ, AB, 49; Univ Mich, spring 49. Polit & Govt Pos: Actuary, US RR Retirement Bd, 52-70, chief actuary, 70-72, chmn, 72- Bus & Prof Pos: Actuarial trainee, Boston Mutual Life Ins Co, 51-52. Mil Serv: Entered as Pvt, Army Air Force, 43, released as 1st Lt, 45, after serv in 8th Air Force in Eng, 44-45; Air Medal with Four Oakleaf Clusters. Publ: Auth, Occupational Differences and Separation Rates, 54-56, RRB Female Mortality and Remarriage Tables, 65 & co-auth, 11th Actuarial Valuation of the Assets and Liabilities under the Railroad Retirement Acts as of December 31, 1968 with Technical Supplement, 70, US RR Retirement Bd. Mem: Am Acad Actuaries; Assoc Soc of Actuaries (comt on self-administered retirement plans); fel Conf Actuaries in Pub Practice; YMCA. Honors & Awards: Superior Accomplishment Awards, US RR Retirement Bd, 56 & 60, Outstanding Efficiency Rating, 60; Nominated for Arthur S Flemming Awards Prog, Downtown Jaycees of Washington, DC & Metrop Life Ins Co, Nat Savings & Trust Co, Potomac Elec Power

Co, 59-63; Nominated Outstanding Prof Employee in Chicago Area, Chicago Fed Exec Bd, 62. Relig: Jewish. Legal Res: 7506 Kildare Skokie IL 60076 Mailing Add: US RR Retirement Board 844 Rush St Chicago IL 60611

COWEN, JOE N (D)
Chmn, Castro Co Dem Exec Comt, Tex
b Clifton, Tex, Apr 26, 10; s John R Cowen & Florence McFadden C; m 1939 to Alice Russell Hamilton; c Joe Hamilton. Educ: Univ Tex, BA; Tejas Club; wrestling champion. Polit & Govt Pos: Alt deleg, Dem Nat Conv, 56; exec committeeman, State Dem Exec Comt, Tex, 56-57; mayor, Dimmitt, Tex, 57-59; chmn, Castro Co Dem Exec Comt, 58-59 & 66- Mem: Castro Co Fair Asn; Castro Co CofC; Dimmitt Lions Club; Dimmitt PTA; Dimmitt Libr Bd. Relig: Presbyterian; Clerk of the Session & Elder, Presby Church, Dimmitt, Tex, 59- Legal Res: 600 Southwest Tenth St Dimmitt TX 79027 Mailing Add: Drawer 247 Dimmitt TX 79027

COWMAN, WILLIAM HENRY (BILL) (D)
Mem, Ga State Dem Exec Comt
b Brunswick, Ga, Nov 10, 10; s Frederick Phillip Cowman & Sabine Marie Goette C; m 1934 to Betty Ruth Drake; c Alice Josephine (Mrs Jesse E Hash), Robert William. Educ: Glynn Acad, Brunswick, Ga, 12 years. Polit & Govt Pos: Staff mem, Gov Sanders, Ga, 63-66; mem adv comt, Congressman W S Stuckey, 67-73; mem exec comt, Glynn Co Dem Exec Bd, 67-; staff mem, Gov Carter, Ga, 71-75; mem, Ga State Dem Exec Comt, 74- Bus & Prof Pos: Brunswick Pulp & Paper Co, 41-75. Mem: Pulp & Sulphite Union; Brunswick Cent Labor Coun. Honors & Awards: Outstanding Dedicated Serv award, Brunswick Cent Labor Coun, 74. Relig: Episcopal. Mailing Add: RFD 6 Box 312 Brunswick GA 31520

COWPER, STEVE (D)
Alaska State Rep
Mailing Add: 210 Nerland Bldg Fairbanks AK 99701

COX, ARCHIBALD (INDEPENDENT)
b Plainfield, NJ, May 17, 12; s Archibald Cox & Frances Bruen Perkins C; m 1937 to Phyllis Ames; c Sally, Archibald & Phyllis. Educ: Harvard Univ, BA, 34, LLB, 37. Polit & Govt Pos: Attorney, Off Solicitor Gen, US Dept Justice, 41-43; assoc solicitor, Dept Labor, 43-45; chmn, Wage Stabilization Bd, 52; co-chmn, Construction Indust Stabilization Comt, 51-52; Solicitor Gen, US Dept Justice, 61-65; spec prosecutor for Watergate Hearings, 73. Bus & Prof Pos: Attorney, Ropes, Gray, Best, Coolidge & Rugg, Boston, 38-41; lectr law, Harvard Univ, 45-46, prof, 46-61, mem, Bd Overseers, 62-65, Williston Prof Law, Harvard Law Sch, 65- Publ: Cases on Labor Law, Sixth Ed, 65; Civil Rights, the Constitution and the Courts, 67; The Warren Court, 68; plus others. Mem: Am Bar Asn; Am Acad Arts & Sci. Legal Res: 31 Glezen Lane Wayland MA 01778 Mailing Add: Langdell Hall Harvard Law Sch Cambridge MA 02138

COX, DEAN F (D)
Chmn, Wayne Co Dem Party, Iowa
b Corydon, Iowa, May 13, 27; s John Anderson Cox & Myrtle Annis Dent C; m 1947 to Willa Jeane Grimes; c C Christine, Joyce Ann (Mrs Bob Hysell, Jr) & Jeffrey Keene. Educ: Cambria High Sch, Iowa, grad, 45. Polit & Govt Pos: Committeeman, Dem Party, Corydon, Iowa, 65-66; chmn, Wayne Co Dem Party, Dist 93, 67-; secy legis comn, Dept Iowa, currently; cand, Iowa State Rep, Dist 96, 70; chmn, SCent Iowa Community Action Prog, 71- Bus & Prof Pos: Owner, Cox's Body Repair, Corydon, 57- Mil Serv: Entered as A/S, Navy, 45, released as Storekeeper 3/C, 46, after serv in Logistic Support Co 175, Asiatic & Pac Theatres, 45-46; Sgt Maj, Army Res, 69- Mem: Am Legion; 40 et 8; VFW; Iowa Vet Coun (exec comt, 70-); Asn US Army Res (nat vpres, 73-74). Relig: Baptist. Mailing Add: 406 S DeKalb Corydon IA 50060

COX, ERNIE E (D)
b WVa, Apr 27, 15; s Harve Cox & Virgie Johnson C; wid; c Elizabeth A (Mrs McNelley) & Joyce C (Mrs Butler). Educ: WVa Univ, 41-42; Anderson Sch Phys Therapy, Princeton, Ill, 68-72. Polit & Govt Pos: Deleg, Dem Nat Mid-Term Conf, 74. Bus & Prof Pos: Coal mining supvr, State of WVa, 44-71 & State of Ohio, 68-71; regional dir, Monitrex of Am, 73- Mil Serv: Pvt, Army, serv in 10th Armored Div, Pac Theatre, 44-46; Good Conduct Medal; Two Bronze Stars. Mem: Moose; Eagles; Kanawha Valley Mining Inst. Honors & Awards: Leadership in Safety & Accident Prev, US Dept of Interior; Phys Therapy Technicians Awards in Coal Mining Safety Training. Relig: Protestant. Mailing Add: 1816 County Rd Weirton WV 26062

COX, GILBERT W, JR (R)
Mass State Rep
b Stoneham, Mass, Feb 28, 33; s Gilbert W Cox & Verna O Linscott C; m 1959 to Helen D Pillsbury; c Gilbert, David, Carol & Elizabeth. Educ: Northeastern Univ, AB; Boston Univ Law Sch, LLB. Polit & Govt Pos: Pres, Needham Young Rep Club, Mass, 63-64; asst dist attorney, 66; chmn, Needham Rep Town Comt, 66-69; Mass State Rep, 68- Bus & Prof Pos: Lawyer, 62- Mil Serv: Entered as Ens, Navy, 55, released as Lt(jg), 59 after serv in US-31; Comdr, Naval Res, currently. Mem: Mass & Norfolk Co Bar Asns; Needham Taxpayers Asn; Needham YMCA (dir, 64-). Mailing Add: 49 Colonial Rd Needham MA 02192

COX, GRACE NORTHROP (R)
Treas, Carroll Co Rep Comt, NH
b Madison, NH; d Fred Arthur Northrop & Gertrude Dorothy Bickford N; m 1926 to George Washington Cox; c Brandon P. Educ: Kennett High Sch, Conway, NH, grad. Polit & Govt Pos: Treas, North Conway Lighting Precinct, NH, 30 years; treas, Conway Town Rep Club, 15 years; treas, Carroll Co Rep Comt, 62-, treas, Conway Women's Rep Club, 62-; deleg, NH State Rep Conv, 63, 65, 67 & 69; NH State Rep, 69-74; mem, Dist 2 Selective Serv Bd, Carroll Co. Mem: NH Order Women Legislators (parliamentarian, 71-); Nat Order Women Legislators; PTA; North Conway CofC; Eastern Star. Relig: Protestant. Mailing Add: Intervale Rd Box 341 North Conway NH 03860

COX, GUY JACKSON (R)
b West Vienna, Ill, Oct 17, 06; s Jackson Mier Cox & Ollie May Cover C; m 1930 to Bernice Estelle Smith; c Garland Don, Zoe Ann (Mrs C J Miller) & Karen Sue (Mrs Jack Cummins). Educ: Salt City Bus Col, 1 year. Polit & Govt Pos: Secy, Gunnison Co Rep Cent Comt, Colo, 64-67, chmn, 67-73; alt deleg, Rep Nat Conv, 72. Bus & Prof Pos: Sta agent helper, MoPac RR, Ordway, Colo, 28-33; city clerk, Ordway, Colo, 33-35; bookkeeper, Zirkle Motor Co, La Junta, 36-38; staff, Powerine Oil Co, 38-41; sta mgr, Continental Air Lines, 42-46; sta mgr, Monarch Air Lines, Gunnison, 47-49, dist mgr, Salt Lake City, Utah, 49-51; mgr, CofC, Gunnison, Colo, 51-55; owner & mgr, Wildwood Motel, 55-62; real estate salesman, Clarke Agency, Gunnison, 62- Mem: Rotary; CofC. Relig: Protestant; Community Church. Mailing Add: PO Box 777 Gunnison CO 81230

COX, HARDIN CHARLES (D)
Mo State Sen
b Rockport, Mo, Mar 4, 28; s Hardin Charles Cox & Frieda Anna Stapel C; m 1952 to Virginia Ann Heifner; c Charles Bryan & Mark Hardin. Educ: Univ Mo, BA in Bus, 51; QEBA; Omicron Delta Kappa; Alpha Phi Omega; Sigma Chi. Polit & Govt Pos: Mo State Rep, 65-74, chmn legis research comt, Mo House Rep, formerly; Mo State Sen, 75- Bus & Prof Pos: Treas, Farmers Mutual Hail Ins Co, Columbia, Farmers Mutual Windstorm Ins Co, Mo Farmers Hail Ins Co & secy-treas, Farmers Mutual Ins Co, Rockport, 60- Mil Serv: Entered as Pvt, Army, 46, released as Cpl, 48, reentered as Lt, 51, released, 53, after serv in Army Artil, Korea; Korean Campaign Ribbon with 3 Battle Stars; Victory Medal; Orient Occup Medal. Mem: Group Millionaire Club Equitable Life, NY; AF&AM; Am Legion; CofC; Boy Scouts (pres coun). Honors & Awards: Univ Mo Cotton Bowl Team, 45, Gater Bowl Team, 48. Relig: Lutheran. Legal Res: 605 Bluff St Rockport MO 64482 Mailing Add: 300 Main St Rockport MO 64482

COX, HAROLD R (D)
Maine State Rep
Mailing Add: 12 Penobscot Ave Brewer ME 04412

COX, JAMES NELSON (D)
Chmn, St Charles Co Dem Cent Comt, Mo
b St Louis, Mo, July 9, 30; s James Neri Cox & Georgia Waters C; m 1952 to Betty Jean Buckley; c Susan, Christy, Martha & Laura. Educ: St Charles High Sch, grad, 47. Polit & Govt Pos: Alderman, O'Fallon, Mo, 64-66; chmn planning & zoning, O'Fallon, 66-69; mem, St Charles Co Bldg Code Comn, 66-68; committeeman, Dardenne Twp Dem Comt, 68-; treas, Ninth Cong Dist Dem Party, Mo, 72-; chmn, St Charles Co Dem Cent Comt, Mo, 74- Bus & Prof Pos: Pres, St Charles Co Elec Co, Inc, 68- Mil Serv: Entered Navy, 50, released as 1/C Aviation Electrician, 54, after serv in Fighter squadron 34, Sixth Fleet, 51-54; Good Conduct; European Theater & Korean Emergency Ribbons. Mem: Kiwanis; IBEW Local 1. Honors & Awards: Clarence Cannon Award, Mo Dem Days Inc, 74. Relig: Methodist. Mailing Add: 724 Winston Pl O'Fallon MO 63366

COX, KENNETH ROGER (D)
Ohio State Rep
b Barberton, Ohio, Oct 8, 28; s Dexter Lafayette Cox (deceased) & Ila Blanche Cox C; m 1949 to Marjorie Lillian Phelps; c Timothy Brian & Patricia Ann. Educ: Univ Akron, 47-48. Polit & Govt Pos: Councilman, Barberton, Ohio, 60-66, mayor, 66-73; Ohio State Rep, 41st Dist, 73-; deleg, Dem Nat Mid-Term Conf, 74. Bus & Prof Pos: Mgr advert prod, BF Goodrich Co, Akron, 46-, on leave of absence since 66. Mem: Kiwanis; Elks; Akron Bd Realtors; Portage Path Ment Health Clin (trustee); Summit Co Ment Health Asn. Relig: Protestant. Mailing Add: 668 E Park Ave Barberton OH 44203

COX, LOREN CHARLES (D)
b Ontario, Ore, May 5, 38; s Charles O Cox (deceased) & Helen M Jackson C; m 1960 to Keith Mayo Capen; c Hilary. Educ: Linfield Col, 56-57; Ottawa Univ, BA, 60; Univ Ore, MA, 62. Polit & Govt Pos: Peace Corps vol, Nigeria, 63-65, dep country dir, Peace Corps, Seoul, Korea, 66-68, dep dir, EAsia & Pac Region, Peace Corps, Washington, DC, 68-70; admin asst to US Rep Al Ullman, Ore, 70-75; prof staff mem, Ways & Means Comt, US House Rep, 75- Bus & Prof Pos: Instr, Univ Ore, 60-63. Mem: Soc Int Develop. Mailing Add: 7813 Moorland Lane Bethesda MD 20014

COX, PATRICIA ANN SWAGGERTY (R)
Committeewoman, Tenn Rep State Exec Comt
b Asbury, Tenn, June 1, 37; d Garrette Hobart Swaggerty & Lula Jane Doane S; m 1964 to Kenneth Kyle Cox. Educ: St Mary's Sch Nursing, Knoxville, Tenn, dipl, 55; Barry Col Women, 59-62; Univ Miami, BS in Nursing, 63; Emory Univ, MS in Nursing, 70; Univ Tenn, Knoxville, EdD, 75; Phi Lambda Theta. Polit & Govt Pos: Committeewoman, Tenn Rep State Exec Comt, 75- Bus & Prof Pos: Staff nurse, St Mary's Hosp, Knoxville, Tenn, 58-59, asst head nurse, 62-67, assoc dir inserv educ, 67-68, instr sch nursing, 71-72; assoc dir nursing serv, Ft Sanders Hosp, Knoxville, 72- Mem: Eighth Dist Rep Club; ETenn Heart Asn; Thorngrove Community Club. Relig: Methodist. Mailing Add: Rte 1 Strawplains TN 37871

COX, ROBERT EMMETT (R)
Chmn, Talbot Co Rep State Cent Comt, Md
b Lakewood, Ohio, Feb 17, 19; s Christopher P Cox & Cecel Davidson C; m 1947 to Mary Louise Collier; c Christopher, Susan & William. Educ: Princeton Univ, class of 41. Polit & Govt Pos: Chmn, Talbot Co Rep State Cent Comt, Md, 60-; alt deleg, Rep Nat Conv, 68; mem, Dept of State Planning Comn; chmn, First Cong Dist Rep Comt, Md, currently. Mil Serv: Entered as A/S, Naval Res, 40, released as Lt Coast Guard, 46, after serv in NAtlantic & Southwest Pac. Mem: Elks. Relig: Protestant. Legal Res: St Michaels MD 21663 Mailing Add: Box 759 Easton MD 21601

COX, STEVE DON (R)
b Garden City, Tex, Dec 29, 28; s John H Cox & Eva Calverley C; m 1962 to Carolyn Graham; c Kimberley, Kerry, Steve R & John W. Educ: Hardin Simmons Univ, 46; Tex Tech Univ, BS, 51; Tau Beta Pi. Polit & Govt Pos: Chmn, Dawson Co Rep Party, Tex, formerly. Bus & Prof Pos: Owner & mgr, ranch, Glasscock Co, Tex, 51-53; salesman, Farmers Supply, Lubbock, 54-56; engr & draftsman, Bridges & Paxton, Albuquerque, NMex, 56-57; owner & mgr, Cox Implement, Lamesa, Tex, 57- Mem: CofC; Farm Bur. Relig: Presbyterian. Legal Res: 104 N 23rd Lamesa TX 79331 Mailing Add: 1017 S Dallas Lamesa TX 79331

COX, WALTER E (D)
Ga State Rep
Mailing Add: 202 West St Bainbridge GA 31717

COX, WILLIAM HARVEY, JR (D)
Md State Deleg
b Edgewood, Md, July 15, 42; s William Harvey Cox & Bertha Ellen Hanna C; m 1969 to Bernice Paige Malkus; c William Harvey, III. Educ: Univ Baltimore, 60-62; Univ Md, 62-63; Am Inst Banking, 65-69; LaSalle Univ, 70-73. Polit & Govt Pos: First vpres, Young Dem Md, 68-69; mem, Tax Appeals Court Harford Co, 68-70; pres, Young Dem Harford Co, 69; mem, Gov Comn Study Md Gen Assembly, 69-70; Md State Deleg, 71- Bus & Prof Pos: Teller,

Equitable Trust Co, Aberdeen, Md, 64-68; new acct mgr, Equitable Trust Co, Bel Air, 68; assoc real estate broker, Paul L Glackin, Inc, Bel Air, 68- Mem: Nat Bd Realtors; Md Asn Real Estate Bd; Harford Co Bd Realtors; Jr CofC; Optimist Club. Honors & Awards: Outstanding Young Man, Jr CofC, 69. Relig: Methodist. Mailing Add: 815 Rockspring Rd Bel Air MD 21014

COY, CHARLES RUSSELL (R)
Chmn, Rep Party of Ky
b Madison Co, Ky, Jan 12, 26; s Charles Henson Coy & Maudie Sowers C; m 1951 to Gay Alley; c Russie Gay & Reba Jane. Educ: Eastern Ky Univ, 46-48; Univ Ky, LLB, 51. Polit & Govt Pos: Exec vpres, Ky Young Rep, 52-53; chmn, Madison Co Rep Exec Comt, Ky, 52-56; campaign chmn, Madison Co, 59; commonwealth attorney, 25th Judicial Dist, Ky, 69-70; area coordr, Nixon-Nunn Campaign, 72; chmn, Ky Lawyers To Reelect the President, 72; chmn, Rep Party of Ky, 73-; mem, Rep Nat Comt, 73- Bus & Prof Pos: Partner, Coy & Coy, Attorneys, 51; instr, Sch Law Enforcement, Eastern Ky Univ, 71. Mil Serv: Entered as Pvt, Army, 44, released as T/Sgt, 46, after serv in 90th Inf Div & Off Mil Govt, Bavaria, ETO, 45-46; Combat Inf Badge; ETO with Two Battle Stars. Mem: Madison Co, Ky & Am Bar Asns; Nat Asn of Defense Lawyers in Criminal Cases; Int Asn Ins Counsel. Relig: Church of Christ. Legal Res: Rte 2 Milford Estates Richmond KY 40475 Mailing Add: 212 N Second St Richmond KY 40475

CRABB, DELBERT ELMO (R)
Chmn, McPherson Co Rep Party, Kans
b McPherson, Kans, Sept 27, 16; s Paul C Crabb & Louise Molzen C; m 1937 to Georgana Oelrich; c Gary Conn. Educ: McPherson Col, 34-36; Univ Kans, BS in Educ, 38, MS in Educ, 46; Phi Delta Kappa. Polit & Govt Pos: Chmn, McPherson Co Rep Party, Kans, 68- Bus & Prof Pos: Mem, McPherson City Sch Bd of Educ, 49-61, pres, 3 years. Mil Serv: Entered as Pvt, Army Air Corps, 42, released as 2nd Lt, 45, after serv in 64th Combat Cargo Group, 12th Air Force, ETO, 45, Maj, Res, 442nd Mil Airlift Wing, RG MO; European Campaign, Po Valley, Appenines, Am Theatre & SAm Ribbons. Publ: Master's Thesis on Guidance, Univ Kans, 46. Mem: ROA; Nat Asn Music Merchants; Kans Music Merchants Asn; Elks; VFW. Relig: Protestant. Mailing Add: 1532 N Walnut McPherson KS 67460

CRABB, FRANK ABEL, JR (R)
Iowa State Rep
b Decatur, Ill, May 23, 03; s Frank Abel Crabb, Sr & Blanche Davis C; m 1931 to Dorothy Ward; c Susan (Mrs Johnson). Educ: DePauw Univ; Univ Chicago; Sigma Chi; Kudos, DePauw Univ. Polit & Govt Pos: Iowa State Rep, 75- Bus & Prof Pos: Plant mgr, Am Store, Pueblo, Colo, 45-47; gen supt, Tobin Packing Co, Ft Dodge, Iowa, 47-51; plant mgr, Kingan-Hy Grade Food, Indianapolis, 51-54; vpres & dir, Stark-Wetzel, Indianapolis, 54-59; meat packing consult, various meat plants in NY territory, 59-62; vpres & gen mgr, Farmland Food, Inc, Denison, Iowa, 62-68. Mem: Farm Bur; Mason; Consistory; Shrine; Rotary. Relig: Presbyterian. Mailing Add: Fairway Heights Denison IA 51442

CRABIEL, J EDWARD (D)
Secy of State, NJ
m to Doris Young; c Lynda. Educ: Rutgers Univ, BS, 36. Polit & Govt Pos: Mayor, Milltown, NJ, 47-51; alt deleg, Dem Nat Conv, 48; borough engr, Milltown, 52; mem, State Air Safety Comn, 54-62; NJ State Assemblyman, 53-65, asst majority leader, NJ Gen Assembly, 62, majority leader, 63 & minority leader, 64-65; mem, NJ Comn Interstate Coop, 60-65; NJ State Sen, 65-74, minority leader, NJ State Senate, 68-74; Secy of State, NJ, 74- Bus & Prof Pos: Pres & dir, Franklin Contracting Co, 67-73. Mil Serv: Lt, Naval Res, serv in 70th Naval Construct Bn. Mem: Am Soc Civil Engrs; Raritan Valley Soc Prof Engrs; Rutgers Engr Soc. Legal Res: 11 Kearney Dr Milltown NJ 08850 Mailing Add: State Capitol Trenton NJ 08625

CRABTREE, BURNIE R (D)
WVa State Deleg
Mailing Add: State Capitol Charleston WV 25305

CRABTREE, GRANVILLE H, JR (R)
Fla State Rep
b Chattanooga, Tenn, Nov 29, 29; s Granville H Crabtree & Gladys Wynn C; m 1956 to Paulette Vitrier; c Michelle & John G. Educ: Univ Calif, 53; Mex City Col, 54; Univ Mo, BS, 56; George Washington Univ, LLB, 60; Lambda Chi Alpha; Student pres, Pub & Bus Admin, Univ Mo. Polit & Govt Pos: Pres, Rep Party League, Sarasota, Fla, 61; attorney, Sarasota Co Planning Comt, 61-62; Fla State Rep, 119th Dist, 66-72, 73rd Dist, 72- Bus & Prof Pos: Practicing attorney, 60- Mil Serv: Entered Officer Cand Sch, Army, 48, released as Capt, 53, after serv in numerous units in Europe, Occup of Ger, Korean War & Occup of Japan, Res, 53-59; Grad, Officer Cand Sch, 50; Occup Ger Medal; Occup Japan Medal; Korean Serv Medal with 5 Campaign Stars; Korean Serv Unit Citation; Commendation Ribbon with Metal Pendant; Airborne Medal. Mem: Am & Sarasota Co Bar Asns; Elks; Am Legion; VFW. Relig: Episcopal. Mailing Add: 4700 Camino Real Sarasota FL 33581

CRABTREE, PAUL LEONARD (D)
b South Webster, Ohio, Sept 1, 29; s Trella R Crabtree & Margaret Leonard C; m 1949 to Rita Mae Anderson; c Margaret V, Jon A, Vyvyanne L, Matthew W & Carole V. Educ: Rio Grande Col; Marshall Univ; WVa State Col, AB, 66. Polit & Govt Pos: Exec asst to US Rep Ken Hechler, 58-61; spec asst to Gov, WVa, 61-65; mem comt on resolutions, WVa Young Dem Clubs, 63, chmn, 64; deleg, Dem Nat Conv, 64 & 68; admin asst to Gov Hulett C Smith, 65-66, exec asst, 66-69; consult to Speaker, WVa State House of Deleg, 69- Bus & Prof Pos: Staff mem, Charleston Gazette, WVa, 51-57, news ed, 57-58; pres, Paul Crabtree & Assocs, Inc, 69- Mil Serv: Entered as Pvt, Army, 46, released as Sgt, 47, after serv in 8th Army Hq, US Japanese Occup Forces. Honors & Awards: Newspaper honors for editorial writing, features and page make-up. Relig: Protestant. Legal Res: 511 McNeill Ave Point Pleasant WV 25550 Mailing Add: PO Box 106 Point Pleasant WV 25550

CRADDICK, THOMAS RUSSELL (TOM) (R)
Tex State Rep
b Beloit, Wis, Sept 19, 43; s Russell Francis Craddick & Beatrice Eleanor Kowalick C; m 1969 to Nadine Nayfa; c Christi Leigh. Educ: Tex Tech Col, BBA, 65, MBA, 66, study, 66-; Phi Alpha Kappa; Alpha Kappa Psi; Saddle Tramps; Tex Tech Finance Asn. Polit & Govt Pos: Tex State Rep, 69- Bus & Prof Pos: Vpres & dir, CBC Inc, Midland, Tex, 67-; vpres & dir, Gulf States Enterprises, Inc, 67-; pres & dir, Field Creek Pecan Farms, Inc, 69; vpres & dir, Tri-City Dr Pepper Bottling Co, Inc, 70-; partner, Mud Supply, Inc, currently. Mem: Jr CofC; Lions Club (dir); Nat Tex Tech Univ Ex-Students Asn (dir); Boys' Club, Midland (dir); Midland Co Livestock Asn. Relig: Catholic. Mailing Add: Box 2910 Capitol Station Austin TX 78767

CRADDOCK, ROBERT GLEN (D)
Nev State Assemblyman
Mailing Add: 6090 E Lake Mead Blvd Las Vegas NV 89110

CRAFT, JERRY DAVID (D)
Committeeman, Tex Dem Exec Comt
b Jacksboro, Tex, Apr 17, 37; s J D Craft & Helen Louise Johnson C; m 1960 to Mary Sue Moore; c Jay David, Sue Helen & Clint Creighton. Educ: Tex Tech Col, BS, 59; Block & Bridle Club; Sigma Alpha Epsilon. Polit & Govt Pos: Deleg, Dem State Conv, Tex, 66-74, mem party officer's comt, 66; alt deleg, Dem Nat Conv, 68; committeeman, Tex Dem Exec Comt, 68 & 69-, chmn youth activities subcomt, 69-74; deleg, Tex Dem Conv, 70; mem, Jacksboro Sch Bd, 70, pres, 74. Bus & Prof Pos: Rancher, Tex, Okla & NMex; secy bd & part-owner, Bowie Cable TV, Inc; dir & pres, P-K Cable TV & Jacksboro Cable TV Co, currently; dir & secy bd, Jacksboro Nat Bank, 72- Mil Serv: Capt, 504th Bn Mil Police, Army Reserve. Mem: Tex Angus Asn; Am Polled Hereford Asn; Am Quarter Horse Asn; Tex & Southwestern Cattle Raiser's Asn. Honors & Awards: Outstanding Citizen of Jacksboro, 70. Relig: Methodist; chmn bd, Jacksboro Methodist Church. Mailing Add: Rte 1 Newport TX 76254

CRAGGY, ERNEST (D)
NH State Rep
Mailing Add: Groveton NH 03582

CRAIG, EARL (DFL)
Dem Nat Committeeman, Minn
Mailing Add: 400 Groveland Ave Minneapolis MN 55403

CRAIG, HARRY E (D)
Chmn, Maricopa Co Dem Party, Ariz
b Friendship, Tenn, Jan 5, 29; s Robert G Craig & Eula Mays C; m 1953 to Joyce Corbin; c Mitzi Lynn, Harry Randall & Kevin Corbin. Educ: Memphis State Univ, BS, 61; Univ Ariz, JD, 64; Student Bar Asn. Polit & Govt Pos: Chmn, Dem Legis Dist 8-L, Phoenix, Ariz, 68-70; mem, Ariz State Dem Exec Comt, 68-70; chmn, Maricopa Co Dem Party, 72- Bus & Prof Pos: State trooper, Tenn, 51-61; motel mgr, Tucson, Ariz, 62-64; dep co attorney, Maricopa Co Attorney's Off, 64-65; attorney, pvt practice, Phoenix, 65- Mem: State Bar Ariz; Maricopa Co Bar Asn; Am & Ariz Trial Lawyers Asns; Elks. Relig: Unitarian. Mailing Add: 1407 E Echo Lane Phoenix AZ 85020

CRAIG, JACK A (R)
Publ Chmn, Boise Co Rep Party, Idaho
b Red Bluff, Calif, July 20, 22; s Dee S Craig & Lorena Robison C; m 1942 to Evelyn A Whyte; c Larry D & Jack A. Educ: DePaul Univ, 44. Polit & Govt Pos: Assessor, Boise Co, Idaho, 75-; publ chmn, Boise Co Rep Party, currently. Bus & Prof Pos: Co-owner, E S Robison Co, currently. Mil Serv: Entered as Pvt, Army, 43, released as Cpl, 46, after serv in Inf, Pac Theatre, 44-45. Legal Res: Box 127 Idaho City ID 83631 Mailing Add: Box 338 Placerville ID 83666

CRAIG, JAMES DONALD (R)
b New York, NY, Mar 6, 21; s Thomas Andrew Craig & Edith Carlson C; m 1942 to Eleanor Tully; c Jeffrey T. Educ: Bucknell Univ, BS, 41; Cap & Dagger; Phi Kappa Psi. Polit & Govt Pos: Mem, Bethel Town Rep Comt, justice of peace, Conn, 49; chmn, Brookfield Town Rep Comt, Conn, formerly. Bus & Prof Pos: Pres, Hunting Ridge, Inc, 58-62; US Develop Corp, 60-66, Wooster Co Inc, 60-66 & White Elephant Corp, 65-66. 65-66. Mil Serv: Entered as Pvt, Army Air Force, 41, released as Lt, 44, after serv in 5th Air Force, Pac Theater, 42-43. Mem: Nat Asn Home Builders; Brookfield CofC; Red Cross; Exchange Club; Nat Coun of Salesmens Orgns. Relig: Presbyterian. Mailing Add: Stony Hill Rd Brookfield CT 06804

CRAIG, LARRY EDWIN (R)
Idaho State Sen
b Council, Idaho, July 20, 45; s Elvin Oren Craig & Dorothy McCord C; single. Educ: Univ Idaho, BA Polit Sci & Speech, 69; George Washington Univ, MA US Foreign Policy, 71; Delta Chi; Silver Lance; Blue Key. Polit & Govt Pos: Idaho State Sen, Dist Ten, 75- Bus & Prof Pos: Salesman, Erickson Real Estate Agency, Weiser, Idaho, 73-; vpres, Craig Ranches Inc, Midvale, 74-; field rep & sales rep, Courtright Irrigation, La Grande, Ore, 74- Mil Serv: Idaho Nat Guard. Mem: Lions Int; Elks; Nat Fedn Independent Bus. Honors & Awards: Am Farmer Degree, Future Farmers Am, 66; Greek Man of the Year, Univ Idaho, 69; Theoaphlus Outstanding Sr, Univ Idaho, 69; Outstanding Student Leader, Idaho Asn Student Govt, 69. Relig: Methodist. Mailing Add: Midvale ID 83645

CRAIG, LELIA BURKS (D)
b Garner, Ark, Jan 14, 98; d Eugene Burks & Eddie Wallen B; m 1921 to Horace Wise Craig, wid; c Daniel Burks. Educ: William Woods Col, Fulton, Mo, 4 years; Southeast Mo State Col, 3 years. Polit & Govt Pos: VChmn, Callaway Co Dem Cent Comt, Mo, formerly. Bus & Prof Pos: Teacher, 27 years. Mem: Delta Kappa Gamma; Dem Woman's Club; DAR; Callaway Co Hist Soc; Woman's Club of McCredie. Honors & Awards: Honored for 40 years of active work with Dem Comt. Relig: Protestant. Mailing Add: Kingdom City MO 65262

CRAIG, PLEZZY HARBOR, JR (R)
Treas, Second Cong Dist Rep Party, NC
b Rockingham Co, NC, Nov 6, 37; s Plezzy Harbor Craig & Mary Thornton C; single. Educ: Univ NC, BS in indust rels, 59, MBA, 63, Sch Law, 61 & 63-65, Realtors Inst, grad, 69; cert real estate appraiser, Nat Asn Real Estate Appraisers; Nat Beta Club; Lambda Chi Alpha; Phi Alpha Delta. Polit & Govt Pos: Precinct chmn & elec judge, Orange Co, NC, 60-67; pres, Orange Co Young Rep, 66-68; chmn, Fourth Cong Dist Bipartisan Cong Adv Comt for Rep James C Gardner, 66-68; chmn, Orange Co Rep Exec Comt, 67-71; mem, Fourth Cong Dist Rep Exec Comt, 67-71; sustaining mem, Nat Rep Party, 67-; Rep nominee, NC State Rep, 22nd Dist, 68 & 70; treas, Fourth Cong Dist Rep Party, 69-71; finance chmn, Second Cong Dist, NC Rep Party, 70-72, treas, 71-; mem, NC Rep Exec Comt, 71-; deleg, Nat Rep Conv, 72; Rep nominee for NC State Sen, 16th Dist, 72. Bus & Prof Pos: Grad counr, Univ NC, 62-63; real estate broker, Chapel Hill, 62-65; realtor & assoc, Foushee Realty, 65-70; compliance inspector & appraiser, Fed Housing Admin, 70 & Dept Housing & Urban Develop, Vet Admin, 70-; owner, P H Craig Real Estate Assocs, 71- Mil Serv: Entered as Ens, Naval Res, 59, released as Lt(jg), 61, after serv in USS Purdy (DD-734), 6th Fleet,

Mediter, 59-61; Lt, Naval Res, 65; grad, 3rd Naval Pub Speaking Sem, 69; cmndg officer, Naval Res Unit MTD, 6-25, Durham, NC, 68-70; mem, Chief of Naval Opers/Commandants Sea Power Presentation Team, 68-74; mem, Naval Res Off Sch 6-2, Raleigh, 71- Mem: Chapel Hill-Carrboro Bd Realtors; Masters Appraisal Inst; Naval Res Asn; Nat Asn Realtors; Chapel Hill-Carrboro Jaycees. Relig: Baptist. Legal Res: PO Box 1 Hillsborough NC 27278 Mailing Add: PO Box 553 Chapel Hill NC 27514

CRAIG, ROBERT (BOB) (D)
Ill State Sen
b Oakwood, Ill, Oct 28, 21; married; c one. Educ: Utterback Bus Col; Reppert's Sch Auctioneering, Decatur, Ind. Polit & Govt Pos: Precinct committeeman, Dem Party, Ill, 46-; secy, Dem Cent Comt, 2 years; twp supvr, 49, reelected, 53; Ill State Rep, formerly; Ill State Sen, 75- Bus & Prof Pos: Auctioneer; operates grain, dairy, livestock farm. Mailing Add: 1628 Franklin Danville IL 61832

CRAIG, ROBERT EMMET (D)
Mem Exec Bd, NH State Dem Comt
b New York, NY, Sept 24, 33; s Joseph Peter Craig, Sr & Florence Anita Conroy C; m 1960 to Patricia Marie Lynch; c Sean Francis, Anne Marie & Siobhan Marie. Educ: Adelphi Univ, BA, 60; Univ NC, Chapel Hill, PhD, 71; Chi Sigma. Polit & Govt Pos: Mem, Dem Town Comt, Durham, NH, 66-68; chmn, Strafford Co Dem Comt, 68-70; mem, NH State Dem Comt, 68-71; mem exec bd, NH State Dem Comt, 71-; alt deleg, Dem Nat Conv, 72. Bus & Prof Pos: Asst prof polit sci, Univ NH, 66- Mil Serv: Entered as Seaman, Navy, 52, released as Radarman 1/C, 56, after serv in Destroyers, Pac; China Serv. Publ: Presidential Primaries in New Hampshire; New Hampshire Democratic Presidential Primary, 68, Am Polit Sci Asn; New Hampshire, In: Encycl Americana Yearbook, 72; plus others. Mem: Am Polit Sci Asn; NH Vet Against Vietnam War. Relig: Roman Catholic. Mailing Add: 107 Madbury Rd Durham NH 03824

CRAIG, WILLIAM H (D)
b Manchester, NH, Aug 26, 27; married; c four. Educ: St Anselm's Col; Boston Univ. Polit & Govt Pos: Chmn, NJ Dem Party, 67-72; deleg, Dem Nat Conv, 68 & 72. Bus & Prof Pos: Attorney-at-law. Mil Serv: Navy. Relig: Catholic. Mailing Add: 250 Purdue St Manchester NH 03103

CRAIGHEAD, DAVID CAPERTON (D)
Okla State Rep
b Galatz, Romania, Mar 8, 31; s Walter Eugene Craighead & Hazel Anna Thomson C; m 1964 to Betty Jo Durham; c Gail Patricia & Ruth Amy. Educ: Baylor Univ, BA, 56; Sigma Delta Chi. Polit & Govt Pos: Okla State Rep, Dist 95, 72- Bus & Prof Pos: News ed, Nowata Daily Star, Okla, 59-61; copy ed, Tulsa Tribune, 61-62; assoc ed & polit writer, Okla J, Oklahoma City, 66-72. Mil Serv: Entered as Pvt, Army, 52, released as Cpl, 54, after serv in First Armored Div, Ft Hood, Tex, 52-54. Mem: Tinker Toastmasters Club; Midwest City Quarterback Club; Rotary; CofC; Tinker Area YMCA. Honors & Awards: Nominated for Newsman of Year, Cent Okla Chap, Sigma Delta Chi, 69; Sponsor, Midwest City Interact Club, 73. Relig: Baptist; secy bd deacons & chmn, Men's Breakfast, First Baptist Church, Midwest City. Mailing Add: 116 E Northrup Dr Midwest City OK 73110

CRAIGHEAD, WILLIAM WADELL, JR (D)
b Richmond, Va, Jan 24, 53; s William Wadell Craighead Sr & Ramona Johnson C; single. Educ: Va State Col, presently. Polit & Govt Pos: Mem, Young Dem of Va, 70; campaign mgr, Klein, Craighead Campaign for City Coun, 72; deleg, Va Dem State Conv, 72; deleg, Dem Nat Conv, 72. Bus & Prof Pos: Student dir educ tel prog, Learning Resources Ctr, Va State Col. Mil Serv: ROTC Res, Squad Sgt. Mem: Student Nat Educ Asn; Human Rels Club of Richmond; North Richmond Recreation Asn. Relig: Catholic. Mailing Add: 2711 Northumberland Ave Richmond VA 23220

CRAIN, BILLY RAY (D)
Mem, State Dem Cent Comt La
b Franklinton, La, Aug 6, 29; s Henry Crain & Zodia Duncan C; m 1957 to Rose Worden; c Randy & Brian. Educ: Southeastern La Univ, BS, 50; La State Univ, MS, 56; Ariz State Univ, 51; Alpha Tau Alpha; Phi Lambda Chi. Polit & Govt Pos: Mem, State Dem Cent Comt La, 75th Dist, 68- Bus & Prof Pos: Agr teacher, Washington Parish Sch Bd, 56- Mil Serv: Entered as Pvt, Air Force, 50, released as S/Sgt, 54, after serv in 5th Air Force, Far East, 51-53; Good Conduct, Sigman Ree, Japanese Occupation, Korean Conflict & UN Medals. Publ: Co-auth, Farm Mechanics Basic to Dairy Farming, La State Dept Educ, 68. Mem: Am & La Voc Asns; La Teachers Asn; Nat Voc Agr Teachers Asn; Mason. Relig: Baptist. Mailing Add: Rt 5 Box 331 Franklinton LA 70438

CRALEY, NATHANIEL NEIMAN, JR (D)
b Red Lion, Pa, Nov 17, 27; s Nathaniel Neiman Craley, Sr & Alverta Peters C; m 1968 to Janet Weeks; c Cynthia, Patricia, Sarah, Edward, Nathaniel, Harry & Stacy. Educ: Gettysburg Col, BA, 50; Lambda Chi Alpha. Polit & Govt Pos: Chmn, York Co Dem Comt, Pa, 62-64; US Rep, 19th Cong Dist, Pa, 65-67; dir pub affairs, Trust Territory of Pac Islands, 67-72, Spec Asst to High Comnr for Legis Affairs, 72-, exec dir, Mariana Islands Plebiscite, 75- Bus & Prof Pos: Sales mgr, Red Lion Furniture Co, Pa, 50-53; pres, 53-65. Mem: Saipan CofC (dir, 67-). Relig: Protestant. Legal Res: RD 1 Dallastown PA 17313 Mailing Add: Box 241 Capitol Hill Saipan Mariana Islands 96950

CRAMER, ALLAN P (D)
VChmn, Westport Dem Town Comt, Conn
b Norwich, Conn, Mar 8, 37; s E L Cramer & Dorothy Pasnik C; m 1961 to Doris Ann Dickler; c Peter Alden & Alison Jane. Educ: Univ Pa, BA cum laude, 58; Univ Conn Sch Law, LLB, 64; Zeta Beta Tau. Polit & Govt Pos: Attorney, Off of the Gen Counsel, US Dept Health, Educ & Welfare, Washington, DC, 64-65; treas, Westport Dem Town Comt, Conn, 68-70, chmn, 70-72, vchmn, 72-; justice of the peace, Town of Westport, 73- Bus & Prof Pos: Attorney, Westport, Conn, 65- Mil Serv: Conn Air Nat Guard, 58-61. Publ: International copyright and the Soviet Union, Duke Univ Law J, 65. Mem: Am, Conn & Westport Bar Asns; Univ Pa Alumni Club of Fairfield Co (pres, 70-72); Westport Pub Libr (bd mem, 74-). Relig: Jewish. Legal Res: Yankee Hill Rd Westport CT 06680 Mailing Add: 38 W State St Westport CT 06680

CRAMER, ANN MARIE JOAN (D)
Chmn, Fla State Dem Party
b Buffalo, NY, Nov 1, 25; d Lawrence Nicholas Bowman & Barbara Herman B; m 1941 to Hugh Bernard Michael Cramer; c Ann Marie, Mary Beth, Cathleen Bridget & Twins, Hugh Skiffington & Lawrence Robert. Educ: Rollins Col. Polit & Govt Pos: Dem Precinct committeewoman, Fla, 54-58; state committeewoman, Broward Co, 58-; deleg, Dem Nat Conv, 60-72, mem credentials comt, 64, mem platform comt, 68; vchmn, Dem Exec Comt, Fla, 62-; asst, Pres Comt Voting Participation & Registr, 63; mem, US Adv Coun World's Fair, Toronto, 67; chmn, Fla State Dem Party, 70-71 & 75-, vchmn, 71-74; mem, Dem Nat Comt, Fla, 71-, dir womens activities & vchmn credentials comt, 72-; deleg, Dem Nat Mid-Term Conf, 74. Bus & Prof Pos: Real estate broker, 58- Mem: Am Legion Auxiliary; West Hollywood CofC; Women's CofC of Hollywood; Gtr Hollywood CofC; Women of the Moose. Honors & Awards: Named Fla Dem Woman of the Year, Dem Nat Comt, 60; First woman chmn of a polit party in Fla hist. Relig: Catholic; Former choir dir, Little Flower & St Stephens Church. Mailing Add: 6249 SW 27th St Miramar FL 33023

CRAMER, WILLIAM C (BILL) (R)
Rep Nat Committeeman, Fla
b Denver, Colo, Aug 4, 22; s Walter B Cramer & Doreen Emma Walters C; m 1951 to Alice Janet Jones; c William C, Jr, Mark C & Allyn Walters. Educ: St Petersburg Jr Col; Univ NC, 46; Harvard Law Sch, LLB, 48; Class Pres, St Petersburg Jr Col; Phi Beta Kappa; Sigma Chi, Significant Sig, 70; Phi Alpha Delta. Hon Degrees: DJurisp, Tampa Univ, 57. Polit & Govt Pos: Rep campaign dir, Pinellas Co, Fla, 50; minority leader, Fla State Legis, 50-52; regional dir, Young Rep Nat Fedn, 51-53; chmn, Fla Col Electors, 52; vchmn Fla deleg, Rep Nat Conv, 52-60, chmn host comt, 68, deleg & chmn rules comt, 72; co attorney, Pinellas Co, 53-54; vchmn, Young Rep Nat Fedn, 53-55; US Rep, Fla, 54-70; Rep Nat Committeeman, Fla, 64-; counsel to Rep Nat Comt, currently, mem exec comt, formerly. Bus & Prof Pos: Partner, Law Firm of Bradham, Lyle, Skipper & Cramer, St Petersburg, Fla, currently; attorney & sr partner, Cramer, Haber & Becker, Washington, DC & Cramer & Matthews, Miami, Fla, currently. Mil Serv: Navy, 43-46, Lt(jg); Citation, Invasion of Southern France; Naval Res. Mem: VFW; Am Legion; Amvets; Shrine; Am Bar Asn. Relig: Methodist. Legal Res: 1448 Lake Tarpon Ave Tarpon Springs FL 33589 Mailing Add: 475 L'Enfant Plaza Suite 4100 Washington DC 20024

CRAMPTON, SCOTT PAUL (R)
Asst Attorney Gen, Tax Div, Dept Justice
b Cleveland, Ohio, Sept 1, 13; s Paul Scott Crampton & Mary Runnells Fayram C; m 1963 to Harriet Yenne; c Don Paul, Scott Charles, Susan Runnells & Lucinda Ann & Louis Harlan Lommasson. Educ: Am Univ, BA, 35; George Washington Univ, LLB, 39; Phi Alpha Delta. Polit & Govt Pos: Asst Attorney Gen, Tax Div, Dept Justice, 71- Bus & Prof Pos: Lawyer, George E H Goodner Law Off, Washington, DC, 39-51, Prince, Taylor & Crampton, 51-61 & Korner, Doyle, Worth & Crampton, 61-71. Mem: Am Bar Asn (chmn sect taxation, 69-70); Metrop Club; Nat Lawyers Club; Kiwanis, Woodbridge, Va; Mason. Relig: Episcopal. Mailing Add: 11701 River Dr Lorton VA 22079

CRAMTON, LOUIS KAY (R)
Mich State Rep
b Lapeer, Mich, Dec 5, 15; s Louis Convers Cramton & Fame Kay C; m 1945 to Dorothy Ellen Chapman; c Margie Kay (Mrs Louis F Wojnaroski). Educ: Alma Col, AB, 38; Tau Kappa Epsilon. Polit & Govt Pos: Pres, Lapeer Co Young Rep, Mich, 39-41; Rep precinct chmn, 18th Precinct Saginaw; bd mem, Saginaw Co Rep Club; co deleg, Rep State Conv; Rep precinct deleg, Lapeer Co Conv, 39-41, Saginaw Co Conv, 49-53 & Midland Co Conv, 53-; treas, Midland Co Rep Breakfast Club, 53, pres, 53-64, mem exec bd, 65-; mem, Rep State Exec Comt, currently; Mich State Rep, 103rd Dist, 71- Mil Serv: Entered as Pvt, Army, 41, released as Cpl, 45, after serv in 14th Signal Corps, Aleutians; Pac Theater Ribbon with 2 stars; Am Theater Ribbon. Publ: Columnist, This is how I see it. Mem: Kiwanis; Elks; Benevolent Protective Order of Wolves; VFW (legis comt); Am Legion. Honors & Awards: Citizenship Award, Midland Co Rep Breakfast Club, 65. Relig: Presbyterian. Mailing Add: 3315 W Nelson St Midland MI 48640

CRANDALL, EARLE P (R)
Mem, Rep State Cent Comt, Calif
b Rayne, La, May 31, 04; s Jesse Lawrence Crandall & Lela E Dodge C; m 1929 to Margarethe Kroeck; c Dr Peter L & Nancy (Mrs J Robert Foster). Educ: Col of Pac, AB, 27, Sec Credential, 31 & Sec Admin, 36; Stanford Univ, MA, 42 & EdD, 46; charter mem, Local Field Chap, Phi Delta Kappa. Polit & Govt Pos: Calif State Assemblyman, 25th Dist, 66-72; mem, Calif Rep State Cent Comt, 69- Bus & Prof Pos: Teacher, Lodi Union High Sch, 31-36, vprin, 36-42, prin, 42-46; dir curriculum, San Jose Unified Sch Dist, 46-50, supt, 50-66. Mem: Col Pac Alumni Asn; life mem Nat Educ Asn; Bay Area Curriculum Coun; Am Asn Sch Adminr; Calif Teachers Asn. Relig: Methodist Episcopal. Mailing Add: 1175 Roycott Way San Jose CA 95125

CRANDALL, ETHEL LEANNA (D)
Treas, Fayette Co Dem Exec Comt, WVa
b Gauley Bridge, WVa, Apr 20, 11; d Willis Oscar Crandall & Mary Robson C; single. Educ: WVa Inst Technol, AB, 34; WVa Univ, summer 34; Phi Mu Gamma. Polit & Govt Pos: Treas, Fayette Co Dem Exec Comt, WVa, 60-; WVa State Deleg, 62-70; mem, Falls Dist Dem Woman's Club, 62-; assoc chmn, Dem Campaign, Fayette Co, 66. Bus & Prof Pos: Teacher, Fayette Co Schs, WVa, 34-55; pres & owner, W O Crandall Hardware Co, Gauley Bridge, 55- Mil Serv: Entered as Pvt, WAAC, 43, released as S/Sgt, 46, after serv in 12th Mapping & Charting Squadron, 311th Photo Wing, Lowery Field, Colo; Victory Medal; Am Theatre Medal; Good Conduct Medal. Mem: Am Asn Univ Women; WVa & Fayette Co Hist Socs; Order of Women Legislators; Hon Order of Ky Colonels. Honors & Awards: Selected as Dem Woman of the Year, Fifth Dist, WVa, 63. Relig: Methodist. Mailing Add: Gauley Bridge WV 25085

CRANE, BRUCE (R)
Rep Nat Committeeman, Mass
b Dalton, Mass, July 27, 09; s W Murray Crane & Josephine Boardman C; m 1932 to Winnie Davis Long; c two daughters, Mrs William Greene & Mrs William Mackey. Educ: Yale Univ, 31. Polit & Govt Pos: Mem, Mass Gov Coun, 53-56; Rep Nat Committeeman, Mass, currently; deleg, Rep Nat Conv, 64-68. Bus & Prof Pos: Pres, Crane & Co, Inc, 51- Relig: Congregational. Mailing Add: 45 Main St Dalton MA 01226

CRANE, EDWARD THURSTON (R)
Vt State Rep
Mailing Add: Box 19 East St Johnsbury VT 05838

CRANE, HENRIETTA PAGE (R)
Rep Nat Committeewoman, Maine
b Skowhegan, Maine; d Blin Williams Page & Edith Nay P; div; c Kennedy Crane, III, Trude (Mrs Arthur E Housman) & Tobey Campbell. Educ: Wellesley Col, BA, 35; Tau Zeta Epsilon. Polit & Govt Pos: Vchmn, Rockport Rep Comt, 62-64, chmn, 64-67; alt deleg, Rep Nat Conv, 68; vchmn, Knox Co Rep Comt, 68-70; committeewoman, Maine Rep Exec Comt, Knox Co, 69-72; Rep Nat Committeewoman, Maine, 72- Bus & Prof Pos: Maine chmn, Develop Fund of Wellesley Col, 52-56; mem exec comt, Gov Adv Comt Educ, 56-61; trustee & mem exec comt, Knox Co Gen Hosp, 58-; assoc dir, Mid-Coast Ment Health Asn, 66-; adv bd, Mid-Coast Home Health Asn, 66-; house of deleg, Pine Tree Soc for Crippled Children & Adults, 67- Relig: Congregational. Mailing Add: 30 Shaw Ave Rockland ME 04841

CRANE, KENT BRUCE (R)
b North Hornell, NY, July 25, 35; s Willard L Crane & Beth Ewart C; m 1956 to Linda Bradfield; c Jeffrey & Andrew. Educ: NY Mil Acad, 53; Dartmouth Col, AB cum laude, 57; Class Treas & Pres; pres, Int Club; Green Key Soc. Polit & Govt Pos: Third secy, Am Embassy, Djakarta, Indonesia, 61-63; with Dept of State, 63-64; vconsul, Am Consulate, Zanzibar, Tanzania, 64-65; second secy, Am Embassy, Accra, Ghana, 65-67; sr research assoc, Rep Nat Comt, 67-68; spec asst to US Sen George Murphy, Calif, 68-69; asst to vpres, Nat Security Affairs, 69-71; asst dir for EAsia & Pac, US Info Agency, 72- Mil Serv: Entered as 2nd Lt, Army, 57, released as 1st Lt, 59; Capt, Army Res. Mem: Inst Strategic Studies, London; Am Polit Sci Asn; Metrop Club NY; Mt Kenya Safari Club; African Safari Club Washington. Relig: Baptist. Legal Res: MD Mailing Add: c/o US Info Agency 1776 Pennsylvania Ave Washington DC 20547

CRANE, PHILIP MILLER (R)
US Rep, Ill
b Chicago, Ill, Nov 3, 30; s Dr George W Crane, III & Cora Miller C; m 1959 to Arlene Catherine Johnson; c Catherine Anne, Susanna Marie, Jennifer Elizabeth, Rebekah Caroline, George Washington, V, Rachel Ellen, Sarah Emma & Carrie Esther. Educ: DePauw Univ, 48-50; Hillsdale Col, BA, 52; Univ Mich, 52-54; Univ Vienna, 53 & 56; Ind Univ, MA, 61, PhD, 63; Phi Alpha Theta; Pi Gamma Mu. Polit & Govt Pos: Pub rels expert, Rep Party, 62; dir research, Ill Goldwater for President Comt, 64; adv on polit & nat issues to Richard Nixon, 64-68; US Rep, Ill, 69-, mem ways & means comt, US House of Rep, 74- Bus & Prof Pos: Teaching asst, Ind Univ, 59-62; asst prof, Bradley Univ, 63-67; dir schs, Westminster Acad, 67-68. Mil Serv: Entered as Pvt, E-2, Army, 54, released as SP-3, 56, after serv in 9th Inf Div, Europe, 55-56. Publ: The Democrat's Dilemma, Henry Regnery Co, 64. Mem: Am Hist Asn; Orgn Am Historians; Acad Polit Sci; Am Acad Polit & Social Sci; Univ Prof for Acad Order. Relig: Methodist. Legal Res: Mt Prospect IL 60056 Mailing Add: 1407 Longworth House Off Bldg Washington DC 20515

CRANE, ROBERT Q (D)
Mass State Treas & Receiver Gen
b Providence, RI, Mar 21, 26; m; c five. Educ: Boston Col Sch Bus Admin. Polit & Govt Pos: Mass State Rep, 57-64, asst majority leader, Mass House of Rep, 2 years; Mass state treas & receiver gen, 64, 65-; chmn, Mass State Dem Party, 71-; chmn, Mass State Lottery Comn, 72- Bus & Prof Pos: Food broker & sales mgr, 15 years; ins broker, 8 years. Mil Serv: Marine Corps. Mem: Am Legion; KofC; DAV; VFW; Elks. Mailing Add: State House Boston MA 02133

CRANE, WILLIAM ALEXANDER (R)
Chmn, Eighth Cong Dist Rep Caucus, Mich
b Saginaw, Mich, Sept 1, 40; s William Erastis Crane, Jr & Lillian Van Tassel C; m 1965 to Janet Carol Johnson; c Ellen Elizabeth & William Andrew. Educ: Albion Col, BA, 62; Univ Mich Law Sch, Ann Arbor, JD, 65; Phi Delta Phi; Sigma Chi. Polit & Govt Pos: Rep, Mich Rep State Cent Comt, 72-75; mem steering comt, Saginaw Co Rep Party, 72-; chmn, Eighth Cong Dist Rep Caucus, Mich, 75- Bus & Prof Pos: Attorney-at-law, Crane, Kessel & Crane, 65- Mem: Saginaw Exchange Club (pres, 74-75); Saginaw Co & Mich Bar Asns; Univ Mich Club of Saginaw. Honors & Awards: Boss of the Year, Nat Secy Asn, Saginaw Chap, 73. Relig: Congregational. Legal Res: 4711 Sudbury Saginaw MI 48603 Mailing Add: 702 Second Nat Bank Saginaw MI 48607

CRANFILL, STEVEN R (D)
Wyo State Rep
b Greybull, Wyo, June 11, 50; s Joe Paul Cranfill & Ola Watson C; single. Educ: Weber State Col, BS in Psychol, 72. Polit & Govt Pos: Sch bd trustee, Washlakie Co Sch Dist One, 72-73; Wyo State Rep, 75- Bus & Prof Pos: Bd mem, Wyo Human Resources Confederation, 72-73. Mem: Wyo Corrections Asn; League of Women Voters. Relig: Episcopal. Mailing Add: Box 651 Worland WY 82401

CRANGLE, JOSEPH F (D)
Mem, Dem Nat Comt, NY
b Buffalo, NY, June 12, 32; s Edward J Crangle & Margarita Anastasia McNutt C; m to Rita J Henry; c Mary Elizabeth, Catherine Ann, Elizabeth Ann, Brigid Marie & Joseph Patrick. Educ: Canisius Col, AB, 55; Univ Buffalo Law Sch, LLB, 59; Alpha Sigma Nu. Polit & Govt Pos: Committeeman, Erie Co Dem Comt, NY, 58-, ward chmn, 60-65, chmn, 65-; exec asst to Speaker of NY State Assembly, 66-68; deleg, Dem Nat Conv, 68 & 72; exec asst & spec counsel to Minority Leader, NY State Assembly, 69-; exec mem, NY State Dem Comt, currently, chmn, 71-75; mem exec comt, Dem Nat Charter Comn, 73-; deleg, Dem Nat Mid-Term Conf, 74. Bus & Prof Pos: Attorney. Mil Serv: 2nd Lt, Army, 56; Capt, Army Res, 56- Relig: Roman Catholic. Legal Res: 69 Starin Ave Buffalo NY 14214 Mailing Add: 575 Genesee Bldg Buffalo NY 14202

CRANSTON, ALAN MACGREGOR (D)
US Sen, Calif
b Palo Alto, Calif, June 19, 14; s William MacGregor Cranston & Carol Dixon C; m 1940 to Geneva McMath; c Robin MacGregor & Kim MacGregor. Educ: Stanford Univ, BA, 36; Sigma Nu; Track Team, 35-36. Polit & Govt Pos: Chief foreign lang div, Off War Info, US Govt, 42-44; pres, Calif Dem Coun, 53-58; mem exec comt, Dem State Cent Comt, 54-; state controller, Calif State Govt, 59-67; US Sen, Calif, 69-, mem budget & nutrition & human needs comts, US Senate, currently, chmn subcomt prod & stabilization, Banking, Housing & Urban Affairs, chmn subcomt human resources, Labor & Pub Welfare & chmn subcomt health & hosps, Vet Affairs, currently. Bus & Prof Pos: Foreign correspondent, Int News Serv, 36-38; owner, Cranston Co, 47-50; pres, Homes for a Better Am Inc, 67-68; vpres, Carlsberg Financial Corp, 68; columnist, Los Angeles Times & other newspapers, 67-68. Mil Serv: Entered as Pvt, Army, 44, released as Sgt, 45, after serv in Inf in US. Publ: Mein Kampf (Anti-Hitler version), Noram Co, 39; The Killing of the Peace, Viking & Compass, 45; A million dollar loser looks at campaigning, Fortune, 64; plus many others. Mem: United World Federalists. Relig: Protestant. Legal Res: Riverside County CA Mailing Add: 452 Old Senate Off Bldg Washington DC 20510

CRANWELL, C RICHARD (D)
Va State Deleg
Mailing Add: 220 E Washington Ave Vinton VA 24179

CRAPO, TERRY LAVELLE (R)
Chmn, Dist 29 Rep Party, Idaho
b Idaho Falls, Idaho, July 2, 39; s George LaVelle Crapo & Melba Olsen C; m 1958 to Valeria Hatch; c David John, Christa Ann, Karen Marie, Jennifer Lynn & Joan Michelle. Educ: Brigham Young Univ, BA & MA, 60; Harvard Univ Law Sch, LLB, 63; ed, Harvard Law Rev. Polit & Govt Pos: Idaho State Rep, 66-72, majority leader, Idaho State House Rep, 68-72; chmn, Dist 29 Rep Party, 73- Bus & Prof Pos: Attorney-at-law & partner, Holden, Kidwell, Hahn & Crapo, 63-; visiting assoc prof law, J Reuben Clark Sch Law, Brigham Young Univ, Provo, Utah, 75- Mem: Idaho State & Am Bar Asns; Idaho Farm Bur. Relig: Latter-day Saint. Legal Res: Rte 4 Box 72 Idaho Falls ID 83401 Mailing Add: PO Box 129 Idaho Falls ID 83401

CRAVALHO, ELMER F (D)
Mayor, Maui Co, Hawaii
b Feb 19, 26; single. Educ: Univ Hawaii. Polit & Govt Pos: Mem, Hawaii Territorial House, 55-59; Hawaii State Rep & Speaker, Hawaii State House of Rep, 59-67; Mayor, Maui Co, 67-; deleg, Dem Nat Conv, 68 & 72; deleg, Dem Nat Mid-Term Conf, 74. Bus & Prof Pos: Teacher, Dept of Pub Instr, Hawaii, 46-54; exec vpres & gen mgr, Maui Supply Inc; organizer & mgr, Kula Commun Fed Credit Union; off mgr, Companion Ins Co. Mem: Independent Ranchers of Maui. Mailing Add: RR 1 Box 742 Kula HI 96790

CRAVEN, JAMES J, JR (D)
Mass State Rep
b Boston, Mass; m to Olivia M Bartels; c James Michael, Theresa & Sheila. Educ: Boston Univ. Polit & Govt Pos: Mass State Rep, 49-50 & 57-; secy, Boston Dem City Comt, 8 years; mem, Ward 19 Dem Comt; deleg, Dem Nat Conv, 68. Mil Serv: Army, discharged as Capt. Mem: Amvets; DAV; KofC; Boy's Club, Inc of Jamaica Plains (dir). Relig: Catholic; Our Lady of Lourdes Holy Name Soc. Mailing Add: 9 St John St Boston MA 02130

CRAVEN, WILLIAM A (R)
Calif State Assemblyman
Mailing Add: 550 W Broadway Vista CA 92083

CRAW, NICHOLAS WESSON (R)
Assoc Dir, ACTION
b Governor's Island, NY, Nov 14, 36; s Col Demas T Craw & Mary Victoria Wesson C; div; c Nicholas W, II. Educ: Princeton Univ, BA cum laude, 59; Johns Hopkins Sch Advan Int Studies, 59-61; Princeton Charter Club. Polit & Govt Pos: Consult, expert, VISTA, 70, spec asst to dir, 70-71, dir training div, 70-71, dir manpower div, 70-71; Assoc Dir, ACTION, 71-73; dir, Peace Corps, 73-74. Bus & Prof Pos: Dir Logistics, Proj HOPE, 60-62, dir opers & logistics, 62-66, dir pub rels, 65-66, dir develop, 66-68. Mem: Princeton Alumni Coun. Relig: Episcopal. Mailing Add: 3724 Cumberland St NW Washington DC 20016

CRAWFORD, ABBOTT LINTON (D)
b Hampton, Ga, Apr 6, 95; s George Milton Crawford & Corrie Farmer C; m 2nd time, 1959 to Ernestine Thompson; c Linton Kimsey, Kathleen C (Mrs Tucker) & Anne C (Mrs Early). Educ: Boston Col, 1 year. Polit & Govt Pos: Comnr, Cornelia, Ga, 35-40 & 63-68; mayor, Cornelia, 36-39 & 69-; chmn, Habersham Co Dem Exec Comt, formerly. Bus & Prof Pos: Mgr, Cornelia Coca-Cola Bottling Co, 19-63. Mil Serv: Entered as Pvt, Army, 17, released as 2nd Lt, 19, after serv in 1st Div, Ger, 18-19; Meuse-Argonne Unit Citation. Mem: Hon lifetime mem Ga Bottlers Asn; hon lifetime mem Ga Coca-Cola Bottlers Asn; 4-H Club; Mason (past Master); Am Legion (past Comdr). Relig: Baptist. Mailing Add: 820 Wayside St Cornelia GA 30531

CRAWFORD, ALEX (R)
Chmn, Hale Co Rep Comt, Ala
b Coleman, Tex, Nov 8, 24; s Alexander Crawford & Ada Oliver C; m 1951 to Helen Maxton; c Helen Cecile & Alexander Bruce. Educ: Greensboro Pub Schs, 12 years. Polit & Govt Pos: Chmn, Hale Co Rep Comt, Ala, 62-; mem, Ala Rep Exec Comt, 62- Bus & Prof Pos: Owner & mgr, cattle & gen farming oper, 45- Mem: Ala Cattlemen's Asn; Am Nat Cattlemen's Asn; Ala Soybean Producers Asn. Relig: United Methodist. Mailing Add: Rte 3 Box 40 Greensboro AL 36744

CRAWFORD, ARNOLD H (R)
Vt State Rep
Mailing Add: PO Box 237 South Royalton VT 05068

CRAWFORD, CAROL FORSYTH (R)
Mem, Rep State Cent Comt Calif
b Okanogan, Wash, Apr 14, 11; d John William Forsyth & Caroline Anderson F; m 1935 to Hugh Eric Crawford; c Camilla (Mrs Hammond). Educ: Univ Ore, BS, 32. Polit & Govt Pos: Div chmn, 46th Assembly Dist Rep Party, Calif, 52, Westchester co-chmn, 54, Westchester chmn, 56, precinct co-chmn, 58; area chmn, 39th Assembly Dist Rep Party, 60, precinct vchmn, 62, precinct chmn, 64, 66, 68; pres, Lakewood-Long Beach Rep Women Fedn, 61-62 & 71-72; mem, Rep State Cent Comt Calif, 66-; precinct chmn, '70 Steering Comt, Reagan Team, 70; precinct chmn, Comt to Reelect the President, 72. Bus & Prof Pos: Prof social worker, RSW State Relief Admin, 34-40; vol social worker, Am Red Cross, 50-64. Mem: Univ Women's Club; charter mem Long Beach Children's Theatre; assoc mem Family Serv; Camp Fire Girls. Relig: Episcopal. Mailing Add: 4417 E Harvey Way Long Beach CA 90808

CRAWFORD, CHARLES S (CHUCK), III (D)
b Tacoma, Wash, Oct 30, 45; s Charles S Crawford, Jr & Naoma Norrie C; single. Educ: Univ Nev, Las Vegas, BA, 68; George Washington Univ, 68; Univ Calif, Los Angeles, 73; Delta Sigma Phi. Polit & Govt Pos: Aide, US Sen Cannon, Nev, 68-71; vpres, Las Vegas Young Dem, 71-72; mem, Clark Co Dem Cent Comt, 72; pres, Nev Young Dem, 72; deleg, Dem Nat Conv, 72. Bus & Prof Pos: Dir publicity, Tropicana Hotel & Country Club, Las Vegas, 71-72; dir pub rels, A&W Restaurants Int, Santa Monica, Calif, 72-73. Mil Serv: Entered as

Pvt, Army Res, 69, Sgt, serv in 301st Civil Affairs Unit, Los Angeles, currently. Mem: Los Angeles Pub Rels Soc; Am Soc Pub Rels; Common Cause; Beverly Hills Young Dem. Honors & Awards: Life membership, Univ Nev Student Body, 68; Student of the Year, Univ Nev, 68. Mailing Add: 4025 Via Marina E211 Marina Del Rey CA 90291

CRAWFORD, GARY WELDON (D)
b Washington, DC, Dec 29, 49; s Lawrence Weldon Crawford & Marie Butler C; single. Educ: Northern Va Community Col, 67-69; Va Western Community Col, 69-70. Polit & Govt Pos: Secy, Eighth Dist Dem Comt, Va, 71-72; mem, Va Dem State Cent Comt, 71-72; mem temporary resolutions comt, Va State Dem Conv, 72; deleg, Dem Nat Conv, 72; mem, Prince William Co Young Dem, 72- Bus & Prof Pos: Purchasing agt, Fed Home Loan Bank Bd, 73- Mem: Am Fedn Fed Employees; Moose. Relig: Protestant. Legal Res: 9506 Spotsylvania St Manassas VA 22110 Mailing Add: 7404 Centreville Rd Manassas VA 22110

CRAWFORD, HAZLE REID (D)
Asst Secy Housing Mgt, Dept Housing & Urban Develop
b Winston-Salem, NC, Jan 18, 39; s Hazle Crawford & Mary Reid C; m 1956 to Eleanora Braxton; c Leslie, Hazle, George, Gregory & Lynne. Educ: Howard Univ, 61-63; DC Teachers Col, 63-65; Am Univ, 67. Polit & Govt Pos: Asst secy housing mgt, Dept Housing & Urban Develop, 73- Bus & Prof Pos: Resident mgr, Frederick W Berens, 64-66; property mgr, Polinger Co, 68-69; vpres, Kaufmann & Broad Asset Mgt, 71; vpres, Polinger & Crawford, 72-73. Mil Serv: Enlisted Air Force, 56, released as Sgt, 65. Publ: Auth, For the use of registered apartment managers, RAM, 5/73; auth, The Crawfordian philosophy of low rent housing, Realtor, 10/73; auth, Counseling families—The homeownership counseling programs, HUD Challenge, 2/74. Mem: Inst Real Estate Mgt; Builders, Owners & Mgrs Asn; Nat Asn Housing & Redevelop Off; Prof Property Mgrs Asn. Honors & Awards: Presidential Citation for Exceptional Serv to Others in Finest Am Tradition, 70; J Wallace Paletou Award, Inst Real Estate Mgt, 74; Career Excellence Award, Push, 74; One of the One Hundred Most Influential Black Men in the Country, Ebony Mag, April, 75. Relig: Roman Catholic. Legal Res: 3195 Westover Dr SE Washington DC 20020 Mailing Add: 451 Seventh St SW Rm 9100 Washington DC 20410

CRAWFORD, IRVIN COOPER (D)
NC State Sen
b Bryson City, NC, Sept 1, 05; s Gordon Law Crawford & Mary Jane Cooper C; m 1935 to Evelyn Gregory; c Stephen G. Educ: Duke Univ; Wake Forest Col. Polit & Govt Pos: Chmn, Swain Co Dem Exec Comt, NC, 32-40; mem, Swain Co Bd Educ, 33-34; mayor, Bryson City, NC, 35-36; NC State Rep, 57-66; NC State Sen, 71- Bus & Prof Pos: Lawyer. Mem: Elks; Moose. Relig: Methodist. Legal Res: 10 Hampshire Circle Asheville NC 28804 Mailing Add: 409 Jackson Bldg Asheville NC 28804

CRAWFORD, JAMES FRANCIS, SR (D)
Ala State Rep
b Abbeville, Ala, Dec 1, 13; s Albert Nickolas Crawford & Neomia Skipper C; m 1968 to Martha Williams; c James Francis, Jr. Educ: Abbeville High Sch. Polit & Govt Pos: Mayor, Abbeville, Ala, 55-63; pres, Ala League Munic; Ala State Rep, Henry Co, 63-67, Henry & Huston Co, 67- Bus & Prof Pos: Farming, quick freeze & meat processing. Mil Serv: Army, 43-45. Relig: Baptist. Mailing Add: PO Box 129 Abbeville AL 36310

CRAWFORD, JAMES LAIRD (R)
b Colorado City, Tex, Sept 22, 08; s Monroe Turner Crawford & Ida May Adair C; m 1932 to Anna Louise Ragan; c Norma Louise (Mrs Shem Ray, Jr), Margaret (Mrs Hinton), Ida Sue (Mrs Putman). Educ: Wesley Col, 1 year; Asbury Col, 1 year; ETex Univ, BA; Northern Ill Col Optom, OD; Tomb & Key. Polit & Govt Pos: Deleg, Rep Nat Conv, 40; chmn, Hopkins Co Rep Party, Tex, formerly. Mem: Rotary. Honors & Awards: 25 years perfect attendance, Rotary. Relig: Church of the Nazarene. Legal Res: 645 Gilmer St Sulphur Springs TX 75482 Mailing Add: PO Box 487 Sulphur Springs TX 75482

CRAWFORD, PATRICIA A (R)
Pa State Rep
b Middletown, Pa, Sept 6, 28; d Patrick Francis Farren & Florence Long F; m 1947 to Robert J Crawford; c Janet & John. Educ: Murphy High Sch, Mobile, Ala, grad, 46; West Chester State Col, 65-66. Polit & Govt Pos: Pa State Rep, 69-; deleg, 1970 White House Conf on Children; comnr, Gov Comn on Women, 72- Mem: Goshen Grange 121, Westchester; hon mem, Jr Women's Club of Malvern; Berwyn-Paoli-Malvern Bus & Prof Women; hon mem Para Med Soc, West Chester State Col; Valley Forge Hist Soc. Honors & Awards: Good Fel Cert Outstanding Contrib to Chester Co Ambulance Asn. Relig: Lutheran. Mailing Add: 341 Oakwood Lane Devon PA 19333

CRAWFORD, REID W (R)
Iowa State Rep
Mailing Add: 1117 Arizona Ave Ames IA 50010

CRAWFORD, VICTOR LAWRENCE (D)
Md State Sen
b Richmond, Va, Apr 19, 33; s Joseph Crawford & Elizabeth Lawrence C; m 1958 to Clare Wootten; c Victor Lawrence, Jr & Charlene Elizabeth. Educ: Univ Md, BA, 57; Georgetown Law Ctr, LLB, 60; Phi Alpha Delta. Polit & Govt Pos: Attorney, Montgomery Elec Bd, 66; vpres, Eastern Montgomery Dem, 66; Md State Deleg, 67-69; Md State Sen, 69- Mem: Am Bar Asn; Isaac Walton League; VFW. Relig: Roman Catholic. Legal Res: 1116 Nora Dr Silver Spring MD 20904 Mailing Add: Suburban Trust Bldg 255 N Washington St Rockville MD 20850

CRAWFORD, VON RUE (R)
NMex State Rep
Mailing Add: 113 W Ash Deming NM 88030

CRAWFORD, WILLIAM A (D)
Ind State Rep
Mailing Add: 3429 N Capitol 5 Indianapolis IN 46208

CRAWFORD, WILLIAM REX (INDEPENDENT)
US Ambassador, Cyprus
b Philadelphia, Pa, Apr 22, 28; s William Rex Crawford & Dorothy Buckley C; m 1950 to Virginia Vollrath Lowry; c Sarah Lowry. Educ: Harvard Col, AB cum laude, 48; Univ Pa, MA, 50; Inst of Modern Oriental Lang, 50-51; Foreign Serv Inst, Arabic lang & area specialization, 54-56; Hasty Pudding Inst; Iroquois Club. Polit & Govt Pos: Foreign Serv Officer, Dept State, 51-, polit officer, Jidda, Saudi Arabia, 51-53, consular officer, Venice, Italy, 53-55, lang trainee, Washington, DC, 55-56; Arab lang area trainee, Beirut, Lebanon, 56-57, Aden prin officer, SYemen, 57-59, Taiz charge d'affaires, NYemen, 57-59, internal rels officer, Washington, DC, 59-62, officer-in-charge, Lebanon-Israel Affairs, Washington, DC, 62-63, officer-in-charge, Arab-Israel Affairs, 63-64, counr/polit officer, Rabat, Morocco, 64-67, Woodrow Wilson fel, Princeton Univ, 67-68, counr, Dept Chief of Mission, Nicosia, Cyprus, 68-72; US Ambassador, Sanaa, Yemen Arab Repub, 72-74, US Ambassador to Cyprus, 74- Mil Serv: Entered as Ens, Navy, 48, released as Ens, 49, after serv in US Naval Aviation Flight Training, Pensacola, Fla. Mem: MidE Inst; Am Foreign Serv Asn. Honors & Awards: Meritorious Serv Award, Dept of State, 59; Award for Distinguished Fed Serv, William A Jump Found, 63. Legal Res: c/o P M Cope 230 Biddulph Rd Radnor PA 19087 Mailing Add: Am Embassy FPO New York NY 09530

CREASEY, DANIEL FREDRICK (D)
b Richland Center, Wis, Feb 6, 43; s Dougal H Creasey & Helen Johnson C; m 1967 to Carolyn Shelley; c Laura. Educ: Univ Wis, BS, 64; Harvard Univ, MBA, 67; Theta Chi. Polit & Govt Pos: Admin asst, US Rep Matthew F McHugh, NY, 75- Bus & Prof Pos: Asst to pres, Banco Nicaraguense, Managua, Nicaragua, 67-68; securities analyst, Lionel D Edie & Co, New York, 68-69; assoc for anal studies in Off Pres, Mass Inst Technol, 69-72; exec dir, NY-PENN Health Mgt Corp, Binghamton, NY, 72-75. Mailing Add: 625 S Carolina Ave SE Washington DC 20003

CREDLE, LOLA FISH (D)
VChmn, Chesapeake Dem Town Comt, Va
b Louisville, Ky, Jan 3, 22; d Ivan Montez Fish & Ella Noakes F; m 1940 to Byron Elwood Credle; c Burnley (Mrs R D Ganus). Educ: Cradock High Sch, dipl, 39; Kee's Bus Col, 51-52. Polit & Govt Pos: Dep comnr revenue, Chesapeake, Va, 53-64; deleg, Dem Nat Conv, 68; vchmn, Chesapeake Dem Town Comt, 68-; mem bd, Va Fedn Dem Women's Club, 72- Mem: Chesapeake Dem Women's Club (pres, 72-73); Am Red Cross (chmn vol, Portsmouth Chap, 72-); CofC (bd, womens div, 71-); Portsmouth Gen Hosp Auxiliary. Relig: Episcopal. Mailing Add: 1224 Boxwood Dr Chesapeake VA 23323

CREECH, WILLIAM AYDEN (D)
NC State Rep
b Smithfield, NC, Aug 5, 25; s Charles Alderman Creech & Corrie Emelia Hollingsworth C; m 1968 to Sally Wood; c Laurence, Ezekiel & Charles. Educ: Univ Oslo, summer 47; Univ NC, AB in Polit Sci, 48; George Washington Univ, 49 & 52-53; Near East Area Specialization Course, Foreign Serv Inst, Dept State, 52-53; City London Law Sch, cert Eng & comp law, summer 54; Georgetown Univ, JD, 58. Polit & Govt Pos: Chmn comt permanent orgn, NC Dem Conv, 60; aide, Sen Sam Ervin, Jr, 64; cand, US Rep, NC, 66 & 72; alt deleg, Dem Nat Conv, 68; NC State Rep, 75- Bus & Prof Pos: Econ asst, Am Embassy, Baghdad, Iraq, 49-51; int economist, Near East & African Div, Bur Foreign Com, US Dept Com, 52-54; econ officer, Am Embassy, London, Eng, 54-55; prof staff mem, US Senate Comt Small Bus, Washington, DC, 55-58, counsel, 58-59; pvt law practice, Smithfield, NC, 59-61; chief counsel & staff dir, Subcomt Const Rights of US Senate Judiciary Comt, Washington, DC, 61-66; pvt law practice, Raleigh, NC, 65- Publ: Auth, Congress looks to the serviceman's rights, Am Bar Asn J, 11/63; auth, Psychological testing & constitutional rights, Duke Law J, 66; The privacy of government employees, Law & Contemporary Probs, 66; plus others. Mem: NC Bus & Econ Improv Corp (adv comt, 73-); Cameron Park Asn (pres, 73-); Raleigh Little Theatre (pres, 75-); NC Ment Health Asn (bd dirs & exec comt, 71-); NC Am Revolution Bicentennial Comn (vchmn, 67-). Honors & Awards: Jr CofC Distinguished Serv Award, 61; Cert Appreciation, Nat Found, 61; Johnston Co Hist Soc Outstanding Serv Award, 65; Campbell Col Achievement Award, 66. Relig: United Methodist. Legal Res: 1208 College Pl Raleigh NC 27605 Mailing Add: PO Box 826 Raleigh NC 27602

CREEDON, MICHAEL C (D)
Mass State Rep
Mailing Add: State Capitol Boston MA 02133

CREEKMORE, FREDERICK HILLARY (D)
Va State Deleg
b Norfolk, Va, Nov 12, 37; s Allie Robert Creekmore, Sr & Ruth Lilly C; m 1961 to Margery Keith Buchanan; c Mary Stuart, Frederick Hillary, Jr & Carla Ruth. Educ: Univ Richmond, BS, 60; T C Williams Sch Law, JD, 63; Sigma Phi Epsilon. Polit & Govt Pos: Va State Deleg, 74- Bus & Prof Pos: Attorney-at-law, Kellam & Kellam, Norfolk, Va, 63-67, sole practitioner, Chesapeake, Va, 67-72, partner, Creekmore & Rinehart, 72- Mem: Great Bridge Masonic Lodge 257; Great Bridge Royal Arch, Chap 82; Chesapeake Giddeon Camp; Chesapeake & Va State Bar Asns. Honors & Awards: Outstanding Pres, Region 1, Va Jaycees, 66. Relig: Presbyterian; elder, Great Bridge Presby Church. Mailing Add: 261 Bridgeview Circle Chesapeake VA 23320

CREGO, DORIS IMOGEN (R)
b Skaneateles, NY, Mar 1, 14; d Merton Gillett & Dora Herrling G; m 1939 to Ernest A Crego. Educ: Syracuse Univ, BA, 37; Pi Beta Phi. Polit & Govt Pos: Vchmn, Rep Town Comt, Skaneateles, NY, 56-63; coordr, Onondaga Co Rep Comt, NY, 63-69, vchmn, 69-72; deleg, Rep Nat Conv, 72. Mem: Onondaga Co Women's Rep Club; Van Dyne Hosp Guild; Community Gen Hosp Auxiliary; Soc Skaneateles Bus Women. Relig: Episcopal. Mailing Add: 2 East St Skaneateles NY 13152

CREIGHTON, THOMAS EDMUND (D)
Mass State Rep
b Uxbridge, Mass, Feb 1, 22; s Thomas Francis Creighton & Bridie Rice C; m 1947 to Dorothy Helen Departie; c Thomas E, II, Mary Anne, Peter E, Cynthia Jane & William E. Educ: Univ NC, 1 year. Polit & Govt Pos: Mem, Uxbridge Dem Town Comt, Mass, 48-; mem, Uxbridge Bd Selectmen, 50-53 & 54-66; mem various local & area study comts; Mass State Rep, Eighth Worcester Dist, 69-; mem, Mass Comt on Pub Serv, 69-; mem, Mass Comn on Marine Boundaries & Resources, 70- Bus & Prof Pos: Owner, Creightons Paint Serv, Uxbridge, Mass, 47-65; sonic technician, Eastern Div, Wyman-Gornon Co, 67-69. Mil Serv: Entered as Pvt, Marine Corps, 42, released as Cpl, 46, after serv in 1-A-14, 4th Div. Mem: Am Legion; VFW; KofC; Uxbridge Progressive Club; Uxbridge Firemens Asn. Relig: Catholic. Legal Res: 81 Douglas St Uxbridge MA 01569 Mailing Add: State House Boston MA 02133

CREIGHTON, TOM (D)
Tex State Sen
b Mineral Wells, Tex, Feb 26, 27; s John Roy Creighton & Flora Boynton C; m 1950 to Sue

Sparks; c Will, Kenneth & Mark. Educ: Univ Tex, Austin, LLB, 50; Phi Alpha Phi; Delta Chi. Polit & Govt Pos: Co attorney, Palo Pinto Co, Tex, 53-60; Tex State Sen, 22nd Dist, 60- Bus & Prof Pos: Practicing attorney, Creighton & Creighton, 50-65; practicing attorney, Creighton & Cleveland, 65- Mil Serv: Entered as Seaman, Navy, World War II. Mem: State Bar of Tex; Palo Pinto Co Bar Asn; Mineral Wells Lions Club; Am Legion; CofC (mil affairs comt). Honors & Awards: Distinguished Serv Award for outstanding serv to community, Mineral Wells Jaycee Club, 52 & 54; Distinguished Serv Award for community serv, Mineral Wells CofC, 65. Relig: Baptist. Legal Res: Rte 2 Box 208 Mineral Wells TX 76067 Mailing Add: PO Box 546 Mineral Wells TX 76067

CRENSHAW, ANDER **(R)**
Fla State Rep
Legal Res: 4569 Huntington Rd Jacksonville FL 32210 Mailing Add: 329 The Capitol Tallahassee FL 32304

CRENSHAW, THOMAS WILLIAM **(R)**
Chmn, Jasper Co Rep Party, Tex
b Silverton, Tex, July 3, 31; s Leslie Crenshaw & Opal Brock C; m 1954 to Norma Dean Petty; c Kathleen & Leslie Robert. Educ: Univ Houston, 1 year. Polit & Govt Pos: Chmn, Jasper Co Rep Party, Tex, 67- Bus & Prof Pos: Data processing supvr, Tex Elec Serv Co, Ft Worth, Tex, 57-63; head data processing dept, The Visador Co, Jasper, 63- Mil Serv: Entered as Recruit, Army, 49, released as S/Sgt, 52, after serv in 5th Machine Rec Unit, 5th Army Area, 50-52. Publ: Data Processing Opens Doors, J Data Processing, 68; reprinted in NSDJA J, 68. Mem: Data Processing Mgt Asn; Kiwanis. Relig: Church of Christ. Mailing Add: 155 Cinnamon Oaks Jasper TX 75951

CRESIMORE, JAMES LEONARD **(R)**
Chmn, Wake Co Rep Party, NC
b Statesville, NC, Jan 24, 28; s Fred Clayton Cresimore & Cleo Edison C; m 1956 to Mary Josephine Conrad; c James Conrad, Jennifer Cheryl & Joel Clayton. Educ: High Point Col, BS in Bus Admin, 49. Polit & Govt Pos: Deleg, Rep Nat Conv, 64 & 68, mem platform comt, 68; mem, NC Rep Exec Comt, 64-; chmn, Wake Co Rep Party, NC, 64-66 & 72-; mem, NC Rep Cent Comt, 66-; chmn, Fourth Dist Rep Party, NC, 66-70; Rep cand, Wake Co Comnr, 70; chmn, Mayor's Comt on Manpower Develop, Raleigh, currently. Bus & Prof Pos: Exec dir, Home Serv Stores, Inc, High Point, NC, 49-50; co-founder & secy, Consol Wholesale Corp, 53-56; owner & operator, Village Super Mkt, 53-56; chmn bd, Bunker Hill Packing Corp, Bedford, Va, currently; pres, Assoc Brokers, Inc, NC, currently; founding dir, State Bank of Raleigh, 72- Mil Serv: Entered as Pvt, Army, 50, released as Sgt 1/C, 52, after serv in Psychol Warfare Unit, Dept Army in US, 50-52. Mem: Raleigh Food Brokers Asn; Raleigh Sales & Mkt Execs Club; Nat Food Brokers Asn; Raleigh CofC (bd mem, 72-73 & bd dirs, 73-74); Rotary. Relig: Protestant; former Supt of Sunday Sch, Ridge Road Baptist Church, Raleigh. Mailing Add: 3720 Williamsborough Ct Raleigh NC 27609

CRESON, THOMAS KYLE, JR **(R)**
b Memphis, Tenn, Feb 25, 31; s Thomas Kyle Creson & Celeste Walters C; m 1959 to Jayne Suess; c Thomas Kyle, III & Barry Franklin. Educ: Washington & Lee Univ, 49-51; Southwestern Univ, summers 50-52; Univ Tenn Med Sch, MD, 55; internship, residency & fel, Cook Co Hosp, Chicago, Ill, 55-59; Sigma Alpha Epsilon; Royal Club; Univ Club; dipl, Am Col Physicians. Polit & Govt Pos: Vpres, SCoast Young Rep, Calif, 59-61; mem steering comt, Memphis & Shelby Co Rep Party, 65-67, chmn, formerly; pres, Memphis & Shelby Co Young Rep Club, 67-68; chmn, Am Med Polit Action Comt, 67-; cand, Tenn State Rep, 66; deleg, Rep Nat Conv, 68; presidential elector, Ninth Dist, 68 & 72; mem, Pub Health Rev Bd, Memphis & Shelby Co, 68- Bus & Prof Pos: Practice of medicine, Memphis, Tenn, 61-; asst clin prof med, Univ Tenn, 67- Mil Serv: Entered as Lt, Navy, 59, released as Lt Comdr, 61, after serv in Med Corps, El Toro Marine Hosp Base, 59-61. Publ: Treatment of duodenal ulcer, Am J Gastroenterology, 61; What to do before prescribing a hematinic, Consult J, 66; Vagaries of jaundice, Memphis & Mid South Med J, 67. Mem: Am & Tenn Med Asns; fel Am Col Physicians; Physicians & Surgeons J Club; Boy Scouts. Honors & Awards: Gold Trumpet, Boy Scouts. Relig: Presbyterian; Chmn Deacons, Evergreen Presbyterian Church. Mailing Add: 257 S Belvedere Blvd Memphis TN 38104

CRESPO PEREZ, AGAPITO **(POPULAR DEMOCRAT, PR)**
Rep, PR House of Rep
Mailing Add: State Capitol San Juan PR 00901

CRESSOTTI, RICHARD DAVID **(D)**
Conn State Rep
b Hartford, Conn, Nov 6, 36; s John Baptist Cressotti & Adeline Nigora C; m 1959 to Lorraine Sikut; c Terri, Richard, Lisa & Karen. Polit & Govt Pos: Dist chmn, Conn Dem Party, 70-72; city councilman, Enfield, 72-75; Conn State Rep, 75- Bus & Prof Pos: Gen mgr, Frank X Griffin Realty, 70-73; pres, Team Realty, 73- Mil Serv: Entered Marine Corps Res, 58, released as Lance Cpl, 64, after serv in 70th Rifle Co. Mem: Rotary; Elks; Unico; Amvets. Relig: Catholic. Mailing Add: 18 Guild Enfield CT 06082

CRESSWELL, WILLIAM EPHRAIM **(D)**
b Valley, Miss, March 30, 26; s Walter Franklin Cresswell & Charlotte Louise Welch C; m 1946 to Catherine Moore; c Catherine Rosalie, William Ephraim & Stephen Edward. Educ: Univ Miss, 43-48, LLB; Phi Alpha Delta; Sigma Alpha Epsilon. Polit & Govt Pos: Miss State Rep, 52-54; asst attorney gen, Miss, 54-56; exec asst, Gov, 56-57; admin asst to US Sen Stennis, 58- Bus & Prof Pos: Attorney, pvt law practice, Durant, Miss, 48-54. Mil Serv: Air Force, 44-45. Mem: Miss State Bar Asn. Relig: Methodist. Legal Res: MS Mailing Add: 1208 Westgrove Blvd Alexandria VA 22307

CRESSY, ELLEN MARY **(D)**
NH State Rep
b Concord, Mass, July 12, 17; d Patrick Joseph McManus & Mary B White M; m 1935 to Horace Tyler Cressy; c Patricia E (Mrs Sayer) & Brian G. Educ: Cambridge Jr Col, 34-35; Northern Essex Community Col & Univ NH Div Continuing Educ, 68-73; NH Teacher Cert. Polit & Govt Pos: Libr trustee, South Hampton, NH, 50-62, mem const conv, 64-74, mem co conv of gen court, 65-67; mem const conv, South Hampton & Seabrook, NH, 74-, mem gen court, 75-; NH State Rep, 75- Bus & Prof Pos: Owner, Registered Beagle Kennel, 50-75. Mem: Exeter Bus & Prof Women's Club; South Hampton Conserv Comn (chmn, 65-75); Fidelity Grange (chaplain, 68-75); Friends of Odiorne Point State Park (educ chmn, 71-75); life mem NH Cong Parents & Teachers. Relig: Catholic. Legal Res: Main St South Hampton NH 01913 Mailing Add: RFD 1 Amesbury MA 01913

CREW, WILLIAM LUNSFORD **(D)**
b Northamton Co, NC, Oct 29, 17; s James Winfield Crew, Sr & Texas S C; m 1940 to Nancy Horney; c Nancy A (Mrs Butler) & William Lunsford, Jr. Educ: Univ NC, AB, Law Sch, LLB; Phi Gamma Delta. Polit & Govt Pos: NC State Sen, 53-63, pres pro tem, NC State Senate, 61; chmn, NC State Dem Exec Comt, 63-64. Mil Serv: Entered as A/S, Navy, 43, released as Lt(jg), 46, after serv in Pac Area; Presidential Unit Citation. Mem: NC & Am Bar Asns; NC State Bar; Am Legion; VFW. Relig: Episcopal. Legal Res: Sunset Ave Roanoke Rapids NC 27870 Mailing Add: Box 160 Roanoke Rapids NC 27870

CREWS, JACK **(D)**
Wyo State Rep
Mailing Add: Box 892 Cheyenne WY 82001

CREWS, JOHN ROBERT **(R)**
Chmn, Kings Co Rep Comt, NY
b Brooklyn, NY, July 4, 94; s John Collins Crews & Emma Woolley C; m 1917 to Florence Marie Specht. Educ: Heffley Inst. Hon Degrees: LLD, St Francis Col, 69. Polit & Govt Pos: NY State Assemblyman, 21-22; deleg, Rep Nat Conv, 24-68; chief clerk, Munic Court, New York, 26-29, tax comnr, 29-33, comnr elec, 43-66; mem exec comt, NY Rep State Comt, 33-; chmn, Kings Co Rep Comt, currently. Bus & Prof Pos: Trustee, Hamburg Savings Bank; adv comt, Bank of Com. Mem: Brooklyn Real Estate Bd; Mason (33 degree); Shrine; Brooklyn Club; Munic Club. Relig: Episcopal. Legal Res: 25 Monroe Pl Brooklyn NY 11201 Mailing Add: 16 Court St Brooklyn NY 11201

CREWS, JON THOMAS **(D)**
b Waterloo, Iowa, Oct 30, 46; s Thomas Leo Crews & Burdene Livingstone C; m 1969 to Pamela Sue Sommer. Educ: US Mil Acad, 65-67; Univ Northern Iowa, BA, 70; Phi Mu Alpha; Sinfonia. Polit & Govt Pos: Mayor, City of Cedar Falls, Iowa, 71-; deleg, Dem Nat Conv, 72. Mem: Jaycees; Optimist Club; CofC. Honors & Awards: Distinguished Serv Award, Jaycees, 73. Relig: Methodist. Mailing Add: 2417 Main St Cedar Falls IA 50613

CRIBBS, THEO **(D)**
Kans State Rep
b Vernon, Ala, Mar 11, 15; c Charlie Cribbs & Isabella Marchbank C; m 1949 to Vera Lee Boone; c Theo, Jr, Tommie Horace & Lois Jean. Educ: Lamar Co Training Sch, grad. Polit & Govt Pos: Kans State Rep, 73- Bus & Prof Pos: Asst supvr, LL 834 Machinist Union, 55-72, shop steward, 65- Mem: John Chiuneth Lodge 109; Le Flambeau Club; Penhouse Club. Relig: Methodist; trustee, African Methodist Episcopal Church, 60- Mailing Add: 3801 S Oliver Wichita KS 67210

CRICHTON, JACK ALSTON **(R)**
Mem, Dallas Co Rep Finance Comt, Tex
b Crichton, La, Oct 16, 16; s Tom J Crichton & Mary Boyleston C; m 1952 to Marilyn Berry; c Anne & Cathy. Educ: Tex A&M Univ, BS, 37, Prof Degree, 52; Mass Inst Technol, MS, 38; Southern Methodist Univ, 48; Tau Beta Pi; Sigma Alpha Epsilon; varsity basketball, tennis & cross country, Tex A&M Univ. Polit & Govt Pos: Deleg, Rep Nat Conv, 64; cand for Gov, Tex, 64; former Tex State Rep Comt; chmn, Ronald Reagan Luncheon Comt, Dallas, 67; mem, Dallas Co Rep Finance Comt, 67-; deleg, Dallas Co Rep Conv, 68 & 72, deleg, Tex State Rep Conv, 68, 70 & 72; designated mem, Electoral Col, Tex, 68; mem, Tex Rep Comt on Fed Employ, 68- Bus & Prof Pos: Vpres, DeGolyer & MacNaughton, 46-50; vpres, San Juan Oil Co, 51-53, pres, Oil & Gas Mgt, 53-59, Nafco Oil & Gas, 59-63, Crichton & Co, 63-, Dallas Resources, Inc, 63- & Arabian Shield Develop Co, 67-; mem bd dirs, Dorchester Gas Producing Co, 55-; Am Petroleum Inst Deleg to Rumania, 63; mem bd gov, Northwood Country Club, Dallas, 72; bd dirs, Clark Oil & Ref Co, 72-; mem bd dirs, Fla Gas Co. Mil Serv: Entered as 1st Lt, Army Air Force, 41, released as Maj, 46, after serv in 487th Heavy Bomb Group, ETO, 44-45; Col, Army Res, 46-53, Army Intel Res, 53-67, Col (Ret); Bronze Star; Air Medal; ETO Medal with Six Battle Stars; Pre Pearl Harbor Ribbon; Legion of Merit. Publ: The Dynamic Natural Gas Industry, Univ Okla, 63; Critical Review Estimating Gas Reserves, Petroleum Technol, 58. Mem: Am Asn Petroleum Geologists; Soc Petroleum Engrs; Soc Petroleum Eval Engrs; Dallas Petroleum Engrs; Am Legion. Honors & Awards: Nominated for Tex A&M Athletic Hall of Fame; Jimmy Williams Award for Distinguished Serv, 71. Relig: Presbyterian; Elder, Preston Hollow Presbyterian Church. Mailing Add: 7027 Orchid Lane Dallas TX 75230

CRIM, BOBBY D **(D)**
Mich State Sen
b Kennett, Mo, Dec 10, 31; m 1953 to Lila F Vogel; c Donald Wayne, Douglas William & David Warren. Educ: Univ Mich, Flint, BA. Polit & Govt Pos: Mem zoning bd appeals, fire comnr, mayor pro tem & councilman, Davison, Mich, formerly; Mich State Rep, 64-66; Mich State Sen, 75- Bus & Prof Pos: Teacher. Mil Serv: Navy, 4 years. Mem: Lions; Flint & Mich Educ Asns; Am Fedn Teachers; Am Legion. Honors & Awards: Davison Jr CofC Young Man of Year Award, 64. Relig: Protestant. Mailing Add: 223 Juniper Dr Davison MI 48423

CRISLER, ROBERT MORRIS **(D)**
La State Rep
b Columbia, Mo, Jan 5, 21; s Otto Smith Crisler & Ruby Buckman C; m 1943 to Shirley Spohn; c Charles Robert & John Allen. Educ: Univ Mo, AB, 41; Northwestern Univ, MS, 47 & PhD, 49; Sigma Xi; Delta Theta Phi; Delta Upsilon. Polit & Govt Pos: La State Rep, 72- Bus & Prof Pos: Asst prof geog, Washington Univ, 48-54; assoc prof geog, Univ Southwestern La, 54-57, head dept social studies, 56-72, prof geog, 57-74. Mil Serv: Entered as Pvt, Army, 42, released as 1st Lt, 46, after serv in 88th Div, Italy, 44-45; recalled as 1st Lt, Army, Mil Intel, 50-52; Purple Heart with cluster. Publ: Republican areas in Missouri, Mo Hist Rev, 1/48; The regional status of Little Dixie in Missouri & Little Egypt in Illinois, J Geog, 11/50; co-auth, The rivers & bayous of Louisiana, La Educ Research Asn, 68. Mem: Asn Am Geogr; Nat Coun Geog Educ; Southwestern Social Sci Asn; La Hist Asn; La Consumers League. Relig: Presbyterians. Mailing Add: 154 Ronald Blvd Lafayette LA 70501

CRISP, JACK W **(D)**
b Omar, WVa, Sept 2, 30; s James Crisp, Sr & Nell Jarrell C; m 1947 to Glenna Ruth Ratliff; c James J, Glen T, Thomas A & Carlanell. Educ: Massey Tech Inst, Jacksonville, Fla, grad in electronics, 60; Am Detective Training Sch, Chicago, grad in criminal invest. Polit & Govt Pos: Precinct committeeman, Meigs Co Dem Exec Comt, Ohio, 64; chmn, Leading Creek Watershed Asn, 66-; pres, Leading Creek Conserv Dist, 66-; participating mem, Dem Nat Comt, formerly. Mem: Aircraft Owners & Pilots Asn; Odd Fellows; F&AM; Dist Six Ancillary Manpower Planning Bd. Honors & Awards: Gov Comt Voc Rehabilitation Cert

Outstanding Serv by both Local & State Odd Fellows. Relig: Church of Christ; minister. Mailing Add: Rte 1 Langsville OH 45741

CRISP, MARY D (R)
Rep Nat Committeewoman, Ariz
b Allentown, Pa, Nov 5, 23; m 1948 to William E Crisp, MD; c William, Barbara & Anne. Educ: Oberlin Col, BA, 46; Ariz State Univ, MA in Polit Sci, 75; Ariz Acad; Ariz Town Hall. Polit & Govt Pos: Dep registr, Ariz, 61-; mem, Ariz State Rep Cent Comt, 62-68, vchmn, 71-; vpres, Scottsdale Rep Women, 62, chmn educ comt, 63-65; Rep precinct committeewoman, Maricopa Co Rep Cent Comt, 62-, precinct capt, 64-68, chmn precinct educ comt, 68, vchairwoman, 68-70; chmn prog & educ comts, Ariz Fedn Rep Women, 66-68, educ adv coordr, 70; vpres, Ariz Rep Workshops, 67, bd mem, 67-, pres, 68-70; mem, Goldwater State Comt, 68; state chmn, 17th Annual Rep Women's Conf, 68; chmn educ comt, Paradise Rep Women, 68-69; co-chmn, Host & Hostess Comt, Gov Inaugural Ball, 71; chmn women's div, Rep Nat Finance Comt, 71-; regional conf chmn, 18th Nat Rep Women's Conf, 72; Rep Nat Committeewoman, Ariz, 72- Bus & Prof Pos: With, Children's Aid Soc, Lehigh Co, Allentown, Pa, 47; asst dir admissions, Cedar Crest Col, 47, assoc dir admissions, 50; cryptographer, US Army Intel, Washington, DC, 49; asst dir personnel-social security, Harvard Univ, 52. Mem: Nat Found March of Dimes; Gov Comn Status Women; charter mem Trunk & Tusk; charter mem Early Birds. Relig: Unitarian. Mailing Add: 6051 E Cactus Wren Rd Scottsdale AZ 85253

CRIST, BETTY JOANNE (D)
Mem, Colo State Dem Exec Comt
b Bonaparte, Iowa, Aug 17, 35; d Arthur Walter Roberts & Roberta Easter R; m 1956 to Ronald Dean Crist, div; c Shari Lynn, Jaye Ronald, Tracy Elizabeth & Jennifer Anne. Educ: Univ Northern Iowa, AEd, 55; Community Col of Denver, 70; Elementa-Ki. Polit & Govt Pos: Kennedy vol, Arvada, Colo, 68; committeewoman, Jefferson Co Dem Party, Colo, 68-69, vcapt, 69, capt, 69-; registration co-chmn, Jefferson Co, 71-72; mem Colo State Cent Dem Comt, 71-72; deleg, Dem Nat Conv, 72; co-chmn, McGovern Womens Nat Adv Coun, 72; off mgr, Vollack US Senate Campaign, 72; staff aide, Colo State Senate, 73-; vchmn, Second Cong Dist Dem Comt, 73-; mem, Colo State Dem Exec Comt, 73- Bus & Prof Pos: Elem teacher, Washington, Iowa, 55-57, Keosauqua, 58-60 & Keokuk, 61-64. Publ: Articles in Colo Dem Weekly. Mem: Arvada Group Home Bd (acting secy, 71-); Joint Homeowner's Coun (vpres, 74-75); Arvada Housing Task Force; Eastern Arvada Concerned Citizens Asn (secy, 72); Lutheran Church Women (prog dir, 72-73). Relig: Lutheran. Mailing Add: 6772 Quay Ct Arvada CO 80003

CRIST, HAROLD HOWARD (R)
Chmn, Scott Co Rep Comt, Kans
b Scott City, Kans, May 18, 08; s John Eli Crist & Mattie Shores C; m 1934 to Alam F Rodabaugh; c Nancy (Mrs Templeton), Robert D & Richard J. Educ: McPherson Col, BS, 30; Colo State Univ, MS, 39. Polit & Govt Pos: Mem, Scott Co Rep Comt, Kans, 42-, chmn, 48-; mem, Scott City Rep Comt, 42-, chmn, 48-; mem, Kans State Bd of Educ, 69- Bus & Prof Pos: Coach, Zook High Sch, Kans, 30-31; prin, Roxbury High Sch, 32-40; supt of schs, Enterprise, 40-42; owner & mgr, Garden Bowl, Garden City, 55-; mgr, Crist Farms, Scott City, 42- Mem: State High Sch Activities Asn; Kans State & Nat Teacher's Asns; Elks; CofC. Honors & Awards: Man of the Year, Farm Bur, 56; Kans Bankers Award, 58; Master Farmer of Kans, 61. Relig: Church of Brethren; Minister. Mailing Add: 1302 Church Scott City KS 67871

CRISTOBAL, ADRIAN L (D)
Sen, Guam Legis
b Agana, Guam, Dec 10, 21; s Adriano M Cristobal (deceased) & Carmen De Leon Untalan C (deceased); m 1953 to Concepcion T Finona; c Carmen J J F, Adrian L F, Jr & John G F. Educ: Guam Eve Sr High, dipl, 40. Polit & Govt Pos: Sen, Guam Legis, 53-64 & 71-, chmn comt agr & natural resources, 56-64, chmn comt gen govt opers, 71-74, mem comt on rules, 71-, mem comt ethics & standards, comt judiciary & consumer protection, comt pub safety, mil & vet affairs, comt youth & sr citizens & minority leader, 75-; chmn, Popular Dem Party Guam, 56-58; chmn, Guam Econ Develop Comn, 60-62; Dem Nat Committeeman, Guam, 60-64; mem exec comt, Dem Party Guam, 70-; mem, Intergovt Rels Comt, Nat Conf State Legis, 75- Bus & Prof Pos: Proprietor & mgr, Nito Store & Market, Barrigada, Guam, 50-67; pub rels officer, Commercial Port Guam, Govt Guam, 67-69; exec asst, Ricky Auto Co, Agana, 69-72. Mil Serv: Entered as Seaman 2/C, Navy, 41, released as Musician 1/C, 46, after serv in Pac Fleet; Good Conduct Medal; Am Pac-Asiatic Campaign Victory Medal; World War II Medal. Mem: Young Men's League Guam; PTA; Elks. Relig: Roman Catholic. Legal Res: Block 12 Lot 10 Ungaguan St Barrigada GU 96913 Mailing Add: PO Box 5001 Barrigada GU 96913

CRITCHLOW, RONALD GLENN (D)
Chmn, Daviess Co Dem Party, Ind
b Washington, Ind, Aug 15, 47; s William James Critchlow & Joyce Moore C; m 1968 to Dora Regina Daily; c Brian Joseph & Rhonda Jean. Educ: Washington High Sch, grad, 65. Polit & Govt Pos: Chmn, Daviess Co Dem Party, Ind, 74- Bus & Prof Pos: Sports ed, Washington Times-Herald, Ind, 65- Mil Serv: E-4, Army Res, 66-72. Mem: Am Legion; 40 et 8. Relig: Christian. Mailing Add: 518 NW Sixth St Washington IN 47501

CRIVELLA, BARBARA ANN (R)
b Washington, DC, Jan 6, 38; d Joseph Cavalier Crivella, Sr & Annette Erdesky C; single. Educ: Notre Dame Acad, Washington, DC, 4 years. Polit & Govt Pos: Exec secy, US Rep Albert W Johnson, Pa, 67- Mem: Rep Women of Capitol Hill; Cong Staff Club. Relig: Catholic. Mailing Add: 8309 Donoghue Dr New Carrollton MD 20784

CROASDALE, CARL PALMER (R)
Chmn, First Cong Dist Rep Party, Va
b Palmer, Va, Aug 22, 16; s Thomas Starr Croasdale & Edna Robertson C; m 1953 to Betty Bartelt; c Elizabeth P, Edward B & Carolinda. Educ: Bus Training. Polit & Govt Pos: Secy, Lancaster Co Rep Party, Va, 50-65, chmn, 65-70; alt deleg, Rep Nat Conv, 68; mem, Am Fisheries Adv Comt, 70-; chmn, First Cong Dist Rep Party, Va, 71- Bus & Prof Pos: Owner & operator, Hardware & Gen Merchandise Store, Palmer, 20 yrs; owner & operator, C P Croasdale Seafood, Palmer, presently; dealing in oysters primarily as planter & packer; mem bd trustees, Va Inst Marine Sci, 72- Mil Serv: Entered as Pvt, Army, 42, released as S/Sgt, in supply, 45, after serv in 552 Engrs, European Theater-landed, Omaha Beach, Normandy; Five Battle Campaigns. Mem: Shellfish Inst NAm; Am Legion. Mailing Add: Box 280-B Rte 1 White Stone VA 22578

CROCE, LEWIS HENRY (R)
Chmn, Blue Earth Co Rep Party, Minn
b Washington, DC, Dec 21, 33; s Robert Croce & Bessie V Johnson C; m 1958 to Nancy Lee Bowen; c James, Robert, Nancy, Linda & Edward, Educ: George Washington Univ, AA, 56; Univ Md, BA, 58, MA, 65, PhD, 68; Omicron Delta Kappa; Phi Alpha Theta; Sigma Chi. Polit & Govt Pos: Judge of elections, Montgomery Co, Md, 60-64; mem, Minn Rep State Cent Comt, 71-; chmn, Blue Earth Co Rep Party, 73- Bus & Prof Pos: Prof hist, Mankato State Col, 68-; sr lectr hist, Univ London, 72-73; tutorial fel, Oxford Univ, summer 73. Mil Serv: Entered as Airman, Air Force, 58, released as Airman 1/C, 61. Mem: Am & Southern Hist Asns; Orgn Am Historians. Relig: Lutheran. Mailing Add: 1117 Marsh St Mankato MN 56001

CROCKER, KENNETH WAYNE (R)
b Union City, Tenn, Nov 3, 33; s Birchie Crocker & Lillie McCartney C; m 1952 to Sue Belew; c Mark Wayne & Suzanne. Educ: Union Univ (Tenn), BS, 55; Alpha Tau Omega. Polit & Govt Pos: Pres, Gibson Co Young Rep, Tenn, 67-68; chmn, Gibson Co Rep Party, formerly; Tenn State Rep, 70-74; deleg, Rep Nat Conv, 72; vchmn local adv comt, Off Econ Opportunity, 72-73. Bus & Prof Pos: Co-owner, Crocker's Lucky Food Store, 45- Mil Serv: Entered as Pvt, Army, 56, released as SP-5, 57, after serv in 28th Inf Regt, 8th Div, Ger, 56-57. Mem: Nat Soc State Legislators (bd gov, 72-); Bradford CofC; Am Legion; Farm Bur. Honors & Awards: Distinguished Serv Award, Jaycees. Relig: Baptist. Mailing Add: Box 13 Bradford TN 38316

CROCKER, VIRGINIA LEAMAN (GINGER) (D)
VChmn, Laurens Co Dem Party, SC
b Clinton, SC, Sept 9, 51; d Claude Arthur Crocker & Myra Adair C; single. Educ: Columbia Col, SC, BA, speech & drama, 73; Columbia Col Dance Co. Polit & Govt Pos: Chmn, Clinton High Sch Teen Dem, 65-69; vchmn, Columbia Col Young Dem, 70-71, chmn, 71-73; deleg, Nat Young Dem Conv, 71 & 73; chmn, Youth Involvement Activities, 72; deleg, SC State Dem Conv, 72; alt deleg, Dem Nat Conv, 72; vchmn, Laurens Co Dem Party, 72-; mem, Comt to Study Reorgn of Dem Party SC, 73. Publ: Co-ed, South Carolina Speech Communication Association Newsletter, 73. Mem: SC & Laurens Co Dem Women's Couns; SC Speech Commun Asn (youth chmn, 70-); Columbia Col Players (pres, 72-73); Columbia Col Alumnae Asn. Relig: Presbyterian. Mailing Add: Merrie Oakes Clinton SC 29325

CROCKETT, J ALLAN
Justice, Utah Supreme Court
b Smithfield, Utah, 1906; s John Allan Crockett & Rachel Maretta Homer C; m 1934 to Eulalia Smith; c Calvin; two granddaughters. Educ: Univ Utah, LLB, 31 & BA, 46; Order of the Coif. Polit & Govt Pos: Asst attorney, Salt Lake Co, Utah, 33-38; dist judge, 40-50; justice, Utah Supreme Court, 51-, chief justice, 59-60 & 67-72; chmn, Judicial Conf of Utah, 67- Publ: Initiated writing & publ of manual for Justices of the Peace & edited & published Jury Instr Forms for Utah. Mem: Utah Legal Aid Soc; Nat Legal Aid & Defender Asn; Regional Traffic Court Conf of Utah; Regional Safety Confs; Nat Conf of Chief Justices. Mailing Add: Utah Supreme Court State Capitol Salt Lake City UT 84114

CROCKETT, KATHERINE WELSH (R)
Chmn, NC Fedn of Young Rep
b Cham, Ger, Nov 17, 46; d Robert Brownlee Welsh & Marie-Luise Osmers W; m 1966 to James Allen Crockett, Jr; c James Allen, III. Educ: Queens Col, NC, BA, 68. Polit & Govt Pos: Mem steering comt, Doug Wheeler for the House, Mecklenburg Co, NC, 68; adv, TAR, Mecklenburg Co, 68-71; awards chmn exec bd, NC Fedn Young Rep, 71, vhcmn, Fedn, 71-73, chmn, 74-; chmn subcomt attracting new people, NC Rep Forum Panel, 71; orgn chmn, Mathis for the House Comt, Mecklenburg Co, 72; Nixonette chmn, Young Voters for the President in NC, 72; alt deleg, Rep Nat Conv, 72; secy, Precinct 57, Mecklenburg Co, 72-73; research asst, NC Rep Carolyn Mathis, Mecklenburg Co, currently; mem, NC Rep State Cent Comt, 74-; training chmn, Mecklenburg Co Exec Bd, 74-; orgn chmn, Crockett for Senate, Mecklenburg & Cabarrus Co, 74- Bus & Prof Pos: Model, June Agar Models & Trim Modeling Agency, 61-, instr, June Agar Models, 68-70; acct rep, Mkt Assocs, 68-69, mkt asst, 69-71; model dir, Trim Modeling Agency, 72- Mem: Mecklenburg Young Rep Club (exec bd, liaison officer to TAR, 68-71, secy, 70-72, vchmn, 72-73, exec bd leadership chmn); Mecklenburg Asn Retarded Children; Mecklenburg Womens Polit Caucus (exec bd). Relig: Presbyterian. Mailing Add: 4719 Rounding Run Rd Mathews NC 28105

CROCKETT, KENNEDY MCCAMPBELL
b Kingsville, Tex, Jan 1920; s Frank H Crockett & Alice Kennedy C; m 1943 to Mary Campbell; c John Kennedy, Laura (Mrs Wendell Loftis), Judy (Mrs Federico Faerron), Mary Melinda & Teresa Alice. Educ: NTex Agr Col, 37-39; Univ Tex, Austin, 39-42. Polit & Govt Pos: With Foreign Serv, 43-72, with Consulate, Nuevo Laredo, Mex, 43-44, vconsul, 44-47, prin officer, Consulate, La Ceiba, Honduras, 47-48, vconsul, Embassy, Mexico City, Mex, 48-51, prin off & Am Consul, Tampico, 51-55, staff asst & spec asst on consular affairs, Dept of State, 55-56, officer in charge of Mex Affairs, 56-57, first secy, Embassy, Guatemala, 57-60, Am consul gen, Tijuana, Mex, 60-62, dep dir, Off of Mex & Caribbean Affairs, 62-63, dir, Off Caribbean Affairs, Dept of State & Agency Int Develop, 64-65, counr, Embassy, San Jose, Costa Rica, 65-67, US Ambassador, Nicaragua, 67-72. Bus & Prof Pos: Consult, Standard Fruit Co of Nicaragua & cattle rancher, Nicaragua, 71- Honors & Awards: Superior Honor Award, Dept of State, 66. Legal Res: 1602 Washington St Laredo TX 78040 Mailing Add: Apartado 18 Rivas Nicaragua

CROCKETT, SAM L (D)
Chmn, Bristol City Dem Comt, Va
b Chilhowie, Va, Mar 2, 34; s Sam B Crockett & Gladys Merrihue C; m 1957 to Sally Allen; c Suzanne & Kathleen. Educ: Emory & Henry Col, BA, 55. Polit & Govt Pos: Liaison asst, Rep W Pat Jennings, 64-66; chmn, Bristol City Dem Comt, Va, 74- Bus & Prof Pos: Dir personnel, Bristol Steel & Iron Works, Inc, 71- Mil Serv: SP-4, Army, 56-59, after serv in finance & acct, BASEC, COM 2, 57-59. Relig: United Methodist. Mailing Add: 78 Clover Lane Bristol VA 24201

CROCKETT, STEPHEN ROBERT (D)
Treas, Kennebec Co Dem Comt, Maine
b Livermore Falls, Maine, Nov 23, 33; s Robert Edward Crockett & Kathleen Richmond C; m 1957 to Sandra Jane Wheelock; c Ned Stephen, Lynn Toby & Belinda Alice. Educ: Gates Bus Col, 68. Polit & Govt Pos: Treas, Kennebec Co Dem Comt, Maine, 69- Bus & Prof Pos: Vpres, Bank of Maine, 66- Mil Serv: Entered Navy, 62, released as E-5, 66, after serv in Patrol Squadron 23, Brunswick Naval Air Sta, Maine; Good Conduct Medal; Korean Conflict

Medal. Mem: Lions; Elks; State of Maine Park & Recreation Comt; Nat Asn of Acct; Am Inst Banking. Relig: Protestant. Mailing Add: Two Orchard St Augusta ME 04330

CROFOOT, JOHN WILLIAM (R)
Kans State Sen
b Newton, Kans, Mar 24, 27; s Ray Freeman Crofoot & Louise Grimwood C; m 1948 to Marian Lucille Hurst; c David, Pamela (Mrs Steve Hett) & James. Educ: Kans State Univ, 45-48; Alpha Gamma Rho. Polit & Govt Pos: Rep precinct committeeman, Cottonwood Twp, 50-71; chmn, Chase Co Rep Party, 58; Kans State Sen, 12th Dist, 71-72, 17th Dist, 72- Bus & Prof Pos: Pres, Western Assocs, Inc, 52-; vpres, Crofoot & Robinson, Inc, 53-; vchmn, Specialty Advert Asn Int, currently. Mil Serv: Entered as A/S, Navy, 45, released as S/C, 46, after serv in Seabees. Mem: Am Legion; Elks; Automobile Club of Kans (vpres). Relig: Methodist. Mailing Add: Cedar Point KS 66843

CROFT, LELAND CHANCY (D)
Alaska State Sen
b Jennings, La, Aug 21, 37; s Leland Reynolds Croft & Dorothy Elizabeth Chancy C; m 1963 to Anita Toni Ruth Williamson; c Eric Chancy, Kimberly Geraldine & Lee Conwell. Educ: Univ Tex, BA, 59, LLB, 61; Phi Gamma Delta. Polit & Govt Pos: Mem bd dirs, Alaska Legal Serv Corp, 68-; Alaska State Rep, 69-70; Alaska State Sen, 71-, pres of senate, 75- Bus & Prof Pos: Partner, Croft & Bailey, currently. Mil Serv: Entered as Seaman Recruit, Naval Res, 54, released as A/S, 62. Publ: Revisor, Alaska Law Sect, Probate Counsel, 68-71. Mem: Tex, Alaska & Anchorage Bar Asns. Relig: Protestant. Legal Res: 1511 G St Anchorage AK 99501 Mailing Add: 425 G St Suite 710 Anchorage AK 99501

CROMER, ELLA MAE (R)
b Bozeman, Mont, June 19, 16; d Gordon Milton Mandeville & Millie Burtch M; m 1937 to John William Cromer; c Edward Gordon, Donald William & Richard Frank. Educ: Mont State Univ, 35-37. Polit & Govt Pos: Vchmn, Gallatin Co Rep Party, Mont, 59-62; mem, Bd of Insts, 63-71; budget & finance chmn, Mont Fedn of Rep Women, 64-67, 72-74; conv chmn, Mont Fedn of Rep Clubs, 65; deleg, Rep State Conv, 68; alt deleg, Rep Nat Conv, 68; Cong committeewoman, Silver Bow Co, 70- Mem: Int Christian Univ of Japan (trustee, 54-); Mont Heart Asn; Mont Asn for Ment Retarded; Mont Asn for Ment Ill; Mont Tuberc Asn. Honors & Awards: Int Peace Scholar given to student from Philippines known as Ella Mae Cromer Scholar, 59. Relig: Presbyterian; First Woman Elder in Butte Church. Mailing Add: 3025 Moulton Butte MT 59701

CRONAN, IRENE M (D)
Chmn, Cheboygan Co Dem Party, Mich
b Detroit, Mich, Mar 20, 36; d James E Gardner & Irene M Penoyer G; div; c John W, Joseph E & Anne Elizabeth. Educ: Cheboygan Cath Cent High Sch, grad, 55; Inst Childrens Lit, 73-75. Polit & Govt Pos: Chmn, Grant Twp Dem Party, 62-66, deleg, 64-; vchmn, Cheboygan Co Dem Party, Mich, 62-75, chmn, 75-; chmn, Voter Regist/Get Out the Vote Campaign, 68-; Dem cand, Cheboygan Co Comnr, Dist 2, 72 & 74. Publ: Annexation vs consolidation, Questions & Answers, School Millage, Questions & Answers, Cheboygan Daily Tribune, 63-65; Alverno, social column, Cheboygan Daily Tribune, 74-; Young people's book review, Cheboygan News, 75- Mem: Mich Asn for Children with Learning Disabilities (publicity chmn, 73-); 4-H Orgn; Daughters of Isabella; St Francis Alverno Rosary Soc; Cheboygan High Sch Choir (hon mem, 75-). Honors & Awards: Five Year Leadership Pin, 4-H Orgn, 74; Selected honorary deleg to 25th Jefferson-Jackson Day Dinner at Cobo Hall, 11 Dist, 75. Relig: Roman Catholic. Mailing Add: Rte 2 Owens Rd Cheboygan MI 49721

CRONIN, PAUL WILLIAM (R)
b Boston, Mass, Mar 14, 38; s William Joseph Cronin & Anna Murphy C; m 1957 to Kathleen Sears; c Kevin P & Kimberley A. Educ: Merrimack Col, 56-58; Boston Univ, BA, 62; fel, John F Kennedy Grad Sch Govt, Harvard Univ, 68-69, MPA, 69; SBK. Polit & Govt Pos: Mem & precinct capt, Andover Rep Town Comt, Mass, 60-; deleg, Rep State Convs, 62-66 & 70; selectman, Town of Andover, 63-66; admin asst, Cong F Bradford Morse, 63-67; Mass State Rep, 67-69; deleg, Rep Nat Conv, 68 & 72; northeast regional dir, Rep Cong Campaign Comt, 69-70; US Rep, Fifth Dist, Mass, 73-74. Mem: Mass Selectmans Asn; Mass Legis Asn; Nat Asn State Legis; Partners of Alliance; Elks. Honors & Awards: Outstanding Young Man award, Jaycees; Foreign Policy Asn Future Leader; Paul Revere Leadership Medal; Young Rep Outstanding Citizen Award; DAV Distinguished Serv Award. Relig: Roman Catholic. Mailing Add: 8 Punchard Ave Andover MA 01810

CROOK, MAUREEN CATHERINE (R)
b Detroit, Mich, Sept 4, 48; d William Francis Crook & Madeline Rita Kenney C; single. Educ: Nazareth Col, BA, 70; Univ Detroit, 71; Student Educ Asn; Dean's List; Drama Club; Nat Student Asn. Polit & Govt Pos: Dist vchmn, Mich Rep State Youth Coun, 71-72; precinct deleg, Oakland Co Rep Party, 72-; deleg, Rep Nat Conv, 72; nat committeewoman, Mich Fedn of Young Rep, 72; chmn, Nixon Youth Spokesman Bur, 72; co vchmn, Mich Young Rep, 72- Bus & Prof Pos: Employ interviewer, Detroit Bank & Trust Co, 72-; admin asst house Rep staff, Mich House Reps, currently. Honors & Awards: Outstanding Young Rep of Year, Mich Fedn of Young Rep, 70-71. Relig: Catholic. Mailing Add: House Rep Off The Capitol Lansing MI 48902

CROOK, ROBERT LACEY (D)
Miss State Sen
b Bolton, Miss, Apr 22, 29; s Walter Barber Crook & Louise Lacey; m 1953 to Brigita V Nerings; c Robert Lacey, II & Hubert William. Educ: Univ Miss, 52-53; Jackson Sch Law, LLB, 65. Polit & Govt Pos: Deleg, Dem State Conv, Miss, 60 & 64; state dir, Miss Civil Defense Coun, 60-63; admin asst to Gov, Miss, 63; Miss State Sen, 64- Mil Serv: Entered as Pvt, Marine Corps, 49, released as Cpl, 52. Mem: Sunflower Co & Miss State Bar Asns; Am Legion; Sons of Confederate Vets; 40 et 8. Relig: Episcopal. Mailing Add: PO Box 85 Ruleville MS 38771

CROOKS, SAMUEL COULTER (D)
RI State Rep
b Belfast, NIreland, Nov 11, 14; nat citizen; s James Crooks (deceased) & Margaret Coulter C; m 1942 to Gladys Catherine Priestley; c Bruce Philip, Barry James, Samuel C, Jr & Brian William. Educ: Brown Univ, AB, 48. Polit & Govt Pos: RI State Rep, 59th Dist, 69- Bus & Prof Pos: Asst personnel mgr, Collyer Insulated Wire Co, Lincoln, RI, 48-50, asst sales mgr, 53-56, plant supt, 56-61, gen traffic & distributional mgr, 61- Mil Serv: Entered as Pvt, Army, 42, released as Col, 52, after serv in Korea, 50-52, Army Res & Nat Guard, 52-67 (Ret); Commendation Medal; Bronze Star. Mem: Elks; F&AM; VFW; Am Legion. Relig: Protestant. Mailing Add: 67 Chapel St Lincoln RI 02865

CROSBY, JANE A (R)
Mem, Rep State Cent Comt, Calif
b Pasadena, Calif, March 31, 20; d Robert Frederick Aldridge & Florence Elizabeth Scott A; m 1938 to Joseph Marshall Crosby; c Joseph Scott & William Marshall. Educ: Pasadena City Jr Col; Woodbury Bus Col. Polit & Govt Pos: Mem bd, South Pasadena Rep Women, Federated, Calif, 60-68, pres, 71-72; assoc mem, Rep State Cent Comt Calif, 60-69, mem, 69-; one of many founders, United Rep Calif, 63, vol state off mgr, 66-68; registr of voters, Los Angeles Co, 64-69; vol state off mgr, Max Rafferty for US Senate Campaign, 68; mem exec comt to Elect John Rousselot to Cong, 70 & 72. Mem: South Pasadena Americanism Ctr. Honors & Awards: Betsy Ross Award, First Congregational Church of Los Angeles, 62; Woman of the Year, South Pasadena Bus & Prof Women's Club, 66-67. Relig: Congregational. Mailing Add: 316 Alta Vista Dr South Pasadena CA 91030

CROSBY, JOSEPH MARSHALL (R)
Mem Exec Comt, Rep State Cent Comt Calif
b Bishop, Calif, Dec 7, 19; s Joseph Junius Crosby & Mary Elizabeth Gibson C; m 1938 to Margaret Jane Aldridge; c Joseph Scott & William Marshall. Polit & Govt Pos: Pres, Calif Rep Assembly, 54th Assembly Dist, 62; one of many founders, United Rep Calif, 63, state chmn, 66-68; mem exec comt, Max Rafferty for US Sen Campaign, 68; deleg, Rep Nat Conv, 68; pub mem, Bd State Calif Dept Prof & Voc Standards, 69-; pub mem, Calif State Bd Registr for Geologists, 69-; mem exec comt, Rep State Cent Comt, Calif, 70-; treas, US Rep John Rousselot, Calif, 70- Mil Serv: 1st Lt, Army Air Force. Mem: Am Legion. Relig: Congregational. Mailing Add: 316 Alta Vista Dr South Pasadena CA 91030

CROSBY, ROBERT BERKEY (R)
b North Platte, Nebr, s Mainard Elery Crosby & Cora May Berkey C; m 1971 to LaVon Kehoe; c Robert Mainard & Susan Mary (Mrs Frank D Smith). Educ: Hastings Col, 27-29; Univ Minn, BA, 31; Harvard Law Sch, LLD, 35. Polit & Govt Pos: Nebr State Sen, 41-45, Speaker of Legis, 43-45; Lt Gov, Nebr, 47-49, Gov, 53-55; deleg, Rep Nat Conv, 56, 60, 64 & 72. Bus & Prof Pos: Sr partner, Crosby, Guenzel, Daris, Kessner & Kuester, Lincoln, Nebr, 55- Mil Serv: Entered as Lt(jg), Navy, 44, released as Lt, 46, after serv in Supply Corp, Pac, 44-45. Publ: Why I Want to Get Rid of My Job, State Govt, 47. Mem: Am & Nebr Bar Asns; Am Judicature Soc; Am Col Trial Lawyers. Mailing Add: 3720 S 40th St Lincoln NE 68506

CROSBY, WILLIAM DUNCAN, JR (R)
b Louisville, Ky, Sept 1, 43; s Dr William Duncan Crosby & Lucille Edwards C; m 1973 to Constance Frederick. Educ: Yale Univ, BA, 65; Columbia Univ Law Sch, LLB, 68. Polit & Govt Pos: Minority counsel, Comt Rules, US House Rep, 72- Mil Serv: Entered as officer candidate, Navy, 68, released as Lt(jg), after serv in USS Shangri-la, CVS-38 & Naval Invest Serv, Washington, DC, 68-71. Mem: Am & Ky Bar Asns. Mailing Add: Apt 1319 4901 Seminary Rd Alexandria VA 22311

CROSHAW, GLENN RANDALL (D)
Nat Exec Dir, Asn Dem State Chmn
b Petersburg, Va, July 4, 50; s Ernest R Croshaw & Charlotte Barnes C; single. Educ: ECarolina Univ, BSBA, 72; Univ Va Sch Law, JD, 75; Omicron Delta Epsilon; Beta Gamma Sigma; Phi Sigma Pi; Kappa Sigma. Polit & Govt Pos: Asst treas, Va Dem Party, 73-75; deleg, Dem Nat Mid-Term Conf, 74; vchmn, Colonial Heights Dem Party, Va, 75; nat exec dir, Asn Dem State Chmn, 75- Publ: Auth, The demise of politics as usual and the expanding Democratic majority, Va Law Weekly, 2/75; ed, Municipal zoning: the past in brief, the future in perspective, Univ Va Newsletter, 5/75. Relig: Methodist. Legal Res: 112 Appomattox Ct Colonial Heights VA 23834 Mailing Add: 1625 Massachusetts Ave Washington DC 20036

CROSS, DONALD MELVIN (D)
Miss State Rep
b Meridian, Miss, Aug 14, 35; s William Joe Cross & Eula Mae Todd C; m 1961 to France Lanelle Abernathy; c Julianne & Donald Joseph. Educ: E Miss Jr Col, 1 year; Meridian Jr Col, 1 year; Miss Col, BS, 57. Polit & Govt Pos: Miss State Rep, 66- Bus & Prof Pos: Asst chief engr, R G LeTourneau, Inc; pres, LeTourneau Vicksburg Fed Credit Union, 64-66; pres, LeTourneau Activities Asn, 65-67. Mil Serv: Entered as Pvt, Army, 58, released as Spec 4, 60, after serv in Eighth Army Honor Guard, Korea, 59-60. Mem: Am Soc Mech Engrs; Jaycees; CofC; VFW. Relig: Baptist. Mailing Add: Rte 2 Box 3 Vicksburg MS 39180

CROSS, HOPE HOFFMAN (D)
Statutory Chmn, Washington Co Dem Party, Wis
b South Amboy, NJ, March 27, 31; d Harold Giles Hoffman & Lillie Moss H; m 1951 to Robert Clarol Cross; c Rebecca, David, Michael, Allen, Roger, Priscilla & Sarah. Educ: Purdue Univ, Lafayette, BS, 52; Univ Wis-Madison, 61; pres, Wood Hall, Student-Staff. Polit & Govt Pos: Co-chmn, Washington Co McCarthy for President, Wis, 67-68 & co-chmn, Lucey for Gov, 69; corresponding secy, Washington Co Dem Party, 69-70, statutory chmn, currently; deleg, Wis State Dem Conv, 69-72; co-chmn, Washington Co McGovern for President, 70-72; deleg, Dem Nat Conv, 72; mem, Soc Serv Adv Bd, Washington Co, 72-; mem, Gov Equal Rights Comn, 72-; second vchmn, Ninth Dist Dem Party; mem, Wis State Dem Party Comt on Deleg Selection; deleg, Dem Nat Mid-Term Conf, 74. Bus & Prof Pos: Correspondent, Sheboygan Press, 70. Mem: Am Field Serv (host home publicity chmn, 71-73); League Women Voters; Washington Co Environ Coun (publicity chmn, 72-73); 4-H Leaders Asn, Washington Co (secy, 70-71); Washington Co Writers (co-chmn, 72-73). Honors & Awards: Outstanding Young Woman, Wis Jr CofC Auxiliary, 62; State Painting Award, Wis Regional Artists, 64. Mailing Add: Rte 4 Box 346 West Bend WI 53095

CROSS, JOHN MELVIN (D)
Committeeman, Dawson Co Dem Cent Comt, Mont
b Alexander, NDak, June 15, 18; s Melvin L Cross & Olive Iverson C; m 1943 to C Louise Jarussi; c Melvin L, Gregory J, Catherine L, Brian R, Justin M & Mark A. Educ: Rocky Mt Col, BS, 41; Harvard Grad Sch Bus Admin, summer 43. Polit & Govt Pos: Chmn, Dawson Co Dem Cent Comt, 56-60, committeeman, 62-; mem, Mont Indust Develop Adv Bd, 58-63; coordr, Kennedy-Johnson Campaign, Dawson Co, 60; mem adv comt, Mont Small Bus Admin, 62-66; mem, Mont Bd Inst, 63-; coordr, Hubert H Humphrey for President, 16 Eastern Counties, 68; alt deleg, Dem Nat Conv, 68; exec committeeman, Melcher for Cong, Eastern Mont Dist, 69. Bus & Prof Pos: Research & statist officer, Vet Admin, Ft Harrison, Mont, 46-51; off mgr, Watson Mfr Co, Helena, Mont, 51-52; CPA, Cross & Rigg, Glendive, Mont, 52- Honors & Awards: Small Businessman of Year, Small Bus Admin, 71; Mont CPA of Year Award, 71. Mailing Add: PO Box 1388 Glendive MT 59330

CROSS, WAYLAND (D)
Ala State Rep
Mailing Add: Box D Courtland AL 35618

CROSS, WILLIAM A (RORY) (D)
Wyo State Rep
Mailing Add: Box 400 Douglas WY 82633

CROSSLAND, PETER NELSON (D)
Ohio State Rep
b Cleveland, Ohio, May 8, 37; s David Harris Crossland & Dorothy Nelson C; div; c David & Andrew. Educ: Miami Univ, BA 59, MA, 62; Yale Univ, BD, 63; Duke Univ, PhD, 66. Polit & Govt Pos: Dem precinct committeeman, Akron, Ohio, 68-; mem, Summit Co Dem Exec Comt, 70-; Dem ward leader, Akron, 72-; Ohio State Rep, 42nd Dist, 72- Bus & Prof Pos: Assoc prof polit sci, Kent State Univ, 66- Mem: Am, Midwest & Ohio Polit Sci Asns; Common Cause. Relig: Methodist. Mailing Add: 29 Borton Ave Akron OH 44302

CROSSLEY, RANDOLPH ALLIN (R)
b Cupertino, Calif, July 10, 04; s John P Crossley & Elizabeth C Hall C; m 1928 to Florence Pepperdine; c Meredith (Mrs Jack E Young). Educ: Univ Calif, Berkeley, 23-25. Polit & Govt Pos: Hawaii Terr Rep, 43-47; chmn, Rep Party Hawaii, 50-53; Hawaii State Sen, 59-64; cand for Gov Hawaii, 66 & 74; Rep Nat Committeeman, 67-69; coordr, Nixon-Agnew Campaign Hawaii, 68; Presidential Elector, 72. Bus & Prof Pos: Pres, Hawaiian Fruit Packers, Ltd, 36-53; pres, Pac Savings & Loan, 62-65; chmn, Am Pac Group, Inc, 69-72; pres & chief exec officer, Hawaii Corp, 69-73; chmn & chief exec officer, 73-; chmn, Medi-Fund Corp, San Francisco, 72- Mem: Newcomen Soc NAm (trustee); Nat Asn Mfg (dir); Rancheros Visitadores; Bohemian Club. Legal Res: 3073 Noela Dr Honolulu HI 96815 Mailing Add: 480 Alexander Young Bldg Honolulu HI 96813

CROTTY, PETER JOHN (D)
b Buffalo, NY, Jan 29, 10; s Peter J Crotty & Delia Agnes Keane C; m 1938 to Margaret M McMahon; c Peter J, Paul A, Robert E, Mary Jo (Mrs Shapiro), Kevin M, Gerald C & James E. Educ: Canisius Col, PhB, 32; Univ Buffalo Sch Law, JD, 36; Phi Delta Phi. Polit & Govt Pos: Pres, Common Coun, Buffalo, NY, 48-52; chmn, Erie Co NY Dem Comt, 54-65; deleg, NY State Const Conv, 67 & Dem Nat Conv, 72. Bus & Prof Pos: Practicing lawyer, 36- Mem: Erie Co, NY State & Am Bar Asns; Bar Asn of City of New York; NY Athletic Club. Honors & Awards: Outstanding Citizen, Buffalo Eve News, 51; LaSalle Medal, Canisius Col, 52. Relig: Roman Catholic. Legal Res: 78 Milford St Buffalo NY 14220 Mailing Add: 1028 Liberty Bank Bldg Buffalo NY 14202

CROUCH, ERNEST (D)
Tenn State Sen
Mailing Add: 111 Rivermont Dr McMinnville TN 37110

CROUCH, GEORGE O'BRIEN (D)
SDak State Rep
b Ulmer, Iowa, Aug 24, 01; s Abram Crouch & Mary Wiseman C; m 1950 to Etta Mae Newkirk; c John, Keith & Barth. Educ: High sch educ. Polit & Govt Pos: SDak State Rep, 71-73 & 75- Bus & Prof Pos: Farmer-rancher, 26-67; dir, West River Elec Asn, Wall, SDak, 46- & Rushmore Elec Co, Rapid City, 52-68; mem, Co Bd Educ, 55-; dir, State Rural Electrification Asn, 68- Mem: Masons; Knight Templar; Lions; CofC; Farmers Union. Relig: Presbyterian. Mailing Add: Wall SD 57790

CROUCH, THOMAS GENE (R)
b Ft Worth, Tex, June 29, 33; s Lloyd Thomas Crouch & Vesta Hardin C; m 1955 to Dorothy Adams; c Kelly, Kippie & Thomas. Educ: Abilene Christian Col, BS in Bus Admin, 54; Southern Methodist Univ, JD, 57; Phi Beta Kappa. Polit & Govt Pos: Cand, Tex State Sen, Dist 16, 66; campaign chmn, Paul Eggers For Gov, Dallas Co, 68; chmn, Dallas Co Rep Party, formerly. Mil Serv: Entered as Pvt, Army Nat Guard, 57, released as Maj, 68, after serv in 49th Armored & 72nd Inf Brigade; Commendation Medal. Mem: Am Judicature Soc; Dallas, Tex & Am Bar Asns; Fed Power Bar Asn. Relig: Church of Christ. Legal Res: 4916 Goodfellow Dallas TX 75229 Mailing Add: 2630 Republic Bank Tower Dallas TX 75201

CROUSE, RUBY ROSE (R)
Secy, 11th Judicial Dist Rep Party, Colo
b Merritt, Ill, Jan 16, 00; d Albert John Newman & Nellie Ann Rufus N; wid; c Albert LeRoy. Educ: Salida High Sch. Polit & Govt Pos: Secy-treas, Chaffee Co Rep Cent Comt, Colo, formerly; Rep precinct committeewoman, Precinct 4, Chaffee Co, 58-62; secy, 11th Judicial Dist Rep Party, 58-; pres, Chaffee Co Rep Women's Club, 66-70, 72-, chmn achievement awards, 67-; finance chmn, Chaffee Co Rep 1200 Club, 67- Bus & Prof Pos: Owner, Crouse's Honey, 66- Relig: Protestant. Mailing Add: 7735 N Hwy 285 Salida CO 81201

CROW, HERSHAL HILLIAR, JR (D)
Okla State Sen
b Olustee, Okla, Mar 30, 35; s Herschal Hilliar Crow & Nova Hensley C; m 1957 to Elizabeth Kay Small; c David Thomas & Michael Carter. Educ: Okla State Univ, AB, 57; Beta Theta Pi. Polit & Govt Pos: Okla State Sen, 68-; Asst Majority Leader, Okla State Senate, 73- Mil Serv: Entered as E-1, Army, 58, released as E-2, 58. Mem: Okla Wheat Growers Asn; Mason (32 degree); Elks. Honors & Awards: Outstanding Young Farmer, Jackson Co, Okla, 66. Relig: Methodist. Mailing Add: 900 E Cypress Altus OK 73521

CROWE, PHILIP KINGSLAND (D)
US Ambassador, Denmark
b New York, NY, Jan 7, 08; s Earl Crowe & Kathleen McClellan Higgins C; m 1937 to Irene Pettus; c Phillippa, Irene & Mary. Educ: St Paul's Sch, Concord, NH, 28; Univ Va, 32. Polit & Govt Pos: Spec rep, Econ Coop Admin, China, 48-49; US Ambassador, Ceylon, 53-56; US deleg to Econ Comn Asia & the Far East Conf of UN, 54; spec asst to Secy of State, 57-59; US Ambassador, Union of SAfrica, 59-61; US Ambassador, Norway, 69-73; US Ambassador, Denmark, 73- Bus & Prof Pos: Reporter, New York Eve Post, 33; chief of customers dept, Milmine Bodman, broker, New York City, 34-35; explorer & hunter of big game, French Indo-China, 35-37; dir travel advert, Life Mag, 37-38; mem advert staff, Fortune Mag, 38-41 & 44-48; leader, wildlife mission to Near East, 63, SAm, 64, Far East, 65 & Mid East, 66. Mil Serv: Lt Col, Army Air Force, 41-44; chief of intel, Off of Strategic Serv, China-Burma-India Theater; Bronze Star; Order of Yun-Hui, Repub of China; Officer French Legion of Honor; Grand Officer, Mil Order of Christ, Portugal, 63. Publ: The Empty Ark, 67; World Wildlife: The Last Stand, 70; Out of the Mainstream, 70; plus others. Mem: Foreign Serv Educ Found (trustee); Fletcher Sch Diplomacy, Tufts Univ (trustee); Sch of Advan Int Studies, Johns Hopkins Univ (bd adv); World Wildlife Fund, African Wildlife Leadership Found; fel Royal Asiatic Soc. Honors & Awards: Knight Comdr, Int Order St Hubert. Legal Res: Easton MD 21601 Mailing Add: US Ambassador to Denmark Dept of State Washington DC 20521

CROWE, RAY P (R)
Ind State Rep
b Franklin, Ind, May 30, 15; s Morten E Crowe & Tommie Ann Burris C; m 1952 to Betty Jean Ewing; c Larry R, Linda J & Lloyd E. Educ: Ind Cent Col, AB, 38; Ind Univ, 49-51; Butler Univ, 64-67; Omega Psi Phi. Hon Degrees: LLD, Ind Cent Col, 62. Polit & Govt Pos: Ind State Rep, Dist 42, 67- Bus & Prof Pos: Mem bd, Ind Cent Col, 66-; mem bd, Ind Basketball Hall of Fame, 74-; mem personnel & labor rels comn, Ind State CofC, 74- Mem: Bachelor Benedict Club; Nat Asn Personnel Admins; Ind Retired Teachers Asn. Honors & Awards: Ind Basketball Hall of Fame, Ind Hall of Fame Found, 69. Relig: Protestant. Mailing Add: 4555 Clover Lake Dr Indianapolis IN 46208

CROWE, ROBERT T (BOBBY TOM) (D)
Ala State Rep
Mailing Add: Box 2308 Jasper AL 35501

CROWELL, DONALD REX (R)
Kans State Rep
b Independence, Kans, Sept 4, 43; s Charles B Crowell, Sr & Anna Guenther C; single. Educ: Independence Community Col, AA, 63; Emporia Kans State Col, BSE, 65, MS, 73. Polit & Govt Pos: Kans State Rep, 76th Dist, 75- Bus & Prof Pos: Acct off supvr, Southwestern Bell Tel, Topeka, Kans, 69-71 & acct mgr, 71. Mil Serv: Entered as E-1, Army, 65, released as 1st Lt, 68, after serv in MAAG, Vietnam, 67-68; Silver Star; Purple Heart; Bronze Star; Vietnam Serv Medal; Vietnam Campaign Medal; Combat Infantryman Badge. Mem: VFW; Am Legion. Mailing Add: RD Longton KS 67352

CROWELL, GENTRY (D)
Tenn State Rep
Mailing Add: RFD 5 Lebanon TN 37087

CROWLEY, ARTHUR EDWARD, JR (R)
b Rutland, Vt, Oct 18, 28; s Arthur E Crowley & Mildred Patricia Gilfeather C; m 1961 to Marcia Colby Smith; c Robert Arthur, David Stevens, Andrew Coppinger & Christopher Smith. Educ: Boston Univ Law Sch. Polit & Govt Pos: Dep Attorney Gen, Vt, 60-61; state's attorney, Rutland Co, 61-65; chmn, Rutland Co Rep Comt, 61-67; mem exec comt, Vt Rep State Comt, 61-67, chmn, 63-67; mem, Vt Rep State Comt, 61-71; city attorney, Rutland, Vt, 65-67. Mil Serv: Entered as Pvt, Army, 51, released as 2nd Lt, 53, after serv in 82nd Airborne Div, US. Mem: Vt & Am Bar Asns; Vt Jr Bar Asn; KofC; Rotary. Relig: Roman Catholic. Legal Res: 12 Foster Pl Rutland VT 05701 Mailing Add: 27 S Main St Rutland VT 05701

CROWLEY, MARY V (R)
Chmn, Derby Rep Town Party, Conn
b Derby, Conn, Apr 16, 19; d Martin G Chromik & Anna Matosha C; m 1949 to Marvin Crowley, wid; c Kathleen (Mrs Joseph Monaco) & Margaret (Mrs Robert Yocher). Educ: McKeown's Secretarial Sch, grad, 37. Polit & Govt Pos: Pres, Derby Rep Women's Club, Conn, 64-67; Rep registr of voters, Derby, 67-; secy, Comn on Elderly, City of Derby, 68-, secy, Charter Comn, 70-71; secy, Naugatuck Valley Registr Asn, 70-71; chmn, Derby Rep Town Party, 71- Bus & Prof Pos: Legal secy, Yudkin, Yudkin & Coppeto, 37-; legal educ chmn for Conn Asn Legal Secretaries Seminars for Legal Secretaries, Yale Univ Law Sch, 67-68. Mem: Registr of Voters Asn; Lower Naugatuck Valley Coun of Cath Women (legis chmn, currently); Nat Rep Comt (sustaining mem); Lower Naugatuck Valley Registr Asn; New Haven Legal Secretaries Asn (prog chmn). Honors & Awards: Legal Secy of Year, New Haven Legal Secretaries Asn, 68-69; Hon Membership, Derby Rep Women's Club, 71; Valley Profile, Eve Sentinel, 71; Distinguished Work for Rep Party, 74. Relig: Roman Catholic. Mailing Add: 170 Elizabeth St Derby CT 06418

CROWLEY, THOMAS M (D)
Vt State Sen
Polit & Govt Pos: VT State Sen, 67-; chmn, Burlington Traffic Comn, Chittenden Co Dem Comt & Young Dem. Bus & Prof Pos: Pres, Crowley Ins Agency, Inc. Mem: New Eng Asn of Mutual Ins Agents; Med Ctr Hosp Assocs; Cathedral Church, Burlington, Vt (mem exec comt); Burlington Jaycees; Fanney Allen Hosp Assocs (dir). Mailing Add: 36 N Willard St Burlington VT 05401

CROWTHER, BILLY LAMAR (D)
Secy, Fourth Dist Dem Party, Miss
b Forest, Miss, May 29, 25; s Fletcher Crowther & Parilee Denham C; m 1943 to Mildred Evelyn Ward; c Billye Jean (Mrs Rhodes), Donald A, Milton Lamar, Jacqueline Elaine (Mrs Thames), Dennis Monroe & Linda Faye. Educ: Jackson State Col, BS, 50; Jackson State Alumni Asn. Polit & Govt Pos: Chmn, Newton Co Dem Party, Miss, 68-72; secy, Fourth Dist Dem Party, 68-; alt deleg, Dem Nat Conv, 72. Bus & Prof Pos: Pres, Fifth Educ Miss Teachers Asn/Nat Educ Asn, 68-70. Mil Serv: Entered as Pvt, Army Air Force, 43, released as Pfc, 46, after serv in 186th Third Aviation Engr, ATO; Good Conduct; ATO Ribbon; World War II Victory Medal. Publ: Human Relations in Mississippi Education, Miss Teachers Asn, 70. Mem: Newton, Fifth Educ Dist & Miss Teachers Asns; Nat Educ Asn; Newton Co Civic Asn. Honors & Awards: Am Legion Adj 100% Award, 69; NAACP Teacher of Year Award, 70; Fifth Educ Dist Teacher of Year Award, 70. Relig: Baptist; Deacon, Pleasant Grove Missionary Baptist Church, Newton, Miss. Mailing Add: PO Box 75 Newton MS 39345

CRUM, ROGER CLARK (R)
b Jeffersonville, Ind, June 10, 11; s John Fry Crum & Paulina Willey C; m 1937 to Edna Louise Everett; c Dr Roger C, Jr; Michael Ray, Diane (Mrs Hozendorf) & Robert Nelson. Educ: Ark Polytech Col, 2 years; Univ Ark, Fayetteville, BSA, 35; Alpha Zeta; Alpha Gamma Rho. Polit & Govt Pos: Secy-treas, Ark Co Rep Orgn, 68-69, chmn, 69-74; mem, Ark Co Elec Comn, 70-, chmn, 70. Bus & Prof Pos: Co agent, Ark Agr Exten Serv, 37-40; vpres, Stuttgart Prod Credit Asn; mem, Dist Credit Bd of Prod Credit Asns, Ark, Mo & Ill, 43-45; research asst, Rice Br Exp Sta, Stuttgart, 57-62; owner, Bamento Plantation, Humphrey. Mem: Univ Alumni Orgn; Farm Bur; CofC; Riceland Foods; Ark Grain Corp. Relig: Methodist; Admin Bd. Mailing Add: 1812 Coker-Hampton Dr Stuttgart AR 72160

CRUMBAKER, DON E (R)
Kans State Rep
Mailing Add: Box 36 Brewster KS 67732

CRUMPACKER, SHEPARD J (R)
b South Bend, Ind, Feb 13, 17; s Shepard J Crumpacker & Grace Dauchy C; m 1950 to Marjorie Patton; c Richard Owen. Educ: Northwest Univ, BS in Engr, 38; Univ Mich, JD, 41; Polit & Govt Pos: US Rep, Third Cong Dist, Ind, 51-56; city attorney, South Bend, Ind, 69-71. Bus & Prof Pos: Assoc, Crumpacker, May, Beamer, Levy & Searer, 46-49, partner, 50; partner, Crumpacker, May, Levy & Searer, 56- Mil Serv: Entered as Pvt, Army Air Corps, 41, released as 1st Lt, 46, after serv in Fighter & Bomber Units; Maj (Ret), Air Force Res. Mem: Am, Ind State & St Joseph Co Bar Asns; Bar Asn of the Seventh Fed Circuit; Am Judicature Soc. Relig: Presbyterian. Mailing Add: 237 Timber Lane South Bend IN 46615

CRUMPLER, GUS H (D)
Secy, Boone Co Dem Cent Comt, Ark
b Lowry, Ark, Mar 7, 11; s Thomas Newton Crumpler & Phebe Sue Dunlap C; m 1942 to Mary Afton Chappelle; c Anna Jean (Mrs Smith) & Saundra Kay (Mrs Villines). Educ: Univ Mo-Columbia, 29-31. Polit & Govt Pos: Postmaster, Lowry, Ark, 33-42; secy, Boone Co Dem Cent Comt, 70- Bus & Prof Pos: Operator gen merchandise store, Lowry, Ark, 33-42; salesman commercial candy co, Harrison, 46-53; adv mgr, Times Publ Co, Harrison, 53- Mil Serv: Entered as Pvt, Army, 43, released as Cpl, 46, after serv in 5th Base PO, China-Burma-India Theatre, 44-46; 2 Battle Stars. Publ: Auth, The Wilkerson Graveyard, Cent States Archaeol Soc, 1/69; auth, Cooch-Behar, India, Ex-CBI RoundUp, 3/75; auth, Under the Burmese Pagoda, Sch of the Ozarks, 75. Mem: Northwest Ark Archaeol Soc (vpres, 72-); Am Legion; VFW; Ex-CBI Vet Asn. Mailing Add: 413 N Center St Harrison AR 72601

CRUMPLER, SHIRLEY ANN (R)
Pres, Nev Fedn Rep Women
b San Francisco, Calif, Jan 21, 35; d Frederick Lloyd Rakeman & Marguerite Linez R; m 1975 to Robert McGill; c Linda, Laura, Jerry & Kimberly. Educ: San Francisco State Univ, 52-53. Polit & Govt Pos: Med adv bd, Small Bus Admin, 73-; Pres, Nev Fedn Rep Women, 73-; Rep nominee for Gov Nev, 74. Bus & Prof Pos: Real estate broker & tax acct, Shirley Crumpler & Assocs, 63-75. Mem: Nat Asn Realtors; Nev Asn Tax Consultants; Am Bus Womens Asn. Legal Res: 1937 Caballera Way Las Vegas NV 89109 Mailing Add: 4141 Maryland Pkwy Las Vegas NV 89109

CRUPPER, CLAY (D)
Ky State Rep
Mailing Add: 25 Wilron Dr Dry Ridge KY 41035

CRUPPER, GORDON (R)
b Denver, Colo, Oct 7, 20; s John Clayton Crupper & Christine Grace Sutherland C; m 1943 to Ellen Elizabeth Keen; c Gordon, Jr, Burton Keen & Jean Elizabeth. Educ: Colo State Univ, BS in Forestry, 42; Yale Univ, 45-46; Forestry Sch Hon Fraternity; Scabbard & Blade. Polit & Govt Pos: Chmn, Lemhi Co Rep Comt, Idaho, formerly. Bus & Prof Pos: Mgr Idaho Div, Intermountain Co. Mil Serv: Entered as 2nd Lt, Army, 42, released as 1st Lt, 46, after serv in Field Artil as Liaison Pilot; Air Medal. Mem: Soc of Am Foresters; West Wood Prod Asn; Mason; Elks; CofC. Relig: Episcopal. Mailing Add: PO Box 1208 Salmon ID 83467

CRUTCHER, HARRY, III (BUZZ) (D)
b San Antonio, Tex, June 16, 38; s Maj Gen Harry Crutcher, Jr & Ruth Gibbons C; m Aug 28, 65 to Carolyn Joyce Burnett; c Dodd, Libby & Catherine. Educ: Rice Univ, AB, 60; Southern Methodist Univ, LLB, 63. Polit & Govt Pos: Attorney, Dept Justice, 63 & 64; campaign mgr for Earle Cabell, US Rep, Tex, 64 & 66, admin asst, 65-67; campaign mgr for 15 Dallas Co Dem state legislators, 68; Dallas Co campaign mgr for US Sen Lloyd Bentsen, 70; campaign chmn, Judge Fred Harless, 14th Dist Court, Tex, 72; mem, Dem Nat Party Charter Comn, currently; deleg, Dem Nat Mid-Term Conf, 74. Bus & Prof Pos: Practicing attorney. Mil Serv: 1st Lt, Air Force Res, 56. Mem: Tex, Fed & Am Bar Asns. Relig: Roman Catholic. Legal Res: 5355 Nakoma Dallas TX 75209 Mailing Add: Suite 400 1307 Pacific Dallas TX 75202

CRUTCHER, JOHN WILLIAM (R)
Dir Div State & Local Govt, Off Econ Opportunity
b Ensign, Kans, Dec 19, 16; s O W Crutcher & Orpha Middleton C; m 1971 to Edith Colyard Koen. Educ: Univ Kans, AB, 40. Polit & Govt Pos: Kans State Sen, 53-57; mem foreign bd, US Coun State Gov, 65-67; mem bd, Midwestern Gov Conf, 65-67; Lt Gov, Kans, 65-69; dir div of state & local govt, Off Econ Opportunity, Washington, DC, 69-; admin asst to US Sen Bob Dole, Kans, currently. Bus & Prof Pos: Pres, Hutchinson Investment Co, 55-; pres, Countryside West, Inc, 60-; pres, Asn Fed Intergovt Execs, 72- Mil Serv: Entered as A/S, Navy, 41, now Capt Naval Res. Publ: The satellite countries, serial in Wichita Eagle & Beacon, Sept, 65. Mem: Am Royal, Kansas City, Mo; Red Cross; Jr CofC; Am Legion; VFW. Relig: Methodist; Mem, Off Bd. Legal Res: 200 E 12th St Hutchinson KS 67501 Mailing Add: 2440 Virginia Ave NW Washington DC 20037

CRUTCHFIELD, WILLIAM WARD (D)
Chmn, Hamilton Co Dem Party, Tenn
b Chattanooga, Tenn, Dec 6, 28; s Thomas Crutchfield & Nel Ward C; m 1966 to Joan Nunley; c Candis Ward & Margie Nel. Educ: Univ Chattanooga; Univ Tenn; Phi Alpha Delta. Polit & Govt Pos: Tenn State Rep, 57 & 61; Tenn State Sen, 63 & 65-67; chmn, Hamilton Co, Dem Party, 71-; asst co attorney, Hamilton Co, 71-; chmn, Third Cong Dist Dem Party, 73- Mil Serv: Entered as Pvt, Army, 53, released as Pfc, 54. Mem: Chattanooga & Am Bar Asns; Am Trial Lawyers Asn; Mason; Sertoma Club of Chattanooga. Honors & Awards: One of Outstanding Young Men in Tenn, 65. Relig: Methodist. Legal Res: 503 Battery Pl Chattanooga TN 37403 Mailing Add: 509 Cherry St Chattanooga TN 37402

CRUZ, VICTOR D (D)
b San Juan, PR, Oct 16, 19; s Isaac Cruz & Maria Selles C; m 1942 to Ida Maria Bloodworth; c Victor D, Jr, Ida Maria (Mrs Herron) & James Vincent. Educ: Textile High Sch, New York, 36; Mechanics Inst, New York, grad, 54; NY Naval Shipyard Apprentice Sch, grad, 58. Polit & Govt Pos: Treas, Robert F Kennedy Dem Club, 65-, admin asst, 69-; judicial deleg, 77th Assembly Dist, 70; first vchmn, Bronx Comt for Dem Voters, 71-72; deleg, Dem Nat Conv, 72; admin asst to NY State Assemblyman Armando Montano, 77th Dist, currently. Bus & Prof Pos: Able body seaman, NY Port of Embarkation, 46-49; elec engr draftsman & designer, NY Naval Shipyard, New York, 54-64; exec bd mem, Am Fedn Tech Engrs, Local Two, 60-64; elec inspector, City of New York, 66-71. Mil Serv: Entered as A/S, Navy, 43, released as Signalman 2/C, 45, after serv in a mine sweeper, Asiatic Theatre, 43-45; Am & Asiatic Theater Ribbon with Two Combat Stars. Honors & Awards: Community Award, Pondiac Dem Club & Robert F Kennedy Dem Club, 70. Relig: Catholic. Mailing Add: 743 Hunts Point Ave Bronx NY 10474

CRUZ DE NIGAGLIONI, OLGA (POPULAR DEM, PR)
Rep, PR House Rep
b Rio Piedras, PR, July 31, 33; d Manuel Cruz Horta & Dolores Jimenez Barredo C; m 1971 to Jose E Nigaglioni; c Olga Isabel. Educ: Univ PR, BA, cum laude, 54, Sch Law, LLB, 57. Hon Degrees: JD, Col Sacred Heart, PR, 72. Polit & Govt Pos: Legal adv, Pub Works Dept, San Juan, PR, 57-58; legal adv, PR Corp of Housing & Urban Renewal, 58-60; dist judge, PR Justice Dept, 60-62, spec dist attorney, 62-63; Rep, PR House Rep, 68-, majority whip, currently. Mem: PR Bar Asn; Am Judicature Soc; Civic Clubs of Prof & Businesswomen PR; Alumni Asn of Univ PR; Kappa Beta Pi. Honors & Awards: Award for Achievement, PR Bar Asn; First woman lawyer to be elected to PR Legis; Award for Polit Achievement Exchangetts Club; Award of Achievement, Nu Sigma Beta, San Patricio Chap; Most Distinguished Women of 1974, PR House of Com; Most Distinguished Young Women, PR Jaycees, 72. Relig: Catholic. Legal Res: Calle Navarra 313 Rio Piedras PR 00923 Mailing Add: House of Rep Capitol San Juan PR 00903

CRUZE, CHESTER T (R)
Ohio State Rep
b Cincinnati, Ohio, May 27, 38; s Jack Harvey Cruze & Fay Chryss C; single. Educ: Univ Cincinnati, BA, 60, grad study, 65-67; Salmon P Chase Col Law, JD, 64; Xavier Univ, grad study, 66-67; Salmon P Chase Col Law Deans List Student; Phi Delta Theta; Phi Alpha Delta. Polit & Govt Pos: Campaign mgr, Gordon H Scherer for Ohio State Rep, 64; campaign coordr, Taft for Senate Comt, 64; campaign mgr, Frank H Mayfield for City Coun, 65; conv chmn, Ohio State Young Rep, 65; vchmn, Ohio League Young Rep Club, 65; campaign chmn, Hamilton Co Rep Party, 66 & 67; mem, Rep Nat Comt Campaign Chmn Conf, 67; chmn, Hamilton Co Youth for Nixon, 68; mem, Richard M Nixon Rep Nat Conv Staff, 68; Ohio State Rep, 68th Dist, 69- Bus & Prof Pos: Advert publicity, Am Laundry Machines, Cincinnati, Ohio, 60-62; mortgage-investment, Union Cent Life Ins, Co, 62-64, assoc counsel, 64-65; asst co prosecutor, Hamilton Co, Ohio, 65-66; instr law, Univ Cincinnati, 67-69; asst attorney gen, Ohio, 68; attorney, Purcell, Sullivan & Young, currently. Publ: Art & politics, Mt Adams Rev, 9/67. Mem: Am Bus Law Asn; Kiwanis; Scottish Rite; Shrine; Eagles. Honors & Awards: Cincinnati's Outstanding Young Man of the Year Award, 64; Key Man Award, Cincinnati Jaycees, 65; Background for Leadership Award, Ohio Jaycees, 66; Jaycee Sound Citizen Award, 66; Gtr Cincinnati CofC Award of Appreciation. Legal Res: 880 Lafayette Ave Cincinnati OH 45220 Mailing Add: 2213 Carew Tower Cincinnati OH 45202

CRUZ-SOLANO, JUAN A (D)
b Mayaguez, PR, July 12, 36; s Adelaido Cruz-Lopez & Maria Solano Arce C; m 1955 to Dolores Gonzales; c John A, Maria R, Sylvia M, Reinaldo A, Orlando, Maria Dolores & Minerva. Educ: High sch & bus admin sch grad. Polit & Govt Pos: Coordr, McGovern for President, 72; alt deleg, Dem Nat Conv, 72; mem, Latino Caucus Steering Comt, Off Spanish Speaking, Washington, DC, 72- Bus & Prof Pos: Pres, Cruz-Solano, Inc, 69- Mil Serv: Entered as Airman 3/C, Air Force, 54, released as S/Sgt, after serv in 832nd Air Div Hq, Tactical Air Command, 53-61; Good Conduct Medal; Air Defense Medal; Presidential Unit Citation. Mem: Nat Asn Minority Contractors (bd dirs, currently); Am GI Forum; Community Asn. Relig: Catholic. Mailing Add: 516 Connelly St Clovis NM 88101

CRYER, CLIFFORD EUGENE (R)
b Morris, Ill, Oct 29, 02; s John Henry Cryer & May Lutzow C; m 1925 to Carol Ruth Cherry; c Barbara (Mrs Bowermaster), Carol J (Mrs Tiemann) & Philip E, MD. Educ: Kirksville Col of Osteopathy & Surg, DO, 26. Polit & Govt Pos: Secy, Woodford Co Rep Cent Comt, Ill, 50-58, chmn, formerly; coroner, Woodford Co, Ill, 52-64. Mem: Am, Ill & Fourth Dist Ill Osteopathic Asns; Am Osteopathic Soc of Radiologists; Masonic Lodge 246 (Mackey Chap 130, Couer De Leon Commandery 43, Mohammed Temple Shrine). Relig: Protestant. Mailing Add: 39 E Front St El Paso IL 61738

CUALCO, EUGENE T (D)
Calif State Assemblyman
Mailing Add: State Capitol Sacramento CA 95814

CUBIT, JAMES (R)
Kans State Rep
Mailing Add: RR 2 Garnett KS 66032

CULBERTSON, DONNA KAY (D)
Second VPres, Young Dem Clubs Am
b Spartanburg, SC, Jan 15, 41; d Shelton Young Culbertson, Jr & Catherine May C; single. Educ: Univ SC, 1 year; Converse Col, 2 years; Zeta Tau Alpha; Cotillion Club. Polit & Govt Pos: Vpres, Spartanburg Co Young Dem, SC, 63-65; third vpres, SC Young Dem, 65-67; Nat Young Dem Exec Committeewoman, 67-73; secy, Young Dem Clubs of Am, 69-71, second vpres, 71-, regional dir, 73-; womens dir, SC Dem Party, 70-; mem, Comn Status Women, 71-, chmn, currently; participant, Outstanding Young Women Am Prog, 73. Bus & Prof Pos: Secy, Spartanburg Co Auditors Off, 62-70. Mem: Pilot Club; Converse Alumni Asn. Relig: Methodist. Legal Res: Apt 712 Tree Top Lane Columbia SC 29210 Mailing Add: PO Box 5965 Columbia SC 29250

CULBERTSON, STUART A (D)
Committeeman, Pa State Dem Comt
b Meadville, Pa, Apr 16, 96; s James L Culbertson & Elizabeth Edmeston C; m 1964 to Katherine E Swisher; c Barbara (Mrs Royston), Stuart A, Jr & Mary Beth. Educ: Dickinson Sch of Law, LLB, 24. Polit & Govt Pos: Deleg, Dem Nat Conv, 52; chmn, Crawford Co Dem Comt, Pa, 58-66; committeeman, Pa State Dem Comt, currently. Bus & Prof Pos: Attorney-at-law, currently. Mem: Crawford Co, Pa State & Am Bar Asns; Rotary; Mason. Relig: Presbyterian. Legal Res: 1141 Lakemont Dr Meadville PA 16335 Mailing Add: 349 Center St Meadville PA 16335

CULBREATH, JOHN RICHARD (D)
Fla State Rep
b Tampa, Fla, June 27, 26; s Hugh Lee Culbreath & Daphne Elizabeth Jackson C; m 1950 to Barbara Jean Council; c Sharron Lynne & Candi Elizabeth. Educ: Baylor Sch, Tenn, 44; Univ Tampa, summers 47 & 48; Univ Ga, BBA, 49; Kappa Sigma. Polit & Govt Pos: Mem,

Hernando Co Dem Exec Comt, Fla, 62-64, chmn, 64-66; Fla State Rep, Dist 69, 67- Bus & Prof Pos: Mgr, Firestone Stores, St Petersburg, Fla, 51-52; owner, Bar Bet Farms, Largo, Tampa & Brooksville, 53-; secy-treas, Little Manatee Acres, Inc, Tampa, 55-; pres, Hernando Indust, Inc, Brooksville, 59-; owner, Agr Consult, 60-; dir, First Nat Bank, 69- Mil Serv: Entered as PAC, Army Air Corps, 44, released as Sgt, 46, after serv in Fifth Air Force, Pac Theater, 45-46; 1st Lt, Res, Inf; Victory Medal; Good Conduct Medal; Pac Theater of Opers, Japan Occup, & VJ Medals. Mem: Am-Int Charolais Asn; Fla Cattlemen's Asn; Farm Bur; Kiwanis; CofC. Honors & Awards: Fla Outstanding Young Farmer of the Year, Fla Jr CofC, 60. Relig: Presbyterian. Mailing Add: Rte 8 Box 1255 Brooksville FL 33512

CULHANE, THOMAS J (D)
NY State Assemblyman
Mailing Add: 2533 Grand Ave Bronx NY 10468

CULLEN, MIKE (D)
Calif State Assemblyman
b Phillipsburg, Mont, Apr 9, 27; s Harold Michael Cullen & Iris Juanita Belden C; m 1953 to Rita Joyce Beane; c Lisa Carol, Tamara Shawn Leolani, Erin Natasha & Merritt Christian. Educ: George Washington Univ, AB, 55; Yale Univ, LLB, 59. Polit & Govt Pos: Calif State Assemblyman, 67- Mil Serv: Entered as A/S, Navy, 44, released as Lt, 57, after serv in Pac Area, 46-56; Letter of Commendation, Asiatic-Pac Theater; China Serv Medal; Navy Occupation Medal; Korean Medal; Viet Nam Medal; Am Expeditionary Force Medal; Capt, Naval Res, 67. Mem: Nat Exchange Club; Long Beach CofC; Calif State Bar Asn; US Naval Inst; Navy League. Relig: Protestant. Mailing Add: Suite 1044 444 W Ocean Blvd Long Beach CA 90802

CULLEN, TIMOTHY F (D)
Wis State Sen
b Janesville, Wis, Feb 25, 44; s William F Cullen & Margaret Ford C; m 1969 to Sally Brownson; c Michele & Mark. Educ: Univ Wis-Whitewater, BS, 66. Polit & Govt Pos: Mem, Janesville City Coun, 70-71; staff, US Rep Les Aspin, 71-74; Wis State Sen, 75- Legal Res: 3273 Hampshire Janesville WI 53545 Mailing Add: 323 S State Capitol Madison WI 53702

CULLINAN, ANNA J (D)
Ariz State Rep
Mailing Add: 8330 E Shiloh St Tucson AZ 85710

CULLIPHER, GEORGE P (D)
NC State Rep
Mailing Add: 102 Christina Ave Williamston NC 27892

CULLISON, ROBERT VIRL (D)
Okla State Rep
b Turley, Okla, Dec 22, 36; s O G Cullison & Lucille Gideon C; m 1963 to Cleo Francilla Cranford; c Robin Lynn & Robert Gene. Educ: Baylor Univ, BBA, 59. Polit & Govt Pos: Okla State Rep, 75- Bus & Prof Pos: Owner, Cullison Grocery, Tulsa, 61-68; partner, Cullison Hardware & Lumber, Tulsa, 68- Mil Serv: Entered as Pvt, Marine Corps Res, 60, released as Sgt, 66, after serv in 1st Motorized Transport. Relig: Baptist. Mailing Add: 6044 N Owasso Tulsa OK 74126

CULLITY, WILLIAM J (D)
NH State Rep
b Manchester, Vt; married. Educ: Manchester Schs. Polit & Govt Pos: NH State Rep, 59- Bus & Prof Pos: Owner heating & appliance bus. Relig: Catholic. Legal Res: NH Mailing Add: 338 Laurel St Manchester NH 03102

CULP, CARL LESTER (D)
Chmn, Armstrong Co Dem Party, Pa
b Manor Twp, Ford City, Pa, Aug 12, 22; s Charles Lawrence Culp & Jessie Heilman C; m 1947 to Beulah Marie Grafton; c Bonnie Kay, Robert & Christopher. Educ: Ford City High Sch, Pa, 36-40. Polit & Govt Pos: Twp supvr, Manor Twp, Pa, 53-65, secy-treas, 10 years; mem planning comn, Armstrong Co, 59-; secy-treas, Co Asn Twp Officers, 60-65; committeeman, Armstrong Co Dem Party, 61-, chmn, 69-; committeeman, Armstrong Co Agr Stabilization & Conserv Serv, currently; supt, Pa Dept Highways, Armstrong Co, 71- Mem: Elks; Lions; Pa Farmers Asn; Pa Farmers Milk Judging Asn (dir, currently); Agr Exten Asn. Relig: Presbyterian. Mailing Add: 2074 Hobson Dr Ford City PA 16226

CULPEPPER, BRYANT (D)
Ga State Rep
Mailing Add: PO Box 471 Ft Valley GA 31030

CULVER, JOHN CHESTER (D)
US Sen, Iowa
b Rochester, Minn, Aug 8, 32; s William C Culver & Mary Miller C; m to Ann T Cooper; c Christina, Rebecca, Catherine & Chester. Educ: Harvard Col, AB cum laude, 50-54; Lionel de Jersey Harvard Scholarship to Cambridge Univ, Eng, 54-55; Harvard Law Sch, LLB, 59-62. Polit & Govt Pos: Legis asst, Sen Edward M Kennedy, 62-63; US Rep, Second Dist, Iowa, 65-74; deleg, Dem Nat Conv, 68; US Sen, Iowa, 75- Bus & Prof Pos: Bus mgr, Culver-Rent-A-Car, 59; attorney-at-law, McGuire, Bernau & Culver, 63-65. Mil Serv: Marine Corps, 55, released as 1st Lt, 58, after serv in 1st Marine Div. Mem: Fed, Iowa & Linn Co Bar Asns. Relig: Presbyterian. Legal Res: 298 Red Fox Rd SE Cedar Rapids IA 52403 Mailing Add: 2327 Dirksen Bldg Washington DC 20510

CULVER, LOUIS P (D)
Iowa State Sen
Mailing Add: PO Box 27 Dunlap IA 51529

CUMBERLAND, JAMES L (R)
Pa State Rep
Mailing Add: Capitol Bldg Harrisburg PA 17120

CUMISKEY, THOMAS BERNARD (D)
Md State Deleg
b Cumberland, Md, Nov 7, 16; s Thomas Bernard Cumiskey & Cecilia Mills C; m 1939 to Helen Agnes Stakem; c Thomas Bernard, III, James Edward, Alice Marie (Mrs Harman), Michael Patrick & Katherine Ann (Mrs Fishell). Educ: LaSalle High Sch, Cumberland, grad, 36. Polit & Govt Pos: US Postal Inspector, 42-46; asst postmaster, Cumberland Post Off, 46-71; mem & chmn, Cumberland Citizens Adv Comt, 61-62 & 68-69; mem, Civil Serv Comn, Cumberland, 73-74; Md State Deleg, 75- Mil Serv: Entered as 1st Lt, Army, 49, released as Maj, 69, after serv in 729th Army Postal Unit, Active Duty Res, 61-62; Maj (Ret), Army Res, 69; Army Commendation Medal. Mem: KofC (Past Faithful Navigator 4 Degree); Cath War Vet (vcomnr, currently); Am Red Cross (mem bd, local chap, currently). Relig: Catholic. Mailing Add: 219 Schley St Cumberland MD 21502

CUMMINGS, CHARLES EVERETT (R)
NH State Rep
Mailing Add: RFD Fremont NH 03044

CUMMINGS, FRANK (R)
b New York, NY, Dec 11, 29; s Louis Cummings & Florence Bonime; m 1958 to Jill Schwartz; c Peter Ian & Margaret Anne. Educ: Hobart Col, AB, 51; Columbia Univ, MA, 55; Columbia Law Sch, LLB, 58; Phi Beta Kappa; Tau Kappa Alpha; Articles Ed, Columbia Law Rev; Phi Alpha Delta. Polit & Govt Pos: Minority counsel, US Senate Comt on Labor & Pub Welfare, Washington, DC, 65-67; admin asst to US Senator Jacob K Javits, NY, 69-71; Minority Gen Coun, US Senate Comt on Labor & Pub Welfare, 72; pub mem, Adv Coun on Employee Welfare & Pension Benefit Plans, US Dept Labor, 72-74; Bus & Prof Pos: Attorney, Cravath, Swaine & Moore, New York, NY, 58-63; Gall, Lane & Powell, Washington, DC, 63-65 & partner, Gall, Lane & Powell, 72-; attorney, Poletti Freidin Prashker Feldman & Gartner, New York, NY, 67-69; lectr in law, Columbia Law Sch, 70-74. Mil Serv: Entered as Pvt, Army, 62, released as Cpl, 65, after serv in US Army, Europe, 62-64. Publ: Miscellaneous articles on labor law, Labor Law J; book rev, Psychiatric Justice, Columbia Law Rev, 66; Remarks on Private Pension Plans, Symp on Pvt Pension Plans, Am Enterprise Inst of Pub Policy Research, Washington, DC & Proc of NY Univ 22nd Annual Inst on Labor, 69. Mem: Am Bar Asn; Asn of the Bar of City of New York; Bar Asn of DC (chmn comt on labor, 72-73); Columbia Univ Seminar on Labor. Mailing Add: 4305 Bradley Lane Chevy Chase MD 20015

CUMMINGS, GAYLORD G (R)
NH State Rep
Mailing Add: 25 School St Bristol NH 03222

CUMMINGS, JAMES R (R)
Okla State Sen
Mailing Add: State Capitol Oklahoma City OK 73105

CUMMINGS, MINNETTE HUNSIKER (R)
Maine State Sen
b Washington, DC; d Harold Whiting Hunsiker & Florence M Lufkin H; m 1942 to H King Cummings, separated; c Stephen H, Wende (Mrs Robert A Richter), Lee L & Jennifer. Educ: Bennington Col, BA, 40. Polit & Govt Pos: Maine State Rep, 69-73; deleg, Rep Nat Conv, 72; Maine State Sen, 73- Bus & Prof Pos: State of Maine agent, Sch & Col Adv Ctr, 65- Mem: Newport Woman's Club; Bangor Theol Sem (trustee); Portland Symphony Women's Comt. Relig: Protestant. Mailing Add: 24 High St Newport ME 04953

CUMMINGS, RICHARD MARSHALL (D)
b New York, NY, Mar 23, 38; s Albert Martin & Betty Benjamin M; m 1965 to Mary A Johnson; c Benjamin & Orson. Educ: Princeton Univ, AB, 59; Columbia Univ Law Sch, JD, 62; Cambridge Univ, MLit, 64; Keyr Seal Club; Univ Pitt Club; Columbia Law Rev. Polit & Govt Pos: Dem cand, Suffolk Co Legis, NY, 71; deleg & mem credentials comt, Dem Nat Conv, 72-; committeeman, Suffolk Co Dem Comt, 73-74; committeeman, Southampton Town Dem Comt, 73-74. Bus & Prof Pos: Assoc, Breed, Abbott & Morgan, 64-65; attorney-adv, Agency for Int Develop, 65-66; prof, Sch Law, Univ Louisville, 66-70; vis prof int law & chmn, J Ethiopian Law, Haille Sellassie Univ, 67-69; vis prof polit sci & dir environ ctr, Southampton Col, LI Univ, 70-71; partner, Ross & Cummings, 71-; columnist, East Hampton Star, 71-; prof law, Univ West Indies, 74-; prof, Prog in Youth & Community Studies, State Univ NY Stony Brook; moderator, Free Speech, WRCN Radio, Riverhead, NY; gen counsel, Press Club of Long Island. Publ: Trade secrets & their protection, Univ Ky Law J, 65-66; The political trial, justice & the preservation of freedom, Cath Lawyer, 70; The Rhodesian unilateral declaration of independence & the position of the international community, NY Univ J Int Law & Polit, 71; plus others. Mem: NY Bar; East Hampton Dem Club; South Fork New Dem Coalition. Honors & Awards: James Kent Scholar, Columbia Univ Law Sch, 62; Buchanan Prize in Polit, Princeton Univ, 59; Cert of Honor, Am Asn Trial Lawyers, 70. Relig: Unitarian. Mailing Add: Box 349 Bridgehampton NY 11932

CUMMINGS, ROBERT E, JR (D)
Vt State Sen
Mailing Add: Bennington VT 05201

CUNDALL, DONALD R (R)
Wyo State Sen
Mailing Add: Uva Rte Wheatland WY 82201

CUNDIFF, EDWIN RUSSELL (D)
Chmn, Adair Co Dem Comt, Ky
b Adair Co, Ky, Jan 12, 30; s Henry Allen Cundiff & Rilda Russell C; m 1952 to Thelma Miller; c Robert Russell, Ann Harper & Todd Allen. Educ: Columbia High Sch, grad, 48. Polit & Govt Pos: Chmn, Adair Co Dem Comt, Ky, 75- Bus & Prof Pos: Salesman, Adair Home Supply, 52-57; mgr, WAIN Radio, 57- Mem: Columbia Masonic Lodge; Columbia-Adair Co CofC. Relig: Protestant. Mailing Add: 415 Young St Columbia KY 42728

CUNNINGHAM, ERNEST (D)
Ark State Rep
Mailing Add: 206 Rose Circle Helena AR 72342

CUNNINGHAM, GLENN C (R)
b Omaha, Nebr, Sept 10, 12; s George Cunningham & Emma C; m 1941 to Janis Thelen; c Glenn, Jr, Judy, Mary, James R, David & Ann Melissa. Educ: Univ Omaha, BA, 35. Polit & Govt Pos: Mgr, Omaha Safety Coun, Nebr, 42-47; mem, Omaha City Coun & supt, Dept Fire Protection & Water Supply, 47-48; mayor, Omaha, 48-54; Nebr state dir, Savings Bonds Div, US Treas Dept, 54-56; US Rep, Nebr, 56-72; mem, Omaha Bd Educ; mem, Rep Nat Cong Comt, formerly. Mem: Omaha Jr CofC; Pi Kappa Alpha; Eagles. Honors & Awards:

Legion of Honor, DeMolay; Named Outstanding Young Man, Nebr, 46. Relig: Episcopal. Mailing Add: 6421 Glenwood Rd Omaha NE 68132

CUNNINGHAM, JOHN (JACK) (R)
Wash State Sen
Mailing Add: 23207 Marine View Dr Seattle WA 98188

CUNNINGHAM, LARRY JACK (D)
Chmn, Taylor Co Dem Exec Comt, Tex
b McLean, Tex, Oct 10, 16; s Russ O Cunningham & Linnie Craig C; m 1941 to Geneva Huddleston; c Beverley, Larry Lyonal & Barry Dean. Educ: Hardin-Simmons Univ, BS, 40, MA, 50; Letterman's Club. Polit & Govt Pos: Chmn, Taylor Co Dem Exec Comt, Tex, 68- Bus & Prof Pos: Coach football & boxing, Dennison & Childress High Schs, 40-42; coach football, McMurry Col & Hardin-Simmons Univ, 47-54; real estate oil opers, farming & ranching, racing & raising running horses, 54- Mil Serv: Entered as Ens, Navy, 42, released as Lt, 46, after serv in SW Pac Theatre; VFW Medal. Relig: Baptist. Legal Res: 760 Mulberry St Abilene TX 79604 Mailing Add: 1632 Parramore St Abilene TX 79604

CUNNINGHAM, LOUISE WARE (D)
Chairperson, Lynchburg City Dem Comt, Va
b Lynchburg, Va, Mar 25, 45; d Fontaine Poindexter Ware & Beatrice Roach W; m to Samuel Eugene Cunningham. Educ: Lynchburg Col, BS, 66, MAT, 72; Kappa Delta Pi. Polit & Govt Pos: Chairperson, Lynchburg City Dem Comt, Va, 74- Mem: Nat, Amherst & Va Educ Asns; Va Polit Action Comt; League Women Voters. Honors & Awards: Virginians for Howell Comt Award, 73. Relig: Methodist. Mailing Add: 333 College St Lynchburg VA 24501

CUNNINGHAM, OVAL H (D)
Okla State Rep
Mailing Add: 9 Meadowheel Dr Bristow OK 74010

CUNNINGHAM, PATRICK JOSEPH (D)
Mem, Dem Nat Comt, NY
b New York, NY, Mar 12, 28; s Hugh Cunningham & Julia Martyn C; m 1951 to Mary T O'Donoghue; c Stephen Patrick, Philip Edward, Christine, Peterpaul & Patrick Joseph, II. Educ: Fordham Univ, BS in Educ, 49; NY Law Sch, LLB, 56. Polit & Govt Pos: Counsel, House Comt Fed Hwys, US House Rep, 63-65; counsel, Comt Labor, NY State Const Conv, 67; alt deleg, Dem Nat Conv, 68; chmn, Exec Comt, Bronx Co Dem Comt, 69-72; mem, Dem Nat Comt, 72- & Dem Exec Comt, 74-; chmn, NY State Dem Comt, currently; deleg, Dem Nat Mid-Term Conf, 74. Bus & Prof Pos: Pres, Emerald Lawyers Soc NY, 65; arbitrator, Am Arbit Asn, 69; mediator, NY State Mediation Bd, 69. Mil Serv: Entered as Seaman, Navy, 45, released as Boatswain 3/C, 46, after serv in Pac & Atlantic; Lt Res, 49-53. Mem: Bronx Co Bar Asn; Nat Dem Club. Relig: Roman Catholic. Legal Res: 6048 Fieldston Rd Bronx NY 10471 Mailing Add: 2488 Grand Concourse Bronx NY 10458

CUNNINGHAM, PAUL JOHNSTON (R)
Committeeman, Tex Rep Party
b Princeton, Ky, Oct 10, 28; s Paul C Cunningham & Marie Johnston C; m 1952 to Billie Jane Freeman; c Suzanne, Cynthia Marie & Paul Raymond. Educ: Univ Ky, BS, 50; Univ Louisville Sch Med, MD, 55; Pi Kappa Alpha; Phi Chi. Polit & Govt Pos: Committeeman, Tex Rep Party, 17th Dist, 74- Bus & Prof Pos: Pres, Galveston Surg Group Assoc, currently. Mil Serv: Entered as 1st Lt, Air Force, released as Capt, 59, after serv as Chief of Surg, 935th TAC Air Force Hosp, Sewart AFB & Ganor AFB. Mailing Add: 907 Sealy-Smith Prof Bldg Galveston TX 77550

CUNNINGHAM, RONALD LEROY (R)
Mem Exec Comt, Ohio Rep Finance Comt
b Cambridge, Ohio, Nov 10, 12; s Leroy R Cunningham & Mary Ada Johnston C; m 1934 to Arlene Elizabeth Peffer; c Nancy Jane (Mrs Ramsayer), Ronald Lee & Lawrence B. Educ: McKinley High Sch, Canton, Ohio. Polit & Govt Pos: Regional finance chmn, Ohio Rep Comt, 63-; mem, exec comt, Ohio Rep Finance Comt, 64-; deleg, Rep Nat Conv, 68. Bus & Prof Pos: Pres, Ohio Ferro-Alloys Corp, 48-; dir, Citizens Savings Asn, 55-; dir, First Nat Bank, Canton, Ohio, 56- Mem: Mfg Chem Asn; Am Soc of Metals; Am Iron & Steel Inst; Duquesne Club, Pittsburgh, Pa; Eldorado Country Club, Palm Desert, Calif. Relig: United Church of Christ. Mailing Add: Congress Lake East Dr Hartville OH 44632

CUNNINGHAM, ROSCOE D (R)
Ill State Sen
Mailing Add: 904 State Lawrenceville IL 62439

CUNNINGHAM, ROY (D)
Chmn, Camden Co Dem Comt, Mo
b Montsaratt, Mo, Aug 5, 17; s Roy Lee Cunningham & Berdena VanLieu C; m 1939 to Lillian Faye Roofener; c Judith Anne (Mrs Fuller), Wallace, Curtis, Maurice, Floy & David. Educ: Cent Mo State Col High Sch. Polit & Govt Pos: Treas, Camden Co Dem Comt, Mo, 68-72, chmn, 72- Relig: Baptist. Mailing Add: Roach MO 65787

CUNNINGHAM, WILFRED R (R)
NH State Rep
Mailing Add: 349 Ocean Blvd Hampton NH 03842

CUOMO, MARIO MATTHEW (D)
Secy of State, NY
b Queens, NY, June 15, 32; s Andrea Cuomo & Immaculata Giordano C; m 1954 to Matilda N Raffa; c Margaret I, Andrew M, Maria C, Madeline C & Christopher C. Educ: St John's Col (NY), BA summa cum laude, 53; St John's Univ Sch Law (NY), LLB cum laude, 56; Skull & Circle; Dean's List; Pi Alpha Sigma; Delta Theta Phi. Polit & Govt Pos: Secy of State, NY, 75- Bus & Prof Pos: Confidential legal asst to Hon Adrian P Burke, Court of Appeals, Albany, NY, 56-58; partner, Corner, Finn, Cuomo & Charles, Brooklyn, 58-74; prof law, St John's Univ Sch Law (NY), 63-74. Publ: Appellate advocacy: some observations & suggestions, New York Law J Revista, 10-11/63; New York City secondary school system, St Thomas Moore Inst, 66; Forest Hills Diary: The Crisis of Low-Income Housing, Random House, 74. Mem: Am Bar Asn; St John's Univ Alumni Fed (bd dirs); Big Bros Am (regional bd dirs); Fedn Ital-Am Dem Orgns; Columbian Lawyers Asn. Honors & Awards: Outstanding Young Man in the Professions, Brooklyn Jr CofC, 63; Pietas Medal, St John's Univ, 72; Man of the Year, Glendal Chap UNICO Nat, 74; Humanitarian Award, Long Beach Lodge B'nai B'rith, 75.

Relig: Roman Catholic. Legal Res: 196-07 Pompeii Ave Holliswood NY 11423 Mailing Add: Dept of State 162 Washington Ave Albany NY 12231

CUPP, ORVAL S (R)
b Columbus Grove, Ohio, Jan 9, 96; s Samual Cupp & Catherine J Sprat C; m 1918 to Mary Henrietta Bussing; c Orval C, Richard N, Charles L, Kenrith E & Marylou (Mrs Scheckelhoff). Educ: Ind Cent Col, 2 years. Polit & Govt Pos: Councilman, village of Leipsic, Ohio, 31-49, precinct committeeman, 31-, mayor, 49-53; vchmn, Putnam Co Rep Exec Comt, 49-64, chmn, Cent Comt & Exec Comt, formerly; mem bd elec, Putnam Co, 58-64. Bus & Prof Pos: Mgr & owner, locker plant & meat mkt, 31-62, abattoir, 31-68; chmn membership, Ohio Locker Asn, 47-53. Mil Serv: Entered as Pvt, Army, 17, released as Provo Sgt, 19, after serv in 331 Hq Co 83 Div, England & France; Victor. Mem: Boy Scouts of Am; Inst Rep Co; Am Legion (serv officer, 32 years); KofP; (50 years mem); Odd Fellows (50 years mem). Honors & Awards: Scouts Silver Beaver award, 57. Mailing Add: 304 Center St Leipsic OH 45856

CURBOW, DERYL CRAWFORD (D)
Mem, Tenn State Dem Comt
b NC, Oct 8, 22; d George Oliver Crawford & Letitia Crowe C; m 1939 to John Donovan Curbow; c Gary Donovan, Angelyn (Mrs Sanford) & John Timothy. Educ: Univ Tenn, Knoxville; Cleveland State Community Col. Polit & Govt Pos: Mem, Polk Co Dem Exec Comt, Tenn; deleg, many dist & state dem conv; gen sessions, criminal & circuit court clerk, Polk Co, 62-; chmn, US Sen Albert Gore's Polk Co Campaign, 66 & 70; alt deleg, Dem Nat Conv, 72; mem, Tenn State Dem Comt, currently. Mem: State Court Clerks' Asn ETenn; 24th Judicial Circuit Clerks' Asn (pres, 69-71); Tenn Dem Women's Federated Club; Tenn Dem Women's Roundtable; Polk Co Dem Women's Club (pres, 73). Honors & Awards: First woman elected to office of Criminal court clerk in Polk Co. Relig: Southern Baptist. Mailing Add: Rte 1 Benton TN 37307

CURLEY, LUCY ALFORD (D)
Co-Chmn, Erie Co Dem Exec Comt, NY
b Ft Smith, Ark; d Lambert M Alford & Lena Hammer A; m to Edward P Curley; c Lucy L (Mrs Paul Teresi), D Patrick & Michael E. Educ: Univ Ark. Polit & Govt Pos: Mem exec comt, NY State Dem Coun, 47-; mem exec comt, Erie Co Dem Comt, NY, 47-, vchmn, Comt & Dem women's div, 62-; dep treas, City of Buffalo, 54-55, treas, 55-61 & 66-; mem speakers bur, NY Dem Gubernatorial Campaign, 54 & 58 & Dem Sen Campaign, 64; deleg, NY State Dem Conv, 60, 62 & 64; Eighth Judicial Dist Dem Conv, 62, 63, 64 & 65 & Dem Nat Conv, 64 & 68; co-chmn, Erie Co Dem Exec Comt, 62- Mem: Cancer Soc (dist chmn, 49 & 70-72); Cath Charities of Buffalo; United Fund of Buffalo & Erie Co (dist chmn, 70-73, mem budget, 71, trustee, 72-73); United Fund. Relig: Roman Catholic. Legal Res: 1306 Delaware Ave Buffalo NY 14209 Mailing Add: City Hall Buffalo NY 14202

CURLIN, WILLIAM P, JR (D)
Mem Rules Comt, Ky State Dem Party
b Paducah, Ky, Nov 30, 33; s William P Curlin, Sr & Margaret Flatt C; m 1959 to Elizabeth Richardson; c William P, III, Elizabeth Caroline, Margaret Rowden & Dorothy Richardson. Educ: Univ Ky, AB, 58, LLB, 62; Phi Delta Theta. Polit & Govt Pos: Pres, Franklin Co Young Dem, Ky, 65-67; Ky State Rep, 57th Dist, 68-71; mem rules comt, Ky State Dem Party, 69-; US Rep, Ky, by spec elec, 71-72. Bus & Prof Pos: Chmn, jour comt & three others, Ky Bar Asn, 63-68. Mil Serv: Entered as Cpl, US Army, released as Sgt, 57, after serv in 1st Armored Div, La, 55-57. Mem: Jaycees. Relig: Presbyterian. Mailing Add: 218 Raintree Rd Frankfort KY 40601

CURLS, PHILLIP B (D)
Mo State Rep
b Kansas City, Mo, Apr 2, 42; s Fred A Curls & Velma E Wagner C; m 1964 to Melba Jean Dudley; c Phillip B, II, Michael Jay & Monica Joy Bianca. Educ: Rockhurst Col, BS & BA, 65. Polit & Govt Pos: Mo State Rep, Dist 28, 73- Relig: Roman Catholic. Mailing Add: 3108 Chestnut Kansas City MO 64128

CURRAN, BARBARA A (R)
NJ State Assemblyman
Mailing Add: State House Trenton NJ 08625

CURRAN, FRANK E (D)
b Cleveland, Ohio, Dec 19, 12; s William E Curran & Anna Hayer C; m 1936 to Florence Ann McKenney. Educ: San Diego Jr Col; Balboa Law Sch; San Diego State Col; Univ Calif Exten. Polit & Govt Pos: Dep assessor, San Diego Co, Calif, 35-41; supvr procurement for critical materials, Navy, 40-49; councilman, San Diego, 55-63, vmayor, 57-58 & 61-62, mayor, 63-71; vpres, Nat League of Cities, 69, pres, 70, mem bd dirs, 71- Bus & Prof Pos: Former laborer, stevedore, co-owner produce mkt, painter & decorating contractor, storekeeper, Oceanside, Calif, 37-38; secy-mgr, Eagles, San Diego, 49-60 & Shoreline Ins Co, 60-63. Mem: Gov Adv Comt on Aviation; Gov Comn of Calif (spec rep); Nat Ctr Vol Action (bd dirs); Coop Area Manpower Planning Syst (chmn); Local Govt Task Force Coastline Preservation. Relig: Catholic. Legal Res: 4901 Westover Pl San Diego CA 92102 Mailing Add: 631 Home Tower Bldg 707 Broadway San Diego CA 92101

CURRAN, GERALD JOSEPH (D)
Md State Deleg
b Baltimore, Md, Mar 20, 39; s James W Curran, Sr (deceased) & Sadenia A Brown C; m 1957 to Anna Jeanette Brown; c Kathleen Ann, Gerald Joseph, Jr, John F X, Margaret Ann & Elizabeth Ann. Educ: Univ Baltimore Undergrad Sch, 58-60, Sch Law, LLB, 63; Sigma Delta Kappa. Polit & Govt Pos: Md State Deleg & mem, Md Gen Assembly, 67-; mem, Mayor's Task Force on Educ, Baltimore City, 68-; deleg, Dem Nat Mid-Term Conf, 74. Bus & Prof Pos: Casualty Claim Rep, Fireman's Fund Am Ins Co, 59-69; bus & financial adv, Nat Life Ins Co of Vt, 69-; sales rep, Coastal Claims Serv, 69- Mil Serv: Entered as Pvt, Md Nat Guard, 57, released as Pfc, 60. Mem: York Dem Club (dir & founder); Friendly Sons of St Patrick; KofC; Ancient Order of Hibernians Baltimore City (past pres); Holy Name Soc Baltimore City (past pres). Honors & Awards: President's Club, Nat Life Ins Co Vt, 70. Relig: Roman Catholic. Mailing Add: 2530 N Charles St Baltimore MD 21218

CURRAN, HUGH C (D)
Mem, Conn State Dem Cent Comt
b Bridgeport, Conn, Jan 20, 24; s Hugh A Curran (deceased) & Mary Ennis C; m 1952 to Eleanor Reagan; c Maura, John E, Hugh, Mary Pat, Mary Kate & Mary Ellen. Educ: Col Holy Cross; Boston Col Law Sch. Polit & Govt Pos: Conn State Rep, 55-57; city attorney,

Bridgeport, Conn, 58-65; mayor, 65-72; comnr, Dept Aeronaut, State Conn, pres, Conn Conf Mayors, mem, Conn Dept Community Affairs, mem, Gov Traffic Comn Comt Standardization Traffic Control Devices, mem Bridgeport Dem Town Comt & mem, Conn State Dem Cent Comt, currently. Mil Serv: Serv as Fighter Pilot, Air Force, ETO, 95 combat missions, 1st Lt; Distinguished Flying Cross; Air Medal with 12 Oak Leaf Clusters; European Theatre Ribbon with two Battle Stars; Presidential Citation with two Oak Leaf Clusters. Mem: VFW (Raymond W Harris Post 145); Am Legion (Harry W Congdon Post 11); CWV (past dept judge advocate, Gold Star Mem Post); Elks; Moose. Relig: Catholic. Mailing Add: 1776 Noble Ave Bridgeport CT 06610

CURRAN, J JOSEPH (D)
City Councilman, Baltimore, Md
b Baltimore, Md, Sept 5, 04; s James Patrick Curran & Theresa Larkins C; m 1930 to Catherine Mary Clark; c J Joseph, Jr, Margaret, Martin Edward & Robert Walter. Educ: Loyola Col, Md, 23. Polit & Govt Pos: Chmn, Dem State Cent Comt, Md, 51-55; vchmn, United Third Dist Dem Orgn, Baltimore, 51-; city councilman, Third Dist, Baltimore, 53-59 & 63-; deleg, Dem Nat Conv, 68 & 72. Mem: KofC; Northwood Asn; Community Asn Govans. Relig: Catholic. Mailing Add: 4222 Kelway Rd Baltimore MD 21218

CURRAN, J JOSEPH, JR (D)
Md State Sen
b West Palm Beach, Fla, July 7, 31; m. Educ: Univ Baltimore, Law Sch, LLB, 59. Polit & Govt Pos: Mem, Regional Planning Coun, Md State Deleg, 59-63; Md State Sen, 63-73 & 75-. Bus & Prof Pos: Bd dirs, Md Higher Educ Loan Corp. Mil Serv: Air Force, 51-55. Mem: Baltimore & Jr Bar Asns; Friends Sons of St Patrick. Legal Res: 5203 Springlake Way Baltimore MD 21212 Mailing Add: 807 W R Grace Bldg Baltimore MD 21202

CURRAN, MICHAEL (D)
SDak State Rep
Mailing Add: Jefferson SD 57038

CURRAN, PETER J (D)
Maine State Rep
Mailing Add: 8 Sandyhill Rd South Portland ME 04106

CURRAN, RAYMOND JOSEPH (D)
Maine State Rep
b Bangor, Maine, Mar 5, 98; s Dennis J Curran & Ann Varley C; m 1935 to Mary Veronica Griffith; c Raymond J, Jr & Thomas N. Educ: Univ Maine, BS; Alpha Tau Omega. Polit & Govt Pos: Chmn, Bangor Dem City Comt, Maine, 34-36; mem, Maine Dem State Comt, 36-38 & 40-42; Maine State Rep, 65- Bus & Prof Pos: Rep, Select Pictures, 21-24, Universal Pictures, 24-26 & Metro-Goldwyn-Mayer, 26-62. Mil Serv: Pvt, Army, 18. Mem: KofC (4 degree); Univ of Maine Alumni Asn. Relig: Roman Catholic. Mailing Add: 188 Maple St Bangor ME 04401

CURRIE, MALCOLM R
Dir, Defense Research & Eng, Dept Defense
Legal Res: CA Mailing Add: Dept of Defense Pentagon Washington DC 20301

CURRIER, DAVID P (R)
NH State Rep
Mailing Add: Box 161 Henniker NH 03242

CURRIER, PHILIP R (R)
NH State Rep
Mailing Add: Windham Rd Pelham NH 03076

CURRIER, RAYMOND A, JR (R)
Chmn, Naugatuck Rep Town Comt, Conn
b Naugatuck, Conn; s Raymond A Currier, Sr & Marguerite O'Brien C; m 1963 to Judith Loring; c Raymond A, III & Melissa B. Educ: Univ Conn, 2 years; Univ New Haven, Assoc in Elec Engr. Polit & Govt Pos: Chmn, Naugatuck Rep Town Comt, Conn, 74- Bus & Prof Pos: Vpres, Currier Elec Co, 49-75; pres, CM Co, currently. Mil Serv: Entered as Pvt, Army, 46, released as Cpl, 47, after serv in Engr Corps Japan; recalled, 50-51, serv in Signal Corps, Korea. Mem: Am Inst Elec & Electronics Engr; Gtr Waterbury Elec Control Asn; Elks; Naugatuck CofC (dir, currently). Relig: Catholic. Legal Res: Naugatuck CT 06770 Mailing Add: 662 Chestnut Tree Hill Rd Oxford CT 06483

CURRLIN, WILLIAM EGON (R)
Chmn, Middlefield Rep Town Comt, Conn
b Brooklyn, NY, Jan 5, 45; s Egon E Currlin & Murian Wilson C; m to Nancy Jean Lilienthal. Educ: Univ Bridgeport, BS, 68; Army Officer Cand Sch; Kappa Beta Rho. Polit & Govt Pos: Mem, Planning & Zoning Comn, Middlefield, Conn, 73-; chmn, Middlefield Rep Town Comt, 73- Bus & Prof Pos: Pres, Currlin Camera Co, Inc & The Floor Store, 74- Mil Serv: Entered as Pvt, Army, 68, released as 1st Lt, 71, after serv in 101st Airborne, Vietnam, 70-71; 1st Lt, Army Res, currently; Bronze Star; Air Medal; Army Commendation; Good Conduct; Repub Vietnam Serv; Combat Inf Badge. Mem: Lions (dir, 74-); Cent Conn Asn Football Officials. Relig: Protestant. Mailing Add: RFD 291 Rte 1 Middlefield CT 06455

CURRY, RICHARD CHARLES (R)
Assoc Dir for Legis, Nat Park Serv
b Detroit, Mich, Apr 18, 37; s Fillmore Smith Curry & Geraldine Grant C; m 1958 to Susan Helen MacMillan; c Michael Reid, Peter Evans, Andrew Blake & Bryan Eliot. Educ: Eastern Mich Univ, BA, 60; Univ Mich, MA, 61, PhD, 65; Phi Gamma Delta. Polit & Govt Pos: City chmn, Williamsburg Rep Party, Va, 67-69; dir arts & sci div, Rep Nat Comt, 69-70, dir spec progs div, 70-71; spec asst to Secy of Interior, 71-72; spec asst to Asst Secy for Fish & Wildlife & Parks, 72-74; assoc dir for legis, Nat Park Serv, 74- Bus & Prof Pos: Instr polit sci, East Mich Univ, 63-65; asst prof govt, Col of William & Mary, 65-69, assoc prof, 69-70. Relig: Presbyterian. Legal Res: 1734 Susquehannock Dr McLean VA 22101 Mailing Add: Nat Park Serv Dept of Interior Washington DC 20240

CURRY, WILLIAM SEERIGHT (R)
Wyo State Rep
b Beason, Ill, Jan 18, 08; s George A Curry & Anna Alexandre C; m 1937 to Peggy Simson; c Michael M. Educ: Lincoln Col, 26-28; Ill Wesleyan Univ, AB, 30; Univ Wyo, MA, 39. Polit & Govt Pos: Wyo State Rep, 67- Bus & Prof Pos: Teacher & coach, Morrisonville High Sch, Morrisonville, Ill, 31-39; teacher, Natrona Co High Sch, Casper, Wyo, 39-43; supt of schs, Midwest Pub Schs, Midwest, Wyo, 43-46; retired chmn, Div of Eng, Casper Col, Wyo. Publ: This I tried & found helpful, Jr Col J. Mem: AF&AM; Elks; Lions. Honors & Awards: Awarded, Centennial Award for Meritorious Serv to Educ, by Lincoln Col, 65. Relig: Presbyterian. Mailing Add: 3125 Garden Creek Rd Casper WY 82601

CURTIN, MARGARET MARY (D)
Pres, Young Dem Clubs, Conn
b New London, Conn, Sept 28, 34; d William Joseph Curtin & Mary Satti C; single. Educ: Williams Mem Inst, 4 years. Polit & Govt Pos: Justice of the Peace, New London, Conn, 55-; secy, treas & vpres, Young Dem of New London, 55-59, first woman pres, 60; deleg, Young Dem State Conv, 57-71, Nat Conv Young Dem, 57-71, Probate Conv, 58, Cong Conv, 60, State Sen Conv, 62, Dem State Conv, 64, 66 & 68; mem, Dem Town Comt New London, 60-, secy, 64-; deleg, state bd, Conn Young Dem, 66- nat committeewoman, 66-71; first woman pres, 69-71; alt deleg, Dem Nat Conv, 68, deleg & mem credentials comt, 72; mem, Conn Platform Comt, 68-74; deleg, UN Youth Coun, Dem Am, 68-; pres, Young Dem Clubs Conn, 69-; nominated for Conn State Secy of State, 70; admin asst, Secy of State, 72-; admin aide, Gov, 75. Bus & Prof Pos: Vpres, Care Homes, Inc, mem, Parish Coun; pres local 300, Am Fedn State, Co & Munic Employees, AFL-CIO, currently, mem exec bd, Coun 16, state organizer, 75. Mem: Taxicabs Conn; Am Ambulance Asn; Ambulance Asn Conn; Confraternity of Christian Doctrine; United Way (union-counr, 74-). Relig: Roman Catholic. Mailing Add: 314 Ocean Ave New London CT 06320

CURTIN, WILLARD S (R)
b Trenton, NJ, Nov 28, 05; s William Smith Curtin & Edna Grace Mountford C; m to Geraldine A Hartman; c Lawrence B & Jeffrey H. Educ: Pa State Univ, AB, 29; Univ Pa Law Sch, LLB, 32; Sigma Chi. Polit & Govt Pos: First asst dist attorney, Pa, 38-49; dist attorney, Bucks Co, 49-54; US Rep, Eighth Dist, Pa, 57-67. Bus & Prof Pos: Former sr partner, Curtin & Heefner Law Firm, Morrisville, Pa. Mem: Rotary; Elks. Relig: Episcopal. Mailing Add: 250 N Pennsylvania Ave Morrisville PA 19067

CURTIS, BOB (R)
Wash State Rep
Mailing Add: PO Box 0188 East Wenatchee WA 98801

CURTIS, CARL T (R)
US Sen, Nebr
b Near Minden, Nebr, Mar 15, 05; m 1931 to Lois Wylie-Atwater (deceased); m 1972 to Mildred Genier Baker; c Clara Mae (Mrs James A Hopkins) (deceased) & Carl T, Jr (Tom); two grandchildren. Educ: Nebr Wesleyan Univ; Theta Chi; hon mem, Phi Delta Phi & Pi Kappa Delta. Polit & Govt Pos: Co attorney, Kearney Co, Nebr, 31-35; US Rep, Nebr, 39-55; US Sen, Nebr, 55-; chmn senate Rep conf, 75; chmn, Nebr deleg & floor mgr for Sen Barry M Goldwater, nominee, Rep Nat Conv, 64. Mem: Mason; Odd Fellows; Elks. Relig: Presbyterian Church of USA. Legal Res: Minden NE 68959 Mailing Add: 2213 Dirksen Senate Off Bldg Washington DC 20510

CURTIS, DAVID WILLIAM (R)
Vt State Rep
Mailing Add: PO Box 367 Shelburne VT 05482

CURTIS, DENNIS REX (D)
State Committeeman, Cassia Co Dem Cent Comt, Idaho
b Declo, Idaho, Aug 5, 37; s Blaine D Curtis & Ruth Brower C; m to Lois Jeanette Sorensen; c Randy D, Rodney Blaine, Travis Marlin, Denette & Justin Dennis. Educ: Utah State Univ. Polit & Govt Pos: Precinct committeeman, Cassia Co Dem Cent Comt, Idaho, 61-63, state committeeman, 64-65 & 68-, chmn, 65-68. Bus & Prof Pos: Mgr, Pella Farms, Ore-Ida Inc, 59-63; mgr, Blaine Curtis & Sons, Registered Herefords, 57-63; instr agr, Col Southern Idaho, 67-68; gen mgr, Lost River Ranch, 69- Mem: Cassia Co Cattlemens Asn; Idaho Hereford Asn; Livestock Agr Exten Agent; SIdaho CofC; Idaho Jr Hereford Asn. Honors & Awards: Idaho State Farmer Award, 55; Hon Future Farmers Am Award, 66. Relig: Latter-day Saint. Legal Res: Burley ID 83318 Mailing Add: Lost River Ranch Rte 2 Box 796-B Klamath Falls OR 97601

CURTIS, DOUGLAS W (R)
Maine State Rep
Mailing Add: 115 Summer St Rockland ME 04841

CURTIS, FLOYD EARL (R)
b Forrest City, Ark, Dec 29, 98; s Thomas F Curtis & Ann Larkin C; m 1935 to Carolyn Hornor; c Frances (Mrs Howe) & Caroline (Mrs William P Bond, Jr). Educ: Ferris State Col, 18-19; Univ Mich, BS, 23; Columbia Univ, 30-33; Univ Ill, 48; Univ Conn, MS, 50; Phi Delta Theta. Polit & Govt Pos: Chmn, Phillips Co Rep Comt, Ark, 46-68, chmn, 68-74; mayor, Helena, 50-58; jury comnr, Fed Court, Eastern Dist Ark, currently; mem, Phillips Co Elec Comn, currently. Bus & Prof Pos: Pres, Curtis & Co, Helena, Ark, 31-70. Mem: Nat Asn Ins Agents; Southern Agents Conf; Rotary; Helena Country Club; Phillips Co CofC. Relig: Episcopal. Mailing Add: 217 Beech St Helena AR 72342

CURTIS, KENNETH MERWIN (D)
b Leeds, Maine, Feb 8, 31; s Archie M Curtis (deceased) & Harriet Turner C; m 1956 to Pauline Brown; c Susan (deceased) & Angela. Educ: Maine Maritime Acad, Castine, BS, 52; Portland Univ Law Sch, LLB, 59. Polit & Govt Pos: Former asst to US Rep, James C Oliver; Legis Res Serv, Legal Res, US Libr of Cong; State coordr, Area Redevelopment Admin, Maine, 61-63; Secy of State, 65-66; Gov, Maine, 67-74; deleg, Dem Nat Conv, 68 & 72; chmn, New Eng Gov Conf, 69-70; state co-chmn, New Eng Regional Comn; mem steering comt, Dem Comn of the States, 70; mem exec bd, Nat Gov Conf, chmn, Environ Task Force, 71; co-chmn, New Eng Regional Comn, currently. Bus & Prof Pos: Attorney-at-law. Mil Serv: Entered as Ens, Navy, 53, released as Lt(jg), 55, after serv in Korea; Lt Comdr, Naval Res, 52-72. Mem: Amvets; Am Legion; Southern Maine Chap, Nat Cystic Fibrosis Research Found; Nat Found March of Dimes. Honors & Awards: Admitted to practice law before US Supreme Court, 65- Relig: Protestant. Mailing Add: One Bay Rd South Portland ME 04106

CURTIS, LAURENCE (R)
b Boston, Mass, Sept 3, 93; s Louis Curtis & Fanny LeLand Richardson C; m to Helen Schryver. Educ: Harvard, AB, 16, LLB, 21; Phi Beta Kappa. Polit & Govt Pos: Secy to Mr Justice Holmes, 21-22; asst US Attorney, Boston, 23-30; Boston City Coun, 30-33; Mass State Rep, 33-36; Mass State Sen, 36-41; Mass State Treas, 47-48; US Rep, Mass, 83rd-87th Cong;

Rep Cand, US Rep, Mass, 68. Bus & Prof Pos: Attorney-at-law, Boston, 22- Mil Serv: Lt, Air Corps, US Naval Res Force, 17-20; Silver Star Citation; Chevalier of Legion of Honor. Mem: DAV (Past Comdr, Mass Dept & Past Nat Sr Comdr); Am, Mass, & Boston Bar Asns; Harvard (Boston, New York). Mailing Add: 53 State St Boston MA 02109

CURTIS, SAM VICTOR, JR (D)
Chmn, San Bernardino Co Dem Cent Comt, Calif
b Birmingham, Ala, Aug 21, 22; s Sam Victor Curtis & Mary Elizabeth Caruso C; m 1948 to Eileen Louise Oehl; c Victor Alan, David Brian, Philip Daniel & Patricia Diane. Educ: Univ Southern Calif, 48-49; Calif State Univ, Los Angeles, BA, 52, MA, 55; Univ Calif, Riverside, 56-60; Rho Delta Chi. Polit & Govt Pos: Vchmn, San Bernardino Co Dem Cent Comt, 70-71, chmn, 72-; pres, Rialto Dem Club, 70-72; beautification comnr, Rialto City Govt, 74- Bus & Prof Pos: Bldg rep, San Bernardino Teachers Asn, 55-56; law & legis chmn, San Bernardino Fedn Teachers, 73-; mem faculty coun, San Bernardino High Sch, 74- Mil Serv: Entered as A/S, Navy, 42, released as Storekeeper 2/C, after serv in Fleet Air Wing Four, Aleutian Islands, 43-45; World War II Victory Medal; Asiatic-Pac Campaign Medal. Mem: Am Legion; VFW; Common Cause; Rialto Hist Soc; Wilsonian Club (bd dirs, 74-). Relig: Episcopal; mem, Bishop's Comt. Mailing Add: 164 W Van Koevering Rialto CA 92376

CURTIS, THEODORE S, JR (R)
Maine State Sen
b Bangor, Maine, Sept 23, 40; s Theodore S Curtis, Sr & Augusta Tolman C; m 1969 to Rose Marie Montero. Educ: Bowdoin Col, LLB, 62; Harvard Law Sch, JD, 66; Alpha Delta Phi. Polit & Govt Pos: Maine State Rep, 71-74; Maine State Sen, 75-, chmn, State Govt Comt, Maine State Senate, 75- Bus & Prof Pos: Attorney, Orono, Maine, 72-; mem bd trustees, Unity Col, currently. Mil Serv: Entered as Officer Cand, Navy, 66, released as Lt, 70, after serv in USS Henry W Tucker (DD-875), Pac & as Naval Adv in Vietnam, 67-70; Lt, Naval Res, 70-; Bronze Star with Combat V; Meritorious Unit Commendation; Vietnam Serv Medal with three Silver Stars; Nat Defense Medal; Republic of Vietnam Campaign Medal; Vietnamese Staff Serv Medal; Vietnamese Navy Serv Medal. Publ: Ed, From Disaster to Distinction, Pocket Books Inc, 65; Maine Political Yearbook, Maine Rep State Comt, 62-66. Mem: Am Legion; Maine State & Am Bar Asns; VFW; Eastern Maine Develop Dist. Relig: Protestant. Legal Res: Woodhaven Rd Orono ME 04473 Mailing Add: Box 272 Orono ME 04473

CURTIS, THOMAS B (R)
b Webster Groves, Mo, May 14, 11; s Edward Glion Curtis & Isabel Wallace C; m to Susan Ross Chivvis; c Elizabeth (Mrs Thomas Allen), Leland, Allan, Charles & Jonathan. Educ: Dartmouth Col, AB; Washington Univ, JD, Alumni Citation, 60. Hon Degrees: MA, Dartmouth Col, 51; LLD, Westminster Col, Mo, 62 & Washington Univ, 69. Polit & Govt Pos: Mem bd, St Louis Co Elec Comnr, Mo, 42; committeeman from Gravois Twp, St Louis Co Rep Comt, 46-50; mem, Mo Bd Law Examr, 48-50; US Rep, Second Dist, Mo, 51-68; Rep nominee for US Sen, Mo, 68 & 74; mem, President's Comn on All-Vol Armed Force, 69-70; chmn, Ozark Nat Scenic Riverways Adv Comn, 69-72; President's Task Force on Int Develop, 70-71; Task Force on Financing Cong Campaigns; chmn, 20th Century Found, 71; Spec Comt Real Estate Taxation & Educ Financing; mem, Educ Comt, US CofC, chmn spec panel foreign trade policy, 69-74; mem, US Territorial Expansion Mem Comn; sr exec coun, Conf Bd; app by President, US, Adv Comn Int Educ & Cult Affairs, 71-75, chmn, Rent Adv Bd, 71 & bd dirs, Corp Pub Broadcasting, 72, chmn bd, 72-73; chief, Fed Elec Comn, 75- Bus & Prof Pos: Trustee, Dartmouth Col, 51-72, William Woods Col, Westminster Col, Cent YMCA Community Col, 70-73 & Nat Col Educ; attorney-at-law, Biggs, Curtis, Casserly & Barnes; vpres & gen counsel, Encycl Britannica, Inc & vpres, gen counsel & mem bd dirs, Encycl Britannica, Educ Corp, 69-73, retired; bd dirs, Pub Media, Inc, Libr Resources, Inc & Lincoln Found; chmn bd, Lafayette Fed Savings & Loan, St Louis, 74- Mil Serv: Entered as Lt(jg), Navy, 42, released as Lt Comdr, 45. Publ: 87 million jobs, a dynamic solution for unemployment; The Kennedy round & after. Mem: St Louis City, St Louis Co & Mo Bar Asns. Honors & Awards: Ellis Forshee Award, Mo Fedn Blind, 58; Newel Perry Award, Nat Fedn Blind, 61; Cong Distinguished Serv Award, Am Polit Sci Asn, 63; Silver Beaver Award, Boy Scouts, Distinguished Eagle Award, Nat Coun Boy Scouts Am, 72. Relig: Unitarian. Legal Res: 230 Brentwood Blvd Clayton MO 63105 Mailing Add: Biggs Curtis Casserly & Barnes 319 N Fourth St St Louis MO 63102

CURTIS, WARREN EDWARD (R)
Iowa State Sen
b Doon, Iowa, Jan 19, 14; s William H Curtis & Nora D Rogers C; m 1935 to Emily E Ericksen; c Stephen J & Susan M (Mrs Shakman). Educ: State Univ Iowa, BSC, 36; ALpha Tau Omega. Polit & Govt Pos: Agt, Internal Revenue Serv, 41-43 & 46-47; Iowa State Rep, 25th Legis Dist, 71-73; Iowa State Sen, Third Dist, 73- Bus & Prof Pos: CPA, Cherokee, Iowa, 47-70. Mil Serv: Entered as Ens, Navy, 43, released as Lt, 46, after serv in Naval Res, Pac Theatre & Bur Naval Personnel, 43-46. Mem: Am Inst CPA (mem coun); Iowa Soc CPA; Rotary; Am Legion; KofC. Relig: Catholic. Mailing Add: 734 Walnut Cherokee IA 51012

CURTISS, SIDNEY Q (R)
Mass State Rep
Mailing Add: State Capitol Boston MA 02133

CURWOOD, WILLIAM B (D)
Treas, Luzerne Co, Pa
b Shickshinny, Pa, Nov 15, 10; s Ray Curwood & Florence Bredbenner C; m 1933 to Mary A Sharretts; c Sally Rae & William B, Jr. Educ: Wyo Sem. Polit & Govt Pos: Tax collector, Pa, 4 years; Pa State Rep, 52-67; borough treas, Burgess of Shickshinny, borough councilman; mem, adv bd, Wyo Nat Bank, Shickshinny Borough, currently; treas, Luzerne Co, currently. Bus & Prof Pos: Ins bus. Mem: F&AM; Elks; Rotary. Relig: Methodist. Mailing Add: 51 N Main St Shickshinny PA 18655

CUSACK, GREGORY DANIEL (D)
Iowa State Rep
b Davenport, Iowa, May 6, 43; s Daniel I Cusack & Jeannette Heaney C (deceased); single. Educ: Georgetown Univ, 61-62; St Ambrose Col, BA, 65; Univ Iowa, MA, 67. Polit & Govt Pos: City councilman, Davenport, Iowa, 70-73; Iowa State Rep, 73- Bus & Prof Pos: Teacher hist & polit sci, Briar Cliff Col, 67-69; teacher hist & polit sci, Marycrest Col, 69-70; dir, State Iowa Youth in Govt Proj, 71-72; salesman real estate, Cusack & Assocs, Davenport, 73- Mem: Am Civil Liberties Union; Am Hist Asn; Asn Advan Slavic Studies; Davenport Inner-City Housing Corp (co-founder); Davenport Cent & Western Neighborhood Develop Corp (co-founder). Relig: Roman Catholic. Mailing Add: 825 Taylor Davenport IA 52802

CUSACK, JOHN FRANCIS (D)
Mass State Rep
b Medford, Mass, Oct 5, 37; s Gerald J Cusack & Francis M Carter C; m 1960 to Janet L Kimball; c Sonya Jean, Margaret Helen, John Francis, Jr, Kimberly Ann & Katherine Mary. Educ: Boston Col, BSBA, 60; Boston Col Varsity Club; Pikes Peak Club. Polit & Govt Pos: Mem, Arlington Town Meeting, Mass, 60-; mem, Arlington Dem Town Comt, 69-; mem, Arlington Housing Authority, 69-; Mass State Rep, Seventh Middlesex Dist, 71- Mem: Arlington Jaycees; Boston Col Downtown Club; KofC; Mass Secondary Sch Hockey Coaches Asn. Relig: Catholic. Mailing Add: 20 Pine Ridge Rd Arlington MA 02174

CUSANOVICH, LOU (R)
Calif State Sen
b Los Angeles, Calif, 1912; m 1937 to Elizabeth McElroy (deceased); m 1969 to Elleen Cairns; c Michael & Gerald. Educ: Southwestern Univ. Polit & Govt Pos: Calif State Assemblyman, 57-66; Calif State Sen, 67- Bus & Prof Pos: Mgr, Lumber Bus; asst supt & dir of activities, McKinley Home for Boys. Mem: Valley Area Welfare Bd; Community Chest; Red Cross; Kiwanis; Elks. Relig: Lutheran. Legal Res: 1128 Nottingwood Circle Westlake Village CA 91361 Mailing Add: State Capitol Sacramento CA 95814

CUSHINGBERRY, GEORGE, JR (D)
Mich State Rep
b Detroit, Mich, Jan 6, 53; s George Cushingberry & Edna James C; single. Educ: Wayne State Univ, 71-74. Polit & Govt Pos: Mich State Rep, 75-, mem judiciary, consumers & House policy comts & co-chmn mil & vet affairs comt, Mich House Rep, 75- Bus & Prof Pos: Supvr, Sanit Serv, 72-73. Publ: Community ed, South End Newspaper, 73-74. Mem: Int Afro Am Mus (trustee, 74-); Concerned Citizens Coun (bd mem, 73-); Black Causes Asn; Asn Black Students. Honors & Awards: Outstanding Youth Leader, EBONI Women, 74. Relig: Baptist. Mailing Add: 19789 Santa Rosa Detroit MI 48221

CUSHMAN, KATHRYN M (D)
NH State Rep
Mailing Add: Box 26 Canterbury NH 03224

CUTILLO, LOUIS SABINO (D)
Conn State Sen
b Mansfield, Mass, Sept 2, 34; s Louis Nunzio Cutillo & Elizabeth Antosca C; m 1958 to Roberta Doyle; c Brian, Diane Alane, Judy & Jacqueline. Educ: Univ Bridgeport. Polit & Govt Pos: Constable, Waterbury, Conn, 64-66, mem town comt, 66-68; Conn State Rep, 88th Dist, 67-71; Conn State Sen, 15th Dist, 71- Bus & Prof Pos: Ins salesman, Prudential Ins Co, 60-72; owner, L S Cutillo Agency, 72- Mem: Gtr Waterbury Labor Coun; Int Ins Workers Union; Eagles; Nat Life Underwriters. Relig: Roman Catholic. Mailing Add: 22 Birchwood St Waterbury CT 06708

CUTLER, GOLDIE (D)
Mem, Dem Nat Comt, Calif
Mailing Add: 37 W Clay Park San Francisco CA 94121

CUTLER, PAUL HARLEY (R)
Chmn, Shelby Co Rep Orgn, Ill
b Moweaqua, Ill, Jan 31, 19; s William H Cutler & Katie A Coultas C; m 1946 to Georgia W Condon; c Debra Lynn, Garry Ken & Larry Paul. Educ: Moweaqua High Sch, grad, 38; LaSalle Exten Univ, Farm Eng & Mgt, 41; Dale Carnegie Course, 71. Polit & Govt Pos: Conservation officer, Shelby Co Rep Orgn, Ill, 57-62; mem, Rep Precinct Comt, Penn Twp, 57-, assessor, 69-; grain warehouse examr, Shelby Co Rep Orgn, 69-74; chmn, Shelby Co Rep Orgn, 74- Mem: AF&AM; Springfield Consistory; Ansar Temple; Twp Officials Ill; Farm Bureau. Honors & Awards: Master Farmer Cert of Achievement, AylcoLiquid Fertilizer, 66; Future Farmer of America Citation, Moweaqua Chap, 66; Voluntary Reporter for 10 years, Ill Coop Crop, Gov Otto Kerner, 67. Relig: Christian. Mailing Add: RR 2 Box 54 Moweaqua IL 62550

CUTTING, HAROLD D (R)
RI State Rep
Mailing Add: 465 Boston Neck Rd North Kingstown RI 02852

CUTTING, WENDELL RILEY (R)
Mem, Rep State Cent Comt, Calif
b Hemet, Calif, Aug 24, 46; to Bert Allen Cutting & Alice Patricia Riley C; single. Educ: Chapman Col, BA in Hist & Govt, 70. Polit & Govt Pos: Pres, Hemet-San Jacinto TAR, Calif, 62; pres, Hemet-San Jacinto Young Rep, 65; dir, Riverside Co Young Rep Bd, 65; precinct chmn, San Jacinto Rep Party, 66-; assoc mem, Rep State Cent Comt, Calif, 67-68, mem, 69-; dep cong dist dir, Calif Rep Assembly, 68, mem polit strategy & educ comts, 68, state dir-at-lg, 68 & 70-71, cong dist dir, 38th Dist, 69-, & chmn state & nat affairs comt, 70-71; campaign aide & strategist, Hunter for Cong Campaign Comt, 68; city councilman, City of San Jacinto, 70-, chmn, Parks & Recreation Comn, 70- Bus & Prof Pos: Radio newscaster, KCIN, Victorville, 66. Mil Serv: PFC, Calif Army Nat Guard. Mem: Am Polit Sci Asn; Am Hist Asn; CofC; Young Am for Freedom; World Youth Crusade for Freedom. Honors & Awards: Voice of Democracy Award, VFW. Relig: Methodist. Mailing Add: 1231 S Santa Fe San Jacinto CA 92383

CUTTS, ROYAL BARTLETT (R)
Vt State Rep
b Shelton, Conn, Feb 27, 10; m to Caroline Cate; c one son & two daughters. Educ: Vt State Sch of Agr. Polit & Govt Pos: Mem sch bd, Townshend, Vt, auditor, 38-47, town moderator, 43-65 & lister, 45-48; Vt State Rep, Townshend, 47-49 & 64-65, Dist 72, 66-, chmn, Natural Resource Comt, Vt House Rep, currently; committeeman, Vt Rep State Comt, currently. Bus & Prof Pos: Ins; tree farm; maple sugar orchard. Mem: Asn to Preserve Vt Const Govt; Grange; Townshend Vol Firemen's Asn; W River Valley Develop Asn. Relig: Congregational. Mailing Add: Townshend VT 05353

CYPERT, JAMES DEAN (D)
Committeeman, Washington Co Dem Comt, Ark
b Springdale, Ark, May 24, 34; s Burl Cypert & Opal Sisco C; m 1956 to Gaye Annette Warren; c Julie Jan & Jamie Ann. Educ: Univ Ark, BS & BA, 55, Sch Law, LLB, 58; Alpha Kappa Psi; Sigma Nu. Polit & Govt Pos: Pres, Washington Co Young Dem, Ark, 60; committeeman, Washington Co Dem Comt, 62-; sec elec comnr, 62-; deleg, Dem Nat Conv, 64. Mil Serv: Entered as 2nd Lt, Army, 56, released as Capt in Artil, 58. Mem: Kiwanis;

Commun Fund; Young Lawyers Asn; Ark Bar Asn; CofC. Honors & Awards: Outstanding Young Men of Am; Distinguished Serv Award, Jaycees, 63. Relig: Methodist. Legal Res: 111 Holcomb St Springdale AR 72764 Mailing Add: 1512 Circle Dr Springdale AR 72764

CYR, EDWARD P (D)
Maine State Sen
Mailing Add: Box 249 Madawaska ME 04756

CZARNECKI, MARIAN ANTHONY (D)
b Sept 18, 27; s Sigmund Czarnecki & Rose Sawicki C; m 1954 to Joan Humphreys; c John R, Andrew W & Julie Rose. Educ: Georgetown Univ Sch Foreign Serv, BSFS, 52, Grad Sch, 53-58. Polit & Govt Pos: Legis-admin asst to US House Rep, 49-59, staff consult, Comt on Foreign Affairs, 59-72, chief of staff, Comt on Int Rels, 72- Mil Serv: Entered as Pvt, Army, 46, released as Sgt, 48. Mailing Add: 1701 Juniper St NW Washington DC 20012

CZERWINSKI, JOSEPH C (D)
Wis State Rep
Mailing Add: 914 S Fourth St Milwaukee WI 53204

CZULOWSKI, EDWARD JOSEPH (D)
Committeeman, Dem Exec Comt, Fla
b Jackson, Mich, Apr 23, 14; s Paul Czulowski & Augustine Wnukowski C; m 1941 to Helen Valkuchak. Educ: Jackson Jr Col, 34-35; Sales Training Inc, 54. Polit & Govt Pos: State committeeman, Jackson, Mich, 46-48; committeeman, Dem Exec Comt, Fla, 75- Bus & Prof Pos: Vpres, Jr CCC, 41-47; owner & mgr, Restaurant & Bar, Jackson, Mich, 49-55 & Bldg & Construction, 52-55; FHA & GI Inspector, Jackson, Mich, 52-56; restaurant & tavern owner, Apalachicola, Fla, 56-71; dept store mgr, Fed Dept Stores, Detroit, Mich, 59-65; retired. Mailing Add: PO Box 204 Eastpoint FL 32328

D

DABROWSKI, EDWARD J, JR (D)
Md State Deleg
Mailing Add: 17 N Highland Ave Baltimore MD 21224

DADDARIO, EMILIO QUINCY (D)
b Newton Center, Mass, Sept 24, 18; m 1940 to Berenice Carbo; c Edward, Stephen & Richard. Educ: Wesleyan Univ, BA, 39; Boston Univ Law Sch, 39-41; Univ Conn, LLB, 42. Polit & Govt Pos: Mayor, Middletown, Conn, 46-48; judge, Middletown Munic Court, 48-50; US Rep, Conn, 59-70; deleg, Dem Nat Conv, 68; Cand Gov, 70. Bus & Prof Pos: Lawyer, 45-50, 52; bd trustees, Wesleyan Univ. Mil Serv: Army, 43, Mediterranean Theater; US Legion of Merit, Ital Medaglia d'Argento Medal; Nat Guard; Korean Conflict, 43rd Div, Maj, Far East Liaison Group, Korea, Japan. Mem: Conn & Mass Bars. Mailing Add: 1462 Asylum Ave Hartford CT 06105

DAGENHART, EWELL MARTIN (R)
Chmn, Alexander Co Rep Party, NC
b Taylorsville, NC, July 12, 24; s Edward Dagenhart & Clara Warren D; m 1944 to Evelyn Elder; c Neal Gene & James Lynn. Educ: Correspondence High Sch. Polit & Govt Pos: Rep precinct chmn, 60-66; chmn, Alexander Co Rep Party, NC, 66-, finance chmn, 69- Mil Serv: Entered as Seaman, Navy, 43, released as Seaman 1/C, 45; Asian & European Theater Ribbons. Mem: Community Develop; 4-H Club; VFW; Am Legion. Relig: Methodist. Mailing Add: Rte 2 Hiddenite NC 28636

DAGGETT, HORACE (R)
Iowa State Rep
Mailing Add: RR 1 Kent IA 50850

D'AGOSTINO, CARL JOSEPH, JR (D)
Mem, Orange Co Dem Cent Comt, Calif
b Socorro, NMex, Jan 1, 35; s Carl Joseph D'Agostino & Emily Fraissinet D; m 1955 to Evelyn Gonzales; c Carl, III, Ellen, Michael, Steven & Mark. Educ: NMex Inst Mining & Technol, BS, 55; Mass Inst Technol, PhD, 61; Sigma Xi. Polit & Govt Pos: Mem, Orange Co Dem Cent Comt, Calif, 67-; consult, Joint Comt Pub Domain, Calif State Legis, 68-69; prin consult Dem Caucus, Calif State Assembly, 70-74, chief consult majority caucus, 71-74; deleg, Dem Nat Conv, 72; campaign dir, Cory for Controller Campaign, 74; chief dep state controller, 75- Bus & Prof Pos: Sr scientist, Res Lab, Aeronutronic Div, Philco/Ford, 61-68. Publ: Co-auth, Biomolecular lipid membranes, In: Biophysics & Cybernetic Systems, Spartan Bks, 65; auth, The price of crude oil in California, Joint Comt Pub Domain, Calif State Legis, 69. Relig: Catholic. Legal Res: 602 E Palmdale Ave Orange CA 92665 Mailing Add: Off of Controller State Capitol Sacramento CA 95814

DAHL, ALLEN W (R)
b Waldheim, Sask, Apr 17, 28; s Henry S Dahl & Marie Berg D; m 1954 to Dolores M Weeks; c Charles A & Susan M. Educ: Univ of Wash, BS, 51, Med Sch, MD, 57. Polit & Govt Pos: Rep precinct committeeman, Snohomish Co, Wash, 65-73; deleg, Wash State Rep Conv, 66 & 68; chmn, Snohomish Co Rep Party, 66-69 & 73-74; chmn, Wash State Non-Partisan Comt Against A State Income Tax, 69-70 & 73. Bus & Prof Pos: Research instr, Univ of Wash Med Sch, 52-63; physician & surgeon, E Edmond Med Clin, Edmonds, Wash, 57-; vol speaker, Edmonds Schs; US Naval War Col, 72. Mil Serv: Entered as Pvt, Army, 44, released as S/Sgt, 46, after serv in Inf Spec Serv Unit, Pac, 44-45; Pac Theatre Ribbon; World War II Victory Medal. Publ: Derivatives of fluorene, J Organic Chem, 55; Decreased gastric activity with lignin, In: Proc Soc Exp Biol & Med, 57; Analysis of homografts, Arch of Path, 60. Mem: Wash State & King Co Med Socs; Am Med Asn. Relig: Protestant. Mailing Add: 21810 117th Pl W Edmonds WA 98020

DAHL, ARDEN (DFL)
Mem, Minn Dem-Farmer-Labor State Exec Comt
b Cottonwood, Minn, Aug 22, 13; s J B Dahl & Bertha Anderson D; m 1933 to Mabel Johnson; c Robert J & Janet M. Educ: Cottonwood High Sch & Cottonwood Bus Sch. Polit & Govt Pos: Secy-treas, Lyon Co Dem-Farmer-Labor Comt, Minn, 58-64; third vchmn, Minn State Dem-Farmer-Labor Party, 60, second vchmn, 62; vchmn, Sixth Dist Dem-Farmer-Labor Party, 60, chmn, 66-72; alt deleg, Dem Nat Conv, 64, deleg, 68; mem, Minn Dem-Farmer-Labor State Exec Comt, currently. Mem: Tracy CofC; Kiwanis. Relig: Lutheran. Mailing Add: 249 Elm St Tracy MN 56175

DAHL, CURTIS (R)
Mem, Norton Town Rep Comt, Mass
b New Haven, Conn, July 6, 20; s George Dahl & Elizabeth Curtis D; m 1952 to Mary Huntington Kellogg; c Julia Curtis & Winthrop Huntington. Educ: Yale Univ, BA, 41, MA, 42, PhD, 45; Phi Beta Kappa; Elizabethan Club; Berzelius; Chi Delta Theta. Polit & Govt Pos: Fence-viewer, Norton, Mass, 64-, mem town comt, 65-66 & 68-69; mem, Norton Town Rep Comt, 64-, chmn, 64-65 & 69-72, treas, 68-69; selectman, Norton, 69-72, mem hist comn, 72-, chmn hist dist study comt, 74-, vchmn charter comn, 74-75. Bus & Prof Pos: Eng, Wheaton Col, Mass, 48-; Fulbright lectr, Univ Oslo, 65-66. Publ: Robert Montgomery Bird, Twayne Publishers, 63; The Victorian wasteland, Col Eng, 55; Mr Smith's American Acropolis, Am Heritage, 58. Mem: Mod Lang Asn; Col Eng Asn; Am Studies Asn; Norton Hist Soc; Am Asn Univ Prof (pres, Wheaton Col chap, 72-73). Honors & Awards: Guggenheim & Carnegie fels, gen educ. Relig: Protestant. Mailing Add: 189 N Washington St Norton MA 02766

DAHL, HAROLD J (DFL)
Minn State Rep
Mailing Add: Howard Lake MN 55349

DAHL, JOHN L (D)
Okla State Sen
Mailing Add: State Capitol Oklahoma City OK 73105

DAHLIN, MELBA R (D)
b Emmetsburg, Iowa, Apr 9, 17; d Lloyd L Schaeffer & Hattie Anderson S; m 1948 to Alvin C Dahlin; c Herbert, Angela & Alvin, Jr. Educ: Univ Minn, 1 year. Polit & Govt Pos: Chmn, Isanti Co Democrat-Farmer-Labor Party, Minn, formerly; alt deleg, Dem Nat Conv, 68; vchmn, Third Dist Democrat-Farmer-Labor Party, chmn; vchmn, Eight Dist Democrat-Farmer-Labor Party. Bus & Prof Pos: Mem staff, Control Data. Mem: VFW Auxiliary; 4-H Club Leader; Co Nursing Auxiliary; Farmers Union. Relig: Lutheran. Mailing Add: Rte 1 Cambridge MN 55008

DAHM, MARION (DFL)
Treas, Stevens Co Dem-Farmer-Labor Party, Minn
b Stockport, Iowa, July 20, 18; s John Dahm & Ida Peterson D; m 1941 to Beulah Opal Bang; c Judy (Mrs Dale Webb), Lynn Ellen (Mrs Jack Lowrey) & Jonna Karlane. Educ: Clay Co Schs, Iowa. Polit & Govt Pos: Precinct deleg, Stevens Co Dem-Farmer-Labor Party, Minn, 66-, treas, 70-; chmn, Humphrey for Sen, Stevens Co, 70; mem, Sixth Dist Dem-Farmer-Labor Party, 70-; chmn, Minn State Dem-Farmer-Labor Party, 70-, state deleg, Duluth, 70; action officer, Farmer's Union, Minn, Stevens Co, 70-, deleg, Nat Meeting, Omaha, 73; coordr, Hon Sen Walter Mondale Reelec, 72, Hon Congressman Bob Bergland Elec, 72 & Hubert H Humphrey for President, 72; alt deleg, Minn Seventh Dist Conv, 72. Bus & Prof Pos: Automobile, diesel & elec mechanic, Spencer, Iowa & Chokio, Minn, 39-; farmer, 41-; custom combine contractor, Great Plains State & Can, 49-61; car racer, 54-69; scuba diver, Viking research work, 60- Mem: Stevens Co Hist Soc (pres, 70-); Farmers Union; Chokio Coop Elevator; Sportmans Club. Honors & Awards: Viking research work recognized on radio & TV progs & in many newspaper articles; Recognized Work in aerial infrared photography used in research work on Viking habitation site, Minn Hist Soc, 75. Relig: Lutheran. Mailing Add: Box 103 Main St Chokio MN 56221

DAIKER, DONALD ARTHUR (D)
Mem, Butler Co Dem Cent Comt, Ohio
b Passaic, NJ, Jan 20, 38; s Arthur Winfred Daiker & Dorothy Bridgeman D; m 1962 to Victoria Ann Galotta; c Pamela Ann, Stephen Barrett, Paul Bryan & Matthew Melville. Educ: Lyndhurst High Sch, NJ, 51-55; Rutgers State Univ, BA summa cum laude, 59; Ind Univ, Bloomington, PhD, 69; Phi Beta Kappa; Psi Chi; Delta Kappa Epsilon (pres). Polit & Govt Pos: Committeeman, Butler Co Dem Cent Comt, Ohio, 68-, chmn, 70-72; chmn, Butler Co Citizens for John Gilligan for Sen, 68; chmn, Butler Co Citizens for John Gilligan for Gov, 70; bd trustees, Butler Co Action Comn; chmn, Eighth Dist Ohio Orgn Comt for Muskie for President, 72; Dem Party Registr Drive, Eighth Dist, 72; canvassing dir, McGovern for President Campaign, Butler City, 72; mem, Gov Comt to Screen Univ Trustees, 72- Bus & Prof Pos: Instr Eng, Miami Univ, 64-69, asst prof, 69-74, assoc prof, 74- Mil Serv: Entered as 2nd Lt, Army, 60, released as 2nd Lt, 60, after serv in Adj Gen Sch, Ft Benjamin Harrison, Indianapolis, Ind, 60; Capt, Army Res. Mem: Modern Lang Asn; Melville Soc; Am Civil Liberties Union (Oxford-Hamilton Chap). Honors & Awards: Woodrow Wilson Nat Fel Found fel, 60-61; Ind Univ fel, 61-63. Mailing Add: 19 E Spring St Oxford OH 45056

DAILEY, MITCH R (D)
Exec VPres, Wash State Young Dem
b Yakima, Wash, Dec 12, 53; s Lynn H Dailey & Vivian Goatz D; single. Educ: Yakima Valley Community Col, AA, 73; Cent Wash State Col, Myron Davies Mem Scholar, 73, polit sci dept honors prog, 73, BA with distinction, 74; Gonzaga Univ, 74-75. Polit & Govt Pos: Spec proj coordr, US Sen Magnuson's Appreciation Comt, 74; eastern vpres, Wash State Young Dem, 74-75, exec vpres, 75-; deleg, Dem Nat Mid-Term Conf, 74; adv mem, Wash State Co Chmn & VChmn Asn, 75-; vchmn, Fifth Cong Dist Affirmative Action Comt, 75; adv mem, McCormick Cong Campaign Comt, 75- Mem: Asn Am Indian Affairs; Gonzaga Univ Student Bar Asn; Nat Hist Soc; Mason; Nat Asn Parliamentarians. Relig: Protestant. Mailing Add: 2003 S Cornell Ave Yakima WA 98903

DAILEY, OLLIE LEE (D)
Chmn, Winston Co Dem Party, Miss
b Macon, Miss, Dec 31, 03; s Tilman Dailey & Louisa Mattha D; m 1922 to Gertie Lee Hickman; c Ruthie Mae (Mrs Montgomery), Leonard Eugene, Lawrence & Burton Lee. Educ: Miss Baptist Sem, Jackson, 4 years; spec seminar, Univ Atlanta, 61; Cent Miss Col, DD, 66. Polit & Govt Pos: Chmn, Winston Co Dem Party, Miss, 67- Bus & Prof Pos: Minister, Mt Olive Missionary Asn, 37-, moderator, Winston Co & moderator & chmn, Baptist Training Union Cong, 59-; trustee & bd mem, Cent Miss Col, 42-; pres, Cent Miss Educ Conv, 62- Mem: Missionary Baptist Ministers & Deacons Coun; Mason; Miss Farm Bur Asn; NAACP; Miss Voter & Registr Educ League (pres, 62-). Honors & Awards: Presidential

Citation for Meritorious Leadership & Serv under admin of President Lyndon B Johnson. Relig: Baptist. Mailing Add: Rte 2 Box 364 Louisville MS 39339

DAILY, FRANK EDWARD, JR (R)
b Ashland, Kans, Apr 5, 16; s Frank Edward Daily & Georgia Dale D; m 1942 to Edith May Railsback; c Michael Robert & Nicholas Scott. Educ: Washburn Univ, AB & LLB, 40. Polit & Govt Pos: Co attorney, Comanche Co, Kans, 41-42, 46-55 & 59-; clerk, Common Sch Dist 1, Coldwater, 49-54; chmn, Comanche Co Rep Cent Comt, 56-74. Mil Serv: Entered as Pvt, Air Force, 42, released as S/Sgt, 45. Mem: Am Legion; Mason (Wichita Consistory, Midian Shrine); Southwest Kans Bar Asn; Coldwater Country Club; Lions; Coldwater Quarter Back Club. Relig: Methodist. Mailing Add: 311 N Philadelphia St Coldwater KS 67029

DAILY, O R (BUD) (D)
Wyo State Sen
b Logan, Kans, Nov 24, 17; s Otto Pierce Daily & Tessa Mae Clark D; m 1942 to Iona Bernice Burton; c Dianne Alice. Educ: Rawlins High Sch, grad. Polit & Govt Pos: Wyo State Rep, 61-74, Wyo State Sen, 75- Bus & Prof Pos: Shift supt, Sinclair-Atlantic Richfield, 40- Mil Serv: Entered as Pvt, Army, 41, released as 1st Sgt, 45, after serv in 45th Inf Div, ETO, 43-45; Purple Heart. Mem: Elks; Odd Fellows; VFW; Ansul Firefighters. Relig: Presbyterian. Legal Res: 723 13th St Rawlins WY 82301 Mailing Add: Box 1101 Rawlins WY 82301

DAIN, EVELYN RANDOLPH (R)
VChmn, Bay Co Rep Exec Comt, Fla
b Lineville, Ala, Sept 6, 27; d Henry Bachelor Randolph & Mildred Bell R; div; c Margaret Howell, Rebecca Lee & James Warren, III. Educ: Univ Wash, BS in Eng, 51; Delta Delta Delta. Polit & Govt Pos: Vchmn, Bay Co Rep Exec Comt, Fla, 67-, secy, 69-70; asst to chmn, First Cong Dist Fla Nixon Campaign, 68; pres, Women's Rep Club, Bay Co, 68-69; coordr, First & Second Cong Dist, Cramer for Senate, 70; Rep State committeewoman, Bay Co, 70-; alt deleg, Rep Nat Conv, 72; publicity chmn, Comt to Reelect Nixon, Bay Co, 72; vchmn, First Dist Rep Party, 72- Bus & Prof Pos: Pub rels dir, WJHG-TV, 68-71; mem eng staff, Int Paper Co, 73- Publ: Ed, Keeping Tab, 67-68. Mem: Mem Hosp Auxiliary; Salvation Army Bd; Am Cancer Soc (bd mem, Bay Co Chap, 68-). Relig: Episcopal. Mailing Add: 1207 W Tenth St Panama City FL 32401

DALBEY, JANET CAROL (R)
Young Rep Nat Committeewoman, Ill
b Evanston, Ill, Dec 1, 35; d James Millington Dalbey & Florence Johnson D; single. Educ: Northwestern Univ, 53-55; Alpha Chi Omega. Polit & Govt Pos: Exec dir, Ill Spec Events Comn, 70-72; tech adv, Gov Off Human Resources, 71-73; committeewoman, 50th Ward Regular Rep Orgn, 72-; Young Rep Nat Committeewoman, Ill, 71- Bus & Prof Pos: Exec secy, Lyric Opera of Chicago, 63-70, artistic coordr, 73- Mem: Women's Nat Rep Club of Chicago. Honors & Awards: Woman of the Year, Ill Young Rep Orgn, 69. Relig: Methodist. Mailing Add: 2003 W Touhy Chicago IL 60645

DALE, CLARENCE TAYLOR (R)
Chmn, Chariton Co Rep Cent Comt, Mo
b Milo, Mo, Dec 4, 11; s Charles Beard Dale & Cora Banta D; m 1935 to Goldie Pearl Johns; c James L. Educ: Park Col, 29-30; Cent Bus Col, 31. Polit & Govt Pos: Chmn, Mendon Twp Bd, Chariton Co, Mo, 52-62, Mendon Twp committeeman, 54-; vchmn, Chariton Co Rep Cent Comt, 60-64, chmn, 64- Bus & Prof Pos: Pres, Chariton Co Farmers Mutual Ins Co, 54- Mem: Mason. Relig: Methodist. Mailing Add: Mendon MO 64660

DALE, FRANCIS LYKINS (R)
Permanent US Rep to European Off UN
b Urbana, Ill, July 13, 21; s Charles Sherman Dale (deceased) & Sarah Lykins D (deceased); m 1948 to Kathleen Hamlin Watkins; c Mitchell W, Myron L, Kathleen Hamlin & Holly Moore. Educ: Duke Univ, AB, 43; Univ Va, LLB, 48; Omicron Delta Kappa; Order of the Coif; Phi Kappa Psi; Sigma Nu Phi; Univ Club; Queen City Club; Cincinnati Country Club; Commercial Club; Bankers Club; Recess Club; Optimist Club of Queen City Club; Cincinnati Lit Club. Hon Degrees: LLD, Eastern Ky Univ, 67, Univ Cincinnati, 67, Ohio Wesleyan Univ, 68, Chase Law Sch, 68 & Bloomfield Col (NJ), 73. Polit & Govt Pos: Permanent US Rep to European Off of UN, Geneva, Switz, 74- Bus & Prof Pos: Mem & partner, Frost & Jacobs, Law Firm, Cincinnati, Ohio, 48-65; pres & publ, Cincinnati Enquirer, 52-73; vchmn & pres, Cincinnati Reds, Inc, 67-73. Mil Serv: Entered as V-7, Navy, 43, released as Lt(jg), 46, after serv in Antisubmarine Warfare Unit, Atlantic, 44-46; Unit Citation. Mem: Nat Coun Crime & Delinquency (vchmn int rels); Boy Scouts (mem nat bd, mem exec bd, Transatlantic Coun); Boys' Club Am (nat assoc). Honors & Awards: Cincinnati's Outstanding Young Man of Year, 51; Gov Award for Advan of Prestige of Ohio, 67; Ohio Info Comt Award for Distinguished Leadership, 69. Relig: Methodist. Legal Res: 1421 Herschel Ave Cincinnati OH 45208 Mailing Add: US Mission 80 rue de Lausanne Geneva Switzerland

D'ALEMBERTE, TALBOT (SANDY) (D)
Mem Exec Comt, Dade Co Dem Party, Fla
b Tallahassee, Fla, June 1, 33; s Dan W D'Alemberte & Eleanor Whitfield D; m 1968 to Linda Sears; c Gabrielle Lyn & Joshua. Educ: Univ of the South, BA, 55; Rotary Found fel, Univ London, 58-59; Univ Fla, LLB with honors, 62; Omicron Delta Kappa; John Marshall Bar Asn; Order of the Coif; Fla Blue Key; Alpha Tau Omega. Polit & Govt Pos: Fla State Rep, formerly; Fla State Coordr for Robert F Kennedy Presidential Campaign, 68; state chmn, McGovern for President Campaign, 72; mem exec comt, Dade Co Dem Party, Fla, currently. Mil Serv: Lt, Navy, 55-58. Publ: Comments on Florida's constitution: Florida Statutes Annotated, West Publ Co, 69; Ombudsman, Nat Civic Rev, 12/66; Journalists under the axe: protection of confidential sources, Harvard J on Legis, 3/69; plus others. Mem: Am Bar Asn (chmn spec comt elec reform); Am Judicature Soc (bd dirs). Relig: Episcopal. Legal Res: 7741 SW 51st Ave Miami FL 33143 Mailing Add: First Nat Bank Bldg 14th Floor Miami FL 33131

D'ALESANDRO, THOMAS, JR (D)
b Baltimore, Md, Aug 1, 1903; s Thomas D'Alesandro & Mary Antoinette Foppiano D; m 1928 to Annunciata M Lombardi; c Thomas, III, Franklin D Roosevelt, Nicholas J, Hector, Joseph, Annunciata. Educ: Calvert Bus Col, Baltimore. Polit & Govt Pos: Md State Deleg, 26-33; mem, US Conf of Mayors & chmn, Standing Comt on Legis; gen dep collector, Internal Revenue, 33-34; mem, Baltimore City Coun, 35-38; US Rep, Md, 76th to 80th Cong; mayor, Baltimore, 47-59; Dem Nat Nat Committeeman, Md, 52-56; mem, US Renegotiation Bd, 61-69; deleg, Dem Nat Conv & mem, Platform & Rules Comts, seven convs; mem, Md State Bd of Parole, 71- Bus & Prof Pos: Owner, Thomas D'Alesandro Jr & Sons, Inc, Ins & Real Estate, Baltimore. Mem: Elks; KofC; Moose; Eagles; Holy Name Soc. Relig: Catholic. Mailing Add: 245 Albemarle St Baltimore MD 21202

DALEY, ANNE BELISLE (D)
b Lawrence, Mass, June 10, 07; d Hector Louis Belisle & Grace Potter B; m to James Alan Daley (deceased); c James Alan, Jr, Eliot Alexander, Walter Louis & Eugene Belisle. Educ: Middlebury Col, AB, 28; Fresno State Col; Univ Mass Exten, Boston; Kappa Kappa Gamma. Polit & Govt Pos: Mem, Fresno Co Adv Comt, US Wage & Price Controls, 52-53; mem, Dem Cong Dist Coun, Fresno, Merced & Madera Counties, 54-64; chmn arrangements for issues conf, Calif Dem Coun, 57-59, conv arrangements secy, 61 & dir, Fifth Cong Dist, 70; secy, Fresno Co Dem Coun, 57-62; secy, Fresno Co Dem Cent Comt, 60-64; mem, Calif Dem State Cent Comt, 60-64 & 68-70; mem, Calif Dem Key Women, 60-; vpres, Fresno Dem Women's Club, 64; chmn, Women Vol for Pat Brown, 66; pres, San Francisco Dem Women's Forum, 66-68; mem, Calif Adv Coun Bd Nurse Educ & Registr, 66-71, secy exec comt, NCalif Women's Div, 67-69; pres, San Francisco Coun Dem Clubs, 72-73; admin asst to Sheriff of San Francisco, 73-; deleg, Dem Nat Mid-Term Conf, 74. Bus & Prof Pos: Secy, United Farm Agency, San Francisco, 68-73. Publ: Poet, publ in periodicals, mag, newspapers & anthologies. Mem: Calif Coun Women's Archit Leagues; Friends of Dep & Inmates of San Francisco Jails (trustee & founder, 72-); San Francisco Tomorrow (founder); Nat Womens Polit Caucus; Calif Dem Coun (trustee, 73-). Honors & Awards: NCalif Key Vol Woman for Year, 66. Relig: Catholic. Mailing Add: 795 Geary St Apt 604 San Francisco CA 94109

DALEY, KATHERINE FAY (R)
Mem, Santa Clara Co Rep Cent Comt, Calif
b San Mateo, Calif, Sept 9, 26; d John Peter Daley (deceased) & Minerva Bosse D (deceased); single. Educ: Stanford Univ, AB, 48; Theta Sigma Phi. Polit & Govt Pos: Mem various campaign comts; mem, Santa Clara Co United Rep Finance Comt, Calif; founder & pres, Los Altos Young Rep, 52; mem, Palo Alto & Los Altos Chap, Calif Rep Assembly, 54-64, secy, Palo Alto chap, 60-62, vpres, Los Altos chap, 63; mem steering comt, US Rep Charles S Gubser, 54-72; vol staff mem, Young Rep Comt Arrangement, Rep Nat Conv, 56; chmn, Santa Clara Co Young Rep, 56; regional vpres, Calif State Young Rep, 56-57, state conv chmn, 56, newspaper ed, 57-58 & membership chmn, 58-59, alt & assoc mem, Santa Clara Co Rep Cent Comt, 6 years, mem, 62-, chmn, precinct comt, 4 years, chmn pub rels comt, currently; mem steering comt, Assemblyman George W Milias, 62-68; mem, Los Altos Rep Women Federated, 63-; vol staff mem, pub rels off, Rep Nat Comt for Rep Nat Conv, 64; founder & vpres, Los Altos Chap, Calif Rep League, 65, mem, 67-; secy, Stanford Rep Club, 68-; assoc mem, Calif Rep State Comt, 4 years, mem, currently; mem steering comt for precinct comt & youth activities comt; alt deleg, Rep Nat Conv, 72. Bus & Prof Pos: Research writer, Pathfinder News Mag, Washington, DC; assoc ed, Stanford Alumni Asn, 52- Mem: Los Altos Hist Comn; Theta Sigma Phi; Am Asn Univ Women. Relig: Methodist. Legal Res: 760 Dixon Way Los Altos CA 94022 Mailing Add: PO Box 387 Los Altos CA 94022

DALEY, PETER JOHN, II (D)
b Brownsville, Pa, Aug 8, 50; s Peter J Daley (deceased) & Gladys Linn Moyer D; single. Educ: Calif State Col, California, Pa, BS, 72, grad work in polit sci, currently; Pi Delta Epsilon; Tau Kappa Epsilon. Polit & Govt Pos: Chmn & SW Pa Dir, Col Young Dem of Pa, 70-72, mem, exec comt, 72; mem exec comt, Voters Rally for Pittsburgh, 72; western Pa chmn, Youth Coalition for Muskie, 72; alt deleg, Dem Nat Conv, 72; chmn, Washington Co Youth for McGovern, 72; chmn, Washington Co Young Dem, 72; cand, Mayor of the Borough of California, Pa, 73. Bus & Prof Pos: Secy-mem, Bd Trustees, Calif State Col, California, Pa, 72-, vpres, Alumni Asn, 72- Mem: Nat, Pa State & California Area Educ Asn; Lions. Honors & Awards: Distinguished Serv Award, Calif State Col, California, Pa, 72. Relig: Protestant. Legal Res: California PA 15419 Mailing Add: E Malden Dr Coal Center PA 15423

DALEY, RICHARD JOSEPH (D)
Mayor, Chicago, Ill
b Chicago, Ill, May 15, 02; s Michael Daley & Lillian D; m 1936 to Eleanor Guilfoyle; c Patricia, Eleanor, Richard, Michael, Mary Carol (Mrs Vanecho), John & William. Educ: DePaul Univ Law Sch, LLB, 33 & St Vincent DePaul Award, 66. Hon Degrees: LLD, Loyola Univ, 66. Polit & Govt Pos: Ill State Rep, 36-38; Ill State Sen, 38-46, minority leader, 41-46; dir revenue, State of Ill, 49, dep comptroller, Cook Co, Ill, 46-49, clerk, 50-55; chmn, Cook Co Dem Party, 53-; mayor, Chicago, Ill, 55-; Relig: Roman Catholic. Mailing Add: Rm 507 City Hall Chicago IL 60602

DALEY, WILLIAM JOSEPH (R)
b Parsons, Kans; s George Edward Daley & Willa Therese Holland D; single. Educ: Washburn Univ, BA, 70, Sch Law, JD, 74; Alpha Kappa Lambda. Polit & Govt Pos: Staff fieldman, Dole for Senate Comt, Topeka, 68; chmn, Washburn Univ Col Rep, 68-69; staff, Seaton for Attorney Gen, Topeka, summer 70; deleg & mem platform comt, Rep Nat Conv, 72; research asst, Sen Bob Dole, Washington, DC, 73-74, staff, Kansans for Sen Dole, Topeka, 74, field rep for Sen Bob Dole, Southeast Kans Off, Parsons, 75- Mem: Rotary Int. Relig: Roman Catholic. Mailing Add: 1730 Morgan Apt 3-W Parsons KS 67357

DALLAS, DEVAN (D)
Miss State Rep
b Okolona, Miss, Mar 4, 26; married. Polit & Govt Pos: Miss State Rep, currently. Bus & Prof Pos: Automobile & implements dealer. Mem: Am Legion; VFW; 40 et 8; Lions; Farm Bur. Relig: Baptist. Mailing Add: Box 538 Pontotoc MS 38863

DALLEY, GEORGE ALBERT (D)
b Havana, Cuba, Aug 25, 41; s Cleveland E Dalley & Constance Powell D; m 1970 to Pearl Elizabeth Love. Educ: Columbia Col, AB, 63, Columbia Univ Sch Law, LLB, 66, Grad Sch Bus, MBA, 66. Polit & Govt Pos: Asst counsel, Comt on Judiciary, US House Rep, 71-72; admin asst to US Rep Charles B Rangel, NY, 72- Bus & Prof Pos: Adminr, Metrop Appl Research Ctr, New York, 66-69; assoc counsel, Stroock & Stroock & Lavan, Washington, DC, 70-71. Mem: Am, DC & Nat Bar Asns. Relig: Presbyterian. Legal Res: 1328 Vermont Ave NW Washington DC 20005 Mailing Add: 107 Cannon House Off Bldg Washington DC 20515

DALTON, HERMAN UDELL (R)
b Reyno, Ark, Jan 10, 29; s David Lawrence Dalton & Irene Lamb D; m 1950 to Eula Mae King; c Sandra Lou, Daniel David & John Elijah. Polit & Govt Pos: Chmn, Randolph Co Rep Cent Comt, Ark, 64-74. Relig: Church of Christ. Legal Res: 500 Maple St Pocahontas AR 72455 Mailing Add: PO Box 87 Pocahontas AR 72455

DALTON, JOHN NICHOLS (R)
Lt Gov, Va
b Emporia, Va, July 11, 31; s Ted Dalton & Mary Turner D; m 1956 to Edwina Panzer; c Katherine S, Mary Helen, Ted E & John N, Jr. Educ: Col William & Mary, BA, 53; Univ Va, LLB, 57; Omicron Delta Kappa; Sigma Alpha Epsilon. Polit & Govt Pos: Chmn, Va Young Rep Fedn, 59-61; mem, Rep State Cent Comt, 59-72; gen counsel, Va Rep Party, 62-72; deleg, Rep Nat Conv, 60, alt deleg, 64 & 72; chmn, Radford City Rep Comt, 62-66; Va State Deleg, 66-72; Va State Sen, 72-73; Lt Gov, Va, 74- Bus & Prof Pos: Mem, First & Merchants Nat Bank, Radford Adv Bd, 65-72, bd dirs, 72- Mil Serv: Entered as 2nd Lt, Army, 54, released as 1st Lt, 56, after serv in 547th Armored Field Artil Bn, Ft Knox, Ky. Mem: Mason; KCCH (32 degree); Shrine; Am Legion; Moose. Relig: Baptist. Legal Res: 411 Fourth St Radford VA 24141 Mailing Add: PO Box 1089 Radford VA 24141

DALTON, MARY MILDRED (R)
Chmn, Caldwell Co Rep Exec Comt, Ky
b Princeton, Ky, Dec 27, 25; d Albert Hewlett Sigler & Mina Jones S; m 1946 to Basil Loyd Dalton. Educ: Cobb High Sch, grad, 44. Polit & Govt Pos: Secy, Caldwell Co Rep Exec Comt, Ky, 68-70, chmn, 70- Bus & Prof Pos: Secy, Princeton Hosiery Mills, 44- Relig: Protestant. Mailing Add: Rte 1 Princeton KY 42445

DALTON, SAMMY DALE (D)
WVa State Deleg
b West Hamlin, WVa, Aug 29, 51; s Howard Dalton & Georgia Dingess D; single. Educ: Marshall Univ, AB, 73. Polit & Govt Pos: WVa State Deleg, 74- Bus & Prof Pos: Sch teacher, Logan Co Bd Educ, 73- Mem: WVa Educ Asn. Mailing Add: RR1 Box 92 Harts WV 25524

DALY, EDNA M (R)
VChmn, Monroe Co Rep Party, NY
b Medford, Mass, Jan 21, 06; d Warren Leslie Faulkner & Rachel Kennedy F; m 1936 to Charles Bennett Daly; c Charles B, II & Edna M (Mrs Conley). Educ: Russell Sage Col, BA, 28. Polit & Govt Pos: Past pres, 18th Ward Womens Club; past pres, Rep Bus & Prof Women's Club; state committeewoman, Monroe Co Rep Party, 61-67; secy, Monroe Co Rep Party, 63-69, vchmn, 69-; deleg, NY Rep State Conv, 69; deleg, Rep Nat Conv, 72; treas, NY State Women's Rep Fedn, 72- Bus & Prof Pos: Sci teacher, Bd of Educ, Rochester, NY, 28-67. Mem: NY State & Rochester Teachers Asn; Sci Teachers Asn; Nat Educ Asn; Eastern Star. Relig: Presbyterian. Mailing Add: 143 Vermont St Rochester NY 14609

DALY, JOHN B (R)
NY State Assemblyman
Mailing Add: 430 Dutton Dr Lewiston NY 14902

DALY, JOSEPHINE FRANCIS (JO) (D)
Mem, Calif Dem State Cent Comt
b Washington, DC, June 6, 46; d Joseph Francis Daly & Charlotte Gartner D; single. Educ: Northern Va Community Col, 68-70; Phi Beta Lambda. Polit & Govt Pos: Pres, Alice B Toklas Mem Dem Club, Calif, 73-75, vpres, 75-; chairperson statewide Gay caucus, Calif Dem Coun, 73-75, northern chairperson, 75-; pres, Cable TV Task Force, San Francisco, 73-74; deleg-at-lg, Dem Nat Mid-Term Conf, 74; founder, Susan B Anthony Dem Club, 74; Gay Community liaison, Human Rights Comn, San Francisco, 75; mem, Calif Dem State Cent Comt, 75- Mem: Commonwealth Club Calif; Nat Orgn for Women, Golden Gate chap; Whitman-Radclyffe Found (dir); Soc for Individual Rights; Bay Area Womens Coalition. Honors & Awards: Feminist Party Media Workshop Award, 75. Relig: Roman Catholic. Mailing Add: 4080 20th St San Francisco CA 94114

DALY, MICHAEL JOHN (D)
Mass State Rep
b Boston, Mass, July 18, 40; s Jeremiah C Daly (deceased) & Bridget O'Mahony D; m 1966 to Elizabeth A Buckley; c 4. Educ: Boston State Col, BS in Educ, 64; Alpha Psi Omega, Rho Beta Chap; Newman Club; pres, Sr Class. Polit & Govt Pos: Deleg, Mass Dem State Conv, 64 & 66; mem, 22nd Ward Dem Comt, 64-67 & 72-; mem, Boston City Dem Comt, Mass, 64-67; Mass State Rep, 67-, chmn, Joint Comt Educ, Mass House Rep, 71-; alt deleg, Dem Nat Conv, 68. Bus & Prof Pos: Teacher, Boston Pub Sch Syst, 64-66. Mem: Allston Civic Asn; Allston Brighton Citizens' Coun; KofC (4 degree); Gtr Boston Jr CofC; Gtr Boston Young Dem. Relig: Roman Catholic. Mailing Add: 15 Burton St Brighton MA 02135

DAM, C EVERETT (D)
Maine State Rep
Mailing Add: 102 Beech St Skowhegan ME 04976

D'AMANTE, CARMINE F (D)
NH State Rep
Mailing Add: 174 North St Claremont NH 03743

D'AMATO, ARMAND P (R)
NY State Assemblyman
b Newark, NJ, May 30, 44; s Armand Michael D'Amato & Antionette Cioffari D; single. Educ: St John's Univ, BBA, 66; Suffolk Univ, Sch Law, JD, 69. Polit & Govt Pos: Legis counsel, NY State Legis, 71-72, NY State Assemblyman, 73- Bus & Prof Pos: Attorney, McGinnity, Bernstein & D'Amato, 71- Mem: Nassau Co Bar Asn; Freeport Cancer Soc (hon pres); Bellmore-Merrick Cancer Soc (hon pres); Sons of Italy (charter mem, Rocky Marciano Lodge). Relig: Catholic. Legal Res: 15 Ostend Rd Island Park NY 11518 Mailing Add: 30 Grove Court Baldwin NY 11510

DAMBORG, PETER MARTIN (R)
Dep Secy of State, Maine
b Augusta, Maine, May 18, 19; s Peter Martin Damborg & Augusta Molbeck D; m 1970 to Phyllis Boudreau; c Karen (Mrs Andrew Allen) & Kirk M. Educ: Gates Bus Col, 38. Polit & Govt Pos: Dir, Vet Serv Ctr, Augusta, Maine, 46; mem, Augusta City Coun, 47-48; campaign coordr, James S Erwin for Gov, 70; Dep Secy of State, Maine, 71- Bus & Prof Pos: Polit-legis writer, Gannett Newspapers, Maine, 62-69; coun, 72-; dir info & publ, Conn State Employees Asn, 69-70; mem, Maine State Personnel Bd, 72- Mil Serv: Entered as Pvt, Air Force, 42, released as S/Sgt, 45. Mem: Assembly of Govt Employees; Pub Rels Soc Am; Pub Personnel Asn; Maine Press Asn; Maine Snowmobile Asn (dir, 73-74). Relig: Protestant. Legal Res: Little Cobbossee Ave East Winthrop ME Mailing Add: State House Augusta ME 04330

D'AMBROSA, ARNOLD J (D)
NJ State Assemblyman
Mailing Add: State House Trenton NJ 08625

DAME, C CECIL (R)
NH State Rep
Mailing Add: 93 Colonial Dr Portsmouth NH 03801

DAMES, GEORGE P (D)
Mo State Rep
b O'Fallon, Mo, June 12, 37; s Omer J Dames & Madeleine McAtte D; m 1970 to Millie M Heppermann; c Teresa Lynette & Tammy Lee. Educ: Assumption High Sch, grad. Polit & Govt Pos: First vpres, Dardenne Dem Club, Mo, 69-71; Mo State Rep, 71-, vchmn, Const Amendments Comt, mem, Econ Comt, Interior Affairs Comt & Workmans Compensation Comt, Mo House Rep, currently. Mem: Carpenters Local 1987; Lions. Relig: Catholic. Mailing Add: 8 S Boxwood O'Fallon MO 63366

D'AMICO, JOHN C (D)
RI State Sen
Mailing Add: 10 Grape Ct Cranston RI 02920

DAMMAN, JAMES J (R)
Lt Gov, Mich
b Grosse Pointe Park, Mich, Jan 16, 33; m 1956 to Margaret A; c James J, Jr, Joan E, Stephen C, Susan M, Mark L & Sandra M. Educ: Univ Detroit Col Com & Finance, BS, 54; Mkt Club (pres, 53-54). Polit & Govt Pos: Mem, Zoning Bd of Appeals, Troy, Mich, 67-68; city comnr, 69-70; Mich State Rep, 71-74; Lt Gov, 74- Bus & Prof Pos: Past nat exec secy, Allied Hardware Distributors Asn; vpres, A L Damman Hardware Co, Sterling Heights, Mich, 56- Mil Serv: Army, 54, released as SP-4, 56. Mem: Troy Rotary Club; Troy Drug Alert Comt. Honors & Awards: Cert of Appreciation for Outstanding Serv as City Comnr, Troy, Mich, 69-70. Relig: Catholic. Legal Res: 2751 Lake Charnwood Blvd Troy MI 48084 Mailing Add: Rm 128 Capitol Bldg Lansing MI 48901

DAMON, HENRY EUGENE (R)
Mem, Exec Comt, Miss Rep Party
b Meridian, Miss, Dec 20, 26; s Henry Eugene Damon & Em Neville Cochran D; m 1950 to Wilhelmine Streater Tew; c Sarah Neville, Wilhelmine Tew & Ann Amelia. Educ: Georgia Inst Technol, BCE, 49; Tau Beta Pi; Chi Epsilon; Omicron Delta Kappa; Sigma Alpha Epsilon. Polit & Govt Pos: Mem exec comt, Miss Rep Party, currently; alt deleg, Rep Nat Conv, 68. Bus & Prof Pos: Asst city engr, Meridian, Miss, 49-51; pres & consult engr, Assoc Consult, Inc, 53- Mil Serv: Entered as Pvt, Army, 45, released as Pfc, 46, after serv in Hq Third Army, Ger; re-entered as 2nd Lt, Corps Engrs, 51, released as 1st Lt, 53, after serv in 336th EUD, Hq, Eighth Army, Korea; Capt, Army Res (Ret); Good Conduct, Am Theater, World War II Victory, Army of Occupation, UN Command, Korea & Commendation Medal. Mem: Am Soc Civil Engrs; Nat & Miss Soc Prof Engrs; Consult Engrs Coun; Miss Asn Land Surveyors. Honors & Awards: Miss Engr of the Year, 71. Relig: Episcopal. Mailing Add: 1300 23rd Ave Meridian MS 39301

D'AMOURS, NORMAN EDWARD (D)
US Rep, NH
b Holyoke, Mass, Oct 14, 37; s Albert L D'Amours & Edna Laplant D; m 1965 to Helen E Manning; c Danielle Ann, Susan Ellen & Norman Manning. Educ: Assumption Col (Mass), AB, 60; Boston Univ Law Sch, LLB, 63. Polit & Govt Pos: Asst Attorney Gen, State of NH, 66-69; city prosecutor, Manchester, 70-72; alt deleg, Dem Nat Conv, 72; chmn, First Cong Dist Dem Party, 72-; mem, Dem Nat Charter Comt, currently; US Rep, NH, 75- Bus & Prof Pos: Pvt law practice, Manchester, 69-; instr criminal evidence, St Anselm's Col, 71- Mil Serv: Entered as E-1, Army Res, 64, released as E-4, 67. Mem: Manchester, NH & Mass Bar Asns; Manchester Optimist Club; Elks. Relig: Catholic. Legal Res: 617 Coolidge Ave Manchester NH 03102 Mailing Add: 922 Elm St Manchester NH 03101

DAMRON, CHARLES HOADLEY (D)
WVa State Deleg
b Kermit, WVa, Mar 18, 44; s George Hoadley Damron & Pauline Mills D; m 1966 to Carolyn Sue Smith; c Charles Hoadley, Jr. Educ: Marshall Univ, AB, 65; Western Md Col, MEd, 69; WVa Univ, JD, 71. Polit & Govt Pos: Admin asst, State Supt Schs, WVa Dept Educ, 71-72; mem, WVa State Dem Exec Comt, 72-; pres, Putnam Co Young Dem, WVa, 74-76; alt deleg, Dem Nat Mid-Term Conf, 74; WVa State Deleg, 74-, vchmn educ comt, WVa House Deleg, 74-; chmn, State Young Dem Conv, 74. Bus & Prof Pos: Teacher, WVa, 64-65; job corps instr, US Dept Interior, 65-66; teacher, Md, 66-68; attorney-at-law, Point Pleasant, WVa, 71- Mil Serv: Entered as Seaman Recruit, Naval Res, 61, released as Seaman, 65. Mem: Mason Co Farm Bur; Am Legion; Phi Alpha Delta; Am Judicature Soc; Am Bar Asn. Honors & Awards: Lectr to WVa State Bar & WVa Acad Sch Adminr, WVa Sch Law, 73. Relig: Methodist. Legal Res: Evergreen Ridge Fraziers Bottom WV 25082 Mailing Add: 232 1/2 Main St Point Pleasant WV 25550

DAMRON, IRVINE KEITH (D)
WVa State Deleg
b Williamson, WVa, July 27, 47; s George Hoadley Damron (deceased) & Pauline Mills D; m 1968 to Pamela Kay Adams; c Irvine Keith, II. Educ: Marshall Univ, AB Admin, 69; SWVa Community Col, spring 73; Marshall Univ, fall 73; Soc for Advan Mgt; Phi Kappa Sigma; WVa Univ Varsity Track Team Letterman. Polit & Govt Pos: WVa State Deleg, 75- Bus & Prof Pos: Sales rep, IBM, Pittsburgh, Pa & New York, NY, 69-70; dept mgr, Finlay Depts, New York, 70-72; owner & mgr, Damron's Cash Store, Lenore, WVa, 73- Mil Serv: Entered as Pvt, Marine Corps Reserve, 69, released as Lance Cpl, 72; 2nd Lt, WVa Nat Guard, 72- Mem: Mingo Co Young Dem Club (pres); Moose; 5-23 Flying Club. Relig: Methodist. Mailing Add: Box 44 Lenore WV 25676

DAMRON, WILLIAM ORVILLE (R)
Mem, Hancock Co Rep Cent Comt, Ill
b Basco, Ill, Oct 27, 07; s William Henry Damron & Lucy Agnes Peter D; m 1941 to Bernice Louise Schilling, c John Milton, Richard Alan & James David. Educ: Univ Ill, AB, 29. Polit & Govt Pos: Twp supvr, Bear Creek, Ill, 37-43 & 49-57; pres bd trustees, Basco, 46-; mem, Hancock Co Rep Cent Comt, 35-, chmn, 50-68. Bus & Prof Pos: Owner, Damron Radio, 33-; field investr, Ill Com Comn, 54-61; secy, Wythe Twp Mutual Fire Ins Co, 65-; owner, Damron Ins Agency, 65- Mil Serv: Entered as A/S, Navy, 43, released as Radio Tech, 2/C, 45, after serv with Amphibious Forces, Pac Theatre; Am Theatre Ribbon; Asiatic-Pac Ribbon; Victory

Medal. Mem: Basco Lodge 618, AF&AM; Scottish Rite; Ralph Parker Post 682, Am Legion. Relig: Baptist. Mailing Add: Basco IL 62313

DAMSCHRODER, GENE (R)
Ohio State Rep
b Ohio, Jan 14, 22; m 1945 to Lu Hufford; c Bonnie, Annette, Rex, Cheri & David. Educ: High sch grad, 40. Polit & Govt Pos: Ohio State Rep, 73- Bus & Prof Pos: Owner, Fremont Progress Airport, Ohio, 45- Mil Serv: Entered as Cadet, Navy, 42, released as Ens, 46, after serv in Air Force, WI. Mem: Am Legion; Farm Bur; Kiwanis Int. Relig: Lutheran. Mailing Add: 365 Star Rte 53 Fremont OH 43420

DAMSEY, JOAN ROBERTA (D)
Mem, Dem State Exec Comt Fla
b Jamestown, NY, Sept 12, 31; d Fred V Landy & Sara Caccamise L; m 1955 to Lloyd Damsey, MD; c Eve, Laurie, Lloyd, Jr & J Landy. Educ: Col of St Elizabeth, Convent, NJ & Catholic Univ Am, BA & MA. Polit & Govt Pos: Mem, Dem State Exec Comt Fla & mem adv comt, State Dem Comt Fla, 62-; mem platform & policy comt & exec comt, platform comt, Dem Nat Conv, 64; chmn, 12th Cong Dist Dem Party, Fla, 62-68. Bus & Prof Pos: Dir & personnel mgr, Marathon Med Clin, 57- Mem: Women of the Moose; Does; Am Legion Auxiliary; Beta Sigma Phi. Honors & Awards: Selected by Lyndon B Johnson to make his nomination by acclamation motion from rostrum at Atlantic City, Dem Nat Conv, 64. Relig: Catholic. Mailing Add: 2805 Overseas Hwy Marathon FL 33050

DANA, DEANE, JR (R)
Mem, Rep State Cent Comt Calif
b New York, NY, July 9, 26; s Deane Dana & Dorothy L D; m 1951 to Doris Weiler; c Deane, III, Marguerite, Diane W & Dorothy W. Educ: Stevens Inst Technol, Hoboken, NJ, ME, 51; Khoda; Chi Phi. Polit & Govt Pos: Pres, Long Beach Suburban Rep Club, Calif, 62; Pres, Lincoln Rep Club, 67-69; alt, 39th Assembly Dist Rep Co Cent Comt, 62-63; Alt, 46th Assembly Dist Rep Co Cent Comt, 67-70, mem & chmn, 70-; assoc mem, Rep State Cent Comt Calif, 64-67, mem, 67-; chmn, Nixon for President Comt, Palos Verdes Peninsula, 68; Los Angeles Co chmn, State Sen George Deukmejian for Attorney Gen, 70. Bus & Prof Pos: Engr through dist engr, Pac Tel & Tel Co, Los Angeles, Calif, 51- Mil Serv: Entered as 2nd Lt, Air Force, 51, released as 1st Lt, 53, after serv in Air Defense Command. Mem: Lincoln Rep Club; Long Beach Suburban Rep Club; Peninsula Coun for Youth. Relig: Episcopal. Mailing Add: 1633 Espinosa Circle Palos Verdes Estates CA 90274

DANAHER, JOHN ANTHONY (R)
b Meriden, Conn, Jan 9, 99; s Cornelius Joseph Danaher & Ellen Ryan D; m 1921 to Dorothy King; c John, Jr, Robert C & Jeanne (Mrs Lennhoff). Educ: Yale Col, AB, 20; Yale Law Sch, 21; Beta Theta Pi; Elihu; Corbey Court. Polit & Govt Pos: Asst US Attorney, Dist Conn, 23-34; Secy of State, Conn, 33-35; US Sen, Conn, 39-45; US Circuit Judge, DC Circuit, 53-69, Sr Circuit Judge, 69- Mil Serv: Entered as Pvt, Field Artil, 17, released as 2nd Lt, 18. Mem: Metrop Club, Washington, DC. Relig: Roman Catholic. Mailing Add: 622 Fed Bldg Hartford CT 06103

DANCE, JAMES HAROLD, JR (R)
Mem, Alameda Co Rep Cent Comt, Calif
b New London, Wis, Aug 30, 32; s James H Dance & Bessie Somers D; m 1973 to Janet Rene Marler. Educ: Univ Wis, BS Met Eng, 55; Prog for Mgt Develop, Harvard Grad Sch Bus, 69; Phi Eta Sigma; Pi Kappa Alpha. Polit & Govt Pos: Rep precinct worker, San Francisco, Calif, 61-65; Rep precinct chmn, 14th Assembly Dist, 67; vpres, Alameda Rep Assembly, 67 & 68, pres, 69; mem, Rep State Cent Comt Calif, 69-; mem, Alameda Co Rep Cent Comt, 69-, treas, 70-74; pres, Alameda Co Coord Rep Assembly, 70- Bus & Prof Pos: Salesman, Kaiser Aluminum & Chem Corp, Oakland, Calif, 57-61, sr mkt analyst, 61-65, mgr corp invest anal, 66-70, mgr bus planning & develop, Kaiser Chem Div, 70-72, mgr financial planning, Kaiser Aetna, 72- Mil Serv: Entered as 2nd Lt, Air Force, 55, released as Capt, 57, after serv in Research & Develop, Lewis Flight Propulsion Ctr, NASA, Cleveland, Ohio. Publ: Rupture strength of several nickel base alloys, Nat Adv Comt for Aeronaut, 57. Mem: F&AM. Relig: Methodist. Mailing Add: 1234 Crimson Ct Walnut Creek CA 94596

DANDENEAU, MARCEL (D)
Wis State Rep
b Racine, Wis, June 28, 31; s Albert Dandeneau & Justine Breland D; m 1954 to Marjorie Pier; c Renee. Educ: Dom Col, BA; Col at Racine, MS; Epsilon Alpha Beta. Polit & Govt Pos: Town Bd Supvr, Racine, 71-; Wis State Rep, 75- Bus & Prof Pos: Teacher, Racine United Schs, 60-75. Mil Serv: Entered as Pvt, Army, 51, released as Sgt, 54, after serv in 45th Div, Korea, 52-53. Mem: KofC; VFW; Caledonia Prof Men; Developmental Disabilities Bd; Pop Estimating Coun. Honors & Awards: Racine Jaycees Man of Year, 67; Wis Asn for Retarded Citizens Spec Award, 73. Relig: Catholic. Mailing Add: 4210 N Main St Racine WI 53402

D'ANDREA, ROBERT ANTHONY (R)
NY State Assemblyman
b Elizabeth, NJ, Aug 17, 33; s Domenic D'Andrea & Jean Farone D; m 1959 to Theresa DelVecchio; c Domenic, Mary Grace, Faust, Jean & Louise. Educ: Bentley Sch Acct, 51-52; Siena Col, 52-54; Siena Alumni. Polit & Govt Pos: Supvr, City of Saratoga Springs, NY, 68-74; vchmn, Capital Dist Regional Planning Comn, 72-75, pres-chmn, 75-; NY State Assemblyman, 75- Bus & Prof Pos: Co-owner, Kaydeross Park, Saratoga Springs. Mem: KofC; Elks; Ital-Am War Vet; Siena Col Alumni Asn. Honors & Awards: Hon mem, Saratoga Springs Fire Dept, Middle Grove Fire Dept & Greenfield Auxiliary. Relig: Roman Catholic. Mailing Add: RD 1 Kaydeross Park Saratoga Springs NY 12866

DANEKAS, WILLIS W (D)
SDak State Rep
Mailing Add: Raymond SD 57258

DANFORTH, BONNIE LEWIS (R)
NH State Rep
b High Point, NC, Mar 31, 24; d Dorsey Marvin Lewis & Bonnie Inez Justice L; m 1947 to Paul Dow Danforth; c Sherry, Debra, Susan & Paula. Educ: High Point Col, BS, 44; Sigma Alpha Phi. Polit & Govt Pos: Deleg, NH Const Conv, 74; deleg, NH Rep Conv, 74; NH State Rep, 75- Relig: Protestant; lay leader, Peoples United Methodist Church. Mailing Add: Scribner Rd Fremont NH 03044

DANFORTH, JOHN CLAGGETT (R)
Attorney Gen, Mo
b St Louis, Mo, Sept 5, 36; s Donald Danforth & Dorothy Claggett D; m 1957 to Sally B Dobson; c Eleanor, Mary, Dorothy, Johanna & Thomas John. Educ: Princeton Univ, AB, 58; Yale Univ Divinity Sch, BD, 63; Yale Univ Law Sch, LLB, 63. Hon Degrees: LLD, from various cols; DD, Lewis & Clark Col; LHD, Lindenwood Col. Polit & Govt Pos: Mem, President's Task Force on Prisoner Rehabilitation, 69-70; Attorney Gen, Mo, 69-; chmn, Mo Law Enforcement Assistance Coun, 73-74. Bus & Prof Pos: Asst rector, Church of the Epiphany, New York, 63-66; attorney, Davis Polk Wardwell Sunderland & Kiendl, 64-66; attorney, Bryan, Cave, McPheeters & McRoberts, St Louis, Mo, 66-68; assoc rector, Church of St Michael & St George, Clayton, Mo, 66-68; assoc rector, Grace Episcopal Church, Jefferson City, currently. Publ: The Christian in politics—the politician as a leader, Theol Today, 1/70. Mem: St Louis Country Club; Bogey Club; Jefferson City Country Club. Honors & Awards: Distinguished Service Award, St Louis Jaycees, 69; Outstanding Young Man, Mo Jaycees, 68. Relig: Episcopal; Hon Canon, Christ Church Cathedral, 71. Legal Res: 340 Fox Creek Rd Jefferson City MO 65101 Mailing Add: Supreme Ct Bldg Jefferson City MO 65101

DANG, MARVIN SECK CHOW (R)
b Honolulu, Hawaii, Feb 11, 54; s Brian Kwong Toong Dang & Flora Yuen D; single. Educ: Univ Hawaii, BA, with distinction, 74; Phi Beta Kappa; Phi Kappa Phi; Phi Eta Sigma; assoc justice, Student Court, 72-73; chmn, Young Voters Hawaii, 73-75; mem, Faculty Promotions Comt, Dept Polit Sci, 73; debater, Lincoln-Douglas Debate Tournaments, 74. Polit & Govt Pos: Precinct pres & Sen Dist treas, Rep Party Hawaii, 73-74; legis intern, State Senator Wadsworth Yee, 74; co-chmn & eval officer, Youth for the reelection of Sen Wadsworth Yee Comt, 74; vol, Campaigns for Lt Gov Nelson Doi & US Sen Dan Inouye, 74; state comnr, State Comn Children & Youth, 74-, chmn action comt for young adults & legis comt, 74-; admin aide, State Rep Dan Hakoda, 75- Bus & Prof Pos: Asst city ed & admin affairs ed, Ka Leo O Hawaii, 71-72; clerk typist, Fed Aviation Admin, summers, 71-75; surv asst & field supvr, Pub Affairs Adv Serv, Inc, 74- Publ: Co-auth, A descriptive analysis of the persuasive strategies used in a state senate campaign, Communication, 6/75. Mem: Panahou Alumni Asn; Univ Hawaii Alumni Asn; Hawaii Bicentennial Comn Horizons Comt; Common Cause. Honors & Awards: Spec Achievement Award, Fed Aviation Admin, 71, 72, 73 & 74; Cert of Appreciation, YMCA, 75; Cert in recognition of outstanding achievement & contrib to Univ Hawaii, Assoc Students Univ Hawaii, 73. Mailing Add: 2216 Sea View Ave Honolulu HI 96822

DANGERFIELD, CLYDE MOULTRIE (D)
SC State Rep
b Oakley, SC, Feb 24, 15; s Obie J Dangerfield, Sr & Abbie Locklair D; m 1946 to Pauline E Nelson; c Clyde, Jr, Dolores Elizabeth, Shirley Ann, Timothy Nelson & Susan Marie. Educ: Clemson Col, 39-40. Polit & Govt Pos: SC State Rep, 54-, chmn, Labor, Commerce & Indust Comt, SC House Rep, currently. Bus & Prof Pos: Owner, Gas & Elec Appliance Store; pres, Suburban Gas & Appliance Co, Inc. Mil Serv: S/Sgt, Army, 42-45, serv in Hq Inf Replacement Training Ctr, Camp Croft, SC. Mem: Exchange Club; Mason; Am Legion; Vol Fire Dept, Isle of Palms (capt). Relig: Methodist; trustee, First Methodist Church, Isle of Palms. Mailing Add: 896 America St Charleston SC 29403

DANIEL, BRUCE B (D)
RI State Rep
Mailing Add: 144 Grace St Cranston RI 02910

DANIEL, EDWARD C (R)
Vt State Rep
Mailing Add: 57 Canada St Swanton VT 05488

DANIEL, JAMES EDWARD (R)
Mem, McNairy Co Rep Exec Comt, Tenn
b Jackson, Tenn, Sept 9, 35; s Bedford Eugene Daniel & Jesse Ardell Blankenship D; m 1957 to Peggy Jewell Williams; c James Michael & Melanie Michelle. Educ: Univ Tenn Exten, 65; Jackson State Col, 68. Polit & Govt Pos: McNairy Co chmn, Ken Roberts Senate Primary, 66; McNairy Co vchmn, Howard Baker Senate Elec, 66; chmn, McNairy Co Young Rep, 67-68, dir, 69-; chmn, Seventh Dist Young Rep, 67-70; co-chmn, Seventh Dist Cong Campaign John T Williams, 68; Seventh Dist coordr, Sen Bill Brock Campaign, 70; mem, McNairy Co Rep Exec Comt, 70-; chmn, Tenn Young Rep Fedn, formerly; dist chmn, Tom Garland for Pub Serv Comnr Campaign. Bus & Prof Pos: Asst engr, SCent Bell Tel, Selmer, Tenn, 65- Mil Serv: Entered as Pvt, Army Res, 57, released as M/Sgt, 66, after serv in 230th Signal Bn, Tenn Army Nat Guard, 57-66; Co A, 230th Signal Bn, 30th Armored Div Commendation Award; nominee for Gen Trophy. Mem: Cubmaster, Pack 32, 67-70, Webelos leader, 69-70; scout master, Troop 232, currently; McNairy Co Young Rep Club. Honors & Awards: Outstanding Young Rep, Tenn, 69; Hon Col, Staff of Gov Winfield Dunn, 71; plaque from US Sen Howard Baker for serv to Rep Party & people of Tenn, 71; Past Chmn Award, Tenn Fedn Young Rep, 71; adult rep to Nat Boy Scout Jamboree E, Pa, 73. Relig: Baptist; team teacher, Young Adult Sunday Sch, First Baptist Church, Selmer. Legal Res: 311 Morningside Dr Selmer TN 38375 Mailing Add: Box 383 Selmer TN 38375

DANIEL, MICHAEL R (D)
SC State Rep
Mailing Add: Box 249 Gaffney SC 29340

DANIEL, PRICE (D)
Assoc Justice, Tex Supreme Court
b Dayton, Tex, Oct 10, 10; s Marion Price Daniel & Nannie Partlow D; m 1940 to Jean Houston Baldwin; c Price, Jr, Jean (Mrs David Murph), Houston Lee & John Baldwin. Educ: Baylor Univ, AB, 31, JD, 32; Sigma Delta Chi. Hon Degrees: LLD, Baylor Univ; Howard Payne Col & ETex Baptist Col. Polit & Govt Pos: Tex State Rep, 38-45, Speaker, Tex House Rep, 43-45; Attorney Gen, Tex, 47-53; US Sen, Tex, 53-57; Gov, Tex, 57-63; mem, Tex State Libr & Hist Comn, 64-69; deleg, Dem Nat Conv, 68; assoc justice, Tex Supreme Court, 71- Bus & Prof Pos: Attorney-at-law, Liberty, Tex, 32-47 & 63-71. Mil Serv: Entered as Pvt, Army, 43, released as Capt, 46, after serv in Security Intel Corps, Judge Adv Gen Corps, US & Pac. Publ: Publication Laws of Texas, 48 & Sovereignty & Ownership in the Marginal Sea, 50, State of Tex; Mansions & Capitols of America, G P Putnam's Sons, 68. Mem: Tex State Bar; Am Bar Asn; Int Law Asn; Am Soc of Int Law; Mason (33 degree). Relig: Baptist. Legal Res: Holly Ridge Ranch Liberty TX 77575 Mailing Add: Tex Supreme Ct Austin TX 78711

DANIEL, ROBERT WILLIAMS, JR (R)
US Rep, Va
b Richmond, Va, Mar 17, 36; s Robert W Daniel & Charlotte Bemiss D; m 1964 to Sally Chase; c Robert W, III, Charlotte B & Nell L. Educ: Univ Va, BA, 58; Columbia Univ, MBA, 61; Phi Kappa Psi. Polit & Govt Pos: Officer, US Cent Intel Agency, 64-68; secy, Prince George Co Planning Comn, Va, 72; mem, Va Bd of Conserv & Econ Develop, 72; deleg, Rep Nat Conv, 72; US Rep, Fourth Cong Dist, Va, 72- Bus & Prof Pos: Financial analyst, Wheat & Co, Richmond, Va, 61-62; instr econ, Univ Richmond, 63; owner & operator, Brandon Plantation, Spring Grove, 68- Mil Serv: Entered as 2nd Lt, Army, 59, released as 2nd Lt, 59, after serv in Qm Corps. Mem: Phi Beta Kappa; Va Farm Bur; Hopewell Moose; Metrop Club, Washington, DC. Legal Res: Spring Grove VA Mailing Add: US House of Rep Washington DC 20515

DANIEL, W C (DAN) (D)
US Rep, Va
b Chatham, Va, May 12, 14; s Reuben Earl Daniel & Georgie Grant D; m to Ruby McGregor; c Jimmie Foxx. Educ: Va schs; Dan River Textile Sch. Polit & Govt Pos: Civilian adv to the Second Army; mem, Reemploy Rights Comt, US Dept of Labor & Selective Serv adv, formerly; permanent mem, President's People to People Comt, 57-; Va State Deleg, 59-68; US Rep, Fifth Dist, Va, 68-, elected pres, Cong Freshman Class & mem, Comt on Armed Serv, US House of Rep. Bus & Prof Pos: With Dan River Mills, 39-57, asst to pres, 57-66, asst to bd chmn, 66-68. Mil Serv: Navy, World War II. Relig: Baptist. Legal Res: Danville VA Mailing Add: 1705 Longworth House Off Bldg Washington DC 20515

DANIELL, EUGENE S, JR (D)
b 1904. Educ: Harvard Univ, SB, LLB; Boston Univ, LLB; Command & Gen Staff Sch, Ft Leavenworth, Kans. Polit & Govt Pos: NH State Sen; NH State Rep, 4 terms, Asst Minority Leader, NH House Rep, 73-74; city solicitor, Franklin, NH; deleg, Dem Nat Conv, 52, 56, 64 & 68; mayor & mem sch bd, Franklin, NH, currently. Bus & Prof Pos: Lawyer. Mil Serv: Lt Col, Army Res, World War II, SE Asia, Battery Comdr; two Battle Stars. Mem: Am Legion; Rotary; Boys Scouts; VFW. Relig: Unitarian. Mailing Add: Daniell Point Franklin NH 03235

DANIELS, BILL (R)
b Greeley, Colo, July 1, 20; s Robert William Daniels & Adele D; m 1967 to Devra Carol Fox; stepchildren, Cindy & Mitchell Fox. Educ: NMex Mil Inst, Roswell, 2 years. Polit & Govt Pos: Region Eight finance chmn, Rep Nat Finance Comt, 69-71; treas, Denver Co Rep Cent Comt, Colo, 69-72; Rep Nat Committeeman, Colo, 72-75. Bus & Prof Pos: Pres, Nat Cable TV Asn, 53-54; pres-owner, Daniels Properties, Inc, 55-; owner, Utah Stars Basketball Club, 70-; pres, Am Basketball Asn, 71-73; dir, Cenikor Found, Inc, 72- Mil Serv: Entered as Second Seaman, Navy, 41, released as Lt Comdr, 45, after serv in Advan Carrier Training, Pac Theatre, 43-45, recalled, 50, released as Comdr, 52; Navy Cross; Bronze Medal; Purple Heart. Mem: Cherry Hills Country Club; Elks; Mason (32 degree); Shriner. Relig: Episcopal. Legal Res: 4190 Shangri-la Dr Denver CO 80222 Mailing Add: 2930 E Third Ave Denver CO 80206

DANIELS, CARY (D)
Committeeman, Ill State Dem Cent Comt
b Marshall, Tex, Mar 29, 12; s John Daniels & Bertha Gray D; m 1938 to Amanda Heretha Chatman. Educ: Wiley Col, 30-32. Polit & Govt Pos: Precinct committeeman, Lake Co Dem Party, Ill, 50-69; treas, Lake Co Dem Cent Comt, 60-64; chmn, Human Rels Comt & Fair Housing Bd, North Chicago, 67-69; secy, North Chicago Dem Munic Comt, 69; committeeman, Ill State Dem Cent Comt, 68-; deleg, Dem Nat Conv, 72; deleg, Dem Nat Mid-Term Conf, 74. Mil Serv: Entered as Pvt, Army Air Force, 42, released as Pfc, 46, after serv in 1889th AEB, 20th Air Force, Cent Pac Theatre, 44-46; Presidential Unit Citation; Good Conduct Medal. Mem: Int Elks (past exalted ruler); Barwell Settlement House (chmn bd). Relig: Methodist. Mailing Add: 1425 Greenfield North Chicago IL 60064

DANIELS, DENNIS RAY (D)
b Alva, Okla, Jan 14, 47; s Archie Ray Daniels & Peggy Beard D; m 1967 to Suzanne Monique Swilley. Educ: Butler Co Community Jr Col, El Dorado, Kans, AA, 72; Wichita State Univ, 73-; Collegiate Young Dem; Polit Sci Club. Postdoctoral Fels & Grants: Chmn, Butler Co Jr Col Young Dem, Kans, 71-72; pres, Butler Co Young Dem, 71-72; deleg, Fifth Cong Dem Conv & Kans Dem State Conv, 72; alt deleg, Dem Nat Conv, 72; area coordr, McGovern for President, Macoupin Co, Ill, 72. Mil Serv: Entered as Airman Basic, Air Force, 67, released as Sgt, 71, after serv in 49th & 36th Tactical Fighter Wing, Europe, 67-70; Outstanding Unit Award, Nat Defense Medal; Good Conduct Medal; Outstanding Non-Commissioned Officer of the Month Ellsworth Air Force Base, Rapid City, SDak. Mem: Am Legion; Nat Farmer's Union. Relig: Methodist. Mailing Add: RR 1 Winfield KS 67156

DANIELS, DOMINICK V (D)
US Rep, NJ
b Jersey City, NH, Oct 18, 08; s John Daniels & Carmela DeStefano D; m 1935 to Camille Curcio; c Dolores (Mrs Maragni) & Barbara (Mrs Coleman). Educ: Rutgers Univ, LLB, 30. Polit & Govt Pos: Vchmn, Jersey City Civil Rights Comn, NJ, 52-55; magistrate, Jersey City Munic Court, 52-58; US Rep, NJ, 58-; deleg, Dem Nat Conv, 68 & 72. Mem: Hudson Co Bar Asn; Univ Club Hudson Co; Elks; KofC (4 degree); Jersey City Lions Club. Legal Res: Union City NJ 07087 Mailing Add: 2370 House Off Bldg Washington DC 20515

DANIELS, FORSAITH (R)
NH State Rep
b Manchester, NH, Mar 11, 04; s Joel Selman Daniels & Caroline Forsaith D; m 1946 to Madeline Hanson; c Joel H. Educ: Univ NH, 2 years; Delta Pi Epsilon. Polit & Govt Pos: NH State Rep, 71-, vchmn, Pub Works Comn, NH House Rep, 73-75, chmn, 75- Bus & Prof Pos: Engr, admin & mgt pos, New Eng Tel Co, Maine, Mass, Vt & NH, 26-69, asst to gen mgr NH area, 66-69; retired. Mil Serv: Entered as 1st Lt, Army, 42, released as Maj, 45, after serv in Signal Construction Bn & Air Forces Bd, Orlando, Fla & Mediterranean Theatre, 42-44; Bronze Star. Mem: NH Soc Prof Engrs (nat dir); Elliot Hosp, Manchester (bd trustees); Serv Corps Retired Exec; Masonic Blue Lodge (Coun, Chap & Commandery); Manchester Country Club. Honors & Awards: Registered Prof Engr, NH. Relig: Congregational. Mailing Add: 1080 Ray St Manchester NH 03104

DANIELS, JONATHAN WORTH (D)
b Raleigh, NC, Apr 26, 02; s Josephus Daniels & Addie Worth Bagley D; m 1923 to Elizabeth Bridgers, wid, 1929; m 1932 to Lucy Billing Cathcart; c Elizabeth Bridgers (Mrs C B Squire), Lucy (Mrs Thomas P Inman), Adelaide (Mrs B J Key) & Mary (Mrs Cleves Daniels Rich). Educ: Univ of NC, AB, 21, MA, 22; Columbia Law Sch, 22-23; Delta Kappa Epsilon. Hon Degrees: Univ NC, Duke, NC State & Shaw Univs, Rollins & Elon Cols. Polit & Govt Pos: Asst dir, Off Civilian Defense, 42; trustee, Vassar Col, 42-48; admin asst to the President, 43-45, press secy, 45; US mem, UN subcomt, Prev of Discrimination & Protection of Minorities, 47-53; mem pub admin bd, ECA & Mutual Security Agency, 48-53; Dem Nat Committeeman, NC, 49-52; mem, Fed Hosp Coun, 49-53. Bus & Prof Pos: Former reporter, Louisville Times, Ky; reporter, Raleigh News & Observer, NC, Washington correspondent, 25-28, assoc ed, 32-33, ed, 33-42, exec ed, 47, ed, 48-70, emeritus ed, 70-; mem ed staff, Fortune Mag, NY, 30-32; contrib of weekly page, A Native at Large to the Nation, 41-42. Publ: The Man of Independence, a Biography of Harry Truman, 50; The End of Innocence, 54; Ordeal of Ambition, 70; plus others. Mem: Nat Press Club, Washington DC. Relig: Episcopal. Mailing Add: News & Observer Raleigh NC 27602

DANIELS, LEE A (R)
Ill State Rep
b Lansing, Mich, Apr 15, 42; s Albert Lee Daniels & Evelyn Bousfield D; m to Susan Kay Spencer; c Laurie Lynn, Rachael Lee, Stephen & Jeffrey. Educ: Univ Iowa, BA, 63; John Marshall Law Sch, JD, 67. Polit & Govt Pos: Mem bd auditors, York Twp, Ill, 66-73; Rep precinct committeeman, 65-74; vchmn, York Twp Rep Comt Orgn, 73-74; Spec Asst Attorney Gen, 73-75; Ill State Rep, 40th Dist, 75- Bus & Prof Pos: Partner, Daniels, Hancock, Faris, Ltd, Attorney-at-law, 67- Mem: DuPage Co & Am Bar Asns; Am & Ill Trial Lawyers Asns; AF&AM. Relig: Protestant. Legal Res: 226 Claremont Elmhurst IL 60126 Mailing Add: 579 W North Ave Elmhurst IL 60126

DANIELS, MARVIN KERMIT (D)
Chmn, Powell Co Dem Cent Comt, Mont
b Deer Lodge, Mont, Nov 28, 16; s Joseph E Daniels & Elma Long D; m to Judith Elizabeth Wilson; c Robert C, Margaret J (Mrs Altenbrun), Nancy E (Mrs Ronald Kelley) & John J. Educ: Mont State Univ; Univ Mont Law Sch, 46; Phi Delta Phi. Polit & Govt Pos: Attorney, Powell Co, Mont, 46-50; Mont State Rep, 55-61; chmn, Powell Co Dem Cent Comt, 62-; co attorney, Powell Co, 71-74; city attorney, Deer Lodge, 75- Bus & Prof Pos: Attorney-at-law, 53- Mil Serv: Entered as A/S, Naval Res, 42, released as Lt, 45, re-entered as Lt Comdr, 52-53; European-Africa & Asiatic-Pac Theater Ribbons. Mem: Mont Bar Asn; Mont Trial Lawyers Asn; Rotary; VFW; Am Legion. Relig: Protestant. Mailing Add: 313 Missouri Ave Deer Lodge MT 59722

DANIELS, MELVIN R, JR (D)
NC State Sen
Mailing Add: 1618 Rochelle Dr Elizabeth City NC 27909

DANIELS, ROBERT VINCENT (D)
Vt State Sen
b Boston, Mass, Jan 4, 26; s Robert Whiting Daniels & Helen Hoyt D; m 1945 to Alice May Wendell; c Robert H, Irene L, Helen L & Thomas L. Educ: Harvard Univ, AB, 45, MA, 47, PhD, 51. Polit & Govt Pos: Mem, Chittenden Co Dem Comt, Vt, 59-; chmn policy & planning comt, Vt Dem Party, 62-66 & 69-73; mem bd visitors, US Air Force Acad, 65-67; mem, Burlington Dem City Comt, 65-; alt deleg, Dem Nat Conv, 68; Vt State Sen, 73- Bus & Prof Pos: Mem faculty social sci, Bennington Col, Vt, 52-53 & 57-58; asst prof Slavic studies, Ind Univ, Bloomington, 53-55; prof hist, Univ Vt, 56-57 & 58-, chmn dept, 64-69, dir exp prog, 69-71; US-Soviet Cultural Exchange scholar, Univ Moscow, 66; mem bd ed, J Mod Hist, 70-73; Nat Endowment for Humanities sr fel, 71-72. Mil Serv: Entered as A/S, Naval Res, 44, released as Ens, Supply Corps, 46, after serv in USS Albany, 45-46. Publ: The Conscience of the Revolution, Harvard Univ, 60; The Nature of Communism, Random, 62; Red October, Scribner, 67. Mem: Am Asn Univ Prof; Am Hist Asn; Am Asn Advan Slavic Studies; Vt Hist Soc; Northeast Slavic Conf. Mailing Add: 195 S Prospect St Burlington VT 05401

DANIELSON, GEORGE ELMORE (D)
US Rep, Calif
b Wausa, Nebr, Feb 20, 15; s August Danielson & Ida Youngner D; m to Gladys Ohanian. Educ: Wayne State Teachers Col, 33-35; Univ of Nebr, BA, 37, Col of Law, JD, 39; Phi Alpha Delta. Polit & Govt Pos: Spec agent, Fed Bur of Invest, 39-44; asst US Attorney, Southern Dist of Calif, 49-51; Calif State Assemblyman, 63-66, chmn, Majority Caucus, 64-66; mem, Calif 'Little Hoover' Comn, 65-67; Calif State Sen, 67-71; past chmn, Comt on Pub Utilities & Corp; deleg, Dem Nat Conv, 68; US Rep, Calif, 71-, Asst Majority Whip, US House Rep, 71- Bus & Prof Pos: Lawyer. Mil Serv: Entered as Ens, Naval Res, 44, released as Lt, 46, after serv in Amphibious Forces, Pac Fleet, Pac Theater, World War II; Pac Theater, Am Defense & Victory Medal. Publ: Facts & Figures Concerning Executions in California, 1937-1963, privately publ, 63; Cable antenna television in California, 1971, McGeorge Sch Law, 71. Mem: Am Bar Asn; Soc of Former Spec Agents of the Fed Bur of Invest. Legal Res: Monterey Park CA Mailing Add: House of Rep Washington DC 20515

DANIELSON, GEORGE G (R)
Idaho State Rep
Mailing Add: Box 57 Cambridge ID 83610

DANKER, ARLYN E (R)
Iowa State Rep
Mailing Add: RR 1 Minden IA 51553

DANNEKER, HENRY LOUIS (R)
Chmn, Beaver Co Rep Party, Pa
b Osceola Mills, Pa, Jan 6, 19; s Henry George Danneker & Mary Griffey D; m 1944 to Geraldine Ann O'Donnell; c Cecilia A (Mrs Goggin), Genevieve M (Mrs McGee), Henry L, Jr, Gerald T, Mary Ann, Patricia L, Catherine A & Carol J. Educ: Tri-State Col, BS in Mech Eng, 41; Alpha Gamma Omega. Polit & Govt Pos: Councilman, Borough of Beaver, Pa, 55-, vpres, currently; chmn, First Ward Rep Party, 62-; chmn, Beaver Rep Town Party, 64-; chmn, Beaver Co Rep Party, 71- Bus & Prof Pos: Draftsman, Ambridge Plant, Am Br Div, US Steel, 46-58, engr, 58-63, chief draftsman, mech eng dept, 63-70, design engr, Pittsburgh, 70- Mil Serv: Entered as 2nd Lt, Army, 42, released as 1st Lt, 46, after serv in 80th Inf Div, 3rd Army, European Theatre, 44-45; Lt Col(Ret), Res, 70; Bronze Star Medal; Meritorious Serv Medal; Combat Infantryman Badge. Mem: Am Legion; Asn Iron & Steel Engrs; Elks; ROA; KofC (Adv, 73-). Relig: Roman Catholic. Mailing Add: 334 Fifth St Beaver PA 15009

DANNER, PAT **(D)**
Chmn, Macon Co Dem Comt, Mo
b Louisville, Ky, Jan 13, 34; d Henry Joseph Berrer & Catherine Shaheen Berrer Stuart; m 1951 to Lavon Eugene Danner; c Stephen Lavon, Stephanie Anne, Shane Michael & Shavonne Leigh. Educ: Hannibal-LaGrange Col, 52; Northeast Mo State Univ, BA, 72. Polit & Govt Pos: Secy, Macon Co Young Dem, Mo, 60-68; committeewoman & chmn, Macon Co Dem Comt, 70-; vchmn, Ninth Cong Dist Dem Party, 70-; asst to US Rep Jerry Litton, Sixth Cong Dist, Mo, 73- Bus & Prof Pos: Tax consult, Danner-Maddy Tax Serv, Macon, Mo. Relig: Catholic. Mailing Add: 4242 NE Davidson Rd Kansas City MO 64116

DANOVITCH, ALAN PAUL **(R)**
Mass State Rep
Mailing Add: State Capitol Boston MA 02133

DANTON, PETER W **(R)**
Maine State Sen
Mailing Add: 7 Beach St Saco ME 04072

DARBY, HARRY **(R)**
b Kansas City, Kans, Jan 23, 95; s Harry Darby & Florence Isabelle Smith D; m 1917 to Edith Marie Cubbison; c Harriet (Mrs Thomas H Gibson, Jr), Joan (Mrs Roy A Edwards, Jr), Edith Marie (Mrs Ray Evans) & Marjorie (Mrs Eugene D Alford). Educ: Univ Ill, BS, 17, ME, 29. Hon Degrees: LLD, St Benedict's Col, Westminster Col, Kansas State Univ & Washburn Univ. Polit & Govt Pos: Deleg, Rep Nat Conv, 40-60, chmn, Credentials Comt, 44, chmn, Kans Deleg, 48, 52 & 56, chmn, Ticket Comt, 56 & 60; mem, Rep Nat Comt, Kans, 40-64, chmn, Rural Vote Comt, 41; mem, Exec Comt of 15, 44; US Sen, Kans, 49-50. Bus & Prof Pos: With Mo Boiler Works Co, Kansas City, 11-19; dir numerous corp; founder & chmn bd, Leavenworth Steel, Inc & Darby Rwy Cars, Inc; with Darby Corp, 20-, now chmn of bd & owner. Mil Serv: Capt, Field Artil, Army, 17-19, AEF. Mem: Kans Heart Asn; Navy League of US; Kans Registr Bd of Prof Engrs; Am Soc Civil Engrs; fel Am Soc Mech Engrs. Relig: Episcopal. Legal Res: 1220 Hoel Pkwy Kansas City KS 66102 Mailing Add: First St & Walker Ave Kansas City KS 66110

DARBY, HOWARD DARREL **(D)**
WVa State Sen
b Quinwood, WVa, Jan 8, 28; s Robert Buren Darby & Loraine Richards D; m 1948 to Laura Grace Boggs; c Michael Wayne, Laura Ann, Mary Beth, Sandra Lynn, Howard Darrel, II & Linett Lee. Educ: Marshall Univ; Anderson Col, 50-52; Ohio Col of Podiatric Med, DPM, 56. Polit & Govt Pos: Mem, Med Licensing Bd WVa, 60-72; WVa State Sen, 73-, chmn, Health Comt, WVa State Senate, 73- Bus & Prof Pos: Podiatrist. Mil Serv: Entered as Seaman, Coast Guard, 45, released, 47. Publ: Casting-treatment of congenital pronation in infants, J Am Podiatry Asn; Unilateral hammer toes, an early clue to brain tumor, J Foot Surg; Podiatry, an important aid to the medical profession, WVa Med J. Mem: WVa Pub Health Asn; Am Pub Health Asn; WVa Podiatry Asn; Am Podiatry Asn (chmn coun legis affairs, 72-, chmn liaison comt, Am Med Asn, Asn Acad Health Ctrs, 72-, pres elect). Relig: Protestant. Legal Res: 1600 S Jefferson Dr Huntington WV 25701 Mailing Add: 1038 Sixth Ave Huntington WV 25701

DARBY, LLOYD HUBERT, III **(R)**
VChmn, First Cong Dist Rep Comt, Ga
b Metter, Ga, June 18, 37; s Lloyd Hubert Darby, Jr & Carolyn Hale D; m 1958 to Loretta Wilkes; c Carolyn Leslie, Jennifer Wilkes & Pamela Elaine. Educ: Medill Sch Jour, Northwestern Univ, 55-57; Emory Univ, BA, 59, Sch Dent, Emory Univ, DDS, 64; pres, Student Am Dent Asn, Emory Univ, 63-64; Phi Delta Theta. Polit & Govt Pos: Precinct capt, Toombs Co Rep Party, 68; chmn, Toombs Co Rep Comt, formerly; vchmn, First Cong Dist Rep Comt, 70-; alt deleg, Rep Nat Conv, 72. Bus & Prof Pos: Pvt dent practice, Vidalia, Ga, 66- Mil Serv: Entered as Ens, Naval Res, 60, released as Lt, 66, after serv in Dent Sect, Marine Corps Supply Ctr, Albany, Ga, 64-66. Mem: Cent Dent Soc of Am Dent Asn; Am Acad Gen Practice; Am Prof Practice Asn; Psi Omega; Elks. Relig: Presbyterian; Deacon, Vidalia Presby Church. Legal Res: 202 W Ninth St Vidalia GA 30474 Mailing Add: 308 Jackson St Vidalia GA 30474

DARBY, LORENA EVA **(D)**
Colo State Sen
b Longmont, Colo, Sept 31, 14; d Peter Jacobsen & Olene Johnson J; m 1938 to John Harold Darby; c James Peter & Sally Ann (Mrs David Sauer). Educ: Longmont High Sch, grad, 32; Parks Sch Bus, grad, 36. Polit & Govt Pos: Colo State Sen, 73- Bus & Prof Pos: Secy, Boulder Co Exten Agt, 35-38; reporter, Longmont Ledger, Longmont, Colo, 54-64, ed & publ, 64-68. Publ: Assorted articles & stories, Empire Mag & Denver Post, 69-72; Mountains & molehills, Community Publs, 71. Mem: Colo Press Women; Colo Mountain Club. Mailing Add: 820 Martin St Longmont CO 80501

D'ARCO, JOHN A, JR **(D)**
Ill State Sen
Mailing Add: 836 S Morgan St Chicago IL 60607

D'ARCY, JAMES ANDREW **(D)**
b Philadelphia, Pa, Apr 8, 37; s Anthony Michael D'Arcy & Mary Brennan D; m 1974 to Beatrice Valencia; c Monica Elena. Educ: Villanova Univ, BEE, 59; Univ Pa, MSEE, 64; Radio Corp of Am Grad Study Prog, 61-63. Polit & Govt Pos: Committeeman, Philadelphia, 64th Ward Dem Exec Comt, Pa, 62-74, treas, 66-75; alt deleg, Dem Nat Conv, 68 & 72. Bus & Prof Pos: Elec engr, Radio Corp of Am Astro Electronics Div, Princeton, NJ, 59-; Registered prof engr, State of Pa, 65-; registered prof engr, State of NJ, 72- Publ: Logic & control system for a dielectric tape camera to be used in a meteorological satellite, Thesis, Univ Pa, 5/64; Logic & control system for a Panoramic TV camera, Third Space Cong, 3/66; Photo dielectric tape camera systems, Fifth Space Cong, 3/68 & RCA Engr, 12/68 & 1/69. Mem: Engrs Club of Philadelphia; Inst of Elec & Electronics Engrs; Pa Soc Prof Engrs; Tau Beta Pi; Eta Kappa Nu. Honors & Awards: Outstanding Jr Award, Engrs Club of Philadelphia, 66-67. Relig: Roman Catholic. Mailing Add: 1063 Claire Ave Huntingdon Valley PA 19006

DARDEN, COLGATE WHITEHEAD, JR **(D)**
b Southampton Co, Va, Feb 11, 97; s Colgate W Darden & Catherine Pretlow D; m 1927 to Constance S du Pont; c Colgate W, III & Irene du Pont (Mrs Field). Educ: Univ Va; Columbia Univ; Oxford Univ, Eng; Phi Beta Kappa; Raven Soc. Polit & Govt Pos: Va State Deleg, 30-33; US Rep, Va, 33-36 & 39-41; Gov, Va, 42-46; mem, US Deleg to UN, 55; mem, Pub Libr Bd, Norfolk, 62-; mem, State Bd Educ, Va, 63- Bus & Prof Pos: Dir, DuPont Co, Life Ins Co of Va Newport News Ship & Merchants & Farmers Bank; chancellor, William & Mary Col, 46-47; pres, Univ Va, 47-59, emer pres, 59- Mil Serv: Serv in Am Ambulance Serv with French Army, 16-17; with Naval Aviation, 17, Marine Corps Aviation, 18, released as 2nd Lt after serv in 1st Marine Sq, Northern Bombing Group. Relig: Episcopal. Mailing Add: 7438 Flicker Point Norfolk VA 23505

DARDEN, CONRAD LYNN **(D)**
b Tyler, Tex, June 3, 34; s Robert Webster Darden & Oleta Jones D; m 1956 to Margaret Alice Furr; c Kimberly Denise, Victoria Diane & Sally Ann. Educ: Baylor Univ, BA, 56; Univ Tex Sch Law, LLB, 59; Delta Sigma Pi; Delta Theta Phi; Taurus Soc; Geol Club. Polit & Govt Pos: Chmn, City of Wichita Falls Civil Defense Investigating Comt, 56, chmn, City Planning Bd, 61-65; admin asst to Congressman Graham Purcell, 61; mem bd & chmn, Wichita Falls Community Ment Health & Ment Retardation Ctr, 67-; mem adv bd, Community Ctrs, State of Tex, 73; mem bd, Tex Dept Ment Health & Ment Retardation, 73-; deleg, Dem Nat Conv, 72; deleg, Dem Nat Mid-Term Conf, 74; chmn, Tex Dem Party Finance Coun, 75. Bus & Prof Pos: Partner, R W Darden Drilling Co, 56-68; partner, Kouri, Banner & Darden, Attorneys, 59-61; with Lynn Darden, Attorney, Wichita Falls, Tex, 62; partner, Humphrey, Gibson & Darden, 62-69, Gibson & Darden, 69-72 & Gibson, Darden & Hotchkiss, 72- Publ: Ed, Pergrinus, Univ Tex, 58 & 59. Mem: Am & Wichita Co Bar Asns; Shrine; Rotary (dir, 62-); Mason (32 degree). Honors & Awards: Univ Tex Bar Asn Award, 58, Consel Award, Univ Tex Sch Law, 59. Relig: Presbyterian. Legal Res: 2100 Berkeley Wichita Falls TX 76308 Mailing Add: 912 City Nat Bldg Wichita Falls TX 76301

DARDEN, GEORGE H, JR **(D)**
Committeeman, Tenn State Dem Exec Comt
b Rutherford Co, Tenn, July 11, 30; s George H Darden, Sr & Mary Wade D; m 1952 to Ruby Jean Dartis; c George Beene Fanchetter, Drusilla L, Janet D & George H, III. Educ: Holloway High Sch. Polit & Govt Pos: Committeeman, Davidson Co Dem Party, Tenn, 74- & Tenn State Dem Exec Comt, 74- Mil Serv: Entered as Pvt, Air Force, 51, released as Airman 1/C, 55, after serv in food serv. Mem: Metro Action Comn; Meharry Ment Health. Relig: Church of Christ. Mailing Add: 1724 22 Ave N Nashville TN 37208

DARDEN, WILLIAM BOONE **(D)**
Committeeman, Dem Party Fla
b Atlanta, Ga, Aug 16, 25; s Joseph Darden & Willie Mae Boone D; m to RoseMerry Myers; c Kimberly, William, Jr & Darrell. Educ: WVa State Univ, 46; Fla Atlantic Univ, 73; Fla Int Univ, BS Criminal Justice, 74; Alpha Phi Alpha. Polit & Govt Pos: Chmn, 11th Dist Dem Comt, 74; committeeman, Dem Party Fla, 74- Bus & Prof Pos: Lt, West Palm Beach Police Dept, 48-65; chief investr, South Fla Migrant Legal Serv, 66-68; chief of police, Riviera Beach, Fla, 71. Mil Serv: Pfc, Army Mil Police, ETO, 43-46. Mem: Ment Health Palm Beach Co (bd dirs); Heart Asn (bd dirs); Palm Beach Co Urban League; Christian Businessman's Comt; Int Asn Chiefs of Police (pub rels comt). Honors & Awards: Cert of Commendation, Am Legion, 72; Cert of Appreciation, Am Red Cross, 72; Law Enforcement Man of Year, VFW, 74. Mailing Add: 1468 Eighth St West Palm Beach FL 33401

DARLING, RONALD L **(D)**
Del State Rep
Mailing Add: RD 1 Box 342 Wyoming DE

DARNELL, RILEY CARLISLE **(D)**
Tenn State Rep
b Clarksville, Tenn, May 13, 40; s Elliott Sinclair Darnell & Mary Anita Whitefield D; m 1963 to Mary Penelope Crockarell; c Neil Whitefield, Duncan Edward & Mary Eve. Educ: Austin Peay State Univ, BS, 62; Vanderbilt Univ, Law Sch, JD, 65; Phi Alpha Theta. Polit & Govt Pos: Tenn State Rep, 67th Legis Dist, 71-, treas, Dem Caucus, Tenn House Rep, 71-, secy, Finance Ways & Means Comt, mem, Calendar & Rules Comt, Judiciary Comt & chmn, Fiscal Rev Comt, 75- Bus & Prof Pos: Attorney-at-law, 65-66 & 69-71. Mil Serv: Entered as 1st Lt, Air Force, 66, released as Capt, 69, after serv in Judge Adv Gen Corps, Turkey, 67-69. Mem: Montgomery Co & Am Bar Asns; CofC. Relig: Church of Christ. Legal Res: 175 E Glenwood Clarksville TN 37040 Mailing Add: 221 S Third St Clarksville TN 37040

DARROW, CLARENCE ALLISON **(D)**
Ill State Rep
b Dubuque, Iowa, Mar 22, 40; s Clarence Darrow & Joan Reinhart D; m 1963 to Lili Ruja; c Elizabeth, John, Antoinette, Clarence & Jennifer. Educ: Loras Col, BS, 62; Univ Ill, MSW, 66; Chicago Kent Col Law, JD, 71. Polit & Govt Pos: Asst state's attorney, Rock Island Co, Ill, 71-74; Ill State Rep, 36th Dist, 75- Mem: Ill & Rock Island Co Bar Asns; Rotary; Elks. Legal Res: 2515 36th St Rock Island IL 61201 Mailing Add: 402 Safety Bldg Rock Island IL 61201

DARROW, PETER P **(D)**
Mem, Mich State Dem Comt
b Glen Cove, NY, Sept 12, 19; s Vasili Podorowski Darrow & Michelena D; m; c Duncan Noble & Peter Vasili; remarried 1972 to Susan Tuttle Parker; c John, Sara & Elizabeth Parker. Educ: NY Univ, BS, 42; Univ Mich Law Sch, JD, 48. Polit & Govt Pos: Mem, Co Dem Comts, Mich, 46-; mem, Mich State Dem Comt, 46-; city, co & dist chmn, Dem Party of Mich, 48-66; pub adminr, Washtenaw Co, State of Mich, 56-; city chmn, Ann Arbor Dem Comt, 57-60; chmn, Washtenaw Co Dem Comt, 60-64; deleg, Dem Nat Conv, 64; chmn, Second Cong Dist Dem Comt, 64; mem nat bd, Am for Dem Action, currently; mem, Ann Arbor Planning Comn, Model Cities Bd & mem bd, Mich Narcotics Comn, currently; hearing referee, State of Mich Civil Rights Comn, 72- Bus & Prof Pos: Guest lectr, Univ Mich, formerly, lectr law, 72-; secy & mem bd, Int Automated Machines, Inc, 64-; organizer & founder, Ann Arbor Community Develop, Inc, 65; partner, Mann, Lipnik & Darrow, Attorneys, currently. Mil Serv: Entered as A/S, Navy, 41, released as Lt(sg), 45, after serv in Amphibious Forces, Mediter-Europe-Africa; Am Theater Ribbon; European-African Serv Ribbon with 11 Battle Stars; Presidential Citation. Mem: Washtenaw Co, Mich & Am Bar Asns; Am Trial Lawyers Asn; Episcopal Soc for Cult & Racial Unity. Honors & Awards: Created first nonprofit housing 221 (d) (3) proj in US, 60. Relig: Episcopal; Warden, St Andrews Episcopal Church; bd mem, Nat Episcopal Student Found. Legal Res: 251 Orchard Hills Dr Ann Arbor MI 48104 Mailing Add: 700 Ann Arbor Trust Bldg Ann Arbor MI 48108

DARSEY, ELTON A **(D)**
Mem, La Dem State Cent Comt
b Houma, La, Jan 26, 08; s Aurestile O Darsey & Angele Malbrough D; m 1940 to Clothilde Ostendorf. Educ: Loyola Univ, LLB, 35, JD, 68; Sigma Nu Phi. Polit & Govt Pos: Mem,

Terrebonne Parish Dem Exec Comt, La, 40-, chmn, 50-; city attorney, Houma, 46-62; mem, La Dem State Cent Comt, 64- Mem: La State & Terrebonne Bar Asns. Legal Res: 125 Cedar St Houma LA 70360 Mailing Add: PO Box 982 Houma LA 70361

DART, STEPHEN PLAUCHE (D)
Mem, Dem State Cent Comt La
b New Orleans, La, Sept 21, 24; s Benjamin W Dart & Clarabel C D; m 1951 to Elisabeth Ann Kelbourne; c James K & Ann H. Educ: Tulane Univ, BBA, 46; La State Univ, BSEE, 51, LLB, 51; Phi Delta Phi; Delta Kappa Epsilon. Polit & Govt Pos: Mem, Dem State Cent Comt La, currently; mem, West Feliciana Parish Dem Exec Comt, currently. Bus & Prof Pos: Sr partner, Kilbourne & Dart, 51- Mil Serv: Entered as A/S, Naval Res-ROTC, Tulane Univ, 42, released as Lt(jg), 46, after serv in European & Pac Theatres, US Amphibious Forces; Battle Ribbons, European Invasion of Southern France, Invasion of Okinawa. Mem: La State & Am Bar Asns. Relig: Episcopal. Legal Res: Westerlie Plantation St Francisville LA 70775 Mailing Add: PO Drawer 489 St Francisville LA 70775

DARY, LEON LEONARD (R)
b Taunton, Mass, June 19, 29; s Leon L Dary & Eleanor Josselyn D; m 1952 to Pauline Saunders; c Jacqueline, Virginia Lee, Stewart Curtis & Elizabeth Ann. Educ: Bentley Col, Boston, 47-48. Polit & Govt Pos: Police comnr, mem bd pub welfare & mem bd selectmen, Raynham, Mass, 58-62; field coordr, Rep Party, Mass, 63-66; mem bd dirs, Precinct, Inc, Mass, 64-69; nat bd dirs, Rep Workshop Educ Prog, 65-69, nat vpres, 69-; chief, Citizens Aid Bur, Off of Mass Attorney Gen Richardson, 66-69; exec dir, Mass Rep State Comt, 70-72. Bus & Prof Pos: Buyer & purchasing agent, Jowall Electronics, Philadelphia, Pa, 49-54; mgr, Life Ins & Bus Planning, 54-63; owner, Sparkling Pools & Supplies, Barnstable, 56- Mem: Nat Asn Purchasing Agents; New Eng Swimming Pool Asn; Mass Jaycees; YMCA (dir); Cancer Soc (dir). Relig: Protestant. Mailing Add: Box 583 Barnstable MA 06230

DASSINGER, ERNEST N (D)
Mont State Rep
b Dickinson, NDak, June 6, 31; s Lorenz Dassinger & Katherine Schmidt D; m 1951 to Jacqueline Gartner; c Dan & Darren. Educ: Dawson Co Col, Glendive, Mont; Dickinson State Col, degree, 58. Polit & Govt Pos: Mont State Rep, Dist 50, 75- Mem: United Transportation Union (chmn); CofC; Elks. Relig: Catholic. Legal Res: 1490 Oak St Forsyth MT 59327 Mailing Add: Box 753 Forsyth MT 59327

DAUB, HAROLD JOHN, JR (R)
Chmn, Douglas Co Rep Party, Nebr
b Fayetteville, NC, Apr 23, 41; s Harold John Daub, Sr & Eleanor M Hickman D; m to Cindy S Shin; c Natalie Ann & John Clifford. Educ: Washington Univ, BS in Bus Admin, 63; Univ Nebr, Lincoln, JD, 66; Thurtene Jr Men's Hon; Omicron Delta Kappa; Alpha Kappa Psi; Kappa Sigma. Polit & Govt Pos: Staff intern, US Sen Roman Hruska, Nebr, 66; jr pres, Nebr Rep Founders Day, 71; treas, Douglas Co Rep Party, 71-74, chmn, 74-; mem, Nebr State Rep Cent Comt, 74- Bus & Prof Pos: Attorney, Fitzgerald, Brown, Leahy, McGill, 68-71; vpres & gen counsel, Standard Chem Mfg Co, Omaha, Nebr, 71- Mil Serv: Entered as 2nd Lt, Army Res, 63, released as Capt, 68, after serv in 2nd Inf Div, Korea, 66-68; Army Commendation Medal. Mem: Nat Asn Credit Mgt (treas, Nebr-West Iowa Unit, 75); Mason (32 degree); Scottish Rite; Am Judicature Soc; Nebr Bar Asn. Honors & Awards: Outstanding Nat Officer, Am Law Student Asn, 66; Most Outstanding Student Mem in Nation, Delta Theta Phi, 66; Jr Press Plaque, Nebr Rep Party Founders Day, 71. Relig: Presbyterian. Mailing Add: 1604 N 58th St Omaha NE 68104

DAUGHERTY, J C (D)
Ga State Rep
Mailing Add: 202 Daugherty Bldg 15 Chestnut St Atlanta GA 30314

DAUGHERTY, MICHAEL DENNIS (R)
Nat Committeeman, La Young Rep Fedn
b Tyler, Tex, May 27, 48; s John Wayne Daugherty & Frances Reynolds D; m 1973 to Janet Mary Laird. Educ: La State Univ, BA, 70, Westminster fel, Law Sch, JD, 73; Omicron Delta Kappa; Phi Kappa Phi; Mu Sigma Rho; mem gov bd, La State Univ Union, 68-71. Polit & Govt Pos: Asst to state chmn, La Rep Party, 69; dist mgr, US Bur Census, Lake Charles, 70; nat committeeman, La Young Rep Fedn, 73-; legis asst, US Rep David Treen, La, currently. Bus & Prof Pos: Attorney, Camp, Carmouche, Palmer, Carwile & Barsh, Lake Charles, La, 73-74. Mem: La State & Am Bar Asns. Relig: Presbyterian. Legal Res: 1523 McNutt Dr Alexandria LA 71301 Mailing Add: 404 Cannon House Off Bldg Washington DC 20515

DAUGHETEE, CHERYL ANN (D)
Nat Committeeman, Ky Young Dem
b Somerset, Ky, Feb 27, 51; d James M Daughetee & Anna Jean McClure D; single. Educ: Somerset Community Col, 69-71; Univ Philippines, 72-73; Univ Ky, BS in Educ, 73; Phi Theta Kappa. Polit & Govt Pos: Fifth Dist chairwoman, Ky Young Dem, 70-71, secy, 71-72, nat committeewoman, 74-; staff, Ford for Gov, 71. Bus & Prof Pos: Teacher, Fayette Co Schs, 73-74; sr admin asst, UK Dent Sch, 74- Honors & Awards: Outstanding Young Woman, Ky Young Dem, 72; Rotary Int Scholar to Philippines, 72. Relig: First Christian Church. Legal Res: 104 Koosp St Somerset KY 42501 Mailing Add: 140 Cochran Rd Apt 2 Lexington KY 40502

DAUPHINAIS, MARGUERITE THERESE (DFL)
VChmn, Nicollet Co Dem-Farmer-Labor Orgn, Minn
b Duluth, Minn, Dec 15, 26; d John Jacob Stangl & Bertha Therese Merkel S; m 1948 to Franklin Allen Dauphinais; c Franklin James, Patrick George, Mary Elizabeth, Paul Gerard & Catherine Ann. Educ: Col St Scholastica Dept of Nursing, RN, 47. Polit & Govt Pos: Prog chmn, Nicollet Co Dem-Farmer-Labor Women's Club, Minn; first vchmn, Nicollet Co Dem-Farmer-Labor Orgn, 70- Mem: Nicollet Co Nurses Bd; Minn League for Nursing; Nicollet Co Ment Health Bd (treas, 67-); Mothers' Club, Good Counsel Acad; Holy Rosary Sodality. Relig: Catholic; Mission chmn, Holy Rosary Church. Mailing Add: 845 Stewart St North Mankato MN 56001

D'AURORA, MINO ROCCO (D)
b Pettorano sul Gizio, Italy, Aug 12, 09; s Giovano D'Aurora & Maria DeStefano D; m 1961 to Pauline Mary Rhodes; c Mary Ann, Giovino John, Joseph Anthony, Robert Martin & Paul Michael. Educ: Steubenville Bus Col; Theta Chi Alpha. Polit & Govt Pos: Dep assessor, Brooke Co, WVa; mem, Follansbee City Coun, 8 years; WVa State Deleg, 58-74, deleg, Dem Nat Conv, 72. Bus & Prof Pos: Employee steel co, 35 years, Ohio Indust Plant. Mem: Eagles (past Worthy pres); Moose; Sons of Italy; KofC; Knights of St Anthony. Relig: Catholic. Mailing Add: 937 Jefferson St Follansbee WV 26037

DAVEE, LINDA JOAN (R)
Secy, Ind Young Rep Fedn
b Martinsville, Ind, Oct 10, 46; d Fredrick Melvin Albertson & Elsie Briant A; m 1965 to Roger Dale Davee; c Misty & Michael. Educ: Martinsville High Sch, Ind, grad, 64. Polit & Govt Pos: Engrossing & enrolling clerk, Ind State Senate, 73, 74 & 75; deleg, Ind Young Rep Fedn Conv, 73 & 74; secy, Morgan Co Young Rep, Ind, 73-74; Young Rep coordr, Ind Rep State Comt, 73-; secy, Ind Young Rep Fedn, 74-; deleg, Nat Young Rep Conv, 75. Bus & Prof Pos: Off clerk, Vernon Ins, 64-65; individual letter writer, Ind Blue Cross/Blue Shield, 68-70. Mem: Neil A Armstrong Parent-Teacher Orgn; Lambda Nu chap, Delta Theta Tau; Morgan Co Rep Women's Club; Morgan Co Farmers Union; United Consumers Club. Honors & Awards: Page, Ind Fedn Rep Women's Conv, 73; Appreciation Award, Neil A Armstrong Parent-Teacher Orgn, 74. Relig: Church of Christ. Mailing Add: RR 2 Box 211 Mooresville IN 46158

DAVENNY, ROBERT ALTON (R)
b Edmonds, Wash, Dec 16, 14; s Alton Davenny & Olive Meyer D; m 1971 to Dorothy McGinn; c Diane Dee & Robert Alton. Educ: Univ Wash, 31-34. Polit & Govt Pos: Senate dist Rep finance chmn, Fairbanks, Alaska, 56-57; state Rep finance chmn, 58-65; Rep state chmn, 65-69; Rep Nat Committeeman, Alaska, 69-72. Bus & Prof Pos: Pres, Thermo-Engr Corp, 46-52, R A Davenny & Assoc, Inc, 53-, Equip Leasing Corp, 66- & Insulating & Fiberglass, Inc, 69- Mil Serv: Entered as Seaman, Navy, 42, released as Metalsmith 1/C, 46, after serv in ETO & Pac Theatre. Mem: Elks; Shrine. Relig: Presbyterian. Legal Res: 2414 Susitna Dr Anchorage AK 99503 Mailing Add: Box 4-2050 Anchorage AK 99509

DAVENPORT, CLYDIA ANN (D)
Nat Committeewoman, La Young Dem
b El Paso, Tex, Jan 2, 50; d Arthur Clyde Davenport & Dorothea Irma Doyle D; single. Educ: Cath Inst Paris, Coun for Develop of French in La scholar, 70-71; St Mary's Dominican Col, BA, 72; Loyola Univ Sch Law, JD, 75; Phi Alpha Delta; Alpha Mu Gamma; Int Club. Polit & Govt Pos: Nat committeewoman, La Young Dem, 75- Bus & Prof Pos: Law clerk, New Orleans Dist Attorney's Off, New Orleans, La, 74-; staff attorney, Probe, 75- Mem: Inst of Polit (fel, 74-); Coun for Develop of French in La (treas, 72-); Alliance Good Govt (secy, 75-); League of Women Voters (chmn comt on water quality, 75-). Honors & Awards: First place in La State Competition in Spanish Interpretive Reading, Spanish Extemporaneous Speaking & Latin II. Relig: Catholic. Mailing Add: 3232 Laurel St New Orleans LA 70115

DAVENPORT, JOHN EDWIN (D)
NC State Rep
b Nashville, NC, Apr 28, 28; s Louis Ludford Davenport & Bybe Rogers D; m 1959 to Mary Elizabeth Pope; c Mary Elizabeth & Wynn Newman. Educ: Univ NC, Chapel Hill, AB, 48 & LLB, 51; George Washington Univ, summer 50; Delta Theta Phi. Polit & Govt Pos: Col organizer, NC Young Dem, 54; pres, Nash Co Young Dem, 55; solicitor, Recorder's Court, Nash Co, 56-57; real property attorney, State of NC, 57-59; mem, NC State Dem Exec Comt, 66 & 70-; chmn, Nash Co Dem Exec Comt, 66-70; NC State Rep, 72- Bus & Prof Pos: Dist chancellor, Delta Theta Phi, NC, 57-; pres, Nashville Indust Develop Corp, currently; pres, Sharpsburg Properties Inc, 71 & Regency Estates Inc, 72- Mil Serv: Entered as Pvt, Air Force, 51, released as 1st Lt, 53, after serv in Hq Squadron, Parks AFB, 52-53; Air Force Res, Capt (Ret). Mem: Am Judicature Soc; NC Acad Trial Lawyers; Am Legion; AF&AM; NC Jr CofC (vpres). Honors & Awards: Outstanding Young Man of Year, 56. Relig: Methodist. Legal Res: Hwy 64 E Nashville NC 27856 Mailing Add: PO Drawer 988 Nashville NC 27856

DAVENPORT, JOSEPH HOWARD (D)
Chmn, Salem Co Dem Party, NJ
b Penns Grove, NJ, June 28, 34; s Frank W Davenport & Mary Friant D; m 1956 to Shirley Ann Prough; c Lori Lynn, Scott Joseph, Debra Mary & Tara Elisabeth. Educ: Glassboro State Col, BA, 60, MA, 70; Social Studies Club. Polit & Govt Pos: Dist committeeman, Pennsville Dem Club, NJ, 65-70, secy, 66-68; bldg inspector, Pennsville Twp, 68-69; chmn, Salem Co Dem Comt, 69- Bus & Prof Pos: Teacher Mannington Twp Sch, 60-66; teacher, Penns Grove-Upper Penns Neck Regional Sch Dist, 66-69, prin, 69- Mil Serv: Entered as Pvt, Army, 54, released as Pvt, 56, after serv in 168th I F C, Alaska, 55-56; Nat Defense & Good Conduct Medals. Mem: NJ Educ Asn; Co Dem Clubs; Tri-Co Heart Asn, (bd dirs); Heart Fund Drive Salem Co. Relig: Methodist. Mailing Add: Supawna Rd RD 3 Salem NJ 08079

DAVENPORT, ROBERT RAMBO (R)
b Philadelphia, Pa, Nov 30, 27; s Joseph Woerner Davenport & Florence Rambo D; single. Educ: Rutgers Univ, 45-46, 47-48; Ohio Univ, BS, Jour, 51. Polit & Govt Pos: Admin asst, Mayor, Wilmington, Del, 55-56; admin asst to US Rep Harry G Haskell, Jr, Del, 57-58; pub rels dir, Del Rep State Comt, 58-59; legis asst, US Sen John J Williams, 59-69, admin asst, 69-71; admin asst to US Sen William V Roth, Jr, 71-72; admin asst to US Rep Robert McClory, 13th Dist, Ill, 73- Bus & Prof Pos: Prod asst, WDEL TV, Wilmington, Del, 51-53, news dir, 54-55. Mil Serv: Entered as Pvt, Army, 46, released as T-5, 47, after serv in Basic Training Unit, US. Relig: Protestant. Mailing Add: 11 Third St NE Washington DC 20002

DAVID, JEANETTE WALLACE (D)
First VChmn, Cumberland Co Dem Exec Comt, NC
b Hamptonville, NC, June 15, 38; d Gurney Clifton Wallace & Effie Whitlock W; m 1958 to Edward Joseph David. Educ: Wake Forest Univ, 56-58; Delta State Univ, BA, 62; Univ Md, Crete Br, 63; Univ NC, Fayetteville, 69; Kappa Delta Pi. Polit & Govt Pos: Mem, Wake Forest Univ Young Dem Fedn, 56-58; pres, Cumberland Co Young Dem Club, 69; secy, Seventh Dist Young Dem, 70; first vchmn, Cumberland Co Dem Exec Comt, 70-; organizer & bd mem, Cumberland Co Dem Womens Orgn, 70-; bd mem, NC Dem Exec Comt, 71-; secy & bd mem, Cumberland Co Human Rels Coun, 71-; nat committeewoman, NC Young Dem Club, formerly; deleg, Dem Nat Conv, 72. Bus & Prof Pos: Case worker, Cumberland Co Social Serv, 65-67; court counr, 12th Judicial Dist Court, Fayetteville, NC, 67-69. Mem: NC Young Dem Club (bd mem); Young Dem Club Am (bd mem); Fayetteville Exchangette Club (past pres); Myrover-Reese Fellowship Home, Inc (secy & bd mem); Cumberland Co Ment Health Asn. Honors & Awards: Recognition of outstanding pub serv, Cumberland Co Bd Comnrs, 70. Relig: Baptist. Mailing Add: 1942 Forest Hill Dr Fayetteville NC 28303

DAVID, NORMA (D)
Chmn, Mono Co Dem Cent Comt, Calif
b Springfield, Mass, 1931; d Maurice Ashley & Mae Weinberg A; div; c Rachel & Jonathan. Educ: Santa Monica Col, AA, 69; Ecole Viticult, Lausanne, Switz, 73-74. Polit & Govt Pos:

Chmn, Mono Co Dem Cent Comt, Calif, 74- Bus & Prof Pos: Commentator, WTTH, Mich; announcer, WAAB, Mass & WNAB, Conn; copy writer, William B Remingon; proprietor, Minors & Majors, 74-; columnist, The Mono Herald; owner, The Tourist Trapper, Mammoth Lakes. Mem: Mammoth Lakes CofC; Mammoth Adv Comn (alt); Mammoth Lakes Tennis Club. Legal Res: Sherwin Villas Mammoth Lakes CA 93546 Mailing Add: Box 8720 Mammoth Lakes CA 93546

DAVIDOFF, PAUL **(D)**
Committeeman, Westchester Co Dem Party, NY
b New York, NY, Feb 28, 30; s Bernard Davidoff & Mildred Cohn D; m 1964 to Linda Greenberg; c Susan, Carla & Daniel. Educ: Allegheny Col, AB, 52; Univ Pa, MCP, 56, LLB, 61. Polit & Govt Pos: Chmn, Center City Reform Dem, Philadelphia, Pa, 63-64; committeeman, Westchester Co Dem Party, NY, 67-; Dem cand, US House Rep, 68; chmn, Concerned Dem Larchmont-Mamaroneck, 68-69. Bus & Prof Pos: Town planner, New Canaan, Conn, 56-57; planner, Voorhees, Walker, Smith & Smith, New York, 57-58; assoc prof city & regional planning, Univ Pa, 58-65; prof & dir grad prog in urban planning, Hunter Col, 65-69; dir, Suburban Action Inst, 69-; research dir, Urban Policy Proj, 20th Century Fund, 69- Publ: A choice theory of planning, 61, Advocacy & pluralism in planning, 65 & Suburban action: advocate planning for an open society, 1/70, J Am Inst Planners. Mem: Am Inst Planners (bd gov, 70-); Planners for Equal Opportunity (mem policy comt). Mailing Add: 18 Forest Park Ave Larchmont NY 10538

DAVIDS, CRAIG E **(D)**
Ariz State Rep
b Charlotte, Mich, Apr 7, 19; s Ernest G Davids & Mary Craig D; m 1944 to Kathleen Hembroff. Educ: Eastern Mich Univ, 38-40; Univ Mich, AB, 42, Law Sch, scholar, 43-45, JD with distinction, 45; Pi Kappa Delta; Phi Kappa Phi; Barristers Soc. Polit & Govt Pos: Dem precinctman, Precinct 23, Pinal Co, Ariz, 66-68; Ariz State Rep, Dist Five, Pinal & Gila Co, 68-, Minority Leader, Ariz House of Rep, 73- Publ: Equity clean hands doctrine, 10/44 & Resulting trusts & statute of frauds, 12/44, Mich Law Rev; Legal limitations on use of chemical analysis to determine intoxication, Mich Bar J, 4/46; plus others. Mem: Mich & Mich Jr Bar Asns; Am Judicature Soc; Phoenix Exec Club; Ariz Farm Bur. Honors & Awards: Distinguished Serv Award, Mich Jr Bar Asn, 54-55; Voice of Democracy Award, VFW. Relig: Presbyterian. Legal Res: 432 Orlando Circle Coolidge AZ 85228 Mailing Add: PO Box 246 Coolidge AZ 85228

DAVIDSON, CARLTON E **(R)**
Chmn, Lawrence Co Rep Orgn, Ohio
b Ironton, Ohio, June 26, 08; s Frank P Davidson & Rebecca Baker D, both deceased; single. Educ: Tri-State Col of Eng, BA in eng, 31; Univ Cincinnati, BS in educ, 33; Rio Grande Col, 45; Ohio Univ, 60; Marshall Univ, 60-65; Beta Phi Sigma. Polit & Govt Pos: Mem, Precinct Rep Cent Comt, Ohio, 32-42; engr on construct & survey, Ohio Hwy Dept, 39-42; comnr, Lawrence Co, 49-61; Ohio State Rep, 26th Dist, 60-72; vchmn, Lawrence Co Rep Orgn, formerly, chmn, currently; mem, Tri Co Ment Health & Retardation Bd; mem, Sch Bd for Ment Retarded; mem, Bicentennial Comn. Bus & Prof Pos: High sch teacher & coach, Ohio Pub Schs, 45-52; sch adminr, Lawrence Co Sch Dist, 52-60. Mil Serv: Entered as Pvt, Army, 42, released as Cpl, 45, after serv in 6th Inf Div, SPac Theater, 43-45; Capt, Ohio Defense Corps, 57-61; Am & Asiatic Pac Theater Campaign Ribbons; Good Conduct & Victory Medals. Mem: Vet Rep Club; DAV; Mason; Grange; Am Bantam Asn. Honors & Awards: Commissioned by Gov to do official bronze sculpture of Neil Armstrong for museum, Wapakoneta, Ohio; Ky Col & Ky Admiral. Relig: Protestant. Mailing Add: 1816 Campbell Dr Ironton OH 45638

DAVIDSON, CURTIS VERNON **(D)**
Mo State Rep
b Albany, Mo, Dec 12, 12; s Charles Edward Davidson & Maude E Hern D; m 1935 to Mary Elizabeth Catley; c Donna Ruth (Mrs Hutson), Patricia Elizabeth (Mrs Vaughn) & Mary Kathleen. Educ: Henry Co Pub Schs; Mo Auction Sch, Kansas City, Mo. Polit & Govt Pos: Mo State Rep, 57- Bus & Prof Pos: Auctioneer & real estate broker, currently. Mem: Mason; Shrine; Optimists; Elks. Relig: Baptist. Mailing Add: 612 S Second St Clinton MO 64735

DAVIDSON, EUGENE ERBERT (GENE) **(D)**
Tenn State Rep
b Springfield, Tenn, Jan 1, 47; s John E Davidson & Georgia Belle Goodman D; m 1970 to Suzanne Pinson. Educ: Austin Peay State Univ, BS, 69; Nashville Law Sch, JD, 75. Polit & Govt Pos: Justice of the Peace, Robertson Co Court, Tenn, 72-74; Tenn State Rep, 66th Dist, 74- Bus & Prof Pos: Teacher, Robertson Co Schs, Tenn, 69-72 & 73-74; field rep & pub rels dir, Robertson Cheatham Farmers Coop, 72-73; law clerk, Joe K Walker, 72-75. Mil Serv: Airman Basic, Air Force; Vol in Time of Mil Crisis Award. Publ: Co-auth, Historical Sketches of Adams & Port Royal, 68. Mem: Mason; Tenn Grand Lodge; Tenn-Ky Thresherman's Asn; Robertson Co Laymen's Club. Honors & Awards: Outstanding Educator, Jaycees, 74; Distinguished Serv Award, 75. Relig: United Methodist. Mailing Add: Rte 2 Adams TN 37010

DAVIDSON, GENE D **(D)**
Tenn State Rep
Mailing Add: PO Box 248 Waynesboro TN 38485

DAVIDSON, IRWIN DELMORE **(D)**
b New York, NY, Jan 2, 06; s Lafayette Davidson & Tillie Bechstein D; m 1965 to Marion Doniger; c James Sylvan & Mark Lewis. Educ: Washington Sq Col, BS, 27; NY Univ Law Sch, LLB, 28; Tau Delta Phi. Polit & Govt Pos: NY State Assemblyman, 37-48; justice, Court of Spec Sessions of NY, 49-54; US Rep, NY, 55-56; justice, Supreme Court of NY, 57- Publ: The Jury is Still Out, Harper's, 59. Mem: NY Co Lawyers' Asn; Asn of the Bar of the City of New York; Am & NY State Bar Asns; Harmonic Club. Relig: Jewish. Legal Res: 180 East End Ave New York NY 10028 Mailing Add: 100 Centre St New York NY 10013

DAVIDSON, JOHN A **(R)**
Ill State Sen
b Westpoint, Miss, Aug 31, 24; s Homer F Davidson & Anna Grosboll D; m 1953 to Shirley Beard; c Ann, Jane & John. Educ: Nat Col Chiropractic, DC, 52; Sigma Phi Kappa. Polit & Govt Pos: Mem & asst supvr Capital Twp, Sangamon Co Bd Supvr, Ill, 59-72, chmn, 70-72; Ill State Sen, 73- Bus & Prof Pos: Trustee, Found Chiropractic Educ & Research, 67- Mil Serv: Entered as A/S, Navy Air Corps, 43, released as Aviation Ordnanceman 1/C, 46, after serv in VT 80, SPac, USS Ticonderoga, 43-45; Air Medal; Unit Citation; Air Crewman Wings-3 Battle Stars; Philippine Campaign-2 Battle Stars; SPac-4 Battle Stars. Mem: Am Chiropractic Asn; Ill Chiropractic Soc; Mason; Am Legion; Elks. Honors & Awards: Outstanding Jaycee, Springfield, 54-55; Fel Int Col Chiropractic, 61; Ill Chiropractor of Year, Ill Chiropractic Soc, 62; Chiropractor of Year, Am Chiropractic Asn, 73. Relig: Methodist. Legal Res: 2509 S Glenwood Springfield IL 62704 Mailing Add: 718 Myers Bldg Springfield IL 62701

DAVIDSON, LUCY **(D)**
Ariz State Sen
b New York, NY, Nov 11, 26; d Morley S Wolfe & June Lurie W; remarried 1962 to Edward S Davidson; c Timothy, Christopher & Jamie Lynn. Educ: Mt Holyoke Col, BA; Columbia Univ, MA; Univ Ariz. Polit & Govt Pos: Ariz State Sen, 75- Bus & Prof Pos: Sch teacher, Jr High, Tucson, Ariz, 58-68. Mem: Am Civil Liberties Union; Ariz Womens Polit Caucus & Nat Womens Polit Caucus. Mailing Add: 2915 Indian Ruins Rd Tucson AZ 85715

DAVIDSON, MARION **(D)**
Idaho State Rep
Mailing Add: Rte 1 Bonners Ferry ID 83805

DAVIDSON, ROBERT CLARKE **(R)**
Rep Nat Committeeman, NMex
b Springfield, Nebr, July 25, 16; m 1939 to Mary Elizabeth (Betty); c Robert C, II, Mary Beth (Mrs McGill), Patricia Ann, Susan Anne (Mrs Putland), Michael Scott & Kathryn Louise. Educ: Boyles Bus Col, Omaha, Nebr, 34-35; Am Inst Banking, 35; Baker Univ, 36-37; Southern Methodist Univ, 41-42. Polit & Govt Pos: Coordr, State Rep Campaign Off, NMex, 62; chmn, Bernalillo Co Rep Cent Comt, 62-65; deleg-at-lg & vchmn NMex deleg, Rep Nat Conv, 64; Rep cand, US Rep, 66; chmn, Rep State Cent Comt NMex, 68-; mem, Do Comt, 69-71; finance chmn, NMex Comt to Reelect the President, 72; Rep Nat Committeeman, NMex, currently. Bus & Prof Pos: With Fed Land Bank, Omaha, Nebr, 34-36, summer 37 & Mutual & United of Omaha, 37-41; Ernest Hundahl Agency & Mutual & United of Omaha, Dallas, Tex, 41-51; gen agent, State of NMex, Mutual & United of Omaha, Albuquerque, 51- Mem: NMex Health & Accident Asn (pres); NMex Life Underwriters Asn (secy); NMex deleg, White House Conf Aging, 61; St Charles' Boy Scout Troop; Albuquerque Baseball Club (secy-treas). Relig: Roman Catholic. Mailing Add: 932 McDuffie Circle NE Albuquerque NM 87110

DAVIDSON, ROBERT W **(R)**
b Colfax, Wash, Sept 18, 49; s William M Davidson & Lena Joyce Soli D; single. Educ: Harvard Univ, BA, 71. Polit & Govt Pos: White House intern, President's Adv Coun on Exec Orgn, 69; admin asst to US Rep Joel Pritchard, Wash, 73- Mem: Ripon Soc. Legal Res: 26307 34th Ave S Kent WA 98031 Mailing Add: 133 Cannon House Off Bldg Washington DC 20515

DAVIDSON, WILLIAM JOHN **(R)**
Mem, Seventh Cong Dist Rep Comt, Ga
b Norfolk, Va, Sept 24, 28; s Lloyd Wallace Davidson & Sophia Schaeffer D; m 1970 to Darlene Smiley; c Dale Lee, Toni Leigh, Don Le & Terry L, stepchildren, Judith Elise, Barry Wayne, William Wallace, Debra Darlene, Daniel Lawrence & Glenn Marshall Wood. Educ: Ga State Col, 65. Polit & Govt Pos: Rep precinct chmn, Smyrna, Ga, 66; mem, Cobb Co Rep Comt, 66-73, first vchmn, 68; mem, Ga State Rep Comt, formerly; Mem, Seventh Cong Dist Rep Comt, 67-; alt deleg, Rep Nat Conv, 68; second vchmn, Ga Rep Party, 70-72. Bus & Prof Pos: Dept mgr, Lockheed-Georgia Co, Marietta, 52- Mil Serv: Entered as A/S Navy, 46, released as Aviation Photographer 3/C, 48, after serv in Utility Squadron Four, US Atlantic Fleet, 47-48. Mem: Civitan Int; Moose. Relig: Methodist. Mailing Add: 891 Brentwood Dr SE Smyrna GA 30080

DAVIE, JOHN TURNEY **(D)**
Chmn, Fulton Co Dem Comt, Ky
b Hickman, Ky, May 28, 11; s Jones Roper Davie & Faye Saunders D; m 1941 to Esther Jane Byrd; c John Wayne & Joyce Lynn. Educ: Sylvan Shade High Sch, 30. Polit & Govt Pos: Fulton Co Sheriff, Ky, 50-54; field agent, Ky State Alcoholic Dept, State Dept, 56-60; supvr, Fulton Co Road Dept, 66-68; chmn, Fulton Co Dem Comt, 54- Bus & Prof Pos: Farm owner & operator, 30-; agent, Davie Ins Agency, 62- Mem: Ky Sheriffs Asn (hon mem); CofC; Ky Farm Bur; Moose; Hickman Recreational Club. Relig: First Christian Church. Mailing Add: 205 Clinton St Hickman KY 42050

DAVIES, D O **(R)**
b New Castle Pa, Nov 1, 20; s Matthew H Davies & Sarah Johns D; m 1968 to Carol Wilkins; c Nicole Lynn & David O. Educ: New Castle High Sch, 46. Polit & Govt Pos: NW div chmn, State Outdoorsmen for Schwecker for US Senate, 66; secy-treas, State Outdoorsmen for Hugh Scott for US Senate, 68-70; adv, Young Rep of Pa, 68-73; adv, Appalachian Trail Conf, Nat Park Serv, 69-; mem exec comt, Lawrence Co Rep Party, 70-73; deleg, Rep Nat Conv, 72; bd mem, Hist Am Bldg Survey, Dept of Interior, 72-; West Pa coordr, Drew Lewis for Gov, 74. Bus & Prof Pos: Pres, Davies Shoe Co, 55-; vpres, Silver Maple Foods, 70. Mil Serv: Entered as Pvt, Marine Corps, 41, released as Sgt, 45, after serv in 5th Amphibian, 1st Marine Div, Pac Theatre, 42-45; Letter of Commendation; Presidential Unit Citations; Asiatic Pac Clusters; Three Battle Stars. Mem: VFW; Pa Fedn of Outdoorsmen Clubs; 1st Marine Div Asn (life mem); Ruffed Grouse Soc of Am (life mem, nat treas, 68-71 & bd gov currently); Allegheny River Conserv Asn. Honors & Awards: Sportsman of the Year, Lawrence Co Conserv Clubs, 61; Outdoorsman of Year, 70; Golden Eagle Award, Outdoorsmen of Pa, 72. Mailing Add: RD 3 Kingswood Dr New Castle PA 16105

DAVIES, JOHN S **(R)**
Pa State Rep
b Spring Twp, Sept 4, 26; s William M Davies & Caroline Boas D; m 1950 to Marguerite Elizabeth Spankle; c Lynn M & Michael J. Educ: Gettysburg Col, AB Polit Sci, 50; Kutztown State Col, Educ Cert, 57; Alpha Tau Omega. Polit & Govt Pos: Pa State Rep, 129th Legis Dist, 75-, mem house educ comt & labor rels comt, Pa House Rep, 75- Bus & Prof Pos: Dept head social sci, Kutztown Sch Dist, 54-63; teacher econ & govt, Wilson Sch Dist, 63-74. Mil Serv: Entered as Seaman, Navy, 44, released as Signalman 1/C, 46, after serv in Anti Sub Warfare, Div 4, Atlantic & Pac Theatres, 44-45. Mem: Pa State Educ Asn; Wilson Educ Asn (pres). Legal Res: 2422 Cleveland Ave West Wyomissing PA 19609 Mailing Add: State Capitol B-8 Harrisburg PA 17120

DAVIES, JOHN THOMAS (JACK) **(DFL)**
Minn State Sen
b Harvey, NDak, Jan 6, 32; s Charles Evan Davies & Marian Healy D; m to Patricia Ann McAndrews; c Elizabeth Ann, Ted Elliott & John Thomas. Educ: Itasca Jr Col, AA, 52; Univ

Minn, BA, 54, JD, 60. Polit & Govt Pos: Minn State Sen, 59-; comnr, Uniform State Laws, 66- Bus & Prof Pos: Sports ed, KSTP-TV, 56-57; pvt law practice, Minneapolis, Minn, 61-65; attorney, Fine, Simon & Schneider, 62-65; registr & prof, William Mitchell Col of Law, 65- Mil Serv: Entered as Pvt, Army, 54, released as Pfc, 56, after serv in Army Intel, Japan & Korea. Publ: Legislative Law & Process in a Nutshell, West Publ Co, 75. Mem: Am, Hennepin Co & Minn Bar Asns. Mailing Add: 3424 Edmund Blvd Minneapolis MN 55406

DAVIES, RICHARD (D)
Maine State Rep
Mailing Add: 53 N Maine St Orono ME 04473

DAVIS, ALFRED, IV (R)
Mem Exec Comt, Rep Party Tex
b Baltimore, Md, Oct 24, 45; s Alfred Davis, Jr & Imogene Stevenson D; single. Educ: Univ Tex, Austin, BA, 67; Univ Houston, MA, 69. Polit & Govt Pos: Campaign mgr, Lee for Senate Campaign, 72; admin asst to co chmn, Harris Co Rep Party, 72-73; admin asst to Tex State Rep Milton Fox, 73-; state chmn, Tex Young Adult Rep Coun, 74-; mem exec comt, Rep Party Tex, 74- Bus & Prof Pos: Instr, Houston Community Col, 72. Mil Serv: Entered as Pvt, Army, 69, released as Specialist 5/C, 71, after serv in Hq, Vietnam, 70-71; Bronze Star Medal; Nat Defense Serv Medal; Vietnam Serv Medal; Vietnam Campaign Medal; Good Conduct Medal; Two Campaign Stars. Mem: Univ Houston Alumni Asn; Gtr Houston Young Adult Rep Club (officer & dir, 72-); life mem Univ Tex Ex-Students Asn. Relig: Disciples of Christ. Mailing Add: 929 Waxmyrtle Houston TX 77024

DAVIS, ALICE (R)
NH State Rep
Mailing Add: Shaker Rd RFD 8 East Concord NH 03301

DAVIS, ANN M (R)
Mem, Sixth Cong Dist Rep Exec Comt, Tenn
b Humphreys Co, Tenn, Apr 24, 14; d Andrew J James & Annie Gray J; m 1954 to William Claude Davis; c Glynn K, Wayne L & Bond Dell Jackson. Educ: High Sch, 31-32. Polit & Govt Pos: Mem, Humphreys Co Rep Exec Comt, Tenn, 55-, secy, 62, chmn, formerly; mem, Co Elec Comn Humphreys Co, 65-66; campaign mgr, Rep Campaign for Sen Howard Baker, Jr, Humpreys, Perry, Lewis & Hickman Co, 66; campaign mgr, President Nixon for Humphreys Co, 60 & 68; US Comnr, Mid Dist Tenn, 68; mem, Sixth Cong Dist Rep Exec Comt, 68- Honors & Awards: Army Navy E Award, 43. Relig: Baptist. Mailing Add: Hurricane Mills TN 37078

DAVIS, BENJAMIN OLIVER, JR
Asst Secy Environ Safety & Consumer Affairs, Dept of Transportation
b Washington, DC, Dec 18, 12; s Benjamin Oliver Davis & Sadie Overton D; m 1936 to Agatha Scott. Educ: Western Reserve Univ, 29-30; Univ Chicago, 30-32; US Mil Acad, BS, 36; Air War Col, 50. Hon Degrees: DMil Sci, Wilberforce Univ, 48; DSc, Morgan State Col, 63; LLD, Tuskegee Inst, 63. Polit & Govt Pos: Dir, Off Civil Aviation Security, Dept Transportation, 70-71, asst secy for safety & consumer affairs, 71- Mil Serv: Army, 32; Air Force, 42-70, serv as Comdr, 99th Fighter Squadron, NAfrica, Sicily, 43; Comdr 332nd Fighter Group, Italy, 43-45; Comdr, 51st Fighter Intercpetor Wing, Korea, 53; VComdr, 13th Air Force & Comdr, Air Task Force 13, 55-57; Chief of Staff, 12th Air Force, 57; Dep Chief Staff for Opers, Hq, Ger, 57-61; Chief Staff, UN Command Korea, 65-67; Comdr, 13th Air Force, 67-68; Dep Comdr, US Strike Command, 68-70, Ret Lt Gen, 70; Distinguished Serv Medal with 2 Oak Leaf Clusters; Silver Star; Distinguished Flying Cross; Legion of Merit with 2 Oak Leaf Clusters; Air Medal with 5 Oak Leaf Clusters. Legal Res: 1001 Wilson Blvd Arlington VA 22206 Mailing Add: Dept of Transportation 400 Seventh St SW Washington DC 20590

DAVIS, BOB (D)
Tenn State Rep
Mailing Add: 1107 Curleque Dr Chattanooga TN 37411

DAVIS, CHARLES RUSSELL (D)
Chmn, Cass Co Dem Exec Comt, Tex
b Paris, Tex, Feb 1, 09; s Henry Bert Davis & Lou Elizabeth Moseley D; m 1941 to Leita Mary Reeder; c James Henry & Ernestine Elizabeth (Betsy). Educ: Marshall Col, AA, 31; Am Inst Banking, Rutgers Univ, 4 years, cert; Dallas Inst Mortuary Sci, 1 year, licensed mortician. Polit & Govt Pos: Chmn, Cass Co Dem Exec Comt, Tex, 64-; former mayor, Hughes Springs, Tex. Bus & Prof Pos: Teller, First Nat Bank, Marshall, Tex, 32-42; partner, Reeder-Watson-Davis Gen Merchandise, 46-50; partner & mortician, Reeder-Watson-Davis Funeral Home, 40-67, owner, 68- Mil Serv: Entered as Pvt, Army Ord Corps, 42, released as Cpl, 45, after serv in 66th Ord, NAfrica & ETO, 42-45. Mem: Lions; Cass Co Cattlemens Asn; ETex Funeral Dirs Asn. Relig: Methodist. Legal Res: 113 N Keasler St Hughes Springs TX 75656 Mailing Add: PO Box 488 Hughes Springs TX 75656

DAVIS, CHESTER J (R)
Chmn, Trousdale Co Rep Party, Tenn
b Red Boiling Springs, Tenn, Oct 19, 03; s Thomas Wayne Davis & Margaret Bastou D; single. Educ: George Peabody Col & Vanderbilt Univ, 28. Polit & Govt Pos: Rural letter carrier, Hartsville, Tenn, 58-59, postmaster, 59-61; chmn, Trousdale Co Rep Party, Tenn, 61- Bus & Prof Pos: Pres, Hartsville Broadcasting Corp, 66- Mem: Hartsville-Trousdale CofC (dir); Farm Bur; Tenn Asn Broadcasters. Mailing Add: Rte 2 Hartsville TN 37074

DAVIS, CLAUDINE (D)
Dem Nat Committeewoman, Wash
b Bridgeport, Wash, June 22, 28; d Frederick George Buckingham & Della Jaynes B; m 1945 to Thomas R Davis; c Kathleen Joanne, Jacky Lynn & Thomas James. Educ: Mansfield High Sch, Mansfield, Wash, grad, 45. Polit & Govt Pos: Committeewoman, Wash Dem State Cent Comt, 67-73; vchmn, Fifth Cong Dist Dem Orgn, Wash, 67-73; finance chmn, Wash State Fedn Dem Women's Clubs, 67-73; deleg, Dem Nat Conv, 72; Dem Nat Committeewoman, Wash, 72-; deleg, Dem Nat Mid-Term Conf, 74. Bus & Prof Pos: Self-employed wheat grower, 45-73. Mem: Wash State Grange Asn; Wash Wheat Growers Asn; Big Bend Basin Water Prog (comt mem); Fla Fedn of Art; Flying Farmers Orgn. Relig: Presbyterian. Legal Res: 402 Walnut Coulee City WA 99115 Mailing Add: Box 258 Coulee City WA 99115

DAVIS, CORNEAL A (D)
Ill State Rep
b New Vicksburg, Miss, Aug 28, 00; s Dudly D Davis & Pearl D; m 1921 to Elma Howell; c Yvonne (Mrs Maule). Educ: Tougaloo Col, 17; John Marshall Sch Law, 48; Moody Bible Inst; Omega Psi Phi. Polit & Govt Pos: Ill State Rep, 15 terms, Asst Minority Leader, Ill House of Rep, 71-; pres, Second Ward Dem Orgn, Ill; mem, Ill Dem State Cent Comt, currently; mem, Bd of Local Improv, 66- Mil Serv: Entered as Pvt, Army, 17, released as Cpl, 19, after serv in Eighth Inf, Ill Nat Guard Co D, Machine Gun Bn, Meuse Argonne Offense, 18. Mem: Mason (33 degree); Wabash YMCA (bd dirs); McKinley Community Serv (bd dirs); Prince Hall Shrines (past Imperial Potentate). Relig: Methodist; asst minister. Mailing Add: 3223 S Calumet Ave Chicago IL 60616

DAVIS, DAVE QUENTIN (DFL)
Chmn, Hubbard Co Dem-Farmer-Labor Party, Minn
b Bay City, Mich, June 25, 21; s Roscoe D Davis & Gertrude Reid D; m 1940 to Beatrice H Schulz; c Ronald Q, Bonnie B (Mrs Allen Friedland), Joan Marie (Mrs Peter Kieffer), David R, Jack R & Deborah Ann. Educ: Ind Bus Col, 37-40; Mich State Univ, 45-47; Univ SDak, 66-67. Polit & Govt Pos: Dem field man & pub rels, Mich, 50-56; Dem pub rels work, Fla, 56-59; Dem pub rels work, Iowa, 59-63; asst for econ develop, Gov Rolvag, Minn, 66; mem exec bd & publicity dir, Hubbard Co Dem-Farmer-Labor Party, 66-72, chmn, 72- Bus & Prof Pos: Gen mgr, Murray Broadcasting Corp, Fla & Iowa, 56-63; mgr, Delehunt Broadcasting Corp, Minn, 63-65; exec dir, Leech Lake Community Action Prog, Cass Lake, 66-68; exec dir, Minn Br, Humane Soc of US, 68- Mil Serv: Entered as Pvt, Army, 42, released as T/Sgt, 45, reentered 50-52, served in Merrills Marauders, China-Burma-India Theatre, 43-45 & Korean War, 50-52; Presidential Citation, 2 Bronze Stars; 2 Purple Hearts; Combat Inf Badge; various theatre ribbons. Publ: Feature articles, Leech Lake Newsweekly, 66-68 & Minn Humane News, 68- Mem: Am Fedn TV & Radio Artists; Radio Press Club; Lions; VFW; Am Legion. Honors & Awards: Outstanding Broadcaster Award, Nashville, Tenn, 58; Manpower Prog Award, US Dept Labor, 67. Relig: Methodist. Mailing Add: Lake Lodge Star Rte Box 41 Laporte MN 56461

DAVIS, DEANE CHANDLER (R)
b East Barre, Vt, Nov 7, 00; s Earl Russell Davis & Lois Hillary D; m 1924 to Corinne Eastman (deceased); c Deane (deceased), Marian (Mrs Frank R Calcagni) & Thomas C; m 1952 to Marjorie Smith Conzelman. Educ: Boston Univ Law Sch, LLB, 22; Delta Theta Phi. Hon Degrees: LLD, Univ Vt, 57, Middlebury Col, 64 & Boston Univ, 69; LittD, Norwich Univ, 63. Polit & Govt Pos: Mem city coun, Barre, Vt, 23-24, city attorney, 24-26 & 28-30; states attorney, Washington Co, 26-28; Superior Judge, Vt, 31-36; deleg, Rep Nat Conv, 48; mem resolutions comt, deleg, Rep Nat Conv, 72; Gov, Vt, 69-72. Bus & Prof Pos: Attorney-at-law, Barre, Vt, 22-31; partner law firm, Wilson, Carver, Davis & Keyser, 36-40; gen coun, Nat Life Ins Co, Montpelier, Vt, 40-43, vpres & gen counsel, 43-50, pres & dir, 50-66, chief exec off, 66-67, chmn bd dirs, 66-68, dir, 68-, mem finance & mgt comts, currently. Publ: Life insurance & business purchase agreements, 45. Mem: Vt Bar Asn (pres & chmn bd of bar exam); Life Ins Asn Am; Inst Life Ins; Am Judicature Soc; F&AM (Past Potentate, Mt Sinai Temple 3); plus many other civic & prof orgns. Honors & Awards: Man of the Year Award, Ins Field Publ, 61; Vt Bankers Asn Award, 62; Cert of Merit, SAR. Relig: Methodist. Mailing Add: 5 Dyer St Montpelier VT 05602

DAVIS, DON CLARENCE (D)
Okla State Rep
b Ardmore, Okla, June 7, 43; s Clarence L Davis & Wilma Henson D; m 1969 to Beverly Jean Gearheard. Educ: Cameron Col, 61-62; Univ Okla, BA, 65, Col of Law, JD, 69; Phi Theta Kappa; Sigma Delta Chi; Phi Alpha Delta; Sigma Alpha Epsilon. Polit & Govt Pos: Staff asst for US Sen Fred R Harris, Okla, 65; Okla State Rep, 71- Bus & Prof Pos: Staff writer, Okla J, Oklahoma City, Okla, 64-69; gen counsel, Page Aircraft Maintenance, Inc, Lawton, 69-71; attorney & counselor at law, 70-; gen counsel, Northrup Worldwide Aircraft Serv, Inc, 71- Mil Serv: Entered as Cadet, Army ROTC, 61, released as Cadet E-1, 65, after serv in Univ Okla. Mem: Rotary Int; Lawton YMCA; Lawton CofC; Cameron Col Former Students Asn; Lawton Community Action Prog (bd dirs). Relig: Baptist. Legal Res: 823 N 41 Lawton OK 73501 Mailing Add: Box 262 Lawton OK 73501

DAVIS, DONALD M (D)
Pa State Rep
b Fairchance, Pa, June 6, 15; s Albert Callatin Davis & Bessie Myers D; m 1936 to Frances Hudock; c Marlene (Mrs Joseph Juriga) & Donald L. Educ: Georges Twp High Sch, 28-32. Polit & Govt Pos: Pa State Rep, 69- Bus & Prof Pos: Ins agent, Metrop Life, NY, 39-51; credit mgr, Cohen Furniture Co, Brownsville, Pa, 51- Mil Serv: Entered as Pvt, Army, 44, released as 1st Sgt, 46, after serving in Inf K-9 Corps. Mem: Optimist Int; Am Legion. Relig: Lutheran. Mailing Add: RD 2 Box 415A Uniontown PA 15401

DAVIS, DORIS ANN (D)
Mayor, Compton, Calif
b Mt Vernon, Ga, Nov 5, 35; d Cornelius Collins & Pearl C; m to Earnest Preacely; c Ricky & John Davis. Educ: Univ Ill, BA; Northwestern Univ, MA; Lawrence Univ, currently; Alpha Kappa Alpha. Hon Degrees: LLD, Windsor Univ, 74. Polit & Govt Pos: City clerk, Compton, Calif, 65-73, mayor, 73- Bus & Prof Pos: Owner & pres, Dee Employ Agency, Compton, Calif; dir, Daisy Child Develop Ctr, Compton, currently. Publ: Arts in Time, African Affairs, Govt Exec, Essence & Ebony. Honors & Awards: Award of Merit, Urban Space Indust, 73; Resolution, Calif Legis Assembly Rules Comt, 68. Mailing Add: 409 W Palmer Compton CA 90220

DAVIS, DREW ANTHONY (D)
Ore State Rep
b Portland, Ore, Feb 9, 51; s Andrew Gus Davis & Evelyn Chapman D; m 1969 to Diane Catherine Van Cleve; c Drew, Jr & Darla. Educ: Mt Hood Community Col, 72-73. Polit & Govt Pos: Ore State Rep, Dist 20, 75- Bus & Prof Pos: Comput specialist, Nationwide Ins, 69- Mem: Willamette Dem Soc; Ore Consumer League; Moose; Dem Gavel Club. Mailing Add: 10812 SE Stark Portland OR 97216

DAVIS, E LAWRENCE, III (D)
NC State Sen
b Winston-Salem, NC, Dec 30, 37; s Egbert Lawrence Davis, Jr & Eleanor Layfield; m 1962 to Alexandra Fortune Holderness; c Alexandra Fortune, Egbert Lawrence, IV, Adelaide Lucinda & Pamela Layfield. Educ: Princeton Univ, AB, 60; Duke Univ Law Sch, LLB, 63; George Washington Univ, MBA, 66. Polit & Govt Pos: NC State Rep, 71-74, chmn, Comt on Social Serv, NC House Rep, 73-74; NC State Sen, 75-, chmn, Comt on Local Govt & Regional Affairs, NC State Senate, currently. Bus & Prof Pos: Assoc, Womble, Carlyle, Sandridge & Rice, 65-69, partner, 69- Mil Serv: Entered as 1st Lt, Army, 63, released as Capt, 65, after serv in 902nd Intel Corps, Washington, DC, 64-65. Mem: Am & NC Bar Asns;

Winston-Salem Rotary Club; Winston-Salem Jaycees; Winston-Salem CofC. Honors & Awards: Young Man of Year Award, Winston-Salem Jaycees, 72; Freedom Guard Award, NC & US Jaycees, 73. Relig: Baptist. Mailing Add: PO Drawer 84 Winston-Salem NC 27102

DAVIS, EDITH PANCOAST (R)
Committeewoman, NJ Rep Party
b Salem Co, NJ, July 6, 11; d Dudley Crowther Pancoast & Florence Emma Shute P; m 1930 to William Ralph Davis; c Dudley Pancoast. Educ: Bucknell Univ, 29-30; Glassboro State Col, exten courses; Debating Soc. Polit & Govt Pos: Mem, Salem Co Rep Comt, NJ, 20 years; committeewoman, NJ Rep Party, 61- Mem: Woodstown Woman's Club; Salem Co Hosp Auxiliary; Woodstown-Pilesgrove Libr Asn; Salem Co Fedn Rep Women; Eastern Star; Salem Co Red Cross. Honors & Awards: Rep Woman of Year, Salem Co Fedn Rep Women. Relig: Soc of Friends. Mailing Add: Eldridges Hill Rd RD 1 Woodstown NJ 08098

DAVIS, EDWARD R (NED) (D)
Dem Nat Committeeman, Del
b Laurel, Del, July 7, 28; s Henry Clay Davis & Mary Carey D; m 1965 to Ivyane Fitzpatrick; c Deborah Carter, Mary Carey, Jessica Terry & stepchildren Vickie (Mrs Plerhoples) & Robb Carter. Educ: Gettysburg Col, 48-50; Kenyon Col, 50. Polit & Govt Pos: Exec press secy, Gov of Del, 65-69; Dem Nat Committeeman, Del, 72- Bus & Prof Pos: Reporter-columnist, Del State News, Dover, 56-62; columnist-exec, News-Jour Papers, Wilmington, 62-65; vpres corp rels, Rollins Int, Inc, 69- Mil Serv: Entered as Pvt, Marine Corps, 46, released as Cpl, 47, after serv in Air Corps. Mem: Del Heart Asn (dir, 72-); Del Arthritis Found; Am Legion. Relig: Episcopal. Mailing Add: 4 The Green Dover DE 19901

DAVIS, EDWIN SPARLING (D)
Chmn, Walker Co Dem Party, Tex
b St Louis, Mo, Sept 7, 40; s Edwin P Davis & Evelyne Sparling D; m 1960 to Beverly Wey; c Kimberly & Edwin, Jr. Educ: NTex State Univ, BA, 62, MA, 64; Tex Tech Univ, PhD, 72. Polit & Govt Pos: Admin asst to city mgr, Irving, Tex, 62-63; Dem precinct chmn, Walker Co, 68-70; deleg, Tex State Dem Conv, 68-74; local coordr, Common Cause, Walker Co, 71-; mem state bd dirs, Common Cause of Tex, 72-; chmn, Walker Co Dem Party, 72-; chmn, Walker Co Redistricting Comt, 73- Bus & Prof Pos: Instr, Celina High Sch, Tex, 63; Irving High Sch, 63-66; instr, Sam Houston State Univ, 66-67, asst prof, 68-75, assoc prof, 75-; part-time instr, Tex Tech Univ, 67-68. Publ: Texas County Government: officers & institutions, Sam Houston State Univ, 72. Mem: Am Soc Pub Admin; Am & Southern Polit Sci Asns; Southwestern Soc Sci Asn; Pi Sigma Alpha. Relig: Episcopal. Legal Res: Box 2149 Huntsville TX 77340 Mailing Add: Box 2149 Sam Houston State Univ Huntsville TX 77340

DAVIS, EMIL L (D)
Chmn, Logan Co Dem Exec Comt, Ohio
b Jackson Co, Ohio, Sept 5, 92; s William McK Davis & Clara McKinniss D; m 1933 to Lelia A Hull; c Virginia (Mrs George R Shafer). Educ: Lima Cent High Sch, grad, 11. Polit & Govt Pos: US Postmaster, Lakeview, Ohio, 14-21, mem, Village Coun, 46-49, mayor, 50-65; chmn, Logan Co Dem Cent Comt, 50-54; chmn, Logan Co Dem Exec Comt, 60-; mem, Logan Co Elec Bd, 66- Mem: Mason; Scottish Rite. Relig: United Methodist. Mailing Add: Corner Market & Place Lakeview OH 43331

DAVIS, ERNEST BURROUGHS (INDEPENDENT)
State Auditor, Ga
b Danielsville, Ga, Sept 12, 19; s James Wylie Davis & Lora Evelyn Burroughs D; m 1946 to Mary Louise Walton; c Lane Nannette & Lauren Patricia. Educ: Ga State Univ, BSC, 48. Polit & Govt Pos: Secy-treas, Ga State Health Dept, 61; aide to State Auditor, Dept of Audits, 61-62; State Budget Off, Budget Bur, 62-64; State Auditor, Ga, 64- Mil Serv: Entered Army, 42, released as M/Sgt, 45, after serv in 103 Inf Div, ETO, 44-45; Five Battle Stars; Combat Inf Badge. Mem: Elks; Atlanta Athletic Club; Univ Ga Gridiron Club. Relig: Baptist. Mailing Add: 1679 Timberland Rd NE Atlanta GA 30345

DAVIS, FLINT (D)
b Jackson, Ky, Aug 3, 27; s Cleve Davis & Maggie Campbell D; m 1947 to Christine Gibson; c Sandra J & Russell K. Educ: Lee Col, 1 year. Polit & Govt Pos: Staff mem, Gov Carl E Sanders, Ga, 62-66; staff mem, Gov Lester Maddox, 66-70; chmn, Fannin Co Dem Exec Comt, formerly; mem Ga Dem State Exec Comt, formerly; deleg, Ga State Conv, 70, 50th Sen Dist, 70 & Ninth Cong Dist, 71. Mil Serv: Entered Maritime, 45, released 45, after serv in Atlantic Theatre. Mem: F&AM; R&SM. Relig: Baptist. Mailing Add: Box 5098 McCaysville GA 30555

DAVIS, FRANK H (R)
Treas, Vt
b New York, NY, June 13, 10; m to Virginia Hewitt; c six; five grandchildren. Educ: Night courses, Columbia Univ & Univ Vt. Polit & Govt Pos: Chmn & treas, Burlington, Vt, formerly; treas, Chittenden Co, formerly; mem, Burlington Housing Comt, 62-70, vchmn, 62-64, chmn, 64-69; Vt State Rep, 67-68, mem Com Comt, Vt State House of Rep; Treas, Vt, 69- Bus & Prof Pos: With, E I Du Pont de Nemours, 29-31; chmn, Fuller Rodney, 31-33; Brokerage, Carlisle Jacquelin, 33-42; owner, Self-Serv Laundry, Vt, 47-55; acct exec A M Kidder & Co, 55-60, E I Du Pont, 60-63 & W E Hutton, 63-66. Mil Serv: Entered as Ens, Coast Guard Res, 42, released as Lt(sg), 45, after serv in Atlantic & Pac; commanding officer, Coast Guard Cutter. Mem: Mallets Bay Boat Club (former dir); Lake Champlain Yacht Club. Relig: Congregational; former deacon, Col St Congregational Church, pres, 68-70. Mailing Add: State House Montpelier VT 05401

DAVIS, FRANK W (R)
Committeeman, Okla State Rep Party
b Ada, Okla, Aug 24, 36; s Roscoe Gladstone Davis & Neva Peck D; m 1961 to Kay Higginbotham; c David & Paul. Educ: Univ Ill, 56-57; East Cent State Col, AB, 58; Univ Okla, LLB, 59; Pi Kappa Delta. Polit & Govt Pos: Pres, League of Young Conservatives, East Cent State Col, 55-56; chmn, Pontotoc Co Rep Party, Okla, 57-59; vpres, Univ Okla Young Rep, 59; acting postmaster, Ada, 59-61; co attorney, Logan Co, 61-65; chmn, Logan Co Rep Party, 64-69, committeeman, Okla State Rep Party, 69- Bus & Prof Pos: Attorney-at-law, 65- Mem: Okla & Logan Co Bar Asns; Lions. Relig: Methodist. Mailing Add: 1445 Fogarty Guthrie OK 73044

DAVIS, GILBERT RAY (D)
NC State Rep
b Randolph Co, NC, Mar 18, 36; s James Ernest Davis & Anna Hohn D; m 1954 to Leola Marie Webster; c Kathryn Diane (Mrs Linthicum), Steven Eddie & Tammy Luane. Educ: Trinity High Sch, NC, grad, 54. Polit & Govt Pos: NC State Rep, 75- Mem: Mason; Shrine; Civitan; Grange; Farm Bur. Honors & Awards: Outstanding Young Farmer of Year, Duke Power Co, 65; Civitan of Year, New Mkt Civitan, 67; Highest Milk Prod Among Holstein Cattle, Dairy Herd Improv Asn, 69; Outstanding Salesman for Tractors, Massey Ferguson Co, 70; Salesman of Year in Dairy Feed, Ralston Purina Co, 71. Legal Res: Rte 1 Randleman NC 27317 Mailing Add: NC Gen Assembly Raleigh NC 27611

DAVIS, GLENN ROBERT (R)
b Mukwonago, Wis, Oct 28, 14; s Charles W Davis & Jennie Wachendorf D; m 1942 to Dr Kathryn McFarlane; c Kathleen, Margaret, Janet, James & Elizabeth. Educ: Wis State Univ, Platteville, BEd, 34, Law Sch, LLB, 40; Phi Delta Phi; Order of the Coif. Polit & Govt Pos: Wis State Assemblyman, 41-42; US Rep, Wis, 47-57 & 65-74; deleg, Rep Nat Conv, 56, 60, 68 & 72. Bus & Prof Pos: Attorney-at-law, Waukesha, Wis, 40-42, 45-47 & 57-65; pres & bd mem, New Berlin State Bank, 59-65. Mil Serv: Entered as Ens, Navy, 42, released as Lt(sg), 45, after serv aboard USS Sangamon in Pac Theater, 43-45; Pac Campaign Ribbon; Nine Battle Stars; Presidential Unit Citation; Lt(sg), Naval Res (Ret), 54. Mem: Waukesha Co Bar Asn; Waukesha CofC; State Bar of Wis; Am Legion; Kiwanis. Honors & Awards: Col awards in baseball & debate; selected One of Am Outstanding Young Men by Nat Jr CofC, 48. Relig: United Church of Christ. Mailing Add: 2729 S Grove St Arlington VA 22202

DAVIS, GUY GAYLON (D)
Okla State Rep
b Yarnaby, Okla, Apr 16, 41; s James Madison Davis & Lela Alma Vines D; m 1962 to Shirley Ruth Green; c Karen Ann, Guy Gaylon, Jr & Donna Arlene. Educ: Christian Col of Southwest, AA; Southeastern Okla State Univ, BA; Pi Kappa Delta. Polit & Govt Pos: Okla State Rep, 75- Bus & Prof Pos: Minister, Church of Christ, Calera, Okla, 70-74; faculty mem, Southeastern Okla State Univ, Durant, 72-74. Mil Serv: Entered as Pvt, Army, 60, released as Sgt, 68; after serv in Mil Police; Nat Defense Serv Medal. Mem: DAV; Bryan Co Livestock Asn. Relig: Church of Christ. Mailing Add: PO Box 486 Calera OK 74730

DAVIS, HARRY L, JR (R)
Treas, Geauga Co Rep Cent & Exec Comts, Ohio
b Cleveland, Ohio, Oct 26, 15; s Harry Lyman Davis & Lucy V Fegan D; m 1955 to Dorothy M Bailey; c Harry L, III. Educ: Case Western Reserve Univ, AB, 37; Harvard Univ, MBA, 39. Polit & Govt Pos: Rep precinct committeeman, Russell Twp, Ohio, 66-70; vchmn, Geauga Co Rep Cent Comt, 68-69, chmn, 69-70, mem exec comt, 69-, chmn selection comt, 71-74, treas cent & exec comts, 74- Bus & Prof Pos: Pres, Harry L Davis Co, Cleveland, 52- Mil Serv: Entered as Ens, Naval Res, 41, released as Lt Comdr, 46, after serv in Supply Corps, Pac Theatre, 42-45; Lt Comdr (Ret), Naval Res. Mem: Ohio Asn Ins Agents; Ins Bd of Cleveland; Harvard Bus Sch Club of Cleveland; Cleveland-W Rotary; Am Legion (vcomdr, Army Navy Shaker Post, 52). Relig: Protestant. Mailing Add: 15156 Hemlock Point Rd Chagrin Falls OH 44022

DAVIS, HAZEL RIVERS (R)
Chmn, Chesterfield Co Rep Party, SC
b Chesterfield, SC, Oct 13, 37; d Mayo Moore Rivers & Fannie Brooks R; m 1955 to Rayson L Davis, Sr; c Patti (Mrs James Eslick) & Rayson L, Jr. Educ: Chesterfield High Sch, grad. Polit & Govt Pos: Chmn, Chesterfield Co Rep Party, SC, 75- Mem: Eastern Star (assoc conductress, 74-75). Relig: Freewill Baptist. Mailing Add: Rte 1 Box 277 Cheraw SC 29520

DAVIS, HELEN GORDON (D)
Fla State Rep
b New York, NY; d Harry Gordon & Doree Goldblatt G; m to Gene Davis; c Stephanie, Karen & Gordon. Educ: Brooklyn Col, BA; Univ SFla; Zeta Phi. Polit & Govt Pos: Judicial chmn, Local Govt Study Comn, Fla, 63-64; mem, Tampa Comn on Juv Delinquency, 66-69; mem, Employ Comt of Comn of Community Rels, 66-69; mem, Mayor's Citizen's Adv Comt, Tampa, 66-69; mem, Qual Educ Comn, 66-68; mem, Arts Coun Tampa, 70-74; mem, Governor's Citizen Comt for Court Reform, 72; comnr, Hillsborough Co Planning Comn, 73-74; Fla State Rep, Dist 70, 75- Publ: Auth, Administration of Justice in Florida, 71, Florida Juries, 72 & You're Under Arrest, 73, League Women Voters Fla. Mem: League Women Voters; PTA; Temple Guild Sisterhood; Tampa Symphony Guild (vpres). Honors & Awards: Univ SFla Young Dem Humanitarian Award, 74. Legal Res: 45 Adalia Tampa FL 33606 Mailing Add: 732 First Fed Bldg Tampa FL 33602

DAVIS, JACKSON BEAUREGARD (D)
La State Sen
b Lecompte, La, Mar 27, 18; s Jesse Octo Davis & Litha Pittman D; m 1944 to Rosemary Slattery; c Jackson B, Jr, Robert Slattery, Rosemary & Susan Patricia. Educ: La Col, 32-33; Northwestern State Col, 33-34; La State Univ, AB, 36, MA, 37, LLB, 40. Polit & Govt Pos: La State Sen, 25th Sen Dist, 56- Bus & Prof Pos: Attorney-at-law, 40- Mil Serv: Entered as Ens, Navy, 41, released as Lt Comdr, 46, after serv in Pac Theater. Publ: Biography of Confederate General Richard Taylor, La Hist Asn, 40. Relig: Baptist. Legal Res: 975 Thora Blvd Shreveport LA 71106 Mailing Add: 1605 Slattery Bldg Shreveport LA 71101

DAVIS, JACOB ERASTUS (D)
b Beaver, Ohio, Oct 31, 05; s George O Davis & Kathryn Leist D; m 1929 to Minnie Eleanor Middleton; c Jacob Erastus & Eleanor Middleton. Educ: Ohio State Univ, BA, 27; Harvard Univ, LLB, 30. Polit & Govt Pos: Spec Asst Secy Navy & asst gen counsel, Navy Dept, 43-44; US Rep, Ohio, 41-43; judge, Court of Common Pleas, Pike Co, Ohio, 37-40; Ohio State Rep, 35-37, speaker pro tem & majority floor leader, Ohio House of Rep, 36-37; prosecuting attorney, Pike Co, Ohio, 31-35. Bus & Prof Pos: Vpres, Kroger Co, Cincinnati, Ohio, 45, exec vpres, 61, pres, 62, chmn bd, 69-70, retired, 70. Mem: Cincinnati & Queen City Country Clubs. Mailing Add: 2002 DuBois Tower 511 Walnut St Cincinnati OH 45202

DAVIS, JAMES ADAIR (R)
Ky State Rep
b Ashland, Ky, Dec 15, 41; s James Harry Davis & Pauline Burton D; m 1963 to Barbara Calvert; c Leigh Adair & Christi Anne. Educ: Morehead State Univ, BS, 63; pres, Circle K & Collegiate Knights. Polit & Govt Pos: Mem, Grayson Utilities Comn, Ky, 67-68; Ky State Rep, 96th Dist, 68-, mem, Legis Audit Comt, Ky House Rep, 72- Bus & Prof Pos: Owner & mgr, Davis & Davis Distributors, Inc, 63-; agent LP gas prod, Williams Energy Co, 71- Mem: Ky Traffic Safety Coordr Comt; Carter Co Develop Asn; Rotary; Jaycees; CofC. Honors & Awards: Outstanding Young Man Award, Grayson, Ky, 68. Relig: Christian Church; Deacon; chmn church bd. Mailing Add: 201 N Court St Grayson KY 41143

DAVIS, JAMES L (D)
WVa State Sen
Mailing Add: State Capitol Charleston WV 25305

DAVIS, JAMES W (R)
b Sept 17, 30; s John W Davis & May B D; m 1955 to Charlotte Gregory; c Kathleen, Debra, William & James. Educ: Univ Wis, Madison, 2 years; Miami Univ, BS, 56; Phi Delta Theta. Polit & Govt Pos: Co-chmn, Milwaukee Co Youth for Eisenhower-Nixon, 52, chmn, Dane Co, 52; campaign coordr, Goldwater Campaign, Racine Co, 64; chmn, Racine Co Young Rep, 65; cand coordr, Racine Co, 66; vchmn, Racine Co Rep Party, 67-69, chmn, 69-72; mem platform comt, Wis Rep Party, 67; coordr for Southern Wis, Boyle for Attorney Gen Comt, 68; mem exec comt, First Cong Dist Rep Comt, 69-71; mem rules comt, Rep Dist Caucus, 69- Bus & Prof Pos: Mgr specialties div, C J Koenig Co, 56-57; territory mgr for Wis, Minn & Mich, Holo-Krome Co, 57-61; vpres & gen mgr, Tools & Abrasives of Racine, 61-63; engr & salesman, Davis Tools, 63-65; process engr, J I Case, Racine, Wis, 65-66, tool control coordr, 66-67, process engr supvr, 67-68, gen machining & welding, 68-70; mfg eng, Racine Hydraulics, Div of Rex Chainbelt, 70- Mil Serv: Entered as Pvt, Army, 53, released as Cpl, 55, after serv in 9466 Tech Serv Unit; Korean Conflict Ribbon; Good Conduct Medal. Mem: Soc Mfg Engrs. Relig: Protestant. Mailing Add: 1007 Lombard Racine WI 53402

DAVIS, JOHN EDWARD (R)
Dir Defense Civil Preparedness Agency, Dept of Defense
b Minneapolis, Minn, Apr 18, 13; s James Ellsworth Davis (deceased) & Helen Wilson D (deceased); m 1938 to Pauline Huntley; c John Edward, Jr, Richard James & Kathleen Anne (deceased). Educ: Univ NDak, BS, 35; Beta Theta Pi. Polit & Govt Pos: Mayor, McClusky, NDak, 46-52; NDak State Sen, 52-56; Gov, NDak, 56-60; chmn, Rep Nat Comt NDak, 61; Dir of Civil Defense, Off of Secy of Army, 69-72; Dir Defense Civil Preparedness Agency, Dept of Defense, 72- Bus & Prof Pos: Engaged in farming, ranching & investments, NDak; dir, Provident Life Ins Co, Bismarck, 59-; pres, First Nat Bank, McClusky, 59- Mil Serv: Entered as Lt, Army, 41, released as Lt Col, 45, after serv in 35th Div, 134th Inf, ETO, 44-45; Silver Star for Valor; Bronze Star; Purple Heart; Combat Infantryman's Badge; Distinguished Unit Citation; Battle Stars for Four Campaigns in ETO. Mem: Mason (33 degree); Shrine; Elks; Am Legion (nat comdr, 67-68); DAV. Honors & Awards: Sioux Award for Distinguished Serv & Outstanding Achievements, Univ NDak, 66; Dept of Defense Distinguished Civilian Serv Medal, Secy of Defense Laird, 73. Relig: Lutheran. Legal Res: 216 W Owens Ave Bismarck ND 58501 Mailing Add: 2000 S Eads St Arlington VA 22202

DAVIS, JOHN EUGENE (R)
Nat Committeeman, Md Fedn Young Rep
b Erie, Pa, Feb 14, 36; s John Luther Davis & Beatrice Carichoff D; c Philip, Cathlyn & Amy. Educ: Univ Mich, Ann Arbor, BS, 57; Johns Hopkins Univ, 59-62; Am Univ, MA, 70; Sigma Phi; Phi Alpha Delta. Polit & Govt Pos: Rep precinct chmn, Montgomery Co, Md, 70-; vpres, Montgomery Co Young Rep, 71-72, pres, 72-73; nat committeeman, Md Fedn Young Rep, 74- Bus & Prof Pos: Physicist, E I du Pont de Nemours & Co, 57-59; sr engr, Bendix Corp, 59-65; proj mgr, Booz, Allen & Hamilton, 65-70; prog mgr, Exotech Systs, Inc, 70-74; sr consult, Nat Sci Corp, 74- & Auerbach Assocs, Inc, 74-; partner, Mgt Technol Assocs, 75- Publ: Co-auth, Mechanization in libraries, Datamation, 69; auth, Cost Effectiveness Study of Optical Character Readers in the US Postal Service, Booz, Allen & Hamilton, 70 & Study of the Causes of Astronaut Weight Loss During Space Flight, Exotech Systs Inc, 72. Mem: Proj Mgt Inst; Asn Comput Mach; Washington Opers Res Coun. Honors & Awards: Achievement Award, Montgomery Co Rep Cent Comt; Serv Award, Montgomery Co Young Rep. Relig: Unitarian. Legal Res: 4214 McCain Ct Kensington MD 20795 Mailing Add: Box 107 Garrett Park MD 20766

DAVIS, JOHN OLIVER (R)
Chmn, Hughes Co Rep Comt, SDak
b Port Hueneme, Calif, Jan 6, 49; s Bert Oliver Davis & Ruth Penne D; m 1974 to Nancy Ellen Askwig. Educ: Univ SDak, Vermillion, 67-68 & 69-70; Dakota State Col, 68-69; Black Hills State Col, BS Hist, 73. Polit & Govt Pos: Mem adv coun, SDak Small Bus Admin, 74-; chmn, Hughes Co Rep Comt, SDak, 75- Mem: Pierre Elks; Pierre CofC (bd dirs). Relig: Catholic. Mailing Add: 633 N Highland Pierre SD 57501

DAVIS, JOHN W (D)
b Rome, Ga, Sept 12, 16; s John Camp Davis & Era DeLay D; m 1944 to Vivian Hawkins, wid 1969; c Katherine DeLay, John W, Jr & Mary Ellen; m 1971 to Bridget O'Sullivan; c Norman & Paul Chrisman. Educ: Univ of Ga, AB, 37, LLB, 39. Polit & Govt Pos: Former Judge Juvenile Courts, Catoosa, Dade, Chattanooga & Walker Cos, Ga; solicitor gen, Rome Circuit, Ga, 50-53; Judge, Lookout Mt Judicial Circuit, 55-60; US Rep, Ga, 60-75, mem, House Comt on Sci & Astronaut & House Admin Comt, formerly; Dem cand for Sen, 74. Bus & Prof Pos: Practice of law, Rome, Ga, 39-42; practice of law, Summerville, 46- Mil Serv: Entered Army, 42, released 46, after serv in Counterintel Corps, SAm. Mem: Ga Bar Asn; Lions; Mason; Elks; Am Legion. Honors & Awards: Licensed private pilot. Relig: Presbyterian. Mailing Add: 100 Espy St Summerville GA 30747

DAVIS, JOHN WILLIAMS (R)
Treas, Buncombe Co Rep Party, NC
b Milwaukee, Wis, June 8, 14; s Price Morgan Davis & Maud Tompkins D; m 1940 to Evelyn June Thatcher; c John W, Jr, Elizabeth S, Gwyneth M & Sara H. Educ: Dartmouth Col, 3 years; Phi Gamma Delta. Polit & Govt Pos: Chmn, Monroe Co Exec Comt, Fla, 64-67; finance chmn, Buncombe Co Rep Party, NC, 68-70, treas, 70-; pres, Buncombe Co Rep Club, 68- Bus & Prof Pos: Stock clerk & salesman, Shadbolt & Boyd Co, Milwaukee, Wis, 33-40; salesman, Repub Steel Corp, 40-61; pres, Cay Casa Corp, 63- Mil Serv: Pvt, Army, 42-45, served with First Spec Serv Force, ETO; Asiatic-Pac, Kiska, Aleutian Islands, Italy-Naples-Foggia & Rome-Arno Campaign Ribbons; Prisoner of War in Germany. Mem: Milwaukee Jr CofC; Toastmasters. Relig: Episcopal. Mailing Add: 62 Maney Ave Asheville NC 28804

DAVIS, JORDAN RAY (R)
Chmn, White Co Rep Party, Ga
b Manchester, Ga, Nov 16, 21; s George Jordan Davis & Jessie Belle Tidwell D; m 1953 to Edna Ruth Clayton. Educ: Southern Tech Inst, 44-48. Polit & Govt Pos: Precinct vchmn, Gwinnette Co Rep Party, 73-74; precinct chmn, White Co Rep Party, Ga, 75-, co chmn, 75- Bus & Prof Pos: Assoc engr, Scientific-Atlanta, Ga, 65-66; prin electronics technician, Southern Tech Inst, 70-74; owner & electronics designer, Callas Mill, 74-; real estate salesman, 74- Mil Serv: Entered as Pvt, Marine Corps Res, 42, released as Pfc, 45, after serv in VMF216, Pac Theatre, 43-44. Mem: White Co Farm Bur. Honors & Awards: US Letters Patent, Electronic Device, 71; Outstanding Serv Award, Southern Tech Inst Elec Dept, 74. Mailing Add: Rte 1 Callas Mill Rd Lula GA 30554

DAVIS, KEN W (R)
VChmn, Park Co Rep Cent Comt, Colo
b Chicago, Ill, Nov 17, 36; s M L Davis & Dorothy Klunder D; div. Educ: Univ Denver, 56-60; Kappa Sigma. Polit & Govt Pos: Chmn, Park Co Rep Cent Comt, formerly, vchmn, currently; mem, Park Co Planning Comn, 73- Bus & Prof Pos: Bd chmn, Colo London Mining Co, 65-70; secy, London Fault Mining Co, 71- Mem: Colo Mining Asn. Relig: Protestant. Mailing Add: Box 35 Fairplay CO 80440

DAVIS, LANNY JESSE (D)
b Jersey City, NJ, Dec 12, 45; s Dr Mortimer C Davis & Frances Goldberg D; m 1966 to Elaine Joyce Charney; c Marlo & Seth. Educ: Yale Col, BA, 67; Yale Law Sch, LLB, 70; Delta Kappa Epsilon; chmn, Yale Daily News. Polit & Govt Pos: Aide, US Sen Abraham Ribicoff, 68; exec secy, Mayor Richard C Lee, New Haven, Conn, 69-70; nat youth coordr, US Sen Edmund Muskie, 70-72; mem, Dem Party Charter Reform Comt, 73-75; deleg, Dem Nat Mid-Term Conf, 74. Bus & Prof Pos: Assoc, Arnold & Porter, Washington, DC, 72-75; assoc, Patton, Boggs & Blow, 75. Publ: Auth, Emerging Democratic Majority, Stein & Day, 74; co-ed, The Democratic Review, 75- Mem: DC Bar Asn; Olney Kiwanis Club. Honors & Awards: Thurman Arnold Moot Court Prize, Yale Law Sch. Relig: Jewish. Legal Res: 11812 Selfridge Rd Silver Spring MD 20906 Mailing Add: 1200 17th St NW Washington DC 20036

DAVIS, LAWRENCE T (LARRY) (D)
Alaska State Rep
Mailing Add: PO Box 172 Nome AK 99762

DAVIS, MABLE WILSON (R)
Committeewoman, Rep State Exec Comt of Fla
b Champaign Co, Ohio, Oct 14, 02; d Edward Isreal Wilson & Jennie Butcher W; m 1941 to Earl Lee Davis, wid; stepchildren, Virginia Lee & Richard Earl. Educ: Springfield Bus Col, Ohio, 22; Northwestern Univ, Chicago, CPA training, 46-47. Polit & Govt Pos: Dir & chmn, 47th Ward, Northside Unit, Rep Women Vols, Chicago, Ill, 51-53; committeewoman, Precinct 20, Manatee Co, Fla, 60-68; supvr elec, Manatee Co, 61-73; committeewoman, Rep State Exec Comt of Fla, Manatee Co, 70-; alt deleg, Rep Nat Conv, 72. Bus & Prof Pos: Off responsible pos, Steel Prod Eng Co, Springfield, Ohio, 22-26 & Elliott Co, 26-40; inspector of Naval materials, US Navy, Chicago, Area, Ill, 42-46. Mem: Nat Fedn Rep Women; Sr Rep Club Manatee; Int Platform Asn; Eastern Star; Aurora Rebekah Lodge. Honors & Awards: Cert of Serv, Dept of Navy, 45; Ky Col, 70; Name enshrined on lasting Rep mem plaque, Nat Mus, Gettysburg, Pa, 72. Relig: Methodist; Steward. Mailing Add: 433 49th St W Bradenton FL 33505

DAVIS, MARY WRIGHT (D)
b Washington, DC, Dec 18, 18; d Calvin Crawford Davis & Irene Douglass D; single. Polit & Govt Pos: Staff & admin pos with various Mem of Cong, 39-; admin asst to US Rep Benjamin S Rosenthal, NY, 62- Relig: Roman Catholic. Mailing Add: 3505 Inverness Dr Chevy Chase MD 20015

DAVIS, MENDEL JACKSON (D)
US Rep, SC
b North Charleston, SC, Oct 23, 42; s Felix C Davis, Sr & Elizabeth Jackson D; m Nov 25, 65 to Suzanna Henley; c Lila Salisbury. Educ: Col of Charleston, SC, BS, 66; Univ SC Sch Law, Columbia, JD, 70; Phi Alpha Delta (Charles Cotesworth Pinckney Chap). Polit & Govt Pos: Aide to late US Rep L Mendel Rivers, SC, formerly; US Rep, SC, 71-; ex officio, Dem Nat Mid-Term Conf, 74. Mem: Mason (32 degree); Scottish Rite; Shriner; Navy League; Air Force Asn. Relig: Methodist. Legal Res: 4342 Patricia St Charleston Heights SC 29405 Mailing Add: 1726 Longworth Bldg Washington DC 20515

DAVIS, MILDRED LOUISE (D)
Mem, Pickaway Co Dem Cent Comt, Ohio
b Belfast, Ohio, Sept 24, 19; d Thomas Homer Sprinkle & Ocie Spruance S; m 1944 to William Lamar Davis; c Janet (Mrs Paul Ray), Joyce (Mrs John Beathard), James William & Jeffrey Eugene. Educ: Wilmington Col (Ohio), 37-39; Ohio State Univ, BS, 72. Polit & Govt Pos: Mem, Pickaway Co Dem Cent Comt, 60-, secy, 62-63, vpres, 63-64; mem, Dem Women's Club of Pickaway Co, 60-; mem, Dem Exec Comt, Pickaway Co, 71-; deleg, Dem Nat Conv, 72; vpres, Pickaway Co Dem Women, 72-; mem, Dem Federated Women's Club Ohio, 72- Bus & Prof Pos: Teacher, Scioto & Westfall Sch Dists, Pickaway Co, 41-46 & 54- Mem: Ohio Educ Asn; Westfall Educ Asn (exec comt, 68-); State Bd of Nat Farmers Orgn (secy, 63-); Farmers Union; Grange. Honors & Awards: Scholarship, Wilmington Col, 37. Relig: Methodist. Mailing Add: Rt 1 Mt Sterling OH 43143

DAVIS, NADA (R)
Mem, Rep State Cent Comt of Calif
b Montpelier, Idaho, Nov 20, 20; d Phillip D Miller & Nada A Hendricks M; m 1942 to William Irving Davis; c Nadette (Mrs William West), Lynne Irene, Laurie Lee & William Richard. Educ: Santa Monica Jr Col, 39-41. Polit & Govt Pos: Mem, Rep State Cent Comt of Calif, 63-; area chmn, Los Angeles Co Rep Fedn, 65, conv chmn, 67 & 68; pres, GOP Jr, Long Beach, 66; realtors chmn for Reagan for Gov, Teague for Cong & Hayes for Assembly, 70; mem, tenth dist steering comt, Reagan '70 Team. Bus & Prof Pos: Part owner, Davis Paint Co, Long Beach, Calif, 49-; real estate broker, Real Estate Store, 69- Mem: Los Angeles Co Fedn of Rep Women; Opti Mrs Club; Ebell Club; Long Beach Dinner Club; Old Ranch Golf Club. Honors & Awards: Assoc Realtor of the Year, Long Beach Dist Bd of Realtors, 67. Relig: Unity. Mailing Add: 1050 El Mirador Ave Long Beach CA 90815

DAVIS, NATHANIEL
Asst Secy of State for African Affairs
b Boston, Mass, Apr 12, 25; s Harvey Nathaniel Davis & Alice Marion Rohde D; m 1956 to Elizabeth K Creese; c Margaret Morton, Helen Miller, James Creese & Thomas Rohde. Educ: Phillips Exeter Acad, AB, 42; Brown Univ, AB, 44; Fletcher Sch of Law & Diplomacy, MA, 47, PhD, 60; student Russian lang, Columbia Univ, Cornell Univ & Middlebury Col, 53-54; Phi Beta Kappa. Hon Degrees: LLD, Brown Univ, 70. Polit & Govt Pos: Entered US Foreign Serv, 47; vconsul, Florence, Italy, 49-52; second secy, Rome, 52-53 & Moscow, 54-56; Soviet Desk Officer, State Dept, 56-60; first secy, Caracas, Venezuela, 60-62; spec asst dir, Peace Corps, 62-63; dep assoc dir, 63-65; Minister to Bulgaria, 65-66; sr staff, Nat Security Coun, 66-68; Ambassador to Guatemala, 68-71; US Ambassador to Chile, 71-73; dir gen, US Foreign Serv, 73-75; Asst Secy of State for African Affairs, 75- Bus & Prof Pos: Asst

in hist, Tufts Col, 47; lectr in US Hist, Centro Venezolana-Americano, 61; lectr Russian & Soviet Hist, Howard Univ, 62-68. Mil Serv: Lt(jg), Naval Res, 44-46. Mem: Am Foreign Serv Asn; Am Hist Asn; Coun Foreign Rels, NY. Honors & Awards: Recipient, Cinco Aguilas Blancas Alpinism Award, Venezuelan Andean Club, 62. Relig: United Church of Christ. Legal Res: c/o Fife 613 Hudson St Hoboken NJ 07030 Mailing Add: Dept of State 2201 C St NW Washington DC 20520

DAVIS, PAULINE L (D)
Calif State Assemblywoman
b Verdigre, Nebr, Jan 3, 17; m to Lester T Davis, Sr, wid; c Karen Joyce (Mrs Mier), Marlene Kaye (Mrs Bryan) & John Rodney. Educ: Sacramento Col. Polit & Govt Pos: Calif State Assemblywoman, 52-, mem, Wildlife Conserv Bd, mem, Ways & Means, Water, Natural Resources & Conserv, Joint Legis Budget & chmn, Joint Fairs Allocation & Classification Comts, chmn Conserv & Wildlife Comt, Calif State Assembly. Bus & Prof Pos: Dispatcher, Western Pac RR, Stockton; former traffic operator, Bell Tel Co, Omaha. Mem: Eastern Star, Portola; White Shrine of Jerusalem, Beckwourth; Bus & Prof Women's Club, Yreka; Brotherhood Locomotive Firemen & Enginemen Ladies Auxiliary. Honors & Awards: Longest record of serv by any woman, Calif State Assembly. Mailing Add: Rm 4148 State Capitol Portola CA 96122

DAVIS, PERCY TERRY (R)
VPres, Wyo State Senate
b Lisco, Nebr, Oct 11, 17; s Percy R Davis & Mary Herfert D; m 1943 to Beth Elaine Corliss; c Terry Eugene, Rebecca Jane (Mrs Black), Mary Ann, C Joe & Bob B. Educ: Lisco Nebr Col of Mortuary Sci, 46. Polit & Govt Pos: Co coroner, Wyo, 51-67, dep co coroner, 67-; Wyo State Sen, 63-, chmn, Corp & Polit Subdiv, Wyo State Senate, 69-, chmn, Corp, Elec & Polit Subdiv Comt & mem, Revenue Comt, currently, chmn, Corp Elec & Policy Comt, 73-76, vpres, Senate, 73- Bus & Prof Pos: Secy & treas, State Bd Embalming, 65-67. Mil Serv: Entered as Pvt, Army, 41, released as T-3, 45, after serv in 134th Inf Div, European Theatre, 44-45. Mem: Kiwanis; Mason; Shrine; Elks; Am Legion. Relig: Episcopal. Mailing Add: 2203 W Main Riverton WY 82501

DAVIS, ROBERT EUGENE (R)
Tex State Rep
b Ft Worth, Tex, Aug 19, 41; s William Cecil Davis & Muriel McCarty D; m 1964 to Abbie Compton Leavitt; c Robert Eugene, Jr, Douglas Carter, Wesley Joseph, Paul Harrison & Matthew Peyton. Educ: Vanderbilt Univ, BE, 63, LLB, 66; Phi Kappa Phi. Polit & Govt Pos: Tex State Rep, Dist 33-A, 73-, chmn rules subcomt, Tex House Rep, 73-, vchmn appropriative matters, revenue & taxation comt & calendar & ins comts, 75-; pres, United Tex Young Rep Fedn, 75- Mem: State Bar Tex; Irving Bar Asn; CofC; Irving Rep Club. Relig: Episcopal. Legal Res: 1010 N Gloucester Irving TX 75062 Mailing Add: 1770 W Irving Blvd Suite 5 Irving TX 75061

DAVIS, ROBERT W (R)
Mich State Sen
Mailing Add: Mich State Senate State Capitol Lansing MI 48903

DAVIS, ROSS E (R)
Chmn, Rep State Cent Comt of Wash
b Centralia, Wash, Sept 5, 40; s Charles W Davis; m Sarah Jane; c Susan & Elizabeth. Educ: Lower Columbia Col, 59-60, 61-62; Univ Wash, BA in Hist, 66, MBusAd, 70; pres, MBA Asn, 69-70. Polit & Govt Pos: In campaigns, Dan Evans for Gov, 64, 68 & 72, Art Fletcher for Lt Gov, 68, Richard Nixon, 68 & 72, Slade Gorton for Attorney Gen, 68 & 72, Lud Kramer for Secy of State, 68 & 72, Chris Bayley for Prosecuting Attorney, 70, numerous house & senate campaigns, 70-72; state bd mem, Action for Wash, 71-72; chmn, Rep State Cent Comt Wash, 73-; Rep Nat Committeeman, 73- Bus & Prof Pos: Announcer, KGW Radio, Portland, Ore, 60-62; prog dir, KEDO Radio, Longview, Wash, 62-63; asst prog dir, KING Radio, Seattle, Wash, 63-69; assoc dir govt affairs, Boise Cascade, Idaho, 70-73; pres, Fireside Lodge Corp, Seattle, Wash. Publ: Governmental relations, information systems & the state legislature, Univ Wash Grad Sch Bus, 70. Mem: Wash Athletic Club. Honors & Awards: Lyons Mem Scholarship, Lower Columbia Col, 59-60; MBA Distinguished Serv Award, Univ Wash, 70, Boise Cascade Fel, 70. Legal Res: 29401 Ninth Place S Federal Way WA 98002 Mailing Add: 595 Industry Dr Tukwila WA 98188

DAVIS, ROY W (R)
NH State Rep
Mailing Add: Chester Rd Auburn NH 03032

DAVIS, RUSSELL C (D)
Mayor, Jackson, Miss
b Rockville, Md, Aug 13, 22; married. Polit & Govt Pos: Miss State Rep, 60-69; mayor, Jackson, 69- Bus & Prof Pos: Gen Ins. Mem: Sons of Confederate Vet; Sertoma; CofC; YMCA; Am Legion. Relig: Methodist. Mailing Add: PO Box 2450 Jackson MS 39205

DAVIS, SHELBY CULLOM (R)
b Peoria, Ill, Apr 1, 09; s George Henry Davis & Julia Mabel Cullom D; m 1932 to Kathryn Edith Waterman; c Shelby Moore, Diana & Priscilla Alden (deceased). Educ: Princeton, AB, 30; Columbia Univ, AM, 31. Polit & Govt Pos: Econ adv to Thomas E Dewey Presidential Campaigns, 40 & 44; chief, foreign requirements sect, War Prod Bd, 42, div of statist & research, Region II, 43; first Dep Supt of Ins, NY State, 44-47; US Ambassador to Switz, formerly. Bus & Prof Pos: Former bus ed, Current Hist & Forum Mags; spec correspondent & assoc with Columbia Broadcasting Co, Geneva, Switz, 32-34; economist, Investment Corp of Philadelphia, 34-37; treas, Delaware Fund, Inc, 37-39; mem, NY Stock Exchange, 41-; managing partner, Shelby Cullom Davis & Co, 47- Publ: Your Career in Defense, 42; contrib to several jour. Mem: Hist Alumni Adv Coun, Princeton (chmn); Financial Analysts Soc; Gen Soc SR; Soc Colonial Wars (Lt Gov); Mayflower Soc. Mailing Add: Crestwood Northeast Harbor ME 04662

DAVIS, STEPHEN ALAN (R)
Ariz State Sen
b Wilmington, Del, Feb 28, 46; s Thomas Crawley Davis & Alice Jeanette McWhorter D; m 1968 to Ann Black; c Christopher Ian & Bryan Thomas. Educ: Davidson Col, 64-66; Kappa Alpha. Polit & Govt Pos: Exec dir, southern dist, Ariz Rep Party, 72-73; Ariz State Sen, 75- Bus & Prof Pos: Musical dir, Up with People, Tucson, Ariz, 66-67; sr co-pilot & admin asst, Cochise Airlines, Tucson, 71-72. Mil Serv: Entered as Pvt, Army, 67, released as E-5, 1970, after serv in MedC, Vietnam, 69-70. Legal Res: Box 337 Tumacacori AZ 85640 Mailing Add: 2053 W Hazelwood Pkwy Phoenix AZ 85015

DAVIS, SYLVAN S (R)
Secy, Scioto Co Rep Exec Comt, Ohio
b Nauvoo, Ohio, Apr 22, 25; s W E Davis, Sr & Essie L Jenkins D; m 1963 to Katheryn Ann Burris; c Anna E & Gloria A. Educ: Ohio Univ, MA in Govt, 55; Ohio Univ Independents Asn; Methodist Student Fraternity. Polit & Govt Pos: Secy, Scioto Co Rep Exec Comt, 48-; orgnr of polit rallies for late US Sen Robert A Taft. Bus & Prof Pos: Real estate broker, Stockham Relaty Co, Ohio, 51-; ins broker, Berndt Ins Agency, Portsmouth, 55-; prin, Jenkins Elem Sch, 58- Mil Serv: Entered as Pvt, Army, 43, released as Sgt, 45, after serv in Air Force, Good Conduct Medal. Mem: Ohio Educ Asn (mem exec comt); Ohio Elem Sch Prin Asn; Southeastern Ohio Educ Asn; Portsmouth Bd of Realtors; James Dickey Post 23. Relig: Methodist. Mailing Add: 1633 Galena Pike West Portsmouth OH 45662

DAVIS, TED MILLER (R)
Utah State Rep
b St Anthony, Idaho, Aug 8, 35; s Afton Earl Davis & Leona Janett Miller D; m 1958 to Lucretia Terry; c Brett Miller, Marci & Steward Earl. Educ: Brigham Young Univ, BA, 66. Polit & Govt Pos: State deleg, Utah Rep Party, 70, precinct chmn, 70-; Utah State Rep, 71-, chmn, Pub Safety Comt, Utah House Rep, 73-; mem, Gov Comt Occup Safety & Health, 72- Bus & Prof Pos: Sales rep, Newbro Drug Co, Idaho Falls, Idaho, 58-62; owner-mgr, Home Appliance, Provo, Utah, 62-66; dist mgr, Allyn & Bacon, Inc, 66-69; coordr bus affairs, Brigham Young Univ, 69-, col pres, Safety & Health Research Inst, 73- Mil Serv: Cpl, Idaho Nat Guard & Res Units, 116th Engr Bn, 54-62. Mem: Utah Bookman's Asn; Am Soc Training Dirs; Utah Safety Coun; Utah Co United Fund. Honors & Awards: Jr CofC Outstanding Young Man nominee, 71. Relig: Latter-day Saint. Mailing Add: 927 E 460 S Provo UT 84601

DAVIS, W LESTER (D)
Chmn, Harford Co Dem State Cent Comt, Md
b Savage, Md, June 25, 09; s George Henry Davis & Bertha Shipley D; m 1938 to Virginia Reamy; c Marie (Mrs McCraw), Virginia (Mrs Ulehla), Leslie (Mrs Hyatt), W Lester, II, Debbie Kay (Mrs James Haywood), Vickie Lynn & Sheree Gail. Educ: Col, 2 years. Polit & Govt Pos: Chmn, Harford Co Dem State Cent Comt, Md, currently; Md State Deleg, Harford Co, 58-59. Bus & Prof Pos: Pres, Davis Concrete Co, 30 years, pres, Davis Concrete of Del, 25 years; pres, Sparton Concrete Co, Bel Air Concrete Co, Joppa Concrete Co & Aberdeen Concrete Co, 9 years; first vpres, First Nat Bank of North East, 58-; dir, Aberdeen Nat Bank, Md, 63-; hon dir, Harford Mem Hosp, Havre de Grace, 63- Mem: Md Golf & Country Club; Swan Creek Country Club; Bush River Yacht Club; Moose; Elks. Relig: Methodist. Mailing Add: RD 2 Box 35 Aberdeen MD 21001

DAVIS, WALLACE ROBERT (D)
Committeeman, Calif Dem State Cent Comt
b Orange Co, Calif, Mar 21, 35; s Wallace Charles Davis & Margaret Kirker D; m 1961 to Irmgard Wally Hermann; c Anja, Mark, Luke, Marisa, Erik, Sabrina & Nadia. Educ: Calif State Col, Long Beach, BA; Univ Calif, Los Angeles, JD; Gemini Club & Woman's Jr Civic Club scholarships, 54; Phi Alpha Delta. Polit & Govt Pos: Pres, Long Beach Young Dem, Calif, 60, 74th Assembly Dist Young Dem, 60-61 & LBJ Dem Club, Orange Co, 64-65; chmn, Orange Co Viva Johnson Comt, 64; committeeman, Calif Dem State Cent Comt, 68-; mem, Orange Co Dem Comt, 73-; co chmn, Brown for Gov, 74. Bus & Prof Pos: Assoc attorney, James E Walker, Attorney, 64; partner, Walker & Davis Attorneys-at-law, Santa Ana, Calif, 65-; partner, Cohen Stokke Owen & Davis, 72-; chmn, Legal Aid Soc of Orange Co; founder & legal counsel, Banco Del Pueblo Commercial Bank, Santa Ana, Calif, formerly. Mil Serv: Entered as Pvt, Army, 56, released as Pfc, 58, after serv in Spec Serv, Ft Ord, Calif; Good Conduct Medal. Mem: Orange Co Bar Asn (mem & chmn comt on fees); CofC; Disabled Am Vet Charitable Found (bd mem); Mex Am Polit Asn; League of United Latin Am Citizens (State Legal Counsel). Honors & Awards: Am Legion Leadership Award, 54. Relig: Roman Catholic. Mailing Add: 9912 Aster Circle Fountain Valley CA 92708

DAVIS, WALTER LAMAR (R)
Ga State Rep
b Atlanta, Ga, Dec 27, 37; s Walter Lamar Davis & Charlie Parker D; m 1958 to Bertha Kate Thompson; c Terry & Linda. Educ: Ga State Col, BBA, 59. Polit & Govt Pos: Ga State Rep, 67- Bus & Prof Pos: Real estate saleman & investor, 62- Mil Serv: Entered as 2nd Lt, Army, 59, released as 1st Lt, 62; Army Commendation Medal. Relig: Baptist. Mailing Add: 3782 Snapfinger Rd Lithonia GA 30058

DAVIS, WILL DAVID (D)
b Houston, Tex, July 18, 29; s David Davis & Nita Barnett D; m 1954 to Ann Byargeon; c Lisa Ann, Mary Lynn & Will David, Jr. Educ: Lamar Col, AA, 50; Baylor Univ, BBA, JD, cum laude, 54; Omicron Delta Kappa; Phi Alpha Delta; ed, Baylor Law Rev; pres, Baylor Univ Student Body; vpres, Am Law Students Asn; pres, Southwest Conf Sportsmanship Comt; Varsity Football. Polit & Govt Pos: Asst Attorney Gen, Tex, 54-57; gen counsel, Tex State Bd of Ins, 57-59; deleg, Tex State Dem Conv, 58-70; deleg, Dem Nat Conv, 64 & 68; cong dist coordr, Kennedy-Johnson Campaign, 60; Cong Dist Coordr, Johnson-Humphrey Campaign, 64; mem, Tex Dem State Exec Comt, 62-64, secy, 64-65, chmn, 65-72; mem & vchmn, Tex State Hist Surv Comt, 63-; mem, Tex Elec Law Study Comt, 66; chmn, State Dem Conv, 66 & 68; chmn, Gov Inaugural Comt, 67; mem & chmn, Austin Independent Sch Bd of Trustees, 67-; state chmn, Humphrey-Muskie Campaign, 68; mem, Tex Col & Univ Syst Coord Bd, 68-; Presidential Elector, 68; mem, Nat Dem Comt Conv Reform & Party Deleg Selection, 69. Bus & Prof Pos: Partner, Heath, Davis & McCalla, 59- Mem: Am, Tex & Local Bar Asns; Fedn of Ins Counsel; Jaycees. Honors & Awards: Selected as Outstanding Young Man of Austin, Tex, One of Five Outstanding Young Texans & Outstanding Young Lawyer Tex, 63; One of Five Outstanding Young Men of Am, 65. Relig: Baptist. Legal Res: 2407 Woodmont Austin TX 78703 Mailing Add: 202 Perry-Brooks Bldg Austin TX 78701

DAVIS, WILLIAM JAMES (INDEPENDENT)
Tenn State Sen
b Memphis, Tenn, Aug 31, 20; s Jesse Hedrick Davis & Johnnie Hutson D; m 1946 to Jean King; c Billie Jean & Deborah. Educ: Byars-Hall High Sch, 34-38. Polit & Govt Pos: Former vchmn, Am Party; Tenn State Sen, 70- Bus & Prof Pos: Ins agent, State Farm Ins Co, 57- Mil Serv: Entered as A/S, Navy, 39, released as Lt (jg), 46, after serv in USS Helena-Hornet LST 343, SPac Theatre, 41-46; Lt Comdr (Ret), Naval Res, 59; SPac Campaign Ribbons with 13 Battle Stars. Mem: VFW; Am Legion; Pearl Harbor Survivors Asn; Retired Officers Asn. Relig: Methodist. Mailing Add: PO Box 99 Covington TN 38019

DAVISON, ARWILLA HUFF (D)
b Bessemar, Ala, Mar 19, 21; d Billy Huff & Annie Belle Lane H; m 1951 to Frank Davison; c Billy Herman Brown, Ruby I & Michael Davison. Educ: Oak Park High Sch, grad, 40. Polit & Govt Pos: Mem state exec comt, Loyalist Dem Party, 71-; deleg, Dem Nat Mid-Term Conf, 74. Bus & Prof Pos: Adminr, Davison Nursing Home, 68- Mem: NAACP; Community Coalition; Southern Christian Leadership Conf; Nat Negro Bus & Prof Women's Club. Honors & Awards: Businesswoman of the Year, Local Bus Women's Club, 74. Relig: Baptist. Mailing Add: 616 E 19th St Laurel MS 39440

DAVISON, DENVER N (D)
Chief Justice, Supreme Court of Okla
b Rich Hill, Mo, Oct 9, 91; s Benjamin P Davison & Lottie Jones D; m 1917 to Barbara A Wilhelm. Educ: Univ Okla, LLB; Alpha Tau Omega; Phi Delta Phi. Hon Degrees: JD, Univ Okla, 72. Polit & Govt Pos: Justice, Supreme Court of Okla, 37-49, Chief Justice, 49 & 50, 59 & 60, 73- Mil Serv: Entered as Pfc, Army, 17, released as 2nd Lt, 19. Mem: Mason; Rotary; Elks; KofP; Am Legion. Relig: Methodist. Mailing Add: State Capitol Bldg Oklahoma City OK 73105

DAVOREN, JOHN FRANCIS XAVIER (D)
Secy of the Commonwealth, Mass
b Milford, Mass, July 27, 15; s Thomas F Davoren (deceased) & Ellen A Casey D (deceased); m 1943 to Eleanor L Comolli; c Ellen Ann & Susan Mary. Educ: Col of the Holy Cross, BS, 40; Portia Law Sch, LLB, 63. Hon Degrees: DSc, Pol, Calvin Coolidge Col; HHD, Mass Col of Optometry. Polit & Govt Pos: Mass State Rep, Ninth Worcester Dist, 55-67, asst majority leader, Mass House of Rep, 61-62, majority leader & acting speaker 63-64, speaker, 65-67; Secy of the Commonwealth, 67-; deleg, Dem Nat Conv, 68. Bus & Prof Pos: Pub rels dir, Vet Admin, Boston, Mass, 46-52; Pub Rels Dir, Off of Price Stabilization, 52-54. Mil Serv: Entered as A/S, Navy, 40, released as Lt(sg), 46, after serv at Naval Base, San Juan, PR, Naval Air Sta, Lakehurst, NJ, with GROPAC 8, SPac, Naval Beachmaster, Saipan & Tinian & at Naval Base, Saipan; Lt, Naval Res (Ret); Presidential Unit Citation; ETO & Caribbean Defense Command Ribbons; Pac Theatre Ribbon with Two Battle Stars. Publ: Constitutional Reform: the Continuing Dialogue on the Ways & Means to its Achievement, Munic Voice, 2/67. Mem: Nat Asn of Secy of State; Nat Inst of Munic Clerks; Mass Legislators Asn; Catholic Charitable Bur of Boston (dir); Portia Law Sch Alumni (dir). Honors & Awards: Cited for Outstanding Interest in & Serv to Vet—a Nation's Defender, Superior Statesman, Nat Dept VFW, 66; hon mem, Ital-Am War Vet, Kiwanis, Armenian-Am Vet, Foggiano Club, Portuguese Club of Milford & Marchegiano Club. Relig: Roman Catholic. Mailing Add: 180 Purchase St Milford MA 01757

DAWAHRE, HOOVER (D)
Ky State Rep
Mailing Add: Box 540 Whitesburg KY 41858

DAWKINS, MAURICE ANDERSON (R)
b Chicago, Ill, Jan 29, 21; s Anderson M Dawkins & Marie Von Dickersohn D; m 1948 to Doris Scott; c Maurice Kimball & Susan Scott. Educ: Columbia Col, BA, 43; Union Theol Sem, MS, 50; Univ Va, EdD cand, 69-70; Alpha Phi Alpha. Hon Degrees: DD, Union Theol Sem, 64. Polit & Govt Pos: Vchmn, NY State Vol for Stevenson, 52; mem, Southern Calif Campaign Comt for Stevenson, 56; mem, Southern Calif Campaign Comt for Kennedy, 60; vchmn, Citizens for Gov Brown, 58 & 62; mem, Gov Comn Metrop Area Probs, 59-63; mem, Mayor's Comt Human Rels, Los Angeles, 62-64; mem, Southern Calif Campaign Comt for Johnson, 64; mem, Attorney Gen Adv Comt on Const Rights, Calif, 59-65; state comnr, Urban Policy, Calif, 59-65; assoc dir, VISTA, 64-67; asst dir, Off Econ Opportunity, 67-69; prof educ, President's Exec Training Prog, Fed Exec Inst, 69-70; exec vchmn, Opportunities Industrialization Ctr & related enterprises for Rev Leon H Sullivan, 70-73, nat dir govt & cong rels, OIC-ZIA Profit & Nonprofit Enterprises, Washington, DC, 73-; mem, Coun 100 Black Rep; mem, Ctr for Study of Presidency, currently. Bus & Prof Pos: Assoc minister & educ dir, Community Church NY, 48-54; minister & dir, First Community Church Los Angeles, 54-65; founder & first pres, First Community Church Home Sr Citizens, Los Angeles; mem bd dirs, Pub Nat Bank; adv, Nat Bus League, DC & Nat Coun Negro Women, NY, 67-; chmn bd, Opportunities Develop Corp, Calif, 67- Publ: Love in action: a challenge to the American Negro, Union Theol Rev, 44; Can religion be democratic, Thesis, Columbia Univ, 50; A Christian Answer, Calif Eagle Newspaper, 55. Mem: Am Acad Polit Sci; Am Psychol Asn; Fed Prof Asn; Am Negro Leadership Conf on Africa; Nat Urban League. Honors & Awards: George Washington Carver Award; Urban League Award; Los Angeles Award; Nat Coun Negro Women Award. Legal Res: 827 Westchester Pl Los Angeles CA 90005 Mailing Add: 1625 I St NW Washington DC 20006

DAWSON, BARBARA ANN (R)
b Washburn, NDak, June 17, 27; d Hans C Nelson & Irene Haugeberg N; m 1949 to James R Dawson; c Debra Ann, Virginia Lynn, Patricia Sue & Judith Jane. Educ: NDak State Univ, BS, 49; Sigma Alpha Iota; Alpha Gamma Delta. Polit & Govt Pos: Mem arrangements comt, Vice President Nixon's Visit to Fargo, NDak, 60; campaign off, mgr & mem steering comt, Andrews for Gov Campaign, 62, mem steering comt, Andrews for Cong Campaign, 63; Rep precinct committeewoman, Cass Co, 62-66; mem, Cass Co Rep Exec Comt, 63-66; alt deleg, NDak State Rep Conv, 62, 63 & 68, deleg, 64, 66 70 & 72, mem arrangements comt & prog chmn, 68, secy, 68, 70 & 72, mem & secy platform comt, 70; mem, NDak Rep State Cent & Exec Comts, 66, secy, formerly; legis chmn, 21st Dist Rep Womens Club, 66, vchmn, 67; mem, 21st Dist Rep Exec Comt, 66-68; Rep precinct committeewoman, 21st Dist, 66-; vchmn, Rep State Publicity Comt, 67-, chmn, 69; comnr & co-chmn, counting comt, US Annual Assay Comt, 70. Mem: Jr League of Am; PTA; PEO. Relig: Presbyterian. Mailing Add: 1749 S Ninth St Fargo ND 58102

DAWSON, ERIC EMMANUEL (D)
Sen, VI Legis
b St Thomas, VI, Dec 26, 37; s Joseph Emmanuel Dawson & Olivia Forbes D; m 1966 to Betty Jean Vanterpool; c Diane Olivia & David Eric. Educ: Sch of Com, NY Univ, BS, 64; Grad Sch Pub Admin, NY Univ, 1 year; Mu Gamma Tau. Polit & Govt Pos: Exec secy, VI Senate, 65-; secy, Dem Party, VI, 66-68, vchmn, 68-70; Sen, VI Legis, 73- Bus & Prof Pos: Mgr, NY Univ Campus Store, 62-65. Mil Serv: Entered as Airman, Air Force, 55, released as Sgt, 59, after serv in Air Force Materiel Command, Far East, Japan, Tripoli, Libya, Europe, 56-59; reentered as Sgt, 69- Publ: Virgin Islands (Polit Hist of the VI), 69. Relig: Episcopal. Legal Res: 19-5 Estate Hope St Thomas VI 00801 Mailing Add: PO Box 3536 St Thomas VI 00801

DAWSON, TOM HENRY (D)
b Fort Dodge, Iowa, Nov 20, 37; s Dr Emerson Blanton Dawson & Pauline Breen D; single. Educ: Univ Wyo, BA, 60; Univ Northern Iowa, teaching cert, 66; Sigma Chi. Polit & Govt Pos: Pres, Young Dem, Univ Wyo, 57-60; youth chmn, Campaign for Sen Gale McGee, US Sen, 58; asst to youth dir, Youth for Kennedy-Johnson, Washington, DC, 60; asst campaign mgr, Dr E B Smith for US Sen, 62, campaign mgr, 66; finance chmn, Dem Party Iowa, 67-69; deleg, Dem Nat Conv, 68; admin asst to US Rep Neal Smith, 69- Bus & Prof Pos: Mgr, Dawson Farms, 50- Mil Serv: Entered as 2nd Lt, Army, 63, released as 1st Lt, 65, after serv in G2 off of Security, 7th Army, ETO, 63-65; Cert of Achievement by 7th Army, presented by Gen Quinn. Mem: Am Polit Sci Asn; Elks; Am Legion; New Frontier Club of Iowa. Relig: Roman Catholic. Legal Res: 227 S 12th St Fort Dodge IA 50501 Mailing Add: 3001 Branch Ave Hillcrest Heights MD 20031

DAY, CATHERINE-ANN (D)
NH State Rep
b Manchester, NH, Dec 21, 42; d Mildred K Smith (Zebnik); m 1969 to John P Day; c Sean Patrick. Educ: Mt St Mary Col, NH, BA, 64; Bread Loaf Sch of English, Middlebury Col, Vt, MA, 69; Sigma Phi Sigma. Polit & Govt Pos: Selectman, Ward Two, Manchester, 73-75; NH State Rep, Ward Two, 75- Bus & Prof Pos: Teacher English, Mem High Sch, Manchester, 64-70; teacher adult basic educ/English as a second language, Cent High Sch-Manchester Eve Prog, 72-75. Mem: NH Women's Polit Caucus; Orgn of Women Legislators, NH. Mailing Add: 284 Hawthorne St Manchester NH 03104

DAY, J EDWARD (D)
b Jacksonville, Ill, Oct 11, 14; s James Allmond Day & Frances Wilmot D; m 1941 to Mary Louise Burgess; c Mary Louise & James Edward. Educ: Univ Chicago, AB, 35; Harvard, LLB, cum laude, 38; Ill Col, LLD; Univ Nev, LLD; Phi Kappa Psi; ed, Harvard Law Rev, 36-37. Polit & Govt Pos: Legal & legis asst, Gov Adlai Stevenson, Ill, 49-50; secy, Ill Comn Intergovt Coop, 49-53; ins comnr of Ill, 50-53; chmn, Dem Assocs, Los Angeles, Calif, 58-61; dir, Nat Capitol Coun, Boy Scouts; vchmn Gov Comn Metrop Area Probs & mem, Gov Bus Adv Coun, Calif, 50-61; deleg, Dem Nat Conv, 60; Postmaster Gen US, 61-63; mem, Montgomery Co Exec Comt for Reelec of Gov Mandel, Md, 70. Bus & Prof Pos: Assoc, Sidley, Austin, Burgess & Harper, 39-41, 45-49; assoc gen solicitor, Prudential Ins Co, 53-56, assoc gen counsel, 56, vpres, Western Opers, Los Angeles, Calif, 57-61; dir, People's Life Ins Co & five co of Zurich Ins group; bd fels, Claremont Col, Calif, 58-66; gen campaign chmn, Los Angeles YMCA, 59; partner, Sidley, Austin, Burgess & Smith, Attorneys, 64-73; partner, Cox, Langford & Brown, Attorneys, 73-; dir, Macke Corp, currently. Mil Serv: Naval Res, Lt, 40-45; Navy Commendation Ribbon. Publ: My Appointed Round—929 Days as Postmaster General, Bartholf Street, 65; Humor in Public Speaking, 65. Mem: Nat Civil Serv League; Nat Asn Ins Comnrs; DC Bar Asn; Citizens Conf on State Legislators (chmn); Montgomery Co Farm Bur. Relig: Methodist. Legal Res: 5804 Brookside Dr Chevy Chase MD 20015 Mailing Add: 21 Du Pont Circle Washington DC 20036

DAY, JAMES MACDONALD (R)
Adminr Mining Enforcement & Safety, US Dept of Interior
b Stamford, Conn, June 19, 30; s James Day & Catherine Nichols Clark D; m 1955 to Nancy Carolyn Payne; c Catherine & James, II. Educ: Piedmont Col, BA, magna cum laude, 56; Am Univ, Washington, DC, LLB, 59; Delta Theta Phi. Polit & Govt Pos: Comptroller & off mgr, Vol for Nixon-Lodge, Washington, DC, 60; dir admin, Goldwater for Pres Comt & Citizens for Goldwater-Miller, San Francisco, Calif & Washington, DC, 63-64; asst gen counsel, Young Rep Nat Fedn, Washington, DC, 65-67; dir admin, United Citizens for Nixon, Washington, DC, 68; chmn, Arlington Co Rep Comt, Va, 68-69; dir Off of Hearings & Appeals, US Dept of Interior, 70-73, adminr mining enforcement & safety, 73- Bus & Prof Pos: Mem, Cent Intel Agency, Washington, DC, 56-60; attorney-at-law, 60-69. Mil Serv: Entered as Pvt, Army, 51, released as Cpl, 53, after serv in 13th Airborne Rangers & 187th Airborne RCT, Far East Theatre. Publ: Auth, Administrative procedures in the Department of the Interior, Rocky Mountain Mineral Law Inst, 72. Mem: Am Bar Asn (sections admin & natural resources law). Honors & Awards: Honor Award for Outstanding Serv, Dept of Interior. Relig: Presbyterian. Mailing Add: 2232 N Madison St Arlington VA 22205

DAY, JAMES V (R)
b Brewer, Maine, Nov 24, 14; s Thomas Patrick Day & Mary Ellen Ryan D; m 1946 to Delma Irene McCormick; c Teresa (Mrs Lynch), Daniel O, James V, Jr, Timothy T, Thomas D & Mary D. Educ: Univ Maine, Machias. Hon Degrees: PhD, Univ Maine. Polit & Govt Pos: Rep cand for Cong, First Dist, Maine, 56; comnr, Fed Maritime Comn, Washington, DC, 62- Bus & Prof Pos: Sales supvr, H J Heinz, 36-41; mgr, Days Hotel, Maine, 46-50; pres, Spillers, Inc, Kennebunk, 50-56. Mil Serv: Entered as Pvt, Navy, 41 released as 1st Lt, after serv in 1st Army Corps. Mem: Kenwood Golf & Country Club; Am Legion; Rotary; Lions; Nat Press Club. Honors & Awards: Big M Award, Maine State Soc; Golden Record Award, Nat Defense; Supreme Merit Award & Man of the Year, Am Legion; Meritorious Serv Citation, Maine Maritime Acad. Relig: Catholic. Legal Res: Kennebunk ME Mailing Add: 5524 Westbard Ave Bethesda MD 20016

DAY, JOAN THOMSON (R)
Mem, Rep State Cent Comt Calif
b Boston, Mass, Sept 17, 19; d Stuart Thomson & Dorothy Faunce T; div; c April (Mrs Richard Eberle), Susan (Mrs Bernard Ledieu), Robert W, III & Linda. Educ: Bennington Col, 37-39. Polit & Govt Pos: Mem, Rep State Cent Comt Calif, 67- Relig: Episcopal. Mailing Add: 1440 Westhaven Rd San Marino CA 91108

DAY, JOHN J (D)
Ind State Rep
Mailing Add: 25 E 14th St Indianapolis IN 46202

DAY, JUDITH OLGA (R)
Rep Nat Committeewoman, Del
b Watts, Calif, Mar 16, 26; d Carl Ragnar Johnson & Dorothy Florence Rivenburg J; m 1948 to Bruce Frederick Day; c Michael Bruce & Jonathan Ragnar. Educ: Univ Calif, Los Angeles, BA, 48; Kappa Delta, Delta Phi Upsilon. Polit & Govt Pos: Mem, New Castle Co Rep Comt, Del, 50-; mem exec comt, Rep Women's Fedn, New Castle Co, 52-55; mem, Young Rep Bd Dirs New Castle Co, 52-56; election dist chmn, Brandywine Region, 60-67; vchmn, Ninth Rep Dist, 67-69; vchmn, New Castle Co Rep Party, 69-71; Rep Nat Committeewoman, Del, 71- Bus & Prof Pos: Elem teacher, Los Angeles Sch Dist, 47-48; elem teacher, Wilmington City Schs, Del, 49. Mem: Del League for Planned Parenthood (mem bd); DuPont Country Club. Relig: Unitarian. Mailing Add: 35 Indian Field Rd Wilmington DE 19810

DAY, LAURENCE JAMES (D)
Wis State Rep
b Elderon, Wis, Oct 18, 13; s Roy A Day & Eleanor McPeck D; m 1935 to Florence M King; c Elaine (Mrs Robert Hanke), Marvel (Mrs Leonard Adams), Sharon (Mrs William Wright), Lois (Mrs Kenneth Karpf), Daniel P, Kenneth L, Warren J, Laurence J, Jr & Carla A. Educ: Wittenberg High Sch, Wis, grad, 32. Polit & Govt Pos: Clerk, Elderon, Wis, 40-; chmn, Marathon Co Agr Stabilization & Conserv Serv, 54-68; Wis State Rep, 69- Bus & Prof Pos: Second vpres, Consol Badger Coop, 48-68. Mem: Elks. Relig: Catholic. Mailing Add: Rte 1 Eland WI 54427

DAY, WALTER (D)
Ark State Rep
Mailing Add: 1100 Chickasawba Blytheville AR 72315

DAY, WILLIAM M (WILLIE) (D)
Mont State Rep
Mailing Add: Bloomfield Rte Glendive MT 59330

DAY, WILLIAM S (BILL) (D)
Wash State Sen
b Rockford, Ill, 1923; m to Lucille; c five. Educ: Palmer Col of Chiropractic, Davenport, Iowa. Polit & Govt Pos: Former Wash State Rep & Speaker, Wash House of Rep; Wash State Sen, 69- Bus & Prof Pos: Chiropractor. Mil Serv: Army. Mem: Rotary; VFW. Mailing Add: 723 Glenn Rd Spokane WA 99206

DEALAMAN, DORIS W (R)
First VChmn, Somerset Co Rep Party, NJ
b Hagerstown, Md, Mar 1, 19; d Dr Irvin M Wertz & Ruth D Barnhart W; m 1942 to Laird Wilson Dealaman; c Frederic J & Laird Wertz. Educ: Duke Univ, AB, 40; Columbia Univ, MS, 43; Phi Beta Kappa & Pi Gamma Mu. Polit & Govt Pos: Munic chmn, Rep Party, Bernardsville, NJ, 60-66, borough councilwoman, 64-66; first vchmn, Somerset Co Rep Party, 66-; freeholder, Somerset Co, 67-; mem, NJ Co Munic Govt Study Comn, 73; NJ Comn Children & Youth, currently. Bus & Prof Pos: Soc group work, YMCA, Germantown, Pa, 42-45, New York, NY, 45-48, Jersey City, 48-50 & Plainfield, 50-52. Mem: NJ Asn Chosen Freeholders; NJ State Bd Pub Welfare (vchmn, 72-); Nat Asn Co Off (chmn steering comt); Somerset Co Coun Community Serv (vpres); Somerset Hills YMCA. Relig: Episcopal. Mailing Add: Round Top Rd Bernardsville NJ 07924

DEAN, ALAN L (D)
Polit & Govt Pos: Asst secy admin, Dept Transportation until 71; dep asst dir, orgn & mgr systs div, Off Mgt & Budget & coordr, President's Departmental Reorgn Prog, formerly; spec adv to Undersecy, Dept Health, Educ & Welfare, until 74. Mem: US Rwy Asn (vpres admin). Mailing Add: 3037 N Stafford St Arlington VA 22207

DEAN, C KENNETH, JR (D)
b St Albans, Vt, July 4, 54; s Calvin Kenneth Dean, Sr (deceased) & Jean Margaret Lafayette Dean Jasman; single. Educ: Fairleigh Dickinson Univ, 73- Polit & Govt Pos: Washington Co student coordr, Gov Philip H Hoff for US Senate Comt, 70; student adv, Gov Comn Children & Youth, 71-72; spec consult sch finance, Vt Educ Dept, 72; deleg, Dem Nat Conv, 72; Dem nominee, Vt State Rep, 72; student adv, Washington Workshop Cong Sem, 72-; mem, Waterbury Dem Town Comt, 72- Mem: Common Cause; Vt Tomorrow; Vt Pub Interest Res Group; Vt Natural Resources Coun; Pub Citizen, Inc. Relig: Roman Catholic. Legal Res: 24 N Main Waterbury VT 05676 Mailing Add: PO Box 595 Waterbury VT 05676

DEAN, CARROLL W (R)
Idaho State Rep
Mailing Add: Box 486 Notus ID 83656

DEAN, DOUGLAS C (D)
Ga State Rep
Mailing Add: 356 Arthur St SW Atlanta GA 30310

DEAN, ERNEST H (D)
Utah State Sen
b American Fork, Utah, May 17, 14; s Owen Dean & Amy Dickerson D; m 1935 to Mildred Glissmeyer; c Connie Ann (Mrs Haws), Donna (Mrs Larsen), Ernest H, Jr & Millicent (Mrs Penovich). Educ: Brigham Young Univ, BS, 37, MEdAdmin, 57; Univ Utah, EdD, 68; 4-year letterman, Track; Phi Delta Kappa. Polit & Govt Pos: Utah State Rep, 49-51 & 59-63, Speaker, Utah House of Rep, chmn, Legis Coun, Majority Leader, Minority Leader & officer, Nat Legis Leaders Conf, formerly; city judge, American Fork, Utah, 58-59; Utah State Sen, 67-, Minority Leader, Utah State Senate, 72-, Pres, currently; exec committeeman, Coun State Govt, 67-, chmn, Human Resource Comt, Western Div, 67-69; vpres, Western Conf, formerly, pres, 71; mem, Fed-State Rels Comt, Nat Legis Conf, 67-71, mem intergovt rel comt, currently; alt deleg, Dem Nat Conv, 68; mem gov bd, Coun State Govts; mem bd, Western Conf State Govts. Bus & Prof Pos: Dir & chmn bd, Savings & Loan Co; contractor, Dean Construction Co, 61-67; dir, Western Nat Investment Co, 64-67. Publ: Junior College & Vocational Education, Utah Trade Tech Inst, 66; Accreditation of Vocational & Technical Education, State of Utah, 67; Factors a Manufacturing Company Consider as They Select Their New Plant Site Locations, 68; plus many others. Mem: Nat Panel of Consult on Voc Educ; Utah Adv Comt for Handicapped Children (chmn); Utah Adv Coun on Juv Delinquency; Ment Retardation Asn Am (pres); Univ Utah Alumni Bd. Relig: Latter-day Saint. Mailing Add: 165 S Third East American Fork UT 84003

DEAN, HENRY LAMAR (R)
Chmn, Gordon Co Rep Party, Ga
b Gordon Co, Ga, Apr 26, 38; s Henry Esco Dean & Martha Pearl Williams D; m 1959 to Margaret Ann Long; c LaRae. Educ: Dale Carnegie & Assocs Human Rels, 70. Polit & Govt Pos: Chmn, Gordon Co Rep Party, Ga, 72-; justice of the peace, 856th Dist, Calhoun, 73- Bus & Prof Pos: Sales, Scoggins-McBrayer Furniture, Calhoun, 63- Mil Serv: Entered as Pvt E-1, Army, 56, released as Pfc, 58, after serv in 95th Med Co, 7th Army, 57-58; Good Conduct Medal; Unit Citation. Mem: Calhoun Lions (pres, 74-75); Red Bud Athletic Booster Club. Relig: Baptist. Mailing Add: Rte 6 Poplar Dr Calhoun GA 30701

DEAN, HERSHEL EDWIN (D)
Secy, Williams Co Dem Cent Comt, Ohio
b Center Twp, Williams Co, Ohio, May 25, 04; s Charles M Dean & Nora Belle Davis D; m 1949 to Leona Mae Hicks; c Doris (Mrs Goldsberry). Educ: Int Col, Ft Wayne, Ind, Gen Bus, 22-23. Polit & Govt Pos: Village letter carrier, US Post Off, Montpelier, Ohio, 24-25, city letter carrier, 25-46, rural letter carrier, 46-64; hunting & fishing license agt, Williams Co Conserv League, 37-48 & 74-; Dem precinct committeeman, Montpelier, 65-, mem city coun & chmn street comt, 66-69; secy, Williams Co Dem Cent Comt, 66-; mem, Williams Co Elec Bd, 66-; mem, Montpelier Planning Comn, 66-70 & 74-; mem, Williams Co Regional Planning Comn, 68-70. Mil Serv: Entered as 3/C PO, Navy, 42, released as Mail Man 1/C, 45, after serv in 53rd Naval Construction Bn, 1st Marine Amphibious Corps, New Caledonia, Guadalcanal, Vella La Vella, Eniwetok & Guam, 43-45; Naval Unit Citation for first Marine Amphibious Corps; Presidential Unit Citation. Publ: Published newspaper for Williams Co Conserv League, 38-42; write hunting & fishing column for Montpelier newspaper, 56- Mem: Nat Asn Letter Carriers; VFW; DAV; Eagles; Am Legion. Relig: Presbyterian. Mailing Add: 207 W Water St Montpelier OH 43543

DEAN, J THOMAS (R)
b Cleveland, Ohio, Feb 22, 33; s John Ladd Dean & Margaret Blakely D; m 1960 to Patricia Whitmore; c Thomas Whitmore, Carol Margaret & Joan Gail. Educ: Ohio Wesleyan Univ, BA, 56; Western Reserve Univ, LLB, 59; Sigma Chi. Polit & Govt Pos: Asst Co Prosecutor, Lake Co, Ohio, 60, mem, Bd Elec, 64-; mem, Painesville Planning Comn, 68-, chmn, 72-; vchmn, Lake Co Rep Cent Comt, 68-70, chmn, 70-74. Bus & Prof Pos: Partner, Blakely & Dean, Painesville, Ohio, 68- Mem: Lake Co, Ohio & Am Bar Asns; Kiwanis. Relig: United Methodist. Legal Res: 35 Forest Dr Painesville OH 44077 Mailing Add: 309 Lake County Nat Bank Bldg Painesville OH 44077

DEAN, JOHN (D)
Dir Minorities Div, Dem Nat Comt
b Baltimore, Md, Oct 17, 30; m to Maryann Franklin; c Kenneth, Phyllis, Michael & Carole. Educ: Howard Univ, 56-60; Phi Beta Kappa. Polit & Govt Pos: Foreign serv officer, Am Embassy, Repub of Sudan, US Info Agency, 60-61, foreign serv officer & press attache of Am Embassy, Liberia & Sierra Leone, 61-62, desk officer, WAfrican Affairs, 63-; dir, Spec African Student Progs, African Am Inst, 63-65; Hq Community Action Progs desk officer for Mid-Atlantic & Southeast Regional Off, Off of Econ Opportunity, 65-66, regional adminr of Community Action Progs, Southeast Region, 66-68; assoc dir & mem local coalition staff, Southeast Region, Urban Coalition, 68-69; dir minorities div, Dem Nat Comt, 69-; first dep adminr, Human Resources Admin, 70-71; spec adv to chmn & vchmn, Cong Black Caucus, 71- Mil Serv: Air Force, 51-55. Mailing Add: Dem Nat Comt 1625 Massachusetts Ave NW Washington DC 20036

DEAN, JOHN GUNTHER
US Ambassador to Khmer Repub
b Ger, Feb 24, 26; s Dr Joseph Dean & Lucy Askenaezy D; m 1952 to Martine Duphenieux; c Catherine, Paul & Joseph. Educ: Harvard Univ, AB, 47, MA, 50, fel, 69; Univ Paris, PhD, 49. Hon Degrees: Hon Degree, Univ Hue, 72. Polit & Govt Pos: Consul, Lome, Togo, 59-60; charge d'affaires, Am Embassy, Bamako, Mali, 60-61; adv US deleg, UN 18th Gen Assembly, New York, 63; first secy, Am Embassy, Paris, France, 65-69; dep to corps comdr, 24th Corps, Mil Region 1, Vietnam, 70-72; dep chief of mission, Am Embassy, Vientiane, Laos, 72-74; US Ambassador to Khmer Repub, 74- Mil Serv: Entered as Pvt, Army, 44, released as Lt, after serv in Mil Intel, European Theatre, 46; Lt, Res, 47; Army Commendation Medal. Mem: Am Foreign Serv Asn. Honors & Awards: Meritorious Honor Award, Dept of State, 63 & Superior Honor Award, 73. Relig: Catholic. Mailing Add: Dept of State Washington DC 20520

DEAN, NATHAN D (D)
Ga State Rep
b Rockmart, Ga, May 9, 34; s Thomas James Dean & Ellen Brooke D; m 1961 to Norma Ann Carpenter. Educ: Shorter Col, BBA, 62. Polit & Govt Pos: Mem, City Coun, Rockmart, Ga, 60-; Ga State Rep, 63- Bus & Prof Pos: Employee, Lockheed Aircraft Corp. Mil Serv: Cpl, Army, Research & Eng Command, 56-58. Mem: Shrine; Jaycees (bd dirs); Touchdown Club (bd dirs). Relig: Baptist. Mailing Add: 340 Wingfoot St Rockmart GA 30153

DEAN, ROBERT WILLIAM
US Ambassador to Peru
b Hinsdale, Ill, May 25, 20; m 1948 to Doris Mary Wilkins; c James William, Karen Anne (Mrs Opalek), Shelley Elizabeth & Virginia Lee. Educ: Univ Chicago, AA, 40, MA, 48; Univ Sao Paulo, 41; Nat War Col, 62-63; Alpha Delta Phi. Polit & Govt Pos: Econ clerk & analyst, US Consulate Gen, Sao Paulo, Brazil, 42-44; admin asst, NY Reception Ctr, Dept State, 49; Kreis resident officer, Kitzingen am Main, Ger, 50-52; vconsul, US Consulate, Belem, Brazil, 52-54; polit officer, US Embassy, Rio de Janeiro, 54-57; chief polit div for Latin Am, Bur Intel Research, Dept State, 57-60; exchange officer, Dept Defense, 61-62; counr embassy, Brasilia, Brazil, 63-65 & Santiago, Chile, 65-69; country dir, Off Brazilian Affairs, Bur Inter-Am Affairs, Dept State, 69-71; minister-counr, US Embassy, Mex, DF, 71-74; US Ambassador, Lima, Peru, 74- Mil Serv: Entered as Seaman, Navy, 45, released as Radar Operator, 46, after serv in Pac Theatre. Legal Res: 369 Marion St Elmhurst IL 60126 Mailing Add: Am Embassy Apartado 1995 Lima Peru

DEAN, ROSCOE EMORY, JR (D)
Ga State Sen
b Jesup, Ga, Sept 2, 36; s Roscoe Emory Dean & Lilly Ellis D; single. Educ: Univ Ga, BA in Jour, 60; John Marshall Univ, JD, 63; Delta Theta Phi; Theta Chi. Polit & Govt Pos: Campaign mgr for Congresslady Iris Blitch, Ga, 54; mem, Ga Cong Dem Exec Comt, 54; state-wide pres, Young Adults for Herman Talmadge for US Sen, 56; Ga State Sen, Sixth Dist, currently. Bus & Prof Pos: Self employed in turpentine, farming, pub rels & bus interests. Mil Serv: Entered as Basic Trainee, Ga Air Nat Guard, 59, released as S/Sgt, 65, after serv in Inactive Res; Outstanding Grad, Lackland AFB, Tex. Publ: Anti-suicide centers, Atlanta J Newspaper, 65; Ga Law of Garnishment, John Marshall Univ, 63. Mem: Ga & Wayne Co Farm Bur; Moose; WOW; Ga Jaycees. Relig: Baptist. Mailing Add: 612 Cherry St Jesup GA 31545

DEAN, WALTER RALEIGH, JR (D)
Md State Deleg
b Baltimore, Md, Dec 12, 34; s Walter Raleigh Dean & Ruth Annette Alston D; single. Educ: Morgan State Col, BA, 62; Univ Md Grad Sch Social Work, MSW, 68; Phi Sigma Tau. Polit & Govt Pos: Md State Deleg, 71- Bus & Prof Pos: Reporter, Afro-Am Newspapers, 62-64; street club worker, Bur of Rel, 64-66; assoc planner, Health & Welfare Coun, Baltimore, Md, 68-69; asst dir, Model Urban Neighborhood Develop, 69-70; asst prof, Community Col Baltimore, 69- Mil Serv: Entered as Airman, Air Force, 54, released as A/1C, 58, after serv

in 25th Community Squadron, ETO, 54-58. Mem: Nat Asn Social Workers; Nat Asn Black Social Workers; Citizens Planning & Housing Asn; Fifth Dist Urban Dem Orgn; Md Conf Social Welfare. Relig: Baptist. Mailing Add: 4308 Liberty Heights Ave Baltimore MD 21207

DEAN, WILLIAM DUBOIS (R)
Minn State Rep
b Mankato, Minn, Sept 1, 40; s William Burdette Dean & Isis Edith DuBois D; m 1973 to Christine Ann Lohr. Educ: Univ of Pac, AB, 62; Univ Minn, Minneapolis, MA, 74; Alpha Epsilon Rho; Phi Kappa Tau. Polit & Govt Pos: Vchmn, Hennepin Co Young Rep League, 70-71; deleg, State Rep Conv, 73-75; Minn State Rep, 75-, mem legis audit comn, Minn State Legis, 75- Bus & Prof Pos: Reporter, Tampa Times, Fla, 67-68; instr & dir TV prod, Univ Minn, Minneapolis, 68-73; studio mgr, VCI, Inc, Minneapolis, 73-74; pres, Dean & Assoc, Media Consult Firm, 74- Mil Serv: Entered as Pvt, Army, 63, released as SP-5, after serv in Army Inf Sch, Ft Benning, Ga, 64-66; Army Commendation Medal for Meritorious Serv; Good Conduct Medal; Nat Defense Serv Medal; Vietnam ERA. Publ: Our Korean Children (16 mm film prod & written by W D Dean), VCI, Inc, 74. Mem: Minn Easter Seals Soc (bd dirs, 73-75); Minn Prof Chap, Sigma Delta Chi; Citizens League; Minn Videomedia Soc. Honors & Awards: Awarded grant to study in Korea, Univ Minn, 72; Past Pres Award, Minn Videomedia Soc, 72. Relig: Methodist. Mailing Add: 5225 York Ave S Minneapolis MN 55410

DEANE, MILDRED OLETA (D)
b Canalou, Mo, June 8, 11; d Seth Thomas Nelson & Dora Midkiff N; m 1930 to William Harrison Deane, Jr; c William Harrison, III. Educ: Canalou High Sch, Mo, two years; Roosevelt High Sch, East Chicago, Ind, 2 years. Polit & Govt Pos: Vchmn, New Madrid Co Dem Comt, Mo, formerly. Mem: Eastern Star; New Madrid Co Bess Truman Club (charter mem). Relig: United Methodist. Mailing Add: RFD 3 Sikeston MO 63801

DEANGELIS, JOSEPH (D)
RI State Rep
Mailing Add: 2 Whitman St Esmond RI 02917

DEARIE, JOHN C (D)
NY State Assemblyman
Mailing Add: 1735 Purdy St Bronx NY 10462

DEAS, STEPHEN CANTRELL, JR (R)
b Atlanta, Ga, Jan 17, 38; s Stephen Cantrell Deas & Christine Boring D; m 1962 to Kenya Diane Windham; c Stephen Cantrell, III, Dana Kendall & William Kirk. Educ: Mercer Univ, AB in econ, 62; Phi Delta Theta. Polit & Govt Pos: Campaign mgr, Callaway for Gov, Eatonton & Putnam Co, Ga, 66; secy, Putnam Co Rep Party, 68-70, chmn, formerly; mem, Small Bus Admin, Ga, 71- Bus & Prof Pos: Secy & treas, Deas Furniture, Inc, 62-; pres, Dealer Coop Systs, Inc, 69-; owner, The Country House, currently. Mil Serv: Entered as Pvt, Army, 60, released as S/Sgt, 66, after serv in Ga Nat Guard. Mem: Mason (32 degree); Scottish Rite; Shrine; Eatonton Exchange Club. Relig: Methodist. Mailing Add: 307 Carriage Way Eatonton GA 31024

DEATHERAGE, CLETA B (D)
b Oklahoma City, Okla, Sept 16, 50; d J H Deatherage & Modean Lane D; m 1970 to E Duane Draper. Educ: Univ Okla, BA, with high honors, 73; Alpha Lambda Delta; Mortar Bd; BWOC, Chi Omega. Polit & Govt Pos: Mem nat bd, Am for Dem Action, Washington, DC, 71-; nat field staff, Sen Edmund Muskie Presidential Campaign, 72; deleg, Dem Nat Conv, 72; Okla rep, McGovern's Adv Coun Women, 72; exec dir, Gov Comn Status Women, 72-; mem nat bd, Dem Planning Group, Washington, DC, 73-; Fourth Dist Rep, Okla Const Rev Comt, summer 73; chmn, Precinct 12, Cleveland Co, 73- Mem: Fedn Dem Women's Clubs Okla; Nat Women's Polit Caucus of Okla (convener); League Women Voters; PEO (FB chap); Am Civil Liberties Union. Honors & Awards: Outstanding pledge, Chi Omega Sorority, 69; Top Ten Freshman Women, Univ Okla Mortar Bd, 69; Outstanding Sr Women, Univ Okla Dad's Asn, 71; Okla Outstanding Young Career Woman, Okla Bus & Prof Women, 75. Relig: Protestant. Mailing Add: 816 S Flood Norman OK 73069

DEATHERAGE, PRISCILLA JEAN (D)
Committeewoman, Mo Dem State Comt
b Troy, Mo, Apr 13, 32; d Frank Dewey Weston (deceased) & Jessie Childers W; m 1953 to William Howard Deatherage; c Mark, Jaye Lea & Jim. Educ: Southwest Mo State Col, BS Educ, 68. Polit & Govt Pos: Secy, Shannon Co Dem Comt, Mo, 70-; committeewoman, Mo State Dem Comt, 70- Bus & Prof Pos: Elem teacher, Winona, Mo, 62-64; elem teacher, Eminence, Mo, 65-, elem prin, 70- Mem: Mo State Teachers Asn. Relig: Protestant. Mailing Add: Box 276 Eminence MO 65466

DEATON, CHARLES M (D)
Miss State Rep
b Hattiesburg, Miss, Jan 19, 31; s Ivan Dean Deaton & Martha Fortenberry D; m 1951 to Mary Dent Dickerson; c Beverly Diane & Dara Lane. Educ: Millsaps Col, BA; Univ Miss, LLB; Omicron Delta Kappa; Phi Delta Phi. Polit & Govt Pos: Miss State Rep, 60-, mem bd dirs, Miss Research & Develop Coun, Miss House of Rep, 64-, chmn, Leflore Co Rural Area Develop, 66- Bus & Prof Pos: Partner, Law Firm of Brewen, Deaton & Evans, 60-; mem bd dirs, Rivers & Harbors Asn, Miss, 62-; secy, Fish & Farms Inc, 66- Mil Serv: Entered as Seaman, Navy, 51, released as PO 2/C, 54; Nat Defense Serv, Korean Serv, UN Serv & Good Conduct Medals. Mem: VFW; Am Legion; Farm Bur; CofC; Lions. Honors & Awards: Received letters in football & basketball, Millsaps Col. Relig: Episcopal. Legal Res: 501 E Harding Greenwood MS 38930 Mailing Add: Drawer B Greenwood MS 38930

DEAVERS, GILBERT L (GIL) (R)
Ill State Sen
Mailing Add: 1001 Porter Lane Normal IL 61761

DEBAR, FRANK RICHARD (R)
Chmn, Peabody Rep City Comt, Mass
b Flushing, NY, July 17, 30; s Frank L E Debar & Julia Fleming D; m 1951 to June E Burgess; c June Leslie, John Francis & Nancy-Jeanne. Educ: Eastern Nazarene Col, Mass. Polit & Govt Pos: Peabody City campaign chmn, Comt to Reelect Gov John Volpe, Mass, 66; mem, Peabody Draft Bd, Planning Bd & Redevelop Adv Comt, 66-; chmn, Peabody Rep City Comt, currently. Bus & Prof Pos: Ins underwriter, John Hancock Ins, 54-; real estate broker & Notary Pub, 66- Mem: Peabody Jaycees; Mason (Lynnfield). Relig: Protestant. Mailing Add: 10 Leonard Rd Peabody MA 01960

DEBERARD, FAY F (R)
Colo State Sen
b Sedgwick, Colo, Mar 15, 05; s Fred F DeBerard & Myrtle Miller D; m to Chloe Decker (deceased); m 1966 to Beverly Burford; c Fay, Jr, Marilyn (Mrs Curry) & Robert; seven grandchildren. Educ: Colo Agr Col, 1 year. Hon Degrees: MA, Rangely Col. Polit & Govt Pos: Former co comnr, Grand Co, Colo, 7 years; mem & pres, Sch Bd, Mid Park Hosp Bd, 25 years; Colo State Sen, 53-, former Majority Leader, Colo State Senate, 4 years, Pres Pro Tem, 68-72 & 75-, chmn, Comt Interstate Coop, currently. Bus & Prof Pos: Owner & breeder, Registered Hereford Cattle. Mem: Nat Conf State Legislators (bd); Bur Land Mgt (adv coun); Rotary; Coun State Govt (Colo chmn); Interstate Coop (chmn); Farm Bur. Honors & Awards: Award of Merit, Colo State Univ, 69. Relig: Episcopal. Mailing Add: Box 188 Kremmling CO 80459

DEBERRY, LOIS M (D)
Tenn State Rep
Mailing Add: 1373 Valse Memphis TN 38106

DE BLASI, PASQUALE, SR (R)
Chmn, Kings Co Rep Comt, NY
b Alcamo, Italy, Jan 18, 10; s Joseph De Blasi & Giovanna Impastate D; m 1934 to Marion Genco; c Joseph, Pasquale, Jr & Frank. Educ: City Col of New York, 3 years. Polit & Govt Pos: Pres, Canarsie Rep Club, NY, 34-38; pres, Canarsie Young Rep Club, 36-40; deleg, NY Rep State Conv, 40-66; chmn, Kings Co Rep Comt, 13th Assembly Dist, NY, 56-64, chmn, 40th Assembly Dist, 66-; pres, 40th Assembly Dist Rep Club, 65-; deleg, Rep Nat Conv, 68 & 72. Bus & Prof Pos: Acct, 20th Century Fox Film Corp, New York, NY, 40-64; self-employed acct, 64- Mem: Empire State Asn of Pub Acct; Unico; KofC. Relig: Catholic. Mailing Add: 1021 Remsen Ave Brooklyn NY 11236

DE BLIEUX, JOSEPH DAVIS (D)
La State Sen
b Columbia, La, Sept 12, 12; s Honore Louis De Blieux, Sr & Ozet Perot D; m 1946 to Dorothy Mary LePine; c Paul Louis. Educ: Ouachita Parish Jr Col, 34; La State Univ, LLB, 38; Theta Kappa Phi. Polit & Govt Pos: Mem, Dem State Cent Comt, Ouachita Parish, 38-40, E Baton Rouge Parish, 60-; deleg, Dem Nat Conv, 56, 64 & 68; La State Sen, 56-60 & 64-; chmn, La State Adv Comt, US Comn on Civil Rights, 60-; mem, La State Dem Const Conv, 72- Mil Serv: Entered as Pvt, Army, 42, released as S/Sgt, 45, after serv in 9th Port Hq, Army Transportation Corps, Middle E Command, Iran, 43-45. Mem: Am Legion; Baton Rouge CofC; Pub Affairs Research Coun; EBaton Rouge Lions; KofC (3 & 4 degree). Honors & Awards: Made a Knight of St Gregory by Pope Pius XII, 58. Relig: Catholic. Legal Res: 3755 Churchill Ave Baton Rouge LA 70802 Mailing Add: PO Box 3071 Baton Rouge LA 70821

DEBOLT, EDWARD S (R)
b Sacramento, Calif, Sept 17, 38; s Merrill E Debolt & Frances Schooler D; m 1960 to Sharron Ann Hoggard; c Ed, Jr & Eric J. Educ: Stockton Col, AA; San Francisco State, 2 years. Polit & Govt Pos: Exec dir, Rep Assoc, Stockton, Calif, 63-64; exec dir, Rep Assoc, Sacramento, 64-65; area dir, Rep State Cent Comt of Calif, 65-66, field dir, 67-68, exec dir, 69-71; dir polit & research divs, Rep Nat Comt, 71-73. Bus & Prof Pos: Vpres, George Young & Assoc, 73-; nat polit sales dir, Reuben H Donnelley Co, currently. Mailing Add: 4050 41st St North Arlington VA 22207

DEBONIS, ANTHONY, JR (D)
b Gary, Ind, Oct 14, 50; s Anthony DeBonis, Sr & Isabella Fabiani D; single. Educ: Purdue Univ, Lafayette, BA with distinction, 72; Syracuse Univ, MA, 73; De Paul Univ Col Law, currently. Polit & Govt Pos: Vpres, Lake Co Collegiate Young Dem, Ind, 69-71; vpres, Purdue Univ Young Dem, 69-72; Dem precinct committeeman, West Lafayette, 70-71; pres, Ind Collegiate Young Dem, 71-72; deleg, Ind Dem State Conv, 72 & 74; deleg, Dem Nat Conv, 72; dir educ & research, Lake Co Frontlash, Gary, Ind, 72; Dem precinct vcommitteeman, Gary, 75- Bus & Prof Pos: Proj rev officer, Northwest Ind Comprehensive Health Planning Coun, Inc, currently. Mem: Phi Beta Kappa; Phi Kappa Phi; Pi Sigma Alpha; Lake Co Young Dem (pres, 75-); Gary Young Dem (exec bd, 71-72), Honors & Awards: Pres Acad Awards Purdue Univ, 70-72; Mellon fel polit sci, Maxwell Grad Sch Pub Affairs, Syracuse Univ, 72-73. Relig: Roman Catholic. Mailing Add: 309 E 43rd Ave Gary IN 46409

DEBONIS, DANIEL VINCENT, JR (D)
Vt State Rep
b Poultney, Vt, Nov 2, 14; m to Teresa Daniels; c three sons. Educ: Poultney High Sch, Troy High Sch, NY. Polit & Govt Pos: Chmn, Town Tax Separation, Poultney, Vt; Vt State Rep, 65-; alt deleg, Dem Nat Conv 68; chmn, Rutland Co Dem Party, Vt, 69- Bus & Prof Pos: Quarrying; farmer. Mem: Farm Bur; PTA; St Raphaels Men's Club; Vt Dairy Asn Coun. Relig: Catholic. Mailing Add: RFD 1 Poultney VT 05764

DE BONIS, JOHN RALPH (D)
b Bellaire, Ohio, Oct 14, 38; s Sam De Bonis & Josephine Di Santis D; m 1962 to Carol Louise Williams; c John Ralph, Jr, Joseph Robert & Jill Renee. Educ: Ohio Univ, St Clairsville, currently. Polit & Govt Pos: Chmn polit action comt, United Steel Workers of Am Local 5760, 68-, chmn legis comt, 70-, chmn, gen grievance comt, 72-; pres, Belmont Co Young Dem, Ohio, 71-72; mem, McGovern for President Steering Comt, 72; alt deleg, Dem Nat Conv, 72. Bus & Prof Pos: External vpres, Shadyside Jaycees, 66-67; chmn, Concerned Citizens about Strip Mining, 71-72; mem adv comt, Ohio Univ Adult & Continuing Educ, 71-; mem adv comt, Belmont Co Joint Voc Sch, 72; chmn, Wage & Price Control Watch Dog Comt, 72; mem bd trustees, Belmont, Harrison, Monroe Co Tech Col, 72-; personnel mgr, Picoma Industs, Inc, 74- Mil Serv: Entered as Pvt, Army Res, 56, released as Sgt E-5, 62, after serv in 983rd Eng Bn, Berlin Crisis, 61-62. Mem: Fraternal Order of Police Lodge 6; Wheeling Area Labor Rels, Personnel Mgt Club; Elks; Bellaire Ital Am Citizen Club; Belmont & Monroe Co AFL-CIO Trades & Labor Coun (pres, 71-). Relig: Methodist. Mailing Add: 15 W 48th St Shadyside OH 43947

DEBRUHL, GARRY GLENN (D)
Va State Deleg
b Alexander, NC, Sept 14, 36; s Glenn Edward DeBruhl & Virginia West D; m 1958 to Carol Cooper; c Mark Reagan, Christopher Dean & Traci Leigh. Educ: Univ NC, AB, 58; Univ Va, MA, 63. Polit & Govt Pos: Mem bd supvr, Patrick Co, Va, 66-68; Va State Deleg, 68-72 & 75- Bus & Prof Pos: Teacher, Henry Co, Va, 58-63; sales rep, Holt, Rinehart & Winston, Inc, NY, 63-; pres, Jay Mark & Assocs, Stuart, Va, 70- Mil Serv: Entered as Pvt, Army, 60, released as E-4, 61, after serv in Artil. Mem: Va Bookmans Asn; Mason; Rotary; Moose.

Honors & Awards: One of Outstanding Young Men of Am, 70. Relig: Disciples of Christ. Mailing Add: Critz VA 24082

DEBRUYN, WILLIAM EDWARD (R)
b Norway, Mich, Jan 16, 22; s Edward De Bruyn & Edwilda Asselin D; m 1946 to Florence Lemyra Brown; c Lemyra, Sidonie, Edwilda, Eduard & Florence. Educ: Northern Mich Univ, BA, 47; Tri Mu. Polit & Govt Pos: Secy, Iron Co Rep Party, Mich, 62-68, chmn, formerly. Bus & Prof Pos: Teacher, Mather High Sch, Munising, Mich, 46-48; self-employed, Fergus Falls, Minn, 48-57; teacher, Bates Twp Sch, Iron River, Mich, 57-69, teaching prin, 69- Mil Serv: Entered as Pvt, Air Force, 42, released as S/Sgt, 46, after serv in 610th Army Air Force Base Unit, Proving Ground Command, Eglin Field, Fla, 43-46. Mem: Iron Co Engrs Club; Bates Sch PTA; Dickinson-Iron Co Sch Adminr Asn; Iron River Country Club. Relig: Catholic. Mailing Add: RR 1 Iron River MI 49935

DEBUSKEY, CHARLOTTE CHIPPER (D)
Nat Committeewoman, Md Young Dem
b Baltimore, Md, Nov 28, 45; d Charles B Debuskey & Harriett Weiner D; single. Educ: Univ of Md, BS, 66; Gamma Sigma Sigma (first vpres, second vpres, parliamentarian & soc chmn, Xi chap); People to People Club; Commuters Orgn. Polit & Govt Pos: Mem, Univ Md Young Dem, 64-66, parliamentarian, 65; mem, Baltimore City Fifth Dist Young Dem, 64-72, parliamentarian, 64, first vpres, 65 & 69, second vpres, 66, ed-in-chief, 67-68, pres, 70, treas, 71; mem, West Baltimore City Young Dem, corresponding secy, 73, pres, 74, treas, 75; mem, Md Young Dem, 64-, state conv deleg, 66-75, mem exec bd, 67-69, 71-73 & 73-75, ticket chmn Jefferson Jackson Day, 71-73, alt nat committeewoman, 67-69 & 70-71, nat committeewoman, 71-, liaison to orgn labor, 72-; mem, Mid-Atlantic Region Young Dem, 73-, regional conf deleg, 73, Bylaws Comt, 73; mem, Young Dem Clubs Am, 66-, nat conv deleg, 67, 71 & 73, nat comt meeting rep, 68-69, 71-, mem credentials comt, 68, mem resolutions comt, 69, mem const comt, 71-75, mem charter comn, 74 & 75; mem statewide hq staff, Gubernatorial Primary Campaign, 66; mem, City-Co Dem Club, 66-70; mem, Baltimore Co Young Dem, 67-69, parliamentarian, 68; admin asst to a state sen, 67-70; Baltimore City coordr, Young Citizens for Humphrey-Muskie, 68; mem, Fifth Dist Reform Dem, 69-73; Citizens to reelect Mandel, Lee, Goldstein & Burch, gubernatorial primary & gen elec campaigns, 74; official page, Dem Nat Mid Term Conv, 74. Bus & Prof Pos: Off dir, United Labor, Annapolis, Md, 71- Publ: Ed, The Pledge Handbook, 71 & 73; ed, The Staff, 72; Introducing Gamma Sigma Sigma, Gamma Sigma Sigma, 72 & 74. Mem: Health Security Action Coun Md (planning bd, 73-); Common Cause; Univ Md Alumni Asn; US Youth Coun; Baltimore City Bicentennial Comt (dir vol, coordr pub, 74-). Honors & Awards: Key for outstanding serv to sch as leader in legis, Student Govt Asn Univ Md, 65; Cert Merit, Gamma Sigma Sigma, 71; Outstanding Sister, Gtr Baltimore Alumnae chap, Gamma Sigma Sigma, 70, 71 & 72; Outstanding Young Dem Md, 74. Legal Res: 2816 Taney Rd Baltimore MD 21209 Mailing Add: 6960 Greenvale St NW Washington DC 20015

DECAMP, JOHN WILLIAM (R)
Nebr State Sen
b Neligh, Nebr, July 6, 41; s William Hewitt Decamp & Marian Siren D; m 1965 to Linda K Bollwitt; c Gary, Richard, Floyd & Eugene. Educ: Univ Nebr, BA, 60, JD, 67; mem legal fraternity. Polit & Govt Pos: Nebr State Sen, 71- Mil Serv: Entered as 2nd Lt, Army, 68, released as Capt, 70, after serv as Inf Capt, Mekong Delta, Vietnam, 69-70; Capt, Army Nat Guard; Bronze Star; Vietnamese RD Medal for Heroism; Presidential Citation; Army Commendation Medal. Relig: Christian. Mailing Add: D&D Plaza Neligh NE 68756

DECAS, GEORGE CHARLES (R)
Chmn, Wareham Rep Town Comt, Mass
b New Bedford, Mass, July 1, 37; s Charles John Decas & Georgia Fotinou D; single. Educ: Yale Col, AB, 59; Univ Pa Law Sch, LLB, 62. Polit & Govt Pos: Master in Chancery, Commonwealth of Mass, 67-; chmn, Wareham Planning Bd, 71-73; alt deleg, Rep Nat Conv, 72; chmn, Wareham Rep Town Comt, 72-; pres, Plymouth Co Rep Club, 72-74. Bus & Prof Pos: Town counsel, Middleborough, Mass, 67-; vpres, Plymouth Co Bar Asn, 74-; incorporator, Tobey Hosp Corp, 73- Mil Serv: Entered as E-1, Army, 62, released as 1st Lt, 68, after serv in 441st Civil Affairs Unit. Relig: Greek Orthodox. Mailing Add: 18 High St Wareham MA 02571

DECCIO, ALEX A (R)
Wash State Rep
b Walla Walla, Wash, Oct 28, 27; s Louis Deccio & Josephine D; m 1946 to Lucille P Dexter; c Barbara Jean Ogle, Janet Marie, Carol Ann, James Paul, Richard A, Patricia E, Teresa M & Catherine Joanne. Educ: Moxee High Sch, four years; Air Force Officer Sch, 41. Polit & Govt Pos: Precinct committeeman, Yakima Rep Party, Wash, 48-; treas, Young Rep Club, Yakima Co, 48, secy, 50; deleg, Yakima Co Rep Conv, 55-, chmn platform comt, 60-66; deleg, Wash State Rep Conv, 55-, mem platform comt, 60-66; treas, Yakima Co Rep Cent Comt, 56-58, secy, 58-60, chmn, 71-72; campaign mgr, Wash State Rep Harold Petrie, 56, Robert Brachtenbach, 60, Keith J Spanton, 66, Wash State Sen James T Matson, 68 & Co Assessor Charles A Riemcke, 70; chmn, fund raising dinners, Barry Goldwater, 60, Richard M Nixon, 62 & Thomas E Dewey, 64; alt deleg, Rep Nat Conv, 60 & deleg, 72; chmn, Yakima Co Rep Campaign Comt, 60 & 72; Yakima Co chmn, Catherine May for Cong Campaign, 64; Yakima Co mem, Gov Daniel Evans' Task Force Comt, 68; trustee, Yakima Valley Commun Col, 67-; State Committeeman from Yakima Co & mem exec bd for Fourth Cong Dist, Wash State Rep Cent Comt, 73-; Wash State Rep, 15th Dist, currently. Bus & Prof Pos: Mem various comts, Yakima CofC, 57-65, bd dirs, 66-68; drive chmn, United Good Neighbors, Yakima Co, Wash, 63; mem, comt to consolidate Yakima Cath Schs, 67; mem bd dirs, Yakima Indian Mus, 68-; pres, Yakima Valley Visitors & Conv Bur, 68-69, mem bd dirs, 69-; mem adv bd, Pac Nat Bank Wash, Tacoma; mem, Sun Dusters, Yakima, 69-; mem bd dirs, Cath Charities, Yakima Diocese. Mil Serv: Entered as Pvt, Air Force, 40, released as 1st Lt, 46, after serv in Troop Carrier Command, ETO, 43-44; Maj, Air Force Res, 56-; Presidential Citation. Mem: Wash State Ins Brokers Asn (legis chmn, 70-); Yakima Co Ins Brokers Asn; Elks; CWV. Relig: Catholic. Legal Res: Rte 1 Box 414 Yakima WA 98901 Mailing Add: PO Box 1343 Yakima WA 98901

DECELL, HERMAN BRISTER (D)
Miss State Sen
b Yazoo City, Miss, Sept 26, 24; s John Eldridge DeCell & Lucile Brister C; m 1951 to Harriet Causey; c Alice, Brister & Causey. Educ: Univ Miss, BBA, 48; Harvard Univ, LLB, 50; Phi Eta Sigma; Beta Gamma Sigma; Sigma Alpha Epsilon; Lincoln's Inn. Polit & Govt Pos: Deleg, Miss State Dem Conv, 60, 64, 68 & 72; mem, State Sovereignty Comt, Miss, 60-72; Miss State Sen, 15th Dist, 60-; deleg, Dem Nat Conv, 64. Bus & Prof Pos: Assoc, Henry & Barbour, 50-57, partner, Henry, Barbour & DeCell, 57- Mil Serv: Entered as Pvt, Army, 43, released as 1st Lt, 46, after serv in 108th Engr Bn, Pac, 45-46; Pac Theater & Philippine Liberation Medals. Publ: Oil & gas law, 51 & Federal crop insurance, 56, Miss Law J. Mem: Am Bar Asn; Lions; Elks; Yazoo Country Club; Am Legion. Relig: Methodist. Mailing Add: Yazoo City MS 39194

DECESARE, DONALD H (R)
NH State Rep
Mailing Add: 33 Cove Rd Salem NH 03079

DECESARE, GRACE L (D)
NH State Rep
Mailing Add: Sandy Beach Rd Salem NH 03079

DE CHABERT, ANSETTA (D)
Mem, VI Dem Party
b Christiansted, St Croix, VI, Feb 11, 08; m to Ralph de Chabert (deceased); c Ralph, Austin, Mario, Rita (Mrs Schuster) & Shirley (Mrs Highfield). Polit & Govt Pos: Mem, Pub Welfare Bd & Bd of Educ, VI; mem, VI Dem Party, 55-; Dem Nat Committeewoman, VI, 64-72; deleg & mem Majority Platform Comt, Dem Nat Comt, 68; finance chmn, St Croix Dem Party. Mem: Red Cross; Welfare; Charles Howard Hosp Auxiliary; Ment Health; Bus & Prof Womens Club. Mailing Add: PO Box 157 Christiansted St Croix VI 00820

DECHAINE, JAMES ANTHONY (D)
b Omaha, Nebr, Dec 13, 43; s James Peter DeChaine & Mary Schmidt D; m 1965 to Theresa Marie Adair; c Christopher & Rebecca. Educ: St John's Univ, BA, 65; Duke Univ, MA, 71, PhD, 72. Polit & Govt Pos: Admin asst, US Rep Richard Nolan, Minn, 75- Bus & Prof Pos: Acct adminr, Honeywell, Minn, 65-67; asst dir admissions, St John's Univ, 67-69, dir research, 72-73. Legal Res: 908 St Germain St Cloud MN 56301 Mailing Add: 2419 Tunlaw Rd NW Washington DC 20007

DECK, STANLEY THEODORE (R)
b Great Falls, Mont, Sept 7, 35; s Earl H Deck & Vivian Hegna D; m 1956 to June Darlene Steele; c Cheree, Valarie, Stanley, Jr & Stacy. Educ: Col Great Falls, BA, 56; Univ San Francisco, 56-57; Mont State Univ, 57-59; Phi Delta Phi. Polit & Govt Pos: Regional finance dir, NDak Rep Party, 69-70, chmn, 37th Dist Rep Party, formerly; dir, Dickinson Airport Authority, 69- Bus & Prof Pos: Prog dir, KMSO-TV, Missoula, Mont, 57-58, mgr, 58-59; gen mgr, KDIX-AM-TV, Dickinson, NDak, 59-68, pres, KDIX-AM-TV-CATV, 68- Mem: Nat Asn Broadcasters; NDak Broadcasters Asn; CBS TV Affiliates; Rotary; Dickinson CofC. Mailing Add: 833 11th Ave W Dickinson ND 58601

DECKER, CLARENCE (D)
Colo State Sen
Mailing Add: 2680 S Zurich Ct Denver CO 80219

DECKER, GLORIA ANN (D)
Chmn, Warren Co Dem Comt, NJ
b Phillipsburg, NJ, Oct 16, 32; d Alfred Rudolf Bates & Maeon Smith B; m 1953 to Jay Roland Decker; c Jay Bradley & Jan Leslie. Educ: Churchman Bus Col, 50-51; Prof Sch Bus, 72. Polit & Govt Pos: Alt deleg, Dem Nat Conv, 68, deleg, 72; mem, Phillipsburg Bd Educ, 68-73, vpres, 72-73; secy, Warren Co Dem Comt, 69-70, vchmn, 70-72, chmn, 72-; comnr, Warren Co Bd Taxation, 73-74. Bus & Prof Pos: Exec secy, Freeman Vliet, Real Estate & Ins, 54-60; real estate salesman, Curzi Real Estate, 72; confidential aide, NJ Lottery Comn, currently. Publ: Series of articles on what a woman does at a nat conv, Easton Express, Pa, 8/68. Mem: Eastern Star; Cederettes of Warren Co; Jr Auxiliary, Warren Hosp; Hillcrest Tennis Club; Mary T Norton Dem Club. Relig: Presbyterian. Mailing Add: 161 Pickford Ave Phillipsburg NJ 08865

DECLUITT, DOUGLAS RONALD (R)
Mem, Tex Rep State Exec Comt
b Port Arthur, Tex, Feb 9, 35; s Samuel Joseph DeCluitt & Margie Chaisson D; m 1957 to Eleanor Grace Roberts; c Sherri Lyn & Christopher Douglas. Educ: Tex A&M Univ, BS, 57; Harvard Univ, MBA, 62. Polit & Govt Pos: Chmn, McLennan Co Rep Party, Tex, 66-68; mem, Tex Rep State Exec Comt, 66-; chmn, Tex State Voter Registr, 67-68; Rep nominee for Lt Gov, 68; deleg, Rep Nat Conv, 68 & 72. Bus & Prof Pos: Pres, Sovereign Corp, Waco, Tex, currently. Mil Serv: Entered as 2nd Lt, Army, 58, released as 1st Lt, 60, after serv in Guided Missile Battery, Air Defense Command; Outstanding Lt, First Army Air Defense Command, 59. Relig: Unitarian. Mailing Add: 200 Castle Waco TX 76710

DECONCINI, DENNIS (D)
Mem, Ariz Dem State Exec Comt
b Tucson, Ariz, May 8, 37; s Evo A DeConcini & Ora Webster D; m 1959 to Susan Margaret Hurley; c Denise, Christina & Patrick Evo. Educ: Univ Ariz, BA, 59, Law Sch, LLB, 63; Phi Delta Rho; Phi Delta Theta. Polit & Govt Pos: Precinct committeeman, Precinct 53, Pima Co, 58-; mem, Pima Co Dem Cent Comt, 58-67; mem, Ariz Dem State Exec Comt, 58-; deleg, Dem Nat Conv, 64; vchmn, Ariz State Dem Comt, 64-70; spec coun, former Gov Samuel P Goddard, Ariz, 65, admin asst, 65-67; Pima Co Attorney, 73- Bus & Prof Pos: Legal research, Evo DeConcini, Attorney & real estate & property mgt, Shopping Centers, Inc, 59-63; attorney-at-law, 63-65; partner, DeConcini & McDonald, Attorneys, 68- Mil Serv: 2nd Lt, Adj Gen Corps, Army, 59-60; 15th Control Group, Army Res, 60-64, Judge Adv Gen Corps, 64-67, 1st Lt. Mem: Ariz & Am Bar Asns; Young Dem of Tucson; Delta Sigma Rho; Phi Alpha Delta. Relig: Catholic. Legal Res: 243 N Norton Tucson AZ 85719 Mailing Add: 510 Valley Nat Bldg Tucson AZ 85701

DECONCINI, ORA (D)
Dem Nat Committeewoman, Ariz
Mailing Add: 3203 E Third St Tucson AZ 85716

DE COSTER, RICHARD J (D)
Mo State Rep
b Ewing, Mo, July 10, 21; m to Jane Herst; c Patricia, Miles, Jules, Timothy, Thomas & Richard. Educ: St Louis Univ, 39-41; Univ Mo, 45-48. Polit & Govt Pos: Mo State Rep, Lewis Co, 55-66, 94th Dist, 66-72 & First Dist, 73-, Speaker Pro Tem, Mo House Rep, 73- Bus & Prof Pos: High sch teacher, California, Mo, 48-51; attorney-at-law, Canton, Mo, 51-; lectr in govt, Culver-Stockton Col, 66-67. Mil Serv: Entered as Seaman 2/C, Navy, 41, released as Lt(jg), 45, after serv in Naval Air Corps, Pac Theatre, 45. Relig: Catholic. Legal Res: Canton MO 63435 Mailing Add: House of Rep PO Jefferson City MO 65101

DEDDEH, WADIE PETER **(D)**
Calif State Assemblyman
b Bagdad, Iraq, Sept 6, 20; s Peter Joseph Deddeh & Hannai Mona D; m 1951 to Mary-Lynn Drake; c Peter Charles. Educ: Univ Bagdad, AB, 46; Univ Detroit, MA, 56. Polit & Govt Pos: Calif State Assemblyman, 77th Dist, 67-, chmn, Comt on Pub Employees & Retirement, Calif State Assembly, 68-70 & 74, Comt on Transportation, 71-73 & Comt on Finance & Ins, 73-74. Bus & Prof Pos: Teacher Arabic lang, Army Lang Sch, Monterey, Calif, 49-54; teacher, Sweetwater High Sch, National City, 59-62; prof polit sci, Southwestern Col, Chula Vista, 62-66. Mem: Calif Teachers Asn; Nat Educ Asn; Calif Jr Col Faculty Asn; KofC; G I Forum. Relig: Catholic. Legal Res: 1152 Melrose St Chula Vista CA 92011 Mailing Add: 815 Third Ave Suite 219 Chula Vista CA 92011

DEDOMENICO, PAUL DOMENIC **(D)**
Mem, Alameda Co Dem Comt, Calif
b San Francisco, Calif, Dec 23, 34; s Paskey DeDomenico & Merrial Redenbaugh D; m 1960 to Anita Ludovici; c Paul & Gina. Educ: Univ Wash, grad. Polit & Govt Pos: Dem co-chmn for local cand, 64 & 66; chmn, Golden Assocs; state co-chmn, Businessmen's Comt for Sen Robert Kennedy for Pres, 68; state chmn, Businessmen's Comt for Alan Cranston for Sen, 68; deleg, Dem Nat Conv, 68; mem, Alameda Co Dem Cent Comt, 69- Bus & Prof Pos: Vpres & mem bd dirs, Golden Grain Macaroni Co, formerly; pres & mem bd dirs, Ghirardelli Chocolate Co, currently; mem bd dirs, Mission Macaroni Co, Seattle, Manteca Bean Co, Manteca, Major Italian Foods Co, Seattle & Buffalo Breeding Asn, Burlingame, currently; owner & pres, Hawaiian Holiday Macadamia Nut Co, Honokaa, currently; adv, Sen Subcomt Antitrust Monopoly. Mil Serv: Entered as 2nd Lt, Army, 56, released as 1st Lt, 57; Letter of Commendation. Mem: Commonwealth Club; San Francisco Press Club; Nat Asn Advert; San Francisco Advert Club; San Francisco CofC. Relig: Christian. Mailing Add: Box 707 Honokaa HI 96727

DEEB, RICHARD JAMES **(R)**
Fla State Sen
b Tallahassee, Fla, Sept 8, 24; s George J Deeb & Mary Shaheen D; m 1950 to Catalina Panayotti; c Alex Richard, Richard George, Teresa Marie & Thomas Patrick. Educ: Univ Notre Dame, BS, 47. Polit & Govt Pos: Fla State Rep, 63-64; chmn, St Petersburg Minimum Housing Standards Bd, Fla, formerly; Fla State Sen, 22nd Dist, 66-; vchmn, Nat Comt for Const Amendment to Prohibit Forced Busing, currently; deleg, Rep Nat Conv, 72; mem, Intergovt Rels Comt, Nat Legis Conf, currently. Mil Serv: Army, 44. Mem: KofC; Am Legion; Exchange Club; Amvets; Contractors & Builders Asn. Relig: Catholic. Mailing Add: 5675 Fifth Ave N St Petersburg FL 33710

DEEBEL, GEORGE FRANKLIN **(R)**
b Ringtown, Pa, Mar 27, 11; s William Cyrus Deebel & Elizabeth Catherine Laudig D; m 1946 to Ellouise Bundy; c Mary Joel (Mrs John Herlitz), Linda Lou (Mrs Robert Graham, Jr) & Kay Elizabeth (Mrs Allan Devine). Educ: Maryville Col, AB, 35; Univ Tenn, MS, 36; Univ NC, PhD, 41; Phi Kappa Phi; Sigma Xi; Alpha Chi Sigma. Polit & Govt Pos: Mem, Ohio Rep Finance Comt, 52-; precinct committeeman, Precinct B, Third Ward, Kettering, Ohio, 64-, ward committeeman, 66-; alt deleg, Rep Nat Conv, 72. Bus & Prof Pos: Res chemist, Monsanto, 41-49, group leader, 49-61, res specialist, Monsanto Res Corp, 61- Publ: Numerous chem patents. Mem: Am Chem Soc. Honors & Awards: Monsanto Civic Award, 65; Outstanding Rep Montgomery Co Men's Rep Club, 68. Relig: Presbyterian. Mailing Add: 4466 Mapleridge Pl Kettering OH 45429

DEEM, J FRANK **(R)**
WVa State Sen
b Harrisville, WVa, Mar 20, 28; s F S Deem & Lila Matheny D; m 1946 to Hilda Marie Snyder; c Deborah Ann, Pamela Ann, Michael Stephen, Patti Carol & Cathy. Educ: Mountain State Bus Col; Marietta Col, BS. Polit & Govt Pos: WVa State Deleg, 54-62; WVa State Sen, 64- Bus & Prof Pos: Oil & gas & retail mercantile bus. Mil Serv: Navy, 45-46. Mem: Alpha Sigma Phi; Pi Epsilon Tau; Ritchie Co Libr Bd; Young Rep Club; PTA. Relig: Protestant. Mailing Add: 602 Second St St Marys WV 26170

DEEN, JESSE C **(D)**
La State Rep
Mailing Add: Rte 2 Box 199 Benton LA 71106

DEERING, FREDERICK HENRY **(D)**
Ohio State Rep
b Erie Co, Ohio, May 9, 23; s Frederick Deering & Nellie Mae Smith D; m 1945 to Dorothy Leona Hartley; c Daryl Lee, Diane Elizabeth (Mrs Karle Nolte), Stephen Joel & Brian Frederick. Educ: Ohio State Univ, 41-44; Phi Eta Sigma. Polit & Govt Pos: Mem, Perkins Sch Bd, Sandusky, Ohio, 52-61; comnr, Erie Co, 61-73; Ohio State Rep, 84th Dist, 73- Mem: Erie-Ottawa Guid Ctr, Inc (bd dirs, 68-); Family Serv of Erie Co (bd dirs, 66-); Farm Bur; Grange; Perkins CofC. Honors & Awards: Am Farmer Degree, Future Farmers of Am, 44; Ohio's Outstanding Young Farmer, Ohio CofC, 55; Serv Award, Erie Co 4-H Clubs, 72. Relig: United Church of Christ. Mailing Add: Rte 1 Ransom Rd Monroeville OH 44847

DEFALAISE, LOUIS GAYLORD **(R)**
Mem, Kenton Co Rep Exec Comt, Ky
b Covington, Ky, Apr 27, 45; s Docteur Jaimes De Falaise & Mildred Howard D; m 1968 to Susan Jane Court; c David Henry & Mary. Educ: Thomas More Col, AB, 68; Univ Ky Law Sch, 68-; Phi Alpha Theta; Phi Alpha Delta. Polit & Govt Pos: Pres, Northern Ky Student Young Rep Club, 63-65; chmn, Fourth Cong Dist TAR, 64-65; chmn Region IV, Ky Col Rep Fedn, 65-66, parliamentarian, 68; state col chmn, Reelect Campaign Sen John Sherman Cooper, 66; chmn, Fourth Cong Dist Young Rep Fedn, 66-67; mem, Ky Rep State Cent Comt, 66-67 & 69-70, asst to exec dir, summer 68 & 69; presiding chmn, Ky Young Rep Fedn State Conv, 66-69 & 70-74; mem staff, US Sen John Sherman Cooper, summer 67; campaign mgr, Ronald B Turner for City Comnr, Covington, 67; vchmn, Ky Young Rep Fedn, 67-68, parliamentarian, 68-69, chmn, 69-70; chmn, Young Kentuckians for Reagan, 68; chmn, Commonwealth Young Rep Club, 68-69; mem, Kenton Co Rep Exec Comt, 68-69 & 74-; mem exec comt, Nat Young Rep Fedn, 69-71, chmn voter registr, 69-71; Asst US Attorney, 72-73. Bus & Prof Pos: Attorney, Adams, Brooking, Stephen & Mitchell, 74- Publ: Campus unrest: a sociological & legal analysis, Univ Ky Law J, winter 70; Brevit Major General Stephen Gano Burbridge Military Commander of Kentucky Feb 1864-Feb 1865, Register of Ky Hist Soc, 4/71. Mem: Am, Fed & Ky Bar Asns; Jaycees; Thomas More Alumni Asn. Honors & Awards: Outstanding Freshman & Jr Man, Thomas More Col, 64-65 & 66-67; Second Nat Winner, VFW Ladies Auxiliary Americanism Essay Contest, 65; Outstanding Ky Col Rep, 66-67; Nat Young Rep Citation, 69-70. Mailing Add: 500 First Nat Bank Bldg Covington KY 41011

DEFEBAUGH, JAMES ELLIOTT **(R)**
Mich State Rep
b Chicago, Ill, Oct 8, 26; s Carl Wright Defebaugh & Martha Barker D; m 1953 to Lois Arlene; c James Elliott, Lynne Ann & Jean Carol. Educ: Knox Col, BA, 50. Polit & Govt Pos: Dir, Birmingham Rep Party, Mich, 64-65; finance chmn, Oakland Co Rep Party, 65, organizational dir, 67-68; dir, 65th Dist Rep Party, 66-67; mem, Oakland Co Rep Exec Comt, 66-; mem, Oakland Co Rep Comt, 66-, chmn, 68-70; mem, 18th Dist Cong Comt, 70-; Mich State Rep, 65th Dist, 71-, Rep Whip, 73-; mem, Mich Bicentennial Comn, currently. Bus & Prof Pos: With Foote, Cone & Belding Advert, New York, NY, 50-52, Grant Advert, New York, NY & Chicago, 52-54, Campbell-Ewald Advert, Chicago, Cincinnati & Detroit, 54-69 & NW Coughlin Direct Mail Mkt, Detroit, 69-; instr direct mail mkt, Wayne State Univ, 62-64. Mil Serv: Entered as Pvt, Army Air Force, 44, released as Pfc, 46, after serv in Tech Training Command, Am Theatre. Mem: Am Asn Advert Agencies; Direct Mail Club of Detroit. Relig: Presbyterian. Legal Res: 580 Lahser Rd Birmingham MI 48010 Mailing Add: PO Box 119 Lansing MI 48901

DEFIELD, FRED **(D)**
Mo State Rep
Mailing Add: 203 N Tenth St Charleston MO 63834

DE GAUTIER, FELISA RINCON **(D)**
Dem Nat Committeewoman, PR
m to Jenaro Gautier. Educ: High sch, dipl; Pharm, 1 year. Polit & Govt Pos: Mayoress, San Juan, PR, formerly; mem, Popular Dem Party; pres, Popular Dem Cent Comt, San Juan; deleg, Dem Nat Conv, 60-72; Dem Nat Committeewoman, PR, currently; mem, Dem Nat Charter Comt, currently. Mem: Am Red Cross; YMCA; YWCA; Am Womans Union. Legal Res: Calle de San Juan 51 San Juan PR 00902 Mailing Add: Box 6607 Loiza Station San Juan PR 00914

DEGENARO, ALFRED **(D)**
b New Haven, Conn, Oct 30, 23; s Ralph DeGenaro & Madeline Pediccini D; m 1947 to Eleanor P Dumas; c David, Gary B & Ellen M. Educ: Univ Conn, 45-46, 49-50; Math Club. Polit & Govt Pos: Mem, Sixth Dist Dem Party, Hamden, Conn, 55; mem, Hamden Dem Exec Comt, 56; mem, Hamden Zoning Bd, 57-59; chmn nominating comt, Madison Dem Town Comt, 60-70, chmn, formerly; mem, Madison Zoning Bd, 60-65; mem, Madison Bd Finance, 65-68; area coordr, Mim Daddario for Gov Campaign, 70. Bus & Prof Pos: Registered rep, Hincks Bros, Gruntal & Co, ER Davenport & Co & Amott Baker & Co, 56-; pres, Technol Investments, Inc, Hamden, Conn, 71- Mil Serv: Enlisted as Pvt, Army Air Force, 42. Mem: Soc Advan Mgt; Security-Traders Asn Conn; Eastside Civic Asn Hamden. Relig: Catholic. Mailing Add: 119 Neck Rd Madison CT 06443

DEGNAN, JUNE OPPEN **(D)**
Mem Finance Comt, Calif State Dem Cent Comt
b New York, NY, Jun 7, 18; d George August Oppen & Seville Shainwald O; div; c Aubrey (Mrs Orley Lindgren). Educ: Sorbonne, Paris, Univ Calif; Univ San Francisco. Polit & Govt Pos: Mem finance comt, Calif State Dem Cent Comt, 56-; nat bd mem, Am for Dem Action, DC, 62-; nat finance co-chmn, Sen Eugene McCarthy's Presidential Campaign, 67-68; nat vchmn, Sen George McGovern's Presidential Campaign, 67-68; bd mem, New Dem Coalition, 68-69; deleg, Dem Nat Conv, 68 & 72. Bus & Prof Pos: Publisher, San Francisco Rev, New York & San Francisco, 59-; consult, Int Learning Inst, San Francisco, 69; investor; dir, Int Child Art Ctr, 70; dir, Oceanic Soc, 73; publ, Océans Mag, 74- Mailing Add: 1000 Mason St Apt 1002 San Francisco CA 94108

DEGRAVELLES, CHARLES CAMILLE **(R)**
b Morgan City, La, June 4, 13; m 1935 to Virginia Wheadon; c Mary Alix (Mrs W P Begneaud, Jr), Elizabeth Claire (Mrs Robert A Cloninger), Virginia Ann (Mrs Charles W McBride), and twins Charles Nations & John Wheadon; four grandchildren. Educ: La State Univ, BA, 36. Polit & Govt Pos: Active in pres campaigns, 56-68; state dir, La Rep Party, 67, chmn, 68 & 70-72; deleg, Rep Nat Conv, 68; Rep cand for various local & dist off; Rep Nat Committeeman, La, until 72; chmn, Lafayette Parish Rep Party, formerly. Bus & Prof Pos: Mem staff, land dept, oil co, 37-68; teacher of oil & gas law, Univ of Southwestern La, 55-62; mem of staff, land dept, Pan Am Petroleum Co, currently. Mem: Phi Delta Phi; Kappa Alpha Alumni; Salvation Army. Relig: Episcopal. Mailing Add: 409 Azalea St Lafayette LA 70501

DEGROAT, FRANK HAMILTON **(R)**
Minn State Rep
b Redwood Falls, Minn, May 7, 16; s Frank Isarah DeGroat & Anna Kronk D; m 1935 to Anna Adeline Bengtson; c Marlys (Mrs William Johnson), Barbara (Mrs Raymond Brown), Janice (Mrs Ed Cyr), Joan (Mrs Ron Wilson) & Cheryl. Polit & Govt Pos: Clerk, Becker Co Sch Bd; vchmn, Natural Resources Comt & Agr Comt; chmn, Agr Comn League; Minn State Rep, 63- Mem: Becker Co Farm Bur (pres); Elks; Mason; Eagles; Conserv Club. Honors & Awards: Appreciation Award, Detroit Lakes CofC; Award for Top Herd, Dairy Herd Improv Asn; Extra Yield Award in Corn Prod. Relig: Lutheran. Mailing Add: Lake Park MN 56554

DEGROW, ALVIN JAMES **(R)**
Mich State Sen
b Pigeon, Mich, June 1, 26; s Russell James DeGrow & Vera Harneck D; m 1946 to Judith Haist; c Jane, Michael & David. Educ: Alma Col, 1 year. Polit & Govt Pos: Mich State Sen, 69- Mil Serv: Entered as A/S, Navy, 44, released as Qm 3/C, 46, after serv aboard Landing Ship, Tank, Pac Theatre, 45-46. Mem: Rotary Int; Pigeon CofC. Relig: Methodist. Mailing Add: 600 Camelot Lane Pigeon MI 48755

DEIBERT, RICHARD RAY **(R)**
Chmn, McPherson Co Rep Comt, SDak
b Eureka, SDak, Jan 30, 40; s Raymond Deibert & Christine Sindelar D; m 1962 to Lois Clausen; c Michele & Ryan. Educ: Northern State Col, 58-61. Polit & Govt Pos: Chmn, McPherson Co Rep Comt, SDak, 72-; first ward alderman, Eureka, 73- Bus & Prof Pos: Dir, SDak Auto Dealers Asn, 75- Mil Serv: Entered as Pvt, Army, 62, released as Sgt, 64, after serv in Hq Div Artil, Korean Theatre, 63-64. Mem: Acacia Lodge 108 Mason (Master); Yelduz Shrine; Am Legion Post 186; 40 et 8. Relig: United Church of Christ. Mailing Add: 401 11th St Eureka SD 57437

DEIFE, MARCINE DELORES (R)
Mem, Spokane Co Rep Cent Comt, Wash
b Odessa, Wash, Feb 23, 27; d David Hardung & Mary Hoff H; m 1949 to Robert Deife; c Linda Jo, Julie Ann Evavold, William R, Mark David, Jan Marie & Jean Louise. Educ: Wash State Univ, BA, with distinction, 49; Eastern Wash State Col, MA, 71; Pi Sigma Alpha; Pi Lambda Theta; Delta Gamma. Polit & Govt Pos: Precinct committeewoman, Lincoln Co Rep Cent Comt, 64-68, state committeewoman, Wash State Rep Comt, 67-69; pres, Lincoln Co Rep Women's Club, 66-67; fifth dist dir, Wash Fedn Rep Women, 71-72, mem exec bd, 71-72; campaign coordr, Goldsworthy for State Senate, 72; deleg, Rep Nat Conv, 72; vchmn, Spokane Co Rep Cent Comt, 73- Bus & Prof Pos: Substitute teacher, Odessa Sch Dist, Wash, 49-60; co-owner & co-operator, wheat & cattle ranch, Odessa, 49-; secy-treas, Deife, Inc, 73-; part-time instr, Spokane Community Col, currently. Publ: Auth, A History of the Russian-Germans, Wash State Univ, 49. Mem: League of Women Voters; Delta Gamma Alumnae; Spokane Symphony Women's Asn; Wash Asn Wheatgrowers; PTA. Relig: Protestant. Mailing Add: E 11211 23rd Spokane WA 99206

DEITZ, WILLIAM THOMAS (D)
b Matawan, NJ, June 13, 26; s Harold Gregory Deitz (deceased) & Vincena Kennedy D; m 1950 to Mary Elizabeth Creamer; c Alissa & Randolph. Educ: Rutgers Univ, LittB, 53; George Washington Univ Sch of Law, JD, 68; Phi Beta Kappa; Kappa Tau Alpha. Polit & Govt Pos: Admin asst to US Rep Frank Thompson, Jr, NJ, 63- Bus & Prof Pos: Third & second deck officer, Standard Oil Co, NJ, 46-49; reporter, Asbury Park Press, NJ, 53 & 54, state house correspondent, 54-63. Mil Serv: Entered as A/S, Navy, 43, released as Qm 1/C, 46, after serv in Naval Training Sta, RI & USS LST 656, Atlantic, Mediter & Pac Theatres; Battle Star; Invasion Southern France. Mem: Bar of the Dist of Columbia; NJ Legis Correspondents Club. Relig: Roman Catholic. Legal Res: 589 Bellevue Ave Trenton NJ 08618 Mailing Add: 3300 Elmore Dr Alexandria VA 22302

DE KOSTER, LUCAS JAMES (R)
Iowa State Sen
b Hull, Iowa, June 18, 18; s John De Koster & Sarah K Poppen D; m 1942 to Dorothea LaVonne Hymans; c Sarah Kay, Jacqueline Anne, John Gordon, Claire Ellen & Mary Denise. Educ: Iowa State Univ, BS in Mech Eng, 39; Cleveland Marshall Law Sch, LLB cum laude, 49; Phi Kappa Phi; Delta Theta Phi. Polit & Govt Pos: Iowa State Sen, 65- Mem: Am & Iowa State Bar Asns; Kiwanis. Relig: Reformed Church in America. Legal Res: 404 Center St Hull IA 51239 Mailing Add: 1106 Main St Hull IA 51239

DE LA GARZA, E (KIKA) (D)
US Rep, Tex
b Mercedes, Tex, Sept 22, 27; s Dario De La Garza & Elisa Villarreal G; m 1953 to Lucille Alamia; c Jorge, Michael & Angela. Educ: Edinburg Jr Col, Tex; St Mary's Univ, LLB, 52; Delta Theta Phi. Polit & Govt Pos: Tex State Rep, 52-64; US Rep, Tex, 65- Bus & Prof Pos: Attorney. Mil Serv: Seaman 1/C, Navy, 44; 2nd Lt, Army, 50-52. Mem: Mission, McAllen & Rio Grande Valley CofC; Am Legion; CWV (past Nat Judge Advocate). Relig: Catholic. Legal Res: 1812 Cummings Mission TX 78572 Mailing Add: US House of Rep Washington DC 20515

DELAHANTY, GEORGE EMMETT (R)
Mem, Orange Co Rep Cent Comt, Calif
b San Francisco, Calif, Feb 3, 16; s George Emmett Delahanty, Sr & Myrtle May Herlitz D; m 1943 to Dorothy Ella Steigerwald; c Kathleen (Mrs Emanuele) & Richard George. Educ: Am Inst Banking, grad, 38. Polit & Govt Pos: Mem, Orange Co Rep Cent Comt, Calif, 64-, chmn, formerly; mem, Rep State Cent Comt, 64-69; gov, Orange Co United Rep Calif, 66-68, state treas, 66-68; mem, Rep Assocs, 66-69; mem, Calif Collection Agency Adv Bd, 67-69, chmn, 69-; alt deleg, Rep Nat Conv, 72; mem adv bd, Bur Collection & Investigative Serv, State of Calif, currently. Bus & Prof Pos: Banker, Bank of Am, 35-38 & 46-51; banker, United Calif Bank, Los Angeles, 38-42; pres, Transcontinental Credit Serv, Inc, Fullerton, Calif, 51- Mil Serv: Entered as Pvt, Air Force, 43, released as S/Sgt, 46, after serv in 25th Bomb Group, 69th Bomb Squadron, Sixth Air Force, 43-44; Victory Medal; Am Theater Ribbon; Serv Stripe; Good Conduct Medal. Mem: Calif Asn Collectors; Am Collectors Asn; CofC; Kiwanis; Elks. Honors & Awards: Outstanding Citizen Award, Fullerton CofC, 54, Cert of Merit, 56-57; Outstanding Citizen Award, Orange Co Fedn Community Chests, 55; Merit Citation; Assoc CofC Orange Co, 60; Cert Award, Orange Co Rep Cent Comt, 66. Relig: Catholic. Legal Res: 2500 Coronado Dr Fullerton CA 92632 Mailing Add: 213 N Pomona Fullerton CA 92632

DELAHUNT, WILLIAM D (D)
Mass State Rep
Mailing Add: State Capitol Boston MA 02133

DELANEY, CHARLES LAWRENCE (D)
Vt State Sen
b Swanton, Vt, Nov 14, 23; m to Carolyn Strauch; c two sons, five daughters. Educ: Miss State Col. Polit & Govt Pos: Vt State Rep, 59; Vt State Sen, 61-72 & 75-; secy, Colchester Fire Dist Two; mem, Colchester Zoning Bd of Adjust & Reapportionment Comn. Bus & Prof Pos: Restaurant owner. Mil Serv: Army Med Corps, SPac Theatre, World War II, S/Sgt. Mem: Elks; VFW; KofC (4 degree); Burlington Downtown Athletic Club. Relig: Catholic. Mailing Add: RD 3 Winooski VT 05404

DELANEY, FRANCES I (DFL)
Vice Chairwoman, Second Cong Dist Dem-Farmer-Labor Party, Minn
b Pipestone, Minn, May 21, 00; d Peter Casper Haubrich & Clara Bell Riffel H; wid; c James B & Francis D. Educ: High Sch; Bus Col, Sioux Falls, SDak. Polit & Govt Pos: Chairwoman, Pipestone Co Dem-Farmer-Labor Party, 40-66; past chairwoman, Seventh Dist Dem-Farmer-Labor Party; vice chairwoman, Second Cong Dist Dem-Farmer-Labor Party, currently; alt deleg, Dem Nat Conv, 68. Bus & Prof Pos: Former secy for Co Treas, Mitchell, SDak; teacher; census supvr, Nine Counties, Minn, 50; ins secy, Nat Mutual Benefit, Madison, Wis, currently. Mem: Catholic Daughters; Am Legion Auxiliary; VFW Auxiliary; Dem-Farmer-Labor Women's Club. Relig: Catholic. Mailing Add: 18 Elbon Dr Pipestone MN 56164

DELANEY, JAMES J (D)
US Rep, NY
b New York, NY, Mar 19, 01; married; c Patrick. Polit & Govt Pos: Asst dist attorney, Queens Co, NY, 9 years; US Rep, NY, 44-45 & 48-; deleg, Dem Nat Mid-Term Conf, 74. Bus & Prof Pos: Lawyer. Legal Res: Long Island City NY Mailing Add: 2267 Rayburn House Off Bldg Washington DC 20515

DE LA VERGNE, HUGHES JULES, II (R)
b New Orleans, La, Feb 18, 31; s Charles Edouard de la Vergne & Marcelle Menard V; m 1966 to Beatrice Blanche Badger; c Hugues J, III. Educ: Univ Notre Dame, 48-49; Tulane Univ, BA, 53, LLB, 57; Delta Kappa Epsilon. Polit & Govt Pos: Committeeman, Orleans Parish Rep Party, Wards 12 & 13, 58-, chmn, Ward 14, 72-; chmn, Young Rep Fedn La Inc, 59-62; deleg, Rep Nat Conv, 60, deleg & mem rules comt, 64, alt deleg, 68; secy, La State Rep Cent Comt, 63-72. Bus & Prof Pos: Partner, de la Vergne & Meyers, 57-; secy-treas, Bd of Comn of Liberty Place, 59-; vpres, Mentab, Inc, partner, Lake Properties & partner, Lake Develop Co, currently. Mil Serv: Entered as Ens SC, Navy, 53, released as Lt(jg), 55, after serv in Amphibious Forces, Atlantic Fleet, 54-55. Mem: New Orleans & La Bar Asns; Statford Club; Pickwick Club; Sons of the Revolution. Relig: Roman Catholic. Mailing Add: 4010 St Charles Ave New Orleans LA 70115

DEL BANE, MICHAEL (D)
Ohio State Rep
Mailing Add: 125 Christian Ave Hubbard OH 44425

DELCO, WILHELMINA RUTH (D)
Tex State Rep
b Chicago, Ill; d William Patrick Fitzgerald & Juanita Heath F; m 1952 to Exalton A Delco, Jr; c Deborah Diane, Exalton A, III, Loretta Elmirle & Cheryl Pauline. Educ: Fisk Univ, BA, 50; Alpha Kappa Delta; Delta Kappa Gamma; Alpha Kappa Alpha. Polit & Govt Pos: Trustee, Austin Independent Sch Dist, Tex, 68-72; deleg, Dem Nat Mid-Term Conf, 74; Tex State Rep, Travis Co, 75- Bus & Prof Pos: Serv rep, Ill Bell Tel Co, 50-52. Publ: Auth, Opportunities and responsibilities for developing human resources, Lib Educ, 69. Mem: Jack & Jill of Am. Honors & Awards: Outstanding Woman, Austin Am Statesman, 69; Liberty Bell Award, Austin Jr Bar Asn, 69; Appreciation Award, NAACP, 71, Arthur DeWitty Award, 72. Relig: Catholic. Legal Res: 1805 Astor Pl Austin TX 78721 Mailing Add: PO Box 2910 Capitol Sta Austin TX 78767

DELCOUR, DAVID W (R)
b St Louis, Mo, Dec 27, 43; s W T Delcour & Mary Eiermann; m 1970 to Susan Kathleen Johnson. Educ: Univ Colo, BA, 65, JD, 68; Pi Sigma Alpha; Phi Alpha Delta. Polit & Govt Pos: Law clerk, Hon Orie Phillips, Judge US Court of Appeals, Tenth Circuit, 68-69; legis asst to US Rep Don Brotzman, Colo, 69-72, admin asst, 73-74. Bus & Prof Pos: Attorney, Amav, Inc, currently. Mem: Am & Colo Bar Asns. Mailing Add: 11042 W Oregon Pl Denver CO 80226

DELEO, JAMES ANTHONY (D)
b Port Townsend, Wash, June 26, 22; s Antonio DeLeo & Grace Sofie D; m 1943 to Dorothy Leadie Sisson; c Terrance J & Linda Ann (Mrs Frank Cassalary). Educ: High sch grad. Polit & Govt Pos: Precinct committeeman, Wash Dem Party, 55-; chmn, Jefferson Co Dem Party, 56-65; committeeman, Wash State Dem Party, formerly; alt deleg, Dem Nat Conv, 68. Bus & Prof Pos: Partner, DeLeo Bros, 47- Mil Serv: Entered as A/S, Coast Guard, 40, released as BM 1/C, 46, after serv in Pac; Pre-Pearl Harbor, Pac Theatre, Good Conduct & Asiatic Theatre Medals. Mem: Elks; Am Legion; Vol Fire Dept; VFW; CofC. Honors & Awards: Man of Year, CofC, 64. Relig: Catholic. Mailing Add: 1005 Quincy Port Townsend WA 98368

DELEZENE, LARRY KEITH (R)
b Kirksville, Mo, Apr 6, 33; s Dr Edward William Delezene & Marian Beatrice Watson D; m 1960 to Martha Lou Snider; c Stephen Craig & Diana Sue. Educ: Southeast Mo State Col, 51; Univ of Mo, 52; Gradwohl Sch of Med Technol, 57; Kappa Alpha. Polit & Govt Pos: Chmn, Madison Co Rep Party, Mo, formerly. Bus & Prof Pos: Pres, Khoury League, Madison Co, Mo, 61-62; co-owner, bowling alley. Mil Serv: Entered as Airman 3/C, Air Force, 53, released as Airman 2/C, 57, after serv in Northeast Air Command, NAtlantic, 55; Good Conduct Medal; Air Force Res, 57-61. Mem: Boy Scouts; Mo Med Technologists Soc; Am Soc Med Technologists; Am Med Technologists; Int Registry Med Technologists. Honors & Awards: Serv Award, Bd of Gov, Khoury Asn of Baseball. Relig: Christian Church; Deacon. Mailing Add: Box 446 Fredericktown MO 63645

DELGADO, VERNON THOMAS (R)
Chmn, Sublette Co Rep Cent Comt, Wyo
b Rock Springs, Wyo, Apr 3, 32; s Thomas Charles Delgado & Florence Kenyon D; m 1953 to Mildred Arlene Logan; c Thomas, Mark, David & Michael. Educ: Univ Utah, BS in Bus Admin, 50; Kappa Sigma. Polit & Govt Pos: Vpres, Wyo State Bd Educ, 63-66, chmn, 66-68; chmn, Sublette Co Rep Cent Comt, 67- Bus & Prof Pos: Chmn bd, First Nat Bank of Pinedale, 63-; pres, West Utility Co, Inc, 69- Mil Serv: Army, 54. Mem: Nat Asn State Bd Educ; Elks; VFW. Relig: Protestant. Mailing Add: PO Box 66 Pinedale WY 82941

DEL GRECO, JOSEPH FRANCIS (R)
Chmn, Revere Rep City Comt, Mass
b Revere, Mass, Mar 27, 40; s Elio Del Greco & Josephine M Vellucci D; m 1963 to Marie Elizabeth Mastrain; c Adriana. Educ: Harvard Univ, Adult Educ, 68; La Salle Exten Univ, 70- Polit & Govt Pos: City chmn, Comt to Elect John A Volpe Gov of Mass, 64; mem comt on parties & polit, Rep Nat Conv, 64 & 68; deleg, Mass Rep State Conv, 67-73; city chmn, Comt to Elect John W Sears Sheriff of Suffolk Co, Mass, 68; city chmn, Comt to Elect Francis W Sargent Gov of Mass, 72; chmn, Revere Rep City Comt, 72- Bus & Prof Pos: Dep sheriff, Suffolk Co, Mass, 68-69; investr, Dept of Pub Utilities, 69-70; inspector, Metrop Dist Comn, 70-73. Mil Serv: Entered as Pvt, Army, 59, released as SP-4, 62, after serv in 56th Brigade Hq, First Army Area, 60-62; Good Conduct Medal; Expert in Rifle. Mem: Order of Sons of Italy in Am; Italian-Am New Deal; St Anthony Holy Name Soc. Honors & Awards: Generous contributions and coop in assisting our children, PTA, 64. Relig: Roman Catholic. Mailing Add: 2 Burnham St Revere MA 02151

DELK, JOSEPH CLAY, III (D)
Third VChmn, Randolph Co Dem Party, NC
b Asheboro, NC, July 2, 50; s Joseph Clay Delk, Jr & Lillian Hodgin D; single. Educ: Oxford Univ, 71; Davidson Col, BA, 72; NC State Univ, MPA, 73; Sigma Chi; Alpha Phi Omega. Polit & Govt Pos: Deleg, Dem Nat Conv, 72; third vchmn, Randolph Co Dem Party, NC, 72-; bill clerk, NC Gen Assembly, 73- Honors & Awards: Dana Scholar, Davidson Col, 70-72. Relig: Methodist. Mailing Add: 1825 Raleigh Rd Asheboro NC 27203

DELLA, GEORGE WASHINGTON (D)
b Baltimore, Md, Feb 9, 08; s George W Della, Jr, & Ida M Hill D; m 1936 to Agnes Helene Mattare; c George W, IV, Mary E & Howard R. Educ: Univ Baltimore, BBA & LLB. Polit & Govt Pos: Md State Sen, 39-51 & 55-58, pres, Md State Senate, 51-54 & 59-62; deleg, Dem Nat Conv, 68 & 72. Mem: Md, Baltimore City & Am Bar Asns; Boumi Temple (past potentate, 59); AF&AM (past master, Corinthian Lodge 93, 43). Relig: Episcopal. Legal Res: 403 Warren Ave Baltimore MD 21230 Mailing Add: Della & Wyatt Suite 1115 10 Light St Baltimore MD 21202

DELLENBACK, JOHN (R)
b Chicago, Ill, Nov 6, 18; s William H Dellenback & Margaret Albright D; m 1948 to Mary Jane Benedict; c Richard, David & Barbara. Educ: Yale Univ, BS in Appl Econ Sci, 40; Univ Mich Law Sch, JD, 49; Phi Beta Kappa; Order of the Coif. Polit & Govt Pos: Ore State Rep, Jackson Co, 61-66; US Rep, Ore, 66-74; deleg, Rep Nat Conv, 64, 68 & 72; assoc dir, ACTION for Int Opers, 75- Bus & Prof Pos: Bus training student, Gen Elec Co, 40-42; asst prof bus law, Ore State Univ, 49-51; partner, Van Dyke, Dellenback, McGoodwin & DuBay, 51-66. Mil Serv: Entered as Ens, Navy, 42, released as Lt Comdr, 46, after serv in USS Yorktown, Pac; Pac Ribbon & Two Battle Stars; Presidential Unit Citation. Mem: Lewis & Clark Col (bd trustees); Yale Alumni Rep for Southwestern Ore; Mason; Elks; Ore State Soc (pres, 72-73). Relig: Presbyterian; Mem Permanent Judicial Comn Gen Assembly & Comn on Ecumenical Mission and Rels, United Presbyterian Church. Legal Res: 300 Windsor Ave Medford OR 97501 Mailing Add: ACTION for Int Opers 806 Connecticut Ave Washington DC 20525

DELLIBOVI, ALFRED A (R)
NY State Assemblyman
b Queens Co, NY, Feb 1, 46. Educ: Fordham Col, BA, 67; Baruch Col, MPA, 73. Polit & Govt Pos: Admin asst, NY State Assemblyman, Alfred D Lerner, 66-69; asst, Assembly Speaker, Perry B Duryea, Jr, 69; mem research staff, Joint Legis Comt on Problems of Aging, NY Gen Assembly; NY State Assemblyman, 71-, mem, Child Abuse, Commercial Indust & Econ Develop, Social Serv & City of NY Comts, NY Gen Assembly; mem, Queens Co Rep Comt, 72- Bus & Prof Pos: Mem faculty, Mater Christi Diocesan High Sch, Astoria, NY. Mem: Queens Co Taxpayers Asn, Inc (md dirs); Richmond Hill Rep Club; Sons of Italy (bd trustees, Bus & Prof Lodge 2269); NY Gen Attorney Task Force to Protect the Wetlands; Brookwood Gunners & Anglers Asn. Honors & Awards: Nominated to attend conf of young polit leaders in Soviet Union, Sen James L Buckley, 72. Legal Res: 114-13 111th Ave Ozone Park NY 11420 Mailing Add: Cent Dist Off 119-06 101st Ave Richmond Hill NY 11419

DELLINGER, RICHARD M (R)
Ind State Rep
Mailing Add: 140 N 15th St Noblesville IN 46060

DELLUMS, RONALD V (D)
US Rep, Calif
b Oakland, Calif, Nov 24, 35; m to Leola Roscoe Higgs; c 5. Educ: Oakland City Col, AA, 58; San Francisco State Col, BA, 60; Univ Calif, MSW, 62. Polit & Govt Pos: Mem, Berkeley City Coun, Calif, 67-71; US Rep, Calif, Eighth Dist, 71- Bus & Prof Pos: Psychiat social worker, Dept Ment Hygiene, 62-64; prog dir, Bayview Community Ctr, 64-65; from assoc dir to dir, Hunters Point Youth Opportunity Ctr, 65-66; planning consult, Bay Area Social Planning Coun, 66-67; dir, Concentrated Employment Prog, San Francisco Econ Opportunity Coun, 67-68; sr consult, Social Dynamics, Inc, 68-70; part-time lectr, San Francisco State Col, Univ Calif & Berkeley Grad Sch Social Welfare. Mil Serv: Marine Corps, 2 years. Legal Res: 53 Fairlawn Dr Berkeley CA 94708 Mailing Add: US House of Rep Washington DC 20515

DELOGU, ORLANDO E (D)
Mem, Cumberland Co Dem Comt, Maine
b New York, NY, Feb 4, 37; s Mr Delogu (deceased) & Magdalene Drummer D; m 1960 to Judith Sara Darke; c Sara, Jon, Joseph & Daisy. Educ: Univ Utah, BS, 60; Univ Wis, MS, 63 & JD, 66; Sigma Chi. Polit & Govt Pos: Bd mem, Dept Environ Protection, Maine, 69-; alt deleg, Dem Nat Conv, 72; mem, Portland Dem City Comt, 72-; mem, Cumberland Co Dem Comt, 72- Bus & Prof Pos: Prof law, Univ Maine, 66- Mil Serv: Entered as 2nd Lt, Army, 60, released as 1st Lt, 62, after serv in 5th Army, Ft Leonard Wood, Mo, Inf Training Post. Publ: Legal aspects of air pollution control & proposed state legislation of such control, Wis Law Rev, 69; Land use control principles applied to offshore coastal waters, Ky Law J, 71; A state implementation approach to effluent charge, Maine Law Rev, 71. Legal Res: 33 Storer St Portland ME 04102 Mailing Add: 246 Deering Ave Portland ME 04102

DELONG, DELMAR (R)
Wis State Rep
b Clinton, Wis, June 7, 31; s William DeLong; m to MaryBelle. Educ: Univ Wis, BA, 52 & JD, 66. Polit & Govt Pos: Pres, Clinton Bd Educ, Wis, 68-73; vchmn, Bd Control, Coop Educ Serv Agency, 72-73; mem, Rock Co Bd of Adjust; mem, Clinton Village Bd, 58-60; Wis State Rep, 73- Mil Serv: 1st Lt, Army, served in Transportation Corps. Mem: Kiwanis Club; Jaycees; Am Bar Asn; Wis Cattlemen's Asn; Sinnissippi Coun of Boy Scouts (vpres). Relig: Lutheran. Legal Res: Rte 2 Clinton WI 53525 Mailing Add: Assembly Chambers State Capitol Madison WI 53702

DEL PADRE, DONALD EDWARD (R)
Chmn, West Warwick Rep Town Comt, RI
b Providence, RI, Oct 21, 36; s John Henry Del Padre, Sr & Isabel Leamy D; m 1966 to Ann Anastasia Esposito; c Michael Anthony & Mark Edward. Educ: Johnson & Wales Col, dipl, 60. Polit & Govt Pos: RI State Rep, 71-72; chmn, West Warwick Rep Town Comt, 75- Bus & Prof Pos: Comptroller, Guill Tool & Eng Co, Inc, 74- Mil Serv: Entered as Pvt, Marine Corps Res, 54, released as Cpl, 60, after serv in 2nd 155 Howitzer Bn, Fields Point, Providence, RI. Relig: Roman Catholic. Mailing Add: 92 Shady Hill Dr West Warwick RI 02893

DELPERCIO, MATTHEW D (D)
Conn State Rep
Mailing Add: 114 Maple St Bridgeport CT 06608

DELPHEY, JULIEN PAUL (R)
Md State Deleg
b Frederick, Md, Dec 16, 17; s Joseph Paul Delphey & Ethel Hemp D; m 1944 to Laura Roe; c Jay Paul & Julia Ruth. Educ: Frederick High Sch, grad, 37; Spec Bus Courses, 44-45. Polit & Govt Pos: Md State Deleg, 71- Bus & Prof Pos: Owner & mgr, Delphey's Sport Store, Frederick, Md, 39-; dir adv bd, Md Nat Bank. Mil Serv: Entered as Pvt, Army, 43, released as Tech 5th Grade, 46, after serv in Signal Corps, Hq & Hq Detachment, 1341st Serv Command Unit, 43-46; Good Conduct Medal; Am Theatre Ribbon; World War II Victory Ribbon. Mem: Lions; Isaac Walton League; Frederick Co Farm Bur; CofC; Agr Soc & Fish & Game Protective Asn. Relig: Methodist. Mailing Add: 222 Carroll Pkwy Frederick MD 21701

DEL TORO, ANGELO (D)
NY State Assemblyman
b New York, NY, Apr 16, 47; s Dionisio Del Toro & Virginia Hernandez D; single. Educ: City Col New York, BA, 68; NY Law Sch, JD, 72. Polit & Govt Pos: Dist leader & vchmn, New York Co Dem Comt, NY, 73-; NY State Assemblyman, 75- Relig: Episcopal. Mailing Add: 129 E 106th St New York NY 10029

DEL TUFO, GERARDO L (R)
b Newark, NJ, Nov 6, 09; s Gerardo Del Tufo & Carmella Luongo D; m 1936 to Josephine Ceraso; c Gerard A & Ronald J. Polit & Govt Pos: Property supvr, NJ Dept Pub Welfare; secy to Majority Leader, NJ State Assembly; secy to State Sen, NJ State Senate; NJ State Assemblyman, Trenton; mem, Newark Bd of Educ; NJ State Sen, Trenton, 68-74; deleg, Rep Nat Conv, 72. Bus & Prof Pos: Lawyer. Relig: Catholic. Mailing Add: 510 Highland Ave Newark NJ 07104

DE LUGO, RONALD (D)
VI Deleg, US House of Rep
b Englewood, NJ, Aug 2, 30; s Angelo de Lugo & Adelaide de L; m 1958 to Maria Morales; c Maria Cristina & Angela Maria. Educ: Colegio San Jose, PR & St Peter & Paul High Sch, St Thomas, VI. Polit & Govt Pos: Campaign mgr, Dem Party of VI, 54; deleg, Dem Nat Conv, 56-68; VI State Sen, 56-66; mem, Dem Nat Comt, 59-61; mem, Presidential Inaugural Comt, 60; adminr, Island of St Croix, VI, 61; VI Rep, Washington, DC, 69-73; VI Deleg, US House of Rep, 73-; ex officio, Dem Nat Mid-Term Conf, 74. Bus & Prof Pos: Prog dir, WSTA Radio, Charlotte Amalie, St Thomas, 50-54 & WIVI, Christiansted, St Croix, 55- Mil Serv: Entered Army, 48, released, 50, after serv in Armed Forces Radio Serv. Mem: Nat Capital Dem Club. Honors & Awards: Man of the Year, NY Prof League, 52; Distinguished Serv Award, US VI Mainland Soc, 69. Legal Res: Christiansted VI Mailing Add: 1217 Longworth House Off Bldg Washington DC 20515

DELURY, BERNARD EDWARD (R)
Asst Secy Employ Standards, Dept Labor
b Brooklyn, NY, Apr 1, 38; s John Joseph DeLury & Margaret Teresa Donnelly D; m 1959 to Jane Frances Sheldon; c Bernard E, Kevin J, Laura J & John B. Educ: St John's Univ (NY), BA, 60; C W Post Col, 67-71; Alpha Sigma Lambda; Pi Gamma Mu. Polit & Govt Pos: Spec proj asst to Comnr Labor, New York, NY, 67-70, Asst Indust Comnr, 70-72, Dep Indust Comnr, 72; mem, Queens Co Rep Comt, 72-73; asst secy employ standards, Dept Labor, 73- Bus & Prof Pos: Foreman, Local 46 Lather's Int Union, New York, 59-55; asst adminr, Local 831 Int Brotherhood Teamsters, 66-67; dir orgn, Queens Community Labor Comn, 68-72; mem labor adv bd, Nassau Co Voc Educ Exten Bd, 70-73. Mem: Nassau Civic Club; Republican Club; NY State Gov Club. Legal Res: NY Mailing Add: Dept of Labor Washington DC 20210

DEL VALLE ESCOBAR, MIGUEL A (POPULAR DEMOCRAT, PR)
Rep, PR House of Rep
Mailing Add: State Capitol San Juan PR 00901

DELYANNIS, LEONIDAS T (R)
Mem, Arlington Co Rep Comt, Va
b Athens, Greece, Nov 8, 26; s Theodore L Delyannis & Xanthi Mamouri-Goura D; m 1957 to Georgia H Alexander; c Theodore L & Harry L. Educ: Greek Mil Acad, Athens, BS, 47; Greek Tech Mil Col, Athens, BSCE, 54; Univ Ill, Urbana, MS, 58. Polit & Govt Pos: Mem, Broyhill for Cong Campaign Comt, Tenth Dist, Va, 64-72; chmn, Greek-Am for Nixon-Agnew in Va, 68; chmn, Greek-Am for Holton for Gov, Va, 69; mem hospitality comt, Nixon-Agnew Inaugural Comt, 69; chmn, Va State Nationalities Coun, 70-; mem, Arlington Co Rep Comt, 70-, mem finance comt, 72; alt deleg-at-lg, Rep Nat Conv, 72; mem, Scott-for-Senate & Broyhill-for-Cong Finance Comt, 72; mem, Nixon-Agnew Inaugural Comt, & chmn comt on mkt & distribution & co-chmn liaison comt for Agnew reception, 73; second vchmn, Nat Rep Heritage Groups Coun, 73- Bus & Prof Pos: Chief struct engr, Ben Dyer & Assoc, Hyattsville, Md, 58-60; chief bridge engr, David Volkert & Assoc, Washington, DC, 60-70; prin owner, L T Delyannis & Assocs, Arlington, Va, 70- Mil Serv: Entered Greek Army, released as Capt, 56, after serv in Corps of Engrs. Publ: Co-ed, First international symposium on concrete bridge design, 67, ed, Second international symposium on concrete bridge design, 69 & auth, Past & future in the design & construction of concrete bridges, 67, Am Concrete Inst. Mem: Am Soc Civil Engrs; Soc Am Mil Engrs; Am Concrete Inst; Va & Nat Soc of Prof Engrs. Relig: Greek Orthodox; Bd mem, St Katherine's Greek Orthodox Church. Mailing Add: 2350 N Taylor St Arlington VA 22207

DELYRE, ELVA W (R)
b Urbana, Ill, Nov 14, 08; d Luther Albert Martin & Bertha Scovil M; m 1948 to Dr Wolf Robert DeLyre. Educ: Univ Ill, Urbana, BS, 30, MS, 37; Delta Zeta. Polit & Govt Pos: Mem bd dirs, Los Angeles Co Rep Women Federated, Calif, 60, 72-; pres, Long Beach Coun Rep Women, 68 & 72; mem bd dirs, Southern Calif Rep Women, Federated, 69-70; assoc mem, Rep State Cent Comt Calif, 69-72, mem, 73-; deleg, Rep Nat Conv, 72; alt mem, 32nd Cong Dist Rep Cent Comt, 73; women's chmn, Flournoy for Gov, 74. Bus & Prof Pos: High sch teacher, Ill, 30-47. Mem: Beta Gamma Sigma; Gamma Epsilon Pi; Phi Chi Theta; Assistance League of Long Beach; Harbor Dent Auxiliary. Honors & Awards: Award Cert for Serv to Rep Party, Los Angeles Co Rep Cent Comt, 73. Relig: United Methodist. Mailing Add: 1100 El Mirador Ave Long Beach CA 90815

DE MARCO, JAMES GARFIELD (R)
Chmn, Burlington Co Rep Comt, NJ
b Hammonton, NJ, July 29, 38; s Anthony R De Marco & Gladys C Alloway D; single. Educ: Dartmouth Col, BA, 59; Yale Law Sch, LLB, 64; Phi Beta Kappa. Polit & Govt Pos: Mem, Water Policy & Supply Coun, NJ Dept Environ Protection, 68-75; chmn, Pinelands Environ Coun, NJ, 72-; chmn, Burlington Co Rep Comt, 74- Bus & Prof Pos: Dir, Ocean Spray Cranberries, Inc, 70-73 & Guarantee Bank & Trust Co Inc, 70- Mem: Nat Cranberry Mkt Comt (chmn, 74-); Am Cranberry Growers Asn (pres, 69-70, dir, 69-); Atlantic Co Blueberry

Growers Asn (dir, 69-); Am Bar Asn; Burlington Co Bd Agr. Legal Res: Barnegat Rd Chatsworth NJ 08019 Mailing Add: PO Box 204 Hammonton NJ 08037

DEMARCUS, WILLIAM HAROLD (R)
Ky State Rep
b Wilton, Ky, Feb 4, 13; s John A DeMarcus & Dorthy Brock D; m 1932 to Elizabeth Edwards; c William Harold, Jr, John Preston, Frank Edwin & David Russell. Educ: Sue Bennett Col, Ky; Univ Ky. Polit & Govt Pos: Councilman, London City Coun, Ky, 34-46; deleg, Rep Nat Conv, 64; Ky State Rep, 64-, Rep Whip, Ky House Rep, 64-65; Rep Floor Leader, 71-72; chmn, Lincoln Co Rep Party, currently; mem, Ky Rep State Comt, 66- Mem: Stanford Rotary Club; Stanford CofC; Mason; Farm Bur. Honors & Awards: Chosen as best orator in House, Capital Press, 70-72. Relig: Christian Church. Mailing Add: Rte 2 Stanford KY 40484

DEMAREE, GERALDINE (D)
b Hamilton Co, Ind, Oct 9, 26; d Paul Nightenhelser & Clarice Dunn N; m 1946 to Herald A Demaree; c Jason Kirk. Educ: Ball State Teachers Col, BS, 48; Univ Mont, MA, 51. Polit & Govt Pos: Precinct committeewoman, Hamilton Co Dem Party, Ind, 68-; deleg, Ind Dem State Conv, 70; Dem nominee, Ind State Sen, 70; deleg & mem platform comt, Dem Nat Conv, 72; deleg, Dem Nat Mid-Term Conf, 74. Bus & Prof Pos: Teacher & chmn dept social studies, Tipton High Sch, Ind, 63- Mem: Nat & Ind Coun Social Studies; Ind State Teachers Asn; Nat Educ Asn; Delta Kappa Gamma. Relig: Protestant. Mailing Add: RR 1 Box 48 Atlanta IN 46031

DEMASO, HARRY A (R)
Mich State Sen
b Battle Creek, Mich, Feb 24, 21; m 1947 to Mary Jayne Hocott; c David, Ray & Thomas Eugene. Educ: Argubright Col; Mich State Univ. Polit & Govt Pos: Supvr, Battle Creek Twp, Mich, 52-65; mem, Calhoun Co Bd of Supvrs, 52-65; Mich State Rep, 56-66; Mich State Sen, 67-; past pres & secy-treas, Calhoun Co Chap, Mich Twp Asn; former chmn, Calhoun Co Planning Comt, Calhoun Co Civil Defense Comt, Battle Creek Area Govt Coun & Coord Coun on Govt Prob; exec dir & former chmn, Calhoun Co Safety Comt; gen chmn, Mich State Asn of Supvrs Comt on the Const Conv; chmn, Community Armory Site Comt; mem, Health & Welfare Comt of Nat Asn of Co Officials & Mich Crime & Delinquency Coun Tech Comt. Mil Serv: Army Air Corps. Mem: F&AM (past Master, Battle Creek Lodge 12); Eastern Star; Mason (32 degree); life mem VFW. Honors & Awards: Outstanding Serv Awards, Fraternal Order of Police, Mich, 62; Mich Probate Judges & Juvenile Officers Asn, 62 & Keep Mich Beautiful, Inc, 64; Selected Alumni of the Year, Argubright Col, 62; hon Legion of Honor, DeMolay, 64. Relig: Methodist. Mailing Add: 40 S LaVista Blvd Battle Creek MI 49015

DEMBLING, PAUL GERALD
Gen Counsel, US Gen Acct Off
b Rahway, NJ, Jan 11, 20; s Simon Dembling & Fannie Ellenbogen D; m 1947 to Florence Brotman; c Ross Wayne, Douglas Evan & Donna Stacy. Educ: Rutgers Univ, BA, 40, MA, 42; George Washington Univ Law Sch, JD, 51; Phi Delta Phi; Tau Kappa Alpha; Scarlet Barbs. Polit & Govt Pos: Mem staff indust rels, War Dept, 42-45 & NACA, 46-51; spec counsel legal adv & gen counsel, Nat Adv Comt Aeronaut, 51-58; chmn bd contract appeals, NASA, 58-61; asst gen counsel, 58-61; vchmn inventions & contrib bd, 59-63; asst admin legis affairs, 61-63, dep gen counsel, 63-67; gen counsel, 67-69; gen counsel, US Gen Acct Off, 69- Bus & Prof Pos: Grad asst & teaching fel, Rutgers Univ, 40-42; ed-in-chief, Fed Bar J, 62-69; prof lectr, George Washington Univ Nat Law Ctr, 65- Publ: Space law and the United Nations, Vol 32, No 3, 66 & The evolution of the outer space treaty, Vol 33, Nov 3, 67, J Air Law & Com; The treaty on rescue & return of astronauts & space objects, Col of William & Mary Law Rev, Vol 9, No 3, 68. Mem: Am & Fed Bar Asns; Int Inst Space Law (pres, 70-72); Am Trial Lawyers Asn; fel Am Inst Aeronaut & Astronaut. Honors & Awards: Army Civilian Meritorious Award; NASA Distinguished Serv Medal; Nat Civil Serv League Award. Legal Res: 6303 Tone Dr Bethesda MD 20034 Mailing Add: 441 G St NW Washington DC 20548

DEMEDIO, A J (D)
Pa State Rep
Mailing Add: Capitol Bldg Harrisburg PA 17120

DEMENNATO, PAUL C (D)
Conn State Rep
Mailing Add: 27 Fortune Dr North Haven CT 06473

DEMERELL, JOHN N (R)
Conn State Rep
Mailing Add: PO Box 252 Essex CT 06426

DEMERS, DANIEL J (D)
Nev State Assemblyman
Mailing Add: 231 Edelweiss Pl Mt Charleston Las Vegas NV 89100

DEMERS, RICHARD H (D)
Mass State Rep
b Chicopee, Mass, Jan 19, 28; s Harry Demers & Josephine Babala D; m 1950 to Lauria C Piquette; c Richard F, Lynette C, Robert Paul, Kenneth Edward & Thomas Alan. Educ: Holyoke Jr Col, AA, 52; Western New Eng Col, 3 years. Polit & Govt Pos: Mem sch comt, City of Chicopee, Mass, 58-60, assessor, 60-66; mayor, 66-70; Mass State Rep, 71- Bus & Prof Pos: Owner, Glenwood Hardware Co, 58-66. Mil Serv: Entered as Pvt, Marine Corps, 46, released as Pfc, 47, after serv in 2nd Marines. Mem: Elks; League of Sacred Heart, Moose; Polish Am Vets. Relig: Catholic. Mailing Add: State House Boston MA 02133

D'EMIC, MATTHEW JUDE (D)
b Brooklyn, NY, Dec 16, 52; s John Joseph D'Emic, Jr & Margaret Hannan D; single. Educ: Fordham Univ, 70- Polit & Govt Pos: Deleg, Dem Nat Conv, 72; coordr, McGovern Campaign, 49th & 50th Assembly Dist, NY, 72. Mem: Bridge, Cent Brooklyn & Bay Ridge Independent Dem; exec mem New Era Independent Dem. Honors & Awards: Robert F Kennedy Mem Award for Community Serv, Nat Info Bur for Jewish Life, 72. Relig: Roman Catholic. Mailing Add: 7523 Narrows Ave Brooklyn NY 11209

DEMICHELE, MARGARET MARY (D)
b Denver, Colo, Mar 3, 21; d Lawrence Connelly & Elizabeth O'Connell C; m 1946 to Joseph Anthony DeMichele. Educ: St Patrick's Acad, Washington, DC, 39. Polit & Govt Pos:

Clerk-stenographer, US Rep James F O'Connor, 40-45; secy to US Rep Mike Mansfield, Mont, 45-52, secy to US Sen Mike Mansfield, 53, admin asst, 55- Relig: Catholic. Legal Res: Great Falls MT 59401 Mailing Add: 9409 Old Marlboro Pike Upper Marlboro MD 20870

DEMOULIN, CHARLES JOSEPH, JR (D)
Colo State Rep
b Denver, Colo, July 6, 29; s Charles Joseph Hookey DeMoulin & Josephine Wareham D; div; c Victoria Marie, Michelle Marie, Theresa Ann, Charles Joseph, III & James Arthur; remarried to Josephine Joy; stepsons, Scott Mathew & Steven Michael Robb. Educ: Local Union 68, Int Brotherhood of Elec Workers, 4 years accredited apprenticeship; Denver Univ Exten Ctr; Colo Univ Exten Ctr. Polit & Govt Pos: Dist co-capt, Dem Party, Colo, 62-63; precinct committeeman, 62-66; Colo State Rep, 65- Bus & Prof Pos: Pres & asst bus mgr, Local Union 68, Int Brotherhood of Elec Workers, 61-63. Mil Serv: Entered as Pvt, Marine Corps, 46, released as Pfc, 47. Mem: Int Brotherhood of Elec Workers (Local Union 68); Int Odd Fellows; AF&AM (South Denver Lodge 93, Colo Consistory, AS&AR); Elec Craftsman (Denver Lodge 86); Adult Educ Coun. Honors & Awards: All City & All State Swimming Letterman. Relig: Episcopal. Mailing Add: Box 19010 Denver CO 80219

DEMPSEY, AMBROSE L (D)
Kans State Rep
Mailing Add: RR 3 Box 258 Leavenworth KS 66048

DEMPSEY, JOHN N (D)
b Cahir Co, Tipperary, Jan 3, 15; m Mary Frey; c Rev Edward, John, Jr, Margaret & Kevin. Hon Degrees: LLD, St Anselm's Col, 62, Providence Col, 63, Univ Hartford, 63, Fairfield Univ, Am Int Col, Trinity Col, 67 & Univ Bridgeport, 67; LHD, Am Int Col. Polit & Govt Pos: City Councilman, Putnam, Conn, mayor, six terms; Conn State Rep, 49-53, minority leader, Conn House of Rep, 53; exec aide to Gov, 56-58; Lt Gov, 58-61; mem, Adv Comn on Intergovt Rels, Gov of Conn, 61-71; Nat Gov Comn on Juv Decency; mem exec comt, Nat Gov Conf; chmn, NEng Gov Conf, 63-65; deleg, Dem Nat Conv, 72. Bus & Prof Pos: Consult environ policy, Southern New Eng Tel Co, 71-; dir, Guarantee Bank & Trust Co, Hartford & several other directorships. Mem: KofC; Rotary; Elks; Foresters of Am; Putnam Irish Am Club. Honors & Awards: Adult Americanism Award, Conn DAR; Silver Beaver Award, Charter Oak Coun, Boy Scouts; St Jude Man of Year, 66; Conn Newsboys Award, 70; Photographers of Conn Highest Award, 71. Mailing Add: 53 Neptune Dr Groton CT 06340

DEMUSE, AMELIA (MILLIE) (DFL)
b Minneapolis, Minn; d Michael DeMuse & Lucia Pitassi D; single. Educ: Dale Carnegie Sales & Leadership Grad; Minneapolis Eve Sch courses. Polit & Govt Pos: Trustee, First Ward Dem-Farmer-Labor Party, Minneapolis, Minn, 60-64, vchairwoman, 67 & 69; alt deleg, Dem-Farmer-Labor State Conv, 60, 65 & 72-73; alt deleg, Fifth Dist Conv, 60, 65, 72 & 73; chmn, 11th Precinct, First Ward, 60-71 & Eighth Precinct, First Ward, 57th Sen Dist, 72-; deleg, City of Minneapolis, Co of Hennepin, Legis Dist, 60-; first vchairwoman, 41st Sen Dist Dem-Farmer-Labor Party, 70-72. Bus & Prof Pos: Switchboard operator, receptionist & billing clerk, Lewis Bolt & Nut Co, Minneapolis, Minn, 37-39, billing clerk, 39-43, pvt secy to pres, 43-48, exec secy, 48-52, secy-admin asst to pres, 52-59, secy-purchasing agent, 59- Mem: Beltrami Park Citizens League (secy, 58-); Pub Charities Minneapolis (adv comt, 74-); Police Dept, Precinct Two, East Side Sta (adv comt, 75). Honors & Awards: Grad from high sch with honors & mem, Nat Honor Soc. Relig: Catholic. Mailing Add: 618 Buchanan St NE Minneapolis MN 55413

DEMUSE, TONI ANN (D)
Mem Exec Comt, Dem-Farmer-Labor Party 55th Dist
b Minneapolis, Minn, Nov 21, 47; d Anthony DeMuse & Olga Krish D; single. Educ: Univ Minn, summer 65. Polit & Govt Pos: Chmn, Women for Sarna for Minn State Rep, 72; alt deleg, Dem Nat Conv, 72; mem exec comt, Dem-Farmer-Labor Party 55th Dist, 72- Relig: Catholic. Mailing Add: 3511 NE McKinley St Minneapolis MN 55418

DEMUZIO, VINCE (D)
Ill State Sen
Mailing Add: 4 Valley Lane Carlinville IL 62626

DENARDIS, LAWRENCE JOSEPH (R)
Conn State Sen
b New Haven, Conn, Mar 18, 38; s Lawrence Alfred DeNardis & Elena Battaglia D; m 1961 to Mary Louise White; c Lawrence, Jr, Mark & Lesley. Educ: Holy Cross Col, BS, 60; NY Univ, MA, 64. Polit & Govt Pos: Deleg, Conn Const Conv, 65; Conn State Sen, 34th Dist, 71- Bus & Prof Pos: Asst prof polit sci & chmn defp, Albertus Magnus Col, 64- Mil Serv: Entered as Ens, Navy, 60, released as Lt(jg), 63, after serv in Eastern Sea Frontier, New York, NY. Publ: Little man's watchdog: the case for an ombudsman in Connecticut, Conn State J, 7-8/65; Metropolis at the crossroads, Conn Community, spring 67. Mem: Am Polit Sci Asn; Am Soc for Pub Admin; Nat Munic League. Honors & Awards: Outstanding Young Man of Conn, Jaycees, 65. Relig: Roman Catholic. Mailing Add: 383 Broadway Hamden CT 06514

DENBO, SETH THOMAS (R)
Chmn Exec Comt, Ind Rep State Cent Comt
b English, Ind, Apr 8, 10; s Robert L Denbo & Estella Jones D; m 1928 to Muriel Marie Pavey; c Ronald Ray, Myrna Yvonne (Mrs Howard Goldman) & Delma Murdean (Mrs James Eckerty). Educ: English High Sch, Ind, 26-29. Polit & Govt Pos: Chmn, Crawford Co Rep Comt, Ind, 58-; chmn, Eighth Cong Dist Rep Party, 62-; campaign coordr, Ind Rep Party, 64; chmn exec comt, Ind Rep State Cent Comt, 64-, mem budget & finance comts, 68-, asst state chmn, 69-70. Bus & Prof Pos: Mem bd dirs, Crawford Co Coop Asn, Ind, 44-48; mem town bd, English, 52-; pres, Kentuckiana Egg & Poultry Asn, 58-62; pres bd dirs, Crawford & Dubois Co REMC, 59-60; dir, Marengo State Bank, 67- Mem: Order of Ky Col; Sagamore of the Wabash; Columbia Club, Indianapolis; Conserv Club Crawford Co; Press Club Indianapolis. Honors & Awards: Mgr baseball club, Ind Kiwanis League; scout for Minn Twins. Relig: Protestant. Mailing Add: S Main St English IN 47118

DENCZAK, RAY (D)
Committeeman, Ohio State Dem Exec Comt
b Canton, Ohio, Jan 4, 25; s Nicholas John Denczak & Mary Katherine Temsic D; m 1951 to Ethel Maxin; c Pamela Kay & Raymond Eric. Educ: Ohio State Univ, 47-50; Pi Kappa Alpha. Polit & Govt Pos: Fourth ward councilman, Canton, Ohio, 61-62; precinct committeeman, ward four, precinct M, 61-64 & ward 11, precinct R, 69-; mem, Stark Co Dem Exec Comt, 70-; committeeman, Ohio State Dem Exec Comt, 70-; pres, Canton City Coun,

72- Bus & Prof Pos: Design engr, Ford Motor Co, 53- Honors & Awards: Citizen of the Year Award, Ford Motor Co. Relig: Catholic. Legal Res: 2416 38th St NW Canton OH 44711 Mailing Add: PO Box 8384 Canton OH 44711

DENDE, HENRY JOHN (D)
Mem, Lackawanna Co Dem Comt, Pa
b Scranton, Pa, Oct 21, 18; s John Dende & Mary Borowski D; m 1958 to Prospine Kathryn Storace; c Diane, Henry, John David, Neil Thomas & Christopher S. Educ: Alliance Col, AA, 38; Univ Warsaw, Poland, AA, 39; Univ Scranton, BA, 41; Alpha Sigma Nu. Polit & Govt Pos: Mem, Scranton Sch Bd, Pa, 51-; chmn, Polish Div of Nationalities Sect, Pa Dem State Comt, 54-58; vpres, Lackawanna Co Sch Bd, 61-67; mem, Lackawanna Co Dem Comt, 66-; pres, Lackawanna Co Voc-Tech Sch Bd; chmn steering comt for formation of Community Col, Lackawanna Co; mem adv comt to Pres, Alliance Col; pres, Scranton Sch Bd, 69. Bus & Prof Pos: Pres, Dende Press, Inc, Scranton, Pa; ed & co-publ, Polish Am J, bi-weekly, 4/45- Mil Serv: Entered as Pvt, Army, 42, released as Sgt, 45; Good Conduct Medal. Mem: Anthracite Club of Printing House Craftsmen; Nat Alumni Soc, Univ Scranton; Am Legion; CofC; Advert Club. Honors & Awards: Named printing man of the year, 62. Relig: Roman Catholic. Mailing Add: 105 Rhonda Dr Scranton PA 18505

DENECKE, ARNO H (R)
Assoc Justice, Ore Supreme Court
b Rock Island, Ill, May 7, 16; s Harry Denecke & Gertrude Etzel D; m 1945 to Selma Rockey; c Virginia (Mrs David Hackett), David, John, William & Anne. Educ: Augustana Col, 33-35, Univ Ill, AB, 37, Col of Law, SJD, 39; Phi Beta Kappa; Order of the Coif. Polit & Govt Pos: Circuit judge, Multnomah Co, Portland, Ore, 59-62; assoc justice, Ore Supreme Court, 63- Bus & Prof Pos: Mem legal dept, Montgomery Ward & Co, Chicago, Ill & Oakland, Calif, 39-41; asst prof, Univ Ore Sch Law, 46; mem legal firm, Mautz, Souther, Spaulding, Denecke & Kinsey, Portland, Ore, 47-58. Mil Serv: Entered as Pvt, Army, 41, released as Maj, 45, after serv in Field Artil, ETO, 41-45; Col, Army Field Judiciary, 64-75; Ret. Publ: Discovery in state & federal courts, Ore Law Rev, No 31, 52, Surety & fidelity bonds, No 37, 58; The judiciary needs your help, teachers, No 22 J of Legal Educ, 70. Mem: Ore State & Am Bar Asns; Am Judicature Soc; Am Legion; AF&AM. Relig: Episcopal. Legal Res: 2830 Bolton Terr S Salem OR 97302 Mailing Add: Supreme Court Bldg Salem OR 97310

DENHAM, MITCHEL B (D)
Ky State Rep
Mailing Add: 506 Forest Dr Maysville KY 41056

DEN HERDER, ELMER HANS (R)
Iowa State Rep
b Sioux Center, Iowa, Aug 14, 08; s Gerrit E Den Herder (deceased) & Jeanette Grotenhuis D (deceased); m 1931 to Christine Vreeman; c James (deceased), Roger, Paul, Phil, Mary (Mrs Vande Berg), Carol (Mrs De Ruyter); 15 grandchildren. Educ: Orange City Acad; Hope Col; Cosmopolitan. Polit & Govt Pos: Iowa State Rep, 67-, mem, Iowa Develop Comt, Iowa House of Rep, mem, Iowa Comprehensive Health Planning Coun, Iowa Regional Med Prog & Iowa Hosp Adv Comn. Bus & Prof Pos: Realtor. Mem: CofC; Farm Bur. Honors & Awards: Award, Future Farmers of Am; hon mem 4-H Girls. Relig: Protestant. Mailing Add: 291 12th St SE Sioux Center IA 51250

DENHOLM, FRANK EDWARD (D)
b Scotland Twp, SDak, Nov 29, 23; s John J Denholm & Laura A Mathias D; m 1950 to Mildred Theresa Niehaus. Educ: SDak State Univ, BS; Sch Law, Univ SDak, LLB; Univ Minn; Univ Calif, JD; Pi Kappa Delta; Phi Delta Phi; past pres, Blue Key. Polit & Govt Pos: Sheriff, Day Co, 50; agent, Fed Bur Invest, 56-61; former city attorney, 8rookings, Volga & White; past mem, Brookings City Planning Comn; US Rep, First Dist, SDak, 70-74; ex officio, Dem Nat Mid-Term Conf, 74. Bus & Prof Pos: Owner & operator farm, Day Co, 45-56; owner & operator ICC Trucking Bus; former legal coun to several farm coops; lectr econ, law & polit sci, SDak State Univ, 62-64; founder, Denholm Law Firm, 62- Mem: SDak & Am Bar Asns; Am Judicature Soc; Am Trial Lawyers Asn; Nat Sheriff's Asn. Honors & Awards: First place winner, Univ SDak & nat winner, Men's Original Oratory, 55. Relig: Catholic. Mailing Add: 2127 Elmwood Dr Brookings SD 57006

DENIGER, ROBERT J (BOB) (R)
Chmn, Walker Co Rep Party, Tex
b Yankton, SDak, Feb 15, 39; s Alfred M Deniger & Louise H Keller D; m to Karen A Krueger. Educ: Univ Nebr, Lincoln, 66; San Jacinto Col, 70-71; Sam Houston State Univ, BBA, 73; Phi Theta Kappa; pres, Mkt Club; vpres, League of Student Voters. Polit & Govt Pos: Chmn, Walker Co Rep Party, Tex, 72- Bus & Prof Pos: Dir, Tex Arboretum Found, Inc, 74- Mil Serv: Entered as Pvt E-1, Marine Corps, 57, released as Cpl E-4, 61, after serv in 1st Marine Air Wing, Iwakuni, Japan, 60-61; Good Conduct Medal; Nat Defense Serv Medal. Mem: Tex Bd Realtors (pres, 75); Elks (Loyal Knight, Huntsville Lodge, 75-76); Huntsville Rotary; Huntsville CofC (chmn legis comt, 75); Tex Asn Realtors. Honors & Awards: Outstanding First Year Jaycee, Region 410, 73; Outstanding Local Dir, Huntsville Jaycees, 73; Outstanding State VPres, Tex Jaycees, 74. Relig: Catholic. Legal Res: 1105 1/2 12th St Huntsville TX 77340 Mailing Add: PO Box 1442 Huntsville TX 77340

DENMAN, DON CURRY (R)
Okla State Rep
b Oklahoma City, Okla, Sept 7, 46; s Earl Smith Denman & Velma Curry D; m 1967 to Kendra Jane Harris. Educ: Yale Univ, BA, 69; Cornell Univ Law Sch, 71-72; Yale Polit Union. Polit & Govt Pos: Okla State Rep, Dist 88, 72-, secy Rep caucus, Okla House Rep, currently, chmn appropriations subcomt on univ hosp; mem exec comt, Rep State Comt, Okla, 72-; mem exec comt & legis dist chmn, Oklahoma Co Rep Comt, 72-, comput comt chmn, 73-74. Bus & Prof Pos: Comput systs rep, Burroughs Corp, Oklahoma City, 69; comput programmer, Okla State Dept Instnl Social & Rehabilitative Serv, 70-71; comput systs analyst, self-employed, 72- Mem: CofC; Speck Homes for Delinquent Children (bd dirs); Okla Heritage Asn; Vols in Corrections; Oklahoma City-Co Community Action Agency. Honors & Awards: Am Legion Legis Award, 73. Relig: Disciples of Christ. Mailing Add: 2629 NW 11th Oklahoma City OK 73107

DENNIS, DANIEL S (R)
Utah State Rep
Mailing Add: 203 N First East Roosevelt UT 84066

DENNIS, DAVID WORTH (R)
b Washington, DC, June 7, 12; s William Cullen Dennis & Agnes Barker D; m 1938 to Tresa Justice; c William C, II & Martha Ellen. Educ: Earlham Col, AB, 33; Harvard Law Sch, LLB, 36. Polit & Govt Pos: Prosecuting attorney, Wayne Co, Ind, 39-43; Ind State Rep, Wayne Co, 47-49, Wayne & Union Co, 53-59; US Rep Tenth Dist, Ind, 69-74. Bus & Prof Pos: Assoc, Rupe, Brown & Reller, Richmond, Ind, 36-39; assoc, Ross, McCord, Ice & Miller, Indianapolis, 43-44; partner, Dennis & Dennis, Richmond, 47-62, Dennis, Dennis & Puckett, 62-67, Dennis, Dennis & Reinke, 67-69 & Dennis, Dennis, Reinke & Vertesch, 69-71. Mil Serv: Entered as Pvt, Army, 44, released as 1st Lt, 46, after serv in Judge Adv Gen Div, Southwest Pac, 45-46. Mem: Am, Ind & Wayne Co Bar Asns; Am Trial Lawyers Asn; Nat Asn Defense Lawyers Criminal Cases. Relig: Society of Friends. Mailing Add: 111 Wescott Hotel Richmond IN 47374

DENNIS, MAX HALE (R)
Ohio State Sen
b Dayton, Ohio, Aug 9, 25; s Paul B Dennis & Josephine Hale D; m 1943 to Ethel Barrett; c Jeffrey, Dianne, Jody & Meredith. Educ: Washington & Lee Univ, AB, 47, LLB, 48; Phi Delta Phi. Polit & Govt Pos: Asst Attorney Gen, Ohio, 51; city solicitor, Wilmington, Ohio, 54-55; Ohio State Rep, 55-63; Ohio State Sen, 63-, mem, Criminal Law Study Comt, Ohio Legis Serv Comn, Ohio State Senate, 66, mem, Tax Study Comn, 66. Bus & Prof Pos: Attorney-at-law, Wilmington, Ohio, 49- Mem: Clinton Co & Am Bar Asns; Mason; Eagles; Rotary. Relig: Church of Christ. Legal Res: 245 N South St Wilmington OH 45177 Mailing Add: State Capitol Columbus OH 43215

DENNIS, REMBERT CONEY (D)
SC State Sen
b Pinopolis, SC, Aug 27, 15; s Edward J Dennis & Ella Mae Coney D; m 1944 to Natalie Brown D; c six. Educ: Furman Univ, AB, 36; Georgetown Univ Law Sch, 36-37; Univ of SC, LLB, 40. Polit & Govt Pos: SC State Rep, 39-42; SC State Sen, 43-; mem, SC Dem State Exec Comt, 44; deleg, Dem Nat Conv, 44, 48, 52, 56 & 60. Bus & Prof Pos: Lawyer, Dennis & Dennis. Mem: Blue Key; Mason (32 degree); Shrine; Lions; WOW. Relig: Baptist; bd of Deacons. Mailing Add: State House Columbia SC 29211

DENNISON, DAVID SHORT, JR (R)
b Poland, Ohio, July 29, 18; s David Short Dennison & Cordelia Whitman D; m 1973 to Dorothy Kelsey Houlette; c David Whitman & Jennie. Educ: Williams Col, AB, 40; Western Reserve Sch of Law, LLB, 45; Order of the Coif; Delta Upsilon; Phi Delta Phi. Polit & Govt Pos: US Rep, Ohio, 57-58; consult, US Civil Rights Comn, 59; chmn, Trumbull Co Rep Exec & Cent Comts, Ohio, 64-66; mem, Ohio Rep State Cent Comt, formerly; mem, Bd of Elec, 64-68; deleg, Rep Nat Conv, 68; mem, Fed Trade Comn, 70-74. Bus & Prof Pos: Vpres, gen counsel & secy, Wheeling-Pittsburgh Steel Corp, Pa, currently, trustee Western Reserve Acad, Hudson. Mil Serv: Vol ambulance driver, Am Field Serv, Libya & NAfrica, 42-43; Africa Star. Mem: Trumbull Co, Ohio State, Am & Fed Bar Asns; Capitol Hill Club. Relig: Episcopal. Mailing Add: 109 Pheasant Dr Pittsburgh PA 15238

DENOMME, ERNEST FRANCIS (R)
Mem, Portsmouth Rep Town Comt, RI
b Fiskeville, RI, Feb 2, 04; s Napoleon Joseph Denomme & Melina De Tonnancour D; m 1938 to Jeanette Nilda Richmond. Educ: Bryant Col, 2 years; Boston Univ, 1 year; Brown Univ Exten, 3 years. Polit & Govt Pos: Mem welfare bd, Portsmouth, RI, 30-35, pub rels rep, 30-69, moderator, 35-39, chmn budget comt, 35-45, mem zoning & hurricane study, 38-42; chmn, Rep Gubernatorial Finance, RI, 50-52; chmn, Eisenhower Local Campaign, 52; mem, Portsmouth Sch Comt, 54-58; mem, RI Real Estate Comn, 58-61; secy, Portsmouth Rep Town Comt, 60-69, chmn, 64-71, mem, 70-; chmn, Nixon Local Campaign, 60 & 68; secy, RI Legis Hosp Comn, 64-66. Bus & Prof Pos: Acct, Pawtuxet Valley Dyeing Co, 21-25; secy strategy dept, US Naval War Col, 25-26; secy, Weyerhaeuser Timber Co, 26-30, asst sales mgr, 30-36, sales mgr, 36-62. Publ: Romance of the lumber industry, Weyerhaeuser News, 30; The Portsmouth Free Library, RI Libr Asn, 66; Stone Bridge & other historical stories, Sakonnet Times, 68-69. Mem: Newport Eng Soc; Int Order Lumbermen; New Eng Coun Econ Develop; KofC (4 degree, advocate, Father Christopher Rooney Coun, 72-73); Am Asn Retired Persons. Honors & Awards: Medal of St George, Bishop McVinney; Selective Serv World War II Medal; Capt George Bucklin Award, 40 years, Boy Scout; Am Red Cross Award, 15 years treas Portsmouth Chap. Relig: Roman Catholic. Mailing Add: 160 Bristol Ferry Rd Portsmouth RI 02871

DENSFORD, CHARLES FRANCIS (R)
b Oklahoma City, Okla, Jan 26, 07; s James Washington Densford & Pearl May Lutes D; m 1932 to Cora Esperanza Giano; c Dolores (Mrs J R Fender), Maj C F, Jr, USA, James T, William H, Cora Elena (Mrs W C Watkins) & Daniel D. Educ: US Mil Acad, BS, 31. Polit & Govt Pos: Chmn, Bandera Co Rep Comt, Tex, formerly. Bus & Prof Pos: Owner-operator, Densford Ranch, 58-; real estate broker, Densford Realty Co, 62-; columnist, The root of the matter, in various Tex newspapers & for subscribing individuals nationwide, currently. Mil Serv: Pvt, Kans Nat Guard, 26; Air Force, 31, retired as Col, 59; Air Medal; Am Defense Serv Ribbon; Am Theater Ribbon; Victory Medal; Grado de Comendador Orden de Boyaca, Colombia. Publ: Auth, The My Lai tragedy and the Calley trial, 71, Whose side is McGovern on?, 72 & Welfare, our Frankenstein monster, 72, Circle M Bus Corral; plus others. Mem: Nat Rifle Asn; Asn of Grads, US Mil Acad; Am Legion; Am Security Coun; Daedalians. Honors & Awards: Pistol Marksmanship, various nat records & state & regional championships; Adjutant, US Rifle & Pistol Team, World Shooting Championships, Buenos Aires, 49. Legal Res: Ranch Home Pipe Creek TX 78063 Mailing Add: Box 174 Pipe Creek TX 78063

DENSMORE, ALBERT HARRY (D)
Ore State Rep
b Portland, Ore, Sept 9, 46; s Harry Darwin Densmore & Ethel P Forrester D; m to Susan Jean Ogle. Educ: Portland State Univ, BS, 68; Southern Ore Col, MS, 74. Polit & Govt Pos: Dem precinct committeeman, Jackson Co, Ore, 68-70; Ore State Rep, 71-, Asst House Majority Leader, Ore State House of Rep, 73-, Speaker Pro Tem, 75-; deleg & mem credentials comt, Dem Nat Conv, 72; deleg, Dem Nat Mid-Term Conf, 74. Bus & Prof Pos: Teacher social sci, Medford Sr High Sch, Ore, 68- Mil Serv: Entered as Pvt, Army, 69; 1st Lt, Army Res, 69- Mem: Ore Law Enforcement Coun; Eastern Star; Grange; Retired Sr Vol Prog (bd dirs, 72-); ROA. Honors & Awards: Boy of the Month, Portland Exchange Club, 65; Outstanding Young Man of Am, 71 & 72. Relig: Presbyterian. Legal Res: 1909 Roberts Rd Medford OR 97501 Mailing Add: 1909 Roberts Rd Medford OR 97501

DENSON, WOODY RAY (D)
Tex State Rep
b Beaumont, Tex, Mar 24, 40; m 1971 to Patricia Vigil. Educ: Univ Houston, LLB, 66; Lamar Univ, BA in Econ, 72; Phi Alpha Delta. Polit & Govt Pos: Tex State Rep, 73-; deleg, Tex State Dem Const Conv, 74. Bus & Prof Pos: Lawyer, 66- Mem: Tex State & Houston Bar Asns; Criminal Defense Lawyers of Harris Co. Legal Res: 5311 W Bellfort Houston TX 77035 Mailing Add: 3220 Louisiana Houston TX 77006

DENT, FREDERICK BAILY (R)
Spec Rep for Trade Negotiations
b Cape May, NJ, Aug 17, 22; s Magruder Dent & Edith Houston Baily D; m 1944 to Mildred Harrison; c Frederick B Jr, Mildred H, Pauline H, Diana G & Magruder H. Educ: Yale Univ, BA, 43. Polit & Govt Pos: Chmn, Spartanburg Co Planning & Develop Comn, SC, 60-72; mem, President's Comn All Volunteer Army, 70-71; Secy of Com, 73-75; Spec US Rep for Trade Negotiations, 75- Bus & Prof Pos: Asst treas, Mayfair Mills, 49-52, exec vpres, 52-58, pres, 58-73. Mil Serv: Entered as Midshipman, Naval ROTC, 40, released as Lt(jg), 46, after serv in USS PCE-873; PC-1547, Pac, 43-46. Relig: Episcopal. Legal Res: SC Mailing Add: Off Spec Rep for Trade Negotiations 1800 G St Washington DC 20506

DENT, HARRY SHULER (R)
b St Matthews, SC, Feb 21, 30; s Hampton Nathaniel Dent, Sr (deceased) & Sally Prickett D (deceased); m 1951 to Elizabeth Inez Francis; c Harry S, Jr, Dolly N, Virginia M & John R. Educ: Presby Col, SC, BA, cum laude, 51; George Washington Univ, LLB, 57; Georgetown Univ, LLM, 59; Blue Key; Phi Alpha Delta; Pi Kappa Alpha. Hon Degrees: LLD, Presby Col, SC; DPSc, Baptist Col Charleston. Polit & Govt Pos: Admin asst to US Sen Strom Thurmond, SC, 55-65; chmn, Thurmond Speaks for Goldwater Comt, 64; state chmn, SC Rep Party, 65-68; mgr, SC Rep State-Wide Campaign, 66; mgr, Thurmond Speaks for Nixon-Agnew Comt, 68; deleg, Rep Nat Conv, 68; Dep Counsel to the President of US, 68-69, Spec Counsel, 69-72; Gen Counsel, Rep Nat Comt, 73-74. Bus & Prof Pos: Formerly, Washington correspondent for several SC newspapers & radio sta; partner, Dent & Kennedy, 65-68; partner, Whaley, McCutchen, Blanton & Dent, Columbia, SC, 73-74; sr partner, Dent, Kirkland, Taylor & Wilson, currently. Mil Serv: Entered as 2nd Lt, Army, 51, released as 1st Lt, after serv in 24th Inf Div, Far East Command, 52-53; Maj, Army Res, currently. Mem: Freedoms Found, Valley Forge (bd trustees); SC Bar Asn. Honors & Awards: Outstanding Sr & Founder's Medal, Presby Col, SC & Distinguished Alumnus Award, 70; Distinguished Achievement Award, Pi Kappa Alpha, 70. Relig: Southern Baptist. Legal Res: 2030 Bermuda Hills Rd Columbia SC 29204 Mailing Add: Box 11300 Bankers Trust Tower Columbia SC 29211

DENT, JOHN H (D)
US Rep, Pa
b Johnetta, Pa, Mar 10, 08; s Samuel Dent & Genevieve D; m 1929 to Margaret R; c Patricia (Mrs Donald Sharp), John Frederick; seven grandchildren. Educ: Great Lakes Naval Aviation Acad; correspondence sch courses. Polit & Govt Pos: Pa State Rep, 36; Dem Floor Leader, Pa State Senate, 17 years; Pa State Sen, 36-58; US Rep, Pa, 58- Bus & Prof Pos: Newspaperman; exec, coal, coke, bldg & transportation co. Mil Serv: Marine Air Corps, 24-28. Mem: United Rubber Workers. Publ: Auth unemploy, workmen's compensation laws, parliamentary & legis procedures, int trade & coal mine health & safety; written for mag & labor publ. Legal Res: Ligonier PA 15658 Mailing Add: 2104 House Off Bldg Washington DC 20515

DENT, R A (D)
Ga State Rep
Mailing Add: 2043 Rosalie St Augusta GA 30901

DENTON, ASHTON LYLE (R)
b Holton, Kans, Oct 6, 09; s James Edgar Denton & Della Pierce D; m 1937 to Maxine Barber; c James Everett & Glenna Lyle. Educ: Morehead State Univ, AB, 39; MA, 53; pres, Morehead State Univ Alumni Asn, 41-42. Polit & Govt Pos: Supvr, Agr Stabilization & Conserv Serv, Fleming Co, Ky, 62-63; chmn, Fleming Co Rep Exec Comt, formerly; admin asst, State Dept Ins, 68- Bus & Prof Pos: Teacher, Fleming Co Schs, Ky, 27-33; elem prin, Hillsboro, Ky, 34-43 & 47-59. Mil Serv: Entered as Pvt, Army, 43, released as T-4, 46, after serv in 233rd Army Postal Unit, Asiatic-Pac Theatre, 44-46; Good Conduct Medal; Battle Star. Mem: Mason; Am Legion; CofC; Farm Bur; Ky Retired Teachers Asn. Relig: Protestant. Mailing Add: PO Box 87 Hillsboro KY 41049

DENTON, HERBERT JACKSON, JR (R)
Tenn State Rep
b Kingsport, Tenn, Dec 13, 41; s Herbert Jackson Denton, Sr & Mayme Ellen Campbell D; m 1966 to Judith Gail Trent; c Hereward Trent & Alaric Campbell. Educ: Tenn Technol Univ, BS, 64; Nat Soc Prof Engrs; Mech Engrs Club; Eta Epsilon Sigma; Scabbard & Blade. Polit & Govt Pos: Tenn State Rep, 68- Bus & Prof Pos: Mech engr, Tenn Eastman Co, 64 & 67- Mil Serv: Entered as 2nd Lt, Army, 65, released as 1st Lt, 67, after serv in 102 Engr Co, Construction Support, Dominican Repub; Vietnam Serv Medal with Bronze Star. Mem: Am Soc Mech Engrs; Mason; Am Legion; VFW; Farm Bur. Relig: Baptist. Mailing Add: Rte 4 Blountville TN 37617

DENTON, LANE (D)
Tex State Rep
b Axtell, Tex, Dec 18, 40; s John Thomas Denton & Fannie Lee Ables D; m 1963 to Betty Kirbo; c Dee Ann. Educ: Baylor Univ, BS, 62, MS, 64; Univ Tex, 2 years; Phi Delta Kappa. Polit & Govt Pos: Precinct chmn, Bellmead Dem Party, Tex, 67; Tex State Rep, 71- Bus & Prof Pos: Teacher, Mart High Sch, 62-63 & Connally High Sch, 63-65; teacher, Waco Independent Sch Dist, 65-67, asst prin, 67-69, dir spec serv, 69- Mem: Waco Kiwanis Club; Boy Scouts (bd mem); Ment Health Asn (bd mem). Relig: Baptist. Mailing Add: 1200 Lewis Waco TX 76705

DENTON, SUE M (R)
Chairwoman, Henderson Co Rep Orgn, Ky
b Barlow, Ky, Oct 16, 19; d Robert E Lee Pate & Sudie May Walton P; m 1945 to Julius Elmus Denton; c Eric Neel & Gary Ivan. Educ: Henderson Co High Sch, dipl, 38. Polit & Govt Pos: Chairwoman, Henderson Co Rep Orgn, Ky, 69-, mem exec comt, 70-; pres, Henderson Co Rep Womens Club, 69 & 70; vice gov, Ky Fedn Rep Women, 70-, third vpres, 71- Bus & Prof Pos: Off mgr, Chem Assocs Ind, Inc, 68- Relig: Disciple of Christ. Mailing Add: Rte 1 Cherry Hill Busby Station Rd Robards KY 42452

DEPALMA, SAMUEL
b Rochester, NY, June 22, 18; s Nicholas DePalma & Rose Freda D; m 1941 to Grace E Kilbourne; c Cynthia M & Winifred R. Educ: Univ Rochester, AB, 40; Am Univ Grad Sch, 40-41; Phi Beta Kappa. Polit & Govt Pos: Expert int orgn affairs, Dept of State, 45-54; officer in charge UN Polit Affairs, 55-56; dep dir, Off UN Polit & Security Affairs, 56-58; foreign serv officer, Am Embassy, Paris, 58-61; counr polit affairs, The Hague, Holland, 61-63; chief officer polit affairs, US Arms Control & Disarmament Agency, 63-66, asst dir, 66-69; asst secy, Bur Int Orgn Affairs, Dept of State, 69-73; adv US delegs numerous int conf. Bus & Prof Pos: Dir, Int Anal Unit, Int Tel & Tel Corp, NY, 73- Mem: Am Foreign Serv Asn; Coun Foreign Rels. Legal Res: 6707 Rannoch Rd Bethesda MD 20034 Mailing Add: ITT World Hq 320 Park Ave New York NY 10022

DEPIANO, SALVATORE C (D)
Conn State Sen
Mailing Add: 56 Lyon Terr Bridgeport CT 06604

DEPRIEST, C E (D)
Tenn State Rep
Mailing Add: 1017 Wilson Lane Pulaski TN 38478

DERAMUS, JUDSON DAVIE, JR (D)
NC State Rep
b Mecklenburg Co, NC, Jan 6, 45; s Judson Davie DeRamus & Nina Jerome D; m 1969 to Sarah Lane Ivey; c Sarah Ivey. Educ: Duke Univ, BS in bus, 65; Univ NC, Chapel Hill, JD, 68; Alpha Kappa Psi; Phi Delta Phi; Kappa Alpha. Polit & Govt Pos: Mem, Winston-Salem Parks & Recreation Comn, NC, 73-; NC State Rep, 75- Bus & Prof Pos: Partner, Jenkins, Lucas, Babb & DeRamus, Winston-Salem, currently. Mem: Odd Fellows; Rotary; Exchange Club; Elks. Relig: Methodist. Legal Res: 792 Arbor Rd Winston-Salem NC 27104 Mailing Add: 350 NCNB Bldg Winston-Salem NC 27101

DERELI, MARGARET ULRICKA (D)
Ore State Rep
b Bemidji, Minn, Feb 18, 37; d Elmer Gainey & Ellen Haapaniemi G; m 1957 to Atila Hasan Dereli; c Ali Ihsan & Suzan Miriam. Educ: Corvallis High Sch, grad, 55. Polit & Govt Pos: Ore State Rep, Dist 32, 73- Mailing Add: 260 15th St SE Salem OR 97301

DEREZINSKI, ANTHONY A (D)
Mich State Sen
b 1942; s Dr Clement Derezinski & Mrs Donald Nutt. Educ: Marquette Univ, BA, magna cum laude; Univ Mich Law Sch, JD, cum laude, 67; Harvard Law Sch, advan degree in urban legal studies. Polit & Govt Pos: Attorney-adv, Nat Labor Rels Bd; Mich State Sen, currently, chmn, Joint Admin Rules Comt, vchmn, Senate Judiciary Comt, vchmn, Senate Bus Comt, mem, Senate Corps & Econ Develop Comt & Comt on Comts. Bus & Prof Pos: Dep, Muskegon Co Sheriff's Dept, formerly; bailiff, US Dist Court, Grand Rapids, formerly; mem faculty, Boston Univ Law Sch, formerly; asst to city attorney, Norton Shores, Mich, formerly; pvt law practice. Mil Serv: Naval Officer, Off Judge Adv Gen & Secy Navy's off legal & legis counsel; served as mil judge & defense counsel, Vietnam. Mem: NAACP; Cath War Vets; Fraternal Order Police; Polish Falcons; Polish Roman Cath Union. Mailing Add: 11 Muskegon Blvd Muskegon MI 49442

DERGE, DAVID RICHARD (R)
b Kansas City, Mo, Oct 10, 28; s David R Derge & Blanche Butterfield D; m 1951 to Elizabeth Anne Greene (deceased); m 1972 to Patricia J Williams; c David & Dorothy. Educ: Univ Mo, AB, 50; Northwestern Univ, AM, 51 & PhD, 55; Phi Beta Kappa; Pi Sigma Alpha; Alpha Pi Zeta; Kappa Sigma. Hon Degrees: LLD, Hanyang Univ, Korea, 73. Polit & Govt Pos: Rep precinct committeeman, Monroe Co, Ind, 62-66; councilman-at-lg, Bloomington City Coun, 63-67; dir, surv research, Nixon-Agnew Campaign Comt, 68; research consult, Rep Nat Comt, 69-71; mem, US Adv Comn on Int Educ & Cult Affairs & Ind Adv Comn to US Civil Rights Comn; consult int & higher educ, Dept Health, Educ & Welfare, 71-72; White House consult, 70-71. Bus & Prof Pos: Instr polit sci, Univ Mo, 54-56; prof, Ind Univ, Bloomington, 56-, assoc dean grad sch, 65-67, assoc dean faculties, 67-69; exec vpres, pres & dean admin, Southern Ill Univ, Carbondale, formerly, prof polit sci, currently; pres, Behavioral Research Assocs, 64- Mil Serv: Entered as Pvt, Army, 46, released as Cpl, 48, after serv in 21st Ord Medium Maintenance Co, Army of Occup, Japan, 47-48; Comdr, Naval Res, 52- Publ: The World of American Politics, Bobbs-Merrill, 68; Institution Building & Rural Development, Ind Univ, 68; Public Leadership in Indiana, Inst of Pub Admin, Ind Univ, 69. Mem: Am Polit Sci Asn; Midwest Conf of Polit Scientists; Soc for Int Develop; Midwest Univ Consortium for Int Activities, Inc. Honors & Awards: Ulysses G Weatherly & Brown Derby Awards for Distinguished Teaching, Ind Univ; Outstanding Young Man of Ind, Ind Jaycees, 64. Relig: Presbyterian. Mailing Add: Rte 1 Carbondale IL 62901

DERHAM, RICHARD ANDREW (R)
Chmn, Wash Young Rep Fedn
b Seattle, Wash, May 29, 40; s Andrew James Derham & Helen Dahl D; single. Educ: Harvard Col, AB cum laude, 62; Columbia Law Sch, JD cum laude, 65, ed, Columbia Law Rev, 65; Phi Alpha Delta. Polit & Govt Pos: Mem bd dir, Young Am for Freedom, Inc, 63-66 & 69-73, treas, 71-73; state chmn, Wash Young Am for Freedom, 65 & 68-70; pres, Downtown Young Rep Club, Seattle, Wash, 71-72; nat committeeman, Wash Young Rep Fedn, 73-75, chmn, 75-; asst gen counsel, Young Rep Nat Fedn, 73-; mem adv bd, King Co Rep Cent Comt, 73- Bus & Prof Pos: Attorney, Davis, Wright, Todd, Riese & Jones, 65-72, partner, 72-; instr commercial law, Am Inst Bankers, 69-70; counsel, Wash State House Rep Judiciary Comt, 69 & 71. Mil Serv: Entered as 1st Lt, Army, 65, released as Capt, 67, after serv in 1st Bn, 39th Inf, 7th Army, 66-67; Maj, Army Res; Army Commendation Medal; Nat Defense Serv Ribbon. Mem: Wash Justice Found (treas, 74-); Charles Edison Mem Youth Fund (trustee, 70-, secy, 75-); Waldo Hosp Asn (trustee, 73-); Am & Wash Bar Asns. Honors & Awards: Best State Orgn, Young Am for Freedom, 70; Man of the Year, Wash Interment Asn, 74. Relig: Congregational. Legal Res: 524 W Comstock Seattle WA 98119 Mailing Add: 4200 Seattle First Nat Bank Bldg Seattle WA 98154

DERIAN, PATRICIA MURPHY (D)
Dem Nat Committeewoman, Miss
b New York, NY; d Ronald Thomas Murphy & Ruby Haridman M; m 1953 to Paul S Derian, MD; c Michael Tabore, Thomas Craig & Renee Brooke. Educ: Palos Verdes Col; Millsaps Col; Univ Va Sch Nursing, grad. Polit & Govt Pos: Dem Nat Committeewoman, Miss, 68-, mem credentials comt, Dem Nat Comt, 73-; mem bd dirs, Miss Coun Human Rels, Operation Shoestring & Mississippians for Pub Educ; chmn, Women in Miss for Humphrey-Muskie, 68;

mem exec comt, Dem Policy Coun, 69; bd dirs, Southern Regional Coun, 69; deleg, Dem Nat Conv, 72, vchmn, Rules Comt; mem, Dem Party Charter Comn, 72-; chmn, McGovern/Shriver Campaign, Miss, 72; vchmn, Miss State Dem Party, currently; mem, Domestic Affairs Task Force Dem Policy Coun, 72-; mem steering comt, Dem Nat Comt Woman's Caucus & Dem Women for Affirmative Action; mem bd dir, Ctr for Correctional Justice, currently. Bus & Prof Pos: Participant, Brandeis Univ Conf on Violence, 65; White House Conf to Fulfill these Rights, 66; Lear-Sigler consult, Off Econ Opportunity, 66, head start consult, 67; proj officer, Miss Action for Progress; vpres, Southern Regional Coun, Atlanta, 72-; bd dirs, Delta Ministry, Nat Coun Churches, currently. Mem: Am Civil Liberties Union (nat bd dirs & mem nat exec comt, currently), bd dirs, Miss chap, 72-); Children's TV Workshop, Miss (bd dirs, 69-); Gallery Guild; League of Women Voters. Mailing Add: 2349 Twin Lakes Circle Jackson MS 39211

DERIZOTIS, PARIS C (D)
Mem, NMex Dem State Cent Comt
b Argos, Greece, Mar 15, 31; s Christos Derizotis & Vasiliki Blatsou D; m 1953 to Minnie Esparza; c Christina, Mona, Paris & Dino. Educ: Col of Polit & Econ, Athens, Greece, 2 years. Polit & Govt Pos: NMex State Rep, McKinley Co, 69-73; vchmn & chmn, McKinley Co Dem Party, formerly; mem, NMex Dem State Cent Comt. Bus & Prof Pos: Restaurant owner, 55- Mem: Odd Fellows; Ahepa. Relig: Greek Orthodox. Mailing Add: 610 Zecca Gallup NM 87301

DERMODY, JOHN DANIEL (D)
Assoc Committeeman, Calif State Dem Cent Comt
b Pleasantville, NY, Sept 21, 09; s John Joseph Dermody & Catherine Susannah Gallegher D; m 1938 to Mary Louise Turkal; c John Paul & Mary Kathleen (Mrs McGrath). Educ: Fordham Univ, 27-29; Clarkson Col Technol, BS Chem Eng, 31. Polit & Govt Pos: Dem committeeman, Mt Pleasant, NY, 32-33; deleg, Dem Nat Conv, 68; mem, Calif State Dem Comt, 68-69; asst coordr, Antelope Valley Dem Campaigns, formerly; assoc committeeman, Calif State Dem Cent Comt, 73- Bus & Prof Pos: Civil engr, Pub Works Admin, 33-38; construction engr, Panama Canal Zone, 38-41; projs mgr, P J Walker Co, Calif, 46-58; gen contractor, J D Dermody Co Inc, Lancaster, 58- Mil Serv: Entered as Lt(jg), Navy, Civil Eng Corps, 41, released as Lt Comdr, 46, after serv in 33rd NC Regt, Philippines, 44-46; Comdr, Res, 59, (Ret). Mem: Soc Am Mil Engrs; Bldg Indust Asn; Rotary; Elks; KofC. Honors & Awards: Los Angeles Co Award of Merit. Relig: Catholic. Mailing Add: 44856 15th St W Lancaster CA 93534

DERMODY, MARY LOUISE (D)
Committeewoman, Calif Dem State Cent Comt
b Zookspur, Iowa, June 18, 17; d John Andrew Turkal & Rose Pozega T; m 1938 to John Daniel Dermody; c John Paul & Mary Kathleen (Mrs McGrath). Educ: Bus Col, Des Moines, Iowa, 35. Polit & Govt Pos: Precinct worker, Presidential Elec, Altadena, Calif, 52; precinct worker, Lancaster, 56; precinct chmn, Gubernatorial Elec, Lancaster, 58; chmn precincts, Presidential State & Cong Elec, 60; chmn, Women for Gov Brown & mgr, Assembly Cand, 62; mem, Calif Dem State Cent Comt, 62-, committeewoman, 73-; 62nd Assembly campaign mgr, Pierre Salinger & Assembly Cand, 64; co-chmn, Dollars for Democrats, 62nd Assembly Area, 65; Dem Women's Forum Adv Comt, 65-; campaign chmn, Gov Brown, Antelope Valley, 66; observer, Dem Nat Conv, 68; co-chmn, Robert Kennedy Campaign, 68; Dem cand, Calif State Assemblyman, 62nd Dist, 68; mem, Dem Co Comt, 68-; chmn cong cand, John Van De Kamp, 69; campaign coordr for Antelope Valley, Sen John Tunney; over-all campaign coordr for Dem Slate, Antelope Valley; campaign coordr, Sen Cranston, 74 & Gov E Brown, Jr, 74. Bus & Prof Pos: Acct, Panama Canal Zone, 41; corp secy, J D Dermody Co Inc, Lancaster, Calif, 58- Mem: Bus & Prof Women's Club; Women's Div CofC; Lancaster Woman's Club; Rotary Anns; Antelope Valley Med Ctr (gifts found bd, 75). Lancaster CofC. Honors & Awards: Key Award, Dem Campaign, 64; Women in Community Serv Outstanding Vol, 67; Vol of the Year, Los Angeles Co Heart Asn, 69, 70 & 71, Spec Vol of the Year, 71, Highest Div Vol of the Year, Verdugo Br, 72; 1969 Serv Award, SCalif Dem Women's Forum; nominee for 1970 Women of the Year, Lancaster CofC. Relig: Catholic. Mailing Add: 44856 15th St W Lancaster CA 93534

DEROECK, WALTER A (D)
Mem, Ark Dem State Comt
b St Nicholas, Belgium, June 8, 42; s George DeRoeck, mother deceased; m 1963 to Judith Ann McAdams; c Kathryn Ann, Melinda Ruth & Walter Brian. Educ: Univ Ark, Fayetteville, BS Econ, 65. Polit & Govt Pos: Mem, Ark Dem State Comt, 74-; dir, Ark Indust Develop Comn, 75- Bus & Prof Pos: Adv bd mem, St Bernard's Hosp, currently; bd mem, Imperial Dynamics, Gen Am Enterprises, Craighead Investment & Home Fed Savings & Loan, currently. Mem: Civic Improvement Comt; Rotary; Jonesboro CofC; Industrial Comt. Relig: Catholic. Mailing Add: 1424 Redbud Circle Jonesboro AR 72401

DEROSA, PASQUALE JOSEPH (R)
b Derby, Conn; s Pasquale DeRosa & Josephine Riccio D; m 1952 to Bernadine Edna Groth; c Linda Susan, Patricia Ann & David Joseph. Educ: Bridgeport Eng Inst, 3 years; Univ Bridgeport, AS. Polit & Govt Pos: Mem, Bd Apportionment & Taxation, Derby, Conn, 54-64; chmn, Derby Rep Town Comt, formerly; Sinking Fund Comnr, Derby, Conn, 68-69. Bus & Prof Pos: Design engr; Farrell Co, Div of USM, 52- Mem: KofC. Relig: Catholic. Mailing Add: 106 Olivia St Derby CT 06418

DEROUNIAN, STEVEN B (R)
b Sofia, Bulgaria, Apr 6, 18; s Boghos Derounian & Eliza Aprahamian D; m 1947 to Emily Ann Kennard; c Ann Ashby, Steven Blake, Eleanor Kennard. Educ: NY Univ, AB, 38; Fordham Univ, LLB, 42; Delta Theta Pi. Polit & Govt Pos: Councilman & mem bd, North Hempstead, NY, 48-52; US Rep, NY, 83rd-88th Cong; Justice, Supreme Court, NY, 69- Mil Serv: Capt, Army Inf, 42-46, serv in 103rd Div; Maj, Res; Purple Heart; Bronze Star with Cluster; Combat Infantrymans Badge. Mem: Am, NY State & Nassau Co Bar Asns; VFW; Am Legion. Mailing Add: Supreme Court Chambers Mineola NY 15001

DERRICK, BUTLER CARSON, JR (D)
US Rep, SC
b Sept 30, 36; s Butler Carson Derrick & Mary English Scott D; m Suzanne Gile Mims; c Lydia Gile & Butler Carson, III. Educ: Univ SC, 54-58; Univ Ga, LLB, 65. Polit & Govt Pos: SC State Rep, 69-74; US Rep, SC, 75- Bus & Prof Pos: Partner, Derrick & Byrd. Mem: SC Bar Asn; SC Jaycees (pres); Edgefield Co Fish & Game Asn (pres); Masons; Lions. Relig: Episcopal; mem & sr warden, Trinity Episcopal Church. Legal Res: 311 Brooks St Edgefield SC 29824 Mailing Add: US House Rep Washington DC 20515

DERRICKSON, HARRY E (R)
Del State Rep
Mailing Add: School Lane Rehoboth Beach DE 19971

DERRICKSON, VERNON BLADES (D)
VChmn, Del State Dem Comt
b Frankford, Del, Apr 25, 00; s Joshua Walter Derrickson & Nancy Blades D; m 1930 to Jean Madelyn Riveles; c Vernon Blades & Joann (Mrs Joseph Rowe Slights, Jr). Educ: Wilmington Conf Acad; Mercersburg Acad; Duke Univ, AB, Law Sch; Kappa Alpha; Gamma Eta Gamma. Polit & Govt Pos: Aide de camp to Gov, Del, 48-52, 61-69, 72-76; mem, Del Comn for the Feeble-Minded, 49-51; mem, Del Pub Serv Comn, 49-69, chmn, 61-69; chmn, Kent Co Dem Comt, 51-69, emer chmn, 69-; mem, Del Dem State Comt & Policy Comt, 50-69; cand for Lt Gov, Del, 52 & 56; deleg, Dem Nat Conv, 52-68; mem, Bldg Comn for State Off Bldg, 64-69; chmn, Emergency Motor Transport Bd, 65-; mem, Del State Parole Bd, 69-72; vchmn, Del State Dem Comt, 69- Bus & Prof Pos: Pres, V & W Hotel Corp, 38-65, Derrickson Hotels, 40-54 & Derrickson, Inc, 54-; vpres & dir, Brandywine Raceway, Wilmington, Del, 52-76; dir, Farmer's Bank, Del, 55-68; chmn bldg & grounds comt, Wesley Col, 60-; mem, Indust Develop Corp, 63- Mem: Ocean Hwy Asn (chmn, 55-); Great Lakes Asn of RR & Utilities; Friends of Old Dover; Wesley Col (trustee); Del State Fair. Honors & Awards: Certificate for Meritorious Serv in Football & Varsity D in Swimming, Duke Univ. Relig: Congregational; Trustee, Mem Bd Ministries & Mem Bd Deacons, Peoples Congregational Church, Moderator, 69- Mailing Add: 128 Hazel Rd Dover DE 19901

DERRY, WILLIAM STEPHENS (R)
Chmn, Van Wert Co Rep Cent & Exec Comts, Ohio
b Lancaster, Ohio, Jan 21, 25; s Lawrence R Derry & Florence Stephens D; m 1950 to Rondalee Ricketts; c Christopher James, Lisa Anne, Elaine & Joseph Stephens. Educ: Ohio Northern Univ, BS in Pharm, 50; Sigma Phi Epsilon. Polit & Govt Pos: Councilman, Van Wert City Coun, Ohio, 58-63, pres, 64-65; chmn, Van Wert Co Rep Cent & Exec Comts, 72- Bus & Prof Pos: Pres, Derry Drugs, Inc, 53-; chmn, Action for Balanced Community Develop, 65-70; vpres, Van Wert Indust Develop Bd, 65-; bd mem, Van Wert Co Found, 67- & Van Wert Nat Bank, 67- Mil Serv: Entered as Pvt, Air Force, 43, released as Sgt, 46, after serv in Air Transport Command, SPac. Mem: Northwestern Ohio Pharmaceutical Asn; Van Wert Rotary; Elks; Am Legion. Relig: Methodist. Mailing Add: 909 Elm St Van Wert OH 45891

DERRYBERRY, LARRY DALE (D)
Attorney Gen, Okla
b Altus, Okla, Apr 22, 39; s Willis Landrum Derryberry & Willene Faye Woodall D; m 1963 to Marcia Gale Brazil; c Darren Bret. Educ: Univ Okla, BA, 61, LLB, 63; Phi Eta Sigma; Phi Delta Phi; Pi Kappa Alpha. Polit & Govt Pos: Okla State Rep, 62-70, asst majority floor leader, Okla House Rep, 67-68, speaker pro-tempore, 69-70; Attorney Gen, 71- Bus & Prof Pos: Attorney-at-law, Oden, Oden & Derryberry, 63- Publ: Insurance: rain as accident within, Okla Law Rev, 5/64. Mem: Jackson Co, Okla, & Am Bar Asns; Altus Jr CofC; Elks. Relig: Methodist. Legal Res: 2412 Apache Pass Altus OK 73521 Mailing Add: State Capitol Oklahoma City OK 73105

DERWINSKI, EDWARD J (R)
US Rep, Ill
b Chicago, Ill, Sept 15, 26; s Casimir Ignatius Derwinski & Sophie Smijewski D; m 1960 to Patricia Ann VanDerGiessen; c Maureen & Michael Stephen. Educ: Loyola Univ, Chicago, BS in Hist, 51; Alpha Delta Gamma. Polit & Govt Pos: Mem, Ill-Ind Bi-State Port Study Comn, 57-58; Ill State Rep, 24th Dist, 57-58; US Rep, Fourth Dist, Ill, 59-; mem exec comt, Rep Nat Comt, currently. Bus & Prof Pos: Pres, West Pullman Savings & Loan Asn, Chicago, 51- Mil Serv: Entered as Pvt, Army, 45, released as Technician, 46; Pac Theater & Japanese Occup Ribbons; Maj, Army Res. Mem: Kiwanis; Moose; Am Legion; VFW; Polish Legion of Am Vets. Honors & Awards: Selected by Chicago Jr Asn of Com & Indust as one of the Ten Outstanding Young Men in Chicago Metrop Area, 59 & 61. Relig: Roman Catholic. Legal Res: Flossmoor IL 60422 Mailing Add: US House of Rep Washington DC 20515

DERZAI, AMY RUTH (D)
b Eveleth, Minn, Sept 4, 04; d John Derzai & Mary Panyan D; single. Educ: Duluth State Teachers' Col, 2 year dipl, 27; Wash Univ, summers 32 & 33; Cent Wash State Col, BA, 41, MA, 54; Honor Student. Polit & Govt Pos: Treas, Dem J, Wash, 60-; deleg, Yakima Co & Wash State Dem Conv, 66 & 70, Dist, Co & Nat Dem Conv, 68 & Dist, Co & State Dem Conv, 72; treas, Yakima Co McCarthy for President, 67-68; chmn, Yakima Co McGovern for President Fund Raising Comt, 71-72; co dir, 14th Dist Dem Party, 75- Mem: Wash Educ Asn; League of Women Voters; Wash Art Asn Allied Arts; Yakima Co Retired Teachers Asn (pres, 75-, chmn legis comt, 73-); Wilson Jr High Sch PTA (pres, 75-). Mailing Add: 7 N 32nd Ave Yakima WA 98902

DESALVIO, LOUIS F (D)
NY State Assemblyman
b New York, NY; m to Elvira Mongillo; c John A & Maria B. Educ: DeWitt Clinton High Sch. Polit & Govt Pos: NY State Assemblyman, 40-, dean & speaker pro tem, NY State Assembly; dep collector of internal revenue. Mem: Holy Name Soc; NY Soc; Elks; KofC; Sons of Italy. Relig: Catholic. Mailing Add: 90 Beekman St New York NY 10038

DE SANTIS, CARL ROBERT (R)
Chmn, Warren Co Rep Comt, NY
b Passaic, NJ, Sept 1, 26; s Joseph De Santis & Irene M Van Hine D (deceased); m 1952 to Barbara Wands Ettinger; c Jonathon M, Carl R Jr, Joseph B, Holly B & William A. Educ: Skidmore Col, 3 years. Polit & Govt Pos: Town councilman, Lake George, NY, 60-64; committeeman, Lake George Rep Comt, 60-64, chmn, 62-64; chmn, Warren Co Rep Comt, 64- Bus & Prof Pos: Pres & treas, De Santis Enterprises Inc, Lake George, NY, 53-, Northway Restaurant & Catering Co Inc, Glens Falls, NY, 57- & Ontario Restaurants Inc, Oswego, NY, 60-; pres, Aviation Rd Develop Co Inc, Glens Falls, NY, 67-; pres, Herkimer Restaurants Inc, Herkimer, NY, 68-; dir, First Nat Bank of Glens Falls, 67- Mil Serv: Entered as Pvt, Army Air Force, 44, released as Sgt, 46, after serv in Fifth Air Force, Pac Theater, 46. Mem: Howard Johnson's Nat Agents Coun; Nat Restaurant Asn; NY State Restaurant Asn (dir, 71-); F&AM; Rotary Int. Honors & Awards: Recipient of Howard Johnson Nat Spotlight Award. Relig: Episcopal. Mailing Add: 113 Aviation Rd Glens Falls NY 12801

DESCANS, ROLAND EUGENE (D)
Chmn, Carter Co Dem Cent Comt, Okla
b Royal Center, Ind, July 10, 23; s John Evertt Descans & Mary Petit D; m 1944 to Ora Lee Albin; m 1972 to Catherine Allen Benjamin; c Janice (Mrs Naylor), Vicki (Mrs Keck) &

Roland Eugene. Educ: Columbia Sch Bus, 2 years. Polit & Govt Pos: Chmn, Precinct 10, Ardmore, Okla, 64-70; chmn, Carter Co Dem Cent Comt, 70-; mem, Third Cong Dist Dem Cent Comt, 70-; mem, Okla State Dem Cent Comt, 70- Bus & Prof Pos: Owner, Retail Bus, 46-54; exec mgr, Ardmore CofC, 54-58; owner, Ins & Real Estate Agency, 58- Mem: Nat Homebuilders Asn; Independent Ins Agents; Kiwanis. Honors & Awards: Distinguished Serv Award, US Jaycees; Silver Beaver, Boy Scouts. Relig: Protestant. Legal Res: 803 Bixby Ardmore OK 73401 Mailing Add: Box 353 Ardmore OK 73401

DESCHALIT, RONALD LEE (D)
VChmn, Ariz Dem Party
b Tucson, Ariz, Apr 29, 52; s Jack DeSchalit & Louise Virginia Shamie D; single. Educ: Pima Col, AA, 72; Univ Ariz, BA, 74, grad work, currently. Polit & Govt Pos: Dem precinct committeeman, Dist 10, Tucson, 70-; state committeeman, Ariz Dem Party, 72-, vchmn, 74-, mem state exec comt, 74-; dep registr, Pima Co, 73-; mem, Pima Co Exec Comt, 74- Bus & Prof Pos: Piano teacher, Tucson, Ariz, 71-; investr, Pima Co Attorney's Off, Tucson, 73-74. Mem: DeMolay (Chevalier); F&AM. Honors & Awards: Broken Arrow Bowmen Award, Tucson Safari, 65 & 66; Third Place Award, State Championship Roller Skating Competition, 65. Relig: Presbyterian. Mailing Add: 2819 E 19th St Tucson AZ 85716

DESCHAMBEAULT, FREDERIC (D)
Treas, York Co Dem Comt, Maine
b Biddeford, Maine, May 19, 00; s Frederic Deschambeault & Camille Giguere D; m M Antoinette Poisson. Educ: High sch, 2 years. Polit & Govt Pos: Mem, Gov Pub Safety Co, York Co & Superior Messenger Court, Maine, 60-; deleg, Dem Nat Conv, 60, 64 & 68; treas, York Co Dem Comt, 63- Bus & Prof Pos: Retail grocer, 20-60. Mem: Life mem Elks; Eagles. Relig: Catholic. Mailing Add: 33 Crescent Biddeford ME 04005

DES CHAMPS, WILLIAM GREEN, JR (D)
SC State Rep
b Bishopville, SC, Aug 29, 17; s William Green Des Champs & Etta Hearon D; m 1944 to Elizabeth N Davall. Educ: Clemson Col, BS, 38. Polit & Govt Pos: Mem, Bishopville City Coun, SC, 47-58; Mayor, Bishopville, 58; SC State Sen, 63-67; SC State Rep, 71- Bus & Prof Pos: Shell Oil Jobber; pres, Bishopville Petroleum Co, Inc; co-partner, Des Champs & Webb Ginning & Delinting Plant; owner, Shell Transport Co; dir, The Peoples Bank. Mil Serv: Army, 47th Field Artil, 41; Hon Med Discharge. Mem: Home Fed Savings Loan Asn; CofC; Clemson Rotary Club (bd of dirs); Elks; Am Legion. Honors & Awards: Clemson Col Alumni Distinguished Serv Award, 62. Relig: Methodist; off bd, Bethelem Methodist Church, 56-58. Mailing Add: Drawer 347 Bishopville SC 29010

DESCHLER, LEWIS
b Chillicothe, Ohio, Mar 3, 05; s Joseph Anthony Deschler & Lillian Lewis D; m 1931 to Virginia Cole; c Lewis, II & Joan Mari (Mrs William B Eddy). Educ: Miami Univ, 22-25; George Washington Univ, 25; Nat Univ, DJ, 32, MPL, 32; Delta Tau Delta. Hon Degrees: LLD, Nat Univ, 47, George Washington Univ, 49 & Miami Univ, 63. Polit & Govt Pos: Asst parliamentarian, US House of Rep, 27, parliamentarian, 28-74, parliamentary consult, 74- Publ: Ed, House Rules & Manual, 29-74; auth, Deschler's Procedures in the US House of Representatives, 74; auth, Deschler's Precedents of the House of Representatives, 75. Mem: DC & Supreme Court Bars; Am Group of Interparliamentary Union Cong, London. Honors & Awards: Delta Tau Delta Distinguished Serv Chap, 64; Ohio Gov Award for Advan of Prestige of Ohio, 71; John W McCormack Annual Award of Excellence, 71. Mailing Add: 101 Lucas Lane Bethesda MD 20014

DESKINS, HERBERT, JR (D)
Pres, Ky Young Dem
b Dublin, Va, Nov 26, 43; s Herbert Deskins, Sr & Grace Houndshell D; m 1965 to Kathy Ileen Hinkle; c Herbert, III, Jennifer & Suzanne. Educ: Univ Ky, 61-64, Law Sch, JD, 67; Phi Delta Phi. Polit & Govt Pos: Pres, Univ Ky Young Dem; co chmn, Humphrey-Muskie-Peden Campaign, 68; co attorney, Pike Co, Ky, 69-; nat committeeman, Ky Young Dem, 70-72; pres, Ky Young Dem, 72-; deleg, Dem Nat Mid-Term Conf, 74. Bus & Prof Pos: Attorney-at-law. Mil Serv: Sgt E-6, Army Res. Mem: Pike Co, Ky & Am Bar Asns. Honors & Awards: Outstanding Young Dem, Seventh Cong Dist, 68; Outstanding Pub Serv Award, WTCR Radio, Ashland, Ky. Relig: Church of Christ. Mailing Add: PO Box 423 Pikeville KY 41501

DESLER, DIANNE KAY (R)
Nat Committeewoman, Nebr Fedn Young Rep
b Omaha, Nebr, July 30, 47; d Harlan D Desler (deceased), stepfather, Robert C Thompson & Norma Zingerli Desler T; single. Educ: Univ Nebr Omaha, BS, 69, MS, 71; Kappa Delta Pi; Waokiya Sr Women's Hon; Chi Omega. Polit & Govt Pos: Secy, Nebr Fedn Young Rep, 73-74, nat committeewoman, 74-; asst chmn, Douglas Co Rep Party, 74-; mem cent comt, Nebr Rep Party, 74-, mem const revisions comt, 74- Bus & Prof Pos: Math teacher, Brownell-Talbot Sch, Omaha, Nebr, 70-, math dept chmn, 72-, head of the Upper Sch, 75- Mem: Omaha Women's Chap Freedoms Found of Valley Forge (bd dirs); Nat Coun Teachers Math; Chi Omega Alumni. Honors & Awards: One of Five Finalists, Outstanding Young Educator Award, Omaha Jaycees, 74; Outstanding Young Rep Woman, Douglas Co Young Rep, 74. Relig: Presbyterian. Mailing Add: 13792 Pierce Omaha NE 68144

DESMARAIS, RAYMOND WILFRED (R)
Chmn, Rep State Sen Dist 35 Comt, RI
b Central Falls, RI, Nov 12, 07; s Wilfred Adelard Desmarais & Laura Gervais D; m 1929 to Laura Anna Cartier; c Laura Leona (Mrs Breault). Educ: Sacred Heart Acad, Central Falls, 4 years; Lincoln Exten Inst, Correspondent Course, Cleveland, Ohio. Polit & Govt Pos: Treas & pres, Central Falls Rep Club, 44-46; founder & pres, Central Falls Good Govt Club, 46-48; chmn, Central Falls Rep City Comt, 67-73; chmn, Rep State Sen Dist 35 Comt, 67-; mem, Econ Stabilizing Comt, State of RI, 67-; chmn, Central Falls Ward Two Comt, 73-; mem, RI Rep State Cent Comt, 75- Bus & Prof Pos: Machinist-toolmaker, 24-70; part-time local ins mgr, Asn Canado-Am, Manchester, NH, 70- Mil Serv: Entered as Pvt, RI Militia, 41, released as Pfc, 43, after serv in Co M, 1st Regt. Mem: Int Asn Machinists; Le Foyer Club, Pawtucket; Toastmasters Int; Sr Citizens RI Action Group; Club Marquette, Inc, Woonsocket, RI. Honors & Awards: Citation, Asn Canado-Am for Outstanding Serv as Secy-Treas, 68. Relig: Roman Catholic. Mailing Add: 78 Tremont St Central Falls RI 02863

DESMARAIS, WALTER J (D)
NH State Rep
Mailing Add: 71 Walnut St Rochester NH 03867

DESMARAIS, WILLIAM A (D)
NH State Rep
Mailing Add: 14 Fifth St Nashua NH 03060

DESNOYER, ALTON G (D)
NH State Rep
Mailing Add: 8 Maple Heights Claremont NH 03743

DESPOL, JOHN ANTON (R)
b San Francisco, Calif, July 22, 13; s Anton Despol & Bertha Mary Balzer D; m 1937 to Jeri Kay Steep; c Christopher Paul & Anthony John. Educ: Los Angeles Jr Col, 30-31; Univ Southern Calif, 31; Calif Inst Technol Exten, Training within Indust, 40-41; Univ Calif, Los Angeles Adult Exten, cert, 68. Polit & Govt Pos: Pub mem, Calif State Defense Coun, 39-41; mem, Los Angeles Co Dem Cent Comt, 42-44; mem, Tenth Regional War Man Power Comn, 42-45; panel mem, Tenth Regional War Labor Bd, 42-45; nat steel panel mem, Nat War Labor Bd, 44; mem exec comt, Calif Dem State Cent Comt, 52-56; chmn, 15th Cong Dist Dem Cent Comt, 54-56; mem, Calif Legis Adv Comn to State Legis, 56-59; deleg, Dem Nat Conv, 48-60; mem, Calif adv comt, US Civil Rights Comn, 58-61; mem, Tech Adv Comt to Calif Econ Develop Agency, 61-65; mem, Rep Assocs of Los Angeles Co, 66-; pub mem, Calif Job Training & Placement Coun, 67-68; secy labor comt, Calif Rep State Cent Comt, 67-68; deleg, Rep Nat Conv, 68; comnr, Fed Mediation & Conciliation Serv, 72-73; consult, mediator & arbitrator, labor rels, economics & polit, 73- Bus & Prof Pos: Registered rep, Dempsey-Tegeler & Co, Inc, 68-70; registered rep, Bache & Co, Inc, 70-72. Publ: California Legislative Analysis & Candidates Questionnaire, 52-54 & 56-58 & Collective Bargaining Strategy, 53, Calif CIO Coun; California Election Analysis, Calif Summer Community Orgn & Polit Educ Prog, 56. Mem: Comt for Econ Develop; retired mem United Steelworkers of Am; Calif CIO; Calif Labor Fedn, AFL-CIO; Los Angeles World Affairs Coun (bd dirs, 53-); Los Angeles Comt on Foreign Rels. Honors & Awards: Cert for Community Leadership. Relig: Protestant. Mailing Add: Suite 3 252 S Mariposa Ave Los Angeles CA 90004

DESPOT, GEORGE JOSEPH (R)
Chmn, Fourth Dist Rep Comt, La
b Shreveport, La, Jan 28, 27; s George Gregory Despot & Katherine Vlahovich D; m 1953 to Pearla Alice Tinsley; c Susan Alicia & Rebecca Ann. Educ: Univ Notre Dame, AB, 47; La State Univ Law Sch, LLB, 50. Polit & Govt Pos: Mem, Rep State Cent Comt, La, 63-, asst to state chmn, 63 & 65-66; mem, Caddo Parish Rep Exec Comt, La, 63-; bd mem, Rep State Action Coun, 64-65; Rep state finance chmn, 67; chmn, Fourth Dist Rep Comt, La, currently. Bus & Prof Pos: Partner, Mecom, Scott & Despot, 54-57; pres, Petroleum Investments, Inc, 59- Mil Serv: Entered as Pvt, Army, 45, released as T-5, 47, after serv in ETO. Mem: Independent Petroleum Asn of Am. Relig: Catholic. Mailing Add: 705 Beck Bldg Shreveport LA 71101

DESROCHER, ARTHUR L (R)
Mass State Rep
Mailing Add: State Capitol Boston MA 02133

DESTEFANIS, RAYMOND H (D)
RI State Rep
Mailing Add: 120 Cumberland St Providence RI 02908

DESTEFANO, C GEORGE (R)
b Providence, RI, Aug 2, 12; s Luke D DeStefano & Amalie Repole D; m to Janet L Harrower; c Richard P, William G & George O. Polit & Govt Pos: Pres, Town Coun, Barrington, RI, 46-49; RI State Rep, 48-54, Dep Minority Leader, RI House of Rep, 51-52; chmn, Barrington Rep Town Comt, 51-56; RI State Sen, 55-68, Dep Minority Leader, RI State Senate, 58-60, Minority Leader, 60-68; chmn, RI State Rep Comt, 68-71; pres, Nat Conf State Legis Leaders, formerly; first vpres & chmn bd, Nat Coun State Govt, formerly; mem, President's Adv Comn Intergovt Rels, formerly; Rep Nat Committeeman, RI, 68-71; deleg, Rep Nat Conv, 72. Bus & Prof Pos: Mem adv comt, Eagleton Inst Polit, Rutgers Univ, formerly; pres, DeStefano Ford Sales Inc, Barrington, RI, currently; pres, DeStefano Investment Corp, currently; ins agt, George DeStefano Agency, currently. Mem: Lions; Salvation Army; Am Red Cross; Bald Mt Ski Corp, Rangley, Maine; Fraternal Order of Police. Relig: Catholic. Mailing Add: 15 Pinetop Rd Barrington RI 02806

DESTIGTER, MELVIN (R)
Mich State Rep
b Sioux Center, Iowa, Nov 21, 28; m 1950 to Carole Jean Schultze; c Melanie, Kurt, Kim, Todd & Heidi. Educ: Calvin Col, AB; Univ Mich. Polit & Govt Pos: Mich State Rep, 64- Bus & Prof Pos: Sales mgr; teacher. Mil Serv: Army, Japan. Mem: Hudsonville City Comn, 59-64. Relig: Christian Reformed. Mailing Add: 10235 42nd Ave Allendale MI 49401

DEUKMEJIAN, GEORGE (R)
Calif State Sen
b Albany, NY, June 6, 28; s C George Deukmejian & Alice Gairdan D; m 1957 to Gloria M Saatjian; c Leslie Ann, George Krikor & Andrea Diane. Educ: Siena Col, BA; St John's Univ Law Sch, JD. Polit & Govt Pos: Calif State Assemblyman, 62-66; Calif State Sen, 67-, minority leader, Calif State Senate, currently. Bus & Prof Pos: Attorney-at-law, 52- Mil Serv: Entered as Pvt, Army, 53, released as Cpl, 55, after serv in US Army Claims Team, Europe, 55. Mem: Lions; Elks; Navy League; CofC; Relig: Episcopal. Legal Res: 5366 E Broadway Long Beach CA 90903 Mailing Add: 444 W Ocean Blvd Long Beach CA 90802

DEUSTER, DONALD EUGENE (R)
Ill State Rep
b Milwaukee, Wis, Sept 26, 29; s Sarto Lewis Deuster & Dorothy M Sanders D; m 1953 to Katharine Brigitti Brink; c Mary Katharine, Ruth Elizabeth, Jane Marguerite & Anne Britta. Educ: Ripon Col, BA, 52; Univ Calif, Los Angeles, LLB, 57; Phi Kappa Pi. Polit & Govt Pos: Admin asst to US Rep Robert McClory, Ill, 36-69; pres, Libertyville Young Rep, 59-60; Rep precinct committeeman, Fourth Precinct, Libertyville Twp, 60-62; educ chmn, Lake Co Rep Cent Comt, Cong Rels Officer, Dept of Transportation, 69-72; Ill State Rep, 72- Bus & Prof Pos: Asst counsel, Legal Dept, Kemper Ins Group, Chicago, Ill, 57-62, asst to chmn bd, 62-63. as 2nd Lt, Army, 52, released as 1st Lt, 54, after serv in 5th Inf Training Div, Indiantown Gap Mil Reservation, Pa & 45th & 24th Inf Div, Korea. Publ: Our national purpose, Libertyville Independent Register, 62; Get into politics, Kemper Ins Mag, 60; Saving the passenger train, Railroad Transportation Inst J, 11/70. Mem: Calif Bar Asn; Ill State Bar. Relig: Presbyterian. Mailing Add: 132 N Sylvan Lake Dr Mundelein IL 60060

DEUTSCH, PETER (R)
Treas, Kings Co Rep Comt, NY
b Brooklyn, NY, July 6, 06; s Joshua Deutsch & Rose Lapidus D; m 1930 to Mae Edelstein; c Judith (Mrs Schneider) & Charles. Educ: St John's Univ Sch of Law, LLB, 28. Polit & Govt Pos: Rep state committeeman, 39th Dist, NY, 44-69; mem research coun, NY State Sen, 46-48; dep state tax comnr, Brooklyn, NY, 67-68, dist tax suprv, 68-; treas, Kings Co Rep Comt, currently. Bus & Prof Pos: Attorney-at-law. Mem: Am, NY State & Brooklyn Bar Asns; NY Trial Lawyers Asn; KofP; Gtr NY Civic Asn. Relig: Jewish. Legal Res: 3137 Fulton St Brooklyn NY 11208 Mailing Add: 32 Court St Brooklyn NY 11201

DEVANE, HARVEY E (D)
Maine State Rep
Mailing Add: Box 673 Ellsworth ME 04605

DEVERIN, THOMAS J (D)
NJ State Assemblyman
Mailing Add: State House Trenton NJ 08625

DEVERTER, WALTER F (R)
Pa State Rep
Mailing Add: Capitol Bldg Harrisburg PA 17120

DEVINE, JOHN WILLIAM (D)
Mont State Sen
b Great Falls, Mont, May 13, 26; s Oshey Devine & Ann Johns D; m 1946 to Elizabeth Ann Little; c Daniel J, Timothy O, Shaun, Kevin, Padraic T & Barry C. Educ: Great Falls High Sch, Mont. Polit & Govt Pos: Mont State Rep, 71-72, mem, Fish & Game Comt, Mont House Rep, 71-72; Mont State Sen, 73-, mem, Bus & Indust Comt & Bill & Jour Comt, Mont State Senate, 73- Bus & Prof Pos: Dir, Five State-Regional Beer Asn, Mont Beer Wholesalers Asn & Anheuser Busch Ecology Region Panel; vpres, Devine & Asselstine Inc & Dale Stapp Fashions. Mil Serv: Entered as Seaman, Navy, 43, released as Coxswain, 46, after serv in Pac Theatre, 44-46; Good Conduct Medal; Asiatic Pac Medal with 1-Star. Mem: VFW; Elks; Meadowlark Country Club; Mont Club. Relig: Catholic. Mailing Add: Park Garden Lane Great Falls MT 59404

DEVINE, SAMUEL L (R)
US Rep, Ohio
b South Bend, Ind, Dec 21, 15; s John F Devine, Jr (deceased) & Kittie M Leeper D; m 1940 to Betty M Galloway; c Lois, Joyce & Carol. Educ: Colgate Univ, 33-34; Ohio State Univ, 34-37; Univ Notre Dame, LLB cum laude, 40; Sigma Nu; Delta Theta Phi; Varsity O Asn. Polit & Govt Pos: Spec agent, Fed Bur of Invest, 40-45; Ohio State Rep, 51-55; prosecuting attorney, Franklin Co, Ohio, 55-58; US Rep, Ohio, 59- Bus & Prof Pos: Attorney-at-law, Metcalf, King, Ramey & Devine, 45-48; attorney-at-law, Hamilton & Kramer Law Off, 48-55. Publ: Various articles, Notre Dame Lawyer, 38-40. Mem: Mason (33 degree); Scottish Rite; Shrine; Charity Newsies; Ohio Asn of Football Officers. Relig: Methodist. Mailing Add: 195 N Roosevelt Ave Columbus OH 43209

DEVINE, TERENCE D (R)
b Grand Forks, NDak, Aug 5, 37; m 1960 to Mary Catherine Bondy; c Theodore Patrick & Stacey Catherine. Educ: Univ NDak, BSBA, 62, LLB, 65. Polit & Govt Pos: Chmn, 17th Legis Dist Rep Party, NDak, 65-70; mem, NDak Rep Exec Comt, 67-70; state attorney, Nelson Co, 67-; deleg, NDak Const Conv, 70; chmn, Nelson Co Rep Party, formerly. Mil Serv: Entered as Pvt, Army, 56, released as SP-4, 68. Mem: NDak State Bar Asn; Lions; KofC. Relig: Catholic. Mailing Add: Lakota ND 58344

DEVITT, JAMES C (R)
Wis State Sen
b La Crosse, Wis, Oct 12, 29; s John J Devitt, Sr & Mary Mullen D; m 1950 to Rita Kosmicki; c Patricia Ann & Brian James. Educ: Marquette Univ, 47-50. Polit & Govt Pos: Wis State Assemblyman, 66-68; state vpres, Nat Defense Transportation Asn, 66-69; Wis rep to Four-State Legis Comt on Pollution of Lake Mich, 67-70; Wis State Sen, 28th Dist, 68-, secy majority caucus, Wis State Senate, 69-, mem, Comt Legis Procedure, currently, chmn, Comt Health, Educ & Welfare, 73-, vchmn, Joint Survey Comt Retirement Systs, currently. Bus & Prof Pos: Pres, Devitt Cartage Co, Inc, 64-65; chmn bd & pres, Devitt Leasing, Inc, 65-68; mem bd dirs, Bank of Greenfield, 65-70; pres, S T C Leasing Corp, 66-68; partner, S D & H Co, 69- Mem: Metrop Jaycees' Pres Coun; Am Legion Post 416; Lions; KofC; Farm Bur. Honors & Awards: Nat Distinguished Serv Award to Am Small Bus, 70; Man of the Year, Milwaukee Police Off, 70; life mem, Am Legion, 70; Rep of the Year, Wis Col Rep, 71; Individual & Outstanding Serv Award, United Asn Retarded Children, 72. Relig: Catholic; Mem Ushers Soc, St Mary's Catholic Church, 64- Mailing Add: 8565 W Waterford Ave Greenfield WI 53228

DEVLIN, GERARD FRANCIS (D)
Md State Deleg
b Boston, Mass, May 29, 33; s James Joseph Devlin & Ann Meldon D; m 1959 to Mary Carol Dailey; s Kathleen Ann, Christine Ellen, James Joseph, II & Mary Elizabeth. Educ: Boston Col, 51-52 & 53-54; Suffolk Univ, AB cum laude, 59; Univ Md Law Sch, Baltimore, JD, 69; Univ Md Grad Sch, College Park, AM, 70; Pi Sigma Alpha. Polit & Govt Pos: Staff mem, Sen Carl Hayden, Ariz, Washington, DC, 64-65; mem, Bd of Elec Suprv, Prince Georges Co, Md, 64-69, chmn, 65-67 & 69; legis asst to US Rep Dominick V Daniels, NJ, Washington, DC, 65-69, admin asst, 72-75; Md Nat Rels Officer, Exec Dept, Annapolis, Md, 69-72; mem, Md Comt on the Concerns of Spanish Speaking, 70-72; chmn, Prince Georges Co Task Force on Fire Serv, 72-73; Md State Deleg, 74-, mem ways & means comt, Md House Deleg, currently. Bus & Prof Pos: Partner, Ross, Lochte, Murray, Redding & Devlin, currently. Mil Serv: Entered as Pvt, Marine Corps, 55, released as Sgt, 57, after serv in Marine Corps Inst, Marine Barracks, Washington, DC, 55-57. Mem: Am & Md Bar Asns; Cong Staff Club; KofC; Marine Corps League. Relig: Roman Catholic. Legal Res: 2505 Kitmore Lane Bowie MD 20715 Mailing Add: Rm 208 House Off Bldg Annapolis MD 20414

DEVLIN, L PATRICK (D)
b Paterson, NJ, Apr 11, 39; m 1964 to Suzanne Zellers; c Kathleen, Cristin & Matthew. Educ: William Paterson Col NJ, BA, 61; Columbia Univ, MA, 63; Wayne State Univ, PhD, 68. Polit & Govt Pos: Deleg, Dem Nat Conv, 72. Bus & Prof Pos: Assoc prof, Univ RI, 67-, pres, Univ RI-AAUP Faculty Union, currently. Publ: Auth, Contemporary Political Speaking, Wadsworth, 71; Hubert H Humphrey: the teacher-preacher, 70 & The McGovern Canvass: a study in interpersonal political campaign communication, 73, Cent States Speech J. Mem: Am Asn Univ Prof; Speech Commun Asn; Eastern States Speech Asn; Comt on Polit Commun. Mailing Add: 31 Lake St Wakefield RI 02879

DEVLIN, PHILIP, JR (R)
Chmn, Putnam Co Rep Exec Comt, Fla
b New Orleans, La, May 1, 16; s Philip A Devlin & Frances Moore D; m 1972 to Marguerite W; c Philip F, Cecily Anne, Paul F, Sheila M, Maureen E & Ellen L. Educ: L H Edwards High Sch, Asheville, NC, grad, 34. Polit & Govt Pos: Chmn, Putnam Co Rep Exec Comt, Fla, 66-; mem, Fla Rep State Exec Comt, 66-; former chmn, Zoning Bd of Appeals, Palatka, Fla. Bus & Prof Pos: Formerly engaged in mortgage banking field, Jacksonville, Miami & Pensacola, Fla; asst mgr, Palatka Abstract & Title Guaranty, Inc, 60- Mil Serv: Entered as Pvt, Army, 42, released as Chief Warrant Officer, 46, after serv in Finance Dept, Army Air Forces, Continental US; Army Commendation Medal; Am Theatre Medal. Mem: Am & Fla Land Title Asns; Mortgage Banking Asn of Am; charter mem Palatka Little Theatre; Putnam Co CofC. Relig: Catholic. Legal Res: Rte 3 Box 1201 Palatka FL 32077 Mailing Add: PO Box 83 Palatka FL 32077

DEVOURSNEY, MARTIN THOMAS (D)
Treas, Bergen Co Dem Coalition, NJ
b Jersey City, NJ, Nov 2, 20; s Frederick DeVoursney & Anne Fleming D; m 1939 to Elizabeth Irene Cargill; c Elizabeth (Mrs Caubet), Susan (Mrs Ganley), Martin, Jr, William & Robin. Educ: Regis High Sch, NY, 33-35. Polit & Govt Pos: Deleg, Nat Dem Conv, 68 & 72; treas, Bergen Co Dem Coalition, NJ 69-; chmn exec comt, Ridgefield Park Dem Club, 73-; deleg, Dem Nat Mid-Term Conf, 74. Bus & Prof Pos: Maintenance mech, Westinghouse Elec Elevator Co, Jersey City, NJ, 42- Mil Serv: Entered as Pvt, Army, 44, released as S/Sgt, 46, after serv in I Co 21st Inf Regt, 24th Inf Div, Southeast Asia; Bronze Star Medal; Two Battle Stars. Mem: IUE, AFL-CIO; Westinghouse Conf Bd; NJ State AFL-CIO Conv; NJ State IUE, AFL-CIO Conv; Hudson & Bergen Co Cent Labor Coun. Mailing Add: 127 Brinkerhoff St Ridgefield Park NJ 07660

DEWALD, GRETTA MOLL (D)
Mem, Ga State Dem Exec Comt
b Kutztown, Pa, Oct 26, 29; d Lloyd Alvin Moll & Olga Wuchter M; m 1951 to Charles Frederick Dewald; c Michael Steven, Jonathan Glenn, Henry Lloyd, Jane Patricia & Joseph Charles. Educ: Agnes Scott Col, BA, 50. Polit & Govt Pos: Precinct chmn, 77th Dist, DeKalb Co Dem Party, Ga, 70-72; mem, DeKalb Co Dem Exec Comt, 70-; pres, Dem Women of DeKalb, 70-72; mem, North DeKalb Dem, 71-72; mem, Fourth Cong Dist, Ga State Exec Comt, 71-, chmn, Speaker's Bur, Ga Women's Polit Caucus, currently, chmn, DeKalb Co Dem Party, formerly; chmn legis observer desk & corp, Ga Environ Coun, 71-; mem, Gov Comn on Volunteerism, 72-; mem, Gov Comn Status of Women, 72-; deleg, Dem Nat Mid-Term Conf, 74. Bus & Prof Pos: Teacher, Eastman High Sch, Ga, 50-51; teacher, Bass High Sch, Atlanta, 51-52. Mem: Ga & DeKalb Co Conserv; Citizens for Clear Air; Nat Wildlife Fedn; Nat Geog Soc. Relig: Presbyterian; Elder, North Decatur Presby Church. Mailing Add: 2231 Kodiak Dr NE Atlanta GA 30345

DEWBERRY, DOLORES DAVENPORT (DEE) (D)
b Indianapolis, Ind, May 15, 32; d Edward Davenport & Jean Hardy D; div; c Dean Daven. Educ: St Petersburg Jr Col, AA, 53; Phi Theta Kappa; Nat Jr Col Players. Polit & Govt Pos: Bd dirs, Iowa Dem Conf, 68-72, publicity chmn, 70; advert dir, William Albrecht Cong Primary, First Dist, Iowa, 70, Fred Moore, Sixth Dist Cong Campaign, 70 & Roger Blobaum, Fourth Dist Cong Campaign, 70; mem state steering comt, Iowans for McGovern, 72; coordr, Barron Co McGovern Primary, Wis, 72; orgn mem & interim chmn, Iowa Dem Women's Caucus, 72; deleg & mem rules comt, Dem Nat Conv, 72; prog coordr & advert dir, Paul Franzenberg Iowa Gubernatorial Campaign, 72. Bus & Prof Pos: Managing dir, Media Methods Advert, 70- Mem: Nat Orgn Women. Honors & Awards: Award for TV Commercials, TV Bur Advert & Nat Retail Merchants Asn, 70. Relig: Unitarian. Mailing Add: 2918 Johnson Ave NW Cedar Rapids IA 52405

DEWBERRY, J H (JIM) (D)
Ariz State Rep
Mailing Add: 5962 E 22nd St Tucson AZ 85711

DEWEES, ELAINE MACDONALD (R)
Mem, Rep State Cent Comt Calif
b Philadelphia, Pa, Aug 5, 22; d William Park MacDonald & Beatrice Boswell M; m 1948 to Roland Robinson Dewees; c David William & Scott MacDonald. Educ: Drexel Inst of Technol, Philadelphia, Pa, 40-42. Polit & Govt Pos: Div chmn, Los Angeles Co Rep Precinct Orgn, 58-62; mem, Rep State Cent Comt Calif, 64-; pres, E Pasadena-Sierra Madre Fedn Rep Women, 65 & 66; 20th Cong Dist chmn, Los Angeles Co Bd Fedn Rep Women, 67-68; mem bd dirs, Pasadena Rep Club, Inc, 68-; dep registr, Los Angeles Co Registr of Voters, 68-70; dist secy, Assemblyman Frank Landerman, 47th Assembly Dist, 68-70, admin asst, currently. Bus & Prof Pos: Real estate clerk, Girard Trust Co, Philadelphia, Pa, 42; clerk, Philgas Div, Phillips Petrol Co, 43-47; clerk, Solgas Div, Sun Oil Co, 47-48. Mem: DAR. Relig: Episcopal. Mailing Add: 3657 Ivydale Ct Pasadena CA 91107

DEWEY, GILES W (R)
Vt State Rep
Mailing Add: RFD 2 Stowe VT 05672

DEWEY, WILLIAM L (R)
Chmn, Isabella Co Rep Party, Mich
b Mt Pleasant, Mich, Apr 30, 51; s William A Dewey & Elva June Osborn D; div. Educ: Odessa State Col, 69-71; Mid Mich Col, Harrison, AA, 73; Mid Mich Student Govt Asn. Polit & Govt Pos: Exec comt mem, Clare Co Rep Party, Mich, 71-73; state conv deleg, Clare & Isabella Co, 71-75; precinct deleg, 71-76; exec comt mem, Tenth Cong Dist Rep Party, 73-76, Rep issues comt chmn, 75-76; exec comt mem, Isabella Co Rep Party, 73-, chmn, 75-; Rep issues comt mem, State of Mich, 74-76. Mem: Lions Int; Optimist Int. Legal Res: 3300 E Deerfield Ave Mt Pleasant MI 48858 Mailing Add: PO Box 372 Mt Pleasant MI 48858

DE WILDE, DAVID
Asst Secy Housing Prod & Mortgage Credit—FHA
Mailing Add: Dept Housing & Urban Develop Washington DC 20410

DEWITT, ELLEN LOUISE (D)
Secy, Piscataquis Co Dem Comt, Maine
b Milo, Maine, Feb 20, 46; d Joseph Patrick Reardon & Eleanor Mitchell R; m 1967 to Edwin

Arthur Dewitt. Educ: Milo High Sch, grad, 64. Polit & Govt Pos: Co deleg, Piscataquis Co, Maine, 70-; secy, Piscataquis Co Dem Comt, 70-; notary pub, Maine, 70-, justice of peace, 70- Bus & Prof Pos: Secy, Employers Liability Ins, Co, Bangor, Maine, 64-67; secy-clerk, B&A RR, Derby, 67; clerk, Pullen's Clothing Store, Milo, 68-69; legal secy, F Davis Clark, Attorney-at-law, 69- Mem: Eastern Star (Esther); Ins Women of Eastern Maine; Milo Jr League. Relig: Baptist; teacher, Sunday Sch, choir mem, Bd Christian Educ. Legal Res: Reardon Rd Milo ME 04463 Mailing Add: RFD 1 Milo ME 04463

DEWITT, FRANKLIN ROOSEVELT **(D)**

b Conway, SC, May 25, 36; s Mathew A DeWitt & Rebecca Hughes D; m 1960 to Willa Waylis Johnson; c Rosalyn Abrevaya & Sharolyn Renee. Educ: SC State Col, BS, 62, Sch Law, LLB, 64; Kappa Alpha. Polit & Govt Pos: Councilman, Conway, SC, 69-; deleg, Dem Nat Conv, 72; secy, Race Path Precinct, 72- Bus & Prof Pos: Trial attorney, US Civil Serv Comn, Washington, DC, 65-67; city attorney, Atlantic Beach, 66-; pvt law practice, Conway, 67- Mil Serv: Entered as Airman Basic, Air Force, 55, released as Airman 1/C, 59, after serv in 305 Bomb Wing, Strategic Air Command; Good Conduct Ribbon. Mem: SC, Fed & Am Bar Asns; Horry-Georgetown Econ Opportunity Coun (treas); Horry-Georgetown Ment Health Coun (bd dirs). Relig: Baptist. Legal Res: 1708 Hwy 378 Conway SC 29526 Mailing Add: 510 Hwy 378 Conway SC 29526

DEWITT, JOHN ALLEN **(D)**

Committeeman, Sixth Cong Dist Dem Comt, Mo

b Gilman City, Mo, Feb 20, 09; s John William DeWitt & Jennie S Robertson D; m 1928 to Amber Gladys Artrip; c June Ann (Mrs Marvin Meadows). Educ: Northeast Mo State Teachers Col, 28; Phi Sigma Epsilon. Polit & Govt Pos: Road comnr, Twp One, Mo, 48-60; Dem committeeman, Sixth Cong Dist, currently; chmn, Harrison Co Dem Cent Comt, formerly; deleg, Dem Nat Conv, 72. Polit & Govt Pos: Owner of Ins Agency, Bethany, Mo, 56-; mgr, Bob Broyles & Assoc, 59-64; assoc, Bethany Realty, 64-65; mgr, United Farm Agency, 65-; owner, H & R Block Franchise, 66- Mem: AF&AM, Gilman City; Odd Fellows, Bethany. Mailing Add: Gilman City MO 64642

DEZINNO, BENJAMIN NICHOLAS, JR **(D)**

Conn State Rep

b Waterbury, Conn, Dec 9, 24; s Benjamin Nicholas DeZinno, Sr & Maye Martone D; m 1943 to Grace Cofrancesco; c Roger Charles, Benjamin N, III, Wm Francis & Margaret Patrice. Educ: Univ Conn Col Pharm, 49. Polit & Govt Pos: Comnr health, Meriden, Conn, 66-75, Dem town committeeman, 72-75, cand for mayor, 73; Conn State Rep, 84th Dist, Meriden-Yalesville, 75- Bus & Prof Pos: Licensed pharmacist, Conn, 49-; owner, Graeber's Pharm, Meriden, 50- Mil Serv: Entered as A/S, Navy, 43, released as Pharmacist Mate 1/C, 46, after serv in US Submarine Force, SPac, 44-46; Letter of Commendation from President of US. Mem: Eagles 35, Meriden; KofC 2; Unison Club; Am & Meriden Pharmaceut Asns. Honors & Awards: Man of the Year Award, Conn Pharmaceut Asn, 73. Relig: Roman Catholic. Mailing Add: 174 Bradley Ave Meriden CT 06450

D'GEROLAMO, EDWARD J **(D)**

La State Rep

Mailing Add: 916 Williams Blvd Kenner LA 70062

DIAL, GERALD O **(D)**

Ala State Rep

Mailing Add: Box 275 Lineville AL 36266

DIAMOND, HARVEY JEROME **(D)**

Chmn, Mecklenburg Co Dem Party, NC

b Charlotte, NC, Dec 7, 28; s Harry B Diamond & Jeaneatte Davis D; m 1952 to Betty Lou Ball; c Michael Alan, Leah Beth, David Arthur & Abby. Educ: Univ NC, Chapel Hill, BS, 52; Tau Epsilon Phi. Polit & Govt Pos: Chmn, Sharon Precinct No Two, NC, 64-70; vchmn, Mecklenburg Co Dem Party, 70-72, treas, 72-74, chmn, 74-; mem, NC Dem State Exec Comt, 70-72; NC & SC regional chmn, Dem Nat Telethon, 72; deleg, Dem Nat Conv, 72. Bus & Prof Pos: Sales mgr, Dixie Neon Supply House, Charlotte, NC, 52-61; owner & mgr, H & D Agency, 62-; pres, Plasti-Vac, Inc, 61-; pres, Diamond Supply Inc, 70- Mil Serv: Entered as Pvt E-1, Army, 52, released as E-4, 54, after serv in Recruiting Duty, NC Mil Dist Hq. Mem: Soc of Plastics Engrs; Soc of Plastics Indust; AF&AM; Scottish Rite; Cotswald Optimist Club. Honors & Awards: Distinguished Serv, March of Dimes, 66; Cert of Appreciation, US Dept of Com, 67; Dist Serv Award, Hon Hubert H Humphrey, 70; Cert of Appreciation, Nat Elec Sign Asn, 70. Relig: Jewish. Legal Res: 6929 Folger Dr Charlotte NC 28211 Mailing Add: PO Box 5543 Charlotte NC 28205

DIAMOND, LLOYD WEBB **(R)**

Mem, Caddo Parish Rep Exec Comt, La

b Shreveport, La, Jan 8, 37; d Robert Lee Webb & Jean Guynemer W; m 1958 to Anthony John Diamond; c John Webb & Robert Anthony. Educ: Col of William & Mary, BA, 59; Theta Alpha Phi. Polit & Govt Pos: Pres, Career Women's Rep Club, 66-67; mem-at-lg, La Fedn of Rep Women, 67-69; precinct orgn coordr, Caddo Parish Rep Polit Action Coun, 67-69 & ballot security coordr, 69-; alt deleg, Rep Nat Conv, 68; secy, Rep Party of La Polit Action Coun, 69-; mem, Caddo Parish Rep Exec Comt, La, 69- Bus & Prof Pos: Chmn, St Paul's Espiscopal Day Sch, 69- Mem: PTA; Women's Symphony Guild; Gas Light Players Summer Theater. Relig: Episcopal. Mailing Add: 237 Pierremont Rd Shreveport LA 71105

DIAMONSTEIN, ALAN ARNOLD **(D)**

Va State Deleg

b Newport News, Va, Aug 20, 31; s William Diamonstein & Lillian Becker D; m 1972 to Beverly Hicks. Educ: Univ Va, BS in Com, 55, LLB, 58. Polit & Govt Pos: Mem, Human Rels Coun, Newport News, Va; mem, Gov Coun for Ment Retardation; past pres, Hampton Roads Young Dem Club; pres, Young Dem Clubs of Va, 68; deleg, Dem Nat Conv, 68; Va State Deleg, 67-, chmn, Va Housing Study Comn, Va House Rep, 73- Bus & Prof Pos: Partner, Diamonstein & Drucker, currently. Mil Serv: Air Force, 50. Mem: Hampton Roads Boys Club; Peninsula Asn for Retarded Children. Relig: Jewish. Legal Res: 540 Hallmark Dr Newport News VA 23606 Mailing Add: 103 28th St Newport News VA 23607

DIAMONT, DAVID HUNTER **(D)**

NC State Rep

b Greensboro, NC, Feb 9, 46; s David Elijah Diamont & Hyacinth Hunter D; single. Educ: Wake Forest Univ, BA, 68; Appalachian State Univ, MA, 72; Lambda Chi Alpha. Polit & Govt Pos: Pres, Surry Co Young Dem Club, NC, 73-74; NC State Rep, 28th Dist, 74- Bus & Prof Pos: Am hist teacher & football coach, Mt Airy Sr High Sch, NC, 68-71 & 72- Mem: NC Coaches Asn; Nat Educ Asn; NC Asn Educators. Relig: Methodist. Mailing Add: PO Box 784 Pilot Mountain NC 27041

DIAZ DE VILLEGAS, OSCAR **(R)**

VPres, Nat Rep Party, PR

b Havana, Cuba, Oct 11, 31; s Oscar Diaz de Villegas y Martinez & Amparo Mederos Pastor D; m 1955 to Elvia Ugartemendia. Educ: Havana Bus Col, BA, 52. Polit & Govt Pos: Vpres, Nat Rep Party of PR, 70-; chmn, Rep Nationalities Comt of PR, 70-; alt deleg, Rep Nat Conv, 72. Publ: Promotion of the book in Latin America, Superior Coun of Cent Am Univs, 68; Marketing of the Book in Latin America, Franklin Book Progs, 68. Mem: Rotary; Inter Am Businessmen Asn; Serra Club of San Juan (vpres, 71-73); UN Assoc of the US (vpres, PR Chap, 71-73). Relig: Catholic. Legal Res: 46 Esmeralda St San Juan PR 00920 Mailing Add: 355 De Hostos Ave San Juan PR 00918

DIAZ GARCIA, LUIS FELIPE **(POPULAR DEMOCRAT, PR)**

Rep, PR House of Rep

Mailing Add: State Capitol San Juan PR 00901

DIBRITO, SANDY LOUIS **(DFL)**

Treas, Otter Tail Co Dem-Farmer-Labor Party, Minn

b Dilworth, Minn, June 21, 35; s Sandy DiBrito & Lena Boit D; m 1960 to Theresa Ann Heck; c Maria Annette, Kevin John, Deanne Marie & Kyle Joseph. Educ: Moorhead State Col, BS, 57, MS, 68; Nat Dramatic Fraternity; Phi Mu Alpha Sinfonia; Alpha Epsilon; Newman Club. Polit & Govt Pos: Mem exec comt, Otter Tail Co Dem-Farmer-Labor Party, Minn, 65-68, treas, 68-; deleg, Minn State Dem-Farmer-Labor Conv, 66-72; village councilman, Perham, Minn, 70-, mem hosp bd dirs, 71-; secy, East Otter Tail Co Fair Bd, 71-; deleg, Nat Dem Conv, 72. Bus & Prof Pos: Vocal music teacher, Belle Fourche, SDak, 57-58, Biwabik, Minn, 58-62 & Perham, 62- Mil Serv: Entered as Pvt, Minn Army Nat Guard, 53, released as Sgt 1/C, 62. Mem: Am Fedn Teachers; Minn Music Educators Asn; KofC (past grand knight); Perham Lakeside Gold Club; Perham CofC. Relig: Roman Catholic. Mailing Add: 633 Second Ave SW Perham MN 56573

DICARLO, DAVID COSIMO **(D)**

Pa State Rep

b Erie, Pa, Sept 21, 45; s Cosimo P DiCarlo & Evelyn Demchak D; m 1965 to Beverly Heintz; c David Jon & Erin Ann. Educ: Gannon Col, BS in Mkt, 71; Pi Kappa Alpha. Polit & Govt Pos: Pa State Rep, 73- Bus & Prof Pos: Job develop specialist, Opportunities Industrialization Ctr, 69-72. Mem: Summit Lions. Honors & Awards: Exec Dir's Serv Award, Opportunities Industrialization Ctr, 73. Relig: Catholic. Mailing Add: 1181 Robison Rd Erie PA 16509

DICARLO, DOMINICK L **(R)**

NY State Assemblyman

b Brooklyn, NY, Mar 11, 38; m to Esther Hansen; c four. Educ: St John's Col, BA, 50; St Johns Sch Law, 53; NY Univ Grad Sch La, LLM. Polit & Govt Pos: Asst US Attorney, Eastern Dist & chief, Organized Crime & Racketeering Sect, NY, 59-62; spec asst to US Attorney, 62; counsel to Minority Leader, A J Arwleo, New York Coun, 62-64; NY State Assemblyman, 64-; mem 12 Assembly Dist Regular Rep Club & Bay Ridge Rep Club. Bus & Prof Pos: Attorney-at-law. Mem: Dyker Heights & Narrows Civic Asn; Men's Asn of Bay Ridge; NY Dist Attorney Asn; St Bernadettes Holy Name Soc; KofC. Mailing Add: 1345 83rd St Brooklyn NY 11228

DICARLO, JOSEPH CARMINE **(D)**

Mass State Sen

b Somerville, Mass, Mar 21, 36; s Peter DiCarlo, Sr & Amalia DeMartino C; m 1958 to Joanne Marie Signore; c Stephen, Denise & Leanne. Educ: Boston Col, AB in Polit Sci; Boston Univ, ME in Educ Admin. Polit & Govt Pos: Mass State Rep, 64-68; Mass State Sen, 69- Bus & Prof Pos: Sch teacher, 58-64. Mem: KofC; Sons of Italy. Relig: Roman Catholic. Mailing Add: 81 Pearl Ave Revere MA 02151

DICE, RICHARD ARLING **(R)**

Conn State Rep

b Mason City, Iowa, July 3, 26; s Arling J Dice & Lila Davis D; married; c Kirk Arling, Dee Ann, Shelley Lyn, Deborah Kay & Richard Kent. Educ: Univ Iowa, BA, 50; Yale Univ Law Sch, JD; pres, Iowa Region & mem nat exec comt, Nat Student Asn; Omicron Delta Kappa; Alpha Tau Omega. Polit & Govt Pos: Co-chmn, Citizens for Ike, New Haven Co, Conn, 56; mem, Cheshire Rep Town Comt, 56-66; Rep campaign chmn, Cheshire, 57-59, prosecutor, 57-59, moderator, 60-68; chmn, Rep Recruit for '60 Comn, New Haven Co, 60; finance chmn, Conn State Rep Party, Cheshire, 69; Conn State Rep, 83rd Dist, 71-73, Conn State Rep, 89th Dist, 73-, chmn appropriations comt, Conn State Senate, 73-74, ranking mem appropriations comt, 75- Bus & Prof Pos: Law practice, New Haven, Conn, 55-60 & Cheshire, Conn, 60; law partnership, Dice, Bohan & Hitt, Cheshire, Conn, 61-71, Dice & Fazzone, Cheshire, 71-73 & Dice, Fazzone & Nuzzo, Cheshire, 74-; secy & gen counsel, Cott Beverage Corp, 60-63, dir, 62-63; legal vpres & secy, Cott Corp (ASE), 63-68; mem adv bd, Colonial Bank & Trust Co. Mil Serv: Entered as A/S, Navy, 44, released as Mailman 3/C, 46, after serv in Pac Theatre, 45-46. Mem: Am & Conn Bar Asns; Yale Alumni Asn; Univ Iowa Alumni Asn; Farms Country Club. Legal Res: 250 Platt Lane Cheshire CT 06410 Mailing Add: 420 Highland Ave Cheshire CT 06410

DICK, LAWRENCE **(R)**

NDak State Rep

b Nebr, Aug 31, 05; married; c six. Educ: Pub schs. Polit & Govt Pos: NDak State Rep, 53-61 & 69- Bus & Prof Pos: Farmer; dir, Farmers State Bank of Lisbon. Mem: Lutheran Home of the Oakes Circuit (pres). Mailing Add: State Capitol Bismarck ND 43215

DICK, NANCY E **(D)**

Colo State Rep

Mailing Add: Box 3466 McSkimming Rd Aspen CO 81611

DICKERMAN, CHARLES PINGREY **(D)**

Mem, Va State Dem Cent Comt

b Chicago, Ill, Oct 15, 09; s Judson Charles Dickerman & Adella Miller D; m to Brooke Benton; c Anne Brooke & William Roberts. Educ: Oberlin Col, BA, 30; Philadelphia Col Osteopathic Med, DO, 34. Polit & Govt Pos: Chmn, Augusta Co Dem Comt, Va, formerly; chmn, 19th Sen Dist Dem Comt, formerly; mem, Sixth Cong Dist Dem Comt, currently; mem, Va State Dem Cent Comt, currently. Bus & Prof Pos: Practicing osteopathic physician, Staunton, Va, 34- Mem: Am Col Gen Practitioners in Osteopathic Med & Surg; Am

Osteopathic Asn; Va Osteopathic Med Asn (pres, currently); Acad Appl Osteopathy; YMCA. Relig: Episcopal. Legal Res: Box 47 Rte 1 Swoope VA 24479 Mailing Add: 15 Terry Ct Staunton VA 24401

DICKERSON, FRANK ARTHUR (R)
Mem, Mo Rep State Comt

b Iberia, Mo, June 3, 12; s Thomas Wesley Dickerson & Annie Hill D; m 1932 to Grace Thelma Snelling; c Brenda (Mrs Norwood Clark, Jr) & Judy (Mrs Lawson). Educ: Iberia Jr Col, 2 years. Polit & Govt Pos: Treas, Miller Co, Mo, 39-42, clerk, 43-46; mem, Electoral Col, Eighth Dist, Mo, 44; mem, city coun, Iberia, 48-50; mem, Miller Co Rep Cent Comt, 50-52; deleg, Rep Nat Conv, 68; treas, Eighth Dist, Nixon-Agnew Campaign Comt, 68; deleg to several State & Dist Convs; mem, Mo Rep State Comt, 70- Bus & Prof Pos: Exec vpres, Bank of Iberia, 47-69, pres, 73- Mem: AF&AM; Lions. Relig: Baptist. Mailing Add: Iberia MO 65486

DICKERSON, HARVEY (D)
b Ely, Nev, June 3, 05; s Denver S Dickerson & Una Reilly D; m 1938 to Virginia Shephard; c Carol, Denver Shephard, Valerie & Donald Charles. Educ: Univ Nev, 30-31; Southeastern Univ, LLB, 41. Polit & Govt Pos: Chief dep US Marshall, Nev, 33-34; floor secy to Sen McCaran, 35-38; jr tax expert, Civil Aeronaut Admin, 39; admin asst, Works Progress Admin, 40; city attorney, Las Vegas, 42-43, Henderson, 53 & North Las Vegas, 56-62; cand Lt Gov, Nev, 50; Attorney Gen, Nev, 54-58 & 62-70; cand for US Sen, Nev, 56; cand for Gov, Nev, 58; mem exec comt, Nev State Dem Party, 60-61; mem, Gov Crime Comn, 69. Mem: Nev State Bar (dist gov, 44-49, pres, 54); Am Bar Asn; Am Judicature Soc; Nat Asn Attorneys Gen; Las Vegas Shrine Club. Relig: Protestant. Mailing Add: 302 Carson Las Vegas NV 89101

DICKERSON, JAMES RALPH (R)
Chmn, Camden Co Rep Cent Comt, Mo

b Camdenton, Mo, Oct 6, 52; s Jack Dickerson & Machir Vincent D; single. Educ: Univ Mo at Columbia, BA, 74. Polit & Govt Pos: Chmn legis action, Univ Mo Col Reps, 72-74, state chmn, 74-75; chmn Camden Co Rep Cent Comt, Mo, 74-; treas, Mo Eighth Cong Dist Rep Comt, 74-; admin asst, Mo State Senate, 75- Mem: Camden Co Bicentennial Comn (chmn); Camden Co Hist Soc (vpres). Honors & Awards: Presidential Commendation, Richard M Nixon, 70; Best Comt Chmn Award, Mo Col Reps, 74; Award of Merit, Mo Heart Asn, Ozark Region. Relig: Christian. Mailing Add: South Highway Five Camdenton MO 65020

DICKEY, CHARLES HARDIN, JR (D)
Chmn, Audrain Co Dem Comt, Mo

b Mexico, Mo, Aug 7, 07; m; c Betty; one grandchild. Polit & Govt Pos: Mem, Mexico City Coun, Mo, 50-57, mayor, formerly; Mo State Rep, 60-72; chmn, Audrain Co Dem Comt, Mo, 75- Bus & Prof Pos: Former auto dealer. Mem: CofC; Mo Asn of Social Welfare; Mason (Hebron Lodge 354); Royal Arch Chap 27, Mexico, Mo; Scottish Rite. Relig: Presbyterian; elder, First Presby Church, Mexico, Mo. Mailing Add: PO Box 22 Mexico MO 65265

DICKEY, DAVID JERRY (D)
Chmn, McNairy Co Dem Exec Comt, Tenn

b Corinth, Miss, July 14, 39; s Cecil Dickey & Rubye Newell D; m 1957 to Anita Lou Garrison; c David Jerry, II. Educ: Adamsville High Sch, Tenn, 4 years. Polit & Govt Pos: Chmn, McNairy Co Dem Exec Comt, Tenn, 72- Bus & Prof Pos: Owner, Adamsville Tel Co, Inc & Custom Concrete Co, Inc, currently. Mem: Tenn Tel Asn (pres, 71); Mason (master, 68); Adamsville Jaycees; Tenn Jaycees. Honors & Awards: JCI Sen, Tenn Jaycees, 65. Relig: Baptist. Mailing Add: PO Box 68 Adamsville TN 38310

DICKEY, DONALD FLOYD (R)
Chmn, Ripley Co Rep Party, Ind

b Batesville, Ind, May 14, 27; s Herschel C Dickey & Elsie Freeland D; m 1949 to Cathryn Marie Fries; c Beverly, John, Glenn, Mary, James, Donald, Jr & Janine. Educ: Batesville High Sch, grad, 45. Polit & Govt Pos: Rep Precinct committeeman, Ind, 48-; trustee, Laughery Twp, Ripley Co, 66-; vol dep sheriff, Ripley Co, 66-; vpres, Ind Twp Trustee Asn, 67-; chmn, Ripley Co Rep Party, 68-; supvr license br, Ninth Cong Dist, 69- Mil Serv: Entered as Apprentice, Seabees, 45, released as 2C CM 3/C, 46, after serving in 1066, 747 Construction Bn Maintenance Unit, Guam. Mem: VFW; Am Legion; F&AM; Eagles. Relig: Methodist. Mailing Add: 705 S Park Ave Batesville IN 47006

DICKEY, GRADY (D)
Mem, Dem Nat Comt, Ga

Mailing Add: 312 E Oglethorpe Ave Savannah GA 31401

DICKEY, RAYMOND, III (R)
b San Antonio, Tex, Sept 4, 41; s Raymond Dickey, Jr & Alice Winkins D; m 1967 to Lois Marie Graham; c Tamara Marie & Raymond, IV. Educ: Southwest Tex State Univ, BS, 68; St Mary's Univ, Tex, MA, 72; Businessman's Club; Eng Lit Club. Polit & Govt Pos: Deleg, Tex Rep State Conv, 68 & 70; treas, Bexar Co Rep Party, 70-, precinct chmn, 70-, dir state sen dist, 72-; coordr, Nixon-Tower-Grover Elect, 72; deleg, Rep Nat Conv, 72. Mil Serv: Entered as Seaman Recruit, US Coast Guard, 60, released as Leading Seaman, 64, after serv in US Coast Cutter Clematis, Galveston, Tex, 61-64; Good Conduct Medal. Mem: Tex State Teachers Asn; Harlandale Adminr Asn; STex Personnel & Guidance Asn; San Antonio CofC (Ambassador's Comt & Educ Comt, 72-); Lions. Relig: United Methodist. Mailing Add: 207 W White San Antonio TX 78214

DICKINSON, FRED OTIS, JR (D)
State Comptroller, Fla

b West Palm Beach, Fla, March 28, 22; s Fred O (Bud) Dickinson, Sr & Georgia Bell D; m 1952 to Mildred (Boots) Goddard; c Cathy, Danny, Douglas, Dwight & Fred Otis, III. Educ: Univ Fla, 41-42; John B Stetson Univ Sch Law, LLB, 48; Pi Kappa Phi; Phi Alpha Delta. Polit & Govt Pos: Fla State Rep, 54; Fla State Sen, 57-58; mgr, Fla Dem Presidential Campaign, 60; spec counsel, State Dem Educ Comt, 65; state comptroller, Fla, 65-; deleg, Dem Nat Conv, 68. Bus & Prof Pos: Law practice, Fisher, Dickinson & Prior, West Palm Beach, 48-65. Mil Serv: Entered as Pvt, Marines, 42, released as Cpl, 45, after serv in SPac, 42-45; Res, 45-57, 2nd Lt; Citation for Bravery. Mem: Fla & Am Bar Asns; NAm Securities Comn; State Banking Comn; Nat Conf of State Bank Supvr. Honors & Awards: Outstanding Young Man of the Year, West Palm Beach Jr CofC, 56, Fla Outstanding Young Man, 57; Allen Morris Awards; Outstanding First Term Legislator, Outstanding Fla Citizen of the Year, 62; Ben C Williard Award, Stetson Univ; Legion of Honor for excellence in govt, Supreme Coun,

DeMolay. Relig: Methodist, Lay Leader. Legal Res: 7500 Buck Lake Rd Tallahassee FL 32301 Mailing Add: The Capitol Tallahassee FL 32304

DICKINSON, HOWARD C, JR (R)
NH State Rep

Mailing Add: Center Conway NH 03813

DICKINSON, JAMES A
Nebr State Sen

Mailing Add: Rte 4 Millard NE 68043

DICKINSON, MILLIE LOCKHART (D)
Regional Dir, Nat Fedn Dem Women

b Honaker, Va, Mar 27, 13; d Dr John H Lockhart & Minnie Nancy Settle L; m 1949; c Bobbie Lee (Mrs Wilson), John J Rankin & James Lockhart. Educ: Col William & Mary, AA; George Washington Univ; Kappa Theta. Polit & Govt Pos: Pres, Somerset-Pulaski Co Dem Women, 64-66; state pres, Ky Dem Woman's Club, 68-72; deleg, Dem Nat Conv, 72; dist pres, Mid-SAtlantic Region, Nat Fedn Dem Women, 73-75, regional dir, currently. Bus & Prof Pos: Woman's dir, WTLO, Somerset, Ky, 59- Mem: Bus & Prof Club; Somerset Garden Club (vpres, 61-). Relig: Episcopal. Mailing Add: Holly Hill Lakeshore Dr Burnside KY 42519

DICKINSON, R DOROTHEA (R)
b Brooklyn, NY, July 1, 15; d Martin Richard Dickinson & Marion Haviland D; single. Educ: San Diego State Col, AB in Econ, 38; Benjamin Franklin Univ, BCS in Acct, 56; Pi Phi Epsilon; Sigma Phi Omega. Polit & Govt Pos: Secy, Mayoralty Campaign, San Francisco & US Navy & Marine Corps Res Training Ctr, Los Angeles, 42; secy, House Govt Oper Comt, 54; secy to US Rep Glenard P Lipscomb, Calif, 65; exec secy to US Rep John E Henderson, Ohio, 56-60, US Rep Tom V Moorehead, Ohio, 61-62, US Rep Louis C Wyman, NH, 63-64 & 67- & to US Rep Wm L Dickinson, Ala, 65-66. Bus & Prof Pos: Clerk, San Diego Gas & Elec Co, Calif, 38-41; secy, Gaylord & Gaylord, Attorneys, Calif, 47-49; secy, Newmyer & Bress, Attorneys, Washington, DC, 54; secy-off mgr, Galland & Kharasch, Attorneys, Washington, DC, 55-56. Mil Serv: Entered as A/S, Navy, 42, released, 45, after serv in Co 13, Seattle, Wash; reentered 51, released as Lt Comdr, 54, after serv in Off Chief Naval Oper, Washington, DC; Am Theater Ribbon; Victory Medal; Korea Serv & Naval Res Medals; Lt Comdr (Ret), Res. Mem: Capitol Hill Club, Washington, DC; Army-Navy Club; ROA; Naval Reserve Asn. Mailing Add: 4105 Mesa Way Alexandria VA 22312

DICKINSON, SPENCER (D)
RI State Rep

b Annapolis, Md, Nov 7, 43; s Dwight Dickinson & Eleanor Hoge D; m 1970 to Avery Halsey. Educ: Harvard Univ, BA, 66. Polit & Govt Pos: Deleg, Dem Nat Conv, 72; RI State Rep, 73- Mil Serv: Entered as E-1, Army, released as E-5, 69, after serv in 241 MID, 5th Mech Div. Mailing Add: Bay St Jamestown RI 02835

DICKINSON, VIVIAN EARL (D)
Va State Deleg

b Spotsylvania, Va, July 7, 24; s Vivian Greenhow Dickinson & Edna McLeod D; m 1950 to Mary Louise Walton; c V Earl, Jr, Martha Day & Howard Walton. Educ: Univ Richmond, BS in Bus Admin, 48; Univ Va Law Sch, 49-50; Phi Delta Theta. Polit & Govt Pos: Councilman, Mineral Town Coun, Va, 61-63; supvr, Louisa Co Bd Supervisors, 63-70; Va State Deleg, 71- Bus & Prof Pos: Pres, V Earl Dickinson Lumber Co, 49-59 & Dickinson Bros Lumber Co, Inc, 59- Mil Serv: Entered as Pvt, Army, 43, released as S/Sgt, 46. Mem: Va Forests, Inc; Lumberman Mfg Asn; Am Legion; Lions Int. Honors & Awards: One Hundred Per Cent Dist Gov, Lions Int, 66. Relig: Baptist. Mailing Add: Box 2B Rte 2 Mineral VA 23117

DICKINSON, WILLIAM LOUIS (R)
US Rep, Ala

b Opelika, Ala, June 25, 25; s Henry Kline Dickinson & Bernice Lowe D; c Christopher, Michael, Tara & William L Jr. Educ: Univ Ala Law Sch, LLB, 50; Sigma Alpha Epsilon. Polit & Govt Pos: Judge, Fifth Judicial Circuit, Ala; Lee Co Juv Court & Lee Co Court of Common Pleas & Opelika City Judge, formerly; US Rep, 65- Mil Serv: Air Force Res. Mem: Elks; Mason. Relig: Methodist. Legal Res: PO Box 4275 Montgomery AL 36101 Mailing Add: 2436 Rayburn House Off Bldg Washington DC 20515

DICKS, NORMAN DEVALOIS (D)
b Bremerton, Wash, Dec 16, 40; s Horace D Dicks & Cora Eileen D; m 1967 to Suzanne Callisan; c David Devalois & Ryan Callisan. Educ: Univ Wash, BA in Polit Sci, 63, JD, 68; Sigma Nu; Phi Delta Phi; Oval Club; Fir Tree Honoraries. Polit & Govt Pos: Legis asst to US Sen Warren G Magnuson, Wash, 68-73, admin asst, 74- Mem: Wash State Bar Asn. Honors & Awards: Scholar/athlete award, Univ Wash, 63; Outstanding male students, Fir Tree, 63. Relig: Lutheran. Legal Res: 4200 E 42nd Seattle WA 98102 Mailing Add: 6223 30th St NW Washington DC 20015

DICKSON, EDITH BRATSCHI (R)
VPres, Christian Co Rep Women's Club, Ky

b Erin, Tenn, Jan 22, 10; d John Wilson Bratschi & Lavella Shelton B; m 1934 to James Wiley Dickson; c Bratschi. Educ: Tenn State Col, 28-29; Austin Peay State Col, 29-30. Polit & Govt Pos: Chairwoman, Christian Co Rep Party, Ky, 60-68; alt deleg, Rep Nat Conv, 64; vpres, Christian Co Rep Women's Club, Ky, 65- Mem: Christian Co Red Cross; Rep Women's Club, Nashville. Relig: Methodist. Mailing Add: Greenfields Farm Oak Grove KY 42262

DICKSON, EDWARD M (D)
Mass State Rep

Mailing Add: State Capitol Boston MA 02133

DICKSON, ELLA IRENE (D)
VChmn, Howard Co Dem Comt, Mo

b Olmsted, Ill, June 28, 14; d James Arthur Scruggs & Millie Goff S; m 1962 to James Randall Dickson; c Ruth Ann (Mrs Lundell) & Betty Jo (Mrs Pierce). Educ: Mound City Pub Schs, 12 years. Polit & Govt Pos: Matron, Howard Co Jail, 42-50, dep sheriff, Howard Co, 42-54; case worker, Welfare Dept, 57-62; dep city marshall, New Franklin, Mo, 67-; pres, Howard Co Dem Club, currently; committeewoman, Franklin precinct, New Franklin Dem Party, currently; vchmn & secy, Howard Co Dem Comt, Mo, currently. Mem: 4-H Club; Keller Auxiliary Bd Hosp of Fayette; Eastern Star (past matron); Womens Auxiliary, Brotherhood

Firemen & Enginemen. Relig: Methodist; Sunday Sch teacher, 40-58. Mailing Add: 210 W Broadway New Franklin MO 65274

DICKSON, ERNEST C (R)
Mem, DC Rep Comt
b Orangeburg, SC, Mar 21, 95; s William L Dickson & Clarisa A D; m 1960 to Mabel T Terry; c Vermuta (Mrs Morris). Educ: SC State Col, LI, 20; Howard Univ, LLB, 24, LLD, 25; Pig Skins. Polit & Govt Pos: Mem, DC Rep Comt, 72- Bus & Prof Pos: Civil lawyer, Washington, DC, 24-; owner of Dickson's Realty Co, 24- Mem: Nat Rep Club; Nat & Washington, DC Bar Asns. Relig: Presbyterian. Mailing Add: 913 U St NW Washington DC 20001

DICKSON, HAROLD (R)
Mo State Rep
b near California, Mo, June 2, 06; m 1934 to Lorene Gentzsch; c Robert H. Educ: William Jewell Col, AB. Polit & Govt Pos: Mem exec comt, State Sch Bd Asn, Mo, formerly; mem sch bd, California Sch Dist, 12 years, pres, 10 years; mem, Co Bd Educ, 12 years; past vpres, Eighth Dist Mo Asn Rep; mem, Moniteau Co Rep Club; Mo State Rep, Dist 112, 62-, mem, Comts on Appropriations, Ins, Traffic Rules & Regulations, Mo House Rep, currently; deleg, White House Conf Aging, 71; mem, Coun Pub Higher Educ, 73. Bus & Prof Pos: Coach & sci teacher, California High Sch, Mo, 27-31; inspector, Nat Battery Co, 31-37; serv sta operator, 38-62; part-time ins agent, 24 years. Mem: Charter mem Local Indust Develop Comt; Conserv Fedn Mo (Mid-Mo Chap); Calif Alumni Asn (pres, 75); Moniteau Co Hist Soc. Honors & Awards: Spec Citations for work for pub libr, Mo Libr Asn, 67, work for Scouts of Am, 71 & work for the elderly, Gov Task Force on Older Missourians, 72. Relig: Methodist; mem, Bd Stewards, chmn, Comn of Missions, past pres, Methodist Men & instr, Bible Class, 15 years. Mailing Add: 400 W Russell California MO 65018

DIDONATO, ANTHONY, JR (D)
Pa State Rep
Mailing Add: Capitol Bldg Harrisburg PA 17120

DIDONATO, S LEONARD (D)
b Lawrenceville, NJ, May 23, 30; s Clarence DiDonato & Lena DiPerna D; m 1954 to Mary Eva Knighten; c Dale Leonard, Debra Camille & John Brooks. Educ: Princeton High Sch, grad, 48. Polit & Govt Pos: Mem, Robert F Kennedy State Comt, NJ, 67-68; committeeman, Mercer Co Dem Comt, NJ, 69-75, chmn, 69; deleg, Dem Nat Conv, 72 & Dem Nat Mid-Term Conf, 74; Dem cand for State Sen, NJ, 73; dir, Div Bldg & Construction, Dept Treas NJ, 74- Mil Serv: Entered as Pvt, Army, 47, released as 1st Lt, 64, after serv in Inf, Ft Benning, Ga, 63-64. Mem: Kiwanis Int; Italian-Am Sportsmen's Club; NJ Soc Archit. Honors & Awards: Cavalier, Govt of Italy. Mailing Add: 2 Tall Timbers Dr Princeton NJ 08540

DIEHL, CYNTHIA BARRE (R)
b Springfield, Mass, May 28, 33; d Charles Stanley Barre & Constance Greenan B; m 1954 to Ricky William Diehl; c Carole Ann, Nancy Elizabeth & Jane Ellen. Educ: Simmons Col, 51-53. Polit & Govt Pos: Chmn, Women for Volpe, Marshfield, Mass, 60; first vpres, Park Cities Rep Women, Dallas, Tex, 64-65; first vpres, Rep Women of Newport, Conn, 66-67, pres, 67-68; mem, Westport Rep Town Comt, 67-68; co-chmn, Women for Nixon, Westport, 68; coordr, Meskill for Gov, Wilton, Conn, 70; pres, Fourth Cong Dist Rep Women, Conn, 71-72; chmn, Nixon for President Campaign, Wilton, 72; deleg & secy credentials comt, Rep Nat Conv, 72; chmn polit educ, Conn Fedn Rep Women, 72- Relig: Roman Catholic. Mailing Add: 48 Topfield Rd Wilton CT 06897

DIEHL, PAUL W (R)
Chmn, Coventry Rep Town Comt, Conn
b Pa, Apr 6, 33; s Paul Walter Diehl & Mary Mullen D; m 1956 to Virginia Trump; c Christopher, Paul, Fred, Bill & Heidi. Educ: Univ Hartford, 59-62; Dale Carnegie Course, 64-65. Polit & Govt Pos: Chmn, Coventry Rep Town Comt, Conn, 73- Bus & Prof Pos: Owner, Diehl Qual Builders, 70- Mil Serv: Entered as Pvt, Army, 49, released as Sgt, 51, after serv in NATO, 50-51. Mem: Teamsters; Elks; Am Legion. Mailing Add: Shore Dr Rte 2 Box 247 Coventry CT 06230

DIEHM, VICTOR CHRISTIAN (R)
b Sparrows Point, Md, Nov 7, 02; s Christian O'B Diehm & Mary L Hackman D; m 1936 to Hazel Virginia Loose; c Elizabeth Anne (Mrs Richard I Bernstein) & Victor C, Jr. Educ: Peabody Conservatory of Music, Baltimore, 19-25; Univ Md, 25. Hon Degrees: Dr Art of Oratory, Staley Col, Boston, 55. Polit & Govt Pos: Mem, Pa Indust Develop Authority, Harrisburg, Pa, 55-; deleg, Rep Nat Conv, 72. Bus & Prof Pos: Mem bd trustees, Bloomsburg State Col, Pa, 48-55; owner & mgr, Vic Diehm Radio Group, 49-; pres, Mutual Broadcasting System, Inc, New York, 69-72; pres, Dolly Madison Ice Cream Co, Inc, Philadelphia, 72- Publ: Various articles in Broadcasting Mag & Sponsor Mag on various aspects of broadcasting. Mem: Radio Advert Bur, Inc, NY; Nat Asn of Broadcasters, Washington, DC (dir, 69-72); Pa Asn of Broadcasters; Hazleton CofC; Pa State CofC (pres, 71-). Honors & Awards: Statewide Vic Diehm Day, Rep Gov Ray Shafer, Pa, 69 & Dem Gov Milton Shapp, 72; George Washington Mem Medal, Freedoms Found, Inc, 72; Bronze Medal, highest award, by Nat Cancer Orgn to layman, 72; Commander-In-Chief Medal, VFW, 72. Relig: United Methodist. Legal Res: Frederick Dr Conyngham PA 18219 Mailing Add: Sta WAZL Hazleton Nat Bank Bldg Hazleton PA 18201

DIELEMAN, WILLIAM W (D)
Iowa State Rep
b Oskaloosa, Iowa, Jan 19, 31; s Garret Jan Dieleman & Jozena DeGeus D; m 1951 to Emily June Langstraat; c Wendell Earl, Cynthia Elaine (Mrs Dennis DeYoung) & Kristen Eileen. Educ: Calvin Col, BA, 59; Univ Iowa, MA, 66; Univ SDak, post grad, summer 72. Polit & Govt Pos: City councilman-at-lg, Pella, Iowa, 70-75; Iowa State Rep, 75- Bus & Prof Pos: High sch teacher, South Holland, Ill & Pella, Iowa, 63-74; life ins underwriter, Bankers Life Nebr, Oskaloosa, Iowa, 74- Mil Serv: Entered as Pvt, Army, 53, released as Sgt E-5, after serv in 37th Inf & Tenth Div, 53-55; Nat Defense Serv Medal & Good Conduct Medal. Relig: Christian Reformed Church. Mailing Add: 518 Woodlawn Dr Pella IA 50219

DIERDORFF, ARDEN (R)
Kans State Rep
Mailing Add: 613 N Main Smith Center KS 66967

DIES, MARTIN, JR (D)
b Greenville, Tex, Dec 21, 21; s Martin Dies & Myrtle McAdams D; m 1946 to Ruth Marie White; c Martin W, IV, Dianne & David. Educ: Stephen F Austin State Univ, BS, 42; Southern Methodist Univ Law Sch, JD, 48; Barrister; Pi Kappa Alpha. Polit & Govt Pos: Tex State Sen, 59-67, pres pro tempore, Tex State Sen, 63; Gov of Tex, 63; Secy of State, Tex, 69-71; Chief Justice, Ninth Court of Appeals, 71- Bus & Prof Pos: Attorney, Lufkin, Tex, 48- Mil Serv: Entered as A/S, Navy, 43, released as Lt(jg), 46, after serv in USS Richard W Suesens in Pac Theater; Area Combat Ribbons; Presidential Unit Citation. Mem: Tex Bar Asn; fel Tex Bar Found; VFW; AF&AM; Mason. Honors & Awards: Plaque & rifle, Sportsmen's Asn; Most Distinguished Alumni Award, Stephen F Austin State Univ, 67; State park at Jasper, Tex named Martin Dies, Jr State Park. Relig: Episcopal. Mailing Add: 1340 Sheridan Lane Beaumont TX 77706

DIETER, ELSIE (R)
Chmn, Mahoning Co Rep Orgn, Ohio
b Youngstown, Ohio; d Bernard Sharsu & Marie Schnell S; m to Henry W Dieter, wid; c Jerry C & Bernard S Wegendt. Educ: Chaney High Sch, Youngstown, Ohio, grad. Polit & Govt Pos: Rep precinct committeeman, Mahoning Co, Ohio, 58-; secy, Mahoning Co Rep Women's Club, 66-67, pres, 68-69; chmn tel comt, Mahoning Co Rep Orgn, 67-68, chmn, 70-; mem, Consumer Adv Comt & Citizens Adv Comt Community Develop, Youngstown, currently; tel chairwoman, Nixon Campaign, 72; Mayor Jack Hunter, 73 & for Gov James A Rhodes, 74. Bus & Prof Pos: Off clerk, Off Price Admin, Youngstown, Ohio, 42-45; cashier, GM McKelveys, 45-52; teller, Dollar Savings & Trust Co, 52-53; off mgr, Oakite Prod, Inc, 53-68 & Tri-State Prod, 68- Mem: Am Bus Womens Asn; Eastern Star; Ladies Oriental Shrine; West Side Merchants & Civic Asn (pres, 75-); Youngstown Area CofC (educ, nat affairs, taxation & community awards comts). Honors & Awards: Diamond Achievement Award, Mahoning Co Rep Women's Club, 68. Relig: Methodist. Mailing Add: 410 Wilkinson Ave Youngstown OH 44509

DIETERICH, NEIL (DFL)
Minn State Rep
Mailing Add: 2171 Knapp St St Paul MN 55108

DIETZ, CLARENCE E (R)
Pa State Rep
Mailing Add: Capitol Bldg Harrisburg PA 17120

DIETZ, ELMER (D)
Ky State Rep
Mailing Add: 514 Linden St Ludlow KY 41106

DIETZ, LEW (D)
Mem, Knox Co Dem Comt, Maine
b Pittsburgh, Pa, May 22, 07; s Louis Andrew Dietz & Bertha Staiger D; m 1950 to Denny Sonke. Educ: NY Univ, 3 years. Polit & Govt Pos: Mem, Knox Co Dem Comt, Maine, 64-; chmn, Rockport Dem Town Comt, 66-; deleg, Dem Nat Conv, 68; mem, Maine Comn Arts & Humanities, currently. Bus & Prof Pos: Writer. Publ: Pines for the Kings Navy, 55 & the Year of the Big Cat, 69, Little; The Allagash, Holt, 68. Mailing Add: Rockport ME 04856

DIETZ, NANCY FENN (D)
State VChmn, CZ Regional Dem Party
b San Diego, Calif, May 6, 44; d Robert Dwight Fenn & Elizabeth Huntsberger F; m 1966 to William Harry Dietz, Jr; c Jonathan Shoemaker. Educ: Smith Col, BA, 66. Polit & Govt Pos: Alt deleg, Dem Nat Conv, 72; coordr, McGovern-Shriver Campaign, CZ, 72; vchmn, CZ Regional Dem Party, 72- Bus & Prof Pos: Teacher, Camden, NJ, 66-70; vol staff, Community Rels Div, Am Friends Serv Comt, Philadelphia, 70-71. Mem: Common Cause; Nat Women's Polit Caucus. Relig: Society of Friends. Legal Res: RR 9 Harrison Lake Columbus IN 47201 Mailing Add: Box 699 Balboa CZ

DIETZEN, WALTER C (D)
Chmn, Madison Co Dem Cent Comt, Ind
b Anderson, Ind, Jan 31, 27; s Louie S Dietzen & Katherine Bartlett D; div; c Lisa (Mrs Reddin) & Marla. Educ: Ariz State Univ, 48-49; Ball State Univ, BS, 55, MA, 58; Ind Univ, Indianapolis, Law Sch, JD, 61. Polit & Govt Pos: Chmn, Madison Co Dem Cent Comt, Ind, 74- Bus & Prof Pos: Dep prosecutor, Madison Co, Ind, 63-65, co attorney, 66-68 & juv court referee, 71-72; probation officer, City of Anderson, 72-73 & pub defender, 73- Mil Serv: Entered as Pvt, Air Force, 45, released as Pfc, 46, after serv in Pac Air Serv Command, Manila, Philippines. Legal Res: 111 E Ninth St Anderson IN 46014 Mailing Add: PO Box 676 Anderson IN 46014

DI FALCO, ANTHONY G (D)
NY State Assemblyman
b New York, NY, July 14, 38; s S Samuel D Falco & Emma Sutera D; div; c Christina Jean & Anthony Samuel. Educ: Holy Cross Col, Worcester, Mass, BA in Econ, 60; NY Law Sch, LLB, 63; Phi Delta Phi. Polit & Govt Pos: Mem, Metrop Area Study, NY Joint Legis Comt, 64; assoc counsel to Pres-Pro-Tem, NY State Senate, 65 & to Minority Leader, NY State Senate, 66-; NY State Assemblyman, 69- Bus & Prof Pos: Counsel, Century Nat Bank & Trust Co, New York, NY, chmn bd dirs, Italian Cultural Found, Ltd & mem bd dirs, Cent Foundry Co, currently; lectr, Practicing Law Inst, Brooklyn Bar Asn, Rockland Co Community Col, Rockland Co Bar Asn, Bank Lawyers Conf, Orange Co Community Col & Orange Co Bar Asn. Mem: Consular Law Soc; Nat Italian-Am League to Combat Defamation (exec secy); Elks; KofC; Holy Cross Col Club NY. Honors & Awards: Community Humanitarian Award, Stuyvesant Chap Cancer Care, 68; Rockland Co Community Col Award, 68; Rockland Co Bar Asn Award; Nat Jewish Hosp Distinguished Vol Serv Award; Man of the Year Award, Stuyvesant Polyclin, 68. Relig: Catholic. Mailing Add: 103 E Tenth St New York NY 10003

DIGBY, DORA MAE (D)
b Brentwood, Md, Apr 15, 20; d Leslie Rowe & Melissa Rice R; m 1942 to Dr Robert Henry Digby; c Robert H Jr, MD & Roger W. Educ: Univ Md, College Park, 37-40; Belmont Col, Nashville, Tenn, 42; Mich State Univ, part time, 62- Polit & Govt Pos: Fed govt secy, Dept Interior, formerly; typist, US Sen Schall, Minn, 37-38; worker, US Sen Poole, Tex, 65-66; Wallace Hq Coordr, Ingham, Eaton & Clinton Co, Mich, 72; deleg, Dem Nat Conv, 72; mem, Charter Comt, Dem Party, 72. Bus & Prof Pos: With British Ministry, Washington, DC, World War II; hearings reporter, US Air Force, Palm Beach, Fla, 41-43; part time writer, Lansing State J, Mich, 65-; pub rels rep, Insts for Achievement of Human Potential, 67-; substitute teacher spec educ, Lansing Schs, 72-; vol in phys therapy rehabilitation for brain

damaged patients & with parents of disabled children. Mem: Int Platform Asn; Friends of the Insts for Achievement of Human Potential; Silva Mind Control Grad; Cent Dist Dent Auxiliary; Lansing Pro-Symphony. Relig: Christian Science. Legal Res: 1554 N Michigan Rd Eaton Rapids MI 48827 Mailing Add: 601 S Grand Ave Lansing MI 48933

DIGBY, JAMES KEITH **(R)**
b Bay City, Mich, June 18, 50; s Charles Digby & Sheila Murphy D; single. Educ: Mich State Univ, BA, 72. Polit & Govt Pos: Chmn, Bay Co, Mich Teen Rep, 67-68; spec courier, Rep Nat Conv, 68; co-chmn, Mich Teens for Nixon-Agnew, 68; mem, Mich Task Force for Values, Ethics & Cult, White House Conf on Youth, 71; mem adv coun, Comt on Youth & Student Partic, Mich House Rep, 71; deleg, Rep Nat Conv, 72; vchmn, Tenth Cong Dist Rep Comt, 71-72; dist liaison rep to US Rep James Harvey, Mich, 72-74; campaign coordr & co-mgr, James Sparling, Jr for Congress, 74. Bus & Prof Pos: Mem, Acad Governance Comt, Mich State Univ, James Madison Col Curric Comt & Socio-Econ Core Curric Comt, 71-72; off mgr, Bay Co Coun on Aging, 75- Mem: Mich State Univ Alumni Asn. Honors & Awards: Practical Politics Award, Bay City, Mich CofC, 68; 1972 Club of 50 outstanding grad, Mich State Univ Alumni Asn, 72. Relig: Congregational. Mailing Add: 401 N Sheridan Bay City MI 48706

DIGGS, ANNA KATHERINE JOHNSTON **(D)**
b Washington, DC, Dec 9, 32; d Virginius Douglass Johnston & Hazel Bramlette J; div; c Douglass Johnston & Carla Cecile. Educ: Barnard Col, BA, 54; Yale Univ Law Sch, LLB, 57. Polit & Govt Pos: Attorney, US Dept of Labor, Washington, DC, 57-60; asst prosecutor, Wayne Co, Mich, 61-62; asst US Attorney, Detroit, 66-67; legis asst to US Rep Charles C Diggs, Mich, 67-71; co-chmn, Lawyers for Humphrey, Mich, 72 & Lawyers for McGovern, Mich, 72; mem, Mich Dem Party Appeals Comt, 71-72; deleg, Dem Nat Conv, 72. Bus & Prof Pos: Attorney & partner, Zwerdling, Maurer, Diggs & Papp, Detroit, 71- Mem: Mich & Nat Bar Asns; Women Lawyers of Mich; Neighborhood Serv Asn, Detroit (vpres, 69-73); Planned Parenthood League, Detroit (bd, 70-). Relig: Episcopal. Mailing Add: 1361 Joliet Pl Detroit MI 48207

DIGGS, BETTY JEAN **(D)**
b Savannah, Ga, Sept 12, 42; d Willie C Johnson & Leila Mae McClain J; m 1965 to Benjamin Diggs; c Sonia & Stephanie Marques. Educ: Mandl Med Sch, New York, 60-61; Harris AT Sch, Savannah, Ga, cert, 63; Del State Col, 70- Polit & Govt Pos: Parent rep, Kent Co Head Start, Del, 71, secy bd trustees, 72-; alt deleg, Del Dem State Conv & Dem Nat Conv, 72; mem, Black Caucus, Del, currently. Bus & Prof Pos: Secy, Del State Col Dept Educ, 68- Mem: Kent Co Educ Secretaries Asn; Capitol Green Community Ctr, Dover (bd mem, 71-). Relig: Baptist. Mailing Add: 715 River Rd Dover DE 19901

DIGGS, CHARLES COLES, JR **(D)**
US Rep, Mich
b Detroit, Mich, Dec 2, 22; s Charles C Diggs, Sr (deceased) & Mayme Jones D; c Charles C, III, Alexis, Denise, Douglass & Carla. Educ: Univ Mich, 40-42; Fisk Univ, 42-43; Wayne State Univ, grad, 46; Detroit Col Law, 50-51. Hon Degrees: Dr, Cent State Col & Wilberforce Univ. Polit & Govt Pos: Mich State Sen, 51-54; US Rep, Mich, 54-, chmn, House Comt on DC & House Foreign Affairs Subcomt on Africa, currently, past chmn, Cong Black Caucus; ex officio, Dem Nat Mid-Term Conf, 74. Bus & Prof Pos: Pres, House of Diggs, Inc, Funeral Homes. Mil Serv: Entered as Pvt, Army, 43, released as 2nd Lt, 45. Legal Res: Detroit MI Mailing Add: 2208 Rayburn House Off Bldg Washington DC 20515

DIGGS, ESTELLA B **(D)**
NY State Assemblywoman
b St Louis, Mo, Apr 21, 16; div; c Edward A, Lawrence C, Jr & Joyce D; two grandchildren. Educ: NY Inst Dietetics, grad; Pace Col, NY; City Col of New York; NY Univ. Polit & Govt Pos: Committeeman & judicial deleg, NY State, currently; NY State Assemblywoman, 73-, mem housing, ment health, social serv & child care comts, spec rep to Speaker Stanley Steingut on Ment Health, chmn subcomt child care, prime sponsor, Equal Rights Amendment; founder & chmn, Bronx Citizens Comt for Housing. Bus & Prof Pos: Teacher, job developer, placement & careeer coun, NY State Career Develop, Adult Educ, formerly; free lance writer, Amsterdam News; confidential aide, NY State Supreme Court; real estate & pub rels. Mem: NAACP (bd mem); Negro Bus & Prof Women (charter mem, Bronx Chap); Nat Coun of Negro Women; Cath Interracial Coun of the Bronx; Women Grand Jurors Asn. Honors & Awards: Spec Salesmanship Awards, Cushman Bakery Co; Hon Parade Marshall, Afro-Am Day Parade; Hon Parade Marshall, Dr Martin Luther King Day Parade. Relig: Catholic. Legal Res: 592 E 167 St Bronx NY 10456 Mailing Add: State Assembly Rm 430 State Capitol Albany NY 12224

DILL, CLARENCE C **(D)**
b Fredericktown, Ohio, Sept 21, 84; s Theodore M Dill & Amanda M Kunkel D; m 1940 to Mabel Aileen Dickson. Educ: Ohio Wesleyan Univ, LLB; Phi Kappa Psi. Polit & Govt Pos: Dep prosecuting attorney, Spokane Co, Wash, 10-12; secy, Gov Ernest Lister, 13; US Rep, 15-19; US Sen, 23-35; spec asst to Attorney Gen US, 45-52. Publ: Communications Act, 1935; Our Government, 1945 Edition; Government of State of Washington, 1945. Mem: Elks; Moose; Athletic Round Table; CofC; Int Platform Asn. Honors & Awards: Persuaded Franklin D Roosevelt to start Grand Coulee Dam on Columbia River; Columbus Day Citizen Award from Am Ital Club of Spokane, 69. Relig: Methodist-Unitarian. Mailing Add: 763 Lincoln Bldg Spokane WA 99201

DILL, J ANTHONY **(R)**
Mo State Rep
b St Louis Co, Mo, Aug 31, 39; s Alfred J Dill & Helene M Reibestein D; m 1972 to Donna Mae Raskevice. Educ: Rockhurst Col, AB, 61; St Louis Univ, LLB, 64; Alpha Sigma Nu; Alpha Phi Omega. Polit & Govt Pos: Precinct capt, Gravois Twp Rep Orgn, St Louis Co, Mo, 61-; alt deleg, Mo State Rep Conv, 64, deleg, 68 & 72; Mo State Rep, Dist 44, 67-72, Dist 102, 73-, minority caucus chmn, Mo House Rep, 75- vpres, Mo Asn of Rep, 68-70. Bus & Prof Pos: Lawyer, Millar, Schaefer & Ebling, 66-70; pvt practice, 70- Mil Serv: Mo Air Nat Guard, 64-70. Mem: Phi Delta Phi; Am & Mo Bar Asns; Gravois Kiwanis; Am Legion. Relig: Roman Catholic. Mailing Add: 7723 Ravenhill Dr Affton MO 63123

DILLARD, GEORGE DOUGLAS **(D)**
b New York, NY, May 14, 42; s George P Dillard & Mary Elizabeth Elarbee D; m 1966 to Myra Gail Huggins; c Karen Asheley & George Douglas, Jr. Educ: Furman Univ, BA, 64; Walter F George Sch Law, Mercer Univ, JD, 67; Kappa Alpha Order; Phi Delta Phi. Polit & Govt Pos: VChmn & mem exec comt, State Dem Party, Ga, formerly; area precinct chmn, DeKalb Co Dem Party, 70-; mem adv bd, DeKalb Co Dept Parks & Recreation, 71- Mem: Am Bar Asn; DeKalb Co Jaycees (internal vpres, 69-70, exec vpres, 70-71, legal counsel, 71-, legal counsel, fifth region, 71-); Decatur-DeKalb Boys Club (bd dirs, 70-, treas, 70-, dir & legal counsel); Furman Univ Alumni Asn (bd dirs, 71-, exec comt, 72, vpres, Atlanta chap, 71-72, pres, 72-73); Am Judicature Soc. Honors & Awards: Outstanding Jaycee, DeKalb Co Jaycees, 68-69. Relig: Methodist; Bd dirs, First United Methodist Church, 72. Legal Res: 643 Clairmont Ave Decatur GA 30030 Mailing Add: 558 Church St Decatur GA 30030

DILLARD, JAMES H, II **(R)**
Va State Deleg
Mailing Add: 4709 Briar Patch Lane Fairfax VA 22030

DILLINGER, DELORES MARIE **(D)**
Mem, Mich Dem State Cent Comt
b Muskegon, Mich, Jan 11, 36; d William Dell Hogan & Sigme Moane H; m 1955 to Patrick Vernon Dillinger; c Kurt, Koleen, Khristopher & Kara. Educ: Muskegon Bus Col. Polit & Govt Pos: Mem, Mich Dem State Cent Comt, 72-; deleg, Dem Nat Conv, 72; mem, Ottawa Co Dem Comt, currently. Bus & Prof Pos: Vpres, Dillinger Bus Equip, 63-; sales rep & mgr, Sarah Coventry Jewelry, 73- Mem: Right to Life Orgn. Relig: Baptist. Mailing Add: 615 Washington Grand Haven MI 49417

DILLINGHAM, BENJAMIN FRANKLIN, II **(R)**
b Honolulu, Hawaii, Oct 14, 16; s Walter Francis Dillingham & Louise Olga Gaylord D; m 1941 to Frances Andrews, div; c Ceseli, Benjamin Franklin III, Gaylord & Bernice. Educ: Harvard, BS, 39. Polit & Govt Pos: Mem bd supvrs, City & Co Honolulu, Hawaii, 46-48; US Sen, Hawaii, 48-56; cand for US Sen, 62; Rep Nat Committeeman, 63-70. Bus & Prof Pos: Dir, Dillingham Corp, 61- Mil Serv: Maj, Army, 41-45; Air Force Res; Bronze Star. Mem: Am Legion; VFW; Mil Order World Wars; Mason (jester); Harvard Club, New York. Honors & Awards: Distinguished Serv Award, Civil Air Patrol; Col Byrd Leadership Award; Serv Award, Jr CofC, Honolulu. Relig: Episcopal. Mailing Add: PO Box 3468 Honolulu HI 96801

DILLON, CLARENCE DOUGLAS **(R)**
b Geneva, Switz, Aug 21, 09; s Clarence Dillon & Anne McE Douglas D; m 1931 to Phyllis C Ellsworth; c Phyllis Ellsworth (Mrs Mark Collins) & Joan Douglas (Princess Joan of Luxembourg). Educ: Harvard, AB, 31. Hon Degrees: LLD, NY Univ, 56, Lafayette Col, 57, Univ Hartford, 58, Columbia Univ, 59, Harvard Univ, 59, Williams Col, 60, Rutgers Univ, 61, Princeton Univ, 61, Univ Pa, 62, Bradley Univ, Middlebury Col & Wash Univ. Polit & Govt Pos: Dir, US & Foreign Securities Corp, 37-53, chmn, currently; dir, US Int Securities Corp, 37-53; Ambassador to France, 53-57; Under Secy of State for Econ Affairs, 58-59; Under Secy of State, 59-61; secy of deleg, Rep Nat Conv, 68. Bus & Prof Pos: Mem bd of gov, NY Hosp & Metrop Mus; mem, NY Stock Exchange, 31-36; vpres & dir, Dillon, Reed & Co, 38-53, chmn of the bd, 46-53. Mil Serv: Lt Comdr,. Naval Res, 41-45; Air Medal; Legion of Merit. Mem: Soc Colonial Wars, NY; Racquet & Tennis, Knickerbocker, Links, & Recess Century Clubs. Legal Res: Far Hills NJ 07931 Mailing Add: 767 Fifth Ave New York NY 10022

DILLON, J C, JR **(D)**
Chmn, WVa Dem State Cent Comt
Mailing Add: 2106 Kanawah Blvd Charleston WV 25311

DILLS, RALPH C **(D)**
Calif State Sen
b Texas, 1910. Educ: Univ Calif, Los Angeles; Univ Southern Calif; Loyola Univ Sch Law. Polit & Govt Pos: Calif State Assemblyman, 38-49; munic judge, 4 terms; Calif State Sen, 67-, chmn comt on govt orgn, Calif State Senate, currently. Mem: Nat Soc of State Legislators. Mailing Add: 16921 S Western Ave Gardena CA 90247

DILUGLIO, THOMAS ROSS **(D)**
Chmn, Johnston Dem Town Comt, RI
b Providence, RI, Nov 25, 31; s Thomas DiLuglio & Elvira Rossi D; m 1952 to Loretta Agnes Migliaccio; c Thomas A, Mark W, Anthony R, Vera H & Beth E. Educ: Brown Univ, AB; Boston Univ Law Sch, LLD; Phi Delta Theta. Polit & Govt Pos: Treas, Johnston Dem Town Comt, RI, 58-64, chmn, 64-, town solicitor, 70-; RI State Sen, 60-64; chmn legis comt, RI Const Conv, 64-67. Bus & Prof Pos: Pres, Highland Orchards Inc, 72- & Queen Restaurant, 72- Mem: United Commercial Travelers. Relig: Catholic. Mailing Add: 1239 Hartford Ave Johnston RI 02919

DIMON, JOHN EDWARD **(R)**
b Roebling, NJ, May 14, 16; s George Dimon & Mary Vrabel D; m 1946 to Virginia Lee Treece; c Patricia, Blake, David, Mark & Mathew. Educ: Villanova Univ; Temple Univ, LLB, 40. Polit & Govt Pos: Deleg, Rep Nat Conv, 64, 68 & 72; deleg & secy, NJ Const Conv, 66, secy continuing comt, 66-; campaign co chmn, Nixon for President, NJ, 68 & chmn, Nixon for President, NJ Adv Comt, 72; chmn, NJ Apportionment Comn, Burlington Co Bridge Comn & NJ Platform Conv; SJersey chmn, Cahill for Gov, NJ; chmn, NJ State Rep Comt, formerly. Bus & Prof Pos: Dir, Roebling Savings & Loan Asn, 52-; dir, Bank of Mid Jersey, 54- Mil Serv: Entered as Pvt, Army, 40, released as Maj, 46, after serv as Commanding Officer, Separate Ord Unit & War Crimes Unit, ETO. Mem: Florence Twp CofC; Roebling Am Legion; Florence Twp VFW; Elks; KofC. Relig: Byzantine Rite Catholic. Mailing Add: Ashurst Mansion Mt Holly NJ 08060

DI MONDI, FRANCIS ANTHONY **(R)**
Chmn, Kent Co Rep Comt, Del
b New Castle, Del, Oct 8, 32; s John A Di Mondi & Speranza Casalena D; remarried 1973 to Jane Pfeil; c William, Gayle, Diane & Francis. Educ: Georgetown Univ, 50-52; La Salle Col, 54; Villanova Univ Law Sch, 54-55; Temple Univ Law Sch, 54-55 & 57. Polit & Govt Pos: Chmn, Standard Brad Develop Bd, 70-; chmn, Kent Co Rep Comt, Del, 73- Bus & Prof Pos: Pres, Wyoming Black Co Inc, Del Block Co Inc & Edgewood Pipe & Block Co, currently. Mil Serv: Entered as E-1, Army, 55, released as E-5, 57, after serv in 1st Armor Div. Mem: Elks; Moose; Maple Dale Country Club. Relig: Roman Catholic. Legal Res: 1371 S State St Dover DE 19901 Mailing Add: Box 113 Wyoming DE 19934

DINELLO, GILBERT JOHN **(D)**
Mich State Rep
b Detroit, Mich, Feb 28, 35; s Carl A DiNello & Carla Paiano D; single. Educ: Univ Detroit, BS in Bus Admin, 59. Polit & Govt Pos: Deleg, 14th Precinct, East Detroit, Mich, 70-72; Mich State Rep, 73rd Dist, 73- Bus & Prof Pos: With Mich Nat Bank of Detroit, 69-72; real estate broker, East Detroit, 72- Mil Serv: Entered as Recruit, Mich Army Nat Guard, 59,

released as Pfc, 62, after serv in Missile Bn. Relig: Roman Catholic. Mailing Add: 18050 Toepfer Rd East Detroit MI 48021

DINGELL, JOHN D (D)
US Rep, Mich
b Colorado Springs, Colo, July 8, 26; s John D Dingell & Grace Bigler D. Educ: Georgetown Univ, BS in Chem, 49, Georgetown Univ Law Sch, JD, 52; Delta Theta Phi. Polit & Govt Pos: Law clerk, US Dist Judge, 52-53; Asst Wayne Co Prosecutor, 53-55; US Rep, 16th Dist, Mich, currently; deleg, Dem Nat Conv, 68. Bus & Prof Pos: Attorney. Mil Serv: Entered as Pvt, Army, 44, released as 2nd Lt, 46, after serv in Panama Canal Zone, Am Theater. Mem: KofC; Moose; CofC; VFW; Am Legion. Relig: Catholic. Legal Res: Trenton MI Mailing Add: 2210 Rayburn House Off Bldg Washington DC 20515

DINGER, MARVIN L (D)
Mo State Sen
b Ironton, Mo, Sept 30, 21; m 1947 to Peggy Ruth McCabe; c Paula Kaye & Mary Kathryn. Educ: Univ Mo, Columbia; Wash Univ, JD. Polit & Govt Pos: Prosecuting attorney, Iron Co, Mo, 63-64; Mo State Rep, 64-72 & 75- Bus & Prof Pos: Attorney-at-law, 55- Mil Serv: Army Air Corps, 43-46; Air Force, 47-52. Mem: Lions; VFW; PTA; Am Judicature Soc. Relig: Lutheran. Mailing Add: Rte 1 Ironton MO 63650

DINGMAN, RICHARD B
b Baltimore, Md, Feb 9, 35; s Briggs P Dingman & Gladys Hazelton D; m 1957 to Ann Wade; c Mark, Jeffrey, Linda Marie & Patricia Ann. Educ: Univ Md, College Park, BS, 62; Am Univ, MBA, 70. Polit & Govt Pos: Staff asst, Dept Army, 52-65, computer admin, 65-69 & 70-71; councilman, Vienna, Va, 64-74, vmayor, 68-69 & 73-74; cong fel, Washington, DC, 69-70; staff counsel to US Rep Peter A Peyser, NY, 71-72; staff dir to US Rep Edwin B Forsythe, NJ, 72; admin asst to US Rep John B Conlan, Ariz, 73- Mil Serv: Entered as Cpl, Army, 55, released as SP-5, 57, after serv in 304th Signal Bn, Korea, 56. Honors & Awards: Cert of Achievement, Dept Army, 68; Distinguished Serv Award, Jaycees, Vienna, Va, 69; Cong Fel, US Civil Serv Comn & Am Polit Sci Asn, 69. Relig: Protestant. Mailing Add: 312 Westview Ct NE Vienna VA 22180

DINI, JOSEPH EDWARD, JR (D)
Nev State Assemblyman
b Yerington, Nev, Mar 28, 29; s Guiseppe Dini & Elvira Castellani D; m 1949 to Jeanne Marion Demuth; c Joseph, George, David & Michael. Educ: Univ Nev, BA, 51; Phi Sigma Kappa. Polit & Govt Pos: Dir, Mason Valley Swimming Pool Dist, Nev, 63-67; mem, Lyon Co Dem Cent Comt, 66-; Nev State Assemblyman, Lyon Co, 67- Mem: Nev Gaming Asn, Inc; Lions; Eagles; Nev Farm Bur; CofC. Relig: Catholic. Mailing Add: Box 968 Yerington NV 89447

DINIELLI, JOSEPH J (D)
Conn State Sen
Mailing Add: 78 Tulip St Bristol CT 06010

DININNI, RUDOLPH (R)
Pa State Rep
b Harrisburg, Pa, Oct 19, 26; s Valentine Dininni & Assunta Pagano D; m 1953 to Arlene M Keiser; c Rudolph V Dininni, William B & Craig D Bush. Educ: Swatara Twp Schs. Polit & Govt Pos: Committeeman, Fifth Ward Rep Orgn, Swatara Twp, Pa, 58-70; chmn, Swatara Twp Rep Asn, 60-; Pa State Rep, 66-, chmn, Subcomt Hwy, Pa House Rep, 73-; treas, Dauphin Co Rep Comt, 70- Bus & Prof Pos: Pres, R Dininni Construction Co, Harrisburg, Pa, 50-; dir, Farmers Bank & Trust Co, Hummelstown, 60-, vpres, 70- Mem: Assoc Gen Contractors of Am; Harrisburg CofC; charter mem Rutherford Heights Lions Club (pres, 70-71); Sons of Italy; VFW. Relig: Catholic. Legal Res: 435 N 69th St Harrisburg PA 17111 Mailing Add: 5090 Franklin St Harrisburg PA 17111

DINSMORE, ROBERT W (D)
WVa State Deleg
Mailing Add: State Capitol Charleston WV 25305

DIPAOLO, ROGER FULVIO (D)
Chmn, Portage Co Dem Exec Comt, Ohio
b Barisciano, Aquilla, Italy, Jan 1, 25; s Carlo DiPaolo & Maria D'Alessandro D; m 1947 to Pauline Martha Siciliano; c Roger Joseph & Linda Marie. Educ: Kent State Univ, 46-48; Akron Univ Law Sch, LLB, 52. Polit & Govt Pos: Vchmn, Portage Co Bd Elecs, 60-; mem, City Charter Comt, Kent, Ohio, 63, safety dir, 64, Dem cent committeeman, Precinct Two-E, 64-, mem, Charter Rev Comt, 69, chmn civil serv comn, 71-72; chmn, Portage Co Dem Exec Comt, 64-; deleg, Dem Nat Conv, 68; mem, Ohio State Dem Exec Comt, 74- Bus & Prof Pos: Dep sheriff, Portage Co, 50; attorney, Ravenna, Ohio, 52-; pres, Roger F DiPaolo Co, 73- Mil Serv: Entered as Pvt, Army, 43, released as T-5, 46, after serv in 496th Antiaircraft Artillery, Pac Theatre, 44-46; Pac Theatre Ribbon with two Battle Stars; World War II Victory Medal. Mem: Ohio Bar Asn; Dem Co Chmn Asn Ohio (pres, 74-); Elks (presiding justice, 57-); Am Legion; VFW. Relig: Roman Catholic. Legal Res: 1147 Norwood Kent OH 44240 Mailing Add: 221 W Main St Ravenna OH 44266

DI PASCA, ALBIN WILLIAM (R)
Chmn, Citrus Co Rep Exec Comt, Fla
b New York, NY, Nov 26, 17; s Roger Di Pasca & Eleanor Duszynski D; m 1940 to Gladys Virginia Young; c Verne R, Lourie (Mrs Joseph Schultz), Yvonne C Beelman & Dorreen R (Mrs Dan Thomas). Educ: Golden Gate Col, 50. Polit & Govt Pos: Various indust mgr pos, Dept of Navy, NY, Calif, Hawaii, Panama, PR & Fla, 41-66; foreign staff officer, Dept of State, Washington, DC, 66-72; chmn, Citrus Co Rep Exec Comt, Fla, 74- Bus & Prof Pos: Secy-treas, Do-All Bus Serv Inc, 72- Mil Serv: Pvt, Army, 36-38, serv in 3rd Engrs. Mem: Shriners (treas, Citrus Shrine Club); Royal Patron of Amaranth; Elks; Homosassa Area CofC (dir); Businessmen's Asn Citrus Co. Relig: Protestant. Mailing Add: Drawer D Homosassa Springs FL 32647

DIPRIMA, LAWRENCE (D)
Ill State Rep
b Chicago, Ill, June 24, 10; s Salvatore DiPrima & Josephine Faulisi D; m 1950 to Elizabeth Corvo; c Robert. Educ: Carnegie Inst. Polit & Govt Pos: Asst adminr, Ill Vet Comn, formerly; mem, 28th Ward Regular Dem Orgn, 37 years & 36th Ward, currently; Ill State Rep, currently. Mil Serv: 83rd Inf Div; Combat Badge; Bronze Star. Mem: Life mem Am Legion (founder, Pat Petrone Post); DAV (life mem chap 47); VFW; Amvets, 83rd Div Asn; CMV. Relig: Catholic. Mailing Add: 2759 N Newcastle Ave Chicago IL 60635

DIRCK, EDWIN L (D)
Mo State Rep
Mailing Add: 10740 St Xavier St Ann MO 63074

DIRCKS, DURWOOD WILLIAM (R)
b Clarence, Iowa, Feb 16, 28; s Arthur Henry Dircks & Edna Dresselhaus D; m 1950 to Susan Mae Goltman; c William D, Russell A & David J. Educ: Univ Iowa, BA, 50; Drake Univ Law Sch, JD, 55; Delta Theta Phi; Theta Xi. Polit & Govt Pos: City attorney, Davenport, Iowa, 58-; chmn, Davenport Rep City Cent Comt, 61-; chmn, Scott Co Rep Cent Comt, formerly; mem, Comt to Select Deleg to Rep Nat Conv, 68. Bus & Prof Pos: Attorney-at-law, 55-; sr partner, Dircks, Berger & Saylor Law Firm, currently. Mil Serv: Entered as Pvt, Army, serv in World War II Occup Army, 45-46 & Korean War, 51-52; Lt Col, Army Res, currently; World War II Victory Medal; Army of Occup Japan Medal; Korean War Medal. Mem: Iowa Munic Attorneys Asn; Am Legion; Mason; Shrine; Optimists. Relig: Congregational. Mailing Add: 315 Union Arcade Davenport IA 52803

DISBROW, JOAN FOSTER (D)
VChairwoman, Pinal Co Dem Comt, Ariz
b Harrisburg, Ill, Feb 15, 30; d William Jennings Foster & Adria Creigmile F; m 1974 to Alan Eastman Disbrow; c Theodore John & William Ronald Koenig. Educ: Miami Univ, BS, 51; Ariz State Univ, MA, 67; Mortar Bd; Pi Lambda Theta; Les Politiques; Kappa Delta Pi; Kappa Kappa Gamma; pres, Panhellenic Coun, 50-51. Polit & Govt Pos: Chmn, Dist 6 Dem Comt, Ariz, 72-74; mem, State Dem Exec Comt, 72-; vchairwoman, Pinal Co Dem Comt, 72-; recording secy, Ariz Fed Dem Women's Clubs, 74-75; pres, West Pinal Co Dem Women's Club, 74-75. Bus & Prof Pos: Stewardess, Am Airlines, Inc, 51-52; mkt research investigator, Procter & Gamble, 52-53; co-owner, vpres & secy, Koenig Aviation, Inc, 53-69. Mem: Casa Grande Town Hall; Hoemako Hosp Auxiliary (bd dirs); Girls Ranch, Inc (bd dirs, 74-); Am Asn Univ Women; Desert Woman's Club. Honors & Awards: Women's Flight Achievement Award, Int Flying Farmers Asn, 64. Relig: Episcopal; mem vestry, St Peter's Episcopal Church, 70- Mailing Add: Rte 1 Box 469 Val Vista Rd Casa Grande AZ 85222

DISCHLER, LOUIS, JR (D)
La State Rep
Mailing Add: 1500 Nile St Eunice LA 70535

DISIMONE, RITA LOUISE (INDEPENDENT)
b Paulsboro, NJ; d Pasquale DiSimone & Carolina Guerrieri D; single. Educ: Univ Ill, Urbana-Champaign, AB, 63; Georgetown Univ, MSFS, 67. Polit & Govt Pos: Exec asst to vpres, Army Times Publ Co, Washington, DC, 65-66; researcher & secy, Near E Report, 67; personal secy, US Rep Julia Butler Hansen, 67-69; legis asst to US Rep Roman C Pucinski, 69-72; legis asst to US Rep Henry Helstoski, NJ, 72-74; legis asst to US Rep Albert W Johnson, Pa, 74- Bus & Prof Pos: Secy, mgt, planning & rev div, Philadelphia Naval Shipyard, Pa, 55-58; adminr & supvr, div biophys, dept physiol & biophys, Univ Ill, Urbana, 58-63; research asst, Nat Rehabilitation Asn, Washington, DC, 64. Publ: Speeches and statements written in capacity as legis asst to various mem of Cong. Mem: Alumni Asns of Univ Ill & Georgetown Univ; Cong Staff Club. Honors & Awards: Scholar, Univ Ill, 58. Relig: Roman Catholic. Legal Res: 120 W Jefferson St Paulsboro NJ 08066 Mailing Add: 2000 N St NW Apt 509 Washington DC 20036

DISPONETT, WILLIAM DAVID (R)
b Lawrenceburg, Ky, Sept 4, 35; s James Tyler Disponett & Nora Searcy D; m 1957 to Brenda Sue Hawkins; c Lois Ann. Educ: Anderson High Sch, 4 years. Polit & Govt Pos: Chmn, Anderson Co Rep Party, Ky, 68-75. Bus & Prof Pos: Lab technician, Kraft Foods, Lawrenceburg, 55-69; subdiv owner & developer, 65-; farm owner & housing contractor, Lawrenceburg, 69- Mem: Ky Colonel; Young Rep. Relig: Baptist. Mailing Add: 300 Forrest Dr Lawrenceburg KY 40342

DISSTON, HARRY (R)
Chmn, Louisa Co Rep Comt, Va
b Red Bank, NJ, Nov 23, 99; s Eugene John Kauffmann & Frances Matilda Disston K; m 1930 to Valerie Duval, wid 1950; m 1960 to Catherine Sitler; c Robin John Duval & Geoffrey Whitmore. Educ: Amherst Col, AB, 21; Phi Beta Kappa. Polit & Govt Pos: Vchmn & finance comt chmn, Louisa Co Rep Comt, Va, 62-63, chmn, currently; campaign mgr for Barry Goldwater, 64; alt deleg, Rep Nat Conv, 68; chmn finance comt, mem cent comt & exec comt, Rep Party of Va, formerly, state finance chmn, 68-72; mem, Nat Rep Finance Comt, currently; chmn Electoral Bd, Louisa Co, Va, 69-; mem Bd of Mil Affairs, Commonwealth of Va, 70-; chmn, Gov Comt for Observance of Vet Day, 70- Bus & Prof Pos: Exec, NY Tel Co & Am Tel & Tel Co, 21-41, mem exec adv staff, Am Tel & Tel Co, 46-60; placement adminr, Univ Va Grad Sch Bus Admin, 66-70; dir horse & cattle leasing, Amvest Leasing Corp, Charlottesville, Va, 72- Mil Serv: Entered as Pvt, Army, 18, Cent Officers Training Camp; 2nd Lt to Capt, Inf & Cavalry, Army Res; reentered as Maj, 41, released as Col, 46, after serv in Cavalry & Gen Staff Corps; Brig Gen (Ret), NY Nat Guard, 21-57, serv comdr, 107th Regimental Combat team, 47-57; Legion of Merit; Bronze Star with Oak Leaf Cluster; NY State Distinguished Serv Medal; Order of Bolivar, Venezuela; Gold Cross, Free Polish Forces; Occup of Japan, Philippine Liberation, SW Pac & Am Theaters, Victory & Am Defense Serv Medals. Publ: Know about horses, Devin, 61; Handbook for the novice horseman; elementary dressage, AS Barnes, 70; plus others. Mem: Keswick Hunt Club, Va; Farmington Country Club; Red Land Club; Jack Jouett Bridle Trails Club; Mil Order of World Wars. Relig: Episcopal; Vestry, Grace Episcopal Church, Cismont; exec comt, Diocese of Va. Mailing Add: Hidden Hill Farm Keswick VA 22947

DI STEFANO, JOSEPH ROBERT (D)
RI State Sen
b Providence, RI, Feb 4, 38; s Joseph Di Stefano & Anita Gaudieri D; m 1936 to Barbara D'Ambra; c David, Gregory & Michael. Educ: Providence Col, AB, 59; Georgetown Univ, JD, 62; Delta Theta Phi. Polit & Govt Pos: Councilman, Town of N Providence, RI, 72-73; RI State Sen, Dist 36, 73- Bus & Prof Pos: Attorney-at-law, RI, 62-66; secy & gen coun, Providence & Worcester Co, 66- Mem: Am & RI Bar Asns; United Commercial Travelers; KofC. Relig: Catholic. Mailing Add: 28 Oak Grove Blvd North Providence RI 02911

DITMER, WARD NELSON (R)
Secy, Miami Co Rep Cent & Exec Comts, Ohio
b Covington, Ohio, Dec 12, 02; s Ulysses Grant Ditmer & Katherine Anna Sowers D; m 1922

to Grace Irene Snavely; c Lt Col Robert A & Clyde Arthur (deceased). Educ: Nat Security Seminar, Ideal Bus Sch, Piqua, Ohio; Univ Dayton Workshops. Polit & Govt Pos: City comnr, Piqua, Ohio, 66-; secy, Miami Co Rep Cent & Exec Comts, currently; Chief Warrant Off, Civil Air Patrol, 69-; secy, Miami Co Munic Asn, 69- Bus & Prof Pos: Owner-operator, letter shop, 40-67; free lance pub speaker; asst to Piqua funeral dir. Mil Serv: Pvt, Army, 19-20. Mem: Ohio Rural Letter Carriers Asn; Lions; CofC; hon Jaycee; Boy Scouts. Honors & Awards: Outstanding Citizen Award, Jaycees, 67. Relig: United Methodist. Legal Res: 502 E Green St Piqua OH 45356 Mailing Add: PO Box 713 Piqua OH 45356

DITRAPANO, RUDOLPH LIDANO (D)
Dem Nat Committeeman, WVa
b Charleston, WVa, July 25, 28; s Luigi DiTrapano & Amelia Filigenzi D; m 1957 to Martha Caroline Veazey; c Luisa Caroline, Louis Dante, Lidano Albert & Lia Marta. Educ: Notre Dame Univ, BS, 50, LLB, 51. Polit & Govt Pos: City attorney, East Bank, WVa, 58; chmn, WVa State Dem Exec Comt, formerly; Dem Nat Committeeman, WVa, currently; deleg, Dem Nat Mid-Term Conf, 74. Mil Serv: Entered as A/S, Navy, 51, released as Seaman, 53, after serv in Naval Operating Base. Mem: WVa Tri-Lawyers Asn; Am Legion; Serra Club; Rotary; KofC. Relig: Roman Catholic. Mailing Add: 604 Virginia St E Charleston WV 25301

DITTEMORE, BETTY ANN (R)
Colo State Rep
Mailing Add: 2239 E Floyd Pl Englewood CO 80110

DIVELY, MICHAEL AUGUSTUS (R)
b Cleveland, Ohio, Dec 30, 38; s George Samuel Dively & Harriett Grace Seeds D; single. Educ: Williams Col, AB, 61; Univ Mich, JD, 64; Delta Kappa Epsilon; Phi Alpha Delta. Polit & Govt Pos: Peninsula Twp deleg, Rep Party, Mich, 66-68; secy-treas, Grand Traverse Rep Exec Comt, 66-68; deleg, Rep State Conv, 66-; secy, Ninth Cong Dist Rep Comt, 67-73; dir, State TAR, 68-69; spec adv youth activities to state chmn, Rep State Cent Comt, 69-70; Mich State Rep, 69-74; alt deleg, Rep Nat Conv, 72; dep dir, Mich Dept Com, 75- Bus & Prof Pos: Partner, Murchie, Calcutt & Brown, Traverse City, Mich, 67-71. Mem: State Bar of Mich; Traverse City Indust Fund (dir, 70-); Mason; Kiwanis. Honors & Awards: Outstanding Achievement Award, Kiwanis Club, Traverse City; Distinguished Serv Award, Traverse City, Jaycees; Five Outstanding Young Men Award, Mich Jaycees. Relig: United Church of Christ. Mailing Add: 10895 Peninsula Dr Traverse City MI 49684

DIXON, ALAN JOHN (D)
Ill State Treas
b Belleville, Ill, July 7, 27; s William Gerard Dixon & Elsa Tebbenhoff D; m 1954 to Joan Louise Fox; c Stephanie Jo, Jeffrey Alan & Elizabeth Jane. Educ: Univ Ill, BS, 46; Wash Univ, LLB, 49; Delta Upsilon. Polit & Govt Pos: Police magistrate, Belleville, Ill, 49; asst state attorney, St Clair Co, 50, chmn, Judicial Adv Coun, 3 terms; Ill State Rep, 49th Dist, 50-62; Ill State Sen, 49th Dist, 63-66 & 54th Dist, 68-71, Minority Whip, Ill State Senate, 65-71; deleg, Dem Nat Conv, 68; Ill State Treas, 71- Mil Serv: Air Cadet, Navy, 45-46. Mem: Ill & Am Bar Asns; Am Legion; CofC; St Clair Country Club. Relig: Presbyterian. Legal Res: 53 Country Club Pl Belleville IL 62223 Mailing Add: 25 W Main St Belleville IL 62221

DIXON, FRED L (R)
Mem, Nat Rep Finance Comt
b Pueblo, Colo, July 18, 22; s Fred L Dixon & Ella Alacia Crowley D; single. Educ: Pueblo Col, AA, 42; Univ Colo, BS in bus, 46; Wharton Col, Univ Pa, Invest Bankers Inst, grad. Polit & Govt Pos: Mem, Nat Rep Finance Comt, 57-; treas, Young Rep Nat Fedn, 58-59; secy, DC Rep Comt, 58-68; asst chmn, Nat Conv, 60-64; chief page, 56; ticket chmn, Eisenhower & Nat Dinners, DC, 60-65; chmn protocol & introd, Nat Fedn Rep Women, 60-70 & 72; tour dir, Wm Miller, VPresident Campaign, 64; first vpres, Capitol Hill Club, 64-67; mem bd dirs & treas, Rep Ctr, 66-, mem exec comt, 69-; mem, Spec Nixon-Agnew Finance Comt, 68; exec coordr, Nixon Inaugural & vchmn & dir Gov Reception, 69; deleg, President's Comn on Handicapped, 69; mem, Wolf Trap Farm Finance Comt, 69-70; chmn protocol & introd, Salute to Vice President Dinner, 70; mem, Nixon, Agnew Finance Comt, 72; deleg, Rep Nat Conv & mem rules comt, 72; co-chmn, VPresidential Reception, Inaugural Comt, 73, vchmn, Finance Comt, 73; mem, Salute to the States Comt, 73; Capitol Hill Assocs, 73. Bus & Prof Pos: Chmn, Investments in Am, 61; vchmn speaker bur, New York Stock Exchange, 61-64; pres & chief exec officer, Dwight D Eisenhower Mem Ctr, Washington, DC, 74- Mil Serv: Served as Pvt, Army, 42-45, in Inf & Army Air Corp. Mem: Lions; CWV; Amvets; Nat Interfraternity Conf; Capitol Hill Club. Honors & Awards: Named Man of the Year, US Jaycees, Washington, DC, 56. Relig: Catholic. Mailing Add: 725 15th St NW Washington DC 20005

DIXON, HARRY DONIVAL (D)
Ga State Rep
b Waycross, Ga, Mar 24, 25; s Hughie Dixon & Mattie Woodard D; m 1946 to Ruth Starling; c Harry Donival (Donnie). Educ: Wacona High Sch, 42. Polit & Govt Pos: Ga State Rep, 62- Bus & Prof Pos: Locomotive Engineman, 46-52; RR engr, 52- Mil Serv: Maritime Serv, 43-46. Mem: Elks; Brotherhood of Locomotive Firemen & Enginemen. Relig: Baptist. Mailing Add: 1303 Coral Rd Waycross GA 31501

DIXON, HUGH B (D)
Tenn State Rep
Mailing Add: South Main St Carthage TN 37030

DIXON, ISAIAH (IKE), JR (D)
Md State Deleg
b Baltimore, Md, Dec 23, 22; s Isaiah Dixon & Evelyn Phillips D; m 20 years to Miriam Millard; c Isaiah, III. Educ: Howard Univ, 3 years. Polit & Govt Pos: Md State Deleg, 67-; deleg, Dem Nat Mid-Term Conf, 74. Bus & Prof Pos: Ins broker & real estate broker. Mem: Realtist; Small Bus Asn. Relig: Catholic. Mailing Add: 1607 W North Ave Baltimore MD 21217

DIXON, JULIAN C (D)
Calif State Assemblyman
Mailing Add: 2907 W Vernon Los Angeles CA 90008

DIXON, KATIE LOOSLE (R)
Recorder, Salt Lake Co, Utah
b Logan, Utah; Oct 10, 25; d Rueben O Loosle & Syliva Griffiths L; div; c Jerry, Michael, Todd & Darcy. Educ: Utah State Univ, BS, 45; grad work, Am Univ, Univ Southern Calif, Univ Utah & Brigham Young Univ; Kappa Delta; Theta Alpha Phi. Polit & Govt Pos: Secy, Voting Dist 16 Utah Rep Party, 60-62, vchmn, 64-74; vchmn, Rep Legis Dist, 64-74; vchmn, Second Cong Dist Rep Comt, 66-; bd dirs, Women's Fedn Utah, 68-69; vchmn, Utah Rep Lincoln Day Dinner, 71, chmn, 72-74; recorder, Salt Lake Co, 75- Bus & Prof Pos: Teachers instr, Univ Utah, 68; field supvr, US Census for Utah, 70; exec dir, Utah Asn for Retarded Citizens, 71-74; develop dir, Pine Canyon Ranch for Boys, 74. Publ: Articles in Life, Time & Newsweek. Mem: Salt Lake Co Bar Auxiliary (organizer); Equal Rights Amendment Coalition; Univ Utah Theatre Guild; Assistance Guild of Salt Lake (pres); Utah Symphony (dir, pres). Honors & Awards: A Award, Utah State Univ. Legal Res: 3781 Lois Lane Salt Lake City UT 84117 Mailing Add: 205 City & Co Bldg Salt Lake City UT 84111

DIXON, PAUL RAND (D)
Comnr, Fed Trade Comn
b Nashville, Tenn, Sept 29, 13; s James David Dixon & Sarah Munn D; m 1939 to Doris Busby; c David Leslie & Paul Randall. Educ: Vanderbilt Univ, AB, 36; Univ Fla, LLB, 38; Phi Delta Phi; Alpha Tau Omega. Polit & Govt Pos: Trial attorney, Fed Trade Comn, 38-57, chmn, 61-70, comnr, currently; chief counsel, staff dir subcomt antitrust & monopoly, US Sen, 57-61. Bus & Prof Pos: Asst football coach, Univ Fla, 36-38. Mil Serv: Naval Res, 42-45. Mem: Vanderbilt Univ Alumni Asn; Fed Bar Asn; Nat Lawyers Club; Mason. Relig: Methodist. Legal Res: 5911 Carlton Lane Glen Mar Park Washington DC 20016 Mailing Add: Fed Trade Comn Washington DC 20580

DIXON, R EARL (R)
Fla State Rep
b Bronson, Fla, Mar 11, 27; s Joseph Dewey Dixon & Edythe Roberson D; m 1948 to Louise Wenzel; c Robert & Carolyn. Educ: Univ Fla, BSA, 51, grad work in entomology, 51; Alpha Gamma Rho. Polit & Govt Pos: Chmn, Pest Control Comn of Fla, 59-62; Fla State Rep, Dist 25, 68- Bus & Prof Pos: Dir, Jacksonville Nat Bank, Fla. Mil Serv: Entered as Tech 3, Army, 46, released, 48, after serv in Armored Cavalry & Signal Corps. Mem: Entomological Soc of Am; Nat Pest Control Asn; Downtown Kiwanis Club (dir); Jacksonville Area CofC (bd dir); Gtr Jacksonville Fair Asn. Relig: Lutheran. Legal Res: 4848 Redbud Lane Jacksonville FL 32207 Mailing Add: Drawer F Jacksonville FL 32203

DIXON, ROBERT GALLOWAY, JR (R)
b Canajoharie, NY, Apr 24, 20; s Robert Galloway Dixon, Sr & Ruth Beverly Spencer D; m 1948 to Claire Bracken; c Janet, Barbara & Laurie. Educ: Syracuse Univ, AB summa cum laude, 43, PhD in Polit Sci, 47; George Washington Univ, JD, 56; Phi Beta Kappa; Order of the Coif. Polit & Govt Pos: Consult, NY State Off Local Govt, 66-67; consult, Rep State Const Conv, NY, 66, Pa, 67, Md, 68 & Ill, 70; consult, Nat Comn of Reform of Fed Criminal Laws, 68-71; consult, Admin Conf of US, 69-71; Asst Attorney Gen Off Legal Counsel, Dept of Justice, 73-74. Bus & Prof Pos: From instr to assoc prof, Univ Md, 46-56; assoc prof, George Washington Univ, 56-60, prof, Law Sch, 60-74; Daniel Noyes Kirby Prof law, Washington Univ, 75- Publ: Democratic representation; reapportionment in law & politics, Oxford Univ, 68; Social Security Disability & mass justice—a problem in welfare adjudication, Praeger, 73; The Warren Court Crusade for the Holy Grail of one man-one vote, Supreme Court Rev, 69. Mem: Asn Am Law Schs; Am Bar Asn; Am Polit Sci Asn. Honors & Awards: Maxwell fel, Syracuse Univ, 43-46; Ford Found faculty fel, 51-52 & grant, summer 71; Rockefeller Found fel, 64-65; Am Philos Soc Grant, summer 65; Book Award for Best Book on Govt, Woodrow Wilson Found, 68; Nat Endowment for Humanities sr fel, 71-72. Relig: Presbyterian. Mailing Add: 7415 Buckingham Clayton MO 63105

DIXON, WALTER THOMAS, SR (D)
City Councilman, Baltimore, Md
b Columbia, SC, Aug 13, 93; s William Dixon & Mary Thompson D; m 1941 to Olivia Pierce; c Walter T, Jr. Educ: Benedict Col, LI, 12; Howard Univ, Commercial Dipl, 15; Cent Col Chiropractic, DC, 18; Columbia Univ, BS, 28, MA, 32; Am Sch of Law, Dipl, 35; Alpha Phi Alpha. Hon Degrees: LHD, Kittrell Col, 70. Polit & Govt Pos: City councilman, Fourth Dist, Baltimore, Md, 55-; mem, Md Interracial Comn & mem, Hosp Comt, Baltimore, 60. Bus & Prof Pos: Dean, Peters Bus Sch, 36-66. Mem: Mason (32nd Degree); Shrine (Past Master Corinthian Lodge 18), Odd Fellows; Elks. Relig: Episcopal. Mailing Add: 1933 McCulloh St Baltimore MD 21217

DIZE, CARLTON YANK (R)
b Fairmount, Md, Dec 6, 13; s James Edward Dize & Arinthia Revell D; m 1937 to Becky Justice. Educ: Crisfield High Sch. Polit & Govt Pos: Mem, State Rep Cent Comt, Md, 46-66; Md State Sen, 66-67; Md State Deleg, 67-74; alt deleg, Rep Nat Conv, 68 & 72. Bus & Prof Pos: Owner, Chesapeake Motor Sales, Crisfield, Md, 50-67; pres & owner, Crisfield CATV Inc, 62-73. Mem: Rotary; Elks; CofC; Mason; Shrine. Relig: Methodist. Legal Res: Troy Rd Crisfield MD 21817 Mailing Add: PO Box 510 Crisfield MD 21817

DMITRICH, MIKE (D)
Utah State Rep
b Murray, Utah, Oct 23, 36; s Dan Dmitrich & Mary Milovich D; m 1958 to Georgia Lorraine Hatsis; c Stephanie, Michael Anthony & Dana. Educ: Utah State Univ, 1 year; Col Eastern Utah, 1 year. Polit & Govt Pos: Utah State Rep, Dist 65 & 69- Bus & Prof Pos: Off & credit mgr, Price Trading Co, Utah, 61-63; asst vpres & asst mgr, Walker Bank & Trust Co, Price, 64- Mem: Carbon CofC; Price Elks; F&AM; AF&AM. Relig: Greek Orthodox. Mailing Add: 735 N Sixth East Price UT 84501

DOAK, HARLAN EVERETT (D)
Maine State Rep
b Rangeley, Maine, July 30, 18; s John Leslie Doak & Gladys Stewart D; m 1940 to Louise Grant; c Thomas H & Toby A. Educ: Rangeley High Sch. Polit & Govt Pos: Maine State Rep, 75- Bus & Prof Pos: Plumbing & heating contractor, 56- Mil Serv: Entered as Pvt, Army, 44, released as Pvt, 44, after serv in Tank Destroyers. Mem: Mason; Am Legion; Eastern Star; CofC. Honors & Awards: Citizen of the Year, CofC, 74. Relig: Episcopal. Mailing Add: PO Box 565 Rangeley ME 04970

DOAR, WILLIAM WALTER, JR (D)
SC State Sen
b Rock Hill, SC, Mar 9, 35; s William Walter Doar & Julia Poag D; m 1957 to Louise Davis; c Elizabeth Beckhan & Julia Terrell. Educ: Univ SC, BS, 57, LLB, 59; Omicron Delta Kappa; Kappa Alpha. Polit & Govt Pos: SC State Rep, 68-72; SC State Sen, 72- Mil Serv: Entered as 2nd Lt, Air Force, 59, released as Capt, 62, after serv in Judge Adv Gen Dept. Mem: Am & SC State Bar Asns; Rotary. Relig: Episcopal. Mailing Add: State House Columbia SC 29211

DOBBIN, TILTON HEMSLEY (R)
Asst Secy Domestic & Int Bus, Dept Com
b Lawyers Hill, Md, Apr 9, 17; s Robert A Dobbin & Maria Kerr Hemsley D; m 1942 to Julia Morris Bruce; c Mary Greeley, Robert, Douglas Seddon, Elizabeth Hemsley & Frances Key. Educ: Boy's Latin Sch, grad, 36. Polit & Govt Pos: Asst secy domestics & int bus, Dept Com, 73- Bus & Prof Pos: With Baltimore Nat Bank, 36-40 & 45-49; asst cashier, Mellon Nat Bank, Pittsburgh, 49-53; asst treas, Olin Mathieson Chem Corp, Baltimore, 53-57; vpres, Baltimore Nat Bank, 57-60; pres, Md Nat Bank, 60-73 & chmn exec comt & dir. Mil Serv: Naval Res, 40-45. Mem: Maryland Club; Green Spring Valley Hunt Club. Relig: Episcopal. Legal Res: Golf Course Rd Owings Mills MD 21117 Mailing Add: Dept of Commerce Washington DC 20230

DOBELLE, EVAN SAMUEL (R)
Mayor, Pittsfield, Mass
b Washington, DC, Apr 22, 45; s Martin Dobelle, MD & Lillian Mendelsohn D; m 1970 to Edith Huntington Jones. Educ: The Citadel, 62-65; Am Univ Sch Govt, 65; Univ Mass, Amherst, BS, 70, MEd, 71, EdD, 75; Phi Delta Kappa. Polit & Govt Pos: Spec asst to US Sen Hugh Scott, Wash, 65; legal asst to former Attorney Gen E W Brooke, Mass, 66-67; asst secy to former Gov John A Volpe, Mass, 67-68; research asst, Presidents Comn on Campus Unrest, summer 70; exec asst to US Sen E W Brooke, 71-73; Mayor, Pittsfield, Mass, 74- Bus & Prof Pos: Mem faculty, Harvard Univ Kennedy Sch Govt, 71-73; pres, Wilmington, Stonewall Assocs, Pittsfield, Mass, 73-74; chmn sch comt, Pittsfield, currently; chmn bd adv, Berkshire Community Col, 72-; chmn, Berkshire Regional Transportation Authority, currently, chmn, Berkshire Training & Employ Consortium, currently. Publ: Co-ed, Campaign, 72, Harvard Univ Press, 73. Mem: Am Asn Univ Prof; B'nai B'rith (pres, Abdullam Lodge, 75-); Mason; Lions; Eagles. Relig: Jewish. Legal Res: 114 Ridge Ave Pittsfield MA 01201 Mailing Add: City Hall 66 Allen St Pittsfield MA 01201

DOBIE, GERTRUDE AGNES (R)
Mem, Second Cong Dist Rep Comt, Mich
b Wilkes Barre, Pa, July 10, 20; d Norman A Getz & Gertrude Loughney G; m 1938 to Edward Raymond Dobie; c Patricia (Mrs Fiore Custode) & Edward R, Jr. Educ: Rocky River, Ohio High Sch, grad, 38. Polit & Govt Pos: Former Rep precinct chmn & deleg, Mich; former secy, Monroe Co Rep Exec Comt; vchmn, Monroe Co Rep Comt, 66-74; deleg, Mich Rep State Conv, 66-; mem, Second Cong Dist Rep Comt, currently. Bus & Prof Pos: Partner, Dobie Co, 47- Mem: Am Red Cross, Monroe Co, Mich. Relig: Methodist; Sunday Sch secy & mem, Comn of Educ, St Paul's United Methodist Church, Monroe, Mich. Mailing Add: 3617 Lakeshore Dr Erie Shores Monroe MI 48161

DOBIS, CHESTER F (D)
Ind State Rep
b Gary, Ind, Aug 15, 42; s Jack F Dobis & Veronica Kordys D; m 1971 to Darlene Zimmerman. Educ: Ind Univ Northwest, 61. Polit & Govt Pos: Vpres, Ross Twp Dem Club, Merrillville, Ind, 68; bd mem, Lake Co Young Dem, 69-70; pres, Ross Twp Young Dem, 70; Ind State Rep, 71-, chmn pub policy & vet affairs comt, Ind House Rep, currently. Bus & Prof Pos: Sales rep, Standard Liquors; asst cashier, Gary Nat Bank, 72- Mil Serv: Entered as Pvt, Nat Guard, 63, released as Sgt, 69, after serv in Co E, 113th Engr Bn. Mem: Nat Soc State Legislators; Isaak Walton League; Lake Area United Way (chmn commercial div); Lake Co Asn for Retarded (bd mem); Polish Am Dem Club. Honors & Awards: One of Top Freshman Legislators, Ind Gen Assembly, 71. Relig: Roman Catholic. Mailing Add: 5425 Lincoln Ct Merrillville IN 46410

DOBKIN, M ADLER (R)
b Rockville, Conn, Jan 8, 31; s Leon Dobkin & Rebecca Levy D; m 1957 to Elsa Wallack; c Lori Sue & Glenn Michael. Educ: Univ Conn, 2 years. Polit & Govt Pos: Mem, Citizens Adv Coun, 64-67; mem, Manchester Town Plan & Zone Comn, 66-70, chmn, 67-70; mem, Manchester Charter Rev Comn, 67-68; chmn, Manchester Town Rep Comt, 68-74; mem, Capitol Region Adv Comt, 69-; mem, Small Bus Adv Coun, 70- Mil Serv: Entered as Airman 3/C, Air Force, 51, released as Airman 1/C, 55, after serv in Air Defense Command, Korea, 53-54. Mem: Am Electroplaters Soc; Manchester Mem Hosp; Savings Bank of Manchester. Relig: Jewish. Mailing Add: 153 Shallow Brook Lane Manchester CT 06040

DOBLER, NORMA MAE (D)
Idaho State Rep
b Haines, Ore, May 2, 17; d Lester Woodhouse & Bessie Bircket W; m 1941 to Clifford Irvin Dobler; c Sharon (Mrs Roger Vega); Carol (Mrs Gene Harris) & Terry Lee. Educ: Univ Cincinnati, 35-37; Univ Idaho, BS in Bus, 39; Alpha Lambda Delta; Phi Chi Theta; Kappa Phi. Polit & Govt Pos: Trustee, Moscow Sch Dist, Idaho, 63-69; Idaho State Rep, 72- Bus & Prof Pos: Secy, Univ Idaho Registr, 39-41, lab technician, Col of Forestry, 60-70, secy, Exten Forester, 71-; secy, Am Express Co, Seattle, Wash, 43 & Judge S Ben Dunlap, Caldwell, Idaho, 45-46. Mem: League of Women Voters; life mem Women's Soc for Christian Serv; Univ Idaho Faculty Women's Club; life mem PTA. Relig: Methodist. Mailing Add: 1401 Alpowa St Moscow ID 83843

DOBSON, CLYDE HERMAN (D)
Miss State Rep
Mailing Add: Box 114 Buckatunna MS 39322

DOCKING, ROBERT BLACKWELL (D)
b Kansas City, Mo, Oct 9, 25; s George Docking & Mary Virginia Blackwell D; m 1950 to Meredith Gear; c William Russell & Thomas Robert. Educ: Univ Kans, BS with honors, 48; Univ Wis Grad Sch of Banking, grad; Beta Gamma Sigma; Delta Sigma Pi; Beta Theta Pi. Polit & Govt Pos: Chmn, Douglas Co Dem Party, Kans, 54-56; vpres, Kans Dem Vet, 57; treas, Fifth Dist Dem Comt, formerly; mayor & city comnr, Arkansas City, Kans, formerly; Gov, Kans, 67-74; mem, Am Asn of Criminology, currently; chmn, Interstate Oil Compact Comn, formerly; state co-chmn, Ozarks Regional Comn, formerly; chmn, Midwest Gov Conf, 71-72; deleg, Dem Nat Conv, 72; ex officio deleg, Dem Nat Mid-Term Conf, 74. Bus & Prof Pos: Credit analyst, William Volker Co, 48-50; cashier & asst trust officer, First Nat Bank, 50-56; vpres, Union State Bank, 56-59, pres, 59-; owner, Docking Ins Agency, currently; asst treas & dir, Kans Pub Serv Co, currently. Mil Serv: Cpl, Army Air Corps, 43-46; 1st Lt, Air Force Res, 46-51. Mem: Local Govt Research Corp; Kans League of Munic; Ark Basin Develop Asn in Kans & Cowley Co; United Serv Orgn; CofC. Honors & Awards: Named Young Man of Year, Kans State Jr CofC, 59. Relig: Presbyterian. Mailing Add: State House Topeka KS 66612

DOCKING, VIRGINIA (D)
b Columbus, Miss; d Thomas Grant Blackwell & Annie Strong Duncan B; m to Gov George Docking, wid; c Robert & George Richard. Educ: Wichita State Univ; Univ Kans, BS; Gamma Phi Beta. Polit & Govt Pos: Deleg, Dem Nat Conv, 68, alt deleg, 72. Publ: Column in 100 Kans newspapers. Mem: Women's Nat Dem Club; Daughters of the Cincinnati; Int Platform Asn; Nat Asn Am Pen Women; Kans Authors Club. Relig: Protestant. Mailing Add: 1444 Westover Rd Topeka KS 66604

DOCKINS, RANDI TORGESEN (R)
Secy, Ninth Dist Rep Party, Ga
b Teaneck, NJ, Mar 16, 41; d Walter T Torgesen & Elizabeth Creel T; div; m 1972 to Charles Landrum Dockins; c Goodney, Gary & Gia Hulsey & Kathleen, Keith & Aubrey Dockins. Educ: South Habersham High Sch, Ga, grad cum laude, 58. Polit & Govt Pos: Rep precinct chmn, Habersham Co, Ga, 66-68; mem, Habersham Co Rep Exec Comt, 66-; mem, Ga State Rep Comt, 68-70; chmn, Habersham Co Rep Party, 68-70, vchmn, 72-73; co campaign mgr, Ninth Dist Cong Cand, 70; deleg, Ga Rep Conv, 70 & 72; secy, Ninth Dist Rep Party, Ga, 70- Bus & Prof Pos: Income tax acct & bookkeeper. Relig: Presbyterian. Mailing Add: Rte 2 Ridgewood Estates Cornelia GA 30531

DOCTER, CHARLES ALFRED (D)
Md State Deleg
b Hamburg, Ger, Aug 5, 31; s Alfred J Docter & Annie Rothschild D; m 1958 to Marcia Kaplan; c Will Henry, Michael Warren & Adina Jo. Educ: Kenyon Col, BA, 53; Univ Chicago Law Sch, JD, 56; Tau Kappa Alpha. Polit & Govt Pos: Staff asst to US Sen Paul H Douglas, 52; pres, Western Suburban Dem Club, Montgomery Co, Md, 64-66; vchmn, Dem Precinct 6-1, 64-66; Md State Deleg, 67- Bus & Prof Pos: Trustee in Bankruptcy, Mutual Security Savings & Loan Asn, Inc, 62-73; mem, Docter, Docter & Salus Law Firm, Washington, DC, currently. Mil Serv: Entered as Seaman, Navy, 56, released as Lt, 59; Lt, Naval Res. Mem: DC & Md State Bar Asns; B'nai B'rith; Montgomery Co Civic Fedn; Lions. Relig: Jewish. Mailing Add: 9810 Hillridge Dr Kensington MD 20795

DODD, CHRISTOPHER JOHN (D)
US Rep, Conn
b Willimantic, Conn, May 27, 44; s Thomas J Dodd & Grace Murphy D; m 1970 to Susan Mooney. Educ: Providence Col, 62-66; Univ Louisville Sch Law, 70-72. Polit & Govt Pos: Deleg, Dem Nat Mid-Term Conf, 74; US Rep, Conn, 75- Bus & Prof Pos: Spec proj coordr, Off of Selection, Peace Corps, Washington, DC, 69; attorney, Suisman, Shapiro, Wool & Brennan, New London, Conn, 69-74. Mem: Big Bros of Southeastern Conn; US Coast Guard Acad (bd of visitors). Relig: Roman Catholic. Legal Res: Mulberry Hollow North Stonington CT 06359 Mailing Add: 429 Cannon House Off Bldg Washington DC 20515

DODD, FRANK J (PAT) (D)
Pres, NJ State Sen
b Orange, NJ, Feb 4, 38; single. Educ: Upsala Col; Seton Hall Univ. Polit & Govt Pos: Mem, Essex Co Young Dem; NJ coordr for US Rep J G Minish campaigns; NJ State Assemblyman, 64-70; mem, State Tax Policy Comn; chmn, Gov Youth Task Force; app platform comt, NJ Dem State Conv; mem, Solid Waste Disposal Study & Welfare Study Comn, NJ Clear Air Comn & NJ Pesticide Comn, 70-72; NJ State Sen, Essex Co, 72-, mem agr & environ comt, law, pub safety & defense comt, ad hoc comt on energy & the environ & law revision & legis serv comt, NJ State Senate, 72-73, chmn senate rules comt, senate pres, 74-; Bus & Prof Pos: Businessman; pres, Dodd Enterprises, currently. Mil Serv: Essex Troop, NJ Nat Guard, six years. Mem: Orange CofC (bd gov); Am Cancer Soc; Elks; Am Legion; KofC. Honors & Awards: Alumni Serv Award for Serv to Upsala Col, 72; Outstanding Legislator Award, Eagleton Inst Polit. Legal Res: Mountain Ave Llewellyn Park West Orange NJ 07052 Mailing Add: Senate Chambers State House Rm 40 Trenton NJ 08625

DODD, ISABEL R (R)
Secy, Nassau Co Rep Comt, NY
b Glasgow, Scotland, Oct 14, 19; d Duncan Robb & Isabelle Curtis R; m 1947 to Duncan O Dodd. Educ: Sea Cliff High Sch; Brownes Bus Sch, Jamaica, NY. Polit & Govt Pos: Legis aide to NY State Assemblyman, Albany, NY, 51-65; research & scheduling, Nassau Co Rep Comt, 66-68, secy, currently; dep comnr, Nassau Co Bd of Elec, Mineola, 69-71, comnr, 73-; town clerk, Oyster Bay, 72; alt deleg, Rep Nat Conv, 72; committeewoman, NY Rep State Comt, currently; vchmn, Oyster Bay Town Rep Comt, currently. Mem: Rep Exec Leader of Sea Cliff; Nassau Co Fedn of Rep Women. Honors & Awards: First Woman to be elected Town Clerk of Oyster Bay in Town's 311 year history, 72. Relig: Protestant. Mailing Add: 43 Hawthorne Rd Sea Cliff NY 11579

DODD, WILMA NEVILLE BEARDSLEE (D)
Mem, Dem Nat Comt, Tenn
b Ridgely, Tenn, Jan 2, 09; d Grover Cleveland Beardslee & Charlie Lou Gullette B; m 1929 to Claude Dodd. Educ: Southwestern at Memphis, 28. Polit & Govt Pos: Dir, Lake Co Civil Defense Tenn, 50-66; dir, Women's Activities, State Off Civil Defense, 58-59; state rep, Region III Civil Defense, 62-63; pres, Lake Co Dem Women's Club, 58-60; chmn, Lake Co Dem Women, 58-66; state pres, Fedn Dem Women, 60-61, parliamentarian, 65-66; chmn publicity, State of Tenn Deleg, Dem Nat Conv, 64, deleg, secy Tenn deleg & rep credentials & rules comt, 68, alt deleg, 72; mem exec comt, WTenn State Travel & Tourist Prom Coun, 64-; vchmn, WTenn Opers Support, 65-66; mem adv comt, President's US Civil Defense Coun, 65-66, state rep, 67-69; secy-treas, State Civil Defense Asn, 65-66, pres, 66-69; committeewoman, Eighth Cong Dist, Tenn State Dem Exec Comt, currently & vchmn, 67-; coordr, Women Eighth Cong Dist for Dem Nominee Ed Jones, 68; secy, Lake Co Dem Exec Comt, 70-; vchmn, Tenn State Dem Party, 72-; mem, Nat Fedn Dem Women's Clubs, 72-; mem, Dem Nat Comt, 73- Mem: Lake Co Bus & Prof Women's Club; Nat Am Legion Auxiliary; Eastern Star (Past Worthy Matron & Tenn chmn, Int Peace Garden); Muscular Dystrophy Asn Am; Nat Found Muscular Dystrophy Asn. Relig: Presbyterian. Mailing Add: Sans Souci Farms Ridgely TN 38080

DODERER, MINNETTE FRERICHS (D)
Iowa State Sen
b Holland, Iowa, May 16, 23; d John A Frerichs & Sophie Sherfield F; m 1944 to Fred H Doderer; c Dennis H J & Kay Lynn. Educ: State Col Iowa; Univ Iowa, BA in Econ, 48; Tau Sigma Delta. Polit & Govt Pos: Vchmn, Johnson Co Dem Cent Comt, Iowa, 53-58 secy, Iowa Citizens for Const Conv, 58-60 & vpres, Iowa Citizens for Fair Representation, 60-62; jury comnr, Johnson-Iowa Dist Court, 62-65; Iowa State Rep, Johnson Co, 64-68; mem coun, State Govt Midwestern Standing Comt on Higher Educ, 65-66; vpres, Iowa Comn on Interstate Coop, 65-67; deleg, Dem Nat Conv, 68; Dem Nat Committeewoman, 68-69; Iowa

State Sen, 68-, pres pro tem, Iowa State Senate, 75-; mem, Dem Nat Policy Coun of Elected Off, 73- Mem: Nat Soc State Legislators; League of Women Voters; UN Asn of US; Nat Order Women Legislators; Iowa Univ Sch Relig (dir, 69-). Honors & Awards: Distinguished Serv in Iowa Gen Assembly Award, Iowa State Educ Asn, 69. Relig: Methodist. Mailing Add: 2008 Dunlap Ct Iowa City IA 52240

DODGE, CARL F (R)
Nev State Sen
Mailing Add: PO Drawer 31 Fallon NV 89406

DODSON, NEWTON B (R)
Chmn, Coahoma Co Rep Party, Miss
b Shattuck, Okla, Aug 25, 26; s Frank F Dodson & Myrtle Newton D; m 1948 to Edwina Montgomery; c Frances (Mrs Marion), Newton Montgomery & Louisa Moss. Educ: Univ Tex, BBA, 50; Sigma Chi. Polit & Govt Pos: Chmn, Coahoma Co Rep Party, Miss, 60-; chmn, Second Cong Dist Rep Party, 66-71; deleg, Rep Nat Conv, 68; dist dir, 1970 Census; mayor, Clarksdale, Miss, 71-; mem, Miss Rep Exec Comt, 74- Bus & Prof Pos: Self-employed farmer, Miss Delta, 50- Mil Serv: Entered as Pvt, Army, 45, released as Sgt, 47, after serv in Mid-Pac Theatre, Hawaii, 45-47. Mem: Miss Munic Asn; VFW; Am Legion; Farm Bur. Relig: Presbyterian. Mailing Add: 434 W Second St Clarksdale MS 38614

DOERR, RAY E (R)
Chmn, Jackson Co Rep Cent Comt, Ill
b Elkville, Ill, Sept 3, 26; s Clyde Doerr & Ida Easterling D; m 1944 to Imogene Schimpf; c Jeffrey Ray. Educ: High Sch. Polit & Govt Pos: Mayor, Vergennes, Ill, trustee, 52-60, pres, 60-; Rep precinct committeeman, Vergennes, 61-; chmn, Jackson Co, Rep Cent Comt, 64-; mem, Ill Rep State Cent Comt. Bus & Prof Pos: Practicing auctioneer; territory mgr, Berry Tractor Co, Inc, 50-57; dist mgr, Massey Ferguson, Inc, 57-64, sales supvr, 63-64, sales mgr, 64- Mil Serv: Entered as A/S, Navy, 44, released as RT 3, 46, after serv in Pac; Four Ribbons & Two Battle Stars. Mem: Mason (Blue Lodge, Consistory); Farm Bur. Relig: Evangelical United Brethren. Mailing Add: Box 27 Vergennes IL 62994

DOGGETT, LLOYD ALTON, II (D)
Tex State Sen
b Austin, Tex, Oct 6, 46; s Lloyd A Doggett & Alyce Freydenfeldt D; m 1969 to Elizabeth Belk; c Lisa. Educ: Univ Tex, Austin, BBA, 67, Sch Law, JD, 70; Order of Coif; Lambda Chi Alpha. Polit & Govt Pos: Tex State Sen, 73- Bus & Prof Pos: Attorney-at-law, Doggett & Jacks, Austin, Tex, 75- Mem: Tex Consumer Asn (pres, 73). Relig: Methodist. Legal Res: 1906 Sharon Lane Austin TX 78703 Mailing Add: PO Box 12068 Austin TX 78711

DOGOLE, SAUL HARRISON (D)
Mem Finance Coun, Dem Nat Comt
b Philadelphia, Pa, Jan 16, 22; s Irving M Dogole & Ethel Kreager D; m 1967 to Marilyne Zucker; c James E & Ian M. Educ: Univ Pa, BA, 43. Polit & Govt Pos: Mem finance coun, Dem Nat Comt, Washington, DC, 70-; nat finance dir, Sen Hubert H Humphrey Presidential Campaign, 72; deleg, Dem Nat Conv, 72; mem bd Coalition for a Dem Majority, Washington, DC, 72-; mem exec comt, Jackson for President, 75. Bus & Prof Pos: Partner, Globe Int Detective Syst, Inc, Philadelphia, Pa, 50-60; pres, Globe Security Syst, Inc, 60-72, chmn, 72- Mem: World Bus Coun; B'nai B'rith; Variety Club, Tent 13; Mason (32nd Degree); Univ Pa (agent). Honors & Awards: Humanitarian Award, Am Cancer Soc, Kain Moses Group, 61; Year of the Negev Award, State of Israel, 62, Commendation Award, 66; Philadelphia Community Serv Award, Jewish Theol Sem of Am, 66; Cyrus Adler Community Serv Award, 69. Relig: Jewish. Legal Res: Apt D 1207 Madison House City Line Philadelphia PA 19131 Mailing Add: 2503 Lombard St Philadelphia PA 19146

DOHERTY, PATRICK WILLIAM (D)
b Amityville, NY, May 24, 51; s Patrick John Doherty & Catherine Lydon D; single. Educ: Hofstra Univ, 69- Polit & Govt Pos: Mem, Nassau Co Dem Comt, NY, 71-; mem, Comt on Voter Registr, NY State Dem Comt, 71-72; youth coordr, Nassau Co McGovern for President, 71-72; mem exec comt, Nassau Co Am for Dem Action, 71-73; deleg, Dem Nat Conv, 72; Dem nominee, NY State Assembly, 11th Dist, 72; mem exec comt, Nassau Co New Dem Coalition, 72-; mem exec coun, NY State New Dem Coalition, 73- Relig: Roman Catholic. Mailing Add: 84 Michigan Ave Massapequa NY 11758

DOHERTY, WALTER GERARD (R)
Press Secy, Mich Rep State Cent Comt
b Cincinnati, Ohio, Sept 24, 34; s David Louis Doherty & Mary Bundy D; m 1965 to Mary Ann Kennett; c Justin Michael, Ian Patrick & Kathleen Elizabeth. Educ: St John's Univ, NY, BA, 56; Sigma Rho. Polit & Govt Pos: Press Secy, Mich Rep State Cent Comt, 69- Bus & Prof Pos: Gen ed, NCAA Serv Bur, 56-59; sports info dir, Univ Detroit, Mich, 60-63; asst pub rels dir, Detroit Race Course & racing officer, Hazel Park Race Course, 63; asst pub rels dir, Arlington Park Race Course, Ill, 64; dir pub rels, Sinai Hosp of Detroit, Mich, 65-69. Mil Serv: Entered as Pvt, NY Nat Guard Army Res, 52, released as SP-4, 59, after serv in 42nd Signal Co, 365th Field Artil Bn. Relig: Roman Catholic. Mailing Add: 27840 Berkshire Southfield MI 48075

DOHNAL, ROBERT LEO (R)
b Mankato, Minn, May 31, 40; s Leo Joseph Dohnal & Evelyn Ario D; m 1970 to Jean Ellen Buckley; c Darcie Jean & David Edward. Educ: Univ Wis, BS, 72; Sigma Chi. Polit & Govt Pos: Chmn, West Allis Citizens for Nixon, Wis, 68 & 72; chmn, West Allis Rep Unit, 68-70; Rep committeeman, West Allis & Wauwatosa, 68 & 72; alt deleg, Rep Nat Conv, 72; Milwaukee coordr, Dyke for Gov, 74. Bus & Prof Pos: Pres, Dohnal Drug Co, Inc, 64-72; vpres, West Allis Spartans Pro Football Team, 70-72; asst pres, Milwaukee Co Pharmacists Soc, 71-72. Publ: Polit columnist, West Allis Star, 68-72; polit writer, Wis State Rev. Mem: Nat Asn Retail Druggists; Rotary; Jaycees; Am Conserv Union; West Allis Western Days. Honors & Awards: Rep of Year, West Allis Rep Unit, 71. Relig: Catholic. Legal Res: 11324 W Potter Rd Wauwatosa WI 53226 Mailing Add: 11138 W Greenfield Ave West Allis WI 53214

DOI, NELSON KIYOSHI (D)
Lt Gov, Hawaii
b Pahoa, Hawaii, Jan 1, 22; s Tadaichi Doi & Chieno Kurata D; m 1949 to Eiko Oshima; c David Tadashi & Katherine Aido. Educ: Univ Hawaii; Univ Minn Law Sch, JD, 48; Gamma Eta Gamma. Polit & Govt Pos: Co attorney, Hilo, Hawaii, 53-54; Hawaii State Sen, 59-69; sr judge, Third Circuit Court, Hilo, 69-74; Lt Gov, Hawaii, 74- Bus & Prof Pos: Attorney-at-Law, pvt practice, Hilo, 54-68. Mem: Hawaii Co, State & Am Bar Asns. Honors & Awards: Hon mem Club 100 (Infantry); hon life mem Hilo Jr CofC. Legal Res: 1179 Kahoa Rd Hilo HI 96720 Mailing Add: State Capitol Honolulu HI 96813

DOKUCHITZ, PETER S (R)
NY State Assemblyman
Mailing Add: 1 Main St Unadilla NY 13849

DOLAN, JOSEPH M (D)
Chmn, Lonoke Co Dem Cent Comt, Ark
b Chicago, Ill, May 12, 17; s Patrick T Dolan & Grace E McElroy D; m 1942 to Edna Carllee; c J Michael, P E Terrence, R Kevin, Elizabeth, Christopher, John & Daria (Mrs Coffield). Educ: Univ Ill, BS, 41; Univ Ark, MS, 41; Phi Kappa Theta. Polit & Govt Pos: Chmn, Lonoke Co Dem Cent Comt, Ark, 71- Mil Serv: Entered as Cadet, Air Force, 42, released as 1st Lt, 46, after serv in Air Transport Command. Legal Res: Rte 2 Box 122 Scott AR 72042 Mailing Add: PO Box 186 England AR 72046

DOLAN, THOMAS FRANCIS (R)
Chmn, Middleton Town Rep Party, Mass
b Newton, Mass, Feb 18, 24; s Thomas F Dolan, Jr & Eleanor Sullivan D; m 1957 to Judith W; c Thomas F, Jr, Sean C & Ellen C. Educ: Mass Inst Technol, SB, 44; pres, 5:15 Club. Polit & Govt Pos: Mem, Bd of Appeals, Middleton, Mass, 61-67, chmn, 66-67; mem, Middleton Town Rep Comt, 64-, chmn, 68-; selectman, Middleton, 67-73, chmn, 69-70 & 72-73, mem, Bd Health, 73- Bus & Prof Pos: Jr technologist, Boston Woven Hose & Rubber Co, 44-46, sr technologist, 47-55, dept mgr, 56-57, Boston Woven Hose & Rubber Div, Am Biltrite Rubber Co, 57-72, Occup Safety & Health Admin coordr, Boston Indust Prod Div, 72- Mem: Am Chem SOc; Div Rubber Chem, Boston Rubber Group; Rubber Reclaimers Asn; Middleton Hist Soc; Middleton KofC. Relig: Catholic. Mailing Add: 238 Essex St Middleton MA 01949

DOLE, HOLLIS M (R)
b Paonia, Colo; m to Ruth Josephine Mitchell; c two. Educ: Ore State Univ, BS in Geol, 40, MS, 42; Univ Calif, Los Angeles & Univ Utah, econ geol. Hon Degrees: DEng, Mont Col Mineral Sci & Technol, 72. Polit & Govt Pos: Mem staff, Bur of Mines, Scappoose, Ore, 42; mem staff, Geol Surv, Tucson, Ariz, 46; former Ore State geologist & dir, Ore Dept of Geol & Minerals Industs; former gen reporter for Ore, Interstate Oil Compact Comn; testified before House & Senate Interior Comts on hearings regarding gold & chrome probs; Asst Secy for Mineral Resources, Dept of the Interior, 69-73. Bus & Prof Pos: Mem staff, Bohemia Mines, Cottage Grove, Ore, 34-35; mem staff, Am Trust Co, Palo Alto, Calif, 35-37; former col instr geol, Portland & Salt Lake City; gen mgr, Colony/C-B Oil Shale Opers, Atlantic Richfield Co, 73- Mil Serv: Entered Navy, 42, released as Lt, 45. Publ: Numerous tech publ on mineral resources. Mem: Am Asn Petroleum Geologists; Asn of Am State Geologists; Ore Acad of Sci; Soc Mining Engrs. Honors & Awards: Distinguished Serv Award, Dept of Interior, 72; Award of Merit, Am Asn Cost Engrs, 72; Distinguished Serv Award, Ore State Univ, 73. Relig: Protestant. Legal Res: 4725 S Forest Ct Denver CO 80237 Mailing Add: 1500 Security Life Bldg Denver CO 80202

DOLE, ROBERT J (R)
US Sen, Kans
b Russell, Kans, July 22, 23; s Doran R Dole & Bina D. Educ: Univ Kans, Lawrence; Washburn Munic Univ, Topeka, AB & LLB magna cum laude, 52; Kappa Sigma. Hon Degrees: LLD, Washburn Univ, 69. Polit & Govt Pos: Kans State Rep, 51-53; co attorney, Russell Co, 53-61; US Rep, First Cong Dist, Kans, 60-68; US Sen, Kans, 69-, mem, Agr & Forestry Comt, Finance Comt, Select Comt Nutrition & Human Needs, Budget Comt & Post Off Civil Serv Comt, US Senate; chmn, Rep Nat Comt, 71-73. Mil Serv: Entered as 2nd Lt, Army, 43, released as Capt, 48, after serv in 10th Mt Div, Italy; Bronze Star with Oak Leaf Cluster; Combat Inf Badge; Purple Heart with Oak Leaf Cluster. Mem: Russell Co, Kans & Am Bar Asns; Kans Co Attorney's Asn; Washburn Alumni Asn. Honors & Awards: Named Outstanding Kansan to overcome a handicap, DAV; Nat Easter Seal Award. Relig: Methodist. Legal Res: Russell KS Mailing Add: 4213 New Senate Off Bldg Washington DC 20510

DOLL, BERNARD THOMAS (R)
b Sault Ste Marie, Mich, Dec 30, 20; s Edward Doll & Mary Elizabeth Tardiff D; m 1945 to Elizabeth Donna Ploegstra; c Nancy Elizabeth (Mrs Joe Carter), Phyllis Kathryn (Mrs Loren Jones), Bernard Edward, Teresa Anne, Patricia Jean, Connie Marie & Mary Kay. Educ: Mich State Univ grad course dairy mfg. Polit & Govt Pos: Deleg, Rep State Comt; mem, Chippewa Co Rep Exec Comt; local Rep deleg, chmn, Chippewa Co Rep Comt, formerly; supvr, Bruce Twp, 59- Bus & Prof Pos: Dairy farmer. Mem: Nat Milk Prod Fedn; State Asn Supvr & State Asn Assessors; Mich Milk Prod Asn; Chippewa Co-Sault Ste Marie Airport Bd; War Mem Hosp Bd. Honors & Awards: Serv award as past mem & chmn, Chippewa Co Bd Supvr. Relig: Catholic; Bldg Comt; mem, Barbeau Catholic Church. Mailing Add: Rte 1 Dafter MI 49724

DOLL, DOROTHEA HELEN (DOTTY) (D)
Mo State Rep
b Chicago, Ill, July 20, 36; d Clarence Louis Stein, Sr & Dorothea Margaret Hunter S; m 1958 to Russell Charles Doll; c Karin Merietta. Educ: Chicago Teachers Col, BE, 58. Polit & Govt Pos: Mo State Rep, 29th Dist, 75- Bus & Prof Pos: First grade teacher, Chicago Sch Dist, 59-64; savings & loan & bank teller, Chicago & Kansas City, 58-63 & 69-70; psychiat social worker trainee, Chicago State Hosp, 64-65. Mem: 49-63 Neighborhood Coalition, Inc; Citizens Asn. Relig: Methodist. Mailing Add: 5400 Rockhill Rd Kansas City MO 64110

DOLLINGER, CHARLES R, JR (R)
Committeeman, Tex Rep Exec Comt
b Beaumont, Tex, July 10, 35; s Charles R Dollinger, Sr & Artie Grammier D; m 1957 to Katherine Anne Barbour; c Lilli, Scot, Brodie & Steve. Educ: Tex A&M Univ, BS in Civil Eng, 57. Polit & Govt Pos: Chmn, Jefferson Co Rep Exec Comt, 70-73; committeeman, Tex Rep Exec Comt, Dist Four, 73- Bus & Prof Pos: Asst shop supt, John Dollinger Jr Inc, Beaumont, 57-64, sales engr, 64-74, secy-treas, 74- Mil Serv: Entered as 2nd Lt, Army, 57, released as 1st Lt, 59, after serv in Ord Missile Command, 58-59. Mem: Tex Structural Steel Inst; Am Inst Steel Construction; Beaumont A&M Club; Rotary Club; Tex Mfrs Asn. Relig: Fundamental. Legal Res: 630 22nd St Beaumont TX 77706 Mailing Add: Box 5365 Beaumont TX 77702

DOLLIVER, JAMES I (R)
b Park Ridge, Ill, Aug 31, 94; s Robert Henry Dolliver & Mary Elle Barrett D; m 1928 to Rachel McCreight; c James M, Arthur M, Margaret E & Robert H. Educ: Morningside Col, Iowa, AB, 15; Univ Chicago, JD, 21. Polit & Govt Pos: Regional legal counsel, Int Coop Admin, Iran, Iraq, Lebanon, Jordan, Egypt & Lybia; US Rep, Iowa, 45-57. Mil Serv: Entered as Pvt, Army, 18, released as 2nd Lt, 18. Mem: Iowa Bar Asn; Mason; Am Legion; Farm Bur; Rotary. Relig: Methodist. Mailing Add: RFD 3 Spirit Lake IA 51360

DOLLIVER, JAMES MORGAN (R)
b Ft Dodge, Iowa, Oct 13, 24; s James Isaac Dolliver & Margaret Elizabeth Morgan D (deceased); m 1948 to Barbara Jean Babcock; c Elizabeth, James, Peter, Keith, Jennifer & Nancy. Educ: Swarthmore Col, BA, 49; Univ Wash, LLB, 52; Phi Delta Theta; Delta Theta Phi. Polit & Govt Pos: Law clerk, Wash State Supreme Court, 52-53; admin asst to Congressman Jack Westland, 55-60; caucus attorney, Wash House Rep, 63-; admin asst to Gov, Wash, 65- Bus & Prof Pos: Lawyer, Port Angeles, Wash, 53-54, lawyer, Everett, 61-65. Mil Serv: Entered as Aviation Cadet, Navy, 43, released as Ens, 46, after serv in Coast Guard. Relig: Methodist. Legal Res: 4603 Westview Dr Everett WA 98201 Mailing Add: 312 N Sherman Olympia WA 98501

DOMBI, LAURAINE MARY (D)
Mem, Torrington Dem Town Comt, Conn
b Torrington, Conn, Oct 2, 51; d William John Dombi & Doris Alexander D; single. Educ: Wheaton Col, 69-71; Univ Conn, BA, 73; Nat Honor Soc. Polit & Govt Pos: Deleg, Dem Nat Conv, 72; mem, Torrington Dem Town Comt, Conn, 72-; research asst, Conn State Legis, 73- Honors & Awards: State of Conn Scholar, 69. Mailing Add: 508 Brightwood Ave Torrington CT 06790

DOMBROWSKI, BERNARD JOSEPH (D)
Pa State Rep
b Erie, Pa, May 11, 29; Boleslaus Dombrowski (deceased) & Michalene Rutecki D; m 1952 to Eleanor Mary Lukaszewski; c Donald, Mark & Marian. Educ: Alliance Col, union seminar, cert; Am Sterilizer Night Sch, cert, 59; Gannon Col, cert, 64. Polit & Govt Pos: Pa State Rep, 71- Bus & Prof Pos: Financial secy, Foresters Beneficial Asn, Erie, Pa, 54-71; dir, Maco, 70-71. Mil Serv: Entered as Pvt, Air Force, 50, released as S/Sgt, 53, after serv in 3380th Air Police Squadron, Keesler AFB, 50-53. Mem: Polish Nat Alliance; Am Legion; Model Cities; Erie Stadium Comn; UAW Local 832. Honors & Awards: Life membership in Foresters Beneficial Asn, 66; East Side Boys Club (secy, 68-). Relig: Roman Catholic. Mailing Add: 618 E 14th St Erie PA 16503

DOMENICI, PETE V (R)
US Sen, NMex
b Albuquerque, NMex, May 7, 32; s Churubino Domenici & Alda Vichi D; m 1959 to Nancy L Burk; c Lisa, Peter, Nella, Clare, David, Nannette, Helen & Paula. Educ: Univ Albuquerque, 52-54; Univ NMex, BS, 54; Univ Denver, JD, 58. Polit & Govt Pos: City comnr, Albuquerque City Comn, NMex, 66-67, chmn, 67-69; US Sen, NMex, 73- Bus & Prof Pos: Attorney, Albuquerque, NMex. Relig: Catholic. Legal Res: 402 15th St SW Albuquerque NM 87104 Mailing Add: 11110 Stephalle Lane Rockville MD 20852

DOMINICK, PETER HOYT (R)
b Stamford, Conn, July 7, 15; s Gayer G Dominick (deceased) & Eleanor Hoyt D (deceased); m 1940 to Nancy Parks; c Peter, Jr, Sandy, Michael & Lynne. Educ: Yale Univ, BA, 37, Law Sch, LLB, 40; Phi Delta Phi; Fence Club; Scroll & Keys. Polit & Govt Pos: Colo State Rep, 57-61; US Rep, Colo, 61-63; US Sen, Colo, 63-74; deleg, Rep Nat Conv, 64, 68 & 72; Ambasador to Switz, 75. Bus & Prof Pos: Partner, Holland & Hart, Denver, Colo, 47-61. Mil Serv: Entered as Cadet, Army-Air Corps, 42, released as Capt, 45, after serv in Training & Transport Command & China-Burma-India Theatre; Air Medal with Cluster; Distinguished Flying Cross; Col, Air Force Res, 61- Mem: Am, Colo, Denver & Arapahoe Co Bar Asns; CofC. Relig: Episcopal. Mailing Add: 5050 E Quincy Englewood CO 80110

DOMINOWSKI, WAYNE VICTOR (D)
Chmn, O'Brien Co Dem Party, Iowa
b Chicago, Ill, June 19, 41; s Frank Lawrence Dominowski & Wanda N Praiss D; m 1967 to Linda L Uhl; c Rick L & Jennifer L. Educ: Northern Ill Univ, 59-61; Wright Jr Col, Chicago, 61-63; Briar Cliff Col, BA, 71. Polit & Govt Pos: Pub info officer, Iowa Nat Guard; chmn, O'Brien Co Dem Party, Iowa, 74- Bus & Prof Pos: Broadcaster-reporter, KTIV-TV, Sioux City, Iowa, 68-71; Eng-jour instr, Woodbury Cent High Sch, 71-73; assoc ed, Sheldon Mail-Sun Newspapers, 73- Mil Serv: Entered as Airman Basic, Air Force, 63, released as Airman 1/C, after serv in Security Serv, Mediter Theatre, 63-65; Good Conduct Medal; Nat Defense. Publ: After they've gone. . ., 4/74, Chicago still says hello, 8/74 & Teaching language, poetry, 9/75, Sheldon Publ Co, Iowa. Mem: Sheldon Tennis Club; Sheldon Country Club; Iowa Press Asn; assoc mem PEN Am Ctr. Honors & Awards: Hon Police Chief, Sioux City Police Dept, 70; Best Feature Story & Second Place, Best Editorial, Iowa Press Asn, 75. Relig: Roman Catholic. Mailing Add: 815 Tenth St Sheldon IA 51201

DONAHEY, GERTRUDE WALTON (D)
State Treas, Ohio
b Tuscarawas Co, Ohio, Aug 4, 08; d George Sebastian Walton & Mary Ann Thomas W; m 1930 to John W Donahey (deceased); c John William, Jr. Educ: Bus Col. Hon Degrees: DPS, Rio Grande Col, 74. Polit & Govt Pos: Field aide in Cent & Southern Ohio for US Sen Stephen M Young, Ohio, 63-69, exec asst, 64-; mem-at-lg, State Platform Comt, Ohio Dem Party, 64 & 68; deleg, Dem Nat Conv, 64 & 68 & Ohio rep, platform & resolutions comt, 68; State Treas-Elect, Ohio, 70-71, State Treas, 71- Bus & Prof Pos: Pvt secretarial work until 30; vol work for community orgn, Ohio, 30- Mem: Bus & Prof Women's Club of Ohio; Nat Asn Auditors, Comptrollers & Treas; Munic Finance Officers Asn; Ment Health Asn Ohio; Cent Ohio Rose Soc. Honors & Awards: First woman elected to state admin off in Ohio. Relig: Episcopal. Mailing Add: 2838 Sherwood Rd Columbus OH 43209

DONAHOE, J MICHAEL (R)
Mem Exec Comt, Okla State Rep Comt
b Kansas City, Mo, May 24, 38; s Daniel J Donahoe, Jr & Helen Clarke D; single. Educ: Georgetown Univ, BS, 62; Univ Okla, JD, 70; Phi Alpha Delta; Sigma Alpha Epsilon. Polit & Govt Pos: Advanceman, Rep Nat Goldwater campaign, 64; advanceman participation polit, Citizens for Nat Nixon-Agnew campaign, 68; dir, Off Intergovt Rels Study, 69-70; Rep nominee, Secy of State, Okla, 70; mem exec comt & chmn, registr, Okla State Rep Comt, 70- Bus & Prof Pos: Attorney, Donahoe Law Off, Ponca City, Okla, 70-, law officer, Washington, DC, 71- & Warner & Angle, Phoenix, 72- Mem: Am Bar Asn (vchmn law day, 73); Am Judicature Soc; Lawyer-Pilots Asn; State Bars of Okla & Ariz. Relig: Catholic. Mailing Add: 143 Whitworth Ave Ponca City OK 74601

DONAHUE, DANIEL FRANCIS (D)
b Pittsburgh, Pa, Sept 1, 40; s Daniel George Donahue & Margaret Dusch D; m 1963 to Barbara Vissing; c Angela Danielle & Daniel Francis, Jr. Educ: John Carroll Univ, AB, 62; Univ Louisville, JD, 69. Polit & Govt Pos: Chmn, Clark Co Dem Cent Comt, Ind, 70-75; prosecuting attorney, Clark Co, 71- Mil Serv: Entered as 2nd Lt, Army, 64, released as 1st Lt, 66, after serv in Sixth Army Combat Develop Command Exp Ctr, Ft Ord, Calif, 64-66; Army Commendation Medal. Mem: Ind & Clark Co Bar Asns. Relig: Catholic. Mailing Add: 511 Hemlock Rd Jeffersonville IN 47130

DONALD, ROBERT HICKS, II (D)
Miss State Rep
b Quitman, Miss, Sept 7, 25; s Robert Hicks Donald & Mae Alice Martin D; m 1949 to Julia Sue Patton; c Kathy Sue, Betty N, Mae Alice, Robert H, III & James Patton. Educ: Miss State Univ, 3 years & 6 months; Sigma Alpha Epsilon; Scabbard & Blade. Polit & Govt Pos: Alderman, Quitman, Miss, 65-67; Miss State Rep, 25th Dist, 68- Bus & Prof Pos: Mgr, Quitman Motor Co, Miss, 51-66; owner, Donald Construction, 66-69; ins agent, State Farm Ins, 67- Mil Serv: Entered as Pvt, Air Force, 43, released as Cpl, 46, after serv in 489th Bomb Group, USA, 45-46. Mem: Am Legion. Relig: Methodist. Legal Res: 203 S Jackson Ave Quitman MS 39355 Mailing Add: PO Box 183 Quitman MS 39355

DONALDSON, CHARLES RUSSELL (NON-PARTISAN)
Chief Justice, Supreme Court of Idaho
b Helena, Mont, Feb 2, 19; s Charles M Donaldson & Mabel King D; m 1944 to Jeanne Coleman; c Karen Elliott, Holly, Jean, Laurel, Sarah & Charles. Educ: Willamette Univ, 37-38; Univ Idaho, BA & LLB, 48; Delta Tau Delta; Phi Alpha Delta. Polit & Govt Pos: Idaho State Rep, Ada Co, 55-57; dist judge, Ada, Elmore, Boise & Valley Co, 64-68; assoc justice, Supreme Court Idaho, 69-73, chief justice, 73- Bus & Prof Pos: Pvt practice law, Boise, 48-64. Mil Serv: Entered as Pvt, Army, 42, released as Capt, 45, after serv in Signal Intel, Italy, 44-45. Relig: Methodist. Mailing Add: 621 Highland View Dr Boise ID 83702

DONALDSON, JERRY (NUB) (D)
Tex State Rep
b Gatesville, Tex, Feb 3, 43; s Marshall Lucky Donaldson & Esther Ellison D; m 1966 to Carolyn McClellan; c Trudy Aileen, Wendi Lee & Kelli Grace. Educ: Univ Tex, Austin, 61-65; Delta Theta Phi. Hon Degrees: JD, Baylor Univ Sch Law, 72. Polit & Govt Pos: Tex State Rep, 73- Bus & Prof Pos: Partner, Cummings & Donaldson, Attorneys-at-Law, Gatesville, Tex, 72- Mil Serv: Entered as Pvt E-1, Army Nat Guard, 65, released as E-4, 72. Publ: Military court jurisdiction, Baylor Law Rev, summer 71. Mem: Mason. Relig: Baptist. Mailing Add: Rte 2 Gatesville TX 76528

DONALDSON, JOHN WEBER (R)
Ind State Rep
b Lebanon, Ind, Oct 13, 26; s Fred Raymond Donaldson & Esther Ann Coombs D; m 1953 to Sara Jane Rudolph; c Carmen Jane, Cathy Ann & John Bradford. Educ: US Naval Acad, 45-48; DePauw Univ, AB, 51; Ind Univ Sch Law, JD, 54; Delta Theta Phi; Beta Theta Pi. Polit & Govt Pos: Co chmn, Young Rep, Ind, 54-56; Ind State Rep, 57-58 & 61-; mem, Ind Judicial Study Comn, 65-; city attorney, Lebanon, 66-68; chmn, Ind Criminal Law Study Comn, 74- Mil Serv: Entered as A/S, Navy, 44, released as Midn, 1/C, 49; Am Theatre & Victory Medals. Mem: Kiwanis; Elks; Am Legion; Jaycees; DAV. Honors & Awards: Distinguished Serv Award, Outstanding Community Serv, Lebanon Jaycees, 57. Relig: Presbyterian; ordained elder & deacon. Mailing Add: RR 5 Lebanon IN 46052

DONALDSON, MICHAEL CLEAVES (R)
Treas, Rep State Cent Comt Calif
b Montclair, NJ, Oct 13, 39; s Wyman Cleaves Donaldson & Ernestine Greenwood D; m 1969 to Diana Dooley; c Michelle & Amy. Educ: Univ Fla, BS, 61; Univ Calif, Berkeley, Sch Law, JD, 67; Sigma Chi. Polit & Govt Pos: Vchmn, Los Angeles Co Rep Cent Comt, Calif, 68-72; mem dept rev panel, Dept Health, Educ & Welfare, 70-72; mem, Dist Attorney's Adv Comt, Los Angeles Co, 72-; chmn, Civil Serv Comn, City of Torrance, 72-; chmn, Van Camp for Secy of State, 74; mem, Attorney's Adv Comt, Calif Elec Code Rev Comt, 75-; treas, Rep State Cent Comt Calif, 75- Bus & Prof Pos: Partner, MacCabe, George & Donaldson, currently; attorney, Harris & Hollingsworth; dep dist attorney, Los Angeles Co. Mil Serv: Entered as Pvt, Marine Corps, 61, released as Capt, 69, officer in charge, Detachment A, 3rd Reconnaissance Bn, 3rd Marine Div, Vietnam. Mem: Calif & South Bay Bar Asns; Los Angeles Co Bar Asn Jr Barristers; Phi Delta Phi. Honors & Awards: City chmn, March of Dimes, 71-; Outstanding Young Man of Year, Torrance Jaycees, 72; Distinguished Serv Award, City of Torrance, 72; Quota Buster, Torrance Family YMCA, 73. Relig: Protestant. Mailing Add: 1229 Acacia Torrance CA 90501

DONART, JAMES B (D)
Dem Nat Committeeman, Idaho
Mailing Add: PO Box 730 Ketchum ID 83340

DONHAM, WILLIAM (R)
Ohio State Rep
Mailing Add: 113 Lylburn Rd Middletown OH 45042

DONIS, JACK ANDREW (R)
Chmn, Elkhart Co Rep Cent Comt, Ind
b Madison, Wis, Feb 4, 23; s Peter A Donis & Kathryn Grey D; m 1944 to Maureen P White; c Annette (Mrs Hardy), Helen (Mrs Keller), Andy, Nicholas & Bruce. Educ: Univ Wis, 40-41 & 48-50; Northwestern Univ Sch Financial Pub Rels, grad, 54; Univ Wis Sch Banking, grad, 58, refresher course, 69; Am Inst Banking, grad, 60. Polit & Govt Pos: Rep precinct committeeman, Elkhart, Ind, 56-66; pub & advert chmn, Elkhart Co Rep Cent Comt, 58-66, chmn, 70-; deleg, Ind Rep State Conv, 62-70; treas, Bucks for Bontrager & Weaver for Mayor Comt; campaign mgr, Vite for State Rep; chmn, Erwin for Cong, Elkhart; treas, Troyer for Co Comnr Comt. Bus & Prof Pos: Asst cashier, First Nat Bank, Madison, Wis, 41-55; asst vpres, First Nat Bank, Elkhart, Ind, 55-58, vpres, 58-70; owner, Jack A Donis & Assocs, 70- Mil Serv: Entered as Pvt, Army, 42, released as T/Sgt, 45, after serv in 14th Port of Embarkation, ETO, 43-45. Publ: Problem: Winning Community Goodwill & Acceptance, Burroughs Clearing House, 4/61; Women in banking, Woman Banker, 7-8/66; A friend in deed-your banker, The Innovator, summer 66. Mem: Am Soc Personnel Adminr; Bank Admin Inst; Gtr Elkhart Personnel Asn; CofC; Better Bus Bur. Honors & Awards: Madison's

Outstanding Young Man, 52; Outstanding Local Pres, Wis Jaycees, 53; Elkhart's Outstanding Young Man, 58; Jr Achievement Award, 63; Distinguished Friend Award, Elkhart Co Asn for retarded, 72. Relig: Presbyterian. Mailing Add: 620 S Main St Elkhart IN 46514

DONLEY, CHARLES EARL (D)
WVa State Deleg
b Wellsburg, WVa, May 12, 21; s John Baxley Donley & Mary Christine Jones D; m 1946 to Mattie Lang; c Edward L, Linda Louise, John B, II & David Ray. Educ: WVa Wesleyan Col, BS, 49; Kappa Alpha; Varsity Football & Baseball; capt, All Conf Football Team. Polit & Govt Pos: WVa State Deleg, 71-, chmn, Roads & Transportation Comt, WVa House of Deleg, currently. Mil Serv: Entered as Pvt, Marine Corps, 42, released as Gunnery Sgt, 45, after serv in Pac; Presidential Unit Citation; Navy Unit Citation; Bronze Star; Purple Heart with Cluster; Asiatic Pac Ribbon; Marine Corps Medal. Mem: Elks; VFW; Moose; Am Legion Post 34; Independent Steel Workers of Am. Honors & Awards: Ideas for Improv, Weirton Div, US Steel Corp. Relig: Christian Church; mem bd. Mailing Add: 301 Washington Pike Wellsburg WV 26070

DONLEY, RUSS (R)
Wyo State Rep
b Salt Lake City, Utah, Feb 3, 39; s R Lee Donley & Leona Sherwood D; m 1960 to Karen Kocherhans; c Tammera, Tonya & Christina. Educ: Univ Wyo, BSCE with honors, 61; Univ Fla, MSE; Phi Epsilon Phi; Omicron Delta Kappa; Sigma Tau; Iron Skull; Sigma Polit & Govt Pos: Chmn, Young Rep Club, Thermopolis, Wyo, 62-64; Rep precinct committeeman, Thermopolis, 63-65 & Powell, 66-68; chmn, State Young Rep Club, Wyo, 66-68; Wyo State Rep, 69-, chmn appropriations comt, Wyo House Rep, 75- Bus & Prof Pos: Prin, Western Engrs-Architects, Inc, 62- Mem: Wyo Asn Consult Engrs & Surveyors; Consult Eng Coun; Wyo Soc Prof Engrs; Wyo Eng Soc; Am Water Works Asn. Relig: Methodist. Legal Res: 1140 Ivy Lane Casper WY 82601 Mailing Add: 2111 E Second Casper WY 82601

DONNELL, FORREST C (R)
b Quitman, Mo, Aug 20, 84; s John Cary Donnell & Barbara Waggoner D; m 1913 to Hilda Hays; c Ruth & John Lanier. Educ: Univ of Mo, AB, 04, LLB, 07; Phi Beta Kappa; Kappa Sigma; Phi Delta Phi; Order of the Coif. Hon Degrees: LLD, Westminster Col, 41 & Univ of Mo, 60. Polit & Govt Pos: Pres, Asn of Young Rep of Mo, 16; Gov Mo, 41-45; US Sen, Mo, 45-51. Bus & Prof Pos: With Selden P Spencer, 07-11; lawyer, Spencer & Donnell, 11-25, Spencer, Donnell & McDonald, 25-28, Holland, Lashly & Donnell, 28-33 & Donnell & McDonald, 33-41; attorney-at-law, St Louis, 51-56; lawyer & mem firm, Donnell, Schoenbeck & Donnell, 56- Mem: Downtown YMCA; St Louis World Court Comn; Am, Mo & St Louis Bar Asns. Relig: Methodist. Legal Res: 245 Union Blvd St Louis MO 63108 Mailing Add: 611 Olive St St Louis MO 63101

DONNELL, JOHN DICKSON (R)
Mem, Santa Fe Co Rep Cent Comt, NMex
b Santa Fe, NMex, Aug 26, 25; s Dee H Donnell & Elda Dickson D; m 1949 to Jimmie N Gryder; c Jack, Nancy, William & Catherine. Educ: Univ NMex, JD, 51; Pi Kappa Alpha. Polit & Govt Pos: Mem, Santa Fe Co Rep Cent Comt, NMex, 62-; deleg, Rep Nat Conv, 64; mem, NMex State Rep Cent Comt, 65; cand, Attorney Gen, 66, spec asst to Attorney Gen, 67- Mil Serv: Entered as Pvt, Marine Corps, 43, released as Cpl, 46, after serv in G Co, 2nd Bn, 24th Marines, Pac Area; Asiatic-Pac Ribbon with Three Battle Stars; Good Conduct Medal; Purple Heart. Mem: Am, NMex & Santa Fe Co Bar Asns; Santa Fe Vol Fire Dept. Relig: Episcopal. Legal Res: 428 Camino de Los Animas Santa Fe NM 87501 Mailing Add: 209 E Marcy Santa Fe NM 87501

DONNELLON, EDWARD JAMES (D)
VChmn, Hamilton Co Dem Cent Comt, Ohio
b Cincinnati, Ohio, Mar 22, 24; s Andrew Joseph Donnellon & Loretta Kroger D; m 1948 to Mary Margaret Nolan; c Thomas Edward, Terrence Michael, Stephen James & Daniel John. Educ: St Vincent's Col, 43-44; Univ Cincinnati, 46-47; Chase Col Law, LLB & JD, 51; vchancellor, Kappa Psi Delta. Polit & Govt Pos: Solicitor, Deer Park, Ohio, 61-66; referee, Juv Court, Hamilton Co, 61-66; Domestic Rels, 65-68; exec dir, Hamilton Co Dem Party, 64-66; vchmn, Hamilton Co Dem Cent Comt, 65-; alt deleg, Dem Nat Conv, 68; solicitor, Golf Manor, Ohio, 69-; prepared city charter, 70; mem, Sycamore Twp Charter Dem Party, 70; Asst Attorney Gen, Ohio, 71- Bus & Prof Pos: Attorney-at-law, Cincinnati, Ohio, 51-; treas, Cincinnati Claims Asn, 60, mem bd dirs, 61-62, pres, 63; legal adv, Americana Ins Adjusting, 69- Mil Serv: Entered as Pvt, Air Force, 43, released as Sgt, 46, after serv in 495th Bomb Squadron, 344th Bomb Group, ETO, 45; Air Medal with Two Oak Leaf Clusters. Mem: Cincinnati & Am Bar Asns; Cincinnati Claims Asn; Moeller High Sch (bd dirs, 67-69); KofC. Relig: Catholic. Legal Res: 7584 Trailwind Dr Cincinnati OH 45242 Mailing Add: 8005 Plainfield Rd Cincinnati OH 45236

DONNELLY, BRIAN J (D)
Mass State Rep
Mailing Add: State Capitol Boston MA 02133

DONNELLY, HELENE ROSALYN (R)
NH State Rep
b Dover, NH, Aug 23, 03; d Frank Charles Stone & Mary R Casey S; wid; c two. Educ: Lawrence & Newton, Mass. Polit & Govt Pos: Mem, Dover Third Ward Dem Comt; publicity chmn, Strafford Co Dem Women; chmn, Strafford Co Dem Women's Disaster Prog to Help Flood Victims & Dover Dem Women's Comt; vchmn, State Dem Women's Orgn; mem exec bd, Dover Citizen's for Fair Taxes; NH State Rep, formerly & 72-; secy & treas, Ward II Dem Comt, 68-; Strafford Co chmn, Signature Campaign for 20% Raise of Social Security. Bus & Prof Pos: Housewife. Mem: Granite State Milk Consumers League (treas & founder); NH Heart Asn (dir); Dover Pollution Cleanup Prog (chmn); Petition for Return of Prayer to Dover Schs (chmn); Am Heart Asn. Honors & Awards: Co-sponsor, Amendment for Prayer in Schs, 65. Relig: Catholic. Mailing Add: 2 Broadway Apt 5 Dover NH 03820

DONNER, SALLY SEARS (INDEPENDENT)
b Troy, NY, May 9, 41; d Ward Smith Donner (deceased) & Hilda DeCamp D; single. Educ: Mt Holyoke Col, BA, 63. Polit & Govt Pos: Staff asst to US Rep Silvio O Conte, Mass, 63-68, off mgr, 71-73 & admin asst, 73- Bus & Prof Pos: Financial develop asst, Nat Urban Coalition, 68-70; acct assoc, Lawson & Williams Assocs, Inc, 70-71. Relig: Unitarian. Mailing Add: 2616 P St NW Washington DC 20007

DONNERMEYER, WILLIAM I, SR (D)
Ky State Rep
b Dayton, Ky, Sept 19, 24; s Frank John Donnermeyer & Bertha Schlereth D; m 1948 to Shirley Snyder, wid 1967; remarried 1970 to Mary Ruth Hill; c William I, Jr, James R, Thomas A & Theresa M. Educ: Villa Madonna Col, 2 years. Polit & Govt Pos: Mem, Bellevue City Coun, Ky, 64-69; Ky State Rep, 68th Dist, 70- Mil Serv: Entered as A/S, Navy, 42, released as 1/C PO Radioman, after serv in European & SPac Destroyers & Destroyers Escorts, 42-46; recalled, Radioman 1/C, SPac, 50; Am Theatre Ribbon; Asiatic Theatre Ribbon; Good Conduct Medal; European Theatre Ribbon; Occupation Japan. Mem: Pipe Fitters; Bellevue Vet; Newport Cath Boosters; KofC; Fraternal Order of Police. Honors & Awards: Outstanding Serv to the City of Bellevue, Bellevue City Coun, 69. Relig: Catholic. Mailing Add: 333 Bonnie Leslie Ave Bellevue KY 41073

DONNEWALD, JAMES H (D)
Ill State Sen
b Carlyle, Ill, Jan 29, 25; m to Ruth Evelyn; c Eric John, Craig James & Jill Yvonne. Educ: St Louis Univ, 42-44, Lincoln Col of Law, 49. Polit & Govt Pos: Committeeman, Precinct 1, Dem Party, Carlyle, Ill, 48-50; supvr, Carlyle Twp, 49-51; Ill State Rep, 2 terms; Ill State Sen, 64-, Asst Majority Leader, Ill State Senate, 71-73, Asst Minority Leader, 73-; alt deleg, Dem Nat Conv, 68 & 72. Bus & Prof Pos: Attorney-at-law, currently. Mil Serv: Korean Vet. Mem: Lions; Elks; Moose; KofC. Relig: Catholic. Mailing Add: 340 N 11th St Breese IL 62230

DONOGHUE, JULIA SHEEHAN (R)
Wis State Rep
b Hamilton, Ohio, Dec 13, 43; d Leonard Anson Donoghue & Julia Kelley D; single. Educ: Univ Colo, 62-63; Univ Wis, BS in Polit Sci, 67. Polit & Govt Pos: Research assoc, Rep Nat Comt, 68-69; asst coordr, White House Conf Food, Nutrit & Health, 69-70; Wis State Rep, 73- Bus & Prof Pos: Asst mgt analyst, Bur Lead Poisoning Control, New York City Dept Health, 70-72. Mem: Bus & Prof Women's Club. Relig: Roman Catholic. Mailing Add: 102 Cottage St Merrill WI 54452

DONOGHUE, PATRICK JOSEPH (D)
b Holyoke, Mass, July 29, 24; s Patrick F Donoghue & Alice C D. Educ: Georgetown Univ, BS. Polit & Govt Pos: Admin asst to US Rep Boland, Mass, currently. Bus & Prof Pos: News reporter, Providence, RI, 47-50; news reporter, Springfield Daily News, Mass, 51-55. Mil Serv: Navy, Radarman 3/C, antisubmarine & convoy duty, Atlantic Theater, & radar-picket destroyer in USS Higbee (DD-806), 3rd, 5th Fleets, Pac. Legal Res: Springfield MA Mailing Add: 215 C St SE Washington DC 20003

DONOHUE, HAROLD D (D)
b Worcester, Mass, June 18, 01; single. Educ: Northeastern Univ of Law. Polit & Govt Pos: With Worcester City Govt, Mass; US Rep, Mass, 46-74; deleg Dem Nat Conv, 68. Bus & Prof Pos: Lawyer. Mil Serv: Lt Comdr, Navy. Mem: Mass Bar Asn. Relig: Roman Catholic. Mailing Add: 82 Forest St Worcester MA 01609

DONOHUE, HUBERT FRANCIS (D)
Wash State Sen
b Dayton, Wash, Sept 24, 21; s Dewey C Donohue & Marguerite Hopkins D; m 1944 to Evelyn Barclay; c Randall, Timothy, Ryan & Kelly. Educ: Wash State Univ, 3 years; Phi Sigma Kappa. Polit & Govt Pos: Mem, Columbia Co Planning Comn, Wash, 62-69; Wash State Sen, 69- Bus & Prof Pos: Farmer, 20 years. Mil Serv: Entered as Aviation Cadet, Air Force, 42, released as Capt, 45, after serv in 323rd Bomber Squadron, Eighth Air Force, ETO, 43-45; Lt Col, Air Force Res, currently; Air Medal with four Clusters; ETO Medal; three Battle Stars; Am Theater Medal. Mem: Elks; Eagles; Farm Bur; Wheat Asn; Kiwanis. Relig: Protestant. Mailing Add: Rte 2 Box 13 Dayton WA 99328

DONOHUE, MARGARET MARY (R)
b Liberty, NY, Feb 19, 14; d Frank G Lyons & Delia Gordon L; m 1947 to Thomas F Donohue. Educ: Hunter Col, BA, 35; New Eng Sch of Law, LLB, 54; Gamma Tau Kappa; Newman Club; Glee Club; Hist Club. Polit & Govt Pos: Dir women's activities, United Citizens for Nixon-Agnew, Mass, 68; secy, Ward One Rep Comt, Boston, 68-72; vchmn, Mass Rep State Comt, 69-72; deleg, Rep Nat Conv, 72. Bus & Prof Pos: Attorney, self-employed, 54- Mil Serv: Entered as Pvt, Army, 43, released as Capt, 46; reentered, 51-52; Maj (Ret), Army Res; Good Conduct, WAAC, Am Theatre & Defense Medals. Mem: Mass Asn Women Lawyers; Boston Rep Bus & Prof Women's Club. Relig: Roman Catholic. Mailing Add: 94 St Andrew Rd East Boston MA 02128

DONOVAN, DANIEL PAUL (D)
Chmn, Freestone Co Dem Party, Tex
b Fairfield, Tex, Feb 13, 54; s Daniel Patrick Donovan & Faye Marie Bailey D; single. Educ: Navarro Col, grad, 74; Sam Houston State Univ, 74-; Phi Delta Kappa. Polit & Govt Pos: Coordr, McGovern Campaign, Freestone Co, Tex, 72; regional coordr, Tex Dem, 73-74; chmn, Freestone Co Dem Party, 75- Mem: CofC. Honors & Awards: Jones Govt Award, Navarro Col. Relig: Catholic. Legal Res: Box 541 Fairfield TX 75840 Mailing Add: 405 E Main Madisonville TX 77864

DONOVAN, EILEEN ROBERTA
b Boston, Mass, Apr 13, 15; d William Francis Donovan & Mary Barry D; single. Educ: Girls Latin Sch, Boston, Grad, 32; Boston Teachers Col, BS in Educ, 36 & MEd, 37; Sch Mil Govt, Univ Va; Civil Affairs Training Sch, Univ Mich, 44-45; Harvard, Foreign Serv Inst fel, 56 & MPA, 57. Polit & Govt Pos: Career officer, US Foreign Serv, 48-; second secy & vconsul, Off of US Polit Adv, Tokyo, Japan, 48-49; mem staff, Bur of Far Eastern Affairs, Japan-Korea Pub Affairs, 49-52; State Dept mem, Educ Exchange Surv Mission to Japan, summer 49; second secy & consul, Am Embassy, Manila, Philippines, 52-54; consul, US Consulate Gen, Milan, Italy, 54-56; chief of Southern Europe br, Bur of Intel & Research, 57-59; sr seminar in foreign policy, State Dept, 59; prin officer, Am Consul-Gen, Barbados, 60-62; US consul gen, Barbados & the Windward & Leeward Islands, WI, 62-65; asst dir, Off of Caribbean Affairs, 65-69; US Ambassador, Barbados & spec rep to WI Assoc States, formerly. Bus & Prof Pos: Teacher hist, Boston Pub Schs, 38-43. Mil Serv: Entered as Pvt, WAC, 43, released as Capt, 46; civilian adv, Japanese women's & secondary educ to Supreme Comdr Allied Powers, Tokyo, 46-48. Legal Res: MA Mailing Add: Dept of State Washington DC 20521

DONOVAN, JAMES HUBERT (R)
NY State Sen
b Holland Patent, NY, Nov 12, 23; s Francis John Donovan & Lena Hurley D; m 1947 to Esther Moretti; c Gary, James, Karen, Jerome, Michael, Barry & Kim. Educ: Whitesboro Cent High Sch, 4 years. Polit & Govt Pos: Town councilman, New Hartford, NY, 62 & 63, town supvr, 64 & 65; NY State Sen, 44th Dist, 66- Bus & Prof Pos: Pres & specialty contractor, J H Donovan & Sons, Inc, 49- Mil Serv: Entered as Pvt, Marines, 42, released as Sgt, 45, after serv in Marine Aviation, Pac Theatre, 43, 44 & 45; Pac Combat Ribbon with one Star; Good Conduct Medal. Mem: Oneida Co Farm Bur, NY; Chadwicks Am Legion; KofC (Utica Coun); Clinton VFW; Christian Appalachian Proj (ex officio dir, Lancaster, Ky). Relig: Roman Catholic. Mailing Add: 9409 Elm St Chadwicks NY 13319

DONOVAN, ROBERT F (D)
Mass State Rep
Mailing Add: State Capitol Boston MA 02133

DOOLEY, ALBERT JOHN (D)
SC State Sen
b Chapin, SC, June 10, 30; s Oscar Lee Dooley & Velma O Cannon D; m 1951 to Connie E Spoon. Educ: Univ SC, BS, 51, LLB, 54. Polit & Govt Pos: SC State Rep, 58-66; SC State Sen, 72- Bus & Prof Pos: Lawyer. Mem: Lions; Merchants Asn; Phi Alpha Delta; Mason; Lexington CofC. Honors & Awards: Inst of Mil Subj. Relig: Lutheran. Mailing Add: State House Columbia SC 29211

DOOLEY, EDWIN BENEDICT (R)
b Brooklyn, NY, Apr 13, 05; s Joseph Augustus Dooley & Isabelle Delaney D; m 1926 to Harriette M Feeley; m 1955 to Anita M Gillies (deceased); m 1964 to Margaret Sheefel; c Edwin Benedict. Educ: Dartmouth, AB, 27; Fordham Univ, LLB, 30. Polit & Govt Pos: Mayor, Mamaroneck, NY, 50-56; mem, NY State Comt of Nat Capitol Sesquicentennial Commemoration, 51; US Rep, 57-62. Bus & Prof Pos: Feature writer, NY Sun, 27-38; vpres, Don Spencer Co, Advert Agency, 38-42; dir pub rels, Gen Foods Corp, 42-46; assoc, Inst Pub Rels, 46-48. Mem: Boy Scouts; NY Div, Am Cancer Soc; Dartmouth Club; Touchdown Club; Orienta Beach Club. Mailing Add: 810 Oakwood Rd Mamaroneck NY 10543

DOOLIN, DENNIS JAMES (R)
Dep Asst Secy of Defense for EAsian & Pac Affairs
b Omaha, Nebr, Oct 28, 33; s Russell James Doolin & Sarah Pickard D; m 1971 to Kathryn Marie Truex; c Maureen Elizabeth, David Hamer & Sarah Ellen. Educ: Univ San Francisco, BS summa cum laude, 58; Stanford Univ, MA, 60, PhD, 64. Polit & Govt Pos: Sr analyst, Asian Affairs, US Cent Intel Agency, 67-69; Dep Asst Secy of Defense for EAsian & Pac Affairs, Dept of Defense, 69- Bus & Prof Pos: Research curator, EAsian Collections, Hoover Inst, Stanford Univ, 64-67. Mil Serv: Entered as Seaman Recruit, Navy, 50, released as QMQ 2/C, 54, after serv in USS Albuquerque & USS Laws, Pac Fleet; Korea Medal; UN Medal; China Serv Medal; Japan Occup Medal; Nat Defense Medal. Publ: Auth, Territorial Claims in the Sino-Soviet Conflict, 65, The Chinese People's Republic, 66 & co-auth, The Making of a Model Citizen in Communist China, 71, Hoover Inst; plus others. Mem: Am Polit Sci Asn; Asn Asian Studies. Honors & Awards: Woodrow Wilson fel; Ford Foreign Area fel; Distinguished Civilian Serv Medal, Dept of Defense. Relig: Catholic. Legal Res: 409 11th St SE Washington DC 20003 Mailing Add: Off of the Asst Secy of Def The Pentagon Washington DC 20301

DOORLEY, JOSEPH ALOYSIUS, JR (D)
b Providence, RI, Oct 12, 30; s Joseph A Doorley & Nora Cannon D; m 1953 to Claire Walsh; c Joseph, III, Michael, Brian, Dennis, Carleen & Patricia. Educ: Notre Dame Univ, AB, 53; Boston Col Law Sch, LLB, 58. Polit & Govt Pos: Research technician, RI Develop Coun, 55; mem, Young Dem, RI, 55-; admin asst to Gov of RI, 56-58, legis counsel, 61-62; state chmn, Kennedy for President Comt, 60; city councilman, Providence, RI, 63-65, mayor, formerly; mem, Dem City Comt, 65; Dem Nat Committeeman, 66-70; deleg, Dem Nat Conv, 68 & 72; spec deleg, Dem Nat Mid-Term Conf, 74. Bus & Prof Pos: Attorney-at-law. Mem: Am & RI Bar Asns; KofC; Ancient Order of Hibernians. Relig: Roman Catholic. Mailing Add: City Hall Providence RI 02903

DORAN, PHILIP D (D)
Conn State Rep
Mailing Add: PO Box 75 Berlin CT 06037

DORFF, EUGENE JOSEPH (D)
Wis State Rep
b Kenosha, Wis, Feb 25, 30; s Edward George Dorff & Minnie Manty D; m 1948 to Donna C Lupi; c Donald E, Gerald G & Allan K. Educ: Mary D Bradford High Sch. Polit & Govt Pos: City alderman, Kenosha, Wis, 64-70; Wis State Rep, 71- Mil Serv: Naval Res. Relig: Catholic. Legal Res: 8045 19th Ave Kenosha WI 53140 Mailing Add: State Capitol Madison WI 53702

DORGAN, BYRON LESLIE (D)
Tax Comnr, NDak
b Dickinson, NDak, May 14, 42; s Emmett Patrick Dorgan & Dorothy Bach D; c Scott Michael & Shelly Lynn. Educ: Univ Denver, MBA, 66; Univ NDak, BSBA, 64; Sigma Alpha Epsilon. Polit & Govt Pos: Dep tax comnr, NDak, 67-69, tax comnr, 69-; mem exec comt, NDak Dem Party, 69-; mem, NDak State Bd of Equalization, 69-; chmn bus liaison comt, Multi State Tax Comn, 70. Bus & Prof Pos: Financial specialist, Martin/Marietta Corp, Denver, Colo, 66-67; instr econ, Bismarck Jr Col, 69; adv, Col of Bus Admin, Mary Col, 69-70. Publ: Revenue Sharing—Reality or Rhetoric, Taxes, Com Clearing House, 6/70. Mem: Am Mgt Asn; Nat Asn Tax Adminr; Multistate Tax Comn (chmn, 72-); Midwest States Assoc Tax Adminr (pres, 70); Elks. Honors & Awards: NDak Nat Leadership Award of Excellence. Relig: Lutheran. Mailing Add: 121 W Interstate Bismarck ND 58501

DORIS, FRANCIS D (D)
Mass State Rep
Mailing Add: State Capitol Boston MA 02133

DORMAN, ARTHUR (D)
Md State Sen
b New York, NY, Nov 21, 26; s Harry Dorman & Stella D; m 1949 to Betty Jean Twery; c Pamela Ruth, Janet Louise, Barbara Susan & Matthew Michael. Educ: George Washington Univ, AA, 49; Pa Col Optom, OD, 53; Beta Sigma Kappa. Polit & Govt Pos: Pres, Langley Park Dem Club, 63-65; mem, Vansville Dem Club, 65-; mem, Co Coun of Dem Clubs, 65-; Md State Deleg, 65-74, speaker pro-tem, Md House Deleg, 72-74; vchmn, Prince George Deleg to Annapolis, 66-70, chmn, 70-; mem, First Dist Dem Club, 69-; Md State Sen, 75- Bus & Prof Pos: Pres, Vision Care Serv, 65-68; pres, Vision Inst of Am, 67-70. Mil Serv: Entered as Draftee, Army, 45, released as T/5, 47, after serv in Engrs, Korea. Publ: Vision care-a new benefit, Nat Found, 9/68. Mem: Am Optom Asn; Kiwanis; Chestnut Hill PTA; Nat Soc of State Legislators; VFW. Honors & Awards: Named Maryland Optometrist of the Year, 67; Nat Optometrist of the Year, 68. Relig: Hebrew. Mailing Add: 11107 Montgomery Rd Beltsville MD 20705

DORMAN, HENRY (D)
Wis State Sen
b Racine, Wis, Sept 24, 16; s Zachary Dorman & Eva Nosalevitch D; m 1949 to Jean Phillips; c Robin, Wendy, Lynne & Heidi. Educ: Univ Wis, PhB in Am Insts, 39, Law Sch, JD, 47; Tau Epsilon Rho. Polit & Govt Pos: Secy, Dem Party of Racine Co, Wis, 7 years; Racine Co supvr, 2 years; mem, Racine Co Bd, 56-58; secy, Mayor's Comt on Human Rights, 5 years; Wis State Sen, 21st Dist, 65-, mem, Sen Pub Welfare Comt, Wis State Senate, 65, mem, Joint Comt on Finance & Joint Comt on Rev, Repeals & Uniform Laws, 65, mem, Legis Coun Local Govt Comt, 65-67; mem task force on local govt finance & orgn, Gov Comt on Law Enforcement; Wis legis rep, Nat Conf on Law Enforcement & Crime Control, 67. Mil Serv: Entered as Pvt, Army Air Force, 42, released as 1st Lt, 45, after serv in Army Airways Commun Syst, US. Mem: Wis State Bar Asn; Nat Soc State Legislators (mem bd dirs); B'nai B'rith; Church Bd of Dirs; Jaycees. Relig: Jewish. Mailing Add: 422 16th St Racine WI 53403

DORN, FRANCIS EDWIN (R)
b Brooklyn, NY, Apr 18, 11; s Jacob J Dorn & Adelaide Leman D; m 1943 to Dorothy E McGann; c Thomas, Therese, Karen Patricia, Steven & Vincent. Educ: Fordham Col, AB, 32; Fordham Law Sch, LLB, 35. Polit & Govt Pos: NY State Assemblyman, 40-42; Asst Attorney Gen, NY, 45-50; US Rep, NY, 52-60; referee, Supreme Court, NY, 60-73, Comnr of Conciliation, 72-73. Mil Serv: Entered as Lt(jg), Navy, 42, released as Lt Comdr, 45, Comdr, Naval Res. Publ: Samuel Chester Reid, Am Legion Mag, 2/58. Mem: Eagles; Elks; Am Legion; VFW. Relig: Roman Catholic. Legal Res: 17 Prospect Park W Brooklyn NY 11215 Mailing Add: 32 Court St Brooklyn NY 11201

DORN, WILLIAM JENNINGS BRYAN (D)
b Greenwood Co, SC, Apr 14, 16; s T E Dorn, Sr & Pearl Griffith D; m 1949 to Millie Johnson; c Briana Pearl (Mrs Wade T Batson, Jr), Olivia Byrd, Debbie Gail, William Jennings Bryan, II & Johnson Griffith. Hon Degrees: LLB, Lander Col, 65, Clemson Univ, 70 & Erskine Col, 73. Polit & Govt Pos: SC State Rep, 39-40; SC State Sen, 41-43; US Rep, Third Dist, SC, 47-49 & 51-74; Dem nominee, Gov, SC, 74. Bus & Prof Pos: Cattleman & tree farmer. Mil Serv: Entered Army Air Force, 42, released as Cpl, 45. Honors & Awards: Rotary Community Serv Award; Young Man of Year Award, SC Jr CofC; Silver Helmet Award, Amvets; Meritorious Pub Serv Award, Vet Adminr, 74; Edward A McDowell Distinguished Serv Award, SC Baptist Conv. Relig: Baptist. Mailing Add: Rte 1 Greenwood SC 29646

DORR, DONALD W (R)
Pa State Rep
Mailing Add: Capitol Bldg Harrisburg PA 17120

DORRIS, WILTON HOWARD (R)
Chmn, Arthur Co Rep Comt, Nebr
b Arthur, Nebr, Jan 18, 30; s Lawrence Milton Dorris & Alice Shaw D; m 1952 to Ruby Joan Ward; c Stephen Clint, Richard Lawrence, William Howard & Michael Eugene. Educ: Arthur Co High Sch, grad, 48. Polit & Govt Pos: Co clerk, Arthur Co, Nebr, 52-; secy-treas, Arthur Co Rep Comt, 55-63, co-chmn, 63-70, chmn, 70- Mil Serv: Entered as Recruit, Navy, 48, released as YNSN, 52, after serv in USS Rochester CA 124, Korea, 50-51; Korean, Good Conduct, UN, China Serv & Japanese Occup Medals. Mem: Mason; Am Legion; VFW. Relig: Protestant. Mailing Add: Arthur NE 69121

DORSEY, ROBERT SCHULT (D)
Mem, Mo State Dem Comt
b Caruthersville, Mo, Dec 26, 17; s William Henry Dorsey & Edna Ann Schult D; m 1942 to Lulagene Johnson; c Bobbiegene, Barbara Ann & William Johnson. Educ: Mo Sch of Mines, BS in Chem Eng, 42. Polit & Govt Pos: Mayor, City of Brookfield, Mo, 54-56; chmn, Linn Co Dem Comt, 56-66; chmn, Mo Sixth Cong Dist Dem Comt, 61-66; mem, Mo State Dem Comt, 66- Bus & Prof Pos: Owner, Gen Ins Agency, 45-56; cashier, Security State Bank, 56-58, pres, 58- Mil Serv: Entered as Flying Cadet, Air Force, 41, released as 1st Lt, 45, after serv as Multiengine Pilot, Training Command. Mem: Lions; Am Legion; KofC (Third Degree); Eagles; Elks. Relig: Roman Catholic. Legal Res: 921 N Main Brookfield MO 64628 Mailing Add: 216 N Main Brookfield MO 64628

DOSEK, EDWIN FRANCIS (D)
Mem All Am Coun, Dem Nat Comt
b Ulysses, Nebr, Oct 9, 20; s Edward A Dosek & Philomene Kabourek D; m 1945 to Betty Rees Scott; c J Richard, Kathryn Ann, E Scott & Teresa Rees. Educ: Univ Nebr, BS, 42; Creighton Univ Col of Law, LLB, 48; Delta Theta Phi; Delta Sigma Rho; Delta Tau Delta. Polit & Govt Pos: Pres, Young Dem of Lancaster Co, Nebr, 49-50; deleg, Lancaster Co Dem Conv, 52-54 & Nebr State Dem Conv, 54; mem, Mayors Comt on Youth Crime Prev, 54-59; deleg, Dem Nat Conv, 60 & 64; mem All Am Coun, Dem Nat Comt, 64- Bus & Prof Pos: Attorney-at-law, 49- Mil Serv: Entered as Pvt, Army, 42, released as Capt, 46, after serv in Army Transportation Corps, Asiatic-Pac Theater Medals; Victory Medal; Army Commendation, Good Conduct & Reserve Medals; Brig Gen, Army Res. Mem: Lincoln, Lancaster Co, Nebr State & Am Bar Asns; Nat Parole & Probation Asn. Relig: Roman Catholic. Legal Res: 1725 Skyline Dr Lincoln NE 68506 Mailing Add: 1566 Farlow Ave Crofton MD 21113

DOSS, CHRISS HERSCHEL (D)
Counsel, Jefferson Co Dem Exec Comt
b Cullman, Ala, May 28, 35; s Herschel A Doss & Dorothy Pauline Blalock D; m 1957 to Faye Williams, MD; c William Blalock, Reuben Herschel Verlon, Nonna Dorothea & Faye Dorothea. Educ: Samford Univ, AB, 57, Cumberland Sch Law, JD, 68; Drexel Inst Technol, MSLS, 62; Eastern Baptist Theol Sem, BD, 62; Omicron Delta Kappa. Polit & Govt Pos: Exec dir, Ala State Dem Exec Comt, 67-69; mem, Jefferson Co Dem Exec Comt, 67-, counsel, 69-; treas, Ala Young Dem, 68-; spec adv to Dem chmn, Ala, 69-; Ala State Rep, 70-74. Bus & Prof Pos: Instr, Eastern Baptist Col, 62-64; asst prof & librn, Cumberland Sch Law, Samford Univ, 64-67. Publ: Early settlement of bearmeat cabin frontier, Ala Rev, 10/69. Mem: Am

& Ala Bar Asns; Ala Hist Asn; Mayor's Coun for Betterment of Handicapped, Birmingham, Ala; Jaycees. Relig: Baptist. Mailing Add: 433 Golf Dr Birmingham AL 35226

DOSS, SAMUEL WELCH, JR (D)
Ga State Sen
b Thomasville, Ga, Dec 3, 27; s Samuel Welch Doss, Sr & Mildred Groover D; m 1948 to Carolyn Camp; c Freda (Mrs Michael C Adams) & Samuel David. Educ: WGa Col, 46-47; Emory Univ, 47; Atlanta Ctr, Univ Ga, 47-48. Polit & Govt Pos: Asst dir, Ga Dept Com, 59; Ga State Sen, 52nd Dist, 69- Bus & Prof Pos: Pres, Harvey-Given Co, Realtors & Mortgage Bankers, 48- Mil Serv: Entered as Hosp Apprentice, Navy, 45, released as Pharmacist Mate 3/C, after serv in Hosp Corps; Am Area Medal; Victory Medal. Mem: Mortgage Bankers Asn Am; Am Legion; Am Cancer Soc; Elks (Past Exalted Ruler); Floyd Co Farm Bur. Honors & Awards: Realtor of Year; Distinguished Serv Award, Rome Jaycees; One of Five Outstanding Young Men, Ga Jaycees. Relig: Presbyterian. Legal Res: 356 Mount Alto Rd Rome GA 30161 Mailing Add: PO Box 431 Rome GA 31061

DOTSON, BOBBY JOE (R)
Treas, Wise Co Rep Party, Va
b Pound, Va, Sept 3, 31; s Edward S Dotson & Pearl Beverly D; m 1957 to Nancy Carol Collins; c Lisa Ellen & Elizabeth Carol. Educ: Emory & Henry Col, BA, 54; Univ Va, MEd, 63; Phi Delta Kappa. Polit & Govt Pos: Treas, Wise Co Rep Party, Va, 68-; admin asst to US Rep William C Wampler, Va, 69. Bus & Prof Pos: High sch teacher & coach, Coeburn, Va, 54-60, prin, 61-68; supt, Norton City Schs, 69-72; pres, Dotson Chevrolet-Olds, Inc, 73- Mem: Dist O, Va & Nat Sch Adminr Asns; Va & Nat Educ Asns. Honors & Awards: Named to Outstanding Men of the South, 66. Relig: Protestant. Legal Res: Dotson Ave Wise VA 24273 Mailing Add: PO Drawer HH Big Stone Gap VA 24219

DOTSON, J RAY (R)
b Pound, Va, July 4, 24; s Edward S Dotson & Pearl Beverly D; m 1974 to Kay Lang. Educ: ETenn State Univ, BS, 55; Univ Tenn, LLB, 57, JD, 64; Law Sch Student Bar Asn (pres); Pi Kappa Delta; Phi Alpha Delta (justice, McReynolds Chap). Polit & Govt Pos: Admin asst to US Rep William C Wampler, Va, 69- Bus & Prof Pos: Asst secy & attorney, Govt Employees Ins Co, 58-69. Mil Serv: Entered as Pvt, Air Force, 48, released as S/Sgt, 52, after serv in Hq OSI, Washington, DC. Mem: Bar of State of Tenn & Va; Bar of Supreme Court of US; Mason. Relig: Protestant. Legal Res: Rte 2 Pound VA 24279 Mailing Add: 2422 Rayburn House Off Bldg Washington DC 20515

DOTSON, WILLIAM FRANCIS (D)
Chmn, Lyon Co Dem Cent Comt, Kans
b San Antonio, Tex, Nov 6, 15; s William Harrison Dotson & Carrie Adel Strittmatter D; m 1935 to Dorothy Lea Bruner; c Mary (Mrs Marchetti), William David, Jane (Mrs Clabattari) & Denise Lea. Educ: Bethel Col, 2 years. Polit & Govt Pos: Chmn, Lyon Co Dem Cent Comt, Kans currently; deleg, Dem Nat Mid-Term Conf, 74. Bus & Prof Pos: Locomotive engr, Santa Fe RR. Mem: Brotherhood Locomotive Engrs; CofC; United Transportation Union. Relig: Congregational. Mailing Add: 1242 Luther Emporia KS 66801

DOTY, GARY (DFL)
Minn State Rep
Mailing Add: 116 Parkland Ave Duluth MN 55805

DOTY, RALPH R (DFL)
Minn State Sen
b Duluth, Minn, July 20, 41; s Russell Carl Doty & Naomi Dewey D; m 1962 to Diane Mary Gooder; c Grant Russell, Tani Ann & Corey William. Educ: Univ Minn, Duluth, BA, 63, EdD, 68; Univ Notre Dame, MA, 65; Pi Gamma Mu; Alpha Phi Omega. Polit & Govt Pos: Vpres, Duluth Community Action Bd, Minn, 68-69; mem, Duluth Head Start Adv Bd, 68-70; mem, Duluth Charter Comn, 69-70; Minn State Sen, 61st Dist, 71- Bus & Prof Pos: Teacher, Duluth Pub Schs, Minn, 65-66; admin asst to dep comnr educ, Minn Dept Educ, 67-68; assoc prof, Col St Scholastica, 68-; mem bd dirs, Duluth United Day Activity Ctr, 72- & Duluth Boys Club, 72- Publ: Pupil Expulsion: Handbook for Administrators, Univ Minn, Duluth, 67; History of Minnesota Department of Education, 67 & A Summary of Minnesota Attorney Generals' Opinions, 68, Minn Dept Educ. Mem: Phi Delta Kappa; United Northern Sportsmen; Save Lake Superior Asn. Relig: Baptist. Mailing Add: 4107 Dodge St Duluth MN 55804

DOTZENROD, RALPH CLARENCE (D)
NDak State Rep
b Leroy, Minn, Mar 23, 09; s Rudolph A Dotzenrod & Ellen Gustafson D; m 1945 to Erma Martha Feistner; c Lt James A, Marjorie, Dan, William, Patricia & Steven. Polit & Govt Pos: Councilman, Wyndmere, NDak, 50-71; NDak State Rep, 70-, mem, Judiciary & Agr Comts, NDak House Rep, currently. Mil Serv: Entered as Seaman, Navy, 42, released as Machinist Mate 2/C, 45, after serv in Destroyer USS Mustin, 7th Pac Fleet, 43-45. Mem: Am Legion; VFW; Odd Fellows; Farm Bur; Wyndmere Commercial Club. Relig: Lutheran. Mailing Add: State Capitol Bismarck ND 43215

DOUB, WILLIAM OFFUTT (R)
b Cumberland, Md, Sept 3, 31; s Albert Alvin Doub, Jr & Fannabelle Offutt D; m 1959 to Mary Graham Boggs; c J Peyton & Albert Alvin. Educ: Washington & Jefferson Col, BA, 53; Univ Md Law Sch, JD, 56; Delta Tau Delta; Delta Theta Phi. Polit & Govt Pos: Mem, Md Rep State Cent Comt, 63-66; chmn, Baltimore City Minimum Wage Comn, 64-66; peoples counsel, Md Pub Serv Comn, 67-68, chmn, 68-71; comnr, US Atomic Energy Comn, 71-74; deleg, World Energy Conf, 74; vchmn US nat comt. Bus & Prof Pos: Assoc, Bartlett, Poe & Claggett Law Firm, Baltimore, 58-61; partner, Niles, Barton & Wilmer Law Firm, 61-71; partner, LeBoeuf, Lamb Leiby & MacRae, 74- Mil Serv: Md Nat Guard. Mem: Md Club of Baltimore; Metrop Club of Washington, DC; Am, Fed & Md State Bar Asns. Relig: Episcopal. Mailing Add: 6 Warde Ct Potomac MD 20854

DOUBLE, BARBARA TURNER (D)
b Miami, Fla, Dec 3, 26; d Ernest Cecil Turner & Lilian Darracott T; m 1948 to Harry McCallister Double; c Addison Turner. Educ: Pasadena Playhouse Sch of the Theatre, 2 years plus grad work. Polit & Govt Pos: Mem, Calif Dem State Cent Comt, 56-58, 62-63, 66-67 & 68-69; pres, Hollywood Hills Dem Club, 58-59; polit action chmn, Calif Dem Coun, 59 & 60, secy, 60-63; alt deleg, Dem Nat Conv, 60; vchmn, Calif Common Cause, 74- Bus & Prof Pos: Corp secy, Double Elec, Inc, 64- Mem: League of Women Voters; Pasadena-Foothill Urban League. Relig: Episcopal. Mailing Add: 310 Linda Vista Ave Pasadena CA 91105

DOUCET, EDDIE A (D)
La State Rep
Mailing Add: 9404 Citrus Lane Jefferson Parish LA 70121

DOUGHERTY, CHARLES F (R)
Pa State Sen
Mailing Add: 1313 Friendship St Philadelphia PA 19111

DOUGHERTY, DANIEL D (D)
Ill State Sen
b Chicago, Ill, Apr 26, 06; married; c two sons & one daughter. Educ: Bowen High Sch; courses in blast furnaces & power plant eng. Polit & Govt Pos: Secy, Tenth Ward Dem Orgn, Ill; Ill State Sen, currently. Bus & Prof Pos: Chief dep clerk, Co Court of Cook Co. Mem: KofC (4 degree); Am Red Cross (col rep); Ahepi; Boy Scout Activities; 50 Fund Raising Drives. Mailing Add: 1957 E 93rd St Chicago IL 60617

DOUGHERTY, JEAN MARIE CORDINER (R)
VChmn, Hillsborough Co Rep Exec Comt, Fla
b Seattle, Wash, June 10, 27; d Ralph Jarron Cordiner & Gwyneth Lewis C; m 1949 to John Ward Dougherty; c Sharon Cordiner (Mrs Walter Aye), Diane Jean, Jonathan Maynard, Ralph Cordiner, Leslie Ann, Janet Lee, Joseph Wardle & Ward Lewis. Educ: Northwestern Univ, BS, 49; Univ SFla, 67-69; Gamma Phi Beta. Polit & Govt Pos: Vchmn, Conn Fedn Rep Women, 64-65; finance chmn, Hillsborough Co Women's Rep Club, Fla, 67-68, rec secy, 68-69, treas, 69-; deleg, Rep Nat Conv, 68; mem, Hillsborough Co Charter Comn, 69-; chmn, Lincoln Day Dinner, 71; mem, Hillsborough Co Rep Exec Comt, 71-, vchmn, 72-; west coast chmn, Women for Responsible Legis, currently; mem, Hillsborough Co Parks & Recreation Bd, 72-73; mem bd, Fla Conserv Union; committeewoman, Rep State Exec Comt Fla, 74-, chmn, Dist 7, currently; prog chmn & second vpres, Carrollwood Women's Rep Club, currently. Mem: Easter Seal Guild; GOPers (pres, 72-); Girls Club of Tampa (second vpres, 71-73); Inner Wheel (pres, 75-); Hillsborough Co Rep Club. Relig: Presbyterian. Mailing Add: Van Dyke Rd Rte 2 Box 1212 Lutz FL 33549

DOUGHERTY, WILLIAM JOSEPH (D)
b Sioux Falls, SDak, Apr 6, 32; s Wm J Dougherty & Alice Walsh D; m 1953 to Louise Hulsabus; c Patrick, Jennifer & Timothy. Educ: SDak State Univ, BS, 54. Polit & Govt Pos: Pres, SDak Young Dem, 59; chmn, Kennedy for President, 60; deleg, Dem State Conv, 60-68; cand, SDak State Sen, 62; chmn, Herseth for Gov, 62; treas, Minnehaha Co State Cent Comt, 66-68; cand, SDak State Rep, 68; chmn, Kennedy for President, 68; chmn, SDak deleg, Dem Nat Conv, 68, deleg, 72; nat chmn, McGovern for President, 68; Dem Nat Committeeman, SDak, formerly; Lt Gov, SDak, formerly. Bus & Prof Pos: Pres & gen mgr, Adams-Dougherty Livestock, 61-; pres, Sioux Falls Livestock Exchange, 63; pres, Sioux Falls Livestock Found, 64; bd dirs, River Mkt, 65. Mem: KofC; Elks; SDak Multiple Sclerosis Soc; SDak Livestock Feeders Asn. Relig: Catholic. Mailing Add: 2901 S Fourth Sioux Falls SD 57105

DOUGHTY, WARREN BROWE (D)
Mem, Mich Dem State Cent Comt
b Detroit, Mich, May 20, 21; s Lloyd William Doughty & Bertha L Browe D; m 1947 to Thelma Jean Wiltz; c Brent Walker, Gregory Lloyd & Sandra Jean (Mrs Alexander Mann). Educ: Wayne State Univ, BA & MA; plus additional grad work. Polit & Govt Pos: Dem precinct deleg, Trenton, Mich, 62-; mem, Mich Dem State Cent Comt, 65-, by-laws comt, 67-; alt deleg, Dem Nat Conv, 68; mem, Haber Comn on Polit Reform, 69-; mem, Wayne Co Dem Comt, currently; mem, 16th Cong Dist Dem Party & mem, exec bd, currently; mem, Wayne Co Dem Finance Comt, currently; mem, Trenton Dem Club, currently. Bus & Prof Pos: Student activities coordr, Detroit Bd of Educ, Mich, 49- Mil Serv: Entered as Pvt, Army, 42, released as T/Sgt, 46, after serv in 12th Armored Div, ETO, 43-46; Purple Heart; ETO Medal with Three Battle Stars. Mem: Nat Coun of Social Studies; Detroit Fedn of Teachers; Mason; Knights Templar; DAV. Relig: Protestant. Mailing Add: 1847 Edsel Dr Trenton MI 48183

DOUGLAS, BOB W (D)
Ark State Sen
b Texarkana, Ark, July 30, 34; s Elbert D Douglas & Jessie Bearden D; m 1957 to Mary Glynn Day; c Stephen Wayne & Mary Susan. Educ: Okla State Univ, BS, 58. Polit & Govt Pos: Mem bd, Texarkana Sch Dist, Ark, 63-72; Ark State Sen, 65- Bus & Prof Pos: Meat packer & gen bus; gen mgr, D & W Packing Co, Inc, 60-71. Mil Serv: Entered as 2nd Lt, Army, 58, released as 1st Lt, 60, after serv in 3rd Army, Training Command, 58-60. Mem: Tex Meat Packers; Kiwanis; Shrine; Farm Bur; Ark Sch Bd Asn. Relig: Church of Christ. Legal Res: 2801 Linden Texarkana AR 75501 Mailing Add: PO Box 1097 Texarkana AR 75501

DOUGLAS, CHARLES GWYNNE, III (R)
Mem, NH Rep State Comt
b Abington, Pa, Dec 2, 42; s Charles G Douglas, Jr & Elizabeth Graham D; m 1965 to Martha Ritzman; c Charles G, IV & Thomas A. Educ: Univ NH, BA, 65; Boston Univ Sch Law, LLB, 68; Phi Beta Kappa; Beta Theta Pi; Pi Gamma Mu. Polit & Govt Pos: Deleg, NH State Rep Conv, 64; co-chmn, NE Col Young Rep, six northeastern states, 64-65; admin asst, Majority Leader, NH House Rep, 65; co coordr, Reelect the President Comt, 72; alt deleg, Rep Nat Conv, 72; mem, NH Rep State Comt, 72-; legal counsel to Gov, NH, 73- Bus & Prof Pos: Assoc, McLane, Carleton, Graf, Greene & Brown, Attorneys, Manchester, NH, 68-70; partner, Perkins, Douglas & Brock, Concord, 70-73. Mil Serv: E-1, NH Army Nat Guard, 68; Res Capt, NH Army Nat Guard, currently; Nat Defense Ribbon. Publ: Are we legally in Vietnam?, Western Politica, 66; New Hampshire stamps, NH Profiles, 71. Mem: Am & NH Bar Asns; Merrimack Co Bar Asn; NH Med-Legal Soc; ROA. Relig: Episcopal. Legal Res: Rollins Rd Hopkinton NH 03301 Mailing Add: Rte 1 Concord NH 03301

DOUGLAS, JAMES HOLLEY (R)
Vt State Rep
b Springfield, Mass, June 21, 51; s Robert James Douglas & Cora Elizabeth Holley D; m 1975 to Dorothy Ann Foster. Educ: Middlebury Col, AB, 72. Polit & Govt Pos: Chmn, Vt Fedn Young Rep, 71-72; Vt State Rep, 73- Mem: Addison Co CofC (dir); Addison Co Dent Clinic (trustee); United Way Addison Co (dir & 75 campaign chmn); Vt State Bicentennial Comn; F&AM (officer Union Lodge 2). Relig: Congregational. Legal Res: Middlebury VT 05753 Mailing Add: RD 3 Middlebury VT 05753

DOUGLAS, LARRY DUANE (D)
Ark State Sen
b Stockton, Calif, Nov 4, 45; s Elmer Douglas & Chloe Parsons D; m 1968 to Mary Elizabeth

Bryant. Educ: Ark Polytech Col, BA, 68; Univ Ark Sch Law, JD, 71. Polit & Govt Pos: State Sen, Ark, 73- Bus & Prof Pos: With Davis, Reed & Douglas, Attorneys-at-law, Springdale, Ark, 71- Mem: Am & Washington Co Bar Asns; Phi Alpha Delta. Honors & Awards: Youngest Sen, State of Ark, 73. Relig: Methodist. Mailing Add: Box 284 Springdale AR 72764

DOUGLAS, PAUL H (D)
b Salem, Mass, Mar 26, 92; m to Emily Taft; c Helen (Mrs Paul Klein), John, Dorothea (Mrs Robert John), Paul & Jean (Mrs Ned Bandler). Educ: Bowdoin Col, AB; Columbia Univ, PhD, 21. Polit & Govt Pos: Alderman, Fifth Ward, Chicago City Coun, 39-42; adv to President Roosevelt on NY Social Security Probs; deleg, Dem Nat Conv, 48, 52, 56, 64 & 68; US Sen, Ill, 48-66; chmn, Nat Comn on Urban Probs, 67-68. Bus & Prof Pos: Prof dept econ, Univ Chicago, 20-48. Mil Serv: Entered as Pvt, Marine Corps, 42, released as Lt Col, 46, after serv in 1st Marine Div, Peleliu & Okinawa; wounded in Peleliu & Okinawa; Bronze Star. Publ: In our time; America in the market place; The theory of wages; plus others. Mem: Am Econ Asn. Honors & Awards: Drafted first Ill Old Age Pension Act; helped draft Ill Unemploy Ins Law; helped revise Fed Social Security Act, 39. Legal Res: Chicago IL Mailing Add: 2909 Davenport St Washington DC 20008

DOUGLAS, PAUL L (R)
Attorney Gen, Nebr
b Sioux Falls, SDak, Sept 19, 27; s Louis P Douglas & Victoria Karavaseles; single. Educ: Univ Nebr-Lincoln, BS, 51, LLB, 53; Delta Theta Phi. Polit & Govt Pos: Mem, Pvt Security Task Force to Nat Adv Comt on Criminal Justice Standards & Goals, 75; chmn, Nebr Comn on Law Enforcement & Criminal Justice, 75; Attorney Gen, Nebr, 75- Bus & Prof Pos: Attorney, Lancaster Co, Nebr, 60-75; pres, Lincoln Bar Asn, 73-74; pres, Co Attorney's Asn, formerly; bd dirs, Nat Dist Attorneys Asn, formerly. Mil Serv: Entered as Pfc, Marine Corps, 44, released as Pfc, 47. Mem: Scottish Rite; Shrine; Nebr State Bar Asn; Elks; Am Legion. Relig: Greek Orthodox. Legal Res: 720 S Cotner Lincoln NE 68510 Mailing Add: Dept Justice State House Lincoln NE 68509

DOUGLAS, WILLIAM ORVILLE (D)
Assoc Justice, US Supreme Court
b Maine, Minn, Oct 16, 98; s William Douglas & Julia Bickford Fiske D; m 1966 to Cathleen Heffernan; c Mildred Riddle (Mrs Norman T Read) & William Orville. Educ: Whitman Col, Wash, BA, 20; Columbia Univ, LLB, 25; Beta Theta Pi; Phi Alpha Delta; Delta Sigma Rho; Phi Beta Kappa. Hon Degrees: LLD, Whitman Col, 38, Wesleyan Univ, 40, Washington & Jefferson Col, 42, William & Mary Col, 43, Nat Univ, 49, New Sch for Social Research, 52, Univ Toledo, 56, Dalhousie Univ, 58, Colby Col, 61, Fairleigh Dickinson Univ & Colgate Univ, 73; plus others. Polit & Govt Pos: Bankruptcy studies, Yale Inst Human Rels & Dept of Com, 29-32; secy comt on bus fed courts, Nat Comn on Law Observance & Enforcement, 30-32; dir protective comt studies, Securities & Exchange Comn, 34-36, comnr, 36-39, chmn, 37-39; assoc justice, US Supreme Court, 39- Bus & Prof Pos: Attorney-at-law, New York, 25-27; mem faculty, Columbia Univ, 25-28, Yale Univ, 28-34. Mil Serv: Pvt, Army, 18. Publ: Democracy's Manifesto, 62; The Anatomy of Liberty, 63; Mr Lincoln & the Negroes, 63; plus many others. Mem: Royal Geog Soc, London; Mason; Yale Club; Himalayan Club, Delhi, India; Univ Club, Wash; Overseas Press Club. Relig: Presbyterian. Legal Res: Goosepraire WA 98929 Mailing Add: US Supreme Ct Washington DC 20543

DOUGLASS, CALVIN ALBERT (D)
b Baltimore, Md, Sept 1, 09; s George Henry Douglass & Florence Butler D; m 1969 to Dorthy Lewis; c Calvin, Jr & Mercedes (Mrs Rankins). Educ: Shaw Univ, BS, 28; Univ Md, College Park, LLB; Phi Beta Sigma. Polit & Govt Pos: Asst city solicitor, Baltimore, Md, 48-59; magistrate, Western Police Ct, Baltimore, Md, 59-61; Md State Deleg, Fourth Dist, formerly. Mem: Urban League; Trenton Dem Club; NAACP; Fourth Dist Dem Orgn. Relig: Presbyterian. Legal Res: 901 N Freemont Ave Baltimore MD 21217 Mailing Add: 1531 Pennsylvania Ave Baltimore MD 21217

DOUGLASS, GUS R (D)
Comnr of Agr, WVa
b Mason Co, WVa, Feb 22, 27; s Gus R Douglass & Fanny Elizabeth D; m 1947 to Anna Lee Roush; c Mary Lee, Stephen Ruben, Thomas Oscar & Cynthia Sue. Educ: Pub schs. Polit & Govt Pos: Mem bd dirs, Pub Land Corp & Agr Hall of Fame, Kans; chmn agr adv comt, Educ Develop Conf, Glenville State Col; supvr, Western Soil Conserv Dist, 10 years; chmn, Geol Surv Comn, Econ Opportunity Comn & State Soil Conserv Comt; mem, WVa Manpower, Tech & Training Comn & Air Pollution Control Comn; mem bd, Pub Works; Asst Comnr of Agr, WVa, 57-64, Comnr of Agr, 64- Mem: Mason; Mason Co Farm Bur (dir & secy); Mason Co Agr Stabilization Comt; Farmers Home Admin; Future Farmers of Am. Honors & Awards: WVa State Farmer Award. Relig: Baptist. Mailing Add: Grimms Landing WV 25095

DOUGLASS, JOHN WILLIAM (D)
Md State Deleg
b Princess Anne, Md, Mar 19, 42; s John W Douglass, Sr & Elsie D; m 1969 to Evelyn Archer. Educ: Lincoln Univ, BA cum laude, 64; Johns Hopkins Univ, MA, 66; Beta Kappa Chi; Alpha Phi Alpha. Polit & Govt Pos: Vpres, Young Dem Md, 69-70; treas, Eastside Dem Orgn, Baltimore, Md, 69-; Md State Rep, 70-, chmn, Joint Budget & Audit Comt. Mem: Model Cities Prog; Assoc Builders & Contractors; Baltimore Bus League; CofC; Glenwood Country Club. Honors & Awards: Am Chem Soc Award; Am Legion Award. Relig: Baptist. Legal Res: 1311 N Central Ave Baltimore MD 21202 Mailing Add: 1535 E North Ave Baltimore MD 21213

DOUGLASS, ROBERT LEE (D)
Md State Sen
b Winnsboro, SC, June 23, 28; s John Douglass & Jannie B Stevenson D; m 1947 to Bernice Viola Sales; c Beverly E, Ronald K, Eric L & Loren R. Educ: Morgan State Col, BS, 53; Johns Hopkins Univ, BS in Elec Eng, 62; Omega Sigma Chi. Polit & Govt Pos: Mem city coun, Baltimore City, 67-74; Md State Sen, 45th Dist, 75- Bus & Prof Pos: Instr, Baltimore City Pub Schs, Md, 55-64; elec design engr, Bendix Corp, Towson, 62-64; syst engr, IBM Corp, Gaithersburg, 65-67; pres & founder, Baltimore Electronics Assoc, Inc, 68- Mil Serv: Entered as 2nd Lt, Army, 53, released as 1st Lt, 55, after serv in 61st AAA Bn, 3rd Armored Div; Nat Serv Medal. Mem: East Baltimore Community Corp (adv & exec dir); Eastside Dem Orgn (pres); Nat Asn Black Mfrs; Baltimore Urban Coalition; Paul Laurence Dunbar Community Sch. Relig: African Methodist Episcopal. Legal Res: 2111 Homewood Ave Baltimore MD 21218 Mailing Add: 2503 E Preston St Baltimore MD 21213

DOUMAR, ROBERT GEORGE (R)
Chmn, Norfolk Rep Town Party, Va
b Norfolk, Va, Feb 17, 30; s George Joseph Doumar & Margot Meshaka D; m 1962 to Dorothy Mundy; c Robert G, Jr & Charles C. Educ: Univ Va, BA, 51, LLB, 53; Raven Soc; Order of the Coif; Delta Upsilon; Phi Delta Phi. Polit & Govt Pos: Chmn, Norfolk Rep Town Party, Va, 60-62 & 66-; mem, Va Rep State Cent Comt, 66-68 & 73-; deleg, Rep Nat Conv, 68 & 72. Bus & Prof Pos: Sr partner, Doumar, Pincus, Knight & Harlan, 58- Mil Serv: Entered as 2nd Lt, Army, 53, released as 1st Lt, 55, after serv in Transportation Mil Rwy Serv, Korea, Far East Command, 54-55; Res, Maj. Mem: KofC; Norfolk-Ports Bar Asn (pres-elect, 75); Optimist; Am Legion; Navy League. Relig: Roman Catholic. Legal Res: 1400 Armistead Bridge Rd Norfolk VA 23507 Mailing Add: 1350 Virginia National Bank Bldg Norfolk VA 23510

DOUTHIT, JACKSON SHERROD (D)
Chmn, Sterling Co Dem Exec Comt, Tex
b Rockwall, Tex, July 19, 12; s William Lee Douthit & Anna Elizabeth Jackson D; m 1941 to Mary Evelyn Herridge; c Mary Lee & Collin Jackson. Educ: Angelo State Col. Polit & Govt Pos: Justice of the Peace, Irion Co, Tex, 38-44; chmn, Sterling Co Dem Exec Comt, 47-; dir, Upper Colo River Authority, 60- Bus & Prof Pos: Publ, Mertzon Star, 37-44, Sterling News-Rec, 44- Mem: Lions (secy, Sterling City Club, 69-). Relig: Methodist. Mailing Add: Box 608 Sterling City TX 76951

DOUTHWAITE, GEOFFREY K (JEFF) (D)
Wash State Rep
b Montreal, Can, Sept 7, 29; s Kingsley Douthwaite & Dorothy Isabel Welsh D; m 1952 to Mary Louise Somerville; c Charles Kingsley, John Winston & Julia Belle. Educ: Univ Wash, BS in EE, 52, MS in EE, 63. Polit & Govt Pos: Wash State Rep, 71- Bus & Prof Pos: Staff engr, Boeing Aircraft Co, Seattle, Wash, 56-58; control syst engr, United Control Corp, Redmond, 58-61; assoc prof eng, Univ Wash, 61- Mil Serv: Entered as 2nd Lt, Army, 52, released as 1st Lt, 54, after serv in Signal Corps, US Theater, 53-54. Publ: Introductory Engineering Problems by Computer Method, Pac Bks, 64, rev ed, 65. Mem: Am Asn Engr Educ; Am Asn Univ Prof; Wash Soc Prof Engrs. Relig: Unitarian. Mailing Add: 5518 31st Ave NE Seattle WA 98105

DOUVILLE, ARTHUR (R)
Kans State Rep
Mailing Add: 9600 Woodson Overland Park KS 66204

DOUZANIS, DAVID B (D)
NH State Rep
Mailing Add: 15 Raleigh Dr Nashua NH 03060

DOVE, FRANKLIN EDWARD (D)
b Chicago, Ill, Feb 1, 36; s Robert I Dove & Elizabeth Heil D; m 1961 to Meredith Sayle; c Andrew F & Ashley G. Educ: Ohio Wesleyan Univ, AB, 58; Northwestern Univ Sch Law, JD, 64; Phi Delta Phi; Beta Theta Pi. Polit & Govt Pos: Mem, Sixth Const Conv, Ill, 69-70; deleg, Dem Nat Conv, 72. Bus & Prof Pos: Asst states attorney, Decatur, Ill, 64-67; partner, Dove & Dove, Attorneys, Shelbyville, 67- Mil Serv: Entered as 2nd Lt, Air Force, 58, released as 1st Lt, 61, after serv in Air Control & Warning, NAfrica; Capt, Air Force Res. Mem: Ill State Bar Asn; Shelby Co Bar Asn; Shelby Country Club. Relig: Methodist. Mailing Add: 143 E Main St Shelbyville IL 62565

DOVE, MEREDITH SAYLE (D)
b Cleveland, Ohio, Feb 2, 37; d Gilbert Edward Sayle & Marjorie Gale S (deceased); m 1961 to Franklin Edward Dove; c Andrew Franklin & Ashley Gale. Educ: Ohio Wesleyan Univ, AB, 59; Kappa Kappa Gamma. Polit & Govt Pos: Deleg, Dem Nat Conv, 72; coordr for McGovern, Shelby Co, Ill, 72; dir, Shelby Co Ment Health Ctr, 73- Bus & Prof Pos: Research asst, Stein Roe & Farnham, Chicago, 61-63. Mem: Am Guild of Organists. Relig: Methodist. Legal Res: 1 Moulton Dr Shelbyville IL 62565 Mailing Add: Box 347 Shelbyville IL 62565

DOVER, J MICHAEL (D)
Mem, Ga State Dem Exec Comt
b Toccoa, Ga, Nov 6, 44; s Howard Quintin Dover & Mary Ariail D; m 1967 to Martha Jennings. Educ: Univ Ga, AB, 66, JD, 69; Phi Delta Phi; Blue Key; Kappa Sigma. Polit & Govt Pos: Dem govt affairs comt, Valdosta-Lowndes Co CofC, 75-; mem, Ga State Dem Exec Comt, 75- Bus & Prof Pos: Partner, McLane & Dover, 71-74; partner, McLane, Dover & Sherwood, 75- Mem: Southern Judicial Circuit Bar Asn; Valdosta Country Club; Gridiron Secret Soc; Azalea City Kiwanis; Univ Ga Alumni Soc (bd mgrs, 73-). Relig: Baptist. Legal Res: 2213 Riverside Dr Valdosta GA 31601 Mailing Add: PO Box 505 Valdosta GA 31601

DOVER, WILLIAM J (D)
Ga State Rep
Mailing Add: Timbrook Hollywood GA 30524

DOW, CHARLES G (D)
Maine State Rep
Mailing Add: RFD 3 Gardiner West Gardiner ME 04345

DOW, JOHN GOODCHILD (D)
b New York, NY, May 6, 05; s Joy Wheeler Dow & Elizabeth Goodchild D; m 1930 to Harriet; c Thomas G, Timothy T (deceased), Diantha E (Mrs Walter B Schull) & A Sophia (Mrs Giorgio Baratto). Educ: Harvard Col, AB, 27; Columbia Univ, MA, 37. Polit & Govt Pos: Chmn, Orangetown Dem Comt, NY, 57-62; chmn, Grand View Zoning Bd of Appeals, 64-65; US Rep, 27th Dist, NY, 65-68 & 71-72; deleg, Dem Nat Conv; staff aide to group of US Rep, 69-70. Bus & Prof Pos: Asst mgr systs & procedures, ACF Industs, Inc, New York, 54-65. Relig: Episcopal; mem int peace adv comt, Episcopal Church, 65-68. Mailing Add: 56 Grand Ave Newburgh NY 12550

DOW, R LEO (R)
NMex State Sen
Mailing Add: 1123 Candelaria NW Albuquerque NM 87107

DOWDEN, FAYE HAYWOOD (R)
Secy, Greene Co Rep Comt, Ind
b Bloomfield, Ind, Oct 18, 10; d Perry Mason Haywood & Destie N Murphey H; m 1929 to R Farrell Dowden. Polit & Govt Pos: Rep precinct vchmn, Ind, 46-; secy, Greene Co Rep

Comt, currently. Mem: Eastern Star; Rebekah (past dist dep); Bus & Prof Club; USNAD; Crane Ind Conserv Club; Nat Fedn Rep Women. Relig: Christian Church. Mailing Add: 219 R R Ave Bloomfield IN 47424

DOWDS, JAMES ALEXANDER (R)
Mem Exec Comt, Mass Rep State Comt
b Holyoke, Mass, July 11, 43; s James Patrick Dowds & Martha Paterson D; m 1970 to Helen Jones Duff. Educ: Harvard Univ, AB, 69, Bus Sch, 71-73. Polit & Govt Pos: Coordr for E L Richardson for Lt Gov Campaign, Mass, 64; deleg, Rep State Conv, 67; mem, Mass Rep State Comt, 68, mem exec comt, 69- Bus & Prof Pos: Banker, New Eng Merchants Nat Bank, Boston, Mass, 69- Mil Serv: Entered as E-1, Army, 61, released as E-4, 68, after serv in Mass Army Nat Guard. Mem: Eagle Scout. Relig: Roman Catholic. Mailing Add: 31 Charpentier Blvd Chicopee MA 01013

DOWDY, JOHN (D)
b Feb 11, 12; m to Johnnie Deana (J D) Riley; c Carol Sue (Mrs Forrest Earle Roberts, Jr) & John (Skip), Jr. Polit & Govt Pos: Dist attorney, Third Judicial Dist, Tex, 44-52; US Rep, Tex, 52-72. Bus & Prof Pos: Lawyer. Mailing Add: 400 Cayuga Dr Athens TX 75751

DOWELL, RICHARD A (D)
Chmn, Kiowa Co Dem Party, Kans
b Wellsford, Kans, Sept 16, 19; s Frank E Dowell & Eva Thomas D; m 1941 to Shirley Faye Asher; c John Michael, James Phillip, Mary Ann (Mrs Cukjati) & Peggy Jane. Educ: Wichita State Univ, AB, 40; vpres, Pi Sigma Alpha. Polit & Govt Pos: Dem precinct committeeman, Brenham Twp, Kans, 50-69; chmn, Kiowa Co Dem Party, 69- Bus & Prof Pos: Mem bd trustees, Haviland Farmers Coop, Kans, 50-65; mem, Kans State Hwy Adv Comt, 64-66. Mem: Farmer's Union; Nat Farmer's Orgn; Rotary. Relig: Methodist. Mailing Add: RFD 1 Haviland KS 67059

DOWLING, YOUNG DANIEL (R)
Chmn, Geneva Co Rep Party, Ala
b Hartford, Ala, Aug 31, 22; s Elder Leon Dowling & Lela Stewart D; m 1940 to Katherine Peters; c Daniel F, Terry S & Jean (Mrs Sammons). Polit & Govt Pos: Chmn, Geneva Co Rep Party, Ala, 66-; mem, Ala State Rep Exec Comt, currently. Bus & Prof Pos: Owner-mgr, Dowling Lumber Co, 55. Mem: Mason; Bus & Prof Men's Orgn. Relig: Protestant. Mailing Add: 500 Seventh Ave Hartford AL 36344

DOWNEN, CLIFFORD LEROY (R)
Mem Exec Bd, Young Rep Nat Fedn
b Columbia, Mo, Feb 3, 44; s Clifford T Downen (deceased) & Billie Strunck Granneman D; single. Educ: Univ Wyo, 64-65; McKendree Col, BA, 68. Polit & Govt Pos: Deleg, Sixth Ill Const Conv, 69; coordr 24th Dist, Ill Comt to Reelect the Pres, 72; mem exec bd, Young Rep Nat Fedn, 73-; campaign mgr to Oshel for Cong, Ill, 74. Bus & Prof Pos: Livestock farmer, Southern Ill, 63-; Herrin Drug Co, Herrin, Ill, 69; partner, D&G Enterprises, 74- Mem: Williamson Co Farm Bur; Southern Ill Inc; Boy Scouts (exec bd Egyptian Coun); Ment Health Serv of Franklin-Williamson Counties, Inc. Honors & Awards: Area Appreciation Award for Govt, Southern Ill Inc, 71. Relig: Christian Church. Legal Res: RR 1 Herrin IL 62948 Mailing Add: 116 N Park Herrin IL 62948

DOWNEND, PAUL EUGENE (R)
Chmn, Crawford Co Rep Comt, Ohio
b Toledo, Ohio, Aug 16, 07; s William Joseph Downend & Della M Keller D; m 1952 to Mary B Butler. Educ: Pub schs. Polit & Govt Pos: Chmn, Bucyrus City Planning Comn, Ohio; chmn, Crawford Co Rep Comt, currently; mem, Dist Three, Ohio Hwy Dept Transportation, currently. Bus & Prof Pos: Supvr, Ernst & Ernst, Toledo, Ohio, 30-42; secy, controller & dir, Ohio Locomotive Crane Co, Bucyrus, 42; exec vpres & dir, Superior Equip Co, Bucyrus, 43; vpres & dir, Gen Hydraulics Co, Bucyrus, 44-; pres & dir, Channel Grove Land Improv Co; mgr, Mar-Nol Co; dir, Second Nat Bank, Bucyrus. Mem: Am Inst Acct; Ohio Soc CPA; Am Ord Asn; Mason (Shriner, Jester); Elks. Legal Res: 325 Joan Dr Bucyrus OH 44820 Mailing Add: Box 21 Bucyrus OH 44820

DOWNEY, THOMAS JOSEPH (D)
US Rep, NY
b Queens, NY, Jan 28, 49; s Thomas Anthony Downey & Norma Rita Morgillo D; single. Educ: Cornell Univ, BS, 70; St John's Univ Law Sch, 72-; Sigma Alpha Mu. Polit & Govt Pos: Deleg, Dem Nat Conv, 72; Committeeman, NY State Dem Party, 72; Suffolk Co Legislator, 72-74; US Rep, Second Dist, NY, 75- Bus & Prof Pos: Employ interviewer, Macy's, New York, 70-72. Publ: My diary, Newsday, 1/72. Relig: Methodist. Legal Res: 42 Sequams Lane West Islip NY 11795 Mailing Add: 4 Udall Rd West Islip NY 11795

DOWNING, DELBERT F (D)
Minority Leader, NH State Senate
b Malden, Mass, Nov 18, 31; s Michael J Downing & Mary E Dewling D; m 1953 to Teresa S Crimlisk; c Michael W, Karen Bean, Patricia A, Delbert G, Brian F, Michele M, Mark C, Teresa M & Suzanne C. Educ: Burdett Col; Emerson Col & Portia Law Sch. Polit & Govt Pos: Mem & chmn, Salem, NH Sch Bd, formerly; mem, Salem, NH Munic Budget Comt, formerly; mem, Selective Serv Bd No 8, 66-; NH State Sen, currently, chmn ways & means comt, NH State Senate, 73-, minority leader, NH State Sen, 75- Mil Serv: Army Signal Corps. Mem: KofC; Elks; DAV. Honors & Awards: Man of the Year, Enrico Fermi Lodge, Sons of Italy; Outstanding Performance, Salem, NH Bd Trade, 73. Relig: Roman Catholic. Mailing Add: 112 N Policy St Salem NH 03079

DOWNING, FENWORTH M (R)
Wyo State Rep
Mailing Add: 1567 Big Horn Ave Sheridan WY 82801

DOWNING, THOMAS N (D)
US Rep, Va
b Newport News, Va, Feb 1, 19; s Dr Samuel Downing (deceased) & Mrs Joseph Phillips; m to Virginia Dickerson Martin; c Susan Nelms & Samuel Dickerson Martin. Educ: Va Mil Inst, BS; Univ Va, LLB. Polit & Govt Pos: US Rep, Va, 58-, mem comt sci & technol, energy resources & develop subcomt, space, sci & appln subcomt, Merchant Marine & fisheries comt, chmn Merchant Marine subcomt, mem oceanog & Panama Canal subcomts, US House Rep, currently. Bus & Prof Pos: Attorney. Mil Serv: Army, World War II, combat troop comdr, Mechanized Cavalry, Third Army; Silver Star. Mem: Hampton, Va State & Am Bar Asns; Am Legion; VFW; Lions; plus many others. Relig: Episcopal. Legal Res: 27 Indigo Dam Rd Newport News VA 23606 Mailing Add: Suite 2135 Rayburn House Off Bldg Washington DC 20515

DOWNING, VIC (D)
Mo State Rep
Mailing Add: Rte 1 Bragg City MO 63827

DOWNS, ROBERT K (D)
Ill State Rep
Mailing Add: 340 N Grove Ave Oak Park IL 60657

DOYEN, ROSS O (R)
Kans State Sen
Mailing Add: 434 W Ninth Concordia KS 66901

DOYLE, ANNA MARIE (D)
Secy, Broward Co Dem Exec Comt, Fla
b Bronx, NY, May 22, 31; d Frank Michael Lapicola & Theresa Saturno L; m to Frank Joseph Doyles; c Marth Ann, Vincent, Faith, Rudolph & Frank, Jr. Educ: Christopher Columbus High Sch, Bronx, NY, 48. Polit & Govt Pos: Mem, Broward Co Dem Exec Comt, Fla, 72-; campaign mgr to Gary Southworth Hollywood City Comt, Hollywood, 73; in charge of Gov Rueben Askew, Campaign Off, South Broward, 74; chmn, Broward Co Dem Telethon, 74; deleg, Dem Nat Mid-Term Conf, 74; secy, Broward Co Dem Exec Comt, 74- Mem: Polit Consultants Am; South Broward Dem Club; Broward Dem Womans Club; Broward Civic & Polit Club. Relig: Catholic. Mailing Add: 4820 SW 59 Terr Davie FL 33314

DOYLE, CLEMENT J (D)
RI State Rep
Mailing Add: Tern Rd Green Hill South Kingstown RI 02881

DOYLE, DANIEL G (D)
Chmn, Santa Cruz Co Dem Cent Comt, Ariz
b Sonora, Mex, July 12, 35; s Thomas F Doyle & Marina Carmen Bravo Carillo; m 1960 to Elisa Moraga; c Cindy, Danny, Terrance Eli, Gabriel A & Kenneth Douglas. Educ: 24 months correspondence entomology courses with dipl, Purdue Univ, 61; Univ Ariz, 60- Polit & Govt Pos: Alderman, Nogales, Ariz, currently; chmn, Santa Cruz Co Dem Party, 72-; chmn, Planning & Zoning Comt, Int Rels Comt, Nogales CofC Comt & Nogales Environ Protection Agency & OSHA Rep, currently. Bus & Prof Pos: Committeeman mem, Nogales Recreation Comt, Financial Comt, St & Pub Works Comt & Ord Comt; land speculator; owner & pres, Doyle Exterminating & Fumigating Co, Inc. Mil Serv: Entered as A/S, Navy, 35, released as Seaman 1/C, after serv in 7th Fleet Aboard Destroyer USS DDR-830 Everett Larson, Steaming Demon, 57-59; Nat Overseas Ribbon. Mem: Nogales Jaycees; Lions; KofC; Am Legion; Santa Cruz Co Ment Retarded Asn (second vpres). Honors & Awards: Outstanding Local Jaycee Pres, State of Ariz, Jaycees, 67 & Dist Gov Southern Dist Ariz, Jaycees, 68. Relig: Catholic. Legal Res: 125 Smelter St Nogales AZ 85621 Mailing Add: PO Box 417 Nogales AZ 85621

DOYLE, DONALD VINCENT (D)
Iowa State Rep
b Sioux City, Iowa, Jan 13, 25; s William E Doyle & Nelsine E Sparby D; m 1963 to Janet E Holtz; c Dawn Renee. Educ: Colo Agr & Mech Col; Univ Nebr; Morningside Col, BS, 51; Univ SDak State Univ Cert for Radiological Defense & Radiological Monitor Instr; Delta Theta Phi & Scholarship Key. Polit & Govt Pos: Iowa State Rep, Woodbury Co, 57-60, 65-67 & 68- Bus & Prof Pos: Lawyer, 53- Mil Serv: Entered as Pvt, Army Air Corps, released as Cpl, 46, after serv in India; China-Burma-India & NAm Ribbons. Mem: China-Burma-India Vet Asn (state comdr Iowa); China-Burma-India Vet Asn Photog & Radio Commun; Civil Defense for State of Iowa (radiological defense officer). Legal Res: 1109 S Fairmount St Sioux City IA 51106 Mailing Add: 437 Ins Exchange Bldg Sioux City IA 51101

DOYLE, JOHN AUGUSTINE (D)
Mem, Calif Dem State Cent Comt
b Dublin, Ireland, Aug 29, 26; s Richard Doyle & Roseanna Murray D; m 1949 to Harriette Elizabeth Montague; c Eileen, Mary, John, Kevin, Brigid, Sheila & Michael. Educ: St Mary's Col, BS in Econ, 50; Univ San Francisco Law Sch, JD, 56; Phi Alpha Delta. Polit & Govt Pos: Mem, Alameda Co Dem Cent Comt, Calif, 64-66, vchmn, 66-68; admin asst to Congressman, George P Miller, 66-; Calif State Dem Cent Comt, 68- Bus & Prof Pos: Attorney-at-law, 57- Mil Serv: Army Air Corp, 45-47. Mem: Alameda Co, East Oakland & Southern Alameda Co Bar Asns; State Bar Calif; Am Legion. Relig: Roman Catholic. Mailing Add: 15341 Inverness St San Leandro CA 94579

DOYLE, JOSEPH TED (D)
Pa State Rep
b Ridley Park, Pa, Oct 6, 31; s Frank J Doyle & Mary Bellwoar D; m 1955 to Elizabeth Kavanaugh; c Louise Ann, Meghan Aine, Kimberly Anne & Rebecca. Educ: LaSalle Col, Philadelphia, BS cum laude, 53; Villanova Univ Law Sch, JD, 58; Sigma Beta Kappa; Varsity Club; Acct Soc. Polit & Govt Pos: Pa State Rep, 163rd Dist, 70-; deleg, Dem Nat Mid-Term Conf, 74. Mil Serv: Entered as Pvt, Army, 53, released as Pfc, 55, after serv in Finance Corps, US & Ger. Mem: Pa & Del Co Bar Asn; Pa Trial Lawyers Asn; KofC; Aldan Civic Asn (bd dirs). Relig: Roman Catholic. Legal Res: 129 W Providence Rd Aldan PA 19018 Mailing Add: 327 W Front St Media PA 19063

DOYLE, MARJORIE POOR (R)
b Arlington, Vt, May 9, 18; d Raymond John Poor & Florence Hurd P; m 1945 to Edward J Doyle; c John, Kathryn, Jo Ann, Kevin (deceased) & Mark. Educ: Middlebury Col, BS, 40. Polit & Govt Pos: Vt State Rep, 65-66; secy, Bennington Co Rep Comt, Vt, 66; mem, Gov Adv Comt on Ment Retardation, 66-68; mem, Comprehensive Health Planning Comt, 67-70; vchmn, Arlington Rep Town Comt, 68-70 & 71-73; sch bd mem, Arlington Sch Dist, 69; chmn, Arlington Community Pub Health Study Comt, 70; trustee, Brandon Training Sch Assocs, 70-74, pres, 72-73; mem, Vt State Health Planning Adv Coun, 70-73; asst clerk, Town of Arlington, 71-; mem, Vt State Develop Disabilities Coun, 72-; bd mem, United Coun Serv, 73-; secy, Arlington Area Bicentennial Comt, 73- Bus & Prof Pos: Sec sch teacher, 40-46. Mem: Arlington PTA; Red Cross Blood Bank; Arlington Community Pub Health Nursing Serv; Bennington Friends of Retarded Children (dir); Vt Asn Retarded Citizens (pres & mem adv coun). Relig: Catholic. Mailing Add: Main Arlington VT 05250

252 / DOYLE

DOYLE, RICHARD D (D)
Ind State Rep
Mailing Add: 602 Odd Fellows Bldg South Bend IN 46601

DOYLE, ROBERT JOHN (D)
b Covington, Va, Mar 31, 42; s Robert Francis Doyle & Harriet Hankins D; single. Educ: Shepherd Col (WVa), BS in Polit Sci, 66; Phi Sigma Epsilon. Polit & Govt Pos: Pres, Jefferson Co Young Dem, WVa, 71-; state youth coordr, West Virginians for McGovern, 72; deleg, Dem Nat Conv, 72. Bus & Prof Pos: Recreation dir, Grafton Sch, Boyce, Va, 66-67; classification counr, Md Correctional Inst, Hagerstown, 67-68; enumerator, WVa Univ, 72-73. Mil Serv: Entered as Pvt, Army, 68, released as 1st Lt, 70, after serv in 4th Bn, 21st Inf, 11th Light Inf Brigade, I Corps, SVietnam, 69-70; 1st Lt, Army Res, 3 years; Bronze Star; Army Commendation Medal; Vietnam Serv Medal; Vietnam Campaign Medal; Repub of Vietnam Cross of Gallantry. Mem: Am Fedn of Musicians Local 770, Hagerstown. Legal Res: German St Shepherdstown WV 25443 Mailing Add: Gen Delivery Shepherdstown WV 25443

DOYLE, ROY H (D)
Chmn, Fannin Co Dem Exec Comt, Tex
b Cooper, Tex, Mar 30, 07; s William H Doyle & Mary Eva Kyle D; m 1932 to Mattie Cunningham; c Billy Roy & Jimmy Lynn. Polit & Govt Pos: Dem precinct officer, Tex, 36-40; weight inspector, State Dept of Agr, 41-42; dep sheriff, 42-44; chmn, Fannin Co Dem Exec Comt, 64-; app mem, Gov Adv Coun on Aging. Bus & Prof Pos: Salesman, Hunts Dept Store, Bonham, Tex, 45. Mem: Kiwanis. Relig: Baptist; deacon; Sunday sch teacher. Mailing Add: 209 S 14th Honey Grove TX 75446

DOYLE, WILLIAM THOMPSON (R)
Vt State Sen
b New York, NY, May 8, 26; s Edward Thompson Doyle & Irene Wagner D; m 1956 to Olene May Ottaway; c Kelly Irene, Keith Brian & Lee William. Educ: Princeton Univ, BA, 49; Columbia Univ Teachers Col, 54-60, MA & EdD; Cannon Club, Princeton Univ. Polit & Govt Pos: Mem sch bd, Montpelier, Vt, 64-68, chmn, 67-68; mem, Wage Labor Bd, Vt, 66-69, chmn, 68-69; mem, Union Dist High Sch Bd, 67-68; Vt State Sen, 69-, mem, Educ Comt, Vt State Senate, 69-71, Govt Opers Comt, 69-71 & Interstate Coop Comt, 69-71; mem, Coun of State Govts, 69-71, Gov Coun Student Interns, 70-71 & Eastern Regional Comt on Consumer Protection, 70-71. Bus & Prof Pos: Teacher, Lawrenceville Sch, NJ, 49-50 & Montclair Acad, 55-58; dir educ resources proj, Johnson State Col, Vt, 58-60, assoc prof social sci, 60-. Publ: Unified School Districts in Vermont, Vt State Dept Educ, 68; ed, 1968 Vermont Almanac, Queen City Printers, Burlington, 68. Mem: Am Hist Asn; Am Polit Sci Asn; Vt Educ Asn; Vt Farm Bur; Green Mt Club. Honors & Awards: Distinction of Merit, Vt Coun Social Studies, 68; Outstanding Serv Award, Montpelier Sch Bd, 68. Relig: Congregational. Mailing Add: Rte 1 Murry Rd Montpelier VT 05602

DRAGO, CHARLES GRADY (R)
b Jamaica, NY, Feb 8, 37; s Louis Charles Drago & Ava Gayle Anderson D; m 1964 to Kate Blundell; c Alexander Grady & Andrea Gayle. Educ: Fla State Univ, 2 years; Md Univ, 2 years; Theta Chi. Polit & Govt Pos: Clerk, Clerk's Doc Rm, US House Rep, 52; on staff of various US Rep, 62-68; legis asst, US Rep G William Whitehurst, Va, 69-72; admin asst, US Rep Stanford E Parris, Va, 73- Mailing Add: 6 Bancroft Bay Ridge Annapolis MD 21403

DRAGO, EUGENE JOSEPH (D)
Chmn, 29th Dist Dem Party, Ky
b Morgantown, WVa, Oct 19, 26; s Anthony Drago & Pearl Shero D; m 1950 to Patricia Sue Blanton; c Michael, Becky & Anthony. Educ: Univ Louisville, BS, 57. Polit & Govt Pos: Chmn, 29th Dist Dem Party, Ky, 69-; dir bldg dept, Jefferson Co, 72- Mil Serv: Entered as Pvt, Army, 45, released as Sgt, 47, after serv in Philippines. Mailing Add: 10307 Sunlight Way Louisville KY 40272

DRAHEIM, ED D (DFL)
Chairperson, Steele Co Dem-Farmer-Labor Party, Minn
b Austin, Minn, Jan 20, 42; s Edmund Draheim & Gladys Quandt; div; c Peter Christian & Heidi Christine. Educ: Mankato State Col, BS, 64, MS, 67. Polit & Govt Pos: Chairperson, Steele Co Dem-Farmer-Labor Party, Minn, 73- Bus & Prof Pos: Instr, Backus, Minn, 64-65, Grand Meadow, 65-68, Owatonna, 68- Mem: Minn Educ Asn (bd dirs); Elks; Eagles; Ducks Unlimited; Owatonna Educ Asn. Relig: Lutheran. Mailing Add: 326 13th St SW Owatonna MN 55060

DRAJEM, IRENE THERESA (D)
VChmn Womens Div, Erie Co Dem Comt, NY
b Dillonvale, Ohio, Nov 23, 20; d Felix Golebiewski & Agnes Andrzejewski G; m 1936 to Victor A J Drajem; c Victor A, Jr & Robert A. Educ: Villa Maria Acad, NY, 4 years; Bryant & Stratton Bus Sch, NY, 4 years. Polit & Govt Pos: Committeewoman, NY State Rep Party, 48-58; organizer & pres, Gtr Buffalo Dem Women's Club, 55-; mem, NY State Dept Com, 57-61; mem, Buffalo Bd Community Rels, 61-63; mem, Battle of Lake Erie Sesquecentennial Celebration Comt, 62; alt deleg, Dem State Conv, 62; deleg, State Judicial Conv, 64; alt deleg, Dem Nat Conv, 68; vchmn womens div, Erie Co Dem Comt, NY, currently. Bus & Prof Pos: Off mgr, Polish Am Trading Co, 39-49; off mgr, Peoples Clothing Co, 49- Mem: Am Heart Asn (dir); Polish Union Am; Polish Roman Cath Union Am; Villa Maria Alumnae Asn. Honors & Awards: Awards from March of Dimes, Police Athletic League, Red Cross, Cath Charities & Heart Fund; Mother's Day Award, Am Polish Eagle Paper, Kiwanis, Buffalo & Citizen of the Year, 71. Relig: Roman Catholic. Mailing Add: 35 Gerald St Buffalo NY 14215

DRAKE, ARTHUR MILES (R)
NH State Rep
b Copiague, NY, Dec 18, 15; s Joseph Miles Drake & Eva Baldwin D; m 1942 to Margaret Elaine Ellis; c Miles Ellis. Educ: NY State Merchant Marine Acad. Polit & Govt Pos: Chmn, Lancaster Rep Comt, NH, 53-61; NH State Sen, 61-65, chmn, State Legis Coun, 63-65; co-chmn, Coos Co Rep Comt, NH, 65-68; NY State Rep, 67-, mem, House Appropriations Comt, 67-71, chmn, 71-, chmn, House Rules Comt & Joint House-Senate Rules Comt, 69-70, chmn, NH Legis Fiscal Comt, 71-; NH rep to Gen Court, currently. Bus & Prof Pos: Owner & operator, Drake's Home, 46-; asst fire chief, Lancaster Fire Dept, 55-65, chief, 65-70. Mil Serv: Entered as Ens, Navy, 41, released as Lt Comdr, 45, after serv in Asiatic-Pac Area; Am Defense & Asiatic-Pac Ribbons. Mem: Lancaster CofC; Kiwanis; White Mountains Region Asn. Relig: Protestant. Mailing Add: Stevens Terr Exten Lancaster NH 03584

DRAKE, GARY (D)
SDak State Rep
Mailing Add: 1325 N Broadway Watertown SD 57201

DRAKE, GLEN LYMAN (R)
Mont State Sen
b Billings, Mont, Sept 29, 27; s George Walker Drake & Verna Faye Williams D; m 1954 to Jo Mae Chase; c Leslie Jo, Glen Curtis, Charles Marshall, Jeffrey Thomas, Joel Victor, Patricia Cathrine & Carl Lyman. Educ: Northwest Nazarene Col, 1 year; Eastern Mont Col, 2 years; Univ Mont, BA & JD. Polit & Govt Pos: Mont State Sen, 71- Mil Serv: Entered as Seaman, Navy, 45, released as RDM 2/C, 48, after serv in Ground Control Approach, Asiatic Pac Theatre, 45-48. Mem: Mont & Lewis & Clark Co Bar Asns; Phi Alpha Delta; Billings Heights Lions Club. Relig: Protestant. Mailing Add: 860 Hiawatha Helena MT 59601

DRAKE, JAMES ELLSWORTH (D)
b Garden City, Kans, Nov 11, 32; s Robert James & Helen Lucille Young D; m 1955 to Nancy Garrott; c Jennifer, Leslie & Robert Drake & Michael, David & Lydia Garrott. Educ: Northwestern Univ, BS & MSJ; Univ Tenn. Polit & Govt Pos: Admin asst, US Rep Richard Fulton, Tenn, currently. Mil Serv: Army, Sgt E-5, Good Conduct Medal, 54. Mem: Jr CofC; Sigma Delta Chi (charter mem, vpres); Mason; Davidson Co Young Dem. Legal Res: 1104 Clifton Lane Nashville TN 37204 Mailing Add: 6912 Southridge Dr McLean VA 22101

DRAKE, JERRY (D)
Mo State Rep
Mailing Add: Box 400 Grant City MO 64456

DRAKE, RICHARD FRANCIS (R)
Iowa State Rep
b Muscatine, Iowa, Sept 28, 27; s Frank Drake & Gladys Young D; m 1950 to Shirley Jean Henke; c Cheryll Dee & Ricky Lee. Educ: Iowa State Univ; US Naval Acad, grad, 50; Sigma Chi; Navy Crew Team. Polit & Govt Pos: Chmn, Young Rep Orgn, Iowa, 54-56; admin asst, Muscatine Co Rep Comt, 56-58, chmn, 58-66; First Dist chmn, Rep State Cent Comt, Iowa, 66-; Iowa State Rep, 71st Dist, 69-73, 76th Dist, 73-; chmn, Nat Task Force on Rail Line Abandonment & Curtailment & Rural Develop for the Coun of State Govts. Bus & Prof Pos: Gen farm operator & mgr, 54- Mil Serv: Entered as Midn, Navy, 46, released as Lt Comdr, 54, after duty in over 50 countries; Capt of Minesweeper, USS Crow; Naval Res (Ret); Victory Medal; Am Defense & China Theater Ribbons; Korean Serv Ribbon with two Stars; UN Korean Serv Medal; Korean Presidential Unit Citation. Mem: AF&AM; Scottish Rite Shrine (32 degree); Elks; Eastern Star; Iowa Farm Bur. Relig: Lutheran. Mailing Add: 420 Parkington Dr Muscatine IA 52761

DRAKE, ROBERT BERT (D)
b Breckenridge, Tex, July 13, 36; s Jack Drake & Peggy Eaton D; m 1961 to Virginia Mae Singleton; c Dina Anjanette & Robert Jack. Educ: Tex Tech, 1 year; Tex Christian Univ, 1 year. Polit & Govt Pos: Chmn, Stephens Co Dem Comt, Tex, formerly. Mem: Jaycees. Relig: Baptist. Mailing Add: Rte 1 Box 324 Breckenridge TX 76024

DRAKE, TOM (D)
Ala State Rep
b Falkville, Ala, Dec 5, 30; m to Christine McCoy; c one daughter. Educ: Univ Chattanooga; Univ Ala. Polit & Govt Pos: Ala State Rep, 63- Bus & Prof Pos: Lawyer. Mil Serv: Army, World War II. Mem: Elks. Relig: Baptist. Mailing Add: State Capitol Montgomery AL 36104

DRAMBERGER, A L (TONY) (D)
Tex State Rep
Mailing Add: 216 Lorita St San Antonio TX 78214

DRANE, DAVIS CLARK (R)
Mem, Rep State Cent Comt Calif
b Columbia, Mo, Aug 27, 21; s J C Drane & Mary Dinkle D; m 1945 to Mildred Janssen; c Mary Margaret (Mrs Matza) & Susan. Educ: Univ Calif, Los Angeles Sch Exten; Valley Jr Col. Polit & Govt Pos: Comnr Rep zoning appeal, Los Angeles, Calif; comnr water appeals bd, Los Angeles Co; mem, Rep State Cent Comt Calif, currently. Bus & Prof Pos: Owner, Clark Drane Ins Agency. Mil Serv: Entered as Seaman, Navy, 43, released as PO, 46, after serv in SPac Theatre; various medals. Mem: Ins Asn; Am Legion; Lions; Mason; Scottish Rite. Relig: Baptist. Mailing Add: 6914 Grenoble St Tujunga CA 91042

DRAPEAU, WILLIAM LAWRENCE (D)
RI State Rep
b Seekonk, Mass, May 11, 29; s Albert Alfred Drapeau & Grace Mullen D; m 1959 to Elaine Dorothy Spinella; c Deborah, Donna, Diane (deceased) & Edward. Educ: Johnson & Wales Bus Sch, Providence, RI, 50. Polit & Govt Pos: Mass Young Dem State Comt, 49-59; mem, East Providence City Dem Comt, 73-, mem exec comt, 73-75; vchmn, 82nd Dist Dem Comt, 74-; vchmn, East Providence Ward One Dem Comt, 75-; RI State Rep, Dist 82, 75- Bus & Prof Pos: Pres, Dial-A-Maid, Inc, 72-; United Janitorial, 74-; Dial Employ Serv, 74- Mil Serv: Entered as Pvt, Army, 51, released as Pfc, 53, after serv in Mil Police, Europe, 52-53; Naval Res, 48-51. Mem: Leukemia Soc Am (bd trustees, RI Chap); Rumford Lions; Audubon Soc RI; RI Asn for Retarded Children, John E Fogarty Ctr. Relig: Catholic. Mailing Add: 17 Case St East Providence RI 02916

DRAPER, DANIEL DAVID, II (D)
Okla State Rep
b Elk Point, SDak, June 26, 11; s Jesse Sylvester Draper & Bertha Sawtelle D; m 1937 to Elva Anderson; c Shirley (Mrs Don Gard), Kay (Mrs William E Miller) & Daniel D, Jr. Educ: Northeastern State Col, 37; Okla State Univ, 49; Univ Ark, 50-54. Polit & Govt Pos: Okla State Rep, Cherokee Co, 38-42; chmn, McIntosh Co Dem Party, Okla, 46-54; chmn, Delaware Co Dem Party, 65-72; mayor, Colcord, Okla, 69-72; Okla State Sen, 72-74; Okla State Rep, 75- Bus & Prof Pos: Pres, Cherokee Co Educ Asn, 37; pres, McIntosh Co Educ Asn, 48; chmn sch adminr, Northeastern Dist Okla, 56; supt, Colcord Pub Schs, 53-; pres, Delaware Co Educ Asn, 61. Publ: The Draper family history, 63 & The Carpender family history, Delaware Co J, 63. Mem: Okla & Nat Educ Asns; Colcord CofC (pres, 67-); Mason. Relig: Methodist. Legal Res: W Blocker St Colcord OK 74388 Mailing Add: Box 1042 Stillwater OK 74074

DRAPER, WILLIAM HENRY, III (R)
b White Plains, NY, Jan 1, 28; s William Henry Draper, Jr (deceased) & Katharine Baum D; m to Phyllis Culbertson; c Rebecca Starr, Polly Carey & Timothy Cook. Educ: Yale Univ, BA; Harvard Grad Sch Bus, MBA; Torch Honor Soc. Polit & Govt Pos: Campaign chmn, Lee Kaiser for Sen, Calif, 64; assoc mem, Calif Rep State Cent Comt, 64-66; dir, San Mateo Co Rep Finance Comt, 64-; mem, Calif Rep League, 64-; campaign chmn, Lt Gov Robert Finch, 66; San Mateo Co chmn, Nixon for President, 68. Bus & Prof Pos: Sales rep, Inland Steel Co, Chicago, Ill, 54-59; assoc, Draper, Gaither & Anderson, Palo Alto, Calif, 59-62; pres, Draper & Johnson Investment Co, 62-65; pres, Sutter Hill Capital Co, 65-; trustee, Crystal Springs Sch Girls, 67-73; dir, Measurex Corp, 68-; partner, Sutter Hill Ventures, 70-; dir, Lexitron Corp, 71- Mil Serv: 1st Lt, Army, serv in 25th Inf Div, 52; Combat Infantryman's Badge; Meritorious Combat Serv Ribbon with Medal Pendant; Airborne Infantryman's Badge. Mem: Western Asn Venture Capitalists; Palo Alto-Stanford United Fund (pres & dir, 67-); Bohemian Club; Pac Union Club. Relig: Presbyterian. Legal Res: 91 Tallwood Ct Atherton CA 94025 Mailing Add: Suite 700 2 Palo Alto Sq Palo Alto CA 94304

DREA, ARTHUR S, JR (D)
Md State Deleg
b Chicago, Ill, Dec 27, 37; s Arthur S Drea, Sr & Jessie M Thompson D; m 1965 to Marilyn Conroy; c Erin & Tracy. Educ: St Joseph's Col (Ind), BA, 59; Univ Baltimore, JD, 66; Phi Alpha Delta. Polit & Govt Pos: Asst co attorney, Montgomery Co, Md, 67-70; zoning hearing examr, 70-72; Md State Rep, 75- Mil Serv: Entered as Pvt, Army, 60, released as E-5, 67, after serv in Civil Affairs. Mem: Md, Montgomery Co & Am Bar Asns; Fed & Supreme Court Bars. Legal Res: 7809 Rydal Terr Gaithersburg MD 20855 Mailing Add: 7901 Wisconsin Ave Bethesda MD 20014

DREBENSTEDT, FRANCES SAMS (D)
Secy, Marion Co Dem Cent Comt, Mo
b Marion Co, Mo, Apr 23, 09; d Jacob Burditt Sams & Anna Maria Frances Leake S; m 1941 to William E Drebenstedt. Educ: Culver-Stockton Col; Hannibal-LaGrange Col; Kirksville State Teachers Col; Univ Mo. Polit & Govt Pos: Caseworker, Marion Co Welfare Dept, Mo, 41-45; dep circuit clerk, Hannibal Court of Common Pleas, 46-55; vchmn, Ninth Cong Dist Dem Comt; secy, Marion Co Dem Cent Comt, 48-; deleg, Dem Nat Conv, 64. Bus & Prof Pos: Elem teacher, Hannibal Pub Sch, 55- Mem: Nat Educ Asn; Mo State Teachers Asn; Am Asn Univ Women; Marion Co Womens Dem Club; Mo Historical Soc. Relig: Baptist. Mailing Add: Star Rte Philadelphia MO 63463

DREES, JANE W (R)
b LaJara, Colo, Apr 3, 07; d Walter LeRoy Wilson & Pearl Glenn W; m 1944 to Anthony Herbert Drees. Polit & Govt Pos: Precinct committeeman, Gila Co Rep Cent Comt, Ariz, 52-; pres, Ariz Fedn Rep Women, 57-58; chmn, Gila Co Rep Comt, 58-65; mem bd dirs, Ariz Community Col Bd, 67-; asst treas, Ariz Rep State Comt, formerly. Bus & Prof Pos: Social worker, Ariz Welfare Dept, 33-42 & Social Serv Ctr, Phoenix, 42-46; partner, Retail Paint & Floor Covering, Miami, Ariz, 46- Relig: Protestant. Legal Res: 3008 Latham Blvd Miami AZ 85539 Mailing Add: 26 Miami Ave Miami AZ 85539

DREHER, RONALD FREDERICK (R)
Chmn, Prospect Rep Town Comt, Conn
b Waterbury, Conn, Apr 10, 36; s Frederick E Dreher & Evelyn Green D; m 1958 to Judith Anne Lahey; c Frederick Ronald, Daniel Edward, Jeffrey Scott, Michael David, Christine Marie & David Joseph. Educ: The Citadel, 56. Polit & Govt Pos: Secy, Prospect Rep Town Comt, Conn, 65-66, chmn, 75-; vchmn, Prospect Town Coun, 66-68, chmn, 68-70. Bus & Prof Pos: Salesman, SealTest, Hartford, Conn, 58-69 & Borden, Stratford, 75-; sales mgr, Diamond, Canada Dry, Hudson, NY, 69-74. Mil Serv: Entered as Pvt, Army Res, 59, released as SP-4, after serv in 12th Det, 59-65. Mem: Festivals of Prospect Bicentennial Comn (co-chmn); Prospect Little League (vpres orgn, chmn fund raising). Relig: Roman Catholic. Mailing Add: 75 Klein Dr Prospect CT 06712

DREIBELBIS, GALEN E (D)
Pa State Rep
b State College, Pa, Jan 3, 35; s Bruce E Dreibelbis & Ruth Herman D; m to Nancy Jean Souloff; c Martin L, Linda J & Gregory E. Educ: State College Area High Sch. Polit & Govt Pos: Pa State Rep, 70- Relig: Protestant. Mailing Add: 100 Hill Pl State College PA 16801

DREILING, NORBERT R (D)
Chmn, State Dem Comt, Kans
b Gorham, Kans, Apr 7, 25; s Richard A Dreiling & Mollie Eichman D; m 1948 to Donna Jean Myerly; c Jan Margaret, Mark Myerly, Curtis Richard & Kathy Jean. Educ: Ft Hays Kans State Col, BA, 46; Washburn Law Sch, LLB, 49. Polit & Govt Pos: Pres, Kans Collegiate Dem, 48; co attorney, Ellis Co, Kans, 51-55; precinct committeeman, 51-; chmn, Ellis Co Dem Cent Comt, 57-68; chmn, Sixth Cong Dem Comt & mem, Kans Dem State Exec Comt, 58-62; campaign chmn, Elmo Mahoney Sixth Dist Cong Race, 58; original Kennedy organizer in Kans before 1960 presidential campaign; deleg, Dem Nat Conv, 60-72; co-chmn, Operation Support, Johnson Presidential Campaign, Kans; chmn, State Dem Comt, Kans, 66-74; mem, Dem Nat Comt, 70-74. Bus & Prof Pos: Attorney-at-law, Hays, Kans, 49- Mem: Phi Alpha Delta; Am Bar Asn; Am Trial Lawyers Asn; KofC; Kiwanis. Legal Res: 2900 Willow St Hays KS 67601 Mailing Add: PO Box 579 Hays KS 67601

DRENGLER, WILLIAM ALLAN JOHN (D)
b Shawano, Wis, Nov 18, 49; s William John Drengler & Vera Simmonds D; single. Educ: Univ Wis-Madison, 68-70; Am Univ, BA, 72; Marquette Univ Law Sch, 72-; Phi Delta Phi. Polit & Govt Pos: US Sen staff, Washington, DC, 70-72; nat comt staff, Dem Nat Conv, 72; deleg, Dem Nat Mid-Term Conf, 74; mem resolutions comt, Wis Dem Party, 74; mem city attorney staff, Milwaukee, 75- Mem: Badger Amateur Baseball Asn (dir, 74-); Future Bus Leaders of Am. Honors & Awards: Mr FBLA, Wis Future Bus Leaders of Am, 68; Eagle Scout, Ad Altare Dei & Order of the Arrow, Boy Scouts Am. Relig: Catholic. Mailing Add: 920 S Andrews Shawano WI 54166

DRENKOW, RODNEY DEAN (D)
Chmn, Lyon Co Dem Party, Iowa
b Sibley, Iowa, Nov 5, 53; s Raymond Drenkow & Lillian Stueven D; single. Educ: Augustana Col, BA, 75; Phi Alpha Theta. Polit & Govt Pos: Chmn, Lyon Co Dem Party, Iowa, 74- Mailing Add: RR 1 Hull IA 51239

DRESSEN, JOHN JOSEPH (DFL)
b Shakopee, Minn, Oct 12, 24; s Frank Dressen & Mary Martinson D; m 1948 to Josephine Schmelzle; c Daniel, Nicholas, Frederick & Mary. Educ: St Thomas Col, BA, 49. Polit & Govt Pos: City councilman, Browerville, Minn, 60-66; chmn, Todd Co Dem-Farmer-Labor Party, Minn, 68-70; deleg, Minn State Dem-Farmer-Labor Conv, 68 & 70; field rep, Seventh Cong Dist Dem-Farmer-Labor Orgn, Minn, 71- Mil Serv: Entered as Pvt, Army, 43, released as Cpl, 45, after serv in 273rd Field Artil, Third Army, ETO, 44-45; Bronze Star Medal. Mem: Nat Educ Asn; State Coaches Asn; State Football Coaches Asn; Minn KofC; Am Legion. Honors & Awards: Todd Co Teacher of Year, 66. Relig: Catholic. Mailing Add: Browerville MN 56438

DREW, DAVID CLIFTON (D)
Vt State Rep
b Lyndonville, Vt, Mar 10, 40; s Clifton Luther Drew & Ann Couture D; m 1969 to Clare Mary Luchini; c Ann Eleana & Clifton Peter. Educ: Univ Vt, 61-62; St Michaels Col, AB, 62; Cornell Univ, Nat Sci Found fel, 62, MA, 64; Villanova Law Sch, Dougherty Law fel, 64, JD, 67; Delta Epsilon Sigma; Phi Eta Sigma. Polit & Govt Pos: Dir, Vt Model Cities Prog, Winooski, 67-74; Vt State Rep, 75- Bus & Prof Pos: Real estate broker, Hickok & Boardman, Burlington, Vt, 73-; attorney-at-law, 75- Mem: Am Bar Asn; Nat Asn Real Estate Brokers; KofC; Winooski Community Develop Corp; Jericho Planning Comn. Relig: Catholic. Mailing Add: Hanley Lane Jericho VT 05465

DREW, JACK HUNTER (D)
Mem Exec Comt, Dem Party Ga
b Thomasville, Ga, Apr 16, 25; s Hardy Hunter Drew & Alvis Wilson D; m 1950 to Mary Frances Sculley; c Jack Hunter, Jr, Michael Brinson & Frances Abigail. Educ: High sch grad. Polit & Govt Pos: Mem exec comt, Clayton Co Dem Party, Ga, currently; mem exec comt, Dem Party Ga, 74- Bus & Prof Pos: Bd mem, Clayton Co Water Authority, Ga, 75- Mil Serv: Entered as A/S, Navy, 42, released as Electrician Mate 3/C, 46, after serv in Amphibious Forces, SPac; 1st Sgt, Army Nat Guard; Several Campaign Medals. Mem: IBEW (chmn exam bd, Local Union 613); Clayton Co Ga Labor Comt (vchmn); Jonesboro Cardinal Booster Club (pres). Relig: Baptist. Mailing Add: 7207 Maple Ave Jonesboro GA 30236

DREW, R HARMON (D)
La State Rep
Mailing Add: 1005 Elm St Minden LA 71055

DREWNIAK, DOROTHY J (D)
NH State Rep
Mailing Add: 768 Page St Manchester NH 03103

DREYER, DARRELL H (D)
Nev State Assemblyman
Mailing Add: 5309 Masters Ave Las Vegas NV 89122

DRIGGS, DON WALLACE (D)
Mem, Washoe Co Dem Cent Comt, Nev
b Phoenix, Ariz, Sept 26, 24; s Golden Kenneth Driggs & Maude Macdonald D; div; c Deborah Eileen, Pamela Elaine & Christopher Golden. Educ: Brigham Young Univ, BS, 50; Harvard Univ, MA, 55, PhD, 56. Polit & Govt Pos: Deleg, Nev Dem State Conv, 60 & 66-74; deleg, Dem Nat Conv, 68; mem, Washoe Co Dem Cent Comt, 68- Bus & Prof Pos: Instr & prof polit sci, Univ Nev, 56-61; chmn div social sci, Stanislaus State Col, 61-63, asst to pres, 64-65; assoc prof polit sci, Univ Nev, 65-68, prof & chmn dept, 68- Mil Serv: Entered as Aviation Cadet, Air Force, 43, released as 1st Lt, 46, after serv in Fifth Air Force, Pac Theatre; reentered Air Force, 51-52; Lt Col, Air Force Res, 69; Seven Battle Stars; Air Medal. Publ: Constitution of State of Nevada: A Commentary, Univ Nev Press, 61; The president as chief educator on foreign affairs, Western Polit Quart, 12/58; Nevada politics, chap in: Western Politics, Univ Utah Press, 61. Mem: Western & Am Polit Sci Asns. Honors & Awards: Speaker of faculty, Stanislaus State Col, 62-63; chmn faculty senate, Univ Nev, 68-69. Mailing Add: 945 Joshua Dr Reno NV 89502

DRIGGS, JOHN DOUGLAS (R)
b Douglas, Ariz, June 16, 27; s Douglas H Driggs & Effie Killian D; m 1956 to Patricia Gail Dorsey; c John D, Jr, Andrew James, Thomas Dorsey, Adam Dorsey & Peter Dorsey. Educ: Stanford Univ, AB, 52, MBAd, 54; Phi Gamma Delta. Polit & Govt Pos: Mayor, Phoenix, Ariz, 70-74. Bus & Prof Pos: Exec vpres, Western Savings & Loan Asn, 67- Mil Serv: Entered as Seaman 1/C, Navy, 45, released as Mate 3/C, 46, after serv in US. Mem: Savings & Loan League of Ariz; Am Legion. Relig: Latter-day Saint. Mailing Add: 7301 N Central Ave Phoenix AZ 85020

DRIGOTAS, FRANK MARTIN (D)
Maine State Rep
b Auburn, Maine, Nov 25, 09; s Martin Drigotas & Caroline Stelmok D; first wife deceased 1958; remarried 1965 to Lauretta Jones; c Frank M, Jr, Carolyn (Mrs Thomas) & Martin D. Polit & Govt Pos: Vchmn, Auburn Dem Comt, 61, chmn, 63-64 & 66-67; mem, Androscoggin Co Dem Comt, 63-67; Maine State Rep, 65-; chmn, House Taxation Comt, 75- Bus & Prof Pos: Owner, Frank's Store for Men, 39-61, now semiretired; corporator, Peoples Saving Bond, Androscoggin Co Savings Bank. Mem: Elks (Past Exalted Ruler, Lewiston, Maine Lodge); Lewiston-Auburn CofC. Relig: Catholic. Mailing Add: 402 Court St Auburn ME 04210

DRINAN, ROBERT FREDERICK (D)
US Rep, Mass
b Boston, Mass, Nov 15, 20; s James Joseph Drinan & Ann Flanagan D. Educ: Boston Col, AB, 42, MA, 47; Georgetown Univ Law Ctr, LLB, 49, LLM, 50; Weston Col, STL, 54. Hon Degrees: LLD, Long Island Univ & Worcester State Col. Polit & Govt Pos: US Rep, Fourth Cong Dist, Mass, 70-, mem, house judiciary & govt opers comts, 70-; deleg & chmn Mass deleg, Dem Nat Conv, 72. Bus & Prof Pos: Dean, Boston Col Law Sch, Brighton, Mass, 56-70. Publ: Religion, the Courts & Public Policy, McGraw Hill, 63; Democracy, Dissent & Disorder, Seabury Press, 69; Vietnam & Armageddon, Sheed & Ward, 70. Mem: Am Judicature Soc; Am Bar Found (fel); Asn Am Law Schs; Am Law Inst; Am Acad Arts & Sci. Honors & Awards: Mass Bar Gold Medal Award, 66. Relig: Catholic; ordained Jesuit priest, 53. Legal Res: 140 Commonwealth Ave Newton MA 02167 Mailing Add: 224 Cannon House Off Bldg Washington DC 20515

DRISCOLL, EDWARD MAURICE (D)
Chmn, Norfolk Dem Town Comt, Conn
b Norfolk, Conn, Apr 24, 36; s Edward M Driscoll & Sara Murphy D; m 1959 to Solveig Kolby; c Ingrid, Peter, Edward, III, D Neil, John & Steven. Polit & Govt Pos: Mem, Norfolk Dem Town Comt, Conn, 66-, chmn, 72- Bus & Prof Pos: Field serv rep, Rowen-Leadgy Co, 63- Mil Serv: Entered as Pvt, Army, 53, released as SP-4, 56, after serv in 7th Inf Div, Korea, 55-56. Relig: Catholic. Mailing Add: Old Goshen Rd Norfolk CT 06058

DRISCOLL, JOHN BRIAN (D)
Mont State Rep
b July 14, 46; s John Bryan Driscoll & Lorraine Green D; m 1969 to Claudia Jo McMahon; c Chanda Maureen & Tamara Jo. Educ: Gonzaga Univ, BA in Polit Sci, 68; Columbia Univ, Sch of Int Affairs, NY, MIA, 70; Univ Mont, Grad Bus Sch, 72-; Alpha Sigma Mu; Nat Honor Soc; Intercollegiate Knights. Polit & Govt Pos: Mont State Rep, Dist 91, 74-, House Majority Leader, 75- Bus & Prof Pos: Trail foreman & lookout, Bitteroot Nat Forest, US Forest Serv, summers 65, 66, 67 & 69, smoke jumper, Aireal Fire Depot, Missoula, Mont, 68. Mil Serv: Entered as 2nd Lt, Army, 70, released as 1st Lt, 72, after serv in 14th MI Bn, Fla, Continental Army Command Intel Ctr, 71-72; 1st Lt, Res, 1 year. Relig: Roman Catholic. Mailing Add: 424 S Second Hamilton MT 59840

DRISCOLL, JOHN J (D)
Mem, Dem Nat Comt, Conn
Mailing Add: 137 Tesiny Ave Bridgeport CT 06606

DRISCOLL, JOHN R (R)
Mass State Rep
Mailing Add: State Capitol Boston MA 02133

DRISCOLL, RICHARD M (D)
Chmn, Russell Co Dem Party, Kans
b Russell Co, Kans, May 9, 19; s James J Driscoll & Elizabeth Miller D; m 1969 to C Marie Wiltse; c Tim J, Jerry E & Kelly P. Educ: Kans Univ, 37-40; Washburn Munic Univ & Sch Law, AB & LLB, 43; Phi Delta Theta. Hon Degrees: LLD, Washburn Univ Sch Law, 70. Polit & Govt Pos: Attorney, Russell Co, Kans, 46-48; chmn, Russell Co Dem Party, 48-; city attorney, Luray, 50-; judge, Munic Court, Russell, 52-68; state hwy comnr, 52-68 & 73-; mem, Kans Econ Develop Comn, 69-73. Mil Serv: Entered as Pvt, Marine Corps, 43, released as Cpl, 45, after serv in 1st Div, Pac Theatre. Mem: Am & Kans Bar Asn; VFW; Elks; KofC; Russell Co Bar Asn (pres, 73-). Relig: Catholic. Mailing Add: 308 Wisconsin Russell KS 67665

DRISCOLL, WILFRED COTE (D)
Mayor, Fall River, Mass
b Fall River, Mass, Dec 31, 26; s Arthur R Driscoll & Maria E Cote D; m 1950 to Gladys Shea; c Wilfred, Jr, Arthur R, Nancy & Jean. Educ: Brown Univ, AB, 49; Bridgewater State Col, EdM, 53. Polit & Govt Pos: Mem, Fall River Sch Comt, Mass, 59-, chmn, 72-; Mass State Rep, 65-72; mayor, Fall River, 72- Bus & Prof Pos: Pres-treas, D D Sullivan-Wilfred C Driscoll Funeral Home; teacher, Fall River Pub Schs. Mil Serv: Entered as Apprentice Seaman, Navy, 45, released as Seaman 1/C, 46, after serv in Am & Caribbean Theater. Mem: Fraternal Order of Eagles (Lodge 118); Mayor's Asn of Mass; Nat League of Cities; US Conf of Mayors (mem community development comt). Relig: Roman Catholic. Mailing Add: 536 Hood St Fall River MA 02720

DRIVER, MARJORIE M (R)
b Maple City, Mich, Aug 30, 19; d Henry W Cork & Bertha E Salisbury C; m 1942 to Louis B Driver; c Jo Ann (Mrs La Pree). Educ: Rochester High Sch, Commercial, grad, 36. Polit & Govt Pos: Prog chmn, Green Oak Rep Club, Mich, 65-69, treas, 67 & 68; secy, Livingston Co Rep Exec Comt, 67-68; vchmn, Livingston Co Rep Party, formerly; precinct deleg, Green Oak Twp Rep Party, dep clerk, 67- Mem: Farm Bur. Relig: Methodist. Mailing Add: 9235 Silverside Dr South Lyon MI 48178

DRIVER, RICHARD JOHN (D)
Mem, NJ State Dem Comt
b Brooklyn, NY, June 22, 37; s Dr Daniel Milton Driver & Julia M Dreyer D; m 1957 to Margarete K M Schumacher; c Deana M. Educ: Rutgers Univ, BA, 63, MA, 65, PhD, 70; Pi Sigma Alpha. Polit & Govt Pos: Councilman, Franklin Twp Dem Party, Somerset Co, NJ, 67-; deleg, Dem Nat Conv, 68; chmn Somerset Co deleg, NJ New Dem Coalition Conv, 69; mem, NJ New Dem Coalition State Steering Comt, 69; mayor, Franklin Twp, NJ, currently; mem, Gov Liaison Comt & dir, NJ Conf Mayors, 70-; mem, NJ State Dem Comt, Somerset Co, 70- Bus & Prof Pos: Research asst, Rutgers Univ, 63-64, teaching asst, 64-65, research fel, 66- Mil Serv: Entered as Airman, Air Force, 54, released as S/Sgt, 60. Publ: Now that you've been elected, Proc 1967 munic orientation conf, Bur Govt Research, Rutgers Univ, 68; The United States Supreme Court and the chronic drunkenness offender, Quart J Studies on Alcohol, 69. Mem: Am Polit Sci Asn; NAm Asn Alcoholism Prog. Relig: Protestant. Mailing Add: Box 405 E RD 3 Somerset NJ 08873

DRIVER, ROBERT FARR (D)
b Ogden, Utah, July 25, 08; s George William Driver & Mary Louena Farr D; m 1935 to Fredricka Beulah Brown; c Robert James, George Fredrick, Sandra Louise (Mrs Milton Gordon) & Mary Lynn (Mrs Patrick Fix). Educ: San Diego High Sch, grad, 27; Pi Delta Kappa. Polit & Govt Pos: Pres, Young Dem, San Diego, Calif, 32-35; Dem nominee, Calif State Assemblyman, 80th Assembly Dist, 44 & 57; chmn, Calif Dem State Cent Comt, 46-48; mem, San Diego Co Grand Jury, 53; pres, Commun Welfare Coun, 54-55; mem, Calif Horse Racing Bd, 60-64, pres; deleg, Dem Nat Conv, 68. Bus & Prof Pos: Pres, Robert F Driver Co, 46-49. Mil Serv: Asst field dir, Am Red Cross, 45, with serv in 82nd Seabee Bn, Okinawa. Mem: Calif Ins Brokers Asn; San Diego Ins Agts Asn; Lions; Univ Club, San Diego; Mason. Honors & Awards: Spec Award, Commun Welfare Coun. Relig: Latter-day Saint. Legal Res: 2938 Ocean Front Del Mar CA 92014 Mailing Add: 400 Cedar St San Diego CA 92101

DROGE, LESLIE A (R)
Kans State Sen
Mailing Add: RR 1 Seneca KS 66538

DRUMHELLER, HELEN E (BETTY) (D)
Secy, Wash State Dem Cent Comt
b Spokane, Wash, Oct 21, 31; d Merrill Burton Chamberlain & Verna Alice Bratt C; m to Joseph Drumheller, wid; stepchildren F C & Mary Katharine (Mrs William J McAllister). Educ: Gonzaga Univ, 54-55. Polit & Govt Pos: Mem campaign comt for Warren G Magnuson, Thomas S Foley & Henry M Jackson, 52-72; deleg, co & state convs, 58-72; alt deleg, Dem Nat Conv, 68, deleg & mem credentials comt, 72; mem adv comt, Munic Comt, Wash State Legis, 66-72; app Munic Res Coun, 70-72; co-chmn, Citizens for Jackson-Wash State, 72; cand, Wash State Legis, 72; mem Sanford Comn, Dem Nat Comt, 73-; mem exec comt, Wash State Dem Cent Comt, 73-, secy, currently. Bus & Prof Pos: Bd mem, Pac Northwest Indian Ctr, 66-71; writer & dir, Off Educ Spec Proj Indian Educ, Dept Health, Educ & Welfare, 70-71; bd mem, Educ Opportunities Prog, Univ Wash, 71; mem bd trustees, Ft Wright Col, 71; bd mem, Expo '74, Spokane Int Exposition, 73. Mem: St Joseph's Childrens Home Auxiliary (bd mem, 57-); Gonzaga Univ Guild (bd mem, 59-); League of Women Voters; CofC; United US Golf Asn. Relig: Protestant. Mailing Add: PO Box 13276 Spokane WA 99213

DRUMMOND, CECIL G (D)
b Stillwater, Okla, Apr 1, 40; s Gent Drummond & Leva Swim D; m 1965 to Mary Carol Chamlee; c Susan Lorraine, Carolyn Blake & Cecil Gentner, II. Educ: Okla State Univ, BS in Agr, 63; Univ Okla, JD, 67; Beta Theta Pi. Polit & Govt Pos: Judge, Munic Court, Hominy, Okla, 68-69; asst dist attorney, Osage & Pawnee Co, 68-69 & 70-71; deleg, Dem Nat Conv, 72; deleg, Dem Nat Mid-Term Conf, 74. Mil Serv: Entered as Pvt, Army Nat Guard, 63, released as 1st Lt, 69. Mem: Phi Alpha Delta. Relig: Protestant. Legal Res: Red Eagle Rte Pawhuska OK 74056 Mailing Add: Box 1211 Pawhuska OK 74056

DRUMMOND, JOHN (D)
SC State Sen
b Greenwood, SC, Sept 29, 19; s James William Drummond & Fannie Smith D; m 1947 to Holly Self. Educ: Aviation Cadet Training Sch, 43. Polit & Govt Pos: SC State Rep, 64-66; SC State Sen, 66- Bus & Prof Pos: Gulf Oil Distributor; pres, Drummond Oil Co; pres, Greenwood Petroleum Co; bd of trustees, Brewer Hosp; bd of trustees, Baptist Col at Charleston, SC, 68- Mil Serv: 262nd CA, 39-41; Air Force, 43-47, Fighter Pilot, Capt 405th Fighter Bomber Group, Eng, France & Ger, 44-45; Distinguished Flying Cross; 2 Purple Hearts; 9 Air Medals; 3 Battle Stars; Presidential Citation. Mem: PTA; Lions (pres); Mason (32 degree); Shrine; Am Legion (Comdr); CofC (vpres). Honors & Awards: Young Man of Year, 60. Relig: Baptist; chmn Forward Prog & Plans Comt; supt, Sunday Sch; bd of deacons. Mailing Add: State House Columbia SC 29211

DRURY, SUSIE B (R)
b Lawrenceburg, Ky, Aug 31, 27; d James Tyler Disponett & Nora Searcy D; m 1946 to Charles Myron Drury, wid; c Sherwin (Mrs Jimmy Cox), Wanda (Mrs Mark Gritton) & Barry; three grandchildren. Educ: Western High Sch, Sinai, Ky, grad. Polit & Govt Pos: Chmn, Anderson Co Rep Party, Ky, 56-60 & 64-74. Bus & Prof Pos: Plant supvr, Ky Overall Serv, 56- Honors & Awards: Ky Col. Relig: Baptist. Mailing Add: 312 Forrest Dr Lawrenceburg KY 40342

DRYFOOS, GEORGE ELLIS (D)
Committeeman, Westchester Co Dem Comt, NY
b New York, NY, June 16, 19; s Walter Dryfoos & Lucy Feibleman D; m 1949 to Joy Abby Gidding; c Paul Rene. Educ: Columbia Univ, 37-39. Polit & Govt Pos: Committeeman, Westchester Co Dem Comt, NY, 55-65 & 69-; village trustee, Hastings-on-the-Hudson, 58-60; co-chmn, Westchester Concerned Dem, 67-69; alt deleg, Dem Nat Conv, 68. Bus & Prof Pos: Sales engr, Picker X-Ray, NY, 45-60; vpres & sales mgr, L Gidding & Co, 61- Mil Serv: Entered as Pvt, Army, 39, released as 1st Lt, 43, after serv in Army Med Unit, ETO, 40-43. Relig: Jewish. Mailing Add: 20 Circle Dr Hastings-on-Hudson NY 10706

DRYFOOS, ROBERT (D)
Mem, Dem Nat Comt, NY
Mailing Add: 501 Fifth Ave New York NY 10036

DUBIN, MARTIN DAVID (D)
Chmn, DeKalb Co Dem Party, Ill
b New York, NY, Aug 7, 31; s Harry Dubin & Rose Nenner D; m 1953 to Eileen Latterman; c Aaron Stuart & Deborah Lynn. Educ: City Col New York, BA with honors, 52; Columbia Univ, 52-53; Ind Univ, Bloomington, MA, 55, PhD, 60; Pi Sigma Alpha; Phi Alpha Theta; Alpha Phi Omega. Polit & Govt Pos: Chmn, DeKalb Co Dem Party, Ill, 68-; deleg, Dem Nat Conv, 72; deleg, Dem Nat Mid-Term Conf, 74. Bus & Prof Pos: Teaching assoc & lectr, Ind Univ Calumet Ctr, 56-59; from asst to assoc prof, Roosevelt Univ, 59-65; assoc prof, Northern Ill Univ, 65-, coordr, Int Rels Prog, 70- Mem: Am Polit Sci Asn; Int Studies Asn; Am Asn Univ Prof; Comt on Ill Govt; Am Fedn TV & Radio Artists. Relig: Jewish. Mailing Add: 1627 Schifly Lane DeKalb IL 60115

DUBINO, HELEN MARY (R)
b Greenfield, Mass, July 18, 26; d John Dubino & Carrie Kucher D; single. Polit & Govt Pos: Secy, US Rep John W Heselton, 50-56; res asst, US Sen Thomas Kuchel, 56; off mgr, US Rep Florence Dwyer, 57; admin asst to US Rep Hubert Scudder, 57-59; confidential asst, Dep Admin Financial Assistance Prog, Small Bus Admin, 59-60; admin asst to US Rep John B Bennett, 60-64; admin asst to US Rep William L Springer, 64-72; staff asst to House Interstate & Foreign Com Comt, 64-73; tech asst to Comnr William L Springer, Fed Power Comn, 73- Mem: Capitol Hill Club; Capitol Hill Restoration Soc. Relig: Catholic. Mailing Add: 234 12th St SE Washington DC 20003

DUBINSKY, DAVID (LIBERAL, NY)
b Brest-Litovsk, Poland, Feb 22, 92; s Bezallel Dubinsky & Shaine Wishingrad D; m 1915 to Emma Goldberg; c Jean (Mrs Appleton). Educ: Schs in Poland; eve schs, New York. Hon Degrees: Doctorate, Bard Col; LHD, Temple Univ, 64, Brandeis Univ, 66 & Roosevelt Univ, 67; LLD, Columbia Univ, 68. Polit & Govt Pos: One of founders, Am Labor Party, NY, 36; Am Labor Party & Dem Party presidential elector, 36; mem, War Dept Bd, 41; mem bd dirs, Nat War Fund; mem bd dirs, Joint Distribution Comt; mem bd dirs, Am Overseas Aid-UN Appeal for Children; mem, Trade Union Adv Comt on Int Labor Affairs, US Dept of Labor; founder & vchmn, Liberal Party, NY State, 44; mem bd dirs, Wilkie Mem, 45; mem, Spec Comt on Labor Standards & Social Security; AFL consult, UN Econ & Social Coun, 46; mem bd dirs, F D Roosevelt Mem Fund; founder, Am for Dem Action, 47. Bus & Prof Pos: Joined Local 10, ILGWU, 11, mgr-secy, 21-29, vpres, 22-29, gen secy treas, 29-32, pres, 32-65, adminr retiree serv dept, 66, retired as pres & named hon pres, 66; vpres, AFL, 34 & 45-69, mem exec coun, 45-69; AFL rep, Gov Body Int Labor Off, Geneva, Switz, 35; mem, Conf on Workers Educ called by IFTU, London, 36; mem, Conf Int Clothing Workers Fedn, 36; mem, Wage & Hour Ladies Apparel Indust Comn, 38-41; mem, Spec Wage & Hour PR Comn, 40; vchmn, Am Labor Conf on Int Affairs; labor rep, Nat Coat & Suit Indust Rev Recovery

Bd, 42; AFL rep, Mgt & Labor Conf, 45; mem bd dirs, Gtr NY Fund; vpres, AFL-CIO. Mem: Gtr NY for United Negro Col Fund; Nat Sponsors Comt of Am Heart Asn; Am Acad Arts & Sci (fel); Nat Conf Christians & Jews (mem nat labor coun). Honors & Awards: King's Medal, Gt Brit; Golden Door Award, Am Coun for Nationalities Serv, 65; Freedom Award, Int Rescue Comt, 66; Medal of Freedom, President Lyndon B Johnson, 69; Sr Citizen of the Year, Gov Nelson A Rockefeller, NY, 70. Legal Res: 24 Fifth Ave New York NY 10011 Mailing Add: ILGWU 201 W 52nd St New York NY 10019

DUBUQUE, LOUIS THEODORE (R)
b Amarillo, Tex, Oct 29, 40; s Louis Clifford Dubuque & Josphine Crabtree D; m 1966 to Phylis Ann Brandon. Educ: Tex Tech Col, BBA, 62; Baylor Univ, LLB, 66; Phi Alpha Delta. Polit & Govt Pos: Chmn, Moore Co Rep Party, Tex, formerly. Mem: 69th Judicial Dist Bar Orgn; State Bar Asn Tex. Relig: Baptist. Mailing Add: PO Box 1085 Dumas TX 79029

DUCI, FRANK JOSEPH (R)
Mayor, Schenectady, NY
b Schenectady, NY, June 24, 21; s John Duci & Nancy Di Pietro D; m 1943 to Elizabeth Kelly; c Nancy (Mrs Donald Denofio) & Patrick. Educ: Nott Terrace High Sch, grad, 40. Polit & Govt Pos: Mem, Schenectady Co Bd Supvr, 59-67; mem, Co Bd Rep, 67-71; mayor, Schenectady, 72- Bus & Prof Pos: Lab specialist metallurgy, Gen Elec Co, Schenectady, 40-75. Mil Serv: Entered as Seaman 1/C, Navy, 44, released 45, after serv in Navy Metalsmith. Mem: Mentally Retarded; KofC; Polish Nat Alliance; Sons of Italy; Am Legion Post 1005. Honors & Awards: Jaycee Plaque hon mem for local efforts in Jaycee work; Spiritual Plaque; Plaque for Spearheading Drive to Defeat Three Million Dollar Unneeded Unwanted Road; Cert for Civil Contrib to Community. Relig: Catholic. Mailing Add: 1775 Ave A Schenectady NY 12308

DUCKETT, THOMAS ROSS (D)
Okla State Rep
b Stuttgart, Ark, Oct 23, 24; s Thomas Ross Duckett, Sr & Mabel Ann Henderson D; m 1946 to Beulah Charline Miller; c Charolette Ann & Thomas Ross, III. Educ: Okla State Univ, BS, 47, MS, 51; Univ Okla, doctoral course work completed, 61. Polit & Govt Pos: Mayor, City of Mustang, Okla, 65-69; Okla State Rep, 72- Bus & Prof Pos: Pub sch adminr, 48-64; pres, Great Plains Life Ins Co & Zool Concession, Inc, 64- Mem: Nat Blue Key; Mason; Lions; CofC. Relig: Baptist. Legal Res: 1886 West Lake Park Dr Mustang OK 73064 Mailing Add: Rm 537A State Capitol Bldg Oklahoma City OK 73105

DUCKETT, WARREN BIRD, JR (D)
b Annapolis, Md, Aug 28, 39; s Warren B Duckett & Mary Knight Linthicum D; m 1961 to Judith Livingstone; c Pamela Bennett, Stephanie Knight & Warren B, III. Educ: Univ Md, AB, 62, JD, 66; Omicron Delta Kappa; Delta Theta Phi; Alpha Tau Omega. Polit & Govt Pos: Asst states attorney, Anne Arundel Co, Md, 67-69, co councilman, 70-73, states attorney, 73-; mem, Md Comt on Capital City, 73-; deleg, Dem Nat Conv, 72; mem, Gov Comt on Criminal Justice & Law Enforcement, 75- Bus & Prof Pos: Partner, Turk, Manis & Duckett, Annapolis, Md, 68- Mem: Lions; Elks; Jaycees; Md States Attorney Asn (1st vpres); Bar Asns. Honors & Awards: Outstanding Young Man Annapolis, 69. Relig: Episcopalian. Mailing Add: 1615 Cedar Park Rd Annapolis MD 21401

DUCOMB, ROBERT JAMES, JR (R)
Ind State Rep
b South Bend, Ind, Sept 3, 43; s Robert J DuComb, Sr & Lucy Cotter D; m 1966 to Jane Jackson; c Darby Nicole & Dana Marie. Educ: Ind Univ, Bloomington, AB, 64, Sch Law, JD, 67; Sigma Alpha Epsilon. Polit & Govt Pos: Dep City Attorney, South Bend, Ind, 69-71; Rep Precinct Committeeman, St Joseph Co, 70; Ind State Rep, 72- Bus & Prof Pos: Attorney, South Bend, Ind, 69- Mil Serv: Entered as 2nd Lt, Army, 67, released as 1st Lt, 69, after serv in 4th Mil Police Group CI, Fourth Army Hq, Ft Sam Houston, Tex, 67-69. Publ: Craft severance: NLRB's new approach, Ind Law J, spring 67. Mem: Ind & St Joseph Co Bar Asns. Relig: Protestant. Legal Res: 16329 State Rd 23 Granger IN 46530 Mailing Add: 511 W Colfax South Bend IN 46601

DUDEK, MICHAEL MATTHEW (D)
b Brooklyn, NY, July 21, 46; s Stanley Francis Dudek & Catherine Hanak D; single. Educ: Univ Scranton, BS, 68, MA, 72; Pi Gamma Mu; French Club; Educ Club; Karate Club. Polit & Govt Pos: Deleg, Dem Nat Mid-Term Conf, 74. Bus & Prof Pos: Teacher, Our Lady of Mt Carmel Sch, Carbondale, Pa, 69-70; teacher social studies, Mid-Valley Sr High Sch, Olyphant, 70- Mem: Nat Educ Asn; Pa Educ Asn (secy, Mid-Valley Sch Dist br, 74-); Jednota; Mid-Valley Chess Club. Relig: Roman Catholic. Mailing Add: 205 Phillips St Throop PA 18512

DUDLEY, DUDLEY W (D)
NH State Rep
Mailing Add: 25 Woodman Rd Durham NH 03824

DUDLEY, EDWARD RICHARD D (D)
b South Boston, Va, Mar 11, 11; s Edward R Dudley & Nellie Johnson D; m 1942 to Rae Elizabeth Olley; c Edward, Richard & Dudley. Educ: Johnson C Smith Univ, BS, 32; St John's Univ Law Sch, LLB, 41; Alpha Phi Alpha. Polit & Govt Pos: Asst Attorney Gen, NY, 42-43; coun to Gov, VI, 45-47; US Ambassador, Liberia, 48-53; judge, Domestic Rels Court, New York, NY, 55-61; borough pres, Manhattan, 61-64; chmn, New York Co Dem Comt, 63-65; justice, NY Supreme Court, 65-, admin judge criminal courts, 65-71, admin judge, NY Supreme Court, Manhattan & Bronx, 71- Mem: Nat Bar Asn. Relig: Presbyterian. Mailing Add: 549 W 123rd St New York NY 10027

DUDLEY, GUILFORD, JR (R)
b Nashville, Tenn, June 23, 07; s Guilford Dudley & Anne Dallas D; m to Jane Anderson; c Guilford, Robert Lusk & Trevania Dallas. Educ: Loomis Inst, Peabody Col; Vanderbilt Univ, AB, 29. Polit & Govt Pos: US Ambassador to Denmark, until 72; former chmn, Tenn Rep Finance Comt; mem, Rep Nat Finance Comt, formerly. Bus & Prof Pos: Chmn & dir, Life & Casualty Ins Co; dir, Radio Sta WLAC, Third Nat Bank, Nashville, Am Gen Ins Co, Houston, Tex, Channing Mutual Funds, New York, Am Century Mortgage Investors, Jacksonville, Fla, STP Corp, Ft Lauderdale, M&W Land Inc, Nashville, Tenn, Vanderbilt Univ & Ensworth Sch, Nashville; trustee, 72 Campaign Liquidation Trust. Mem: Phi Delta Theta. Relig: Episcopal. Mailing Add: Harding Pl & Hillsboro Rd Nashville TN 37215

DUDLEY, JAMES T (D)
Maine State Rep
Mailing Add: West Enfield Enfield ME 04493

DUDLEY, TILFORD ELI (D)
Mem, DC Dem Cent Comt
b Charleston, Ill, Apr 21, 07; s Dr Gerry Brown Dudley & Esther Shoot D; m 1937 to Martha Fairchild Ward; c Donica Ward, Gerric Ward & Martha Fairchild. Educ: Wesleyan Univ, PhB, 28; Harvard Law Sch, LLB, 31; Delta Sigma Rho. Polit & Govt Pos: Chief legal sect, land prog, Fed Emergency Relief Admin, 34-35; chief land sect, Suburban Resettlement Admin, 35-37; chief land acquisition, Nat Park Serv, 36-37; trial examr, Nat Labor Rels Bd, 37-42; principle mediation officer, Nat War Labor Bd, 42-43, regional dir, Disputes, 43-44; deleg, Dem Nat Conv, 48, 52, 60 & 68; alt mem, Dem Nat Comt, 48-68; mem, DC Dem Cent Comt, 48-68, 72-, treas, 61-64, vchmn, 64-67, chmn, 67-68; chmn, Citizens Coun of DC Govt, 62-67. Bus & Prof Pos: Partner, Law firm of Mighell, Gunsul, Allan & Latham, Aurora, Ill, 31-34; assoc gen counsel, United Packinghouse Workers, 44-45; asst to Sidney Hillman, chmn of CIO-PAC, 45-46; asst dir, Comt on Polit Action, CIO, 46-55, asst dir, Comt on Polit Educ, AFL-CIO, 55-58; dir, Speakers Bur, 58-69; assoc dir, CCSA, United Church of Christ, 69-; ed, Washington Report, 69- Publ: The Harvard Legal Aid Bureau: Its History & Purposes, 31; Digest of Decisions of the National Labor Relations Bd, 40; Poverty & Hunger—The Whence & the Whither, 70. Mem: Nat Coun Churches (exec bd, Div of Christian Life & Mission, 65-); Am for Dem Action; NAACP; Urban League; YMCA (bd mgt, Washington, DC). Relig: Methodist & United Church of Christ. Legal Res: 2942 Macomb St NW Washington DC 20008 Mailing Add: 110 Maryland Ave NE Washington DC 20002

DUE, MARY JANE CARTER (D)
b Salt Lake City, Utah, June 20, 22; d Irvin R Carter & Rhoda Bryant C; m 1941 to John Fitzgerald Due, div; c Nancy (Mrs McCormick). Educ: Univ Utah, JD, 56; Phi Delta Delta. Polit & Govt Pos: Vpres, Young Dem of Utah, 47-50; exec secy, Utah Dem State Comt, 47-52; attorney solicitor, Dept of Interior, 61-71; counsel, US Senate Comt Minerals, Materials, Fuels, Interior, 71-72, chief clerk, US Senate Comt Aeronaut & Space Sci, 72-73; admin asst to US Sen Frank E Moss, Utah, 73- Bus & Prof Pos: Counsel, Anaconda Co, Salt Lake City, 71. Publ: Auth, Effect of Dawson Act on leasing, Utah Bar J, 58; P L 585 in retrospect, Rocky Mountain Law Rev, 60; Access over public lands, Rocky Mountain Mineral Law Found, 65 & 74. Mem: Am Asn Univ Women; League of Women Voters. Legal Res: 1772 Yalecrest Ave Salt Lake City UT 84105 Mailing Add: 905 Sixth SW Washington DC 20024

DUEHOLM, HARVEY L (D)
Wis State Rep
b Bone Lake, Wis, Jan 29, 10. Educ: Luck High Sch. Polit & Govt Pos: Community committeeman, Agr Conserv Serv, 38-53; town chmn, 45-59; chmn, Co Bd, 57-59; Wis State Rep, 58- Bus & Prof Pos: Dairy farmer; mem various coop exec bds. Mailing Add: Rte 2 Luck WI 54853

DUENAS, CRISTOBAL CAMACHO (R)
Judge, Dist Court Guam
b Agana, Guam, Sept 12, 20; s Jose Castro Duenas & Concepcion Martinez C; m 1954 to Juanita Castro Calvo; c Christopher Joseph, Therese, Vincent, Zerlina, Joanna, Ricardo & David. Educ: Aquinas Col, Grand Rapids, Mich, 46-48; Univ Mich, AB, 50, JD, 52; Student Bar Asn. Polit & Govt Pos: Asst Attorney Gen, Govt of Guam, 52-57, dir land mgt, 57-60; judge, Island Court Guam, 60-69; judge, Dist Court, Guam, 69- Mem: Am Bar Asn; Guam Bar Asn; Am Judicature Soc; KofC; Nat Lawyers Club. Relig: Catholic. Legal Res: O'Hara St Agana GU Mailing Add: PO Box 203 Agana GU 96910

DUENAS, EDWARD RAMIREZ (R)
b Agana, Guam, May 11, 36; s Jesus C Duenas & Juliana T Ramirez D; m 1963 to Lourdes Fe Unpingco; c Michele Carmelin. Educ: Col of St Thomas, 55-57; Marquette Univ, BS, 59; Int Club; Drama Club; Press Club; Marquette Jour Alumni Asn; St Thomas Col Alumni Asn. Polit & Govt Pos: Pub rels officer, Eighth Guam Legis, 65-66, staff dir, 66; Vista supvr & asst to adminr, Guam Econ Opportunity Comt, 67-69; admin officer & pub rels officer, Guam Housing & Urban Renewal Authority, 69; press secy, Off of the Gov, 69- Mil Serv: Entered as Pvt, Army, 61, released as SP-4, 63, after serv in Garrison Co, Army, Hawaii; ed, Hawaii Lightning News, Defense Dept Merit Award, 63. Mem: Int Platform Asn; Guam Press Asn; Guam Jr CofC; Pac Jaycees; Guam Rifle & Pistol Asn. Honors & Awards: Dean's List, Col of St Thomas; Commendation from Guam Legis; Merit of Achievement, Guam Jaycees. Relig: Catholic. Legal Res: Mongmong GU 96910 Mailing Add: PO Box 373 Agana GU 96910

DUENAS, JOSE RAMIREZ (D)
Sen, Guam Legis
b Agana, Guam, Oct 17, 30; s Jesus Camacho Duenas (deceased) & Juliana Torres Ramirez D; m 1954 to Rosario Cruz Perez; c Joseph, Danny, Anthony, Gerardlyn, Carina, Thomas, Marcella & Julienne. Educ: Aquinas Col, BA, 55. Polit & Govt Pos: Sen, Guam Legis, 70- Bus & Prof Pos: Auditor, Dept Admin, Govt Guam, 57-58, chief acct, 62-65, acct supvr, 67; vpres financial affairs, Univ Guam, 66-70. Mem: Jaycees; Fifth SPac Games Coun (treas). Relig: Catholic. Legal Res: Dededo GU 96911 Mailing Add: PO Box 333 Agana GU 96910

DUENAS, ROY PAULINO (D)
Sen, Guam Legis
b Inarajan, Guam, Oct 31, 42; s Manuel Mendiola Duenas & Ana Cepeda Paulino D; m 1968 to Mildred Therese; c Anna Marie, Michael & Roy. Educ: US Merchant Marine Acad, BS, 66. Polit & Govt Pos: Mem, Guam Dem Cent Exec Comt, 72-; Sen, Guam Legis, 75- Bus & Prof Pos: Mgr, Flores Poultry Farm, currently. Mem: Marianas Poultry Asn (pres); Committeeman for Boy Scouts; Mem Adv Coun-Univ Guam. Relig: Catholic. Legal Res: Malojloj Inarajan GU 96916 Mailing Add: PO Box 991 Agana GU 96910

DUERK, JAMES ALLEN (R)
b Defiance, Ohio, July 13, 30; s Karl Duerk & Alice Bybee D; m 1951 to Dolores M Hempstock; c Karla Annette (Mrs Spencer C Lang), Kathryn Jeanne & Kristin Elizabeth. Educ: Centre Col Ky; Bowling Green State Univ; Sigma Chi. Polit & Govt Pos: Press asst, Congressman Oliver P Bolton, Ohio, 64; pub rels dir, Campaign of Congressman Clarence J Brown, Jr, 65; dir pub rels, Ohio Rep State Hq, 65-69; press secy to Gov James A Rhodes, Ohio, 69-71; dir press rels for US Sen William B Saxbe, Ohio, 73- Bus & Prof Pos: Sports ed, Sentinel-Tribune, Bowling Green, Ohio, 51-52; reporter & columnist, Crescent-News, Defiance, 52-55; pub rels rep, Columbia Gas of Ohio, Inc, 55-63; pres, James A Duerk &

DUFF, BRIAN B (R)
Ill State Rep
Mailing Add: 618 Maple Ave Wilmette IL 60091

DUFF, JOHN BERNARD (D)
Committeeman, Essex Co Dem Party, NJ
b Orange, NJ, July 1, 31; s John B Duff & Mary Cunningham D; m 1955 to Helen Mezzanotti; c Michael, Maureen, Patricia, John & Robert. Educ: Fordham Col, BS, 53; Seton Hall Univ, MA, 58; Columbia Univ, PhD, 64. Polit & Govt Pos: Deleg, NJ State Const Conv, 66; committeeman, Essex Co Dem Party, 67-; Dem cand for cong, 12th Cong Dist, 68; vchmn bd trustees, Essex Co Col, 66-70; chmn, Livingston Dem Comt, 72- Bus & Prof Pos: Sales rep, Remington-Rand Corp, Newark, NJ, 55-57; dist mgr, Jersey City, 57-60; from instr to assoc prof, Seton Hall Univ, 60-69, prof, 69-, acad vpres, 70-, provost, 72- Mil Serv: Entered as Pvt, Army, 53, released as Pfc, 55, after serv in 74th Regt Combat Team, Ft Devens, Mass, 53-55; Nat Defense Medal; Good Conduct Medal. Publ: Co-auth, The Immigrants' Influence on Wilson's Peace Policies, Univ Ky Press, 67; auth, The Irish in the United States, Wadsworth Publ, 71; The Nat Turner Rebellion (w P M Mitchell), Harper & Row, 71; plus others. Mem: Am Hist Asn; Orgn of Am Historians; Am Asn Univ Prof; Immigration Hist Research Group; Phi Alpha Theta. Relig: Catholic. Mailing Add: 8 Laurel Ave Livingston NJ 07032

DUFFEY, JOSEPH D (D)
Mem Nat Policy Coun, Dem Nat Comt
b Huntington, WVa, July 1, 32; s Joseph I Duffey & Ruth Wilson D; m 1952 to Patricia Fortney; c Michael Robert & David King. Educ: Marshall Univ, AB, 54; Andover Newton Theol Sch, BD, 57; Yale Univ, STM, 63; Hartford Sem Found, PhD, 69; Omicron Delta Kappa; Rockefeller Found doctoral fel, 64-65. Polit & Govt Pos: Chmn, Conn Campaign for Eugene McCarthy, 68; mem, Dem State Platform Comt, Conn, 68; deleg, Dem Nat Conv, 68 & 72; nat chmn, Am for Dem Action; Dem cand for US Sen, 70; mem, nat policy coun, Dem Nat Comt, currently. Bus & Prof Pos: Fel, J F Kennedy Sch Govt, Harvard Univ, 71-72; adj prof, Yale Univ, 71- Publ: The Supreme Court decision regarding church & state, United Church Herald, 63; The Liberals plight, Christianity & Crisis, 11/57. Relig: United Church of Christ. Mailing Add: c/o Dem Nat Comt 2600 Virginia Ave NW Washington DC 20037

DUFFIELD, JOHN RICHARD (D)
b Elizabeth, NJ, May 17, 30; s Stuart Duffield & Mary Horning D; m 1955 to Mary Rose Carroll; c Christopher, John, Jennifer & Marjorie. Educ: Williams Col, BA, 52; Yale Law Sch, LLB, 57; Phi Beta Kappa, Order of the Coif; Phi Gamma Delta. Polit & Govt Pos: Chmn, Pima Co Dem Cent Comt, Ariz, 64-66; chmn, Dem Party, Ariz, 66-70. Bus & Prof Pos: Partner, Spaid, Fish, Briney & Duffield, Lawyers, 63- Mil Serv: Entered as 2nd Lt, Air Force, 52, released as 1st Lt, 54. Mem: Am, Pima Co & Ariz Bar Asns. Relig: Episcopal. Legal Res: 4125 Camino Encerrado Tucson AZ 85718 Mailing Add: 711 Transamerica Bldg Tucson AZ 85701

DUFFIN, DENNIS J (D)
Mass State Rep
Mailing Add: State Capitol Boston MA 02133

DUFFY, F RYAN (D)
b Fond du Lac, Wis, June 23, 88; s Francis Fee Duffy & Hattie E Ryan D; m 1918 to Louise Haydon; c Mrs Ann L, Judge F Ryan, Jr, Dr Haydon R & Rev James H. Educ: Univ Wis, BA, 10, BBL, 12, LLD, 52; De Paul Univ, LLD, 55; Delta Sigma Rho. Polit & Govt Pos: US Sen, Wis, 33-39; US Dist Judge, 39-49; US Circuit Judge, 49-; chief judge, US Court of Appeals, Seventh Circuit, 54-59. Mil Serv: Entered Army, 17, released as Maj, 19, after serv in Motor Transport Corps, AEF. Mem: Milwaukee Legal Aid Asn; Am Legion; Milwaukee Athletic Club; Milwaukee Club. Honors & Awards: Alumni of the Year Award, Univ Wis Law Sch, 68. Relig: Roman Catholic. Legal Res: 3107 N Hackett Ave Milwaukee WI 53211 Mailing Add: 718 Federal Bldg Milwaukee WI 53202

DUFFY, GORDON W (R)
Calif State Assemblyman
b Hanford, Calif, Apr 24, 24; s Carl Henry Duffy & Fannie Andersen D; m 1958 to JoAnn Mary Hein; c Brian Edwin, Mark Carl, Eric Nathaniel, Sean Christian & Nancy Jean. Educ: Univ Calif, Berkeley, AB, 44, BS, 48; Kappa Sigma. Polit & Govt Pos: Mem & chmn, Hanford Planning Comn, Calif, 52-55; mem, Hanford Elem Sch Bd, 55-61; vmayor, Hanford, 62-64 & mayor, 64; Calif State Assemblyman, 21st Dist, 65-, chmn, Comt on Health & Welfare, Calif State Assembly, 69- Bus & Prof Pos: Optometrist, 58- Mil Serv: Entered as A/S, Navy, 44, released as Lt(jg), 46, after serv in SPac & Philippine Theaters. Mem: Fel Am Acad Optom; fel Am Sch Health Asn; Moose; Am Legion; Mason. Honors & Awards: Selected, Man of the Year, Univ Calif Optom Alumni Asn, 68. Relig: Presbyterian; elder, First Presby Church. Legal Res: 253 Cortner Hanford CA 93230 Mailing Add: Rm 8 321 N Douty St Hanford CA 93230

DUFFY, J HOWARD (D)
RI State Rep
b East Providence, RI, Jan 4, 06; m to Mary S. Educ: Bryant Col; Brown Univ, exten courses; Univ RI. Polit & Govt Pos: Mem, 24th Dist Dem Comt; labor rep, Minimum Wage Bd, 53; RI State Rep, 61-; mem, Providence & House Steering Comt. Bus & Prof Pos: Bus agt, Hotel & Restaurant Serv Employees & Bartenders Union 285. Mem: Legis Comt of State Coun, CIO. Mailing Add: 171 Reynolds Ave Providence RI 02905

DUFFY, JAMES EVAN (R)
b White Plains, NY, July 1, 32; s James Evan Duffy & Pearl Kath D; m to Carol Letitia Brugh; c Jacquelyn Carol & James Evan, III. Educ: Clemson Univ, 50-54; Phi Chi Eta; bus mgr, Sr Platoon, Clemson Univ; Pershing Rifles; Scabbard & Blade. Polit & Govt Pos: Mem speakers bur, SC Rep Party, 60; deleg, Co Rep Conv, SC, 61, 62, 64, 66 & 68; Rep state committeeman, Anderson Co, 61-65; deleg, SC State Rep Conv, 62-68; chmn, Steering Comt 64 & 68, vchmn, Steering Comt & chmn, Agenda & Order of Bus Comt, 66; deleg, 13-State Regional Rep Conv, 63; Third Dist Ballot Security Officer, SC, 63; chmn, Third Dist Rep Party, 63-65; mem, SC State Rep Finance Comt, 63-68; mem, SC State Rep Cent Adv Comt, 63-68; presidential elector, 64; deleg & mem, credentials comt, Rep Nat Conv, 64; state ballot security chmn, 64, 66, 68 & 72; state finance chmn, SC Rep Party, 65-66; mem, Nat Rep Finance Comt, 65-66; mem, SC State Personnel Comt, 65-66; vchmn, SC State Rep Finance Campaign Comt, 66-68; co committeeman, Arcadia Precinct, Richland Co, 66; mem, Richland Co Rep Adv Comt, 66; secy, Second Cong Dist Rep Comt, 66; chmn, Second Cong Dist Rep Party, 66-68; orgn dir, SC State Rep Party, 68; chmn, Ravenel for Gov, SC, 69-70; pres, Mission Precinct Club, Greenville Co Rep Party, 69-71; mem, SC Rep State Cent Adv Comt, 71; mem, SC Reelect the President Comt, 72; state chmn ballot security, Reelect the President Comt & SC Rep Party, 72. Bus & Prof Pos: Personnel dir, Orr-Lyons Mills, 57-59; asst dir qual control, Cent Mfg Div, M Lowenstein & Sons, 59-65; asst to gen mgr, Pac, Columbia Mills, 65-66; tech supt, 66-68; syst analyst, United Merchants & Mfrs, Greenville, SC, 68-69, chief proj engr, 70- Mil Serv: Entered as 2nd Lt, Army, 55, released as 1st Lt, 57. Mem: Textile Qual Control Asn; Anderson Co Personnel Club; Civil Rights & Foreign Affairs Comt, Columbia; CofC; Merrifield Park Community Action Comt (chmn). Relig: Episcopal; past jr warden, vestryman, Bible teacher, treas & law reader, currently, vestryman, St Peter's Episcopal Mission, 69-71; jr warden, St Peter's Episcopal Church, 71; deleg, Diocesan Conv, 71-72. Mailing Add: 105 Seabury Dr Greenville SC 29607

DUFFY, JOHN P (D)
Chmn, Bristol Dem Town Comt, Conn
b Bristol, Conn, May 24, 24; s William J Duffy & Rena O'Connell D; single. Educ: Univ Conn, BA, 52; Univ Mass, 65-67; Trinity Col, Hartford, MA, 66; Kappa Sigma; Irish Am Soc. Polit & Govt Pos: City councilman, Bristol, Conn, 61-63, chmn, Pub Works Bd, 68-72; mem, Bristol Dem Town Comt, Conn, 60-74, chmn, 74- Bus & Prof Pos: Eng teacher, Univ Conn, 67- Mil Serv: Entered as Pvt, Army, 45, released as Cpl, 46, after serv in 410th Engrs. Mem: Am Asn Univ Prof; Thoreau Soc; Emerson Soc; Irish-Am Cult Inst. Relig: Roman Catholic. Mailing Add: 96 South St Bristol CT 06010

DUFOUR, E JAMES (D)
Committeeman, Maine Dem State Comt
b Old Town, Maine, June 2, 34; s P Paul DuFour & Audelie Brodeur D; m 1957 to Pauline Gilbert; c Michael J, Anne Marie & David Donald. Educ: Univ Maine, BA. Polit & Govt Pos: Chmn, Somerset Co Dem Party, 59-60; committeeman, Maine Dem State Comt, 70- Bus & Prof Pos: Vpres & dir, William Philbrick Co, currently. Mil Serv: Entered Maine Air Nat Guard, 57, released as Airman 1/C, 63. Mem: Independent Agts Asn Maine; Rotary; KofC. Relig: Catholic. Mailing Add: Star Rte Skowhegan ME 04976

DUGAN, JAMES (D)
Chmn, NJ Dem State Comt
Mailing Add: 601 Broadway Bayonne NJ 07002

DUGGER, RONNIE EDWARD (D)
b Chicago, Ill, Apr 16, 30; s William LeRoy Dugger & Mary King D; m 1951 to Jean Williams; c Gary McGregor & Celia Williams. Educ: Univ Tex at Austin, BA, 50, grad work, 50-51, 54; Oxford Univ, 51-52; Phi Beta Kappa; Phi Eta Sigma; Pi Sigma Alpha; Tejas Club. Polit & Govt Pos: Deleg, Dem Nat Mid-Term Conf, 74. Bus & Prof Pos: Ed & gen mgr, The Texas Observer, 54-61, 65-66, ed-at-lg & publ, 66-; numerous others. Publ: Dark Star, Hiroshima Reconsidered in the Life of Claude Eatherly, World, 67; ed, Three Men in Texas, Bedichek, Webb & Dobie, Univ Tex Press Austin, 67; Our Invaded Universities, Form, Reform & New Starts, W W Norton, 74. Mem: Am Civil Liberties Union; Authors Guild; Tex Inst Letters & others. Honors & Awards: Rockefeller Found grant, 69-70. Mailing Add: 1017 W 31st St Austin,TX 78705

DUGUID, ROBERT LEE (R)
Mem, State Rep Cent Comt Calif
b Humboldt, Ariz, July 28, 17; s William Duguid & Lola Carey D; m 1939 to Zell Frances Lanyon; c Charles William & James Francis. Educ: Clarkdale High Sch, Ariz, grad, 37. Polit & Govt Pos: Pres, Employee Mgt Coun, China Lake, Calif; vmayor & city councilman, Ridgecrest; mem, State Rep Cent Comt Calif, 69- Bus & Prof Pos: Dist mgr, Farmers Ins Group, 57-65; pres, Desert Ins Agency, Ridgecrest, Calif, 65- Mem: Mason; Kiwanis; Elks; Shrine; Ridgecrest CofC. Relig: Protestant. Mailing Add: 330 Lenore St Ridgecrest CA 93555

DUHAMINE, ROGER M (D)
NH State Rep
Mailing Add: 47 Eldridge St Lebanon NH 03766

DUHE, LESTER ANTOINE (R)
Mem-at-Lg, St John Parish Rep Exec Comt, La
b Reserve, La, Apr 8, 24; s Paul Duhe & Louise Millet D; m 1946 to Estelle N Hymel; c Jeanette, Joycelyn, Joanne, Judith, Lester A, Jr & Jeffery. Educ: Isaac Delgado Col, 2 years; La State Police Acad, grad, 52. Polit & Govt Pos: Vet serv officer, La Dept Vet Affairs, 49-52; mem-at-lg, St John Parish Rep Exec Comt, 64-, chmn, formerly; polit action dir, St John Parish, 71. Mil Serv: Entered as Pvt, Army, 41, released as Sgt, 45, after serv in 760 Tank Bn, GHQ, Africa & Italy, 42-44; Purple Heart with 2 Oak Leaf Clusters; ETO, Victory, Am Theatre & Good Conduct Medals. Mem: VFW (nat asst inspector gen); Am Legion; DAV. Honors & Awards: Outstanding DAV Award; Outstanding Serv Award, Red Cross. Relig: Catholic. Legal Res: 146 E 12th St Reserve LA 70084 Mailing Add: Rte 1 Box 802 Reserve LA 70084

DUIS, HERBERT J (R)
Nebr State Sen
b Gothenburg, Nebr, Apr 26, 16; s John H Duis & Anna Schram D; m 1944 to Mary Jane Trusdale; c John Robert & Mary Elizabeth. Educ: Gothenburg Pub Schs, 12 years. Polit & Govt Pos: Nebr State Sen, 39th Legis Dist, 51-54 & 69- Bus & Prof Pos: Pres, Duis & Co, Nebr, 33- Mil Serv: Entered as Pvt, Signal Corps, Army, 41, released as M/Sgt, 45, after serv in 3145th Signal Base Group, Pac Theater, 44-45. Mem: AF&AM; Kiwanis. Relig: Presbyterian. Mailing Add: 2013 Lake Ave Gothenburg NE 69138

DUKAKIS, MICHAEL S (D)
Gov, Mass
Mailing Add: 85 Perry St Brookline MA 02146

DUKE, A DON (D)
Okla State Rep
b Madill, Okla, Dec 7, 33; s Arville B Duke & Vina Mae Bartee D; m 1953 to Donnell Gorrell; c Donna (Mrs Waggoner), Denita (Mrs Plyler) & DeLinda Sue. Educ: Southeastern State Univ, BA, 63; Okla Univ & Okla City Univ; Young Dem; Red Red Rose; Student Senate. Polit & Govt Pos: Okla State Rep, Dist 48, 70- Bus & Prof Pos: Real estate broker & sch counr,

Ardmore, Okla. Mem: Eastern Star; York Rite Mason; Shrine; Optimist Club; Cattlemen's Asn. Mailing Add: 114 Seventh NW Ardmore OK 73401

DUKE, ANGIER BIDDLE (D)
b New York, NY, Nov 30, 15; s Angier Buchanan Duke & Cordelia Biddle D; m 1962 to Robin Chandler Tippett; c A St George, Maria-Luisa, Dario & Angier Biddle, Jr. Educ: Yale Univ, 34-37; Delta Kappa Epsilon. Hon Degrees: DH, Long Island Univ, 68; LLD, Duke Univ, 69. Polit & Govt Pos: Second secy, US Foreign Serv, Buenos Aires, 49-51; spec asst to US Ambassador to Madrid, 51-52; US Ambassador to El Salvador, 52-53; chmn, NY State Dem Conv Comt, 54; comnr, Long Island State Park, 55-59; chmn, Nationalities & Intergroup Rels Comt, NY State Dem Comt, 60; chief of protocol, Dept of State, 61-65; US Ambassador to Spain, 65-68; US Ambassador, Denmark, 68-69; comnr civic affairs & pub events, City of New York, currently. Bus & Prof Pos: Pres, Int Rescue Comt, 55-60; chmn, Newwirth Investment Fund, 70-73. Mil Serv: Entered as Pvt, Army Air Force, 41, released as Maj, 46, after serv in Air Transport Command, Europe, 43-46; Am Defense Medal; European Campaign Medal with Four Stars; Victory Medal. Mem: Coun on Foreign Rels; Foreign Serv Asn; Am Immigration & Citizenship Conf (hon chmn); Overseas & Nat Press Clubs; Am Legion. Honors & Awards: Commandeur, Nat Order of Viet Nam; Order of Merit, Haiti; Grand Cross of the Order of Malta; Order of George I, Greece. Legal Res: 435 E 52nd St New York NY Mailing Add: 521 Fifth Ave New York NY 10017

DUKE, MERLIN (R)
Chmn, Washington Parish Rep Exec Comt, La
b Mamou, La, Feb 27, 41; s Clarence Shockley Duke & Emily Pommier D; m 1963 to Eleanor Elaine Watson; c David Merlin & Damon Michael. Educ: La Col, BA, 62; La State Univ, Baton Rouge, 63; Southeastern La Univ, ME, 71 & MT, 72; Sigma Alpha Eta; Circle K; John Quincy Adams Forensic; Alpha Sigma Kappa; Athenian Lit Soc. Polit & Govt Pos: Mem elect comn, St Landry Parish, Opelousas, La, 64; youth chmn, Washington Parish, Nixon Campaign, 68-69; chmn orgn & registr, Washington Parish Rep Polit Action Coun, 69-72, chmn, 72-; alt deleg, Rep Nat Conv, 72; co-chmn, Reelect President Nixon, 72-73; deleg, La Rep State Conv, 72-73; mem, Washington Parish Rep Exec Comt, 72-, chmn, currently. Bus & Prof Pos: Pub sch teacher, Opelousas High Sch, La, 62-66; speech pathologist, Bogalusa City Schs, 66- Mem: La Teachers Asn; Bogalusa Classroom Teachers; La Speech & Hearing Asn (exhibits chmn, 66-); Phi Kappa Delta; La Ment Health. Honors & Awards: Outstanding Mem, La Col Legionnaires, 62; Outstanding Orator, Alexandria Kiwanis Club, 62; Yearbook Dedication, Opelousas High Sch Annual Staff, 66; Handbook Dedication, Opelousas High Sch Student Coun, 66; nominee, Young Man of the Year, Washington Parish Rep Party, 70. Relig: United Methodist. Mailing Add: 1318 Colorado Bogalusa LA 70427

DUKERT, JOSEPH MICHAEL (R)
b Baltimore, Md, Sept 19, 29; s Andrew Joseph Dukert & Margaret Przybyl D; m 1952 to Virginia Linthicum (deceased); m 1968 to Betty Cole. Educ: Univ Notre Dame, BA magna cum laude, 51; Georgetown Univ, grad study int rels, 51-52; Hopkins Sch Adv Int Studies, Bologna, Italy, 55-56; Johns Hopkins Univ, grad study int rels, 56-57; Wranglers; Ger Club. Polit & Govt Pos: Deleg, Rep Nat Conv, 60 & 68;, alt deleg, 64, vchmn Md deleg, 68; vchmn, Rep State Cent Comt Md, 62-66, chmn, 66-69; mem, Baltimore City Jail Bd, 63-68; founder & pres, Second Dist Citizen Action Orgn, 65-66; coordr, Md Rep Conv, 72. Bus & Prof Pos: Dir pub rels, Research Inst Advan Studies, 62-65; free lance consult, mkt & indust commun, 65-; intermittent consult, US Info Agency, Energy Res & Develop Admin & Dept of Com, currently. Mil Serv: Entered as 2nd Lt, Army Air Force, 51, released as 1st Lt, 53, after serv in 13th Air Force, Philippines. Publ: Atompower, 61, This is Antarctica, 65, 2nd ed, 71 & Nuclear Ships of the World, 73, Coward-McCann. Mem: Nat Assoc Sci Writers; Aerospace Writers Asn; Antarctican Soc; Atomic Indust Forum's Comt Pub Understanding. Honors & Awards: Exec producer, Power for Continent 7 (voted best indust sales film of the year, Rome Film Festival); exec producer, Atoms for Space (voted outstanding TV news released film, 62). Relig: Roman Catholic. Legal Res: Crestview MD Mailing Add: 4709 Crescent St Washington DC 20016

DUKES, GENE W (D)
SC State Rep
b Reevesville, SC, July 13, 43; s Henry L Dukes & Roberta Reeves D; m 1966 to Geraldine Dorman. Educ: Clemson Univ, BS, 65, MS, 67; Univ SC Sch Law, JD, 71; Sigma Phi Epsilon. Polit & Govt Pos: Chmn, Dorchester Co Dem Party, SC, 72-; SC State Rep, 72- Bus & Prof Pos: Attorney-at-law, Berry & Dukes, St George, SC, 71- Mil Serv: Entered as Pfc, Army Res, 67, released as SP-5, 73, after serv in Hq First Brigade 108, 67-73. Publ: Co-auth, South Carolina law policies & program pertaining to water & related land resources, Water Resources Research Inst, 68. Mem: Am Judicature Soc; Alpha Zeta; AF&AM; Am Legion; Farm Bur. Honors & Awards: Am Jurisp Award, Excellence in Wills, 62; Student Achievement Award, Wall Street J, 65. Relig: Baptist. Legal Res: 302 Minus St St George SC 29477 Mailing Add: PO Box 368 St George SC 29477

DUKES, HAZEL NELL (D)
Dem Nat Committeewoman, NY
b Montgomery, Ala, Mar 17, 32; d Edward Johnson & Alice Bunch J; div; c Ronald L. Educ: Ala State Teachers Col, 49-50; Nassau Community Col, 68-70. Polit & Govt Pos: Deleg, Dem Nat Mid-Term Conf, 74; Dem Nat Committeewoman, NY, 75- Bus & Prof Pos: Vpres, NY State Conf, NAACP, 74; rec secy, Coun Black Elected Dem NY State, 74; mem, Roslyn League Women Voters; bd dirs, New York City Off Track Betting Credit Union, 75. Mem: NAACP (vpres, NY State Conf of Branches, 74); Econ Opportunity Comn (comnr, Nassau Co, 74). Honors & Awards: Woman of the Year Award, presented by Ray Heatherton, 74; Econ Opportunity Comn Award, 74; Award for Outstanding Leadership, Great Neck NAACP, 74; Award of Merit, Westbury Nat Asn Negro Bus & Prof Women, 75. Relig: Baptist. Mailing Add: 300 Edwards St Roslyn Heights NY 11577

DULANEY, SIM CLARENCE, JR (R)
b Clarkdale, Miss, Feb 7, 28; s Sim Clarence Dulaney, Sr & Arizona Tims D; m 1952 to Mary Catherine Gunn; c Dara Ryan, Sim Clarence, III & Deborah Elizabeth. Educ: Delta State Col, BS, 50; Univ Miss, 1 year; Jackson Sch Law, LLB, 69; Sigma Delta Kappa; Men's Honor Coun; Class Officer; Col Newspaper Staff; Col Annual Staff. Polit & Govt Pos: Secy, Madison Co Rep Party, Miss, 64-67, chmn, formerly; dir, Canton Acad Sch Bd, 65-; secy & comnr, Bear-Tylda Bogue Comn, 67- Bus & Prof Pos: Pres, New Evans Gin, Inc, 71-; secy-treas, Para-Plex, Inc, 71-; pres, New Ballard Gin Co, Inc, 72- Mil Serv: Pvt, Army, 50. Mem: Canton Area CofC (dir, 69-, chmn agr comt, 68-, mem comt on state & local govt & comt on educ, 71); Mason; Miss Farm Bur; Miss Cattlemens Asn; Am Soybean Asn. Relig: Baptist; deacon & former chmn bd deacons. Mailing Add: Rte 3 Box 14 Canton MS 39046

DULLEA, EDWARD JAMES, JR (D)
Mem, Peabody Dem City Comt, Mass
b Peabody, Mass, Oct 13, 31; s Edward James Dullea (deceased) & Elizabeth Walsh D; m 1957 to Marie Splaine Dullea; c Kathleen, Edward, III, Eileen, Michael, Anne Marie, Maureen & Suzanne. Educ: Boston Univ, BS, 57; Suffolk Univ, 1 year; Salem State Col, grad work. Polit & Govt Pos: Mem, Dem City Comt, Peabody, Mass, 60-; vchmn, Peabody Sch Comt, 66- Bus & Prof Pos: Self-employed. Mil Serv: Entered as Airman, Air Force, 51, released as Airman 1/C, 54, after serv in 517th Materiel Squadron Training Command-Air Defense Command, 51-54; Air Defense Command Medal; Good Conduct Medal. Relig: Catholic. Mailing Add: 59 Gardner St Peabody MA 01960

DULSKI, THADDEUS J (D-LIBERAL)
b Buffalo, NY, Sept 27, 15; married; c five. Educ: Canisius Col; Univ Buffalo. Polit & Govt Pos: With Bur Internal Revenue, Treas Dept, 40-47; spec agt, Price Stabilization Admin, 51-53; Walden Dist Councilman, 53; mem, Finance Coun Comt, chmn, Taxation Comt & Wage Classification Comt; councilman-at-lg, Buffalo, NY, 57; US Rep, NY, 58-74, chmn post off & civil serv comt, US House Rep, 67-74, mem house vet affairs comt, formerly; deleg, Dem Nat Mid-Term Conf, 74. Bus & Prof Pos: Acct, tax consult, 47. Mil Serv: World War II. Mailing Add: 50 Peace St Buffalo NY 14211

DUMAIS, THOMAS A (D)
NH State Rep
Mailing Add: 229 High St Somersworth NH 03878

DUMAS, WOODROW WILSON (WOODY) (D)
Mayor, Baton Rouge, La
b Opelousas, La, Dec 9, 16; s J E Dumas & Margaret A Jernigan D; m 1940 to Carol E Epperson; c Diane & Woodrow Huntley. Educ: East Baton Rouge Parish Schs. Polit & Govt Pos: Mayor-Pres, Baton Rouge & Parish of East Baton Rouge, La, 64-; chmn, secy & vpres, Fed Projs Comt, Gtr Baton Rouge Port Comn; mem, Nat Adv Comt for Hwy Beautification, formerly; mem, Nat Hwy Safety Adv Comt, formerly; mem, Nat Adv Comt for Youth Opportunity, formerly; vpres-at-lg, La Munic Asn, 67-, mem exec bd, currently; mem, City-Parish Coun, 12 years; pres, La Police Jury Asn, formerly; pres, Sixth Cong Dist Police Jury Asn, 3 years; mem, Dem State Cent Comt, La, formerly; mem, La Air Control Comn, formerly. Mil Serv: Navy, 11 years, grad of US Submarine Sch, New London, Conn, with submarine forces in SPac, World War II & Korean War. Mem: Nat Asn Counties; Am Legion; VFW; Eagles; Moose. Honors & Awards: Named Outstanding Police Juror, La, 63 & Outstanding Police Juror of Sixth Dist; Outstanding Layman Award, La Hosp Asn, 72; Citizen of the Year Award, Easter Seal Soc Crippled Children & Adults of La, Inc, 72. Relig: Methodist, former mem bd stewards, Baker Methodist Church. Legal Res: Rte 1 Box 3 Baker LA 70714 Mailing Add: Rm 208 Munic Bldg Baton Rouge LA 70801

DUMM, LUCILLE (R)
Secy-Treas, Pickaway Co Rep Cent & Exec Comts, Ohio
b Circleville, Ohio, Oct 3, 13; d Leroy H Dumm & Lillie Martin D; single. Educ: Circleville High Sch, Ohio, 4 years. Polit & Govt Pos: Pres, GOP Booster Club, 43-; secy, Pickaway Co Rep Cent Exec Comt, Ohio, 52-; mem, Pickaway Co Bd of Elec, 62- Mem: Pickaway Co Women's Rep Club; Pickaway Co Hist Soc. Relig: Protestant. Mailing Add: 340 Walnut St Circleville OH 43113

DUMMER, ARLETTE ELAINE (DFL)
VChairwoman, Renville Co Dem-Farmer-Labor Party, Minn
b Fairfax, Minn, Oct 6, 28; d John Richard Borth & Ida Dallmann B; m 1949 to Ralph George Dummer; c Gary John, Steven William, Kristine Kay, Richard Ralph, Jennifer Jane & twins, Jean & Joan. Educ: Fairfax Pub High Sch, grad, 46. Polit & Govt Pos: Vchairwoman, Renville Co Dem-Farmer-Labor Party, Minn, 69- Bus & Prof Pos: Owner & mgr, Ralphies Drive In, 67 & Ralphies Self Serv, 71- Mem: Am Legion Auxiliary; VFW Auxiliary. Relig: Lutheran. Mailing Add: 206 NW Second St Fairfax MN 55332

DUMONT, ROLAND A (R)
Chmn, Providence Rep City Comt, RI
b Providence, RI, Mar 15, 30; s Albert J Dumont & Leosa Gilman; m 1950 to Louise R Tougas; c John, Ronald, Alan & Michael. Educ: LaSalle Acad, 48. Polit & Govt Pos: Dep sheriff, State of RI, 68-70; committeeman, Eighth Ward Rep Party, 68-, chmn, 69-71; chmn, Providence Rep City Comt, 71-; supt weight & measures, Providence, 75- Bus & Prof Pos: Roland Dumont Watch Crystals, Providence, 49-74 & Artif Advert Co, 72-75. Relig: Catholic. Mailing Add: 144 Superior St Providence RI 02909

DUMONT, WAYNE, JR (R)
NJ State Sen
b Paterson, NJ, June 25, 14; s Wayne Dumont & Sallie I Hunt D; m 1938 to Helen S Williamson; c Wayne Hunt. Educ: Lafayette Col; Univ Pa Law Sch. Hon Degrees: DLitt, Glassboro State Col, 64. Polit & Govt Pos: Mem, NJ Rep State Comt, 48-52; NJ State Sen, 52-65 & 69-; mem, NJ State Tax Policy Comt, 54-65 & chmn, 64-65; dist deleg, Rep Nat Conv, 60; Rep nominee for Gov, NJ, 65. Bus & Prof Pos: Practicing attorney, Phillipsburg, NJ, 41- Mil Serv: Entered as Pvt, Army, 43, released as 1st Lt, 46, after serv in Pac; Maj, NJ Army Nat Guard; dir of instr, NJ Mil Acad, Sea Girt; G-5, 50th Armored Div, Hq, E Orange, at present. Mem: Elks; KofP; Moose; Mason (32 degree); Am Legion. Honors & Awards: Phillipsburg Outstanding Citizen Award, B J Donovan Post 203, Am Legion, 56; Man of Year Award, Phillipsburg CofC, 62; Award for Outstanding Serv to Warren Co Agr, Warren Co Bd of Agr, 63; Shield Plaque for Outstanding Achievements in Cause of Civil Serv, NJ Farm Bur, 64 & Honored for Distinghished Serv to NJ Agr, 64. Relig: Presbyterian. Legal Res: 701 Hillcrest Blvd Phillipsburg NJ 08865 Mailing Add: 97 S Main St Phillipsburg NJ 08865

DUNAVANT, LEONARD CLYDE (R)
Tenn State Sen
b Ripley, Tenn, Oct 29, 19; s Harvey Maxie Dunavant & Chloris Akin D; m 1940 to Deloris Marie Anderson; c Janene (Mrs Pennel), Leonard C, Jr & Suzanne (Mrs Ripski). Educ: Union Univ, 37; Memphis State Univ, 38-39. Polit & Govt Pos: Alderman, City of Millington, Tenn, 56-68; Tenn State Rep, 67-72; Tenn State Sen, 72- Bus & Prof Pos: Pres, Millington Furniture Co, 50- Mil Serv: E-5, Navy, 44-46. Mem: Rotary; Shelby State Tech Inst (adv bd); Lambuth Col (bd trustees). Honors & Awards: Man of Year, City of Millington, 70. Relig: Methodist. Mailing Add: 4625 Cedar Rose Millington TN 38053

DUNCAN, C WOODROW, JR (D)
b Montebello, Calif, July 23, 43; s Charles Woodrow Duncan & Hazle Moffat D; m 1963 to Frances Kuzmic; c James Robert & Timothy Joseph. Educ: Univ Kans, 62-64 & 73-; Kansas City Art Inst, Mo, 65-71; Penn Valley Community Col, Kansas City, 71-72. Polit & Govt Pos: Chmn, Wyandotte Co New Dem Coalition of Kans, 69-71; Kans mem nat steering comt, New Dem Coalition, 70-72; local organizer, McGovern for President, 72; deleg, Dem Nat Conv, 72; manpower chmn, McGovern-Shriver Campaign, Wyandotte Co, 72. Mem: UAW Local 31; Kans Young Dem. Mailing Add: 1712 S 31st Kansas City KS 66106

DUNCAN, CYRIL DOUGLASS (D)
Chmn, Simpson Co Dem Exec Comt, Ky
b London, Eng, Jan 2, 03; s George Duncan & Isabella Annand D; m 1931 to Jewell Dobbs; c Duane Andrews & Diane (Mrs Baldwin). Educ: Max Morris Sch Pharm, Registered Pharmacist, 22. Polit & Govt Pos: Councilman, Franklin, Ky, 72-74; chmn, Simpson Co Dem Exec Comt, 72- Mem: Mason (Past Master); Ky Pharmaceutical Asn; Lions; Franklin-Simpson CofC. Relig: Presbyterian. Mailing Add: 503 Hillcrest Rd Franklin KY 42134

DUNCAN, DAVID L (D)
State Treas, Utah
b Greenup Co, Ky, June 13, 33; s Charles Edward Duncan & Grace Raynor D; m 1956 to Leah H Stuart; c Charles, Ruth & David. Educ: Stevens Henager Bus Col, ACS, 64. Polit & Govt Pos: Dep treas, Weber Co, Utah, 58-62, chief dept treas, 62-65, treas, 65-72; treas, Weber Co Young Dem, 62-65; deleg, Co & State Dem Conv, 62-; dist chmn, Weber Co Dem Party, 65-; treas, Utah State Dem Party, 65-; mem, Utah State Welfare Bd, 67-72, chmn, 69-71; deleg, Dem Nat Conv, 68; State Treas, Utah, 73- Bus & Prof Pos: Pres & dir, Ogden Munic Employees Credit Union, 66-70. Mil Serv: Entered as Airman, Air Force, 52, released as Airman 1/C, 56, after serv in Tactical Air Command; Korean, Nat Defense & UN Serv Medals; Good Conduct Medal. Mem: Utah State & Nat Asns of Co Off; Nat Asn Treas & Finance Off; Kiwanis. Relig: Baptist. Legal Res: 1062 Hudson St Ogden UT 84404 Mailing Add: Rm 215 State Capitol Salt Lake City UT 84114

DUNCAN, HERMAN HENRY (R)
b New Tazwell, Tenn, Aug 21, 88; s James Wesley Duncan & Martha Lewis D; m 1909 to Vivian Alvis; c James Horace & Pauline (Mrs Galloway). Educ: ETex Normal Col, teachers cert. Polit & Govt Pos: Chmn, Kaufman Co Rep Party, Tex, formerly; deleg, Tex State & Kaufman Co Rep Convs, 14-; postmaster, Kaufman, 22-34; mem, Tex Rep State Exec Comt, 34-54; presidential elector-at-lg, Tex, 36 & 48; asst campaign mgr for Tex, Dewey-Warren Campaign, 48; crew leader, Census of Agr, Kaufman Co, 54 & Bur of Census, 60; deleg or alt, Rep Nat Conv, 7 times, asst sgt-at-arms, 3 times. Bus & Prof Pos: Teacher, Hoffer & Abner Schs, Kaufman, Tex, 11-12; merchant & farmer, 13-22; merchant, 35-68; retired. Publ: Texas Under Many Flags, Am Hist Soc, 30; The Texas Republican, Tex Rep Party, 66. Mem: Odd Fellows; WOW; Lions; ETex CofC; Odd Fellow-Rebekah Asn of Tex. Honors & Awards: Name on Eisenhower Mem, Gettysburg, Pa; 60 year Jewel, Odd Fellows, 50 year Elders Jewel, United Presby Church; 45 year Jewel, Lion & Commercial Club, 50 year Charter Monarch, Lions. Relig: Presbyterian; elder. Legal Res: 400 W Mulberry St Kaufman TX 75142 Mailing Add: 460 W Mulberry St Kaufman TX 75142

DUNCAN, J EBB (D)
Ga State Sen
Mailing Add: PO Box 26 Carrollton GA 30117

DUNCAN, J SANTFORD (SANDY) (R)
Kans State Rep
Mailing Add: 2355 S Hillside Wichita KS 67211

DUNCAN, JAMES WENDELL (D)
Alaska State Rep
b Muscatine, Iowa, May 4, 42; s Paul Revere Duncan & Hazel Brayton D; m 1962 to Carol Jean Aceveda; c James, Desiree, Michelle, Derek, Jon & Marc. Educ: Sheldon Jackson Col, AA, 61; Ill State Univ, BS, 65; Ore State Univ, MBA, 70; Beta Gamma Sigma. Polit & Govt Pos: City & borough assemblyman, Juneau, Alaska, 72-74; Alaska State Rep, 75- Bus & Prof Pos: Acct instr, Juneau-Douglas Community Col, 70-74; audit supvr, Alaska Dept Revenue, 72-74; acct, Tlingit-Haida Housing Authority, 74- Legal Res: Birch Lane Mendenhaven Juneau AK 99803 Mailing Add: RR 4 Box 4316 Juneau AK 99803

DUNCAN, JASON CHARLIE (D)
SC State Rep
b Lyman, SC, June 27, 29; s William Jason Duncan & Arry Nodine D; m 1953 to Patricia Miller; c Kimber Lee & Jason Charlie, Jr. Educ: Wofford Col, AB, 51; Univ SC & Furman Univ, grad work in psychol. Polit & Govt Pos: SC State Rep, Spartanburg Co, 69-72 & 75- Bus & Prof Pos: Teacher, Blue Ridge High Sch, Greenville, 51-59; teacher Palmetto High Sch, Anderson, 59-60; asst prin & dir guid, Boiling Spring High Sch, Spartanburg, 60-66. Mem: WOW; Ruritan; Sertoma; Mason; Shrine. Honors & Awards: Most Inspiring Teacher Award, Chapman High Sch, 68-69. Relig: Methodist. Mailing Add: Rte 1 Lyman SC 29365

DUNCAN, JOHN JAMES (R)
US Rep, Tenn
b Scott Co, Tenn; m to Lois Swisher; c Beverly, James, Joe & Becky. Polit & Govt Pos: Asst Attorney Gen, Tenn, 47-56; dir, Legal Dept, Knoxville, 56-59; Mayor, Knoxville, 59-64; US Rep, Tenn, 64-; deleg, Rep Nat Conv, 68, alt deleg, 72. Mil Serv: Army, 42-45. Mem: Am Bar Asn; Am Legion; Knoxville Prof Baseball Club; Knoxville Baseball Club (dir). Honors & Awards: Good Govt Award, Jaycees; Nat Conf Christians & Jews Annual Citizenship Award, 63; Annual City Salesman Award. Relig: Presbyterian; elder, Eastminister Presby Church, Knoxville, Tenn. Legal Res: TN Mailing Add: US House of Rep Washington DC 20515

DUNCAN, LATON EARL (D)
Mem, Ga State Dem Exec Comt
b Jasper, Ga, Mar 26, 29; s John McLeroy Duncan & Viola Collins D; div; c Gregory Allen, Susan Christine & Prilla Ann. Educ: Southern Col Pharmacy, BS, 50. Polit & Govt Pos: Mem, Ga State Dem Exec Comt, 70-, mem rules & regulations comt, 70- Bus & Prof Pos: Mgr & pharmacist, Atherton Drug, Smyrna, Ga, 52-54 & 61-63; mgr & pharmacist, Dunaway Drug, Marietta, 54-59; partner & asst mgr, People Drug, Dallas, 59-61; owner & operator, Earl Duncan's Drug Store, 63- Mil Serv: Entered as Recruit, Army, 50, released as M/Sgt, 52, after serv in 2nd Div, 9th Regt, Korea, 51-52; First Sgt, Army Res, 52-56; Commendation Ribbon with Medal Pendant, Korea; Outstanding Reservist. Mem: Ga Pharmaceutical Asn; Paulding Co Jaycees; Rotary; CofC; Downtown Merchants Asn (pres). Honors & Awards: Outstanding Citizen Award, Paulding Co CofC, 69. Relig: Baptist. Mailing Add: 318 Main St Dallas GA 30132

DUNCAN, ROBERT BLACKFORD (D)
US Rep, Ore
b Normal, Ill, Dec 4, 20; s Eugene Frank Duncan & Katheryn K Blackford D; m to Marijane Dill; c Nancy Jane, Robert Angus, David Bruce, James Douglas, Laurie Ann, Bonnie Dee & Jeannie Elizabeth. Educ: Univ Alaska; Ill Wesleyan Univ, BA; Univ Mich Law Sch, LLB. Polit & Govt Pos: Ore State Rep, 56-58, Speaker, Ore State Legis, 58-62; US Rep, Fourth Dist, Ore, 62-67, Third Dist, 75-; mem, Adv Comn on Intergovt Rels; cong adv, World Food Conf, Food & Agr Orgn, 63; Dem nominee for US Sen, Ore, 66. Bus & Prof Pos: Attorney; partner, Lindsay, Nahstoll, Hart, Duncan, Dafoe & Krause, 66- Mil Serv: Entered as Aviation Cadet, Navy, 42, released as Lt(jg), 45, after serv in Atlantic & Pac Theaters; Comdr, Naval Res. Relig: Methodist. Legal Res: OR Mailing Add: 330 Cannon Bldg Washington DC 20515

DUNCAN, ROBERT MICHAEL (R)
Chmn, Ky Young Rep Fedn
b Oneida, Tenn, Apr 14, 51; s Robert C Duncan & Barbara Taylor D; m 1972 to Joanne Kirk. Educ: Cumberland Col, BA, 71; Univ Ky, JD, 74; Delta Theta Phi; pres, Student Govt Asn; chmn, Ky Col Rep; dir, Col Rep Region III, 71-72. Polit & Govt Pos: Mem, Ky Rep State Cent Comt, 70-72 & 74-75; youth chmn, Kentuckians for Nixon, 72; deleg, Rep Nat Conv, 72; chmn, Ky Young Rep Fedn, 74- Bus & Prof Pos: Legis intern, Ky Gen Assembly, 69-70; grad asst, Ky Secy State, 71; instr, Cumberland Col, 74; asst vpres & dir, Inez Deposit Bank, 74-; assoc, McCoy-Marcum Law Firm, 74- Mem: Am Bar Asn; Cumberland Col Alumni Asn (dir). Honors & Awards: Outstanding Male Grad, Cumberland Col, 71; Man of Year, Ky Col Rep, 71; Man of Year, Ky Young Rep, 72. Relig: Baptist. Mailing Add: Box 331 Inez KY 41224

DUNCAN, T MARVIN (R)
Chmn, Duval Co Rep Exec Comt, Fla
b Baltimore, Md, Feb 7, 16; s Andrew Thomas Duncan & Mildred Wheatley D; m 1936 to Dorothea B Markley; c Irene (Mrs Rousseau); Sandra (Mrs Rose) & Patricia (Mrs Kloeppel). Educ: US Coast Guard Acad, New London, Conn. Polit & Govt Pos: Chmn, numerous mayor's study comts, Fla, 58-; cand, Fla State Senate, 68; exec dir, Duval Co Rep Party, 73-74; campaign mgr & dir, Ed Guerney for Fla State Senate, 74; chmn, Duval Co Rep Exec Comt, Fla, 75- Bus & Prof Pos: Security dir, Prudential Ins Co, Jacksonville, Fla, 56-59; div mgr, Channing Co Inc, 61- Mil Serv: Entered as A/S, Coast Guard, 35, retired as Lt Comdr, 56, after serv in all theatres of war; Expert Rifle, Expert Pistol, Am, European, African, Pac & Asiatic Theatre Medals; Good Conduct Medal; Command Afloat Ribbon. Mem: Southside Bus Mens Club (chmn bd); Retired Commissioned Officers Asn, NFla; Jacksonville Area Golf Asn (bd gov, currently); South Coun CofC (bd mem, currently); Bull Snort Forum Inc (pres & chmn bd). Honors & Awards: Million Dollar Round Table in Investment Sales. Relig: Baptist. Legal Res: 7847 San Jose Blvd Jacksonville FL 32217 Mailing Add: 2809 Art Museum Dr Suite 5 Jacksonville FL 32207

DUNFEY, ROBERT JOHN (D)
Mem, Dem Finance Comt, Maine
b Lowell, Mass, Feb 9, 28; s LeRoy William Dunfey & Catherine Agnes Manning D; m 1950 to Shirley Mae Corey; c Robert J, Jr, Roy, Eileen, Brian & Maryanne. Educ: Keith Acad, Lowell, Mass. Polit & Govt Pos: Advance work, John F Kennedy Campaign, 60; campaign mgr, Curtis for Gov, 66; mem, Maine Recreation Authority, 66-; mgr, Robert F Kennedy Campaign, Maine, 68; campaigned for Robert F Kennedy in Ore, Calif & SDak Primaries, 68; state chmn, Businessmen for Humphrey-Muskie, Maine, 68; deleg, Dem Nat Conv, 68, set up & organized Draft Ted Campaign Hq, 68; mem, Maine Comn on Party Structure & Deleg Selection, 69; mem, Dem Finance Comt, 69-; coordr, Curtis Reelec Campaign, 70; finance dir, Muskie for President, 72; mem finance comt, Hathaway for Sen, 72 & George Mitchell for Gov, 74; dir, Portland Chap, Nat Comt for Sane Nuclear Policy, currently. Bus & Prof Pos: Vpres & dir, corporate develop, Dunfey Family Hotels & Motor Inns of New Eng, 40-; mem, Gtr Boston Real Estate Bd, 69-; pres, Susan L Curtis Found; dir, Depositors Trust Co; state dir, Cystic Fibrosis Found. Mem: NH Asn Realtors; New Eng Innkeepers Asn (dir, 65-); Cumberland Club; KofC; Gtr Portland CofC. Honors & Awards: Maine Hotel Man of Year, 65. Relig: Catholic. Legal Res: Running Tide Rd Cape Elizabeth ME 04107 Mailing Add: 157 High St Portland ME 04101

DUNFORD, CHARLES DONALD (D)
Va State Deleg
b Tazewell Co, Va, Jan 15, 36; s Charles W Dunford & Clara Condle D; m 1962 to Nancy Bowman; c Donna. Educ: Va Polytech Inst & State Univ; Concord Col. Polit & Govt Pos: Va State Deleg, 72- Legal Res: Dial Rock Tazewell VA 24651 Mailing Add: Box 549 Tazewell VA 24651

DUNKLE, FRANK H (R)
Mont State Sen
b Oakmont, Pa, Oct 12, 24; s Frank Harper Dunkle, Sr & Isabel Reed D; m 1947 to Carol Jane Seebart; c Lesley Jane, Richard Frank, Marilyn Diane & Bruce Harper. Educ: Mont State Univ, BS, 50, MS, 55; Sigma Chi. Polit & Govt Pos: Ranger, Nat Park Serv, 51-53; educ asst, Mont Fish & Game Dept, 55-57, chief info & educ div, 59-63 & state dir, 63-72; conserv supvr, Mont Dept Pub Instr, 57-59; Mont State Sen, Dist 15, 75- Mil Serv: Entered as Seaman Recruit, Navy, 43, released as Gunners Mate 2/C, 46, after serv in 116 CB, USS Iowa, SPac, 43-46; Comdr, Naval Res, 46-, Korean Campaign, 50-52. Mem: Mason; Shrine; Am Soc Photogrammetry; Lion Int. Honors & Awards: Water Conserv Award for Mont, Sears Found, 68; ROMCOE Award for Outstanding Environ Achievement, 70; Green Leaf Award, Nature Conservancy, 71; Award, Am Motors, 71. Relig: Protestant. Mailing Add: 1725 Golden Ave Helena MT 59601

DUNLAP, CARTER WESLEY (PAT) (R)
Mem, State Rep Cent Comt Calif
b Licking, Mo, Aug 29, 14; s Edward Franklin David Dunlap & Ethel Mitchell D; m 1949 to Barbara Jeanne Albertson; c Natilee Ann & Carter Wesley, Jr. Educ: Univ of the Pac, AB, 40; Harvard Grad Sch Bus, 40-41; Rho Lambda Phi. Polit & Govt Pos: Mem & deleg, Calif Rep Assembly, 64-69; co chmn, Reagan for Gov, 66, area chmn & mem state adv comt, 70; mem, San Joaquin Rep Cent Comt, 67-68, chmn, 69-; assoc mem, Rep State Cent Comt Calif, 67-68, mem, 68-; chmn, Nixon for Pres, 68; vchmn, Kuechle for Sen Primary Campaign, 68; alt deleg, Rep Nat Conv, 68. Bus & Prof Pos: Pres & chmn, Dunlap Electronics, Inc, 46-; dir,

Advan Ross Corp, Chicago, currently. Mil Serv: Entered as Ens, Navy, 42, released as Lt, 46, after serv in SPac & Serv Squadron, 43-45; Lt, Naval Res; Commendation Ribbon. Mem: Nat Electronic Distributors Asn; Electronic Indust Show Corp; Rotary; Tennis Club; Yosemite Club. Relig: Protestant; deacon, First Congregational Church. Mailing Add: 1460 W Alpine St Stockton CA 95204

DUNLAP, FRED EVERETT (R)
Chmn, Linn Co Rep Party, Kans
b Carlyle, Kans, Oct 21, 03; s A M Dunlap & Sadie Jones D; m 1932 to Ermalea Hart; c Lynn (Mrs E D Marshall) & Wallace H. Educ: Kans State Univ, 2 years; Col Osteop Med & Surg, DO; Delta Tau Delta. Polit & Govt Pos: Chmn, Linn Co Rep Party, Kans, 44-; presidential elector, 48; deleg, Rep Nat Conv, 52; secy-treas, Cong Dist Rep Party, Kans, 52-56, chmn, 60-64; co health officer & dep coroner for Linn Co. Mem: Five Co Health Asn (dir); Rotary Int; Mason (33 degree); Shrine. Relig: Presbyterian. Mailing Add: Pleasanton KS 66075

DUNLAP, JOHN FOSTER (D)
Calif State Sen
s Harry Crum Dunlap & Amy Louise Coombs D; m 1946 to Janet Louise Jack; c Jill Bonner, David Anderson, Peter Trask & Jane Hamilton. Educ: Univ Calif, BA, 46; Univ Calif, Hastings Col of Law, LLB, 49; Zeta Psi. Polit & Govt Pos: Dep city attorney, City of Napa, Calif, 50; sch dist trustee, Mt George Union Sch Dist, 50-61; mem, Napa Co Dem Cent Comt, 56-66, chmn, 62-66; dir, Calif Dem Coun, 60-64; asst dist attorney, Napa Co, 61-; mem, Calif Dem Cent & Calif State Dem Cent Com Exec Bd, 62-66; chmn, Napa Co Ment Health Serv Adv Bd, 64-66; Calif State Assemblyman, Fifth Dist, 67-74; Calif State Sen, Fourth Dist, 75-, mem educ, revenue & taxation, natural resources & wildlife & govt orgn comts, Calif State Senate, currently; deleg, Dem Nat Conv, 72. Mil Serv: Entered as Pvt, Army Air Corps, 42, released as Sgt, 46, after serv at Training Schs & as a combat gunnery instr at Muroc Army Air Base. Mem: Am Legion; Sons of Italy; Sierra Club; NAACP; Am Civil Liberties Union. Legal Res: 2087 Third Ave N Napa CA 94558 Mailing Add: 583 Coombs St Napa CA 94558

DUNLAP, PEGGY MAYFIELD (R)
Mem Exec Comt, Rep Party of Tex
b Austin, Tex, Mar 24, 27; d Ike N Mayfield & Ella Lockwood M; m 1955 to Dr I Ray Dunlap, wid. Educ: Univ Tex, Austin, BS Chem, 48, PhD, 52, postdoctoral, 52-53. Polit & Govt Pos: Precinct chmn, Dallas Co Rep Party, Tex, 68-, secy exec comt, 70-73; mem exec comt, Rep Party of Tex, 71-; deleg & mem platform comt, Rep Nat Conv, 72. Bus & Prof Pos: Spec instr chem, Univ Tex, Austin, 52-53; research assoc, Mobil Research & Develop Corp, Dallas, 53-; dir & secy, Stone Gap Indust Corp, Duncanville, 67- Publ: Co-auth, Waterflooding employing surfactant solution, US Patent 3, 468, 377, 69, Multistep method of waterflooding, US Patent 3, 437, 141, 69 & Pentammineiridium (O), J Am Chem Soc, 53. Mem: Am Chem Soc (women chemists comt, 72-); Mobil Mgt Asn; Sigma Xi; Iota Sigma Pi; Sigma Pi Sigma. Relig: Methodist. Mailing Add: 2018 Elmwood Blvd Dallas TX 75224

DUNLAP, RALPH W (R)
NH State Rep
Mailing Add: 192 N Main St Rochester NH 03867

DUNLAP, RON (R)
Wash State Rep
b South Bend, Ind, Oct 31, 37; s Claude D Dunlap & Thelma Sanner D; m 1966 to Allison Marie Dale; c Marcia & Lynne. Educ: Purdue Univ, BS, 59, MS, 61; Harvard Univ, 61-62. Polit & Govt Pos: Wash State Rep, 75- Bus & Prof Pos: Structural engr, Boeing Co, 62-74, financial analyst, 74- Mem: CofC; Boeing Mgt Asn. Mailing Add: 3129 109th SE Bellevue WA 98004

DUNLOP, JOHN THOMAS
Secy of Labor
b Placerville, Calif, July 5, 14; s John W Dunlop & Antonia Forni D; m 1937 to Dorothy Webb; c John Barrett, Beverly Claire & Thomas Frederick. Educ: Univ Calif, AB, 35; PhD, 39; Univ Chicago, LLD, 68. Polit & Govt Pos: Vchmn, Boston Regional War Labor Bd, 44-45; chmn, Nat Joint Bd Settlement Jurisdictional Disputes Bldg & Construction Indust, 48-57; consult, Off Econ Stabilization, 45-47 & Nat Labor Rels Bd, 48-52; mem, Atomic Energy Labor Panel, 48-53; pub mem, WSB, 50-52; arbitrator, Emergency Bd, 54, 55, 60 & 66; mem, Presidential RR Comt, 60-62 & Missile Sites Labor Comt, 61-67; mem, Presidential Comt Equal Employ Opportunity, 64-65; impartial chmn construction, Indust Joint Conf, 59-68; dir, Cost of Living Coun, 73-74; Secy of Labor, 74- Bus & Prof Pos: Instr, Stanford Univ, 36-37; instr, Harvard Univ, 38-45, assoc prof econ, 45-50, prof econ, 50-74, dean faculty arts & sci, 70-73; mem bd inquiry, Bituminous Coal Indust, 50. Mem: Am Acad Arts & Sci; Am Philos Soc. Polit & Govt Pos: Collective Bargaining: Principles & Cases, 49; Industrial Relations Systems, 58; Labor & the American Community (with D C Bok), 70. Legal Res: 509 Pleasant St Belmont MA 02178 Mailing Add: Dept of Labor Washington DC 20210

DUNMIRE, GEORGE Q (R)
b Kennett, Mo, Feb 6, 15; s John H Dunmire & Maggie Quertermous D; m 1969 to Gordyne McLendon; c Martha Anne (Mrs John Perry White) & Susan H. Educ: Southeast Mo State Col, AB, 35; Univ Tenn Col Med, MD, 40. Polit & Govt Pos: Chmn, Dunklin Co Rep Cent Comt, Mo, formerly. Mil Serv: Entered as 1st Lt, Army, 42, released as Capt, 46, after serv in Med Corps, 42-46. Mem: Dunklin Co Med Soc; Mo & Am Med Asns; Am Acad Gen Practice; Mason (32 degree). Relig: Disciples of Christ. Mailing Add: 504 S Baker Dr Kennett MO 63857

DUNN, AUBREY L (D)
NMex State Sen
b 1928. Educ: NMex Western Univ, 3 years. Polit & Govt Pos: NMex State Sen, currently. Bus & Prof Pos: Newspaper bus mgr. Mil Serv: Navy. Mem: Am Legion; CofC; Lions. Relig: Protestant. Mailing Add: Box 93 Mountain Park NM 88325

DUNN, BARBARA BAXTER (R)
b Danbury, Conn, Oct 24, 26; d William Charles Baxter & Dorthea Oestmann B; div; c Joanne, Kimberly & James Scott. Educ: Univ Conn, BA, 48; Delta Zeta. Polit & Govt Pos: Mem, East Hartford Rep Town Comt, Conn, 52-71, treas, 59, secy, 60; mem, Charter Revision Comn, 62; councilman, East Hartford Town Coun, 63-67; mem, Comn on Necessity & Feasibility of Metrop Govt, Gen Assembly, 65-67; mem personnel bd, East Hartford Ord Comt, 66-67; Conn State Rep, 67-71; Conn Comnr Consumer Protection, 71-75, mem, Gov Cabinet, 71-75, State Adv Coun on Aging, 71-75, State Drug Adv Coun, 71-75 & Conn Comprehensive Health Planning Coun, 71-75; chmn, Health Serv Industs Comt, app by President Nixon, 71-73; mem adv bd, Cost of Living Coun, Wage Bd & Price Bd; chmn state rels comt, US Consumer Prod Adv Coun, 73-; mem, Meat & Poultry Adv Bd, US Dept Agr, 73-75. Bus & Prof Pos: Bd trustees, Conn Educ TV, 73-; vpres sales & consumer rels, Pepsi Cola, Hartford, Springfield & New Haven, 75- Mem: Univ Conn Alumni Coun; League of Women Voters; Gtr Hartford CofC (mem aviation comt, 74-); Greater Hartford Panhellenic Asn. Relig: Episcopal. Mailing Add: 1203 Silver Lane East Hartford CT 06118

DUNN, BRYANT WINFIELD CULBERSON (R)
b Meridian, Miss, July 1, 27; s Aubert C Dunn & Dorothy D Crum D; m 1950 to Betty Jane Prichard; c Charles Winfield, Donna Gayle & Julie Claire. Educ: Univ Miss, BBA, 50; Univ Tenn Col Dent, DDS, 55; Omicron Delta Kappa; Scabbard & Blade; Delta Sigma Pi; Omicron Kappa Upsilon; Kappa Alpha; Delta Sigma Delta. Polit & Govt Pos: Chmn, Shelby Co Rep Party, Tenn, 64-68; vchmn, Tenn Young Rep, 64-65; deleg, Rep Nat Conv, 68 & 72; Gov, Tenn, 71-75; chmn bd trustees, Univ Tenn, 71-; chmn, Educ Comn of the States, 72-73; vchmn, Rep Gov Asn, 72-73; chmn, Tenn-Tombigbee Waterway Develop Authority, 73; ex-officio mem exec comt, Rep Nat Comt, 74- Bus & Prof Pos: Practicing dentist, 56-70. Mil Serv: Entered as Hosp Apprentice 1/C, Navy, 46, released as Pharm Mate 3/C, 47, after serv in Asiatic-Pac Theatre, 47; 2nd Lt, Air Force Res, Inactive, 50-; Good Conduct Medal; Asiatic-Pac Theatre Ribbon. Mem: Am & Tenn Dent Asns; Farm Bur Fedn; Kiwanis. Honors & Awards: Tenn Man of Year, 70 & 71. Relig: Methodist. Legal Res: 249 St Andrews Fairway Memphis TN 38111 Mailing Add: 822 Curtiswood Lane Nashville TN 37204

DUNN, CLARE (D)
Ariz State Rep
Mailing Add: 4751 E Linden Tucson AZ 85712

DUNN, EDGAR M, JR (D)
Fla State Sen
b Daytona Beach, Fla, Feb 14, 39; s Edgar M Dunn, Sr & Charlotte Galloway D; m 1960 to Margaret McCurry; c Wesley R, Kathleen S, Christine M & Julie A. Educ: Univ Fla, BA, 62, JD, 67; Phi Delta Phi; Phi Delta Theta. Polit & Govt Pos: Asst city attorney & prosecutor, Daytona Beach, Fla, 67-70; gen counsel to Gov Reubin Askew, Fla, 71-73; asst state attorney, Seventh Judicial Circuit of Fla, 73-74; mem, Gov Coun on Criminal Justice, Fla, 73-; chmn, Fla Organized Crime Coord Coun, 74-; Fla State Sen, Dist Ten, 74- Bus & Prof Pos: Law Ctr coun mem, Univ Fla Col Law, 74- Mil Serv: Entered as 2nd Lt, Army, 62, released as 1st Lt, after serv in Inf & Counter-Intel, 62-64; Capt, Army Res, 64-73; Army Commendation Medal. Mem: Civic League of Halifax Area; Nat Prosecuting Attorneys Asn; Am, Fla & Volusia Co Bar Asns; Am Legion. Honors & Awards: Outstanding Young Man of Year, Daytona Beach Jaycees, 70; Man of Year, KofC Daytona Beach Coun, 70; Man of Year, Daytona Beach Civitan Club, 70; Meritorious Serv Award, US Nat Guard, 73; Furtherance of Justice Award, Fla Prosecuting Attorneys Asn, 73. Relig: Roman Catholic. Legal Res: 450 N Yonge St Ormond Beach FL 32074 Mailing Add: 523 N Halifax Ave Daytona Beach FL 32018

DUNN, FORREST (D)
La State Rep
Mailing Add: 4001 Jewella Rd Shreveport LA 71109

DUNN, FRANCIS GILL (D)
Chief Justice, SDak State Supreme Court
b Scenic, SDak; s Thomas Bernard Dunn & Mary Gill D; m 1942 to Eldred Elizabeth Wagner; c David, Rebecca (Mrs Smith), Thomas & Carol (Mrs Norbeck). Educ: Dakota State Col, 31-34; Univ SDak, LLB, 37; George Washington Univ, LLM, 48; Delta Theta Phi. Polit & Govt Pos: Secy to US Sen W J Bulow, 41-42; trial attorney, US Dept Justice, 46-50; Asst US Attorney, SDak, 50-54; munic judge, Sioux Falls, 56-59; circuit judge, 59-73; justice, SDak State Supreme Court, 73-74, chief justice, 74- Bus & Prof Pos: Pvt law practice, Madison, SDak, 37-41 & Sioux Falls, 54-56. Mil Serv: Entered as Pvt, Army, transferred to Navy, 42, released as Lt, after serv in Naval Intel, Pac Theatre, 43-46; Lt Comdr, Naval Res, 50. Mem: Am Bar Asn (judicial sect); SDak Bar Asn; VFW; Elks. Relig: Roman Catholic. Legal Res: 320 N Summit Sioux Falls SD Mailing Add: 1100 E Church St Pierre SD 57501

DUNN, JAMES B (R)
SDak State Sen
b Lead, SDak; s William B Dunn & Lucy Mullen D; m 1955 to Elizabeth Ann Lanham; c Susan Marie, Thomas William, Mary Elizabeth & Kathleen Ann. Educ: Black Hills State Col, BS in Bus Admin & Econ, 62. Polit & Govt Pos: State & co chmn, Citizens for Goldwater, 64; deleg, SDak Rep State Conv, 68; SDak State Rep, 70-72; alt deleg, Rep Nat Conv, 72; SDak State Sen, 73- Bus & Prof Pos: Staff asst pub affairs, Homestake Mining Co, 62-64, asst dir pub affairs, 64- Mil Serv: Entered as Pvt, Army, 45, released as Pfc, 47, after serv in Signal Corps, 92nd AFA Bn, 2nd Armored Div. Mem: Am Inst Mining, Metallurgical & Petroleum Engrs; Am Legion (Post Comdr, 50); KofC (Grand Knight, Black Hills Coun, 56); SDak Farm Bur; Lead CofC. Relig: Roman Catholic. Legal Res: 619 Ridge Rd Lead SD 57754 Mailing Add: 203 W Main St Lead SD 57754

DUNN, JAMES R (D)
Ky State Rep
Mailing Add: 5009 Maryman Rd Louisville KY 40258

DUNN, JOHN F (D)
Ill State Sen
Mailing Add: 523 Sheffield Decatur IL 62526

DUNN, RALPH (R)
Ill State Sen
Mailing Add: Box 107 Rte 3 DuQuoin IL 62832

DUNN, ROBERT G (R)
Minn State Sen
wid; five children; m 1972 to Bette J Hendenstrom; c Robert & Mary. Educ: Amherst Col, 48. Polit & Govt Pos: Chmn, Mille Lacs Co Rep Comt, Minn; Minn State Rep, 64-72; Minn State Sen, 73- Bus & Prof Pos: Lumber dealer; bldg contractor. Mil Serv: Marine Corps, 42-46, 50-52. Mem: Princeton Planning Comn (chmn); Mille Lacs Co Red Cross; CofC. Mailing Add: 708 Fourth St Princeton MN 55371

DUNN, THOMAS G **(D)**
NJ State Sen
Mailing Add: State House Trenton NJ 08625

DUNN, VERNON **(D)**
Okla State Sen
Mailing Add: State Capitol Oklahoma City OK 73105

DUNNE, ISABELLE MARY **(D)**
Chmn, Wayne Co Dem Comt, Pa
b Honesdale, Pa, Sept 20, 01; d Thomas J Canivan & Catherine Ryan C; wid; c Margaret C (Mrs McCullough), Patricia (Mrs O'Neill), Rita D (Mrs Soete), Ann Marie (Mrs Bursis) & Thomas F (deceased). Educ: Pa State Col. Polit & Govt Pos: Mem, Wayne Co Dem Comt, Pa, 32-, secy, 32-44 & 46-63, chmn, 63-72 & 75-; co auditor, Wayne Co, 44; dep collector, Internal Revenue Serv, 44-46; regional dir, Pa Fedn Dem Women, Harrisburg, 58-62 & 64-; appraiser, Inheritance Tax Div, Co of Pa, Harrisburg, 59 & 62; alt deleg-at-lg, Dem Nat Conv, 60, deleg-at-lg, 64; pres, Wayne Co Dem Women's Club, 61-66. Bus & Prof Pos: Acct & tax consult, 46- Mem: Northern Wayne Dem Club. Relig: Roman Catholic. Mailing Add: 962 Main St Honesdale PA 18431

DUNNE, JOHN RICHARD **(R)**
NY State Sen
b Baldwin, NY, Jan 28, 30; s Frank Dunne & Virginia Heckman D; m 1958 to Denise C Maher; c Joanne, Peter, Timothy & Hilary. Educ: Georgetown Univ, AB, 51; Yale Law Sch, LLB, 54. Polit & Govt Pos: NY State Sen, 65- Bus & Prof Pos: Partner, Doran, Colleran, O'Hara, Pollio & Dunne, Attorneys-at-Law, 66- Mem: Nassau Co, NY State & Am Bar Asns. Relig: Roman Catholic. Legal Res: 109 Fifth St Garden City NY 11530 Mailing Add: 1461 Franklin Ave Garden City NY 11530

DUNNELL, MILDRED HAZEL **(R)**
Chmn, 12th Dist Rep Party, Mich
b Wampum, Pa, May 15, 11; d George H Evans & Anna Ault E; wid; c Nancy Mae (Mrs Morehouse). Polit & Govt Pos: Womens finance chmn, Macomb Co Rep Party, Mich, 58-62; deleg, Rep State & Co Conv, 58-69; alt deleg-at-lg, Rep Nat Conv, 60, deleg, 72; chmn, Macomb Co Rep Party, formerly; chmn, 12th Dist Rep Party, 69-; first vchmn, Mich Rep State Cent Comt, formerly. Bus & Prof Pos: Pres, Bristol Corp, Detroit, 40-69; secy, Wayne Leasing, Detroit, 67- Mem: Detroit Tooling Asn; Detroit CofC; Nat Tool & Die Mfg Asn; Zonta Club of Detroit. Relig: Protestant. Mailing Add: 34304 Jefferson Mt Clemens MI 48043

DUNNING, JEAN DOUGLAS **(D)**
Mem, Va State Dem Cent Comt
b Lakeland, Fla, Feb 1, 27; d James Gordon Douglas & Louise Deadwyler D; div; c Robin, Merry, Donna, Douglas & Eve. Educ: Fla State Univ, AB, 48; Am Univ & George Washington Univ, 2 years. Polit & Govt Pos: Recording & corresponding secy, Young Dem Clubs DC, 49-53; dir, Region III, Young Dem Clubs Am, 52; conv aide, Dem Nat Conv, 52; staff mem, Vol for Stevenson, Tampa, Fla, 52; staff mem, pub affairs dept, Dem Nat Comt, 59-62; deleg, Va Eighth Cong Dist Dem Conv, 62 & 64; deleg, Va State Dem Conv, 68 & 72; scheduler & press asst, Rawlings for Cong Campaign, 66; co-chmn, Humphrey-Muskie Comt, Stafford, Va, 68; mem steering comts, primary, gen & gubernatorial campaign, 69; chmn, Stafford Co Dem Comt, 69-72; press secy, Rawlings for US Sen Campaign, 70; mem, Eighth Cong Dist Dem Comt, 72-; mem, Va State Dem Cent Comt, 72- Bus & Prof Pos: Research analyst foreign affairs, US Army Security Agency, 48-50; asst clerk, majority staff, US Sen Comt Agr & Forestry, 50-53; tech ed, Research Anal Corp, McLean, Va, 67-70, Ernst & Ernst, Washington, DC, 71 & Northrop, Arlington, 72. Relig: Episcopal. Mailing Add: Rte 2 Box 631 Stafford VA 22554

DUNSMORE, ELIZABETH MARGARET **(D)**
Vt State Rep
b Brockton, Mass, June 24, 13; d Ernest Sigfried Johnson & Margareta Miller J; m 1939 to Donald Collins Dunsmore, wid; c Margaret (Mrs Bernard Coon), George Murray, Dorothy Jean & Carol Elizabeth. Educ: Salem Mass State Col, BScEd, 36. Polit & Govt Pos: Trustee, St Albans Free Libr, St Albans, Vt, 67-; Vt State Rep, 73- Bus & Prof Pos: Recorder, Sylvania Research & Eng, Salem, Mass, 36-37; elem teacher, Rochester, Vt, 37-38; jr high teacher, St Albans, Vt, 38-39; farmer, 39-74. Mem: Order Women Legislators; Vt Ayrshire Asn; Vt Farm Bur; Vt Exten Serv; Vt Libr Trustees Asn (secy, 70-). Relig: Methodist. Legal Res: Dunsmore Rd St Albans Town VT Mailing Add: RFD 1 Swanton VT 05488

DUNTON, FRANKLIN ROY **(R)**
Chmn, Mojave Co Rep Party, Ariz
b North Port, Wash, Aug 3, 21; s Franklin J Dunton & Freida Ferningle Utes D; m 1949 to Peggy Josephine Rogers; c Scott Roy & Debra (Mrs Blake). Polit & Govt Pos: Chmn, Rep Party Finance Comt, Kingman, Ariz, 68-74; chmn, City Bd Adjustments, Kingman, 70-73; vchmn gov adv bd, Off Econ Planning & Develop, 72-75; chmn, Mojave Co Rep Party, 74- Bus & Prof Pos: Pres, Roy Dunton Motors, 49-; pres, Dunton Ins & Leasing, 56-; pres, Well Dunn Inc, 62- Mil Serv: Entered as A/S, Navy, 42, released as PO 1/C, 46, after serv in SE Asia & SPac. Mem: Elks; Rotary; Ariz Auto Dealers Asn; F&AM; Am Legion. Honors & Awards: Ariz First Time Mag Qual Dealer Award, 70. Relig: Methodist. Legal Res: 2651 Ricca Dr Kingman AZ 86401 Mailing Add: 119 Andy Devine Ave Kingman AZ 86401

DUNTON, HAROLD HARTLEY **(R)**
Finance Chmn, Clearwater Co Rep Party, Minn
b Buffalo, Minn, Oct 1, 96; s Arthur Mayo Dunton & Kate Norton D; single. Educ: Crookston Sch Agr, Minn, grad. Polit & Govt Pos: Chmn, Clearwater Co Rep Party, Minn, 65-68, finance chmn, currently. Bus & Prof Pos: Secy, Clearwater Co Farm Bur, 32-62, pres, 62-68, secy, currently; bd mem, Bagley Coop Creamery, 18 years; pres, Bagley Coop Elevator, currently. Mailing Add: Rte 2 Bagley MN 56621

DUNTON, KEITH H **(D)**
Iowa State Rep
b Poseshiek Co near Deep River, Iowa, Mar 20, 15; s Le Roy Dunton & Sarah Faye D; m 1937 to Ethel Cowan; c Cynthia Kay. Educ: Thornburg High Sch, 32. Polit & Govt Pos: Chmn, Keokuk Co Sch Bd, Iowa, 10 years; Iowa State Rep, currently. Bus & Prof Pos: Farming; livestock; former hardware & implement merchant. Mem: Nat Comt for Support of Pub Schs; Mason; Eastern Star; Shrine; Elks. Relig: Methodist; lay leader, Thornburg. Mailing Add: Box 477 Thornburg IA 50255

DU PONT, PIERRE SAMUEL, IV **(R)**
US Rep, Del
b Wilmington, Del, Jan 22, 35; s Pierre Samuel du Pont & Jane Holcomb d; m 1957 to Elise Ravenel Wood; c Elise Ravenel, Pierre S, Benjamin Franklin & Eleuthere Irenee. Educ: Phillips Exeter Acad, 52; Princeton Univ, BSE, 56; Harvard Law Sch, LLB, 63. Polit & Govt Pos: Del State Rep, 68-70; US Rep, Del, 71- Bus & Prof Pos: Tech rep, E I du Pont de Nemours & Co, 63-70. Mil Serv: Entered as Ens, Navy, 57, released as Lt, 60, after serv in Civil Engr Corps. Mem: Del Bar. Relig: Episcopal. Legal Res: DE Mailing Add: 127 Cannon House Off Bldg Washington DC 20515

DUPONT, ROBERT LOUIS (JR)
Dir, Spec Action Off for Drug Abuse Prev, Exec Off President
b Toledo, Ohio; s Robert Louis DuPont & Martha Lancashire; m 1962 to Helen Spink; c Elizabeth (Mrs Hamilton) & Caroline (Mrs McDonald). Educ: Emory Univ, BA, 58; Harvard Med Sch, MD, 63; Sigma Pi Epsilon; Phi Delta Theta. Polit & Govt Pos: Acting assoc dir for community servs, Dept Corrections, 68-70; adminr, Narcotics Treatment Admin, 70-73; dir, Nat Inst on Drug Abuse, Dept Health, Educ & Welfare, 73-; dir, Spec Action Off for Drug Abuse Prevention, Exec Off President, 73- Bus & Prof Pos: Teaching fel in psychiat, Harvard Med Sch, 64-66; asst clin prof psychiat, George Washington Univ, 67-72; assoc clin prof psychiat, 72- Mil Serv: Entered as Surgeon Maj, US Pub Health Serv, 66, released 68, after serv in Nat Insts Health. Publ: Profile of a heroin addiction epidemic and an initial treatment response, New Eng J Med, 285: 320-324, 71; Coming to grips with an urban heroin addiction epidemic, J Am Med Asn, 223: 46-48, 72; co-auth, The dynamics of a heroin addiction epidemic, Science, 181: 716-722, 73. Mem: Am & World Psychiat Asns; Washington Psychiat Soc; Am Pub Health Asn; Pan Am Med Asn. Honors & Awards: Melvin C Hazen Award to the Outstanding Young Man in the DC Govt, Downtown Jaycees, 71, 72; Meritorious Serv Award, DC Govt, 73. Legal Res: 8708 Susanna Lane Chevy Chase MD 20015 Mailing Add: 726 Jackson Pl NW Washington DC 20506

DUPRE, MICHAEL **(D)**
b Lafayette, La, Mar 3, 43; s Hayward Joseph Dupre & Gladys Guillory D; m 1965 to Maxine Green; c Monicita Marie & Jacques Mickel. Educ: Grambling Col, BS, 65; Ariz State Univ, MAEd, 74; Kappa Alpha Psi. Polit & Govt Pos: Deleg, Dem Nat Conv, 72. Bus & Prof Pos: Chmn, Voters League, Eunice, La, 72-75; mem, Polit Action Comt, St Landry Parish, 73-75; vpres, Local Educ Asn, St Landry Parish, 74-75. Mem: Young Voters League; NAACP; Polit Action Comt; La Educ Asn; Sattalite Club. Honors & Awards: Outstanding Young Voters League Mem of the Year, 72. Relig: Baptist. Mailing Add: Rte 2 Box 81-G Eunice LA 70535

DUPREY, STEPHEN MICHAEL **(R)**
NH State Rep
b North Conway, NH, June 1, 53; s William Gerard Duprey, Jr & Natalie McCrillis D; single. Educ: New Col, Fla, grad, 74. Polit & Govt Pos: NH State Rep, 73-, chmn legis admin comt, NH House Rep, currently, mem comt exec dept & admin, mem House Rep caucus comt & mem youth caucus, currently. vchmn, NH Rep State Comt, 73- Bus & Prof Pos: Mem bd trustees, New Col Found Inc. Mem: Youth Horizons Inc; NH State YMCA Youth & Govt Prog (adv comt, 73-75). Relig: Episcopal. Mailing Add: North Conway NH 03860

DUPUIS, JOSEPHINE MABEL **(D)**
Chmn, Hartford Dem Town Comt, Vt
b Boston, Mass, Apr 3, 20; d William Ely (deceased) & Mabel Horne (deceased); m 1947 to Henri Victor Dupuis; c Regina Helen & Michael Henri. Educ: Pierce Secretarial Sch, Boston, 39-41. Polit & Govt Pos: Vchmn, Hartford Dem Town Comt, 58-59, mem, currently, chmn, 59-67 & 74-; justice of peace, Hartford Bd Civil Authority, 58-, vchmn, 62-72; treas, Windsor Co Dem Comt, 65-69, chmn, 70-73, mem, currently; mem, Hartford Tax Study Comt, 69-71; mem, Vt State Dem Comt, 70-73; mem, Hartford Bicentennial Comn. Bus & Prof Pos: Med secy, Dartmouth Eye Inst, Hanover, NH, 41-46; secy, Vet Admin Hosp, White River Junction, Vt, 46-53; court reporter, Hartford Munic Court, 63-67. Relig: Roman Catholic. Legal Res: Gilson Ave Quechee VT 05059 Mailing Add: RFD 1 Box 117 White River Junction VT 05001

DUPUIS, STEVEN J **(D)**
La State Rep
Mailing Add: Rte 1 Box 23 Opelousas LA 70570

DUPUIS, SYLVIO LOUIS **(D)**
Mem, NH Dem State Cent Comt
b Manchester, NH, June 2, 34; s Arthur E Dupuis & Alma Lizotte D; m 1956 to Cecile Dupuis-Pellerin; c Jeanne-Marie, Michelle, Marc & Mary-Carol. Educ: St Anselm's Col, 54-55; Ill Col Optom, BS & OD; Phi Theta Upsilon. Hon Degrees: LLD, Notre Dame Col (NH), 75. Polit & Govt Pos: Mayor, Manchester, NH, 72-75; mem, NH Dem State Cent Comt, 74-; alt deleg, Dem Nat Mid-Term Conf, 74. Bus & Prof Pos: Optometrist, Manchester, NH, 57-71; pres & chief exec officer, Cath Med Ctr, Manchester, 75- Mil Serv: Entered as 2nd Lt, Air Force, 57, released as 1st Lt, 64, after serv in 157th Dispensary. Mem: Manchester Exchange Club; Am Optom Asn; Am Acad Hosp Adminr; Manchester Bank (bd dirs); Currier Art Gallery (dir). Honors & Awards: Beta Sigma Kappa Scholar, 57; Distinguished Serv Award, US Jaycees, 68; Layman of Year, Coun Clergymen, 74; Nat Alumnus of Year, Ill Col Optom, 75. Relig: Catholic. Mailing Add: 451 Coolidge Ave Manchester NH 03102

DURAN, BOBBY F **(D)**
NMex State Rep
b Taos, NMex, Nov 18, 39; s Serapio Duran & Bertha M D; div. Educ: NMex Highlands Univ, 59-62. Polit & Govt Pos: NMex State Rep, Dist 42, 73- Bus & Prof Pos: Owner, Duran's Ins Agency, 64- Mem: Eagles; Jaycees. Mailing Add: PO Box 1684 Taos NM 87571

DURAN, JUNE CLARK **(R)**
Mem, Rep State Cent Comt Calif
b Los Angeles, Calif, June 10, 19; d Willis Winfield Clark & Ethel May King C; m 1940 to Frank Michael Duran; c Timothy Clark & Patricia Ellen. Educ: Santa Monica City Col, 35-37; Univ Calif, Los Angeles, 37-39; Univ Southern Calif, BA, 49; Univ Calif, Berkeley, 53. Polit & Govt Pos: Pres, Hollywood Rep Women's Club, Los Angeles, Calif, 58-60; vpres, Monterey Bay Rep Women's Club, 62-65; mem, Rep State Cent Comt Calif, 62-; mem, Monterey Co Rep Cent Comt, 63-; mem bd dirs, Seventh Dist Agr Asn, 68- Bus & Prof Pos: Dir opers, Calif Test Bur, Los Angeles, 55-59, admin vpres, 59-65; secy-treas, Clark Develop Co, Monterey, 60-65; asst vpres, CTB/McGraw Hill Book Co, 65-; pres, Clark Found, Monterey, Calif, 69- Mem: Am Personnel & Guid Asn; Calif Educ Research Asn; Monterey

Peninsula CofC (bd dirs); Alliance on Aging; Calif Asn Measurement & Guid. Relig: Protestant. Mailing Add: Box 23 Pebble Beach CA 93953

DURANT, PHIL SAMUEL (R)
Chmn, SCent Dist Nine Rep Party, Alaska
b St Charles, Ill, Feb 15, 98; s Harvel Lee Durant & Esther Borg D; m 1946 to Mildred Harriet Sallows; c Phil, Jr & John. Educ: Univ Ill, BS, 23; Nat Jour Soc; Chi Phi. Polit & Govt Pos: Investr, Ill Dept Conserv, 24-25; councilman, mem utility dist, planning & zoning & harbor comn, Seward, Alaska, 53-70; chmn, SCent Dist Nine Rep Party, Alaska, 68-70 & 73- Bus & Prof Pos: Ed & publ, Wheaton Illinoisan newspaper, 23-40. Mil Serv: Entered as Pvt, Army 18, released as Cpl, 19, after serv in 42nd AEF, France, 18-19; Sharpshooter Award. Mem: Mason; Legion; Elks; Coast Guard Auxiliary. Relig: Lutheran. Legal Res: 517 Sixth Ave Seward AK 99664 Mailing Add: Box 737 Seward AK 99664

DURBIN, ELIZABETH D (R)
VChmn, Washtenaw Co Rep Comt, Mich
b Pontiac, Mich, Aug 27, 39; d Frances Ernest Arnoldi & Emma V Dodson A; m 1959 to Harry E Durbin; c Bradley, Laura & Anne. Educ: Univ Mich, 57-59. Polit & Govt Pos: Deleg, Washtenaw Co to State & Co Rep Conv, 72-; mem orgn & ways & means comt, Mich Rep State Cent Comt, Mich, 73-; vchmn, Washtenaw Co Rep Comt, 74- Mailing Add: 3058 Lexington Dr Ann Arbor MI 48105

DUREN, JOANNE M (D)
Wis State Rep
Mailing Add: Box 234 Cazenovia WI 53924

DURFEE, LYNDA MARGARET (R)
Asst Secy, Young Rep Nat Fedn
b Newport, RI, Feb 8, 51; d Ray Huntington Durfee & Iva Guthrie D; single. Educ: Brown Univ, AB, 73. Polit & Govt Pos: Treas, Middletown TAR Club, RI, 65-66, secy, 66-67, co-chmn, 67-68; research asst, Miska for Cong Comt, 70; Nat Committeewoman, RI Fedn Young Rep, 70-71, state co-chmn, 71-73; state secy, RI Fedn Col Rep, 71-72; deleg, Young Rep Nat Conv, 71, 73 & 75; first vpres, New Eng Coun Young Rep, 71-73; Region One co-dir, Young Rep Nat Fedn, 71-73, asst secy, 73-75; exec secy & canvass dir, RI Comt for Reelec of the President, 72; mem, Middletown Rep Town Comt, 72-74; mem, Rep State Representative Dist Comt, Dist 96, 72-74; research asst to speechwriting staff, Exec Off of the President, 73- Mem: DAR; RI Soc Mayflower Descendents; Am Conservative Union; Young Am for Freedom; Sino-Am Coord Coun (asst secy-treas). Honors & Awards: RI State Scholar, 69. Legal Res: 46 Bliss Mine Rd Middletown RI 02840 Mailing Add: Young Rep Nat Fedn 310 First St SE Washington DC 20003

DURFEE, RAYMOND M (R)
RI State Sen
b Cranston, RI, Apr 25, 22; m to Elizabeth G. Educ: Brown Univ, 44. Polit & Govt Pos: RI State Rep, 63-71; RI State Sen, 71- Bus & Prof Pos: Mgr & treas, Durfee Hardware, Inc. Mil Serv: Entered as Ens, Navy, 42, released as Lt (jg), 46, after serv as asst to Pac Fleet Disbursing Off; Lt (sg), Naval Res, Jacksonville Naval Air Sta, Fla, 51-52. Mailing Add: 29 Glenmere Dr Cranston RI 02920

DURGIN, LENA C (R)
Maine State Rep
Mailing Add: 6 Cook St Kittery ME 03904

DURHAM, RICHARD C (D)
Chmn, PR Dem Party
Mailing Add: Banco de Ponce Bldg Suite 713 Ponce de Leon Ave Santurce PR 00907

DURHAM, STEVEN JACKSON (R)
Colo State Rep
b Wichita, Kans, July 15, 47; s B Jack Durham & Marcine Gilberson D; single. Educ: Univ Northern Colo, BA, 69; Univ Miss, 71-72. Polit & Govt Pos: Colo State Rep, Dist 22, 75- Bus & Prof Pos: Mgr Cottage Corp, 64- Mem: Manitou Springs CofC (mem bd dirs); Christmas Unlimited (chmn bd); Colorado Springs CofC (mem travel marketing comt). Mailing Add: 1514 W Cheyenne Blvd Colorado Springs CO 80906

DURKAN, MARTIN JAMES (D)
b Great Falls, Mont, June 30, 23; s Martin James Durkan & Jen O'Neill D; m 1951 to Lorraine Noonan; c Kathleen, Martin James, III, Ryan, Jenny, Matthew, Timothy & Meagan. Educ: Univ Wash Law Sch, LLB, 53. Polit & Govt Pos: Legal counsel to speaker, Wash House Rep, 55, Wash State Rep, 56-57; Wash State Sen, 58-74; deleg, Dem Nat Mid-Term Conf, 74. Bus & Prof Pos: Attorney. Mil Serv: Enlisted in Marine Corps & transferred to Navy, World War II, released as Ens, after serv in Atlantic, Mediter & Pac Theatres. Mem: Seattle & Am Bar Asns; DAV; Am Legion; VFW. Legal Res: 4049 W Lake Sammish Blvd South Issaquah WA 98027 Mailing Add: 1212 Pacific Bldg Seattle WA 98104

DURKIN, JOHN A (D)
Polit & Govt Pos: Cand US Sen, 74. Mailing Add: 60 Lenz St Manchester NH 03102

DURNELL, GERALD LEE (R)
Mo State Rep
b Santa Paula, Calif, Apr 27, 42; s Homer Robert Durnell & Iva Lucile Van Hooser D; m 1963 to Oleta Pearl Werner; c Meranie Elizabeth, John Christopher & Amber Katherine. Educ: Southwest Mo State Univ, BS, 65, pre-med, 71-72; Kappa Alpha Order. Polit & Govt Pos: Mo State Rep, 149th Legis Dist, 73- Bus & Prof Pos: TV prod, KYTV, Springfield, Mo, 60-61; radio announcer, KICK, Springfield, 61-65; pres, Coffee Cup Prod, 72- Mil Serv: Entered as 2nd Lt, Army, 65, released as Capt, after serv in 245th Sac, 122nd Avn Co & 212th Combat Spt Avn Bn, 66-71; Capt, Mo Nat Guard; Bronze Star, Air Medal & 11 Oak Leaf Clusters, Army Aviator; Defense Medal; Vietnam Serv Medal; Vietnam Campaign & three Stars. Mem: Am Army Aviation Asn; Am Aviation Hist Soc; AF&AM; Springfield Advert Club; Mason (Melville Chap, Dadeville). Relig: Protestant. Mailing Add: 825 E Portland Springfield MO 65807

DURNO, EDWIN RUSSELL (R)
b Albany, Ore, Jan 26, 99; s John P Durno & Clara Estell Waddell D; m 1929 to Evelyn Baker; c Anne (Mrs Richard Hensley), Janet (Mrs Brian Stringer) & Kaye (Mrs Ronald Louis). Educ: Univ Ore, BS; Harvard Med Sch, MD, cum laude; Mass Gen Hosp, surg training; Phi Delta Theta; Nu Sigma Nu. Polit & Govt Pos: Mem, State Bd Med Examr, Ore, 47-59; Ore State Sen, 59-60, mem ways & means comt, fiscal comt & taxation comt, 59-60; alt deleg, Rep Nat Conv, 60, deleg, 64; US Rep, Ore, 61-63, mem interior comt, 61-63. Mil Serv: Sgt, Army, 18, reentered serv as Capt, Army, 42, released as Maj, 45, after serv in First Auxiliary Corps, ETO; Purple Heart; 3 Campaign Ribbons. Mem: Nat Med Soc; Am Col Surgeons; Mason; Scottish Rite; Shrine. Honors & Awards: All-Am basketball, Univ Ore, 21. Relig: Protestant. Mailing Add: 2512 E Main St Medford OR 97501

DURRETTE, WYATT BEAZLEY, JR (R)
Va State Deleg
b Richmond, Va, Feb 21, 38; s Wyatt Beazley Durrette, Sr & Beulah C Showker D; m 1962 to Cheryn Coller; c Deborah, Dawn, Dea & Wyatt, III. Educ: Va Mil Inst, BS in Math, 61; Washington & Lee Univ, LLB, 64; Johns Hopkins Univ, MA in Polit Sci, 66; Omicron Delta Kappa; Pi Sigma Alpha. Polit & Govt Pos: Exec dir, Youth for Goldwater, Md, 64; Va State Deleg, 71-; state co-chmn, Young Voters for the President, Va, 72. Bus & Prof Pos: Attorney, 69- Mil Serv: Entered as 1st Lt, Air Force, 66, released as Capt, 69, after serv in 432nd Combat Support Group, Pac Air Command, 68-69. Mem: Va Trial Lawyers Asn; Vienna Jaycees (dir, 69-); VFW (chaplain, 71-); Northern Va Asn for Retarded Children; Northern Va Conserv Coun. Honors & Awards: Outstanding Young Man, Vienna Jaycees, 70. Relig: Protestant. Mailing Add: 9849 Marcliff Ct Vienna VA 22180

DURYEA, PERRY BELMONT, JR (R)
Speaker, NY State Assembly
b East Hampton, NY, Oct 18, 21; s Perry Belmont Duryea & Jane Stewart D; m 1944 to Elizabeth Ann Weed; c Lynn & Perry B, III. Educ: Colgate Univ, BA; Delta Upsilon. Hon Degrees: LLD, Dowling Col, 63, Southampton Col, 68; LHD, Siena Col, 72. Polit & Govt Pos: Mem, Suffolk Co & NY State Rep Comts & Montauk Fire Dept, pres bd trustees, Montauk Pub Schs, 54-60; NY State Assemblyman, 61-, Minority Leader, NY State Assembly, 66-68 & 74- & Speaker, 69-74; deleg, Rep Nat Conv, 68 & 72; mem, Long Island State Park Comn, 63-, pres, 63-69; mem, Bethpage Park Authority, 63-, pres, 63-69; mem, Jones Beach State Pkwy Authority, 63-, pres, 63-69; vpres, NY State Const Conv, 67. Bus & Prof Pos: Pres, Perry B Duryea & Sons. Mil Serv: Entered as Ens, Navy, 42, released as Lt Comdr, 45, after serv in Naval Air Transport, Pac Theatre; Atlantic, Pac & Philippine Campaign Ribbons. Mem: CofC; Lions; Am Legion; VFW; Nat Conf State Legis Leaders (exec comt). Relig: Presbyterian. Mailing Add: Old Montauk Hwy Montauk NY 11954

DURYEE, HAROLD TAYLOR (R)
b Willoughby, Ohio, Feb 11, 30; s Gerald Fancher Duryee & Margaret Grace Taylor D; m 1966 to Phyllis Annette Painter. Educ: Kenyon Col, BA, 51; Archon. Polit & Govt Pos: Precinct committeeman, Stark Co Rep Cent Comt, Ohio, 58-72; mem, North Canton City Planning Comn, 58-65, vchmn, 61-67; chmn, North Canton City Charter Comn, 60; chmn, North Canton Rep Comt, 60-72; mem, Stark Co Rep Exec Comt, 60-72; pres, Stark Co Young Rep Club, 61-62; campaign chmn for reelec of US Rep Frank T Bow, Ohio, 62; state chmn, Ohio League of Young Rep Clubs, 62-63; vchmn, Young Rep Nat Fedn, 63-65; campaign coordr, US Rep, Oliver P Bolton, 64; legis & field dir, Ohio Rep State Cent & Exec Comt, 65-70; exec asst to Ohio Rep State Chmn, 70- Bus & Prof Pos: Dist exec, Mahoning Valley Coun, Boy Scouts, Youngstown, 51-56; off mgt, Nationwide Ins Co, Canton, 56-64. Mem: Am Acad Polit & Social Sci; North Canton Area CofC. Honors & Awards: North Canton Rotary Club Civic Serv Award in field of govt; North Canton Jaycees Distinguished Serv Award. Relig: Episcopal. Legal Res: 6220 Fernwood NW Canton OH 44718 Mailing Add: Rep State Headquarters Suite 3300 50 W Broad St Columbus OH 43215

DUSSAULT, ANN MARY (D)
Mont State Rep
b Missoula, Mont, May 23, 46; d Edward T Dussault & June R Myers D; single. Educ: Seattle Univ, 63-64, 65-67; Univ Mont, 64-65, 67-68; Mich State Univ, BA in music therapy, 71. Polit & Govt Pos: Mont State Rep, 75- Bus & Prof Pos: Primary therapist perceptual motor prog, St Lawrence Hosp Community Ment Health Ctr, Lansing, Mich, 71-73, acting coordr child & adolescent serv, 72-73; coordr, Child Develop Ctr, Missoula, Mont, 75- Mem: Nat & Regional Asns for Music Therapy; Child Abuse Educ Team (state app); Title IV Adv Coun (state app). Relig: Catholic. Mailing Add: Rte 2 Mullan Rd Missoula MT 59801

DUTKO, DENNIS M (D)
Mich State Rep
Mailing Add: 29338 Hoover Rd Apt 338 Warren MI 48093

DUTREMBLE, RICHARD DONALD (D)
b Biddeford, Maine, Oct 1, 31; s Honore Dutremble (deceased) & Rose Anna Binette D (deceased); m 1954 to Anne Marie Seymour; c Pamela, Judith, Richard H, Kenneth & David. Educ: St Louis High Sch, Biddeford, grad. Polit & Govt Pos: Sheriff, York Co, Maine, 63-; chmn, Biddeford City Dem Comt, 67; deleg, Dem Nat Conv, 68 & 72. Mil Serv: Entered as Pvt, Army, 55, released as Cpl, 57, after serv in Southern European Task Force, Hq Italy, 56-57. Mem: Elks; KofC; Eagles; Amvets. Relig: Catholic. Mailing Add: 3 Greenwood Ave Biddeford ME 04005

DUTTON, FREDERICK G (D)
b Julesburg, Colo, June 16, 23; s Dr F G Dutton & Lucy Elizabeth Parker D; m to Nancy Hogan; c Christopher, Lisa, Eve, Stacy & Christina. Educ: Univ Calif, BA, 46; Stanford Law Sch, LLB, 48; Delta Tau Delta. Polit & Govt Pos: Chmn, Stevenson-Kefauver Presidential Campaign, Southern Calif, 56; chief asst attorney gen, Calif, 57-58; state dir, Brown for Gov Campaign, 58; exec secy to Gov, Calif, 59-60; dep nat chmn, Citizens for Kennedy & Johnson, 60; spec asst to President John F Kennedy & secy to the Cabinet, 61-62; Asst Secy of State, US Dept of State, 62-64; Regent, Univ Calif, 62-; dir research & planning, Presidential Campaign, Dem Nat Comt, 64 & dir platform comt; personal campaign asst to Robert F Kennedy, Presidential Primaries, 68; personal campaign asst to Sen George McGovern, Presidential Primaries, 72. Bus & Prof Pos: Assoc, Wilson, Kirkbridge, Wilson & Harzeld, 49-50; chief asst gen counsel, Southern Counties Gas Co of Calif, 52-56; organizing dir, John F Kennedy Mem Libr Oral Hist Proj, 63-65; partner, Dutton, Zumas & Wise, Attorneys, DC, 64-; exec dir, Robert F Kennedy Mem Found, 68-70; chmn, Nat Town Meetings, 74- Mil Serv: Entered as Pvt, Army, 42, released as 1st Lt, 45, after serv in Inf, Europe; Ger Prisoner of War; serv as 1st Lt, 51-52, Judge Adv Gen Corps, Japan, Korean Conflict; Bronze Star; Combat Inf Badge; Purple Heart; 3 Battle Stars. Publ: American Politics in the 1970's, McGraw-Hill, 71; Election Guide to '72, Playboy Press, 72. Mailing Add: 1990 M St NW Washington DC 20036

262 / DUTTON

DUTTON, JUDSON DUNLAP (R)
Chmn, Morgan Co Rep Party, Ind
b Martinsville, Ind, Nov 13, 08; s Harry Freeman Dutton & Hazel Dunlap D; m 1932 to Nina Pauline Hayes; c Carolyn Hayes. Educ: Wabash Col, AB, 30; Beta Theta Pi. Polit & Govt Pos: Rep precinct committeeman, Ind, 36-48; city councilman, Martinsville, 40-43; chmn, Morgan Co Rep Party, 46-; clerk & treas, Martinsville, 62- Bus & Prof Pos: Mgr, Artesian Laundry, 34-62. Mem: Kiwanis; Mason; Scottish Rite; Elks; Moose. Relig: Presbyterian. Legal Res: 410 S Jefferson St Martinsville IN 46151 Mailing Add: PO Box 407 City Hall Martinsville IN 46151

DUVAL, CLAUDE BERWICK (D)
La State Sen
b Houma, La, Oct 24, 14; s Stanwood R Duval & Mamie Richardson D; m 1938 to Betty Bowman; c Dorothy. Educ: La State Univ, Baton Rouge, 1 year; Tulane Univ Col Law, LLB; Pi Kappa Alpha. Polit & Govt Pos: La State Sen, 20th Sen Dist, 68- Bus & Prof Pos: Attorney, Houma, 37-; chmn bd dirs, First Nat Bank & Trust Co of Houma; mem bd dirs, Pelican Lake Oyster & Packing Co, Ltd & Duval, Whitney Stevenson, Inc; sr partner, Duval, Arceneaux, Lewis & Funderburk, Attorneys-at-law; mem bd dirs, Sundulyn Corp, 69- Mil Serv: Entered as Pfc, Marines, 42, released as Capt, 45, after serv in Co K, Third Bn, 23rd Marines, Fourth Marine Div, four Pac Theater land operations, 42-45, Res, 44-55, Lt Col (Ret); Bronze Star & Am Defense Medals; Purple Heart Medal, Iwo Jima; Letter of Commendation; two Presidential Unit Citations; Asiatic Pac Ribbon with four Stars. Mem: Am Judicature Soc; Am Legion (Past State Comdr); La State CofC; Elks; Mason. Honors & Awards: Outstanding Young Man Award, Jr CofC, 47. Relig: Episcopal. Legal Res: 18 Country Club Dr Houma LA 70360 Mailing Add: 504 Belanger St Houma LA 70360

DUVAL, CLIVE L, 2D (D)
Va State Sen
b New York, NY, June 20, 12; m 1940 to Susan Holdrege Bontecou; c Susan, Clive III, David & Daniel. Educ: Yale Univ, BA & LLB; Phi Beta Kappa; ed, Yale Law J. Polit & Govt Pos: Asst Gen Counsel of Defense, Washington, DC, 53-55; gen counsel, US Info Agency, 55-59; Va State Deleg, 66-72; Va State Sen, Arlington & Fairfax Co, 72- Bus & Prof Pos: Lawyer. Mil Serv: Lt Comdr, Naval Res, 42-46. Mem: Arlington & Fairfax CofC; Nat Press Club of Washington; Am Legion; VFW (Judge Advocate, Post 8241, McLean, Va, 66-). Honors & Awards: Award by Nat Wildlife Fedn as Top State Legislator in US in Field of Conserv Achievement, 69. Relig: Presbyterian. Legal Res: 1214 Buchanan St McLean VA 22101 Mailing Add: 2007 N 15th St Arlington VA 22201

DUVAL, MERLIN K (INDEPENDENT)
Polit & Govt Pos: Asst secy health & sci affairs, Dept Health, Educ & Welfare, 70-72. Bus & Prof Pos: Dean col med & dir Ariz Med Ctr, Univ Ariz, 64-72, vpres health sci, 73- Mailing Add: Col of Med Univ of Ariz Tucson AZ 85724

DUVALL, CHARLES RAYMOND, JR (D)
Mem, Va State Dem Cent Comt
b Frederick Co, Va, June 14, 44; s Charles Raymond Duvall, Sr & Emma Swimley D; m 1969 to Glenne Withers. Educ: Randolph-Macon Col, BA, 66. Polit & Govt Pos: Mem, Frederick Co Dem Exec Comt, Va, 67-68; deleg, Va Dem State Conv, 68, 71 & 72; treas, Winchester-Frederick Co Young Dem, 69-70, vpres, 70 & 71; membership chmn, Winchester Dem Comt, 71-72, treas, 72-; coordr mayor & six councilmen elec, Winchester, 72; deleg, Dem Nat Conv, 72; chmn, Va Seventh Dist Young Dem Club, 72-; mem, Va Seventh Dist Cent Comt, 73-; mem, Va Dem State Cent Comt, 73- Bus & Prof Pos: Teacher, D G Cooley Elem Sch, Clarke Co, Va, 67-68, asst prin, 68-70; personnel dir, Educ Tour Consult, Winchester, summers 68-70; in family auction bus, 70-; polit consult, 70-; tour dir, Nat Educ Asn, 72. Mem: Northwestern Community Action Inc (bd dirs, 72-). Relig: Methodist. Mailing Add: 327 N Braddock St Winchester VA 22601

DUVALL, LESLIE (R)
Ind State Sen
b Indianapolis, Ind, Feb 23, 24; s John L Duvall & Maud E Buser D; m 1945 to Carolyn S Coxen; c John Allen & David Blanton. Educ: Butler Univ, AB, 48; Ind Univ, LLB, 49; Sigma Delta Kappa; Sigma Chi. Polit & Govt Pos: Chmn, 11th Dist Young Rep, Ind, 54; probate comnr, Marion Co Probate Court, 55-56; chmn, Ind State Young Rep, 57-58; attorney examr, Ind Pub Serv Comn, 57-58, comnr, 58-60; committeeman, Rep Precinct, 58-; chmn, Ind Draft Goldwater Comt, 63, Ind Goldwater for President Comt, 64 & Ind Citizens for Goldwater Comt, 64; Ind State Sen, currently. Mil Serv: Pvt, Army, 43, 1st Lt, Judge Adv Gen Corps, 55. Mem: Sigma Delta Kappa; Indianapolis Bar Asn; Am Legion. Relig: Presbyterian. Mailing Add: 731 Nottingham Ct Indianapolis IN 46240

DVORAK, CHARLES VINCENT (D)
Chmn, Dist 36 Dem Orgn, NDak
b Dickinson, NDak, Oct 4, 17; s Vincent Dvorak & Mary Kovash D; m 1939; c Edith (Mrs Ludwig Meduna), Robert, Richard, Susan & Sandra. Educ: Grade & 2 years correspondence sch. Polit & Govt Pos: Co chmn, Dem Party, NDak, 58-68; co comnr, NDak, 61-68; chmn, Dist 36 Dem Orgn, NDak, 68- Bus & Prof Pos: Dir, Farmers Union Oil, Killdeer, NDak, 55-, Dunn Co Farmers Union, 61-, Consol Tel & Coop, Dickinson, 64- & West Plains Electric Coop, Dickinson. Mem: Elks; Eagles; KofC; US & State Farmers Unions. Honors & Awards: Community Leader of America, 68. Relig: Catholic. Mailing Add: Manning ND 58642

DWIGHT, DONALD RATHBUN (R)
b Holyoke, Mass, Mar 26, 31; s William Dwight, Sr & Dorothy Rathbun D; m 1952 to Susan N Russell; c Dorothy, Laura, Eleanor, Arthur & Stuart. Educ: Princeton Univ, AB, 53. Polit & Govt Pos: Mem, South Hadley Town Meeting, Mass, 57-69; deleg, Mass Rep Pre-Primary Conv, 60 & 62; assoc comnr, Mass Dept Pub Works, 63-66; Comnr of Admin, Mass, 69-70, Lt Gov, 71-75. Bus & Prof Pos: Reporter, Holyoke Transcript-Telegram, Mass, 55-57, asst to publ, 57-63, assoc publ, 66-69; dir, Greenfield Recorder; dir, Concord Monitor, NH, 66-; trustee, Community Savings Bank Holyoke, 59-72. Mil Serv: Entered as 2nd Lt, Marine Corps, 53, released as Capt, 55, after serv in 3rd Div, Marine Corps Res, 55-61. Mem: Citizens' Scholar Found of Mass (hon chmn, 72-); Sigma Delta Chi; Mass Newspaper Info Serv; Mass Audubon Soc. Relig: Episcopal. Mailing Add: 46 Decatur Lane Wayland MA 01778

DWIGHT, JAMES S, JR (R)
b Pasadena, Calif, Mar 9, 34; s James S Dwight, Sr & Natalie Phelps D; m 1953 to Elsa Fae Hardy; c Catherine, Janet, Dianne & James S, III. Educ: Pomona Col; Univ Southern Calif, BS, 56; Beta Alpha Psi; Phi Delta Theta. Polit & Govt Pos: Chief dep dir, Calif Dept Finance, 66-72; assoc dir, Off Mgt & Budget, Exec Off of the President, 72-73; adminr, Social & Rehabilitation Serv, Dept Health, Educ & Welfare, 73-75. Bus & Prof Pos: CPA, Haskins & Sells, 55-59; controller, Sunkist Growers, Inc, Calif, 59-66; acct, currently. Mem: Calif Soc CPA; Am Inst CPA. Honors & Awards: Outstanding Young Men, US Jaycees, 66. Mailing Add: 4109 N River St Arlington VA 22207

DWINELL, LANE (R)
b Nov 14, 06; m 1932 to Elizabeth Cushman. Educ: Dartmouth Col, AB; Amos Tuck Sch, MBA; Theta Delta Chi. Hon Degrees: DCS, Suffolk Univ; MA, Dartmouth Col; LLD, Univ NH; DCL, New Eng Col. Polit & Govt Pos: Mem, State Bd Educ, NH; speaker, NH House Rep & pres, NH Senate, formerly; deleg, Rep Nat Conv, 52-56, 68 & 72; Gov, NH, 55-58; Asst Secy of State, 59-60; asst adminr, Agency Int Develop, 69-71. Bus & Prof Pos: Pres, Carter & Churchill Co, Inc, 36-66; pres, Nat Bank of Lebanon, 60-67, chmn bd, 67- Mem: SAR; Rotary Int; Moose; Grange. Relig: Congregational. Mailing Add: 94 Bank St Lebanon NH 03766

DWINELL, RICHARD J (D)
Mass State Rep
Mailing Add: State Capitol Boston MA 02133

DWORAK, DONALD N (R)
Nebr State Sen
b David City, Nebr, Dec 3, 34; s Anthony R Dworak (deceased) & Matilda M Morbach D; m 1963 to Judith Lynne Kosch; c Donald Paul & Anthony John. Educ: Univ Nebr, Lincoln, BSEd. Polit & Govt Pos: Nebr State Sen, 75- Bus & Prof Pos: Group supvr, Travelers Ins Co, 59-65; research coordr, Bankers Life Nebr, 65-69; pres, Nebraskaland Allied Securities & Nebraskaland Allied Agency, 68- Mem: Am Col Chartered Life Underwriters; Optimists; Elks; KofC (4 degree); Friends of Music (bd dirs). Legal Res: 2973 N Parklane Columbus NE 68601 Mailing Add: PO Box 818 Columbus NE 68601

DWORKIN, RONALD MYLES (D)
b Worcester, Mass, Dec 11, 31; s David Dworkin & Madelaine Tabor D; m 1958 to Betsy Ross; c Anthony & Jennifer. Educ: Harvard Col, BA, 53, Law Sch, JD, 57; Oxford Univ, BA, 55; Phi Beta Kappa. Hon Degrees: MA, Yale Univ, 64 & Oxford Univ, 69. Polit & Govt Pos: Co-chmn, Dem Abroad, 72-; mem, Dem Nat Charter Comn, 74. Bus & Prof Pos: Prof law, Yale Law Sch, 61-69; prof jurisprudence, Oxford Univ, 69- Publ: Taking Rights Seriously, Duckworth, 76. Mailing Add: 17 Chester Row London England

DWYER, BERNARD J (D)
NJ State Sen
Mailing Add: 31 Mason Dr Edison NJ 08817

DWYER, CLAIRE BUCKLEY (D)
Mem, Mass Dem State Comt
b Somerville, Mass, May 9, 30; d Hugh E Buckley & Grace M Fife B; m 1948 to James J Dwyer; c James J, II. Educ: Col. Polit & Govt Pos: Mem, Mass Dem State Comt, Seventh Middlesex Dist, 64-; exec secy, Humphrey Campaign, 68; deleg, Dem Nat Conv, 68; mem, Mass Electoral Col, 68; clerk, Middlesex Co Court, currently; alt deleg, Dem Nat Mid-Term Conf, 74. Mem: DAV Auxiliary; Dem Women on Wheels; Fedn Dem Women, Mass; Mass State & Co Employees Asn. Relig: Catholic. Mailing Add: 16 Frederick Dr Woburn MA 01801

DWYER, DONALD R (D)
NH State Rep
Mailing Add: Box 666 Merrimack NH 03054

DWYER, FLORENCE P (R)
b Reading, Pa; m to M Joseph Dwyer (deceased); c one son. Polit & Govt Pos: Mem, NJ Legis, 49-56; US Rep, NJ, 56-72, ranking minority leader govt oper comt, US House Rep, until 72; mem, US Adv Comn on Intergovt Rels, 59- Mem: NJ Fedn Bus & Prof Women's Clubs. Mailing Add: 320 Verona Ave Elizabeth NJ 07208

DWYER, HENRY W (R)
NY State Assemblyman
Mailing Add: 81 Cypress St Floral Park NY 11001

DWYER, JOHN WILLIAM (R)
b Williston, NDak, Jan 2, 48; s Tim Dwyer & Marjorie Skarsgard D; m 1970 to Barbara Lynn Greene; c Dana Lynn. Educ: St Olaf Col, BA, 70; Univ NDak Sch Law, Burtness scholar, 70, JD, 73; Deans List, 71 & 73, articles ed, NDak Law Rev, 72-73; Sigma Delta. Polit & Govt Pos: Legis intern, former US Rep Tom Kleppe, summer 69; col coordr, NDak Rep Party, 69-70, new voter chmn, 71-73; deleg, Rep Nat Conv, 72; legis asst, US Rep Mark Andrews, 73-74, admin asst, 75- Bus & Prof Pos: Intern & comt counsel, NDak Const Conv, 72; trustee in bankruptcy, Gordon Thompson, Bankruptcy Judge, 72-73. Mil Serv: 1st Lt, Air Force, 73, serv in 321 CS Group, Judge Adv, Strategic Air Command; 1st Lt, Air Force Res, 70; Judge Adv Gen Officer, Air Nat Guard, currently. Publ: Judicial selection in North Dakota—is constitutional revision necessary?, 48 NDak Law Rev 327, winter 72. Mem: Elks; Phi Alpha Delta; Am & NDak Bar Asns; House Admin Asst Asn. Honors & Awards: Am Jurisprudence Award, NDak Law Sch, 71. Relig: Lutheran. Legal Res: Alexander ND 58831 Mailing Add: 2411 Rayburn House Off Bldg Washington DC 20515

DWYER, THEODORE JOHN (R)
Chmn, Jackson Co Bd Comnr, Mich
b Jackson, Mich, Nov 26, 26; s William A Dwyer & Mildred Jennings D; m 1950 to Anne Marie Bakken; c Elizabeth, Martha Mary & Laura Jean. Educ: Jackson Community Col, 46-48; Univ Mich, 48-49; Cent Mich Univ, 50-51. Polit & Govt Pos: Supvr, Liberty Twp, Jackson Co, Mich, 61-68; deleg, Rep Nat Conv, 68; chmn, Jackson Co Bd Comnr, Mich, 65-; chmn, Jackson Co Rep Party, formerly. Bus & Prof Pos: Ins salesman, John Dobben Agency, 61-69. Mil Serv: Entered as Pvt, Air Force, 43, released as Cpl, 45, after serv in Am Theatre. Mem: Am Legion; Jackson Co Fair Bd; Jackson Hillsdale Community Ment Health Serv Bd (chmn). Relig: Roman Catholic. Mailing Add: 6211 Springbrook Rd Horton MI 49246

DWYER, WILLIAM F (R)
b Rochester, NY, Mar 30, 35; s Leo F Dwyer & L Mayfield Costello D; m 1975 to Constance M Drath; c Elizabeth Clark & Geoffrey Cooke. Educ: Princeton Univ; Univ Rochester; Delta Kappa Epsilon. Polit & Govt Pos: Campaign mgr, Monroe Co Rep Comt, NY, 61, chmn,

70-72; chmn, Monroe Co Rep Forum, 62-63; admin asst to US Rep Frank Horton, NY, 63-67; deleg, Rep Nat Conv, 72; presidential elector, 72; consult, US Dept Labor, 72; news coordr, Inaugural Comt, 72-73; spec asst to Asst Secy Labor, John H Stender, 73-74; commun dir, Gen Serv Admin, 74. Bus & Prof Pos: Staff announcer, WGVA, Geneva, NY, 54-55; mem news staff, WBBF, Rochester, 55-56; mem news staff, WHAM, Rochester, 56-61; vpres & dir, Astro Agency, 61-62; vpres pub affairs & dir, Darcy Commun, Inc, 67-71; partner, Rochester News Serv, 71-73; asst to pres, Tobacco Inst, Washington, DC, 75- Mem: Pub Rels Soc Am; Am Fedn TV & Radio Artists; AFL-CIO; Capitol Hill Club; Gov Club. Mailing Add: 4450 MacArthur Blvd NW Washington DC 20007

DYAL, KEN W (D)
Wid; remarried to Barbara Winkelman; c Kyrna Gay (Mrs Gordon Lyman), Karen Rae (Mrs Ken Cory), Timothy & Terence. Polit & Govt Pos: Secy, Co Bd Supvr; chmn, Mayor's Adv Planning Comt; postmaster, San Bernardino, 47-54; former mem bd dirs, San Bernardino Co Supplemental Water Asn; campaign mgr for US Rep Harry R Sheppard; mem adv bd, State Feather River Proj Asn & Comts; US Rep, 33rd Cong Dist, Calif, 64-67; mem pub works comt, US House Rep; regional dir, US Post Off, San Francisco, 65-69, regional progs coordr, Western Region, 69-70. Bus & Prof Pos: Mem bd dirs, Los Angeles Airways, Inc, 58-64; former mem bd dirs, Nat Orange Show, former chmn govt exhibits div & entertainment of guests comt, aide, Citrus Inst & Co Bd Trade events, secy-mgr & treas, 60-64; trustee, Patton State Hosp. Mil Serv: Lt Comdr, Naval Res, 42-46. Mem: Kiwanis; Retired Postmasters Asn; Am Legion. Honors & Awards: DAR Annual Citizen Award; Bd of Trade Award for Meritorious Serv to Co; Citizen of the Month Award, Exchange Club. Relig: Latter-day Saint. Mailing Add: 6907 Dwight Way San Bernardino CA 92404

DYAR, ROSWELL E (R)
Mem, Maine Rep State Comt
b Strong, Maine, June 19, 31; s Colin Dyar & Orra Welch D; m 1951 to Ethel Haley; c Walter, Thomas, Colin & Scott. Educ: Becker Col, AS, 51; Phi Theta Pi. Polit & Govt Pos: Mem, Co Rep Comt, Maine, 64-; deleg, Young Rep Conv, 65 & deleg & mem platform comt, 67; chmn, Maine Fedn Young Rep, 66-67; mem, Second Cong Dist Rep Comt, 68-69; Maine State Rep, 69-74; vchmn, Maine Rep State Comt, formerly, mem, 73- Bus & Prof Pos: Mgr, J J Newberry Co, 51-62; pres, Dyar's Northland Trading Ctr, Strong, 63- Mil Serv: Entered as Sgt, Army Res, 55, released as Sgt, 57, after serv in First Armored Div, Tex & La. Mem: CofC; Grange; AF&AM (Past Master); Royal Arch Mason (High Priest Chap); Lions Int; Shrine (Potentates Ambassador). Relig: Protestant. Mailing Add: Strong ME 04983

DYAS, HESS (D)
b Omaha, Nebr, Apr 18, 37; s Sandford Miller Dyas & Edith Lee Dearmont D; m 1959 to Carol Ann Johnson; c Heidi, Keating Hess & Kyle Arthur. Educ: Nebr Wesleyan Univ, BA, 59; Illif Theol Sch, Denver, Colo, 59-60; Univ Colo, 60-63; Blue Key; Phi Kappa Tau. Polit & Govt Pos: Precinct committeeman, Lancaster Co Dem Comt, 64-70; chmn, Lancaster Co Buck-A-Month Club, 65-66; field rep, State of Nebr Tech Assistance Agency, 66-67; admin asst, Nebr Dem State Cent Comt, 67-69, exec dir, 69, chmn, formerly; mem, Dem Nat Comt, formerly; Dem cand for US Rep, Nebr, 74. Bus & Prof Pos: Eng teacher, Lincoln Pub Schs, 63-66. Mem: Dem Midwest Conf (chmn). Relig: Unitarian. Mailing Add: 1688 Otoe Lincoln NE 68502

DYCK, ALICE NADINE (D)
b Frankfort, Kans, Sept 11, 29; d Donald Farrar Sitler & Gladys Mary Carver S; m 1948 to Herbert Cornelius Dyck; c D Frederick, Maria Louisa, Christine Elisa, Justin Jacob & Nathan Philip. Educ: Butler Co Community Col, Kans, 66-67. Polit & Govt Pos: Dem capt, Bonhomme Twp-Precincts 67 & 76, Mo, 58-66; treas, Bonhomme Twp Dem Club, 63; Dem co-capt, Queeny Twp Precincts, 26-28, 68-; Queeny Twp capt, McGovern for President, 71-72; deleg, Second Cong Dist Caucus, 72, Mo State Dem Conv, 72 & Dem Nat Conv, 72; secy, Queeny Twp Dem Club, 73- Mem: St Louis & Kans State Genealogical Socs; New Neighbors (adv bd, 72-); Manchester Methodist Woman's Soc of Christian Serv. Honors & Awards: Outstanding Young Woman, Ballwin Jaycee Wives, 63. Relig: Methodist. Mailing Add: 37 James Ct Winchester MO 63011

DYCK, HAROLD PETER (R)
Kans State Rep
b Hesston, Kans, Sept 2, 20; s Jac H Dyck & Fannie Elizabeth Yost D; m 1942 to Elva Mae Hershberger; c Gary, Joycelyn (Mrs Terry Koppenhaver), Tom & Julia. Educ: Am Mgt Asn & Sales Mkt Exec Int. Polit & Govt Pos: Mem, Hesston Sch Bd, Kans, 58-60; mayor, Hesston, 69-71; Kans State Rep, 71-, chmn, Educ Comt, Kans House Rep, 73-75, chmn, Commercial & Financial Inst, 75- Bus & Prof Pos: Dir sales & vpres, Hesston Corp, Kans, 50-68; dir, Hesston State Bank, 65-; vchmn, Hesston Corp Bd, 68-; Mid-West area dir, Estate Planning Consult, Mennonite Found, 68-; dir, First Fed Savings & Loan Asn, Newton, 70- Mem: Farm Equip Mfrs Asn; Schowalter Villa Retirement Home, Hesston; CofC; charter mem Lions; Kiwanis. Relig: Mennonite. Legal Res: 226 Hess Ave Hesston KS 67062 Mailing Add: Box 160 Hesston KS 67062

DYE, JAMES KERRY (R)
Chmn, Young Rep League Colo
b Julesburg, Colo, Sept 5, 49; s William L Dye & Phyllis Hanley D; m 1969 to Connie L Sellers; c Richard & Sarah. Educ: Colo State Univ, BSBA, 74, MS, 75; Beta Epsilon; Lancers; Student Senate. Polit & Govt Pos: Chmn, Colo State Univ Col Rep, 71-72; mem state exec bd, Young Rep League Colo, 71-; chmn, currently; deleg, Rep Nat Conv, 72; chmn, Colo Col Rep League, 72; mem exec bd, Colo State Rep Cent Comt, currently; bonus mem, Larimer Co Rep Comt, precinct committeeman, currently. Mil Serv: Entered as E-1, Navy, 67, released as E-4, 70, after serv in USS Isle Royale (AD-29), 68-69. Mem: Civil Air Patrol. Honors & Awards: Outstanding Male Young Rep, 73. Relig: Christian. Mailing Add: Apt 154 4412 E Mulberry Ft Collins CO 80521

DYE, MARILYN SUE (D)
Ariz State Sen
b Terre Haute, Ind, Jan 28, 28; d James McNaught & Helen Shelby M; div; c Linda (Mrs Larry Roesch) & Nicholas. Educ: Ind State Univ, BA, 51; Ind Univ, MA, 68; Univ Ariz, 65-74. Polit & Govt Pos: Ariz State Sen, 75- Mailing Add: 1141 N Norton St Tucson AZ 85719

DYER, DONALD E (R)
Maine State Rep
Mailing Add: 32 Fickett St South Portland ME 04106

DYER, DONALD JAMES (R)
Chmn, Townsend Rep Town Comt, Mass
b Greenfield, Mass, Aug 16, 34; s Charles Henry Dyer & Valentine Rosalie Papillon D; m 1969 to Diane Lois Fournier. Educ: Nichols Jr Col, Dudley, Mass, ABA, 54. Polit & Govt Pos: Mem, Townsend Zoning Adv Comt, Mass, 60-65; Townsend Planning Bd, 60-66; chmn, Townsend Rep Town Comt, 60-; chmn, Volpe for Gov Comt, 62, 64 & 66; deleg, Rep State Conv, 62-70; mem, Townsend Bd Assessors, 65-; Townsend Water Comnr, 67-; Townsend Bd Selectmen, 69-; chmn, Sargent for Gov Comt, 70. Bus & Prof Pos: Head eng dept, Sprague & Carleton, Inc, Milford, NH, 58-62; gen mgr, Merrivale Mfg, Inc, Nashua, 62-68; personnel & off mgr, United Sterilite Corp, Townsend, Mass, 68- Mil Serv: Entered as Pvt, Army, 57, released as SP-4, 59, after serv in Third Inf Div, Ger. Mem: Mass Selectmen's Asn; Middlesex Country Selectmen's Asn; Mass Assessors Asn; Rep Club Mass. Relig: Roman Catholic. Mailing Add: 18 Scott Rd Box 441 Townsend MA 01469

DYER, FREDERICK T (R)
Mo State Rep
b O'Fallon, Mo, Mar 7, 41; s Lawrence M Dyer (deceased) & Teresa Burkamper D; m 1964 to Rose Duraski; c Sherry Rose. Educ: Northeast Mo State Col, BS in Bus Admin, 63; Univ Mo Sch Law, 63-64; Southern Ill Univ; Pi Kappa Delta Debate Fraternity. Polit & Govt Pos: Mo State Rep, 51st Dist, St Charles Co, 73- Bus & Prof Pos: Local cartage co owner, St Charles, Mo. Mem: KofC; Grand Order of Pachyderms; St Charles Jaycees. Relig: Catholic. Mailing Add: 1025 Sherbrook St Charles MO 63301

DYER, HAROLD J (D)
Fla State Rep
Mailing Add: 3225 Harrison St Hollywood FL 33021

DYER, MRS ROBERT C (GIDDY) (R)
Ill State Rep
b Atlanta, Ga, May 28, 19; d Edward Jones Erwin & Mary Louisa Browne E; m 1940 to Robert Campbell Dyer; c Robert C & Wynn. Educ: Agnes Scott Col, AB, 38. Polit & Govt Pos: Pres, Western Springs League Women Voters, Ill, 55-56; pres, Du Page Co Rep Workshops, 57-58; legis chmn, PTA Coun, Hinsdale, 58; state bd mem, Ill Rep Workshops, 58-60; nat bd mem, Nat Coun Rep Workshops, 60-61; Rep precinct committeeman, 62-69; asst supvr, Downers Grove Twp, 61-68; mem, Du Page Co Bd Supvrs, 61-68; Ill State Rep, 41st Dist, 68- Mailing Add: 441 E Third St Hinsdale IL 60521

DYER, ROSS WATKINS (D)
Chief Justice, Tenn Supreme Court
b Halls, Tenn, Mar 10, 11; s Clarence Watkins Dyer & Zona Smith D; m 1938 to Agnes Rebecca Moss; c Thomas Ross. Educ: Univ Tenn, 29-30; Cumberland Univ, 30-31; YMCA Law Sch, LLB, 37; Phi Delta Phi. Polit & Govt Pos: Mayor, Halls, Tenn, 46-48; mem, Limited Tenn Constitutional Conv, 53; Tenn State Sen, 57-59; exec asst to Gov, Tenn, 59-61; assoc justice, Tenn Supreme Court, 61-69, Chief Justice, 69- Mil Serv: Entered as Pvt, Army, 43, released as 1st Lt, 46, after serv in Third Army, ETO, 44-46. Mem: Mason; Am Legion. Relig: Methodist. Mailing Add: Halls TN 38040

DYER, WILBUR (D)
La State Rep
Mailing Add: Box 426 Cheneyville LA 71325

DYKE, WILLIAM D
b Princeton, Ill, Apr 25, 30; s Alfred D Dyke & Vinnie Thompson D; m 1953 to Joan Piper; c Wade, Sarah & Kathryn. Educ: Bradley Univ, 49-50; DePauw Univ, BA, 52; Univ Wis-Madison, LLB, 59; Alpha Tau Omega. Polit & Govt Pos: City attorney, Jefferson, Wis, formerly; asst to Lt Gov, Wis, 63-64; mayor, Madison, Wis, 69-74; adv to comt human environ, US Secy State, formerly; mem urban transportation adv coun, US Dept Transportation, currently; adv, Housing & Urban Develop Dept Urban Dynamics Proj, Mass Inst Technol, currently; bd dirs & comt intergovt rels, Nat League of Cities, currently; bd dirs & finance & taxation comt, Wis League Munic, currently; vpres, Wis Alliance Cities, formerly, bd dirs, currently; cand for Gov, Wis, 74. Bus & Prof Pos: Radio & TV announcer, 56-59; pvt law practice, 60-; instr taxation, Madison Voc, Tech & Adult Sch, 64-68. Mil Serv: Pvt, Army, 52-55, serv as Spec Agt in Counter Intel Corps, ETO. Mem: Am Judicature Soc; Wis & Dane Co Bar Asns. Honors & Awards: Man of Year, Wis Reserve Off Asn, 71. Legal Res: 3826 Council Crest Madison WI 53711 Mailing Add: PO Box 65 Mt Horeb WI 53572

DYKES, W E (BILL) (D)
La State Sen
Mailing Add: PO Box 126 Montpelier LA 70422

DYMALLY, MERVYN M (D)
Lt Gov, Calif
b Trinidad, WI, May 12, 26; s Hamid Dymally & Andreid Richardson D; m to Alice Gueno; c Mark & Lynn. Educ: Calif State Col, Los Angeles, BA; Calif State Univ, Sacramento, MA, 69; Kappa Alpha Psi; Phi Kappa Phi. Hon Degrees: LLD, Univ West Los Angeles. Polit & Govt Pos: Chmn, Youth for Kennedy, 60; state treas, Calif Fedn Young Dem, 60-61; mem, Dem State Cent Comt, Calif, 62-; Calif State Assemblyman, 53rd Dist, 62-66; Calif State Sen, 29th Dist, 67-75; deleg, Dem Nat Conv, 68; Lt Gov, Calif, 75- Bus & Prof Pos: Teacher elem & spec sec educ, Los Angeles City Schs, 54-60; vis fel, Metrop Appl Research Ctr, 67-; co-chmn, Nat Conf Black Elected Off, 67-; lectr polit sci, Univ Calif, Davis, 69-; lectr govt & educ, Claremont Cols, 69-; lectr, Whittier Col & Claremont Cols; mem adv bd, Joint Ctr Polit Studies; mem bd dirs, Lincoln Univ & Univ WLos Angeles. Publ: Auth, Outline—the Black Man in American Politics, 69; ed, The Black Politician—His Struggle for Power, Doxbury, 71; auth, The rise of Black political leadership in California, In: What Black Politicians Are Saying, 72; plus others. Mem: Am Acad Polit & Social Sci; Am Asn Univ Prof; Am Polit Sci Asn; Acad Polit Sci; NAACP. Honors & Awards: Am specialist of US Dept of State, East & Cent Africa, 64, Caribbean & Guyana, 65, guest of Ditchley Found, Eng, 70. Outstanding Freshman Legislator, Women for Legis Action, 63. Relig: Episcopal. Mailing Add: State Capitol Sacramento CA 95814

DYPSKI, CORNELL N (D)
Md State Sen
Mailing Add: 638 S Decker Ave Baltimore MD 21224

DYPSKI, RAYMOND A (D)
Md State Deleg
Mailing Add: 2824 Dillon St Baltimore MD 21224

DYRLAND, TERRY EUGENE (D)
Iowa State Rep
b Cedar Rapids, Iowa, Apr 15, 43; s Lester Eugene Dyrland & Opal Hodge D; m 1963 to Cherryl Diane Moon; c Christina & Lindsay. Educ: Univ Northern Iowa, BA, 68; Iowa State Univ, 70; Theta Alpha Phi; Kappa Delta Pi. Polit & Govt Pos: Iowa State Rep, 75- Bus & Prof Pos: High sch Eng teacher, Cent Community Schs, Elkader, Iowa, 68- Mem: Iowa State Educ Asn; Clayton Co Opera House Players. Honors & Awards: Outstanding Young Educator, Elkader Jaycees, 70; deleg, Nat Human Rels Conf, Washington, DC, Iowa State Educ Asn. Mailing Add: 408 E Bridge Elkader IA 52043

DYSON, JOHN STUART (D)
Chmn Adv Coun, NY State Dem Comt
b Washington, DC, Mar 7, 43; s Charles H Dyson & Margaret MacGregor D; m 1971 to Kathe Marie Bova; c Leigh. Educ: Cornell Univ, BS, 65; Woodrow Wilson Sch Pub & Int Affairs, MPA, 67; Phi Eta Sigma; Phi Kappa Phi; Alpha Delta Phi. Polit & Govt Pos: Legis asst to J Y Resnick, NY, 66-68; campaign mgr, Robert Fouhy, Dutchess Co Exec Cand, 67; cand, US House Rep, 28th Cong Dist, 68; chmn rural affairs task force, Adv Coun Community & Pub Affairs, NY State Dem Comt, 69, chmn adv coun, 73-; mem, Dem Nat Comt Policy Coun, 71- Bus & Prof Pos: Publisher, Millbrook Round Table, 68-; pres, Dymer Commun, Inc, New York, 68- Mil Serv: Entered as 2nd Lt, Army, 68, released as 1st Lt, 70, after serv in Hq, Mil Assistance Command, Vietnam, 69-70; Bronze Star; Joint Serv Commendation; Vietnam Serv Medals. Publ: Our Historic Hudson, James B Adler, 68. Mem: Wilderness Soc; Nat Trust for Historic Preservation; Am Acad Polit Sci; Asn Am Indian Affairs. Relig: Presbyterian. Mailing Add: Hickory Glen Millbrook NY 12545

DYSON, MRS LORRAY (D)
Mem, Dem Nat Comt, Okla
Mailing Add: PO Box 566 Guthrie OK 73044

DYSON, ROYDEN (ROY) (D)
Md State Deleg
b Great Mills, Md, Nov 15, 48; s Leroy B Dyson & Marie Meise D; single. Polit & Govt Pos: Md State Deleg, 75- Mailing Add: Box 5 Great Mills MD 20634

DZIALO, RAYMOND JOHN (D)
Conn State Rep
b Middletown, Conn, July 24, 31; s John Joseph Dzialo & Adela Berdysz D; m 1961 to Irene Biernacki; c Jodel. Educ: Quinnipiac Col, BS, 57. Polit & Govt Pos: Conn State Rep, Middletown, 58-; admin asst to US Rep Frank Kowalski, 59-61; pres, Pulaski Dem Club, 59-; mem, Middletown Dem Town Comt, 60-, chmn, 72-; admin asst to mayor, Middletown, 65-; mem, Conn Transportation Authority, 67- Bus & Prof Pos: Owner, Dzialo Ins Agency, Conn, 62-; consult, Achenbach Realty Co; corporator, Middlesex Mem Hosp; chmn, Middletown Community Develop Action Plan Agency; corporator, Middletown Savings Bank, 69-; mem adv comt, Laurel Bank & Trust Co, currently. Mil Serv: Entered as Pvt, Army, 52, released as 2nd Lt, 54; Lt Col, 103rd SCRAO, CTARNG, currently; Good Conduct & Korean Serv Medals; UN Serv Ribbon. Mem: Am Legion; VFW; Polish Falcons of Am; CWF; Elks. Honors & Awards: distinguished Serv Award, Middletown Jaycees, 64. Relig: Catholic. Mailing Add: Lisa Lane Middletown CT 06457

E

EADS, EDNA C (R)
Secy, Mo State Rep Comt
b Farmington, Mo, Aug 8, 13; d Alfred Montgomery Burch & Minnie Dietzler B; m 1934 to Charles Paul Eads; c Ronald Wayne, James David & Robert Eugene. Educ: Elvins High Sch; St Louis Bus Col. Polit & Govt Pos: Committeewoman & secy, Perry Twp Rep Comt, 48-54; secy, Eighth Cong Dist Rep Comt, 50-54, Tenth Cong Dist, Rep Comt, 62-; postmaster, Bonne Terre, 54-58; secy, Mo Rep State Comt, 66-; Mo State Rep, 66-74. Bus & Prof Pos: Real estate, 49- Mem: Bus & Prof Women's Club; Co Heart Fund; Ment Health; Cancer Soc; Bonne Terre Centennial Corp (pres). Relig: Congregational. Mailing Add: 112 Pine St Bonne Terre MO 63628

EADS, FELIX (BUCK) (D)
Chmn, Adair Co Dem Party, Okla
b Stilwell, Okla, Feb 20, 11; s Fred Lewis Eads & Penelope Ross E; m 1932 to Jewell Worley; c Patsy Lynn (Mrs W Neil Morton) & James Louis. Educ: Northeastern State Col, MA, 58. Polit & Govt Pos: Chmn, Adair Co Dem Party, 60-; deleg, Dem Nat Conv, 68. Bus & Prof Pos: Prin, Bell Sch, Stilwell, 33-; Co Supt of Schs, Adair Co, 70- Mem: Okla Educ Asn. Relig: Baptist. Mailing Add: Box 602 Stilwell OK 74960

EAGAN, FREDERICK LEITZ (D)
La State Sen
Mailing Add: 1127 Philip St New Orleans LA 70130

EAGAN, JAMES JOSEPH (D)
Mayor, Florissant, Mo
b St Louis, Mo, Mar 4, 26; s Patrick Eagan & Margurite Franey E; m 1948 to Frances May Regan (deceased); c Kathleen, J Regan, Kevin, Margaret, Patrick, Michael, Mary Frances & Timothy. Educ: St Louis Univ, LLB, 54. Polit & Govt Pos: Trustee, Woodson Terr, Mo, 54-55; prosecuting attorney, Florissant, 54-58; city attorney, 57-58, mayor, 63-; village attorney, Hazelwood, 57-58; Judge, St Louis, Co, 58-63. Mil Serv: Yeoman 2/C, Navy, 44-46. Relig: Catholic. Mailing Add: 955 Rue St Francois Florissant MO 63031

EAGLEBURGER, LAWRENCE SIDNEY (R)
Dep Under Secy State
b Milwaukee, Wis, Aug 1, 30; s Leon Sidney Eagleburger & Helen Van Ornum E; m 1966 to Marlene Ann Heinemann; c Lawrence Scott, Lawrence Andrew & Lawrence Jason. Educ: Cent State Col, Wis, 48-50; Univ Wis, BS, 52, MS, 57; Alpha Sigma Phi. Polit & Govt Pos: Mem, Wis Young Rep Exec Comt, 49-51; vchmn, Seventh Dist Young Rep, Wis, 50-51; foreign serv officer, 57-, third secy, Tegucigalpa, Honduras, 57-59, assigned, Dept State, 59-62 & 65-66; second secy, Belgrade, Yugoslavia, 62-65, mem staff, Nat Staff Col, 66-67; spec asst to Under Secy State, 67-69; exec asst to asst to President for Nat Security Affairs, 69; polit adv & counr polit affairs, US Mission, NATO, 69-71; dep asst secy, Dept Defense, 71-73; dep asst to President for Nat Security Opers & exec asst to Secy State, 73-74, Dep Under Secy State, 75- Bus & Prof Pos: Teaching asst, Univ Wis, 56-57. Mil Serv: 1st Lt, Army, 52-54. Legal Res: 2111 Jefferson Davis Hwy Arlington VA 22202 Mailing Add: Dept of State Washington DC 20520

EAGLES, ALOHA TAYLOR (R)
NDak State Rep
b Duluth, Minn, Nov 8, 16; d Edward R Browne & Belle Taylor B; m 1939 to Donald Emmett Eagles; c Donald Taylor & Keehn Emmett. Educ: Univ Minn, 34-35; Hibbing Jr Col, grad, 36; Va Jr Col, 36-37. Polit & Govt Pos: Secy exec comt, SE Region Community Action Prog, NDak, 65-71; NDak State Rep, 66-; mem adv bd, Alcohol Comn, currently; mem, Regional Bd Voc Rehabilitation, currently; mem, Law Enforcement Coun, currently; bd dirs, Comn on Status of Women, currently. Mem: League of Women Voters (local pres & dir local & state bd); Shrine Auxiliary; Voc Rehabilitation Auxiliary. Relig: Presbyterian. Mailing Add: State Capitol Bismarck ND 43215

EAGLES, FAYE BURNS (R)
VChmn, Second Dist, NC Rep Party
b Hickory, NC, June 27, 26; d David Reuben Burns & Alma Yoder B; div; c Robert Kirk & Landyce (Mrs Robert Eugene Boone). Educ: Lincoln Col, 2 years; Logan Chiropractic Col, DC, 53. Polit & Govt Pos: Mem exec comt, Nash Co Rep Party, 68-; coordr, Henderson Census Dist NC, 69-70; secy, Local Precinct Rep Party, 70-; mem platform Comt, NC Rep Party, 70 & 72; vchmn, Second Dist Rep Party, 70-, mem conv site comt, 71; mem, Gov Coord Coun on Aging, 71; NC Women's Polit Caucus, 72; Nat Women's Polit Caucus, 72; deleg, Rep Nat Leadership Conf, 72; alt deleg, Rep Nat Conv, 72; app, NC Comn Health Servs, 73- Bus & Prof Pos: Mem steering comt, Cong Chiropractic State Asns, 74-; mem, United Chiropractic Comn, currently. Publ: Digest of Chiropractic Economics, State Reporter, 3 years; Women in chiropractic, Chiropractic Yearbook, 72. Mem: Am Chiropractic Asn (alt NC deleg); NC Chiropractic Asn (bd dirs, 72-); Am Coun of Women Chiropractors; Int Col Chiropractors (fel); Am Coun of Chiropractic Roentgenologists. Honors & Awards: NC Chiropractor of the Year, 72; Distinguished Achievement Award, Am Chiropractic Asn, 73. Relig: Lutheran. Legal Res: 3206 Sunset Ave Rocky Mount NC 27801 Mailing Add: 124 N Franklin St Rocky Mount NC 27801

EAGLES, LARRY P (D)
NC State Rep
Mailing Add: 806 St Patrick St Tarboro NC 27886

EAGLETON, THOMAS F (D)
US Sen, Mo
b St Louis, Mo, Sept 4, 29; s Mark D Eagleton & Zitta Swanson E; m 1956 to Barbara Ann Smith; c Terence & Christin. Educ: Amherst Col, AB; Harvard Law Sch, LLB. Hon Degrees: JD, Suffolk Univ, 58, Park Col, 69, Amherst Col, 70 & Rockhurst Col, 70. Polit & Govt Pos: Circuit attorney, St Louis, Mo, 56; Attorney Gen, Mo, 60, Lt Gov, 64-68; US Sen, Mo, 69-; deleg, Dem Nat Conv, 72. Mil Serv: Navy, 48-49. Mem: Mo Prosecuting Attorneys Asn (Pres); Nat Dist Attorneys Asn (mem bd dir); Nat Asn of Attorney Gen. Honors & Awards: Distinguished Serv Award, Clayton Jr CofC, 62; Civic Award, Alpha Kappa Psi of St Louis Univ Sch of Com & Finance; recognized by Life Mag as One of Top 100 Young Leaders in the US; nominated by St Louis Jr CofC as One of the Country's Ten Outstanding Young Men; Bicentennial Award of Pub Serv, St Louis Bar Asn, 64. Legal Res: MO Mailing Add: Senate Off Bldg Washington DC 20510

EAMES, CHARLES BURTON (R)
b Oneida, NY, Sept 19, 20; s David K Eames & Vera Burton E; m 1942 to Harriet Allyn; c Charles B, Jr, Frederick A, David K, II & Thomas R. Educ: Hamilton Col, BA, 42, Maxwell Grad Sch, Syracuse Univ, MS, 47. Polit & Govt Pos: Dir res, Oneida Co, NY, 64-66; asst dir, NY; State Off Planning Coord, 67-69; spec asst to chmn, NY Rep State Comt, 69-; dep comnr, NY State Off for Local Govt, 71- Bus & Prof Pos: Prof polit sci, Utica Col, Syracuse Univ, 47-63. Mil Serv: Entered as Aviation Cadet, Air Force, 43, released as 1st Lt, 45, after serv in 379th Bomb Group, 8th Army Air Force, UK, 44; Air Medal with Four Oak Leaf Clusters; Distinguished Flying Cross; Presidential Unit Citation. Relig: Presbyterian. Mailing Add: 10 Pine Ridge Dr Guilderland NY 12084

EARDLEY, RICHARD ROY (D)
Mayor, Boise, Idaho
b Denver, Colo, Dec 23, 28; s Walter B Eardley & Pearl Wessels E; m 1950 to Patricia L Engum; c Rick B, Randall S & Ronald R. Educ: Eastern Ore State Col, 47-48. Polit & Govt Pos: Mem city coun, Boise, Idaho, 70-74, mayor, 74- Bus & Prof Pos: City reporter, Dem-Herald, Baker, Ore, 51-52; news dir, KBKR Radio, Baker, 52-55; reporter & sports ed, Daily Statesman, Boise, Idaho, 55-59; news dir, KBOI Radio-TV, Boise, 59-74. Mem: Asn Idaho Cities; Ada Coun Govts. Honors & Awards: Community Affairs Reporting Award, Radio-TV News Dir Asn, 63. Relig: Methodist. Legal Res: 522 Cashmere Rd Boise ID 83702 Mailing Add: City Hall Box 500 Boise ID 83701

EARL, ANTHONY SCULLY (D)
b Lansing, Mich, Apr 12, 36; s Russel K Earl & Ethlynne Scully E; m 1962 to Sheila Coyle; c Julia, Anne, Mary & Catherine. Educ: Mich State Univ, BA, 58; Univ Chicago Law Sch, JD, 61; Phi Kappa Phi; Phi Eta Sigma; Beta Theta Pi. Polit & Govt Pos: Asst dist attorney, Marathon Co, Wis, 65-66; city attorney, Wausau, 66-69; Wis State Rep, Marathon Co, Second Dist, formerly, majority leader, Wis State Assembly, formerly. Bus & Prof Pos: Mem law firm, Crooks, Low & Earl, 69- Mil Serv: Entered as A/S, Navy, 62, released as Lt, 65, after serv in COM Five, 62-65. Mem: Am & Wis Bar Asns; Am Legion; KofC; Optimists Int. Relig: Roman Catholic. Mailing Add: 917 Graves Ave Wausau WI 54401

EARLE, ERNEST JOSEPH (STUB) (R)
Vt State Rep
Mailing Add: Eden VT 05653

EARLE, JOHN K (R)
SC State Rep
Mailing Add: 7 Bartram Grove Greenville SC 29605

EARLE, LEWIS SAMUEL (R)
Mem, Orange Co Rep Exec Comt, Fla
b Gibbstown, NJ, Aug 22, 33; s Lewis Reade Earle & Alice Freas Richie E; m 1972 to Barbara Borrows Richardson; c Eric Dwight & Lewis Reade. Educ: St Petersburg Jr Col, Fla, AA, 53; Univ Fla, 53-54; Emory Univ, DDS, 58; Omicron Kappa Upsilon; Psi Omega. Polit & Govt Pos: Mem, Orange Co Rep Exec Comt, Fla, 62-, finance chmn, 66-67; bd mem, Orange Co Econ Opportunity, Inc, 67-69; Fla State Rep, 43rd Dist, Orange Co, 68-74, Minority Floor Leader, 72-74. Bus & Prof Pos: Lab aide, Fed Bur Invest, 51-52; partner, Earle Elec Co, 53-58; lab research asst, Emory Univ, 56-58; self employed dentist, 61- Mil Serv: Entered as Ens, Naval Res, 58, released as Lt, 61, after serv in Fleet Air Serv Squadron 51 & Sanford Naval Air Sta, Fla, Comdr, Naval Res; Award of Merit, Mil Order of the World Wars. Mem: Int Asn Dent Research; Rotary; CofC; Audubon Soc; Mason. Honors & Awards: Univ Scholarship Awards; Award of Excellence, Am Security Coun. Relig: Methodist. Legal Res: 630 S Lake Sybelia Dr Maitland FL 32751 Mailing Add: 255 N Lakemont Ave Winter Park FL 32789

EARLE, RONALD DALE (D)
Tex State Rep
b Ft Worth, Tex, Feb 23, 42; s Charles C Earle & Lowleta Muse E; m 1963 to Barbara Leach; c Elisabeth Ashlea & Charles Jason. Educ: Univ Tex, Austin, BA, 64, Univ Tex Sch Law, JD, 67; Asn Criminal Law Studies; Student-Faculty Rels Comt; Texas Club; Univ Coop Bd Dirs; Nat Students Asn. Polit & Govt Pos: Legal asst to Tex Gov John Connally, 67-69; judge, Munic Court of Austin, Tex, 69-72; counsel, Tex Civil Judicial Coun, 72-73; Tex State Rep, 73- Publ: Numerous periodical publ on subj of court reform over three-year period, 72-75. Mem: Travis Co Bar Asn (bd dirs); Tex State Bar Asn; Capital Area Planning Coun criminal justice comt); Travis Co Legal Aid & Defender Soc; Tex Adv Comn on Intergovt Rels. Relig: Baptist. Legal Res: 6810 Glen Ridge Dr Austin TX 78731 Mailing Add: PO Box 2910 Austin TX 78767

EARLEY, ROBERT EMMETT (D)
Mem, NH State Dem Comt
b Nashua, NH, July 3, 96; s John M Earley & Nellie Harrington E; m 1938 to Evelyn C Blankenberg; c Robert E, Jr & Eleanor B (Mrs McGinn). Educ: Harvard Col, Boston Univ, LLB, 24; pres, Boston Univ grad class of 24. Polit & Govt Pos: NH State Rep, 20-21; chmn, Dem City Comt, Nashua, 23, solicitor, Nashua, 28-32; deleg, Dem Nat Conv, 32, 44, 48 & 62, chmn, 44; attorney, Fed Home Loan Asn, 36; chmn, NH State Dem Comt, 40-44, mem, currently. Bus & Prof Pos: Mem, NH Judicial Coun; & New Eng Law Inst, 47- Mil Serv: Seaman, Navy, 17-21. Mem: NH & Am Bar Asns; Elks; Am Legion (comdr, James E Coffey Post 3, 26); Nashua Country Club. Relig: Roman Catholic. Mailing Add: 5 Lincoln Ave Nashua NH 03060

EARLY, EDWARD J, JR (D)
Mass State Rep
Mailing Add: State Capitol Boston MA 02133

EARLY, EDWARD M (D)
Pa State Sen
Mailing Add: 101 Oxbridge Dr Pittsburgh PA 15237

EARLY, JOSEPH DANIEL (D)
US Rep, Mass
b Worcester, Mass, Jan 31, 33; s George F Early & Mary Lally E; m 1955 to Marilyn Powers; c Joseph D, Jr, Mark, Colleen, Maureen, Lynn, Sean, Eileen & Patrick. Educ: Col of the Holy Cross, BS, 55; Capt, Holy Cross Basketball Team, 54-55; mem, Team that won the Nat Intercollegiate Tournament, 54; participated in Sugar Bowl Tournament in New Orleans, 53, 54. Polit & Govt Pos: Mass State Rep, 63-74, vchmn, Ways & Means Comt, Mass House Reps, 73-74; US Rep, Third Dist, Mass, 75- Bus & Prof Pos: Teacher, St John's Prep Sch, Shrewsbury, Mass, 57-59; teacher-coach, David Prouty High Sch, Spencer, Mass, 59-63. Mil Serv: Entered as Ens, Navy, 55, released as Lt(jg), 57, after serv in USS Dashiell as an Intel Officer. Mem: Holy Cross Club of Worcester; Holy Cross Varsity Club, Worcester, Mass; KofC (Alhambra Coun 88); Spencer Teachers Asn; Collegiate Basketball Off Asn. Relig: Roman Catholic. Legal Res: 36 Monroe Ave Worcester MA 01602 Mailing Add: 34 Mechanic St Rm 203 Worcester MA 01608

EARLY, MICHAEL P (D)
Wis State Rep
b New Richmond, Wis, Mar 10, 18; s James J Early & Julia O'Neill E; m 1945 to Dorothy Burke; c Timothy Patrick, Dennis Michael, Michael Sean, Mary Shannon, Patrick Thomas, Daniel Joseph & Brian Hugh. Educ: Washburn Tech Col, 46. Polit & Govt Pos: Wis State Rep, 30th Dist, 70-, chmn vet & mil affairs comt, Wis House Rep, 71, chmn higher educ subcomt, 75-, mem comt hwys & comt tourism, 75-; mem, Wis-Minn Boundary Area Comt, 71; mem, Gov Hwy Safety Task Force, 71; mem, Coun Alcohol & Other Drug Abuse, 74; mem, Wis Bldg Comn, 75. Mil Serv: Entered as Pvt, Army, 41, released as Pfc, after serv in 503rd Parachute Inf, SW Pac, 42-44; Combat Inf Badge; SW Pac Theatre Ribbon. Mem: Am Legion; VFW; Moose; KofC; DAV. Honors & Awards: Lions Int Man of Year Award. Relig: Catholic. Legal Res: 1052 South Ford Dr River Falls WI 54022 Mailing Add: 125 N Main River Falls WI 54022

EARNHART, MILT (D)
Ark State Sen
b St Louis, Mo, Apr 1, 18; s Charles Stanley Earnhart & Anna Sullivan E; m 1943 to Mary Elizabeth Robben; c Anne Cecile, Thomas P & Dave M. Educ: High Sch & Domestic & Serv Schs. Polit & Govt Pos: Ark State Rep, 59-66; Ark State Sen, Fourth Sen Dist, 66- Bus & Prof Pos: Sales mgr, Encycl Britannica, Cincinnati, Ohio, 49-50; vpres, Armbruster & Co, Inc, 50- Mil Serv: Entered as Pvt, Army, 42, released as Sgt, 45, after serv in 3137 Sig Mtr Message Co, ETO; ETO, Battle of Bulge, Ger Campaign Ribbons; plus others. Mem: Lions; Am Legion; KofC; Elks. Honors & Awards: TV news personality, KFSA-TV Channel 5, Ft Smith, 53- Relig: Catholic. Legal Res: 2319 S Greenwood Ave Ft Smith AR 72901 Mailing Add: Box 1178 Ft Smith AR 72901

EARNHEART, E DANE (D)
Pres, Young Dem Ga
b Sapulpa, Okla, Apr 24, 51; s Dane Earnheart & Billie Joan Pierce E; single. Educ: Univ Fla, 69-71; Atlanta Law Sch, 75- Polit & Govt Pos: Pres, Young Dem Ga, 74-, pres state steering comt, 74; mem, State Affirmative Action Comn, 74-; mem, Charter Comn, Dem Party Ga, 74-, mem drafting comt, 75-; alt deleg, Dem Nat Mid-Term Conf, 74; mem, Ga Dem Exec Comt, 74- Bus & Prof Pos: Advert layout artist, Sears, Roebuck & Co, Atlanta, Ga, 71-72; sr graphics asst, Southern Railway Co, Atlanta, Ga, 72- Mem: Save America's Vital Environ; Ga Conservancy. Mailing Add: 1765 Peachtree Rd NE Apt D-3 Atlanta GA 30309

EASLEY, BETTY (R)
Fla State Rep
b Victoria, Tex, Aug 5, 29; d Clifford P Chapman & Inez Cary C; m 1966 to Kenneth E Easley; c Cary, Barbara, Katherine, Virginia & Bill (deceased). Educ: Univ Tex, 49; Alpha Delta Pi. Polit & Govt Pos: Mem, Study Comn Pinellas Co Charter, Fla, 71 & Citizens' Adv Comt to Pinellas Co Charter Comn, first vchmn, Pinellas Co Rep Exec Comt, currently; liaison asst to Pinellas Co Legis Deleg, 71; Fla State Rep, 72- Bus & Prof Pos: Med illustrator, Walter Reed Med Ctr, Washington, DC; med secy, legal secy & acct, Hillsborough Co, Fla; columnist for local newspaper, Pinellas Co. Mem: Clearwater Bus & Prof Women's Club; Zonta Int; Clearwater Women's Rep Club; Belleair Women's Rep Club; Seminole Rep Club. Relig: Episcopal. Legal Res: 801 Camellia Dr Harbor Bluffs Largo FL 33540 Mailing Add: 314 S Missouri Ave Suite 304 Clearwater FL 33515

EASLEY, SIDNEY HUGH (R)
Chmn, Webster Co Rep Exec Comt, Miss
b Mathiston, Miss, Jan 2, 47; s Vernon Webster Easley & Susie Gammill E; m 1969 to Betty Jo Cook. Educ: Miss State Univ, BS, 69. Polit & Govt Pos: Chmn, Webster Co Rep Exec Comt, Miss, 73- Mem: Jaycees; Mathiston Develop Found; Lions. Relig: Baptist. Mailing Add: PO Box 82 Mathiston MS 39752

EASOM, JERRY DON (D)
Mem, Ark Dem State Comt
b Dallas, Tex, July 3, 46; s James Clayton Easom & Ellen Hargis E; m 1968 to Donna Sears; c Anndi D. Educ: El Centro Univ, 66; Southwest Mo State Univ, 74-75. Polit & Govt Pos: Mem, Ark Dem State Comt, 72-; mem, Pulaski Co Dem Comt, 74-; vpres, Ark Young Dem, 74-; mem, Pulaski Co Young Dem, 74- Mil Serv: Entered as Airman Basic, Air Force, 61, released as Airman 1/C, 64, after serv in Air Materiel Command. Mem: CofC; Jaycees; Kiwanis. Legal Res: Apt 1 8913 Morriss Manor Little Rock AR 72204 Mailing Add: PO Box 971 Little Rock AR 72201

EAST, JOHN PORTER (R)
b Springfield, Ill, May 5, 31; s Laurence John East & Virginia Porter E; m 1953 to Priscilla Sherk; c Kathryn P & Martha Ellen. Educ: Earlham Col, BA, 53; Univ Ill, Urbana, LLB, 59; Univ Fla, MA, 62, PhD, 64; Phi Beta Kappa; Pi Sigma Alpha. Polit & Govt Pos: Deleg, Rep Nat Conv, 68; Mem Electoral Col, NC, 72. Bus & Prof Pos: Assoc prof polit sci, ECarolina Univ, 67-72, prof polit sci, 72- Mil Serv: Entered as Pvt, Marine Corps, 53, released as 1st Lt, 55. Publ: Auth, Intellectual decline on the American campus, Human Events, 11/71; Political relevance of St Augustine, Modern Age, spring 72; Political thought of Willmoore Kendall, Polit Sci Rev, 73; plus others. Mem: Am Polit Sci Asn; Southern Polit Sci Asn; Am Hist Asn; Fla Bar Asn. Relig: Protestant. Mailing Add: 212 Longmeadow Rd Greenville NC 27834

EASTERLY, CHARLES THOMAS (D)
Ky State Sen
b Columbus, Ohio, Apr 21, 40; s Edgar Ernest Easterly & Ethel K E; single. Educ: Carleton Col, BA; Univ Paris, France dipl d'etudes; Univ Nuremberg, Ger, Fulbright Scholar; Univ Ky, MA; Univ Tenn, Knoxville, JD; Phi Beta Kappa; pres, Student Bar Asn. Polit & Govt Pos: Ky State Sen, 20th Dist, 74-, vchmn judiciary comt, Ky State Legis, 74-, mem appropriations & revenue comt & health & welfare comt, 74- Bus & Prof Pos: Teacher polit sci, French, Span & Ger, Univ Ky & Ky State Univ, 64-65; attorney, State Dept Ins, 71-72; legal consult & dir research & educ, State AFL-CIO, 73; attorney, Frankfort, 72- Mil Serv: Entered as Pvt, Army, 65, released as 1st Lt, 68, after serv in 4th Inf Div, Spec Forces; Bronze Star; Air Medal; Army Commendation Medal. Mem: Am Legion; Optimists; Ky Voc Teacher Educ Adv Comt (bd dirs, 75-). Honors & Awards: Outstanding Young Man of Ky, Ky Jaycees, 74. Relig: Lutheran. Mailing Add: 210 W State St Frankfort KY 40601

EASTIN, JANE WHITE (R)
Committeewoman, Rep State Cent Comt Iowa
b St Louis, Mo, July 3, 15; s Warren Abel White & Helen Vandiver W; m 1941 to Kent DeVaughn; c Todd V, Jill V & Rand W. Educ: Columbia Col, AA, 34. Polit & Govt Pos: Pres, Scott Co Rep Women, Iowa, 59-60; legis chmn, Iowa Fedn Rep Women, 61-63; committeewoman, Rep State Cent Comt Iowa, First Dist, 74- Mem: League Women Voters; Quad-Cities World Affairs Coun (pres, 74-75). Relig: Christian Science. Mailing Add: 300 River Dr Bettendorf IA 52722

EASTLAND, JAMES OLIVER (D)
US Sen, Miss
b Doddsville, Miss, Nov 28, 04; s Woods Caperton Eastland & Alma Austin E; m 1932 to Elizabeth Coleman; c Nell, Ann Sue & Woods Eugene. Educ: Univ Miss, 22-24; Vanderbilt Univ, 25-26; Univ Ala, 26-27. Polit & Govt Pos: Miss State Rep, 28-32; US Sen, Miss, 41-, chmn, Judiciary Comt, US Senate, currently, Pres Pro Tem, 72-, ranking mem, Comt on Agr & Forestry, currently. Bus & Prof Pos: Attorney & farmer. Relig: Methodist. Legal Res: Doddsville MS 38736 Mailing Add: 2241 Dirksen Off Bldg Washington DC 20510

EASTMAN, EDWIN WINTER (R)
NH State Rep
b Exeter, NH, June 18, 94; married. Educ: Phillips Exeter Acad; Kimball Union Acad. Polit & Govt Pos: NH State Rep, 53-; deleg, Const Conv, 56-64. Bus & Prof Pos: Retired mfrs rep; trustee, Trust Funds, Exeter Cemetery, Exeter Hosp, Gilman Park & Robinson Fund & Kinsington Libr. Mil Serv: 189 Aero Squadron, World War I. Mem: NH Soc Colonial Wars; NH Hist Soc; SAR; Exeter Hist Soc; KT. Relig: Congregational. Mailing Add: 76 Court St Exeter NH 03833

EASTMAN, JOHN LESLIE (R)
Chmn, Barkhamsted Rep Town Comt, Conn
b Winsted, Conn, Nov 27, 16; s Leslie Howard Eastman & Amelia Moore E; m 1939 to Lina Florio; c Carole (Mrs William C Zegel), Cynthia (Mrs Kenneth H Williams) & Susan (Mrs Harold M Scheintaub). Educ: Gilbert Sch, Winsted, Conn, 31-35. Polit & Govt Pos: Mem, Bd Educ, Barkhamsted, Conn, 46-54, mem bd assessors, 53-55, mem bd selectmen, 67-; chmn, Barkhamsted Rep Town Comt, 73- Bus & Prof Pos: Nat serv mgr, Waring Prod Div, 45- Mem: Union Agr Soc (treas, 50-); Winsted Area Ambulance Serv (dir & past pres). Relig: Protestant. Legal Res: Riverton Rd Riverton CT 06065 Mailing Add: PO Box 25 Riverton CT 06065

EASTMAN, RUTH ANN (R)
b Webster, SDak; d Warren Lester Lakin & Mary Perkins L; m 1947 to Frederic Philip Eastman; c Warren & Catherine. Educ: Am Inst of the Air, Brown Inst, Minneapolis, Minn. Polit & Govt Pos: Chairwoman, Hopkins Rep Comt, 55-56; mem, Hennepin Co Rep Comt, Minn, 55-58; mem campaign staff, Third Dist Rep Cong Campaign, 56; mem, Mayor's Transit Comn, Minneapolis, 58-61; state chairwoman, GROW Labor Comt, 63-64; mgr, Minneapolis Aldermanic Campaign, 65 & 67; pres, Minn Fedn Rep Women, 65-69, mem bd dirs, 65-; bd mem, Nat Fedn Rep Women, 65-71, chmn community serv, Mid West, 69-71; mem, Minn State Rep Cent Comt, 65-69, chairwoman's appointee, 69-71; mem, Fifth Cong Dist Rep Comt, Minn, 66-67, coordr legis campaigns, 66; mem adv comt, State Dept Welfare, 66-69; chmn, Candidate Search Comt, Minneapolis, 67; campaign scheduler, Minneapolis Mayorality Campaign, 69; vchairwoman, Statewide Legis Campaign Comt, 69-70; consult, Action Now, Rep Nat Comt, 69-70. Bus & Prof Pos: Broadcaster, woman's prog dir, continuity dir, pub rels, writer & ed, 47-; ed, Something of Significance, Seventh Ward Rep Comt, 60-63 & Hennepin Rep. Mem: City Youth Ctr (bd dirs). Relig: Methodist. Mailing Add: 4605 Heritage Hills Dr Bloomington MN 55437

EATON, CLYDE S (R)
NH State Rep
Mailing Add: Greenville NH 03048

EATON, JOSEPH MARCH (R)
NH State Rep
b Salisbury, Mass, Dec 1, 01; s Stephen J Eaton & Ellen C Merrill E; m 1930 to Mildred P Pehrson; c Joseph M, Jr, Nancy W (Mrs Whitelaw) & Pauline M (Mrs Attridge). Educ: Boston Univ, BBA, 26. Polit & Govt Pos: Chmn, Regist of Voters, Fairhaven, Mass, 30-42; fed investr, Travel Status, 42-47; NH State Rep, 61-, chmn, Comt on Appropriations & Adv Budget Comt, NH House of Rep, 65-, chmn, Joint House & Senate Fiscal Comt, 65-, mem, Legis Serv Comt, 65 & Coord Comt, 69- Mailing Add: 11 Walnut St Hillsboro NH 03244

EATON, LEWIS WILMOT, JR (D)
Mem, La Dem State Cent Comt
b Baton Rouge, La, July 11, 22; s Lewis Wilmot Eaton, Sr & Grace Bahm E; m 1945 to Mary Gallaher Frey; c Lewis Wilmot, III, Gregory McCarroll, Mary Frey, Susan Martin & Barbara Anne. Educ: Ga Sch Technol, 43-44; La State Univ, BS, 54; Omicron Delta Kappa; pres, Kappa Alpha Order; Daggers; pres freshman class, La State Univ, 41-43; representative, Marine Corps, Student Coun, Ga Sch Technol, 43-44. Polit & Govt Pos: Dir, Civil Defense, La, 51; city councilman, Baton Rouge, 53-56; La State Sen, 68-72; mem planning & zoning comn & auditorium comn, East Baton Rouge Parish; mem, La Dem State Cent Comt, 75- Bus & Prof Pos: Owner, real estate investments, 47-71; pres, L W Eaton Construction Co, Inc, currently; bd dirs, Fidelity Nat Bank, Commercial Securities & Baton Rouge Savings & Loan, currently. Mil Serv: Entered as Pvt, Marine Corps, 42, released as 2nd Lt, 46, recalled as 1st Lt, 51-52, serv in 4th Regt, 6th Div, Pac, 45-46 & Korean Conflict, 51-52. Mem: Red Cross (bd mem, currently); La State Univ Alumni Asn; YMCA Capitol Improvement Fund Raising Drive (chmn, 73-); Baton Rouge Civil Ctr Comn (chmn, 73); Capitol Region Planning Comn. Honors & Awards: Distinguished Serv Award, Jaycees, 50. Relig: Methodist; former chmn off bd, Univ United Methodist Church. Legal Res: 2855 McCarroll Dr Baton Rouge LA 70809 Mailing Add: 408 Fidelity Nat Bank Bldg Baton Rouge LA 70809

EATON, MYRL R (R)
NH State Rep
Mailing Add: Wilson Mobilehome Park Auxiliary Rte 2 Enfield NH 03748

EAVES, JOHN ARTHUR (D)
Miss State Rep
Mailing Add: 101 Bakers Trust Plaza Bldg Jackson MS 39201

EAVES, MARY MARIE (D)
VChmn, NMex State Dem Party
b Wichita Falls, Tex, June 30, 39; d James Pinkney Hines & Mary Edna Hughes H; m 1960 to Joe Clell Eaves; c Christie Jo & Lea Ann. Educ: Farmington High Sch, grad, 57. Polit & Govt Pos: Precinct officer, San Juan Co Dem Party, NMex, 64-74, co chairwoman, 66-67; mem, NMex State Dem Cent Comt, 67-; vchmn, NMex State Dem Party, 67-; alt deleg & mem platform comt, Dem Nat Conv, 68, alt deleg & mem rules comt & charter comn, 72; mem, Dem Nat Comt, 70-73; mem, Dem Charter Comn, 72-; state chairperson, Women for McGovern-Shriver, 72. Bus & Prof Pos: Secy, Southern Union Gas Co, 57-60, admin asst to sr vpres, 75-; vpres, W & C Rouseabout Co, 69-; Vpres, Chaparral Oil & Gas Co, 70-; pres, M E D Tankers, Inc, 70- Mem: Salvation Army, (Secy Adv Bd, 69-); Daughters of the Nile; League Women Voters; CofC. Honors & Awards: Appreciation Awards, NMex State Dem Party & NMex State Dem Women, 74. Relig: Presybterian. Legal Res: 5508 Cedarwood Dr Farmington NM 87401 Mailing Add: 351 E Garcia Santa Fe NM 87501

EBBESEN, JOSEPH B (R)
Ill State Rep
b De Kalb, Ill, Jan 12, 25; s Maynard E Ebbesen & Elsie E; m 1951 to Janice R Sanderson; c Jay R & Jane C. Educ: Northern Ill Univ, 46-49; Ill Col Optom, OD. Polit & Govt Pos: Mem bd educ, De Kalb, Ill, 6 years; councilman, City of De Kalb, 61-65, mayor, 65-69; vpres, Ill Munic League, 66-69; pres, Northern Ill Mayors Asn, 68-69; Ill State Rep, 37th Legis Dist, 73- Mil Serv: Entered as Pvt, Marine Corps, 43, released as Cpl, 46. Mem: Am Optom Asn; Am Acad Optom; Am Legion; Eagles; Elks. Relig: Protestant. Mailing Add: 212 Forsythe Lane De Kalb IL 60115

EBERHARD, OGRETTA (D)
Committeewoman, Dem Exec Comt Fla
b White Co, Ill, July 30, 09; m 1927 to Eugene Eberhard. Educ: High sch grad, 26. Polit & Govt Pos: Precinct committeewoman, Dem Exec Comt Fla, 68-70, vchmn, 70-74, committeewoman, 74- Relig: Catholic. Mailing Add: 2225 54th Ave Vero Beach FL 32960

EBERT, MIKE (R)
SC State Rep
Mailing Add: PO Box 632 Columbia SC 29202

EBNER, BEVERLY JONES (R)
VChmn, SC Rep Party
b Lancaster, Pa, Apr 8, 33; d Pierce Roy Jones, Sr & Irene Howe J; div. Educ: Lander Col, 51-53; bus mgr col newspaper; Glee Club; Christian Asn. Polit & Govt Pos: With Charleston Co Rep Party, SC, as canvass worker, Workman for Senate, 62, helped organize Meggett Rep Precinct, 62, treas, 62-68, exec committeewoman, 70-72, vpres, 72, deleg, Charleston Co Rep Conv, 62, 64, 66, 68, 70 & 72, mem, Credentials Comt, 70 & 72, canvass worker, Goldwater for President, 64, helped organize Adams Run, Edisto & Ravenel Precincts, 64, co-sponsor, Meggett TAR, 64, campaign secy, Charleston Co Rep Hq, 66, treas, Charleston Co Rep Party, 66-69, cand, State Senate, 67, co-chmn, Charleston Co Women for Nixon, 68, chmn, Charleston Co Elephant Fun-A-Rama, 72, Charleston Co Elec Day Chmn for Nixon, 72; charter mem, Charleston Rep Women's Club, 63, vpres, 63-64 & 72, pres, 65-66 & 73-75, deleg, SC Fedn Rep Women Biennial Conv, 65, 67, 69, & 71, parliamentarian, 67, chaplain, 68, legis chmn, 69, awards chmn, 70, membership chmn, 71, prog chmn, 72; mem bd dirs, SC Fedn of Rep Women, 65-66, mem-at-lg, Exec Comt, 66, pres, 66-71, campaign activities chmn, 72-73, chmn, A Day for the President, 72, pub rels chmn, 74-75, dist dir & chmn conv comt, 75-; Chmn, State Workshop for Nat Speakers, 73; participant, Nat Rep Women's Conf, Washington, DC, 65, 66, 69 & 70, Little Rock, Ark, 68, SC Conf Chmn, Washington, DC, 67; participant, Southern Regional Leadership Conf, New Orleans, La, 69; Participant, Regional Rep Leadership Conf Memphis, Tenn, 71; mem bd dirs, Nat Fedn Rep Women, 65-66, deleg & mem, Elections Comt, Biennial Convs, 67, 69 & 71; with SC Rep Party as deleg, SC Rep Conv, 64, 66, 68, 70 & 72, decorations chmn, 70, mem, State Steering Comt, Women for Nixon, 68; Mem State Steering Comt, Parker for Senate, 68, state campaign mgr, Eddings for State Supt of Educ, 70, off mgr, Edwards for Cong, 71, mem, SC State Rep Steering Comt, 71, mem, Order of Bus & Conv Comts, SC Rep Conv, 72, mem state steering comt & state vol chmn, Reelect Nixon Comt, 72, cand for SC Nat Committeewoman, 72, deleg, Delegation Co-VChairwoman & mem, Nat Credentials Comt, Rep Nat Conv, 72; vchmn, SC Rep Party, 74-; app, Gov Comt to Study Interest Rates, 75- Bus & Prof Pos: Teller, Citizens & Southern Nat Bank, Charleston, SC, 53-56; head ins dept, Arthur Ravenel Jr & Co Real Estate Agency, 64-69; secy, Rand Industs, Inc, 71-73; secy-bookkeeper, L C J Construction Co, 73- Mem: Jaycee-ettes; Charleston Opera Co; Southern Region VChmn Asn (secy-treas, 75-); Carolina Art Asn. Honors & Awards: SC Rep Woman of the Year, 69; Jaycee-ette of the Year Award, three times. Relig: Baptist. Mailing Add: Apt 202 210 Royal Palm Blvd Charleston SC 29407

ECHOLS, ALVIN EDWARD (R)
Dep Chmn, State Rep Comt Pa
b Philadelphia, Pa, Dec 5, 30; s Alvin Edward Echols, Sr & Rhudine Parker E; m 1959 to Gwendolyn Granderson; c Donna & Alison. Educ: Va Union Univ, BA cum laude, 55; Howard Univ, LLB, 57; Alpha Phi Alpha. Polit & Govt Pos: Comnr, Pa Human Rels Comn, 69-; vchmn, Philadelphia Rep City Comt, 70-; dep chmn, State Rep Comt, 73- Bus & Prof Pos: Exec dir, North City Congress, 63- Publ: Deadline, vengeance & tribute, Crime & Delinquency, 70. Mem: Med Col Pa (bd mem, 72-); Friends of Free Libr (exec comt, 72-); Community Leadership Sem Prog (steering comt, 62-); Health & Welfare Coun (bd mem, 74-). Honors & Awards: Philadelphia Achievement Award, 66; Nat Conf Christians & Jews Distinguished Merit Citation, 67; US Jaycees Leadership Series Award, 68. Relig: Methodist. Legal Res: 1429 Dondill Pl Philadelphia PA 19122 Mailing Add: 1428 N Broad St Philadelphia PA 19121

ECHOLS, GENE (D)
Nev State Sen
s Alvin Dean Echols & Willie Chestnut E; m 1962 to Wanda Earline Benge. Educ: Stonewall High Sch, Okla, grad, 39; Humphrey's Bus Col, Calif, 51-53; Am Inst Banking, Stanislaus Co Chap, Calif, 51-62; Inst Orgn Mgt, Univ Santa Clara, 67-68. Polit & Govt Pos: Mayor, City of North Las Vegas, Nev, 69-73; Nev State Sen, Dist Two, 73- Bus & Prof Pos: Asst mgr, Valley Nat Bank, Escalon, Calif, 51-62; officer, First Nat Bank of Nev, Las Vegas, 62-64; with Findlay Oldsmobile & Friendly Ford, Las Vegas, 70-72. Mil Serv: Entered Army, 41, released, 45. Mem: Am Legion; VFW; Am CofC Exec; Lions; Elks. Relig: Methodist. Mailing Add: 1832 Renada Circle North Las Vegas NV 89030

ECHOLS, M PATTON, JR (R)
Mem, Va Rep State Cent Comt
b Honolulu, Hawaii, Oct 1, 25; s Marion Patton Echols & Nancy McArthur E; m 1956 to Susanne Stokes; c R Carter, M Patton, III, T Tucker & S Campbell. Educ: Va Mil Inst, BS in civil eng, 45; Univ Del Sch Chem Eng, grad student, 54; George Washington Univ, JD, 58; George Washington Univ Law Rev Registered Prof Engr, Va. Polit & Govt Pos: Mem, Dept Com, Exec Res, 55-63; cand, Va State Legis, 63; vchmn, Arlington Co Rep Comt, 63-64, chmn, 64-66; mem campaign comt, Joel T Broyhill for Cong, 64, 66, 68, 70 & 72; mem, Va Rep State Cent Comt, 66-; Va State Sen, Ninth Dist, 69-72; chmn, Arlington Co Comt to Reelect the President, 72; Rep nominee for Attorney Gen of Va, 73. Bus & Prof Pos: Instr & trainee, York Corp, York, Pa, 45-47, appln engr, Atlanta, Ga, 47-50, br mgr, Wilmington, Del, 53-55, asst to vpres corp, DC, 55-58; assoc, Ball & McCarthy, Attorneys, Arlington, Va, 58-62; attorney-at-law, Echols & Hyman, Arlington, 62- Mil Serv: Entered as Recruit, Army, 50, released as Lt, 53, after serv in 928th Engr Aviation Group, 52-53; Lt Col, Army Res, 72- Publ: Air conditioning hospitals, Hosp Mgt, 57. Mem: Am Soc Prof Engrs; Am Soc Civil Engrs; Am Soc Refrigerating Engrs; Am Soc Heating, Ventilating & Air Conditioning Engrs; Soc Am Mil Engrs. Relig: Episcopal; Former Vestryman, St Andrews Episcopal Church, Arlington. Legal Res: 2824 24th St N Arlington VA 22207 Mailing Add: 1419 N Courthouse Rd Arlington VA 22201

ECHOLS, ODIS L (D)
NMex State Sen
b Clovis, NMex, May 28, 30; s Odis L Echols, Sr & Grace Traweek E; m 1955 to Pat Haws; c Danny. Educ: Tex Tech Univ, BS in Educ, 54; Phi Mu Alpha; Kappa Sigma. Polit & Govt Pos: NMex State Sen, 67-; treas, Dem Party of NMex, 74- Bus & Prof Pos: Owner of KCLV Radio, Clovis, NMex, 53-71 & KINT Radio, El Paso, Tex, 61-62; owner of Studio City Shopping Ctr, Clovis, 66-; pres, KMXN-TV, Albuquerque, 74- Mil Serv: Entered as Pvt, Air Force, 51, released as Cpl, 52. Mem: Rotary; NMex Amigos. Honors & Awards: Outstanding Young Man in NMex, State Jaycees, 64; NMex Broadcaster of Year, Broadcasters Asns, 65;

One of Nations Outstanding Legislators, Rutgers Univ, 75. Relig: Methodist. Mailing Add: PO Box 916 Clovis NM 88101

ECHOLS, ROBERT LYNN (R)
b Memphis, Tenn, Jan 13, 41; s James Robert Echols & Carrie Elizabeth E; m 1967 to Marcia Marie Austin; c Susan Marie & Robert Lynn, Jr. Educ: Southwestern at Memphis, BA, 62; Univ Tenn, JD, 64; Sigma Alpha Epsilon; Phi Delta Phi. Polit & Govt Pos: Law clerk, Judge Marion S Boyd, 65-66; legis asst, US Rep Dan Kuykendall, Tenn, 67-69; exec dir Davidson Co, Gov Winfield Dunn, Tenn, 70; gen counsel, Tenn Young Rep Fedn, 70-73; state-fed liaison dir, US Sen Bill Brock, Tenn, 71; state campaign mgr, Tenn State Sen Tom Garland, 72; gen counsel, Tenn Rep Party, 73-74. Mil Serv: Entered as E-1, Army Nat Guard, 66, released as E-3, 69, after serv in Mil Police; Capt, Res, 4 years. Mem: Tenn & Nashville Bar Asns; Tenn Trial Lawyers Asn; Jr CofC; Cumberland Club. Relig: Presbyterian. Legal Res: 125 Vossland Dr Nashville TN 37219 Mailing Add: 1912 Parkway Towers Nashville TN 37219

ECHTMAN, IRWIN M (D)
Mem, Nassau Co Dem Comt, NY
b New York, NY, June 21, 37; s Harry Echtman & Celia Manas E; m 1961 to Leila Goldberg; c Steven Jay, Barry Theodore & Elyse Debra. Educ: Hunter Col, BA, Yale Law Sch, LLB; APO. Polit & Govt Pos: Deleg, Dem Nat Conv, 68; mem, Nassau Co Dem Comt, NY, 68- Bus & Prof Pos: Partner, Easton & Echtman, NY, 67- Legal Res: 30 Bluebird Dr Roslyn Heights NY 11577 Mailing Add: 6 E 39th St New York NY 10016

ECKART, DENNIS EDWARD (D)
Ohio State Rep
b Euclid, Ohio, Apr 6, 50; s Edward J Eckart & Mary D Luzar E; m 1975 to Sandra J Pestotnik. Educ: Xavier Univ, BA; St Louis Univ Law Sch; Cleveland State Univ, JD. Polit & Govt Pos: Ohio State Rep, Dist 18, 75- Bus & Prof Pos: Attorney-at-law, 74- Mem: Slovenian Nat Benefit Soc; United Slovenian Soc. Relig: Roman Catholic. Legal Res: 396 E 272 Euclid OH 44132 Mailing Add: 22578 Lake Shore Blvd Euclid OH 44123

ECKELBERRY, ROBERT LEE (R)
Colo State Rep
b Cameron, Mo, Aug 11, 38; s William Loren Eckelberry & Opal Cousins E; m 1971 to Mary Jane Holwerda. Educ: Am Univ, BA, 59; Cent Mo State Univ, MA, 61; Univ Nebr, Lincoln, PhD, 64; Univ Denver, JD, 68; Alpha Sigma Phi; Omicron Delta Kappa. Polit & Govt Pos: Rep precinct committeeman, Arapahoe Co, Colo, 67-72; Colo State Rep, Arapahoe Co, 73- Bus & Prof Pos: Instr, Univ Nebr, 61-63; asst prof, Kans State Teachers Col, 63-64; assoc prof, Univ Denver, 64-73; attorney-at-law, Englewood, Colo, 69-73. Mem: Am, Colo, Denver & Arapahoe Co Bar Asns; Am Polit Sci Asn. Relig: Methodist. Mailing Add: 3429 E Easter Pl Littleton CO 80122

ECKELS, CHARLES ELMER (R)
Chmn, Stillwater Co Rep Cent Comt, Mont
b Fishtail, Mont, Mar 15, 18; s Charles Elmer Eckels & Nita Beers E; single. Educ: Absarokee High Sch, 4 years. Polit & Govt Pos: Deleg, Mont State Rep Cent Comt, 68-; chmn, Stillwater Co Rep Cent Comt, 68-72 & 75- Bus & Prof Pos: Rancher, 38- Mem: Mason; Scottish Rite; Shrine; Farm Bur. Mailing Add: Fishtail MT 59028

ECKENSBERGER, WILLIAM H, JR (D)
Pa State Rep
b Cementon, Pa, Apr 29, 28; s William H Eckensberger & Hilda Rebecca Gruver E; m to Louise A Wolbach; c Gail Patricia, Jill Louise & William Henry, III. Educ: Muhlenberg Col, BA; George Washington Univ Law Sch, LLB; Phi Alpha Delta. Polit & Govt Pos: Pa State Rep, 64-, chmn, Standing Comt on Law & Order, Pa House of Rep, 69- Bus & Prof Pos: Attorney-at-law. Mil Serv: Army, 50-52. Mem: Lehigh Co Bar Asn; Whitehall Exchange Club. Mailing Add: 839 Fairmont Ave Whitehall PA 18052

ECKER, PEDER KALOIDES (D)
b Sioux City, Iowa, Oct 21, 29; s Peder K Ecker, Sr & Amalia Kaloides E; m 1951 to Dorothy Severson; c Diane, Debra, Dorothy, Dawn & Donna. Educ: Univ SDak, AB, 54, JD, 55; Phi Delta Phi; Alpha Tau Omega. Polit & Govt Pos: Chmn, Lawyers for John F Kennedy, 60; chmn, Minnehaha Co Young Dem, SDak, 60-61; committeeman, SDak Dem State Cent Comt, 60-62; nat committeeman, SDak Young Dem, 62; state chmn, Young Citizens for Johnson-Humphrey, 64; chmn, Minnehaha Co Dem Party, 66 & 68; chmn, Minnehaha Co Dem for Robert F Kennedy, 68; deleg & mem rules comt, Dem Nat Conv, 68; chmn, SDak Dem Party, 68-69; part-time referee in bankruptcy, US Dist Court, SDak, 69- Bus & Prof Pos: Bd mem & pres, SDak Young Lawyers, 64-65; mem bd comrs, State Bar SDak, 65-68. Mil Serv: Army, 48-49, serv in 2nd Inf Div; Judge Adv Gen Corps, Army Res, 62-68, Capt. Mem: Nebr Bar Asn; Am Trial Lawyers Asn; Eagles; Kiwanis; Shrine. Relig: Lutheran Legal Res: 721 E 21st St Sioux Falls SD 57105 Mailing Add: 131 N Main Ave Sioux Falls SD 57102

ECKERLE, PAULINE AUGUSTA (NASH) (R)
Secy, Greene Co Rep Cent & Exec Comts, Ohio
b Xenia, Ohio, Aug 19, 07; d Walter Leigh Nash & Nellie Avis Ireland N; m 1930 to George Clark Eckerle; c Elaine (Mrs Philip E Anderson) & Eloise (Mrs Dale W Shipley). Educ: Greene Co Normal, Cedarville Col, Ohio, 25-27; YWCA; Speech & Drama Club. Polit & Govt Pos: Mem, Pub Employees Retirement Systs, Ohio, 56-; mem, Greene Co Rep Cent Comt, 58-; secy, Greene Co Rep Cent & Exec Comts, 58-64 & 66-; mem, Ohio Asn Elec Off, 58-, mem bd trustees, 62-66, mem legis & retirement comts, 69- Bus & Prof Pos: Elem Teacher, Northridge Schs, Montgomery Co, Ohio, 27-35; dir elec, Greene Co, Ohio, 58- Mem: Ohio Fedn of Rep Women's Orgn, Inc; Xenia Women's Rep Club; Young Men's Christian Asn of Xenia & Greene Co, Ohio; La Sertoma Int & Local Club; Greene Co Coun on Alcoholism. Honors & Awards: Elem Sch Life Cert for Teaching, State of Ohio; Red Cross Vol Serv Award for serv in Air Force Hosp, 9 years. Relig: Presbyterian. Mailing Add: 996 Monroe Ct Xenia OH 45385

ECKERT, FRED J (R-CONSERVATIVE)
NY State Sen
b Rochester, NY, May 6, 41; s Fred J Eckert, Sr & Vera A Costello E; m 1964 to Karen F Laughlin; c Douglas, Brian & Cynthia. Educ: NTex State Univ, BA, magna cum sonitus, 64; NY Univ & New Sch Social Research, eve postgrad courses. Polit & Govt Pos: Town supvr, Greece, 70-72; NY State Sen, Monroe Co, 73- Bus & Prof Pos: Asst dir mass commun, Cath Foreign Mission Soc Am, Ossining, NY, 64-65; pub rels specialist, Gen Foods Corp, Plains, 65-67; acct exec, Rumrill-Hoyt, Inc, Rochester, 67-69; pres, Eckert Assocs, Inc, 73- Publ: Ed, What's So Funny, Padre?, Maryknoll Publ, 65; auth, Playboy interview with H L Hunt, Playboy, 8/66 & The Catholic who didn't want to be President, Cath Digest, 11/72. Honors & Awards: John J McLoughlin Good Citizenship Award, McLoughlin Found, 69; Newell-Boily Award, Tobin Club, 72; Flynn-Formicola Award, 73; Stupp Citation, 74. Relig: Roman Catholic. Mailing Add: 141 Ledgewood Circle Rochester NY 14615

ECKES, J KENNETH (D)
Mem, Dist 36 Exec Comt, NDak
b Wahpeton, NDak, Nov 9, 09; s William F Eckes & Magdaline Pahl E; m 1939 to Martha Worth; c M Kaye (Mrs Hoffert) and Toni M (Mrs Worden). Educ: State Sch Sci, 2 years; Dickinson State Col, 6 months; Univ NDak, JD; Sigma Alpha Epsilon. Polit & Govt Pos: Co & dist secy, Dem Party, NDak, 34-; mem, Dist 36 Exec Comt, currently; state committeeman, NDak Dem Party, Dunn Co, 20 years; states attorney, Dunn Co; City Attorney; City Judge; mem, Dunn Co Exec Comt, currently; mem, first NDak State Parole Bd; chmn, first two war loan drives, Dunn Co; regional dir & mem, NDak State Exec Comt, 8 years; chmn deleg, Dem Nat Conv, 56, deleg, 60. Bus & Prof Pos: General law practice, NDak, 32-; mem several adv bds & dir several corp. Mem: NDak State Bar Asn; NDak Fireman's Asn; Killdeer KofC (grand knight); Elks; Farmers Union. Honors & Awards: Medal for Selective Serv Work; Marksman Award. Relig: Catholic. Mailing Add: Killdeer ND 58640

ECKHARDT, ROBERT CHRISTIAN (D)
US Rep, Tex
b Austin, Tex, July 16, 13; s Joseph Carl Augustus Eckhardt & Norma Wurzbach E; m to Orissa Stevenson (deceased); m 1962 to Nadine Ellen Cannon; c Orissa S (Mrs Lawrence L Arend), Rosalind, Willie, Sidney, Shelby & Sarah. Educ: Univ Tex, BA, 35, LLB, 39. Polit & Govt Pos: Southwestern Rep coordr on Inter-Am Affairs, 44-46; Tex State Rep, 58-66; US Rep, Eighth Dist, 67-, mem interstate & foreign com comt, US House Rep, 69-, mem interior & insular affairs comt, 75-; chmn, Dem Study Group, 75. Bus & Prof Pos: Attorney-at-law, 46- Mil Serv: Pfc, Army Air Corps, 42-44, serv as Primary Flying Sch Instr, 42-44. Relig: Presbyterian. Legal Res: 18710 Bamwood Houston TX 77090 Mailing Add: 1741 Longworth House Off Bldg Washington DC 20515

ECKHART, HENRY WORLEY (D)
Mem Exec Comt, Franklin Co Dem Party, Ohio
b Columbus, Ohio, Nov 12, 32; s Jay Vincent Eckhart & Alice Worley E; m 1963 to Claudine Lalli; c Anne Elizabeth & Robert Alan. Educ: Ohio State Univ, BS in BA, 54; Univ Mich, JD, 58; Kappa Sigma; Phi Delta Phi. Polit & Govt Pos: Cent committeeman, & mem exec comt, Franklin Co Dem Party, Ohio, 67-; alt deleg-at-lg, Dem Nat Conv, 68; chmn speakers bur, Ohio Dem Party, 68-, chmn const & by-laws comt, 70-71, treas exec comt, 71, legal counsel, 73-74; treas, Gilligan for Gov Comt, 70; deleg, Ohio Dem Conv, 70-74; mem, Dem Charter Comn, 71-74; chmn, Pub Utilities Comn, Ohio, 71-73. Bus & Prof Pos: Attorney-at-law, 58-; field counsel, Fed Nat Mortgage Asn, 67-69; mem, Zacks, Luper & Durst, 74-; mem, Ad Hoc Comt on Energy Research & Develop, Nat Asn of Railroad & Utilities Comnrs, 73 & Power Siting Comn, Ohio, 73. Mem: Ohio State Bar Asn; Jr CofC; Univ Mich Club of Columbus (pres); Kappa Sigma Alumni Asn (treas); Dem Lawyers Club (treas). Mailing Add: 1850 Upper Chelsea Rd Upper Arlington OH 43212

ECKHART, JAMES F (D)
Fla State Rep
b Camden, NJ, June 7, 23; s Joseph Eckhart & Mary E E; m 1950 to Alicia Moreno; c John, James, Debora, Eva & Daniel. Educ: Univ Miami, JD, 50; Omicron Delta Kappa; Iron Arrow; Phi Kappa Delta; Phi Alpha Delta. Polit & Govt Pos: Gen counsel, Govt Opers Comt, Mil Opers Subcomt, US House Rep, Washington, DC, 53-57; gen counsel, Dade Co Port Authority, Fla, 58-66; Fla State Rep, Dist 115, 74- Bus & Prof Pos: Attorney, pvt practice, Coral Gables, Fla, 66- Mil Serv: Entered as Pvt, Air Force, 43-46 & 50, released as 1st Lt, 53, after serv as Base Legal Officer, NAfrica, 50-53. Mem: Coral Gables Lions; United Way (various off, 58-); SDade CofC. Honors & Awards: Cert of Merit, Fed Aviation Agency, 64; Cert of Appreciation, Dade Co Comn, 67. Relig: Catholic. Legal Res: 8530 SW 16th St Miami FL 33155 Mailing Add: 370 Minorca Ave Coral Gables FL 33134

ECKLES, STANLEY HEURICH (R)
Treas, Montgomery Co Rep Cent Comt, Md
b Washington, DC, Sept 4, 29; s Charles Ellison Eckles & Anita Heurich E; m 1955 to Ruth Rowe; c Ivy Victoria, Gail Marie, Laurie Lee & David James. Educ: Univ Mo-Columbia, 49-52. Polit & Govt Pos: Deleg, Md Rep State Conv, 64; mem, Montgomery Co Rep Cent Comt, 66-, chmn, 70, treas, currently; deleg, Rep Nat Conv, 72. Bus & Prof Pos: Farmer, Montgomery Co, Md, 52-57; asst mgr, Riverside Car Wash, Washington, DC, 57; off mgr, C E Eckles & Co (real estate), 58-; partner, P R E P (pub rels), 67- Mem: Lakewood Country Club, Rockville, Md; Garrett Park Estates Citizens Asn; Columbia Hist Soc, Washington, DC. Relig: Episcopal. Mailing Add: 5201 White Flint Dr Kensington MD 20795

ECKSTEIN, A J (TONY) (DFL)
Minn State Rep
Mailing Add: 411 S State New Ulm MN 56073

EDDINGS, INEZ C (R)
Rep Nat Committeewoman, SC
b Richland Co, SC, Nov 14, 09; m 1935 to B Ray Eddings. Educ: SC, AB, MEd, PhD. Polit & Govt Pos: Richland Co Supt Educ, SC, 65-69; Rep nominee, State Supt Educ, 66 & 70; alt deleg, Rep Nat Conv, 68; Rep Nat Committeewoman, SC, 31-65. Relig: Baptist. Mailing Add: 832 Kipling Dr Columbia SC 29205

EDDLEMAN, RICHARD E (R)
Chmn, Bexar Co Rep Party, Tex
b Graham, Tex, Aug 3, 21; s Virgil C Eddleman & Julia Pitman E; m 1952 to Carol Stevenson; c Ann, Margaret & John. Educ: Tarleton State Col; Tex Univ; pres, Lords & Commoners; vpres, student coun, Tarleton State Col. Polit & Govt Pos: Campaign canvas coordr, Bexar Co Rep Party, Tex, 72, orgn dir, 73, chmn, 74- Mil Serv: Entered as Pvt, Army, 42, released as Col, 71, after serv in Europe, Korea; Legion of Merit, plus many others. Mailing Add: 618 Richfield Dr San Antonio TX 78239

EDDY, DONNA M (D)
Second VChairperson, 26th Assembly Dist Dem Comt, Wis
b Milwaukee, Wis, Nov 20, 52; d John Eddy & Dorothy C Connors E; single. Educ: Univ Wis-Milwaukee, 70-; Acad Affairs Comt; FOCUS; United Students; Vote 72. Polit & Govt

Pos: Coordr, Univ Wis-Milwaukee Student Comt for Landry, formerly; vchairperson, Univ Wis-Mailwaukee Students for McGovern Campaign, 71-72; deleg, Dem Nat Conv, 72 & Dem Nat Mid-Term Conf, 74; second vchairperson, 26th Assembly Dist Dem Comt, Wis, 73-; off mgr, Friends of Jacobson for Attorney Gen Campaign, 74; committeeperson, Third Aldermanic Dist, Milwaukee, 75. Mem: Nat Comt for Sane Nuclear Policy; Concerned Consumers League; Milwaukee Dem Co Coun; Dem Women's Comt; Nat Women's Polit Caucus. Relig: Christian. Mailing Add: 615 E Wright Milwaukee WI 53212

EDDY, FRANK VINCENT (R)
Chmn, Newington Rep Town Comt, Conn
b New Britain, Conn, Aug 15, 22; s Vincent Luce Eddy & Charlotte M Rowley E; m 1946 to Esther Kathleen Mangone; c Joshua Frank & Norah Esther. Educ: Moody's Bus Sch, 45; Univ Conn, Dairy Mfg, 47. Polit & Govt Pos: Mem, Newington Rep Town Comt, Conn, 49-, chmn, 67-; selectman, Newington, Conn, 62- Bus & Prof Pos: Owner, Eddy Dairy, 51-65; vpres, Red Rock Develop Corp, 62-; secy, Mowhawk Farms Inc, 66-68; dir local bd, New Britain Bank & Trust Co, 67-; pres, F V Eddy Inc, Car Rental, 68-72; Frank V Eddy Real Estate Co, 73- Mil Serv: Entered as Pvt, Army, 42, released as Pfc, 45, after serv in 102nd Inf Div, ETO, 44-45; Expert Combat Infantry Badge; Purple Heart; Bronze Star. Mem: Am Legion; Mason; Kiwanis; Conn Farm Bur; DAV. Honors & Awards: Kiwanian of Year, 74. Relig: Congregational. Mailing Add: 200 Church St Newington CT 06111

EDELEN, MARY BEATY (R)
SDak State Rep
b Vermillion, SDak, Dec 9, 44; d Donald William Beaty & Marjorie Louise Heckel B; m 1968 to Joseph Ruey Edelen, Jr. Educ: Cottey Col, 63-64; Black Hills State Col (SDak), summer 65; Univ SDak, Vermillion, BA, 67; Trinity Univ (Tex), MA, 71; Phi Alpha Theta; Phi Theta Kappa; Chi Omega. Polit & Govt Pos: Page, SDak State Senate, 63; research intern, SDak Legis Research Coun, summer 66; co chmn, Robert Hirsch for US Senate, 72; SDak State Rep, 72-, mem, Judiciary Comt, vchmn, Com Comt, chmn, Subcomt on Ins, vchmn, Investigating Comt, mem, Legis Research Coun Exec Bd. Bus & Prof Pos: Lectr hist, Univ SDak, Vermillion, 69-71; part time instr hist, Yankton Col, 74-75. Publ: Bryan Callaghan, II: His Earlier Political Career, 1885-1899, Trinity Univ (Tex), 71. Mem: Am Asn Univ Women; Nat Orgn Women Legislators; Eastern Star (Worthy Matron); PEO (pres); Mortar Bd (hon mem). Honors & Awards: Grace E Burgess Book Award, Univ SDak, 66. Relig: United Church of Christ. Mailing Add: 301 Lewis St Vermillion SD 57069

EDELMAN, ALMA ANN (D)
Chmn, Grant Co Dem Party, Nebr
b Hecla, Nebr, Dec 31, 18; d William Tecumpseh Gottlob & Rebekah Osborn G; m 1936 to Floyd Franklin Edelman; c Margaret (Mrs Applegarth), Frances Davis & Thelma. Educ: Chadron High Sch, Nebr; Hyannis High Sch, grad, 36. Polit & Govt Pos: Mem Eisenhower's Youth Comn, spring 61; Co coordr for Robert F Kennedy, Nebr, 68; Co coordr for Gov J J Exon, 70; chmn, Grant Co Dem Party, 68-; mem, Nebr State Dem Cent Comt, 70- Bus & Prof Pos: Bus assoc & clerk, Floyd Edelman Ranching & Custom Opers, 36- Mem: Order of Eastern Star (past Matron, Golden Rules chap); Nebr Stockgrowers Asn; Nebr Cowbelles; Calvary Episcopal Guild; Am Legion Auxiliary. Relig: Episcopal. Mailing Add: Box 164 Hyannis NE 69350

EDELMAN, EDMUND DOUGLAS (D)
b Los Angeles, Calif, Sept 27, 30; s Nathan Edelman & Buddie Rothman E; m 1968 to Mari Mayer Kogus; c Erica Nancy & Emily Rose. Educ: Univ Calif, Los Angeles, BA, 54, LLB, 58; Phi Beta Kappa; pres, Phi Sigma Alpha. Polit & Govt Pos: Arbitrator, Fed Mediation & Conciliation List; dep legis counsel, Calif State Legis, 61-62; spec asst to gen counsel, Nat Labor Rels Bd, 63-64; councilman Fifth Dist, Los Angeles City Coun, 65-74, chmn charter & admin code comt, 69; pres, Beverly Hills Young Dem; supvr, Third Dist, Los Angeles Co, 74- Bus & Prof Pos: Law clerk to US Dist Court judge, 58-60; attorney, 58-; teacher, Fairfax Eve High Sch, 59-61; lectr, Inst Indust Rels, Univ Calif, Los Angeles, 63. Mil Serv: Entered as Yeoman Seaman, Navy, 51, released as Yeoman 3/C, 52. Mem: Medic Alert, Los Angeles (mem bd); Jewish War Vets; Town Hall; B'nai B'rith; Anti-Defamation League (mem regional adv bd). Relig: Jewish. Legal Res: 1110 Chantilly Rd Los Angeles CA 90024 Mailing Add: 500 W Temple St Rm 821 Los Angeles CA 90012

EDEN, JANET JONES (R)
Co-Chmn, Washita Co Rep Comt, Okla
b Cordell, Okla, Sept 30, 38; d Ray Lockwood Jones, Sr & Ellen Jones J; m 1960 to Jimmie Winfred Eden; c Angela & Jimmie, Jr. Educ: Am Univ, 56-57; Univ Okla, BS, 60; Southwestern Okla State Univ, MEd, 68; Kappa Delta Pi. Polit & Govt Pos: Mem, Sen Henry Bellmon's Orgn, 68; committeewoman, Rep State Comt, Okla, 69-70; co coordr, Jay Wilkinson's Cong Campaign, 70; co-chmn, Washita Co Rep Comt, Okla, 70-72 & 75-, chmn, 72-75; co coordr, Sen Dewey Bartlett's Sen Campaign, 72; mem, Comt to Draft Reagan for President, 75. Bus & Prof Pos: Clerk typist, Small Bus Admin, Washington, DC, summers, 57-59; asst dormitory counr, Univ Okla, 59-60; high sch teacher, Perryton, Tex, 60-62 & Okla, 64-; counr, Foreign Study League, European Campus, 69 & 74. Mem: Okla Educ Asn (Washita Co secy-treas, 70-71, 72-73, co pres, 74-); Delta Kappa Gamma; Washita Co Farm Bur (vpres, Woman's Bd dirs, 73-74); Washita Co Develop Coun (vchmn, 75); Okla Coun Teachers English. Honors & Awards: Okla Cherry Blossom Princess, 57; Okla Farm Bur Family of Year, 74; first person to have her United Daughters of Confederacy membership issued before age 16. Relig: Baptist. Mailing Add: Rte 1 Rocky OK 73661

EDENS, J DRAKE, JR (R)
b Columbia, SC, May 13, 25; s J Drake Edens, Sr & May Youmans E; m 1946 to Ferrell McCracken; c Jenny & Robert M. Educ: Univ SC, BS in bus admin, 49; Eta Mu Pi. Polit & Govt Pos: State exec committeeman, Richland Co Rep Party, SC, 62-63; state chmn, SC Rep Party, 63-65; deleg, Rep Nat Conv, 64 & 68, chmn, SC deleg, 64; chmn, SC Presidential Campaign for Sen Barry Goldwater, 64; campaign chmn for reelection of US Rep Albert W Watson, 65; Rep Nat Committeeman, vchmn, Rep Nat Comt, mem exec comt & Nat Rep Coord Comt, 65-72; mem, Nixon for President Nat Adv Comt & Nat Finance Comt & State Finance Chmn for SC, Nixon Campaign, 68; app by President Nixon & Secy of Interior as mem, Nat Adv Bd for Sport Fisheries & Wildlife, 70-, elected chmn bd, 70- Bus & Prof Pos: Vpres, Edens Food Stores Inc, 49-55; pres & gen mgr, Edens-Turbeville Gen Ins Agency, 56-64; self-employed, securities, real estate investments, farming and timber mgt, 64- Mil Serv: Entered as Pvt, Marine Corps, 43, released as Cpl, 46, after serv in 6th Marine Div & various other units with duty in Pac Theatre, 44-45. Mem: Gtr Columbia & SC State CofC; Columbia Community Rels Coun, Inc; Alston Wilkes Prisoner Aid Soc, (bd mem, currently); Audubon Soc. Relig: Methodist. Mailing Add: 905 Arbutus Dr Columbia SC 29205

EDGAR, JOSEPH T (R)
Secy of State, Maine
b Jersey City, NJ, Apr 1, 10; s Joseph A Edgar & Alice C Tappen E; m 1939 to Margaret Sanford; c Margaret. Educ: Princeton Univ, AB, 32; Univ Pa Law Sch, 2 years. Polit & Govt Pos: Mem town coun, Bar Harbor, Maine, 48-49; Maine State Rep, 55-60, speaker, Maine House of Rep, 57-60; Maine State Sen, 61; Dep Secy of State, 61-65, Secy of State, 67- Mem: Bar Harbor CofC (pres, 50-52). Relig: Protestant. Legal Res: 31 Ridgeway Dr Hallowell Post Off ME 04347 Mailing Add: State House Augusta ME 04330

EDGAR, ROBERT WILLIAM (D)
US Rep, Pa
b Philadelphia, Pa, May 29, 43; s Leroy Edgar & Marion E; m 1964 to Merle Deaver; c Robert William, Jr, Thomas David & Andrew John. Educ: Lycoming Col, BA, 65; Drew Univ, MD, 68. Polit & Govt Pos: US Rep, Pa, 75-, mem pub works & transportation comt & vet affairs comt, US House Rep, 75- Bus & Prof Pos: Pastor, Pa, 61-74; United Protestant chaplain, Drexel Univ, 71-74; assoc pastor, Lansdowne United Methodist Church, 73-74. Mem: Cong Dem Study Group; Mem of Cong for Peace Through Law; Environ Study Conf; Nat Wildlife Fedn. Honors & Awards: NAACP Award Courage & Humanitarianism, 75. Relig: Methodist. Legal Res: 221 S Sproul Rd Broomall PA 19008 Mailing Add: 117 Cannon House Off Bldg Washington DC 20515

EDGECOMB, ROBERT LEE (R)
b Dallas, Tex, Feb 28, 38; s James Delbert Edgecomb & Charleyne Bryan; m 1964 to Patricia Ann Neely. Educ: Tex A&M Univ, BBA, 69; Alpha Delta Sigma. Polit & Govt Pos: Chmn voter groups, Brazos Co Rep Party, 68, chmn pub rels, 68-70, chmn primary comt, 70, chmn exec comt & chmn party, 70-72; chmn Reelect the President Comt, 72; chmn, finance comt, 72; chmn, ballot security, 72; deleg, Tex State Rep Conv, 72, mem permanent orgn comt, 72. Bus & Prof Pos: Educ dir, Am Mkt Schs, Dallas, Tex, 60-61; material order analyst, Ryan Aeronaut Co, San Diego, 61-62; outside salesman, Ducommun Metals & Supply Co, Dallas, 62-66; mgr, United Fidelity Life Ins Co, Bryan, 69-71; rep & acct exec ANCO/The Anderson Co, currently. Mil Serv: Entered as Pvt, Army, 57, released as SP-5, 60, after serv as instr, Army Engr Sch, Ft Belvoir, Va, 57-60; Good Conduct Medal. Mem: Cent Tex Asn Life Underwriters (secy); Sul Ross Lodge 1300 AF&AM (Past Master); Houston Consistory; Arabia Temple Shrine; Scottish Rite. Relig: Episcopal. Mailing Add: 1200 Berkeley College Station TX 77840

EDGERTON, JOHN PALMER (R)
Chmn, Warren Co Rep Cent Comt, Ind
b Rock Island, Ill, Dec 27, 17; s Palmer Ray Edgerton & Zoe McConnell E; m 1942 to Florence Smith; c Heather (Mrs Ray Slaby), Celeste, Dia & Darci. Educ: Purdue Univ, BSA, 39; Kappa Sigma. Polit & Govt Pos: Trustee, Pine Twp, Warren Co, Ind, 63-70; chmn, Warren Co Rep Cent Comt, Inc, currently. Bus & Prof Pos: Farmer, Warren Co, Ind, 49- Mil Serv: 1st Lt, Army, 41-46, 135th Anti Aircraft Gun Bn, ETO, 44-46. Mem: Lions; Ind Farm Bur. Relig: Protestant. Mailing Add: Box 151 RR 1 Pine Village IN 47975

EDGERTON, ROBERT ALBERT, SR (R)
Chmn, Stratford Rep Town Comt, Conn
b Milford, Conn, Aug 22, 27; s Bryant Clinton Edgerton & Lillian Engval E; m to Dorothy Firmender; c Robert Albert, Jr & Donna Beth. Educ: Milford Prep, Conn, 47. Polit & Govt Pos: Chmn, Stratford Rep Town Comt, Conn, 71- Bus & Prof Pos: Vpres, Lawrence Transport Inc, Stratford, 61- Mil Serv: Entered as enlistee, Navy, 45, released as Seaman 1/C, 46, after serv in Washington, DC. Mem: Mill River & H B Brownson Country Clubs; Third Cong Dist Rep Orgn; Conn Rep Key Club. Mailing Add: 230 Twin Oak Terr Stratford CT 06497

EDINGTON, PATRICIA GENTRY (D)
Committeewoman, Young Dem of Ala
b Mobile, Ala, Mar 17, 38; d Curtis A Gentry, Jr & Mildred Delchamps G; m 1962 to State Sen Robert Sherard Edington; c Sherard Caffey & Virginia Ellen. Educ: Auburn Univ, BS, 60. Polit & Govt Pos: Deleg & mem, Credentials Comt, Dem Nat Conv, 68; committeewoman, Young Dem of Ala, 72- Bus & Prof Pos: Exec dir, Mobile Historic Develop Comn, 72- Mem: Mobile Historic Develop Comn (pres); Jaycettes; Historic Mobile Preservation Soc; various other Historic Preservation Groups. Honors & Awards: Distinguished Young Woman of Mobile, 67; Arthritis Foundation's Distinguished Serv Award. Relig: Presbyterian. Mailing Add: 307 Conti St Mobile AL 36602

EDISON, DEBRA DENISE (D)
b Parsons, Kans, Mar 2, 54; d Creo Edison & Mildred Delores Warren E; single. Educ: Labette Community Jr Col, 71-72; Kans State Col, Pittsburg, BS, 75; Phi Theta Kappa; Psi Chi. Polit & Govt Pos: Sen, Labette Community Jr Col Student Senate, Parsons, Kans, 71-72; Sen, Kans State Col, Pittsburg, 72-73; deleg, Dem Nat Conv, 72; mem, Kans Platform Subcomt, 72. Bus & Prof Pos: Secy, Millie's Fashions Inc, 72- Mem: Pittsburg Black Student Movement; NAACP. Honors & Awards: Neewollah Queen Cand, Parsons CofC, 71; Voice of Dem Medal, VFW, 71 & 72. Relig: United Methodist. Mailing Add: 1305 Morton Parsons KS 67357

EDMISTEN, RUFUS LIGH (D)
Attorney Gen, NC
b Watauga Co, NC, July 12, 41; s Walter F Edmisten & Nell Hollar E; m 1963 to Martha Jane Moretz; c Martha Rebecca. Educ: Univ NC, BA, 63; George Washington Univ Law Sch, JD, with honors, 67; KA Fraternity; Soc Janus; Order of the Old Well; Robert Linher Award. Polit & Govt Pos: Counsel, Judiciary Subcomt Const Rights, US Senate, 67-69, chief counsel & staff dir, Judiciary Subcomt Separation of Powers, 69-74, dep chief counsel, Select Comt Presidential Campaign Activities, 73-74; Attorney Gen, NC, 74- Mil Serv: Pvt, Army Res, 66-67, serv in Transportation C. Mem: Mason; Am, Fed & NC Bar Asns. Honors & Awards: Wildlife Conserv Award, Watauga Wildlife Club, 62; Good Govt Award, State of NC, 69; Hon Mem, NC Fraternal Order of Police, 74. Relig: Baptist. Legal Res: 1533 Shadowood Rd Raleigh NC 27609 Mailing Add: PO Box 629 Raleigh NC 27602

EDMONDSON, BETTY LAVERN (R)
b Camarillo, Calif, Feb 23, 24; d Dr Charles Allen Laws & Zina Shumway L; m 1943 to Merwin Paul Edmondson; c George Henry, Kelley Allen (deceased) & Brian Paul. Educ: Univ Wash; Alpha Chap, Chi Omega. Polit & Govt Pos: Bd mem pub rels & chmn mem comt, Wash Fedn Rep Women, 59-65, arrangement chmn for conv, 68, dir, Fourth Cong Dist, 68-70, second vpres, 71-73; vchmn, Yakima Co Rep Cent Comt, 60-64; State Committeewoman, 64-69; precinct committeewoman, Yakima Co Rep Party, 60-; deleg & panel mem pub rels, Biennial Meeting, Nat Fedn Rep Women, Phoenix, 63, & deleg,

Washington, DC, 67; alt deleg-at-lg, Rep Nat Conv, 64; secy, Wash State Rep Cent Comt, 66-69; arrangements chmn, Rep State Conv, 66 & 70, mem rules & orders comt, 68; mem, Gov Task Force Comt, 66-; chmn rules & order comt, Yakima Co Rep Conv, 68; treas, Yakima Co Citizens Comt Nixon-Agnew, 68; mem, Wash State Am Revolution Bicentennial Comn, 70-73; pres, Yakima Woman's Rep Club, 71-72; city councilman, Yakima, 73-; mem, Yakima Co Alcohol Abuse & Alcoholism Comn, 73-; mem, Yakima Co Dist Bd Health, 73- Bus & Prof Pos: Secy, Douglas Aircraft Co, Los Angeles, 43; Bookkeeper & typist, Fairway Finance, Yakima, 44-46; Cascade TV Homemaker, KIMA-TV, Yakima, KLEW-TV, Lewiston, Idaho & KEPR-TV, Tri-Cities, 56-58; field rep, McCall's Mag, 58-68; commentator, style shows, People's Store & Serv Orgns, 58- Publ: Manual on public relations, adopted & published by Nat Fedn of Rep Women, 61. Mem: Allied Arts Coun Agenda Club; Woman's Fed Club; Wash State Pub Health Asn; Alma Graham Hosp Guild; Wash State Fedn Women's Clubs (adv jr mem & interaction liaison). Honors & Awards: Distinguished Citizen Award, Yakima Co United Good Neighbors, 70; Citizen's Salute Host City Award, Yakima Valley Visitors & Conv Bur, 70; Distinguished Serv Award, Wash State Rep Cent Comt, 71; Woman of Achievement, Yakima Bus & Prof Women's Club, 73. Relig: Latter-Day Saint; Dir of Drama & Speech, Mutual Improv Asn, 58-68. Mailing Add: 624 S 34th Ave Yakima WA 98902

EDMONDSON, ED (D)

b Muskogee, Okla, Apr 7, 19; s Edmond Augustus Edmondson & Esther Pullen E; m 1944 to June Maureen Pilley; c James Edmond, William, John, June & Brian. Educ: Univ Okla, AB, 40; Georgetown Univ Law Sch, LLB, 47; Phi Beta Kappa; Phi Delta Phi; Delta Sigma Rho; Phi Gamma Delta. Polit & Govt Pos: Fed Bur Invest, 40-43; attorney-at-law, Muskogee, Okla, 47-49; Muskogee Co attorney, 49-53; US Rep, Okla, 53-72; Dem cand for US Sen, 74. Bus & Prof Pos: Newspaperman, Muskogee Daily, Okla; newspaperman, United Press, 36-38; Washington correspondent, Muskogee Phoenix, Sapulpa Herald, Holdenville News & Daily Ardmoreite, 46-47; admitted to DC & Okla Bars, 47; assoc, J Howard Edmondson, 48. Mil Serv: US Navy, 43-46. Mem: Am Legion; VFW; Mason; Elks; Kiwanis. Mailing Add: 219 N 14th St Muskogee OK 74401

EDMONDSON, W A DREW (D)

Okla State Rep

b Washington, DC, Oct 12, 46; s Ed Edmondson & June Pilley E; m 1967 to Linda Larason; c Mary Elizabeth & Robert Andrew. Educ: Northeastern State Col, BAE, 68; Dean's & Pres Honor Rolls; Phi Sigma Epsilon; Young Dem; Student Educ Asn. Polit & Govt Pos: Staff mem, US Sen Mike Monroney, Okla, summers 64 & 65; staff mem, US Rep Carl Albert, Okla, summer 66; deleg, Okla Dem Conv, 68; Okla State Rep, 74- Bus & Prof Pos: Teacher, Muskogee High Sch, Okla, 73-74. Mil Serv: Entered as E-1, Navy, 68, released as E-5, after serv in Saigon, 71-72; Vietnam Campaign Ribbon; Navy Achievement Medal; Joint Serv Commendation Medal. Mem: Okla Educ Asn; Am Legion; VFW. Honors & Awards: Outstanding Debator, Cent High Sch, Muskogee, Okla, 64; Finalist, Nat Collegiate Debate Tournament, Brooklyn, NY, 68. Relig: Presbyterian. Mailing Add: 2017 Columbus Muskogee OK 74401

EDMONSON, JAMES HOWARD (D)

Committeeman, Tenn State Dem Exec Comt

b Sylacauga, Ala, May 19, 31; s Cecil Howard Edmonson (deceased) & Flora Owings Coleman E; m 1954 to Frances Royala Tucker; c Betty Faith, Deborah Lynn & James David. Educ: Jacksonville State Univ, 50-51; Samford Univ, BA, 57; Southern Theol Sem, BD, 61; La State Univ, Baton Rouge, MA, 63, PhD, 71; Phi Alpha Theta. Polit & Govt Pos: Deleg, Madison & Gibson Co, Tenn Const Conv, 71-72; committeeman, Tenn State Dem Exec Comt, Madison & Gibson Co, 74-; committeeman, Jackson-Cent-Merry High Sch Adv Comt, 72- Bus & Prof Pos: Tabulator operator, Hayes Aircraft Corp, Birmingham, Ala, 55-57; engr-TV technician, WAVE-TV, Louisville, Ky, 57-61, WHBT-TV, Baton Rouge, La, 61 & WBRZ-TV, Baton Rouge, La, 62-65; chmn & assoc prof, Union Univ (Tenn), 65- Mil Serv: Entered as Pvt, Army, 51, released as 2nd Lt, 54, after serv in 75th Field Artil Bn, Korea, 53-54; Lt Col, Army Res, 54-; Korean Serv Medal; UN Serv Medal; Nat Defense Serv Medal. Publ: Auth, Desertion in the American Army During the Revolutionary War, McCowart-Mercer, 75. Mem: West Tenn Hist Soc (ed, Papers, 75-); Am Hist Asn; Orgns Am Historians; Southern Hist Asn; Exchange Club, Jackson, Tenn. Honors & Awards: Research grant, Union Univ, 75; Outstanding Educator of Am, 74; WJAK Radio Action Award, 73, 74 & 75. Relig: Southern Baptist. Mailing Add: 15 Franwood Cove Jackson TN 38301

EDMUNDS, JAMES T (D)

Va State Sen

Mailing Add: PO Box 387 Kenbridge VA 23944

EDSELL, RALPH JAMES, JR (R)

b Far Rockaway, NY, Oct 11, 23; s Ralph James Edsell & Geraldine V Dulfer E; m 1945 to Mary Elizabeth Essig; c Lisa Jane, Ralph James, III & John Charles. Educ: Cornell Univ, AB, 46, Law Sch, LLB, 49; Phi Gamma Delta. Polit & Govt Pos: Trial attorney, Internal Security Div, Dept Justice, 53-55; chief counsel to Speaker Joseph F Carlino, NY State Assembly, 55-65; Rep cand for US Rep, NY, 64; admin asst to US Rep Norman F Lent, NY, 71-75. Bus & Prof Pos: Attorney, Cedarhurst, NY, currently; pres, The Edsell Agency, Ins, currently. Mil Serv: Entered as Pvt, Air Force, 43, released, 46, reentered as 1st Lt, 50-52, serv in Mil Intel, 43-46 & Judge Adv Gen Corps, Japan, 50-52. Mem: Nassau Co Bar Asn; Capitol Hill Club; Am Legion; VFW; Lawrence-Cedarhurst Rep Club. Honors & Awards: Nassau Co Regional Scholarship, 42. Relig: Methodist. Mailing Add: 572 Atlantic Ave Lawrence NY 11516

EDSTROM, RONALD DWIGHT (DFL)

b Oakland, Calif, Mar 21, 36; s Dwight A Edstrom & Edna M Stamps E; m 1959 to Patricia Jean Ponten; c John R, Robert G & Jennifer P. Educ: Univ Calif, Berkeley, AB, 58; Univ Calif, Davis, PhD, 62; Sigma Xi; Abracadabra; Delta Chi. Polit & Govt Pos: Chmn, 25th Ward, Hennepin Co Dem-Farmer-Labor Party, 69-71; chmn, 31st State Sen Dist Dem-Farmer-Labor Party, 70-71, chmn, Third Cong Dist Dem-Farmer-Labor Party, formerly; mem, Golden Valley Planning Comn, 71-; deleg, Dem Nat Conv, 72. Bus & Prof Pos: Research assoc, Univ Mich, 62-63; research assoc, Johns Hopkins Univ, 63-65; asst prof, Univ Minn, Minneapolis, 65-71, assoc prof, 71- Publ: Contrib to sci lit on biochem. Mem: Am Chem Soc; Am Soc Microbiol; Am Asn Advan Sci; Am Asn Univ Prof. Relig: Protestant. Mailing Add: 2303 Xerxes Ave N Golden Valley MN 55422

EDWARDS, ATTICUS FITZGERALD (D)

Chmn, Wichita Co Dem Exec Comt, Tex

b Waxahachie, Tex, May 4, 90; s Henry Batte Edwards & Mary Strickland E; m 1925 to Louise Wright. Educ: Ft Worth Polytech Col, 08-12; Trinity Univ, 14-16; Univ Tex, BA, 20; Southern Methodist Univ, fel, 21-23, MA; Univ Calif, Los Angeles, summer, 26; Univ Colo, summer, 27; Phi Kappa Gamma. Polit & Govt Pos: Precinct chmn, Dem Party, 38-64; secy, Wichita Co Dem Exec Comt, Tex, 60-64, chmn, 64-; admin asst to Maurice Doke, Tex Legislator, 63; alt deleg, Dem Nat Conv, 68, deleg, 72. Mil Serv: Home Guard in World War II. Mem: Wichita Falls City Teachers Asn; Col Classroom Teachers Asn; Retired Teachers Asn; Mason; charter mem, Knife & Fork Club. Relig: Methodist; mem off bd & Sunday Sch teacher. Mailing Add: 2160 Ave H Wichita Falls TX 76309

EDWARDS, BINGHAM DAVID (D)

Ala State Sen

b Decatur, Ala, Apr 6, 43; s Dr Mike E Edwards & Julia Bingham E; m 1968 to Elizabeth Watson; c Bingham David, Jr & Elizabeth Reynolds. Educ: Univ of the South, BA, 65; Univ Ala Law Sch, JD, 68; Phi Alpha Delta; Sigma Nu; Highlanders. Polit & Govt Pos: Asst dist attorney, Morgan Co, Ala, 72-73; Ala State Sen, Lawrence & Morgan Co, 74- Bus & Prof Pos: Partner, Hutson, Elrod, Edwards & Belser, attorneys-at-law, 72- Mil Serv: Lt, Naval Res, 67- Mem: Decatur Jaycees; Kiwanis Club; Morgan Co Young Dem; Am Bar Asn; Ala Trial Lawyer's Asn. Honors & Awards: Nominated Decatur's Outstanding Young Man, 74-75. Relig: Protestant. Legal Res: 2408 Crestview Dr SE Decatur AL 35601 Mailing Add: PO Box 632 Decatur AL 35601

EDWARDS, CHARLES CORNELL (R)

b Overton, Nebr, Sept 16, 23; s Charles Busby Edwards & Lillian Margaret E; m to Sue Cowles Kruidenier; c Timothy K, Charles C, Jr, Nancy Cornell & David B. Educ: Princeton Univ, 41-43; Univ Colo, BA, 45, MD, 48; St Mary's Hosp, Minneapolis, internship, 48-49; Univ Minn, MS in Surg, 56. Hon Degrees: Doctor of Laws, Fla Southern Col, 73. Polit & Govt Pos: Mem, Polk Co Rep Finance Comt, Iowa, 59-60; Comnr, Food & Drug Admin, 68-73; Asst Secy Health, Dept Health, Educ & Welfare, 73-74. Bus & Prof Pos: Teaching fel physiol, Univ Minn, 49-50; staff asst surg, Mayo Clin, Rochester, 55-56; pvt practice, surg, 56-61; teaching staff, Iowa Methodist Hosp & Mercy Hosp, Des Moines, 58-61; instr surg, Georgetown Univ Med Sch, 61-62; asst dir, Georgetown Surg Serv, DC Columbia Gen Hosp, 61-62; consult, US Pub Health Serv, 61-62; secy, residency rev comt gen surg, obstetrics & gynecology, plastic surg, otolaryngology & urology, Coun Med Educ & Hosp, Am Med Asn, 62-63, asst dir, Div Environ Med & Med Serv, 63-64, secy, Coun Med Serv, 63-64, dir, Div Socio-Econ Activities, 65-67; mem faculty, Northwestern Univ Med Clin, 63; vpres & managing off, Booz Allen & Hamilton, 67-69; sr vpres, Becton, Dickinson & Co, Rutherford, NJ, currently. Mil Serv: Navy, 42-46; Lt Med Corps, Navy, assigned to Marine Corps, Korea, 49-50. Mem: Iowa Children's Homes Soc; Metrop Club of Washington, DC; Econ Club of Chicago; Kenwood Club of Bethesda, Md. Honors & Awards: Silver & Gold Award, Med Ctr, Univ Colo, 72; Founders Award, Grant Hosp, Chicago, 72; Hon Chancellor of Fla Southern Col for 73. Relig: Protestant. Mailing Add: Becton Dickinson & Co Rutherford NJ 07070

EDWARDS, CHARLES MARVIN (D)

Chmn, Carroll Co Dem Comt, Tenn

b Nov 11, 25; s Robert Lee Edwards & Donnie Gooch E; m 1946 to Bula Lee Cobb; c Phyllis, Brian & Sheila. Polit & Govt Pos: Chmn, Carroll Co Dem Comt, Tenn, 74- Mil Serv: Entered as Pvt, Army, 44, released as T/5, 46, after serv in Field Artil, ETO; Good Conduct; Marksman; ETO Ribbon with two Battle Stars; Army Occup Medal. Mem: Nat Farmers Orgn (co chmn); Farm Bur (dir, 51-52, 71-72 & 74). Relig: Protestant. Mailing Add: Rte 1 Box 139 Hollow Rock TN 38342

EDWARDS, CHARLES WADE (CHUCK) (D)

Ga State Rep

b Ramseur, NC, Mar 13, 34; s Wade Baxter Edwards & Lillie May York E; m 1959 to G Nadine Pulley; c Charlene Duke & Cathy York. Educ: NC State Univ, BS, 61; Alpha Gamma Rho. Polit & Govt Pos: Ga State Rep, 75- Bus & Prof Pos: Pres, Willis-Wade Co, Inc, 64-, C W Edwards & Co, Inc, 67-, Home Builders Asn, Metro Atlanta, 70-71 & C W E & Supply Co, Inc, 73- Mil Serv: Entered as E-1, Coast Guard, 53, released as E-5, 57; Good Conduct Medal; Nat Defense Ribbon. Mem: Nat Asn of Home Builders (chmn, State Govt Affairs Comt); Home Builders Asn of Ga (first vpres, 74-75). Relig: Presbyterian. Mailing Add: 4416 Paper Mill Rd Marietta GA 30060

EDWARDS, DEIGHTON OCTAVIUS, JR (R)

Committeeman, NY Rep Party

b Jamaica, NY, June 17, 36; s Deighton O Edwards, Sr & Marion Wilson E; m 1955 to Gail Pricilla Robinson; c Marc Deighton & Derek Wilfred. Educ: New York City Community Col. Polit & Govt Pos: Chmn bd gov, John V Lindsay Young Rep, NY, 64-68; committeeman, NY Rep Party, 65-; alt deleg, Rep Nat Conv, 68; bd mem, Creedmoor State Ment Hosp, Queens Co, 68- Bus & Prof Pos: Clerical asst, Off of the Messrs Rockefeller, 54-55; asst to off mgr, Ibec Housing Corp, 55-59; asst off mgr, Off of Gov Nelson Rockefeller, 59-67; pres, Promon Assocs, Inc, 63-66; vpres, Aroco Import & Exports, Inc, 64-69; asst mgr, Franklin Nat Bank, 67-70, asst vpres, 70; bd mem, treas & vpres admin, Burnett Int Develop Corp, 71-; chmn & pres, Devco Mgt Inc, New York, 71- Mem: Soc for Prevention of Cruelty to Children; Queens Hearing Aid Asn; St Peter Claver; Jamaica Community Corp; Jamaica Community Develop Coun Corp. Honors & Awards: Named Man of the Year by the 26th Assembly Dist Regular Rep Asns. Relig: Episcopal. Mailing Add: 138-20 175th St Springfield Gardens NY 11434

EDWARDS, DON (D)

US Rep, Calif

b San Jose, Calif; c Leonard Perry, II, Thomas Charles, Samuel Dyer, Bruce Haven & William Don. Educ: Stanford Law Sch, 36-38; Stanford Univ. Polit & Govt Pos: US Rep, Calif, 62-; mem judiciary comt, US House Rep, currently, mem comn bankruptcy laws & comn individual rights, mem nat comn rev fed & state laws relating to wiretapping & electronic surveillance; deleg, Dem Nat Conv, 68, alt deleg, 72. Bus & Prof Pos: Spec Agent, Fed Bur Invest, 40-41; pres, Valley Title Co. Mil Serv: Navy, 42-45. Legal Res: CA Mailing Add: US House of Rep Washington DC 20515

EDWARDS, DONALD EVERETT (D)

Vt State Rep

b Bellows Falls, Vt, June 15, 37; s Ralph Everett Edwards & Anne Edmunds E; m 1965 to Julie Schmid; c William & Edmund. Educ: Norwich Univ, BS, 59; Univ Tenn, MS, 68; Beta Gamma Sigma. Polit & Govt Pos: Mem sch bd, Grafton, Vt, 73-74, chmn, Planning Comn, 74-; mem, Windham Co Dem Comt, 73-; Vt State Rep, 75- Mil Serv: Entered as 2nd Lt, Army, 59, released as Maj, 71, after serv in Ger, Vietnam & Eng; Maj, Army Res, 71; Bronze

Star; Army Commendation Medal; nine Campaign Awards. Mem: Grafton Grange; ROA; Grafton Vol Fire Dept (sr warden). Mailing Add: Box 123 Grafton VT 05146

EDWARDS, DOROTHY BEATRICE (R)
RI State Rep
b Fall River, Mass, Mar 22, 24; d George Albert Jackson & Esther Holland J; m 1944 to Edwin B Edwards, Jr; c E Branford, III, Gary Charles & twins Debbi Suzanne & Cindy Joanne. Educ: Rogers High Sch, Newport, RI, grad. Polit & Govt Pos: Mem, Portsmouth Rep Town Comt, RI, 62-; mem, Rep State Cent Comt, RI, 66-; RI State Rep, Dist 94, 67-; legis chmn, RI Fedn of Rep Women, Providence, 68-69. Bus & Prof Pos: Tel operator, New Eng Tel, Newport, RI, 41-42 & US Navy Dept, 42-45. Mem: Portsmouth Rep Women's Club. Relig: Episcopal. Mailing Add: 25 Cove St Portsmouth RI 02871

EDWARDS, EDWIN ARMSTRONG (R)
First VChmn, Kershaw Co Rep Party, SC
b Staunton, Va, Sept 25, 10; s Marvin Jackson Edwards & Lucy Carver E; m 1956 to Marion Kemp; c Edwin Milton. Educ: Beverley Manor High Sch, grad; correspondence in construction eng. Polit & Govt Pos: First vchmn, Kershaw Co Rep Party, SC, 70-; chmn, Camden City Rep Party. Bus & Prof Pos: Supvr, E I du Pont de Nemours & Co, Camden, SC, retired. Mem: Lions; Toastmasters; Shrine. Relig: Baptist. Legal Res: 96 Upton Ct Camden SC 29020 Mailing Add: PO Box 393 Camden SC 29020

EDWARDS, EDWIN W (D)
Gov, La
b Marksville, La Aug 7, 27; s Clarence W Edwards & Agnes Brouillette E; m 1949 to Elaine Schwartzenburg; c Anna Laure (Mrs Richard Hensgens), Victoria Elaine, Stephen Randolph & David Edwin. Educ: La State Univ, LLD, 49. Polit & Govt Pos: Mem City Coun, Crowley, La, 54-62; La State Sen, 64-65; US Rep, La, 65-72; deleg, Dem Nat Conv, 72; Gov, La, 72-; chmn, Interstate Oil Compact Comn, 75-; host, Nat Gov Conf, 76. Bus & Prof Pos: Sr partner, Edwards & Edwards Law Firm. Mil Serv: Navy Air Corps, 44. Mem: Lions (past pres); Int Rice Festival (past pres); Gtr Crowley CofC; Am Legion (past adjutant). Honors & Awards: Nat Thomas Jefferson Award, 74. Relig: Catholic. Legal Res: Crowley LA 70526 Mailing Add: State Capitol Baton Rouge LA 70806

EDWARDS, F ROBERT (R)
Mich State Rep
b Newberry, Mich, Mar 26, 40; both parents deceased; m 1972 to Mary Ruth Visser. Educ: Gen Motors Inst, Flint, Mich, grad design, 63; pres, Soc Automotive Engrs, 62-63. Polit & Govt Pos: Vpres, Flint Young Rep, Mich, 65, pres, 66; city dir, Rep Precinct Orgn, 67; mem, Genesee Co Rep Exec Comt, 68-70; Mich State Rep, 79th House Dist, 71- Bus & Prof Pos: Design engr, Buick Div, Gen Motors, 64-71. Honors & Awards: God & Country Award & Eagle Award, Boy Scouts; One of Outstanding Young Men of Am, 71 & 72. Relig: Protestant. Mailing Add: 413 W Witherbee Flint MI 48503

EDWARDS, GEORGE H (D)
Mich State Rep
b Brunswick, Ga, Feb 13, 11; married; c Harry, Verne, Robert & Pamela. Educ: Morehouse Col, Atlanta, Ga, AB in Bus Admin & Acct; Atlanta Univ & NY Univ, grad study. Polit & Govt Pos: Mich State Rep, 54-; precinct deleg & dist exec bd mem. Bus & Prof Pos: Bus admin. Mem: Elks (Metrop Lodge 962). Relig: Episcopalian. Mailing Add: 87 Woodland Detroit MI 48202

EDWARDS, JACK (R)
US Rep, Ala
b Birmingham, Ala, Sept 20, 28; s William J Edwards, Jr & Sue Fuhrman E; m 1954 to Jolane Vander Sys; c Susan Lane & Richard Arnold. Educ: US Naval Sch, Acad & Col, 47-48; Univ Ala, BS, 52, Sch Law, LLB, 54; pres, Kappa Alpha Fraternity, 51-53 & Univ Ala Student body, 52-53; Omicron Delta Kappa. Polit & Govt Pos: US Rep, Ala, 64-, secy, House Rep Conf, US House Rep, 72-; deleg, Rep Nat Conv, 72. Bus & Prof Pos: Attorney-at-law, Mobile, Ala, 54-58; legal counsel, Gulf, Mobile & Ohio RR, Mobile, 58-64. Mil Serv: Marine Corps, 46-48, 50-51. Mem: Mobile Jr CofC. Honors & Awards: Chosen Outstanding Local Pres of Ala Jr CofC, 61-62; one of Outstanding Young Men of Am by US Jr CofC, 64. Relig: Presbyterian. Legal Res: Mobile AL Mailing Add: 2439 House Off Bldg Washington DC 20515

EDWARDS, JAMES BURROWS (R)
Gov, SC
b Hawthorne, Fla, June 24, 27; s O Morton Edwards & Bertie Ray Hieronymus; m 1951 to Ann Norris Darlington; c James Burrows, Jr & Catherine Darlington. Educ: Col Charleston, BS, 50; Univ Louisville Sch Dent, DMD with honors, 55; Univ Pa Grad Med Sch, 57-58; Henry Ford Hosp, Detroit, oral surg residency, 58-60; Am Bd Oral Surg, dipl, 63; Omicron Delta Kappa; Phi Delta; Phi Kappa Phi; pres, Dent Class; pres, Student Body, Univ Louisville. Polit & Govt Pos: Fund raising, Goldwater Campaign, Charleston Co, SC, 64; chmn, Charleston Co Rep Party, 64-69; deleg, Rep Nat Conv, 68 & 72; SC Dent Asn Rep, Gov Statewide Comt for Comprehensive Health Care, Planning, 68-72; presidential appointee, Fed Hosp Coun, 69-73; chmn, First Cong Dist Rep Party, 70-71; cand, US House Rep, 71 & 74; mem, Comt for the Reelec of the President, 72; mem, SC Statewide Steering Comt for the Rep Party; chmn, Rep Steering Comt, Charleston Co, currently; SC State Sen, formerly; Gov, SC, 75- Bus & Prof Pos: Deck officer, Alcoa Steamship Co, 50-51; lectr oral surg, Royal Soc of Oral Surgeons, Gt Brit. Mil Serv: Entered as Seaman, Navy, 44, released as Deck Officer, 47, after serv in World War II, US Maritime Serv; recalled as Dent Off, Navy, 55-57, Korea; Lt Comdr, Naval Res, 67. Mem: Am Dent Asn; Am Bd Oral Surg; Int Dent Fedn; fel Am Col Dent; Am Soc Oral Surgeons. Honors & Awards: Outstanding Grad in Class, Two Alumni Orgns. Relig: Methodist; mem admin bd, Hibben United Methodist Church, 2 terms. Legal Res: 1 Darlington Lane Mt Pleasant SC 29464 Mailing Add: State Capitol Columbia SC 29211

EDWARDS, JAMES HARRELL (D)
NC State Rep
b Pitt Co, NC, Nov 25, 26; s James Josiah Edwards & Ella Stokes E; m to Trelby Bumgarner; c James Loren, Charles Thomas, Ella Ann (Mrs Larry Compton), Johnny Harrell, Keith Charles & Greta Lynn. Educ: Atlantic Christian Col; ECarolina Univ; Phi Kappa Alpha. Polit & Govt Pos: Precinct chmn, Swift Creek Twp, Greenville, NC, 47-49; mem, Gov Scott's Ins Study Comt, NC Legis, 71-72; NC State Rep, 75- Bus & Prof Pos: Mgr & owner, Southeastern Adjustment Co, Hickory, NC, 59-, pres, Carolinian Investors, 70-; vpres, Southeastern Adjustment Co, Inc, Greensboro, 73-; owner, Edwards & Assocs, Hickory, NC, 73- Mil Serv: Entered as Cadet, Naval Res, 45, released as engr, 46, after serv in European Theatre, 45-46. Mem: Nat Asn Independent Ins Adjusters (regional vpres); NC Adjusters Asn; Int Asn of Arson Investigators; Int Asn Stress Analysis; Scottish Rite Mason. Honors & Awards: Nominee Adjuster of the Year, Northwestern NC Claimsmens Asn; Nominee Claimsmens of the Year, Atlanta Claims Asn; Hon Award, Am Fedn Police. Relig: Lutheran. Legal Res: Rte 3 Box 118 Granite Falls NC 28630 Mailing Add: PO Box 1601 Hickory NC 28601

EDWARDS, JIMMIE C, III (D)
Tex State Rep
Mailing Add: PO Box 1630 Conroe TX 77301

EDWARDS, JOSEPH ROBERT (R)
Exec Secy, Nebr Rep Party
b Auburn, Nebr, June 9, 32; s Charles Harold Edwards & Pearl Moody E; m 1954 to Paula Jean Scharman; c Kathleen Sue, Beth Yvonne & David Charles. Educ: Univ Nebr, BS in Agr, 54; Block & Bridle Club; Farm House. Polit & Govt Pos: Finance chmn, Nemaha Co Rep Cent Comt, Nebr, 62, chmn, formerly; dist chmn, More Prog, 66; exec secy, Nebr Rep Party, currently. Bus & Prof Pos: Pres, Adv & Develop Serv, Inc, 71- Mil Serv: Entered as 2nd Lt, Army, 54, released as 1st Lt, 56, after serv in 134th Inf, Nat Guard; Capt, Army Res, 61. Mem: Mason; Elks; Farm Bur; Am Legion. Relig: Methodist. Mailing Add: 2132 S 24th Lincoln NE 68502

EDWARDS, JULIAN WARD (D)
Mem, State Dem Exec Comt, Ga
b Howard, Ga, Feb 28, 30; s Julian Willis Edwards & Lillian Brown E; m 1956 to Billie Salmon; c Hallie Ward. Educ: Gordon Mil Col; Univ Ga; John Gupton Sch of Mortuary, Nashville, Tenn. Polit & Govt Pos: Aide to Lt Gov of Ga, 58-62; liaison officer, State Hwy Dept, 63-64; Ga State Rep, 66-72, Dem Majority Whip, Ga House Rep, 70-71, secy, 73-; deleg, Ga State Dem Exec Comt, 70-; mem, State Dem Exec Comt, Ga, 74-; pres, Third Dist Legis Caucus, 75. Bus & Prof Pos: Mortician, Edwards Funeral Home, Butler, Ga. Mil Serv: Entered as Pvt, released as S/Sgt, after serv in Northeastern Air Command, 52-54. Mem: VFW; Elks; Kiwanis. Relig: Methodist. Legal Res: Garward Circle Butler GA 31006 Mailing Add: PO Box 427 Butler GA 31006

EDWARDS, MARTIN K (R)
Ind State Sen
Mailing Add: Ind State Senate State Capitol Indianapolis IN 46204

EDWARDS, MICHAEL DEAN (D)
b San Antonio, Tex, Oct 4, 46; s Harvey Edwards & Anne Louise Josephson E; single. Educ: Univ Calif Berkeley, AB Honors; London Sch Econ & Polit Sci, Griffiths fel. Polit & Govt Pos: Spec asst, US Sen Charles E Goodell, 69-71; exec asst, US Rep William F Ryan, 71-73; admin asst, US Rep Robert H Steele, 73-75 & US Rep Peter A Peyser, 75- Bus & Prof Pos: Polit consult, Washington, DC, 73. Publ: Military branding iron, New Republic, 10/74; The children are still waiting, 9/74 & Golden threads to the Pentagon, 3/75, The Nation. Mem: Nat Acad Polit Sci; Int & Am Polit Sci Asns; Nat Trust for Historic Preservation; Int Inst Community Serv. Honors & Awards: Recipient Donald M Severy Mem Award for Community Serv. Mailing Add: 4201 Cathedral Ave NW Washington, DC 20016

EDWARDS, NANCY HARRINGTON (PENNY) (D)
b Jackson, Tenn, Nov 21, 45; d Judge Joseph Lawrence Harrington, Jr (deceased) & Nancy Griffin H (deceased); m 1967 to Elbert Edwin (Bo) Edwards, III. Educ: Mid Tenn State Univ, BS, 67. Polit & Govt Pos: Supply coordr, Ellington for Gov Campaign, Tenn, summer 66; State Committeewoman, Young Dem of Tenn, Seventh Dist, 66-68, Nat Committeewoman, 71-73; mem personnel, Off of Treas, State of Tenn, 67, extraditions secy, Off of Gov, 67; out of state coordr, Robert Kennedy Campaign, Ky, 68; head speaker's bur & supply mgr, Hooker for Gov, Tenn, 70; secy, Dem Women of Davidson Co, 71-72; asst dir, Dem Caucus Campaign, Tenn House Rep, 72, admin aide to Speaker of the House, 73-74; press secy, Lt Gov, 74-; mem, Young Dem Tenn; mem, Community Develop Bd, currently. Bus & Prof Pos: Teacher French, Hillsboro High Sch, Nashville, Tenn, 68-71; secy-treas, Info Retrieval & Anal, Inc, 70-72; capitol correspondent, Knoxville News Sentinel, 71. Publ: Auth & ed, The Tennessee Report (weekly newsletter on state govt & polit), Info Retrieval & Anal, Inc, 70-72. Mem: Am Civil Liberties Union; Nashville Women's Polit Caucus; Dem Women of Tenn; YMCA; Concerned Dem. Honors & Awards: Young Career Woman of the Year, Nashville Bus & Prof Women's Club, 73. Relig: Roman Catholic. Legal Res: 4217 Wallace Lane Nashville TN 37215 Mailing Add: Suite One Legis Plaza Nashville TN 37219

EDWARDS, RICHARD G (R)
Chmn, Hawaii Co Rep Party, Hawaii
b Elkhart, Ind, Apr 13, 29; s Joseph Oliver Edwards & Helen Baker E; div; c Cyndie Ann (Mrs Holmes). Educ: Ind Univ, AB; Trinity Univ, 50-51; Georgetown Univ, 53-55; Acacia Fraternity. Polit & Govt Pos: First dist chmn, Hawaii Rep Party, 65-66; chmn platform comt, Hawaii Co, 66; deleg, Rep Nat Conv, 68; mem, Nat Comt on Party Orgn, 68; chmn, Hawaii Co Rep Party, 73- Bus & Prof Pos: Broker & partner, Hawaii-Hilo Realty, 67-75. Mil Serv: Air Force, 52. Mem: CofC; Volcano Isle Develop Asn (dir); Puna Lions Club. Relig: Protestant. Mailing Add: SR Box C-10 Keaau HI 96749

EDWARDS, TOM W, JR (D)
SC State Rep
b Nashville, Tenn, Nov 11, 29; s Tom W Edwards, Sr & Mary Hill E; m 1964 to Dorothy Ballew; c Anita Dawn. Educ: Presby Col, 3 years; Univ Denver, 1 year; Sigma Nu; Block P Club. Polit & Govt Pos: SC State Rep, Spartanburg Co, 67-, mem, Ways & Means Comt, SC House of Rep, 68- Bus & Prof Pos: Sales mgr, Crawford Door Co, 60-69. Mil Serv: Entered Navy, 51, released as Adv Navigator 1/C, 55, after serv in Comdr Air Force, Pac Fleet, San Diego, Calif. Mem: Prof Sales Engrs Asn; Southern Conf Football Off Asn; Boy Scouts (adv bd); Jaycees; Nat Co Found (bd dir). Relig: Methodist. Legal Res: 504 Perrin Dr Spartanburg SC 29302 Mailing Add: Box 1911 Spartanburg SC 29301

EDWARDS, WARD (D)
Ga State Rep
b Howard, Ga, Feb 28, 30; s Julian Willis Edwards & Lillian Ethel Brown E; m 1956 to Billie Salmon; c Hallie Ward. Educ: Ga Mil Col, 48-49; Ga State Col; Gupton Sch Mortuary Sch, grad. Polit & Govt Pos: Hosp contact rep, Vet Serv, Dept Ga, 54-58; aide to Lt Gov Ga, 58-62, liaison officer, 62-64; permit officer, State Hwy Dept, 64-66; Ga State Rep, 67-, Dem Majority Whip, Ga State House, 71-; deleg, Dem Nat Conv, 72. Bus & Prof Pos: Owner, dir & mortician, Edwards Funeral Home, currently. Mil Serv: Entered as Pvt, Air Force, 50,

released as S/Sgt, 54, after serv in Northeastern Air Command, St Johns, Nfld. Mem: Am Legion; Kiwanis; Elks; Moose; Farm Bur. Relig: Methodist; mem bd trustee. Mailing Add: PO Box 146 Butler GA 31006

EDWARDS, WILLIAM CHARLES (D)
Wyo State Rep
b Waukegan, Ill, May 17, 34; s Henry Charles Edwards & Lillian Yockey E; m 1961 to Nancy Beal; c Jonathan Charles & Benjamin Ralph. Educ: Carleton Col, BA, 56; Univ Wyo, MS, 58; Univ Nebr, PhD, 66; Univ Mich & Univ Northern Colo; Sigma Xi. Polit & Govt Pos: Wyo State Rep, 75-, secy, Joint Interim Mines, Minerals & Indust Develop Comt, Wyo House Rep, 75- Bus & Prof Pos: Asst prof, Mankato State Col, 66-70; instr ecology, Laramie Co Community Col, 70-; dir ecology lab, Cheyenne Sch Dist, 71-73. Publ: Antelope Reproduction in Wyoming, Wyo-Colo Acad Sci, 57; Bog Birch in Grand Teton, Nebr Acad Sci, 64; Bog Birch in Minnesota, Minn Acad Sci, 69. Mem: Phi Delta Kappa; Kiwanis; Cheyenne High Plains Audubon Soc (bd dirs); Laramie Co Community Col Faculty Asn (pres, 75). Honors & Awards: Hon mention as the outstanding Biol Teacher, Wyo, 63; Outstanding Serv Award, Mankato, Minn CofC, 69. Relig: Episcopal; mem vestry. Mailing Add: 520 Harvard Lane Cheyenne WY 82001

EDWARDS, WILLIAM DEARA (D)
Ala State Rep
b Eclectic, Ala, July 7, 16; s Oscar Parker Edwards & Annie Chapman E (deceased); m 1939 to Virginia Spencer; c Spencer Chapman & William Parker. Educ: Auburn Univ, BA, 37; Sigma Chi. Polit & Govt Pos: Ala State Rep, 29th Dist, 62-66 & 70-; legis agent, 67-71. Bus & Prof Pos: Owner farm implement bus, 37-58; cattle farmer & owner, 56- Mem: Mason (Master); Civitan; Quarterback Club; Cattlemen's Asn; Farm Bur. Relig: Methodist. Mailing Add: Rte 1 Box 180-A Ft Deposit AL 36032

EGAN, MARY KATHERINE (D)
b Springfield, Mass, May 21, 39; d James Francis Egan & Mary Collins E; single. Educ: Newton Col of the Sacred Heart, BA, 60; Boston Col Law Sch, LLB, 65. Polit & Govt Pos: Staff, Off of Gov Calvin L Rampton, Utah, 65; deleg & mem rules comt, Dem Nat Conv, 72; City Coun, Springfield, Mass, 72-, pres, 73- Bus & Prof Pos: Attorney, Egan, Flanagan & Egan, Springfield, 65- Mem: Mass Bar Asn; Springfield Libr & Mus Asn; Legal Aid Soc; Mercy Hosp; Springfield Inst for Savings. Honors & Awards: Fel, Nat Ctr for Educ in Polit, 65. Relig: Roman Catholic. Mailing Add: 72 Yorktown Dr Springfield MA 01108

EGAN, MICHAEL JOSEPH (R)
Ga State Rep
b Savannah, Ga, Aug 8, 26; s Michael Joseph Egan & Elise Robider E; m 1951 to Donna Jean Cole; c Moria, Michael, Donna, Cole, Roby & John. Educ: Yale Univ, AB, 50; Harvard Law Sch, LLB, 55. Polit & Govt Pos: Ga State Rep, 66-, Minority Leader, Ga House Rep, 71-; deleg, Rep Nat Conv, 68. Bus & Prof Pos: Assoc, Sutherland, Asbill & Brennan, 55-61, partner, 61- Mil Serv: Entered as Pvt, Army, 45, released as 2nd Lt, 47; recalled to active duty, 50, released as 1st Lt, 52, after serv in Pac Theater with 86th Inf Div, 46 & in Korea with 2nd Inf Div, 9th Inf Regt, 51-52. Publ: Problems of Federal Taxation of Estates-Gifts-Trusts, Am Law Inst & Am Bar Asn, 66. Mem: Am & Atlanta Bar Asns; State Bar of Ga; Piedmont Driving Club; Commerce Club. Relig: Roman Catholic. Legal Res: 97 Brighton Rd NE Atlanta GA 30309 Mailing Add: First National Bank Tower Atlanta GA 30303

EGAN, RENA ADELE (R)
b New York, NY, Sept 14, 23; d Dr Reginald B Weiler & Effie May Russell W; m 1940 to Walter Steve Egan; c Janet Susan & Bernard Steve. Educ: Pueblo Jr Col, AA; Colo Col, BS, Biol, 70; St Francis Hosp, Colo Springs, Registry of Med Technologist. Polit & Govt Pos: Admin asst to co chmn, Colo, 64-68; voting machine instr, Pueblo, Colo, 66-68, educ chmn, 69-; mem, Rep State Cent Comt Colo, 67-69; deleg, Rep Nat Conv, 68; lobbyist, Med Technol Bill, 72; campaign coordr & mem vacancy comt, Pueblo Co Rep Cent Comt, 72- Bus & Prof Pos: Head hematology technologist, lab, St Francis Hosp, 59-62; head technologist, lab, Alamosa Community Hosp, 62-63; head technologist, Lab, Parkview Episcopal Hosp, 63-67; head technologist, lab mgr, Marsh Path Labs, 67-69; admin asst & para-med couns dept biol, Southern Colo State Col, 69-; Speaker symposium licensure & legis, Nat Med Technol Conv, 73. Publ: Five articles in Colo Med Technologist on Hematology; Burketts Lymphoma, Colo Med Technologist, summer 70. Mem: Pueblo Soc Med Technologists; Colo Soc Med Technologists; Am Soc Med Technologists (chmn legis comt, 73-); Am Soc Clin Pathologists; Am Bus Women's Asn. Honors & Awards: Woman of the Year, Am Bus Women's Asn Rocky Mt Chap; Med Technologist of the Year, Colo State Soc Med Technologists, 71. Relig: Episcopal. Mailing Add: 2520 Seventh Ave Pueblo CO 81003

EGAN, RICHARD EDWARD (D)
b Syracuse, NY, Aug 28, 37; s Edward Thomas Egan & Marie Stowell E; m 1955 to Eva M Carmer; c Martin J, Marcelle I, Alexander R, Richard J & Nancy E. Educ: Eastwood High Sch, Syracuse, NY. Polit & Govt Pos: Deleg, Dem Nat Conv, 72; deleg, Dem Nat Mid-Term Conf, 74. Bus & Prof Pos: Cable splicer, New York Tel Co, 55-67; fund raiser, City of Hope Nat Med Ctr, 67- Mil Serv: Entered as Pvt, Army Res, 55, released as SP E-5, 67. Mem: New Dem Coalition Philadelphia. Mailing Add: 1317 Greeby St Philadelphia PA 19111

EGAN, ROBERT JOSEPH (D)
Ill State Sen
b Elmhurst, Ill, Nov 11, 31; s Mathias C Egan & Elizabeth Rose Quill E; m 1958 to Marie Terese Gillespie; c Elizabeth, Margaret, Sarah, Robert & Frank. Educ: St Norbert Col, BA, 53; Loyola Univ Sch Law, JD, 59; Phi Alpha Delta. Polit & Govt Pos: Ill State Sen, 71- Mil Serv: Entered as 2nd Lt, Army, 54, released as 1st Lt, 56, after serv in Infantry, 3rd Div. Mem: Chicago & Ill Bar Asns. Relig: Roman Catholic. Legal Res: 6200 N Meredith Ave Chicago IL 60646 Mailing Add: One N LaSalle St Chicago IL 60602

EGAN, WILLIAM ALLEN (D)
b Valdez, Alaska, Oct 8, 14; s William Edward Egan & Cora Allen E; m 1940 to Neva McKittrick; c Dennis William. Educ: Alaska Methodist Univ, LLD. Hon Degrees: LLD, Univ Alaska, 72. Polit & Govt Pos: City Councilman, Valdez, Alaska, 37-38 & 41-45, mayor, 46; Alaska State Rep, 41-51, speaker, Alaska House Rep, 51; Alaska State Sen, 53-55; pres, Alaska Const Conv, 55-56; Alaska Tenn Plan Sen in Statehood Effort, Washington, DC, 57-58; Gov, Alaska, 59-66 & 71-74; chmn, Western Gov Conf, 61; Dem cand for US Rep, 74; ex officio, Dem Nat Mid-Term Conf, 74. Bus & Prof Pos: Owner, Valdez Supply, Alaska, 46-; dist mgr, Equitable Life Assurance, 67-70. Mil Serv: Entered as Pvt, Army, 43, released as Sgt, 46. Mem: Pioneers of Alaska; VFW; Am Legion; CofC (pres, 48); Moose. Honors & Awards: First Gov, Alaska; pilot, pvt flying. Relig: Catholic. Mailing Add: 716 Calhoun Ave Juneau AK 99801

EGBERT, RICHARD ALEXANDER (D)
Idaho State Sen
b Tetonia, Idaho, Aug 23, 06; s Hyrum S Egbert & Annie McGhie E; m 1932 to Alta Phillips; c LaRae (Mrs Merrill Wilson) & Richard Phillips. Educ: Ricks Col. Polit & Govt Pos: Idaho State Rep, 41-48 & 60-62, Asst Minority Leader, Idaho House of Rep, 47-48; Idaho State Sen, 63-69 & 71-, Asst Minority Leader, Idaho State Senate, 63-66. Bus & Prof Pos: Owner & mgr livestock ranch. Mem: Targhee Nat Forest (adv coun); Bur of Land Mgt (adv bd); Targhee Woolgrowers Asn (pres). Relig: Latter-day Saint. Mailing Add: Tetonia ID 83452

EGEBERG, ROGER O (D)
b Chicago, Ill, Nov 13, 03; m to Margaret McEchron Chahoon; c Dagny (Mrs William Hancock), Sarah (Mrs Robert Beauchamp), Roger Olaf & Karen (Mrs Richard Warmer). Educ: Cornell Univ, BA, 25; Northwestern Univ, MD, 29. Polit & Govt Pos: Chmn, Gov Comt for Study of Med Care & Health, Calif, 59-60; mem, Calif State Bd Pub Health, 61-68, pres, 66-68; Asst Secy of Health & Sci Affairs, Dept of Health, Educ & Welfare, 69-71, spec asst to the Secy Health Policy, 71-; Spec Consult to the President on Health Affairs, 71-; chmn, Advan Health Care Delivery Pilot Proj, Comt Challenges Mod Soc, NATO, 71-; co-chmn, US-USSR Joint Comt Health Coop, 72-74. Bus & Prof Pos: Intern, Wesley Hosp, Chicago, Ill; resident, Univ Hosp, Ann Arbor, Mich; pvt practice internal med, Cleveland, Ohio, 32-42; chief of med serv, Vet Admin Hosp, Los Angeles, Calif, 46-56; med dir, Los Angeles Co Hosp, 56-58; staff mem, Los Angeles Co Gen Hosp & Rancho Amigos Hosp, Downey; prof med, Univ Calif, Los Angeles, 48-64; prof med, Col Med Evangelists, 56-64; prof med, Univ Southern Calif, 56-69, dean sch of med, 64-69. Mil Serv: Entered as Maj, Med Corps, Army, 42, released as Col, 46, after serv as personal physician & aide-de-camp to Gen Douglas MacArthur, 44-45; Bronze Star; Legion of Merit; St Olaf's Medal, Norway. Publ: Regional medical programs, Calif Med, 1/68; Balance between medical education and medical service in medical schools, J Am Med Asn, 5/68; Discussion of group practice in the education of medical students, J NY Acad of Med, 11/68; plus others. Mem: Nat Adv Cancer Coun; Calif Bd of Pub Health; Am Col Physicians (master); Am Clin & Climatological Asn; Calif Soc of Internal Med. Honors & Awards: Dipl, Am Bd Internal Med. Legal Res: PO Box 333 Cambria CA 93428 Mailing Add: 2909 Garfield Terr NW Washington DC 20008

EGELAND, LEONA HELENE (D)
Calif State Assemblywoman
b New York, NY, Apr 29, 38; d Charles Shapiro & Estelle S; m 1961 to Gilbert Kenneth Egeland; c Ilaan & Hylah. Educ: Univ Ariz, BA, 60; San Jose State Univ, MA, 65; Beta Beta Beta; Pi Lambda Theta; Phi Kappa Phi; grad with high distinction. Polit & Govt Pos: Calif State Assemblywoman, 24th Dist, 74-, vchairwoman, Assembly Comt Health, mem, Assembly Comt on Agr & Assembly Comt on Educ, Joint Comt on Legal Equality, Comn on Status of Women, Subcomt on Post Sec Educ, Subcomt on Health Manpower & Joint Comt on Spec Educ, 75- Bus & Prof Pos: Legis consult, State of Calif, 70-73; teacher, San Jose Unified Sch Dist, 7 years. Mem: Nat Orgn for Women; Am Asn Univ Women; Nat Women's Polit Caucus; Zero Pop Growth; San Jose Mus of Art Asn. Honors & Awards: Outstanding Young Women of Am Award, San Jose, 72; Nominee Women of Achievement Award, Mercury News, 72-73; regional finalist, White House Fel Prog, 73; Susan B Anthony Award, Nat Orgn for Women, 75; Award, Redevelop Agency of San Jose, 75. Relig: Jewish. Mailing Add: 1924 Barry Rd Davis CA 95616

EGENES, SONJA (R)
Iowa State Rep
Mailing Add: 905 Lafayette Story City IA 50248

EGGERS, FLOYD MARTIN (D)
Chmn, Gasconade Co Dem Comt, Mo
b Owensville, Mo, Oct 2, 09; s Thomas J Eggers & Ida Palmer E; m 1930 to Ragien Louise Plassmeyer; c Joyce D (Mrs Sieckmann), Thomas E & Lawrence N. Educ: Owensville Pub Sch. Polit & Govt Pos: Committeeman, Gasconade Co Dem Comt, 56-70, vchmn, 70-72, chmn, 72- Bus & Prof Pos: Car dealer, Eggers Dodge, Owensville, Mo, 55- Mem: Lions; KofC; Moose; Eagles. Relig: Catholic. Mailing Add: 305 E Jefferson Owensville MO 65066

EGGERS, JEAN ETHALEN (R)
VChmn, Minnehaha Co Rep Cent Comt, SDak
b Sioux Falls, SDak, Apr 19, 28; d Russell Glenn Bachtell & Ethalen Johnson B; m 1946 to Curtis Ordell Eggers; c Sandra Dean (Mrs Sorum), Kathleen (Mrs Paul Evenson), Lanette, Timothy & Michael; 4 grandchildren. Educ: Washington High Sch, Sioux Falls, SDak, 4 years. Polit & Govt Pos: Rep precinct committeewoman, Mapleton Twp, SDak, 52-; vchmn, Minnehaha Co Rep Cent Comt, 60-; mem recount bd, Minnehaha Co, 70 & 74; mem, Minnehaha Co Local Draft Bd, 72- Mem: Rep Women's Club 3, Sioux Falls (pres, 74-); Am Legion Auxiliary (pres, Baltic, 75-). Honors & Awards: Cert Appreciation, Minnehaha Co Rep Cent Comt. Relig: Lutheran; pres, Renner Lutheran Church Womans Group. Mailing Add: Renner SD 57055

EGGLE, DORIS E (R)
b Adrian, Mich, Mar 14, 23; m 1944 to Robert J Eggle; c Robert J, Jr, David J, Randall L & Marsha A. Polit & Govt Pos: Chmn, Osceola Co Rep Party, Mich, formerly; pres, Osceola Co Rep Women, 5 years. Bus & Prof Pos: Homemaker. Mem: Farm Bur. Relig: Baptist. Mailing Add: Rte 2 Tustin MI 49688

EHLERS, THOMAS MARTIN (R)
Mem, Rep State Cent Comt, Minn
b Worthington, Minn, Feb 6, 37; s Martin Andrew Ehlers & Genevieve Ellen Rust E; m 1964 to Sandra Joan McCartney; c Joseph Martin & Genevieve Elizabeth. Educ: Am Univ, 57; Hamline Univ, BA, 59; NY Univ, MSR, 60; Pi Gamma Mu; Pi Kappa Delta; Eta Mu Pi; Tau Kappa Epsilon. Polit & Govt Pos: Chmn, Redwood Co Rep Party, Minn, 65-67; mem, Rep State Cent Comt, Minn, 65-; area chmn, Sixth Cong Dist Rep Party, 67-70; city chmn, Redwood Falls; chmn, Sixth Dist Dinner. Bus & Prof Pos: Exec trainee, Abraham & Straus, Minneapolis, Minn, 59; exec trainee, Daytons, 60; buyer, Ehlers, Inc, 61-63, vpres & merchandise mgr, 64- Relig: Episcopal. Mailing Add: 521 E Third St Redwood Falls MN 56283

EHLERS, WAYNE (D)
Wash State Rep
Mailing Add: 13203 S J St Tacoma WA 98444

EHLMAN, CAROLYN (JEAN) (R)
b Woodstock, Va, Jan 7, 40; d Charles Thomas Sollenberger, Sr & Elizabeth Dalke S; m 1971 to William George Ehlman. Educ: Radford Col, BS in educ, 62; Univ NC, Chapel Hill, summer 66; Sigma Sigma Sigma; Cotillion Club. Polit & Govt Pos: Pres, Radford City Young Rep Club, Va, 60-62; vpres, secy & dist rep, Young Rep Clubs, Staunton & Arlington, 62-70; mem, Nixon & conv staff, Citizens for Nixon, Washington, DC, 68; chmn youth activities for N Va, Nixon Campaign, 68; vol work transition off, President-Elect Nixon, 68; acting personnel dir, Rep Nat Comt, 69; vol work patronage area, White House, 69; mem, Va State Rep Cent Comt, 69-; nat committeewoman, Young Rep Fedn Va, 69-73; mem, Fairfax Co Polit Action Comt Educ, currently; Eighth Dist rep, Legis Rels Comt Va, currently; mem, Young Rep Exec Bd Va, 69-; chmn teachers & shopping ctr activities, for Congressman Broyhill, 70 & 72; co-chmn campaign, Va Del, Callahan, 71; mem, Fairfax Co Rep Comt, 72- Bus & Prof Pos: High sch teacher, Staunton, Va, 62-66; high sch teacher polit sci, Fairfax, 67- Mem: Radford Col Alumnae; Va Educ Asn; Harbor View Yacht Club; Nat & Va Coun of Social Studies; Red Fox Civic Asn. Honors & Awards: Outstanding Young Rep of Va, Young Rep Fedn, Va, 71; Invitation to represent Va, State Dept Inst for Young Polit Leaders, 71 & 72; Outstanding Young Educator, Springfield, Va Jr CofC, 73. Relig: Catholic. Mailing Add: 5033 Linette Lane Annandale VA 22003

EHRLICH, ROY MELVEN (R)
Kans State Rep
b Hoisington, Kans, Dec 6, 28; s George Ehrlich & Katherin Bitter E; m 1950 to Lila Jean Ochs; c Jolene (Mrs Don Morgenstern), Karla, Lonney & Rox Ann. Educ: Univ Corpus Christi, 46-47; Barton Co Jr Col, Kans, 71-72. Polit & Govt Pos: Mem twp bd, Barton Co, Kans, 61-66, co comnr, 67-70; Kans State Rep, Dist 112, 71-72 & 73-, vchmn, Pub Health & Welfare Comt, Kans House Rep, mem, Judiciary Reapportionment, Claims & Accts & Legis Coord Comt. Bus & Prof Pos: Farmer-rancher, Hoisington, Kans, 49-72. Mil Serv: Entered as Guard Pvt, Army, 62, released as Cpl, 63, after serv in Co Clerk Unit. Publ: Weekly news reports in two local papers; legis reports. Mem: Barton Co Community Ment Retardation Ctr, Inc, (pres, 72-); Eagles; Mason (32 degree); Consistory; Shrine. Relig: Lutheran. Mailing Add: Rte 1 Box 84 Hoisington KS 67544

EHRMANN, PETER NICHOLAS (R)
b Milwaukee, Wis, Dec 23, 50; s Arthur Steven Ehrmann & Frances Pertzborn E; single. Educ: Milwaukee Area Tech Col, 69-71; Univ Wis-Milwaukee, grad, 74; Beta Phi Gamma. Polit & Govt Pos: Summer intern, US Rep Glenn R Davis, Wis, Washington, DC, 71; summer ed, Battle Line, Am Conservative Union, Washington, DC, 72; alt deleg, Rep Nat Conv, 72; first vchmn, Wauwatosa Rep Club, Wis, 72-73. Bus & Prof Pos: Summer intern, Human Events, Washington, DC, 74. Publ: No to reduced age of majority, 2/10/72 & Commission biases account for police indictments, 1/22/73, Milwaukee Jour; God and counter-culture, Nat Rev, 11/24/72. Mailing Add: 524 N 64th St Wauwatosa WI 53213

EIDSON, WANDA CARROLL (R)
b Weldon, Tex, Aug 15, 22; d Ira Lee Carroll & Wera Keeling C; m 1944 to Jack L Eidson; c Jack, Jr, Mark, Scott, Carroll & Jon. Educ: Tex State Col for Women, BS in Music, 43; Univ Tex, MA in Music, 45; Mary Eleanor Breckenridge Club; Mod Choir. Polit & Govt Pos: Vchmn, Parker Co Rep Party, Tex, 62-64, chmn, 64-73; alt deleg, Rep Nat Conv, 64; state committeewoman, Dist 22, 72- Bus & Prof Pos: Choir dir & soloist, Presby Church Choir, Weatherford, Tex, 50- Mem: Cecilian Music Club; Confrerie St Etienne, Alsace, France; Tex life mem, PTA; Rep Womens Club; Ft Worth Woman's Club. Relig: Presbyterian. Mailing Add: 607 W Columbia Weatherford TX 76086

EIKENBERRY, KENNETH OTTO (R)
Wash State Rep
b Wenatchee, Wash, June 29, 32; s Otto Kenneth Eikenberry & Florence Markham E; m 1962 to Beverly Jane Hall. Educ: Wenatchee Valley Col, AA, 52; Wash State Univ, BA, 54; Univ Wash, LLB, 59; Delta Theta Phil; Alpha Tau Omega. Polit & Govt Pos: Precinct committeeman, Precinct 92, Dist 36, 62-66; Wash State Rep, 36th Legis Dist, 71- Bus & Prof Pos: Spec agent, Fed Bur Invest, Washington, DC, San Diego, Calif & Oklahoma City, Okla, 60-62; dep prosecuting attorney, King Co, Seattle, Wash, 62-67; lawyer, Richey & Eikenberry, 67-68 & Clinton, Moats, Andersen & Fleck, 68- Mil Serv: Entered as Pvt, Army, 54, released as Sp-3, 56, after serv in Combat Eng Bn, Ft Lewis, Wash, 54-56; Good Conduct Medal. Mem: Soc Former Spec Agents of FBI; Yarrow Bay Yacht Club; Elks; Seattle-King Co Cougar Club. Relig: Protestant. Mailing Add: 1644 32nd Ave W Seattle WA 98199

EILBERG, JOSHUA (D)
US Rep, Pa
b Philadelphia, Pa, Feb 12, 21; s David B Eilberg (deceased) & Miriam Jaspan E; m 1944 to Gladys Greenberg; c William H & Amy B. Educ: Wharton Sch, Univ Pa, BS; Temple Univ Law Sch, JD. Polit & Govt Pos: Asst dist attorney, Philadelphia, Pa, 52-54; Pa State Rep, 54-66, mem exec bd, Gen State Authority, exec bd, Joint State Govt Comn, Interstate Coop Comn, Pa House of Rep, 54-66, Minority Whip & Majority Leader, 64-66; Dem leader, 54th Ward of Philadelphia, 57-; deleg, Dem Nat Conv, 60, 64 & 68; US Rep, Pa, 67-, mem Judiciary Comt & chmn subcomt, Immigration & Nationality, US House of Rep, 73- Mil Serv: Entered as Ens, Navy, 41, released as Lt(sg), 45, after serv in Fleet Air Wing One, Pac Area; Pac Theater Ribbon. Mem: Am Bar Asn; Am Judicature Soc; VFW; Am Legion; Jewish War Vets. Relig: Jewish. Legal Res: 1522 Longshore Ave Philadelphia PA 19149 Mailing Add: 2429 Rayburn House Off Bldg Washington DC 20515

EILERT, DAVID DEWITT (D)
Secy, Eighth Dist Dem Party, Ind
b Stendal, Ind, Aug 21, 06; s William H Eilert & Rosina C Egbert E; m 1940 to Edna L Wellemeyer; c Donald E & Lois Jean. Educ: Oakland City Col, 2 year cert; Am Inst of Banking, course in Pub Rels. Polit & Govt Pos: Chmn, Pike Co Dem Cent Comt, Ind, 52-72; secy, Eighth Dist Dem Party, 62- Bus & Prof Pos: Sch teacher, 25-54, coach, 4 years; recreation supvr, Works Progress Admin, five co in Southern Ind, 39-42; asst cashier, Holland Nat Bank, 54-62, cashier, 64-; cashier, First Nat Bank, Spurgeon, 62-64. Mem: Quad-Co Bankers Asn; Kiwanis; Methodist Men's Orgn (originator & first pres local orgn). Relig: Methodist; Off Bd Mem, 20 years. Mailing Add: Stendal IN 47585

EILTS, HERMANN FREDERICK (R)
US Ambassador to Egypt
b Ger, Mar 23, 22; s Friedrich Alex Eilts & Meta Dorothea Prüser E; nat, 1930; m 1948 to Helen Josephine Brew; c Conrad Marshall & Frederick Lowell. Educ: Ursinus Col, BA, 42, LLD, 60; Johns Hopkins Univ Sch Adv Int Studies, MA, 47. Polit & Govt Pos: Career officer, US Dept of State Foreign Serv, 47-70, career minister, 70-; mem staff, Am Embassy, Tehran, 47-48, mem staff, Jidda, 48-50, vconsul & consul, Aden, 51-53; second secy, Baghdad, 54-56; officer-in-charge, Baghdad Pact & SEATO Affairs, 57-60; officer-in-charge, Arabian Peninsular Affairs, 60-61; with Nat War Col, 61-62; first secy, London, 62-64; dep chief of mission & counr, Tripoli, 64-65; US Ambassador to Saudi Arabia, 65-70; diplomatic adv, US Army War Col, 70-73; US Ambassador to Egypt, 73- Mil Serv: 1st Lt, Army, 42-45. Mem: Fel Royal Geog Soc; fel Royal Asiatic Soc; fel Royal Cent Asian Soc; MidE Inst; Am Foreign Serv Asn. Honors & Awards: Arthur S Flemming Award for Govt Serv, 58. Relig: Protestant. Legal Res: PA Mailing Add: Am Embassy Cairo Egypt

EINSCHUTZ, LOUIS E (D)
Md State Deleg
Mailing Add: 1307 Chapel Hill Dr Baltimore MD 21221

EISENBERG, WARREN WOLFF (R)
b Newark, NJ, Dec 22, 32; s Samuel Sydney Eisenberg & Ann Grace Wolff E; m 1961 to Rita Ann Muir; c Adam Muir, David Wolff & Eric Reid. Educ: George Washington Univ, BS, 54, grad work, 55-56. Polit & Govt Pos: Research asst, US Rep Harrison A Williams, Jr, NJ, 55-56; exec asst, US Rep William J Green, Pa, 67-71; admin asst, US Rep H John Heinz, III, Pa, 71- Bus & Prof Pos: Ed, Fed Reserve Bank, New York, 59-62; ed, Pa Guardian, Philadelphia, 62-63; assoc ed, Philadelphia Mag, 63-66; ed, Population Reference Bur, Washington, DC, 66-67. Mil Serv: Pvt E-2, Army, 57; Sgt, Res, Ft Sam Houston, Tex, 63. Publ: Book rev, City Mag, 71; Populations and areas, In: Encycl Britannica, 67-73; United States Farm Bureau Lobby, Progressive Mag, 70; plus one other. Relig: Jewish. Mailing Add: 3215 Coquelin Terr Chevy Chase MD 20015

EISENHOWER, JOHN SHELDON DOUD (R)
b Denver, Colo, Aug 22, 22; s Dwight David Eisenhower & Mamie Geneva Doud E; m 1947 to Barbara Jean Thompson; c Dwight David, II, Barbara Anne (Mrs Fernando Echavarria-Uribe), Susan Elaine (Mrs Alexander Hugh Bradshaw) & Mary Jean; two grandchildren. Educ: US Mil Acad, BA, 44; Columbia Univ, MA in Eng & Comp Lit, 50; Command & Gen Staff Col, 55. Hon Degrees: LHD, Norwood Inst, 70. Polit & Govt Pos: Asst staff secy, White House, 58-61; chmn, Citizens for Nixon, Pa, 68; US Ambassador to Belgium, 69-71. Bus & Prof Pos: Dir & trustee, Eisenhower Fel. Mil Serv: Entered as 2nd Lt, Army, 44, released as Lt Col, 63, after serv in Europe, 45 & Korea, 52-53; Brig Gen, Army Res, 74; Legion of Merit; Bronze Star; Army Commendation Ribbon; Combat Inf Badge. Publ: The Bitter Woods, G P Putnam's Sons, 69; Strictly Personal, Doubleday, 74. Relig: Presbyterian. Mailing Add: 111 White Horse Rd Phoenixville PA 19460

EISENHOWER, MILTON STOVER (R)
b Abilene, Kans, Sept 15, 99; s David Jacob Eisenhower & Ida Stover E; m 1927 to Helen Elsie Eakin, wid; c Milton Stover & Ruth Eakin (Mrs Snider). Educ: Kans State Univ, BS, 24; Pi Kappa Phi; Phi Beta Kappa; Sigma Alpha Epsilon; Alpha Zeta. Hon Degrees: From 37 cols & univs. Polit & Govt Pos: Am vconsul, Edinburgh, Scotland, 24-26; Asst to Secy of Agr, 26-28; dir info, Dept of Agr, 28-41, coordr progs, 37-42; mem various govt comns, 40-; dir, War Relocation Authority, 42; assoc dir, Off of War Info, 42-43; mem, Famine Emergency Relief Comt, 46; mem exec bd, UNESCO, 46, chmn, US Nat Comn for UNESCO, 46-48, deleg, UNESCO Conf, 46, 47, 48 & 49; trustee, Nat Comt Econ Develop, 47-51; chmn, Gen Awards Jury, 50; mem, President's Comt on Govt Orgn, 53-60; spec ambassador & personal rep of President, Latin Am Affairs, 53 & 57-60; chmn, President's Comn Causes & Prevention of Violence, 68-69; mem bd vis, US Naval Acad, 58-61; mem bd vis & gov, Washington Col; chmn, President's Comn Int Broadcasting, currently. Bus & Prof Pos: Dir, Freedoms Found Inc, 51-, Geisinger Mem Hosp, 52- & Fund for Adult Educ, 53-61; chmn, Am Korean Found, 52-53; dir, B&O RR, C&O RR, Commercial Credit Co, Am Gen Convertible Securities, Inc & Windsor Life Ins Co; emer pres, Johns Hopkins Univ. Publ: The wine is bitter, 63; The President is Calling, 74; numerous fed leaflets. Mem: Fel Am Acad Arts & Sci; hon mem, Acad Polit Sci; Kans Acad Sci. Honors & Awards: Received several awards from foreign govt. Relig: Episcopal. Legal Res: 12 E Bishop Rd Baltimore MD 21218 Mailing Add: 4545 N Charles St Baltimore MD 21210

EISS, ROGER (D)
b Lowville, NY, Sept 1, 37; s Albert F Eiss & Grace Rogers E; m 1963 to Francoise Beaujour Bourget. Educ: Alfred Univ, BS, 58, MS, 64; Mass Inst Technol, PhD, 67; Keramos; Lambda Chi Alpha. Polit & Govt Pos: Chmn, Topics Res, Demoforum, 69; Washington Co Dem Task Force, Ore, 69-70; Citizens Comt for AuCoin, 70; mem, Ore State Dem Cent Comt, 70-72; chmn, Washington Co Dem Cent Comt, 70-72; vchmn, Comt for State Conv Reform, 71; pres, Campaigners, 73; mem strategy comt, AuCoin for Cong, 74; mem steering comt, Straub for Gov, 74; legis asst, Cong Les AuCoin, 75- Bus & Prof Pos: Res chemist, AMP, Inc, Harrisburg, Pa, 60-63; instr, Univ Pittsburgh, 64; asst prof, Ore Grad Ctr, Portland, 67-72, dir educ, 72-74. Publ: Auth of seventeen publ in assorted chem jour. Mem: Am Chem Soc; Am Asn Univ Prof; Am Crystallog Asn; Am Asn Advan Sci; fel Am Inst Chem. Legal Res: OR Mailing Add: A719 101 G St SW Washington DC 20024

EIZENSTAT, STUART ELLIOT (D)
VChmn, Fulton Co Dem Party, Ga
b Chicago, Ill, Jan 15, 43; s Leo Eizenstat & Sylvia Medintz E; m 1967 to Frances Carol Taylor; c Jay Laurence, Brian Lee. Educ: Univ NC, Chapel Hill, AB, 64; Harvard Law Sch, LLB, 67; Phi Beta Kappa; Phi Eta Sigma; Pi Sigma Alpha; Order of Old Well; Zeta Beta Tau; Carolina Forum; Carolina Political Union; Daily Tar Heel; Student Attorney Gen Staff; Col rep to Model UN; Naval Acad Foreign Affairs Conf; Nat Student Asn. Polit & Govt Pos: Summer intern, US Rep G Elliott Hagan, Ga, 63; research & speechwriting staff, Postmaster Gen John Gronousky, summer 64; spec asst to pres Nat Young Dem Am, summer 64; summer intern, Off Gen Counsel, Dept Health, Educ & Welfare, 66; White House staff, 67-68; dir cand res staff, Hubert Humphrey Presidential Campaign Staff, 68; adv, San Massell Mayoral Campaign, 68; law clerk, US Dist Judge Edenfield, 68-70; adv, Jimmy Carter Gubernatorial Campaign, 70; adv, Andy Young for Congress Campaign, 70; precinct chmn, Fulton Co Dem Party, 70-, vchmn, 71-; mem, Ga State Dem Exec Comt, 71-; aide-de-camp, Gov Jimmy Carter, 71-74; issues dir, Congressman Andrew Young's Campaign, 72; mem, Citizens Adv Comt, Atlanta Charter Comn, 72-; mem, Nat Comn on VPresidential Selection, Dem Nat Comt, 73. Bus & Prof Pos: Attorney, Powell, Goldstein, Frazer & Murphy, 70- Publ: Co-auth, Accountants' professional liability: expanding exposure, Fed of Ins Coun Quart, 72

& Andrew Young: the path to history, Voter Educ Proj, 73; An expanding era of protected civil rights, Mercer Law Rev Vol 23, No 759. Mem: Ga & Atlanta Bar Asns; Am Judicature Soc; Atlanta Bur Jewish Educ (vpres, mem exec comt & vpres 72-74); Atlanta Jewish Community Ctr (bd dirs). Honors & Awards: Freshman Merit Cert, Col; High Sch All-Am Basketball; Fed Meritorious Serv Award. Relig: Jewish. Mailing Add: 2249 Havenridge Dr NW Atlanta GA 30305

EKBALD, ART (R)
NDak State Rep
Mailing Add: State Capitol Bismarck ND 58501

EKEN, WILLIS (DFL)
Minn State Rep
b Ada, Minn, Apr 12, 31; s Bernhard Eken & Hazel Hokestra E; m 1954 to Betty Lou Skaurud; c Loren Wayen, Lee Rodger, Kyle Jay & Bernhard Kent. Educ: Twin Valley High Sch, grad, 49. Polit & Govt Pos: Vchmn, Norman Co Dem-Farmer-Labor Party, Minn, 67-70; Minn State Rep, 71- Bus & Prof Pos: Farmer. Mem: Farmers Union; Nat Farmers Orgn; Retarded Children's Asn. Relig: Lutheran. Legal Res: Twin Valley MN 56584 Mailing Add: State Capitol St Paul MN 55101

ELAM, PAMELA LYNN (D)
b Ashland, Ky, Apr 28, 50; d James Harve Elam, Jr & Mildred Elizabeth Hayes E; single. Educ: Univ Ky, BA in Polit Sci, 72, Col of Law, currently. Polit & Govt Pos: Founder & mem steering comt, Lexington Women's Polit Caucus, Ky, 71-72; coordr, Univ Ky Students for McGovern, 71-72; mem, Nat Women's Polit Caucus, 71-, deleg, conv, 73; mem steering comt, Citizens for McGovern, 72; deleg, Ky Dem State Conv, 72; alt deleg, Dem Nat Conv, 72; mem state policy coun, Ky Women's Polit Caucus, 72-; staff asst, Ky Comn Women, 73-74; coordr, Women's Ctr Lexington, Inc, 74; mem, Univ Ky Women's Studies Comt; co chairwoman, Int Women's Year Comt. Mem: Univ Ky Coun on Women's Concerns (chairwoman, 73). Relig: Methodist. Legal Res: 2511 Woodland Ave Ashland KY 41101 Mailing Add: 307 Euclid Ave Lexington KY 40508

ELBRICK, C BURKE
b Louisville, Ky, Mar 25, 08; s Charles J Elbrick & Lillian Burke E; m 1932 to Elvira Lindsay Johnson; c Alfred Johnson & Valerie Burke. Educ: William Col, BA, 29; Phi Delta Theta. Hon Degrees: LLD, Hartwick Col. Polit & Govt Pos: Vconsul, Panama, 31-32; vcounsul, Southampton, Eng, 32-34; 3rd secy, Port-au-Prince, Haiti, 34-37, Warsaw, Poland, 37-38, Praha, 38-39, Warsaw, Poland, 39, Bucharest, 39, Warsaw (Angers, France), 39-40 & Madrid, Spain, 40; vconsul, Lisbon, Portugal, 40-41, 3rd secy, 41, 2nd secy, 41-43; 2nd secy, Tangier, 43-44; 2nd secy, Div of African Affairs, Dept of State, 44-45; 1st secy, Warsaw, Poland, 45; asst chief, Div East European Affairs, Dept of State, 46-48; student, Nat War Col, 48-49; counr, Havana, 49-51; counr, NAtlantic Coun Deleg, London 51 & Paris, 52-53; Dep Asst Secy of State, 53-56; Asst Secy of State, 57-58; US Ambassador to Portugal, 59-63; US Ambassador to Yugoslavia, 64-69; US Ambassador to Brazil, 69-70. Mem: Metrop & Chevy Chase Clubs. Legal Res: 2137 R St NW Washington DC 20008 Mailing Add: Dept of State Washington DC 20520

ELCONIN, MICHAEL HENRY (D)
Wis State Rep
b Cleveland, Ohio, June 20, 53; s Arnold Norman Elconin & Jane Rose E; single. Educ: Univ Wis-Milwaukee, 71 & 73; Brown Univ, 71-72. Polit & Govt Pos: Wis State Rep, 73- Bus & Prof Pos: Computer programmer, 72. Mem: Dem Party of Wis; Wis Coalition for Balanced Transportation (mem steering comt, 73-). Mailing Add: 4246 N Sercombe Rd Milwaukee WI 53216

ELDER, CHARLES (D)
Okla State Rep
b Purcell, Okla, Feb 23, 33; s Arthur Revere Elder & Helen Gold E; m 1957 to Beverly Beck; c Charles, II & Todd Hester. Educ: Univ Okla, BA in Polit Sci, 55, JD, 58; Delta Sigma Rho; Phi Eta Sigma; Phi Alpha Delta. Polit & Govt Pos: Secy-treas, Okla League of Young Dem, 52-55; deleg, Dem Nat Conv, mem Platform Comt & exec comt of the Platform Comt, 64; asst to chmn of the State Dem Cent Comt, Okla, 64; Okla State Rep, Garvin, Grady & McClain Co, 70- Bus & Prof Pos: Pres, Purcell CofC, 69; chmn, Okla Rural Affairs Coun, 70. Mem: Am & Okla Bar Asns; Tenth Circuit Judicial Conf; Purcell Rotary Club. Relig: Episcopal. Mailing Add: PO Box 667 Purcell OK 73080

ELDER, DAVID MAYNE (D)
b Watkinsville, Ga, Sept 19, 18; s David M Elder & Ola Edwards E; m 1949 to June Carol Anthony. Educ: Univ of Ga, BSAgrE, 40. Polit & Govt Pos: Councilman, Watkinsville, Ga, 49-58; Ga State Rep, 55-59; admin asst to US Rep Robert G Stephens, Jr, Ga, 62- Bus & Prof Pos: Coordinator & off mgr, Dept of Vet Serv, Ga, 47-61. Mil Serv: Entered as Ens, Naval Res, 41, released as Lt Comdr, after serv in European & Pac Theatres, 41-46; Coast Guard Res, Capt. Mem: Elks; Am Legion; VFW. Relig: Protestant. Legal Res: Watkinsville GA 30677 Mailing Add: 3389 S Stafford St Arlington VA 22206

ELDRIDGE, DON D (R)
b Mt Vernon, Wash, Dec 26, 19; s Raymond L Eldridge & Blanche E Thorpe E; m 1973 to Nanci J Williams; c Raymond E, Jean M, Sally A & Jon D. Educ: Western Wash State Col, BA in educ, 44; Phi Delta Theta; Alpha Phi Omega. Polit & Govt Pos: Past field adv, Small Bus Admin, 10 years; past mem bd trustee, Western Wash State Col, 10 years, chmn bd, 57-59; Wash State Rep, 53-70, mem interim comt on educ, Wash House Rep, 59-63, vchmn, 59-60, Speaker of the House, 67-70; mem, Wash-Ore Boundary Comn, 55-56; mem, Wash State Legis Coun, 57-58 & 65-70, chmn, 67-70; bd mem, Wash State Liquor Control Bd, 70- Bus & Prof Pos: Mem exec comt, Wash Retail Coun, 62-64; mem bd dirs, Asn of Wash Indust, 64-70. Mil Serv: Army Air Corps, 43, Pvt. Mem: Skagit Develop Asn; US Jr CofC (vpres); Wash State Jr CofC (pres); Mt Vernon CofC; Rotary. Honors & Awards: Distinguished Serv Award Jr CofC, 47; Silver Beaver, Boy Scouts, 60, Silver Antelope, 62. Relig: Episcopal. Legal Res: 621 Blvd Rd Olympia WA 98501 Mailing Add: Wash State Liquor Control Bd Olympia WA 98504

ELDRIDGE, FRANK, JR (D)
Ga State Sen
Mailing Add: Box 1141 Waycross GA 31501

ELDRIDGE, NANCI JANE (R)
Chmn, Thurston Co Rep Cent Comt, Wash
b Shawnee, Okla, Sept 11, 39; d Charles William Mooney & Mary Jane Jones M; m 1973 to Donald Delos Eldridge; c John Charles Williams, III. Educ: Bellevue Community Col, 65-66; Centralia Community Col, 73-75. Polit & Govt Pos: Speaker's secy, Wash State House Rep, 67-70; vchmn, Thurston Co Rep Cent Comt, Wash, 69-70, chmn, 75-; admin asst, Rep State Cent Comt, 70-71; proj coordr, Comt for Reelec of President, 72. Bus & Prof Pos: Secy to pres, Puget Sound Power & Light Co, 63-66; ins agt, 72-73; real estate salesman, Hearthstone Realty, 75- Mem: United Way Thurston Co (pres, 75); Thurston Co YWCA (bd mem, 72-75); League Women Voters, Wash; Olympia CofC; Thurston Co Coun on Aging (bd, 72-). Honors & Awards: Jr Altrusan Award, 56. Mailing Add: 621 Blvd Rd Olympia WA 98501

ELDRIDGE, RONNIE MYERS (D)
b New York, NY, Jan 30, 31; d Clifford Luckstone Myers & Aimee Fleck M; m 1955 to Dr Lawrence Eldridge, wid; c Daniel, Emily & Lucy. Educ: Barnard Col, AB, 52. Polit & Govt Pos: Dist leader, New York Co Dem Comt, NY, 64-68; dir, Coalition for Dem Alternative, 68; vchairperson, Citizen's Comt for Robert F Kennedy, 68; dir, Dem for Lindsay, 69; spec asst to mayor, New York, 69-72, dep city adminr, 72; dep campaign mgr, Lindsay for President, 72; campaign mgr, Bella Abzug for Cong, 72; vchairperson platform comt, Dem Nat Conv, 72; deleg, Dem Nat Mid-Term Conf, 74. Bus & Prof Pos: Pres, Ms Marketing, 73-74; dir spec prod, Ms Mag, 73-74; exec producer, WNET, New York, 74- Mailing Add: 149 W 93rd St New York NY 10025

ELESER, GOLDA EASLEY (R)
Mem, La State Rep Cent Comt
b Magnolia, Miss, Nov 10, 27; d Augusta Easley & Gladys Johnson E; m 1946 to Louis Peter Eleser, Jr; c Glynn Barry, Ronald Wayne, Pamela Jean, Cynthia Ann & Deborah Lynn. Educ: Southeastern La Col, Hammond, 2 years. Polit & Govt Pos: Co-chmn, Nixon Campaign, Hammond, La, 60; chmn, Tangipahoa Parish Rep Exec Comt, 60-69; mem, La State Rep Cent Comt, 64-; mem, Sixth Dist Rep Polit Action Coun, 64-; chmn, Goldwater Hq, Tangipahoa Parish & Lyons Campaign, 64; deleg, Rep Nat Conv, 64; sponsor, Young Rep Camp Meet, 65. Mem: League of Women Voters; Am Legion Auxiliary; Clio Sportsman League; Hammond High & Hammond Jr High PTA; Hammond High Boosters Club. Honors & Awards: Recipient of Farm Bur Freedom Award, for promoting the causes of Am Patriotism, 63. Relig: Catholic. Legal Res: 129 Florence Dr Hammond LA 70401 Mailing Add: PO Box 7 Hammond LA 70401

ELEVELD, ROBERT JAY (R)
Chmn, Fifth Cong Dist Rep Party, Mich
b Grand Rapids, Mich, Aug 3, 36; s John H Eleveld & Dena Klooster E; m 1961 to Lynn Keister; c Robert J, Jr & Karen L. Educ: Dartmouth Col, BA, 58; Univ Mich Law Sch, LLB, 61; Kappa Sigma. Polit & Govt Pos: City comnr, East Grand Rapids, Mich, 71-73; chmn, Kent Co Rep Party, 73-75; chmn, Fifth Cong Dist Rep Party, 75- Bus & Prof Pos: Partner law firm, Varnum, Riddering, Wierengo & Christenson, 68- Mil Serv: Entered as 1st Lt, Mich Air Nat Guard, 61, released as Capt, 67. Mem: Am, Mich & Grand Rapids Bar Asns; Int Asn Ins Counsel. Legal Res: 1120 Plymouth SE Grand Rapids MI 49506 Mailing Add: 666 Old Kent Bldg Grand Rapids MI 49502

ELIASON, LARRY BILL (R)
Chmn, SDak Young Rep
b Pierre, SDak, Jan 25, 49; s William Edward Eliason & Dorothy Briscoe E; single. Educ: Univ SDak, BA, 71. Polit & Govt Pos: State secy, Teen-Age Rep, SDak, 66-67; secy, SDak Young Rep, 73- Bus & Prof Pos: Press secy, US Senate Campaign, Sioux Falls, SDak, 73-74; state ed, Mitchell Daily Repub, 75- Mil Serv: Entered as 2nd Lt, Army, 71, released as 1st Lt, 73, after serv in Logistics Ctr; 1st Lt, Army Res, currently; Nat Defense Serv Medal; Army Commendation Medal. Mem: Am Legion; ROA; Young Rep. Relig: Catholic. Mailing Add: 307 E Fifth Ave Mitchell SD 57301

ELIASON, RICHARD J (DICK) (R)
Alaska State Rep
Mailing Add: PO Box 143 Sitka AK 99835

ELIASSEN, HERB O (R)
b Colgan, NDak, Sept 2, 15; s Peter Eliassen & Thea Wold E; m 1940 to Cecile; c Robin, Thea & Gary. Polit & Govt Pos: Chmn, Okanogan Co Rep Cent Comt, Wash, formerly. Mil Serv: Entered in Navy, 45, released, 46, after serv in Fleet Ship Salvage, Pac Theatre. Mem: Am Legion (Americanism chmn); Okanogan & Nat CofC; Toastmasters. Relig: Presbyterian; Deacon. Legal Res: 446 S Fir Omak WA 98840 Mailing Add: 338 S Second Box 822 Okanogan WA 98840

ELICH, JACK FRANK (D)
Mem Exec Bd, Pierce Co Dem Party, Wash
b Pueblo, Colo, Sept 27, 04; s Anton Elich & Mary Svetich E; m 1930 to Frances Marie Hugg. Educ: Marquette Univ, 1 year; Fed Bur Invest & Interserv Training Schs. Polit & Govt Pos: Coord chmn, Pierce Co Dem Cent Comt, Wash, 65-70, chmn, 69-70; pres, 26th Dist Dem Club, 3 years; Humphrey Presidential Campaign, 68; mem exec bd, Pierce Co Dem Party, currently. Bus & Prof Pos: Spec agent, Fed Bur Invest, 37-44; asst treas, Sperry Gyroscope Corp, 44-52; chief of police, Tacoma, Wash, 52-54; mgr, Kefauver Invest Crime, New York; jail supt, Pierce Co, Wash. Mil Serv: Entered as Pvt, Marine Corps, 24, released as 1st Sgt, 28, after serv in USS Md, 2 years & China, 1 year; Good Conduct Medal. Publ: Espionage & Sabotage, McGraw Hill, 44. Mem: Wash Athletic Club; Boys' Club; Grange; Elks; Dem Club. Relig: Presbyterian. Mailing Add: 3909 N 36th Tacoma WA 98407

ELIOT, THOMAS HOPKINSON (D)
b Cambridge, Mass, June 14, 07; s Samuel Atkins Eliot & Frances Stone Hopkinson E; m 1936 to Lois A Jameson; c Samuel Atkins & Nancy. Educ: Harvard, AB, 28, LLB, 32; Emmanuel Col, Cambridge, Eng, 28-29. Hon Degrees: LLD, Drury Col; LHD, Hobart & William Smith Col & St Louis Univ; Dr Humanities, Wash Univ, 71. Polit & Govt Pos: Asst solicitor, US Dept Labor, 33-35; counsel, Pres Comn Econ Security, 34-35; gen counsel, Soc Security Bd, 35-38; regional dir wage & hour div, US Dept Labor, 39-40; US Rep, Mass, 41-43; spec asst to ambassador & head of Brit div, London Off War Info, 43; with Nat War Labor Bd, 43-44, Off Strategic Serv, 44; chief counsel div power, Dept of Interior, 44-45; exec dir, Spec Comn on Structure of State Govt, 50-52; vchmn, US Adv Comn Intergovt Rels, 64-67. Bus & Prof Pos: Assoc, Kenefick, Cooke, Mitchell, Bass & Letchworth, Buffalo, 32-33; lectr govt, Harvard Univ, 37-38 & 48-51, mem bd overseers, 64-70; partner, Foley, Hoag &

Eliot, 45-52; prof & chmn dept polit sci, Wash Univ, 52-61, prof const law, law sch, 58-62, dean col liberal arts, 61-62, Chancellor, 62-71; vis prof, Princeton Univ, 58-59; pres, Salzburg Seminar in Am Studies, 71- Publ: American government problems for analysis, 59; Governing America, 60; co-auth, State politics and the public schools, 63 plus one other. Mem: United Negro Col Fund; Monticello Col; Am Civil Liberties Union; Am Polit Sci Asn; Am Acad of Arts & Sci. Relig: Unitarian. Mailing Add: 986 Memorial Dr Cambridge MA 02138

ELKINS, JAMES E (BUZZ) (R)
Tenn State Rep
Mailing Add: 305 Westbury Dr Clinton TN 37716

ELKINS, RANDALL SCOTT (D)
b Morgantown, WVa, Sept 29; 54; s Eugene Randall Elkins & Joan Goff E; single. Educ: WVa Univ, currently. Polit & Govt Pos: Alt deleg, Dem Nat Conv, 72. Mailing Add: 316 Wagner Rd Morgantown WV 26505

ELLENBOGEN, HENRY (D)
b Vienna, Austria, Apr 3, 00; s Samson Ellenbogen & Rose Franzos E; m 1927 to Rae Savage; c Naomi & Judith. Educ: Royal-Imperial Univ Vienna, Austria, 18-21; Duquesne Univ, AB, 23, LLB, 24, JD. Polit & Govt Pos: US Rep, Pa, 32-38; judge, Court of Common Pleas, Allegheny Co, 38-, pres judge, 63-; permanent mem, Judicial Coun, Commonwealth of Pa, currently. Publ: Report of the sub-committee on judicial administration of the Pennsylvania Bar Association regarding administrator for the courts in Pennsylvania, Pa Bar Asn, 59; Automation in the courts, Am Bar Asn J, 7/64; The English courts as seen by an American judge, Pa Bar Asn Quart, 3/67. Mem: Fel Int Acad Law & Sci; Am Judicature Soc; Pa Conf State Trial Judges; Asn Former Mem Cong; Span Nat Asn Forensic Med. Mailing Add: 618 City-County Bldg Pittsburgh PA 15219

ELLER, ARMENA MORSE (R)
b Santa Ana, Calif; d Thomas Oliver Morse & Leila Dawes M; m 1917 to Dr Williard H Eller; c Willard Morse. Educ: Univ of Calif, Berkeley, BS, 17; Univ of Hawaii, 32-33 & 48. Polit & Govt Pos: Mem, Rep Women's Club of Honolulu, 48-58; tel chmn, 14th Rep Precinct Club, Honolulu, 50-54, secy, 54-56; deleg, State Rep Conv, Honolulu, 50, 52, 54 & 56; co-dir, Rep Sch of Polit, Manoa Sch, 52; vpres, Oroville Area Rep Women's Club, Calif, 58, pres, 58-60, bull ed, 58-74; mem, Butte Co Rep Cent Comt, Calif, 60-62, 64-66, 68-70 & 72-74; chmn, Oroville Dist, 66-68 & 73-74; mem, Calif Rep State Cent Comt, 62-64 & 68-74; deleg, Calif Rep Asn Conv, 62 & 64. Bus & Prof Pos: Sci illustrator, Univ of Calif, Berkeley, 25-28 & Pineapple Research Inst, Honolulu, 28-29, illustrator, 37-38; archit designer, Lake Bldg Corp, 28-35; art instr, Cent & Stevenson Schs, Honolulu, 35-36; designer for Gump's Roosevelt High Sch, Honolulu, 40-56, head of art dept, 40-46 & 48-57. Publ: Illustrator, Kinetic Theories of Gases, Leonard Loeb, McGraw-Hill, 28; Star Over the Pacific, Grove Day & Carl Stroven, 56; Illustrator of innumerable sci articles in various journals, 25-55. Mem: Maui Womens Rep League. Honors & Awards: Cert Merit, Gov Ronald Reagan, 73. Relig: Protestant. Mailing Add: 1204 Bridge St Oroville CA 95965

ELLERD, ROBERT A (R)
Mont State Rep
Mailing Add: 2206 Bridger Dr Bozeman MT 59715

ELLETT, ALBERT HAYDEN
Justice, Supreme Court of Utah
b Huntsville, Ala, Feb 4, 98; s Isaac William Ellett & Martha Catherine Green E; m 1924 to Florence Rowe; c Kenneth William, Walter Rowe & Jeanne (Mrs Clifford Parks). Educ: Univ Utah, BA; Blackstone Col Law, LLB, 30; Phi Kappa Phi; Phi Beta Kappa; Order of the Coif. Polit & Govt Pos: Co dep attorney, Salt Lake City Utah, 33-34; city judge, Salt Lake City, 34-40; Dist Court Judge, Utah, 41-66; justice, Supreme Court of Utah, 67- Bus & Prof Pos: Sch teacher, Tex, 16-18 & 19-20, Utah, 20-21 & 22-23, La, 21-22. Mil Serv: Pvt, ROTC, East Tex State Normal Col, 18. Mem: Salt Lake Co Bar Asn; Utah State Bar; Am Judicature Soc. Relig: Latter-day Saint. Legal Res: 3910 Luetta Dr Salt Lake City UT 84117 Mailing Add: 332 State Capitol Salt Lake City UT 84114

ELLINGER, CAROL ELOISE (R)
Chmn, Cole Co Rep Comt, Mo
b Pittsburgh, Pa, Apr 8, 31; d Robert Russell Thompson & Lillian Schirra T; m 1962 to John Winfield Ellinger; c Marc Henry & Daniel Patrick. Educ: Bethany Col (WVa), AB, 53; Smith Col, MA, 54; Univ Colo, Boulder, summer 56; Univ Wis-Madison, summer 57; Zeta Tau Alpha. Polit & Govt Pos: Mem, Mo Fedn Rep Women, currently, conv chmn, 75; vchmn, Cole Co Rep Comt, Mo, 70-72, chmn, 74-; mem, Mo Rep State Comt, 72-74. Bus & Prof Pos: Instr, Holton-Arms Sch & Jr Col, Washington, DC, 54-57 & Stephens Col, 57-62. Mem: Cole Co Hist Soc (suitcase lady); Church Women United. Honors & Awards: Outstanding Jr Girl, Bethany Col, 52, Oreon E Scott Award, 53; nominee, Outstanding Young Women, Jefferson City, Mo, 65; Outstanding Rep Women (one of several), Mo Fedn Rep Women, 68. Relig: United Church of Christ; mem, Women's Fel, Cent United Church of Christ. Mailing Add: 5003 Henwick Lane Jefferson City MO 65101

ELLINGSON, BERTRUM EDWIN (D)
SDak State Rep
b Rosholt, SDak, Apr 17, 21; s Bert Ellingson & Esther Stanley E; m 1943 to Nilda Renfroe; c Robert, Faye Marie & Linda Sue. Polit & Govt Pos: SDak State Rep, 69- Mil Serv: Entered as Pvt, Air Force, 41, released as Lt Col, 63, after serv in various overseas & stateside units; Silver Star; Distinguished Flying Cross with two Oak Leaf Clusters; Air Medal with six Oak Leaf Clusters; Army Commendation Medal. Mem: Am Legion; VFW. Relig: Lutheran. Mailing Add: Rte 1 Box 135 Sisseton SD 57262

ELLIOTT, CARL (D)
b Vina, Ala, Dec 20, 13; s George W Elliott & Lenora Massey E; m 1940 to Jane Hamilton; c Carl, Jr, Martha Owen, John Hamilton & Lenora Jane. Educ: Univ Ala, AB, 33, LLB, 36; Omicron Delta Kappa; Philomathic Lit Soc; Jasons; Phi Alpha Delta; pres, Student Body, 35-36. Hon Degrees: LLD, Tufts Univ, 65, Univ Ala, 72. Polit & Govt Pos: Mem, Franklin Co Dem Exec Comt, Ala, 36; US Comnr, 38-39; recorder, City Court of Jasper, Ala, 39-42 & 44-46; secy, Walker Co Dem Exec Comt, 42; mem, Ala State Dem Exec Comt, 42-50; city attorney, Jasper, Ala, 45-46; US Rep, Ala, 49-65, chmn, Select Comt on Govt Res, US House Rep, 63-65; mem, President's Comn on Libr, 66-68; chmn, Comt to Investigate Admin of State Tech Serv Act, app by Secy of Com, 67-68, mem tech adv bd, US Dept Com, 68-70; cand for Dem Elector, Ala, 72. Bus & Prof Pos: Attorney, Elliott, Elliott, O'Rear & Robinson, Jasper, Ala. Mil Serv: Entered as Pvt, Army, 42, released as 1st Lt, 44, after serv in Inf. Publ: Annals of northwest Alabama, privately publ, Vols I, II & III, Vol IV, 72. Mem: Lions; Mason; Odd Fellows; Am Legion; life mem DAV. Relig: Methodist. Mailing Add: 1700 Birmingham Ave Jasper AL 35501

ELLIOTT, DAISY (D)
Mich State Rep
b Filbert, WVa; c three. Educ: Detroit Inst of Com, grad; Wayne State Univ; Univ Detroit. Polit & Govt Pos: Deleg, Mich State Dem Const Conv, 61-62; Mich State Rep, Eighth Dist, 62-, mem, Educ, Labor & Admin Rules Comts, Mich House Rep, chmn, Comt on Cols & Univs & Const Rev & Women's Rights, currently; alt deleg, Dem Nat Conv, 72; Asst Majority Dem Caucus Chmn, currently; mem, Coun on Postsec Educ & Joint Legis Liaison Comt of Gov Comn on Higher Educ, currently. Publ: Civil rights provision, Mich State Const. Mem: Order of Women Legislators; charter mem Nat Soc State Legislators; Mich Dem Black Caucus (secy); United Black Coalition (secy). Honors & Awards: One of the Most Outstanding Black Women in Politics, Alpha Kappa Heritage Series, 70; Community Serv Award, People's Community Church; Meritorious Serv Award, Most Worshipful Prince Hall Lodge; Woman of the Year, Mich Federated Dem Club; Distinguished Serv Award, Black Legislators Clearing House. Relig: People's Community Church; mem trustee bd. Mailing Add: 8701 LaSalle Blvd Detroit MI 48206

ELLIOTT, DAVID H (R)
Del State Sen
Mailing Add: Rte 1 Box 154 Laurel DE 19956

ELLIOTT, EWELL H (HANK), JR (R)
Ga State Rep
b Cedartown, Ga, Mar 22, 36; s Ewell Herman Elliott, Sr & Reva Treadaway E; m 1959 to Jane Senn; c Laura Lee & Scott. Educ: Auburn Univ, BS in Indust Mgt, 59; Emory Univ Sch Law, JD, 71; Omicron Delta Kappa; Kappa Sigma (pres). Polit & Govt Pos: Ga State Rep, 73- Bus & Prof Pos: Attorney, Harvey, Willard & Elliott, Decatur, 72- Mil Serv: Entered as 2nd Lt, Army Res, 59, released as Capt, 68, after serv in 310th Civil Affairs, 60-68; Hon Mil Grad, Auburn Univ, 59. Mem: Am, Ga & Decatur-DeKalb Bar Asns. Relig: Methodist. Mailing Add: The Exec Bldg Decatur GA 30030

ELLIOTT, FRANK, JR (R)
b Bonnieville, Ky, Apr 19, 20; s Frank Elliott & Birdie Hatfield E; m 1946 to Mary Stella Carter; c Demetra (Mrs Lester M Bradway), Regina (Mrs Fredrich W Hodges), Belinda (Mrs Gary Walters), Michael R & Deborah Rene. Educ: Bonnieville Grade Sch, grad, 34. Polit & Govt Pos: Campaign chmn, Hart Co, Ky, 63; Chmn, Hart Co Rep Party, formerly. Bus & Prof Pos: Retail merchant. Mil Serv: Entered as Pvt, Army, 42, released as T-5, 43, after serv in 25th Engr Bn. Mem: Mason; Farm Bur; Optimist Club. Relig: Protestant. Mailing Add: Bonnieville KY 42713

ELLIOTT, HUMPHREY TAYLOR (R)
Chmn, Casey Co Rep Party, Ky
b Gilpin, Ky, Mar 12, 33; s Green Lee Elliott & Manilla Taylor E; single. Educ: Eastern Ky State Col, BS, 59, MA, 61. Polit & Govt Pos: Chmn, Casey Co Rep Party, Ky, 64-; deleg, Rep Nat Conv, 72. Mil Serv: Entered as Airman, Air Force, 52, released as S/Sgt, 56, after serv in Fla, Japan, Formosa & Ga. Mem: Mason; Kiwanis; Farm Bur; Am Legion. Relig: Christian. Mailing Add: Box 113 Liberty KY 42539

ELLIOTT, JACK MARK (R)
Chmn, Ringgold Co Rep Cent Comt, Iowa
b Mount Ayr, Iowa, Sept 25, 27; s Mark Elliott & Ilah Spencer E; m 1945 to Mildred Ellen Dixon; c Craig, Richard, Kirk & Karen. Educ: Mount Ayr High Sch, grad, 45. Polit & Govt Pos: Chmn, Ringgold Co Rep Cent Comt, Iowa, 60-; pres, Mount Ayr Community Sch Bd, 64-72. Mem: Mason (32 degree); Shrine; Eastern Star; Lions; Farm Bur. Honors & Awards: Iowa Master Swine Producer, 67; Iowa Master Farmer, 70. Relig: United Methodist. Mailing Add: 107 Shellway Dr Mount Ayr IA 50854

ELLIOTT, JAMES ALTON (D)
Ariz State Rep
b Blandville, Ky, Sept 30, 04; s Ernest Edwin Elliott & Atha Swindle E; m 1931 to Ruth Katheryn Donohoe; c Ruth (Mrs Ralph Aldridge), Martha & Veronica Ann (Mrs Thomas E Price). Educ: Northern Ariz Univ, BA, 30; Univ Ariz, MA, 42; Sigma Alpha; Phi Delta Kappa. Polit & Govt Pos: Ariz State Rep, Cochise Co, 45-47, 49-50 & 61-69; mem, State Retirement Bd, 55-60; Ariz State Sen, Dist 2, 69-71; Ariz State Rep, Dist 8, 75- Bus & Prof Pos: Teacher, McNary Schs, Ariz, 30-33; teacher, Douglas Schs, 34-47, elem sch prin, 47-70; retired. Mem: Nat Educ Asn; KofC; Ariz Town Hall; Elks; Cochise Co Hist & Archeol Soc. Honors & Awards: Douglas High Sch Yearbk Copper Kettle dedicated to him, 47; Sterling Silver State Seal, Ariz State Univ; Distinguished Serv Plaque Award, Ariz Educ Asn, 72; Distinguished Citizen of Year Award, Northern Ariz Univ Alumni Asn, 72. Relig: Catholic. Mailing Add: 1450 13th St Douglas AZ 85607

ELLIOTT, MILDRED ELLEN (R)
b Des Moines, Iowa, Feb 11, 27; d Otho Glen Dixon & Madge Wallace D; m 1945 to Jack Mark Elliott; c Craig, Richard, Kirk & Karen. Educ: Mt Ayr High Sch, grad, 45. Polit & Govt Pos: Mem, Iowa Gov Comn on Youth & Children, 61-71; deleg, White House Conf on Children, 70; pres, Fifth Dist Rep Women of Iowa, 73-; alt deleg, Rep Nat Conv, 72; mem, Iowa Rep State Platform Comt, 70; mem, State Exten Adv Coun, 72-74; mem, Rep State Const Revisions Comt, 74; mem, Iowa Rural Develop Adv Comt, 74- Mem: Eastern Star (Worthy Matron, 61); Federated Women's Club; Order of Rainbow for Girls (Grand Dept, 69-). Relig: United Methodist. Mailing Add: 107 Shellway Dr Mt Ayr IA 50854

ELLIOTT, RICHARD WYATT (D)
Va State Deleg
b Richmond, Va, Mar 29, 44; s Cecil Irvin Elliott & Annie Elizabeth Wood E; m 1967 to Patricia Carroll Davis; c Carrington Wyatt. Educ: Univ Richmond, BSBA, 66; Univ Va, LLB, 69; Omicron Delta Kappa; Alpha Kappa Psi; Phi Gamma Delta. Polit & Govt Pos: Va State Deleg, 72-; deleg, Dem Nat Mid-Term Conf, 74. Mil Serv: SP-4, Army Res. Mem: Cent Va Ment Health Asn; Gtr Lynchburg Legal Aid Soc (dir); Lynchburg, Va & Am Bar Asn; Va Trial Lawyers Asn. Honors & Awards: Norman Award, Univ Richmond, 66. Relig: Baptist. Legal Res: Rte 2 Box 177 Gladys VA 24554 Mailing Add: PO Box 250 Rustburg VA 24588

ELLIOTT, ROBERT AMOS (R)
b Portland, Ore, Oct 13, 16; s Harry Clayton Elliott & Beatrice Janet Parsons E; m 1943; c John Douglas & Robin Leigh. Educ: Univ Ore, BS, 40; Phi Delta Theta. Polit & Govt Pos: State chmn, Ore State Young Rep, 46; deleg-at-lg, Rep Nat Conv, 48, 52 & 56; chmn, Multnomah Co Rep Cent Comt, 48-50 & 61-62; chmn, Rep State Cent Comt, Ore, 50-52; state campaign chmn, Tom McCall for Gov, 66; Ore State Rep, 67-74. Mil Serv: Entered as Pvt, Army, 41, released as Capt, 46, after serv in 104th Div, ETO; Lt Col, Army Res, 46-58; Bronze Star; Armed Forces Res, Occup, Am Campaign, Europe-Africa-Mid East, Cent Rhineland & Victory Medals; Combat & Expert Infantryman Badges. Mem: Lions Int. Relig: Episcopal; former key layman, Episcopal Diocese of Ore. Mailing Add: 11036 NE Everett St Portland OR 97220

ELLIOTT, ROBERT R (R)
Gen Counsel, Dept Housing & Urban Develop
b Buffalo, NY, Feb 26, 41; s Charles Alexander Elliott & Evelyn Charlot Wahl E; m 1968 to Maria Gloria Romero; c Thomas Andrew & Andrea Faye. Educ: Harvard Col, AB magna cum laude, 63; Harvard Law Sch, JD, 66; Univ Chile, 66-67. Polit & Govt Pos: Dep gen counsel, Dept Housing & Urban Develop, 73-74, gen counsel, 74- Bus & Prof Pos: Assoc attorney, 67-71; partner, Hill, Christopher & Phillips, 71-73. Mem: Nat Economists Club; Am & DC Bar Asns. Legal Res: 7500 Cerro Gordo Rd Gainesville VA 22065 Mailing Add: Suite 10214 451 Seventh St SW Washington DC 20410

ELLIOTT, ROLAND L (R)
b Bremerton, Wash, Sept 27, 36; m to Dorothy Case; c Mark, Shannon & Sarah. Educ: Univ Calif, Los Angeles, BA, 61. Polit & Govt Pos: Spec asst to President, 71- Legal Res: VA Mailing Add: 1600 Pennsylvania Ave Washington DC 20005

ELLIOTT, RONALD D (R)
Colo State Rep
Mailing Add: 1860 Iris St Lakewood CO 80915

ELLIOTT, THOMAS EDWARD (D)
Treas, Richland Co, SC
b Columbia, SC, Aug 2, 29; s David Onslow Elliott & Nora Stevens E; m 1948 to Gertrude Agnes Bultman; c Robert Cone, Thomas Edward, Jr, Stevens Bultman & Lyon Lambert. Polit & Govt Pos: SC State Rep, 58-61; treas, Richland Co, SC, 61-; alt deleg, Dem Nat Conv, 64, deleg, 68. Bus & Prof Pos: Deleg, Nat Food Retailers Conv, 60. Mailing Add: Rte 1 Box 7 Eastover SC 29044

ELLIOTT, TYRON CLIFFORD (R)
Chmn, Third Cong Dist Rep Party, Ga
b Cordele, Ga, Oct 27, 42; s Seniamon Byron Elliott & Bertie Williams E; m 1965 to Pinky Marilyn Gill; c Clifford Douglas & Jennifer Anne. Educ: Mercer Univ, AB, 64, LLB, 66; Blue Key; Alpha Psi Omega; Sigma Nu; Phi Delta Phi. Polit & Govt Pos: Chmn, Tift Co Rep Party, Ga, 68-70; vchmn, Second Cong Dist Rep Party, 68-70; chmn, Meriwether Co Rep Party, 70-72; chmn, Third Cong Dist Rep Party, 72- Bus & Prof Pos: Assoc, Law Firm of Reinhardt, Ireland, Whitley & Sims, 66-70; partner, Elliott & Turner, 70- Mem: Am, Ga & Meriwether Co Bar Asns; Manchester Kiwanis; Woodbury Lions. Relig: Baptist. Mailing Add: 225 Jones Mill Rd Woodbury GA 30293

ELLIS, BRAXTON CRAIG (D)
Chmn, Scotland Co Dem Exec Comt, NC
b Wilmington, NC, Jan 13, 41; s Braxton Ellis & Nettie May Craig E; m 1964 to Patricia Phillips; c Jennifer Craig & Elizabeth Anne. Educ: Univ Va, BS Educ, 64; Univ NC, Chapel Hill, JD, 70; Sigma Pi. Polit & Govt Pos: Co-chmn, Scotland Co Comt to Reelect US Sen B Everett Jordan, NC, 72; chmn, Scotland Co Dem Exec Comt, NC, 72- Bus & Prof Pos: Partner, Cashwell & Ellis, Attorneys-at-Law, Laurinburg, NC, currently. Mil Serv: Entered as Ens, Navy, 64, released as Lt, 68, after serv in Mine Forces, Atlantic & Pac Fleets, 64-68; Secy of the Navy Commendation for Achievement Award; Nat Defense Medal. Mem: NC, Am & Scotland Co Bar Asns; Jaycees; Laurinburg-Scotland Co CofC (dir, 72-). Relig: Presbyterian. Mailing Add: Box 1339 Laurinburg NC 28352

ELLIS, CLYDE T (D)
b Garfield, Ark, Dec 21, 08; s Cecil Oscar Ellis & Minerva Jane Taylor E; m 1970 to Camille Waldron Fitzhugh; c Patricia Suzanne (Mrs Marti) & Mary Lynn (Mrs Duty). Educ: Univ Ark, BS in Bus Admin. Polit & Govt Pos: Ark State Rep, 33-35; Ark State Sen, 35-39; US Rep, Ark, 39-43; mem, Nat Water Comn, 68-; mem prof staff, US Sen John L McClellan, Ark, 71- Bus & Prof Pos: Attorney, admitted to bar, 33. Mil Serv: Entered as Lt(jg), Naval Res, 43, released as Lt, 45, after serv in North Atlantic Command. Publ: A Giant Step, Random House, 66. Mem: Washington, DC Bar; Cosmos Club; Author's Guild; Congressional Country Club. Mailing Add: 5317 Kenwood Ave Chevy Chase MD 20015

ELLIS, DAVID LLOYD (R)
b Owensboro, Ky, Dec 19, 46; s Norman B Ellis & Ruth Lloyd E; m 1969 to Sheila Nonaka. Educ: Univ Hawaii, BA, 74; Tau Kappa Epsilon. Polit & Govt Pos: Precinct pres, 12th Dist, Hawaii, 69-71; alt deleg, Rep Nat Conv, 72; aide, Hawaii State Senate, 72-74; security consult, HEDCO, Model Cities Prog, 74- Bus & Prof Pos: Sky marshall, US Customs Air Security, Honolulu, 71-72. Mil Serv: Entered as Pvt, Army, 64, released as E-5, 67, after serv in 319th MI Bn, USAR Pac & MACV, 65-67; Purple Heart, Vietnam Serv Award; Vietnam Govt Award, Army Commendation Award, Good Conduct Award. Mem: Civil Air Patrol (Search & Rescue Commun Coordr); Nat Rifle Asn; Am Bowling Congress; Barons. Honors & Awards: Outstanding Vol Worker, Shriners Hosp Honolulu, 66. Relig: Southern Baptist. Mailing Add: 2755 Kapiolani Blvd Apt 32 Honolulu HI 96814

ELLIS, EDWARD DALE (D)
Mem, Venango Co Dem Exec Comt, Pa
b Franklin, Pa, Apr 19, 14; s Edward Luke Ellis & Mazie Mitchell E; m 1946 to Antionette Marie Leta; c Edward Dale, Frank Thomas, James Paul, Mary Helen & William Lewis. Educ: Int Commercial Sch, Scranton, Pa; Univ Ky; home study in architecture & law. Polit & Govt Pos: Mem, Venango Co Dem Exec Comt, Pa, 65-, chmn for Franklin, currently; founding mem, Citizens for Humphrey, 68; deleg, Dem Nat Conv, 68. Bus & Prof Pos: Consult Engr, 56-; dealer, Walker/Parkensburg Steel Bldgs, Div of Textron, 68-; dealer, Lyco Sewage Treatment Plants, 68- Mil Serv: Entered as Pvt, Army, 43, released as 2nd Lt, 45, after serv in 12th Army Group, ETO; 1st Lt, Res, 45-54; ETO & Good Conduct Medals; Five Battle Stars. Mem: Venango Co ROA; Catholic War Vets; Am Legion. Relig: Catholic. Mailing Add: 411 15th St Franklin PA 16323

ELLIS, FRANK C (D)
Mo State Rep
b Lithium, Mo, Dec 11, 13; m 1937 to Jewel Bollinger; c Gregory, Pamela, Anthony & Patrick. Educ: High sch, Sedgewickville, Mo. Polit & Govt Pos: Mo State Rep, 62-69 & 72-; mem, Co Health Unit, Fed Housing Admin, formerly. Bus & Prof Pos: Farmer. Mem: Odd Fellows; Black River Elec Coop (bd mem); Sedgewickville Sch Bd; active in civic & co orgns. Relig: Methodist. Mailing Add: RR Sedgewickville MO 63781

ELLIS, HARRELL VICTOR (D)
Tenn State Rep
b Madison, Tenn, May 12, 23; s Sam Polk Ellis & Metta Garrett E; m 1964 to Hazel Moss; c Victor, Jr. Educ: High sch. Polit & Govt Pos: Mem, Tenn Legis, 57-59; Tenn State Rep, 73- Mil Serv: Entered as Pvt, Marine Corps, 42, released as Pfc, after serv in Third Marine Div, Pac, 43-45. Mem: Am Legion (Past Comdr); VFW; mem unions for 27 years. Mailing Add: 635 Ermac Dr Nashville TN 37210

ELLIS, HOWARD L (R)
Mont State Rep
Mailing Add: Rte 4 Missoula MT 59801

ELLIS, JOHN HAGOOD (R)
Chmn, Lowndes Co Rep Party, Ala
b Ft Deposit, Ala, Dec 15, 28; s Hense Reynolds Ellis & Ellen Hagood E; m 1954 to Rose Herlong; c Eric Herlong, Joana Salley, Hense Reynolds, II & Clara Rose. Educ: Univ Ala, BS, 50. Polit & Govt Pos: Chmn, Lowndes Co Rep Party, Ala, 62-; mem, Lowndes Co Soil Conserv Dist, 64-; mem, Ala Forestry Coun, 65- Mil Serv: Entered as Pvt, Army, 50, released as M/Sgt, 52, after serv in 28th Inf Div, Ger, 51-52. Mem: Farm Bur; Lowndes Cattlemen's Asn; Forest Farmers Asn; Mason. Relig: Baptist. Mailing Add: Drawer L Ft Deposit AL 36032

ELLIS, MICHAEL G (R)
Wis State Rep
Mailing Add: 315 1/2 N Commercial Neenah WI 54956

ELLIS, RICHARD I (R)
NH State Rep
Mailing Add: 559 Portsmouth Ave PO Box 161 Greenland NH 03840

ELLIS, ROBERT LAWSON, JR (D)
Ala State Sen
b Birmingham, Ala, Mar 27, 22; s Robert Lawson Ellis, Sr & Evelyn Donahoo E; m 1943 to Mary Florence Thomas; c Don Wayne, Mary Gail & Sherry Elen. Educ: Auburn Univ; Univ Ala, mech eng. Polit & Govt Pos: Mem, Jefferson Co Bd Educ, Ala, 60-66; mem, Birmingham-Jefferson Co Regional Planning Comt, 64-; Ala State Rep, 14th Dist, 66-74; Ala State Sen, 14th Dist, 74- Bus & Prof Pos: Draftsman, US Steel, TCI Div, 45-48 & James A Evans, 48-50; engr & planning engr, SNat Gas Co, 50-71, indust develop rep, 71-73, area develop rep, 73- Mil Serv: Entered as Pvt, Air Force, 42, released as Sgt, 45, after serv in Training Command. Mem: Am Soc Heating & Refrig Engrs; Lions; Indust Develop Asn Ala; Southern Indust Develop Coun; Am Legion. Honors & Awards: Personally organized 20 Lions' Clubs in Ala; Silver Beaver Award, Boy Scouts; Selected Best Citizen Western Section, 54. Relig: Methodist. Mailing Add: Rte 1 Box 509 Poplar Lane Adamsville AL 35005

ELLIS, T W, JR (D)
NC State Rep
Mailing Add: 70 Forrest Rd Henderson NC 27536

ELLIS, VERNA JEANNE (R)
VChmn, Iowa State Rep Coun
b Cedar Falls, Iowa, Feb 15, 26; d Hans C Smith & Edna Nielsen S; m 1946 to Lynn Milford Ellis; c Sherilyn Kay (Mrs Ronald Foster) & Stephen Ross. Educ: Univ Northern Iowa, BS, 58; Upper Iowa Col, summer 68; Univ Womens League Bd; Univ Sr Counr; Sigma Sigma Sigma; Womens Athletic Asn; Womens Phys Educ Club. Polit & Govt Pos: Committeewoman, Black Hawk Co Rep Party, Iowa, 58-60; campaign activities chmn, Black Hawk Co Rep Women, 60-66; secy, Clayton Co Rep Women, 65-66; chmn & adv, Clayton Co TAR, 65-67; adv, currently; vchmn, Clayton Co Rep Cent Comt, Iowa, 67-; mem, Second Dist Iowa Cent Comt, 67-; chmn, Clayton Co Women for Nixon-Agnew, 68; vchmn, Iowa State Rep Coun, currently. Mem: Florana Flower Club; Am Asn Univ Women; Am Asn Health, Phys Educ & Recreation; Iowa State Educ Asn; Univ Northern Iowa Alumni Asn. Honors & Awards: Pins for serv, Black Hawk Co Rep Party, Iowa. Relig: Lutheran. Mailing Add: 306 Prairie Ave Strawberry Point IA 52076

ELLISON, CHARLES E, JR (DFL)
b Elbow Lake, Minn, Feb 13, 07; s Charles E Ellison, Sr & Roxy Stillman E; m 1931 to Evalyn D Larson; c C Eugene & Barbara R. Educ: Univ Minn. Polit & Govt Pos: Town clerk, Delaware Twp, Minn, 29-38; mem sch bd, Dist 39, 42-48; supvr town bd, Elbow Lake, 50-; deleg, all Co, Dist & State Dem-Farmer-Labor Conv, 54-; secy, Grant Co Minn Dem-Farmer-Labor Party, 54-66, chmn, 66-72; mem exec comt, Seventh Cong Dist, 58-64; dist chmn, Dem-Farmer-Labor Comt for Kennedy, 60; mem, Farmers Home Admin Co Comt, 60-; deleg, Dem Nat Conv, 64. Mem: Farmers Union; Nat Farmers; Odd Fellows. Relig: Lutheran. Mailing Add: RR 1 Elbow Lake MN 56531

ELLISON, ORVAL S (R)
Mont State Rep
Mailing Add: W Boulder Rte McLeod MT 59052

ELLISON, PETER KEMP (R)
Utah State Rep
b Cincinnati, Ohio, Sept 21, 42; s Harris Adams Ellison & Jane Weber E; m 1967 to Elizabeth Sloan; c Ann Elizabeth & Rebecca Adams. Educ: Univ Cincinnati, BA in Econ, 65; Univ Utah Col Law, JD, 68; Northwestern Univ Nat Grad Trust Sch, 69-71; Sigma Chi. Polit & Govt Pos: Deleg & voting dist chmn, Salt Lake Co Rep Party, Utah, 69-; Utah State Rep, 72- Bus & Prof Pos: Vpres & trust officer, Zions First Nat Bank, Salt Lake City, 68- Mem: Am & Utah State Bar Asns. Relig: Latter-day Saint. Mailing Add: 2438 Cardinal Way Salt Lake City UT 84121

ELLSWORTH, JAMES (R)
Idaho State Sen
Mailing Add: Box 27 Leadore ID 83464

ELLSWORTH, ROBERT F (R)
Asst Secy Int Security Affairs, US Dept Defense
b Lawrence, Kans, June 11, 26; s W Fred Ellsworth & Lucile Rarig E; m 1957 to Vivian Esther Sies; c Robert William & Ann Elizabeth. Educ: Univ Kans, BSME, 45; Univ Mich, JD, 49; Beta Theta Pi. Hon Degrees: LLB, Boston Univ, 70. Polit & Govt Pos: US Rep, Kans, 61-67; asst to the President, Washington, DC, 69; US Ambassador to NATO, Brussels, Belgium, 69-71; Asst Secy Int Security Affairs, US Dept Defense, Washington, DC, 74- Bus & Prof Pos: Gen partner, Lazard Freres & Co, New York, 71-74. Mil Serv: Entered as A/S, Navy, 44-46, reentered, 50, released as Lt Comdr, 53. Publ: Co-auth, Off dead center: A proposal to reform the international monetary system, Joint Econ Comt, US Cong, 65; auth, Europe, America & The era of negotiation, Survival, 71; auth, Deterrence in Europe in the 1970's, Round Table, 72. Mem: Int Inst Strategic Studies; Coun Foreign Rels; Am Legion; VFW; Mason. Mailing Add: 11601 Springridge Rd Potomac MD 20854

ELMORE, MARY LOUISE (D)
Pres, Ark Dem Women's Club
b St Louis, Mo, Mar 28, 42; d William Warren Bolinger & Dorinda Mae Ginocchio B; m 1962 to Jackie Marion Elmore; c Michael Marion. Educ: Little Rock Univ, 60-61. Polit & Govt Pos: Recording secy, Ark Dem Women's Club, 69-71, pres, 71-, couns, 73-; mem, Ark Dem Party, 71. Bus & Prof Pos: Div secy, Ark Blue Cross & Blue Shield, Inc, 67-72, sales mgt asst, 72- Mem: Am Bus Women's Asn; Pulaski Co Unit-Ark Dem Women's Club. Honors & Awards: Appreciation Award, Greene Co Unit-Ark Dem Women's Club, 73. Relig: Baptist. Mailing Add: 12 Forest Dale Rte 2 North Little Rock AR 72118

ELMS, CHRISTOPHER WILLIAM (D)
b Oklahoma City, Okla, May 9, 54; s Richard Alden Elms & Ann West E; single. Educ: Stanford Univ, 72- Polit & Govt Pos: McCarthy campaign worker, Calif, 68; city campaign dir, McGovern campaign, 72; deleg, Dem Nat Conv, 72. Relig: Presbyterian. Mailing Add: 910 Valencia Mesa Dr Fullerton CA 92635

ELROD, A DON (D)
Committeeman, Nebr Dem State Cent Comt
b Loup City, Nebr, May 8, 25; s Lawrence Ray Elrod & Adelia Minnie Bichel E; m 1947 to Helen Dorothy Niemoth; c Mary Jo & James Alan. Polit & Govt Pos: Secy-treas, Grand Island Fedn Labor & Comt on Polit Educ, AFL-CIO, Nebr, 57-; chmn, Hall Co Dem Cent Comt, 62-64; exec bd mem, Nebr State AFL-CIO, 63-; committeeman, Nebr Dem State Cent Comt, 35th Dist, 64-; pres, Typographical Union 31, 65-; Nebr State Sen, 66-72. Mil Serv: Entered as A/S, Navy Seabees, 43, released as Ship Serviceman 3/C, 46; Am Theater Medal; Asiatic Pac Medal with Two Battle Stars; Victory Medal. Mem: Am Legion; VFW; YMCA; Eagles. Relig: Lutheran. Legal Res: 2327 N Sheridan Grand Island NE 68801 Mailing Add: PO Box 17 Grand Island NE 68801

ELVIN, DAVID N
Mayor, Augusta, Maine
b Brunswick, Maine, Nov 14, 42; s Kenneth L Elvin & Doris I Moody E; m 1961 to Nancy A Malone; c Andrew W & Susan E. Educ: Cony High Sch, grad, 60. Polit & Govt Pos: Councilman, Ward Eight, Augusta, Maine, 68-72 & 73-74, mayor, 75- Bus & Prof Pos: Customer Rep, Postal Serv, formerly. Mil Serv: Entered as E-1, Navy, 60, released as E-5, 63, after serv in Aviation. Mailing Add: 37 Highland Ave Augusta ME 04330

ELWOOD, IRA ELMER (D)
b Creighton, Nebr, Feb 9, 93; s Henry Clay Elwood & Alzura Mary Campbell E; m 1934 to Emma Lafuer; c Francis, Elmer, Troy, Wesley & stepchild, Deloris Casper. Polit & Govt Pos: Chmn, Shannon Co Dem Party, SDak, formerly; comnr, Shannon Co; with Agr Stabilization & Conserv; mem, Housing Bd; SDak State Rep, 65-73. Mem: Nat Farmers Union (co chmn, 30 years). Mailing Add: Batesland SD 57716

ELY, HERBERT LEONARD (D)
b Brooklyn, NY, Nov 13, 33; s Jacob Ely & Edith Marcus E; m 1955 to Elayn J Goldberg; c Daymon, Zane & Elise. Educ: Lebanon Valley Col, BA, 55; Univ Pa Law Sch, LLD, 57. Polit & Govt Pos: Mem, Ariz State Dem Exec Comt, 64-68; chief counsel & parliamentarian, Ariz State Dem Party, 65-, state chmn, 70-72; counsel, Maricopa Co Dem Cent Comt, 66-68; deleg, Dem Nat Conv, 68 & 72, mem, Platform Comt, 68; co-chmn, Humphrey Campaign, Phoenix, Ariz, 68. Bus & Prof Pos: Attorney-at-law, Gorey & Ely, Phoenix, Ariz, currently. Mem: Ariz Bar Asn; Am & Ariz Trial Lawyers Asn; Am Arbit Asn; Am Civil Liberties Union. Honors & Awards: Nat Honor Soc; Grad Honors from Univ Pa Law Sch, 69. Relig: Jewish. Mailing Add: 6745 N Central Ave Phoenix AZ 85012

ELY, JOHN HART
Gen Counsel, Dept of Transportation
Mailing Add: Dept of Transportation Washington DC 20410

EMANUEL, MEYER M, JR (D)
Md State Sen
b Washington, DC, Apr 4, 19; s Meyer Emanuel, Sr & Julia Cohen E; m to Louise Vorlander. Educ: City Col of New York, BBA, 40. Polit & Govt Pos: Md State Deleg, 63-66; Md State Sen, 67- Bus & Prof Pos: CPA, 47- Mil Serv: Entered as Pvt, Army Corps of Engrs, 42, released as Chief Warrent Officer, 46, after serv in Continental US; Meritorious Serv Award. Mem: Am & DC Insts of CPA's; Md Fiscal Officer's Asn; City Col of New York Alumni Asn. Relig: Jewish. Legal Res: 3319 Gumwood Dr Hyattsville MD 20783 Mailing Add: Suite 1100 1156 15th St NW Washington DC 20005

EMANUELLI, EDUARDO RAFAEL (R)
Nat Committeeman, Young Rep Nat Fedn
b Santurce, PR, Apr 7, 46; s Aurelio J Emanuelli Perez & Selma Belaval Mercado E; single. Educ: Boston Col, BS in Finance; Col Ins, New York; Beta Gamma Sigma. Polit & Govt Pos: Nat committeeman, Young Rep Nat Fedn, 71- Bus & Prof Pos: Acct exec, Trigo Ins Agency Inc, 70-72; asst vpres bonding, Benitez & Assocs, Inc, Santurce, PR, 71, vpres bonding, 72-73, vpres opers & dir, 73-; dir, Builders Ins Co, Inc, 73- Mil Serv: Entered as Airman, Air Nat Guard, 68, released as Sgt, 74, after serv in 140th AC&W Squadron. Mem: PR CofC; Berwind Country Club; AFDA Fraternity; ROA Beach & Tennis Club. Mailing Add: 617 Belaval St Santurce PR 00909

EMBRY, CARLOS BROGDON, JR (R)
Chmn, Ohio Co Rep Party, Ky
b Louisville, Ky, July 29, 41; s Carlos Brogdon Embry, Sr (deceased) & Zora Romans E; m 1962 to Wanda Lou Ralph; c Laura Ann, Barbara Ann & Carlos Brogdon, III. Educ: Western Ky Univ, BS, 63; Alder Univ, BD, 70; Edison Col, MA, 72; Col Young Rep, pres, 61 & 73; Geography Club, pres, 62. Polit & Govt Pos: Mayor, Beaver Dam, Ky, 70-73; judge, Ohio Co, Ky, 74-; co chmn, Local & State Progs, Young Rep Nat Fedn; nat committeeman, Ky Young Rep, 75-; chmn, First Dist Rep Party, 75-; chmn, Ohio Co Rep Party, Ky, 75- Bus & Prof Pos: Gen mgr, Embry Newspapers, Inc, 63-73. Publ: Auth, History of Beaver Dam Government, 70 & The right to make a profit, 70, Ohio Co Messenger. Mem: Green River Health Planning Coun (vchmn, 74-); Beaver Dam Jaycees; Ohio Co Hosp (mem bd); Beaver Dam Lions Club. Honors & Awards: Beaver Dam's Outstanding Young Man, Beaver Dam Jaycees, 69 & 73; George Washington Hon Medal, Nat Freedoms Found, 70; Outstanding Young Rep in Ky, Ky Young Rep Fedn, 73-74; Outstanding Young Rep in Nation, Nat Young Rep Fedn, 73-75. Relig: Baptist. Legal Res: Box 202 Cromwell Rd Beaver Dam KY 42320 Mailing Add: Ohio Co Courthouse Hartford KY 42347

EMERLING, MURIEL BERGSON (D)
Committeewoman, Ohio State Dem Exec & Cent Comts
b New York, NY, Mar 7, 31; d Samuel Bergson & Dora Deutschman B; m 1953 to Kenneth Lloyd Emerling; c Sandra Gail, David Martin & Lawrence Charles. Educ: Ohio Univ, BSEd cum laude, 53; Kappa Delta Pi. Polit & Govt Pos: Chmn, Dem Registr Comt, Cuyahoga Co, Ohio, 70; chmn, Dem Women's Comt, Cuyahoga Co, 70-72; vchmn, Cuyahoga Co Dem Exec Comt, 70-; committeewoman, Ohio State Dem Exec & Cent Comts, 70- Bus & Prof Pos: Teacher & chmn faculty, Cleveland Bd of Educ, Ohio, 53-56; teacher, South Euclid-Lyndhurst Bd of Educ, 67-70; dep registr, Cuyahoga Co, 71- Publ: Past, Present and Future Structures of County Government, Radio Station WCLV-FM, 66 & Changing the Voting Age-Pros & Cons, 69. Mem: Northeastern Ohio Teachers Asn; South Euclid-Lyndhurst League of Women Voters (vpres); Adrian PTA (legis chmn); Cleveland Coun of Jewish Women; Cleveland Coun on World Affairs. Relig: Jewish. Mailing Add: 933 Glenside Rd South Euclid OH 44121

EMERY, DAN D (D)
Idaho State Rep
b Woodland, Idaho, June 26, 22; s Leroy Emery & Bessie W Wolley E; m 1946 to Lorainne Adamson; c Dana (Mrs Terrell Fuhriman), Rae Ann (Mrs Joel Flake), Lanae (Mrs Bruce Connolly), Douglas, Stacy & Scott. Educ: Northern Col Educ, BA. Polit & Govt Pos: Idaho State Rep, Dist 14, 75- Bus & Prof Pos: Owner-mgr, Emery Ins Agency, Boise; treas, Tex Longhorn Cattle Breeders Asn, San Antonio. Mil Serv: Entered as Buck Sgt, Army, 39, released as Buck Sgt, 45, after serv in 194th Tank Bn; Prisoner of War, Japan, over 3 years; Five Purple Hearts; Distinguished Serv Award; Unit Badge with Two Stars; GO149 Seven Overseas Serv Bars. Relig: Latter-day Saint. Mailing Add: 5514 State St Boise ID 83703

EMERY, DAVID FARNHAM (R)
US Rep, Maine
b Rockland, Maine, Sept 1, 48; s Albert O Emery & Georgia Elizabeth Farnham E; single. Educ: Worcester Polytech Inst, BSEE, 70; Shield. Polit & Govt Pos: Maine State Rep, Rockland Dist, 71-74; deleg, Rep Nat Conv, 72; US Rep, First Dist, Maine, 75- Mem: Jaycees; AF&AM; AASR. Honors & Awards: Fel, John F Kennedy Inst Polit, 74. Relig: Congregational. Mailing Add: 192 N Main St Rockland ME 04841

EMERY, EUGENE MARSHALL (D)
Mem, Androscoggin Co Dem Comt, Maine
b Poland, Maine, Jan 31, 24; s Marshall Fields Emery & Ruth Elizabeth Hunt E; m 1967 to Ida Frenchette Lemieux; c Arthur R Lemieux. Educ: Int Correspondence Schs, 57-61, Machine Tools; Maine Apprenticeship Coun, 57-61. Polit & Govt Pos: Auburn city councilman, 67-; mem, Auburn City Dem Comt, Maine, 68-; mem, Androscoggin Co Dem Comt, 69-; Maine State Rep, 69-72, mem, Pub Utilities Comt, Maine House of Rep, 69-70. Bus & Prof Pos: Tool specialist, Bath Iron Works, 64- Mil Serv: Entered as A/S, Navy, 43, released as Machinist Mate, 46, reentered, 51, released as Machinist Mate 2/C, 52, after serv in US Seabees, ETO, Atlantic-Pac-Japanese Occupation for 49 months; Citation from Commandant Adm Towers, Atlantic Fleet; Combat Stars. Mem: United Shipbuilding & Marine Workers of Am-AFL-CIO. Relig: Methodist. Mailing Add: 20 Towle Ave Auburn ME 04210

EMERY, JAMES LOUIS (R)
NY State Assemblyman
b Lakeville, NY, July 22, 31; s James B Emery & Ruth Wamser E; m 1974 to Jill Houghton; c James L, Jr & Jon Scott. Educ: Univ Cincinnati, BBA, 53. Polit & Govt Pos: Sheriff, Livingston Co, NY, 60-64; NY State Assemblyman, 65-, Dep Majority Leader, NY State Assembly, 69-74, asst minority leader, 75- Mil Serv: Entered as 2nd Lt, Air Force, 53, released as Lt, 55; Lt Col, Air Force Res. Mem: Livingston Co Exten Serv; Am Legion; Rotary; Livingston Co Asn Town Hwy Supts; Am Red Cross. Mailing Add: 6112 Lakeville Rd Livonia NY 14487

EMETT, ROBERT LYNN (R)
Chmn, Los Angeles Co United Rep Finance Comt, Calif
b Oxnard, Calif, Aug 9, 27; s Edward Llewellyn Emett & Isabel Vaughan E; m to Carole Hopkins; c Michael Scott, Robert Charles, Lindy Louise & James Stewart. Educ: Claremont Men's Col, BA, 50. Polit & Govt Pos: State finance chmn, Young Rep, 56-57, Budget & Finance Comt, 57-69; mem exec comt, Calif Goldwater Adv Comt, 63; mem, Calif State Rep Finance Comt, 64-; mem exec comt & budget & expenditures comt, Los Angeles Co United Rep Finance Comt, 64-, chmn, currently; deleg, Rep Nat Conv, 64, alt deleg, 68; mem exec comt, Reagan Campaign Comt, 70. Bus & Prof Pos: Dir, Emett & Chandler, 60-, vpres, 61-63, pres, 63-68; chmn, Pinehurst Corp, 68- Mil Serv: Naval Res, SPac, 45-46; 1st Lt, Air Force Res, 51-59. Mem: Young Pres Orgn; Claremont Men's Col (bd trustees); Calif Cong Recognition Proj; Calif Club; Los Angeles Country Club. Relig: Presbyterian. Mailing Add: 1800 Ave of the Stars Century City Los Angeles CA 90067

EMMONS, DALE CLIFTON (D)
Nat Committeeman, Ky Young Dem
b Maysville, Ky, Aug 1, 52; s Lowell Lee Emmons & Theresa Alice Fay E; m 1973 to Marilyn Rose Benge. Educ: Morehead State Univ, BS; Delta Tau Alpha; Delta Tau Delta; prog dir, Student Govt Asn, 72-73, admin asst, 73-74. Polit & Govt Pos: Chmn, Seventh Dist, Ky Young Dem, 73-74, nat committeeman, 74- Bus & Prof Pos: Mgr trainee, Southern States Coop, Inc, 74; park supvr, Ky Dept Parks, 75- Mem: Future Farmers Am Alumni Asn;

Morehead State Univ Alumni Asn; Delta Tau Delta House Corp Morehead (treas). Honors & Awards: Am Farmer Degree, Future Farmers Am, 72; Outstanding Col Young Dem, Ky Young Dem, 74. Relig: Methodist. Legal Res: 708 Greenbriar Dr Harrodsburg KY 40330 Mailing Add: Rte 7 20 Country Sq Apts Frankfort KY 40601

EMORY, RICHARD W, JR (D)
Md State Deleg
Mailing Add: 735 Equitable Bldg Baltimore MD 21202

EMROCH, WALTER H (D)
Va State Deleg
Mailing Add: 696 Seaboard Bldg Richmond VA 23230

EMSHWILLER, THOMAS C (D)
Chmn, Fountain Co Dem Cent Comt, Ind
b Montpelier, Ind, May 14, 14; s Fred Owen Emshwiller & Elma Inez Craven E; m 1939 to Jean Hammond; c Jon A, Mary Joan & Jane Kay (Mrs Moore). Educ: Univ Wis, 1 year; Delta Chi. Polit & Govt Pos: Vpres, Wells Co Young Dem, Ind, 36-38; city councilman, Covington, 52-60; treas, Troy Twp Dem, 56-; secy-treas, Ferguson Dem Club, 56-; chmn, Fountain Co Dem Cent Comt, 66- Bus & Prof Pos: Mgr personnel & acct, ballast dept, Gen Elec, Danville, Ill, 46-67; vpres, Covington Swimming Pool Inc, 46-49; dir indust rels, ATI Continental Div, Danville, 67- Mem: Danville Personnel Asn; F&AM; Eastern Star (past Worthy Patron); Covington Band Parents; Covington CofC. Relig: Methodist. Mailing Add: 808 E Third St Covington IN 47932

ENCINIAS, FRANK T (D)
Chmn, Guadalupe Co Dem Party, NMex
b Las Vegas, NMex, Jan 20, 91; s Anacleto Encinias & Agustina Trujillo E; m 1912 to Elvira Padilla; c J Eloy. Educ: Highlands Univ, 21-22. Polit & Govt Pos: NMex State Rep, 32-35; co assessor, Guadalupe Co, 39-43; police justice, Santa Rosa, 48-51; probate judge, Guadalupe Co, 68-72; chmn, Guadalupe Co Dem Party, 70- Mil Serv: Entered as Pvt, Army, 17, released as Cpl, 19, after serv in 42nd Div, ETO, 17-19; Sharpshooter Medal. Publ: Billy the Kid narrative, Santa Rose News, 69. Mem: Am Legion. Honors & Awards: Nat Achievement Award, Am Legion, 69; Life Mem Cert, Int Asn Probate Judges, 72; Dem Polit Award, State Dem Cent Comt, 74. Relig: Catholic. Mailing Add: 357 Ninth St Santa Rosa NM 88435

ENDERS, THOMAS OSTROM
Asst Secy State Econ & Bus Affairs
b Hartford, Conn, Nov 28, 31; s Ostrom Enders & Alice Dudley Talcott E; m 1955 to Gaetana Marchegiano; c Domitilla Elena, Alice Talcott, Claire Whitmore & Thomas Ostrom, III. Educ: Philips Exeter Acad, 49; Yale Univ, BA, 53; Univ Paris, DUniv, 55; Harvard Univ, MA, 57. Polit & Govt Pos: Foreign serv officer, 58-, assigned Washington, 58-60 & 63-69, assigned, Stockholm, 61-63, spec asst to Under Secy State Polit Affairs, 66-68, Dep Asst Secy State Int Monetary Affairs, 68-69, dep chief mission, Belgrade, 69-70 & Phnom Penh, 71-74; Asst Secy State Econ & Bus Affairs, 74- Honors & Awards: Arthur S Flemming Award, 69. Mailing Add: Dept of State Washington DC 20520

ENDRIS, GLENN EDWIN (D)
Miss State Rep
b Biloxi, Miss, May 6, 38; s Leo J Endris & Frances Quackenbush E; m 1960 to Brenda Marie Cuevas; c Glenn, Jr, Kerry, Andrea & Darren. Educ: Univ Southern Miss, BS, 60, MS, 62; Order of Artus. Polit & Govt Pos: Miss State Rep, 72- Bus & Prof Pos: Instr econ, Jefferson Davis Col, 67- Mil Serv: Entered as Pvt, Army Nat Guard, released as Pvt. Mem: Lions; Jaycees; Miss Soc Economists; Miss Asn Educators. Relig: Catholic. Mailing Add: 103 Martin Rd Biloxi MS 39531

ENEBO, STANLEY A (DFL)
Minn State Rep
b Hennepin Co, Minn, 1926; m to Lois; c Nancy (Mrs Larry Solheim) & Stanley David. Educ: Univ Minn. Polit & Govt Pos: Minn State Rep, 58-66 & 71-, chmn, Labor-Bus Rels, Minn House Rep, currently. Bus & Prof Pos: Electrician. Mil Serv: World War II; Bronze Star Medal. Mem: IBEW (Local 292); Sons of Norway. Relig: Lutheran. Mailing Add: 2801 43rd Ave S Minneapolis MN 55406

ENEGUESS, DANIEL FRANCIS (R)
Exec Comt Mem, Peterborough Rep Town Comt, NH
b Steubenville, Ohio, Oct 24, 22; s Daniel Francis Eneguess & Mary M E; m 1950 to Ann Cavanaugh; c David M, Daniel F, III, Katharine Ann & John M. Educ: Boston Col, AB Econ, 47. Polit & Govt Pos: Finance chmn, Hillsboro Co Rep Comt, NH, 62-66; exec comt mem, Peterborough Rep Town Comt, 64-; deleg, NH State Rep Conv, 66 & 70; alt deleg, Rep Nat Conv, 68. Bus & Prof Pos: Owner, Eneguess Publ Co; owner, Daniel F Eneguess Assocs. Mil Serv: Entered as Pvt, Marine Corps, 43, released as 1st Lt, 47, after serv in Third Marine Div, Pac, 44-46; Am & Pac Theater Ribbons. Mem: Rotary; Am Legion; NH Vacation Travel Coun; Conn River Watershed Coun; Swiftwater Girl Scout Coun. Relig: Catholic. Mailing Add: Old Dublin Rd Peterborough NH 03458

ENFIELD, CLIFTON WILLIS (R)
b Watertown, NY, Nov 26, 18; s George Hyson Enfield & Anna Humerick E; m 1948 to Mary Verone Sullivan; c Douglas George & Brian Michael. Educ: NC State Col, BS with honors, 38; Univ Va, JD, 48; Sigma Tau Sigma; Delta Theta Phi; Order of the Coif. Polit & Govt Pos: Asst attorney gen, State of Ore, 48-56; asst counsel, Ore State Hwy Dept, 48-51, chief counsel, 51-56; gen counsel, US Bur Pub Rds, Washington, DC, 56-61; minority counsel, Comt Pub Works, US House of Rep, 61- Mil Serv: Entered as 2nd Lt, Army, 40, released as Maj, 46, after serv in 9th Inf Div & 40th Inf Div, Pac & Far East Theatres, 42-45; Army Res, Lt Col (Ret); Bronze Star with Oak Leaf Cluster; Purple Heart; Combat Infantryman's Badge. Publ: Special benefits & right of way acquisition, Appraisal J, 59; Limitations of Access in Partial Takings, Condemnation Appraisal Practice, 61; Federal Highway Beautification: Outdoor Advertising History & Regulation, 69. Mem: Am Right of Way Asn; Am Rd Builders Asn; Legal Resources Group Coun; Transportation Research Bd, Nat Acad Sci; Md State Bar Asn. Relig: Presbyterian. Mailing Add: 1706 Tilton Dr Silver Spring MD 20902

ENG, JOHN SY (D)
Wash State Rep
b Hong Kong, Brit Crown Colony, Jan 21, 42; s Bing Chong Eng & Lim Tan Yin E; single. Educ: Univ Wash, BA, 66. Polit & Govt Pos: Mem, US Peace Corps, 66-68; Wash State Rep, 73- Mailing Add: PO Box 18088 Seattle WA 98118

ENGDAHL, CHARLES F (D)
Mass State Rep
Mailing Add: State Capitol Boston MA 02133

ENGEBRETSON, GARY DUANE (R)
b Cresco, Iowa, June 24, 37; s Henry Tuttle Engebretson & Edna Thompson E; m 1954 to Margaret Frances Brown; c Gary Allen, Janet Lee, David Mark & Margie Sue. Educ: DeVry Inst, 2 years; Alexander Hamilton Inst, 2 years. Polit & Govt Pos: Winneshiek Co Young Rep chmn, 63 & 64; Winneshiek Co Rep organizational chmn, 64 & 65; chmn, Winneshiek Co Rep Cent Comt, Iowa, formerly; mem, Iowa-Miss River Pkwy Comn, 69-; mem, Winneshiek Co Cancer Soc Bd, 69-72; mem, Nat Miss River Pkwy Exec Bd, 70-; co-pilot, Nat Miss River Pkwy Comn, 73- Bus & Prof Pos: Pres, Brown Elec & Appliance Inc, 19 years. Mem: Minn Elec Contractors Asn; Iowa State Hist Soc; Great River Road Asn; Elks. Relig: Protestant. Mailing Add: RR 2 Blue Ridge Stables Decorah IA 52101

ENGEL, AUSTIN GEORGE, JR (D)
Mem, NDak State Dem Comt
b Little Falls, Minn, Aug 9, 28; s Austin George Engel & Eugenia Donahue E; m 1950 to Mary Berwick Roessel; c David James, Michael Robert, Peter Clarke, Paul Monteath & Steven Johnstone. Educ: Macalester Col, BA, 50; Yale Divinity Sch, BD, 54; Univ Mich, summer 60. Polit & Govt Pos: Mem campaign comt, NDak Dem Non-Partisan League, 62, regional dir, 64; mem, Mountrail Co Dem Non-Partisan League Exec Comt, 62-66; deleg, Dem Nat Conv & mem, Credential Comt, 64; precinct committeeman, Burleigh Co, 66-; mem, Burleigh Co Dem Exec Comt, 66-; chmn, Burleigh Co Dem Party, 68-; mem, NDak State Dem Comt, 68-; mem, NDak State Dem Finance Comt, 68-; Burleigh Co Dem Non-Partisan League cand for NDak Legis, 70. Bus & Prof Pos: Pastor, United Church of Christ, New Town, NDak, 54-61; spec worker, Indian Work in NDak, United Church of Christ, 61-65, adminr, 65-67; exec dir, NDak Indian Affairs Comn, 65-; mem bd dirs, Charles L Hall Youth Serv, 65-; secy, United Tribes of NDak Develop Corp, 68-71. Publ: On the move at Ft Berthold, Children's Relig, 2/62. Mem: NDak Conf United Church of Christ. Relig: United Church of Christ. Mailing Add: 1324 N Second St Bismarck ND 58501

ENGEL, DAVID CHAPIN (R)
b New York, NY, Oct 6, 31; s Robert Albert Engel & Mabel Gretchen Eshbaugh E; m 1972 to Priscilla Stevens; c Karen Chapin, Kathleen Christy, Julie Talbot, Peter Otis, Rebecca Eaton & Heidi May Stevens. Educ: St Lawrence Univ, BA, 54; NY Univ, LLB, 56; Sigma Chi; Student Union; Student Gov Rep. Polit & Govt Pos: Attorney, NH Attorney Gen Off, 56-58; pres, Kensington Rep Club, 60-62; state campaign vchmn, Perkins Bass for US Sen, 62; deleg-at-lg, Rep Nat Conv, 64; mem, Rockingham Co Rep Exec Comt, NH, 65-68; Rep Co Finance Chmn, 65-; mem bd appeals, Kensington, 65-; deleg, Rep State Conv, 66, 68 & 70. Bus & Prof Pos: Secy, Rockingham Co Bar Asn, 61; chmn, NH Bar Asn Legis Comt, 68-69. Mem: Am & NH Co Bar Asns; Am Judicature Soc; Am Trial Lawyers Asn; Am Arbit Asn. Honors & Awards: Eagle Scout with Four Palms. Relig: Congregational; bd dirs, Greenland Congregational Church, 75- Mailing Add: 47 Park Ave Greenland NH 03840

ENGEL, ELIOT L (D)
Committeeman, Bronx Co Dem Comt, NY
b New York, BA, 69, MS, 73; Pi Lambda Phi (pres, 68 & 69). Polit & Govt Pos: Vpres, Park-East Independent Dem Club, NY, 70-71; deleg, Bronx Comt for Dem Voters, 71-; deleg & mem steering comt, Youth Caucus, Dem Nat Conv, 72; vpres, Independent Dem of Co-op City, 72-; committeeman, Bronx Co Dem Comt, 72-; mem exec coun, NY State New Dem Coalition, 73- Bus & Prof Pos: Counr & adv, New York Urban Corps, 68; teacher & dept chmn, New York Bd of Educ, 69- Publ: A delegate's diary, Co-op City News, 7/72. Mem: United Fedn of Teachers; Bronx Citizens for Peace (steering comt, 71-); B'nai B'rith. Relig: Jewish. Mailing Add: 4100-11 Hutchinson River Pkwy E Bronx NY 10475

ENGEL, JOHN A (D)
Committeeman, SDak State Dem Cent Comt
b Avon, SDak, Oct 27, 09; s Joseph Engel & Elizabeth Rueb E; m 1939 to Thelma Mitchell; c Patricia D (Mrs Odens), Mary J (Mrs Hewett) & Jan A (Mrs Johnson). Educ: Univ SDak, LLB, 38; Delta Theta Phi. Polit & Govt Pos: City attorney, Avon, SDak, 46-58, mayor, 58-64; chmn, Bon Homme Co Dem Party, 50-58, finance chmn, 58-65; chmn, State Hwy Comn, 59-61; chmn, SDak Dem Party, 62-64; committeeman, SDak State Dem Cent Comt, Bon Homme Co, 62-; mem platform comt, Nat Dem Party, 64; chmn, SDak deleg, Dem Nat Conv, 64; SDak State Rep, formerly; app mem, SDak Judicial Qualifications Comn, 73- Bus & Prof Pos: Attorney-at-law, 40- Mil Serv: Pvt, Army, 43; entered as Lt(jg), Navy, 43, released as Lt Comdr, 45, after serv in ETO & Am, Asiatic-Pac & NAfrican Theaters; Lt, Naval Res (Ret); ETO, Am, Asiatic-Pac & African Campaign Ribbons. Mem: State Bar of SDak; Am Bar Asn; Am Legion; Lions. Relig: Presbyterian. Mailing Add: Avon SD 57315

ENGELBRECHT, MARLENE VIVIAN (R)
VChairwoman, Hand Co Rep Comt, SDak
b St Lawrence, SDak, Oct 27, 24; d Henry George Rettmer & Alta Keyser R; m 1948 to Myrl Arthur Engelbrecht; c Mark Arthur & Marilee Kim. Educ: SDak State Univ, BS, 46; Sigma Lambda Sigma; Theta Sigma Phi. Polit & Govt Pos: VChairwoman, Hand Co Rep Comt, SDak, 66- Bus & Prof Pos: Assoc ed, SDak Exten Ed Staff, Brookings, 46; advert mgr, Herberger's Dept Store, Watertown, 46-48; case worker, Douglas Co Welfare Off, Alexandria, Minn, 48; rural sch teacher, Hand Co, Miller, SDak, three terms, teacher's aide, two terms. Mem: Am Legion Auxiliary; Exten Club; 4-H Club Leader. Relig: Methodist. Mailing Add: RR 1 Zell SD 57483

ENGELHARD, ROBERT JOHN (R)
b Milwaukee, Wis, May 16, 27; s Aloys August & Ora Krebs A; m 1960 to Karen Beebe; c Daniel Robert & Diane Mary. Educ: Utah State Univ, BS, 50; Univ Denver, MS, 52; Mich State Univ, PhD, 69. Polit & Govt Pos: Chmn, Portage Co Chilsen for Cong Comt, 69; mem, Portage Co Rep Party, 69-71, vchmn, formerly; mem, Seventh Dist Rep Exec Comt, 69-71; chmn, Portage Co Warren for Attorney Gen, 70. Bus & Prof Pos: Forester, US Forest Serv, Southern Region, 52-56; Trees for Tomorrow, Inc, Merrill, Wis, 56-65; instr, Wis State Univ-Stevens Point, 65-66, assoc prof, 67- Mil Serv: Entered as Pvt, Army, 45, released as Cpl, 46, after serv in Med Detachment, 85 Ord Bn, ETO; reentered as Pfc, Army, 50, released as Sgt, 51, after serv in 469th Field Artil; World War II Ribbon, ETO Occup Ribbon; Korean Serv Ribbon. Publ: Role of Wood Procurement in Paper Indust, NCent Forest Exp Sta, 71.

Mem: Soc Am Foresters; Elks; Kiwanis. Relig: Roman Catholic. Mailing Add: 4309 Janick Circle N Stevens Point WI 54481

ENGEN, GERALD BOB **(R)**
Wyo State Rep
b Laramie, Wyo, June 11, 22; s Ernest J Engen & Olga Bothen E; m 1950 to Rose Y Arant; c Gary, Paul, Juanita & Robin. Educ: Univ Wyo, BS, 49 & 53. Polit & Govt Pos: Vchmn, Albany Co Rep Cent Comt, Wyo, 61-65 & chmn, Wyo State Rep, 69-, chmn, Wyo House of Rep Transportation & Hwy Comt & Wyo Transportation & Hwys Interim Comt, 73- Bus & Prof Pos: Rancher, Centennial, Wyo, 53-63; orgn dir, Wyo Farm Bur Fedn, 60-64; retail merchant, Laramie, 64-; real estate salesman, 65- Mil Serv: Entered as Pvt, Army Air Force, 42, released as Pfc, 46, after serv in Eighth Air Force, ETO, 44-46. Mem: Am Legion (past Post Comdr); VFW: Mason; Elks; Farm Bur. Relig: Lutheran. Mailing Add: PO Box 727 Laramie WY 82070

ENGESSER, EMMETT HENRY **(DFL)**
Publicity Chmn, Waseca Co Dem-Farmer-Labor Party, Minn
b St Peter, Minn, May 24, 12; s John Engesser, Sr & Martha Heyne E; m 1946 to Margaret Anne Robinson; c John, III, Cheryl (Mrs Timothy Kortuem), Thomas & Sandra. Polit & Govt Pos: Publicity chmn, Waseca Co Dem-Farmer-Labor Party, Minn, 57-62, 66- Bus & Prof Pos: Vpres, New Richland Develop Group, 56, pres, 56-59; dir, Waseca Co Hist Soc, 56-58; secy-treas, Quad Co Rotary Press, Inc, 67-69, pres, 70- Mil Serv: Entered as Seaman, Navy, 42, released as EM 1/C & CPO, 45, after serv in USS Enterprise, Pac Theatre; Presidential Unit Citation; Naval Unit Citation; Commendation Medal; 19 Battle Stars while in USS Enterprise. Publ: Tax Equality, Cong Rec; auth of ed in various Minn newspapers on Domian Report. Mem: Minn & Nat Newspaper Asn; Am Legion; VFW; DAV. Honors & Awards: Typographical Award, Minn Newspaper Asn, 69; Community Serv Award, Nat Newspaper Asn, 70. Relig: Protestant. Mailing Add: New Richland MN 56072

ENGLANDER, SOPHIA **(D)**
b Atlanta, Ga, July 24, 24; d Joseph Tendrich & Bessie Miller T; m 1943 to Judge Malvin Englander; c Nicki Yverne (Mrs Mel Grossman), Donna Lynn (Mrs Mark Fleishman), Patti Lu, Tobie Sue, Marla Chanelle & Joseph Robert. Educ: Univ Miami. Polit & Govt Pos: Dist committeewoman, Dade Co Opers Support Chmn, Fla; alt deleg, Dem Nat Conv, 60 & 68, deleg, 64; vchmn, Third Cong Dist Dem Party; co-chmn, Oper Clean Sweep; Dade Co Four for 64 Chmn; fifth dist chmn, Kennedy-Johnson Campaign; chmn, 11th Cong Dist Dem Party; chmn, Miami Beach Div Dem Exec Comt; chmn, Adlai Stevenson Mem Fund Dinner; state chmn, Fla Dollars for Dem Drive, 66; committeewoman, Fla Dem Party, formerly; original mem, Fla Consumers Coun, 68, reappointed, 68-; vchmn, Miami Beach Housing Authority, currently. Mem: Am Legion Auxiliary; Jewish War Vet Auxiliary; Eastern Star; Anna Miller Circle; Hadassah. Honors & Awards: Elected Dem Mother of the Year, 66; Nominated Dem Woman-Doer for Dade Co, Fla, 68-69. Originator of Cabinet Level Secy of Youth Affairs Bill introduced by US Rep Claude Pepper into US House Rep, 69. Relig: Jewish. Mailing Add: 4620 Pinetree Dr Miami Beach FL 33140

ENGLE, JAMES BRUCE
US Ambassador to Dahomey
b Billings, Mont, Apr 16, 19; s Bruce Wilmot Engle & Verbeaudah Morgan E; m 1950 to Priscilla Joyce Wright; c Stephen, Judith, Philip, Susan, John & Peter. Educ: Burlington Jr Col, Iowa, dipl, 38; Univ Chicago, BA, 40; Harvard Univ Grad Sch Bus Admin, dipl, 45; Rhoades scholar, Oxford Univ, 47-50, BA with hons, 50, MA with hons, 54; Univ Stranieri, Perugia, Italy, dipl, 49; Univ Naples, 50-51; Fulbright scholar, Inst Stud Storici, Naples, 50-53; Am Univ, Washington, DC, 56-58; Cambridge Univ, 58-59; Goethe Inst, Ger, dipl, 58; US Dept State Sr Sem in Foreign Policy, 67-68; Phi Beta Kappa. Polit & Govt Pos: Liaison officer, Bd Econ Warfare, US Dept State, 41-42; vconsul, Quito, Ecuador, 42-44, Rio de Janeiro, Brazil, 46-67 & Naples, Italy, 51-53; second secy Embassy & vconsul, Rome, 53-54; officer-in-chg Ital affairs, Washington, DC, 55-58; first secy Embassy, London, Eng, 58-59; consul, Frankfurt, Ger, 59 & Duesseldorf, 59-60; labor attache, Am Embassy, Bonn; first secy Embassy & consul, Accra, Ghana, 61-62, acting dep chief mission, 62-63, charge d'affaires, 63; dep chief mission, counr Embassy & consul, Managua, Nicaragua, 63-67, charge d'affaires, 67; dep chief reports & anal div, Mil Assistance Command, Saigon, Vietnam, 68; Phy Yen province sr adv, Tuy Hoa, 69-70; dir Vietnam working group, Washington, DC, 70-71; spec asst to Secy Treas & Ambassador-at-Lg David M Kennedy, Washington, DC & overseas, 71-72; spec asst to US Ambassador to NAtlantic Coun, Brussels, Belgium, 72; exec secy interdept task force on Indochina, Washington, DC, 72-73; consul gen, Nha Trang, Vietnam, 73; dep chief mission, counr Embassy & consul, Phnom Penh, 73-74, charge d'affaires, 74; US Ambassador to Dahomey, 74- Mil Serv: Entered as A/S, Navy, 44, released as Lt(jg), 46, after serv in 83rd Mil Govt Hq, Japan & Pac Theatre, 45-46. Publ: Co-auth, The Next Ten Years in American Foreign Policy (won nat prize), Inst Nat Policy, Col William & Mary, 41. Mem: Oxford Union; Exeter Col, Oxford Univ (permanent mem); King's Col, Cambridge Univ (permanent sr mem). Honors & Awards: Rockefeller Pub Serv Award, Princeton Univ, 58. Relig: Episcopal. Mailing Add: RFD 2 Groton VT 05046

ENGLEHART, HARRY A, JR **(D)**
Pa State Rep
s Harry A Englehart & Esther Davis E; m to Mercedes Parsons; c four. Educ: US Naval Acad; Yale Law Sch; holds BS & LLB. Polit & Govt Pos: Pa State Rep, 65-, majority caucus chmn, Pa House of Rep, 69-72, chmn, Minority Policy Comt, 73- Bus & Prof Pos: Attorney-at-law. Mil Serv: Navy, Lt(jg), World War II; Pac Theater; Korean War. Mem: Elks; Eagles; Moose; Am Legion; KofC. Mailing Add: Capitol Bldg Harrisburg PA 17120

ENGLER, COLLEEN HOUSE **(R)**
Mich State Rep
b Bay City, Mich, Mar 17, 52; d James D House & Kathleen A McGill H; m 1975 to John Mathias Engler. Educ: Mich State Univ, BA, 73. Polit & Govt Pos: Mich State Rep, 74- Mem: Am Asn Univ Women; Zonta Int. Relig: Catholic. Legal Res: 2109 McKinley Ave Bay City MI 48706 Mailing Add: PO Box 119 State Capitol Lansing MI 48901

ENGLER, JOHN M **(R)**
Mich State Rep
b Mt Pleasant, Mich, Oct 12, 48; s Mathias John Engler & Agnes Neyer E; m 1975 to Colleen House. Educ: Mich State Univ, BS in Agr Econ, 71; Enzian Honorary. Polit & Govt Pos: Mich State Rep, 71-; deleg, White House Conf on Youth. Bus & Prof Pos: Agent, Am United Life Ins Co, 68- Mem: YMCA (bd dirs); US Jaycees; Farm Bur. Honors & Awards: Youngest mem ever elected to Mich House Rep. Relig: Roman Catholic. Mailing Add: 1798 W River Rd Mt Pleasant MI 48858

ENGLERT, KENNETH EDWARD **(R)**
b Lodge Pole, Nebr, Feb 28, 11; s Frank Englert & Lois Lough E; m 1941 to Lorene Baker; c Kendra (Mrs Earl Bowers), Steven & Holly (Mrs Steven Leewaye). Educ: Lodge Pole & Sunol High Schs, Nebr. Polit & Govt Pos: Committeeman, Colorado Springs Rep Comt, 50-65; chmn, Chaffee Co Rep Party, formerly. Bus & Prof Pos: Owner, restaurant & lounge, Colorado Springs, Colo, 38-42, owner, package liquors, 46-65; raising buffalo, Salida, Colo, currently. Mil Serv: Entered as A/S, Navy, 42, released as Gunner 2/c, 45, after serv in Armed Guard, SPac Theatre, 42-45. Publ: Raids by Reynolds, 56 & Milling All Around, 60, Westerners Brand Books; Oliver Perry Wiggings, Filter Press, 68. Mem: Colo State Hist Soc; Colo Archaeol Soc; Hist Soc of the Pikes Peak Region; Elks; DAV (pres currently, past comdr, Colorado Springs). Relig: Methodist. Mailing Add: 9095 W County Rd 120 Salida CO 81201

ENGLISH, ELEANOR JEAN **(D)**
Chmn, Shoshone Co Dem Party, Idaho
b Wallace, Idaho, June 16, 21; d Sam Hammer & Ellen Ottem H; m to William F English; c William P. Educ: Univ, Idaho, 39-40. Polit & Govt Pos: Dem precinct committeeman, Shoshone Co Cent Comt, Idaho, 65-68; chmn, Shoshone Co Dem Party, 68- Bus & Prof Pos: Secy, Am Smelting & Refining Co, 49- Relig: Lutheran. Mailing Add: Idaho Bldg Wallace ID 83873

ENGLISH, GLENN **(D)**
US Rep, Okla
b Cordell, Okla, Nov 30, 40; s Glenn English, Sr & Marcella E; m to Jan. Educ: Southwestern State Col, degree in Gen Bus & Acct & Econ, 64. Polit & Govt Pos: Exec dir, Okla Dem Party, 69-73; US Rep, Sixth Dist Okla, Mem, House Agr Comt & subcomts on Livestock & Grains, Conservation & Credit & Cotton, Govt Opers Comt & subcomts on Intergovt Rels & Human Resource & Transportation; mem, Cong Rural Caucus, currently. Mil Serv: S/Sgt, US Army Res, 65-71. Legal Res: 1100 N Grant Cordell OK 73632 Mailing Add: 1108 Longworth House Off Bldg Washington DC 20515

ENGLISH, JOHN FRANCIS **(D)**
Chmn, Nassau Co Dem Comt, NY
b Brooklyn, NY, Apr 21, 26; s Thomas English & Anne Daley E; m 1951 to Dolores Hofler; c Danette. Educ: Iona Col, BA, 52; Fordham Law Sch, 55; Hofstra Univ Citizens Comt. Polit & Govt Pos: Committeeman, Franklin Sq Dem Orgn, NY, 47; secy, Nassau Co Dem Comt, 53, chmn, 58-; Dem zone leader, Franklin Sq, 54; leader & state committeeman, First Assembly Dist, Nassau Co, 55; town leader, Hempstead, NY, 56; law secy to Hon Mario Pittoni, 56-58; comnr, Bd Elecs, 61-64; dir, Muskie Campaign, 71-72; Dem Nat Committeeman, NY, formerly, gen counsel, Dem Nat Comt, 72, mem comn on party structure & deleg selection, formerly. Bus & Prof Pos: Attorney-at-law, English, Cianciulli & Reisman, 61- Mil Serv: Entered as Sailor, Navy, 43, released as Qm 3/C, 47; Navy Unit Citation with Four Battle Stars; Philippine Liberation Medal. Mem: Nassau Co Bar Asn; Legal Aid Soc Nassau Co; Friends of Mercy Hosp; LI Chap, Nat Conf Christians & Jews; United Cerebral Palsy Asn, LI. Honors & Awards: Recipient of LI Daily Press Distinguished Serv Award, for bringing a strong two-party system to Nassau Co, 63. Relig: Catholic. Legal Res: Split Rock Rd Syosset NY 11791 Mailing Add: 160 Mineola Blvd Mineola NY 11501

ENGLISH, WILLIAM CONRAD **(R)**
Chmn, Hillsborough Co Rep Comt, NH
b Concord, NH, Apr 27, 37; s Raymond Edward English & Helen Tasker E; div; c Stuart Morgan. Educ: Cushing Acad, grad, 56; Norwich Univ, BS, 60; Sigma Nu. Polit & Govt Pos: Chmn, Hillsborough Co Rep Comt, NH, 75- Mil Serv: Entered as 2nd Lt, Army, 61, released as 1st Lt, 61, after serv in Army Terminal Command/Atlantic. Relig: Protestant. Mailing Add: 11 Union St Milford NH 03055

ENGLUND, MERRILL WAYNE **(D)**
s Elbert M Englund & Leona Hazel Bussard E; m 1946 to Geraldine Mildred Lando; c Eric, Gretchen & Karl. Educ: Univ Nebr, BS. Polit & Govt Pos: Exec Asst to US Rep Metcalf, 53-60; admin asst, Staff of Sen Metcalf, 61-; instr on admin opers for cong assts, Grad Sch, US Dept Agr, 67-; cong staff adv to US deleg, UN Seabed Comt, Geneva, Switz, 73. Mil Serv: Navy, Lt Comdr, Patrol Bombing Squadron 102, Naval Air Transport Serv, Pac. Mem: Sigma Delta Chi; Innocents; Kappa Sigma; Montgomery Co Oratorio Soc; Am Newspaper Guild. Relig: Unitarian. Mailing Add: 11703 College View Dr Silver Spring MD 20902

ENGMAN, LEWIS AUGUST **(R)**
Chmn, Fed Trade Comn
b Grand Rapids, Mich, Jan 6, 36; s H Sigurd Engman & Florence C Lewis E; m 1961 to Jacqueline Ransford Graham; c Geoffrey Ponton, Jonathan Lewis & Richard Ransford. Educ: Univ Mich, Ann Arbor, AB, 57; Univ London Sch Econ, 57-58; Harvard Univ Law Sch, LLB, 61; Phi Beta Kappa; Delta Sigma Rho; Phi Kappa Phi; Phi Eta Sigma. Polit & Govt Pos: Dir legis affairs, President's Comt on Consumer Interests, Off of Consumer Affairs, Washington, DC, 70, gen counsel, 70-71; asst dir, Domestic Coun, 71-73, chmn, Fed Trade Comn, 73- Bus & Prof Pos: Assoc, Warner, Norcross & Judd Law Firm, 61-65, partner, 65-70. Mem: Life mem Sixth Circuit Judicial Conf of the US; Am, Grand Rapids & DC Bar Asns; State Bar of Mich. Relig: Presbyterian. Legal Res: Grand Rapids MI Mailing Add: Fed Trade Comn Pennsylvania Ave at Sixth St NW Washington DC 20580

ENNA, IRVING **(R)**
b New York, NY, July 26, 14; m 1937 to Margaret; c Carol & twins, David & Ronald. Educ: Franklin High Sch, Portland, Ore, grad, 32. Polit & Govt Pos: Chmn, Hatfield Comts, Multnomah Co, Ore, 56 & 58; chmn, Multnomah Co Rep Cent Comt, 64-67; chmn, Ore Rep State Cent Comt, 67-71; alt deleg, Rep Nat Conv, 68 & 72. Bus & Prof Pos: Life ins underwriter, Standard Ins, 52- Mem: Portland & Ore Life Ins Underwriters Asns. Honors & Awards: Life mem, Million Dollar Roundtable, Standard Ins Co; Ins Man of the Year for Ore, 59 & 61; Portland Jr First Citizen, 49. Legal Res: 6224 SE 31st Ave Portland OR 97202 Mailing Add: Standard Ins 200 SW Market Portland OR 97201

ENNIS, DONALD S **(INDEPENDENT)**
Vt State Rep
Mailing Add: Box 226 Graniteville VT 05654

ENNIS, JOHN D **(R)**
Ind State Rep
Mailing Add: 800 S Ninth St Terre Haute IN 47807

ENNIS, PATRICIA MARY (D)
Mem, Bronx Co Dem Comt, NY
b Teaneck, NJ, May 15, 52; d George Joseph Ennis & Teresa Mary Perrone E; single. Educ: Marymount Manhattan Col, BA, 74; Student Govt. Polit & Govt Pos: Mem, Bronx Co Dem Comt, NY, 72-; deleg, Dem Nat Mid-Term Conf, 74. Honors & Awards: Polit Achievement Award, Bronx Comt Dem Voters, 74. Mailing Add: 4632 Carpenter Ave Bronx NY 10470

ENNIS, ROBERT TAYLOR (R)
Chmn, Prince George's Co Rep Cent Comt, Md
b Washington, DC, Jan 5, 39; s Robert Ellsworth Ennis & Blanche Lurene Taylor E; m 1960 to Ella Elizabeth Steele; c Robyn Steele. Educ: Univ Md, College Park, BS, 66. Polit & Govt Pos: City councilman, Capitol Heights, Md, 66-68; pres, Southern Prince George's Rep Club, 71-73; chmn, Prince George's Co Rep Cent Comt, 74- Bus & Prof Pos: Mgr, Computer Sci Corp, 67- Mil Serv: Entered Navy, 59, released as Missile Technician 2/C, 63, after serv in USS Proteus, 60-63; Navy Unit Citation. Mem: Odd Fellows; NAACP; Ft Washington Estates Citizens Asn (dir). Mailing Add: 712 Calvert Lane Silisia MD 20022

ENSMINGER, JOHN (R)
La State Rep
Mailing Add: Rte 4 Box 138-A Monroe LA 71201

EPPS, WILLIAM DOUGLAS (R)
b Athens, Ga, Mar 9, 29; s Ben T Epps & Omie Williams E; m 1958 to DeLette Wingfield; c Lawrence Edward, Carolyn Diane & Susan Claire. Educ: Univ Ga, BBA, 52. Polit & Govt Pos: Rep precinct chmn, Jonesboro, Ga, 64-70; chmn, Clayton Co Rep Party, 70-72; alt deleg, Rep Nat Conv, 72. Bus & Prof Pos: Pilot, Delta Air Lines, Atlanta, Ga, 56-, capt, 66- Mil Serv: Entered as 2nd Lt, Air Force, 52, released as Capt, 56, after serv in 363 Air Base Group, 11th TSC Reconnaisance Squadron, Korea, 54-55. Mem: Air Line Pilots Asn. Relig: Baptist. Mailing Add: 2747 Emerald Dr Jonesboro GA 30236

EPSTEIN, BARBARA K (D)
b Cleveland, Ohio, June 7, 45; d Edward A Katz & Gwendolyn Kamellin K; m 1966 to Barry Joel Epstein. Educ: Miami Univ, 63-65; Ohio State Univ, 65-66; Cleveland State Univ, BA, 67, grad study, 72- Polit & Govt Pos: Dem precinct committeeperson, Precinct R, Shaker Heights, Cuyahoga Co, Ohio, 72-; alt deleg, Dem Nat Conv, 72. Bus & Prof Pos: Employ counr, Ohio Bur Employ Serv Work Incentive Prog, Cleveland, 69-70; field investr, Ohio Civil Rights Comn, Cleveland, 70-71. Mem: Am Sociol Asn. Mailing Add: 3635 Norwood Rd Shaker Heights OH 44122

EPSTEIN, ELISSA (D)
VChairperson, Nassau Dem Co Comt, NY
b New York, NY, Jan 4, 33; d Charles Gottfried & Lola Mishkin G; m 1953 to Herbert Epstein; c Jill, Mark & Debra. Educ: New York Univ, BA, 54; Hofstra Law Sch, currently. Polit & Govt Pos: Committeewoman, NY Dem State Comt, 70-74, assembly dist leader, 72-74; chairperson, Nassau Co Chmn's Club, 72-; vchairperson, Nassau Dem Co Comt, 74-; deleg, Dem Nat Mid-Term Conf, 74. Bus & Prof Pos: Dir, R K Baking Corp, New York, 58- Mem: Encampment for Citizenship (bd dirs, 62-); Five Towns Martin Luther King Asn (bd dirs, 69-); South Shore United Jewish Appeal; Nat Jewish Hosp, Denver (bd dir). Honors & Awards: Five Towns Dem Club Award, 72; Award, Hofstra Law Sch, 74. Relig: Jewish. Mailing Add: 301 Pepperidge Rd Hewlett Harbor NY 11557

EPSTEIN, SEYMOUR FRANCIS (D)
Mem, Sharon Dem Town Comt, Mass
b Providence, RI, Nov 7, 19; s Louis Epstein & Jennie Fine (deceased); m 1944 to Pearl Fine; c Marlene Enid. Educ: Boston Eng High Sch, grad, 38; Bridgton Acad, Maine, 39. Polit & Govt Pos: Treas, Dem Ward Comt, Mass, 60-64, mem, 68-; mem, Boston City Dem Comt, 60-64 & 68-72; Mass State Rep, Tenth Suffolk Dist, 69-70; mem, Sharon Dem Town Comt, currently. Bus & Prof Pos: Ins examr, Div of Ins, Commonwealth of Mass, 56-68, research analyst, 70- Mem: Temple Beth Hillel Brotherhood; King Solomon Humanitarian Found for Crippled Children; King Solomon Lodge, KofP; Gtr Boston Lions Club (first vpres, pres, 70-71); Heart Fund. Relig: Hebrew. Mailing Add: 25 Glendale Rd Sharon MA 02067

EPTON, BERNARD E (R)
Ill State Sen
Mailing Add: 5555 S Everett Ave Chicago IL 60637

ERB, LILLIAN EDGAR (R)
b Stonington, Conn, July 28, 22; d Edward Matthew & Lillian Ellis M; m 1943 to David Charles Erb; c David Lawrence, Dana Louise & Gregory Barron. The educ: Eastern State Col, Conn, 65-66; Univ Conn, 67-70. Polit & Govt Pos: Justice of the peace, Groton, Conn, 54-58 & 62-64; mem, Rep Town Comt, Groton, 54-, vchmn, 54-58; Conn State Rep, 62-71, asst minority leader, Conn House Rep, formerly; dir & secy, Conn Student Loan Found, 66-; first vpres, Conn Order Women Legis, 69-; judge, Probate Court, Groton, 123rd Dist, 71-; chmn legis comt, Conn Probate Assembly, 71-; co-chmn, Conn Rep State Platform Comt, 72; deleg, Rep Nat Conv & mem platform comt, 72. Bus & Prof Pos: Owner-mgr, Erb Cleaners & Laundry, Noank, Conn, 47-60 & Erb Apts, 52-; regional adv coun, Moheugen Community Col, 70- Mem: Nat Col Probate Judges; Am Judicature Soc; Child & Family Agency Southeastern Conn (vpres, 72-); Nat Coun Women US; Prof & Bus Women's Club. Relig: Catholic. Mailing Add: 51 Front St Noank CT 06340

ERBE, NORMAN ARTHUR (R)
b Boone, Iowa, Oct 25, 19; s Otto L Erbe & Louise Festner E; m 1942 to Jacqueline D Doran; c DeElda, Jennifer & Kevin. Educ: Univ Iowa, BA, 46; JD, 47. Polit & Govt Pos: Chmn, Boone Co Rep Cent Comt, 52-57; spec asst attorney gen, Iowa Hwy Comn, 55-57; attorney gen, Iowa, 57-61, Gov, 61-63; regional rep, US Secy of Transportation, Seattle, Wash, formerly, Chicago, Ill, 71-; chmn, Fed Regional Coun, 72- Bus & Prof Pos: Exec dir, Nat Paraplegia Found. Mil Serv: Army, Co-Comdr Inf, 41-42; Air Force Pilot, 43-45; Maj, Iowa Nat Guard, 47, Col (Ret); Distinguished Flying Cross; Air Medal with Clusters. Publ: Iowa Highway Road & Street Laws, 56; Iowa Drainage Laws, 57. Mem: E Boone Co Chap, Am Red Cross; Boone CofC; Am, Iowa & Boone Co Bar Asns. Relig: Lutheran. Legal Res: 509 S Story St Boone IA 50036 Mailing Add: 450 E Park St Arlington Heights IL 60005

ERDAHL, ARLEN INGOLF (R)
b Blue Earth, Minn, Feb 27, 31; s Christian A Erdahl & Inga Fosness E; m 1958 to Ellen Marie Syrdal; c Rolf, Eric, John, Lars & Laura. Educ: St Olaf Col, BA, 53; Harvard Univ, MPA, 66; Toastmaster's Club. Polit & Govt Pos: Deleg, State & Dist Rep Conv, 63-64; Minn State Rep, 63-70; chmn, Dist Young Rep Coun, 64; chmn, Twp Rep Party, 64-65; cong fel with US Rep Gerald R Ford & US Sen Mark Hatfield, 67-68; Secy of State, Minn, formerly; comnr, Minn Pub Serv Comn, currently. Bus & Prof Pos: Farm owner, mgr & operator. Mil Serv: Entered as Pvt, Army, 54, released as Spec, 56, after serv in Spec Category Army with Air Force in Japan, 54-56. Mem: St Olaf Col Alumni Letterman's Club; Farm Bur; St Olaf Co Alumni Assoc. Honors & Awards: Freedoms Found Award, 56; Distinguished Serv Award, Blue Earth Jr CofC, 64; One of Ten Outstanding Young Men of Minn, 64; Bush Found Leadership Fel, 65; Distinguished Alumnus Award, St Olaf Col, 72. Relig: Lutheran, mem Church Coun, Dell Lutheran Church. Mailing Add: 20 W Imperial Dr West St Paul MN 55118

ERDIE, ROMEO D (D)
WVa State Deleg
Mailing Add: State Capitol Charleston WV 25305

ERDMAN, DAVID WILLIAMS (D)
b Camp LeJeune, NC, July 4, 49; s Lawrence Huntington Erdman & Marian Williams E; single. Educ: Duke Univ, BSE, 71; Georgetown Univ Law Sch, JD, 75. Polit & Govt Pos: Pres, Eng Sch Student Govt, Duke Univ, 70-71; deleg, Dem Nat Conv, 72; mem staff, NC Dept Labor, 73; mem, US Senate Select Comt Presidential Campaign Activities, 73; mem, NC Inst Govt, 74. Bus & Prof Pos: Asst to chancellor, Duke Univ, 71-72; nat pres law student div, Am Bar Asn, 74-75; nat dir, Juriscan Job-Search Syst, 74-75. Publ: Juriscan—Smart hiring is more than an art—it's a science, Am Bar Asn J, 1/75; Summing up, Student Lawyer, 10/74-9/75. Honors & Awards: Angier B Duke Scholar, Duke Univ, 67. Relig: Methodist. Legal Res: 520 Craven St New Bern NC 28560 Mailing Add: Box 908 New Bern NC 28560

ERDMAN, WALTER CLARENCE (D)
NDak State Sen
b Willow City, NDak, Dec 2, 11; s Otto Erdman & Emma Voigt E; m 1936 to Ruth L Siebert; c Kenneth (deceased), Karen (Mrs Dave Johnson) & Kathleen (Mrs William Harris). Polit & Govt Pos: NDak State Sen, 70-, mem, Senate Appropriation Comt, 73rd Session; mem, Legis Research Coun for Biennium, currently; dir, Int Peace Garden, currently. Mem: Farmers Union; Bottineau CofC. Relig: Lutheran. Mailing Add: State Capitol Bismarck ND 58501

ERHARD, VIRGINIA W (GINNIE) (DFL)
VChairwoman, Third Cong Dist Dem-Farmer-Labor Party, Minn
b Chicago, Ill, Mar 21, 38; d James Francis Weldon & Blanche K Keller W; m 1963 to Leander Remigius Erhard; c Christopher W & Alison M. Educ: Clarke Col, BA, 60; Univ Iowa & Univ Minn, part-time; Mankato State Col, MS, 72; Art Club (pres); Legis Bd (mem). Polit & Govt Pos: Secy, Legis Dist Ward Dem-Farmer-Labor Party, Minn, 65-66; chairwoman, New Hope Village Dem-Farmer-Labor Party, 66-70; third vchairwoman, Third Cong Dist Dem-Farmer-Labor Party, 67-68, second vchairwoman, 69-70, vchairwoman, currently; chairwoman, 33rd Sen Dist Dem-Farmer-Labor Party, 70-72; mem, Minn State Cent Dem-Farmer-Labor Comt, 70- Bus & Prof Pos: Teacher art & Eng, Williamsburg Jr Sr High Sch, Iowa, 60-61; teacher art, Minneapolis Pub Schs, 61-67; teacher & artist, Proj Upward Bound, Univ Minn, summers 68-73. Mem: Minn Artist Asn; Minn Artist Asn Gallery; Nat Art Educ Asn; Nat Educ Asn; Minneapolis Teachers Union. Honors & Awards: Hill grant to Minneapolis Sch of Art, summer 65; Spec Merit Award on painting at Tweed Gallery; many art exhibits. Relig: Catholic. Mailing Add: 4140 Flag Ave N New Hope MN 55427

ERICKSON, LEIF (D)
Dem Nat Committeeman, Mont
b Cashton, Wis, July 29, 06; s Oluf Erickson & Dora B Swanson E; m 1932 to Huberta B Brown; c Katherine (Mrs David Mitchell), Leif Barton & Elizabeth Ruth. Educ: Univ NDak, 25-26; Univ Chicago, PhB, JD. Polit & Govt Pos: Co attorney, Richland Co, 26-37; assoc justice, Mont Supreme Court, 38-46; Dem nominee for Gov, Mont, 44 Dem nominee for US Sen, 46; mem presidential emergency bd, Rwy Labor Bd, 45-52; mem platform drafting comt, Dem Nat Conv, 52, 56 & 60, deleg, 68 & 72; chmn, Mont Dem Party, 56-57; Dem Nat Committeeman, 62- Bus & Prof Pos: Attorney-at-law, Helena, Mont. Mem: Helena Community Chest; Am, Mont, & Lewis & Clark Bar Asns; Mont Club. Mailing Add: 1230 11th Ave Helena MT 59601

ERICKSON, LEROY (R)
NDak State Rep
m to Lila Moxness. Polit & Govt Pos: NDak State Rep, 67-69 & 72-; deleg, NDak Const Conv, 69-71. Bus & Prof Pos: Farmer. Mailing Add: DeLamere ND 58022

ERICKSON, ORBIN A (R)
b Hoople, NDak, Oct 28, 17; s Gustav Erickson & Molly Gjevre E; m 1947 to Mary Jane Gillespie; c Molly Ann & Richard. Educ: NDak State Univ, 3 years; Kappa Sigma Chi. Polit & Govt Pos: Chmn, 16th Dist Rep Party, NDak, formerly. Mil Serv: Entered as Pvt, Air Force, 42, released as Sgt, 45, after serv in 311th Fighter Bomber Group, China-Burma-India, 43-45. Mem: Mason; Am Legion; Farm Bur. Relig: Lutheran. Legal Res: Dundee Twp Hoople ND 58243 Mailing Add: RR 1 Hoople ND 58243

ERICKSON, PHYLLIS K (D)
Wash State Rep
Mailing Add: PO Box 44487 Parkland WA 98444

ERICKSON, STEPHEN PAUL (R)
b Newport, RI, May 1, 51; s Norman Hilmer Erickson & Miriam Feroline Reason E; m 1974 to Bonnie Lee King. Educ: Univ RI, BA, 73; Boston Univ Sch Law, currently; Phi Kappa Phi; Delta Sigma Rho. Polit & Govt Pos: Mem exec bd, RI Fedn Young Rep, 71-73; deleg, Rep State Cent Comt, 71-74; deleg & mem rules comt, Rep Nat Conv, 72; campaign aide, Feeley for Congress, RI, 72; dir research proj, Louise Kazanjian for Lt Gov, RI, 74. Relig: Roman Catholic. Mailing Add: 119 Purgatory Rd Middletown RI 02840

ERICKSON, WENDELL O (R)
Minn State Rep
b Isanti Co, 1925; m 1953 to Kathryn Ann Thorsgard; c Margaret, Kirsten, Charles, Anna & Hans. Educ: Univ Minn, BS. Polit & Govt Pos: Minn State Rep, Dist 26B, 65- Bus & Prof Pos: Teacher; mem bd dirs, MIKOTA Opportunities, Inc, 69- Mem: Minn Voc Agr Inst Asn; Minn Voc Asn (deleg, Nat Conv, 63-); Nat Voc Agr Teachers Asn; Am Voc Asn; Am Legion. Honors & Awards: Rock Co Sec Teacher of Year, 65; Minn Teacher of Excellence, 67; Nat

4-H Alumni Award, 69. Relig: Am Lutheran. Legal Res: Hills MN 56138 Mailing Add: Box 134 State Capitol St Paul MN 55155

ERICKSTAD, RALPH JOHN (R)
Chief Justice, NDak Supreme Court
b Starkweather, NDak, Aug 15, 22; s John T Erickstad & Anna Myklebust E; m 1949 to Lois Katherine Jacobson; c John Albert & Mark Anders. Educ: Univ NDak, 3 years; Univ Minn, BScL & LLB. Polit & Govt Pos: Munic Judge, Devils Lake, NDak; state's attorney, Ramsey Co; NDak State Sen, Ramsey Co, 57-62, Asst Majority Floor Leader, NDak State Senate, 59-61; Assoc Justice, Supreme Court, NDak, 63-73, Chief Justice, 73- Mil Serv: Entered as Pvt, Air Corps, 43, released as Sgt, 45, after serv in Eighth Air Force, ETO. Mem: Am Bar Asn; State Bar Asn NDak; Nat Judicature Soc; Am Legion; VFW. Honors & Awards: Univ NDak Sioux Award, 73. Relig: Lutheran. Legal Res: 1266 W Highland Acres Rd Bismarck ND 58501 Mailing Add: NDak Supreme Court Bismarck ND 58501

ERICSON, EVERETT FARM (R)
Chmn, Mercer Co Rep Comt, Ill
b Millersburg, Ill, Oct 7, 13; s John Ludwig Ericson & Emma Farm E; m 1942 to Alta Schloeter; c Janice Lee (Mrs Jerry Hall). Educ: Aledo High Sch, Ill, grad, 31; Roosevelt Mil Acad, 2 years. Polit & Govt Pos: Chmn, Mercer Co Rep Comt, Ill, 71- Mem: 1200 Club Ill; United Rep Orgn; Mercer Co Farm Bur. Relig: Lutheran. Mailing Add: RR 3 Aledo IL 61231

ERIKSEN, GERALD BRUCE (R)
Chmn, Burt Co Rep Party, Nebr
b Oakland, Nebr, Jan 4, 51; s Gerald B Eriksen & Luella Ann Palmer E; single. Educ: Nebr Wesleyan Univ, BS, 75; Gamma Phi Theta Chi. Polit & Govt Pos: Chmn, Burt Young Rep, 73-74; legis asst, Sen Gerald Stromer, 72-74; mem cent comt, Nebr Fedn Young Rep, 73; coordr, US Rep Charles Thone, 74; chmn, Burt Co Rep Party, Nebr, 74-, mem exec comt, 74-; admin asst, Nebr State Sen, 74-; standby Sen, Nebr State Senate, 75- Mem: Mason; Farm Bur. Relig: Presbyterian. Legal Res: RR 1 Craig NE 68019 Mailing Add: 1025 N 63rd Apt 1-126 Lincoln NE 68505

ERIKSEN, LU DEAN (D)
b Downey, Idaho, Oct 12, 19; d S Albert Christensen & Phoebe M Bowman C; m 1940 to Warren Eriksen; c Tim, Stephan & Kevin. Educ: Univ Idaho, South Br. Polit & Govt Pos: Pres, Bannock Co Dem Women's Club, Idaho, 58-60; precinct committeewoman, Bannock Co Dem Cent Comt, 57-64 & 66-, vchmn, 58-60 & state committeewoman, formerly; secy, Idaho Fifth Dist Citizens for Kennedy Comt, 60-63; vchmn, Idaho State Dem Cent Comt, 60-72; alt deleg, Dem Nat Conv, 68. Bus & Prof Pos: Social worker, Bannock Co Welfare Dept, 67-69, Bannock Co Community Ctr, 69-70. Mem: Bannock Mem Hosp, Jr Div Co Fair Bd; Am Heart Asn, Honors & Awards: Individual Award, Young Women's Mutual Improv Asn Gen Bd, 59. Relig: Latter-day Saint; mem stake bd, Young Women Mutual Improv Asn, 58-64. Mailing Add: 4325 Hawthorne Rd Pocatello ID 83201

ERKERT, ROGER WILLIAM (R)
Treas, Winnebago Co Rep Cent Comt, Ill
b Peoria, Ill, Aug 28, 31; s William Christian Erkert & Mary Hanna Sommer E; m 1956 to Joan Elizabeth Matthews; c Matthews Sommer, Elizabeth Lyn & John Graham. Educ: Northwestern Univ Sch of Bus, BS, 53; Phi Kappa Psi. Polit & Govt Pos: Mem, Young Rep, Rockford, Ill, 58; precinct committeeman, Rockford, 62; Rep Nat Committeeman, 66; secy, Winnebago Co Rep Cent Comt, 64, treas, 66-; clerk, treas & mem bd trustees, Rockford Sanitary Dist, 66, pres bd trustees, 70-75; mem exec comt, Winnebago United Rep Fund, 66; co campaign chmn for John Altorfer Gubernatorial Primary, 68; treas, Winnebago Co Rep Finance Comt, 70- Bus & Prof Pos: Customer serv mgr, Nat Lock Co Div Keystone Consol Industs, 57-60, dir materials, 60-64, asst to pres, 64-68; vpres fastener sales, 68-70, vpres mfg, 70- Mil Serv: Entered as Officers Cand, Navy, 53, released as Lt(jg), 57, after serv in Com Serv Ron 3, 53-55; Combat Info Ctr Officer, USS Lake Champlain, 55-57. Mem: Rotary; CofC; Univ Club of Rockford. Relig: Congregational. Mailing Add: 4713 White Oak Ave Rockford IL 61111

ERKINS, ROBERT ALTER (R)
b Ft Lauderdale, Fla, Jan 20, 24; s Albert W Erkins & Charlotte Alter E; m 1949 to Bernardine Morris; c Gregory, Melissa, Melinda, Marla, Melanie, Randolph, Mara, Melonni, Megan & Timothy. Educ: Univ of Notre Dame, BS Naval Sci & Tactics & BS Bus Admin. Polit & Govt Pos: State finance chmn, Idaho Rep Party, formerly. Bus & Prof Pos: Pres, Thousand Spring Trout Farms, Inc, 52-; part-time lectr, Col of Fisheries, Univ of Wash. Mil Serv: Naval Officer, World War II, Pac Theatre, Japan & North China; ret, Naval Res, 67. Mem: Rotary Club; CofC; Red Cross; Boy Scouts; Idaho State CofC. Publ: Articles on Thousand Springs Trout Farms, Inc published in Reader's Digest, Saturday Evening Post, Sunset Mag, Friends Mag, Trailways Mag, Garret Topics & Am Fish Farmer also coverage of farm on Nat Broadcasting Co prod, Tomorrow's World: Feeding the Billions. Honors & Awards: Selected by President Johnson's Coun of Small Bus as one of the top ten small businessmen in US. Mailing Add: Box 108 White Arrow Ranch Buhl ID 83314

ERLENBORN, JOHN NEAL (R)
US Rep, Ill
b Chicago, Ill, Feb 8, 27; s John H Erlenborn & Veronica M Moran E; m 1952 to Dorothy C Fisher; c Debra Lynn, Paul Nelson & David John. Educ: Univ Notre Dame, 44; Ind State Teachers Col, 44-45; Univ Ill, 45-46; Loyola Univ Chicago Sch Law, JD, 49. Hon Degrees: LLD, Elmhurst Col, 68 & St Procopius Col, 69. Polit & Govt Pos: Asst states attorney, DuPage Co, Ill, 50-52; pres, Elmhurst Young Rep, Ill, 54; Ill State Rep, 56-64; US Rep, Ill, 65- Bus & Prof Pos: Lawyer, Joseph Sam Perry, Wheaton, Ill, 49-50; partner, Erlenborn & Bauer, 52-63; partner, Erlenborn, Bauer & Hotte, 63-71. Mil Serv: Naval Res, 44-46. Mem: DuPage Co & Ill Bar Asns; Elmhurst Am Legion; Lions; Elmhurst CofC. Relig: Roman Catholic. Legal Res: 448 Raintree Ct Glen Ellyn IL 60137 Mailing Add: 2236 House Off Bldg Washington DC 20515

ERLER, ROBERT C (R)
NH State Rep
Mailing Add: Langford Rd Raymond NH 03077

ERLING, JACQUE J (R)
Committeewoman, SDak Rep State Cent Comt
b Sheridan, Wyo, Sept 7, 25; d Jozef Depner & Clementine Bianchi D; m 1947 to C H Erling; c Michael, Bridget Cook (Mrs Thomas) & Ernest. Educ: St Benedict's Col, BA, 45. Polit & Govt Pos: Secy, Rep Federated Women, 65-67; vchairwoman, Berry for Cong, East River, SDak, 66; committeewoman, SDak Rep State Cent Comt, 68-; co-chmn, Abnor for Cong, Beadle Co, 72; alt deleg, Rep Nat Conv, 72. Relig: Missouri Synod Lutheran. Mailing Add: 1580 Utah SE Huron SD 57350

ERNST, DON WILLIAM (D)
Chmn, Jefferson Co Dem Exec Comt, Ky
b Louisville, Ky, Aug 5, 37; s William P Ernst & Hattie Walls E; m to Rose Ann Childress; c Don William, Jr & John Phillip. Educ: Ind Univ, 65; Bellarmine Col, Ky, 72-73. Polit & Govt Pos: Dem precinct capt, Louisville, Ky, 65-71, group capt, 71-72; deleg, Ky Dem State Conv, 72; chmn, Jefferson Co Dem Exec Comt, 72- Mem: E End Dem Club; Jefferson Little League (pres, 72-73). Honors & Awards: Ky Col, Gov, State of Ky, 71. Relig: Catholic. Mailing Add: 156 Chenoweth Lane Louisville KY 40207

ERNST, JOSEPH MICHAEL, SR (D)
Mem, Dem State Cent Comt Md
b Baltimore, Md, Oct 7, 22; s Austin Alfred Ernst & Nellie Coyne E; m 1944 to Gloria F Bates; c Joseph M, Jr, William A, Mary E, Regina A, Charles F, Thomas P & Felicia K. Educ: Univ Baltimore, ABA, 50. Polit & Govt Pos: Mem, Dem State Cent Comt Md, 74- Bus & Prof Pos: Off mgr, Clifton Conduit Div, Gen Cable, 48-57; salesman, off mach & supplies, Monroe Div, Litton Industs, 57-61; acct, Westinghouse Elec Corp, 61-71; off mgr, Allied Metal Finishing Corp, Baltimore, 72- Mil Serv: Entered as Pvt, Army, 43, released as S/Sgt, 46, after serv at Ft G G Meade. Mem: Lauraville Improv Asn (vpres, 72-); HARBEL (exec comt, 74-); Third Dist Citizens Good Govt; Herring Run Club (bd mem); Baltimore City League Women Voters. Relig: Catholic; mem finance comt & coun mem. Mailing Add: 4801 Morello Rd Baltimore MD 21214

ERRECA, ROBERT CRONWELL (D)
Mem Exec Comt, Calif State Dem Cent Comt
b Los Banos, Calif, Feb 2, 36; s John Erreca & Ida May Cronwell E; m 1963 to Marie Accardo; c Mark Joseph & Chuck Anthony. Educ: St Mary's Col, Moraga, Calif, BS, 57; Int Rels Club. Polit & Govt Pos: Dir, Merced Co Fair, Calif, 62-, pres, 67-68; mem exec comt, Calif State Dem Cent Comt, 66-; chmn, Merced Co Dem Cent Comt, 66-70. Mem: Sportsmen's Club; 20-30 Club; Los Banos Community Chest; Elks; Lions. Relig: Catholic. Mailing Add: 139 North Santa Rosa Los Banos CA 93635

ERVIN, EDWARD SINGLETON (D)
Chmn, Sumter Co Dem Party, SC
b Manning, SC, Dec 15, 25; s Edward Singleton Ervin, Jr & Thelma Eadon E; m 1949 to Irene Y Ervin; c Lillian Augusta & Edward Singleton, IV. Educ: Wofford Col, AB, 49; Pi Kappa Phi. Polit & Govt Pos: Chmn, Sumter Co Dem Party, SC, 72- Bus & Prof Pos: Pres, Ervin Adjustment Co, Sumter, SC, 67- Mil Serv: Navy, 43. Mem: Nat Asn of Independent Adjusters; SC Claims Mgt Asn; Atlanta Claims Asn. Relig: Presbyterian. Legal Res: 732 Henderson St Sumter SC 29150 Mailing Add: Box 734 Sumter SC 29150

ERVIN, SAM J, JR (D)
b Morganton, NC, Sept 27, 96; m 1924 to Margaret Bruce Bell; c Sam J, Mrs Gerald M Hansler & Mrs William Smith. Educ: Univ NC, AB, 17; Harvard Law Sch, LLB, 22. Hon Degrees: LLD, Univ NC, 51, Western Carolina Col, 55, Wake Forest Univ, 71, George Washington Univ, 72, Davidson Col, 72 & St Andrews Presby Col, 72; DPA, Suffolk Univ, 57. Polit & Govt Pos: NC State Rep, 23, 25 & 31; chmn, Burke Co Dem Exec Comt, 24; trustee, Morganton Graded Schs, 29-30; mem, NC State Dem Exec Comt, 30-37; trustee, Morganton Graded Schs, 29-30; mem, NC State Dem Exec Comt, 30-37; trustee, Univ NC, 32-35, 45-46; trustee, Davidson Col, 48-58; judge, Burke Co Criminal Court, 35-37; judge, NC Superior Court, 37-43; mem, NC State Bd of Law Examr, 44-46; US Rep, NC, 46-47; chmn, NC Comn for Improv of the Admin of Justice, 47-49; assoc justice, NC Supreme Court, 48-54; US Sen, NC, 54-74; deleg, Dem Nat Conv, 56, 60, 64 & 68; deleg, Dem Nat Mid-Term Conf, 74. Bus & Prof Pos: Lawyer. Mil Serv: World War I, First Div, France; Nat Guard; Awarded French Fourragere; Purple Heart with Oak Leaf Clusters; Silver Star; Distinguished Serv Cross. Mem: Am & NC Bar Asns; Am Judicature Soc; NC State Bar; Newcomen Soc. Honors & Awards: Grand Orator, Grand Lodge of Masons of NC, 63; Awarded Cross of Mil Serv, UDC; Good Citizenship Medal, SAR; Distinguished Citizenship Cert, NC Citizens Asn; Patriotic Serv Medal, Am Coalition of Patriotic Soc. Relig: Presbyterian; Elder, Morganton Presby Church. Mailing Add: 515 Lenoir St Morganton NC 28655

ERVIN, WILLIAM J (D)
Okla State Sen
Mailing Add: State Capitol Oklahoma City OK 73105

ERWIN, FRANK CRAIG, JR (D)
b Waxahachie, Tex, Jan 25, 20; s Frank Craig Erwin & Margaret Edwards E; married to June Carr (deceased); c Frank Craig. Educ: Univ of Tex, 48; Kappa Sigma; Phi Beta Kappa; Phi Eta Sigma; Phi Sigma Alpha; Phi Delta Phi. Polit & Govt Pos: Vchmn, Citizens Comn, Tex, 42; chmn, Travis Co Dem Conv, 62; past chmn & past secy, Tex Dem State Exec Comt; deleg & vchmn Tex deleg, Dem Nat Conv, 64, deleg, 68; mem, Dem Nat Comt, formerly. Bus & Prof Pos: Partner, firm of Brown, Erwin, Maroney & Barber, Austin, Tex; chmn bd of regents, Univ Tex; former mem, Nat Adv Gen Med Sci Coun; chmn, Comt of Gov Bds of State-Supported Cols & Univs, currently. Mil Serv: Naval Res, 41-46; PTO. Mem: Am & Travis Co Bar Asns; State Bar of Tex; Int Asn of Ins Attorneys; Defense Research Inst. Relig: Episcopal. Legal Res: 2307 Woodlawn Blvd Austin TX 78703 Mailing Add: 900 Brown Bldg Austin TX 78701

ERWIN, JAMES SHREWSBURY (R)
b New York, NY, Nov 27, 20; s James Robinson Erwin & Elizabeth Mathilda Davidson E; m 1947 to Charlotte Anne Ruprecht; c Charlotte Elizabeth, Sarah Anne, James Robinson & Martha Jane. Educ: Dartmouth Col, AB, 42; Columbia Univ Law Sch, LLB, 49; Alpha Delta Phi; Sphinx. Polit & Govt Pos: Trustee, York Sch Dist, Maine, 51-62; chmn, York Co Rep Comt, 54-58; mem, Maine State Rep Comt, 58-64; Maine State Sen, 61-62; Maine State Rep, 65-66; Attorney Gen, Maine, 67-72; Rep cand for Gov, Maine, 74. Bus & Prof Pos: Partner, Sewall, Strater, Erwin & Winton, 53-66; dir, Portsmouth Trust Co, Portsmouth, NH, 60-66; attorney-at-law, Augusta & York, Maine, currently. Mil Serv: Entered as Pvt, Army, 42, released as 2nd Lt, 45, after serv in 6th Port Hq, European-African-Mid East Theater; Campaign Ribbon with Four Stars; European-African-Mid Eastern Theater Ribbon. Mem: Am Bar Asn; Am Judicature Soc; Mason; Shrine; Am Legion. Honors & Awards: First Annual Recipient, Progress with Promise Award, Columbia Law Sch Alumni, 70. Relig: Congregational. Mailing Add: RFD 4 Gardiner Pittston ME 04345

ERWIN, JOHN PRESTON (R)
Chmn, Hill Co Exec Comt, Tex
b Hemphill, Tex, Mar 16, 39; s John Preston Erwin, Sr & Clemence Buckley E; m 1965 to Martha Jo Phillips; c John Preston, III, Bryan Phillips, Mark Christopher & Brant Travis. Educ: Lamar State Univ, BS, 60; Univ Tex, Galveston, MD, 64; Am Bd Family Practice, dipl; Phi Rho Sigma; Mu Delta. Polit & Govt Pos: Treas, Young Rep Club, Galveston, Tex, 62-64; co chmn, Bush for Senate Campaign, 70; chmn, Hill Co Exec Comt, 71-; mem steering comt, Physicians for Tower, 72; mem bd trustees, Hillsboro Independent Sch Dist, 73-, pres, currently. Bus & Prof Pos: Partner, Family Diag Med Ctr, Hillsboro, Tex, 68- Mil Serv: Capt, Air Force, 66-68, serv in 831st TAC Hosp. Mem: Am Med Asn; Am Acad Family Physicians; Lions (dir); Mason. Relig: Episcopal; mem vestry. Mailing Add: 201 Falcon Hillsboro TX 76645

ERWIN, RICHARD C (D)
NC State Rep
Mailing Add: PO Box 995 Winston-Salem NC 27102

ERWIN, WILLIAM WALTER (R)
Asst Secy Agr for Rural Develop
b Plymouth, Ind, Sept 28, 25; s Lewis Erwin & Eleanor Fribley E; m 1948 to June Bramlet; c Hope Ellen, Lewis, II & James William. Educ: Univ Ill, BS, 49; Scabbard & Blade; Beta Theta Pi. Polit & Govt Pos: Chmn, Ind Young Rep, 52-56; mem, Nat Young Rep Exec Comt, 54-56; farm rep for Eisenhower, 56; farm rep for Nixon, 60; mem, Conserv Study Comt, Dept of Agr, 58; mem, Rep Comt on Prog & Progress, 59; chmn, Ind Adv Comt, US Civil Rights Comn, 64; pres, Comt on Community Rels, 64; Ind State Sen, 65-69; Rep nominee for US Rep, Ind, 68; mem, President Nixon's White House Task Force on Rural Develop, 70; consult to adminr, Environ Protection Agency, 71; Dep Undersecy Agr for Rural Develop, 72; Asst Secy Agr Rural Develop, 72- Bus & Prof Pos: Mem, Field Crops Adv Comt, Am Farm Bur Fedn, 60-; mem bd, Found for Am Agr, 62-; pres & gen mgr, Triple E Farm, Inc. Mil Serv: Entered as Pvt, Air Force, 44, released as Cadet, 45, commissioned 2nd Lt, 48. Mem: Am Legion; Am Soc of Farm Mgrs & Rural Appraisers; Mason; Lions; Purdue Farm Policy Study Group. Relig: Methodist. Legal Res: RR 2 Bourbon IN Mailing Add: Dept of Agr Washington DC 20250

ESAU, GILBERT D (CONSERVATIVE)
Minn State Rep
b Mt Lake, Minn, 1919; married; c four. Educ: Mt Lake pub schs. Polit & Govt Pos: Councilman, Mt Lake, Minn, 54-63; Minn State Rep, 62- Bus & Prof Pos: Automobile garage owner. Mil Serv: Army, 41-45, ETO & Asiatic Theatre. Mailing Add: Mt Lake MN 56159

ESCH, MARVIN L (R)
US Rep, Mich
b Flinton, Pa, Aug 4, 27; s Paul J Esch & Susan M Gill E; m 1950 to Olga Jurich; c Emily, Leo & Thomas. Educ: Univ Mich, AB, 50, MA, 51, PhD, 57. Polit & Govt Pos: Mich State Rep, 65-66; US Rep, Mich, 67-, mem, Educ & Labor Comt, US House of Rep, 67-, mem, Comt Sci & Technol, 71-; mem, UNESCO Adv Bd, 70-; chmn, Rep Task Force on Energy, 71-72; mem, Technol Assessment Bd, currently. Bus & Prof Pos: Assoc prof speech, Wayne State Univ, 55-64; lectr, Univ Mich-Wayne State Univ Inst Labor & Indust Rels, 55-64; mem bd trustees, John F Kennedy Ctr Performing Arts, currently. Publ: The Need for Reform, Rep Papers, Anchor Bks, 68. Relig: Presbyterian. Legal Res: Ann Arbor MI Mailing Add: 2353 Rayburn House Off Bldg Washington DC 20515

ESELY, WILLIAM JOSEPH (R)
b Stewartsville, Mo, Feb 29, 32; s Roy H Esely & Josephine Grimes E; m 1958 to Glenda Carol Greis. Educ: Univ Mo, AB in Polit Sci, 54 & LLB, 59; Phi Delta Phi; Law Rev. Polit & Govt Pos: City attorney, Gilman City & New Hampton, Mo; city attorney, Bethany, 62-; alt deleg, Rep Nat Conv, 64 & 72, deleg & mem Platform Comt, 68; mem & secy, Sen Reapportionment Comn, 65; prosecuting attorney, Harrison Co, 60-; co-chmn, Harrison Co Rep Comt, formerly; mem, Mo State Rep Comt, 66-70, mem budget comt, 68-70; Mo State Sen, 12th Dist, 70-74. Bus & Prof Pos: Practicing attorney, 59-70; owner & pres, Harrison & Mercer Co Abstract Co, Inc, 65-; farming interests; mem bd dirs, Calhoun Mfg Co, 68- & Rep Clipper, 69- Mil Serv: Entered as Airman 3/C, Air Force, 54, released as Lt, 56, after serv in Training Command. Mem: Mason (32 degree); Shrine; CofC; Farm Bur; Rotary. Relig: Methodist. Legal Res: 518 S 15th Bethany MO 64424 Mailing Add: Box 410 Bethany MO 64424

ESEROMA, LIGOLIGO KURESA (R)
VSpeaker, Am Samoa House Rep
b Fitiuta, Am Samoa, Oct 5, 28; s Paopao Eseroma & Vasalealofi Mikaio Moliga E; m 1957 to Saini Muamua Utu; c Jean Susan, Esther Maopu, Janet Sinasaumane, Faafetai L, Colleen Lauli'i, Diego Faresa, Dean Rusk, Thomas Stafford Eliu & Richard Kuresa. Educ: Frederick Barstow Found High Sch, Am Samoa, grad, 49. Polit & Govt Pos: Asst chief immigration off, Govt Am Samoa, 65-69, chief weights & measures inspector, 69-; secy, Fitiuta Youth Orgn, Am Samoa, 66-67, vpres, 67-; Rep, Am Samoa House Rep, First Dist, 67-, vspeaker, 69-; chmn, Comprehensive Health Planning, 73- Mil Serv: Entered as Seaman Recruit, Navy, 54, released as PO 2/C, 64, after serv in USS Inglesol, Pac Fleet, 63-64; Nat Defense Serv Medal; Two Navy Good Conduct Medals. Publ: 40 Consecutive Days of the Legislature of American Samoa, Samoa Times, 5/69. Mem: VFW; Fleet Reserve Asn (secy, 67-); Tepatasi VFW (comdr, Post 9781, Am Samoa, 73-74). Relig: Congregational Christian; secy, Samoan Congregational Christian Church. Legal Res: Fitiuta Manua American Samoa Mailing Add: PO Box 208 Pago Pago American Samoa

ESHELMAN, JOHN LEO, JR (D)
Chmn, Licking Co Dem Cent & Exec Comts, Ohio
b Newark, Ohio, July 15, 27; s John L Eshelman, Sr & Mary Olive Eshelman Hoskinson; m 1947 to Geraldine M Kaercher; c Jennifer K (Mrs Long), Leslie Anne & John L, III. Educ: Ohio State Univ, Newark Br, currently; Realtors Inst, Grad. Polit & Govt Pos: Committeeman, Licking Co Dem Cent Comt, 62-66 & 69-; mem, Licking Co Bd Elec, 70-; chmn, Licking Co Cent & Exec Comts, 70- Bus & Prof Pos: Staff mgr, Monumental Life Ins Co, Newark, Ohio, 52-55; staff mgr Prudential Life Ins Co, 55-65; regional dir, Nat Old Line Ins Co, Ohio & Ky, 65-68; with Jones & Hupp Real Estate, Newark, Ohio, 68-71; owner, Zodiac Real Estate, 71- Mil Serv: Entered as A/S, Naval Res, 45, released as S 1/C, 46. Mem: Ohio Asn Real Estate Bd; Ohio Asn Elec Officer; F&AM; Dem Co Chairmen of Ohio; Licking Co Bd Realtors. Relig: Baptist. Mailing Add: 219 Quentin Rd N Newark OH 43055

ESHLEMAN, EDWIN D (R)
US Rep, Pa
b Lancaster Co, Pa, Dec 4, 20; s Reeder L Eshleman (deceased) & Mary B E (deceased); m to Kathryn E Dambach; c E Bruce & R Lee. Educ: Franklin & Marshall Col, BS in polit sci; US Coast Guard Acad, Res Officer Training Course; Temple Univ, grad study in polit sci. Polit & Govt Pos: Dir Bur Co audits, Dept Auditor Gen, Pa, 49-53; mem bd dirs, Young Rep Lancaster Co, 50-53 & 55-57, pres, 51, 52 & 54; exec asst, State Treas Dept, 53-55; Pa State Rep, 54-66, majority whip, Pa House of Rep, 64, minority whip, 65-66; vchmn, Pa Higher Educ Assistance Agency, 64-; US Rep, Pa, currently. Bus & Prof Pos: Pub sch teacher, 45-49. Mil Serv: Entered as Lt, Coast Guard Res, 42, released 54, after 38 months active duty, 18 months overseas; commendations for conduct-in-action at Salerno, Anzio & Normandy. Mem: Am Legion; Lancaster Co Sportsmen Asn; F&AM; Elks; Lancaster Co Hist Soc. Honors & Awards: Distinguished Serv Award as Outstanding Young Man of Year, Lancaster Jr CofC, 56; VFW Nat Silver Merit Medal; Elk of Year, 74. Relig: Lutheran. Mailing Add: 2173 W Ridge Dr Lancaster PA 17603

ESKENS, ESTHER P (R)
Wyo State Rep
b Manhattan, Kans, Nov 30, 24; d Paul George Brown & Viola McDowell B; m 1954 to Henry R Eskens, MD; c Joan & Henry, II. Educ: St Mary Sch Nursing, dipl, 45. Polit & Govt Pos: Wyo State Rep, 75- Bus & Prof Pos: Head nurse, St Lukes Hosp, Kansas City, Mo, 48-51, clin instr, 51-56; head nurse & off mgr, Lovell, Wyo, 62- Publ: Co-auth, New concepts in nursing & diet, Am J Nursing, 53. Mem: Bus & Prof Women (pres, currently); Fedn Women's Clubs (local treas, currently); Nurses Asn; Wyo Med Soc Auxiliary. Honors & Awards: Woman of the Year, Lovell Bus & Prof Women, 73-74. Relig: Catholic. Mailing Add: 15 E Tenth St Lovell WY 82431

ESKIND, JANE GREENEBAUM (D)
Mem, Tenn State Dem Exec Comt
b Louisville, Ky, May 18, 33; d Samuel Lewis Greenebaum, Jr (deceased) & Doni Sturm Selligman; m 1954 to Richard Jerome Eskind; c Ellen Katz & William Herbert. Educ: Brandeis Univ, 52-54; Univ Louisville, BA, 56. Polit & Govt Pos: Mem, Comt of 100, Tenn Found for Better Govt, 68-; secy, Tenn Citizens Comn on Compensation, 69-70; mem platform comt, Dem Nat Comt, 72; pres, Dem Women's Club of Davidson Co, Tenn, 73; mem, Tenn State Dem Exec Comt, 21st Dist, 74- Mem: Citizen's for Court Modernization (vpres, 73); Am Judicature Soc; Coun of Jewish Women; League of Women Voters; Outlook Nashville Inc (bd mem, 75-). Honors & Awards: Mem, Pres Coun, Brandeis Univ, 73. Relig: Jewish. Mailing Add: 6000 Dunham Springs Rd Nashville TN 37205

ESPALDON, ERNESTO (R)
Sen, Guam Legis
Mailing Add: Guam Legis Box 373 Agana GU 96910

ESPARZA, MOCTESUMA DIAZ (D)
b Los Angeles, Calif, Mar 12, 49; s Francisco Esparza & Ester Diaz E; single. Educ: Univ Calif, Los Angeles, BA, 72, MFA, 73; Acad TV Arts & Sci; MECHA. Polit & Govt Pos: Deleg, co-chmn Calif youth deleg & co-chmn Chicano caucus, Dem Nat Conv, 72; mem rules comt, Dem Nat Comt, 72-73, comnr deleg selection & party reform, 73-; co-chmn Southern Calif McGovern for President, Chicago Dem Coalition Caucus, 72-75. Bus & Prof Pos: Pres, Moctesuma Esparza Prods, Los Angeles, Calif, 72- & Euclio Holding Co, 73-; producer, Villa Allegre, Bilingual Children TV, Oakland, 73-74. Publ: Producer & writer, Cinco Vidas (documentary), KNBC, 1/73; Survival (documentary) & Celebracion (documentary), McGraw-Hill Broadcasting, 75. Mem: Euclid Found (vpres, 69-75); Am Fedn TV & Radio Artists; Nat Latino Media Coalition (chmn, cable TV comt, 73-75). Honors & Awards: Bronze Medal, producer, Requiem 29, Atlanta Film Festival, 73; Emmy, producer Cinco Vidas, Acad TV Arts & Sci Best Documentary, 74; City of Los Angeles Plaque, 74; Cert of Appreciation, City of Los Angeles, 74; East Los Angeles Health Task Force Achievement Award, 74. Mailing Add: 2036 Lemoyne Ave Los Angeles CA 90026

ESPICH, JEFFREY K (R)
Ind State Rep
Mailing Add: Box 152 Uniondale IN 46791

ESPOSITO, ALBERT C (R)
WVa State Deleg
b Pittsburgh, Pa, Nov 9, 12; s Charles A Muzio Micali Esposito & Elizabeth Cuda E; m 1940 to V Elizabeth Dodson; c Bettina (Mrs Peter F Kelly), Mary Alice & Gregory Charles J. Educ: Univ Pittsburgh, BS; Loyola Univ, MD cum laude, 50; Am Bd Ophthal, dipl, 50; Alpha Omega Alpha; Alpha Phi Delta. Polit & Govt Pos: WVa State Deleg, 75-, mem comt health, educ & welfare, WVa House Deleg, 75- Bus & Prof Pos: Instr ophthal & chmn dept, St Mary's Sch Nursing & St Mary's Hosp, Marshall Univ, 50-; chief ophthalmologist, Doctors Mem Hosp, currently; instr ophthal, Ohio State Col Med, 7 years; consult, Chesapeake & Ohio RR, currently; attending ophthalmologist, Cabell Huntington Hosp & Huntington Hosp, currently. Mil Serv: Entered as Lt, Army, 42, released as Maj, 46, after serv in MedC. Publ: Auth, Esposito erisophake & cataract extraction, Brit J Ophthal, 11/62; auth, Surgical management of a free floating iris cyst in the anterior chamber, Am J Ophthal, 11/65; Complications of cataract surgery, Trans Am Diopter & Decible Soc, 74; plus many others. Mem: Int Col Surgeons (fel); Am Med Asn; Am Asn Ophthal (pres-elect); Am Diopter & Decibel Soc; Marshall Found (bd trustees, 73-). Honors & Awards: Outstanding Ophthalmologist in the South Award, Southern Med Asn, 72; City Huntington Appreciation Award, 74; Distinguished Serv Award, Marshall Univ, 74; George Van Zant Pub Serv Award, Jaycees, 75; Stritch Medal Award, 74. Relig: Roman Catholic. Legal Res: 171 Woodland Dr Huntington WV 25705 Mailing Add: 420 11th St Huntington WV 25701

ESPOSITO, DONALD F (D)
Conn State Rep
Mailing Add: 4 Mountainville Rd Danbury CT 06810

ESPOSITO, FRANCIS JAMES (D)
Chmn, Rutland Co Dem Comt, Vt
b Lebanon Springs, NY, Dec 30, 13; s Ralph Esposito & Maria Stella E (deceased); m 1945 to Eileen Joy Warner; c Francis J, Jr & Michael J. Educ: Mt St Joseph's Acad, Rutland, Vt, 4 years. Polit & Govt Pos: Mem, Rutland City Dem Comt, 61-; mem, Rutland Co Dem Comt, 65-, chmn, 72-; Vt State Rep, 66-74; chmn Rutland deleg, Vt Dem Conv, 68; state chmn, Vt Dem Party, 68-73; alt deleg, Dem Nat Conv, 72. Bus & Prof Pos: Trainman, Rutland Rwy Corp, 40-62, conductor, 50-62, gen chmn, Rutland Rwy Corp, BRT, 52-62; self-employed in

real estate & ins, 61- Mil Serv: Entered as Pvt, Army Air Force, 42, released as Warrant Officer, 45, after serv in Pac Theatre, 42-45. Mem: Mt St Joseph Athletic Bd; KofC (4 degree & past Grand Knight); Am Legion; Kiwanis Int (first vpres, Rutland Club); BRT Lodge 704. Relig: Catholic. Mailing Add: 20 James St Rutland VT 05701

ESPOSITO, JOHN A **(R-CONSERVATIVE)**
NY State Assemblyman
b Brooklyn, NY, Sept 19, 27; married; c three. Educ: Manhattan Col; Fordham Univ & Brooklyn Law Sch. Polit & Govt Pos: Asst Dist Attorney, Queens Co, 66; exec secy, Pub Serv Comn, 68; asst welfare inspector gen to George Berlinger, 71; NY State Assemblyman, 23rd Dist, 71-, mem, Judiciary, Govt Opers & Cities Comt; mem, 23rd Assembly Dist Rep Co Comt, currently. Bus & Prof Pos: Law secy, Court of Claims, 71. Mil Serv: Army, hon discharge, 47. Mem: Ameritał Asn; Home Sch Asn; Wayanda Civic Asn; Local Rep Clubs. Mailing Add: 222-01 101st Ave Queens Village NY 11429

ESPOSITO, MEADE H **(D)**
Mem-At-Lg, Dem Nat Comt
b Brooklyn, NY, Jan 1, 10; s Guiseppe Esposito & Felicia Visone E; m 1928 to Anna Deconzo; c Felicia (Dr Joseph Zito). Educ: Pub schs. Polit & Govt Pos: Mem exec comt, 39th Assembly Dist, NY, 60-; chmn, Kings Co Dem Exec Comt, 69-72; mem-at-lg, Dem Nat Comt, 72-; deleg, Dem Nat Mid-Term Conf, 74. Bus & Prof Pos: Vpres, Grand Brokerage & Brooklyn Carpet Co, Brooklyn, NY, currently. Mem: B'nai B'rith; NAACP; Italian Am Civil Rights League. Honors & Awards: Man of the Year, B'nai B'rith & NAACP. Relig: Catholic. Mailing Add: 2035 Royce St Brooklyn NY 11234

ESPOSITO, MICHAEL P **(D)**
NJ State Assemblyman
b Jersey City, NJ, Jan 22, 13; s John Esposito & Marianna Delisa E; m 1936 to Theresa Orrico; c Marianne (Mrs Costello). Educ: Bucknell Univ, 4 years; Alpha Phi Delta. Polit & Govt Pos: Mem & dir, Jersey City Bd of Educ, 65-68; NJ State Assemblyman, 68- Bus & Prof Pos: Pres, John Esposito & Sons Inc, Hardware Co, 47- Mem: Friendly Merchants Businessmens Asn; Columbus Triangle Bus & Prof Mens Asn (pres); Holy Rosary Holy Name Soc; Paul Revere Boys' Club; Boys' Club of Am. Honors & Awards: Recipient of Outstanding Am Award, 59; Medallion Award, Boys' Club of Am, 61. Relig: Catholic. Legal Res: 366 Second St Jersey City NJ 07301 Mailing Add: 275 Newark Ave Jersey City NJ 07302

ESQUER, CECILIA D **(D)**
Mem-at-lg, Dem Nat Comt
b Superior, Ariz, May 18, 42; d Ramon R Denogean & Bertina Teyechea D; m 1965 to Elias Yescas Esquer; c Andrea & Marc. Educ: Ariz State Univ, BA, 63, MA, 66; Pi Omega Pi; Alpha Pi Epsilon. Polit & Govt Pos: Campaign coordr, Esquer for Sch Bd, 69 & 70; campaign coordr, Arredondo for City Coun, 70; dep registr, Dem Party, Ariz, 70-; campaign coordr, Eliza Carney for State Legis, 72; Cent Ariz coordr, UNIDOS con McGovern, 72; precinct committeeperson, Dist 27, Dem Party, 72-; mem exec comt, Ariz Dem Party, 72-; first vchairperson, Maricopa Co Dem Party, 72-; vpres, UNIDOS, 73-; mem-at-lg, Dem Nat Comt, 73- Bus & Prof Pos: Teacher, Ray High Sch, Kearny, Ariz, 63-64, McClintock High Sch, Tempe, 65-66 & 68-70 & Baker Jr High, Tacoma, Wash, 66-68; eve instr, Mesa Community Col, Mesa, Ariz, 70-71; faculty assoc, Ariz State Univ, 71-72. Mem: Mexican Am Educ Adv Comt (secy, 72-73). Honors & Awards: Outstanding Bus Educ Student, Nat Bus Educators Asn, 63. Relig: Catholic. Mailing Add: 1720 E Palmcroft Dr Tempe AZ 85282

ESSER, HAROLD JOSEPH **(R)**
Mo State Rep
b Boonville, Mo, Feb 11, 23; s John Lawrence Esser & Elizabeth Fischer E; m 1953 to Lorraine Joan Anderson; c David Anderson. Educ: St Benedict's Col, 40-41; Univ Mo, Columbia, 46-48; Kappa Alpha. Polit & Govt Pos: Mo State Rep, 69- Mil Serv: Entered as Pvt, Army, 43, released as Cpl, 46, after serv in Med Corps, Europe & Asia. Mem: South Kansas City CofC. Relig: Catholic. Mailing Add: 3 W Glen Arbor Rd Kansas City MO 64114

ESSEX, PAULA HIGASHI **(D)**
Dem Nat Committeewoman, Calif
b San Pedro, Calif, Feb 8, 49; d Paul Masata Higashi & Mary Kinoshita H; m 1969 to James Douglas Essex. Educ: Univ Calif, Los Angeles, BA, 71. Polit & Govt Pos: Alt deleg, Dem Nat Conv, 72; deleg, Dem Nat Mid-Term Conf, 74; Western States coordr, Dem Planning Group, 74; mem, Los Angeles Co Dem Comt, Calif, 74-; mem, Mayor's Adv Comt on Status of Women, Los Angeles, 75; co-chmn, Calif State Dem Party Affirmative Action Comt, 75-; Dem Nat Committeewoman, Calif, 75- Legal Res: 531 N Bandini St San Pedro CA 90731 Mailing Add: Dem Party 6022 Wilshire Blvd Los Angeles CA 90036

ESTEE, PAUL N **(D)**
NH State Rep
Mailing Add: 6 Frances St Franklin NH 03235

ESTES, KATE REED **(D)**
b Trenton, Tex, June 28, 17; d Charles Burgher Reed & Lucile Morrow R; div. Educ: ETex State Univ, BS, 37, MS, 50; Univ Tex, Austin; NTex State Univ; Tex Women's Univ; Phi Mu Epsilon; Marpessa Club; Chaparral Club. Polit & Govt Pos: Deleg, Tex State Dem Conv, 54-, Dem Nat Conv, 64, Nat Dem Womens Conf, 66, Dem Nat Mid-Term Conf, 74; educ consult, Tex State Sen Ray Roberts, 61 & Sen Ralph M Hall, 63-65. Bus & Prof Pos: Co sch supvr, Fannin Co, Tex, 44-58, 65-66 & Grayson Co, 70-71; spec consult, Elem Educ, World Book Co, Dallas, 58-59; consult admin serv, Educ Serv Ctr, Region X, Richardson, 66-70; spec serv teacher, Tom Bean & Bells, Tex, 71-74. Mem: Fannin Co Dem Women's Club; Delta Kappa Gamma; Prof Musicians Union, Austin & Ft Worth. Relig: Methodist. Legal Res: US Hwy 69 E Trenton TX 75490 Mailing Add: Box 245 Trenton TX 75490

ESTES, SUE HORN **(D)**
b Louisville, Ky, May 18, 38; d George Horn & Bessie Walker H; m 1961 to Dr Ralph W Estes. Educ: Ky Wesleyan Col, 56-58; Univ Ky, BA in Jour, 60, grad work, 62-63; Univ Tex, Arlington, 66-67. Polit & Govt Pos: Publicity chmn, Johnson for President, Bloomington, Ind, 64 publicity chmn, McCarthy for President, Ft Worth, Tex, 68; mem bd dirs, Tarrant Co Dem Woman's Club, Tex, 67-72; state co-chmn, Texans for McGovern, 71-72; chmn, McGovern for President, Tarrant Co, 72; deleg, Dem Nat Conv, 72; acting pres, Dem Clubs of Tarrant Co, 73- Bus & Prof Pos: Reporter, The Evansville Press, Ind, 60-61; reporter, The Wheaton Daily J, Ill, 61-62; writer, News Bur, Ind Univ, Bloomington, 63-65; reporter, The Herald-Tel, Bloomington, 65 & The Press, Ft Worth, Tex, 66; contrib ed, The Tex Observer, Austin, 66-73. Publ: The new left in Dallas, 10/67 & Cesar Chavez in Texas, 12/69, The Tex Observer; What the poor are up against in Texas, The New Repub, 6/19/69. Mem: Am Civil Liberties Union (secy, Ft Worth Chap, 69-70, bd dirs, 69-73). Honors & Awards: Ky Col, The Hon Order of Ky Col, 64. Relig: Unitarian. Mailing Add: 2007 Warwick Arlington TX 76015

ETCHART, MARK S **(R)**
Mont State Sen
b Glasgow, Mont, Aug 31, 23; s John Etchart & Catherine Urquilux E; m 1949 to Delores Stroble; c Colette, Kathy, Brian, Diane & Denise. Educ: St Thomas Col, St Paul, Minn, 40-41; Carroll Col, Helena, Mont, 41-42; Mont State Univ, BS in Animal Indust, 51; Alpha Zeta; Lambda Chi Alpha. Polit & Govt Pos: Mont State Rep, Valley Co, 61-65; Mont State Rep, Dist 5B, 67-69; deleg, Mont Const Conv & chmn, Gen Govt Comt, 72; Mont State Sen, 75- Bus & Prof Pos: Partner, Etchart Ranch, 43-; dir, Buggy Creek State Grazing Dist, 64-; pres, Glasgow Irrigation Dist, 66. Mil Serv: Entered as A/S, Navy, 45, released as AMM 3/C, 46, after serv in Fleet Air Wing 14, Hq Squadron 14-1, San Diego, Calif. Mem: Mont Pilots Asn; Am Legion; Elks; KofC; Nat Water Resources Asn. Relig: Catholic. Legal Res: 514 Sixth Ave N Glasgow MT 59230 Mailing Add: Box 229 Glasgow MT 59230

ETHERTON, TRUDY SLABY **(R)**
Mem Bd Dirs, Young Rep Nat Fedn
b South Bend, Ind, June 6, 42; d Frank A Slaby & Alice E Michalec S; m 1967 to William M Etherton. Educ: Butler Univ, BS, 64; Ind Univ, postgrad studies; Delta Gamma; Panhellenic. Polit & Govt Pos: Vpres, Butler Univ Young Rep, 62, pres, 63-64; region co-chmn, Col Young Rep, 63; deleg, Rep Nat Conv, 64; dir, Young Rep South Bend, Ind, 65, vpres, 66; auditor, Ind, 68-70; comnr, Bur of Motor Vehicles, Ind, 70-71; mem bd dirs, Young Rep Nat Fedn, currently; dir, State of Ind Washington, DC Liaison Off, 71-72; acting assoc dir state & local govt opers, Off Econ Opportunity, 72-73; spec asst to Secy Dept Housing & Urban Develop as dir of area liaison for Off Exec Mgt, 73- Bus & Prof Pos: Teacher, Penn-Harris-Madison Sch Corp, 64-68; dep registr officer, St Joseph Co, Ind. Mem: Ind State Teachers Asn; Nat Educ Asn; Nat Asn Social Studies Teachers; Notre Dame Faculty Club; Butler Univ Alumni Asn. Honors & Awards: First Woman Comnr in Ind. Relig: Catholic. Legal Res: 23721 State Rd No 2 South Bend IN 46619 Mailing Add: Apt 614 501 Slaters Lane Alexandria VA 22314

ETZELL, GEORGE FERDINAND **(R)**
b Clarissa, Minn, Feb 1, 09; s George Adolph Etzell & Ida Hammer E; m 1934 to Ione Margaret Koch; c Peter, Gretchen, Paul, Mary & Martha. Polit & Govt Pos: Mem, Minn Rep Nat Comt, until 72; village clerk, Clarissa, Minn, 30-34; mem, Young Rep League, Sixth Cong Dist Rep Orgn, 36-38; printer, State of Minn, 39-43; chmn, Sixth Cong Dist Rep Orgn, 46-51; spec adv, Gov C Elmer Anderson, 51-52; vchmn, Rep Nat Conv Rules Comt, 56, chmn, 60 & 64; mem, Rep Nat Comt, 52-71. Bus & Prof Pos: Pres, Etzell Publ, Inc, 63-72; ed & publ, The Clarissa Independent, 39-73. Publ: Auth of children's stories, articles, etc publ in about 100 mag since 1930. Mem: Nat Ed Asn; Minn Newspaper Asn; charter mem Minn Press Club; Minneapolis Athletic Club; KofC. Relig: Roman Catholic. Mailing Add: Clarissa MN 56440

EU, MARCH FONG **(D)**
Secy of State, Calif
b Oakdale, Calif; d Yuen Kong & Shiu Shee K; m; c Matthew Kipling & Marsha Suyin. Educ: Univ Calif, Berkeley, BS; Mills Col, MEd; Stanford Univ, EdD, 54; post grad study, Columbia Univ & Calif State Col, Hayward; Delta Kappa Gamma. Polit & Govt Pos: Mem, Alameda Co Bd Educ, Calif, 56-66, pres, 61-62, legis advocate, 63; co-chmn, Richards for Senate Campaign, Alameda Co, 62; women's chmn, Petris for Assembly Campaign, 62 & 64; dir, Key Women for Kennedy, 63, dir, Key Women for Alameda Co, 64; dir & vpres, Eighth Cong Dist Dem Coun, 63; mem, Calif Dem State Cent Comt, 63-70; mem, Gov Adv Comn Compensatory Educ, 63-; spec consult, Bur Intergroup Rels, Calif State Dept Educ; mem exec comt, 47 Million Dollar Bond Campaign, Peralta Jr Col; mem, Alameda Co Elected Off Comt, Johnson for President, 64; women's vchmn, Northern Calif Johnson for President Campaign, 64; East Oakland chmn, No on Proposition 14, 64; Calif State Assemblywoman, 15th Dist, 67-74; deleg & asst secy Calif deleg, Dem Nat Conv, 68; Alameda Co co-chmn, Robert Kennedy for President, 68; mem, Adv Compensatory Educ Comn; Task Force, Educ Comn of State on Early Childhood Educ; White House Conf on Youth, 71; Calif Econ Develop Comn; exec comt, Calif State Dem Cent Comt; Alameda Co co-chmn, Wilson Riles for Supt Pub Instr; Secy of State, Calif, 75- Bus & Prof Pos: Legis advocate, Alameda Co Bd Educ, 63; educ & legis consult, Sausalito Pub Schs, Santa Clara Co Off Educ, Jefferson Elem Union Sch Dist, Santa Clara High Sch Dist, Santa Clara Elem Sch Dist & Live Oak Union High Sch Dist; lectr health educ, Mills Col, Oakland; supv dent health educ, Alameda Co Schs; dent hygienist, Oakland Pub Schs; chmn div dent hygiene, Univ Calif Med Ctr, San Francisco. Mil Serv: Dent Hygienist, World War II, Presidio, San Francisco. Mem: Life mem Am Dent Hygienists' Asn; Am Asn Univ Women (area rep educ); hon mem Southern Calif Dent Asn; hon mem Zero Pop Growth; life mem Howard Elem Sch PTA. Honors & Awards: Recipient, Ann Award for Outstanding Achievement, Eastbay Intercultural Fel, 59; Phoebe Apperson Hearst Distinguished Bay Area Woman of the Year Award; Woman of the Year, Calif Retail Liquor Dealers Inst, 69; Loyalty Day Award, VFW, 70; Merit Citation, Calif Asn Adult Educ Adminr, 70; Art Educ Award. Relig: Unitarian. Mailing Add: 111 Capitol Mall Sacramento CA 95814

EURE, THAD **(D)**
Secy of State, NC
b Gates Co, NC, Nov 15, 99; s Tazewell A Eure & Armecia Langstun E; m 1924 to Minta Banks; c Thad, Jr & Mrs J Norman Black. Educ: Univ NC, 19; Univ Law Sch, 22; Elon Col, LLD, 58. Polit & Govt Pos: Chmn bd trustees, Elon Col; mayor, Winton, NC, 23-28; co attorney, Hertford Co, 23-31; NC State Rep, 29; prin clerk, NC House of Rep, 31-36; escheats agent, Univ NC, 33-36; Secy of State, NC, 36-; keynote speaker, Dem State Conv, 50, permanent chmn, 62. Bus & Prof Pos: Attorney-at-law. Mem: Ahoski Kiwanis; Theta Chi Jr Order; Elks (Grand Lodge Chair Officer, 56); Am Legion; 40 et 8. Relig: Congregational. Legal Res: Winton NC 27986 Mailing Add: State Capitol Raleigh NC 27602

EUSTAQUIO, GEORGE CASTRO **(D)**
b Agana, Guam, Feb 21, 31; s Jose Garrido Eustaquio & Ana Leon Guerrero Castro E; m 1957 to Rosita San Nicolas Flores; c George, Jr, Geordette Rose, Geoward, Jacques, Georanna Carmen, Leonisa Geonesa, Norene Nathajia & Geocinda Angelica. Educ: Loyola Univ, Los Angeles, BS, 55; Georgetown Univ, BSFS, 56; Int Rels Club. Polit & Govt Pos: Pub rels officer, Guam Legis, 58-; adminr, Econ Opportunity, Gov Off, 65-67; asst area develop officer, US Dept State/Agency Int Develop, 68-69; cand for Sen, Guam Legis, 70; dir research, 11th Guam Legis, 70-73; campaign dir & chmn, Elec Comt for State Chmn, Dem

Party of Guam, admin asst to Del US House of Rep Antonio B Won Pat, Guam, 73- Mil Serv: Entered as Pvt, Army, 57, released as Pfc, 58, after serv in 21st Inf, Hawaii, 57-58; Good Conduct Medal. Publ: Legislative Digest (syntopics), Fifth Guam Legis, 59 & ed, Legislative Briefing Folder, 11th Guam Legis, 72; auth, Guam social development since the Organic Act of 1950, Chammoro Week, 72. Mem: Elks; St Francis Sch PTA; Boy Scouts; Holy Name Soc; Nat Capital Dem Club, Washington, DC. Relig: Catholic. Legal Res: Yona GU 96910 Mailing Add: 216 Cannon House Off Bldg Washington DC 20515

EVANGER, JACQUELINE RUTH (D)
Chmn, Summit Co Dem Cent Comt, Colo
b Cedaredge, Colo, Aug 11, 26; d Scott Davis Gorsuch & Zella Ione G; div; c W Scott & J Rudd Pyles. Educ: Univ Colo, 43-45; Western State Col Colo, 45-46 & 61-63; Tri-Sigma; Kappa Phi. Polit & Govt Pos: Trustee, Town of Frisco, Colo, 54-60, 71-74, chmn admin comt, 72-74; bd mem & secy, Summit Co Sch Dist RE-1, 59-61; chmn, Summit Co Dem Cent Comt, 72-; mem, Colo State Dem Exec Comt, 75- Bus & Prof Pos: Tech librn, Climax Molybdenum Co, Climax, Colo, 55-56 & 59-73; owner & mgr, Totem Pole, Sporting Goods Store, 56-59; adminr rec & tech info, Indust Mineral Ventures, Inc, Golden, 73- Publ: Frisco news reporter, Summit Co J, 54-59; Poem (from a thankful librarian), World Mining, 2/64; letters-to-editor, various newspapers. Mem: Soc Mining Engrs; Am Rec Mgt Asn (mem-at-lg); Indust Rels Research Asn; Spec Libr Asn (historian, Colo chap, 69-, chmn elect, metals/materials div, 75-76, chmn, 76-77). Legal Res: 702 Frisco St Box 37 Frisco CO 80443 Mailing Add: Apt 501 95 Emerson Denver CO 80218

EVANS, BILLY L (D)
Ga State Rep
Mailing Add: 1844 Flintwood Dr Macon GA 31201

EVANS, CHARLES WESLEY (D)
Tex State Rep
b Jacksonville, Fla, Feb 19, 39; s Robert Lee Evans & Leona Evelyn E; m 1963 to Patricia Anne; c Lisa Anne & James Wesley. Educ: Arlington State Col, BA, 65; Southern Methodist Univ, JD, 67; Phi Alpha Delta. Polit & Govt Pos: Mem city coun, Hurst, Tex, 70-72; Tex State Rep, 73-, vchmn local govt comt during Tex Const Conv, vchmn House admin comt, Tex House Rep, 74- Mil Serv: AE2 Navy, 57-61; Good Conduct Medal. Mem: Am & Ft Worth-Tarrant Co Bar Asns; Hurst-Euless-Bedford CofC; Lions. Honors & Awards: Man of Month, Hurst Jaycees, 72; Distinguished Serv Award, State Bar Tex, 73. Relig: Baptist. Legal Res: 809 Bedford Ct W Hurst TX 76053 Mailing Add: Suite 200 First State Bank Bldg Bedford TX 76021

EVANS, COOPER (R)
Iowa State Rep
Mailing Add: 1009 H Ave Grundy Center IA 50638

EVANS, DANIEL JACKSON (R)
Gov, Wash
b Seattle, Wash, Oct 16, 25; s Daniel Lester Evans & Irma Ida E; m 1959 to Nancy Ann Bell; c Daniel Jackson, Mark Lawrence & Bruce McKay. Educ: Univ Wash, BS, 48, MS, 49. Polit & Govt Pos: Wash State Rep, 56-65, Rep Floor Leader, Wash State House of Rep, 61-65; Gov, Wash, 65-; chmn campaign comt, Nat Rep Gov, 65-66, mem policy comt, 67-68 & 72; mem exec bd, Nat Gov Conf, 66-67 & 73-75, chmn const rev comt, 66-68, chmn comt exec mgt & fiscal affairs, 69, chmn transportation, com & technol comt, 69-72; deleg & keynote speaker, Rep Nat Conv, 68 & del, 72; chmn, Western Gov Conf, 68-69; mem exec comt, Rep Gov Asn, 69, chmn policy comt, 70-71; mem, Rep Gov Adv Bd to the President, 69; mem, Comn of Cities in 70's, Nat Urban Coalition, 71-72; mem, Adv Comn Intergovt Rels, 72-; app, Proj Independence Adv Comt, 74; app, Nat Comn Productivity & Work Qual, 75; pres, Coun State Govts, 72- Bus & Prof Pos: Asst mgr, Mt Pac Chap of Assoc Gen Contractors, 53-59; partner, Gray & Evans struct & civil engrs, 59-65. Mil Serv: Naval Res, 43-46, recalled to active duty, 51-53, Lt. Mem: Boy Scouts; Urban Coalition. Honors & Awards: Human Rights Award, Pac Northwest Chap, Nat Asn Intergroup Rels Off, 68; Scales of Justice Award, Nat Coun Crime & Delinquency, 68; Silver Beaver Award, Boy Scouts & Silver Antelope Award, 70; Award for Serv to the Profession, Consult Engrs Coun, 69; Distinguished Eagle Award, 73. Relig: Congregational. Mailing Add: State Capitol Olympia WA 98504

EVANS, DAVID VERNON (D)
b Holdrege, Nebr, Dec 9, 41; s Charles Vernon Evans & Mildred Frost E; single. Educ: Grinnell Col, BA, 64; Eagleton Inst, Rutgers Univ, MA, 65; Pa State Univ, 66-67; Pi Sigma Alpha; Young Dem. Polit & Govt Pos: Campaign secy, Whelan for Cong, Nebr, 60; Adams Co youth chmn, Kennedy for President, 60; campaign asst, Nebraskans for Morrison, 62; coordr, Downing for Attorney Gen, 64; deleg, Dem State Conv, 64; spec asst to Gov Frank Morrison, 65-66; secy, Dem State Adm Coun on Educ, 67-69, chmn, 69; state chmn, McCarthy for President, 68; deleg, Dem Nat Conv, 68; research analyst, Gov Frank Licht, RI, 69, admin asst, 69-72; deleg & chmn, RI Deleg, Dem Nat Conv, 72; state campaign dir, McGovern for President, RI Primary, 72; regional coordr, McGovern for President, Gen Elec Campaign, NY State, 72. Bus & Prof Pos: Instr polit sci, Wayne State Col, 67-68; vpres, Harney Advert, Lincoln, Nebr, 68-69; consult, Jamestown, RI, 72- Relig: Presbyterian. Mailing Add: 28 Green Lane Jamestown RI 02835

EVANS, DAVID W (D)
US Rep, Ind
b Lafayette, Ind, Aug 17, 46; s I Walter Evans & Margaret Reppert E; m to Darlene Ginder. Educ: Ind Univ, Polit Sci Degree, 67. Polit & Govt Pos: Deleg, Dem Nat Mid-Term Conf, 74; US Rep, Sixth Dist, Ind, 75- Bus & Prof Pos: Asst prin, St Ann Parochial Sch, Ind, 68-72; teacher polit sci, St Andrews Parochial Sch, 72-74. Relig: Catholic. Mailing Add: PO Box 41709 Weir Cook Airport Indianapolis IN 46241

EVANS, DONALD D (R)
b Seattle, Wash, Feb 4, 47; s Donald D Evans & Vivian Berkshire E; single. Educ: Univ Wash, BA, 69; Univ Calif, Berkeley, JD, 72; Phi Beta Kappa; Delta Chi. Polit & Govt Pos: Legis asst, US Rep John Ashbrook, Ohio, 73- Mem: Calif State Bar. Relig: Presbyterian. Mailing Add: 110 D St SE Apt 303 Washington DC 20003

EVANS, E CHRIS (R)
Chmn, Licking Co Rep Cent Comt, Ohio
b Granville, Ohio, Sept 14, 28; s Chris N Evans & Naomi Clark E; m 1953 to Patsy Meadows; c Rodney, Vicki, Jeffrey, Sandra & Leslie. Educ: Newark High Sch, grad, 46. Polit & Govt Pos: Pres, Heath Bd Pub Affairs, Ohio, 60-62; mem, Small Bus Admin Regional Adv Bd, Columbus, Ohio, 70-; chmn, Licking Co Rep Cent Comt, 72- Bus & Prof Pos: Owner, Evans Ins Agency, Newark, Ohio, 59- Mil Serv: Entered as E-1, Army Paratroops, 54, released as SFC, 58, after serv in 101st ABN Div, Japan; Good Conduct; Am Defense Ribbon; Sr Parachutist Badge; Commendation Medal. Mem: Licking Co Independent Ins Agt Asn (pres, 72-74); Sertoma Club; Mason; Shrine. Mailing Add: 1158 Ramp Lane Heath OH 43055

EVANS, EARL WESLEY (R)
b Barlow, Ky, Aug 17, 06; s John Wesley Evans & Carrie Lancaster E; m 1936 to Lawanda Williamson; c Ellen (Mrs Phillip Noth) & John E. Educ: Georgetown Col, 1 year; Bowling Green Col Com, BS, 26. Polit & Govt Pos: Mayor, Barlow, Ky, 40-44; chmn, Ballard Co Rep Comt, Ky, formerly. Bus & Prof Pos: Elec comnr, Ballard Co, 40-44; dir, Citizens State Bank, 60- Mem: Barlow Lions Club; CofC; Ballard Co Country Club (dir, 67-); Axe Lake Hunting & Fishing Club. Relig: Baptist; Treas, Barlow First Baptist Church, 40-, Deacon, 44- Mailing Add: Barlow KY 42024

EVANS, ERNESTINE DURAN (D)
Secy of State, NMex
b Alamosa, Colo, Sept 5, 17; d Gilberto Duran & Maria de Garcia Martinez D; wid; c Stanley G. Educ: NMex Highlands Univ, 3 years. Polit & Govt Pos: NMex State Rep, 40-42; head, Royalty Div, State Land Off, 46-52; off mgr, Bd Educ Finance, 53-60; Admin Secy to Gov, 60-61 & 63-66; off mgr, Legis Coun, 61-62; Secy of State, 67-70 & 75- Bus & Prof Pos: Teacher, Rio Arriba Co Schs, 37-39; Secy, State Hwy Dept, 40-42; mem staff, Bruns Gen Hosp, Santa Fe, 42-45; saleswoman, Evans Realty Co, Santa Fe, 72-74. Mem: Orgn for Women Legis (life mem). Legal Res: 520 Acequia Madre Santa Fe NM 87501 Mailing Add: PO Box 5412 Santa Fe NM 87501

EVANS, F MAURICE (D)
Chmn, Yellowstone Co Dem Cent Comt, Mont
b El Paso, Tex, Nov 7, 30; s Leslie Schrandt (stepfather) & Berniece Burger S; m 1961 to Joan Matchette; c John & Bruce. Educ: Northern State Col, BS, 52, MSEd, 57; Stanford Univ, MA, 61; Pi Mu Epsilon. Polit & Govt Pos: Mem precinct comt, Yellowstone Co Dem Cent Comt, Mont, 65-, third vchmn, Co Comt, 69-71, chmn, 71-; Eastern Dist co-chmn, Mont State Dem Exec Comt, 71; co-chmn, Mont State Dem Educ Comt, 71; vchmn educ comt, Mont State Dem Platform Conv, 72; alt deleg, Dem Nat Conv, 72. Bus & Prof Pos: Teacher, Leola High Sch, SDak, 56-60; instr, Fullerton Jr Col, Calif, 61-63; assoc prof math, Eastern Mont Col, 63- Mil Serv: Entered as Seaman, Navy, 53, released as ETR 2, 55, after serv in Mobile Electronic Tech Unit, Pac, 54-55. Mem: Math Asn Am. Honors & Awards: Fels, Gen Elec, 58 & Nat Sci Found, 59-61 & 67-69. Relig: Protestant. Mailing Add: 400 Beverly Hill Blvd Billings MT 59101

EVANS, FAITH PATRICIA (R)
Hawaii State Rep
b Honolulu, Hawaii, May 11, 37; d Freeman Ernesto & Marie Rodrigues E; m 1962 to Noel D Evans; c Tricia, Kathleen & John. Educ: St Francis Hosp Sch Nursing, RN, 58. Polit & Govt Pos: Hawaii State Rep, 24th Dist, 74- Mem: Hawaii State PTA (third vpres); Kailua Community Coun (dir); Spec Educ Ctr of Oahu (dir); Girl Scouts Coun of Pac (mem pub rels comt); Nat Fedn Rep Women. Relig: Roman Catholic. Mailing Add: 687 Ululani St Kailua HI 96734

EVANS, FRANK EDWARD (D)
US Rep, Colo
b Pueblo, Colo, Sept 6, 23; s Frank Edward Evans (deceased) & Mildred Hoag E; m 1952 to Eleanor Trefz; c Peter, Susan, Frances & Charles. Educ: Pomona Col, Calif, 41-43; Denver Univ, BA & LLB, 46-49. Polit & Govt Pos: Colo State Rep, 61-65; US Rep, Third Cong Dist, Colo, 65- Mil Serv: Entered as Cadet, Naval Res, 43, released as Ens, 46. Mem; Am Colo & Pueblo Co Bar Asns. Relig: Presbyterian. Legal Res: Beulah CO Mailing Add: 4935 Quebec St NW Washington DC 20016

EVANS, HARRY KENT (D)
b Long Beach, Calif, July 16, 35; s Harry Carlton Evans & Elizabeth Wedelin E; m 1955 to Theresa Marie Maure; c Harry Carlton, II, Cindy Lou, Laura Lynn & Scott Kent Eugene. Educ: Univ Denver, 54-56. Polit & Govt Pos: Mem, Crime & Juv Delinquency Comn, Los Angeles Co, Calif, 68-70; deleg, Dem Nat Conv, 72. Bus & Prof Pos: Bargaining comt chmn, Local 887, UAW, 60-64, western commun dir, 64-73; western dir, Am Fedn State, Co & Munic Employees, AFL-CIO, 73- Mil Serv: Entered as Pvt, Army, 53, released as 1st Lt, 56, after serv in ChemC. Publ: Auth, Killer oil . . . still killing, 6/69 & East Los Angeles: urban vineyards, UAW Solidarity; auth, Retirement to poverty, AFL-CIO Agenda, 5/69. Mem: Calif Labor Press Asn; Los Angeles Press Club. Honors & Awards: Front Page Award, Int Labor Press Asn, 63. Mailing Add: 14503 Longworth Ave Norwalk CA 90650

EVANS, HAZEL ATKINSON (D)
Dem Nat Committeewoman, Fla
b Atlanta, Ga, Aug 16, 31; d Alex Pierce Robert & Hazel Thomas R; div; 2nd m 1968 to Robert Winfield Evans; c W Reed, Jr & Allex R Talley. Educ: Wash Sem, Atlanta, Ga, 45-49; Marjorie Webster Jr Col, Washington, DC, 49-51; Beta Sigma Phi. Polit & Govt Pos: Pres, Manatee Co Dem Women's Club, Fla, 57-60; vchmn, Manatee Co Dem Exec Comt, 62-64; state secy, Young Dem Clubs of Fla, 62-63, state vpres, 63-64; deleg, Dem Nat Conv, 64, 68 & 72, mem credentials comt, 68; state Dem committeewoman, Pinellas Co, Fla; Dem Nat Committeewoman, Fla, 68-, mem exec comt, 73-; exec dir, Inauguration of Reubin Askew as Gov of Fla, 71; comnr, Pinellas Co Housing Authority, 72- Mem: Nat Found of March of Dimes; Fla Heart Asn; Fla Ment Health Asn; Pinellas Co United Fund (bd dirs, 67-); Suncoast Heart Asn. Honors & Awards: US Sen George Smathers Award, 62, Franklin D Roosevelt Award, 63 & President's Awards, 63 & 64, Young Dem Clubs of Fla; Am Heart Asn Meritorious Serv Awards, 60, 64 & 66. Relig: Baptist. Mailing Add: 1146 41st Ave NE St Petersburg FL 33703

EVANS, HELEN WITTEN (R)
b Tazewell, Va, Aug 5, 05; d Joseph Witten & Sallie W; m 1927 to John Clyde Evans; c John Robert. Educ: Bluefield Teachers Col, 23; Va State Col, Educ Degree, 27; Ohio State Univ. Polit & Govt Pos: Field reviewer, Dept of Welfare, Ohio, 39-51; asst cashier, State Treas, 51-60; mem, Ohio Rep Coun, Rep State Comt, 52-, exec secy, 71-; dep auditor, Ohio, 60-62; dept dir, Indust Rels, Ohio, 62-71, consult, 71; alt deleg, Rep Nat Conv, 72. Mem: Women's Rep Fedn. Relig: Methodist. Mailing Add: Rte 5 Marysville OH 43040

EVANS, HOWARD DAVID (D)
b Mystic, Iowa, Apr 24, 91; s Lee Edgar Evans & Minnie Haines E; m 1914 to Jessie Lee Long; c Byron Long, Enid (Mrs Jack Beattie) & Claud Richard. Educ: Mystic High Sch, 11. Polit & Govt Pos: Clerk, Dist Court, Centerville, Iowa, 32-40; chmn, Appanoose Co Dem Cent Comt, formerly. Bus & Prof Pos: Farmer & livestock shipper, Mystic, 14-28; auto & machinery dealer, Centerville, until 51; owner, real estate agency, 51- Mem: Elks; Mason; Rotary Int. Relig: Methodist. Mailing Add: Country Club Rd Centerville IA 52544

EVANS, HUBERT CAROL (D)
Treas, Tenth Cong Dist Dem Comt, Mich
b Beaverton, Mich, Dec 25, 21; s A C P Evans & Edna E Walke; m 1946 to Delaine A Boske; c Mark Brian. Educ: Univ Mich, 56; Mich State Univ, 57; Cent Mich Univ, 58. Polit & Govt Pos: Councilman, Gladwin, Mich, 61; cand for State Senate to fill vacancy, 28th Sen Dist & Const Conv, 28th Sen Dist, 61; chmn, Gladwin Co Dem Comt, 61-72; cand, US Rep, Tenth Dist, 62, 64 & 66; treas, Tenth Cong Dist Dem Comt, 67-; alt deleg, Dem Nat Conv, 68; mayor pro tem & mem police comt, Gladwin, 69. Mil Serv: Entered as Pvt, Army, 42, released as Pfc, 45, after serv in 49th Combat Engr, European-African-Mid Eastern Theatres, 43-45; Good Conduct Medal; Am Theatre Serv Medal; European, African, Mid Eastern Theatre Medals with Five Bronze Stars. Mem: United Mine Workers of Am; Mich Munic League. Relig: Lutheran. Mailing Add: 529 N Antler Gladwin MI 48624

EVANS, JAMES LARKIN (D)
Mem, Calif Dem State Cent Comt
b Mallakaoff, Tex, Aug 10, 21; s Frank Lewis Evans & Clyde Kennedy E; c Janice Louise, Larry Ray Joyce & James L, Jr. Educ: Mallakaoff High Sch, Tex, grad, 36. Polit & Govt Pos: Campaign chmn of various Dem cand, 56-64; chmn, Co Dem Cent Comt, Calif, 58-60; mem civil & const rights comt, Attorney Gen Comn, 59-62; mem & dir, 28th Agr Dist Asn, 59-63; sgt-at-arms, Calif Dem Deleg, 60; mem, San Bernardino City Civil Serv Comn, 60-62; mem, Calif Dem State Cent Comt, 68- Bus & Prof Pos: Locomotive fireman & engr, San Bernardino, 44-64; coach, mgr & founder, East Baseline Little League, 53-57; Calif state legis dir, United Transportation Union, Sacramento, 64-73, dir, 73- Mem: Arrowhead United Fund; Mason; Elks; Roofers Local; Teamsters. Relig: Protestant. Mailing Add: Rm 552 1127 11th St Sacramento CA 95814

EVANS, JAMES WELDON (R)
Chmn, Terry Co Rep Party, Tex
b Post, Tex, Feb 14, 26; s Charles Cranfil Evans; m 1950 to Janelle Jo Turner. Educ: Tex Tech Univ, BBA, 50; Tech Mgt Asn; Saddle Tramps. Polit & Govt Pos: Chmn, Terry Co Rep Party, Tex, 60-; alt deleg, Rep Nat Conv, 68. Bus & Prof Pos: With Amoco Prod Co, 50-; part-time instr, South Plains Col, currently. Mil Serv: Entered as Pvt, Marines, 43, released as Cpl, 45, after serv in 3rd Marine Div, Pac Theater; Lt Col (Ret), Air Force Res; Asiatic-Pac Ribbon with Two Stars; Naval Unit Citation; Presidential Unit Citation; Victory, Am Theater & Air Force Res Ribbons. Mem: ROA; Am Legion; Third Marine Div Asn; Optimist Club; Tex Tech Alumni Asn. Relig: Baptist. Legal Res: 1204 E Warren Brownfield TX 79316 Mailing Add: PO Box 3 Brownfield TX 79316

EVANS, JOHN F (R)
Chmn, Champaign Co Rep Exec Comt, Ohio
b Mechanicsburg, Ohio, July 3, 18; s Earl E Evans (deceased) & Florence Frank E (deceased); m 1941 to Ruth Iloh Rasmussen; c Jane E, Margaret A & John E. Educ: Ohio State Univ, 37-38. Polit & Govt Pos: Pres, Mechanicsburg Bd Educ, Ohio, 51-55; exec secy, Ohio Rep Farm Div, 54-; vchmn, Champaign Co Rep Exec Comt, 57-59, chmn, 59-; mem, Ohio Expos Comn, 64-, secy, 70-72; mem, Champaign Co Elec Bd, 66-; chmn, Champaign Co Rep Cent Comt, 70-; deleg, Rep Nat Conv, 72. Mem: Ohio Shorthorns Breeders Asn; Ohio Jr CofC; US Jr CofC; Urbana Area CofC (bd dirs, 69-72). Mailing Add: RFD 2 Mechanicsburg OH 43044

EVANS, JOHN MARION (R)
b Sumter, SC, Jan 15, 22; s John Lynwood Evans & Mildred Boone E; m 1942 to Elizabeth Dingle; c John Dickey, Ingrid Elaine & Henry Pitts. Educ: Presby Col, Clinton, SC. Polit & Govt Pos: Mem, Sumter Co Planning Comn, Va, 61-62, secy, 62-63, chmn, 63-64; chmn, Sumter Co Rep Party, 63-66; vchmn, Comn for Higher Educ, 65-69; Sumter Co Rep campaign dir; adv to Cent Adv Comt; former mem, SC State Rep Comt; exec dir, SC Rep Party, 67-68; exec asst to Sen Strom Thurmond, SC, 69- Bus & Prof Pos: Pres, John Evans Sales Co, 52-56; pres, Evans Realty Co, 56-68 & Broad St Realty Co, 64-68. Mil Serv: Entered as Pvt, Air Force, 42, released as S/Sgt, 45, after serv with 1st Air Force. Mem: Mason; Shrine; Jester; Kiwanis; Am Legion. Relig: Methodist. Mailing Add: 8512 Canterberry Dr Annandale VA 20003

EVANS, JOHN VICTOR (D)
Lt Gov, Idaho
b Malad City, Idaho, Jan 18, 25; s David Lloyd Evans & Margaret Thomas E; m 1945 to Lola Daniels; c David L, John V, Jr, Martha Anne, Susan Dee & Thomas Daniels. Educ: Idaho State Univ; Stanford Univ. Polit & Govt Pos: Idaho State Sen, 53-57 & 67-74, majority leader, Idaho State Senate, 57-59, minority leader, 69-74, mayor, Malad, 60-66; chmn, Law Enforcement Planning Comt, 75-; chmn, Subcomt, State Land Bd Lease Rates & Policies, 75-; Lt Gov, 75- Bus & Prof Pos: Vpres & dir, J N Ireland & Co, Bankers, 55-75; vpres, B B Water Users, 63-65; pres, Deep Creek Irrigation Co, 65-73; pres, Oneida Co RC&D, 68-74. Mil Serv: Entered as Pvt, Army Inf, 44, released as T/Sgt, after serv in 7th Div, Asiatic Pac, 45-46; Asiatic Pac Ribbon; Good Conduct Medal. Mem: Mason; Am Legion; Eagles; VFW; Farm Bur. Honors & Awards: Distinguished Serv Award, Asn Idaho Cities, 74. Mailing Add: Rte 1 Box 1 Malad City ID 83252

EVANS, LLOYD RUSSELL, JR (RUSS) (R)
Mem, Rep State Cent Comt Conn
b Danbury, Conn, Apr 21, 47; s Lloyd Russell Evans & Ada Lee Nichols E; single. Educ: Univ Md, 67; Wesleyan Univ, BA, 70; Alpha Delta Phi. Polit & Govt Pos: Rec & control clerk, Agency Int Develop, 66-67; staff asst, May for US Senate, 68; campaign asst, Steele for Cong, 69-70, campaign dir, 72; admin asst to US Rep Robert H Steele, Conn, 70-75; campaign mgr, Steele for Gov, 74; polit consult, 75-; mem, Rep State Cent Comt Conn, currently. Bus & Prof Pos: Asst to mgr, H L Reynolds Co, Lyme, Conn, 63-67; mgr, Star & Crescent Club, Middletown, 68-69; computerization rec chief, Wesleyan Univ, 69; wildlife consult, Northeast Utilities, Haddam, 69; gen partner, Conn Consults, 74- Publ: In re Gault: Juv Court Proc, 70. Mem: Adelphic Lit Soc (bd trustees); Adelphic Educ Fund, Inc (bd trustees); New Hope Manor, Inc (dir, 71-); hon mem Eastern Conn Develop Coun, Inc. Relig: Congregational. Legal Res: 68B Prospect St Willimantic CT 06226 Mailing Add: PO Box 365 Willimantic CT 06226

EVANS, MELVIN H (R)
Gov, VI
b Christiansted, St Croix, VI, Aug 7, 17; s Charles Herbert Evans & Maude Rogers E; m 1945 to Mary Phyllis Anderson; c Melvin Herbert Jr, Robert Rogiers, William Charles & Cornelius Duncan. Educ: Howard Univ Col Lib Arts, BS, 40, Howard Univ Col Med, MD, 44; Univ Calif, Berkeley, MPH, 67. Hon Degrees: DHL, Morgan State Col, 71; LLD, Howard Univ, 72. Polit & Govt Pos: Physician-in-charge, Govt of the VI, Frederiksted, 45-48 & 50-51; sr asst surgeon, US Pub Health Serv, Washington, DC, 48-50; chief munic physician, Govt of VI, St Croix, 51-56 & 57-59, Comnr of Health, 56-67; Gov of VI, 69-; deleg, Rep Nat Conv, 72. Bus & Prof Pos: Intern, Harlem Hosp, New York, 44-45; fel cardiol, Johns Hopkins Hosp, Md, 56-57; pvt practice internal med, St Croix, 67-69. Mil Serv: 2nd Lt (inactive) in Med Admin Corps A, US, 42-45. Publ: The late hemo dynamic effects of the Blaylock-Taussig Operation for the tetralogy of fallot, Circulation, 57. Mem: VI Med Soc; Am & Nat Med Asns; charter mem Am Asn of Pub Health Physicians; Am Pub Health Asn. Honors & Awards: Howard Univ Alumni Award; Am Legion Citizenship Award, 70; Trustees' Distinguished Achievement Serv Award, Fairleigh Dickinson Univ, 72; Pub Health Award, NJ Health Indust Comt, 72. Relig: Wesleyan. Legal Res: Gov House Charlotte Amalie St Thomas VI 00801 Mailing Add: PO Box 599 Charlotte Amalie St Thomas VI 00801

EVANS, PATRICIA ANNE (PATTY) (D)
VChairperson, Ind Dem State Cent Comt
b Koleen, Ind, Aug 4, 29; d Victor L Wright & Mary Lucas W; m 1947 to Floyd O Evans, Jr; c Christine (Mrs Rodney B Miller), Nancy (Mrs Larry R Patterson) & Barbara. Educ: Ind State Univ, 63-64, 65-66. Polit & Govt Pos: Vchairperson, Greene Co Dem Party, Ind, 68-74; vchairperson, Seventh Cong Dist Dem Party, 70-; deleg, Dem Nat Mid-Term Conf, 74; vchairperson, Ind Dem State Cent Comt, 74-; dir women's activities, Ind Fedn Dem Women, 74- Relig: First United Methodist. Legal Res: 78 First St SE Linton IN 47441 Mailing Add: 311 W Washington Indianapolis IN 46204

EVANS, R G (RON) (R)
Minn State Rep
Mailing Add: 1104 Woodland Ave Mankato MN 56001

EVANS, RACHEL WIEGMAN (R)
Co-Chmn, Webster Co Rep Cent Comt, Iowa
b Rolfe, Iowa, Mar 19, 23; d Henry Cyrus Wiegman & Marie Hauck W; m 1944 to John Hedrick Evans; c Linda Sue & Jeffery John. Educ: Grinnell Col, 41-42; Iowa State Univ, BS, 45; Gamma Phi Beta. Polit & Govt Pos: Co-chmn, Webster Co Rep Cent Comt, Iowa, 68-; deleg, Rep Nat Conv, 72; co-chmn, Sixth Dist Rep Party, 73- Mem: PEO; Fedn Rep Women; Forward Ft Dodge; YWCA; Cyclone Club. Relig: Presbyterian; Deaconess, First Presby Church. Mailing Add: 1142 N 19th St Ft Dodge IA 50501

EVANS, RICHARD FULTON (R)
Nat Committeeman, Ky Young Rep
b Owensboro, Ky, Jan 3, 49; s Benjamin Fulton Evans & Anna Lou May E; m 1972 to Joanne Wood Fore. Educ: Ky Wesleyan Col, BS, 71; Sigma Alpha Mu. Polit & Govt Pos: Region III chmn, Col Rep Nat Comt, 71-72; chmn, McLean Co Rep Party, Ky, 71-72; chmn, Ky Col Rep Fedn, 72-73; treas, Col Rep Nat Comt, 72-73, vchmn, 73-74; mem, Ky Rep State Cent Comt, 74-; nat committeeman, Ky Young Rep, 75- Mem: Lions Club; Owensboro Jaycees; Livermore Island CofC. Honors & Awards: Ky Col, Ky Gov Louie B Nunn, 69; Dwight David Eisenhower Award, Nat Rep Party, 70. Relig: Baptist. Mailing Add: 517 Maple Ave Owensboro KY 42301

EVANS, RICHARD H (R)
b Philadelphia, Pa, Sept 26, 34; s Francis C Evans & Dorothy Hamilton E; m 1962 to Arlene Joan Ewer; c Cynthia Joan, Richard H, Jr & Scott Allen. Educ: Pa State Univ, 1 year; Univ Pa, grad. Polit & Govt Pos: Rep committeeman, Dover, Del, 66, Wilmington, 68; dist elec chmn, Wilmington, 68; deleg, Del Rep State Conv, 68 & 70; admin asst to US Rep Pierre S duPont, IV, 71- Bus & Prof Pos: Mgr, Diamond State Tel Co, 63-70. Mil Serv: Entered as Pvt, Army, 55, released as Spec-3, 57, after serv in 22nd Tank Bn, 1st Armored Div, Ft Knox, Ky. Mem: Del State CofC; Rotary; Brandywine Hundred Kiwanis Club. Relig: Episcopal. Mailing Add: 1510 Flynt Pl Crofton MD 21113

EVANS, THOMAS BEVERLEY, JR (R)
Rep Nat Committeeman, Del
b Nashville, Tenn, Nov 5, 31; s Thomas Beverley Evans & Hannah Hundley E; m 1961 to Mary Page Hilliard; c Thomas Beverley, III, Robert Speir & Mary Page. Educ: Univ Va, Charlottesville, BA, 53, LLB, 56; Student Coun; capt, Golf Team; Phi Alpha Delta; Delta Phi. Polit & Govt Pos: Mem, Del Finance Comt for Goldwater for President, 64; mem, Del Finance Comt for Roth for Cong, 66; mem, Del Rep Finance Comt & Del Rep State Comt, 66-; chmn, Nixon-Agnew Campaign Comt, Del, 68; chmn, Nixon for President Comt, Del, 68; regional chmn, Nixon-Agnew Finance Comt, 68; chmn, Del Inaugural Comt, 69; dir, Del State Develop Dept, 69-70; regular chmn & mem exec comt, Rep Nat Finance Comt, 69-71, dep chmn, 69-71; chmn, Agnew Dinner Comt, Del, 70; Rep Nat Committeeman, Del, 70-; co-chmn, Rep Nat Comt, 71-, mem exec comt, currently; deleg, Rep Nat Conv, 72; hon chmn, 1973 Nat Inaugural Comt, 73. Bus & Prof Pos: Pres, Evans & Assocs, Inc, Del, 62- Mil Serv: Entered as Pvt, Del Army Nat Guard, 56, released as Sgt, 60, after serv in Battery A 1 Bn. Publ: Various speeches & guest ed & articles. Mem: Million Dollar Round Table; Wilmington Country Club; Wilmington Club; Pine Valley Golf Club; Vicmead Hunt Club. Honors & Awards: Nat Hiring-the-Handicapped Award, 70. Relig: Episcopal. Legal Res: 1111 Brandon Lane Westover Hills Wilmington DE 19807 Mailing Add: Evans & Assocs Delaware Trust Bldg Wilmington DE 19801

EVANS, WARREN D (D)
Ga State Rep
Mailing Add: PO Box 670 Thomson GA 30824

EVANS, WILLIAM ROBERT (D)
Mem, Dem State Cent Comt Md
b Baltimore, Md, Apr 3, 45; s William Thomas Evans & Mary Smith E; m 1968 to Judith Ann Bock. Educ: John Carroll Univ, BS, 67; Univ Baltimore Law Sch, JD, 73; Alpha Kappa Psi; Phi Alpha Beta. Polit & Govt Pos: Mem, Dem State Cent Comt Md, 74- Bus & Prof Pos: Attorney, Dundalk, Md, 73- Mil Serv: Entered as Airman, Air Nat Guard, 67, released as

S/Sgt, 73. Mem: Lions (bd dirs); YMCA (bd mgrs). Relig: Protestant. Legal Res: 1617 Four Georges Ct Baltimore MD 21222 Mailing Add: 2 N Dundalk Ave Dundalk MD 21222

EVARTS, KATHARINE AVERY (R)
Mem, Kent Town Rep Comt, Conn
b Oyster Bay, NY, Oct 29, 98; d Edwin Denison Morgan & Elizabeth Moran M; m to Jeremiah Maxwell Evarts, div; c Mary (Mrs Steele), Maxwell, Katharine (Mrs Albert W Merck), Elizabeth (Mrs Casimir de Rham, Jr) & Jasper Morgan. Educ: Brearley Sch, New York; Merchants & Bankers Bus Sch, New York, Radcliffe Col, studies hist. Polit & Govt Pos: Former mem, Kent Park & Recreation Comn; Conn State Rep, Kent, 59-67; former mem & vchmn, Kent Town Planning Comn, chmn, 61; pres, Litchfield Co Rep Women's Asn, 62-63; mem, Kent Town Rep Comt, currently, vchmn, 66-69; chmn state fund drive, Conn Child Welfare Asn, formerly, vpres & bd dirs, several years. Bus & Prof Pos: Dairy farmer, Conn, 42- Mem: Grange; Litchfield Co Farm Bur; League of Women Voters; Housatonic Valley Asn. Relig: Congregational; mem, Bd Deacons, 1st Congregational Church, Kent, formerly. Mailing Add: Cobble Rd Kent CT 06757

EVATT, HARMON PARKER (R)
SC State Rep
b Greenville, SC, Aug 27, 35; s Haskell Dewey Evatt & Ruby Parker E; m 1960 to Jane Mangum; c Kathy & Alan. Educ: Univ SC, BS in ME, 58; Pi Kappa Alpha. Polit & Govt Pos: SC State Rep, 75- Bus & Prof Pos: Mech engr, SC State Hwy Dept, 60-66; exec dir, Alston Wilkes Soc, 66- Mil Serv: Entered as Ens, Navy, 58, released as Lt(jg), 60, after serv in USS Skagit, AKA 105; Comdr, Naval Res; Armed Forces Medal; Expeditionary Award-Taiwan Straits. Mem: Five Points Rotary (treas); Int Halfway House Asn (vpres); Carolina Naval Res Asn (pres); Mid-Carolina Coun on Alcoholism (bd dirs); Columbia Res Officers Asn (vpres). Honors & Awards: Faith in God Award, SC Jaycees, 69; Distinguished Serv Award, St Andrews Jaycees. Relig: United Methodist. Legal Res: 258 Chartwell Rd Columbia SC 29210 Mailing Add: PO Box 363 Columbia SC 29202

EVE, ARTHUR O (D)
NY State Assemblyman
b New York, NY, Mar 23, 33; s Arthur B Eve & Beatrice Clark E; m 1956 to Lee Constance Bowles; c Arthur, Jr, Leecia R, Eric V & twins Martin K & Malcolm X. Educ: WVa State Col, 50-53; Erie Co Tech Inst, 57; Canisius Col, evening sch, 62-63. Polit & Govt Pos: Founder & vpres, Masten Dist Young Dem, NY, 58; committeeman, 13th Ward Dem Comt, 60-, vchmn, 60-62 & chmn, 62-; NY State Assemblyman, 143rd Dist, 67-; deleg, Dem Nat Conv, 72. Bus & Prof Pos: Engr, City of Buffalo Civil Serv, 59-; ed & pres, Buffalo Challenger News Weekly, 62- Mil Serv: Entered as Pvt, Army Signal Corps, 53, released as Cpl, 55, after serv in Ger. Mem: Amvets; NAACP; Urban League; United Auto Workers. Honors & Awards: Basketball: All City & State, Miami, Fla, 48; All CIAA, WVa State Col, 52; All Army, Ger, 54. Relig: Episcopal; vestryman. Mailing Add: 14 Celtic Pl Buffalo NY 14208

EVELTI, MARY M (D)
Vt State Rep
Mailing Add: 4 Scarff Ave Burlington VT 05401

EVERETT, ANNABELLE SMITH (BELLE) (D)
b Marydel, Md, Oct 15, 98; d Frank S Smith & Mary E Bickling S; m 1916 to Levi L Everett, Jr; c Franklin L & T Marvel. Polit & Govt Pos: State Treas, Del, 59-67; Dem Nat Committeewoman, formerly; vchmn, Kent Co Dem Party, 18 years, state vchmn & mem state comt, 8 years; organizer & pres, Kent Co Women's Den Club, 7 years; mem bd, State Dept Welfare, 10 years; deleg, Dem Nat Conv, 68. Bus & Prof Pos: Former bd mem, Childrens Bur, Del. Relig: Methodist; mem bd & treas, Kenton Methodist Church. Mailing Add: Kenton DE 19955

EVERETT, DONN JAMES (R)
Majority Leader, Kans House Rep
b Emporia, Kans, Apr 29, 29; s Harry Willard Everett & Nelle Batchelor E; m 1956 to Fredrica Voiland; c Brinton, Bradford, Brooke, Brian Brock & Bridget. Educ: Col Emporia, 47-49; Univ Kans, AB, 51, LLB, 56; Sigma Alpha Epsilon. Polit & Govt Pos: Asst city attorney, Manhattan, Kans, 58-63, city comnr, 68-69; co attorney, Riley Co, 64-68; Kans State Rep, 69-, Majority Leader, Kans House Rep, 73- Mil Serv: Entered as Pvt, Marines, 51, released as 1st Lt, 53, after serv in First Marine Div, Korea, 52-53; Marine Corps Res; Bronze Star; Combat V Medal. Mem: Judicature Soc; Am Legion; Elks; VFW; Manhattan CofC. Honors & Awards: Distinguished Serv Award, City of Manhattan, 63. Relig: Episcopal. Legal Res: 1730 Fairview Manhattan KS 66502 Mailing Add: PO Box 816 Manhattan KS 66502

EVERETT, JESSE HERBERT (R)
Ariz State Rep
b Inverness, Miss, Mar 28, 07; s Jesse Jones Everett & Lula Till E; m 1930 to Nell Jester; m 1966 to Kathryn Wilson Doom; c Shirley Deane (Mrs Bowden); Marilyn (Mrs Thompson). Educ: Miss Col, 25-27; Wash Univ, BS, 29. Polit & Govt Pos: Alderman, Tutwiller, Miss, 47-49; mem, Planning Comn, Youngtown, Ariz, 67-71, mem, Zoning Bd, 71-72; Ariz State Rep, Dist 15, 73- Bus & Prof Pos: Wholesale & retail grocer, Tutwiller, Miss, 31-49; farm operator, 41-66; chem sales engr, 50-66; realtor, Youngtown, Ariz, 66-74. Mem: Farm Bur; Kiwanis; Mason & Shrine; Lions; Acacia Club. Honors & Awards: Kiwanis Outstanding Leadership Award, 72; Best Sales Award, Delta Chem Corp, 53, 55, 56 & 60. Relig: Southern Baptist; deacon. Legal Res: 11454 114th Dr Youngtown AZ 85363 Mailing Add: Drawer 218 Youngtown AZ 85363

EVERETT, REYNOLDS MELVILLE (R)
b Atkinson, Ill, Aug 1, 07; s Melville M Everett & Maude Reynolds E; m 1935 to Annette Young; c Reynolds M, Jr. Educ: Knox Col, 24-26; Univ Ill, LLB, 26-29; Delta Sigma Rho; Zeta Psi; Gamma Eta Gamma. Polit & Govt Pos: States attorney, Henry Co, Ill, 44-52; Asst Attorney Gen, Ill, 53-60 & 69-; chmn, Henry Co Rep Party, Ill, formerly. Bus & Prof Pos: Mem bd gov, Ill State Bar Asn, 60-63. Mem: AF&AM: Elks; Consistory; Shrine; Odd Fellows. Relig: Congregational. Legal Res: 412 NW Fourth St Galva IL 61434 Mailing Add: Yocum Bank Bldg Galva IL 61434

EVERETT, RUTH C (DEMING) (R)
b Colebrook, Conn, Jan 25, 15; d Homer P Deming & Harriet Moore D; m 1951 to Donald Ernest Everett. Educ: Gilbert Sch, Winsted, Conn, grad & 2 years postgrad. Polit & Govt Pos: Registr, Rep voters, Colebrook, Conn, 54-; chmn, Colebrook Rep Town Comt, formerly. Bus & Prof Pos: Secy, J C Burwell, Inc, Winsted, Conn, 36-45; secy, Carnell Co, 45-61. Mem: Riverton Grange; P of H; Rebekah; Conn Package Stores Asn; DAR. Relig: Protestant. Legal Res: Deer Hill Rd Colebrook CT 06021 Mailing Add: RFD 4 Winsted CT 06098

EVERIDGE, MARY JAMES (JIM) (D)
b Tampa, Fla, Dec 16, 30; d James Franklin Smith & Mary Ellen Hancock Miles S; m 1946 to James Ralph Everidge, Sr; c Mary Elizabeth (Mrs Peters) & James Ralph, Jr. Educ: Fla Southern Col; Fla State Univ; Univ Fla. Polit & Govt Pos: Dist committeewoman, Young Dem Fla, 67-69; treas, Hillsborough Co Young Dem, 68-69; precinct committeewoman, Hillsborough Co Dem Comt, 11 years; treas, Hillsborough Co Dem Exec Comt, 68-71, vchairperson, 71-74; pres, Dem Women's Club Fla, Inc, 73-75; deleg, Dem Nat Mid-Term Conf, 74. Bus & Prof Pos: Owner & operator day nursery, Plant City, Fla, 58-61; dir, Mary Jim Show, Radio Sta WPLA, Plant City, 61-64; exten worker, Plant City Neighborhood Serv Ctr, 67-69; tax info clerk & East Hills off mgr, Hills Co Tax Assessor, 69-72; vol coordr, Hills Co Dept Children's Serv, 73- Mem: Dem Women's Club Fla, Inc; Fla Bus & Prof Women's Club; Fla Cong PTA. Honors & Awards: Community Serv Award, Plant City Jr Woman's Club, 49-50; Woman of Year, Plant City Bus & Prof Women's Club, 64 & 65; Commendation for Outstanding Vol Serv, Women in Community Serv, Inc, 68; Good Govt Award, Plant City Jaycees, 74. Relig: United Methodist. Mailing Add: 502 E DeVane St Plant City FL 33566

EVERIX, MURIEL KATHERINE (R)
VChmn, Wis Rep Party
b Chicago, Ill, Oct 19, 14; d Henry Arthur Marsh & Lillian Groetzinger M; m 1937 to Mark Peter Everix; c M DeWitt. Educ: Chicago Art Inst, scholar, 33; Univ Wis-Madison, statist course, 36. Polit & Govt Pos: Vchmn, Calumet Co Rep Party, Wis, 60-70; organizer, Calumet Co Fedn Rep Women, 64; Wis chmn, Wash Women's Conf, Washington, DC, 65-67; first vpres, Wis Fedn Rep Women, 67-68, pres, 69-75; secy, Sixth Cong Dist Rep Orgn, 67-69; fifth vchmn, Wis Rep Party, 69-; deleg, Rep Nat Conv, 72. Mem: New Holstein Hist Soc. Relig: Presbyterian. Mailing Add: 718 S Madison St Chilton WI 53014

EVERS, JAMES CHARLES (D)
Dem Nat Committeeman, Miss
b Decatur, Miss, Sept 11, 22; s Jim Evers & Jessie Wright E. Educ: Alcorn A&M Col, BA. Polit & Govt Pos: Dem cand for US Rep, Miss, 68; Dem Nat Committeeman, Miss, 68-, mem exec comt, Dem Nat Comt, currently; mayor, Fayette, Miss, 69-; nominee for Gov, Miss, 71; deleg, Dem Nat Conv, 72. Bus & Prof Pos: Exec dir, Medgar Evers Shopping Ctr, 65-; pres, Medgar Evers Fund, 69- Mil Serv: Entered as Pvt, Army, released as M/Sgt. Relig: Baptist. Mailing Add: PO Box 605 Fayette MS 39069

EVERSON, HARLAND E (D)
Wis State Rep
Mailing Add: Box 750 RR 3 Edgerton WI 53534

EVINS, JOE LANDON (D)
US Rep, Tenn
b Smithville, Tenn, Oct 24, 10; s James Edgar Evins & Myrtie Goodson E; m 1935 to Ann Smartt; c Joanna (Mrs Carnahan), Jane Fancher (Mrs Leonard) & Mary Adelaide. Educ: Vanderbilt Univ; Cumberland Univ Law Sch; George Washington Univ Post Grad Sch; Phi Kappa Sigma; Phi Delta Phi. Polit & Govt Pos: Past chmn, DeKalb Co Dem Exec Comt; mem legal staff & asst secy, Fed Trade Comn, 35-41; deleg, Dem Nat Conv, 56, 58, 60, 64 & 68; US Rep, Fourth Dist, Tenn, 57-, mem, Comt on Appropriations, US House Rep, chmn, Small Bus Comt, chmn, Independent Off & Housing & Urban Develop Appropriations Subcomt, 64-70, chmn, Subcomt on Pub Works Appropriations, 71- Bus & Prof Pos: Chmn bd, First Nat Bank, Smithville, Tenn, 60-73. Mil Serv: Entered as 1st Lt, Army, 42, released as Maj, 46, after serv in Judge Adv Gen Corps, ETO; Cross of Mil Serv. Publ: Understanding Congress, Clarkson Potter, 62. Mem: Tenn & Am Bar Asns; Am Legion; VFW; Mason (33 degree). Relig: Church of Christ. Legal Res: 300 E Main St Smithville TN 37166 Mailing Add: 2300 Rayburn Bldg Washington DC 20515

EWALD, DOUGLAS R (DOUG) (R)
Minn State Rep
Mailing Add: 15025 Highland Trail Minnetonka MN 55343

EWELL, RAYMOND WHITNEY (D)
Ill State Rep
b Chicago, Ill, Dec 29, 28; s Whitney Ewell & Severine Ray E; m 1953 to Joyce Marie Haywood; c David Raymond & Marc Whitney. Educ: Univ Ill, BA, 49, MA, 51; Univ Chicago, JD, 54. Polit & Govt Pos: Adv, 17th Ward Young Dem, Ill, 64-; Ill State Rep, 29th Dist, 67- Bus & Prof Pos: Teacher, Chicago Bd of Educ, 49-57; attorney-at-law, Ewell, Graham, McCormick, Davidson & Ross, 56- Mil Serv: Pfc, Army, 54-55. Relig: Episcopal. Mailing Add: 52 W 78th St Chicago IL 60620

EWEN, WARREN GAIL (R)
Co-Chmn, Webster Co Rep Comt, Iowa
b Milford, Iowa, Apr 1, 25; s Roscoe W Ewen & Freida Erickson E; m 1946 to Veneta DeWitt; c Teresa Bailey, Eric DeWitt & Kristin L. Educ: Univ Iowa, BSEE, 49. Polit & Govt Pos: Co-chmn, Webster Co Rep Comt, Iowa, 74- Bus & Prof Pos: Engr, IIG&E Co, Davenport, Iowa, 49-57, asst supt elec distribution, 57-59, supt elec distribution, Ft Dodge, 59- Mil Serv: Entered as Pvt, Air Force, 43, released as Flight Officer, 46. Mem: Inst Elec & Electronics Engrs; Elks; Am Legion; Rotary. Relig: Methodist. Mailing Add: 1432 N 16th St Ft Dodge IA 50501

EWING, BAYARD (R)
b Sorrento, Mo, Aug 19, 16; s Thomas Ewing & Anna Cochran E; m 1939 to Harriet M Kelley; c Linda L (Mrs Hamlin), Gillian C (Mrs M W Ehrich), Bayard C, Gifford P & Harriet K. Educ: Yale Univ, AB, 38; Harvard Univ, LLB, 41. Polit & Govt Pos: Mem, Rep State Cent Comt, RI, 48-70; deleg, Rep Nat Conv, 48-68; mem, RI Pub Expenditures Coun; RI State Rep, 50-52; cand for US Sen, 52 & 58; Rep Nat Committeeman, RI, 55-68; mem, RI Rep State Cent Comt, 49-71; mem, Rep Nat Finance Comt, 70-71. Bus & Prof Pos: Partner, Tillinghast, Collins & Graham, Providence, 49-; dir, Old Stone Bank & Old Stone Realty Trust; chmn, RI Sch of Design. Mem: Am & RI Bar Asns; Mason (32 degree); United Way of Am, Inc. Relig: Episcopal. Legal Res: 41 Waterman St Providence RI 02906 Mailing Add: 2000 Hosp Trust Tower Providence RI 02903

EWING, JOHN H (R)
NJ State Assemblyman
Mailing Add: State House Trenton NJ 08625

EWING, LYNN MOORE, JR (D)
Committeeman, Mo State Dem Cent Comt
b Nevada, Mo, Nov 14, 30; s Lynn Moore Ewing & Margaret Rae Blair E; m 1954 to Peggy Patton Adams; c Margaret Grace, Melissa Lee & Lynn Moore, III. Educ: Univ Mo, AB, 52; LLB, 54; Phi Beta Kappa; Order of the Coif; Sigma Nu. Polit & Govt Pos: Mo House of Rep, 59-64; city councilman, Nevada, Mo, 67-, mayor, 69-70 & 71-72; committeeman, Mo State Dem Cent Comt, 68-; chmn, Vernon Co Dem Comt, 70-72. Bus & Prof Pos: Vpres & trust officer, Citizens State Bank, Nevada, Mo, currently; dir & gen counsel, Farm & Home Savings Asn, currently. Mil Serv: Entered as 2nd Lt, Air Force, 54, released as 1st Lt, 56, after serv in 475th Fighter Interceptor Group, Air Defense Command, 54-56. Publ: Missouri condominium law, Mo Bar J, 63. Mem: Vernon Co, Mo & Am Bar Asns; US Savings & Loan League; Mo Savings & Loan League. Relig: Episcopal. Mailing Add: 146 Country Club Dr Nevada MO 64772

EWING, THOMAS W (R)
Ill State Sen
Mailing Add: 324 S Mill St Pontiac IL 61764

EWING, WAYNE S (R)
Pa State Sen
Mailing Add: 148 Poplar Dr Mt Lebanon PA 15228

EXLER, JOHN J (D)
Mem, Pa Dem State Exec Comt
b Pittsburgh, Pa, Mar 29, 17; s John E Exler & Elizabeth McConnell E; m 1944 to Ruth Haberman; c Ellen (Mrs Lavender), Janice & John J, Jr. Educ: High sch. Polit & Govt Pos: Recorder of Deeds, Allegheny Co, Pa, 47-; agent, Sale of Pa Realty Transfer Tax Stamps, Commonwealth of Pa, 52-; deleg, Dem Nat Conv, 68; mem, Pa Dem State Exec Comt, currently; agent, Sale of Munic Stamps, Co of Pa, 72- Mil Serv: Army, 42-46. Mem: Pa Recorders Asn; KofC; KofE; VFW; Am Legion. Honors & Awards: Pa Most Outstanding Disabled Vet Award, 62. Relig: Catholic. Legal Res: 10 Mt Hope St Pittsburgh PA 15223 Mailing Add: County Off Bldg Pittsburgh PA 15219

EXON, JOHN JAMES (D)
Gov, Nebr
b Geddes, SDak, Aug 9, 21; s John James Exon, Sr & Luella Johns E; m 1943 to Patricia A Pros; c Stephen James, Pamela Ann & Candace Lee. Educ: Univ Omaha, 39-41. Polit & Govt Pos: Active on state comts for Lt Gov Sorensen, 54, US Rep Callan, 54 & Gov Brooks, 57; state campaign mgr, Morrison for Gov Comt, 59; deleg, Dem Nat Conv, 64, alt deleg, 72; state coordr, Johnson-Humphrey Campaign, 64; chmn, Nebr Jefferson-Jackson Day Dinner, 65; mem exec comt, Nebr Dem State Dem Party, 64-; vchmn, Nebr State Dem Cent Comt, 64-68; Dem Nat Committeeman, Nebr, 68-70; Gov, Nebr, 71-; mem, Educ Comn of the States, currently; mem exec comt, Nat Gov Conf, 71 & Dem Gov, 71 & 74; vchmn, Midwest Gov Conf, 73, chmn, 74; co-chmn, Old West Regional Comt, 74-75. Bus & Prof Pos: Br mgr, Universal Finance Corp, 46-54; pres, Exon's Inc, 54- Mil Serv: Entered as Pvt, Army Signal Corps, 42, released as M/Sgt, 45, after serv in New Guinea, Philippines & Japan, 43-45; Southwest Pac & Philippine Campaign Ribbons; M/Sgt, Army Res, until 49. Mem: Lincoln CofC; Nat Off Prod Dealers Asn; Mason (32 degree); Shrine; Elks. Relig: Episcopal. Legal Res: 1615 Brent Blvd Lincoln NE 68506 Mailing Add: State Capitol Bldg Lincoln NE 68509

EZZARD, CLARENCE GRAY (D)
b Atlanta, Ga, Apr 16, 05; s Dock S Ezzard & Rena Alexander E; m 1930 to Etta Mae Green; c Clarence G, Jr, Merian T, Myrtle V, Joel G & Wesley P. Polit & Govt Pos: Ga State Rep, 69-74; deleg, Dem Nat Conv, 72. Bus & Prof Pos: Letter carrier, US Post Off, Atlanta, 29-68. Relig: Episcopal. Mailing Add: 245 Atlanta Ave SE Atlanta GA 30315

EZZELL, MICHAEL HERMAN (D)
Tex State Rep
b Wharton, Tex, May 25, 44; s James Ezra Ezzell & Genevive Barbara Scholz E; m to Betty Sorrells; c Michael & Marla Kay. Educ: Abilene Christian Col, BS, 66, MA, 69. Polit & Govt Pos: Tex State Rep, 75-, state affairs comt, Tex House of Reps, 75 & health & welfare comt, 75- Bus & Prof Pos: Sch counr, Snyder Independent Schs, 69-75; mgr & co-owner, Basin Weed Control, Snyder, Tex, currently; minister, Dunn Community Church of Christ, currently. Mem: Scurry Co Asn for Retarded Children; Rotary. Relig: Church of Christ. Legal Res: 3009 Crockett Snyder TX 79549 Mailing Add: PO Box 1124 Snyder TX 79549

F

FABREGA, WENCESLAO JAY (R)
Mont State Rep
b San Jose, Costa Rica, May 17, 33; s Wenceslao Jose Fabrega & Lotty Proesch; m 1959 to Julianne Preda; c Wendy Julia, Wences John & Wynette Lotty. Educ: Dunwoody Indust Inst, Archit Drafting & Estimating, 58. Polit & Govt Pos: Mont State Rep, 75- Bus & Prof Pos: Archit draftsman & estimator, Forman-Ford, Minneapolis, Minn, 58-60, Forman-Ford, Great Falls, Mont, 60-62, mgr, 62-65; contract mgr archit div, House of Glass, 65-66, vpres, 67- Mil Serv: Entered as Pvt, Army, 54, released as Cpl, 56, after serv in 82nd Airborne Div; Good Conduct Medal; Paratrooper Wings. Mem: AF&AM; Elks; The Montana Club; Scottish Rite; Shrine. Honors & Awards: Outstanding Freshman Rep in Mont House of Rep, United Press Int, 75. Relig: Congregational. Mailing Add: 2207 Beech Dr Great Falls MT 59404

FABRIZIO, JOHN ARTHUR (R)
Mem, Norwalk Rep Town Comt, Conn
b Norwalk, Conn, Nov 17, 23; s John Joseph Fabrizio & Mary Elizabeth Perella F; m 1962 to Dr Tuula Irja Jokinen; c John Arne & Robert Arthur. Educ: NY Univ Sch Com, BS, 46; NY Law Sch, LLB, 60; NY Univ Mgt & Hon Clubs; Phi Theta Phi. Polit & Govt Pos: Mem, Norwalk Zoning Bd of Appeals, Conn, 62-; mem, Norwalk Rep Ward A Comt, 65-; mem, Norwalk Rep Town Comt, 68-; Conn State Rep, 140th Dist, 69-74; mem adv bd, Conn Heritage Group for Reelec of the President, 72. Bus & Prof Pos: Owner & operator, Norwalk Auto Transit Co & Fabrizio Bus Co, 62- Mem: Am Platform Asn; Am Judicature Asn; Easter Seal Rehabilitation Ctr (bd dirs, Stamford, 72-); Long Shore Country Club. Relig: Roman Catholic. Mailing Add: 42 Stevens St Norwalk CT 06850

FACE, ALBERT RAY (R)
b Aberdeen, SDak, Mar 31, 19; s Ray James Face & Elsie Sloan F; m 1942 to Ellenore Ambur; c Carol (Mrs Clark) & Ray Jay. Educ: SDak State Col, BC, 41; Colo State Col, 45; Alpha Zeta; Agr Club; Col 4-H. Polit & Govt Pos: Dist 4-H leader, SDak Agr Exten Serv, 43-45; co 4-H exten agent, Yuma Co, Ariz, 45-49, co agr exten agent, 49-55; pres, Yuma Co Citizens for Goldwater, 64; chmn, Laguna Precinct Rep Party, 67-69; treas & campaign chmn, Goldwater for US Sen, Yuma Co, 68; committeeman, Gov Williams Adv Comt, 68-70; chmn, Yuma Co Rep Cent Comt, formerly, vchmn, 70-73. Bus & Prof Pos: Cattle supt, Bruce Church, Inc, Yuma, 55-, ranch mgr, 59- Mil Serv: Entered as 2nd Lt, Army, 41, released as 1st Lt, 43, after serv in Transportation Corps, Caribbean Theater, 42-43. Mem: Int Brangus Breeders Asn; Ariz Cattle Feeders; Ariz Cattle Growers; Rotary; Farm Bur. Honors & Awards: Yuma Co Man of the Year, 52. Relig: Lutheran, Mo Synod. Mailing Add: Rte 3 Box 310-A Yuma AZ 85364

FACKLER, ERNEST CARL, III (R)
Chmn, 15th Cong Dist Rep Comt, Mich
b Detroit, Mich, Aug 5, 43; s Ernest Carl Fackler, Jr & Emma Engel F; m 1967 to Karen Anne Wagner; c Anne Wagner & William James, II. Educ: Condordia Sr Col, BA, 65; Wayne State Univ, MA, 73. Polit & Govt Pos: Asst dir, United Rep Fund, Detroit, Mich, 70-71; Rep nominee, US House of Rep, 15th Dist, 70 & 72; mem, Tech Comt, 1972 White House Conf on Aging, 71-72; chmn, 15th Cong Dist Rep Comt, 72-; dir, Bur of Workmen's Compensation, State of Mich, 72-; alt deleg, Rep Nat Conv, 72. Bus & Prof Pos: Dir, Peoples Community Hosp Authority, Mich, 70-71; pub info asst, Mich Consolidated Gas Co, Detroit, 71-72. Mem: Am Polit Sci Asn; Pub Rels Soc of Am; Dearborn Heights Goodfellows (vpres, 71); Dearborn Heights Jaycees (dir, 70); Lutheran Luncheon Club of Detroit (pres, 70). Honors & Awards: Outstanding Young Man of Year 1970, Dearborn Heights Jaycees, 71. Relig: Lutheran. Mailing Add: 26740 Timber Trail Dearborn Heights MI 48127

FADELEY, EDWARD NORMAN (D)
Ore State Sen
b Williamsville, Mo, Dec 13, 29; s Robert Sylvester Fadeley & Nelle Norman F; m 1953 to Nancie Newell Peacocke; c Charles Norman & Shira Nannette. Educ: Univ Mo, AB, 51; Univ Ore, JD, 57; Order of the Coif; Alpha Pi Zeta; Phi Alpha Delta; Varsity debater; ed, Ore Law Rev. Polit & Govt Pos: Precinct committeeman, Dem Party, Eugene, Ore, 56-, area chmn, 58-64; Ore State Rep, Lane Co, 61-63; Ore State Sen, Lane Co, 63-, chmn, Disclosure of Influences on Govt Comt, Ore State Senate, 64-66 & mem, 5-man State Steering Comn, Comt to Repeal the Death Penalty, chairperson, Ore Senate Educ Comt, 73-, Ways & Means & Appropriations Comt & subcomt govt, 73-; permanent chmn, Dem State Platform Conv, 64-66; chmn, Dem Party Ore, 67-68; deleg, Dem Nat Conv, 68; Dem nominee for US Rep, Ore, 68; chmn, Ore Legis Counsel Comt, 71-73; mem intergovt rels comt, Nat Legis Conf, 73- Bus & Prof Pos: Secy-treas, Ore Research Inst, Inc, 60-; chmn, Uniform Laws Comt, Ore State Bar, 63-65; presiding chmn, State Conv, Ore State Bar. Mil Serv: Entered as Midn, Navy, 47, released as Lt (jg), 54, after serv in Mediterranean, Atlantic & Caribbean, 52-53; European Occup & Nat Defense Ribbons; Lt, Naval Res, 66. Publ: Capital credits, Lawyers Reporting Serv, 1/72; Criminal law revision, Ore Law Rev, spring 72; OSHA checklist, Nat Rural Elec Coop Asn, 12/72; plus others. Mem: Am Acad Polit & Social Sci; Am Judicature Soc; CofC; Am Civil Liberties Union; Metrop Civic Club. Honors & Awards: All conf tackle, Conf Championship Team, Grant City, Mo, 46; nominated Distinguished Jr Citizen, Eugene, 63 & 64. Relig: Methodist. Mailing Add: 260 Sunset Dr Eugene OR 97401

FADELEY, NANCIE PEACOCKE (D)
Ore State Rep
b St Louis, Mo, July 11, 30; d Charles Sidney Peacocke & Nannette Wood P; m 1953 to Edward Norman Fadeley; c Charles Norman & Shira Nannette. Educ: Cent Methodist Col, BA, 52; Duke Univ, 52-53; Univ Ore, MA, 74; Kappa Tau Alpha. Polit & Govt Pos: Various pos in Dem Party Orgn, Lane Co, Ore; alt deleg, Dem Nat Conv, 68; secy to Ore State Sen Ed Fadeley, 61-70; Ore State Rep, 71-, chmn, Environ & Land Use Comt, Ore House Rep, 72-, chmn, Environ & Energy Comt. Bus & Prof Pos: Former sch teacher; freelance writer, currently. Publ: The Wizardy of Os, Emerald Empire Mag, 1/68; Cycling through summer, Parents' Mag, 6/73; Challenge to the throwaway ethic, Sierra Club Bull, 5/74. Mem: Church Women United of Ore (state legis chmn, presently). Relig: Methodist. Mailing Add: 260 Sunset Dr Eugene OR 97403

FADEM, JERROLD ALAN (D)
Mem, Los Angeles Co Dem Cent Comt, Calif
b St Louis, Mo, Jan 19, 26; s Samuel H Fadem & Betsy Sparks F; m 1951 to Joyce Abrams; c Cheryl Marlene & Judith Allison. Educ: Wash Univ, 43-44; Univ Calif, Los Angeles, BS in Econ, 47; Loyola Univ, JD, 53; Zeta Beta Tau. Polit & Govt Pos: Spec consult, State Lands Comn, 64-65; mem, Calif Dem State Cent Comt, 64-66; consult airport noise, Comt on Transportation, Calif State Assembly, 68-69; mem, Los Angeles Co Dem Cent Comt, 68-; consult eminent domain, Calif Law Rev Comn oral examr, Los Angeles City Civil Serv Dept, 69. Bus & Prof Pos: Partner, Fadem & Kanner, 53- Mil Serv: Entered as Pvt, Army, 44, released as S/Sgt, 46, after serv in Hq Sect, Fourth Army. Publ: Ed & co-auth, Condemnation Practice Handbook, Continuing Education of the Bar of Calif, 62; auth, Negative Argument on Proposition D, November Election, 68. Mem: Calif State Bar; Mason (32 degree); Scottish Rite; Justice Lodge, B'nai B'rith; Town Hall. Relig: Jewish. Mailing Add: 427 S McCadden Pl Los Angeles CA 90005

FADEM, JOYCE A (D)
Mem, Calif Dem State Cent Comt
b Los Angeles, Calif, Feb 25, 32; d Arthur J Abrams & Regina Goodman A; m 1951 to Jerrold A Fadem, div; c Cheryl Marlene & Judith Allison. Educ: Univ Calif, Los Angeles, BA in polit sci, 52, Gen Secondary Teaching Credential, 53 & MA, 61; Phi Beta Kappa; Pi Lambda Theta; Pi Gamma Mu; Pi Sigma Alpha; Alpha Epsilon Phi. Polit & Govt Pos: Coordr vol serv, Dem Nat Conv, 60; mem, Calif Dem State Cent Comt, 60-64 & 66-; secy, Calif Dem Coun, 63-67; alt deleg, Dem Nat Conv, 64 & 68; mem, Los Angeles Co Cent Comt, 66-; coordr, Educators for Alan Cranston, Sen Elec, 68; secy, Calif Dem State Conv, 71; comnr, Los Angeles Housing Authority, 74-; comnr, Los Angeles Bicentennial; mem adv comt, Elec Code Revision Comt, 75- Bus & Prof Pos: Instr, Los Angeles City Col, 62-69; lectr educ, Exten, Univ Calif, Los Angeles, 63-65; consult, Calif State Dept Educ, 64-66; mem faculty, Immaculate Heart Col, Los Angeles, 67-69; lectr, US Int Univ, Calif Western Campus, summer 71 & 72; dir polit action & legis, Calif Teachers Asn, Southern Sect, 69-72, polit educ exec, 71- Publ: Bill of Rights: a Source Book for Teachers, Calif State Dept Educ, 66; We

Teach Freedom, Const Rights Found, Los Angeles, 65; co-auth, Registration of young voters: an ongoing responsibility, Social Educ, 10/72; plus others. Mem: Calif Teachers Asn; Nat Coun Social Studies (chmn acad freedom comt, 65 & 68-69, mem nat citizens comt, 72-); Nat Educ Asn; SCalif Social Sci Asn (dir-at-lg, 64-); Const Rights Found. Relig: Jewish. Mailing Add: 427 S McCadden Pl Los Angeles CA 90020

FAGAN, JAMES W **(D)**
Dem State Committeeman, Wyo
b Casper, Wyo, July 13, 27; s Thomas M Fagan & Josephine Warner F; m 1950 to Lita Kaan; c Curtis Page, Patrick Lance, Thomas Mathew & Nora Lynn. Educ: Univ Wyo, BA & BSL, 53, LLB, 55; Sigma Alpha Epsilon. Polit & Govt Pos: Dem precinct committeeman, Natrona Co, Wyo, 59-70; Wyo rep, US Sen Gale McGee, 59-69; mem exec bd, Wyo Young Dem, 62; bus mgr & organizer, The Spokesman, 63-; mem finance comt, Wyo Dem Party, 66; deleg, Dem Nat Conv, 68; Dem State Committeeman, Wyo, 71- Legal Res: 123 S Kimball Casper WY 82601 Mailing Add: 142 N Center Casper WY 82601

FAGAN, LAWRENCE JAMES **(R)**
Mem, Berlin Rep Town Comt, Conn
b New Britain, Conn, Dec 24, 30; s Edward Joseph Fagan & Margaret Fitzsimmons F; m 1963 to Mary Ann Milewski; c John A & Christopher J. Educ: Fairfield Univ, BS, 53; Boston Col Law Sch, LLB, 56. Polit & Govt Pos: Mem, Bd Finance, Marlborough, Conn, 62-66; Conn State Rep, 63-67; mem, Berlin Rep Town Comt, Conn, 69- Mil Serv: 1st Lt, Air Force, 57, serv in Judge Adv Gen Dept. Mem: Am, Conn & Hartford Co Bar Asns; Am Trial Lawyers Asn; Blackledge Country Club. Relig: Roman Catholic. Mailing Add: 233 Main St New Britain CT 06051

FAGERHOLT, LEONARD B **(D)**
NDak State Rep
b Grafton, NDak, Dec 9, 23; s Albert Christian Fagerholt & Clara Brende F; m 1972 to Elizabeth Jackson; c Roberta (Mrs Earl Burger); Bruce & Bette. Educ: Hoople High Sch, grad, 41. Polit & Govt Pos: Clerk, Glenwood Twp, 60-75; NDak State Rep, Dist 16, 74- Bus & Prof Pos: Farmer, 41- Mem: Eagles; Farmers Union. Relig: Lutheran. Mailing Add: RR 1 Hoople ND 58243

FAGG, HARRISON GROVER **(R)**
Mont State Rep
b Billings, Mont, Oct 27, 31; s Mearl Leonard Fagg & Frances Soule F; m 1952 to Darlene Rae Bohling; c Sherril Soule, Russel Charles & Grantland Mearl. Educ: Mont State Univ, 1 year; Univ Ore, BS in Archit; Sigma Chi. Polit & Govt Pos: Mont State Rep, Dist Eight, Yellowstone Co, 69- Bus & Prof Pos: Proj designer, Orr Pickering & Assocs, 56-58; proj designer, Nordquist & Sundell, 58-59; owner archit firm, Harrison Fagg & Assocs, 59-; partner, Beartooth Planning Enterprises, 72- Mil Serv: Entered as 2nd Lt, Air Force, 54, released as 1st Lt, 56, after serv as an Air Installations Engr, Larson AFB, Moses Lake, Wash. Mem: Mont State & Am Inst Architects; AF&AM; Shrine; Elks. Honors & Awards: Outstanding Young Man of Billings, Mont, 58; Outstanding Young Man of Mont, 59. Relig: Presbyterian. Legal Res: 1414 Mystic Dr Billings MT 59101 Mailing Add: 214 N 32nd St Billings MT 59101

FAHEY, JOSEPH EDMUND **(D)**
b Syracuse, NY, June 30, 49; s James J Fahey & Mary McGuire F; single. Educ: Onondaga Community Col, Syracuse, NY, AA, 69; Univ Tenn, Knoxville, BS, 71; Syracuse Univ Col Law, JD, 75; Am Civil Liberties Union & Instr in Confraternity of Christian Doctrine, Tenn. Polit & Govt Pos: Deleg, Dem Nat Conv, 72; chmn platform comt, Onondaga Co Young Dem, 72; chmn, 12th Ward Dem Comt, Syracuse, NY, 74-75. Bus & Prof Pos: Admin asst to comnr, Ernest W Speach, Dept Pub Works, Syracuse, NY, 72-73. Mem: Ancient Order of Hibernians. Relig: Roman Catholic. Mailing Add: 2005 S Geddes St Syracuse NY 13207

FAHRENKAMP, BETTYE **(D)**
Dem Nat Committeewoman, Alaska
Mailing Add: 4013 Evergreen Fairbanks AK 99507

FAHRENKOPF, FRANK J, JR **(R)**
Chmn, Nev Rep Party
b Brooklyn, NY, Aug 28, 39; s Frank J Fahrenkopf, Sr & Rose Freeman F; m 1962 to Mary Ethel Bandoni; c Allison Marie, Leslie Ann & Amy Michelle. Educ: Univ Nev, BA, 62; Boalt Hall Sch Law, Univ Calif Berkeley, JD, 65; Blue Key; Alpha Tau Omega. Polit & Govt Pos: Pres, Reno Young Rep, 68-69; mem, Washoe Co Rep Cent Comt, 68-; deleg, Nev Rep Conv, 68-74, chmn, 72 & 74; Young Rep Nat Committeeman, Nev, 69-72, chmn, Nat Young Rep Awards Comt, Young Rep Nat Fedn, 69-71, mem exec bd, 69-72; chmn, Robert List for Attorney Gen, Nev, 70 & 74; gen counsel, mem, Nev State Rep Cent Comt, 72-75, chmn, Nev Rep Party, currently; Nev co-chmn, Comt for Reelect of the President, 72; deleg, Rep Nat Conv, 72; munic court judge pro-tem, Reno, 73- Bus & Prof Pos: Attorney, Breen & Young, Reno, Nev, 65-68; instr criminal law, Univ Nev, Reno, 67-; attorney, Sanford, Sanford, Fahrenkopf & Mousel, 68- Mil Serv: Entered as Pvt, Army, 57, released as SP-3, after serv in 338th Chem Co, Reno, Nev, Army Res. Publ: The value and use of motions in limine, 1/67 & The trap for the unwary or Article 9 of the Nevada Commercial Code, 7/68, Nev State Bar J. Mem: Washoe Co Bar Asn (pres, 73-); Am Bar Asn; Nev Bd Bar Examr (bd mem, 71-); State Bar of Nev; Nev Trial Lawyers Asn. Honors & Awards: Distinguished Serv Award, Jr CofC, 73. Relig: Roman Catholic. Mailing Add: 1040 LaRue Ave Reno NV 89502

FAILOR, EDWARD DALE, SR **(R)**
Adminr Social & Econ Statist Admin, Dept Com
b Marion, Iowa, Oct 22, 27; s William Ernest Failor & Harriet Rhode F; m 1956 to Isobel Maurene Julius; c Michelle L, Patrice L & Edward D, Jr. Educ: Univ Wyo, 45; Univ Dubuque, BS, 50; Univ Iowa, JD with distinction, 55; Phi Alpha Delta. Polit & Govt Pos: Regional dir, Goldwater for President, Iowa, 64; assoc to dir bur mines, Dept Interior, Washington, DC, 71-72; spec asst to campaign dir strategy, Comt to Reelect the President, 72; adminr social & econ statist admin, Dept Com, 73- Bus & Prof Pos: Lawyer, O'Connor, Thomas, McDermott & Wright, Dubuque, Iowa, 55-60; vpres, Page Hotels, Inc, Dubuque, 60-63; munic court judge, Dubuque, 65-67; campaign mgr, Iowans for Stanley, 67-68; vpres polit div, Fred A Niles Commun, Inc, Chicago, Ill, 69-70. Mil Serv: Entered as Pvt, Army, 45, released as Sgt, 47, after serv in Army Air Corps; entered as Sgt, Air Force, 51, released as S/Sgt; Am Theatre Medal; Good Conduct Medal. Publ: Co-auth, State Sales Tax on Services, 54 & co-auth & co-ed, Iowa Handbook of Model Ordinances, 54, Univ Iowa; auth, Judicial standards, Iowa Asn Munic Judges, 66. Mem: Am & Iowa Bar Asns; Am Legion; Mason. Honors & Awards: Iowa Jaycees Outstanding Polit Activities Award, 60; Mem Iowa Young Rep Hall Fame, 62; Outstanding Serv to Youth Award, Dubuque Optimists, 63; Al DuPont Award, Dubuque Jr CofC, 63; Distinguished Civic Serv Award, Dubuque CofC, 65. Relig: Presbyterian. Mailing Add: 1919 Rhode Island Ave McLean VA 22101

FAIN, DAVID C **(D)**
Chmn, Dimmit Co Dem Party, Tex
b Houston, Tex, July 24, 29; s David Crockett Fain & Eddie Dixon F; m 1948 to Edwina Taylor; c David T, Pamela Kay & Gwendolyn. Educ: Carrizo Springs Sch, 12 years. Polit & Govt Pos: Precinct chmn, Dimmit Co Dem Party, Tex, 66-70, chmn, 70- Bus & Prof Pos: Comn agent, Atlantic Richfield Co, 51- Mil Serv: Entered as Pvt, Tex Nat Guard, 48, released as Sgt 1/C, 51, after serv in Co D 141st Ins 36th Div. Mem: Masonic Lodge 566 (past Master); Carrizo Springs Lions Club; Tex Tech Dad's Asn. Relig: Baptist. Legal Res: 1908 Johnson St Carrizo Springs TX 78834 Mailing Add: 200 Houston St Carrizo Springs TX 78834

FAIR, ROBERT J **(D)**
Ind State Sen
Mailing Add: Ind State Senate State Capitol Indianapolis IN 46204

FAIRBANKS, LINDA GAY **(D)**
VPres, Va Young Dem
b Richmond, Va, Sept 17, 48; d Horatio Gano Fairbanks & Sally Stewart F; single. Educ: Marymount Jr Col, Arlington, Va, AA, 68; NC State Univ, BA, 70; Social Serv Club, 67; Polit Action Comt, 70. Polit & Govt Pos: Secy, Richmond Area Young Dem, Va, 71-72, vpres, 72-; deleg, Dem Nat Conv, 72; secy, Richmond Area Dem Women's Club, 72-, vpres, 74-75; committeewoman, Henrico Co Dem Comt, 72-75; pres, Richmond Area Young Dem, 73-74; vpres, Va Young Dem, 74- Bus & Prof Pos: Legal research asst, Allen, Allen, Allen & Allen Law Firm, 71- Mem: League of Women Voters. Relig: Protestant. Mailing Add: 9201 Waterloo Ct Richmond VA 23229

FAIRBANKS, MADGE H **(R)**
b Washington, DC; m 1947 to Bryce J Fairbanks; c Bryce, J, II, Jeffrey M, Jerald R, Jan L & James A. Educ: St Joseph's High Sch, Manchester, NH, 43; Margaret Pillsbury Sch of Nursing, RN, 47. Polit & Govt Pos: State vchmn, Young Rep, 57-59; Salt Lake Co vchmn, Young Rep, Utah, 65-67; mem state bd, Rep Women's Fedn, 59-61; deleg, Rep Nat Conv, 60, alt deleg, 64; Rep Nat Committeewoman, Utah, 67-72. Bus & Prof Pos: Nurse, 47-49. Mem: UN Asn of US; UN High Sch Model Assembly; League of Women Voters; Salt Lake Med Auxiliary; Ment Health Comn. Relig: Latter-day Saint. Mailing Add: 1215 Catherine Salt Lake City UT 84116

FAIRCHILD, RUTH **(D)**
Chmn, Haakon Co Dem Party, SDak
b Pierre, SDak, May 19, 18; d Mervin Curtis Sherwood & Fleta May Weeks S; m 1938 to Wayne Leo Fairchild; c Kent Leo, Bruce Wayne & Marsha May (Mrs Billy Ray Sumpter). Educ: Philip High Sch, Grad, 37, Valedictorian; Aberdeen Bus Col, 37-38. Polit & Govt Pos: Chmn, Haakon Co Dem Party, SDak, 64-68 & 74-, vpres, 70-74; mem exec comt, SDak Dem Party, 68-70. Mem: Haakon Co Farmers Union; Get Together Home Exten Club; Tri-Co Exten Clubs (chmn, 75-); SDak Grazing Asn (secy-treas). Relig: Presbyterian. Mailing Add: Star Rte Philip SD 57567

FAISON, DAVID JOHN **(DFL)**
Third VChmn, 35th Legis Dist Dem-Farmer-Labor Party, Minn
b Louisville, Ky, July 16, 18; s James William Faison & Rosa Lee Scott F; wid; c Shirley (Mrs Edward Sanders); Dorothy (Mrs Eugene Dixon) & David J, Jr. Educ: Roosevelt High Sch, grad, 37. Polit & Govt Pos: Third vchmn, 35th Legis Dist Dem-Farmer-Labor Party, Minn, 70-; city, co & state deleg, Dem-Farmer-Labor Party, 70- Bus & Prof Pos: Prof musician, 34-; dry cleaning-indust specialist, Minneapolis Modelett Corp, 58- Mil Serv: Worked in defense plants, 41-44. Mem: A Philip Randolph Continuation Comt; Am Fedn Musicians Local 73 & 30; Elks Lodge Ames 106 (exalted ruler). Relig: Lutheran. Mailing Add: 4000 Fifth Ave S Minneapolis MN 55409

FAISON, LEE VELL **(D)**
Mem, Ark Dem State Comt
b ElDorado, Ark, Apr 14, 33; s Lelus Faison & Essie Evans F; m 1951 to Annie Lean Herts; c Patricia Ann (Mrs Lidell); Sandra, Cathy & David. Educ: Oil Belt Voc Tech Sch, grad, 69. Polit & Govt Pos: Committeeman, Ark Dem State Comt, 67-; mem, Union Co Welfare Bd, 70-71; justice of the peace, Union Co, 73- Bus & Prof Pos: Pumper, Lion Oil Co, ElDorado, Ark, currently. Mem: Fair Deal Vote League; NAACP. Relig: Baptist. Mailing Add: Rte 4 Box 40 ElDorado AR 71730

FALASCO, EDA **(D)**
Chairperson, Merced Co Dem Cent Comt, Calif
b Los Banos, Calif, Aug 18, 26; d Domenico Falasco & Teresa Bottafuco F; single. Educ: Univ Calif, AA, 47; San Jose State Col, BA, 49; Fresno State Col, grad work, 50- Polit & Govt Pos: Chairperson, Merced Co Dem Cent Comt, 71-; chairperson, Calif Rural Caucus, Region III, 75-; mem steering comt, Calif Dem Party, 73-, mem exec comt, currently; deleg, Dem Nat Mid-Term Conf, 74. Bus & Prof Pos: Teacher, Los Banos Jr High Sch, 49- Mem: CTA-NEA-ABC-Los Banos Teachers Asn; Delta Kappa Gamma. Honors & Awards: John Swett, Teacher in Polit, CTA & Merced-Mariposa Co Couns, 73. Relig: Catholic. Mailing Add: 958 J St Los Banos CA 93635

FALCEY, ROBERT M **(D)**
b Trenton, NJ, June 15, 13; s Edward J Falcey & Sara Marie Bird F; m 1947 to Kathryn Borne Falcey; c Robert M Falcey, Jr. Educ: Cathedral Prep Sch, Trenton, NJ, grad, 31. Polit & Govt Pos: Asst Secy of State, NJ, 54-74, exec officer, 55-, Acting Secy of State, 72-74. Bus & Prof Pos: Info clerk, Supreme Court of NJ, 38-47; clerk judgement sect, Superior Court of NJ, 47-54. Mem: Nat Asn Secy of US; Gov Exec Comt on Ethical Standards in State Serv; Coun of State Employees; Mercer Coun, Civil Serv Employees. Relig: Roman Catholic. Legal Res: 18 Woodside Ave Trenton NJ 08618 Mailing Add: State House Trenton NJ 08625

FALCON, MARGARET MARY **(D)**
Mem, Dem State Cent Comt, La
b New Orleans, La, Aug 30, 41; d Millard Louis Falcon & Regina Kroeper F; single. Educ: Barat Col, 59-61; Loyola Univ (La), BS, 63, MSEd, 67; Kappa Delta Pi; Phi Phi Phi. Polit & Govt Pos: Admin asst to mayor, New Orleans, 70-; mem, Dem State Cent Comt, La &

Dem Charter Comn, 74- Mem: New Orleans Country Club; Independent Women's Orgn; Kappa Delta Pi. Relig: Catholic. Mailing Add: 4239 S Prieur St New Orleans LA 70125

FALCONE, ERNANI CARLO (D)
Chmn, Del Co Dem Comt, Pa
b Upper Darby, Pa, July 16, 28; s Nicholas Falcone & Julia Di Georgio F; m 1952 to Rachel Bateman Rogers; c Julia C, Ernani C & Claude D. Educ: Princeton Univ, BA, 50; Univ Pa, MA, 55. Polit & Govt Pos: Worker, Haverford Twp Dem Comn, Pa, 55-57; committeeman, Marple Twp Dem Assoc, 57-64; comnr, Marple Twp, 63-65; chmn, Del Co Dem Comt, 64-; deleg, Dem Nat Conv, 68. Bus & Prof Pos: Instr social sci, Swarthmore High Sch, 57- Mil Serv: Entered as Pvt, Army, 51, released as 2nd Lt, 55, after serv in Eng Depot, Kaiserslautern Ger, ETO, 55; Maj, Res. Mem: Res Officers Asn; Nat Educ Asn. Relig: Roman Catholic. Mailing Add: 42 E Baltimore Pike Media PA 19063

FALKENBURG, FRANCIS (D)
Ala State Rep
Mailing Add: 3001 Argyle Rd Birmingham AL 35213

FALKNOR, RICHARD WILLIAM CONDON (D)
b Seattle, Wash, Apr 1, 35; s Judson Fahnestock Falknor & Dorothy Condon F; m 1972 to Gilda M Iriarte; c Catherine Marie, Christopher Condon & Jon-Erik. Educ: Univ Calif, Berkeley, AB, 57; Harvard Univ, MPA, 67; Sigma Chi. Polit & Govt Pos: Legis asst to US Sen Henry M Jackson, Wash, 61-63; prof staff mem, Comt on Interior & Insular Affairs, US Senate, 63-66; spec asst to US Rep Thomas S Foley, Wash, 67-71; dir, Fed Plans & Progs, Off of Gov of PR, Washington, DC, 72; admin asst to Resident Comnr Jaime Benitez, US House Rep, PR, 73-74; spec asst, House Com Oversight & Investigations Subcomt, 75- Bus & Prof Pos: Consult arms-control matters, Hudson Inst, Croton-on-Hudson, NY, 72- Mil Serv: Entered as E-1, Army, 57, released as E-5, 61, after serv as Ed-in-Chief, Seventh Army Paper, Seventh Army Hq, Stuttgart, Fed Repub of Ger; Army Commendation Medal. Publ: The broad perspective: Congress & the environment—some modest proposals for the 1970's, In: Proc of the 1970 Symp on Natural Areas, Northwest Sci Asn; co-auth & ed of several Cong Comt Reports. Mem: World Future Soc; Am Soc for Pub Admin. Honors & Awards: Cong Staff Fel, Am Polit Sci Asn, 65. Relig: Episcopal. Mailing Add: 4454 Reservoir Rd NW Washington DC 20007

FALLIN, JAMES HOLDER (D)
b Louisville, Ky, Sept 13, 45; s James Taylor Fallin & Frances Irene Holder F; m 1968 to Sharon Faye Simmons; c Angela Lynn & John Matthew. Educ: Brescia Col, BS, 67; Delta Phi Omega; Midwest Model UN. Polit & Govt Pos: Pres, Brescia Col Young Dem, Ky, 64-66; admin asst to Wendall Ford for Lt Gov, 67; chmn, Ky Deleg, Young Dem of Am Conv, 67; committeeman, Ky Young Dem, 68; admin asst state youth chmn, Katherine Peden for US Sen, 68; alt deleg, Dem Nat Conv, 68; chmn exec comt, Hancock Co Dem Exec Comt, Ky, 71-73; chmn Hancock Co, Walter (Dee) Huddleston for US Sen Comt, 72; chmn, Hancock Countians for Wendall Ford for US Sen, 74; elec judge, Hancock Co, 74-; secy & bd mem, Green River Area Develop Dist, 74-; chmn, Green River Dist Bd Health, 74-; mem, Green River Crime Coun, 74-; mem, Audubon Area Community Serv, 74- Bus & Prof Pos: Pub rels mgr, Am Olean Tile Co, Lewisport & Cloverport plants. Mil Serv: 1st Lt, Army Res, currently; Direct Comn, into the Army Res as a Civil Affairs Officer, Co Comdr, Army Res, currently. Mem: Brescia Col Alumni (pres, 74-75); Lions. Honors & Awards: Chosen by the Young Dem of Am as one of five Young Dem to lead Pledge of Allegiance before the Dem Nat Conv, Chicago, 68; Outstanding Dem During 72, Ky State Dem Hq; Outstanding Young Man, Hancock Co Jaycees, 74. Mailing Add: RR 2 Box 174B Lewisport KY 42351

FALLIN, PAT FINLEY (D)
Chairperson, Pitkin Co Dem Party, Colo
b Pryor, Okla, Sept 5, 41; d William Marshall Finley & Gay Worsham Rychel F; m 1964 to Richard Alden Fallin; c Brooks & Ashley Adair. Educ: Univ Okla, BA, 63; Gamma Phi Beta. Polit & Govt Pos: Chairperson, Pitkin Co Dem Party, Colo, 73-; vchairperson, Fourth Dist Dem Comt, 75-; mem, Gov Comn Status Women, 75- Mem: League Women Voters; Nat Orgn Women. Relig: Protestant. Mailing Add: Box 2711 Aspen CO 81611

FALLON, CLAUDIA ANN (D)
b New York, NY, Feb 2, 53; d Bernard R Fallon & Rita Rosica F; single. Educ: Rockland Community Col, 71-72; Ohio Univ, 72- Polit & Govt Pos: Deleg, Dem Nat Conv, 72. Relig: Catholic. Mailing Add: 131 Parkway Dr S Orangeburg NY 10962

FALLON, GEORGE H (D)
b Baltimore, Md, July 24, 02; s Lawrence Fallon Sr & Mary Dempsey F; m 1929 to Willa Thomas; c Mary Joyce. Educ: Calvert Bus Col; Johns Hopkins Univ. Polit & Govt Pos: Chmn, Md Dem State Cent Comt, 38; Baltimore City councilman, 39-44; US Rep, Md, 44-70; deleg, Dem Nat Conv, 68. Mailing Add: 3806 Hadley Sq E Baltimore MD 21218

FALLON, JOHN JOSEPH (D)
Md State Deleg
b Baltimore, Md, Feb 2, 24; m 1948 to Lauretta Mary Betourne; c John J, Jr & Shawn-Marie. Educ: Baltimore parochial & pub schs. Polit & Govt Pos: Anne Arundel Dem Coun; Lake Shore Dem Club Inc; recreation comnr, Ann Arundel Co, Md, 61-62; Mo State Deleg, 63-66 & 71- Bus & Prof Pos: Partner, Fallham Enterprises; clerk, Baltimore & Ohio RR Co, Baltimore, Md, 29 years; pres, Brotherhood RR Clerks Union, 61-62; pres, Brotherhood Air-Line Clerks Union, 68-70. Mil Serv: Entered as A/S, Naval Res, 43, released as Yeoman 1/C, 46, after serv in USS Mettawee, Pac. Mem: Int Traders; Elks (Lodge 2266); VFW (Post 2562); Am Legion (Post 252); Lake Shore Dem Club. Relig: Catholic. Mailing Add: 14 Park Dr Pasadena MD 21122

FALLON, THOMAS F (D)
Mass State Rep
Mailing Add: State Capitol Boston MA 02133

FALLS, ARTHUR JOSEPH (R)
Asst State Treas, Ill
b Astoria, NY, Aug 27, 26; s Joseph Francis Falls (deceased) & Estelle C Branigan F; m 1951 to Nancy Ann Stribling; c Robert Arthur, Betsy Ann & Joseph Stribling. Educ: Fla Southern Col, BS in Jour, 52; Lambda Chi Alpha. Polit & Govt Pos: Asst state safety coordr, Ill, 55-59; downstate dir, United Rep Fund, Ill, 59-64; Rep precinct committeeman, 61-; alt deleg, Rep Nat Conv, 64; chmn, Cass Co Rep Cent Comt, 64-69; Asst State Treas, Ill, 64- Bus & Prof Pos: Dir student financial aid, Univ Ill, Chicago Circle, 67- Mil Serv: Entered as A/S, Navy, 44, released as Seaman 1/C, 46. Mem: Lions Int, Ashland; Elks; Am Legion; Lions. Relig: Roman Catholic. Mailing Add: c/o Off of State Treas State House Springfield IL 62706

FALLS, C FRANK (D)
Chmn, First Cong Dist Dem Comt, Ark
b Jonesboro, Ark, Oct 27, 34; s George Franklin Falls & Willie Wood F; m 1957 to Anna Lee Collins; c Cynthia Ann, Brian Douglas & Derek Charles. Educ: Ark State Univ, BS, Bus Admin, 59. Polit & Govt Pos: Comnr, Metrop Planning Comn, Ark, 67-; co coordr, Dale Bumpers for Gov Campaign, 70; chmn, First Cong Dist Dem Comt, 70-; mem exec bd, Ark Dem Party, formerly; comnr, Ark State Police, 71- Bus & Prof Pos: Pres, Jonesboro Merchants Asn, 66- Mil Serv: Pvt, Army Nat Guard Artil, 57. Mem: Kiwanis; YMCA. Mailing Add: 803 Parkview Jonesboro AR 72401

FALLS, ROBERT ZEMRI (D)
NC State Rep
b Cleveland Co, NC, Apr 15, 12; s Alfred Falls & Lula Crowder F; m 1935 to Jennie Blanton. Educ: Gardner-Webb Jr Col. Polit & Govt Pos: NC State Rep, 63- Bus & Prof Pos: Farmer. Mem: Rotary; Shelby CofC; Cleveland Co Agr Comt. Relig: Baptist; deacon, Westview Baptist Church, Shelby, NC, 53. Mailing Add: 1308 Wesson Rd Shelby NC 28150

FALSTAD, WILLIAM JAMES (R)
b Superior, Wis, Jan 5, 34; s Ralph Leonard Falstad & Patricia Calhoun; m 1958 to Diane Hollis, div; c David, Daniel, Julie & Robert. Educ: Carleton Col, 52-53; Univ Wis, BA, 56; Pi Kappa Alpha; Beta Alpha Psi. Polit & Govt Pos: Mayor, Fredonia, Kans, 68-71; chmn, Kans Rep State Comt, 70- 73; mem, Rep Nat Comt, 70-73. Bus & Prof Pos: CPA, Arthur Andersen & Co, Chicago, Ill, 56-61; pres, Kans Bank Note Co, Fredonia, 62-; dir, First Nat Bank, Fredonia, 69- Mem: Am Inst CPA; Ill Soc CPA; Elks; Lions; Shrine. Relig: Methodist. Mailing Add: Box 360 Fredonia KS 66736

FANNIN, PAUL JONES (R)
US Sen, Ariz
b Ashland, Ky, Jan 29, 07; s Thomas Newton Fannin & Katharine Davis F; m 1934 to Elma Addington; c Tom, Bill, Bob & Linda; eight grandchildren. Educ: Univ Ariz; Stanford Univ, BA, 30; Kappa Sigma. Polit & Govt Pos: Gov, Ariz, 59-64; chmn, Western Gov Conf, 63; mem exec comt, Nat Gov Conf, 3 terms, chmn, Comt on Roads & Hwy Safety; mem, Pres Civil Defense Adv Coun, 63-65; US Sen, Ariz, 64- Bus & Prof Pos: Vpres, Fannin's Gas & Equip Co, 32-56, pres, 56-58. Mem: Nat Coun, Boy Scouts; Elks; Moose; Rotary; Maricopa Co Better Bus Bur. Relig: Methodist. Legal Res: Phoenix AZ Mailing Add: 3121 Senate Off Bldg Washington DC 20510

FANNING, CHARLES THEODORE (R)
Finance Chmn, Whitman Co Rep Cent Comt, Wash
b Oakesdale, Wash, Jan 24, 30; s Charles L E Fanning & Bernice Slate F; m 1953 to Shirley Jean Jones; c Louise Ann, Steven Gary, Crystal Marie & Timothy Charles. Educ: Eastern Wash State Col. Polit & Govt Pos: Deleg, Whitman Co Rep Conv, Wash, 64, deleg & chmn rules comt, 68, deleg & permanent chmn, 70 & 72; dist chmn, Whitman Co Rep Cent Comt, 66-68, chmn, 68-72, finance chmn, 74-; deleg & mem rules comt, Wash State Rep Conv, 68, deleg & co del chmn, 70-72; precinct committeeman, Whitman Co Rep Party, 68-; mem nominating comt, Fourth Cong Dist Rep Club, 71; deleg, Rep Nat Conv, 72; mem citizens adv comt, Region X, Off Econ Opportunity, 72-73. Bus & Prof Pos: Farmer, Garfield, Wash, 52-74; pres, Garbel, Inc, 74- Mil Serv: Entered as Seaman Recruit, Navy, 48, released as Airman, 49, after serv in Catapult Crew, USS Princeton & Fighter Squadron VF111, 13th Naval Dist, 48-49; mem Naval Res, Naval Auxiliary Air Sta, Spokane, Wash, 49-50; activated, Airman, Navy, 50, Fleet Air Serv Squadron, 50-51; returned to VF111, USS Valley Forge, Korean Theatre, 51-52; discharged, Aviation Machinist Mate 2/C, Naval Res, 53; Asian Occup Medal. Mem: F&AM; Whitman Co Rural Libr (trustee, 71-); Boy Scouts (chmn adult comt, 72-73); Am Legion; Am Farm Bur Fedn. Relig: Protestant; Trustee, Garfield Methodist Church. Mailing Add: Rte 1 Box 6 Garfield WA 99130

FANNING, HERMAN J (D)
Ind State Sen
Mailing Add: 6504 Clinton Rd Terre Haute IN 47805

FANNING, JOHN PATTON (D)
WVa State Sen
b Iaeger, WVa, Aug 14, 34; s James Patton Fanning & Gertrude Neal F; m 1956 to Marianna Young; c Brenda Jean, Deborah Ann & John William. Educ: Davis & Elkins Col, degree, 55; Cincinnati Col Embalming, degree, 59; Alpha Sigma Phi; Phi Sigma Eta. Polit & Govt Pos: Mayor, Iaeger, WVa, 64-66; WVa State Sen, Sixth Dist, 68-72 & 75- Bus & Prof Pos: Mgr, Fanning Funeral Home, 59- Mem: Rotary (pres, 69-); AF&AM. Relig: Methodist. Mailing Add: Box 68 Iaeger WV 24844

FANTASIA, MARY E (D)
Mass State Rep
b Arlington, Mass; m to Anthony; c Patricia M (Mrs James Stewart), Kevin Paul & Joanne Mary. Educ: Bryant Stratton Bus Sch. Polit & Govt Pos: Precinct worker, every election; head of women's div & vchmn, Mass Dem State Comt; chmn, Middlesex Co Dem Party, currently; deleg, Five Mass State Dem Conv; Dem State Committeewoman, Mass, 57-; Presidential Elector, 60 & 64; Dem Nat Committeewoman, Mass, 62-; deleg, Dem Nat Conv, 64, 68 & 72; mem, Somerville Dem Ward & City Comt; Mass State Rep, 70- Bus & Prof Pos: Liaison officer between the State & Fed Govt for the Mass Dept of Com & Develop, 64-66; exec secy to Mayor of Somerville, 66- Mem: Mass Women on Wheels (hon pres); Mass Legislators Asn; PTA; Somerville Hosp Ladies Comt; League of Cath Women. Relig: Roman Catholic. Mailing Add: 181 Hudson St Somerville MA 02144

FANTASIA, NICK (D)
WVa State Deleg,
b Kingmont, WVa, Jan 3, 23; s Louis Fantasia & Rose DiGiacama F; m 1949 to Carmella Simonetti; c Georgeanna, Rosemary, Nicolena, Gina, Annette & Nick Louis. Educ: Fairmont State Col, BA, 49; WVa Univ, MA, 53. Polit & Govt Pos: WVa State Deleg, 54-58, 64-72 & 75- Bus & Prof Pos: Vpres & gen mgr, WTCS Radio Sta, Fairmont; prin & teacher, Marion Co Schs, 16 years. Mil Serv: Army, 3 years serv. Mem: Life mem Nat Educ Asn; Classroom Teachers Asn; Moose; Am Legion; Eagles. Relig: Catholic. Mailing Add: Box 64 Kingmont WV 26578

FARABEE, RAY (D)
Tex State Sen
b Wichita Falls, Tex, Nov 22, 32; s Jack Wortham Farabee & Annie Sneed F; m 1958 to Helen Rehbein; c Steve Ross & David Lee. Educ: Univ Tex, Austin, BBA, 57, Law Sch, LLB, 61; Phi Alpha Delta; Phi Gamma Delta. Polit & Govt Pos: Tex State Sen, 30th Dist, 75- Bus & Prof Pos: Lawyer, Wichita Falls, Tex, 61- Mil Serv: Entered as 2nd Lt, released as Capt, Air Force Res. Mem: Wichita Co Bar Asn; State Jr Bar of Tex; State Bar of Tex. Relig: Baptist. Legal Res: 1512 Buchanan Wichita Falls TX 76309 Mailing Add: PO Box 5147 Wichita Falls TX 76307

FARBER, EARL CLARENCE (R)
Chmn, Hamilton Co Rep Comt, NY
b Norway, NY, June 19, 02; s Henry C Farber & Rosilda Grassel F; m 1931 to Elizabeth Nancy Butler; c Gene Earl. Educ: Herkimer High Sch. Polit & Govt Pos: Supvr, Town of Morehouse, NY, 36-43; co clerk, Hamilton Co, NY, 43-; vchmn, Hamilton Co Rep Comt, 44-63, chmn, 45 & 63-; Rep committeeman, Town of Morehouse, 45-; trustee, Sch Dist Three, 52- Bus & Prof Pos: Agent, Travelers Ins Co, 29-; agent, Am Surety Co, Transamerica Ins Co, 36-66. Mem: F&AM; Mohawk Valley Consistory; Ziyara Shrine; Herkimer Lodge, Elks. Relig: Baptist. Mailing Add: Town of Morehouse Hoffmeister NY 13353

FARBSTEIN, LEONARD (D)
b New York, NY; s Louis Farbstein & Yetta Schlanger F; m to Blossom Langer; c Louis Jacob. Educ: City Col of New York; NY Univ Law Sch, LLB. Polit & Govt Pos: NY State Assemblyman, 33-56; US Rep, NY, 56-72. Mil Serv: Coast Guard Res, World War II. Mem: Am Judicature Soc; NY Co Lawyers Asn; Am & NY Bar Asns; Asn of Bar of New York, NY. Legal Res: 830 Shore Rd Long Beach NY 11561 Mailing Add: 276 Fifth Ave New York NY 10001

FARENTHOLD, FRANCES TARLTON (D)
b Corpus Christi, Tex, Oct 2, 26; d Benjamin Dudley Tarlton & Catherine Bluntzer T; m 1950 to George E Farenthold; c Dudley Tarlton, George E, Jr, Emilie, James Dougherty & Vincent Bluntzer (deceased). Educ: Vassar Col, AB, 46; Univ Tex Law Sch, JD, 49; Woman's Hon Legal Soc. Hon Degrees: LLD, Hood Col & Boston Univ, 73. Polit & Govt Pos: Mem, Corpus Christi Human Rels Comn, Tex, 63-68; mem, Tex Adv Comt to US Comn on Civil Rights, 68-; Tex State Rep, Dist 45, Pl 1, 69-72; Dem cand for gov, 72; deleg, Dem Nat Conv, 72, received 420 votes for nomination US vice president; co-chmn, Citizens for McGovern, 72; chmn, Nat Women's Polit Caucus, currently. Bus & Prof Pos: Asst prof law, Univ Houston, currently. Mem: Tex & Nueces Co Bar Asns; Nat Coalition Human Needs & Budget Priorities; Am Civil Liberties Union; Tax Action Campaign. Relig: Roman Catholic. Legal Res: 4034 Piping Rock Lane Houston TX 77027 Mailing Add: 3935 Westheimer Houston TX 77027

FARGHER, LAWRENCE LEROY (R)
Mem, Rep State Cent Comt, Calif
b Helena, Mont, Sept 16, 32; s Lawrence Arthur Fargher & Maude Lauson F; m 1953 to Camille Marie Augusta; c Larry Lee, Leighton Lynn, Lauson Layne, Lindel Lee & Laure Lynne. Educ: Univ Omaha, BS in eng, 54; Univ Santa Clara, MBA, 65. Polit & Govt Pos: Dir, Santa Clara Co Sanit Dist Four, Calif, 63-69; councilman, Santa Clara, 62-71, mayor, 64-65, mayor protem, 69; cand, US House of Rep, Ninth Cong Dist, Calif, 68; mem, Gov Comt on Hiring the Handicapped, 68-; mem, Calif & Santa Clara Co Rep Cent Comts, currently. Bus & Prof Pos: Engr, Boeing Airplane Co, 58; eng writer, Westinghouse Elec Corp, 58-62; head systs eng, United Tech Ctr, 62-; realtor-partner, Realcom Assocs. Mil Serv: Entered as 2nd Lt, Air Force, 54, released as 1st Lt, 58, after serv in 9th Bomb Sq, 7th Bomb Wing, Heavy Strategic Air Command, 55-58. Mem: Calif & Nat Socs of Prof Engrs; Nat Asn Real Estate Bds; Calif Real Estate Asn; founder Darvon Civic Club of Calif. Relig: Catholic. Legal Res: 3347 Villanova Ct Santa Clara CA 95051 Mailing Add: City Hall 1500 Warburton Ave Santa Clara CA 95051

FARICY, RAYMOND WHITE, JR (DFL)
Minn State Rep
b St Paul, Minn, Nov 26, 34; s Ray W Faricy & Frances Corcoran F; m 1959 to M Sidney Beahan; c Tara M, Raymond W, Megan L, Brigid M & Patrick M. Educ: St Thomas Col, BA, 56; William Mitchell Col Law, BSL & LLB, 60; Delta Theta Phi. Polit & Govt Pos: Minn State Rep, 71- Bus & Prof Pos: Assoc, Schultz & Springer, 60-62 & D D Wozniak, 62-65; partner, Faricy & Green, 65-72 & Fallon, Faricy, Green, Battis & Wolf, 72- Mem: Minn State & Ramsey Co Bar Asns. Relig: Catholic. Mailing Add: 2240 Goodrich St Paul MN 55105

FARIES, MCINTYRE (R)
b Wei Hsien, Shantung Province, China, Apr 17, 96; s Dr William Reid Faries & Priscilla Ellen Chittick F; m 1922 to Margaret Lois Shorten, wid; m 1965 to Geraldyne Brewer Bergh; c Barbara Lois (Mrs Kenneth J Simpson) & Marjorie Ann (Mrs John William Gaines). Educ: Occidental Col, AB, 20; Univ Southern Calif, 19-22; Southwestern Univ (Calif), JD, 26; Phi Beta Kappa; Olive Crown; Phi Delta Phi; Phi Gamma Delta; Econ Club; Blackstonian. Polit & Govt Pos: Deleg, Rep Nat Conv, 36, 40, 44, 48 & 52; vchmn, Rep State Cent Comt, Calif, 38; pres, Calif Rep Assembly, 38; chmn, Rep Campaign Comt South Calif, 40 & 42, mem exec comt, 47-52; chmn, Sen William F Knowland Campaign, 46 & 52; mem, Rep Nat Comt, 47-53, mem exec comt & vchmn, 48-53; mem exec comt, Calif Campaigns, Gen Dwight D Eisenhower, 52, Richard M Nixon for Congressman, Sen & VPresident, Thomas F Kuchel for Senate twice & Earl Warren for Gov, three times; judge, Superior Court, Calif, 53-, pretrial div, 60, presiding judge, 61-64 & appellate dept, 65. Bus & Prof Pos: Pres & mem exec comt, El Pueblo de Los Angeles, Inc, Calif, 53-68; dir, United Financial Corp of Calif, 71- Mil Serv: Entered as Seaman 2/C, Navy, 17, released as Ens, Naval Res, 19, after serv in Pac, 17-19; Naval Res, 19-20, (Ret). Mem: Am Acad Polit & Social Sci; Judicature Soc; Mason; F&AM; Am Legion. Relig: Presbyterian. Mailing Add: Apt 5-C 400 S Burnside Los Angeles CA 90036

FARIS, JANE THERESA CANTWELL (D)
VChmn, Washington Co Dem Cent Comt, Mo
b St Louis, Mo, Sept 9, 31; d Harry James Cantwell & Jane Cummings C; m 1950 to Rubin Faris; c Jane Kevin (Mrs Glen Jones), Monica Helen (Mrs James Lands), Victoria Ellen, Kimberly Kay, Lisa Jean, Abby Michelle & Amy Marie. Educ: Mineral Area Jr Col, night courses, 68-69. Polit & Govt Pos: Committeewoman, Mo State Dem Cent Comt, 66-; secy, Washington Co Dem Cent Comt, Mo, formerly, vchmn, currently; treas, Washington Co Dem Club, 72-; committeewoman, Bellevue Twp, 72-; trustee, Caldonia Town Bd, 72- Bus & Prof Pos: Income tax consult, Interstate Securities Co, Potosi, Mo, 73. Mem: 4-H; Valley High PTA; Caledonia Stitch in Time Club; Caledonia Saddle Club; Caledonia Community Betterment Org. Relig: Catholic. Mailing Add: Box 85 Caledonia MO 63631

FARLAND, JOHN FRANCIS (D)
Mass State Rep
b Southbridge, Mass, May 14, 40; s John E Farland & Rita Duffy F; m 1962 to L Jane DiBonaventura; c Wynne Anne & Gregory John. Educ: Boston Univ, BS in Pub Rels, 62; Sigma Phi Epsilon. Polit & Govt Pos: Mass State Rep, 75-, clerk, Comn on State Admin, Contracts Comn & Surplus Land Comn, Mass House Rep, 75- Bus & Prof Pos: Teacher & coach, several communities, 62-73; Northeast regional supplies mgr, Double Eagle Golf Co, 73-74; assoc publ, Sports Dig of Boston, 74- Legal Res: 70 Cole Ave Southbridge MA 01550 Mailing Add: State House Rm 38 Boston MA 02133

FARLEY, BRUCE A (D)
Ill State Sen
Mailing Add: 3730 N Marshfield Chicago IL 60609

FARLEY, GEORGE EDWARD (D)
WVa State Deleg
b McFarland, WVa, Dec 23, 29; s Charles William Farley (deceased) & Sweetlyn Roberts F (deceased); m 1954 to Lora Jean Dye; c Brenda Lynn & Lynda Jean. Educ: WVa Wesleyan Col, 2 years. Polit & Govt Pos: Pres, Wood Co Young Dem Club, WVa, 64; mem, Parkersburg Charter Bd, 70; WVa State Deleg, 71-72 & 75- Bus & Prof Pos: Rep, State Farm Ins, 62- Mil Serv: Entered as Seaman, Navy, 48, released as PO 2/C, 52, after serv in Naval Patrol Squadron, Far East, 50-52; Good Conduct Medal. Mem: PTA; Farm Bur; YMCA; Jr CofC; AFL-CIO Dist 50 UMW. Relig: Baptist; chmn bd deacons. Legal Res: 2313 36th St Parkersburg WV 26101 Mailing Add: 1007 Division St Parkersburg WV 26101

FARLEY, JAMES A (D)
b Grassy Point, NY, May 30, 88; s James Farley & Ellen Goldrick F; m to Elizabeth A Finnegan (deceased); c Elizabeth (Mrs Glenn D Montgomery), Ann (Mrs Edward J Hickey, III) & James A. Educ: Packard Commercial Sch, New York, NY, 06. Hon Degrees: DCL, Univ of the South, 33, Lincoln Mem Univ, 35, St Ambrose Col, 41, & Villanova Col, 42; LLD, Canisius Col, Manhattan Col, John Marshall Col of Law, 34, Niagara Univ, 35, Hendrix Col, 39, Oglethorpe Univ, 40, Seattle Univ, 50, Ithaca Col, Loras Col, St Anselm's Col, 51, St Joseph's Col, 55 & LI Univ, 57; DCS, NY Univ, 50 & Suffolk Univ, 56; citation, Univ of Fla, 50; DSS, Duquesne Univ, 53. Polit & Govt Pos: Town clerk, Stony Point, NY, 12-19; port warden, Port of NY, 18-19; chmn, Rockland Co Dem Comt, 19-29; supvr, Rockland Co, 20-23; past vpres, Nat Dem Club, New York, NY; NY State Assemblyman, 23; mem, NY State Athletic Comn, 23-33, chmn, 25-33; deleg, Dem Nat Conv, 24, 28, 32, 36, 40, 44, 48 & 68; secy, NY Dem State Comt, 28-30, chmn, 30-44; chmn, Dem Nat Comt, 32-40; Postmaster Gen of US, 33-40; mem, Comn on Orgn Exec Br of Govt, 53; mem, NY State Banking Bd, 55- Bus & Prof Pos: Bookkeeper, Merlin Heilholtz Paper Co, New York, NY, 06; sales mgr, Universal Gypsum Co, 26; organizer, James A Farley & Co, 26, merged with five other bldg materials firms to form Gen Builders Supply Corp, 26, pres & dir, 29-33 & 49; dir, Coca Cola Co, dir, Campania Embotelladora Coca-Cola, S A, pres & dir, Coca-Cola Int, chmn bd & dir, Coca-Cola Co of Can, Ltd, chmn of bd, Coca-Cola Export Corp, 40. Publ: Behind the Ballots, 38; Jim Farley's Story, 48. Mem: Pan-Am Soc, Inc; NY State Hist Asn; Am Soc of Polit & Social Sci; Am Acad Polit & Social Sci; Albany Soc NY. Honors & Awards: Capt Robert Dollar Mem Award; Freedoms Found Award, 53; Cardinal Newman Award, 56; Am Irish Hist Soc Award, 56; Cross of Isabel la Catolica, Spain. Relig: Catholic. Mailing Add: 301 Park Ave New York NY 10022

FARLEY, JAMES WALLACE (D)
Lee Twp Committeeman, Platte Co Dem Cent Comt, Mo
b Kansas City, Mo, July 31, 28; s Wallace J Farley & Idabelle Vanlandingham F; div; c Emma Susan, James Wallace, Jr & John Walter. Educ: Univ Mo, Columbia, BS in Bus Admin, 49, JD, 52; Phi Alpha Delta. Polit & Govt Pos: Lee Twp committeeman, Platte Co Dem Cent Comt, Mo, 50-, chmn, 60-68; mem & secy, Platte Co Planning Comt, 52-54; treas, Mo Young Dem Clubs, 54-55, pres, 55-56; Mo State Rep, 56; deleg, Dem Nat Conv, 56, 68 & 72; mem, Mo State Dem Comt, 60-68; mem, Sixth Cong Dist Dem Comt, Mo, 60-68 & 72-; co-chmn, Mo Sen Redistricting Comt, 61. Bus & Prof Pos: Mem, Kansas City Metrop Planning Comn, 68- Mem: Mo Bar Asn; Platte Co Bar Asn (pres, 65 & 73); Mason; RAM; Shrine. Relig: Disciples of Christ; Deacon, First Christian Church, Platte City, Mo. Mailing Add: Box 33 Farley MO 64028

FARLEY, ROBERT M (D)
Maine State Rep
Mailing Add: 45 Myrtle St Biddeford ME 04005

FARMER, DONALD FRANCIS (D)
b Chicago, Ill, Feb 12, 47; s Robert Paul Farmer, Sr (deceased) & Laura Louise Allred F; single. Educ: Univ Tenn, Martin, 65; Jackson State Col, 66-72. Polit & Govt Pos: Hon mayor, Lavinia, Tenn, 63-69; deleg, Dem Nat Mid-Term Conf, 74. Bus & Prof Pos: Prod control scheduler, ITT Telecommun, Milan, Tenn, 65- Mem: Jaycees (admin asst, Tenn Jaycees). Honors & Awards: Outstanding Award, Gibson Co Sesquicentennial Orgn, 73; Outstanding Young Man Award, Milan, 74 & Tenn, 75. Relig: Baptist. Mailing Add: 368 Hunter Heights Milan TN 38358

FARMER, JAMES (INDEPENDENT)
Asst Secy, Dept Health, Educ & Welfare
b Marshall, Tex, Jan 12, 20; s James Leonard Farmer & Pearl Marion Houston F; m 1949 to Lula A Peterson; c Tami & Abbey. Educ: Wiley Col, BS, 38; Howard Univ, BD, 41. Hon Degrees: HHD, Morgan State Col, 64; LLD, Muhlenberg Col. Polit & Govt Pos: Founder, Cong of Racial Equality, 42, nat chmn, 42-44 & 50, nat dir, 61-66, leader, Freedom Ride, 61; race rels secy, Fel of Reconciliation, 44-45; organizer, Upholsterers' Int Union of NAm, 45-47; lectr race, educ & labor probs, 48-; student field secy, League for Indust Democracy, 50-54; int rep, State, Co & Munic Employees Union, 54-59; vchmn, Liberal Party of NY Co, 54-61; prog dir, NAACP, 59-61; mem nat exec bd, Am Comt on Africa, 59-64; sponsor, Am Negro Leadership Conf on Africa; chmn, Coun of United Civil Rights Leadership, 63-; head, Ctr for Community Action Educ, 66-; asst secy, Dept Health, Educ & Welfare, 69-70 & 72-; pres, Coun Minority Planning & Strategy, 72- Publ: Freedom—When?, 65. Mem: League for Indust Democracy; Am Civil Liberties Union; Am for Dem Action. Honors & Awards: Omega Psi Phi Award, 61, 63; Amvets Community Award, 62; John Dewey Award, League for Indust Democracy, 62. Mailing Add: 5129 Chevy Chase Pkwy NW Washington DC 20008

FARMER, MERLE LOUISE (D)
b Tularosa, NMex, Oct 23, 06; d Arthur Lincoln Douglass & Blanche Rachael Parker; m to Paul R Farmer, div. Educ: Tularosa High; Bus Col, grad, 23. Polit & Govt Pos: Pres, Ariz Fedn Dem Women Clubs, 61-62; chmn, Yavapai Co Dem Cent Comt, 62-72; deleg, Dem Nat Conv, 64 & 68; alt deleg, Dem Nat Mid-Term Conf, 74; mem, State Personnel Comn, 75- Bus & Prof Pos: Yavapai Co Welfare Bd, Prescott, Ariz, 16 years; owner, Wholesale Bread, 49-59; supvr, Legis Post Off, Phoenix, 60-65; supt, Ariz Pioneer Home, Prescott, 65-67. Mem: Bus & Prof Womens Club; Soroptimist Club (charter mem); Am Legion Auxiliary; VFW Auxiliary; Am Cancer Soc (mem bd dirs). Honors & Awards: 35 Years Vol Work, Am Cancer Soc. Relig: Methodist. Mailing Add: 607 Country Club Dr Prescott AZ 86301

FARMER, ROBERT L (D)
NC State Rep
b Johnston Co, NC, July 23, 33; s Thomas Albert Farmer & Oma Martha Adams F; m 1959 to Martha Caroline Lassiter; c Joseph Robert, James Thomas & Caroline Marie. Educ: Univ NC, Chapel Hill, BS in Bus Admin, 55, LLB, 50. Polit & Govt Pos: Solicitor, Wake Co Domestic Rels Court, NC, 63-65; NC State Rep, 71- Bus & Prof Pos: Attorney, 60- Mil Serv: Entered as Pvt, Army, 55, released as SP-3, 57. Mem: NC State Bar; NC & Wake Co Bar Asns; Raleigh Jaycees; Raleigh Kiwanis. Relig: Methodist; chmn bd trustees, Hayes Barton United Methodist Church, 68- Mailing Add: 107 Kipling Pl Raleigh NC 27609

FARMER, THOMAS LAURENCE (D)
b Berlin, Ger, July 26, 23; s Laurence Farmer & Else Dienemann F; div; c Daniel Fairchild, Sarah Bennett & Elspeth Lanham. Educ: Harvard, BA, 43, LLB, 50; Brasenose Col, Oxford Univ, BA in Jurisprudence, 48, MA, 50; Lincoln's Inn Soc. Polit & Govt Pos: Chmn adv bd, Nat Capitol Transportation Agency, 61-64; gen counsel, Agency Int Develop, 64-68. Bus & Prof Pos: Clerk to Judge Manley O Hudson, Int Law Comn of Gen Assembly of UN, Geneva, Switz, 50; assoc, Simpson, Thacher & Bartlett, New York, NY, 54-57, assoc, Simpson, Thacher & Bartlett, Wash, 58-64; partner, Kominers, Fort, Schlefer, Farmer & Boyer, 68-70; partner, Prather, Levenberg, Seeger, Doolittle, Farmer & Ewing, Wash, 70- Mil Serv: Entered as Pvt, Army, 43, released as M/Sgt, 46, after serv in Mil Intel Rec Sect, War Dept Gen Staff, 44-46. Mem: DC, NY, Am & Fed Bar Asns; Am Soc Int Law. Relig: Episcopal. Legal Res: 3456 Macomb St NW Washington DC 20016 Mailing Add: 1101 16th St NW Washington DC 20036

FARNHAM, RODERICK EWEN (R)
Maine State Rep
b Brownville Junction, Maine, Jan 23, 10; s Willard C Farnham & Marion Morrison F; m 1938 to Margaret Davis Sprague; c Alden C Sprague (stepson), Patricia (Mrs Russell), R Ewen, M Jane (Mrs Rabeni) & Barbara M (Mrs Briggs). Educ: Colby Col, BS, 31; Lambda Chi Alpha. Hon Degrees: MA, Colby Col, 60. Polit & Govt Pos: Maine State Rep, 69- Mem: Am Soc Personnel Adminr (past pres, Maine Chap); Mason; Hampden Kiwanis (dir); Hampden Regional Libr (dir); Hampden Conserv Comn (chmn). Relig: Protestant. Legal Res: Sunset Ave Hampden ME 04444 Mailing Add: MRC Box 17 Bangor ME 04401

FARNIK, JOE F (D)
Chmn, Knox Co Dem Party, Nebr
b Pischelville, Nebr, June 19, 10; s Joseph Farnik & Anna Dobriehousky F; m 1935 to Helen Jerman; c Joseph Charles, Dennis D, John A, Gary L & Jo Ellen (Mrs Miller). Educ: Colo State Barber Col, 32. Polit & Govt Pos: Precinct committeeman, Verdigre Dem Party, Nebr, 50-72; vchmn, Knox Co Dem Party, 70-72, chmn, 72-; mem, Judicial Nomination Comn, Ninth Dist, 72- Bus & Prof Pos: Self-employed barber, Verdigre, Nebr, 46-; laundromat owner, 60- Mem: Verdigre Improv Club; Mason; Housing Authority Bd. Relig: Methodist; Chmn of admin bd, United Methodist Church, 69- Mailing Add: Verdigre NE 68783

FARNSLEY, CHARLES ROWLAND PEASLEE (D)
b Louisville, Ky, Mar 28, 07; s Burrel Hopson Farnsley & Anna May Peaslee F; m 1937 to Nancy Hall Carter; c Mrs Robert Bird, Jr, Mrs Ann Farnsley, Douglass Charles Ellerbe, Alexander, IV & Burrel Charles. Educ: Univ Louisville, LLB, 30, AB, 42; Delta Upsilon; Omicron Delta Kappa. Hon Degrees: LLD, Univ Louisville, 50, Wesleyan Univ, 59. Polit & Govt Pos: Ky State Rep, 36-40; Mayor, Louisville, 48-54; US Rep, Third Dist, Ky, 64-66. Bus & Prof Pos: Law practice, 30-48 & 54-64; mem bd trustees, Louisville Free Pub Libr, 43-48; trustee, Univ Louisville, 46-48, secy bd trustees, 47-48, mem bd overseers, 47-58; curator, Transylvania Univ, 47-58; pres, Lost Cause Press Co, currently. Mem: Am, Jefferson Co & Ky Bar Asns; Sons of Confederate Vet; Louisville Philharmonic Soc. Relig: Episcopal. Mailing Add: Lost Cause Press Co 455 S Fourth Louisville KY 40202

FARNSWORTH, LEE WINFIELD (R)
Utah State Rep
b Salt Lake City, Utah, Mar 6, 32; s Walter J Farnsworth & Ethel Loveridge F; m 1953 to Zona Gayle Smith; c Carol, David, Kenneth, Ellen, Leonard, Bryan, Steven, Janis & Mary. Educ: Stanford Univ, 60-61; Mt San Antonio Col, AA, 53; Univ Calif, Berkeley, BA, highest hons, 57, MA, 60; Claremont Grad Sch, PhD, 63; Pi Sigma Alpha; student body pres, Mt San Antonio Col. Polit & Govt Pos: Sch bd mem, Provo City Schs, Utah, 73-74; Utah State Rep, 75- Bus & Prof Pos: Teacher, Claremont City Schs, Calif, 58-60; asst prof govt, Fla State Univ, 62-64; asst prof polit sci, Brigham Young Univ, 64-66, assoc prof, 66-71, prof, 71-; vis assoc prof, Int Christian Univ, Tokyo, 70-71. Mil Serv: Entered as Pvt, Army, 53, released as Sgt, 56. Publ: Auth, Story of Japan, McCormick-Mathers, 70; co-ed, Security In a World of Change, Wadsworth, 69; auth, Political Factions & Political Conflict: Japan as a Case Study, General Learning Press, in press. Mem: Am Polit Sci Asn; Asn for Asian Studies; Scholars Specializing on Japanese Politics (chmn & ed, 69-); Western Conf Asian Studies. Honors & Awards: Nat Sci Found Award, summer 69; Fulbright-Hays Lectr in Philippines, summer 71; Fulbright-Hays Research Award in Japan, 70-71; Japan Found Fel, 75-76. Relig: Latter-day Saint. Mailing Add: 3147 Apache Lane Provo UT 84601

FARNSWORTH, NORMA KIMBER (R)
VChmn, Millard Co Rep Comt, Utah
b Delta, Utah, Nov 16, 31; d Albert Latham Kimber & Lucille Strong K; m 1953 to Frank Gale Farnsworth; c Janet, Kathleen, LuAnne, Michael, Neil & Owen. Educ: Southern Utah State Col, BS, 53. Polit & Govt Pos: Vchmn, Millard Co Rep Comt, Utah, 74- Bus & Prof Pos: Teacher, Millard Co Sch Dist, Utah, 57-58 & 67-70, Clark Co Sch Dist, Nev, 60-65 & Weber Co Sch Dist, Utah, 65-66. Relig: Latter-day Saint. Legal Res: 243 W 200 North Delta UT 84624 Mailing Add: PO Box 277 Delta UT 84624

FARR, HAROLD P (R)
Chmn, Wyoming Co Rep Party, Pa
b Pa, July 16, 17; s Stanley W Farr & Evangeline Phillips F; m 1941 to Dorothy Bickos; c Thomas A (deceased), Stanley W & Kenneth A. Educ: Wyoming Sem Bus Sch, Kingston, Pa, grad, 34; Univ Fla, Tallahassee. Polit & Govt Pos: Chmn, Wyoming Co Rep Party, Pa, 72- Bus & Prof Pos: Field underwriter sales, Monarch Life Ins Co, 69- Mil Serv: Entered as Aviation Cadet, Army Air Force, 42, released as Maj(Ret), 67, after serv in WWII & Korea; Two Distinguished Flying Crosses; Four Air Medals & various others. Mem: Mason; Temple Lodge 248; Keystone Consistory; Trew Temple. Relig: Protestant. Mailing Add: Rte 2 Box 107 Meshoppen PA 18630

FARR, LOUISE ROSE (R)
Secy, Rep State Cent & Exec Comts, Ohio
b Cleveland, Ohio, Feb 13, 18; d Carmine Conte & Mary Giammaria C; m 1937 to Louis N Farr; c John Anthony, Carmen Joseph & Louis Nicholas, Jr. Educ: John Hay High Sch, grad, 36. Polit & Govt Pos: Alt deleg, Ohio Rep State Conv, Columbus, 48 & 49, deleg, 50-65 & deleg-at-lg, 66-70; precinct committeewoman, 3-E, Cleveland Heights, 46-58; woman sect leader, Cleveland Heights, 50-60; mem, Cuyahoga Co Rep Cent Comt, 56-69; dep registr, Bur Motor Vehicles, State of Ohio, 57 & 58 & 66-70; mem, Cuyahoga Co Rep Exec Comt, 60-, precinct committeewoman, 72-; asst dist supvr, 1960 Decennial Census app by Rep Frances P Bolton, 60; mgr, Robert Grogan for State Rep Campaign, Cuyahoga Co, 64; temporary dep co auditor, 64-70 & 72-; mem bd mgr, Ohio Fedn of Rep Women's Orgn, Inc, 66-; mem, Rep State Cent & Exec Comts of Ohio, 22nd Cong Dist, 66-, secy, 72-; bd trustees, Ohio Rep News, Inc, 66-, secy bd, 73-; mem, Cuyahoga Co Women's Rep Adv Bd, 68-; vchmn, Ohio Rep State Conv Arrangements Comt, 70; secy, Donald W Gropp for Cong Comt, 22nd Dist, 72. Bus & Prof Pos: Sales mgr, Snedeker's Toy Shoppe, Cleveland Heights, Ohio, 52-60, owner-mgr, 60-69; notary pub, Cuyahoga Co. Mem: 19th Ward Rep Club of Cleveland, Ohio; Western Reserve Women's Rep Club, Shaker Heights; Cleveland Heights Rep Club, Civic Club & Rep Orgn; St Ann's Guild, Cleveland Heights; Cuyahoga Co Rep Ward Club. Relig: Roman Catholic. Mailing Add: 1012 Hereford Rd Cleveland Heights OH 44112

FARR, WILLIAM MORRIS (D)
Ariz State Sen
b Kansas City, Mo, Oct 20, 38; s Glenn Levi Farr & Ruth Toliver F; m 1960 to Pi A D Irwin; c Jefry & Katherine. Educ: Rice Univ, BS, 60; Univ Mich, PhD, 66; Sigma Chi. Polit & Govt Pos: Pres, Anderson Co Young Dem, Tenn, formerly; chmn, Dist 13 Dem Club, Tucson, Ariz; Ariz State Sen, 75- Bus & Prof Pos: Asst prof nuclear eng, Univ Ariz, 70- Publ: Numerous sci articles. Mem: Am Phys Soc; Am Nuclear Soc; Am Asn Univ Prof. Relig: Unitarian. Mailing Add: 3812 Ensenada Tucson AZ 85716

FARR, WILLIAM S, JR (R)
Mem, Kent Co Rep Party Exec Comt, Mich
b New York, NY, Mar 10, 35; m 1957 to Kay C Cougill; c Gregory William, Sheryl Lynn & Cynthia Kay. Educ: Wash Univ, AB; Univ Mich, LLB. Polit & Govt Pos: Chmn, Mich Teachers Tenure Comn, 68-72; chmn, Kent Co Rep Party, 69-70; Rep cand for Attorney Gen, Mich, 70; chmn, Fifth Dist Rep Comt, 71-72; chmn, Mich Rep State Conv, 71; deleg & mem platform comt, Rep Nat Conv, 72; mem, Kent Co Rep Party Exec Comt, 73- Bus & Prof Pos: Attorney-at-law. Mem: Kent Co United Fund Dr; Grand Rapids Area Coun of Churches; Grand Rapids Bar Asn (trustee, 73-); Proj Rehab (bd dirs, 73-). Honors & Awards: Grand Rapids Young Man of the Year, Jaycees, 70. Relig: Presbyterian; Elder & former Deacon, Eastminster Presby Church. Legal Res: 2102 Griggs SE Grand Rapids MI 49502 Mailing Add: 430 Federal Sq Bldg Grand Rapids MI 49502

FARRAND, CHRISTOPHER GEORGE (R)
b Detroit, Mich, Mar 18, 41; s David O Farrand & Jean Russel True F; m 1966 to Christa Schneidawind; c Stephan & Alexander. Educ: Univ Mich, BLitt, 63; Psi Upsilon. Polit & Govt Pos: Peace Corps vol, Repub of Guinea, 65-66; legis asst to US Rep Philip E Ruppe, Washington, DC, 67-71, admin asst, 71- Bus & Prof Pos: Copywriter, D P Brother & Co, Advert, Detroit, Mich, 64-65. Mem: Bull Elephants; Ripon Soc. Relig: Protestant. Legal Res: 1406 First Ave S Escanaba MI 49829 Mailing Add: 3523 Albemarle St NW Washington DC 20008

FARRAR, FRANK L (R)
b Britton, SDak, Apr 2, 29; m to Patricia Henley; c Jeanne M, Sally A, Mary S, Robert J & Ann M. Educ: Univ SDak, BS, 51, LLB, 53; pres Univ Student Asn, Inter-Fraternity Coun, Alpha Tau Omega; Phi Delta Phi. Polit & Govt Pos: Fed internal revenue agent, judge & states attorney, Marshall Co, SDak; former chmn, Marshall Co Young Rep; former mem sch bd; chmn, Marshall Co Sr Rep; asst sgt-at-arms, Rep Nat Conv, 60; pres, SDak States Attorneys Asn, 61; Attorney Gen, SDak, 62-69, Gov, 69-70. Bus & Prof Pos: Attorney-at-law. Mil Serv: Korean Vet; Capt, Army Res (Ret). Mem: Boy Scouts (pres, Pheasant Coun); Lions; Elks; Mason; Shrine. Honors & Awards: Citizenship Award, Jaycees; SDak Young Rep Man of the Year, 63. Relig: Presbyterian; Adult Sunday Sch teacher & former deacon, Presbyterian Church. Mailing Add: Britton SD 57430

FARRAR, KEITH (R)
Kans State Rep
Mailing Add: Rte 2 Hugoton KS 67951

FARRAR, REGINALD WARREN, JR (R)
b El Dorado, Ark, Aug 2, 22; s Reginald Warren Farrar, Sr & Katherine Grigsby F; m 1949 to Ann Mills, div; c Gail, Katherine & Cynthia. Educ: La Polytech Inst, BA, 43; La State Univ JD, 48; Alpha Lambda Tau; Gamma Eta Gamma. Polit & Govt Pos: US comnr, West Dist La, 54-72, US Magistrate, 72-; chmn personnel comt, Lake Charles, La, 56-59; dep dir, DeLesseps S Morrison Campaign Gov, 59; chmn, Lake Charles Munic Fire & Police Civil Serv Bd, 67-70; deleg, Rep Nat Conv, 68 & 72; mem, La State Rep Cent Comt, 68-72. Bus & Prof Pos: Partner, Raggio, Farrar, Cappel & Chozen, Attorneys, 50- Mil Serv: Entered as A/S, Coast Guard, 43, released as SigM 3/C, 46, after serv in Atlantic & Pac Theatres, 43-46. Mem: La Defense Counsel Asn; Defense Res Inst; Int Asn Ins Counsel; La State Bar Asn (bd gov, comt law reform, 62-, comt no-fault, 72-); Southwest La Bar Asn. Relig: Episcopal. Legal Res: 2960 Lake St Apt 169 Lake Charles LA 70601 Mailing Add: PO Box 820 Lake Charles LA 70601

FARRAR, WILLIAM HAROLD (R)
Chmn, Linn Co Rep Comt, Mo
b Highland, Ill, Aug 8, 26; s Joseph Vernon Farrar & Viola Schwend F; m 1949 to Elizabeth Moore; c William H, Jr, Nancee Jane (Mrs Linebaugh), Kathleen & Patricia. Educ: Ofallon

High Sch. Polit & Govt Pos: Chmn, Linn Co Rep Comt, Mo, 69- Mil Serv: Entered as Seaman 3/C, Navy, 44, released as MMO 3/C, 46, after serv in 23rd Seabee Bn, SPac, 45-46. Relig: Protestant. Mailing Add: 619 Skyline Dr Brookfield MO 64628

FARRELL, GEORGE JOSEPH, JR (R)
VChmn, Nassau Co Rep Party, NY
b Brooklyn, NY, Sept 27, 30; s George J Farrell (deceased) & Mae Travers F; m 1957 to Patricia Carney; c Kathleen, Joseph, Kevin, Elizabeth & Margaret. Educ: Fordham Col, AB, 52; Brooklyn Law Sch, JD, 57. Polit & Govt Pos: Mem zoning bd of appeals, Village of Floral Park, NY, 60-63, trustee, 63, & mayor, 63-65; NY State Assemblyman, 21st Assembly Dist, 66-74; alt deleg, Rep Nat Conv, 68 & 72; mem, Rep Exec Comt, 68-; vchmn, Nassau Co Rep Party, 68-; mem, Long Island State Parks & Recreation Comn, 74- Mil Serv: Entered as Pvt, Army, 52, released, 54, after serv in 25th Inf Div, 53-54. Mem: Bar Asn of Nassau Co; Am Bar Asn; Elks; Lions; Nassau Hosp (mem bd dirs). Honors & Awards: 1968 Friendship Award, Nat Info Bur for Jewish Life. Relig: Roman Catholic. Legal Res: 116 Carnation Ave Floral Park NY 11001 Mailing Add: 114 Old Country Rd Mineola NY 11501

FARRELL, HERMAN D, JR (D)
NY State Assemblyman
Mailing Add: 522 W 157th St New York NY 10032

FARRELL, JOHN CHARLES (D)
b Vallejo, Calif, Aug 3, 49; s Ambrose Michael Farrell & Helen Cecile DeGrenier F; single. Educ: Providence Col, BA, 71. Polit & Govt Pos: Deleg, Dem Nat Conv, 72; sr vpres, Young Dem Club of RI, 72-73. Bus & Prof Pos: Mkt coordr, Gripnail Corp, East Providence, RI, 71-72. Mem: RI Workers Asn. Relig: Catholic. Mailing Add: 225 Orms St Providence RI 02908

FARRELL, JOSEPH ALOYSIUS, III
b Long Beach, Calif, June 29, 29; s Joseph Aloysius Farrell, Jr & Alice Edwards F; m 1971 to Claudia Bourne; c Monica, Kevin, Stephen, Maureen, Kathleen, Dennis & Linda. Educ: Brown Univ, 46-48; US Naval Acad, BS, 52, Naval Officers Submarine Course, 55, Naval Advan Reactor Eng, 58-59; Sigma Nu. Polit & Govt Pos: Dir, Peace Corps, Honduras, 64-66, dir, Peace Corps Sch Partnership Prog, DC, 66-67 & Peace Corps Vol Selection, 67-69; admin asst to US Sen Charles H Percy, Ill, 69- Mil Serv: Entered as Midn, Navy, 48, released as Lt Comdr, 64, after serv 7 of 12 years in nuclear submarines mainly in Pac Fleet, last pos was exec officer of Polaris Submarine; Navy Unit Citation for first Atlantic to Pac Polar Trip. Legal Res: 2315 Swainwood Dr Glenview IL 60025 Mailing Add: 618 E St NE Washington DC 20002

FARRELL, PHYLLIS CHASE (D)
Committeewoman, Ga State Dem Exec Comt
b Washington, DC, June 15, 30; d Ralph Henry Chase & Ruth Weihe C; m 1953 to John James Farrell; c Maureen, John James, III, Patrick Kelly & Timothy. Educ: Univ Md, BS in home econ, 52; Omicron Nu. Polit & Govt Pos: Committeewoman, Ga State Dem Exec Comt, 70-; Ga First Cong Dist deleg, Dem Nat Conv, 72; chmn, Ga Dem Charter Comn, Second Sen Dist, 74-; mem, Ga Crime Info Ctr Adv Coun, 74- Mem: DAR (corresponding secy, Lachlan McIntosh chap, 70-); Peace Officers Ga (assoc mem); League Women Voters; Mayfair Park, Inc (secy, 71-); Mayfair Gardeners (Garden Club of Ga, Inc). Mailing Add: 1418 N Camden Circle Savannah GA 31406

FARRELL, THOMAS FRANCIS (D)
Chmn, DeKalb Co Dem Party, Ga
b Bronxville, NY, Apr 14, 45; s John Thomas Farrell & Anna-Marie Krieg F; m 1968 to Melissa Ann DeFreese; c Thomas Damian. Educ: Ga Inst Technol, BSIM, 71; Ga State Univ, MBIS, 75; Alpha Kappa Psi. Polit & Govt Pos: Mem exec comt, DeKalb Co Dem Party, Ga, 72-, chmn, 74-; mem exec comt, Dem Party Ga, 74- Bus & Prof Pos: Systs consult, Comprehensive Planning Group, 71-72; systs consult, Interactive Syst, 72-73; city admin asst, Atlanta, Ga, 73-74, supvr gen acct, 74- Mil Serv: Entered as Pvt E-1, Army, 68, released as Sgt E-5, 69, after serv in 7th Army, Europe; Legion of Dragoons. Relig: Catholic. Mailing Add: 3003 Catalina Dr Decatur GA 30032

FARRELLY, ALEXANDER (D)
Chmn, VI Dem Party
Mailing Add: PO Box 1239 St Thomas VI 00801

FARRICIELLI, JOSEPH J (D)
Conn State Rep
Mailing Add: Cherry Hill Brandford CT 06504

FARRINGTON, ELIZABETH PRUETT (R)
b Tokyo, Japan, May 30, 98; d Robert Lee Pruett & Josephine Baugh P; m 1920 to Joseph Rider Farrington, wid; c Beverly (Mrs Hugh F Richardson) & John. Educ: Univ Wis, BA, 18; Theta Sigma Phi; Alpha Omicron Pi. Polit & Govt Pos: Prog chmn, League of Rep Women, DC, 45-46, pres, 47-48; nat chmn pub rels, Nat Fedn Rep Women, 47-49, pres, 49-53; US Rep, Hawaii, 54-57; deleg, Hawaii State Rep Conv, 54-66; deleg, Rep Nat Conv, 56; mem, Hawaii State Comn, NY World's Fair & Hawaii rep, Nat Bd Dirs, 64 & 65; dir, Off of Territories, Dept of Interior, 69-72. Bus & Prof Pos: Reporter, Wis State J, Madison, 18-20; Washington, DC Cong correspondent & columnist, Lee Syndicate Newspapers, 20-23; founder, Wash Press Serv, 23; art & music critic for Honolulu papers, 27-36; originator & ed, Wash Newsletter, 45-54; pres & chmn bd dirs, Honolulu Star Bull, Ltd & subsidiary corps, Star Bull, Commercial Printing Co, Hilo Tribune-Herald, KGMB Radio & TV & Honolulu Lithograph Co, 57-62. Mem: Pan-Pac Union; 78th Cong Club 45, 1925 F St Club; Capitol Hill Club; Am Asn Univ Women. Honors & Awards: Named one of Ten Most Powerful Women in Politics in Nation, McCall's Mag, 51; Named one of Twelve Outstanding Women in Nation in Any Field of Endeavor, Gen Fedn Women's Clubs, DC, 52; Outstanding Grad in Field of Jour, Univ Wis Col Jour, 55; selected to debate, NY Herald Tribune Forum, 48. Relig: Disciples of Christ. Mailing Add: Royal Hawaiian Hotel 2259 Kalakaua Ave Honolulu HI 96815

FARRINGTON, STEPHEN HUGH (R)
NDak State Rep
b Fessenden, NDak, Mar 16, 26; s S Hugh Farrington & Ruth Olson F; m 1952 to JoAnn Goetz; c Mary & Hugh. Educ: Univ NDak, BS, 50; Phi Alpha Theta; Lambda Chi Alpha. Polit & Govt Pos: NDak State Rep, Dist 14, 74- Bus & Prof Pos: Newspaper publ, Fessenden, NDak, 52-63; US Civil Serv personnel investr & mgt specialist, Des Moines, Iowa & Washington, DC, 63-66; newspaper publ, Harvey, NDak, 66- Mil Serv: Entered as A/S, Navy, 44, released as Signalman 3/C, 46, after serv in Pac Theatre. Mem: NDak Newspaper Asn (third vpres, 74-75); Gtr NDak Asn (dir); Am Legion; VFW; Kiwanis. Mailing Add: 4 Advent Ave Harvey ND 58341

FARRINGTON, THOMAS (D)
Dem Nat Committeeman, Md
Mailing Add: 12000 Kingfield Ct Upper Marlboro MD 20807

FARRIS, NORMAN EDWIN (R)
Minority Floor Leader, Ky State Sen
b Ware, Ky, Apr 11, 21; s William Ernest Farris (deceased) & Sina Frances Hodge F (deceased); m 1972 to June Bargo; c Frances Ann (Mrs Jerry Ray Girdler) & Mark Edwin. Educ: Univ Louisville; Ky Sch Mortuary Sci, grad, 48. Polit & Govt Pos: Coroner, Pulaski Co, Ky, 62-67; Ky State Sen, 15th Dist, 68-, Minority Whip, Ky State Senate, 68-70, Minority Floor Leader, 70-; treas, Ky Rep State Comt, 70- Bus & Prof Pos: Vpres, Southern Belle Dairy, Somerset, 69-; vpres, Southern Food Corp, Somerset, 69- Mil Serv: Entered as Pvt, Air Force, 42, released as Maj, 45, after serv as pilot. Mem: Ky Funeral Dir Asn; Kiwanis; F&AM (past Master, 225); Mason (32 degree); Shrine. Relig: Baptist. Mailing Add: PO Box 831 Somerset KY 42501

FARY, JOHN G (D)
US Sen, Ill
Mailing Add: 3600 S Damen Ave Chicago IL 60609

FASBENDER, LAWRENCE WILLIAM, JR (LARRY) (D)
Majority Leader, Mont House Rep
b Great Falls, Mont, Aug 18, 42; s Lawrence William Fasbender & Hazel M Blossom F; m 1965 to Retta Rae Greenup; c Lisa Marie, Laura Ann & Bradley Todd. Educ: Gonzaga Univ, BA, 64; Univ Mont Law Sch, 1 year; Alpha Sigma Nu; Jesuit Scholastic Soc; Knights of the Kennel. Polit & Govt Pos: Mont State Rep, Dist 18, 67-, Dem Minority Whip, Mont House Rep, 71-73, Majority Leader, 73- Bus & Prof Pos: Farm mgr, Family Farm, Ft Shaw, Mont, 65-66, owner, 66- Mem: Lions; Farmers Union. Honors & Awards: Jaycees Outstanding Young Man of the Year; selected to partic in Eagleton Inst of Polit. Relig: Catholic. Mailing Add: Rte 1 Box 23 Ft Shaw MT 59443

FASCELL, DANTE B (D)
US Rep, Fla
b Bridgehampton, NY, Mar 9, 17; m to Jeanne-Marie Pelot; c Sandra Jeanne, Toni & Dante Jon. Educ: Univ of Miami, JD, 38; Kappa Sigma. Polit & Govt Pos: Pres, Dade Co Young Dem Club, Fla, 47-48; legal attache, State Legis Del from Dade Co, 47-50; Fla State Rep, 50-54; US Rep, Fla, 54-, mem, House Comt on Int Rels & Comt on Govt Opers; alt deleg, Dem Nat Conv, 68; mem, US Del to UN 24th Gen Assembly, 69. Mil Serv: With Fla Nat Guard, 41, 2nd Lt, 42, released as Capt, 46, after serv in African, Sicilian & Italian Campaigns. Mem: Iron Arrow Soc; Italian-Am Club; Lions; Am & Fed Bar Asns. Honors & Awards: Selected as One of Five Outstanding Men in State, Fla Jr CofC, 51. Legal Res: Miami FL Mailing Add: US House of Rep 2160 Rayburn House Off Bldg Washington DC 20515

FASI, FRANK FRANCIS (D)
Mayor, Honolulu, Hawaii
b East Hartford, Conn, Aug 27, 20; s Carmelo Fasi & Josephine Lupo F; m 1958 to Joyce Miyeku Kono; c Toni Anne, Kathleen Helen, Carl Frederick, Francesca Maria, Paul Francis, Charles Francis, Frank Francis, II, Gina Marisa, David Francis, Gioia Melissa & Salvatore Francis. Educ: Trinity Col, BS, 42; Sigma Nu. Polit & Govt Pos: Dem precinct pres & secy, Hawaii Dem State Cent Comt, 50; Dem Nat Committeeman, Hawaii, 52-56; Hawaii State Sen, 59; councilman-at-lg, Honolulu, 65-69, mayor, 69-; deleg, Hawaii Dem Nat Conv, 68. Bus & Prof Pos: Owner, Frank F Fasi Supply Co, 47-66. Mil Serv: Entered as Pfc, Marine Corps, 42, released as 1st Lt, 46, after serv in Pac Area, 42-46; Capt, Marine Res, until 56. Mem: AFTRA of AFL-CIO; Kalihi Businessmen's Asn; VFW; Am Legion; Boy Scouts. Relig: Catholic. Mailing Add: Off of the Mayor Honolulu HI 96813

FASSER, PAUL, JR (D)
Asst Secy for Labor Mgt Rels, Dept Labor
Legal Res: VA Mailing Add: Dept of Labor Washington DC 20210

FAST, ROBERT ERWIN (D)
VChmn, Franklin Co Dem Comt, Maine
b Woodbury, NJ, Sept 10, 32; s Fred L Fast & Helen Justice F; m 1955 to Joan Elizabeth Henderson, div; c Robert Erwin, Jr & Linda Joan. Educ: Princeton Univ, AB, 54; Rutgers Univ, MEd, 59, EdD, 67; Cloister Inn Club. Polit & Govt Pos: Treas, Johnson for President Campaign, Woodstown, NJ, 64; vpres, Woodstown Dem Club, 65-67; cand for freeholder, Salem Co, 66; deleg, Maine Dem State Conv, 68, 70 & 72; chmn, Strong Dem Comt, 68-; mem, Franklin Co Dem Comt, 68-, chmn, 70-72, vchmn, 72-; mem, Maine State Dem Comt, 70-74. Bus & Prof Pos: Teacher, Woodstown High Sch, NJ, 56-59, guid dir, 56-61; teaching asst, Rutgers Univ, 61-62; asst to dir, Salem Tech Inst, 62; sch psychologist & guid dir, Washington Twp Schs, Sewell, 63; assoc prof educ, Glassboro State Col, 63-67, asst dir students, 63-66, assoc dean admin, 66-67; prof educ & psychol, Univ Maine, Farmington, 67-, chmn dept prof educ & psychol, 70- Mil Serv: Entered as Pvt, Army, 55, released as Pvt, 55, after serv in Hq Co 48th Group, Ft Eustis, Va. Mem: Am Personnel & Guid Asn; Am Asn Univ Prof; Am Asn Higher Educ; Nat Asn Teacher Educ; New Eng Teacher Preparation Asn. Relig: Protestant. Mailing Add: Box 23 Strong ME 04983

FATH, EDNA EVANS (R)
Committeewoman, Ohio State Rep Comt
b Minneapolis, Minn, May 10, 07; d William Orson Evans & Emma Jarvis E; m to James Place Fath, wid. Educ: Hennepin Co Bus Col, 1 year. Polit & Govt Pos: Chairwoman, Butler Co Rep Party, Ohio, formerly; treas, Ohio Fedn, Rep Women's Orgn, 56-68; dir, Butler Co Bd Elec, 63-; committeewoman, Ohio State Rep Comt, 66- Mem: Ft Hamilton-Hughes Mem Hosp Ctr (bd trustees, 72-); Eastern Star; Woman's City Club of Hamilton. Mailing Add: 1340 Park Ave Hamilton OH 45013

FATZER, HAROLD R (R)
Chief Justice, Kans Supreme Court
b Fellsburg, Kans, Aug 3, 10; s John R Fatzer (deceased) & Rella Shannon F (deceased); m 1936 to Frances Josephine Schwaup; c John Richard. Educ: Kans State Univ, 2 years; Washburn Col Law Sch, LLB, JD, 71; Dean's Honor Roll; Tau Delta Phi; Kappa Sigma. Hon

Degrees: LLD, Washburn Univ, 71. Polit & Govt Pos: Co attorney, Edwards Co, Kans, 34-41; chief counsel, State Bd Welfare, 41-43; Asst Attorney Gen, Kans, 43 & 45-49, Attorney Gen, 49-56; Chief Justice, Kans Supreme Court, 56- Bus & Prof Pos: Mem, Appellate Judges Seminar, NY Univ, 59; mem bd trustees, Washburn Col, 67; lectr legal ethics, Washburn Law Sch, 64-68. Mil Serv: Entered as Pvt, Army, 43, released as Sgt, 45, after serv in FARTC, Ft Sill, Okla; Good Conduct Medal. Mem: Kans & Am Bar Asns; Kans Co Attorneys Asn; Nat Asn Attorneys Gen; Am Judicature Soc. Honors & Awards: Herbert Lincoln Harley Award, Am Judicature Soc, 72; Kans Dist Court Judges Asn Award, 72. Relig: Protestant. Legal Res: Kinsley KS Mailing Add: State House Topeka KS 66612

FAUBUS, ORVAL EUGENE (D)
b Combs, Ark, Jan 7, 10; s John Samuel Faubus & Addie Joslin F; m 1931 to Alta Mozell Haskins; m 1969 to Elizabeth Drake Thompson; c Farrell Eugene, Kim & Ricci. Educ: Huntsville Vocational Sch, grad, 34; Exten course, Univ Ark; Lone Scouts; Boy Scouts; Future Farmers of Am. Polit & Govt Pos: Circuit clerk & recorder, Madison Co, Ark, 38-42; acting & permanent postmaster, Huntsville, 46-54; hwy comnr, dir & admin asst to Gov, 49-53; Gov, Ark, 55-67. Bus & Prof Pos: Sch teacher, 28-38; ed-publ, Madison Co Rec, Huntsville, Ark, 46-69; ed-publ, The Spectator, Ozark, Ark, 68-69; pres, Dogpatch, USA Recreational Enterprises, 69-70. Mil Serv: Entered as Pvt, Army, 42, released as Maj, 46, after serv in 35th Inf Div, ETO; Maj (Ret), Army Res; Combat Inf Badge; Bronze Star; Six Battle Stars. Publ: In This Faraway Land. Mem: Combs 4-H Club; Huntsville Lions; Ozark Playground Asn; Madison Co CofC; Am Legion. Honors & Awards: Am Legion Man of Year, 57; One of the Ten Men in the World Most Admired by Americans, 58; Munic Man of Year, 65; Conservationist of Year, 66. Relig: Baptist. Mailing Add: Rte 5 Governor's Hill Huntsville AR 72740

FAUCHER, RAYMOND N (D)
Maine State Rep
Mailing Add: Solon Hotel Solon ME 04979

FAULISE, DOROTHY (D)
Conn State Rep
b New York, NY, May 12, 29; d Paul Abramchuk & Mary Danyluk A; m 1947 to John Faulise; c John Urick, Paula (Mrs Mikutel), Mary Donita & Theodore Anthony. Educ: High sch. Polit & Govt Pos: Mem bd educ, Griswold, Conn, 70-; Conn State Rep, 45th Assembly Dist, 74- Bus & Prof Pos: Restaurant mgr, Jewett City, Conn, 60. Mem: New London Federated Dem Women's Club; Pauchaug Grange. Relig: Catholic. Legal Res: Bethel Rd Griswold CT 06360 Mailing Add: RFD 3 Norwich CT 06360

FAULISO, JOSEPH J (D)
Conn State Sen
Mailing Add: 67 Lafayette St Hartford CT 06106

FAULKNER, RALPH EDWARD (D)
Secy-Treas, Ouachita Co Dem Cent Comt, Ark
b ElDorado, Ark, Apr 1, 39; s Cy Faulkner & Stella Fugitt F; m 1970 to Susan Reeves Burnham; c Joseph Harlan. Educ: Southern State Col, BA, 68; Univ Ark Law Sch, JD, 71. Polit & Govt Pos: Secy-treas, Ouachita Co Dem Cent Comt, Ark, 72- Mil Serv: Entered as Pvt, Air Force, 61, released as Airman 2/C, 65, after serv in Security Serv & 15th Air Force. Mem: Am & Ark Bar Asns; Kiwanis Int; Ouachita Co Bar Asn (vpres, 71-74); Am Trial Lawyers Asn. Relig: Methodist. Legal Res: 1721 Woodcliff Dr Camden AR 71701 Mailing Add: PO Box 516 Camden AR 71701

FAULSTICH, JANET KAY (D)
b Washington, DC, Dec 17, 42; d Robert Charles Faulstich & Ruth Olson F; single. Educ: Col William & Mary, BA, 64. Polit & Govt Pos: Spec asst to James Roosevelt, 65-66; spec asst to US Rep, Thomas M Rees, 66-69, admin asst, 69- Mailing Add: 700 Seventh St SW Washington DC 20024

FAUNTROY, WALTER E (D)
DC Deleg, US Congress
b Washington, DC, Feb 6, 33; s William T Fauntroy & Ethel V F; m to Dorothy Simms; c Marvin Keith. Educ: Va Union Univ, AB, cum laude, 55; Yale Divinity Sch, BD, 58. Hon Degrees: DD, Va Union Univ, 68 & Yale Univ, 69; LLD, Muskingum Col, 71. Polit & Govt Pos: DC coordr, March on Washington for Jobs & Freedom, 63; coordr, Selma to Montgomery March, 65; chmn, DC Coalition of Conscience, 65-66; chmn, Wash Metrop Area Transit Authority, 67; vchmn, DC City Coun, 67-69; nat coordr, Poor People's Campaign, 69; DC Deleg, US Congress, 71-; chmn, platform comt, Nat Black Polit Conv, Gary, Ind, 72; chmn, Cong Black Caucus Task Force for Dem Nat Conv, 72; deleg, Dem Nat Conv, 72. Bus & Prof Pos: Mem univ coun, Yale Univ; chmn bd dirs, Martin Luther King, Jr Ctr for Social Change, Atlanta, Ga; past chmn bd dirs, Model Inner City Community Orgn; pastor, New Bethel Baptist Church, 59- Mem: Bd mem various civic, relig & civil rights orgns; Inter-Rel Comt Race Rels (bd mem); Leadership Conf Civil Rights (bd mem). Relig: Baptist. Mailing Add: 326 Cannon House Off Bldg Washington DC 20515

FAUST, MARY JANE (D)
Chmn Finance Comt, Wapello Co Dem Party, Iowa
b New Ulm, Minn, Apr 23, 31; d Carl Sanford Monson & Viola Swenson M; m 1952 to Richard Chandler Faust; c Richard Fredrick & James Chandler. Educ: NDak State Univ, BA; Drake Univ, MSE; Kappa Delta Pi. Polit & Govt Pos: Deleg, Dem Nat Conv, 72; Wapello Co coordr, McGovern for President, 72; chmn finance comt, Wapello Co Dem Party, Iowa, 72- Bus & Prof Pos: Teacher, Des Moines, Iowa, 69-71; sch counr, Ottumwa, 71-; bd dirs, Lutheran Social Serv of Iowa, 72-; mem, Fourth Cong Dist Farm Labor Comt on Polit Educ, 72-73. Mem: Am Personnel & Guid Asn; Nat & Iowa State Educ Asns; Am Asn Univ Women. Relig: Lutheran. Mailing Add: 122 N Jefferson Ottumwa IA 52501

FAUST, WILLIAM PAUL (D)
Mich State Sen
b Bucyrus, Ohio, Mar 29, 29; s Paul Joseph Faust & Teresa Johnson F; single. Educ: Univ Ind, 48-49; Univ Mich, AB, 52; Eastern Mich Univ, 55-56. Polit & Govt Pos: Trustee, Nankin Twp, Mich, 60-63; supvr, 63-65; chmn, Nankin Twp Planning Comn, 65-66; Mich State Sen, 13th Dist, 67- Bus & Prof Pos: Managing ed, Wayne Eagle, Wayne, Mich, 60-62. Mem: CofC; Civitan Club. Relig: Roman Catholic. Mailing Add: 8228 Ravine Dr Westland MI 48185

FAUVER, SCRIBNER L (R)
Ohio State Rep
b Elyria, Ohio, June 1, 31; s King E Fauver & Annie Lee Scribner F; m 1956 to Ann Babbitt; c Scribner K, Cole M & Grace. Educ: Dartmouth Col, BA, 53; Harvard Law Sch, LLB, 56. Polit & Govt Pos: Vchmn & mem, Elyria City Charter Comn, Ohio, 65; councilman-at-lg, Elyria City Coun, 70-74, pres, 71; Ohio State Rep, 54th Dist, 75- Mem: Am & Ohio State Bar Asns; Elyria Mem Hosp (trustee); Rotary. Relig: Congregational. Mailing Add: 252 Hamilton Ave Elyria OH 44035

FAVOR, BONNIE ALVINA (R)
Secy, Kootenai Co Rep Cent Comt, Idaho
b Spokane, Wash, June 9, 56; d Franklin Joseph Favor & Donna Sands F; single. Educ: NIdaho Col, 74-; Phi Theta Kappa. Polit & Govt Pos: Page, Idaho State Senate, 74; secy, Kootenai Co Rep Cent Comt, 74- Mem: Kootenai Co Comt Coun Youth; Nat Asn Retarded Citizens; Young Rep; Col Rep. Relig: Presbyterian. Mailing Add: 1036 N 23rd St Coeur d'Alene ID 83814

FAVREAU, ROBERT J (R)
NH State Rep
Mailing Add: 181 Sagamore St Manchester NH 03104

FAWCETT, CHARLOTTE D (R)
Pa State Rep
b Delaware Co, Iowa, Apr 20, 11; d Floyd A Durey & Cora Rolfe D (deceased); m 1930 to Cecil C Fawcett; c Kay c (Mrs Benson) & Dr Kennedy C. Educ: Upper Iowa Col, 28-29. Polit & Govt Pos: Committeewoman, Lower Moreland Rep Comt, 60-70, munic leader, 63-70; mem adv comt, Montgomery Co Rep Comt, 62-70; deleg, Pa State Const Conv, 67-68; vpres & chmn legis comt, Eastern Montgomery Co Rep Women, 68, third vpres, currently; Pa State Rep, 152nd Dist, 70-, mem, State Govt Comt, Health & Welfare Comt & Prof Licensure Comt, currently. Publ: Personnel management for public libraries, Pa Libr Asn, 2/67. Mem: Am & Pa Libr Asns; Coun State Govt; Ambler Bus & Prof Women's Club; Citizens Coun Montgomery Co. Relig: Presbyterian. Mailing Add: Capitol Bldg Harrisburg PA 17120

FAWELL, HARRIS W (R)
Ill State Sen
b West Chicago, Ill, Mar 25, 29; s Walter R Fawell & Mildred Nelson F; m 1952 to Ruth Johnson; c Richard, Jane & John. Educ: NCent Col, Naperville, 47-51; Chicago-Kent Col Law, LLB, 52. Polit & Govt Pos: Pres, Naperville Young Rep, Ill, formerly; asst state attorney, DuPage Co, 53-57; Ill State Sen, 63-, chmn, Welfare Comn, Ill State Senate; deleg, Rep Nat Conv, 68. Bus & Prof Pos: Mem law firm, Fawell & Larson, 52-70. Mem: Am Trial Lawyers Asn; WChicago Jaycees; YMCA (mem bd); Kiwanis; DuPage Co Family Serv Asn. Honors & Awards: Outstanding Freshman State Sen, 73rd Gen Assembly, Newsman Awards, Best Freshman State Sen, Ill Polit Reporter; John Howard Award, 67; Best Legislator Award, Independent Voters Ill, 67 & 70; Ill Distinguished Serv Award, Ill Welfare Asn, 67; Ill Hosp Asn Award, 70. Relig: Methodist. Mailing Add: 444 S Sleight St Naperville IL 60540

FAXON, JACK (D)
Mich State Sen
b Detroit, Mich, June 9, 36. Educ: Wayne State Univ, BS & MEd; Univ Mich, MA in Hist. Polit & Govt Pos: Mich State Rep, until 70; Mich State Sen, 71- Bus & Prof Pos: Teacher of Am govt & hist, Southwestern High Sch, formerly; headmaster & pres bd trustees, City Sch of Detroit. Mem: Anti-Defamation League of B'nai B'rith (Mich regional adv bd); Am Civil Liberties Union of Mich; Theol Inst of Episcopal Diocese of Mich; Mich Hist Soc; Bagley Community Coun. Mailing Add: 15343 Warwick Detroit MI 48223

FAY, MRS JOHN (D)
Mem, Dem Nat Comt, RI
Mailing Add: 197 Indiana Ave Providence RI 02906

FAY, JOHN J, JR (D)
NJ State Sen
b Elizabeth, NJ, June 8, 27; s John Logan Fay & Ann Mulcahy F; m 1951 to Elizabeth Stankunas. Educ: Set on Hall Univ, BA, 58, MA, 60. Polit & Govt Pos: Councilman, Woodbridge Twp, NJ, 62-64; freeholder, Middlesex Co, 64-67; NJ State Assemblyman, Middlesex Co, 67-74; NJ State Sen, 75- Bus & Prof Pos: Stillman's helper, Esso Standard Oil, Bayway, NJ, 49-58; high sch teacher, Linden High Sch, 58- Mil Serv: Entered as A/S, Navy, 44, released as Seaman 1/C, 46, after serv in Underwater Demolition; Victory Medal. Mem: Am Fedn Teachers; KofC. Honors & Awards: B'nai B'rith Citizenship Award; Eagleton fel grant. Relig: Roman Catholic. Mailing Add: 115 Amherst Ave Colonia NJ 07067

FAY, THOMAS FREDERIC (D)
RI State Rep
b Central Falls, RI, Oct 13, 40; s Joseph A Fay & Ethel Lupton F; m 1965 to Paulette R Demers; c Kelly Ann & Thomas Joseph. Educ: Providence Col, AB, 62; Boston Univ Law Sch, LLB, 65. Polit & Govt Pos: Mem Dem Comt, Lincoln, RI, 63-66; RI State Rep, 72nd Dist, 69- Bus & Prof Pos: Partner, Oster, Espo, & Fay, 69-; legal counsel, Pawtucket Jr CofC, 69- Mem: Trial Lawyers Asn; Am Judicature Soc; Jr CofC; Lions; charter mem Lincoln Kiwanis. Relig: Roman Catholic. Legal Res: 97 Clay St Central Falls RI 02863 Mailing Add: 936 Smithfield Ave Lincoln RI 02865

FAYARD, CALVIN C, JR (D)
Chmn, Livingston Parish Dem Exec Comt, La
b Baton Rouge, La, Aug 12, 43; s Calvin C Fayard, Sr & Katherine Abels F. Educ: Southeastern La Univ, BS, 65; La State Univ, JD, 69; Phi Kappa Phi; Delta Tau Alpha; 13 Club; Sigma Tau Gamma; Gleaners Club. Polit & Govt Pos: City attorney, Denham Springs, La, 70-; deleg, La Const Conv, 72; asst dist attorney, 21st Judicial Dist, 73-; chmn, Livingston Parish Dem Exec Comt, currently. Bus & Prof Pos: Attorney, Livingston, La, 69- Mil Serv: Air Nat Guard, 68-, T/Sgt. Mem: Am & La State Bar Asns; 21st Judicial Dist Bar Asn (secy-treas, 72-); Denham Springs CofC (bd mem, 71-). Relig: Methodist. Legal Res: South Range Ave Denham Springs LA 70726 Mailing Add: PO Box 233 Livingston LA 70754

FAZZINO, ALEX J (D)
Mo State Rep
Mailing Add: 1809 Pendleton Kansas City MO 64124

FEARS, WILLIAM EARL (D)
Va State Sen
b Jonesboro, Ark, Sept 28, 21; s Arthur Earl Fears & Mary Catherine Scarry F; m 1944 to Betty Belle DeCormis; c Barbara Anderson & Richard Bradford. Educ: Yale Univ, BE, 42; Univ Cincinnati, LLB & JD, 48; Phi Delta Phi. Polit & Govt Pos: Commonwealth's attorney, Accomack Co, Va, 55-59; Va State Sen, First Dist, 68- Bus & Prof Pos: Vpres, Avemco Ins Co, Bethesda, Md, 64-66. Mil Serv: Entered as Aviation Cadet, Army Air Corps, 43, released as 1st Lt, 46, after serv in 92nd Bombardment Group, Eng, Eighth Air Force, ETO, 45-46; Maj Army Res, currently; Occup Europe Medal with three Battle Stars; Va Serv Medal; ETO & Am Theater Medals; Presidential Unit Citation. Mem: Am Trial Lawyers Asn; Shrine; Mason (32 degree); Elks; Moose. Relig: Baptist. Legal Res: Box 38 Accomac VA 23301 Mailing Add: Box 247 Accomac VA 23301

FECHTEL, VINCE (R)
Fla State Rep
Mailing Add: Tomato Hill Leesburg FL 32748

FEDERER, ESTELLE ANASTATIA (D)
Mem Exec Bd, Sheboygan Co Dem Party, Wis
b Rossiter, Pa, Apr 4, 15; d John Moskewich & Mary Rinkavich M; m 1935 to Robert W Federer; c Patricia (Mrs Donnel Lee Hanson) & Susanne (Mrs James E Kuhn). Educ: Sheboygan Cent High Sch, grad, 33; Sheboygan Tech Sch Adult Educ. Polit & Govt Pos: Treas, Sch Bd, Wis; chmn, Women's Comt, Dem Party of Wis; secy & chmn, Dem Party, Wis; mem exec bd, Sixth Cong Dist Dem Party; mem, exec bd, Sheboygan Co Dem Party, 69- Mem: League of Women Voters; Red Cross; Rocky Knoll Health Care Facility (trustee); Wis TB Control Adv Comt; Regional Consumer Coun. Honors & Awards: Cert or pins for Serv from Dem Nat Comt, Red Cross, March of Dimes, Univ Wis Exten Homemaker Coun & Cath Daughters Am. Relig: Catholic. Mailing Add: 622 Maine Adell WI 53001

FEDERICO, JAMES JOSEPH, JR (D)
RI State Sen
b Westerly, RI, Apr 26, 46; s James J Federico, Sr & Florence Giannoni F; m 1970 to Nancy K Sisk; c James J, III & David William. Educ: Harvard Univ, BA, 68; Fordham Univ, AM, 71. Polit & Govt Pos: Deleg, RI Const Conv, 73; RI State Sen, Dist 26, 75- Bus & Prof Pos: Instr polit sci, RI Jr Col, 72- Mem: Elks; RI Educ Asn; Westerly Bocce Club; Calabrese Soc. Mailing Add: 15 Lovat Lane Westerly RI 02891

FEDERICO, ROBERTO M (D)
Mont State Rep
Mailing Add: 313 S 32nd Billings MT 59101

FEE, THOMAS J (D)
Pa State Rep
Mailing Add: Capitol Bldg Harrisburg PA 17120

FEEHAN, THOMAS (R)
Chmn, Will Co Rep Cent Comt, Ill
b Joliet, Ill, Mar 1, 26; s Leo M Feehan & Zita Broderick F; m 1953 to Beverly Long; c Colleen, Kathleen, Thomas, Brian & Kevin. Educ: Loyola Univ, BS, 49, JD, 53. Polit & Govt Pos: Chmn, Will Co Rep Cent Comt, Ill, 64-; dir, Ill State Toll Hwy Authority, 69; mem community adv coun, Small Bus Admin. Mil Serv: Navy, 44-46. Mem: Ill State & Am Bar Asns; Am Trial Lawyers Asn; United Crusade, Will Co, Ill; George W Buck Boys Club, Joliet. Relig: Catholic. Mailing Add: 5 E Van Buren St Joliet IL 60431

FEENEY, MICHAEL PAUL (D)
Mass State Rep
Mailing Add: State Capitol Boston MA 02133

FEGGANS, EDWARD LELAND (R)
Mem, DC Rep Comt
b Atlantic City, NJ, Mar 5, 19; s Edward L Feggans & Ethel McIntyre F; m 1950 to Ozra Kimus Young; c James E Kearney & Helen A Thombani. Educ: Howard Univ; Suffolk Univ; La Salle Exten Univ, Law, 1 year. Polit & Govt Pos: Mem, DC Rep Comt, 62-, chmn, 68-70, vchmn, 71-72; precinct coordr, Rockefeller for President, 63; mem, Ed Brooke for US Sen Comt, 66; consult to dir, Off Minority Bus Enterprise, US Dept Com, 70; alt deleg, Rep Nat Conv, 72. Bus & Prof Pos: Asst sales mgr, Kaplan & Crawford, 53-57; sales mgr, Fuller Prod Co, 57-64; bus consult, Small Bus Develop Ctr, Washington, DC, 64-66, asst dir, Small Bus Guid & Develop, 66-; secy, Nat Bus League & first vpres, DC CofC, 69-; exec dir, Washington Area Contractors Asn; pres-owner, Ed Feggans Oldsmobile, Inc, 72- Mil Serv: Entered as Pvt, Army, 41, released as Technician, 45, after serv in 449th Army Serv Force Band; Good Conduct, Am Defense Serv & Victory Medals; Am Theatre Campaign Ribbon. Publ: Business Talk, Wash Afro Am, 68. Mem: Life mem, Local 161-710 AFM DC Fedn of Musicians; life mem Capitol Hill Club; Kiwanis; DC Coun Adv Comt Indust & Commercial Develop; Pi Sigma Epsilon. Honors & Awards: Received Man of the Year Award, Neptune Yacht Club. Relig: Episcopal; Licensed layreader, Episcopal Church. Mailing Add: 2504 South Dakota Ave NE Washington DC 20018

FEIGENBAUM, BOB (D)
Mo State Rep
Mailing Add: 605 St Marie Florissant MO 63031

FEIGHAN, EDWARD FARRELL (D)
Ohio State Rep
b Cleveland, Ohio, Oct 22, 47; s Francis X Feighan & Rosemary Elizabeth Ling F; single. Educ: Loyola Univ, New Orleans, BA, 69. Polit & Govt Pos: Ohio State Rep, 73-, chmn comt housing, Ohio House Rep, 75- Mailing Add: 2805 Clinton Ave Cleveland OH 44113

FEIGHAN, MICHAEL A
b Lakewood, Ohio, m 1930 to Florence J Mathews; c William M & Fleur M. Educ: Princeton Univ, AB, 27; Harvard Univ, LLB, 31; Princeton Elm Club. Polit & Govt Pos: Ohio State Rep, 37-40, Dem leader, Ohio House Rep, 39-40; US Rep, 20th Dist, Ohio, 43-70. Mem: Burning Tree Club; Cong Country Club; City Tavern Asn. Relig: Roman Catholic. Mailing Add: 4000 Cathedral Ave NW Washington DC 20016

FEIL, PAUL ARNOLD (R)
Mem, NMex State Rep Cent Comt
b Albuquerque, NMex, Oct 22, 22; s Paul Julius Feil & Erna Bertha Schulze F; m 1949 to Alma Ruth Barr; c Paul Alan, Nancy Ruth, David Arnold & Anita Louise. Educ: Univ NMex, BS, 44; Baylor Univ, MD, 48; Phi Sigma. Polit & Govt Pos: Chmn, Luna Co Rep Cent Comt, NMex, 65-71; mem, NMex State Rep Cent Comt, 71- Bus & Prof Pos: Mem city coun, Deming, NMex, 58-62; mem sch bd, 59-65, secy, 61-63, pres, 63-65. Mil Serv: Entered as A/S V-12, Navy, 41, released as Lt(jg), 50. Mem: Luna Co & NMex Med Soc; Am Med Asn; Am Acad Family Physicians (charter fel, 72); Lions. Relig: Methodist. Legal Res: 719 W Ash St Deming NM 88030 Mailing Add: PO Box 670 Deming NM 88030

FEILD, KAY CAROL (R)
Secy, Sebastian Co Rep Comt, Ark
b Somerset, Pa, Feb 9, 38; d Earl William Barclay & Velma Ankney B; m 1960 to Theophilus A Feild, III, MD; c Katherine Bolling, Elizabeth Barclay, Anne Gardner & Janie Duckett. Educ: Johns Hopkins Hosp Sch of Nursing, RN, 60. Polit & Govt Pos: Secy, Sebastian Co Rep Women, 65-66, vchmn, 66-67; chmn, Sebastian Co Rep Comt, 66-68, secy, 68-; committeewoman, Ark State Rep Comt, formerly, asst secy, 70; alt deleg, Rep Nat Conv, 68. Bus & Prof Pos: Staff nurse, Henry Ford Hosp, Detroit, Mich, 60-61. Mem: Johns Hopkins Hosp Nurses Alumnae Asn; St Edward Mercy Hosp Auxiliary; Sparks Mem Hosp Womens Bd; Sebastian Co Ment Health Asn; Sebastian Co Med Auxiliary. Relig: Episcopal. Mailing Add: 4823 S Cliff Dr Ft Smith AR 72901

FEINBERG, ELI MICHAEL (D)
b Charleroi, Pa, July 2, 41; s Joseph T Feinberg & Rose Levitan F; m 1971 to Andi Honig. Educ: Temple Univ, BA, 63; Univ Miami, MA, 72; Pi Sigma Alpha; Tau Epsilon Phi. Polit & Govt Pos: Legis asst, Fla State Senate, 67-70; dep secy state, Fla Dept State, 70-74; admin asst, US Sen Richard Stone, Fla, 75- Legal Res: FL Mailing Add: Apt 1416 700 New Hampshire Ave Washington DC 20037

FEINSTEIN, ELIZABETH COOKE (D)
b New York, NY, May 29, 47; d John A Cooke & Elizabeth Bassett C; m 1969 to Paul D Feinstein; c Emily Cooke. Educ: Col of St Rose, BS Econ & Bus, 69. Polit & Govt Pos: Mem pub affairs, New York Dept Consumer Affairs, 69-70, mem adv coun, 74-; researcher, New York Consumer Protection Bd, 70-71; deleg, Dem Nat Mid-Term Conf, 74. Bus & Prof Pos: Asst dir, Polit Action Dept, Am Fedn State, Co & Munic Employees, 71- Mailing Add: 4 East 95 St New York NY 10028

FEINSTEIN, OTTO (D)
Mem Exec Bd, 13th Cong Dist Dem Orgn, Mich
b Vienna, Austria, May 18, 30; s Abraham Feinstein & Bella Silber F; m 1961 to Nicolette Margaret Cecelia Carey; c Sara Rebecca Michelle. Educ: Univ Chicago, BA, 50, PhD, 65; Grad Inst Int Studies, Univ Geneva, Licenciate, 53. Polit & Govt Pos: Precinct deleg, 13th Dist Dem Orgn, Mich, 64-, vchmn, 66-69, mem resolutions comt, Mich Dem Party, 65-69, mem polit reform comt, 69, cand for chmn, 69; deleg, Dem State Conv, 65, 66, 67, 68 & 69; mem Comt of 99 on Co Home Rule Wayne Co, 67-68; alt deleg, Dem Nat Conv, 68; exec secy & chmn, McCarthy for President Campaign, 68. Bus & Prof Pos: Asst prof, Monteith Col, Wayne State Univ, 60-64, assoc prof, 64- Mil Serv: Entered as Pvt, Army, 53, released as Pfc, 55; Good Conduct medal. Publ: Two Worlds of Change, Anchor Press, 65; Scholars look at US foreign policy, Bull Atomic Scientist, 59-60. Mem: Am & Int Polit Sci Asns; Nat Planning Asn; Latin Am Studies Asn; Int Studies Asn. Mailing Add: 709 W Hancock Detroit MI 48203

FELDER, JOHN GRESSETTE (D)
SC State Rep
b Orangeburg, SC, Sept 4, 44; s Clarence Bates Felder, Jr & Helen Gressette F; m 1966 to Jane Schuford Nelson; c John Gressette, Jr, Theodore Baskin & Bates Nelson. Educ: Wofford Col, AB, 66; Univ SC Law Sch, JD, 69; Kappa Alpha Order, Phi Delta Phi. Polit & Govt Pos: Chmn sch bd, Calhoun Co, St Matthews, SC, 70-72; officer, Calhoun Co Dem Party, 70-; SC State Rep, 75-, mem spec comn to study interest rates, judiciary comt & statutory laws comt, SC House of Rep, 75- Bus & Prof Pos: Attorney, St Matthews, SC, 69- Mem: Am & SC Bar Asns; Lions (pres); Elks. Relig: Methodist. Legal Res: Pine Hill Rd St Matthews SC 29135 Mailing Add: 101 Herlong Ave PO Box 437 St Matthews SC 29135

FELDER, WILLIE W (D)
b Birmingham, Ala, Mar 19, 27; s Anderson H Felder & Lera Trammel F; m 1947 to Mabel Byrd; c Cameron, Claudette, Celester, Anderson H, Willie W, Roderick & Trunell D. Educ: Carlisle War Col, cert, 50; Booker T Washington Bus Col, Assoc Degree, 52; Univ Calif, Los Angeles, exten courses, 64; LaSalle Exten Univ, 69. Polit & Govt Pos: Dem Precinct Deleg, 68-; mem, Mich Dem State Cent Comt, 70-72; mem exec bd, 17th Cong Dem Dist, 70-73; mem, Mich Black Dem Caucus, 70-, polit coordr, 73-; bd mem, Community United for Action, 70-; bd mem, Mayor's Comt for Human Resources Develop, 71-73; deleg, Dem Nat Conv, 72. Bus & Prof Pos: Mem Local 148, UAW, Douglas Aircraft, Long Beach, Calif, 56-, chmn, 62-67; mem, Aerospace Dept, UAW, 67-70; exec dir, UAW SEMCAP, 70-73, int rep, UAW Nat CAP Dept, 73-; bd dirs, Cath Social Serv, 72. Mil Serv: Entered as Pvt, Army, 45, released as Cpl, 47, after serv in Inf, European Theatre, 45-46; recalled as Cpl, Korean Conflict, 50-51; Theatre Ribbon; Good Conduct Medal; Occup Reward. Mem: Southeastern Mich Transportation Authority; Dem Nat Comt Black Caucus; life mem NAACP (chmn voter registr & educ & bd mem, Detroit Br, 73-). Relig: Protestant. Legal Res: 17515 Cherrylawn Detroit MI 48221 Mailing Add: 8000 E Jefferson United Auto Workers NATCAP Detroit MI 48214

FELDMAN, GEORGE JOSEPH (D)
b Boston, Mass, Nov 6, 03; s Harry Feldman & Bessie Alpert F; m 1948 to Marion Schulman; c George J, Jr & Margot. Educ: Boston Univ Law Sch, LLB, 25. Hon Degrees: LLD, Holy Cross Col, 67 & Boston Univ, 68. Polit & Govt Pos: Admin asst to US Sen David I Walsh, 26-30; attorney, Fed Trade Comn, 30-32; litigation attorney, Nat Recovery Admin, 34-35; dir & chief counsel, Select Comt on Astronaut & Space Exploration, US House of Rep, 58-59, mem adv comt, Select Comt on Govt Research, 63-64; mem US deleg, UN Gen Assembly, 59; consult to legal adv, State Dept, 59-60; mem US deleg, UN Conf on Law of Sea, Geneva, 60; mem, US NATO Citizens Comn, 61-62; one of original incorporators & dir, Commun Satellite Corp, 62-65; US Ambassador, Malta, 65-67; US Ambassador, Luxembourg, 67-69; consult to Asst Secy European Affairs, State Dept, 70- Bus & Prof Pos: Pvt practice of law, 32-34 & 35-65; lectr, Boston Univ Law Sch, 32-34 & Practicing Law Inst, New York, NY, 47-50. Mil Serv: Entered as Capt, Air Force, 42, released as Maj, after serv in 355th Fighter Group, ETO, 43-45. Publ: Business Under New Price Laws, Prentice Hall, 36; Advertising

& Promotional Allowances, Bur Nat Affairs, 48; The Reluctant Space Farers, New Am Libr, 64; plus others. Mem: Am & NY State Bar Asns; Am Foreign Serv Asn; Coun, Holy Cross Col; Bd Fels Boston Univ. Relig: Jewish. Legal Res: 1010 Fifth Ave New York NY 10028 Mailing Add: 516 Fifth Ave New York NY 10036

FELDMAN, HENRY LEE (D)
Chmn, Putnam Co Dem Party, Mo
b Warrensburg, Mo, May 15, 03; s Henry Feldman & Mary O'Brian F; m 1942 to Mary Louzann Hayes McKimstray; stepsons; Jerry D & Jackie Z. Polit & Govt Pos: Chmn, Putnam Co Dem Party, Mo, 46-; mem, Mo Dem State Comt, 58-64. Bus & Prof Pos: Pres, Lake Thunderhead, recreational lake, Mo, 65- Mem: Lions Int; Elks. Relig: Catholic. Mailing Add: 109 S 16th Unionville MO 63565

FELDMAN, MARTIN L C (R)
b St Louis, Mo, Jan 28, 34; s Joseph Feldman & Zelma Bosse F; m 1958 to Melanie Pulitzer; c Jennifer & Martin, Jr. Educ: Tulane Univ, BA, 55, JD, 57; Order of the Coif; Tulane Law Rev; Sigma Alpha Mu. Polit & Govt Pos: Pres, New Orleans Young Rep Club, 59-60; dist mgr, Nixon-Lodge Campaign, 60; vchmn & gen counsel, La Young Rep Fedn, 61; vchmn, Orleans Parish Rep Exec Comt, 62-67; election day chmn, Goldwater-Miller Campaign, 64; gen counsel, Rep Party, La, 65-72; mem, Orleans Parish Election Reforms Coun, 66-68; finance chmn, Rep Party, New Orleans, 67; parliamentarian, La Rep State Cent Comt, 67-71; chmn spec events, Nixon-Agnew Campaign, 68; deleg-at-lg, Rep Nat Conv, 68 & 72; adv to Secy Health Educ & Welfare, Region VI, 73- Bus & Prof Pos: Partner Bronfin, Heller, Feldman & Steinberg, New Orleans, dir & vpres, Wembley Indust Inc, secy, Textile Realty Corp, secy, 1st Chestnut St Corp & secy, Advance Planning Consult, Inc, currently. Mil Serv: Entered as Pvt, Army, 57, released as Pfc, 57, after serving in Adj Gen Corps; Capt, Army Res, 57-69. Publ: Trafficking in net operating loss corporations—revisited, 68 & The shareholders' agreement, 71, La Bar J; Planning for employee's payments to widows, Tulane Tax Inst, 70; plus others. Mem: Am, La & Mo Bar Asns; New Orleans Estate Planning Coun; Int House, New Orleans. Honors & Awards: Nat winner, Nathan Burkan Mem Copyright Law Competition, 57; Lemann-Stern Leadership award, New Orleans Jewish Welfare Fedn, 60. Relig: Jewish. Mailing Add: 12 Rosa Park New Orleans LA 70115

FELDMAN, MATTHEW (D)
Majority Leader, NJ State Senate
b 1920; m to Muriel Gunsberg; c Beth Ellen, Rachel & Daniel. Educ: Univ NC; Panzer Col of Phys Educ. Polit & Govt Pos: Former mayor, Teaneck, NJ; NJ State Sen, 66-67 & 75-, majority leader, NJ State Senate, 75-; chmn, Bergen Co Dem Party, 71-74; alt deleg, Dem Nat Mid-Term Conf, 74. Bus & Prof Pos: Vpres, Fedway Assocs, Kearny. Mil Serv: Capt, Army Air Corps, 5 years; Awarded Citation for Skilled Training of Bombardiers, Cadets & Parachutists by Comdr, 8th AF. Mem: Am Legion; Jewish War Vet; Hebrew Home & Hosp of NJ; Sch of Nursing, Holy Name Hosp. Honors & Awards: Brotherhood Award, Bergen Co Chap, Nat Conf of Christians & Jews, 63. Mailing Add: Box 131 Kearny NJ 07032

FELDMAN, MYER (D)
b Philadelphia, Pa, June 22, 17; s Israel Feldman & Bella Kurland F; m 1941 to Silva Moskovitz; c Jane Margaret & James Alan. Educ: Girard Col, Philadelphia, 22-31; Wharton Sch, Univ Pa, BS, 35, fel, 38-39, LLB, 38. Polit & Govt Pos: Spec counsel, exec asst to chmn, Securities Exchange Comn, 46-54; counsel, Banking & Currency Comn, US Senate, 55-57; legis asst to Sen John F Kennedy, 58-61; dep spec counsel to Presidents Kennedy & Johnson, 61-64; counsel to President Johnson, 64-65; deleg, Dem Nat Conv, 68; vchmn, Cong Leadership for Future, 70; pres, McGovern for President Comt, Inc. Bus & Prof Pos: Attorney-at-law, Philadelphia, 39-42; lectr law, Univ Pa, 41-42; prof, Am Univ, 55-56; pres, Radio Assocs, Inc, 59; partner, Key Sta, 60; bd overseers, Virgin Islands Univ, 62-; trustee, Eleanor Roosevelt Mem Found, 63-; trustee, United Jewish Appeal; bd dirs, Weitzman Inst, 63-; partner, Ginsburg & Feldman, Washington, DC, 65-; dir, Flying Tiger Line, Inc; dir, Flame of Hope, Inc; chmn bd, Speer Publ, Capital Gazette & Bay Publ; dir, Music Fair Enterprises, Inc. Publ: Standard Pennsylvania Practice, four Vols, 58; plus articles. Mil Serv: Army Air Force, 42-46. Mem: Tau Epsilon Rho; Univ Pa Law Alumni Asn, Washington. Mailing Add: 1700 Pennsylvania Ave Suite 300 Washington DC 20006

FELECIANO, PAUL, JR (D)
Kans State Rep
Mailing Add: 2815 Euclid Wichita KS 67217

FELIEN, ALICE MILDRED (DFL)
Treas, Fifth Dist Dem-Farmer-Labor Party, Minn
b Manila, Philippines, Nov 23, 13; d Rudolph Stellbar & Mary Jane Devitt S; m 1937 to Edwin E Felien; c Edwin, Jr, Patrick Brian, William Charles & Michael John. Educ: Voc High Sch, dipl, 31. Polit & Govt Pos: Membership chmn, 12th Ward Dem-Farmer-Labor Club, Minneapolis, Minn, 67-68; chairwoman, 12th Ward Dem-Farmer-Labor Caucus, 68-69; precinct chmn, 12th Ward Dem-Farmer-Labor Party, 68-69; deleg, Minn State Dem-Farmer-Labor Party, 68-71, 72-, mem, State Cent Comt, 72-, treas, Fifth Dist Dem-Farmer-Labor Party, 70-, chmn credentials, 70-; mem credentials comt, Minn State Dem-Farmer-Labor Conv, 70- Mem: John Ericsson PTA; Cath Fedn Home & Sch (pres); VFW Auxiliary; St Helena's Benevolent Soc; Intermediate Cath League. Relig: Roman Catholic. Mailing Add: 4213 29th Ave S Minneapolis MN 55406

FELIX, FRANCISCO JAVIER (FRANK) (D)
Ariz State Sen
b Tucson, Ariz, Jan 29, 47; s Ernesto R Felix & Jesusita F; m 1972 to Diana Perez. Educ: Mesa Community Col, 67-68; Univ Ariz, BA, 71, MA, 73, PhD work, 73- Polit & Govt Pos: Summer intern, US Rep Morris K Udall, Ariz, 71, asst dist aide, 71-72; Ariz State Sen, 73- Bus & Prof Pos: Counselor-evaluator, Univ Ariz Financial Aides Off, 70-71; elem sch teacher, Tucson Dist One, Tully Elem, 72-73. Mem: Los Changuitos Feos (bd dir, 71-); Tucson & Ariz Educ Asns; Mex-Am Unity Coun. Relig: Catholic. Legal Res: 1302 W Ajo Way Apt 401 Tucson AZ 85713 Mailing Add: Capitol Bldg Ariz Senate Wing Phoenix AZ 85007

FELIX, OTIS L
Sen, VI Legis
Mailing Add: PO Box 902 Charlotte Amalie St Thomas VI 00801

FELL, GEORGE HENRY (R)
Secy, Lucas Co Rep Exec Comt, Ohio
b Toledo, Ohio, Sept 28, 08; s George Nicholas Fell & Anna McDonald F; div; m 1972 to Virginia A Urbanski; c George N, Madelyn L, Richard A, James F, Charles F & John E. Educ: St John's Col, Toledo, Ohio, AB, 30; Harvard Law Sch, LLB, 33. Polit & Govt Pos: First asst, Legal Sect Bank Liquidation, Toledo, Ohio, 39-42; Rep precinct committeeman, Toledo, 42-; secy, Lucas Co Rep Exec Comt, Ohio, 43-; Asst Attorney General, Ohio, 51-57; mem, Toledo Regional Bd Rev, Workman's Compensation Law, 57-59, attorney examr & original hearing officer, 59. Mem: Am, Ohio & Lucas Co Bar Asns; Toledo Bar Asn; KofC. Relig: Roman Catholic. Legal Res: 2444 Scottwood Ave Toledo OH 43620 Mailing Add: 730 Nat Bank Bldg Toledo OH 43604

FELS, MARGARET KATHERINE (R)
b Erie, Pa, Apr 29, 27; d Charles Porter McGeary, Sr & Chelsie Schenck M; m 1949 to Raymond Lee Fels; c Bryan Lee & Brett Garey. Educ: Grove City Col, 45-47; Chatham Col, BA, 49. Polit & Govt Pos: Pres, Erie Coun Rep Women, Pa, 61-63; Erie Co chmn, Women's Polit Activities, 62-63; mem exec comt, Erie Co Rep Party, 62-64; NW regional chmn membership, Pa Coun Rep Women, 62, state chmn membership, 63-65, state chmn prof, 65-67, dir, 65-69; mem resolutions comt, Pa Coun Rep Women Conv, 63; pres, Erie Co Fedn Rep Women's Coun, 63-64; alt deleg, Rep Nat Conv, 64; dir, Fairview Coun Rep Women, 66-68; deleg for Pa, Nat Fedn Rep Women Conv, 67-; deleg, Rep Nat Leadership Conf, 72. Bus & Prof Pos: Teacher, Erie Bus Ctr, 49-53 & Behrend Ctr of Pa State Univ, 50-51; curriculum coordr, Erie Bus Ctr, 67-, coordr mock conv, 72, co-owner & co-dir, 73-, vpres, corp bd, 73- Mem: Am Asn Univ Women; Soroptimist Club; YWCA (bd dirs); Ment Health Asn Pa; PEO. Honors & Awards: Delivered Party-to-People Forum Report to Gen Eisenhower, 64; Honorarium, Comn on Ecumenical Mission Rels, 65; name enshrined, Rep Mem in Nat Mus at Gettysburg Battlefield, 69. Relig: Presbyterian; deacon, United Presbyterian Church of the Covenant; Elder on Session of Church of the Covenant, 72; mem, Ministerial Rels Comt, Lake Erie Presbytery, 72. Mailing Add: Manchester Rd Fairview PA 16415

FELTNER, RICHARD LEE (R)
Asst Secy Mkt & Consumer Serv, Dept Agr
b Crawfordsville, Ind, Oct 16, 38; s Denver Doyal Feltner & Marcella Turner Nees F; m 1959 to Karen Ann Sommer; c Richard Arthur & Susan Sommer. Educ: Purdue Univ, BS, 60, MS, 61; NC State Univ, Kellogg Found fel, 61-64, PhD, 65; Phi Eta Sigma; Alpha Zeta; Gamma Sigma Delta; Alpha Gamma Rho. Polit & Govt Pos: Asst Secy Mkt & Consumer Serv, Dept Agr, 74- Bus & Prof Pos: Asst prof agr econ, Mich State Univ, 65-68, asst dean col agr, 68-70; prof agr econ & head dept, Univ Ill, 70- Mem: Am Agr Econ Asn; Rotary. Legal Res: 703 Silver St Urbana IL 61801 Mailing Add: Dept of Agr Washington DC 20250

FELTON, DANIEL HENRY, JR (D)
Chmn Lee Co Dem Cent Comt, Ark
b Felton, Ark, July 1, 20; s Daniel Henry Felton & Felecia Curtis F; m 1944 to Counts McCollum; c Daniel Henry, III, Martha Counts & Richard Trent. Educ: Univ Ariz, 39-41. Polit & Govt Pos: Chmn, Lee Co Elec Comt, Ark, 54-70 & 72-; mem, Lee Co Dem Cent Comt, 54-, chmn, 54-70 & 72-; mem, Ark State Dem Comt, 62-70; mem, Ark State Comn Coord Higher Educ Finance, 62-72. Bus & Prof Pos: Dir, First Nat Bank, Marianna, Ark, 53-; dir, Forrest City Cotton Oil Co, 64-; owner, Dan Felton Jr Farms; operating partner, Dan Felton & Co; owner, Felton Angus Farms. Mem: Farm Bur; Ark Agr Coun (dir); Ark-Mo Ginners Asn; Am Angus Asn; Oakwood Club, Inc. Relig: Methodist. Legal Res: Felton AR Mailing Add: PO Box 555 Marianna AR 72360

FELTON, DOROTHY WOOD (R)
Ga State Rep
b Tulsa, Okla, Mar 1, 29; d George Fetter Wood & Ima Chronister W; m 1953 to Jethro Jerome Felton, Jr; c Jethro Jerome, III & Frank Bryan. Educ: Univ Ark, Fayetteville, BA, 50; Delta Gamma. Polit & Govt Pos: Mem personnel bd, Fulton Co Govt, 73-75; Ga State Rep, Dist 22, 75- Bus & Prof Pos: Reporter & soc ed, Tulsa Tribune, Okla, 50-53; freelance pub rels, 53-74. Mem: League of Women Voters; United Methodist Women. Relig: Methodist. Mailing Add: 465 Tanacrest Dr NW Atlanta GA 30328

FENDLER, ERNST JOSEPH (D)
Mo State Rep
b St Louis, Mo, Sept 29, 35; s Ernst Joseph Fendler, Sr & Marie Doran F; m 1958 to Carol Ann Klose; c Paul Joseph, Timothy Julius, Ernie Joseph, Jill Marie & Robert John. Educ: Christian Bros Col, grad, 54. Polit & Govt Pos: Mo State Rep, 73- Mil Serv: Entered Air Force, 53, released as S/Sgt, 58, after serv in 110th Bombardment Squadron, US. Relig: Catholic. Mailing Add: 527 Hoffmeister St Louis MO 63125

FENDLER, OSCAR (D)
Committeeman, Mississippi Co Dem Cent Comt, Ark
b Blytheville, Ark, Mar 22, 09; s Alfred Fendler & Rae Sattler F; m 1946 to Patricia Shane; c Frances Shane & stepson Tilden P Wright, III. Educ: Univ Ark, BA, 30; Harvard Law Sch, LLB, 33. Polit & Govt Pos: Committeeman, Mississippi Co Dem Cent Comt, Ark, 47-; spec trial judge, Circuit Court, Mississippi Co Ark, 52; deleg, Dem Nat Conv, 68; spec assoc justice, Ark Supreme Court, formerly; mem, Ark Bd Pardons & Paroles, 70-71. Bus & Prof Pos: Attorney-at-law, Blytheville, Ark, currently. Mil Serv: Entered as Lt (jg), Naval Res, 41, released as Comdr, 46, after serv in Continental US, Southwest Pac, China & Philippines; Res, 46-, Comdr. Publ: Uniform limited partnership act, 56 & Arkansas judicial system at the crossroads, 63, Ark Law Rev; The legal profession & the anti-poverty program, NH Bar J, 66. Mem: Am Judicature Soc; Am Col Probate Counsel; Scribes; Ark Judicial Coun; fel Am Bar Found. Relig: Jewish. Legal Res: 1062 W Hearn St Blytheville AR 72315 Mailing Add: PO Box 548 Blytheville AR 72315

FENLASON, A HAROLD (R)
Maine State Rep
Mailing Add: Danforth ME 04424

FENN, DAN HUNTINGTON, JR (D)
b Boston, Mass, Mar 27, 23; s Rev Dan Huntington Fenn & Anna Yens F; m 1969 to Lenore Ornston Sheppard; c Peter H, Anne H, David E, Thomas O, W Gregory, W Marie & Christopher G. Educ: Harvard Col, AB, 44; Harvard Univ, AM, 72; Phi Beta Kappa. Hon Degrees: LLD, Nasson Col, 72. Polit & Govt Pos: Deleg, Mass State Dem Conv, 54-60; chmn, Dem Town Comt, Lexington, 56-61; secy, Lexington, Mass Sch Comt, 58-61; alt deleg, Dem Nat Conv, 60; spec asst to US Sen Benjamin A Smith, Mass, 61; staff asst to the President, 61-63; comnr, US Tariff Comn, 63-67, vchmn, 64-65; dir, John F Kennedy Libr, 71- Bus & Prof Pos: Asst dean freshmen, Harvard Col, 46-49; exec dir, World Affairs Coun Boston, 49-54; mem faculty, Harvard Bus Sch, 55-61, lectr, 69-, asst ed, Harvard Bus Rev, 55-61; pres, Ctr Bus-Govt Rels, 67-; prof lectr, Am Univ, 67-69. Mil Serv: Entered as Pvt,

Army Air Force, 43, released as Warrant Officer (jg), 45, after serv in 767th Bomb Squadron, 461st Bomb Group, Italy, 44-45. Publ: Ed, Seven-Vol Series on Management, McGraw-Hill, 55-61; Cases in Business & Government (w Donald Grunewald & Robert Katz), Prentice Hall, 66; co-auth, The Corporate Social Audit, Russell Sage, 72; plus others. Mem: Am Soc Pub Admin. Honors & Awards: Decorated by Govt of Morocco, 52. Relig: Unitarian. Mailing Add: 130 Worthen Rd Lexington MA 02173

FENNELL, MELVIN (R)
Mem, Rep Town Comt, Fairfield, Conn
b New York, NY, June 24, 12; s Herman Fennell & Minnie Sanders F; m 1942 to Estelle Murov; c Gary Ritchie. Educ: Yale Col, BA, 32; Harvard Law Sch, LLB, 35. Polit & Govt Pos: Clerk, Fairfield Town Court, Conn, 50; mem, Fairfield Rep Town Meeting, 47-61; Conn State Rep, 61-67; mem, Rep Town Comt, Fairfield, 62- Bus & Prof Pos: Lectr, Univ Bridgeport, 40-42 & 65-66. Mil Serv: Entered as Pvt, Army, 44, released as T/4, 45, after serv in Army Signal Corps. Mem: Fla & Conn Bar Asns; Red Cross; Am Legion; Stratfield Vol Fire Dept 3. Relig: Hebrew. Mailing Add: 1217 Stratfield Rd Fairfield CT 06604

FENNELLY, ROBERT (D)
NH State Sen
Mailing Add: Box 193 10 Portland Ave Dover NH 03820

FENNER, BERTINE LORRAINE (D)
Mem, Mich Dem State Cent Comt
b Thompson, Mich, Aug 10, 15; d Edward John Miller & Ida M; m 1941 to Milford Sherman Fenner; c Richard Lloyd. Educ: High Sch. Polit & Govt Pos: Mem, Dem Nat Comt; vchmn, MacKinac Co Dem Party, Mich, 56, chmn, 58-72; mem, MacKinac Co Planning Comt, 65; mem, Mich Dem State Cent Comt, 73- Mem: Am Legion Auxiliary; Moose. Mailing Add: Rte 2 St Ignace MI 49781

FENNESSEY, JOSEPH (D)
Ill State Sen
Mailing Add: Rte 2 Ottawa IL 61350

FENSTER, LEO (D)
Mem, Calif Dem State Comt
b New York, NY, May 20, 22; s Morris Fenster & Bessie Geffner F; m 1945 to Maryann Weinstein; c Alan, Stephen & Michael. Educ: Santa Monica City Col, AA, 42; Univ Calif, Los Angeles, 42; Univ Southern Calif Law Sch, 45-46; Southwestern Univ Law Sch, LLB, 50. Polit & Govt Pos: Vchmn, 16th Cong Dem Coun, Los Angeles, Calif, 56; Dem nominee, Calif State Assembly, 60th Dist, 64, 66 & 68, chmn 60th Assembly Dist Dem Coun, Los Angeles, 67; mem, Calif Dem State Comt, 64- Bus & Prof Pos: Attorney, Los Angeles, 51-69. Mil Serv: Entered as Air Cadet, Army Air Force, 43, released as 1st Lt, 45, after serv in 9th Air Force, ETO, 44-45; Purple Heart; Air Medal with 12 Oak Leaf Clusters. Mem: Santa Monica Bar Asn; CofC; B'nai B'rith; Optimist. Relig: Jewish. Mailing Add: 961 Bluegrass Way Los Angeles CA 90049

FENTON, ISABELLE B (R)
VChmn, Delaware Co Rep Comt, NY
b New Rochelle, NY, May 13, 22; d Bertram Ormand Bentley & Louise McCumber B; m 1944 to Donald McLean Fenton; c Andrea (Mrs William J Campbell), John Donald & James Thomas. Educ: State Univ Col at Oneonta, NY, BEd, 43, 27 hours of grad work; Arethusa Sorority; Glee Club. Polit & Govt Pos: Committeewoman, Delaware Co Rep Comt, NY, 51-, vchmn, 59-69, 70-, chmn, 69-70; secy, Rep Town Comt of Middletown, 56-; chmn, Housewives Comt for Gov Rockefeller, Delaware Co, 70; mem col coun, State Univ NY Agr & Tech Col Delhi, 72- Bus & Prof Pos: Teacher, Bayport Sch, Long Island, NY, 43-45, Margaretville Cent Sch, 49-52 & 58-; pres col coun, State Univ NY Agr & Tech Col, Delhi, 74-; mem bd dirs, Asn Coun Mems & Trustees, State Univ NY, 74- Mem: NY State Teachers Asn; Eastern Star; Middletown Women's Rep Club; Women's Soc of Presby Church; Delaware Co Women's Rep Club. Relig: Presbyterian. Mailing Add: Mountain Ave Margaretville NY 12455

FENTON, JACK R (D)
Calif State Assemblyman
Mailing Add: 1601 W Beverly Blvd Montebello CA 90640

FENWICK, MILLICENT HAMMOND (R)
US Rep, NJ
b New York, NY, Feb 25, 10; d Ogden Haggerty Hammond & Mary Picton Stevens H; div; c Mary (Mrs Reckford) & Hugh. Educ: Foxcroft Sch, Middleburg, Va, 2 years; Columbia Univ Exten Sch; New Sch for Social Research, NY. Polit & Govt Pos: Mem bd educ, Bernardsville, NJ, 38-41; borough coun, 58-64; vchmn, NJ Adv Comt to US Comn on Civil Rights, 58-72; NJ State Assemblyman, 70-73; dir, Div Consumer Affairs, Dept Law & Pub Safety, 73-74; US Rep, NJ, 75- Bus & Prof Pos: Assoc ed, Conde Nast Publ, NY, 38-50. Publ: Vogue's Book of Etiquette, Simon & Schuster, 48. Legal Res: Mendham Rd Bernardsville NJ 07924 Mailing Add: US House of Rep Washington DC 20515

FERDINANDO, RICHARD (R)
VPres, NH State Senate
b Manchester, NH, July 15, 34; s Vincent Ferdinando & Germaine Normand F; m 1960 to Barbara Byrne; c Mark, Greg & Keith. Educ: St Anselm's Col, BA in bus admin. Polit & Govt Pos: NH State Sen, 69-, vpres, NH State Senate, 75- Bus & Prof Pos: Pres & owner, Ferdinando Ins Assoc, Inc, 65- Mil Serv: Entered as Pvt, Army, 53, released as Pfc, 55, after serv in 82nd Airborne Unit; Sharpshooter Award. Mem: Exchange Club; Sacred Heart Sch of Nursing (bd dirs); St Anselm's Century Club; Manchester Senate Deleg (chmn). Honors & Awards: Honored as Community Leader, St Anselm's Col Alumni Asn, 74. Relig: Roman Catholic. Mailing Add: 77 Madeline Rd Manchester NH 03104

FERDON, JULIE (D)
b Santa Fe, NMex, Dec 25, 50; d Edwin Nelson Ferdon, Jr & Constance Potter Etz F (deceased); single. Educ: Univ Oslo, Int Summer Sch, summer 70; Univ Ariz, BA, 72. Polit & Govt Pos: Secy, Univ Ariz Dem Alliance, 70-71, pres, 71-72; voter regist coordr for Univ Ariz, Young Dem Am, 71-72; deleg, Ariz Dem State Conv, 72; alt deleg, Nat Dem Conv, 72; staff asst, US Rep Morris K Udall; vol coordr, Udall '76 Comt, 75- Mem: UN Asn, Tucson, Ariz. Relig: Unitarian. Mailing Add: 2141 E Juanita St Tucson AZ 85719

FERGUSON, BILL B (D)
Ore State Rep
Mailing Add: 1379 SE 40th Hillsboro OR 97123

FERGUSON, CHARLES WRIGHT, JR (R)
NH State Rep
b Quincy, Mass, Mar 7, 27; married; c seven. Educ: Univ Ala, BA; Boston Univ Law Sch, LLB. Polit & Govt Pos: Mem, Comt on Serv for Older Persons, NH Social Welfare Coun; chmn, Milford Sch Bd; NH State Rep, 63- Bus & Prof Pos: Owner of grocery store & nursing home. Mil Serv: Army, released 47, serv in Korea, 10 months. Mem: Lions; NH Nursing Home Asn. Relig: Congregational. Mailing Add: Foster Rd Milford NH 03055

FERGUSON, CLARENCE CLYDE, JR (R)
Dep Asst Secy of State for African Affairs
b Wilmington, NC, Nov 4, 24; s Clarence Clyde Ferguson, Sr & Georgeva Owens F; wid; c Claire, Hope, & Eve. Educ: Wilberforce Univ, 42-43; Ohio State Univ, AB cum laude, 48; Harvard Law Sch, LLB cum laude, 51; Phi Beta Kappa; Alpha Phi Alpha. Polit & Govt Pos: Gen counsel, Civil Rights Comn, 62-63; spec legal adv, US Mission to the UN, Dept of State, 63; asst US attorney, Dept of Justice, 54-55; spec coord for Nigerian relief, Dept of State, 69-70; US Ambassador to Uganda, 70-72; Dep Asst Secy of State for African Affairs, 72- Bus & Prof Pos: Teaching fel & teaching asst, Harvard Univ, 50-52; law firm assoc, Baltimore, Paulson & Canudo, 52-54; asst gen counsel & chmn, Comt on Invest of Harness Racing, State of NY, 53-54; prof, Rutgers Univ Law Sch, 55-63 & 69; dean, Howard Univ Law Sch, 63-69. Mil Serv: Army, 42-46; ETO & Pac Theatre of Opers Decorated Bronze Star. Publ: Desegregation & the Law: the Meaning and Effect of the School Segregation Cases (w A P Blaustein), 60; Enforcement & Collection of Judgments & Liens, 61; Secured transactions, Article IX Uniform Commercial Code in New Jersey, 61. Mem: Am, Fed & Nat Bar Asns; Harvard Law Sch Alumni. Honors & Awards: Numerous honors & awards. Legal Res: DC Mailing Add: US Mission to the UN 799 UN Plaza New York NY 10017

FERGUSON, FRANK (D)
Alaska State Sen
Mailing Add: Box 131 Kotzebue AK 99752

FERGUSON, GEORGE ROBERT, JR (D)
Miss State Rep
b Learned, Miss, Aug 13, 33; s George Roberts Ferguson (deceased) & Eugenia Williams F; m 1959 to Martha Gillespie; c Martha Elizabeth, George Robert, III & Cade Drew. Educ: Hinds Jr Col, Raymond, Miss, 1 year; Miss State Univ, BS, 55; Jackson Sch Law, LLB, 65; Blue Key; Pi Delta Epsilon; Sigma Delta Kappa; Pi Kappa Alpha; Delta Sigma Pi. Polit & Govt Pos: Miss State Rep, Hinds Co, 68-; mem, Miss Classification Comn, 70-74. Bus & Prof Pos: Rep, Procter & Gamble Co, 58-60; dir advert & pub rels, Standard Life Ins Co, Jackson, Miss, 60-64; vpres, L E Davis & Assocs, 64-65; attorney-at-law, Raymond, 65-; owner & publisher, Miss Valley Stockman Farmer, 65-; mem bd dirs, Bankers Trust Savings & Loan Asn, Raymond, 70- Mil Serv: Entered as Pvt E-1, Army, 56, released as Pfc, 58, after serv in 23rd Anti-aircraft Artillery Bn, US & Ger. Mem: Mason; Shrine; Lions; Moose; Farm Bur. Honors & Awards: Named to Outstanding Young Men of Am, 69. Relig: Presbyterian; elder, Presby Church, Raymond. Mailing Add: PO Drawer 89 Raymond MS 39154

FERGUSON, GLENN W (D)
b Syracuse, NY, Jan 28, 29; s Forrest E Ferguson & Mabel Walker F; m to Patricia Lou Head; c Bruce Walker, Sherry Lynn & Scott Sherwood. Educ: Cornell Univ, BA, 50, MBA, 51; Georgetown Univ, 51-52; Univ Santo Tomas, Philippines, 52-53; George Washington Univ Law Sch, 53-55; Univ Chicago Law Sch, 55-56; Univ Pittsburgh, JD, 57; Phi Beta Kappa; Phi Delta Phi; Psi Upsilon; Phi Kappa Phi; Beta Gamma Sigma. Hon Degrees: Worcester Polytech Inst & Sacred Heart Univ. Polit & Govt Pos: Consult, Int Coop Admin, Pakistan, 59; rep, Peace Corps, Bangkok, 61-63, assoc dir, Washington, DC, 63-64; dir, VISTA, 64-66; US Ambassador to Kenya, 66-69. Bus & Prof Pos: Asst secy-treas & asst ed, Am Judicature Soc, 55-56; admin asst to chancellor & asst dean, Grad Sch Pub & Int Affairs, Univ Pittsburgh, 56-60; mgt consult, McKinsey & Co, Washington, DC, 60-61; chancellor, Long Island Univ, 69-70; pres, Clark Univ, 70-73 & Univ Conn, 73-; mem bd dirs, New Eng Bd Higher Educ; mem bd dirs, Pvt Export Funding Co, New York; bd trustees, Cornell Univ. Mil Serv: 1st Lt, Air Force, Korea & Philippines, 52-53. Publ: Various pub admin & comp govt articles for prof jour. Mem: Fed Bar Asn; Am Polit Sci Asn; Coun on For Rels; Int Club, Washington, DC; Century Asn, New York. Honors & Awards: Arthur Flemming Award, 68. Mailing Add: Oak Hill Rd Storrs CT 06268

FERGUSON, HOMER (R)
b Harrison City, Pa, Feb 25, 88; s Samuel Ferguson & Margaret Bush F; m 1913 to Myrtle Jones; c Amy (Mrs Charles R Beltz). Educ: Univ Pittsburgh, 10-11; Univ Mich, LLB, 13; Sigma Delta Kappa. Hon Degrees: LLD, Univ Mich, 51; hon degrees, Detroit Col Law, Kalamazoo Col & Muhlenberg Col. Polit & Govt Pos: Mem, Second Hoover Comn; spec attorney for Dept of Defense; judge, Circuit Court, Wayne Co, 29-43; US Sen, Mich, 43-55; US Ambassador to Philippines, 55-56; assoc judge, US Court of Mil Appeals, 56-71, sr judge, 71- Bus & Prof Pos: Attorney, pvt practice, 13-29. Mem: Am Bar Asn; Wash Inst of Foreign Affairs; Interparliamentary Union (hon mem); Inst of Fiscal & Polit Educ; Metrop Club, Washington, DC. Relig: Presbyterian. Legal Res: 5054 Millwood Lane NW Washington DC 20016 Mailing Add: US Ct of Mil Appeals Washington DC 20442

FERGUSON, JO O (R)
b Willow Springs, Mo, June 29, 89; s David S Ferguson & Martha Isabel Young F; m 1920 to Anna Stogsdill; c David Jo, Dolores Ann (Mrs Frank Hooper) & Larry Ross. Educ: Univ Mo Law Sch, 1 year. Polit & Govt Pos: Mem city coun, Pawnee, Okla, 22-24; Okla State Sen, Tenth Dist, 24-32; Rep nominee for Cong, 36, Lt Gov, 42 & Gov, 50; deleg, Rep Nat Conv, 40 & 52; chmn, Pawnee Co Rep Party, Okla, formerly. Bus & Prof Pos: Ed-publ, Pawnee Courier-Dispatch, Okla, 22-30, Cleveland Am, 34-62 & Pawnee Chief, 41-52. Mil Serv: Entered Army, 17, released as 1st Lt, 19, after serv in 140th US Inf, European Theatre, 18-19; Combat & Serv Badges. Mem: Okla Press Asn; Mason; Am Legion; VFW. Relig: Protestant. Mailing Add: 1111 Pawnee Bill Trail Pawnee OK 74058

FERGUSON, JOHN DUNCAN (INDEPENDENT)
b Tacoma, Wash, Jan 12, 46; s James D Ferguson & Audrey Colceck F; single. Educ: Univ Ore, BA Hist, 68; Acad IntLaw, The Hague, 69; Univ Ore Grad Sch, 71. Polit & Govt Pos: Legis aide, US Rep Floyd V Hicks, 72-73; admin aide, US Rep Don Young, Alaska, 73- Mem: Soc Int Law. Legal Res: P.O Box 1175 Anchorage AK 99510 Mailing Add: 318 Second St SE Washington DC 20003

FERGUSON, JOHN P **(D)**
Del State Rep
Mailing Add: 10 Addison Dr Newark DE 19702

FERGUSON, MARGARET OSBORNE **(D)**
Committeewoman, Brevard Co Dem Comt, Fla
b Morrowville, Kans, June 29, 03; d Ernest Richard Osborne & Jessie Ethel MacFarland O; m 1920 to Virgil O Ferguson, wid; c George W & Virginia M (Mrs William L VanSandt). Educ: Univ Mo-Columbia, AB, 40; Columbia Univ, MA, 45; Univ Southern Calif & Univ Hawaii, grad work; Pi Lambda Theta. Hon Degrees: DHL, Sioux Empire Col, 66. Polit & Govt Pos: Treas, 15th Dist Dem Party, Hawaii, 60-68; vchmn, Gov Libr Comn, 65-68; mem, Clark Co Dem Comt, Nev, 68-70; committeewoman, Brevard Co Dem Comt, Fla, 72-, off mgr, Dem Hq, 74; deleg, Dem Nat Mid-Term Conf, 74. Bus & Prof Pos: Teacher hist & chmn dept, Kansas City Sec Schs, Mo, 27-54; teacher hist & chmn dept, Radford High Sch, Honolulu, Hawaii, 54-65; prof hist, Univ Hawaii, 65-68; teacher hist, Las Vegas Sec Schs, Nev, 68-71; retired. Mem: South Brevard Dem Women's Club; Geneal Soc South Brevard. Relig: Protestant. Mailing Add: Apt B5 2186 Hwy A1A Indian Harbour Beach FL 32937

FERGUSON, ROBERT EARL **(D)**
Lt Gov, NMex
b Pineland, Tex, Aug 5, 24; s Jim L Ferguson & Myrtle Gilchrist F; m 1947 to Rosemary Martin; c Robert E, II, Debra Lee, James Ray & Candace. Educ: Baylor Univ, BBA, 49. Polit & Govt Pos: NMex State Rep, 62-66, NMex State Sen, 66-75; Lt Gov, 75- Bus & Prof Pos: Vpres & mgr, Ferguson Trucking Co, 49-59; owner, Bob Ferguson Real Estate & Ins, 59- Mil Serv: Entered as Pvt, Air Force, 44, released as S/Sgt, after serv in Western Pac, 44-46; Battle Stars. Mem: Mason (32 degree); Shrine; Elks; Am Legion. Relig: Methodist. Legal Res: 713 Clayton Rd Artesia NM 88210 Mailing Add: PO Box 350 Artesia NM 88210

FERGUSON, ROBERT ERNEST **(DFL)**
Chmn, Dakota Co Dem-Farmer-Labor Party, Minn
b Rochester, Minn, Sept 13, 37; s Victor Brent Ferguson & Josephine Irene Anderson F; m 1964 to Karen Marie Swanson; c Kari Josephine. Educ: Brainerd Jr Col, Minn, 58-59; Bemidji State Col, BS, 62, MA, 68. Polit & Govt Pos: Chmn, 12B Legis Dist Dem-Farmer-Labor Party, Minn, 69-71; chmn, Dakota Co Dem-Farmer-Labor Party, 70-72 & 75- Bus & Prof Pos: Elem sch teacher, Sch Dist 196, Minn, 62-65, prin, 65- Mem: Nat & Minn Elem Sch Prin Asns; AF&AM; Scottish Rite; Shrine. Relig: Methodist. Mailing Add: 855 Cliff Rd Eagan MN 55123

FERGUSON, ROSETTA **(D)**
Mich State Rep
b Florence, Miss, July 1, 20; d Gabriel Sexton & Earnie S; m 1939; c Linda Henderson (Mrs Burton), Prince Michael, Huey A & Maurice. Educ: Detroit Inst Technol. Polit & Govt Pos: Mem, Mich Dem State Cent Comt, 2 years, mem exec bd & precinct deleg, First Cong Dist, 10 years; recording secy, 13th Cong Dist, formerly; mem, Wayne Co Dem Rep Human Rels Coun Civil Rights; organized & sponsored Youth Civic Eagles; founder & financial secy, People's Community Civic League, 8 years; app, Loyalty Investigating Comt; Mich State Rep, 9th Dist, 64-72, 20th Dist, 72-, treas, Wayne Co Dem Deleg, Mich House Rep, currently, chmn, Civil Rights Comt, formerly, vchmn, currently, mem, Comts on Pub Safety & Roads & Bridges, currently, chief sponsor of Fair Textbook Law, 66, chmn social servs & corrections comt, currently. Bus & Prof Pos: Gen mgr staff, Real Estate Firm, Detroit, currently. Mem: Nat Order Women Legislators; Nat Soc State Legislators; Cong Nat Orgn Black Elected Off; NAACP; Trade Union Leadership Coun. Honors & Awards: Key to the City of New Orleans, 68; Mich House resolution for her far-sighted vision & dedication to the full maturity of the human family, 70. Relig: Baptist. Mailing Add: 2676 Arndt Detroit MI 48207

FERGUSON, WILLIAM ALVAH **(D)**
b Knoxville, Tenn, Nov 15, 35; s Alvah Asco Ferguson & Ova Young F; div; c Gregory Vance. Educ: Univ Tenn, 60-61. Polit & Govt Pos: Press secy, US Rep J Edward Roush, Ind, 74-75, admin asst, 75- Bus & Prof Pos: Polit reporter, The Elkhart Truth, Ind, 61-64 & The Ft Wayne New-Sentinel, 64-74. Mil Serv: Entered as E-1, Army, released as SP-4, after serv in 518 Combat Engrs Bn, CZ, 58-60. Mem: Ft Wayne Press Club (past pres); Admin Asst Asn. Honors & Awards: Conserv Writer of the Year, Ind Izaak Walton League, 68; Two nominations for the Pulitzer Prize. Legal Res: 3301 Portage Blvd Apt 42 Ft Wayne IN 46804 Mailing Add: 326 Fed Bldg Ft Wayne IN 46802

FERN, BENJAMIN R
b NJ. Educ: Queens Col, AB, 42; George Washington Univ Law Sch, JD, 57. Polit & Govt Pos: Chief counsel, Select Comt on Standards & Conduct, US Senate, Washington, DC, 65- Mil Serv: Entered as A/S, Navy, 42, released as Capt, 65. Mem: Am Bar Asn. Legal Res: McLean VA Mailing Add: Select Comt Standards & Conduct US Senate Washington DC 20510

FERNANDEZ, JOACHIM OCTAVE **(D)**
b New Orleans, La, Aug 14, 96; s Octave Gonzales Fernandez & Mary Benson F; remarried 1946 to Jessie Josephine Nosacka; c Florau J, Joachim Octave, Jr, Mercedes & June Rose. Educ: Sophie Wright High Sch. Polit & Govt Pos: Mem, La Const Conv, 21; La State Rep, 24-28; La State Sen, 28-30; US Rep, La, 31-41; collector, Internal Revenue, Dist of La, 43-46; head, Income Tax Sect, State of La, 51-63, retired. Mil Serv: Lt Comdr, Naval Res, 41-43; Victory Medal. Mem: Am Legion. Relig: Catholic. Mailing Add: 3110 Derby Pl New Orleans LA 70119

FERNANDEZ, RUTH **(POPULAR DEMOCRAT, PR)**
Sen, PR Senate
Mailing Add: State Capitol San Juan PR 00901

FERRALL, GRACE LOIS **(D)**
Chmn, Shawano Co Dem Comt, Wis
b Weyerhauser, Wis, June 29, 13; d Michael J Ellison & Pauline Goodness E; m 1935 to Russell Brown Ferrall; c R Michael & Ellison W. Educ: Sch of Cosmetology, 32-33; Wis State Col-Stevens Point, 59-60. Polit & Govt Pos: Secy, Shawano Co Dem Comt, Wis, 60-64, chmn, 64- Mem: Fel Poets, Wis; Nat Fedn State Poetry Socs; Eastern Star (Past Matron); Bus & Prof Women's Club; Gresham Women's Club. Relig: Methodist. Mailing Add: 126 River Heights Box 493 Shawano WI 54166

FERRALL, R MICHAEL **(D)**
Wis State Rep
b Minneapolis, Minn, Oct 3, 36; s Russell Brown Ferrall & Grace Ellison F; c Gregory, Allison, Paul, James & Bruce. Educ: Wis State Univ, Stevens Point, BA in Polit Sci, 62; Univ Calif, Berkeley, 67; Univ Wis, Milwaukee, MA in Polit Sci, 70; Hon Social Sci Fraternity. Polit & Govt Pos: Chmn, Wis State Univ, Stevens Point Young Dem, 59-62; vchmn, Wis State Young Dem, 61; bd dirs, Racine Civil Liberties Union, 66-71; Wis State Rep, 71-, chmn, State Comt on Admin Rules, 73-75, chmn, Assembly Educ Comt, 74- Bus & Prof Pos: Educator, William Horlick High Sch, Racine, Wis, 62-70 & Washington Park High Sch, 70- Mil Serv: Navy, Korean Conflict, 54-57. Mem: Racine Jaycees. Relig: Protestant. Legal Res: 1816 Wisconsin Ave Racine WI 53403 Mailing Add: State Capitol Madison WI 53702

FERRARI, RAYMOND CHARLES **(D)**
Conn State Rep
b Brooklyn, NY, May 4, 48; s Raymond A Ferrari & Margaret Lugar F; m 1974 to Lila North. Educ: Univ Hartford, BA, 72. Polit & Govt Pos: Dist capt, Windsor Dem Town Comt, Conn, 70-; First Dist chmn, Young Dem Conn Inc, 72-74; mem, Zoning Bd Appeals, Windsor, 74-75; Conn State Rep, 75- Mailing Add: 32 Corey St Windsor CT 06095

FERRARO, ANTHONY MICHAEL **(D)**
RI State Rep
b Everett, Mass, Oct 18, 35; s Michael Ferraro & Mary Capone F; m 1961 to Sheila Mae Murphy; c Aileen Marie, Anthony M, Jr & Christopher Alan. Educ: Providence Col, AB; Suffolk Univ Law Sch, 1 year; Royal Inst Chem, ITE & EdM; Year Book Staff; Ship & Scales Club; Providence & Cranston Club; St Thomas More Club; social chmn, Student Coun. Polit & Govt Pos: Chmn, State Correspondence Schs, RI, 67; mem, State Comt to Study Open Dumping, 67; vchmn, Comt to Study State Scholarships, 67; vchmn, State Dept of Health, Educ & Welfare, 69; mem state comt, Motor Vehicle Code, 69; mem, State Comt to Study Exec Sch Year, 69; RI State Rep, Dist 25, 69- Mil Serv: Entered as Airman Basic, Air Force, 59, released as A/2C, 60, after serv in Air Nat Guard; Cert of Merit; Supply Sch Award; Honors Award. Mem: RI Educ Asn; Warwick Teachers Union; Community Caucus; Boy Scouts (committeeman); Stoney Brook Civic Asn. Relig: Catholic. Mailing Add: 86 Stone Dr Cranston RI 02920

FERRARO, ROSEMARY FLORENCE **(R)**
b Terra Haute, Ind, Sept 7, 19; d Robert Cushman Winningham & Edna Mae Shaffer W; m 1938 to Nat Ferraro; c Dr Kenneth Nat, Stephen Charles, Cheryl Jean (Mrs Baker) & Michael James. Polit & Govt Pos: Hq chmn, Reelec of Gov Reagan, 38th & 52nd Assembly Dist, Calif, 70; area chmn, Comt for Reelec of the President, 72; deleg, Rep Nat Conv, 72; alt, Los Angeles Co Cent Comt, 38th Assembly Dist, Calif, 72; campaign chmn, Dr Robert McLennan, Rep cand for 38th Assembly Dist Seat, 73. Bus & Prof Pos: Vpres, Downey Vendors, 60- Mem: Los Angeles Co Women's Chap, Freedoms Found at Valley Forge (vpres educ, 72-); Am Cancer Soc (chmn annual dinner & bd dirs, Los Angeles, currently); Downey Rep Women Federated (membership chmn, 72-73); Assistance League of Southern Calif. Relig: Christian Science. Mailing Add: 9504 Gallatin Rd Downey CA 90240

FERRE, LUIS A **(R)**
b Ponce, PR, Feb 17, 04; s Antonio Ferre & Mary Aguayo F; m 1931 to Lorencita Ramirez de Arellano; wid; c Antonio Luis & Rosario. Educ: Mass Inst Technol, BS, & MS; LLD, Springfield Col. Hon Degrees: DCL, Cath Univ PR; LHD, Inter-Am Univ PR, Pace Col & NY Univ; LLD, Harvard Univ & Amherst Col, 70. Polit & Govt Pos: Mem, PR Const Conv, 50-51; PR State Rep, 52-56; cand for Gov PR, 56, 60 & 64; mem, USPR Status Comn, 64-66; mem, State Adv Comt on Sci, Eng & Specialized Personnel; mem citizens adv comt, Comn on Govt Security; pres, New Progressive Party; Rep Nat Committeeman, PR; Gov, PR, 69-72. Bus & Prof Pos: Mem corp, Mass Inst Technol. Publ: Industrial Democracy; The American Citizenship. Mem: PR Acad of Arts & Sci; Am Soc Mech Engrs; Elks (Exalted Ruler); Lions Club (past pres, int counsr); Fedn YMCA's PR. Honors & Awards: Puerto Rican of the Year, Knights of St John of Chicago, 58; Named to the Knights of the Holy Sepulcher by Pope John XXIII, 59; Eugenio Maria de Hostos Award, 62; Order of Vasa, 63; Freedom Award, Order of Lafayette, 69. Relig: Roman Catholic. Mailing Add: GPO Box 6108 San Juan PR 00936

FERREIRA, FRANCIS JOSEPH, JR **(R)**
Chmn, Rockingham Co Rep Comt, NH
b Salem, Mass, Nov 18, 38; s Francis Joseph Ferreira & Catherine Holland F; m 1960 to Anne Marie Archambault; c Cathrina Maria, Jonathan David & Gretchen Brianna. Educ: Mass State Col Salem, BSEd, 60, MEd, 64; Footlighters Drama Club (publicity chmn); Student Nat Educ Asn (secy-treas). Polit & Govt Pos: Co-founder & treas, Exeter Young Rep Club, 64-67; mem exec comt, NH Fedn Young Rep Clubs, 65-67; deleg, NH Rep State Conv, 66, 68 & 70; area coordr, in primary elec of Congressman Louis C Wyman, 66, 68 & 70, President Richard M Nixon, 68 & Gov Walter R Peterson, 68 & 70; mem exec comt, Rockingham Co Rep Comt, 67-68, chmn, 69-70 & 75-, vchmn, 71-75; chmn, Hampton Falls Rep Town Comt, 67-; town auditor, Hampton Falls, 68-, supvr checklist, 70-; chmn, Rockingham Co Comt for Reelec of the President, 72; mem adv comt, NH State Rep Comt, 73- Bus & Prof Pos: Teacher, Pentucket Regional Sch Dist, Mass, 60-65; asst prin, Pentucket Jr High Sch, 65-68, prin, 68- Mem: Nat Asn Sec Sch Prin; Mass Jr High & Mid High Sch Prin Asn; Mass Asn Supv & Curriculum Develop; Boy Scouts (treas, troop comt 377, inst rep Boy Scouts & Cub Scouts, 72-); Seacoast Youth Ctr (bd dirs, 72-). Relig: Roman Catholic. Mailing Add: Exeter Rd Hampton Falls NH 03844

FERRELL, J FRED, JR **(D)**
Okla State Sen
Mailing Add: State Capitol Oklahoma City OK 73105

FERRELL, WILLIAM FRANKLIN (BILL) **(D)**
Nat Committeeman, Mo Young Dem
b Morehouse, Mo, Dec 7, 39; s John Frank Ferrell & Henrietta Steinbeck F; m 1962 to Sharon Lee Watson; c William Franklin, II, (Buzz), John Fitzgerald, Lee Watson & Stefani Nicole. Educ: Cent Col, 2 years; Southeast Mo State Univ, six months. Polit & Govt Pos: Treas, Mo Young Dem, formerly, vpres, formerly, nat committeeman, currently; assessor, Scott Co, 73- Bus & Prof Pos: Gen mgr, Tire Co; construction foreman; off mgr, State License; self employed, Ferrell Auto Salvage, currently. Mem: State Young Dem Club (exec bd, 72-73); Mo Independent Auto Dealers Asn; Jaycees; Elks; Mason. Honors & Awards: Outstanding Young Dem, Scott Co, Mo. Relig: Baptist. Legal Res: Rte 2 Sikeston MO 63801 Mailing Add: PO Box 187 Sikeston MO 63801

FERRIS, CHARLES DANIEL (D)
b Boston, Mass, Apr 9, 33; s Henry Joseph Ferris & Mildred MacDonald F; m to Patricia Brennan; c Caroline & Sabrina. Educ: Boston Col, AB, Physics, 54, Law Sch, LLB, 61; Harvard Univ, AMP, 71. Polit & Govt Pos: Trial attorney, US Dept Justice, 61-63; assoc gen counsel, Dem Policy Comt, US Senate, 63-64, chief of staff & gen counsel, 64- Bus & Prof Pos: Asst prof naval sci, Harvard Univ, 58-60. Mil Serv: Entered as Ens, Navy, 55, released as Lt, 60, after serv in USS Brinkley Bass (DD887), Western Pac, 55-58, Lt, Naval Res (Ret). Legal Res: Dorchester MA Mailing Add: 8802 Mansion Farm Place Mt Vernon VA 22121

FERRIS, JOSEPH (D)
NY State Assemblyman
Mailing Add: State Assembly State Capitol Albany NY 12224

FERRIS, ROBERT CHARLES (R)
b Waterville, Maine, Dec 12, 43; s Joseph Emy Ferris & Sadie Thomas F; m 1972 to Mary Elizabeth Reggie. Educ: Brown Univ, BA, 65; Theta Delta Chi. Polit & Govt Pos: Chmn, Waterville Rep Town Comt, Maine, formerly; Maine State Rep, 73-74. Bus & Prof Pos: Vpres, Ferris Bros Jeep Sales, 71- Mil Serv: Entered as 2nd Lt, Marine Corps, 68, released as 1st Lt, 71, after serv in 2nd Bn, 5th Regt, 1st Marine Div, Vietnam, 69; Purple Heart. Mem: VFW; Elks; Am Legion. Relig: Roman Catholic. Mailing Add: 11 Averill Terr Waterville ME 04901

FERRY, MILES YEOMAN (CAP) (R)
Utah State Sen
b Brigham City, Utah, Sept 22, 32; s John Yeoman Ferry, Jr & Alda Cheney F; m 1952 to Suzanne Call; c John Yeoman, Suzanne, Jane & Benjamin Call. Educ: Utah State Univ, BS, 54; Phi Kappa Phi; Pi Kappa Alpha. Polit & Govt Pos: Chmn, Corinne Rep Voting Dist, Utah, 62-64; deleg, Rep State Conv, 62, 64 & 66; Utah State Rep, 65-66; Utah State Sen, 67-, chmn, Bus, Labor & Agr Comt, Utah State Senate, 73- Mem: Utah Farm Bur; Agr Stabilization & Conserv Dist; Brigham City Jaycees; Corinne PTA; Nat Golden Spike Asn. Honors & Awards: Selected as One of Ten Outstanding Nat Dirs, US Jr CofC, 62; One of Three Outstanding Young Men, Utah, 62. Relig: Latter-day Saint. Mailing Add: Box 70 Corrine UT 84307

FERST, JEANNE ROLFE (R)
Treas, Ga Rep Party
b Chicago, Ill, Sept 6, 18; d Mark A Rolfe & Rose Kominsky R; m 1940 to Robert H Ferst; c Suzanne F (Mrs Nelson Neiman) & Robin H. Educ: Univ Chicago, 36-38. Polit & Govt Pos: Co-chmn, Nixon Rally, Atlanta, Ga, 60; precinct chmn, Fulton Co Rep Party, 60, mem exec comt, 60-68; deleg, co & state conv, 60-; vchmn, Ga Rep State Finance Comt, 61-66; co-chmn finance comt, O'Callaghan for Cong, Atlanta, 62; co-chmn, Circle R & Comt of 100, Fulton Co, 62-64; asst treas, Fulton Co Rep Party, 64-68; chmn, Calloway for Gov Rally, 66; chmn, Dirksen Dinner, Atlanta, 67 & Nixon Dinner, 68; alt deleg, Rep Nat Conv, 68, deleg, 72; adv & mem, US Deleg to Gov Coun of the UN Develop Prog, Geneva, Switz, June-July, 69, mem, June-July, 70; treas & finance chmn, Ga Rep Party, 70-; Ga chmn, Nat Rep Finance Comt, 71; mem, President's Adv Panel S Asian Relief, 71-; women's chmn for Ga, Nat Finance Comt to Reelect the President, 72. Mem: Atlanta Comt Foreign Rels; Southern Coun Int & Pub Affairs; Atlanta Symphony Mem Guild; Multiple Sclerosis Soc (mem bd); Nat Rep Womens Club, New York. Relig: Jewish. Mailing Add: 3585 Woodhaven Rd NW Atlanta GA 30305

FESSLER, RICHARD DONALD (R)
Mich State Rep
b Detroit, Mich, May 17, 43; s John Arthur Fessler, Sr & Lily Thompson F; m 1971 to Marilyn Elizabeth Meissner; c Richard Donald, II, Katherine Elizabeth & Robert Harrison. Educ: Oakland Community Col, 65-67; Oakland Univ, BA, 69; Univ Detroit Sch Law, JD, 72; Gamma Eta Gamma. Polit & Govt Pos: Chief dep treas, Oakland Co, Mich, 72; asst prosecutor, 73; asst twp attorney, Waterford Charter Twp, 73-74; Mich State Rep, 24th Legis Dist, 75- Bus & Prof Pos: Attorney-at-law, Pontiac, Mich, 72- Mem: Am, Mich & Oakland Co Bar Asns. Honors & Awards: Scholastic Award, Oakland Univ, 68-69; First Place Moot Court Competition, Moot Court Bd Dirs, Univ Detroit Sch Law, 70. Mailing Add: 1760 Marylestone Dr Union Lake MI 48085

FETRIDGE, WILLIAM HARRISON (R)
Mem, Rep Nat Finance Comt
b Chicago, Ill, Aug 2, 09; s Matthew Fetridge & Clara Hall F; m 1941 to Bonnie Jean Clark; c Blakely (Mrs Harvey H Bundy, III) & Clark. Educ: Northwestern Univ, BS, 29; Beta Theta Pi; Deru; Sargent Scholar. Hon Degrees: LLD, Cent Mich Univ, 54. Polit & Govt Pos: Founder & first pres, Evanston Young Rep Club, Ill; mem bd gov, United Rep Fund of Ill, 47-, vpres, 60-67, pres, 67-73; campaign mgr, Merriam for Mayor, 55; alt deleg, Rep Nat Conv, 56, deleg, 68; chmn, Midwest Vol for Nixon-Lodge, 60; chmn, Nixon Recount Comt, 60; mem, Rep Nat Finance Comt, 66- Bus & Prof Pos: Vpres, Popular Mech Mag, 45-53, exec vpres, 53-59; vpres, Diamond T Motor Truck Co, 59-61, exec vpres, 61-65; pres, Dartnell Corp, 65-; pres, US Found Int Scouting, 71- Mil Serv: Entered as Lt, Naval Res, 42, released as Lt Comdr after serv in Am & European Theatre, 42-45. Publ: The Navy Reader, Bobbs-Merrill, 43; Republican Precinct Workers Manual, 46 & Am Political Almanac, 52, Capitol House. Mem: Boy Scouts (nat vpres); Lake Forest Col (mem bd trustees); Chicago Club; Union League; Capitol Hill Club, Washington, DC. Honors & Awards: Silver Buffalo, Silver Antelope & Silver Beaver, Boy Scouts. Relig: Episcopal. Legal Res: 2430 Lake View Ave Chicago IL 60614 Mailing Add: 4660 N Ravenswood Chicago IL 60640

FETTINGER, GEORGE EDGAR (D)
NMex State Rep
b Rochester, NY, Feb 27, 29; m 1962 to R Nell Lankford; c George Michael & Douglas Patrick. Educ: Hobart Col, BBA, 50; Univ NMex Law Sch, JD, 58. Polit & Govt Pos: NMex State Rep, 64-, Majority Floor Leader, NMex House of Rep, 69-70, chmn, Judiciary Comt, 71-72; mem, Bd Bar Comnrs, 72-73. Bus & Prof Pos: Attorney-at-law. Mil Serv: Entered as Pfc, Air Force, Jet Fighter Pilot, 4 years, released as Capt, Res, 7 years. Mem: Am Legion; Alamogordo CofC; Lions; Elks (Lodge 1897); Boy Scouts. Relig: Presbyterian. Legal Res: 1501 Juniper Dr Alamogordo NM 88310 Mailing Add: PO Drawer M Alamogordo NM 88310

FEUER, ALAN CRAIG (D)
b Detroit, Mich, Jan 3, 53; s Arthur Feuer & Regina Landau F; single. Educ: Bennington Col, 72; Polit & Govt Pos: Precinct deleg opers, McCarthy for President, Mich, 68; campaign coordr, Annetta Miller for Cong, 18th Cong Dist, 70; staff organizer, Emergency Conf New Voters, Washington, DC, 71; Ozaukee Co coordr, Lindsay '72 Wis Primary, 72; advan man, Lindsay '72, 72; Oakland Co coordr, McGovern for President, Mich Primary, 72; Greenpoint Area of Brooklyn elec day coordr, Lowenstein for Cong, NY, 72; deleg, Dem Nat Conv, 72; co-campaign mgr, Michael Einheuser for Wayne Univ Bd Gov, 72; elec day coordr, McGovern for President, 14th Cong Dist, Mich, 72. Bus & Prof Pos: Res asst, The Almanac of Am Polit, 71-; correspondent, WABX-FM, 72- Mem: Am Civil Liberties Union; Am Dem Action; Mich Dem Youth Caucus; Temple Israel of Detroit. Relig: Jewish. Legal Res: 23210 Harding Oak Park MI 48237 Mailing Add: c/o Bennington College Bennington VT 05201

FEULNER, EDWIN JOHN, JR (R)
b Evergreen Park, Ill, Aug 12, 41; s Edwin John Feulner, Sr & Helen Franzen F; m 1969 to Linda C Leventhal; c Edwin John, III & Emily Victoria. Educ: Regis Col (Colo, BS, 63; Wharton Grad Sch, Univ Pa, MBA, 64; London Sch Econ, 65; Georgetown Univ, 65-68; Alpha Kappa Psi. Polit & Govt Pos: Pub affairs fel, Ctr for Strategic & Int Studies, Georgetown Univ, 65-67 & Hoover Inst, Stanford Univ, 67-68; research analyst, Rep Conf, US House Rep, 68-69; Spec Asst to Secy of Defense, Pentagon, 69-70; legis asst to US Rep Philip M Crane, Ill, 70-71, admin asst, 71-73; campaign mgr, Crane for Cong Comt, 72; exec dir Rep study comt, US House Rep, 74- Publ: Co-auth, Trading with the Communists, Wash Ctr for Strategic Studies, 68; Revenue sharing, South Econ J, 68; Evolving Attitudes Toward the United Nations, Washington, 74; plus many others. Mem: Transportation Research Forum; Am Econ Asn; Am Polit Sci Asn; Asn for Soc Econ; Philadelphia Soc (treas). Honors & Awards: Outstanding Young Man of Am, US Jr CofC, 67 & 73. Relig: Catholic. Legal Res: 305 Elm Park Ave Elmhurst IL 60126 Mailing Add: 6216 Berkeley Rd Alexandria VA 22307

FEWELL, SAMUEL BRUCE, JR
SC State Rep
b Rock Hill, SC, July 8, 39; s Dr Samuel B Fewell & Rebecca Reed F; m 1966 to Kerrina Cramer; c Karen Sloan & Samuel B, III. Educ: Univ SC, BS, 61 & LLB, 65; Sigma Chi; Block C Club; Phi Delta Phi. Polit & Govt Pos: SC State Rep, currently. Mem: Jr CofC; Moose; Elks. Relig: Presbyterian. Mailing Add: Box 929-CSS Rock Hill SC 29730

FEYEN, KATHLEEN ANN (D)
VChmn, Miss Dem Party
b Fond du Lac, Wis, Aug 17, 33; d Henry Feyen & Alma Schmitz F; single. Educ: Badger Green Bay Bus Col, Wis. Polit & Govt Pos: Secy, First Dist Dem Party, Miss, 68-72; secy, Leflore Co Dem Party, 68-; vchmn, Miss Dem Party, 72-, mem, Dem Nat Comt, formerly. Bus & Prof Pos: Ed, Ctr Light Newspaper, Greenwood, Miss, 69- Mem: NAACP (br secy, 66-). Relig: Catholic. Mailing Add: 708 Ave I Greenwood MS 38930

FICHTER, JOSEPH WILLIAM (D)
b Aberdeen, Ohio, July 12, 94; s Andrew Fichter & Sarah Hiett F; m 1917 to Orveda Beckett; c Jean (Mrs Warner H Shugert), Robert B, Richard H & J Hal. Educ: Miami Univ, AB, 15; Univ Cincinnati, grad study, 35-36; Phi Beta Kappa; Tau Kappa Alpha; Phi Kappa Tau. Polit & Govt Pos: Deleg-at-lg, Dem Nat Conv, 40, 64 & 68; mem, Nat Adv Bd to US Surgeon Gen under the Hosp Surv & Construction Act, 47-51; agr consult & price analyst, Econ Stabilization Admin, 51; mem, Gov Task Force on Tax Reform, Ohio, 71; mem, Gov Adv Coun on Malabar Farm, 72-; state chmn, Rural Am for Voter Action, Ohio Farmers Union, 72; mem, Ohio Comn on Aging, 73-; alt deleg, Dem Mid Term Conf, 74. Bus & Prof Pos: Prin, Hanover Twp High Sch, Butler Co, Ohio, 15-21; teacher Eng, Hamilton High Sch, Ohio, 21-23; supt, Butler Co Schs, Ohio, 23-31; asst state dir educ, Ohio, 31-35; mem faculty, Miami Univ, 36-58; spec asst to pres, Nat Farmers Union, 71- Publ: Diamond Jubilee History of Ohio State Grange, 47 & Handbook for Grange leaders, 50; columnist, The law of the land, weekly newspapers, 53- Mem: Ohio Div Nat Farmers Union (legis rep, 72-, emer pres, 74-); Ohio State Grange (Past Master, mem exec comt, 26-); Nat Planning Asn (bd trustees, 45-); Mason (32 degree). Honors & Awards: Meritorious Serv Award, Nat Farmers Union, 72 & Citation on behalf of Ohio State Senate for above award, 72. Relig: United Methodist, deleg, Gen Conf, United Methodist Church, 72. Mailing Add: 28 E Vine St Oxford OH 45056

FICKETT, LEWIS PERLEY, JR (D)
Va State Deleg
b Winthrop, Mass, May 28, 26; s Lewis P Fickett, Sr & Phyllis Macpherson; m 1969 to Martha Elaine VanZandt; c Lewis P, III, Sybil A & Karin A. Educ: Bowdoin Col, AB, 48; Harvard Law Sch, LLB, 52; Harvard Grad Sch, PhD, 56; Phi Beta Kappa; Zeta Zsi. Polit & Govt Pos: Chmn, Fredericksburg City Dem Party, 69-; Va State Deleg, 74-, mem house educ comt, Va House Deleg, 74- Bus & Prof Pos: US Foreign Servs Officer, US State Dept, Washington, DC, Bonn, Ger & Algiers, Algeria, 56-63. Mil Serv: Entered as A/S, Naval Res, 44, released as Yeoman 2/C, 46, after serv in Pac, 45-46; comdr, Naval Res, currently. Publ: Auth, Problems of the Developing Nations, Thomas Y Crowell Co, 66, plus articles on Indian Politics. Mem: Am Polit Sci Asn; Asn for Asian Studies; Va Bar Asn. Honors & Awards: Admin Fel; Fund for the Rep Fel; Fulbright Fel to India, 65 & 67-68. Relig: Unitarian. Legal Res: 191 Longstreet Ave Fredericksburg VA 22401 Mailing Add: Law Bldg 910 Princess Anne St Fredericksburg VA 22401

FICKLE, WILLIAM DICK (D)
Mo State Rep
b Kansas City, Mo, Oct 29, 43; s William Fickle & Elvarea Dick F; m 1969 to Jane Thompson Jones; c Tara Elizabeth & William Dick, Jr. Educ: Westminster Col, BA, 65; Univ Mo-Columbia, JD, 68; Phi Delta Phi; Kappa Alpha Order. Polit & Govt Pos: Prosecuting attorney, Platte Co, Mo, 72-74; Mo State Rep, 17th Dist, 75- Bus & Prof Pos: Attorney-at-law, Fickle & Hull, Platte Co, Mo, 72-75, Klibinger, Fickle & McGinness, 75- Mil Serv: Entered as Pvt, Army, 69, released as Sgt, 71, after serv in Judge Adv Gen Correctional Training Facil. Mem: Mason; Jr CofC; Am Legion; Optimists. Honors & Awards: Outstanding Young Man of Platte Co, 73; Legion of Honor, 75. Relig: Episcopal. Mailing Add: 1102 Main St Parkville MO 64152

FIDEL, JOSEPH A (D)
NMex State Sen
b Bibo, NMex, Oct 14, 23; s Abdoo Habeeb Fidel & Latife Hanosh F; m 1949 to Aurora Baca; c Barbara, Donna Marie, Marcia, Anna Marie, Mary Lee & Mark. Educ: St Michael's High Sch, Santa Fe, NMex, 35-39. Polit & Govt Pos: City councilman, Grants, NMex, 54-60; co assessor, Valencia Co, 50-54 & 62-66; mem sch bd, Grants Munic Schs, 59-71; NMex State Sen, Dist 30, Socorro-Valencia Co, 73- Bus & Prof Pos: Vpres, Fidel & Moleres, Inc, Ins-Real Estate, Grants, 45- Mem: Elks Lodge 2053 (charter mem); KofC (charter mem); Rotary. Relig: Catholic. Legal Res: 1034 E High St Grants NM 87020 Mailing Add: PO Box 968 Grants NM 87020

FIEDLER, BETTY MAE (R)
State Committeewoman, Pa Rep Comt
b Cleveland, Ohio, Mar 3, 25; d Maurice Glenroy Miles & Grace Hodgson M; m 1944 to Edwin Gustav Fiedler, Jr; c Edwin, III, Eric & William. Educ: Hahnemann Sch of Nursing, Philadelphia, 2 years. Polit & Govt Pos: Committeewoman & secy exec comt, Lancaster Co Rep Comt, Pa, 62-64, precinct orgn chmn, 69-70, vchmn research & training, 71-74; Rep regist chmn, Lancaster Co, 64; pres, Lancaster Co Women's Rep Club, 65-66; mem, Cong Campaign Comt, 66, 68 & 70; TAR coordr, Pa Coun Rep Women, 67-70, asst treas, 71-72; alt deleg, Rep Nat Conv, 68; chmn, Fund Raising Dinner Comt, 69, mem, 75; state committeewoman, Pa Rep Comt, 70-; mem, Co Campaign Comt, 74; Rep vol co-chmn, 74 & 75. Mem: Lancaster Gen Hosp Auxiliary; Lancaster Br, Am Cancer Soc (dir, 72-); Iris Club; Presby Women (hon mem comn ecumenical mission & rels). Relig: Presbyterian. Mailing Add: 1515 Country Club Dr Lancaster PA 17601

FIEDLER, EDGAR R (R)
b Milwaukee, Wis, Apr 21, 29; s Albert Charles Fiedler & Blanche Tolman F; m 1956 to Jessie McKeith Lichtfeldt; c William Frederick & Carol Blanche. Educ: Univ Wis, BBA with honors, 51; Univ Mich, MBA with high distinction, 56; NY Univ, PhD, 70. Polit & Govt Pos: Dep asst secy econ affairs, Dept of Com, 70-71; dep dir, Cost of Living Coun, 71; asst secy econ policy, Dept of the Treas, 71- Bus & Prof Pos: Statist analyst, Eastman Kodak Co, Rochester, NY, 56-59; sales analyst, Doubleday & Co, New York, 59-60; asst economist, Bankers Trust Co, New York, 60-69; mgr gen econ dept, Nat Indust Conf Bd, 69-70. Mil Serv: Naval Res, 52-55. Mem: Am Econ Asn; Nat Asn Bus Econ; Am Statist Asn. Legal Res: NY Mailing Add: Dept of the Treas Washington DC 20220

FIELD, ANDREW ROBERT (R)
Mem Exec Comt, Vt State Rep Comt
b Cleveland, Ohio, Dec 22, 26; s George Howard Field & Louise Hamm F; m 1947 to Juanita Virginia Baird; c Nora, Sarah, Elizabeth & Emily. Educ: Western Reserve Univ, BBA, 50; Cleveland Marshall Law Sch, LLB, cum laude, 58; Delta Theta Phi. Polit & Govt Pos: Mem exec comt from Washington Co, Vt State Rep Comt, 67-; chmn, Washington Co Rep Comt, formerly. Bus & Prof Pos: Asst mgr, Bond Dept, Otis & Co, Cleveland, Ohio, 47-52; investment security salesman, Singer, Deane & Scribner, 52-53; asst dist supvr, Nat Life Ins Co, Cleveland, Ohio, 53-58, counsel Montpelier, Vt, 58- Mil Serv: Entered as Pvt, Army, 45, released as Pfc, 47, after serv in Mil Police, Third Army, Germany, 45-47. Mem: Vt, Washington Co, Ohio & Am Bar Asns; Am Land Title Asn; KofC; Elks. Honors & Awards: Delta Theta Phi Scholarship Key. Relig: Roman Catholic. Mailing Add: Spring Hollow Lane Montpelier VT 05602

FIELD, DONALD WILLIAM (R)
Mem City Adv Coun, San Leandro, Calif
b Portland, Ore, Mar 21, 20; s Leslie William Field & Clara Lutes F; m 1944 to Beverly Eileen Hacker; c Jeffery B & Gregory C. Educ: Willamette Univ, 42-43; Calif Podiatry Col, DPM, 49; Theta Upsilon Tau. Polit & Govt Pos: Vchmn, San Leandro Unit, Calif Rep Assembly, 60; pres, Alameda Co Rep Coord Coun, 61-62; chmn, Bay Area Co Goldwater for Pres Clubs, 63-64; deleg, United Rep of Calif, 63-64; mem, Alameda Co Rep Cent Comt, 63-65; co-chmn, Alameda Co, Goldwater-Miller Campaign, 64; deleg, Rep Nat Conv, 64; mem finance comt, Alameda Co for Ivy Baker Priest & for Ronald Reagan, 66; San Leandro chmn, Richard M Nixon for Pres Campaign, 68; finance chmn, Max Rafferty for US Sen, 68; mem, San Leandro City Adv Coun, 69-; city chmn, Reagan for Gov Comt, 70. Bus & Prof Pos: Mem, Hosp Comt, Calif Podiatry Asn, 63-64; chief, Podiatry Serv, Levine Gen Hosp, Hayward, 64-66. Mil Serv: Entered as Pvt, Army, 43, released as S/Sgt, 46, after serv in Enlisted Res Corps, QM; Good Conduct Medal; ETO Ribbon; Battle Star for Invasion France. Publ: Podiatry, NY Podiatry J, 56; Dignity-Stature-Recognition, Calif Podiatry Asn Newsletter, 56. Mem: Am Podiatry Asn; Am Asn Hosp Podiatrists; Am Legion Post 117; San Leandro CofC (bd dirs, 67-68, pres, 71-); Calif State Podiatry Exam Comt (mem, 68-). Honors & Awards: Outstanding Citizen, San Leandro Optimist Clubs, 55; San Leandro Kiwanis Club's Outstanding Citizen, 53; Outstanding Young Man of the Year Award, San Leandro Jr CofC, 54; Leader in Int Campaign to change name of profession from Chiropody to Podiatry, 55-59. Relig: Catholic. Mailing Add: 1446 Daily Dr San Leandro CA 94577

FIELD, FREDERICK GORHAM, JR (R)
NY State Assemblyman
b Albany, NY, Apr 13, 32; s Frederick G Field, Sr & Elizabeth A Loucks F; m 1949 to Patricia Bak; c Frederick John, Linda Patrice, Jeffery Donald, Ronald David & Kimberly Ann. Educ: Rensselaer Polytech Inst, 58-59. Polit & Govt Pos: Councilman, Town of Colonie, NY, 60-67, Rep committeeman, 60-; NY State Assemblyman, 103rd Dist, Albany Co, 69-, mem standing comts on Housing, Labor, Local Govt & Com, Indust & Econ Develop & chmn subcomt, Consumer Credit, NY State Assembly, chmn, Spec Comt, Youth & Govt, currently, chmn, Joint Legis Comt State's Econ, currently, mem, Joint Legis Comt, Metrop & Regional Area Studies & Consumer Protection, currently. Bus & Prof Pos: Indust engr, Allegheny Ludlum Steel Corp, Watervliet, NY, 50-63, indust engr supvr, 63- Mem: YMCA (bd dirs, Troy); Urban League of Albany Area; Albany Regional Med Prog Adv Group; Int Narcotic Enforcement Officers Asn; Elks (Colonie Lodge, 1292). Relig: Dutch Reformed. Mailing Add: 16 E Newton Rd Newtonville NY 12128

FIELD, H JAMES, JR (R)
Chmn, Rep State Cent Comt RI
Mailing Add: Turks Head Bldg Suite 501 Providence RI 02903

FIELD, LEON B (D)
Okla State Sen
b San Augustine, Tex, Sept 21, 02; s Jerry R Field & Katherine Horn F; m 1926 to Velma L Heary; c Albert Ray & Larry L. Educ: Hills Bus Col, Okla, 21; Panhandle State Col, AB, 26. Polit & Govt Pos: Chmn, Co Dem Party, 41-45; mem, Texhoma Sch Bd, 42-50; mem, Okla State Bd Agr, 44-47; Okla State Rep, 47-51, Asst Majority Floor Leader, Okla House Rep, 61 & 65; Okla State Sen, currently. Bus & Prof Pos: Coach & athletic dir, Panhandle State Col, 30-35; supt schs, Texhoma, Okla, 35-40; pres, Texhoma CofC, 45-46. Mem: Okla Ins Agents Asn; Real Estate Comn Texhoma Lodge 382; India Temple Shrine; Eastern Star (Consistory Orient of Okla). Relig: Methodist. Legal Res: 510 N Second Texhoma OK 73949 Mailing Add: Box 307 Texhoma OK 73949

FIELD, PETER (D)
Chmn, Weston Co Dem Party, Wyo
b Fuerth, Ger, Mar 23, 26; s Else Borchardt; m 1950 to Margaret Elizabeth Farnham; c Christopher B & Lisa A. Educ: Univ Calif, Berkeley, AB, 50. Polit & Govt Pos: Alt deleg, Dem Nat Conv, 68 & 72; chmn, Weston Co Dem Party, Wyo, 68- Mil Serv: Entered as Pvt, Army, 44, released as Cpl, 46, after serv in 502nd Parachute Regt, 101st Airborne Div, ETO, 44-46. Mem: Mason; Lions. Relig: Unitarian. Mailing Add: Box 684 Newcastle WY 82701

FIELDING, ELIZABETH MAY (R)
b New London, Conn, May 16, 17; d Frederick James Fielding & Elizabeth Martin F; single. Educ: Conn Col for Women, BA, 38; Am Univ Sch Pub Affairs, MA in pub admin, 44; Phi Beta Kappa. Polit & Govt Pos: Postmaster, Substation One, New London, Conn, 36-38; spec agt, Census Bur, 38-39; personnel clerk, Labor Dept, 39, govt economist & personnel asst, 41-42; sci asst, Nat Insts Health, 39-40; campaign & research writer, Rep Nat Comt, 40 & 42-48, acting dir research, 44, asst dir research, 48-53 & assoc dir research, 54-57; speech writer & consult to several US Congressmen, 48-54; legis asst to US Sen Wiley, Wis, 53-54; pub rels dir, Nat Fedn Rep Women, 61-68; dir spec activities, Women's Div, United Citizens for Nixon-Agnew, 68; finance coordr, 69 Inaugural Comt, 68-69; spec & confidential asst to Asst Postmaster Gen, 69-71; pub affairs dir, President's Coun on Youth Opportunity, 70-72; asst adminr pub affairs, Nat Credit Union Admin, 71-72, ed, Nat Credit Union Admin Quart & Report, 71-, acting asst adminr pub affairs, 73- Bus & Prof Pos: Staff writer, Nat Asn of Elec Co, Wash, DC, 57-60. Publ: Ed, The Republican clubwoman, Nat Fedn Rep Women, 61-68; auth, numerous Rep Party publ, campaign manuals & study papers including, A History of the Republican Party, 1854-1948; ed, Nat Credit Union Admin Bull, 71-73. Mem: Am Asn Advan Sci; Am Acad Polit & Soc Sci; Am Soc Pub Admin; Nat Press Club, Washington; Am Newspaper Women's Club Washington. Honors & Awards: Hon citizen of several US cities; Outstanding Serv Award, Nat Fedn Rep Women Pres, 63 & 67; Medal of Achievement for Outstanding Govt-Party Serv, Conn Col, 71. Relig: Methodist. Mailing Add: 3701 Thornton Pkwy Oxon Hill MD 20022

FIELDS, LOWELL (R)
Treas, Randolph Co Rep Cent Comt, Ind
b Randolph Co, Ind, Nov 25, 20; s Weldon Fields & Orpha Fetters F; m 1962 to Ann Hogue. Educ: Ind Col Embalming, 41. Polit & Govt Pos: Councilman, Randolph Co, Ind, 71-; treas, Randolph Co Rep Cent Comt, currently. Bus & Prof Pos: Personnel mgr, Standard Brands, Inc, Saratoga, Ind, 46-48; asst plant mgr, Campbell Soup Co, Saratoga, 48-53, plant mgr, 53- Mil Serv: Entered as Pvt, Army, 42, released as S/Sgt, 46, after serv in 94th Signal Bn, ETO; Bronze Star Medal. Mem: F&AM; Scottish Rite; Shrine. Relig: Protestant. Mailing Add: 133 E North St Winchester IN 47394

FIELDS, RICHARD EARL (D)
b Charleston, SC, Oct 1, 20; s John Fields & Mary Cook F; m 1950 to Myrtle Thelma Evans; c Mary Diane & Richard Earl, Jr. Educ: WVa State Col, 40-44; Howard Univ, 44-47; Alpha Phi Alpha. Polit & Govt Pos: Mem, Bd Parks & Playgrounds, Charleston, SC, munic judge, currently; deleg, City, Co & State Dem Conv, 68; deleg, Dem Nat Conv, 68 & 72. Bus & Prof Pos: Mem bd trustees, Claflin Univ, 56-; mem bd dirs, United Fund, 62-67, Charleston Co Family Serv, 62- & McClennan Banks Hosp, 62- Mem: Am & SC Bar Asns; F&AM; Alpha Phi Alpha; Charleston Trident CofC (bd dir). Honors & Awards: Civic Award for Lawyers. Relig: Methodist; Mem gen bd of Soc Christian Concern, United Methodist Church. Legal Res: 1734 Heritage Park Rd Charleston SC 29407 Mailing Add: 65 Spring St Charleston SC 29403

FIELDS, VIRGINIA A (R)
Chairwoman, Lorain Co Rep Comt, Ohio
b Lorain, Ohio, Nov 7, 32; d Alfred H Basore & Helen M Tirpak B; m 1955 to Donald W Fields; c David W, Michael W, Richard W & Deborah A. Educ: Lorain Co Community Col. Polit & Govt Pos: Mem, Lorain Co Rep Exec Comt & Lorain Co Rep Finance Comt, currently; chairwoman, Lorain Co Rep Comt, 73- Relig: Catholic. Mailing Add: 39035 Detroit Rd Avon OH 44011

FIENBERG, GEORGE MITCHELL (D)
Chmn, Bennington Co Dem Party, Vt
b New York, NY, Aug 26, 10; s Harry Fienberg & Anna Goldman F; m 1936 to Nesbith Perelman; c Rosalind (Mrs Kaplan). Educ: Univ Vt; Albany Law Sch. Polit & Govt Pos: Mem, Bennington Dem Town Comt, Vt, 52-66, chmn, 59-61; secy, Bennington Co Dem Party, 55-59, chmn, 59-61 & 71-; mem, Bennington Co Dem Comt, 55-66; chmn, Gov Hoff Inaugural Dinner, 63; munic judge, Bennington, 63- Mem: Bennington CofC; Mason; Shrine; Elks; Mt Anthony Country Club. Relig: Jewish. Legal Res: Convent Ave Bennington VT 05201 Mailing Add: Box 83 Main St Bennington VT 05201

FIENE, CHESTER OLAN (R)
Chmn, Lafayette Co Rep Cent Comt, Mo
b Alma, Mo, Feb 28, 35; s Henry Fiene & Lena Marie Vogt F; m 1958 to Arleen Louise Bergman; c Randall, Michael & Deborah. Educ: Cent Mo State Col, BS, 61. Polit & Govt Pos: Chmn, Lafayette Co Rep Cent Comt, Mo, 74- Bus & Prof Pos: Revenue agt, Internal Revenue Serv, 61-67; auditor, Off Econ Opportunity, 67-68; off mgr & auditor, Larry Hutchison, CPA, 69-73; self-employed, Chester O Fiene, Tax Consult & Bookkeeping Serv, 74- Mil Serv: Entered as Pvt, Army, 53, released as SP 4/C, 56, after serv in Transportation; Good Conduct & Overseas Medals. Mem: Concordia Fall Festival (secy, exec bd); Concordia Civic Club; Concordia Lions; Concordia Bus Men's Asn; Nat Asn Enrolled Agts. Honors & Awards: Vet Scholar Award, Vet Orgn of Cent Mo State Col. Relig: Lutheran. Legal Res: 202 E Rundee Concordia MO 64020 Mailing Add: PO Box 167 Concordia MO 64020

FIFIELD, ELWOOD B (R)
Ind State Rep
Mailing Add: 12512 Buchanan St Crown Point IN 46307

FIKE, EUDORA A (R)
VChmn, Middlesex Co Rep Orgn, NJ
b Brockway, Pa, Sept 21, 29; d William Feldman & Laura Buskirk F; m 1946 to William Charles Fike; c Robert Wayne & Dawn Robin. Educ: Brockway Snyder High Sch, grad, 47. Polit & Govt Pos: Committeewoman, Piscataway Twp Rep Orgn, NJ, 66-, munic vchmn, 67-68, munic chmn, 68-70; vchmn, Middlesex Co Rep Orgn, 70-; alt deleg, Rep Nat Conv, 72. Mem: Eastern Star; United Cerebral Palsy of Middlesex Co; Elks Ladies Auxiliary; NJ Fedn Rep Women's Orgn; NJ Rep VChmn Asn (secy, 72-). Honors & Awards: Distinguished Citizen Citation, Middlesex Co Young Rep, 71. Relig: Methodist. Mailing Add: 5323 Foster St Piscataway NJ 08854

FIKE, STANLEY REDFIELD (D)
b Warrensburg, Mo, June 7, 13; s Lyman Walter Fike & Bethana Redfield F; m 1935 to Mildred Curry; c Margaret (Mrs Anthony Gray), Bethana (Mrs John Cartland, Jr) & Joann Dorace. Educ: Kans City Jr Col, 30-31. Polit & Govt Pos: Mem, Kansas City, Mo Bd Educ, 52; admin asst to US Sen Stuart Symington, Mo, 53-; exec dir, Symington for President Campaign 60. Bus & Prof Pos: Gen mgr & ed, Inter-City Press, Inc, Mo, 30-53; pres, Lee's Summit Journal Inc, 49-65; vpres, Jackson Co Times, Inc, 52-53. Mem: Hon mem Univ Mo Sch Journalism Alumni Asn; Sigma Delta Chi; Mo Press Asn; Kansas City Area Coun, Boy Scouts (bd dirs); Mo-Kans-Ark Dist, Kiwanis. Honors & Awards: Academy of Mo Squires, 67. Relig: Reorganized Latter-day Saint. Legal Res: 610 N Delaware Independence MO 64050 Mailing Add: 229 Senate Office Bldg Washington DC 20510

FILAN, JAMES KIERAN (D)
b Bohola, Ireland, July 28, 28; s Patrick Joseph Filan & Katherine Judge F; m 1955 to Nancy Lillis; c Patrick Joseph, Deirdre Mary, James Kieran, Jr & Joan Katherine. Educ: St Nathy's Col, LS, 47; Univ Col, Nat Univ of Ireland, MD, 54; Dramatic Club; Lit & Debating Soc. Polit & Govt Pos: Chmn, Derby Bd Educ, Conn, 67-70; deleg, Dem State Conv, 70; chmn, Derby Town Dem Party, formerly. Bus & Prof Pos: Physician. Mil Serv: Irish Army. Mem: Am Med Asn; Am Acad Gen Practice; Elks; Knights of St Patrick; KofC. Relig: Roman Catholic. Mailing Add: 17 Fairview Terr Derby CT 06418

FILLBACK, ARMAS WALFRED (R)
NH State Rep
b Fitchburg, Mass, Nov 13, 12; s Nicholas Fillback & Elena Benson F; m 1937 to Annie Louise Geiger; c Donna Lee (Mrs Docekal). Educ: Clark Univ, 31-32; Fitchburg State Col, BSE, 35. Polit & Govt Pos: Mem, Sch Bd, Rindge, NH, 58-61; liaison finance comt, Bd Selectmen, 62-63; health officer, 72-75; NH State Rep, 75- Bus & Prof Pos: Teacher, Fitchburg Sch Syst, Mass, 35-74. Mem: Elks. Relig: Protestant. Mailing Add: Box 145 RD 1 Rindge NH 03461

FILLMORE, LILLIAN GARNET (R)
VChmn, Lawrence Co Rep Party, SDak,
b Redfield, SDak, Apr 3, 01; d Charles William Waterfall & Maud Connor W; m 1922 to William Orlo Fillmore; c LaEtta (Mrs Heltibridle), Lineal (Mrs Falk), Billie June (Mrs Bradshaw), Sarah (Mrs Buittner) & Charles William. Educ: Redfield High Sch, SDak, grad, 18; MacPhail Sch Music, Minneapolis, Minn, 21. Polit & Govt Pos: Vchmn, Lawrence Co Rep Party SDak, 58-; committeewoman, Rep State Cent Comt, 60-66. Bus & Prof Pos: Secy, Fillmore & Co, Inc, Spearfish, SDak, 51-, Am Mining & Smelting, Inc, 52- & Beardsley & Fillmore, Inc, 67- Mem: Eastern Star (past matron); Rebekah (past state assembly pres); Spearfish Federated Women's Club (past local & dist pres); Community Concert Asn (dir). Relig: Methodist. Legal Res: 344 Fifth St Spearfish SD 57783 Mailing Add: Box 328 Spearfish SD 57783

FILOSA, PHILIP FRANK (D)
Mass State Rep
b Norwood, Mass, July 6, 48; s Frank G Filosa & Victoria M Bartolomei F; single. Educ: Goethe Insts, WGer, 68; Int Sch, Univ Vienna, 68-69; St Anselm's Col, BA History, 70; Univ Miami Sch Law, JD, 73; Nat Hon Soc; Phi Delta Phi. Polit & Govt Pos: Mass State Rep, 75- Bus & Prof Pos: Assoc mem, Saphire & Saphire Law Firm, Westwood, Mass, 74- Mem: Mass, Norfolk Co & Western Norfolk Co Bar Asns. Honors & Awards: Bancroft Whitney Best Brief Award, Bancroft Whitney Publs, 71; Second Prize Essay Contest, Lawyers Title Guaranty Fund Fla. Mailing Add: 134 Cumberland Rd Wrentham MA 02090

FIMLAID, EINO O (R)
NH State Rep
Mailing Add: RFD Lisbon NH 03574

FINA, EUNYCE ALOYS (R)
Treas, 16th Cong Dist Rep Comt, Mich
b Kittanning, Pa, Sept 26, 39; d Carl William Johnson & Anna R Fry J; m to Kenneth Michael Fina; c Lynda & Carole Ann. Educ: Henry Ford Community Col, 2 years. Polit & Govt Pos: Deleg, Rep State Conv, Mich, 62-69; Rep precinct deleg, Dearborn, 62-; asst campaign mgr, Sen N Lorraine Beebe, 66; statutory mem, 16th Cong Dist Rep Comt, 66-67, secy, 67-68 & vchmn, 69-73, treas, 73-; vol coordr, Nixon Hq, 68; alt deleg, Rep Nat Conv, 68. Mem: West Dearborn Rep Club. Relig: Roman Catholic. Mailing Add: 23331 Oak Ave Dearborn MI 48128

FINAN, RICHARD H (R)
Ohio State Rep
Mailing Add: 3068 Stanwin Pl Cincinnati OH 45241

FINAN, THOMAS B (D)
b Cumberland, Md, June 30, 14; m 1941 to Isabel Jean North; c two. Educ: Georgetown Univ, BA, 36; Univ Md Sch of Law, LLB, 39. Polit & Govt Pos: Chmn, Allegany Co Dem Cent Comt, Md, 54-59; deleg, Dem Nat Conv, 56, 60 & 72; chmn, Md Dem State Cent Comt, 59; Secy of State, Md, 59-61 & Attorney Gen, 61-65; Judge, Md Court of Appeals, 66-69; Assoc Justice, Md Supreme Court, formerly. Bus & Prof Pos: Officer, bus firms. Mil Serv: Capt, Army, 41-45, serv in ETO; Prisoner of War; Legion of Merit; Maj, Army Res. Mailing Add: 316 Mountain View Dr Cumberland MD 21502

FINCH, ROBERT HUTCHISON (R)
b Tempe, Ariz, Oct 9, 25; s Robert L Finch & Gladys Hutchison F; m 1946 to Carol Crothers; c Maureen, Kevin, Pricilla & Cathleen. Educ: Occidental Col, BA in Polit Sci, 46; Univ Southern Calif, JD, 51; Kappa Sigma; Phi Alpha Delta. Hon Degrees: LLD, Occidental Col, Lincoln Univ, Univ Calif, Los Angeles, Univ Southern Calif, Ohio State Col, Wash & Jefferson Col, Univ Pac, Westminster Col, Rockford Col, Western State Univ Col of Law & Univ San Fernando Valley Col of Law. Polit & Govt Pos: Exec secy, US Rep Poulson, Calif, 47-48; deleg, Rep Nat Conv, 48-56, 60 & 68; Rep nominee for US Rep, 52 & 54; chmn, Los Angeles Co Rep Cent Comt, 56-58; trustee, Rep Assocs of Los Angeles, 58-66; admin asst to VPres Richard Nixon, 58-60; mgr, Richard Nixon's Presidential Campaign, 60; Lt Gov, Calif, 66-69; former pres, Calif State Senate, chmn, Calif Job Training & Placement Coun, Interagency Coun for Ocean Resources, Bicentennial Celebration Comn, Comn of the Californias & Electronic Data Processing Policy Comt, Gov Cabinet & Gov Coun, 66-69; mem bd regents, Univ Calif & trustee, Calif State Cols, 66-69; mem exec comt, Nat Conv Lt Gov, 67; Secy of Health, Educ & Welfare, 69-70; mem, President's Adv Comn Intergovt Rels, 69-72; mem, Comn White House Fels, 69-; Counsr to the President, 70-72; mem, President's Cabinet Vol Action & Environ Qual Comts & Urban Affairs Coun; chmn, President's Coun on Aging & Comt on Retardation, Interdept Comt on Children & Youth, Air Qual Adv Bd & Fed Radiation Coun, currently; mem, Domestic Coun & Cabinet Comt Educ, currently. Bus & Prof Pos: Instr & trustee, Palos Verdes Col, Calif, 52-56; partner, Finch, Bell, Duitsman & Margulis, 53-69; organizer & pres, Palos Verdes Fed Savings & Loan, 56-58; chmn bd, Marine Fed Savings & Loan Asn, 58-59; attorney-at-law, McKenna, Fitting & Finch, 72-74 & Stroock & Stroock & Lavan, 75-; instr, Univ Southern Calif & Occidental Col, 73. Mil Serv: Marine Corps, 43-45, recalled in 51 & released as 1st Lt, 53- Publ: The New Conservative Liberal Manifesto, Viewpoint Books, 68. Mem: Legion Lex; Calif Commonwealth Club; Town Hall; CORO Found (mem adv bd); Los Angeles Dist Attorney's Adv Comt. Relig: Presbyterian. Legal Res: Pasadena CA Mailing Add: 707 Wilshire Blvd Los Angeles CA 90017

FINCHER, W W, JR (D)
Ga State Sen
Mailing Add: PO Box 149 Chatsworth GA 30705

FINCHUM, FRANK DEWAYNE (R)
b Port Arthur, Tex, May 18, 32; s Frank Edward Finchum & Jessie Lorraine Hunt F; m 1955 to Nancy Jo Benfield; c Tab Damon, Frank Dewayne, Jr & Barbara Nan. Educ: Univ Tex, Austin, BBA; Int Correspondence Sch, Pulp & Paper Making Degree; Scabbard & Blade; Col Independents. Polit & Govt Pos: Rep precinct chmn, Orange, Tex, 67-68, finance chmn, 68; chmn, Orange Co Rep Party, formerly. Bus & Prof Pos: Prod supvr, Equitable Bag Co, Inc, Orange, Tex, 55-58, safety dir, 58-60, dir personnel & safety, 60-62, prod mgr, 62- Mil Serv: 2nd Lt, Army, 67, serv in Res Officers Prog, Ft Lee, Va, 6 months; Capt, Army Res, 54-62. Mem: United Fund (second vpres bd dirs); CofC (mem bd dirs); Sunset Grove Country Club (pres bd dirs). Relig: Methodist. Mailing Add: 1809 Decker Orange TX 77630

FINDLEY, PAUL (R)
US Rep, Ill
b Jacksonville, Ill, 1921; m; c Craig & Diane. Educ: Ill Col, BA; Phi Beta Kappa. Hon Degrees: DHL, Lindenwood Col; LLD, Ill Col. Polit & Govt Pos: US Rep, 20th Dist, Ill, currently, mem, Foreign Affairs & Agr Comts, US House Rep; deleg, NATO Parliamentarian Conf, 65, 66 & 67; deleg to NAtlantic Assembly, Brussels, 68, 69, 70 & 72, deleg to European Parliament, 75. Bus & Prof Pos: Pres & publ, Pike Press, Inc, Pittsfield, Ill. Mil Serv: Navy, World War II, served as Supply Corps Off, Seabees, Guam invasion & Japanese occupation. Publ: Federal Farm Fable, Arlington House. Mem: Am Soc Int Law; Am Legion; VFW; Lions; Fed Union, Inc (mem bd dirs). Relig: Congregational. Legal Res: 115 W Jefferson St Pittsfield IL 62363 Mailing Add: 2133 Rayburn House Off Bldg Washington DC 20515

FINDLEY, SUSAN HANCOCK (D)
b Okeechobee, Fla, June 17, 30; d James Thomas Hancock & Ruby Shuler H; m 1955 to Marshall Ewing Findley; c James Eric & Thomas Marshall. Educ: Agnes Scott Col, BA, 52; Emory Univ, MA, 53. Polit & Govt Pos: Alt deleg, Dem Nat Mid-Term Conf, 74. Bus & Prof Pos: Hist teacher, Fairfax Hall, Waynesboro, Va, 53-54; student counr, Univ Fla, 54-55; hist instr & arch asst, Auburn Univ, 60-62 & 63-64; English teacher, US Info Serv, Alexandria, Egypt, 62-63; student counr, Fulbright Comn, Kuala Lumpur, Malaysia, 69-70. Publ: Alexander J Bondurant: American agricultural adviser to Australian tobacco growers, 1896, Agr Hist, 4/66. Mem: League Women Voters; Rolla People to People Prog; Audubon Soc; UNA-USA Asn; Natural Mus Hist, NY. Relig: Episcopal. Mailing Add: 1004 Lynwood Dr Rolla MO 65401

FINE, FRANKLIN MARSHALL (D)
b Cleveland, Ohio, Sept 29, 47; s Herbert D Fine & Helma Kay F; c Daria Joy. Educ: Boston Univ, BA, 69; Univ NMex, MArch, 75; Delta Honor Soc; Tau Kappa Epsilon. Polit & Govt Pos: Pres, Univ NMex Students for McGovern, 72; mem, State Steering Comt, Citizens for McGovern, 72; alt deleg, Dem Nat Conv, 72; deleg, NMex Dem State Conv, 72 & 73; mem, Bernalillo Co Selective Serv Bd Ore, 73-; treas, NMex Dem Coun, 73- Bus & Prof Pos: Bus mgr, The Boston Tea Party, Boston, Mass, 69; mgr, Select Beverage Co, Cleveland, Ohio, 71; planning coordr, Pub Serv Co of NMex, currently. Mem: Regional Sci Asn; Inst Elec & Electronic Engrs; Am Inst Planners; Am Soc Planning Off. Relig: Jewish. Mailing Add: 2638 Morrow Rd NE Albuquerque NM 87103

FINE, JOSEPH LOYD (D)
Ala State Sen
b Hanceville, Ala, Jan 1937; s Joseph Loyd Fine, Sr & Bertha Thompson F (deceased); m 1955 to Gayle Nuss; c Craig & Clark. Educ: Univ Ala, BS, Sch Law, LLB; Sigma Delta Kappa. Polit & Govt Pos: Dist attorney, 34th Judicial Circuit, Ala; asst comnr ins, State of Ala; Ala State Sen, Fifth Dist, 71- Mem: Rotary Club; Jaycees; Elks. Relig: Church of Christ. Legal Res: 1205 College Ave Russellville AL 35653 Mailing Add: PO Box 818 Russellville AL 35653

FINEMAN, HERBERT (D)
Speaker, Pa House Rep
b Philadelphia, Pa, July 4, 20; s Joseph Fineman & Esther Best F; m to Frances Brownstein; c two. Educ: Temple Univ, BS; Temple Sch of Law, LLB. Hon Degrees: LLD, Sch Osteopathic Med, 68; LHD, Pa Col Podiatric Med, 69. Polit & Govt Pos: Secy & mem exec bd, Gen State Authority; exec bd, Joint State Govt Comn Commonwealth Pa; mem, Pa Hwy & Bridge Authority; mem, Pa Pub Sch Bldg Authority; mem, Pa Higher Educ Facilities Authority; investigator, Illegal Use of Wire Tapping in Pa; Pa State Rep, 54-, Majority Whip, Pa House Rep, 65-66, Minority Floor Leader, 67-68, Speaker, 69-70 & 71-, chmn, Joint State Govt Comn Task Force on Proc Against Juveniles, Eminent Domain & Rev of Penal Code, mem, Pa Transportation Assistance Authority, Pa Pub TV Network Comn & Legis Budget & Finance Comt; leader, 52nd Ward Dem Exec Comt; mem, Dem Party Speakers Bur; deleg, Dem Nat Conv, 68 & 72; deleg, Dem Nat Mid-Term Conf, 74. Bus & Prof Pos: Practicing attorney, 46-; partner, Fineman & Fineman. Mem: B'nai B'rith; Gamma Lodge; Col Podiatric Med (trustee); Philadelphia Col Podiatry (trustee); Nat Conf State Legis Leaders (exec bd). Mailing Add: 2291 Bryn Mawr Ave Philadelphia PA 19131

FINEMORE, LOUIS F (R)
Maine State Rep
Mailing Add: Bridgewater ME 04735

FINGER, HAROLD B
b New York, NY, Feb 18, 24; s Ben Finger & Anna Perelmutter F; m 1949 to Arlene Karsch; c Barbara Lynn, Elyse Sue & Sandra Ruth. Educ: City Col NY, BS in Mech Eng, 44; Case

Inst Tech, MS in Aeronaut Eng, 50. Polit & Govt Pos: Aeronaut research scientist, Lewis Research Ctr, Nat Adv Comt for Aeronaut, Cleveland, Ohio, 44-52, head axial flow compressor sect, 52-54, assoc chief, Compressor Research Br, 54-58, head nuclear radiation shielding group & nuclear rocket design analysis group, 58; chief nuclear propulsion, NASA, 58-60, asst dir nuclear applns, 60-61, dir nuclear syst, 61-64, dir space power & nuclear syst, 64-67, assoc adminr for orgn & mgt, 67-69; mgr, Atomic Energy Comn-NASA Space Nuclear Propulsion Off, 60-67; dir, Space Nuclear Syst Div, Atomic Energy Comn, 65-67; Asst Secy for Research & Technol, Dept of Housing & Urban Develop, 69-72. Bus & Prof Pos: Gen mgr, Ctr Energy Syst, Gen Elec Co, Washington, DC, 72- Publ: Numerous tech reports & papers. Mem: Am Inst of Aeronaut & Astronaut; Am Soc Pub Admin; Nat Acad Pub Admin. Honors & Awards: Co-winner, Manley Mem Award for the best paper on aeronaut, Soc Automotive Engrs, 57; Outstanding Leadership Medal, NASA, 66; James H Wyld Propulsion Award, Am Inst for Aeronaut & Astronaut, 68. Mailing Add: 6908 Millwood Rd Bethesda MD 20034

FINGER, SEYMOUR MAXWELL (D)
b New York, NY, Apr 30, 15; s Samuel Finger & Bella Spiegel F; m 1956 to Helen Kotcher; c Mark. Educ: Ohio Univ, BS, 35; Univ Cincinnati, 42; Littauer Sch Pub Affairs, Harvard Univ, 53-54; Phi Beta Kappa; Kappa Delta Pi. Polit & Govt Pos: Second secy, Am Embassy, Paris, France, 49-51; second secy & econ off, Am Legation, Budapest, Hungary, 51-53; mem staff, Econ Defense Off, Rome, Italy, 54-55; first secy, Am Embassy, Vientiane, Laos, 55-56; ambassador & sr adv to permanent rep to UN, US Mission to UN, 56-71. Bus & Prof Pos: Prof polit sci, City Univ New York, 71-; dir, Ralph Bunche Inst & pres, Inst for Mediter Affairs, currently. Mil Serv: Entered as Pvt, Army, 43, released as S/Sgt, 45, after serv in ETO. Publ: Breaking the deadlock on UN peacekeeping, Orbis, summer 73; A new approach to colonial problems at the United Nations, Int Orgn, Vol XXVI, No 1; The New World Balance & Peace in the Middle East, Assoc Univs Press, 75. Mem: Am Acad Polit & Soc Sci; Am Soc Int Law; Coun on Foreign Rels. Honors & Awards: Cert of Merit, Ohio Univ Alumni Asn, 67. Mailing Add: 476 Morris Ave Rockville Center NY 11570

FINK, EARL BARTON (D)
b Granville, Pa, July 7, 19; s Earl Truman Fink & Jessie Barton F; m 1945 to Betty Jane Moist; c Earl Barton, Jr & Todd Patrick. Polit & Govt Pos: Sch dir, Granville Twp Sch Dist, Pa, 50-54; tax collector, Granville Twp, 54-; regist chmn, Mifflin Co Dem Comt, 60-64, chmn, formerly. Bus & Prof Pos: Owner, Grocery Store, Granville, Pa, 45-55. Mem: F&AM; Shrine; United Commercial Travelers; Methodist Men's Club; Elks. Relig: Protestant. Mailing Add: Box 41 Granville PA 17029

FINK, STANLEY (D)
NY State Assemblyman
Mailing Add: 2249 E 70th St Brooklyn NY 11234

FINK, THOMAS A (D)
Dep VChmn, Monroe Co Dem Comt NY
b Albany, NY, Oct 15, 34. Educ: Cornell Univ, BA, 57, Law Sch, LLB, 59. Polit & Govt Pos: Mem, Monroe Co Dem Comt, NY, 60-, dep vchmn, 73-; pres, Brighton Dem Club, 66-68; deleg, Dem Nat Conv, 68; chmn, Dem Action Comt, 70-; mem exec comt, NY State Dem Comt, 72-, committeeman, 131st Dist, currently. Bus & Prof Pos: Partner, Beckerman, Davidson, Cook & Fink, 73- Mailing Add: 157 Monteroy Rd Rochester NY 14618

FINK, TOM (R)
Alaska State Rep
Mailing Add: 1350 W 23rd Ave Anchorage AK 99503

FINKELSTEIN, JERRY (D)
b New York, NY, Jan 26, 16; s Albert A Finkelstein & Ethel Kaufman F; m 1942 to Shirley Marks; c Andrew Jay & James Arthur. Educ: NY Univ; NY Law Sch, LLB, 38. Hon Degrees: LLD, NY Law Sch, 69. Polit & Govt Pos: Research dir, NY State Senate, 38-41; mem aviation comt pub schs, NY State Bd Regents, 41; mem off comt exten civil serv, NY State Legis, 41; campaign mgr, Mayoralty Campaign, New York, NY, 49; chmn planning comt, City Planning Comn, New York, NY, 50-51; deleg, Dem Nat Conv, 68; chmn finance comt, NY State Dem Comt, formerly; chmn, New York City Dem Comt, 70-72; comnr, Port Auth, NY & NJ, 72-; mem, Nat Adv Coun Drug Abuse Prev. Bus & Prof Pos: Mem of staff spec prosecutor Thomas E Dewey, 35-36; reporter civil serv ed, NY Mirror, 37-39; founder, Pub Civil Serv Leader, NY, 39-; dir, Struthers Sci & Int Corp; chmn bd & chmn exec comt, Struthers Wells Corp; publ, NY Law J, 64-; chmn bd, Struthers Capital Corp, ABC Industs, & Sci & Govt Publs, Inc; pres & chmn bd, NY Law Pub Co; dir, Commercial Bank NAm, New York, NY. Mil Serv: Coast Guard Res, 43-45. Mem: Nat Cult Ctr (chmn fine arts gifts comt); Am Jewish Comt, Soc Silurians; Newspaper Reporters Asn; Overseas Press Club; Hall of Sci of the City of New York (mem exec comt & chmn finance comt). Honors & Awards: Scroll for Outstanding Efforts Civic Betterment, Comt of 1000, 51; Recipient Knickerbocker Award for Outstanding City Planning, 51; Decorated Knight, Order of Merit, Italy, 58. Legal Res: 812 Park Ave New York NY 10021 Mailing Add: 630 Fifth Ave New York NY 10020

FINLEY, BOB (D)
Mont State Rep
b Houghton, Mich, June 8, 18; s Arthur Finley & Elizabeth Berry F; m 1946 to Marion Fyanne Miles; c Jack Arthur, James Ray & Jon Miles. Polit & Govt Pos: Mont State Rep, 75- Bus & Prof Pos: In prod control, Atlas Press Co, 36-41; prod mgr, Fuller Mfg Co, 45-46; hwy engr, State of Mont, 47-74; retired. Mil Serv: Entered as Air Cadet, Army Air Corps, 41, released as Capt, after serv in 366th Fighter Bomber, ETO, 43-45; Air Medal; Bronze Star; Unit Citation. Relig: Unitarian. Mailing Add: 221 Spring Creek Dr Kalispell MT 59901

FINLEY, BYRON BRUCE (D)
Chmn, Clay Co Dem Exec Comt, Ala
b Dudleyville, Ala, Aug 26, 01; s Augustus Haygood Finley & Elah Roberts F; m 1926 to Lucille House; c Dr Wayne House, Dixie (Mrs Lester Roberts) & Robert Byron. Educ: Jacksonville State Univ, BS, 38; Auburn Univ, MEd, 57. Polit & Govt Pos: Chmn, Clay Co Dem Exec Comt, Ala, 70- Bus & Prof Pos: Gospel minister, Primitive Baptist Church, Ala, 25-; prin & teacher, Coosa Co Bd Educ, Goodwater & Rockford, 27-42 & Lineville, 47-57; supt schs, Ashland, 57-65; moderator, Hillabee Primitive Baptist Asn, 59-73; teacher, Talladega, 55-66. Relig: Primitive Baptist. Mailing Add: Box 255 Rte 3 Lineville AL 36266

FINLEY, JOSEPH CALDWELL (R)
b Marion, NY, May 31, 16; s Fremont Finley & L Blanche Rich F; m 1946 to Lorraine Blanchard; c Gary L & Lee B. Educ: Newark Collegiate Ctr, 34-35. Polit & Govt Pos: Committeeman, Dist One Rep Party, NY, 44-64; mem bd educ, Walworth Union Free Sch, 45-49; town supvr, Walworth, 51-55; co clerk, Wayne Co, 56-60; chmn, Wayne Co Rep Party, 57-64; NY State Assemblyman, 129th Assembly Dist, 61-73; chmn, Transportation Comt, NY State Assembly, 68-73; mem adv comt, Rochester-Genesee Transportation Auth, 73-; chmn, Walworth Rep Town Party, 72- Bus & Prof Pos: Co-owner, Newark Stationery, Newark, NY, 63-71. Mem: United Way, Wayne Co (campaign chmn & mem bd dirs, 73-); F&AM; Farm Bur; NY State Asn of Co Clerks; CofC. Relig: Methodist. Mailing Add: 38 Sherburne Rd Walworth NY 14568

FINLINSON, FRED W (R)
Utah State Rep
Mailing Add: 720 Shiloh Way Murray UT 84107

FINN, JOHN PATRICK (D)
b Seattle, Wash, July 25, 41; s James William Finn & Helen Allison F; m 1961 to Janet N Ellingsen; c Lise M, Lori A & Erin J. Educ: Univ Wash, 59-61; Harvard Univ, Trade Union Prog, 69; Delta Chi. Polit & Govt Pos: Polit coordr, Congressman Lloyd Meeds, Skagit Co, Wash, 70-; deleg, Dem Nat Mid-Term Conf, 74. Bus & Prof Pos: Secy-treas, Meat Cutters Local 247, Wash, 66- Mem: Wash State Labor Coun (exec bd mem); Comt Polit Educ. Mailing Add: 731 Gull Dr Burlington WA 98233

FINN, JOHN RODERICK (D)
b St Albans, Vt, Oct 9, 23; s James Grover Finn & Marieanne Limoges F; m 1949 to Elmerine Bove (deceased); c Michael John. Educ: Norwich Univ, BA in Eng, 48; Dean's List; pres, Theta Chi; Commencement Week Chmn; pres, Intrafraternity Coun; vpres, Skull & Swords; vpres, NUVA; Marshall, Theta Chi; Glee Club; Newman Club; chmn, Homecoming Week. Polit & Govt Pos: Party organizer & trailer operator, Vt Dem Campaign, 54; party organizer, 55 & 56; sheriff, Franklin Co, Vt, 56-69; chmn, St Albans City Dem Comt & campaign mgr, St Albans & Franklin Co, 60-65; advan, Hoff For Gov Campaign, 66; former vchmn, Franklin Co Dem Comt, chmn, 65-73; alt deleg, Dem Nat Conv, 68; St Albans city grand juror, currently. Bus & Prof Pos: Pres, Franklin Co Develop Asn, Inc, 62-69; chmn, Champlain Valley Off Econ Opportunity, Inc, 64-68. Mil Serv: Entered as Pvt, Army, 43, released as Sgt, 45, after serv in Mil Police & Armored Inf; ETO Ribbon with Three Battle Stars; Purple Heart; Good Conduct Ribbon. Mem: Am Legion; VFW; Elks (Past Exalted Ruler); Moose; KofC. Honors & Awards: Singing scholar, Univ Vt, 42; Hon mention, All-State Football, 41. Relig: Roman Catholic. Mailing Add: Box 741 St Albans VT 05478

FINNEGAN, JOHN J (D)
Mass State Rep
Mailing Add: 128 Neponset Dorcester MA 02122

FINNEY, DAVE (D)
Tex State Rep
Mailing Add: 4819 Hope St Ft Worth TX 76114

FINNEY, ERNEST ADOLPHUS, JR (D)
SC State Rep
b Isle of Wight, Va, Mar 23, 31; s E A Finney, Sr & Caroline Godwin F; m 1955 to Frances Annetta Davenport; c Ernest Adolphus, III, Lynn Carol & Jerry Leo. Educ: Claflin Col, AB, 52; SC State Col, LLB, 54; Alpha Kappa Mu; Alpha Phi Alpha. Polit & Govt Pos: Chmn, SC Civil Rights Comn, 60-62; mem, Sumter Citizens Adv Comt, 61-64; SC State Rep, 72- Bus & Prof Pos: Chmn, Buena Vista Develop Corp, 67- Mem: Southeastern Lawyers Asn (pres, 65-67); NAACP (comt chmn Sumter Br, 60-); Black Polit Caucus of Sumter (chmn, 72-); Masons; Shrine. Honors & Awards: Serv award, City of Sumter; serv award, Citizens of Sumter, 72; citizenship award, SC State Col, 73. Relig: Methodist. Mailing Add: 110 S Sumter St Sumter SC 29150

FINNEY, FLORENCE DONADY (R)
Dep Majority Leader, Conn State Senate
b Long Island City, NY, 03; m 1923 to James A Finney; c James A, Jr. Polit & Govt Pos: Mem, Greenwich Representative Town Meeting, Conn, 41-; Conn State Rep, 49-55; Conn State Sen, 55-, Dep Majority Leader, Conn State Senate, 73- Bus & Prof Pos: Businesswoman. Mem: Nat Order of Women Legislators. Relig: Episcopal. Legal Res: 10 Riverside Lane Riverside CT 06878 Mailing Add: 59 River Rd Cos Cob CT 06807

FINNEY, JOAN (D)
Kans State Treas
b Topeka, Kans, Feb 12, 25; d Leonard McInory & Mary Sands M; m 1957 to Spencer W Finney, Jr; c Sally, Dick & Mary. Educ: Kans City Conservatory of Music, 46; Col of St Theresa, Kansas City, Mo, 50; Washburn Univ, 4 years; Sigma Alpha Iota. Polit & Govt Pos: Asst, US Sen Frank Carlson, Kans, 53-69; comnr of elec, Shawnee Co, 70-72; cand for US Cong Second Dist, 72; admin asst, Mayor of Topeka, currently; Kans State Treas, currently; mem, Kans Fedn Dem Women & Kans Womens' Polit Caucus, currently. Mem: Big Bros-Big Sister Prog (bd dirs); Girls Club of Topeka, Inc; Latin-Am Dem Club (bd dirs); Century Club; YWCA. Relig: Catholic; mem bd admin & finance, Most Pure Heart of Mary Church. Mailing Add: 4600 W 19th Topeka KS 66604

FINNIGAN, RICHARD F (D)
Mass State Rep
Mailing Add: State Capitol Boston MA 02133

FINO, PAUL A (R)
b New York, NY, Dec 15, 13; s Isidoro Fino (deceased) & Lucia Patane F; m 1939 to Esther Claudia Liquori; c Lucille (Mrs Dimuro) & Paul A, Jr. Educ: St John's Univ, 33-35, Sch Law, LLB, 37. Polit & Govt Pos: Asst Attorney Gen, NY, 43-44; NY State Sen, 45-50; Civil Serv Comnr, New York, 50-52; US Rep, NY, 53-68; mem-at-lg, NY State Rep Comt & chmn, Bronx Co Rep Comt, 61-68; deleg, Rep Nat Conv, 64 & 68; justice, NY Supreme Court, 68-72. Publ: My fight for a national lottery, 60. Mem: Bronx Lodge, Elks; Senate Club; Former Mems of Cong; Civil Air Patrol. Relig: Roman Catholic. Mailing Add: 85 Suffolk Rd Atlantic Beach NY 11509

FIORENTINI, JAMES JOHN (D)
Mem, Haverhill Dem City Comt, Mass
b Haverhill, Mass, Apr 14, 47; s John A Fiorentini & Lucy Scamporino F; single. Educ: Tufts Univ, BA Polit Sci, 69; Northeastern Univ Sch Law, JD, 73; Phi Epsilon Pi. Polit & Govt Pos: Coordr, Sen Eugene McCarthy, Tufts & Haverhill, Mass, 68; pres, Tufts Young Dem, Tufts Univ, 68-69; mem, Haverhill Dem City Comt, 68-, chmn policy subcomt, 68-; research asst, Boston City Coun, 68; VISTA Vol, Waterloo, Iowa, 69-70; chmn, Merrimack Valley Peace Coalition, Mass, 71-; cand, Haverhill City Coun, 71; del, Mass Dem State Conv, 72; alt deleg, Dem Nat Conv, 72; student clerk, Neighborhood Legal Serv, Lynn, 72; coordr for Fourth Essex Sen Dist, McGovern Campaign, 72. Bus & Prof Pos: Mgr, Educ Enterprises, Medford, Mass, 69; mgr, Tufts Coop Soc, 67-69; student clerk, Mahoney, McGrath, Atwood & Goldings, Boston, 71; staff asst, Criminal Div, Mass Attorney Gen, 73- Mil Serv: Entered as Seaman 1/C, Naval Res, 69, released as Seaman, after serv in Tufts Univ ROTC, 69-71. Relig: Catholic. Mailing Add: 19 Flora St Haverhill MA 01830

FIORINA, BETTY (D)
b El Paso, Tex, 1925; d Jules A Vicknair & Delphine Souders V; m to A J Fiorina; c Tom & Gary. Educ: Bus admin, 2 years. Polit & Govt Pos: Admin staff, NMex Legis, 49-57; Secy of State, NMex, 59-62 & 71-73; chief clerk, NMex Const Conv, 69. Mem: State Voting Machine Comn; NMex Am Revolution Bicentennial Comn; Am Red Cross (bd); Nat Secretaries Asn, Int; Albuquerque Humane Asn (bd). Honors & Awards: Am Heritage Found Award; Only NMex Secy of State to be elected to third term. Mailing Add: 713 Don Diego St Santa Fe NM 87501

FIRESTONE, GEORGE (D)
Fla State Sen
b New York, NY, May 13, 31; s Benjamin Firestone & Sally Gollon F; m 1952 to Helene A Eiserman. Polit & Govt Pos: Econ Adv Bd, Miami, Fla, 60-62; chmn, Dade Co Personnel Adv Bd, 62-64; Fla State Rep, 67-72; Fla State Sen, 72-, vchmn, Senate Rules Comt, formerly; chmn, Exec Suspensions, currently; mem, Govt Opers, Judiciary-Criminal, currently; co-chmn, Fla Energy Comt, 73-75. Mil Serv: Entered as Pvt, Army, 48, released as Sgt 1/C, 52, after serv in 519th Field Artil Bn, ETO, 49-52. Mem: Nat Soc State Legis (mem exec comt); Dade CofC; Dade Young Dem; Miami Progress Club; Jewish War Vet. Honors & Awards: Outstanding Young Man of Am, US Jr CofC, 65; Good Govt Award, Miami Jaycees, 72; Outstanding First Term Mem of Senate, 74. Relig: Jewish. Legal Res: 630 SW Eighth Ave Miami FL 33130 Mailing Add: 2424 S Dixie Hwy Miami FL 33133

FIRLEY, CARL FRANKLIN (D)
Chairperson, Marquette Co Dem Party, Mich
b Riverside, Ill, Sept 22, 33; s Carl F Firley, Sr & Marthana Johnson F; m 1966 to Sirkka Sinikka Hohtari; c Sinikka Susan, Aulikki Angela (deceased) & Carl Henry August. Educ: Lyons Twp Jr Col, 51-52; Ill State Univ, BS in educ, 57; Univ Ill, grad work in commun, 57-61. Polit & Govt Pos: Cand, US Rep, 22nd Cong Dist, Ill, 68; chairperson, Marquette Co Dem Party, Mich, 73- Bus & Prof Pos: Civics teacher, Edison Jr High Sch, Champaign, Ill, 61-64; Fulbright grantee, Helsinki, Finland, 64-65; Am Finnish loan grant, Tampere, 65-66; asst dean of men, Univ Ill, Champaign, 66-67, asst dean of student progs & serv, 67-69; dir of housing, Northern Mich Univ, 69-72; assoc prog dir, Upper Peninsula Regional Interagency Coord Comt on Ment Retardation & Related Disabilities, 72- Mil Serv: Entered as Pvt, E-2, Army, 54, released as Pfc, 56, after serv in Fifth Div, Ger; Good Conduct Medal. Mem: Nat Asn Stud Personnel Adminr; Asn of Col & Univ Housing Off; Nat Educ Asn. Relig: Methodist. Mailing Add: 613 Mountain St Marquette MI 49855

FISCHBACH, DELORIS R (R)
Chairwoman, Auglaize Co Rep Cent Comt, Ohio
b Auglaize Co, Ohio, Mar 30, 23; d Edward E Kipp & Sarah Stienecker K; m 1941 to Richard M Fischbach; c Jean (Mrs Gordon Coffin). Educ: Wright State Univ, BS in educ, 73; Kappa Delta Pi. Polit & Govt Pos: Mayor, New Knoxville, Ohio, 72-; mem exec bd, Ohio Mayors Asn, 74-; precinct leader, New Knoxville, 74-; chairwoman, Auglaize Co Rep Cent Comt, 74- Mem: New Knoxville Civic Asn (pres, 74-75); Auglaize Co Civil Defense (bd dirs, 72-); Auglaize Co Health Adv Bd (secy, 72-73); Am Legion Auxiliary (adv, Buckeye Girls State, 75); Soroptimist Int. Relig: United Church of Christ. Legal Res: 511 S Main St New Knoxville OH 45871 Mailing Add: PO Box 378 New Knoxville OH 45871

FISCHER, DONALD FREDERICK (R)
b Oil City, Pa, Aug 15, 27; s William F Fischer & Susie Fox F; m 1957 to Elaine Winger; c Curtis Lee, Tracey Lynn & Donald Christian. Educ: Franklin Bus Sch; LaSalle Univ. Polit & Govt Pos: Vchmn, Venanago Co Young Rep, Pa, 59-61, chmn, 61-63; chmn, Venanago Co Rep Comt, formerly; co prothonotary, Venanago Co, 68-; clerk courts, 68- Mil Serv: Entered as Pvt, Army, 45, released as T-5, 47, after serv in Ord Corps, Pac Theatre, 46-47. Mem: Lions. Relig: Lutheran. Mailing Add: 1135 Allegheny Ave Oil City PA 16301

FISCHER, FRANCES M (D)
Treas, Munic Co Dem Comt, NJ
b Syracuse, NY, Apr 30, 02; m 1924 to Anthony Fischer; c Mabel, Anthony & Frances A; five grandsons; two great grandchildren. Educ: Schs, Newark, NJ. Polit & Govt Pos: Committeewoman & secy, Dem Club Cranford, NJ, formerly; corresponding secy, Union Co, formerly; chairlady, Brick Twp Munic Comt, formerly; committeewoman, Dist 21, Brick Twp, currently; treas, Munic Co Comt, currently; deleg, Dem Nat Conv, 72. Mem: Brick Twp Dem Club (secy); Lake Riviera Beach Club (past secy); Lake Riviera Property Owners Asn (secy); Deborah (treas, Brick Twp Chap); Brick Twp Hosp Asn. Relig: Catholic. Mailing Add: 310 Heritage Dr Brick Town NJ 08723

FISCHER, GLENNON JOHN (R)
Chmn, Ste Genevieve Co Rep Party, Mo
b Ste Genevieve, Mo, Nov 8, 27; s Charles Ludwig Fischer & Philamena Fritch F; m 1954 to Mary Magdalen Klein; c Constance, Paulette, Lisa, Mary, Edward, Geraldine, Joseph, John, Rita, Julie & George. Educ: River Aux Vases Grade Sch, 8 years. Polit & Govt Pos: Chmn, Ste Genevieve Co Rep Party, Mo, 68-; mem sch bd, Ste Genevieve Dist R-11, 69- Mil Serv: Pvt, Army, 46, serv in Antiaircraft, reentered as Pvt, 50, released as Sgt, 52, after serv in Combat Engrs. Mem: United Glass & Ceramic Workers of NAm; AFL-CIO-CLC; Am Legion. Relig: Catholic. Mailing Add: Star Rte 1 Ste Genevieve MO 63670

FISCHER, HELEN MARIE (D)
Alaska State Rep
b Sleepy Eye, Minn, June 2, 12; d William John Schmid & Anna Loretta Nelson S; m 1932 to Edward A Fischer; c Linda Ann (Mrs Parr), David Anthony & Richard William. Educ: Univ Minn, 3 years; Northwest Col Speech, 1 year; St Mary's Col (Minn), 3 years. Polit & Govt Pos: Deleg, Alaska Const Conv, 55-56; Dem Nat Committeewoman, Alaska, 55-62; Alaska State Rep, 57-61 & 71-, mem, Legis Coun & chmn, State Affairs, Alaska State House of Rep, currently; chmn, 13 Western States Foreign Trade Comt, 57-60, vchmn, 13 Western States Conf, 59-62; hon mem, President Kennedy's Inaugural Comt. Bus & Prof Pos: Advert mgr, Anchorage Daily News, 47-51; merchandise mgr, Mil Post Exchanges, 51-55; state dir, US Treasury Savings Bond Div, 62-70. Mem: Women's Med Col Pa (bd dirs, 60-71); Bus & Prof Womens Club; VFW Auxiliary; NAACP; 55 Club. Honors & Awards: US Govt Award for Outstanding Serv, 65; Alaska Centennial Award, 67; Gtr Anchorage, Inc Award, 69; US Treasury Flying Eagle Award, 69; William Strandberg Award for Civil Serv, 70. Mailing Add: 2023 Wildwood Lane Anchorage AK 99503

FISCHER, HENRY FRED (DFL)
Chmn, Minn Dem-Farmer-Labor Party
b Fair Haven, Minn, Nov 9, 38; s Fred H Fischer & Anna Steenlage F; m 1964 to Janet Marie Torgerson; c Jennifer & Christopher. Educ: Univ Minn, 56-57. Polit & Govt Pos: Chmn, Tenth Ward, Dem-Farmer-Labor Party, Minn, 66-68; exec dir, Minn Dem-Farmer-Labor Party, 68-70, chmn, 72-; dep dir, Anderson for Gov Comt, 70; spec asst, US Sen Walter Mondale, 70-72; secy, Midwest Dem Conf, 73- Mem: Asn Dem State Chmn (vpres); Am Asn Campaign Consults. Relig: Lutheran. Legal Res: 4309 Williston Rd Minnetonka MN 55343 Mailing Add: 730 E 38th St Minneapolis MN 55407

FISCHER, JOHN M (D)
Wash State Rep
Mailing Add: 23424 88th W Edmonds WA 98020

FISCHER, ROGER M (D)
Chmn, Erie Co Dem Party, Pa
b Erie, Pa, June 28, 34; s Sebastian Fischer & Josephine Daubler F; m 1959 to Gloria Ann Deegan; c Julie M, Eric A & Joan M. Educ: Pa State Univ, BA, 55; Univ Pittsburgh Sch Law, JD, 58. Polit & Govt Pos: Legal aid attorney, Erie Co, Pa, 62 & 63, register of wills, 64-; mem, Young Dem Pa, 64; del, Dem Nat Conv, 68 & 72; mem, Dem State Policy Comt, 68; chmn, Erie Co Dem Party, 68-; mem, Dem Nat Comt, presently. Mil Serv: Entered as Pvt, Army, 58, released as Cpl, 60, after serv in First Army, Ft Dix, NJ, 58-60. Mem: Phi Alpha Delta; Am Bar Asn; Am Judicature Soc; Am for Dem Action; Am Civil Liberties Union (state rep). Relig: Roman Catholic. Legal Res: 353 E 41st St Erie PA 16504 Mailing Add: 332 E Sixth St Erie PA 16507

FISCHER, ROGER RAYMOND (R)
Pa State Rep
b Washington, Pa, June 1, 41; s Raymond Luther Fischer & Louise Gartley F; m 1972 to Catherine Louise Trettel; c Roger Raymond, II. Educ: Washington & Jefferson Col, BA, 63; Carnegie Inst Technol, grad work in nuclear eng; Delta Epsilon; Lambda Chi Alpha; Letterman's Club. Polit & Govt Pos: Sch dir, Washington Sch Bd, Pa, 65-; mem, legis coun Pa State Bd Asn, 66-67; Pa State Rep, 66-, chmn, police subcomt, Pa Crime Comn Region V Planning Coun, mem, Joint State Govt Task Force to Investigate State Prisons, Pa State House of Rep, mem Prof Licensure Comt, Indust Develop Comt & Pub Utilities Comt, 67-69, mem, Educ Comt, 67-, mem, Law & Order Comt, 69-71, chmn, Basic Educ Subcomt, 73-, chmn, Appropriations Comt, 73-, chmn, Mil Affairs Comt, 73- Bus & Prof Pos: Research engr, Jones & Laughlin Research, 66-67. Mil Serv: Entered as Airman Basic, Air Force, released as 2nd Lt, 66, after Officers Training Sch; Capt, Air Force Res, 66- Mem: Am Inst Physics; Am Nuclear Soc; Am Legion; Jaycees; 40 et 8. Honors & Awards: Red Cross Water Safety Instructor. Relig: Lutheran. Legal Res: Overlook Dr Washington PA 15301 Mailing Add: Box 195 State House of Rep Harrisburg PA 17101

FISCHER, WILLIAM RAYMOND (D)
Chmn, Wallingford Dem Town Comt, Conn
b Bound Brook, NJ, Aug 31, 26; s Harold Clifford Fischer (deceased) & Florence Gatto F; m 1952 to Anna Mae Francolino; c William Raymond, Jr, David Thomas, Marianne, Diana & Harold Clifford, II. Educ: Lyman Hall High Sch, 4 years. Polit & Govt Pos: Mem, Wallingford Dem Town Comt, Conn, 55-, chmn exec bd, 60, chmn, 64-; treas, W Side Dem Club, 57; chmn, Bd Assessors, Wallingford, 59; staff researcher, Gen Assembly Comt for Aid To Non-Pub Schs, 69-70; mem, Mayor's Ad Hoc Comt on Aviation, 71- & on Elec Power, 71- Bus & Prof Pos: Barber, Ralph Roudi's Barber Shop, 41-61; owner, Fischer's Barber Shop, 61-70; sales rep, Teletronics, Inc, Hamden, Conn, 70-; partner, Conn Intruder Alarms, Inc, 71-; pres, DiNatale Realty Co, 75- Mil Serv: Entered as Pvt, Army, 44, released as T-4, 46, after serv in Vienna Area Command Hq Co, ETO, 45-46; Army Occup Medal; Europe-Africa-MidE Campaign Medal; World War II Victory Medal; Good Conduct Medal. Mem: Am Legion; Holy Name Soc; Wallingford Kiwanis (vpres); KofC. Honors & Awards: Community Leader Award, 67. Relig: Catholic; former trustee, Holy Trinity Church. Mailing Add: 31 Sunrise Circle Wallingford CT 06492

FISH, HAMILTON, JR (R)
US Rep, NY
b Washington, DC, June 3, 26; m to Julia Mackenzie (deceased); c Hamilton III, Alexa, Nicholas S & Peter L. Educ: Harvard Univ, AB, 49; NY Univ Sch Law, LLB, 57; John F Kennedy Sch Pub Admin. Polit & Govt Pos: Vconsul, Ireland, US Foreign Serv; attorney, NY Assembly Judiciary Comt; dir, Civil Defense & former bd mem, Comt for Econ Opportunity, Dutchess Co; US Rep, NY, 68- Mil Serv: Naval Res, 44-46. Mem: Dutchess Co Coun, Boy Scouts (mem exec comt); F&AM; Elks; Am Legion; VFW. Relig: Episcopal; Mem bd of missions, Episcopal Diocese of NY. Legal Res: Millbrook NY 12545 Mailing Add: 1230 Longworth House Off Bldg Washington DC 20515

FISH, ODY J (R)
Rep Nat Committeeman, Wis
b Sauk Centre, Minn, June 16, 25. Polit & Govt Pos: Rep Nat Committeeman, Wis, currently; state chmn, Wis Rep Party, formerly; chmn, Midwest & Nat Rep State Chmn Asns, currently; deleg, Rep Nat Conv, 68 & 72, dir security & chief sgt at arms, 72. Bus & Prof Pos: Pres, Pal-O-Pak Insulation Co, Inc, Hartland, Wis & Woodland Mfg Co; chmn bd, Pal-O-Pak Mfg Co, Ltd, Whitby, Ont. Mem: Rotary; Lions; Milwaukee Athletic Club; Waukesha YMCA. Legal Res: 323 Main St Pewaukee WI 53072 Mailing Add: 547 Progress Ave Hartland WI 53029

FISHBAUGH, FRED (D)
Mont State Rep
Mailing Add: Carter MT 59420

FISHER, ARNOLD R (R)
Chmn, Madison Co Rep Comt, NY
b Hamilton, NY, Oct 31, 23; s Seymour A Fisher (deceased) & Flora Faulkner F (deceased); m 1950; c Daphne & Denise. Educ: Cornell Univ. Polit & Govt Pos: Former chmn, Sixth Judicial Dist Young Rep Clubs, NY; pres, Madison Co Young Rep Club, formerly; mem, Madison Co Rep Comt, 50-, chmn, 61-; Comnr of Jurors, Madison Co, 57-, Clerk, 58-; mem, NY State Rep Exec Comt, 72- Bus & Prof Pos: Dir, Chenango Coop Ins Co, 71- Mem: NY Asn Co Clerks; Madison Co Farm & Home Coun (dir); Madison Co Farm Bur; F&AM. Honors & Awards: NY State 4-H Alumni Award, 59 & Dept of State Distinguished Serv Award, 65. Legal Res: Lebanon St Hamilton NY 13346 Mailing Add: Box 57 Hamilton NY 13346

FISHER, AUDREY HORN (R)
b Waynesfield, Ohio; m 1929 to Robert Bradley Fisher. Educ: Henry Ford Hosp Sch Nursing, grad; Sch Neuropsychiat Nursing, Dibble Army Hosp, Calif. Polit & Govt Pos: Mem, Los Altos Rep Women Federated, Calif, 52-, pres, 54-55; mem, Santa Clara Co Rep Cent Comt, 55-65, treas, 2 years, vchmn, 3 years, chmn precinct orgn, acting chmn, 60; mem, United Rep Finance Comt Santa Clara Co, 5 years; mem bd dirs, Calif Fedn Rep Women, 9 years, vpres, 59-60 & 66-67, gen chmn, biennial conv, 61-67, parliamentarian Northern Div, 7 years; mem, Calif Rep State Cent Comt, 54-74, mem precinct comt, mem platform comt, auth, Preamble to 58 & 60 State Rep Platforms & mem exec comt, formerly; alt deleg, Rep Nat Conv, 60; cand for Rep nomination, Calif State Assembly, 22nd Dist, 62; campaign coordr, Co Cent Comt, 62; mem city coun, Los Altos, Calif, 64-, mayor pro-tem, 66 & 73, mayor, 67-69; state chmn women's activities, Spencer Williams for Attorney Gen, 66; deleg, Nat Rep Women's Conf, 5 times; deleg, Nat Fedn Rep Women's Conv, 5 times; mem, State Health Planning Coun, mem, Health Admin Comt & Health Facil Comt, 67-73; mem citizens comt to form El Camino Hosp Dist; consult, Dept Comprehensive Health Planning, Region IX, Dept Health, Educ & Welfare, 70-73; bd mgt, Pilgrim Haven Retirement Home, 74-; bd mgt, Palo Alto Area Chap, Am Red Cross, 74-; bd mem, San Francisco Bay Regional Water Qual Control Bd, 75- Bus & Prof Pos: Registered nurse, pvt duty, gen hosp & doctor's off; secy-treas, Western Sales Co, 38- Mil Serv: Army Nurse Corps, 45, 2nd Lt, Res, 46-49. Mem: El Camino Hosp Auxiliary (bd dirs, 3 years); Quota Club Los Altos; League of Women Voters; Los Altos Chap United Fund (bd dirs & allocations comt); Am Legion. Legal Res: 120 Hawthorne Ave Los Altos CA 94022 Mailing Add: PO Box 415 Los Altos CA 94022

FISHER, CHARLES OSBORNE, JR (D)
VChmn, Carroll Co Dem Cent Comt, Md
b Ocean Port, NJ, Sept 1, 43; s Charles Osborne Fisher & Margaret Gunther F; m 1967 to Christine Parsons; c Maura Christine, Stephen Blair & Matthew Osborne. Educ: Loyola Col (Md), AB, 65; Univ Md Sch Law, JD, 69. Polit & Govt Pos: Asst states attorney, Baltimore, Md, 69-72; vchmn, Carroll Co Dem Cent Comt, 74- Mem: Am, Md & Carroll Co Bar Asns; Carroll Co Heart Asn (bd dirs, 75-). Relig: Roman Catholic; pres parish coun, St John Church, 73-75. Mailing Add: 137 E Green St Westminster MD 21157

FISHER, D MICHAEL (R)
Pa State Rep
b Pittsburgh, Pa, Nov 7, 44; s C Francis Fisher & Dolores Darby F; m 1973 to Carol A Hudak. Educ: Georgetown Univ, AB Govt, 66, Law Ctr, JD, 69; Collegiate Club. Polit & Govt Pos: Vchmn, Allegheny Co Young Rep, 71-73 & Upper St Clair Rep Club; Pa State Rep, 75- Mil Serv: Entered as E-1, Army, 69, released as SP-5, 75, after serv in 2073rd Res Sch. Mailing Add: 360 Lorlita Lane Upper St Clair PA 15241

FISHER, ETHEL VIRGINIA (R)
Chmn, Clay Co Rep Cent Comt, Ind
b Brazil, Ind; d William H Hill & Emma Maria Young H; m to Raymond C Fisher, wid; c Phyllis (Mrs Melvin Francis). Educ: High Sch & Bus Col grad. Polit & Govt Pos: Vprecinct committeeman, Rep Cent Comt, Ind, 45-50; pres, Women's Rep Club, 50-60; vchmn, Clay Co Rep Cent Comt, 60-68, chmn, 68-; mgr, Brazil License Br 17, Brazil, Clay Co, currently. Bus & Prof Pos: Buyer, Ideal Ladies' Dept Store, Clay City, Ind, 56- Mem: Clay Co Women's Rep Club; Harrison Twp Women's Rep Club; Eastern Star; Women's Bus Club Clay City; Ind Women's Rep Federated Clubs (corresponding secy, 70-). Honors & Awards: Ind Rep Woman of the Year, Nat Rep Women's Fedn, 69. Relig: Methodist. Mailing Add: 604 Main St Clay City IN 47841

FISHER, GEORGE WATSON (D)
b Norristown, Pa, Feb 16, 20; s Harry Anderson Fisher & Irene Rosenberger F; m 1947 to Julia Bongart; c Steven Anderson & Robert Gregg. Educ: Pierce Sch Bus, 37. Polit & Govt Pos: Admin asst to US Rep Olin Teague, Tex, Washington, DC, 49- Mil Serv: Entered as Pvt, Army, 42, released as Sgt/Maj, after serv in 1st Bn, 314th Inf, 79th Div, ETO, 44-46; Bronze Star with Two Oakleaf Clusters; Purple Heart; French Fourragerre. Mem: Nat Capitol Dem Club (bd dir); Ponte Vedra Country Club; Columbia Country Club. Relig: Protestant. Mailing Add: 10403 Royalton Terr Silver Spring MD 20901

FISHER, JOEL MARSHALL (R)
Dir New Majority Div, Rep State Cent Comt Calif
b Chicago, Ill, June 24, 35; s Dr Dan Fisher & Nell Kolvin F; m 1970 to Linda Joyce Buss; c Sara Melinda. Educ: Univ Southern Calif, AB, 55; Univ Calif, Berkeley, LLB, 61; MA, 62; Claremont Grad Sch & Univ Ctr, PhD, 68; Pi Sigma Alpha; Blue Key; Delta Phi Epsilon; Phi Beta Kappa; Blackstonian; Phi Alpha Delta. Polit & Govt Pos: Pres, Trojan Young Rep, Univ Southern Calif, 57; mem bd dirs, Calif Young Rep, 58 & 60-62; campaign dir, Rep Cong Campaigns, 60 & 66; pres, Calif Young Rep Col Fedn, 61; fieldman, First & 12th Cong Dists, 62; regional campaign dir, Keating for Senate Comt, 64; orgn dir & acting exec dir, Rep Citizens Comt of US, 64-65; chmn arts & sci, Rep State Cent Comt Calif, 68, dir new majority div, 73-; dir arts & sci, Rep Nat Comt, 68-69; asst to the Dep Counsel to the President, 69-70; Dep Econ & Soc Affairs, Dept State, 69-71, consult, Dept State & Agency Int Develop, 71-73; dir spec comts, Calif Comt Reelect of the President, 72; consult, Calif State Assembly, 72-73. Bus & Prof Pos: Dir pub rels, World Peace Through Law, Rhyne & Rhyne, 65; assoc prof polit, Calif State Col, Fullerton, 66-73; secy, South Calif Ctr Educ Pub Affairs, Inc, 67-72; pres, Int, Forum, Los Angeles World Affairs Coun, 72- Mil Serv: Entered as 2nd Lt, Army, 54, released as 1st Lt, 57, after serv in Army Intel, Europe, 56-57. Publ: Co-auth, The legislative process in California, Am Polit Sci Asn, 73 & British electoral politics in 1970, Verfassung und Verfassungswirklichkeit, spring 71; auth, The campaign, In: To be a Congressman: Promise and the Power, Acropolis Bks, 73; plus others. Mem: Am Polit Sci Asn; Am Soc Int Law; Polit Studies Orgn; Claremont Grad Coun (bd dirs, 73-); SPIR (bd dirs, 71-). Honors & Awards: Noble Found Grantee; Falk Fel Am Polit; Rep Nat Conv Faculty Fel; Am Polit Sci Asn Comt Fel, formerly & State Legis Fel, 70-73; Danforth Found Research Grant, 72. Relig: Episcopal. Legal Res: 2660 Woodstock Rd Los Angeles CA 90046 Mailing Add: 1326 W Sixth St Los Angeles CA 90017

FISHER, JOSEPH LYMAN (D)
US Rep, Va
b Pawtucket, RI, Jan 11, 14; s Howard C Fisher & Caroline Nash F; m to Margaret W. Educ: Bowdoin Col, BS in Econ, 35; Harvard Univ, PhD(econ), 47; George Washington Univ, MA in Educ, 51; Phi Beta Kappa. Hon Degrees: DSc, Bowdoin Col, 65; LLD, Allegheny Col, 66. Polit & Govt Pos: Mem, Arlington Co Bd, 63-, chmn, 65 & 71; pres, Metrop Washington, DC Coun Govt, 69, chmn bd dirs, 70, mem bd dirs, 73-; chmn, Arlington Planning Comn; US Rep, Tenth District, Va, 75-, mem, Ways & Means Comt, US House Rep, 75- Bus & Prof Pos: Pres, Resources for the Future, Inc; exec officer, Coun Econ Adv; planning technician, Nat Resources Planning Bd. Mil Serv: Entered Army, 43, released as T/Sgt, 46, after serv in Pac. Publ: Resources in America's Future, Johns Hopkins Press, 63; World Prospects for Natural Resources, 64. Mem: Am Econ Asn; Am Soc for Pub Admin; Am Forestry Asn (dir). Relig: Unitarian; moderator & chmn bd, Unitarian-Universalist Asn. Legal Res: 2608 24th St N Arlington VA 22207 Mailing Add: 1755 Massachusetts Ave NW Washington DC 20036

FISHER, LEO FRANK (DFL)
VChmn, Steele Co Dem-Farmer-Labor Party, Minn
b Owatonna, Minn, Mar 5, 17; s Henry Leo Fisher & Elizabeth Renchin F; single. Polit & Govt Pos: Precinct chmn, Dem-Farmer-Labor Party, Minn, 57-; deleg, Minn Dem State Conv, 57; deleg, Minn Dem State Cent Comt, 63; vchmn, Steele Co Dem-Farmer-Labor Party, Minn, 65-; del, Dem Nat Conv, 68. Mil Serv: Entered as Pvt, Army, 42, released as Pfc, 45, after serv in 576 Ambulance Bn, ETO, 44-45; Seven Major Campaign Ribbons. Mem: VFW; Am Legion; Int Brotherhood of Carpenters & Joiners Am. Relig: Catholic. Mailing Add: 225 Linden Owatonna MN 55060

FISHER, M BYRON (R)
Utah State Rep
b Honolulu, Hawaii, Dec 5, 36; s Milton b Fisher & Louise Larsen F; m 1960 to Joan Peterson; c Debra Joan, Michael Byron, Janae, Sharlene & Peter. Educ: Brigham Young Univ, BA, 61; George Washington Univ, JD, 64. Polit & Govt Pos: Utah State Rep, 67-; mem, Utah Legis Coun, 69-71. Bus & Prof Pos: Partner, Law Firm of Fabian & Clendenin. Mem: Salt Lake Co & Am Bar Asns; Utah State Bar. Relig: Latter-day Saint. Mailing Add: 1264 E 3700 S Salt Lake City UT 84106

FISHER, MELVIN LESLIE (R)
Chmn, Williamson Co Rep Cent Comt, Ill
b Crowder, Mo, Mar 22, 35; s Earl Fisher & Eathel Tubbs F; m 1956 to Mary Emma Crawford; c Michael Duane, Mark Leslie & Melanie Michele. Educ: Malden, Mo High Sch. Polit & Govt Pos: Precinct committeeman, Williamson Co, 69-; chmn, Williamson Co Rep Cent Comt, 74- Bus & Prof Pos: Owner, Melvin Fisher & Sons Painting Contractors, 62-75; partner, Fisher Painting Co, 75-; systems div mgr, F E Holmes & Son Construction Co, 75- Mem: Am Quarter Horse Asn; Nat Cutting Horse Asn; Little Egypt Cutting Horse Asn (pres, 75-). Relig: Protestant. Legal Res: Rte 4 Marion IL 62959 Mailing Add: PO Box 532 Marion IL 62959

FISHER, MERWYN T (D)
Ind State Rep
b Pekin, Ind, May 5, 37; s Hugh Thomas Fisher & Gertrude Terrell F; m 1962 to Darlene Constance Haub; c Trindy & Brock. Educ: Pekin High Sch, Ind. Polit & Govt Pos: Twp trustee & assessor, Pekin, Ind, 67-74; Ind State Rep, currently. Bus & Prof Pos: Grain & beef farmer, currently. Mil Serv: Sgt, Nat Guard. Mem: Farm Bur; Lions. Relig: United Methodist. Mailing Add: RR 2 Pekin IN 47165

FISHER, NORRIS (D)
b Barksdale, Tex, Dec 29, 25; s Jack Emesly Fisher & Mabel Belle Howard F; m 1947 to JoAnn Brice; c Clinton Norris & Lisa Lynette. Educ: High Sch. Polit & Govt Pos: Chmn, Real Co Dem Comt, Tex, formerly. Bus & Prof Pos: Mgr, Local Grocery Store, 48-54; owner, Leakey Drug Store, 54- Mil Serv: Entered as A/S, Navy, 44, released as Coxswain, 46, after serv in Amphibious Forces in SPac; Saipan & Guam Invasion Ribbons. Mem: Leakey Sch Bd Trustees, (pres, 8 years); Frio Canyon CofC (mem bd). Relig: Protestant. Mailing Add: PO Box 255 Leakey TX 78873

FISHER, O CLARK (D)
b Junction, Tex, Nov 22, 03; s Jobe B Fisher & Rhoda Clark F; m 1927 to Marian DeWalsh; c Rhoda. Educ: Univ Tex; Baylor Univ, LLB, 29. Polit & Govt Pos: Co Attorney, Tom Green Co, Tex, 31-35; Tex State Rep, 35-37; Dist Attorney, 51st Judicial Dist, Tex, 37-43; US Rep, Tex, 42-74. Bus & Prof Pos: Attorney. Publ: It Occurred in Kimble, Texas Heritage of Fishers & Clarks, King Fisher—his Life and Times; co-auth, Great Western Indian Fights. Mem: Mason; KofP; Eastern Star; Rotary. Legal Res: San Angelo TX 76901 Mailing Add: Watergate East Apt Washington DC 20013

FISHER, ROBERT (R)
Tenn State Rep
Mailing Add: Seiler Bldg Elizabethton TN 37643

FISHER, ZACK BUCHANAN (R)
Chmn, Hall Co Rep Party, Tex
b Dennison, Ohio, Nov 7, 41; s Zack Fisher & Helen Buchanan F; m 1962 to Texie Ann Barkley; c Kelli Dawn & Zack Kevin. Educ: Univ Tex, 1 year; Panhandle Agr & Mech Col, 1 year. Polit & Govt Pos: Chmn, Hall Co Rep Party, Tex, 69-; cand for Tex State Rep, 70; agr adv, US Sen John Tower, Tex, 71-72, campaign mgr, 72; exec dir, Tex Rep Party, 72 & 75-; app mem tech adv comt on livestock & livestock prod for trade negotiations, US Dept Agr, Washington, DC, 75-; mem agr adv comt for US Rep Bob Price, Tex, dist rep, 73-74. Bus & Prof Pos: Owner & mgr, Fisher-Red River Ins Agency, currently. Mem: Tex Asn Ins Agt; Ins Councilors Asn Tex; Memphis Rotary Club; CofC; Tex Farm Bur. Relig: Methodist. Legal Res: 720 S Eighth Memphis TN 79245 Mailing Add: PO Box 638 Memphis TX 79245

FISHMAN, ALVIN (D)
VChmn, New Dem Coalition of Mich
b Los Angeles, Calif, Nov 18, 27; s Harry C Fishman & Bertha Berkenfeld F; m 1951 to Margaret Radulovich; c Marcia & Daniel. Educ: NY Univ, 1 year; Univ Mich, 2 years; Wayne State Univ, BS. Polit & Govt Pos: Precinct deleg, Detroit Dem Party, Mich, 55-; mem, Mich State Dem Cent Comt; vchmn, Mich Conf of Concerned Dem, 67-68; state chmn, New Dem

Coalition of Mich, 68-71, vchmn, 71-; alt deleg, Dem Nat Conv, 68; bd mem, Mich Comt Against Repression. Mailing Add: 18995 Warrington Detroit MI 48221

FISHMAN, SAM (D)
Mem, Dem Nat Comt, Mich
Mailing Add: 8000 E Jefferson Detroit MI 48214

FITHIAN, FLOYD J (D)
US Rep, Ind
b Vesta, Nebr, Nov 3, 28; m 1952 to Marjorie Heim; c Cindy, Judy & John. Educ: Peru State Col, BA, 51; Univ Nebr, MA, 55, PhD, 64. Polit & Govt Pos: US Rep, Ind, 75- Bus & Prof Pos: Teacher, high sch; prof, Nebr Wesleyan Univ; assoc prof hist, Purdue Univ. Mem: Ind Cattlemen's Asn; Lafayette Farm Coop; Am Hist Asn; Orgn Am Hist; State Coun Social Studies. Relig: Methodist; law speaker & past chmn admin bd & youth dir, Grace United Methodist Church. Legal Res: 3711 N 500 E Lafayette IN 46202 Mailing Add: US House Rep Washington DC 20515

FITZ, HERBERT GEORGE (R)
Idaho State Rep
b Spirit Lake, Iowa, Apr 28, 08; s George G Fitz & May Thatcher F; m 1930 to Ruth Toolson; c George H. Educ: Idaho State Univ, PhG, 29; Phi Delta Chi. Polit & Govt Pos: Chmn, Village Bd, New Meadows, Idaho, 55-62; Idaho State Rep, Dist Nine, 73- Bus & Prof Pos: Pres, Idaho State Bd of Pharm, 62-70. Mem: Mason (Master); Masonic York Rite; Scottish Rite; Shrine; Odd Fellows. Honors & Awards: Outstanding Serv, Idaho State Pharmaceutical Asn, 57, A H Robbins Bowl of Hygea, 68. Relig: Methodist. Mailing Add: PO Box 317 New Meadows ID 83654

FITZGERALD, GEORGE S (D)
b Troy, NY, Dec 26, 01; m to Jane M Gignac; c William B. Educ: Holy Cross Col, Worcester, Mass, BA; Univ Detroit, JD; Gamma Eta Gamma. Polit & Govt Pos: Dem Nat Committeeman; mem, Mich Soc Welfare Comt, formerly; Asst Prosecuting Attorney, Wayne Co, Mich; Asst US Dist Attorney; legal adv, US Customs; Mich State Sen, 64-68 & 70-74. Bus & Prof Pos: Lawyer; instr, Univ Detroit Law Sch, formerly. Mem: Mich Aeronaut & Space Club; KofC; Elks; Holy Cross Varsity Club; Detroit Press Club. Relig: Roman Catholic. Legal Res: 1334 Buckingham Grosse Pointe Park MI 48230 Mailing Add: 1714 Guardian Bldg Detroit MI 48226

FITZGERALD, JEROME (D)
Iowa State Rep
Mailing Add: 1008 S 17th St Ft Dodge IA 50501

FITZGERALD, JOHN E (D)
WVa State Deleg
Mailing Add: State Capitol Charleston WV 25305

FITZGERALD, KEVIN W (D)
Mass State Rep
Mailing Add: State Capitol Boston MA 02133

FITZGERALD, TOM (D)
Nebr State Sen
Mailing Add: 8104 N Ridge Dr Omaha NE 68112

FITZGERALD, WILLIAM B (D)
Mich State Sen
b Troy, NY, Feb 3, 14; married; c William B, Jr & Timothy E. Educ: Univ Detroit; Detroit Col Law; completed the Wayne State Univ Exec Develop Course sponsored by Detroit Civil Serv Comn; Delta Theta Phi. Polit & Govt Pos: Mich State Rep, formerly; precinct deleg; Mich State Sen, 75- Bus & Prof Pos: Licensed real estate salesman; former legal investr, Detroit Dept of St Rwy. Mem: Nat Rwy Hist Soc (hon mem); AFSCME, AFL-CIO. Relig: Catholic. Mailing Add: 5550 Courville Detroit MI 48224

FITZGIBBON, JOSEPH EUGENE (D)
Okla State Rep
b Bardstown, Ky, Nov 22, 37; s Patrick Antony Fitzgibbon & Lila Linder F; m 1958 to Pearle Ann Bowyer; c Mary Jo & Daniel Joseph. Educ: Northeastern Okla A&M Col, 58-61. Polit & Govt Pos: Precinct chmn, Miami Dem Party, Okla, 68-; Okla State Rep, Dist 7, 75- Bus & Prof Pos: Partner, Fitz Freight, Miami, Okla, 55- Mil Serv: Entered as Seaman, Navy, 54, released as YN2, 58, after serv in Pac & Far East, 56-58; China Serv Medal; Good Conduct Medal. Mem: KofC; Lions; VFW; Elks. Relig: Catholic. Mailing Add: 1806 H St NW Miami OK 74354

FITZMORRIS, JAMES E, JR (D)
Lt Gov, La
Mailing Add: State Capitol Baton Rouge LA 70806

FITZPATRICK, CHARLES HENRY (R)
b Lowell, Mass, Dec 22, 45; s William J Fitzpatrick & Shirley Donnelly F; m 1966 to Johanna Levenson; c William E. Educ: Tufts Univ, AB, 68; Cath Univ Law Sch, JD, 72. Polit & Govt Pos: Attorney, Dept Health, Educ & Welfare, 70-73; admin asst to US Rep G William Whitehurst, 73- Mem: Am & DC Bar Asns. Mailing Add: 8316 Garfield Ct Springfield VA 22152

FITZPATRICK, EDWARD JOSEPH (DFL)
Assoc Chairperson, Fifth Cong Dist Dem-Farmer-Labor Party, Minn
b Foreston, Minn, Aug 13, 25; s Charles M Fitzpatrick & Margaret Smith F; m 1953 to Charlotte Berg; c Charles Edward, James William, Richard Henry & John Berg. Educ: St John's Univ (Minn), 46-48; Univ Minn, Minneapolis, BA, 50, MA, 56; Phi Delta Kappa. Polit & Govt Pos: Secy, Fridley Dem-Farmer-Labor Club, Minn, 64-65, chmn, 65-67; mem, Civic Adv Coun on Children & Youth, 65-67; secy, Anoka Co Dem-Farmer-Labor Exec Comt, 65-74; deleg, Minn State Dem-Farmer-Labor Conv, 66, 68, 70, 72 & 74; chmn, Anoka Co Statesman's Dinner, 68; chmn, Fridley Parks & Recreation Comn, 68-73; mem, Fridley Planning Comn, 68-73, chmn, 73; state exec comt, Dem-Farmer-Labor Party, Minn, 72-; assoc chairperson, Fifth Cong Dist, Dem-Farmer-Labor Party, Minn, 72- Bus & Prof Pos: Teacher, Minneapolis Pub Schs, Minn, 52- Mil Serv: Navy, 45-46. Mem: Nat Coun Teachers Eng; Am Fedn Teachers; AFL-CIO. Mailing Add: 5273 Horizon Dr Fridley MN 55421

FITZPATRICK, JOHN HITCHCOCK (R)
Mass State Sen
b Quincy, Mass, Apr 5, 23; s Clarence E Fitzpatrick & Clara Hitchcock F; m 1944 to Jane Pratt; c Nancy Jane & Jo Ann. Educ: Middlebury Col, BA, 48; Boston Univ Law Sch, LLB, 51. Polit & Govt Pos: Mass State Sen, 73- Bus & Prof Pos: Owner, Country Curtains Inc, 56 & Red Lion Inn, 67- Mil Serv: Entered as Pvt, Army, 43, released as Cpl, 46, after serv in Inf, ETO, 44-46; Bronze Star. Mem: Am Legion. Relig: Protestant. Legal Res: Main St Stockbridge MA 01262 Mailing Add: Red Lion Inn Stockbridge MA 01262

FITZPATRICK, JOHN JOSEPH (D)
b Wheeling, WVa, Mar 19, 43; s John R Fitzpatrick & Nell Gonot F; m 1966 to Elizabeth Pickens. Educ: Georgetown Univ, BSFS, 65; State Univ NY Buffalo, PhD, 72; Pi Sigma Alpha. Polit & Govt Pos: Admin asst to US Rep Tom Harkin, Washington, DC, 75- Bus & Prof Pos: Asst prof polit sci, Iowa State Univ, 69-74. Relig: Roman Catholic. Legal Res: 2324 Knapp St Ames IA 50010 Mailing Add: 223 Ninth St NE Washington DC 20002

FITZPATRICK, JOHN LEO (D)
Mem, Lincoln Co Dem Comt, Maine
b Quincy, Mass, Nov 29, 22; s John Leo Fitzpatrick & Lillian Gleason F; m 1947 to June R Reilly; c John L, Kevin P, James T, June R, Kerry E, Melinda M & Melissa A. Educ: Quincy High Sch, Mass, grad, 41. Polit & Govt Pos: Chmn, Bristol Dem Town Comn, Maine, 66-72; mem, Lincoln Co Dem Comt, 66-, chmn, 70-72; mem, First Dist Dem Comt, 68-70; Justice of Peace, 68- Mil Serv: Entered as A/S, Navy, 42, released as AM 1/C, 45, after serv in Asiatic Pac Campaign, 45; Purple Heart; Asiatic Pac Campaign Medal; Am Theatre Medal; Victory Medal. Mem: Nat Geog Soc; VFW; Samoset Fire Co; Samoset Fish & Game Club; St Patricks Mens Club. Relig: Catholic. Legal Res: Bristol ME Mailing Add: Southside Rd New Harbor ME 04554

FITZPATRICK, JOSEPH (D)
Chmn, Va State Dem Cent Comt
Mailing Add: 701 E Franklin St Richmond VA 23219

FITZPATRICK, MARK WILLIAM (R)
b Twiggs Co, Ga, Dec 12, 89; s William Hart Fitzpatrick & Thulia Massey F; m 1933 to Jane Lippincott Duross, wid; c Duross, Jane Lippincott (Mrs Turner), Loxley Childs & Barry Kelly. Educ: Gordon Inst; Univ Ga, BSCE, cum laude; Sr Round Table; Gridiron Iron Secret Soc; Sigma Chi. Polit & Govt Pos: Research engr & asst div engr, Ga Hwy Dept, 34-46; tax comnr, Twiggs Co, 49-60; Ga State Sen, 61-62; chmn, Twiggs Co Rep Party, formerly. Bus & Prof Pos: Civil engr, Southern Rwy, 13-18; gen mgr of saw mill & bookkeeper for farm, I & M W Fitzpatrick, 19-34. Mil Serv: Entered as Acting 1st Sgt, Army, 18, released as 1st Sgt, 19, after serv with 20th Engrs, France; Citation for Exceptionally Meritorious & Conspicuous Servs at Cambrai, France. Mem: Am Legion; Ga Farm Bur; Idle Hour Golf & Country Club, Macon, Ga. Relig: Baptist. Mailing Add: Tarversville Jeffersonville GA 31044

FITZPATRICK, ROSALYN M (R)
Mem, Rep State Cent Comt Calif
b Marshfield, Wis, Apr 19, 11; d Antone J Meidl & Mary C Streveler M; m to Edward J Fitzpatrick, wid; c Karalyn (Mrs James D Belcher). Educ: San Mateo Col, 33-34. Polit & Govt Pos: Mem, Pajaro Valley Fedn of Rep Women, Watsonville, Calif, 58-; mem, Rep State Cent Comt Calif, 58-; co-chmn for Calif State Assemblyman Alan G Pattee, Monterey Co, Calif for Calif Sen George Murphy, 64 & for Robert E Finch for Lt Gov, 66; mem, 12th Cong Dist Rep Comt, 68-; mem, Co Nixon Steering Comt, 72. Bus & Prof Pos: Secy, Valley Packing, Watsonville, Calif, currently. Mem: Am Cancer Soc (mem co bd dirs, 68-, secy-treas, 72-74). Honors & Awards: Outstanding Citizen Award, Pajaro Valley Fedn of Rep Women. Relig: Catholic. Mailing Add: 21 Secondo Way Watsonville CA 95076

FITZSIMONS, RICHARD W (CONSERVATIVE)
Minn State Rep
b Argyle, Minn, Jan 19, 22; m to Janice; c Mark Patrick & Lori Anne. Polit & Govt Pos: Minn State Rep, 52-72; Minn State Sen, 72- Bus & Prof Pos: Grain farmer. Mailing Add: 192 S Sixth St Warren MN 56762

FITZWATER, BETH THOMAS (R)
Idaho State Rep
b Driggs, Idaho, Jan 31, 20; d Thomas Vernerd Thomas & Mary Elizabeth Heiner T; wid; c D Scott & Kevin Thomas. Educ: Brigham Young Univ, 38; Boise Bus Univ, cert, 39-40; Univ Utah, 41-42. Polit & Govt Pos: Idaho State Rep, 74- Mailing Add: 6407 Robertson Dr Boise ID 83705

FIX, GEORGE ARTHUR (D)
Chmn, Yuma Co Dem Cent Comt, Colo
b Wray, Colo, Nov 28, 25; s George Fix & Julia Shivley F; m 1947 to Betty Jeanne Reed (deceased); m 1959 to Cleora Louvetta Welp; c Vikki Lorraine, Douglas Lane, Margaret Grace, Amy Collen, Curtis Dale, Dixie Lynette, James Albert, Nancy Elaine & Janette Lyn Witte. Educ: Colo A&M Col, 47. Polit & Govt Pos: Dem committeeman, McGee Precinct, Colo, 53-58; capt, Comnr Dist Two, 55-59; treas, Yuma Co, 59-70; mem exec comt, Yuma Co Dem Cent Comt, 60-66, chmn, 69-; pres, Yuma Co Young Dem, 66. Bus & Prof Pos: Partner, Yuma Co Abstr Co, 68- Mil Serv: Entered as Pvt, Army Air Corps, 43, released as S/Sgt, 46, after serv in 19th Bomb Group 21st Bomber Command, Pac Theater, 45-46; Good Conduct Medal; Am Serv Medal; Asiatic Pac Serv Medal; Victory Medal; Presidential Unit Citation with Oak Leaf Cluster; Aerial Gunner Badge. Mem: Land Title Asn Colo; Lions; Am Legion; VFW; Lutheran Laymen's League. Relig: Lutheran. Mailing Add: 1030 W Seventh St Wray CO 80758

FIX, HELEN HERRINK (R)
Ohio State Rep
b Richmond, Va, Sept 21, 22; d Louis Shepard Herrink, Sr & Virginia Wardwell H; m 1944 to John C Fix, Sr; c John C, Jr, Carol (Mrs Thomas Brown) & Marian (Mrs Charles Van Slaars). Educ: Univ Richmond, BA; Phi Beta Kappa; Tau Kappa Alpha; Pi Delta Epsilon. Polit & Govt Pos: Mem coun, Amberley Village, Ohio, 67-75; Ohio State Rep, 26th Dist, 75- Bus & Prof Pos: Ed, Reporter, Cincinnati, Ohio, 55-57; ed, Northeastern Suburban Life, Cincinnati, 61-71. Mem: Women in Commun; Ohio Newspaper Women's Asn; Cincinnati Women's Polit Caucus; Univ Cincinnati Alumni Col Adv Bd; Hamilton Co Police Asn. Relig: Methodist. Mailing Add: 3141 Esther Dr Cincinnati OH 45213

FJOSLIEN, DAVE (R)
Minn State Rep
Mailing Add: Rte 2 Brandon MN 56315

FLACK, JOHN T (R)
NY State Assemblyman
Mailing Add: 78-14 64 Pl Glendale NY 11227

FLACK, WILLIAM PATRICK (D)
b Anderson, SC, Mar 19, 27; s Pinder Alfred Flack & Alma E Burriss F; m 1951 to Thomasenia Mattison. Educ: Tuskegee Inst, 43-46. Polit & Govt Pos: Mem, SC Bd Social Serv, currently; mem elec comt, Anderson Co, currently; deleg, Dem Nat Mid-Term Conf, 74. Bus & Prof Pos: Coordr for NC, R T P Inc, New York, currently; chmn bd, ANECP, Anderson, SC, currently. Mem: Elks; Am Fed State, Co & Munic Employees; SC Human Rights Coun; Anderson Co Hosp Asn. Relig: Presbyterian. Mailing Add: Rte 8 Box 247-A Anderson SC 29621

FLADAGER, MILTON WALLACE (R)
State Committeeman, Mont Rep Party
b Scobey, Mont, Sept 26, 18; s Wilhelm Paul Fladager & Marie Lavanger F; m 1945 to Lois Loraine Lowthian; c Loren Stanley, Brian Milton, Warren Irwin, Wallace Archie, Kathleen Georgetta, Willard Keven & Armand Lee. Educ: Peerless High Sch. Polit & Govt Pos: Dep assessor, Daniels Co, Mont, 45-46; Crop Ins Adjuster, Fed Crop Ins Corp, 46-55; mem, Agr Soil Conserv Comt, Daniels Co, 53; Mont State Rep, Daniels Co, 59-60; mem, State Land Use Comt, 61-64; chmn, Daniels Co Rep Cent Comt, Mont, formerly; state committeeman, Mont Rep Party, 69- Mil Serv: Entered as Cadet, Air Force, 42, released as Cpl, 44, after serv as Radio Operator in 9th Air Force. Mem: Am Legion; Farm Bur; Farmers Union; Mason; AF&AM. Relig: Lutheran. Mailing Add: Peerless MT 59253

FLAGG, MORGAN (D)
b Oakland, Calif, Mar 13, 26; s A J Flagg & Mabel Yeagel F; m 1950 to Claire E Barker; c Lawrence Jay, Brian Edward, James Morgan, John Patrick, Janine Alaine, Lori Ruth, Kerri Louise & Mary Claire. Educ: Fremont High Sch, Oakland, Calif, 40-43. Polit & Govt Pos: File clerk, Calif State Senate, 47, 48 & 49; alt deleg, Dem Nat Conv, 64, deleg, 72; mem, Comn on Housing & Community Develop, State of Calif, 65, 66 & 67; mem & chmn, Monterey Co Dem Cent Comt, 68-70; cand, US Rep, 16th Dist, 74; chmn, ARB Finance Comt, Monterey, 74. Bus & Prof Pos: Deleg, Home Builders Cong of Calif, 64 & 65. Mil Serv: Cadet, Army Air Corp, 44-45, serv in OLT Prog, Continental US. Mem: Commonwealth Club of San Francisco; Robert Louis Stevenson Sch Boys (trustee, 72-); Pacheco Club; Pebble Beach Beach & Tennis Club; Olympic Club. Relig: Christian. Legal Res: 1450 Manor Rd Monterey CA 93940 Mailing Add: 400 Camino Aguajito Monterey CA 93940

FLAHERTY, CHARLES FRANCES, JR (D)
Mass State Rep
b Boston, Mass, Oct 13, 38; s Charles Francis Flaherty & Anna Coughlin F; m 1962 to Evelyn Ann Walsh; c Charles Thomas, Timothy Richard, Maureen & Daniel Paul. Educ: Boston Col, BS in BA, 60; Boston Col, Grad Sch of Arts & Sci polit sci, 67-68. Polit & Govt Pos: Mass State Rep, 67-; chmn, Mass Dem State Legis Com, 71-; Mass Presidential Elector & pres, Mass Electoral Col, 72; Dem state committeeman, Second Middlesex Dist, Mass, 72-; mem, Dem Nat Comt, Mass, 72-; deleg, Dem Nat Mid-Term Conf, 74. Bus & Prof Pos: Asst dir univ research, Boston Col, 65-70, dir research admin, 70-, dir environ ctr, 72- Mil Serv: Entered as Ens, Navy, 60, released as Lt, 65, after serv in USS Bearss (DD-654), Atlantic Fleet, 60-65; Lt, Naval Res, 65-; Naval & Armed Forces Expeditionary Medal; Nat Defense Medal. Publ: ASW-Are we missing the boat?, US Naval Inst Proc, 2/66; Toward a uniform state building code in Massachusetts, The Bldg Inspector, 6/67; Adopt a tot-lot, Mag of Cambridge, 7/68. Mem: Am Legion; VFW; KofC; Holy Name Soc; Jr CofC. Honors & Awards: Freedoms Found Award, 64 & 65; Ten Outstanding Young Leaders Award, Boston Jaycees, 73. Relig: Catholic. Mailing Add: 14 Woodbridge St Cambridge MA 02140

FLAHERTY, MICHAEL FRANCIS (D)
Mass State Rep
b Boston, Mass, Sept 6, 36; s John James Flaherty & Mary E Joyce F; m 1961 to Margaret Joanne McGlone; c Margaret J, Michael F, Jr & John J. Educ: Boston Col, AB, 63; New Eng Sch of Law, LLB, 68; Ballermine Speakers Club. Polit & Govt Pos: Chmn, Spec Comn Studying Drug Abuse in Mass, 70-; Mass State Rep, 67-, asst majority leader, Mass House of Rep, 69-, chmn, House Comt Social Welfare & chmn, House Judiciary Comt, currently; deleg, Dem Nat Conv, 68; mem, Ward Seven Dem Comt, South Boston-Dorchester, 68- Bus & Prof Pos: Acct clerk, Boston Edison Co, Mass, 60-63; ins claim adjuster, Travelers Ins Co, 63-67; attorney, Boston, 70- Mil Serv: Entered as Seaman Recruit, Navy, 54, released as PN-2, 57, after serv on USS Northampton, 55-57; Nat Defense & Good Conduct Medals; selected Honor Man by fellow recruits while in basic training. Publ: Minority Report: Third Interim Report of the Spec Comn Studying Illegal Drugs in Mass, Commonwealth Mass, 2/70. Mem: Mass State Legis Asn; Am, Mass & Boston Bar Asns; KofC. Honors & Awards: Kiwanis Citation for Combating Drug Abuse; Boston Firefighters Appreciation Award; South Boston Outstanding Citizen's Award, 62 Club, 69. Relig: Catholic. Mailing Add: 833 E Third St South Boston MA 02127

FLAHERTY, PETER F (D)
Mayor, Pittsburgh, Pa
b Pittsburgh, Pa, June 24, 25; s Pete Flaherty & Anne O'Toole F; m 1958 to Nancy Houlihan; c Shawn, Pete, Brian, Maggie & Greg. Educ: Notre Dame Univ, LLB, 51; Univ Pittsburgh, MPA, 67. Polit & Govt Pos: Asst dist Attorney, Allegheny Co, 57-64; City Councilman, Pittsburgh, 66-69; Mayor, Pittsburgh, 70- Bus & Prof Pos: Attorney, Pa Bar, 52- & Fla Bar, 66- Mil Serv: Entered as Pvt, Air Force, 42, released as Capt, 46 after serv in 20th Air Force, Guam, Pac, 45-46; Air Medal; Distinguished Unit Citation, Two Battle Stars. Mem: Am Bar & Pa Bar Asns; Pa League of Cities (pres, 72-73); Nat League of Cities (mem bd). Honors & Awards: Man of Year, Jr CofC, Pittsburgh, Pa. Relig: Catholic. Legal Res: 5033 Castleman St Pittsburgh PA 15232 Mailing Add: City-County Bldg Pittsburgh PA 15219

FLAHERTY, THOMAS EDWARD (D)
Pa State Rep
b Pittsburgh, Pa, June 18, 50; s John Steven Flaherty & Lucille Rodan F; single. Educ: Duquesne Univ, BA, 72. Polit & Govt Pos: Pa State Rep, 75- Mem: VFW; United Steelworkers & Teamsters; Retail Clerks Union; Hibernians. Relig: Catholic. Mailing Add: 380 Lehigh Ave Pittsburgh PA 15232

FLANAGAN, JAMES E (D)
Maine State Rep
Mailing Add: 77 Torrey St Portland ME 04103

FLANAGAN, JOHN JOSEPH (R)
NY State Assemblyman
b Bronx, NY, Sept 11, 36; s Peter Flanagan & Ann Higgins F; m 1959 to Barbara Jeanne Falk; c Eileen Ann, John J, Jr, Maureen Ann & Matthew Daniel. Educ: St Francis Col(Pa), BS, 58; St John's Univ (NY), JD, 64; Phi Kappa Theta. Polit & Govt Pos: NY State Assemblyman, 72- Bus & Prof Pos: Partner, Flanagan, Kelly, Ronan & Spollen, Greenlawn, NY, 65- Mem: Elks; Kiwanis; KofC. Honors & Awards: Serv Award, Kiwanis. Relig: Roman Catholic. Legal Res: 52 Dunlop Rd Huntington NY 11743 Mailing Add: 52 Broadway Greenlawn NY 11740

FLANAGAN, JOHN PATRICK (D)
Ind State Rep
b Indianapolis, Ind, Oct 5, 44; s John P Flanagan & Mary Hittle F; m 1966 to Ellen Jean Shimer; c Michael Timeothy, Brian Patrick & Kerry Colleen. Educ: Ind Univ, BS, 68. Polit & Govt Pos: Precinct committeeman, Indianapolis Dem Party, 68-; deleg, Ind State Conv, 72-74; deleg, Dem Nat Mid-Term Conf, 74; Ind State Rep, 75- Bus & Prof Pos: Mgt, Blue Cross & Blue Shield, 68- Mailing Add: 280 S Downey Indianapolis IN 46219

FLANAGAN, NATALIE SMITH (R)
NH State Rep
b Bradford, Mass, Aug 6, 13; d Forrest Van Zandt Smith & Blanche Robbins S; m 1943 to John Francis Flanagan. Educ: Oak Grove Jr Col, 28-29. Polit & Govt Pos: Mem, NH Rep State Rep, currently; NH State Rep, 75- Mem: Atkinson Garden Club; Child & Family Serv; NH Fedn Women's Rep Clubs. Relig: Protestant. Mailing Add: Maple Ave Atkinson NH 03811

FLANAGAN, RUTH WALLACE (D)
VChmn, Windsor Locks Dem Town Comt, Conn
b Windsor Locks, Conn, Dec 29, 16; d George M Wallace (deceased) & Sarah Fitzpatrick W (deceased); m 1938 to James Joseph Flanagan; c Maryellen (Mrs Robert A Andersen) & Faith (Mrs Edmund M Casarella). Educ: High Sch. Polit & Govt Pos: Conn State Rep, 59-67; mem & vchmn, Windsor Locks Dem Town Comt, currently; mem, Selectmens Adv Bd, Windsor Locks, 64-67; vchmn, Housing Comn of Windsor Locks. Mem: Jeffersonian Club; Windsor Locks Coun Cath Women; St Mary's Parish Club (vchmn coun). Relig: Roman Catholic. Mailing Add: 2 James St Windsor Locks CT 06096

FLANAGAN, SID (R)
Wash State Rep
b Bellingham, Wash, 1909; m to Vyvien F; c three. Educ: Univ Wash. Polit & Govt Pos: Wash State Rep, currently. Bus & Prof Pos: Farmer, cattleman. Mem: Elks; Moose. Mailing Add: Rte 1 Box 205 Quincy WA 98848

FLANDERS, JOHN THOMPSON (R)
b Concord, NH, May 12, 26; s Ralph Winthrop Flanders & Bessie Thompson F; m 1975 to Diane M Rule; c Susan Jean, John Thompson, II, Richard Smalldon & James Robert. Educ: Univ NH, BS, 49; Beta Kappa Chap of Kappa Sigma. Polit & Govt Pos: Munic Accounts Auditor, State Tax Comn, NH, 50-52, asst, 52-57, dir, Div of Accounts, 57-61; admin asst to Gov Wesley Powell, 61; Asst Hwy Comnr, 61-70; Comptroller, NH, 70-73; mem sch bd, Concord Union Sch Dist, 72-74; Assoc Hwy Comnr, NH, 73- Bus & Prof Pos: Trustee, Merrimack County Savings Bank, Concord, NH, 67-; trustee, Concord Hosp, 72- Mil Serv: Entered as Pvt, Air Force, 44, released as Aviation Cadet, 45. Mem: Am Asn State Hwy & Transportation Officials; Am Pub Works Asn; Am Road Builders Asn; Eureka Lodge 70 F&AM; Concord Kiwanis Club. Relig: Congregational. Legal Res: 119 Warren St Concord NH 03301 Mailing Add: J O Morton Bldg Concord NH 03301

FLANDERS, WILLIAM D (R)
Vt State Rep
Mailing Add: Prospect St Essex Junction VT 05452

FLANERY, WILLIAM S (D)
Colo State Rep
b Sioux Falls, SDak, July 3, 35; s William S Flanery & Carol Bagstad F; single. Educ: Univ Colo, Boulder, BS, 59, grad study, 68-69; Union Theol Sem, MDiv, 63; Tau Beta Pi; Sigma Pi Sigma. Polit & Govt Pos: Planner, Model Cities Prog, Santa Fe, NMex, 69-70, dir, 70-71; admin asst, Pikes Peak Area Coun Govts, Colorado Springs, Colo, 71-74; Colo State Rep, Dist 20, 75- Bus & Prof Pos: Test engr, North Am Aviation, Downey, Calif, 59; teaching asst, Univ Ariz, 59-60; asst pastor, United Methodist Church, Cincinnati, Ohio, 63-65; pastor, United Methodist Church, Denver, Colo, 65-68. Mem: Am Soc Pub Admin. Relig: United Methodist. Legal Res: 4211 Forest Hill Rd Apt 7 Colorado Springs CO 80907 Mailing Add: House of Rep State Capitol Denver CO 80203

FLANIGAN, PETER MAGNUS (R)
b New York, NY, June 21, 23; s Horace C Flanigan & Aimee Magnus F; m 1954 to Brigid Snow; c Brigid Snow, II, Sheila Magnus, Timothy Palen, Megan Adams & Robert White. Educ: Princeton Univ, BA, 47. Polit & Govt Pos: Spec foreign serv officer, Econ Coop Admin Mission, UK, 49-50; mem exec comt, Ninth Assembly Dist Club, NY, 55-59; chmn, New Yorkers for Nixon, 59; chmn, Vol Nixon-Lodge, 60; dep campaign mgr, Nixon for President, 68; asst to the President, 69-73, asst to President for Int Econ Affairs, 73-74; dir, Coun on Int Econ Policy, 73-74. Bus & Prof Pos: Vpres, Dillon, Read & Co, Inc, New York, 50-69. Mil Serv: Navy, 43-46, Lt(jg), serv as Carrier Pilot, Pac. Honors & Awards: Brotherhood Award, Nat Conf Christians & Jews, 63. Relig: Roman Catholic. Mailing Add: American Embassy Serrano 75 APO New York NY 09285

FLANIGAN, ROBERT M (R)
b Sept 25, 30; m 1954 to Joan; c Ned, Stan, Chris, Aimee & Kevin. Polit & Govt Pos: Chmn, Summit Co Rep Party, Colo, 65-69 & 73-75; chmn, Cong Dist Rep Party, 67-69; chmn, Colo Rep Party, 68-72; mem, Rep Nat Comt, 68-72. Bus & Prof Pos: Rancher. Relig: Roman Catholic. Mailing Add: Summit City Blue Ridge Rte Kremmling CO 80459

FLATH, DON EDGAR (R)
Chmn, Wayne Co Rep Cent Comt, Ohio
b Wadsworth, Ohio, Aug 28, 22; s Leonard Flath & Theresa Garbett F; m 1948 to Barbara Ann Timmerman; c Richard C, Ian Douglas & Penelope Ruth. Educ: Wittenberg Univ, AB,

47; William McKinley Law Sch, LLB, magna cum laude, 52; Dean's List for Scholarship; Phi Kappa Psi; Delta Theta Phi. Polit & Govt Pos: Solicitor, Dalton Village, Ohio, 58-; Rep precinct committeeman, 58-; vchmn exec comt & chmn, Wayne Co Rep Cent Comt, 62-; mem, State Bd Educ, 65. Bus & Prof Pos: Adjuster, Travelers Ins Co, 51-54; asst to pres, Erie Ins Exchange, 54-56; Attorney-at-law, 56- Mil Serv: Entered as Pvt, Air Force, 43, released as Aviation Cadet, 46, after serv in Med Dept, 2nd Air Force, US. Mem: Wayne Co Libr (trustee); Mason; Scottish Rite; Shrine; Rotary (past pres). Honors & Awards: Edward Hardie Roche Nat Award, Ins Knowledge. Relig: Lutheran. Mailing Add: 130 W Main St Dalton OH 44618

FLECK, CHARLES JAMES, JR (R)
Ill State Rep
b Evanston, Ill, May 1, 40; s Charles Joseph Fleck & Genevieve Kanause F; single. Educ: Northwestern Univ, BA, 62; Valparaiso Univ, JD, 67. Polit & Govt Pos: Asst Attorney Gen, Ill, 68-70; pres, 33rd Ward Rep Orgn, 70; Ill State Rep, 71-; vchmn, Ill Ment Health Comn, 72-; chmn, Spanish Speaking Peoples Study Comn, 72- Mem: Am Trial Lawyers Asn; Chicago & Ill Bar Asns; Union League Club; Ill Athletic Club. Mailing Add: 3415 N Seeley Chicago IL 60618

FLECK, LEON J (D)
Chmn, Dubois Co Dem Cent Comt, Ind
b Jasper, Ind, Jan 19, 34; s Albert J Fleck, Sr & Emily Hopf F; m 1959 to Elfrieda I Schwinghammer; c Noel John, Madonna Rose, Kevin Leon, Karen Marie, Denise Ann & Jon Albert. Educ: Evansville Univ, 2 years. Polit & Govt Pos: Treas, Dubois Co Young Dem, Ind, 59-61; pres, 61-63; pres, Dubois Co Elec Bd, 61-69; pres, Eighth Dist Young Dem, 63-65; chmn, Dubois Co Dem Cent Comt, 69-; asst to US Sen Birch Bayh, Ind, currently; mem, Jasper Housing Authority, 74- Mil Serv: Entered as Pvt, Army, released as Sgt, 56, after serv in 82nd Airborne Div; 2nd Lt, Army Res, 60. Mem: Jr CofC; Kiwanis; KofC (3 degree & 4 degree); CofC; Region E Jr CofC. Honors & Awards: Ind Outstanding Local Pres Jaycee's Award, 63; Distinguished Serv Award, Jr CofC, 65; Nat Found March of Dimes Serv Award, 68. Relig: Catholic. Mailing Add: RR 4 Box A 72 Jasper IN 47546

FLECKNER, ANN (D)
Mem, Dem Nat Comt, Ohio
Mailing Add: 96 S Remington Rd Columbus OH 43209

FLEETWOOD, THIRVIN DOW (D)
Mem, Calif Dem State Cent Comt
b Henryetta, Okla, Oct 4, 22; s Sanford Cal Fleetwood & Willie Mae Pendergrass F; m 1944 to Norma Lasters; c Sharron (Mrs Paul Noland), Karen (Mrs Robert Gilson) & Ronald Gene. Educ: St Louis Univ, 46; Long Beach City Col, Tech Dipl, 50; Harbor Jr Col, 65-66. Polit & Govt Pos: Planning comnr, Torrance City Hall, Calif, 54-62; mem, Los Angeles Co Dem Cent Comt, 56-66; mem, Inter City Hwy Comt, SBay, Los Angeles Co, 59-62; mem, Calif Dem State Cent Comt, 66-; spec asst to Calif State Assemblyman Le Townsend, 67th Assembly Dist, 68- Bus & Prof Pos: Utility worker, Southern Calif Gas Co, 48-; financial secy, Local 132, Utility Workers, AFL-CIO, 52-56, chief steward, 58-60, vpres, 60-61; area chmn southwestern div, 62-64. Mil Serv: Entered as A/S, Coast Guard, 42, released as BM 3/C, 45, after serv in Southwest Pac Theatre, 44-45; Am Defense Medal; Pac Theatre Medal; Good Conduct Medal; Bronze Star. Mem: Lions (pres, N Torrance Club, 71-72); Club 67, Gardena, Calif, Dem Party (chmn); 67th Assembly Dist Dem Coun (chmn). Honors & Awards: Resolution from Calif State Assembly. Relig: Baptist. Mailing Add: 3637 W 182 St Torrance CA 90504

FLEGEL, ALBERT GORDON (D)
Comnr, Douglas Co, Ore
b Portland, Ore, May 14, 06; s Austin Finck Flegel & Dora Dawley F; m 1939 to Margaret Louise Mahoney; c Alice Anne (Mrs Daniel G Schaefer). Educ: Willamette Univ, 24-25; Univ Ore, 25-27; Beta Theta Pi. Polit & Govt Pos: Mayor, Roseburg, Ore, 46-52; mem, Bur Land Mgt Adv Bd, 52-69; Ore State Rep, Douglas Co, 57-60; Ore State Sen, 61-69; comnr, Douglas Co, Ore, 69- Bus & Prof Pos: Dir, Ore Trucking Asn & Ore Draymen & Warehousemen's Asn, 57-69. Mil Serv: Entered as Pvt, Army, 43, released as S/Sgt, 45, after serv in 261st Field Artil Bn, 401st Field Artil Group, ETO; Rhine & ETO Ribbons. Mem: Am Legion; VFW; Mason; Shrine; Elks. Relig: Episcopal. Legal Res: 1376 SE Lane Ave Roseburg OR 97470 Mailing Add: PO Box 1633 Roseburg OR 97470

FLEISCHER, ALFRED J (R)
Finance Chmn, Mo Rep State Comt
b St Louis, Mo; s M I Fleischer; m to Eva Davidson; c Margaret (Mrs Herbert Kaufman), Alice (Mrs Norman Davis) & Alfred J, Jr. Educ: Washington Univ, BS; Omicron Delta Kappa; Zeta Beta Tau. Polit & Govt Pos: Mem sch bd, University City, Mo, 68; mem, Educ Comn of States, 73-; finance chmn, Mo Rep State Comt, 72- Bus & Prof Pos: Pres, Assoc Gen Contractors, St Louis, Mo, formerly. Mil Serv: Army, Corps Engrs. Honors & Awards: Construction Man of Year, 72 & President's Award of Year, Assoc Gen Contractors. Mailing Add: 3 Westwood Country Club St Louis MO 63131

FLEISCHLI, GUS (R)
Wyo State Rep
Mailing Add: 518 Dartmouth Lane Cheyenne WY 82001

FLEISHER, HILDA W (R)
NH State Rep
Mailing Add: 251 N Bay St Manchester NH 03104

FLEISHER, RISSELLE ROSENTHAL (D)
b Baltimore, Md, Dec 12, 34; d Jerome Rosenthal & Adele Salzman; m 1962 to Leon Fleisher, div; c Paula Beth & Julian Ross. Educ: Univ Pa, 53-54; Johns Hopkins Univ, BS, 61, MLA, 68; Univ Md Law Sch, JD, 75. Polit & Govt Pos: Secy, Mt Royal Dem Club, Baltimore, 61-63; admin asst, Md State Sen Julian R Lapides, 67-70; alt deleg, Dem Nat Conv, 68 & 72; corresponding secy, New Dem Coalition of Md, 68-71, mem-at-lg, Exec Bd, 71-75; campaign aide, Deleg, Leonard S Jacobson, Baltimore Co, 70; campaign aide, State Sen Royal Hart, Fifth Cong Dist, Md, 70; chmn, Progressive Action Lobby, Annapolis, 70-71; exec bd, Women's Polit Caucus, Baltimore City, 71-72; mem bd dirs, New Dem Club, Second Dist, Baltimore City, 72-74; mem polit ethics comt, Md Dem Party, 75. Publ: Race in Baltimore, Nov 71 & McGovern's hidden win, Apr 72, The New Democrat. Mem: Women's Law Ctr; Baltimore Area SANE (bd mem & newsletter ed, 71-); Am Civil Liberties Union; Am for Dem Action; Common Cause. Relig: Jewish. Mailing Add: 1723 Park Ave Baltimore MD 21217

FLEMING, CHARLES FRANK (D)
NDak State Rep
b Grafton, NDak, Oct 11, 45; s Charlie Frank Fleming & Nina Elizabeth Geiger F; m 1972 to Arliss Faye Halldorson. Educ: NDak State Univ, BS, 67; Sigma Nu. Polit & Govt Pos: Pres, Pembina Co Teen Dem, 62-63; regional dir, NDak Young Dem, 64-65; pres, NDak State Univ Young Dem Club, 65-66; vpres, Young Dem Club NDak, 66, pres, 66-67; NDak State Rep, 11th Dist, Pembina Co, 70- Bus & Prof Pos: Asst mgr bus off, Northwestern Bell Tel Co, Fargo, NDak, 69-70; farmer, Hamilton, NDak, 70- Mil Serv: Entered as 2nd Lt, Army, 67, released as 1st Lt, 69, after serv in 360th Signal Bn, Strategic Commun Command, ETO, 68-69; Commendation Medal for Meritorious Serv. Mem: Am Legion; Pembina Co Mus (trustee). Honors & Awards: Outstanding freshman mem NDak House Rep, 71. Relig: Presbyterian. Mailing Add: Hamilton ND 58238

FLEMING, GEORGE (D)
Wash State Sen
Mailing Add: 1100 Lake Washington Blvd S Seattle WA 98144

FLEMING, GEORGE GAINS (R)
b Jacksonville, Fla, Feb 5, 12; s Frank Fleming & Georgiana Hopkins F; m 1944 to Katherine Louise Biot; c LaVerne Estella. Educ: Bordentown Mil Acad; Life Ins Mgt Inst; Life Underwriters Training Coun. Polit & Govt Pos: Mem, Gov Bipartisan Coun, NJ; chmn, Pub Assistance Div, Bd Pub Welfare, DC; state Comnr, NJ Educ Facility Authority; treas, NJ Rep State Comt, formerly. Bus & Prof Pos: Assoc, Progressive Life Ins Co, 30 Years, regional vpres, 63-66, sr vpres, 66- Publ: Dollars Down the Drain. Mem: Life Ins Officers Mgt Asn; Washington, DC NAACP; Boy Scouts of Monmouth Co, NJ (bd dirs & exec comt); Urban League; Nat Conf of Christians & Jews, DC. Honors & Awards: Winner, Afro-Am Outstanding Citizen Award, Washington, DC, 54; United Givers Found Oscar Awards. Relig: Protestant. Mailing Add: 95 Bamm Hollow Rd Middletown NJ 07748

FLEMING, JAMES F, JR (D)
Mont State Rep
Mailing Add: Box 116 Pablo MT 59855

FLEMING, JAMES PRESTON (D)
Chmn, Polk Co Dem Exec Comt, Fla
b Opp, Ala, June 14, 44; s Preston Fleming & Loette Bedsole F; m 1972 to Beverley Wynn; c James Preston, Jr. Educ: St Leo Col, Fla, 63-64. Polit & Govt Pos: Legis aide to Fla House of Rep, 70-; mem, Polk Co Dem Exec Comt, Fla, 74-, chmn, 75- Bus & Prof Pos: Sports ed, Dade City Banner, Fla, 61-65; ed, Hawaiian Falcon, Hickam AFB, Hawaii, 67-68; bur chief, New Port Richey & Dade City, Tampa Tribune, Fla, 69-70. Mil Serv: Entered as Airman, Air Force, 65, released as S/Sgt, 69, after serv at Hickam AFB Command, Hawaii, Pac Air Forces, 66-69; Marksmanship; Good Conduct Medal. Relig: Baptist. Mailing Add: 4921 Marla Ave Lakeland FL 33803

FLEMING, JOHN GRANT (D)
Chmn, Woodbury Dem Town Comt, Conn
b North Tarrytown, NY, July 7, 14; s Robert Wilson Fleming & Elizabeth Grant F; m 1939 to Marlice J Buner; c Deryl Marlice. Educ: NY Univ, BS in elec eng, 36; Brooklyn Polytech Inst, grad work, 37; NY Univ & Trinity Col, Conn, 48; Tau Beta Pi; Iota Alpha. Polit & Govt Pos: Mem, Gov Fact Finding Comt in Educ, 48-50; chmn, Woodbury Dem Town Comt, Conn, 52-57 & 60-; pres, Small Town Dem, 53-57; mem, Conn Dem Party Rules Comt, 56, 70 & 71; Dem State Cent Committeeman for 32nd Dist, 70-; chmn, Fifth Cong Conv, 56, Sixth Cong Conv, 64 & 68, mem, Conn Dem Platform Comt, 72. Bus & Prof Pos: Develop engr, Cambridge Instrument Co, Ossining, NY, 36-45; mgr product planning, Bristol Co, Waterbury, 45-57; mgr new bus planning, IBM Corp, Conn, 57- Publ: Man Runs a Power Plant, Pa Elec Assocs Conf, 52; Human engineering in power plant instrumentation, Proc Instrument Soc Am, 53. Mem: Inst Elec & Electronics Engrs; Asn Comput Machinery; Lions; NY Univ Club; Wash Club. Honors & Awards: Outstanding Eng Achievement Citation, NY Univ, 55. Relig: United Church of Christ. Mailing Add: 17 Cowles Rd Woodbury CT 06798

FLEMING, NEIL WAYNE (D)
Eastern VPres, NDak Dem Non-Partisan League
b Hamilton, NDak, Apr 22, 43; s Charlie F Fleming & Nina Geiger F; m 1966 to Charlotte Conner; c James Conner, Robert Charles & Thomas Wayne. Educ: Univ NDak, PhB, 65, JD, 68; Delta Tau Delta; Phi Alpha Delta. Polit & Govt Pos: Pres, Univ NDak Young Dem, 63-65; vpres, NDak Young Dem, 65-66; secy-treas, 66-67 & 68; Dem precinct committeeman, Grand Forks, NDak, 66-68; deleg, Dem Nat Conv, 68; eastern vpres, NDak Dem Non-Partisan League, 72- Bus & Prof Pos: Asst states attorney, Pembina Co, NDak, 68-70; states attorney, 70-74. Mil Serv: Entered as 1st Lt, Army, 68, released as Capt, 70, after serv in Hq XXIV Corps, Repub Vietnam, 69-70; Vietnam Campaign Medal; Vietnam Serv Medal; Army Commendation Medal; Bronze Star Medal. Publ: House Bill 628, An analysis of North Dakota's anti corporation farming law, Univ NDak Law Rev, 1/68. Mem: NDak & Am Bar Asns; Am Legion. Honors & Awards: Numerous scholarships; selected as NDak Outstanding Young Dem, 67. Relig: Catholic. Mailing Add: Box 388 Cavalier ND 58220

FLEMING, RICHARD LEO (D)
Treas, Webster Co Dem Cent Comt, Iowa
b St Paul, Minn, July 22, 12; s Richard Leo Fleming & Delia Agnes Foley F; m 1965 to Corinne Marion Hastings; c Phyllis. Educ: SDak State Col, 1 year. Polit & Govt Pos: Chmn, Webster Co Dem Cent Comt, Iowa, 66-69; treas, 69-; Justice Peace, Ft Dodge, 71-; alt deleg, Dem Nat Conv, 68. Bus & Prof Pos: Various positions with Ft Dodge, Des Moines & Southern RR in Des Moines leading to terminal supt, Ft Dodge, 39-69; salesman, Lincoln Life & Casualty, Ft Dodge, 69-; salesman, Walt Brown Realty Co, 70- Mem: Ft Dodge, Iowa Realtors; Moose (fel degree); Elks; Brotherhood of Rwy & Airline Clerks; Am Legion Country Club (assoc mem). Relig: Catholic. Mailing Add: 1751 14th St Ft Dodge IA 50501

FLEMING, RICHARD THORPE (R)
b Melrose, Mass, Feb 7, 32; s Herbert Paul Fleming (deceased) & Sally Thorpe F; single. Educ: Dartmouth Col, AB, 53; Amos Tuck Sch Bus Admin, Dartmouth Col, MBA, 58. Polit & Govt Pos: Research dir, F Bradford Morse for Cong Comt, Mass, 60; research dir, Mass Rep State Comt, 61-64, admin asst to chmn, 62, exec secy, 63; schedules dir, Elliot L Richardson for Lt Gov Comt, Mass, 64; legis asst to Lt Gov, Commonwealth of Mass, 65-66;

assoc research dir, Rep Nat Comt, 66-67; exec dir, Rep Gov Asn, 67-69; dir of staff serv, Mass Dept of Health, 69- Bus & Prof Pos: Mkt trainee, Gen Elec Co, 58-59, sales rep, 59-61; sr admin analyst, ABT Assocs, Inc, 69. Mil Serv: Entered as Officer's Cand A/S, Navy, 53, released as Lt(jg), 57, after serv in USS Hale & USS Brister, Combat Info Ctr Officer's Sch, Atlantic Theatre, Naval Air Tech Training. Mem: US Naval Inst; Rep Club of Mass; Ripon Soc; Middlesex Club. Relig: Episcopal. Mailing Add: 1572 Massachusetts Ave Cambridge MA 02138

FLEMING, ROBERT D **(R)**
b Sharpsburg, Pa, Mar 8, 03; s Robert H Fleming & Daisy Doty F; m to Jean Varner; c Jean Frances. Educ: Univ of Pittsburgh, BS. Polit & Govt Pos: Pa State Rep, 38-50; Pa State Sen, 50-74; mem, Port Authority, Allegheny Co, 58-; mem, Pa Const Rev Comn, 59; deleg, Rep Nat Conv, 60 & 72, alt deleg, 68. Bus & Prof Pos: Ins, real estate broker. Mem: Kiwanis; Mason; Elks; Sportsmen's Club. Mailing Add: 405 Freeport Rd Pittsburgh PA 15215

FLEMING, ROBERT HENRY **(D)**
b Madison, Wis, Jan 30, 12; s Robert H Fleming & Mabel Scanlon F; m 1936 to Jean E Heitkamp; c Robert H, Jr & Frederick H. Educ: Univ Wis, BA, 34; Harvard Univ, 49; George Washington Univ, 72-73; Sigma Delta Chi; Nieman Fel, 49. Polit & Govt Pos: Dep press secy, Off of the President, 66-68; asst dir, US Info Agency, 68-69; info dir, House Select Comt on Crime, 69-70; admin asst, US Rep Abraham Kazen, Tex, 70- Bus & Prof Pos: Reporter, Capital Times, Madison, Wis, 31-43; reporter, Milwaukee Jour, 45-53; bur chief, Newsweek, Chicago, 53-57; correspondent, Am Broadcasting Co, Washington, DC, 57-60, bur chief, 60-66. Mil Serv: Entered as Pvt, Army, 43, released as Lt, 45, after serv in Infantry, Replacement & Schs Command. Relig: Presbyterian. Mailing Add: 2711 Jenifer St NW Washington DC 20015

FLEMINS, FRANCES G (FRANKYE) **(D)**
Chmn, Torrance Co Dem Orgn, NMex
b Moriarty, NMex, Aug 11, 26; d Earl Gordon Gilmer & Bodie Long Gilmer Gloss; m 1961 to Donald Leon Flemins; c Betty Kaye Wright Davis (Mrs Damon Kennard). Educ: Albuquerque High Sch, NMex, grad, 43. Polit & Govt Pos: Secy, Torrance Co Dem Orgn, NMex, 60-72, chmn, 72-; court clerk, Seventh Judicial Dist, Estanicia, 68- Bus & Prof Pos: Postal clerk, US Post Off, Moriarty, NMex, 48-66; asst city clerk, Moriarty, 67- Mem: Big Valley Rebekah (noble grand, Lodge 41, 72, secy & treas, 69-70, vgrand, 71); Torrance Co Exten Coun (held off from secy to chmn, 48-72). Relig: Methodist. Mailing Add: PO Box 303 Moriarty NM 87035

FLEMISTER, ELIZABETH SMARTT **(D)**
b Atlanta, Ga, Aug 20, 53; d Carl West Flemister, Jr & Ida Chapman Morris F; single. Educ: Southern State Col (Ark), 70-74; Army Col Jr Prog, summer 73; Col Activities Bd; co-chmn, Lect Comt. Polit & Govt Pos: Deleg & mem platform Comt, Ark Dem State Conv, 72; alt deleg, Dem Nat Conv, 72; vpres, Young Dem of Southern State Col (Ark), 72- Bus & Prof Pos: Sales clerk, Murphy's Jewelry, 70-71; student-secy, Southern State Col (Ark), 72, dissertation & resident asst, 72-73; personalized serv dept, Union Nat Bank, Little Rock, currently. Mem: Student Govt Asn (rep, 70-73, pres, 73-74). Honors & Awards: Nat Girl Scout Event, Girl Scouts, 69; one of top ten deleg, Ark Model UN, 72; chmn deleg, Midwest Model UN, 73; Ark Col Girl of the Year, 74. Relig: Episcopal. Mailing Add: 621 Cumberland Apt 3 Little Rock AR 72202

FLEMMING, ARTHUR SHERWOOD **(R)**
b Kingston, NY, June 12, 05; s Harry H Flemming & Harriet Sherwood F; m 1934 to Bernice Virginia Moler; c Elizabeth Anne (Mrs George Speese), Susan Harriet (Mrs John Parker), Harry Sherwood & twins, Arthur Henry & Thomas Madison. Educ: Ohio Wesleyan Univ, AB, 27; Am Univ, AM, 28; George Washington Univ, LLB, 33; Alpha Sigma Phi; Delta Sigma Rho; Omicron Delta Kappa. Hon Degrees: From 40 insts in the US. Polit & Govt Pos: Mem, US Civil Serv Comn, 39-48; chief labor supply, Labor Div, Off of Prod Mgt, 41-42; chmn, Adv Comt on Personnel Mgt, Atomic Energy Comn, 43-53; mem, Adv Coun, Retraining & Reemploy Admin, Dept Labor, 44-47; mem, First & Second Hoover Comns on Orgn Exec Br of Govt, 47-49 & 53-55; dir, Off of Defense Mobilization, 53-57; mem, Int Civil Serv Adv Bd, 50-64; Secy of Health, Educ & Welfare, 58-61; mem, Nat Adv Comt, Peace Corps, 61-68; chmn, White House Conf on Aging, 71; spec consult to President on Aging, 72; Comnr on Aging, US Dept Health, Educ & Welfare, 73-; chmn, Comn on Civil Rights, 75- Bus & Prof Pos: Instr govt & debate coach, Am Univ, 27-30, dir, Sch Pub Affairs, 34-39, exec officer, 38-39; ed staff, US Daily, 30-34; ed, Uncle Sam's Diary, weekly current events newspaper for high sch students, 32-35; pres, Ohio Wesleyan Univ, 48-53 & 57-58; vpres, Nat Coun Churches of Christ in Am, 50-54 & 64-66, pres, 66-69; pres, Univ Ore, 61-68; pres, Macalester Col, 68-71. Mem: Ore Coun Churches (pres, 64-66). Honors & Awards: Awarded traveling fel, Wash Br, Eng-Speaking Union, 28; Medal of Freedom, 57; Alexander Meiklejohn Acad Freedom Award, 62. Relig: Methodist. Legal Res: VA Mailing Add: Rm 3086 S Admin on Aging US Dept of Health Educ & Welfare Washington DC 20201

FLEMMING, HARRY S **(R)**
b Washington, DC, Sept 15, 40; s Arthur S Flemming & Bernice Moler F; div. Educ: Ohio State Univ; Am Univ; Phi Gamma Delta. Polit & Govt Pos: Vchmn, Tenth Dist Rep Comt, Va, 66-68; spec asst to the chmn, Rep Nat Comt, 68; co-chmn, Nixon for President, Va, 68; alt deleg, Rep Nat Conv, 68; city councilman, Alexandria, Va, 68-69; Spec Asst to the President, 69-70; mem bd dirs, Metrop Washington Urban Coalition, 70-; mem bd dirs, Atlantic Coun Young Polit Leaders, 70-; spec asst to campaign mgr, Comt for Reelec of the President, 71-72; pres, Am Coun Young Polit Leaders, 72-; comnr, US Adv Comn Int Educ & Cultural Affairs, currently. Bus & Prof Pos: Vpres, Madigan Electronic Corp, 66-68; secy-treas, J Newspapers, Inc, 68-69; pres, Northern Va Community, Inc, 68-; chmn bd, Weadon Printing Co, Inc, 71-; pres, Leeway Develop Co, Alexandria, 73-; pres, Inverness Capital Corp, 73- Legal Res: 1 Potomac Ct Alexandria VA 22314 Mailing Add: PO Box 1355 Alexandria VA 22313

FLETCHALL, LORAN CLYDE **(D)**
Committeeman, Third Cong Dist Dem Party, Iowa
b Duncombe, Iowa, Aug 4, 34; s Clyde Harvey Fletchall & Evelyn Rhodes F; m 1959 to Josephine Virginia Gauley; c Michael & Marcia. Educ: Iowa State Univ, BS Civil Eng, 56; Kans Univ, MA Pub Admin, 61; Arnold Air Soc; Sigma Pi. Polit & Govt Pos: Asst engr, Hamilton Co, Iowa, 56-57; admin asst, city mgr, Hutchinson, Kans, 60-61; chmn, Hamilton Co Dem Party, Iowa, 69-71; mem, Const Revision Comt, 70; chmn, Third Dist Eval & Coord Comt, 71; committeeman, Third Cong Dist Dem Party, Iowa, 71-; mem budget subcomt, Iowa State Dem Cent Comt, 73-; State Interim Comt Party Reform, 73-; State Canvass & Registr Comt, 73- Bus & Prof Pos: Farmer, self employed, 61- Mil Serv: Entered as 2nd Lt, Air Force, 57, released as 1st Lt, 59, after serv in Installations Squadron, Strategic Air Command, Capt, 67. Mailing Add: Rte 3 Webster City IA 50595

FLETCHER, ARTHUR ALLEN **(R)**
Asst Secy for Wage & Labor Standards, Dept of Labor
b Phoenix, Ariz, Dec 22, 24; s Andrew A Fletcher & Edna Miller F; m 1965 to Bernyce Ayesha Hasson; c Phyliss, Sylvia, Arthur, Jr, Paul, Phillip & Joan. Educ: Washburn Univ, BA, 50; Kans State Univ, 53-54; San Francisco State Col, 64-65. Hon Degrees: Doctorate, Malcolm X Col, City Col of Chicago, 69; LLD, Kent State Univ, 72; LHD, Wilberforce Univ, 72. Polit & Govt Pos: Vchmn, Kans Rep State Comt, 54-56; vchmn, Schawnee Young Rep, Calif, 56-57; chmn adv comt on civil rights, Calif Rep Assembly, 62-64; committeeman, Alameda Co Rep Cent Comt, 62-65; Rep cand, City Coun, Pasco, Wash, 67; Rep cand for Lt Gov, Wash, 68; city councilman, Pasco, 68-69; Asst Secy for Wage & Labor Standards, Dept of Labor, 69-; alt deleg, 26th Assembly, UN, 71. Bus & Prof Pos: Exec dir, United Negro Col Fund, 71-73. Mil Serv: Army, 43-45. Mem: Kans & Calif Teachers Asns; Northwest Asn of Personnel Off; Am Legion; NAACP. Honors & Awards: Nat Freedom Found Award, 68; Citation, Publ & Ed of Eng News Record, 69. Legal Res: 628 North Beech St Pasco WA 99301 Mailing Add: 5101 W Running Brook Rd Columbia MD 21044

FLETCHER, CHARLES KIMBALL **(R)**
b San Diego, Calif, Dec 15, 02; s Ed Fletcher & Mary Catherine Batchelder F; m 1926 to Jeannette Toberman; c Charles K, Jr, Peter T & Dale (Mrs Lingenfelder). Educ: Stanford Univ; Pembroke Col, Oxford Univ; Phi Delta Theta. Polit & Govt Pos: US Rep, Calif, 46-48; deleg, Rep Nat Conv, 68. Bus & Prof Pos: Chmn bd, Home Fed Savings & Loan, San Diego, Calif, 34-; chmn bd, Pioneer Fed Savings & Loan, Hawaii, 63- Mil Serv: Lt, Navy, 3 years. Relig: Congregational. Mailing Add: 2940 Ocean Front Del Mar CA 92014

FLETCHER, GEORGE A **(R)**
b Peotone, Ill, Nov 1, 09; s Allison Fletcher & Lula Pillem F; m 1935 to Ruth Johnson; c Roger L, George A, II & James D. Educ: Ore State Univ, BS, 33; Alpha Zeta; Delta Sigma Rho; Sigma Phi Epsilon. Polit & Govt Pos: Mem, Hartland Planning & Zoning Comn, Conn, 57-64, chmn, 57-61; mem, Hartland Bd Finance, 62-; chmn, Hartland Rep Town Comt, Conn, formerly. Bus & Prof Pos: Farm supt, Travelers Ins Co, Salem, Ore, 33-52, mgr farm div, Hartford, Conn, 52-66, second vpres, Mortgage Loan Dept, 66- Publ: Articles on farm credit in Am Banker, Mortgage Banker & Forest Farmer. Mem: Am Soc Farm Mgrs & Rural Appraisers. Relig: Protestant. Mailing Add: South Rd East Hartland CT 06027

FLETCHER, JAMES CHIPMAN
Adminr, NASA
b Millburn, NJ, June 5, 19; s Dr Harvey J Fletcher & Lorena Chipman F; m 1946 to Fay Lee; c Virginia Lee, James Stephen, Barbara Jo & Mary Susan (Mrs Bruce K Hammond). Educ: Columbia Univ, BA, 40; Calif Inst Technol, PhD, 48; Sigma Xi; Phi Kappa Phi. Hon Degrees: DSc, Univ Utah, 71. Polit & Govt Pos: Adminr, NASA, 71- Bus & Prof Pos: Dir, Hughes Aircraft Co, Los Angeles, Calif, 48-54; assoc dir, Ramo-Wooldridge Corp, 54-58; pres, Space Electronics Corp, El Monte, 58-61; pres, Space Gen Corp, 61-62; vpres systs, Aerojet-Gen Corp, 62-64; pres, Univ Utah, Salt Lake City, 64-71. Mem: Am Inst Aeronaut & Astronaut; fel Inst Elec & Electronics Engrs; Nat Acad Eng; Tau Beta Pi; Cosmos Club. Honors & Awards: First recipient, Distinguished Alumnus Award, Calif Inst Technol. Relig: Latter-day Saint. Legal Res: 7721 Falstaff Rd McLean VA 22101 Mailing Add: NASA 400 Maryland Ave SW Washington DC 20546

FLETCHER, MARY LYNN **(D)**
VPres, Tenn Young Dem
b Knoxville, Tenn, Oct 15, 46; d Robert James Fletcher & Mary Evelyn Wilson F; single. Educ: Univ Tenn, Knoxville, BS, 72, MA, 73; pres, Alpha Xi Delta; pres, Col Young Dem, 70-71; chmn, Student Health Comt. Polit & Govt Pos: ETenn press rels dir, Sen Albert Gore Campaign, 70; chmn, Debate on Nat Health Ins, Conf for Southeastern Students, 71; dist comt person, Tenn Young Dem, 71-72, vpres, 72-; deleg, Dem Nat Conv, 72; chmn, Knox Co Vol for McGovern, Tenn, 72. Publ: Debate on National Health Insurance, Dept Health, Educ & Welfare, 10/71; Effects of private health insurance on the physically handicapped, Senate Subcomt on Antitrust & Monopoly, 5/72. Mem: Student Am Med Asn; Psi Sigma Alpha; Am Civil Liberties Union; Vol Women's Roundtable. Relig: Episcopal. Mailing Add: PO Box 69 Lenoir City TN 37771

FLETCHER, THOMAS WILLIAM **(D)**
b Portland, Ore, Mar 1, 24; s Irving Archibald Fletcher & Florence Ada Cooper F; m 1945 to Margerie Frances Muller; c Thomas Franklin, Heidi Ann & Dean Thurston. Educ: Army Specialized Training Prog in Pre-Med, Stanford Univ, 43-45 & Univ Nebr, 45-46; Univ Calif, Berkeley, BA, 51. Polit & Govt Pos: Asst to city mgr, San Leandro, Calif, 51-52; city adminr, Davis, 52-55; asst to city mgr, San Diego, 55-61, city mgr, 61-66; dep asst secy, Housing Assistance Admin, Dept of Housing & Urban Develop, 67; dep mayor-comnr, Washington, DC, 67-70; city mgr, San Jose, Calif, 70-72; pres, Nat Training & Develop Serv, 72- Bus & Prof Pos: Pres, Foodmaker Franchise Corp, San Diego, Calif, 66-67. Mil Serv: Entered as Pvt, Army, 43, released as Pfc, 46, after serv in Army Specialized Training Prog, US Theatre. Publ: Innovation & Change: A City's Management on the Move, Inst for Local Self Govt; Organizing cities to cope with change, In: Annual Proc, Nat League of Cities, 66; Decision making in government, Eng Mgt. Mem: Nat Acad Pub Admin; Western Govt Research Asn; League of Calif Cities; Int City Mgrs Asn; Nat Munic League. Relig: Episcopal. Legal Res: 4740 Connecticut Ave NW Apt 407 Washington DC 20008 Mailing Add: 1140 Connecticut Ave NW Washington DC 20036

FLETCHER, VIRGIL T **(D)**
Ark State Sen
b Benton, Ark, Dec 1, 16; s John T Fletcher & Lula Ballard F; m 1941 to Eda S Kruse; c John Karl, William Ferral & Mark Edward. Polit & Govt Pos: Ark State Rep, 54-62; Ark State Sen, 62-, chmn, Legis Joint Audit, Ark State Senate & mem, Ark Legis Coun, currently. Bus & Prof Pos: Owner, Real Estate & Ins Bus. Mem: Lions; Mason (32 degree); Shrine. Relig: Baptist. Mailing Add: PO Box 604 Benton AR 72015

FLETCHER, VIRGINIA CAROL **(D)**
b Norton, Va, Nov 17, 44; d Ada Fugate F; single. Educ: J I Burton High Sch. Polit & Govt Pos: Exec secy, US Rep Dan Rostenkowski, Ill, 63- Relig: Methodist. Mailing Add: Apt 831 1900 S Eads Arlington VA 22202

FLETCHER, W FRED (D)
b Colonial Heights, Va, Aug 13, 28; s James Kilby Fletcher & Mary Estelle Wharton F; m 1954 to Catherine Elaine Wade; c Karen Elaine & Barbara Suzanne. Educ: Wash Bible Col, 52-55; Am Univ, BA, 60, MA, 64. Polit & Govt Pos: Admin asst, US Rep W M Abbitt, Va, 52-73; admin asst, US Rep Dan Daniel, Va, 73- Bus & Prof Pos: Reporter & assoc ed, The Progress-Index, 47-52. Honors & Awards: Distinguished Serv Award, Petersburg Jr CofC, 52; Jaycee Key Award, 52. Relig: Baptist. Mailing Add: 3701 Lyons Lane Alexandria VA 22302

FLETT, NANCY W (D)
Colo State Rep
b Wadena, Minn, Sept 27, 36; d William Wallace Wolf & Teresa L Smith W; m 1958 to Charles T Flett; c Michael Eric & Marguerite Ann. Educ: Univ Minn, Minneapolis, BBA, 58; Phi Delta. Polit & Govt Pos: State chairwoman, Minn Young Dem-Farmer-Labor Party, 59-60; Dem precinct committeewoman, vcapt, capt-at-lg, capt, Jefferson Co Dem Party, Colo, 60-72; Colo State Rep, Dist 27, 75- Mailing Add: 9105 W 73rd Pl Arvada CO 80005

FLINN, MONROE LAWRENCE (D)
Ill State Rep
b Batesville, Ark, Dec 17, 17; s Monroe Jesse Flinn & Rue Hanks F; m 1940 to Freda Florence Tullock; c Donald L, Carol (Mrs Samuel Millati) & Debra S (Mrs Ronald Lobsinger). Educ: High sch grad. Polit & Govt Pos: Supvr, St Clair Co, Ill, 61-; deleg, Dem Nat Conv, 68; Ill State Rep, 70- Bus & Prof Pos: Dir community affairs, Granite City Steel Co, Ill, 56-; chmn bd trustees, Cahokia Pub Water Dist, 67- Mem: Moose; Mason; Scottish Rite; Shrine. Relig: United Church of Christ. Mailing Add: 2746 Camp Jackson Rd Cahokia IL 62206

FLINTROP, RICHARD A (D)
Wis State Rep
Mailing Add: 1119 Cherry St Oshkosh WI 54901

FLIPPO, RONNIE G (D)
Ala State Sen
Mailing Add: 114 Lane Ln Florence AL 35630

FLOOD, DANIEL J (D)
US Rep, Pa
b Hazleton, Pa, Nov 26, 03; m 1949 to Catherine H Swank. Educ: Syracuse Univ, AB, MA; Harvard Law Sch; Dickinson Sch Law, LLB, 29. Hon Degrees: LLD, Dickinson Sch Law. Polit & Govt Pos: Secy, Dem Soc, Pa; counsel for Pa Liquor Control Bd, 35-39; dep attorney gen; exec asst to State Treas, 41-44; dir, Bur of Pub Assistance Disbursements, State Treas; US Rep, Pa, 44-46, 48-52 & 54-; deleg, Dem Nat Mid-Term Conf, 74. Bus & Prof Pos: Spec master RR Reorganization, US Circuit Court; bd trustees, Col Misericordia; bd dirs, Kingston Nat Bank; attorney-at-law, 30-; attorney, Home Owner's Loan Corp, 34-35. Mil Serv: Chmn, Marine Corps Vol Res Comt. Mem: Luzerne Co, Pa & Am Bar Asns; Wilkes-Barre CofC (pres); Wyo Valley Motor Club (bd dirs). Legal Res: Wilkes-Barre PA Mailing Add: The Congressional Hotel Washington DC 20003

FLORENCE, BUCK (D)
Tex State Rep
Mailing Add: FR 161 N Hughes Springs TX 75656

FLORES, ROSALE (D)
Mem, Dem Nat Comt, Guam
Mailing Add: PO Box 2797 Agana GU 96910

FLORIO, ANITA (D)
Mem, Dem Nat Comt, NY
Mailing Add: 2060 Tenbroeck Ave Bronx NY 10458

FLORIO, JAMES JOSEPH (D)
US Rep, NJ
b Brooklyn, NY, Aug 29, 37; s Vincent Joseph Florio & Lillian Hazel F; m 1960 to Maryanne Spaeth; c Christopher, Gregory & Catherine. Educ: Trenton State Col, BA, 62; Columbia Univ, 62-63; Rutgers Univ Law Sch, JD, 67; Vets Club. Polit & Govt Pos: Borough attorney, Woodlynne, Runnemede, Audubon Park, Somerdale & Oaklyn; solicitor, Runnemede Sewage Authority; NJ State Assemblyman, 69-, chmn, State, Fed & Interstate Rels Comt; attorney, Lindenwold & Pennsauken Bd Educ; US Rep, NJ, 75- Bus & Prof Pos: Attorney, NJ Bar Asn, 67- Mil Serv: Entered as Seaman, Navy, 55, released from active duty after serv in Korean Conflict; Lt Col, Naval Res, 58-; Korean Serv Medal; Good Conduct Medal. Mem: NJ & Camden Co Bar Asns; NJ League of Munic Attorneys; Sons of Italy; hon mem NJ Fraternal Order of Police. Honors & Awards: NJ Bell Tel Award; Woodrow Wilson Fel; Eagleton Fel; Trenton State Col Mem Award. Relig: Catholic. Mailing Add: 62 S 28th St Camden NJ 08103

FLORIO, MICHEL PETER (D)
b Fremont, Ohio, Feb 19, 52; s Pasquale Peter Florio & Bernadine Foreman F; single. Educ: Bowling Green State Univ, BA, 74; NY Univ Sch Law, 74-; Princeton Univ, 75-; Omicron Delta Kappa; Phi Eta Sigma; Pi Sigma Alpha; Resident adv, Rodgers Quadrangle. Polit & Govt Pos: Alt deleg, Dem Nat Conv, 72; mem, Wood Co Dem Exec Comt, Ohio, 73-74; mem exec bd, New Dem Coalition Ohio, 74. Mem: Am Civil Liberties Union; Wood Co Dem Club. Honors & Awards: Sophomore Man of the Year, Phi Eta Sigma, Bowling Green State Univ, 72, Harold Anderson Mem Scholar, 73; Root-Tilden Scholar, NY Univ Law Sch, 74- Relig: Humanist. Mailing Add: 2821 S State Rte 590 Elmore OH 43416

FLOURNOY, HOUSTON IRVINE (R)
Mem, Rep State Cent Comt Calif
b New York, NY, Oct 7, 29; s William Raymond Flournoy & Helen Horner F; m 1954 to Marjorie Elsie Westerkamp; c David Houston, Jean Douglas & Ann Horner. Educ: Cornell Univ AA, 50; Princeton Univ, MA, 52, PhD, 56; Pi Sigma Alpha; Lambda Chi Alpha. Polit & Govt Pos: Research asst, div law rev & legis info, NJ Legis, 54-55; legis asst to US Sen H Alexander Smith, NJ, 55-57; Calif State Assemblyman, 61-66, secy, Assembly Rep Caucus, 61-62; mem, Los Angeles Co Rep Cent Comt, 61-; mem, Rep State Cent Comt Calif, 61-; chmn, Arts & Sci & Platform & Prin Comt, 63; Calif State Controller, 66-74; deleg, Rep Nat Conv, 68 & 72; Rep nominee for Gov, Calif, 74. Bus & Prof Pos: Assoc prof govt, Pomona Col & Claremont Grad Sch, 57-67; prof polit sci, Univ Southern Calif, 75- Mil Serv: Entered as 2nd Lt, Air Force, 52, released as 1st Lt, 54, after serv in 474th Fighter Bomber Group, Korea, 53-54; Lt Col, Calif Air Nat Guard, currently; Korean Theater & Am Defense Ribbons; UN Serv Medal. Publ: Legislative Bodies in California, Dickinson Publ Co, 66; The role of the California Republican delegation, in Inside politics: the national conventions, 1960, ed by Paul Tillett, Oceana, 62. Mem: Western & Am Polit Sci Asns. Relig: Congregational. Legal Res: 4280 Offham Court Sacramento CA 95825 Mailing Add: Rm 1114 State Capitol PO Box 1019 Sacramento CA 95805

FLOURNOY, ROBERT LANE (R)
Committeeman, Rep Party Tex
b Lufkin, Tex, Mar 26, 41; s Morgan Mitchell Flournoy & Ruby Pitre F; m 1962 to Genie Louise Walton; c Lisa Lynn, Erin Ashley & Derek Christian. Educ: Southern Methodist Univ, 59-61; Univ Tex, BA, 64, Law Sch, JD, 67; Alpha Tau Omega; Student Body Pres & Student Sen, Southern Methodist Univ. Polit & Govt Pos: Area chmn, Nixon for President, 68; mem, Angelina Co Rep Exec Comt, Tex; dist ballot security chmn, Rep Party Tex, 72, committeeman, currently; Rep precinct chmn, currently. Bus & Prof Pos: Pvt law practice; city judge, Lufkin, Tex, city attorney, currently; pres, Rural Water Bd, 72-75; dir & incorporator, United Bus & Indust, currently. Mem: Rotary (bd dirs); Jr Bar Asn; Salvation Army (bd dirs); Univ Tex Exec Asn. Relig: Methodist. Legal Res: Rte 1 Box 378 Diboll TX 75901 Mailing Add: PO Box 190 Lufkin TX 75901

FLOWERS, WALTER WINKLER, JR (D)
US Rep, Ala
b Greenville, Ala, Apr 12, 33; s Walter Winkler Flowers, Sr & Ruth Swaim F; m to Margaret Pringle; c Vivian, Walter W, III & Victor. Educ: Univ Ala, AB, 55; Univ Ala, LLB, 57; Rotary fel, Univ London, Eng, 58; Phi Beta Kappa; Omicron Delta Kappa; Jasons Soc; Phi Delta Phi; Sigma Alpha Epsilon; pres, Student Govt Asn, Univ Ala. Polit & Govt Pos: Mem & chmn, Tuscaloosa City Civil Serv Bd, Ala, formerly; US Rep, Ala, 69-, mem judiciary comt, sci & technol comt, select comt on aging & comn revision of Fed Court Appellate Syst, US House Rep, currently. Mil Serv: Res officer, Mil Intel, Army, 55, released as Lt, 59. Mem: Am Bar Asn; YMCA; Tuscaloosa Co Red Cross & Tuberc Asn; Tuscaloosa Co Ment Health Asn; Rotary. Relig: Episcopal. Legal Res: Tuscaloosa AL 35401 Mailing Add: House Off Bldg Washington DC 20515

FLOYD, ELDRA MOORE, JR (D)
Committeeman, Darlington Co Dem Exec Comt, SC
b Robeson Co, NC, July 19, 20; s Eldra Moore Floyd & Sarah Augusta Blake F; m 1942 to Eugenia Chandler; c Michael Hinnant, Cindy Moore, Eldra M, III (Chip), Eugenia (Genie) & Ruth H. Educ: Univ SC, JD, 48; Wake Forest Univ, BA, 50. Polit & Govt Pos: Comnr, Darlington Co, SC, 61-64, mem bd educ, 68-; committeeman, Darlington Co Dem Exec Comt, 64-; deleg, Dem Nat Mid-Term Conf, 74. Mil Serv: Entered as A/S, Navy, 40, released as Lt Comdr, 45, after serv in Seventh Fleet, SW Pac, 44-45; Lt Comdr (Ret), Naval Res; Atlantic & Pac Serv Ribbons with Five stars. Mem: Am Bar Asn; SC Bar (exec committeeman, 73-); Mason; Scottish Rite; Shrine. Relig: Episcopal. Legal Res: 411 Kenwood St Hartsville SC 29550 Mailing Add: PO Drawer 909 Hartsville SC 29550

FLOYD, ERVIN RICHARD (R)
Exec Committeeman, Jasper Co Rep Party, SC
b Tillman, SC, Mar 29, 34; s Clarence Wilson Floyd (deceased) & Flossie Ivey F; m 1955 to Shirley Ann Jones; c Ervin R, Jr & Clarence Mitchell. Educ: Ridgeland High Sch. Polit & Govt Pos: Finance chmn, Goldwater for Pres Campaign, SC, 64; chmn, First Cong Dist Voter Registrn, SC Rep Party, 65; chmn, Jasper Co Rep Party, SC, formerly, exec committeeman, currently, cand, US House of Rep, 66; clerk of court, Jasper Co, 70- Bus & Prof Pos: Sales rep, Coastal Paper Co, 59- Mil Serv: BM-3, Navy, 57-59; Naval Res, 6 years. Mem: Ridgeland Jaycees; Civitan Club; Jasper Co CofC; Am Lodge 98, AFM. Honors & Awards: Organized the first Rep Party in the hist of Jasper Co, 65; received following awards from Jaycees; Spoke, Spark Plug, Speak-up Jaycee; selected Outstanding Young Man of the Year in Jasper Co, 64. Relig: Baptist. Mailing Add: PO Box 602 Ridgeland SC 29936

FLOYD, GLENN ELDON (D)
Okla State Sen
Mailing Add: State Capitol Oklahoma City OK 73105

FLOYD, HENRY F (D)
SC State Rep
Mailing Add: Box 978 Pickens SC 29671

FLOYD, LANUE (D)
SC State Sen
Mailing Add: Kingstree SC 29556

FLOYD, NOAH EUGENE (D)
Chmn, Mingo Co Dem Exec Comt, WVa
b Chattaroy, WVa, June 10, 17; s William Troy Floyd, Sr & Lillie Adair F; m 1937 to Thelma Farley; c Janith Sue (deceased), Patricia Jane (Mrs D E Staker) & Alana Jean (Mrs Thomas J Mearns). Educ: Glenville State Col, AB, 48; Marshall Univ, MA, 54. Polit & Govt Pos: WVa State Delg, 54-62; WVa State Sen, Sixth Dist, 56-70; chmn, Mingo Co Dem Exec Comt, 63- Bus & Prof Pos: Prin & asst supt schs, Mingo Co, WVa, 54-62; dist mgr & consult, Charles E Merrill Publ Co, 62- Mil Serv: Pvt, Army, 43. Mem: WVa & Ky Bookmens Asn; Mingo Co Prin Asn; Int Platform Comt; Moose. Relig: Baptist. Mailing Add: 210 W Oak Williamson WV 25661

FLOYD, RICHARD THOMAS (R)
Chmn, Torrance Co Rep Party, NMex
b Bell, NMex, Aug 15, 07; s Thomas Floyd, Jr & Lovica Young F; m 1927 to Mary Edith McClernon; m 1950 to Ethel Lorena Cummings; c Steward Frances, Richard Thomas, Charles Patrick, MD & Gretchen Ellen Floyd & stepsons, Perry Lee & Gene duMar White. Educ: NMex State Univ, BS in Agr, 31; Gamma Sigma. Polit & Govt Pos: Probate judge, Torrance Co, NMex, 69-73; chmn, Torrance Co Rep Party, 71- Bus & Prof Pos: Elem prin, Kiowa Sch, Colfax Co, NMex, 29-30; teacher, Estancia Pub Schs, 31-41; supvr, Farmers Home Admin, 41-42 & 46-49; agronomist, Base Engr Off, Sandia, 51-52; adminr, Willard & Estancia Pub Schs, 54-67. Mil Serv: Entered as 1st Lt, Army, 42, released as Capt, 46, after serv in 20th Armored Div, ETO; Maj, Army Res, 54-; Bronze Star; Combat Infantryman's Badge. Mem: Rotary; KofP (Golden Spur, 4-); Mid-Rio Grande Coun Govts; Hope Med Ctr (pres bd, 64-). Honors & Awards: Col Aide-de-Camp, Gov, NMex, 73. Relig: Protestant. Mailing Add: Box 271 Estancia NM 87016

FLOYD, SIDNEY THOMAS (D)
SC State Rep
b Horry Co, SC, Aug 25, 29; s William Cater Floyd & Ruth Smith F; m 1956 to Alice Anne Skinner; c Frances Mozelle, Patricia Ann, Anita Ruth & William Thomas. Educ: Univ SC, 47-50; Univ SC Law Sch, LLB, 56; Pi Kappa Phi; Alpha Delta Phi. Polit & Govt Pos: City judge, Conway, SC, 59-64; US Comnr, 64-67; SC State Rep, 69- Mil Serv: Pvt, Qm Corps, Army, ETO, 51-53. Mem: SC State & Horry Co Bar Asns; CofC; Jaycees. Relig: Baptist. Mailing Add: 1115 Third Ave Conway SC 29526

FLYNN, ANN DOLORES (D)
Committeewoman, NJ Rep State Comt
b Asbury Park, NJ, Oct 17, 12; d John De Sarno & Carmel Vacchiano D; m 1946 to John Doyle Flynn; c Angela T & Ellen E. Educ: Beans Bus Col, Asbury Park. Polit & Govt Pos: Committeewoman, Monmouth Co Rep Comt, NJ, 42-; vchmn, Monmouth Co Exec Comt, 59-; pres, Monmouth Co Fedn Rep Women, 62-64, chmn, Co Bd Elec, 63-; alt deleg, Rep Nat Conv, 64, deleg-at-lg, 68, mem credential comt, 68; pres, NJ Fedn Rep Women, 68-71; mem, Monmouth Co Finance Comt, 67-; Asst State Campaign Mgr Nixon, 68; committeewoman, NJ Rep State Comt, Monmouth Co, 69-; admin secy, Div Tax Appeals, State NJ, 71-; mem Presidential adv comt, Nat Fedn Rep Women; chmn, NJ State Cong Financial Comt, 72-; mem, Adv Comt to Reelect the President, 73; chmn, NJ Inaugural Ball, 73. Bus & Prof Pos: Mem publicity dept, City of Asbury Park, 41-42, from secy bur health to registr vital statist, 43-50; owner & operator, Flynn's Luncheonette, 45-55 & Flynn's Gift Shop, 50-70. Mem: PTA (treas, Mt Carmel, vpres, St Rose); Co Civil Serv Orgn (pres, Coun 9); Bus & Prof Women Shore Area; Princess Marie Jose Lodge Asbury Park; Women's Columbia League Monmouth Co. Honors & Awards: Award, Deborah Jewish Orgn, 65; Testimonial dinner given by citizens in recongnization to serv to charitable orgns, 68; First Prize, NJ State Fedn Rep Women, 70, Diamond Achievement Award, 71, Rep Women of the Year, 71. Relig: Catholic. Mailing Add: 133 Norwood Ave Deal NJ 07723

FLYNN, BERNARD D (D)
Mass State Rep
Mailing Add: State Capitol Boston MA 02133

FLYNN, BILL (D)
Fla State Rep
Mailing Add: 12900 Old Cutler Rd Miami FL 33156

FLYNN, DICK (R)
Ariz State Rep
Mailing Add: 2210 S Mill Ave Tempe AZ 85282

FLYNN, G ELMER (D)
Mont State Sen
b Missoula, Mont, Jan 2, 19; s John J Flynn & Mary Helterline F; m 1939 to Mary A Ahern; c Marifrances (Mrs Edward K Courtney) & Colleen Carol. Educ: Missoula Schs, 12 years. Polit & Govt Pos: Mont State Rep, 63-67; Mont State Sen, 67-72 & 75- Bus & Prof Pos: Mem, Hellgate Sch Bd, 10 years; dir, Hellgate Valley Irrigation Co, 17 years. Mem: Moose; Eagles; KofC. Relig: Catholic. Mailing Add: Rte 2 Flynn Lane Missoula MT 59801

FLYNN, GERALD THOMAS (D)
b Racine, Wis, Oct 7, 10; s John Joseph Flynn & Margaret Williams F; m 1938 to Mary Cecilia McAvoy; c Ellen, Dennis, Gerald, Jr & Agnes. Educ: Marquette Univ Law Sch, JD, 33; Delta Theta Phi. Polit & Govt Pos: Wis State Sen, 21st Dist, 50-54; US Rep, First Dist, Wis, 59-61. Bus & Prof Pos: Attorney-at-law, 33- Mem: Elks; Eagles. Relig: Catholic. Legal Res: 3065 Ruby Ave Racine WI 53403 Mailing Add: 310 Fifth St Racine WI 53402

FLYNN, GWENDOLYN KAY (DFL)
VChmn, Yellow Medicine Co Dem-Farmer-Labor Party, Minn
b Turtle Lake, NDak, June 11, 35; d Justin Oliver Simonson & Ingeborg Hauge S; m 1961 to Michael David Flynn; c Shawn & Terry. Educ: Valley City State Col, BS, 60; Mankato State Col, grad study, 70-71; Gamma Theta Upsilon; Atheneum Soc. Polit & Govt Pos: Secy, NDak Young Dem, 59-60; vchmn, Yellow Medicine Co Dem-Farmer-Labor Party, Minn, 70- Mil Serv: Entered as Pvt, Womens Army Corps, 54, released as Sgt, 56, after serv in Dent Corps. Mem: Granite Falls Educ Asn; Coun Exceptional Children; Am Asn Univ Women (membership chmn, 69-). Honors & Awards: Teacher of the Year, Granite Falls Pub Schs, 71. Relig: Lutheran. Mailing Add: 786 Seventh Ave Granite Falls MN 56241

FLYNN, JAMES P (D)
RI State Sen
Mailing Add: 155 Oakdale Rd North Kingstown RI 02852

FLYNN, JAMES T (D)
Wis State Sen
Mailing Add: 1432 S 86th St West Allis WI 53214

FLYNN, JOHN E (R)
NY State Sen
married; c four daughters. Educ: NY Univ; Columbia Univ. Polit & Govt Pos: Mayor, Yonkers, NY, 61-66; NY State Sen, 67- Bus & Prof Pos: Partner & vpres, Bleakley & Tobin, Inc, Oil Distributors; trustee, Yonkers Savings Bank, currently. Mem: Jr CofC (past pres); Catholic Youth Orgn; United Givers Fund. Honors & Awards: Distinguished Serv Award, NY State Jr CofC; B'nai B'rith Brotherhood Award, 64. Relig: Catholic. Mailing Add: 15 Huron Rd Yonkers NY 10710

FLYNN, JOSEPH P (D)
Conn State Sen
Mailing Add: 4 Finney St Exten Ansonia CT 06401

FLYNN, LEO H (D)
Conn State Rep
Mailing Add: 76 Providence St Taftville CT 06380

FLYNN, LUCY ANN (D)
State Committeewoman, Mass Young Dem
b Boston, Mass, July 27, 53; d John B Flynn & Roseanne Dawson F; single. Educ: Emmanuel Col, BA, 75. Polit & Govt Pos: Committeewoman, Framingham Dem Town Comt, 72-; pres, Framingham Young Dem, 72-75; state committeewoman, Mass Young Dem, 74-; staff mem, Cong Richard F Vander Veen, Mich, summer 74. Bus & Prof Pos: Staff, Gerald F O'Leary, Pres Boston City Coun, 72-75. Mem: Framingham & Mass Young Dem; Framingham Dem Town Comt. Honors & Awards: Top Ten Col Women, Glamour Mag, 75. Mailing Add: 2 Longview Rd Framingham MA 01701

FLYNN, PETER Y (D)
Mass State Rep
Mailing Add: State Capitol Boston MA 02133

FLYNN, RAYMOND L (D)
Mass State Rep
Mailing Add: State Capitol Boston MA 02133

FLYNN, WILLIAM EDWARD (D)
NJ State Assemblyman
b Perth Amboy, NJ, Feb 3, 38; s William Edward Flynn & Mary Cappaccione; m 1963 to Elaine Czech; c Erin, Colleen, Tara & Bonnie. Educ: Trenton State Col, BA, 60, deans list; Rutgers Univ Law Sch, JD, 63; Theta Nu Sigma. Polit & Govt Pos: Planning bd attorney, Sayreville, NJ, 68-69; councilman, Madison Twp, 72-74, mayor, 74-; NJ State Assemblyman, 74- Bus & Prof Pos: Attorney, Antonio & Flynn, Perth Amboy, NJ, 63- Mem: Am & NJ State Bar Asns; Elks Lodge 724 (Justice of Subordinate Forum, 70-); Madison Twp Jaycees; NJ Comprehensive Planning Agency (steering comt). Honors & Awards: Am Jurisprudence Prize for Excellence in civil rights & civil liberties, Rutgers Law Sch; Cert of Merit, Madison Twp. Relig: Roman Catholic. Legal Res: 30 Buttonwood Dr Old Bridge NJ 08857 Mailing Add: PO Box 515 Old Bridge NJ 08857

FLYNN, WILLIAM J, JR (D)
Mass State Rep
Mailing Add: State Capitol Boston MA 02133

FLYNT, JOHN J, JR (D)
US Rep, Ga
b Griffin, Ga, Nov 8, 14; s John J Flynt, Sr & Susan Banks F; m 1942 to Patricia Bradley; c Susan Banks, John James, III & Crisp Bradley. Educ: Univ Ga, AB, 36; George Washington Univ Law Sch, LLB, 40; Sigma Alpha Epsilon; Phi Delta Phi. Polit & Govt Pos: Asst US attorney, Northern Dist Ga, formerly; Ga State Rep, 47-48; solicitor gen, Griffin Judicial Circuit, 49-54; US Rep, Ga, 54- Bus & Prof Pos: Attorney-at-law, 41-45; grad, Command & Gen Staff Sch & Air Corps Adv Flying Sch, Brooks Field, Tex; Col, Army Res; Bronze Star Medal. Mem: Solicitors Gen Asn of Ga; VFW; Mason; Shrine; Am Legion. Relig: Methodist; chmn, Bd of Stewards. Legal Res: Griffin GA Mailing Add: 2110 Rayburn House Off Bldg Washington DC 20515

FLYTE, CHARLES E (D)
SDak State Sen
Mailing Add: Oral SD 57766

FOERSTER, THOMAS JOSEPH (D)
Co Comnr, Allegheny Co, Pa
b Pittsburgh, Pa, Apr 17, 28; s J Edward Foerster & Eleanor Heyl F; single. Educ: Slippery Rock State Col, 45-47; Univ Pittsburgh, BS, 50. Polit & Govt Pos: Admin asst, Pittsburgh City Coun, 55-57; staff mem, Civil Serv Comn, Pittsburgh, 57-59; Pa State Rep, 56-68, vchmn, State Govt Comt, Pa State House of Rep, 61-62, chmn, Fisheries Comt, 65-66 & Spec Clean Streams Comt, 66; admin asst, Pittsburgh, 59-; co comnr, Allegheny Co, 67-; deleg, Dem Nat Conv, 68. Mem: Water Pollution Control Asn of Pa; Moose; Eagles; Lions; Perry Athletic Asn. Honors & Awards: Varsity Football, Slippery Rock State Col. Relig: Catholic. Mailing Add: 3714 Ruggles St Pittsburgh PA 15214

FOGEL, HERBERT ALLAN (R)
b Philadelphia, Pa, Apr 20, 29; s Frank Fogel & Ethel Weinstein F; m 1957 to Alexandra Wolf; c Alexa & Marya Jennifer. Educ: Univ Pa, BA, 49, Sch Law, JD, 52; Harvard Univ Law Sch, 49-50; Zeta Beta Tau. Polit & Govt Pos: Pres, Germantown Chestnut Hill Young Rep Club, Pa, 53-55; dep attorney gen, Gen Counsel to Pa Harness Racing Comn, 63-70; alt deleg, Rep Nat Conv, 72; judge, US Dist Court, Eastern Dist of Pa, 73- Bus & Prof Pos: Law clerk, Judges of Common Pleas Court 2, Philadelphia Co, Pa, 52-54 & Pres Judge Vincent A Carroll, 54-55; vol on staff, Vol Defender, Philadelphia, 53; with Obermayer, Rebmann, Maxwell & Hippel Law Firm, Philadelphia, 54-73. Publ: Commonwealth vs Silver & Schwartz, its problems and ramifications, Pa Bar Asn Quart, 4/56; Developments in the field of CPA-attorney-client privilege, Pa CPA Spokesman, 6/65; Doctrine of uniformity of ratio of tax assessments; Deitch v Board of Property Assessments, Revisited, 4/70. Mem: Philadelphia Orchestra Pension Fund Found (trustee); Libr Co Philadelphia; Locust Club. Honors & Awards: Edwin L Keady Moot Court Award, Univ Pa Law Sch, 52. Legal Res: 6540 Wissahickon Ave Philadelphia PA 19119 Mailing Add: 2102 US Courthouse Philadelphia PA 19107

FOGEL, JERRY PAUL (R)
Chmn, Jackson Co Rep Comt, Mo
b Kansas City, Mo, June 11, 40; s Morris S Fogel & Helen Rowlette F; m 1963 to Julianna Arnold; c Brooke & John Paul. Educ: Univ Mo-Columbia, BS in Econ & Real Estate, 62; Sigma Chi. Polit & Govt Pos: Chmn, Jackson Co Rep Comt, Mo, 74- Bus & Prof Pos: Partner, B A Karbank & Co, Kansas City, Mo, 65- Mil Serv: Entered as 2nd Lt, Army, 62, released as Capt, 64, after serv in 7th Div, Korea, 62-63; Army Commendation Medal; Cert of Achievement. Mem: Soc Indust Realtors; Real Estate Bd of Kansas City (comt chmn); Mid Am Coun Boy Scouts (dir); Boys Clubs of Gtr Kansas City (dir). Relig: Christian Church; deacon, Country Club Christian Church. Legal Res: 826 W 59th Terr Kansas City MO 64113 Mailing Add: 922 Walnut Kansas City MO 64106

FOGLEMAN, JOHN ALBERT (D)
Assoc Justice, Ark Supreme Court
b Memphis, Tenn, Nov 5, 11; s John Franklin Fogleman & Julia McAdams F; m 1933 to Annis Adell Appleby; c John Albert, Jr, Annis Adell (Mrs Henry M Rector) & Mary Barton (Mrs Charles L Williams, Jr). Educ: Univ of Ark, 27-31; Univ of Memphis Law Sch, LLB, 34; Sigma Chi; Alpha Chi Sigma; Delta Theta Phi; Scabbard & Blade. Polit & Govt Pos: Dep Circuit Court Clerk, Crittenden Co, Ark, 33-34; chmn, Crittenden Co Dem Cent Comt, 37-44, secy, Bd Elec Comnrs, 37-44; dep prosecuting attorney, Crittenden Co, 46-57; chmn, Ark Judiciary Comn, 63-65; mem Ark Constitutional Rev Study Comn, 67; Assoc Justice, Ark Supreme Court, 67-; mem, Ark Criminal Code Revision Comn, 72-74. Bus & Prof Pos:

Pvt practice, Marion, Ark, 34-44; partner, Hale & Fogleman, West Memphis, Ark, 44-66. Mil Serv: Entered as Pvt, Army, 44, released as 1st Lt, 46, after serv in Judge Adv Gen Dept, Western Pac, 45-46. Mem: Fel Am Col Trial Lawyers; Rotary; Mason; Am Legion, VFW. Honors & Awards: Man of Year, West Memphis, Ark, 61. Relig: Methodist. Legal Res: Cherry St Marion AR 72364 Mailing Add: Justice Bldg State Capitol Little Rock AR 72201

FOGLIETTA, THOMAS M (R)
City Councilman, Philadelphia, Pa
b Philadelphia, Pa, Dec 3, 28; s Michael Foglietta & Rose F; single. Educ: St Joseph's Col, BS in polit sci, 49; Temple Univ Sch Law, LLB, 52; Univ Pa, Fels Inst State & Local Govt, 58 & 62. Hon Degrees: LHD, Philadelphia Col Podiatry, 69. Polit & Govt Pos: First vpres, Young Rep Club Philadelphia, Pa, 54-; city councilman, Philadelphia, 55-, minority floor leader, city coun, 59-, Rep cand for mayor, 75; deleg, Rep Nat Conv, 56, alt deleg, 68; mem, Mayor's Freedom Week Comt, 62; mem, Adv Comt to Supt Pub Schs on Integration & Inter-Group Activities. Bus & Prof Pos: Attorney-at-law, Philadelphia, Pa, 53- Mem: Justinian Soc Philadelphia; Loyal Legion; Temple Law Sch Alumni Asn; St Thomas Moore Soc; Sons of Italy. Relig: Roman Catholic. Legal Res: 708 Clymer St Philadelphia PA 19147 Mailing Add: 592 City Hall Philadelphia PA 19107

FOLEY, DANIEL J (D)
Mass State Sen
Mailing Add: State Capitol Boston MA 02133

FOLEY, EILEEN (D)
NH State Sen
b Portsmouth, NH, Feb 27, 18; d Charles A Dondero & Mary Ellen Carey D; m 1948 to John J Foley; c Mary Carey, John J & Barry C. Educ: Syracuse Univ, BA; Univ NH; Beta Sigma Phi. Polit & Govt Pos: Vchmn, State Dem Comt, NH; vchmn, Rockingham Co Dem Orgn, formerly; city clerk, Portsmouth, 5 years; secy, Portsmouth Dem City Comn, chmn, formerly; mem, Portsmouth Sch Bd, second term; NH State Sen, 65-, Minority Leader, NH State Senate, formerly; app to Gov Comn on Status of Women; mayor, Portsmouth, 68-; deleg, Dem Nat Conv, 72; mem adv coun, Dem Nat Comt, 73- Bus & Prof Pos: Bd dirs, Portsmouth Rehabilitation Ctr, 61-; spec serv work, Navy; vchmn, St Thomas Aquinas Regional High Sch; incorporator, NH Charitable Fund, 73- Mil Serv: Women's Army Corp, 44-45. Mem: Portsmouth Col Women's Club; KofC Auxiliary; St Thomas Aquinas Mother's Guild; Immaculate Conception Altar Soc; Nat Defense Adv Comt on Women in Serv. Honors & Awards: Jaycees Distinguished Serv Award, 68; Women Doer's Award in the Field of Politics, Nat Dem Women's Div; Rose of Honor Award, League of Women Voters. Relig: Catholic. Mailing Add: 39 Sunset Rd Portsmouth NH 03801

FOLEY, JOHN FIELD (R)
Mem, Santa Clara Co Rep Cent Comt, Calif
b Tulsa, Okla, Aug 6, 31; s Lyndon Lyman Foley & Margaret Cray F; m 1969 to Shirley L Brancato. Educ: Univ of Mich, 49-51; Stanford Univ, AB, 53, JD, 56; Chi Phi. Polit & Govt Pos: Mem, Santa Clara Co Rep Cent Comt, Calif, 62-, chmn, formerly. Mem: Santa Clara Co & Am Bar Asns; Barristers Club of Santa Clara Co; San Jose Stanford Club; Univ Club of San Jose. Relig: Episcopal. Mailing Add: 18441 Hernandez Lane Monte Sereno CA 95030

FOLEY, THOMAS STEPHEN (D)
US Rep, Wash
b Spokane, Wash, Mar 6, 29; s Ralph E Foley & Helen F; m 1968 to Heather Strachan. Educ: Univ Wash, BA, 51, LLB, 57. Polit & Govt Pos: Dep prosecuting attorney, Spokane Co, Wash, 58; asst attorney gen, Wash, 60; asst chief clerk, Spec Counsel, US Senate Comt on Interior & Insular Affairs, 61-63; US Rep, Wash, 64-, chmn agr comt, US House of Rep, currently; deleg, Dem Nat Conv, 68 & 72. Bus & Prof Pos: Mem, Law firm of Higgins & Foley, 57-; instr const law, Gonzaga Univ Law Sch. Legal Res: 1229 E 29th Spokane WA 99204 Mailing Add: 1201 Longworth House Office Bldg Washington DC 20515

FOLGER, STANLEY RALPH (R)
Committeeman, Tenn Rep State Exec Comt
b Wayne Co, Tenn, Nov 6, 20; s Paul K Folger & Myrtle Gower F; m 1946 to Jennie Belle Skelton. Polit & Govt Pos: Mem, Wayne Co Court, Tenn, 54-62; committeeman, Tenn Rep State Exec Comt, currently. Mil Serv: Entered as Seaman, Navy, 41, released as CPO, after serv in Amphibian Force, Europe & Pac Theatres, 42-46; numerous awards. Mem: Lions; Am Legion; CofC; VFW. Relig: Church of God. Mailing Add: Box 235 Waynesboro TN 38485

FOLKES, W D (D)
La State Rep
Mailing Add: PO Box 369 St Francisville LA 70775

FOLLETT, MURIEL (R)
b East Jamaica, Vt; m to Robert C Follett; c Robert, Jr & Jean (Mrs Harold Willard). Educ: Leland & Gray Sem, Townshend, Vt; Univ Vt. Polit & Govt Pos: Mem Weathersfield Town Comt, Vt; worked for State of Vt on War Hist Comn, 44; mem & secy, Springfield Town Planning Comn, 53-62; second vpres, Vt Fedn Rep Women, 67-69; mem, Vt Rep State Comt; secy, Windsor Co Rep Comt, Vt, 65-73; mem, State Bd Ment Health, 69-75. Bus & Prof Pos: Elem sch teacher; farmer, 42- Publ: Auth, New England year; A drop in the bucket; Springfield, the machine tool town, Vt Anthology. Mem: Hist Soc; Assoc Country Women of the World; Grange. Relig: Ascutney Union Church. Mailing Add: PO Box 26 Ascutney VT 05030

FOLMAR, JOEL MICHAEL (D)
Ala State Rep
b Pike Co, Ala, Jan 19, 36; s George Williamson Folmar (deceased) & Lois Graves F; m 1957 to Annie Dorman; c Mike, Jon & Matt. Educ: Troy State Univ, BS, 62; Sanford Univ Cumberland Sch Law, JD, 67; Sigma Delta Kappa; Theta Xi. Polit & Govt Pos: Judge Inferior Court, Pike Co, Ala, 69-74; Ala State Rep, 74- Bus & Prof Pos: Mem, State of Ala Youth Servs Bd, 75- Mil Serv: Entered as Pvt, Army, 53, released as Sgt, 56, after serv in Atomic Energy Comn, 55-56; Good Conduct Medal. Mem: Troy CofC; Troy Lodge 56, Mason; Scottish Rite (32 degree); Alcazar Shrine Temple; Troy Shrine Club. Honors & Awards: One of the Outstanding Young Men of Am, Bd Adv Editors, 71. Relig: Methodist. Mailing Add: PO Box 325 Troy AL 36081

FOLSOM, HENRY RICHARD (R)
b Wilmington, Del, July 19, 13; s Henry Richard Folsom & Elizabeth Jones F; m 1937 to Grace Broadway. Educ: Univ Del, BS in ME, 36. Polit & Govt Pos: City councilman, Newark,

Del, 62-67; councilman, New Castle Co Coun, 67-73, pres, 73-; alt deleg, Rep Nat Conv, 72. Relig: Methodist. Legal Res: 25 Amstel Ave Newark DE 19711 Mailing Add: Public Bldg Wilmington DE 19801

FOLTZ, JOHN C
Dep Under Secy Legis Affairs, Dept Agr
Mailing Add: Dept of Agriculture Washington DC 20250

FONDREN, ELMER LOUIS, JR (D)
Miss State Rep
b Colony Town, Miss, May 16, 32; s Elmer L Fondren & Mary Hull F; m 1963 to Bobbie Joyner; c Suzanne & Michael. Educ: Yale Univ, 50-52; Univ Miss, LLB, 55; Phi Alpha Delta; Sigma Alpha Epsilon. Polit & Govt Pos: City attorney, Moss Point, Miss, 66-68, mayor, 69-72; Miss State Rep, 72- Mil Serv: Entered as Pfc, Army, 55, released as Sgt, 57, after serv in 3rd Army Hq, Atlanta, Ga; Good Conduct Medal. Mem: Odd Fellow; VFW. Relig: Baptist. Mailing Add: 1321 Griffin St Moss Point MS 39563

FONG, HIRAM L, JR (R)
Hawaii State Rep
Mailing Add: House Sgt-at-Arms State Capitol Honolulu HI 96813

FONG, HIRAM LEONG (R)
US Sen, Hawaii
b Honolulu, Hawaii, Oct 1, 07; s Lum Fong & Chai-Ha Shee Lum F; m 1938 to Ellyn Lo; c Hiram Leong, Jr, Rodney, Merie Ellen & Marvin Allan. Educ: Univ Hawaii, BA, 30; Harvard Law Sch, LLB, 35; Phi Beta Kappa. Hon Degrees: LLD, Univ Hawaii, 53, Tufts Univ, 60, Lafayette Col, 60, Lynchburg Col, 70 & Lincoln Univ, 71; LHD, LI Univ, 68. Polit & Govt Pos: Clerk supply dept, Navy Shipyard, Pearl Harbor, 24-27; chief clerk, Suburban Water Syst, 30-32; dep attorney, City & Co of Honolulu, Hawaii, 35-38; Hawaii State Rep, 38-54, vspeaker, Hawaii House of Rep, 44-48, speaker, 48-54; vpres, Hawaii State Const Conv, 50; deleg, Rep Nat Conv, 52-72; favorite son nominee for President, 64 & 68; US Sen, Hawaii, 59-, mem, Rep Policy Comt; US Deleg, 150th Anniversary Celebration of Argentine Independence, 60; mem, US Deleg Can-US Interparliamentary Conv, 61 & 65; US Observer, Commonwealth Parliamentary Asn Meeting, Wellington, NZ, 65; Off US Deleg, 55th Interparliamentary Union Conv, Tehran, Iran, 66. Bus & Prof Pos: Operator, banana farm & fish pond; chmn bd, Hwy Construction Co, Ltd; Ocean View Cemetery, Ltd; founder & chmn bd, Finance Factors Grand Pac Life Ins, Finance Realty, Finance Home Builders, Finance Investment, Finance Factors Found & Market City; founder, Cosmopolitan Law Firm, Fong, Miho, Choy & Robinson, Honolulu, Hawaii. Mil Serv: Entered as 1st Lt, Army Air Corps, 42, released as Major, 44, after serv as Judge Adv, Seventh Fighter Command, Seventh Air Force; Col (Ret), Air Force Res. Mem: Am Legion; VFW; Kalihi Community Improv Club; Downtown Improv Club. Honors & Awards: Elector for Hall of Fame; Outstanding Nat Award, Nat Conf Christians & Jews, 60; Citation for Meritorious Serv, Nat Asn Retired Civil Employees, 63; Horatio Alger Award, 70; Golden Plate Award, Am Acad Achievement, 71. Relig: Congregational. Legal Res: 1102 Alewa Dr Honolulu HI 96817 Mailing Add: 9 Highboro Ct Bethesda MD 20034

FONNER, PAUL E (DOC) (R)
b Newman, Ill, Mar 28, 96; s Charles Fonner & Dora Gertrude Cameron F; m 1920 to Millie Holier; c Carmin (Mrs Robert W Huisinga). Educ: High Sch, Newman, Ill, 2 years. Polit & Govt Pos: Rep committeeman, Twp, Ill, 30-69; chmn, Piatt Co Rep Comt, formerly; mem, Ill Rep State Cent Comt, 46-52. Bus & Prof Pos: In mercantile bus, DeLand, Ill, 16-45; dir & vpres, DeLand State Bank, 45- Mil Serv: Sgt, Army, 17-19, with serv in Coast Artil, overseas, 18-19. Mem: Am Legion; AF&AM; Shrine; Farm Bur. Relig: Protestant. Mailing Add: DeLand IL 61839

FONSECA, MARY L (D)
Mass State Sen
Mailing Add: 400 David St Fall River MA 02720

FONSECA JIMENEZ, ANGEL (NEW PROGRESSIVE, PR)
Rep, PR House of Rep
Mailing Add: State Capitol San Juan PR 00901

FONTANA, A M (TONY) (D)
Fla State Rep
Mailing Add: 14601 Lake Candlewood Ct Miami Lakes FL 33014

FONTENOT, JAMES E (D)
La State Sen
b Kaplan, La, Oct 14, 44; s Tenes Fontenot & Maudry Marie Marceaux F; single. Educ: Univ Southwestern La, BA, 67; La State Univ, JD, 70. Polit & Govt Pos: La State Sen, Acadia & Vermilion Parishes, 72- Bus & Prof Pos: Attorney, 70- Mem: Phi Kappa Phi; Rotary Int. Mailing Add: PO Box 137 Abbeville LA 70510

FOOTE, ELLSWORTH BISHOP. (R)
Mem, North Branford Rep Town Comt, Conn
b North Branford, Conn, Jan 12, 98; s Frank Foote & Ellen Bishop F; m 1925 to Ruth Magill; c Robert M, Richard B, Roberta (Mrs Koontz) & Anne Marie (Mrs Floyd). Educ: Yale Univ Bus Col, 16; Georgetown Univ Law Sch, LLB, 23. Polit & Govt Pos: US Rep, Third Dist, Conn, 47-48; asst legis comnr, Conn Gen Assembly, 53; mem, North Branford Rep Town Comt, currently. Bus & Prof Pos: Practicing attorney before all Courts in Conn, 24-; practicing attorney before US Supreme Court, 29-; attorney, North Branford, 24-46 & 49-63; spec asst to the US Attorney Gen, Washington, DC, 25-26; chmn, Bd of Finance, North Branford, 34-46 & 49-63; judge of probate, North Branford, 38-46; attorney, New Haven Co, 42-46 & 49-60; acting judge of probate, New Haven, 44-45; secy & dir, Bank & Trust Co of North Branford, 61. Mil Serv: Capt, Gov Foot Guard, former mem of Troop A Cavalry, Conn Nat Guard. Mem: Conn & New Haven Co Bar Asns; New Haven Choral Club; Totoket Grange PofH; hon mem, Exchange Club. Relig: Congregational. Legal Res: Twin Lake Rd North Branford CT 06471 Mailing Add: 265 Church St New Haven CT 06501

FOOTE, MARGIE ELLEN (D)
Nev State Sen
b Reno, Nev, Dec 23, 29; d Harry Stephen Foote & Marie Alice Williams F; single. Educ: Cottey Jr Col, AA, 49; Univ Nev, BA, 51; Delta Delta Delta. Polit & Govt Pos: Alt deleg, Dem Nat Conv, 64; vchmn, Washoe Co Dem Cent Comt, Nev, 64-66; Nev State

Assemblyman, 67-74; Nev State Sen, 75- Bus & Prof Pos: Owner & operator, children's apparel shop, 55- Mem: PEO; Eastern Star; Daughters of the Nile. Relig: American Baptist. Mailing Add: 5585 Wedekind Rd Sparks NV 89431

FORAN, JOHN FRANCIS (D)
Calif State Assemblyman
b San Francisco, Calif, July 11, 30; s James Edward Foran & Kathleen Egan F; m 1958 to Costanza G Ilacqua; c David John, Mary Carmel & Thomas Edward. Educ: Univ San Francisco, BS, 56; Univ San Francisco Law Sch, LLB, 59. Polit & Govt Pos: Calif State Assemblyman, 63-, chmn, Transportation Comt, Calif State Assembly; mem, Calif State Transportation Bd; intergovt rels comt & task force comt on com & transportation, Coun of State Govts. Mil Serv: Entered as Pvt, Army, 51, released as Cpl, 54, after serv in 32nd Inf Regt, 7th Div, Korea; Purple Heart; Combat Infantrymans Badge; Korean Campaign Medal; UN Medal. Mem: Lawyers Club of San Francisco; DAV; VFW; Ancient Order Hibernians; Sons of Italy. Relig: Catholic. Mailing Add: 350 McAllister St San Francisco CA 94102

FORAN, WALTER E (R)
NJ State Assemblyman
Mailing Add: State House Trenton NJ 08625

FORBES, CLINTON D (R)
Ore State Rep
Mailing Add: 755 W Hills Way Salem OR 97304

FORBES, EUREKA BERNICE (R)
b Ft Worth, Tex, Oct 17, 04; d Ambrose Eugene Ryan & Gladys Bates R; m 1932 to Frederick Blatchford Forbes; c Doris Leone, David William & Kathleen (Mrs Russell F Coover). Educ: Univ Calif, Los Angeles, Teacher's Cert, 24; Univ Hawaii, BA, 33, MA, 38; grad work in govt & admin; former pres, Theta Chap, Delta Kappa Gamma; Alpha Phi; Prytannean Soc. Polit & Govt Pos: Mem, Adult Adv Coun, Dept of Pub Educ, 52-56; teacher, Honolulu Pub Schs, 51-59; deleg, Hawaii Territorial Rep Conv, 52-; mem, Territorial Comn on Children & Youth, 53-59; mem, City & Co Honolulu Charter comn, 55-58; secy, Oahu Co Rep Comt, 57-61; Hawaii State Rep, 59-66; alt deleg, Rep Nat Conv, 64 & 68, deleg, 72; corresponding secy, Hawaii State League of Rep Women, 66-67; Hawaii State Sen, 66-74. Bus & Prof Pos: Music instr, Univ Hawaii, 37-40; admin & owner, Pokii Kindergarten & Nursery Sch, 37-41; teacher, Kamehameha Schs, 42-43; counr & prof govt, polit sci & hist, Jackson Col, Honolulu, 62-65; semi-weekly Radio Commentary Prog, 62-66; part owner dress shop, My House, 64-; mem bd trustees, Hawaii Pac Col, Honolulu, 65-, pres, 65, secy & prof polit sci, 65-66. Publ: Life and work of Cochran Forbes, Univ Hawaii, 38. Mem: Acad Polit Sci; League of Women Voters; Honolulu Art Acad; Women's Symphony Soc; Nat League Am Pen Women (treas, Hawaii Br, 70). Honors & Awards: Outstanding Alumni Award, Univ Hawaii, 65; Kuokoa Award for Outstanding Merit, Young Am for Freedom, 69; Mother of the Year Award, Hawaii, 70. Relig: Protestant. Mailing Add: 3607 Woodlawn Dr Honolulu HI 96822

FORBES, JOHN ROBERT (D)
Fla State Rep
b Jacksonville, Fla, Feb 12, 40; s Robert Grady Forbes & Lola Haddock F; m 1963 to Elfreda M Heida; c Jean H, Lisa Lynn & John, Jr. Educ: Univ Fla, BS, 63, JD, 67; Pi Mu; Blue Key; Sigma Chi. Polit & Govt Pos: Fla State Rep, 70- Bus & Prof Pos: Attorney at law. Mil Serv: Entered as E-1, Army Nat Guard, 62, released as E-3, 62. Mem: Mason; Scottish Rite; Shrine; Am Legion; Lions. Relig: Baptist. Legal Res: 8040 Holiday Rd S Jacksonville FL 32216 Mailing Add: 320 E Adams St Jacksonville FL 32202

FORBES, JOSEPH (D)
Mich State Rep
Mailing Add: 24541 Harding Oak Park MI 48237

FORBIS, JAMES EDWIN (D)
Chmn, Wise Co Dem Party, Tex
b Ft Worth, Tex, Dec 4, 31; s Tommy Tillman Forbis & Sarah Jane McKinnis F; m 1962 to Althea Clara Nielsen; c Christopher & Nancy Jane & stepchildren, Thomas Nielsen Long & Jana (Mrs Martin Bennett Woodruff). Educ: Arlington State Col, 50-51; Univ Tex at Austin, BBA, 53, JD, 55; Phi Alpha Delta; Tejas Club. Polit & Govt Pos: Chmn, Wise Co Dem Party, Tex, 74- Bus & Prof Pos: Attorney, Sewell & Forbis, Attorneys-at-law, Decatur, Tex, 57- Mil Serv: Entered as Lt, Air Force, 55-57; served in Mountain Home AFB, Idaho. Mem: State Bar Tex; Decatur CofC; Decatur Independent Sch Dist (mem bd trustees, 67-); Decatur Hosp Authority (secy bd dirs, 67-74, pres, 74-); Wise Co Bar Asn (secy-treas, 57-). Honors & Awards: Citizen of the Year, Decatur CofC Poco Graphite Award, 72. Relig: Episcopal. Legal Res: Box 534 Decatur TX 76234 Mailing Add: 102 W Walnut Decatur TX 76234

FORD, BARBARA LOUISE (R)
Chmn, Merced Co Rep Cent Comt, Calif
b Vicksburg, Miss, Jan 28, 44; d Charles Edward Green & Margarette Newman G; m 1962 to Douglas Gary Ford; c Terrilynn, Pamala & Camile. Educ: High Sch, grad, 61; Merced Jr Col, 70-; Alpha Gamma Sigma. Polit & Govt Pos: Dept register, Merced Co, Calif, 71-; area chmn, Comt to Elect Carol O Harner to Cong, 72, campaign coordr, 74; mem, Rep State Cent Comt, currently; treas, Merced Co Rep Cent Comt, 74-75, chmn, 75-; mem, Calif Rep Assembly, currently. Bus & Prof Pos: Owner, DoBar Bake Shop, Atwater, Calif, 62- Mem: Merced Rep Women's Club; Atwater Women's Club; Merced Co Young Rep. Relig: Protestant. Mailing Add: 401 Drakeley Ave Atwater CA 95301

FORD, BECKY JANE (D)
b Fairfield, Iowa, Aug 9, 47; d Robert Edward Williams & Martha Lee Hoenshel W; m 1969 to Jon Ronald Ford. Educ: Okla State Univ, 65-66; Chapman Col World Campus Afloat, fall 67; Univ Okla, BS, 69, MA, 71; Univ Hawaii, summer 71; Alpha Gamma Delta. Polit & Govt Pos: Chmn, Garfield Co McGovern for President Comt, 72; mem, State Steering Comt, Okla McGovern for President Comt, 72; alt deleg, Dem Nat Conv, 72. Bus & Prof Pos: Free-lance photographer, Enid, Okla, 72-73; claims rep, Soc Security Admin, 73- Mem: Asn for Asian Studies; Nat Women's Polit Caucus; Enid Women's Polit Caucus; YWCA. Honors & Awards: Acad achievement scholar award, Chapman Col World Campus Afloat, 67; Hon Midn Capt, Navy Reserve Off Training Corps, 68; Outstanding geol student scholar award, Okla Univ Dept of Ecol, 68. Relig: Presbyterian. Mailing Add: 501 S Grant Enid OK 73701

FORD, CHARLES REED (R)
Minority Floor Leader, Okla House Rep
b Tulsa, Okla, Aug 2, 31; s Juell Reed Ford & Marzee Lane F; m 1951 to Patricia Ann Ojers; c Christopher Reed, Roger Howard, Karin Rebecca & Robyn Ann. Educ: Okla State Univ, 49-51; Alpha Sigma Eta. Polit & Govt Pos: Trustee, Tulsa Exposition & Fair Corp, 55-67; vchmn, Tulsa Metrop Area Planning Comn, 60-65; past officer, Tulsa Co Young Rep; Okla State Rep, Dist 80, 67-, minority floor leader, Okla House Rep, currently; deleg, Rep Nat Conv, 72. Bus & Prof Pos: Engr, aide, Corps of Engrs, 51-53; designer, Sunray-DX, 53-55; asst mkt engr, Tidewater Oil Co, 55-58; archit designer; pres, Gothic Investments, Inc. Mil Serv: Naval Res, 48-53. Mem: Jr CofC (Okla pres, 59-60, US vpres, 60-61 & Int vpres, 63). Honors & Awards: Selected Outstanding Young Man, Okla, 60. Relig: Protestant. Mailing Add: 4100 E 51st St Tulsa OK 74135

FORD, CLARENCE VERGE, JR (D)
Ark State Rep
b Wynne, Ark, Sept 24, 38; s Clarence Verge Ford, Sr & Lavonne Glenn F; m 1958 to Carol Ann DeBusk; c David Anthony, Douglas Alan & Claiborne Caldwell. Educ: Univ Ark, Little Rock, BA in Finance, 69, Grad Sch Educ & Sch Law, currently; Alpha Kappa Psi; Delta Theta Phi. Polit & Govt Pos: Ark State Rep, 75- Mil Serv: Entered as Cpl, Army, 61, released as Sgt, after serv in 49th Armored Div, 61-62; Maj, Army Res, 73. Mem: Am & Ark Bar Asns; F&AM; Ark Farm Bur; CofC. Relig: Methodist. Mailing Add: 18020 Hwy Ten Little Rock AR 72207

FORD, DALE HARRIS (D)
Miss State Sen
Mailing Add: PO Box 277 Taylorsville MS 39168

FORD, EMMITT H (D)
Tenn State Rep
Mailing Add: 580 W Mitchell Rd Memphis TN 38109

FORD, GERALD R (R)
President of the US
b Omaha, Nebr, July 14, 13; m to Elizabeth Bloomer; c Michael Gerald, John Gardner, Steven Meigs & Susan Elizabeth. Educ: Univ Mich, BA, 35; Yale Univ Law Sch, LLB, 41. Hon Degrees: LLD, Mich State Univ, Albion Col, Aquinas Col & Spring Arbor Col, 65; degrees, Western Mich Univ & Grand Valley State Col, 73. Polit & Govt Pos: US Rep, Mich, 48-73, Minority Leader, US House of Rep, 65-73, Vice President US, 73-74, President, 74-; permanent chmn, Rep Nat Conv, 68 & 72; ex officio mem, Rep Nat Comt, 72- Bus & Prof Pos: Attorney. Mil Serv: Navy, 42-46. Honors & Awards: Recipient Grand Rapids Jaycees Distinguished Serv Award, 47; US Jaycee Distinguished Serv Award, 49; Distinguished Cong Serv Award, Am Polit Sci Asn, 61; George Washington Award, Am Good Govt Soc, 66; Nat Football Found & Hall of Fame Award, 72. Legal Res: 1624 Sherman SE Grand Rapids MI 49502 Mailing Add: The White House 1600 Pennsylvania Ave Washington DC 20515

FORD, HAROLD EUGENE (D)
US Rep
b Memphis, Tenn, May 20, 45; s Newton Jackson Ford & Vera Davis F; m 1969 to Dorothy Jean Bowles; c Harold Eugene, Jr & Newton Jake. Educ: Tenn State Univ, BS & MS; Gupton Col, LFD & LED; Pi Omega Pi; Alpha Phi Alpha. Polit & Govt Pos: Tenn State Rep, 71-74, Majority Leader, Tenn House Rep, until 74; deleg, Dem Nat Conv, 72; cand, US Cong, 74; chmn, Black Tenn Polit Conv, formerly; mem bd dirs, Nat Legis Clearinghouse, currently; US Rep, 75- Bus & Prof Pos: Vpres & mgr, Ford & Sons Funeral Home, 69- Mem: CofC; Nat Funeral Dirs & Morticians Asn; Mason; 35th, 50th & 51st Civic Clubs. Honors & Awards: Tenn Mr Esquire; Man of Year, 71. Relig: Baptist. Legal Res: 219 Joubert Ave Memphis TN 38109 Mailing Add: US House of Rep Washington DC 20515

FORD, HOBART (R)
Tenn State Rep
Mailing Add: Box 487 Newport TN 37821

FORD, JEAN E (R)
Nev State Assemblyman
b Miami, Okla, Dec 28, 29; d Clarence N Young & Daisy Flook Y; m 1955 to Samuel M Ford; c Janet Lynn & Carla Marie. Educ: Okla Col Women, 47-49; Southern Methodist Univ, BA in sociol, 51. Polit & Govt Pos: Comnr, Nev State Park Adv Comn, 67-73; mem, Gov Policy Bd Rehabilitation Planning, 70-71; Nev State Assemblyman, 74- Mem: League of Women Voters (pres, Las Vegas Valley, 65-67, bd, State Nev, 67-69, pres, 69-71); Parents Group, Orr Jr High Sch (chmn, 70-71); Sierra Club; Nev Open Spaces Coun; Nev Wildlife Fedn (bd mem, 73-). Relig: Unitarian. Mailing Add: 3511 Pueblo Way Las Vegas NV 89109

FORD, JOE M (D)
Ala State Rep
Mailing Add: 117 Arcade St Gadsden AL 35903

FORD, JOE T (D)
Ark State Sen
b Conway, Ark, June 24, 37; s A W Ford & Ruby Watson F; m 1959 to Jo Ellen Wilbourn; c Alison & Scott. Educ: Ark State Univ; Univ Ark, BS, BA; Alpha Kappa Psi; Blue Key; Pi Kappa Alpha. Polit & Govt Pos: Ark State Sen, Fourth Dist, Pulaski Co, 67- Bus & Prof Pos: Vpres, Allied Tel Co, Little Rock, Ark, 59-, Allied Tel Co of Ark, Inc, Allied Tel Co of Okla, Inc, Allied Utilities Corp & Allied Tel Co of Mo, Inc, currently; Mil Serv: Capt & Unit Comdr, Ark Nat Guard, 62-67. Mem: Fifty for the Future. Relig: Baptist. Legal Res: 321 Colonial Ct Little Rock AR 72205 Mailing Add: PO Box 2177 Little Rock AR 72203

FORD, JOHN NEWTON (D)
Tenn State Sen
b Memphis, Tenn, May 3, 42; s Newton Jackson Ford & Vera Davis F; m to Maxine Foster; c Kemba Nyja & Sean. Educ: Tenn State Univ, BS, 64; Univ Chicago Law Sch, 66-68; Alpha Phi Alpha. Polit & Govt Pos: City councilman, Memphis, Tenn, 71-; Tenn State Sen, 74- Mem: NAACP; Nat League Cities; Nat Black Caucus Local Elected Officials; Regional Sickle Cell Anemia Coun (bd mem). Honors & Awards: Outstanding Citizens Award, Mallory Knights Charitable Orgn, 74; Outstanding Accomplishment, Civil Liberty League Inc, 75. Relig: Baptist. Legal Res: 1911 Todd Dr Memphis TN 38109 Mailing Add: 219 Joubert Ave Memphis TN 38109

FORD, KEITH JOHN (DFL)
Mem, Dem-Farmer-Labor Party State Cent Comt, Minn
b London, Eng, May 19, 44; s Robert Reuben Ford & Marjorie Wilson F; m 1967 to Elizabeth

Ann Warner. Educ: Univ Minn, 2 years. Polit & Govt Pos: Campaign asst, Anderson for Gov, Minn, 69-70; chmn, 36th Sen Dist Dem-Farmer-Labor Party, 70-72; asst press secy to Gov, Minn, 71; dep dir, Minn Off Consumer Serv, 71-; mem, Dem-Farmer-Labor Party State Cent Comt, Minn, 72- Mil Serv: Entered as Pvt, Army, 64, released as SP-5, 67, after serv in Hq Co, 1st Bn, 34th Inf, 24th Inf Div, Ger, 64-66; Army Commendation Medal; Nat Defense Medal; Army Occupation Medal. Mem: Am Legion; Citizens League; Minneapolis Asn for Retarded Children. Mailing Add: 4053 Lyndale Ave S Minneapolis MN 55409

FORD, SEABURY H (R)
Chmn, Portage Co Rep Exec Comt, Ohio
b Burton, Ohio, Sept 26, 02; s Carl Boughton Ford & Eluzabeth Hurd F; m 1941 to Helen Paar Sherrick. Educ: Western Reserve Univ, 6 years; Sigma Delta Chi; Alpha Delta Phi. Polit & Govt Pos: Precinct committeeman, Aurora Rep Party, Ohio, 36-58; councilman, Aurora, 41-44, law dir, 66-; committeeman, Ohio Rep State Cent Comt, 43-48; prosecuting attorney, Portage Co, 45-53; chmn, Portage Co Rep Exec Comt, 68-; mem, Bd Elec, Portage Co, currently. Bus & Prof Pos: Pres, Portage Co Title Co, currently; pres, First Portage Corp, currently; dir, First Nat Bank & Trust Co, Ravenna, currently. Mem: Portage Co Bar Asn; Fel Ohio State Bar; Am Judicature Soc; Elks; F&AM. Relig: Protestant. Legal Res: 12 W Garfield Rd Aurora OH 44202 Mailing Add: 200 W Main St Ravenna OH 44266

FORD, WENDELL H (D)
US Sen, Ky
b 1924; m to Jean Neel; c Steve & Shirley (Mrs Dexter). Educ: Univ Ky; Md Sch Ins. Polit & Govt Pos: Chmn, Ky Turnpike Authority; chmn, Ky State Property & Bldg Comn; mem, President's Coun Youth Fitness; chief asst to Gov, Ky, 59-61; Ky State Sen, 65-67; deleg, Dem Nat Conv, 68 & 72; chmn, Daviess Co Dem Comt, 69; Lt Gov, Ky, 68-71, Gov, 71-74; vchmn comt natural resources & environ mgt, Nat Gov Conf, formerly; mem, Nat Dem Adv Coun Elected Pub Off, formerly; chmn comt law & order, Southern Gov Conf, 71-75; chmn, Nat Dem Gov Conf, 71-75. Bus & Prof Pos: Ins. Mil Serv: Vet, World War II. Mem: Am Legion; Nat Coun Relig in Am Life; Owensboro Jaycees; State Jaycees. Honors & Awards: Outstanding Young Man, Owensboro, 54 & Ky, 55; Minerva Award for Merit, Univ Louisville. Relig: Baptist. Legal Res: 2017 Fieldcrest Dr Owensboro KY 43201 Mailing Add: US Senate Washington DC 20510

FORD, WILLIAM DAVID (D)
US Rep, Mich
b Detroit, Mich, Aug 6, 27; c William D, Jr, Margaret & John. Educ: Wayne Univ; Univ Denver, BS, LLB, JD; Phi Delta Phi. Hon Degrees: Doctorate, Westfield State Col, 70. Polit & Govt Pos: Precinct deleg, Dem Party & vchmn & chmn, Taylor Twp Dem Club, Mich, formerly; justice of the peace, Taylor Twp, 55-57, attorney, 57-64; city attorney, Melvindale, 57-59; mem exec bd, 16th Dist Dem Orgn, 59-64, corresponding secy, 60-62; deleg, Constitutional Conv, 61-62; Mich State Sen, 62-64; US Rep, Mich, 64-; deleg, Dem Nat Conv, 68. Bus & Prof Pos: Attorney-at-law, 52- Mil Serv: Navy, 44-46; Air Force Res, 50-58, discharged as 1st Lt (legal officer). Mem: Taylor Twp Businessmen's Asn; Mich & Downriver Bar Asns; Nat Inst of Munic Law Officers; Rotary. Honors & Awards: Distinguished Serv Award, Jr CofC, 62. Legal Res: Taylor MI 48180 Mailing Add: 2238 House Off Bldg Washington DC 20515

FORELL, ORA E (R)
Treas, Lyman Co SDak
b Chester, Nebr, Dec 28, 88; s Adolph Carl Forell & Catherine Daley F; m 1912 to Julia Woodward; c Caryl (Mrs David Rearick), Melba (Mrs Wayne Quinn), Kenneth, Ardith (Mrs William S Moore) & Darlene (Mrs Robert Iosty). Educ: Hubbell High Sch, grad. Polit & Govt Pos: Auditor, Lyman Co, SDak, 49-52, treas, 69-; bill clerk, SDak Senate, 55-61, sergeant at arms, 61-72; chmn, Lyman Co Rep Party, 62-68. Bus & Prof Pos: Farmer & rancher, 18-49; treas, Lower Brule Sch, 28-48; pres, Hill Tel Co, 30-34; owner, Ins agency, 56-68. Mem: Mason. Honors & Awards: Award, State Orgn Co Officers Orgn. Relig: Methodist. Mailing Add: Kennebec SD 57544

FORELLA, JUNE B (R)
Chmn, Portland Rep Town Comt, Conn
b New Rochelle, NY, Feb 13, 27; d Harold F Blanchard & Edith Garfield B; c Peter, John, Thomas & Ann. Educ: Bates Col, 2 years. Polit & Govt Pos: Mem, Conn Rep State Adv Comt on Educ & Training of Party Workers, 65-, vchmn, 69-; chmn, Portland Rep Town Comt, 70-; justice of peace, Portland, 73-; pub rep, Conn State Adv Coun for Unemployment Compensation, 73- Bus & Prof Pos: Lab technician, Dept Biol, Wesleyan Univ, 73- Mailing Add: 5 Highland Ave Portland CT 06480

FOREMAN, E DAVID, JR (R)
Chmn, Fairfax Co Rep Comt, Va
b Norfolk, Va, Mar 31, 37 s Edgar David Foreman & Genivive Collins F; m 1960 to Rosemary Constance Colachicco; c Sheryl Lynn & E David, III. Polit & Govt Pos: Goldwater vol, Orange Co Rep Comt, Va, 64; precinct chmn, Fairfax Co Rep Comt, 68, chmn polit educ, 69, chmn finance comt, for chmn race, 69 & deleg race, 69-70, vchmn, Comt, 71, chmn, 72-; deleg, Fairfax Co & Va Rep State Conv, 69-72; chmn, Salute Dinners for Gov & President, 70 & 71; chmn, all Fairfax Co races, 71; deleg, Rep Nat Conv, 72. Bus & Prof Pos: Design engr trainee, Melpar Inc, Falls Church, Va, 58-59; electronic engr, Jansky & Bailey, Alexandria, 60-61; govt rep, Atlantic Research Corp, 61-68; vpres, Jaycees, Springfield, 64; Washington off mgr, Ogden Corp, New York, 68-70; pres, Foreman & Assocs, 70-; bd dirs, Fairfax Co Opportunities Unlimited, 72. Relig: Protestant. Mailing Add: 6800 Seton Ct Springfield VA 22152

FOREMAN, ED (R)
b Portales, NMex, Dec 22, 33; s Edgar F Foreman, Sr & Lillian Childress F; m 1955 to Barbara Southard; c Kirk & Rebecca. Educ: NMex State Univ, BS in civil eng, 55; Sigma Tau. Polit & Govt Pos: US Rep, 16th Dist, Tex, 63-64, mem, House Armed Serv Comt; chmn, NMex Rep Cong Campaign Comt, formerly; US Rep, Second Dist, NMex, 69-72. Bus & Prof Pos: Pres, Valley Transit Mix, Foreman Oil, Inc & Atlas Land Co, 65- Mil Serv: Entered Corps Engrs, Navy, 56, released, 62, after 6 months active duty & 5 years, 6 months Res; Capt, Air Force Res, 66. Mem: Soc Civil Engrs; Am Petrol Inst; NMex Ready-Mix Concrete & Sand & Gravel Asn; Rotary; CofC. Honors & Awards: Outstanding Young Man of Odessa, 60; one of five Outstanding Young Men in Tex, 62; one of ten Outstanding Young Men of Am, US Jr CofC, 64. Relig: Methodist. Mailing Add: PO Drawer L Las Cruces NM 88001

FORGASH, MICHAEL A (R)
b Bay City, Mich, Mar 27, 42; s Ambrose F Forgash & Emily A Sajdak F; m 1970 to Judith L O'Tool; c Craig Allen & Mark Thomas. Educ: Holy Cross Sem, AB in philos; Cath Univ Am, AB in theol; Sigma Pi Delta, Cath Univ Am. Polit & Govt Pos: Legis asst, US Rep E A Cederberg, 68-69, admin asst, 70- Mem: Cong Secy Club; Bull Elephants; Capitol Hill Jaycees; Mich State Soc (pres, 70-71); Capitol Hill Club. Relig: Roman Catholic. Legal Res: 909 Columbus Ave Bay City MI 48706 Mailing Add: 2306 Rayburn House Off Bldg Washington DC 20515

FORKNER, RICHARD E (R)
b Langdon, NDak, May 29, 09; s Mark Isaac Forkner & Jeanette Ethel Braithwaite F; m 1935 to Joyce May Rasmusson; c Richard Earl, Mark Otto & Susan Claire. Educ: Dacotah Bus Col, Fargo, NDak, 30. Polit & Govt Pos: NDak State Sen, Tenth Dist, 62-72, mem transportation comt, NDak State Senate, 62-72, vchmn, 65-67, chmn, 69-72, vchmn, Indust, Bus & Labor Comt, 63, 65 & 67, chmn, Legis Coun Interim Transportation Comt, 69-72; mem transportation comt, Midwest Coun of State Govt, 69- Bus & Prof Pos: Co-owner & co-publ, Cavalier Co Rep, 35-69. Mil Serv: Platoon Sgt, Army, 26-29, serv in Citizens Mil Training Camp, Ft Snelling, Minneapolis, Minn, 26, 27 & 29 & Ft Lincoln, Bismarck, NDak, 28; Army Enlistees Res, 29-39. Mem: Langdon CofC (chmn transportation comt, 35-); Cavalier Co Fair Asn; Tri-State Harness Horse Asn; Scottish Rite (Knight Comdr of the Court of Honor, 50-); AF&AM. Honors & Awards: Awarded life membership, Langdon City Fire Dept, 52; Hon Chap Farmer Degree, local chap, Future Farmers of Am, 54; Good Citizen Award, Langdon KofC, 66; Outstanding Citizen Award, Langdon City Jaycees, 68. Relig: United Methodist; treas of the bd, Methodist Church, 38-39, mem, bd trustees, 46-47, mem, bd stewards, 40- Mailing Add: 1005 Sixth St Langdon ND 58249

FORNOS, WERNER H (D)
b Leipzig, Ger, Nov 5, 33; s Jaime Fornos & Lilly E Warmbold F; m 1961 to Margaret Lynn Sampson; c Werner H, Jr, Elizabeth Ann & Jaime Martin. Educ: Univ Md, BS in Govt & Polit, 65; Sigma Delta Chi. Polit & Govt Pos: Pub info officer, Ft George Meade, Md, 58-60; dir info, Army, Rocket & Guided Missile Agency, Huntsville, Ala, 60-62; pub affairs officer, President's Missile Sites Labor Comn, 62-63; chief of spec activities, Off of Secy of Labor, 63-65; dep asst manpower adminr, US Dept of Labor, 65-66; deleg, Md Const Conv, 68; Md State Deleg, until 72; deleg, Dem Nat Mid-Term Conf, 74. Bus & Prof Pos: Ed apprentice, Boston Post Publ Co, 50-54; Pan Am World Airways, currently. Mil Serv: Entered as Pvt, Army, 54, released as Sgt, 58, after serv in Ger; Army Commendation Medal; Nat Defense Serv Medal; Good Conduct Medal. Mem: Nat Press Club; Press Club of Anne Arundel Co; Univ Md Alumni Asn (bd dirs); Univ Col Chap, Univ Md Alumni (pres); Young Dem of Anne Arundel Co; Ruritan; Southern States Farm Coops (bd); Community Chest of Anne Arundel Co (bd). Honors & Awards: Gold Award, United Appeal of Baltimore for Serv, 58-60; chmn, 1966 Non-Partisan Voter Registrn Dr; Young Man of the Year for Md, Jaycees, 68. Relig: Methodist. Mailing Add: Hilltop Farm Davidsonville MD 21035

FORSTADT, JOSEPH LAWRENCE (R)
Asst Nat Legal Counsel, Young Rep Nat Fedn
b New York, NY, Feb 21, 40; s Hyman Forstadt & Ciele Polansky; m 1972 to Sally Louise Beckerman; c Jonathan & Andrew. Educ: City Col New York, AB, 61; NY Univ Sch Law, Judge Jacob Markowitz scholar, 63-64, LLB, 64; Aeropagus; vpres, Govt & Law Soc; pres, Student Bar Asn, 63-64. Polit & Govt Pos: Mem exec comt, Metrop Rep Club, New York, 63-; asst legal counsel, Citizens Comt on Reapportionment, 64; mem, New York Co Borough Pres Planning Bd Six, 64-74; spec legal counsel & law asst, Bd Justices, Supreme Court of NY, First Dept, 65-67; dep comnr, New York Dept Licenses, 67-68; acting comnr, New York Dept Licenses & Consumer Affairs, 68-69; asst adminr, New York Econ Develop Admin, 69-70; pres, New York Young Rep Club, 70-71; alt deleg, Rep Nat Conv, 72; vchmn, NY State Comt to Reelect President Nixon, 72; pres, NY State Asn of Young Rep Clubs, 72-74; mem exec comt, NY State Rep Comt, 72-74; asst nat legal counsel, Young Rep Nat Fedn, 75- Bus & Prof Pos: Assoc with Stroock, Stroock & Lavan, 70- Publ: Co-auth, Report of the Citizens Comt on Reapportionment, NY State Gov Off, 12/64. Mem: Coun NY Law Assocs; Am Judicature Soc; Fed Bar Coun; NY Ripon Soc (bd govs). Honors & Awards: Benjamin F Butler Mem Prize, NY Univ Sch Law, 64. Relig: Hebrew. Mailing Add: 205 E 63rd St New York NY 10021

FORSTER, DIANNA RUTH (R)
Pres, Rep Women's Fedn Mich
b Detroit, Mich, Apr 26, 37; d Louis Ray Batson & Frances Ruth Broome B; m to Charles Morton Forster; c Jamie. Educ: Hillsdale Col, 55-56; Wayne State Univ, BA, 60, MA, 64; Kappa Kappa Gamma. Polit & Govt Pos: Chmn Rep women's activities, Grand Traverse Co Rep Comt, Mich, 66-71, mem exec comt, 68-71; bd mem, Rep Women's Fedn Mich, 67-, pres, 74-; mem exec comt, Antrim Co Rep Comt, Mich, 72-; bd mem, Nat Fedn Rep Women, 74- Bus & Prof Pos: Pub sch teacher, Livonia, Mich, 60-62, Detroit, 63-64, Traverse City, 64-69; debate coach, Livonia, Mich Pub Schs, 60-62 & Traverse City, 67-69; real estate salesman, 69-70. Mem: Traverse Bay Area Rep Women; Traverse City Civic Players; Lawyer's Wives; Traverse Area Found (bd mem, 74-75). Relig: Protestant. Legal Res: 11268 S US 31 Elk Rapids Twp MI Mailing Add: Rte 2 Williamsburg MI 49690

FORSYTHE, EDWIN B (R)
US Rep, NJ
b Westtown, Pa, Jan 17, 16; s Albert H Forsythe & Emily Matlack F; m 1940 to Mary McKnight; c Susan. Educ: Westtown Sch grad, 33. Polit & Govt Pos: Secy, Bd of Adjust, Moorestown, NJ, 48-52, mem, Bd of Health, 53-62, Mayor, 57-62, chmn, Planning Bd, 62-63; committeeman, Moorestown Twp, 53-62; bd mem, NJ State League of Munic, 58-62; NJ State Sen, 64-70; deleg, Rep Nat Conv, 68; US Rep, NJ, 70- Bus & Prof Pos: Gen mgr, Locust Lane Farm Dairy, 33-60, secy-treas, 60-; pres, S Jersey Milk Dealers Asn, 58-61; pres, NJ Milk Indust Asn, 60-62. Mem: Burlington Co YMCA. Relig: Society of Friends. Legal Res: 265 W Second St Moorestown NJ 08057 Mailing Add: US House of Rep Washington DC 20515

FORSYTHE, JOHN EDWARD (R)
Chmn, Montgomery Co Rep Exec Comt, Miss
b Memphis, Tenn, Mar 19, 37; s Arthur Harold Forsythe & Elizabeth Ann Ingram F; m 1968 to Eleanor Elizabeth Salveson; c Elizabeth Ann. Educ: Univ Miss, 5 years; Kappa Alpha. Polit & Govt Pos: Chmn, Montgomery Co Rep Exec Comt, Miss, 64-; chmn, City of Winona Planning Comn, currently. Bus & Prof Pos: Exec vpres, Fidelity Underwriters, Inc, Winona, Miss, 70- Mil Serv: Sgt, Air Nat Guard Res, 60-69; Am Spirit of Honor Medal. Mem: Independent Miss Agents Asn; Winona Rotary Club. Relig: Methodist. Mailing Add: 604 Summit St Winona MS 38967

FORSYTHE, MARY MACCORNACK (R)
Minn State Rep
b Whitehall, Wis, May 23, 20; d Robert L MacCornack, Sr & Gladys Fry M; m 1942 to Robert Ames Forsythe; c Robert Ames, II, Mary Pauline (Mrs Johnson), Jean Louise, Ann Maureen & Joan Carol. Educ: St Olaf Col, BMus, 42. Polit & Govt Pos: Mem state bd dirs, Rep Workshop Minn, 65-70; precinct chairwoman, Edina Rep Party, 67-71; mem, Edina Rep Village Comt, 67-; mem, Minn Rep State Cent Comt, 71-; Minn State Rep, 73- Mem: Citizens League. Relig: Lutheran. Mailing Add: 4605 Edina Blvd Edina MN 55424

FORSYTHE, ROBERT AMES (R)
Mem, Minn State Rep Cent Comt
b Menomonie, Wis, Oct 22, 21; s Robert Alvin Forsythe & Elvera Hovlid F; m 1942 to Mary MacCornack; c Robert Ames, Mary Pauline, Jean Louise, Ann Maureen & Joan Carol. Educ: Univ Cambridge, Eng, 46-47; St Olaf Col, BA, 47; Univ Minn, LLB, 49; Blue Key; Pi Kappa Delta; Phi Delta Phi. Polit & Govt Pos: State chmn, Minn Rep Fedn Col Rep Clubs, 47-48; nat committeeman, Minn Young Rep League, 51-53; chief counsel, US Senate Small Bus Comt, 53-55; admin asst to US Sen Edward J Thye, 55-59; cong liaison officer, Dept Health, Educ & Welfare, 59, asst secy, 59-61; chmn, Minn State Rep Cent Comt, 61-65, mem, currently; comnr, President Kennedy's Voter Registrn & Participation Comn, 63; nat voter registration chmn, Rep Nat Comt, 64; mem, Minn State Rep Exec Comt; alt deleg, Rep Nat Conv, 68. Bus & Prof Pos: Mem law firm, Thompson, Hessian, Fletcher, McKasy, 73- Mil Serv: Entered as Pvt, Air Force, 42, released as Capt, 46, after serv in Ninth Air Defense Command, ETO; Bronze Star. Mem: Hennepin Co & Minn Bar Asns; Minneapolis CofC; Citizens League of Gtr Minneapolis; St Olaf Col Alumni Asn (bd dirs). Relig: Lutheran. Mailing Add: 4605 Edina Blvd Edina MN 55424

FORTAS, ABE (D)
b Memphis, Tenn, June 19, 10; s William Fortas & Ray Berson F; m 1935 to Carolyn Eugenia Agger. Educ: Southwestern Col, Memphis, AB, 30; Yale Univ, LLB, 33; Omicron Delta Kappa; Order of the Coif. Polit & Govt Pos: Dir div power, Dept Interior, 31-42, Under Secy of the Interior, 42-46; asst dir corporate reorgn study, Securities Exchange Comn, 34-37, consult, 37-38, asst dir pub utilities div, 38-39; gen counsel, Pub Works Admin, 39-40; acting gen counsel, Nat Power Policy Comn, 41; mem, President's Comn to Study Changes in Organic Law of Puerto Rico, 43; adv to US deleg, UN, San Francisco, 45; adv to US deleg, UN, London, 46; Assoc Justice, US Supreme Court, 65-69. Bus & Prof Pos: Asst prof, Yale Univ, 33-37, vis prof, 46-47; trustee, Carnegie Hall & Kennedy Ctr for Performing Arts; partner, Fortas & Koven. Mailing Add: 1054 31st St NW Washington DC 20007

FORTENBERRY, HAROLD C (D)
Miss State Rep
Mailing Add: Box 756 Monticello MS 39654

FORTES, ROBERT L (D)
Mass State Rep
Mailing Add: State Capitol Boston MA 02133

FORTIER, GUY JOSEPH
NH State Rep
b Livermore Falls, Maine, Jan 13, 93; s Patrick Fortier & Eva Lofrance F; wid; c Dr Milton & Dr Norman. Polit & Govt Pos: Mem, Berlin City Coun, NH, 46-56, mayor, 56-58; NH State Rep, currently. Bus & Prof Pos: Real estate, 20-60; owner, restaurant, 32-35; owner, Cocala Bottling Co, 35-38. Mem: Club Joliette; Milfield Sporting Club; AFL. Relig: Catholic. Mailing Add: 49 Mt Forist St Berlin NH 03570

FORTINBERRY, TOXEY THOMAS (R)
Chmn, Yalobusha Co Rep Party, Miss
b Tylertown, Miss, May 15, 08; s Thomas Calvin Fortinberry & Irene Magee F; m 1937 to Martha Reeves Costen; c Sylvia L, Merle I, Martha C, Toxie Ann, Sabrina S G, Marjorie E, Thomas A, Luther W & Mary Lu. Educ: Holmes Jr Col, 31; Southwest Col, 33; Univ Tenn, cert in real estate, 55; Reports Sch Auctioneering, 58; Nat Asn Real Estate Bds, GRI, 72; pres, Freshman Class; bus mgr, Weekly Paper; Glee Club. Polit & Govt Pos: Chmn, Yalobusha Co Rep Party, Miss, 63-; alt deleg, Rep Nat Conv, 72; state chmn, Realtors Polit Action Comt, currently. Bus & Prof Pos: Park dir, Memphis, Tenn, 33-34; salesman, Nat Life Ins Co, 34-40; real estate broker, builder & auctioneer, 41-73. Mem: Mason (32 degree); Rotary (sgt at arms, 72-, vpres northern region, currently); Northwest Miss Real Estate Bd; Miss State Real Estate Bd; Nat Real Estate Bd. Honors & Awards: Awarded Football Scholarship to Holmes Jr Col & Southwestern Col; Realtor of the Year, 72. Relig: Baptist; Deacon & Sunday Sch Teacher; music dir for Yalobusha Co Baptist Asn. Legal Res: 555 Air Ways Dr Water Valley MS 38965 Mailing Add: PO Box 70 Water Valley MS 38965

FORTSON BEN W, JR (D)
Secy of State, Ga
b Tignall, Ga, Dec 19, 04; s Benjamin Wynn Fortson & Lillie Wellborn F; m 1926 to Mary Cade, wid; c Ann McNeill (Mrs George Mandus). Educ: Starks Univ, 20-23; Ga Inst Technol, 23-24; hon mem, Alpha Kappa Psi, Pi Sigma Alpha. Hon Degrees: DDL, John Marshall Law Sch. Polit & Govt Pos: Ga State Sen, 50th Dist, 39-42; Ga State Rep, Wilkes Co, 42-44; Secy of State, Ga, 46- Bus & Prof Pos: Mem staff, Citizens Nat Bank, Wash, 24-26; mem staff, Atlanta & Lowry Nat Bank & Trust Co Ga & Wash Loan & Banking Co, Ga, 26-29. Mem: Nat Asn of Secy of State; Mason; Moose; Kiwanis; Gridiron Club. Honors & Awards: Smiling G Award, Goodwill Industs, 71; Outstanding Serv to Youth Award, Ga Dist, Key Club Int, 71; Outstanding Georgian Award, Exchange Clubs, 72; Good Citizenship Gold Medal, SAR, 73; Americanism Medal & Medal Honor, Ga Soc, DAR, 75. Relig: Methodist. Legal Res: Tignall Rd Washington GA Mailing Add: 214 State Capitol Atlanta GA 33034

FORTSON, ELEANOR ANN (D)
Wash State Rep
b Renton, Wash, Mar 7, 04; d Peter Dullahant & Emma Pothecary D; m 1925 to William Felton Fortson; c Barbara (Mrs Donald Wise), George Peter & Stephen Michael. Educ: Cent Wash Col Educ, elem teacher cert, 25; Western Wash Col Educ, BA in Educ, 56, MA in Educ, 60; Honor Roll, 2 years; pres sr class, Cent Wash Col Educ; Herodetean. Polit & Govt Pos: Pres, Camano Island Dem Party, Wash, 54-67, secy, 67-68; secy, Second Dist Dem Coun, 58-; chmn, Co Comt to Elect Dem Gubernatorial, Wash State Rep & US Rep Nominees, 66 & 68; committeewoman, Wash State Dem Party, 66-, chairperson rules comt, Cent Comt, currently; deleg, Dem Nat Conv, 68 & 72; deleg, many Co & State Dem Conv; Dem cand for Wash State Rep, 70, Wash State Rep, 72-; mem, Wash Oceanog Comn, currently. Bus & Prof Pos: Elem teacher, Kennydale, Wash Sch Dist, 22-24, Bur Indian Affairs, Shungnak, Noorvik, Alaska, 25-28, Deering, 31-36, Snohomis Co, 45-46 & Stanwood, Wash, 51-59, elem prin, 60- Mem: Delta Kappa Gamma Int Soc; Wash Educ Asn (legis state comt, deleg state conv, 3 terms); Camano Island Educ Asn (pres, 2 terms); Wash State Grange (state intern comt educ, master & lectr exec bd); Rebekah. Honors & Awards: Received Spec Serv Award in Educ from Stanwood Sch Dist & Snohomish Co Educ Asn, 70. Relig: Protestant. Mailing Add: 4008 SW Camano Dr Camano Island WA 98292

FORTUNE, EDMOND M (D)
Fla State Rep
b Milton, Fla, Nov 23, 32; s Perry Fortune & Nora Lowery F; m 1956 to Erma Ruth Stewart; c Felicia Ann, Edmond Dwayne & Terry Leon. Educ: Pensacola Jr Col, 2 years; Howard Col, BS, 58; Phi Delta Chi. Polit & Govt Pos: Fla State Rep, 66-, mem, State Appropriations Comt, Fla House Rep, 69-, vchmn, 71, chmn subcomt dealing with pub funding, 69-, chmn, Dem Policy Comt, 73-, mem & vchmn, Comt Health & Rehabilitation Serv, 73-, mem, Rules Comt, 73- Bus & Prof Pos: Mem bd of trustees, WFla Tuberc Asn, 66-; Fla State Welfare Bd, Dist One, 67- Mil Serv: Entered as Pvt, Army, released after serv in ETO. Mem: Fla, Am & Santa Rosa Pharmaceut Asns; Pace Civitan Club. Honors & Awards: Man of the Year Award, Fla Legis, 67. Relig: Baptist; mem & Sunday sch teacher, Imanuel Baptist Church. Mailing Add: Rte 2 Box 78A Chumuckla Hwy Pace FL 32570

FORTUNE, THOMAS R (D)
NY State Assemblyman
Mailing Add: 190 Ralph Ave Brooklyn NY 11233

FORWARD, DAVID ROSS (R)
Chmn, Rep State Cent Comt, Md
b Geneva, NY, Aug 23, 34; s Robert T Forward & Mildred Lull F; m 1956 to Gail Henderson; c Diane Katherine & David Sydney. Educ: Univ Md, College Park, BS, 56. Polit & Govt Pos: Vchmn, Young Rep Nat Fedn, Md, 71; chmn, Gore for Gov Comt, 74; chmn, Rep State Cent Comt, Md, 74-; mem, Rep Nat Comt, 74- Bus & Prof Pos: Acct exec, Merrill Lynch, Pierce Fenner & Smith, Baltimore, Md, 63-67; mgr, E F Hutton & Co Inc, Washington, DC, 68-71, asst vpres, 71-74, vpres, 74- Mil Serv: Entered as 2nd Lt, Air Force, 57, released as Capt, 62, after serv in 56th Fighter Wing, Air Defense Command, 59-62. Mem: Charles Edison Mem Youth Fund (dir); Metrop Washington Bd Trade; Conn Ave Asn. Relig: Protestant. Mailing Add: 12301 Overpond Way Potomac MD 20854

FOSHEE, E C (D)
Ala State Sen
Mailing Add: PO Drawer J Red Level AL 36474

FOSHEE, KATHERINE ALMIRA (R)
b Garber, Okla, Nov 24, 26; d Richard Oril Hill & Myrtle Jane Ernst H; m 1963 to Roy Edmond Foshee; c Richard Allen Hughes; three grandchildren. Educ: Hughes Beauty Acad, Tulsa, Okla, 58. Polit & Govt Pos: Precinct chmn, Allen Precinct, Creek Co Rep Party, Okla, 57-65; precinct elec judge, 64-; vchmn, Creek Co Rep Party, 67-68, chmn, formerly. Bus & Prof Pos: Ticket cashier, Criterion Theatre, Sapulpa, 45-46; waitress, Liberty Cafe, 46-47, Loraine Hotel Coffee Shop, 47-49 & Western Chicken House, 49-53; waitress & cafe owner, Park Inn Cafe, 54; glass tester, Liberty Glass Lab, 55-58; Beauty shop owner & operator, 59- Mem: Am Legion Auxiliary; Nat Fedn Rep Women; Dorcas Kelly Chap Rep Women's Club Creek Co. Honors & Awards: Rep Women of the Year, Dorcas Kelly Chap Rep Women's Club Creek Co. Relig: Protestant. Mailing Add: Rte 3 Box 83 Sapulpa OK 74066

FOSHEE, PAUL (D)
La State Sen
Mailing Add: PO Box 2147 Natchitoches LA 71457

FOSS, JOSEPH JACOB (R)
b Sioux Falls, SDak, Apr 17, 15; s Frank Foss (deceased) & Mary F (deceased); m to Donna Wild Hall; c Mrs Ward Johnson, Harry Dean Hall, Mrs Robert King, Mrs John Finke & Frank. Educ: Sioux Falls Col; Augustana Col; Univ SDak, BS, 40; Sigma Alpha Epsilon. Polit & Govt Pos: SDak State Rep, 48-50 & 51-53; Gov, SDak, 54-58. Bus & Prof Pos: Pres, Joe Foss, Inc; dir, Raven Indust; comnr, Am Football League, 60-66; dir pub affairs, KLM Royal Dutch Airlines, currently. Mil Serv: Maj, Marine Corps, World War II; Col, Air Force, Korea; Distinguished Flying Cross; Cong Medal of Honor; Brig Gen & Chief of Staff, SDak Air National Guard, currently. Mem: Air Force Asn; Air Force Acad (bd dirs); Nat Soc Crippled Children & Adults (bd trustees); Outdoor Writer's Asn; Am Legion. Relig: Methodist. Mailing Add: PO Box 566 Scottsdale AZ 85252

FOSTER, ALFRED CARVILLE, JR (R)
Pa State Rep
b Parkton, Md, Oct 21, 32; s Alfred Carville Foster, Sr & Dorothy Jane Early F; m 1960 to Ilene Frances Miller. Educ: Sparks High Sch, Sparks, Md, grad, 49. Polit & Govt Pos: Mem coun, Shrewsbury Borough, Pa, 62-68; Pa State Rep, 73- Bus & Prof Pos: Farmer, Shrewsbury, Pa, 49-67; supvr, Bur of Liquid Fuels Tax, Harrisburg, 67-71; ins salesman, Equitable Life Assurance Soc, 71-72. Mil Serv: Entered as Seaman Recruit, Navy, 55, released as Seaman, 57, after serv in Comtransphibron IV aboard USS Olmsted, 56-57. Mem: Lions; Red Lion Grange. Relig: United Methodist. Legal Res: RD 2 Seven Valleys PA 17360 Mailing Add: Capitol Bldg Harrisburg PA 17120

FOSTER, BEN (R)
Kans State Rep
b Hutchinson, Kans, Mar 31, 26; s True E Foster & Leta Brady F; m 1955 to Lucinda Stevens. Educ: Kans Univ, AB, 48, LLB, 51; Phi Delta Phi; Kappa Sigma. Polit & Govt Pos: Judge, Court of Common Pleas, 59; Kans State Rep, 65-69, 75-; munic judge, Wichita, 67-69; Kans State Sen, 69-72. Mil Serv: Cadet, Navy, 44-46; entered as 2nd Lt, Air Force, 51, released as 1st Lt, 52, after serv in Thule, Greenland; Lt Col, Air Force Res, 52-65; Am Theater & Korean Serv Ribbons; Victory Medal. Mem: Wichita & Kans Bar Asns; Am Legion. Relig: Episcopal. Legal Res: 600 Longford Lane Wichita KS 67206 Mailing Add: 420 Olive W Garvey Bldg Wichita KS 67202

FOSTER, DANNY O'NEIL (D)
b Hawkinsville, Ga, Sept 17, 51; s Dan Foster & Minnie Johnson F; single. Educ: Ft Valley State Col, Ga, BS in Soc Sci, 73; Soc Sci Club. Polit & Govt Pos: Alt deleg, Dem Nat Conv, 72; mem, Planning & Zoning Comn, Hawkinsville, Ga, 73- Bus & Prof Pos: Salesman, Imperial Int Life Ins Co, 73- Mem: Dem Club Pulaski Co; Young Dem of Mid Ga; Eighth

Dist Voter League of Ga. Relig: Methodist. Mailing Add: 117 Lovejoy St Hawkinsville GA 31036

FOSTER, DONALD R (D)
Mont State Sen
b Gooding, Idaho, Apr 18, 37; s Howard W Foster & Eva M F; m 1963 to Rosalie A Levitte; c Laura, Michael, Bryan, Mae Lynn & Elisa. Educ: Stanford Univ, AB in Psychol, 58, Med Sch, 59-60; Alpha Sigma Phi. Polit & Govt Pos: Deleg, Mont State Dem Const Conv, 72; Mont State Sen, 75- Mil Serv: Entered as Ens, Navy, 61, released as Lt(jg), 64. Mem: Am & Mid US Honey Producers Asn; Rotary Int; Northwest Mkt Asn (pres, 74-); Elks; KofC (Dep Grand Knight, 74-75). Honors & Awards: Outstanding Serv Award, Jaycees, 73. Relig: Catholic. Mailing Add: Rte 2 Lewistown MT 59457

FOSTER, ECKORD LEWIS (D)
Secy, Fannin Co Dem Exec Comt, Ga
b McCaysville, Ga, Feb 1, 20; s Org Foster & Montine Stuman F; m 1941 to Curtistine Ward; c Karen (Mrs Steven Taylor), Douglas & Michael. Educ: Ducktown High Sch, Tenn, grad, 39. Polit & Govt Pos: Secy, Fannin Co Dem Exec Comt, Ga, 72-; chmn, 50th Dist Charter Comn, 74-; mem, Ga State Dem Exec Comt, 74- Mil Serv: Entered as A/S, Navy, 44, released as Seaman 1/C, 46, after serv in Am Theatre. Mem: Mason. Relig: Baptist. Legal Res: E Second St Blue Ridge GA 30513 Mailing Add: PO Box 904 Blue Ridge GA 30513

FOSTER, ELEANOR CORINNE (R)
Chmn, Lowell Rep City Comt, Mass
b Lowell, Mass, May 12, 19; d Wilbrod Lagasse & Donia Lequin L; div; m 1952 to Lyndwood D Foster, Jr; c Patricia Ann (Mrs Leo Stromvall); Roland Laural, Jr & Kenneth R Hughes & Gertrude A, Frederick A, Linda D & John J Foster. Educ: Lowell High Sch, dipl, 38. Polit & Govt Pos: Publicity chmn, Gtr Lowell Rep Women, Mass, 64-66 & 69-71, mem bd, 66-; second vpres, 68-72; chmn, Lowell Rep City Comt, Ward Five, 67- Mem: Mothers & Wives of War Vet; Merrimack Valley Goodwill Industs; Middlesex Womens Club; Int Platform Asn; Varnum-Ribinson PTO (pres, 70). Honors & Awards: Award for Gtr Lowell Area Fund Raising Drive, Nat Kidney Found, 70. Relig: Catholic. Mailing Add: 186 Tenth St Lowell MA 01850

FOSTER, JAMES MILTON (D)
b Brooklyn, NY, Nov 19, 34; s Milton Whiteside Foster & Elizabeth S Macdonald F; single. Educ: Brown Univ, BA, 57. Polit & Govt Pos: Polit dir, Soc for Individual Rights, 70; pres, Alice B Toklas Mem Dem Club, 71; deleg, Dem Nat Conv, 72; prog secy, Calif Dem Coun, 73-; co-chmn credentials comt, Calif Dem State Cent Comt, currently. Bus & Prof Pos: Dir, Whitman-Radclyffe Found, 72- Relig: Episcopal. Legal Res: 544 Noe St San Francisco CA 94114 Mailing Add: 2131 Union St 4 San Francisco CA 94123

FOSTER, JIM (D)
Fla State Rep
Mailing Add: Foster's Lazy Acres Lutz FL 33549

FOSTER, JOHN CLAYTON (D)
Ga State Sen
b Habersham Co, Ga, Apr 2, 35; s H C Foster & Essie Mae Purcell F; m 1958 to Bobbie Carpenter; c John Clayton, Jr & David Carpenter. Educ: Piedmont Col, grad. Polit & Govt Pos: Ga State Sen, 50th Dist, 75- Bus & Prof Pos: Co-owner, vpres & gen mgr, Washington Broadcasting Co, Radio Sta WSNT, Sandersville, Ga, 57-60; owner, Radio Sta WKLE, Washington, 60; co-owner & pres, Radio Sta WCON, Cornelia, 60-; pres, Habersham Broom Co, Cornelia, 71- Mil Serv: Entered as Pvt, Army, 53-55. Mem: Ga Mountains Planning & Develop Comn Exec Comt (dir); Habershan Co Resource Conserv & Develop Proj Steering Comt (chmn); Chattahoochee River Soil & Water Conserv Dist (dist supvr & vchmn); Rotary. Honors & Awards: Distinguished Serv Award, Habersham Co Jaycees, 69-70. Relig: Baptist. Mailing Add: PO Box 100 Cornelia GA 30531

FOSTER, LEWIS (D)
Ky State Rep
Mailing Add: Rte 2 Lewisburg KY 42256

FOSTER, MIRL A (D)
Chmn, Marshall Co Dem Party, SDak
b Wakonda, SDak, Feb 17, 21; s Alonzo Marion Foster & Wanda Myrtle Hartshorn F; m 1949 to Eunice Opal Gronseth; c Curtis, David, Joanne & Richard. Educ: Claremont High Sch, grad, 39. Polit & Govt Pos: Chmn, Marshall Co Dem Party, SDak, 70- Mem: Mason; Farmers Union; Marshall Co Sportsmans Club. Relig: Lutheran. Mailing Add: Waverly Precinct Britton SD 57430

FOSTER, PAUL W (D)
Ga State Rep
Mailing Add: PO Box 679 Blackshear GA 31516

FOSTER, R L (D)
Ga State Rep
Mailing Add: 4899 Tibbs Bridge Rd SE Dalton GA 30720

FOSTER, RETHA REYNOLDS (D)
Chmn, Dickinson Co Dem Party, Kans
b Arlington, Tex, Sept 13, 18; d Weeks Reynolds & Gertrude Davison R; m 1936 to Amos Harold Foster. Educ: High sch, grad, 38. Polit & Govt Pos: Precinct committeewan, Abilene, Kans, currently; chmn, Dickinson Co Dem Party, 66-; dist committeewan, Second Dist, 74- Mem: Kans Dem Club; Am Legion Auxiliary; Kans Womens Golf Asn. Relig: Lutheran. Mailing Add: 1013 NW Second St Abilene KS 67410

FOSTER, ROLAND RAYMOND (R)
Vt State Rep
b Claremont, NH, May 1, 21; m to Mavis; c Two daughters. Educ: West Springfield High Sch. Polit & Govt Pos: Trustee, Wash Elec Coop, Inc; selectman, 52-; Vt State Rep, 61-63, 65-66 & 71- Bus & Prof Pos: Carpenter; contractor. Mil Serv: Air Force, 42-45, Sgt. Mem: Mason; F&AM; Shrine; Am Legion. Relig: Methodist. Mailing Add: RFD Moretown VT 05660

FOSTER, ROY GUYLUS, JR (R)
Chmn, Jefferson Co Rep Comt, Ga
b North Wilkesboro, NC, Oct 9, 26; s Roy Guylus Foster & Lula Lee Stokes F; m 1946 to Parkie Leigh Camp; c Roy G, III, Terri Leigh, William Hayes & Parkie Camp. Educ: Univ Ga; US Mil Acad; Kappa Alpha. Polit & Govt Pos: Nat treas, Nat Fedn Young Rep, 55-57; chmn, Southern Coun Young Rep, 57-59; councilman, Wadley, Ga, 57-64; mem, Jefferson Co Bd of Educ, 62-64; Ga State Sen, 21st Dist, 65-66; chmn, Jefferson Co Rep Comt, 68- Bus & Prof Pos: Pres, Savannah Terminals, Inc, Ga & R G Foster & Co, Wadley, Ga, 62- Mil Serv: Entered as Pvt, Army, 46, released as Cpl, 48, after serv in Army Occupation, Ger. Mem: Am Legion; Mason; PTA; Farm Bur; Lions. Relig: Methodist. Mailing Add: Dalmatian Plantation Wadley GA 30477

FOSTER, THOMAS HENRY (R)
Vt State Rep
b Bennington, Vt, July 24, 07; s Thomas Henry Foster & Nettie Burnell Potter; m 1937 to Catharine Osgood Foster. Educ: Bennington High Sch, 25; Bread Loaf Sch Eng, summer 28. Polit & Govt Pos: Chmn, Scenery Preservation Coun, 70-73; Vt State Rep, 72- Mem: Am Ornithologists Union; Nature Conservancy (life mem); Vt Acad Arts & Sci; Wilderness Soc; Zero Population Growth. Honors & Awards: Governor's Award, received jointly with wife for outstanding contribution to conservation, Conservation Soc Southern Vt, 73. Relig: Episcopal. Legal Res: Monument Rd Bennington VT 05201 Mailing Add: PO Box 397 Bennington VT 05201

FOSTER, W F (BILL) (D)
Ark State Rep
Mailing Add: 323 Irvy Rd England AR 72046

FOSTER, WILLIAM CHAPMAN (R)
b Westfield, NJ, Apr 27, 97; s Jed S Foster & Anna Louise Chapman F; m 1925 to Beulah Robinson; c Seymour Robinson. Educ: Mass Inst Tech, 18. Hon Degrees: LLD, Syracuse Univ, 57, Bowdoin Col, Rutgers Univ, 68 & Yale Univ, 69; DPubServ, George Washington Univ, 63; DHL, Kenyon Col, 68. Polit & Govt Pos: Consult, War Prod Bd, 41; spec rep, Under Secy War on Procurement for Army Air Force, World War II; dir purchases, Div Army Serv Forces; Under Secy of Commerce, 46-48; dep spec rep, Marshall Plan, Econ Coop Admin, Europe, 48-49, dep adminstr, 49-50, adminstr, 50-51; Dep Secy of Defense, 51-53; co-chmn, Security Resources Panel, 57; with Nat Planning Comn, 60-61; dir, US Arms Control & Disarmament Agency, 61-69, mem gen adv comt, 69- Bus & Prof Pos: Officer & dir, Pressed & Welded Steel Prod Co, Inc, 22-46; pres, Mfg Chemists Asn, Inc, 53-55; exec vpres & dir, Olin Mathieson, 55-58; dir, vpres & sr adv, Olin Mathieson Chem Corp, 58-61; chmn bd & pres, United Nuclear Corp, 61; chmn bd, Porter Int Co, 69- Mil Serv: Army, World War I; US Medal of Merit; Commendations for Civilian Serv, War Dept, Dept of Defense, World War II. Mem: Cosmos Club; Metrop & Chevy Chase Clubs, Washington, DC. Honors & Awards: Distinguished Honor Award, Arms Control & Disarmament Agency, 69. Mailing Add: 3304 R St NW Washington DC 20007

FOSTER, WILLIAM EDWARD (R)
Chmn, Fourth Cong Dist Rep Orgn, Colo
b Laramie, Wyo, Feb 24, 31; s Edward Horatio Foster & Beaulah Cook F; m 1951 to Margaret Florence Evans; c Ann Therese, Elizabeth Marie, William Edward, Laura Ellen, Timothy Evans, Peter Ryan & Michael. Educ: Univ Wyo, LLB cum laude, 55; Omicron Delta Kappa; Sigma Chi. Polit & Govt Pos: Pres, Wyo Young Rep, 52-53; secy-treas, Mesa Co Rep Party, Colo, 58-60; precinct committeeman, 62-64; Colo State Rep, 64-66; chmn, Fourth Cong Dist Rep Orgn, 70-; mem, Colo Comn Higher Educ, 70- Bus & Prof Pos: Attorney & partner, Foster & Farina, 56-; dir, Best Plastic Container Corp, 62-; vpres & dir, Dixson, Inc, 63-; vpres & dir, Mesa Sanitary Supply Co, 64-; dir, Powderhorn Ski Corp, 65-; vpres & dir, Thermo Dynamics Corp, Shawnee Mission, Kans, 68-; pres & dir, CBW Builders Inc, Grand Junction, Colo, 69-; vpres & dir, DEA Prod, Inc, Tempe, Ariz, 69-; dir, Energy Leasing, Inc. Mil Serv: Entered as Pvt, Army, 50, released as Cpl, 51, after serv in 141st Tank Bn. Mem: Am Bar Asn; KofC; Farm Bur; Lions; Am Legion. Honors & Awards: Selected Outstanding Young Man, Mesa Co & One of Three Outstanding Young Men, Colo, 66, Jr CofC. Relig: Catholic. Mailing Add: 1701 Orchard Ave Grand Junction CO 81501

FOSTER, WILLIAM WALTER (R)
Pa State Rep
b Cherry Ridge, Pa, July 22, 22; s John A Foster & Charlotte C Dirlam F; m 1946 to Alice C Rutledge; c Deborah A (Mrs Brian Leidy), William Brian & Constance D. Educ: Honesdale High Sch, 4 years. Polit & Govt Pos: Pres, Wayne Co Young Rep Club, formerly; mem, Wayne Co Rep Comt; comnr, Wayne Co, 60-71; Pa State Rep, 139th Dist, 71- Bus & Prof Pos: Owner, Wayne Tractor & Equip Co, 46- Mil Serv: Entered as Pvt, Marines, 42, released as Sgt, 45, after serv in 4th Marine Div, Pac, 43-45; Purple Heart; Bronze Star; Letter of Commendation. Mem: F&AM; Am Legion; VFW; Irem Temple Shrine; Indian Orchard Grange. Relig: Lutheran. Legal Res: 1245 Bridge St Seelyville PA 18431 Mailing Add: Capitol Bldg Harrisburg PA 17120

FOUCHE, PETER JAMES (D)
b Springfield, Mass, Jan 21, 48; s Gerald James Fouche & Clair Moore; m 1972 to Katherine Mary Zecher. Educ: St Leo Col, Fla, BA, 69; Univ Mass, Amherst, MA, 70. Polit & Govt Pos: Deleg, Dem Nat Conv, 72; ward chmn, Westfield Dem City Comt, Mass, 72-73; city councilman, Westfield, 72- Bus & Prof Pos: Salesman, Matt's Sports, Inc, 70-72; teacher, Springfield Sch Syst, Mass, 72-73. Relig: Roman Catholic. Mailing Add: 220 Bates Rd Westfield MA 01085

FOUDY, MICHAEL L (D)
Mem Exec Comt, Nat Col Young Dem
b Douglas, Ariz, Apr 12, 51; s Michael J Foudy, Jr & Olga Markovich F; m 1974 to Terry Jean Shield. Educ: Univ Ariz, BA in Govt, 73, JD, 76; Beta Phi Delta. Polit & Govt Pos: Organizer, Lindsay for President, Ariz & Wis, 72; organizer, McGovern for President, Calif & Ariz, 72; alt deleg, Dem Nat Conv, 72; chmn, Cochise Co Dem Party, Ariz, 72-; mem exec comt, Nat Col Young Dem, 73-; mem, Castro for Gov Comt; dir, Ariz Dem Telethon, 74 & 75; campaign mgr, Jonathan Marshall for US Sen, 74. Bus & Prof Pos: Partner, Trademark Assocs, currently. Legal Res: Box 4292 Bisbee AZ 85603 Mailing Add: Box 4692 Tucson AZ 85717

FOULK, JACK M (R)
b Columbus, Ohio, June 29, 41; s (father deceased) Evelyn Day F; single. Educ: Bliss Col; Phi Theta Pi, Gamma Kappa chap. Polit & Govt Pos: Admin asst to US Rep Chalmers P

Wylie, Ohio, 66- Mem: F&AM; Bull Elephants. Relig: Methodist. Legal Res: 64 E Mithoff St Columbus OH 43206 Mailing Add: 2447 Rayburn House Off Bldg Washington DC 20515

FOUNTAIN, L H (D)
US Rep, NC
b Leggett, NC, Apr 23, 13; s Lawrence H Fountain & Sallie Barnes F; m 1942 to Christine Dail; c Nancy Dail. Educ: Univ NC, AB, 34, JD, 36; Wiley P Mangum Oratorical Medal; Mary D Wright Debate Medal; pres, Univ NC Philantropic Lit Soc. Polit & Govt Pos: Reading clerk, NC State Senate, 36-41; pres, Edgecombe Young Dem Club, 40; east organizer Young Dem Clubs NC, 41; NC Sen, 47-52; US Rep, NC Second Dist, 53-, past chmn exec comt, Second Dist, chmn intergovernmental rels subcommittee, House Govt Opers Comn, House Foreign Affairs Comt; US Deleg, UN Gen Assembly, 67; ex officio, Dem Nat Mid-Term Conf, 74. Bus & Prof Pos: Attorney-at-law; officer, Coastal Plains Broadcasting Co, radio sta WCPS, Tarboro, NC, 49-69, vpres, 69- Mil Serv: Entered as Pvt, Army, 42, released as Maj, 46, after serv in Inf & Judge & Adv Gen Off; Lt Col, Army Res. Mem: Elks; Kiwanis; NC Bar Asn; Farm Bur; Grange. Honors & Awards: Distinguished Serv Award, Man of the Year, Tarboro Jr CofC, 48; Distinguished Pub Serv Award, NC Citizens Asn, 71; Distinguished Serv Award, Sch Med, Univ NC, 73. Relig: Presbyterian; Elder. Legal Res: 1102 Panola St Tarboro NC 27886 Mailing Add: 2188 Rayburn House Off Bldg Washington DC 20515

FOUNTAIN, NINA WALSTON (D)
Chmn, Edgecombe Co Dem Exec Comt, NC
b Scotland Neck, NC, Jan 5, 13; d William Amos Walston & Lillian Deborah Walston W; m 1938 to Joseph Emerson Fountain, wid. Educ: East Carolina Teachers Col, AB, 32; East Carolina Univ, MA, 69; Kappa Delta Pi. Polit & Govt Pos: Town comnr, Leggett, NC, 73-; chmn, Edgecombe Co Dem Exec Comt, 74- Bus & Prof Pos: Reading supvr, Edgecombe Co Bd Educ, 66-; trustee, Edgecombe Tech Inst, 71- Mem: Delta Kappa Gamma; Nat Educ Asn; Asn Supvrs & Curriculum Dir; Pilot Club Tarboro (dir, 75-); Edgecombe Co Red Cross. Relig: Presbyterian. Mailing Add: RFD 2 Box 141 Tarboro NC 27886

FOUSHEE, ROGER BABSON (D)
Mem, NC Dem Exec Comt
b Haw River, NC, July 29, 38; s Joseph Baxter Foushee & Elsie Jenkins F; single. Educ: Univ NC, Chapel Hill, AB in European hist, 60, grad work in polit sci, 60-64; Phi Eta Sigma; Phi Alpha Theta; Order of the Golden Fleece. Polit & Govt Pos: Dem judge, Country Club Precinct, Orange Co, NC, 66-68, precinct chmn, 68; chmn, Orange Co Dem Exec Comt, 68-72; mem, NC Dem Exec Comt, 70-; chmn, Orange Co Comt, NC Comn Bicentennial of the Am Revolution, 71- Bus & Prof Pos: Serials asst, Wilson Libr, Univ NC, 60-62, research asst, Gov Comn on Educ Beyond High Sch, 62; research assoc, Inst Govt, Univ NC, 63; publ rep, George F Scheer, 64- Mem: Chapel Hill Hist Soc (pres); Rotary; L Q C Lamar Soc. Honors & Awards: One of Ten Outstanding Young Dem in NC, 69 & 72. Relig: Protestant. Legal Res: 735 Raleigh Rd Chapel Hill NC 27514 Mailing Add: PO Box 1145 Franklin Street Sta Chapel Hill NC 27514

FOUST, MARY LOUISE (D)
Auditor of Pub Acct, Ky
b New Albany, Ind, Oct 15, 09; d The Rev David Taylor Foust & Mary Margaret Rippel F; single. Educ: Martin Jr Col, grad, 28; Georgetown Col, AB, 38; Univ Louisville Law Sch, JD, 44; Beta Alpha Psi; Int Rels Club; Jr Col Honor Roll. Polit & Govt Pos: Chief acct, Div Pub Assistance, Frankfort, Ky, 45-49; Auditor of Pub Acct, Ky, 56-60 & 69 Bus & Prof Pos: Tax control clerk, E I du Pont de Nemours, Charlestown, Inc, World War II; staff acct, CPA firms, San Francisco, Calif & Louisville, Ky, 49-53; attorney-at-law & CPA, 53-70. Publ: Mag articles. Mem: Ky Bar Asn; Am Inst CPA; Am Women's Soc CPA; Am Soc Women Acct; Georgetown Col Women's Club. Honors & Awards: Pub Serv Award, Am Woman's Soc CPA, 72; Outstanding Alumnus, Georgetown Col, 72. Relig: Baptist. Mailing Add: Midland Trail W Shelbyville KY 40065

FOWLE, ELEANOR CRANSTON (D)
State Women's Chmn, Calif Dem State Cent Comt
b Palo Alto, Calif; d William MacGregor Cranston & Carol Dixon C; m to John Miller Fowle; c Michael & Linda (Mrs Burke). Educ: Stanford Univ, 2 years; Alpha Phi. Polit & Govt Pos: Chmn, Santa Clara Co Key Women for President Johnson, 64; Co-Chmn, Tenth Cong Dist, 64-65; mem exec & steering comts, Calif Dem State Cent Comt, 64-, state women's chmn, 66-68 & 71-; mem Northern Calif Exec Comn, West State Conf, 65; women's chmn, Northern Calif Dem State Cent Comt, 65-66 & 68-71; mem exec comt, Gov Brown's Campaign, 66; mem exec comt, Alan Cranston's Campaign for US Sen, 68 & 74; alt deleg, Dem Nat Conv, 68; mem exec comt, Dem State Chmn Adv Comt, 68-; mem exec comt, John Tunney for US Senate Campaign, 70. Mem: North Santa Clara Co Community Coun; League of Women Voters; UN Asn; Family Serv Asn, Los Altos & Palo Alto; United World Federalists (mem Nat Exec Coun). Relig: Congregational. Mailing Add: 27060 Old Trace Rd Los Altos Hills CA 94022

FOWLER, BEN B (R)
Legal Counsel, Ky Rep State Cent Comt
b Christian Co, Ky, Mar 9, 16; s William T Fowler & Ila Earle F; m 1940 to Eleanor Randolph. Educ: Univ Ky, BS in Com, 37; Univ Va, LLB, 40; Phi Alpha Delta; Delta Tau Delta. Polit & Govt Pos: Asst Attorney Gen of Ky, 45-48; city solicitor, Frankfort, 57-60; legal counsel, Ky Rep State Cent Comt, 63- Bus & Prof Pos: Pres & dir, Community Serv, Inc, Frankfort, Ky, 52-; gen counsel & chmn bd dirs, Frankfort & Cincinnati RR, Frankfort, 61-; mem bd dirs, Frankfort Cemetery Co, 68-; sr partner, Law Form of Stites, McElwain & Fowler, Frankfort & Louisville, 72- Mil Serv: Entered as 2nd Lt, Army, 41, released as Maj, 45, after serv in 33rd Inf Div, 3rd Army Corps, Pac Theatre, 43, European Theatre, 44-45; Bronze Star Medal. Mem: Am Judicature Soc; Frankfort Country Club; Frankfort CofC; VFW; Am Legion. Honors & Awards: Outstanding Serv Award, Ky State Bar Asn, 54. Relig: Presbyterian. Legal Res: 110 Reservoir Rd Frankfort KY 40601 Mailing Add: 500 McClure Bldg Frankfort KY 40601

FOWLER, CALVIN W (INDEPENDENT)
Va State Deleg
Mailing Add: Box 1077 Danville VA 24541

FOWLER, DONALD LIONEL (D)
Chmn, Dem Party SC
b Spartanburg, SC, Sept 12, 35; s James W Fowler, Sr & Enoma Polk F; m to Septima Twyford Briggs; c Donald Lionel, Jr & Cynthia Twyford. Educ: Wofford Col, AB, 57; Univ Ky, MA, 61, PhD, 66. Polit & Govt Pos: Exec dir, Dem Party SC, 67-74, chmn, 71-; pres & mem exec comt, Asn State Dem Chmn, 75- Bus & Prof Pos: Asst prof polit sci, Univ SC, 64-68; mem prin staff, Hellams & Ullman, Columbia, SC, 75- Mil Serv: Entered Army, 58, released 60; recalled, Army, 61-62; Maj, Res. Mem: Southern & Am Polit Sci Asns; Am Soc Advan Pub Admin; ROA; Wofford Col Alumni (bd dirs). Relig: Methodist. Legal Res: 1698 Woodlake Dr Columbia SC 29206 Mailing Add: PO Box 5965 Columbia SC 29250

FOWLER, H M (D)
La State Rep
Mailing Add: PO Box 405 Coushatta LA 71019

FOWLER, HAMMOND (D)
Mem, Roane Co Dem Exec Comt, Tenn
b Rockwood, Tenn, Apr 6, 01; s Hammond Fowler, Sr & Zoe Leland F; m 1952 to Netha McCorkle. Educ: Univ Tenn; Maryville Col; Cumberland Univ Law Sch, LLB; Lambda Chi Alpha. Polit & Govt Pos: Mem, Roane Co Dem Exec Comt, Tenn, 22-; city attorney, Rockwood, Tenn, 33-53; Tenn State Sen, 34-36; chief counsel, Employ Security Dept, Tenn, 39-47; comnr, Tenn Pub Serv Comn, 48-72, chmn, 51-54, 59-60, 65-66 & 71-72. Bus & Prof Pos: Pres, Times Printing Co, Rockwood, Tenn, 22-42; dir, Rockwood Fed Savings & Loan Asn, 34-, vpres & gen counsel, 46-; attorney-at-law, Rockwood, 72-; vpres & dir, Tenn-Val Realty, Inc, 73- Mil Serv: Pvt, Army, 41, entered Naval Res as Lt, 42, released as Lt Comdr, 45; Comdr, Naval Res, 45-63; Am Defense Serv, Am Theater & Victory & Naval Res Medals. Mem: Am Bar Asn; Am Legion; VFW; Mil Order of World Wars; SAR. Relig: Presbyterian. Legal Res: 421 S Douglas Ave Rockwood TN 37854 Mailing Add: PO Box 167 Rockwood TN 37854

FOWLER, HENRY HAMILL (D)
b Roanoke, Va, Sept 5, 08; s Mack Johnson Fowler & Bertha Browning F; m 1938 to Trudye Pamela Hathcote; c Mary Anne (Mrs Roy C Smith IV), Susan Maria (Mrs Gallagher) & Henry H (deceased). Educ: Roanoke Col, AB, 29; Yale Univ, LLB, 32, JSD, 33; Pi Kappa Phi; Phi Delta Phi; Tau Kappa Alpha. Hon Degrees: LLD, Roanoke Col, 62, Wesleyan Univ, 66, William & Mary Univ, 66. Polit & Govt Pos: Counsel, Tenn Valley Authority, 34-38, asst gen counsel, 39; spec asst to US Attorney Gen as chief counsel, subcomt of Sen Comt on Educ & Labor, 39-40; counsel, Fed Power Comn, 41; asst gen counsel, Off of Prod Mgt, 41, asst gen counsel, War Prod Bd, 42-44, spec econ adv, US Mission Econ Affairs, 44; spec asst to Adminr, For Econ Admin, 45; dep adminr, Nat Prod Auth, 51, adminr, 52; dir, Off of Defense Mobilization & adminr, Defense Prod Admin, 52-53; deleg, Dem Nat Conv, 56; under secy of treas, US Dept of Treas, 61-64, Secy of Treas, 65-68; chmn, Atlantic Coun US; chmn, Inst Int Educ, currently. Bus & Prof Pos: Partner, Fowler, Leva, Hawes & Symington, 46-51, 53-61 & 64-65; Investment Banker, partner, Goldman, Sachs & Co, 69-; trustee, Roanoke Col, Alfred P Sloan Found, Carnegie Endowment for Peace; mem bd dirs, Corning Glass Works, US Indust, Inc, US & Foreign Securities Corp & Norfolk & Western Rwy Co. Mem: Coun on Foreign Rels; Recess, Pinnacle & Links Club, Wash; Nat Capital Dem Club; Metrop Club. Honors & Awards: Named Distinguished Alumnus, Roanoke Col & Tau Kappa Alpha; Alexander Hamilton Award, US Treas, 64. Relig: Episcopal. Legal Res: 209 S Fairfax St Alexandria VA 22314 Mailing Add: c/o Goldman Sachs & Co 55 Broad St New York NY 10004

FOWLER, HUGH CHARLES (R)
Colo State Sen
b Chicago, Ill, May 21, 26; s Frank Parker Fowler & Dorothy Hinckley F; m 1949 to Shirley Sprague; c Laurie Lynn & Hugh Charles, Jr. Educ: Univ Wis, 1 year; Univ Colo, BS in Bus, 48; Phi Kappa Tau. Polit & Govt Pos: Various app jobs, Arapahoe Co Rep Cent Comt, Colo, 56-66, secy, 66-68; Colo State Sen, Dist 20, 69- Bus & Prof Pos: Sales & gen mgt in mfg & publ, 48-58; acct exec, advert agencies in Denver, 58-64; owner, Fowler & More Advert Agency, Englewood, Colo, 64-73. Mil Serv: Entered as A/S, Naval Res, 43, retired as Lt, 58, after serv in SPac; recalled in 51 for Korean duty on USS Bremerton, 51-52. Mem: Mason; Shrine; Scoutmaster. Relig: Presbyterian; elder. Mailing Add: 5399 S Clarkson St Littleton CO 80120

FOWLER, JAMES DARWIN (R)
Mem, Ga State Rep Cent Comt
b Toombsboro, Ga, Nov 10, 27; s H G Fowler & Emma Lee Brantley F; m 1947 to Sue Johnson Allen; c E Joanne & James D. Educ: Swainsboro High Sch, grad, 45. Polit & Govt Pos: Chmn, Emanuel Co Rep Party, Ga, formerly; mem, First Dist Rep Comt, currently; mem, Ga State Rep Cent Comt, currently. Bus & Prof Pos: Home builder, currently. Mil Serv: Entered as Seaman, Navy, 45, released as Seaman 1/C, 48, after serv in Atlantic Fleet. Mem: VFW; Moose. Relig: Episcopal. Legal Res: Allen Dr Swainsboro GA 30401 Mailing Add: PO Box 438 Swainsboro GA 30401

FOWLER, LEONARD (D)
b Arcadia, Nebr, Sept 15, 05; s Morris Fowler & Laura Ellen Middaugh F; m 1925 to Faye Erna Jensen; c Darlene (Mrs Schultz, deceased) & Gilbert. Polit & Govt Pos: Chmn, Loup Co Dem Party, Nebr, formerly. Bus & Prof Pos: Farmer-rancher. Relig: Protestant. Mailing Add: Taylor NE 68879

FOWLER, LESLIE R (R)
Colo State Sen
b 1924; m to Jane; c Three. Educ: Univ Colo, BS, 48. Polit & Govt Pos: Precinct capt & committeeman, Colo Rep Party, mem, Boulder City Coun, 56-62; Colo State Rep, 67-69; Colo State Sen, 69-, chmn, Finance Comt & mem, local Govt & Educ Comts, Colo State Senate, currently. Mil Serv: Navy, 43-46. Mem: Jr Achievement (bd dirs); Boulder United Fund (former pres); Univ Colo Golf Team (coach). Relig: Methodist. Mailing Add: 7273 Old Post Rd Boulder CO 80301

FOWLER, R LYNN (R)
Chmn, Third Cong Dist Rep Comt, Mich
b Eaton Rapids, Mich, May 27, 23; s Rice C Fowler & Gladys I Scott F; m 1948 to Kathleen M Mikesell; c Mindy A, Rice T & Dort E. Educ: Mich State Univ, 1 year; US Naval Acad, BS, 45. Polit & Govt Pos: Held various co Rep orgn off, Eaton Co, Mich, 58-64; city councilman, Charlotte, 60-66; mem, Third Cong Dist Rep Comt, 64-66, chmn, 66- Bus & Prof Pos: Owner, Fowler's Inc, Chevrolet-Oldsmobile, Charlotte, 51- Mil Serv: Entered as Ens, Navy, 45, released as Lt(jg), 47, after serv on USS North Carolina, BB-55 & USS Manchester, CL-83, Pac & Mediterranean Theatre, Lt, Res, 51-53, serv on USS Black, DD-666 & USS Zellars, DD-777 as Gunnery Officer. Mem: Rotary; CofC; Charlotte Country Club; Mason.

Relig: Congregational. Legal Res: 1182 E Clinton Trail Charlotte MI 48813 Mailing Add: 1616 Lansing Rd Charlotte MI 48813

FOWLER, RAYMOND WILLIAM (BILL) (D)
VChmn, Cherokee Co Dem Comt, Kans
b Arcadia, Kans, June 8, 22; s James Thomas Fowler & Ada M Davenport F; m 1943 to Wadean Davis; c Joseph William. Educ: Ft Scott Jr Col, 2 years. Polit & Govt Pos: Vchmn, Cherokee Co Dem Comt, Kans, 66-; mem, Kans Mined Land Bd & Kans Export Coun, 68-; comnr, Kans Forestry, Fish & Game Comn, 68- Bus & Prof Pos: Pres, Citizens Bank of Weir, Kans, 51-; pres, Home State Bank, Arcadia, 60-; dir, Weir Grain & Supply, 67-; treas, Jarboe Lackey Feedlots, Inc, currently; pres, Bar Brand Cattle Co Inc, currently. Mil Serv: Entered SpD, Coast Guard, 42-45. Mem: Mason; Scottish Rite; Shrine; Commandery; Elks. Relig: Protestant. Legal Res: RR 1 Weir KS 66781 Mailing Add: c/o Citizens Bank of Weir Weir KS 66781

FOWLER, STEVE
Nebr State Sen
Mailing Add: 1039 S 11th St Lincoln NE 68508

FOX, ABIJAH UPSON (R)
Conn State Rep
b Brooklyn, NY, Jan 20, 05; s Abijah Charles Fox & Helen Manlove Shawhan F; m 1935 to Isabel Place Sullivan; c Abijah Shawhan, Jarvis Powell & Suzanne Angevine. Educ: Rutgers Col, LittB cum laude, 26; Beta Theta Pi. Polit & Govt Pos: Dep dir foreign funds control, US Treas Dept, Washington, DC, 41-44, dir, Off Surplus Property, 45, dep dir finance div, Mil Govt, Frankfurt, Ger, 45-46; mem, Greenwich Rep Town Comt, Conn, 57-, seventh dist leader, 64-68; mem, Greenwich Representative Town Meeting, 60-65; mem, Conn Rep Finance Comt & Conn Rep Budget Comt, 64-68; mem, Greenwich Bd of Estimate & Taxation, 65-68; chmn, Greenwich Rep Finance Comt, 68-; Conn State Rep, 152nd Assembly Dist, 69-72, 149th Dist, 73-, vchmn, Finance Comt, Conn House Rep, 73-74, ranking mem, 75- Bus & Prof Pos: Exec, Nat City Bank of NY, Tokyo, Japan, 27-34; partner, Swan, Culbertson & Fritz, Shanghai, Hong Kong & Manila, 34-41; chmn, Mathieson Alkali Works, New York, 46-48; vpres & dir, Am Thread Co, 48-59; vpres, Hayden, Stone, Inc, 59-72; sr investment exec, Riter, Pyne, Kendall & Hollister, 72-73; investment exec, Harris Upham & Co, 73- Mem: Am Arbit Asn; Belle Haven Club; Indian Harbor Yacht Club, Greenwich; Navy League. Honors & Awards: Silver Beaver, Greenwich Boy Scouts Coun. Relig: Episcopal. Mailing Add: 200 North St Greenwich CT 06830

FOX, EUNICE JANE (R)
Secy, Lexington Co Rep Party, SC
b Orangeburg, SC, June 18, 53; d Joseph Carl Fox & Adele Bates F; single. Educ: Coker Col, BA; Sch Med Technol, SC Baptist Hosp. Polit & Govt Pos: First vchmn, Orangeburg Co TAR, SC, 68-69; co-chmn, Orangeburg Youth for Spence, Cong Race, 70; deleg, SC TAR Conv, 70; deleg, Orangeburg Co Rep Conv, 72; deleg, SC Rep State Conv, 72; alt deleg, Rep Nat Conv, 72; chmn, Orangeburg Co Youth for Thurmond, US Senate Race, 72; campaign chmn, Mrs J Carl Fox for SC House Rep, 72; Coker Col coordr, Reelect the President & Nixonettes, 72; Coker Col coordr, for US Sen J Strom Thurmond, 72; vol, Spence for Cong, 74; secy, Lexington Co Rep Party, 75- Bus & Prof Pos: Tutor, Orangeburg Dyslexia Found, SC, summer 72. Mem: Coker Col Rep Club; SC Col Rep Club; Lexington Co Rep Club; PEO; Am Soc Med Technol. Relig: Episcopal. Legal Res: 310 Brewton Orangeburg SC 29115 Mailing Add: 524 Treetop Lane Columbia SC 29210

FOX, FRANCES FARNSWORTH (R)
b Olean, NY, Nov 8, 28; d Vane Launce Farnsworth & Ednah Hill F; m 1961 to William Fox; Nancy Erline & James Lee Collins. Educ: Fredonia State Teachers Col, 46; Westbrook Acad, 48-49; pvt music study, Buffalo, 44-51. Polit & Govt Pos: Alt deleg, Rep Nat Conv, 72; trustee, Cuba Bd of Educ, NY, 72-; vpres, 74-; vpres, Allegany Co Rep Women, 73-75, pres, 75- Bus & Prof Pos: Pres, Farnsworth's Cookies, Inc, 56- Relig: Anglican. Legal Res: RD 1 Cuba NY 14727 Mailing Add: PO Box 51 Cuba NY 14727

FOX, GEORGE F, JR (D)
La State Rep
Mailing Add: Rte 2 Box 456 Lake Providence LA 71254

FOX, HARRY M (R)
b New Castle, Pa, Apr 29, 24; s Homer F Fox & Thelma Whitfield F (deceased); m 1957 to Pauline Baculik, wid; c Suzanne M & Patricia A. Polit & Govt Pos: Admin asst to US Rep John P Saylor, Pa, 49-74; Rep nominee for Cong, 74; cand for co comnr, Armstrong Co, Pa. Bus & Prof Pos: Secy, Valley Novelty Co, 41-42; teller, Armstrong Co Trust Co, 42-43; secy, Pittsburgh Plate Glass Co, 46-49. Mil Serv: Entered as A/S, Navy, 43, released as Yeoman 1/C, 46, after serv in Pac Theater, 43-46; Am Theater Ribbon; Asiatic-Pac Theater Ribbon with 2 Stars. Mem: Am Legion; VFW; Eagles; Jednota. Relig: Catholic. Mailing Add: Rural Valley PA 16249

FOX, MICHAEL ALLEN (R)
Ohio State Rep
b Hamilton, Ohio, Dec 15, 48; s Benjamen A Fox & Nora J Bowling F; single. Educ: Miami Univ, BSEd in Polit Sci, 71; Delta Tau Delta. Polit & Govt Pos: Asst to Secy of Agr Earl Butz, 73; spec asst to US Sen Robert Taft, Jr, Ohio, 73-74; Ohio State Rep, 58th Dist, 75- Mem: Fraternal Order of Police Assocs; Butler Co Youth Serv Bur (bd mem). Relig: Church of Christ. Mailing Add: 606 Haldimand Ave Hamilton OH 45013

FOX, MILTON E (R)
Tex State Rep
b Tulsa, Okla, July 28, 26; s Stanley S Fox & Florence Stephens F; m 1947 to Ruth Huffmaster; c Bryan D, Martin E, Helen A, Susan E & Clayton A. Educ: Univ Tex, BS in Petroleum Eng, 46. Polit & Govt Pos: Mem, LaFayette Parish Sch Bd, La, 64-67; Tex State Rep, Dist 93, 73- Bus & Prof Pos: Engr, Carter Oil Co, 46-59; engr supt, Tenneco Oil Co, 59-70; vpres, Ryder-Scott Int, 70-72. Mil Serv: Entered as A/S, USNR, 44, released as Lt(jg). 46. Relig: Presbyterian. Mailing Add: Box 2910 Austin TX 78767

FOX, THOMAS P (D)
Chmn, Bayfield Co Dem Party, Wis
b Appleton, Wis, May 27, 46; s Jerome F Fox & Rosemary Bachhuber F; m 1969 to Susan Mary Kasimor; c Bridget. Educ: Col St Thomas, BA; Univ Wis Law Sch, Madison, JD; pres, student body. Polit & Govt Pos: Vchmn, Wis Natural Resources Bd; assembly chief clerk, Wis State Assembly, 71-73; chmn, Bayfield Co Dem Party, 73- Mem: State Bar Wis. Relig: Roman Catholic. Mailing Add: Rte 1 Washburn WI 54891

FOXHOVEN, ELOISE FAITH (D)
Chairperson, Page Co Dem Comt, Iowa
b Riverton, Iowa, May 17, 20; d Samuel John Lewis & Daisy Rippy L; m 1951 to Bernard Conrad Foxhoven. Educ: Riverton Consolidated High Sch, 38. Polit & Govt Pos: Chairperson, Page Co Dem Comt, Iowa, 74- Mem: Des Moines Diocesan Catholic Coun Women (community affairs comnr); West Page Improvement Ctr (bd dirs); Nishna Productions (bd dirs); Governor Traffic Safety Coun (dir dist 13). Relig: Catholic. Mailing Add: 1301 W Lowell Shenandoah IA 51601

FOY, THOMAS PAUL (D)
NMex State Rep
b Silver City, NMex, Oct 19, 14; s Thomas J Foy & Mary V F; m 1948 to Joan Carney; c Thomas P, Jr, Celia, Mary Ann, Joe Carney & James B. Educ: Univ Notre Dame Col Com, BCS, 38, Univ Notre Dame Col Law, JD, 39. Polit & Govt Pos: Village attorney, Bayard, NMex, 48-; dist attorney, Sixth Judicial Dist, 49-57; committeeman, Grant Co Dem Cent Comt, 49-; village attorney, Central, 56-66; town attorney, Hurley, 59-71; NMex State Rep, Dist 39, 71- Bus & Prof Pos: Dir, sr vpres & gen counsel, Grant Co Bank, Silver City, NMex, 46-, chmn bd, 69-; attorney-at-law, Foy & Vesely, 49-65, Foy & Sprecher, 66-67 & Foy & Keith, 68- Mil Serv: Entered as Pvt, Army, 41, released as 1st Lt, 46, after serv in 200th CA (aa), Philippines, prisoner of war, 42-45; Purple Heart; Good Conduct Medal with Clasp; Presidential Unit Citation with 3 Oak Leaf Clusters; Philippine Liberation Medal; Philippine Defense Medal; Am Defense Medal with 1 Bronze Serv Star; Asiatic Pac Campaign Medal with 2 Bronze Serv Stars; Am Theatre Campaign Medal; World War II Victory Medal. Mem: Elks; KofC (Grand Knight); Am Legion; Bataan Vets; VFW. Honors & Awards: Citizen of the Year, Grant Co, NMex, 66. Relig: Catholic. Legal Res: 2 Kilian Dr Bayard NM 88023 Mailing Add: PO Box 190 Silver City NM 88061

FOYLE, DOLORES HARTLEY (R)
Third VChairwoman, Ariz State Rep Comt
b Charleston, SC, June 17, 28; d David Hartley Dewitt (deceased) & Lillian Thompson Dewitt Galpine; m 1953 to Charles Martin Foyle; c Edward, Charles M, III, Michael Kevin & Donna Marie. Educ: Scottsdale Community Col, AA, 74; Ariz State Univ, 74- Polit & Govt Pos: Third vchairwoman, Ariz State Rep Comt, 72-; second vpres, Ariz Fedn Rep Women, 75- Mem: Ariz Bicentennial Comn; Cocopah PTA (state & nat parliamentarian); Camp Fire Girls Paradise Women Unit. Mailing Add: 5030 E Mockingbird Lane Scottsdale AZ 85253

FRALEY, VANCE LEVOY (R)
Committeeman, 52nd Ill Rep Representative Comt
b Taylorville, Ill, May 11, 34; s Everett Leonel Fraley & Ethel Lipe F; m 1967 to Mary Kate Reeder; c Karen & Lenee. Educ: Univ Ill, BS, 56, JD, 58; Sigma Phi Epsilon; Phi Delta Phi. Polit & Govt Pos: Corresponding secy, Christian Co Young Rep, Ill, 64-65; deleg, Ill Rep Conv, 64 & 66; fund raising dinner chmn, Christian Co Rep Party, 66, 67 & 68; committeeman, 52nd Ill Rep Representative Comt, 66- Bus & Prof Pos: Partner, Tipsword & Fraley, Taylorville, Ill, 61-67; partner, Coale, Taylor, Tipsword & Fraley, 67- Mil Serv: 1st Lt, Army, 58-61, with serv in Judge Adv Gen Corps, Judge Advocates Off, Ft Eustis, Va, 59-61; Capt, Res, 61-66. Mem: Ill State Christian Co & Am Bar Asns; Kiwanis. Relig: Methodist. Mailing Add: 104 S Othelle Taylorville IL 62568

FRAME, RICHARD C (R)
Pa State Sen
b Franklin, Pa, July 16, 26; s Thomas C Frame & Martha Crawford F; m Josephine German; c Three. Educ: Yale Univ, AB; Univ Va Law Sch, LLB. Polit & Govt Pos: Mem, Rep State Exec Comt, Pa; chmn, Venango Co Reps; Pa State Sen, 62-, Rep Leader, Pa Senate, 72-; chmn, Rep State Comt Pa, 74- Bus & Prof Pos: Attorney; dir, Exchange Bank & Trust Co & other corps. Mil Serv: Army, Sgt. Publ: Rep campaign manual. Mem: Am Bar Asn; Supreme & Superior Courts of Pa; Venango Co Indust Develop Corp (dir); Franklin Area CofC (past pres). Mailing Add: 1514 Liberty St Franklin PA 16323

FRANCIS, KATHRYN GENE (R)
Conn State Rep
b Philadelphia, Pa, Aug 30, 20; d Dr Harold Wells Gilbert & Florence Dietrich G; m 1969 to Robert E Francis; c Bonnie L (Mrs McCoy), Robert T, Kathryn C, Sandra G & Terri G Raney. Educ: Goucher Col, BA, 42; Pi Beta Phi. Polit & Govt Pos: Secy, Rep Town Comt, Conn, 61-64, vchmn, 65-67; transcriber, Conn Gen Assembly, 63-69; Conn State Rep, 75- Bus & Prof Pos: Secy, Regional Sch Dist 13, Conn, 69- Relig: Protestant. Mailing Add: Maple Ave Durham CT 06422

FRANCIS, LESLIE C (LES) (D)
Mem, Orange Co Dem Cent Comt, Calif
b San Jose, Calif, Feb 13, 43; s Leonard C Francis & Dorothy Bernard F; m 1963 to Pamela Lane Hecker; c Kirsten Louise, Renee Lane & Matthew Crane. Educ: San Jose State Univ, BA, 65, gen sec teaching credential, 66. Polit & Govt Pos: Mem, Orange Co Dem Cent Comt, Calif, 74-; admin asst to US Rep Norman Y Mineta, Calif, 75- Bus & Prof Pos: Consult on student progs, Calif Teachers Asn, 67-69 & regional consult, 72-74; dir, Proj 18, Nat Educ Asn, 69; asst prof/student personnel, San Jose State Univ, 69-70; exec dir, Orange Unified Educ Asn, 70-72. Mem: Calif Teachers Asn; Nat Educ Asn; Am Wilderness Soc; Amnesty Int. Legal Res: 1128 Linda Vista Orange CA 92669 Mailing Add: 3106 McGeorge Terr Alexandria VA 22309

FRANCIS, NADINE WEBBER (R)
Dep State Chmn, Rep Party Tex
b Cold Springs, Okla, Feb 20, 25; d Sanford Webber & Erie Emma Rose W; m 1944 to Edgar Burnett Francis; c Linda Carol (Mrs Joe Ray Cross), Sharon Gayle (Mrs Raymond L Vickrey), Aubin Phyllis (Mrs Wm Aubrey Canon) & Edgar Burnett, Jr. Educ: Hills Bus Univ, 42-43. Polit & Govt Pos: Pres, Ector Co Rep Womens Club, 61-62; chmn, Women for Ed Foreman for Cong, 62 & 64; co-chmn, Ector Co Re-elect Sen John Tower, 66; mem, Tex State Rep Exec Comt, 70-, dep state chmn, Rep Party, Tex, currently; mem field staff orgn, Sen Tower's campaign to re-elect, 73. Mem: Odessa CofC; Eastern Star; Odessa Bd Realtors. Relig: Baptist. Legal Res: 3510 Mercury Odessa TX 79760 Mailing Add: Box 731 Odessa TX 79760

FRANCIS, PETER DAVID (D)
Wash State Sen
b Seattle, Wash, Oct 28, 34; s Jack Albert Francis & Alice Scudder F; m 1959 to Lillian Elva Green; c Thomas Michael & Daniel Green. Educ: Stanford Univ, BA, Polit Sci, 56; Stanford Law Sch, JD, 61; Kappa Sigma; Phi Delta Phi. Polit & Govt Pos: Dem precinct committeeman, 92nd Precinct, Wash, 67-; Wash State Rep, 32nd Dist, 69-70; Wash State Sen, 70- Bus & Prof Pos: Law clerk, Wash State Supreme Court, Olympia, 61-62; instr, Univ Wash Law Sch, Seattle, 62-63; attorney-at-law, 63-; owner, Francis & McFarlane, currently. Mil Serv: Entered as 2nd Lt, Marine Corps, 56, released as 1st Lt, 59; Capt, 61-68. Mem: Am, Wash & Seattle Bar Asns; Greenlake CofC; Lions. Relig: Presbyterian. Legal Res: 4324 Dayton Ave N Seattle WA 98103 Mailing Add: 7300 E Greenlake Dr N Seattle WA 98115

FRANCIS, ROBERT ELSWORTH (R)
Chmn, Durham Rep Town Comt, Conn
b Middletown, Conn, Jan 19, 16; s Frank J Francis & Maude LeCompt F; m 1965 to Kathryn Gene Gilbert. Educ: Wesleyan Univ, 35-36. Polit & Govt Pos: Registrar voters, Durham Rep Party, Conn, 37-57; chmn, Durham Rep Town Comt, 57-67 & 73-; Conn State Rep, 61-69. Bus & Prof Pos: Owner, Durham Tool & Die Co, Conn, 57-; corp, Berlin Savings Bank, 73- Publ: Auth, Am Tool, Die & Stamping News, 73. Mem: AF&AM; Shrine. Relig: Protestant. Mailing Add: Maple Ave Durham CT 06422

FRANCIS, ROBERT TALCOTT, II (D)
b Springfield, Mass, Feb 5, 38; s George Churchill Francis & Carolyn Hunter Russell F; m 1965 to Judith Ann Clark; c Carolyn Louise & Allison Churchill. Educ: Williams Col, AB, 60; Boston Univ, 62-63; Univ Ibadan, 63-64. Polit & Govt Pos: Foreign affairs off, Dept of State, Washington, DC, 65-68; staff asst, Am Embassy, Lusaka, Zambia, 68-70; polit officer, Am Embassy, Algiers, Algeria, 71-72; admin asst, US Rep Gerry E Studds, Mass, 73- Relig: Protestant. Legal Res: 90 Howard Gleason Rd Cohasset MA 02025 Mailing Add: 1430 Woodacre Dr McLean VA 22101

FRANCIS, THOMAS EDWARD (R)
b Arkadelphia, Ark, Dec 4, 33; s John Thomas Francis & Fairy Wilson F; m 1953 to Billie Dean; c Barry, Brian & Steeve. Educ: Henderson State Col, 3 years. Polit & Govt Pos: Chmn, Clark Co Rep Comt, Ark, formerly. Bus & Prof Pos: Plant scheduler, Reynolds Metals Co, currently; owner, SCent Termite Control Co, currently. Relig: Baptist. Mailing Add: 2619 Golden Arkadelphia AR 71923

FRANCIS, WILMER J (D)
Chmn, Shelby Co Dem Cent & Exec Comt, Ohio
b Russia, Ohio, Apr 24, 04; s Felix Francis & Anna Voisara F; m 1927 to Cora E Kelch; c Norma Jean (Mrs John Magoto), Carolyn Ann (Mrs James Barga), Lawrence F, Linda L (Mrs Thomas Monnin) & Judith S (Mrs Anthony Monnin). Educ: Russia Schs, Ohio. Polit & Govt Pos: Chmn, Shelby Co Dem Cent & Exec Comt, Ohio, 68-; chmn, Shelby Co Bd Elec, currently. Bus & Prof Pos: Partner-owner, Francis Bros Chevrolet Dealer, 33- Mem: KofC; Shelby Co Motor Club (dir); Shelby Co Tuberc & Health Asn (dir). Relig: Roman Catholic. Mailing Add: PO Box 435 Russia OH 45363

FRANCISCO, DOUGLAS LLOYD (R)
b Wilmington, Del, Apr 6, 42; s Lawrence William Francisco & Shirley B Del, BA, 65. Polit & Govt Pos: Legis asst, US Rep Daniel E Button, NY, 67-71; admin asst, US Rep Tim Lee Carter, Ky, 71- Relig: Presbyterian. Mailing Add: 11021 Belton St Upper Marlboro MD 20870

FRANCISCO, JAMES LEE (D)
Kans State Sen
b Lamar, Colo, Oct 10, 37; s James Rufus Francisco & Wilma G White F; m 1958 to Sharon Lynn Maddux; c James D, Brenda L, Debra M & Jerald L. Educ: Wichita State Univ; Friends Univ. Polit & Govt Pos: Committeeman, Dem Party, Kans; Kans State Rep, 69th Dist, formerly; deleg, Dem Nat Conv, 68; Kans State Sen, 73- Mil Serv: Entered as Pvt, Marine Corps, 57, released as Pfc, 60. Mem: Am Legion; Int Asn of Machinists; Kans State Fedn of Labor; Kans State Coun of Machinists; Lions. Relig: Methodist. Legal Res: 604 N First Mulvane KS 67110 Mailing Add: 9709 E Central Wichita KS 67206

FRANCISCO, KENNETH DALE (D)
Kans State Rep
b Lamar, Colo, Nov 16, 41; s James Francisco & Wilma White F; m 1964 to Everell D Baldwin; c Darren L, Sean D, Shanna D. Educ: Wichita State Univ, 65. Polit & Govt Pos: Kans State Rep, 90th Dist, 75- Bus & Prof Pos: Owner, Classic Floors, Wichita, Kans, 67-75; salesman, Boyd Powell Floors, currently. Mil Serv: Entered as Pvt, Army, 60, released as Pfc, 63, after serv in Combat Support Co. Mem: Moose. Mailing Add: 4043 Dale Wichita KS 67204

FRANCOIS, EVAN A (R)
Polit & Govt Pos: Rep Nat Committeeman, formerly. Mailing Add: PO Box 276 St Thomas VI 00802

FRANCOIS, TERRY ARTHUR (D)
Mem, Calif Dem State Cent Comt
b New Orleans, La, Aug 28, 21; s Terry A Francois & Leona Keller F; m 1947 to Marion Claire Leblanc; c Wade Adrian, Gary Anthony, Brian Andrew, Eric Alfred & Carol Ann. Educ: Xavier Univ, BA, 40; Atlanta Univ, MA, 42; Hastings Col of Law, Univ Calif San Francisco, LLB, 49; Alpha Phi Alpha. Polit & Govt Pos: Mem, San Francisco Fair Employ Practices Comn, Calif, 57-59; mem, San Francisco Interim Human Rights Comt, 63-64; mem, San Francisco Bd Supvr, 64-; mem, Calif Ment Retardation Adv Bd, 66-; mem, Dem Co Comt, 67-; mem, Calif Dem State Cent Comt, 68-; chmn, Regional Criminal Justice Adv Bd, 69- Bus & Prof Pos: Attorney-at-law, San Francisco, Calif, 50-; pres, Multi-Cult Inst, currently. Mil Serv: Entered as Pvt, Marines, 42, released as Platoon Sgt, 45, after serv in 51st Defense Bn, SPac Theater, 44-45. Mem: State Bar of Calif; San Francisco Bar Asn; San Francisco Lawyers Club; Charles Houston Law Club; NAACP. Honors & Awards: Served as Acting Mayor of San Francisco on several occasions during Mayor's absence. Relig: Catholic. Legal Res: 20 Taraval St San Francisco CA 94116 Mailing Add: 497 Fulton St San Francisco CA 94102

FRANDSEN, LLOYD WAYNE (R)
Utah State Rep
b Panguitch, Utah, Feb 16, 48; s Lawrence Wayne Frandsen & Margaret Sevy F; m 1974 to Suzanne Holt. Polit & Govt Pos: Utah State Rep, Dist 73, 75- Bus & Prof Pos: Real estate, currently. Relig: Latter-day Saint. Mailing Add: Box 394 Panguitch UT 84759

FRANGELLA, JOSEPH CARMEN (R)
Secy, NY Rep State Comt
b Albany, NY, July 9, 28; s Nicholas Joseph Frangella & Frances Mayone F; m 1956 to Theresa Dolores Ryan; c Nicholas Joseph, Frances Amelia, Faith Mary, Michael James, Felice Ann & Alexia Mary. Educ: Cornell Univ, 2 years; Siena Col, 3 years; Albany Law Sch, 1 year; Alpha Phi Delta. Polit & Govt Pos: Chmn, Rep Orgn Town of Coeymans, 60-66; chmn, Albany Co Rep Comt, 66-; secy, NY Rep State Comt, 68-; deleg, Rep Nat Conv, 68 & 72. Bus & Prof Pos: Owner & operator, Fran Mushroom Co, Inc, currently. Mil Serv: Entered as Pvt, Army, 54, released as Cpl, 56, after serv in 503rd Transportation Corps, European Theatre US ERA, 55-56; Good Conduct Medal; European Theatre Serv Ribbon; German Occup Serv Ribbon. Mem: Am Farm Bur; Lions Int; KofC; Elks; Wolfert's Roost Country Club. Relig: Roman Catholic. Mailing Add: Forest Hill Rd Slingerlands NY 12159

FRANK, ALFRED SWIFT, JR (R)
b Dayton, Ohio, Feb 9, 24; s Alfred Swift Frank, Sr & Mary Conover F; single. Educ: Cornell Univ, 1 year; Miami Univ, Ohio, BS, 48; Univ Cincinnati, LLB, 51; Delta Sigma Pi; Phi Delta Phi; Beta Theta Pi. Polit & Govt Pos: Attorney adv, Fed Communications Comn, 61-69; admin asst, US Rep Charles W Whalen, Jr, Ohio, 70- Bus & Prof Pos: Partner, Brumbaugh, Corwin & McDonnell, 51-61; ed staff, Cincinnati Law Rev. Mil Serv: Army, 43-46, serv in ETO, 44-46; Lt, Naval Res, 50- Publ: Habeas Corpus, Cincinnati Law Rev, 1/51. Mem: Dayton & Fed Bar Asns; English-Speaking Union; Ohio State Soc; Washington Performing Arts Soc. Relig: Protestant. Legal Res: 321 Harman Blvd Dayton OH 45419 Mailing Add: 700 New Hampshire Ave NW Washington DC 20037

FRANK, BARNEY (D)
Mass State Rep
b Bayonne, NJ, Mar 31, 40; s Samuel Frank & Elsie Golush F; single. Educ: Harvard Col, AB, 62. Polit & Govt Pos: Exec asst to Mayor, Boston, 68-71; admin asst, US Rep M J Harrington, Mass, 71-72; Mass State Rep, 73- Mem: Phi Beta Kappa; Am for Dem Action (secy, 71-72). Mailing Add: 18 Commonwealth Ave Boston MA 02116

FRANK, GERALD WENDEL (R)
b Portland, Ore, Sept 21, 23; s Aaron M Frank (deceased) & Ruth Rosenfeld F (deceased); single. Educ: Stanford Univ, 41-42; Loyola Univ of Los Angeles, 43-44; Cambridge Univ, BA, 48, MS, 53. Hon Degrees: DBA, Greenville Col, 71. Polit & Govt Pos: Mem, Gov Adv Comt Econ Develop Comn, Ore, 57-73, chmn 8 years; gen chmn, Gov Mark Hatfield for US Sen Comt, Ore, 66, spec asst to US Sen Mark Hatfield, Ore, 67-75, admin asst, 75-; deleg-at-lg, Rep Nat Conv, 68; gen chmn, Reelect Sen Mark Hatfield Comt, 72. Bus & Prof Pos: Vpres & store mgr, Meier & Frank Co, Portland & Salem, Ore, 48-65. Mil Serv: Entered as Pvt, Army, 43, released as Sgt, 46, after serv in 89th Inf Div, ETO, 44-46. Mem: Salem Area CofC; Salem League of Women Voters; Rotary; Am Legion; Elks. Honors & Awards: Pac Northwest Serv to Mankind Award, Sertoma, 67; Named State of Ore Outstanding Salesman of 61; Silver Beaver Award, Boy Scouts, 63; Named Admiral, Astoria Regatta, 64; Named Salem First Citizen of 64. Legal Res: 3250 Crestview Dr Salem OR 97302 Mailing Add: Standard Ins Bldg Salem OR 97301

FRANK, GERARD VINCENT (D)
Colo State Rep
b New York, NY, May 24, 37; s Otto H Frank & Mary Brennan F; m 1967 to Marian J Culbert; c Magdaline Marie & Dagmar Denise. Educ: Fordham Univ, BA, 58; Univ Colo, MA, 70. Polit & Govt Pos: Colo State Rep, 73- Relig: Catholic. Mailing Add: 9890 E Fifth Ave Aurora CO 80010

FRANK, HELEN JOYCE (D)
Committeewoman, SDak Dem State Cent Comt
b Manchester, SDak, Mar 3, 32; d Elmer O Grotta & Lottie Beachler G; m 1950 to Stanley Richard Frank; c Blair Stanley, Rhonda Lee & Brenda Kay. Educ: Wash High Sch, Sioux Falls, grad. Polit & Govt Pos: Dem precinct committeewoman, Minnehaha Co, SDak, 65-69; committeewoman, SDak Dem State Cent Comt, 66-; deleg, Dem Nat Conv, 68; chmn, Minnehaha Co Dem Party, 73- Mem: AFL-CIO Auxiliary (pres, Sioux Falls Coun, past secy-treas, SDak State Coun); Eastern Star; United Commercial Travelers. Honors & Awards: Woman Doer of the Year, Minnehaha Co Dem Party, 67. Relig: Methodist. Mailing Add: 827 S Euclid Ave Sioux Falls SD 57104

FRANK, KURT A (D)
Wis State Sen
Mailing Add: 933 E Ohio Ave Milwaukee WI 53207

FRANKEL, CHARLES (D)
b New York, NY, Dec 13, 17; s Abraham Philip Frankel & Estelle Edith Cohen F; m 1941 to Helen Beatrice Lehman; c Susan & Carl. Educ: Columbia Col, New York, AB with honors, 37, Columbia Univ, PhD, 46; Cornell Univ, 37-38; Phi Beta Kappa. Hon Degrees: LLD, Mercer Univ, 68. Polit & Govt Pos: Asst secy of State, Washington, DC, 65-67; mem, NY State Comn on Quality & Cost of Educ, 69- Bus & Prof Pos: Faculty mem, Columbia Univ, 39-, prof philos, 56-; host, TV Prog, World of Ideas, 59; chief consult ed, Current Mag, 60-65; ed-at-lg, Saturday Rev, New York, 68-71; Old Dominion Prof of philos & pub affairs, Columbia Univ, 70- Mil Serv: Lt(sg), Naval Res, 42-46. Publ: Auth, High on foggy bottom, Harper & Row, 69; The pleasures of philosophy, 72 & A stubborn case, 72, W W Norton & Co; plus others. Mem: Am Philos Asn; Am Asn Univ Prof; fel, Am Acad of Arts & Sci; Authors League of Am; Coun on Foreign Rels. Honors & Awards: Fulbright Research Prof, Univ Paris, 53-54; Guggenheim Fel, 53-54; Carnegie Corp Reflective Year Fel, 59-60; vis scholar, Russell Sage Found, 71-72. Legal Res: 317 Phillips Hill Rd New City NY 10956 Mailing Add: 3 E 71st St New York NY 10021

FRANKEN, JOHN H (D)
Chmn, Carroll Co Dem Cent Comt, Mo
b Norborne, Mo, Jan 14, 15; s Joseph H Franken & Anna Barkley F; m 1952 to Priscilla Tatro; c John C & Dennis T. Educ: Northwest Mo State Col, 33-35; Univ of Mo, 35-36. Polit & Govt Pos: Mayor, Norborne, Mo, 50-56; chmn, Carroll Co Dem Cent Comt, currently; deleg, Dem Nat Conv, 68. Bus & Prof Pos: Mo Bar Asn, 40- Mil Serv: Entered as Aviation Cadet, Army Air Corps, 41, released as 1st Lt, 45, after serv in Training Command. Mem: KofC. Relig: Catholic. Mailing Add: 6 S Folger Carrollton MO 64633

FRANKENBURG, RICHARD JAMES (R)
Committeeman, Allegheny Co Rep Comt, Pa
b Pittsburgh, Pa, June 3, 29; s George Frankenburg & Ethel Shepherd Cunningham F; m 1954 to Sue Anna Ward; c Cheryl Anne & Linda Sue. Educ: Wilkinsburg High Sch, Pa, grad, 48; Univ Pittsburgh Inst Local Govt, 65; Nat Honor Soc. Polit & Govt Pos: Committeeman, Allegheny Co Rep Comt, Pa, 62-; borough councilman, Wilkinsburg, 65-71; Pa State Rep, 71-74. Bus & Prof Pos: Mem, Int Union Operating Engrs Local 66B, 22 years. Mil Serv: Entered as Constructionman 3/C, Seabee Res, 50, released as PO 1/C, 60, after serv in McKeesport, Pa. Mem: Am Legion; F&AM; John Birch Soc; Friends of Scouting; Nat Rifle Asn. Relig: Protestant; bd mem & financial secy of church. Mailing Add: 1637 Doyle St Pittsburgh PA 15221

FRANKLIN, GOLDA BRIDGES (D)
b Monticello, Miss, Feb 10, 38; d Edgar Bridges & Willie Mae Newman B; m 1961 to Jimmie L Franklin; c Elizabeth Renee & Marvin Lewis. Educ: Jackson State Univ, BS, 61; Alpha Kappa Alpha. Polit & Govt Pos: Deleg, Dem Nat Conv, 72. Mailing Add: 502 Coolidge Ave Charleston IL 61920

FRANKS, VAUDRY LEE (D)
Chmn, Franklin Co Dem Exec Comt, Ala
b Guin, Ala, Mar 27, 21; s Willie O Franks & Mertie Stowe F; m 1940 to Vaudine Pickens; c Jerry L & Larry J. Educ: Glen Allen High Sch, Ala, 12 years; col bus course, 1 year 6 months. Polit & Govt Pos: Chmn, Franklin Co Dem Exec Comt, Ala, 60-; co Dem campaign mgr, 60- Bus & Prof Pos: Merchant, Russelville, Ala, 56-61; agent, Metropolitan Life Ins Co, 64- Mil Serv: Entered as Pvt, Army, 44, released as Cpl, 46, after serv in 82nd Air Borne Div, Berlin Occupation, Europe, 45; Good Conduct Medal; Unit Presidential Citation; French & Belgian Unit Awards; European Medal. Mem: Civitan; VFW; Am Legion. Honors & Awards: Hon Lt Col, Gov Lurleen B Wallace's Staff, Ala. Relig: Baptist. Mailing Add: PO Box 69 Russelville AL 35653

FRAPPIER, J H (R)
Mo State Sen
b Milwaukee, Wis, Aug 8, 31; s Francis S Frappier & Dorothy Ihrig A; m 1955 to Marian Joyce Pridgen; c Bettina Jo, Michelle Rae & Lisa Rene. Educ: Ind Univ, BS, 57, MBA, 58. Polit & Govt Pos: Councilman, Florissant, Mo, 63 & 65; Mo State Rep, 56th Dist, 67-75; Mo State Sen, Second Dist, 75- Bus & Prof Pos: Methods coordr, Laclede Gas Co. Mil Serv: Entered as Pvt, Marine Corps, 51, released as Sgt, 53, after serv in Korea, 52-53; Presidential Unit Citation; UN Medal; Korean Medal with two Stars. Relig: Christian. Mailing Add: 2665 Sorrell Dr Florissant MO 63033

FRASER, DONALD H (D)
Ga State Rep
Mailing Add: PO Box 472 Hinesville GA 31313

FRASER, DONALD MACKAY (DFL)
US Rep, Minn
b Minneapolis, Minn, Feb 20, 24; m to Arvonne Skelton; c Six (one deceased). Educ: Univ Minn, BA, cum laude, 44, LLB, 48; Naval ROTC. Polit & Govt Pos: Dem-Farmer-Labor Activities, 47-; Minn State Sen, 54-62; chmn, Minn Citizens for Kennedy, 60; secy, Minn Deleg to Dem Nat Conv, 60, deleg, 64 & 68; US Rep, Minn, 62-, mem int rels comt & chmn subcomt int orgns, US House Rep, currently, mem, DC Comt, currently; participation mem, Anglo-Am Parliamentary Conf on Africa, 64-; vchmn, Comn on Dem Selection of Presidential Nominees, 68; chmn, Dem Study Group, 69-71; chmn, Comn on Party Structure & Deleg Selection, Dem Party, 71-72; nat chmn, Am for Dem Action, 73- Bus & Prof Pos: Partner, Law Firm of Lindquist, Fraser & Magnuson, 54-62. Mil Serv: Navy, radar off, Pac Theatre, World War II. Mem: Minn Law Alumni Asn (bd); Minneapolis Foreign Policy Asn; Minneapolis Citizens' League; Minneapolis Citizens' Comt on Pub Educ; Legal Aid Soc (bd). Legal Res: Minneapolis MN Mailing Add: 1253 Fourth St SW Washington DC 20024

FRASER, EMILE J (D)
Maine State Rep
Mailing Add: 47 Osgood Ave Mexico ME 04257

FRASER, THOMAS JEFFERSON (D)
Chmn, Chase Co Dem Party, Nebr
b Bonne Terre, Mo, Dec 23, 32; s John M Fraser & Velma M Highley F; m 1956 to Virginia Helen Reeves; c Thomas L, Theodore P, Laurel Elizabeth & Paul Jon (deceased). Educ: Flat River Jr Col, AA, 52; Cent Col, Mo, BA, 54; Perkins Sem, Southern Methodist Univ, BD, 57; Jr Col Scholastic Hon; Church Scholarships. Polit & Govt Pos: Mem, Knox Co Dem Comt, Nebr, 64; mem, Nebr State Dem Comt, 68; alt deleg Dem Nat Conv, 68; mem, Scotts Bluff Co Dem Comt, Nebr, 68-72; mem, Nebr Dem State Cent Comt, 68-; mem, Nebr State Manpower Planning Bd, 72-; chmn, Chase Co Dem Party, Nebr, 72- Bus & Prof Pos: United Methodist minister, Genoa, Nebr, 57-61, Norfolk, 61-64, Bloomfield, 64-67, Gering, 67-69, Wauneta, 69-75 & Pawnee City, 75-; conducted youth summer camping progs, 6 summers. Mem: Chase Co Ministerial Asn; Am Friends Serv Comt; Lions; Optimists; Rotary. Honors & Awards: Boys State Award, 49; Danforth Award 50. Relig: United Methodist. Legal Res: c/o T C Reeves RFD 1 Central City NE 68826 Mailing Add: Methodist Church Pawnee City NE 68420

FRASER, WILLIAM CHARLES (R)
Mem, Nebr Rep State Cent Comt
b Walnut, Iowa, June 20, 87; s William E Fraser & Dora Burton F; m 1909 to Mabel Gray; c Dorothy (Mrs Samuel), Mary (Mrs Nicholson), Robert G & Barbara (Mrs Martin). Educ: Creighton Univ, LLB, 08. Polit & Govt Pos: Mem, Post War Planning Comn; treas, Nebr Rep State Comt, 36-46; mem, Nebr Rep State Cent Comt & Finance & Budget Comt, 36-; chmn, Rep Founders Day, 55; deleg, Rep Nat Conv, 60 & 64; Presidential Elector from Nebr, 68. Bus & Prof Pos: Mem bd dirs, Musser-Mosler Cattle Co & Fawn Lake Ranch Co, 35 years; pres, Omaha Bar Asn, 24-25; pres Omaha Community Chest, 30-31; mem bd dirs, Omaha CofC, 36-46, pres, 40-41; regional chmn, Nebr Develop Comt, 41-45; regional chmn, Nebr Adv Defense Comt, 41-46; Nebr State Capitol Bldg Chmn, 12 years; mem Nebr State Bd of Bar Exam, 5 years; mem adv bd, St Catherine's Hosp, 60- Mil Serv: World War I; mem, US Navy State Selection Comt & Air Corps Civilian Comt, World War II. Mem: Boys Clubs of Omaha; Omaha Urban League; fel Am Bar Asn; Nat Conf of Christians & Jews; KofC (Grand Knight, 17-18). Honors & Awards: Received plaque for outstanding serv, Founders' Day State of Nebr, 67 & sixty years serv, Douglas Co Rep Party, 70; Recognition as mem US Supreme Court for fifty years, 68. Relig: Catholic. Legal Res: Radisson-Blackstone Hotel Apt 525 302 S 36th St Omaha NE 68131 Mailing Add: 510 Electric Bldg Omaha NE 68102

FRASSINELLI, ATTILIO (D)
Chmn, Stafford Springs Town Dem Party, Conn
b Stafford, Conn, Aug 7, 08; s John D Frassinelli & Josephine Dell'Agnese F; m to Mildred M McLagan; c Gordon, David, Claire (Mrs Wilmer West), Nancy (Mrs Richard Bilyak) & Virginia (Mrs Richard Pisciotta). Educ: Metrop Schs of Acct, Boston; LaSalle Univ. Polit & Govt Pos: Mem sch bd, Conn, 40-48; chmn town comt, 44-48; Conn State Rep, 46-56; selectman, 47-59; Comnr of Food & Drugs, 55-59; Comnr of Consumer Protection, 59-66; Lt Gov, Conn, 66-71; mem, Civil Defense Adv Coun & chmn, Exec Comt on Human Rights & Opportunities, 67-; mem, Viet Nam Bonus Appeals Bd & Inter-govt Coop Comn, 68-; chmn, Stafford Springs Town Dem Party, Conn, 71-; alt deleg, Dem Nat Conv, 72. Bus & Prof Pos: Ins & Real Estate Broker. Mem: Rotary (pres); KofC; Cent Atlantic States Asn. Honors & Awards: Italian Execs William Paca Award. Mailing Add: 1 Grant Ave Stafford Springs CT 06076

FRATE, GENNARO W (R)
Conn State Rep
Mailing Add: 47 Hecker Ave Darien CT 06820

FRATES, KENT F (R)
Okla State Sen
Mailing Add: State Capitol Oklahoma City OK 73105

FRAZEE, CLYDE L (R)
b Hugoton, Kans, July 18, 23; s William Forrest & Juanita Moser F; m 1944 to Margaret L Patton; c Forrest Wayne, Dennis Gene & Robert Allen. Educ: Eads Pub Sch. Polit & Govt Pos: Chmn, Kiowa Co Rep Cent Comt, Colo, formerly. Bus & Prof Pos: Rancher, currently. Mem: Elks Lodge 1319. Relig: Protestant. Mailing Add: RR 2 Eads CO 81036

FRAZIER, BERT LEE (R)
b Burem, Tenn, Nov 13, 26; s Dana Frazier & Mattie Mitchell F; m 1953 to Joan Price; c Margaret Ann & William Dana. Educ: ETenn State Univ, BS in mkt, 51; grad study, Univ Tenn & Univ Miss. Polit & Govt Pos: Mem, Lee Co Rep Exec Comt, Miss, 62-63; chmn, Lee Co Rep Comt, formerly; alt deleg, Rep Nat Conv, 68. Bus & Prof Pos: Lab staff & time keeper, Eastman Kodak, 47 & 51-52; ins adjuster, Commercial Credit Corp, 52-54; ins adjuster, Gen Adjustment Bur, 54-57; claims mgr, Hartford Fire Ins Co Group, 57-59; owner, One Hour Martinizing Drycleaning & Robo Car Wash, presently. Mil Serv: Entered as Pvt, Army, 45, released as Pfc, 47, after serv in Aviation Engrs, Philippines. Mem: Blue Goose Int; Am Legion; VFW; Flying Club; Aircraft Owners & Pilots Asn. Relig: Baptist. Legal Res: 123 Enoch Ave Tupelo MS 38801 Mailing Add: PO Box 721 Tupelo MS 38801

FRAZIER, CAROLINE HOLLINGSWORTH (R)
b Carroll Co, Ga, Mar 31, 26; d James Fred Hollingsworth & Cleo Patra Morgan H; div. Educ: WGa Col, Normal Dipl, 45; Univ Ga, AB, 47; Emory Univ, 50; Ga State Univ, MAT, 67; Phi Kappa Phi; Phi Beta Kappa. Polit & Govt Pos: Deleg, DeKalb Co Rep Conv, Ga, 66, 68 & 70; deleg, Nat Young Rep Conv, Omaha, Nebr, 67; precinct leader, DeKalb Co, Ga, 68; poll mgr, DeKalb Co Bd Registr, 68; honor guard, Rep Nat Conv, 68, alt deleg, 72; pres, DeKalb Fedn of Rep Women, Ga, 69 & 72-; deleg, DeKalb Co Rep Exec Comt, 70; deleg & mem rules comt, Ga Fedn of Rep Women Conv, 70; deleg, Nat Fedn Rep Women Conv, Washington, DC, 70. Bus & Prof Pos: Research asst, State of Ga Agency, 47-48; educator, Atlanta Sch Syst, 48-73; chmn dept social studies, Smith High Sch, 60-63; educator, Roosevelt High Sch, Atlanta, Ga, 73- Publ: Resolutions adopted by National Education Association Convention, Nat Educ Asn, 70. Mem: Atlanta Asn Educators; Ga Asn Educators. Relig: Christian & Missionary Alliance. Mailing Add: 2931 Mt Olive Dr Decatur GA 30033

FRAZIER, JAMES BERIAH, JR (D)
b Chattanooga, Tenn, June 23, 90; s James Beriah Frazier & Louise Douglas Kieth F; m 1939 to Elizabeth Hope; c Elizabeth Hope. Educ: Univ Va; Chattanooga Col, LLB, 14. Polit & Govt Pos: US Attorney, Eastern Dist, Tenn, 33, 37 & 41-48; US Rep, Tenn, 49-62. Bus & Prof Pos: Lawyer with firm Frazier & Frazier. Mil Serv: Maj, World War I. Relig: Methodist. Mailing Add: Frazier & Frazier 622 Georgia Ave Chattanooga TN 37403

FRAZIER, LINCOLN B (R)
Chmn, 11th Cong Dist Rep Party, Mich
b Aurora, Ill, Sept 20, 05; s Lincoln B Frazier & Bertha Plumb F; m 1939 to Anne Maxwell Reynolds; c Julia, Peter W & Lincoln B, Jr. Educ: Univ Wis, BS, 27; Delta Kappa Epsilon. Polit & Govt Pos: Finance chmn, Marquette Co Rep Party, Mich, 58-68; chmn, 11th Cong Dist Rep Party, 69- Bus & Prof Pos: Pres, Campbell Supply Co, 40- Mil Serv: Entered as Lt, Navy, 42, released as Lt Comdr, 46, after serv as Inspector of Naval Material, USA. Mem: CofC. Relig: Protestant. Mailing Add: 460 E Ridge St Marquette MI 49855

FRAZZINI, MARY (R)
Mem, Nev Rep Cent Comt
b Oakland, Calif, d Hugh Cort Cameron & Johanna Vollmar C; m 1939 to E Carson Frazzini; c Carson Cameron. Educ: Glendale City Col, Calif, 2 years; Glendale Bus Col, 8 months. Polit & Govt Pos: Clerk, Co Sch Bd, 40-44; mem, Washoe Co Rep Cent Comt, Nev, 57-; mem, Nev Rep Cent Comt, 61-; deleg, Rep Nat Conv, 64; Nev State Assemblyman, 64-72; vchmn, Gov Comn Status Woman, 67-71. Bus & Prof Pos: Dir, Sr Citizens Ctr, Reno, 73- Mem: Rep Women's Club, Reno; Nev Fedn Rep Women (vchmn, Reno Comn Status Women, 70-); Northern Nev Women's Polit Caucus (vchmn, 71-); Int Soc for Women Teachers; Delta Kappa Gamma. Honors & Awards: Woman of the Year Award, Reno Bus & Prof Women's Club; One of Three Outstanding Rep Women in US, 69. Mailing Add: 9345 Fleetwood Dr Reno NV 89508

FREAR, JOSEPH ALLEN, JR (D)
b Rising Sun, Del, Mar 7, 03; s Joseph Frear & Clara Lowber F; m 1933 to Esther Viola Schauer; c Fred, Clara, Louise. Educ: Univ of Del, BS, 24; Sigma Nu. Polit & Govt Pos: State comnr, State Col, 36-41, Old Age Welfare, 37-48 & Del State Hosp, 46-48; US Sen, Del, 49-61; mem, Securities & Exchange Comn, 61-63. Bus & Prof Pos: Agriculturist, 22-; dir & chmn bd, Fed Land Bank, Baltimore, 46-48; dir, Farmer's Bank, Dover & Baltimore Trust Co, Camden; past pres, Kent Gen Hosp; vpres, Wilmington Trust Co, Dover. Mil Serv: World War I & Lt Col, Officer Res Corps, World War II. Mem: CofC; Am Legion; Del State Farm Bur; Mason; KT. Mailing Add: 622 S State St Dover DE 19901

FREBORG, LAYTON WALLACE (R)
NDak State Rep
b Underwood, NDak, May 13, 33; s Samuel Arnold Freborg & Laura Gayle Caldwell F; m 1951 to Delilah Jane Walcker; c Terry, Candace, Lisa, Michelle & Dawn. Educ: Underwood Pub Schs, NDak. Polit & Govt Pos: NDak State Rep, 73- Bus & Prof Pos: Owner gen contracting firm, Underwood, NDak, currently. Relig: Methodist. Mailing Add: 300 Third Underwood ND 58576

FREBURG, CHARLES RAYMOND (R)
b Walnut Grove, Ill, Jan 16, 12; s Ernest Victor Freburg & Laura Beatrice Raymond F; m 1939 to Mary Josephine Snell; c Lindsay Mark. Educ: Eureka Col, AB. Polit & Govt Pos: Admin asst to US Rep Fred Schwengel, Iowa, 55-64; admin asst to US Rep Chester L Mize, Kans, 65-71; admin asst to US Rep LaMar Baker, Tenn, 71- Bus & Prof Pos: Sch teacher, Prairie City, Ill, 35-38; prog dir, WOC, WOC-TV, Davenport, Iowa, 38-52; asst to pres, KWWL-TV, Waterloo, 53-54; radio-TV dir, Sperry-Boom, Inc Davenport, 54-55. Mil Serv: Army, Sgt, Inf, 43-46; Inf Replacement Training Cent, Camp Roberts, Calif. Mem: Tau Kappa Epsilon. Mailing Add: 2000 Stirrup Lane Alexandria VA 22308

FREDA, ALDO (D)
RI State Rep
b Providence, RI, July 18, 21. Educ: Cent High Sch; courses in Life Ins Off Mgt. Polit & Govt Pos: Chmn, 12th Rep Dist Comt, RI, formerly; RI State Rep, Dist 14, 61-, Dep Majority Leader, RI House of Rep, 69-, vchmn, Corp Comt & mem, Joint Comt Hwy Safety, currently; mem, 14th Rep Dist Comt, currently; spec asst to chmn, RI Dem State Comt, 73- Bus & Prof Pos: Dist off supvr, John Hancock Life Ins Co. Mil Serv: Sgt, Air Force, 42-46, Chief Clerk, Radar Sect. Relig: Catholic; past pres, Holy Name Soc, Our Lady of Mt Carmel Church, Providence, RI. Mailing Add: 115 Vinton St Providence RI 02909

FREDA, CARMINE (R)
Chmn, Rockland Co Rep Party, NY
b Manhattan, NY, May 4, 01; s Louis Alfonse Freda & Sophia Mellucio F; m 1937 to Hazel Loretta Burnie; c William C & Louis J. Educ: First Inst Podiatry; Long Island Col, DP, 21; Fordham Univ, 22. Polit & Govt Pos: Village trustee, Grand View on the Hudson, NY, 48-56; sch bd trustee, Cent Sch Dist 1, 48-66; mayor, Grand View Nyack, 55-66; mem adv comt, Hudson River Valley Scenic Comn, 64-; chmn, Rockland Co Rep Party, 66-; alt deleg, Rep Nat Conv, 68 & 72; mem med adv comt, NY State Dept of Soc Serv, 68-; comnr, NY State Comn on Pure Waters, 69, mem bd, Pure Waters Auth, currently; mem & dir, Environ Facil Corp, currently. Mil Serv: Lt, Coast Guard Auxiliary, 41-42; entered as Lt, Navy, 42, released as Comdr, 47, after serv in Naval Aviation as officer in charge of aviation training, Corpus Christi, Tex & US Marine Corps Air Sta, Cherry Point, NC, 42-43; Comdr (Ret), Naval Res, 47-62; Pearl Harbor Medal; Am Theatre Medal; 10 Year & 20 Year Good Conduct Medals; Presidential Commendation Medal with Pendant; plus others. Publ: Articles & booklet. Mem: Asn Am Foot Specialists (chmn); Affiliated Podiatrists of NY (mem polit action comt); US Naval Aviation Asn; Naval Order of the US; Retired Officers Asn. Relig: Catholic. Mailing Add: 85 River Rd Grand View on the Hudson Nyack NY 10960

FREDERICK, BEEBE RAY, JR (R)
Mem Exec Comt, Montgomery Co Rep Comt, Ala
b Ft Deposit, Ala, Oct 12, 38; s Beebe Ray Frederick & Emma Lou Golson F M; single. Educ: Auburn Univ, BS, 60; Delta Sigma Pi; Pi Kappa Alpha. Polit & Govt Pos: Dir, Young Rep Nat Fedn, 71-73; chmn, Montgomery Co Young Rep, Ala, 71-73; mem exec comt, Montgomery Co Rep Comt, 71-; alt deleg, Rep Nat Conv, 72. Bus & Prof Pos: Salesman, Liberty Mutual, 62-64; Universal Underwriters, 64-65; mgr, Auerbach Jordan Co, 66-72; partner, H & F Cattle Co, 70-; pres, C Ward Hall Ins Agency, Inc, 72-; pres, Auerbach Jordan Agency, Inc, 72- Mil Serv: Entered as 2nd Lt, Army, 60, released as 2nd Lt, 61, after serv in 2nd Medium Tank Bn, 69th Armor Div, Ft Benning, Ga, 60-61. Mem: Independent Ins Agents of Montgomery (pres, 71); Jaycees (vpres & dir, 71-72); Ala Jr Miss Pageant, Inc (vpres & dir, 71-73); Montgomery Riverboat Comn, Inc (dir, 71-73); Ala Cattlemen's Asn. Relig: Methodist. Legal Res: 3144 Old Dobbin Rd Montgomery AL 36111 Mailing Add: PO Box 669 Montgomery AL 36101

FREDERICK, CAROLYN ESSIG (R)
SC State Rep
b Atlanta, Ga; d Philip Martin Essig & Lillian Margaret Hall E; m 1933 to Holmes Walter Frederick; c Lynn (Mrs John Grant Williamson) & Rosa Margaret (Mrs Glen Clayton Smith). Educ: Agnes Scott Col, AB, 28. Polit & Govt Pos: SC State Rep, US Comt for UNICEF, 63-65; SC State Rep, 66-, vchmn, Educ & Pub Works Comt, SC House Rep, 67-; secy, Greenville Co Deleg, 67 & 68; vchmn, State-Wide Planning Comt Nursing Educ, 71-; mem, SC Higher Educ Comn Tuition Grants Comt, 72- Bus & Prof Pos: Pub rels consult, 54-; mgr, Greenville Symphony Orchestra, 54-70; pub rels dir, YWCA Develop Prog, 58-64; newspaper writer; former dir advert & sales prom, Burdine's, Miami, Fla. Mem: Nat League Am Pen Women; Am Asn Univ Women (SC State Bd, nat mass media comt, pres, SC Div, 59-61, past pres, Ithaca, NY & Greenville, SC br, nat topic comt media, 73-); White House Conf Children & Youth Youth; Converse Col Master Arts in Teaching Prog (adv comt, 61-66); Alliance for Arts Educ Comt. Honors & Awards: Named SC Woman of the Year, 70; App by President Nixon to Adv Comt to John F Kennedy Ctr for the Performing Arts, 70-; Carolyn Frederick Educ Found Fel Grant estab by Am Asn Univ Women, 71 & 74; Robert W Beatty Outstanding Serv to Youth Award, SC Youth Worker's Asn, 74; Citizen of Year, Cent Chap, Nat Asn Social Workers, 75. Relig: Presbyterian; mem, Long-Range Planning Comt, First Presby Church, 72- Mailing Add: 326 Chick Springs Rd Greenville SC 29609

FREDERICK, MELVIN LYLE (R)
Minn State Sen
b West Concord, Minn, Nov 24, 29; s Elmer J Frederick & Martha E Pagel F; m 1956 to Donna M Christopherson; c Mitchell Scott, Debra Leigh & Michael Alan. Educ: West Concord High Sch, Minn, 4 years. Polit & Govt Pos: Rep precinct chmn, West Concord, Minn, 61-67; vchmn, Dodge Co Rep Comt, 65-67, chmn, 67-69; first vchmn, First Dist Rep Party, 69-; Minn State Sen, 71- Bus & Prof Pos: Registered rep, Dain, Kalman & Quail, Inc, mem, New York Stock Exchange, currently. Mil Serv: Entered as Pvt, Army Nat Guard, 48, released as M/Sgt, 52, after serv in Co E, 19th Inf Regt, 24th Div, Korea, Far East Command, 51-52; Japan Occup & UN Medals; lo/s Bar; Combat Infantrymans Badge; Korean Serv Medal with One Bronze Serv Star. Mem: Minn Food Retailers Asn; West Concord Businessmens Asn; Mason; Am Legion; Lions Int. Relig: United Methodist. Mailing Add: 414 Clyde St West Concord MN 55985

FREDERICK, WILLARD D (D)
b Winter Haven, Fla, July 6, 34; s Willard D Frederick & Lucille Adams F; m to Joanne Race; c Charles Rogers, Virginia Adams & John Thomas. Educ: Duke Univ, AB, 52-56; Univ Fla, JD, 67; Phi Beta Kappa; Omicron Delta Kappa; Beta Omega Sigma; Sigma Delta Phi; Phi Delta Phi. Polit & Govt Pos: Pub defender, Ninth Judicial Circuit Court, 63-68; mem, Gov Select Comt on POW/MIA, 71; mem bd, Dept Pollution Control, Fla, 73-74, chmn, 74-; mem, Dem Charter Comn, 74. Bus & Prof Pos: Attorney; partner, Billings, Frederick, Wooten & Honeywell, PA, 66-; mem ex-officio, Fla Coun 100, 75- Mem: Fla Bar; Am Bar Asn; Acad Fla Trial Lawyers; Am Trial Lawyers Asn; Univ Club Orlando. Honors & Awards: Distinguished Serv Award, Orlando Jaycees, 64-65; Man of the Week, Orlando Sentinel Sun Mag, 66; Outstanding Young Men of Am, Jaycees Int, 68. Relig: Presbyterian. Legal Res: 105 W New Hampshire Ave Orlando FL 32803 Mailing Add: 236 S Lucerne Circle Orlando FL 32801

FREDERICKSON, LYLE L (R)
b Norma, NDak, Nov 20, 05; s Harry Frederickson & Pauline Tredt F; m 1929 to Margaret Marie Carstens; c Harold (deceased). Educ: Minot State Teachers Col, 6 months; NDak State Univ, 1 year. Polit & Govt Pos: Precinct Three committeeman, Third Dist Rep Party, NDak, 62-, chmn, 67-72, finance chmn, currently. Bus & Prof Pos: Owner grocery store, 30-57; farmer, owner & operator, 38- Mem: Farm Bur; Farmers Union; Kenmare Asn Commerce. Honors & Awards: Membership Awards. Relig: Lutheran. Mailing Add: 204 NW Sixth St Kenmare ND 58746

FREDLUND, RAY (R)
Chmn, Iberville Parish Rep Exec Comt, La
b Valley Stream, NY, July 31, 25; s Nils Victor Fredlund & Alice Mason F; m 1947 to Lorene Hilda Jesse; c Loren Raymond, Alice Marie, Susan Lee, Glen George & Taffie Ruth. Educ: Rensselaer Polytech Inst, BChE, 50. Polit & Govt Pos: Mem, Rep State Cent Comt, La, 66-; chmn, Parish Polit Action Coun, Iberville Parish, 67-68, vchmn, 69; chmn, Iberville Parish Rep Exec Comt, 67-; alt deleg, Rep Nat Conv, 68. Bus & Prof Pos: Chem engr, Austin Co, Tex, 50; proj leader, Dow Chem Co, Tex, 51-56, plant supt, Plaquemine, La, 57-67 & mgr plant tech serv, 67-70; div purchasing mgr, 70- Mil Serv: Entered as Pvt, Army Air Force, 43, released as 2nd Lt, 45, after serv in 487th Bomb Group, 8th Air Force, ETO, 45. Mem: Am Inst Chem Engrs; Registered Prof Engr, La; Gtr Baton Rouge Purchasing Agents Asn; Elks. Relig: Methodist. Mailing Add: 204 Pecan Tree Lane Plaquemine LA 70764

FREDMAN, SAMUEL GEORGE (D)
Chmn, Westchester Co Dem Comt, NY
b Reading, Pa, Mar 9, 24; s Nathan Fredman & Bessie Falkowitz F; m 1946 to Miriam Imber; c Neil Allen & Andrew David. Educ: Pa State Univ, BA, 42; Columbia Univ Law Sch, LLB, 47; Delta Sigma Rho; Beta Sigma Rho. Polit & Govt Pos: Pres, White Plains Dem Club, NY, 59-61; chmn, White Plains City Dem Comt, 64-65; vchmn, Westchester Co Dem Comt, 71-75, chmn, 75- Bus & Prof Pos: Attorney, Firm of Fink, Weinberger, Fredman & Charney, New York & White Plains, NY, 61- Mil Serv: Entered as Pvt, Air Force, 43, released as T/Sgt, 46, after serv in Far Eastern Air Forces, 45-46. Mem: Am Bar Asn (mem family law comt); Am Acad Matrimonial Lawyers (mem bd dirs, New York chap); Fedn Jewish Philanthropies (mem bd trustees & vpres, Synagogue Rels Comn); Westchester Co Bar Asn (mem bd dirs, family law sect). Relig: Jewish. Legal Res: 29 Colonial Rd White Plains NY 10605 Mailing Add: 551 Fifth Ave New York NY 10017

FREDRICKS, CONRAD BRADLEY (R)
Cong Committeeman, Mont State Rep Cent Comt
b Helena, Mont, Apr 10, 34; s William Henry Fredricks & Mabel DeKay F; m 1967 to Patricia Corleen Pettichord; c Bradley Earl & William Conrad. Educ: Mont State Univ, BS Chem, 55; Univ Mont, JD, 62; Phi Delta Phi; Alpha Chi Sigma; Sigma Alpha Epsilon. Polit & Govt Pos: Attorney, Sweet Grass Co, Mont, 71-74, pub adminr, 75-; mem, Mont Criminal Law Comn, 72-73; cong committeeman, Mont State Rep Cent Comt, 73- Bus & Prof Pos: Chemist, Anaconda Aluminum Co, 55-59; attorney-at-law, 62- Mil Serv: Entered as 2nd Lt, Army, 55, released as 1st Lt, 64. Publ: Class actions in Montana under Rule 23(a) (3), Mont Law Rev, spring 62. Mem: Am Bar Asn; State Bar Mont; Elks; Mason; Lions. Honors & Awards: Outstanding Grad, Univ Mont Law Sch, Phi Delta Phi, 62. Relig: Protestant. Legal Res: 901 Hooper St Big Timber MT 59011 Mailing Add: Box 520 Big Timber MT 59011

FREDRICKS, EDGAR JOHN (R)
Mich State Rep
b Holland, Mich, June 27, 42; s Russell Fredricks & Audrey Beckman F; single. Educ: Calvin Col, AB, 64; Western Mich Univ, MA in Hist, 67, MA in Sociol, 68. Polit & Govt Pos: Vconsul, Am Embassy, Seoul, Korea, 70-72; polit officer, US State Dept, 72-74; Mich State Rep, 75- Publ: MacArthur: His Mission & Meaning, Whitmore, 68; Moral myopia of US foreign policy, Human Events, 6/74. Mailing Add: 392 W 35th St Holland MI 49423

FREE, VICTORIA ELLEN (D)
Committeewoman, Manhattan Co Dem Comt, NY
b New York, NY, Nov 30, 49; d Stan Free & Jean Marcus F; single. Educ: Brandeis Univ, BA cum laude, 71; Columbia Univ Grad Sch Jour, MS, 73; Sigma Delta Chi. Polit & Govt Pos: Committeewoman, Manhattan Co Dem Comt, NY, 71-; deleg, Dem Nat Conv, 72; exec bd mem, Community Free Dem, 72-73. Bus & Prof Pos: Admin asst, Dept Soc Serv, New York, 72. Publ: A delegate's diary, NY Daily News, 7/72. Relig: Jewish. Mailing Add: 251 W 92 St New York NY 10025

FREED, ELAINE EILERS (D)
Mem, Colo State Dem Exec Comt
b Hinton, Iowa, Jan 14, 34; d Fred Eilers & Frieda Borchers E; m 1953 to Douglas Freed; c David & Casey. Educ: Univ Minn, BA, 58. Polit & Govt Pos: Mem, Colo Dem Cent Comt, 61-65; mem, El Paso Co Exec Comt, 61-65; co-chmn, Frank Evans Cong Comt, 64; deleg, Dem Nat Conv & mem platform comt, 68; mem, Colo State Dem Exec Comt, 72- Bus & Prof Pos: Teacher elem sch, Colo, 58-60; teacher nursery sch, 67-68; dir, Colorado Springs Community Sch, 69- Honors & Awards: Outstanding Young Women Am, 68. Mailing Add: 2111 N Tejon Colorado Springs CO 80907

FREED, HOWARD A (R)
NDak State Sen
b Dickinson, NDak, Mar 14, 26; s Amos Freed & Ella Stenerson F; m 1952 to Barbara Day; c Mary Beth, Bob, Tom & Kathleen. Educ: NDak State Univ, 46-47; St Thomas Univ, BS, 50; Marquette Univ, JD, 53; Delta Theta Phi. Polit & Govt Pos: State's attorney, Stark Co, NDak, 54-58; NDak State Sen, 66-; mem exec comt, Dist 37 Rep Party, 68- Mem: Fel Am

Col Probate Counsel; Am Trial Lawyers Asn; Am Bar Asn; Mary Col, NDak (regent, 68-). Relig: Catholic. Legal Res: 926 Seventh Ave W Dickinson ND 58601 Mailing Add: State Capitol Bismarck ND 43215

FREEDMAN, SAMUEL SUMNER **(R)**
b Bridgeport, Conn, July 5, 27; s Harry Freedman & Estelle Bernstein F; m 1964 to Judith Hoffman Greenberg; c Martha Ann. Educ: Univ Conn, 46-48; George Washington Univ Sch Govt-Foreign Affairs, AB in Govt, 50; Yale Univ Law Sch, JD, 54; Phi Beta Kappa; Pi Gamma Mu; chmn & moderator, Yale Law Forum. Polit & Govt Pos: Justice of the Peace, Bridgeport, Conn, 54-62; writer & vol for Meskill, Conn Gubernatorial Campaign, 70; chmn, Rules Rev Comt, mem Finance & Pub Rels Comt, chmn, Liaison Comt with State Cent Comt; mem, Westport Rep Town Comt, 72-73; Conn State Rep, 135th Dist, 73-74, chmn judiciary comt & subcomts on criminal justice, court reform & pub defenders, Conn House Rep; dep clerk, Rep State Conv, 74; State Legis Comnr, 75- Bus & Prof Pos: Partner, Freedman, Peck & Freedman Law Firm, Bridgeport, Conn, 55-; spec pub defender, Fairfield Co, Conn, 59-61; instr polit sci, Sacred Heart Univ, 74. Mil Serv: Entered as A/S, Navy, 45, released as Yeoman 3/C, 46, after serv in Atlantic Fleet, USS Frost (DE 144) and USS Melville (AD 2), 45-46; Yeoman 3/C, Naval Res, 46-51; Victory Medal; Am Theatre Ribbon. Publ: Auth of Column on the theatre, specializing in Shakespearian Drama, Lakeville J, 63- & Westport News, 68- Mem: Western Conn Asn of Phi Beta Kappa; Algonquin Club; Yale Club of NY; Yale Club of Eastern Fairfield Co. Honors & Awards: Voted Outstanding Legislator, 73. Relig: Jewish. Mailing Add: Crawford Rd Westport CT 06880

FREELS, WILLARD DUDLEY **(R)**
Chmn, Morgan Co Rep Exec Comt, Tenn
b Sunbright, Tenn, Jan 7, 24; s Joe Edward Freels & Lucy Human F; m 1948 to Norma Nitzschke; c Janet Aneita (Mrs Joe Dan Galloway); two grandchildren. Educ: Univ Tenn, 1 year; Tenn Tech Univ, 70; Tenn Cert Appraisers, cert, 72. Polit & Govt Pos: Assessor of property, Morgan Co, Tenn, 68-; chmn, Morgan Co Rep Exec Comt, 69- Bus & Prof Pos: Vet trainee instr, Morgan Co Bd Educ, 48-55; owner-operator, Freels Hardware & Grocery, Sunbright, 48-; fire chief, Sunbright Vol Fire Dept, 21 years. Mil Serv: Entered as Pvt, Army, 45, released as Sgt, 46, after serv in Mil Police; Sgt, Army Res, 46-49. Mem: Nat Asn Property Assessors; Eastern Star (Past Patron); Kiwanis; life mem, Nat PTA; Mason (32 degree). Relig: Methodist; Chmn Off Bd, 12 years. Mailing Add: Box 89 Sunbright TN 37872

FREEMAN, BRUCE N **(R)**
Mass State Rep
b Watertown, Mass, Mar 4, 21; s Forrest Ervin Freeman & Ethel V Noyes F; m 1945 to Daphne Grace Russell; c Bruce R, Gary R, Deborah A & Dale H. Educ: Newton High Sch, Mass, grad, 39. Polit & Govt Pos: Mem, Rep Town Comt, Chelmsford, Mass, 61-; pres, Chelmsford Rep Club, 65-66; Mass State Rep, 32nd Middlesex Dist, 69- Bus & Prof Pos: Salesman, Liggett & Myers Tobacco Co, 46-50, div sales mgr, 50-58; ins agt, Prudential Ins Co Am, 58- Mil Serv: Entered as Pvt, Army, 42, released as T-4, 46, after serv in 96th Machine Unit, Adj Gen Dept, European & Pac Theatres, 42-46; Good Conduct Medal; European African Mid Eastern Theatre Campaign Ribbon; Asiatic Pac Theatre Ribbon; Am Theatre Campaign Ribbon; Philippine Liberation Ribbon; Victory Medal; Meritorious Award. Mem: Millionaire Club, Prudential Ins Co; Mason; Am Legion; VFW; Elks. Honors & Awards: Pres Citation, Prudential Ins Co. Relig: Protestant. Legal Res: 7 Kenwood St Chelmsford MA 01824 Mailing Add: State House Rm 146 Boston MA 02133

FREEMAN, GLENN R **(D)**
Ky State Rep
Mailing Add: 1209 Lynn St Cumberland KY 40823

FREEMAN, JAMES MARION **(D)**
Chmn, Presidio Co Dem Comt, Tex
b Sierra Blanco, Tex, June 18, 14; s James Massey Freeman (deceased) & Ollie B Mercer F (deceased); m 1951 to Mary Marie Scidmore; c William Robert Lewis. Educ: Marfa High Sch, Tex, dipl. Polit & Govt Pos: Comnr, Presidio Co, Marfa, Tex, 51-61; mem, Presidio Co Independent Sch Bd, 63-65; dep sheriff, Presidio Co, 65-66; city police, Marfa, 66-; chmn, Presidio Co Dem Comt, 70- Bus & Prof Pos: Mem staff surveying & triangulation, US Coast & Geodetic Survey, Dept of Commerce, 42-44; with restaurant bus, Marfa, Tex, 44- Mem: Marfa Lodge 596 AF&AM; Big Bend Area Law Enforcement Off Asn; Tex Comn on Law Enforcement Off Standards & Educ. Honors & Awards: App by Lt Gov Ben Barnes to go to Europe regarding Am War Prisoners, 8/71. Relig: Baptist. Legal Res: 716 W San Antonio St Marfa TX 79843 Mailing Add: PO Box 1102 Marfa TX 79843

FREEMAN, JO **(D)**
b Atlanta, Ga, Aug 26, 45; d William Maxwell Freeman & Helen Mitchell F; single. Educ: Univ Calif, Berkeley, BA, 65; Univ Chicago, PhD, 73; Nat Honor Soc. Polit & Govt Pos: Nat staff, McCarthy for President Campaign, 68; alt deleg, Dem Nat Conv, 72. Bus & Prof Pos: Research dir, Southern Christian Leadership Conf, 65-66; co-ed, West Side Torch, 67; asst ed, Mod Hosp, 67-68; research asst, Univ Chicago, 68-70, lectr exten, 71; asst prof Am studies, State Univ NY Col Old Westbury, 73-74; asst prof polit sci, State Univ NY Col Purchase, 74- Publ: The social construction of the second sex, In: Roles Women Play (ed Michele Garshof), 71; ed, Women: A Feminist Perspective, Mayfield, 75; auth, The Politics of Women's Liberation, McKay, 75. Mem: Am Polit Sci Asn; Policy Studies Orgn; Nat Orgn Women; Women's Caucus for Polit Sci; Nat Women's Polit Caucus. Honors & Awards: Nat Inst Ment Health fel, 68-73; State Univ NY Res Found Grant, 75-76. Legal Res: NY Mailing Add: State Univ NY Lincoln Ave Purchase NY 10577

FREEMAN, KEMPER, JR **(R)**
Wash State Rep
Mailing Add: PO Box 1012 Bellevue WA 98009

FREEMAN, MICHAEL JOHN **(D)**
b Canton, Ohio, Jan 24, 51; s Robert D Freeman & Betty Lynch F; single. Educ: Case Western Reserve Univ, BA & MA, 73; Phi Beta Kappa. Polit & Govt Pos: Deleg, Dem Nat Conv, 72; exec mem, Young Dem of Ohio, 73- Bus & Prof Pos: Trust adminr, Harter Bank & Trust Co, Canton, 73- Relig: Catholic. Mailing Add: 803 Colonial Blvd NE Canton OH 44714

FREEMAN, ORAL E **(D)**
Alaska State Rep
Mailing Add: 2743 Third Ave Ketchikan AK 99901

FREEMAN, ORVILLE LOTHROP **(D)**
b Minneapolis, Minn, May 9, 18; s Orville E Freeman; m 1942 to Jane Charlotte Shields; c Constance Jane & Michael Orville. Educ: Univ Minn, BA, 40, LLB, 46; Phi Beta Kappa; Delta Theta Phi; Iron Wedge; M Club; Alpha Zeta. Hon Degrees: LLD, Univ Seoul, St Joseph's Col, Fairleigh Dickinson Univ & Am Univ. Polit & Govt Pos: Deleg Dem Nat Conv, 44, 48, 52, 56, 60, 64 & 68; chmn, Civil Serv Comn, Minneapolis, Minn, 46-49; state chmn, Dem-Farmer-Labor Party, 48-50; Gov, Minn, 56-60; Secy of Agr, 61-69; mem, Int Task Force for Dem Adv Coun, currently. Bus & Prof Pos: Law partner, Larson, Loevinger, Lindquist, Freeman & Fraser, 47-54; pres, EDP Tech Int, Inc, 69-70; pres, Bus Int, New York, currently. Mil Serv: Entered as Pfc, Marine Corps, 42, released as Capt, 45, after serv in Ninth Regt, Third Div, Pac; Col, Marine Corps Res; Purple Heart; Pac Campaign Ribbon. Publ: World Without Hunger, Praeger, 67. Mem: Coun Foreign Rels; Minn State Bar Asn; Univ Minn Alumnae Asn; Univ Club New York; Int Club Washington, DC. Relig: Lutheran; former deacon, Ebenezer Lutheran Church; mem exec comt, Lutheran Church Am. Mailing Add: Hudson House Ardsley-on-Hudson NY 10503

FREEMAN, RAYMOND ROBERT, JR **(R)**
Nat Committeeman, NC Fedn Young Rep
b Hendersonville, NC, Nov 30, 41; s Raymond Robert Freeman, Sr & Elizabeth Bryant F; m 1971 to Malinda Huss; c Raymond Robert, III. Educ: Western Carolina Univ, BS, 65, MA, 67; Phi Delta Kappa. Polit & Govt Pos: Vpres, Western Carolina Univ Young Rep, 62-63, pres, 63-64; mem western dist, NC Fedn Young Rep, 63-64, Nat Committeeman, 73-; mem 11th dist state exec bd, NC Rep Party, 65-66, mem ninth dist state exec bd, 72-; chmn, Mecklenburg Young Rep, NC, 70-73; dist asst to US Rep James G Martin, NC, Ninth Dist, 73- Bus & Prof Pos: Teacher & counr, Polk Cent High Sch, NC, 65-67; counr, W Mecklenburg High Sch, 67-69 & Union Co Schs, 70-72. Mem: Cong Staff Club; Rotary. Honors & Awards: Outstanding Club Membership for State, NC Fedn Young Rep, 72-73; Young Rep Man of Year, NC Fedn Young Rep, 73. Mailing Add: E-1 2700 Eastway Dr Charlotte NC 28205

FREEMAN, ROBERT DECORPS **(D)**
Ohio State Sen
b Canton, Ohio, Nov 20, 21; s Robert Emmet Freeman & Pauline DeCorps F; m 1946 to Betty Lynch; c Robert, James, Michael, Elizabeth & Christopher. Educ: Univ Firenze, Italy, 45; Mt Union Col, BA in Hist, 48; Univ Calif, Los Angeles, MA in Hist, 50; NY Inst Finance, 68-69; Pi Gamma Mu; Pi Sigma Alpha; Psi Kappa Omega; Student Coun; Signet; Vet; Int Rels Club; Young Dem. Polit & Govt Pos: Comnr, Stark Co, Ohio, 71-75; Ohio State Sen, 75- Bus & Prof Pos: Alumni secy, Mt Union Col, 50-55; dir & lectr, Case Western Reserve Univ, 56-60 & dir spec projs, 70-71; exec secy, Ohio Scholar Funds, 60-61; mgr, Am Soc Metals, 61-63; pres, RDF & Assocs, 63-70. Mil Serv: Entered as Pvt, Army Air Corps, 42, released as S/Sgt, 45, after serv in 461st Bomb Group, MTO, 44-45; Capt(Ret), Res; Eight Battle Stars; Victory Medal; Presidential Unit Citation; MTO-ETO Medal. Mem: Stark Co Hist Soc; Am Legion; ROA; Ohio Hist Preserv (adv bd, 71-74). Honors & Awards: Conserv Award, Am Sportsmens Club, 73. Relig: Roman Catholic. Mailing Add: 803 Colonial Blvd NE Canton OH 44714

FREEMAN, ROBERT L **(D)**
La State Rep
Mailing Add: 811 Sherburne St Plaquemine LA 70764

FREEMAN, SYLVIA **(D)**
Polit & Govt Pos: Mem, Dem Nat Comt, Wyo, formerly. Mailing Add: 804 E Eighth St Sheridan WY 82801

FREEMAN, TRAVIS **(R)**
Mem Exec Comt, Tulsa Co Rep Comt, Okla
b Chicago, Ill, Jan 19, 25; s Raymond A Freeman & Dawn Thorman F; m 1950 to Lucia Johnson; c Teri G (Mrs James Winkleman) & Eric T. Educ: Univ Okla, 44-45; Univ Ill, BS, 47; Delta Chi. Polit & Govt Pos: Co-chmn, Nixon for President, Tulsa Co, 67; chmn, Bellmon for Senate, Tulsa Co, 68; chmn, Tulsa Co Rep Comt, 69-73, mem exec comt, currently; vchmn, Tulsa City-Co River Parks Authority, currently; deleg, Rep Nat Conv, 72. Bus & Prof Pos: Freeman Builders Supply, Inc, 54- Mil Serv: Entered as Seaman, Naval Reserve, 43, released as Ens, 46, after serv in Underwater Demolition & Landing Craft, Inf, US & Pac, 43-46. Mem: Construction Specifications Inst; Toastmasters Int; Rotary (club pres). Relig: Presbyterian. Mailing Add: 4836 S Peoria Tulsa OK 74105

FREEMAN, WILLIAM A, JR **(D)**
Fla State Rep
Mailing Add: 724 Eaton St Key West FL 33040

FREER, LYLE LEROY **(R)**
Chmn, Wadena Co Rep Party, Minn
b Isle, Minn, Apr 1, 25; s Edward Eugene Freer & Inez Windsor F; m 1953; c Janet, David, Mark, Paul & Jonathan. Educ: Brown Radio Inst, grad, 49; Ga Southwest Col, 49-50. Polit & Govt Pos: Chmn, TAR, Wadena Co, Minn, 67-68; first vchmn, Wadena Co Rep Party, 67-68, second precinct chmn, 68-69, chmn, 69- Bus & Prof Pos: Pres, Wadena Jr CofC, 59-60; regional vpres, Minn Jr CofC, 60-61; pres, Wadena CofC, 62; dir, Minn Baseball Asn, 70- Mil Serv: Entered as Pvt, Army, 45, released as S/Sgt, 46, after serv in 1st Inf Div, ETO, 45-46; reentered as S/Sgt, 50, released as M/Sgt, 51, after serv in Korean War; ETO Ribbon; Good Conduct Medal. Mem: Wadena Lions Club; Am Legion; VFW; Wadena CofC. Relig: Lutheran. Mailing Add: 317 SW Seventh Wadena MN 56482

FRELINGHUYSEN, PETER H B **(R)**
b New York, NY, Jan 17, 16; s Peter H B Frelinghuysen, Sr (deceased) & Adaline Havemeyer F (deceased); m 1940 to Beatrice S Procter; c Peter, Beatrice, Rodney, Adaline & Frederick. Educ: Princeton Univ, BA, magna cum laude in hist, 38; Yale Law Sch, LLB, 41. Polit & Govt Pos: Staff mem, Hoover Comn Foreign Affairs Task Force, 48; US Rep, Fifth Dist, NJ, 53-75; deleg, UN 20th Gen Assembly, 65; US Cong Deleg, NATO Parliamentarians' Conf; mem, Rep Truth Squad, 64 & 68; mem, Rep Platform Comt, 64, 68 & 72; deleg, Rep Nat Conv, 64, 68 & 72; Cong adv, 18 Nation Disarmament Conf, 67, 68 & 69. Bus & Prof Pos: Mgr family bus; with law firm of Simpson, Thacher & Bartlett, 41-42; dir, Metrop Mus Art, NY; mgr, Howard Savings Bank, Newark, NJ; dir, Am Nat Bank & Trust, Morristown, NJ, currently; mem bd trustees, John F Kennedy Ctr for Performing Arts, currently; dir, North Jersey Conserv Found. Mil Serv: Entered Navy, 42, released as Lt, 45, after serv in Naval Intel, Off Chief Naval Opers. Mem: Am Bible Soc (vpres); Morristown Mem Hosp (trustee). Relig: Episcopal; Former Vestryman, St Peter's Episcopal Church. Mailing Add: Sand Spring Lane Morristown NJ 07960

FREMMING, G JAMES (D)
NY State Assemblyman
Mailing Add: 2349 Kensington Ave Snyder NY 14226

FRENCH, ELEANOR CLARK (D)
b Philadelphia, Pa, June 29, 08; d Herbert Lincoln Clark & Elizabeth Conway Bent C; m 1950 to John French; stepchildren, John, III, Roberts W & Mary (Mrs Moore). Polit & Govt Pos: Cand for NY State Sen, 56; vchmn, NY State Dem Comt, 57-60; chmn, Women for Kennedy, 60; chmn, Vol, Wagner Campaign, 61; comnr, City Comn on Human Rights, New York, 61-; city comnr, UN, 62-66; Dem & Liberal cand for US Rep, 17th Cong Dist, NY, 64; deleg, Dem Nat Conv, 64, 68 & 72; co-chmn, NY State Comt for Dem Alternative, 68; NY State co-chmn, McGovern for President, 70-72. Bus & Prof Pos: Teacher & supvr elem sch, 32-43; Off Inter-Am Affairs, 43-46; assoc dir, France Unitarian Serv Comt, 46, 47-; women's news ed, NY Times, 49-55. Publ: Women in politics, NY Times Mag, 56. Mem: Foreign Policy Asn; Am for Dem Action. Relig: Unitarian. Mailing Add: 144 E 38th St New York NY 10016

FRENCH, MARSHALL ADAMS (R)
NH State Rep
b Manchester, NH, Dec 19, 16; s Frank A French & Ethel Adams F; m 1937 to Susan Hagland; c Peter, David & John. Educ: New Eng Col of Embalming & Sanit Sci, Boston, Mass. Polit & Govt Pos: Selectman, Town of Meredith, NH, 69-71; NH State Rep, 71-, chmn, Educ Comt, NH House, 73, chmn, Rules Comt & Majority Leader, 75- Mem: AF&AM (Past Master, Bible Lodge 27); NH Consistory SPRS (32 degree); Mt Horeb Royal Arch Chap 11 Adoniram Coun 3; Meredith Rotary Club. Relig: Episcopal. Mailing Add: 108 Pleasant St Meredith NH 03253

FRENCH, ROBERT BRYANT, JR (R)
Mem, Ala State Rep Exec Comt
b Howell, Tenn, Sept 16, 33; s Robert B French, Sr & Nina Sibley F; m 1955 to Celeste I Mongiello; c Michelle. Educ: Univ Ala Sch Commerce & Bus Admin, BS, Law Sch, LLB. Polit & Govt Pos: Dir of orgn, Tuscaloosa Co Rep Party, Ala, 62-63; co-chmn, Tuscaloosa Young Rep Club, 62-63; state chmn, Ala Young Rep Fedn, 63-65; mem, Ala State Rep Exec Comt, 63-; deleg, Rep Nat Conv, 64, 68 & 72; precinct chmn, Beat Nine, Ft Payne, 66-; mem, DeKalb Co Rep Exec Comt, 66-; vchmn, Ala Rep Party, 69-73; cand, Lt Gov, Ala, 70. Mil Serv: Enlisted Air Force, 53, released as Sgt, 57, after serv in Eastern Air Defense Force; Good Conduct Medal. Mem: Farrah Law Soc; Am Judicature Soc; Ala Mt Lakes Asn (mem bd dirs); DeKalb Co Arts Coun (pres); DeKalb Co Tourist Asn (pres). Honors & Awards: Selected One of Outstanding Young Men of Am, Nat Jr CofC, 65; One of Ten Outstanding Young Rep State Chairmen, 65; Man of the Year, Ft Payne, 68; One of Four Outstanding Young Men of Ala, 68; nominated Ten Outstanding Young Men of Am, 68. Relig: Baptist. Legal Res: Scenic Hwy Ft Payne AL 35967 Mailing Add: PO Box 596 Ft Payne AL 35967

FRENCH, WARREN B, JR (R)
First VChmn, Seventh Cong Dist, Va
b Woodstock, Va, Apr 14, 23; s Warren B French & Lena Sheetz F; m 1949 to Patricia Teale; c Anne E, Cynthia E, Warren B III & Christopher E. Educ: Univ of Va, BSEE, 47; Trigon. Polit & Govt Pos: First secy, Tenth Dist Rep Comt; precinct chmn, Rep Party of Arlington, Va, during 40's; pres, Electoral Col of Va, 52; campaign mgr, State Sen J Kenneth Robinson, Va, 65; deleg, Rep Nat Conv, 68; chmn, Va Seventh Dist Rep Comt, 66-70; chmn, State Personnel Comt, 70; chmn, Rep Party Va, formerly; campaign chmn, Congressman J Kenneth Robinson, Seventh Cong Dist, Va, 72; first vchmn, Seventh Cong Dist, Va, currently. Bus & Prof Pos: With Am Tel & Tel, Long Lines Dept, 47-54; pres & dir, Shenandoah Tel Co, Edinburg, Va, 54-, vpres, 63-; dir, Farmers Bank of Edinburg, 58-; dir, Shenandoah Indust Develop Corp, 63, former pres; dir & vpres, Shenandoah Co Mem Hosp, 58-; dir, Va Eng Found, Univ of Va. Mil Serv: Navy, 43-46, serv as Exec Off LCI-684 & Commanding Off, LCI-976; Lt Naval Res. Mem: Va Independent Tel Asn; Univ Va Bd Visitors; Boy Scouts, Shenandoah Area Coun (exec bd mem); Woodstock Rotary Club. Honors & Awards: Commercial Award, Woodstock CofC, 72. Relig: Methodist; past chmn admin bd, trustee & finance chmn, Woodstock United Methodist Church. Mailing Add: Rte 2 Box 209-A Edinburg VA 22842

FRENZEL, WILLIAM ELDRIDGE (BILL) (R)
US Rep, Minn
b St Paul, Minn, July 31, 28; s Paul William Frenzel & Paula Schlegel F; m 1951 to Ruth Purdy; c Deborah Anne, Pamela Ruth & Melissa Lee. Educ: Dartmouth Col, BA, 50, MBA, 51; Sigma Nu. Polit & Govt Pos: Minn State Rep, 30th Dist, 63-70; transportation dir, Hennepin Co Civil Defense, Minn & mem exec reserves, Off of Emergency Transportation, Dept of Commerce, 65; US Rep, Minn, Third Dist, 71-, mem ways & means comt, US House Rep, 74- Bus & Prof Pos: Employee, Minneapolis Terminal Warehouse Co, 54-57, mgr, 57-60, pres & dir, 60-70. Mil Serv: Entered as Ens, Naval Res, 51, released as Lt(jg), 54, after serv in Amphibious Forces, Korea; Lt(Ret), Naval Res. Mem: Nat Rivers & Harbors Cong; Citizen's League. Honors & Awards: Selected as One of Outstanding Young Men Am, US Jr CofC, 64; citation for work in Civil Defense, Minneapolis, 63. Legal Res: MN Mailing Add: 1026 Longworth House Off Bldg Washington DC 20515

FRERICHS, KENT ELMER (D)
SDak State Rep
b Ortonville, Minn, Feb 16, 46; s Elmer John Frerichs & Elnora Ione Christenson F; single. Educ: SDak State Univ, BS, 72; Alpha Zeta; Pi Kappa Delta; Alpha Gamma Rho; Block & Bridle; Agr-Educ Club. Polit & Govt Pos: Pres, SDak State Univ Young Dem, 67; chmn, Roberts Co Dem, SDak, 68-; pres, SDak Young Dem, 69-; regional dir, Young Dem Clubs Am, currently; deleg, Dem Nat Conv, 72; SDak State Rep, 75- Mem: SDak Pork Producers Coun (dir, 70-71); SDak SPF Swine Asn (treas, 68-); SDak Duroc Swine Asn (vpres, 68). Honors & Awards: Int Future Farmers Am deleg, England, 67. Relig: Lutheran. Mailing Add: Rte 2 Wilmot SD 57279

FREUND, BARBARA LEA (R)
Research Dir, Kans Rep Party
b Kansas City, Mo, Dec 7, 46; d L F Springer & Florence Feitz S; div. Educ: Univ Kans, BS, 68; Univ Mo, Kansas City, MA in Commun, 71; Alpha Omicron Pi. Polit & Govt Pos: Precinct committeewoman, Johnson Co Rep Comt, Kans, 72-74; nat committeewoman, Kans Young Rep, 73-74, chmn, currently; research dir, Kans Rep Party, 74- Bus & Prof Pos: Teacher, Kansas City Pub Schs, Kans, 68-74. Relig: Protestant. Mailing Add: 2825 Prairie Rd Topeka KS 66614

FREY, LOUIS, JR (R)
US Rep, Fla
b Rutherford, NJ, Jan 11, 34; s Louis Frey & Mildred Engel F; m 1956 to Marcia Turner; c Julie, Lynn, Louis III, Lauren & Chris. Educ: Colgate Univ, BA, cum laude, 55; Univ Mich Law Sch, JD with honors, 61; asst ed, Univ Mich Law Rev; Order of the Coif. Polit & Govt Pos: Asst co solicitor, Orlando, Fla, 61-63; acting gen counsel, Fla State Turnpike Authority, 66-67; former mem, Fla Rep State Exec Comt; former treas, Fla State Rep Party; former chmn, Fla Fedn Young Rep; US Rep, Ninth Dist, Fla, 68-, mem, Sci & Astronaut Comt & Manned Spaceflight, US House Rep, mem Interstate & Foreign Commerce Comt & power & commun subcomt, currently, pres, 91st Club, mem, Rep Task Force on Campus Unrest & chmn, Rep Task Force on Drug Abuse; mem, Peace Corps Adv Bd; deleg, Rep Nat Conv, 72. Bus & Prof Pos: Attorney-at-law, Orlando, Fla, 61-63; partner, Mateer, Frey, Young & Harbert, Orlando, 67-71. Mil Serv: Entered Navy, 55, released as Lt(jg), 58, after serv in Naval Aviation; Comdr, Naval Res. Mem: RETRO (founder); Phi Gamma Delta; Phi Delta Phi; dir, Winter Park Youth Ctr & Am Cancer Soc, Orange Co; assoc bd, Fla Symphony. Legal Res: Winter Park FL 32789 Mailing Add: 214 Cannon House Off Bldg Washington DC 20515

FREY, ROBERT G (R)
Kans State Rep
Mailing Add: 451 Harold Blvd Liberal KS 67901

FREY, THOMAS R (D)
NY State Assemblyman
Mailing Add: 308 Merchants Rd Rochester NY 14609

FRI, ROBERT WHEELER (R)
Dep Adminr, Energy Research & Develop Admin
b Kansas City, Kans, Nov 6, 35; s Homer Fri & Ruth Wheeler F; m 1965 to Jean Landon; c Perry Leigh, Robert Sean & Stephen Kirk. Educ: Rice Univ, BA, with distinction, 57; Harvard Univ Bus Sch, MBA, with distinction, 59; Phi Beta Kappa; Sigma Xi. Polit & Govt Pos: Dep adminr, Environ Protection Agency, 71-73, acting adminr, 73; dep adminr, Energy Research & Develop Admin, 74- Bus & Prof Pos: Principal, McKinsey & Co, 63-71 & 73-75. Mil Serv: Entered as officer, Naval Officers Cand Sch, 59, released as Lt, 62, after serv in Bur Naval Weapons, 59-62. Mem: President's Comn Personnel Interchange (comnr). Relig: Presbyterian. Mailing Add: 5105 Baltan Rd Washington DC 20016

FRICK, JOSEPH B (R)
Chmn, Armstrong Co Rep Comt, Pa
b Adrian, Pa, Mar 12, 20; s James M Frick & Lettie Montgomery F; m 1939 to Goldie Eva Hooks; c Joseph J, Sally Ann, Jerry Linn & Sandi Lee (Mrs Russel Toy). Polit & Govt Pos: Chmn, Armstrong Co Rep Comt, Pa, 73- Bus & Prof Pos: Sheriff, Armstrong Co, 66- Mil Serv: Entered as Pvt, Army, 44, released as Pvt 1/C, 45, after serv in 5th Inf Div; ETO; Purple Heart; World War Victory Medal; European-African Eastern Serv Medal with Three Bronze Stars. Honors & Awards: J Edgar Hoover Mem Award for Pub Safety & Law Enforcement; Armstrong Co Conserv Award, Armstrong Co Conserv League. Relig: Protestant. Mailing Add: E Market St Kittanning PA 16201

FRICKS, ROBERT PRICE (D)
Ariz State Rep
b Tucson, Ariz, Jan 4, 33; s Henry Edgar Fricks & Ethel Price Fricks Thomas; m 1956 to Roberta Ann Crabtree; c Robert Lynn, Carrie Ann & Richard Scott. Educ: Univ Ariz, 3 years. Polit & Govt Pos: Ariz State Rep, 67- Mil Serv: Entered as Airman Basic, Air Force, 52, released as Airman 2/C, 56, after serv in Far East Air Force, 53-55; UN Ribbon; Korean Ribbon. Mem: VFW; Am Legion; Tucson Rod & Gun Club; Mason. Relig: Baptist. Mailing Add: 3810 W Ironwood Hill Dr Tucson AZ 85705

FRIED, JIM (D)
Okla State Rep
b Oklahoma City, Okla; s John B Fried & Ruby Marie Hood F; m 1968 to Barbara Jean Riggs; c Bryan Scott. Educ: Univ Wyo, 67-69; Univ Okla, BS in Polit Sci, 72. Polit & Govt Pos: Okla State Rep, 74-, vchmn vet & mil affairs, Okla House Rep, 74- Bus & Prof Pos: Teacher, Highland Park Elem Schs Okla, 72-74. Mem: South Oklahoma City CofC. Relig: Southern Baptist. Mailing Add: 828 SE 68th Oklahoma City OK 73149

FRIEDEL, SAMUEL NATHANIEL (D)
b Washington, DC, Apr 18, 98; s Philip Friedel & Rose Franklin F; m 1939 to Regina B Johnson. Educ: Pub Schs, Baltimore. Polit & Govt Pos: Md State Deleg, 34-38; mem, Baltimore City Coun, 39, 43 & 51; US Rep, Md, 53-70, chmn, House Admin Comt, Joint Comt on the Libr, Transportation & Aeronautics Subcomt of House Interstate & Foreign Commerce Comt & vchmn, Joint Comt on Printing, US House of Rep, formerly; deleg, Dem Nat Conv, 68. Mem: Wash Improv Asn; Elks; Am Israel Soc; Safety First Club of Md; Md Law Enforcement Officers Asn. Mailing Add: 2201 South Rd Baltimore MD 21209

FRIEDEMANN, ZYGMUNT JERZY (D)
RI State Rep
b Poland, Feb 15, 22; s Dr Leon Friedemann & Lilli Friszer F; m 1946 to Ruth B Avots; c Gail K & Glenn R. Educ: Jagiellonski Univ, 33-39; Goethe Univ, 45-47; Boston Univ, BA, 54; Brown Univ, MA, 58, PhD, 66; Pi Sigma Alpha. Polit & Govt Pos: RI Deleg, US Rivers & Harbors, 64-; chmn, Retirement Pension Bd, Warwick, RI, 64-69; deleg, Const Conv, Dist 37, 73; chmn, Charter Study Comn, 75-; RI State Rep, 75- Bus & Prof Pos: Instr, Providence Col, 56-59, asst prof, 59-63, assoc prof, 63-68, chmn dept polit sci, 65-74 & prof, 69- Mem: Foreign Affairs Coun (bd dirs, 74-); Int Inst (bd dirs, 75-). Mailing Add: 355 George Arden Ave Warwick RI 02886

FRIEDERSDORF, MAX LEE (R)
Asst to President for Legis Affairs
b Grammer, Ind, July 7, 29; s John L Friedersdorf & Lola Francis Fox F; m 1953 to Priscilla Marion Jones; c Kristine & Fritz. Educ: Franklin Col, AB, 52; Am Univ, MA, 69. Hon Degrees: Degree, Franklin Col, 75. Polit & Govt Pos: Spec asst to President for legis affairs, White House, 71-72, dep asst, 72-75, asst, 75- Mailing Add: 7617 Leith Pl Alexandria VA 22307

FRIEDHEIM, JERRY WARDEN (R)
b Joplin, Mo, Oct 7, 34; s Volmer Havens Friedheim & Billie Warden F; m 1956 to Shirley Margarette Beavers; c Daniel, Cynthia & Thomas. Educ: Univ Mo, BJ, 56, AM, 62; Indust

Col of Armed Forces, 68; Omicron Delta Kappa; Kappa Tau Alpha. Polit & Govt Pos: Asst to US Rep Hall, Mo, 62; asst to US Sen Tower, Tex, 63-69; Dep Asst Secy of Defense for Pub Affairs, 69-70, Prin Dep Asst Secy Pub Affairs, 70-73, Asst Secy of Defense for Pub Affairs, 73-74. Bus & Prof Pos: Reporter & ed, Neosho Daily News, Mo, Joplin Globe & Columbia Missourian, 58-61; instr, Univ Mo, 61-62; vpres govt & pub affairs, Amtrak, 74-75. Mil Serv: Entered as 2nd Lt, Army, 56, released as 1st Lt, 58, after serv in Second & Tenth Inf Div, Europe; Capt, Army Res, 58-69. Publ: Where are the voters, Nat Press, Inc, 68. Mem: Sigma Delta Chi; Am Polit Sci Asn. Honors & Awards: Award for Distinguished Reporting of Pub Affairs, Am Polit Sci Asn, 61, cong fel; Dept of Defense Medal for Distinguished Pub Serv. Relig: Protestant. Mailing Add: 1116 Allison St Alexandria VA 22302

FRIEDLAND, JOHN E (R)
Ill State Sen
Mailing Add: 224 Virginia Dr South Elgin IL 60177

FRIEDMAN, ALAN RICHARD (D)
Mem, Md Dem State Cent Comt
b Baltimore, Md, May 29, 51; s Jack Friedman & Zelda Roth F; single. Educ: Univ Md, College Park, BA with high honors, 73, Univ Md, Baltimore, JD, 75; Omicron Delta Kappa; Zeta Beta Tau; Kalegathos Soc. Polit & Govt Pos: Admin asst to Md State Sen Peter A Bozick, Off Law, Prince George's Co, 72; mem, Young Dem of Md, currently; mem, Young Dem of Prince George's Co, currently, legis chmn, 73-; mem, Md Dem State Cent Comt, 74- Mem: Am Bar Asn; Phi Alpha Delta. Honors & Awards: Outstanding Leadership Award, YMCA, 70; Outstanding Serv Award, Gov Comt Student Affairs, 71. Relig: Jewish. Legal Res: 7302 Yale Ave College Park MD 20740 Mailing Add: PO Box 181 College Park MD 20740

FRIEDMAN, DON (R)
Colo State Rep
b Denver, Colo, Mar 21, 30; married; c three. Polit & Govt Pos: Colo State Rep, currently, chmn, appropriations comt, vchmn, joint budget comt; mem, Gov Local Affairs Study Comn, Colo House Rep. Mem: B'nai B'rith (past pres, Denver Lodge 171); Hemophilia Found (mem bd). Mailing Add: 1888 S Jackson St Denver CO 80210

FRIEDMAN, EDWARD DAVID (D)
b Chicago, Ill, May 2, 12; s Jacob Friedman & Bessie Levison F; m 1947 to Mary Louise Melia; c Michael John, Daniel Shay, Maryel & Elizabeth Anne. Educ: Univ Chicago, AB with honors, 35, James Nelson Raymond fel, 37; Univ Chicago Law Sch, JD cum laude, 37; Order of the Coif; assoc ed, Univ Chicago Law Rev, 36-37; Order of the Wig & Robe. Polit & Govt Pos: Mem gen counsel's staff, Securities & Exchange Comn, 39-43; chief counsel, Off of Price Admin, 42-43; spec asst to Archibald Cox, dep solicitor, Dept of Labor, 43-44, spec asst to Solicitor of Labor Tyson, 44-48, spec asst foreign farm labor prog, Secy of Labor, 65, dep solicitor, Dept of Labor, 65-69, acting solicitor, 69; exec asst to assoc gen counsel, Div of Law, Nat Labor Rels Bd, 48-57, chief law officer, Fifth Regional Off, 57-59, asst gen counsel, Nat Labor Rels Bd, 59-60; mem, Garrett Park Town Coun, Md, 54-58; labor counsel to US Sen John F Kennedy, Mass, 60-61; mayor, Garrett Park, Md, 60-66; labor counsel to US Sen Wayne Morse, Ore, 61-65; labor counsel, US Senate Labor & Pub Welfare Comt & counsel subcomts on labor, manpower & railway retirement, 61-65; counsel, majority & minority floor mgrs for US Sen Clark, Pa & US Sen Case, NJ, Civil Rights Bill, 64; US deleg, Orgn for Econ Coop & Develop, Paris, France, 68; consult comn on rules, Dem Nat Conv, currently. Bus & Prof Pos: Assoc, Rosenberg, Toomin & Stein, Chicago, Ill, 38-39; partner, Bernstein, Alper, Schoene & Friedman, Washington, DC, 69- Publ: Racial Problems in Labor Relations: The Civil Rights Act, NY Univ, Eighteenth Annual Conf on Labor, 66; various law rev articles, Univ Chicago Law Rev. Mem: Am & Fed Bar Asns. Legal Res: 10702 Weymouth St Garrett Park MD 20766 Mailing Add: 818 18th St NW Washington DC 20006

FRIEDMAN, JEFFREY MARK (D)
Mayor, Austin, Tex
b Forest Hills, NY, Jan 20, 45; s Sidney Martin Friedman & Evalyn Oken F; m 1973 to Carole Schwartz. Educ: Univ Wis, 62-64; Rockhurst Col, 65-66; Univ Mo-Kansas City, BA in psychol, 67; Univ Tex Sch Law, JD, 70; Delta Theta Phi. Polit & Govt Pos: City councilman, Austin, Tex, 71-75, mayor, 75-; deleg, Dem Co Conv, 72; deleg, Dem State Conv, 72; deleg, Dem Nat Conv, 72. Bus & Prof Pos: Attorney, 70-72, Friedman & Burroughs, 72-73 & Friedman, Burroughs & Hansen, 73- Mem: Nat Asn Criminal Defense Lawyers; Tex Trial Lawyers; Austin Coun, United Serv Orgn (bd mem, 73-); B'nai B'rith; Common Cause. Honors & Awards: Cert of Appreciation, Austin Police Dept, 68; Consul, Univ Tex Sch Law, 70; Appreciation Plaque, Austin Police Asn, 72. Relig: Judaism. Mailing Add: 1602 Rock Cliff Rd Austin TX 78746

FRIEDRICH, DONALD LAWRENCE (R)
Minn State Rep
b Rochester, Minn, July 7, 29; s William Edward Friedrich & Gladys Lull F; m 1953 to Betty Lou Kach. Educ: Rochester High Sch, grad, 47. Polit & Govt Pos: Supvr, Marion Twp Bd, Minn, 65-74; planning comnr, Olmsted Co, 66-74; Minn State Rep, 75- Mil Serv: Entered as Seaman, Navy, 47, released as Seaman 2/C, 51, after serv in Med Field Research. Mem: Am Legion. Relig: Lutheran. Mailing Add: RR 3 Rochester MN 55901

FRIEDRICH, DWIGHT P (R)
Ill State Sen
Mailing Add: 915 Frazier Centralia IL 62801

FRIEND, HARLAN DILLMAN (D)
b Flora, Ill, Jan 20, 24; s Harlan Downs Friend & Erba Dillman F; m 1970 to Karen Lee Shannon; c Shelley Anne, Harlan Jefferson, Shannon Lee, Sean Arthur & Patrick Dillman. Educ: Baylor Univ, BBA, 49, LLB, 56; Sigma Delta Chi; Delta Sigma Phi; Phi Delta Phi. Polit & Govt Pos: Deleg, Tex Dem State Conv, 56 & 66; deleg, Dem Nat Conv, 64; chmn, Planning & Zoning Comn, Liberty, Tex, 58-62; City Attorney, Dayton, 60-; chmn, Liberty Co Dem Exec Comt, formerly. Bus & Prof Pos: Attorney-at-law, Zbranek & Friend, currently. Mil Serv: Entered as Seaman, Navy, 42-46, serv in SPac Theater, 45-46; Asiatic Theater Ribbon; Good Conduct Medal. Publ: Tex Talks, a polit column, Waco Record, 47-48. Mem: Mason; Elks; VFW; Am Legion; Liberty Co Recover Unit. Relig: Methodist. Legal Res: 1505 Bowie St Liberty TX 77575 Mailing Add: PO Box 151 Liberty TX 77575

FRIEND, HAZEL IRENE (R)
Mem, Calif Rep State Cent Comt
b Ray, Kans, Sept 25, 06; d William Orvel Frazer & Mary Rice F; m 1929 to Cecil William Friend, wid; c Mary Love (Mrs Frederic P Burnside) & Delores Darlene (Mrs Herbert W Speck). Educ: Southwestern Col, 24-25; Kans State Teachers Col, Teachers Cert, 25; Kans Teachers Normal, Co Cert, 2 years; Delta Kappa Chi. Polit & Govt Pos: Asst postmaster, Rolla, Kans, 25; vol chmn, Bellflower & 23rd Cong Dist Women for Knowland for Gov, 58 & chmn, Women for Nixon for President, 60 & 68; chmn, Bellflower Women for Nixon for Gov of Calif, 62; mem, Calif Rep State Cent Comt, 67-, mem arts & sci comt; chmn, Bellflower Women for Murphy, 70; chmn, Bellflower Bus & Indust for Reelec of the President, 72. Bus & Prof Pos: Piano teacher, pvt lessons, Rolla, Kans, 25-30 & teacher, Rolla Grade Sch, 26-30; manage own property, Bellflower, Calif, Morton & Stevens Co, Kans & Fla, 65- Mem: Bellflower Coun of Rep Women, Federated; Women's Club of Bellflower; PEO; Rep Party Nat Hq (sustaining mem); YMCA (Century Club Mem, Los Cerritos Chap). Honors & Awards: Plaque, Los Cerritos YMCA Century Club; Several cert for vol work in philanthropic orgn such as Red Cross & Heart Found. Relig: Presbyterian. Mailing Add: 16910 S Bixby Ave Bellflower CA 90706

FRIEND, KAREN LEE (D)
Committeewoman, Tex State Dem Exec Comt
b Mercedes, Tex, Feb 15, 42; d H A Buster Shannon & Clara Goodrich S; m 1970 to Harlan Dillman Friend; c Shelley Anne, Harlan Jefferson, Shannon Lee, Sean Arthur & Patrick Dillman. Educ: Univ Tex, Austin, BJ, 64. Polit & Govt Pos: Chmn, Precinct 213, Harris Co, Tex, 66-70; mem, Harris Co Dem Exec Comt, 66-70; VIP guest, Dem Nat Conv, 68; state coordr, Yarbrough for Gov Campaign, Tex, 68; deleg, Tex Dem State Conv, 68 & 72; Harris Co coordr, McGovern for President, 72 & Farenthold for Gov Campaign, 72; committeewoman, Tex State Dem Exec Comt, Fourth Sen Dist, 72- Bus & Prof Pos: With pub rels dept, Young & Rubicam Advert Agency, NY, 64-65 & Houston Chronicle, Tex, 65-66; free lance pub rels agent, Tex Fishing & Camping Mag, 69 & Odd Fellows & Rebekah's of Tex, 69. Mem: Gamma Alpha Chi (charter mem); Ladies Auxiliary, VFW & Elks, Liberty, Tex; Valley Players Theatrical Soc, Liberty; Doberman Pinscher Club, Houston. Honors & Awards: Woman of the Year, Downtowner Optimist-Mrs Club, Houston, 68. Relig: Methodist. Legal Res: 1505 Bowie St Liberty TX 77575 Mailing Add: PO Box 151 Liberty TX 77575

FRIEND, KELSEY E (D)
Ky State Sen
b Pikeville, Ky, Mar 18, 22; s J P Friend & Clarissa Mullins F; m 1945 to Margaret Jones Earp; c Kelsey E, Jr, Joe Jett & Clarissa Mauree. Educ: Pikeville Col, Teacher's Cert, 42; Univ Ky Law Sch, LLB, 49; Duke Univ, LLM, 50. Polit & Govt Pos: Master comnr, 35th Judicial Dist, Pike Co, Ky, 50-52, commonwealth attorney, 58-63; co attorney, Pike Co, 54-57; chmn, Pike Co Dem Exec Comt, 64-67, secy, 68-; Ky State Sen, 75- Bus & Prof Pos: Attorney-at-law, 49- Mil Serv: Entered as Pvt, Army, 42, released as 1st Lt, 46, after serv in Co E, 357th Regt, 90th Inf Div, ETO, 44-45; Maj, Army Res; Inf Combat Badge; Purple Heart; Bronze Star Medal & First Oak Leaf Cluster; Victory Medal; ETO Medal with 3 Battle Stars. Mem: Ky State Bar Asn; Mason; Noble, Mystic Shrine, El Hasa Temple, Ashland, Ky. Relig: Methodist. Legal Res: Rte 1 Pikeville KY 41501 Mailing Add: Box 512 Pikeville KY 41501

FRIERSON, CHARLES DAVIS, III (D)
Chmn, Craighead Co Dem Cent Comt, Ark
b Jonesboro, Ark, July 5, 32; s Charles Davis Frierson, Jr & Margaret Purifoy F; m 1954 to Carolyn Rhea; c Sandra & Terry. Educ: Ark State Univ, BS, 53; Univ Ark, Fayetteville, JD, 58; Phi Alpha Delta; Blue Key; Pi Kappa Alpha. Polit & Govt Pos: City attorney, Jonesboro, Ark, 56-62; deleg, Ark Const Conv, 70-71; chmn, Craighead Co Dem Cent Comt, 71-; chmn, Craighead Co Elec Comn, 71- Bus & Prof Pos: Partner, Frierson, Walker, Snellgrove & Laser Law Firm, Jonesboro, Ark, 58-; pres, Mercantile Bank, Jonesboro, 71-; chmn bd, Monette State Bank, 71- Mil Serv: Entered as 2nd Lt, Army, 53, released as 1st Lt, 55, after serv in 64th Field Artil Bn, 25th Inf Div, Korea & Hawaii. Mem: Elks; Ark Bankers Asn (chmn legis comt); Ark Bar Asn; Rotary; Boy Scouts. Honors & Awards: Outstanding Young Man, Jonesboro Jaycees, 64, Boss of Year Award, 74. Relig: Presbyterian. Mailing Add: 1507 Frierson Jonesboro AR 72401

FRIES, THOMAS LOUIS (D)
Ohio State Rep
b Dayton, Ohio, Sept 28, 42; s Robert L Hawley & Charlotte Van Ostrand H; m 1963 to Esther Carole Stookey; c Thomas Louis, Jr & Melissa Susanne. Educ: Ohio State Univ, 3 years; Bowling Green State Univ, 1 year; Univ Dayton, 2 years; Phi Delta Theta. Polit & Govt Pos: Ohio State Rep, 86th Dist, 71- Bus & Prof Pos: Prof baseball player, Minn Twins, 60-64 & Washington Senators, 64-66; sales & mkt, Gulf Oil Corp, 66-70; acct exec, Land Mortgages, Inc, 70- Mem: Citizens Clear Air Asn; Huber Heights-Wayne Twp Jaycees. Relig: Catholic. Mailing Add: 5210 Markey Rd Dayton OH 45415

FRINK, GARY R (D)
b Pontiac, Mich, Jan 22, 33; s Wayne C Frink (deceased) & Helen Snyder F; m 1955 to Sherry Lou Rood; c Christopher Rood & Geoffrey Richard. Educ: Mich State Univ, 51-54; Univ Americas, Mexico City, BA, 55; Univ Mich, JD, 63; Lambda Chi Alpha. Polit & Govt Pos: Legal asst, Off Gen Counsel, Dept Com, 63-64; legis asst, US Rep Weston E Vivian, Mich, 65-66; spec counsel task force on environ health, Dept Health, Educ & Welfare, 66-67; staff dir & counsel postal facilities & modernization subcomt, Post Off & Civil Serv Comt, US House Rep, 67-68; Dem cand, US Rep, 19th Dist, Mich, 68; spec counsel, Sen Frank E Moss, 69-70; spec counsel to US Rep William Anderson, 71. Bus & Prof Pos: Attorney-at-law, Elliott & Naftalin, Washington, DC, 68-69; secy & counsel, Linton, Mields & Coston, Inc, 68-71; chmn, Delta Group, Ltd, 72-; exec dir, Nat Comt for Effective No-Fault, 73- Mem: Mich, DC, Am, Fed & Interam Bar Asns. Relig: Protestant. Legal Res: Rochester MI Mailing Add: 2535 Massachusetts Ave NW Washington DC 20008

FRISBY, ROBERT W (R)
Wyo State Rep
b Casper, Wyo, Sept 23, 20; s J E Frisby & Bessie Snyder F; m 1943 to Peggy Holm; c Robert E, Donald R & Gloria J. Educ: Univ Wyo, 38-41. Polit & Govt Pos: Co assessor, Park Co, Wyo, 55-60; precinct committeeman, Park Co Rep Party, 60-64; co chmn, Park Co Rep Cent Comt, 64-66; Rep State Committeeman, Park Co, 66-68 & 70-72; Wyo State Rep, 71- Bus & Prof Pos: Sr vpres, First State Bank, Cody, Wyo, 60-73. Mil Serv: Entered as Pvt, Air Force, 42, released as Capt, 46, after serv in Air Transport Command, China-Burma-India, 45; India-Burma Campaign Ribbon. Mem: AF&AM; Rotary; Am Legion. Relig: Methodist. Mailing Add: 2007 Newton Ave Cody WY 82414

FRISKE, RICHARD **(AMERICAN PARTY)**
Chmn, Am Independent Party, Mich
b Josephine, Poland, June 16, 25; s Ferdinand Friske & Martha Rosenthal F; m 1950 to Olga Kottke; c Judith, Richard Wilfred S & Kornelius Wolfram. Educ: High Sch, Deutscheneck, Ger, grad. Polit & Govt Pos: Mich State Rep, 106th Dist, 71-73; chmn, Am Independent Party, Mich, 73- Bus & Prof Pos: Tool & die maker, 54-62; orchardist, 62- Mil Serv: Entered Ger Air Force, 43, released as Aviation Instr, 46. Mem: John Birch Soc; Farm Bur; Friends of Mich Schs; Nat Asn Keep & Bear Arms; Nat Adv Bd, Am Security Coun. Relig: Pentecostal; Lay preacher. Legal Res: Rte 1 Box 196 Charlevoix MI 49720 Mailing Add: Box 119 Lansing MI 48901

FRITSCHEL, TED C **(D)**
Committeeman, Oahu Co Dem Party, Hawaii
b Greeley, Colo, Mar 10, 32; s Dr Erwin G Fritschel & Irma Hast F; m 1955 to Nancy Graese. Educ: Wartburg Col, BA, 54; Wartburg Theol Sem, BD, 58; Univ Hamburg, ThD, 63; Sigma Delta Chi; Student Senate; Athletes' Lettermen's Club. Polit & Govt Pos: Vpres, Crosslines Coun, Kansas City, Kans, 65-66; bd mem, Fair Housing Coun, Metrop Kansas City, 66; deleg, Hawaii Dem State Conv, 68, deleg, & mem rules comt, 70 & 72; pres, Precinct Dem Party, Hawaii, 68-70, councilman, 72-; chmn, Ninth Dist Dem Party, 70-72; committeeman, Oahu Co Dem Party, 70-72 & 74-; pres, Hawaii Chap, Am for Dem Action, 71 & 72; alt deleg, Dem Nat Conv, 72; deleg, Dem Nat Mid-Term Conf, 74. Bus & Prof Pos: Pastor, Westwood Lutheran Church, Kansas City, Kans, 63-67 & Lutheran Campus Ministry, Univ Hawaii, 67- Mem: Lutheran Campus Ministers' Asn; Citizens for Hawaii; John Howard Asn; Am for Dem Action. Relig: Lutheran. Legal Res: Apt Makai-9 1325 Wilder Ave Honolulu HI 96822 Mailing Add: 2039 Vancouver Dr Honolulu HI 96822

FRITTER, LINDBERGH ALEXANDER **(R)**
Chmn, Stafford Co Rep Party, Va
b Stafford Co, Va, May 25, 28; s Thomas Alexander Fritter & Grace Bell Randall F; m 1949 to Edna Catherine DeShields; c Elizebeth (Mrs Daniel Burton), Wendy Marie & Patricia Ann. Educ: Stafford High Sch, Va, 3 years. Polit & Govt Pos: Chmn, Stafford Co Rep Party, Va, 64- Mem: Moose. Relig: Methodist. Mailing Add: Rte 3 Box 541 Stafford VA 22554

FRITZ, GEORGE H **(R)**
Chmn, Barber Co Rep Comt, Kans
b Lake City, Kans, Dec 31, 19; s George Louis Fritz & Eliza Lane F; m 1942 to Dorothy A Kimball; c Janis Louise & Randy. Educ: Kans State Univ, grad, 46; Farm House. Polit & Govt Pos: Mem sch bd, Brookville, Kans, 58-66; precinct committeeman, Brookville Rep Party, 60-66; chmn, Barber Co Rep Comt, 68- Bus & Prof Pos: Co agr agt, Hodgeman Co, Kans, 46-48; ranch mgr, CK Ranch, Brookville, 57-66; rancher, Lake City, 66- Mil Serv: Entered as Pvt, Army, 42, released as T-4, 46, after serv in Med Corps, ETO, 44-46; Good Conduct Medal. Mem: Mason; Am Royal Bd Gov; Kans Livestock Asn (pres, 70); Barber Co Cattlemen's Asn (secy-treas); Kans Nat Livestock Show (mem bd dirs, 71-72). Honors & Awards: Diamond Award, Kans Livestock Asn, 57; Kans Banker Award for Soil Conserv, 72. Relig: Methodist. Mailing Add: Star Rte Box 9 Lake City KS 67071

FRITZELL, STELLA H **(R)**
NDak State Sen
b Bucyrus, NDak, Oct 3, 09; d Gunder Houge & Carrie Engen H; m 1933 to Kenneth E Fritzell, wid; c Peter, Sara (Mrs Hanhan), Erik & Anne (deceased). Educ: Univ Minn, BS, cum laude, 31, Univ Minn Hosps, dietetic internship, 32; Omicron Nu; Phi Upsilon Omicron; Alpha Xi Delta. Polit & Govt Pos: Pres, Park Bd Comn, Grand Forks, NDak, 61-; deleg, NDak Const Conv, 70-72; mem, NDak State Bd Park Comn, 71-; mem, Grand Forks City Planning & Zoning Comn, 71-; NDak State Sen, 72- Bus & Prof Pos: Research technician, Univ Minn Hosps, 33-35; nutritionist, Minneapolis Welfare Dept, 35-40; stock broker, Piper, Jaffray & Hopwood, Grand Forks, 59-71. Mem: NDak Recreation & Park Asn (legis comt, 60-); Bus & Prof Womens Club (youth conf, legis comt, 67-); Grand Forks CofC (chmn environ & beautification comt, 71-); Natural Sci Soc; Audubon Soc (issue comt, 70-); United Hosp Corp. Honors & Awards: Trap Shooting Champion, NDak State Women, 69; Pub Serv Award, Univ Students for Environ Defense, 70; Cert of Appreciation, Badlands Environ Asn, 73. Mailing Add: 1120 Cottonwood Grand Forks ND 58201

FRIZZELL, DALE KENT **(R)**
Solicitor, Dept Interior
b Wichita, Kans, Feb 11, 29; s Elton Sanderson Frizzell (deceased) & Irma A Hays F; m 1955 to Shirley Elaine Piatt; c Gregory, Damon, Kirsten, Angela & Blaine. Educ: Friends Univ, BA, 53; Washburn Univ Law Sch, LLB, 55; Phi Alpha Delta; Phi Kappa Psi. Polit & Govt Pos: Precinct committeeman, Co Rep Cent Comt, Kans, 50-64; pres, Wichita Bd Educ, 59-65; mem, State Munic Acct Bd, 61-64; Kans State Sen, 25th Sen Dist, 65-69; Attorney Gen, Kans, 69-71; asst attorney gen, Land & Natural Resources Div, 72-73; Dept Justice, solicitor, Dept Interior, 73- Bus & Prof Pos: Pvt law off, 55-63; partner, McCarter, Frizzell & Wettig, 63-68. Mil Serv: Entered as Cpl, Marine Corps, 48, released as Sgt, 52. Mem: Am Bar Asn; Am Legion. Honors & Awards: Am Legion Nat Oratorical Contest winner & Methodist Church Nat Pub Speaking Contest winner, 47. Relig: Methodist. Legal Res: 3268 Juniper Lane Falls Church VA 22044 Mailing Add: Dept of Interior Washington DC 20240

FRIZZELL, MARTHA MCDANOLDS **(R)**
NH State Rep
b Branchville, NJ, Nov 18, 02; d George A McDanolds & Kate E Roe M; m 1927 to Theodore J Frizzell; c Katharine (Mrs Edwin E Blaisdell), Theodora (Mrs Gordon Duke Duncan), Elizabeth (Mrs Allyn M Bascom), Robert T & James A; 15 grandchildren. Educ: Univ NH, BS, 24; Columbia Univ. Polit & Govt Pos: Libr trustee, Charlestown, NH, over 25 years; NH State Rep, 51-, chmn, Judiciary Comt, NH House Rep; deleg, Const Conv, 56 & 64; women's chmn, Rep Party, Sullivan Co, 56-58 & 72-; mem, New Eng Bd of Higher Educ, 57-65 & 69-, exec comt, 60-64 & 69-70; chmn, Sullivan Co Deleg, 59, 63, 69 & 71, clerk, 61. Publ: Second history of Charlestown, NH, 55; History of Walpole. Mem: NH Libr Trustee Asn; NH Fed Women's Clubs (legis chmn); NH OWLS (pres, 63); Women's Club (pres); Farm Bur. Honors & Awards: Univ NH Citation for Community Serv. Relig: Congregational; trustee, NH Congregational Christian Conf; moderator, 73. Mailing Add: Box 245 RFD Charlestown NH 03603

FROEHLICH, HAROLD VERNON **(R)**
Chmn, Eighth Dist Rep Party, Wis
b Appleton, Wis, May 12, 32; s Vernon W Froehlich (deceased) & Lillian Wohlfeil; m 1970 to Sharon Ross; c Jeffrey Scott & Michael Ross. Educ: Univ Wis, BBA, 59, Law Sch, LLB, 62; Phi Kappa Phi. Polit & Govt Pos: Co-chmn & treas, Outagamie Co Young Rep, Wis, 56-57; dist chmn, Wis Fedn Young Rep, 58, state treas, 59; precinct committeeman, Outagamie Co Rep Party, 56-62; chmn, Outagamie Co Statutory Comt, 58-62; Wis State Rep, 63-73, chmn Rep Caucus, Wis House of Rep, 65-67, speaker, 67-71, minority leader, 71-73; deleg, Rep Nat Conv, 72; US Rep, Wis, 73-75; chmn, Eighth Dist Rep Party, 75- Bus & Prof Pos: Staff acct, Reuschlein & Storteon, CPA, 61; partner, Froehlich & Jensen, attorneys-at-law & Patterson, Froehlich, Jansen & Wylie, 64-73; assoc, Patterson, Jensen, Wylie & Silton; comnr, Outagamie Co Family Court, 75- Mil Serv: Entered as A/S, Navy, 51, released as Aviation Electronics Technician 1/C, 55, after serv in 30th Antisubmarine Squadron, European Occup, 52-55; European Occup & Good Conduct Medals. Mem: Wis Soc CPA; Am Inst Cert Pub Accts; Am Asn of Attorney-CPA; Am Legion; VFW. Honors & Awards: One of Wis Five Outstanding Young Men, Wis Jaycees, 67. Relig: Lutheran. Mailing Add: 907 N State St Appleton WI 54911

FROEHLKE, ROBERT FREDERICK **(R)**
b Neenah, Wis, Oct 15, 22; s Herbert O Froehlke & Lillian P Porath F; m 1946 to Nancy Jane Barnes; c Bruce, Jane, Ann & Scott. Educ: Univ Wis Law Sch, Madison, LLB, 49; Order of the Coif. Polit & Govt Pos: Asst Secy of Defense for Admin, 69-71; Secy Army, 71-73. Bus & Prof Pos: Assoc lawyer, McDonald & MacDonald, Madison, Wis, 49-50; prof, Univ Wis Law Sch, 50-51; legal adv, Sentry Ins Co, 51-59, vpres sales, 67-68; exec vpres, Sentry Life Ins Co, 59-67; resident vpres, Sentry Ins, Boston, Mass, 68-69; pres, Sentry Corp, currently. Mil Serv: Entered as Pvt, Army, 43, released as Capt, 46, after serv in Inf, ETO. Mem: Am & Wis Bar Asns. Relig: Presbyterian. Mailing Add: 1201 Soo Marie Ave Stevens Point WI 54481

FROHNMAYER, DAVID BRADEN **(R)**
Ore State Rep
b Medford, Ore, July 9, 40; s Otto J Frohnmayer & Marabel Fisher Braden F; m 1970 to Lynn Dianne Johnson; c Kirsten Lori. Educ: Harvard Col, AB, magna cum laude, 62; Oxford Univ, BA, 64, MA, 71; Univ Calif Berkeley, Sch Law, JD, 67; Phi Beta Kappa; Order of Coif; bd ed, Calif Law Rev, 65-67; grad class speaker, 67. Polit & Govt Pos: Assoc mem & gen counsel, San Francisco Co Rep Cent Comt, 68-69; mem, Calif Rep State Cent Comt, 68-69; asst to the Secy, US Dept of Health, Educ & Welfare, 69-70; mem, Ore Field Burning Comt, 73; vchmn, Lane Co Rep Cent Comt, Ore, 73-; Ore State Rep, 75- Bus & Prof Pos: Law clerk, Frohnmayer, Lowry & Deatherage, Ore, 65; Law clerk, Pillsbury, Madison & Sutro, Calif, 66 & assoc, 67-; consult, Adv Comt Probate Law Rev, State of Ore, 66-69; asst prof law & spec asst to the univ pres, Univ Ore, 71- Publ: The university & the public: the right of access by non-students to public university property, Calif Law Rev, 66; These parchment barriers: an essay in the vitality of a constitutional idea, Cong Record, 10/72; The constitutional doctrine of Serrano v Priest: some reservations & caveats, In: Restructuring School Finance, 72; plus others. Mem: Am & San Francisco Bar Asns; State Bar Calif; Barrister's Club San Francisco; Harvard Club San Francisco. Honors & Awards: Rhodes Scholar; Detur Prize, Harvard Col; Samuel Pool Weaver Const Law Essay Prize, Am Bar Found, 72 & 74. Relig: Presbyterian. Mailing Add: 2875 Baker Blvd Eugene OR 97403

FROSCH, ROBERT ALAN
b Bronx, NY, May 22, 28; s Herman Louis Frosch & Rose Bernfeld F; m 1957 to Jessica Rachel Denerstein; c Elizabeth Ann & Margery Ellen. Educ: Columbia Col, AB, 47; Columbia Univ, AM, 49, PhD, 52; Zeta Beta Tau; Phi Beta Kappa; Sigma Xi. Polit & Govt Pos: Dir nuclear test detection, Advan Research Projs Agency, Dept Defense, Washington, DC, 63-65, dep dir, 65-66; Asst Secy of the Navy for Research & Develop, 66-73; asst exec dir, UN Environ Prog, 73-75. Bus & Prof Pos: Teacher, Pupin Physics Lab, Columbia Univ, 50-51; scientist, Hudson Labs, NY, 51-54, assoc dir, 54-56 & dir, 56-63; assoc dir appl oceanog, Woods Hole Oceanog Inst, Mass, 75- Publ: Numerous scientific & technical articles. Mem: Fel Am Asn Advan Sci; fel Inst Elec & Electronics Engr; Seismological Soc Am; Soc Explor Geophysicists; Cosmos Club. Honors & Awards: Arthur S Flemming Award, 66. Relig: Jewish. Legal Res: MD Mailing Add: Woods Hole Oceanog Inst Woods Hole MA 02543

FROST, E DOUGLAS **(D)**
b Windsor, Ont, Sept 7, 44; s Earl L Frost & Inez White F; single. Educ: Wayne State Univ, BA, 66; Omicron Delta Kappa; Tau Kappa Alpha. Polit & Govt Pos: Staff dir, Comt House Admin, US House Rep, 75- Bus & Prof Pos: Staff, Wayne Co Health Dept, Detroit, Mich, 68-73; staff, Marttila, Payne, Kiley & Thorne, Inc, Boston, Mass, 73-74. Mailing Add: 225 Tenth St NE Washington DC 20002

FROST, JACK WESLEY **(R)**
Committeeman, Johnson Co Rep Cent Comt, Kans
b Kansas City, Mo, Mar 14, 33; s Earl W Frost & Esther Houston F; m 1954 to Doris Sites, div; c Leigh C, Laura J, Lizabeth A & John L. Educ: Univ Kans, BA in Elec Eng, 55; Sigma Tau; Phi Delta Theta. Polit & Govt Pos: Co campaign mgr, Gov William Avery, Kans, 64; committeeman, Johnson Co Rep Cent Comt, 65-, chmn, 68-72; campaign mgr, Congressman Larry Winn, Third Dist, 66; city councilman, Prairie Village, 67-71. Bus & Prof Pos: Vpres, Nationwide, Inc, Chicago, Ill, 63-; pres, Hardin & Stockton Co, Kansas City, 64-; chmn, Kans Real Estate Comn, 66-70; dir, Ranchmart State Bank, Overland Park, 67-; vpres, Lawyers Title Co, Kansas City, Olathe, 68- Mil Serv: Entered as 2nd Lt, Air Force, 55, released as 1st Lt, 57, after serv in 1885 AACS, Far East Command, Tokyo, 55-57, Res, 57-63. Mem: Nat Asn Real Estate Bd; Real Estate Bd Kansas City, Mo; Real Estate Bd Johnson Co, Kans; Cosmopolitan Club. Relig: Presbyterian. Mailing Add: 7301 Mission Rd Prairie Village KS 66208

FROST, JAMES L (JACK) **(R)**
Recorder, Brown Co, Ohio
b Georgetown, Ohio, Mar 14, 06; s Willie A Frost & Mary J Snider F; m 1940 to Florence Payne (deceased); m 1973 to Mildred N Kennedy; c Carol Ann (Mrs Dreyling) & James L, Jr. Educ: Millers Bus Col, 25-26; Univ Cincinnati, 31-32. Polit & Govt Pos: Treas, Brown Co, Ohio, 45-61, recorder, 69-; Ohio State Rep, Brown Co, 61-67; state examr, Co & Twps, 68. Bus & Prof Pos: Jack Frost's Ins Agency, 35-; teller, Bank of Russellville, 43-45; real estate salesman, Moore & Howser, 47- Mil Serv: Entered as Pvt, Army, 42, released as Cpl, 43; Sharp Shooters Medal. Mem: DAV; Am Legion; CofC; Farm Bur; Farmers Union. Relig: Protestant; Elder for 25 years. Mailing Add: 410 S Main St Georgetown OH 45121

FROST, NORMA W **(R)**
Mem Bd Dirs, Nat Fedn Rep Women
b Miami Co, Ohio, Aug 26, 27; d Fred J Webster & Hazel Jones W; m 1947 to John E Frost; c Marcia, Lynn & James. Educ: Otterbein Col, 1 year 6 months; Tau Epsilon Mu. Polit & Govt Pos: Mem, Fairfield Rep Town Comt, Conn, 63-72; dist leader, 64-66, voter regist

chmn, 65-66 & vchmn, 66-70; state affairs chmn, Fairfield Co Rep Women's Asn, 64-66; first vpres, Fairfield Rep Women's Club, 66-68, acting pres, 68; state affairs chmn, 4th Cong Dist Rep Women's Asn, 66-69; mem, Fairfield Co Rep Orgn & 4th Cong Dist Rep Orgn, 66-72; alt deleg, Rep Nat Conv, 68, deleg, 72; first vpres, Conn Fedn of Rep Women's Clubs, 68, pres, 69-74; mem bd dirs, Nat Fedn Rep Women, 69-, vchmn prog comt, 73-; mem, Conn Rep State Platform Comt, 72, & Subcomt on Narcotics, 70; mem, Meskill for Gov Strategy Comt, 70; deleg, Rep State, State Sen, Sheriff & 4th Cong Dist Conv, 72; mem, Conn Reelect the President Comt, 72. Bus & Prof Pos: Asst med lab technician, 63. Mem: League of Women Voters; PTA; Fairfield Oratorio Soc; Fairfield Hills State Hosp (adv comt, 70-). Relig: Protestant; former mem, First Church of Christ choir. Mailing Add: 30 Morning Glory Dr Easton CT 06612

FROST, STANLEY F (D)
Chmn, Quay Co Dem Cent Comt, NMex
b Clovis, NMex, June 1, 41; s Lloyd Frost & Mary Helen Rose F; m 1959 to Bonnie Gay Duke; c Warren, Wade & Teresa. Educ: NMex Highlands Univ, AB, 62; George Washington Univ Law Sch, JD, 67; Pi Gamma Mu. Polit & Govt Pos: Nat committeeman, NMex Young Dem, 62; chmn, Quay Co Dem Cent Comt, NMex, 68-; Judge, Tenth Judicial Dist Court of NMex, 73- Bus & Prof Pos: Position classification specialist, Libr of Cong, Washington, DC, 62-67; attorney, Tucumcari, NMex, 67- Mem: Kiwanis; Elks. Legal Res: 1505 S Fourth Tucumcari NM 88401 Mailing Add: Box 784 Tucumcari NM 88401

FROUDE, JOHN H (D)
NJ State Assemblyman
Mailing Add: State House Trenton NJ 08625

FRUECHTENICHT, THOMAS ERIC (R)
Ind State Rep
b Ft Wayne, Ind, Apr 8, 40; s Walter John Fruechtenicht & Clara VonGunten F; m 1961 to Sharon Gail Guy; c Beth Ann & Robert Douglas. Educ: Ind Univ, Bloomington, BS, 62 & JD, 65; Phi Delta Phi; Sigma Nu; Ind Univ Found. Polit & Govt Pos: Justice of the peace, Wayne Twp, Ind, 67-70; dep prosecuting attorney, Allen Co Juv Court, 70-71 & Allen Co Circuit Court, 71-72; Ind State Rep, 73- Bus & Prof Pos: Mem bd dirs, Ft Wayne Construction Trade, Inc, 72, mem bd dirs, Child Care Study Comt, 72; mem bd dirs, Young Lawyers Sect, Ind State Bar Asn, 74, Ind Lawyers Comn, 74-, Ind Criminal Justice Planning Agency, 74- & Ft Wayne Art Sch, 74- Mem: Am, Ind State & Allen Co Bar Asns; Anthony Wayne Lions (bd dirs, 72); Ment Health Asn. Relig: Presbyterian. Legal Res: 2314 Indian Village Blvd Ft Wayne IN 46807 Mailing Add: 2410 Ft Wayne Bank Bldg Ft Wayne IN 46802

FRY, CHARLES E (R)
b Greenville, Ohio, July 26, 16; s Charles William Fry & Virginia Wills F; m 1940 to Marjorie; c Charles R, Beatrice Jane (Mrs Darre), Marmee Joan & Robin L. Educ: Ohio State Univ, BS, 38; Beta Gamma Sigma; Phi Eta Sigma; Beta Alpha Psi; Phi Kappa Psi; Toastmasters. Polit & Govt Pos: Ohio State Sen, 60-62; Ohio State Rep, 75th Dist, 64-74, chmn, Govt Opers Comt, Ohio House Rep, Speaker Pro Tem, 69-74; deleg, Rep Nat Conv, 72. Bus & Prof Pos: Former spec agt, Fed Bur Invest; chmn bd & chief exec officer, Fry, Inc. Mem: Nat Soc State Legislators (pres-elect, pres, 71-72); Home Mfrs Inst (former bd mem); Rotary (dist gov); Ohio State Univ Asn (nat bd); Children's Home Levy Comt (chmn). Honors & Awards: Outstanding First-Termer, Ohio State Senate, 60-62. Relig: Presbyterian; elder & pres bd trustee, Covenant Presby Church. Mailing Add: 2430 St Paris Pike Springfield OH 45504

FRY, HOWARD M (R)
Chmn, Rep Finance Comt of Berks Co, Pa
b Reading, Pa, Feb 7, 31; s Samuel R Fry & Margaret Thun F; m to Nancy L Nickerson; c Victoria Lee, Allison Brooks, Julia Nickerson & Howard Morton, III. Educ: Yale Univ, BA, 53; Harvard Law Sch, LLB, 57. Polit & Govt Pos: Deleg, Rep Nat Conv, 68 & 72; chmn, Rep Finance Comt Berks Co, Pa, currently. Legal Res: 1156 Old Mill Rd Wyomissing PA 19610 Mailing Add: PO Box 679 Reading PA 19603

FRY, LESLIE MCGEE (R)
Mem, Nev Rep State Cent Comt
b Louisiana, Mo, Mar 13, 13; s Octa McGee Fry & Sallie Wilcoxen F; m 1936 to Jean Sauer; c Leslie Mack, Maralyne (Mrs Mallott), Sally (Mrs Woycichowsky), Robert James & Stanley Preston. Educ: Univ Mo, pre-law, 30-35; Univ Louisville, LLB, 40; Kappa Alpha. Polit & Govt Pos: Chmn, Washoe Co Rep Party, Nev, 56-58 & 64-66; mem, Nev Rep State Cent Comt, 56-; alt deleg, Rep Nat Conv, 58 & 68; mem, Am Battle Monuments Comn, 70- Bus & Prof Pos: Attorney, Reno, Nev, 39- Mil Serv: Entered as 1st Lt, Army, 41, released as Maj, 46, after serv in 37th Div Field Artil, Pac Theater, 42-45, Res, 45-66, Lt Col (Ret); Bronze Star. Mem: Am Bar Asn; Future Farmers Am (nat pres); Lions; Boy Scouts; VFW (nat comdr-in-chief). Honors & Awards: Silver Beaver & Order of Antelope, Boy Scouts. Relig: Presbyterian. Legal Res: 991 Whitaker Dr Reno NV 89503 Mailing Add: 105 N Sierra St Reno NV 89501

FRY, LUCIAN (D)
Chmn, Wayne Co Dem Exec Comt, WVa
b Stiltner, WVa, Nov 5, 06; s Andrew J Fry & Mary Frances Napier F; m 1967 to Willa Fae Sanders. Educ: Marshall Univ, 27-31. Polit & Govt Pos: Dep US Marshal, Southern Dist, WVa, 34-40; sheriff & treas, McDowell Co, WVa, 41-43; chmn, McDowell Co Dem Exec Comt, 42-43; treas, Wayne Co Dem Comt, 55-56; chmn, Wayne Co Dem Exec Comt, 57-; investr, WVa Beverage Comn, 61-64. Bus & Prof Pos: Owner & pres, Trace Fork Coal Co, 46-61, vpres & dir, 52 Gas Line, 49-70; dir, Wayne Co News, 61-; secy, Wayne Co Planning Comt, 60-; dir & treas, Wayne Co Bank, 57-; pres, Wayne Mobile Homes, Inc, currently. Mil Serv: Entered as Pvt, Army, 43, released as Sgt, 45, after serv in 119th Inf Regt, 30th Div, ETO, 43-45; Purple Heart; Good Conduct Medal. Mem: Am Legion; DAV; CofC; Lions. Relig: Protestant. Mailing Add: 2395 Fry Lane East Lynn WV 25512

FRYE, CHARLES ALTON (R)
b Nashville, Tenn, Nov 3, 36; c Edgar Alton Frye & Kathleen Hannah F; m 1953 to Patricia Ann Davis; c Wesley Andrew & Emily Hannah. Educ: St Louis Univ, BS summa cum laude, 58; Woodrow Wilson nat fel, Yale Univ, 58-59, Gen Elec Found Owen D Young fel, 59-61; Jr Sterling fel, 60-61, PhD, 61. Polit & Govt Pos: Personnel supvr, City of St Louis, Mo, 56-58; consult various off, Dept of State & Dept Defense, 62-; consult, Nat Adv Comn on Civil Disorders, 67; Dept of Housing & Urban Develop, 67; lectr, State Dept Sr Seminar in Foreign Policy, 65; lectr, Air War Col, 65 & Cent Intel Agency Advan Intel Seminar, 70; foreign policy adv, Brooke for Senate Campaign, 66, admin asst, US Sen Edward W Brooke, Mass, 68-71, consult, 71- Bus & Prof Pos: Reporter-announcer, WNAH & WMAK, Nashville, 53-54, WTMV, KXLW, WEW, St Louis, Mo, 54-56 & WELI, New Haven, 58-61; staff mem, Rand Corp, Santa Monica & Washington, DC, 62-68; vis asst prof, Univ Calif, Los Angeles, 64; research fel, Ctr for Int Affairs & lectr dept govt, Harvard Univ, 65-66; fel, Woodrow Wilson Int Ctr for Scholars, 70-; int fel, Coun on Foreign Rels, 70-71, sr fel, 72-; consult, Comt for Econ Develop, 72-; lectr, US Naval War Col, 73. Publ: Auth, Congress: the virtues of its vices, Foreign Policy, summer 71; One way out: a ceiling on busing, Washington Post Outlook, 4/72; Arms Limitation Treaty: the price and the value, Los Angeles Times Opinion, 6/72; plus others. Mem: Inst for Strategic Studies; Am Polit Sci Asn; World Future Soc; Am Acad Polit & Social Sci; Coun Foreign Rels. Honors & Awards: Am Polit Sci Asn cong fel, 61-62; Pulitzer Prize nominee, 67. Relig: Congregational. Legal Res: 1242 Titania Lane McLean VA 22101 Mailing Add: Woodrow Wilson Int Ctr Scholars Smithsonian Bldg Washington DC 20560

FRYE, HENRY E (D)
NC State Rep
b Ellerbe, NC, Aug 1, 32; s Walter A Frye (deceased) & Pearl A Motley F; m 1956 to Shirley Taylor; c Henry Eric & Harlan Elbert. Educ: A&T State Univ, BS, 53; Syracuse Univ Law Sch, summer 58; Univ NC, Chapel Hill, JD, 59; Alpha Kappa Mu; Beta Kappa Chi; Kappa Alpha Psi. Honorary Degrees: LLD, Shaw Univ, 71. Polit & Govt Pos: Asst US dist attorney, US Dept of Justice, 63-65; NC State Rep, 69-; deleg, Dem Nat Conv, 72. Bus & Prof Pos: Prof, NC Cent Univ Law Sch, 65-67; partner, Frye, Johnson & Barbee, Attorneys, 68-; organizer & pres, Greensboro Nat Bank, 71-; mem bd dirs, NC Mutual Life Ins Co, 71- Mil Serv: Entered as 2nd Lt, Air Force, 53, released as 1st Lt, 55, after serv in 8th Fighter Bomber Wing, Korean Theatre, 54; Capt, Air Force Res. Mem: Am & Nat Bankers Asns; Am & Nat Bar Asns; Southeastern Lawyers Asn; CofC. Honors & Awards: First Negro State Representative in NC since 1899; A&T State Univ Alumni Excellence Award, 73. Relig: Baptist. Mailing Add: 1920 Drexmore Ave Greensboro NC 27406

FRYER, LESTER K (D)
Pa State Rep
b Colebrookdale Twp, Pa; s William B Fryer & Edna Hoffman F; m to Mary Ellen Wolfe; c Charles E. Educ: Army Finance Sch, Ft Harrison. Polit & Govt Pos: Pres, Boyertown Dem Club; chmn bldg comt, Boyertown Area Schs; sch dir, Colebrookdale Twp, 54-57; pres of bd & sch dir, Boyertown Borough, 58-63; Pa State Rep, 62- Bus & Prof Pos: Beverage distributor. Mil Serv: Army, S/Sgt, 42-45; 8th Inf Div, Normandy, NFrance, Rhineland, Cent Europe Campaigns. Mem: VFW (Past Comdr); Am Red Cross (chmn, Boyertown Chap); Boyertown Area United Fund (vchmn); Boyertown Businessman's Asn (past pres). Legal Res: 402 E Third St Boyertown PA 19512 Mailing Add: Capitol Bldg Harrisburg PA 17120

FRYMIRE, RICHARD L (D)
b 1931; m 1955 to Phyllis Taylor; c Richard, III, Anne, John, Betsy, Jane & David. Educ: Centre Col, AB; Univ Ky, JD. Polit & Govt Pos: Ky State Rep, 62-65; Ky State Sen, 66-69, Majority Leader, Ky State Senate, 68-69; Adj Gen, Ky, 71- Bus & Prof Pos: Attorney-at-law. Mil Serv: Lt Col, Marine Corps; Ky Air Nat Guard. Relig: Methodist. Legal Res: 125 Montrose Dr Madisonville KY 42431 Mailing Add: Moore Morrow Frymire & McGaw Box 695 Madisonville KY 42431

FU, SING (R)
b Honolulu, Hawaii, Feb 9, 09; s Chan Fu & Chang Shee F; m 1929 to Rose Chow; c Helene (Mrs Okamoto), Denis, Linda, Deanna (Mrs Park), Patricia & Francis. Educ: Dietz Commercial Col. Polit & Govt Pos: Chief warden, Precinct 25, Zone 2, Hawaii, 41-45; precinct officer, Precinct Two, Fourth Dist, Hawaii, 53-56; mem, Territorial Tax Appeal Court, 53-63; mem, Hawaii State Rep Cent Comt, 53-69; State Treas, Rep Party Hawaii, formerly; chmn, Hawaii Regional Adv Coun, Small Bus Admin, 70-; app to Nat Adv Coun, Small Bus Admin, 71 & 73-; alt deleg, Rep Nat Conv, 72. Bus & Prof Pos: Vpres & mgr mkt br, Bank of Hawaii, 62- Mem: Cult Chinese Plaza (treas); F&AM, York Rite Bodies, Scottish Rites & Aloha Temple Shriners. Relig: Christian. Mailing Add: 4124 Harding Ave Honolulu HI 96816

FUCHS, JOSEPH HERMAN (D)
Mem-at-lg, Ariz Dem Exec Comt
b Brooklyn, NY, Jan 15, 17; s Samuel Fuchs & Esther Farber F; single. Educ: City Col New York, 35-37. Polit & Govt Pos: Treas, Nucleus Club, Maricopa Dem Party, 69-; vchmn, Legis Dist 25, Dem Party Ariz, 74-; mem, Gov Screening Comt, currently; mem, Nat Finance Coun, 75; mem-at-lg, Ariz Dem Exec Comt, 75- Bus & Prof Pos: Co-owner, Davids Shoes, Phoenix, 41-61; self-employed, Bus Consult, 61- Mil Serv: Pvt, Army, 43. Mem: Phoenix Realtors; Phoenix Art Museum; Phoenix Symphony Asn. Relig: Jewish. Mailing Add: 1205 E Thomas Rd Phoenix AZ 85014

FUDRO, STANLEY J (DFL)
Minn State Rep
b Minneapolis, Minn, 1918; m to Ramona; c Beth, Angelle, Lisa. Educ: St Thomas Col; Univ Minn. Polit & Govt Pos: Minn State Rep, 57- Bus & Prof Pos: Union bus agt. Mil Serv: Vet, World War II. Mem: Northeast Neighborhood House (boys' dir); Margaret Barry Settlement House (boxing coach); Golden Gloves Boxing Comt; Corker Club; Northeast Boosters Club. Mailing Add: 2322 Second St NE Minneapolis MN 55418

FUGINA, PETER X (DFL)
Minn State Rep
m to Virginia Britt; c Britt. Educ: Hamline Univ, BS; Univ Minn; Univ Wash; Stanford Univ; Purdue Univ; Princeton Univ. Polit & Govt Pos: Minn State Rep, 55-66 & 71-; mem, Minn Adv Comt on Compact for Educ. Bus & Prof Pos: Pub sch instr; ins & real estate; deleg, Va Cent Labor Union; dir, Iron Range Rehabilitation Ctr & Range Ment Health Ctr. Mil Serv: Navy, Amphibious Forces, SPac Mil Govt, Japan & Korea. Mem: KofC; Elks; Moose; VFW; Am Legion. Mailing Add: 5 Merritt Dr Virginia MN 55792

FUHRMAN, MARK J (D)
Chmn, Thurston Co Dem Cent Comt, Nebr
b Pender, Nebr, Oct 1, 36; s Robert G Fuhrman & Leone Johnsen F; m 1963 to Mary Gunderson; c Sheryl, Lori, Janel & Robert G, III. Educ: Creighton Univ, JD, 64; Phi Alpha Delta. Polit & Govt Pos: Co attorney, Thurston Co, Nebr, 66-70; chmn, Thurston Co Dem Cent Comt, Nebr, 72; mem, Nebr Dem State Cent Comt, 74- Mil Serv: Entered as E-1, Army, 58, released as SP-5, after serv in 8th Army Hq, Korea, 58-59. Legal Res: 608 Norris Pender NE 68047 Mailing Add: Box 340 Pender NE 68047

FUJITA, BEN MAMORU (R)
b Long Beach, Calif, Oct 10, 35; s Harry Satoru Fujita & Fusae Kanamaru F; m 1974. Educ: Boise City High Sch, Okla, grad, 53. Polit & Govt Pos: Alt deleg, Rep Nat Conv, 72. Bus & Prof Pos: Owner & partner, Fujita Bros, 59-, Baker Refuse Co & AAA-1 Products Co, currently. Mem: Automotive Serv Coun (secy, unit three, 66-73, pres, 72); Japanese Am Rep (pres, 71 & 72); Univ Relig Conf (pres, 71-73); Toastmasters (pres, 74-). Relig: United Church of Christ. Legal Res: 6537 Hereford Dr Los Angeles CA 90022 Mailing Add: 4469 E Olympic Blvd Los Angeles CA 90023

FULBRIGHT, JAMES WILLIAM (D)
b Sumner, Mo, Apr 9, 05; s Jay Fulbright & Roberta Waugh F; m 1932 to Elizabeth Kremer Williams; c Elizabeth (Mrs John Winnacker) & Roberta (Mrs Thaddeus Foote). Educ: Univ Ark, BA, 25; Oxford Univ, Pembroke, Rhodes Scholar, BA, 28 & MA, 31; George Washington Univ Law Sch, LLB with distinction, 34; Sigma Chi. Hon Degrees: Doctorate, Oxford Univ, 53. Polit & Govt Pos: Spec attorney, Anti-Trust Div, Dept of Justice, 34-35; US Rep, Ark, 43-44; US Sen, Ark, 45-74, chmn, Comt Foreign Rels & Banking & Currency Comt, US Senate; US deleg to UN Gen Assembly, 54. Bus & Prof Pos: Lectr law, George Washington Univ, 35-36; instr law, Univ Ark, 36-39, pres, 39-41. Publ: Old Myths and New Realities, 64 & Arrogance of Power, 66, Random House; The Pentagon Propaganda Machine, Liveright, 70; plus one other. Relig: Disciples of Christ. Mailing Add: Fayetteville AR 72701

FULCOMER, JAMES JOSEPH (R)
Rep Nat Committeeman, Young Rep Nat Fedn
b Elizabeth, NJ, Nov 20, 43; s James Samuel Fulcomer & Josephine Mary Decker F; m 1967 to Katherine Eleanor Harms. Educ: Newark State Col, BA Hist, 66; NY Univ, MA Polit Sci, 72; Humanist Club. Polit & Govt Pos: Chmn & founder, Union Twp TAR, NJ, 60-62; chmn & co-founder, TAR of Union Co, Inc, 61-62; deleg, Union Co Young Rep Coun, 62-; chmn, Newark State Rep Club, Inc, 63-66; treas, Mid-Atlantic Coun of Col Rep Clubs, 63-64; chmn, Union Co Youth for Nixon, 68-71; deleg, Young Rep of NJ, Inc, 68-, assoc vchmn, 71-; chmn, Young Rep of Union Co, Inc, 70-72; mem, Exec Comt, Union Co Rep Comt, 70-; chmn, Environ Health Comt, Union Co Govt, 71-; alt deleg, Rep Nat Conv, 72; Rep nat committeeman, Young Rep Nat Fedn, currently. Bus & Prof Pos: US hist teacher, Edison High Sch, Elizabeth, NJ, 68-72; US hist & polit sci teacher, Jefferson High Sch, 72- Publ: GOP view—a weekly column on political events, The Independent, 9/62-5/65. Mem: Elizabeth Educ Asn (coun rep, 69-71); Edison Faculty Orgn (chmn, 71-73); Union Co AFL-CIO Coun (deleg, 71-); Newark State Col Alumni Asn (rep, 69-); Am Fedn Teachers (vpres, Local 733, 72-). Honors & Awards: Distinguished Serv Award, Newark State Rep Club, Inc, 67. Relig: Lutheran. Mailing Add: 384 Raleigh Rd Rahway NJ 07065

FULFORD, WILLIAM EDMOND (D)
Fla State Rep
b Orlando, Fla, July 9, 23; s Jesse Curtis Fulford & Effie Hansel F; m 1943 to Mary Ramsey; c Danny, Mickey, Pat & Jeff. Educ: Univ Fla, 41. Polit & Govt Pos: Fla State Rep, 66-, chmn, House Comt Natural Resources & Subcomt Appropriations, 73-; mem, Comt Rules & Calendar, Appropriations, Transportation, Fla House Rep, 73- Bus & Prof Pos: Pres, Fulford Van & Storage Co, Inc, Orlando, Fla, 48- Mil Serv: Entered as Aviation Cadet, Army Air Corps, 42, released as 1st Lt, 45, after serv in 26th Fighter Squadron, 14th Air Force, China-Burma-India, Theatre, 43-44; Air Medal; Distinguished Flying Cross. Mem: Orange Co Sportsmen's Asn (past pres & hon life mem); Fifty Dist Sportsmen's Asn (past pres); Fla Wildlife Fedn (past pres); CofC; Farm Bur. Honors & Awards: Fla Outstanding Legis Conservationist, Nat Wildlife Fedn. Relig: Protestant. Legal Res: 3221 Alamo Dr Orlando FL 32805 Mailing Add: PO Box 1226 Orlando FL 32802

FULKERSON, JEWETT MONROE (R)
Rep Nat Committeeman, Mo
b Weaubleau, Mo, Oct 2, 13; s Jewett Hayden Fulkerson & Dovie Monroe F; m 1940 to Carolyn Elizabeth Jenkins; c Judith (Mrs John H Ferguson), Janet (Mrs Eldon L Boisseau) & Joan (Mrs Lawrence P Tompkins). Educ: Univ Mo, Columbia, BS in agr, 36; Farmhouse Fraternity. Polit & Govt Pos: Committeeman, Clay Co Rep Cent Comt, Mo, 58-, chmn, 70-; deleg, Rep Nat Conv, 60 & 64; committeeman, Mo Rep State Comt, 68-; Rep Nat Committeeman, currently. Bus & Prof Pos: Fieldman, Am Hereford J, 36-46; farmer & purebred Hereford & polled Hereford breeder, 42-; fieldman, Southern Stockman, 46-48; co-owner & founder, Polled Hereford World, 48-50; founder & owner, Fulkerson Sale Serv, 48-; registered Hereford & polled Hereford auctioneer, 49- Mem: Am Polled Hereford Asn (dir, 72-); Nat Auctioneers Asn; Farm Bur. Relig: Presbyterian. Mailing Add: 1011 W Ten Hwy Liberty MO 64068

FULLAM, ARTHUR W (R)
NH State Rep
Mailing Add: RFD Ossipee NH 03864

FULLE, FLOYD THEODORE (R)
Chmn Exec Comt, Cook Co Rep Cent Comt, Ill
b Chicago, Ill, Feb 15, 21; s Fred A Fulle & Bernice Rasch F; m to Patricia Ruth Lowry; c Ricky, Talbert & Michael. Educ: Knox Col, AB, 42; Phi Delta Theta. Polit & Govt Pos: Asst precinct capt, precinct capt & twp coordr, Maine Twp Regular Rep Orgn, 49-61, chmn twp Rep reorgn comt, 61, committeeman, 63-; co-comnr, Cook Co, 64-; pres, Suburban Committeemen's Asn, 64-; chmn audit & budget comt, Cook Co Rep Cent Comt, 64, chmn exec comt, 66-; deleg, Rep Nat Conv, 68 & alt deleg, 72. Bus & Prof Pos: Founder & publ, Suburban Progress; owner, Rosemont Publ. Mil Serv: Entered as 2nd Lt, Army, 42, released as Maj, 47, after serv in 379th Transportation Corps & 248th TRK Bn, Mediter, European & Philippine Theaters, 42-45, Lt Col, Res; Bronze Star. Mem: Lions; Mason; Shrine; Am Legion; VFW. Honors & Awards: Best Ed Award, Ill Press Asn, 55; Am Legion Americanism Award for Ed, 58; Outstanding Serv Award, Jr CofC, 60; Ill Award for Prom Traffic Safety, 65; Knox Col Alumni Achievement Award, 66. Relig: Protestant. Mailing Add: 666 Laurel Ave Des Plaines IL 60016

FULLER, ALBERT CLINTON (D)
b Henderson, NC, June 14, 20; s Butler Vance Fuller & Chloe Wrenn F; m 1945 to Louise Burnette; c Albert Lawrence (Larry). Educ: NC State Univ, 37. Polit & Govt Pos: From vchmn to chmn, Franklin Co Bd Educ, Louisburg, NC, 61-72; chmn, Second Cong Dist Dem Campaign Comt, 68-70; chmn, Franklin Co Dem Party, 68-72; commun asst to US Sen Jesse Helms, NC, 73-74, exec asst, 74- Bus & Prof Pos: Super mkt owner, Louisburg, NC, 52-63; news-sports dir, WYRN Radio, Louisburg, 63-64; ed, Franklin Times, Louisburg, 64-73. Mil Serv: Entered as Pvt, Army Air Corps, 42, released as S/Sgt, 45, after serv in Air Transport Command, European & African Theatre, 43-45; Theatre Ribbon; Good Conduct Medal. Publ: Auth of newspaper articles & editorials. Mem: Rotary Club, Louisburg; Bus Asn, Louisburg; Senate Staff Club. Honors & Awards: Americanism Award, Am Legion; Journalist & Educator Award, Quill & Scroll Soc; Man of the Year, Louisburg Rotary, 66; Tarheel of the Week, Raleigh News & Observer, 67; First Investigative Reporter, NC Press Asn, 73. Relig: Baptist. Legal Res: 944 Henderson Rd Louisburg NC 27549 Mailing Add: 3830 N 30th St Arlington VA 22207

FULLER, CHARLES EUGENE, JR (D)
Mem, Ala Dem State Exec Comt
b LaFayette, Ala, July 26, 09; s Charles Eugene Fuller, Sr & Daisy Schuessler F; m 1934 to Mary Faye Riser; c Frieda (Mrs Gibbons), Charles Eugene, III, Mary Faye, Cecilia, Roseanne & William Riser. Educ: Univ Ala, BA, 31; Auburn Univ, 32; Phi Gamma Delta. Polit & Govt Pos: Dep solicitor, Chambers Co, Ala, 37-38 & 50-56; mem, Interstate Com Comn, 40; chmn, Chambers Co Dem Exec Comt, 42-71; mem, Ala Dem State Exec Comt, currently; mem, League of State Dem Exec Comts of the Co Dem Comts of Ala. Bus & Prof Pos: Attorney-at-law, LaFayette, Ala, 31- Mem: State of Ala Bar Asn; LaFayette Rotary Club. Relig: Methodist. Legal Res: 308 S LaFayette St LaFayette AL 36862 Mailing Add: Court House LaFayette AL 36862

FULLER, DON EDGAR (R)
Chmn, Ross Co Rep Cent Comt, Ohio
b Columbus, Ohio, Aug 9, 28; s Francis Edgar Fuller & Irene Hagerson F; m 1953 to Virginia Rose Ashmore; c John, Leslee, Ralph, Donna, Ginger, Frank & Christi. Educ: Ohio State Univ, BA, 50; Capital Univ, JD, 54; Beta Theta Pi; Phi Delta Phi. Polit & Govt Pos: Mem, Ross Co Rep Cent Comt, Ohio, 62-, chmn, 66-; secy, Ross Co Rep Exec Comt, 62-68; asst city solicitor, Chillicothe, 65-67, city solicitor, 68- Bus & Prof Pos: Attorney-at-law, Chillicothe, Ohio, 54- Mem: Lions; Ohio State & Ross Co Bar Asns; Ross Co YMCA (bd dirs & pres); Ross Co Community Improv Corp (bd dirs). Relig: Presbyterian; past pres bd deacons & bd elders, First Presby Church. Mailing Add: 19 W Second St Chillicothe OH 45601

FULLER, LARRY DEAN (D)
Chmn, Malheur Co Dem Comt, Ore
b Island City, Ore, Mar 2, 37; s C Lowell Fuller & Nettie Lee Whittenberg F; m 1959 to Linda Dickson; c Lowell Dean, Jon Bradley, Dana Colleen, Jana Carol & Krystol Lynn. Educ: Brigham Young Univ, 55-57; George Washington Univ, BBusAdmin, 62; pres, Young Dem Club. Polit & Govt Pos: City councilman, Baker, Ore, 66-67, budget bd mem, 67; chmn, Malheur Co Dem Comt, 70- Mem: US Jaycees (vpres, 70-71); Ore Jaycees. Honors & Awards: Outstanding State VPres, Ore Jaycees. Relig: Latter-day Saint. Mailing Add: 1468 NW Third Ave Ontario OR 97914

FULLER, MARGARET E (D)
b Salt Lake City, Utah, May 14, 49; d Forrest Wayne Fuller (deceased) & Judith Ivins Hyde F; single. Educ: Utah State Univ, 67-68; Univ Utah, 70-; student body officer, legis rels, student affairs, adv cabinet & Hinckley intern. Polit & Govt Pos: Student coordr, Bob Nance for Cong, Utah, 70; deleg, Nat Emergency Conf, Chicago, 71; student coordr, McGovern for President, Utah, 71-72; chmn, Emergency Voter Conf, Utah, 72; co-chmn, Delaney for Comn, Utah, 72; mem platform comt, Utah State Dem Party, 72; deleg, Salt Lake Co & Utah State Dem Conv, 72; alt deleg, Dem Nat Conv, 72; admin asst, McGovern for President, 72. Mem: Help Line, Univ Utah (adv, 71-72). Relig: Catholic. Mailing Add: 231 Tenth Ave Salt Lake City UT 84103

FULLER, WAYNE P (D)
b Buhl, Idaho, Aug 19, 32; s Wesley M Fuller & Elsa Rosenbaum F; m 1954 to Margaret Denison Cathcart; c Douglas, Leslie, Neal, Hilary & Stuart. Educ: Stanford Univ, BA, 54, LLB, 57; Phi Beta Kappa; Los Arcos Club; Alpha Phi Omega; Phi Alpha Delta; Stanford Polit Union. Polit & Govt Pos: Dep prosecuting attorney, Canyon Co, Idaho, 59-60; precinct committeeman, Dem Party, 62-66; finance chmn, Canyon Co Dem Cent Comt, 64-65, chmn, 66-72; state finance chmn, Idaho Dem Party, 65-66; chmn, Legis Dist 11, 72- Bus & Prof Pos: Partner, Brauner & Fuller, Attorneys, Caldwell, Idaho, 59-66; partner, Brauner, Fuller & Doolittle, 66- Mil Serv: Entered as Pvt, Army Res, 55, released as Capt, 66, after serv in Judge Adv Gen Detachment, 6th Army, US, 59-66. Publ: Defining a liberal, Caldwell News Tribune, 11/66; A review of legal insurance, Advocate, 2/69; Farm labor relations, Idaho Law Rev, fall 71. Mem: Am, Idaho & Third Dist Bar Asns; Canyon Co Lawyer's Club; Boy Scouts. Relig: Presbyterian. Legal Res: 1910 Ray Ave Caldwell ID 83605 Mailing Add: PO Box 130 Caldwell ID 83605

FULLERTON, BERT (R)
Iowa State Rep
b Correctionville, Iowa, Oct 11, 02; s Alex H Fullerton & Elsie Bower F; m 1967 to Francis Keller; c Mary (Mrs Gary Meyers) & Rev Dean Fullerton. Polit & Govt Pos: Dir, Bd of Educ, Correctionville, Iowa, 32-40; twp clerk, 32-54; Rep precinct committeeman, 34-40; mem, City Coun, 40; bd mem, Woodbury Co Selective Serv, 40-48; Iowa State Rep, 67- 69 & 73- Bus & Prof Pos: Dir, Farmers Coop Elevator, 44-52. Mem: Mason; Eastern Star; Scottish Rite; Shrine; Western Iowa Exp Farm Asn. Honors & Awards: W G Shelly Agr Achievement Award. Relig: Methodist. Mailing Add: Correctionville IA 51016

FULLERTON, ROBERT L (R)
Chmn, Bedford Co Rep Party, Tenn
b Petersburg, Tenn, Jan 25, 30; s Eugene Fullerton & Daisy Holt F; m 1953 to Nobuko Kanno. Educ: Freed-Hardeman Col, 55-56; Draughons Bus Col, 68-69. Polit & Govt Pos: Exec comt mem, Bedford Co Rep Party, 70-72, treas, 72-74, chmn, 74- Bus & Prof Pos: Salesman, Nat Dairies, Shelbyville, Tenn, 56-62, US Tobacco Co, Knoxville, 62-68; controller, Eaton Corp, Shelbyville, 69- Mil Serv: Entered as Pvt, Army, 51, released as Sgt 1/C, 53, after serv in 24th Inf Div, Far East Theatre, 51-53; Korean Defense, Japanese Occup & Good Conduct Medals. Mem: Nat Asn Accts; Am Legion; VFW. Honors & Awards: Colonel Aide-de-Camp, Gov Winfield Dunn, Tenn, 74. Relig: Church of Christ. Legal Res: 500 Hillcrest Shelbyville TN 37160 Mailing Add: 111 Eaton Dr Shelbyville TN 37160

FULLMER, DONALD K (R)
b Rockyford, Colo, Apr 11, 15; s Clinton G Fullmer & Florence Kitchen F; m 1934 to Ardyth N Creesy; c Robert E, Maxine (Mrs Duffield) & Phyllis (Mrs Danielson). Educ: Am Col Life Underwriters, CLU, 62. Polit & Govt Pos: Chmn, Gray's Harbor Co Rep Party, Wash, formerly, precinct committeeman, 64-69, state committeeman, Wash Rep Party, 69-71. Bus & Prof Pos: Life underwriter, NY Life, 54- Mil Serv: Entered as Pfc, Army, 45, released as Pfc, 45, after serv in Ground Forces. Mem: Twin Harbor Life Underwriters Asn; Wash State

Asn Life Underwriters (pres); Kiwanis; Mason. Relig: Methodist. Mailing Add: PO Box 611 Montesano WA 98563

FULSTONE, DAVID HILL, II **(R)**
Chmn, Lyon Co Rep Cent Comt, Nev
b Yerington, Nev, Dec 23, 50; s David Hill Fulstone & Angie Magaroli F; single. Educ: Sierra Jr Col, 69; Univ Nev, Reno, 70; Alpha Tau Omega. Polit & Govt Pos: Chmn, Lyon Co Rep Cent Comt, Nev, 74- Bus & Prof Pos: Owner & mgr, Fulstone Ranches, 70- Mem: Lions Int; Toastmasters Int; Nat Hot Rod Asn; Future Farmers Alumni Asn. Relig: Catholic. Mailing Add: 513 West Bridge St Yerington NV 89447

FULTON, CURTIS RAY **(R)**
b Adaton, Miss, Oct 21, 26; s Eddie O Fulton & Anna Elizabeth S F; m 1952 to Pauline Pettus; c Charles A & David W. Educ: Miss State Univ, BS, 49; Air Force Inst Technol, MBA, 60. Polit & Govt Pos: Finance dir, Nat Rep Cong Comt, 67-72. Mil Serv: Entered as Pvt, 43, Marines, released as Sgt, 46; Air Force, 49-67, Maj (Ret); Distinguished Flying Cross; Air Medal with Four Clusters. Relig: Baptist. Mailing Add: 6734 Bostwick Dr Springfield VA 22151

FULTON, RICHARD HARMON **(D)**
US Rep, Tenn
b Nashville, Tenn, Jan 27, 27; s Lyle Houston Fulton & Labina Plummer F; m to Sandra Fleisher; c Richard, Michael, Donna & Linda & Cynthia & Charles Fleisher. Educ: Univ Tenn. Polit & Govt Pos: Tenn State Sen, 59; US Rep, Tenn, 63-, mem, House Ways & Means Comt, US House of Rep, Asst Dem Whip & mem, Dem Steering Comt, currently; deleg, Dem Nat Conv, 68. Bus & Prof Pos: Real estate broker. Mil Serv: Seaman 1/C, Navy, 45-46. Mem: Mason (32 degree); Shrine; Civitan; Sertoma; Am Legion. Relig: Methodist. Legal Res: 1250 Genelle Dr Goodlettsville TN 37072 Mailing Add: 2305 Rayburn Off Bldg Washington DC 20515

FULTON, ROBERT D **(D)**
Dem Nat Committeeman, Iowa
b Waterloo, Iowa, May 13, 29; s Lester Charles Fulton & Fern Ryan F; m 1955 to Rachel Breault; c Susan, Mary, Jack & James. Educ: State Univ Iowa, BSC, 52 & JD, 58; Phi Delta Phi. Polit & Govt Pos: Iowa State Rep, 58-60; Iowa State Sen, 62-64; Lt Gov, State of Iowa, 64-68; deleg, Dem Nat Conv, 68 & 72; Dem Nat Committeeman, Iowa, 68- Bus & Prof Pos: Attorney, Black Hawk Co Legal Aid, 59-61. Mil Serv: Entered as Pvt, Air Force, 53, released as Cpl, 55. Mem: Iowa State & Black Hawk Co Bar Asns; Amvets; Am Legion; CofC. Legal Res: 616 Lafayette St Waterloo IA 50702 Mailing Add: 141 Hillcrest Rd Waterloo IA 50701

FUNDERBURK, KENNETH LEROY **(R)**
Chmn, Russell Co Rep Party, Ala
b Phenix City, Ala, Sept 13, 36; s Lemuel LeRoy Funderburk & Ruth Duke F; m 1958 to Judy Barbee; c Rebecca Lee, Kimberly Ann & Eric Barbee. Educ: Howard Col, AB, 57; Miss State Univ, 57-58; Univ Ala, LLB, 65; Trident; Bench & Bar; Lambda Chi Alpha; Kappa Pi; Mu Alpha Chi; Sigma Delta Kappa. Polit & Govt Pos: Chmn, Russell Co Rep Party, Ala, 66- Bus & Prof Pos: Credit mgr, Cobb Hosp, 58; rep, Canned Meat Div, Armour & Co, 58-60; partner, Phillips & Funderburk, Law Off, 65- Mil Serv: Entered as E-1, Army Res, 58, released, 58, recalled, 61 & released as E-3, 62, after serv in MedC & as a Chaplain Asst. Mem: Ala Bar Asn; Russell Co Bar; Lions; Jr CofC. Relig: Baptist. Legal Res: 3303 Fifth Ave Phenix City AL 36867 Mailing Add: Phenix Nat Bank Phenix City AL 36867

FUNKHOUSER, RICHARD
b Trenton, NJ, Sept 10, 17; s Edgar Bright Funkhouser & Evelyn Hayes F; m 1944 to Phyllis Parkin; c Phillip (deceased), Bruce Bedford & Blaine. Educ: Princeton Univ, BA summa cum laude, 39; Nat War Col, grad, 54. Polit & Govt Pos: Joined Foreign Serv, 45; assigned Am Embassies, Paris, Bern, Brussels & Luxembourg, 45-47; officer-in-charge, Iraq, Syria & Lebanon Affairs, Dept of State, 50-52; polit officer, dep chief of mission & charge d'affaires, Am Legation, Bucharest, Rumania, 54-55; chief, polit & econ sect, Am Embassy, Damascus, Syria, 56-58; spec asst to Asst Secy of State, 59-60; counr econ affairs, Am Embassy, Moscow, USSR, 61-64; counr polit affairs, Am Embassy, Paris, France, 65-69; US Ambassador to Gabon, 69-70; mem policy planning staff, Dept of State, 72-74; Consul Gen, Scotland, 74- Bus & Prof Pos: Consult, Bethlehem Steel Co, 39, Shell Union Oil Co, 39 & Standard Oil Co, Venezuela, 40-42. Mil Serv: Entered Air Force, 43, released as 1st Lt, 45; Distinguished Flying Cross with three Oak Leaf Clusters; Air Medal with four Oak Leaf Clusters. Mem: Phi Beta Kappa; Chevy Chase, Metrop & Princeton Clubs, Washington, DC. Relig: Presbyterian. Legal Res: Washington DC 20007 Mailing Add: 3 Regent Terr Edinburgh Scotland

FUNSTON, BOB **(D)**
Okla State Sen
b Tulsa, Okla, Sept 17, 38; s Louis Robert Funston & Mary Anne Scott F; m 1963 to Karen Kay Tanner. Educ: Okla Baptist Univ, BS in Chem, 61; Univ Tulsa Col Law, JD, 65; Delta Theta Phi. Polit & Govt Pos: Pub defender, Tulsa Co, Okla, 66; Okla State Sen, 72-, chmn bus, indust & labor rels comt, Okla State Senate; chmn, Okla Dem Party, 75- Bus & Prof Pos: Chemist, Federated Metals, Sand Springs, Okla, 60-62; chief chemist, Standard Magnesium, Tulsa, 62-64; Ford Found intern, Okla Legis Coun, 65; pvt law practice, 66- Mil Serv: Entered as Airman, Okla Nat Guard, 66, released as S/Sgt, 72. Mem: Tulsa Co & Okla Bar Asns; Okla Trial Lawyers; Broken Arrow CofC. Relig: Unitarian. Mailing Add: 2401 S Elm Pl Broken Arrow OK 74012

FUQUA, DON **(D)**
US Rep, Fla
b Jacksonville, Fla, Aug 20, 33; s J D Fuqua & Lucille Langford F; m 1955 to Doris Akidakis; c Laura & John Eric. Educ: Univ Fla, 51-53, BS, 57; Alpha Gamma Rho; Gamma Sigma Delta. Polit & Govt Pos: Fla State Rep, 58-62; US Rep, Fla, 62-; deleg, Dem Nat Mid-Term Conf, 74. Bus & Prof Pos: Dairy & gen farm operator, currently. Mil Serv: Entered as Pvt, Army, 53, released as Sgt, 55; Capt Army Res. Mem: Am Legion; Elks; KT; Mason (32 degree); Shriner, Red Cross of Constantine & Royal Order of Jesters. Honors & Awards: Named One of Five Outstanding Young Men, Fla Jaycees, 63. Relig: Presbyterian; Elder. Legal Res: Altha FL 32421 Mailing Add: Rm 2266 Rayburn Off Bldg Washington DC 20515

FUQUA, J B **(D)**
b Prince Edward Co, Va, June 26, 18; m 1945 to Dorothy Chapman; c Rex. Educ: Pub schs, Va. Hon Degrees: LLD, Hampden-Sydney Col. Polit & Govt Pos: Ga State Rep, 58-62, chmn banking comt, Ga House Rep, 58-62; chmn, Ga State Dem Exec Comt, 62-66; Ga State Sen, 63-64, chmn banking comt, Ga State Senate, 63-64; mem, Ga State Adv Coun & Ga Sci & Technol Comn. Bus & Prof Pos: Pres, Fuqua Nat Inc, 49-; chmn bd & chief exec officer, Fuqua Industs, Inc, 65-; dir, Gable Industs, Inc, Cent Ga RR Co & Winston Develop Corp; owner, Fuqua Invest Co, Cablevision Augusta & Rentavision Augusta; mem bd trustees, Med Col Ga Found, Hampden-Sydney Col & World Bus Coun. Mem: Ga Asn Broadcasters; Young Pres Orgn; Augusta CofC; Augusta Exchange Club; Augusta Aviation Comn; Atlanta CofC. Honors & Awards: Boss of the Year, Augusta Jaycees, 59; Ga Broadcaster-Citizen of the Year, Ga Asn Broadcasters, 62. Relig: Presbyterian. Legal Res: 3574 Tuxedo Rd NW Atlanta GA 30305 Mailing Add: 3800 First Nat Bank Tower Atlanta GA 30303

FUQUA, L P **(D)**
Tenn State Rep
Mailing Add: College St Milan TN 38358

FUQUA, THOMAS EDWARD **(D)**
Mem, DeKalb Co Dem Finance Comt, Tenn
b Detroit, Mich, Dec 16, 42; s Thomas Edward Fuqua & Rose Lee Meadows F; m 1967 to JoNell Amonette. Educ: Tenn Polytech Inst, BS, 64; Soc Bus; Acct Club; Young Col Dem. Polit & Govt Pos: Chmn, Smithville City Planning Comn, Tenn, 68-74; mem, DeKalb Co Quarterly Court, 69-; mem, DeKalb Co Budget Comt, 72-; mem, DeKalb Co Dem Finance Comt, 74- Bus & Prof Pos: Acct, Cumberland Feed Mills, 64-65; dir acct, Middle Tenn Utility Dist, 65- Mem: Tenn Gas Asn (chmn, subcomt on acct & finance, 72, co-chmn, personnel comt, 74); Magistrates Asn Tenn. Relig: Baptist. Mailing Add: 611 W Broad St Smithville TN 37166

FURCOLO, FOSTER **(D)**
b New Haven, Conn, July 29, 17; s Dr Charles L Furcolo & Alberta Foster F; m to Kay Foran, wid, 64; m to Lucy Carra; c Charles Mark, David, Foster, Jr, Hope & Richard. Educ: Yale Col, AB, 33, Law Sch, LLB, 36; Yale Labor Mgt Ctr, cert, 47. Hon Degrees: Various hon degrees including LLD, LHD & DrAdmin from several cols & univs. Polit & Govt Pos: US Rep, Second Dist, Mass, 48-52; Treas & Receiver Gen of Mass, 52-54; Gov of Mass, 57-61. Mil Serv: Navy, 42-46. Publ: Let George do it, Harcourt-Brace, 58; The story of Katyn, Marlboro Press, 72; Pills, people, problems, Research Publ, 73. Mem: Hampden Co Barristers, Mass; Mass Bar Asn; Hampden Co Bar Asn. Relig: Catholic. Mailing Add: 1111 Stearns Hill Waltham MA 02154

FURLONG, FRANK J **(D)**
Chmn, Luce Co Dem Comt, Mich
b Sault Ste Marie, Mich, Sept 3, 28; s Francis Patrick Furlong & Margaret K Jordan F; m 1961 to Jane C Turner; c Frank T, Patrick M, Kate M, Courtney A & Carrie E. Educ: St Norbert Col, BSc in hist & econ; Varsity Club; Collegiate Players. Polit & Govt Pos: Chmn, Luce Co Dem Comt, Mich, 62-; mem, Mich State Adv Coun, Small Bus Admin, 66-67. Bus & Prof Pos: Mem, Luce Co Planning Comn, 63-64; mem, St Gregory Sch Bd, 65-; dir, Child & Family Serv Comt, Upper Peninsula Mich, currently; dir, Eastern UP Manpower Consortium, currently. Mil Serv: Entered as Ens, Naval Res, 51, released as Lt, 55, after serv afloat several commands in the Atlantic & Far East Theatres, 51-55, Lt Comdr, Naval Res, Retired; Presidential Unit Citation. Mem: Am Legion; VFW; US Naval Acad Found; KofC; Luce Co CofC. Relig: Catholic. Mailing Add: 306 W Harrie St Newberry MI 49868

FURNISS, SUSAN WEST **(D)**
Chmn, Larimer Co Dem Party, Colo
b Minneapolis, Minn, Aug 8, 24; d David Ripley West & Blanche Sheffield W; wid; c David West, Edgar Stephenson, III & Robert French. Educ: Smith Col, BA, 46; Yale Univ Sch Nursing, 46-48; Univ Minn, MA in libr sci, 66; Colo State Univ, MA in polit sci, 67; Univ Colo, PhD in polit sci, 70. Polit & Govt Pos: Secy, Larimer Co Dem Party, Colo, 69-71, vchmn, 71-72, chmn, 72-; deleg, Dem Nat Conv, 72; dir Colo off, US Sen Gary Hart; deleg, Dem Nat Mid-Term Conf, 74. Publ: The response of the Colorado General Assembly to attempts at metropolitan reform, Western Polit Quart, 12/73. Mem: Am & Western Polit Sci Asns; Pi Sigma Alpha; Phi Kappa Phi; League of Women Voters of Colo. Mailing Add: 1901 W Mohawk Ft Collins CO 80521

FURR, DOROTHY PRESSER **(R)**
Mem, Mecklenburg Co Rep Exec Comt, NC
b Milwaukee, Wis, Aug 9, 29; d Erwin Joseph Presser & Erna Splavec P. Polit & Govt Pos: Treas, vpres & comt chmn, Mecklenburg Young Rep, NC, 49-63; asst secy, NC State Rep Party, 53-66, secy, 66-74; exec secy, NC Young Rep, 53-54, mem exec comt, 53-66, Nat Committeewoman, 55-57; mem, Mecklenburg Co Rep Exec Comt, 53-; asst secy, Nat Young Rep Fedn, 59-61; alt deleg-at-lg, Rep Nat Conv, 60 & 64; chmn, State Plan of Orgn Comt, 60, 62, 64, 66 & 68; organizing pres, Mecklenburg Co Eve Rep Women's Club, 62; Presidential elector, 68 & 72. Bus & Prof Pos: Vpres, E J Presser & Co, Advert Agency. Mem: Charlotte Toastmistress Club. Mailing Add: PO Box 4286 Charlotte NC 28204

FURTH, FREDERICK PAUL **(D)**
Dem Nat Committeeman, Calif
b Harvey, Ill, Apr 12, 34; s Frederick Paul Furth & Mamie Stelmach F; m 1961 to Donna Wickham; c Alison Darby; Ben Anthony & Megan Louise. Educ: Drake Univ & Mich Univ, BA, 56; Univ Mich Law Sch, JD, 59; Univ Berlin & Univ Munich, 59-60. Polit & Govt Pos: Secy, State Citizen Comt on Elec Reform, currently; mem, Exec Comt, Calif State Cent Comt, currently; co-chairperson, Calif Affirmative Action Task Force, currently; mem, Dem Nat Comt, 75-, mem by-laws comt, currently. Bus & Prof Pos: Attorney, Cahill, Gordon, Reindel & Ohl, New York, 60-64; staff mem, Kellogg Co, Battle Creek, Mich, 65-66; Law Off of Joseph Alioto, San Francisco, 65-66; pvt practice, San Francisco, 66- Publ: The anatomy of a seventy million dollar Sherman Act settlement—a law professor's tape-talk with plaintiff's trial counsel, DePaul Law Rev, spring, 74. Mem: Bar Asn San Francisco; Int Bar Asn (antitrust comt); NAACP Legal Defense Fund (bd mem); San Francisco Lawyer's Comt for Urban Affairs. Legal Res: 710 El Camino del Mar San Francisco CA 94121 Mailing Add: 235 Montgomery St Suite 1300 San Francisco CA 94104

G

GAAR, NORMAN EDWARD (R)
Kans State Sen
b Kansas City, Mo, Sept 29, 29; s William Edward Gaar & Lola McKain G; m 1953 to Joanne Rupert; c Anne Elizabeth, James Rupert, William Edward & John Lawrence. Educ: Baker Univ, 47-49; Univ Mich, AB, 55, Law Sch, JD, 56; Delta Theta Phi; Kappa Sigma. Polit & Govt Pos: Munic judge, Westwood, Kans, 59-63, mayor, 63-65; Kans State Sen, 65- Mil Serv: Entered as Aviation Midn, Navy, 49, released as Lt(jg), 53, after serv in 111th Fighter Squadron Task Force 77, 7th Fleet, Korea, 51-52; Japanese Occup & UN Serv Medals; Korean Theater Ribbon with 2 Battle Stars; Korean Presidential Unit Citation; Navy Unit Citation; 2 Air Medals; Letter of Commendation for Valor with Combat Distinguishing Device; Naval Res Ribbon. Mem: Kansas City & Am Bar Asns; US Supreme Court Bar; Am Judicature Soc; Optimists Int. Relig: Presbyterian. Mailing Add: 2340 W 51st Westwood KS 66205

GABALDON, TONY (D)
Ariz State Rep
Mailing Add: 208 W Dale Flagstaff AZ 86001

GABRIEL, FANNIE R (R)
Chmn, Bloomfield Rep Town Comt, Conn
b Rutland, Vt, Aug 17, 22; d Philip S Rockefeller & Jessie Stone R; wid. Educ: Univ Bridgeport, AA; Beaver Col, BA. Polit & Govt Pos: Deleg, State Conv, 53-; secy, Torrington Rep Town Comt, Conn, 53-55, vchmn, 55-58; secy, Bloomfield Rep Town Comt, 62-64, vchmn, 64-72, chmn, 72-; vchmn, Conn Young Rep, 54-55; pres, Women's Rep Fedn, 62-64, dist reg, 75. Mem: Wintonbury Chap, Eastern Star; Wintonbury Hist Soc; Bloomfield Woman's Club (rec secy, 74-); Conn State Fedn Women's Clubs. Relig: Protestant. Mailing Add: 43 Prospect St Bloomfield CT 06002

GABRIELSON, GUY GEORGE (R)
b Sioux Rapids, Iowa, May 22, 91; s Frank August Gabrielson & Ida Jansen G; m 1918 to Cora M Speer; c Guy George; Nancy G (Mrs Owens). Educ: Univ of Iowa, BA, 14; Harvard Univ, JD, 17. Hon Degrees: LLD, Upsala Col, 32, Colby Col, 53. Polit & Govt Pos: Rep Nat Committeeman for NJ; NJ State Assembly, 26-30, majority leader, 28, Speaker, 29; chmn, Rep Nat Comt, 49-52. Bus & Prof Pos: Attorney, pvt practice, NJ, 19-; attorney, pvt practice, New York, 31-; chmn bd dirs, Nicolet Industs, Inc; dir, Somerset Hills Nat Bank; trustee, Drew Univ; trustee, Colby Col. Mem: NJ Bar Asn; NY Co Lawyers Asn; Am Legion; SAR; NY Union League. Relig: Methodist. Mailing Add: Bernardsville NJ 07924

GACKLE, WILLIAM FREDERICK (R)
NDak State Rep
b Kulm, NDak, Dec 7, 27; s Otto Gackle & Alice Higdem G; m 1950 to Marilyn Bernice Goehner; c Frederick, David, Mary Alice & Jonathan. Educ: San Angelo Jr Col, 48-49. Polit & Govt Pos: NDak State Rep, 63- Mil Serv: Entered as Pvt, Army Air Force, 46, released as Sgt, 49, after serv in Training Command; M/Sgt, NDak Nat Guard, 54-60. Mem: Elks; Lions. Relig: Protestant. Mailing Add: Kulm ND 58456

GADDIS, WILLIAM FINLEY (BILL) (R)
Chmn, Harper Co Rep Comt, Okla
b Ashland, Kans, June 7, 50; s William Everet Gaddis & Neoma Joy Thrasher G; single. Educ: Cent State Univ (Okla), 69-70. Polit & Govt Pos: Campaign asst, Harper Co Rep Comt, summer 72, campaign aide, 72-, chmn, 73- Bus & Prof Pos: Asst, Drive Inn Bus, Buffalo, Okla, 63-72; vpres, Gaddis & Sons Inc, 72- Mem: Capitol Club. Honors & Awards: OKIE, 73. Relig: Baptist. Mailing Add: Box 492 409 NW First Buffalo OK 73834

GADDY, CAROLYN C (D)
Mem, NC Dem State Exec Comt
b Rock Hill, SC, June 15, 10; d William Thomas Caldwell & Nancy McAteer C; m 1946 to Samuel Roy Gaddy, wid. Educ: Winthrop Col, AB, 31, MA, 32; Univ NC, Chapel Hill, 40; Sophia Univ, Japan, 65; Duke Univ, 66 & 73. Polit & Govt Pos: From vchmn to chmn, Wingate Precinct Dem Party, NC, formerly; vchmn, Union Co Dem Party, formerly; mem, NC Dem State Exec Comt, 71-; Bus & Prof Pos: Prof, Wingate Col, 32-75. Mem: Southern Hist Soc; NC Lit & Hist Soc; Historic Preservation Soc; Eastern Star (Worthy Matron); Heart Bd Union Co. Legal Res: Rte 1 Wingate NC 28174 Mailing Add: Box 365 Wingate NC 28174

GAETH, M BEN (R)
Ohio State Sen
Mailing Add: 304 Third St Defiance OH 43512

GAFFNEY, BETTY JANE (D)
Mem Credentials Comt, Dem Nat Comt
b Toledo, Ohio, Apr 17, 28; d John J Gaffney & Helen Quinn G; single. Educ: Ursuline Acad, grad; St Louis Univ; Mary Manse Col, grad. Polit & Govt Pos: Col coordr, Young Students for Truman; exec asst to Frazier Reams, Jr, titular head, Ohio Dem Party; chmn press & publicity, Federated Dem Women's Clubs of Ohio; deleg, Ohio Young Dem; state cent committeewoman, Ninth Cong Dist; mem & vchmn, Lucas Co Dem Exec Comt; Dem committeewoman, Precinct 10-M; mem, Lucas Co Dem Policy Comt; nat committeewoman, Ohio Young Dem, 62-66; nat chmn, Young Women Activities, Young Dem Clubs Am, 62-66; field rep, Dem Nat Comt on Block Worker Prog, Ohio, Ind & Wis, 66; state coordr, Reams for Gov Campaign, 66; deleg, Dem Nat Conv, 68 & 72; Dem Nat Committeewoman, 68-72; co-chmn, Nat Regist Drive; mem credentials comt, Dem Nat Comt, 69- Bus & Prof Pos: Pub affairs & prom dir, WCWA, Radio, Toledo. Mem: League of Women Voters (co-dir, You the Voter Prog); Women's Advert Club Toledo; Cath Conf Ohio (dept commun); Zonta Club Int; Commun & World Serv Asn. Relig: Catholic. Mailing Add: 2848 Rockwood Pl Toledo OH 43610

GAFFNEY, J BRIAN (R)
b New Britain, Conn, Mar 25, 33; s Cyril F Gaffney & Helen M Downes Sullivan G; m 1959 to Mary Lou Blinn; c Mary Alicia, Laura Anne, Kateri Ellen, Cyril F, John Brian, Jr & Michael Thomas. Educ: Univ Notre Dame, BA, 55; Fordham Sch Law, LLB, 58; Irish Club; Conn Club. Polit & Govt Pos: Mem, Coun New Britain, Seventh Dist, Conn, 62-64; Alderman-at-lg, 64-65; chmn, New Britain Rep Town Comt, 65-74; asst corp counsel, City of New Britain, 66-68; Conn State Rep, 29th Dist, 67-72; chmn, Conn Rep State Cent Comt, 71-74; mem, Rep Nat Comt, formerly; deleg, Rep Nat Conv, 72. Bus & Prof Pos: Clerk of Superior Court, 60-62; dir, Burritt Mutual Savings Bank. Mil Serv: Pvt, Army, 59; Army Res, 3 years. Mem: Am, New Britain, Hartford Co & Conn Bar Asns; Lions. Relig: Roman Catholic. Legal Res: 36 Westwood Dr New Britain CT 06052 Mailing Add: 30 Bank St New Britain CT 06051

GAFFNEY, JAMES J, III (INDEPENDENT)
Mass State Rep
Mailing Add: State Capitol Boston MA 02133

GAFFORD, ROBERT C (BOB) (D)
Ala State Rep
Mailing Add: 5345 Division Ave Birmingham AL 35212

GAGE, BEVERLY ANNE (R)
NH State Rep
b Tewksbury, Mass, Feb 1, 34; d Wilfred Vaughn Richardson & Catherine Thelma Lafoe R; m 1951 to Clarence W Gage; c Virginia (Mrs Richard N Kimball), Frank Joseph & Diane Helen. Educ: Haverhill High Sch, 51. Polit & Govt Pos: Vchmn, Salem Rep Town Comt, NH, 60-62, treas, 72-75; mem, Rep State Comt, 75-; NH State Rep, 75- Relig: Protestant. Mailing Add: 45 Pelham Rd Salem NH 03079

GAGE, DARLEEN NOTEBOOM (R)
b Brookings, SDak, Mar 9, 25; d Mike Noteboom & Lillian Husman N; m 1944 to Dale Jesse Gage; c Gary Gene, Michael Jay, Christopher Dale & Patricia Anne. Educ: Nettleton Commercial Col, Sioux Falls, SDak, 41. Polit & Govt Pos: Rep precinct woman, Hughes Co, SDak, 57-67; pres, Hughes Co Rep Women, 59-60; mem, State Bd of Educ, 61-74; deleg, SDak Rep State Conv, 64; alt deleg, Rep Nat Conv, 72; staff mem, SDak Rep State Cent Comt, 70-74; Hughes Co Rep Cent Committeewoman, 70-74. Bus & Prof Pos: Secy, Comts of SDak Legis, 55-59 & 68-71; secy, SDak Taxpayers Asn, 60-62; stringer, Rapid City J, 65-69. Mem: Nat Secy Asn Int (secy, Oahe Chap, 71-72); Nat Fedn Press Women; SDak Presswomen; Oahe YMCA (secy & mem bd dirs, 73-74); SDak Coun Econ Educ. Second place for ghost written speech, Nat Fedn of Press Women, 72; first place for ghost written speech, SDak Presswomen, 72, first place for personal column, 72. Relig: Methodist. Mailing Add: 425 Fifth Ave Brandon SD 57005

GAGNE, DAVID LAWRENCE (D)
NH State Rep
b Gardner, Mass, Mar 23, 47; s Ronald J Gagne & Constance Mary Lawrence G; single. Educ: Keene State Col, BA, 73. Polit & Govt Pos: Mem, Mayors Task Force Vet, Keene, NH, 72; mem, Gov Comt Children & Youth, 72; mem, Cheshire Co Exec Comt, 75-; mem, Cheshire & Sullivan Co Crime Comn, 75-; NH State Rep, 75- Bus & Prof Pos: Trustee, Univ NH, 71-72; coordr vet affairs, Keene State Col, 73- Mil Serv: Entered as Pvt E-1, Army, 67, released as Sgt E-5, 70, after serv in Vietnam, 68-70; Good Conduct Medal; Army Commendation Medal; Bronze Star; plus others. Mem: Nat Asn Vet Prog (adminr). Honors & Awards: Student of Year, Keene State Col, 73. Mailing Add: 31 Dunbar St Keene NH 03431

GAGNON, GABRIELLE VIRGINIA (D)
NH State Rep
b Nashua, NH, Mar 5, 13; d Joseph A Boilard & Kathleen V Brousseau B; m 1937 to Sylvio A Gagnon; c Sylvia E (Mrs Kapsack); Beverly V (Mrs Murray). Educ: Nashua High Sch, 32. Polit & Govt Pos: Mem, NH State Const Conv, 74; vchmn, Nashua Rep State Const Comt, 74-75; NH State Rep, 75- Bus & Prof Pos: Laser operator, Sprague Electric, 64-75. Mem: Nashua Dem Womens Club; Nashua Emblem Club 170; Am Legion Auxiliary (James E Goffey Unit Three); NH State Asn Emblem Clubs (3rd vpres); Order Women Legislators. Honors & Awards: Two Publicity Awards, Plaque Dist Dep & Americanism Award, Supreme Emblem Club, USA; Outstanding Award for Welfare Chmn & Publicity Award, CWV Auxiliary 1406; Plaque for Work Appreciation, Nashua Dem Women Club. Mailing Add: 22 Maurice St Nashua NH 03060

GAGNON, REBECCA A (D)
NH State Rep
b Berlin, NH, Nov 11, 94; wid; c Five. Educ: St Regis Acad. Polit & Govt Pos: Mem, Women's Dem Club, NH; deleg, Const Conv, 38, 48, 56 & 64; NH State Rep, 39- Mem: Am Legion Auxiliary; Women's Relief Corps Auxiliary; Club Raquetteurs Joliette; Costumes & Soc. Relig: Catholic. Mailing Add: 511 Goebel St Berlin NH 03570

GAHAGAN, HAYES EDWARD (R)
Maine State Sen
b Presque Isle, Maine, Nov 6, 47; s John Edward Gahagan & Chrystal Smith G; m 1973 to Linda Stone; c Erin C Stone. Educ: Harvard Univ, 67; Oxford Univ, 68-69; Univ Maine, Orono, BA, 70, MA in Pub Admin; law student, currently; Phi Gamma Delta. Polit & Govt Pos: Dist dir, Comt to Reelect the President, Maine, 72; alt-at-lg, Rep Nat Conv, 72; Maine State Rep, Caribou, 73-74; Maine State Sen, 75-; comnr, Title III Educ Funding Admin, currently. Bus & Prof Pos: Exec dir, Int Exchange, Inc, formerly, pres, currently; registered rep, NY Stock Exchange, currently; dir, Heritage Found, currently. Mem: Am Soc Pub Admin. Relig: The Way Ministry. Mailing Add: 27 Hammond St Caribou ME 04736

GAIA, PAM (D)
Tenn State Rep
Mailing Add: 3093 N Watkins Memphis TN 38127

GAILLARD, JOHN PALMER, JR (D)
Mayor, Charleston, SC
b Charleston, SC, Apr 4, 20; s John Palmer Gaillard & Eleanor Ball Lucas G; m 1944 to Lucy Huguenin Foster; c John Palmer, III, William Foster & Thomas Huguenin. Polit & Govt Pos: Alderman, Charleston, SC, 51-59, mayor, 59-; pres, Munic Asn SC, 64-65; mem adv bd, US Conf of Mayors, 69-; cand, US Rep, 71. Mil Serv: Entered as Seaman 1/C, Navy, 41, released as Lt, 45. Mem: Elks; Carolina Yacht Club; Hibernian; CofC; St Andrews Soc; Charleston Club. Honors & Awards: Good Neighbor Award, Navy Times, 61. Mailing Add: 77 Montagu St Charleston SC 29401

GAINER, CARL E (D)
WVa State Sen
b Montrose, WVa; s Marvin J Gainer & Pearle Poling G; m 1948 to Clarise Smith; c Frewen,

Carl, Jr & Grace Ann. Educ: Alderson-Broaddus Col, BA; Duke Univ, grad work. Polit & Govt Pos: WVa State Sen, 58-; deleg, Dem Nat Conv, 64 & 68. Bus & Prof Pos: Oil co distributor; former sch prin in Barbour Co. Mil Serv: Naval Res, Cmndg Officer of USS LSM 556. Mem: Shrine; Elks; Moose; Am Legion; VFW. Relig: Methodist. Mailing Add: Box 670 Richwood WV 26261

GAINES, CHARLES ELLIS **(R)**
Ill State Rep
b Chicago, Ill, Jan 16, 24; s Harris Barrett Gaines & Irene McCoy G; m 1957 to Lena Patton; c Cheryl & Michael Ellis. Educ: Fisk Univ, 42-44; Univ Ill, Urbana, BA, 47; John Marshall Law Sch, 47-49; Delta Sigma Rho; Alpha Phi Alpha. Polit & Govt Pos: Mem Rep comt, First Dist, 54-56; vchmn, Young Rep Nat Fedn, 56-59; Ill State Rep, 29th Dist, 75- Bus & Prof Pos: Hearing officer, Consumer Fraud, Attorney Gen, Ill, 69-71; dir, South Side Consumer Fraud Off, 71-74. Mem: Dixon Elem Sch Coun; Chatham Avalon Park Community Coun (civic chmn, 72-); South Cent Community Health Serv Orgn (bd mem, 71-); Chatham Avalon Ment Health Ctr (adv bd, 74-). Honors & Awards: Humanitarian Award, Chatham Businessmen Asn, 74; Citizen of Distinction Citation, Rosa Geff Federated Womens Club, 75. Relig: Protestant; bd mem, Commonwealth Community Church. Mailing Add: 8235 S Calumet Ave Chicago IL 60619

GAINES, FRANK D **(D)**
Kans State Sen
Mailing Add: 1713 Meadowlake Dr Augusta KS 67101

GAINES, ROBERT E **(D)**
Wash State Rep
b Harlowtown, Mont, Feb 22, 23; s Earl E Gaines & Cecile A Boifeuillet G; m 1945 to Dorothy A Goldsberry; c David C, Diane M & Annette C. Educ: Auburn High Sch, Wash, grad. Polit & Govt Pos: City councilman, Auburn, Wash, 60-64, mayor, 64-69; Wash State Rep 30th Dist, 73- Bus & Prof Pos: Owner & mgr, Gen Refrigeration, Auburn, Wash, 50-; mgr, Auburn Area CofC, 70- Mil Serv: Entered as SM 2/C, Naval Res, 42, released as MOM 2/C, after serv in US Submarine, Pac Theatre, 42-45. Mem: Rotary; Am Legion; Elks (Past Exalted Ruler, Lodge 1808, 64-65); Eagles. Relig: Methodist. Mailing Add: 24 B St NE Auburn WA 98002

GALBRAITH, FRANCIS J
b Timber Lake, SDak, Dec 9, 13; m to Martha Townsley Fisher; c Susan, Kathleen & Kelly Francis. Educ: Col Puget Sound, BA, 39; Univ Wash, BA, 40; Yale Univ, 48-49. Polit & Govt Pos: Career officer, US Dept of State Foreign Serv, 46-, vconsul, Hamburg, Ger, 46-48, Batavia, 49-50, Djakarta, 50-51; officer-in-charge, Indonesian & Pac Island affairs, 51-55, US consul, Medan, Indonesia, 55-56, Air War Col, 57-58, London, Eng, 58-62, dep chief of mission to Djakarta, 62-65, Foreign Serv inspector, 66, US Ambassador to Singapore, 66-69; US Ambassador to Indonesia, 69-74. Mil Serv: Capt, Army, 41-46, serv in Artil, WNew Guinea. Mem: Am Acad Polit Sci; Am Foreign Serv Asn; Cosmos Club, Washington, DC; Yale Club of Washington; Circumnavig Club. Legal Res: 2242 Decatur Pl NW Washington DC 20008 Mailing Add: Dept of State Washington DC 20521

GALBRAITH, J KENNETH **(D)**
b Iona Station, Ont, Oct 15, 08; s William Archibald Galbraith & Catherine Kendall G; m 1937 to Catherine Atwater; c Alan, Peter & James. Educ: Univ Guelph, BS, 31; Univ Calif, MS, 33 & PhD, 34; Cambridge Univ, 37-38. Hon Degrees: LLD, Bard Col, 58, Miami Univ, 59, Univ Mass, Brandeis Univ & Univ Toronto, 63, Univ Guelph & Univ Sask, 65. Polit & Govt Pos: Econ adv, Nat Defense Adv Comn, 40-41; asst admin, Price Div, Off Price Admin, 41-42, dep adminr, Off of Price Admin, 42-43; dir, US Strategic Bombing Surv, 45; dir, Off of Econ Security Policy, State Dept, 46; US Ambassador, India, 61-63; nat chmn, Am for Dem Action, 67-69; deleg, Dem Nat Conv, 72. Bus & Prof Pos: Economist; Social Sci Research Coun fel, 37-38; instr & tutor, Harvard Univ, 34-49, lectr, 48-49, prof econ, 49-, Paul H Warburg Prof econ, 59-61 & 63-; asst prof econ, Princeton Univ, 39-42; mem bd ed, Fortune Mag, 43-48. Publ: A China Passage, 73; Economics & Its Public Purpose, 73; Money: Whence It Came, Where It Went, 75; plus others. Mem: 20th Century Fund (trustee); Am Acad Arts & Sci (fel); Am Econ Asn; Am Farm Econ Asn; Century Club. Honors & Awards: Medal of Freedom, 46. Mailing Add: 30 Francis Ave Cambridge MA 02138

GALBRAITH, JAMES RONALD **(R)**
Exec Dir, Rep Gov Asn
b Crystal Falls, Mich, Mar 18, 36; s Edwin Galbraith & Lillian Robichaud G; m 1962 to Mary Redington; c Richard Lee, Timothy Scott & John Redington. Educ: Pasadena City Col, 53-55; Univ Southern Calif, 55-56; Calif State Univ, Los Angeles, 56-60; Omicron Mu Delta; Beta Phi Gamma; Pi Kappa Delta. Polit & Govt Pos: Cong admin asst, US Rep E W Hiestand, 60-62; asst dir pub rels, Nat Rep Cong Comt, 64-69; dir pub rels, Rep Gov Asn, formerly, exec dir, currently. Bus & Prof Pos: Columnist & asst news ed, Pasadena Independent Star News, 55-60; broadcaster, Three Star Extra, NBC Radio, 62-64; managing ed, Washington World Mag, 62-64. Mem: Capitol Hill Club; Nat Press Club; Bull Elephants Club; Toastmasters Int. Honors & Awards: Hon grad, Pasadena City Col, 55; Outstanding Toastmaster of the Year Award, Capitol Hill Toastmasters Club, 69; First Place Winner of Club, Area & Div Serious Speech Competition, Toastmasters Int, 69; Nat & Western States Oratory Championships. Relig: Roman Catholic. Mailing Add: 1518 Tuba Court Vienna VA 22180

GALBRAITH, JOHN ALLEN **(R)**
Ohio State Rep
b Toledo, Ohio, Aug 23, 23; s Evan G Galbraith & Nina Allen G; m 1950 to Cynthia Finn; c John Michael, Geoffrey, Cynthia & Tenley. Educ: Univ Mich, LLB, 49; Phi Delta Phi; Chi Psi. Polit & Govt Pos: Pres, Young Rep Lucas Co, Ohio, 63-65; asst attorney gen, Ohio, 63-67; Ohio State Rep, 67- Bus & Prof Pos: Legal dept, Electric Auto Lite, 49-56; gen mgr, Community Sanitation, 56-62; pres, Maumee Construction Co, 63- Mil Serv: Entered as A/S, Navy, 42, released as Lt Comdr, 53, after serv in World War II; Lt Comdr, Naval Res, 66; Am, European & Pac Theater Campaign Ribbons; Philippine Victory Medal; Naval Res Medal; Victory Medal; Korean Serv Medal; China Serv Medal; Philippines Commendation Medal. Mem: Rotary; Toledo Zoo, Orchestra & Museum. Mailing Add: 602 Pierce St Maumee OH 43537

GALBRAITH, SAMUEL G **(D)**
Mem, Ga State Exec Comt
b St Louis, Mo, Sept 7, 46; s Dr James R Galbraith & Wilma Meinhardt G; m 1967 to Sue Valentine; c James Robert (Jay). Educ: DeKalb Jr Col, Decatur, Ga, AA. Polit & Govt Pos: Chmn, Fulton Co Dem Party, Ga, 74-; mem, Ga State Exec Comt, 74- Mil Serv: Army, 66, released as E-5, 69. Mem: KofC; Civitan Club. Relig: Catholic. Mailing Add: 140 Port Antonio Ct Atlanta GA 30349

GALE, JOHN ALAN **(R)**
Gen Counsel, Nebr State Rep Party
b Omaha, Nebr, Oct 23, 40; s John C Gale, Jr & Faye Lane; m 1966 to Linda Lou Lyman; c David Douglas & Elaine Elizabeth. Educ: Oberlin Col, summer 61; Carleton Col, BA, 62; Univ Chicago, JD, 65. Polit & Govt Pos: Legis asst to Sen Roman Hruska, 68-70; asst US attorney, Dist of Nebr, 70-71; asst state chmn, Nebr State Rep Party, 73-75, gen counsel, 75- Bus & Prof Pos: Chmn, Nebr State Adv Comt to US Civil Rights Comn, 72-; bd mem, North Platte United Way, 73- Publ: Co-auth, Preventive detention—the constitution and the congress, Creighton Law Rev, 69. Mem: North Platte Rotary Club; Nebr Asn Trial Attorneys; Am Bar Asn; North Platte CofC (bd mem, 75-); Lincoln Co Bar Asn (pres). Honors & Awards: Outstanding Young Man, North Platte Jaycees, 74. Relig: Unitarian. Mailing Add: 2011 West C St North Platte NE 69101

GALIBER, JOSEPH LIONEL **(D)**
NY State Sen
b New York, NY, Oct 26, 24; s Joseph F Galiber & Ethel Bowser G; m 1946 to Emma Evangeline Shade; c Pamela Susan & Ruby Dianne (Mrs Karlton Wint). Educ: City Col NY, BS, 50; NY Law Sch, LLB, 62. Polit & Govt Pos: Deleg & asst majority leader, NY State Const Conv, 67; vchmn, NY State Dem Comt; chmn, Bronx Co Dem Comt, NY; deleg, Dem Nat Conv, 68; NY State Sen, 69- Bus & Prof Pos: Attorney-at-law, 65- Mil Serv: Entered as Pvt, Army, 43, released as S/Sgt, 45, after serv in 4010 Qm Truck Co, ETO, 43-45; European-African-Mid Eastern Serv Medal; Good Conduct Medal; World War II Victory Medal. Mem: Bronx Bar Asn; NY Trial Lawyers; NAACP; Am Legion. Honors & Awards: Outstanding Serv Human Rels, City Univ New York, 70; Amerigo Vespucci Award, 72; Awards in Black, 73; Outstanding Legislator Year, Morrisania Educ Coun, 75; Citizen Year, Bronx Boys Club, 75. Relig: Presbyterian. Mailing Add: 800 Concourse Village W Bronx NY 10451

GALIFIANAKIS, NICK **(D)**
b Durham, NC, July 22, 28; s Mike Galifianakis (deceased) & Sophia Kastrinakis G; m 1963 to Louise Cheatham Ruggles; c Stephenie, Katherine & Jon Mark. Educ: Duke Univ, AB, 51, Law Sch, LLB, 53; Delta Theta Phi. Polit & Govt Pos: NC State Rep Durham Co, 61-65, chmn, Judiciary & Ment Insts Comts, NC Gen Assembly, formerly; US Rep, Fourth Dist, NC, 66-72. Bus & Prof Pos: Partner, Upchurch & Galifianakis; asst prof bus law, Duke Univ, 60-67. Mil Serv: Marine Corps, 53-56, Maj, Marine Corps Res, Cmndg Officer, 41st Rifle Co, 60-63; Lt Col, Civil Air Patrol. Mem: Durham Co & 15th Judicial Dist Bar Asns; Jaycees; Kiwanis; Young Dem Club. Honors & Awards: Outstanding Young Man of the Year, NC Jr CofC, 63; Distinguished Serv Award, Durham Jaycees; named among Outstanding Young Men in Am, 64. Relig: Greek Orthodox; Trustee, St Barbara's Church, Durham. Mailing Add: 2648 University Dr Durham NC 27707

GALLAGHER, CORNELIUS E **(D)**
Mem, Hudson Co Dem Exec Comt, NJ
b Bayonne, NJ, Mar 2, 21; s Cornelius E Gallagher & Ann Murphy G; m 1943 to Claire Richter; c Diane, Christine, Patrice & Bridget. Educ: John Marshall Law Sch, LLB cum laude, 48. Hon Degrees: DLitt, Chungang Univ, Korea, 70. Polit & Govt Pos: Organizer & first pres, Hudson Co Young Dem, NJ, 49; deleg, Dem Nat Conv, 52, 56, 60, 64 & 68; mem, Hudson Co Dem Exec Comt, 50-; freeholder, Hudson Co, 53-55; comnr, NJ State Turnpike Authority, 55-57, vchmn, of 57-61; US Rep, 13th Dist, NJ, 59-72, chmn, Asian & Pac Subcomt, US House of Rep, 62-72, chmn, Spec Comt on Invasion of Privacy, US House of Rep, formerly. Bus & Prof Pos: Prof mil sci & tactics, Rutgers Univ, 46-47; attorney-at-law, 49- Mil Serv: Entered as Enlisted Res, Army, 41, released as Capt, 46, after serv in 80th Div, 318th Inf; re-entered for 1 year in Korean War; Army Res, until 52; Two Bronze Stars; Three Purple Hearts; Presidential Citation; Commendation Ribbon; Combat Inf Badge; Three Battle Stars. Mem: Am Bar Asn (chmn spec subcomt invasion of privacy); KofC; Am Legion; DAV; Elks. Honors & Awards: Award, Nat Coun Christians & Jews, 60. Relig: Catholic. Mailing Add: 102 W Fifth St Bayonne NJ 07002

GALLAGHER, DENNIS JOSEPH **(D)**
Colo State Rep
b Denver, Colo, July 1, 39; s William Joseph Gallagher & Ellen Philomena O'Flaherty G; single. Educ: Regis Col, BA, 61; Cath Univ Am, MA, 68; Denver Club; Aquinas Acad; Lit Club; Debate Soc. Polit & Govt Pos: Chmn, Dem Fund Drive, Dist 1, Denver, Colo, 69; mem consumer & educ subcomts, Denver Dem Cent Comt, 68-71; moderator, Regis Col Young Dem, 69-71; Colo State Rep, 71- Bus & Prof Pos: Teacher Latin & Eng, St John's Col (DC), 64-66; asst prof speech & classics, Regis Col, 67-71. Mem: Am Asn Univ Prof; James Joyce Found; Am Fedn Teachers; Irish Fellowship Club. Relig: Roman Catholic. Mailing Add: 3820 Urain Denver CO 80212

GALLAGHER, HAROLD MILTON **(R)**
Chmn, Richmond Co Rep Party, Va
b Warsaw, Va, July 4, 06; s John Edward Gallagher & Rosa Belle Mothershead G; m 1933 to Katherine Louise Beauchamp; c Sarah Louise. Educ: Warsaw High Sch, 12-22. Polit & Govt Pos: Chmn, Richmond Co Rep Party, Va, 35-; mem, Va Rep State Cent Comt, 50-60; city councilman, Warsaw, 56-60. Bus & Prof Pos: Construction rep, H M Gallagher Co, 25-, real estate appraiser, 46-, state cert auctioneer, 62-; Ins underwriter, Rappahannock Gen Ins Agency, Warsaw, 60- Mil Serv: Entered as CPO, Navy, 43, released as CPO, 44, after serv in Seabees, Pac Theater, 43-44. Mem: Rappahannock Baptist Asn; Va Baptist Children's Home (bd trustees, 60-); Eastern Star; Mason. Relig: Baptist; Trustee, Warsaw Baptist Church, 45- Mailing Add: 118 Hamilton Blvd Warsaw VA 22572

GALLAGHER, J (JACK) **(D)**
NJ State Assemblyman
b Haddonfield, NJ; s John J Gallagher, Sr & Dorothy Hodrus G; m 1966 to Christine Fessler; c Christine & Shawn. Educ: Valley Forge Mil Sch, AA, 65. Polit & Govt Pos: NJ State Assemblyman, 74-, co-chmn co govt comt & mem agr comt, NJ State Assembly, 74- Bus & Prof Pos: Vpres, Gallagher Assocs, 4 years; pres, Associated Ins Mgt, 75- Mem: NJ Jaycees; Valley Forge Alumni Asn. Honors & Awards: US Jaycees Presidential Leadership Award, 70-71; NJ Jaycees Govt Involvement Award, 73. Legal Res: 1612 Kresson Rd Cherry Hill NJ 08034 Mailing Add: 2167 Rte 70 Cherry Hill NJ 08002

GALLAGHER, JAMES J A (D)
Pa State Rep
b Philadelphia, Pa, Sept 19, 27; m 1948 to Lavinia E Sismore; c James, Sharon Ann, Shiela Ann & Kathleen Marie. Educ: US Marine Corps Inst; St Joseph's Col Indust Rels Sch. Polit & Govt Pos: Past chmn, Bristol Twp Sch Dist Authority, Pa, 6 years; first treas & trustee, Bucks Co Free Libr, 58-; mem, State Libr Adv Coun on Develop, 61-62; Pa State Rep, Dist 141, 59-, chmn, Higher Educ Comt & mem, Elec & Apportionment, Pub Utilities, Hwy, Munic Corp, Hwy Safety, Community Col, Dem Policy Comts, Joint State Govt Comn Task Force Comts & Comt on Intermediate Units, State Bd Educ & chmn, House Educ Comt, Pa State House of Rep; alt deleg, Dem Nat Conv, 68. Mil Serv: Marine Corps, 45-46. Mem: Marine Corps League; Bucks Co AFL-CIO (past secy-treas, Comt Polit Educ, hon chief steward, Local 282, Transport Workers Union Am, past pres 8 years). Mailing Add: 26 Flower Lane Levittown PA 19055

GALLAGHER, JAMES V (D)
Iowa State Sen
Mailing Add: 4710 Spring Creek Rd Jesup IA 50648

GALLAGHER, MARY CECELIA (D)
VChmn, Lawrence Co Dem Exec Comt, Ohio
b Pine Grove, Ohio, Nov 11, 98; d Cornelius Gallagher, MD & Elizabeth F Goldcamp G; single. Polit & Govt Pos: Chmn, Lawrence Co Bd of Elec, Ohio, 46-; secy, Ohio Dem State Cent & Exec Comts, 48-68, mem, 70-; chmn, Lawrence Co Dem Exec Comt, Ohio, 68-75, vchmn, 75- Bus & Prof Pos: Owner, Mary C Gallagher, Ins. Relig: Catholic. Mailing Add: 1705 S Third St Ironton OH 45638

GALLAGHER, P J (JIM) (D)
Wash State Rep
b Taylor, Wash, 1915; m to Mabel; c Six. Educ: Wash State Univ. Polit & Govt Pos: Wash State Rep, currently. Bus & Prof Pos: Pub rels officer, LeMay Enterprises, Inc, currently. Mem: Tacoma Sportsmen (dir); KofC; Eagles. Mailing Add: 125 S 72nd St Tacoma WA 98408

GALLAGHER, TOM (R)
Fla State Rep
Mailing Add: 1794 Opechee Dr Coconut Grove FL 33133

GALLAHAN, RUSSELL WAYNE (D)
Chmn, Fifth Cong Dist Dem Party, Ind
b Mexico, Ind, Nov 17, 20; s Floyd Nathan Gallahan & Isa Leora Fishburn G; m 1950 to Gertrude Stanton; c Dawn. Educ: Mexico High Sch, Ind, 4 years. Polit & Govt Pos: Deleg, Dem Nat Conv, 68 & alt deleg, 72; chmn, Miami Co Dem Party, Ind, 68-; chmn, Fifth Cong Dist Dem Party, Ind, 72- Bus & Prof Pos: Broker, Moore Real Estate Agency, Peru, Ind, 67- Mil Serv: Entered as Pvt, Air Force, 42, released as Pvt, 46, after serv in ASCS, Caribbean. Mem: Elks; Am Legion; Mason; Scottish Rite; Shrine. Relig: Church of the Brethren. Legal Res: Mexico IN 46958 Mailing Add: 8 E Second St Peru IN 46970

GALLAHER, JOHN K (D)
Mem, NC State Dem Exec Comt
b Mexico, Mo, Sept 12, 24; s James William Gallaher & Iona Melvina Smith G; m 1950 to Christine Gray; c John K, Jr, Christine L, David N, Thomas G & James. Educ: Univ Mo; Univ Wis. Polit & Govt Pos: Local precinct chmn, Dem Party, NC, 60-61; bd mem, Winston-Salem, Forsyth Co Planning & Zoning Bd, 61; chmn, Forsyth Co Dem Exec Comt, 61-65; mem, NC State Dem Exec Comt, 62-; deleg & mem, Credentials & Appeals Comt, Dem Nat Conv, 64 & deleg, 72; mem from 21st Dist, State Dem Judicial Dist Exec Comt, 64-66; mem from 23rd Dist, State Dem Sen Exec Comt, 64-66; chmn, NC Real Estate Licensing Bd, 64-66; mem, Platform & Resolutions Comt, NC Dem Conv, 66; campaign mgr for Gov Robert Scott, Fifth Cong Dist, 68; chmn, Fifth Cong Dist Exec Comt, NC, 70- Bus & Prof Pos: Pres, Gallaher Realty Co, NC, 57-; pres, Winston Develop Co, 60-; pres, Winston-Salem Bd of Realtor, 70. Mem: Nat Asn of Real Estate Bds; Twin City Mens Club; CofC (legis comt); NC Realtors Legis Comt & Speakers Bur; Lions. Relig: Presbyterian. Legal Res: 1056 Kent Rd Winston-Salem NC 27107 Mailing Add: Box 3082 Winston-Salem NC 27102

GALLEN, HUGH (D)
Mem, Dem Nat Comt, NH
Mailing Add: Woodside Ave Littleton NH 03561

GALLEN, JAMES J (R)
Pa State Rep
b Reading, Pa, Aug 15, 28; s A Joseph Gallen & Anna V Strain G; m to Sara C Boyle; c Eight. Educ: Villanova Univ, BS. Polit & Govt Pos: Mem, Young Rep Club, Pa; Pa State Rep, 64-; chmn, Berks Co Rep Party, currently. Bus & Prof Pos: Ins agt. Mil Serv: Army, Korean War. Mem: Clubmaster; Berks Co Comt Probs Older Workers (chmn); Am Legion; Shillington Keystone Fire Co. Mailing Add: 150 N Sixth St Reading PA 19601

GALLEN, THOMAS M (D)
Fla State Sen
b Tampa, Fla, Dec 28, 32; s Thomas M Gallen & Mary Ellen Satterfield G; m to Linda C Pruitt; c Thomas M, Jr, Mary P, Kathleen & Michael P. Educ: Univ Tampa, 50-52; Fla State Univ, BS, 57; Univ Fla Col Law, LLB, 60; Dean's List, Fla State Univ; Phi Delta Phi; Phi Delta Theta; John Marshall Bar Asn. Polit & Govt Pos: Fla State Rep, Manatee Co, 66-72; Fla State Sen, 24th Dist, 72- Mil Serv: Entered as Pvt, Army, 52, released as Sgt, 55, after serv in 10th Spec Forces Airborn, ETO. Mem: KofC (4 degree); Hernando-DeSoto Hist Soc; DAV; Am Legion; VFW. Honors & Awards: Key Man Award, Bradenton Jaycees. Relig: Catholic. Legal Res: 5508 Ninth Ave Dr W Bradenton FL 33505 Mailing Add: 701 11th St W Bradenton FL 33505

GALLI, AMERICO JOHN (D)
Vt State Rep
b Crenna, Italy, Apr 12, 03; s Giovanni Galli & Luigia Marelli G; m 1926 to Lina Eva Calcagni; c Elizabeth G Calcagni & Alelia M (Mrs Burns). Educ: Spaulding High Sch, Barre, Vt, 4 years. Polit & Govt Pos: Sch comnr, Barre, Vt, 42-65; chmn, Barre City Sch Comnr, 5 years; justice of the peace & mem bd of civil authority, Barre, Vt, 61-65; Vt State Rep, Dist 7-4, 67- Bus & Prof Pos: Apprentice, journeyman, plant foreman & owner, granite bus, 23-67. Mem: Granite Cutters Int Asn; F&AM; MWA. Relig: Methodist. Mailing Add: 97 Berlin St Barre VT 05641

GALLIZA, CARLOS (PR INDEPENDENCE)
Rep, PR House of Rep
Mailing Add: State Capitol San Juan PR 00901

GALLO, THOMAS A (D)
NJ State Assemblyman
Mailing Add: State House Trenton NJ 08625

GALLOGLY, RAYMOND J (D)
RI State Rep
Mailing Add: 31 Bourbon Pl Warwick RI 02888

GALLOGY, E PETER, JR (D)
RI State Sen
Mailing Add: 136 Miller Ave Providence RI 02905

GALLOWAY, CHARLES RAYMOND (D)
Chmn, Orange Co Dem Comt, Ind
b Orange Co, Ind, Aug 17, 29; s Charles Galloway & Carrie Slaybaugh G; m 1950 to Selma Violet Simmons; c Larry Ray, Eric Brooks & Anthony Rex. Educ: French Lick High Sch, Ind, grad, 47. Polit & Govt Pos: Chmn, Orange Co Dem Comt, Ind, 73- Bus & Prof Pos: Farmer & owner of Twin City Feed Mill, 47- Relig: Protestant. Mailing Add: 506 College St French Lick IN 47432

GALLOWAY, RITA L (R)
Chmn, Caldwell Co Rep Comt, Mo
b New Hamburg, NY, June 28, 30; d Louis L Herles & Elizabeth Huther H; m 1953 to J W Galloway; c Sue (Mrs Moore), Bill, Janice M, Daniel & Michele. Educ: Wappingers Falls Cent High Sch, NY, grad, 48. Polit & Govt Pos: Secy, Caldwell Co Rep Women's Club, 74-75, pres, 75-; chmn, Caldwell Co Rep Comt, Mo, 75- Bus & Prof Pos: Bookkeeper, Poughkeepsie New Yorker, Poughkeepsie, NY, 48-49, Vassar Col, 49-50 & Galloways Standard Serv, Cameron, Mo, 70- Mil Serv: Entered as Recruit, Air Force, 51, released as Airman 2/C, 54. Mem: Am Legion; Caldwell Co Rep Womens Club (pres, 75-). Relig: Catholic. Mailing Add: Rte 2 Cameron MO 64429

GALLUGI, ANTHONY MICHAEL (D)
Mass State Rep
Mailing Add: State Capitol Boston MA 02133

GALM, ROBERT WOODS (R)
VChmn, Young Rep Nat Fedn
b Indianapolis, Ind, Dec 15, 42; s Kenneth John Galm & Marie Roach G; m 1963 to Tamra McCready; c Brian Woods & Christopher Edwards. Educ: Ind Univ, Bloomington, BS, 64. Polit & Govt Pos: Treas, Co Rep Comt, 66-72; chmn, Young Rep Dist Comt, 68-70; mem exec comt, Young Rep Nat Fedn, 69-71, vchmn, 75- chmn, Ind Young Rep Fedn, 71-; chmn, Co Rep Cent Comt, 72- Bus & Prof Pos: Teacher, Owen Co Schs, Spencer, Ind, 64-66 & Bartholomew Co Schs, Columbus, 66-69; dir, Ind Youth Coun, 69-73; realtor-owner, Bill Gore Realty, Nashville, 72- Mem: Brown Co Bd of Realtors (vpres, 72-); Ind Real Estate Asn; Boy Scouts (chmn troop adult comt, 71-); Brown Co Art Gallery Asn; Brown Co CofC. Honors & Awards: Named Distinguished Hoosier, 70 & Sagamore of the Wabash, 71, Gov of Ind. Relig: Protestant. Mailing Add: PO Box 546 Nashville IN 47448

GALOTTI, EDWARD FRANCIS (D)
Mass State Rep
b Everett, Mass, May 11, 25; s Rocco C Galotti & Gertrude Blay G; m 1955 to Carol Crocker; c Edward M & Edward F, Jr. Educ: Boston Col, BSBA, 49; Nat Students Asn. Polit & Govt Pos: Mem, Belmont Dem Town Comt, Mass, 65-72; town meeting & mem, Belmont, 66-, selectman, 67- & munic light comnr, 67-; Mass State Rep, 69- Bus & Prof Pos: Pres, Ambassador Aluminum Prod, Inc, 54-; proprietor, Edward F Galotti Realty, 65- Mem: Nat Asn Acct; Elks; Sons of Italy; KofC; Am Legion. Relig: Roman Catholic. Mailing Add: 80 Clark St Belmont MA 02178

GALPERIN, SI HIRSCH, JR (D)
WVa State Sen
b Charleston, WVa, Aug 5, 31; s Simon H Galperin & Fan Lavenstein G; m 1958 to Rose Marie Rogers; c Stephen Hirsch & Gregory Lee. Educ: Washington & Lee Univ, BS in com, 53; Alpha Kappi Psi; Zeta Beta Tau. Polit & Govt Pos: Committeeman, Kanawha Co Dem Exec Comt, WVa, 65-66; WVa State Deleg, 67-70; WVa State Sen, 71-; deleg, Dem Nat Conv, 72; campaign dir, McGovern for President, WVa, 72. Bus & Prof Pos: Pres, Galperin Music Co, 63-72; real estate, 72- Mil Serv: Entered as Seaman, Navy, 53, released as Lt(jg), 56 after serv in Potomac River, Naval Command Hq, 54-56. Mem: Nat Asn Young Music Merchants (pres); Nat Asn Music Merchants (bd dirs); WVa Music Teachers Asn (vpres, 71-72); Pub Affairs Conf of WVa (secy-treas, 67-73); Isaac Walton League of Am (pres, Mountain State chap, 72-73). Relig: Jewish. Mailing Add: 827 Beaumont Rd Charleston WV 25314

GALT, JACK E (R)
Mont State Sen
Mailing Add: Martinsdale MT 59053

GALVIN, JOHN RAYMOND (D)
RI State Rep
b Pawtucket, RI, Feb 5, 16; s Patrick J Galvin & Annie V Elwood G; m 1940 to Catherine Doris Fogarty; c Barry John & Brian David. Educ: Pawtucket High Sch, 4 years. Polit & Govt Pos: Dem ward committeeman, Pawtucket Second Dist, RI, 38-69; RI State Rep, 81st Dist, 67- Mem: Painter & Decorating Contractors of Am; KofC; Elks; Boy Scouts (committeeman). Relig: Catholic. Mailing Add: 78 Warwick Rd Pawtucket RI 02861

GAMACHE, OVILA (D)
NH State Rep
Mailing Add: 22 Ferry St Suncook NH 03275

GAMBILL, BRUCE WARREN (R)
Chmn, Osage Co Rep Party
b Carlsbad, NMex, Nov 22, 30; s Oren Bain Gambill & Wilma Ally G; m 1952 to Patricia Hill; c Bruce David, Dan Alan & Linda Michelle. Educ: Univ Okla, BS, 52, LLB, 57; Scabbard & Blade; Lambda Chi Alpha. Polit & Govt Pos: Pres, Tulsa Co Young Rep, Okla, 59, Tulsa Co Rep Exec Comt, 59-61 & Osage Co Rep Exec Comt, 63-64; chmn, Osage Co Rep Party, 64-72 & 75- committeeman, Rep State Comt Okla, 69- Bus & Prof Pos: Asst co attorney, Wash Co, 57-; indust rels mgr, Sinclair Oil & Gas, Tulsa, 58-63; partner, McCoy, Kelly & Gambill Law Firm, 63-64; partner, Kelly & Gambill Law Firm, 64- Mil Serv: Entered as 2nd Lt, Army, 52, released as 1st Lt, 54, after serv in 7th Inf Div, Korea, 52-54; Korean Campaign Medal; Battle Ribbons. Mem: Mason; Rotary; Am Legion; Osage Co Bar Asn (pres); Co Bar Pres (pres). Relig: Episcopal. Legal Res: RR 1 Pawhuska OK 74056 Mailing Add: PO Box 329 Pawhuska OK 74056

GAMBLE, MICHAEL P (D)
b 1907; married; c seven. Polit & Govt Pos: Councilman-at-lg, Canton, Ohio, 2 terms & councilman, 2 terms, city treas, 70-; Ohio State Rep, 67-70; deleg, Dem Nat Conv, 72; deleg, Dem Nat Mid-Term Conf, 74. Bus & Prof Pos: Salesman. Mailing Add: 2618 Clyde Pl SW Canton OH 44710

GAMBRELL, DAVID HENRY (D)
b Atlanta, Ga, Dec 20, 29; s E Smythe & Kathleen Hagood G; m 1953 to Luck Coleman Flanders; c Luck Coleman, David Henry, Alice Kathleen Hagood & Mary Latimer. Educ: Davidson Col, BA, 49; Harvard, LLB cum laude, 52. Polit & Govt Pos: Chmn, Ga State Dem Cent Comt, until 71; US Sen, Ga, 71-72. Bus & Prof Pos: Pvt practice, Atlanta, 52-54 & 56-; teaching fel, Harvard Law Sch, 54-55; partner, Gambrell & Mobley, 63-; mem bd dirs, Ga YMCA, 65-, vpres, 65-66; trustee, Metrop Atlanta Comn Crime & Juv Delinquency, 66-68. Mem: Am Bar Asn; NC Soc Cincinnati; Sigma Alpha Epsilon; Omicron Delta Kappa; Kiwanis. Relig: Presbyterian. Mailing Add: 3820 Castlegate Dr NW Atlanta GA 30327

GAMEL, JACK F (R)
Chmn, Douglas Co Rep Party, Ga
b Frankfurt, Ger, Apr 13, 48; s T R Gamel & Rosemarie Kuhne G; m 1967 to Donna Gordon. Educ: Ga State Univ, BBA. Polit & Govt Pos: Chmn, Douglas Co Rep Party, Ga, 75-; committeeman, Ga Rep State Comt, 75- Bus & Prof Pos: Staff acct, Webb & Dreher CPA, Atlanta, Ga, 69-70 & LKH&H CPA, 70-74; self-employed CPA, 74- Mil Serv: Entered as Pvt, Army, 64, released as Pfc after serv in various units, Europe & Vietnam. Mem: Rotary (secy, Douglas Co Club, currently); Douglasville Jaycees (treas & dir); Region 20 Jaycees (secy-treas, currently). Legal Res: 3050 Bomar Rd Douglasville GA 30134 Mailing Add: 8479-A Price Ave Douglasville GA 30134

GAMMAGE, OLIN LYNN, JR (D)
Ga State Rep
b Albany, Ga, July 13, 45; s Olin Lynn Gammage, Sr & Doris Tony G; m 1964 to Letitia Zuker; c Olin Lynn, III, Laura Camell & Michael Zuker. Educ: Univ Tenn; John A Gupton Col Mortuary Sci, grad. Polit & Govt Pos: Ga State Rep, Dist 17, 75-; city comnr, Cedartown, Ga, 75- Bus & Prof Pos: Dir, Gammage Funeral Home, 70- Mem: Lions (bd dirs). Relig: Baptist. Legal Res: 106 N College St Cedartown GA 30125 Mailing Add: PO Box 718 Cedartown GA 30125

GAMMAGE, ROBERT ALTON (BOB) (D)
Tex State Sen
b Houston, Tex, Mar 13, 38; s Paul Gammage & Sara Ella Marshall G; m 1962 to Judy Ann Adcock; c Terry Lynne, Sara Noel & Robert A, Jr. Educ: Del Mar Col, AA, 58; Univ Corpus Christi, BS, 63; Sam Houston State Univ MA, 65; Univ Tex Sch Law, JD, 69; Pi Gamma Mu; Phi Alpha Delta; Dean's List. Polit & Govt Pos: Tex State Rep, 71-73; Tex State Sen, Dist Seven, 73-; chmn gen provisions comt, Tex Const Conv, 74. Bus & Prof Pos: Teaching fel & dir fraternities, Sam Houston State Univ, 63-65; dean men & dir student activities, Univ Corpus Christi, 65-66; instr law, STex Col Law, 71-73. Mil Serv: Entered as Pvt, 59, released as SP-4, 60, after serv in Korea Mil Adv Group, 59-60; Lt Comdr, Naval Res, 65- Mem: State Bar Tex; Am Bar Asn; Am Judicature Soc; Tex & Am Trial Lawyers Asns. Honors & Awards: Outstanding Lineman Award, High Sch; Consul Award, Univ Tex Sch Law; Outstanding Sen, 63rd Legis, Tex Intercol Student Asn; Distinguished Alumnus, Univ Corpus Christi, 75. Legal Res: 7903 Glenheath Houston TX 77017 Mailing Add: 7718 Bellfort Houston TX 77017

GAMMAL, ALBERT ABRAHAM, JR (R)
b Lynn, Mass, Dec 31, 28; s Albert A Gammal & Jenny Shaker G; m 1955 to Margaret Ann Romley; c Candith Ann, Sandra Ann, Gayle Ann & Joseph Albert. Educ: Clark Univ, BBA, 52; Suffolk Univ, LLB, 66; Delta Sigma; Clark Univ Players Soc. Polit & Govt Pos: Pres, Young Rep Club, Worcester, Mass, 52-54; deleg, Mass Rep State Conv, 56-68; chmn, Mass Coun Young Rep Clubs, 58-59; Rep Jr Nat Committeeman, 60-61; chmn, Worcester Rep Ward Comt, 60-62; state rep, Mass Gen Court, 61-68; admin asst, US Sen E W Brooke, 67-69; deleg, Rep Nat Conv, 68; US Marshall, Dist of Mass, 69-70; New Eng regional adminr, US Gen Serv Admin, 70-; chmn, Boston Fed Exec Bd, 72- Bus & Prof Pos: Treas-dir, Gammal Chem Co Inc, 53-62; trustee, Gardner State Hosp, 54-69; attorney, 67- Mil Serv: Entered as Pvt, Army, 46, released as Pfc, 48, after serv in 17th Inf, 1st Bn, 24th Corp, Far East, Korea, 46-47; Inf Reserves, 48-50; Cpl, Air Force Reserves, 50-52. Mem: Mass Bar Asn; Mass Legislators Asn; Mason (32 degree); Shrine; Am Legion. Honors & Awards: Outstanding Young Man award, Gtr Worcester Jr CofC; Serv Award & Red Triangle award, YMCA. Relig: Greek Orthodox. Mailing Add: 73 Sagamore Rd Worcester MA 01609

GAMMELL, RICHARD A (R)
RI State Rep
Mailing Add: 84 Fordson Ave Cranston RI 02910

GAMSER, HOWARD GRAHAM (D)
Counsel, Compliance Rev Comn, Dem Nat Comt
b New York, NY; s Gustave Gamser & Rose Harris G; m 1952 to Doris P Gold; c Matthew Simon & Diana Marion. Educ: City Col New York, BSS, 40; Columbia Univ, MA, 41; NY, LLB, 52; Phi Beta Kappa. Polit & Govt Pos: With Nat Labor Rels Bd, 46-52; with Wage Stabilization Bd, 52-53; chief counsel, Comt on Educ & Labor Rels, US House of Rep, 61-63; mem, Nat Mediation Bd, 64-67, chmn, 67-69; counsel, Comn on Rules, Dem Nat Comt, 69-74, parliamentarian, currently, counsel, Compliance Rev Comn, currently; counsel, Rules Comt, Dem Nat Conv, 72. Bus & Prof Pos: Attorney & arbitrator, New York, 52-61; partner, Bobroff, Olonoff & Scharf, 52-; lectr labor law, Columbia Univ, 57-61; adj prof labor law, Georgetown Univ, 64-; counsel, Dutton, Gwirtzman, Zumas & Wise, Washington, DC, 69- Mil Serv: Pvt to Capt, Army, 41-46. Publ: Articles in various legal & econ periodicals; Call to order, narrative report on work of Comn on Rules, Dem Nat Comt, 72. Mem: Nat Acad Arbitrators (bd gov, 68-); Indust & Labor Rels Asn; Am Econ Asn; NY & DC Bar Asns. Mailing Add: 3022 Cambridge Pl NW Washington DC 20007

GANDY, EDYTHE EVELYN (D)
Comnr of Ins, Miss
b Hattiesburg, Miss, Sept 4, 22; d Kearney C Gandy & Abbie Whigham; single. Educ: Univ Southern Miss, 39-41; Univ Miss, Law Sch, JD, 44; pres, Student Body. Polit & Govt Pos: Mem, State Bond Comn, State Depository Comn, State Mineral Lease Comn, State Tag Comn & Comn on Status of Women, formerly; chmn, Pub Employees Retirement Bd & State Bd of Savings & Loan Asns, formerly; mem, State Bd of Savings & Loan Asns & State Ins Comn, currently; chmn, State Fire Fighters Sch Bd, currently; Miss State Rep, Forrest Co, 48-52; attorney, Miss State Dept Pub Welfare, 52-58; Asst Attorney Gen, Miss, 59; State Treas, 60-64 & 68-72; Comnr Pub Welfare, 64-68; Comnr of Ins, 72- Bus & Prof Pos: Mem bd dirs, Miss Cong PTA, 64-67; bd dirs, Miss Hosp & Med Serv, 67-69. Mem: Miss Women's Cabinet of Pub Affairs; Miss Off Women's Club; Hattiesburg Bus & Prof Women's Club; Miss Fedn of Bus & Prof Women's Clubs. Honors & Awards: One of Top Ten Women of Mid-S for Decade of Sixties; Woman of Year, Jackson, Miss, 64; First woman to serve in many Miss state offices. Relig: Baptist. Legal Res: Rte 1 Hattiesburg MS 39401 Mailing Add: 727 Arlington St Jackson MS 39202

GANIM, GEORGE WANIS (R)
Mem, Bridgeport Town Rep Comt, Conn
b Bridgeport, Conn, July 15, 27; s Wanis Ganim & Rose Bagdaady G; m 1957 to Josephine Tarick; c Roseanne, Joseph, George, Jr, Laura, Raymond, Paul, Mary & Thomas. Educ: Univ Bridgeport, 46-48; Boston Univ Sch Law, LLB, 51; Boston Univ Law Rev. Polit & Govt Pos: Rep cand for mayor, Bridgeport, Conn, 61; mem, Bridgeport Town Rep Comt, 65-, chmn, 69-73; mem, Conn Rep State Cent Comt, 68-69. Bus & Prof Pos: Attorney-at-law, Ganim, Ganim & Ganim, 51-; counsel to Bridgeport & Conn Bar Asns; Lions; KofC. Relig: Catholic. Mailing Add: 349 Center Rd Easton CT 06425

GANLEY, BARBARA T (D)
NH State Rep
Mailing Add: 10 Elliot St Exeter NH 03833

GANN, DONALD L (R)
Mo State Rep
b Sparta, Mo, June 16, 40; m 1962 to Marilyn Joyce Kehr. Educ: Southwest Mo State Col, BS in educ. Polit & Govt Pos: Mo State Rep, 64-; mem, Christian Co Young Rep Club. Bus & Prof Pos: Pub sch teacher. Relig: Baptist. Mailing Add: 706 N Tenth St Ozark MO 65721

GANNETT, ANN COLE (R)
Mass State Rep
b Brookline, Mass, Nov 7, 16; d Benjamin Edwards Cole & Ann Sheafe C; m 1936 to Thomas B Gannett, wid; c Thomas B, Jr, Ann G (Mrs Hurlbut), Benjamin H, Deborah G (Mrs Brooks) & Peter C. Educ: Abbot Acad, cum laude, 33; Vassar Col, 33-35. Polit & Govt Pos: Chmn, Wayland Rep Town Comt, Mass, 49-52, mem, 46-; trustee, State Hosp, 50-56; mem, Gov Herter Adv Comt, 52-54; mem, Mass Rep Finance Comt, 52-60; mem, Mass Rep State Comt, 52-67; mem, Civil Defense Comn, 60-; deleg, Rep Nat Conv, 64 & 72; Mass State Rep, 69- Relig: Roman Catholic. Mailing Add: 85 Old Connecticut Path Wayland MA 01778

GANNETT, ROBERT T (R)
Vt State Sen
Mailing Add: RFD 2 West Brattleboro VT 05301

GANNON, CLIFFORD W (JACK) (D)
Mo State Sen
Mailing Add: 725 Wine St DeSoto MO 63020

GANNON, JOSEPH A (D)
b Jersey City, NJ, June 1, 34; s William Patrick Gannon & Loretta Norris G; m 1954 to Lois Massarelli; c Joseph Aloyious, Mary Lois, Shawn Ann, Timothy Francis, Amy Elaine & Christopher Charles. Educ: Seton Hall Univ, 57-59; St Peter's Col, BS, 58. Polit & Govt Pos: Deleg, NJ Const Conv, 66; mem, Gov Comn on Rehabilitation, 66-67, mem Planning Bd, Scotch Plains, 68-69, mem planning bd, Indust Comn, 68-70; Dem munic chmn, Scotch Plains, 68-69; State committeeman, Union Co Dem Party, 69-73, chmn, formerly; exec dir, NJ Dem State Comt, 70-72; coordr, NJ legis Elec, 71; staff dir, NJ Dem Assembly Deleg, 72- Bus & Prof Pos: With NJ Bell Tel, 52-61; pres, Commercial Tel Workers, 54-55; staff, Commun Workers Am, AFL-CIO, 61-67; pres, Indust Rels Personnel Co, Washington, DC & NJ; mem faculty, Rutgers Univ Labor Sch, 67-70. Mil Serv: Entered as Pvt, NJ Nat Guard, 56, released as S/Sgt, 59. Publ: Auth & ed, The Commentator, Commun Tel Workers, 55 & The New Priority, NJ Dem State Comt, 71. Mem: Int Labor Press Asn. Honors & Awards: Outstanding Teacher Award, Rutgers Univ, 70. Relig: Roman Catholic. Legal Res: 444 Stelle Ave Plainfield NJ 07060 Mailing Add: Rm 115 State House Trenton NJ 08625

GANSER, URBAN E
Mayor, West Allis, Wis
b West Allis, Wis, Sept 1, 13; s John J Ganser & Adeline K Specht G; div; c John U & James H. Educ: Marquette Univ & Univ Wis, Milwaukee, 46-49. Polit & Govt Pos: Mem, Mayors Nat Comt Energy, 73-74; mayor, West Allis, Wis, 73-; mem effective govt comn, Nat League Cities, 75. Bus & Prof Pos: Realtor. Mem: Elks; Kiwanis; Soc Real Estate Appraisers; KofC (4 degree). Relig: Catholic. Mailing Add: 7128 W Orchard St West Allis WI 53214

GANT, BOBBIE ANNA (D)
Committeewoman, Fla Dem State Exec Comt
b LaBelle, Fla, Jan 27, 34; d Perry G Frierson & Grace Cross F; m 1956 to George Albert Gant; c George Albert, Jr. Educ: Pahokee High Sch, Palm Beach Co, Fla, dipl, 52; voc postgrad courses, 53. Polit & Govt Pos: Chmn of women's div, Fla Gov Campaign, 66, co-chmn, 66; chmn & mem, Osceola Co Children's Home Bd of Visitors, 67-75; mem, Gov Adv Comt, 73; vchmn, Fla Dem State Exec Comt, 73-75, committeewoman, 74- Bus & Prof Pos: Secy to chmn, Palm Beach Co Comn, Fla, 52-56; secy to off mgr, Foster's Off Supply, Miami, 56-58; secy to bus mgr, Abel Stationers, Austin, Tex, 58-59; pres, Osceola CHACO, Inc, 70-76. Mem: Cent Civic Coun Woman's Club (charter pres, 70, club adv, currently); Beta Sigma Phi; Boys Clubs of Am (local dir, 74-); Osceola Co Med Soc Auxiliary; CofC Legis Comt (chmn, 73-). Honors & Awards: First Prize Entry, Cent Fla Community Projs, Sentinel

Star Co, 67; Membership Award as Jr Dist Dir, Fla Fedn Women's Clubs, 70, New Clubs Award, 70. Relig: Baptist. Mailing Add: 9 Glendale Dr Kissimmee FL 32741

GANT, JACK E (D)
Mo State Sen
Mailing Add: 9417 E 29th St Independence MO 64052

GANT, JOSEPH ERWIN, JR (D)
NMex State Sen
b Alamance Co, NC, Feb 4, 12; s Joseph Erwin Gant & Mary Gilmer Banner G; m 1938 to Opal Martin; c Joseph Erwin, III & Mary Martin. Educ: Univ NC, BS chem, 34; Alpha Tau Omega. Polit & Govt Pos: Chmn, Eddy Co Dem Party, NMex, 48-; mem, NMex State Dem Exec Comt, 53-54; pub mem, NMex State Invest Coun, 59-60; chmn, Eddy Co Bd Comnr, 67-68; NMex State Sen, Dist 34, 68-, mem, Legis Univ Study Comt, 70- & Legis Environ Health Study Comt, 73-, chmn, NMex Sen Conserv Comn, 73- & NMex Sen Majority Party Caucus, 73-; mem, NMex State Dem Cent Comt, 74- Bus & Prof Pos: Chemist, US Borax & Chem Co, 34-67; mem, Southwestern Regional Energy Coun, 75- Mem: Am Chem Soc; NMex Asn Co; Elks. Relig: Episcopal. Legal Res: 602 Riverside Dr Carlsbad MN 88220 Mailing Add: PO Box 909 Carlsbad NM 88220

GANT, MARY L (D)
Mo State Sen
Mailing Add: 5804 E 14th St Kansas City MO 64126

GANTS, ROBERT MONTE (R)
b Aug 19, 37; m to Norma Eneim; c two sons & one daughter. Educ: US Mil Acad, BS, 61; Am Univ Washington Col Law, JD, 67. Polit & Govt Pos: Minority & asst counsel, House Comt on Interior & Insular Affairs, Washington, DC, 71-72; admin asst, US Rep John B Anderson, III, 72-73 & 75-; admin & legis asst, US Rep Ralph S Regula, Ohio, 73-75. Bus & Prof Pos: Partner, Partridge, Gants & Perkins, Washington, DC, 67-71. Mil Serv: Entered as enlistee, Army, 56, released as 1st Lt, 64, after serv as Commissioned Officer in Inf, 61-64. Mem: Am & DC Bar Asns; Barristers; Phi Delta Phi; West Point Soc, DC. Legal Res: 103 Pommander Walk Alexandria VA 22314 Mailing Add: Off of Hon John B Anderson 1729 Longworth House Off Bldg Washington DC 20515

GAON, DAVID M (D)
Colo State Rep
Mailing Add: 885 Dexter St Denver CO 80220

GARABEDIAN, ARAM GEORGE (R)
RI State Rep
b Providence, RI, May 13, 35; s Harry Garabedian & Irene Nalbandian G; m 1957 to Jane Sarah Bliss; c Lisa Beth & Gary. Educ: Univ Maine, Orono, BS in Ed, 57; Kappa Sigma. Polit & Govt Pos: Sch committeeman, Cranston, RI, 67-72; RI State Rep, 26th Dist, Cranston, 73- Bus & Prof Pos: Sales, Ortho Pharmaceuticals, Raritan, NJ, 59-62, Smith, Miller & Patch, New York, 63-66, Travelers Inst, Providence, RI, 66-67 & Arco Pharmaceuticals, Plainview, NY, 67-; wholesale mgr, second vpres & bd dirs, Natures Bounty, currently. Mil Serv: Entered as 2nd Lt, Army, 57, released as 1st Lt, 59, after serv in 2nd Battle Group, 60th Inf; Capt(Ret), Army Res. Mem: RI Traveling Mens Auxiliary; Cranston Mens Rep Club. Mailing Add: 73 Belvedere Dr Cranston RI 02910

GARAMENDI, JOHN R (D)
Calif State Assemblyman
Mailing Add: 218 W Pine St Lodi CA 95240

GARBETT, RICHARD WALKER (R)
b Gary, Ind, Aug 18, 26; s Roy Arthur Garbett & Evelyn Walker G; m 1955 to Mary Elizabeth Welford; c Barbara Lee, Margaret Elizabeth, Richard Welford & Mary Hannah. Educ: Yale Univ, BA, 49; Yale Polit Union. Polit & Govt Pos: Pub rels dir, Yale Young Rep Club, 49-50; nat committeeman, Active Young Rep of Delege, Inc, 49-53; nat committeeman, pub rels adv comt, NJ Rep Comt, 61-62; pres, Florham Park Rep Club, 61; munic Rep chmn, Florham Park, 62; dist chmn, Morris Co Rep Comt, 63-64, mem exec comt, 63-67; pub rels dir, US Rep Peter Frelinghuysen, NJ, 62 & 64, campaign mgr, 66; vchmn, NJ Nixon Now Comt, 68; nat field advert dir, Nixon-Agnew Campaign Comt, 68; dir commun, Rep Nat Comt, 69-70; consult govt rels & polit commun, Richard Garbett Assoc, Washington, DC, 70-; mem, Regional Export Expansion Coun, Dept of Com, 72- Bus & Prof Pos: Mkt exec, Vick Chem Co, New York & Manila, PI, 50-57; acct exec, Compton Advert Inc, New York, 57-59; prod mkt mgr, Thomas J Lipton, Inc, Englewood Cliffs, NJ, 59-62; vpres & acct supvr, Kenyon & Eckhardt, Inc, New York, 62-69. Mil Serv: Entered as A/S, Navy, 44, released as Radioman 2/C, 46, after serv in USS LCI 682, Asiatic-Pac Theater, ADCOMPHISFOR PAC-Guam, 45-46; Ens, Naval Res, 46-55; Victory Medal, Am Theater & Pac Theater Medals. Mem: Export Mgrs Club NY; Yale Club New York; Capitol Hill Club, Washington, DC. Relig: Protestant. Mailing Add: 11116 Luxmanor Rd Rockville MD 20852

GARBOSE, DORIS RHODA (R)
State Committeewoman, Mass Rep State Comt
b Bridgeport, Conn, Mar 11, 24; d David Lewis Lesser & Betty Lessler; m 1945 to Judge William Garbose; c Daniel Marvin, James Lesser, David Lewis & Susan Beth. Educ: Univ Mich, Ann Arbor, BA, 45; Zeta Phi Eta; Sigma Delta Tau. Polit & Govt Pos: State committeewoman, Mass Rep State Comt, 60-; mem, Athol Town Rep Comt, Mass, 60-, vchmn, 62-66; alt deleg, Rep Nat Conv, 68 & 72; dir, Western Mass Health Planning Coun, currently. Bus & Prof Pos: Dir & clerk, Keystone Nursing Home, Inc, Leominster, Mass, 60-67, adminr & dir, 67-; adminr & dir, Franklin Nursing Home, Inc, Greenfield, 64- Mem: Am Col of Nursing Home Adminrs (comnr, Mass Bd Registr, 71-); Hadassah. Relig: Jewish. Mailing Add: 1192 Main St Athol MA 01331

GARCIA, A C (TONY) (D)
Tex State Rep
Mailing Add: 522 S Cage Pharr TX 78577

GARCIA, ALEX P (D)
Calif State Sen
b El Paso, Tex, June 22, 29; s Jerry R Garcia & Cecilia G; m 1948 to Blanche Alvarez; c Alex g, twins Daniel A & Thomas A, Cecilia A & Catherine A. Educ: Southern Calif Col; Univ Calif Exten, Los Angeles; East Los Angeles Jr Col. Polit & Govt Pos: Calif State Assemblyman, 68-74; Calif State Sen, 75-, mem comts elec & reapportionment, health & welfare, Calif State Senate, currently, vchmn transportation, currently; mem, Comn of the Californias, 71- Mil Serv: Army. Mem: Thomas Jefferson Dem Club; Mex-Am Polit Asn; Optimist Club; Boy Scouts; Am Cancer Soc (dist chmn). Relig: Catholic. Legal Res: 1166 S Calada St Los Angeles CA 90023 Mailing Add: Rm 5095 State Capitol Sacramento CA 95814

GARCIA, CLOTILDE (D)
Committeewoman, Tex State Dem Exec Comt
b Victoria, Tampaulipas, Mex, Jan 11, 17; d Jose G Garcia & Faustina Perez G; m 1943 to Hipolito Canales, div; c Jose Antonio Canales. Educ: Univ Tex, Austin, BA, 38, MEd, 50; Univ Tex Sch Med, Galveston, MD, 54; Edinburg Jr Col, AA, 56; Sigma Delta Pi. Polit & Govt Pos: Mem, Tex Const Revision Comn & Adv Comt on Aging, 73; committeewoman, Tex State Dem Exec Comt, 74- Bus & Prof Pos: Regent, Del Mar Col, Corpus Christi, Tex, 60- Publ: An Indian Uprising in Camargo, Southwestern Hist J, Univ Tex, 75. Mem: Am Med Asn; Am Asn Physicians & Surgeons; Tex & Nueces Co Med Asns; Tex Rehabilitation Asn. Honors & Awards: Outstanding Citizen Award, Am GI Forum Tex, 72. Relig: Catholic. Legal Res: 3017 Ocean Dr Corpus Christi TX 78404 Mailing Add: 2601 Morgan St Corpus Christi TX 78405

GARCIA, LABRE RUDOLPH (R)
b Antonito, Colo, Apr 21, 10; s Celestino Garcia & Sidelia Trujillo G; m 1948 to Anne Mildred Royce; c Kim, Kristine & Judith. Educ: Barnes Bus Col, 2-year cert; George Washington Univ, 34-35; Washington Col Law, Am Univ, LLB & JD, 40; Mussey Law Cong; Sigma Delta Kappa. Polit & Govt Pos: Presiding dist judge, High Comnr Ger, Nurnberg, 46-51; attorney, Off Price Stabilization, 51-53; legis attorney, Secy of Air Force, 53-57, 60-67; dir procurement, Hq US Air Force, Europe, 57-60; counsel, House Armed Serv Comt, US House Rep, 67-69; minority counsel, Sen Armed Serv, US Senate Comt, 69- Mil Serv: Entered as Pvt, Army, 41, released, 46, after serv in NAfrica, Sicily & Italy, 43-45; recalled, 53, Col, Air Force Res, retired 67; Legion of Merit with Oak Leaf Cluster; Bronze Star Medal; Campaign Ribbons; Ger Occup Medal & Brazilian War Medal. Mem: Air Force Asn. Relig: Catholic. Mailing Add: 10020 Cedar Lane Kensington MD 20795

GARCIA, MARIA DE LOURDES (D)
Committeeperson, Adams Co Dem Party, Colo
b Matanzas, Cuba, June 20, 53; d Segundo Nicolas Garcia & Esther Marina Menes G; single. Educ: Nebr Wesleyan Univ, 71; Univ Colo, Denver, 72. Polit & Govt Pos: Deleg, Dem Nat Conv, 72; co-coordr, Register Youth, Denver, Colo, 72; coordr, Unidos con McGovern-Shriver, 72; comt chairperson, Colo Dem Womens' Caucus, 72-; mem & initiator, Adams Co Dem Womens' Caucus, 73-; committeeperson, Adams Co Dem Party, 73- Mem: Common Cause; Nat Orgn for Women; Mountain State Abortion Coalition; Cuban Circle of Denver (secy, 73). Relig: Catholic. Mailing Add: 7850 Valley View Dr Denver CO 80221

GARCIA, RICHARD (D)
Hawaii State Rep
b Tokyo, Japan; s Labriano Garcia & Aya Hattori G; m 1970 to Kerrianne Kau. Educ: Univ Hawaii, 65-70. Polit & Govt Pos: Hawaii State Rep, 17th Dist, 70- Mem: Delta Sigma Rho; Tau Kappa Alpha. Honors & Awards: One of Ten Outstanding Young Men of Hawaii, Hawaii State Jaycees, 71. Legal Res: 814-6 Bannister St Honolulu HI 96819 Mailing Add: Rm 318 State Capitol Honolulu HI 96813

GARCIA, ROBERT (D)
NY State Sen
b Bronx, NY, Jan 9, 33; s Rafael Garcia & Rosa Rodrigues G; m 1959 to Anita Theresa Medina; c Rosalind, Robert & Kenneth. Educ: RCA Inst, EE, 57; Community Col New York, 1 year; City Col New York, BA. Polit & Govt Pos: Cong asst to Congressman James H Scheuer, 21st Cong Dist, 65-66; NY State Assemblyman, 83rd & 77th Assembly Dist, 66-67; NY State Sen, 29th Sen Dist, 67-; mem, NY State Temporary Comn to Evaluate Drug Laws; mem, Dem Charter Comn, 74. Bus & Prof Pos: Ins consult. Mil Serv: Entered as Pvt, Army, 50, released as Sgt, 53, after serv in 3rd Inf Div, Korea, 51-52; Korean Serv Ribbons; Korean Combat Ribbon; 2 Bronze Stars; Good Conduct Medal. Mem: Adlai Stevenson Club; PR Vet Asn; PR Nat Asn for Civil Rights; NAACP. Relig: Protestant. Legal Res: 540 Concord Ave Bronx NY 10455 Mailing Add: 221 1/2 St Ann's Ave Bronx NY 10454

GARCIA, ROBERT N (D)
NMex State Rep
b Albuquerque, NMex, Aug 17, 37; s Antonio S Garcia & Maria Garcia de Gutierrez; m 1959 to Gloria Christine Garcia Fajardo; c Eric Lee & Stephanie Marisa. Educ: Univ NMex, BA Bus, 72. Polit & Govt Pos: NMex State Rep, 75- Bus & Prof Pos: Realtor, broker & secy-treas, G&G Realty Ltd, Inc, 75- Relig: Catholic. Mailing Add: 3615 Rio Grande Blvd NW Albuquerque NM 87107

GARCIA, ZARAGOZA D, JR (D)
Chmn, Jim Wells Co Dem Party, Tex
b Ben Bolt, Tex, Nov 3, 25; s Zaragoza Garcia, Sr & Concepcion Gonzales de G; m 1970 to Auora Gonzales. Educ: Ben Bolt High Sch, grad, 43. Polit & Govt Pos: Chmn, Jimm Wells Co Dem Party, Tex, 60-70 & 73- Bus & Prof Pos: Rancher, 50-70. Mil Serv: Entered as Pvt, Army, 44, released as Sgt, 46, after serv in 65th Inf Div, ETO, 45-46; three Battle Stars; Inf Combat Badge; Presidential Citation; Good Conduct Medal; two Bronze Stars. Mem: VFW. Relig: Catholic. Mailing Add: PO Box 1359 Alice TX 78332

GARCIA-MENDEZ, MIGUEL A (R)
b Aguadilla, PR, Nov 17, 02; s Juan Bautista Garcia-Figueroa & Carmen Mendez-Elias G; m 1926 to Fredeswinda Ramirez de Arellano-Bartoli; c Ileana (Mrs Carr) & Fredeswinda (Mrs Frontera). Educ: Univ PR, LLB, 22; Princeton Univ, Dipl on Const Law; pres, Grad Class of 1922; Res Officers Training corps. Polit & Govt Pos: Judge, Court of San German, PR, 23; Rep, PR House of Rep, 28-32, Speaker of House, 33-41; mem, Const Conv, 51-52; Sen-at-lg & Floor Leader Statehood Party, PR Legis Assembly, 52-69; mem, US-PR Comn on the Status of PR; pres & state chmn, Statehood Rep Party, PR, 52-68; deleg, Rep Nat Conv, 68. Bus & Prof Pos: Pres, Mayaguez Ins Serv, Inc, 43; pres, Western Fed Savings & Loan Asn, Super-A Fertilizer Works, Inc & El Imparcial Newspaper, currently; chmn bd, Mayaguez Motors Corp, Atlantic Quality Construction, Cent Eureka, Ins & Domican Ventures, Inc. Publ: Constitutional decisions of Chief Justice Marshall; Political and parliamentary speeches; Saturday Column El Imparcial. Mem: Lawyers' Asn of PR; Am Bar Asn; Asn of the US Army; Ateneo de PR; Lions. Relig: Catholic. Legal Res: Cerro de Las Mesas Mayaguez PR Mailing Add: PO Box 599 Mayaguez PR 00709

GARCZYNSKI, JOSEPH, JR (D)
Mass State Rep
Mailing Add: State Capitol Boston MA 02133

GARDINER, SHERRY BIGGERS (R)
Secy, Marion Co Rep Cent Comt, Ind
b Toledo, Ohio, Dec 30, 18; d John David Biggers & Mary Kelsey B; m 1941 to Sprague H Gardiner, MD; c John Biggers, William Sprague, Thomas Kelsey & Ann Sherret. Educ: Vassar Col, AB, 40. Polit & Govt Pos: Deleg, Rep State Conv, Ind, 54, 60, 62, 68 & 70-74; precinct committeeman, Marion Co Rep Party, 60-, vol chmn, 64, vice ward chmn, 66-72, assoc vol chmn, 66 & 67, vol worker at Rep Hq, 66-; area capt, Rep Action Comt, Marion Co, 66; alt deleg, Rep Nat Conv, 68, deleg, 72; mem, Campaign Coord Comt, Marion Co, Ind, 68; mem, Ind Inaugural Comt, Marion Co, Ind & Washington, DC, 68-69; spec asst to chmn, Marion Co Rep Cent Comt, Ind, 68-70, secy, 70-; mem, Region Five Health Adv Comt on Comprehensive Health Planning, 71-73. Mem: Jr League of Indianapolis; Marion Co Rep Workshop; Day Nursery Asn of Indianapolis; League of Women Voters; Meridian Hills Country Club. Relig: Protestant. Mailing Add: 330 W 62nd St Indianapolis IN 46260

GARDINER, TERRY (D)
Alaska State Rep
Mailing Add: Box 1092 Ketchikan AK 99901

GARDNER, EDITH B (R)
NH State Sen
Mailing Add: RFD 5 Laconia NH 03246

GARDNER, HOYT DEVANE (R)
Mem, Ky Rep State Cent Comt
b Paragould, Ark, Aug 2, 23; s Hoyt Landis Gardner & Grayce Grady G; m 1945 to Rose Brakmeier; c Hoyt Devane, Jr, Thomas George & Nicholas Grady. Educ: Westminster Col, 42-43; Univ Louisville, AB, 47, Med Sch, MD, 50; Univ Mich Grad Sch, 54-55; Omicron Delta Kappa; Delta Tau Delta. Polit & Govt Pos: Mem, Mayor's Citizens' Adv Comt, Louisville, Ky, 60-64; mem, Ky Rep State Cent Comt, 64-; chmn, Louisville & Jefferson Co Bd Health, 65-; mem, Ky State Comprehensive Health Planning Comt, 68- Bus & Prof Pos: Gen surgeon, 51-; chmn, Ky Educ Med Polit Action Comt, 62-63; chmn, Am Med Action Comt, 71; mem bd trustees, Univ Louisville, 71- Mil Serv: Entered as Seaman, Navy, 43, released as Pharmacist Mate 1/C, 46, after serv in Fleet Hosp 116, Okinawa; entered as 1st Lt, Air Force, 51, released as Capt, 53, after serv in Strategic Air Command, Korean Conflict. Mem: Am Med Asn (bd trustees); Southeastern Surgical Cong; fel Am Col Surgeons; Rotary; Big Springs Country Club. Honors & Awards: Outstanding Graduating Sr Award, Omicron Delta Kappa, 50; dipl, Am Bd Surgery. Relig: Presbyterian. Legal Res: 2707 Lamont Rd Louisville KY 40218 Mailing Add: 508 Watterson City Bldg W Louisville KY 40218

GARDNER, J M (D)
NC State Rep
Mailing Add: 825 Vermont St Smithfield NC 27577

GARDNER, JACK CRANDALL (D)
Mem, Ark State Dem Comt
b Parkdale, Ark, June 12, 28; s Leroy Gardner & Jewell Allen G (deceased); divorced. Educ: Univ Ark, 51. Polit & Govt Pos: Mem, Ark State Dem Comt, 74- Mil Serv: Entered as A/S, Navy, 46, released as Sgt 1/C, 47, after serv in Navy Supply, SPac Theatre, 46-47. Mem: F&AM, Tyrian Lodge 553; Am Legion, M M Eberts Post 1. Relig: Baptist. Mailing Add: 5503 B St Apt 23 Little Rock AR 72205

GARDNER, JAMES A (R)
Ind State Sen
Mailing Add: RR 3 Fowler IN 47944

GARDNER, JAMES CARSON (R)
b Rocky Mount, NC, Apr 18, 33; s James C Gardner & Sue T G; m 1957 to Marie Tyler; c Beth, Terry & Christopher. Educ: NC State Univ, 53-56. Polit & Govt Pos: NC Cong cand, 64; chmn, NC State Rep Party, 65; US Rep, NC, 67-68; deleg, Rep Nat Conv, 68; cand for Gov of NC, 68. Bus & Prof Pos: Vpres, Gardner Dairy Prod, 56-61; exec vpres, Hardee's Food Systems, Inc, 62-66; pres & chmn of bd, Quick Food Syst, Inc, 68; pres, Gardner Properties, Rocky Mount, ND, 68-70; pres & chmn bd, Southern Sports Corp, 68-70; pres, Carolando Corp, 68- Mil Serv: Entered as Pvt, Army, 54, released as Pfc, 56, after serv in Signal Corps. Publ: A Time to Speak, 68. Honors & Awards: Young Man of the Year Award, Rocky Mount Jr CofC, 67. Mailing Add: 3820 Woodlawn Dr Rocky Mount NC 27801

GARDNER, JANE KENDALL (D)
Vt State Rep
Mailing Add: Arlington VT 05250

GARDNER, JAY D (R)
Chmn, Chatham Co Rep Comt, Ga
b Camilla, Ga, Sept 23, 29; s Bernard Clay Gardner & Annie Williams G; m 1951 to Ruth Carleen Gaulden; c James Robert, Jay D, Jr & Katherine. Educ: Emory Univ; Univ Ga, BBA, 51, LLB, 56; Chi Phi; Phi Beta Kappa. Polit & Govt Pos: Chmn, Chatham Co Rep Comt, Ga, 66-67, 75-, counsel & mem, 71-74; former Ga State Rep Sen; mem, First Cong Dist Rep Exec Comt, Ga, currently; parliamentarian, Ga State Rep Party, 69-71; chmn, Ga State Rep Conv, 70. Bus & Prof Pos: Partner, Adams, Adams, Brennan & Gardner, 59- Mil Serv: Entered as 2nd Lt, Air Force, 51, released as 1st Lt, 53, after serv in 20th Fighter Bomber Wing, ETO; Maj (Ret), Air Force Res. Mem: Am & Ga Bar Asns; Rep Club, First Cong Dist of Ga (bd dirs); F&AM; Optimist (past Lt Gov). Relig: Episcopal. Legal Res: 4614 Lansdowne Savannah GA 31405 Mailing Add: PO Box 1208 Savannah GA 31402

GARDNER, JOHN WILLIAM (R)
b Los Angeles, Calif, Oct 8, 12; s William Gardner & Marie Flora G; m 1934 to Aida Marroquin; c Stephanie (Mrs Philip Trimble) & Francesca (Mrs John R Reese). Educ: Stanford Univ, AB, 35, AM, 36; Univ Calif, PhD, 38, LLD, 59. Hon Degrees: Various cols & univs. Polit & Govt Pos: Head Latin-Am Sect Foreign Broadcast Intel Serv, Fed Commun Comn, 42-43; chmn, Social Sci Panel, Sci Adv Bd, US Air Force, 51-55; chmn, US Adv Comn Int Educ & Cult Affairs, 62-64; chmn, White House Conf on Educ, 65; Secy, Health, Educ & Welfare, 65-68; chmn, Urban Coalition, 68-70; chmn, Common Cause, 70- Bus & Prof Pos: Asst psychol teacher, Univ Calif, 36-38; instr, Conn Col, 38-40; asst prof psychol, Mt Holyoke Col, 40-42; staff mem, Carnegie Corp, NY, 46-47, exec-assoc, 47-49, vpres, 49-55, pres, 55-65; pres, Carnegie Found, 55-65; mem, Adv Comt Social Sci, Nat Sci Found, 58-65; trustee, Stanford Univ, 68-; Rockefeller Bros Found, 68-; dir, Woodrow Wilson Found, 60-63. Mil Serv: Capt, Marine Corps, 43-46, with serv in Off Strategic Serv, Mediter & ETO, 44-45; Air Force Exceptional Serv Award, 56; Presidential Medal of Freedom, 64. Publ: Excellence; Self-Renewal; No Easy Victories; Recovery of Confidence; In Common Cause. Honors & Awards: Democratic Legacy Award, Anti-Defamation League; Soc Justice Award, UAW; Murray Green Award, AFL-CIO. Mailing Add: 5325 Kenwood Ave Chevy Chase MD 20015

GARDNER, PAUL E (D)
b Peoria, Ill, Sept 11, 28; s Charles Alva Gardner & Anna Kelch G; m 1951 to Maxine Sylvia Miller; c Thomas, Gerald, Christine, Daniel, Benjamin & Elizabeth. Educ: Labor Studies Inst, 73; Bradley Univ, Ill Cent Col, Univ Ill. Polit & Govt Pos: Precinct committeeman, Peoria Co, 55-; secy, Peoria Co Dem Cent Comt, 68-72; committeeman & chmn, 46th Dist Dem Party, 69-73; mem elec comn, Peoria, Ill, 70-, mem zoning comn, 73-; chmn, COPE Comt, Peoria Tazewell Labor Coun, 71-; deleg, Dem Nat Conv, 72. Bus & Prof Pos: Elec & gen foreman, Oberlander Elec, 51-55; elec foreman, Aborac Elec, 65-71; asst bus agt, IBEW Local 34, 71- Mil Serv: Entered as Seaman, Navy, 46, released as AT-3, 49; Good Conduct Medal. Mem: Inst of Elec & Electronic Engrs; Int Asn Elec Inspectors. Relig: Catholic. Mailing Add: 406 W Lawndale Peoria IL 61604

GARDNER, REECE B (R)
Mem, Lenoir Co Rep Exec Comt, NC
b Bennettsville, SC, Sept 27, 32; s John Tilghman Gardner & Amy Lee Shaw G; m 1960 to Emma V; c Jessica & Reece B, Jr. Educ: Clemson Col, 2 years; Univ SC, 2 years; Pi Kappa Alpha. Polit & Govt Pos: State chmn, Am for Independent Action, NC, 64-65; Second Dist Rep cand for US Cong, 66, First Dist cand, 68; vchmn, Second Dist Young Rep, 67; aide to President Nixon, 69; mem, Lenoir Co Rep Exec Comt, 69-; chmn, Lenoir Co Bd Elec, 74- Bus & Prof Pos: Vpres & treas, Gardner Construction Inc, 64-; bd dirs, Lenoir Plumbing & Heating Co, Inc, 68-; instr, Dale Carnegie Course, 71-; pres, Lenoir Contractors Inc, 72- Mil Serv: Entered as Seaman, Navy, 51, released as PN-1, 55, after serv in Mediter Theatre, 53-54; Award for outstanding leadership, Naval Air Sta, Pensacola, Fla. Publ: For Love of Country, Hallmark Mag, 6/56. Mem: Rotary; Am Legion; Local & Nat CofC. Relig: Baptist. Legal Res: 2003 Cambridge Dr Kinston NC 28501 Mailing Add: PO Box 1536 Kinston NC 28501

GARDNER, STEPHEN S
Dep Secy of the Treas
Mailing Add: 15th St & Pennsylvania Ave NW Washington DC 20220

GARDNER, STEVE (D)
Mo State Rep
Mailing Add: 609 Twigwood Ballwin MO 63011

GARDNER, WILLARD HALE (R)
Utah State Rep
b Logan, Utah, Dec 22, 25; s Willard Gardner & Rebecca Viola Hale G; m 1956 to Lillian DeAnn Rich; c Julie Lynn, Bonnie, Wendy, Scott Willard, Craig Eugene & Paul Rich. Educ: Colo Col, 44; Col Pac, 45; Univ Calif, Berkeley, 46; Utah State Agr Col, BS, 48; Univ Utah, 49-52; Brigham Young Univ, MS, 56; Blue Key; Scabbard & Blade; Pi Kappa Alpha. Polit & Govt Pos: Utah State Rep, 73- Bus & Prof Pos: Systs analyst, Ramo-Wooldridge Corp, 56-61 & Informatics Inc, 61-63; sr systs analyst, Brigham Young Univ, 63-70 & asst dir comput serv, 70- Mil Serv: Entered as Seaman 3/C, Navy, 44, released as Seaman 2/C, 46, after serv in V-12 prog, US, 44-46. Publ: Co-auth, Programming on-line systems, Datamation, 5/63. Mem: Asn Comput Mach (nat chmn student chap & mem, 70-72); Utah Valley Coun (chmn, 70-72). Relig: Latter-day Saint. Mailing Add: 1495 Oak Lane Provo UT 84601

GARDNER, WILLIAM MICHAEL (D)
NH State Rep
b Manchester, NH, Oct 26, 48; s William George Gardner & Mildred Claus G; single. Educ: Univ NH, BA, 70; London Sch Econ, cert, 72; Univ NC, ME, 73; Phi Sigma Soc; London Sch of Econ Soc; Phi Mu Delta. Polit & Govt Pos: mem, Dem State Comt; NH State Rep, Manchester, Hillsborough, Dist 30, 73- Relig: Catholic. Mailing Add: 539 Candia Rd Manchester NH 03103

GARFF, KEN D (R)
b Draper, Utah, July 17, 05; s Royal B Garff & Rachael Day G; m 1931 to Marjorie Heiner; c Gary, Robert & Janie. Educ: Univ Utah, grad. Polit & Govt Pos: Mem, local, state & nat campaigns; dist chmn, Rep Party, Utah, 60-64; Rep Nat Committeeman, Utah, 64-72. Bus & Prof Pos: Owner, Ken Garff Co; pres, Ken Garff Trailer Sales & Aetna Trailer Sales; part owner, Deseret Livestock Co; dir, First Security Bank, 60- Mem: YMCA (dir, 62-); Alta Club; Hunting Club; New State Duck Club; Univ of Utah Boosters. Relig: Latter-day Saint. Mailing Add: 531 S State St Salt Lake City UT 84111

GARFIELD, CARROLL L (R)
Vt State Rep
Mailing Add: Cross Rd West Brattleboro VT 05301

GARFIELD, ERNEST (R)
b Ariz, July 14, 32; s Emil Garfield & Carmen Ybarra G; m 1953 to Betty Ann Redden; c Laural & Jeffery. Educ: Univ Ariz, 49-51 & 55-56; Am Inst Foreign Trade, 51-52; Alpha Kappa Psi. Polit & Govt Pos: Mem, Eastside Young Rep, 64-, mem bd dirs, formerly; coordr, Southern Ariz TAR Clubs; precinct committeeman, Pima Co, Ariz, 64-; Ariz State Sen, 66-68, mem, Appropriations, Judiciary, Com & Indust, Labor & Mgt, Natural Resources & Joint Educ Interim Comt, Ariz State Senate, vchmn, Educ Comts; mem, Gov Comt to Investigate Indust Comn, vchmn, Pima Co Rep Club, 69, pres, 70; dep state pres, Ariz, 70, State Treas, 71-75; Corp Comnr, 75- Bus & Prof Pos: Mgr, Americana Corp, 55-58; owner, Gen Serv Agency, 59-60; owner, Nat Credit Act, 61-62; agt, Equitable Life Assurance, 62-64; agt, Occidental Life of Calif, 64-65; owner, Garfield Ins Agency, 66- Mil Serv: Entered as Pvt, Army, 52, released as 2nd Lt, 55, after serv in 37th Field Artil, 7th Div, Korea, 53-54. Mem: Naruc Ad Hoc Comt on Regulatory Reform; Ariz Jaycees (chmn govt affairs); PTA (local pres & coun vpres); Southern Ariz Multiple Sclerosis Soc; Western Conf Pub Serv Comns (secy-treas). Honors & Awards: Educ Leadership Award, Ariz Dept Pub Instr; One of Three Outstanding Young Men of Ariz, 67; Unselfish Serv as Govt Affairs Chmn of Ariz Jaycees, US Jaycees, 67; Orchid Award, Tucson Press Club, 67; Outstanding Serv to

Community of Tucson, Pima Jaycees, 68. Relig: Catholic; secy, Our Mother of Sorrows Cath Church Men's Club, 68. Mailing Add: 4537 N 17th Ave Phoenix AZ 85015

GARLAND, FRANCES VAUGHAN (R)
Pres, Va Fedn Rep Women
b Crewe, Va, Apr 9, 24; d Holmes Arthur Vaughan & Sarah Carr V; m 1943 to Robert Allen Garland, Sr; c Robert Allen, Jr, Rebecca (Mrs Reed), Anita Holmes & Teresa Ann. Educ: Burkeville High Sch, 41; Pan Am Sch Girls, 42. Polit & Govt Pos: Pres, Va Fedn Rep Women, 72- Mem: Woman's Club of Roanoke; Roanoke Sci Museum; Rep Womans Club Roanoke; Joy Sheffey Wesleyan Serv Guild; Roanoke Fine Arts Ctr. Honors & Awards: Mother of Year in Community Activities, Roanoke Merchants Asn, 74; Hon mem, Jr Womans Club, Roanoke Jr Woman's Club, 60. Relig: Methodist. Mailing Add: 1345 Lakewood Dr SW Roanoke VA 24015

GARLAND, RAY LUCIAN (R)
Va State Deleg
b Roanoke, Va, May 20, 34; s Walter Burnham Garland & Minnie Allen G; single. Educ: Roanoke Col, BA; Univ Va, Charlottesville, MA; Univ London, Eng; Jefferson Soc. Polit & Govt Pos: Va State Deleg, 68-; Rep cand, US Senate, 70. Bus & Prof Pos: Asst mgr, Garland Drug Co, 49-60; teacher, Roanoke Col, 60-68. Mem: Moose; United Commercial Travellers; Am Club, London; Roanoke Hist Soc; Va Wildlife Fedn. Relig: Methodist. Mailing Add: 3752 Sunrise Ave NW Roanoke VA 24012

GARLAND, THOMAS JACK (R)
Tenn State Sen
b Kingsport, Tenn, June 16, 34; s Jack Warren Garland & Martha Potter G; m to Helen Patricia Kitchens; c Deborah Ann, Thomas, Jr & Lisa Carol. Educ: ETenn State Univ; Pi Kappa Alpha. Polit & Govt Pos: Chmn, Col Young Rep Club, Tenn, 58; pres, Greene Co Young Rep Club, 63-64; Tenn State Sen, currently, Minority Leader, Tenn State Senate, 73- Bus & Prof Pos: Gen mgr, Chapman Exterminating Co, Inc, 60-; chmn bd trustees, Tusculum Col. Mil Serv: Entered as Pvt, Air Force, 52, released as Airman 1/C, 56, after serv in ETO; Nat Defense & Good Conduct Medals. Mem: Exchange; Elks; VFW; Am Legion; Mason. Relig: Cumberland Presbyterian. Legal Res: 1604 Moore Ave Greeneville TN 37743 Mailing Add: Box 187 Greeneville TN 37743

GARLICK, JAMES GRAHAM (D)
Chmn, Seneca Co Dem Party, NY
b Waterloo, NY, Apr 9, 36; s Graham B Garlick & Hazel Christler G; m 1956 to Helen Frances Cosentino; c Cynthia, James J, Micheal J, Stephen F & Thomas A. Educ: Auburn Community Col, 60. Polit & Govt Pos: Town chmn, Vorich, NY, 57-, supvr, Seneca Co, 66-69; deleg, State Conv, 58-; chmn, Seneca Co Dem Party, 73- Bus & Prof Pos: Farmer & dist mgr, Chem-O-Fert Co, Surveying Farmers & Dealers, NY, currently. Mil Serv: Entered as Pvt, Army, 54, released as Pfc after serv in 499 Eng Bn, Ger. Mem: Coop Exten; NY State Pesticide Asn; NY State Farm Bur; NY State Fertilizer Asn. Relig: Catholic. Mailing Add: RD-3 Box 286 Geneva NY 14456

GARMAN, JACQUELYN MAY (R)
Mem, Rep State Cent Comt, Calif
b San Diego, Calif, Oct 9, 26; d Livingston Henry Chapron & Della Reynolds C; m to Macdonald Grant Garman; c Paul Grant, Chris Stuart & Bonnie Leigh. Educ: Ore Univ, 45. Polit & Govt Pos: Alt deleg, Rep Nat Conv, 72; mem bd southern div, Calif Fedn Rep Women, 73-, mem promotion chmn, 74-, mem exec comt, Los Angeles Co Rep Comt, 75-; alt deleg, 64th Assembly Dist Rep Cent Comt, 75-; mem, Rep State Cent Comt, 75-, 2nd vpres, Los Angeles Co Fedn Rep Women, 72-74, pres, 75- Bus & Prof Pos: Acct, Calif, 63-74. Mem: PEO; Whittier Rep Women Fed. Honors & Awards: Whittier Rep Women of the Year, 72. Relig: Christian Scientist. Mailing Add: 16000 West Rd Whittier CA 90603

GARMATZ, EDWARD A (D)
b Baltimore, Md, Feb 7, 03; m to Ruth Burchard. Educ: Polytech Inst. Polit & Govt Pos: Mem, Md State Racing Comn, 3 years; Police magistrate, 44-47; US Rep, Md, 47-72; deleg, Dem Nat Conv, 68. Bus & Prof Pos: Elec bus. Mailing Add: 2210 Lake Ave E Baltimore MD 21239

GARMENT, LEONARD (R)
US Rep Human Rights Comn, UN Econ & Social Coun
Polit & Govt Pos: Counsel to the President, formerly. Mailing Add: United Nations Human Rights Comn New York NY 10017

GARMEY, RONALD (R)
Chmn, Nahant Rep Town Comt, Mass
b Columbus, Ohio, Apr 9, 37; s Clifford Ronald Garmey & Harriet DeHuff G; m 1962 to Diana Outram Bangs; c Anne Squires & Amory. Educ: Harvard Col, BA, 60, Harvard Law Sch, LLB, 63. Polit & Govt Pos: Mem, Nahant Adv Comt, Mass, 64-68; chmn, Nahant Rep Town Comt, 67-69 & 73-; chmn, Nahant Bd Selectmen, 68- Bus & Prof Pos: Partner, Hutchins & Wheeler, Boston, 63- Mem: Mass & Boston Bar Asns. Relig: Episcopal. Mailing Add: 36 Maolis Rd Nahant MA 01908

GARMISA, BENEDICT (D)
Ill State Sen
Mailing Add: 4157 W Kamerling Ave Chicago IL 60651

GARN, EDWIN JACOB (JAKE) (R)
US Sen, Utah
b Richfield, Utah, Oct 12, 32; s Jacob Edwin Garn & Fern Christensen G; m 1957 to Hazel Thompson; c Jacob Wayne, Susan Rhae, Ellen Marie & Jeffrey Paul. Educ: Univ Utah, BS in Bus Admin & Finance, 55, 1 year grad work; Sigma Chi; Univ Utah Alumni Asn. Polit & Govt Pos: Chmn, Rep Voting Dist, Salt Lake Co, Utah, 60-64; mem, Exec Comt for Congressman Lloyd, 60-68; mem bd dirs, Salt Lake Co Young Rep, 60-66; deleg, Utah Rep State Conv & Salt Lake Co Rep Conv, 62-; mem, Utah Rep State Finance Comt, 64-66; comnr, Salt Lake City, 68-72, mayor, 72-75; mem, Joint Bd Comnr of Salt Lake Models Cities Agency, 68-73, chmn, 73-; mem, Utah League of Cities & Towns, 68-, pres, 71-72; mem bd dirs, Salt Lake Community Action Prog, 68-; mem bd dirs & mem revenue & finance steering comt, Nat League of Cities, 71-, second vpres, 72-, mem comt on intergovt rels, 72-; mem, Gov Adv Coun of Community Affairs, 72-; mem, Wasatch Front Regional Coun Govt, 73-, chmn manpower progs, 73-; mem, Salt Lake Co Coun Govt, 73-; US Senator, Utah, 75-, mem, Banking, Housing & Urban Develop Comt & Aeronaut & Space Sci & DC Comt, US Senate, 75- Bus & Prof Pos: Ins agt, John Hancock Mutual Life Ins Co, Salt Lake City, 60-61; asst mgr Salt Lake Off, Home Life Ins Co of NY, 61-66; gen agt-mgr, Mutual Trust Life Ins Co, Salt Lake City, 66-68. Mil Serv: Entered as Ens, Navy, 56, released as Lt(sg), after serv in Patrol Squadron 50, Pac Theatre, 56-60; Air Force Res, Utah Air Nat Guard, 10 years; Outstanding Unit Award, Air Force; Armed Forces Expeditionary Medal; Vietnam Serv Medal; Combat Readiness Medal; Nat Defense Medal; Armed Forces Res Medal; Expert Pistol; Nat Guard Serv. Mem: Utah Water User's Asn (bd dirs, 68-); Metrop Water Dist (bd dirs, 68-); Am Cancer Soc (bd dirs, Utah Div, 68-); Utahans for Effective Govt (bd dirs, 70); Salt Lake Co Coun of Aging. Honors & Awards: Spoke Award, Salt Lake City Jaycees, 61; Tom McCoy Award, Utah League of Cities & Towns, 72; Outstanding Couple of 72, presented to Mayor & Mrs Garn, Pioneer Chap of the Sons of the Utah Pioneers, 72; Outstanding Munic Officer in the State of Utah, 72. Relig: Latter-day Saint. Legal Res: 1428 Laird Ave Salt Lake City UT 84105 Mailing Add: US Senate Washington DC 20510

GARNER, JOHN BROMLEY (D)
Exec Secy, Madison Co Dem Exec Comt, Miss
b Chicago, Ill, July 21, 37; s Orrin O B Garner & Lillian Bromley G; m 1961 to Margrit Schmid; c Stephen Mark & Evelyn Silvia. Educ: Carleton Col, BA, 59; Univ Ill, Urbana, MS, 62; Brown Univ, 64-65. Polit & Govt Pos: Mem, Miss State Dem Nominating Comt, 68; mem, Madison Co Dem Conv & Fourth Cong Dist Dem Conv, Miss, 68 & 72; deleg, Dem Nat Conv, 68 & 72; exec secy, Madison Co Dem Exec Comt, Miss, 68-; mem, Miss Dem State Conv, 72; mem, Miss Dem State Exec Comt, 72- Bus & Prof Pos: Assoc prof physics, Tougaloo Col, 62- Mem: Am Asn Physics Teachers; Miss Acad Sci; Coun for a Livable World; Am Civil Liberties Union. Relig: Methodist. Mailing Add: Tougaloo Col Tougaloo MS 39174

GARNER, MARIE G (D)
Mem, Pa Dem State Comt
b South Fork, Pa, Mar 6, 24; d Joseph R Grillo & Mary Forest G; m 1947 to John A Garner; c Evelyn A, Margaret Jeanne & twins John A & M Judy. Educ: Pa State Univ, Exten, voc, 3 years. Polit & Govt Pos: Chmn, Calling Comt for J F Kennedy, 59; Dem committeewoman, South Precinct, State College Pa, 56-69; treas, Federated Dem Women's Club, 60-66, adv, currently; chmn, Jane's For Joe, 62; chmn, 4 For 64 Nat Comt, 64; vchmn, Centre Co Dem Comt, 64-66, chmn, 66-72; chmn, 47th Sen Dist Const Nominating Conv, 67; deleg-at-lg, Pa Dem State Cent Comt, 68; deleg, Dem Nat Conv, 68, deleg-at-lg, 72; mem, Pa Dem Platform Comt; state adv, Teen-Dems, chmn, Humphrey Campaign, 34th Dist, Pa, 72; organizer, McGovern Campaign, 72; mem, Comt to Reelect Judge Gen Blatt; mem from 34th Sen Dist, Pa Dem State Comt, 72-; deleg, Dem Nat Mid-Term Conf, 74. Bus & Prof Pos: Lectr on Aeronaut for Army Air Force Air Power Show, Museum of Sci & Indust, Rockefeller Ctr, NY, 44-45; instr, Pa State Sch of Aeronaut, Harrisburg & Olmsted Field, Pa, 44-46; mgr, Family Jewelry Store, Bellefonte, Pa, 46-48. Mil Serv: Citation from Gen Clark & Gen Arnold for outstanding performance as civilian instr with the Army Air Force. Mem: Dem Women's Adv Coun of Pa (charter mem & treas); Int Platform Asn. Honors & Awards: Named One of Ten Outstanding Women in Pa by J F Kennedy, 62; Elected as the Outstanding Co Chmn in Pa by State Teen Dem, 68; Award for outstanding achievements in registration and work with youth, Dem Women's Adv Coun of Pa, 72. Relig: Catholic. Mailing Add: 1214 Old Boalsburg Rd State College PA 16801

GARNSEY, WILLIAM SMITH (R)
Treas, Weld Co Rep Comt, Colo
b Billings, Mont, Nov 5, 11; s William Smith Garnsey & Agnes Sprague Wood G; m 1936 to Louisa Boulton Herrick; c Louisa (Mrs Samuel Waldron Lambert, III), William Herrick & Anson Herrick. Educ: Yale Col, BA, 33; Skull & Bones Hon Soc; Alpha Delta Phi. Polit & Govt Pos: Mem sch bd, Dist Six, Greeley, Colo, 49-55; Colo State Sen, Dist 25, Weld Co, 67-74; mem adv comt, Comn Higher Educ, 67-74; mem, Gov Fiscal Study Comt, 68-74; mem, Legis Coun Study Comt Govt Employee Negotiations, 69, Uniform Consumer Credit Code, 69 & 70 & Child & Women Labor Laws, Farm Labor Comt, 71; Gov Interim Comt State Personnel Syst, 71-73; Ins Study Comt, 72; treas, Weld Co Rep Comt, 74-, bonus mem, 74- Bus & Prof Pos: Property mgr, Van Schaack & Co, Denver, Colo, 34-37; mgr mortgage loan dept, Capitol Life Ins Co, Denver, 37-47; partner, Garnsey & Wheeler Co, Greeley, 47-58, pres, 58-72, chmn bd, currently; vpres, Garnsey & Wheeler Rebuilders Inc, 51- Mil Serv: Entered as Lt(jg), Naval Res, 42, released as Lt Comdr, 45, after serv in Naval Training Sch, Hq Squadron 9-1, Atlantic Fleet. Mem: Colo Automobile Dealers Asn; Elks; Am Legion; VFW; Greeley Country Club. Relig: Episcopal. Legal Res: 1926 23rd Ave Greeley CO 80631 Mailing Add: PO Box D Greeley CO 80631

GAROFALO, ANTHONY JOSEPH (R)
b Detroit, Mich, Oct 25, 36; s Peter Garofalo & Josephine Brucia G; m 1967 to Carol Bea Lennebacker. Educ: Detroit Col Appl Sci, grad, 59. Polit & Govt Pos: Pub rels dir, Ottawa Co Rep Party, 68-, gen campaign chmn, 70-, chmn, formerly; deleg, Rep Nat Conv, 72. Bus & Prof Pos: Mgr, Garofalo Pharmacy, Grosse Pointe Woods, Mich, 59-62; prof serv rep, Warner-Chilcott Labs, Holland, 62-70; key accounts sales rep, Revlon, Inc, 70-71; exec dir, Holland Bd Realtors, 71-; mkt mgr, Interwheel Div, Import Motors, Grand Rapids, Mich, 73- Mem: Detroit Econ Club. Honors & Awards: Rep of the Month. Mailing Add: 978 Forest Hills Dr Holland MI 49423

GARR, ELIZABETH ANN (R)
VChmn, Jay Co Rep Cent Comt, Ind
b Dunkirk, Ind, July 11, 17; d Homer Wilson McDaniel & Hazel Ayres M; m 1938 to Marion Russell Garr; c Robert Dean. Educ: Ball State Univ, 36-37; Alpha Sigma Tau. Polit & Govt Pos: Vchmn, Jay Co Rep Cent Comt, Ind, 68-; secy, Ind Tenth Dist Rep Comt, 72- Bus & Prof Pos: Home serv rep, Ind & Mich Elec Co, Hartford City, Ind, 46-48; license br mgr, Ind Bur Motor Vehicles, 68-73, Tenth dist driver examr supvr, 73-75. Mem: Nat Fedn Rep Women; Eastern Star; Am Legion Auxiliary. Relig: Methodist. Mailing Add: 148 Moore Ave Dunkirk IN 47336

GARR, JOHN M (D)
Utah State Rep
Mailing Add: 151 Denver Ave East Carbon City UT 84520

GARRAHY, J JOSEPH (D)
Lt Gov, RI
b Providence, RI, Nov 26, 30; s John Garrahy & Margaret Neylon G; m 1956 to Margherite DiPietro; c Colleen, John, Maribeth, Sheila & Seanna Margaret. Educ: La Salle Acad, 48; Univ of RI; Univ of Buffalo. Polit & Govt Pos: RI State Sen, 62-68, dep majority leader, RI State Sen, 63-68, chmn, Dem State Comt, RI, 67-68; Lt Gov, RI, 69-; mem adv comt, New

Eng Regional Kidney Prog, 72-; co-chmn, Econ Renewal Coun, 73-74; chmn, Proj Recovery Task Force, 75-; co-chmn, Cancer Control Bd, currently. Relig: Catholic. Legal Res: 31 Elmcrest Ave Providence RI 02908 Mailing Add: Rm 316 State House Providence RI 02903

GARRAMONE, RAYMOND (D)
NJ State Sen
Mailing Add: State House Trenton NJ 08625

GARRARD, ED (D)
Ga State Rep
Mailing Add: 956 Plymouth Rd NE Atlanta GA 30306

GARRETT, CHARLES G (D)
SC State Sen
b Fountain Inn, SC, Nov 9, 18; s C G Garrett & Lucy Pullen G; m 1945 to Martha Inez Jones; c Lucy, Sally & Glenn. Educ: Furman Univ, BA, 41. Polit & Govt Pos: Mayor, Fountain Inn, SC, formerly; SC State Rep, 49-68; SC State Sen, currently. Bus & Prof Pos: Textiles; dir, Fed Savings & Loan Asn. Mem: Rotary. Honors & Awards: Man of the Year, Fountain Inn, SC. Relig: Presbyterian. Mailing Add: Box 535 Fountain Inn SC 29644

GARRETT, HOWARD M (D)
Mo State Rep
b Albany, Ala, June 16, 18; s J Ben Garrett; m 1939 to Bessie C Morris; c Carla Jean, William Joseph & David Wayne. Educ: DeSoto, Mo, pub schs. Polit & Govt Pos: Mo State Rep, 62- Bus & Prof Pos: Wholesale & retail sales of gasoline, oil & tires. Mil Serv: Army, ETO, 44-46; Combat Inf Badge; Bronze Star. Mem: Mason; Scottish Rite; VFW. Relig: Fairview Christian Church, deacon. Mailing Add: 1540 Westvale Festus MO 63028

GARRETT, JOHN L (D)
Okla State Sen
b Wannett, Okla, Oct 12, 17; s Spurgeon Earl Garrett & Sarah Ellen G; m 1939 to Hazel Ann Morris; c Carolyn June (Mrs Pool) & Connie Ann (Mrs Matthews). Educ: Cameron Jr Col, 36-37; Univ Okla, BA, 41, Law Sch, LLB, 42. Polit & Govt Pos: Okla State Sen, 65- Mem: Okla State & Co Bar Asns; Lions. Relig: Christian Church. Mailing Add: 1444 Howard Dr Del City OK 73115

GARRETT, JULIAN BURGESS (R)
Dir Region VII, Young Rep Nat Fedn
b Des Moines, Iowa, Nov 7, 40; s Julian C Garrett & Loyat Bland G; single. Educ: Cent Univ Iowa, BA, 62; Univ Iowa, JD, 67. Polit & Govt Pos: Asst attorney gen in charge of consumer protection div, Iowa Dept of Justice, 67-; dir Region VII, Young Rep Nat Fedn, 73- Mem: Iowa Bar Asn; Iowa Farm Bur. Honors & Awards: Outstanding Iowa Young Rep, 69-70; Award of Merit, Northeast Mo State Univ Law Enforcement Educ Prog, 73. Mailing Add: 609 N Jefferson Indianola IA 50125

GARRETT, MARCELLA (D)
Committeewoman, Pemiscot Co Dem Party, Mo
b Cooter, Mo, Feb 26, 05; d J Ham Smith & Dora Brooks S; m 1924 to Cleo Garrett, wid; c Robert S & Howard H. Educ: Carothersville High Sch, Mo, dipl, 22. Polit & Govt Pos: Committeewoman, Pemiscot Co Dem Party, Mo, 64- Bus & Prof Pos: Teacher, Cooter Pub Sch, Mo, 22-24; mem staff, Garrett Ins Agency, 44-64. Mem: Steele Pub Libr (chmn bd trustees). Relig: Methodist. Mailing Add: 509 S Walnut Steele MO 63877

GARRETT, RAY, JR (R)
Chmn, Securities & Exchange Comn
b Chicago, Ill, Aug 11, 20; s Ray Garrett & Mabel May G; m 1943 to Virginia R Hale; c Nancy (Mrs John T Worcester), Susan (Mrs Neil M Dunn), Anne (Mrs J Roderick Burfield) & Richard H. Educ: Yale Univ, AB, 41; Harvard Law Sch, LLB, 49; Beta Theta Pi. Polit & Govt Pos: Assoc dir & dir div corp regulation, Securities & Exchange Comn, 54-57, assoc exec dir, 57-58, chmn, 73- Bus & Prof Pos: Teaching fel, Harvard Law Sch, 49-50; assoc, NY Univ Sch Law, 50-52; assoc, Gardner, Carton & Douglas, Attorneys-at-law, Chicago, Ill, 52-54; vis lectr, Northwestern Univ Sch Law, 62-66; chmn adv comt, Commentaries on Model Debenture Indentures, Am Bar Found, 67. Mil Serv: Entered as 2nd Lt, Army, 42, released as Capt, 46, after serv in Field Artil, ETO, 9th, 1st & 3rd Armies, 42-46; Maj(Ret), Army Res; Bronze Star Medal. Mem: Am Bar Asn (mem, Bd Ed J, 67-73); Univ Club Chicago. Relig: Episcopal. Mailing Add: 182 Myrtle St Winnetka IL 60093

GARRETT, ROY H (D)
Kans State Rep
Mailing Add: 701 E Walnut Derby KS 67037

GARRETT, TOM (D)
Ky State Sen
b 1921. Educ: Univ Ky Col Law, LLB. Polit & Govt Pos: Ky State Sen, 62-64 & 69- Bus & Prof Pos: Attorney; pres, Co Bar Asn, 73- Mil Serv: Army Air Force. Relig: Baptist. Mailing Add: 700 Hillgate Paducah KY 42001

GARRETT, WAYNE LEE
b Chester, Pa, Sept 30, 50; s Leroy Dacy & Dorothy N Wilhelmi D; single. Educ: Muhlenberg Col, Allentown, Pa, BS, 72; Philadelphia Col of Osteopathic Med, 72-; Omicron Delta Kappa; Phi Sigma Gamma; Tau Kappa Epsilon. Polit & Govt Pos: State chmn, Pa Col Rep, 71-72; deleg, Rep Nat Conv, 72. Mem: DeMolay. Relig: Episcopal. Mailing Add: 105 Robin Hood Lane Aston Twp PA 19014

GARRIGUES, GEORGE LOUIS (R)
Mem, Rep State Cent Comt Calif
b Bishop, Calif, July 25, 26; s Louis Garrigues & Mildred Yaney G; m 1950 to Barbara Robinson; c Sally E, William R, Patricia A & John L. Educ: Stanford Univ, BA, 50; El Tigre Eating Club. Polit & Govt Pos: Mem, Inyo Co Rep Cent Comt, Calif, 60-; mem, Bishop Elem Sch Bd, 65-69, pres, 68; mem, Rep State Cent Comt Calif, 67-; chmn, Inyo Co Rep Comt, formerly. Bus & Prof Pos: Self employed, Pinon Book Store, Bishop, Calif, 58-; dir, Inyo-Mono Nat Bank, Bishop, 64- Mil Serv: Entered as Seaman, Navy, 44, released as RM 3/C, 46, after serv in Asian Theatre, 45-46. Mem: Bishop Rotary (pres, 70-71); CofC (treas & mem bd dirs); Bishop Mus & Hist Soc (trustee, 70-, pres, 72-73). Relig: Episcopal; Treas & mem, Bishops Comt. Mailing Add: 666 Sycamore Dr Bishop CA 93514

GARRIGUS, FOREST ORA, JR (R)
Chmn, Deschutes Co Rep Cent Comt, Ore
b Forest Grove, Ore, Jun 12, 30; s Forest Ora Garrigus & Leatha Sohren G; m 1950 to Patsy Ruth Wasson; c Forest O, III & John P. Educ: Univ Ore, 49-50; Linfield Col, BS, 55; Pi Gamma Mu; Pi Kappa Gamma; Delta Upsilon. Polit & Govt Pos: Chmn, Deschutes Co Rep Cent Comt, Ore, 69- Mil Serv: Entered as Seaman, Navy, 48, released as Radarman 2, 52, after serv in USS Bairoko, CVE-115, Pac Theatre, 50-52; Korean Serv Medal; Presidential Unit Citation. Mem: Elks; Mason; Shrine; Bend Jaycees. Honors & Awards: Senator, Jr Chamber-Inter. Relig: Protestant. Mailing Add: 147 Reed Market Rd Bend OR 97701

GARRISON, JAMES B (D)
NC State Sen
Mailing Add: 819 N Sixth St Albemarle NC 28001

GARRISON, MARY JANE (D)
Committeewoman, Benton Co Dem Cent Comt, Ark
b Fort Smith, Ark, Oct 27, 45; d Charles Richard Hobbs & Mary Eagle H; m 1963 to Donald Leo Garrison; c Richard Hobbs, Mark Edward & Martin Cox. Educ: Mellie's Sch of Cosmetology, grad, 63. Polit & Govt Pos: Deleg, Dem Nat Conv, 72; deleg, Ark Dem State Conv, 72 & 74; pres, Benton Co Dem Women, 72-73; committeewoman, Benton Co Dem Cent Comt, 72-; mem, Ark State Credentials Comt, 72-; state dir, Ark Dem Womens Club, currently; mem, Nat Fedn Dem Women, currently; mem exec comt, Ark Dem State Comt, currently. Bus & Prof Pos: Hairdresser, Ark State License, 63-72; exec secy, Benton Co Judge, 74- Mem: Beta Sigma Phi; CofC Community Fund. Honors & Awards: Outstanding Young Woman of Am, Beta Sigma Phi, Xi Iota Chap, 71; Young Career Woman, Bus & Prof Womens Club, 72. Relig: Roman Catholic. Legal Res: Osage AR 72664 Mailing Add: Rte 4 Box 249 Bentonville AR 72712

GARRISON, THOMAS EDMOND (D)
SC State Sen
b Anderson, SC, Jan 21, 22; s Thomas Edmond Garrison & Nettie C McPhail G; m 1955 to Juanita Bartlett; c Carol Gaye, Thomas Edmond, III, James Bartlett, Anita Lee. Educ: Clemson Univ, BS, 42. Hon Degrees: State Farmer Degree of FFA, Clemson Univ, 55. Polit & Govt Pos: SC State Rep, 59-66; SC State Sen, currently. Bus & Prof Pos: Teacher, Vet Agr Class, Boys' High Sch, Anderson, SC, 46-53; dairy farmer, agr teacher, 54-58. Mil Serv: Air Force, pilot, 42-45; 69th Medium Bombardment Squadron, 13th Air Force SPac, 65 missions; Air Medal with 5 Oak Leaf Clusters. Mem: Anderson Soil Conserv Dist Supvrs; SC Asn Soil Conserv Supvrs; Co Farm Bur; SC Young Farmers Asn; Hejaz Shrine. Honors & Awards: Selected Outstanding Young Farmer of the Year, Anderson Jaycees, 57; Anderson Co Man of Year, 68; Distinguished Serv Award, West Piedmont Asn of Conserv Dist, 71; Distinguished Serv Award, Clemson Univ Alumni Asn, 72; Soil Conserv Award, SC Wildlife Fedn, 72. Relig: Baptist; deacon, Welcome Baptist Church, teacher, Men's Bible Class. Mailing Add: Clemson Hwy RD 2 Anderson SC 29621

GARRUBBO, JOSEPH L (D)
NJ State Assemblyman
Mailing Add: State House Trenton NJ 08625

GARSKE, MARIE KETTELFORDER (R)
Mem, DC Rep Cent Comt
b Richmond, Ind, Dec 13, 34; d Paul Edward Kettelforder & Elsie Foley K; m 1960 to Robert Allen Garske; c Peder Andrew, Joanna Ruth & Sarah Louise. Educ: Valparaiso Univ, BA, 57. Polit & Govt Pos: Mem, DC Rep Cent Comt, 72- Bus & Prof Pos: Teacher, Prince Georges Co Sch Syst, Md, 57-58; teacher, DC Pub Sch Syst, 58-61. Relig: Lutheran. Mailing Add: 152 12th St SE Washington DC 20003

GARSOE, WILLIAM J (R)
Maine State Rep
Mailing Add: Cumberland ME 04021

GARST, RICHARD SYLVESTER (D)
Chmn, Atchison Co Dem Comt, Maine
b Watson, Mo, Dec 23, 36; s Orville Sylvester Garst & Belva Carder G; m 1957 to Lois Jean Walker; c Tammy, Garry & Melinda. Educ: Tarkio Col, 55; Northwest Mo Univ, 56; Alpha Lambda. Polit & Govt Pos: Committeeman, Atchison Co Dem Comt, 71-, chmn, 74- Bus & Prof Pos: Farmer, 56- Mem: Rock Port Tel Bd; Atchison Co ASCS Comt (twp chmn); Sonora Lodge 200 (jr warden); Nat Farmers Orgn. Relig: Lutheran. Mailing Add: Rural Watson MO 64496

GARTEN, MEREDITH (PETE) (R)
Mem, Mo State Rep Comt
b Ottawa Co, Okla, Nov 24, 97; s William Garten & Maud Ellen Meador G; m 1926 to Alice Winifred Amery; c Gretchen (Mrs James Tatum) & Beth (Mrs Forest Brown). Educ: Col of Emporia, Kans, BA; Univs Kans & Mo, grad study; Sigma Delta Chi; Pi Kappa Delta. Polit & Govt Pos: Deleg, Mo Const Conv, 43-44; Mo State Rep, 46-48; Mo State Sen, 48-52, mem, Mo State Senate Reapportionment Comn, 59; chmn, Lawrence Co Rep Comt, Mo, formerly; mem, Mo State Rep Comt, 66- Bus & Prof Pos: Ed & owner, Pierce City Leader J, 33-61; pres, Mo Press Asn, 46 & Ozark Press Asn; pres, Mo Rep Ed Asn, 47. Mem: Mason; Shrine; Kiwanis (Lt Gov, Div 10, Mo-Ark Dist). Relig: Congregational. Mailing Add: 314 Elm St Pierce City MO 65723

GARTLAN, JOSEPH V, JR (D)
Va State Sen
Legal Res: VA Mailing Add: 1801 K St NW Washington DC 20006

GARTLEY, MARKHAM LIGON (D)
Secy of State, Maine
b Mayfield, Ky, May 16, 44; s Gerald Arthur Gartley & Minnie Lee Ligon G; m 1975 to Sherrel Elaine Wilcox. Educ: Ga Inst Technol, BS Physics, 66; Scabbard & Blade; Beta Theta Pi. Polit & Govt Pos: Secy of State, Maine, 75- Bus & Prof Pos: Eastern Airlines, Atlanta, Ga, 72-74. Mil Serv: Entered as Ens, Navy, 66, released as Lt, 73, after serv in VF-142, Vietnam Theatre, 68-72; Lt, Naval Res, 74; Air Medal; Navy Commendation; Nat Defense Serv; Navy Unit Commendation; Combat Action Ribbon; Vietnam Serv Medal; Vietnam Campaign Medal; Vietnam Cross of Gallantry. Mem: Am Vets; Am Legion; DAV; Airline Pilots Asn. Legal Res: Beaver Creek Greenville ME 04441 Mailing Add: RFD 2 Winthrop ME 04364

GARTNER, DAVID G (D)
b Des Moines, Iowa, Sept 27, 35; s Carl D Gartner & Mary M Gay G; m 1965 to Suzanne U Schmidt; c James David, John Martin, Pamela Suzanne & Michael Curtis. Educ: State Univ Iowa, BA, 59; Am Univ, Washington Col Law, JD, 72. Polit & Govt Pos: Mem staff, US Rep Carter, Iowa, 59; mem staff, US Rep Harold Johnson, Calif, 60-61; asst to Vice President Hubert Humphrey, 61-68, admin officer, Former Vice President's Transitional Off, 69, exec asst to US Sen Hubert H Humphrey, Minn, 71-73, admin asst, 74- Bus & Prof Pos: Reporter & correspondent, Des Moines Register, 56-59. Mil Serv: Entered as Seaman Recruit, Navy, 54, released as Aviation Electronics Technician Third Class, 56, after serv in Fleet Aircraft Serv Squadron 106, Argentia, Newf, 55-56. Relig: Roman Catholic. Mailing Add: 3420 N George Mason Dr Arlington VA 22207

GARTON, ROBERT DEAN (R)
Ind State Sen
b Chariton, Iowa, Aug 18, 33; s Dr J Glenn Garton & Irene Wright G; m 1955 to Barbara Arlene Hicks; c Bradford Glenn & Brenda Arlene. Educ: Iowa State Univ, BS, 55; Sch Indust & Labor Rels, Cornell Univ, MS, 59; Beta Theta Pi. Polit & Govt Pos: Chmn, Young Rep Club, Bartholomew Co, Ind, 64-65; mem bd dirs, Nat Rep Workshops, 65-67; mem state & nat exec comt, Young Rep Club, 66-67; Rep cand, US Rep, Ninth Dist, Ind, 68; chmn, Civil Rights Comn, 70; Ind State Sen, 70- Bus & Prof Pos: Temporary field organizer, Dist 50, UMW, summer 57; indust rels trainee, Procter & Gamble, Cincinnati, Ohio, 59; col recruiting adminr, Cummins Engine Co, Inc, Columbus, Ind, 59-61; owner, Robert D Garton Assocs, 61- Mil Serv: Entered as 2nd Lt, Marine Corps, 55, released as 1st Lt, 57, after serv as a Spec Serv Officer & Provost Marshall, Supply Schs, Camp Lejeune, NC, 55-57, Res, 57-63; Outstanding Marine Grad, Iowa State Univ. Publ: Author of articles in NY State Labor Report, 59, Personnel Admin, 60 & J Col Placement, 61. Mem: Nat Mgt Asn (lectr); fel Ind Mgt Insts; Rotary Int; Columbia Club; Harrison Lake Country Club. Honors & Awards: Winner, Toastmasters Int Speech Contest, 62; Distinguished Serv Award, Columbus Jr CofC, 68; Named One of Ind Five Outstanding Young Men, Ind Jaycees, 68; One of Outstanding Legislators, State House Press Corps; Named One of 100 Most Promising Legislators in Nation, Eagleton Inst Govt Affairs, Rutgers Univ, 72-73. Relig: Methodist. Legal Res: RR 9 Columbus IN 47201 Mailing Add: PO Box 1111 Columbus IN 47201

GARVEY, JAMES SUTHERLAND (R)
State Committeeman, Tex Rep Party
b Colby, Kans, Dec 30, 22; s Ray Hugh Garvey & Olive White G; m 1947 to Shirley Fox; c Janet Lee (Mrs J J Sawyer); Carol Jo (Mrs W R Sweat) & Richard Fox. Educ: Wichita State Univ, BA, 47; Beta Theta Pi; Scabbard & Blade. Polit & Govt Pos: State committeeman, Tenth Dist, Tex Rep Party, currently, mem, Exec Comt, currently; alt deleg, Rep Nat Conv, 64, deleg, 68; mem, Nat Mkt Adv Comt, US Dept Com, 72; cong cand, 12th Dist, Tex, 74. Bus & Prof Pos: Pres, Jim Garvey Ranches, Inc, Rafter-J Ranch, Inc & JaGee Corp; partner, Garvey Farms Mgt Co; chmn bd, Garvey Elevators Inc & Serv Oil Co; dir, Ft Worth & Denver RR, Ft Worth Nat Bank, Ft Worth Nat Corp, Garvey Properties, Inc, Garvey Ctr, Inc & Garvey, Inc; vpres & trustee, Garvey Tex Found, Inc; trustee, Garvey Found, Inc. Mil Serv: Reserve Corp, 42; Armored Force, 43-46. Mem: Exchange Club of Ft Worth; Mason; Shrine; Newcomen Soc NAm; Longhorn Coun, Boy Scouts. Mailing Add: PO Box 1688 Ft Worth TX 76101

GARVIN, HAROLD WHITMAN (D)
Mem, Calif Dem State Cent Comt
b Salt Lake City, Utah, Jan 21, 24; s Harold Thomas Garvin & Marguerite Whitman G; m 1947 to Frances E Rhoades; c Linda (Mrs Don Benson), Beth Ann (Mrs Jim Berry) & Buzzy. Educ: Occidental Col, BA, 48; Univ Southern Calif, MA Polit Sci, 54. Polit & Govt Pos: Mem cent comt, Co Dem Party, 50-66; Dem cand for State Sen, 66; dist rep for Congressman Glenn Anderson, 69-71; mem, Calif Dem State Cent Comt, 72-; deleg, Dem Nat Mid-Term Conf, 74. Bus & Prof Pos: Prof polit sci, Los Angeles Harbor Col, 61-, chmn faculty senate, 68-71. Mil Serv: Entered as Pvt, Air Force, 43, released as T/Sgt, 45, after serv in 15th Air Force, Italy, 44; Three Air Medals; Distinguished Flying Cross; Seven Battle Stars. Mem: Am Fedn Teachers Local 1521 (exec bd mem); Los Angeles Community Col (mem Cert Employees Coun). Honors & Awards: Dem of the Year, Gardena Dem Club. Relig: Presbyterian. Mailing Add: 3736 Bluff Pl San Pedro CA 90731

GARY, RAYMOND D (D)
b Madill, Okla, Jan 21, 08; s D R Gary & Winnie Edith Romans G; m 1929 to Emma Mae Purser; c Raymond Jerdy & Mona Mae (Mrs Waymire). Educ: Southeastern State Col, Okla. Polit & Govt Pos: Co supt of schs, Marshall Co, Okla, 32-36; Okla State Sen, 41-54, pres Pro Tem, Okla State Senate, 53-54; Gov, Okla, 55-59. Bus & Prof Pos: Pres, Sooner Corp Co, 45-; mem bd dirs, Kansas City Southern RR, 59-, Kansas City Southern Ind RR, 62- & La & Ark RR; pres, Gary Industs, Inc & Gary Cattle Co, 64-; dir, Southwest Baptist Theol Sem, 64-; chmn bd dirs, Western Heritage Life Ins Co. Mem: Rotary; Marshall Co Indust Found (pres); Okla Farmers Union. Relig: Southern Baptist. Mailing Add: Box 40 Madill OK 73446

GARZIA, RALPH A (D)
Pa State Rep
Mailing Add: Capitol Bldg Harrisburg PA 17120

GASKILL, JOHN ROBERT (R)
b Ogden, Utah, Dec 14, 39; s Carl C Gaskill & Arita Bolin G; m 1963 to Susan Griffin; c John Robert, Jr, David Reid, Stephen Paul & William Griffin. Educ: Univ Utah, BS in acct, 61; Beta Theta Pi. Polit & Govt Pos: Chmn, Voting Dist, 64; chmn, Weber City Young Rep, 66; mem, Utah Rep State Cent Comt, 66-68, treas, formerly; deleg, Utah Rep State Conv, 66-70; campaign mgr, US Rep Laurence J Burton, 68, field asst, 69. Bus & Prof Pos: Prin, Gaskill Ins Agency, 63-70; pres, Pioneer Enterprises, 69-70; partner, Gregersen & Co, 70. Mem: Ogden Asn Ins Agts; Beta Theta Pi Alumni Asn; Ogden CofC; Salt Lake CofC. Relig: Latter-day Saint. Mailing Add: 2060 Marwood Dr Salt Lake City UT 84117

GASKILL, PETER C (R)
NH State Rep
Mailing Add: Box 398 Londonderry NH 03053

GASPARD, MARCUS STUART (D)
Wash State Rep
b Tacoma, Wash, Apr 19, 48; s Gordon Stuart Gaspard & Joanne Johnston G; m 1973 to Jo Anne Crouch. Educ: Univ Ore, BBA, 70; Univ Puget Sound Law Sch, 72-; Sigma Phi Epsilon. Polit & Govt Pos: Admin asst & research analyst, Senate Com & Regulatory Agencies Comt & Legis Interim Comt on Banking, Ins & Utility Regulation, 71-72; Wash State Rep, 73- Mem: Wash State Pub Employees' Union. Relig: Protestant. Legal Res: 728 Second St NW Puyallup WA 98371 Mailing Add: PO Box 295 Puyallup WA 98371

GASPER, ALTON JOSEPH (DFL)
b New Orleans, La, Mar 4, 44; s Felix Henry Gasper & Isabella Leufroy G; m 1966 to Consuella Paulette Steuart; c Nathaniel Patrick & Jennifer Leah. Educ: St Thomas Col, BS, Chem, 66; mem, Young Dem-Farmer-Labor Club; Chem Club. Polit & Govt Pos: First vchmn, 35th Dist Dem-Farmer-Labor Party, Minn, 70-71, chmn, 71-72; chmn, 61st Sen Dist Dem-Farmer-Labor Party, formerly. Bus & Prof Pos: Research chemist, ADM, Minneapolis, 66-68; research chemist, Minn Mining & Mfg Co, St Paul, 68- Mem: Am Chem Soc; NAACP. Honors & Awards: High Sch Valedictorian; Contact Award, Cath Youth. Relig: Catholic. Mailing Add: 4817 Portland Ave S Minneapolis MN 55417

GASQUE, J RALPH (D)
SC State Sen
b Mullins, SC, May 16, 13; s Cordie A Gasque & Jennie Price G. Educ: Nat Univ Law Sch, LLB, 41; LLM, 42. Polit & Govt Pos: US claims examr, US Govt Gen Acct Off; spec agt, US Internal Revenue Serv; chief, Mil Personnel Sect, Provost Marshall Gen Sch; prin custodian officer, DC Penal Inst; SC State Rep, 45-48; SC State Sen, 49-52, 56-62 & 64-; deleg, Dem Nat Conv, 60 & 68; chmn, Marion Co Dem Party, 71- Mem: WOW; Mason; Eastern Star; Sigma Delta Kappa; Shrine. Mailing Add: Box 127 Marion SC 29571

GASQUE, S NORWOOD (D)
SC State Rep
Mailing Add: Latta SC 29565

GAST, HARRY T, JR (R)
Mich State Rep
b St Joseph, Mich, Sept 20, 20; s Harry T Gast, Sr & Fern Shearer G; m 1944 to Vera Jean Warren; c Barbara (Mrs Rob Moray), Linda & Dennis. Educ: Mich State Univ, 39-41. Polit & Govt Pos: Treas, Lincoln Twp, Mich, 46-64, supvr, 65-70; co supvr, Berrien Co, 65-69; mem, Berrien Co Bd Pub Works & Berrien Co Bd Health, 65-70; Mich State Rep, 43rd Dist, 71- Mem: Lions; Farm Bur; hon Jaycee; Mich United Conserv Clubs. Relig: Baptist. Legal Res: 5165 Lincoln Ave St Joseph MI 49085 Mailing Add: PO Box 43 Capitol Bldg Lansing MI 48901

GASTL, EUGENE FRANCIS (D)
Kans State Rep
b Shawnee, Kans, Apr 28, 32; s Bert Joseph Gastl & Bessie Bell G; m 1959 to Deanna J Cordon; c Philip E, Catherine L, David Bruce & Brenda Maria. Educ: Kansas City Jr Col, 50-52; Univ Kans, 52-56, AB & LLB; Delta Theta Phi. Polit & Govt Pos: Committeeman, Johnson Co Dem Cent Comt, Kans, 56-70; Kans State Rep, 11th Dist, 61-65; Kans State Sen, 14th Dist, Johnson Co, 65-69; Kans State Rep, 18th Dist, 71- Mil Serv: Entered as Pvt, Army, 56, released as Specialist 3/C, 58. Mem: Am, Kans & Johnson Co Bar Asns; CofC; Univ Kans Alumni Asn. Relig: Methodist. Mailing Add: 6117 Ballentine Shawnee KS 66203

GASTON, ROBERT CECIL, JR (R)
Tex State Rep
b San Francisco, Calif; s Robert Cecil Gaston, Sr & Lottie Maurine Newsom G; m to Jeanne Clements, div; c Robert Cecil, III & Elisa Paige. Educ: Univ Houston, BS, 51; Southern Methodist Univ; KA; Blue Key; Frontiersmen; Red Masque Players; Radio & Opera Guild. Polit & Govt Pos: Radio-TV-motion picture dir, Nat Rep Campaign Comt, Washington, DC, 64-70, Tex State Rep, 75- Bus & Prof Pos: Pres, Gaston & Assoc; vpres, Merrell & Assoc; news anchorman, WFAA-TV, Dallas, Tex; correspondent, NBC, Washington Bur. Mil Serv: Entered as Pvt, Marine Corps, 45, released as Pfc, 46; Pfc, Air Force, 51, released as 1st Lt, 54. Relig: Methodist. Mailing Add: PO Box 18164 Dallas TX 75218

GATES, MARK THOMAS (R)
b Santa Monica, Calif, Jan 13, 37; s Mark T Gates & Margaret Woods G; m 1960 to Elizabeth Wilson; c Mark T, III, Stephanie & Whitney Elizabeth. Educ: Dartmouth Col, BA, 59; Stanford Univ, LLB, 62; Phi Delta Phi; Beta Theta Pi. Polit & Govt Pos: Los Angeles Co chmn, Reelect of Gov Ronald Reagan, 70; mem, Calif Bd Educ, 71-75; deleg, Rep Nat Conv, 72. Bus & Prof Pos: Assoc, Walker, Wright, Tyler & Ward, 61-64; partner, Dietsch, Gates, Morris & Merrell, 64- Mem: Calif & Am Bar Asns; Beach Club; Riviera Tennis Club; Calif Club. Relig: Methodist. Legal Res: 340 N Cliffwood Los Angeles CA 90049 Mailing Add: 800 Wilshire Blvd Los Angeles CA 90017

GATES, REBECCA TWILLEY (D)
Dem Nat Committeewoman, Del
b Dover, Del, Nov 16, 32; d Edgar Willard Buchanan & Madaline Elliot B; second m 1973 to Joseph Emmanuel Gates, II; c Stephanie, Jeffrey, Linda & Edgar Twilley. Educ: Meredith Col, 50-52; Boston Univ, 52-53; Univ Del, 53-54. Polit & Govt Pos: Human rels comnr, Del, 69-; Dem Nat Committeewoman, Del, 72-; deleg, Dem Nat Mid-Term Conf, 74; legis liaison, Dept Health & Social Serv, Del, 75- Bus & Prof Pos: Pres, Atlantic Develop, Inc, 71- Mem: Geriatric Serv of Del, Inc; Kent Co NOW; Del Women's Polit Caucus. Relig: Episcopal & Am Baptist. Mailing Add: 25 Woodburn Circle Dover DE 19901

GATES, ROBERT E (R)
b Columbia City, Ind, Nov 19, 20; s Ralph F Gates & Helene Edwards G; m 1948 to Harriett K Brown; c Marjorie B, Anne E & Mary Ellen. Educ: Ind Univ, BS, 42, JD, 48; Phi Eta Sigma; Sigma Alpha Epsilon; Phi Delta Phi. Polit & Govt Pos: Chmn, Whitley Co Rep Party, Ind, formerly; chmn, Fourth Dist Rep Party, 61-69; Rep cand gov, 64; deleg, Rep Nat Conv, 68. Mil Serv: Entered as Ens, Navy, 42, released as Lt, 46, after serv in USS NMex, Pac Theatre, 43-45; Eight Battle Stars. Mem: Columbia Club; Ind Soc Chicago; Mason; Scottish Rite; Shrine. Relig: Presbyterian. Legal Res: 701 W Park Dr Columbia City IN 46725 Mailing Add: Gates Gates & McNagny Columbia City IN 46725

GATES, THOMAS S (R)
b Germantown, Pa, Apr 10, 06; s Thomas Sovereign Gates & Marie Rogers G; m 1928 to Millicent Anne Brengle; c Millicent Anne, Patricia S, Thomas S (deceased) & Katharine Curtin. Educ: Univ of Pa, AB, 28; Phi Beta Kappa. Honors & Awards: LLD, Univ of Pa, Yale Univ, Columbia Univ & Univ of Toledo. Polit & Govt Pos: Under Secy of Navy, 53-57; Secy of Navy, 57-59; Dep Secy of Defense, 59; Secy of Defense, 59-61. Bus & Prof Pos: Assoc, Drexel & Co, Philadelphia, Pa, 28, partner, 40-53; dir, Gen Elec Co, Scott Paper Co, Campbell Soup Co, Inc Co NAm, Smith Kline & French Lab & Cities Serv Co; life trustee, Univ of Pa; chmn exec comt, Morgan Guaranty Trust Co, 61-62, pres & dir, 62-65, chmn

bd & chief exec officer, 65-68, chmn exec comt, formerly, dir, 71-; dir, Philadelphia Contributionship for the Ins of Houses from Loss by Fire, 72- Mil Serv: Lt Comdr, Naval Res, 42-45; served Overseas. Mem: Acad Polit Sci; Coun Foreign Rels; Navy League; Colonial Soc of Pa; Philadelphia Racquet, Metrop Links Clubs; Econ Club of New York. Legal Res: Mill Race Farm Devon PA 19333 Mailing Add: 23 Wall St New York NY 10015

GATHINGS, EZEKIEL CANDLER (D)
b Prairie, Miss, Nov 10, 03; s Melville Williamson Gathings & Virgie Eva Garner G; m 1939 to Tolise Kirkpatrick; c Tolise Kirkpatrick & Joseph Royston. Educ: Univ Ala, 23-26; Univ Ark, LLB, 29; Blue Key; Phi Alpha Delta; Pi Kappa Alpha. Polit & Govt Pos: Mem zoning comn, West Memphis, Ark & Crittenden Co Bd Elec Comnrs, formerly; Ark State Sen, 35-39; US Rep, Ark, 39-69. Bus & Prof Pos: Attorney-at-law. Mem: Am Judicature Soc; Ark Trial Lawyers Asn; Mason (32 degree); Shrine; Eastern Star. Relig: Baptist. Legal Res: 421 W Barton West Memphis AR 72301 Mailing Add: Holiday Plaza Mall West Memphis AR 72301

GATHRIGHT, MORRELL (D)
Ark State Sen
Mailing Add: PO Box 5268 Pine Bluff AR 71601

GAUDETTE, DONALD ROGER (D)
Mass State Rep
b Acushnet, Mass, Dec 16, 26; s Charles Ovide Gaudette, Sr & Aurore M R Gregoire G; m 1948 to Theresa Annette Castonguay; c Janice Marie, Donald R, Jr, Rachel J & Robert C. Educ: New Bedford Voc High Sch, 4 years. Polit & Govt Pos: City coun, New Bedford, Mass, 62-67 & city coun pres, 65; Mass State Rep, Boston, 67- Mem: Nat Soc State Legislators; Eagles; KofC (4 degree); Cath Order of Foresters; Mass Legislators Asn. Relig: Catholic. Mailing Add: 1125 Pequot St New Bedford MA 02745

GAUDIN, EDWARD CLARK (R)
La State Rep
b New Roads, La, Dec 26, 31; s Alton F Gaudin & Vida Swindler G; m 1959 to Marianne Hurst; c Allison, Dana & Todd. Educ: La State Univ, BS, 52, JD, 58; Sigma Nu. Polit & Govt Pos: La State Rep, East Baton Rouge Parish, 67-68; alt deleg, Rep Nat Conv, 68; chmn polit action coun, East Baton Rouge Rep Party, 69-; La State Rep, 75- Bus & Prof Pos: Partner, Smith & Gaudin, Attorneys, 61- Mil Serv: Entered as 2nd Lt, Army, 52, released as 1st Lt, 54, after serv in 196th Field Artil Bn; Korean Theatre, 53-54; Res, Judge Adv Gen Corps, 54-68, Maj. Mem: La State Bar Asn; Kiwanis; KofC; Alhambra; Pelican Pioneers. Relig: Roman Catholic. Mailing Add: 3165 Murphy Dr Baton Rouge LA 70809

GAUDINEER, LEE H (D)
b Des Moines, Iowa; married; c four. Educ: Grinnell Col, BA; Univ Mo, LLM; Drake Univ Sch Law, JD. Polit & Govt Pos: Mem staff, Legis Research Bur, Iowa; asst city attorney; asst co attorney; Iowa State Rep, formerly; Iowa State Sen, 67-73; deleg, Dem Nat Conv, 72. Bus & Prof Pos: Lawyer. Mil Serv: Parachutist, Korean War, 3 years. Mailing Add: 312 Hubbell Bldg Des Moines IA 50309

GAULTIER, GERALD DOUGLAS (R)
Chmn, Kalkaska Co Rep Comt, Mich
b South Boardman, Mich, Apr 11, 34; s P Vere Gaultier & Eleanor Johnson G; m 1954 to Elaine Marie Brockway; c Douglas, Shaleen, Toni & Melanie. Educ: Mich Col Mining & Technol, 1 year; Ind Technol Col, 6 months; Northwestern Col, 6 months; col newspaper cartoon ed, Lode, Mich Col Mining & Technol. Polit & Govt Pos: Treas, Bd Educ, South Boardman, Mich, 58-59, secy, 67-73; mem, Kalkaska Co Rep Exec Comt; chmn, Kalkaska Co Rep Comt, 68-, treas, 68; mem, Regional Planning Comn, Kalkaska Co, 72-; mem, Kalkaska Co Zoning Bd, 73-; co comnr, Dist Six, Kalkaska Co, 73- Bus & Prof Pos: Owner, Boardman Valley Construction Co, 65- Mil Serv: Entered as Airman, Air Force, 54, released as S/Sgt, 58, after serv in 98th Bomb Wing 818th Air Div, Strategic Air Command, 54-58; S/Sgt, Res, 58-; Nat Defense Serv Medal; Good Conduct Medal; Outstanding Crew Chief for 98th Bombardment Wing. Mem: Nat Rifle Asn Am; Nat Honor Soc. Relig: Methodist. Mailing Add: Box 93 Mill St South Boardman MI 49680

GAUTHIER, LORENZO P (D)
NH State Rep
Mailing Add: 22 Laval St Manchester NH 03102

GAUTHIER, ROLAND A (D)
Maine State Rep
Mailing Add: 67 North Ave Sanford ME 04073

GAUTIER, AUGUSTO R (D)
Mem, PR Dem Party Comt
b Santurce, PR, Sept 5, 32; s Aurelio R Gautier & Carmen Luisa Mayoral G; m 1955 to Carmen Margarita Lloveras; c Augusto, Carmen Margarita, Carlos & Luis. Educ: Rensselaer Polytech Inst, BArch, 55; Tau Beta Pi; Sigma Xi; Scarab; Am Inst Architects Sch Medal; Pi Kappa Phi; Phi Eta Mu. Polit & Govt Pos: Mem, PR Dem Party Comt, 63-, sgt at arms, currently; mem, Bd of Exam of Engrs, Architects & Surveyors of PR, 63-72, pres, 65-67, 69-72; alt deleg, Dem Nat Conv, 64, deleg, 68; deleg, Popular Dem Party of PR Conv, 64 & 68; pres, Citizens Comt for Humphrey in PR, 68. Mil Serv: Entered as 2nd Lt, Army, 55, released as 1st Lt, 57, after serv in 84th Bn, Conarc; Lt Col, Mil Intel, Army Res, 73. Mem: Engrs, Architects & Surveyors Asn of PR; Inst of Architects of PR; Am Inst of Architects; Pan-Am Fedn of Architects Asn (mem, hon coun, 70-); Lions. Relig: Catholic. Legal Res: DA4 FP Hastings St Garden Hills Bayamon PR 00619 Mailing Add: Box 11591 Santurce PR 00910

GAY, CARLUS DELMAS, JR (D)
b Dublin, Ga, Oct 21, 38; s Carlus D Gay, Sr & Georgia Barrs G; m 1961 to Bertie Watson; c Tammy Delaine, Terrie Denise & Carlus D (Tracy). Educ: Ga Mil Col, 59-60; Univ Ga, 60-61. Polit & Govt Pos: Deleg, Ga State Dem Party, 71; mem, Ga State Dem Exec Comt, formerly. Bus & Prof Pos: Trooper, Dept of Pub Safety, 61-66; owner, Dairy Queens & Braziers, 64-69; pres, G&S Realty Co, currently. Mil Serv: Entered as Airman E-2, Navy, 56, released as E-4, 59, after serv in Naval Security, NAS Brunswick, Ga; Good Conduct Medal. Mem: Jaycees; Elks; Boy Scouts of Am (mem exec comt). Honors & Awards: Outstanding Jaycee, 64. Relig: Baptist. Legal Res: Lee St Rd Americus GA 31709 Mailing Add: PO Box 1399 Americus GA 31709

GAY, CLAY (R)
Ky State Rep
Mailing Add: Box 43 Hyden KY 41749

GAY, JAMES HOYT (R)
Chmn, Chambers Co Rep Comt, Ala
b Lanett, Ala, June 1, 02; s Henry Mitchell Gay & Mattie J Autrey M; m 1921 to Maude Avery; c Gwendolyn (Mrs Rowe Staples), Ernestine (Mrs Jesse Shaddix) & Betty (Mrs Heard). Educ: Lanett High Sch. Polit & Govt Pos: Secy, Chambers Co Rep Comt, Ala, 27-62, chmn, 62-; alt deleg, Rep Nat Conv, 56 & 68; mem, Ala Rep State Exec Comt, 63. Bus & Prof Pos: Shipping clerk, cotton dept, Lanett Mill Div, West Point-Pepperell, Inc, 20-26, mgr cotton dept, 26-55, supvr cotton & waste dept, 55-65, retired. Mem: Moose; WOW; Valley Hexagon Club; Valley Baseball Club; Ga-Ala League. Honors & Awards: Silver Beaver Award, Boy Scouts. Relig: Methodist. Legal Res: 409 S Eighth Ave Lanett AL 36863 Mailing Add: PO Box 271 Lanett AL 36863

GAYDOS, JOSEPH MATTHEW (D)
US Rep, Pa
b Braddock, Pa, July 3, 26; s John Gaydos & Helen Magella G; m 1955 to Alice Ann Gray; c Joseph, Jr, Kelly, Kathleen, Coleen & Tammy. Educ: Duquesne Univ, 46-48; Notre Dame Univ, LLB, 51. Polit & Govt Pos: Asst attorney gen, Commonwealth, Pa, 3 years; asst solicitor, Allegheny Co, 13 years; Pa State Sen, 45th Dist, 1 term; US Rep, Pa, 20th Dist, presently; deleg, Dem Nat Mid-Term Conf, 74. Bus & Prof Pos: Attorney at law. Mil Serv: Entered as Seaman 2/C, Navy, 44, released as S/M-3/C, after serv in Naval Res Amphibious Forces, SPac, Philippines & Far East, 44-46; Two Battle Stars. Mem: Allegheny Co & Pa Bar Asns; all vet orgn. Honors & Awards: Man of the Year Award, Allegheny Co Chap CWV. Relig: Catholic. Mailing Add: 3000 Valley Rd McKeesport PA 15132

GAYLORD, MARY FLETCHER (R)
Finance Chmn, Rep Nat Fedn Women
b Detroit, Mich, June 2, 15; d Harold Fletcher Wardwell (deceased) & Helen Russel W; m to Charles Gaylord; c Edith (Mrs Harrison), Gretchen (Mrs Bering), Henry, III & Helen (Mrs Evans, deceased). Educ: Bennington Col, BS, 36; Simmons Sch Social Work, MA, 43. Polit & Govt Pos: Precinct committeewoman, Denver Co Cent Comt, 48-52, dist capt, 50-54; mem, Denver Community Rels Comn, 48-62; treas, Colo Fedn Rep Women, 52-54; state finance vchmn, Colo Rep State Cent Comt, 54-56; Rep Nat Committeewoman, Colo, 56-68; mem, Denver Libr Comn, 59-65; mem, Nat Adv Ment Health Coun, 69-; mem, Colo Med Adv Comt & Bd Adult Educ; coun, 69-; finance chmn, Rep Nat Fedn Women, 71- Mem: Winter Park Recreational Asn (mem bd, 50-); Ment Health Asn Colo; Vis Nurse Asn; League of Women Voters; Denver Art Mus, Symphony Soc & Libr Found. Relig: Episcopal. Mailing Add: 410 Marion St Denver CO 80218

GAZTAMBIDE, MARIO FRANCISCO, JR (NEW PROGRESSIVE PARTY)
b San Juan, Puerto Rico, Oct 21, 45; s Mario F Gaztambide-Arrillaga & Miriam Aneses G; m 1967 to Lourdes Crusellas; c Mario F, III. Educ: Univ PR, BA in polit sci, magna cum laude, 67, BA law, 70. Polit & Govt Pos: Spec asst to Gov L A Ferre, PR, 70-71; vpres in charge of youth, PR Rep Party, 71-; alt deleg, Rep Nat Conv, 72. Bus & Prof Pos: Pres, Gaztambide Bros, 68-; lawyer, Mario F Gaztambide Law Off, 71- Mem: Global Health Planning Bd; Univ PR Pres Adv Coun; Nu Sigma Beta (vchancellor, 66-67). Honors & Awards: Man of Year, Nu Sigma Beta, 67, Distinguished Serv Award, 70. Relig: Catholic. Legal Res: 1009 Windsor Towers Rio Piedras PR 00923 Mailing Add: Box 1077 Hato Rey PR 00919

GAZZARA, ANTHONY V (D)
NY State Assemblyman
Mailing Add: 31-11 28th Rd Long Island City NY 11105

GEAKE, RAYMOND ROBERT (R)
Mich State Rep
b Detroit, Mich, Oct 26, 36; s Harry Nevill Geake & Phyllis R Fox G; m 1962 to Carol Lynne Rens; c Roger Rens & Tamara Lynne. Educ: Univ Mich, Ann Arbor, BS, 58, MA, 59, PhD, 63. Polit & Govt Pos: Trustee-at-lg, Schoolcraft Community Col Bd, Livonia, Mich, 69-72; Mich State Rep, 73- Bus & Prof Pos: Sch psychologist & coordr child develop research, Henry Ford Mus & Greenfield Village, 62-66; dir psychol, Plymouth State Home & Training Sch, Mich Dept Ment Health, 66-69; psychologist, pvt practice, 69- Publ: Co-ed, The inter-institutional seminar in child development, Edison Inst, annually, 61-66; co-auth, Visual tracking, a self-instructional workbook for perceptual skills in reading, Ann Arbor Publ, 62 & Effects of early institutionalization on growth and development of young children with Down's syndrome, Mich Med, 10/68. Mem: Life mem Nat Educ Asn; Mich Psychol Asn; Mich Asn Sch Psychologists; Rotary Int. Relig: Presbyterian. Mailing Add: 48525 W Eight Mile Rd Northville MI 48167

GEARTY, EDWARD JOSEPH (DFL)
Minn State Sen
b Minneapolis, Minn, Mar 17, 23; s John Edward Gearty & Elletta Newton G; m 1965 to Lorraine Margaret Breher; c Ann Theresa. Educ: Col of St Thomas, BA, 52; Georgetown Univ Law Sch, LLB, 55. Polit & Govt Pos: Park comnr, Minneapolis Park Bd, 59; Minn State Rep, 63-70; Minn State Sen, 71- Bus & Prof Pos: Attorney, Minneapolis Park Bd, 63. Mil Serv: Entered as A/S, Navy, 42, released as AMM 3/C, 48. Relig: Catholic. Legal Res: 3810 Xerxes Ave N Minneapolis MN 55412 Mailing Add: 1102 W Broadway Minneapolis MN 55411

GEBHARDT, JOSEPH DAVIS (D)
b New York, NY, July 14, 45; s Henry Gebhardt & Mary Davis G; m 1971 to Susan Karpel; c Daniel Karpel. Educ: Cornell Col, BA, magna cum laude, 68; Harvard Law Sch, JD, 71; Phi Beta Kappa; Beta Omicrom. Polit & Govt Pos: Ed & summer intern, Staff, Comn on Party Structure & Deleg Selection, Nat Dem Party, 69; pres, Harvard Law Sch Dem Club, 69-70; staff counsel, Nat Voter Regis Drive, Dem Nat Comt, 72, dir, Legal & Ballot Security Prog, 72; dir, McGovern for President Campaign, 72; chairperson, Sub-Task Force on Campaign Reform, Montgomery Co Dem Cent Comn, 73-74; bd mem, Western Suburban Dem Club, Montgomery Co, Md, 73-; precinct vchmn, Montgomery Co Dem Party, 75-; deleg, Dem Nat Mid-Term Conf, 74. Bus & Prof Pos: Citizen participation rep, Dept Housing & Urban Develop, Chicago Region, 70; counsel, Ctr for Polit Reform, Washington, DC, 72; staff attorney, Ctr on Corp Responsibility, 73-; public interest lawyer, 73- Publ: Co-auth, The Offenses of Richard M Nixon: A Guide to His Impeachable Crimes, Quadrangle, 73; auth, The politics & law of Democratic party reform, Harvard Law Sch Bull, 6/73; auth, The

machinery broke down: errors, confusion mark the voting process, Viewpoint, 12/72. Mem: Am & DC Bar Asns. Honors & Awards: Runner Up, Scholar-Athlete Trophy, Assoc Col Midwest, 68. Relig: Catholic. Mailing Add: 5802 Namakagan Rd Bethesda MD 20016

GEE, BILL F (R)
Chmn, Marshall Co Rep Comt, Ind
b Elnora, Ind, Mar 23, 34; s William McKinley Gee & Callie Bales G; m 1956 to Mary Lynn Johnson; c Elizabeth Bales. Educ: Vanderbilt Univ, BA, 56; Alpha Tau Omega. Polit & Govt Pos: Mem, Daviess Co Young Rep, Ind, 58-62; mem, Marshall Co Young Rep, 62-; chmn, Marshall Co Rep Comt, 66-; mgr, Marshall Co Auto License Bur, 69- Bus & Prof Pos: Mgr for Ind, Harper & Row, Publishers, 62-; pres, Ind Prof Bookmen of Am, 67-68. Mil Serv: Entered as 2nd Lt, Marines, 56, released as 1st Lt, 58. Mem: Elks; Mason; Scottish Rite; Kiwanis. Relig: Methodist. Mailing Add: 222 E Shalley Dr Plymouth IN 46563

GEELEN, LESLIE PATRICK (R)
Chmn, Cameron Co Rep Party, Pa
b Emporium, Pa, July 21, 22; s Patrick Dewey Geelen & Jennie Skillman G; div; c Patricia (Mrs Kim E Kelly) & Jean Marie. Educ: High sch grad. Polit & Govt Pos: Tax collector, Shippen Twp, Pa, 56-60; comnr, Cameron Co, 60-72; chmn, Cameron Co Rep Party, 73- Bus & Prof Pos: Receiving tube plant supt, GTE Sylvania Inc, 64-70, traffic supvr, 70- Mil Serv: Entered as Pvt, Army, 42, released as 1st Lt, after serv in 351st Inf, 88th Div, ETO, 43-45; Purple Heart; Combat Inf Badge; Bronze Star; Silver Star; Field Comn. Mem: Am Legion; VFW; Emporium Country Club (pres bd dirs); Guy & Mary Felt Nursing Home (vpres bd dirs). Relig: Protestant. Mailing Add: RD 2 Box 165 Emporium PA 15834

GEERLINGS, EDGAR ALLEN (R)
Mich State Rep
b Zeeland, Mich, Apr 24, 37; s Alvin R Geerlings & Dorothy Otting G; m 1959 to Mary Jane Watterworth; c Derek Edgar. Educ: Cent Mich Univ, BS, 59 & MA, 61; Delta Sigma Phi. Polit & Govt Pos: Mich State Rep, 97th Dist, 67- Mem: Mich Educ Asn; Muskegon Co Educ Asn; Mich Coun Teachers of Math; Mich High Sch Athletic Asn; UAW Local 480. Relig: Reformed Church of Am. Mailing Add: 1280 Edinborough Dr Muskegon MI 49441

GEESEY, EUGENE RONALD (R)
Pa State Rep
b Dallastown, Pa, Dec 1, 31; s Luther Elwood Geesey & Rose Jennings G; m 1954 to Joanne Elizabeth Tarbert; c Cynthia, David, Ann, Beth, Sue & Joe. Educ: Lebanon Valley Col, BS in Econ, 56. Polit & Govt Pos: Auditor, Fairview Twp, Pa, 65-69; Pa State Rep, 92nd Dist, 69- Bus & Prof Pos: Pres, Cent Pa Ins Asn, 66. Mil Serv: Entered as Pvt, Army, 51, released as Cpl, 53. Mem: Lions. Relig: Protestant. Mailing Add: Box 466 RD 1 New Cumberland PA 17070

GEESEY, ORIN G (R)
Wyo State Rep
Mailing Add: 1130 Third W Ave Kemmerer WY 83101

GEHL, CAROLYN GILMORE (D)
Mem, Ga State Dem Exec Comt
b Pensacola, Fla; d Quigley G Gilmore & Harriet Saunders G; m 1966 to John M Gehl; c Thomas & Andrew. Educ: St Mary's Dominican, BA, 59; Fla State Univ, MS. Polit & Govt Pos: Mem, Ga State Dem Exec Comt, 75- Bus & Prof Pos: High sch hist teacher, 59-67; co-ed, Flat Shoals Alliance Newsletter, 73- Mem: Flat Shoals Alliance (commun coordr, 73-); Flat Shoals PTA (cult arts chmn, 74-). Relig: Catholic. Mailing Add: 2884 Norgate Ct Decatur GA 30034

GEHRES, WALTER ARNOLD (D)
Secy, Van Wert Co Dem Cent Comt, Ohio
b Wren, Ohio, Apr 20, 20; s Walter Gehres & Lorena Giessler G; m 1953 to Helen L Roop. Educ: Wren High Sch, Ohio, grad, 38. Polit & Govt Pos: Dem precinct committeeman, Van Wert Co, Ohio, 55-; secy, Van Wert Co Dem Cent Comt, 68- Bus & Prof Pos: Traveling speciality salesman, 5 years; dept mgr, Montgomery Wards, Van Wert, 54-; Genealogist, currently. Mem: Elks; Van Wert Co Men's Dem Club; Van Wert Co Hist Soc. Relig: Methodist; Sunday sch teacher & church historian chmn. Mailing Add: 1026 Elm St Van Wert OH 45891

GEHRETT, VIRGINIA DALTON (R)
Committeewoman, Powell Co Rep Cent Comt, Mont
b Mansfield, Wash, Oct 20, 19; d Stanley Charles Dalton & Anna Graybeal D; m 1946 to Joseph Owen Gehrett; c Virginia Anne, Joseph Owen, Jr & George Dalton. Educ: Univ Wash, 1 year, Univ Va, 6 months; Wilson Teachers Col, BS, 41; George Washington Univ, LLB & JD, 46. Polit & Govt Pos: Chmn, Powell Co Rep Women's Club, Mont, 64-66; chmn, Powell Co Rep Cent Comt, 66-68, committeewoman, 68-; chmn nominating comt, Rep State Cent Comt, 67. Bus & Prof Pos: Teacher, Washington, DC Pub Schs, 42-44; co-publisher & co-ed, The Silver State Post, 63- Mem: PEO; Mont Women's Club. Relig: Presbyterian. Mailing Add: 830 Missouri Deer Lodge MT 59722

GEHRIG, JAMES JOSEPH (D)
b Milwaukee, Wis, Nov 7, 21; s Joseph Phillip Gehrig & Theresa Neuser G; m 1949 to Susan Helen Kleinz; c James Joseph, Jr, Teresa Sue, Leigh Michelle, Renee Lorraine, William Lee, Benjamin Phillip, Helen Kleinz & Paul Neuser. Educ: Colo State Univ, 43-44; Univ Wis, BS, 49, Grad Sch, 50; Univ Del, 51-53; Univ Calif, Los Angeles, 55-59; Pi Mu Epsilon. Polit & Govt Pos: Legis asst, then spec asst to US Sen Stuart Symington, 61-65; staff dir & chief clerk, Senate Comt on Aeronaut & Space Sci, Washington, DC, 65-73, mem prof staff, 73- Bus & Prof Pos: Chief artil effectiveness group, Weapons Systs Lab, Ballistic Research Lab, Aberdeen, Md, 50-54; chief strategic systs group, Systs Anal, Northrop Corp, Hawthorne, Calif, 54-61. Mil Serv: Entered as Pvt, Army, 43, released as 1st Lt, 46, after serv in 24th Inf Div, Philippines & Japan, 44-46; Asiatic Pac Campaign Medal; Combat Infantryman's Badge; Bronze Star Medal for Valor. Mem: Opers Research Soc; Am Asn Math; Am Asn Adv Sci; Am Inst Aeronaut & Astronaut. Relig: Roman Catholic. Legal Res: 1118 Gatewood Dr Alexandria VA 22307 Mailing Add: Rm 231 Russell Senate Off Bldg Washington DC 20510

GEIB, G HARRIET (R)
Deleg-at-Large, Minn Rep State Exec Comt
b Moorhead, Minn, Aug 3, 13; d Olaf Jenson Hagen & Moselle Edna Weld H; m 1939 to Marvin Jacob Geib; c Peter Jacob. Educ: Moorhead State Col, Minn, 31-32; Concordia Col, 32-33 & 34-35; Univ Minn, 33-34 & 35-38; Gamma Phi Beta. Polit & Govt Pos: Rep precinct secy, Moorhead, Minn, 52-56; vchairwoman, Clay Co Rep Party, 58-61, chairwoman, 61-63; appointee, Minn Rep State Exec Comt, 64, deleg-at-lg, 69-; alt deleg, Rep Nat Conv, 64, deleg, 68; chairwoman, Seventh Cong Dist Rep Party, Minn, 65-69. Bus & Prof Pos: Med technologist, Fargo Clin, NDak, 38-39 & 42. Mem: Registry of Med Technologists, Am Soc of Med Pathologists; PEO; YWCA; Sigma Alpha Iota (Patroness); Fedn Rep Women. Relig: Protestant. Mailing Add: 1219 Fourth Ave S Moorhead MN 56560

GEIER, ROBERT ALBERT (R)
b Pittsburgh, Pa, Aug 28, 12; s Bernard Adam Geier & Laurelda Helbling G; m 1942 to Phyllis May White; c Robert W, Corry Leland & Kelly James. Educ: Univ Pittsburgh, 31-33 & 37; Santa Ana & Orange Coast Cols, 40's; Am Univ, 54; LaSalle Exten Univ, LLB, 72. Polit & Govt Pos: Aeronaut inspector, Civil Aeronaut Admin, 43-46; admin asst to US Rep James B Utt, Calif, 53-57 & 67-70, field rep, 58-63; Rep nominee, US Cong, 34th Dist, Calif, 62 & 64; admin asst to US Rep John G Schmitz, Calif, 70-72; admin asst to US Rep Victor V Veysey, Calif, 72-74. Bus & Prof Pos: Owner garage & serv sta, Avalon, Pittsburgh, Pa, 34-35; plant supt, Citrus Juice & Flavor, Santa Ana, Calif, 35-39; chief pilot & instr, Martin Sch Aviation, 40-43, mgr & chief pilot, 46-50; owner pub rels agency, Santa Ana, 50-52, Santa Ana & Orange, 58-66. Mil Serv: Sgt, ROTC. Publ: Various aviation articles in Western Aviation & other periodicals, 40's; Weekly column, Sky-Bobbing, Santa Ana Register, 46-66. Mem: Pilot orgns. Relig: Catholic. Mailing Add: 785 Calle Punta Thousand Oaks CA 91360

GEIGER, RICHARD STUART (D)
Tex State Rep
b Dallas, Tex, Feb 21, 36; s Gilbert A Geiger & Letitia Lewis Wells G; m 1954 to Phyllis Scott McGee; c Richard Scott, Angela Gaye, Margaret Louise, Phyllis Claire & Amy Stuart. Educ: Tex A&M Univ, 53-54; Southern Methodist Univ, 54-58, LLB, 62; Phi Delta Phi. Polit & Govt Pos: Tex State Rep, Dist 33-G, Dallas, 73- Bus & Prof Pos: Assoc attorney, Spafford, Freedman, Hamlin, Gay & Whitham, Dallas, 62-69; attorney, Dallas, 69- Mem: Am & Dallas Bar Asns; Int Platform Asn; Oak Cliff CofC; Oak Cliff Lions. Relig: Episcopal. Legal Res: 647 Bizerte Dallas TX 75202 Mailing Add: 1210 Main Tower Dallas TX 75202

GEIGER, RONALD E (R)
NH State Rep
Mailing Add: Box 42 Merrimack NH 03054

GEIS, GERALD E (R)
Wyo State Sen
Mailing Add: 600 Holly Worland WY 82401

GEISICK, CONSTANCE JEAN (R)
b Torrington, Wyo, Feb 7, 50; d Ronald Geisick & Frances Gates G; single. Educ: Casper Col, 68-69; Univ Wyo, BA, 72; NTex State Univ, 73-; Nat Collegiate Adv, Kappa Delta, 72-73; Phi Theta Kappa; Mortar Board. Polit & Govt Pos: Committeewoman, Casper Col Rep, 68-69; research intern, Sen Clifford P Hansen, 70; chmn, Wyo Col Rep, 71-72; chmn, Wyo Young Rep, 72-73; mem Wyo Adv Coun, Small Bus Admin, 72- Bus & Prof Pos: Panhellenic asst, NTex State Univ, 73-74; community serv, Richland Community Col, 75- Mem: Kappa Delta Pi. Honors & Awards: Outstanding Kappa Delta, Rho Chap of Kappa Delta, 72. Relig: Presbyterian. Legal Res: 2518 E D St Torrington WY 82240 Mailing Add: 200 Ave D Denton TX 76201

GEISLER, JERRY HUBERT (R)
Va State Deleg
b Big Stone Gap, Va, July 6, 34; m to Betty Lou Coyle. Educ: Emory & Henry Col, BA; T C Williams Sch of Law, LLB. Polit & Govt Pos: Chmn, Carroll Co Rep Comt, Va, formerly; mem, Va State Rep Cent Comt, 64-; Va State Deleg, 66-; mem, Commercial Credit Study Comn, 70-; chmn, New River Compact Study Comn, 71-; deleg, Rep Nat Conv, 72. Bus & Prof Pos: Attorney. Mem: Hillsville Jaycees (past pres, vpres & local dir); Izaak Walton League (past pres). Relig: Methodist. Mailing Add: Box 516 Hillsville VA 24343

GEISLER, ROBERT A (R)
Pa State Rep
Mailing Add: Capitol Bldg Harrisburg PA 17120

GEITTMANN, IDA MAE (R)
Publicity Chmn, Beltrami Co Rep Comt, Minn
b Sesser, Ill, Sept 3, 23; d Louie Jones & Carmen Bishop J. Educ: Southern Ill Univ, BS in educ, 44 & MS in educ, 57; Ill State Normal Univ, grad work, 45; Pi Kappa Delta; Sphinx for Outstanding Leadership; received speech Medals; Pi Kappa Sigma. Polit & Govt Pos: Supt of children & youth activities, Ill State Fair, 50-52; capt, 75th precinct, Springfield, 52; chmn, Beltrami Co Dem-Farmer-Labor Party, Minn, 57-61; adv, Beltrami Co Young Dem, 58-60; mem, Minn Dem-Farmer-Labor State Cent Comt & chairwoman, Seventh Dist Dem-Farmer-Labor Party, 58-65; civil defense dir, Beltrami Co & Bemidji, 60-62; mem nominating comt, Minn State Dem-Farmer-Labor Conv, 60; comt mem, State Bd of Prominent Women for Sen Eugene McCarthy, 65; deleg, Dem Nat Conv, 64; mem, Beltrami Co Rep Comt, Minn, 68-, publicity chmn, 70-; Beltrami Co chmn, MacGregor for Sen, Ohman for State Sen, Erdahl for Secy of State & Joakola for Rep, 70. Bus & Prof Pos: Dept mgr, Peers Store, 41-44; personnel interviewer, US Cartridge Co, 43; dean of girls & teaching supvr, Rochester High Sch, 48-53; radio announcer, WCVS, Springfield, Ill, 50-52; camp dir, YWCA, 51-53; dean of girls, drama coach & instr, Christopher High Sch, 53-55; dean of girls & dir of guid, Sesser High Sch, 55-57; asst dean of students & dir of Housing, Bemidji State Col, Minn, 57-69, asst to vpres admin, 69-; partner, Lee's Secretarial Serv, 61-66; gen agt, Planned Future Life Ins Co, 66-69, securities rep, 69-; vpres, Sudan Holding Corp, Minneapolis, 68-69; real estate consult, Horizon Land Corp, 69-; salesman, Viking Div, Franklin Life Ins Co Springfield, Ill, 70- Publ: Health Bibliography, State of Ill, 46; America Today, Minn Bus & Prof Women's Clubs, 71. Mem: Am Personnel & Guid Asn; Nat Dean of Women Asn; Am Asn Univ Women; North Minn Counsr Asn; Minn Fedn Bus & Prof Women's Clubs. Honors & Awards: Woman of the Year, Planned Future Life Ins Co, 68; Woman of the Year, Bemidji Bus & Prof Women's Clubs, 70; Legis Leadership Award & Woman of Achievement, Minn Fedn Bus & Prof Women's Clubs. Relig: Methodist. Legal Res: Birchmont Rd Bemidji MN 56601 Mailing Add: Box 276 Bemidji MN 56601

GEJDENSON, SAMUEL (D)
Conn State Rep
Mailing Add: RFD 1 Fitchville CT 06334

GELBER, LOUISE CARP (D)
Mem Exec Comt, Calif Dem State Cent Comt
b Detroit, Mich, Oct 24, 21; d Jacob Carp & Gusta Schneider C; m 1943 to Milton Gelber; c Jack, Bruce & Julie. Educ: Los Angeles City Col, 1 year; Univ Mich, 1 year; Univ Calif, Los Angeles, 1 year; Univ Calif, Berkeley, BA & JD, 44. Polit & Govt Pos: Dem nominee for Calif State Sen, 19th Dist, 68; asst treas, Los Angeles Co Dem Comt, Calif, 68, mem, 68-; mem exec comt & co-chmn, 24th Cong Dist, Calif Dem State Cent Comt, 68- Bus & Prof Pos: Attorney-at-law, Gelber & Gelber, Attorneys, El Monte, Calif, 45-; legis advocate, Calif Bus & Prof Women's Clubs, 59. Publ: Joint tenancy & safe deposit boxes, 43 & Property settlement agreements, 43, Calif Bar J; Equal rights amendment California analysis, Calif Bus & Prof Women's Clubs, 59. Mem: Am Bar Asn; Eastern Star; League of Women Voters; Southern Calif Women Lawyers; Am Asn of Univ Women. Honors & Awards: Co-Woman of Year Award, El Monte CofC, 68. Relig: Christian Science. Mailing Add: 1225 Rancho Rd Arcadia CA 91006

GELDERMANN, HARLAN STOLP (R)
Mem, Rep State Cent Comt, Calif
b Oakland, Calif, Nov 15, 23; s Alfred Jacques Geldermann & Carmen Stolp G; separated; c James & Joel. Educ: Stanford Univ, BA Econ; Colo Col, 43; Delta Tau. Polit & Govt Pos: Mem, Calif Real Estate Comn, 68-; mem, Rep State Cent Comt, Calif, 69- Bus & Prof Pos: Pres, broker-owner & land developer, Geldermann Realtors, Danville, Calif, 47-; owner-developer, Round Hill Country Club, Alamo, 61-; dir, Oceanic Properties, Inc, Honolulu, Hawaii, 68- Mil Serv: Entered as Midn, Navy, released as Lt(jg), after serv in Submarine Duty, Pac Fleet, 42-46; Successful War Patrol Awards. Mem: Round Hill Golf & Country Club; Sonoma Co Trail Blazers; Elks; VFW; Nat Asn Real Estate Brokers. Relig: Protestant. Legal Res: 19251 San Ramon Rd San Ramon CA 94583 Mailing Add: PO Box 415 Danville CA 94526

GELEGOTIS, PAUL (D)
SC State Rep
Mailing Add: 732 Jim Isle Dr Charleston SC 29412

GELINAS, DAVID L (D)
NH State Rep
Mailing Add: 181 Beech St Rear Manchester NH 03103

GELLERT, RANDALL CLARENCE (DFL)
First VChmn, Goodhue Co Dem-Farmer-Labor Party, Minn
b Fairmont, Minn, Aug 31, 35; s Clarence Walter Gellert & Edna Simmering G; m 1955 to Gay Ann Swink; c William, Shawn, Heather & Lori. Educ: Mankato State Col, BS, 60, MS, 67. Polit & Govt Pos: Mem resolutions comt, Goodhue Co Dem-Farmer-Labor Party, Minn, 66-68, first vchmn, 70-; chmn second ward, Cannon Falls Dem-Farmer-Labor Party, 68, chmn, 70; alderman, Cannon Falls City Coun, 69-, state comnr, Cannon Falls, 69, police comnr, 70, mem ordinance comt, 70, city charter comnr, 70; chmn, Sen Dist 25 Dem-Farmer-Labor Party, 72-; chmn, Cannon Falls City Dem-Farmer-Labor Party, 73-; mem, Minn State Dem-Farmer-Labor Cent Comt, 73- Mil Serv: Entered as Pvt, Army, 55, released as Pfc, 57, after serv in 596th Light Truck Co, ETO, 56-57; Good Conduct Medal. Mem: Cannon Falls, Minn & Nat Educ Asns. Relig: Lutheran. Mailing Add: 201 N First St Cannon Falls MN 55009

GELLHAUS, DERALD B (R)
SDak State Rep
Mailing Add: 502 James Pl Yankton SD 57078

GELSTON, MORTIMER ACKLEY (R)
Chmn, East Haddam Rep Town Comt, Conn
b East Haddam, Conn, Mar 25, 20; s George Hugh Gelston & Marie Forand G; m 1947 to Susan Hale; c Todd H & George W. Educ: High sch, 36. Polit & Govt Pos: State Power Facility Eval Coun, Conn, 73-; chmn, East Haddam Rep Town Comt, 73- Bus & Prof Pos: Owner, Maple Ridge Farm, East Haddam, Conn, 56-; vpres, Green Mountain Liquors, Montpelier, Vt, 74- Mem: Mason; Rotary; Grange; Farm Bur; Conn Milk for Health (vpres). Mailing Add: Maple Ridge Farm East Haddam CT 06423

GEMMILL, JOHN K (R)
NH State Rep
b Philadelphia, Pa, June 29, 43; s Kenneth W Gemmill & Helen Hartman G; m 1973 to Josie Manternach. Educ: Hamilton Col, BA, 65; Columbia Univ, MA, 66; Phi Beta Kappa. Polit & Govt Pos: NH State Rep, currently; mem, NH Am Revolution Bicentennial Comn, 72- Relig: Protestant. Legal Res: Hebron NH Mailing Add: Star Rte Bristol NH 03222

GEMPEL, GORDON LEO (R)
Chmn, Huron Co Rep Party, Mich
b Harbor Beach, Mich, Dec 11, 28; s Leo C Gempel & Irene Hamlin G; m 1950 to Betty Ann Murawske; c Wendy Sue (Mrs Eidenberger), Cheryl Renee & Marsha Leigh. Educ: Univ Mich, 1 year. Polit & Govt Pos: Chmn, Huron Co Rep Party, Mich, 71-, finance chmn, 75-; mem, Dist 8, State Rep Issues Comt, 74; mem, Dist 8, Rep State Cent Comt, 75- Bus & Prof Pos: Pres, Huron Co Asn Independent Ins Agents, 66-67, vpres, 70-71. Mem: Harbor Beach Rotary Club; Mich Asn Independent Ins Agts (mem legis comt); Conserv Club (secy, 11 years); Mich United Conserv Clubs (dist vchmn); Commun Sch Citizens Adv Comt. Relig: Presbyterian; elder. Legal Res: 530 Garden St Harbor Beach MI 48441 Mailing Add: 220 State St Harbor Beach MI 48441

GENDRON, JOSEPH SAUL (D)
RI State Sen
b Pawtucket, RI, Jan 24, 38; s Henry Leonard Gendron & Elizabeth Hughes G; m 1965 to Nancy Kelly; c Patricia, Martha, Anne Elizabeth & Joseph S, III. Educ: Georgetown Univ, BS in Biol, 59; Univ RI, BS in Chem, 63; Suffolk Univ Law Sch, JD, 69. Polit & Govt Pos: RI State Sen, 67- Mil Serv: Sp-5, Army Res, 61-67. Mem: RI Pharmaceut Soc. Relig: Roman Catholic. Mailing Add: 14 Massasoit Ave Pawtucket RI 02861

GENGENBACH, EDWARD CARL (R)
Chmn, Price Co Rep Party, Wis
b Lincoln, Nebr, Mar 9, 50; s Carl Edward Gengenbach & Gloria Ann Evans G; m 1973 to Sylvia Anne Voight. Educ: Wis State Univ-Superior, 69-71; Alpha Psi Omega; Sigma Tau Gamma. Polit & Govt Pos: Chmn, Price Co Rep Party, Wis, 75- Bus & Prof Pos: Gen mgr, Gengenbach Handcrafts, 71-74; sales mgr, WNBI AM-FM Radio, 74- Mem: Lions; CofC; Boy Scouts (chmn troop comt coun). Relig: Unitarian-Universalist. Mailing Add: Rte 2 Box 345 Phillips WI 54555

GENTHNER, GEORGIA CARO (D)
Chmn, Sagadahoc Co Dem Comt, Maine
b Whitefield, Maine, Mar 7, 10; d Warren Edgar Cunningham & Ella Snowdeal C; m 1931 to John Flitner Genthner; c Barbara Hope (Mrs Donald Hinckley), Jean A (Mrs John Davis), Josephine (Mrs David Carr) & Roy Stephen. Educ: Gorham State Teachers Col, BS, 57. Polit & Govt Pos: Mem, Alna Sch Bd, Maine, 36-42; chmn, Sagadahoc Co Dem Comt, currently. Bus & Prof Pos: Teacher, Whitefield, Maine, 27-29, Rockland, 30-31 & Brunswick, 43-44; teacher first grade, Topsham, 44- Mem: Nat Educ Asn; Maine Teachers Asn; Elem/Kindergarten/Nursery Educators; Grange (7 degree) Eastern Star. Relig: Protestant. Mailing Add: Augusta Rd Topsham ME 04086

GENTILE, GEORGE G (D)
Chmn, Canton Dem Town Comt, Conn
b New Britain, Conn, May 29, 21; s Frank L Gentile & Julia Fusaro G; m 1952 to Winifred Bolles; c Beth Ann, Susan & Julia. Educ: Niagara Univ, BS, 47; Georgetown Univ, DDS, 50; Xi Psi Phi. Polit & Govt Pos: Chmn, Canton Police Comn, Conn, 71-; chmn, Canton Dem Town Comt, 74-; mem, Canton Charter Comn, 75-; deleg, Dem Nat Mid-Term Conf, 74. Mil Serv: Entered as Pvt, Marine Corps, 42, released as Cpl, 46, after serv in 4th Marine Div, Pac Theatre, 43-46. Mem: New Britain Dent Soc; New Britain Civitan Club; Conn State Dent Asn; KofC. Honors & Awards: Pierre Fauchard Acad, 73. Relig: Roman Catholic. Mailing Add: 182 Bahre Corner Rd Canton CT 06019

GENTLEMAN, JULIA B (R)
Iowa State Rep
Mailing Add: 2814 Forest Dr Des Moines IA 50312

GENTRY, CHARLES EZELL (D)
Mem, Tenn State Dem Exec Comt
b Cookeville, Tenn, Nov 30, 21; s Carlos B Gentry & Maggie Roberts G; m 1967 to Doris Hobson; c Linda & Phillip. Educ: Altus Jr Col; Wayne Univ, AA, 52. Polit & Govt Pos: Field rep to US Rep Joe L Evins, 60-; mayor, Smithville, Tenn, 72-74; mem, Tenn State Dem Exec Comt, 74- Bus & Prof Pos: Owner, Real Estate & Ins Agency, Smithville, Tenn, 60-; advert mgr, Smithville Rev, 65- Mil Serv: Entered as Pvt, Army, 43, released as Pfc, 45, after serv in Med Corps, South Pac. Mem: Am Legion; Rotary; Nat Youth Camps. Relig: Church of Christ; Minister, DeKalb, Tenn. Mailing Add: 133 Dearman St Smithville TN 37166

GENTRY, JAMES WORTH (D)
NC State Rep
b King, NC, Aug 4, 08; s I G Gentry & Mary Kreeger G; m 1934 to Marguerite Precilla Slate; c Two. Educ: Draughans Bus Col, 29. Polit & Govt Pos: Chmn, Sch Bd, NC, 10 years; co comnr, 56-57; NC State Sen, formerly; NC State Rep, 69-72, 74- Bus & Prof Pos: Farmer; cattle raiser; fertilizer dealer. Mem: Stokes-Reynolds Mem Hosp; Mason; charter mem Kings Lions (past pres); Stokes Co United Fund (past pres); Stokes Co Ind Comt, NW Develop Asn. Honors & Awards: Citizen of the Year, Lions Club Award, 58. Relig: Methodist; steward, 52-64. Mailing Add: King NC 27021

GENTRY, RICHARD HAYDEN (LIBERTARIAN)
b Dodge City, Kans, Nov 16, 33; m to Jean Blair; c Jennifer Lorien & Richard Blair. Educ: Occidental Col, BA; Am Univ, MA. Polit & Govt Pos: Justice of the Peace, Fairfax Co, Va, 63-67; treas, Northern Va State Rep Presidential Campaign Comts, 64 & 68 & Va Rep State Finance Comt, 65-69; cand, Va State Senate, 67; legis asst to US Rep John P Saylor, Pa, 69-75; chmn, Va Libertarian Party, currently. Bus & Prof Pos: Pub rels consult; freelance writer; secy-treas, Everymans Publ Opinion Clearing House Inc. Mil Serv: Army Security Agency, 53-56. Mem: Acad Polit Sci; Am Asn Pub Opinion Res; Pi Sigma Alpha. Mailing Add: 6151 Tompkins Dr McLean VA 22101

GENTRY, WILLIAM R, JR (D)
Ky State Sen
Mailing Add: 110 Westwind Trail Bardstown KY 40004

GENTZ, GERALD THOMAS (D)
VChmn, Onondaga Co Dem Comt, NY
b Syracuse, NY, Aug 26, 49; s Fred John Gentz & Betty Frand G; single. Educ: Syracuse Univ, BA, 71, MBA, 75. Polit & Govt Pos: Pres, Syracuse Univ Action Dem, 70-71; vpres, Onondaga Co Young Dem, 71-72, pres, 72-73; pub rels dir, 73-; alt deleg, Dem Nat Conv, 72; trustee, Village East Syracuse, 75-; vchmn, Onondaga Co Dem Comt, NY, 75-; vchmn, Dewitt Dem Town Comt, 75- Bus & Prof Pos: Regional correspondent, Carrier Int Corp, currently. Mem: Asn of Masters in Bus Admin Exec; East Syracuse Jaycees (chmn govt affairs, 71-); St Martin's Soc. Relig: Episcopal. Mailing Add: 308 McCool Ave East Syracuse NY 13057

GENTZLER, KENNETH C (D)
Chmn, Adams Co Dem Comt, Pa
b Hanover, Pa, Apr 8, 41; c Charles L Gentzler & Ruth Hale G; m 1963 to Catherine Bollinger; c Kimberly Ann. Educ: Shippensburg State Col, 60; Thompson Col, grad, 62. Polit & Govt Pos: Mayor, Borough of East Berlin, Pa, 74-; chmn, Adams Co Dem Comt, 75- Bus & Prof Pos: Self-employed, Gentzler Motors, 2 years; salesman, Shultz Chevrolet Inc, 2 years; clothing mgr, Wiest's Dept Store, 7 years. Mem: Elks; Moose; DeMolay. Legal Res: 118 Abbottstown St East Berlin PA 17316 Mailing Add: Box 35 East Berlin PA 17316

GEO-KARIS, ADELINE JAY (R)
Ill State Sen
Mailing Add: 2803 Eschol Ave Zion IL 60099

GEORGE, ALLAIRE ANN (D)
b Marquette, Mich, Oct 28, 35; d Thurber C George & Virginia Knuth G; single. Educ: Wittenberg Univ, BA, 57; Duke Univ, MA & ABD, 66; Psi Chi, Kappa Delta Epsilon; Alpha Xi Delta. Polit & Govt Pos: Admin asst to US Rep Bob Krueger, 75- Bus & Prof Pos: Asst prof sociol dept, Wittenberg Univ, 69-72; asst to vprovost & dean, Duke Univ, 72-73. Mem: Nat Women's Polit Caucus; Am Sociol Asn. Legal Res: 211 W Lincoln St New Braunfels TX 78130 Mailing Add: 323 D St SE Washington DC 20003

GEORGE, CAMILLE (D)
Pa State Rep
Mailing Add: Capitol Bldg Harrisburg PA 17120

GEORGE, CLAUD REID (D)
Secy, Yell Co Dem Cent Comt, Ark
b Birta, Ark, Nov 12, 06; s John Nathan George & Hulda Strait G; m to Fanny Blanche Compton; c Jan (Mrs Richison) & Lary Compton. Educ: Univ Ark, LLB, 29, JD, 35; Phi Alpha Delta. Polit & Govt Pos: Dep tax assessor, Danville, Yell Co, Ark, 30; city attorney, Danville, 40-; judge, Yell Co, 41; prosecuting attorney, Fifth Dist, 42-46; secy, Yell Co Dem Cent Comt, 70- Mem: Masonic Lodge; United Methodist Church Sch (secy, 35-). Relig: Methodist. Mailing Add: PO Box 246 Danville AR 72833

GEORGE, LLOYD R (D)
Ark State Rep
Mailing Add: PO Box 486 Danville AR 72833

GEORGE, MARY (R)
Hawaii State Sen
b Seattle, Wash, May 27, 16; d William Day Shannon & Agnes Lovejoy S; m 1946 to Flave Joseph George; c Flave Joseph, Jr, Karen (Mrs Van Hook), Christy (Mrs Cebaus) & Shannon (Mrs Lowrey). Educ: Univ Wash, BA, 37; Univ Mich, 37; Columbia Univ, 38; Phi Beta Kappa; Kappa Alpha Theta. Polit & Govt Pos: Vchmn, Hawaii State Ethics Comn, 68; councilman, City & Co of Honolulu, 69-74; chmn, Hawaii State Conf Elected Rep, 73-74; Hawaii State Sen, 74- Bus & Prof Pos: Asst news ed, Pathe News, New York, 39-42; foreign editions staff, Readers Digest, Pleasantville, 43-45; columnist, Caracas Daily J, Venezuela, 50-60. Publ: Auth, A Is for Abrazo, VAAUW, Venezuela, 61. Mem: League of Women Voters Honolulu; Mensa; Am Asn Univ Women. Honors & Awards: Woman of the Year, Hawaii Asn Bus & Prof Women, 70; Woman of the Year, Honolulu Press Club, 69; Annual Brotherhood Award, Jewish Men's Club Hawaii, 74. Mailing Add: 782 G North Kalaheo Ave Kailua HI 96734

GEORGE, MICHAEL JOHN (DFL)
Minn State Rep
b St Paul, Minn, Sept 28, 46; s Norbert John George & Geraldine Macdonald G; m 1973 to Janice Rae MacKenzie. Educ: Univ Minn, 64-68; Delta Tau Delta. Polit & Govt Pos: Minn State Rep, Dist 50-A, 75- Bus & Prof Pos: Div dir, Canvas Prod Asn Int, 71-74. Mem: Wildwood Lions. Legal Res: 1140 Park Ave Mahtomedi MN 55115 Mailing Add: 213 State Off Bldg St Paul MN 55155

GEORGE, NEWELL A (D)
b Kansas City, Mo, Sept 24, 04; s Adolphus K George & Ida Scobee G; m 1934 to Regina Hannan. Educ: George Washington Univ, LLB, 34, LLM, & MPL, 35; Delta Theta Phi. Polit & Govt Pos: Pres, Wyandotte Co Young Dem, 32; pres, Kans Dem Club, Washington, DC, 35 & 36; attorney, Reconstruction Finance Corp, Washington, DC, 35-37; regional attorney, Fed Security Agency, 37-52; regional counsel, War Manpower Comn, 42-43; first asst to Wyandotte Co Attorney, 53-58; US Rep, Kans, 59-60; deleg, Dem Nat Conv, 60; US Attorney, Kans, 61-68; mem, Gov Comt Criminal Admin, Interstate Oil Compact Comn, currently; mem, Civil Serv Comn Kansas City, Kans, currently; mem, State Govt Ethics Comn, currently. Bus & Prof Pos: Practicing anti-trust & probate law, currently; trustee, Law Found, Univ Mo-Kansas City, currently; secy adv coun, Wentworth Mil Acad, currently. Publ: Contrib to Kans Law Rev. Mem: Am, Kans State & Wyandotte Co Bar Asns; US Army Asn; Kansas City Breakfast Optimist Club. Honors & Awards: Knute Rockne Club Award, Law Enforcement Man of the Year, 66; Admiral Nebr Navy; Cert for Outstanding Serv, Am Asn Criminology; Kehoe Publ Citation for Law Enforcement. Relig: Presbyterian. Mailing Add: 1831 New Jersey Ave Kansas City KS 66102

GEORGE, ORLANDO J, JR (D)
Del State Rep
Mailing Add: 2707 Baynard Blvd Wilmington DE 19802

GEORGE, RALPH WEIR (R)
b Milford, Tex, Aug 26, 32; s Van Theodore George, Sr & Mayna Sybol Weir G; m 1961 to Charlsie Sue Terry; c Teresa Sue, Jerry Van & Terry Van. Educ: Tex A&M Col, DVM, 55; Phi Zeta; Phi Kappa Phi. Polit & Govt Pos: Chmn, Hill Co Rep Party, Tex, formerly. Mil Serv: Entered as 1st Lt, Air Force, 55, released as Capt, 57, after serv in Air Force Vet Med Corps. Mem: Am & Tex Vet Med Asns; Rotary; Jaycees; Farm Bur. Relig: Methodist. Legal Res: 1411 Old Brandon Rd Hillsboro TX 76645 Mailing Add: 216 Craig Hillsboro TX 76645

GEORGE, WALTER (R)
Nebr State Sen
b Gudensberg, Apr 23, 29; m 1955 to Ann Harms; c Eric & Stephen. Educ: Univ Heidelberg; Univ Marburg; Univ NC; Univ Nebr, MA Polit Sci, 56. Polit & Govt Pos: Councilman, City of Blair, Nebr, 72-74; Nebr State Sen, Dist 16, 75- Bus & Prof Pos: Prof, Dana Col, Blair, Nebr, 66-74. Mil Serv: Research Asst, Army Research Off, 59-61. Mailing Add: 3065 College Dr Blair NE 68008

GEORGE, WANDA CAROL (R)
VChmn, Polk Co Rep Party, Mo
b Bolivar, Mo, Aug 6, 34; d William Jacob Hocker & Myrtle Ellen Scott H; m 1967 to Collie Robert George; c Patricia Ann & William O'Bryan. Educ: Draughons Bus Col, 67. Polit & Govt Pos: VChmn, Polk Co Rep Party, Mo, 74- Bus & Prof Pos: Broker, Real Estate By George, 73-; broker, Ins By George, 74- Mem: Polk Co Rep Womens Club; Polk Co Summer Sports Prog; Am Cancer Soc (pres, Polk Co Unit, 74-); Red Cross (treas, 75-). Mailing Add: 621 W Broadway Bolivar MO 65613

GERALD, GASTON (D)
La State Sen
Mailing Add: Box 227 Greenwell Springs LA 70739

GERALDS, MONTE R (D)
Mich State Rep
b Huntington, WVa, Sept 10, 34; m 1956 to Barbara Ellen Bunnell; c Jeffrey, Cameron, Scott, Cynthia & Laurie. Educ: Wayne State Univ, JD, 63; Pi Kappa Alpha; Phi Alpha Delta. Polit & Govt Pos: Councilman, Madison Heights, Mich, 65-69, mayor, 69-72; bd supvrs, Oakland Co, 66-69; Mich State Rep, 75- Bus & Prof Pos: Supvr off servs, Chevrolet Div Gen Motors, 58-63; attorney, Madison Heights, 63- Mem: Mich Bar Asn. Honors & Awards: Mackenzie Hon Soc, Wayne State Univ, 63; Distinguished Serv Award, Madison Heights Jaycees, 67. Relig: Presbyterian. Legal Res: 28162 Lorenz Madison Heights MI 48071 Mailing Add: House of Rep Lansing MI 48901

GERAN, DEDRA ELAINE (R)
b Las Vegas, Nev, Dec 14, 53; d Johnus Geran & Hazel Wilburn G; single. Educ: Ariz State Univ, currently; Delta Sigma Theta. Polit & Govt Pos: Mem cent comt, Las Vegas, Nev, 72-73; alt deleg, Rep Nat Conv, 72; dist rep for State Rep David Towell, Las Vegas, 73. Relig: Catholic. Legal Res: 1028 I St Las Vegas NV 89106 Mailing Add: 1705 E Pleasant Lane Phoenix AZ 85040

GERARD, SUMNER, JR (R)
US Ambassador to Jamaica
b Melville, NY, July 15, 16; s Sumner Gerard & Helen Coster G; m 1943 to Louise Grosvenor, div; m Sept, 1968 to Teresa Dabrowska; c Jenny, Molly (Mrs Wheelock), Helen, Anne & Sumner III. Educ: Trinity Col, Cambridge, BA & MA, 37; Univ Wis, post grad work. Polit & Govt Pos: Asst to dir, Wis State Dept Com, 38-39; secy to Rep minority, NY City Coun, 39; asst to adminr, Bur Export Control, Washington, DC, 40-41; Rep precinct, co & state committeeman, 50-54; Mont State Rep, 55-60, Minority Leader, Mont State House of Rep, 59; alt deleg, Rep Nat Conv, 56, deleg, 60, polit secy to Gov Aronson, conv, 56 & 60; chmn, Rep State Finance Comt, 58-60; chmn platform comt, Rep State Conv, 62; asst campaign dir, Nat Rep Cong Comt, 62-64; dep dir tech serv orgn, Rep Nat Comt, 64; Mont State Sen, Madison Co, 62-66, Minority Leader, Mont State Senate, 65-66; dir, US Agency Int Develop Mission, Tunis, Tunisia, 70-74; US Ambassador to Jamaica, 74- Bus & Prof Pos: Asst to dir int div, Radio Corp Am, NY, 45-46; vpres & dir, Aeon Int Corp, 46-70; ranching, oil & land develop, Mont, 48-70; former pres & dir, Aeon Realty Co, Ennis Co, Newmont Resources Corp; former dir, Financial Gen Corp, Washington, DC & Cardinal Petrol Corp, Billings; former exec vpres & dir, Immer Realty Corp; former treas & dir, Shelter Island Farms, Inc. Mil Serv: Entered as Pvt, Army Air Force, 41, released as Capt, Marine Corps Res, 45 after serv in Army, Navy & Marine Corps, NAfrican & China-Burma-India Theaters, 3 years; Army Commendation; Order of British Empire. Relig: Episcopal. Legal Res: Princeton NJ Mailing Add: c/o US Embassy Kingston Jamaica

GERBER, SAMUEL ROBERT (D)
Mem, Cuyahoga Co Dem Exec Comt
b Hagerstown, Md, Aug 22, 98; s Judah Hyman Gerber & Bessie Nachenson G; div; c Roberta Lee. Educ: Valparaiso Univ, 17-18; Cincinnati E Med Col, MD, 22; Cleveland Marshall Law Sch, LLB, 49. Hon Degrees: LHD, Ohio Col of Podiatry, 60; LLD, Cleveland Marshall Law Sch, 61. Polit & Govt Pos: Mem, Cuyahoga Co Dem Exec Comt, Ohio, 36-, secy, 67-69, chmn, 69-70; coroner, Cuyahoga Co, 37-; deleg, Dem Nat Conv, 56, 60, 64 & 68; mem, Ohio Dem State Exec Comt, 68-71, vchmn, 68-70; Dem precinct committeeman, Ward 19, Cleveland, 68-71. Bus & Prof Pos: Physician-in-charge, Warrensville Correction Farms, Dept Pub Health & Welfare, Cleveland, Ohio, 25-27; acting chief physician for med serv-parochial schs, Div Child Hygiene, Dept of Health, Cleveland, 27-33; physician-in-charge, med aid for unattached person, Co, State & Fed Relief Admin, 33-37; assoc in legal med, Dept of Pathology, Sch of Med, Case Western Reserve Univ, 53-68, asst clin prof in legal med, 68-72, consult, currently; co-founder & co-dir, The Law-Med Ctr, Case Western Reserve Univ & Cuyahoga Co, 53- Publ: Practical use of biochemical tests for alcohol, Am Bar Asn J, 5/61; The physician's relations with the medicolegal officer, in The environment of medical practice, Yearbook Med, 63; Causation in death after trauma with preexisting cardiac disease, Cleveland Marshall Law Rev, 9/66. Mem: Int Asn Coroners & Med Examr (Nat Asn Coroners, pres, 37-38, secy-treas, 43-); Comt on Definitions of Home Accidents, Nat Safety Coun, 58-, Comt on Alcohol & Drugs, 60-; Study Group on Medicolegal Cert of Death, US Dept Health, Educ & Welfare, 60-; Shrine. Honors & Awards: Distinguished Alumnus, Cleveland Marshall Law Sch; Distinguished Mem, Acad of Med, Cleveland; Recognition of 50 years of practice of medicine. Relig: Reformed Judaism. Mailing Add: 2112 Acacia Park Dr Lyndhurst OH 44124

GERDING, DONNA ETHEL (D)
Mem, Mo State Dem Party
b Montgomery City, Mo, Nov 1, 22; d John Allen Cobb & Ethel Hudson C; m 1937 to Leroy William Gerding; c Lillian Mae (Mrs Uhlenkott) & Donald William. Educ: Montgomery High Sch, Mo, 2 years; St Charles Key Punch, O'Fallow, 6 months, 70. Polit & Govt Pos: Mem, Mo State Dem Party, 60-; secy & treas, Warren Co Dem Club, 63-65 & 67-69; judge of elec, city, primary & gen, Dem Ward One, Warren Co, 64-68; deleg, Conf Meeting of Five States, Springfield, Ill, 68; chmn, Lt Gov William E Morris Campaign, Warren Co, Mo, 68; pres, Womens Fed Dem Club, 68; vchmn, Warren Co Dem Cent Comt, formerly; field personnel-vision test sect, Dept of Revenue, 69- Publ: Letter of Opinion & Laws of Election, Warrenton Banner, 8/70. Mem: Nat Fedn of Bus & Prof Womens Clubs, Inc; Womens Prog Farm Asn; Commun Betterment Prog; Bus & Prof Working Women; Grange Lodge. Relig: Church of Christ. Mailing Add: 606 W Main Warrenton MO 63383

GERENA, VICTOR M (R)
Exec Secy, Statehood Rep Party, PR
b Quebradillas, PR, Nov 14, 35; s Victor Gerena & Gloria Cancel G; single. Educ: Univ PR, currently. Polit & Govt Pos: Exec secy, PR Rep Party, 63-68, deleg, 66; exec secy, Statehood Rep Party, 66-; asst minority leader, PR Senate, 67-68; alt deleg, Rep Nat Conv, 68. Bus & Prof Pos: Inside salesman, Honeywell, Inc, 57-62; mem claim dept, Lykes Lines, Inc, 63; State Sales Mgr, Taylor Wine Co, Inc, NY, 69- Mem: Asn Univ Student for Statehood; Action for Statehood; Young Rep Club; UN Asn of the US; Capitol Hill Club. Honors & Awards: Award, DAR, 53; three medals & one dipl, Asn of the Hist Mus; dipl, Univ Student for Statehood. Legal Res: Calle 9-E35 Sierra Berdecia Guaynabo PR 00657 Mailing Add: PO Box 285 San Juan PR 00902

GERKE, HAROLD EDWARD (D)
Mont State Rep
b Cherokee, Iowa, May 1, 12; s William H Gerke & Hannah Bredahl G; m 1930 to Vera E Adamson; c Harold Dean. Educ: Globe Bus Col. Polit & Govt Pos: Alderman, Billings, Mont, 59-61, mayor, 61-62; Mont State Rep, 65-, Speaker, Mont House Rep, 73- Bus & Prof Pos: Pres & gen mgr, Midland Propane Co, 46-55; pres, Petrolan Supply Co, 55-63; secy-treas, Am Galloway Asn, 63- Mem: L P Gas Asn; AF&AM. Relig: Lutheran. Mailing Add: 202 Mountain View Billings MT 59101

GERKEN, JOHN RAYMOND, JR (R)
Mem, Huron Co Rep Comt, Ohio

b Norwalk, Ohio, Aug 7, 26; s John Raymond Gerken & Elizabeth Helen Cole G; m 1948 to Norma Eileen Bachman; c James Ethan & Ann Elizabeth. Educ: Colgate Univ, AB, 47; Delta Kappa Epsilon. Polit & Govt Pos: Mem, Huron Co Rep Cent Comt, 56-, secy, 64-66, chmn, 66-70 & 73-74; pres, Norwalk Rep Club, 63; deleg, Rep Nat Conv, 64, alt deleg, 68; chmn Huron Co Rep Finance Comt, currently. Bus & Prof Pos: Pres, Norwalk Furniture Corp, 66- Mil Serv: Entered as Seaman, Naval Air Force, 44, released as Aviation Cadet, 45. Relig: Episcopal. Mailing Add: RD 2 Norwalk OH 44857

GERLACH, CHESTER A (D)
Wis State Rep
Mailing Add: 724 Marion Ave South Milwaukee WI 53172

GERLACH, GAYLE LESLIE (R)
b Oklahoma City, Okla, Apr 26, 53; s Stanley Cleatus Gerlach & Bobbie Jean Roberts G; single. Educ: Stephens Col, fall 71; Okla Col Lib Arts, spring 72; Univ Okla, 72-; Kappa Alpha Theta. Polit & Govt Pos: Deleg, Nat TAR Leadership Conf, Washington, DC, 71, Grady Co Rep Conv, Okla, 72 & Young Rep Leadership Conv, Washington, DC, 72; alt deleg, Rep Nat Conv, 72; contact personnel, Fourth Dist for Bartlett Campaign, 72; deleg, Okla Rep State Conv, 72 & 73. Mem: Col Republicans. Honors & Awards: Citizenship Award, Am Legion, 71; Dean's Honor Roll, Univ Okla, 72. Relig: Methodist. Legal Res: 1016 Kansas Ave Chickasha OK 73018 Mailing Add: RR 2 Box 311 Norman OK 73069

GERLING, WILLIAM CURTIS (D)
Committeeman, Monroe Co Dem Comt, NY

b Rochester, NY, May 13, 37; s G Curtis Gerling & Patricia Moran G; m 1971 to Elizabeth White; c John, Elizabeth, Katie, Peter & Chris Schmitt. Educ: City Col New York, 58; Rochester Inst Technol, AA, 72; Nazareth Col Rochester, 72- Polit & Govt Pos: Vchmn, Monroe Co Young Dem, NY, 57; committeeman, Monroe Co Dem Comt, NY, 58-60, 70-, mem, Monroe Co Adv Comt on Outreach Voter Regist, 75- Bus & Prof Pos: Vpres, Empire State Weeklies, 62- Mil Serv: Entered as E-1, Army, 58, released as SP-4, 62, after serv in Third Div Mil Police, Europe, 60-62; Good Conduct Medal. Mem: Metro-Act Rochester Inc; Genesee Valley Chap Am Civil Liberties Union; Western NY Newspaper Publs Asn; NY Press Asn (bd mem); Canterbury-Harvard Neighborhood Asn (vpres). Mailing Add: 245 Vassar St Rochester NY 14607

GERMINO, DONALD OWEN (R)
b Los Banos, Calif, Oct 1, 39; s D Oliver Germino & Helen King G; m 1974 to Bernadette Faria; c Michelle Lynn. Educ: Univ South Calif, AB, 61; Univ Calif, Berkeley, Law Sch, LLB, 61, JD, 64; Sigma Chi. Polit & Govt Pos: Mem, Calif Young Rep, 59-66; deleg, Calif State Rep Cent Comt, 67-69; vchmn, Merced Co Rep Cent Comt, 67-68, chmn, 69-71; city attorney, Los Banos, Calif, 71- Mem: Am, Calif & Merced Co Bar Asns; Lions; Elks; Sportsman's Asn. Honors & Awards: Outstanding Serv Awards, Los Banos Community Chest & Yosemite Area Coun, Boy Scouts, 65. Relig: Roman Catholic. Legal Res: 1548 Canal Farm Lane Los Banos CA 93635 Mailing Add: PO Box 591 Los Banos CA 93635

GERRARD, M WILLIAM (D)
Polit & Govt Pos: Chmn, Wis State Dem Cent Comt, formerly. Mailing Add: PO Box 1086 La Crosse WI 54606

GERSTELL, GLENN STEVEN (R)
b New York, NY, Nov 9, 51; s Martin H Gerstell & Jean G; single. Educ: New York Univ, BA, 73; Columbia Univ Law Sch, currently; Pi Sigma Alpha. Polit & Govt Pos: Spec asst to city campaign dir, Gov Nelson Rockefeller Reelec Campaign, 70; vpres, Ripon Soc, NY, 71-72; state polit dir, 72-; chmn gov bd, 74-; mem nat gov bd, Ripon Soc, Inc, 72-, nat vpres, 74-; mgr, William Diamond NY State Assembly Campaign, 72; dep campaign dir, New York Comt to Reelect the President, 72; alt deleg-at-lg, Rep Nat Conv, 72; research assoc, NY State Charter Rev Comn for New York, 73-; dep city campaign dir, Gov Malcolm Wilson's Campaign, 74; assoc dist leader, 68th Assembly Dist Rep Party, 74-; mem, NY Rep State Comt Task Force, 74- Publ: Contrib ed, Ripon Forum, 71- Mailing Add: 355 E 72nd St New York NY 10021

GERSTEN, JOSEPH MORRIS (D)
Fla State Rep

b Dade Co, Fla, July 19, 47; s Joseph J Gersten & Kathryn Morris G; single. Educ: NY Univ, BS, 70; Sophia Univ, Japan, 69; Univ Md, MA, 72; Univ Miami, JD, 75. Polit & Govt Pos: Fla State Rep, 74- Mem: Tropical Audubon Soc; Ment Health Asn; League Women Voters. Legal Res: 1025 Spring Garden Rd Miami FL 33136 Mailing Add: 2000 S Dixie Hwy Miami FL 33133

GERVAIS, ROLAND G (D)
Vt State Rep
Mailing Add: Enosburg Falls VT 05450

GERY, L CLAYTON (D)
Chmn, Westbrook Dem Town Comt, Conn

b Nittance, Conn, Jan 6, 36; s Louis Gery & Mildred G; m 1960 to Joan W Wrigley; c Jonathan & Pamela. Educ: Univ Conn, BS; Univ Conn Law Sch, LLB; Sigma Nu. Polit & Govt Pos: Selectman, Clinton, Conn, 65-67; chmn, Westbrook Dem Town Comt, Conn, 73- Bus & Prof Pos: Attorney. Mem: Am & Conn Bar Asns. Mailing Add: Meetinghouse Lane Westbrook CT 06498

GERY, MICHAEL E (D)
Ind State Sen
Mailing Add: 530 Robinson St West Lafayette IN 47906

GESELL, CRANSTON RICHARD (R)
Chmn, Calhoun Co Rep Party, Iowa

b Davenport, Iowa, Jan 9, 13; s Charles Abram Gesell & Armena Barbour G; m 1947 to Elaine Sims Hurt; c Cranston Richard, Jr, John Charles, Frances (Mrs Endreson), Thomas Martin, Mary Elizabeth & David Michael. Educ: Augustana Col, 35-38; Carthage Col, BA, 38; Lutheran Sch Theol, Chicago, BD, 41. Polit & Govt Pos: Chmn, Calhoun Co Rep Party, 71- Bus & Prof Pos: Parish pastor, Immanuel Lutheran Church, Jackson, Mich, 42-44; mgr, Vets Serv, Valdosta, Ga, 47-49; parish pastor, St James Lutheran Church, Vandalia, Ill, 50-55; Grace Lutheran Church, Muscatine, Iowa, 55-63 & Augustana Lutheran Church, Manson,

Iowa, 63- Mil Serv: Entered as Lt(jg), Navy, 45, released, 46, after serv in Pac. Mem: Nat Asn Parliamentarians (pres, Ft Dodge chap); Am Legion; Manson Ministerial Asn. Relig: Lutheran. Legal Res: 1114 Sixth St Manson IA 50563 Mailing Add: Box 207 Manson IA 50563

GETCHELL, EARLE DUNCAN (R)
Mem, Mobile Co Rep Exec Comt, Ala

b Medford, Mass, Dec 15, 16; s George Elmer Getchell & Anne Marie Robertson G; m 1943 to Jean Elder Thompson; c Earle Duncan, Jr & Anne (Mrs Riviere). Educ: Royal Can Air Force & US Army Air Corps Sch. Polit & Govt Pos: Dir, Aircraft Div For Liquidation Comn, Latin Am & Caribbean Div, 46-47; mem, Mobile Co Rep Exec Comt, 66-67 & 68-; alt-deleg, Rep Nat Conv, 68. Bus & Prof Pos: Exec vpres, Mobile Glass Co, Inc, Mobile, Ala, 58-64, pres, 64- Mil Serv: Entered Royal Can Air Force, 40, released, 42, after serv as pilot & navigator; entered Army Air Corps, 42, released as Capt, 46, after serv as pilot. Mem: Construction Indust Asn, Mobile (pres); Rotary. Relig: Methodist. Mailing Add: 4226 Bellevue Lane Mobile AL 36608

GETLER, HELEN (D)
Committeeman, Nassau Co Dem Party, NY

b New York, NY, May 30, 25; d Irving Einhorn & Ilma Greenfield E; m 1947 to Monte W Getler; c Richard & Carol. Educ: Brooklyn Col, 41-43; Bryn Mawr Col, BA, 45; Columbia Univ, 45-46; Delta Sigma Pi. Polit & Govt Pos: Zone leader, Roslyn Dem Party, NY, 69-72; committeeman, Nassau Co Dem Party, 70-; deleg, Dem Nat Conv, 72; vchmn, North Hempstead Dem Party, 72- Bus & Prof Pos: Biochemist, Sloane-Kettering Inst, 46-49; pres, Corp Art Consultants, 71- Publ: Co-auth, A study of the metabolism of hypoxanthine & xanthine in the rat, 49 & A synthesis of isotopic cytosine & a study of its metabolism in the rat, 49 J Biol Chem. Mem: League of Women Voters; Nat Women's Polit Caucus; Better Roslyn Asn. Relig: Jewish. Mailing Add: 475 Bryant Ave Roslyn NY 11576

GETTEL, GERHARD F (R)
Mem, Midland Co Rep Comt, Mich

b Owendale, Mich, Mar 9, 15; s John W Gettel (deceased) & Catherine Schnepp G (deceased); m 1947 to Ruth M Berkenstock. Educ: Mich State Col, BS; Cornell Univ, MS; Mich State Univ, PhD; 4H Club; Dairy Club; Jr Farm Bur; Walther League. Polit & Govt Pos: Rep precinct leader, Midland, Mich, 58; ward chmn, Rep Party, Midland, 58-62; mem, Rep Co Comt & Exec Comt, 62-66; pres, Midland Co GOP Breakfast Club, 68; chmn, Midland Co Rep Comt, 68-70, mem, 72-; mem, Midland Co Rep Exec Comt, 72- Bus & Prof Pos: Dir, Kalos Enterprises, Inc Lepta Asn & Ashton Plantation, Inc, 67-, Frankenmuth Lutheran Home for the Aged, 72- Mil Serv: Entered as Pvt, Army, 42, released as Pfc, 46, after serv in Mil Govt, ETO, 44-46; Rifleman Medal; Good Conduct Medal; ETO Medal with four stars. Publ: Your school district, Nations Schs, 51; several minor articles. Mem: Midland Asn Life Agents (nat committeeman, currently); Lutheran Acad of Scholarship; Midland Co Farm Bur (citizenship chair); People to People, Midland; Boy Scouts, Midland (first aid counr, 60-). Honors & Awards: Citation from Red Cross, Kiwanis Club, Lyons Club & CLU, 67. Relig: Lutheran. Mailing Add: 2309 Burlington Dr Midland MI 49640

GETTO, VIRGIL M (R)
Nev State Assemblyman

b Fallon, Nev, June 19, 24; s Andrew Getto & Desolina Longo G; m to Marilyn Malaney; c Virgil (Mike), Andrea, David M & Marlea. Educ: Churchill Co High Sch, grad. Polit & Govt Pos: Bd mem, Churchill Co Sch Bd, 62-66; dir, Churchill Co CofC, 66-69; Nev State Assemblyman, 66-, mem, Taxation & Hwy Safety Interim Legis Comts, Nev State Assembly, 68-70, chmn, Agr Comt, 68-, mem, 73-, mem, Govt Affairs Comt, 68-70 & 73-74, vchmn, 71-72, chmn, Subcomt Pub Employ Practices, 69-, mem, Environ & Pub Resources Comt & Legis Comt, 71-72, mem, Health & Welfare Comt, First Alt Legis Comn, Legis Comn Subcomt for Study of Probate Laws & Study of Mobile Home Taxation, 73-74, mem, Agr & Com Comts & First Alt Legis Comn, 75-; mem, Comt Future Water Needs, 67-; mem agr comt, Western Conf State Govts, 68-70; state pres, Citizens Adv Comt, Col of Agr, 69-70; dir, Churchill Co Econ Develop, 70-; pre mem exec comt, Churchill Co Bicentennial Comn & chmn finance comt, Rural Health Serv in Nev. Bus & Prof Pos: Owner & mgr, Virgil Getto Dairy Farms. Mem: Rotary; CofC (mem bd, Churchill Co); Churchill Co Econ Develop Bd. Relig: Catholic. Mailing Add: 1400 Lovelock Hwy Fallon NV 89406

GETTY, L MICHAEL (D)
Ill State Sen
Mailing Add: 15401 S Drexel Ave Dolton IL 60419

GETTYS, THOMAS SMITHWICK (D)
b Rock Hill, SC, June 19, 12; s John E Gettys & Maud Martin G; m 1947 to Mary Phillips White; c Julia Martin & Sara Elizabeth. Educ: Clemson Univ; Erskine Col, BA, 33; Duke Univ, Winthrop Col, grad work. Polit & Govt Pos: Rock Hill postmaster, 51-54, secy to Congressman James P Richards, 7 years; US Rep, SC, 64-74. Bus & Prof Pos: Teacher & coach, Rock Hill High Sch; prin, Cent Sch; law practice, 54- Mil Serv: Navy, Pac Theater. Mem: Am Legion; VFW; Elks; Rotary; YMCA. Relig: Presbyterian; former deacon & elder, Assoc Reformed Presbyterian Church of Rock Hill. Mailing Add: Rock Hill SC 29730

GETZWILLER, POLLY (D)
Ariz State Rep

b Luna, NMex, Mar 8, 24; d William T Johnson & Grace Ross Birdwell J; m 1954 to Marion H Getzwiller; c Billie Lou, William Albert & Marion Joe. Polit & Govt Pos: Ariz State Rep, currently; deleg, Dem Nat Conv, 68. Mem: Bus & Prof Women's Club; Dem Women; Woman's Club; Nat Platform Asn; Colo River Water Asn. Relig: Presbyterian. Mailing Add: Box 127 Casa Grande AZ 85222

GEWERTZ, KENNETH A (D)
NJ State Assemblyman
Mailing Add: 4 Cooper St Woodbury NJ 08096

GEYERMAN, PETER THOMAS (D)
Treas, Pennington Co Dem Comt, SDak

b Huron, SDak, Oct 7, 31; s Peter Rudolph Geyerman & Ella Forking G; m 1953 to Frances Darlene Scott; c Clay Scott. Educ: Univ Minn. Polit & Govt Pos: Pres, Pennington Co Young Dem, SDak, 58-60 & 61-64; Dem precinct committeeman, 58-66; treas, Pennington Co Dem Comt, 66- Mil Serv: Entered as Airman Recruit, Navy, 51, released as PO 2/C, 55, after serv in Patrol Squad 46, Philippines. Mem: Downtown Improvement Asn; Rapid City CofC (mem bd, Retail Comt, 58-66); Lions; Elks. Relig: Protestant. Mailing Add: PO Box 1910 Rapid City SD 57701

GHOLSON, ISAAC WILLIAM (D)
Chmn, Stonewall Co Dem Party, Tex
b Aspermont, Tex, Feb 14, 12; s James Monroe Gholson & Lila Elizabeth Hart G; m 1960 to Jenora Kathlyn Davis; c Bobby Roe, William Alec, Carolyn Louise (Mrs Albright) & James W. Educ: High sch, Aspermont, Tex. Polit & Govt Pos: Chmn, Stonewall Co Dem Party, Tex, 42- Bus & Prof Pos: Rancher, currently. Mem: Farm Bur; Odd Fellows. Relig: Baptist. Mailing Add: Rte 1 Box 16 Aspermont TX 79502

GHOLSON, JEROME BUSLER (D)
Committeeman, Ill Dem Cent Comt
b Eldorado, Ill, Apr 30, 35; s Elmo Gholson & Abbie Busler G; m 1962 to Beulah Frances Fowler. Educ: Southern Ill Univ, BS in Bus Admin, 58; Ky Sch of Embalming, 60; MEA Ky Sch of Embalming Award. Polit & Govt Pos: Dep coroner, Hamilton Co, Ill, 64-72 coroner, 72-; committeeman, Ill Dem Cent Comt, 66- Bus & Prof Pos: Funeral dir, Gholson Funeral Home, McLeansboro, Ill, 57-; dir, Off of Econ Opportunity, Wabash Area, 66- Mil Serv: Pvt, Army Res, 58, released as Pfc, 64, after serv in Berlin Crisis, 61-62. Mem: Elks; Odd Fellows; Scottish Rite; AF&AM; Miss Valley Consistory (32 degree). Honors & Awards: Award for one of America's Outstanding Young Men of 1970; Man of Year Award, Hamilton Co Future Farmers of Am. Relig: Baptist. Mailing Add: 107 W Randolph McLeansboro IL 62859

GIADONE, WILLIAM BIAGIO (R)
Chmn, Fitchburg Rep City Comt, Mass
b Italy, Oct 9, 09; s Salvatore Giadone & Domica Guinta G; m 1932 to Beuna Baldarelli; c Dorothy (Mrs Peter C Valeri), Barbara (Mrs Gerald Gallent) & Sandra (Mrs William D Leger). Educ: Several short courses in Merchandising, Advert, & Financing. Polit & Govt Pos: Coordr, Gov Volpe, 62-; chmn, Fitchburg Rep City Comt, 68- Bus & Prof Pos: Pres, Giadone's Furniture Co, 32-69. Mem: Arm of Retail Merchants; Retailers Mkt Guild; Nat Retail Furniture Asn; Sons of Italy; Rotary. Honors & Awards: Man of the Year Award, Sons of Italy, 65; Devoted Serv Award, Fitchburg CofC, 66. Relig: Catholic. Legal Res: 475 Water St Fitchburg MA 01420 Mailing Add: 325 Water St Fitchburg MA 01420

GIAIMO, ROBERT NICHOLAS (D)
US Rep, Conn
b New Haven, Conn; s Rosario Giaimo & Rose Scarpulla G; m to Marion Schuenemann; c Barbara Lee. Educ: Fordham Col, AB, 41; Univ Conn Law Sch, LLB, 43. Polit & Govt Pos: Mem, Bd of Educ, North Haven, Conn, 49-55 & Bd of Finance, 52-55; third selectman, North Haven, 55-57; chmn, Conn Personnel Appeals Bd, 55-58; US Rep, Third Dist, Conn, 59-, mem, Appropriations Comt & its Subcomts on Dept Defense, Housing & Urban Develop, Space-Sci-Vet & Legis Br, US House of Rep, currently, mem, Joint Comt Cong Opers, US Cong, currently, mem, House Comn on Info & Facil & Select Comt on Intel, currently. Bus & Prof Pos: Lawyer, New Haven, 46- Mil Serv: Entered Army, 43, released as 1st Lt, 46; Capt, Judge Adv Gen Corps, Army Res. Mem: Conn Bar Asn. Relig: Roman Catholic. Legal Res: 139 Washington Ave North Haven CT 06473 Mailing Add: Rm 2265 Rayburn House Off Bldg Washington DC 20515

GIAMMARCO, HENRY J (D)
Pa State Rep
Mailing Add: Capitol Bldg Harrisburg PA 17120

GIANGIACOMO, ANTHONY (D)
RI State Rep
b Providence, RI, Sept 19, 26; s Dionino Giangiacomo & Josephine Pronda G; single. Educ: Johnston & Wales Bus Col, acct dipl, 50; Life Ins Mkt Inst, Purdue Univ, dipl, 56. Polit & Govt Pos: Deleg, RI Const Conv, 64-68; RI State Rep, 12th Dist, 67-, mem Finance Comt, Eastern Regional Comt on Policy Prob & Transportation, RI House of Rep, 67-, mem Comt to Study Regionalization of State & Local Serv, 68-, chmn, Pub Rights of Way Comn, 69- Bus & Prof Pos: Licensed pub acct & ins agt & broker, 55- Mil Serv: Entered as Pvt, Army, 44, released as Cpl, 46, after serv in Inf, Pac Theatre, 45-46. Mem: Nat Soc of Pub Acct; Ital-Am War Vet (past comdr, Dept of RI); Am Legion; VFW; St Vincent dePaul Soc. Relig: Catholic. Mailing Add: 24 Melissa St Providence RI 02909

GIANNINI, ANTHONY ALBERT (D)
b Providence, RI, July 17, 22; s Anthony Giannini & Elvira Izzi G; m 1951 to Eleanor Antonette Ruggerio; c Anthony A, Jr, William T, Stephen M & Judith M. Educ: Boston Col, LLB. Polit & Govt Pos: Legal counsel, Div Pub Utilities, RI, 57-59; exec secy, Gov John A Notte, Jr, 61-62; exec committeeman, RI Dem Party, 65-68, chmn, 68-69; Justice, RI Superior Court, 69- Mil Serv: Entered as Pvt, Army Air Force, 42, released as Sgt, 45. Mem: RI Bar Asn; Am Bar Asn; KofC; Lions; Serra Int. Relig: Catholic. Mailing Add: 39 Sheffield Ave Providence RI 02911

GIANULIS, JOHN ANDREW (D)
Chmn, Rock Island Co Dem Cent Comt, Ill
b Moline, Ill, Oct 5, 22; s Andrew John Gianulis (deceased) & Meta Kutselas G; m 1946 to Mary Jane Sandbo; c Andrew John, Sara Ann & Martha Marie. Polit & Govt Pos: Inspector, Ill Liquor Control Comn, 62-69; chmn, Rock Island Co Dem Cent Comt, Ill, 68-; field auditor, State Auditor, 69-73; asst personnel dir, Secy of State, 73-75, asst to Secy of State, 75- Bus & Prof Pos: Staff mem, Quad Cities Realty, 65- Mil Serv: Entered as A/S, Navy, 42, released as PO 1/C, 45, after serv in APA 222 USS Livingston, SPac, 42-45. Relig: Greek Orthodox. Legal Res: PO Box 95 Andalusia IL 61232 Mailing Add: PO Box 428 Rock Island IL 61201

GIARD, HAROLD WALTER (D)
Vt State Rep
b Burlington, Vt, Feb 21, 52; s Walter Louis Giard & Mary Helen G; single. Educ: St Michael's Col (Vt), currently; Arnold Air Soc. Polit & Govt Pos: Vt State Rep, currently. Mil Serv: Air Force ROTC, second year. Relig: Catholic. Mailing Add: Lake St Bridport VT 05734

GIBB, ARTHUR (R)
Vt State Sen
b Brooklyn, NY, Apr 16, 08; s Henry Elmer Gibb & Grace Dwight G; m 1932 to Barbara Lowrie Gibb; c John Dwight, Arthur, Jr, Lowrie, Barbara Grace & Henry F. Educ: Yale Univ, AB, 30. Polit & Govt Pos: Vt State Rep, 63-70, vchmn, Comt on Ways & Means, Vt House of Rep, 65, chmn, 69, chmn, Comt on Natural Resources, 66, 67 & 69, chmn, Legis Coun Tax Study, 67 & 68, chmn, Comt on Equal Opportunity, 68, vchmn, Legis Coun, 68 & 69; chmn, Gov Comn on Environ Control, 69; Vt State Sen, Addison Co, 70-, chmn comt agr, Vt State Senate, 73-74, chmn comt natural resources, 75- Bus & Prof Pos: Farming, Angus cattle breeder; estate trustee; banking & investment counsel. Mil Serv: Entered as Lt, Naval Res, 42, released as Comdr, 45, after serv in USS Lexington, Pac Theater, 43-45; Capt(Ret), Naval Res; Bronze Star with Combat V; Presidential Unit Citation; Pac Area Ribbon with ten Battle Stars. Mem: Nat Pilots Asn; Farm Bur; Porter Hosp (trustee); Vt YMCA (state comt). Relig: Congregational. Legal Res: Weybridge VT Mailing Add: Box 42 Rte 1 Middlebury VT 05753

GIBBONS, ALBERTA JOHANNA (R)
Chairperson, San Juan Co Rep Party, Utah
b Utrecht, Netherlands, Dec 19, 37; d Jan Krommenhoek & Mathilde Lemken K; m 1960 to De Lamar Johnson Gibbons; c Charlotte, De Grant, Robyn, Mignon & Gregory John. Educ: San Bernardino Valley Col, 56-57; Brigham Young Univ, 58, 65, 72 & 73. Polit & Govt Pos: Chairperson, San Juan Co Rep Party, Utah, 73- Mem: Utah Med Asn Women's Auxiliary; Nat, State & Co Rep Women's Fedn. Relig: Latter-day Saint. Legal Res: 639 W 100 South Blanding UT 84511 Mailing Add: PO Box 404 Blanding UT 84511

GIBBONS, ELEANOR KEATING (D)
b Medford, Mass, May 13, 39; d Robert Joseph Keating & Eleanor Plumstead K; m 1961 to Barry Francis Gibbons; c Michael John, Matthew Eric & Maureen Ellen. Educ: Burbank Hosp Sch Nursing, Dipl in Prof Nursing, 60; State Col at Fitchburg, BS, 60; Delta Phi Delta. Polit & Govt Pos: Mem, Reading Dem Town Comt, Mass, 68-; deleg, Dem Nat Conv, 72. Bus & Prof Pos: Surg nurse, Symmes Hosp, Arlington, Mass, 61; asst nurse, private oral surgeon, Washington, DC, 61-62; claims examr, Blue Cross Blue Shield, 62-63; indust nurse, Kimberly-Clark, New Milford, Conn, 63-65. Mem: League of Women Voters. Relig: Roman Catholic. Mailing Add: 86 Red Gate Lane Reading MA 01867

GIBBONS, SAM M (D)
US Rep, Fla
b Tampa, Fla, Jan 20, 20; s Gunby Gibbons & Jessie Kirk Cralle G; m to Martha Hanley; c Clifford, Mark & Timothy. Educ: Univ Fla, LLB; Blue Key; Univ Hall of Fame; Alpha Tau Omega. Polit & Govt Pos: Fla State Rep, 52-58; Fla State Sen, 58-62; US Rep, Fla, 62-; deleg, Dem Nat Conv, 68; deleg, Dem Nat Mid-Term Conf, 74. Bus & Prof Pos: Law firm, Gibbons, Tucker, McEwen, Smith, Cofer & Taub, 47- Mil Serv: Army, 501st Parachute Inf, 101st Airborne Div, in initial assault landing, D-Day, Europe, in Bastogne oper, released as Maj; Bronze Star. Mem: Am, Fla, Tampa & Hillsborough Co Bar Asns; Univ of SFla Found. Honors & Awards: Tampa's Outstanding Young Man of the Year, 54; CofC Pres Award, One of Ten Top State Legislators in both House & Senate. Relig: Presbyterian; Deacon, First Presbyterian Church of Tampa. Legal Res: 940 S Sterling Ave Tampa FL 33609 Mailing Add: 430 Cannon House Off Bldg Washington DC 20515

GIBBS, HENRY LAWRENCE, JR (D)
La State Rep
b Monroe, La, Mar 7, 19; s Henry L Gibbs (deceased) & Annie Kelly G; m 1941 to Bobbie Regenia Hibbard (deceased); c Henry Lawrence, III, Kenneth Lane, Bobby Keith & Gary Dean. Polit & Govt Pos: La State Rep, 56-, chmn, House Educ Comt, La House Rep, currently; mem, La Dem State Cent Comt, 60-68. Mil Serv: Entered as Pvt, Army, 44, released as Sgt, 46, after serv in 28th Inf Div, ETO; ETO Medal with two Battle Stars; Good Conduct Medal; Presidential Unit Citation. Mem: Mason; Consistory; Shrine; Am Legion. Relig: Methodist. Mailing Add: 3718 Grammont St Monroe LA 71201

GIBBS, JUNE NESBITT (R)
Rep Nat Committeewoman, RI
b Newton, Mass, June 13, 22; d Samuel F Nesbitt & Lulu H Glazier N; m 1945 to Donald T Gibbs; c Elizabeth. Educ: Wellesley Col, BA, 43; Boston Univ, MA, 47. Polit & Govt Pos: Vchmn, Rep State Cent Comt, RI, 60-69; deleg, Rep Nat Conv, 68; Rep Nat Committeewoman, RI, 69-, mem, Exec Comt, 73-; mem, Defense Adv Comt Women in the Serv, 70-72, vchmn, 72; councilwoman, Middletown, RI Town Coun, 74- Mil Serv: Entered as Midn, Navy, 43, released as Lt(jg), 46. Relig: Congregational. Mailing Add: 163 Riverview Ave Middletown RI 02840

GIBNEY, ROBERT EMMET (R)
Mem, Rep State Cent Comt, Calif
b Pittsburgh, Pa, Sept 10, 15; s Christopher Arthur Gibney & Anna Haggerty G; m 1946 to Dorothy May Casselman; c Linda Anne, Robert Emmet, Nancy Jean, Mary Susan, William David & Kathleen Louise. Educ: Univ Pittsburgh, BS, 37; Phi Kappa Theta; Newman Club. Polit & Govt Pos: Mem, Eisenhower, Nixon & Goldwater for President Comts; mem, Reagan Finance Comt, Calif; mem, United Rep Finance Comt, Los Angeles Co; capt, 80th Precinct, 23rd Cong Dist; mem, Rep State Cent Comt, Calif, 69- Bus & Prof Pos: Owner & mgr, Robert E Gibney Assocs, Mfgs Rep, Los Angeles, 48- Mil Serv: Entered as 2nd Lt, Army, 42, released as Maj, 46, after serv in several units including Hq, Am, European & Asiatic Theatres, 44-46; Lt Col, Army Res, 46-69; 2 Battle Stars: Ardennes, Rhineland; 2 Commendations from 2 Maj Gen; Citation, President's Interdepartmental Comt. Mem: Los Angeles Athletic Club; Boy Scouts; Am Legion; Mil Order World Wars; Americanism Educ League (trustee). Honors & Awards: Citation for Outstanding Serv to Americanism Educ League, 69. Relig: Roman Catholic. Legal Res: 254 La Paloma San Clemente CA 92672 Mailing Add: PO Box 1102 Downey CA 90240

GIBONEY, BARBARA FAY (D)
b Jefferson City, Mo, Dec 26, 50; d William Donald Giboney & Bonnie Dell Shipman G; single. Educ: Jefferson City Sr High Sch, 68. Polit & Govt Pos: Off mgr, Mo State Dem Comt, 69-; deleg, Dem Nat Conv, 72. Mem: Mo Dem Comt 10,000; Mo Young Dem. Mailing Add: 1224 E Elm St Jefferson City MO 65101

GIBSON, ALEXANDER DUNNETT (R)
Mem, Caledonia Co Rep Comt, Vt
b Lisbon, NH, Oct 6, 01; s Dr John Mitchell Gibson & Clara Belle Dunnett G; m 1929 to May Bess Huberich; c Barbara Jean (Mrs Roth) & Alexander D, Jr. Educ: Middlebury Col, 20-21; Dartmouth Col, AB, 24; Columbia Univ, AM, 28, grad courses, 30-38; Univ Toulouse, France, 28-29; Univ Paris, summer 32; Laval Univ, summer, 59; Kappa Phi Kappa; Gamma Delta Chi. Polit & Govt Pos: Mem, Andover Town Rep Comt, Mass, 52-67, vchmn, 52-54, chmn, 54-58; deleg, Mass Rep State Conv, 54-56; chmn, Barnet Town Rep Comt, Vt, 69-70; chmn, Caledonia Co Rep Comt, 69-71, mem, 69-; mem, Vt Rep State Comt, 69-73; mem liaison comt, 70-71; mem platform comt, Vt Rep State Conv, 70 & 72; mem, Educ Comn of

States, 71-73. Bus & Prof Pos: Teacher French & Eng, Burlington High Sch, Vt, 24-28; instr French, Horace Mann Sch Boys, New York, NY, 29-36; sr master French, William Penn Charter Sch, Pa, 36-39; head lang dept, Mt Hermon Sch, Mass, 39-44; instr French & head bur self-help, Phillips Acad, Andover, 44-67; acting prin & teacher French, McIndoes Acad, Vt, 67-68; teacher, Sterling Sch, 68-69; regular contribr to French Rev & the Andover Bull, currently. Publ: Causeries, Henry Holt, 49; Anthologie, Odyssey Press, 67; History of McIndoes Academy. Mem: Vt Hist Soc; Rotary (pres, 74-75); Barnet Hist Soc (curator); Monroe, NH Men's Club; Vt Congregational Home, Inc (trustee). Honors & Awards: Palmes Academiques, French Govt, 62. Relig: Congregational. Mailing Add: McIndoe Falls VT 05050

GIBSON, ANDREW E (R)
b New York, NY, Feb 19, 22; s Andrew Gibson & Louisa Ann Tozer G; m to Jane Louise Mork; c Janet P, Andrew K, John S, Alexander S & Ann C. Educ: Mass Maritime Acad, 42; Brown Univ, BA cum laude, 51; NY Univ, MBA, 59. Polit & Govt Pos: Asst secy maritime affairs, Dept of Com, 69-72, asst secy domestic & int bus, 72. Bus & Prof Pos: Former capt, US Lines ocean freighter; asst dept mgr, Firestone Latex Prod Co, 46-48; asst to treas, Grace Line, Inc, New York, 53-54, cargo mgr, 54-57, terminal mgr, 57-62, asst vpres, 62-64, vpres of terminal opers, 64-65, sr vpres of opers, 65-67; vpres, Diebold Group, 67-69; pres, Interstate Oil Transport Co Inc, Philadelphia, 72- Mil Serv: Entered as Lt, Navy, 51-53, Asst Controller, Budget, Mil Sea Transportation Serv. Mailing Add: 8315 Seminole Ave Philadelphia PA 19118

GIBSON, BEN J, JR (R)
Mem Exec Comt, Polk Co Rep Cent Comt, Iowa
b Des Moines, Iowa, Mar 18, 22; s Ben J Gibson & Anna Ralston G; m 1942 to Katherine Chase; c Ben J, III, Megan Elizabeth, Chase Fredrick, Wendell Stewart & Brian Charles. Educ: Univ Va, BA, 47, Grad Sch, grad work in Am Hist, 47; Sigma Nu. Polit & Govt Pos: Rep cand for Cong, Fifth Dist, Iowa, 64; chmn resolutions comt, Polk Co Rep Orgn, 66; mem platform comt, State Rep Orgn, 66; campaign mgr, Polk Co Rep Cand, 66; mem exec comt, Polk Co Rep Cent Comt, 66- Bus & Prof Pos: Pres, Gibson Co, Inc & The Book Store, Inc, Des Moines. Mil Serv: Entered as Pfc, Marine Corps, 42, released as 1st Lt, 46, after serv in Inf, 46. Mem: Exec secy, Midland Booksellers Asn, Des Moines; mem, Des Moines CofC. Relig: Presbyterian. Mailing Add: 5324 Grand Ave Des Moines IA 50312

GIBSON, BILLY RANDALL (D)
Miss State Rep
b Schlater, Miss, Nov 17, 37; s Marland Edward Gibson & Eva Mae Smith G; m 1961 to Linda Kaye Simmons; c David Edward & Susan Michelle. Educ: Univ Southern Miss, BS, 60; Univ Miss, JD, 65; Alpha Tau Omega. Polit & Govt Pos: Mem bd trustees, Northwest Miss Jr Col, 72-; Miss State Rep, 72-; pres, Bruce Libr Bd, 73-; mem, Dixie Regional Libr Bd, 73-; mem, Miss Classification Comt, 73-; mem, Miss Post Secondary Educ Planning Bd, 74- Bus & Prof Pos: Attorney-at-law, Bruce, Miss, 65- Mil Serv: Entered as A/S, Navy, 60, released as Lt(jg), 63, after serv in USS Forrest Royal, Atlantic, Caribbean, Middle Eastern, 60-63; Armed Forces Campaign Medal (Cuban Crisis). Mem: Miss & Calhoun Co Bar Asns; VFW; Am Legion; Bruce CofC. Honors & Awards: Outstanding Young Men of Am, 72. Relig: Church of Christ. Mailing Add: S Newburger St Bruce MS 38915

GIBSON, CATHARINE (R)
b Sullivan, Ind, Sept 29, 07; d C Edward Coffman & Alice MacDonald C; m 1924 to Peter Gibson; c Isabel (Mrs Douglas W Taylor). Educ: Wicker Sch Fine Arts, Detroit, 27-30. Polit & Govt Pos: Pres, Rep Women's Fedn, Mich, 48-53, chmn, Campaign Activities Comt, 72-; deleg, Rep Nat Conv, Chicago, 52; deleg, Rep Nat Conv, San Francisco, 56; first vpres, Nat Fedn Rep Women, 52-56; vchmn, Rep Cent Comt, Mich, 53-57; chmn, Rep VChmn Midwest & Rocky Mountain States, 54-57; pres, Nat Fedn Rep Women, 57-60, mem exec comt, 61-63; Presidential app, Assay Comn, 58; mem adv coun, Comt to Reelect the President, 72. Mem: DAR; Eastern Star; Order of Rainbow for Girls; Bus & Prof Women's Clubs; Monroe City Co Fine Arts Coun (pres, 74 & 75). Relig: Presbyterian. Mailing Add: 3265 Parkwood Woodland Beach Monroe MI 48161

GIBSON, CHARLES MACDONALD (D)
b Charleston, SC, Aug 16, 32; s Charles E Gibson & Helen Woodcock G; m 1971 to Shirley Mauldin; c Five. Educ: Univ Va, BA, 54; Univ SC, LLB, 59. Polit & Govt Pos: Mem, Co Elec Comt, formerly; SC State Rep, 61-66; app mem by Gov, Gov Legis Comt on Ment Health & Ment Retardation, 62-; SC State Sen, 67-68; deleg, SC Dem State Conv & Dem Nat Conv, 68 & 72; state elector, Humphrey-Muskie Gen Elec, 68. Bus & Prof Pos: Lawyer; pres, Charleston Cable TV Co, Inc, 70- Mil Serv: Lt, Transportation Corps, 159th Boat Bn, 54-56. Mem: Am, SC & Charleston Co Bar Asns; Wig & Robe; Phi Delta Phi. Legal Res: 15 Wentworth St Charleston SC 29401 Mailing Add: PO Box 1018 Charleston SC 29402

GIBSON, DONALD BANCROFT (D)
Mem, Hampton Dem Exec Comt, Va
b Hampton, Va, Jan 19, 28; s Stuart Mather Gibson & Elizabeth Rowe Souder G; m 1971 to Caroline Elizabeth Christian; c Faith Ann & Wendy Elizabeth. Educ: King Col, 47-49; Univ Richmond, 49-52; Theta Chi. Polit & Govt Pos: Dep clerk, Circuit Court, Va, 59-; deleg, Dem State Conv, 60, 64, 68 & 72; secy, Hampton Roads Young Dem Club, 62-63, vpres, 63-64 & pres, 64-66; deleg, Dem Nat Conv, 64; dep clerk, Court of Law & Chancery, 64-; mem, Hampton Dem Exec Comt, Va, 69- Bus & Prof Pos: Asst underwriter, NAm Assurance Soc, 55-58; Ins agent, Home Beneficial Life Ins Co, 58-59. Mil Serv: Coast Guard, 52-54; Nat Defense Serv Medal; Coast Guard Res, 54-60. Mem: Elks; Peninsula Exchange Club; Va Court Clerks Asn; Va Govt Employees Asn Inc. Relig: Presbyterian. Legal Res: 135 Hanover Hampton VA 23661 Mailing Add: Clerks Off Circuit Court Hampton VA 23669

GIBSON, DONALD JACK (R)
b Spearfish, SDak, Nov 14, 23; s George L Gibson & Irene Adams G; m 1944 to Donna Rae Searls; c Claudia Lea & David John. Educ: SDak State Univ, 41-43; Okla State Univ Army Specialized Training Prog, 44-45; Columbia Univ Sch Bus & Transportation Mgt Sch, 59; Harvard Bus Sch, mgt, 68. Polit & Govt Pos: Mem, Sioux Falls Independent Bd of Educ, SDak, 63-68; chmn, SDak Citizens for Goldwater-Miller, 64; chmn, Karl Mundt for Sen, 65 & 66; chmn, SDak Nixon for Pres Comt, 68; deleg, & secy-treas, SDak Deleg, Rep Nat Conv, 68; chmn, Nixon-Agnew, SDak, 68; Rep Nat Committeeman, formerly. Bus & Prof Pos: Pharm apprentice, Blue Drug Co, Spearfish, SDak, summers 41-42; from various job assignments to opers mgr, Wilson Truck Syst, Sioux Falls, 46-51. Mil Serv: Entered as Pvt, Army, 43, released as T/Sgt, 46, after serv in 409th Inf, ETO, 44-46; Combat Inf Badge; Purple Heart. Mem: Am Trucking Asn (dir & mem exec comt); Elks; Am Legion; Sioux Falls Consistory; Shrine. Honors & Awards: Sioux Falls Citizen of the Week. Relig: Episcopal. Mailing Add: 2900 33rd St Sioux Falls SD 57103

GIBSON, JAMES ISAAC (D)
Nev State Sen
b Golden, Colo, Mar 22, 25; s Fred Daniel Gibson & May Emma Borsberry G; m 1947 to Audrey June Brinley; c James Brinley, David Scott, Robin Lee, Terry Lynn, Cynthia Rae & Holly Jo. Educ: Univ Kans, 43-44; Univ Colo, 44; US Naval Acad, BS, 47; Rensselaer Polytech Inst, BCE, 48, MCE, 50; Sigma Xi. Polit & Govt Pos: Trustee, Henderson Sch Dist, Nev, 54-56; Nev State Assemblyman, 58-66, mem, Interim Finance Comt, Nev State Assembly, 60-66, chmn, 66, mem, Legis Comn, 62-66, chmn, 65; mem adv bd, Bur Land Mgt, Nev & Desert Research Inst, Univ Nev, 60-69; Nev State Sen, First Dist, 67-, mem, Legis Comn, 67 & 71; vpres Western Conf, Coun State Govt, 68, pres, 69, governing bd, 68-71 & 73, exec bd, 73- Bus & Prof Pos: Asst chief engr, Western Electro Chem Co, 53-54, chief engr, 54-55; plant engr, Am Potash & Chem Corp, 55-61, adv engr, 58-61; chief engr, Pac Eng & Prod, 61-66, exec vpres, 66- Mil Serv: Entered as A/S, Navy, 43, released as Lt, 53, after serv in 104th Construction Bn, Provost Marshall, Port Hueneme, Staff, Pub Works Off, Potomac River Naval Command; Am Theater & Korean Campaign Ribbons. Mem: Nat & Nev Soc Prof Engrs; Soc of Mil Engrs; Am Legion Post 40; Boy Scouts (vpres & treas, Boulder Dam Area Coun, 66-). Honors & Awards: Silver Beaver Award, Boy Scouts, 69; Distinguished Nevadan Award, Univ Nev, Las Vegas, 73. Relig: Latter-day Saint; stake pres, Lake Mead Stake, 56-73; regional rep of the Twelve, 73- Mailing Add: 806 Park Lane Henderson NV 89015

GIBSON, JARRETT DEMPSEY (D)
Committeeman, WVa Dem Party
b Dunbar, WVa, Feb 21, 27; s George W Gibson & Susie Pribble G; m 1947 to Maxine Jewel Hager; c Tami Ann. Educ: Morris Harvey Col, 45-46. Polit & Govt Pos: Committeeman, WVa Dem Party, 69-; WVa State Deleg, 69-70; registr, Kanawha Co, WVa, 70-72, assessor, 73-; alt deleg, Dem Nat Conv, 72. Bus & Prof Pos: Owner, Gibson's Furniture Co Inc, Nitro, WVa, 56-61 & St Albans, WVa, 61-69. Mil Serv: Air Force, 51-55, 56, S/Sgt, with serv in Air Defense Command, Colorado Springs, Colo. Mem: CofC (pres, St Albans Chap; state dir, WVa Chap); Lions; Elks; Am Legion. Honors & Awards: Named Businessman of the Year. Relig: Baptist. Legal Res: 924 Helene St St Albans WV 25177 Mailing Add: 2412 Kanawha Terr St Albans WV 25177

GIBSON, JOHN F (MUTT) (D)
Ark State Sen
Mailing Add: PO Box 217 Dermott AR 71638

GIBSON, JOHN S (D)
Pres, Los Angeles City Coun, Calif
b Geneseo, Kans, Aug 11, 02; s John Samuel Gibson & Flora Dix G; m 1923 to Mina Workman; c Marlyn (Mrs Buehler) & Dixie (Mrs Blackwelder), grandchildren, Susan, George, Marlie, John, Becky & Laurie Buehler, Jacqueline, Janis, Jinelle & John Blackwelder. Educ: Kans Univ, 1 year; Am Inst Banking of Los Angeles, grad; Calif Real Estate Asn courses. Polit & Govt Pos: City police judge & mayor, Geneseo, Kans; councilman, 15th Dist, Los Angeles, Calif, 51-, pres coun, 53-61 & 69-, pres pro tem, 67-69; first vpres, Mayor's & Councilmen's Dept, League of Calif Cities. Bus & Prof Pos: With Long Beach Dairy & Creamery Co, 27-28; assoc, George M Bronaugh, Gen Contractor, 34-41; gen contractor in own bus, 41- Mem: Pac Southwest Youth for Christ in Los Angeles (vpres); Mason; Al Malaikan Shrine; Elks; KT. Honors & Awards: Founder, first Boy's Club in Calif, 35; Distinguished Serv Award, Nat Jr CofC, 36; Distinguished Serv Award, Civitan Serv Club Int, 38. Relig: Baptist; Bd Deacons, First Baptist Church, San Pedro. Legal Res: 1604 Sunnyside Terr San Pedro CA 90732 Mailing Add: Rm 375 City Hall Los Angeles CA 90012

GIBSON, KENNETH ALLEN
Mayor, Newark, NJ
b Enterprise, Ala, May 15, 32; s Willie Foy Gibson & Daisy Lee G; m to Muriel Cooke; c Cheryl & Jo Ann. Educ: Newark Col Engr, BS in Civil Eng, 62. Polit & Govt Pos: Mayor, Newark, NJ, 70-; deleg, Dem Nat Mid-Term Conf, 74. Bus & Prof Pos: Licensed Engr. Mailing Add: 92 Rose Terr Newark NJ 07108

GIBSON, KENNETH O, SR (D)
Ky State Sen
Mailing Add: 229 Highland Dr Madisonville KY 42431

GIBSON, PETE JONES (D)
Mem Exec Comt, Ga Dem Party
b Waynesville, Ga, Jan 26, 14; s William Richman Gibson & Sarah Elizabeth Anderson G; m 1940 to Marion Virginia Thran; c William Richard, John Pete & Donald Edward. Educ: Univ Ga, BSAE, 40. Polit & Govt Pos: Dir, Slash Pine Area Planning & Develop Comn, Ga, 63-, chmn, 67; chmn, Brantley Co Airport Comt, 65-; secy, Adv Comt State Planning Bur, 67, vchmn, 68; dir, Slash Pine Community Action Agency, 68; mem exec comt, Ga Dem Party, 71- Bus & Prof Pos: Pres, Brantley Co Med Ctr, Inc, 59- Mil Serv: Entered as Seaman 2/C, Navy Air Corps, 40, released as Aviation Cadet, after serv in Pensacola, Fla Flight Training. Mem: Lions; Aircraft Owners & Pilots Asn. Relig: Baptist. Legal Res: Waynesville GA 31566 Mailing Add: Nahunta GA 31553

GIBSON, ROBERT ALFRED (D)
Chmn, Terry Co Dem Comt, Tex
b Ropesville, Tex, Oct 25, 32; s John Henry Gibson & Ava Beatrice Poole G; m 1958 to Beverly Ann Wartes; c Rebecca Ann & Ruth Allison. Educ: Meadow High Sch, grad, 51. Polit & Govt Pos: Mem, Parks & Recreation Bd, Terry Co, Tex, currently; chmn, Terry Co Dem Comt, Tex, 74- Bus & Prof Pos: Mem bd dirs, Cotton Producers Gin Inc, currently; mem bd dirs, Meadow Farm Store Inc, currently. Mil Serv: Entered as Pvt, Army, 56, released as SP-4, 62. Mem: Tex Farmers Union; South Plains Dem Coun; Meadow Agri-Bus Club. Relig: Baptist. Mailing Add: Box 283 Meadow TX 79345

GIBSON, WILLIAM L (R)
Fla State Rep
b Huntington, WVa, Oct 3, 06; m Ocie A Mossburg; c Patricia (Mrs E Stallings), William L, Jr, Karl B & Gregory T. Educ: Univ Md; George Washington Univ. Polit & Govt Pos: Fla State Rep, 38th Dist, 67- Bus & Prof Pos: Security supvr, Avco Missile Div, Cape Kennedy, 3 years; Air Force dir spec invests, with Scotland Yard, Brit Mil Intel, US Secret Serv, Cent Intel Agency & Fed Bur Invests, London, Eng. Mil Serv: Col, Air Force, World War II,

Col(Ret), 62; Air Force Commendation Medal with two Oak Leaf Clusters; Am Campaign Medal; European-African-Mid East Campaign Medal; Asiatic-Pac Campaign Mgdal; World War II Victory Medal; Medal for Humane Action; Nat Defense Serv Medal & Air Force Serv Award with three Bronze Oak Leaf Clusters. Mem: Mason; Seminole Sojourners; Leaf Soc; ROA; Air Force Asn. Honors & Awards: One of Nation's First Transportation Brokers; Licensed by Atomic Energy Comn as Radiation Control Officer; Fed Aviation Agency Commercial Pilot License; only mem of Fla Legis that has never missed a Roll Call or Vote for past six years. Relig: Methodist. Mailing Add: 1432 Knollwood Circle Orlando FL 32804

GIEBLER, RICHARD OWEN (R)
b Washington, Mo, Jan 22, 38; s John Thomas Giebler & Hilda Marie Gilgrease G; m 1962 to Barbara Ann Block; c Karen Marie & Denise Louise. Educ: Wash Univ, 59; Southeast Mo State Col, BS, 62; Southwest Mo State Col, 66; Sigma Phi Epsilon. Polit & Govt Pos: Twp committeeman, Franklin Co Rep Cent Comt, Mo, 62-, treas, 66-68, chmn, formerly; pres, BOLES-Calvey Rep Club, 65-66. Bus & Prof Pos: Teacher, Rockwood High Schs, 62-67; sr salesman, Addison Wesley Publ, 67- Mil Serv: Entered as Pvt, Army, 56, released as Sgt, 59, after serv in Armor. Mem: Mo State Teachers Asn; Zeta Chap, Prof Bookmen of Am; Pac Jaycees; Mo Jaycees; US Jaycees. Mailing Add: RR 2 Pacific MO 63069

GIESE, KENYON E (R)
Wis State Rep
Mailing Add: 328 Dallas St Sauk City WI 53583

GIESSINGER, PETER W (D)
Treas, Grant Co Dem Party, SDak
b Milbank, SDak, Jan 5, 20; s Ignaty Giessinger & Theresa Lemmer G; m 1942 to Helen L Prevey; c Lawrence C, Sandra K (Mrs White) & Gregory P. Educ: High sch, 2 years. Polit & Govt Pos: Treas, Grant Co Dem Party, SDak, 63- Bus & Prof Pos: Owner/operator, Red Owl Groceries, 53-63 & Sears Catalog Merchant, 64- Mem: KofC (3 degree & 4 degree); Catholic Order Forestors. Relig: Catholic. Mailing Add: 105 S Ninth St Milbank SD 57252

GIFFEE, ROLAND M (D)
Chmn, Platte Co Cent Dem Comt, Mo
b Platte City, Mo, Feb 8, 15; s William M Giffee & Georgie Linney G; m 1937 to Melva Baldwin; c Brenda Ann (Mrs Phillip G Cohen). Educ: Park Col, 32-33 & 47-48; Univ Mortuary Sci, 48-49. Polit & Govt Pos: Coroner, Platte Co, Mo, 53-; committeeman, Carroll Twp Dem Comt, 72-; chmn, Platte Co Cent Dem Comt, 74- Bus & Prof Pos: Printer, Landmark, 29-42, mgr, 53-; draft bd clerk, Platte Co, Mo, 42-43; mgr funeral home, Platte City, 46-53. Mil Serv: Entered as SK 2/C, Navy, 43, released as SK 2/C, 45, after serv in 26th Spec SeaBees, Pac Theatre, 44-45; Good Conduct Medal; Pac Theatre Medal. Mem: Mason; VFW; Platte Co Bus & Prof Club; Mo Peace Officers Asn. Relig: United Methodist. Mailing Add: Box 55 16 Maple Dr Platte City MO 64079

GIFFORD, WILLIAM LEO (R)
b Weston, Conn, Aug 30, 30; s Rolland Wyckoff Gifford & Margaret Mary Clifford G; m 1956 to Marion Frances Mileti; c Margaret Rose, William Leo, Jr & David Wyckoff. Educ: Fordham Univ, AB, 52; Univ Conn Sch Law, 52-55. Polit & Govt Pos: Spec Asst to Secy Labor for Legis Affairs, 69-70; spec asst to the President, 70-72; Asst to Secy Treas for Legis Affairs, 72-73; Adv, Bd Gov, Asian Develop Bank, Inter-Am Develop Bank, 72-73; Dep Under Secy Treas, 73-74; Washington rep, Gen Elec Co, 74- Bus & Prof Pos: Reporter, various newspapers. Relig: Roman Catholic. Legal Res: 43 Walnut St Jamestown NY 14701 Mailing Add: 3908 Terry Pl Alexandria VA 22304

GIGERICH, WILLIAM EDWARD (D)
b Indianapolis, Ind, Sept 10, 44; s Lawrence A Gigerich & Eva Faye Vestal G; m 1965 to Carolyn Sue Vasil; c Lawrence Edward & Lisa Sue. Educ: Nat Cash Register Computer Sch, grad, 63; IBM Computer Programming Sch, grad, 63. Polit & Govt Pos: Campaign worker, Jacobs for Congress, Indianapolis, Ind, 64-72; Dem precinct committeeman, Indianapolis, 68-72; campaign asst, Ind State Dem Comt, 68; campaign asst, Robert Kennedy for President, 68; deleg, Marion Co Conv, 68-74; campaign asst, Beatty for Lt Gov, Ind, 68; state chmn, McGovern for President, 71-72, campaign asst & coordr, 72; deleg, Ind State Dem Conv, 72; asst to Congressman Andy Jacobs, Ind, 68-72; campaign staff, Forestal for Auditor, Ind, 74. Bus & Prof Pos: Data processing supvr, Merchants Bank, Indianapolis, Ind, 62-68; bus mgr, WTLC Radio, Indianapolis, 68-72; dir opers, Aquaterra Inc, Ind & Ohio, 73; dir opers, Contentintal Home Parks, Fla, 74; chief dep auditor, Marion Co, Ind, 75- Relig: Catholic. Legal Res: 7689 N Meridian St Indianapolis IN 46260 Mailing Add: Rm 821 City County Bldg Indianapolis IN 46204

GIGLIO, FRANK (D)
Ill State Sen
Mailing Add: 1326 Mackinaw Ave Calumet City IL 60409

GIGNAC, JUDITH ANN (R)
Chmn, Cochise Co Rep Comt, Ariz
b Detroit, Mich, Mar 21, 39; d Durward Arthur DuPont & Gertrude Maneck D; m 1964 to Paul Ross Gignac; c Beth & Christopher. Educ: Broward Bus Col, 58; Univ Colo, Colorado Springs Ctr, 67-69. Polit & Govt Pos: Treas, Colorado Springs Young Rep, Colo, 64-65; pres, Thunder Mountain Rep Women, Sierra Vista, Ariz, 72-74, campaign chmn, 72-; chmn, Cochise Co Rep Cent Comt, 72-; chmn, Sierra Vista Bd Adjustments, 74- Bus & Prof Pos: Computer programmer, RCA, Colorado Springs, Colo, 62-70. Mem: Huachuca Art Asn (mem chmn, 73-); North Sierra Vista Civic Forum (vpres, 74-); PTA. Honors & Awards: Woman of the Year, Bus & Prof Women, 74-75. Mailing Add: 565 Raymond Dr Sierra Vista AZ 85635

GIGNILLIAT, ARTHUR (D)
Ga State Rep
Mailing Add: PO Box 968 Savannah GA 31402

GILBERT, CHARLES BREED, III (R)
Chmn, Norwich Rep Town Comt, Conn
b New London, Conn, Apr 6, 22; s Charles Breed Gilbert & Helen Lee G; m 1950 to Margaret Fearn; c Margaret Ann (Mrs David S Cook), Dinah & Jane (Mrs D Wesley Peek). Educ: Univ Mich, 40-42; Univ Conn, BS Mech Eng, 49; Univ New Haven, MBA, 74; Chi Psi. Polit & Govt Pos: Chmn, Norwich Rep Town Comt, Conn, 73-; mem bd trustees, State Tech Cols, 74- Bus & Prof Pos: Mem staff, Elec Boat Div, Gen Dynamics, 54-, mgr qual assurance eng, currently. Mil Serv: Entered as Seaman 1/C, Navy, 42, released as Aviation Machinist Mate 1/C, 45, after serv in Pac Theatre, 43-45. Mem: Am Soc Mech Engrs; Am Soc Qual Control; Am Mgt Asn. Mailing Add: 39 Harland Rd Norwich CT 06360

GILBERT, J C (D)
La State Rep
b Gilbert, La, Mar 6, 22; s Jess C Gilbert & Fannie Adams G; m 1946 to Barbara Jane Peck; c Barbara (Mrs Enright) & Jess, Jr. Educ: Northeast Jr Col, 2 years; La State Univ, Baton Rouge, 6 months; La State Univ, Chambers, 1 year. Polit & Govt Pos: Police juror, Catahoula Parish, La, 56-60; La State Sen, 60-72; La State Rep, Catahoula & Concordia Parish, 72- Bus & Prof Pos: Farmer. Mil Serv: Entered as Pvt, Army Air Force, 42, released as Sgt Maj, 46, after serv in 8th Air Force, ETO (Eng & Africa), 43-45. Mem: Am Legion; Farm Bur; Cattlemens Asn; Mason; Shrine. Relig: Methodist. Mailing Add: PO Box 278 Sicily Island LA 71368

GILBERT, JACOB H (D)
b Bronx, NY, June 17, 20; m 1949 to Irma Steuer; c Miriam Sharon, Sandra & Samuel Stephen. Educ: St John's Col; St John's Law Sch, LLB, 43. Polit & Govt Pos: Asst corp counsel, New York, 49-50; NY State Assemblyman, 51-54; NY State Sen, 55-60; US Rep, NY, 60-70, mem comt on ways & means, US House of Rep, formerly. Bus & Prof Pos: Attorney, Foley, Hickey, Gilbert & Currie, New York. Mem: Nat Dem Club; Bronx River YM-YWHA; AFL-CIO; NAACP; Am Jewish Cong. Relig: Jewish. Legal Res: 3801 Hudson Manor Terr Riverdale Bronx NY 10472 Mailing Add: 70 Pine St New York NY 10005

GILBERT, ROBERT BACON, JR (D)
Chmn, Meriwether Co Dem Exec Comt, Ga
b Greenville, Ga, Sept 27, 05; s Dr Robert Bacon Gilbert & Marilu Irvin G. Educ: Mercer Univ, 29-31; Stamford Univ, JD, 33; Blue Key; Sigma Delta Kappa; Lambda Chi Alpha; Cauldron; bus mgr, Col Annual; M Club; mgr football team. Polit & Govt Pos: Mem, Ga State Dem Exec Comt, 44-46 & 63-66; mem, Meriwether Co Dem Exec Comt, 46-71, chmn, 72-; deleg, Dem Nat Conv, 48, 52 & 64, alt deleg, 68; mem, Gov Staff, 63-66; mem, Ga Dem Comt of One Hundred, 65-66; mem, President Club; mem, Fulton Co Dem 500 Club. Bus & Prof Pos: Owner, Greenville Cotton Warehouses, 46-66; dir, Kennesaw Life & Accident Ins Co, 58-66; dir, Atlanta Int Raceway, 60-64; dir, Ga Cotton Warehouse & Compress Asn, 60-66; dir, Md Nat Ins Co, 63-66. Mem: Atlanta Athletic Club; Stadium Club; Piedmont Driving Club; Cherokee Town & Country Club; Elks. Relig: Baptist. Mailing Add: PO Box 236 Greenville GA 30222

GILBERT, THOMAS MARTIN (D)
b Elkmont, Ala; s Van Buren Gilbert & Mary McWilliams G; single. Educ: Athens Col, AB, 49; Am Univ, grad work. Polit & Govt Pos: Admin asst, US Rep Armistead Selden, 53-69, US Rep George Andrews, 69-71, US Rep Elizabeth Andrews, 72 & US Rep Marjorie S Holt, Ala, 73- Mil Serv: Entered as Seaman, Navy, 45, released as PO, 46. Relig: Episcopal. Legal Res: Greensboro AL Mailing Add: 1238 Longworth House Off Bldg Washington DC 20515

GILBERT, WILLIAM LEWIS (D)
b Pelham, NY, Apr 22, 15; s Lewis Gilbert & Betty Stewart G; m 1940 to Margaret Ruth Holmes; c Joann (Mrs R von Sternberg) & Virginia L. Educ: NY Univ, BS cum laude in Indust Eng & Bus Admin; Mass Inst Technol, grad study; Delta Mu Delta. Polit & Govt Pos: Affil mem, Calif State Dem Cent Comt; mem, Dist Attorney's Adv Coun & various local & fed govt comts & comns, including War Labor Bd, 41-; deleg & alt deleg, Dem Nat Conv, 60, 64 & 72; secy, Los Angeles Co Dem Cent Comt, Calif, 61-64. Bus & Prof Pos: Officer & rep, various nat & local unions, 36-50; field rep, Nat AFL-CIO, 50-63, dir, Los Angeles-Orange Co Orgn Comt, 63-68 & asst regional dir for Calif, Ariz, Nev & Utah, 68-74, western regional dir, 74- Mil Serv: Entered as Pvt, Army Air Corps, 44, released as Sgt, 46, after serv with Aviation Engrs; Good Conduct Medal. Publ: Various articles in labor & polit publ. Mem: IAMAW; United Furniture Workers; Indust Rels Asn; NAACP; Urban League. Relig: Protestant. Mailing Add: 2016 Strand Manhattan Beach CA 90266

GILBREATH, JERRY MICHAEL (R)
Chmn, Miss Young Rep Fedn
b Laurel, Miss, Sept 3, 48; s Jimmie B Gilbreath & Mary Jo Cozart G; single. Educ: Univ Miss, BA, 70, Sch Law, currently; Omicron Delta Kappa; officer, Alpha Tau Omega. Polit & Govt Pos: Student coordr, Miss Rep Party, 70-71; state chmn, Young Voters for Reelec of President Nixon, 72; alt deleg, Rep Nat Conv, 72; chmn, Miss Young Rep Fedn, 72- Mil Serv: SP-6, Miss Army Nat Guard, 3 years; Letter of Commendation for serv as legal clerk in off of Staff Judge Advocate, Ft Knox, Ky. Mem: Phi Alpha Delta; Boy Scouts (exec comt, Pine Burr Area Coun, 69-). Relig: Methodist. Legal Res: 811 W Fifth St Laurel MS 39440 Mailing Add: PO Box 1772 Laurel MS 39440

GILCHRIST, CHARLES W (D)
Md State Sen
b Washington, DC, Nov 12, 36; s Ralph Alexander Gilchrist & Eleanor Waters G; m 1961 to Phoebe Royce; c Donald, James & Janet. Educ: Williams Col, AB magna cum laude, 58; Harvard Law Sch, LLB, 61; Phi Beta Kappa; Alpha Delta Phi. Polit & Govt Pos: Md State Sen, 75- Bus & Prof Pos: Partner, Lee, Tooney & Kent, Washington, DC, 67- Mil Serv: Md Nat Guard, 61-67. Mem: Am, DC & Md Bar Asns. Mailing Add: 405 W Montgomery Ave Rockville MD 20850

GILCHRIST, DAVID BRUCE (R)
Chmn, Coos Co Rep Comt, NH
b Cambridge, Mass, Jan 11, 45; s Ross Stanley Gilchrist & Audrey Rohrman Gilchrist Archibald; m 1965 to Judith Peabody Gammon; c Ross Eric & Jason Stewart. Educ: Littleton High Sch, grad, 62. Polit & Govt Pos: Chmn, Groveton Rep Town Comt, NH, 73-; labor rep, Appeals Tribunal, NH Unemploy Dept, 74-; chmn, Coos Co Rep Comt, 75-; mem steering comt, NH Rep State Comt, 75- Bus & Prof Pos: Papermill employee, Groveton Papers Co, 70- Mem: United Paperworkers Int Union (treas, local 61, 73-); Nat Model RR Asn. Relig: Methodist. Mailing Add: 19 Preble St Groveton NH 03582

GILCHRIST, LAWRENCE BARNT (R)
b Denison, Iowa, Aug 13, 32; s L V Gilchrist & Genevieve Barnt G; m 1956 to Wilda Jean Williams; c Lawrence Wesley, Margaret Ann, Julie Diane & Elizabeth Jean. Educ: Coe Col, BA, 54; Iowa Univ Law Sch, JD, 60; Phi Alpha Delta; Alpha Sigma Phi. Polit & Govt Pos: Co attorney, Franklin Co, Iowa, 63-67; chmn, Franklin Co Rep Cent Comt, formerly. Bus & Prof Pos: Lawyer, 60-; mem bd, Hampton State Bank & Latimer State Bank, 70- Mil Serv: Entered as 2nd Lt, Air Force, 55, released as 1st Lt, 58; Capt, Air Force Res, 62. Mem: ROA;

Hampton Jaycees; Hampton CofC; Farm Bur; Forum Club. Relig: Methodist; mem bd, NIACC Found, 68- Mailing Add: Rte 3 Hampton IA 50441

GILES, ABRAHAM L (D)
Conn State Rep
Mailing Add: 2588 Main St Hartford CT 06120

GILES, DENNIS EARL (D)
b Kalispell, Mont, Mar 3, 49; s Lewis Burton Giles & Arta Marion Eastwood G; single. Educ: Spokane Community Col, Wash, 67-69 & 70-72; Eastern Wash State Col, 69-70. Polit & Govt Pos: Alt deleg, Dem Nat Conv, 72; precinct committeeman, Spokane Co Dem Cent Comt, 72-; Int Platform Asn, 75-; mem, Ctr for the Study of the Presidency, 75- Bus & Prof Pos: Telegrapher, Burlington Northern Inc, 68-, train dispatcher, 74- Mem: Young Dem Am (chap pres & charter mem, 75-); F&AM Brotherhood of Rwy, Airline & Steamship Clerks. Relig: Methodist. Mailing Add: N 4727 Walnut Spokane WA 99208

GILHOOLEY, JOHN JOSEPH (R)
b Brooklyn, NY, Oct 9, 21; s Francis Girard Gilhooley & Ann Flynn G; m 1949 to Josephine Ann Bergin; c John J, Jr, Paul Girard, Mark Francis, Thad Phillip, David Martin & James Mitchell. Educ: St John's Univ, NY, BBA, 42; Harvard Univ, 42-43; Cornell Univ, LLB, 49. Polit & Govt Pos: Asst Secy Labor, US Dept Labor, 57-60; comnr, NY Transit Authority, 62-68; deleg, Rep Nat Conv, 68; incorporator & dir, Amtrak, currently; app mem, Nat Hwy Safety Adv Comt, 75- Bus & Prof Pos: Assoc & partner, Whitman & Ransom, 49-53 & 60-61; chmn, Urban Indust Inc, NY, 69-71; chmn & chief exec, Transport of NJ, Inc, currently. Mil Serv: Entered as Ens, Naval Res, 43, released as Lt(sg), 46, after serv in USS Tex, NAtlantic, European, SPac & Japanese Theaters, 43-45; NAtlantic, European, SPac & Japanese Theater Ribbons; 5 Combat Stars; Commendation Medal from Adm Chester Nimitz, Okinawa & Iwo Jima. Publ: Weary Erie, Cornell Law Rev, spring 49; numerous articles & printed speeches, 53-68. Mem: New York & Am Bar Asns. Honors & Awards: Awards from various nat & local civic orgn. Relig: Roman Catholic. Legal Res: 384 Indian Trail Dr Franklin Lakes NJ 07417 Mailing Add: 180 Boyden Ave Maplewood NJ 07040

GILKEY, ROBERT C (D)
Secy, Hawaii State Dem Cent Comt
b Oakland, Calif, Feb 17, 28; s Errol C Gilkey & Katharine Carlton G; m to Conchita Ortiz; c John Henry, Maria Cristina, Maria Victoria, Philip Michael, Daniel Francis, Joseph Errol & Vincent Anthony. Educ: Univ Santa Clara, BS, 52. Polit & Govt Pos: Secy, Oahu Dem Co Comt, Hawaii, 59-60 & 70-72; mem, Hawaii State Dem Cent Comt, 60-70 & 72-, vchmn, 62-68, secy, 72-; state campaign coordr for President Lyndon B Johnson, 64; state vchmn, Citizens for McGovern-Shriver, 72; deleg, Dem Nat Mid-Term Conf, 74. Bus & Prof Pos: Personnel dir, St Francis Hosp, Honolulu, Hawaii, 57-67; dep dir, Hawaii State Dept Labor & Indust Rels, 67- Relig: Roman Catholic. Mailing Add: 427 Kaleimahamu St Honolulu HI 96825

GILL, BETTY (D)
Treas, Nat Fedn Dem Women
b Farmington, WVa, Jan 10, 21; d William Wayne Bainbridge & Nelle Jones B; m 1950 to Joseph Max Gill. Educ: Marion Co High Sch, Farmington, WVa, grad, 37; WVa Bus Col, secy, 38. Polit & Govt Pos: Prog chmn, Marion Co Dem Women's Club, WVa, 60-63; first dist dir, WVa Fedn Dem Women, 63-67, pres, 68-72; alt deleg, Dem Nat Conv, 68- treas, Nat Fedn Dem Women, 72-; comnr, Marion Co, 73-; mem, Marion Co Planning Comn, Health Bd, Coop Shop for Retarded Children & Sr Citizens Bd Dirs. Mem: Gov Adv Coun Drug Abuse; Nat Guard (adv bd); Benedum Airport Authority; YWCA. Relig: Church of Christ. Mailing Add: 1150 Avalon Rd Fairmont WV 26554

GILL, EDWIN MAURICE (D)
State Treas, NC
b Laurinburg, NC; s Thomas Jeffries Gill & Mamie North G. Educ: Trinity Col, 22-24; hon mem, Omicron Delta Kappa, hon mem, Beta Gamma Sigma, Univ NC, 63. Hon Degrees: LLD, Duke Univ, 59. Polit & Govt Pos: NC State Rep, 29-31; private secy, Gov Gardner, NC, 31-33; mem, Comn of Paroles, 33-42; mem, Comn Revenue, 42-49; collector & dir, Internal Revenue, Greensboro, 50-53; State Treas, NC, 53- Bus & Prof Pos: Law firm, Gibson & Gill, 24-31; law firm, Gardner, Morrison & Rogers, 49-50. Mem: Am Parole Asn; Am Prison Asn; Nat Tax Asn; State Banking Comn (chmn); Local Gov Comt (chmn, dir). Relig: Methodist. Mailing Add: State Capitol Raleigh NC 27602

GILL, ELBERT T (D)
Tenn State Rep
Mailing Add: 1007 Crocus St Johnson City TN 37601

GILLELAND, JAMES E (R)
Wash State Rep
Mailing Add: 3234 Hunts Point Rd Bellevue WA 98004

GILLESPIE, JERALD DAN (R)
Chmn, Bay Co Rep Exec Comt, Fla
b Birmingham, Ala, Nov 4, 36; s J D Gillespie & Louise Armstrong G; m 1956 to Carmen Charlene Riha; c Jerald Dan, Jr, Theresa Ann & Charles Joseph. Educ: Sewanee Mil Acad, Sewanee, Tenn, 55; Pensacola Jr Col, Fla, 55-56. Polit & Govt Pos: Treas, Bay Co Young Rep, Fla, 71, chmn, 73-; mem, Bay Co Rep Exec Comt, 72-, mem policy comt, 73-, chmn, currently; nat committeeman, Fla Fedn Young Rep, 72-73. Bus & Prof Pos: Orthotic apprentice, Gillespie Brace & Limb Co, Pensacola, Fla, 58-64, cert orthotist, 64- & mgr, 68-69; owner, Gillespie Orthopedic Ctr, Panama City, 70- Honors & Awards: Key Man, Pensacola Jaycees, 62; Cert of Achievement, Fla Fedn Young Rep, 72, One of Top Ten Young Rep, 73; Cert of Appreciation, Bay Co Rep Exec Comt, 73. Relig: Methodist. Legal Res: 2716 Stanford Rd Panama City FL 32491 Mailing Add: 604 N Cove Blvd Panama City FL 32401

GILLESPIE, PATRICK B (R)
Pa State Rep
Mailing Add: Capitol Bldg Harrisburg PA 17120

GILLESPIE, ROBERT GILL (R)
Chief Justice, Miss Supreme Court
b Madison, Ala, Sept 17, 03; s Philander M Gillespie & Flora Gill G; m 1930 to Margaret Griffith (deceased); c Robert Gill & Virgil Griffith. Educ: Huntsville Jr Col, 23-24; Univ Ala, 24-26; Delta Tau Delta. Polit & Govt Pos: Spec agt, Fed Bur Invest, 34-35; chancellor, Second Chancery Court of Miss, 39; assoc justice, Miss Supreme Court, 54-66, presiding justice, 66-71, chief justice, 71- Bus & Prof Pos: Attorney, Bailey & Gillespie, 39-43, Gillespie & Minniece, 45-48 & Gillespie, Huff & Williams, 48-54. Publ: Some animadversions on land line cases, Miss Law J, 3/62; The matter of perspective, Tenn Bar J, 2/65. Mem: Am Judicature Soc; Miss & Am Bar Asns. Honors & Awards: One of group of agts which killed John Dillinger in Chicago, 34. Relig: Presbyterian. Legal Res: 432 Dunbar St Jackson MS 39216 Mailing Add: PO Box 117 Jackson MS 39205

GILLETTE, HELEN D (D)
Pa State Rep
b Pittsburgh, Pa; d Louis Frederick & Georgia E Mohn F; m to Michael J Gillette; c Michael J, Jr, Georgia A (Mrs Pellegrino) & Rebecca Rae. Educ: Univ Pittsburgh. Polit & Govt Pos: Pa State Rep, 31st Dist, 66- Bus & Prof Pos: Ins agt & acct. Mem: Nat Order Women Legislators; Cath Daughters Am; Bus & Prof Women; Women's Club Allegheny Valley. Relig: Catholic. Mailing Add: 1917 Freeport Rd Natrona Heights PA 15065

GILLETTE, HOWARD F, JR (R)
b Chicago, Ill, June 8, 42; s Howard F Gillette & Mary Hale G; m 1968 to Jane Brown. Educ: Yale Univ, BA, 64, PhD, 70. Polit & Govt Pos: Campaign mgr, Conn 109 Legis Dist, 66; exec dir, Rockefeller for President Comt, Conn, 68; co-chmn, Proj Pursestrings, 70; pres, Ripon Soc, 66- Bus & Prof Pos: Lectr Am civilization, Univ Pa, 69-70; asst prof Am studies, George Washington Univ, 70- Mem: Am Studies Asn; Am Hist Asn. Relig: Episcopal. Mailing Add: 3301 Porter St NW Washington DC 20008

GILLETTE, ROBERT WEST (R)
Mass State Rep
b Weymouth, Mass, Sept 1, 34; s George K Gillette, Jr & Marjorie L West G; m 1956 to June Ryan; c Suzanne M, R West, Jr & Sarah L. Educ: Bates Col, AB, 56. Polit & Govt Pos: Dir civil defense, Pembroke, Mass, 66-71; Mass State Rep, 71- Bus & Prof Pos: Mgr life ins dept, W C Ryan & Co, Inc, 61-; corporator, Rockland Savings Bank, 72-73. Mil Serv: Entered as Pfc, Marine Corps, 56, released as 1st Lt, 61, after serv in 2nd Marine Div, 2nd Air Force Serv Regt & 8th Marine Barracks, Washington, DC, 57-61; Capt, Marine Corps Res. Mem: Mass Asn Independent Ins Agents & Brokers; Mass Legislators Asn; AF&AM; Lions; Pembroke Hist Soc. Honors & Awards: Dist 33S Outstanding Pres Award, Mass Lions Club. Relig: Protestant. Mailing Add: 84 Little's Ave Pembroke MA 02359

GILLEY, SMITH E (D)
Tex State Rep
Mailing Add: 5111 Meadowbrook Dr Greenville TX 75401

GILLIAM, CHARLES (D)
WVa State Deleg
Mailing Add: State Capitol Charleston WV 25305

GILLIAM, HERMAN ARTHUR (D)
b Nashville, Tenn, Mar 6, 43; s Herman Arthur Gilliam, Sr & Leola Caruthers G; single. Educ: Yale Univ, BA, 63; Univ Mich, Ann Arbor, MBA, 67; Omega Psi Phi. Polit & Govt Pos: Admin asst, US Rep Harold Ford, Tenn, 75- Bus & Prof Pos: Asst vpres, Universal Life Ins Co, 71-72, vpres, 72- Mil Serv: Entered as Airman 3rd, Air Force Res, 65, released as Airman 2nd, 70. Mem: Lemoyne Owen Col (trustee bd); Memphis Acad Art (trustee bd). Relig: Protestant. Legal Res: 1283 S Parkway E Memphis TN 38106 Mailing Add: 901 Sixth St SW Apt 913 Washington DC 20024

GILLIAM, JEAN MARIE (D)
Chmn, Gilliam Co Dem Cent Comt, Ore
b Syracuse, NY, June 14, 23; d Charles Martin Cline & Faye Marie Crego C; m 1947 to Louis Leonard Gilliam; c Cheryl Jean, Richard Louis, Mary Jane & Juliann. Educ: Powelson Bus Inst, Syracuse, NY, 1 year. Polit & Govt Pos: Chmn, Gilliam Co Dem Cent Comt, Ore, 64- Bus & Prof Pos: Secy, Syracuse & Rome Air Bases, 43-47; ed, Condon Globe-Times, Ore, 65-; correspondent, East-Oregonian, Pendleton, 65- & Assoc Press, 66- Mem: Ore Press Women's Club; PTA; Altar Soc. Relig: Roman Catholic. Legal Res: 414 E Well St Condon OR 97823 Mailing Add: Box 106 Condon OR 97823

GILLIG, ANN STEPHENSON (D)
b Pikeville, Ky, Dec 19, 24; d Elmer D Stephenson & Emabel Bennett S; m 1949 to J Robert Gillig, wid 1958; c John Stephenson & Robert Bennett. Educ: Ward-Belmont Col, 41-42; Univ Ky, AB with high distinction, 45; Phi Beta Kappa; Delta Delta Delta. Polit & Govt Pos: Parliamentarian, Dem Women's Club of Ky, 68-72, pres, 72-74; state chairwoman, Sen Bill Sullivan for Lt Gov Campaign, currently; resolutions chmn, Ky Dem State Conv, 72. Mem: Jr League of Lexington; Women's Club Cent Ky; Gtr Lexington Dem Women's Club; Opportunity Workshop (adv bd). Relig: Christian Church; Study Dir, Christian Women's Fel, Cent Christian Church, secy admin bd, currently. Mailing Add: 108 Eastin Rd Lexington KY 40505

GILLIGAN, JOHN JOYCE (D)
Dem Nat Committeeman, Ohio
b Cincinnati, Ohio, Mar 22, 21; s Harry J Gilligan & Blanche Joyce G; m 1945 to Mary Kathryn Dixon; c Donald, Kathleen, John & Ellen. Educ: Univ Notre Dame, BA, 43; Univ Cincinnati, MA, 47; J F Kennedy Inst Polit, Harvard Univ, fel, 69; Adlai Stevenson Inst Int Studies, Univ Chicago, 69; Distinguished Woodrow Wilson Fel, Int Ctr for Scholars, Smithsonian Inst, 75- Hon Degrees: Hon doctorates from Univ Akron, Wilberforce Univ, Miami Univ, Xavier Univ, Univ Toledo & Univ Dayton. Polit & Govt Pos: Mem, Cincinnati City Coun, Ohio, 53-64 & 67-68; US Rep, Ohio, 64-66; Dem nominee for US Sen, 68; deleg-at-lg, Dem Nat Conv, 68; Gov, Ohio, 71-75; Dem Nat Committeeman, Ohio, currently. Bus & Prof Pos: Instr, Xavier Univ, 48-53; partner, John J Gilligan Consults, 75- Mil Serv: Navy, 42-45; Silver Star for Gallantry in Action. Relig: Catholic. Mailing Add: 88 E Broad St Columbus OH 43215

GILLIGAN, PETER J, JR (D)
Mont State Rep
Mailing Add: 3330 13th Ave S Great Falls MT 59405

GILLIGAN, ROBERT F (D)
Del State Rep
Mailing Add: 2628 Sherwood Dr Sherwood Park Wilmington DE 19808

GILLIGAN, ROBERT G (D)
Conn State Rep
Mailing Add: 130 Wells Farm Dr Wethersfield CT 06109

GILLIGAN, WILLIAM LEE (R)
WVa State Sen
b Wheeling, WVa, Aug 17, 24; s John Joseph Gilligan, Sr & Emma Eichenberg G; m 1948 to Noca Ruth Boggs; c Thomas L, James M & Robert W. Educ: WVa Univ, BS, 49; La Tertulia; Phi Delta Theta. Polit & Govt Pos: Civil defense dir, Tyler Co, WVa, 60-64, mem, Planning Comn, 66-71; chmn, Tyler Co Rep Exec Comt, 68-; mem, Second Sen Dist, WVa State Rep Exec Comt, 64-72, campaign chmn, 68-; mem, WVa State Rep Finance Comt, 66-72; app by Gov as WVa State Sen, 71, elected, 72- Bus & Prof Pos: Asst off mgr, Owens, Libbey, Owens Gas Dept, Charleston, WVa, 49-56; systs mgr, FMC Corp, South Charleston, 56-57; asst to gen mgr, Ormet Corp, Hannibal, Ohio, 57-; mem bd dirs, Sisterville Gen Hosp, 71-, mem bd dirs, WVa Oil & Gas Festival, 72- Mil Serv: Entered as Pvt, Marine Corps, 42, released as Cpl, 45, after serv in 4th Div, Pac Theatre, 43-45. Mem: Moose; Elks; VFW; Am Legion; Lions Int. Honors & Awards: Distinguished West Virginian Award, Gov WVa, 70; Good Neighbor Award, Tyler Co Fair, 72; Citizen of Year Award, Sisterville Jaycees, 72. Relig: Lutheran. Mailing Add: 920 Maple Lane Sisterville WV 26175

GILLIS, CARL L, JR (R)
Chmn, Johnson Co Rep Party, Ga
b Adrian, Ga, Aug 29, 17; s Carl L Gillis, Sr & Vina Lou Rowland G; m 1953 to Iris Mackey; c Gwenda, Carl, III & Gayla. Educ: Univ Ga, 3 years. Polit & Govt Pos: Mayor, Adrian, Ga, 50-58; deleg, Rep Nat Conv, 68; chmn, Johnson Co Rep Party, Ga, currently. Bus & Prof Pos: Pres, Builtwell Homes, 59-62; pres, Adrian Housing Corp, 63- Mem: Lions; Elks; Ga Farm Bur; Exchange Club. Relig: Methodist. Mailing Add: Box 246 Adrian GA 31002

GILLIS, HUGH MARION (D)
Ga State Sen
b Soperton, Ga, Sept 6, 18; s Jim L Gillis, Sr & Annie Lois Walker G; m 1948 to Jean; c Hugh, Jr, Donald Walker & Jean Marie. Educ: Ga Mil Col, 36; Univ Ga, BS, 39; Sigma Alpha Epsilon. Polit & Govt Pos: Chmn, Treutlen Co Hosp Authority, Ga; Ga State Rep, 41-43 & 49-52; Ga State Sen, 57-58 & 63-, Pres Pro Tempore, Ga State Senate, currently. Bus & Prof Pos: Farmer; Naval Stores. Mem: Livestock Asn (pres); Farmers Coop. Relig: Baptist; deacon, Baptist Church. Mailing Add: Box 148 Soperton GA 30457

GILLIS, LAURENCE JOSEPH (D)
NH State Rep
b Revere, Mass, June 18, 42; s Colin Alphonsus William Gillis & Dorothy Kelley G; m 1970 to Margaretta Thompson Archbald; c Margaretta Kelley & Sarah Archbald. Educ: Harvard Col, AB, 64; Boston Univ Law Sch, LLB, 71; Hasty Pudding Club; Harvard Young Dem. Polit & Govt Pos: Mem, NH Dem State Comt, 74-; NH State Rep, 75- Bus & Prof Pos: Attorney, Avery, Dooley, Post & Avery, Boston, Mass, 71-72; prosecuting attorney, Seabrook Munic Court, NH, 73; attorney, Junkins & Gillis, Hampton, NH, 72- Mil Serv: Entered as 2nd Lt, Army, 64, released as Capt, 67, after serv in 437th Mil Police Co, USACOMZEUR, 65-67. Publ: The California oath controversy, Boston Univ Law Sch, Commentaries Mag, 3/69. Mem: NH & Mass Bar Asns; Am Legion; Hampton Lions Club. Honors & Awards: Harvard Col Scholar, 60-61. Relig: Roman Catholic. Mailing Add: 1 Eastmor Lane Hampton NH 03842

GILLMOR, PAUL EUGENE (R)
Ohio State Sen
b Tiffin, Ohio, Feb 1, 39; s Paul Marshall Gillmor & Lucy Fry G; m 1962 to Brenda Luckey, wid; c Linda Dianne & Julie Ellen. Educ: Ohio Wesleyan Univ, BA, 61; Univ Mich Law Sch, JD, 64; Pi Sigma Alpha; Sigma Alpha Epsilon; Phi Delta Phi. Polit & Govt Pos: Ohio State Sen, 12th Dist, 67-, asst minority leader, Ohio State Senate, 75-; mem, Ohio War Orphans Scholarship Bd, 67-; Interstate Legis Comn Lake Erie, 70-; Ohio Const Rev Comn, 72- Bus & Prof Pos: Attorney-at-law, 67- Mil Serv: Capt, Air Force; served in 314th Combat Support Group, Tactical Air Command. Mem: Am & Ohio State Bar Asns. Relig: Lutheran. Legal Res: 2253 Sand Rd Port Clinton OH 43452 Mailing Add: Ohio Senate State House Columbus OH 43215

GILLMORE, ROBERT HAROLD (R)
b Claremont, NH, Jan 21, 46; s Vern Winslow Gillmore & Helen Tyre G; single. Educ: Williams Col, BA cum laude, 68; London Sch Econ, spring 70; Univ Va, MA, 71 & PhD, 73; Philip Francis Dupont Fel, Univ Va; Gargoyle; class secy; co-ed, The Williams Record; dir, Williams Ripon Soc. Polit & Govt Pos: Mem, Sullivan Co Rep Youth Orgn, 62-64; mem & chmn, Williams Col Young Rep, 64-68; mem, Manchester City Rep Comt, 73-; NH State Rep, 73-74; mem, Comt on Const Rev, NH House Rep, 73-74; deleg, NH State Const Conv, 74, vchmn comt on form & style; mem state adv comt, US Comn Civil Rights. Bus & Prof Pos: Summer employ, reporter and/or ed, The Manchester Union Leader, NH, 64, Claremont Daily Eagle, 65, North Adams Transcript, Mass, 66 & Bennington Banner, Vt, 67; ed staff, The Washington Post, DC, 70; teaching asst, Univ Va, 70-72; prof polit, St Anselm's Col, Manchester, 72-73; writer & ed, NH Times, Concord, 73; prin, Robert Gillmore & Assocs; co-publ, NH Law Weekly, currently. Mil Serv: Enlisted, Army, released as Pub Info Specialist, after serv in Vietnam; Army journalist in I Corps, 68-70. Mem: Williams Alumni Soc; Williams NH Alumni Asn; Gargoyle Alumni Asn; Friends of the London Sch Econ. Honors & Awards: Albert C Newell Prize, Williams Col, 68. Relig: Unitarian. Mailing Add: 50 Rockland Ave Manchester NH 03102

GILLOCK, EDGAR HARDIN (D)
Tenn State Sen
b Savannah, Tenn, July 30, 28; s Edgar Cherry Gillock & Ruth Hardin G; div; remarried 1971 to Joyce Genette Dowell; c Debra Ruth, Lee Hardin, Vicky Denise, Laura Elizabeth, Lorri June, Robert Neils, Ricky, Roger, Sherrie & Edgar H, II. Educ: Memphis State Univ, BS, MA & LLB, Kappa Alpha, Nat Forensic Club; Nat Hist Club. Polit & Govt Pos: Tenn State Rep, 63-66; asst city attorney, Memphis, Tenn, 64-66; Tenn State Sen, 69-; mem, Coun State Govt, Tenn, currently. Bus & Prof Pos: Attorney, Irwin, Owens, Gillock & Colton, 60- Mil Serv: Army, 51, Pfc, serv in 196th Field Artil. Mem: Nat Soc State Legislators; Scottish Rite; Nat Dem Party; East Frayser Civic Club; Exchange Club. Relig: Baptist. Mailing Add: 2925 Springhill Dr Memphis TN 38127

GILLOON, THOMAS J (D)
Iowa State Rep
Mailing Add: 3100 Brunskill Rd 5 Dubuque IA 52001

GILLSON, DEBORAH LYNN (R)
b Baton Rouge, La, Apr 22, 53; d Gordon Earl Gillson & Phyllis Laurine Anderson G; m 1975 to Perry Arthur McAnally. Educ: Adams State Col, Alamosa, Colo, 70-71 & 72; Colo State Univ, BA, 74; Univ Okla Col Law, 74- Polit & Govt Pos: Secy, Colo State Univ Col Rep, 72, chmn, 72-73, treas, 73-74; 1st vchmn, Col Rep League Colo; alt deleg, Rep Nat Conv, 72. Mem: Am Bar Asn; PEO. Relig: Lutheran. Mailing Add: 90 Monterey Ave Alamosa CO 81101

GILMAN, BENJAMIN A (R)
US Rep, NY
b Poughkeepsie, NY, Dec 6, 22; s Harry Gilman & Esther G; m 1952 to Jane Prizant; c Jonathan, Harrison, David, Susan & Ellen. Educ: Univ Pa, Wharton Sch, BS, 46; NY Law Sch, LLB, 50; Phi Sigma Delta. Polit & Govt Pos: Nat committeeman, NY State Young Rep, formerly; asst state attorney gen, NY, 53-55; attorney, NY State Temporary Comn on the Courts, 56-57; NY State Assemblyman, 95th Dist, 67-72, mem, JLC on Real Property Tax Exemptions, 69; mem, Southeastern Water Comn, 69; US Rep, 26th Dist, NY, 73-, mem, House Int Rel & Post Off Comts, US House of Rep, currently; bd visitors, USMA, currently. Bus & Prof Pos: Gilman & Gilman, 55- Mil Serv: S/Sgt, Air Force, 43-45; Distinguished Flying Cross & Air Medal. Mem: VFW; Little League (chmn); Orange Co Health Asn (vpres); Shrine; Elks. Relig: Hebrew. Legal Res: 10 Coolidge Ct Middletown NY 10940 Mailing Add: PO Box 443 Middletown NY 10940

GILMAN, LAWRENCE M (R)
b Bozrah, Conn, Nov 21, 09; m 1938 to Edna Grubner; c Faith (Mrs Robert A Cross), Wallis & Richard. Educ: Col William & Mary; Univ Ala. Polit & Govt Pos: Pres, Shoestring Rep Club, 20th Dist, Conn, formerly; chmn, Bozrah Bd Finance; first selectman, Bozrah, 43-51; mem, Conn Rep State Finance Comt; Conn State Rep, 47-55, chmn rules, incorporations & roads, bridges & rivers comts, Conn House Rep; Conn State Sen, 55-57; chmn, Bozrah Rep Town Comt; mem, President Eisenhower's Conf on Nat Safety; conducted Conn Eisenhower-Nixon Bandwagon, 52, Conn Eisenhower-Nixon Bus, 56 & Conn Nixon-Lodge Trailer, 60; mem, President Eisenhower's Int Orgns Employees Loyalty Bd; presidential elector, Conn, 68; vchmn, Conn Citizens for Nixon-Agnew, 68; chmn, Eastern Conn Nat Alliance Businessmen, currently. Bus & Prof Pos: Pres, Gilman Bros Co, Gilman, Conn; vpres, Bozrah Light & Power Co; dir, Norwich Savings Soc; mem Norwich adv bd, Hartford Nat Bank & Trust Co. Mem: Soc Plastic Engrs; Rotary; Mason (32 degree); Shennecossett Yacht Club; Commerce Club (bd gov). Honors & Awards: Conceived, introduced & carried to passage the bill for construction of Conn Turnpike. Mailing Add: Gilman CT 06336

GILMARTIN, THOMAS P (D)
Ohio State Rep
Mailing Add: 825 S Hazelwood Ave Youngstown OH 44509

GILMORE, EDDIE HUBERT (D)
Ala State Sen
b Gilmore, Ala, June 12, 25; s Eddie Henry Gilmore & Grovie Elizabeth Franklin G; m 1946 to Elizabeth Jackson; c Randall, Joanne, Lea, Julie, Elizabeth & Jane. Educ: Birmingham-Southern Col. Polit & Govt Pos: St supt, Bessemer, Ala, formerly; Ala State Rep, 62-66; Ala State Sen, 67- Bus & Prof Pos: Contracting, 46-51 & 55-; pres, Blue Square Concrete, Inc, 63- Mil Serv: Maj, Ala Nat Guard; Army, World War II & Korea. Mem: Mason; Shrine. Relig: Methodist. Mailing Add: Box 546 Bessemer AL 35020

GILMORE, JAMES STANLEY, JR (R)
b Kalamazoo, Mich, June 14, 26; s James Stanley Gilmore Sr & Ruth McNair G; m 1949 to Diana Holdenreide Fell; c Bethany, Sydney, James S, III, Elizabeth & Ruthie. Educ: Culver Mil Acad; Western Mich Univ; Kalamazoo Col, 45. Polit & Govt Pos: Mem & chmn, Mich Water Resources Comn, formerly; mayor, Kalamazoo, Mich, 59-61; mem, Kalamazoo Co Bd of Supvr, formerly; chmn, Congressman Garry Brown Polit Campaign; pres, Kalamazoo Co Young Rep, formerly; chmn, Kalamazoo City Rep Exec Comt, formerly; chmn exec comt, Rep 100 & One Comt; deleg, Rep Nat Conv, 68; mem bd dirs, Fed Home Loan Bank of Indianapolis; mem Nat Asn Broadcasters Adv Comt to Corp for Pub Broadcasting; app by the President, Nat Adv Cancer Coun, Dept Health, Educ & Welfare, currently; app by President, Citizens Adv Comt on Environ Qual, 72- Bus & Prof Pos: Dir, vpres, secy & treas, Gilmore Bros Dept Store, Inc, 47-58; owner & pres, Jim Gilmore Enterprises, including pres, Sta WEHT-TV, Ind, Gilmore Broadcasting Corp, pres, Sta KODE-TV, Mo, pres, Sta WSVA-TV, Va & pres, Sta WREX-TV, Ill, pres, Jim Gilmore Cadillac-Pontiac, Inc & bd chmn & pres, Gilmore Advert, Inc, currently; sponsor, Gilmore Racing Team, Inc, A J Foyt, Driver; vpres & dir, Holiday Inn-Continental Corp, Mich; dir & mem trust comt, First Nat Bank & Trust Co, Kalamazoo, mem, Holding Co Comt; dir, Mich Carton Co, Battle Creek; dir & asst secy, Fabri-Kal Plastics Corp, Kalamazoo; bd mem, Shakespeare Co, Kalamazoo; mem bd dirs, World Wide Sportsman, Inc, Islamorada, Fla & Southern Mich Inn Corp, Sturgis, Div of Holiday Inns of Kalamazoo. Mil Serv: Army Air Force, World War II, ETO. Mem: Wolverine Charitable Found (pres); Bronson Methodist Hosp (bd trustees & bldg comt); Family Serv Ctr of Kalamazoo (bd dirs); Kalamazoo Co CofC; Episcopal Diocese of Western Mich (bd trustees). Honors & Awards: Young Man of the Year for Kalamazoo Co, 60; One of Mich Five Outstanding Young Men of Year, Nat Jr CofC, 60; Selected by Radio Free Europe to rep US in Ger; Annual Serv to Mankind Award, Sertoma. Relig: Episcopal. Mailing Add: 1550 Long Rd Kalamazoo MI 49001

GILMORE, THOMAS ODELL (D)
NC State Rep
b Randolph Co, NC, Nov 15, 36; s Glenn Gordon Gilmore, Sr (deceased) & Mary Lizzie Harris G; m 1958 to Betty Lou Shoffner; c Thomas Odell, Jr, Dwayne Gordon & Dana Ellen. Educ: Am Landscape Sch, grad, 57; NC State Univ, BS in Hort, 59; Blue Key; Alpha Zeta; Pi Alpha Xi; Farm House; Apollo Club; Agr Club. Polit & Govt Pos: Pres, NC State Univ, Young Dem Club, 58; deleg & mem voting comt, Dem Nat Conv, 64, alt deleg, 68; mem, NC State Dem Exec Comt, vchmn, precinct; NC State Rep, Guilford Co, 73- Bus & Prof Pos: Vpres, Gilmore Plant & Bulb Co, Inc, 59-; chmn hwy comt, Am Asn Nurserymen, 67-; pres, NC Asn Nurserymen, 69; mem, Nat Beautification Clinic, 69; mem adv coun, Sch Agr & Life Sci, 69-72; bd dir, Assoc Landscape Contractors of Am. Mem: Forest Oaks Community Asn (bd dirs); NC State Univ Alumni Asn; Rotary; Forest Oaks Country Club; Wolfpack Club, NC State Univ. Honors & Awards: Most Outstanding NC Col Dem; One of Top Three Young Col Dem in US; Most Outstanding Farmer in Guilford Co; Indust Landscaping Judges Award, Am Asn Nurserymen, 71; Outstanding Young Alumnus Award, Alumni Asn, NC State Univ, 72. Relig: Presbyterian; elder, Commun in Christ. Legal Res: 4503 Ramblewood Greensboro NC 27406 Mailing Add: Gilmore Plant & Bulb Co Inc Julian NC 27283

GILMOUR, JEFF L (D)
Ore State Rep
Mailing Add: Rte 1 Box 108 Jefferson OR 97352

GILREATH, ROWAN (R)
Second VChmn, Seventh Dist Rep Comt, Ga
b Cartersville, Ga, Aug 9, 12; m 1937 to Hazel Dollie Chumley; c Metta R, Linda F & James Rowan. Educ: Ga Inst Technol, BSME, 35. Polit & Govt Pos: Deleg, Rep State Conv; chmn, Bartow Co Rep Comt, Ga, formerly; second vchmn, Seventh Dist Rep Comt, 70-; deleg, Seventh Dist Rep Conv, 73; deleg, Ga Rep State Conv, 73. Bus & Prof Pos: Mgr & stockholder, Gilreath Lumber Yard, Cartersville, Ga, 46- Mem: Bartow Co Farm Bur (dir, currently); Mason. Relig: Baptist. Legal Res: 1 Elm St Cartersville GA 30120 Mailing Add: 233 S Tennessee St Cartersville GA 30120

GINES, RALPH JUNIOR (R)
Idaho State Rep
b Woodland, Utah, May 8, 33; s Ralph Henry Gines & Agnes Lorna Sessions G; m 1958 to Betty Ann Hoover; c Samuel, Ronald, David, Rebecca, Susan & Richard. Educ: Brigham Young Univ, BS, 58; George Washington Univ, JD, 65. Polit & Govt Pos: Idaho State Rep, 72- Bus & Prof Pos: CPA, Utah & Ore, 62-; attorney-at-law, Ore & Idaho, 66-; prof, Boise State Univ, 67-74; dep prosecuting attorney, Canyon Co, Idaho, 70-72. Mil Serv: Entered as 2nd Lt, Air Force, 58, released as 1st Lt, 60, after serv in Cheyenne & Harlingen Tex, Air Training Command & Japan, Air Defense Command, 58-60; Res, Capt, resigned, 66. Mem: Ore & Idaho State Bars. Relig: Latter-day Saint. Mailing Add: Apt D 137 Davis Ave Nampa ID 83651

GINGER, LYMAN VERNON (D)
Supt Pub Instr, State Dept Educ, Ky
b Oscar, Ky, June 21, 07; s G C Ginger & Emma Abel G; m 1932 to Elizabeth Sudduth; c Leslie Thomas & William Wesley. Educ: Ky Wesleyan Col, BA; Univ Ky, MA & EdD; Phi Delta Kappa; Kappa Delta Pi; Pi Kappa Delta; Omicron Delta Kappa. Hon Degrees: LHD, Ky Wesleyan Col, 60. Polit & Govt Pos: Mem, White House Conf Comn, 55-56; chmn, Gov Comn Pub Educ, 60-61; deleg, Int Conf Educ, Washington, DC; US Rep, Third Asian Leadership Training Seminar; secy US deleg, World Conf Orgns Teaching Profession, Dublin, Ireland; mem educ comt, US Nat Comn for UNESCO; supt pub instr, State Dept Educ, Ky, 72- Bus & Prof Pos: Sci teacher & athletic coach, Winchester High Sch, Ky, 29-39; prin, Owingsville Consol Sch, 39-42; prin, Univ High Sch, Univ Ky, Lexington, 42-43; acting dir div instr, Col Educ, 43-46, dir, 46-54, dean col adult & exten educ, 54-56, dean col educ, 56-67, assoc dean, 67-71. Mem: Phi Delta Kappa (pres); Adv Comt Student Publ, Univ Ky (chmn); Nat Educ Asn; PTA; Kiwanis (pres). Honors & Awards: Boss of Year, Am Bus Women's Asn, 68; Serv Award, Phi Delta Kappa, 70. Relig: Presbyterian; elder & teacher young couples class. Mailing Add: 1265 Standish Way Lexington KY 40504

GINGRASS, JACK L (D)
Mich State Sen
Mailing Add: 627 E B St Iron Mountain MI 49801

GINN, RONALD BRYAN (BO) (D)
US Rep, Ga
b Morgan, Ga, May 31, 34; s Elijah Mathis Ginn & Annie Laura Bryan G; m 1956 to Gloria Ann Averitt; c Lauren Kacy, Julie & Ronald Bryan, Jr. Educ: Abraham Baldwin Agr Col, 51-53; Ga Southern Col, BS, 53-56. Polit & Govt Pos: Former admin asst to US Rep Hagan, Ga, admin asst to US Sen Talmadge, Ga, 67-71; US Rep, First Dist, Ga, 73- Bus & Prof Pos: Teacher, Coffee Co High Sch, Douglas, Ga, 56-57; asst mgr pub rels, Planters EMC, Millen. Relig: Baptist; deacon, Millen Baptist Church. Legal Res: 200 W College Millen GA 30442 Mailing Add: 508 Cannon House Off Bldg Washington DC 20515

GINN, ROSEMARY LUCAS (R)
Rep Nat Committeewoman, Mo
b Columbia, Mo, Aug 28, 12; d Reuben E Lucas & Mary Bewick L; m 1934 to Milton Stanley Ginn; c Nancy Bewick & Sally Reuben. Educ: Univ Mo, BA, 33, grad work, 33-34; Phi Beta Kappa; Alpha Kappa Delta; Delta Sigma Rho; Alpha Phi Zeta; Delta Delta Delta. Polit & Govt Pos: Mem, Mo Rep Speakers Bur, 36-54; pres, Lawrence Co Women's Rep Club, 37-39; dist vpres, Mo Young Rep Clubs, 48; pres, Boone Co Women's Rep Club, 48-49; deleg, Co, Dist & State Rep Conv, 48-56; permanent secy, Mo Rep Conv, 56; mem, Columbia Bd Health, 56-59; alt deleg-at-lg, Rep Nat Conv, 56, deleg, 68 & 72; pres, Fedn Rep Women's Clubs of Mo, 59-61; Rep Nat Committeewoman, Mo, 60- Bus & Prof Pos: Dir, Mo Stores Co, Columbia, Mo, 39-; adv, Columbia Coun Clubs, 56-58; trustee, Nat Mortar Bd Found, 56-; bd dirs, Boone Co Hosp Auxiliary Friends of Arrow Rock. Mem: Asn Col Honor Socs; Mortar Bd; Nat Asn Women Deans & Counr; Am Legion Auxiliary (counr, Mo Girls, 56-); League Women Voters. Relig: Baptist. Mailing Add: 303 W Boulevard S Columbia MO 65201

GINSBERG, RONALD ERWIN (D)
VChmn-at-lg, Dem Party Ga
b Savannah, Ga, Jan 7, 46; s Louis Phillip Ginsberg & Rita Nicholson G; m 1972 to Anne Turner McCall. Educ: Armstrong State Col, 63-65; Univ Ga, AB, 67; Univ Ga Sch Law, JD, 71; Tau Epsilon Phi; Phi Delta Phi. Polit & Govt Pos: Vchmn-at-lg, Dem Party, Ga, 74- Bus & Prof Pos: Attorney, Friedman, Haslam & Weiner, 71- Mil Serv: Entered as Pvt, Army Res, 68, released as 1st Lt, 74, after serv in 333rd Med Detachment 1st Res Command. Publ: Unification of the State Bar of Georgia, Georgia State Bar J, 70. Mem: Young Lawyers Sect Savannah Bar Asn (pres, 74-75); Am & Ga Bar Asns; Plaintiff Lawyers Club; Ga Indigent Legal Serv Inc (bd dirs). Legal Res: 15 E 48th St Savannah GA 31405 Mailing Add: PO Box 10105 Savannah GA 31402

GINSBURG, MICHAEL JOSEPH (DFL)
Secy, Renville Co Dem-Farmer-Labor Party, Minn
b Minneapolis, Minn, Feb 7, 40; s Joseph David Ginsburg & Doris Kester G; m 1967 to Marilyn Sophie Anderson; c Lara Mae & Lado Michael. Educ: Univ Minn, AA, 62. Polit & Govt Pos: Secy, Renville Co Dem-Farmer-Labor Party, Minn, 70- Bus & Prof Pos: Farmer, 63- Mem: Hector CofC. Relig: Jewish. Mailing Add: RR 2 Box 154 Hector MN 55342

GIOLITO, CAROLYN HUGHES (D)
b Birmingham, Ala, May 8, 33; d Cecil T Hughes & Eunice Brown H; m 1959 to Caesar Augustus Giolito; c Glenn & Antoinette. Educ: Ala Col, BS, 55; George Washington Sch Law, 56-58; Beta Beta Beta. Polit & Govt Pos: Cong aide to various US Sen & Rep, 55-73; admin asst to US Rep John B Breckinridge, Ky, 73- Mem: Admin Assts Asn of US Cong. Relig: Presbyterian. Mailing Add: 2313 Eastgate Dr Silver Spring MD 20906

GIORDANO, JOHN ANTHONY, JR (D)
Conn State Rep
b New Haven, Conn, June 22, 50; s John Anthony Giordano, Sr & Doris Keeley G; m 1973 to Barbara Ann Piglio. Educ: Univ New Haven, currently; Prelaw Club; Polit Sci Club. Polit & Govt Pos: Councilman, East Haven, Conn, 71-74; Conn State Rep, 99th Dist, 75- Bus & Prof Pos: Owner, Deck 'N' Sand Beach Club, East Haven, Conn, 72- Honors & Awards: Youngest Town Councilman, East Haven, Conn, 71. Mailing Add: 35 Catherine St East Haven CT 06512

GIORGI, E J (ZEKE) (D)
Ill State Rep
b Rockford, Ill, Sept 5, 21; s Gabriele Giorgi & Louise DiMarco G; m 1943 to Josephine Buttacavoli; c Barbara, Beverly & Betty. Educ: Washington & Lee Univ. Polit & Govt Pos: Dep assessor, Rockford Twp, Ill, 46-50, alderman, Fifth Ward City Coun, 55-; Ill State Rep, 64-, mem, Appropriations, Indust & Labor & Traffic & Hwy Safety Comts, Ill House Rep; mem, Comn Ment Health & Comn to Study Not for Profit Corp Legis; mem adv coun, Reference Bur. Bus & Prof Pos: Stove mfg, Roper Inc, 46; sales rep, Midwest Dist Co, 56-66; bd chmn, NISCO Corp. Mil Serv: Entered as Pvt, Army, 42, released as Sgt, 46, after serv in Co C, 742 Tank Bn, Continental Limits, 40 months; Good Conduct & Victory Medals; Am Theater Ribbon. Mem: Am Munic Asn, Washington, DC; Robert Carlson Am Legion Post; St Anthonys Sr Holy Name; St Ambrose Mutual Benefit; Order Sons of Italy. Relig: Catholic. Mailing Add: 1024 Blake St Rockford IL 61102

GIPS, WALTER F, III (TERRY) (D)
VChairperson, Yolo Co Dem Cent Comt, Calif
b Chicago, Ill, Feb 11, 51; s Walter F Gips, Jr & Ann Arenberg G; single. Educ: Ctr Intercultural de Documentacion, Cuernavaca, Mex, summer 70; Am Univ, fall 71; Claremont Men's Col, BA cum laude, 73; Nat Honor Soc. Polit & Govt Pos: Organizer, McGovern for President Campaign, New York, NY, 72; off mgr, Moretti for Gov, Davis, Calif, 74; dir & co-chairperson, Yolo Co Citizens for Brown for Gov, Davis, 74; deleg, Dem Nat Mid-Term Conf, 74; vchairperson, Yolo Co Dem Cent Comt, 75- Bus & Prof Pos: Social worker, Emerson Settlement House, Chicago, 69; stockbrokers asst, New York, 72; res asst, Claremont Men's Col, 72-73; final assemblyline operator, Gulton Europe, Ltd, Brighton, Eng, 73; morning clean-up man, Jack-in-the-Box Restaurant, 74; founder & dir, Sacramento Community Gardens Proj, 75- Mem: Yolo Co Soc Prev Cruelty Animals (secy, 75-); League of Women Voters; Am Dem Action; Sierra Club; Davis Dem Club (exec bd, 75-). Honors & Awards: Recipient Student Citizenship Award, Claremont Men's Col Alumni Asn. Mailing Add: 1205 Fifth St Davis CA 95616

GIUFFREDA, LEON EUGENE (R)
NY State Sen
b Brooklyn, NY, Aug 1, 13; s Joseph Giuffreda & Concetta Daniele G; m 1934 to Rose M Gazzano; c Rosemary (Mrs Mazzei) & Renee (Mrs Anthony LeVigne). Educ: NY Univ, 31-32; Eron Sch Ins, dipl, 34-35; Fordham Law Sch, qualifying cert, Town Justice, 62. Polit & Govt Pos: Town justice, Brookhaven, 54-64; comnr, Centereach Fire Dist, 62-63; NY State Sen, 66-, chmn educ comt, NY State Senate, currently; comnr, Educ Comn of the States, 73- Bus & Prof Pos: Pres, Leon E Giuffreda Agency, 42-75; pres, Selden Heights Bldg Corp, 45-75; dir, Marine Midland Tinker Nat Bank, 60-75, John T Mather Mem Hosp, 64-75 & Cleary Sch for Deaf, 72-75. Publ: Annual legislative report of the Joint Committee on Mental & Physical Handicapped, NY State, 73. Mem: Port Jefferson Elks; Centereach CofC; Centereach Lions Club; NY State & Suffolk Co Magistrates Asns. Honors & Awards: Educ Award, Suffolk Co Orgn for Promotion of Educ, 70; Medal of Good Hope, Little Flower Children's Serv, 73; Educ Award, NY State Speech & Hearing Asn, 74; Distinguished Citizens Award, Maryhaven Ctr of Hope, 75; Rosemary Cleary Founder's Day Award-Man of the Year, Cleary Sch for Deaf Children, 75. Relig: Catholic. Legal Res: 15 N Coleman Rd Centereach NY 11720 Mailing Add: State Off Bldg Veteran's Hwy Hauppauge NY 11788

GIULIANI, PETER (R)
Vt State Rep
Mailing Add: 15 College St Montpelier VT 05602

GIVAN, RICHARD MARTIN (R)
Judge, Ind Supreme Court
b Indianapolis, Ind, June 7, 21; s Clinton Hodell Givan & Glee Bowen G; m 1945 to Pauline Marie Haggart; c Madalyn (Mrs Larry Hesson), Sandra, Patricia (Mrs Michael Gross) & Elizabeth. Educ: Ind Univ, LLB, 51; Sigma Delta Kappa. Polit & Govt Pos: Dep pub defender of Ind, 52-54; dep attorney gen, Ind, 54-65; dep prosecuting attorney, Marion Co, 65-67; Ind State Rep, 67-68; Judge, Ind Supreme Court, 69- Bus & Prof Pos: Partner, Givan & Givan Law Firm, 52-59, Bowen, Myers, Northam & Givan, 59-69. Mil Serv: Entered as Pvt, Army Air Corps, 42, released as 2nd Lt, 45, after serv in 95th Div, Troop Carrier Command, Air Transport Command, SAtlantic Theatre. Mem: Indianapolis & Ind Bar Asns; Ind Trial Lawyers Asn; Ind Judges Asn; Lions Int. Relig: Society of Friends. Mailing Add: RR 2 Box 376 Indianapolis IN 46231

GIVEN, D P (SHERIFF) (D)
b Upperglade, WVa, May 6, 17; s H F Given & Susan R Paugh G; m 1946 to Hazel Cochran; c Donna Jane. Educ: Glenville State Teachers Col. Polit & Govt Pos: Webster Co Court, 46-52; WVa State Deleg, 58-66 & 71-73; deleg, Dem Nat Conv, 72; deleg, Dem Nat Mid-Term Conf, 74. Bus & Prof Pos: Contractor, real estate dealer. Mil Serv: Air Force, World War II, 5 years. Mem: Moose; Am Legion; VFW. Relig: Presbyterian. Mailing Add: 216 Marvin Ct Webster Springs WV 26288

GIVEN, PHYLLIS E (D)
WVa State Deleg
Mailing Add: State Capitol Charleston WV 25305

GIVENS, ARTHUR A, JR (D)
Ark State Rep
b Stuttgart, Ark, Feb 13, 36; s Arthur A Givens & Ina Charlene Skarda; m 1964 to Marna Loy Byram; c Shane. Educ: Ark Polytech Col, BA, 61; Ark Law Sch, LLB, 66; Univ Ark, Fayetteville, JD, 68; Phi Alpha Delta. Polit & Govt Pos: Ark State Rep, 71- Bus & Prof Pos: Claims rep, MFA Ins Co, Little Rock, Ark, 61-65; State Farm Ins Co, 65-68; attorney, pvt practice, 68- Mil Serv: Entered as Pvt, Air Force, 53, released as Sgt, 58, after serv in Mil

Police, 3rd Air Force, Europe, 54-58; Good Conduct Medal; Nat Defense Medal; Korean Conflict Award. Mem: Am Trial Lawyers Asn; Ark Bar Asn; Pulaski Co Bar Asn; Am Bar Asn; Mason. Relig: Church of Christ. Legal Res: 1000 S Longfield (Sherwood) North Little Rock AR 72116 Mailing Add: 1004-300 Spring Bldg Little Rock AR 72201

GIVHAM, THOMAS B (D)
Ky State Rep
Mailing Add: Star Rte Shepherdsville KY 40165

GIVHAN, WALTER COATS (D)
Ala State Sen
b Perry Co, Ala, May 7, 02; s Walter Pope Givhan & Betty Coats G; m 1961 to Mrs Frank James; c Walter Houston, Samuel Pope. Educ: NGa Col, BS, 21. Polit & Govt Pos: Ala State Rep, 30 & 42-50; mem, State Sovereignty Comt; Ala State Sen, 54- Bus & Prof Pos: Planter; chmn, Farmers Mkt Authority; dir, Planters & Merchants Bank, Uniontown. Mem: Ala State Farm Bur Fedn (state bd dirs); CofC (bd dirs, Selma & Dallas City); Kiwanis; Mason; Sigma Nu. Relig: Methodist. Mailing Add: Safford AL 36773

GJESDAL, LARS B, JR (R)
b Plankinton, SDak, Dec 18, 26; s Lars B Gjesdal & Inga M Hoysted G; single. Polit & Govt Pos: Chmn, Aurora Co Rep Party, SDak, formerly; SDak State Sen, 60-62. Mem: Farm Bur. Relig: Lutheran. Mailing Add: Plankinton SD 57368

GLACKIN, PAUL LOUIS (D)
b Delta, Pa, Dec 17, 23; s Charles A Glackin & Mahala McCallister G; m 1951 to Dorothy Marvin; c Susan L. Educ: Univ Baltimore, 5 years. Polit & Govt Pos: Mem, Md State Dem Cent Comt, formerly; mem, Harford Co Planning & Zoning, 58-62; mem, Harford Co Study Comn, 67-; appraiser, Orphans Court, Harford Co; co comnr, Dept Pub Works & Parks & Recreation Comn; deleg, Dem Nat Conv, 68. Bus & Prof Pos: Pres, Paul L Glackin Inc, 62-, Dublin Manor, Inc, 62- & Glackin Umbarger Inc, 62-; dir, Commercial & Savings Bank, 68- Mil Serv: Served in Merchant Marine. Mem: Nat Inst Real Estate Brokers; Nat Asn Realtors; Md Home Builders; KofC; Elks. Relig: Roman Catholic; lay corporator, St Mary's Church, Pylesville, Md. Mailing Add: Chestnut St Cardiff MD 21024

GLADDEN, ZELMA E (D)
VChairperson, Scott Co Dem Cent Comt, Ind
b Scott Co, Ind, Feb 28, 22; d Aaron Hendricks Alsup & Myrtle F MacDonnell A; m 1946 to John Gladden; c Leigh (Mrs Neuhauser). Educ: LaSalle Exten Univ. Polit & Govt Pos: Clerk-treas, Scottsburg, Ind, 64-67 & 72-75; deleg, Dem Nat Mid-Term Conf, 74; vchairperson, Scott Co Dem Cent Comt, currently. Bus & Prof Pos: Pub acct, Scottsburg, Ind, 54-75. Mem: Scott Co Dem Women; Am Legion Auxiliary. Relig: Baptist. Mailing Add: 420 N Highland Scottsburg IN 47170

GLADDING, HARRY TILDEN, JR (R)
Chmn, Essex Co Rep Comt, Va
b Richmond, Va, Aug 24, 36; s Harry Tilden Gladding & Elsie Schmidt G; m 1956 to Ann Montgomery; c Roy M, Allison & Harry T, III. Educ: Hargrave Mil Acad. Polit & Govt Pos: Chmn, Essex Co Rep Comt, Va, 64- Bus & Prof Pos: Employee, Va Farm Bur Mutual Ins Co, 58; employee, Daingerfield Ins Agency, 60-63, owner, 63-; chief, Tappahannock Vol Fire Dept. Mil Serv: Entered as Pvt, Army Res, 54, released as Sgt, 62. Mem: Tappahannock CofC; Lions. Relig: Baptist. Mailing Add: 637 Cradle Ave Tappahannock VA 22560

GLADSON, CHARLES LEE (R)
b Glendale, Calif, Jan 25, 34; s Virgil H Gladson & Marjorie Brewer G; m 1957 to Elizabeth Jane Morgan; c Linda Jayne, Karen Elizabeth, Marcia Ann & Stephen Robert. Educ: San Jose State Col, AB, 57; Univ Calif Hastings Col Law, JD, 63; Phi Delta Phi; Kappa Alpha. Polit & Govt Pos: Co campaign vchmn, San Bernardino Co for Gov Ronald Reagan, 66; campaign chmn, Western San Bernardino Co for Lt Gov Robert Finch, 66 & Congressman Jerry Pettis, 33rd Dist, 66 & 68; mem, Calif Rep State Cent Comt, formerly; asst gen counsel, Agency Int Develop, Dept of State, 69-72. Bus & Prof Pos: Partner Covington & Crowe, Law Firm, 65-, on leave of absence for govt serv, 69- Mil Serv: Entered as Ens, Naval Res, 57, released as Lt, 60, after serv in Naval Commun Sta, Pearl Harbor, Hawaii; Lt, Res, 60-; Letter of Commendation. Publ: Securities regulation, Hastings Law J, 58. Mem: Am Bar Asn; Am Judicature Soc; Kiwanis Int (dir, Upland, Calif); Ontario, Calif CofC (dir). Relig: Protestant. Legal Res: CA Mailing Add: 7820 Birnam Wood Dr McLean VA 22101

GLADSTONE, HERBERT MOREY (D)
NJ State Assemblyman
b New York, NY, Aug 31, 15; s Edward Gladstone & Ethel Wordsman G; m 1947 to Irma Jeanne Robinson; c Jane Ellen, Jonathan Alan & Bart Edward. Educ: NY Univ, Univ Miss, Univ Wash & Brooklyn Col. Polit & Govt Pos: Committeeman, Twp of River Vale, NJ, 58-60, mem, Bd Health, 63-66; mem, Bergen Co Transit Comt, 60-62; mem, Pascack Valley Human Rels Coun, 65-67; chmn, Sewer Comn, 65-68; NJ State Assemblyman, Dist 39, 74- Mailing Add: 577 Egan Terr River Vale NJ 07675

GLADSTONE, WILLIAM (D)
Mem Exec Bd, 17th Cong Dist Dem Party, Mich
b Detroit, Mich, June 21, 25; s Irving Gladstone & Ida Rabinowitz G; m 1950 to Hannah Levin; c Deborah Ann & Judith Ellen. Educ: Wayne State Univ, 43-50; Sigma Alpha Mu. Polit & Govt Pos: Precinct deleg & bd mem, 17th Cong Dist Dem Party, Mich, 64-66 & 68-70, precinct deleg, currently, mem exec bd, 70-, chmn, 17th Dist Dem Orgn, 66-70; deleg, Dem Nat Conv, 68. Bus & Prof Pos: Retailer, 50-54; merchandise mgr, Crown Furniture Co, Detroit, 54-60; retailer, Gladstone's Inc, Wayne, 61- Mem: B'nai B'rith; NAACP; Am Civil Liberties Union; Nat Asn Small Bus; Two-Ten Assocs. Relig: Jewish. Mailing Add: 20287 Greenview Detroit MI 48219

GLADWELL, BEATRICE HOWARD (R)
Committeewoman, Pocahontas Co Rep Exec Comt, Wva
b Buckeye, WVa, July 31, 14; d Judson Luke Howard & Jennie Aurora Barker H; m 1941 to Carl Harry Gladwell; c twins, Sharla Howard & Carla Howard (Mrs James C Totten). Educ: Davis & Elkins Col, AB, 57; Delta Kappa Gamma. Polit & Govt Pos: Committeewoman, Pocahontas Co Rep Exec Comt, WVa, 56- Publ: Poems in co papers, 41-42; Adult education in Pocahontas Co, WVa Sch J, 8/67. Mem: Bus & Prof Women (pres, 72-); WVa Classroom Teachers Asn; Nat Educ Asn; Delta Kappa Gamma; Eastern Star (Worthy Matron). Honors & Awards: All Star Orgn, WVa 4-H Alumni Woman; Pocahontas Co Teacher of Year & WVa Teacher of Year, 70. Relig: Presbyterian. Mailing Add: Buckeye WV 24924

GLAESCHER, KENNITH PARKER (D)
b Mt Summit, Ind, Oct 29, 02; s William J Glaescher & Odessa L Rader G; wid. Educ: Miss State Univ, 23-27; Ball State Univ, 45-46. Polit & Govt Pos: Dep collector, Internal Revenue, Ind, 42-47; town clerk-treas, Mt Summit, 50-55; trustee, Prairie Twp, Henry Co, 55-62; chmn, Henry Co Dem Cent Comt, 65-68; councilman, Henry Co Coun, Ind, 70-72; staff, Ind Secy of State, currently. Bus & Prof Pos: Agt, Standard Oil Co of Ky, Columbus, Miss, 28-35; with Chrysler Corp, New Castle, Ind, 35-41; partner, Reece & Glaescher Ins Agency, Mt Summit, 50-65; retired. Mem: Mason; Scottish Rite; York Rite; Shrine; Optimist. Relig: Protestant. Legal Res: 205 S Willard St Mt Summit IN 47361 Mailing Add: PO Box 206 Mt Summit IN 47361

GLANTON, THOMAS PETTIS (D)
Ga State Rep
b Newnan, Ga, Feb 21, 40; s Thomas Abner Glanton & Judy Baker G; m 1959 to Bess Miller; c Elizabeth Wynn & Thomas Miller. Educ: Auburn Univ, BS, 62; Ga Inst Technol, MS, 70; Phi Kappa Phi; Omicron Delta Kappa; Kappa Sigma. Polit & Govt Pos: Ga State Rep, Dist 66, 75- Bus & Prof Pos: Staff asst, Arthur Andersen & Co, Atlanta, Ga, 65-66; research economist, Ga Inst Technol, 66-70; developer, Roush & Assocs, Carrollton, 70-73; pres, Remco, Inc, Carrollton, 73- Mil Serv: Entered as 2nd Lt, Air Force, 62, released as 1st Lt, 65, after serv in 4500 Air Base Wing, Tactical Air Command; Air Force Commendation Medal. Mem: Kiwanis; Jaycees; Ga Indust Developers Asn. Relig: Methodist. Mailing Add: 539 N White St Carrollton GA 30117

GLASER, NORMAN DALE (D)
Mem, Elko Co Dem Cent Comt, Nev
b Elko, Nev, Apr 4, 21; s Clarence Webster Glaser & Margaret Layer G; m 1943 to Nelda Marie Lancaster; c Steven, Sharon & Brent. Educ: Okla State Univ, BS in Agr Eng. Polit & Govt Pos: Mem, Elko Co Sch Bd, 54-60; Nev State Assemblyman, until 72, Speaker-Pro-Tem, Nev State Assembly, 61-63, Speaker of the Assembly, 64; mem, Elko Co Dem Cent Comt, Nev, currently. Mil Serv: Entered as Ens, Navy, 44, released as Lt(jg), 46, after serv in Pac; Pac Theater & Leyte Gulf Ribbons. Mem: Nev Farm Bur; Elko CofC; Toastmasters; VFW; Farm Bur. Honors & Awards: Outstanding Young Farmer, Nev, 55. Relig: Presbyterian. Mailing Add: Halleck NV 89824

GLASS, BOB (D)
Ala State Rep
Mailing Add: 4723 Bavarian Dr Mobile AL 36619

GLASS, BRADLEY M (R)
Ill State Sen
Mailing Add: 723 Happ Rd Northfield IL 60093

GLASS, JOSEPH EDWARD (D)
Mem, Md Dem State Cent Comt
b Prince George's Co, Md, Apr 17, 40; s William John Glass & Mary King G; m 1962 to Connie Lee Overstreet Crum; c Joseph E, Jr, Tiffany Lee, Katie Lee & Candance Lee. Educ: Towson State Col, BS, 62; Univ Md, JD, 66; Am Univ, Md, Johns Hopkins Univ & Georgetown Univ, 68-; Delta Theta Phi; Nat Honor Soc; Gamma Eta Gamma; Phi Alpha Omega. Polit & Govt Pos: Cand, Md State Deleg, 70; comnr, Dist Court for Baltimore Co, 71-72; mem, Citizens Adv Bd to State Hosp, 72-; deleg, Dem Nat Conv, 72; mem, Md Dem State Cent Comt, Baltimore Co, 74- Bus & Prof Pos: Lawyer, 67-; diversified occup coordr, 70- Mem: Am & Md State Bar Asns; Jr Bar Asn for Baltimore City; Nat Educ Asn; Baltimore Co Dem Club. Honors & Awards: Outstanding Young Civic Worker, Jaycees, 70. Relig: Catholic. Legal Res: 212 Locknell Rd Timonium MD 21903 Mailing Add: 209 Courtland Ave Towson MD 21204

GLASS, PENNY LANE (D)
b Hope, Ark, Jan 3, 54; d A D Glass, Jr & Hazel Teal G; single. Educ: Ouachita Baptist Univ, BA, 75; Kappa Delta Pi; Chi Delta; Baptist Student Union; Ozark Soc; Asn Women Students; Pre-prof Club; Col Young Dem (mem state comt, 72-73); student senate; Student Found. Polit & Govt Pos: Deleg, Desha Co Dem Conv, Ark, 72, Ark Dem State Conv, 72 & 74 & Dem Nat Conv, 72. Mem: Am Legion Auxiliary; Ark Speech & Hearing Asn. Honors & Awards: President's List; ROTC Sponsor. Relig: Southern Baptist. Mailing Add: 216 Brent Dumas AR 71639

GLASSCO, CHARLES KIMBALL, JR (R)
Chmn, Bolivar Co Rep Exec Comt, Miss
b Cleveland, Miss, Apr 8, 21; s Charles Kimball Glassco & Effie Coghlan G; m 1942 to Nell Bond Busby; c Melinda (Mrs Paul Calvert), Mary (Mrs Tom Hubbard), Kim (Mrs Sam Roth) & Charles Kimball, III. Educ: Miss State Univ, BS, 42; Delta State Univ, MA, 68; Univ Miss, EdD, 71; Phi Delta Kappa; Scabbard & Blade; Blue Key; Sigma Alpha Epsilon; Ag Club. Polit & Govt Pos: Chmn, Bolivar Co Rep Exec Comt, Miss, 68-; dir census, Third Cong Dist, 70. Bus & Prof Pos: Farmer, Cleveland, Miss, 46-70; assoc prof educ, Miss Valley State Univ, 71- Mil Serv: Entered as 2nd Lt, Army, 42, released as Capt, 46, after serv in Spec Forces, Pac Theater, 43-46; Pac Campaign Stars; Unit Citation. Mem: Miss Ment Health Asn; Miss Educ Asn; Am Legion; Dist Ment Health Asn (adv bd). Honors & Awards: Award for Outstanding Work, Boy Scouts, 69. Relig: Presbyterian. Mailing Add: 1201 Lamar Cleveland MS 38732

GLASSCOCK, JAMES SAMUEL (D)
Va State Deleg
b Springton, WVa, Nov 19, 31; s Alvin L Glasscock & Ellen Jordan G; m 1955 to Betty Jane Staples; c Thomas Jay, Linda Cate & Lisa Carol. Educ: Hampden-Sydney Col, BA, 52; Univ Va Law Sch, LLB, 55; Omicron Delta Kappa; Chi Beta Phi; Eta Sigma Phi; Order of Coif; Theta Chi; Phi Alpha Delta. Polit & Govt Pos: Va State Deleg, 70- Bus & Prof Pos: Assoc & partner, Godwin & Godwin Law Firm, 59-66; partner, Godwin, Glasscock & Kelly Law Firm, 66-68; partner, Godwin & Glasscock Law Firm, 68-73; partner, Glasscock, Gardy & Savage Law Firm, 74- Mil Serv: Entered as 1st Lt, Army, 56-59, serv in Europe. Mem: Am & Va State Bar Asns; Va Trial Lawyers Asn; Ruritan. Relig: Methodist. Legal Res: Chuckatuck Sta Suffolk VA Mailing Add: PO Box 1876 Suffolk VA 23434

GLASSHEIM, ELIOT ALAN (D)
NDak State Rep
b New York, NY, Feb 10, 38; s Raymond Glassheim & Edith Ruthizer G; m 1969 to Patricia Flagg Sanborn; c A Eagle & Vo Van Dung. Educ: Wesleyan Univ, BA, 60; Univ NMex, MA, 66, PhD, 73; John Wesley Club. Polit & Govt Pos: Mem, Citizens Adv Coun, Revenue Sharing Funds, Grand Forks, NDak, 74; NDak State Rep, 75- Bus & Prof Pos: Book reviews & copy boy, Washington Post, 60-61; proofreading & layout, Wall Street J, New York, NY, 62-63; mgt trainee, Accessory Fashions, New York, 64-65; teacher, Augusta Col, 60-71; teacher, Ctr for Teaching & Learning, Univ NDak, 72- Publ: The Restless Giant, San Marcos, 68; Paul Goodman Bibliography, Bull Bibliog, 70. Mem: Near Northside Neighborhood Asn, Grand Forks. Mailing Add: 619 N Third St Grand Forks ND 58201

GLASSMAN, ABRAHAM
Conn State Rep
b Hartford, Conn, Apr 1, 33; s Max Glassman & Anna Brass G; m 1955 to Beverly Farber; c Amy Karen, Steven Paul, Andrew Charles & Elizabeth Fay. Educ: Univ Conn, BA, 55, MA, 57; Phi Epsilon Pi. Polit & Govt Pos: Mem town coun, South Windsor, Conn, 67-73, mayor, 71-73; Conn State Rep, 14th Dist, 74- Mailing Add: 44 Berle Rd South Windsor CT 06074

GLATZER, HAL (D)
b Manhattan, NY, Jan 31, 46; s Harold Glatzer & Glenna Beaber G; single. Educ: Syracuse Univ, BA, 67. Polit & Govt Pos: Precinct vpres & dist councilman, Dem Party of Hawaii, 72-74, precinct pres, 74-76; deleg, Dem Mid Term Conf, 74. Bus & Prof Pos: Teacher, Sec Sch, Hawaii, 69-70; bur chief, Island of Hawaii, Honolulu Advertiser, 71; ed, Orchid Isle Mag, Hawaii Tribune-Herald, 72-74, writer, news features & commentary for Tribune-Herald, 74; journalist-publisher, Friendly World Enterprises, 75. Publ: Kamehameha County, Friendly World Enterprises, 74; Owner-builder, six part series, Orchid Isle Mag, 74; Along Judd Road, Hawaii Tribune-Herald, 74. Mem: Big Island Press Club; Hawaii Newspaper Guild; Hawaii 2000. Mailing Add: Box 361 Pepeekeo HI 96783

GLAVIN, JAMES HENRY, III (D)
Mem Exec Comt, Saratoga Co Dem Comt, NY
b Albany, NY, Oct 6, 31; s James Henry Glavin, Jr & Elizabeth Gibbons G; m 1963 to A Rita Chandellier; c Helene Elizabeth, James C & Rita Marie. Educ: Villanova Univ, AB, 53; Albany Law Sch, JD, 56; mem ed bd, col newspaper, Villanovan & lit quarterly, Lynx. Polit & Govt Pos: Committeeman & mem exec comt, Saratoga Co Dem Comt, NY, 61-, chmn, 64-68; attorney, Water Comn, Waterford, 61-, mem, Planning Comn, 62-; area campaign coordr, NY State Dem Comt, 65; chmn, Judicial Conv, Fourth Judicial Dist, NY, 67. Bus & Prof Pos: Mem law firm, Glavin & Glavin; mem bd, Saratoga Co Region, Nat Commercial Bank & Trust Co. Mil Serv: 1st Lt, 839th Air Div, Staff Judge Adv Off, Tactical Air Command, 57-60; Capt, Air Force Res, 60-70; Air Force Outstanding Unit Award. Mem: Am Soc Law & Med; Am Arbit Asn (nat panel arbitrators); Int Soc for Gen Semantics; Bellevue Maternity Hosp (mem bd); St Mary's Church (trustee). Relig: Roman Catholic. Legal Res: 66 Saratoga Ave Waterford NY 12188 Mailing Add: PO Box 40 Waterford NY 12188

GLEASON, PATRICK AUGUSTINE (R)
Pa State Rep
b Johnstown, Pa, July 30, 34; s Augustine Martin Gleason, Sr & Helen Elizabeth Rumberger G; m 1962 to Louise Ann Daley; c Helen Catherine, Peter Andrew & Kathleen Alice. Educ: Georgetown Univ, AB, cum laude, 56, Law Ctr, JD, 59; Univ Pittsburgh, Johnstown, 63, 65 & 69; nominee for Woodrow Wilson Fel. Polit & Govt Pos: Solicitor, Johnstown, Pa, 67-70; mem, Johnstown Housing Develop Corp, 68-70; mem, Pa City-State Partnership, 68-70; mem, Johnstown Citizens Adv Coun, 71-; Pa State Rep, 71- Bus & Prof Pos: Counsel, Local 530, Plumbers & Pipe Fitters Union, adminr pension & health & welfare funds. Mem: Pa State Bar Asn; Pa Trial Lawyers Asn; Pittsburgh Inst Legal Med. Relig: Catholic. Legal Res: 1128 Confer Ave Johnstown PA 15905 Mailing Add: 636 Main St Johnstown PA 15901

GLEASON, ROBERT A (R)
Chmn, Cambria Co Rep Party, Pa
b Philipsburg, Pa, Jan 16, 09; s Gus M Gleason & Helen Rumberger G; m to Thelma Kremer; c Robert A, Jr, Christopher K & Pamela J. Educ: St Francis Col, BA, 32; Sigma Chi. Polit & Govt Pos: Alderman, Johnstown, Pa, 34-40; chmn, Cambria Co Rep Party, Pa, 49-; councilman, Westmont Borough, 56-60. Bus & Prof Pos: Pres, Gleason Agency, 32- Mil Serv: Pfc, Air Force, 43-44, serv in Supply Unit, US. Mem: St Francis Col (bd adv); Moose; Am Legion; 40 et 8. Relig: Roman Catholic; mem bd, Our Mother of Sorrows Church. Legal Res: 543 Elknod Lane Westmont Borough PA 15905 Mailing Add: Swank Bldg Johnstown PA 15901

GLEASON, ROBERT REILLY, JR (R)
Pres, DC Young Rep Club
b Jersey City, NJ, Mar 26, 47; s Robert Reilly Gleason & Anne Paul G; single. Educ: Tri-State Col, Angola, Ind, BS, 69; Alpha Phi Gamma; Kappa Sigma. Polit & Govt Pos: Pres, DC Young Rep Club, 73- Bus & Prof Pos: Internal auditor, Kay Jewelry Store, Inc, 70-71; asst to exec dir, Nat Asn Trade & Tech Sch, Washington, DC, 71- Mem: Elks. Honors & Awards: Auth of Best Ed, Ind Collegiate Press Asn, 69. Relig: Catholic. Mailing Add: Apt 117 1100 22nd St NW Washington DC 20037

GLEESON, FRANCIS EDWARD, JR (D)
Pa State Rep
b Philadelphia, Pa, Nov 25, 37; s Francis E Gleeson, Sr & Helen Grace McGee G; m 1966 to Mary Ellen Mallon; c Francis E Gleeson, III. Educ: La Salle Col, AB, 59; Law Sch, Univ Pa, LLB, 62; Wilson Law Club. Polit & Govt Pos: Pa State Rep, 172nd Dist, 69- Bus & Prof Pos: Attorney, self-employed, 64- Mil Serv: Entered as Pvt, Army, 62, released as Pfc, 63, after serv in Inf, Ft Dix, NJ, 62-63; Sp-4, Army Res, Judge Adv Gen, 63-68. Mem: Philadelphia Bar Asn. Legal Res: 7032 Erdrick St Phildelphia PA 19135 Mailing Add: 7055 Frankford Ave Philadelphia PA 19135

GLEIM, IRA KENNY (D)
Mem, Cumberland Co Dem Comt, Pa
b Mt Holly Springs, Pa, Dec 15, 09; s Ira Clarence Gleim & Lue Klepp G; m 1931 to Dorothy Sidsinger; c Doris S. Polit & Govt Pos: Mem, Cumberland Co Dem Comt, Pa, 32-, treas, 66-69; pres, Borough Coun, Mt Holly Springs, Pa, 48-52, treas, 54-58; chmn, South Dist Cumberland Co Dem Party, formerly; alt deleg, Dem Nat Conv, 64; treas, Mt Holly Springs Water & Sewer Authority, 69- Bus & Prof Pos: Foreman, Peter J Schweitzer Div, Kimberly Clark Corp, 42-72. Mem: Eagles; White Circle Lodge; Mt Holly Fish & Game Asn; Mt Holly Springs Dem Club; Mt Holly Springs Fire Co. Relig: Methodist. Mailing Add: 202 Chestnut St Mt Holly Springs PA 17065

GLENN, EARL (D)
Ky State Sen
Mailing Add: Rte 3 Leitchfield KY 42754

GLENN, GENE W (D)
Iowa State Sen
b Wapello Co, Iowa, Nov 13, 28. Educ: State Univ Iowa, BA, 50; Int Grad Sch, Univ Stockholm, Sweden, 55; George Washington Univ Law Sch, LLB, 60. Polit & Govt Pos: Foreign Affairs Asst to US Rep Frances P Bolton, 56-61; Iowa State Rep, formerly; Iowa State Sen, 67- Bus & Prof Pos: Attorney. Mil Serv: Army, Korea, 3 years. Mem: United Packinghouse Workers of Am; Omicron Delta Kappa. Honors & Awards: US deleg nat student YMCA World Conf of Christian Youth, Oslo, Norway, 47. Relig: Christian Church. Legal Res: Rte 7 Ottumwa IA 52501 Mailing Add: 229 W Woodland Ottumwa IA 52501

GLENN, JOHN HERSCHEL, JR (D)
US Sen, Ohio
b Cambridge, Ohio, July 18, 21; m 1942 to Anne Margaret Castor; c David & Lyn. Educ: Muskingum Col, BS. Polit & Govt Pos: US Sen, Ohio, 75- Bus & Prof Pos: Mem bd trustees, Muskingum Col; bus vpres, Royal Crown, 66-68; pres, Royal Crown Int, 67-69; mem bd dirs, Questor Corp, 70-74. Mil Serv: Marine Corps, 42-65, Col(Ret); Astronaut, NASA, 59-65; World War II & Korean War Medals. Honors & Awards: First American to orbit the earth aboard Friendship 7, 62. Relig: Presbyterian; elder. Legal Res: OH Mailing Add: US Senate Washington DC 20510

GLENN, ROBERT EASTWOOD (R)
VChmn, Roanoke City Rep Comt, Va
b Catlettsburg, Ky, Dec 24, 29; s Albert Sydney Glenn & Pauline Elizabeth Eastwood G; m 1956 to Clydenne Reinhard; c Pauline E & Robert E, Jr. Educ: Washington & Lee Univ, BS, 51, LLB, 53; Beta Gamma Sigma; Phi Delta Phi; Alpha Kappa Psi; Pi Kappa Phi. Polit & Govt Pos: Pres, Roanoke City Young Rep, Va, 60; chmn, Roanoke City Rep Comt, 68-70, vchmn, 70- Bus & Prof Pos: Assoc, Eggleston & Holton, Attorneys, Roanoke, 57-59, partner, Eggleston, Holton & Glenn, 60-62, Eggleston, Holton, Butler & Glenn, 62-70 & Eggleston, Butler & Glenn, 70-72; Eggleston & Glenn, 72- Mil Serv: 1st Lt, Air Force, 53-57, Lt Col, Res, currently. Mem: Roanoke, Va State & Am Bar Asns; Newcomen Soc. Relig: Roman Catholic. Legal Res: 3101 Allendale St SW Roanoke VA 24014 Mailing Add: PO Box 2887 City Roanoke VA 24001

GLICK, LESLIE ALAN (D)
Mem, Md Dem State Cent Comt
b New York, NY, May 22, 46; s Leo S Glick & Sylvia Hall G; single. Educ: Cornell Univ, BS, 67, Law Sch, JD, 70. Polit & Govt Pos: Confidential law asst, NY State Supreme Court Appellate Div, 70-71; mem, Montgomery Co Young Dem, Md, 72-, pres, 73; mem, Young Dem of Md, currently, gen counsel, 75-; counsel, select comt on small bus, US House Rep, 73-74; spec asst attorney gen, Md, 74-; mem, Md Dem State Cent Comt, 74- Bus & Prof Pos: Attorney, Graubard, Moskovitz & McCauley, 71-73. Publ: Co-auth, Product Safety and Liability Handbook, McGraw-Hill, in prep; auth, Mutual fund management fees: in search of a standard, Am Bar Asn, The Bus Lawyer, 70 & Independent judicial review of administrative rate-making, Fordham Law Rev, 71. Mem: Montgomery Co Adv Comt on Consumer Affairs. Honors & Awards: Nat Munic League Carl Pforzheimer fel, 67; Barksdale-Morrow lectr, Hood Col, 75; Second prizewinner, Copyright Law Contest, Am Soc Composers, Artists & Producers. Mailing Add: 1220 E West Hwy Silver Spring MD 20910

GLINSEK, GERALD JOHN (D)
b Akron, Ohio, Jan 16, 39; s Rudolph Paul Glinsek & Angela Stanger G; m 1968 to Karen Rosemary Mehen; c David, Rebecca & Kelli. Educ: Univ Akron, BA, 63, JD, 67; Phi Kappa Tau; Omicron Delta Kappa; Phi Alpha Delta. Polit & Govt Pos: Asst Prosecuting Attorney, Summit Co, Ohio, 67-71; pres, Summit Co Young Dem, 70; pres, Ohio Young Dem, 72-74; mem exec comt, Ohio Dem Party, 72-74. Bus & Prof Pos: Attorney, Akron, Ohio, 67- Mil Serv: Pvt, Army, 57, serv in 1st Armored Div. Mem: Am, Ohio & Akron Bar Asns; Am & Ohio Trial Lawyers Asns. Relig: Catholic. Mailing Add: 953 Wye Dr Akron OH 44303

GLISSON, ROMAINE LILLIAN (R)
Chmn, Baldwin Co Rep Party, Ala
b Columbus, Ohio, Sept 12, 28; d Roman John Claprood & Florence Ann Deibel C; m 1948 to Courtney Glisson, Jr; c Damon Christopher, John Tilghman, Wyatt Charles & Camille Romaine. Educ: Ohio State Univ, WS, 48. Polit & Govt Pos: Pres, SBaldwin Fedn Rep Women, 67-71; chmn, Baldwin Co Rep Party, Ala, 71-; mem, Rep State Exec Comt Ala, 71- Bus & Prof Pos: Secy, R J Claprood Co, Fla, 46-, secy-treas, R J Claprood Co, Ala, 53-, secy, R J Claprood Co, Columbus, Ohio, 64-, R J Claprood Co, WVa, 65- & Gulf Beach Corp, Gulf Shores, 69- Mem: Fla Flower Asn. Honors & Awards: Navigator, US Power Squadron. Relig: Catholic. Legal Res: 314 Marigold Ave Foley AL 36535 Mailing Add: PO Box 516 Foley AL 36535

GLOCKNER, EDWARD L (EBB) (D)
Chmn, Scioto Co Dem Cent Comt, Ohio
b Portsmouth, Ohio, Mar 6, 21; s Edward A Glockner & Helen Folz G; m 1950 to Joanne Krick; c Susan, Andrew & Mary Ann. Educ: Xavier Univ, BSBA, 48. Polit & Govt Pos: Chmn, Scioto Co Dem Cent & Exec Comts, Ohio, 69- Bus & Prof Pos: Bd dirs, Ohio Univ Br, 62-73, Mercy Hosp, Portsmouth, 72-73 & Ohio Auto Dealers Asn, 73- Mil Serv: Entered as Cadet, Navy Air Corps, 42, released as Lt, 46, after serv in Torpedo Squadron 8, Task Force 38, Carrier Based, SPac, 43-45; Four Air Medals; Distinguished Flying Cross; SPac Theatre; Presidential Unit Citation. Mem: Scioto Co New Car Dealers (pres); CofC; Am Legion; Elks; Aircraft Owners & Pilots Asn. Honors & Awards: Distinguished Serv Award, Jaycees, 53; Distinguished Alumni, Xavier Univ, 68; Citizens Award, Southwestern Ohio Counties, 71; Distinguished Citizen Award, Jaycees & CofC, 72. Relig: Roman Catholic. Legal Res: 2920 Willow Way Portsmouth OH 45662 Mailing Add: PO Box 1303 Portsmouth OH 45662

GLOVER, ALAN HARNEY (D)
Nev State Assemblyman
b Carson City, Nev, June 10, 49; s John Nelson Glover (deceased) & Peggy Harney G; single. Educ: Univ Nev, Reno, 68-72; Phi Delta Theta. Polit & Govt Pos: Nev State Assemblyman, 72- Mem: KofC. Relig: Catholic. Mailing Add: 230 S Iris St Carson City NV 89701

GLOVER, BILLY JOE (D)
Mem, State Dem Exec Comt, Tenn
b Fayette Co, Tenn, Oct 1, 38; s Joe Franklin Glover & Faye Holmes G; m 1962 to Martha Ann McCullar; c James Adam (Jim), Molly Ann & John Michael (Jack). Educ: Lambuth Col, BS, 61; Memphis State Univ, MA, 65. Polit & Govt Pos: Alderman, Selmer, Tenn, 69-71, mayor, 71-; committeeman, McNairy Co Dem Comt, 73-; mem, State Dem Exec Comt, 75- Bus & Prof Pos: Supvr adult educ, State Dept Educ, Tenn, 65- Publ: Co-auth, Adult Basic Education Curriculum Development, Memphis State Univ, 74. Mem: Tenn Educ Asn; Tenn Asn Pub Sch Adult Educ; Selmer Moose Lodge; Selmer Golf & Country Club; Civitan Club. Honors & Awards: Young Educator of Year, Selmer Jaycees, 65. Relig: Methodist. Mailing Add: 989 E Poplar Selmer TN 38375

GLOVER, BOBBY L (D)
Ark State Rep
Mailing Add: 701 N Center Carlisle AR 72024

GLOVER, DELONE BRADFORD (R)
VChmn, Box Elder Co Rep Party, Utah
b Corinne, Utah, Jan 5, 24; d Alfred Edgar Bradford & Viola Lorina Hansen B; m 1943 to Clyde Lorenzo Glover; c Annette (Mrs Douglas Hunsaker), Rama (Mrs Steve Rasmussen), Marco (Mrs Charles Simonsen) & Bradford. Educ: Box Elder High Sch, Utah, grad, 41. Polit & Govt Pos: Precinct vchmn, Box Elder Co Rep Party, Utah, 47-50, precinct secy, 51-54, precinct vchmn, 55-58 & 67-70, vchmn, 74-; vchmn, Brigham City Rep Party, 63-66 & 70-73; worked on successful campaigns of Gov George Clyde, Sherm Lloyd, Lawrence Burton & Jake Garn. Bus & Prof Pos: Qm acct, US Army Civil Serv, Tex, 43-44; clerk acct, Bushnell Gen Hosp, Brigham City, Utah, 44-45 & GI Prog, Box Elder Co, 45-49; secy to supt, Box Elder Co Schs, 52-68, acct payable clerk, 68-72, payroll clerk, 72-74 & purchasing agt, 74- Mem: Box Elder Co Golden Spike Asn (exec secy, 52-); Nat Golden Spike Soc (exec secy, 57-); Brigham City Mus-Gallery (bd dirs, 70-); Civic Improv Club. Relig: Latter-day Saint. Mailing Add: 106 W First N Brigham City UT 84302

GLOVER, MERTON (R)
Chmn, Shannon Co Rep Party, SDak
b Trinidad, Colo, Feb 15, 18; s John H Glover & Maude Jones G; m 1951 to Mable I Miller; c Brenna L, Kendall M, Craig J & June K. Educ: SDak State Univ Sch Agr, 4 years. Polit & Govt Pos: Mem, Shannon Co Draft Bd, SDak, 47-50; rd comnr, Shannon Co, 48-52; chmn, Shannon Co Rep Party, 52-55 & currently; SDak State Rep, 55-57; committeeman, SDak Rep State Cent Comt, 65- Mil Serv: Entered as Pvt, Army, 41, released as S/Sgt, 45, after serv in 4th Cavalry, ETO, 43-45; Bronze Star; Purple Heart; Presidential Unit Citation. Mem: Elks; Am Legion; SDak Stockgrowers Asn; Am Nat Cattlemens Asn. Mailing Add: Porcupine SD 57772

GLOVER, MICHAEL G (D)
Kans State Rep
Mailing Add: 1308 Summit Lawrence KS 66044

GLOVER, MILDRED (D)
Ga State Rep
Mailing Add: 672 Beckwith St SW Atlanta GA 30314

GLOVER, RUTH CHAMPION (R)
Chmn, Charleston Co Rep Party, SC
b Charleston, SC, Oct 12, 26; d Joseph David Champion & Alice Spell C; m 1947 to Francis St Clair Glover; c Lynda Elizabeth, Lydia Elise & Ruth-Anne. Educ: Stokes Bus Col, 44-45. Polit & Govt Pos: Exec committeeman, Charleston Co Rep Party, SC, 62-66, vchmn, 68-74 & chmn, 74-; state conv secy, SC Rep Party, 70; vpres, James Island Fedn Rep Women, 72-73. Bus & Prof Pos: Serv rep, Southern Bell Tel & Tel Co, Charleston, SC, 45-50; archit reporter & plan rm mgr, F W Dodge Div, McGraw-Hill Info Syst Co, 63- Mem: Nat Asn Women in Construction (charter mem, Charleston Chap); League of Women Voters; Tullian Toastmistress Int (charter mem); Am Bus Women's Asn (charter mem, Swamp Fox Chap); James Island Fedn Rep Women. Honors & Awards: Woman of the Year, Nat Asn Women in Construction, Charleston Chap, 72. Relig: Episcopal. Mailing Add: 450 Maybank Hwy Charleston SC 29412

GLOVER, THOMAS EUGENE, JR (R)
Chmn, Houston Co Rep Party, Ga
b Brunswick, Ga, July 11, 29; s Thomas Eugene Glover & Jose Garcia G; m 1948 to Miriam Jean Merritt; c Thomas Callaway, Beverly Cooper, Donna Lynn, Janice Faye & Laura Susan. Educ: Univ Southern Miss, BS, 65, Grad Sch, 66-68; Pen & Sword. Polit & Govt Pos: Chmn, Houston Co Rep Party, Ga, 72- Bus & Prof Pos: Proj engr, Maxson Electronic, Inc, 68-69 & develop engr, 69-70; teacher, Tabor Jr High Sch, 70-71; graphic arts mgr, Unijax, Inc, Macon, Ga, 71-75; self-employed, Glover-Williamson Printing Co, 75- Mil Serv: Entered as Pvt, Air Force, released as M/Sgt, 68, after serv in Training Command. Publ: Co-auth, Radioisotope Long-Term Timing Device, Tech Report GT-NE-11, Ga Inst Technol; auth, Radioisotope Switch, P-OD 34-20.09, Maxson Electronic, Inc. Mem: Warner Robins CofC; United Fund of Houston Co (bd dirs, 75-); Morning Optimist Club (bd gov); Noncommissioned Officers Asn; Air Force Asn. Relig: Methodist. Legal Res: 427 Alabama Ave Warner Robins GA 31093 Mailing Add: PO Box 911 Warner Robins GA 31093

GLUBA, WILLIAM EVAN (D)
Iowa State Sen
b Davenport, Iowa, Oct 7, 42; s William Lee Gluba & Ellen Conboy G; m 1965 to Patricia Ann Keefe. Educ: St Ambrose Col, BA, 64; Univ Iowa, Grad Work, 65- Polit & Govt Pos: Active in President Kennedy's Campaign, 60; pres, St Ambrose Col Young Dem, 62; exec secy, Young Dem Clubs, Iowa, 62, nat committeeman, 63-64; alt deleg, Dem Nat Conv, 64; pres, Iowa Young Dem, 65; Dem Party Activists, Scott Co, Iowa, 65-69; mem, Eugene McCarthy for President Drive, 66; co-chmn, Scott Co Citizens for Robert Kennedy for President Comt, 67; cand mayor, Davenport, 69; Iowa State Rep, 70-72; Iowa State Sen, 73-, chmn human resources comt, Iowa State Senate, currently, mem appropriations, ways & means & ethics comts, currently. Bus & Prof Pos: Realtor assoc. Mem: Am Dem Action; Jaycees; KofC; Izaak Walton League; Am Acad Polit & Social Sci. Honors & Awards: Outstanding Young Dem, Iowa, 65. Relig: Catholic. Mailing Add: 943 Cimarron Dr Davenport IA 52804

GNIADEK, DONALD RICHARD (D)
Coun Chmn, Stratford, Conn
b Bridgeport, Conn, May 18, 42; s Edward G Gniadek & Ann Stukowski G; m 1964 to Barbara P Boyko; c Joanne, Michelle & Donald, II. Educ: Fairfield Univ, BBA, 63, MA, 74. Polit & Govt Pos: Second Dist councilman, Stratford, Conn, 69-71, councilman-at-large & coun chmn, 73- Bus & Prof Pos: Sr indust engr, Bryant Elec Co, Bridgeport, Conn, 66- Relig: Catholic. Mailing Add: 308 Garibaldi Ave Stratford CT 06497

GNODTKE, LUCILE H (R)
Mem Exec Comt, Berrien Co Rep Comt, Mich
b Richland Center, Wis, July 28, 07; d Edwin Huston & Helen Ray H; m 1931 to William Gnodtke; c Mary (Mrs Ralph Painter) & William Huston. Educ: Univ Mich, Ann Arbor, 26-27. Polit & Govt Pos: Deleg or alt deleg, State, Dist & Co Rep Convs, 60-; mem, Mich Rep State Cent Comt, formerly, mem orgn comt, formerly, mem exec comt, formerly; mem exec comt, Berrien Co Rep Comt, 68-; pres, Berrien Co Rep Womens Club; alt deleg, Rep Nat Conv, 72. Relig: Presbyterian. Mailing Add: 311 W Fourth St Buchanan MI 49107

GOBLE, EDWARD EARL (D)
Ind State Rep
b Aurora, Ind, May 17, 38; s Bernard Goble & Elizabeth Resing G; m 1958 to Clara Cecelia Fledderman; c Lawrence Edward, Lee Ann & Lori Dale. Educ: Aurora High Sch, Ind, 52-56; Data Processing Inst, Cincinnati, Ohio, 63. Polit & Govt Pos: Pres, Ripley Co Young Dem, Ind, 63-67; treas, Ninth Cong Dist Young Dem, 65-67; regional dir, Ind State Young Dem, 67-69; Ind State Rep, 71- Mil Serv: Entered as Pvt, Army, 56, released as Sgt, 61, after serv in 661st Tank Bn Res. Mem: Eagles; KofC; Elks; Tri Twp Conserv Club; United Steelworkers of Am. Honors & Awards: Outstanding Serv Award, Decatur Co Rural Elec Corp; Distinguished Serv Award, Ind Rural Elec Corp; Ind Acad Family Physicians. Relig: Catholic. Mailing Add: 411 S Walnut Batesville IN 47006

GODDARD, RUTH (R)
VChmn, Decatur Co Rep Party, Ind
b Greensburg, Ind, May 25, 23; d Edmund Russell French & Margaret Willeford F; m 1945 to Howard Goddard. Educ: Greensburg High Sch, grad, 41. Polit & Govt Pos: Dep recorder, Decatur Co, Ind, 45-58, dep treas, 69-70 & dep clerk, 71-72; vchmn, Decatur Co Rep Party, 71-; license br mgr, Bur Motor Vehicles, 73- Relig: Presbyterian. Mailing Add: RR 9 Box 29 Greensburg IN 47240

GODDARD, SAMUEL PEARSON, JR (D)
Dem Nat Committeeman, Ariz
b Clayton, Mo, Aug 8, 19; s Samuel Pearson Goddard & Florence Denham G; m 1944 to Julia Hatch; c Terry, Tim & Bill. Educ: Harvard Col, AB, 41; Univ Ariz, LLB, 49; mem, Harvard Varsity Crew, 40-41, pres, Student Bar Asn, Univ Ariz, 49. Polit & Govt Pos: Chmn, Dem Party of Ariz, 60-62; Dem nominee for Gov, Ariz, 62, Gov, Ariz, 65-67; US rep, Inauguration of Pres Leras Restrepo, Colombia, SAm, 66; deleg, Dem Nat Conv, 68 & 72; Dem Nat Committeeman, Ariz, 72-; deleg, Dem Nat Mid-Term Conf, 74. Bus & Prof Pos: Partner, Goddard, Sophy & Ahearn, Attorneys, Tucson & Phoenix, Ariz; officer & dir numerous business enterprises. Mil Serv: Enlisted as Pvt, Army Air Corps, 41, released as Maj, 46, after serv in all theaters of opers; Col, Air Force Res. Mem: Am Bar Asn; United Way of Am (bd gov, 72-); Nat Acad for Volunteerism (chmn); ROA; Phi Alpha Delta. Honors & Awards: Tucson Man of the Year, 59. Relig: Unitarian. Mailing Add: 4724 E Camelback Canyon Dr Phoenix AZ 85018

GODFREY, HELEN MARGARET (R)
VChairwoman, Third Dist Rep Party, NC
b Pittsburgh, Pa, Apr 5, 20; d Elmer David James & Maude Ferner J; m 1941 to William Edward Godfrey; c Mary Frances (Mrs Thomas Watts), James Edward & Thomas William. Educ: Warren High Sch, 34-38. Polit & Govt Pos: Precinct chmn, Raleigh Rep Party, NC, 63-66; prog chmn, Goldsboro Rep Party, 66-67, precinct develop chmn, 66-67, campaign mgr local alderman, 67, gubernatorial candidates, 68; vchairwoman, Third Dist Rep Party, 67-; mem, NC State Rep Cent Comt, 67-; third dist chmn, NC Rep Party, 69-70; mem state steering comt, Gov Holshouser, 72-; app, NC Human Rels Comn, 75- Mem: Goldsboro Art League. Mailing Add: 1611 E Pine St Goldsboro NC 27401

GODIN, WILFRID LUCIEN (D)
RI State Sen
b Woonsocket, RI, May 26, 37; s Wilfrid Antoine Godin & Claire Blanche St Germain G; m to Pauline Jeannine Vary; c Marc Richard, Michelle Marie, Jerome Paul, Denise Anne, Celeste Andree, Daniel Peter & Jules Christian. Educ: Providence Col, BA, 60; RI Col, MEd, 68; Nat Defense Educ Act fel, 68-69, Univ RI, MA, 69. Polit & Govt Pos: Deleg, RI Const Conv, 73; RI State Sen, Dist 32, 75-, mem, Judiciary Comt & Labor Comt, RI State Senate, 75- Bus & Prof Pos: Teacher, Woonsocket Sr High Sch, 62- Mil Serv: Entered as Airman 1/C, Air Force, 61, released, 62, after serv in 102 AC&W Squadron (RIANG), Germany during the Berlin Crisis, 61-62; Sr M/Sgt, RI Air Nat Guard, 56-; Armed Forces Expeditionary Medal; Armed Forces Res Medal; Armed Forces Meritorious Serv Ribbon; Nat Defense Medal; RI XV Serv Medal. Mem: Am & RI Fedn Teachers; Woonsocket Teachers Guild; Am Educ Research Asn; Nat Coun on Educ Measurement. Honors & Awards: Fel, Robert A Taft Inst Govt, RI Col, 74; Freedoms Found fel, Valley Forge, Pa, 74. Relig: Catholic. Mailing Add: 323 Carrington Ave Woonsocket RI 02895

GODLEY, G MCMURTRIE
b New York, NY, Aug 23, 17; m 1966 to Elizabeth McCray; c George McMurtrie, Jr & Nicholas Franchot. Educ: Yale Univ, AB, 39; Univ Chicago. Hon Degrees: LLD, Hartwick Col, Oneonta, NY. Polit & Govt Pos: Career officer, US Dept of State Foreign Serv, 41-, vconsul, Marseille, 41, third secy, Bern, 41-46, second secy, Brussels, 46-48, first secy, Paris, 52-55, counr, Cambodia, 55-57, Sr Seminar in Foreign Policy, Foreign Serv Inst, 60-61, counr, Congo, 61-62, dir, Off Cent African Affairs, 62-64, US Ambassador to the Congo, 64-66, Foreign Serv Inspector, 67, Dep Asst Secy, EAsian Affairs, 68, US Ambassador to Laos, 69-73; US Ambassador to Lebanon, 74. Mil Serv: Ens, Naval Res, 39-41; Marine Corps, 45-46. Relig: Protestant. Legal Res: Morris NY 13808 Mailing Add: Dept of State Washington DC 20520

GODLEY, GENE EDWIN (D)
b Houston, Tex, Oct 6, 39; s Thomas Edwin Godley & Jewel Drain G; m 1964 to Lisbeth Kamborian. Educ: Southern Methodist Univ, Dallas, BA, 60; Univ Chicago Law Sch, JD, 63. Polit & Govt Pos: Counsel vet subcomt, US Senate Labor & Pub Welfare Comt, 64, labor subcomt, 67, gen counsel, 70-; press & research asst to US Sen Ralph Yarborough, 65, legis

asst, 68 & admin asst, 69-; gen counsel, Senate Comt DC, 71-72; admin asst to US Sen Thomas F Eagleton, Mo, 73- Bus & Prof Pos: Consult, Booz, Allen & Hamilton, Washington, DC, 66. Mil Serv: Pvt, Army Res, 64, Capt, Res. Mem: Phi Delta Phi; Tex, DC & Am Bar Asns. Legal Res: 2927 Garapan Dallas TX 75224 Mailing Add: 3008 45th St NW Washington DC 20016

GODSEY, ANDREW EMMETT (D)
Chmn, Cumberland Co Dem Comt, Va
b Cumberland, Va, July 6, 05; s Andrew Emmett Godsey & Mary Courtney Foster G; m 1926 to Eloise Brightwell Blanton, wid. Educ: Cumberland High Sch, grad, 22; LaSalle Correspondence Sch, sponsored by Standard Oil Co, 1 year. Polit & Govt Pos: Pres, Young Dem Club, 39-45; chmn, Cumberland Co Dem Comt, Va, 45-72 & currently; campaign mgr gov elec for Mills Godwin, Albertis Harrison, Tom Stanley & Lindsay Almond & Watkins M Abbitt for Congressman, A Willis Robertson, Harry F Byrd, Sr & Harry F Byrd, Jr for US Sen, 50- Bus & Prof Pos: Salesman, Standard Oil Co, NJ, 25-50, retired; farming & real estate. Mem: Mason (32 degree, Master of Lodge, chmn various comts); Scottish Rite; Shrine; Moose; Kiwanis. Relig: Baptist. Mailing Add: Cumberland VA 23040

GODWIN, MILLS EDWIN, JR (R)
Gov, Va
b Nansemond Co, Va, Nov 19, 14; s Mills Edwin Godwin & Otelia Darden G; m 1940 to Katherine Thomas Beale; c Becky Katherine (deceased). Educ: Col of William & Mary, 31-34; Univ Va, LLB, 38. Hon Degrees: LLD, Elon Col, 54, Col William & Mary, 66, Roanoke Col, 69, Washington & Lee Univ, 70, Elmira Col & Hampden-Sydney Col, 72. Polit & Govt Pos: Chmn, Va Potomac River Comn, formerly; vchmn, Va Comn on Const Govt, formerly; mem, Comn Pub Educ & Va Adv Legis Coun, formerly; Va State Deleg, 48-52; chmn, Nansemond Co Dem Comt, Va, 48-58; Va State Sen, 52-62; Lt Gov, Va, 62-66; Gov, Va, 66-70 & currently; deleg, Dem Nat Conv, 68. Bus & Prof Pos: Asst commonwealth's attorney, Nansemond Co, formerly; spec agt, Fed Bur Invest, formerly; owner & operator 500 acre farm, Nansemond Co; corp dir, Norfolk & Western Rwy Co & Standard Brands, Inc, currently; mem exec comt & bd dirs, Va Nat Bank, currently; dir, Va Real Estate Trust, 71-, Dan River Co, 71- & Union Camp Corp, 72- Mem: Omicron Delta Kappa; Ruritan; KofP; Mason (33 degree); Scottish Rite. Honors & Awards: Va Distinguished Serv Award, 70; Thomas Jefferson Award for Pub Serv, 71. Relig: Christian Church; former chmn bd deacons, Oakland Christian Church. Mailing Add: State Capitol Richmond VA 23219

GOE, WILLIAM ROBERT (D)
Chmn, Lewis Co Dem Exec Comt, WVa
b Weston, WVa, Aug 7, 18; s Norval Douglas Goe & Madge Houghton G; single. Educ: Mountain State Bus Col, Parkersburg, WVa, grad, 36. Polit & Govt Pos: Mem, Lewis Co Bd Educ, WVa, 49-55; chmn, Lewis Co Dem Exec Comt, 60-; mem, Weston Sanit Bd, 65- Bus & Prof Pos: Acct, Danser Hardware & Supply Co, Weston, WVa, 36- Mil Serv: Entered as Pvt, Army, 42, released as Tech-4, 46, after serv in 102nd Machine Rec Unit, 7th Corps, 46; Good Conduct Medal; Victory & Am Campaign Medals. Mem: Am Legion; Weston Jr CofC; Weston Lions Club; Moose Lodge. Relig: Methodist. Mailing Add: 216 E Third St Weston WV 26452

GOEMAERE, WARREN N (D)
Mich State Rep
b Detroit, Mich, Feb 24, 17; m 1941 to Marian Kathryn Dallwitz; c Warren Russell. Educ: High sch, grad. Polit & Govt Pos: Mich State Rep, 64- Bus & Prof Pos: Retired. Mil Serv: 101st Airborne Div, World War II, 4 years serv in Pac & ETO. Mem: Elks; Warren 101st Airborne Div Asn; Sacred Heart Dad's Club. Relig: Roman Catholic. Mailing Add: 27132 Demirick Roseville MI 48066

GOESKE, JANET L (R)
Mem, Rep State Cent Comt Calif
b Kenneth, Minn, Oct 6, 11; d James A Knowlton & Anna Obele K; m 1929 to John Goeske; c Jacqueline (Mrs Fargo) & James. Educ: High sch. Polit & Govt Pos: Polit campaign worker, 46-; city & co pres, Rep Women Orgn, formerly; city & co chmn for many cand; deleg, Rep Nat Conv, 68 & 72; vchmn, Riverside Co Rep Women, Calif, 74; mem, Rep State Cent Comt Calif, currently; mem adv coun, Calif Off on Aging, currently; mem nat adv coun disabled & consult, Dept Health, Educ & Welfare, currently; mem, Riverside Community Rels Comt, currently. Publ: Compiled & ed, Rep Cook Book, 60. Mem: Pac State Hosp Adv Bd (chmn & sec gov adv bd, 69-); Foster Daughters (pres). Honors & Awards: Woman of Year, Parents & Friends Pac State Hosp Coun, 70; Humanitarian Award & Community Leader Award, Mayor, Riverside, 71; Soroptomist Serv Award, 72; Foster Grandparents Adv Coun Spec Chmn Award, 74-75; Vol Serv Award, Pac State Hosp, 74; plus others. Mailing Add: 4025 Rice Rd Riverside CA 92506

GOETZ, JAMES B (JIM) (R)
b Freeport, Ill, May 28, 36; s Thomas Goetz & Marian Isley G; m to Ruth Elbert; c James Jeffrey & Gregory Thomas. Educ: Univ Wis; Mid-Western Broadcasting Sch, Chicago. Polit & Govt Pos: Alderman, Winona, Minn, formerly; chmn, Winona Co Rep Party, formerly; first vchmn & chmn, Minn State Rep Exec Party & State Cent Comt, formerly; deleg, Rep Nat Conv, 64; Lt Gov, Minn, 67-70; Midwest Region Vchmn, Nat Lt Gov Conf, 67- Bus & Prof Pos: Pres & co-owner, KAGE, Winona, Minn, 61-72; pres, Gen TV of Minn, Inc, 71- Mil Serv: Army. Mem: Minn Jaycees; Mason (32 degree); Shrine. Honors & Awards: One of Ten Outstanding Young Men in Minn, 65; One of Ten Outstanding Young Men in Am, 71. Relig: Methodist. Mailing Add: Villa Seeblick Lakeland Shores MN 55043

GOETZ, LILLIAN RUTH (R)
VChmn, Benton Co Rep Cent Comt, Ind
b Fowler, Ind, Mar 5, 18; d William Christian Benner & Ruth Windler B; m 1941 to Cyril Joseph; c James Cyril. Educ: Lafayette Bus Col, 67. Polit & Govt Pos: Precinct vcommitteeman, Benton Co Rep Cent Comt, Ind, 42-70, secy, 44-62, vchmn, 62- Bus & Prof Pos: Dep treas, Benton Co, Ind, 53-56 & 65-67, co treas, 57-64; court reporter, Benton Circuit Court, 67- Relig: Roman Catholic. Mailing Add: 400 N Washington Ave Fowler IN 47944

GOETZ, WILLIAM G (R)
NDak State Rep
b Hazen, NDak, June 6, 44; s Otto E Goetz & Elfrieda Knoop G; m 1970 to Marion R Schock; c Marcia. Educ: Bismarck Jr Col, AA, 64; Minot State Col, BA, 66; Univ NDak, MA, 67; Col Rep. Polit & Govt Pos: NDak State Rep, 75- Bus & Prof Pos: Asst mgr Medora Div, Gold Seal Co, 63-70; asst prof bus, Dickinson State Col, 67- Relig: Lutheran; deacon, Church Coun. Mailing Add: 251 Allen St Dickinson ND 58601

GOFF, ABE MCGREGOR (R)
b Colfax, Wash, Dec 21, 99; s Herbert William Goff & Mary Dorsey G; m 1927 to Florence L Richardson; c Timothy R & Annie McGregor. Educ: Univ Idaho, LLB, 24; Scabbard & Blade; Beta Theta Pi. Polit & Govt Pos: Prosecuting attorney, Latah Co, Idaho, 26-34; comnr, Idaho State Bar Comn, 39-41; Idaho State Sen, 41-43; US Rep, Idaho, 47-48; gen counsel, US Post Off Dept, 54-58; comnr, Interstate Com Comn, 58-67. Bus & Prof Pos: Lawyer; retired. Mil Serv: Pvt, Army, 18; reentered serv as Maj, Army, 41, released as Col, 46, after serv in Judge Adv Corps, Africa, Europe, Pac, Gen McArthur's Staff, Tokyo & Off Under Secy War; Col (Ret), Army Res; Legion of Merit; Commendation & Reserve Medals; World War I & World War II Victory Medals; Am Defense, Am Campaign, Africa-Europe-Mid East & Pac Campaign Ribbons; Army of Occup Medal. Mem: Fed Bar Found (bd dirs); Am Soc Int Law; Judge Adv Asn; Am Bar Asn; Mason. Relig: Episcopal. Mailing Add: 503 East C St Moscow ID 83843

GOFF, ELIZABETH E (D)
NH State Rep
Mailing Add: 259 Main St Salem NH 03079

GOFFENA, SHYLA LEE (D)
Secy, Shelby Co Dem Cent & Exec Comts, Ohio
b Sidney, Ohio, July 7, 38; d William Gerald Freeman & Blanche Elliott F; m 1957 to Peter John Goffena; c Peter Michael, Thomas Joseph & William David. Educ: Sidney High Sch, grad, 56. Polit & Govt Pos: Treas, Shelby Co Women Dem Club, Ohio, 67-71; secy, Shelby Co Dem Cent & Exec Comts, 70-; dep dir, Shelby Co Bd Elections, 71- Bus & Prof Pos: Secy, Copeland Refrigeration, 60-62 & 64-66; secy, Dem Hqs, Sidney, Ohio, 68-70. Mem: Women of the Moose; Shelby Co Dem Club; Women Dem Club of Shelby Co; Sidney High Sch Football Mothers Club. Relig: Catholic. Mailing Add: 310 S Miami Ave Sidney OH 45365

GOFFIN, MIRIAM SUSAN (D)
b Jersey City, NJ, Dec 24, 40; d Harold Gorenberg & Lillian Rosman G; m 1966 to Eugene William Goffin. Educ: Jersey City State Col, BA, 63; NY Univ, MA, 68, completed PhD course work, awarded doctoral candidacy; Kappa Delta Pi; Int Rels Club; chmn, Collegiate Coun for the UN Model Gen Assembly Deleg, 62. Polit & Govt Pos: Vol, Citizens for Sen Joe Clark, 68; alt deleg, Dem Nat Conv, 72; mem policy comt, Del Dist Dem for McGovern-Shriver, Buffalo, NY, 72. Bus & Prof Pos: Teacher, Wantagh High Sch, NY, 66-67; part-time lectr, King's Col, Wilkes-Barre, Pa, 67-68, Marywood Col, Scranton, 68 & Univ Scranton, summer 68; asst prof hist & govt, Niagara Co Community Col, 69-73; sales rep, Dushkin Publ Group, Guilford, Conn, 73- Mem: Am Hist Asn; Conf on Latin Am Hist; Am Asn Univ Prof; Latin Am Studies Asn; Nat Women's Polit Caucus. Honors & Awards: Nat Defense Educ Act Title VI Fel in Portuguese Lang & Brazilian Studies, Dept Health, Educ & Welfare, 63-66. Mailing Add: 64 Irving Pl Buffalo NY 14201

GOFORTH, RAY A (D)
Chmn, Fayette Co Dem Exec Comt, WVa
b Beckley, WVa, June 23, 28; s James Kelley Goforth & Frances Cooper G; m to Betty Jo Wells; c Teresa S & Tina M. Educ: Morris Harvey Col, 59; WVa State Col, 71. Polit & Govt Pos: Chmn, Fayette Co Dem Exec Comt, WVa, 72-; committeeman, Valley Dist, 72- Bus & Prof Pos: Owner & mgr, Goforth Ins Agency, 63- Mil Serv: Entered as Pvt, Army, 55, released as SP-3, 57, after serv in 21st Infantry Div, Korea, 56-57; Good Conduct Medal. Mem: WVa & Nat Asns Mutual Ins Agts; Civitan Club of Montgomery. Relig: Baptist. Mailing Add: PO Box 218 Charlton Heights WV 25040

GOGGIN, TERRY (D)
Calif State Assemblyman
b Los Angeles, Calif, Nov 8, 41; s George T Goggin & Mary Hare G; m 1963 to Jill Ann Tronvic; c Brian, Patrick & Colin. Educ: Georgetown Univ, AB; Univ Southern Calif Sch Law, JD. Polit & Govt Pos: Campaign coordr, Inland Empire, Comt to Reelect Gov Pat Brown, Calif, 66; asst prof, US Mil Acad, West Point, 67-70; spec consult, White House Urban Affairs Coun, 69; cand for cong, 38th Cong Dist, 72; admin asst to US Rep George E Brown, Jr, Calif, 73-74; Calif State Assemblyman, 75- Bus & Prof Pos: Law partner, Goggin, Goggin & Commons, 71- Mil Serv: Entered as 2nd Lt, Army, 66, released as Capt, 70, after serv in West Point; Army Commendation Medal. Publ: Co-auth, Politics American Style, Prentice Hall, 72; auth, The effects of pretrial publicity on a jurors ability to be impartial, 65 & Publicity & partial criminal trial: resolving the Constitutional conflict, 66, Southern Calif Law Rev. Relig: Catholic. Legal Res: 855 Edgemont San Bernardino CA 92405 Mailing Add: State Capitol Sacramento CA 95814

GOGGINS, JUANITA WILLMON (D)
SC State Rep
b Pendleton, SC, May 11, 34; d Willie Rogers Willmon & Lillian Atlee Vandiver W; m 1961 to Dr Horace Goggins; c Horace Willmon. Educ: SC State Col, BSHE, 57; Univ SC; Alpha Kappa Alpha. Polit & Govt Pos: Deleg, SC Dem Conv, 72; deleg, Dem Nat Conv, 72; mem, Legis Comt to Study Changing Method of Electing Sch Bd Off, Rock Hill Sch Dist III, 72-73; mem, State Comt for McGovern Campaign, 72; co coordr, Nick Zeigler for US Senate, 72; Gov app, Comt for Studying Legis Pay Scale, 72-74; mem adv comt, Dem Women's Coun of SC, 73-; SC State Rep, 75-; deleg, Dem Nat Mid-Term Conf, 74. Bus & Prof Pos: Home econ teacher, York Sch Dist 1, SC, 57-64; home econ teacher, Chester Co Schs, 64-65; teacher, Rock Hill Sch Dist III, 65-66. Mem: Piedmont Med, Dent, Pharmaceutical Auxiliary (secy); Palmetto Med, Dent, Pharmaceutical Auxiliary; NAACP; York Co Dem Women. Honors & Awards: First black woman elected to SC Dem Conv & first black woman from SC to go to Dem Nat Conv, 72; honor dinner, Black Citizens of Rock Hill, 72. Relig: Baptist. Mailing Add: 1635 W Main St Rock Hill SC 29730

GOING, PADEN CAWHERN (R)
Chmn, Preston Rep Town Comt, Conn
b Atlanta, Ga, July 5, 27; s James Leonard Going, Sr & Artie Mary Chastain G; m 1945 to Ruth Evelyn App; c Sharon Lee (Mrs Cramer) & Jonathan Perry. Educ: O'Keefe High Sch, 40-44. Polit & Govt Pos: Mem, Preston Rep Town Comt, Conn, 62-69, chmn, 69-, mem bd finance, 63- Mil Serv: Entered as Recruit, Navy, 44, released as Hospitalman Chief, 66, after serv in Submarine & Destroyer Forces, Atlantic & European Theatres. Mem: AF&AM (Master Mason); Fleet Reserve Asn; VFW; Am Cancer Soc (bd dirs). Relig: Seventh Day Adventist. Legal Res: Preston CT Mailing Add: RFD 5 Rte 12 Norwich CT 06360

GOING, ROBERT MORTON (D)
Chmn, Lancaster Co Dem Comt, Pa
b Amsterdam, NY, Aug 31, 27; s John J Going & Marion Morton G; m 1953 to Margaret

M Gunselman; c Patricia Marie, Robert M, Jr, Thomas M, Julia M & Marian E. Educ: Franklin & Marshall Col, AB, 52; Dickinson Sch Law, JD, 55; Phi Kappa Tau. Polit & Govt Pos: Exec dir, Redevelop Authority, Lancaster, Pa, 57-60; comnr, Lancaster City Planning Comn, 57-60, asst city solicitor, Lancaster, 67-73; appeal agt, Selective Serv Syst, 70-73; chmn, Lancaster Co Dem Cent Comt, 72- Bus & Prof Pos: Attorney-at-law, 56-70; partner, Zimmerman & Going, 71-73. Mil Serv: Entered as Seaman, Navy, 45, released as 2/C PO, 48, after serv in Ground Controlled Approach Unit. Mem: Am, Pa & Lancaster Co Bar Asns; Am Trial Lawyers Asn; Am Arbit Asn. Relig: Catholic. Mailing Add: 1120 Wheatland Ave Lancaster PA 17603

GOJACK, MARY LEE **(D)**
Nev State Assemblyman
b Hillsboro, Iowa, Feb 19, 36; d Sam V Whitaker & Leona Semler W; m 1969 to John T Gojack; c Patricia Lee Hixson & John Warner Hixson. Educ: Univ Nev, Reno, BA, 68, Sec Teaching Cert; Phi Alpha Theta. Polit & Govt Pos: Nev State Assemblyman, Assembly Dist 23, 72- Bus & Prof Pos: Partner, Financial Mkt, Family Corp, 69- Mem: Am Asn Univ Women; Nat Arthrogryposis Asn (nat bd secy, 72); Nev Opera Guild (membership chmn, 72); Washoe Co Coun on Alcoholism; Am Legion Auxiliary. Relig: Protestant. Mailing Add: 3855 Skyline Blvd Reno NV 89502

GOLD, EMANUEL R **(D)**
NY State Sen
Mailing Add: 104-40 Queens Blvd Queens NY 11375

GOLD, MICHAEL **(D)**
Chmn, Hunterdon Co Dem Comt, NJ
b New York, NY, Nov 17, 35; s Nat Gold & Sylvia Price G; m 1957 to to Lucienne Kacew; c Pamela, Cathrine & Jennifer. Educ: Columbia Col, AB, 57; Rutgers Univ Law Sch, LLB, 62; Alpha Epsilon Pi. Polit & Govt Pos: Dep Attorney Gen, NJ, 65-67; counsel, NJ Dept Agr, 65-67; counsel, NJ Young Dem, 67-69; first asst prosecutor, Hunterdon Co, 68-70; chmn, Hunterdon Co Dem Comt, 72- Bus & Prof Pos: Prin, Gold Trust, 59-; partner, Gold, Gold & Morland, 66- Mil Serv: Entered as Pvt, NJ Nat Guard, 59, released as Sgt, 66. Mem: Am Judicature Soc; NJ Fedn Planning Off; Lions; NJ Milk Indust Asn (secy, 72-); Am Civil Liberties Union. Mailing Add: Box 252 RD 6 Flemington NJ 08822

GOLD, SHIRLEY ESTELLE **(D)**
Mem, Wake Co Dem Party, NC
b New York, NY, Nov 27, 34; d Abraham Usdansky & Edith Senderoff U; m 1952 to Harvey Joseph Gold; c Linda Riki & Roger Eliot. Educ: Univ Miami, 52-54; Univ Wis, BS, 55. Polit & Govt Pos: Bd mem, League of Women Voters, Winterhaven, Fla, 60-62; co-chmn, Citizens for Johnson-Humphrey, Raleigh, NC, 64 & Citizens for Humphrey-Muskie, 68; exec secy & campaign dir, Wake Co Dem Party, 68-74, mem, currently; bd mem, Wake Co Young Dem Club, 69; deleg, NC State Dem Conv, 70 & 72; deleg, Dem Nat Conv, 72; alt policy coun mem, NC Women's Polit Caucus, 72; bd mem, Wake Co Dem Women's Club, 72- Legal Res: 1209 Mindees Ct Raleigh NC 27609 Mailing Add: PO Box 1372 Raleigh NC 27602

GOLDBERG, ARTHUR JOSEPH **(D)**
b Chicago, Ill, Aug 8, 08; s Joseph Goldberg & Rebecca Pearlstein G; m 1931 to Dorothy Kurgans; c Barbara L & Robert M. Educ: Crane Jr Col, BSL, 29; Northwestern Univ, JD, 30. Polit & Govt Pos: Secy of Labor, 61-62; Assoc Justice, US Supreme Court, 62-65; US Ambassador to the UN, 65-68. Bus & Prof Pos: Attorney-at-Law, 29-41 & currently; mem law firm Goldberg, Devoe, Shadur & Mikva, Chicago, 45-61; gen counsel, USW, 48-61; with Goldberg, Feller & Bredhoff, Wash, 52-61; gen counsel, Indust Union Dept, AFL-CIO, 55-61; sr partner, Paul, Weiss, Goldberg, Rifkind, Wharton & Garrison, 68-71. Mil Serv: Maj, Army, 42-44, OSS, 42-43, serv in ETO. Publ: AFL-CIO Labor United, 56; The defense of freedom: the published papers of Arthur J Goldberg, 66; Equal justice, the Warren Era of the Supreme Court, 72; plus others. Relig: Jewish. Mailing Add: 1101 17th St NW Washington DC 20036

GOLDBERG, ROBERT MICHAEL **(D)**
b Chicago, Ill, Jan 23, 41; s Arthur Joseph Goldberg & Dorothy Kurgans G; m 1966 to Barbara Sproston; c Esther Fiona, Angus Ephraim & Duncan Abraham. Educ: Amherst Col, BA, 63; London Sch Econ, 64; Harvard Law Sch, JD, 67. Polit & Govt Pos: Deleg, Dem Nat Mid-Term Conf, 74. Bus & Prof Pos: Law clerk to Chief Judge David L Bazelon, US Court of Appeals, Washington, DC, 67-68; attorney-at-law, Kay, Miller & Libby, Anchorage, Alaska, 68-70; assoc prof law, Univ Alaska, Anchorage, 70-72; attorney-at-law, Anchorage, 70-; adj prof law, Sch Law, Univ Denver, 73- Publ: Co-auth, Alaska Survey & Report, Research Inst Alaska, Vols I & II, 70 & 72; auth, Ends & means: enforcement analysis & the law of the sea, Am Soc Int Law, 75. Mem: Am, Alaska & Ill Bar Asns. Honors & Awards: Best nonfiction book, Alaska Press Club, 70. Mailing Add: 3312 Madison Way Anchorage AK 99504

GOLDBERG, SAMUEL **(R)**
b Buffalo, NY, Aug 12, 28; s Benjamin N Goldberg & Norma Mendelson G; m 1952 to Barbara Koonin; c Robert, Thomas, Margaret, Karen & Michael. Educ: Univ Va, BA, 51; Georgetown Univ, 51-52. Polit & Govt Pos: Admin officer, US Dept Army, 52-67; foreign serv officer, US Dept State, 67-70; legis asst, US Sen Charles Mathias, Md, 70-72, admin asst, 72- Mil Serv: Entered as Pvt, Army, 55, released as Pfc, 56, after serv in 101 Airborne Div. Relig: Jewish. Mailing Add: 9208 Burning Tree Rd Bethesda MD 20034

GOLDBERG, SHEILA ANN **(D)**
Mem, Los Angeles Co Dem Cent Comt, Calif
b Pasadena, Calif, May 16, 39; d Louis Berkus & Shirley Frank B; m 1960 to Michael Jay Goldberg; c Tracey & Jay. Educ: Univ Calif, Berkeley; Univ Calif, Los Angeles, BA, 62. Polit & Govt Pos: Deleg, Dem Nat Conv, 72; mem, Los Angeles Co Dem Cent Comt, Calif, 72- Bus & Prof Pos: Teacher. Mem: Sherman Oaks Dem Club. Mailing Add: 5401 Oceanfront Walk Venice CA 90291

GOLDBERG, STANLEY B **(D)**
b Boston, Mass, Mar 14, 27; s Samuel Goldberg & Anna Kaplan G; m to Joyce Stocklan; c Sandra Lee & Melody Sue. Educ: Univ Mass, BSCE, 50; Boston Univ Grad Sch, 53; Tau Epsilon Phi. Polit & Govt Pos: Hwy engr, State Hwy Dept, Mass, 50-51; city planner, Boston, 51-53; town engr, Saugus, 53-56; city engr, North Miami, Fla, 56-60, city mgr, 63-65; city mgr, Dania, 66-69; alternate deleg, Dem Nat Conv, 72. Bus & Prof Pos: Instr, Dade Co Sch Bd, Miami, Fla, 69-70; chief planner, Rader & Assocs, 70-72; consult, Goldberg & Assocs, 72- Mil Serv: Entered Navy, 45, released As Sgt 1/C, 46, after serv in Pac Theatre; World War II Victory Medal; Pac Theatre Medal. Publ: Master comprehensive plan, City of Opa-Locka, Fla, 60; Available federal funds will benefit many cities, Munic South, 2/66; The crisis before the silver lining, Nation's Cities, 7/66. Mem: Fla Soc Prof Engrs (sr mem); Nat Soc Prof Engrs (sr mem); Int City Mgr Asn; Am Inst Planners; Mass Munic Engrs Asn (hon life mem). Relig: Jewish. Mailing Add: 11900 Bayshore Dr North Miami FL 33161

GOLDEN, JOHN MATTHEW **(D)**
Dem Nat Committeeman, Conn
b Old Saybrook, Conn, Nov 4, 95; s Matthew J Golden & Alice P Strickland G; m 1920 to Margaret J Stumpf; c Margaret (Mrs John A Berges) & Frances A (Mrs William Krenisky). Educ: Pub schs, Old Saybrook, Conn. Polit & Govt Pos: Dir pub works, New Haven, Conn, 32-45; Dem Nat Committeeman, Conn, 52-; deleg, Dem Nat Conv, 68 & 72. Bus & Prof Pos: Supt, Greist Mfg Co, 15-30; pres, Golden, O'Neill & Gebhardt Inc ins agency, 40; dir, Gen Bank & Trust Co & Winthrop Bank & Trust Co; trustee, St Raphael Hosp, Albertus Magnus Col, Annhurst Col & New Haven Found. Mem: Knights of St Patrick; KofC; Hibernian; Eagle; Union League Club. Relig: Roman Catholic; dir, Cath Diocesan Bur. Mailing Add: 1 Columbus Plaza New Haven CT 06507

GOLDEN, RICHARD A **(R)**
Mem, Mich Rep State Cent Comt
b Detroit, Mich, July 15, 41; s George M Golden & Elsie Zackem G; single. Educ: Wayne State Univ, BSEE, 65, JD, 71. Polit & Govt Pos: Mem, Mich Rep State Cent Comt, 75- Bus & Prof Pos: Engr, Bendix Corp, 65-70; attorney, 71- Mem: State Bar Mich; Inst Elec & Elec Engrs; Am Judicature Soc; Am Bar Asn. Mailing Add: 71 W Hancock Detroit MI 48201

GOLDFARB, ALEXANDER A **(D)**
Counr, Dem State Cent Comt, Conn
b Hartford, Conn, Oct 27, 27. Educ: Trinity Col, Conn, BS, 46; Cornell Univ Sch Law, JD, 49; Yale Grad Sch, 50-51; Pi Gamma Mu. Polit & Govt Pos: Asst corp counr, City of Hartford, Conn, 54-56, corp counsel, 72-; counr, Dem State Cent Comt, 54-; counr, Gtr Hartford Flood Comn of Conn, 56-71; mem, Comt to Revise Elec Laws of Conn, 61-63. Bus & Prof Pos: Faculty mem, Univ Nebr Col Law, 49-50; sr partner, Goldfarb & Reis, currently. Mil Serv: Pvt, Army Inf, 44-45. Relig: Jewish. Mailing Add: 1 Lewis St Hartford CT 06103

GOLDFARB, DAVID **(R)**
Committeeman, Essex Co Rep Party, NJ
b Newark, NJ, Mar 1, 17; s Barney Goldfarb & Rose Fechtner G; m 1960 to Renee Kornreich. Educ: Elon Col, 1 year; NY Univ, 3 years. Polit & Govt Pos: State dir, Ethnic for Nixon, 68; committeeman, Essex Co Rep Party, currently; chmn, South Orange Rep Town Comt, currently; NJ State Assemblyman, 71-73; exec secy, NJ State Bd CPA, 72-; Essex City Campaign Mgr, President Nixon & Ticket, 72; exec adminr, State Off Bldg, Newark, NJ, 73- Bus & Prof Pos: Pres, 6 Transportation Co, Newark, NJ, 41-; pres, Transportation Indust, 44-; consult on aging, Essex Co, 68; secy to dir personnel, Essex Co, 70-71. Mem: Elks; KofP; B'nai B'rith (North Jersey Coun Mem, 72-); NAACP; Urban League. Honors & Awards: Outstanding Athletes Award, High Sch & College. Relig: Judaism. Mailing Add: 39 Glenview Rd South Orange NJ 07079

GOLDFARB, OWEN **(D)**
b Seattle, Wash, July 19, 44; s William Goldfarb & Florence G; single. Educ: Rensselaer Polytech Inst, BEE, 66, MEE, 68; Adelphi Univ, Lawyer's Asst Prog cert, 74. Polit & Govt Pos: Budget dir, Rensselaer Co, NY, 71; admin asst to US Rep Edward W Pattison, NY, 75- Bus & Prof Pos: Systs consult-digital commun, Pattern Recognition, 67-70; bus mgr, Troy Rehabilitation & Improv Prog, NY, 72-73; housing consult, Upstate NY, 72-74. Mailing Add: 1431 33rd St NW Washington DC 20007

GOLDINGER, SHIRLEY **(D)**
Mem, Dem Nat Comt, Calif
Mailing Add: 644 Tiger Tail Rd Los Angeles CA 90049

GOLDMAN, GERALD **(R)**
Mayor, Passaic, NJ
b Brooklyn, NY, Sept 14, 34; s Max Goldman & Rachel G; m 1973 to Susan Ann Heiblim; c Keith, Kevin & Kim & Lance Herner (stepson). Educ: Univ Vt, BS, 55; NY Univ Sch Law, JD, 59; Key & Serpent; Gold Key; Phi Sigma Delta. Polit & Govt Pos: Admin asst, NJ State Legis, 63-64; mayor, Passaic, NJ, 71- Bus & Prof Pos: Founder & sr partner, Goldman, Carlet, Garrison & Bertoni, Attorneys-at-law, Clifton, NJ, 61- Mil Serv: Entered as 2nd Lt, released as 1st Lt, Army. Honors & Awards: Distinguished Serv Award, City of Passaic, 63; Outstanding Young Man in Am, Jaycees, 66. Relig: Jewish. Mailing Add: 77 Brook Ave C5 Passaic NJ 07055

GOLDMAN, SHIRLIE SELMA **(D)**
Assoc Mem, Milton Dem Town Comt, Mass
b Haverhill, Mass, Aug 4, 23; d Joseph Dorff & Bess Cooperman D; m 1950 to David S Goldman; c James Alan & Richard Marc. Educ: Mary Brooks Jr Col, 41-43. Polit & Govt Pos: Deleg, Dem Nat Conv, 72; assoc mem, Milton Dem Town Comt, currently. Mem: Common Cause (bd mem, Mass). Mailing Add: 93 Wendell Park Milton MA 02186

GOLDSTEIN, BLANCHE **(D)**
b Sacramento, Calif; d Morris Goldstein & Lena Berman G; m 1941 to Frank Goldstein; c Laurie C, David M & Michael L. Educ: Univ Calif, Berkeley, AB, 38; Mortar Board; Prytanean. Polit & Govt Pos: Organizer, Sacramento Co Woman's Div, Calif Dem State Cent Comt, 65-72, chmn, 7 years, state women's chmn, 72-73; Northern Calif co-chmn, Campaign to Elect US Sen Alan Cranston, 67; Northern Calif Woman's chmn, Campaign to Elect US Sen John Tunney, 70; co-chmn, Third Cong Dem Dist, 72-74. Bus & Prof Pos: Sr social worker, Sacramento Co Welfare Dept, 38-42. Mem: Haddasah; League of Women Voters. Honors & Awards: Woman of the Year, B'nai B'rith, 65; Action Award for Work with Hunger Task Force, Kennedy Action Corps, 66; Big Brother's Award, 68; Woman of Achievement, Sacramento Union Newspaper, 70; Volunteer of the Year, United Fund, 71. Relig: Jewish. Mailing Add: 6201 S Land Park Dr Sacramento CA 95831

GOLDSTEIN, HERBERT **(D)**
Chmn, Queen Anne's Co Dem State Cent Comt, Md
b Prince Frederick, Md, Nov 18, 14; s Goodman Goldstein (deceased) & Belle Butcher G (deceased); m 1938 to Shirley Fox; c Frances & Alan. Educ: Univ Md, 34. Polit & Govt Pos: Alt deleg, Dem Nat Conv, 60, deleg, 64 & 68; chmn, Queen Anne's Co Dem State Cent Comt, Md, 62-; dir & mem, Adv Comt on Wage Hours Law, Md Phys Fitness Comn & dir, Queen Anne's Co Welfare Bd, 65. Bus & Prof Pos: Dir, Centreville Nat Bank, 66. Mil Serv: Pvt,

Army, 45. Mem: Queen Anne's Co to Employ the Handicapped (chmn); Ment Health Asn (co-dir); Centreville CofC; Am Legion; Shrine. Honors & Awards: Ky Colonel. Relig: Jewish. Mailing Add: RD 1 Box 38 Chestertown MD 21620

GOLDSTEIN, LOUIS L (D)
State Comptroller, Md
b Prince Frederick, Md, Mar 14, 13; s Goodman Goldstein & Belle Butcher G; m 1947 to Hazel Elizabeth Horton; c Philip, Luisa & Margaret. Educ: Washington Col, BS, 35; Univ Md, LLB, 38; Omicron Delta Kappa; Zeta Beta Tau. Polit & Govt Pos: Md State Deleg, 39-42; deleg or alt deleg, Dem Nat Conv, 40 & 48-72; Md State Sen, 47-58, Majority Leader, 4 years, pres, 4 years, chmn, Chesapeake Bay & Tributaries, exec, nominations & finance comts; chmn legis coun & mem, Atlantic State Marine Fisheries Comn; mem, Bd Pub Works, Bd Revenue Estimates & Gov Adv Coun; mem, Employees', Teachers' & State Police Retirement Systs; State Comptroller, Md, 59- Bus & Prof Pos: Lawyer, Prince Frederick, Md; ed, Calvert J-Gazette; real estate broker; mem bd visitors & gov, Washington Col; ex-officio mem bd regents, Univ Md. Mil Serv: Entered as Pvt, Marine Corps, 42, released as 1st Lt, 46, after serv in Asiatic & Pac Theaters; Capt (Ret), Marine Corps Res. Mem: Am Bar Asn; Am Judicature Soc; Nat Asn State Auditors, Comptrollers & Treas; Munic Finance Officers Asn of US & Can; Nat Cong Parents & Teachers. Relig: Jewish. Mailing Add: Oakland Manor Prince Frederick MD 20678

GOLDSTEIN, MAXINE SHAPIRO (D)
Mem, Dem Party Ga
b Augusta, Ga, Aug 25, 26; d Harry Shapiro & Sadie Robbins S; m 1947 to Jacob Louis Goldstein; c Marcia (Mrs Charles Stein) & Harriet. Educ: Jr Col of Augusta, 45; Univ Ga, 46; Di Gamma Kappa; Zata Phi Eta; Delta Phi Epsilon. Polit & Govt Pos: Mem, Status of Women Comn, Ga, 62-70; mem, Dem Party Ga, 74-, mem, Charter Comn, Exec Comt & Affirmative Action Comts, 74- Bus & Prof Pos: Partner, Old Capitol Treasures, Milledgeville, Ga, 72-; dance instr, Milledgeville Recreation Dept, 74- Mem: Milledgeville Civic Women (chmn, Int Affairs, 74-); Garden Clubs Ga (chmn, State Garden Therapy, 75-); Designers Critique (pres, 73-75); Mid Ga Flower Show (judges coun); Adv Comt Mayors Core Comt. Honors & Awards: Judge, Amateur Flower Show, 67. Relig: Jewish. Legal Res: Meriweather Circle Milledgeville GA 31061 Mailing Add: PO Box G Milledgeville GA 31061

GOLDSTROM, ALLEN E (R)
WVa State Deleg
Mailing Add: State Capitol Charleston WV 25305

GOLDWATER, BARRY, JR (R)
US Rep, Calif
b Los Angeles, Calif, July 15, 38; m 1972 to Susan L Gherman; c Barry M, III. Educ: Univ Colo; Ariz State Univ, grad, 62; founder of col bus & mkt newspaper. Polit & Govt Pos: Speaker, Barry Goldwater for President Campaign, 64; mem, Rep State Cent Comt Calif, currently; US Rep, 20th Dist Calif, 69-, mem comt on sci & technol & comt on pub works & transportation, US House Rep, currently. Bus & Prof Pos: Partner, Noble Cooke, Div Gregory & Sons, stock brokers. Mem: SAR; San Fernando Valley Bus & Prof Asn; Rotary; Southeast Los Angeles Youth Coun (vol worker). Relig: Episcopal. Legal Res: Woodland Hills CA Mailing Add: 1421 House Off Bldg Washington DC 20515

GOLDWATER, BARRY MORRIS (R)
US Sen, Ariz
b Phoenix, Ariz, Jan 1, 09; s Baron Goldwater & Josephine Williams G; m 1934 to Margaret Johnson; c Barry Morris, Jr, Margaret Ann (Mrs Holt), Joanne (Mrs Ross) & Michael Prescott. Educ: Staunton Mil Acad; Univ Ariz, 1 year; Sigma Chi. Hon Degrees: LLD, Univ Ariz, 69. Polit & Govt Pos: Mem, Phoenix City Coun, 50-52; US Sen, Ariz, 52-64 & 69-; Rep cand for President, 64. Bus & Prof Pos: Pres, Goldwater's, Inc, 37-50. Mil Serv: Entered as 2nd Lt, Army Res, 30, serv in Asiatic-Pac & China-Burma, retired as Maj Gen, Air Force Res; Air Medal; China-Burna-India Campaign Star. Publ: Down the River of Canyons; Arizona Portraits; Conscience of a Conservative; plus others. Mem: Royal Photog Soc Gt Brit (assoc mem); Am Legion; Mason (33 degree); VFW. Relig: Episcopal. Legal Res: 6250 N Hogan Dr Scottsdale AZ 85253 Mailing Add: 440 Old Senate Off Bldg Washington DC 20510

GOLDWATER, MARILYN (D)
Md State Deleg
b Boston, Mass, Jan 29, 27; m 1948 to William H Goldwater; c Charles A & Diane L. Educ: Mt Sinai Hosp Sch Nursing, RN, 48; Am Univ, 60. Polit & Govt Pos: Md State Deleg, 75- Mailing Add: 5508 Durbin Rd Bethesda MD 20014

GOLDWIN, ROBERT A (R)
b New York, NY, Apr 16, 22; s Alexander Goldwin & Sed Applebaum G; m 1944 to Daisy Lateiner; c Nancy (Mrs Harvey), Jane (Mrs Bandler), Elizabeth & Seth. Educ: St John's Col (Md), BA, 50; Univ Chicago, MA, 54, PhD, 63. Polit & Govt Pos: Spec adv to Ambassador, US Mission to NATO, Brussels, Belgium, 73-74; spec consult to the President, Washington, DC, 74- Bus & Prof Pos: Lectr polit sci & dir pub affairs conf ctr, Univ Chicago, 60-66; assoc prof polit sci & dir pub affairs conf ctr, Kenyon Col, 66-69; dean & Charles Hammond Elliott tutor, St John's Col (Md), 69-73. Mil Serv: Entered as Pvt, Army, 42, released as 1st Lt, 46, after serv in 1st Cavalry, Asia-Pac Theatre. Publ: Auth, John Locke, In: History of Political Philosophy, 59, ed, Readings in American Foreign Policy, 2nd ed, 71 & ed, How Democratic Is America?, 71, Rand McNally. Honors & Awards: Univ Chicago Fel, 51, Hilman Fel, 53; Guggenheim Found Fel, 66. Legal Res: 1565 44th St NW Washington DC 20007 Mailing Add: White House Washington DC 20500

GOLDY, DANIEL LOUIS (D)
b Butler, NJ, Aug 7, 15; s Morris A Goldy & Gussie Silverman G; m 1944 to Genevieve Beatrice Rustvold; c Daniel Rustvold. Educ: Univ Wis, Madison, BA, summa cum laude, 36; grad sch, Univ Chicago, 36-37; Phi Beta Kappa; Phi Kappa Phi; Artus. Polit & Govt Pos: Asst comnr, Placement & Unemploy Compensation, State of Ill, 37-41; asst regional dir, Off Defense, Health & Welfare Serv, Fed Security Agency Cleveland, Ohio, 41-42; asst regional dir, War Manpower Comn, Cleveland, 42-43; spec asst to dir, US Employ Serv, Washington, DC, 46-47; Dep Asst Secy Interior, 47-48; regional adminr, Bur Land Mgt, Portland, Ore, 49-51; off of the spec rep of the President, Econ Coop Admin, Paris, France, 51-52; regional dir, Bur Employ Security, Seattle, Wash & New York, 52-58; dep adminr, Area Redevelop Admin, US Dept Com, Washington, DC, 61-62; adminr, Bus & Defense Serv Admin & Dep Asst Secy Com, 62-64; President's Nat Export Expansion Coordr & exec dir of US Cabinet Comt on Export Expansion, 64-65; alt deleg, Dem Nat Conv, 68; chmn task force capital investment & trade & mem exec comt, Japan-US Coun Econ Rels, currently; exec comt mem & chmn task force world wide shortages, EEC-US Econ Coun; vchmn, Bulgarian-US Econ Coun, currently. Bus & Prof Pos: Lectr, Grad Sch, Northwestern Univ, 38-41; gen partner, Mt Fir Lumber Co, Independence, Ore, 55-61 & 65-; vpres, Pac Northern Lumber Co, Wrangell, Alaska & Portland, Ore, 59-61; vpres & dir, Int Systs & Controls Corp, Houston, Tex & Washington, DC, 65-69, pres & dir, 69-; pres, Rhodes Corp, Oklahoma City, Okla, 67-68; pres, ISC World Trade Corp, Washington, DC, 68-; pres & dir, Capital Shares, Inc & Investors Counsel, Inc, 69-; dir, Otis Elevator Co, New York, 72-; mem, US Deleg & vchmn environ comt, Bus & Indust Adv Comt, Orgn Econ Coop & Develop, currently. Mil Serv: Entered as Ens, Navy, 43, released as Lt, 46, after serv in Pac, 44-45. Mem: Am Econ Asn; US CofC (chmn int comt, mem exec comt, bd dirs & natural resources comt, nat vpres); Nat Economists Club; Int CofC (mem bd trustees, US Coun). Honors & Awards: John Lendrum Mitchel Mem Medal. Legal Res: RR 2 Box 1218 Bend OR 97701 Mailing Add: 2727 Allen Parkway Houston TX 77019

GOLLOTT, THOMAS ARLIN (D)
Miss State Rep
Mailing Add: 1390 E Bay View Ave Biloxi MS 39533

GOLTZ, H A (BARNEY) (D)
Wash State Sen
b Balaton, Minn, Aug 13, 24; s Albert Oscar Goltz (deceased) & Olga Mitzner G (deceased); m 1948 to Marguerite Nauss; c Jeffrey David. Educ: Macalester Col, BA, 45; Univ Minn, Minneapolis, MA, 51. Polit & Govt Pos: Wash State Rep, 42nd Dist, 73-75, Wash State Sen, 75- Bus & Prof Pos: Asst dir student personnel serv, Macalester Col, 47-57; asst to pres & dir planning, Western Wash State Col, 57-75. Mil Serv: Entered as Pvt, Air Force, 45, released as Cpl, 46, after serv in US; Good Conduct Medal. Mem: Soc Col & Univ Planners; St Lukes Hosp, Bellingham (bd dirs); CofC. Honors & Awards: Wash State Arts Comn Award, 69; Dept Housing & Urban Develop Nat Awards, 63 & 65. Mailing Add: 3003 Vallette St Bellingham WA 98225

GOMEZ, BLANCHE M (R)
Mem, Rep State Cent Comt Calif
b El Paso, Tex, Oct 29, 28; d Joseph Marusich & Dolores Bencomo M; m 1947 to Alfonso Gomez, Jr; c Cecilia, Adrian, Joseph & Stefan. Educ: Tex Western Col, 46-47; Mt St Mary's Col (Calif), 66-68. Polit & Govt Pos: Spanish speaking coordr, Viva Nixon, 68; comnr, Housing Authority, Los Angeles, 68-71, comn pres, 70-71, comnr, Human Rels Comn, 71-72, comnr, City Planning Comn, 72-; spec rep, State Comn of the Californias, Gov Off, 68-; city wide women's chmn, Yorty for Mayor, 69; Southern Calif women's chmn, Spanish Speaking Comt to Reelect the President, 72; deleg, Rep Nat Conv, 72; US deleg, Orgn Am States Inter Am Comn on Women, 72-; mem state adv bd, Off Econ Opportunity, San Francisco, 72-; mem, Rep State Cent Comt Calif, 73- Mem: Nat Asn Housing & Redevelop Off; Nat Housing Conf Inc; CofC; VFW Ladies Auxiliary; Latin Am Cult Soc. Honors & Awards: Community Serv Awards, Canoga Park Coord Coun, 67, Los Angeles City Coun, 68 & Mayor Sam Yorty, 68; Key Man Award, League of United Latin Americans, 69; Ambassador George V Allen Commendation, Town Affil, Inc, 69; Human Rels Commendation, Los Angeles Human Rels Comn, 72. Relig: Roman Catholic. Mailing Add: 7062 Lurline Ave Canoga Park CA 91306

GOMIEN, JOHN RICHARD (R)
b Opheim, Mont, May 15, 15; s Harry Gomien & Tressie Anderson G; m 1940 to Glee Devore; c Dee Ann (Mrs Gretz), Danice Lynn & Donna Sue. Educ: Gallagher Sch Bus, Kankakee, Ill, 38-39; Strayer Col Accountancy, BCS, 44; Dale Carnegie Pub Speaking Course, 47. Polit & Govt Pos: Exec secy, Rep Everett M Dirksen, 40-48, admin asst, US Sen Dirksen, 51-69; exec secy, Rep Harold H Velde, 49-50; admin asst, US Sen Ralph Tyler Smith, 69-70; admin asst, Us Sen Robert Taft, Jr, 71- Bus & Prof Pos: Aid, Dr Guy E Seymour, Colfax, Ill, 33-34; attendant, Standard Oil Sta, 34-36, agt, 36-37; clerk, Armour & Co, Peoria, 69. Mem: Senate Admin Assts & Secy Asn; Kenwood Golf & Country Club; Capitol Hill Club; Colfax Community High Sch Alumni. Relig: Methodist. Legal Res: Colfax IL 61728 Mailing Add: 5509 Cromwell Dr Washington DC 20016

GOMPERTS, ROBERT ELLIOT (D)
b San Francisco, Calif, Apr 22, 27; s Jack Gomperts & Ro Fles G; m 1948 to Elizabeth Konstance Schneider; c John Sarto, Mark Alexander & Rosan Elizabeth. Educ: Lowell High Sch, San Francisco, Calif, grad, 45. Polit & Govt Pos: Pres, Menlo Atherton Dem Club, Calif, 68-; Cong dist co-chmn, Calif Dem State Cent Comt, formerly; Dem cand for Cong, 70. Bus & Prof Pos: Vpres, Calagrex, Inc, San Francisco, 61-; pres, Idaho Sales Corp, 61-; pres, Nordisk Andelsforbund Calif Inc, 62- Mil Serv: Seaman 3/C, Navy Air Corps, 45, released as Seaman 1/C, 46, after serv as a combat aircrewman. Mem: World Affairs Coun of Northern Calif (exec comt); Calif Coun for Int Trade (pres); Nat Comt for New China Policy (nat chmn); Vol for Int Develop (chmn); Coun on Foreign Rels (San Francisco Comt). Mailing Add: 132 Tuscaloosa Ave Atherton CA 94025

GONTHIER, EILEEN M (D)
VChairperson, NH Dem State Comt
b Franklin, Maine, Mar 24, 38; d William F Maher & Evelyn Collar M; div; c Gary & Gregory. Educ: Ellsworth High Sch, Maine, grad, 55. Polit & Govt Pos: Vchairperson, NH Dem State Comt, 73-; deleg, Dem Nat Mid-Term Conf, 74; off mgr & head caseworker, Congressman Norman D'Amours, US House Rep, 75-; exec bd mem, Dem Women NH, currently. Mailing Add: 2 Maple St Goffstown NH 03045

GONZALES, ROBERT EUGENE (D)
Mem, San Francisco Co Bd Supvr, Calif
b Fresno, Calif, Nov 13, 36; s Bernard Louis Gonzales & Ramona Ortiz G; single. Educ: Univ Calif, Berkeley, BA, 59; Hastings Col Law, JD, 62; Kappa Alpha; Big C Soc; Circle C Soc. Polit & Govt Pos: Pres, Mexican-Am Polit Asn of San Francisco, 65-67, vpres, Calif Asn, 66-68; mem, Calif Dem State Cent Comt, 66-68; mem bd permit appeals, San Francisco City & Co, 68-69; mem, San Francisco City & Co Bd Supvr, 69-; mem bd dirs, Golden Gate Bridge Hwy, Transportation Dist & Bay Area Sewage Serv Agency, currently. Bus & Prof Pos: Partner, Gonzales, Mitchell & Ortiz, Attorneys. Mem: Am Trial Lawyers Asn. Relig: Catholic. Mailing Add: 19th Floor 100 Van Ness Ave San Francisco CA 94102

GONZALES, ROSA RIOJAS (D)
Secy, Nueces Co Dem Exec Comt, Tex
b McAllen, Tex, Mar 21, 19; d Jose Maria Riojas & Josefa Salinas Garza R; m 1934 to Sabas Betancourt Gonzales; c Rudolph, John Edward & Randolph Joseph. Educ: Corpus Christi Bus Col, 41-45; St Christopher Col, 68; Del Mar Col, 73. Polit & Govt Pos: Elec officer, nat elec,

Precinct 75, Corpus Christi, Tex, 50-56, elec officer, local elec, 51-55; presiding elec judge, 55-69, Dem chairperson, 56-; secy, Nueces Co Dem Exec Comt, 56-; chairperson, Precinct 75 Dem Conv, 64, 66, 68, 70 & 72; dir, Medicare Alert Prog, Nueces Co Community Action Agency, 65; deleg, Nueces Co Dem Convs, 56-72; deleg, Tex Dem State Conv, 64 & 72; deleg, Dem Nat Conv, 72. Bus & Prof Pos: Ladies apparel store mgr, Franklin Stores Corp, Corpus Christi, Tex, 44-50; owner & operator state licensed home for neglected children, 51-58; sales agt, Field Enterprises Educ Corp, Chicago, Ill, 62- Mem: Nat Cath Conf Bishops & US Cath Conf (nat adv coun); Tex Cong Parents & Teachers (hon life mem); Nat Cong Parents & Teachers (hon life mem); Las Hermanas Nat Spanish Speaking Nuns Orgn (exec comt, 72-); Nueces Co Community Comt on Youth Educ & Job Opportunities. Honors & Awards: Outstanding Citizen Award, United Married Couples Social Club, 59; Appreciation for Community Serv Award, United Fund, Corpus Christi, Tex, 60; Distinguished Community Serv Award, Nueces Co Community Agency, 71. Relig: Catholic. Mailing Add: 3246 Greenwood Dr Corpus Christi TX 78405

GONZALEZ, HENRY BARBOSA (D)
US Rep, Tex
b San Antonio, Tex, May 3, 16; s Leonides Gonzalez (deceased) & Genevieve Barbosa G; m 1940 to Bertha Cuellar; c Henry B, Jr, Rose Mary (Mrs Ramos), Charles, Bertha Alice (Mrs Denzer), Stephen, Genevieve (Mrs Singleterry), Francis & Anna Marie; ten grandchildren. Educ: San Antonio Jr Col; Univ Tex; St Mary's Univ Sch Law, LLB. Hon Degrees: LLD, St Mary's Univ Sch Law, 65. Polit & Govt Pos: Probation officer, Bexar Co, Tex, 43-46; family relocation dir, San Antonio Housing Authority, 50-52; city councilman, San Antonio, 53-56, mayor protem, 54; Tex State Sen, 56-61; co-chmn, Viva Kennedy Orgn, 60, Viva Johnson Orgn, 64 & Arriba Humphrey, 68; US Rep, Tex, 61-, chmn subcomt int develop inst & finance, US House Rep, 71-; hon chmn, McGovern Campaign, Bexar Co, 72. Publ: Hope & promise: Americans of Spanish surname, Am Federationist, AFL-CIO Mag; When Pancho Villa rode into legend, Bus Week Mag, 7/25/70; The federal government & bilingual education, NEA J, 11/70; plus others. Mem: Delta Theta Phi. Legal Res: 238 W Kings Hwy San Antonio TX 78212 Mailing Add: 2312 Rayburn House Off Bldg Washington DC 20515

GONZALEZ, JAIME A (D)
Chmn, Zapata Co Dem Party, Tex
b Kingsville, Tex, July 14, 33; s Humberto Gonzalez & Angelica Garcia G; m 1961 to Carmen Benavides; c Annabel, Jaime A, Jr & Daniel A. Educ: Tex A&I Univ, BA, 58, MA, 64. Polit & Govt Pos: Chmn, Parole Bd, Zapata Co, Tex, 58-, chmn, Zapata Co Dem Party, 74- Bus & Prof Pos: Owner, Rex Motel & Drive-In Grocery, 59-; fed progs dir, Zapata Co Independent Sch Dist, 68- Mil Serv: Entered as Pvt, Army, 53, released as Cpl, 55, after serv in 546th Antiaircraft Artil. Mem: Zapata Co CofC; Zapata Optimist Club; PTA; Tex State Teachers Asn; Nat Educ Asn. Honors & Awards: Optimist of the Year Award, Zapata Optimist Club, 75. Relig: Catholic. Mailing Add: PO Box 878 Zapata TX 78076

GONZALEZ, SARITA GALLARDO (R)
Rep Nat Committeewoman, PR
b Caguas, PR, May 12, 32; d Hostos Gallardo & Sara Jimenez G; m 1952 to Wallace Gonzalez-Oliver; c Wallace M & Jorge A. Educ: Col of Mt St Vincent, BS, 52. Polit & Govt Pos: Rep Nat Committeewoman, PR, 72- Bus & Prof Pos: Dir, Bank of San Juan, PR, 72- Mem: Am Translators Asn; Capitol Hill Club. Relig: Catholic. Mailing Add: Blvd Ramirez Arellano Dio Bayamon PR 00619

GOOCH, JAMES THOMAS (D)
Chmn, Clark Co Dem Comt, Ark
b Vanndale, Ark, Dec 10, 13; s Samuel Amos Gooch & Augusta Connelia Halk G; m 1940 to Edris Wyanna Lookadoo; c Edris Johanna (Mrs Quinn) & Marilyn Kay. Educ: Ark State Univ & Ark Law Sch. Polit & Govt Pos: Ark State Sen, 40-44; US Attorney, Eastern Dist, Ark, 45-54; chmn, Clark Co Dem Comt, Ark, 60- Bus & Prof Pos: Pres, US Attorneys Conf, 50-52; pres, Clark Co Bar Asn, 64-65. Mil Serv: Entered as Ens, Navy, 42, released as Lt(sg), 45, after serv as Naval Gunnery Officer, ETO & Pac Theater. Mem: Ark Trial Lawyers Asn (pres, currently); Am Trial Lawyers Asn; Am Judicature Soc. Relig: Methodist; chmn, World Serv & Finance of Little Rock Conf, Methodist Church. Legal Res: 1215 Richardson St Arkadelphia AR 71923 Mailing Add: PO Box 357 Arkadelphia AR 71923

GOOCH, RAYMOND LEROY (R)
b Wood River, Ill, Mar 23, 38; s Raymond Orval Gooch & Mary Dian Miller G (both deceased); single. Educ: Washington Univ, BS, ChE, 60; Georgetown Univ Law Ctr, JD, 64; Tau Beta Pi; Omicron Delta Kappa; Beta Theta Pi. Polit & Govt Pos: Patent examr, Dept Com, Washington, DC, 60-64; legis asst, US Rep Silvio O Conte, 65-67; attorney legis affairs, Agency for Int Develop, Dept State, 67-68; dir cong rels, Off Econ Opportunity, 70; consult, Vista, 70-71; staff counsel, Joint Comt on Cong Opers, 71- Bus & Prof Pos: Assoc, US CofC, Washington, DC, 68-69; attorney, law off, C B Kennedy, 69-70. Mem: VA & DC Bar Asns. Mailing Add: 821 Independence Ave SE Washington DC 20003

GOOD, JOSEPHINE LOUISE (R)
Dir Conv Div, Rep Nat Comt
b Denver, Colo, Mar 10, 18; d George Washington Good & Pearl Wooley G; single. Educ: High Sch & Blair's Bus Col, Denver, Colo. Polit & Govt Pos: Secy, Trading & Exchange Div, Securities & Exchange Comn, 40-42; admin asst, Exec Off Price, Off Price Admin, 42-43; cong secy, House of Rep, 46-53; confidential & admin aide, Postmaster Gen, Post Off Dept, 53-56; dir conv div, Rep Nat Comt, currently. Bus & Prof Pos: Secy to pres, Fageol Motor Sales Co, 39-40. Mil Serv: Entered as A/S, Coast Guard Women's Res, 43, released as Chief Yeoman, 45, after serv in Mil Morale Hq; Am Theater Ribbon. Publ: The History of Women in Republican National Conventions & Women in the Republican National Committee. Honors & Awards: First & thus far only woman dir of Presidential Nominating Convs of either party. Relig: Catholic. Mailing Add: 3900 Tunlaw Rd NW Washington DC 20007

GOOD, ROBERT CROCKER (D)
b Mt Vernon, NY, Apr 7, 24; s Alfred Henry Good & Josephine Crocker G; m 1946 to Nancy Cunningham; c Stephen, Karen & Kathleen. Educ: Haverford Col, BA, 45; Yale Divinity Sch, BD, 51, Yale Grad Sch, PhD, 56; Phi Beta Kappa. Polit & Govt Pos: Research assoc, Washington Ctr of Foreign Policy Research, Johns Hopkins Univ, 58-61; dir, Carnegie Endowment Seminars in Diplomacy, 60-61; coordr, Kennedy's Task Force on Africa, 60-61; dir, Off of Research & Analysis for Africa, State Dept, 61-65; US Ambassador to Zambia, 65-69. Bus & Prof Pos: Dir, Am Friends Serv Comt Neighborhood Ctr, Frankfurt am Main, 47-48; adminr, Int Student Seminars in Philadelphia, 48; faculty, Univ Denver, 53-58; research assoc, Washington Ctr for Foreign Policy Research, Johns Hopkins Univ, with grant from Ford Found to prepare a book on the Rhodesian Rebellion, 69-70; dean, Grad Sch Int Studies & dir, Social Sci Found, Univ Denver, 70- Publ: Co-auth, Neutralism & Nonalignment: The New States in World Politics, Praeger, 62; co-ed, Foreign Policy in the Sixties: The Issues and the Instruments (w Roger Hilsman), Johns Hopkins Univ, 65; auth, UDI: The International Politics of the Rhodesian Rebellion, Faber & Faber, 73; plus others. Mem: Soc Relig in Higher Educ; Am Polit Sci Asn; Int Studies Asn. Honors & Awards: Dept of State Superior Honor Award, 64. Relig: Unitarian. Mailing Add: 1985 Grape St Denver CO 80220

GOOD, ROBERT J (R)
Tenn State Rep
Mailing Add: 1007 Crocus St Johnson City TN 37601

GOODE, JAMES WALTOM (R)
b Albany, Ga, Mar 11, 50; s James Lee Goode & Jeannine Knighton G; single. Educ: Albany Jr Col, AA, 70; Ga Southern Col, BS Educ, 72. Polit & Govt Pos: Secy-treas, Calhoun Co Rep Party, Ga, 68, ballot security chmn, 68, co-chmn, 68, chmn, formerly; chief mgr, first Rep primary in Calhoun Co, 68; polit action & polit educ dir, TAR of Albany, 68; co-founder, Albany Jr Col Young Rep, 68, polit educ & polit action dir, 68, chmn, 68-, chmn eight mem deleg to Ga Fedn of Young Rep Clubs State Conv, 69; off poll observer, Gen Elec, Calhoun Co, 68; first vchmn, Second Dist Rep Party, 69-72; deleg, Dist Conv, 70; deleg, Calhoun Co Rep Party Conv, 70; deleg, Ga State Rep Conv, 70; secy, Leary Rep Elec Dist, Ga, 70- Bus & Prof Pos: Carrier, Albany Herald, Leary, Ga, 61-67; swimming instr, summers 66-68. Publ: Ed, The War Hawk 1968, Taylor Publ Co, 68. Honors & Awards: Cert of Award for boys declamation & Cert of Award for Annual Editorship, Calhoun Co High Sch. Relig: Methodist. Mailing Add: PO Box 125 Leary GA 31762

GOODE, MARY H (D)
Mass State Rep
Mailing Add: State Capitol Boston MA 02133

GOODE, P WAYNE (D)
Mo State Rep
b St Louis, Mo, Aug 20, 37; m 1963 to Jane Margaret Bell. Educ: Univ Mo, BS. Polit & Govt Pos: Mo State Rep, currently. Bus & Prof Pos: Vpres & treas, Be-Mac Transport Co, Inc. Mil Serv: Army, Lt, grad US Army Artil & Missile Sch; active reservist. Mem: Alpha Kappa Psi; Sigma Alpha Epsilon; St Louis CofC; Normandy CofC; Kiwanis. Mailing Add: 7335 Huntington Dr Normandy MO 63121

GOODE, VIRGIL H SR (D)
Chmn, Franklin Co Dem Party, Va
b Franklin Co, Va, July 31, 02; s Benjamin M Goode & Fannie Mildred Ross G; m 1943 to Alice Elizabeth Besecker; c Virgil H, Jr & Elizabeth Ross. Educ: Univ Richmond, BS, 27, LLB, 35; Omicron Delta Kappa; Sigma Delta Psi; Phi Alpha Delta; Lambda Chi Alpha; pres, Law Sch Student Body; pres, Athletic Asn; pres, Freshman Law Class. Polit & Govt Pos: Mem, Franklin Co Dem Comt, Va, 32-72; Va State Deleg, Franklin Co, 40-48, commonwealth's attorney, Franklin Co, 48-72; deleg, Va State Const Conv, 56; state campaign dir, Va Straight Dem Ticket Elec, 60; deleg, Dem Nat Conv, 60, alt deleg, 68; deleg, Am Legion Nat Conv; mem, Va State Bar Coun, 67-; chmn, Franklin Co Dem Party, currently. Bus & Prof Pos: Teacher, coach & athletic dir, Ansted High Sch, WVa, 26-31; attorney, currently. Mil Serv: Entered as Pvt, Army, 42, released as Capt, 45, after serv in QmC; Commendation; Citation for Army Commendation Ribbon. Mem: Va State Bar Asn; Franklin Co Bar Asn (pres, 53-); Am Legion; Rotary; Ruritan Club. Honors & Awards: Capt undefeated track team & held four col track records, mem all varsity teams. Mailing Add: Rte 2 Rocky Mount VA 24151

GOODE, VIRGIL HAMLIN, JR (D)
Va State Sen
b Richmond, Va, Oct 17, 46; s Virgil Hamlin Goode & Alice Besecker G; m 1969 to Martha Sanders Brandt. Educ: Univ Richmond, BA, 69; Univ Va, JD, 73; Phi Beta Kappa; Omicron Delta Kappa; Pi Sigma Alpha; Eta Sigma Phi; Lambda Chi Alpha. Polit & Govt Pos: Mem, Franklin Co Dem Comt, Va, 72-; secy, Fifth Dist Dem Party, 72-; mem, Dem State Cent Comt, 72-; Va State Sen, 73-, mem local govt comt, gen laws comt & rehabilitation & social serv comt, Va State Senate, 74- Bus & Prof Pos: Lawyer. Mem: Ruritan; Jaycees; CofC. Mailing Add: 425 Diamond Ave Rocky Mount VA 24151

GOODELL, CHARLES ELLSWORTH (R)
b Jamestown, NY, Mar 16, 26; s Dr Charles E Goodell & Francesca Bartlett G; m 1954 to Jean Rice; c William Rice, Timothy Bartlett, Roger Stokoe, Michael Charles Ellsworth & Jeffrey Harris. Educ: Williams Col, BA cum laude, 48; Yale Univ Sch Law, LLB, 51, Yale Univ Grad Sch Govt, MA, 52; Phi Beta Kappa. Polit & Govt Pos: Asst to Attorney Gen & Cong Liaison, Dept of Justice, NY, 54-55; councilman, Ellicott Town Bd, 57; chmn, Chautauqua Co Rep Comt, 58; US Rep, 38th Dist, NY, 59-68; deleg, Rep Nat Conv, 64 & 68; US Sen, NY, 68-70. Bus & Prof Pos: Law partner, Van Vlack, Goodell & McKee, Jamestown, 56-58; sr partner, Roth, Carlson, Kwit, Spengler & Goodell, 71-72; counsel, Life Ins Co of NY, 71-; mem bd dirs, Bohack Corp & Presidential Life Ins Co, 71-; partner, Hydeman, Mason & Goodell, 74-; chmn, Presidential Clemency Bd, 74- Mil Serv: Seaman, Navy, World War II; 1st Lt, Air Force, Korean Conflict. Publ: Auth, Political Prisoners in America, Random House, 73. Mem: Am Bar Asn. Honors & Awards: Five varsity letters in baseball & football at Williams Col. Relig: Episcopal. Legal Res: 504 Fairmount Ave Jamestown NY 14701 Mailing Add: 1225 19th St NW Washington DC 20036

GOODHUE, MARY B (R)
NY State Assemblyman
b London, Eng; d Ernest Brier & Marion Hawks B; m 1948 to Francis A Goodhue, Jr; c Francis A, III. Educ: Vassar Col, BA, 42; Univ Mich Law Sch, LLB, 44. Polit & Govt Pos: NY State Assemblyman, 75- Bus & Prof Pos: Lawyer, 55-; mem, Goodhue & Lange, 67- Mem: Am, Westchester Co & Northern Westchester Bar Asns. Mailing Add: McLain St Mt Kisco NY 10549

GOODKNIGHT, DOROTHY WALKER (R)
b Philadelphia, Pa; d Winfield Krotell Reichner & Estelle Evans R; m to Logan Hartzel Goodknight, wid; c Gloria (Mrs Mulcihy), Bruce & Logan C (deceased). Educ: Univ Calif, Los Angeles, 26-27; Alpha Gamma Delta. Polit & Govt Pos: Deleg, Rep Nat Conv, 52, alt, 56, 60 & 60; pres, Long Beach Coun Rep Women, 53 & 58; treas & dist vchmn, Los Angeles Co Rep Cent Comt; pres southern div, Calif Fedn Rep Women, 59-64, pres, 64-65; mem exec comt, State Rep Cent Comt Calif, 64-65; mem-at-lg, Nat Fedn Rep Women, 65-67, exec dir,

68-72; dep nat coordr, President's Environ Merit Awards Prog under Environ Protection Agency, 72-73. Mem: Nat Assistance League: PEO; Nat Fedn Rep Women. Honors & Awards: Named Alpha Gamma Delta Woman of Year, 67; Awarded three citations for dedicated serv to Rep ideals & philosophy, Nat Fedn Rep Women, 64, 66 & 67. Relig: Protestant. Mailing Add: Apt 8 2045 Appleton St Long Beach CA 90803

GOODLETT, BERRY CHRISTOPHER (R)
Second VChmn, Mich Rep State Cent Comt
b Omaha, Nebr, July 16, 31; s Rev Foster Samuel Goodlett & Mary Annett Davis G (deceased); m 1968 to Romona Edna Wright; c LuJuana Lee, Mary Christina & Kimberly Amanti Tulia. Educ: Univ Nebr, BA, 62; Eastern Mich Univ, MA, 75; Kappa Alpha Psi; Stage Crafters. Polit & Govt Pos: Second vchmn, Mich Rep State Cent Comt, 72-; comnr, Civil Rights Comn, 75- Bus & Prof Pos: Admin asst to pres, Mott Community Col, 72- Mil Serv: 2nd Lt, Army Engrs, 55. Mem: United Way (bd mem, 74); Co Econ Develop Comn; Co Community Action Agency. Relig: Baptist. Mailing Add: 1915 Oxley Dr Flint MI 48504

GOODLING, GEORGE A (R)
b Loganville, Pa, Sept 26, 96; s R A Goodling & Jennie K G; m to Annetta J Glatfelter (deceased); c three boys & three girls. Educ: Pa State Univ, BS in Hort; Gamma Sigma Delta. Polit & Govt Pos: Pa State Rep, 42-56; chmn, Joint State Govt Subcomts; US Rep, 19th Dist, Pa, 60-64 & 67-74; mem, Migratory Bird Conserv & Agr & Merchant Marine & Fisheries Comts. Bus & Prof Pos: Teacher voc agr, 2 years; owner & operator, fruit farm, 23-; sch dir, pres bd, treas & mem bldg comts, 28 years; dir, Peoples Bank of Glen Rock; dir, White Rose Motor Club. Mil Serv: Seaman 2/C, Navy. Mem: Pa Hort Asn (exec secy, currently); Agr Exten Asn; Pa Farmers Asn; Alpha Tau Omega; Am Legion. Relig: United Methodist; treas, 25 years. Mailing Add: Loganville PA 17342

GOODLING, WILLIAM FRANKLIN (R)
US Rep, Pa
b Loganville, Pa, Dec 5, 27; s George Atlee Goodling & Annette Gladfelter G; m 1957 to Hilda Wright; c Todd & Jennifer. Educ: Univ Md, BS, 53; Western Md Col, MEd, 57; Theta Chi. Polit & Govt Pos: Mem sch bd, Dallastown Area Schs, Pa, 64-67; US Rep, Pa, 19th Dist, 75- Bus & Prof Pos: Teacher-counr, Southeast Sch Dist, 53-57; high sch prin, West York, 57-67; supt schs, Spring Grove, 67-74. Mil Serv: Entered as Pvt, Army, 46, released as Pfc, 48, after serv in 25th Div, Japan. Mem: Nursing Comt York Hosp; York Co Heart Asn; Spring Grove Lions. Relig: United Methodist. Mailing Add: Box 93 Jacobus PA 17407

GOODMAN, ARTHUR (D)
Committeeman, NY State Dem Comt
b New York, NY, Apr 14, 35; s Jesse J Goodman & Lillian Wisla G; m 1958 to Marian Edelson Van Loen; c Loren & Drew. Educ: Hunter Col, Bronx, NY, 3 years; Empire State Col, BA; Fordham Univ Law Sch, currently; Dramatic Club. Polit & Govt Pos: Chmn, Concerned Dem, Second Cong Dist, 67-68; exec bd, Long Island Dissenting Dem, 67-69; deleg, Dem Nat Conv, 68; Northern Westchester coordr, McGovern for President, 72; vchmn, Concerned Dem of Westchester-Putnam, 72-73; committeeman, NY State Dem Comt, 93rd Assembly Dist, 72-; Westchester regional vchmn, New Dem Coalition of NY, 73. Bus & Prof Pos: Pres, Argood Enterprises, Ltd, NY, currently. Relig: Jewish. Mailing Add: Fancher Rd Pound Ridge NY 10576

GOODMAN, C W (R)
NDak State Sen
Mailing Add: State Capitol Bismarck ND 58501

GOODMAN, JAMES ANTHONY (D)
Pa State Rep
b New Boston, Pa, June 12, 36; s Cornelius Goodman & Anna Holzenthaler G; m 1964 to Joan Margaret Yonosky; c Sharon. Educ: Pa State Univ, BS in Bus Admin, 61. Polit & Govt Pos: Pa State Rep, currently; mgt trainee, City of Philadelphia, Pa, 61-62; alt deleg, Dem Nat Conv, 72. Bus & Prof Pos: Securities salesman, Waddell & Reed, Inc, 62-; owner & mgr, Independent Ins Agency, 63- Mil Serv: Entered as Airman Basic, Air Force, 54, released as Airman 1/C, 57, after serv in Hq, Controllers Br, Washington, DC, France & Morocco. Mem: Amvets; Elks; KofC; Pa State Univ Alumni Asn; Young Dem. Relig: Roman Catholic. Mailing Add: 201 W Pine St Mahanoy City PA 17948

GOODMAN, ROY M (R)
NY State Sen
b New York, NY, Mar 5, 30; s Bernard A Goodman & Alice Matz G; m 1955 to Barbara Furrer; c Claire, Leslie & Randolph. Educ: Harvard Col, AB cum laude, 51; Harvard Grad Sch of Bus Admin, MBA with distinction, 53; Hasty Pudding Club. Polit & Govt Pos: Treas, New York Co Rep Party, NY, formerly; vchmn, Lindsay-for-Mayor Comt; treas, New Yorkers for Lindsay; mem, Community Planning Bd No 8, 64; pres, Ninth Assembly Dist Rep Club, formerly; finance adminr, New York, 66-68, chmn, Temporary State Charter Rev Comn, currently; deleg, NY Rep State Convs, 66, 68 & 70; NY State Sen, 26th Dist, 68-, chmn, Housing & Urban Develop Comt, mem, City of New York Civil Serv & Pensions, Finance, Cities, Educ & Banking Comts, NY State Senate, currently, mem, Select Comt on Environ Conserv, NY State Legis, currently; deleg, Rep Nat Conv, 72. Bus & Prof Pos: Assoc, Kuhn, Loeb & Co, investment bankers, 56-60; pres, drug co including Ex-Lax, Inc, 62-71, chmn bd & dir, Ex-Lax, Inc, 71-; dir, Gen Cigar Co, Inc, 71-; dir, Manhattan Industs, Inc, 69- Mil Serv: Officer, Navy, 53-56. Mem: Inst Philos & Polit of Educ, Teachers Col, Columbia Univ (adv coun); Harvard 1951 Permanent Class Comt; Young Pres Orgn, Inc; Wall St Club; Fort Orange Club. Honors & Awards: Mt Scopus Citation, Hebrew Univ of Jerusalem, 68; Scroll of Hon, United Jewish Appeal, 70; NY State Rep of the Year Award, Ripon Soc, 72; Medal of Merit, City Univ New York, 72; Scroll of Merit, Brotherhood-in-Action, 72. Relig: Jewish. Mailing Add: 1035 Fifth Ave New York NY 10028

GOODNER, ORVAL KERN (D)
Secy, Scott Co Dem Comt, Ark
b Boles, Ark, June 19, 10; s William Robert Goodner & Louisa Walls G; m 1933 to Effie Hanna Taylor; c Hoyt, Harland & Oleta (Mrs Lewis). Educ: Ark Polytech Col, 31-33. Polit & Govt Pos: Treas & recorder, City of Waldron, Ark, 42-; secy, Scott Co Dem Comt, 42- Bus & Prof Pos: Teacher, Boles High Sch, 31-40; exec vpres, Bank of Waldron, Ark, 41- Mem: Farm Bur; CofC; Lions Club; Scott Co Develop Asn. Relig: Freewill Baptist. Legal Res: 950 S Main St Waldron AR 72958 Mailing Add: PO Box 252 Waldron AR 72958

GOODOVER, PAT M (R)
Mont State Sen
b Sheridan, Wyo, Oct 17, 16; s George Goodover & Anna Barna G; m 1941 to Erma Louise Nelson; c Joy Ann (Mrs Mike Root), Pat M, II & B Lynn (Mrs Ken Seiger). Educ: First Nat Radio-TV Inst, grad, 37. Polit & Govt Pos: Mont State Sen, Dist 22, 75- Bus & Prof Pos: Engr-announcer, Radio Sta KGNF, North Platte, Nebr, 37-38; announcer-engr-sales, KGIR, Butte, Mont, 38-39; mgr, KRBM, Bozeman, 39-40; asst mgr news coverage legis, Z Network, Butte-Helena-Bozeman, 40-41; radio engr, US Signal Corps, Washington, DC, 41-42; mgr-part owner, KXLL, Missoula, 48-58; owner, KARR, KOPR-FM, Great Falls, 58-74; owner, Travel Ctr, Great Falls, 74-75. Mil Serv: Entered as Air Cadet, Air Corps, 42, released as 1st Lt, after serv in 10th Air Force, 12th Bomber Group, China-India-Burma, 45-46; Air Medal with Clusters; Silver Star; Bronze Star; Presidential Citation. Mem: Great Falls Shrine Thunderbird Patrol (pres, 75-76); Great Falls Int Airport Authority (vchmn, 75-76); Mont State CofC (exec bd, 73-76); Lions; Mont Broadcasters. Honors & Awards: Theatre Commendation for Pub Rels-CBI-Reporting, 45; Named by UPI as Outstanding Freshman Rep Sen, 75. Relig: Presbyterian. Mailing Add: 803 Forest Ave Great Falls MT 59404

GOODPASTER, MARY J (D)
Jr Nat Committeewoman, Kans Young Dem
b Liberal, Kans, July 17, 46; d Aurelio Andrade & Luz Renteria A; m 1967 to John F Goodpaster; c Nina Maria & John F, III. Educ: St Mary of the Plains Col, 64-67; Wichita State Univ, fall 72. Polit & Govt Pos: Secy, St Mary of the Plains Collegiate Young Dem, Dodge City, Kans, 66-67; secy, Reno Co Young Dem, Hutchinson, 68-71; treas, Kans Young Dem, 70-71, Jr Nat Committeewoman, 71- Bus & Prof Pos: Jr cost acct, Cessna Indust Prod Div, Hutchinson, Kans, 68- Mem: Reno Co Young Dem; Eagles Auxiliary. Relig: Catholic. Mailing Add: 22 E 27th Hutchinson KS 67501

GOODRICH, GLENN A (D)
Nebr State Sen
b Orson, Iowa, Feb 22, 25; s Walter H Goodrich & Susie Gillette; m 1950 to Gaynelle Tusha; c D'Arcy & twins Christopher & Gregory. Educ: Creighton Univ, BS, 49. Polit & Govt Pos: Nebr State Sen, 71- Mil Serv: Entered as Pvt, Army, 43, released as Sgt, 46, after serv in Prov Qm Detachment, Pac. Mem: Rho Epsilon; Centennial Masonic Lodge. Relig: Lutheran. Mailing Add: 4408 Walnut Omaha NE 68105

GOODRICH, MARY LUCILE (R)
Chairwoman, Livingston Co Rep Party, Ill
b Waltonville, Ill, Mar 24, 06; d Charles W Bevis & Nelle Rae Dodds B; m 1932 to Bernell H Goodrich. Educ: Univ Ill, AB, 25, MEd, 54. Polit & Govt Pos: Chairwoman, Livingston Co Rep Party, Ill, 60-, committeewoman, Cent Comt, 60-; chairwoman, 17th Dist Rep Cent Comt, 64-; mem, Livingston Co Adv Comt to Regional Educ Serv Region, 71-; vpres, Livingston Co Rep Womans Club, 72-; alt deleg, Rep Nat Conv, 72. Bus & Prof Pos: Teacher & adminr, Saunemin Schs, Ill, 29-44; asst co supt schs, Livingston Co, 44-47, co supt schs, 47-69, supt educ serv region, 69-71. Publ: History of the country superintendency in Illinois, Ill Educ; History of the schools of Livingston County, Pontiac Daily Leader; coordr, Supervision—an inservice training experience, Ill J Educ, 5/64. Mem: Am Asn Sch Adminr; Nat Educ Asn; Livingston Co Retired Teachers Asn; Delta Kappa Gamma; Kappa Delta Pi. Relig: Methodist; treas, Methodist Church, 71- Mailing Add: Rte 1 Saunemin IL 61769

GOODRICH, PATRICIA A (R)
Wis State Rep
Mailing Add: 159 Oak St Berlin WI 54923

GOODRICH, VERA E (R)
NH State Rep
Mailing Add: PO Box 326 Epping NH 03042

GOODWIN, HARLAND CLARK, JR (D)
Maine State Rep
b Portsmouth, NH, June 22, 48; s Harland Clark Goodwin, Sr & Natalie McLaughlin; single. Educ: Univ Maine, Orono, BA in Polit Sci, 70; Alpha Tau Omega. Polit & Govt Pos: Vchmn, South Berwick Dem Comt, 70-; Maine State Rep, South Berwick-Eliot, 73- Bus & Prof Pos: Job developer, Maine Concentrated Employ Prog, Sanford, Maine, 71-72; dir adult educ, Marshwood High Sch, Eliot, 72- Mem: South Berwick Park, Recreation & Conserv Comt (chmn, 70-73); Camp Waban, North Berwick (bd dirs). Relig: Protestant. Mailing Add: 10 Parent St South Berwick ME 03908

GOODWIN, JOE WILLIAM (D)
Ala State Rep
b Muscle Shoals, Ala, Feb 22, 28; s Jesse Chris Goodwin & Gertrude Kennedy G; m 1954 to Sadie Brock. Educ: Florence State Univ, BS, 56. Polit & Govt Pos: City recorder, Muscle Shoals, Ala, 58, city comnr & mayor, 59-71; Ala State Rep, Dist Five, Place 1, 71- Mailing Add: 310 Ford Rd Muscle Shoals AL 35660

GOODWIN, JOSEPH ROBERT (D)
Chmn, Jackson Co Dem Exec Comt, WVa
b Ripley, WVa, Dec 23, 42; s Robert Booth Goodwin & Lessie Staats G; m 1964 to Kathleen Huffman; c Robert Booth, II. Educ: WVa Univ, BS, 65, JD, 70; Kappa Alpha. Polit & Govt Pos: Chmn rules comt, WVa State Dem Conv, 72; chmn, Jackson Co Dem Exec Comt, 73- Mil Serv: Entered as 2nd Lt, Army, 65, released as Capt, 67, after serv in Army Adj Gen Sch; Army Commendation Medal. Mem: WVa Bar Asn; Am Judicature Soc; Order of the Coif; Phi Alpha Delta. Mailing Add: 500 Church St Ripley WV 25271

GOODWIN, KATHLEEN WATSON (D)
Maine State Rep
b Bath, Maine, Nov 13, 40; d Nathan Wilbur Watson & Kathleen Leonard W; m 1969 to John Raymond Goodwin; c Jonathan Eaton. Educ: Univ Maine, 60-62; Bliss Bus Col, Lewiston, Maine, 63. Polit & Govt Pos: Secy, Bath City Dem Comt, Maine, 63-66; treas, Sagadahoc Co Dem Comt, 64-65; committeewoman, Maine Dem State Comt, 66-, secy, 68-; secy, Gov Task Force Govt Reorgn, 67-68; mem, Maine Comn on Party Struct & Deleg Selection, 69-70; Maine State Rep, 69-, mem & secy Joint Standing Comt, State Govt, Maine House Rep, 69-; vchmn, Maine Dem Platform Comt, 70; mem, Citizens Adv Comt, Bur of Rehabilitation, Dept of Health & Welfare, 70-; chmn, Maine Comt on Aging, 71-; deleg, Dem Nat Conv, 72. Bus & Prof Pos: Secy, Pres of Maine State Sen, 65, Comnr Forestry, 65-66 & Off Gov, 67-68. Mem: Natural Resources Coun, Maine. Relig: Catholic. Mailing Add: 409 High St Bath ME 04530

GOODWIN, MARTIN BRUNE (R)
b Vancouver, BC, Aug 8, 21; s Dr Ray S Goodwin & Emma Augusta Brune G; m 1947 to Bette-Jane W; c Nancijane Margo. Educ: Univ BC, BSA, 43; McGill Univ, MD, CM, 48; Kappa Sigma. Polit & Govt Pos: Mem, State Radiation Tech Adv Coun, NMex, 59-67; chmn, NMex State Cent Comt, 63-64 & 65-67; mem, NMex Bd Pub Health, 67-68; mem, NMex Health & Social Serv Bd, 68-70, chmn, 70-71. Bus & Prof Pos: Radiologist, Scott & White Clin, Temple, Tex, 49-53; pvt practice radiol, Clovis, NMex, 55-75. Mil Serv: Entered as Capt, Army, 53, released as Capt, 55, after serv in Ft Belvoir; Col, Air Force Res, 75- Mem: Am Col Radiol (fel); Am Asn Advan Sci (fel); Radiol Soc NAm (counr); Am Col Chest Physicians (fel); Elks. Honors & Awards: Robins Award, NMex Med Soc; Outstanding Alumni, Kappa Sigma, 66. Relig: Presbyterian; elder & clerk session, First Presby Church, Clovis, NMex. Legal Res: Irisarbor Dr Clovis NM 88101 Mailing Add: PO Drawer 1628 Clovis NM 88101

GOODWIN, RONALD (D)
Mem, DC Dem Cent Comt
b Birmingham, Ala, Dec 18, 43; s William L Goodwin & Cora L G; m 1965 to Mary J Stewart; c Sonya Y. Educ: Am Univ, 72; Univ Md, 72. Polit & Govt Pos: Chmn, Ward 8, DC Dem Cent Comt, 72-, mem, currently; alt deleg, Dem Nat Conv, 72. Bus & Prof Pos: Rep, Field Enterprizes Corp, 65-; asst vpres, Polinger & Crawford Corp, 71-; vpres, H R Crawford Corp, 72- Mil Serv: Entered as E-1, Air Force, 61, released as E-5, 69, after serv in 1002 OMS Hq, Andrews AFB, 65-69. Mem: Wash Bd Realtors; Eastern Br Kiwanis; DC Recreation Dept Adv Bd; Jr Citizens Corp Adv Bd. Mailing Add: 1010 Vermont Ave NW Suite 516 Washington DC 20005

GOODWIN, THOMAS G (D)
WVa State Deleg
b Kanawha Co, WVa, Nov 22, 22; s Charles A Goodwin & Grace B Hudnall G; m 1955 to Shirley Jo Stamper; c Matthew Virlon. Educ: WVa Inst Technol, BS; Morris Harvey Col; WVa Univ; Univ Miami. Polit & Govt Pos: WVa State Deleg, 64- Bus & Prof Pos: Teacher; coach. Mil Serv: Marine Corps, 42-45, Pac Theatre. Mem: VFW; Am Legion; Elks; Lions; PTA. Honors & Awards: Legis Conserv Award, WVa & Nat Wildlife Fedn, 67; Conservationist of the Year Award, Izaak Walton League of Am, WVa Div, 69. Relig: Baptist. Mailing Add: Seth WV 25181

GOODWIN, THOMAS N (D)
RI State Sen
Mailing Add: 325 Smith St Providence RI 02908

GOODWIN, THOMAS N (TOM) (R)
Ariz State Rep
Mailing Add: 1705 W Sunset Rd Tucson AZ 85704

GORDON, ANNE BRADLEY (R)
NH State Rep
b Hartford, Conn, Apr 27, 08; d Mark Spaulding Bradley & Jessie Goodnow B; wid; c Priscilla (Mrs Palmer), Donald Bradley, Peter Upton & George Watson. Educ: Fairmont Jr Col, Washington, DC, 26-27; Boston Sch Occup Ther, grad, 29. Polit & Govt Pos: Chmn, Cheshire Co Rep Comt, NH, 69-73; secy, NH Bicentennial Comn, 69-; mem sch bd & town auditor, Jaffrey, formerly; secy, NH Rep State Comt, 73-74; clerk, Cheshire Co Deleg, 73-; NH State Rep, 75- Publ: Jaffrey view of the general court, weekly column, 73 & Bicentennial comments, series, 74-75, Monadnock Ledger. Mem: Am Legion Auxiliary; Jaffrey Hist Soc; Cheshire Rep Womens Club; Jaffrey Grange. Relig: Protestant. Mailing Add: RFD Box 282 Jaffrey NH 03452

GORDON, B J, JR (D)
SC State Rep
Mailing Add: Box 751 Kingstree SC 29556

GORDON, BARTON JENNINGS (D)
Mem, Tenn State Dem Exec Comt
b Murfreesboro, Tenn, Jan 24, 49; s Robert Jennings Gordon, Jr & Margaret Barton G; single. Educ: Mid Tenn State Univ, BS, 71; Univ Tenn, JD, 73; Phi Alpha Delta; Phi Alpha Theta; Kappa Alpha. Polit & Govt Pos: Mem, Rutherford Co Dem Exec Comt, Tenn, 72-; mem, Tenn State Dem Exec Comt, 74- Bus & Prof Pos: Pvt law practice, 74- Mem: Am & Tenn Bar Asns; Am Trial Lawyers Asn; Tenn Criminal Defense Lawyers Asn. Honors & Awards: Most Outstanding Legis Award, Tenn Intercollegiate State Legis, 70; Student Body Pres, Mid Tenn State Univ, 70. Legal Res: 1515 SE Broad St Murfreesboro TN 37130 Mailing Add: PO Box 1336 Murfreesboro TN 37130

GORDON, BERNARD G (R)
NY State Sen
b Peekskill, NY; m to Leila Mencher; c Elise Ann. Educ: Syracuse Univ; Syracuse Col of Law. Polit & Govt Pos: Corp counsel, Peekskill, NY; counsel, Joint Legis Comt to Study Assessments & Taxation of State Lands; Dep Secy of State in charge of New York Off, 59; NY State Assemblyman, 60-64; NY State Sen, 64- Bus & Prof Pos: Attorney; assoc dir, Co Trust Co; mem bd of dirs, Peekskill Hosp. Mil Serv: Lt & Command Pilot, Navy, World War II. Mem: F&AM (Past Master, Dunderberg Lodge No 1070); Jewish War Vets (Past Comdr, Peekskill Post). Mailing Add: 1420 Riverview Ave Peekskill NY 10566

GORDON, CARL JACKSON, JR (D)
Miss State Rep
b Okolona, Miss, Dec 29, 44; s Carl Jackson Gordon, Sr & Louise Thompson G; m 1967 to Martha Ann Estes; c Natalie Carl & Kimberly Estes. Educ: Univ Miss, 64; Miss State Univ, BS in Bus, 67. Polit & Govt Pos: Miss State Rep, Dist Five, 72- Bus & Prof Pos: Agt, Bankers Life & Casualty, Tupelo, Miss, 64-68 & Lincoln Am Life, Tupelo, 68-71; agt, Sanders Oil Co, Okolona-Tupelo, 72- Mem: Houston Exchange Club; Miss State Univ Alumni Asn; Miss Farm Bur; Okolona CofC. Relig: Baptist. Legal Res: Hwy 41 Okolona MS 38860 Mailing Add: PO Box 377 Okolona MS 38860

GORDON, ELAINE Y (D)
Fla State Rep
b New York, NY, 1931; d Henry Weitzman & Freda Singerman W; div; c Brian, Seth & Pamela. Educ: City Col New York, 49-50; Miami-Dade Jr Col, Fla, 65-66. Polit & Govt Pos: Legis aide to Dade Co Rep George Firestone for Const Rev Session, 68-69; mem, Dade Co Mgr Task Force on Pub Serv Employ; mem, Manpower Area Planning Coun; chairperson, Task Force on Econ Discrimination of Women & Dade Co Comn on Status of Women, currently; Fla State Rep, Dade Co, 72- Bus & Prof Pos: Sales & marketing exec, 69- Mem: Nat & Fla Women's Polit Caucus; Nat Orgn Women; Dade Co Bus & Prof Women; gold honor mem B'nai B'rith Women. Honors & Awards: Outstanding Citizens Award, Dade Co; Cert of Appreciation for Community Serv, from mayor & city comn of Miami & from Metro Comn; Sojourner Truth Award, Nat Orgn Women. Mailing Add: 561 NE 79th St Miami FL 33138

GORDON, GEORGE E, III (R)
NH State Rep
Mailing Add: 139 Main St Suncook NH 03275

GORDON, JACK D (D)
Fla State Sen
Mailing Add: 48 Palm Island Miami Beach FL 33139

GORDON, JOAN (R)
Pres, NMex Fedn Rep Women
b Birmingham, Ala, July 12, 25; d Thomas Murray Wallace & Jeannie Norton W; m 1950 to Joseph Cowan Gordon, Jr; c Jeannette & Joseph Cowan III. Educ: Vanderbilt Univ, Eng, 48; Athenians & Lotus Eaters; Alpha Omicron Pi. Polit & Govt Pos: Pres, Lea Co Rep Women's Club, NMex, 63-67; mem, Lea Co Rep Cent Comt, 63-, chmn voter regist, 66-, mem exec comt, 67-, chairwoman, 71-75; third vpres, NMex Fedn Rep Women, 65-67, first vpres, 67-71, second vpres, 71-73, pres, 73-; mem, Lea Co Bd Voter Regist, 67-75; mem cent comt & party rules comt, NMex State Rep Party, 69-, mem exec comt, 73-; deleg, Nat Fedn Rep Women's Conv, 71, 73 & 75. Mem: Hobbs Panhellenic Soc; Lea Co Engrs Auxiliary (pres). Relig: Episcopal. Mailing Add: 1600 N Penasco Dr Hobbs NM 88240

GORDON, JOAN VERNON (R)
Committeewoman, Park Co Rep Cent Comt, Colo
b Gustline, Tex, Nov 2, 29; d Frank Owen Vernon & Edna Lee Livingston V; m 1952 to Finney Morris Gordon, Jr; c Benjamin Clement & Patrick Wynne. Educ: San Diego Jr Col, 50; Univ NMex, 57; Epsilon Sigma Alpha. Polit & Govt Pos: Committeewoman, Park Co Rep Cent Comt, 67-; deleg, Colo Rep State Conv, 68 & 72; alt deleg, Rep Nat Conv, 72; chmn, Park Co Nixon for President, 72. Bus & Prof Pos: Vpres, Tarryall River Ranch, 61-; vpres-treas, Gordon Guiding & Outfitting, 64-; chmn assoc membership comt, Colo Outfitters Asn, 70-71. Publ: The outfitters wife, Track Mag, 5/72, Colo Mag, 9/72 & Mont Mag 4/73. Mem: Colo Dude Ranch Asn; Dude Ranchers Asn; Colo Outfitters Asn; Int Prof Hunters Asn; Colo Cowbelles. Relig: Presbyterian. Legal Res: Tarryall River Ranch Lake George CO 80827 Mailing Add: Box 122 Lake George CO 80827

GORDON, JOANN CHASE (R)
Committeewoman, Maine State Rep Comt
b Milo, Maine, May 24, 31; d Walter Sargeant Chase & Virginia Buck C; m 1950 to Horace Hunt Gordon, Jr; c Geoffery Hunt, Thomas Ralph, Deborah Ann, Virginia Jean & Peter Call. Educ: Gorham State Teachers Col, 49-50; Univ Maine, BS, 70. Polit & Govt Pos: Mem, Dover-Foxcroft Rep Town Comt, 70; committeewoman, Piscataguis Co, Maine State Rep Comt, 70- Bus & Prof Pos: Dir & teacher, Head Start, Piscataguis Co Off Econ Opportunity, Maine, 67-68; teacher, Guilford Pub Sch, 68; teacher, Dover-Foxcroft Pub Sch, 70- Mem: Nat Educ Asn; Maine Teachers Asn. Relig: Congregational. Mailing Add: Fairview Ave Dover-Foxcroft ME 04426

GORDON, LEONILE (D)
Mem, Dem Nat Comt, VI
Mailing Add: PO Box 3082 St Croix VI 00820

GORDON, MARGARET COHN (D)
Mem, Dem Nat Comt, Ill
b Buffalo, NY, July 5, 28; d Michael Martin Cohn & Margaret Heymann C; m 1948 to Bernard Gordon; c Anne Judith, Jonathan Mark & Alan David. Educ: Wellesley Col, BA, 49; Durant Scholar; vpres, Wellesley Col Forum. Polit & Govt Pos: Bd Educ, Ill, 69-71; deleg, Dem Nat Conv, 72; mem, Dem Nat Comt, Ill, 72-; mem exec comt, New Trier Twp Dem Orgn, Cook Co, 73- Mem: Phi Beta Kappa; Common Cause; Am Civil Liberties Union; Nat Women's Polit Caucus; Urban Coalition. Relig: Jewish. Mailing Add: 1030 Forest Ave Glencoe IL 60022

GORDON, MILTON G (D)
Mem Exec Comt, Dem State Cent Comt, Calif
b Detroit, Mich, June 1, 22; s Abe Gordon & Anna Pragg G; m to Sandra Louise Driver; c Jonathan. Educ: Wayne State Univ, AB in Pub Admin; Univ Calif, Los Angeles, MA in Polit Sci; Pi Sigma Alpha. Polit & Govt Pos: Mem, Los Angeles Co Dem Cent Comt, 58-66, treas, 63-66; mem, Real Estate Comn, Calif, 62-63, Pub Works Bd, 63-64 & Gov Emergency Resources Planning Comt, 64; adminr, Bus & Com Agency, State of Calif; mem exec comt, Dem State Cent Comt, 69-; Dem cand for State Treas, 70; comnr, Los Angeles Co Efficiency & Econ Comn, 71- Bus & Prof Pos: Pres, Milton-Gordon Co, Inc, 51-63; pres, Village-Gordon Co, 63-; vpres-treas, HDC Corp, San Diego, 67-70; consult & real estate counr, 69- Mil Serv: Pfc, Army, 42-44; Good Conduct Ribbon; Marksman. Publ: Race & Property, Univ Calif, 64. Mem: DAV; Am Legion; B'nai B'rith; Beverly Hills & Los Angeles Realty Bd; Nat Asn License Law Officers. Honors & Awards: Outstanding Alumnus Award, Wayne State Univ Club of Southern Calif, 63. Relig: Jewish. Mailing Add: 10504 Cheviot Dr Los Angeles CA 90064

GORDON, SHERRILL LYNN (R)
Nat Committeewoman, Young Rep League Utah
b Salt Lake City, Utah, Apr 20, 48; d Farrell Lynn Gordon & Mary Helen Letson Higgins; single. Educ: Univ Utah, BS, 72, 74-; Phi Mu; Tau Beta Sigma; Golden Hearts of Sigma Phi Epsilon. Polit & Govt Pos: Univ Utah pres, Col Rep, 70-71; Univ Utah student coordr, Burton for Sen Campaign, 70-71; nat committeewoman, Young Rep League Utah, 72-; Region XI dir, Young Rep Nat Fedn, 73-; Salt Lake Co auditor, Women's Rep Club, 75- Bus & Prof Pos: Dept bus secy, Columbia Univ, 69; off mgr & acct, Western Slope Carbon, Inc, Salt Lake City, Utah, 70-; independent interior designer, 72-; part-time tax consult & acct, C P Heiner & Co, Inc, 74- Mem: Girl Scouts (leader, Jr Troop 36); Women's Legis Caucus; Smithsonian Inst. Honors & Awards: Sigma Phi Epsilon Diamond Princess Attendant, 66; Kappa Kappa Psi Fraternity Queen, 66-67. Relig: Latter-day Saint. Mailing Add: 748 N 900 W Apt 302 Salt Lake City UT 84116

GORDON, TINA-JILL (D)
b New York, NY, Aug 2, 50; d Herbert Gordon & Edna Saet G; single. Educ: Monmouth Col (NJ), BS. Polit & Govt Pos: Deleg, Dem Nat Conv, 72; mem, Reform Dem of Madison Twp, NJ, 72- Bus & Prof Pos: Eng teacher, Madison Twp Bd Educ, 72-; actress. Mem: Nat Coun Teachers of Eng; Nat & NJ Educ Asns; Am Fedn TV & Radio Artists; Smithsonian Assocs. Legal Res: 40 Carole Pl Old Bridge NJ 08857 Mailing Add: 56 Ashwood Mall S Old Bridge NJ 08857

GORDON, VIRGIL (R)
Chmn, Austin Co Rep Party, Tex
b Campbellsburg, Ind, Oct 15, 89; s Thomas Gordon & Sarah Catherine Wheat G; m 1914 to Josie Mae Miller. Educ: Ind Univ, MD; Delta Upsilon. Polit & Govt Pos: Chmn, Austin Co Rep Party, Tex, 62- Bus & Prof Pos: Owner, Sealy Hosp, Tex, 50-66. Mil Serv: Entered as Lt, Army Med Corps, 18, released, 19, after serv in 103rd Inf, 26th Div. Mem: Tex State & Am Med Asns; Am Legion. Legal Res: 1031 Meyer St Sealy TX 77474 Mailing Add: 526 Fifth St Sealy TX 77474

GORDY, A PERRY, JR (R)
Mem, Muscogee Co Rep Party, Ga
b Columbus, Ga, Dec 16, 11; s Arthur Perry Gordy, Sr & Edna Spencer G; m 1948 to Martha Louisa Trimble; c Layton Trimble, Louisa Denise & A Perry, III. Educ: Ala Polytech Inst, BS eng, 36; Univ Fla; Ga Inst Technol; Harvard Univ; Univ Ga, MEd, 70; Alpha Tau Omega; Phi Psi; Phi Kappa Phi. Polit & Govt Pos: Mem, Ga Rep State Cent Comt, 63-65; Ga State Sen, 63-66, Rep chmn, Ga State Senate, 64-65; mem, Third Cong Dist Rep Party, 65-; mem, Muscogee Co Rep Party, 65-; mem, Ga Rep State Exec Comt, 70-72. Bus & Prof Pos: Textile engr; advert & pub rels; owner credit bur, 5 years; dir, Columbus Tech, 65-; pres, State Dirs Asn Tech Insts, 70-72. Mil Serv: Navy, Lt(sg), 42-45. Mem: SE Resources Develop Asn; Jaycees; CofC (mem bd dirs); Rotary (exec club bd); Iota Lambda Sigma. Honors & Awards: Outstanding Young Man of Year, Columbus Jaycees, 39; originator, Port Cities Day for Columbus, Ga & Phenix City, Ala, 46; Silver Beaver Award, Outstanding Vol Adult in Boy Scouts, 50; first Rep chmn of Ga State Senate in mod times & first Rep elected to state polit off from Columbus, Ga & Muscogee Co, 63. Relig: Methodist. Mailing Add: 4460 River Rd Columbus GA 31904

GORDY, WILLIAM JOHN (D)
Del State Rep
b Laurel, Del, Feb 20, 25; s Reese O Gordy & Mary Collins G; m 1944 to Marian Lee Hearne; c Mary Ellen, Peggy (Mrs Ronald Williams), Cynthia (Mrs James Whaley), Michael, Judith & Philip. Educ: Laurel High Sch. Polit & Govt Pos: Chief clerk, Del House of Rep, 57-58; committeeman, Fourth & 32nd Rep Dists, Sussex Co, Del, 57-66; chmn, Del Indust Accident Bd, 61-70; deleg, Dem Nat Conv, 68, alt deleg, 72; Del State Rep, 37th Dist, 71-; deleg, Dem Nat Mid-Term Conf, 74. Bus & Prof Pos: Secy, Laurel Grain Co, 64-; pres, Siloam Enterprises, 70- Mem: Farm Bur; Exchange Club; 4-H Club (leader); Lions. Relig: Protestant. Mailing Add: Rte 2 Box 139 Laurel DE 19956

GORE, ALBERT ARNOLD (D)
b Granville, Tenn, Dec 26, 07; s Allen Gore & Margie Denny G; m 1937 to Pauline LaFon; c Nancy & Albert. Educ: State Teachers Col, Tenn, BS, 32; YMCA Night Law Sch, Tenn, LLB, 36. Polit & Govt Pos: Comnr labor, Tenn, 36-37; US Rep, Tenn, 39-53; US deleg UN Gen Assembly; US Sen, Tenn, 53-70; deleg, Dem Nat Conv, 68. Bus & Prof Pos: Lawyer; chmn bd, Island Creek Coal Co, currently; mem bd & vpres, Occidental Petroleum Corp, currently. Mem: Tenn Educ Asn. Relig: Baptist. Mailing Add: Carthage TN 37030

GORE, LOUISE (R)
Rep Nat Committeewoman, Md
b Leesburg, Va, Mar 6, 25. Educ: Finch Col; Bennington Col. Polit & Govt Pos: Head of Dewey Button Girls, Rep Nat Conv & mem staff, Dewey Nat Campaign Hq, Washington, DC, 48; co-chmn, Eisenhower-Nixon Campaign, Montgomery Co, Md, 52; mem of press, Mutual Broadcasting Co, Rep Nat Conv, 52; pres, Rock Creek Rep Women's Club, 53-55; treas, Md Fedn Rep Women, 54-56; prog chmn, Nat Fedn Rep Women, 54-59, chmn, Women Power for Eisenhower, 56; vchmn, Citizens for Nixon-Lodge Campaign, East Coast, 60; Md State Deleg, 63-67, mem educ, banking & ins & metrop affairs comts & legis coun comt tourism, Md House Deleg, formerly; chmn, St Mary's City Comn to Restore First Capitol of Md; co-chmn, Goldwater-Miller Campaign Md, 64; alt deleg, Rep Nat Conv, 64 & 72, deleg, 68; mem, Rep Nat Finance Comt, 64-72; Md State Sen, 67-71, mem econ affairs comt, exec nominations comt & chmn legis coun comt tourism, Md State Senate, formerly; mem, Task Force Govt Labor Rels, Study Comn Educ Needs of Handicapped Children & Comt Alcoholism; chmn, Nixon-Agnew Campaign of Md & chmn women's div, United Citizens for Nixon-Agnew, 68; US mem exec bd, UNESCO, 69; mem, Nat Coun Ment Health, 71; mem bd dirs, Nat Rep Women's Club, 72; Rep Nat Committeewoman, Md, 72- Bus & Prof Pos: Pres, Jockey Club Restaurant. Mem: Muscular Dystrophy Asn Am (vpres, 72-); Potomac Conserv Found (bd dirs). Honors & Awards: Lady of Mercy Award, Mt Carmel Mercy Hosp & Med Ctr, 71. Relig: Methodist. Mailing Add: 11300 River Rd Potomac MD 20854

GORE, MARION ADAMS (R)
b Manchester, NH, June 12, 02; d James Edward Adams & Grace Gibson A; m 1930 to Harry Brigham Gore, wid; c John Adams, James Edward & Judith (Mrs Powers). Educ: Sweet Briar Col, 22-23; Katherine Gibbs Secretarial Sch, 23-24; Boston Univ, 25-26; Boston Conservatory of Music; Glee Club, Sweet Briar Col. Polit & Govt Pos: Vpres, Souhegan Rep Club, 55-57; alt deleg, Nat Rep Conv, 64; advisor, Young Rep Club, Univ NH, 66-; mem, Amherst Rep Town Comt, 67-73. Bus & Prof Pos: Secy to Dr Sherman, Columbia Univ, 27-28; secy, Mass Investment Fund, 28-30; treas, Shoe Rep, 46-56; treas, Adams Bros, 58-61; head resident, Univ NH, 60-67; retired. Mem: Boston Boot & Shoe Traveler's Asn; The Women's Asn, Amherst. Relig: Congregational. Mailing Add: Box 482 Amherst NH 03031

GORMALLEY, JOAN PATRICIA (R)
VChmn, Mass Young Rep Asn
b Salem, Mass, May 11, 38; d Francis P Gormalley & Edith Bates G (deceased); single. Educ: Mass State Col, Salem, BS Educ, 59; Future Teachers Am. Polit & Govt Pos: Organizer, NShore Young Rep Club, Mass, 61, pres, 62-63; mem, Salem Rep City Comt, 61, vchmn, 70-; Young Rep nat committeewoman, Mass Young Rep Asn, 63-67, co-chmn, 65-67, chmn, 67-69, vchmn, 69-70; signer statewide petition drive, State Const Conv, 68; alt deleg, Rep Nat Conv, 68; pres, Salem Women's Rep Club, 60-71; bd trustees, Bates Ctr Pub Affairs, 70-; bd trustees, Essex Co Agr & Tech Sch, 73- Bus & Prof Pos: Teacher, St Pius V Sch, Lynn, 59- Mem: Salem State Col Alumni Asn; North Shore Cath Charity League; NAACP; Mass Comt Const Reform. Honors & Awards: Rep of the Year Award, North Shore Young Rep Club, 65. Relig: Roman Catholic. Mailing Add: 236 Lafayette St Salem MA 01970

GORMAN, DONALD W (R)
NH State Rep
Mailing Add: PO Box 621 Derry NH 03038

GORMAN, EDWARD ARMSTRONG (R)
b Lakeland, Fla, Nov 7, 34; s Edward Amar Gorman & Muriel Floride Davis G; div; c Michelle Elizabeth, Forrest Walton & John Davis. Educ: Univ Fla, 52-53 & 56-58; Med Col Va, DDS, 62; Alpha Tau Omega. Polit & Govt Pos: Rep precinct committeeman, Hillsborough Co Rep Exec Comt, Fla, 66-71, finance chmn, 67-68, chmn, formerly. Bus & Prof Pos: Dent preceptor, Polk Co Health Dept, 62-63; dent practice, Brandon, Fla, 63- Mil Serv: Entered as A/B, Air Force, 54, released as A/3C, 56, after serv in 791st AC&W Squadron, 31st Air Div, 54-56. Mem: Am Dent Asn; Elks; Kiwanis (dir); Jaycees (dir); Brandon Booster Club. Honors & Awards: Young Man of Year, Jaycees, 65; CofC Man of the Month, 68. Relig: Catholic. Mailing Add: 116 S Montclair Brandon FL 33511

GORMAN, FRANCIS JOHN (D)
NJ State Assemblyman
b Gloucester City, NJ, Nov 19, 24; s John Francis Gorman & Mary M Nowrey G; m 1950 to Margaret C McHugh; c Francis X, Regina M, John F, Edward, Bridget, James M, Robert T, Cecilia M, Matthew P & Margaret C. Educ: LaSalle Col, BA, 49. Polit & Govt Pos: Treas, Gloucester City Dem Comt, NJ, 53-66, chmn, formerly; mem city coun, Common Coun, Gloucester City, 54-57, city treas, 58-; committeeman, Camden Co Dem Comt, 64-; deleg, Dem Nat Conv, 68; NJ State Assemblyman, 72- Bus & Prof Pos: Teacher, Mt Ephraim Pub Sch, 49-50; br mgr, Seaboard Finance Co, Hartford, Conn & Bound Brook, NJ, 52-57. Mil Serv: Entered as A/S, Naval Res, 43, released as Yeoman 1/C, 46, after serv in USS Wharton, Pac Theatre, 43-46; recalled, 50-52. Mem: Munic Finance Officers NJ; Tax Collectors, Treas & Receivers NJ; VFW; KofC (4 degree); Gloucester City Savings & Loan Asn (bd dirs). Relig: Roman Catholic. Mailing Add: 921 Hudson St Gloucester City NJ 08030

GORMAN, GEORGE E (D)
Chmn, Goodhue Co Dem Party, Minn
b Goodhue, Minn, Mar 4, 21; s Ernest Gorman & Mary McNamara G; m 1946 to Josephine Heaney; c Helen, Tom, Chas, Mike, Mary, Ernest, Patricia, Donna, Denise & Richard. Educ: High sch. Polit & Govt Pos: Chmn, Goodhue Co Dem Party, Minn, 60- Mil Serv: Entered as Pvt, Army, released as Cpl, 45, after serv in 763rd Tank Div, Pac; Pac Campaign Ribbon with 2 stars; Good Conduct Medal. Mem: Am Legion; VFW; KofC; Farmers Union. Relig: Catholic. Mailing Add: PO Box 38 Goodhue MN 55027

GORMAN, WILLIAM D (R)
Fla State Rep
Mailing Add: Beauclaire Ave Tangerine FL 32777

GORTON, SLADE (R)
Attorney Gen, Wash
b Chicago, Ill, Jan 8, 28; s Thomas Slade Gorton, Jr & Ruth Israel G; m 1958 to Sally Jean Clark; c Tod, Sarah Jane & Rebecca. Educ: Dartmouth Col, AB, 50; Columbia Univ Law Sch, LLB, 53; Phi Beta Kappa; Phi Delta Phi. Polit & Govt Pos: Wash State Rep, 46th Dist, 59-69, Majority Leader, Wash State House of Rep, 67-69; Attorney Gen, Wash, 69-; chmn, State Comt on Law & Justice; chmn, Wash Law Enforcement Officer Training Comt. Bus & Prof Pos: Partner, Seattle law firm, formerly. Mil Serv: Entered as Pvt, Army, 46, released as Pfc, 47, reentered as 1st Lt, Air Force, 53, released, 56; Lt Col, Air Force Res. Publ: Redistricting—a proposal, Nat Munic Rev, spring 64. Mem: Am Bar Asn; Nat Asn Attorneys Gen (vchmn environ control comt & govt opers & fiscal affairs comt); Seattle Tennis Club; Washington Athletic Club, Seattle; Pac Sci Ctr (trustee). Honors & Awards: Dartmouth 1949 Gold Pick Axe Award, 70. Relig: Episcopal. Mailing Add: Temple of Justice Olympia WA 98504

GOSMAN, ROBERT F (BOB) (R)
Rep Nat Committeeman, Wyo
b Butte, Mont, Dec 2, 27; s Frank Gosman & Ruth Weenik G; m Barbara B; c Jeffrey & Deborah. Educ: Mont State Univ, BA; Dartmouth Col, MA. Polit & Govt Pos: Chmn, Natrona Co Rep Comt, Wyo, 63-66; secy, Wyo State Rep Comt, 64-66, chmn, 66-70; Rep Nat Committeeman, Wyo, 70- Mil Serv: Entered as Pvt, Army, 46, released as Sgt, 47, after serv in Sixth Engrs, Korea. Relig: Protestant. Legal Res: 3055 Hamilton Way Casper WY 82601 Mailing Add: PO Box 241 Casper WY 82601

GOSS, BERNARD WAYNE (D)
Chmn, Ashe Co Dem Exec Comt, NC
b Lansing, NC, Feb 11, 32; s Robert Victor Goss & Viller Miller G; m 1957 to Diane Gentry; c Caroline, Carmen, Candace, Randall & Robert. Educ: Mars Hill Col, 51-52. Polit & Govt Pos: Vpres, Ashe Co Young Dem Comt, 72-74; chmn, Ashe Co Dem Exec Comt, NC, 75- Bus & Prof Pos: Mem serv rep, Blue Ridge Elec Mem Corp, 61-74, dir mem rels, 75- Mil Serv: Entered as Pvt, Army, 52, released as Sgt, 54, after serv in 45th Div, Far East, 53-54; Bronze Star. Mem: Blue Ridge Creative Activities Coun (vpres, 75-); Blue Ridge Opportunity Comn (dir, 75-); Ashe Co 4-H Activities, Inc (pres, 75-). Honors & Awards: Hon Lifetime Mem Award, Ashe Jaycees, 69. Relig: Protestant. Mailing Add: West Jefferson NC 28694

GOSSELIN, DAVID (R)
b Wolfeboro, NH, May, 1942; m 1971 to Susan Gauthier. Educ: Olivet Col, BA with honors, 65; Eastern Mich Univ, MA, 66. Polit & Govt Pos: Mgr mayors campaign, Willimantic, Conn, 69; field dir, Robert H Steele, Second Cong Dist, 70; admin asst to speaker, NH House Rep, formerly; exec dir, NH Rep State Comt, 72-73, chmn, formerly; mem, Rep Nat Comt, formerly. Bus & Prof Pos: Teacher social studies, Pittsfield High Sch, NH, 65-; asst to pres, Eastern Conn State Col, 66-69; owner pub rels bus, 70-71. Relig: Congregational. Mailing Add: RFD Center Barnstead NH 03225

GOSSELIN, ERNEST J (D)
Conn State Rep
Mailing Add: 354 Hanover St Bridgeport CT 06605

GOSSETT, ED (D)
b Sabine Parish, La, Jan 27, 02; s Edward L Gossett & Sarah Anne McKinley G; m 1939 to Mary Helen Mosley; c Glenn, Judy, Jane, Melissa, Stephen & Murray. Educ: Univ Tex, AB,

24, LLB, 27. Polit & Govt Pos: Dist Attorney, 46th Judicial Dist, Tex, 32-36; US Rep, 13th Dist, 38-51; mem, Nat Electoral Reform Comt; judge, Criminal Dist Court 5, Dallas Co, 68- Bus & Prof Pos: Jr mem, Berry, Stokes, Warlock & Gossett, Vernon, Tex, 27-32; gen attorney for Tex, Southwestern Bell Tel Co, 51-67; counsel, Strasburger, Price, Kelton, Martin & Unis, 67- Mem: Am & Dallas Bar Asns. Relig: Presbyterian. Mailing Add: Rm 392 County Court House Dallas TX 75202

GOSSETT, JAMES D (R)
Chmn, Upton Co Rep Party, Tex

b Post, Tex, Sept 16, 24; s Ed L Gossett & Sarah McKinley G; m 1959 to Pauline Thompson; c Annie (Mrs Joe Shaffer), Tom, Bryan, Kitty Sue, Linda & Jamie Dee. Educ: Univ Tex, MD, 48; Theta Kappa Psi. Polit & Govt Pos: Chmn, Upton Co Rep Party, Tex, 61- Bus & Prof Pos: Pres, Rankin Sch Bd, 60-69. Mil Serv: 2nd Lt, Army, 42-45, 1st Lt, 48-53. Relig: Methodist. Legal Res: 1000 Elizabeth Rankin TX 79778 Mailing Add: Box 525 Rankin TX 79778

GOTCH, CLIFFORD ROY (R)
b Waterbury, Nebr, Oct 3, 24; s Roy Edward Gotch & Loena Brownell G; m 1944 to Rose Von Minden; c Dwight Eugene. Educ: Allen High Sch, Nebr, grad. Polit & Govt Pos: Treas, Galena Twp Nebr, 52-60; mem, Agr Soil Conserv Bd, 56-60; financial secy, Dixon Co Rep Party, 62-66, chmn, formerly. Bus & Prof Pos: Pres, Big Four Tel, 51-63; agr researcher, Univ Nebr, 57-59. Mem: Iowa Life Ins Underwriters Asn; Dixon Co Farm Bur; Future Farmers of Am; Shrine. Relig: Lutheran. Mailing Add: Box B Allen NE 68710

GOTTFRIED, RICHARD NORMAN (D-LIBERAL)
NY State Assemblyman

b New York, NY, May 16, 47; s Bert A Gottfried & Dorothy Karger G; m 1971 to Louise Rubin. Educ: Cornell Univ Col of Arts & Sci, BA, 68; Columbia Univ Law Sch, JD, 73; Delta Sigma Rho; Tau Kappa Alpha; Forensics. Polit & Govt Pos: Dem leader, 65th Assembly Dist, Part B, 69-71; NY State Assemblyman, 67th Assembly Dist, 71- Bus & Prof Pos: Lawyer, 74- Mem: Am for Dem Action (NY State Bd Dirs); Park-Lincoln Free Dem; New Dem Coalition; Am Civil Liberties Union; Am Jewish Cong. Relig: Jewish. Legal Res: 91 Central Park W New York NY 10023 Mailing Add: 131 W 72nd St New York NY 10023

GOTTLIEB, ROY A (D)
Polit & Govt Pos: Dem Nat Committeeman, VI, formerly; deleg, Dem Nat Conv, 72. Mailing Add: 61 Lindberg Bay St Thomas VI 00801

GOTTLIEB, SANFORD (D)
b Brooklyn, NY, Sept 17, 26; s Sidney Gottlieb & Helen Lipshutz G; m 1947 to Gladys Blumenthal; c Steven, Barbara & Gordon. Educ: Dartmouth Col, BA, 46; Univ Paris, Dr Univ, 52. Polit & Govt Pos: Deleg, Dem Nat Conv, 72; mem, McGovern Panel on Nat Security, Washington, DC, 72. Bus & Prof Pos: Exec dir, SANE, Washington, DC, 60- Mil Serv: Entered as A/S, V-12, Navy, 44, released, 46. Publ: Vietnam: a debate/the road to negotiations, Saturday Rev, 12/65; State within a state: what is the military-industrial complex?, In: The Seventies: Problems & Proposals, Harper & Row, 72; Analyzing the defense budget, New York Times, 5/74. Mailing Add: 11102 Brandywine St Kensington MD 20795

GOUGEON, BYRON C (R)
Chmn, Ontonagon Co Rep Comt, Mich

b Ontonagon, Mich, Oct 29, 32; s Clifford Gougeon & Berniece Goard G; m 1953 to Mary Louise Kelley; c Robert, Sandra, Laura, Dennis & Patrick. Educ: High sch, Rockland, Mich. Polit & Govt Pos: Finance chmn, Ontonagon Co Rep Comt, 68-74, chmn, 74- Bus & Prof Pos: Maintenance foreman, White Pine Copper Co, 65-70; salesman, Burridge Inc, 70-75, sales mgr, 75- Mil Serv: Entered as Pvt, Air Force, 52, released as Airman 1/C, 56. Mem: Am Legion (past Comdr); White Pine Vol Fire Dept (asst chief); White Pine Sch Bd; VFW. Relig: Methodist. Mailing Add: 19 Cedar St White Pine MI 49971

GOULD, GARY HOWARD (D)
Chmn, Bannock Co Dem Cent Comt, Idaho

b Dayton, Ore, Apr 1, 38; s Calvin J Gould & Alice Dobesh G; m 1963 to Marcy Davenport; c Susan & Jon. Educ: Idaho State Univ, BA, 64, MS, 70; Phi Beta Kappa. Polit & Govt Pos: Precinct committeeman, Bannock Co Dem Cent Comt, Idaho, 72-74, chmn, 74- Bus & Prof Pos: Dir, Student Financial Aid & scholar, Idaho State Univ, 72-; mem exec comt, Western Assembly Col Entrance Exam Bd, 75- Mil Serv: Entered as Pvt, Army, 59, released as Pfc, 61. Mem: Elks; Rocky Mountain, Western & Idaho Asns Student Financial Aid Adminr. Mailing Add: 541 S Seventh Pocatello ID 83201

GOULD, KINGDON, JR (R)
US Ambassador, Netherlands

b New York, NY, Jan 3, 24; s Kingdon Gould & Annunziata Lucci G; m 1946 to Mary Thorne; c Lydia (Mrs Barbieri), Kingdon, III, Thorne, Frank, Candida, Caleb, Melissa, Annunziata & Thalia. Educ: Yale Univ, BA, 48; Law Sch, LLB, 51; Phi Beta Kappa. Polit & Govt Pos: Finance chmn, Md Rep Party, formerly; mem, Md Bd Natural Resources, 68-69; US Ambassador, Luxembourg, 69-72; US Ambassador, Netherlands, 73- Bus & Prof Pos: Private law practice, Washington, DC, 51-69; vpres, Parking Mgt Inc, 54-69; dir, Madison Nat Bank, 64-69; bd chmn, Murray Corp, Cockeysville, Md, 64-69. Mil Serv: Entered as Pvt, Army, 42, released as 2nd Lt, 46, after serv in 36th Reconnaissance Squadron Mechanized, Europe, 43-45; Battlefield Comm; 2 Silver Stars; 2 Purple Hearts. Mem: Glenelg Country Sch, Md (founder & chmn trustees, 54-); Millbrook Sch, NY (trustee, 68-). Legal Res: Laurel MD Mailing Add: 1725 De Sales St NW Washington DC 20036

GOULD, R BUDD (R)
Mont State Rep

b Pasadena, Calif, May 10, 37; s John H Gould & Betty Karkeet G; m 1961 to Rosalia Vasecka; c Sheri Anne. Educ: Univ Mont, 55-56. Polit & Govt Pos: Adv counsel, Mont State Libr, 72-; Mont State Rep, 75- Bus & Prof Pos: Owner, Budd Gould Insured Repossession, 56-70. Mailing Add: 2121 35th Ave Missoula MT 59801

GOULD, STEPHEN R (R)
Maine State Rep
Mailing Add: 65 Spring St Stillwater Old Town ME 04489

GOULD, SUE (R)
Wash State Sen
Mailing Add: 19225 92nd W Edmonds WA 98020

GOULDING, PAUL EDMUND (D)
b Providence, RI, Nov 6, 34; s James Simon Goulding & Margaret McCabe G; single. Educ: Providence Col, AB, 57. Hon Degrees: LLD, Mt St Joseph Col, 74. Polit & Govt Pos: Admin asst, US Sen Claiborne Pell, RI, 61-; mem, Dem City Comt, Providence, 64-74. Mem: Wamsutta Club; Aurora Civic Asn. Relig: Catholic. Legal Res: 402 Angell St Providence RI 02906 Mailing Add: Apt 611 2501 Calvert St NW Washington DC 20008

GOULSTON, PAUL MILTON (D)
Mass State Rep

b Boston, Mass, Aug 1, 32; s Joseph Goulston & Elizabeth Goldman G; m 1957 to Elizabeth Ann Rice; c Sandra, Miriam, Stephen & Emily. Educ: NY Univ, 50; Lowell Technol Inst, 51; Mass Col Pharm, BS, 59; Omicron Pi. Polit & Govt Pos: Mass State Rep, 75- Bus & Prof Pos: Pres & treas, Stoughton Drug Co, 70-; pres, Drug Serv Coop Inc, 73- Mil Serv: Entered as Pvt, Army, 54, released as Pfc, 56, after serv in 5th Inf Regt, Ger, 54-56. Mem: Mass State Pharmacy Asn; CofC; Nat Fedn Independent Bus; Nat Asn Retail Druggists. Mailing Add: 1285 Central St Stoughton MA 02072

GOVER, CLARA NELLIE (D)
b Wathena, Kans, Apr 4, 19; d Henry Stewart Scott & Nellie McCahon S; m 1937 to Glen Elmer Gover; c Glenn Michael & David Allen. Educ: Cent High Sch, Kansas City, Mo, grad, 36. Polit & Govt Pos: Vchmn, St Clair Co Dem Cent Comt, Mo, 68-70, chmn, 70-74. Mem: Mo Dem State Club; St Clair Co Women's Dem Club; Eastern Star; Osceola Art Guild; Farm Bur. Relig: Christian. Mailing Add: Rte 1 Osceola MO 64776

GOVERNALI, JOSEPH PAUL (D)
Chmn, New Fairfield Town Dem Comt, Conn

b New York, NY, Oct 22, 34; s Vincent Governali & Santina Trigona G; m 1969 to Wendy Patricia Russell; c Laura Anne, Joseph, Vincent Paul & Kim Joseph. Educ: Columbia Col, AB, 56; Fordham Univ Sch Law, LLB, 59, JD, 68. Polit & Govt Pos: Mem, New Fairfield Town Dem Comt, Conn, 65-, chmn, 68-; justice of peace, New Fairfield, 66-, mem bd finance, 67- Bus & Prof Pos: Attorney-at-law, 60- Mil Serv: Entered as Pvt, Army Nat Guard, 69, released after serv in Hq Co Four Training Unit, Ft Dix, NJ; Sharpshooter Medal. Mem: Bronx Co & NY State Bar Asns. Relig: Roman Catholic. Legal Res: Meeting House Hill Circle New Fairfield CT 06810 Mailing Add: 1443 E Gunhill Rd Bronx NY 10469

GOVRIK, JUDY KAY (D)
Chmn, Lafayette Co Dem Party, Wis

b Austin, Minn, July 15, 46; d Merle Kaster & Margaret Davis; m to Kalman Janos Govrik; c John, Endre, Christopher, Nicholas & Anthony. Polit & Govt Pos: Chmn, Lafayette Co Dem Party, Wis, 75-; mem, Wis Dem Platform Comt, currently. Mailing Add: 543 Ohio Darlington WI 53530

GOWARD, RUSSELL (D)
Mo State Rep

b St Louis, Mo, Aug 25, 35; s William Goward & Zenobia Askew G; m 1957 to Dolores Jean Thornton; c Russell, II. Educ: Hubbard's Bus Col, cert, 59; Harris Teachers Col, currently. Polit & Govt Pos: Div leader, 21st Ward Dem Orgn, Mo, 63-66; Mo State Rep, 76th Dist, 67- Bus & Prof Pos: Spec agt, Prudential Ins Co, 64-65; pres & treas, Goward's & Assocs & Inc, 67-; ins & real estate broker, 67- Mil Serv: Entered as A/S, Navy, 52, released as QmSN, 56, after serv in USS Libra & USS Cambria, Korea & ETO, 52-55; Nat Defense Serv Ribbon; European Occup Medal; Good Conduct Ribbon. Mem: Mason; Boy Scouts; Human Develop Corp Bd. Relig: Congregational. Mailing Add: 4015 Fair Ave St Louis MO 63115

GOWDEY, DWIGHT M (D)
b Ames, Iowa, Feb 17, 17; s Louis V Gowdey & Lenna V Springstun G; m 1945 to Dorothy E Smith; c Kathleen, Christine & Sharon. Educ: Univ Wash, BS in CE, magna cum laude, 38; Yale Univ, MEng, 40; Tau Beta Pi; Sigma Xi. Polit & Govt Pos: Deleg, King Co Dem Exec Bd, Wash, 60-70 & 72-; chmn, 44th Dist, 62-66 & 68; cand, State Rep, 66 & 68; deleg, Dem Nat Conv, 72. Bus & Prof Pos: Engr, Rubens, McClure & Pearson, Seattle, Wash, 48-; owner, Creative Designers, 70- Mil Serv: Lt Col (Ret), Army Res; Purple Heart. Mem: Am Soc Civil Engrs (fel, 38-); Am Concrete Inst; ROA; Nellie Goodhue Group Homes for the Retarded. Relig: Presbyterian. Mailing Add: 11536 Sixth NW Seattle WA 98177

GOWER, JOHN CLARK (R)
Wis State Rep

b Chicago, Ill, Jan 10, 41; s Benjamin Gray Gower & Julie Paradis G; m 1963 to Helen S Coman; c David Coman, Heather Kathleen & Melissa Erin. Educ: Marquette Univ, AB, 63; Marquette Univ Law Sch, JD, 66; Delta Theta Phi. Polit & Govt Pos: Deleg, Annual Wis Fedn Young Rep Conv, 59-; pres, Marquette Univ Young Rep, Wis, 59-60; dep col dir, Wis Fedn Young Rep, 60-61, col dir, 61-62, state committeeman, 66-67, state chmn, 67-69; deleg, Annual Midwest Fedn Col Rep Clubs Conv, 61-65; alt deleg, Young Rep Nat Conv, 61, deleg, 67 & 69; deleg, Wis Rep State Conv, 62, 63, 66, 67, 68, 69, 70-73, alt deleg, 64; secy, Midwest Fedn Col Young Rep, 62-63; chmn, Milwaukee Co Young Rep, 65-66; sixth vchmn, Rep Party, Wis, 67-69; alt deleg, Rep Nat Conv, 68; dist attorney, Brown Co, Wis, 69-71; deleg, Wis State Young Rep Conv, 71 & 73; supvr, Brown Co Bd Supvr, 72-; Wis State Rep, 73- Bus & Prof Pos: Asst gen attorney, Inland Steel Prod Co, 66-67. Mem: Elks; Optimists; Kiwanis; Wis Hist Soc; Wis Guides Asn. Honors & Awards: Dean's Award, Marquette Law Sch. Relig: Catholic. Mailing Add: 312 Terraview Dr Green Bay WI 54301

GOYETTE, MAURICE JOSEPH (D)
NH State Rep

b Laconia, NH, Aug 16, 34; s Horace Christopher Goyette & Leonide Dulac G; m 1955 to Etta May Plante; c Joseph, Paul, & Cheryl. Polit & Govt Pos: NH State Rep, 75- Mem: United Steelworkers Am (int auditor). Relig: Catholic. Mailing Add: 4 Butler St Laconia NH 03246

GOYKE, GARY REGIS (D)
Wis State Sen

b Oshkosh, Wis, May 9, 47; s Robert Edward Goyke & Adeline Gertrude Gronowski G; single. Educ: St Mary's Col (Winona, Minn), BA, 69; Univ Minn, 69-70. Polit & Govt Pos: Mem, City Plan Comn, Oshkosh, Wis, 73-; Wis State Sen, 19th Dist, 74- Bus & Prof Pos: Asst mgr, Shakey's Pizza Parlor, 71-72 & 74-, mgr, 72-74. Mem: Oshkosh Community Coun (bd dirs, 73-); Oshkosh Human Rights Coun; League of Women Voters; Winnebago Conserv

Club. Honors & Awards: Distinguished Serv Award, Oshkosh Jaycees, 74. Relig: Roman Catholic. Legal Res: 1715 Hollister Ave Oshkosh WI 54901 Mailing Add: Rm 700 404 N Main St Oshkosh WI 54901

GRABA, JOSEPH P (DFL)
Minn State Rep
b Wadena, Minn, Mar 3, 38; s Clifford S Graba & Cora B Platten G; m 1967 to Sylvia Gay Eide; c Jess Charles & Jeff Joseph. Educ: Bemidji State Col, BS, 61; Colo State Col, summers 65-68. Polit & Govt Pos: Vchmn, Minn Dem-Farmer-Labor Party, 61; mem, Minn Task Force Environ Educ, 70-71; Minn State Rep, Dist 54-B, 71- Mem: Wadena Fedn Teachers; Minn Fedn Teachers (vpres, 67-71); Minn Sci Teachers Asn; Minn Acad Sci; Nat Sci Teachers Asn. Relig: Methodist. Legal Res: Rte 1 Box 94 Wadena MN 56482 Mailing Add: State Capitol St Paul MN 55101

GRABER, VINCENT JAMES (D)
NY State Assemblyman
b Buffalo, NY, May 14, 31; s Howard J Graber & Eileen Cavanaugh G; m 1955 to Grace Brown; c Judith A, Lynn M, Vincent, Jr, Robert M, James J, Daniel J & Peter T. Educ: South Park High Sch, grad. Polit & Govt Pos: Mem, Zoning Bd Appeals, West Seneca, NY, 66-69, councilman, 70-74; NY State Assemblyman, 75- Bus & Prof Pos: RR brakeman, South Buffalo Rwy, 50-54, RR yardmaster, 54-61 & RR gen yardmaster, 61-74. Mil Serv: Entered as Pvt, Army, released as Cpl, after serv in Transportation Corp, ETO, 52-54. Mem: KofC; Kiwanis Int; VFW; Am Legion; CofC. Relig: Roman Catholic. Legal Res: 248 Elmsford Dr West Seneca NY 14224 Mailing Add: Rm 546 Legis Off Bldg Albany NY 12224

GRABER, WALTER W (D)
Kans State Rep
b Pretty Prairie, Kans, Jan 22, 07; s Jacob K Graber & Mary Graber G; m 1935 to Jean Arbuckle; c Geraldine (Mrs Neil Crane), Mary (Mrs Mark Collins) & Helen (Mrs Wayne Unruh). Educ: Bethel Col, Kans, AB, 29. Polit & Govt Pos: Mem, Pretty Prairie Sch Bd, Kans, 38-69; mem, State Bd Educ, 54-60; adminr, Kans Wheat Comn, 57-63; Kans State Rep, 69-, mem, Comt on Assessment & Taxation, Comt on Agr & Livestock & Comt on Natural Resources, Kans House Rep, 69. Bus & Prof Pos: Exec secy, US Bulgur Processors, 63-64; dir, Kans State Wheat Growers, 67-72; consult, African Land Develop of World Homes, Subsidiary of Garvey Enterprises, Wichita, Kans, currently. Mem: Lions; Farm Bur; Kans Livestock Asn. Honors & Awards: Farm Bur Award for Serv; Award for 31 years Serv on Sch Bd; Distinguished Alumni Award, Bethel Col, Kans. Relig: Mennonite. Mailing Add: Pretty Prairie KS 67570

GRABOWSKI, BERNARD FRANCIS (D)
b New Haven, Conn, June 11, 23; s John Grabowski & Felixa Szydlowski G; m 1953 to Anne J Gorski; c Carol Ann & Diane Marie. Educ: Univ Conn, 46-52, BSc & JD. Polit & Govt Pos: Councilman, Bristol, Conn, 53-55; judge, City Court of Bristol, 55-60; chief prosecutor, Circuit Court, Bristol, Plymouth, Southington & Thomeston, 61; US Rep at-Large, Conn, 62-64, Sixth Cong Dist, 64-66. Bus & Prof Pos: Coordr redevelop, Bristol, Conn, 53-58; mem law firm, Hanrahan, Grabowski & Hayes; admitted to practice before US Supreme Court. Mil Serv: Entered as Pvt, Army, 43, released as Pfc, 45, after serv in 103rd Inf Div, ETO, 43-45; Purple Heart; Good Conduct Ribbon. Mem: DAV; Civitan; Bristol Polish Am Citizens Club; Polish Legion of Am Vets; KofC. Relig: Roman Catholic. Legal Res: 57 George St Bristol CT 06010 Mailing Add: 683 Farmington Ave Bristol CT 06010

GRABOYES, ROBERT FRANCIS (D)
b Petersburg, Va, Jan 11, 54; s Harold Graboyes & Lois Sandler G; single. Educ: Univ Va, 72-; Phi Epsilon Pi. Polit & Govt Pos: Pres, Va Teen Dem Clubs, 71-72; del, Va Dem State Conv, 72; deleg, Dem Nat Conv, 72; chmn, Petersburg Dem Comt, formerly. Honors & Awards: Youth Appreciation Music Award, Optimists, 71; John Philip Sousa Band Award, Petersburg High Sch Band, 72. Relig: Jewish. Mailing Add: 2014 Westover Ave Petersburg VA 23803

GRACE, HARRISON DEARING (D)
Secy, Miller Co Dem Cent Comt, Ark
b El Dorado, Ark, Sept 3, 19; s Walter Garland Grace & Annie Eliza Dearing G; m 1973 to Betty Walters; c Harrison D, Jr. Educ: Texarkana Tex High Sch, grad, 37. Polit & Govt Pos: Secy-pres, Texarkana Sch Bd, Ark, 55-66; officer, Miller Co Soil Conservation Dist, 58-62; secy, Miller Co Dem Cent Comt, 62- Bus & Prof Pos: Pres, Southwest Ark Tel Coop Inc, 52- Mem: Hudson Creek Hunting Club; Miller Co Farm Bur; Ark Farm Bur; Red River & Ark Cattleman's Asn. Relig: Methodist. Mailing Add: Rte 4 Box 718 Texarkana AR 75501

GRACE, JULIAN (D)
NMex State Rep
b Santa Fe, NMex, Nov 23, 31; s Augustine (Tinnie) Grace, Sr & Margaret Zinsser G; m 1953 to Eulogia Garcia; c Kathleen, Julian Ray, Alan C, Pamela R & Venus Ann. Educ: Eastern NMex Univ, Teachers Cert. Polit & Govt Pos: NMex State Rep, Dist 47, 75- Mem: NMex Tech & Indust Voc Asn (pres); Eagles; 20-30 Clubs; NMex Tech Voc Sch Teachers Asn. Relig: Catholic. Legal Res: 647 Cerrillos Rd Santa Fe NM 87501 Mailing Add: PO Box 2245 Santa Fe NM 87501

GRACE, ROBERT WILLIAM (R)
b Ft Worth, Tex, Aug 17, 51; s Russell R Grace & Evelyn Randall G; single. Educ: Tex Wesleyan Col, 70; Tex Christian Univ, 71; Univ Tex, Austin, BBA, Finance & Ins, 73; Ins Soc; Kappa Sigma; Sailing Club. Polit & Govt Pos: Ed, State High Sch Young Rep Newsletter, 67-69; chmn, Tarrant Co High Sch Young Rep, 68-69; chmn, Tarrant Co Young Rep, 68-71; dist committeeman, Tex Young Rep, 69-70; pres, Tex Wesleyan Col Young Rep, 69-70; NCent Tex chmn, Tex Young Rep Fedn, 70-71, chmn, 1970 Conv Comt, 70-71, state conv chmn, 71, Tarrant Co young adult chmn, 74; deleg, Nat Young Am for Freedom Conv, St Louis, Mo, 69 & Nat Young Rep Conv, Phoenix, Ariz, 71; alt deleg, Rep Nat Conv, 72. Bus & Prof Pos: Pres, Ft Worth Pub Rels, currently; secy-treas, Grace Ins Agency, Inc, Grace Co Inc & Grace Excess Lines, currently. Honors & Awards: Ford Future Scientist, Ford Found, 66; Most Outstanding Tarrant Co Young Rep, 68 & Tarrant Young Rep, 71; hon mention, Tex Young Rep, 70 & 71. Relig: Methodist. Legal Res: 3201 Westcliff Rd W Ft Worth TX 76109 Mailing Add: 2304 W Seventh St Ft Worth TX 76107

GRADISON, WILLIS DAVID, JR (R)
US Rep, Ohio
b Cincinnati, Ohio, Dec 28, 28; s Willis David Gradison & Dorothy Benas G; m 1950 to Helen Ann Martin; c Ellen, Robin, Anne, Beth & Margaret. Educ: Yale Univ, BA, 48; Harvard Univ, MBA, 51, DCS, 54. Polit & Govt Pos: Asst to under secy, US Treas Dept, 53-55; asst to secy, US Dept Health, Educ & Welfare, 55-57; city councilman, Cincinnati, Ohio, 61-74, vmayor, 67-71, mayor, 71; US Rep, Ohio, 74- Bus & Prof Pos: Vpres, Gradison & Co Inc, mem, NY Stock Exchange. Publ: Key questions in pension fund investment, Harvard Bus Rev, 7-8/55. Relig: Jewish. Legal Res: 6 Elmhurst Pl Cincinnati OH 45208 Mailing Add: Fed Off Bldg Cincinnati OH 45202

GRADY, THOMAS WESLEY (D)
Vt State Sen
b Gloucester, Mass, July 2, 13; s Robert Alexander Grady & Anna Mae Kelley G; m 1939 to Barbara Davis; c Kevin Albert & Laureen Anne (Mrs Keyes). Educ: Boston Eng High Sch. Polit & Govt Pos: Vt State Sen, currently. Bus & Prof Pos: Salesman & tech rep, Linde Div, Union Carbide Corp, 35-46; pres & treas, Grady's Welding Supply Inc, Burlington, Vt, 46-70. Mem: Vt Asn for Blind (pres); 1690 Shelburne Rd Inc (dir). Relig: Catholic. Mailing Add: Pleasant Valley Rd Underhill Center VT 05490

GRAF, ROBERT E (R)
Vt State Rep
b Rupert, Vt, Nov 5, 15; married; c 3 daughters. Educ: St Lawrence Univ, Canton, NY, BS, 38. Polit & Govt Pos: Auditor, justice of the peace, Pawlet, Vt, 47-; supvr, Bennington Soil Conserv Dist, 50; Vt State Rep, 59- Bus & Prof Pos: Dairy farmer. Mem: F&AM; Eastern Star; Scottish Rite; Alpha Tau Omega. Relig: Congregational. Mailing Add: RD Pawlet VT 05761

GRAFF, PATRICIA HALE (D)
b Philadelphia, Pa, June 16, 29; d James W Hale & Edith Harris H; m 1952 to LeRoy L Graff; c Stephen H, Valerie P & Eric Z. Educ: Philadelphia Officers Training Sch, cert, 54. Polit & Govt Pos: Committeewoman, Sharon Hill, Pa, 53-54; committeewoman, Upper Providence Twp, Pa, 60-, vchmn, 72-; secy, various campaign comts, Delaware Co, Pa, 70-; deleg, Dem Nat Conv, 72. Bus & Prof Pos: Cosmetic demonstrator, Blum Store, Philadelphia, 47-50; clerk, Fine Arts Silver Co, 50; clerk typist, Prudential Ins Co, 54-55; clerk typist, Commonwealth of Pa, Media, 71- Mil Serv: Entered as Pvt, Air Force, 50, released as A/3, 52, after serv in 3700 Instr Squadron, 3700th Air Training Command, 50-52. Mem: Am Fedn State, Co & Munic Employees (shop steward, 72-, exec bd, 72-); Media Fel House; NAACP; Rose Tree Media Parent-Teacher Groups. Mailing Add: 116 W Lincoln St Upper Providence PA 19063

GRAFFAM, LINWOOD E (R)
Maine State Sen
Mailing Add: 6 Park Lane Gorham ME 04038

GRAFTON, A WALLACE, JR (D)
b Louisville, Ky, Dec 30, 37; s Arthur Wallace Grafton, Sr & Poala Copeland G; m 1961 to Donna Carrigan; c Michael, Carolyn & Sarah. Educ: Va Mil Inst, BA, 60; Univ Louisville Law Sch, JD, 65; Delta Theta Phi. Polit & Govt Pos: Deleg, Ky Dem Conv, 68; mem, Louisville & Jefferson Co Exec Comt, 69-73; legis asst to Gov Ford, Ky, 71-72; chmn, Muskie for President Campaign, Jefferson Co, 72; alt deleg, Dem Nat Conv, 72; orgn chmn, Wendell Ford for Senate Comt, 74; mem, Carroll for Gov Comt, 75. Bus & Prof Pos: Secy, Louisville Ctr City Comn, 74-75; chmn of bd dirs, Ky Dance Coun, 75; mem of bd dirs, Louisville Med Ctr, Inc, 74; mem bd dirs, Univ Louisville Found, Inc, 74; mem bd trustees, Univ Louisville, 74-75. Mil Serv: Entered as 2nd Lt, Army, after serv in 29th Unit; Capt, Army Res, 68. Publ: Auth, Deductibility of real estate commissions on federal estate tax returns, 67, co-auth, The Kentucky Tax System: A way to attract new industry to Kentucky, 69, Ky Bar J. Mem: Louisville, Ky & US Bar Asns; Louisville & Jefferson Co Bar Asn (exec comt, 73-74). Relig: Catholic. Legal Res: 4000 Napanee Rd Louisville KY 40207 Mailing Add: Wyatt Grafton & Sloss Citizens Plaza Louisville KY 40202

GRAGG, BILLY HARDIN (R)
Chmn, Anderson Co Rep Party, Tex
b Palestine, Tex, Oct 10, 28; s Oscar Lee Gragg & Inez Hardin G; m 1958 to Jacquelyn Lockey; c Holli Sue & Laura Lee. Educ: Univ Tex, BA in Econ, 50, LLB, 53; Alpha Phi Omega. Polit & Govt Pos: Bd mem, Palestine Civil Serv Comn, Tex, 63-; chmn, Anderson Co Rep Party, 64-; Rep state committeeman, 66. Bus & Prof Pos: Anderson Co Bar Asn; Tex & Am Bar Asns; Rotary. Relig: Methodist. Legal Res: 1020 Hilltop Palestine TX 75801 Mailing Add: PO Box 678 Palestine TX 75801

GRAHAM, ALFRED CURTIS (R)
Chmn, Pulaski Co Rep Comt, Va
b Floyd Co, Va, Nov 17, 22; s Andrew Lester Graham & Annie Pearl Yeatts G; m 1951 to Helen Landrum Smith; c Sandra & Robert. Educ: Va Polytech Inst, BS, 49. Polit & Govt Pos: Chmn, Pulaski Co Rep Comt, Va, 70- Bus & Prof Pos: Asst secy-treas, Southwest Prod Credit Asn Nat Farm Loan Asn, 50-57; self employed, retail sales, Dublin, Va, 57- Mil Serv: Entered as Seaman, Navy, 43, released as PO 2/C, 46, after serv in Pac Theater of Opers. Mem: Am Legion; VFW; Mason; Ruritan Club; Ruritan Nat (dir). Relig: United Methodist. Legal Res: Roseberry St Dublin VA 24084 Mailing Add: PO Box 698 Dublin VA 24084

GRAHAM, ALFRED T (D)
Wyo State Rep
b Lincoln, Nebr, Dec 22, 09; m to Ada; c three. Polit & Govt Pos: Wyo State Sen, formerly; Wyo State Rep, 59-61, 65-71 & 75-; city councilman, Thermopolis, Wyo, 73- Bus & Prof Pos: Contractor. Mem: Elks; KofC; Eagles. Relig: Catholic. Mailing Add: 1115 Clark St Thermopolis WY 82443

GRAHAM, ANNA M (R)
Mem, Rep State Exec Comt Ala
b New Orleans, La, Sept 6, 32; d Jake Montalbano & Josephine Latino M; m 1956 to Dr William Hardin Graham; c Carol Anne, Michael David, Janet Lee, Patrick Hardin & Alan Gleason. Educ: La State Univ, BSEd, 54; Newman Club. Polit & Govt Pos: Treas & pres, Huntsville Fedn Rep Women, Ala, 64; mem, Madison Co Rep Exec Comt, 64-65; membership chmn, Ala Fedn Rep Women, 65-66, fourth vpres, 66-67, mem bd dirs, 67-, pres, 67-69, legis chmn, 70; attended Nat Rep Leadership Conf, Washington, DC, 70; deleg, Ala Rep Conv, 70; deleg-at-lg, 16 Biennial Conv, Nat Fedn Rep Women, 70; co-chmn comt to reelect the president, Upper Dublin Twp, Montgomery Co, Pa, 72; mem, Rep State Exec Comt Ala, currently; Madison Co commun, publicity & pub rels chmn, Ala Rep Fifth Dist Comt, 75- Bus & Prof Pos: Elem teacher, Sacred Heart of Jesus Sch, 54-56; elem teacher, Blessed Sacrament Sch, 56-57. Mem: La State Univ Alumni Asn; Huntsville Cath Charities

Social Serv (bd dirs, 69-). Honors & Awards: Alpha Omega Award, La State Univ, 54; John Henry Newman Award, Nat Newman Club, 54; Ala Fedn Rep Women Outstanding Rep Woman of Year, 66. Relig: Roman Catholic. Mailing Add: 3019 Barcody Rd Huntsville AL 35802

GRAHAM, BETTY JUNE (D)
Chmn, Cowley Co Dem Cent Comt, Kans
b Mt Hope, Kans, Sept 2, 17; d Harley L Caffrey & May Wimp C; m 1941 to Eugene Holt Graham. Educ: Southwestern Col, AB, 39. Polit & Govt Pos: Precinct committeewoman, Dem Party, 48-; chmn, Cowley Co Dem Cent Comt, Kans, 60-; secy, Fifth Dist Dem Party, 62-64, vchmn, 73-; deleg, Dem Nat Conv, 64 & alt deleg, 68; vchmn, Jefferson Jackson Day Dinner, Kans, 66. Mem: Winfield Country Club Golf Asn; Snyder Research Found Auxiliary. Relig: Methodist. Legal Res: 1515 E 13th Winfield KS 67156 Mailing Add: PO Box 632 Winfield KS 67156

GRAHAM, CARROLL ADRIAN (D)
Mont State Sen
b Hardin, Mont, Dec 14, 13; s Joseph Allen Graham & Frances Robinson G; m 1939 to Nelle Yvette Pickard; c Gary Joe & Carroll Allen. Educ: Lodge Grass High Sch; Billings Polytech. Polit & Govt Pos: Mont State Sen, Dist 1, Big Horn Co, 61-, chmn livestock, agr & irrigation comt, Mont State Senate, 75-, pres pro tem, 75-, vchmn hwys & transportation comt, mem comt on comts, mem legis admin & rules comts, mem legis coun, currently. Mem: Mason; RAM; Al Bedoo Shrine; Eastern Star; Elks. Relig: Baptist. Legal Res: 22 Miles SW Lodge Grass MT 59050 Mailing Add: Drawer K Lodge Grass MT 59050

GRAHAM, DANIEL ROBERT (D)
Fla State Sen
b Coral Gables, Fla, Nov 9, 36; s Ernest R Graham & Hilda Simmons G; m 1959 to Adele Khoury; c Gwendolyn Patricia, Glynn Adele, Arva Suzanne & Kendall Elizabeth. Educ: Univ Fla, BA, 59; Harvard Law Sch, LLB, 62; Phi Beta Kappa, Fla Blue Key; Chancellor of Honor Court; Sigma Nu. Polit & Govt Pos: Fla State Rep, 66-70; Fla State Sen, 33rd Dist, 70-, chmn, Senate Educ Comt, Fla State Senate, 72- Bus & Prof Pos: Vpres & secy, Sengra Develop Corp, Miami Lakes, Fla. Mem: Nat Comn on Reform of Sec Educ; Nat Found for Improv of Educ; Southern Regional Educ Bd; Builders Asn of SFla; YMCA. Honors & Awards: Outstanding First Term Mem of the Senate, Allen Morris, 71; Most Valuable Legislator, St Petersburg Times, 72; Lawmaker-Newsmaker of the Year, Tallahassee Dem, 72; Conserv Awards, Sierra Club, Fla Wildlife Fedn & Save Our Bays Asn, 72. Relig: United Church of Christ. Mailing Add: 16141 Aberdeen Way Miami Lakes FL 33014

GRAHAM, DAVID LIVINGSTONE (D)
Maine State Sen
b Philadelphia, Pa, Aug 26, 04; s John Graham & Florence Beale G; m 1956 to Mymie Warrell; c Lani Florence Beale. Educ: Yale Univ, BA, 27; Cambridge Univ, BA & MA, 29; Zeta Psi; Wolf's Head Soc. Polit & Govt Pos: Maine State Rep, 65-66; Maine State Sen, 71-72, 75- Bus & Prof Pos: English instr, Univ Ga, 30-32. Mil Serv: Entered as Lt(jg), Navy, 41, released as Lt Comdr, 45, after serv in Southwest Pac, 44-45. Publ: What progress in the alliance?, Va Quart Rev, autumn 63; Government by freshmen, The Nation, 1/66; As the nation goes, so goes Maine, The Progressive, 2/72; plus others. Mem: Authors League of Am; Am Vets Comt, Water Polo, Boxing, Ice Hockey & Tennis. Relig: Protestant. Mailing Add: RFD 1 Freeport ME 04032

GRAHAM, DEBORAH SUSAN (R)
Nat Committeewoman, Miss Young Rep Fedn
b Mobile, Ala, Feb 18, 53; d Thomas J Graham, Jr & Frances Hethcox G; single. Educ: Univ Southern Miss, Pub Rels, 75; Alpha Lambda Delta; Phi Delta Rho; Pi Gamma Mu; Student Govt Asn, student senate, 72-74, elec comnr, 74-75. Polit & Govt Pos: Secy, Miss Young Rep Fedn. 73-75, nat committeewoman, 75- Mem: Univ Southern Miss Young Reps (pres, 73-75); Univ Southern Miss Student Cong Adv Bd. Relig: Baptist. Legal Res: 1208 W Seventh St Hattiesburg MS 39401 Mailing Add: 1281 Southern Sta Hattiesburg MS 39401

GRAHAM, JAMES LEONARD (R)
Wyo State Rep
b Camden, SC, Mar 20, 21; s James Leonard Graham & Lucie Barry Wilshire G; m 1957 to Gretchen E Swindle; c John Wilshire & Margaret Barry. Educ: Williams Col, 41-42 & 45-47; Psi Upsilon. Polit & Govt Pos: Dir, Sheridan Co Recreation Bd, Wyo, 67-; Wyo State Rep, 73- Bus & Prof Pos: Owner-mgr, Little Tongue Ranch, 57- Mil Serv: Entered as Aviation Cadet, Navy, 41, released, 43. Mem: Mason; Shrine; Elks; Ranchester Rotary; Farm Bur. Relig: Episcopal. Mailing Add: Little Tongue Ranch Dayton WY 82836

GRAHAM, JEAN CHARTERS (D)
Chmn, Second Dist Rep Comt, Colo
b Columbia, Mo, Dec 31, 14; d W W Charters & Jessie Allen C; m 1941 to Charles Andrew Graham (deceased); c Judi Allen, Andy & Margaret M. Educ: Univ Wis, BA, 35; Columbia Univ, MA, 36; Univ Chicago, PhD, 42; Mortar Bd; Pi Beta Phi. Polit & Govt Pos: Dem Nat Committeewoman, Colo, 60-68; deleg, Dem Nat Conv, 64 & 68; chmn, Colo Dem Equal Rights Comn, 69-70; co-chmn, Colo Dem Century Club, 71-73; chmn, Second Dist Rep Comt, currently. Honors & Awards: Colo Dem Woman of the Year, 68. Mailing Add: 2345 Routt St Lakewood CO 80215

GRAHAM, JOHN A (R)
Ill State Sen
b Irving, Ill, Dec 3, 11; m to Inga G; c Vickie Lynn, Steven. Educ: Fillmore High Sch; bus schs, tech schs; grad acct. Polit & Govt Pos: Ill State Sen, 54-; mem, Reg Rep Orgn. Bus & Prof Pos: Owner, appliance bus, 46- Mil Serv: Army Air Force, T/Sgt, World War II, Pac Theatre. Mem: CofC (past pres); Mason (past master); Lions; Am Legion; Moose. Relig: United Church of Christ. Mailing Add: 715 S Cook St Barrington IL 60010

GRAHAM, LLOYD KENNETH (LUKE) (D)
b Cashmere, Wash, July 1, 06; s Fred C Graham & Clara Bollman G; div; c James E, Carol Ann (Mrs John S Edgar) & Fred C. Educ: Int Correspondence Schs. Polit & Govt Pos: First chmn, Polit Action Comt, Clark, Skamamona & W Klickitat Cent Labor Coun, Wash, 34; chmn, Scale Comt, W Klickitat Cent Labor Coun, 41; vpres, Seattle Webb Local, 41; chmn, Clark Co Dem Comt, 47-56; treas, Nine Counties Dem League, 48-53, chmn, 53-54; deleg, Dem Nat Conv, 48-60 & 68, chmn, Wash deleg, 60; chmn, Statewide Jefferson-Jackson Day Dinner, 51; mem, Wash Dem Finance Comt, 53-54, chmn, 57-61; pres, Portland Webb's Pressmans Union, 55-56; mem, Sen Magnuson's Dinner Comt, 63; co-dir, Sen Magnuson's Campaign, 62; mem, Gov Rosellini's Dinner Comt, 63; mem, Sen Jackson's Dinner Comt, 63; co-chmn, Jefferson-Jackson Dinner Comt, 63; mem, King Co Dem Finance Comt, 63-64; co-chmn, Wash Comt Elec Dem House, 64; chmn, President Johnson's Wash Finance Comt, 64; Dem Nat Committeeman, Wash, 64-72. Bus & Prof Pos: Mem staff, Astoria, Budget, Ore, 20-24, Columbian Daily, Vancouver, Wash, 24-25, San Francisco Examr, Calif, 24-25, Vancouver Columbian, 25-37, Ore J, Portland, 37-41, Seattle Post Intelligencer, Wash, 41-42 & 51-55; pressman, Columbian Daily, Vancouver, 55-57; with Int Correspondence Schs, 42-51, supt Ore div, 45-51; mem staff, Bank of Tacoma, Wash, 61-63, secy, 63-64, mem exec bd, 64- Mem: Mason; Elks. Mailing Add: 2649 Walnut St SW Seattle WA 98116

GRAHAM, LORRAINE HUNT (D)
Vt State Rep
b Burlington, Vt, July 20, 25; d Elzor L Hunt (deceased) & Leona M Gelinas H; m 1946 to Foster J Graham; c Lealand Hunt, Foster J, II, Deborah Lorraine, Dana Scott, Darryl Kim, Bryan Keith & Stacy Jo. Educ: Burlington High Sch, grad, 44. Polit & Govt Pos: Vt State Rep, 66-; membership chmn, Chittenden Co Dem Women, 67-; mem, Gov Comt Children with Learning Disabilities; comnr, Burlington Sch Bd, currently; mem, Comt for the Electorate of Tomorrow, 71-; chairperson, Spec Study Comt on Demonstration Sch Dist, 73. Bus & Prof Pos: Typist eng dept, Bell Aircraft, 44-45; typist traffic dept, New Eng Tel & Tel, 45-52; investr, CTI-New Eng Tel & Tel, 62-65. Mem: State Order Women Legislators (legis pres); Nat Guard Officers Wives; Fanny Allen Hosp Auxiliary; Chittenden Co Dem Women; Vt Fedn Dem Women. Honors & Awards: President's Award for Children with Learning Disabilities; deleg from Vt Nat Support of Pub Schs, 67. Relig: Roman Catholic. Mailing Add: 280 N Winooski Ave Burlington VT 05401

GRAHAM, LUKE (D)
Dem Nat Committeeman, Wash
Mailing Add: 2649 Walnut Ave SW Seattle WA 98116

GRAHAM, MACK (D)
Miss State Rep
b Sumrall, Miss, June 12, 24; s O T Graham & Jessie Napier G; m 1948 to Doris; c Douglas, Martha & Mackie. Polit & Govt Pos: Miss State Rep, 61- Bus & Prof Pos: Merchant; farmer. Mil Serv: Entered as Pvt, Army, 42, released as Cpl, 46, after serv in 60th Gen Hosp, SPac, 43-45. Mem: Am Legion; VFW; 40 et 8; Miss Sch for Blind; Ment Health & Retardation Bd (chmn region 12). Relig: Baptist. Mailing Add: Box 205 Sumrall MS 39482

GRAHAM, MILTON HENRY (R)
b Fairfield, Iowa, Mar 23, 19; s Lonnie D Graham & Bertha M Coffman G; m 1969 to Charlotte S Kelley; stepchildren, Brian & Melanie. Educ: Parsons Col, BA, 40. Polit & Govt Pos: Mayor, Phoenix, Ariz, 64-70; vpres, Nat Munic League, 64-71; mem, Nat League of Cities-Am Asn Hwy Off Joint Hwy Study Comt, 66-69; mem bd dirs, Town Affiliation Asn, 66-69, vpres, 70-71; mem bd adv, US Conf Mayors, 67-69; mem steering comt, Nat Urban Coalition, 67-69; vpres, League of Ariz Cities & Towns, 68-69; mem bd dirs, Nat League of Cities, 69. Bus & Prof Pos: Owner, Milt Graham Distributing Co, 46-; secy, World Housing Corp, 73-; pres, Cent Phoenix Bus & Prof Asn, currently; mem bd dirs, Ariz Film Prod, Inc, currently. Mil Serv: Entered as Aviation Cadet, Air Force, 42, released as Capt, 46, after serv in 8th Air Force, ETO. Mem: CofC (Phoenix bd, 72-); Jaycees; Community Coun; Thunderbirds; Theodore Roosevelt Boy Scout Coun. Relig: Protestant. Legal Res: 511 W Ocotillo Ave Phoenix AZ 85013 Mailing Add: 349 N Black Canyon Phoenix AZ 85009

GRAHAM, MORTIMER ELLIOTT (R)
Mem, Pa State Rep Exec Comt
b Oil City, Pa, Oct 18, 01; s Lyman Lincoln Graham & Luella Barnes G; m 1925 to Grace Budd; c Douglas Hume & Nancy Lee (Mrs Brown). Educ: Allegheny Col, AB cum laude, 22; Univ Pa, LLB cum laude, 25; Phi Beta Kappa; Order of the Coif; Sigma Delta Rho; Phi Delta Theta. Polit & Govt Pos: Dist Attorney, Erie Co, Pa, 32-40; chmn, Erie Co Rep Comt, 32-34 & 66-72; alt deleg, Rep Nat Conv, 36, deleg, 64 & 68; mem, Comn on Const Revision, Pa, 64-66; mem exec comt, Pa Rep Primary Campaign Comt, 66; mem, Pa State Rep Exec Comt, 66- Bus & Prof Pos: Attorney-at-law, 25-; secy, Hammermill Paper Co, 48-64, gen counsel, 48-66, vpres, 64- Mil Serv: Entered as Lt, Navy, 42, released as Lt Comdr, 45, after serv in Naval Aviation; Comdr (Ret), Naval Res, 52. Mem: Am Bar Asn; Mason (33 degree). Relig: Episcopal. Mailing Add: 322 Mohawk Dr Erie PA 16505

GRAHAM, PIERRE ROBERT
US Ambassador to Upper Volta
b St Nazaire, France, Aug 10, 22; s William Robert Graham & Jeanne Augerau G; m 1968 to Dr Helgard Planken; c Diane Crisafulli, Katherine & Patricia. Educ: Col Aristide Briand, France, PhB, 40; US Merchant Marine Acad, dipl, 43; Univ Chicago, MA, 49. Polit & Govt Pos: Third secy, Am Legation, Tangier. 51-54 & Am Embassy, Beirut, 54-57; second secy, Am Embassy, Paris, 57-58; first secy, Am Embassy, Dakar, 58-61; personnel officer, Dept State, 62-64; counr, Am Embassy, Conakry, 64-66; dep dir IO/OES, Dept State, 66-69; US permanent rep, UNESCO, Paris, 69-73; dept chief mission, Am Embassy, Amman, 73-74; chief mission, Am Embassy, Ouagadougou, Upper Volta, 74- Mil Serv: Entered as Ensign, Navy, 43, released as Lt(jg), 46, after serv in USS Calvert Pac Theatre, 43-46. Mailing Add: Ouagadougou-Dept of State Washington DC 20520

GRAHAM, PRECIOUS JEWEL (D)
b Springfield, Ohio, May 3, 25; d Robert Lee Freeman & Lulubelle Malone F; m 1953 to Paul Nathaniel Graham; c Robert & Nathan. Educ: Fisk Univ, BA, 46; Howard Univ, 46-47; Case Western Reserve Univ, MSSA, 53; Alpha Kappa Alpha. Polit & Govt Pos: Mem & secy, Human Rels Comn, Yellow Springs, Ohio, 63-67; deleg, Dem Nat Conv, 72. Bus & Prof Pos: Teen-age prog dir, YWCA, Grand Rapids, Mich, 47-50; metrop coordr teen-age prog, YWCA, Detroit, 53-56; social worker, 56-69; dir, Antioch Col Prog Interracial Educ, Yellow Springs, Ohio, 64-69, dir social work prog, 69-, assoc dean, 72-73. Mem: Nat Asn Social Workers; Asn Black Social Workers; YWCA (nat bd, 70-76); Women's Polit Caucus. Honors & Awards: Opportunity Fel, John Hay Whitney Found, 46; Danforth Found fel, 72. Relig: Unitarian. Mailing Add: 1475 Corry St Yellow Springs OH 45387

GRAHAM, ROBERT VINCENT (D)
State Auditor, Wash
b Pacific City, Wash, Apr 12, 21; s Ralph Vincent Graham & Hazel M Smith G; m 1945 to Lloydine C Ryan; c Randall V, Susan L, Paul R, James M & Richard S. Educ: Grays Harbor Col. Polit & Govt Pos: Examr, Budget Dept, Wash, 47-48; chief examr, Auditors Munic Div, Wash, 48-59, Dep State Auditor, 59-64, Asst State Auditor, 64-65, State Auditor, 65- Mil Serv: Entered as Pvt, Air Force, 42, released as T/Sgt, 46, after serv in Air Transport

Command; Good Conduct Medal; Victory Medal; Am & Asiatic-Pac Theater Ribbons. Mem: Nat Asn State Auditors, Controllers & Treasurers; Munic Finance Officers of US & Can; UGN (bd mem). Relig: Presbyterian; elder. Legal Res: 4600 Boulevard Rd Olympia WA 98501 Mailing Add: Legislative Bldg Olympia WA 98502

GRAHAM, WILLARD WOODROW (D)
Chmn, Wayne Co Dem Comt, Mo
b Clubb, Mo, Dec 11, 12; s William Monroe Graham & Elizabeth Durr G; m 1957 to Madalyne Armstrong Hollida; c Carrie Elizabeth (Mrs William G Beckett), Imogene (Mrs James R Roach), B G Hollida, Judith (Mrs Lavern Daves) & R Dan Hollida. Polit & Govt Pos: Committeeman, Cowan Twp Rep Party, Mo, 40-56; chmn, Wayne Co Dem Comt, 56- Bus & Prof Pos: Farmer, 28-69; saw mill operator, 38-56; operator grocery, 57-60; egg inspector, State Dept Agr, Mo, 60- Mem: AF&AM; Scottish Rite. Relig: Missionary Baptist. Mailing Add: Clubb MO 63934

GRAHAM, WILLIAM CLYDE (R)
Chmn, Third Cong Dist Rep Cent Comt, Colo
b Pueblo, Colo, June 18, 48; s William Christopher Graham & Clarice R Smith G; single. Educ: Univ Colo, BA, 71; Pi Sigma Alpha; Student Senate; Assoc Students of Univ Colo. Polit & Govt Pos: Vpres, Univ Rep, 68-70; research dir, Colo Rep State Cent Comt, 70-72; mem, Colo State Platform Drafting Comt, 72; chmn, Third Cong Dist Rep Cent Comt, 73-; mem state bd educ, Colo Third Cong Dist, 73- Relig: Methodist. Mailing Add: PO Box 68 Beulah CO 81023

GRAHAM, WILLIAM THOMAS (R)
Chmn, Forsyth Co Rep Party, NC
b Waynesboro, Va, Oct 24, 33; s James Monroe Graham & Margaret Virginia Goodwin G; m 1958 to Nancy Kent Hill; c William Thomas, Jr & Ashton Cannon. Educ: Duke Univ, AB, 56; Univ Hawaii, 58; Wake Forest Col, 61; Univ Va, LLB, 62; Beta Theta Pi; Phi Alpha Delta. Polit & Govt Pos: Deleg, NC Rep State Conv, 64-73, NC Fifth Cong Dist Rep Conv, 66-73 & Forsyth Co Rep Conv, 64-73; mem exec comt, Forsyth Co Rep Party, 64-69 & 73-, chmn, 66-69 & 73, gen counsel, 72-73; mem, Forsyth Co Bd Elec, 64-66; alt deleg, Rep Nat Conv, 68; asst gen counsel, Dept Housing & Urban Develop, Washington, DC, 69-70; Rep cand for mayor, Winston-Salem, NC, 70; metrop coordr, Holshouser for Gov Comt, 72; mem, NC Comt to Reelect the President, Forsyth Co co-chmn, 72; gen counsel, NC Young Rep, 73-74. Bus & Prof Pos: Assoc, Craige, Brawley, Lucas & Horton, 62-65, partner, Craige, Brawley, Horton & Graham, 65-69; partner, Billings & Graham, 71- Mil Serv: Entered as Pvt, Army, 57, released as Pfc, 58, after serv on staff of the Judge Adv, Hq, Army Security Agency, Pac, in Tokyo, Japan & Helemano, Hawaii. Mem: Am Bar Asn; Va & NC State Bars; Twin City Club; Old Town Club. Honors & Awards: Sr Party Award, NC Young Rep Conv, 71. Relig: Methodist. Legal Res: 1000 Arbor Rd Winston-Salem NC 27104 Mailing Add: 2324 Wachovia Bldg Winston-Salem NC 27101

GRAIG, A H (GUS) (D)
Fla State Rep
Mailing Add: Rte 1 Box 85-F Crescent Beach St Augustine FL 32084

GRAINGER, LEROY CECIL (R)
b Conway, SC, Jan 23, 32; s Joseph LeRoy Grainger & Ruth Graham G; m 1957 to Sarah Elizabeth Graham; c Gavin Glen & Garon Gil. Educ: Clemson Col, BS, 58. Polit & Govt Pos: Chmn, Horry Co Rep Party, SC, 68-73; vchmn, Sixth Dist Rep Party, 73- Bus & Prof Pos: Off clerk & budget dept mgr, Firestone Tire & Rubber Co, Macon, Ga, 58-59, off & credit mgr, Columbus, 59-60, store mgr, Staunton, Va, 60-61; co-owner, vpres & treas, G-H Finance Co, Inc, Conway, SC, 61-68; co-owner, vpres & treas, G-H Ins Agency, Inc, 62-; vpres, Way-Con Investment, Inc, 64-72, pres, 72; vpres & treas, Gee-Paw Corp, 71; builder & broker, G-H Develop & Realty, Inc, 73. Mil Serv: Entered as Pvt, Army, 54, released as Cpl, 56, after serv in 9th Corp Artil, Far East, Korea, Japan, 54-56. Mem: Conway CofC; Mason; Shrine; Kiwanis; Conway Jaycees. Honors & Awards: Jaycee Spoke of Year, Jaycee Spark Plug; Outstanding Nat Dir, SC Jaycees; Outstanding Young Man of Am; Int Leadership Award, Dale Carnegie Alumni Asn. Relig: Baptist; deacon & dir Sunday Sch, North Conway Baptist Church. Mailing Add: 488 Hwy 905 Conway SC 29526

GRALIKE, DONALD J (D)
Mo State Sen
b St Louis Co, Mo, Oct 22, 29; m 1954 to Rita J Simeone; c Donald, David & twins Dennis & Daniel. Educ: Wash Univ. Polit & Govt Pos: Mem, United Young Dem; mem, Regular Legis Dem Club; Mo State Rep, 62-72, majority whip, Mo House Rep, formerly; Mo State Sen, 72- Bus & Prof Pos: Instr, O'Fallen Tech High Sch, 56-60; bus rep, Inst Brotherhood of Elec Workers, 60-62; Sachs Elec Contractors. Mil Serv: Army, 52-54; 185th Eng Combat Battery. Mem: Am Legion. Relig: Catholic. Mailing Add: 648 Buckley Rd St Louis MO 63125

GRAM, LAURENCE CARTER, JR (D)
b Milwaukee, Wis, Feb 17, 32; s Laurence Carter Gram, Sr & Isabel Feistl G; m 1951 to Elizabeth Ann Newell; c Mary Jane, Barbara Jean, Laurence Michael & Nancy Sue. Educ: Univ Wis, BS, 54, JD, 56; Phi Kappa Phi; Alpha Chi Rho; Phi Delta Phi. Polit & Govt Pos: Chmn, West Allis Dem Party, Wis, 57-61 & 63-64; chmn, Fourth Cong Dist Dem Party, 61-63; mem, State Admin Comt, Dem Party, 61-63 & 68-; court comnr, Milwaukee Co, 62-67; exec dir, Milwaukee Co Dem Party, 67-68, chmn, formerly; mem, Urban Renewal & Capital Improv Comts, West Allis, Wis, 67- Bus & Prof Pos: Attorney, private practice, 56-; vpres, Gram & Co, 58- Mem: State Bar Wis; West Allis CofC; South West Allis Advan Asn; Jaycees; KofC. Relig: Catholic. Legal Res: 2330 S 56th St West Allis WI 53219 Mailing Add: 7900 W National Ave West Allis WI 53214

GRAMLING, DAVID KARL (D)
NH State Rep
b Williamsport, Pa, Dec 5, 44; s Karl Eugene Gramling & Mary Welteroth G; m 1972 to Beth Carol Burdick. Educ: Villanova Univ, BA, 67; Univ Ill, Champaign-Urbana, MA, 73. Polit & Govt Pos: Social comt chmn, Nashua Dem Comt, NH, 73-, pres cand reception comt, 74-; NH State Rep, 75- Bus & Prof Pos: Teacher, Austin Prep Sch, Reading, Mass, 67-, chmn social studies dept, 71-; part-time instr econ, New Eng Aeronaut Inst/Daniel Webster Jr Col, Nashua, NH, 75- Mem: Am Fedn Teachers (pres, 72-); Nat Coun for Social Studies; Joint Coun Econ Educ; Quill & Scroll. Mailing Add: 7 Coleridge Rd Nashua NH 03060

GRAMMES, LLOYD EDGAR (R)
City Councilman, Allentown, Pa
b Allentown, Pa, Aug 9, 03; s George P Grammes & Jennie A Wieder G; m 1965 to Florence A Bartholomew; c Roberta J (Mrs Daubenspeck). Educ: Allentown High Sch; LaSalle Exten Univ. Polit & Govt Pos: Alderman, Pa Magistrates Asn, 35-; dir city coun, Allentown, Pa, 49-, councilman, 56- Bus & Prof Pos: Weighmaster, US Steel Corp, 24-27; acct, Mack Trucks, Inc, 27-30, acct, dry cleaners, 30-34. Mem: Odd Fellows; Elks; Fraternal Order of Police; Boys Club of Am; Magistrates Asn. Honors & Awards: Nat Merit Award, Amvets. Relig: Protestant. Mailing Add: 836 N 29th St Allentown PA 18104

GRAMS, WILLIAM LANE (R)
SDak State Sen
b Sturgis, SDak, Apr 5, 12; s Harry William Grams & Edna May Lane G; m 1941 to Geraldine Ethlyn Cooper; c William Henry & Robert Dale. Educ: Sturgis Pub High Sch, grad, 30. Polit & Govt Pos: Treas, Meade Co, SDak, 48-50, comnr, 50-62; SDak State Sen, Dist 21, 66-, mem, Appropriations Comt, SDak State Senate, 67-, mem exec comt, Legis Res Coun, 73- Bus & Prof Pos: Owner & mgr, H Gram & Sons Sawmill, 55- Mil Serv: Entered as Pvt, Army, 42, released as Maj, 46, after serv in Transportation Corps, China-Burma-India Command, 43-46. Mem: Am Legion; VFW; Mason; Shrine; Eastern Star. Relig: Presbyterian. Mailing Add: 848 LaZelle St Sturgis SD 57785

GRANADOS, JOSE (NEW PROGRESSIVE, PR)
Rep, PR House of Rep
b Santurce, PR, Feb 1, 46; s Antonio Granados & Belen Navedo G; m 1971 to Alba Iris Rivera. Educ: Univ PR, 64-69; pres, Gen Studies Student Coun, 65. Polit & Govt Pos: Pres, Univ Students for Statehood, 65-66; pres, PR Statehood Youth, 67-68; chmn, PR Young Rep, 67-68; secy gen, Progressive Action, 69-71; pres, New Progressive Party Youth, 71-; mem exec comt, New Progressive Party, 71-; pres & publ, Decision, 71-72; Rep, PR House Rep, 73- Bus & Prof Pos: Coordr commun orgn, City of San Juan, PR, 69-72. Publ: Auth, Statehood: an alternative to the Puerto Rican status problem, Ed Decision, 73; Fraud in drugs, Advance Mag, 3/73. Mem: Consumers Union. Relig: Roman Catholic. Legal Res: 492 Teruel St Villa Granada Rio Piedras PR 00923 Mailing Add: PO Box 4708 San Juan PR 00905

GRANAI, EDWIN CARPENTER (D)
Vt State Rep
b Barre, Vt, Aug 16, 31; s Cornelius O Granai & Ruth Carpenter G; m 1954 to Joanne Dawson; c Janet, Judith & Matthew. Educ: Antioch Col, Yellow Springs, Ohio, BA, 54; Yale Univ, MDiv, 74. Polit & Govt Pos: Vt State Rep, 75- Bus & Prof Pos: Mgt, Procter & Gamble Co, Cincinnati, Ohio, 57-69; owner-pres, Little Prof Book Ctr Vt, 69-; owner-operator, Lake Champlain Sail Charter, 74- Mem: Lake Champlain CofC; Vt Med Ctr. Relig: Presbyterian. Mailing Add: 106 Killarney Dr Burlington VT 05401

GRANATA, PETER CHARLES (R)
b Chicago, Ill, Oct 28, 98; s Frank Granata & Rose Cairo G; m 1944 to Johanna Wollner; c Peter C, Jr & Paul F. Educ: Pub & bus schs. Polit & Govt Pos: Rep committeeman, First Ward, 18 years; chief dep coroner, Cook Co, 25-28; chief clerk, Prosecuting Attorney, Chicago, 28-30; US Rep, Ill, 30; Ill State Rep, until 74; deleg, Rep Nat Conv, 68; vchmn, Ill Rep State Cent Comt, until 74. Relig: Roman Catholic. Legal Res: 1025 S May St Chicago IL 60607 Mailing Add: 1129 W Taylor St Chicago IL 60607

GRANDE, ANDREW R (D)
Conn State Rep
Mailing Add: 518 Lake Ave Bristol CT 06010

GRANDE, WILLIAM G (D)
RI State Rep
Mailing Add: 270 Mount Pleasant Ave Providence RI 02908

GRANGE, RUSSELL DEAN (R)
Mayor, Provo, Utah
b Huntington, Utah, Aug 14, 21; s Wallace Guy Grange & Vernessa Tullis G; m 1947 to Helen Fullmer; c Mayrene (Mrs Romney M Stewart), Russell Dean, II, Kelly Fullmer & Karen. Educ: Brigham Young Univ, degree in acct & bus admin, 46; Alpha Kappa Psi. Polit & Govt Pos: Mem, Gov Adv Coun, Utah, 72-; comnr, Provo-Jordan Parkway Authority, 72-; mem exec coun, Mountainlands Asn Govts, 72-; comnr, Provo, Utah, 72-73, mayor, 74- Mil Serv: Entered as Pvt, Army Air Force, 42, released as Pilot, 45, after serv in Pac. Relig: Latter-day Saint. Mailing Add: 1020 N 1200 East Provo UT 84601

GRANGER, GUY RICHARD, JR (R)
NH State Rep
b Nashua, NH, July 12, 47; s Guy Richard Granger, Sr & Nellie Urban G; single. Educ: Keene State Col, BA, 70. Polit & Govt Pos: NH State Rep, 75- Mil Serv: Entered as Pvt, Army, 69, released as Sgt, 72, after serv in 90th Replacement Bn, Vietnam, 70-72; Bronze Star. Mem: VFW; Post 8641. Relig: Roman Catholic. Mailing Add: Naticook Rd Merrimack NH 03054

GRANGER, HERBERT CURRY (D)
SC State Rep
b Greenville, SC, May 25, 23; s James H Granger & Lula Myers G; m 1945 to Vera Taylor; c Ronald L & Russell C. Educ: Okla State Teachers Col. Polit & Govt Pos: SC State Rep, 59- Bus & Prof Pos: Textiles, J P Stevens, Inc. Mil Serv: Air Force, 42-45; 8th Air Force, 548th Bomb Sq, 385th Bomb Group, ETO. Mem: Carolina High Sch Booster's Club (treas); W Gantt High Sch (former trustee); Mason; Am Legion. Honors & Awards: Pres Sr Class West Gantt High Sch; Citizenship Award, High Sch. Relig: Baptist; gen supt Sunday sch, West Gantt Baptist Church, past chmn bd of deacons, former pres Brotherhood. Mailing Add: 316 Westcliffe Way Greenville SC 29611

GRANNELL, WILLIAM NEWTON (D)
Ore State Rep
b Denver, Colo, Jan 6, 38; s Clarence Edward Grannell & Margaret Ann Dillon G; m 1960 to Marilyn Elizabeth Adams; c William Newton, II. Educ: Univ Denver, BA, 60, teachers cert, 61, 61-62; Beta Theta Phi; Phi Delta Kappa. Polit & Govt Pos: Chmn, Coos Co Dem Party, Ore, 68-; bd mem, Demoforum, 68-; mem, Ore State Dem Cent Comt, 68-, mem, Comn Deleg Selection & Party Reform, 69; research dir, Ore Dem Party, 69; state chmn, Citizens Opposing Sales Tax, 69; vchmn, Fourth Dist Dem, 70-; bd mem, Coos Co CPL of CAP, 71-; Ore State Rep, 57th Dist, 72-, mem, State & Fed Affairs, Transportation & Labor & Indust Comts, Ore House Rep, 72- Bus & Prof Pos: Teacher, Jefferson Co Schs, Lakewood,

Colo, 62-64, Reedsport Pub Schs, Ore, 64-65 & North Bend Jr High Sch, formerly; Uniserv dir, Ore Educ Asn, 71- Mem: Coastal Acres Inc (pres, 66-); North Bend Consultation Comt; North Bend Educ Asn (co-chmn, econ comt, 70-71); Uniserv Dirs Asn (chmn, 71-72); AF&AM. Honors & Awards: Outstanding Co Chmn, 69. Relig: Presbyterian. Legal Res: 438 Northwood Rd North Bend OR 97459 Mailing Add: Ore State Capitol Bldg Salem OR 97301

GRANNIS, ALEXANDER BANKS (D)
NY State Assemblyman
b Chicago, Ill, Jan 6, 42; s Uri B Grannis & Margorie Banks G; m 1971 to Ainslie Dinwiddie; c Wilcox Snellings. Educ: Rutgers Univ, BA in Econ, 64; Univ Va Law Sch, LLB, 67; Pi Delta Epsilon; Delta Phi. Polit & Govt Pos: Compliance counsel & spec asst to comnr, NY State Dept of Environ Conserv, 70-72; NY State Assemblyman, 68th Dist, 74- Bus & Prof Pos: Mem staff, Parker, Duryee, Zunino, Malone & Carter, New York, NY, 67-70 & Berle, Butzel & Kass, 72-74. Mem: Environ Action Coalition (founder & bd mem, 70-); Coun Environ (gen counsel & mem exec comt, 73-); City Club New York City (mem housing comt, 74-); Yorkville Alliance Block Asns (bd mem, 74-). Legal Res: 501 E 87th St New York NY 10028 Mailing Add: 309 E 85th St New York NY 10028

GRANT, BEN Z (D)
Tex State Rep
b DeRidder, La, Oct 25, 39; s Joseph H Grant & Beatrice Smith G; single. Educ: Panola Jr Col, Carthage, Tex, AA, 59; Northwestern State Univ, BA, 61; Univ Tex, Austin, JD, 68. Polit & Govt Pos: Tex State Rep, 71-, chmn judiciary comt, Tex House Rep, currently. Relig: Church of Christ. Legal Res: PO Box 299 Marshall TX 75670 Mailing Add: PO Box 2910 Austin TX 78767

GRANT, CECIL GREENE (R)
Mem Exec Comt, DC Rep Comt
b Bakersfield, Calif, Feb 20, 22; d Ernest Harry Greene & Minnie M G; m 1953 to Howard Sylvester Grant, Jr; c Jeffrey A Grant & Stephen Clifford Wallace. Educ: Howard Univ, 45; Miner Teachers Col, BS, 47; NY Univ, 52; Phi Sigma Phi. Polit & Govt Pos: Mem exec comt, DC Rep Comt, 72-; mem steering comt, Nat Black Rep Coun, 73-; mem, Nat Comn Observance World Pop, 74-75. Bus & Prof Pos: Secy, Colour Graphics, Inc, 72-75; mem bd dirs, Capital Head Start, 73-75; mem bd dirs, Washington Black Econ Union Develop Co, 73-75. Mem: Sen Hugh Scott Nat Scholar Found (exec bd). Relig: Baptist. Mailing Add: 1820 Shepherd St NE Washington DC 20018

GRANT, DAVID MARSHALL (D)
Dir Legis Research, St Louis Bd Aldermen, Mo
b St Louis, Mo, Jan 1, 03; s William Samuel Grant & Elizabeth Margaret Holliday G; m 1944 to Mildred Hughes; c David Wesley & Gail Milissa. Educ: Univ Mich; Howard Univ Sch Law, LLB, 30; Omega Psi Phi. Polit & Govt Pos: Asst city counr, St Louis, Mo, 33-40, asst circuit attorney, 40-42, mem bd of freeholders, 56-57; dir legis research, St Louis Bd Aldermen, 57-; mem state adv comt, US Comn on Civil Rights, 61-; US deleg, Freedom Celebration, Kampala, EAfrica, 62. Bus & Prof Pos: Practicing attorney, 30- Mem: NAACP; Nat Asn Criminal Defense Lawyers; Lawyers Asn; Bar Asn of St Louis; Mound City Bar Asn. Relig: Episcopal. Mailing Add: 3309 Arsenal St St Louis MO 63118

GRANT, GARY S (D)
Wash State Sen
b Chippewa Falls, Wis, Sept 18, 34; s Merrill E Grant & Kathryn T Lutgen G; m 1960 to Tanya C Olson; c Stephen, Leah, Daniel & Jennifer. Educ: St Martin's Col, BA, 56; Pi Kappa Delta. Polit & Govt Pos: Wash State Rep, formerly; Wash State Sen, 73- Bus & Prof Pos: Pres, Pub Serv Employees Union, 71-73. Relig: Catholic. Mailing Add: 25823 132nd St SE Kent WA 98031

GRANT, GEORGE HENRY (D)
Exec Committeeman, SC State Dem Party
b Ware Shoals, SC, Oct 4, 17; s John A Grant & Pearl Elizabeth Schumpert G; m 1956 to Louise Foust; c George H, Jr & Kelli Reed. Educ: Wofford Col, 46-49; Univ SC, JD, 52; Lambda Chi Alpha; Phi Delta Phi; Omicron Delta Kappa. Polit & Govt Pos: Chmn, Aiken Co Dem Party, SC, 66-68; exec committeeman, SC State Dem Party, 68-; SC State Rep, 69-70. Mil Serv: Entered as Seaman 2/C, Navy, 42, released as PO 1/C, 46, after serv in Navy Med Corps, Pac Theatre, SPac, Tenth Army, 42-46; Good Conduct, Pac Theatre & Am Oper Medals; Distinguished Serv with Combat Device. Mem: Am Trial Lawyers Asn; Am Judicature Soc; Elks; VFW; Am Legion. Relig: Baptist. Legal Res: 111 Gregg Ave Aiken SC 29801 Mailing Add: Box 328 Aiken SC 29801

GRANT, MAYNOR CAMP (D)
Chmn, Floyd Co Dem Exec Comt, Ga
b Rome, Ga, Sept 16, 18; d Fred Elbert Camp & Maynor Ware C; m 1951 to Thomas Hunter Grant, wid; c Maynor Elaine. Educ: Rome High Sch, Ga, grad, 35. Polit & Govt Pos: Chmn, Floyd Co Dem Exec Comt, Ga, 70- Bus & Prof Pos: Treas, J L Todd Auction Co, Rome, Ga, currently. Mem: Rome Bus & Prof Women (pres, 75-); Quota Club; Floyd Co League Dem Women (secy, 75-); State Dem Charter Comn for Dem Party Ga (mem drafting comt, 75-). Legal Res: 4 Westlyn Dr Rome GA 30161 Mailing Add: PO Box 783 Rome GA 30161

GRANT, PHILIP R (BOB) JR (R)
NMex State Rep
Mailing Add: 9720-D Candelaria Rd NE Albuquerque NM 87112

GRANT, ROBERT WILLIAMS, JR (R)
b Saginaw, Mich, July 4, 15; s Robert W Grant & Lucile Brewer G; m 1938 to Patricia Lord; c Robert L, James M & Carolyn. Educ: Northwestern Univ, BS in Com, 37; Lynx; Beta Theta Pi. Hon Degrees: Bus Admin, Saginaw Bus Inst, 63. Polit & Govt Pos: Mem, Police-Fireman Civil Serv Comn, Saginaw, Mich, 44-50; mem bd educ, Saginaw, 50-62; chmn, Saginaw Co Rep Party, formerly; alt deleg, Rep Nat Conv, 68. Bus & Prof Pos: Pres, Grant Grocer Co, Saginaw, 37-; pres, Brewer Co, 38-; dir, Cent Warehouse Co, 40-; dir, Saginaw Properties, 45-; pres, Washington Ave Co, 50-; dir, Brewer Neinstedt Lumber Co, Palmetto, La, 57-; pres, Golden Triangle Cold Storage Co, Saginaw, 59-; dir, Mich Nat Bank, 63-; dir, Midland Terminal Warehouse Co, 64- Mem: Nat Frozen Food Asn; Nat Asn Wholesalers; Saginaw Club; Kiwanis; United Commercial Travelers. Relig: Congregational. Legal Res: 429 Ardussi Ave Saginaw MI 48602 Mailing Add: 2700 Perkins St Saginaw MI 48605

GRANT, WILLIAM (D)
b Estes Park, Colo, Aug 29, 10; s William West Grant & Gertrude Hendrie G; m 1938 to Helen Prindle. Educ: Dartmouth Col, AB, 31; Harvard Law Sch, BL, 38; Phi Beta Kappa. Polit & Govt Pos: Chmn, Colo Dem State Cent Comt, until 69; deleg, Dem Nat Conv, 64 & 68. Bus & Prof Pos: Chmn bd, Metrop TV Co, Colo. Mil Serv: Entered as Lt(jg), Naval Res, 42, released as Lt Comdr, 46, after serv in Pac; Bronze Star. Mem: Colo & Am Bar Asns. Relig: Episcopal. Mailing Add: 101 S Humboldt St Denver CO 80209

GRANTHAM, DON ANTHONY (D)
b Augusta, Ga, Dec 26, 38; s Elijah M Grantham (deceased) & Loucile Carson G (deceased); m 1962 to Carol Willcox; c Zoe Elizabeth & Don Anthony, Jr. Educ: Furman Univ, 56-58; Univ Ga, BBA, 62; Kappa Alpha. Polit & Govt Pos: Richmond Co campaign chmn, Carter for Gov, 70; mem, Ga State Dem Exec Comt, formerly. Bus & Prof Pos: Vpres, Forest Sales Corp, Augusta, Ga, 69- Mil Serv: Entered as Pvt, Air Nat Guard, 61, released as Airman 2/C, 67. Mem: Augusta Country Club; Elks; Univ Ga Alumni Asn; Ga Bulldog Club of Augusta. Relig: Methodist; bd mem, Aldersgate Methodist Church, Augusta. Mailing Add: 744 McClure Dr Augusta GA 30904

GRANTHAM, ROY EMERY (D)
Okla State Sen
b Fairfax, Okla, Jan 26, 07; s Amos Dean Grantham & Flora Lillian McCarty G; m 1933 to Martha Elizabeth Young; c Marcia Lea (Mrs Moore) & Linda Roy (Mrs McNew). Educ: Univ Okla, AB, 34, LLB, 34; EdM, 38; Phi Delta Phi; Univ Okla Debate Team. Polit & Govt Pos: Co attorney, Kay Co, Okla, 41-42; Okla State Sen, Dist 20, 50-, secy, State Sen Dem Caucus, 54, presiding officer, Okla State Senate, sitting as Court of Impeachment, 65, chmn, Comt on Committees & Rules, 65 & Judiciary Comt, 69-; deleg all Dem Convs, 72; alt deleg, Dem Nat Conv, 68. Bus & Prof Pos: Gen practice of law, 47- Mil Serv: Entered as 1st Lt, Army, 42, released as Lt Col, 47, after serv in 78th Div & US Army of Occup, ETO, 45-47; Commendation Ribbon for Outstanding Serv in Judge Adv Sect Hq, Berlin Command; Lt Col, Army Res, 47- Publ: Introduction to symposium on commercial code, Okla Law Rev, 8/62. Mem: Am Bar Asn; Okla Bar Asn (chmn, Comt Admin Justice, 72-); Order of the Coif; CofC; Mason (32 degree). Relig: Christian Church NAm. Mailing Add: 325 S 12th St Ponca City OK 74601

GRASSER, THOMAS W (D)
Conn State Rep
Mailing Add: 174 E Main St Wallingford CT 06492

GRASSIE, CHARLES WESLEY, JR (D)
NH State Rep
b Rochester, NH, Sept 6, 52; s Charles Wesley Grassie, Sr & Geraldine Drapeau G; single. Educ: Univ NH, grad, 75. Polit & Govt Pos: Chmn, Rochester Dem City Comt, NH, currently; Nat Committeeman, NH Young Dem, currently; NH State Rep, 75- Relig: Catholic. Mailing Add: 29 King St Rochester NH 03867

GRASSLEY, CHARLES E (R)
US Rep, Iowa
b New Hartford, Iowa, Sept 17, 33; m to Barbara Ann Spiecher; c Lee, Wendy, Robin Lynn, Michelle Marie & Jay Charles. Educ: State Col Iowa, BA, 55, MA, 56; Univ Iowa, work toward PhD. Polit & Govt Pos: Iowa State Rep, until 74; US Rep, Iowa, 75- Bus & Prof Pos: Farmer; instr polit sci, Drake Community Col, 62; instr polit sci, Charles City Col, 67-68. Mem: Farm Bur; State & Co Hist Socs; Pi Gamma Mu; Kappa Delta Pi; Mason; Eastern Star. Relig: Baptist. Legal Res: RFD 1 New Hartford IA 50660 Mailing Add: US House of Rep Washington DC 20515

GRASSO, ELLA TAMBUSSI (D)
Gov, Conn
b Windsor Locks, Conn, May 10, 19; d James Tambussi (deceased) & Maria Oliva T (deceased); m 1942 to Dr Thomas A Grasso; c Susane & James. Educ: Mt Holyoke Col, BA magna cum laude, 40, MA, 42; Phi Beta Kappa. Hon Degrees: LLD, Mt Holyoke Col & Sacred Heart Univ. Polit & Govt Pos: Asst dir research, War Manpower Comn of Conn World War II; Conn State Rep, 53-57, floor leader, Conn State House of Rep, 55; mem, Long Lane Farm Study Comn & Hwy Finance Adv Comn; chmn, Dem State Platform Comt, 56-; Secy of State, Conn, 59-71; deleg, Dem Nat Conv, 60, 64 & 68, mem, Platform Drafting Comt, 60, co-chmn, Resolutions Comt, 64 & 68; mem, Bd of Foreign Scholar, 61-66; chmn, Comn to Prepare for Const Conv; deleg & Dem floor leader, Conn State Const Conv, 65; chmn planning comt, Gov Comn on Status of Women; vchmn exec comt, Human Rights & Opportunities, 67; US Rep, Sixth Cong Dist, Conn, 71-74; deleg, Dem Nat Mid-Term Conf, 74; Gov, Conn, 75-; mem bd of dirs, Proj Cause, Off Ment Retardation, State Dept Health. Publ: Canal fever, Hartford Courant, 5/69. Mem: Conn Col (bd of trustees); Am Comt on Italian Migration (adv bd, Hartford Chap); Windsor Locks Pub Libr (bd of dirs); Comt of 100, Univ of Hartford Libr (bd); hon mem Urban League of Gtr Hartford (bd dirs). Honors & Awards: Merit Award, Dept Conn, Ital Am War Vet of US; Woman of the Year, Gtr Hartford Chap & New Britain Chap of Am Comt on Ital Migration; Outstanding Serv Award, Conn Cystic Fibrosis Asn; Citation for work on Cooley's Anemia, Grand Lodge of Conn, Order of Sons of Italy; Leadership Citation, Loomis Inst. Relig: Catholic; Elected mem of church coun, St Mary's Church, Windsor Locks. Legal Res: 13 Olive St Windsor Locks CT 06096 Mailing Add: State Capitol 210 Capitol Ave Hartford CT 06115

GRASSO, SALVATORE P (R)
NH State Rep
Mailing Add: 32 Elm St Milford NH 03055

GRAUBART, JUDAH LEON (D)
b Chicago, Ill, May 6, 45; s David Graubart & Eunice Morris G; m 1968 to Alice Diane Vision. Educ: Wright Jr Col, Chicago, 63-63; Univ Ill, BA, 67; Northeastern Ill Univ, MA; Phi Theta Kappa. Polit & Govt Pos: Campaign coordr, 11th Cong Dist Independent Dem, Ill, 68; mem exec bd, Independent Dem Coalition Ill, New Dem Coalition, 69-71; deleg, Ill Dem State Conv, 70; mem exec bd, Independent Voters of Ill, 71-72, alt mem bd dirs, Am for Dem Action, 71-72; deleg, Dem Nat Conv, 72. Bus & Prof Pos: Asst dir, Am Jewish Comt, 68-75; rabbi, Congregation B'nai David, Chicago, 73-75. Publ: Soviet Jews and Christians-different agendas & ecumenical strategies, Christian Century Mag, 2/72; The night of the murdered poets, Reconstructionist, 9/73; Escaping their fate: the historiography of the holocaust, Midstream, 73. Mem: Asn Jewish Community Rels Workers; Nat Asn Jewish Communal Serv; Nat Asn Jewish Rights Workers; Chicago Conf on Relig & Race (exec bd,

73); Ill Comt for Pub Educ & Relig Liberty (exec bd, 72-73). Relig: Jewish. Mailing Add: 314 Dover Lane Des Plaines IL 60018

GRAVEL, CAMILLE F, JR (D)
b Alexandria, La, Aug 10, 15; s Camille F Gravel, Sr & Aline Delvaille G; m 1939 to Katherine Yvonne David; c Katherine Ann (Mrs Stephen J Vanderslice), Mary Eileen (Mrs Richard B Cappell), Martha Louise (Mrs Thomas A Antoon), Camille F, III, Grady David, Eunice Holloman (Mrs Joseph A Mitchell), Virginia Maureen (Mrs Charles Larry Carbo, Jr), Margaret Lynn, Mark Alan & Charles Gregory; 12 grandchildren. Educ: Univ Notre Dame, 31-35; La State Univ, 35-37; Cath Univ Am, 37-39; Kappa Sigma. Polit & Govt Pos: Mem, US Capitol Police Force, 37-39; asst dist attorney, Rapides Parish, La, 42, attorney for inheritance tax collector, 43-45; asst city attorney, Alexandria, 46-48; attorney, La Tax Comn, 48-52; mem, La Dem State Cent Comt, 48-64; Stevenson-Sparkman presidential elector, 52; Dem Nat Committeeman, La, 54-60, rep of 12 southern states, Exec Comt, Dem Nat Comt, 55-60; deleg, Dem Nat Conv, 56, 60, 64 & 72, chmn, La Deleg, 56, chmn, Site Selection Comt, co-chmn, Credentials Comt & mem, Arrangements Comt, 60; mem, Nat Adv Coun, Dem Party, 56-60; co-chmn, La Lawyers for Johnson-Humphrey, Presidential Campaign, 64; app mem by President Johnson, Nat Citizen's Comt for Community Rels, 64-68; mem, Gov Adv Comn on La Workmen's Compensation Laws & Tax Laws of La, 64-65; mem, Nat Adv Bd Community Rels, 65-67; Spec Counsel Medicare to Gov, La, 66-67, Gov Spec Counsel on Health, 67; mem, State La Inter-Dept Health Policy Comn, 67-68; gen counsel, State La Labor Mgt Comn of Inquiry, 67; Spec Legis Counsel to Gov, La, 72; mem, La Bd of Tax Appeals, 72-; app deleg to La Const Conv, 73. Bus & Prof Pos: Sr partner, Gravel, Roy & Burnes, currently. Mem: Am Bar Asn; Am Judicature Soc; Am Trial Lawyers Asn; Int Acad of Trial Lawyers; Notre Dame Law Asn. Honors & Awards: Invested Knight of St Gregory, Pope Pius XII, 54; Outstanding Achievement in Field of Politics, Cath Univ Am, 62. Relig: Catholic. Legal Res: 3214 Carol Ct Alexandria LA 71301 Mailing Add: PO Box 1792 711 Washington St Alexandria LA 71301

GRAVEL, MIKE (D)
US Sen, Alaska
b Springfield, Mass, May 13, 30; s Alphonse Gravel & Maria Bourassa G; m 1959 to Rita Jeannette Martin; c Martin Anthony & Lynne Denise. Educ: Assumption Prep Sch, Worcester, Mass, 4 years; Assumption Col, Worcester, 1 year; Am Int Col, Springfield, 1 year; Columbia Univ, BS Econ. Polit & Govt Pos: Alaska State Rep, until 66, speaker, Alaska House of Rep, 65-66; US Sen, Alaska, 69-, mem, Finance Comt & Pub Works Comt & chmn, Subcomt on Water Resources, US Senate, currently, mem joint comt on cong opers & chmn subcomt energy, currently. Mil Serv: Entered Army, 51, released as 2nd Lt, 54. Publ: Citizen Power, 72. Relig: Unitarian. Legal Res: PO Box 2283 Anchorage AK 99510 Mailing Add: 3315 New Senate Off Bldg Washington DC 20510

GRAVELLE, GENE R (D)
NH State Rep
b Hartford, Conn, May 2, 42; s Sylvio T Gravelle & Cecile M Lavoie G; m 1966 to Lucille R Trudeau; c Nadine C, Gene R K, Raymond G & Justine J. Polit & Govt Pos: NH State Rep, 75-, mem comt banks & ins, NH House Rep, 75- Bus & Prof Pos: Ins underwriter, Latvis Ins Agency, 75- Mil Serv: Entered as E-1, Navy, 59, serv in USS Newport News; E-6, Naval Res, 59- Mem: KofC. Relig: Catholic. Mailing Add: 35 Ferry St Hudson NH 03051

GRAVES, G EUGENE (R)
b Gossett, Ill, Oct 18, 14; s Charles Alexander Graves & Minnie Jane Bruce G; m 1946 to Catherine Lucille Sturgill; c Carolyn Jean (Mrs Keebler). Educ: High sch, 4 years. Polit & Govt Pos: Rep precinct committeeman, Ill, 40-42 & 50-; chmn, East St Louis Rep Comt, 52-66; asst supvr, St Clair Co Bd of Supvr, 53-72; chmn, St Clair Co Rep Comt, formerly. Mil Serv: Entered as Pvt, Army, 43, released as T/Sgt, 46, after serv in 2nd Mil Rwy Serv, ETO, 43-46; Normandy & Rhineland Ribbons with Three Battle Stars; Bronze Star; Three Overseas Bars; Good Conduct & Victory Medals; Mid East-African-European Theater Ribbon with Three Bronze Battle Stars. Mem: BRT (past pres, Lodge 1086); Pari-mutuel Clerk Local 642; AF&AM; Low Twelve Club; High Twelve Club. Relig: Protestant. Mailing Add: 640 N 61st St East St Louis IL 62203

GRAVES, GERALD WILLIAM
Mayor, Lansing, Mich
b Alpena, Mich, July 28, 24; s Joseph Graves & Mary G; m to Donna I Rouleau; c Jeri. Donna, Amy & William G. Educ: US Merchant Marine Acad, BS; Mich State Univ, MA. Polit & Govt Pos: Mich State Rep, 50-54; exec dir, Mich Good Rd Fedn, 54-61; secy, Mich Joint Legis Comt on Hwy Needs, 54-61; mem, Mich State Safety Comn Spec Comt Hwy Control & Gov Pre-Const Conv Fiscal Comt; treas, Lansing, 61-69, mayor, 69-; former secy, Mayor's Comt Human Rels. Mil Serv: Entered Navy, 42, released as Capt, 48, after serv as Sea Capt & Asst Port Capt, NY. Publ: How Expressways Help Michigan & You, Mich Good Rd Fedn; Safety & Economic Aspects of Expressway Construction in Michigan, Am Hwy, Traffic Eng & Better Roads; Michigan's Future Road Program, Bus Topics. Mem: Lansing Old Newsboys Asn (exec secy & chmn ed comt). Legal Res: 1704 W Shiwassee St Lansing MI 48915 Mailing Add: City Hall Ninth Floor Lansing MI 48933

GRAVES, HAZEL CAROLINE (R)
Chmn, Marblehead Rep Town Comt, Mass
b Cambridge, Mass, Mar 1, 02; d John Axel Ohman & Annie Marie Black O; m 1923 to Emerson Arthur Graves; c Jacqueline Mae (Mrs Williams), Emerson Arthur, Jr & Fred Lawrence, II. Educ: Lynn Burdett Col, 21-22. Polit & Govt Pos: Corresponding secy, Women's Rep Club Essex Co, Mass, 54, fourth vpres, 56, third vpres, 58, second vpres, 60, first vpres, 62, pres, 64; legis chmn, Marblehead Women's Club, 62-68; co-chmn, Bill Bates for Cong Comt Marblehead, 63; mem, Marblehead Rep Town Comt, 64-, chmn, 68-; clerk, Clerk of Court's Off, Dist Court Southern Essex; deleg, Mass Rep State Conv. Mem: Marblehead Women's Club; Eastern Star; Marblehead Hosp Asn; St Catherine's Guild (pres, Thrift Shop, 54-); Abbot Hall Assocs. Relig: Episcopal; Vestry, St Michael's Church. Mailing Add: 36 Evans Rd Marblehead MA 01945

GRAVES, J WILSON (D)
SC State Rep
Mailing Add: Star Route Bluffton SC 29910

GRAVES, JAMES THOMAS (R)
b Salina, Kans, Nov 14, 34; s Dwight Lyman Graves & Rita Lavonne Carlin G; m 1957 to Karen Larsen Milner; c Leslie Ann, Sarah Carlin & Amy Katheryn. Educ: Kans State Univ, BS Polit Sci & BS Bus Admin, with honors, 57; Univ Kans, JD, with distinction, 60; Phi Kappa Phi; Order of Coif; Sigma Alpha Epsilon; Phi Delta Phi. Polit & Govt Pos: Chmn, Saline Co Young Rep, Kans, 64-66; chmn, Cent Kans, Avery for Gov Comt, 65-66; chmn, Saline Co Rep Cent Comt, Kans, 66-70, mem, 66-74; mem, Kans State Rep Cent Comt, 66-70; mem, Citizens Urban Renewal Adv Comt, 67-68. Bus & Prof Pos: Asst instr western civilization, Univ Kans, 58-60, assoc ed, Univ Kans Law Rev, 59-60; assoc, Morrison, Hecker, Buck & Cozad, Mo, 60-61; assoc, Clark, Mize & Lillard, Kans, 61-64, partner, Clark, Mize, Graves & Linville, 64-71; dir, Nat Bank Am, Salina, 67-; exec vpres & gen counsel, Graves Truck Line, Inc, 71- Mil Serv: 2nd Lt, Army Res, 61, serv in 48th Transportation Group, Ft Eustis, Va; Distinguished Mil Grad of ROTC; Unit Comdr Letter of Commendation. Mem: Am Judicature Soc; Saline Co, Kans & Am Bar Asns; Salina CofC. Honors & Awards: Outstanding Civic Serv Award, Salina Jr CofC, 66. Relig: Presbyterian; Chmn bd trustees, First Presby Church, Salina. Legal Res: 23 Crestview Salina KS 67401 Mailing Add: Box 1343 Salina KS 67401

GRAVES, JOE (R)
Ky State Sen
Mailing Add: 1306 Fincastle Rd Lexington KY 40502

GRAVES, PARKER (R)
b Champaign, Ill, Mar 8, 21; s Perry H Graves, Sr, (mother deceased); m 1944 to Betty Beryington Benjamin; c John, David & Clifford. Educ: Ind Univ, BS, 42; Alpha Tau Omega. Polit & Govt Pos: Chmn, Crawford Co Rep Cent Comt, Ill, formerly; chmn, 55th Sen Co Comt, 66- Mil Serv: Entered as Officer candidate, Navy, 43, released as Lt(jg), 45. Mem: Ind Univ Alumni Asn (dir exec comt, 65-); Ill Lumber & Material Dealers Asn; Ill-E Iowa Dist, Kiwanis; Ill Fuel Merchants Asn; Elks. Relig: Methodist. Legal Res: 301 N Allen St Robinson IL 62454 Mailing Add: Box 242 Robinson IL 62454

GRAVES, RALPH WAYNE (D)
Okla State Sen
b Elmore, Okla, May 28, 19; s Luther Homer Graves & Wing Park G; m 1942 to Betty Collum (deceased); c Barbara Lippel & Russell Graves. Educ: ECent Col; Okla Baptist Univ, BA, 50. Polit & Govt Pos: City comnr, Shawnee, Okla, 48-50, mayor, 50-54; Okla State Rep, 54-60; Okla State Sen, 60-, chmn, Senate Majority Caucus, 30th Session. Bus & Prof Pos: Owner & mgr, Ralph Graves Ins Agency, 46. Mil Serv: Entered as Pvt, Army, 42, released as S/Sgt, 46, after serv in 96th Inf, Pac; Purple Heart; Bronze Star. Mem: Gtr Oklahoma City Coun Ment Health; Am Legion; VFW; Nat Conserv Asn; Shawnee CofC. Relig: Baptist. Legal Res: 716 W Dewey Shawnee OK 74801 Mailing Add: 130 Broadway Bldg Shawnee OK 74801

GRAY, BARBARA E (R)
Mass State Rep
Mailing Add: State Capitol Boston MA 02133

GRAY, ELMON T (D)
Va State Sen
Mailing Add: Waverly VA 23890

GRAY, FREDERICK THOMAS (D)
Va State Sen
b Petersburg, Va, Oct 10, 18; m 1943 to Evelyn H Johnson; c Frederick T, Jr & Evelyn Cary. Educ: Univ Richmond, BA, LLB, Phi Beta Kappa. Polit & Govt Pos: Mem, South Bd of Regional Educ; mem, Va Const Conv, 56; mem, Va Comn on Const Govt; attorney gen, Va, 61-62; Va State Deleg, 66-72; mem, Va Code Comn, 68-; Va State Sen, 11th Sen Dist, 72- Bus & Prof Pos: Attorney-at-law; dir, Pioneer Fed Savings & Loan Asn & Bank of Chesterfield. Mil Serv: Army Air Force, 1st Lt, Navigator. Mem: Chesterfield Lions Club (past pres); Dale Ruritan Club; Meadowbrook Country Club; Jordan Point Country Club (past pres); Am Col Trial Lawyers. Relig: Methodist. Mailing Add: 510 State-Planters Bank Bldg Richmond VA 23219

GRAY, JAMES H (D)
b Westfield, Mass, c James, Jr, Geoffrey & Constance. Educ: Dartmouth Col; Univ Heidelberg; Phi Beta Kappa. Polit & Govt Pos: Temporary chmn & keynote speaker, Ga Dem Conv, 58; chmn, Ga Dem Exec Comt, 60; delivered Southern minority report to nation-wide TV audience, Dem Nat Conv, 60; chmn, Ga Dem State Exec Comt, 62-70; Dem cand for Gov, 66. Bus & Prof Pos: Ed & feature writer, Courant & NY Herald Tribune, Hartford, Conn; owner, Albany Herald, 46-; chmn bd & pres, Gray Commun Systs Inc. Mil Serv: Entered as 2nd Lt, Army, 42, released as Maj, 46, after serv in Sicily & Europe. Mem: Rotary; CofC. Honors & Awards: Citizens of the Year, Co Comnrs Asn Ga, 59. Relig: Episcopal; vestryman. Mailing Add: Albany GA 31702

GRAY, JO ANNE HASTINGS (R)
Rep Nat Committeewoman, Colo
b Birmingham, Ala, Dec 1, 21; d Littleberry Byrd Haley & Virginia Irene Jenkins Haley Hastings; m 1946 to Daniel Gray; c Daniel Allen & Robert Byrd. Educ: Univ Colo, BA, 43; Univ Denver, grad study, summer 43; rush chmn, Delta Gamma. Polit & Govt Pos: Precinct committeewoman, Rep Party, Colo, 60-; clerk, Colo State Senate, 63-65; mem, Rep Roundtable, Rep Women's Club, 63-, pub rels chmn, 65-; state co-chmn, Goldwater Campaign, 64; co Rep training chmn, City & Co of Denver, 65-; Schauer Campaign, 66; chmn reservations & housing, Western States Rep Conf, 67, secy, Conf, 69, vchmn, 71; Rep Nat Committeewoman, Colo, 68-, mem exec comt, Rep Nat Comt, currently. Bus & Prof Pos: Stewardess, Continental Airlines, 43-46, asst chief stewardess & dir stewardess training, 46; teacher stewardess training, Univ Denver, 47. Mem: Univ Colo Alumni Asn; Univ Colo Develop Found; Bus & Indust Polit Action Comt; Planned Parenthood of Colo; Delta Gamma Alumnae. Honors & Awards: Inaugurated first Univ Colo Alumni Inst. Relig: Presbyterian. Mailing Add: 2850 E Flora Pl Denver CO 80210

GRAY, JOHN DAVID (D)
Va State Deleg
b Newport News, Va, June 8, 28; m to Nancy Louise McMillan. Educ: Univ Va, BS, LLB. Polit & Govt Pos: City attorney, Hampton, 54-63; chmn, Hampton Dem Comt, formerly; Va State Deleg, 66- Bus & Prof Pos: Lawyer. Mil Serv: Army. Mem: Mason; Shrine; Elks; Va State Bar Asn. Relig: Methodist. Legal Res: 501 Harbor Dr Hampton VA 23361 Mailing Add: 5 W Queen St Hampton VA 23669

GRAY, JOHN NICHOLAS (R)
b Maryville, Mo, July 2, 33; s John Borland Gray & Eunice Cox G; single. Educ: Northwest Mo State Col, summer 53; Univ Mo, BS, 56; Delta Chi (vregent, Region Five, 70). Polit &

Govt Pos: Chmn, Nodaway Co Young Rep, Mo, 58-62; secy, Mo Fedn Young Rep, 59-62, mem bd, 66-68, chmn, 69-70; committeeman, Polk Twp Rep Party, 66-; chmn, Nodaway Co Rep Cent Comt, 66-72; vpres, Mo Asn Rep, Sixth Dist, 69-; chmn, Mo Rep State Comt, 70-72; deleg, Rep Nat Conv, 72. Bus & Prof Pos: Salesman, Henry Bernhard & Co, Kansas City, Mo, 58-61; prin, J Nick Gray & Assocs Mfg Rep, Maryville, 61- Mil Serv: Entered as Pvt, Army, 56, release as SP-3, 58, after serv in Specialist Sch Command, Ft Chaffee, Ark, 56-58. Mem: Assoc Midwest Gift Orgn (vpres, 70-); United Commercial Travelers. Relig: Presbyterian. Mailing Add: 320 W Cooper Maryville MO 64468

GRAY, KENNETH ELWOOD (D)
b Saginaw, Mich, Nov 9, 31; m 1960 to Patricia Neal; c Jefferson & Douglas. Educ: Western Mich Univ, AB, 53; Univ Chicago, 55-61. Polit & Govt Pos: Legis asst to US Sen Paul H Douglas, Ill, 61-65; prof staff mem, Comt on Banking & Currency, US Senate, Washington, DC, 65-66; legis asst to Vice President Hubert H Humphrey, 66-67; admin asst to US Sen Joseph D Tydings, Md, 67-71; admin asst to US Sen Hubert Humphrey, 71-73; chief govt div & sr specialist Am govt, Cong Research Serv, Libr Cong, 73- Mailing Add: 7904 Park Overlook Dr Bethesda MD 20034

GRAY, KENNETH J (D)
b West Frankfort, Ill, Nov 14, 24; m 1943 to June Croslin; c Diann. Educ: West Frankfort Community High Sch; Army Adv Sch during World War II. Polit & Govt Pos: US Rep, Ill, 54-74; deleg, Dem Nat Conv, 68 & 72; ex-officio, Dem Nat Mid-Term Conf, 74. Bus & Prof Pos: Auto bus; air serv, Benton, Ill, 6 years; licensed pilot; licensed auctioneer. Mil Serv: Army, Air Forces World War II, overseas, Italy, N Africa, Corsica & S France. Mem: Am Legion; 40 et 8; VFW; Kiwanis; Elks. Relig: Baptist. Mailing Add: 1603 E Main St West Frankfort IL 62896

GRAY, MARCUS J (D)
Clerk, Calhoun Co, Mich
b Kansas City, Mo, Sept 22, 36; s Marcus O Gray & Christina Kaigler G; m 1959 to Abbey Lynette Dowdy; c Marcus, III, Sean & Yolanda. Educ: Kellogg Community Col, currently. Polit & Govt Pos: Co chmn, Young Dem, 59-60; mem, Dem Exec Comt, 59-; dir, Dem Youth Activities, 61-64; co clerk, Calhoun Co, Mich, 64-; dir, Dem Party Orgn, 66-68; chmn, Co Dem Campaign, 68; chmn, Third Cong Dist Dem Party, 66-69; deleg, Dem Nat Conv, 72. Bus & Prof Pos: Secy, Battle Creek Bus & Prof Men's Club, Mich, 69. Mil Serv: Entered as E-1, Air Force, 55, released as A/2C, after serv in Strategic & Tactical Air Commands, Pac Air Command; Good Conduct Medal; Airman of the Month. Mem: Nat & United Co Officers' Asns; Mich Co Clerks' Asn; F&AM; Battle Creek Urban League. Honors & Awards: Les Bon Amie Club Award for Outstanding Community Serv; Cert of Merit, Mich Dem Party & Cert of Merit, Dem Women's Club for Outstanding Work in the Party; Outstanding Man of Year, Battle Creek Bus & Prof Women, 73. Relig: Protestant. Legal Res: 40 Maurer Dr Battle Creek MI 49017 Mailing Add: 315 W Green St County Bldg Marshall MI 49068

GRAY, THEODORE MILTON (R)
Ohio State Sen
b Springfield, Ohio, Sept 3, 27; s Theodore Milton Gray, Sr & Dorothy Whittington G; m 1951 to W Marilyn Kautz; c Scarlett Ann Lewis & Thackery Scott, Timothy Milton & Nathan Theodore Gray. Educ: Wabash Col, fall 45; Ohio State Univ, BA, 50. Polit & Govt Pos: Ohio State Sen, Third Dist, currently; exec secy, Ohio League Young Rep, 54-55; pres pro tem, Ohio Senate, 65-74; co-chmn, Bi-Partisan Comt Reapportionment, 67; co-chmn, $750 Million Bond Issue, 68 & homestead exemption, 68; coordr, Ohio United Citizens for Nixon, 68; deleg, Rep Nat Conv, 68 & 72. Bus & Prof Pos: Pres, Howe-Simpson Co, 61- Mil Serv: Entered as Seaman, Navy, 45-46, serv in 5th Fleet, SPac, 46. Mem: Am Legion. Honors & Awards: Jaycee's State & Local Distinguished Serv Award, 60; Gov Award for the Advan of the Prestige of Ohio, 69; Legis Leadership Citation, Nat Conf State Legis, 71. Relig: Presbyterian. Legal Res: 4735 Widner Ct Columbus OH 43220 Mailing Add: Capitol Bldg Columbus OH 43216

GRAY, WAYNE C (R)
Maine State Rep
Mailing Add: 67 Lawn Ave Rockland ME 04841

GRAYBILL, TURNER CARLISLE (D)
b Great Falls, Mont, Apr 27, 53; s Leo Graybill, Jr & Sherlee Turner G; single. Educ: Yale Univ; Harvard Law Sch, currently. Polit & Govt Pos: Deleg, Dem Nat Conv, 72; deleg, Mont Dem State Conv, 72; mem steering comt, McGovern for President, Mont, 72. Bus & Prof Pos: Dir, Spec Prog Group, 69-73; dir educ progs, KUDI Radio, 71- Publ: An analysis of mass communication in the 1972 Presidential Campaign, 1/73; A theory of communication in politics. Honors & Awards: Nat Forensic League Dist Debate Champion, 70; Abe Lincoln Award, Southern Baptist Radio-TV Comn, 73. Relig: Presbyterian. Legal Res: 3401 Seventh Ave N Great Falls MT 59401 Mailing Add: Harvard Law Sch Cambridge MA 02138

GRAYSON, GEORGE W (D)
Va State Deleg
Mailing Add: 146 Hunting Cove Williamsburg VA 23185

GREANIAS, GUS THOMAS (R)
b Chicago, Ill, Jan 4, 15; s Thomas G Greanias & Ann Wojeck G; m 1940 to Mary Elizabeth Livesay; c Thomas Gregory, John Kenneth & Frances Ann. Educ: James Millikin Univ, 33-35; Univ Ill, Champaign, AB, 38; Loyola Univ, Chicago, JD, 40; Tau Kappa Epsilon. Polit & Govt Pos: Pres, Macon Co Young Rep, Ill, 40-42; deleg, State Conv of Rep Party, 40-72; deleg, Judicial Conv of Rep, 40-72; state officers, Ill Young Rep Club, 41-49; judge, Macon Co, 46-60; deleg, Rep Nat Conv, 72. Bus & Prof Pos: Comnr by app on character & fitness on applicants for admission to practice law, Ill Supreme Court, 63-72; sr partner, Greanias, Booth, Greanias & Burton, currently. Mil Serv: Entered as Ens, Navy, 42, released as Lt Comdr, 46, after serv in USS Pittsburg, Pac & Atlantic Theatres; Naval Reserve, 47-57, commanding officer, Decatur, Ill & Newport, RI & exec officer, Dam Neck, Va Anti-Aircraft Training & Test Ctrs; Seven Serv Medals; Seven Combat Stars. Mem: Am Bar Asn; Ill Bar Asn; Ill Judges Asn (pres); Nat Juv Judges Asn; Airplane Owners & Pilots Asn. Honors & Awards: Good Govt Award, Jr CofC; Pub Serv, James Millikin Univ. Relig: Greek Orthodox. Legal Res: 104 Glencoe Decatur IL 62522 Mailing Add: Suite 330 Millikin Ct Decatur IL 62521

GRECO, STEPHEN R (D)
NY State Assemblyman
b Buffalo, NY, Dec 2, 19; m to Anne L Cherre; c three sons. Educ: Lafayette High Sch, Buffalo. Polit & Govt Pos: Judge, NY State Athletic Comn; mem, Erie Co Bd of Supvrs, 57; NY State Assemblyman, 58- Bus & Prof Pos: Food broker, Joseph Greco & Sons. Mem: KofC; Romulus Club; Eagles; Nat Narcotic Enforcement Officers Asn; Elks. Mailing Add: 795 Richmond Ave Buffalo NY 14222

GREELEY, EDWIN H (R)
Maine State Sen
Mailing Add: Morrill ME 04952

GREELEY, STEPHEN ALONZO (R)
b Franklin, NH, Apr 8, 01; s Loren B Greeley & Clara Stevens G; single. Polit & Govt Pos: Former NH State Rep; chmn, Franklin Rep Club; chmn, Merrimack Co Rep Cent Comt, formerly. Mem: Nat, NH, Merrimack Pomma & Franklin Grange; Odd Fellows. Mailing Add: 26 Pleasant St Franklin NH 03235

GREELY, MICHAEL T (D)
Mont State Sen
b Great Falls, Mont, Feb 28, 40; s Myril J Greely & Laura Harriet Haugh G; m 1972 to Marilyn Jean Myhre. Educ: Yale Univ, BA, 62; Univ Mont Law Sch, JD, 67; Beta Theta Phi. Polit & Govt Pos: Asst attorney gen, Helena, Mont, 67-69; dep co attorney, Cascade Co, 70-; Mont State Rep, 71-75; Mont State Sen, 75-, chmn state admin comt, Mont State Sen, currently. Bus & Prof Pos: Attorney-at-law, Great Falls, Mont, 70- Mil Serv: Entered as Pvt 1/C, Army Res, 63, released as Sp-4, 69; DAR Medal; Am Spirit Medal. Mem: Cascade Co & Mont Bar Asns; Am Trial Lawyers Asn. Relig: Protestant. Legal Res: 2767 Greenbriar Dr Great Falls MT 59401 Mailing Add: 409 Strain Bldg Great Falls MT 59401

GREEN, ALLISON (R)
State Treas, Mich
b Caro, Mich, Oct 28, 11; s James Edward Green & Evelyn Kiteley G; m 1934 to Marjorie Christina Denhoff; c Shirley Joan (Mrs Chapin), James Allison, Thomas Albert, Marjorie May & Robert Frederick. Educ: Cent Mich Univ, AB, 35; Univ Mich, advan studies. Hon Degrees: LLD, Cent Mich Univ. Polit & Govt Pos: Mich State Rep, 50-64, Speaker, Mich House of Rep, 63-64; Auditor Gen, Mich, 65; State Treas, Mich, 65- Bus & Prof Pos: Mem bd, Kingston State Bank, 54-65; teacher, prin & supt of schs, 14 years. Mem: Mich Farm Bur; Lions; Mason; RAM. Relig: Methodist. Mailing Add: Kingston MI 48741

GREEN, DAVID M (DAVE) (R)
Chmn, Ore Rep Party
b Portland, Ore, Jan 27, 35; m 1953 to Jean; c Michael D, Thomas Alan & Patti Sue. Educ: Madras Union High Sch, Ore, grad, 52. Polit & Govt Pos: Rep precinct committeeman, Ore, 68-72; campaign mgr, Marv Root for Cong, Second Cong Dist, 68; Gov Coun Youth, Dist 10, 70-; Ore Comprehensive Health Planning Authority; Region X, Off Econ Opportunity Coun Local Govt, 72-, Legis Interim Comt Educ, 72-; cand, Ore House of Rep, 72; chmn, Ore Rep Party, 72-; mem, Rep Nat Comt, 72- Bus & Prof Pos: Rancher, 52-65; ins agent, 65- Mem: CofC; Cent Ore Community Col Found (chmn, 72-); Ore Jr Chamber; US Jr Chamber; Elks. Honors & Awards: Outstanding Young Man of Jefferson Co, 63; One of Ten Outstanding Young Men of Ore, 63; Outstanding Young Man of Madras, 68; One of Five Outstanding Young Men of Ore, 68; hon life mem, Jr Chamber Int Sen. Relig: Christian Church; Deacon, First Christian Church Madras. Mailing Add: Box 1974 Madras OR 97741

GREEN, EDITH S (D)
b Trent, SDak, Jan 17, 10; d James Vaughn Starrett & Julia Hunt S; div; c James S & Richard. Educ: Willamette Univ; Univ Ore, BS; Stanford Univ, grad work; Delta Kappa Gamma; Delta Sigma Theta. Hon Degrees: LLD, Univ Alaska, 56, Goucher Col, Linfield Col, Gonzaga Univ & Seattle Univ, 64, Hood Col, Regis Col (Mass), Boston Col, St Xavier Col (Ill), Keuka Col & Yale Univ, 65, Reed Col, Georgetown Univ, Oberlin Col & Miami Univ, 66, Beloit Col, 71 & Anderson Col, 72; DH, Culver-Stockton Col, 60, Univ Portland, 69; DHL, Eureka Col, 62; DPA, Bethany Col (WVa), 64, Willamette Univ, Univ S Fla & Tex Christian Univ, 70 & Northeastern Univ, 72; LHD, Marylhurst Col & Warner Pac Col, 72. Polit & Govt Pos: US Rep, Ore, 54-74; deleg-at-lg, Dem Nat Conv, 56, 60, 64 & 68, mem, Platform Comt, 56, mem, Credentials Comt, 64. chmn Ore deleg, 60 & 68, seconded nominations of Adlai Stevenson, 56 & John F Kennedy, 60; deleg, Interparliamentary Conf, Switz, 58, NATO Conf, London, Eng, 59 & UNESCO Gen Conf, Paris, France, 64 & 66; mem, President Kennedy's Comn on Status of Women, 61-63 & US Comn to UNESCO. Bus & Prof Pos: Teacher, Salem Pub Schs, 30-41; free lance writer & mem staff, Women's Half Hour Prog, Radio Sta KALE. Publ: The Federal Government & Education, US Govt Printing Off, 63; Legislating in the age of Science, In: The Scientific Revolution, Pub Affairs, 59. Mem: Ore Educ Asn (dir pub rels). Honors & Awards: Citation of Appreciation, Am Legion, 72; One of Ten Portland Women of Accomplishment, Ore J, 72; Outstanding Serv Award, Nat Asn Student Personnel Adminr, 72; Simon LeMoyne Medal, LeMoyne Col, 73; Nat Am Asn Univ Women Achievement Award, 74. Relig: Christian Church. Mailing Add: 1209 SW Sixth Portland OR 97204

GREEN, FORREST (D)
Tex State Rep
Mailing Add: Rte 2 Box 39 Corsicana TX 75110

GREEN, JAMES A (D)
Pa State Rep
Mailing Add: Capitol Bldg Harrisburg PA 17120

GREEN, JAMES COLLINS (D)
NC State Rep
b Halifax Co, Va, Feb 24, 21; s John Collins Green & Frances Sue Oliver G; m 1943 to Alice McAulay Clark; c Sarah Frances, Susan Clark & James Collins, Jr. Educ: Washington & Lee Univ. Polit & Govt Pos: Precinct vchmn & chmn, Dem Party, 10 years; mem, Bladen Co Dem Exec Comt, NC, formerly; mem, Bladen Co Bd Educ, 55-61; NC State Rep, 61-67 & 69-; NC State Sen, 67-69. Bus & Prof Pos: Farmer & tobacco warehouse operator. Mil Serv: Entered Marine Corps, 44, released as Cpl, 46, after serv in Iwo Jima invasion as machine gunner with 3rd Marine Div. Mem: French Lodge 270, AF&AM; Scottish Rite; Mason (32 degree); WOW; Consol Univ NC (trustee). Relig: Presbyterian; deacon, Clarkton Presby Church; past supt, Sunday sch. Mailing Add: Box 185 Clarkton NC 28433

GREEN, LEO EDWARD (D)
Md State Deleg
b Mt Cuba, Del, Mar 27, 32; s Leo Benedict Green & Grace O'Neal G; m 1956 to Alhen

Ehrensing; c Leo E, Jr, Mary Ehren, Mary Alison, Collin Patrick, Mary Kristin, Gareth Joseph, Mary Gretchen & Mary Michelle. Educ: Mt St Mary's Col, BS, 54; Georgetown Univ, LLB (JD), 62; Univ Va, Charlottesville; George Washington Univ. Polit & Govt Pos: Mayor, Bowie, Md, 68-72; chmn munic officials comt, Citizens for Charter, Prince George's Co, 69-70; trustee, Md State Cols, 72-75; Md State Deleg, 24th Dist, 75- Bus & Prof Pos: Regional counsel, US Post Off Dept, 67-72; pvt law practice, Bowie, Md, 72- Mil Serv: Army, 54-56. Mem: Prince George's Co & Md Bar Asns (legis comts); Diocese of Washington Cath Charities (bd dirs); Bowie Boys Y Girls Club (dir); Am Legion. Honors & Awards: Outstanding Young Man of Year, Jr CofC, 67; Social Action Award, Mt St Mary's Col Alumni, 71. Relig: Catholic. Mailing Add: 3123 Belair Dr Bowie MD 20715

GREEN, LEWIS WESLEY **(D)**
b Boley, Okla, Jan 29, 35; s James Wesley Green & Lillian Marie Porter G; m 1963 to Catherine Martin; c Cotie Debra & Shelley Michelle. Educ: Univ Nebr, BA in Archit, 57; Los Angeles City Col, AA, 68; Calif State Univ, Los Angeles, BA in Pub Admin, 72; Assoc Engrs. Polit & Govt Pos: Coordr, New Image Comt for Robert Kennedy, Calif, 68; dist coordr, Black Calif for McGovern, 72; deleg, Dem Nat Conv, 72; mem, Zephar Dem Club, 73. Bus & Prof Pos: Designer-planner, Green's Drafting Serv, Los Angeles, 65-72; facilities planner, Archit Serv, Univ Southern Calif, 72-; assoc adj prof, Shaw Univ, 72- Mil Serv: Entered as Airman Basic, Air Force, 54, released as Airman Basic, 57, after serv in 92nd Bomb Wing, Strategic Air Command, Lincoln, Nebr. Mem: Am Polit Sci Asn; Am Asn Univ Prof; NAACP; United Neighborhood Orgn of Watts; Citizens Adv Comt of Watts. Relig: Catholic. Mailing Add: 1411 E 100th St Los Angeles CA 90002

GREEN, MARSHALL
US Ambassador, Australia
b Holyoke, Mass, Jan 27, 16; s Addison Loomis Green & Gertrude Metcalf G; m 1942 to Lispenard Seabury Crocker; c Marshall Winthrop, Edward Crocker & Brampton Seabury. Educ: Yale Univ, BA, 39. Polit & Govt Pos: Pvt secy to US Ambassador, Japan, 39-41; career officer, US Dept of State Foreign Serv, 45-; third secy & vconsul, Wellington, NZ, 46-47; officer in charge of Japanese Affairs, Dept of State, 47-50; first secy & consul, Stockholm, 50-55; Nat War Col, 55-56; regional planning adv for the Far East, 56-59; Acting Dep Asst Secy of State for Far Eastern Affairs, 59-60; minister counr, Seoul, 60-61; consul gen, Hong Kong & consul, Macao, 61-63; dep asst secy, Bur of Far Eastern Affairs, 63-65; US Ambassador, Indonesia, 65-69; detached to Viet Nam Peace Mission, Jan to Mar 69; asst secy, Bur of E Asian & Pac Affairs, 69-73; US Ambassador, Australia, 73- Mil Serv: Entered as Ens, Navy, 42, released as Lt, 45, after serv in Naval Intel. Mem: Metrop & Chevy Chase Clubs, DC. Honors & Awards: Meritorious Serv Award, Dept of State, 59; Nat Civil Serv League Career Award, 69. Relig: Episcopal. Legal Res: Washington DC Mailing Add: Am Embassy Canberra Australia

GREEN, MARY LOUISE KATHERINE **(R)**
Mem, San Francisco Co Rep Cent Comt, Calif
b Fresno, Calif, Feb 9, 29; d Edward Hilary Green & Elinor Mary Komes G; single. Educ: Univ Calif, Davis & Berkeley, BS, 50; Univ San Francisco, Gen Sec Teacher's Credential, 56; Newman Club. Polit & Govt Pos: Precinct dir, 20th Assembly Dist for Rep Co Cent Comt, Calif, 60-65; mem, Rep State Cent Comt, 60-66 & 68-70; mem, San Francisco Co Rep Cent Comt, 61-, precinct coordr, 73-; pres, Golden Gate Rep Women's Club, 65-67; mem regional bd dirs, Calif Rep League, 70- Bus & Prof Pos: Chmn, Cert Employees Coun, 70-72. Mem: Calif Teachers's Asn; San Mateo Elem Teachers Asn; Tel Hill Dwellers Orgn. Relig: Roman Catholic. Mailing Add: 566 Vallejo Apt 21 San Francisco CA 94133

GREEN, MAXINE WISE **(R)**
Mem, Calif Rep State Cent Comt
b Vincennes, Ind, Feb 7, 17; d Raymond Franklin Wise & Iva Copple W; m 1938 to Alvin E Green; c William C & Alvin E, Jr. Educ: Lincoln High Sch, Vincennes, Ind, grad, 34; Univ Calif exten classes. Polit & Govt Pos: Hq chmn, Congressman Bob Wilson, 58-60; campaign coordr, Calif State Assemblyman Clair W Burgener, 62, secy, 63-66, campaign chmn, 64, coordr, Calif State Sen Campaign, 66, field rep, Calif State Sen Clair W Burgener, 68-73, dist rep, US Rep Clair W Burgener, 43rd Dist, Calif, 73-; secy, Regional Off for Gov Ronald Reagan, 66-67; field rep, Calif State Sen Jack Schrade, 67-68; alt mem, Rep Cent Comt, San Diego Co, currently; mem, Calif Rep Cent Comt, currently. Mem: Hon life mem PTA; Clairemont Woman's Club; Clairemont Rep Women's Club; United Fund of San Diego Co. Honors & Awards: Woman of the Year, Clairemont Woman's Club, 58; Woman of Valor, City of San Diego, 59. Relig: Presbyterian. Mailing Add: 2847 Arnott St San Diego CA 92110

GREEN, RAYMOND EUGENE (GENE) **(D)**
Tex State Rep
b Houston, Tex, Oct 17, 47; s Garland B Green & Evelyn Clark G; m 1970 to Helen Lois Albers. Educ: Univ Houston, BBA, 71. Polit & Govt Pos: Tex State Rep, Dist 95, 73- Relig: Disciples of Christ. Mailing Add: 423 Sulky Trail Houston TX 77037

GREEN, S WILLIAM **(R)**
b New York, NY, Oct 16, 29; m to Patricia Freiberg; c Catherine Ann & Louis Matthew. Educ: Harvard Col, AB, 50, Harvard Law Sch, 53. Polit & Govt Pos: Law secy to Judge George T Washington, US Court of Appeals for DC Circuit, 55-56; counsel to Joint Legis Comt on Housing & Urban Develop, 61-64; NY State Assemblyman, 65-68; regional adminr, US Dept of Housing & Urban Develop, Region II, 70-; ex officio mem, Tri-State Regional Planning Comn, NY, NJ & Conn, currently; app by President as chmn, Fed Regional Coun, Region II, 72- Bus & Prof Pos: Attorney. Mem: NY State Bar Asn; NY Co Lawyers Asn; Asn of Bar of New York; Fed Bar Asns of NY & NJ. Mailing Add: 26 Fed Plaza New York NY 10007

GREEN, WALTER GUERRY **AMERICAN PARTY**
b Charleston, SC, Jan 1, 07; s Walter Guerry Green & Daisie Holt G; m 1934 to Irma Camman; c Walter Guerry, III. Educ: Univ of the South; Oxford Univ; Phi Beta Kappa. Polit & Govt Pos: Alt deleg-at-lg, Rep Nat Conv, 64; Rep cand for US House of Rep, Sixth Dist, NC, 64; Rep cand for NC State Senate, 66; mem, NC Rep State Exec Comt, 64-68; state chmn, Am Party of NC, 69-72. Bus & Prof Pos: Attorney-at-law. Mil Serv: Entered as Lt(jg), Naval Res, 42, released as Lt Comdr, 45; Am & Asiatic-Pac Theater Ribbons; Philippine Liberation & Victory Medals. Mem: NY Bar & NC Bar Asns. Relig: Episcopal. Mailing Add: PO Box 621 Burlington NC 27215

GREEN, WARREN ERNEST **(R)**
Okla State Rep
b Mannford, Okla, Dec 23, 21; s Clarence Green & Millie P Shoumake G; m 1941 to Betty J Foster; c Sharon Kay (Mrs Cloyd W Childers), Priscilla A (Mrs Kenneth W Davidson), Roberta Susan & Marilyn L. Educ: Draughons Bus Col, Tulsa, Okla, grad, 42. Polit & Govt Pos: Precinct chmn, dist dir & mem, Tulsa Co Rep Exec Comt, Okla, formerly; Okla State Rep, 64-72, 75-, Okla State Sen, 72-74. Bus & Prof Pos: Serv supvr & salesman, Fred Jones Ford & Leasing Co, 48-54; pres & prin owner, Green Auto Serv, Inc, Tulsa, 54- Mem: CofC; Lions. Relig: Disciples of Christ. Mailing Add: 2260 E 39th St Tulsa OK 74105

GREEN, WILLIAM ARTHUR **(D)**
b Marengo, Ind, June 30, 30; s Charles Cletus Green & Inez A Wright G; div; c Peggy (Mrs Patrick Grant) & Janet. Educ: High sch grad. Polit & Govt Pos: Pres, Young Dem, Ind, 61-65; chmn, Crawford Co Dem Party, formerly. Mailing Add: Box 312 Marengo IN 47140

GREEN, WILLIAM JOSEPH **(D)**
US Rep, Pa
b Philadelphia, Pa, June 24, 38; s William Joseph Green (deceased) & Mary Elizabeth Kelly G; m 1964 to Patricia Anne Kirk; c William Joseph, Katherine Kirk & Anne Patricia. Educ: St Joseph's Col, Pa; Villanova Law Sch; Georgetown Univ. Polit & Govt Pos: US Rep, Third Dist, Pa, currently; chmn, Dem Co Exec Comt, 67-69; deleg, Dem Nat Conv, 68. Publ: The Congressman, McGraw-Hill, 68. Mem: Frankford Hosp (trustee); Neighborhood Ctr (bd dirs); Holy Family Col (lay trustee). Relig: Catholic. Legal Res: Wakeling St Philadelphia PA 19124 Mailing Add: Rm 2434 Rayburn House Off Bldg Washington DC 20515

GREENAWAY, ROY FRANCIS **(D)**
b Takoma Park, Md, July 9, 29; s Alfred Roy Greenaway & Lila F Bartlett G; m 1951 to Carol Faye Wagle. Educ: Univ Chicago, BA, 50; Fresno State Col, MA, 56. Polit & Govt Pos: Mem, Fresno Co Dem Cent Comt, 52-65; regional vpres, Calif Dem Coun, 57-60, northern vpres, 65-67; mem, Calif Dem State Cent Comt, 58-60 & 66-70; inheritance tax appraiser, Fresno Co, 59-67; admin asst to US Sen Alan Cranston, Calif, 69- Bus & Prof Pos: Teacher, Kerman Union High Sch, Calif, 55-59; appraiser, Fresno Co & Los Angeles, 67-69. Mil Serv: Entered as Pvt, Army, 52, released as Cpl, 54, after serv in Casual Officers Detachment, Camp Drake, Far E Command, Japan, Korean War; Good Conduct Medal. Relig: Unitarian. Legal Res: 4325 E Madison Fresno CA 93705 Mailing Add: 326 M St SW Washington DC 20024

GREENBERG, MARTIN L **(R)**
NJ State Sen
Mailing Add: State House Trenton NJ 08625

GREENBERG, MARVIN **(D)**
b New York, NY, Mar 15, 19; s Frank Greenberg & Beatrice Lichtenstein G; m 1945 to Lillian Peck Greenberg; c Barbara (Mrs Lichter), Janet & Frank. Educ: NY Univ, 36. Polit & Govt Pos: Deleg, Dem Nat Mid-Term Conf, 74. Mailing Add: 4025 Atlantic Ave Brooklyn NY 11224

GREENE, BILL **(D)**
Calif State Assemblyman
Educ: Lincoln Jr Col; Univ Mich. Polit & Govt Pos: Clerk, Calif State Assembly; labor consult legis advocate; legis asst to Assemblyman Mervyn Dymally; Calif State Assemblyman, 67- Bus & Prof Pos: Radio; television; journalism. Legal Res: 3809 1/2 S Flower Dr Los Angeles CA 90037 Mailing Add: 203 E Vernon Ave Los Angeles CA 90011

GREENE, EDWIN EUGENE **(R)**
b Holly Springs, Miss, July 9, 22; s Edwin E Greene & Lilla Matthews G; m 1942 to Allie Jewell Boatwright; c Edwin E, Jr, Kerry Lawrence, Allen Leroy & Patrice Elizabeth. Educ: Columbia Mil Acad, Tenn, grad; Univ Ala, Col of Com & Bus Admin, grad. Polit & Govt Pos: Mem, City Sch Bd; chmn, Marshall Co Rep Party, Miss, formerly. Mil Serv: S/Sgt, Army, 42-45, serv in 3rd Army, ETO; Normandy & two others. Mem: Rotary Club; Credit Men's Asn; Nat Asn of Cost Accts; Nat Asn of Pub Accts; Miss Cattlemen's Asn. Relig: Presbyterian. Legal Res: Magnolia Gardens Holly Springs MS 38635 Mailing Add: Box 516 Holly Springs MS 38635

GREENE, ELIZABETH A **(R)**
NH State Rep
b North Hampton, NH; m to Leroy Greene; c Three. Educ: Univ NH. Polit & Govt Pos: NH State Rep, 61-, chmn, Environ Qual & Agr Comt, vchmn, Comt Interstate Coop, NH House Rep, currently, Asst Majority Leader, 73-; chmn, NH Air Pollution Comn; mem, Eastern Regional Conf Comt on Environ, currently; mem, Nat Water Bank Adv Bd, 72- Mem: Rye Libr (trustee); NH Oceanographic Found (trustee); Soc Protection of NH Forests (trustee, 72-); Order Women Legislators. Relig: Protestant. Mailing Add: 399 South Rd Rye NH 03870

GREENE, LEROY F **(D)**
Calif State Assemblyman
Mailing Add: 5738 Marconi Ave Carmichael CA 95608

GREENE, NANCY LOUISE **(D)**
b Baltimore, Md, Oct 7, 47; d Bertram Lloyd Edmonston & Alverta Norman E; separated. Educ: Essex Community Col, Baltimore, Md, AA with highest honors, 73. Polit & Govt Pos: Deleg & mem standing rules comt, Dem Nat Conv, 72. Mem: Baltimore Co Womens' Polit Caucus; Baltimore Co League of Women Voters; nat mem Another Mother for Peace; Belmont Townhouse Condominium (coun of co-owners). Relig: Roman Catholic. Mailing Add: 23 Coatsbridge Ct Baltimore Co MD 21236

GREENE, SCOTT E **(R)**
Chmn, Otsego Co Rep Party, NY
b Fleischmanns, NY; m to Helen Whitaker. Educ: Univ Kans; Union Col; Albany Law Sch, LLB, 49. Polit & Govt Pos: Former asst dist attorney, Otsego Co, NY; NY State Assemblyman, 64-68; chmn, Otsego Co Rep Party, currently. Bus & Prof Pos: Attorney, Law Firm, Greene & Kapner, 49- Mil Serv: Army Inf, 41-45. Mem: Am Legion; VFW; Rotary; Elks; Mason. Relig: Presbyterian. Mailing Add: 50 Main St Cooperstown NY 13326

GREENER, WILLIAM ISAAC, JR **(R)**
b Memphis, Tenn, Feb 18, 25; s William Isaac Greener, Sr & Sara Baer G; m 1949 to Charlene McPheeters; c William I, III, Barbara Susan, Charles Vaughn, Candice Ellen & Thomas Max. Educ: Memphis State Univ, 41-42; La State Univ, Baton Rouge, 42-43; Univ Mo-Columbia, BS, 47; Boston Univ, MS, 67; Beta Gamma Sigma; Tau Mu Epsilon. Polit & Govt Pos: Dir pub affairs, Internal Revenue Serv, 70-71 & Cost of Living Coun, 71; asst to comt pub affairs,

Internal Revenue Serv, 71-72; dep spec asst to secy pub affairs, Treas Dept, 72; asst dir pub affairs, Cost of Living Coun, 72-73; asst to secy pub affairs, Dept Housing & Urban Develop, 73-75; asst dir for pub affairs, Off Mgt & Budget, Washington, DC, 75; dep press secy to President, White House, 75- Mil Serv: Entered as 1st Lt, Air Force, 51, released as Lt Col, after serv in 7th Air Force, Vietnam, 67-68; Air Force Commendation Medal; Bronze Star; Vietnamese Medal Honor; Legion Merit. Mailing Add: 6116 Bardu Ave Springfield VA 22152

GREENFIELD, JAMES ROBERT (D)
Chmn, Posey Co Dem Party, Ind
b Evansville, Ind, Sept 1, 22; s James Alexander Greenfield & Esther Niehaus G; m 1957 to Ann Powers; c Amy. Polit & Govt Pos: Chmn, Posey Co Dem Party, Ind, 69- Mailing Add: Box 248 Poseyville IN 47633

GREENFIELD, ROLAND (D)
Pa State Rep
Mailing Add: Capitol Bldg Harrisburg PA 17120

GREENGO, IRVING (R)
Wash State Rep
Mailing Add: 3203 NE 88th Seattle WA 98115

GREENHAGEN, CHARLES RICHARD (D)
b Salt Lake City, Utah, Aug 4, 46; s Charles Ray Greenhagen & Georgia Ruth Powell G; m 1966 to Faye Elizabeth Braithwaite; c Stephanie Ann & Chad Richard. Educ: Univ Utah, 64-66; Western Wyo Col, 69-70. Polit & Govt Pos: Alt deleg, Dem Nat Mid-Term Conf, 74; second vpres, Lincoln Co Dem Club, Wyo, 74- Mem: Int Asn of Bridge, Struct & Ornamental Iron Workers, Local 27. Relig: Latter-day Saint. Legal Res: Diamondville Hill Diamondville WY 83116 Mailing Add: Box 154 Diamondville WY 83116

GREENHILL, JOE R (D)
Chief Justice, Supreme Court, Tex
b Houston, Tex, July 14, 14; s Joseph Robert Greenhill & Violet Stanuell G; m 1940 to Martha Shuford; c Joe Robert, IV & William Duke. Educ: Univ Tex, BA & BBA, 36, LLB, 39; Ed, Cactus, foreman, Cowboys; student mgr, Intramural Sports; Friar; Phi Beta Kappa; Beta Gamma Sigma; Phi Eta Sigma; Order of the Coif; ed, Tex Law Rev; Phi Delta Phi; Phi Delta Theta. Polit & Govt Pos: First asst to Attorney Gen, Tex, 49-50; Justice, Supreme Court, Tex, 57-72, Chief Justice, 72- Mil Serv: Entered as Ens, Naval Res, 42, released as Lt(sg), 46, after serv in Cent Pac. Publ: Articles publ in Baylor Law Rev, Southwestern Law J, Tex Law Rev & St Mary's Law J. Mem: Am & Tex Bar Asns; Am Judicature Soc (dir, 71-); Philos Soc Tex. Relig: Episcopal. Legal Res: 3204 Bridle Path Austin TX 78703 Mailing Add: Supreme Court of Tex Box 12248 Capitol Sta Austin TX 78711

GREENHOLTZ, HERBERT THOMAS, JR (R)
Chmn, Second Cong Dist Rep Party Orgn, Ga
b Westminster, Md, May 9, 34; s Herbert Thomas Greenholtz & Hazel Vinson G; div; c Herbert Thomas, Jr & Cynthia Elizabeth. Educ: Eastern Col, AA, 53; Univ Baltimore, JD, 56. Polit & Govt Pos: Chmn, Dougherty Co Rep Party, Ga, 70-71; chmn, Second Cong Dist Rep Orgn, 70- Bus & Prof Pos: Attorney. Mil Serv: Entered as E-1, Army, 56, released as E-5, 59, after serv in Army Security Agency. Mem: Albany, Ga & Am Bar Asns; Am Trial Lawyers Asn; Elks. Relig: Lutheran. Mailing Add: 127 Court Ave Albany GA 31701

GREENLAW, LAWRENCE PEARL, JR (D)
Maine State Rep
b Boston, Mass, Dec 12, 45; s Lawrence Pearl Greenlaw & Frances Clara Tesch G; single. Educ: Univ Maine, Orono, BA in Polit Sci, 74. Polit & Govt Pos: Maine State Rep, Stonington, 73-, chmn marine resources comt, Maine State Legis, currently, mem energy comt, currently; vchmn, Hancock Co Dem Comt, spring 73, chmn, 73-; mem, Stonington Conserv Comt, 73-; mem, Marine Resources Comn, 73-; mem, Small Grants Adv Comt, 74- Mil Serv: Entered as Pvt, Army, 66, released as S/Sgt, 70, after serv in Security Agency, Europe, 67-70. Relig: Episcopal. Mailing Add: Stonington ME 04681

GREENOUGH, GARY ARNOLD (D)
Mayor, Mobile, Ala
b Pascagoula, Miss, Mar 30, 38; s G Arnold Greenough (deceased) & Vivian Ezell Frazier G; m to Frances Elizabeth Canty; c Kelly & Kimberly. Educ: Univ SAla, BA in Econ & Polit Sci. Polit & Govt Pos: Finance comnr, Mobile, Ala, 73-, mayor, currently. Mil Serv: Entered as Pvt, Marine Corps, 55, released as Lance Cpl, 59. Mem: Optimists; Am Econ Asn; Am Acad Polit & Social Sci; Southern Econ Asn; Asn Evolutionary Econ. Relig: Baptist. Mailing Add: PO Box 1827 Mobile AL 36601

GREENWALT, LYNN ADAMS (R)
Dir US Fish & Wildlife Serv, Dept Interior
b Reno, Nev, Mar 15, 31; s Ernest J Greenwalt & Lyndel Adams G; m 1955 to Judith Ann Cunningham; c Mark L, Scott L & Grant L. Educ: Reedley Jr Col, 49-50; Univ Okla, BS, 53; Univ Ariz, MS, 55. Polit & Govt Pos: Var field assignments, US Fish & Wildlife Serv, Dept Interior, Western US, 57-70, regional supvr law enforcement, Portland, Ore, 70-71, chief div wildlife refuges, Washington, DC, 71-72, acting asst dir, 72-73, dir, 73- Mil Serv: Entered as Pvt, Army, 55, released as Spec 3/C, 57, after serv in 3rd Armored Div, Ger, 56-57; Good Conduct Medal. Mem: Wildlife Soc; Am Fisheries Soc. Honors & Awards: Meritorious Serv Award, US Dept Interior, 73. Relig: Presbyterian. Mailing Add: 16412 Keats Terr Rockville MD 20855

GREENWELL, JESSIE MAY (D)
Chmn, Shelby Co Dem Party, Mo
b Bethel, Mo, Aug 16, 06; d Jess D Taylor & Rhoda Lee Pickett T; m 1925 to George Welch Greenwell; c Joan (Mrs Tom Bierly), Hiram Lee & Carol Taylor. Educ: Shelbina High Sch, Mo, grad, 24. Polit & Govt Pos: Chmn, Shelby Co Dem Party, Mo, 66-; vchmn, Ninth Dist Dem Party, 70-74. Bus & Prof Pos: Bd trustees, Mo Archaeological, Columbia, 72-74. Mem: PEO (pres); Shelby Co Bicentennial Comt; Flag Raising Comt (chmn). Honors & Awards: Fifty Year Pin, PEO; Twenty Year Serv Pin, Co Red Cross. Relig: Methodist; chmn, Admin Bd, United Methodist Church, Shelbina, 70-74. Mailing Add: Broadacres Farm Shelbina MO 63468

GREER, BAYLESS LYNN (D)
Ala State Rep
b Rogersville, Ala, Nov 20, 41; s Odus Clifton Greer & Captola Grisham G; m 1965 to Joan Rebecca Myhan; c Lisa & Lori. Educ: Auburn Univ, BSEE, 64; Univ Ala, 66-68. Polit & Govt Pos: Ala State Rep, Dist 1, 74- Mem: Civitan; Ala Cattlemans Asn. Relig: Baptist. Mailing Add: Rte 3 Box 102 Rogersville AL 35652

GREER, JOHN W (D)
Ga State Rep
Mailing Add: 802 Healey Bldg Atlanta GA 30303

GREGG, DICK HOSKINS, JR (D)
Chmn, Dist 17 Dem Party, Tex
b Houston, Tex, Dec 19, 39; s Dick H Gregg & Katharine Parker G; div; c Dick H, III & Christopher Anderson. Educ: Univ Tex, BA, 61, JD, 64; Sigma Alpha Epsilon; Silver Spurs. Polit & Govt Pos: Asst Attorney Gen, Tex, 64-65; election judge, Nassau Bay, 67-; chmn, Dist 17 Dem Party, 68-; city attorney, Nassau Bay, 70-; alt deleg, Dem Mid-Term Conf, 74; mem, Tex Const Revision Comt, 74. Mem: Rotary; NASA Area Dem (ed, newsletter, 74-); Am & Houston Bar Asns; Earth Awareness Found (dir, 74-). Legal Res: 18290 Upper Bay Rd Nassau Bay TX 77058 Mailing Add: 1102 Broadway LaPorte TX 77571

GREGG, HUGH (R)
b Nashua, NH, Nov 22, 17; s Harry A Gregg & Margaret Richardson G; m 1940 to Catherine Marshall Warner; c Cyrus W & Judd A. Educ: Yale Univ, AB, 39; Harvard Law Sch, LLB, 42; Alpha Sigma Phi. Hon Degrees: Univ NH, New Eng Col & Dartmouth Col. Polit & Govt Pos: Alderman-at-lg, Nashua, NH, 48-50, mayor, 50; Gov, NH, 53-55. Bus & Prof Pos: Attorney-at-law, Sullivan & Gregg, 46-; pres & treas, Gregg & Son, Inc, 47-; chmn bd, Indian Head Nat Bank, Nashua, 48-; pres, Nashua Fresh Air Camp, 48-; dir, Wildcat Corp, 58-, NH Bankshares, 64- & Indian Head Nat Bank, Manchester, 65-; pres & treas, Gregg Cabinets, Ltd, Can, 65-; dir, Can Kitchen Cabinet Asn, 68-; dir, Crotched Mt Found, 70. Mil Serv: Entered as Air Force Cadet, 42, released as Spec Agent, Counter Intel Corps, 52, after serv in Mil Intel Res, ETO, Mediter & China-Burma-India, 43-45 & Korea; usual campaign ribbons. Publ: Co-publ, New Hampshire Profiles, 59-65. Mem: Nashua, NH, Mass & Am Bar Asns; Nat Kitchen Cabinet Asn. Relig: Congregational. Mailing Add: RFD 3 Nashua NH 03060

GREGG, JAMES ERWIN (D)
Mem, Butte Co Dem Cent Comt, Calif
b Harrisburg, Pa, May 3, 27; s Clarence Richard Gregg, Sr & Mabel Elicker G; m 1955 to Lyla Pauline Korb; c William Jason, Richard James, Joan Nancy, Michael Eric & Robert John. Educ: Lebanon Valley Col, BA, 50; Univ Calif, Berkeley, MA, 54; Univ Calif, Santa Barbara, PhD, 64; Pi Gamma Mu. Polit & Govt Pos: Admin asst, US Navy, China Lake, Calif, 51-52; staff secy for educ, Gov Edmund G Brown, Calif, 65-66; deleg, Dem Nat Conv, 68; mem, Butte Co Dem Cent Comt, 68- Bus & Prof Pos: Teacher, counr & head dept, Shasta Union High Sch & Jr Col, Calif, 52-59; asst prof jour, Chico State Col, 59-62, assoc prof jour & polit sci, 64-68, prof & head dept polit sci, 68-71, dean grad sch, 71-; dir student publ, Univ Calif, Santa Barbara, 62-63 & teaching fel polit sci, 63-64. Mil Serv: Entered as A/S, Navy, 45, released as Photo Mate 3/C, 46, after serv in USS Cape Gloucester CVE-109, Pac Theatre, 46. Publ: Auth, Newspaper Endorsements & Local Elections in California, 66 & The Influence of Newspaper Editorial Endorsements on State Ballot Measures Elections in California, 1948-1968, 70, Univ Calif, Davis; The era of Earl Warren, In: The Rumble of California Politics, Wiley, 70. Mem: Am, Western & Northern Calif Polit Sci Asns; Am Fedn Teachers; Calif Col & Univ Faculty Asn. Honors & Awards: Ford Found fel, 54-55; Wall Street J Jour fel, 59; Nat Ctr for Educ in Polit fel, 65-66; Pub Rels Soc Am fel, 65. Mailing Add: 1655 Filbert Ave Chico CA 95926

GREGG, MARIE ELLEN (R)
VChmn, Stevens Co Rep Cent Comt, Kans
b Cherokee Co, Okla, Mar 10, 14; d Thomas Lafayette Manes & Irene Nations M; m 1934 to Elden Marion Gregg; c John Elden, Keith Thomas & Carl Donald. Educ: High sch grad; Nat Honor Soc. Polit & Govt Pos: Precinct committeewoman, Kans, 64; vchmn, Stevens Co Rep Cent Comt, 64-68 & 72, chmn, 68-72; organized, Women's Rep Club, 66; sponsor, Stevens Co TAR, 66-; alt deleg, Rep Nat Conv, 72. Bus & Prof Pos: Cooperator & mgr, E M Gregg Truck Serv, 51-63, traffic mgr, E M Gregg, Inc, 63-68, adv & consult, 68-69; acct, Rowland Construction Co, 68-69. Mem: Kans Acct Coun, Kans Motor Carriers; Nat Fedn Independent Bus; Hugoton CofC; Kans CofC; Home Demonstration Unit, Stevens Co Knife & Fork Club. Relig: Church of God. Mailing Add: Box G Hugoton KS 67951

GREGG, RICHARD (D)
Ala State Rep
Mailing Add: 401 Wynn Dr Huntsville AL 35805

GREGORIO, ARLEN (D)
Calif State Sen
Mailing Add: 1177 University Dr Menlo Park CA 94024

GREGORIO, JOHN T (D)
NJ State Assemblyman
Mailing Add: State House Trenton NJ 08625

GREGORY, CARSON (D)
NC State Rep
Mailing Add: Rte 2 Angier NC 27501

GREGORY, DICK (PEOPLE'S PARTY)
Co-Chmn, People's Party
b St Louis, Mo, 1932; m 1959 to Lillian G; c Michelle, Lynn, Paula, Pamela, Stephanie, Gregory & Miss. Educ: Southern Ill Univ, 51-53 & 55-56; outstanding athlete, 53. Polit & Govt Pos: Chmn, Nat Conf for New Polit, 67-; co-chmn, People's Party, 69- Bus & Prof Pos: Nightclub, TV & rec artist; comedian, appearances at Playboy & Esquire Clubs, Chicago, master of ceremonies, Roberts Show Club, Chicago. Mil Serv: Army, 53-55. Publ: What's Happening, 65; The Shadow That Scares Me, Doubleday, 68; Write Me In, Bantam Bks, 68; weekly nationwide syndicated column; plus others. Mailing Add: 79 W Monroe Chicago IL 60603

GREGORY, DOUGLAS MEIGS (R)
b Charleston, WVa, July 15, 48; s Albert Meigs Gregory & Nancy Watkins G (deceased); single. Educ: St Petersburg Jr Col, AA; Fla State Univ, BS. Polit & Govt Pos: Personnel coordr host comt, Rep Conv, 68; legis asst, Fla State Sen & Minority Leader, C W Bill Young, 69-70; admin asst to US Rep C W Bill Young, 69-70; admin asst to US Rep C W Bill Young, Fla, 71- Relig: Episcopal. Legal Res: 1549 Carson Circle NE St Petersburg FL 33703 Mailing Add: Suite 627 Fed Bldg 144 First Ave S St Petersburg FL 33701

GREGORY, GEORGE WINFIELD, JR (D)
SC State Rep
b Jefferson, SC, June 5, 38; s George W Gregory, Sr & Harriet Venters G; m 1962 to Sharon Bennett; c Sharon Kristen, Avril Elizabeth & Gracen Anne. Educ: Univ SC, BA, 59, Law Sch, LLB, 62, JD, 70; Sigma Chi. Polit & Govt Pos: SC State Sen, Eighth Dist, until 68; SC State Rep, 72- Mil Serv: Entered as 1st Lt, Army, 63, released as Capt, 66; Capt, Army Res. Mem: Am & SC Bar Asns; Chesterfield Co Bar; Am Legion; Jr CofC. Relig: Presbyterian. Legal Res: 143 McIver St Cheraw SC 29520 Mailing Add: 121 Chesterfield Rd Cheraw SC 29520

GREGORY, HARDY, JR (D)
Chmn, Dooly Co Dem Exec Comt, Ga
b Vienna, Ga, Aug 12, 36; s Hardy Gregory, Sr & Mary Wood Gaither G; m 1959 to Carolyn Burton; c Hardy, III & Elizabeth Marywood. Educ: US Naval Acad, BS; Walter F George Sch of Law, Mercer Univ, LLB. Polit & Govt Pos: Chmn, Dooly Co Dem Exec Comt, Ga, 71- Bus & Prof Pos: Attorney, Davis & Gregory, currently. Mil Serv: From A/S, Navy, to Capt, Air Force, 54-64. Relig: Methodist. Mailing Add: PO Box 397 Vienna GA 31092

GREGSON, MARY POAGE (R)
Mem, Roanoke Co Rep Comt, Va
b Roanoke Co, Va, Apr 16, 10; d Harvey Claytor Poage & Lucy Dyer P; m 1944 to Carl Louis Gregson; c Naomi (Mrs Ramsey), Carol (Mrs Mills), Carl L, Jr, Molly Poage (Mrs W C Kelly) & Jeff S. Educ: Radford Col, grad, 29. Polit & Govt Pos: Clerk, Va precinct for 25 years; deleg, Rep Nat Conv, 64; mem, Co Rep Comt; corresponding secy, Roanoke Valley Rep Woman's Club, 65-66; pres, Roanoke Valley Rep Club; mem, Roanoke Co Rep Comt, currently; mem, Rep State Cent Comt, Va, 68-; mem, Sixth Dist Rep Comt, 68-; mem, Roanoke Co Welfare Bd, 69-; vchmn, Roanoke Co Comn, 70-; awards chmn, Va Rep State Fedn Women, 71-73; deleg, White House Conf on Aging, 71. Bus & Prof Pos: Elem sch teacher, Va for 18 years. Mem: Tuberc Asn (bd); PTA; McVitty House Inc (bd dirs). Relig: Presbyterian. Mailing Add: Rte 7 Box 327 Roanoke VA 24018

GREGSON, VERNON JOSEPH (D)
La State Rep
b New Orleans, La, July 30, 12; s Thomas Emile Gregson & Mary Merriman G; m 1937 to Maryfrances Burns; c Vernon J, SJ. Educ: SJ Peters Boys High Sch, grad. Polit & Govt Pos: La State Rep, Dist 21, Orleans Parish, 56- Bus & Prof Pos: Bookkeeper, L A Comiskey; treas, Henri Petetin, Inc, 52-69; vpres, Hansell-Petetin, Inc, 69- Mil Serv: Entered as Pvt, Army, 44, released as Pfc, 46, after serv in 381st Combat Engrs, ETO, 44-46. Mem: KofC; YMBC; VFW. Relig: Catholic. Mailing Add: 3828 Banks St New Orleans LA 70119

GREIGG, STANLEY LLOYD (D)
b Ireton, Iowa, May 7, 31; s Robert D Greigg & Hattie M Torwelle G; m 1965 to Cathryn Olivia Thomson; c Valerie Kay, Heather Marie & Cathryn Louise. Educ: Morningside Col, BA, 54; Maxwell Grad Sch, Syracuse Univ, fel & MA in hist. Polit & Govt Pos: Mem city coun, Sioux City, Iowa, 61-64, mayor, 64-65; US Rep, Iowa, 65-67; exec asst to Asst Postmaster Gen, US Post Off Dept, 67, dir, Off of Regional Admin, 67-69; dir campaigns & party orgn, Dem Nat Comt, 70-71, dep chmn, 71-73. Bus & Prof Pos: Sr assoc, Lawrence F O'Brien Assocs, Washington, DC, currently. Mil Serv: Navy, 57-59. Mem: Northwest Iowa Community Conf; Northwest Iowa Indust Opportunities Conf. Honors & Awards: Distinguished Alumni Award, Morningside Col, 72. Relig: Lutheran. Legal Res: 1526 S Helen St Sioux City IA 51106 Mailing Add: 5300 Wriley Rd Washington DC 20016

GREIMAN, ALAN J (D)
Ill State Sen
Mailing Add: 8545 N Harding Ave Skokie IL 60076

GREINER, KEITH ALLEN (R)
Chmn, Lyon Co Rep Cent Comt, Kans
b Hunter, Kans, Feb 24, 40; s Wendell Whitson Greiner & Lois Jaeger G; m 1963 to Sarah Jane Steerman; c Laura Elaine, Keith Allen, Jr, Sarah Ann & William Samuel. Educ: Wichita State Univ, 58-59; Kans State Teachers Col, BA, 62, study, 62-63; Univ Va, Charlottesville, LLB, 66; Blue Key; Pi Gamma Mu; Kappa Mu Epsilon. Polit & Govt Pos: Pres, Kans Collegiate Young Rep, 62-63; chmn, Lyon Co Rep Cent Comt, Kans, currently. Bus & Prof Pos: Lawyer, Steerman, Greiner & Roach, Emporia, Kans, currently. Mem: Am & Lyon Co Bar Asns; Kans Bar Asn (chmn, Citizen Comt, 72-); Am Judicature Soc; Rotary. Relig: Protestant. Mailing Add: 2000 Briarcliff Lane Emporia KS 66801

GREINER, WILLIAM MERLIN (R)
b Zanesville, Ohio, Jan 31, 26; s William Martin Greiner & Mildred Eddy G; m 1949 to Phyllis C Webster; c William Mark (deceased), Lisa Karen, Jeff Jay, Erin Gale & Eric Martin. Educ: Zanesville High Sch, 4 years. Polit & Govt Pos: Committeeman, Washington Twp Rep Party, Ohio, 66; mem, Muskingum Co Rep Club, 66; chmn, Muskingum Co Rep Cent Comt, formerly. Bus & Prof Pos: Agent, Prudential Ins Co, 63- Mil Serv: Entered as A/S, Navy, 42, released as Signalman 2/C, 46, after serv in LST, SPac, 43-46. Mem: Life Underwriters; AMROV Grotto; Charity Newsies; Old Timers Baseball; Muskingum Co Fair Bd. Relig: Protestant. Mailing Add: Rte 4 East Pike Zanesville OH 43701

GREINKE, GARY ARTHUR (R)
Chmn, Seward Co Rep Cent Comt, Nebr
b Hastings, Nebr, Feb 1, 41; s Arthur Ernest Greinke & Marie MacCauley G; m 1965 to Julie Ann Gouty; c Robyn Lynn & Chad William. Educ: Valparaiso Univ, BA, 63; Baylor Univ Sch Law, 63-64; Univ Nebr Sch Law, JD, 66; Pi Sigma Alpha; Phi Delta Phi; Phi Delta Theta. Polit & Govt Pos: Committeeman, Seward Co Rep Cent Comt, Nebr, 68-70, chmn credential comt, 70-; mem, Nebr Rep Party Const Rev Comt, 70; deleg, Nebr State Rep Conv, 70-74; committeeman, Nebr Rep State Cent Comt, currently. Bus & Prof Pos: Prof polit sci, Concordia Teachers Col (Nebr), 66-71, asst to pres, 70-, dir planning, 72- Publ: Church governance, diagnosis, prognosis, Issues, fall 74. Mem: Am & Nebr Polit Sci Asns; Nebr Bar Asn; Lutheran Human Rels Asn (welfare comt). Relig: Lutheran. Mailing Add: 158 E Hillcrest Seward NE 68434

GRENIER, HENRY R (D)
Mass State Rep
Mailing Add: State Capitol Boston MA 02133

GRENIER, JOHN EDWARD (R)
Mem, Ala Rep State Exec Comt
b New Orleans, La, Aug 24, 30; s Charles Desire Grenier & Elizabeth Schaumburg G; m 1953 to Lynne Dea Youmans; c John Beaulieu. Educ: Tulane Univ, LLB, 53; NY Univ, LLM, 57; Omicron Delta Kappa; Delta Kappa Epsilon. Polit & Govt Pos: Chmn, Jefferson Co Young Rep Club, Ala, 60-61; chmn, Ala Fedn of Young Rep, 61-62; mem, Jefferson Co Rep Exec Comt, 62-72; mem, Ala State Rep Exec Comt, 62-, chmn, 62-65; southern regional dir, Goldwater for President Comt, 63-64; exec dir, Rep Nat Comt, 64. Bus & Prof Pos: Assoc, Burke & Burke, 56-57; attorney, Southern Natural Gas Co, 57-59; mem, Bradley, Arant, Rose & White, 59-66; mem, Lange, Simpson, Robinson & Somerville, currently. Mil Serv: Entered as 2nd Lt, Marine Corps, 53, released as Capt, 56, after serv in 121st Squadron, Korea, 55-56; Capt, Marine Corps Res. Mem: Ala, La & NY Bar Asns. Relig: Episcopal. Legal Res: 90 Country Club Blvd Birmingham AL 35213 Mailing Add: 1800 City Fed Bldg Birmingham AL 35203

GRESHAM, JOHN KENNETH (BUDDY) (D)
Miss State Sen
Mailing Add: PO Box 540 Greenville MS 38701

GRESHAM, ROBERT COLEMAN (R)
b Booneville, Miss, Nov 12, 17; s J F Gresham & Pearl Bellamy G; m 1955 to Katherine Wootten; c Robin & D Jackson. Educ: Sunflower Jr Col, AA, 38; Southeastern Univ, BCS, 42; Delta Theta Phi. Polit & Govt Pos: Spec agent & exec asst, Fed Bur Invest, 38-53; res dir, Coun State CofC, 53-65; rep staff dir, House Appropriations Comt, US House of Rep, 65-69; comnr, Interstate Com Comn, 69- Relig: Episcopal. Mailing Add: 14712 Claude Lane Silver Spring MD 20904

GRESSETTE, LAWRENCE MARION (D)
SC State Sen
b St Matthews, SC, Feb 11, 02; s J T Gressette & Rosa Wannamaker G; m 1927 to Florence Howell. Educ: Univ of SC, LLB, 24. Polit & Govt Pos: SC State Rep, 25-28 & 31-32; SC State Sen, 37-, chmn judiciary & hwy comt, SC State Senate, currently, pres pro tempore, 72-; Col Gov William's Staff; mem, State Dem Exec Comt, SC, 48, chmn, 53-54; chmn, SC Sch Comt, 51-66; ex officio mem, Judicial Coun of SC, 57-, chmn, Steering Comt on Rev State Const, 69- Bus & Prof Pos: Lawyer. Mem: Fel Am Col Trial Lawyers; Mason; Phi Kappa Phi; Blue Key. Relig: Baptist. Mailing Add: Box 346 St Matthews SC 29135

GREWE, ISABELLE MCNAUGHTON (R)
Mem Exec Comt, Rep Party of Wis
b Middleville, Mich, May 10, 10; d Charles Peter McNaughton & Hazel Mitchell M; m 1933 to Raymond Howard Grewe; c Thomas M & John M. Educ: Univ Minn, Minneapolis, BS in Health Supv of Sch Child, 31; Chi Omega. Polit & Govt Pos: Part-time vol case worker, State Dept of Pub Instr, Local Pub & Pvt Agencies & State Dept of Pub Welfare-Div of Children & Youth, Wis, 33-39; mem & officer, Eau Claire Co Children's Bd, 33-53; mem, Eau Claire Co Rep Club, 50; pres, Eau Claire Co Fedn of Rep Women, 53-57; mem, Wis Rep State Cent Comt, 54-60; alt deleg, Rep Nat Conv, 56, 60 & 68; vchmn, Ninth Cong Dist Rep Party, Wis, 57-63; mem exec comt, Rep Party of Wis, 57-, secy, formerly. Bus & Prof Pos: Dir, Health Educ, Hennepin Co Anti-tuberc Asn, Minneapolis, Minn, 31-33, part-time employ, 34-36. Mem: Wis Conf Social Work; Wis Ment Health Asn; Wis Anti-tuberc Asn; Wis Children's Aid Soc; Sacred Heart & Luther Hosp Guilds. Relig: United Church of Christ. Mailing Add: 122 Wold Ct Eau Claire WI 54701

GRIBBS, ROMAN S (D)
b Detroit, Mich, Dec 29, 25; s Roman Grzyb & Magdeline Widziszewski G; m 1954 to Katherine Stratis; c Paula, Carla, Christopher, Rebecca & Elizabeth. Educ: Univ Detroit, BS magna cum laude, 52, Law Sch, grad, 54; Blue Key; Delta Sigma Phi. Polit & Govt Pos: Presiding traffic court referee, Detroit, Mich, 66-68; sheriff, Wayne Co, 68-69; mayor, Detroit, 70-74; mem exec comt & chmn pub safety, Nat League Cities, 70, pres, 72-73; pres, Mich Conf Mayors, 70-; mem adv bd, US Conf Mayors, 70-; mem, Nat Civil Defense Adv Comt, 70-; judge, Third Judicial Circuit Mich, 75- Bus & Prof Pos: Attorney, Shaheen, Gribbs & Shaheen, Detroit, Mich, 64-66; partner, Fenton, Nederlander, Dodge, Barris, Gribbs, Ritchie & Crehan, 74-75. Mil Serv: Entered as Pfc, Army, released as Sgt. Mem: Univ Detroit (bd trustees); Sacred Heart Rehab Ctr (bd dirs); Mich Opera Theatre (bd dirs); Mich Judges Asn. Relig: Roman Catholic. Mailing Add: 401 Old County Bldg Detroit MI 48226

GRICE, BENNING MOORE (D)
Presiding Justice, Supreme Court, Ga
b Hawkinsville, Ga, Sept 16, 09; s Warren Grice & Clara Elberta Rumph G; m 1941 to Mary Flavia Calhoun; c Benning M, Jr, Ann Victoria & Warren C. Educ: Mercer Univ, AB, 31, LLB, 32; Blue Key; Kappa Alpha Order. Polit & Govt Pos: Ga State Rep, 39-42; part-time judge, Juv Court of Bibb Co, 46-59; mem, Ga Bd of Bar Exams, 57-60; assoc justice, Supreme Court of Ga, 61-72, presiding judge, 72- Mil Serv: Entered as Lt(jg), Navy, 42, released as Lt Comdr, 45, after serv in Continental US, 42-44 & in 5th & 3rd Fleets, Pac Theater, 44-45; Lt Comdr (Ret), Naval Res, 45-56; Am & Pac Theater Ribbons; Japanese Victory Medal with Three Battle Stars. Mem: Macon, Ga & Am Bar Asns; Macon Circuit Bar Asn; Mason. Honors & Awards: Selected Macon's Outstanding Young Man, 40. Relig: Baptist. Legal Res: 3065 High Point Dr Macon GA 31204 Mailing Add: 522 State Judicial Bldg Atlanta GA 30334

GRIEB, FRANCES BACCELLI (R)
VChmn, Orange Town Rep Comt, Conn
b New Haven, Conn, Nov 14, 14; d Leone Baccelli & Anita Poli B; m 1939 to Robert Charles Grieb; c Bernadette E (Mrs Henry Barclay), Leona F (Mrs Dana H Heckendorf) & Cheryl Ann (Mrs David P Serfilippi). Educ: Nursing Sch, grad, 36. Polit & Govt Pos: Secy-charter mem, Orange Women's Rep Club, Conn, 57-; treas, Orange Rep Town Comt, 60-62, vchmn, 66-; Rep registr, Orange, 66-; treas, New Haven Co Rep Women's Asn, 64-67; treas, Conn Fedn of Rep Women, 66-72, 2nd vpres, 72-; mem, Gov Consumer Protection Coun, 70-; deleg, Nat Rep Conv, 72; clerk, Orange Probate Court, 75- Bus & Prof Pos: Head nurse obstetrics, Grace-New Haven Hosp, Conn, 36-38; pvt duty nurse, New Haven, 38-40; vol worker, Am Red Cross Nursing Serv, Stamford & New Haven, 41-43 & 66- Publ: Eye on Nixon Julie N Eisenhower, Ed W Clement Stone, 72; ed, President Nixon's Trip to China, Press Corp Bantam, 72 & Interpretation of President Nixon's inaugural speech, David

Lawrence, 1/25/73. Mem: Registr Asn of Conn; Grace Hosp Alumni Asn; New Haven Chap, Am Red Cross Asn; Orange Women's Rep Club; Third Cong Dist Rep Women's Asn. Honors & Awards: President Truman Award for work in home nursing care during World War II, 46. Mailing Add: 235 Riverdale Rd Orange CT 06477

GRIECO, JOSEPH V (R)
Pa State Rep
Mailing Add: Capitol Bldg Harrisburg PA 17120

GRIER, FRANCIS EBENEZER (R)
Exec Committeeman, SC Rep Party
b Abbeville, SC, Oct 23, 48; s Francis Calvin Grier (deceased) & Elizabeth Gutzke G; single. Educ: Erskine Col, BS, 70; Univ SC, 71-74; Philomathean Literary Soc, secy, 70. Polit & Govt Pos: Exec committeeman, SC Rep Party, 73-, third vchmn, Third Dist, SC, 74- Bus & Prof Pos: Owner, McCormick Bookkeeping & Tax Serv, 70-; secy-treas, McCormick Develop Corp, Inc, 73- Mem: McCormick Country Club (treas, 73-); Greenwood Moose; SC Forestry Asn; McCormick Co Bi-Centennial Comn. Relig: Presbyterian. Legal Res: Rte 1 Troy SC 29848 Mailing Add: Box 713 McCormick SC 29835

GRIER, GEORGE EDWARD (D)
Chmn, Clallam Co Dem Cent Comt, Wash
b Seattle, Wash, Aug 7, 34; s George Edward Grier & Phyllis Grace Pruvey G; m 1956 to Nancy Ruth Lumberg; c Kris Edward, Diane Elizabeth, Eric Karl & Michael Ray. Educ: Eastern Wash State Col, BA in Music, 56, BA in Music Educ, 57, MA, 63; Phi Mu Epsilon. Polit & Govt Pos: Chmn, Clallam Co Dem Cent Comt, Wash, 74- Bus & Prof Pos: Music teacher, Bridgeport Schs, Wash, 56-58, Davenport Schs, 58-63 & Port Angeles Schs, 63- Mil Serv: Entered as Airman Basic, Air Nat Guard, 54, released as S/Sgt, 50, after serv in 560th ANG Band. Mem: Am Fedn Musicians; Nat, Wash & Port Angeles Educ Asns. Mailing Add: 1629 W Seventh Port Angeles WA 98362

GRIESHEIMER, RONALD E (R)
Ill State Rep
b Chicago, Ill, Jan 25, 36; s Edward Ray Griesheimer & Carolyn Knapp G; m 1958 to Dourelle J Kweder; c Amy Lynne & David Edward. Educ: Univ Ill, 54-57; Bradley Univ, 57-58; Southern Methodist Univ Law Sch, LLB, 61; Phi Delta Phi; Pi Kappa Alpha. Polit & Govt Pos: Ill State Rep, 73- Bus & Prof Pos: Attorney, Griesheimer & Thompson, 65- Mil Serv: Entered as 1st Lt, Air Force, 61, released as Capt, 65, after serv in Judge Adv Gen Dept, McCord AFB, Wash; Maj, Air Force Res, currently. Publ: With Southwestern Law Jour, Southern Methodist Univ Law Sch, 60. Mem: Lake Co Young Rep Fedn (pres, 71-72); Waukegan Young Rep (past pres); Ill State Young Rep Orgn (12th cong dist gov, 68 & 71); Waukegan City Club (past pres); Northeast Ill Coun Boy Scouts (vchmn, NDist). Honors & Awards: Outstanding Young Rep in US for 1970-71, Nat Young Rep Fedn, 71. Relig: Protestant. Legal Res: 2303 S Bonnie Brook Lane Waukegan IL 60085 Mailing Add: 216 Madison St Waukegan IL 60085

GRIFFEE, WILLIAM B (D)
Iowa State Rep
Mailing Add: RFD Nashua IA 50658

GRIFFIN, BOB FRANKLIN (D)
Mo State Rep
b Braymer, Mo, Aug 15, 35; s Benjamin Franklin Griffin & Mildred Elizabeth Cowan G; m 1957 to Linda Charlotte Kemper; c Julie Lynn & Jeffrey Scott. Educ: Univ Mo, Columbia, BS, 57, LLB, 59, JD, 69; Phi Alpha Delta. Polit & Govt Pos: Prosecuting attorney, Clinton Co, Mo, 63-71; Mo State Rep, Dist 85, 71-73, Dist Ten, 73- Mil Serv: Entered as 2nd Lt, Air Force, 59, released as Capt, 62, after serv in Judge Adv Gen, Air Defense Command; Air Force Commendation Medal. Mem: Mo & Clinton Co Bar Asns; Am Legion; Lions; Cameron Sportsmanship Club. Relig: Methodist. Legal Res: 204 Benjamin Dr Cameron MO 64429 Mailing Add: 223 E Third St Cameron MO 64429

GRIFFIN, CHARLES HUDSON (D)
b Utica, Miss, May 9, 26; s Charles Farris Griffin & Nora Shelton G; m 1953 to Angelina Mary Pedrotti. Educ: Hinds Jr Col, 43-44 & 46-47; Miss State Univ, BS in Pub Admin, 49; Barristers Club. Polit & Govt Pos: Admin asst to US Rep John Bell Williams, Miss, 49-68; admin asst to US Rep, Miss, 68-72. Bus & Prof Pos: Dir, Cong Employees Fed Credit Union, 63-68; pres, Cent Bank of Miss, Brandon, 73- Mil Serv: Entered as A/S, Navy, 44, released as Qm 3/C, 46, after serv in Asiatic-Pac Theater, 45; Asiatic Pac Campaign & Victory Ribbons. Mem: Miss Hist Soc; Mason; Am Legion; VFW; Moose. Legal Res: 5435 Saratoga Dr Jackson MS 39211 Mailing Add: PO Box 27 Brandon MS 39042

GRIFFIN, FRANCIS J (D)
NY State Assemblyman
b Buffalo, NY; married; c Margaret Mary. Educ: Canisius Col. Polit & Govt Pos: NY State Assemblyman, 62-; Erie Co Bd of Supvrs, 15 years. Bus & Prof Pos: Ins broker. Mem: KofC; Am Legion Post 721; Holy Name Soc of St Ambrose Parish; Knights of Equity; Brotherhood of Rwy Clerks. Mailing Add: 56 Morgan Rd Buffalo NY 14220

GRIFFIN, HARMON TERRELL (R)
Chmn, Orange Co Rep Exec Comt, Fla
b Waycross, Ga, Sept 6, 42; s Sion P Griffin & Margaret Royal G; m 1964 to Jean Higgins; c Gregory Terrell, Michael Alden & Christopher David. Educ: Mercer Univ, AB, 66, JD, 68; Delta Theta Phi; Blue Key; Ed, Mercer Law Review, 68. Polit & Govt Pos: Vpres, Orange Co Young Rep Club, Fla, 69-70; gen counsel, Fla Fedn Young Rep, 72-75; chmn, Orange Co Rep Exec Comt, 74-; mem exec comt, Rep Party Fla, 74-, exec bd mem, 75- Bus & Prof Pos: Attorney-at-law, Maguire, Voorhis & Wells, Orlando, Fla, 68-70, Troutman, Griffin & Parrish, Winter Park, 70-74 & Griffin & Jones, 74- Mil Serv: Entered as Pvt, Army, 60, released as SP-4, 63, after serv in 10th Gen Dispensary, Europe, 61-63; Good Conduct Medal. Mem: The Fla Bar; Acad Fla Trial Lawyers; Asn Trial Lawyers Am; Orange Co & Am Bar Asns. Honors & Awards: Scholar Key, Delta Theta Phi, 68; Outstanding Young Men of Am, 72; Meritorious Serv Award, Mercer Univ, 73. Legal Res: 1161 Willowbrook Trail Maitland FL 32751 Mailing Add: 515 Pan American Bldg 250 N Orange Ave Orlando FL 32801

GRIFFIN, JAMES D (D)
NY State Sen
b 1929; single. Educ: Erie Co Tech Inst. Polit & Govt Pos: Ellicott Dist councilman, Buffalo, 61-65; chmn, Council's Port Comt; NY State Sen, currently. Bus & Prof Pos: Engr, Buffalo Creek RR. Mil Serv: Paratrooper, ranger, Korean War; discharged as Lt. Mem: Brotherhood of Locomotive Firemen & Engrs; St Brigid Holy Name Soc; KofC; Downtown YMCA. Mailing Add: 420 Dorrance Ave Buffalo NY 14218

GRIFFIN, JAMES W, SR (R)
Iowa State Sen
Mailing Add: PO Box 391 Council Bluffs IA 51501

GRIFFIN, MARVIN COLLINS (D)
Secy, United Polit Orgn of Tex
b Wichita, Kans, Feb 20, 23; s Jesse Griffin & Beulah Howell G; m 1944 to Lois Jesse King; c Marva Lois (Mrs Carter), Gaynelle (Mrs Jones) & Ria Joy. Educ: Bishop Col, BA magna cum laude, 43; Oberlin Grad Sch of Theol, BD, 47; Southwestern Baptist Theol Sem, MRE, 55; pres, Col YMCA. Polit & Govt Pos: Mem, Grass Roots Comt, Waco, Tex, 54, pres, Progressive Voters League, 56; mem, Action Comt to Implement Needs, Waco, 56-69; secy, United Polit Orgn, Tex, Austin, 63-; vchmn citizens adv comt, Waco Independent Sch Dist, 64; first vpres, Tex Grand Jury Asn, Houston, 65; mem, Waco Park Bd, 66-; vchmn, Econ Opportunity Adv Corp, Waco, 67-68; alt deleg, Dem Nat Conv, 68. Bus & Prof Pos: Chmn bd dirs, Tex Southern Univ, Houston, 63-; pastor, New Hope Baptist Church, Waco, 51-69. Mem: YMCA (bd dirs, Waco, 53-69, chmn, Doris Miller Br, 57-68, vchmn, 68-); Waco United Fund (dir, 66-); Austin Ment Health Ment Retardation; Capitol Area Comprehensive Health Planning (bd mem, 70); Christian Life Comn, Tex Baptist Conv (bd mem, 71). Honors & Awards: Named Alumnus of the Year, Bishop Col; Recipient of Outstanding Leadership Award, West Tex CofC; Shriver Award. Relig: Baptist. Legal Res: 1203 Cotton Austin TX 78702 Mailing Add: 1010 E Tenth St Austin TX 78202

GRIFFIN, MICHAEL GARY (D)
Mem-At-Lg, Dem Nat Comt
b San Francisco, Calif, Apr 4, 48; s John Edward Griffin & Mary Crawford G; m 1971 to Colley Rhodes. Educ: Univ Ala, 66-69; Univ Md, 70-71; Auburn Univ, 71; Alpha Tau Omega. Polit & Govt Pos: Ballot pos adv, Wallace Campaign, Montgomery, Ala, 71-72; dir activities & arrangements for Wallace Campaign, Dem Nat Conv, 72; mem-at-lg & mem exec comt, Dem Nat Comt, 72-; exec asst to Gov George C Wallace, Ala, 72- Mil Serv: Sgt, Ala Air Nat Guard, 5 years. Mem: Young Dem Ala; Ala Cattlemen's Asn; Ala Farmers' Asn; Gov Coun on Drug Abuse. Relig: Presbyterian. Legal Res: 151 Felder Ave Montgomery AL 36104 Mailing Add: Governor's Off State Capitol Montgomery AL 36104

GRIFFIN, MICHAEL J (D)
Mich State Rep
Mailing Add: 505 North Elm Jackson MI 49202

GRIFFIN, OSCAR O'NEAL, JR (R)
b Daisetta, Tex, Apr 28, 33; s Oscar O'Neal Griffin & Myrtle Ellen Edgar G; m 1955 to Patricia Lamb; c Gwendolyn, Amanda, Gregory O'Neal & Marguerite Ellen. Educ: Univ Tex, Austin, BJ, 58. Polit & Govt Pos: Dept info dir, Dept of Transportation, 69-70, asst dir pub affairs, 70-74. Bus & Prof Pos: Pub rels dir, Liberty, Tex, 58-59; ed, Canyon News, 59-60; ed, Pecos Independent, 60-62; spec assignments reporter, Houston Chronicle, 62-66; spec assignments reporter, Washington Correspondent, 66-69; vpres, Griffin Oil Well Serv, Inc, El Campo, Tex, currently. Mil Serv: Entered as Pvt, Army, 53, released as Sgt, 55, after serv as ed, Ft Bliss News, 4052nd Area Serv Unit, Ft Bliss, Tex, 54-55; Armed Serv Newspaper Award, 55. Mem: Nat Press Club; Sigma Delta Chi. Honors & Awards: Tex Newspaper Asn Sweepstakes Award, 60; Pulitzer Prize, 63; Golden Plate Award, Am Acad Achievement for Jour, 64; Tex Headliners Club Award for Journalistic Reality, 65. Relig: Roman Catholic. Mailing Add: 2208 Hutchins Lane El Campo TX 77437

GRIFFIN, PAT (D)
NC State Rep
Mailing Add: 1829 Front St Apt F-2 Durham NC 27705

GRIFFIN, RICHARD THOMAS (D)
Chmn, Ansonia Dem Town Comt, Conn
b Derby, Conn, Aug 18, 38; s Gerald Edward Griffin & Constance Beck G; m 1962 to Jeanne Ellen McWilliams; c Kathleen, Karen & Jeffrey. Educ: Quinnipiac Col, 56-62. Polit & Govt Pos: Mem, Ansonia Dem Town Comt, Conn, 68-, chmn, 74- Bus & Prof Pos: Asst treas, Conn Union of Tel Workers Inc, 68-74; real estate broker, Larkin Realtors, 71-; asst rec supvr, Southern New Eng Tel Co, 74- Mil Serv: Entered as Pvt, Army, 56, released as Specialist Four, 60, after serv in 108th Machine Rec Unit. Relig: Catholic. Mailing Add: 5 Fox Hill Terr Ansonia CT 06401

GRIFFIN, ROBERT PAUL (R)
Minority Whip, US Senate
b Detroit, Mich, Nov 6, 23; s Julius A Griffin & Beulah Childers G; m 1947 to Marjorie Jean Anderson; c Paul Robert, Richard Allen, James Anderson & Martha Jill. Educ: Cent Mich Univ, AB & BS, 47; Univ Mich Law Sch, JD, 50; The Citadel; Shrivenham Univ, Eng; Tau Alpha Upsilon; Sigma Tau Delta. Hon Degrees: LLD, Cent Mich Univ, 63, Eastern Mich Univ, Albion Col, Western Mich Univ, Grand Valley State Col, Detroit Col of Bus, Univ Mich & Detroit Col Law; LHD, Hillsdale Col; JCD, Rollins Col; DEd, Northern Mich Univ; DPS, Detroit Inst Technol. Polit & Govt Pos: US Rep, Ninth Cong Dist, Mich, 57-66; US Sen, Mich, 66-, Minority Whip, US Senate, 69-, mem, Com, Foreign Rels & Rules & Admin Comts, currently; deleg, Rep Nat Conv, 68 & 72; mem, Nat Rep Sen Comt, 70- Bus & Prof Pos: Attorney, Traverse City, Mich, 50-56. Mil Serv: Enlisted man, Army 3 years in World War II, serv in Field Artil, ETO; Medal with Two Battle Stars. Publ: The labor board and section 8(b) (7), Univ Detroit Law J, 12/62; Federal labor policy & the NLRB, Mich State Univ Bar J, 11/68; The Fortas controversy: the Senate's role of advice and consent, Prospectus, a J of Law Reform, 4/69. Mem: Am & Mich State Bar Asns; Alpha Kappa Psi; Phi Alpha Delta; Elks. Honors & Awards: Named One of the Ten Outstanding Young Men in Am, US Jr CofC, 59. Relig: Congregational. Legal Res: Traverse City MI 49684 Mailing Add: 353 Old Senate Off Bldg Washington DC 20510

GRIFFIN, RUTH LEWIN (R)
NH State Rep
b Fall River, Mass, July 9, 25; d Perez Otis Lewin & May Dorothy Bailey L; m 1947 to John Kenneth Griffin; c Joan G (Mrs Maloney), John K, Jr, Michael J, Joyce E & Timothy G. Educ: Wentworth Hosp Sch of Nursing, Dover, NH, RN, 46. Polit & Govt Pos: NH State Rep, 71-; deleg & mem, Platform Comt, NH State Rep Conv, 72; First Dist Deleg & mem, Platform Comt, Rep Nat Conv, 72. Mem: Portsmouth Federated Rep Women's Club; Nat

Fedn Rep Women; Order of Women Legislators; DAR. Relig: Methodist. Mailing Add: 479 Richards Ave Portsmouth NH 03801

GRIFFIN, SAMUEL MARVIN (D)
b Bainbridge, Ga, Sept 4, 07; s Ernest Howard Griffin & Josie Butler G; m 1931 to Mary Elizabeth Smith; c Samuel Marvin, Jr. Educ: The Citadel, AB. Polit & Govt Pos: Ga State Rep, 35-37; Adj Gen, State of Ga, 44-47, Lt Gov, 48-54, Gov, 54-59. Bus & Prof Pos: Publ, The Post-Searchlight, 33- Mil Serv: Entered as Capt, Army, 40, released as Lt Col, 44, after serv in 101st Sep Bn (AA-AW), SW Pac Theatre, 42; Unit Citation. Mem: Ga Press Asn; Mason; Shrine; Lions; CofC. Honors & Awards: Man of the Year, Lions. Relig: Presbyterian. Mailing Add: 809 Lamar St Bainbridge GA 31717

GRIFFIN, WALTER JOSEPH (R)
Chmn, Sudbury Rep Town Comt, Mass
b Brooklyn, NY, Aug 12, 26; S Walter R Griffin & Grace H Kallighan G; m 1954 to Jean A Oates; c Barbara J & Thomas M. Educ: Brooklyn Polytech Inst, BSEE, 52; Northeastern Univ, MSEE, 62; Eta Kappa Nu; Tau Beta Pi; Pi Kappa Phi. Polit & Govt Pos: Chmn, Sudbury Rep Town Comt, Mass, 68- Bus & Prof Pos: Eng sect head, Raytheon Co, Waltham, Mass. Mem: Inst Elec & Electronics Engrs. Relig: Roman Catholic. Mailing Add: 25 Old Coach Rd Sudbury MA 01776

GRIFFIN, WALTER ROLAND (D)
Committeeperson, Iowa Dem State Cent Comt
b Carbondale, Pa, Nov 20, 42; s Walter Joseph Griffin & Maud Boland G; m 1961 to Mary Eleanor Armstrong; c Rebecca, Kathleen & Shawn. Educ: Loyola Col (Md), AB, 63; Univ Cincinnati, MA, 64; Phi Alpha Theta; Pi Gamma Mu. Polit & Govt Pos: City councilperson, Fayette, Iowa, 71-; campaign mgr, Don Avenson for State Rep, 72 & 74; chairperson, Fayette Co Dem Cent Comt, 72-; chairperson, Second Dist Dem Campaign Comt, 74-; committeeperson, Iowa Dem State Cent Comt, 74- Bus & Prof Pos: Lectr hist, Xavier Univ (Ohio), 65-66; asst prof hist, Mt St Mary's Col, 67-68; asst prof hist, Upper Iowa Univ, 66-67 & 68-, chmn dept, 69-, chmn div social sci & bus admin, 69-, chmn faculty, 74- Publ: Auth, Louis Ludlow & the war referendum crusade, 1935-1941, Ind Mag Hist, 12/68; auth, George W Goethals, explorer of the Pacific Northwest, 1882-84, Pac Northwest Quart, 10/71; co-ed, A comprehensive guide to the location of published & unpublished newspaper indexes in Colorado repositories, Colo Mag, fall 72. Mem: Orgn Am Hist; Am Hist Asn; Soc Hist Am Foreign Rels. Honors & Awards: Taft Teaching Fel, Univ Cincinnati, 63, Grad Assistantships, 64-66; Iowa Dem Party Voter Identification Prog Award, 74; Fayette Jaycees Community Serv Award, 74. Relig: Unitarian. Mailing Add: 105 Alexander St Fayette IA 52142

GRIFFITH, CALVIN GRANT, III (R)
Chmn, Blair Co Rep Comt, Pa
b Altoona, Pa, Apr 30, 27; s Calvin Grant Griffith, Jr & Charlotte Williams G; m 1954 to Joan Dobson; c Peter Thompson & Amy Louise. Educ: Washington & Jefferson Col, AB, 50; Pa State Univ, 51; Phi Delta Theta. Polit & Govt Pos: Mem city charter comn, Altoona, Pa, 64-65; dir, Altoona Area Sch Dist, 68-; dir, Blair Co Sch Bd, 70-71; dir, Intermediate Unit Bd, 71-; mem, Blair Co Rep Comt, 72-, asst chmn, 74, chmn, 74- Bus & Prof Pos: Sports ed, Altoona Tribune, Pa, 44-45; secy-treas, Cal G Griffith, Jr Agency, Inc, Altoona, 50-; vchmn, Pa Econ League, Blair Co, 72-74, chmn, 74- Mil Serv: Entered as Seaman 2/C, Naval Res, 45, released as SP-3, 46, after serv in Pub Info Div; Am Theatre Opers Medal; World War II Victory Medal. Mem: Nat & Pa Asns Ins Agts; Blair Co Asn Fire & Casualty Agts. Relig: Episcopal. Legal Res: 3614 Broad Ave Altoona PA 16601 Mailing Add: Suite 432 Cent Trust Bldg Altoona PA 16601

GRIFFITH, DOUGLAS JON (D)
b St Paul, Minn, Sept 25, 48; s David Griffith & Carolyn Nielsen G; m to Eloise E Jensen. Educ: Univ Wis-River Falls, BS, 70; Univ Minn; San Diego State Univ; Sigma Alpha. Polit & Govt Pos: Deleg, Minn State Dem Conv, 72; alt deleg, Dem Nat Conv, 72; chmn, Washington Co Citizens for McGovern, 72; chief admin asst to Rep Stephen G Wenzel, Minn, 75- Bus & Prof Pos: Polit sci instr, Forest Lake Sr High Sch, Minn, 70- Publ: The unmaking of the President 1972, Hopf & Hopf Inc, 72; Miami Beach: the Democrats in review, Forest Lake Times, 72. Mem: Minn & Nat Educ Asns; Am Polit Sci Asn; Am Civil Liberties Union; Minn Coun for Social Sci. Mailing Add: 1634 N Victoria St Paul MN 55117

GRIFFITH, EDWARD (D)
NY State Assemblyman
Mailing Add: 710 Warwick St Brooklyn NY 11207

GRIFFITH, JAMES BRADSHAW (R)
State Auditor, Wyo
b Laredo, Tex, Jan 13, 27; s James Bradshaw Griffith, Sr & Nellie Snyder G; div; c Sally Anne, Laura Nell & Carol Lynn. Educ: Univ Wyo, BS, 50; Alpha Kappa Psi; Sigma Delta Chi; Sigma Nu. Polit & Govt Pos: Chmn, Wyo State Young Rep, 49-50; committeeman, Wyo Rep Party, 55-71, publicity chmn, 63-65, treas, 71-; State Auditor, Wyo, 75- Mil Serv: Entered as A/S, Navy, 44, released as Seaman 1/C, 46, after serv in US. Mem: Wyo Press Asn; Mason; Am Legion; Lions Club. Relig: Congregational. Legal Res: 557 S Elm Lusk WY 82225 Mailing Add: 5464 Walker Rd Cheyenne WY 82001

GRIFFITH, MARGARET RUTH (MARGY) (R)
VChmn, Pike Co Rep Cent Comt, Mo
b Louisiana, Mo, Aug 22, 25; d Lester I Zumwalt & Marie Jones Z; m 1943 to Darwin Bartlett Griffith; c Darwin Bartlett (Bart), Jerry Lester & Randall Lee. Educ: Louisiana High Sch, grad, 43. Polit & Govt Pos: Secy, Pike Co Rep Cent Comt, Mo, 58-68, chmn, 68-70, vchmn, 70-; pres, Federated Rep Women Pike Co, 67-74, chmn, 74-; treas, Ninth Cong Dist Rep Women's Club, 69; vchmn, Ninth Cong Dist Rep Orgn, 70-73, chmn, 73-; rec secy, Mo Federated Rep Women's Clubs, 72- Bus & Prof Pos: Asst 4-H agt, Univ Mo Exten Serv, 75- Mem: Pike Co 4-H Clubs; Farm Bur; PTA. Honors & Awards: Outstanding 4-H Family, 57. Relig: Presbyterian; elder, Calumet Presby Church, 74; treas, Covenant Larger Parish. Mailing Add: McIntosh Angus Farm RR 1 Box 132 Clarksville MO 63336

GRIFFITH, NAOMI REBECCA (R)
Chairwoman, Scott Co Rep Orgn, Ky
b Corinth, Ky, Oct 14, 10; d Kelly Cyrus Dunn & Sudie Francis Smith D; m 1932 to Paul Penn Griffith; c Elizabeth Sue (Mrs R W Elder). Educ: Sadieville High Sch, Scott Co, Ky, dipl, 29; Shannon Sch Music, dipl, 31. Polit & Govt Pos: Dietitian, Ky Village of Reform, Lexington, 44; substitute postman, rural rte, Hinton, Ky, 46; chairwoman, Scott Co Rep Orgn, Ky, 52-; Scott Co campaign chairwoman, Dwight D Eisenhower, 52; pres, Scott Co Rep Woman's Club, 54; enumerator, US Farm Census Bur, 54; crew leader, US Census Bur, Washington, DC, 57; election officer, Georgetown, Ky, 58-68; sr clerk, Safety Div, State Hwy Dept Dist Seven, 68-72; chmn purgation bd, Scott Co, Georgetown, Ky, 68-72; mem staff, State Dept of Econ Security, 71-72; mem exec comt, Local Rep Orgn, currently. Bus & Prof Pos: Teacher music, Renaker High Sch, Cynthiana, Ky, 30. Mem: Bus & Prof Women's Club; Woman's Soc Christian Serv; Hinton Homemaker's Club; Scott Co Rep 100 Club. Honors & Awards: Ky Col, Gov Louie B Nunn. Relig: Methodist. Mailing Add: Glenwood Dr Rte 4 Georgetown KY 40324

GRIFFITHS, EARLE CURTISS, JR (R)
Chmn, Sherman Town Rep Party, Conn
b Philadelphia, Pa, Jan 31, 30; s Earle Curtiss Griffiths & Elizabeth Alexander G; m 1960 to Donna June King; c Robin Ann, Deborah Jean & Earle Curtiss, III. Educ: Univ Wyo, 49-50; Ski Team. Polit & Govt Pos: Justice of peace, Sherman, Conn, 66-; chmn, Sherman Rep Town Comt, 70-72 & 75- Bus & Prof Pos: Owner, independent garage, Williamstown, Mass, 53-57; serv mgr, Gilmer Cadillac & Oldsmobile, North Adams, 57-59; mechanic, Finney's Serv Ctr, 59-60; parts mgr, New Milford Tractor, Conn, 60-66; 2nd Lt, Sherman Fire Dept, 65-66, 1st Lt, 66-68, Capt, 68-70; store mgr, Humphrey Bros, 66- Mil Serv: Entered as Pvt, Army, 51, released as E-3, 53, after serv in 7131 Army Unit JTF 132, First H Bomb Test, Eniwetok, Marshall Islands. Mem: Sherman Boy Scouts (inst rep comt mem & treas, 63-). Relig: Protestant. Mailing Add: Griffiths Hill Sherman CT 06784

GRIFFITHS, MARTHA W (D)
b Pierce City, Mo; m to Hicks G Griffiths. Educ: Univ Mo, BA; Univ Mich Law Sch, JD. Polit & Govt Pos: Mich State Rep, 49-52; recorder & judge, Recorder's Court, 53; US Rep, Mich, 55-74. Bus & Prof Pos: Mem bd dirs, Chrysler Corp, Burroughs Corp, Nat Detroit Corp, Am Automobile Club & Consumers Power. Mailing Add: Suite 120 32985 Hamilton Ct Farmington Hills MI 48024

GRIMALDI, JAMES L (D)
Mass State Rep
Mailing Add: State Capitol Boston MA 02133

GRIMES, RUTH (D)
RI State Sen
Mailing Add: 663 Cranston St Providence RI 02907

GRIMM, ROBERT JOHN (R)
Mem Exec Comt, Young Rep Nat Fedn
b Forest Hills, NY, Feb 6, 37; s John Andrew Grimm & Margaret O'Conner G; single. Educ: Univ Vt, BA, 58; NY Univ Sch Law, LLB, 64; Tau Kappa Alpha; Sigma Nu. Polit & Govt Pos: Mem bd gov, Asn NY State Young Rep Clubs, 64-, mem exec comt, 69-; chmn, Nassau Co Young Rep, NY, 68-69; mem exec comt, Nat Fedn Young Rep, 69- Bus & Prof Pos: Leland Badler, Esq, Hicksville, NY, 64-65; trial attorney, Criminal Div, Legal Aid Soc, Nassau Co, 65-69; attorney, Avon Prod, New York, 69- Mil Serv: Entered as 2nd Lt, Army, 59, released as 1st Lt, 59, after serv in 504th Mil Police Co, Ft Eustis, Va, 59; Capt, Army Res, currently. Mem: NY State & Nassau Bar Asns. Relig: Lutheran. Mailing Add: 1421 Belmont Ave New Hyde Park NY 11040

GRIMSEY, J HERBERT (R)
Dep Dir, NY State Rep Campaign Comt
b East Orange, NJ, Oct 10, 09; s George H Grimsey & Evelyn Terrien G; m 1942 to Ruth Marie Sheridan. Educ: Univ Ky, BS in elec eng, 30. Polit & Govt Pos: Comnr, White Plains Elec Bd, NY, 51-; campaign chmn, Westchester Co Rep Party, 52, 56, 58, 62, 64 & 70, coordr, 69; dep dir, NY State Rep Campaign Comt & co committeeman, Westchester Co, NY, 60-; deleg, Rep Nat Conv, 64; bd of visitors, Wassaic State Sch, 64-; presidential elector, 72; mem exec comt, White Plains Rep Orgn, 75- Bus & Prof Pos: Pres, Eastern Elec Corp, 48-52, chmn & bd dir, 52-; mem bd dirs, Rumarlin Corp, 59; mem bd dirs, Windsor Life Ins Co of Am, 65- Mem: Nat Exchange Clubs (nat pres); Elks; Mason (32 Degree); CofC; Red Cross & Community Chest. Relig: Protestant. Legal Res: 90 Bryant Ave White Plains NY 10605 Mailing Add: 96-98 Fulton St White Plains NY 10606

GRING, HARRY H (R)
Pa State Rep
Mailing Add: Capitol Bldg Harrisburg PA 17120

GRISBAUM, CHARLES, JR (D)
La State Rep
Mailing Add: 3224 N Turnbull Metairie LA 70002

GRISWOLD, ERWIN NATHANIEL (R)
b East Cleveland, Ohio, July 1, 04; s James Harlen Griswold & Hope Erwin G; m 1931 to Harriet Allena Ford; c Hope (Mrs Daniel Murrow) & William Erwin. Educ: Oberlin Col, AB & AM, 25; Harvard Law Sch, LLB, 28 & SJD, 29; Phi Beta Kappa. Hon Degrees: 29 hon degrees. Polit & Govt Pos: Attorney in off of Solicitor Gen & spec asst to Attorney Gen, Dept of Justice, 29-34; consult, Treas Dept, 42; mem, Comn on Civil Rights, 61-67; Solicitor Gen, US Dept of Justice, 67-73. Bus & Prof Pos: Asst prof law, Harvard Law Sch, 34-35, prof, 35-67, dean, 46-67. Publ: The Fifth Amendment Today, 54 & Law and Lawyers in the United States, 64, Harvard Univ Press; Cases on Federal Taxation, Found Press, 6th Ed, 66. Mem: Am, Mass, Fed & Boston Bar Asns; Am Bar Found. Honors & Awards: Hon Bencher, Inner Temple; Corresponding fel, Brit Acad. Legal Res: 36 Kenmore Rd Belmont MA 02178 Mailing Add: 1100 Connecticut Ave Washington DC 20036

GRIZZARD, ROBERT HAROLD (D)
Mem, Fla State Dem Cent Comt
b Winchester, Tenn, May 27, 15; s Thomas M Grizzard & May Saunders G; m 1941 to Mildred Booth; c Carol Ann (Mrs Shull, Jr) & Robert H, II. Educ: Univ of the South, 34-36; Fla Southern Col, AB, 39; Phi Kappa. Polit & Govt Pos: City comnr, Lakeland, Fla, 63-66, mayor, 64-; committeeman, Polk Co Dem Exec Comt, 73-75; mem, Fla State Dem Cent Comt, Polk Co, 74- Bus & Prof Pos: Pres, Sunshine Oil Co Inc, 59-67; sales mgr, H & M Realty Co, 67-75. Mil Serv: Entered as Pvt, Air Force, 42, released as T/Sgt, 46, after serv in 45th Troop Carrier; Purple Heart; Good Conduct Medal; Victory Medal; Theatre of Opers Medals. Mem: Kiwanis; Am Legion; Exchange Club; CofC; Lone Palm Club. Honors & Awards: Exchange Club Good Citizenship Award, 64. Relig: Methodist. Legal Res: 2715 Berkeley Lakeland FL 33803 Mailing Add: PO Box 3186 Lakeland FL 33802

GRIZZLE, MARY R (R)
Fla State Rep
b Lawrence Co, Ohio, Aug 19, 21; m to Ben F Grizzle; c Henry, Polley, Lorena, Mary Alice, Betty & Jeanne. Educ: Portsmouth Interstate Bus Col. Polit & Govt Pos: Town comnr, formerly; Fla State Rep, 63-, mem, Comts on Bus Regulation, Environ Pollution Control & Appropriations, Fla House Rep, currently; chmn, Pinellas Co Deleg, 64-66, mem, Co Civil Serv Comt & Co Planning Coun; Rep Precinct Committeewoman; pres, Clearwater Women's Rep Club & Fla Fedn of Rep Women, formerly; chmn, Fla Comn on Status of Women; Gov Rep to Nat Conf of Women Community Leaders for Hwy Safety. Bus & Prof Pos: Housewife; bus investments. Publ: Co-author & publ, Thimbleful of History. Mem: Anona PTA (past pres); Altrusa & Woman's Clubs of Clearwater; Bus Indust Polit Comt, NY; Nat Soc of Arts & Letters. Honors & Awards: Selected Outstanding Woman of the Year, 66; One of Ten Outstanding Women in 1966 by St Petersburg Times. Relig: Episcopal. Legal Res: 120 Gulf Blvd Belleair Shore Indian Rocks Beach FL 33535 Mailing Add: Rm 505 Coachman Bldg 503 Cleveland St Clearwater FL 33515

GROENER, DICK (D)
Ore State Sen
Mailing Add: 15014 Woodland Way Milwaukie OR 97222

GROENER, T RALPH (D)
Ore State Rep
b Oregon City, Ore, Dec 25, 41; s George Stanton Groener & Mary Ella McKee G; m 1965 to Sharon Diane Rich; c Hilary Annette & Christopher Jon. Educ: Univ Ore, BS, 69; Portland State Univ, 69-70. Polit & Govt Pos: Mem sch bd, Clackamas Community Col, 71-73; Ore State Rep, 72-; mem, Ore Gov Comn on Youth, 73- Mil Serv: Entered as Basic, Air Force, 60, released as A 2/C, 64, after serv in Hq Lowry Tech Training Ctr, Air Training Command, 60-64; Airman's Medal. Mem: Jaycees; Camp Fire Girls (bd dirs, membership chmn, 70-); Clackamas Co Youth Comn (chmn, 70-); Clackamas Co Sr Citizen Coun; Clackamas Co Cancer Soc. Honors & Awards: Outstanding Jaycee, 71-72; Outstanding Youth Leader, Clackamas Co Youth Comn, 71-72; Distinguished Serv Award, Am Asn Retired Persons, 72; Outstanding Youth Leadership, Camp Fire Girls, 72-73. Relig: Protestant. Mailing Add: 210 Elmar Dr Oregon City OR 97045

GROFF, REGIS F (D)
Colo State Sen
b Monmouth, Ill, Apr 8, 35; s Eddie Groff & Fenimore Thomas G; m 1962 to Ada Lucille Brooks; c Traci Lucille & Peter Charles. Educ: Western Ill Univ, BS in Social Sci, 62; Univ Denver, MA in Sec Educ & Hist, 72; Urban Affairs Inst, grad, 72; Alpha Phi Omega. Polit & Govt Pos: Colo State Sen, Dist 3, 74-; mem, Mayor's Comn Human Rels, currently. Bus & Prof Pos: Teacher, Denver Pub Schs, Colo, 63-; instr, Univ Colo, Boulder, 74- Mil Serv: Entered as Airman Basic, Air Force, 53, released as Airman 1/C, 57, after serv in Air Defense Command. Mem: Nat Educ Asn; Malcolm X Ment Health Ctr (bd mem); Denver Classroom Teachers Asn. Honors & Awards: Collegiate Coun of UN, 62; Presidents Educators Award, 69. Relig: African Methodist Episcopal. Mailing Add: 2079 Albion St Denver CO 80207

GROFF, WILLIAM ALBERT (D)
b Victor, Mont, Feb 17, 20; s Houston Clay Groff & Julia Vic G; m 1946 to Phyllis Ann Weisener; c Ann & Kay. Educ: Kemper Mil Sch, AA, 40; Univ Tex, 41; Univ Mont, BA, 42; Delta Tau Delta. Polit & Govt Pos: Mont State Sen, 55-74, chmn, Finance & Claims Comt, Mont State Senate, 57-63, 65-67 & 69-74, Majority Leader, 63, Pres Pro Tem Ad Interim, 67-69; mem, Columbia River Compact Comn, 57-; mem, White House Conf Educ, 59; chmn, Mont Legis Coun, 63-64; deleg, Dem Nat Conv, 68, alt deleg, 72; exec mem, Western States Water Coun, currently, vchmn, 68- Bus & Prof Pos: Cashier, Farmers State Bank, 55-61, pres, 61- Mil Serv: Entered as Pvt, Army, 42, released as 1st Lt, 46, after serv in Hq, Base F, Qm Corps, Southwest Pac; Asiatic-Pac Serv Medal with 2 Bronze Stars; Philippine Liberation Medal with 1 Bronze Star; World War II Victory Medal. Mem: Mason; Elks; Am Legion; VFW; Grange. Relig: Presbyterian. Mailing Add: Box 46 Victor MT 59875

GROGAN, LEE R (D)
b Ball Ground, Ga, Apr 16, 31; s Paul Grogan & Lila Stamper G; m 1954 to Jane Haywood; c Lee R, Jr, Susan, Nancy & Paul Martin. Educ: Emory Univ, Oxford, 48-50; Mercer Univ, AB, 52, Law Sch, JD, 55; Blue Key; Kappa Sigma; Phi Alpha Delta. Polit & Govt Pos: Chmn, Campaign for Gov Jimmy Carter, Muscogee Co, Ga, 70; mem, Ga Port Authority; mem, State Dem Exec Comt, formerly. Bus & Prof Pos: Lawyer, Columbus, Ga, 60-; partner, Grogan, Jones & Layfield, Columbus, currently, pres, 72-73. Mil Serv: Entered as Ens, Navy, 55, released as Lt, 59, after serv in Law Specialists; admitted to practice before US Court of Mil Appeals; cert as Trial & Defense Counsel for Gen Court Martial. Mem: Columbus Lawyers Club; Chattaidoochee Circuit Bar Asn; State Bar of Ga; local & state Bar Asns; Mercer Univ (bd trustees). Honors & Awards: Jr Chamber Int, Senator. Relig: Baptist. Legal Res: 3431 Sue Mack Dr Columbus GA 31906 Mailing Add: PO Box 2607 Columbus GA 31902

GROMALA, JOHN ANTHONY (R)
Mem, Calif State Rep Cent Comt
b Meriden, Conn, Jan 23, 30; s John Anthony Gromala & Anna Wojcik G; m 1956 to Suzanne Thornton Barrie; c Ellen Suzanne, Margaret Ann & John Barrie. Educ: Quinnipiac Col, AS, 49; Univ San Francisco, BS, 56, JD, 58. Polit & Govt Pos: Chmn, San Francisco 22nd Dist Young Rep, Calif, 55; co-chmn, Young Rep Testimonial for Sen Knowland, 55; treas, San Francisco Young Rep, 56; chmn, San Francisco Ike Day, 56; co-chmn, San Francisco Young Voters Comt for Sen Kuchel, 56; chmn, San Francisco Knowland for Gov Clubs, 57-58; campaign mgr, Athearn for Calif State Sen, San Francisco, 58; mem exec comt, Humboldt Co Nixon for President, 60; pres, Eel River Valley Young Rep, 61; mem exec comt & parliamentarian, Humboldt Co Rep Cent Comt, 61-65; finance chmn, Clausen for Cong Primary Campaign, Humboldt Co, 62; parliamentarian, First Cong Dist Rep Comt, 62-63; vpres of Region I, Calif Young Rep, 62-63, gen counsel, 63-64, pres & mem exec bd, 64-65; deleg, Young Rep Nat Conv, 63 & 65; Rep Presidential Elector Nominee & deleg, Rep Nat Conv, 64; mem, Calif State Rep Cent Comt, 64-; successor treas in event of disaster, Calif, 67-; mem exec comt, Ivy Baker Priest for Treas, 70. Bus & Prof Pos: Partner, law firm, Mahan, Harland & Gromala, 60-68; partner, law firm, Mahan, Dunn, Harland & Gromala, 68-; dir, Bank of Loleta, Calif, 61- Mil Serv: Entered as Pvt, Marine Corps, 51, released as S/Sgt, 54, after serv in Continental US. Mem: Am Calif & Humboldt Co Bar Asns; Fortuna Rotary; Humboldt Co Cancer Soc (dir, 61-64 & 67-). Relig: Roman Catholic. Legal Res: 22 Pinecrest Dr Fortuna CA 95540 Mailing Add: PO Box 626 Fortuna CA 95540

GRONEMEIER, RALPH A (R)
Treas, Posey Co Rep Comt, Ind
b Mt Vernon, Ind, June 7, 04; s Alfred S Gronemeier & Mary Tischendorf G; m 1927 to Florence Hufnagel; c Ruth (Mrs Don Miles) & Gary. Educ: Cent Bus Col, 1 year. Polit & Govt Pos: Precinct committeeman, Mt Vernon, Ind, 30-65; treas, Posey Co Rep Comt, Ind, 54- Mem: Kiwanis (secy, 33-); CofC (treas, 67-); Beulah Masonic Lodge (Past Master, treas, 58-); Evansville Stamp Club (treas, 72-). Relig: Methodist. Mailing Add: 504 E Fifth St Mt Vernon IN 47620

GRONHOVD, ERICH ARTHUR (D)
NDak State Sen
b Steele Co, NDak, July 26, 05; s Gilbert Gronhovd & Christine Erickson G; m 1927 to Ruth Prudence Pederson; c Ruth (Mrs Vernon Halda), Carol (Mrs Lee Bjerke), James & Judith (Mrs Gail Groth). Educ: Elem & high sch; trade sch, 1 year. Polit & Govt Pos: Mem, Steele Co Agr Stabilization & Conserv Comt, US Dept Agr, 12 years, chmn, 16 years, mem, NDak Comt, 4 years, chmn, 65-69; NDak State Sen, 70- Mem: Sons of Norway Lodge. Relig: Lutheran. Legal Res: Finley ND Mailing Add: State Capitol Bismarck ND 43215

GRONNEBERG, ARNOLD J (D)
NDak State Rep
b Walum, NDak, Oct 6, 12; s C N Gronneberg (deceased) & Inga Bjornseth G (deceased); m 1941 to Christine Sabby; c Douglas, Carol Ann (Mrs White), Lee Alan & Sandra Avis (Mrs Francis). Educ: NDak State Univ, Assoc BS, 38. Polit & Govt Pos: NDak State Rep, 71- Bus & Prof Pos: Mem staff, Griggs Co & Steele Co Dist, Farmers Home Admin, NDak, 66-69. Mem: Odd Fellows; Eagles; Sons of Norway; Farmers Union. Honors & Awards: Soil Conserv Award, 65. Relig: Lutheran. Mailing Add: Hannaford ND 58448

GRONOUSKI, JOHN AUSTIN (D)
b Dunbar, Wis, Oct 26, 19; s John Austin Gronouski & Mary Riley G; m 1948 to Mary Louise Metz; c Stacy & Julie. Educ: Univ Wis, BA, 42, MA, 47 & PhD, 55. Hon Degrees: DHL, Alliance Col; LLD, Fairleigh Dickinson Univ & Babson Col, 73; DDL, St Edward's Univ, 70. Polit & Govt Pos: Research dir, Wis Dept of Taxation, 59; Wis State Comnr of Taxation, 60-63; Postmaster Gen of US, 63-65; Presidential Rep, Int Trade Fair, Poland, 64; US Ambassador, Poland, 65-68; mem bd trustees, Nat Urban League, 68-73; app mem by President Nixon to Presidential Study Comn on Int Radio Broadcasting, 72-73. Bus & Prof Pos: Dean, Lyndon B Johnson Sch Pub Affairs, Univ Tex, Austin, 69-74. Mil Serv: Entered as Pvt, Army Air Corps, 42, released as 1st Lt, 45, after serv in 8th Air Force. Mem: Am Econ Asn; Nat Tax Asn; Polish-Am Inst Arts & Sci (pres). Honors & Awards: Distinguished Alumnus Award, Wis State Col, Oshkosh, 64; Distinguished Citizen Citation, Creighton Univ, 69; Phi Kappa Phi, Univ Tex, 70. Mailing Add: 610 E 43rd St Austin TX 78751

GROOM, JAMES HAYNES (R)
Mem, Rep State Cent Comt Calif
b Rocky Ford, Colo, July 3, 19; s Elijah Moore Groom & Tina G; m 1946 to Pearl Daisy Andersen; c Charlene (Mrs Scott La Strange) & Ann. Educ: Santa Rosa Jr Col, AA, 39. Polit & Govt Pos: Mem, Rep State Cent Comt Calif, 67-; chmn finance comt, First Cong Club, 67-; dir, Sonoma Co Rep Cent Comt, 67; chmn, Indust Develop Comt, Rohnert Park, 67-69; dir Eel River Asn; dir, Zone 1A Flood Dist; former mem, Santa Rosa City Coun. Bus & Prof Pos: Owner, Groom Equipment Co, Santa Rosa, Calif, 46- Mil Serv: Entered as A/S, Navy, 42, released as CPO, 66, after serv in Pac Theatre; Letter of Commendation; seven combat stars. Mem: Calif State Exchange Clubs; Santa Rosa CofC; Mason; Scottish Rite; Shrine. Honors & Awards: Key to City, Santa Rosa, Calif. Relig: Protestant. Legal Res: 1625 Fair Oaks Ct Santa Rosa CA 95404 Mailing Add: 85 Scenic Ave Santa Rosa CA 95401

GROOVER, DENMARK, JR (D)
b Quitman, Ga, June 30, 22; s Denmark Groover, Sr & Mary McCall G; m 1945 to Kathryn McCaskell Terry; div; c Denmark, III, Charles Terry. Educ: Univ Ga, LLB, 48; Phi Delta Theta. Polit & Govt Pos: Ga State Rep, 53-56 & 63-64, floor leader, Ga House Rep, 55-56. Bus & Prof Pos: Attorney. Mil Serv: Marine Corps Res, Maj, 42-45; Purple Heart; Air Medal. Relig: Presbyterian. Mailing Add: 165 First St Macon GA 31201

GROPPO, JOHN G (D)
Conn State Rep
Mailing Add: 18 Cherry St Winsted CT 06098

GROSBY, ELEANOR (R)
Chmn, 145th Legis Dist Rep Party, Conn
b Boston, Mass; d Jacob Hurwitz & Minnie Slosberg H; m 1947 to Robert N Grosby; c Mark Jonathan & Craig Hollis. Educ: NY Univ; Univ Cincinnati. Polit & Govt Pos: Pres, Norwalk Women's Rep Club, Conn, 56-60; co-chmn, Young Rep, 60; councilwoman, Norwalk Common Coun, 61-67, cand for re-election, 67 & 69; chmn, Conserv Comn, 63-69; Oak Hills Bd of Gov, 65; spec dep sheriff, Fairfield Co, currently; chmn, 145th Legis Dist Rep Party, 69-; campaign staff mem, Sen Lowell P Weicker & Congressman Stewart R McKinney; comnr, Planning & Zoning Comn, 71- Bus & Prof Pos: Publ, Rathkopfon Planning & Zoning, 48-50; realtor, 59-, first vpres, Norwalk Bd Realtors, 69-70, dir, currently; dir, Norwalk Cent Listing, Inc, currently; developer, Rose Estates & Meadowbrook Estates, communities of 175 houses. Mem: Nat Asn of Real Estate Bd; Nat Asn of Home Builders. Legal Res: East Rocks Rd Norwalk CT 06851 Mailing Add: 534 West Ave Norwalk CT 06850

GROSECLOSE, JOHN ROBERT (BOB) (R)
b San Angelo, Tex, Feb 8, 38; s William Buell Groseclose & Adelaide Colvard G; single. Educ: Univ Tex, BA in math. Polit & Govt Pos: Precinct chmn, Tom Green Co Rep Party, Tex, 64-, chmn, 66-72; field rep, Tex Rep State Party, 72- Mailing Add: 114 E Twohig San Angelo TX 76901

GROSHEK, LEONARD ANTHONY (D)
Wis State Rep
b Stevens Point, Wis, June 13, 13; s Leo Groshek & Helen Jablonski G; wid; m 1968 to Regina T Kirschling; c Anita (Mrs Gosh), Audrey (Mrs Piecznyshi) & Dalene. Educ: Col, 2 years, teaching cert, 30. Polit & Govt Pos: Town assessor, Stockton, Wis, 49-51, town clerk, 51-; chmn, Reynolds for Gov Campaign, Portage Co, 64; first vchmn, Portage Co Dem Party, 65, chmn, formerly; Wis State Rep, currently. Bus & Prof Pos: Prod worker & supvr, A O Smith Corp, Milwaukee, 42-48; storekeepers, Groshek Trading Post, 48-; gen ins agt, 49-; comnr, Land Condemnation, Portage Co, 60- Mem: Tomorrow River Conserv Club. Relig: Catholic. Mailing Add: 2125 Indiana Ave Stevens Point WI 54481

GROSJEAN, BARBARA GRACE (D)
b Canton, Ohio, Jan 24, 29; d Robert O Grosjean (deceased) & Irene Markley G; single. Educ: Ohio State Univ, BSc chem, 50. Polit & Govt Pos: Secy, Knox Co Dem Cent & Exec Comts, Ohio, 70-72; deleg, Dem Nat Conv, 72. Bus & Prof Pos: Prin chemist, Battelle Mem Inst, 50-56; mem tech staff, NAm Aviation, Columbus, Ohio, 56-70; teacher, 71- Relig: Presbyterian. Mailing Add: Rte 6 19889 Coshocton Rd Mt Vernon OH 43050

GROSS, BENNY J (R)
SDak State Rep
Mailing Add: Onida SD 57564

GROSS, FRED ALFRED, JR (R)
NMex State Sen
b Fulton, Mo, Apr 2, 23; s Fred Alfred Gross & Florence Marie Hutsel G; m 1943 to Susan Kist; c Joyce (Mrs Michael Costello), Cheryl Ann (Mrs Douglas Boone), Fred A, III & Nara Sue. Educ: Westminster Col, chem, 41-42; Univ Wis, BS in Physics & MS in Nuclear Physics; Univ NMex, theoretical physics, 52-53; Indust Col Armed Forces, 59-60. Polit & Govt Pos: NMex State Sen, Dist 21, 68-, mem, Finance & Conserv Comts, NMex State Senate, currently; mem elec utilities adv comt, Fed Energy Admin, 73-; mem energy task force, Nat Conf State Legislators, 73- Bus & Prof Pos: Asst high sch football coach; vis scientist for NMex Acad of Sci, 60-67; staff mem adv syst research dept, Sandia Corp, 63-66, supvr exp syst div, 66-67; vpres & dir, Nuclear Defense Research Corp of NMex, Inc, 67- Mil Serv: Entered as Pvt, Army Air Corps, 42, retired as Lt Col, Air Force, 63, after serv as navigator, instr & post engr & as nuclear weapons research & develop off; Distinguished Flying Cross; Air Medal with Seven Oak Leaf Clusters; Commendation Medal; Occup of Japan Medal; Am & European Mid East Theatre Medals; World War II Victory Medal; Presidential Unit Citation; Korean Serv Medal. Publ: Effects of Topography on Shock Waves in Air, PVIM-57, 57; Nuclear Weapons Employment Handbook, Air Force Manual 200-8, 58; System Applications of Nuclear Technology & Nuclear Weapon Effects on Air Force Systems, Air Force System Command Manual 500-1, 63. Mem: Am Asn Advan Sci; Nat Wildlife Fedn (bd dirs, 72-); Nat Rifle Asn; Kit Carson Coun Boy Scouts (exec bd, 71-); NMex Wildlife Fedn. Honors & Awards: KOB Conservationist of Year, 71; Air Conservationist of Year, 71; Wildlife Soc Nonprof Award, 75. Relig: Methodist. Mailing Add: 2916 Chama NE Albuquerque NM 87110

GROSS, H R (R)
b Arispe, Iowa, June 30, 99; m 1929 to Hazel E Webster; c Phil & Alan. Educ: Univ Mo Sch Jour. Polit & Govt Pos: US Rep, Iowa, 48-74; deleg, Rep Nat Conv, 68; cand, US House of Rep, 74. Bus & Prof Pos: Newspaper reporter & ed, 21-35; radio news commentator, 35-48. Mil Serv: AEF, World War I; Mexican Border Serv, 16. Mem: Mason; Elks; Am Legion; VFW. Relig: Presbyterian. Legal Res: Waterloo IA Mailing Add: 1600 S Joyce St Arlington VA 22202

GROSS, LOIS IRENE (D)
VChmn, Bucksport Dem Town Comt, Maine
b Rockland, Maine, Apr 30, 20; d Capt Orrin F Lawry & Lilla McFarland L; m 1955 to Lawrence Carter Gross; c Sharon (Mrs Albert Charpentier), stepchildren, Joan (Mrs Ronald Turner) & Frederic S Gross. Educ: Rockland High Sch, grad. Polit & Govt Pos: Elec clerk, Bucksport, Maine, 56-, Justice of the Peace, 67-; secy, Hancock Co Dem Comt, 60-66, legis dist chmn, 68-70; mem, Bucksport Dem Town Comt, 64-66, treas, 66-70, vchmn, 66-; committeewoman, Maine State Dem Comt, 66-74; adv to Bucksport Young Dem, 72- Bus & Prof Pos: Pres, Bucksport Regional Health Ctr, Inc, 73-; corporator, Eastern Maine Med Ctr, 75- Mem: Bucksport Garden Club; Floral Grange; Bucksport October Club; Maine State Fedn Women's Clubs; Civic Club. Honors & Awards: Cert Honor, Dem Nat Comt; App Dedimus Justice, Gov Kenneth M Curtis, 74. Relig: Episcopal; Women's Auxiliary, ST Stephen's Episcopal Church, 72- Mailing Add: 157 Main St Bucksport ME 04416

GROSS, MARTIN LOUIS (D)
Legal Counsel, NH Dem State Comt
b New York, NY, Oct 22, 38; s Walter Woolf Gross & Harriet Shoben G; m 1960 to Caroline Barrett Lord. Educ: Harvard Col, AB, 60, Law Sch, JD, 64; Hasty Pudding Inst 1770. Polit & Govt Pos: Mem, State Bd Bar Examr, 69-73, chmn, 74-; legal counsel, Gov, NH, 70-72; mem city coun, Concord, NH, 70-; mem, State Bd Prison Trustees, 72-; mayor pro-tem, Concord, 74-; legal counsel, NH Dem State Comt, 74- Bus & Prof Pos: Law clerk to US Dist Judge, Concord, 64-65; assoc, Sulloway Hollis Godfrey & Soden, Concord, 65-69, partner, 69- Publ: Condition of New Zealand unions, NZ J Pub Admin, fall 60; co-auth, New Hampshire's business profits tax, NH Bar J, fall 70. Mem: NH Munic Asn (legal counsel & mem exec comt, 70-); Am & NH Bar Asns. Honors & Awards: Frank Knox Mem Fel, Harvard Univ, 60. Mailing Add: 15 Rumford St Concord NH 03301

GROSS, OVAL (D)
Chmn, Lee Co Dem Party, Ky
b Greeley, Colo, Dec 6, 23; s Green B Gross & Alice Crabtree G; m 1946 to Nannie Elizabeth Crabtree; c James David, Diania E, Victoria A (Mrs Robert Moore) & Jackson Oval. Educ: Greeley Sch, 37. Polit & Govt Pos: Sheriff, Lee Co, Ky, 58-61; investigator, Commonwealth of Ky, 62-67; chmn, Lee Co Dem Party, 72- Bus & Prof Pos: Owner, Beattyville Food Store, Ky, 67-71. Mil Serv: Entered as Pvt, Army, 40, released as Sgt, 45, after serv in 1st Armored Div, ETO, 42-45. Mem: Mason (secy, 47-52, master, 52, 68-69, dist dep grand master, 72). Relig: Protestant. Legal Res: Grand Ave Beattyville KY 41311 Mailing Add: Box 486 Beattyville KY 41311

GROSS, SHEILA TOBY SMITH (D)
b Brooklyn, NY, Nov 16, 37; d Rubin Smith & Rose Koch S; m 1956 to Leonard Gross; c Michael Jay, Mark Paul & Robert Lawrence. Educ: Brooklyn Col, 55-57 & 62; Lamb House. Polit & Govt Pos: Campaign coordr, Dem Primary, 13th Cong Dist, Brooklyn, NY, 68; campaign mgr, Mayor & Coun Elect, Marlboro Dem Party, NJ, 69, press secy & campaign mgr, 71; membership chmn, Marlboro Dem Club, 70, rec secy, 71, pres, 72; secy welfare assistance bd, Marlboro Twp, 70, dir welfare, 70-71, admin asst to Mayor Salkind, 72-; mem, Bayshore Dem Orgn, Monmouth Co, 71-; chmn, Monmouth Co Deleg, Dem Nat Conv, 72. Mem: League for Rehabilitation, Kingsbrook Jewish Med Ctr, Brooklyn; Marlboro Chap for Retarded Children, NJ (parliamentarian, 70 & exec bd, 70-72); Marlboro Auxiliary-Freehold Area Hosp; Temple Beth Ohr, Sisterhood. Relig: Jewish. Mailing Add: 2 Lindsay Dr Morganville NJ 07751

GROSSE, GEORGE R (D)
Fla State Rep
Mailing Add: 8560 Commonwealth Ave Jacksonville FL 32220

GROSSMAN, JEROME (D)
Dem Nat Committeeman, Mass
b Boston, Mass, Aug 23, 17; s Maxwell B Grossman & Mary Radin G; m 1942 to Roslyn Gruber; c Daniel Jefferson, Marilyn Jean & Richard Adam. Educ: Harvard Univ, AB, 38. Polit & Govt Pos: Dir, consult & chmn, Minority Employ Comt, Newton Fair Housing & Equal Rights Comt, Mass, 59-67; campaign mgr, Hughes for Senate, 62; founder, Mass Polit Action for Peace, 62, chmn, 62-71; dir, UN Asn of Boston, 65-68; mem exec comt, Civil Liberties Union of Mass, 65-70; dir, Newton Peace Ctr, 65-72; mem steering comt, Thomas B Adams for Senate, 66; chmn, Subcomt on Minority Group Employ, Community Rels Comn of City of Newton, 66-71; mem steering comt, Mass, McCarthy for President, 68, nat dir admin, McCarthy for President Nat Hq, 68; mem steering comt, Joseph G Bradley for Cong, 68; dir, Nat New Dem Coalition, 68-; mem, Charter Reform Comn, Newton, 69-; originator, Vietnam Moratorium Movement, 69; mem bd dirs, Eastern Middlesex Opportunities Coun, 69-70; mem steering comt & chmn finance comt, Drinan for Cong, 70 & 72 & 74; mem steering comt, Mass Citizen's Presidential Caucus, 72; mem steering comt & chmn finance comt, McGovern for President, 72; deleg, Dem Nat Conv, 72; mem exec comt, Citizen's for Participation Polit, 72-; Dem Nat Committeeman, Mass, 72-; dir affirmative action comt, Mass Dem Party, 75-; mem exec comt, People vs Handguns, 75- Bus & Prof Pos: Pres, Mass Envelope Co, Somerville, 42-; pres, Newton Coun of PTA, 50-67; pres, Hull Little League, 52-57; coach, Newton S Minor Baseball League, 53-68, comnr, 55-67; mem, Mass High Sch Prin Asn Scholar Comt, 62-63; mem exec comt, CPPAX, 71- Relig: Jewish. Mailing Add: 115 Dorset Rd Newton MA 02168

GROUBY, EDWARD ARTHUR, SR (D)
b Abbeville, Ala, Sept 20, 02; s Augustus Underwood Grouby & Elizabeth Skipper G; m 1926 to Rose Saunders; c Lt Comdr Edward A, Jr, Betty (Mrs Clarence T Milldrum) & Dianne (Mrs Juhan). Educ: High Sch, Abbeville, Ala, grad, 19; Massey Bus Col, 20. Polit & Govt Pos: Mem, Prattville City Coun, Ala, 41-47; chmn, Prattville Water Works, 48-54; chmn, Autauga Co Dem Exec Comt, formerly; Ala State Rep, 50-66; chmn, Bd of Revenue & Control, Autauga Co, 66-; judge of probate, Autauga Co, 66- Bus & Prof Pos: Owner & operator, Grouby Furniture Co, Prattville, Ala, 34-70; railway express agency, 44- Mem: Lions; Mason (Master); Prattville Country Club; Peace Officers Asn; WOW. Relig: Baptist. Legal Res: 327 Washington St Prattville AL 36067 Mailing Add: PO Box 488 Prattville AL 36067

GROVER, JAMES R, JR (R)
b Babylon, NY, Mar 5, 19; m to Mary Fullerton; c Nancy L, Jean, James R & Jill. Educ: Hofstra Col, AB; Columbia Law Sch, LLB. Polit & Govt Pos: Spec counsel, Babylon, NY; NY State Assemblyman, 57-62; US Rep, Second Dist, NY, 63-74; cand, US House of Rep, 74. Bus & Prof Pos: Attorney. Mil Serv: Army Air Force Coast Artil, World War II, China Theater, discharged as Capt. Mem: Lions; KofC; Holy Name Soc; VFW; Am Legion. Relig: Roman Catholic. Mailing Add: 185 Woodsome Rd Babylon NY 11702

GROVER, LILLIAN EVELIN (R)
Secy, Maine Rep State Comt
b Gardiner, Maine, June 12, 07; d George Edwin Colby & Ernestine Stevens C; m to Harry Michael Grover; wid; c Edith M (Mrs Terry Crone), G Bradford & Marsha E (Mrs Paul Roussel). Educ: Gates Bus Sch; Univ Maine, exten courses. Polit & Govt Pos: Pres, Kennebec Co Women's Rep Club; pres, Maine State Women's Rep Club; chaplain, Nat Rep Women; secy, Maine Rep State Comt, 66- Mem: Eastern Star (matron); DAR (state regent & vpres gen); Daughters of Colonial Wars; Soc of Colonial Clergy; Huguenots of Maine. Relig: Baptist. Mailing Add: 128 Maine Ave Farmingdale ME 04345

GROVES, G MARK (R)
Mem, Rep State Cent Comt Calif
b Long Beach, Calif, May 29, 29; s Gordon L Groves, Jr & Aimee K Bryant G; m 1955 to Bette Jane Lummis; c Keith L. Educ: El Camino Col, Los Angeles Co, 47-49; Ore State Univ, BS, 52. Polit & Govt Pos: Mem, Coffee Creek Elem Sch Dist, Calif, 59-69 & 70-; mem, Trinity Co Sch Dist Orgn Comt, 62-; mem, Trinity Co Rep Cent Comt, 64-65; mem, Rep State Cent Comt Calif, 69- Bus & Prof Pos: Forester, R & G Lumber Co, Trinity Co, 56-60; pvt timber consult, 60-64; vpres, Wyntoon Develop Co, 64- Mil Serv: Entered as Pvt, Army, 53, released as Cpl, 55, after serv in Mil Police, Ft Lewis, Wash. Mem: Soc Am Foresters; Am Philatelic Soc. Mailing Add: Coffee Creek Rte Trinity Center CA 96091

GROVES, JAMES MARTIN (D)
Chmn, Todd Co Dem Comt, Ky
b Elkton, Ky, June 24, 34; s Mike Groves & Viola Blake G; single. Educ: Transylvania Univ, AB; Austin Peay State Univ, 54; Univ Ky Grad Sch, 58-59; Kappa Alpha Order. Polit & Govt Pos: Admin aide to US Rep Frank W Burke, 60-61; dep clerk, Todd Circuit Court, Elkton, 61-64, clerk, 64-; dist mem, Ky State Dem Exec Comt, 67-71; secy, Todd Co Dem Exec Comt, 68-72; chmn, Todd Co Dem Comt, 72- Bus & Prof Pos: Mem bd dirs, Spindletop Research, Inc, Lexington, Ky, currently; mem, Ky Heritage Comn; mem, Pennyroyal Region Ment Health Bd. Mil Serv: Entered as Pvt, Army, 56, released as SP-3, 58, after serv in Security Agency, European Hq, Frankfurt, WGer, 57-58. Mem: Ky Asn Circuit Court Clerks; Am Legion; Elkton Rotary Club; Todd Co Jaycees. Honors & Awards: Outstanding Young Man of Todd Co, Todd Co Jaycees, 69. Relig: Disciples of Christ. Legal Res: 156 Goebel Ave Elkton KY 42220 Mailing Add: Todd County Courthouse Elkton KY 42220

GRUBBS, LAWTON EDISON (D)
b Sharpe, Ky, Sept 19, 98; s Thomas Achel Grubbs & Jennie Johnston G; m 1951 to Louise Simerley. Educ: Ark State Col, 2 years. Polit & Govt Pos: Alderman, Kensett, Ark, 32-34; ward committeeman, White Co Dem Comt, 38-40; chmn, White Co Welfare Bd, 38-42; committeeman, Ark State Dem Comt, 40-44; chmn, White Co Bd Educ, 40-44; chmn, White Co Dem Cent Comt, formerly. Bus & Prof Pos: Traveling salesman, Milburn Johnston Grocery Co, Searcy, 27-42; mgr, New Port Br, Plunkett Jarrell Grocery Co, Little Rock, 42-50, br house supvr, 50-57; vpres, Wood-Freeman Lumber Co, Searcy, 57-; mem, State Bd Collection Agencies, Little Rock, 66; mem, White Co Draft Bd, 66- Mil Serv: Entered as Pvt, Army, 18, released as Pvt, 18, after serv in Student Army Training Corp, St Louis, Mo. Mem: Wholesale Grocery Asn; State Fair Asn; Searcy CofC; Newport CofC; Mason. Honors & Awards: Awards from Am Red Cross & Rotary. Relig: Protestant. Mailing Add: 1805 W Center Ave Searcy AR 72143

GRUENES, BERNARD A (R)
Chmn, Stearns Co Rep Party, Minn

b Richmond, Minn, Dec 11, 33; s Anton A Gruenes & Anna M Kalthoff G; m 1956 to Catherine M Stang; c David B, Donald P, Mary T, Diane L & Robert A. Educ: St Cloud State Col, 56-68; Wis Sch Banking, Madison, Banking Degree; Col Rep Party. Polit & Govt Pos: Chmn, Watkins Pub Sch Bd, Minn, 62-67; chmn, Stearns Co Reelect John Zwach, 70-72; pres, St Michael's Parish Coun, 70-; treas, Opportunity Training Ctr, St Cloud, 71-; chmn, Stearns Co Rep Party, 71- Bus & Prof Pos: Chmn, St Anthony's Parochial Sch Bd, 64-66. Mil Serv: Entered as Pvt, Army, 54, released as Sgt, after serv in 24th Inf Div, Korea, 54-55. Mem: Minn Bankers' Asn (legis comt, 70-); Cent Minn Bankers; Cold Springs KofC (Dep Grand Knight, 63-64 & Grand Knight, 64-65); Am Legion; St Cloud CofC. Relig: Catholic. Mailing Add: 1013 State Aid Rd 4 St Cloud MN 56301

GRUENING, CLARK (D)
Alaska State Rep
Mailing Add: 940 Tyonek Anchorage AK 99501

GRUNSKY, DONALD LUCIUS (R)
Calif State Sen

b San Francisco, Calif, Oct 19, 15; s Eugene Lucius Grunsky & Margaret Koch G; m 1943 to Mary Lou Meidl. Educ: Univ Calif, Berkeley, AB, 36, LLB, 39. Polit & Govt Pos: Calif State Assemblyman, 47-52; Calif State Sen, currently; deleg, Rep Nat Conv, 52 & 68. Bus & Prof Pos: Attorney-at-law, Grunsky, Pybrum, Skemp & Ebey. Mil Serv: Entered as Ens, Navy, 41, released as Lt Comdr, 45. Mem: State Bar of Calif; Am Bar Asn; Elks; Am Legion; VFW. Relig: Protestant. Mailing Add: PO Box 1186 Watsonville CA 95076

GRUNWALDT, DAVID CARL (R)
Mem Exec Comt, Outagamie Co Rep Party, Wis

b Green Bay, Wis, Feb 6, 38; s Carl August Grunwaldt (deceased) & Viola Wussow G; m 1963 to Diane Cory; c Christine, Constance, Cathleen & David Carl August. Educ: Marquette Univ Sch Dent, DDS, 63; Delta Sigma Delta. Polit & Govt Pos: Chmn, Outagamie Co Young Rep, Wis, 64-65; mem exec comt, Outagamie Co Rep Party, 64-, chmn, 68-71; mem resolutions comt, Wis State Rep Party, 69; chmn, Eighth Cong Dist Rep Party, formerly; alt deleg, Rep Nat Conv, 72; mem, Kaukauna Bd Educ, 73- Bus & Prof Pos: Pres, Environ Action Prod, Inc, 70- Mil Serv: Pvt E-2, Army, 56; Army Res, 56-; Reservist of the Year, 84th Div, 58. Mem: Am Dent Asn; Wis State & Outagamie Co Dent Socs; Am Acad Physiologic Dent; Am Analgesia Soc. Relig: Methodist. Legal Res: 1901 Crooks Ave Kaukauna WI 54130 Mailing Add: 11 Escarpment Terr Rte 1 Menasha WI 54952

GUASTELLO, THOMAS (D)
Mich State Sen

b Detroit, Mich, Oct 25, 43; s Peter James Guastello & Barbarose Shaw B. Educ: Mich State Univ, BA, 65; Detroit Col Law, JD, 69; Alumni Asn; Alpha Tau Omega; Student Govt J Coun. Polit & Govt Pos: Former precinct deleg, Sterling Heights, Mich; former chmn, Macomb Co, Young Dem; mem exec bd, Macomb Co Dem Comn; Mich State Rep, 71st Dist, 69-74, Mich State Sen, 74- Bus & Prof Pos: Vpres, Village Inns, Inc, 64-; circuit court law clerk, 67-68; attorney-at-law, Mt Clemens, currently. Mem: Macomb Co Bar Asn; Macomb Co Prosecuting Attorneys Asn; State Bar of Mich; Utica Citizens' Adv Comt; Macomb Co Drug Abuse & Voc Educ Comn. Honors & Awards: Lakeview High Sch Hall of Fame; Mich State Univ Honors Prog; finalist in Ben Probe Moot Court presentation, Detroit Col Law. Relig: Catholic. Mailing Add: 11165 Laurel Ct Sterling Heights MI 48077

GUBBINS, JOAN MARGARET (R)
Ind State Sen

b New York, NY, July 2, 29; d Arthur L Barton & Margaret Hedge B; m 1949 to Dale George Gubbins; c Gregory Dale & Carol Jane. Educ: Univ Ill, 47-49; Alpha Chi Omega. Polit & Govt Pos: Research chmn, Ind Goldwater for President Comt, 64; deleg, Ind Rep State Conv, 66 & 68; Rep precinct committeewoman, Indianapolis, 66-; Ind State Sen, 69- Mem: Ind State Legis Club; Citizens' Forum; Poet's Corner (hon mem); Am Contract Bridge League; Cent Ind Bridge Asn. Relig: Reformed Presbyterian. Mailing Add: 1000 E 81st St Indianapolis IN 46240

GUBBRUD, ARCHIE (R)
b Alcester, SDak; Dec 31, 10; s Marius T Gubbrud & Ella Rommerien G; m 1939 to Florence Dexter; c John D & Maxine (Mrs Roberts). Polit & Govt Pos: Mem, Twp Bd, SDak, 34-50; mem, Local Sch Bd, 47-53; SDak State Rep, 51-60, Speaker of the House, 58-60; Gov, SDak, 61-64; deleg, Rep Nat Conv, 68; state dir, Farmers Home Admin, 69- Bus & Prof Pos: Chmn bd dirs, Beefland Int, Council Bluffs, Iowa, 68-; dir, State Bank, Alcester, SDak, currently. Mem: Nat Livestock Feeders (dir for SDak); Mason (32 Degree); Shrine; Farm Bur. Honors & Awards: Miss Valley Asn Award, Soil Conserv SDak. Relig: Lutheran. Mailing Add: RFD 2 Alcester SD 57001

GUBSER, CHARLES S (R)
b Gilroy, Calif, Feb 1, 1916; s Charles Henry Gubser & Ella Oma Matlack G; m 1972 to Jean E Gordon; c Mrs Raymond Camino; three grandchildren. Educ: Univ Calif, AB, 37; Kappa Alpha. Polit & Govt Pos: Calif State Assemblyman, 50-52; US Rep, Calif, 52-74; cand, US House of Rep, 74; chmn US sect, Am-Can Permanent Joint Bd on Defense, 75- Bus & Prof Pos: Secondary sch teacher, 39-43; operator, truck farm, 40-50; farmer. Mem: Mason; Elks; Rotary. Mailing Add: Gilroy CA 95020

GUDAJTES, EDWARD RAYMOND (D)
Secy, Walsh Co Dem Orgn, NDak

b Warsaw, NDak, July 28, 11; s Anton L Gudajtes & Jane Byzewski G; m 1939 to Marie Slominski; c James, John, Mary & Marjorie. Educ: Minto High Sch. Polit & Govt Pos: NDak State Rep, Dist Four, Walsh Co, 65-67; secy, Walsh Co Dem Orgn, 69-; secy, 16th Dist NDak Dem Non-Partisan League, 70-; munic judge, City of Minto, 72- Bus & Prof Pos: Pres, Minto Co-op Oil Co, NDak, 51-56; pres, Minto Farmers Elevator, 59-63; secy & mgr, Walsh Co Mutual Ins Co of Minto, 67- Mil Serv: Mem, Walsh Co Draft Bd, 51-53. Mem: Farm Bur; Farmers Union; Nat Farmers Orgn; Nat Malting Barley Growers; Walsh Co Crop & Improvement Asn. Relig: Roman Catholic. Mailing Add: Minto ND 58261

GUDE, GILBERT (R)
US Rep, Md

b Washington, DC, Mar 9, 23; s Adolph E Gude (deceased) & Inez Gilbert G (deceased); m 1948 to Jane Wheeler Callaghan; c Sharon (Mrs Al Giraldi), Gregory, Adrienne, Gilbert, Jr & Daniel. Educ: Cornell Univ, BS, 48; George Washington Univ, MA, 58; Pi Kappa Phi; Phi Sigma Kappa. Polit & Govt Pos: Md State Deleg, 52-58; mem, Montgomery Co Rep Cent Comt, Md, 58-62, chmn, 61-62; Md State Sen, 62-66; US Rep, Md, 67-; deleg, Rep Nat Conv, 68 & 72; chmn, World Environ Comt, Mem of Cong for Peace Through Law, 71-74. Relig: Catholic. Legal Res: Bethesda MD Mailing Add: 332 Cannon House Off Bldg Washington DC 20515

GUDGER, LAMAR (D)
NC State Sen
Mailing Add: 189 Kimberly Ave Asheville NC 28804

GUENTHNER, LOUIS ROBERT, JR (R)
Ky State Rep

b Louisville, Ky, Aug 9, 44; s Louis Robert Guenthner & Gladys Longonbahm G; m 1966 to Betty Carol Newcomb; c Melissa Louise & Louis Robert, III. Educ: Bellarmine Col, BA, 69; Univ Louisville, JD, 71; Delta Theta Phi; Delta Sigma Delta. Polit & Govt Pos: Deleg, Rep Leadership Conf, Washington, DC, 71; Ky State Rep, 48th Dist, 73- Bus & Prof Pos: Attorney-at-law, Louis R Guenthner, Jr, 71- Mil Serv: Entered as Pvt, Army, 66, released as SP-4, 68, after serv in Adj Gen Corps. Mem: Am Bar Asn; Ky Bar Asn; Louisville-Jefferson Co Bar Asn; Ky Asn Trial Attorneys (bd dirs); Non-Parti- san Comt for Judiciary (chmn). Relig: Roman Catholic. Mailing Add: 235 S Fifth St Suite 200 Louisville KY 40202

GUERIN, DAVID LLOYD, SR (R)
b San Francisco, Calif, May 27, 22; s Harold Theodore Guerin & Agnes Krogstad G; m 1942 to Jacqueline Natalie Thompson; c David Lloyd, Jr, Paul Emmett, Kathleen (Mrs Ronny Metcalf), Kevin Natalie, Peter Vincent & Bridget Jacqueline. Educ: San Francisco Jr Col, 40-42; Ore State Col, 43; Southern Col Optom, OD, 52; Phi Theta Upsilon. Polit & Govt Pos: Secy, Faulkner Co Elec Comn, 70-; chmn, Faulkner Co Rep Comt, Ark, formerly; consult optometrist, Ark State Dept Pub Welfare, 70- Bus & Prof Pos: Dr Optom, Hope, Ark, 52-66, Conway, 67- Mil Serv: Entered as Pvt, Army, 42, released as Sgt, 45, after serv in 91st Inf Div, NAfrican-Mediter Theatre, 44-45; Combat Infantryman's Badge; Bronze Star; Presidential Unit Citation; Three Battle Stars to Theatre Ribbon; Good Conduct Medal. Mem: Am Optom Asn; Optom Exten Prog Found; Ark Optom Asn; Conway CofC; Conway Country Club. Relig: United Methodist. Legal Res: Lakeview Acres Conway AR 72032 Mailing Add: Con-Ark Village Conway AR 72032

GUERRA, RAMIRO M (D)
b McAllen, Tex, Sept 3, 22; s Guillermo D Guerra & Tomasita Saena G; m 1942 to Enedina Barrera; c Rebecca (Mrs Strong); Jose G & Roberto D. Educ: Edinburg High Sch, grad, 41. Polit & Govt Pos: Bd mem, Edinburg Independent Sch Dist, 51-62; comnr, Hidalgo Co, Tex, 63-74 & judge, 75-; deleg, Dem Nat Conv, 72. Bus & Prof Pos: Pres, Guerra's Land Clearing Co, 49-61 & San Felipe Ranch Inc, 59-75; vpres & co-owner, Baker Guerra Inc, 60-65; pres, Guerra Jones Inc, 63-67; co-owner, R&O Guerra, 71- Mem: Tex Co & Dist Retirement Syst; Lions; Farm Bur; Co Judges & Comnr Asn of Tex; Lower Rio Grande Valley Develop Coun. Honors & Awards: Meritorious Serv, Edinburg Independent Sch Dist, 61; South Most Tex Conserv Dist, 69, 4-H Club, 72 & Tex Co & Dist Retirement Syst, 73. Relig: Catholic. Mailing Add: 1109 S 13th Edinburg TX 78539

GUERRERO, EDWARD GARCIA (D)
Ariz State Rep

b Globe, Ariz, Sept 21, 32; s Ventura S Guerrero & Enriqueta Garcia G; m to Mrs Jessie Ybarra; c Deborrah Lorraine, Michael Francis, Patricia Ann, Anna Marie, Mark Antony, Mario Charles, Mathew James & Benjamin Edward & stepchildren, Linda (Mrs Perez), Dolores (Mrs Verdugo), Richard, Manuel & Yolanda Ibarra. Educ: Globe High Sch, Ariz, grad, 50. Polit & Govt Pos: Dep registr, Gila Co Dem Party, Ariz; precinct committeeman, Globe Precinct Two, Gila Co; mem, Ariz State Dem Exec Comt; councilman, Globe, 66-68, 68-70, 70-; mem, Southwest Conf Interstate-Intergroup Affairs; mem steering comt, Nat Conf on Poverty in Southwest; Ariz State Rep, Dist Seven, 71-72, Dist Four, 72- Bus & Prof Pos: Laborer, Construction, Prod & Maintenance Laborers Local 383, Phoenix, 56, area steward & dispatcher, 5 years, pres, 67- Mil Serv: Entered as Seaman Recruit, Navy, 50, released as SH 3, 53, after serv in USS Abbot DD 629, Destroyer Force Pac & Atlantic; Three Ribbons; Korean War Veteran. Mem: Eastern Ariz Alcoholic Recovery Ctr (fund raising chmn & mem bd dirs); Ariz Acad (Town Hall Panel Mem on Reform of Correctional Insts); Am Legion (Honor Guard); VFW (perpetual life charter mem). Relig: Citizen of the World. Legal Res: 225 Yuma St Globe AZ 85501 Mailing Add: PO Box 521 Globe AZ 85501

GUERRERO, JOAQUIN C (R)
Spec Asst Manpower Resources Develop, Govt Guam

b Agana, Guam, Dec 8, 20; s Joaquin Guerrero & Luisa G; single. Educ: Ind Univ, BS, 58, MS, 59, MBA, 61; Alumni Asn. Polit & Govt Pos: Immigrant inspector, Govt Guam, 51, admin officer, 52-53, asst dir finance, 61-64, dir finance, 65-68, chief of admin, 63, dir revenue & taxation, 68, dir bur budget & mgt research, 69-71; spec asst manpower resources develop, Govt, Guam, 71- Mil Serv: 1st Lt, Guam Militia, 51. Mem: Munic Finance Officers' Asn; Rotary (chmn scholastic comt); FGAA; Guam Chap, Am Red Cross (chmn). Mailing Add: PO Box 2228 Agana GU 96910

GUERRERO, MANUEL FLORES LEON (D)
b Agana, Guam, Oct 25, 14; s Jose L G Leon Guerrero & Maria Lujan Flores G; m to Delfina Tuncap; c Alfred, Lolita, Rudolpho, Evelyna, Teresita, Manuel & Patricia. Educ: High Sch. Honors & Awards: LLD, WVa Inst Technol, 68; LittD, Colo State Col, 68. Polit & Govt Pos: Secy of Guam, 61-63, Gov, 63-69; US Comnr, SPac Comn, 64-70; deleg, Dem Nat Conv, 68. Mil Serv: Civilian internee, 41-44. Mailing Add: PO Box 223 Agana GU 96910

GUESS, SAM C (R)
Wash State Sen

b Greenwood, Miss, 1909; m to Dorothy G; c two. Educ: Univ Miss, BS. Polit & Govt Pos: Wash State Sen, 62- Bus & Prof Pos: Civil Eng. Mil Serv: Maj, Army. Mem: Sigma Nu. Mailing Add: W 408 33rd Ave Spokane WA 99023

GUEST, CALVIN RAY (D)
Chmn, Tex Dem Party

b Strawn, Tex, Nov 18, 23; s James Edgar Guest & Hazel Blanche Bennett G; m 1946 to Jenna V Reeves; c Gwen (Mrs Otis W Bledsoe) & Gary Dean. Educ: Tex A&I Col, BBA cum laude, 48; Tex A&M Univ, 53-54; Alpha Chi. Polit & Govt Pos: Active in precinct, city & co elec, many years; chmn, Tex Dem Party Pres Conv, 72; chmn, Tex Dem Party, 72-; mem, Dem Nat Comt, 72- Bus & Prof Pos: Asst auditor, State of Tex, 48-50; asst auditor, Tex A&M Col, 50-53, auditor, Syst, 53-56; exec vpres, Am Coin-Meter Corp, 56-69, pres, 71-; pres, Bryan

Bldg & Loan Asn, 70-; pres, United Coin Meter Serv, 71- Mil Serv: Entered as Pvt, Marines, 42, released as T/Sgt, SPac, 42-46. Relig: Baptist; Deacon, First Baptist Church. Legal Res: 2907 Rustling Oaks Bryan TX 77801 Mailing Add: 2800 Texas Ave Bryan TX 77801

GUEST, RAYMOND RICHARD, JR (R)
Va State Deleg
b New York, NY, Sept 29, 39; s Raymond Richard Guest & Elizabeth Polk G; div; c Raymond Richard, III & Mary Elizabeth. Educ: Yale Univ, BA, 64; Fence Club. Polit & Govt Pos: Mem, Front Royal & Warren Co Rep Comt, Va, 64-69, chmn, 70-; mem, Warren Co Planning Comn, Va, 65-70, chmn, 71-; Va State Deleg, 73- Mil Serv: Entered as Pvt, Marine Corps Res, 58, hon discharged as Cpl, 64. Mem: Elks; Ruritan. Relig: Episcopal. Mailing Add: Rte 2 Rock Hill Farm Front Royal VA 22630

GUFFEY, JAMES VINCENT (D)
b Goodwin, SDak, July 25, 41, s Boyd V Guffey & Dorothy Kranz G; m 1962 to Karen Marie Gasser; c James V, Jr, Jill Vanessa & John V. Educ: Northern State Col, 59-62; Univ Md, BS, 66; Sigma Delta Chi. Polit & Govt Pos: Treas, SDak Young Dem, 59-62, pres, 67-70; treas, SDak State Dem Party, 69-70, chmn, 70-74; mem, Dem Nat Comt, formerly; deleg, Dem Nat Conv, 72. Bus & Prof Pos: Newspaper owner & publ; owner, Hamlin Co Herald Enterprise & Interstate Publ; mem bd dirs, Harmony Hill Sch, Multi-Co Planning & Northeast Ment Health Ctr, currently. Mem: SDak Press Asn; SDak Heart Asn; Dist Press Asn; NE SDak Lake Region Asn (past pres, bd dirs, currently); Lake Region Ment Health Ctr (treas, 72-73, pres-elect, 73, bd dirs, currently). Honors & Awards: Outstanding Serv Award, SDak Heart Asn; Outstanding Young Dem, 68. Relig: Catholic; Pres, St John's Church, 69-70. Mailing Add: Box 207 Hayti SD 57241

GUGLIEMINI, SAMUEL JOSEPH (D)
b Hazelton, Pa, Mar 1, 36; s Samuel Gugliemini & Angelina Lamanna G; separated; c Angela, Santina, Marco & Vincent. Educ: Rutgers Univ Exten Night Sch, Newark, NJ, 57-58; Fairleigh Dickinson Univ, 59-60. Polit & Govt Pos: Vpres, Morris Co Young Dem, NJ, 63, pres, 65; committeeman, Netcong Dem Comt, 63-, munic chmn, 63; councilman, Netcong Borough Coun, 64-65, 68-69, mayor, 65-67; chmn voter registr, Morris Co Dem Comt, 68, chmn, 69-72; chmn, Robert F Kennedy Campaign Comt, Morris Co, 68; comnr, Morris Co Bd Elec, 70-; mem, Dem Policy Coun, NJ State Dem Comt, 70- Bus & Prof Pos: Pres, Local 5307, United Steelworkers Am, 60-67, legis chmn, Morris Co, 60-67, legis lobbyist, State of NJ & Washington, DC, 60-67; field underwriter, Manhattan Off, NY Life Ins Co, 67-70; field underwriter, Financial Planning & Research Corp, Parsippany, NJ, 70- Mil Serv: Entered as Pvt, Army, 54, released as Pfc, 56, after serv in 50th Ord Co, German Theatre, 55-56; Good Conduct Medal; Nat Defense Medal; European Theatre Serv Medal. Mem: Kiwanis. Honors & Awards: Star Club, NY Life Ins Co, 68; Million Dollar Producer, Financial Planning & Research Corp, 71. Relig: Roman Catholic. Mailing Add: 18 Main St Netcong NJ 07857

GUIDA, BARTHOLOMEW F (D)
Mayor, New Haven, Conn
b New Haven, Conn, July 8, 14; s Fred Guida & Raphaela Curci G; m 1952 to Caroline Frances Scates; c Fred Bartholomew, David Bartholomew & Deborah Ann. Educ: Commercial High Sch, four years. Polit & Govt Pos: Bd of aldermen, City of New Haven, 47-69, bd finance, 12 years, mayor, 70-, chmn, Charter Revision Comn, Comt on Appropriations & Comt on Legis, mem, Personnel Appeals & Rev Bd & City Plan Comn, currently. Bus & Prof Pos: Owner & pres, Guida Real Estate & Ins & pres, Gtr New Haven Bd of Realtors, currently. Mil Serv: Entered Air Force, 42, released, 45. Mem: Life mem New Haven Basketball Officers Asn; Ahepa; Ital Am War Vet; Redmen; Amity Club. Honors & Awards: Musicians & Gold Ring Award; New Haven Boys Club Veritas Award, Providence Col; Distinguished Am Award, New Haven Co Chap. Relig: Catholic. Mailing Add: 100 Foster St New Haven CT 06511

GUIDERA, GEORGE CLARENCE (R)
Conn State Sen
b Norwalk, Conn, July 14, 42; s George Guidera & Janet Krothe G; m 1965 to Linda Anne Gmelch; c Karen Elizabeth, George C, Jr, Barbara Lynne & Suzanne Kathleen. Educ: Colgate Univ, BA, 64; Georgetown Univ Law Ctr, JD, 67; Phi Kappa Psi. Polit & Govt Pos: Mem, Weston Rep Town Comt, 68-, vchmn, 69-70, chmn, 70-72; Conn State Rep, 162nd Assembly Dist, 71-73; mem, Gov Comn on Age of Majority, 71; Conn State Sen, 26th Sen Dist, 73-, chmn Judiciary Comt, Conn State Senate, 73- Bus & Prof Pos: Attorney-at-law, Boyd, McKeon & O'Neil, Westport, Conn, 67-71; attorney-at-law, Sherwood, Garlick & Cowell, 71- Mem: Am, Conn & Westport Bar Asns; Ark Lodge 39, AF&AM; Grange. Relig: Episcopal. Mailing Add: 227 Lyons Plain Rd Weston CT 06880

GUIDO, ROBERT NORMAN (R)
Dep Chmn, Bergen Co Rep Party, NJ
b New York, NY, Jan 25, 35; s Robert Guido & Helen Vega G; m 1957 to Loretta LaRocca; c Robert Christopher, Michele Helene, John David, Paul Andrew & Jane Susan. Educ: Columbia Univ, 1 year; Edward Williams Col, AA. Polit & Govt Pos: Co committeeman & munic chmn, Paramus Rep Party, NJ, 64-; parliamentarian, Bergen Co Rep Party, 66-73, assembly dist chmn, 67-69, dep chmn, 73-; recreation comnr, Paramus, 67-70; mem, Juv Conf Comt, Paramus, 68-71; alt deleg, Rep Nat Conv, 68, deleg, 72; chmn, Bergen Co Young Rep, 69-70; pool comnr, Paramus, 70-72; treas, Bergen Co Sewer Authority, 71- Bus & Prof Pos: Actuarial asst, Mutual Ins Adv Asn, New York, 64-; asst actuary, Automobile Ins Plan Serv Off, 73-75, actuary, 75- Mem: Am Mensa Soc; Paramus Jaycees; KofC; Holy Name Soc. Relig: Roman Catholic. Mailing Add: 71 Knollwood Dr Paramus NJ 07652

GUIDRY, JESSE (D)
La State Rep
Mailing Add: PO Box E Cecilia LA 70501

GUIDRY, RICHARD P (D)
La State Rep
Mailing Add: PO Box 8 Galliano LA 70354

GUILES, JON ROGER (R)
Chmn, Sixth Dist Rep Party, Wis
b Platteville, Wis, Jan 30, 45; s Roger E Guiles & M Margaret Washburn G; single. Educ: Univ Wis-Madison, BS, 67, Law Sch, JD, 70. Polit & Govt Pos: Deleg, Wis Fedn Young Rep Conv, 64-71, mem legal coun, 69-71; deleg, Midwest Col Rep Conv, 64-68; chmn, Univ Wis Col Rep, 65-66; Wis Col Rep, 66-67; secy, Winnebago Co Rep Party, 70-71, chmn, 73-74; deleg, Wis State Rep Party Conv, 70-71; Wis State Rep, First Dist, 71-73; chmn, Sixth Dist Rep Party, 75- Mem: Winnebago Co, Wis & Am Bar Asns; Boy Scouts; United Fund. Relig: Congregational. Legal Res: 2010 Wisconsin St Oshkosh WI 54901 Mailing Add: PO Box 1124 Oshkosh WI 54901

GUILFORD, BARBARA JO (D)
Committeewoman, Wyo Dem State Cent Comt
b Scottsbluff, Nebr, July 21, 39; d Henry Martin & Linda Buxbaum M; m 1966 to Dennis Andrew Guilford; c Jill Denise & Philip Glen. Educ: Univ Northern Colo, BA, 62; Wichita Univ, 63; Univ Wyo, 71-72. Polit & Govt Pos: Precinct committeewoman, Laramie Co Dem Party, Wyo, 67-73; committeewoman, Wyo Dem State Cent Comt, 73- Mem: Am Asn Univ Women; Cheyenne Fedn of Teachers (pres, 69-70). Mailing Add: 1820 Russell Cheyenne WY 82001

GUILLORY, ROBERT K (D)
La State Sen
Mailing Add: 511 S Second St Eunice LA 70535

GUILMETTE, GERARD A (D)
Mass State Rep
Mailing Add: State Capitol Boston MA 02133

GUINN, ROY BENTON (J R) (R)
Chmn, Otero Co Rep Party, NMex
b McCamey, Tex, May 21, 48; s Roy Benton Guinn & Grace Frances G; single. Educ: Odessa Col, 66-67; Eastern NMex Univ, BS, 71; Sigma Chi; Indust Educ Club. Polit & Govt Pos: Chmn, Otero Co Rep Party, NMex, 72- Mem: Alamogordo Classroom Teachers (chmn legis comt, 72-); Toastmasters; Kiwanis; Nat Ski Patrol. Relig: Baptist. Legal Res: 515 16th Alamogordo NM 88310 Mailing Add: PO Box 1327 Alamogordo NM 88310

GUISER, PAUL (R)
Chmn, Bennett Co Rep Comt, SDak
b Idaho, Jan 23, 13; m 1942 to Mae M Spindler Fulton; wid. Educ: SDak State Sch Mines, 37-39. Polit & Govt Pos: Active in Rep polit on precinct & co levels, 34-; chmn, Bennett Co Rep Comt, SDak, 71- Bus & Prof Pos: Originator & first vchmn, Rural Elec Asn; producer wheat & small grain, 46 years. Mem: State Wheat Promotion Asn; State Wheat Comn (chmn); Great Plains Wheat Asn (vchmn). Relig: Protestant. Mailing Add: Box 517 Martin SD 57551

GULLICKSON, DALE DEAN (D)
Committeeman, SDak Dem Party
b Bryant, SDak, Dec 24, 33; s Leo B Gullickson & Edla Johnson G; m 1955 to Beverly J McLain; c Douglas Dean, Randy Gene, Scott Bradley & Bonnie Lou. Educ: SDak State Univ, Brookings, attending. Polit & Govt Pos: SDak State Rep, 65-67; committeeman, SDak Dem Party, 70-; dir, Div of Mkts, SDak Dept of Agr, 71- Bus & Prof Pos: Mem bd dirs, Interlakes Community Action Agency, 67- Mil Serv: Entered as Pvt, Army, 56, released as Pfc, 58, after serv in 14th Army Res. Mem: Kingsbury Co Farm Fedn; Farmers Union; Nat Farmers Orgn. Relig: Lutheran. Mailing Add: 317 N Pierce Pierre SD 57501

GULLICKSON, ROGER WAYNE (D)
Committeeman, SDak State Dem Party
b Bryant, SDak, May 31, 38; s Leo B Gullickson & Edla Johnson G; m 1960 to Sandra Sue Halvorson; c Susan Renae & Darin Wayne. Educ: Huron Col, 56-57. Polit & Govt Pos: Committeeman, SDak State Dem Party, 70-; deleg & mem resolutions comt, SDak Dem State Conv, 72, mem platform comt, 74. Bus & Prof Pos: Self-employed farmer & trucker. Mil Serv: Entered as Airman, Air Force, 60, released as S/Sgt, 66, after serv in Air Nat Guard. Mem: Lake Preston Coop Asn (dir, 68-, chmn bd dirs, currently); Lake Preston Jaycees; Lake Preston Quarterback Club (vpres, 73); Farmers Union (dir, 66-73). Honors & Awards: Outstanding Relig Leader, Jaycees, 71. Relig: Lutheran. Mailing Add: Lake Preston SD 57249

GULLUSCIO, RONALD JOHN (D)
Chmn, Hopkinton Dem Town Comt, RI
b Westerly, RI, June 16, 37; s Patrick F Gulluscio & Angeline Giorno G; m 1963 to Janice Trebisacci. Educ: Univ RI, BS in Bus Admin, 59; Phi Sigma Kappa. Polit & Govt Pos: Treas, Town of Hopkinton, RI, 68-72; chmn, Hopkinton Dem Town Comt, 73- Bus & Prof Pos: Sr financial analyst, Elec Boat Div/Gen Dynamics, Groton, Conn, 59-; tax acct, 59- Mem: KofC (Grand Knight, 63-65); Calabrese Soc; Westerly Asn (secy, 68-); Theatre Workshop of RI. Relig: Catholic; Auditor, Our Lady of Victory Church, 73- Mailing Add: 13 Juniper Dr Ashaway RI 02804

GUMPER, FRANK JOHN (D)
b Manhattan, NY, Nov 1, 42; s Herbert Frederick Gumper & Bertha Siebold G; m 1974 to Dorothy P Caesar Loeb; c Victor Andrew & Eric & Matthew Loeb. Educ: Rensselaer Polytech Inst, BS Physics, 65; Columbia Univ, MA Geophysics, 71; Sigma Xi. Polit & Govt Pos: Alt deleg, Dem Nat Conv, 72; chmn, Bd Comnrs, Rockland Co Sewer Dist, 74-75; co legislator, Rockland Co, 74- Bus & Prof Pos: Grad research asst in seismology, Lamont-Doherty Geological Labs, 65-71; staff asst of forecasting div, NY Tel Co, New York, 71-73, staff supvr, 73- Publ: Co-auth, Seismic wave velocities & earth structure on the African Continent, 4/70, An earthquake sequence & focal mechanism solution, Lake Hopatcong, NJ, 8/70 & Microseismicity & tectonics of the Nevada seismic zone, 10/71, Seismological Soc Am Bull. Mem: Am Asn Advan Sci; Am Geophysical Union; Seismological Soc Am; Sigma Xi; Operations Research Soc Am. Mailing Add: 27 Tammy Rd Spring Valley NY 10977

GUNDERSON, ASTER B J (D)
b Brinsmade, NDak, Sept 10, 03; d Theodore O Geldaket & Julia Halvorson G; wid. Educ: Bemidji State Univ, 2 year cert, 24. Polit & Govt Pos: Asst postmistress, Winger, Minn, 34-43; chairwoman, Mahnomen Co Dem Party, Minn, 66-68, vchairwoman, 68-74. Bus & Prof Pos: Teacher, rural schs, Norman & Polk Co, Minn, 24-33. Mem, Bear Park-Bejou Chap, Minn Farmer's Union. Relig: Lutheran. Mailing Add: Bejou MN 56516

GUNDERSON, ELMER MILLARD
Chief Justice, Nev Supreme Court
b Minneapolis, Minn, Aug 9, 29; s Elmer Peter Gunderson & Carmaleta Oliver G; m 1967 to Lupe Gomez; c John Randolph. Educ: Univ Minn; Univ Omaha, 48-53; Creighton Univ, LLB, 56; McGeorge Sch Law, Univ of the Pac, LLD; Phi Alpha Delta; Alpha Sigma Nu. Polit & Govt Pos: Justice, Nev Supreme Court, 71-74, chief justice, 75- Bus & Prof Pos: Attorney-adv, FTC, 56-57; pvt practice, Las Vegas, 58-71; instr bus law, Southern Regional

Div, Univ Nev; lectr, author bulls, felony crimes, Clark Co Sheriff's Dept; counsel, Sheriff's Protective Asn; mem legal staff, Clark Coun Civil Defense Agency; legal counsel, Nev Jaycees; chmn, Clark Co Child Welfare Bd; compiler, annotator, Omaha Home Rule Charter; adj prof law, McGeorge Sch Law, Univ of the Pac; proj coordr, Judicial Orientation Manual. Mil Serv: Army. Mem: Nat Multiple Sclerosis Soc (Nev Cent Chap); Am Bar Asn; Inst Judicial Admin; Am Trial Lawyers Asn; Rotary. Legal Res: 1240 Custer Circle Carson City NV 89701 Mailing Add: Supreme Court Bldg Carson City NV 89701

GUNDERSON, JACK EDWARD **(D)**
Mont State Rep
b Great Falls, Mont, May 23, 29; s Ole S Gunderson & Effie Bergman G; m 1949 to Corinne Francis Nelson; c Stephen, Dana, Kari & Alan. Educ: Mont State Univ. Polit & Govt Pos: Nat deleg, Mont Young Dem, 62 & 64; Mont State Rep, 65-67 & 69-; app to Gov Adv Comt for Voc-Tech Educ, currently. Bus & Prof Pos: Dir, Power Farmers Elevator Co, 60-65; pres, Farmers Union Coop Creamery, 65-69. Mem: Elks Lodge 214, Great Falls; Mont Farmers Union; Mont Grain Growers Asn. Relig: Lutheran. Mailing Add: Box 187 Power MT 59468

GUNDERSON, OBEN JOHN IVER **(R)**
NDak State Rep
b McCanna, NDak, May 6, 27; s Oben Gunderson & Mildred Nelson G; m 1948 to Janice Adeline Hill; c Bradley John, Cathryn Janelle & Diane Kay. Educ: Concordia Col, 2 years; Delta Rho. Polit & Govt Pos: NDak State Rep, 71- Bus & Prof Pos: Grain farmer, 48-; mem, Bible Camp Bd, 62-69; agr supvr, Selek-Leka Mission, Ethiopia, 68-69. Mem: Crop Improv Asn; Eastern NDak Dist Church Coun; Adult Christian Educ Found (area rep, 73-). Honors & Awards: Winner of Soil Conserv Award in Farming Practices, 72. Relig: Lutheran. Mailing Add: McCanna ND 58253

GUNDERSON, STEVE CRAIG **(R)**
Wis State Rep
b Eau Claire, Wis, May 10, 51; s Arthur Gunderson & Adeline Myren G; single. Educ: Univ Wis, Madison, BA, 73; Brown Sch Broadcasting, Minneapolis, Minn, 74; Beta Theta Pi. Polit & Govt Pos: Wis State Rep, 75- Bus & Prof Pos: Customer rels & advert mgr, Gunderson Chevrolet, 73-74. Mem: Lions. Relig: Lutheran. Legal Res: RR 2 Osseo WI 54758 Mailing Add: 334 N Capitol Madison WI 53702

GUNN, CHARLES WESLEY, JR **(D)**
Va State Deleg
b Tallahassee, Fla, July 31, 22; m to Mary Wilson Sheffied. Educ: Fla State Univ; Washington & Lee Univ, LLB. Polit & Govt Pos: Va State Deleg, 64-; chmn, Rockbridge Co Dem Party, Va, 65-72. Bus & Prof Pos: Lawyer. Mil Serv: Navy. Mem: Am Legion; Kiwanis; Mason; Lexington-Rockbridge Co CofC (past pres); Va State Bar (mem coun). Relig: Methodist. Mailing Add: PO Box 1033 Lexington VA 24450

GUNN, GEORGE, JR **(R)**
Mem, Wash State Rep Finance Comt
b Tacoma, Wash, Apr 10, 91; s George Gunn & Emma Howe G; m 1917 to Cleata Dyer; c Cleata (Mrs McIntosh), Nancy (Mrs Tobiason), Gloria (Mrs Hagen) & JoAnne (Mrs Fennema). Educ: Univ Wash, 12-13. Polit & Govt Pos: Mem, Wash State & King Co Rep Finance Comts, 30-52 & currently; treas, Wash State Rep Cent Comt, 52-64; alt deleg, Rep Nat Conv, 68; chmn finance comt, Gov Daniel E Evans Campaign, 72. Bus & Prof Pos: Vpres, White Motor Car Co, 25-30; pres, Kirsten Pipe Co, 38-49, Pioneer, Inc, 40-44, Webster-Brinkley Co, 41-43 & Tote Eng, Inc, 48-61. Mem: Phi Gamma Delta; Mason; CofC; Gtr Seattle, Inc; Wash Athletic Club. Relig: Protestant. Legal Res: 1100 University St Seattle WA 98101 Mailing Add: 3306 White Bldg Seattle WA 98101

GUNN, HOWARD LEE **(D)**
Chmn, Chickasaw Co Dem Party, Miss
b Egypt, Miss, Sept 19, 31; s Mary Sue Gunn; m 1953 to Doris Louise Jamison; c Willie F, Gloria J, Carolyn G, Howard Lee, Jr, Debra G, Johnnie H & Shelia C. Educ: Okolona Jr Col, Miss, 48-51; Philander Smith Col, 54; Miss Indust Col, BS, 59; Miss State Univ, 67-69. Polit & Govt Pos: Chmn, Chickasaw Co Dem Party, Miss, 70-; alt deleg, Dem Nat Conv, 72. Bus & Prof Pos: Elem sch prin, Palona Co Sch Syst, Batesville, Miss, 55-57; sci teacher, Okolona Sch Syst, 59-64; sci teacher & football coach, Carroll Co Sch Syst, Carrollton, 64-65; baseball coach & teacher, Gwinnett Co Sch Syst, Duluth, Ga, 65-67; dir exten serv, Mary Holmes Col, West Point, Miss, 67. Mil Serv: Entered as Pvt, Army, 51, released as Sgt, 53, after serv in 101st Airborne 2nd Inf Div, Korea & Japan, 51-52; Platoon Sgt E-7, Res, 53-73; Combat Inf Badge; UN Serv Medal with One Bronze Serv Star; Nat Defense Serv Suspension Ribbon; Campaign & Serv Ribbon, Armed Forces Reserve. Publ: Educational Psychology Guide for Study, 69. Mem: Chickasaw Co Voter's League (chmn, 64-); NAACP (vchmn, Chickasaw Co Chap, 70-); NMiss Rural Legal Serv (bd mem, 70); Delta Ministry; Masons. Relig: Baptist. Mailing Add: 406 School St Okolona MS 38860

GUNN, STEVEN IRVING **(R)**
Bonus Mem, Boulder Co Rep Comt, Colo
b Sheridan, Wyo, Mar 8, 39; s William Thomas Gunn & Marjorie Carson G; m 1965 to Susan Kathy Goetz; c Carolyn Louise & William Thomas. Educ: Johns Hopkins Univ, 57-60; Columbia Univ, BArch, 64. Polit & Govt Pos: Colo State Rep, 49th Dist, 73-74; bonus mem, Boulder Co Rep Comt, 74- Bus & Prof Pos: Draftsman, John Shober Burrows, Architect, White Plains, NY, 64-68; furniture designer, Hughes & Co, Denver, 68; architect, Everett & Zeigel Architects, 68-70 & Steven I Gunn, Architect, Longmont, Colo, 70-; pres, State Bd Cosmetology, 74- Mem: Am Inst Architects (lobbyist, 75-), Colo Cent Chap; Moose; Mason; Rotary; Jaycees (dir, Longmont, 72-73). Relig: Protestant. Mailing Add: 1207 Fox Hill Dr Longmont CO 80501

GUNNELLS, JOEL B **(D)**
Mem, Ga State Dem Exec Comt
b Detroit, Mich, Apr 27, 35; s Joel Boyd Gunnells, Sr & Mozell Caldwell G; m 1957 to Emily Sanders; c Gail, Glada & Ginnie. Educ: Abraham Baldwin Col, 53-54; Univ Ga, BSA, 57, MS, 65; Alpha Zeta. Polit & Govt Pos: Exec dir, Cent Iowa Asn Local Govts, Des Moines, 72-74; city mgr, Royston, Ga, 74-75; mem, Ga State Dem Exec Comt, 75- Bus & Prof Pos: Co agr agt, Worth Co, Ga, 57-66; mem, Regional Coun Govts, Aiken, SC, 68-72; Hart Co rep, Ga Mountains Planning Comn & Health Planning Coun, currently. Mem: Rotary; CofC; Farm Bur; Mason; Am Soc Planning Officials. Honors & Awards: Prom Prog of Year, Ga Asn Radio Broadcasters, 65; Conservationist of Year, Ga Wildlife Asn, 63. Relig: Southern Baptist; deacon, Hartwell Baptist Church. Legal Res: Bowman Rd Hartwell GA 30643 Mailing Add: PO Box 768 Hartwell GA 30643

GUNNING, ROSEMARY RITA **(R-CONSERVATIVE)**
NY State Assemblyman
b Brooklyn, NY, Feb 7, 05; d Joseph James Gunning & Annie Carney G; m 1946 to Lester Thomas Moffett. Educ: Brooklyn Law Sch, St Lawrence Univ, LLB, 3 years; Phi Delta Delta. Polit & Govt Pos: Deleg, Const Conv, NY, 67; NY State Assemblyman, 69- Bus & Prof Pos: Attorney-at-law, New York & Mineola, NY, 30-42 & Ridgewood, NY, 53-; attorney, NY Ord Dist, Dept Army, 42-53; attorney, Staff-Pres Pro Tem, NY State Senate, 68. Mem: Queens Co Women's Bar Asn; Queens Co Bar Asn; Assoc Orgn of Gtr Ridgewood; Women's Auxiliary of VFW; Am Legion Women's Auxiliary. Honors & Awards: Outstanding Serv to Community, Sgt Edward Miller Post of VFW & Parent & Taxpayers of Ridgewood-Glendale; Exceptional Polit Leader, Conservative Party of NY State; Citations from Nat Info Comt for Jewish Life, Inc & Dept of NY, VFW, 70. Relig: Roman Catholic. Mailing Add: 1867 Grove St Ridgewood NY 11237

GUNTER, BILL **(D)**
b Jacksonville, Fla, July 16, 34; s William D Gunter, Sr & Ruth Senterfitt G; m to Teresa Arbaugh; c Bart & Joel. Educ: Univ Fla, BSA with high honors, 56; Univ Ga, study govt & hist; Fla Blue Key; Univ Hall of Fame; pres, Baptist Student Union; Sigma Alpha Epsilon; nat pres, Future Farmers of Am, 54. Polit & Govt Pos: Mem, Orlando Rehabilitation & Develop Adv Comt, 66-67; Fla State Sen, 66-72; US Rep, Fifth Dist, Fla, 72-74; cand, US House of Rep, 74. Mil Serv: Army, 57-58; Outstanding Hon Grad of Basic Army Admin Course. Mem: Cent Fla Asn Life Underwriters; Gen Agents & Mgr Asn; Orange Co Farm Bur; Orlando Jaycees; Kiwanis. Honors & Awards: One of Five Outstanding Young Men of Fla, Jaycees, 55, One of Outstanding Young Men of Am, 64, State Jaycee Good Govt Award, 72; Award for distinguished serv to agr, Gamma Sigma Delta, 72. Relig: Baptist; Deacon & Sunday Sch Teacher, First Baptist Church of Orlando. Mailing Add: 3006 Ardsley Dr Orlando FL 32804

GUNTER, CARL N **(D)**
La State Rep
Mailing Add: 621 Main St Pineville LA 71360

GUNTER, CAROLYN MAE **(R)**
b Iowa, May 30, 31; d Delmar Carr & Lucille Whittmer C; m 1958 to Hugh Edd Gunter; c Jeff & Kim. Educ: St Luke's Sch Nursing, RN, 54; Ind Univ Exten, South Bend, 56; Ind Univ, Bloomington, 57. Polit & Govt Pos: Exec mem-at-lg, Maricopa Co Rep Comt, Ariz, 69-70, vchairwoman, 70-74; mem exec comt, Ariz State Rep Comt, 70-74; alt deleg, Rep Nat Conv, 72; adv mem, Ariz State Unemployment, 72-73. Bus & Prof Pos: Ed, Committeeman, Maricopa Co Rep Comt, 65-75. Mem: Phoenix Art Museum; Cactus Wren Rep Women's Club; Trunk 'n Tusk Rep Fund Raising Comt. Mailing Add: 721 W Port Royale Lane Phoenix AZ 85023

GUNTER, PEACHES **(D)**
b Gastonia, NC, Sept 2, 51; d Daniel Cornelius Gunter, Jr & DeNorma Smith G; single. Educ: NC State Univ, BA, 73; Alpha Delta Pi (vpres). Polit & Govt Pos: Deleg, NC Tenth Cong Dist Conv, 72; deleg, Dem Nat Conv, 72; statewide campus coordr, Congressman Nick Galifianakis for US Senate, 72. Bus & Prof Pos: Summer field worker, Nat Asn Student Coun, Washington, DC. Publ: We've got the vote, Student Life Highlights, Nat Asn Student Coun, 11/72. Mem: Gaston Co Young Dem Club. Honors & Awards: Presented at the NC Inaugural Ball, 72. Relig: Methodist. Mailing Add: 509 Hawthorne Lane Gastonia NC 28052

GUNTER, WILLIAM B **(D)**
Assoc Justice, Ga Supreme Court
b Commerce, Ga, Apr 20, 19; s Wm Barrett Gunter & Helen Carson G; m 1946 to Elizabeth Parker; c Marjorie Gay, Barrett & John H. Educ: Univ Ga, AB, Law Sch, LLB. Polit & Govt Pos: Ga State Rep, 52-58; city attorney, Gainesville, Ga, 59-; deleg, Dem Nat Conv, 64; mem, Ga State Dem Exec Comt, 65 & 66; Dem Nat Committeeman, Ga, 71-72; Assoc Justice, Ga Supreme Court, 72- Mil Serv: Entered as 2nd Lt, Army, 42, released as 1st Lt, after serv in 3rd Inf Div, ETO; Silver Star; Purple Heart & Seven Campaign Stars, ETO. Mem: Am Bar Asn; State Bar of Ga. Relig: Presbyterian. Mailing Add: Ga Supreme Court Gainesville GA 30501

GUNTHARP, WALTER ANDREW **(R)**
Adminr, Rural Develop Serv, Dept Agr
b Greenville, SC, Sept 26, 19; s George Oscar Guntharp & Mable Claire Beaman G; m 1945 to Margaret Marie Akers; c Walter, Jr & Robert B. Educ: Univ Fla, BA, 49; George Washington Univ, MA, 62, PhD, 72; Sigma Delta Chi; Los Picaros de Quevedo. Polit & Govt Pos: Exec officer, US Mil Assistance & Adv Group, The Netherlands, 55-58; chief foreign develop off, Chief of R&D, Dept Army, 58-61; chief, Latin Am Mil Assistance, US Army S Canal Zone, 64-65; comdr, Joint US Mil Group, Colombia, SAm, 65-67; dep dir, Int & Civil Affairs, Dept Army, 67-69; consult for rural develop, US Dept Agr, 72-73, adminr, Rural Develop Serv, 72- Mil Serv: Entered as Pvt, Army, 41, released as Col, (Ret), 69, after serv in Inf Command Pos in Europe & Korea, 43-51; Distinguished Serv Medal; Silver Star with Two Oak Leaf Clusters; Legion of Merit, Bronze Star; Purple Heart. Publ: Auth, Waves Into Ripples, Inf J, 48 & Where's tac air, Army Magazine, 60; co-auth, The concept of hemispheric defense, Current Hist, 69. Mem: Am Polit Sci Asn; Retired Officers Asn; Conservative Caucus. Relig: Presbyterian. Mailing Add: 1921 MacArthur Dr McLean VA 22101

GUNTHER, GEORGE LACKMAN **(R)**
Conn State Sen
b Nov 22, 19; s George Gunther & Gwendolyn Clift G; m 1941 to Priscilla Agnes Staples; c Priscilla Karen, Karla Gwen & Lance Inder; 12 grandchildren. Educ: Nat Col of Drugless Physicians, Chicago, Ill, ND, 42; hon mem, Theta Sigma. Polit & Govt Pos: Mem, Conn Bd Natureopathic Exam, 46-49; mem, Bd Educ, Stratford, Conn, 57-61; third dist councilman, Town Coun, Stratford, 60-65; organizer & chmn, Stratford Conserv Comn, 61-71; organizer & first pres, Conn Asn of Conserv Comns, 63-65; mem, Stratford Drug Adv Comt; Conn State Sen, 21st Dist, Milford & Stratford, 67-, mem, Pub Health & Safety, Environ, Long Island Sound Study, Regulation Rev & Bi-State Legis, Long Island Sound Marine Resources Comts, Conn State Senate, currently, mem, Subcomt on Budget Rev, currently, Dep Minority Leader, 71-73. Bus & Prof Pos: Natureopathic physician. Mem: Sigma Phi Kappa; AF&AM; Stratford Antique Gun Collectors Asn (organizer & first pres); Milford CofC (hon mem); Univ Bridgeport (bd assoc). Honors & Awards: Outstanding Civic Leader of Am Award, 67; Legis Conservationist of Year for Conn, Conn State League of Sportsmen, Nat Wildlife Fedn & Sears & Roebuck Found, 69; Citizen of Year Award, Stratford Civitan Club, 70; Rickerby Mem Award, Ecol League of Conn, 72; Legion of Honor Award, Int Order of DeMolay, 72. Relig: Methodist. Mailing Add: 890 Judson Pl Stratford CT 06497

GUREVICH, MAE (D)
Polit & Govt Pos: Mem, Dem Nat Comt, NY, formerly. Mailing Add: 415 Madison Ave New York NY 10017

GURNEY, CHAN JOHN CHANDLER (R)
b Yankton, SDak, May 21, 96; s Deloss Butler Gurney & Henrietta Belle Klopping G; m 1917 to Evelyn Bordeno; c Ida Elaine (Mrs Morgan T Smith), John Bordeno & Deloss Braddock. Educ: Pub schs, Yankton, SDak. Polit & Govt Pos: US Sen, SDak, 39-51; mem, Civil Aeronaut Bd, 51-65, chmn, 54-, vchmn, 57-61. Bus & Prof Pos: Built & operated Radio Sta WNAX, 27-32; secy-treas, Gurney Seed & Nursery Co, 32; pres, Chan Gurney Oil Co, Sioux Falls, 32-36. Mil Serv: Army Engrs, Sgt, World War I, serv in 34th Div, overseas. Mem: Am Legion; VFW; Mason; Goethals Mem Comn, 47. Mailing Add: 802 W Third St Yankton SD 57078

GURNEY, EDWARD JOHN (R)
b Portland, Maine, Jan 12, 14; s Edward John Gurney & Nellie Kennedy G; m 1941 to Eleanor Natalie Ahlborn; c Sarah & Jill (Mrs Lewis Tappen Holt). Educ: Colby Col, BS, 35; Harvard Univ, LLB, 38; Duke Univ, LLM, 48; Biscayne Alpha Tau Omega. Hon Degrees: LLD, Rollins Col & Colby Col; DSc, Fla Inst Technol; LHD, Biscayne Col. Polit & Govt Pos: Comnr, Winter Park, Fla, 52-58, mayor, 61-62; US Rep, Fla, 63-68; US Sen, 68-74; deleg, Rep Nat Conv, 72. Bus & Prof Pos: Lawyer, Barry, Wainwright, Thacher & Symmers, New York, 38-41; lawyer, Gurney & Skolfield, Winter Park, Fla, formerly. Mil Serv: Entered as Pvt, Army, Nat Guard, 41, released as Lt Col, 46, after serv in 8th Armored Div, ETO, 44-45; Silver Star; Purple Heart. Relig: Congregational. Mailing Add: 800 Greentree Dr Winter Park FL 33880

GURNSEY, KATHLEEN W (KITTY) (D)
Idaho State Rep
Mailing Add: 1111 W Highland View Dr Boise ID 83702

GURULE, FRANK P (D)
NMex State Rep
Mailing Add: 744 La Vega Ct SW Albuquerque NM 87105

GURZENDA, TED J (D)
Chairperson, Roscommon Co Dem Party, Mich
b Wyandotte, Mich, Jan 24, 22; s Julius Gurzenda & Mary Sakowski G; m 1943 to Geraldine Trombly; c Bonnie (Mrs Lankford), Richard, Barbara (Mrs Teddy Cyster), Mary Lou & Robert. Educ: Mt Carmel High Sch, grad, 41. Polit & Govt Pos: Chairperson, Roscommon Co Dem Party, Mich, 73-; twp supvr, Richfield, Mich, 74- Bus & Prof Pos: Real estate salesman, Mich, 52; dist ins agt, Prudential Ins Co, 64- Mil Serv: Entered as Pvt, Army, 43, released as Sgt, 46, after serv in Mil Police, European & Pac, 43-46. Relig: Catholic. Legal Res: 1684 Lolich St Helen MI 48656 Mailing Add: Box 147 St Helen MI 48656

GUS SERRA, EMANUEL (D)
Mass State Rep
Mailing Add: State Capitol Boston MA 02133

GUST, GERALD N (D)
Chmn, Polk Co Dem Party, Wis
b Amery, Wis, Dec 26, 46; s Orville E Gust & Lucille Warner G; m 1970 to Susan Jean Dudding; c Shayne Jean & Thomas Jefferson. Educ: Univ Wis-River Falls, BS, 69; Univ Wis-Madison, JD, 72; Phi Nu Chi. Polit & Govt Pos: Dir, Young Dem of Wis, 67-68; chmn, Polk Co Dem Party, 73- Bus & Prof Pos: Attorney, Cwayna, Novitzke, Byrnes & Gust, 72- Mem: Am Wis & Intercounty Bar Asns; Phi Alpha Theta; Jaycees. Relig: Lutheran. Mailing Add: 345 Arlington Dr Amery WI 54001

GUST, WALTER R (D)
Chairperson, Richland Co Dem Party, Wis
b Stratford, Wis, Oct 2, 36; s Otto Gust & Johanna Hagen G; m 1963 to Carolla Paul; c Lisa, Carrie & Amy. Educ: Lakeland Col, 54-56; Wis State Univ, Stevens Point, BS, 64; Univ Minn, MA, 69. Polit & Govt Pos: Chairperson, Richland Co Dem Party, Wis, 74- Bus & Prof Pos: Proprietor, Park View Motel, 72- Mil Serv: Entered as Basic Airman, Air Force, 57, released as Airman 2/C, 59, after serv in 2848 Squadron, Air Materiel Command. Mem: Mason; Wis Innkeepers Asn. Relig: Lutheran. Mailing Add: 511 W Sixth St Richland Center WI 53581

GUSTAFSON, BERNHARD GUSTAF (BEN) (D)
NDak State Rep
b Foxholm, NDak, Sept 8, 03; s Sam A Gustafson (deceased) & Clara Olina Olson G; m 1928 to Ruth Louise Corell; c Bernard Gilbert & Lorna Gail Greta (Mrs Thomas T Berge). Educ: Jamestown Col, BS, 26; Univ NDak, MS, 45; Dept of Defense Staff Col, 62-68. Hon Degrees: DS, Jamestown Col, 74. Polit & Govt Pos: Mem, Gov Comt on Aging, NDak, chmn, 65-73; mem, NDak Coun on Exten, state coordr Title 1-HEA, 65, secy, 69-; mem, NDak Coun on Human Resources, vchmn, 65-73, chmn, 73; mem, NDak Econ Develop Comn, chmn comt educ & research, 66-69; chmn, NDak State Conf on Aging, 71; mem educ tech comt, White House Coun on Aging, 71, consult comt on educ, 71-72; NDak State Sen, 71-72; consult, Comt on Employ of the Handicapped, 74; NDak State Rep, 75- Bus & Prof Pos: Instr chem, NDak State Sch Forestry, Bottineau, 38-40; assoc prof, Univ NDak, 40-64, dir gen exten div, 57-64, dean, Williston Ctr, 58-69, Div Continuing Educ & Ellendale Ctr, 64-69, coordr research & develop, Div Continuing Educ, 69-74, dean emer & assoc prof chem emer, 74-; control chemist, Am Foods, Inc (on leave from Univ NDak), 42-45; research consult, US Bur of Mines, NDak Research Found, US Dept Agr & US Army Qm Corps. Mem: Mason (Grand Master, 59-60); Elks; Nat Univ Exten Asn; Nat Asn State Univs & Land Grant Cols (Sen, 69-72); NDak Acad Sci. Honors & Awards: NDak Adult Educator of the Year, 70; Julius M Nolte Award, Nat Univ Exten Asn, 73. Mailing Add: 421 Princeton St Grand Forks ND 58201

GUSTAFSON, CARL H (R)
Colo State Rep
b Eaton, Colo, Feb 26, 29; m 1971 to Elizabeth Roser (deceased); c four. Polit & Govt Pos: Colo State Rep, 67-, Majority Leader, Colo House of Rep, formerly. Bus & Prof Pos: Vpres & mgr, Quinn & Co, Inc, investment securities firm; mem exec comt, Mid-Continental Dist Securities Indust Asn, 71- Relig: Lutheran. Legal Res: 480 S Marion Pkwy Denver CO 80209 Mailing Add: Suite 710 818 17th St Denver CO 80202

GUSTAFSON, RICHARD (D)
Ore State Rep
Mailing Add: 16901 SE Division Portland OR 97236

GUSTE, WILLIAM JOSEPH (D)
Attorney Gen, La
b New Orleans, La, May 26, 22; s William Joseph Guste, Sr & Marie Louise Alciatore G; m 1947 to Dorothy Elizabeth Schutten; c William Joseph, III, Bernard Randolph, Marie Louise, Melanie Ann, Valerie Eve, Althea Maria, Elizabeth Therese, James Patrick & Anne Duchesne. Educ: Loyola Univ, BA, 42, LLB, 43; Blue Key; pres, Sigma Alpha Kappa; St Thomas More Lawyers Asn. Polit & Govt Pos: Deleg, Dem Nat Conv, 68; La State Sen, 68-72; auth of Urban Renewal Enabling Legis for New Orleans, 66; chmn, Ad Hoc Comt which prepared & secured approval of the city's appln to the Dept of Housing & Urban Develop for a Model City Planning Grant, 67; mem, Gov Comt on Law Enforcement & Admin of Justice, 69-70; Attorney Gen, La, 72- Bus & Prof Pos: Practicing attorney-at-law, 46- Mil Serv: T/Sgt, Army Inf, serv in ETO, 46. Mem: Am & La Bar Asns; Nat Housing Coun; KofC; Nat Asn of Housing & Redevelop Off (mem fed local rels comt). Relig: Catholic. Legal Res: 4 Richmond Pl New Orleans LA 70115 Mailing Add: 1624 Nat Bank of Com Bldg New Orleans LA 70112

GUSTIN, JOE RICHARD (R)
b Cherry Fork, Ohio, June 12, 36; Roy F (Spud) Gustin & Mary Schweickart G; m 1961 to Joyce Lee Thatcher; c Debora Lynn & Roy Frame, II. Educ: Miami Univ, BS in bus admin, 58; Young Rep. Polit & Govt Pos: Campaign mgr, Adams Co, Young Ohions for John Bricker, 58; mem & vpres, Southern Hills Joint Voc Sch Bd, 69-71; mem, Adams Co Bd Educ & Ohio Valley Local Sch Bd, 69-; sustaining mem, Rep Nat Party, 70-; deleg, Rep Nat Conv, 72. Bus & Prof Pos: Mem, Pres Cabinet, Columbia Nat Life Ins Co, Columbus, 67, mem, Chancellors Cabinet, 69, supt agencies, Southern Ohio, 72- Mil Serv: Entered as Seaman Apprentice, Naval Res, 59, released as Seaman, 61, after serv in Radar. Mem: F&AM; Order of Eastern Star; AASR; Elks. Relig: Protestant. Mailing Add: RR 3 West Union OH 45693

GUTHRIDGE, ESTHER BLANCH (R)
VChmn, Second Dist Rep Cent Comt, Ind
b Klemme, Iowa; d James William Scott & Annette Klaus S; m to Emmett O Guthridge; c Garry A & David E. Educ: Ind Bus Col. Polit & Govt Pos: Precinct committeewoman, Rep Party, Benton Co, Ind, 34-42; vchmn, Benton Co Rep Party, 36-62; dist dir, Second Dist, Ind Fedn Rep Women, deleg, Conv, 52-, pres, formerly, mem, Comt Achievement Awards, currently; alt deleg, Rep Nat Conv, 56, deleg, 60, 64 & 68; secy, Second Dist Rep Cent Comt, 56-60, vchmn, 60-; chmn, Coun of Ind Civil Defense, 69-; vchmn, Ind Rep Cent Comt, formerly. Bus & Prof Pos: Clerk circuit court, Benton Co, Ind, 63-67. Mem: Gov Comt on Status of Women; Rep State VChmn Asn (chmn, Midwest Regional Adv Comt); Eastern Star; Delta Sigma Kappa; Rebekah. Honors & Awards: Sagamore of the Wabash. Relig: Protestant. Legal Res: 105 N Grant Fowler IN 47944 Mailing Add: PO Box 189 Fowler IN 47944

GUTHRIE, A B (R)
Mont State Rep
Mailing Add: 311 Yellowstone Ave Billings MT 59102

GUTIERREZ, ALFREDO (D)
Majority Leader, Ariz State Senate
Mailing Add: 334 E Roeser Apt 126 Phoenix AZ 85040

GUTIERREZ, CARL TOMMY CRUZ (D)
Sen, Guam Legis
b Agana, Guam, Oct 15, 41; s Tomas Taitano Gutierrez & Rita Benavente Cruz G; m 1963 to Geraldine Torres; c Carla Helene & Carl Thomas, II. Educ: Univ Guam, 64-70. Polit & Govt Pos: Comput syst supvr, Navy Finance Ctr, Washington, DC, 65; data processing mgr, Govt of Guam, 65-72; precinct chmn, Agana Heights Dem Club, Guam, 71-73; Sen, Guam Legis, 73- Bus & Prof Pos: Owner & mgr, Carltom Construction, 71- Mil Serv: Entered as Airman Basic, Air Force, 60, released as S/Sgt, 65, after serv in Tactical Air Command-Strategic Air Command, 60-65; Good Conduct Medal; Airman of Quarter. Mem: Data Processing Mgt Asn (Int pres, 71-72); Elks; Guam Jaycees. Relig: Catholic. Mailing Add: PO Box 404 Agana Heights GU 96910

GUTIERREZ, ROSENDO (D)
Mem, Ariz Dem State Exec Comt
b El Paso, Tex, Aug 31, 32; s Rosendo C Gutierrez & Caridad Munoz G; div; c Rosendo Carlos & Armando. Educ: Tex Western Col, BS in Civil Eng, 53. Polit & Govt Pos: Chmn, LEAP Comn, Phoenix, Ariz, 65-68; Dem nominee, State Senate, Dist 8-I, 66; Dem precinct committeeman, Madison Precinct Two, 66-; mem, Ariz Dem State Exec Comt, 66-; mem exec comt, Phoenix Charter Govt Comt, 67; mem exec comt, Phoenix Forward Comt, 69-; Dem chmn, Legis Dist 18, 67-72; mem, Maricopa Co Dem Exec Comt, 67-72; initial chmn & then exec dir, City No Ward Campaign, Phoenix, 67; deleg, Dem Nat Conv, 68; dir, Castro for Gov Campaign, 70 & 74; mem, Madison Sch Bd, 70-71; comnr, City of Phoenix Planning Comn, 71-73; city councilman, Phoenix, 74-75. Bus & Prof Pos: Proj engr, L H Bell & Assoc, Phoenix, Ariz, 61-63; proj engr, Ken R White Co, 63-66; owner, Pace Eng, 66- Mil Serv: Entered as S/A, Navy, 53, released as Lt(jg), 57, after serv in Civil Eng Corps, Japan & Miss; Comdr, Naval Res, Seabee; Nat Defense Medal; Korean Theatre Medal; UN Serv Medal; Expert Pistol. Mem: Naval Res Asn; Nat & Ariz Soc Prof Engrs; Am Soc Civil Engrs; Soc Am Mil Engrs; Urban League (bd dirs, Phoenix Chap). Honors & Awards: Outstanding Community Serv Award, Cent Labor Coun, AFL-CIO, 72. Relig: Methodist. Mailing Add: 55 E Weldon Ave Phoenix AZ 85012

GUTMAN, PHILLIP EDWARD (R)
Ind State Sen
b Ft Wayne, Ind, Jan 5, 30; s Froncie Gutman & Beulah M Holman G; m 1955 to Mabel Carolyn Prickett; c Phillip E, Jr, Gretchen K & Kurt A. Educ: Ind Univ, BS in Bus Admin, 52, Law Sch, JD, 57; Phi Delta Phi; Delta Upsilon. Polit & Govt Pos: Asst to co chmn, Ind Rep Party, 57-62; asst to state chmn, 62-64; precinct committeeman, Ft Wayne, Ind, 64-68; ward chmn, 66-67; Ind State Sen, 68-, pres-pro-tem, Ind State Senate, currently. Mil Serv: Air Force, 52-54, 1st Lt, serv as asst finance officer, Park AFB, Calif & Ladd AFB, Alaska. Mem: Rotary; Am Legion; Mason; Scottish Rite; York Rite. Relig: Methodist. Legal Res: 2840 Club Terr Ft Wayne IN 46804 Mailing Add: Mezzanine Floor Ind Bank Bldg Ft Wayne IN 46802

GUTMAN, THEODORE E (TED) (D)
Mem, Calif State Dem Cent Comt
b Gotha, Germany, Dec 24, 09; s Leo Gutman & Henrietta Cosmann G; m to Ruth Pearlman; c Carol Betsy Cosman (Mrs Alter) & Marjorie Ann (Mrs Weiss). Educ: Univ Jena, DL, 32. Polit & Govt Pos: Pres, Sherman Oaks Dem Club, 72; deleg, Dem Mid-Term Conf, 74; vpres, 22nd State Senate Dist Coun, 75; mem, Calif State Dem Cent Comt, 75- Bus & Prof Pos: Superior Court Judge, Germany, retired; partner wholesale bus, The Hays Co, Los Angeles, Calif, 52-73; retired. Mil Serv: Entered as Pvt, Sea Coast Artil, US Army, 43, released as 1st Lt, 45, after serv in Military Intel, 80th Inf Div, ETO, 3rd Army, 44-45; Army Res, Maj (Ret), 54; Inf Combat Badge, Bronze Star with cluster. Mem: Archaeological Inst, UCLA, (fel); Soc for Calif Archaeology. Relig: Jewish. Mailing Add: 4101 Stansbury Ave Sherman Oaks CA 91423

GUTOWSKI, STANLEY L (R)
Chmn, Livingston Co Rep Comt, NY
b Plymouth, Pa, Mar 27, 31; s Stanley Gutowski & Catherine Stadts G; m 1953 to Edythe Mae Hank; c Debra Ann, Darlene Marie & Doreen Sue. Educ: Plymouth High Sch, Pa, grad. Polit & Govt Pos: Pres, Livingston Co Young Rep Club, NY, 65-66, gov, 66-67, co-gov, 68; vchmn, Livingston Co Rep Comt, 66-73, acting chmn, 73, chmn, 73-; admin asst to Dep Majority Leader, NY State Assembly, 71- Bus & Prof Pos: Plant mgr, Dynamic Components Corp, 63-68, vpres, 68- Mil Serv: Entered as Pvt, Air Force, 51, released as S/Sgt, 55, after serv at Sampson AFB. Mem: Caledonia Fire Dept; Hook & Ladder Fire Co; Jaycees. Honors & Awards: Named Outstanding Rep of the Year by Livingston Co Rep Comt, NY, 67 & Outstanding Gov of NY State by Young Rep Club, 68. Relig: Catholic. Mailing Add: 680 W Lake Rd Geneseo NY 14454

GUY, JAMES LINDSAY, II (R)
Exec Committeeman, SC Rep Party
b Charlotte, NC, July 31, 43; s Edwin P Guy & Mary Tilden Hoopes; m 1966 to Frances Jean Keough; c Leslie Keough & James Lindsay, III. Educ: Furman Univ, BA, 65; SC Realtor's Inst, grad, 74; vpres, Tau Kappa Epsilon. Polit & Govt Pos: Exec committeeman, SC Rep Party, 70-; city councilman, Camden, 72-; mem, Santee-Wateree Regional Planning Coun, 73- Bus & Prof Pos: Admin asst, Fed Home Loan Bank, Greensboro, NC, 65-68; mgr, Powe Veneer Co Inc, 68-73; partner, deLoach & Guy Real Estate, 73- Mil Serv: Entered as Cand, Marine Corps, 62, released as Lance Cpl, 64, after serv in Platoon Leaders Class. Mem: Rotary; Navy League; CofC; Kershaw Co Bd Realtors. Relig: Presbyterian. Mailing Add: 110 Union St Camden SC 29020

GUY, PHIL (D)
Alaska State Rep
Mailing Add: Kwethluk AK 99621

GUY, WILLIAM L (D)
b Devils Lake, NDak, Sept 30, 19; m 1943 to Elizabeth Jean Mason; c William, James, Deborah, Holly & Nancy. Educ: NDak State Univ, BS, 41; Univ Minn, MA, 46. Hon Degrees: Dr, Concordia Col, 71 & NDak State Univ, 73. Polit & Govt Pos: NDak State Rep, 58-60; Gov, NDak, 61-73; chmn, Mo State Comn & Midwest Gov Conf, 61-63; chmn, Nat Gov Conf & Coun of State Govts, 67; mem, President Johnson's Elec Observer Team to SVietnam, 67; mem, President Johnson's Nat Health Facilities Adv Comt, 68; deleg, Dem Nat Conv, 68; mem adv bd, NDak Bd of Higher Educ, 73- Bus & Prof Pos: Farmer; former teacher agr econ at NDak State Univ; dir, Fargo Ins Agency, 73- Mil Serv: Navy, World War II. Mem: Amenia Sch Bd; NDak State Univ Alumni Asn; Gate City Toastmasters Club, Fargo; Elks; Am Legion. Honors & Awards: Silver Antelope, Boy Scouts; Nat 4-H Club Alumnae Award; Outstanding NDak State Univ Alumnae Award. Relig: Presbyterian; church trustee, Sunday sch teacher. Mailing Add: Casselton ND 58102

GUY, WILLIAM S (D)
Miss State Rep
Mailing Add: Box 853 McComb MS 39648

GUYANT, GEORGE M (D)
Mem, Portage Co Bd of Supvr
b Milwaukee, Wis, Aug 29, 45; s Wakefield M Guyant & Evelyn Akey G; m 1965 to Patricia Ann Berto; c Albert William & Michele Renee. Educ: Wis State Univ, Stevens Point, 68- Polit & Govt Pos: Chmn & organizer, Portage Co Young Dem, Wis, 62-63; deleg, Seventh Dist Dem Conv, 68; deleg, Wis Dem Conv, 68 & 69; alt deleg, Nat Dem Conv, 68; mem, Portage Co Bd of Supvr, 11th Dist, 72- Mil Serv: Entered as E-1, Air Force, 63, released as E-4, 67, after serv in First Combat Support Unit, First Fighter Wing, 64-67; E-4, Inactive Air Force Res, 67-70; Nat Defense & Good Conduct Medals. Mem: Izaak Walton League; Portage Co Vets for Peace (chmn, 71-72). Relig: Christian. Mailing Add: 349 Second St N Stevens Point WI 54481

GUYER, TENNYSON (R)
US Rep, Ohio
b Findley, Ohio, Nov 29, 13; s William Harris Guyer & Myrtle Emma Hartsock G; m 1944 to Edith Mae Reuter; c Sharon Mae & Rosetta Kae. Educ: Findlay Col, AB, 34; Alpha Club; Letter F Club. Hon Degrees: DLitt, Findlay Col, 53; DCom Sci, Tiffin Univ, 53. Polit & Govt Pos: Councilman, Celina, Ohio, 40-42; mayor, 42-44; mem, Ohio State Rep Cent & Exec Comts, 54-66; Ohio State Sen, 59-73; US Rep, Ohio, 73- Publ: The Church-Institution or Destitution, Post Publ Co, 40; Speech Record-the Miracle Called America, Queen City Rec Co, 63. Mem: Life mem Int Platform Asn; hon mem Exchange Club; Ohio Press Club; Int Lions Clubs; Mason. Honors & Awards: Amvets Community Serv Award; Golden Deeds Award, Nat Exchange Clubs; Hon Chief Sa-Gee-Ya, Cherokee Indians; Ky Col; Outstanding Alumnus, Findlay Col, 66. Relig: Church of God. Mailing Add: 1196 E Sandusky St Findlay OH 45840

GUZZI, PAUL (D)
Secy of State, Mass
b Newton, Mass, June 17, 42; s Alfred R Guzzi & Rose M Gorgone G; m 1970 to Joanne Clarke; c Mark Joseph & Michael Paul. Educ: Harvard Univ, AB, 64. Polit & Govt Pos: Mass State Rep, 71-74; Secy of State, Mass, 75- Mil Serv: Capt, Marine Corps Res. Relig: Catholic. Mailing Add: State House Boston MA 02133

GUZZI, RALPH JOSEPH (D)
Mem, Stratford Dem Town Comt, Conn
b Bridgeport, Conn, Apr 5, 32; s Salvatore Guzzi & Margaret Tempini G; m 1956 to Lorraine Bouchard; c Sharon Marie, Charlene Ann & Allison Marie. Educ: Univ Conn Exten Sch, 56-57; Univ Purdue, 64. Polit & Govt Pos: Mem, Stratford Dem Town Comt, Conn, 57-; Justice of the Peace, Stratford, Conn, 57-58, chmn, Zoning Bd of Appeals, 60-63; mem, Gtr Bridgeport Regional Planning Agency, Bridgeport & Stratford, Conn, 64; Dem cand for state legis, 66; mem, Redevelop Agency, 67; deleg, Dem Nat Conv, 68 & 72; mem, Dem State Cent Comt, Conn, 74- Bus & Prof Pos: Owner, Ralph J Guzzi Agency, Life Gen Agent, part owner, West Haven Manor Convalescent Hosp, Ralton Agency Real Estate & partner, Jar Assocs Develop Co, currently. Mil Serv: Entered as Airman, Air Force, 51, released as Airman 1/C, 55, after serv on Patrol Squadron Duth, Iceland, 53-55; Good Conduct Medal; Spec Unit Citation. Publ: Several articles in Ins Salesman, 60-66. Mem: Bridgeport Life Underwriters; East Bridgeport Lions Club (tailtwister); East Bridgeport Trade & Civic Asn (dir). Honors & Awards: Qualifier Million Dollar Round Table, Nat Asn Life Underwriters, 5 times; Boss of the Year, Bridgeport Jr CofC, 68. Relig: Roman Catholic. Mailing Add: 180 Pilgrim Lane Stratford CT 06497

GVOYICH, GEORGE PAUL (D)
WVa State Deleg
b Weirton, WVa, May 8, 36; s Paul Gvoyich & Susan Lisko G; m 1963 to Viola Mae Riggi; c Kris Ann & Deborah Lee. Educ: Weir High Sch, grad, 66. Polit & Govt Pos: Dem mem & second vchmn, Hancock Co Dem Exec Comt, 74-; WVa State Deleg, 75- Bus & Prof Pos: Steel worker, Weirton Steel Co, 56- Mil Serv: Pvt, Marine Corps, 53-56; Philippine Islands & Atsugi, Japan. Mem: Weirton Coun for Retarded Children & Adults (bd dirs); Weirton Moose; Am Legion; Upper Ohio Valley Dapper Dan Club; Weirton FOPA. Relig: Serbian Orthodox. Mailing Add: 224 Elaine St Weirton WV 26062

GWALTNEY, LAMAR EDWARD (D)
NMex State Sen
b Osceola, Ark, Apr 21, 33; s Louie Edward Gwaltney & Lilian Ward G; m 1965 to Mary Gail Anderson; c Cynthia, Tracy, Rebecca & Lamar. Educ: NMex State Univ, 51-52, 53-54 & 56-58; Eastern Ariz Jr Col, Thatcher, 52-53. Polit & Govt Pos: NMex State Sen, 75- Bus & Prof Pos: Pres, Lamar Liquors Inc, 58- & Gail Inc, 65- Mil Serv: Entered as Pvt, Army, 51, released as M/Sgt, after serv in 525 M1. Relig: Episcopal. Legal Res: 1910 N Alameda Las Cruces NM 88001 Mailing Add: PO Box 1139 Las Cruces NM 88001

GWATHMEY, ROBERT RYLAND, III (D)
Va State Deleg
b Richmond, Va, Dec 21, 17. Educ: Randolph-Macon, BA; Univ Va Law Sch, LLB. Polit & Govt Pos: Commonwealth attorney, Hanover Co, Va, 48-56; pres, Jamestown Festival Comt, 56-58; past asst co judge, Hanover Co; Va State Deleg, 58- Bus & Prof Pos: Lawyer. Mil Serv: Navy. Mem: Ruritans; Hanover Farm Bur; Downtown Club Richmond; Va State & Richmond Bar Asns. Relig: Episcopal. Legal Res: Hanover VA 23069 Mailing Add: 5728 Mechanicsville Pike Mechanicsville VA 23111

GWINN, WILLIAM F (R)
Ore State Rep
Mailing Add: PO Box 923 Albany OR 97321

GWYNN, WILLIAM G (D)
Mont State Rep
Mailing Add: Box 645 Eureka MT 59917

H

HAAG, GEORGE A (R)
b San Antonio, Tex, Aug 18, 39; s G A Haag & Dora Fehlis H; m 1963 to Geneva Ann Tresenriter; c Amber Dawn. Educ: Tex A&I Univ, BA, magna cum laude, 61; Univ Mo-Columbia, MA & MPA, magna cum laude, 64; Alpha Chi; Phi Alpha Theta; pres & vpres, Student Body; Southern Conf Debate Champions; All State Baseball. Polit & Govt Pos: Guest speaker, Rep Nat Comt Campaign Mgt Seminar, admin asst, US Rep Jim Collins, Tex, 68-; campaign mgr, US Senate cand Nelson G Gross, NJ, 70; Washington rep for various business & municipal govt groups. Bus & Prof Pos: Vpres, First Southern Inc, 68; exec asst to pres & dir mkt, Creative Develop Corp, Rockville, Mo, 74- Mil Serv: Entered as 2nd Lt, Air Force, 62, released as Capt, 66, after serv as a Flight Training Officer, Squadron Comdr & General's Aide in ADC & ATC, 62-66; Capt, Res, 66-; Air Force Commendation Medal; Outstanding Unit Award; Vietnam Serv Medal; Marksmanship Award; Selected as Outstanding Junior Officer for Air Defense Command, 64. Publ: Joint chiefs of staff-three problems, Air Force J, 64. Mem: Dallas Junior CofC, (bd dirs); Dallas Summer Job Fair Comt (Div Comdr). Honors & Awards: Outstanding Jaycee in Dallas, 67. Relig: Episcopal. Mailing Add: 12 Infield Court S Rockville MD 20854

HAAS, HARL H (D)
b Cape Girardeau, Mo, Dec 24, 32; s Harl H Haas & Mary Berneice Taylor H; m 1969 to Sharron Rae Burnham; c Amy Taylor. Educ: Southeast Mo State Col, 51-52 & 55-57; Willamette Univ, LLB, 61; Phi Delta Phi. Polit & Govt Pos: Mem, Criminal Law Revision Comn, Ore, 69; orgn chmn, Ore State Dem Party, 69; Ore State Rep, Multnomah Co, 69-71, minority leader, Ore House Rep, 70-71; rep of elected Dem off, Multnomah Co Dem Cent Comt, 69-; Ore State Sen, 71-72; dist attorney, Multnomah Co, Ore, 73-; mem, Dem Charter Comn, 75- Bus & Prof Pos: Mem, Client Indemnity Fund Comt, Ore State Bar, 62-63, Procedure & Practice Comt, 63-64 & Pub Rels Comt, 68-69; lectr on workman's compensation, Willamette Univ, 68-69. Mil Serv: Entered as Pvt, Army, released as Pfc, after serv in 716th Mil Police Bn, 53-55; Good Conduct Medal; Nat Defense Ribbon. Publ: Other insurance clauses, Willamette Law J; auth continuing legal educ articles on evidence, malicious prosecution & workman's compensation. Mem: Am Bar Asn; Am Trial Lawyers Asn; Nat Judiciary Soc. Honors & Awards: Best Oral Argument, Am Trial Lawyers Western Regional Moot & Contest, 60. Relig: Methodist. Mailing Add: 444 N Hayden Bay Dr Portland OR 97217

HABEL, EUGENE JOSEPH (D)
NH State Rep
b Somersworth, NH, May 15, 02; s Joseph H Habel & Delvina Lessard H; div. Polit & Govt

Pos: Moderator & selectman, currently; NH State Rep, 71-72 & 74- Bus & Prof Pos: Orchestra leader, 16-65; guard force, Gen Elec Co, Somersworth, NH, 47-64; police chief, Rollinsford, 65- Mil Serv: Entered as Fireman 1/C, Navy, 42, released as EN 1, 64, after serv in Asia; five mil awards. Mem: Am Legion (past Comdr); 40 et 8 (past Chef de Gare); VFW. Relig: Catholic. Mailing Add: 72 C Washington St Somersworth NH 03878

HABEL, R WILLIAM (D)
b Grand Rapids, Mich, Apr 16, 35; s Lloyd August Habel & Katherine House H; m 1957 to Janice Caroline Edwards; c Shana Lee, Katherine Jean, Justin William & Jennifer Amanda. Educ: Utah State Univ, BS, 60; George Washington Univ Law Sch, JD, 68; Phi Kappa Phi. Polit & Govt Pos: Legis asst, US Rep David S King, 64-66; admin asst, US Rep Allan T Howe, 75- Mil Serv: Entered as Pvt, Marine Corps, 52, released as Sgt, 55, after serv in 1st Marine Div, Pac & Korea; Korean Serv Medal; UN Serv Medal; Good Conduct Medal; 1st Marine Div Unit Citation. Mem: Home Builders Asn; CofC. Relig: Latter-day Saint. Legal Res: 362 W 100 S Logan UT 84106 Mailing Add: 1525 Longworth House Off Bldg Washington DC 20515

HABEN, RALPH H, JR (D)
Fla State Rep
Mailing Add: 608 Seventh St Palmetto FL 33561

HABERMAN, REX STANLEY (R)
Chmn, Chase Co Rep Party, Nebr
b Friend, Nebr, Jan 23, 24; s George C Haberman & Francis Hodek H; m 1946 to Phyllis Kavan; c Mary Lou (Mrs Russell), George, Rex II & Phillip. Educ: Colo State Univ & Univ Nebr, 42-43. Polit & Govt Pos: Chmn, Chase Co Rep Party, Nebr, 73- Mil Serv: Entered as Pvt, Air Force, 43, released as Cpl, 45, after serv in 709 Bomber Squadron, ETO, 42-43. Mem: Tex Longhorn Asn; VFW; Am Legion; Shrine; Elks. Relig: Episcopal. Mailing Add: 440 W 11th Imperial NE 69033

HABIB, PHILIP CHARLES
Asst Secy State EAsian & Pac Affairs
b Brooklyn, NY, Feb 25, 20; s Alex Habib & Mary Spiridon H; m 1942 to Marjorie W Slightam; c Phyllis A & Susan W. Educ: Univ Idaho, BS, 42; Univ Calif, Berkeley, PhD, 52. Polit & Govt Pos: Foreign serv officer, 49-, third secy, Am Embassy, Ottawa, Can, 49-51; second secy, Am Embassy, Wellington, NZ, 52-54; research specialist, Dept State, 55-57; Am Consulate Gen, Port of Spain, Trinidad, 58-60; foreign affairs officer, Dept State, 60-61; counr polit affairs, Am Embassy, Seoul, Korea, 62-65 & Saigon, Vietnam, 65-67; personal rank of minister, 66-67; personal rank of Ambassador, 69-; Dep Asst Secy State EAsian & Pac Affairs, 67-69, Asst Secy State EAsian & Pac Affairs, 74-; mem US deleg to meetings on Vietnam, Paris, 68-71; Ambassador, Repub Korea, 71-74. Mil Serv: Entered as Pvt, Army, 42, released as Capt, 46. Honors & Awards: Rockefeller Pub Serv Award, 69; Nat Civil Serv League Award, 70. Relig: Roman Catholic. Mailing Add: Dept of State Washington DC 20520

HACKEL, STELLA B (D)
State Treas, Vt
Div; c Susan Jane & Cynthia Anne. Educ: Univ Vt, 43-45; Boston Univ, JD cum laude, 48. Polit & Govt Pos: Pres, Rutland League Women Voters, Vt, 51-53; pres, Rutland Co Dem Women's Asn, 56-63; treas, Rutland City Dem Comt, 57-63; comnr, Dept Employ Security, Vt, 63-73; State Treas, 75- Bus & Prof Pos: City grand juror, Rutland, Vt, 57-63; pres, Nat Interstate Conf Employ Security Agencies, 72-73; lawyer, Rutland, 73-75. Mem: Rutland Girl Scout Leaders Asn; Am Asn Univ Women; Vt & Rutland Co Bar Asns; Vt Charitable Found. Mailing Add: 43 North St Exten Rutland VT 05701

HACKNEY, GLENN (R)
Alaska State Rep
Mailing Add: 1136 Sunset Dr Fairbanks AK 99701

HADLEY, DELLA M (D)
Mo State Rep
b Lawrence, Kans, Jan 27, 29; d Will H Hayden & Mary R Hanna H; m 1948 to Stephen D Hadley; c Susan Ellen, Kathleen Mary (Mrs Gordon Milne), Thomas Hayden & Stanton Willard. Educ: Univ Kans, 46-48; Purdue Univ, West Lafayette, BS, 52. Polit & Govt Pos: Vpres, Bd Educ, Kansas City, Mo, 70-74; Mo State Rep, 75- Mem: League Women Voters; Women's Polit Caucus; Fellowship House; Heart of Am Eye Ctr; Mo Am Revolution Bicentennial Comn. Relig: Unitarian. Legal Res: 7345 Belleview Kansas City MO 64114 Mailing Add: House PO Jefferson City MO 65101

HADLEY, FRED B (R)
Ohio State Rep
b Pioneer, Ohio, July 2, 11; s F W Hadley & Ethel M Grannis H; m 1935 to Jean Munro; c James F, Betty. Educ: Hillsdale Col. Polit & Govt Pos: Mem, Bd Pub Affairs, Pioneer, Ohio, formerly; Ohio State Rep, 64- Bus & Prof Pos: Hadley Dept Store, 31-63. Mem: Mason; CofC; Williams Co Develop Corp; Farm Bur. Relig: Methodist. Mailing Add: 611 W South St Bryan OH 43506

HADSEL, FRED LATIMER
b Oxford, Ohio, Mar 11, 16; s Fred Latimer Hadsel & Mary Perine H; m 1942 to Winifred Nelson; c Mary C, Winifred R & Jane L. Educ: Univ Grenoble, 33; Miami Univ, AB, 37; Freiburg Univ, grad student, 38; Clark Univ, MA, 38; Univ Chicago, PhD, 42. Polit & Govt Pos: With Dept of State, 46-, hist researcher, German Affairs Off & exec secretariat, Bur of Near East, SAsian & African Affairs, 46-56, dir, Off of SAfrican Affairs, 56-57, first secy, Am Embassy, London, Eng, 57-61, dep chief of mission, Addis Ababa, Ethiopia, 61-62, adv, Bur of African Affairs, Dept of State, 63-64, dir, Off of Inter-African Affairs, 64-69, US Ambassador to the Somali Repub, 69-71; US Ambassador to Ghana, 71-74. Bus & Prof Pos: Prof lectr polit sci, George Washington Univ, 63-69; lectr African affairs, Johns Hopkins Univ & Howard Univ, 68-69. Mil Serv: Entered as Pvt, Army, 42, released as Maj, 46. Publ: Contrib, articles, prof jour. Mem: Phi Beta Kappa; Beta Theta Pi; Omicron Delta Kappa; Phi Eta Sigma. Relig: Protestant. Mailing Add: Oxford OH 45056

HAEGEN, FLORENCE VIRGINIA (R)
Chmn, Mont Rep State Cent Comt
b Lincoln, Nebr, May 6, 25; d Branson Washburn Stewart & Claudia Chaplin S; m 1946 to Leo Francis Haegen; c Noel (Mrs A J Hauser), Stewart F, Leslie Ruth, Prentice L & Allison Priscilla. Educ: Colo Col, 43-45; Col of Great Falls, BA, 71; Independent Women. Polit & Govt Pos: Secy, Fergus Co Rep Cent Comt, Mont, 61-68, vchmn, 68-71, chmn, 71-73; vchmn, Mont Rep State Cent Comt, 73-75, chmn, 75- Mem: Mont Cowbelles; Mont Fedn Rep Women; Eastern Star. Relig: Protestant. Mailing Add: Three Smokes Ranch Buffalo MT 59418

HAEGEN, STEWART FRANCIS (R)
Chmn, Mont Col Rep League
b Lewistown, Mont, Nov 8, 48; s Leo F Haegen & Florence Stewart H; single. Educ: US Mil Acad, 66-67; Mont State Univ, 67- Polit & Govt Pos: Deleg, Rep Nat Conv, 72; dir, Region IX, Pac Northwest Col Rep Nat Comt, 72; chmn, Mont Col Rep League, 72-; vchmn, Western Fedn Col Rep, 72- Mil Serv: Entered as Cadet, Army, 66, released as SP-5, 71, after serv in 173rd Airborne Brigade, Vietnam, 69-71; Nat Defense Serv Medal; Vietnam Serv Ribbon; Vietnam Campaign Medal; Army Commendation Medal; Bronze Star. Mem: DeMolay. Mailing Add: Buffalo MT 59418

HAERLE, PAUL RAYMOND (R)
Chmn, Rep State Cent Comt Calif
b Portland, Ore, Jan 10, 32; s George W Haerle & Grace Soden H; m 1953 to Susan Ann Wagner, div; m 1974 to Nola Smith; c Karen Joyce & David Arthur. Educ: Yale Univ, AB, 53; Univ Mich Law Sch, JD, 56; Phi Delta Phi; Soc of Barristers; Yale Key; Order of the Coif. Polit & Govt Pos: Mem, Marin Co Rep Cent Comt, Calif, 63-66; pres, Marin Rep Coun, 65-66; mem, Rep State Cent Comt, Calif, 65-, secy, 69, vchmn, 73, chmn, 74-; chmn, Marin Co Reagan for Gov Comt, 66; appointments secy, Gov staff, State of Calif, 67-69; Northern Calif chmn, Comt to Reelect Gov Reagan, 70; deleg, Rep Nat Conv, 72; mem, Rep Nat Comt, 74- Bus & Prof Pos: Assoc, Thelen, Marrin, Johnson & Bridges, 56-64, partner, 65-67 & 69- Publ: Ed-in-chief, Mich Law Rev, 55-56. Mem: Am & San Francisco Bar Asns; The Guardsmen, San Francisco. Relig: Protestant. Mailing Add: 2 Embarcadero Ctr Rm 2200 San Francisco CA 94111

HAESCHE, ARTHUR B, JR (D)
Chmn, Killingworth Dem Town Comt, Conn
b New Haven, Conn, Sept 18, 32; s Arthur B Haesche, Sr & Anne McClure; m 1959 to Geraldine Farley; c Arthur B, III, Meggan Elizabeth, Colleen Patricia & Jennifer Farley. Educ: Univ Notre Dame, AB, 54; Southern Conn State Col, MS, 68; Univ Conn, 57-58; Univ New Haven, currently; Theta Chi. Polit & Govt Pos: Mem & clerk, Bd Finance, Killingworth, Conn, 69-; mem bldg comt, Regional Sch Dist 17, 70-; chmn, Killingworth Dem Town Comt, 73-; secy, 33rd Sen Dist Dem Comt, 74- Bus & Prof Pos: Elem sch teacher, Haddam Conn Bd Educ, 59-61; employee, Southern New Eng Tel Co, Bridgeport, New Haven, Hartford & New London, 61-71; dist equip supt, Waterbury, 71-74, orgn develop spec, 74- Mil Serv: Entered as 2nd Lt, Air Force, 54, released as 1st Lt, 57, after serv in 316 Air Div, NAfrica; recalled as Capt, 61-62, after serv in 152 TAC ConGp, Ger; currently Lt Col, Conn Air Nat Guard; Armed Forces Expeditionary Medal. Mem: Air Force Asn; Nat Guard Asn US; Killingworth Lions Club (bd dir); Clinton Country Club. Relig: Roman Catholic. Mailing Add: RFD 3 Hemlock Dr Killingworth CT 06417

HAFFNER, ANN DUNCAN (R)
VChmn, Alexandria Rep Party, Va
b Iola, Kans, Sept 6, 17; d Clifford Morrell Duncan & Margret Webb D; m 1940 to Bernhard Kinsey Haffner; c John Duncan, Julie Renard & Janette Turnbull. Educ: Los Angeles Art Ctr, 38-39; Queens Univ (Ont), 41; studied portrait painting, Hague, Netherlands, 50-52. Polit & Govt Pos: Mem, Alexandria Bd Archit Rev, Va, 70-; pres, Commonwealth Rep Womens Club, 70-71; alt deleg, Rep Nat Conv, 72; vchmn, Cardinal Club Va, 74-75; mem state bd, Young Am for Freedom, 74-; vchmn, Alexandria Rep Party, currently. Mem: DAR (state chmn, Am Heritage comt, 74-); Capital Speakers; Meridian House Int Found; Alexandria Historic Preservation & Restoration Comn (secy-treas). Mailing Add: 215 N Fairfax St Alexandria VA 22314

HAFSTAD, KATHARINE CLARKE (R)
Mem, Mich State Rep Cent Comt
b Harbor Springs, Mich, Dec 6, 03; d James Turner Clarke & Maud Hartness Bishop C; div. Educ: Northwestern Univ, BS, 26; Clark Univ, MA, 30; Kappa Delta. Polit & Govt Pos: Mem, Gov Comn on the Status of Women, Mich, 63-65; mem bd trustees, Cent Mich Univ, 64-, chmn, 66; vchmn, 11th Cong Dist Rep Comt, Mich, 65-69; chmn, Emmet Co Rep Comt, 65-72; fourth vpres, Rep Women's Fedn, 67-; mem exec comt, Mich State Rep Cent Comt, 69-74, mem, 74- Bus & Prof Pos: Climatologist, Carnegie Inst of Wash, 30-34; meteorologist, Soil Conserv Serv, 34-40 & US Weather Bur, 40-42; research analyst, US Air Force, 42-50; opers analyst, Opers Res Off, Johns Hopkins Univ, 50-58; owner & mgr, Snowberry Farm Lodge, 58- Mem: Am Asn Univ Women. Honors & Awards: Korean Theater Medal for serv in Korea as civilian opers analyst. Relig: Presbyterian. Mailing Add: Snowberry Farm Lodge Rte 2 Harbor Springs MI 49740

HAGAN, FRED (R)
Fla State Rep
b Shamokin, Pa, Dec 16, 33; s Paul C Hagan & Peg Moser H; m 1956 to Charlsie Ann Edwards; c Clifford R, Steven M, Kim Dinese & Pamela Lynn. Educ: Lafayette Col, 53-54; Univ Miami, BSIM, 56, MBA, 57; Tulane Univ, cert electronic comput, 60; pres, Delta Sigma Pi, 56; L'Apache. Polit & Govt Pos: Mem, ECent Fla Regional Planning Coun, 68-70; Fla State Rep, 72- Bus & Prof Pos: Pres, Hagan Mgt Consult, 65-72; vpres, Barnett Bank of Orlando, 73- Mil Serv: Entered as Pvt, Air Force, 50, released as Sgt, 52, after serv in Mil Air Transport Serv, ETO. Mem: Fla Pub Rels Asn (pres, 70); Fla Soc Asn Exec (pres, 69-70); Emergency Med Serv Coun Fla; YMCA (bd dirs, 71-); Fla Coun Econ Educ (pres, 68-70). Honors & Awards: Grad Fel, Univ Miami, 56; Good Govt Award, Maitland Jaycees, 71; Spec Educ Award, Fla State Jaycees, 72. Relig: Protestant. Legal Res: 5712 Eggleston Ave Orlando FL 32810 Mailing Add: Suite 103 988 Woodcock Rd Orlando FL 32803

HAGAN, G ELLIOTT (D)
b Sylvania, Ga, May 24, 16; m to Frances Bryant; c G Elliott, Jr, Charles Franklin & Frances Bryant. Educ: Univ Ga; Emory Univ; John Marshall Law Sch. Polit & Govt Pos: Ga State Rep, 5 terms; Ga State Sen, 1 term; secy-treas & dep dir, State Bd Workmen's Compensation, 46; state mem, Nat Coun State Govt, 2 terms; dist dir, Savannah Dist Off, Off Price Stabilization, 51-53, dep regional dir, Atlanta Regional off, 53; US Rep, Ga, 61-73. Bus & Prof Pos: Formerly engaged in life ins, estate planning & farming; former weekly newspaper ed. Mil Serv: Signal Corps, Army, 2 years in World War II. Mem: Rotary; Am Legion; Elks; Univ Ga Alumni Asn; Moose. Relig: Baptist; vpres, Ga Baptist Conv, 63. Legal Res: 116 Peachtree Circle Sylvania GA 30467 Mailing Add: 4887 N 35th St Arlington VA 22207

HAGAN, JAMES G (D)
RI State Sen
Mailing Add: 530 Woonsocket Hill Rd North Smithfield RI 02895

HAGAN, WILLIAM CLARENCE (D)
Chmn, Marion Co Dem Party, Ky
b Loretto, Ky, Feb 29, 36; s Joseph Guy Hagan, Sr & Adelaide Logsdon H; m 1957 to Ruth Thompson; c Macky, Christopher, Jude A, John F, & Hope M. Educ: Universal Training Sch, 57; Life Underwriters Training Coun, 58; State Farm Sch Ins, 61. Polit & Govt Pos: Treas, Young Dem, Ky, 65-67; chmn, Dem for Ward for Gov, 67; chmn, McGovern for President, Marion Co, 72; chmn, Marion Co Dem Fund Raising, 73; chmn, Marion Co Dem Party, 73- Mem: VFW; Am Legion; Lebanon Optimist Club; KofC (grand dep knight, 57-73); Jr CofC. Honors & Awards: President's Club, Commonwealth Life Ins, 57, 58 & 59; Career Achievement Club, State Farm Ins, 62, 63, 64, 70 & 71, Million Dollar Club, 71. Relig: Catholic. Mailing Add: 496 JoAnn Ct Lebanon KY 40033

HAGEDORN, CLYDE WILLIAM (D)
WVa State Deleg
b Dellslow, WVa, May 24, 06; s Marshall Johnson Hagedorn & Amanda Elizabeth Shaffer H; m 1950 to Edith Leona Rice; c Robert Burl, Norma Elizabeth (Mrs Nuce), Minnie Belle (Mrs Coulson), Janice Mae (Mrs Whittaker), Lorna Joan & Fred Allen. Educ: Morgantown High Sch, grad, 37. Polit & Govt Pos: WVa State Deleg, 75- Mil Serv: Entered as Pvt, Army, 44, released as Pfc, 45, after serv in Army Courier Serv. Mem: Sr Citizens; Postal Workers Am; Odd Fellows; Am Legion; PTA. Relig: Methodist. Mailing Add: 280 Eureka Dr Morgantown WV 26505

HAGEDORN, GARRETT WILLIAM (R)
NJ State Sen
b Midland Park, NJ, Sept 16, 10; s John William Hagedorn & Jennie Klopman H; m 1935 to Hubrine M Hamersma; c Ruth Ann (Mrs Knyfd), Dr Donald W & Dorothy M (Mrs Vander Guchte). Educ: Eastern Christian Sch Syst, 12 years. Polit & Govt Pos: Councilman, Midland Park, NJ, 51-57 & mayor, 58-68; mem exec bd, NJ League of Munic, 62-68; NJ State Sen, Dist 40, 68-, chmn, Insts, Health & Welfare Comt, mem, Gambling Study Comn, Comn to Study Co Penal Syst & Comn to Study Penalties in Dangerous Substances Act, NJ State Senate, 72-, mem, Comn on Correctional Planning, Comn to Study Malpractice Ins & Minority Whip. Relig: Christian Reformed. Mailing Add: 210 Vreeland Ave Midland Park NJ 07432

HAGEDORN, THOMAS M (R)
US Rep, Minn
b Blue Earth, Minn, Nov 27, 43; m 1962 to Kathleen Mittlestadt; c James, Heidi & Tricia. Educ: Blue Earth High Sch, grad, 62. Polit & Govt Pos: Minn State Rep, 70-74; US Rep, Minn, 75- Mil Serv: Navy. Mem: Jaycees; Farm Bur. Relig: Lutheran. Legal Res: MN Mailing Add: US House Rep Washington DC 20515

HAGEL, CHARLES TIMOTHY (R)
b North Platte, Nebr, Oct 4, 46; s Charles Dean Hagel & Elizabeth E Dunn H; single. Educ: Wayne State Col, 64-65; Kearney State Col, 65-66; Brown Inst Radio & TV, 66-67; Univ Nebr, Omaha, BA, 71; Phi Alpha Theta; Phi Phi Phi. Polit & Govt Pos: Dist rep, US Rep John Y McCollister, Nebr, 71-72, campaign dir, 72, admin asst, 72- Bus & Prof Pos: Sales rep, Radio Sta KLMS, Lincoln, Nebr, 67; newscaster, Radio Sta KRCB, Council Bluffs, Iowa, 69; music show host, Radio Sta KBON, Omaha, 69-70; newscaster & talk show host, Radio Sta KLNG, Omaha, 70-71. Mil Serv: Entered as Pvt E-1, Army, 67, released as Sgt E-5, 68, after serv in 9th Infantry Div, SVietnam, 67-68; Combat Infantry Badge; Purple Heart with Oak Leaf Cluster; Army Commendation Medal; Vietnam Campaign Ribbon; Good Conduct Medal; Nat Defense Ribbon; Am Spirit Honor Medal; Outstanding Trainee Award; S Vietnamese Ribbon. Mem: Am Legion; Big Bros Asn (bd dirs, 72-); Capitol Hill Admin Asst Asn; Omaha Press Club; Washington Capitol Hill Club. Relig: Roman Catholic. Legal Res: 11817 Jackson Rd Omaha NE 68154 Mailing Add: 165 D St SE Washington DC 20003

HAGEMAN, ALVIN WILLIAM (D)
Mont State Rep
b Wheatland, Co, Ill, Feb 6, 14; s William J Hageman & Amanda Emma Mary Dannenberg H; m 1939 to Evelyn Marie Conover; c Gayle Marie (Mrs Wayne Long), Richard Alvin & Carol Jeannine (Mrs Craig Brewington). Educ: Billings Pub High Sch, Mont, grad, 35. Polit & Govt Pos: Comnr, Stillwater Co, Mont, 58-64; Mont State Rep, 69-70 & 73-; vchmn, State Admin Comt, 75- Mem: Mason (Worshipful Master, Rapilje Lodge 122, 62); Eastern Star; Elks; Shrine; Mont Grain Growers Asn (dir & secy, 65-73). Relig: Am Lutheran. Mailing Add: Broadview MT 59015

HAGEMEIER, RICHARD JOHN (R)
b Beatrice, Nebr, Feb 25, 37; s John Carl Hagemeier & Bertha Mae Hackert H; m 1960 to Phyllis Ann Stokebrand; c Teresa Ann & Rick John. Educ: Univ Nebr, BS; Innocents Soc; Alpha Gamma Rho. Polit & Govt Pos: Chmn, Ida Co Rep Party, formerly. Bus & Prof Pos: Farm foreman, Kreutz Bros, Inc, Giltner, Nebr, 62-63; field supvr & farm mgr, Farmers Nat Co, Ida Grove, 63-70; salesman, NY Life, 70; farm mgr, G&M Farm Serv, 70- Mil Serv: Entered as 2nd Lt, Army, 59, released as 1st Lt, 62, after serv in 4th Aviation Co, 4th Inf Div, Ft Lewis, Wash, 60-62; Helicopter Pilot. Mem: Iowa Soc Farm Mgr & Rural Appraisers; Am Soc Farm Mgr & Rural Appraisers; Ida Grove Jaycees. Relig: Lutheran. Mailing Add: 501 Fairlane Ida Grove IA 51445

HAGEN, ORVILLE WEST (INDEPENDENT)
Labor Comnr, NDak
b Watford City, NDak, Sept 26, 15; s Oscar Wilhelm Hagen & Carrie Scollard H; m 1939 to Astrid Berg; c Orvis Wayne, Mylo LeRoy, Ellyn Marie & Lana Jo. Educ: Dickinson State Teachers Col, 37-38. Polit & Govt Pos: NDak State Sen, McKenzie Co, 53 & 55; Lt Gov, NDak, 60-62; Labor Comnr, 67- Mem: Asn Labor Mediation Agencies (dir, 72-); Moose; Elks; Sons of Norway; Odd Fellows. Relig: Lutheran. Legal Res: Arnegard ND 58835 Mailing Add: 1528 N 19th Bismarck ND 58501

HAGEN, SYLVIA (D)
Mem, Dem Nat Comt, NDak
Mailing Add: 902 NW Third Mandan ND 58554

HAGER, ELIZABETH SEARS (R)
NH State Rep
b Washington, DC, Oct 31, 44; d Hess Thatcher Sears & Elizabeth Harper S; m 1966 to Dennis Sterling Hager; c Annie Elizabeth & Lucie Caroline. Educ: Wellesley Col, BA, 66; Tufts Univ, 67; Tau Zeta Epsilon. Polit & Govt Pos: NH State Rep, 73-; comnr, NH Comn Status of Women, 73-; mem adv bd, NH Bur Maternal & Child Health, 73-; deleg, Const Conv, 74 & chmn, Bill of Rights Comt. Bus & Prof Pos: Instr, Therapeut Educ Ctr, Concord, NH, 67-69; prin, Philbrook Ctr, Concord, 69-71. Mem: Child & Family Serv NH (bd mem, 70-74); NH Wellesley Club (pres, 71-73); Order of Women Legislators; NH Women's Polit Caucus (steering comt, 74-). Relig: Episcopal. Mailing Add: RFD 8 Loudon Rd Concord NH 03301

HAGER, TOM (R)
Mont State Rep
b Minneapolis, Minn, Feb 2, 38; s Otis A Hager & Hazel Hruska H; m 1963 to Connye L Idstrom; c Gretchen Ann & Van Michael. Educ: Mont State Univ, BS, 60; Pi Omega Pi; Sigma Alpha Epsilon. Polit & Govt Pos: Mont State Rep, Dist 60, 73-, chmn, Environ Qual Coun, Mont House Rep. Bus & Prof Pos: Secy-treas, Hager Bros Eggs, 60- Mem: Billings CofC; Billings Jaycees; Billings Heights Kiwanis; charter mem Northwest Egg Producers. Honors & Awards: Key Man Award, Jaycees, 69. Relig: Lutheran. Legal Res: 1540 Elaine St Billings MT 59101 Mailing Add: Box 1767 Billings MT 59103

HAGLER, CLYDE H (D)
Fla State Rep
Mailing Add: Unit 10 4300 West Francisco St Pensacola FL 32504

HAGNER, ELMER F, JR (D)
Md State Deleg
Mailing Add: Rte 8 Box 7 Annapolis MD 21401

HAHN, GILBERT, JR (R)
b Washington, DC, Sept 12, 21; s Gilbert Hahn & Hortense King H; m 1950 to Margot Hess; c Gilbert, III, Amanda B & Polly K. Educ: Princeton Univ, AB, 43; Yale Law Sch, LLB, 48; Cannon Club; Corbey Court; Fed City Club. Polit & Govt Pos: Pres, DC Young Rep Club, 49; alt deleg, Rep Nat Conv, 52; finance chmn, DC State Rep Comt, 64-68; chmn, Rep Party, DC, 68-69; chmn, DC City Coun, 69-72. Bus & Prof Pos: Partner, Amram, Hahn & Sundground, 54- Mil Serv: Entered as Sgt, Army, 42, released as 1st Lt, 46, after serv in 558th Field Artil, ETO 43-45; ETO Ribbon with Three Battle Stars; Metz & Verdun Medals; Purple Heart. Mem: DC, Md & US Supreme Court Bar Asns. Relig: Jewish. Mailing Add: 3022 University Terr NW Washington DC 20016

HAHNEN, RICHARD YOUNG (R)
b Minneapolis, Minn, Oct 27, 46; s Robert Courtney Hahnen, Sr & Elizabeth Young H; single. Educ: Univ Minn, Minneapolis, 64-67; Concordia Col (Moorhead, Minn), BA, 72; participant, 1972 Nobel Conf; state bd mem, Minn Pub Interest Research Group; pres, Concordia Environ Protection Agency; mem, Vets Club; mem, Col Rep; mem, Jan 19th. Polit & Govt Pos: Alt deleg, Ramsey Co Rep Conv, 68; deleg, Clay Co Rep Conv, 72; US Cong Rep nominee, Minn Seventh Cong Dist, 72; alt deleg, Rep Nat Conv, 72; State House Campaign Mgr, Moorhead, Minn, 72; ward committeeman, Moorhead, 72- Bus & Prof Pos: Asst supvr, Hennepin Co Gen Hosp, 71; ed, Concordian Newspaper, 71-72; writer & photographer, Home Mag, Fargo, NDak, 72; asst to the pres, Westheimer Importing & Mfg, Elk Grove Village, Ill, 72- Mil Serv: Entered as Pvt, Army, 68, released as SP-5, 70, after serv in 600th Qm Co, TUSA, Ft Bragg, NC; Nat Defense Medal; Good Conduct; Brigade Soldier of the Month, Group Soldier of the Year; Brigade Letter of Outstanding Achievement. Mem: Nat Press Photographers Asn; Am Legion Post 34, St Paul (deleg state conv, 71, adjutant, 71-72). Relig: Congregational. Legal Res: 2290 Commonwealth Ave St Paul MN 55108 Mailing Add: Number 23 41-Lane An Tung St Taipei Republic of China

HAIG, ALEXANDER M, JR (R)
Polit & Govt Pos: Chief, White House Staff, formerly; chief NATO, Brussels. Legal Res: PA Mailing Add: 4622 N 38th St Arlington VA 22207

HAILEY, EVELYN MOMSEN (D)
Va State Deleg
b St Paul, Minn, Apr 12, 21; d Charles Bowers Momsen & Anne Offutt M; m 1943 to Robert Hailey; c Anne (Mrs John Harvey Bartee), Robert Harwell & Christopher Thomas. Educ: George Washington Univ; Univ Hawaii, Honolulu; Sigma Kappa; Tau Omicron Phi. Polit & Govt Pos: Va State Deleg, 74- Mem: League Women Voters; PTA; YWCA (bd dirs); Norfolk Theater Ctr (bd dirs); Citizens Asn for Justice in Va. Relig: Methodist. Mailing Add: 1535 Versailles Ave Norfolk VA 23509

HAINES, JOAN RENSHAW (D)
Mem, Ohio State Dem Cent & Exec Comt
b Philadelphia, Pa, July 29, 34; d Harry Francis Renshaw & Laura Hendricks R; m 1956 to John J Haines; c John P, Jason R & Lauren A. Polit & Govt Pos: Mem, Geauga Co Bd of Elec, Ohio, 66-; exec vchmn, Geauga Co Dem Cent & Exec Comts, 66-69, chmn, 69-; mem, Ohio State Dem Platform Comt, 68 & 70; alt deleg, Dem Nat Conv, 68; mem, Ohio State Dem Cent & Exec Comt, 68-; mem, Ohio State Dem Party Reform & Deleg Selection Comt, 69- Bus & Prof Pos: Geauga Observer, 68- Mem: League of Women Voters, Geauga Co; Progress Research Club, Chardon. Relig: Protestant. Mailing Add: 10666 Cedar Rd Chesterland OH 44026

HAINKEL, JOHN JOSEPH, JR (D)
La State Rep
b New Orleans, La, Mar 24, 38; s John Joseph Hainkel & Alida Bonnette H; m 1961 to Kathleen Roth; c John Joseph, III, Juliet Roth & Alida Camors. Educ: Tulane Univ, BA, 58, Law Sch, LLB, 61; Order of Coif; Kappa Alpha. Polit & Govt Pos: La State Rep, 29th Dist, 68- Bus & Prof Pos: Assoc attorney, Porteous & Johnson, New Orleans, La, 61-65; partner, Porteous, Toledano, Hainkel & Johnson, 65- Mem: La Defense Counsel Asn; Exchange Club; Am Farm Bur; Young Men's Bus Club; KofC. Honors & Awards: Most Distinguished Alumni, De La Salle High Sch, 68. Relig: Catholic. Mailing Add: 909 Arabella New Orleans LA 70115

HAINSWORTH, BRAD E (R)
b Salt Lake City, Utah, Oct 27, 35; s Norman Eric Hainsworth & Hattie Hendrickson H; m 1958 to Jacquelin Webster; c Todd Brad, Traci Webster & Julie Webster. Educ: Univ Utah,

BA, 63, MA, 66, PhD, 68; Phi Kappa Phi; Phi Delta Phi; Pi Sigma Alpha; Alpha Kappa Delta; Delta Phi. Polit & Govt Pos: Research assoc, Utah Legis Coun, 66; consult community planning, Mont State Univ, 68-69; admin asst to US Rep Dick Shoup, Mont, 71-72; staff asst to the President, 72-73; asst dir, Off of Econ Opportunity, 73- Bus & Prof Pos: Asst prof, Univ Mont, 68-71. Mil Serv: Entered as draftee, Army, 58, released as SP-4, 60, after serv in First Battle Group, 18th Inf. Publ: Auth, Those damnable sevens, Utah Hist Quart; 1970 elections in Montana's First Congressional District, spring 72 & Montana & the Presidency, Mont Bus Quart. Mem: Am & West Polit Sci Asns; Am Soc Pub Admin; Acad Polit Sci; Int Commun Asn. Honors & Awards: Nat Defense Foreign Lang Fel, Int Commun Asn, 67-68. Relig: Latter-day Saint. Mailing Add: 9302 Shari Dr Fairfax VA 22030

HAIR, MATTOX STRICKLAND (D)
Fla State Sen
b Coral Gables, Fla, Jan 18, 38; s Henry Horry Hair, Jr & Frances Strickland H; single. Educ: Fla State Univ, BS, 60; Univ Fla, JD, 64; Gold Key; Phi Delta Phi; John Marshall Bar Asn; Kappa Alpha (pres, 59-60); Fla State Univ (pres, freshman class, 56, vpres & pres, student body, 59 & 60, permanent class pres, 60). Polit & Govt Pos: Asst Attorney Gen, State of Fla, 64-65; mem, Trial Court Nominating Coun, Fourth Judicial Circuit of Fla, 72; Fla State Rep, Dist 22, 72-74; Fla State Sen, Dist Nine, 74- Bus & Prof Pos: Partner, Marks, Gray, Conroy & Gibbs, Attorneys, 65- Mil Serv: Entered as 2nd Lt, Army, 61, released as 1st Lt; Fla Nat Guard, Capt(Ret). Mem: Jacksonville Bar Asn (bd gov, 68-69 & 71-72); Gateway Residence, Inc, Ment Health Asn (bd dirs, 70-72); West Duval Jaycees; Westside Optimist Club; Fel of Christian Athletes. Honors & Awards: Outstanding Sr Man, Fla State Univ, 60, Hall of Fame, 60. Relig: Baptist. Legal Res: 2950 St Johns Ave Apt 12 Jacksonville FL 32210 Mailing Add: PO Box 447 Jacksonville FL 32201

HAIRSTON, PETER W (D)
NC State Rep
Mailing Add: Rte 2 Advance NC 27006

HAKODA, DAN SHIMAO (R)
Hawaii State Rep
b Holualoa, Hawaii, Oct 6, 19; s Nobujiro Hakoda (deceased) & Chiyo Arakawa H (deceased); m 1946 to Leatrice Fumiko Yamachika; c Orin Fumio & Danette Mitsue (Mrs Chang). Educ: Konawaena High Sch, Kona, Hawaii, grad, 39; Hawaii Dept Educ, supvry training. Polit & Govt Pos: Mem, Gov Task Force Law Enforcement & Juv Delinquency, Hawaii, 69-74; legis intern to Rep Patricia Saiki, 72; Hawaii State Rep, Ninth Dist, 75- Bus & Prof Pos: Div mgr, Sears Roebuck & Co, formerly, chmn, Sears Good Citizenship Prog, 70, polit adv, 72. Mem: St Louis Heights Community Asn (bd dirs); Honolulu CofC; Kona Club (bd dirs). Honors & Awards: Sears Citizen of Year Award, 72; KGU Citizen of Day, 72. Mailing Add: 2695 Peter St Honolulu HI 96816

HALABY, NAJEEB E
b Dallas, Tex, Nov 19, 15; s Najeeb Elias Halaby & Laura Wilkins H; m 1946 to Doris Carlquist; c Lisa, Christian & Alexa. Educ: Stanford, AB, 37; Mich Univ Law Sch, 37-38; Yale Univ, LLB, 40. Hon Degrees: LLD, Allegheny Col, 67 & Loyola Univ, Calif, 68. Polit & Govt Pos: Former mem, Chief Intel Coord Div, Dept of State; foreign affairs adv to Secy of Defense, 48-53; dep, Mutual Security Affairs, Econ Coop Admin, 50-51; Dep Asst Secy of Defense, 52-54; vchmn, White House Aviation Facil Study Group, 55-56; adminr, Fed Aviation Agency, 61-65. Bus & Prof Pos: Gov, Flight Safety Found; lectr civil mil rels, Nat War Col, Air War Col & Univ Calif, Los Angeles, dir & lectr, Aspen Inst; faculty lectr, Sch Bus Admin & dir defense studies prog Univ Calif, Los Angeles; vpres, Janss Corp; trustee, Aerospace Corp; pres, Am Tech Corp; attorney, O'Melveny & Meyers, Los Angeles, 40-42; attorney-at-law, 40-48 & 54-61; test pilot, Lockheed Aircraft Corp, Burbank, 42-43; assoc, L S Rockefeller & Bros, 53-56; exec vpres & Dir, Servomechanisms, Inc, 56-58 & 59; dir & mem exec comt, Pan Am World Airways, Inc, 65-, pres, 68-, chief exec off, 69-; dir, Whirlpool Corp, 68-, Bank of Am, San Francisco, Chrysler Corp, Detroit & Viacom, New York, NY; trustee Aspen Inst & Stanford Univ. Mil Serv: Aviator, Navy; Asst Chief Fighter Sect, Naval Air Test Ctr, Patuxent River, Md. Mem: Am Inst Aeronaut & Astronaut; Soc Exp Test Pilots; Foreign Policy Asn; Stanford Assocs; Stanford Law Sch (bd visitors). Mailing Add: 1120 Fifth Ave New York NY 10028

HALBROOK, DAVID MCCALL (D)
Miss State Rep
b Belzoni, Miss, Aug 8, 27; s John Cullum Halbrook & Ernestine McCall H; m 1949 to Rita Mary Robertshaw; c Ann Loree, David McCall, Jr, Lynn Ernestine & Andrew Lee. Educ: Southwestern Ark Agr & Mech Col, 1 semester; Southwestern Univ, 1 semester; Univ Miss, BA; Tau Kappa Alpha; Delta Psi. Polit & Govt Pos: Pub rels coordr, Miss State Bd Health, 49; Miss State Rep, Dist 18, Humphreys Co, 68-72 & Dist 16, Humphreys & Holmes Co, 72- Bus & Prof Pos: Mgr, Halbrook Motor Co, Belzoni, 50-54; mgr, Belzoni Ins Agency, 54-; secy-treas-agt, Belzoni Realty Co, 58- Mil Serv: Aviation Cadet, 5th Div Naval Air Corps, 45-46. Mem: Rotary Int; Am Legion; Humphreys Co Country Club; CofC; Aircraft Owners & Pilots Asn. Honors & Awards: Mr Mutual Agt. Relig: Episcopal. Legal Res: 169 Cohn St Belzoni MS 39038 Mailing Add: PO Box 653 Belzoni MS 39038

HALE, DOUGLAS VAN (R)
Mem, Ala State Rep Exec Comt
b Birmingham, Ala, Jan 1, 42; s Willard Douglas Hale & Marion Meeter H; m 1963 to Joanne Tyus; c Holly Ann. Educ: Auburn Univ, BS, Mech Eng, 64; Mass Inst Technol, MS, Nuclear Eng, 65; Cumberland Sch Law, currently; Tau Beta Pi; Pi Tau Epsilon; Pi Mu Epsilon; Omicron Delta Kappa; Phi Kappa Phi; Pi Kappa Alpha. Polit & Govt Pos: Ala State Rep, 70-74, mem, Ala State Rep Exec Comt, 71- Bus & Prof Pos: Group leader, Lockheed, 65-71; pres, Lockheed Mgt Asn, 67-68. Mem: Huntsville Indust Expansion Comt (dir, 70-73); Multiple Sclerosis Bd; Huntsville Jaycees. Honors & Awards: Outstanding Eng Grad, Auburn Sch Eng, 64. Relig: Baptist. Mailing Add: 2105 Clubview Ct NW Huntsville AL 35810

HALE, ERNEST A (R)
Idaho State Rep
Mailing Add: 725 E 16th St Burley ID 83318

HALE, EVERETTE (R)
Del State Sen
b Middletown, Ohio, July 13, 20; s Stanley F Hale & Verne McQuinn H; m 1944 to Charlene Haynes; c George Everette & Cheryl. Educ: Va Polytech Inst, BS in Chem Eng; Univ Del, grad study in polit sci. Polit & Govt Pos: Del State Rep, 62-69, Minority Whip, Del House Rep, 62-67, Majority Leader, 67-69; Del State Sen, 69- Bus & Prof Pos: Area supvr, E I du Pont de Nemours, Inc, 48- Mil Serv: Entered as Pvt, Air Force, released as Maj, 45, after serv in ETO; Air Force Res, 68-, Lt Col; Air Medal with 4 Oak Leaf Clusters; ETO Ribbon with 5 Battle Stars; Presidential Citation. Mem: Educ Comn on States; AF&AM; KT; Scottish Rite; Shrine. Relig: Methodist; mem off bd. Mailing Add: 109 Meriden Dr Newark DE 19711

HALE, JAMES CECIL (D)
Chmn, Crittenden Co Dem Cent Comt, Ark
b Blytheville, Ark, Oct 9, 08; s Edward Augustus Hale & Kate Richards H; m 1936 to Jean Allen Robinson; c James C, Jr, Ralph Robinson & Jeanie (Mrs W S Crain). Educ: Univ Ark, Fayetteville, BA, 31, LLB, 33; Sigma Chi; Scabbard & Blade; Delta Theta Phi. Polit & Govt Pos: Ark State Rep, 39-44; chmn, Crittenden Co Dem Cent Comt, 44-; dir, Marion Sch Bd, 44-61; prosecuting attorney, Second Judical Dist, 45-48; chmn, Crittenden Co Bd Elec Comnr, 46-; vchmn, Ark State Police Comn, 53-60; bd gov, Crittenden Mem Hosp, 53-, chmn, 69- Bus & Prof Pos: Pres, Crittenden Publ Co, West Memphis, Ark, 50-; dir, West Memphis CofC, 56-65; pres, West Memphis Indust Develop Corp, 59-; bd dirs, Bank of West Memphis, 61-; chmn, Ark Supreme Court Comt on Prof Conduct, 65- Mem: Am Col Trial Lawyers (fel); Am Bar Asn; F&AM; Little Rock Consistory; Shrine. Honors & Awards: Man of Year, West Memphis CofC, 61; Lawyer-Citizens Award, Ark Bar Asn-Ark Bar Found, 62; award, Univ Ark Endowment & Trust Fund, 62-63. Relig: Methodist. Legal Res: 124 Military Rd Marion AR 72364 Mailing Add: Bank of West Memphis Bldg West Memphis AR 72301

HALE, JOSEPH ROBERT (R)
VChmn, Ill Rep State Cent Comt
b Ridgway, Ill, June 12, 27; s Everett Lee Hale & Grace Jackson H; div; c Susan Lee, Sally Jo & Joseph R, Jr. Educ: Univ Ill, Urbana, BS, 50, LLB, 52; Sigma Nu; Phi Delta Phi. Polit & Govt Pos: Co judge, Gallatin Co, Ill, 54-62; Ill State Rep, 59th Dist, 63-65; committeeman, Ill Rep State Cent Comt, 21st Cong Dist, 66-70, vchmn, 70-; deleg, Rep Nat Conv, 72; mem bd gov, State Univs & Cols Ill, formerly. Bus & Prof Pos: Dir, First Nat Bank, Shawneetown; pres, Tri-Co Bar Asn, formerly. Mil Serv: Entered as Pvt, Army, 45, released as Pfc, 47, after serv in Finance Corps, Fifth Army. Mem: Am & Ill State Bar Asns; Am Judicature Soc; Am Legion; 40 et 8. Honors & Awards: Honors Days, Univ Ill. Relig: Presbyterian. Legal Res: 107 N Webster Harrisburg IL 62946 Mailing Add: Lincoln Blvd E Shawneetown IL 62984

HALE, LOUIS DEWITT (D)
Tex State Rep
b Caddo Mills, Tex, June 10, 17; s Ernest Louis Hale & Ethel Massay H; m 1947 to Carol Gene Moore; c Janet Sue & Nancy Carol. Educ: Univ Tex, BA, 37, MA, 40; Pi Sigma Alpha; Sigma Iota Epsilon; Rusk Literary Soc. Polit & Govt Pos: Asst dist supvr, Work Proj Admin, 40-41; classification analyst, Off Emergency Mgt, 41-43; classification officer, Off Defense Transportation, 43; Tex State Rep, 39-40, 53-62 & 65-, mem, Tex Legis Coun, Tex House Rep, 54-55, Tex Civil Judicial Coun, 61-65 & 69-, Speaker-Pro-Tem, 62; deleg, Tex Const Conv, 74. Bus & Prof Pos: Vpres, Nueces Invest Corp, 55-57; secy, Ulrich Bros, Inc, 60-69; secy, Tex-Trans, Inc, 73- Mil Serv: Entered as Pvt, Army Air Force, 43, released as 1st Lt, 46, after serv in Hq, Strategic Air Command; Lt Col, Air Force Res; Commendation Medal. Publ: Streamlining classification, 6/45 & Let's rewrite the Classification Act, 6/46, Personnel Admin. Mem: Tex State Teachers Asn; ROA; CofC; Am Bar Asn; State Bar Tex. Relig: Baptist. Legal Res: 334 Cape Hatteras Corpus Christi TX 78412 Mailing Add: 203 Wilson Bldg Corpus Christi TX 78401

HALE, PHALE DOPHIS (D)
Ohio State Rep
b Starksville, Miss, July 16, 15; s Church Hale & Lee Ellen H; m to Cleo Marion Ingram; c Phale Dophis, Jr, Janice Ellen, Marna Amoretti & Hilton Ingram. Educ: Morehouse Col, AB, 40; Gammon Theol Sem, MD, 44; Chapel Sch Theol, DD, 48. Polit & Govt Pos: Ohio State Rep, currently, chmn, Health & Welfare Comt, Ohio House Rep, currently. Bus & Prof Pos: Pastor, Union Grove Baptist Church, 50- Mem: NAACP (past pres Columbus chap); Frontiers Int (past pres & mem exec comt, chmn past pres comt); Columbus Area Anti-Poverty Orgn (past pres); Columbus United Community Coun (bd dirs); Ohio Baptist Gen Asn (exec dir social action comn). Relig: Baptist. Mailing Add: 1434 E Long St Columbus OH 45203

HALE, ROBERT (R)
b Portland, Maine, Nov 29, 89; s Clarence Hale & Margaret Rollins H; m 1922 to Agnes Burke; c Patricia. Educ: Bowdoin Col, AB, 10; Oxford Univ, BA in Jurisp, 12; Harvard Law Sch; Phi Beta Kappa; Psi Upsilon. Polit & Govt Pos: Mem of Mission Sent to Finland, Estonia, Latvia & Lithuania by Am Comn to Negotiate Peace, 19; Maine State Rep, 23-30; US Rep Maine, 43-59. Bus & Prof Pos: Lawyer; secy, treas & trustee of various Institutions; overseer, Bowdoin Col, 31-73. Mil Serv: Entered as Pvt, Army, 17, released as 2nd Lt, 19, after serv in various units; Capt, Army Res. Publ: But I Too Hate Roosevelt, Harper, 36; The United States & the War, Speeches printed in book form, 40; Congressional farewell, New Yorker. Mem: Am Legion. Relig: Congregational. Legal Res: Portland ME Mailing Add: 1125 15th St NW Washington DC 20005

HALE, SAMUEL (R)
b Chicago, Ill, Nov 11, 17; s Samuel Hale & Ethel Jackson H; m 1939 to Jane Bozung; c Samuel, Jr & Kathryn Bower. Educ: Univ Calif, Los Angeles, BS, 39; Univ Calif, Berkeley, MBA, 50; Indust Col Armed Forces, grad, 62; Beta Gamma Sigma; Alpha Delta Sigma; Blue Key; Scabbard & Blade; Delta Kappa Epsilon. Polit & Govt Pos: Dir seminars, Price Comn, 72; admin asst to US Rep Walter E Powell, Ohio, 72-74; exec asst, Energy Research & Develop Admin, 75- Bus & Prof Pos: Mgr bus practices, Gen Elec Co, 64-72. Mil Serv: Entered as 2nd Lt, Air Force, 40, released as Col, 64, after serv in 493rd Bomb Group, 8th Air Force, European Theatre, 43-45; Distinguished Flying Cross; Air Medal with Six Oak Leaf Clusters; Commendation Medal; French Croix de Guerre with Palm; plus many theatre ribbons & combat stars. Mem: Air Force Asn; Armed Forces Mgt Asn; Army Navy Club; Nat Aviation Club; Aviation Hall of Fame. Honors & Awards: Publ Serv Award, Small Bus Admin, 68. Relig: Episcopal. Mailing Add: 4913 Ft Sumner Dr Sumner MD 20016

HALEY, FRANCES SHALLER, (R)
VChmn, Sequoyah Co Rep Party, Okla
b Canadian, Tex, Dec 18, 32; d Frank Jamison Shaller & Pauline McMordie S; m 1954 to James Evetts Haley, Jr; c James Evetts, III, Mary Ann, Frank Jefferson & Frances Sabrina. Educ: Stephens Col, 50-51, dipl; Univ Tex, 51-54; Delta Delta Delta. Polit & Govt Pos: Alt deleg, Rep Nat Conv, 68, deleg, 72; mem, Rep State Exec Comt Okla, currently; vchmn, Sequoyah Co Rep Party, 71- Bus & Prof Pos: Owner & mgr, Book Store, 65-68. Relig: Lutheran-Mo Synod. Mailing Add: Rte 4 Sallisaw OK 74955

HALEY, JAMES ANDREW (D)
US Rep, Fla
b Jacksonville, Ala, Jan 4, 99; s Andrew Jackson Haley & Mary Lee Stevenson H; m to Aubrey B Ringling. Educ: Univ Ala, 19-20. Polit & Govt Pos: Chmn, Sarasota Co Dem Exec Comt, Fla, 32-52; Fla State Rep, 48-52; US Rep, Fla, 52-; deleg, Dem Nat Conv, 52 & 60; deleg, Dem Nat Mid-Term Conf, 74. Bus & Prof Pos: Pres & dir, Ringling Bros Barnum & Bailey Circus, 46-48. Mil Serv: Army, World War I. Mem: Am Legion; 40 et 8; VFW; Mason; Elks. Relig: Methodist. Legal Res: Sarasota FL Mailing Add: US House of Representatives Washington DC 20515

HALEY, K DANIEL (D)
NY State Assemblyman
b Ogdensburg, NY, May 25, 29; s Leon Frank Haley & Virginia Baker H; div; c Isabel Virginia. Educ: Harvard Col, AB cum laude. Polit & Govt Pos: Vconsul, Am Embassy, Saigon, 53; training officer, US Aid Mission to Brazil, 58-60; cand, US House Rep, 31st Dist, NY, 68; NY State Assemblyman, 110th Assembly Dist, 71-, chmn, Assembly Dem Prog Comt, 73- Bus & Prof Pos: Mgr, Underwood Dealership, Brazil, 60-62; mgr Brazilian subsidiary, Mosler Safe Co, 62-64, distributor for Brazil, 64-68. Mil Serv: Entered as Pvt, Air Force, 54, released as 1st Lt, 57, after serv in Air Intel Group, Far East Air Force, 55-57. Publ: The rural crisis, privately publ, 68. Mem: Harvard Club of NY. Honors & Awards: First Dem elected NY State Assemblyman from 110th Assembly Dist. Relig: Episcopal. Mailing Add: Waddington NY 13694

HALEY, TED (R)
Wash State Rep
Mailing Add: 5800 100th St SW Apt 30 Tacoma WA 98499

HALL, ALBERT CARRUTHERS (R)
Asst Secy Intel, Dept of Defense
b Port Arthur, Tex, June 27, 14; s Albert Bright Hall & Eva Carruthers H; m 1941 to Barbara Johnson. Educ: Tex A&M Col, BS, 36; Mass Inst Technol, ScD, 43; Eta Kappa Nu; Tau Beta Pi; Sigma Xi. Polit & Govt Pos: Dep for space technol, Off Dir Defense Research & Eng, Washington, DC, 63-65; asst secy intel, Dept of Defense, 71- Bus & Prof Pos: Asst elec eng, Mass Inst Technol, 37-39, instr, 39-43, asst prof, 43-46, assoc prof elec eng & dir dynamic anal & control lab, 46-50; assoc dir research labs, Bendix Aviation Corp, 50-52, tech dir, 53-54, gen mgr, 54-57; dir eng, Denver div, also dir research, Martin Co, 58-60, vpres eng, 60-61, vpres & gen mgr space systs div, Baltimore, 62-63, vpres advan technol, Martin Marietta Corp, 65-67, vpres eng, 67-71; mem torpedo study panel comt undersea warfare, Nat Acad Sci-Nat Research Coun, 63; mem arms control bd, Defense Sci Bd, 68-69; chmn sci adv comt, Defense Intel Agency, 70-71; chmn bd, Severn Sch, Severna Park, Md. Mem: Fel Inst Elec & Electronics Engrs; Am Inst Aeronaut & Astronaut; Nat Acad Eng; Int Acad Astronaut; Cosmos Club. Honors & Awards: Cert of Merit, Naval Ord Dept, 46; Meritorious Civilian Serv Award, Dept Defense, 65, Distinguished Pub Serv Medal, 73, Exceptional Civilian Serv Award, Defense Intel Agency. Legal Res: 1600 S Joyce St Arlington VA 22202 Mailing Add: Dept of Defense The Pentagon Rm 3E 282 Washington DC 20301

HALL, ANTHONY WILLIAM, JR (D)
Tex State Rep
b Houston, Tex, Sept 16, 44; s Anthony William Hall, Sr & Quintanna Wilson Alliniece H; m 1965 to Carolyn Joyce Middleton; c Ursula Antoinette & Anthony William, III. Educ: Howard Univ, BA in Econ, 67. Polit & Govt Pos: Deleg, Tex State Dem Conv, 72 & 74 & Dem Nat Conv, 72; Tex State Rep, Dist 85, 73-; Sen Dist 11 committeeman, Tex State Dem Exec Comt, 73-; deleg, Dem Nat Mid-Term Conf, 74. Bus & Prof Pos: Student asst economist, Fed Trade Comn, Washington, DC; asst to Co Comnr Jamie H Bray, Harris Co, Tex, 71-72; in pvt bus, Houston, 73- Mil Serv: Entered as 2nd Lt, Army, 67, released as Capt, 71, after serv in Berlin Command & 19th Light Inf Brigade, ETO, 68-69 & Vietnam, 69-70; 3 Bronze Stars; Air Medal-Valor in Air Opers, Vietnam; Meritorious Serv, Vietnam; Purple Heart; Vietnam Campaign; Nat Defense Serv; Berlin Occup; Vietnam Serv. Mem: Harris Co Coun of Orgns; YMCA (bd mgrs, SCent Br, Houston); United Negro Col Fund (Houston Exec Bd); Mason; Shrine. Honors & Awards: Black Achiever Award, SCent YMCA, Houston, 72; Citation for outstanding community serv, NAACP, Houston, 72; Cotton Hook of the Year, Int Longshoreman's Asn Local 872, Houston, 73; Distinguished Community Serv Award, Tex Southern Univ Ex-Students Asn, 75. Relig: Baptist. Legal Res: 3709 Rio Vista Houston TX 77021 Mailing Add: 4300 Reed Rd Houston TX 77051

HALL, DAVID MCGIFFERT (R)
Chmn, Greene Co Rep Comt, Ala
b Moundville, Ala, Jan 8, 10; s Dr David M Hall & Louise Elliott H; m 1949 to Lida Meriwether; c Lida Rogers. Educ: Birmingham-Southern Col, AB, 31; Univ Ala, LLB, 36; Omicron Delta Kappa; Phi Alpha Delta; Kappa Alpha. Polit & Govt Pos: Ala State Rep, 35-39; Ala State Sen, 57-59; chmn, Greene Co Rep Comt, currently. Bus & Prof Pos: Attorney. Mil Serv: Entered as Capt, Army, 41, released as Lt Col, 46, after serv in XV Corps, ETO; Am Defense Medal; Am Theatre Serv Medal; European African Medal; Eastern Theater Serv Medal with Two Bronze Stars; Victory Medal; Army Commendation Ribbon; Col, Army Res, 46-61. Mem: Ala Bar Asn; Am Legion; VFW. Relig: Methodist. Legal Res: 314 Eatman Ave Eutaw AL 34562 Mailing Add: PO Box 442 Eutaw AL 35462

HALL, DONALD M (D)
Maine State Rep
Mailing Add: RFD 1 Dover-Foxcroft Sangerville ME 04426

HALL, DONALD ROOTS (R)
Chmn, Pima Co Rep Cent Comt, Ariz
b Little Rock, Ark, June 20, 30; s Graham Roots Hall & Mary Louise Boaz H; m 1957 to Alice Anne Coates; c David Graham, Alison Blakeslee & Ashley Boaz. Educ: Univ Chicago, BA, 58; Univ Colo, MA, 63, PhD, 66; pres, Cloister Inn, Princeton Univ, 56-57. Polit & Govt Pos: Exec secy, Comt for Two Party Syst, Little Rock, Ark, 60-62; chmn, Pima Co Rep Cent Comt, Ariz, 74- Bus & Prof Pos: Mgr indust develop dept, Little Rock CofC & mgr, Better Bus Bur, Little Rock, Ark, 58-60; assoc prof polit sci, Univ Ariz, 66- Mil Serv: Entered as Airman Recruit, Air Force, 50, released as 1st Lt, after serv in Korea, 52-53 & Eng, 53-55; Good Conduct Medal; UN Medal; Korean Serv Medal with Battle Star. Publ: Auth, Cooperative Lobbying: The Power of Pressure, Univ Ariz Press, 69; auth, The 1968 election in Arizona, Western Polit Quart, 9/69; auth, Intergroup & cooperative lobbying, US Capitol Hist Soc, 9/72. Mem: Am Fedn Musicians. Honors & Awards: Guest Scholar, Brookings Inst, summer 65. Relig: Jewish Episcopal. Mailing Add: 6161 E Miramar Dr Tucson AZ 85715

HALL, DURWARD GORHAM (R)
b Cassville, Mo, Sept 14, 10; s Thomas C Hall & Omah Neill H; m 1931 to Mary Elizabeth Turner; c Linda Lea (Mrs Ellison). Educ: Drury Col, AB, 30; Rush Med Sch, Univ Chicago, MD, 34; Theta Kappa Nu scholarship key; Beta Beta Beta; Alpha Omega Alpha; Lambda Alpha Chi. Polit & Govt Pos: US Rep, Seventh Cong Dist, Mo, 61-73. Bus & Prof Pos: Intern, St Elizabeths Hosp, DC, 34-36; physician & surgeon, 36-60. Mil Serv: Entered as 1st Lt, Army, 40, released as Col, 46, after serv as Asst Surgeon Gen, Dept Army & Chief, Personnel Serv, Med Dept; Legion of Honor; Commendation Ribbon & Two Palms; Col (Ret), Army, Res, 65. Publ: Personnel in World War II, Dept of Army Med Dept, 63 & Cong Record. Mem: Dipl, Am Bd Surg; US CofC; MOWW; Nat Coun, Boy Scouts; Rotary. Honors & Awards: Cong adv, XV World Health Assembly, Geneva, 62. Relig: Baptist. Mailing Add: 2422 S Fremont St Springfield MO 65804

HALL, EARL WELLS (R)
Chmn, Jefferson Co Rep Comt, Ala
b Haleyville, Ala, Dec 6, 24; s Oliver Beauregard Hall & Alene Wells H; m 1947 to Mary Jacqueline Brislin; c Earl W, Jr & Murray OB. Educ: Univ Pittsburgh; Birmingham-Southern Col, 3 years; Univ Ala, LLB, 51; Phi Alpha Delta; Kappa Alpha. Polit & Govt Pos: Munic judge, Gardendale, Ala, 64-66; mem, Ala State Rep Comt, 67-; chmn, Jefferson Co Rep Comt, Ala, 67-; deleg, Rep Co, State & Nat Conv, 68. Mil Serv: Entered as Pilot Cadet, Air Force, 43, released as 2nd Lt, 45, after serv in Air Transport Command, Am Theater, 45. Mem: Ala Munic Judges Asn; The Club; VFW; Am Legion; Eagles. Relig: Methodist. Legal Res: 2210 Montreat Circle Vestavia AL 35216 Mailing Add: 2004 13th Ave S Birmingham AL 35205

HALL, EDWARD THOMAS (R)
Minority Leader, Md State Senate
b Calvert Co, Md, Aug 15, 16; s Charles Wesley Hall & Bessie Virginia Bowen H; m 1959 to Irma Bernice Sweeney. Educ: Ottmar Mergenthaler Sch Printing, 34-37; spec course Strayers Col, 35 & City Col, Baltimore, 36. Polit & Govt Pos: Md State Sen, 59-, Minority Leader, Md State Senate, 59-; deleg, Rep Nat Conv, 68. Bus & Prof Pos: Owner & publ, Calvert Independent. Mem: Fire Dept; Lions; Farm Bur; Sportsmen Club; CofC. Relig: Methodist. Mailing Add: Prince Frederick MD 20678

HALL, EDWIN ARTHUR, JR (R)
b Binghamton, NY, Feb 11, 09; s Edwin Arthur Hall & Harriet Babcock H; first wife deceased; m 1958 to Freida Elizabeth Stein; c Eric Ashley, Charles Milton, George Richard, Marlyce, David Reginald, Edwin Arthur, III & Marriet Bowser. Educ: Cornell Univ, 27-28; Chi Phi. Polit & Govt Pos: Mem, Broome Co Rep Comt, NY, 35-37; deleg, NY State Rep Conv, 36; city councilman, Binghamton, 37-39; US Rep, NY, 39-53; admin asst to NY State Assemblyman Richard Knauf, 53-54; acct clerk, Syracuse State Sch, 54-56; admin asst, US Dept Agr, NY, 56-58; dir, Silver Lake Twp Sch Bd, Pa, 62-65, pres, 63-65; dir, Montrose Area Sch Bd, Pa, 65-72. Mem: Am Inst Banking (pres, Binghamton Chap, 36); Preston Grange, NY; Nat Grange; Lawsville Grange, Pa. Honors & Awards: Winner, NY-New Eng Oratorical Contest & participant & rep of NY-New Eng Dist, Nat Oratorical Competition, A P Gianinni Found, 35, served as US Rep from Broome Co, NY longer than any other resident in history. Relig: Episcopal. Mailing Add: Indian Mountian Brackney PA 18812

HALL, GUS (COMMUNIST)
Gen Secy, Communist Party of USA
b Iron, Minn, Oct 8, 10; s Matt Halberg & Susan H; m 1934 to Elizabeth Turner. Polit & Govt Pos: Mem nat comt, Young Communist League, 26-33; mem, Co Farmer Labor Party Comt, Minn, 28; mem, Nat Communist Party USA Comt, 34-, nat secy, 48-, gen secy, 59-; gen secy, Communist Party of Ohio, 47-52; Presidential cand, 72. Mil Serv: Entered as Seaman, Navy, 42, released as Machinist Mate 1/C, 46, after serv in Pac Theatre. Publ: For a Radical Change—the Communist View, 66, On Course—the Revolutionary Process, 69 & Hard Hats & Hard Facts, 70, New Outlook Publ. Mem: Int Union Hod Carriers & Common Laborers; Struct Iron Workers Union; USW (founding mem & int rep, 36-). Legal Res: 230 Van Cortland Park Ave Yonkers NY 10705 Mailing Add: 23 W 26th St New York NY 10010

HALL, HARBER HOMER (R)
Ill State Sen
b Chicago, Ill, Sept 24, 20; s Harry Hall & Dorothy Harber H; m 1959 to Jeanette Buttell; c Heather Anne. Educ: Univ Miami, Fla, 39-41. Polit & Govt Pos: Co treas, McLean Co, Ill, 62-66; Ill State Rep, formerly; deleg, Rep Nat Conv, 72; Ill State Sen, 72- Bus & Prof Pos: Pres, Brookside Farms, Inc. Mil Serv: Entered as Aviation Cadet, Air Force, 42, released as Maj, 56, after serv in Hq Mil Air Transport Serv; Lt Col, Air Force Res; Distinguished Flying Cross with 1 Oak Leaf Cluster; Air Medal with 7 Oak Leaf Clusters; Medal for Humane Action; Berlin Air Lift; Pac, European & Am Theater Ribbons; Presidential Citation. Mem: Mason; Consistory; Shrine; Am Legion; Elks. Relig: Presbyterian. Mailing Add: 1202 E Jefferson Bloomington IL 61701

HALL, JAMES MERWIN (R)
Chmn, Stone Co Rep Comt, Mo
b Clever, Mo, Dec 15, 11; s James Allen Hall (deceased) & Mabelle Sherd H; m 1932 to Frances Dunivant; c Connie Sue (Mrs Dale Stafford) & Jane Ann (Mrs Larry E Cox). Educ: Southwest Mo State Col, BS in Educ, 42; Univ Mo, ME, 47; Phi Delta Kappa. Polit & Govt Pos: Chmn, Stone Co Rep Comt, Mo, 48- Bus & Prof Pos: Teacher rural schs, Stone Co, Mo, 33-39; supt & prin schs, Galena, 40-45; supt schs, Spokane, 45-51 & 64-68; supt schs, Stone Co, 51-55; supt schs, Blue Eye, 55-56, Hurley, 56-63, Chadwick, 63-64 & Fordland Schs, 68-; farmer, 51- Mem: Webster Co Teachers Asn; Mason, AF&AM (past Master, Galena Lodge 515); Shrine; charter mem, Galena Lions Club. Relig: Methodist. Mailing Add: Rte 1 Clever MO 65631

HALL, JOHN EMORY (R)
b Rock Falls, Ill, Jan 9, 13; s Emery John Hall & Ebal Osborn H; m 1937 to Esther Arlene Bley; c Peggy (Mrs Lawrence Dunlap), Ginny (Mrs John Butzer) & John Fredric. Educ: Sterling Twp High Sch, 4 years; bus & sales course under, Nat Recovery Admin, 2 years; typing & shorthad course, 2 years. Polit & Govt Pos: Chief clerk, State Police Dist 1, Ill, 41-49; precinct committeeman, Rep Party, Sterling, 43-; investr, Ill Com Comn, 53-54; chief clerk, State Treas, 54-56; clerk circuit court, Whiteside Co, 56-68; chmn, Whiteside Co Rep Party, formerly; appellate court clerk, Third Dist, 69-; deleg, Rep Nat Conv, 72. Bus & Prof Pos: Employee bus off finance dept, Sterling Daily Gazette, Ill, 49-53; owner restaurant & lounge, NSterling, 52-54. Mem: Mason; Shrine; Elks; Moose; Hist Soc. Relig: Protestant. Mailing Add: 1506 Locust St Sterling IL 61081

HALL, KATIE **(D)**
Ind State Rep
b Mound Bayou, Miss, Apr 3, 38; d Jeff L Greene (deceased) & Bessie Mae Hooper G; m 1957 to John Henry Hall, IV; c Jacqueline Demetris & Junifer Detrice. Educ: Miss Valley State Univ, BS, 60; Ind Univ, Bloomington, MS, 69; Phi Delta Kappa; Gary Cong Concerned Citizens. Polit & Govt Pos: Mem, Comt to Elect Richard G Hatcher, Mayor, Gary, Ind, 67, 71 & 75; mem, Comt to Elect Robert F Kennedy President, Gary, 68; mem, Gary Citizens to Reelect Sen Birch Bayh, Ind, 74; Ind State Rep, Fifth Dist, 74-, ranking majority mem, comt affairs of Lake & Marion Co, Ind House Rep, 75- Bus & Prof Pos: Substitute teacher, Gary Pub Schs, Ind, 61-64; teacher social studies & chairperson dept, Edison Sch, Gary, 64-75. Mem: Gary Coun Social Studies; Gary Housing Bd Comnrs (vchairperson, 73-). Honors & Awards: Outstanding Achievements in Polit Award, Van Buren Baptist Church, 74; Outstanding Woman in Polit Award, Gary, Ind, 75; Outstanding Achievements in Polit & Educ Award, Miss Valley State Univ, 75, Outstanding Serv to Mankind Award, 75 & Outstanding Alumni Award, 75. Relig: Protestant. Mailing Add: 1937 Madison St Gary IN 46407

HALL, KEITH EDWARD **(R)**
b LeRoy, Minn, Jan 6, 29; s Edward Elmer Hall & Irene Smith H; m 1957 to Charlotte Hampton Reed; c Douglas Elliott Reed, Bruce Edward Reese & Charles David. Educ: Macalester Col, BA, 50, MEd, 51; Georgetown Univ, BSFS, 56; Grad Inst Int Studies, 66-67. Polit & Govt Pos: Asst to legis asst for US Sen Edward J Thye, 56-58; legis asst to US Rep Walter Judd, 59-62, US Rep Burt Talcott, 63-69 & US Rep Albert Quie, 69-73; admin asst to US Rep Albert Quie, 73- Mil Serv: Entered as Pvt, Army, 53, released as Pvt 1/C, 55, after serv in Army QmC. Mem: Admin Asst Asn. Relig: Presbyterian. Mailing Add: 8724 Susanna Lane Chevy Chase MD 20015

HALL, KENNETH **(D)**
Ill State Sen
Mailing Add: 1725 Kansas Ave East St Louis IL 62205

HALL, LEONARD WOOD **(R)**
b Oyster Bay, NY, Oct 2, 00; s Franklyn H Hall & Mary Garvin H; m 1934 to Gladys Dowsey; stepchild, H W Carroll. Educ: Georgetown Univ Law Sch, LLB, 20. Hon Degrees: LLD, C W Post Col. Polit & Govt Pos: NY State Assemblyman, 27-28 & 34-38; sheriff, Nassau Co, 29-31, surrogate, 53; US Rep, NY, 39-53; chmn, Nat Rep Cong Comt, 47-53; chmn, Rep Nat Comt, 53-57; campaign chmn, Nixon for President Campaign, 60; chmn, Nassau-Suffolk Regional Planning Bd, 65- Bus & Prof Pos: Partner, Hall, Dickler, Lawler, Kent & Howley; dir, Servo Corp Am, 59- & Beneficial Nat Co, 63-; dir, Madison Sq Garden. Publ: An old pro describes how politics in US has changed, Life, 4/60; What's wrong with the Republican Party, Newsday, 3/65. Mem: Nassau & NY State Bar Asns; Mason; Elks; Metrop Club, Washington, DC. Relig: Episcopal. Legal Res: Feeks Lane Locust Valley NY 11560 Mailing Add: 600 Old Country Rd Garden City NY 11530

HALL, LILBOURNE PRESTON **(R)**
Chmn, Lauderdale Co Rep Comt, Ala
b Florence, Ala, Feb 3, 22; s Lamar Petway Hall & Maude Evelyn Murphree H; m 1949 to Helen Elizabeth Mattox; c Gregory, Jeffrey, Zachary & Peri. Educ: Univ NC, Chapel Hill, 42-43; Florence State Univ, BS, 45; Peabody Col, MA, 47; Southern Methodist Univ Inst Ins Mgt, grad dipl, 55; La State Univ, seminars, 69, 71 & 72-73; Kappa Delta Pi; Kappa Mu Epsilon. Polit & Govt Pos: Vchmn, Lauderdale Co Rep Comt, Ala, 58-62, mem exec comt, 60-, cand recruitment chmn, 64-66, chmn, 64-66 & 73-, chmn legis & issues comt, 70-; cand, Bd of Educ, Lauderdale Co, 62; mem, Rep State Exec Comt Ala, 62-64. Bus & Prof Pos: Teacher math & sci, Leighton High Sch, 45-46 & 47-48; teaching fel, Peabody Col, 46-47; life underwriter, Pilot Life Ins Co, Florence, 53-54 & Jackson Life Ins Co, 54-58, regional mgr, 58-; gen agt, Provident Life & Accident Ins Co, 15 years; broker, Lincoln Nat Ins Co, 18 years & Occidental Life Ins Co of Calif, 15 years. Mil Serv: Pvt, Army Air Force, 42-43. Publ: Various articles in Ins Mag & Ins Jour. Mem: Life Underwriter Asn Ala; Muscle Shoals Life Underwriters; Nat Asn Life Underwriters; Muscle Shoals Concert Asn; YMCA. Honors & Awards: Silver Beaver Award, Boy Scouts; Number One Sales Awards, Jackson Life Ins Co, 18 of last 19 years. Relig: Lutheran; bd elders; pres congregation, teacher, Sunday Sch, Our Redeemer Lutheran Church, supt, 1 year. Mailing Add: 2128 Old Cloverdale Rd Florence AL 35630

HALL, NANCY JOHNSON **(D)**
State Treas, Ark
b Prescott, Ark, Oct 5, 04; d George Sim Johnson & Minnie Bryan J; m 1929 to Claris G Hall; c Nancy (Mrs R Bailey). Educ: High Sch, Little Rock, Ark. Polit & Govt Pos: Asst Secy of State, Ark, 37-61, Secy of State, 61-63, State Treas, 63- Bus & Prof Pos: Head steno, Ark Hwy Dept, 25-30. Mem: Daughter of 1812; Womens Dem Club; Bus & Prof Womens Club; Zonta Int; UDC. Relig: Presbyterian. Mailing Add: State Capitol Little Rock AR 72200

HALL, RICHARD HAROLD **(D)**
VChmn, Midland Co Dem Party, Mich
b Akron, Ohio, Jan 12, 27; s John Silas Hall & Phoebe Mairet H; m 1954 to Wilma Jean Rush; c Richard R & Daniel F. Educ: Univ Akron, 44 & 46; Case Inst Technol, BSChE, 50; Univ Del, MS & PhD, 53; Pi Kappa Epsilon; Alpha Chi Sigma; Alpha Chi. Polit & Govt Pos: Chmn, Homer Twp Dem Party, Mich, 60-; mem, Midland Co Dem Comt, 60-63; mem, Midland Co Bd Canvassers, 63-66, chmn, 63-64; deleg, Midland Co Dem Conv, 67; deleg, Dem Nat Conv, 68; mem exec comt, Midland Co Dem Party, 69-, chmn, 71-72, vchmn, 73- Bus & Prof Pos: Chemist, BF Goodrich Research, Brecksville, Ohio, 52; research chemist, Dow Chem Co, Midland, Mich, 53, group leader, 64 & sr research engr, 68- Mil Serv: Entered as Pvt, Marine Corps, 44, released as Pfc, 46, after serv in US; Am Theatre & Victory Medals. Mem: Sci Research Soc Am; Am Chem Soc; Am Inst Chem Eng; Chem Soc London; Am Inst Chemists. Relig: American Lutheran. Mailing Add: 1187 Stewart Rd Rte 2 Midland MI 48640

HALL, ROBERT ARTHUR **(R)**
Mass State Sen
b Philadelphia, Pa, Apr 15, 46; s Robert Russell Hall & Dorothy Grey H; single. Educ: Mt Wachusett Community Col, AA, 70; Univ Mass, Amherst, BA, 72; Pi Sigma Alpha; Phi Theta Kappa. Polit & Govt Pos: Mass State Sen, Third Worcester Dist, 73- Mil Serv: Entered as Pvt, Marines, 64, released as Cpl, 68, after serv in 26th Marines, Vietnam, 66-67; Good Conduct; Nat Defense; Vietnam Serv; Vietnam Campaign. Mem: VFW; Am Legion; Franco-Am War Vet; Mass Audubon Soc; Lunenburg Town Rep Comt. Relig: Episcopal. Mailing Add: 166 Cross Rd Lunenburg MA 01462

HALL, ROBERT B **(D)**
Ala State Rep
Mailing Add: Rte 2 Box 593-W Pinson AL 35126

HALL, ROBERT HOWELL **(INDEPENDENT)**
Justice, Ga Supreme Court
b Soperton, Ga, Nov 28, 21; s Instant Howell Hall, Jr & Blanche Mishoe H; m 1946 to Alice Coberly; c Carolyn, Patricia & Howell. Educ: Univ Ga, BS in Com, 41; Univ Va, LLB, 48; Delta Tau Delta; Phi Delta Phi; Phi Delta Theta. Hon Degrees: LLD, Emory Univ, 73. Polit & Govt Pos: Asst Attorney Gen, Ga, 53-61; judge, Ga Court of Appeals, 61-74; chmn, Gov Comn on Judicial Processes, 71-73; chmn, Judicial Coun of Ga, 73-74; justice, Ga Supreme Court, 74- Bus & Prof Pos: Prof law, Emory Univ, 48-61. Mil Serv: Entered as 2nd Lt, Army, 42, released as Maj, after serv in Hq, Ft Lee, Va & Asiatic Theatre, 42-46; Lt Col, Judge Adv Gen Corps, Res; Army Commendation Ribbon; Asiatic Theatre Ribbon; DM Battle Star. Publ: Georgia Practice & Procedure, Harrison Co, Atlanta, 57; 23 law rev articles in various periodicals, 49-75. Mem: Am Judicature Soc; Nat Inst of Justice Comn Am Bar Asn (vchmn, 73-75); fel Am Bar Found; Am Acad Judicial Educ. Honors & Awards: Award, Harvard Law Sch Asn of Ga, 67; Herbert Harley Award, Am Judicature Soc, 74; Golden Citizenship Award, Fulton Grand Jurors, 75. Legal Res: 1630 E Clifton Rd Atlanta GA 30307 Mailing Add: 40 Capitol Sq Atlanta GA 30334

HALL, RODNEY MAPLE **(D)**
SDak State Sen
b Parker, SDak, July 25, 28; s Emory Hall & Ethel Hershey H; m 1958 to Sherry Ellen Alberts; c Barbara, Debra, Preston & Randall. Educ: Dakota Wesleyan Univ, BA, 57; Univ SDak, EdM, 59; Phi Delta Kappa. Polit & Govt Pos: SDak State Sen, Ninth Dist, 71-, mem rules rev comt, SDak State Senate, 71-, chmn educ comt, 73-; mem, Educ Comn of States, 73- Mil Serv: Entered as Pvt, Army, 52, released as Cpl, 53, after serv in 354th Eng Unit, Europe. Mem: Am Legion; Farmers Union; Nat & SDak Educ Asns. Relig: Methodist. Mailing Add: Fulton SD 57340

HALL, THOMAS WILLISON **(D)**
Ind State Rep
b Medora, Ind, Oct 2, 04; s George Washington Hall & Emmer Lee Hardy H; m 1937 to Harriett Allegra Goss; c Jane (Mrs Monte Huffman), George Walter, Sara (Mrs Norman M Beck) & Sue. Educ: Medora High Sch. Polit & Govt Pos: Postmaster, Medora, Ind, 32-38, rural letter carrier, 38-45; trustee, Carr Twp, 50-58; comnr, Jackson Co, 62-70; Ind State Rep, 71-, mem, Public Health Comt, Ways & Means Taxation Comt, Ways & Means Educ Comt, Natural Resources Comt & Transportation Comt, Ind House Rep, currently; chmn, Co Twp Bus & mem, Interstate Coop, 75- Mem: Mason; Scottish Rite; Elks; Seymour Country Club; Wabash Valley Asn. Relig: United Methodist. Mailing Add: Box 308 Medora IN 47260

HALL, TIM L **(D)**
US Rep, Ill
b West Frankfort, Ill, June 11, 25; s Grover Cleveland Hall & Mary Carter H; m 1970 to Marianne Ruth Heller; c Bret Tim & Jon Jason. Educ: Iowa Wesleyan Col, BA, 51; Southern Ill Univ, MS, 56. Polit & Govt Pos: US Rep, 15th Dist, Ill, 75- Bus & Prof Pos: Teacher & coach, Pub Schs, Ill, 52-66; educ consult & salesman, D C Cook Publ Co, Elgin, 66-70. Mil Serv: Entered Coast Guard Res, 43, released as Fireman 1/C, 46, after serv in USS Gulfport, Atlantic & Pac Theatre. Publ: In the Spirit of 76, privately publ, 72. Mem: Rotary; VFW; Am Legion. Relig: Methodist. Legal Res: 115 E Seminole St Dwight IL 60420 Mailing Add: 710 Braeburn Dr Tantallon MD 20022

HALL, TONY P **(D)**
Ohio State Sen
b Dayton, Ohio, Jan 16, 42; s Paul Davis Hall & Anna Deve H; single. Educ: Denison Univ, BA, 64; Sigma Chi. Polit & Govt Pos: Vol, US Peace Corps, Thailand, 65-67; Ohio State Rep, 69-73; Ohio State Sen, 73- Bus & Prof Pos: Real estate agt, Paul Tipps Inc, 68; real estate investor. Mem: Sigma Chi Alumni; Gem City Dem Club (vpres); YMCA; Agomis Club. Honors & Awards: All-State Football, Little All-Am Football Team, Denison Univ, 63. Relig: Presbyterian. Mailing Add: 2924 Knoll Ridge Rd Dayton OH 45449

HALL, VIRGINIA MCDANIEL **(D)**
Mem, Martinsville Dem Town Exec Comt, Va
b Erwin, Tenn, Apr 19, 21; d James Oscar McDaniel & Lillie M; m 1939 to Elmo Rush Hall, Jr; c Nancy Kerrigan (Mrs Cosby) & Capt Thomas Elmo. Educ: Marshall Univ, 38-39; John Robert Powers Finishing Sch, 57. Polit & Govt Pos: Mem adv bd for President Lyndon B Johnson; mem, Dem Nat Comt, Va, formerly; alt deleg, Dem Nat Conv, 68; Fifth Dist chmn, Robert F Kennedy Presidential Campaign, Va, 68; Martinsville chmn, Humphrey-Muskie Campaign, 68; mem, Martinsville Dem Town Exec Comt, currently; Martinsville chmn, Andrew Miller for Attorney Gen, Va, 69 & 73; co-chmn, McGovern for President, 72; deleg, Dem State Conv, 73; deleg, Dem Nat Mid-Term Conf, 74. Bus & Prof Pos: Mem staff, Martinsville Bull, 17 years. Publ: Columnist & TV Show, Around Town with Virginia, 17 years. Mem: Gray Ladies, Martinsville Gen Hosp Auxiliary; Elks Auxiliary; CofC (co-chmn cong comt); Am Bus Women's Asn; Marshall Univ Alumni Asn (secy). Honors & Awards: Good Citizenship Medal, DAR; Ky Col, 73. Relig: Protestant. Mailing Add: 1609 Sam Lion Trail Martinsville VA 24112

HALL, WALTER CLARENCE, JR **(D)**
Chmn, Sevier Co Dem Party, Tenn
b Knoxville, Tenn, June 29, 33; s Walter Clarence Hall, Sr & Lissie Wise H; m 1960 to Freeda Idel Bradley; c Walter C, III (Chip). Educ: Stair Technol High Sch; Dale Carnegie Course. Polit & Govt Pos: Chmn, Sevier Co Dem Party, Tenn, 72- Bus & Prof Pos: Owner, Honey Bee Gift Shop, 56-, Wishing Well Gift Ctr, 58-, HallCraft, Inc, 59, & Basket World, 71-; secy-treas, Gatlinburg Ready Mix, Inc, 72. Mil Serv: Entered as Pvt, Army Nat Guard, 49, released as Cpl, 53, after serv in Lt Div, First Combat Bn as Medic. Mem: Elks Lodge No 1925; Kiwanis; Am Legion Post 202; Gatlinburg CofC. Honors & Awards: Col-aid-de-Camp, Ray Blanton Gov, Tenn; hon Lt Col-aid-de-camp, Gov George Wallace; hon Gov, Gov Wendell Ford, Ky. Relig: Forrest Ave Christian Church. Legal Res: Smokey Heights Hill Ave Gatlinburg TN 37738 Mailing Add: Wishing Well Gift Ctr Pkwy PO Box 624 Gatlinburg TN 37738

HALL, WILLIAM N, JR (BILLY) **(D)**
Tex State Rep
Mailing Add: 1811 Market St Laredo TX 78040

HALL, WILLIAM O
Dir Gen, US Foreign Serv, Dept of State
b Roswell, NMex, May 22, 14; s William O Hall & Margaret Barnard H; m 1943 to Jayne Bowerman; c Sarah, William & Robert. Educ: Univ Ore; Univ Minn; Phi Beta Kappa. Polit & Govt Pos: Off dir, Dept of State, 47-51; sr adv, US Mission to UN, 51-56; counsr, Am Embassy, London, 56-57; Dep Asst Secy of State, 57-59; minister counsr, Am Embassy, Karachi, Pakistan, 59-63; asst admin, Agency Int Develop, Dept of State, 63-67; US Ambassador to Ethiopia, 67-71; dir gen, US Foreign Serv, Dept of State, 71- Mil Serv: Entered as Ens, Navy, 44, released as Lt(jg), 46, after serv in ETO. Mem: Am Soc Pub Admin; Am Foreign Serv Off Asn; Int City Mgr; Cosmos Club. Honors & Awards: Nat Civil Serv League Award, 65. Relig: Episcopal. Legal Res: RD 1 Joseph OR 97846 Mailing Add: Rm 7331 Dept of State Washington DC 20520

HALLEY, JAMES WINSTON (R)
Mem, Rep State Cent Comt Calif
b San Francisco, Calif, Mar 17, 21; s James Leopold Halley & Clara Kroehnke H; m 1949 to Isabelle Joyce Finlay; c Janet Elizabeth, James F & John A. Educ: Univ Calif, Berkeley, AB, 43, Law Sch, LLB, 48; Harvard Bus Sch, completion cert, 44; Officers Midn Sch, 44; pres, Alpha Sigma Phi, 43. Polit & Govt Pos: Vchmn, Peninsula Div Rep Alliance, 61, chmn, 62; vchmn, Bay Area Rep Alliance, 63, chmn, 64; chmn, San Mateo Co Rep Party, Calif, 63-64; mem, Rep Nat Comt, 67-69; chmn, Rep State Cent Comt Calif, 67-69, mem, 69-; deleg & vchmn Calif deleg, Rep Nat Conv, 68, hon deleg, 72; Presidential Elector, 68 & 72; chmn, Get Out the Vote Drive, Calif, 72; co-chmn, Flournoy for Gov Campaign, 74; mem, Dept of Justice Unit, Nat Defense Exec Reserve, currently. Bus & Prof Pos: Partner & founder, Halley, Cornell & Lynch, Attorneys, 56-; vchmn, Calif Ctr for Research & Educ in Govt, currently; secy treas & gen counsel, Woodlawn Mem Park Asn, 65- Mil Serv: Entered as Midn, Naval Res, 43, released as Lt(jg), 45, after serv aboard USS Robert F Keller, Pac Theater, 44-45; Philippines, Iwo Jima, Okinawa & Japan Campaign Ribbons. Publ: Monthly signed column on polit & govt commentary, San Mateo Times. Mem: Am Arbit Asn (arbitrator); Am Legion; Commonwealth Club of Calif (bd gov, chmn exec comt); F&AM (Past Master, Richmond Lodge 375); San Mateo Park Improv Asn. Relig: Episcopal. Legal Res: 529 W Poplar Ave San Mateo CA 94402 Mailing Add: 2160 Crocker Plaza San Francisco CA 94104

HALLING, BEVERLY JANE (R)
SDak State Rep
b York, NDak, Sept 16, 31; d William Ralph Silliman & Mayme Hanson S; m 1949 to Hubert Ronald Halling; c Cherise (Mrs Carl Richard Coers, III), Mary Jane, Rhonda Kay & Carol Jean. Educ: High sch, grad, 49. Polit & Govt Pos: SDak State Rep, 73-, mem state affairs, health & welfare comt, SDak House Rep, currently, vchmn transportation comt & interim rules comt, currently; mem, Adv Comt State Indian Bus Develop Orgn, currently; mem, Citizens' Comt Criminal Justice for Juv & Adults, currently. Bus & Prof Pos: Dir, SDak Innkeepers Asn, 72- Mem: Queen City Bus & Prof Club. Relig: Lutheran. Mailing Add: 306 W Kansas Spearfish SD 57783

HALLOCK, JOSEPH THEODORE (TED) (D)
Ore State Sen
b Los Angeles, Calif, Oct 26, 21; s Joseph Homer Hallock & Mary Peninger H; m 1946 to Phyllis Eggert Natwick, div 1968; m 1969 to Jacklyn Louise Goldsmith; c Stephanie Elizabeth, Leslie Mary & Christopher. Educ: Univ Ore, BS in Jour, 48; Sigma Delta Chi. Polit & Govt Pos: Ore State Sen, 62-; deleg, Dem Nat Conv, 68. Bus & Prof Pos: State coordr, Ore Centennial Comn, 58-59; owner, Ted Hallock, Inc, pub rels, 59- Mil Serv: Entered as Aviation Cadet, Army Air Corps, 42, released as Capt, 45, after serv in 306th Heavy Bombardment Group, 8th Air Force, England, 43-44; Distinguished Flying Cross; Air Medal with 3 Oak Leaf Clusters; Purple Heart with Oak Leaf Cluster; Presidential Unit Citation; ETO Theatre Ribbon with Battle Star; Capt, Army Res, 45-50. Mem: Press Club of Ore; Local 99, Am Fedn of Musicians; Portland Local, Am Fedn of TV & Radio Artists. Relig: Presbyterian. Mailing Add: 2445 NW Irving St Portland OR 97210

HALMRAST, GERALD ALLYN (D)
NDak State Rep
b DeLamere, NDak, July 27, 31; s Adolph Otto Halmrast & Lillian Jorgenson H; m 1953 to Beverly Yvonne O'Brien; c Sandra Kay, Tamra Lynn, Jeri Jill & Heidi Marie. Educ: Valley City State Col, BA, 59; Macalester Col, 63; Univ NDak, 67-69. Polit & Govt Pos: Comnr & vpres, Bismarck Park Bd Comn, NDak, 70-; deleg, NDak Dem Conv, 74-; NDak State Rep, 74- Bus & Prof Pos: Instr US hist & wrestling coach, Bismarck Sch Dist, NDak, 59-75, asst prin, 75- Mil Serv: Entered as Pvt, Air Force, 51, released as Airman 1/C, 55, after serv in Air Training Command, 52-55. Publ: Progression drill program for wrestlers, In: Coaching Clin, Prentice-Hall, 64. Mem: Nat High Sch Athletic Coaches Asn (nat sports chmn, 73-); Nat & Bismarck Educ Asn; NDak Educ Asn; NDak Recreation & Park Asn. Honors & Awards: Danforth Leadership Award, Ralston Purina Co, 50; Viking Outstanding Athlete Award, Valley City State Col, 58; Region 7 Wrestling Coach of Year Award, Nat High Sch Athletic Coaches Asn, 72, Nat Wrestling Coach of Year Award, 73; NDak Coach of Year Award, NDak Sportswriters & Sportscasters Asn, 73. Relig: Lutheran. Mailing Add: 816 W Divide Ave Bismarck ND 58501

HALPERIN, DONALD MARC (D)
NY State Sen
b Brooklyn, NY, July 25, 45; s Charles Halperin & Gladys Solomon H; m 1969 to Brenda Stibel. Educ: Rutgers Univ, BA, 67; Brooklyn Law Sch, JD, 70; Chi Phi; Phi Delta Phi. Polit & Govt Pos: Co committeeman, Dem Party, 68-70; NY State Sen, 71- Bus & Prof Pos: Attorney, Fuchsberg & Fuchsberg, 72- Mem: NY Co Lawyers Asn; Brooklyn Bar Asn; B'nai B'rith; Manhattan Beach Community Group; Fedn Jewish Philanthropies. Honors & Awards: Youngest NY State Sen in hist of NY. Relig: Jewish. Legal Res: 40 Girard St Brooklyn NY 11235 Mailing Add: 1515 Sheepshead Bay Rd Brooklyn NY 11235

HALPERN, SEYMOUR (R)
Mem, Queens Co Rep Comt, NY
b New York, NY, Nov 19, 13; s Ralph Halpern & Anna Swanton H; m 1959 to Barbara Margaret Olsen. Educ: Seth Low Col, Columbia Univ, 32-34. Hon Degrees: LLD, St John's Univ, 67. Polit & Govt Pos: Staff asst to Mayor Fiorello LaGuardia, New York, NY, 37; asst to the pres, New York City Coun, 37-40; NY State Sen, 41-54, chmn, Comt on Civil Serv, NY State Senate, 41-46, Comt on Motor Vehicles & Transportation, 46-47 & NY State Joint Legis Comt on Motor Vehicle Probs, 48-54; mem, Mayor's Comt on the Courts, 56-58; mem, Queens Co Rep Comt, presently; US Rep, NY, 59-72; mem, Franklin D Roosevelt Mem Comt, 62-74; cong adv, US Deleg, UN Conf on Psychotropic Drugs, Vienna, 71; US deleg, UN Conf on Drug Abuse, Geneva, 72 & UN Conf on Human Environ, Stockholm, 72. Bus & Prof Pos: Reporter, Long Island Daily Press, 31-32; staff writer, Chicago Herald Exam, 32-33; partner, Halpern & Stone, 45-54; impartial chmn, Moving & Storage Indust of NY, 55-60; vpres, John C Paige & Co, Inc, NY, 64-70; adj prof sociol, St John's Univ, 72-73; sr vpres, Sydney S Baron & Co Inc, 73-; vpres, United Siscoe Mines, Ltd, Toronto, 73-; dir, Geothermal Kinetics, Inc, Phoenix, Ariz, 73- Mil Serv: Lt Col, Civil Air Patrol, Air Force. Mem: Zionist Orgn Am (nat adv coun, Odyssey House, nat exec coun); B'nai B'rith (trustee F D R Chap); KofP (Gavel Lodge); charter mem US Capitol Hist Soc; Ctr for Study of Presidency (nat adv coun). Relig: Jewish. Legal Res: 166-05 Highland Ave Jamaica NY 11432 Mailing Add: 540 Madison Ave New York NY 10022

HALPIN, ROBERT J (D)
Mem, Cumberland Co Bd of Freeholders, NJ
b Vineland, NJ, Dec 8, 22; married; c five. Educ: SJersey Col; Rutgers Univ Law Sch. Polit & Govt Pos: Asst prosecutor, Cumberland Co, NJ, 1 year; mem, Bd Estimates Sch Bd; mem, Vineland City Planning Bd formerly; pres, Vineland City Coun, 56; NJ State Assemblyman, 60-68, Asst Minority Leader, NJ State Assembly, 65, Majority Leader, 66 & Speaker, 67; deleg, Dem Nat Conv, 68; mem, Cumberland Co Bd of Freeholders, 69-; chmn, Cumberland Co Dem Party, currently. Bus & Prof Pos: Attorney-at-law. Mil Serv: Navy, serv in Atlantic & Pac. Mem: Vineland CofC (solicitor); KofC (4 degree); Am Legion; Judge Adv Vineland Cath War Vet (first vcomdr); NJ Cath War Vet. Honors & Awards: Outstanding Young Man, Vineland CofC, 56. Mailing Add: 319 Landis Ave Vineland NJ 08360

HALSTEAD, FRED WOLF (SOCIALIST WORKERS PARTY)
Anti-War Dir, Socialist Workers Party
b Los Angeles, Calif, Apr 21, 27; s Frank Harrison Halstead & Bloomah Buckholtz H; m 1957 to Virginia Garza; c Laura Ellen, Celia Maria & Frank William. Educ: Univ Calif, Los Angeles, 2 years. Polit & Govt Pos: Mem Nat Comt, Socialist Workers Party, 62-, anti-war dir, 65-, Presidential cand, 68. Bus & Prof Pos: Garment cutter, shops in Los Angeles, Detroit & New York, 50-66; staff writer, The Militant, 55-66; anti-war organizer Fifth Ave Vietnam Peace Parade Comt, 66-68. Mil Serv: Entered as A/S, Navy, 45, released as Motor Machinist Mate 3/C, 46, after serv in USS LST 897, Asiatic-Pac Theatre. Publ: Harlem Stirs, Marzani-Munsell, 66; If This Be Revolution, Intercontinental Press, 67; Interviews With Anti-War GIs, Merit, 69. Mem: GI Civil Liberties Defense Comt; Nat Peace Action Coalition (steering comt); Vet for Peace. Mailing Add: c/o Socialist Workers Party 428 S Wabash Ave Chicago IL 60605

HALTOM, ELBERT BERTRAM, JR (D)
VChmn, Ala Dem State Party
b Florence, Ala, Dec 26, 22; s Elbert Bertram Haltom & Elva Simpson H; m 1949 to Constance Boyd Morris; c Emily Morris. Educ: Florence State Teachers Col, 40-42; Univ Ala Sch Law, LLB, 48; Phi Delta Phi; Phi Gamma Delta. Polit & Govt Pos: Ala State Rep, 55-58; Ala State Sen, 59-62; vchmn, Ala Dem State Party, 74- Bus & Prof Pos: Practicing attorney, Florence, Ala, 48-; pres & chmn bd, United Ala Bancshares, Inc, 67-72, mem bd dirs, 67- Mil Serv: Entered as Pvt, Air Force, 43, released as S/Sgt, 45, after serv in 15th Air Force, European Theatre, Italy, 44-45; Air Medal with Four Oak Leaf Clusters. Mem: Am & Ala State Bar Asns; Int Soc Barristers; Am Legion; VFW. Relig: Methodist. Legal Res: 562 Palisade Dr Florence AL 35630 Mailing Add: PO Box H Florence AL 35630

HALTOM, STERLING M (D)
Ind State Rep
Mailing Add: 1145 Orchard Lane Franklin IN 46131

HALVERSON, HAROLD WENDELL (R)
Mem, SDak State Rep Cent Comt
b Burke, SDak, Nov 24, 26; s Reuben Arnold Halverson & Viola Hauge H; m 1948 to Marie Christina Vosika; c James Arnold, Marilyn Marie, Cindy Lou & John Edward. Educ: Burke High Sch, grad. Polit & Govt Pos: Mem, Gregory & Grant Co Rep Party, SDak, 20 years; SDak State Rep, 71-72; mem, SDak State Rep Cent Comt, 75- Bus & Prof Pos: Fieldman, Mo Valley Mutual Ins, Burke, SDak, 57-59; Milbank Mutual Ins Co, 59-60, asst claims supvr, 60-66, agency dir, 66-, mem bd dirs & vpres, 69- Mil Serv: Entered as A/S, Navy, 45, released as Seaman 1/C, 46, after serv in 53rd Construction Bn, Bikini Atoll, 45-46. Mem: Mason (Worshipful Master, Milbank Chap); Eastern Star (Past Patron, Esther Chap); Am Legion (past Comdr); Com & Commun Club; Dale Carnegie Club. Relig: Methodist; Sunday sch teacher, law leader, choir mem, pastoral rels, coun of ministries & admin bd, Parkview United Methodist Church. Mailing Add: 606 S5 Milbank SD 57252

HALVERSON, KENNETH SHAFFER (R)
Pa State Rep
b Somerset, Pa, July 24, 33; s Kenneth Evan Halverson & Alma Shaffer H; m 1956 to Olive Mae Nibert; c David, Daniel, Robert, Barry & William. Educ: Somerset High Sch, Pa, grad, 51; Univ Pittsburgh. Polit & Govt Pos: Justice of the peace, Somerset Twp, Somerset, Pa, 62-67; vchmn, Young Rep, Somerset, 64, chmn, 66; Pa State Rep, 69th Legis Dist, 66-, vchmn, Bus & Com Comt, Pa House Rep, 73-; vchmn, Somerset Twp Munic Sewerage Authority, 71- Bus & Prof Pos: Spec agt & underwriter, Selected Risks Ins Co, Branchville, NJ, 56-59; owner, Ken Halverson Ins Agency, 59-; mem adv bd trustees, Univ Pittsburgh, Johnstown, 72- Mil Serv: Entered as Pvt, Army, 53, released as S/Sgt, 56, after serv in Army Security Agency, Ger. Mem: Tri State Mutual Ins Agents Asn; Jaycees; Am Legion; Somerset Sportsmen; VFW. Honors & Awards: Outstanding Jaycee, Somerset, Pa, Jr Chamber Int Senate 6626. Relig: Protestant. Mailing Add: RD 5 Somerset PA 15501

HALVERSON, RONALD T (R)
Utah State Rep
b Ogden, Utah, Dec 18, 36; s Marlowe Halverson & Hilda Tomlinson H; m 1960 to Linda Kay Jenson; c Brent Ronald, David J, Jannette & Blair T. Educ: Weber Col, AS, 60; Univ Utah, 60-61; Weber Col Excellsior Club. Polit & Govt Pos: Voting dist chmn, Rep Nat Conv, 60, deleg, 64; Utah State Rep, 67-, Majority Whip, Utah State House Rep, 68- Bus & Prof Pos: Pres, Halverson Plumbing & Heating, currently; bd mem, Joint Apprentice Comt, 64- Mil Serv: Entered as Pvt, Army, 60, released as Sgt, 66, after serv in H/H Battery, 83rd Artil. Mem: Utah Plumbing & Heating Contractors Asn; Kiwanis. Relig: Latter-day Saint. Mailing Add: 1540 Burton Ct Ogden UT 84403

HALVORSON, GEORGE CHARLES, SR (R)
Field Rep, Seventh Cong Dist Rep Party, Minn
b Menahga, Minn, June 22, 24; s Arthur B Halvorson & Francis Gustafson H; m 1946 to Barbara T Paulson; c George C, Jr, Linda Sue & Barbara Jean. Educ: Concordia Col

(Moorhead, Minn), BA, 51; Moorhead State Col; St Cloud State Col; Univ NDak; Mondamin Lit Soc. Polit & Govt Pos: Vchmn, Wadena Co Rep Party, Minn, 61-66, 67-, chmn, 66-68; chmn, Educators for Langen, 64; mayor, Village of Menahga, 65-; chmn, Dist Seven Resolutions, 66; mem, State Rep Rules Comt, 66; mem, Menahga Planning Comn, Village of Menahga, 68-; field rep, Seventh Cong Dist Rep Party, 68- Bus & Prof Pos: Secy, Menahga CofC, 46-47; adv, Northern Minn Educator, Newspaper, 65-68; chmn, Faculty Coun, 67-68. Mil Serv: Entered as Pvt, Marine Corps, 43, released as Cpl, 46, after serv in Second Marine Div, SPac, 43-46; four combat awards for serv in SPac; two Presidential Unit Citation Awards; Occup of Japan Award. Publ: Numerous articles on polit & civic subjects in area newspapers. Mem: Minn Bus Educator's Asn; Menahga CofC; Lions; Am Legion; VFW. Honors & Awards: Yearbook Dedication; Dist Commendation. Relig: Lutheran. Mailing Add: Box 177 Menahga MN 56464

HALVORSON, ORA JUANITA (D)
Mont State Rep
b Maxwell, Iowa, Dec 31, 13; d Harry Herbert Johnson & Plona DeWinter J; m 1935 to Stanley Norman Halvorson; c Wayne, Lowell (deceased), Karen Sue (Mrs Tom R Miller), David & Kevin. Educ: Billings Bus Col, dipl, 33; Goddard Col, BA, 73. Polit & Govt Pos: Mem Mont deleg, White House Conf Children & Youth, 60 & 70; Mont State Rep, Dist 16, 73- Bus & Prof Pos: Off mgr, Yellowstone Co Agr Adjust Admin, 33-35. Publ: Charles E Conrad, Daily Inter Lake Great Falls Tribune, 12/57; Charles E Conrad of Kalispell: merchant prince with gentle touch, Mont the Mag of Western Hist, 4/71. Mem: Int Platform Asn; DAR; Fedn of Women's Clubs; Grange; Salvation Army Adv Bd. Honors & Awards: Lady of the Year, Beta Sigma Phi, 63; First Person of the Year, Rocky Mountain Informer, 72. Relig: Presbyterian. Mailing Add: 244 Woodland Ave Kalispell MT 59901

HALVORSON, ROGER A (R)
Iowa State Rep
b Allamakee Co, Iowa, Feb 12, 34; s Victory Leiran Halvorson & Ruby Jenson H; m 1955 to Connie May Rohde; c Tracey Dawn, Rogeta Ann, Jay Allan & Lisa May. Educ: Upper Iowa Univ, BS, 55. Polit & Govt Pos: Chmn, Clayton Co Rep Cent Comt, Iowa, 64-74; chmn, Second Dist Rep Cent Comt, 69-74; Iowa State Rep, 17th Dist, 75- Bus & Prof Pos: Dist dir, Independent Ins Agents of Iowa, past 6 years; vpres, Northeast Iowa Bd Realtors, 74- Mil Serv: Army Nat Guard, 50-59. Mem: Kiwanis; Boy Scouts (troop comt chmn). Relig: Lutheran. Mailing Add: Box 627 Monona IA 52159

HAM, ARLENE HANSEN (R)
VChairwoman, SDak Rep State Cent Comt
b Fruitdale, SDak, Aug 1, 36; d Alfred Hansen & Clara Castleberry H; m 1956 to Donald J Ham; c Jennifer Lynn & Grady Donald. Educ: Bus Col, Omaha, Nebr, dipl, 54. Polit & Govt Pos: Precinct committeewoman, Custer Co Rep Cent Comt, SDak, 62-70; state committeewoman, Mont State Rep Comt, 64-70, chmn credentials comt, 66; co vchairwoman, Pennington Co Rep Cent Comt, SDak, 70-74, precinct committeewoman, 70-; campaign mgr, Barbara Gunderson for US Senate, 74; vchairwoman, SDak Rep State Cent Comt, 74- Bus & Prof Pos: Deleg & secy to vpres, Mont Vet Med Auxiliary, 62-70; secy to pres, Intermountain Vet Med Auxiliary & Hosp Guild, 66-70; pres & second vpres, Rapid City Toastmistress, 70-74. Mem: Rep Women's Club (secy to pres, Mont & SDak Chap & state deleg to nat conv, 68-72); Meade-Pennington Co Ment Health Asn (pres, 73-75). Honors & Awards: Outstanding Young Woman, Jaycettes, 66; Regional Speech Winner, Toastmistress Club. Relig: Lutheran; bd mem, Calvary Lutheran, 71-74. Mailing Add: 3728 Reder Rapid City SD 57701

HAM, ARTHUR CARL (R)
SDak State Rep
b Rapid City, SDak; s Arthur C Ham & Gladys Chapman H; m 1946 to Donna Ballard; c eight. Educ: SDak State Univ, BS, 43; Alpha Zeta; Blue Key. Polit & Govt Pos: Mem, Pennington Co Sch Bd, Rapid City, SDak, 64-73; mem, Assoc Sch Bd SDak, 67-; mem, Rapid City Sch Bd, 69-; SDak State Rep, 75- Bus & Prof Pos: Mem staff exten serv, SDak State Univ, 47-51; rancher, 52- Mil Serv: Entered as Cpl, Army, 42, released as Capt, 47, after serv in 21st Armored Inf, European Theatre, 45-46; Purple Heart; Am Campaign Medal; Europe-Africa-Mid East Medal; 1 Bronze Star. Mem: Elks; VFW; SDak Stockgrowers. Honors & Awards: Outstanding Sch Bd Mem, SDak, 72; Outstanding Young Farmer, Jaycees, 54. Mailing Add: Box 89 Caputa SD 57725

HAM, BENSON (D)
Ga State Rep
Mailing Add: PO Box 677 Forsyth GA 31029

HAM, DONALD JAMIESON (R)
Chmn, Pennington Co Rep Cent Comt, SDak
b Rapid City, SDak, May 30, 34; s Ernest B Ham & Nancy Hannum H; m 1956 to Arlene Hansen; c Jennifer & Grady. Educ: SDak State Univ, 52-53; Colo State Univ, BS & DVM, 58; Omicron Delta Kappa; Farm House Fraternity. Polit & Govt Pos: Vchmn, Mont Young Rep, 65-68; chmn, Custer Co Rep Cent Comt, Mont, 66-69; chmn, Pennington Co Rep Cent Comt, SDak, 75- Bus & Prof Pos: Dr vet med, Custer Vet Clin, 60-69; acct exec, Dain Kalman & Quail, 69- Mil Serv: Entered as 1st Lt, Army, 58, released as 1st Lt, 60, after serv in Vet Corps, Biol Warfare Labs, Ft Detrick, Md, 58-60. Mem: United Way of Rapid City (pres); Boys Club of Rapid City (bd dirs). Honors & Awards: Outstanding Young Man of Mont, Mont Jaycees, 68. Relig: Lutheran. Mailing Add: 3728 Reder St Rapid City SD 57701

HAM, EVERETT ADAMS, JR (R)
Mem, Ark Rep State Exec Comt
b Little Rock, Ark, May 15, 23; s Everett A Ham, Sr & Lena Faisst H; div; c Gretel Christine & Everett A, III. Educ: Univ Dayton, 3 years; Univ Ark, BSA, 50. Polit & Govt Pos: Rep co committeeman, Ark, 50-; exec dir, Party for Two Parties, Little Rock, 61-69; Rep Nat Committeeman & asst to Winthrop Rockefeller, 61-69; mem, Ark Rep State Exec Comt, 63-, vchmn, 71-73; Bolivian consul for Ark, 67-; deleg, Rep Nat Conv, 68. Mil Serv: Entered as Aviation Cadet, Air Force, 42, released as Capt, 45, after serv in 5th Air Force, Southwest Pac, 43-44; Air Medal with Five Oak Leaf Clusters; Southwest Pac Theatre Medal with Four Battle Stars. Mem: ROA; Little Rock Club; Top of the Rock Club; Ark River Yacht Club; Am Legion; VFW; Soc for Preservation & Encouragement of Barbershop Singing in Am. Honors & Awards: Named Outstanding Barbershopper in the South, 63. Relig: Protestant. Mailing Add: 1007 Wildwood North Little Rock AR 72116

HAM, GLEN (D)
Okla State Sen
b Maysville, Okla, Apr 1, 19; s Charles Ova Ham & Stella Melvina Reddell H; m 1964 to Ramona G Garrison; c Paul. Educ: Univ Okla, 37-40; Univ Tulsa Law Sch, 46-47; Oklahoma City Univ Law Sch, LLB, 49; Delta Theta Phi. Polit & Govt Pos: State exec secy, Okla League of Young Dem, 38, Fifth Dist chmn, 39; Okla State Rep, 50-60, Majority Leader, Okla House of Rep, 53; Okla State Sen, 60-, Majority Leader, Okla State Senate, 63. Mil Serv: Entered as Pvt, Army Air Corps, 42, released as Sgt, 45, after serv in 5th Air Force, Australia, New Guinea, EIndies, Philippines & Okinawa; New Guinea, Southern Philippines & Luzon Campaign Ribbons; Good Conduct Medal; Philippines Liberation Ribbon with 1 Star. Mem: Okla State Bar Asn; Mason (32 degree); Am Legion; VFW; CofC. Relig: Southern Baptist. Legal Res: 412 N Ash Pauls Valley OK 73075 Mailing Add: Box 198 Pauls Valley OK 73075

HAM, RAY (R)
SC State Rep
Mailing Add: 3180 Buckeye Dr West Columbia SC 29169

HAMBERGER, MARTIN GEORGE (R)
b Pottsville, Pa, Oct 2, 43; s Calvin Lewis Hamberger & Mary Catherine Snitzer H; m 1966 to Rose Ann Domenici; c Eric Martin & Scott Martin. Educ: Georgetown Univ, BSFS, 65; Georgetown Law Ctr, JD, 69; Alpha Sigma Nu. Polit & Govt Pos: Admin asst to US Sen Hugh Scott, Pa, 69- Bus & Prof Pos: Assoc, Shoemaker & Thompson, York, 71- Relig: Catholic. Legal Res: RD 3 Glen Rock PA 17327 Mailing Add: 260D Russell Sen Off Bldg Washington DC 20510

HAMBLEN, LYONS ALEXANDER (R)
Chmn, Hawkins Co Rep Party, Tenn
b Surgoinsville, Tenn, Nov 9, 22; s Charles H Hamblen, Sr & Flora Johnson H; m 1948 to Muriel Evelyn Bennett; c Carole H (Mrs Fowler) & Lyons A, Jr. Educ: Carson-Newman Col, AB, 48; Univ Tenn, summer 49. Polit & Govt Pos: Trustee, Hawkins Co, Tenn, 50-58; justice of the peace, 66-; chmn, Hawkins Co Rep Party, 71- Bus & Prof Pos: Vpres, Citizens Union Bank, 65- Mil Serv: Entered as Pvt, Army, 43, released as Cpl, 45, after serv in 35th Inf Div; Cert of Merit. Mem: Kiwanis; Shrine; Am Legion; VFW. Honors & Awards: Lt Gov, Kiwanis Int, 65; Col, Gov Winfield Dunn, 73. Relig: Baptist. Mailing Add: 408 Colonial Rd Rogersville TN 37857

HAMERMAN, WILDA SLEVIN (D)
Conn State Rep
b New York, NY, Mar 15, 24; d Theodore Slevin & Katherine Bluh S; m 1952 to Martin Hamerman; c Donald & Paul. Educ: Univ Ill, Urbana, BA, 45; Columbia Univ, summer 44. Polit & Govt Pos: Conn State Rep, 114th Dist, 74- Mem: League of Women Voters. Mailing Add: 815 Tall Timber Rd Orange CT 06477

HAMERSLY, MARJORY ANN (R)
b Monticello, Iowa, Sept 5, 31; d Charles M Luett & Ruth McNeilly L; m 1952 to Winston Charles Hamersly; c James Buchanan & Carla JoAnn. Educ: Univ Northern Iowa, 49-51; Mankato State Col, 65-68; Purple Arrow. Polit & Govt Pos: Chairwoman, First Cong Dist Citizens for Nixon-Agnew, 68 & First Cong Dist GOP Comt, 69-71; vchairwoman, Minn Rep State Cent Comt, 71-74; deleg & mem rules comt, Rep Nat Conv, 72; campaign mgr, Rep Albert H Quie, First Dist, Minn, 74; vol state chairwoman, J Robert Stassen, cand for Minn State Treas. Bus & Prof Pos: Elem teacher, Anamosa, Iowa, 51-52. Mem: Nat Educ Asn; Minn Sch Bd Asn; PEO; Farm Bur Fedn; League Women Voters. Relig: Methodist. Legal Res: RR Glenville MN 56036 Mailing Add: Rte 2 Northwood IA 50459

HAMIL, DAVID ALEXANDER (R)
Adminr, Rural Electrification Admin, Dept of Agr
b Logan Co, Colo, Dec 3, 08; s James Newton Hamil & Ada Walker H; m 1933 to Genevieve Robinson; c Jo Ann (Mrs Donald A Ostwald), Donald William & Jack Robinson. Educ: Hastings Col, AB, 30. Polit & Govt Pos: Colo State Rep, 32nd-36th & 38th-40th sessions, chmn, Joint Budget Comt, Colo House of Rep, 34th & 36th sessions, speaker, 38th-40th sessions; adminr, Rural Electrification Admin, Dept of Agr, 56-61 & 69-; dir, Dept of Insts, Colo, 63-69. Bus & Prof Pos: Owner & operator, Hamil Bros, Inc & Hamil Bros Land Co, Logan Co, Colo, 32- Mem: AF&AM (33 degree); Shrine; Elks (past exalted ruler, Sterling Lodge 1336, past dist dep & grand exalted ruler, Colo N); hon mem, Rotary. Honors & Awards: Citizenship Award, Hastings Col; Cert of Recognition, Colo & US Jr CofC; Merit of Honor Award, Colo State Univ Alumni Asn; Nat 4-H Alumni Award. Relig: Presbyterian; elder. Legal Res: Sterling CO 80751 Mailing Add: Rural Electrification Admin 14th St & Independence Ave SW Washington DC 20250

HAMILTON, A C (SCOTTY) (R)
VChmn, Fourth Cong Dist Rep Party, Colo
b Dalmuir, Scotland, Jan 5, 18; s William M Hamilton (deceased) & Margaret Crawford H (deceased); m 1947 to Lea M Suppes; c Alwyn Charles & David Scott. Educ: Colo State Col, BA; Phi Mu Alpha; Kappa Kappa Psi; Phi Delta Pi. Polit & Govt Pos: Vet Employ rep, Ft Collins, Colo, 46-47; mem, Sch Bd, Bayard, Nebr, 54-59, pres, 58-59; chmn, Morrill Co Rep Cent Comt, Nebr, 57-59; treas, Adams Co Rep Cent Comt, Colo, 61-; chmn, Second Cong Dist Rep Party, Colo, 69-72; vchmn, Fourth Cong Dist Rep Party, 72- Mil Serv: Entered as Pvt, Army, 41, released as M/Sgt, 45, after serv in Hq G-3, XVI Corps, ETO, 44-45; Bronze Star; Victory Medal; Good Conduct Medal; European Theatre Medal. Mem: Am Soc Sugar Beet Technol; Am Legion; Kiwanis. Relig: Presbyterian. Mailing Add: 171 S 15th Ave Brighton CO 80601

HAMILTON, ANN TWYNAM (D)
Committeewoman, Suffolk Co Dem Comt, NY
b Havant, Hampshire, Eng, Aug 22, 22; d Philip Blake & Marjorie Down B; m 1945 to Leonard Derwent Hamilton. Educ: St Hugh's Col, Oxford Univ, BA, 44, MA, 48. Polit & Govt Pos: Zone leader, Concerned Dem of First Cong Dist, NY, 68; committeewoman, Suffolk Co Dem Comt, 68-; chmn, Brookhaven New Dem Coalition, 68-70, chmn law comt, 70-72; campaign mgr, Mildred Steinberg for Suffolk Co Legis, 71; deleg, Dem Nat Conv, 72. Bus & Prof Pos: German & French teacher, Eng Schs, 44-46; asst prof, Mod Lang Dept, Univ Utah, 50. Mailing Add: 6 Childs Lane Setauket NY 11733

HAMILTON, ART (D)
Ariz State Rep
Mailing Add: 405 N 40th Ave Phoenix AZ 85009

HAMILTON, BUFORD GARVIN, II (D)
b Kansas City, Mo, Dec 15, 40; s Dr Buford Bates Hamilton & Eunice Moran H; m 1963 to Camille Laird Cameron; c Scott Cameron & Megan Moran. Educ: Univ Mo-Columbia, BA, 62, Sch Dent, DDS, 66; Beta Theta Phi; Psi Omega. Polit & Govt Pos: Chmn, Comt to elect Thomas Eagleton for Senate, Ray Co, Mo, 68; councilman, Richmond, 69, mayor pro tem, 71; committeeman, Richmond Twp Dem Party, 70; chmn, Ray Co Dem Comt, formerly; chmn, Litton for Cong, Ray Co, 72. Mil Serv: Entered as Ens, Navy, 63, released as Ens, 65, after serv in Res, 63-65; Naval Res Ret, 71. Mem: Am Dent Asn; Kansas City Dent Asn (bd dirs, 73-); Kiwanis Int; CofC (mem bd dirs); Cancer Soc (pres, Ray Co Unit). Am Nat Red Cross Award of Merit, 65. Relig: Episcopal. Legal Res: 306 Park Richmond MO 64085 Mailing Add: 108 S College Richmond MO 64085

HAMILTON, CHARLES T (D)
NY State Assemblyman
Mailing Add: 24 Stone Ave Brooklyn NY 11230

HAMILTON, DWIGHT ALAN (R)
Chmn, Arapahoe Co Rep Cent Comt, Colo
b Denver, Colo, Aug 21, 28; s Alfred H Hamilton, Jr & Emily L Loucks H; m 1952 to Elizabeth Folds; c Camilla L, Dwight Alan, Jr, Elizabeth Ann & Scott Weston. Educ: Colo Col, BA, 50; Univ Denver Col Law, LLB, 54; Beta Theta Pi. Polit & Govt Pos: Mem, Nat Conv of Comnr on Uniform State Laws, Colo, 65-; chmn, Patronage Comt, Colo Rep Party, 68-; chmn, Arapahoe Co Rep Cent Comt, 69-; mem, Rep State Cent Comt, Colo, 69-, chmn, 74-75. Bus & Prof Pos: Attorney-at-law, partner, Fuller & Evan, 55- Mil Serv: Entered as Cpl, Marine Corps, 48, released as Capt, 62, after serv in First Marine Div, Korea, 51; Purple Heart. Mem: Am Bar Asn; Denver Law Club; AF&AM; Rocky Mt Consistory; Shrine. Relig: Christian Science. Mailing Add: 5005 S Lafayette Lane Englewood CO 80110

HAMILTON, ERNEST ROLL (D)
b Chicago, Ill, Mar 12, 27; s Ernest Frank Hamilton & Margarett Etta Stroud H; m 1949 to Dolores D Meyer; c Gary Stephen, Gail Louise, Dale Douglass & Cheryl Laurett. Educ: Ill Inst Technol, 44-45; Purdue Univ, Civil Eng, 53; Chi Epsilon; Delta Tau Delta. Polit & Govt Pos: Statistician, US Dept Army, 44; utility engr, Sanit Dept, City of Indianapolis, Ind, 48; planning engr, Marion Co Plan Comn, 49-50; cand co engr, Marion Co, 52; precinct committeeman, Marion Co Dem Cent Comt, 53-64; deleg, Ind State Dem Conv, 62, 66 & 68; chmn, Washington Twp Award, Indianapolis, 64-70; deleg, Dem Nat Conv, 68 & 72; ward chmn, Washington Twp; treas, Sixth Dist. Bus & Prof Pos: Pres & prof engr, Ernest R Hamilton Assocs, Inc, 55-; consult prof engr & pres, RSH Assocs, Inc, 67-; consult, Whiting, Ind, Fremont, Ft Wayne & Lewisville. Mil Serv: Entered as Pvt, Air Force, 45, released as Sgt, 46, after serv in PACUSA, 13th & Fifth Air Force, Pac, 44-45; Pac Theatre, Occup & Good Conduct Medals. Publ: Water for peace, Vol 4, Industrial reuse of combined sewage treatment plant effluent, Supt Doc, US, 67. Mem: Nat Soc Prof Engrs; Am Soc Mech Engrs (incinerator div); Am Water Works Asn; Water Pollution Control Fedn; Am Pub Works Asn. Relig: Lutheran. Mailing Add: 9420 N Kenwood Ave Indianapolis IN 46260

HAMILTON, GRACE T (D)
Ga State Rep
Mailing Add: 582 University Pl NW Atlanta GA 30314

HAMILTON, HELEN PACKER (D)
Mem, WVa Dem Exec Comt
b Miles City, Mont, Jan 3, 27; d Edward Albert Packer & Beda Carlson P; m 1950 to Patrick R Hamilton; c Patricia Leigh, Debra Lynn, Judith Ann & James Edward. Educ: Univ Mont, BA, 48; Univ Minn, summer 48; Alpha Phi. Polit & Govt Pos: Mem, WVa Dem Exec Comt, 68-; deleg, Dem Nat Conv, 72, mem, rules comt, WVa Dem platform comt & WVa Dem platform drafting subcomt, 72. Bus & Prof Pos: Teacher-libr, Sidney High Sch, Mont, 48-50; libr, San Francisco Pub Lib, Calif, 50-51; teacher, Collins High Sch, Oak Hill, WVa, 54-64. Mem: WVa Educ Asn; PTA; Oak Hill Civic League. Relig: Protestant. Legal Res: 10 Arbuckle Rd Oak Hill WV 25901 Mailing Add: PO Box 115 Oak Hill WV 25901

HAMILTON, HUBERT EARL (BERT), JR (D)
Ga State Sen
b Pickens, SC, July 19, 07; s Hubert Earl Hamilton, Sr & Cynthia Riddle H; m 1949 to Carolyn Dudney; c Hubert Earl, III (Hu) & Bruce Dudney. Educ: The Citadel, AB, 32; George Peabody Col, MA, 35, EdD, 52; Kappa Delta Pi; Phi Delta Kappa; Pi Gamma Mu. Polit & Govt Pos: Alderman, Macon, Ga, 59-63, 67-70; Ga State Sen, 71- Bus & Prof Pos: Teacher, Walhalla High Sch, SC, 32-33 & pub schs, Atlanta, Ga, 35-53; prin elem sch, Easley, SC, 33-34; prof educ, Mercer Univ, 53-, McCommon Prof, 56- Mil Serv: Entered as Lt, Army, 41, released as Maj, 46, after serv in gen staff, SHAEF, 43-45; Lt Col (Ret), Army Res; Rhineland Campaign Battle Star. Mem: Gtr Macon CofC; Moose; Eagles; Am Legion; VFW. Relig: Christian. Mailing Add: 464 W Buford Rd Macon GA 31204

HAMILTON, JAMES E (D)
Okla State Sen
Mailing Add: State Capitol Oklahoma City OK 73105

HAMILTON, JAMES F (R)
Mem, Rep State Cent Comt Calif
b Calexico, Calif, Apr 19, 35; s James W Hamilton & Phillis G Moore H; m 1963 to Sally Sue Trexler; c Debbie Sue & James Russell. Educ: Imperial Valley Col, 55-57. Polit & Govt Pos: Mem, Youth for Ike, Brawley, Calif, 52; mem, Imperial Co Young Rep, 60-66, vchmn, 62, treas, 63, chmn, 64-65; mem, Imperial Co Rep Cent Comt, 66-, precinct chmn, 68-70, chmn, 70-72; mem, Rep State Cent Comt Calif, 70-, youth dir, currently; mem, Calif State Chmn Asn, 70-; campaign mgr, five nonpartisan races & two non-partisan races, mem nine campaign comts. Bus & Prof Pos: Off & credit mgr, Firestone Tire & Rubber Co, 58-65; mgr, Avco Financial Serv, 65- Mil Serv: Entered as Pvt, Army, 56, released as E-4, 58, after serv in Chem Corp. Mem: Lions (bd dirs); 20-30 Club; Imperial Co Camp Fire Girls; Imperial Co City of Hope Chap; Brawley Beautification Comn. Honors & Awards: Founded orphanage while in mil serv in Korea; honored for serv in City of Hope, Camp Fire Girls & 20-30 Club. Relig: Baptist. Mailing Add: 240 W J St Brawley CA 92227

HAMILTON, JAMES RALPH (DUCK) (D)
Ga State Sen
b Atlanta, Ga, June 21, 38; s James Ralph Hamilton, Sr & Cora Bell West H; m 1960 to Mary Katherine Jinks. Educ: John Marshall Univ, LLB, 60; Sigma Delta. Polit & Govt Pos: Dir bd, Metrop Atlanta Rapid Transit Authority, Ga, 72-75; Ga State Sen, Dist 34, 75- Bus & Prof Pos: Pres, Hamilton Construction Co, 60; pilot, Piedmont Air Lines, 69; dir, First Palmetto Bank, 69, chmn bd, 70, pres, 74- Mil Serv: Entered as Pvt, Marine Corps, 56, released as Cpl, 60, after serv in 1st Motor Transport Bn. Mailing Add: 4745 Stonewall Tell Rd College Park GA 30337

HAMILTON, JOHN H, JR (R)
Pa State Rep
b Philadelphia, Pa, Feb 9, 19; s John H Hamilton & Marie Holland H; m to Doris V Johnson; c two. Educ: Wharton Eve Sch; N Philadelphia Realty Sch. Polit & Govt Pos: Exec vpres & treas, Pa Rep State Exec Comt, 17 years; Pa State Rep, currently. Bus & Prof Pos: Ins broker. Mil Serv: Med Corps, 75th Field Hosp, Okinawa, World War II. Mailing Add: 6916 Shalkop St Philadelphia PA 19128

HAMILTON, LAVERNE MCDANIEL (D)
State Dem Committeewoman, NY
b Springfield, Mo, Jan 31, 40; d Rev James Alfred McDaniel & Maxine Johnson M; m 1965 to Dr Harry Lemuel Hamilton, Jr; c David McDaniel & Lisa LaVerne. Educ: Beloit Col, BA, 61. Polit & Govt Pos: Deleg, Dem Nat Conv, 72; secy, Albany Co McGovern for President Campaign, 72; State Dem Committeewoman, NY, 74- Bus & Prof Pos: Teacher, Cleveland, Ohio, 61-63; ed asst, Scott, Foresman & Co, 64-65, ed consult, 69 & 72; ed, Pub Rel Off, State Univ NY, Albany, 66-68. Publ: Ed-consult, Perspectives, 69; Guidebook to perspectives, Scott, Foresman; Thought & Phrase, 74. Mem: NAACP (ed, newsletter, 67- & secy, 68-); Nat Women's Polit Caucus. Honors & Awards: Hon Mention for Newsletter of NAACP, NAACP Nat Conv, 68, 71, 72 & 73, second place, 74. Mailing Add: 5 Morningside Dr Delmar NY 12054

HAMILTON, LEE HERBERT (D)
US Rep, Ind
b Daytona Beach, Fla, Apr 20, 31; s Frank A Hamilton & Myra Jones H; m 1954 to Nancy Ann Nelson; c Tracy Lynn, Deborah Lee & Douglas Nelson. Educ: DePauw Univ, AB, cum laude, 52; Goethe Univ, Ger, study-travel scholarship, 52-53; Ind Univ Sch Law, JD, 56; Gold Key. Hon Degrees: LLD, DePauw Univ, 71. Polit & Govt Pos: Chmn, Citizens for Kennedy Comt, 60; chmn, Citizens for Bayh for Sen Comt, 62; treas, Bartholomew Co Young Dem, Ind, 60-63, pres, 63-64; US Rep, Ninth Dist, Ind, 65-, Foreign Affairs & Post Off & Civil Serv Comts, US House Rep, currently, pres, 89th Cong Club; deleg, Dem Nat Conv, 68; ex-officio, Dem Nat Mid-Term Conf, 74. Bus & Prof Pos: Attorney, Wilkins Witwer & Moran, Chicago, 56-58; attorney & partner, Sharpnack & Bigley, Columbus, Ind, 58-64; instr, Am Banking Inst, 60-61. Mem: Ind Bar Asn; Rotary; DePauw Univ Nat Bequests Comt; CofC; Jr CofC. Honors & Awards: Award for basketball & tennis in col, 65. Relig: Methodist. Legal Res: IN Mailing Add: 4215 Peach Tree Pl Alexandria VA 22304

HAMILTON, LONNIE, III (D)
Exec Committeeman, Charleston Co Dem Party, SC
b Charleston, SC, Nov 14, 27; s Lonnie Hamilton, Jr & Anna Hall H; m 1956 to Clarissa L Hill; c Kendra Y. Educ: SC State Col, BS, 51; Vandercook Col Music, MMed, 63; Omega Psi Phi. Polit & Govt Pos: Councilman, Charleston Co, SC, 70-, chmn, Purchase & Bids Comt, 75; alt deleg, Dem Nat Conv, 72; exec committeeman, Charleston Co Dem Party, SC, 74- Bus & Prof Pos: High sch teacher, Union, SC, 53-55, North Charleston, 55- Mil Serv: Entered as Pvt, Army, 51, released as Cpl, 53, after serv in Antiaircraft Artil, Korea, 52-53. Mem: Nat, SC & Charleston Co Educ Asns. Relig: Episcopal. Mailing Add: 22 Leola St Charleston Heights SC 29405

HAMILTON, MARY ELLEN (R)
b Great Bend, Kans, Aug 4, 21; d Jay Abram Sitterley & Evelyn Buechner S; m 1943 to William H Hamilton; c Mary Ellen (Mrs Joseph Lakin Lockett) & William H, III. Educ: Univ Kans, 40-43. Polit & Govt Pos: Secy, Coconino Co Rep Women's Unit, Ariz, 60, pres, 63 & 64; asst secy, Coconino Co Rep Cent Comt, 61-65, chmn, formerly; campaign off mgr for elections of 62, 64 & 68; state chmn, Mamie Eisenhower Libr Proj, 65, 66 & 67; deleg, Rep Nat Conv, 68. Mem: Beta Sigma Phi. Relig: Protestant. Mailing Add: 24 W Oak Flagstaff AZ 86001

HAMILTON, MILTON HUGH, JR (D)
Tenn State Sen
b Union City, Tenn, Sept 8, 32; s Milton Hamilton, Sr & Novelle Rogers H; m 1953 to Dale White; c Milton, III, Ann Barrett & David Blanton. Educ: Memphis State Univ, 3 years; Murray State Univ, BA; Kappa Alpha; Inter Fraternity Coun. Polit & Govt Pos: Chmn, Union City Sch Bd, Tenn, 60-64; vchmn, Fiscal Rev Comt, State Tenn; comnr, Tenn Educ Compact of States; Tenn State Rep, Obion, Weakley & Lake Co, 64-68; Tenn State Sen, Obion, Weakley, Henry, Carroll & Lake Co, 24th Dist, 68- Mil Serv: Entered as 2nd Lt, Army, 55, released as 1st Lt, 57, after serv in Antiaircraft Artil & Guided Missile Sch, Ft Bliss, Tex; Maj, Army, Nat Guard, 57-; Distinguished Mil Student & Distinguished Mil Grad. Mem: Mason; KT; Rotary; CofC; Tenn Sch Bd Asn. Honors & Awards: Selected Tenn Outstanding Young Man of 64 by Tenn Jaycees; Phillips Petrol Co Mr Phil Award for Community Serv. Relig: Methodist; mem, Bd of Stewards. Mailing Add: 920 Whirmantler Dr Union City TN 38261

HAMILTON, PAT R (D)
WVa State Sen
Mailing Add: PO Box 115 Oak Hill WV 25901

HAMILTON, ROBERT K (D)
b Roswell, NMex, Sept 3, 05; s James C Hamilton & Alma L Ritchey H; m 1945 to Jean Hunt; c William & James. Educ: Pa State Univ, BS; Duquesne Univ, JD; Alpha Zeta; Phi Kappa Sigma. Polit & Govt Pos: Mem, Soil Conserv Comt Beaver Co, formerly; Pa State Rep, 40-72, chmn, Ins Comt, 55-57 & 61-62; Pa House Rep, vchmn, Local Govt Comn, 61-62, vchmn, Comn on Interstate Coop, 61-62, treas, 69-70, mem, Rules & Appropriations Comts, Comt on Higher Educ, Gen State Authority, State Hwy & Bridge Authority, State Pub Schs, Bldg Authority & Legis Budget & Finance Comt, 65-66, treas, Joint State Comn, 65-66, Speaker of the House, 65-66, chmn, Policy Comt, 67-68, chmn Ways & Means Comt, 69-72; mem, intergovt rels comt & task force on com & transportation, Coun State Govt, 70-; legis liaison off, Dept Mil Affairs, Commonwealth of Pa, 73- Bus & Prof Pos: Former farmer; ins agent. Mil Serv: 2nd Lt, ROTC Inf, 28-30; 2nd Lt, Battery B, 107th Field Artil, Off Res Corps & Pa Nat Guard Res. Mem: Nat Soc State Legislators; Mason; Grange; Elks; AFL. Honors & Awards: Outstanding Alumni Award, Dept of Animal Indust & Nutrition, Pa State Univ, 65 & from the Univ, 66. Relig: Methodist; Lay leader, Ambridge First United Methodist Church. Mailing Add: 917 Maplewood Ave Ambridge PA 15003

HAMILTON, THOMAS DEWAYNE (D)
Mem Exec Comt, Dem Party Ga
b Great Falls, Mont, Mar 7, 51; parents deceased; m 1975 to Cynthia Ann Marshall. Educ: Armstrong State Col, grad polit sci & econ, 75; Young Dem; vchmn, Student Adv Coun to Bd of Regents, 74-75, chmn, 75-; pres, Student Govt, 75-; Sigma Nu. Polit & Govt Pos: Mem, Savannah City Dem Exec Comt, Ga, 74-; mem exec comt, Dem Party Ga, 75- Mil Serv: Entered as E-1, Air Force, 69, released as Sgt, 73. Mem: Chatham Co Young Dem (asst to chmn); Ga State Young Dem (asst to dir membership & finance). Honors & Awards: Outstanding Sen, Armstrong State Col Student Govt, 74-75; Outstanding Serv to Student Adv Coun to Bd of Regents, 74-75. Relig: Baptist. Mailing Add: Versailles Apts Apt C-14 10612 Abercorn Savannah GA 31406

HAMILTON, WILLIAM J, JR (D)
NJ State Assemblyman
b New Brunswick, NJ, Dec 26, 32; s William J Hamilton & May V Mulligan H; m 1958 to Barbara Brown; c William Joseph, III, Brian Reedy, Sheila Ann & Michael Sean. Educ: Rutgers Col, AB, 54; Georgetown Univ Law Sch, JD, 60; Phi Delta Phi (pres, 60); Sigma Phi Epsilon; Newman Club. Polit & Govt Pos: First asst US attorney, Mid Dist, Fla, 62-67; dir, Civil Defense-Disaster Control, New Brunswick, NJ, 70-71; NJ State Assemblyman, 72-; mem, NJ State Higher Educ Master Plan Rev Comn, 72-; chmn, Real Estate Title Ins Study Comn, 73- Bus & Prof Pos: Law clerk, US Dist Judge Bryan Simpson, Jacksonville, Fla, 60-61; attorney, Turner & Hamilton, 61-62, Hamilton & Mulligan, 70-; assoc attorney, Pincus, Shamy & Sheehan, New Brunswick, NJ, 67-70. Mil Serv: Entered as Seaman Recruit, Naval Res, 52, released as A/S, 54, recalled as Ens, 54-58, Lt(jg), 58; Comdr & Naval Aviator, Res, currently. Mem: Am Bar Asn; New Brunswick Bar Asn (trustee, 67-); Am Arbit Asn; KofC; Elks. Honors & Awards: Citation, Allied Servicemen/Alpha Sigma Mu, 73. Relig: Roman Catholic. Legal Res: 230 New York Ave New Brunswick NJ 08903 Mailing Add: 96 Bayard St PO Box 1231 New Brunswick NJ 08903

HAMLETT, RAY (D)
Mo State Rep
Mailing Add: PO Box 38 Laddonia MO 63352

HAMLIN, JOHN G (R)
Colo State Rep
Mailing Add: 815 Diana Fort Morgan CO 80701

HAMM, LEE (D)
Kans State Rep
Mailing Add: RR 1 Pratt KS 67124

HAMMER, CHARLES LAWRENCE (D)
Mem, Iowa State Dem Cent Comt
b Buffalo, NY, June 30, 22; s Charles Lawrence Hammer, Sr & Maxine Burdick H; m 1948 to Hazel Churchill Mills; c David Lawrence, Alison Rae Cocks, Carla Louise & Bonnie Sue. Educ: Univ Mich, Ann Arbor, BA, 48, MS, 50, PhD, 53; Sigma Xi; Phi Beta Kappa; Phi Kappa Phi; Gamma Alpha. Polit & Govt Pos: Precinct committeeman, Story Co Dem Party, Iowa, 58-71; exec secy, Iowa Scientists & Engrs for Johnson-Humphrey, 64; chmn, Iowa Dem Conf, 70-72; committeeman, Fifth Cong Dist Dem Party, 74-; mem, Iowa State Dem Cent Comt, 74- Bus & Prof Pos: Instr physics, Univ Mich, Ann Arbor, 53-54; research assoc, Iowa State Univ, 54-55, asst prof physics & assoc physicist, Ames Lab, 55-59, assoc prof physics & physicist, Ames Lab, 59-61, prof physics & sr physicist, Ames Lab, 61- Mil Serv: Entered as Cadet Pvt, Army Air Force, 43, released as 1st Lt, 46, after serv in 330th Bombardment Group, Pac Theatre, 45; Distinguished Flying Cross with Oak Leaf Cluster; Air Medal with 3 Oak Leaf Clusters; Pac Theatre Opers Medal. Publ: Var prof papers publ by Am Phys Soc, 53- Mem: Am Phys Soc (fel); Centro Superiore de Logica e Scienze Comparate (assoc adv). Relig: Unitarian. Mailing Add: 1222 Scholl Rd Ames IA 50010

HAMMER, MARY LOU SIMPSON (R)
Secy, Weber Co Rep Party, Utah
b Syracuse, Utah, July 13, 34; d John George Simpson & Edith Elizabeth Hardy S; m 1958 to Clyde Ross Hammer; c Paul Clyde & Julie. Educ: Weber Col, 53-54; United Airlines, Stewardess Training, 57; Utah State Univ, 59-60. Polit & Govt Pos: Co secy, Young Rep, Utah, 65-67; deleg, Utah Rep Conv, 67-75; secy, Weber Co Rep Party, 74-, mem cent comt & exec comt, 74- Bus & Prof Pos: Admin asst, Thiokol Chem Corp, Ogden & Brigham City, Utah, 58-63; consult, Whittaker Corp, San Diego, Calif, 64-65; prof secretarial serv, Ogden, Utah, 67-; instr shorthand, Ogden City Schs, 68- Mem: Jr League Ogden; Ogden Symphony Guild (secy, 75-, mem bd dirs & exec comt, 75-). Relig: Latter-day Saint. Mailing Add: 4123 Bona Villa Dr Ogden UT 84403

HAMMERSCHMIDT, JOHN PAUL (R)
US Rep, Ark
b Harrison, Ark, May 4, 22; m to Virginia Sharp; c John Arthur. Educ: The Citadel; Univ Ark; Okla A&M. Polit & Govt Pos: Rep State Committeeman, mem, Rep Nat Finance Comn & Harrison City Coun, Ark, formerly, deleg, Rep Nat Conv, 64; chmn, Rep State Cent Comt, 64-66; US Rep, Ark, 66- Bus & Prof Pos: Bd dirs, Harrison Fed Savings & Loan Asn; chmn bd, Hammerschmidt Lumber Co. Mil Serv: Army Air Corps, 2nd Lt, 42; Maj, Air Force Res; Distinguished Flying Cross with Three Oak Leaf Clusters; Air Medal with Four Oak Leaf Clusters; Three Battle Stars. Mem: Nat Lumber & Bldg Material Dealers Asn (bd dir); Mason; Elks; Am Legion; VFW. Honors & Awards: Harrison Man of the Year, 65; Nat Fedn Independent Bus Man of Year for Ark, 71 & 72. Relig: Presbyterian; Bd of Elders, Ordained Elder & Deacon. Mailing Add: Harrison AR 72601

HAMMOCK, CHARLES PAUL (D)
Pa State Rep
s Charles Paul Hammock, Sr & Mary H; single. Educ: Villanova Univ, BS, 63; Howard Sch Law, JD, 66; Blue Key. Polit & Govt Pos: Pa State Rep, 196th Dist, 72- Bus & Prof Pos: Court adminr, Philadelphia Criminal Courts, 67-71; with Boeing Co, Philadelphia, 71-72. Relig: Roman Catholic. Legal Res: 1726 W Atlantic St Philadelphia PA 19140 Mailing Add: 3761 N 17th St Philadelphia PA 19140

HAMMOND, EVERT NEWTON (R)
Chmn, Pike Co Rep Cent Comt, Ohio
b Pike Co, Ohio, Aug 17, 17; s Sherman Eli Hammond & Mary Alice Lowe H; m 1939 to Bernice Edith Dunlap. Educ: Wakefield High Sch, Ohio, 3 years. Polit & Govt Pos: Mem, Pike Co Bd Elect, Ohio; chmn, Pike Co Rep Cent & Exec Comts, 66-; alt deleg, Sixth Cong Dist, Rep Nat Conv, 68. Bus & Prof Pos: Farmer. Mem: Pike Co Rep Club; Farm Bur; Cattlemen's Asn. Relig: Protestant. Mailing Add: Box 416 RR 1 Piketon OH 45661

HAMMOND, F MELVIN (D)
Idaho State Rep
b Blackfoot, Idaho, Dec 19, 33; s Floyd Milton Hammond & Ruby Hoge H; m 1956 to Bonnie Sellers; c Melanie, Lezlee, Stephanie, Todd & Lisa. Educ: Ricks Col, 51-53; Brigham Young Univ, BA, 58, MA, 62; Univ Colo, 63-67. Polit & Govt Pos: Idaho State Rep, 69-, Minority Leader, Idaho House Rep, 73- Bus & Prof Pos: Prof, Ricks Col, Rexburg, Idaho, 66-69. Relig: Latter-day Saint. Mailing Add: 149 Elm Ave Rexburg ID 83440

HAMMOND, JAY STERNER (R)
Gov, Alaska
b Troy, NY, July 21, 22; s Morris A Hammond & Edna Brown Sterner H; m 1952 to Bella Gardiner; c Heidi & Dana. Educ: Pa State Univ, 2 years; Univ Alaska, BS, 48. Polit & Govt Pos: Alaska State Rep, Bristol Bay, 59-65; Alaska State Sen, 67-72, majority leader, Alaska State Senate, 69-71, pres, 71-72; mayor, Bristol Bay Borough, formerly; Gov, Alaska, 75- Bus & Prof Pos: Govt hunter, US Fish & Wildlife Serv, 49-56; mgr, Bristol Bay Borough, 65-66; licensed master guide; owner, Lake Clark Lodge. Mil Serv: Entered as Seaman 2/C, Naval Flight Cadets, 42, released as Capt, Marine Corps Res, 46, after serv in VMF 211 Fighter Pilot, SPac Theatre, 45. Publ: Several outdoor articles; one book of verse. Mem: VFW. Honors & Awards: Legis Conservationist of the Year Award, Alaska, 70. Relig: Protestant. Mailing Add: Pouch A Juneau AK 99801

HAMMOND, NELLIE HANDCOCK (D)
First VChmn, Yuma Co Dem Cent Comt, Ariz
b Okla, Mar 12, 09; d Benjamin Lucas Handcock & Lavina Jones H; m 1937 to Leland Lawrence Hammond; c Lelia Mae (Mrs John Foty), Kathleen (Mrs Earnest Munoz) & Lee Vernon (deceased). Polit & Govt Pos: Pres, Yuma Dem Womans Club, 69-70, courtesy chmn, currently, mem-at-lg, Third Cong Dist Dem Party, 70-71, committeeman, Precinct 1, 8 years; pres, Ariz Fedn Dem Womens Clubs, 71-72; first vchmn, Yuma Co Dem Cent Comt, 75- Bus & Prof Pos: Monitor, Ground Observer Corps, Air Defense Command, 57-58. Mem: Ladies of the Elks 476; Yuma Women Reel & Rifle Club, Mittry Lake (chmn & publicity chmn). Honors & Awards: Woodmen of the World Conservation Award, 68; Salesmanship Award, Yuma Dem Cent Comt, 69-70; Mittry Lake Improvement Award, 70; Dem Woman Doer Award, 71. Relig: Methodist. Mailing Add: 133 Fourth Ave Yuma AZ 85364

HAMMONDS, RICHARD LEE, SR (D)
Mem, Ga State Dem Exec Comt
b Henry Co, Ga, Apr 25, 35; s Emory Howard Hammonds & Willie Richardson H; m 1956 to Katherine Yvonne Ridley; c Terri, Lisa, Tracey, Connie, Jerri & Richard, Jr. Educ: Auburn Univ, 53-56; Emory Univ Sch Med, MD, 60; Phi Chi. Polit & Govt Pos: Chmn, Cobb Co Bd of Health, 64-68; mem, Ga State Dem Exec Comt, 70-; mem, Ga State Bd Offender Rehabilitation, 72- Bus & Prof Pos: Chief staff, Cobb Gen Hosp, 68-70. Mil Serv: Entered as Lt, Air Force, 60, released as Capt, 62; Med Units. Mem: Am & Ga Med Asns; Am Acad Gen Practice; Cobb Med Soc; Rotary. Relig: Baptist. Mailing Add: 4820 Springdale Rd Austell GA 30001

HAMMONS, JOHN LAYNE (R)
b New Orleans, La, Apr 5, 51; s Samuel Dean Hammons & Etoil Adams H; single. Educ: Northeast La Univ, BA, 73; Phi Kappa Phi; Phi Eta Sigma; Phi Alpha Theta; Sigma Tau Gamma; pres, Student Govt, 72-73. Polit & Govt Pos: Deleg, La State Rep Conv, 72; deleg, Rep Nat Conv, 72; mem, La Rules Comt, 72; campaign mgr, Dav Treen, Caldwell Parish, 72. Bus & Prof Pos: Ins clerk, Caldwell Hosp & Clin, 69-72. Honors & Awards: Outstanding Lib Arts Student, Optimist Club, 72-73; Outstanding Sr Man, Northeast La Univ, 72-73. Relig: Baptist. Mailing Add: Box 852 Columbia LA 71418

HAMMONS, MARK EDGAR (D)
Okla State Rep
b Oklahoma City, Okla, Apr 1, 50; s Kenneth Hammons & Trudy Rice H (deceased); single. Educ: Univ Okla, BBA, 73; Lambda Chi Alpha. Polit & Govt Pos: State pres, Okla Young Dem, 71-72; state youth coordr, Okla Dem Party, currently; Okla State Rep, Dist 43, 73- Mil Serv: Army Res, 356th Transportation Co, 71- Mem: Jaycees; Kiwanis. Honors & Awards: Univ Scholar; Nat Merit Scholar; One of Top Ten Freshmen, Univ Okla; State Champion Am Heritage Orator. Relig: Roman Catholic. Mailing Add: 1403 S Miles El Reno OK 73036

HAMMONS, OWEN CECIL (D)
Mem-at-large, Jefferson Co Dem Exec Comt, Ky
b Horton, Ky, Dec 19, 22; s Leslie Thompson Hammons & Ivy Taylor H; m 1940 to Martha Gray Peters; c Martha Katherine (Mrs Hay) & Cecilia Ann (Mrs Finnell). Educ: Purdue Univ. Polit & Govt Pos: Mem, Dem Nat Comt & Dem Club of Ky formerly; deleg, Dem Nat Conv, 68; mem, Mayor's Adv Comt, Louisville, Ky, formerly, comnr, Improv Dist, currently; mem-at-large, Jefferson Co Dem Exec Comt, 73- Bus & Prof Pos: Pres, Local 862, UAW, 48-61; int rep UAW, 61- Mil Serv: Entered as Pvt, Marine Corps, 45, released as Pfc, 46, after serv in 1st Div, SPac. Mem: F&AM; Eastern Star; Scottish Rite; Kosair Shrine; Community Action. Relig: Protestant. Mailing Add: 7307 Nottoway Circle Louisville KY 40214

HAMPTON, LEWIS BURDETT (R)
Chmn, First Dist Rep Party, Ore
b Wenatchee, Wash, June 12, 33; s John Lewis Hampton & Mary Smith H; m 1955 to Jodie Lou Johannaber; c Dane, Molly, Kent & Adam. Educ: Willamette Univ, BA, 55, JD, 60; Phi Eta Sigma; Pi Gamma Mu; Tau Kappa Alpha; Omicron Delta Kappa; Phi Delta Phi. Polit & Govt Pos: Dep legis counsel, Ore State Legis, 60-61; dep dist attorney, Multnomah Co, Portland, 63-66; spec counsel to secy state, 71-72; Ore State Rep, Dist Five, Washington Co, 73-74; chmn, First Dist Rep Party, 75- Bus & Prof Pos: Attorney, Reiter, Day & Anderson, Portland, Ore, 61-63; mem, Myatt, Bolliger, Hampton, PC, Beaverton, Ore, 66- Mil Serv: Entered as 2nd Lt, Air Force, 55, released as 1st Lt, 58 after serv in 49th Fighter Bomber Wing, 5th Air Force PACAF, Pac Air Forces Misawa AFB, Japan, 55-58; Maj Judge Adv Gen Dept, Air Force Res, 55-73; Distinguished Mil Student; Distinguished Mil Grad. Publ: Proof of damages-wrongful death, Willamette Law J, 60; Punitive damages, 73 & Nominal damages, 73, Ore State Bar Continuing Legal Educ. Mem: Ore State Bar; Beaverton Area CofC; Kiwanis. Honors & Awards: First Citizen of Beaverton, 73. Relig: Presbyterian. Legal Res: 1700 NW 137th Portland OR 97229 Mailing Add: 4250 SW Cedar Hills Blvd Beaverton OR 97005

HAMPTON, MASON LILLARD, JR (CONSERVATIVE, NY)
VChmn, NY State Conservative Party
b Westgrove, Pa, Nov 29, 30; s Mason Lillard Hampton & Nora Schuyler H; m 1957 to Jean Sprower; c Linda Jean, John Wade & Katherine Lee. Educ: Va Polytech Inst, BS, 51; Washington & Lee Univ, LLB, 56; Omicron Delta Kappa; Tau Kappa Alpha. Polit & Govt Pos: Nominee, US Rep, NY, 68; vchmn, NY State Conservative Party, 68- Bus & Prof Pos: Assoc lawyer, Townsend & Lewis, NY, 56-61; law partner, Gaylor & Hampton, Lynbrook, NY, 62- Mil Serv: Entered as 2nd Lt, Army, 53, released as 1st Lt, 55, after serv in 24th Inf Div, Korea, 53-55. Mem: Phi Alpha Delta; Nassau Co Bar Asn; Nassau-Suffolk Trial Lawyers. Relig: Lutheran. Mailing Add: 15 Margaret Blvd Merrick NY 11563

HAMPTON, ROBERT EDWARD (R)
Chmn, US Civil Serv Comn
b Chattanooga, Tenn, Sept 21, 22; s Charles Alfred Hampton (deceased) & Mary Lee Plemons H; m 1947 to Geraldyne A Stivers; c Adrienne Ann & Jeffrey Scott. Educ: Univ Tenn, 46-48; Univ Chattanooga, BA in Bus Admin, 49. Polit & Govt Pos: Vice-consul, Dept State, Munich, Ger, 50-52; foreign affairs officer, Exec Secretariat, 52-53; staff asst to Secy of State, 53-55; asst dep manpower, personnel & orgn, Dept Air Force, 55-57; spec asst to under secy for admin, State Dept, 57-58; spec asst for personnel, White House, 58-61; comnr, US Civil Serv Comn, 61-69, chmn, 69- Bus & Prof Pos: Prin, Blackfox Sch, Cleveland, Tenn, 49-50; chmn, Fed Labor Rels Coun; mem, President's Comn on White House Fels, President's Comt on the Handicapped, Int Civil Serv Comn, Bd Foreign Serv; mem, Gen Admin Bd Grad Sch, Dept Agr; mem, President's Econ Adjustment Comt, 73- Mil Serv: Army Air Force, 42-45, ETO. Mem: Nat Acad Pub Admin. Honors & Awards: Named Young Republican of Year, 60; Silver Helmet Award, Amvets, 70; Stockberger Award, Soc for Personnel Admin, 71; Exec Govt Award, Opportunities Industrialization Ctrs, Inc, 72; Award of Merit, Fed Admin Law Judges Conf, 74. Legal Res: 10 Savannah Ct Bethesda MD 20034 Mailing Add: US Civil Serv Comn Washington DC 20415

HAMPTON, ROGER JOE (D)
Chmn, Iron Co Dem Comt, Mo
b Annapolis, Mo, Oct 19, 41; s Richard Winfred Hampton & Irene Jackson H; m July 4 to Janice Marie Nelson; c Barbara Jean & Roger Joe, Jr. Educ: McKinley High Sch, St Louis, Mo, 2 years. Polit & Govt Pos: Committeeman, Union Twp, Mo, 70-; chmn, Iron Co Dem Comt, 70- Mem: United Automobile Workers of Am. Mailing Add: PO Box 296 Annapolis MO 63620

HAMPTON, THELMA A HAYES (D)
Committeewoman, Mo State Dem Comt
b Green Castle, Mo, Sept 12, 08; d Sam M Campbell & Rosetta (Rosa) Schillie C; m to Gail L Hayes, wid; remarried 1972 to Archie Hampton. Educ: Northeast Mo State Col. Polit & Govt Pos: Dep co treas & ex-officio collector, Sullivan Co, Mo, 37-44, co treas & ex-officio collector, 44-57; twp committeewoman & vchmn, Sullivan Co, Dem Comt, 57-70; committeewoman, Mo State Dem Comt, 70-; committeewoman, Liberty Twp, currently. Bus & Prof Pos: Secy, Motor Vehicle Registr, Sullivan Co, Mo. Mem: Am Legion Auxiliary; Bus & Prof Women's Club. Relig: Baptist. Mailing Add: RFD Harris MO 64645

HAMPTON, WAYNE (D)
Ark State Rep
Mailing Add: Star Route Stuttgart AR 72160

HAMRA, SAM F, JR (D)
Chmn, Seventh Cong Dist Dem Comt, Mo
b Steele, Mo, Jan 21, 32; s Sam Farris Hamra, Sr & Victoria H; m 1956 to June S Samaha; c Sam F, III, Karen Escine, Michael Kenneth & Jacqueline Kay. Educ: Univ Mo-Columbia, BS, 54, Law Sch, LLB, 59; Phi Delta Phi (pres, 58-59); Kappa Sigma. Polit & Govt Pos: Secy, Warren E Hearnes for Gov Comt, Greene Co, Mo, 62-64; Hon Col, Gov Warren E Hearnes Staff, 64-72; spec asst, Attorney Gen of Mo, 66-68; southwest Mo campaign mgr, True Davis for US Sen Comt, 68; vchmn, Jackson Day Banquet Comt 70; Southwest Mo finance & campaign chmn, Stuart Symington for US Sen Comt, 70; committeeman, Ward 32, Greene Co Dem Party Mo, 70-; chmn, 141st Legis Dist Dem Party, 70-; chmn, Seventh Cong Dist Dem Comt, 70-; deleg, Dem Nat Conv, 72. Bus & Prof Pos: Partner, Hamra & Crow, Attorneys at Law, Springfield, Mo. Mil Serv: Entered as 2nd Lt, Army, 54, released as 1st Lt, 56, after serv in Field Artil, Command, 55. Publ: Law Student Internship Program, Mo Bar J, 67. Mem: AF&AM; Joplin Consistory Number 3; Shrine; Springfield CofC (bd dirs, 71-); Rotary. Honors & Awards: Henry Giessenbier Award, 64; US Jr CofC Clarence H Howard Award, 64; Springfield's Outstanding Young Man of the Year Award, 66; Mo Outstanding Young Man of the Year Award, 67; nominated for US Jaycee TOYM, 67. Relig: Episcopal; St James Episcopal Church, Bishop's comt, 59-60, first pres, Men's Club, 60, lay reader, 60-, vestryman, 60-63, 70-71. Legal Res: 2704 S Marlan Springfield MO 65804 Mailing Add: 1722 H S Glenstone Springfield MO 65804

HAMZY, JOSEPH AMIN (R)
Mem, Falls Village Rep Town Comt, Conn
b Becket, Mass, Feb 26, 15; s Amin Abu Hamzy & Friede H; m 1940 to Evelyn Ruth Goodrich; c Joseph Amin, Jr & Beth. Educ: Am Univ, Beirut, Lebanon. Polit & Govt Pos: Chmn bd educ, Falls Village, Conn, 39-45, Justice of the Peace, 41-; Conn State Rep, 43-47; co treas, 49-60; chmn, Falls Village Rep Town Comt, 60-70, mem, 70-; Judge of Probate, Dist Canaan, 60- Mem: Mason (32 degree); Consistory; Commandery; Shrine. Relig: Protestant. Mailing Add: RD Beebe Hill Rd Falls Village CT 06031

HANAHAN, THOMAS J (D)
Ill State Sen
Mailing Add: 2012 W Grandview Dr McHenry IL 60050

HANAWAY, G FRANK (D)
RI State Sen
Mailing Add: Box 136 Diamond Hill Rd Cumberland RI 02864

HANAWAY, PAUL E (D)
RI State Rep
Mailing Add: 591 Hines Rd Cumberland RI 02864

HANCE, KENT (D)
Tex State Sen
Mailing Add: 1603 Broadway Lubbock TX 79401

HANCOCK, CHARLES M (D)
Ky State Rep
Mailing Add: 514 Murray St Frankfort KY 40601

HANCOCK, CLARA C (R)
Chmn, York Co Rep Party, Va
b Lexington, Ky, Dec 22, 14; d William Jefferson Clark & A Katherine Snyder C; m 1939 to William Andrew Hancock; c Mark J. Educ: Maryland Inst Art, 35-36; Christopher Newport Col, 63-65; William & Mary Summer Col, 63-64. Polit & Govt Pos: Coordr for census, Counties of York, Gloucester & Mathews, Va, 60; campaign chmn, York Co Rep Party, 60-74; chmn, York Co Rep Party, 60-; pres, York Co Rep Women's Club, 61-63; rep, First Dist Va Fedn Rep Women, 63-64; vchmn, First Sen Dist Rep Orgn, 63-; cand, Va State Sen, 65; mem, Va Rep State Cent Comt, 65-; mem, York Co Prob Study Group & York Co Rep to Hampton Roads Area Comt, 68-; alt deleg, Rep Nat Conv, 68. Bus & Prof Pos: Off mgr, Fuel Distributor, 32-39. Mem: York High PTA; Eastern Star; York Co Rep Assembly; Heritage Rep Womens Club (pres, 73-); VFW Auxiliary. Relig: Lutheran. Mailing Add: Box 204 Robanna Shores Seaford VA 23692

HANCOCK, DON (D)
Mo State Rep
b Pine, Mo, July 28, 34; m 1953 to Avanell Jackson; c Steve, Sherry & Stan. Educ: Southeast Mo State Col; Northern Ill Univ; Ark State Col. Polit & Govt Pos: Mo State Rep, 64- Bus & Prof Pos: Salesman; sch teacher. Mil Serv: Army, Paratroopers, 54-56. Mem: Lions; CofC. Relig: Protestant. Mailing Add: 906 Lafayette Doniphan MO 63935

HANCOCK, JOHN ELLSWORTH (R)
Vt State Rep
Mailing Add: East Hardwick VT 05836

HANCOCK, NOLAN WARD (D)
Chmn, Jefferson Co Dem Comt, Idaho
b Lewisville, Idaho, May 22, 32; s Ward Hancock & Rosetta Fife H; m 1961 to Barbara Ann Clark; c Joan Marie, Robert Nolan, Linda Lee & David Lynn. Educ: Brigham Young Univ, 50, & Idaho, 68; Univ Idaho, 69-70. Polit & Govt Pos: Precinct committeeman, Jefferson Co Dem Comt, Idaho, 70, chmn, 70-; regional campaign coordr, Gov Cecil Andrus Campaign, 70; regional Dem chmn, Dem Orgn, 71; exec secy, Idaho Dem Cent Comt, 72-; deleg, Dem Nat Conv, 72. Bus & Prof Pos: Mem staff, Nuclear Instrument Maintenance, Idaho Nuclear Corp, 65- Mem: Instrument Soc of Am; Oil Chem & Atomic Workers Int Union Local 2-652 (secy-treas, 65-71, 1st vpres, Dist Coun Two, Nine West State Union Orgn, 69-71); Idaho Falls Cent Labor Coun (vpres, 71); Idaho State AFL-CIO; Toastmasters. Relig: Latter-day Saint. Mailing Add: Rte 1 Box 99A Rigby ID 83442

HANCOCK, OSCAR WALKER (D)
Chmn, Pickens Co Dem Comt, Ala
b Ethelsville, Ala, Oct 17, 03; s Thomas Jeremiah Hancock & Iva Pridmore H; m 1923 to Mary Eloise Sanders; c Martha Jean (Mrs William Lang), Oscar Walker, Jr, Charles Sanders & James Turiman. Educ: Birmingham Southern Col, 22-23; Alpha Tau Omega. Polit & Govt Pos: Mem, Selective Serv Bd, Pickens Co, Ala, 41-46; mayor, Ethelsville, 56-; chmn, Pickens Co Dem Comt, 54-69 & 73-; mem, Pickens Co Agr Comt, 61-69; mem, Pickens Co Action Comt, 67-69; legis agent, Pickens Co, 68- Mem: Farm Bur; Pickens Co 4-H (chmn & founder, 63-); Rotary; Civitan Club; Mason. Honors & Awards: Leadership Award, Pickens Co, Ala, 71. Relig: Methodist; Chmn Bd, Lay Leader, Sunday Sch Supt. Mailing Add: PO Box 8 Ethelsville AL 35461

HANCOCK, RICHARD WILSON (D)
b Beeville, Tex, Mar 4, 46; s James M Hancock & Dorothy Wilson H; single. Educ: Univ Houston, BS, 73; Pi Kappa Alpha; vpres, Student Body, 67. Polit & Govt Pos: Aide to Marvin Watson, spec asst to the President, Washington, DC, 68; co-chmn youth records, Young Rep Nat Fedn, formerly; admin asst, State Rep, Sid Bowers, 72; admin dir, Tex Dem Party, 73; Gov Staff Budgetary Affairs, Tex, 73- Bus & Prof Pos: Pub affairs off, Manned Spacecraft Ctr, NASA, Houston, Tex, 68-71; gen mgr, Mitee Electronics, 71-72. Mem: Southwest & Tex Cattle Raisers Asn (legis affairs comt); Tex Elec Officials Asn (pres, 74-). Relig: Catholic. Mailing Add: Westgate Apts Suite 1710 1122 Colorado Austin TX 78701

HAND, CARROLL RAYNER (D)
Chmn, Chambers Co Dem Party, Tex
b Corrigan, Tex, Oct 15, 18; s Lawson Jefferson Hand & Beulah May Raynor H; m 1958 to Lillian Lucille Copehand. Educ: Baylor Univ Law Sch, LLB, 42, JD, 69. Polit & Govt Pos: Chmn, Chambers Co Dem Party, Tex, 75- Bus & Prof Pos: Owner, Carroll R Hand Ins, 55- Mem: Lions; Elks; Mason; Scottish Rite (32 degree); Shrine. Relig: Southern Baptist. Legal Res: 508 Donna Dr Anahuac TX 77514 Mailing Add: Box 1000 Anahuac TX 77514

HAND, LLOYD NELSON (D)
b Alton, Ill, Jan 31, 29; s Nelson T Hand & Robbie Omega Taylor H; m 1952 to Lucy Ann Donoghue; c Catherine Marie, Lloyd Nelson, II, Susan Louise, Bridget Ann & Thomas Lyndon. Educ: Univ Tex, BA, 52, LLB, 57; Friar Soc. Polit & Govt Pos: US Sen, Calif & asst to Vice President Lyndon B Johnson, 57-61; financial coordr for Calif Johnson-Humphrey Campaign, 64; deleg, Dem Nat Conv, 65; mem, Calif Dem Cent Comn, formerly; Chief of Protocol, The White House, 65-66. Bus & Prof Pos: Lawyer, 57-, mem law firm, Wyman, Bautzer, Rothman & Kuchel; vpres & dir, Pierce Nat Life Ins Co, Los Angeles; pres, Worldwide Consults, Inc; dir, Continental Airlines & Continental Air Serv. Mil Serv: Lt, Naval Res, 51-55. Mem: Univ Tex Ex-Students Asn; Burning Tree Country Club; Bel-Air Country Club; Cong Country Club. Legal Res: 166 Groverton Pl Los Angeles CA 90024 Mailing Add: Suite 2000 10100 Santa Monica Blvd Los Angeles CA 90067

HANDLEY, HELEN M (R)
Committeewoman, Tenn Rep State Exec Comt
b Jefferson Co, Ala, Nov 18, 21; d James Oliver Mullins & Carrie Abel M; m 1941 to Thomas H Handley, Sr; c Hetty Patricia (Mrs Hugh Nevin, III); Thomas H, Jr & Mary Catherine. Educ: Bus Col. Polit & Govt Pos: Pres, Oak Ridge Rep Women Club, 68-72; co-chmn, Bill Brock Campaign for US Senate, 70; vchmn, Third Cong Dist Tenn Rep Party, 73-; third dist chmn for Congressman Lamar Baker, 74-; vchmn & mem steering comt, Anderson Co Rep Exec Comt, 68-; committeewoman, Tenn Rep State Exec Comt, 74- Bus & Prof Pos: Pres & founder, Anderson Co Arthritis Clin, 67-; pres, Tenn Collectors Ann, 68-69; int dir, Am Collectors Asn, 70; owner, Anderson Co Adjustment Co, currently. Publ: Ed & publ, Tenn

Collectors Magazine, 69- Mem: Oak Ridge CofC; Oak Ridge Women Club; Beta Sigma Phi; PTA. Relig: Baptist. Mailing Add: 103 Delaware Ave Oak Ridge TN 37830

HANDLEY, WILLIAM J

b Netherlands Guiana, Dec 17, 18; s Am citizens; married. Educ: Univ London, 35-37; Univ Md, BA, 42; Am Univ, 43-44. Polit & Govt Pos: Priority specialist, War Prod Bd, 42-44; analyst, Foreign Econ Admin, 44; econ analyst, Foreign Serv Auxiliary, 44; attache, Cairo, Egypt, 45, Addis Ababa, Baghdad, Beirut, Damascus, Jerusalem, Jidda & Teheran, 47; US observer, 1st Int Labor Orgn meeting for Near E govt, 47; assigned to Dept of State, 48-49, labor adv, Bur Near E, SAsian & African Affairs, 49-51, labor adv, Off of Asst Secy of State, 51; pub affairs officer & attache, New Delhi, India, 51-52, planning officer & attache, 52-53; joined Info Agency, New Delhi, 53, dep chief pub affairs officer & attache, 54-55; assigned to Info Agency, Washington, 55-61, chief, Near E Policy staff, 55-56, dep asst dir, Near E, SAsia & Africa, 56-57, asst dir, 57-61; US Ambassador to Mali, 61-64; dep asst secy for Near Eastern Affairs, Dept of State, 64-69; US Ambassador to Turkey, 69-72. Bus & Prof Pos: Announcer & prog writer, broadcasting sta, 36-39; mgr import co, British Guiana, 37-39. Honors & Awards: Recipient of Superior Serv Award, Info Agency, 56. Mailing Add: c/o Dept of State Washington DC 20525

HANDLON, FOREST, JR (D)

Ind State Rep

Mailing Add: 4264 Burkhart E Dr Apt A Indianapolis IN 46227

HANDY, REX MONTE (D)

b North Wilkesboro, NC, Apr 26, 23; s Alonzo Montgomery Handy & Ella Maude Absher H; m 1942 to Della Leona Welch, div; c Charles Eugene & Larry Michael. Educ: North Wilkesboro High Sch, NC, grad, 40; Clevenger Col, BA, 49; Phi Theta Pi. Polit & Govt Pos: Mem, North Wilkesboro City Coun, NC, 67-; chmn, Wilkes Co Dem Exec Comt, formerly. Bus & Prof Pos: Mgr, Motor Serv Sales Co, Inc, 49- Mil Serv: Entered as Pvt, Air Force, 43, released as T/Sgt, 45, after serv in 15th Air Force Unit, Mediterranean, 44-45; Purple Heart; Air Medal with Five Oak Leaf Clusters; Distinguished Flying Cross; Good Conduct Medal. Mem: North Wilkesboro Optimist Club. Honors & Awards: Man of the Year Distinguished Serv Award, 54-55. Relig: Baptist. Legal Res: 807 D St North Wilkesboro NC 28659 Mailing Add: Box 432 North Wilkesboro NC 28659

HANDY, THOMAS V (R)

b Corbin, Ky, Mar 8, 44; s Conrad F Handy & Lou McCowan H; m Jan 1973 to Bonnie Collier Bledsoe; c Dennie Beth. Educ: Centre Col, AB, 66; Wake Forest Univ Col of Law, 66-67, Univ of Ky Col of Law, JD, 69; Delta Kappa Epsilon; Student Govt; Interfraternity Coun; Letterman. Polit & Govt Pos: Legal aide, Dept of Hwy State of Ky, 67-69; admin legis asst to US Rep T L Carter, Ky, 69-; Asst Commonwealth Attorney, 75. Bus & Prof Pos: Secretary, Town Ctr Motel Inc, 65-67; vpres, Handy Hand Enterprises, Inc, 72- Mem: Laurel Co Bar Asn (pres, 73-74); London Jaycees (pres, 74-75); Civil Air Patrol; Odd Fellows; Young Rep. Honors & Awards: Outstanding Jaycee in Southeast Region, 74. Relig: Christian Church. Legal Res: RR 5 London KY 40741 Mailing Add: 105 E Fourth St London KY 40741

HANDY, WENDELL TAYLOR (R)

Mem, Rep State Cent Comt Calif

b Tyler, Tex, Jan 28, 28; s Taylor Handy (deceased) & Lucy Johnson H; m 1960 to Adelaide Fisher; c Wendell T, Jr, Anthony I & Darryl H. Educ: Univ Calif, Los Angeles Sch Bus Admin, 1 year; Metrop Bus Col, 1 year. Polit & Govt Pos: Mem credentials & rules comt, speaker's bur, Rep State Cent Comt Calif, 66, mem, currently; mem & mem deleg assembly & legis steering comt, Calif Sch Bd Asn, 67; chmn youth employ & recreation, Gov Adv Comt Children & Youth, 67-; deleg, Rep Nat Conv, 68; campaign dir, Nixon-Agnew Hq (3), 68; mem dist attorney's adv coun, Los Angeles Co Legis Comt, 69; Calif State chmn, Nat Coun Concerned Afro-Am Rep, 69; chmn, 55th Rep Assembly Dist, 69; vchmn, Mid-Cities Sch Trustees Asn, 69; mem, 21st Rep Cong Dist Comt, currently; mem, Los Angeles Co Rep Cent Comt, currently; mem, Rep Victory Squad, 69-70; chmn Region I, Gov Reagan's Campaign, 70; cand, Secy of State, Calif, 70; mem, Gov Reagan's Inaugural Comt, 70-71; legis rep, Compton Unified Bd Educ, 70-71, vpres, 72-73; mem, Calif Rep Assembly, currently, treas, 72-, vchmn, 73-; founder-pres, Calif Progressive Club, 72; chmn, Black Citizens' Comt to Reelect the President, 72. Publ: Watts Riot, privately publ, 66. Mem: NAACP (bd mem, Compton Br); Compton Improve Asn; Compton Bus & Prof Mens Asn; Master Mason; St Joseph Grand Lodge AF&AM. Honors & Awards: Award for Outstanding Achievement on Community Activities, Metrop Gazette Newspaper, 68; Outstanding Achievement Award for community serv, Calif Legis; Distinguished Serv Award for sustaining interest in & contrib to pub educ, Compton Teachers Asn; Meritorious Serv Award for distinguished serv to pub educ in Los Angeles Co; Community Serv Merit Award, Compton Br, NAACP. Relig: Protestant. Legal Res: 13716 S Wilmington Ave Compton CA 90222 Mailing Add: 13714 S Wilmington Ave Compton CA 90222

HANEY, JEWELL M (D)

VChmn, Texas Co Dem Cent Comt, Mo

b St Paul, Kans, Mar 17, 27; d Frank Moore & Rosina Seifert M; m 1947 to Leland Chester Haney; c Bradford Lee & Shauna Lynn. Educ: St Paul Pub Schs, Mo. Polit & Govt Pos: Dep co clerk, Texas Co, Mo, 55-66; committeewoman, Piney Twp, 62-; secy, Texas Co Dem Cent Comt, 62-70, vchmn, 70-; secy, US Rep Richard H Ichord Dist Off, 66- Bus & Prof Pos: Secy, Kans Power & Light, 45-47, secy, Off Supply & Equipment Co, 47-53. Mem: Am Legion Auxiliary; Houston Bus Women. Relig: United Methodist. Mailing Add: Star Rte 5 Box 165 Houston MO 65483

HANKINS, FREEMAN (D)

Pa State Sen

b Brunswick, Ga, Sept 30, 18; s Oliver Hankins & Anna Pyles H; m to Dorothy Days; c one. Educ: Friendship Sch, Pittsburgh; Selden Inst, Brunswick; Temple Univ; Dolan's Col Embalming, grad, 45. Polit & Govt Pos: Pa State Rep, formerly; deleg, Dem Nat Conv, 68; Pa State Sen, 69-; deleg, Dem Nat Mid-Term Conf, 74. Bus & Prof Pos: Funeral dir. Mil Serv: Army Med Corps, 44-47. Mem: Am Legion; NAACP; Nat Funeral Asn; Masonic Bodies. Relig: Baptist. Mailing Add: 4075 Haverford Ave Philadelphia PA 19104

HANKS, EMMA JANE (R)

Pres, Md Fedn Rep Women

b Bellefonte, Pa, Feb 14, 16; d John Van Valzah Foster, MD & Emily Hartley F; m 1964 to Fletcher Hanks; c Joan Claire (Mrs Randles). Educ: Pa State Univ, BA, 37; Yale Univ Sch Nursing, MN, 40; Quain, Hon Sophomore Soc; Chi Omega. Polit & Govt Pos: Chmn, Bd Elec, Oxford, Md, 70-; mem, Talbot Co Cent Comt, 70-; pres, Md Fedn Rep Women, 71-; secy, Oxford Bd Zoning Appeals, 74- Bus & Prof Pos: Pub health nurse, Community Health Asn, Minneapolis, Minn, 40-41; asst instr, Yale Univ Sch Nursing, New Haven, Conn, 43-46; health educator, Tuberc & Health Soc, Dauphin & Perry Co, Harrisburg, Pa, 46-54, exec dir, 54-60; exec dir, Pa Health Coun, 60-64. Mil Serv: Am Vol Group, Flying Tigers, China-Burma Area, 41-42. Mem: Fel Am Pub Health Asn; Md Pub Health Asn; League Women Voters; Talbot Co YMCA. Honors & Awards: Cert of appreciation for exceptional serv in the field of pub health from the Md Dept Health & Ment Hygiene, 71; Cert for distinguished citizenship from Gov Marvin Mandel for outstanding leadership in promoting better pub health progs in Md, 71. Mailing Add: Morris St Oxford MD 21654

HANKS, NANCY (R)

Chmn, Nat Found for Arts & the Humanities

b Miami Beach, Fla, Dec 31, 27; d Bryan Cayce & Virginia Wooding H. Educ: Univ Colo, 46; Oxford Univ, 48; Duke Univ, AB, magna cum laude, 49; Phi Beta Kappa; Phi Kappa Delta; Kappa Alpha Theta; Sigma Alpha Iota. Hon Degrees: DFA, Pratt Inst, 70; DHL, Princeton Univ & Hofstra Univ, 71; DL, Mich State Univ, George Washington Univ & Univ Southern Calif, 73. Polit & Govt Pos: Mem staff, Off Defense Mobilization, Dept Defense, 51-52; mem, President's Adv Comt Govt Orgn, 53; asst to undersecy, Dept Health, Educ & Welfare, 53-54; spec asst, Spec Proj Off, 55; asst to Nelson A Rockefeller, Mayor, New York, NY, 56-59; exec secy, Spec Studies Proj, Rockefeller Bros Fund, 56-59; assoc, Laurance S Rockefeller, New York, NY, 59-69; adv Outdoor Recreation Resources Rev Comn, 61-62; chmn, Nat Found for Arts & the Humanities, 69-; vchmn, Arts & Humanities Comt, Am Revolution Bicentennial Comn, 70-; mem, Nat Comn, UNESCO, 70- Bus & Prof Pos: Trustee, Mus Primitive Art, 54-69; trustee, Robert Col, Turkey, 63-69; mem exec comt, Radcliffe Inst, 66-68; mem adv bd, Mary Duke Biddle Gallery Blind, NC Mus Art, 67-69. Mem: Am Asn Mus; Duke Univ Mem Assoc Coun Arts; Cosmopolitan Club; Capitol Hill Club. Honors & Awards: Cult Award, Recording Indust Asn Am, 70. Relig: Protestant. Mailing Add: Shoreham Bldg 806 15th St NW Washington DC 20506

HANLEY, BENJAMIN (D)

Ariz State Rep

b Crownpoint, NMex, Mar 13, 41; s Max Howard Hanley & Sistah Hannah H; m 1964 to Joy Jean Sells; c Andrea Rhae & Theresa Jeannette. Educ: Ariz State Univ, BA, 64, JD, 71. Polit & Govt Pos: Ariz State Rep, 73-74; minority whip, Ariz House Rep, 75-, mem, Health, Banking & Ins & Agr Comts, 73- Bus & Prof Pos: Research chemist, Unidynamics, Phoenix, Ariz, 64-69; attorney-in-chg, DNA Legal Servs, Window Rock, 71-72; legal adv to chief prosecutor, Navajo Tribe, 73- Relig: Presbyterian. Mailing Add: PO Box 247 Window Rock AZ 86515

HANLEY, JAMES MICHAEL (D)

US Rep, NY

b Syracuse, NY, July 19, 20; s Michael Joseph Hanley & Alice Gillick H; m 1950 to Rita Ann Harrington; c Christine Mary & Peter J. Hon Degrees: LLD, LeMoyne Col, 67. Polit & Govt Pos: US Rep, NY, 64-; deleg, Dem Nat Conv, 68; deleg, Dem Nat Mid-Term Conf, 74. Bus & Prof Pos: Owner, Callahan-Hanley-Mooney Funeral Home. Mil Serv: Army, World War II. Mem: CofC; Am Legion; KofC (grand knight); Elks; Syracuse Liederkranz. Relig: Catholic. Legal Res: 316 Coleridge Ave Syracuse NY 13204 Mailing Add: 6614 Melody Lane Bethesda MD 20034

HANLON, CHARLES J (INDEPENDENT)

Ore State Sen

b Pa, Sept 15, 18; s Charles Hanlon & Anna Darby H; m 1943 to Neila Margaret Gaines; c Kathy & Jeff. Educ: Greensburg High Sch, Pa, 35. Polit & Govt Pos: Ore State Sen, 75- Mil Serv: Entered as Pvt, Army, 41, released as 1st Lt, 45, after serv in Aviation Engrs, Southwest Pac & Philippines, 44-46. Mailing Add: Rte 1 Box 221 Cornelius OR 97113

HANLON, NEAL B (R)

Conn State Rep

b Waterbury, Conn, July 20, 45; s Thomas J Hanlon & Catherine Bergin H; single. Educ: Fordham Univ, BA, 67; Univ Conn, JD, 70. Polit & Govt Pos: Burgess, Borough of Naugatuck, Conn, 71-74, vchmn charter revision comn, 73-75; Conn State Rep, 75- Bus & Prof Pos: Attorney, 70- Relig: Catholic. Mailing Add: 101 Radnor Ave Naugatuck CT 06770

HANNA, EDWARD (D)

b Allentown, Pa, Dec 28, 36; s Charles Shahoud Hanna & Levinia Moffit H; m 1962 to Brenda Rae Carl; c Edward C & Bethany Ann. Educ: Kutztown State Col, BS Educ, 62; Temple Univ, MA Hist, 66; Kappa Delta Pi. Polit & Govt Pos: Deleg, Dem Nat Conv, 72; committeeman, Allentown Dem Party, Pa, 73- Bus & Prof Pos: Teacher, Collegeville-Trappe High Sch, 62-66; teacher hist, Allentown Sch Dist, Pa, 66-73. Mil Serv: Entered as Cpl, Marine Corps, 56, released as Sgt, 59, after serv in 8-inch Howitzers, 2nd Marines, Camp Lejeune, NC, 56-59; Good Conduct Medal; Nat Defense Medal. Mem: Am, Pa & Allentown Fedns of Teachers; Lehigh Co Labor Coun, AFL-CIO; Optimists of South Allentown. Honors & Awards: Community Serv Award, United Fund of Lehigh Co, 73. Relig: Syrian Orthodox. Mailing Add: 1606 Coronado St Allentown PA 18103

HANNA, JOE CURRIE (D)

Tex State Rep

b Lawton, Okla, May 19, 21; s Roy Monroe Hanna & Winifred Currie H; m 1942 to Betty Elliott; c Judith Lynn, Stephen Elliott & Mark Monroe. Educ: John Tarleton Jr Col, grad, 40; Univ Tex, grad, 42. Polit & Govt Pos: Tex State Rep, 70- Mil Serv: Entered as Student Pilot, Navy, 41, released as Lt(sg), 45, after serv in Air Corps, Atlantic Submarine Patrol. Mem: Lions; Farm Bur; Am Legion; VFW. Relig: Baptist. Legal Res: 201 N Harding Breckenridge TX 76024 Mailing Add: Tex House of Rep Austin TX 78701

HANNA, KATHERINE MERRITT (D)

NH State Rep

b Keene, NH, Sept 5, 53; d George Russell Hanna & Shirley Garfield H; single. Educ: Mt Holyoke Col, 72-75. Polit & Govt Pos: Deleg, Dem Nat Conv, 72; deleg, NH Const Conv, 74; NH State Rep, 75- Honors & Awards: First 18 year old elected del in open primary. Relig: Protestant. Mailing Add: 693 West St Keene NH 03431

HANNA, MARTIN SHAD (R)

Nat VChmn, Young Rep Nat Fedn

b Bowling Green, Ohio, Aug 4, 40; s Martin Lester Hanna & Julia Loyal Moor H; m 1969 to Sharon Ann Higgins; c Jennifer Lynn, Jonathan Moor & Katharine Anne. Educ: Univ Toledo, summer sch; Bowling Green State Univ, summer sch; Purdue Univ, Lafayette, BS, 62; Am Univ Wash Col Law, JD, 65; Phi Delta Phi; Sigma Alpha Epsilon. Polit & Govt Pos:

Mem, Purdue Univ Young Rep Club, 58-62; mem, Am Univ & DC Young Rep Clubs, 62-65; orientation chmn, Nat Leadership Training Sch, Young Rep Nat Fedn, 65; precinct committeeman, Wood Co Rep Cent Comt, Ohio, 68-; immediate past pres, Wood Co Young Rep Club, 70-72; state vchmn, Ohio League of Young Rep Clubs, 71-72, state chmn, 72-73; first vchmn, Wood Co Rep Policy Comt & Wood Co Rep Exec Comt, 72-; nat vchmn, Young Rep Nat Fedn, 73- Bus & Prof Pos: Partner, Hanna, Middleton & Roebke Law Firm, 65-70; partner, Hanna & Hanna Law Firm, 71-; spec counsel & lectr, Off of Attorney Gen, Ohio, 68-71; instr, Col Bus Admin, Bowling Green State Univ, 70; instr, Trades & Indust Educ Serv, Ohio Div of Voc Educ, 70-, lectr, Ohio Legal Ctr Inst, 73- Publ: What part will I play as a citizen?, Cong Record, 58; co-ed, Am Univ Law Rev, Am Univ Wash Col Law, 65; auth, Ohio rules of criminal procedure—sentence & post-sentence proceedings, Ohio Legal Ctr Inst, 73. Mem: Defense Research Inst; Nat Asn of Criminal Defense Lawyers; Wood Co Cancer Soc; Wood Co Red Cross; Bowling Green Jaycees. Honors & Awards: Ky Col, Gov Breathitt, Ky, 65; One of Ten Outstanding Young Men in Ohio, Ohio Jaycees, 68; George Washington Honor Medal Award, Freedom's Found at Valley Forge, 69; Robert A Taft Distinguished Serv Award, 74. Relig: Presbyterian; Ordained Elder & Lay Minister. Legal Res: 506 Knollwood Dr Bowling Green OH 43402 Mailing Add: 700 N Main St Bowling Green OH 43402

HANNA, MICHAEL A **(D)**
Chmn, Washington Co Dem Party, Pa
b Joffre, Pa, Jan 20, 15; s Samuel Hanna & Susan Albert H; m 1950 to Eliza Jane Gibson; c Michael & Mark. Educ: Villanova Col, BA, 38; Univ Pittsburgh Law Sch, LLB, 41. Polit & Govt Pos: Sch dir, Smith Twp, Washington Co, Pa, 39-42; asst co solicitor, Washington Co, 47-53, chief co solicitor, 53-56 & dist attorney, 56-64; chmn, Washington Co Dem Party, 65- Bus & Prof Pos: Attorney-at-law, 42- Mil Serv: Entered as Pvt, Army, 43, released as M/Sgt, 46, after serv in ETO, 44-46, Five Battle Stars. Mem: VFW; Am Legion; Elks; Eagles; Lions. Relig: Protestant. Mailing Add: RD 2 Washington PA 15301

HANNA, RICHARD T **(D)**
b Kemmerer, Wyo, June 9, 14; s Robert Alexander Hanna & Martha Jane Thomas H; m 1945 to Doris Muriel Jenks; c Pamela, Alexander Harris & Kimberly Grace. Educ: Univ Calif, Los Angeles, LLB, 52; Lambda Chi Alpha; Phi Delta Phi. Polit & Govt Pos: Mem bd dirs, Gemco Scholarship Found, formerly; recreation supvr, Works Progress Admin, WTex, 38-41 & Calif, 46; Calif State Assemblyman 57-62; US Rep, Calif, 62-75; deleg, Dem Nat Mid-Term Conf, 74. Bus & Prof Pos: Newspaper reporter, Sweetwater Reporter, Tex, 37-38; gen law practice, Orange Co, 52-; partner, Launer, Chaffee & Hanna, 58-71. Mil Serv: Air Corps, Naval Res, 41-45. Mem: Am, Calif & Orange Co Bar Asns; Lions; VFW; Am Legion. Relig: Latter-day Saint. Mailing Add: 9461 Grindlay Suite 104 Cypress CA 90630

HANNA, RON **(D)**
Wash State Rep
Mailing Add: PO Box 5313 Tacoma WA 98405

HANNA, THOMAS ASHE **(R)**
NY State Assemblyman
b Rochester, NY, Oct 2, 26; s Thomas Francis Hanna & Beatrice Ashe H; m 1952 to Mary Ann Donaher; c Rebecca, Kevin, Margaret Mary, Brendan, Siobhan, Sean, Ciaran & Thomas. Educ: Boston Col, AB; Harvard Univ, MBA. Polit & Govt Pos: NY State Assemblyman, 73- Bus & Prof Pos: Chmn bd, Empire Sign, Ontario, NY, 66-; pres, Schaefer-Ross Co, Webster, NY, 71- Mil Serv: Entered as A/S, Naval Res, 44, released as Seaman 1/C, 46, after serv in Pac, 45. Mailing Add: 1680 Lake Rd Webster NY 14580

HANNAFORD, MARK WARREN **(D)**
US Rep, Calif
b Woodrow, Colo, Feb 7, 25; s William Townsend Hannaford & Ina Owen H; m 1948 to Sara Jane Lemaster; c Mark William, Kim Karl & Robert Owen. Educ: Ball State Univ, BA, 50; Yale Univ, John Hay fel, 61-62. Polit & Govt Pos: Mem, Planning Comn, Lakewood, Calif, 60-61, city councilman, 66-68, Mayor, 68-70 & 72-; mem, Los Angeles Co Dem Cent Comt, 62-67; mem, Calif Dem State Cent Comt, 66-71; deleg, Dem Nat Conv, 68; spec deleg, Dem Nat Mid-Term Conf, 74; US Rep, Calif, 75- Bus & Prof Pos: Teacher Govt, Lakewood High Sch, 56-57; assoc prof polit sci, Long Beach State Univ, 67- Mil Serv: Entered as Pvt, Air Force, 43, released as T/Sgt, 46, after serv in 43rd Bomb Group, 5th Air Force, Pac Theatre on Bomber Crew, 44-45. Relig: Protestant. Mailing Add: 4944 N Stevely Ave Lakewood CA 90713

HANNAFORD, PETER DOR **(R)**
b Glendale, Calif, Sept 21, 32; s Donald Richardson Hannaford & Elinor Nielsen H; m 1954 to Irene Harville; c Richard Harville & Donald R, II. Educ: Univ Calif, Berkeley, AB, 54; Order of the Golden Bear; Theta Xi. Polit & Govt Pos: Comnr, Piedmont Park Comn, Calif, 64-68; assoc mem, Rep State Cent Comt Calif, 65-67, mem, 68-74; treas, Rep Alliance, EBay Div, Calif, 66, vpres, 67, pres, 68, pres, Alameda Co Div, 69; mem, Alameda Co Rep Cent Comt, 66-74; chmn, 16th Assembly Dist Rep Coord Coun, 69-70; managed several campaigns in Calif; secy, San Francisco Bay Area Rep Alliance, 70; chmn, Sherman for State Senate Comt, 70; Rep nominee for US Cong, Seventh Dist, Calif, 72; vchmn, Gov Consumer Fraud Task Force, 72-73; mem governing bd, Calif & Bi-State, Tahoe Regional Planning Agency, 73-74; asst, Gov & Dir Pub Affairs, Calif, 74; Bus & Prof Pos: Vpres, Kennedy, Hannaford, Inc, 57-62, pres, Kennedy, Hannaford & Dolman, Inc, 62-67; pres, Pettler & Hannaford, Inc, 67-69; vpres, Wilton, Coombs & Colnett, Inc, 69-72; pres, Hannaford & Assocs, Inc, Oakland, 73; vpres, Deaver & Hannaford, Inc, 75- Mil Serv: Entered as 2nd Lt, Army Signal Corps, 54, released as 1st Lt, 56, after serv in 24th Signal Bn, Ft Devens, Mass, 55-56. Publ: Book reviewer, Berkeley Gazette & Richmond Independent, Calif, currently. Mem: Advert Club Oakland; Univ Club, San Francisco; The Guardsmen; Sierra Club; Oakland Symphony Orchestra Asn. Relig: Protestant. Mailing Add: 10960 Wilshire Blvd Los Angeles CA 90024

HANNAH, REBECCA RANSOM **(D)**
b Nuremberg, Ger, Oct 11, 51; d Dr Walter White Hannah (deceased) & Doris Beasley H; single. Educ: St Mary's Jr Col; Univ NC, Chapel Hill, currently. Polit & Govt Pos: Deleg, Dem Nat Conv, 72. Honors & Awards: One of Five Outstanding Col Young Dem, NC Young Dem, 72. Relig: Presbyterian. Legal Res: 90 Cabarrus Ave W Concord NC 28025 Mailing Add: 1605 Smith Level Rd Chapel Hill NC 27514

HANNEMAN, PAUL A **(R)**
Ore State Rep
b Portland, Ore, July 20, 36; s Karl Hanneman & Mary Doerfler H; m 1962 to Sandra Siltanen; c Kurtis & John. Educ: Portland State Col. Polit & Govt Pos: Ore State Rep, 65, 67 & 69-; deleg, Rep Nat Conv, 68 & 72; chmn, Nat Resources Comn, 69; chmn, Rules & Resolutions Comn, 69-70. Mem: Two CofC; Kiwanis. Honors & Awards: Distinguished Serv Award, Jaycees, 61; Outstanding Young Man of Ore, 67. Relig: Congregational. Mailing Add: RR 2 Cloverdale OR 97112

HANNIBAL, ALICE PRISCILLA **(D)**
b Metuchen, NJ, Dec 6, 16; d Charles Joseph Stateman & Hester Roann Robbins S; m 1939 to John Jacob Hannibal, Jr; c Alice Lauretta (Mrs Macon Jones, Jr), John Jacob, III, Marcia Elaine (Mrs Algenia McCall), Myriam Arielle (Mrs George Morrow), Gregor Josef, Charles Jordan & Rhonda Adrienne. Educ: Middlesex Jr Col, Perth Amboy, NJ, 36-39; La Salle Exten Univ, 68-72; ECarolina Univ, BA, 75. Polit & Govt Pos: First councilwoman, Bd of Aldermen, Kinston, NC, 59-61; mem, League of Municipalities, 59-61; mem adv bd, Lenoir Co Ment Health, 60-64; mem bd dirs, Dem Women of Lenoir Co, 62-65; East Carolina rep, Gov Comt on Juvenile Delinquency & Crime, 63-65; precinct chmn, Dem Party of Lenoir Co, 66-67, precinct vchmn, 71-72; alt deleg, Dem Nat Conv, 72; polit educ dir, Grass Roots Organized Woman Power, 72-; mem, North Carolina Women's Polit Caucus, 72- Bus & Prof Pos: Mem exec bd, Asn for Study of Negro Life & Hist, 50-52; mem legal redress comt, NAACP, 52-54; mem exec bd, Lenoir Co Chap, Am Red Cross, 63-64; exhibits & publicity, Nat Libr Week, 65; taxidermist, Kinston, presently; pub speaker & adult educ instr, presently. Publ: Co-auth, Tools of town government, In: Survey Handbook, Kinston League of Women Voters, 54; auth, Racial barriers, Carolina Times, 9/65 & Law, order & justice, The Carolinian, 7/65. Mem: Kinston Arts Coun (charter mem, 68 & life membership); Vol Housewives (chmn voter registr, 65-); Auxiliary Old North State Med Soc (historian, 52-58 & sickle cell consult, 72-73); Neuse River Indust (steering comt). Honors & Awards: Regional Silver Civic Serv Award, Nat Coun Negro Women, 60; Emma V Kelly Achievement Award, Daughters of Elks, 60; Civil Rights Award, United East Dist Baptist Conv, NC, 62; Finer Womanhood Award, Delta Rho Zeta, 66; Civic Serv Award, Vol Housewives of Lenoir Co, 72. Relig: Episcopal. Legal Res: 201 N Rochelle Blvd Kinston NC 28501 Mailing Add: Box 924 Grove Park Kinston NC 28501

HANNON, GEORGE WILLIAM, JR **(D)**
Conn State Sen
b Hartford, Conn, Dec 29, 32; s George W Hannon Sr & Mary Stanton H; m 1953 to Doris Elaine Davy; c Patricia L, David R, Margaret E, Elizabeth J, Kathleen M, Colleen J, Thomas K, James S & Mary Catherine. Educ: St Bonaventure Univ, 2 years; Univ Conn, 1 year. Polit & Govt Pos: Conn State Rep, 69-74, majority whip, Conn House Rep, 69, asst majority leader, 71-74; Conn State Sen, 74- Mem: Elks (charter mem Lodge 2063); Lions. Honors & Awards: Distinguished Serv Award, East Hartford Lions Club, 62. Relig: Roman Catholic. Mailing Add: 9 Ellsworth St East Hartford CT 06108

HANNON, LENN LAMAR **(D)**
Ore State Sen
b Roseburg, Ore, July 4, 43; s Leonard Thomas Hannon & Irene Massey H; m 1966 to Dixie Lynn Gibbs; c Michelle R, Patrick L, Rebecca A & Rachel L. Educ: Southern Ore State Col, 63-64. Polit & Govt Pos: Ore State Sen, 75- Mil Serv: Entered as E-1, Army, 61, released as E-5, 67, after serv in Ore Nat Guard. Mem: AF&AM; Jackson Co Farm Bur; fel Christian Athletes; Mason. Honors & Awards: Outstanding Young Man of Am, US Jaycees, 74. Relig: Nazarene. Mailing Add: 431 Lit Way Ashland OR 97520

HANNUM, ROBERT JOHN **(R)**
Secy, Montgomery Co Rep Comt, Pa
b Philadelphia, Pa, Mar 19, 21; s Edwin Pennell Hannum & Frances Smith H; m 1938 to Esther Nichols; c Robert J, Jr & Sandra Lee (Mrs Dockstader). Polit & Govt Pos: Chmn, Cheltenham Twp Rep Orgn, 64-; secy, Montgomery Co Rep Comt, 66-, area leader, 66-; alt deleg, Rep Nat Conv, 68; 1st vpres, Montgomery Co Asn Twp Off, 68. Bus & Prof Pos: With Bunting Co, Inc, Philadelphia, Pa, 46 & Poloron Prod, Inc, New Rochelle, NY, 66- Mil Serv: Entered as Pvt, Army, 42, released as 1st Lt, 45, after serv in Fourth Armored Div, ETO; Two Purple Hearts; Two ETO Stars. Mem: Am Legion; Mason; Consistory; Shrine; Eastern Montgomery Co Profession-Bus Coun. Relig: Lutheran. Mailing Add: 37 Dewey Rd Cheltenham PA 19012

HANRAHAN, ROBERT P **(R)**
Dep Asst Secy Educ, Dept Health, Educ & Welfare
b Chicago Heights, Ill, Feb 25, 34; s William J Hanrahan & Ida Koenig; m 1957 to Barbara Ann Golletz; c Kevin, Brian & Greg. Educ: Thornton Community Col, Harvey, Ill, AA, 54; Bowling Green State Univ, BS, 56, MEduc, 59; Phi Alpha Theta; Phi Delta Kappa; Delta Upsilon. Hon Degrees: Dr Pedagogy, Bowling Green State Univ, 71. Polit & Govt Pos: Bloom Twp Auditor, Town of Bloom, Ill, 65-67; supt of schs, Cook Co, 67-71; Regional Comnr of Educ for Midwest, States of Minn, Wis, Mich, Ill, Ind & Ohio, 71; US Rep, Third Dist, Ill, 73-75; dep asst secy educ, Dept Health, Educ & Welfare, 75- Bus & Prof Pos: Dir develop, Ingalls Mem Hosp, Harvey, Ill, 72. Publ: Successful leadership in student council elections, Student Life, 1/61; Faculty leadership in elections for student councils, Clearing House, 2/61; Emphasis should be on instruction, Ill Asn of Secondary Sch Principals Bull, winter 66. Mem: Chicago Asn of Commerce & Indust; US Capitol Hist Soc; Nat & Ill Educ Asns; Execs Club of Chicago; Honors & Awards: Award for outstanding internal sch publ, Col & Personnel Asn Inst, 67; Outstanding Young Man of Am, 67; Supt Award, Ill Am Legion, 70; Outstanding Educator Award, Little Flower Men's Soc, Chicago, 70; Chmn Award, Better Bus Bur, Chicago, 73. Relig: Episcopal. Legal Res: 17930 Homewood Ave Homewood IL 60430 Mailing Add: Rm 3001 Fed Off Bldg 300 Maryland Ave SW Dept HEW Washington DC 20202

HANSEN, BETTY ANN **(D)**
Secy, Moscow Dist Dem Cent Comt, Idaho
b Lewiston, Idaho, d A F (Fred) Hansen & Angeline Dvorak H; single. Educ: Univ Idaho, 71-73; Alpha Lambda Delta; polit ed, Idaho Argonaut; Univ Idaho Polit Sci Students. Polit & Govt Pos: Pres, Lewiston High Sch Young Dem, 69-71; vpres, Idaho Young Dem, 71-72; page, Idaho State Legis, 70-71, intern, 73-; deleg Dem Nat Conv, 72; secy, Moscow Dist Dem Cent Comt, 73- Honors & Awards: Voice of Democracy Winner, VFW, 71; Am Legion Oratory Winner, 70 & 71; Girls State Deleg, Am Legion Auxiliary, 70; Young Legis Deleg, YMCA, 70 & 71; Deans List, Univ Idaho, 72 & 73. Relig: Catholic. Mailing Add: 1503 11th Ave Lewiston ID 83501

HANSEN, C R (BALDY) **(DFL)**
Minn State Sen
Mailing Add: 100 SE First St Austin MN 55912

HANSEN, CARL R (R)
VChmn, Cook Co Rep Cent Comt, Ill
b Chicago, Ill, May 2, 26; s Carl M Hansen & Anna Roge H; m 1952 to Christa Marie Loeser; c Lothar. Educ: Univ Chicago, MBA, 54. Polit & Govt Pos: Resident officer, US High Comn for Ger, 48-52; chmn, Young Rep Orgn of Cook Co, Ill, 57-58; mem bd, United Rep Fund of Ill, 58-; deleg, Ill State Rep Conv, 62-74; Rep committeeman, Elk Grove Twp, Cook Co, 62-; primary campaign mgr, Percy for Gov Comt, 63-64; vchmn, Cook Co Rep Cent Comt, 64-66 & 68-, chmn, Third Legis Dist Rep Party, 64-; campaign adv, Ogilvie for Gov Comt, 68; deleg, Rep Nat Conv, 68; Comnr, Cook Co, 70, 74-; chmn, Suburban Rep Orgn Cook Co, 74-; chmn, 12th Cong Dist Rep Orgn, 71-74; presidential elector, 72. Bus & Prof Pos: Serv vpres, Mkt Research Corp Am; dir mkt research, Earle Ludgin & Co & Kitchens of Sara Lee, 56-67; pres, Chicago Assocs, Inc, 67- Mil Serv: Entered as Pvt, Army, 44, released as 1st Lt, 48, after serv in European Command, Res, Maj (Ret). Mem: Am Mkt Asn; Am Statist Asn; Shrine; Scottish Rite; John Ericsson Rep League Ill (state pres). Relig: Lutheran. Mailing Add: 110 S Edward St Mt Prospect IL 60056

HANSEN, CLIFFORD PETER (R)
US Sen, Wyo
b Zenith, Wyo, Oct 16, 12; s Peter Arthur Hansen & Mary Elizabeth Wood H; m 1934 to Martha Elizabeth Close; c Peter Arthur & Mary Elizabeth (Mrs Mead). Educ: Univ Wyo, BS, 34; Alpha Zeta; Delta Sigma Rho; Phi Kappa Phi. Hon Degrees: LLD, Univ Wyo, 65. Polit & Govt Pos: Chmn adv comt livestock research & mkt, Secy of Agr; Teton Co Comnr, Wyo, 43-51; trustee, Univ Wyo, 46-; pres, 56-63; Gov, Wyo, 63-67; mem exec comt, Nat & Western Gov Conf, 65-; US Sen, Wyo, 67-; deleg, Rep Nat Conv, 68. Bus & Prof Pos: Rancher, Jackson, Wyo, 34-; vpres, Jackson State Bank, 52-73. Mem: Wyo Stock Growers Asn; Wyo Farm Bur Fedn; Mason (33 degree); Shrine. Relig: Episcopal. Legal Res: Spring Gulch Ranch Jackson WY 83001 Mailing Add: 3229 Dirksen Off Bldg Washington DC 20510

HANSEN, CONNOR THEODORE
Assoc Justice, Wis Supreme Court
b Freeman, SDak, Nov 1, 13; s William Dayton Hansen & Gladdus G Hall H; m 1939 to Annette P Ferry; c Annette H (Mrs Benjamin E Olson), Peter C, David P & Jane H (Mrs Richard LaRonge). Educ: Wis State Univ, BS, 34; Univ Wis Law Sch, JD, 37; Sigma Nu; Phi Delta Phi. Polit & Govt Pos: Dist attorney, Eau Claire Co, Wis, 39-43; spec agent, Fed Bur Invest, Dept Justice, Washington, DC, 43-45; co judge, Eau Claire Co, 58-67; Assoc Justice, Wis Supreme Court, currently. Bus & Prof Pos: Lawyer, Eau Claire, Wis, 39-58. Mem: Wis State Bar Asn; Am Law Inst; Wis Dist Attorney Asn; Wis State Bd Juvenile Court Judges; Nat Conf Christians & Jews. Honors & Awards: Distinguished Serv Award, Wis Conf, Nat Conf Christians & Jews, 72. Relig: Protestant. Mailing Add: 340 S Main St Lake Mills WI 53551

HANSEN, FRANK (TUB) (D)
Wash State Rep
Mailing Add: 9018-A McConnell Dr Moses Lake WA 98837

HANSEN, FRED
NMex State Sen
Mailing Add: State Capitol Santa Fe NM 87501

HANSEN, FREDERIC JAMES (R)
b Portland, Ore, Mar 22, 46; s Vernon Edward Hansen & Ella Freda Shacher H; m 1967 to Nancy Byrd Ray. Educ: Univ Ore, BA, 68; McMaster Univ, MA, 70; Johns Hopkins Univ, 70-71; Phi Eta Sigma; Phi Beta Kappa; Phi Delta Theta. Polit & Govt Pos: Off asst, Nat Park Serv, summer 70; off mgr, US Sen Charles E Goodell, NY, 70-71; admin asst, US Rep John Dellenback, Ore, 71-75. Mailing Add: 66 Bailey Lane Eugene OR 97401

HANSEN, GEORGE VERNON (R)
US Rep, Idaho
b Tetonia, Idaho, Sept 14, 30; m to Constance Camp; c Steven George, James Vernon, Patricia Sue, William Dean & Joanne. Educ: Ricks Col, BA, 56; Idaho State Univ; Grimms Bus Col, Pocatello, Idaho. Polit & Govt Pos: Pres, Bannock Co Young Rep Club, Idaho, formerly; vchmn, publicity chmn & precinct committeeman, Bannock Co Rep Cent Comt, formerly; mayor, Alameda, 61-62; city comnr, Pocatello, 62-65; US Rep, Idaho, 65-69 & 75-; dep under secy, Dept Agr, 69, dep adminr, Agr Stabilization & Conserv Serv, US Dept Agr, 69-72. Bus & Prof Pos: Agent, life ins. Mil Serv: Air Force, 3 years 6 months; Naval Res Off. Mem: Idaho Munic League; 20-30 Club; CofC; Farm Bur; Am Legion. Honors & Awards: Various distinguished serv awards. Relig: Latter-day Saint. Legal Res: PO Box 671 Pocatello ID 83201 Mailing Add: US House of Rep Washington DC 20515

HANSEN, GLADYS (D)
NMex State Sen
b Bristol, Colo, Jan 29, 20; d Oscar Samuel Strode & Mable Clinger S; m 1939 to Bernard Christian Hansen; c Keith Roger, Harry Lawrence & Thomas Kent. Educ: Los Angeles City Col, 36-38. Polit & Govt Pos: City clerk, Las Cruces, NMex, 60-63; co clerk, Dona Ana Co, 69-72; NMex State Sen, Dist 37, 73-, mem, Senate Finance Comt, Pub Affairs Comt & Interim Tax Study Comt, NMex State Senate, 73- Bus & Prof Pos: Mgr, Credit Bur, Las Cruces, NMex, 52-56; mgr catalog store, Montgomery Ward, 56-60; self-employed realtor, 63- Mem: Nat Asn of Real Estate Bd; NMex Asn of Co (pres, 71); Bus & Prof Women's Club of NMex (legis chmn, 72); Dem Women's Club of NMex & Las Cruces (pres, 73); Las Cruces Bus & Prof Women's Club (legis chmn, 73). Honors & Awards: Realtor of the Year, Las Cruces Bd Realtors, 68; Woman of the Year, Las Cruces Bus & Prof Women's Club, 72. Relig: United Methodist. Mailing Add: 1930 Gladys Dr Las Cruces NM 88001

HANSEN, GRANT LEWIS (R)
b Bancroft, Idaho, Nov 5, 21; s Paul Ezra Hansen & Leona Sarah Lewis H; m 1945 to Iris Rose Heyden; c Alan Lee, Brian Craig, Carol Margaret, David James & Ellen Diane. Educ: Ill Inst Technol, BS in Elec Eng, 48; Univ Calif, Los Angeles; Calif Inst Technol; Tau Beta Pi; Eta Kappa Nu. Polit & Govt Pos: Asst Secy of Air Force for Research & Develop, 69-73; US nat deleg, NATO Adv Group Aerospace Research & Develop, Paris, 69-74; US mem, Sci Comt Nat Rep, Shape Tech Ctr, The Hague, Netherlands, 69-73; mem, NASA Research & Technol Adv Coun, 71-73. Bus & Prof Pos: Former test conductor, Nike Prog, White Sands Proving Grounds, NMex, launched 74 of the earliest Nike research & develop vehicles, responsible for design of Nike Launch Control & Test Equipment, later responsible for all elec & electronic eng for Nike Ajax, Nike Hercules, Honest John, Sparrow, MB-1, Thor, Thor-Delta, Nike Zeus & Skybolt; tech mgr, Sparrow flight test, Naval Air Missile Test Center, Point Mugu, Calif, formerly; participant, research & develop flight test progs, Hollomon & Vandenberg Air Force Bases & Cape Kennedy, formerly; assisted in deployment of the Thor weapon system in Eng; asst chief design engr, Douglas Aircraft Co, 58-60; chief engr, Convair Div, Gen Dynamics Corp, San Diego, Calif, 60-62, vpres & prog dir, Centaur, 62-65, vpres, Launch Vehicle Prog, 65-69, vpres, Gen Dynamics Corp & gen mgr, Convair Div, currently. Mil Serv: Entered as A/S, Navy, 40, released as Chief Radio Tech, 45; Purple Heart; Asiatic-Pac Area Campaign Medal with Nine Bronze Stars; Am Defense Serv Medal with One Star; Am Area Campaign Medal; Good Conduct Medal. Mem: Fel Am Inst of Aeronaut & Astronaut (bd dirs & exec comt, 72-, nat pres, 75-); sr mem Inst of Elec & Electronics Engrs; Nat Soc of Aerospace Prof; fel Am Astronaut Soc; Grossmont-Mt Helix Improv Asn. Honors & Awards: Pub Serv Award, NASA, 66; Recognition Award for leadership & exceptional sci & tech accomplishment in connection with NASA's Surveyor I mission, Ill Inst Tech Alumni Asn, 67; Except Civilian Serv Medal, US Air Force, 73. Relig: Latter-day Saint. Mailing Add: PO Box 80847 San Diego CA 92138

HANSEN, HAROLD D (D)
Conn State Sen
Mailing Add: Barnes Hill Sherman CT 06784

HANSEN, INGWER L (R)
Iowa State Rep
Mailing Add: 201 S Eighth Ave E Hartley IA 51346

HANSEN, JAMES V (R)
Utah State Rep
Mailing Add: 399 E Oak Lane Farmington UT 84025

HANSEN, JOHN ROBERT (D)
b Manning, Iowa, Aug 24, 01; s Herman P Hansen & Laura Karstens H; m 1929 to Mary Louise Osthoff, wid 67; remarried 1969 to Dorothy Meyer; c Robert & John. Educ: State Univ Iowa, 19-21; Alpha Sigma Phi. Polit & Govt Pos: Mem, Carroll Co Dem Cent Comt, Iowa, 32-52, chmn, 44-52; alt deleg, Dem Nat Conv, 44 & 64, del, 48 & 68; mem, Iowa Comn on Interstate Coop & exec coun, Gov Comn on Alcoholism, formerly; dist chmn, State Dem Cent Comt, 52-57; mem, Bd Control State Insts, 57-60; Western Iowa area mgr, Savings Bonds Div, US Treas Dept, 61-62; US Rep, Seventh Dist, Iowa, 64-66; mem, Iowa State Hwy Comn, 67-69. Bus & Prof Pos: Majority owner & pres, Dultmeier Mfg Co, Manning, Iowa, 32-62; gen mgr & prin partner, Dultmeier Sales Co, Omaha, 34-57. Mem: Charter mem Manning Rotary; Manual Lodge 450 AF&AM; Sioux City Consistory; Za Ga Zig Shrine; Salona Chap Eastern Star. Relig: Presbyterian; Elder. Mailing Add: 69 E Lane Winterset IA 50273

HANSEN, JULIA BUTLER (D)
b Portland, Ore, June 14, 07; m to Henry A Hansen; c David K. Educ: Univ Washington, BA. Hon Degrees: LLD, St Mary's Col (Ind), 72. Polit & Govt Pos: Wash State Rep, 39-60, speaker pro tem, Wash House Rep, 55-60; US Rep, Wash, 60-75, chmn, House Appropriations Subcomt on Dept Interior & Rel Agencies, mem, House Appropriations Subcomt Transportation, chmn, House Dem Reform Comt & mem, House Dem Steering Comt, US House Rep, formerly; deleg, Dem Nat Conv, 68; deleg, Dem Nat Mid-Term Conf, 74. Mem: Bus & Prof Women's Clubs, Longview, Wash; Eastern Star. Honors & Awards: Recipient Certificate of Merit, Wash State Chap, Road Building; Wash Outstanding Serv Plaque; Good Roads Assoc Award. Legal Res: Cathlamet WA Mailing Add: 201 Cannon Bldg Washington DC 20515

HANSEN, LOWELL C, JR (R)
SDak State Rep
Mailing Add: 4701 S Minnesota Ave Sioux Falls SD 57105

HANSEN, MATILDA ANNE (D)
Wyo State Rep
b Paullina, Iowa, Sept 4, 29; d Arthur J Henderson & Sada G Thompson H; m 1965 to Hugh G Hansen; c Eric J & Douglas E Michener. Educ: Univ Colo, Boulder, BA, 63; Univ Wyo, MA, 70. Polit & Govt Pos: Chmn host co fund raising comt, Wyo State Dem Conv, 74; Wyo State Rep, 75-, secy judiciary interim comt, Wyo House Rep, 75- Bus & Prof Pos: Dir adult educ, Albany Co Sch Dist 1, Laramie, Wyo, 69- Publ: Auth, Ratmalana, Ceylon: A Developing Central Place, Univ Wyo, 70; sr auth, To Help Adults Learn, Albany Co Dist 1, 71; auth, Community Education Needs Assessment, Mott Found Funds, Wyo Ctr Community Educ, 74. Mem: League Women Voters; Mountain Plains & Wyo Adult Educ Asns; Nat Asn Pub Continuing & Adult Educ. Honors & Awards: Regents Scholar, Univ Colo, 61-63; Gen Elec Scholar in Econ, 65. Relig: Religious Society of Friends. Mailing Add: 1306 Kearney Laramie WY 82070

HANSEN, MEL (R)
Minn State Sen
b Russell, Minn, Sept 20, 15; s Ludvig Hansen & Clara Petersen H; m 1937 to Ethel E Long; c Sharon (Mrs James C Beckstrom), Judy C & Kerry M. Educ: Univ Minn, correspondence, 33-34; Univ Minn, Minneapolis, 34-37, BA, 40, exten, 37-60. Polit & Govt Pos: Treas, 12th Ward Rep Orgn, Minneapolis, Minn, 60-62; Minn State Sen, 34th Dist, 63- Bus & Prof Pos: Chief acct & off mgr, Fiber Div, Archer Daniels, Midland, Minn, 40-52; cost analyst, Ford Motor Co, St Paul, 53-54; off mgr & credit mgr, Buttrey Stores, Minneapolis, 55-57; vpres, Minn Employ Agencies Asn, 66-68; mgr, Careers Placement Serv, 57-65, pres, Careers, Inc, 65- Mil Serv: Entered as Ens, Naval Res, 44, released as Lt(jg), 46, after serv in DD 614, asst to legal assistance officer, 6th Naval Dist, ETO. Mem: Int Inst St Paul (bd mem); RAM (3 degree); Roosevelt PTA (legis chmn); Roosevelt Area Community Asn; Longfellow Field Activities Coun. Relig: Lutheran; secy bd pensions, Lutheran Church in Am; past pres, St Peder's Lutheran Church. Mailing Add: 4505 28 Ave S Minneapolis MN 55406

HANSEN, ORVAL HOWARD (R)
b Firth, Idaho, Aug 3, 26; s Farrell Lawrence Hansen & Lily Walquist H; m 1955 to June Duncan; c Margaret, Elizabeth, James, Katherine, John, Mary & Sarah. Educ: Univ Idaho, BA, 50; George Washington Univ, JD, 54, LLM, 73; London Sch Econs & Polit Sci, Univ London, 54-55; Phi Beta Kappa; Sigma Delta Chi; Phi Alpha Delta; Sigma Chi. Polit & Govt Pos: Vchmn, Idaho Young Rep League, 50; Idaho State Rep, Bonneville Co, 56-62 & 64-66; mem, Rep Cent Comt, Bonneville Co, 56-66; nominee, US House Rep, 62; chmn, Idaho Manpower Adv Comt, 63-; mem, Idaho Comn Constitution Rev, 66; Idaho State Sen, Dist 30, 67-68; US Rep, Second Dist, 69-75. Mil Serv: Entered as A/S, Navy, 44, released as Seaman 1/C, 46, after serv in Pac, 45-46; Am & Asiatic-Pac Theater Ribbons; Victory Medal;

Maj, Air Force Res. Mem: Ninth Dist Bar Asn; Idaho State Bar Asn; Rotary; Am Legion. Honors & Awards: Awarded Rotary Found Fellowship for study at Univ London, 54-55. Relig: Latter-day Saint. Mailing Add: PO Box 396 Idaho Falls ID 83401

HANSEN, WILLARD R (R)
Iowa State Sen
Mailing Add: 411 Main Cedar Falls IA 50613

HANSEN, WILLIS L (R)
Utah State Rep
Mailing Add: 323 W Forest St Brigham City UT 84302

HANSEY, DONALD G (R)
Wash State Rep
b Everett, Wash, Aug 21, 29; s Walter G Hansey & Gladys Myers H; m 1954 to Virginia A Jellison; c Randal G, Mark B, Brent S & Karen M. Educ: Univ Wash, BA in Bus Admin. Polit & Govt Pos: Mem, Wash State Aeronaut Comn, 66-; Wash State Sen, 68-69; Wash State Rep, 42nd Dist, 71-72 & 40th Dist, 73- Mil Serv: Entered as Pvt, Army, 52, released as Cpl 53, after serv in 1903 Eng Aviation Bn, Korean Conflict, 52-53; Korean Theatre Oper Ribbon; Unit Commendations. Mem: Am Poultry & Hatchery Asn (state dir, 68-); Rotary; Bellingham CofC; Am Farm Bur Fedn; Mason. Relig: Presbyterian. Mailing Add: 1551 Lakewood Lane Bellingham WA 98225

HANSON, BERNICE ZILPHA (R)
Mem, York Co Rep Comt, Maine
b Fitchburg, Mass, Dec 11, 01; d Herbert Greenwood Bonney & Annie Amiott B; m 1923 to Howard Hartley Hanson; c Virginia A (Mrs George Stackpole), Robert A & Arthur W. Educ: High Sch; Exten course in pub speaking, Univ NH. Polit & Govt Pos: Moderator, Lebanon Town Meetings, 50-65; Maine State Rep, 51-52, 59-62 & 65-68, mem, Interim Legis Comts Educ & Appropriations to Study Sch Construction, Maine House of Rep, 60; chmn, Lebanon Town Rep Comt, Maine, 53-; pres, Maine State Fedn Rep Women, 59-61; mem, Resolution Comt Educ, Rep Nat Conv, 60; mem, York Co Rep Comt, Maine 72- Bus & Prof Pos: Part-time secy, YMCA, 44-45; clerk, Off Price Admin, Bath Iron Works, Maine, 46. Mem: Eastern Star; Arundel York Co Rep Women's Club; Lebanon Hist Soc; Lebanon Women's Group (secy). Relig: Congregational; treas, Parish & North Lebanon Cemetery Asn. Mailing Add: RD 1 East Lebanon ME 04027

HANSON, CAMILLA RUTH (D)
Treas, Tenth Dist Dem Party, Wis
b Lexington, Ky, Jan 25, 28; d Edgar Zavitz Palmer & Ruth Opal Yarbrough P; m 1965 to J Louis Hanson; c Eric K, Stephen E & Philip J Sorensen. Educ: Univ Wis, 45-46; Univ Nebr, BA, 49; YWCA. Polit & Govt Pos: Chmn, Ashland Co Dem Party, Wis, 67-72; treas, Tenth Dist Dem Party, 67- Bus & Prof Pos: Proj asst, Peace Corps, 62-63; spec asst, Univ Wis, 64-65. Mem: Headstart Parent Adv Bd; League of Women Voters. Legal Res: 137 Tyler Ave Mellen WI 54546 Mailing Add: Box 707 Mellen WI 54546

HANSON, DONALD PAUL (R)
Chmn, Jackson Co Rep Party, Colo
b Laramie, Wyo, Feb 3, 23; s Victor Hanson, Sr & Sigrid Lindhal H; m 1947 to Anna Marie Van Valkinburg; c Kent A, Kirk L, Kelly E, Kevin W & Kale V. Educ: Iowa State Univ. Polit & Govt Pos: Vet serv officer, Jackson Co, Colo, 3 years, civil defense dir, 15 years; chmn, N Park Hosp Dist, Walden, 58-; chmn, Jackson Co Rep Party, 63- Bus & Prof Pos: Owner, Cattle Ranch; chmn bd, N Park Soil Conserv Dist, 69-71; chmn pub lands comt, Colo Asn Soil Conserv Dist, 73- Mil Serv: Entered as Pvt, Marine Corps, 43, released as Pfc, 45, after serv in 28th Marines, Fifth Marine Div, Pac Theatre, 44-45; Bronze Star; Purple Heart; Presidential Unit Citation; Am Theatre & Pacific Theatre Medals. Mem: Charter life mem Nat Cowboy Hall of Fame; Am Nat Cattlemans Asn; Colo Cattlemans Asn; Odd Fellows; North Park Stockgrowers Asn. Relig: Methodist. Mailing Add: Box 428 Walden CO 80480

HANSON, DOYLE ROBERT (D)
Chmn, Dixon Co Bd Supvr, Nebr
b Thurston, Nebr, July 14, 03; s George Lynn Elias Hanson & Jennie H; m 1932 to Katherin Carmen Hull; c Wendall Hull. Educ: Morningside Col, 24-25. Polit & Govt Pos: Chmn, Dixon Co Bd Supvr, Nebr, 50-, chmn, Dixon Co Welfare Bd, 50-; mem, State Welfare Rehabilitation, 62-69; pres, State Asn Co Off, 64-; dir, Law Enforcement & Criminal Justice State Nebr; chmn, Dixon Co Dem Party, 68-72. Bus & Prof Pos: Pres, Newcastle Chevrolet Co, 26-32. Mil Serv: Entered as Pvt, released as Cpl, Civilian Mil Training Camp, 23. Mem: Odd Fellows; MWA. Honors & Awards: Good Sport Award, World Herald, Omaha, Nebr. Relig: Protestant. Mailing Add: New Castle NE 68757

HANSON, FRED (D)
NMex State Sen
Mailing Add: 803 Hermosa Dr Artesia NM 88210

HANSON, HAROLD LESLIE (R)
b Houston, Minn, Dec 3, 04; s Severt Hanson & Emma Omodt H; m 1928 to Ruth Scow (deceased); m 1969 to Mrs Dester Sack; c Duane & Gene S. Educ: Univ NDak, 2 years. Polit & Govt Pos: Mem sch bd, Reeder Sch Dist, NDak, 37-41; mem, City Coun, Reeder, 44-61; co comnr, Adams Co, 50-66, mem, Welfare Bd, 64-70; chmn, Adams Co Rep Party, 61-65; chmn, Dist 39 Rep Party, formerly. Bus & Prof Pos: Livestock dealer, 44-68. Mil Serv: Entered as Pvt, Army, 22, released as Capt, 32, after serv in Army Res. Mem: Mason; Elks; Shrine; Lions; Farm Bur. Relig: Congregational. Mailing Add: Reeder ND 58649

HANSON, J LOUIS (D)
b Chicago, Ill, Sept 25, 25; s Martin J Hanson & Ann E Carroll H; m 1965 to Camilla R Palmer. Educ: Northwestern Univ. Polit & Govt Pos: Chmn, Tenth Dist, Dem Party Wis, 61-63, Dem Party Wis, 63-67, Seventh Dist, Dem Party Wis, 72-75; home secy, US Sen Gaylord Nelson, Mellen, Wis, 67-75, admin asst, Washington, DC, 75- Bus & Prof Pos: Secy-treas, Louis Hanson Co, Chicago, Ill, 45-50; pres, Bad River Lumber, Mellen, Wis, 45-50; self-employed, 51-67. Legal Res: Box 707 Mellen WI 54546 Mailing Add: 1435 Fourth St SW Washington DC 20024

HANSON, LEO OLIN (R)
VChmn, Bannock Co Rep Party, Idaho
b Hyrum, Utah, Nov 2, 1896; s Hans Peter Hanson & Randah Olsen H; m 1924 to Mary Shumway; c LeMar Olyn, Lois Ruth (Mrs Davis) & Wendell Reed. Educ: Utah State Univ,

18. Polit & Govt Pos: Chmn, Dist 33 Rep Party, Idaho, 70-; city councilman, McCammon, Idaho, currently; vchmn, Bannock Co Rep Party, currently. Bus & Prof Pos: Dairy farmer, McCammon, Idaho, 22-65. Mil Serv: Entered as Pvt, Army, 18, released after serv in Students Army Training Corps. Mem: Farm Bur. Honors & Awards: Serv Award, Bannock Co Farm Bur, 75. Relig: Latter-day Saint. Mailing Add: 320 Center St McCammon ID 83250

HANSON, NORMA LEE (DFL)
Treas, Marshall Co Dem-Farmer-Labor Party, Minn
b Brainerd, Minn, Feb 3, 30; d Fred Kruckow & Lena Sawyer K; m 1953 to Lynn C Hanson; c Michael Lynn. Educ: Minn pub schs, 12 years. Polit & Govt Pos: Pres, Marshall Co Women's Dem-Farmer-Labor Fedn, 67-69, vpres, 69-; chmn, Twp Caucus, 68-70; chmn sustaining fund, Marshall Co Dem-Farmer-Labor Party, Minn, 68-, mem dist resolutions comt, 70, treas, 70-; deleg, Dem Nat Conv, 72; mem, Gov Zoo Bd, Minn, currently. Bus & Prof Pos: Society reporter, Thief River Falls newspaper, 57-58, bookkeeper, 58-61; off mgr, Kiewel Bottling Co, 61-70; lobbyist, Minn Farmers Union, 71- Mil Serv: Entered Navy, 49, released as Seaman, 53, after serv in Naval Air Res, Minneapolis, Minn. Publ: Newspaper articles on farming, 68 & educ, 70. Mem: Off Econ Opportunity (bd dirs); Minn Farmers Union. Honors & Awards: Writer award, Minn Farmers Union; Silver Pin, five-year 4-H adult leader; Alumni award for 10 years as 4-H adult leader. Relig: Lutheran. Mailing Add: RR 3 Goodridge MN 56725

HANSON, RHODA E (D)
Chmn, Custer Co Dem Party, Mont
b Dedham, Mass, June 20, 12; d Chester Mayo Pratt & Grace Joy White P; m 1935 to Roy A Hanson; c Andrew Mayo, Kurt Ahan, Erika Pratt (Ms Edward Brown) & Thora Elizabeth. Educ: Col William & Mary, BA, 35. Polit & Govt Pos: Precinct committeeman, Custer Co Dem Party, Mont, 60-71, vchmn, 68-71, chmn, 71- Bus & Prof Pos: Secy, Berlitz Sch of Lang, Boston, 34-37; journalist, Boston Globe, Assoc Press, 42-45; life underwriter, Western Life Ins Co, 48-; teacher, Custer Co High Sch, 62-63. Mem: Am Asn Univ Women; Soroptimist Club. Mailing Add: Box 867 Miles City MT 59301

HANSON, RICHARD D (R)
NH State Rep
b Bow, NH, June 12, 27; s Oscar V Hanson & Lillian Morgan H; m 1949 to Betty Mae Morse; c Susan C, Tina J, Richard D, Jr, Jonathan K & Heidi E. Educ: Concord High Sch, 4 years. Polit & Govt Pos: Selectman, Bow, NH, 54-; NH State Rep, 58-; chmn, Merrimack Co Rep Party, 60-62, deleg chmn, 62; pres, NH Assessors Asn, 64; alt deleg, Rep Nat Conv, 68, deleg, 72; comt chmn, Munic & Co Govt, NH, 69- Bus & Prof Pos: Owner, Hanson Bldg Co, 59-; owner, Bow Trucking Co, 60- Mil Serv: Entered as Seaman, Navy, 45, released as 1/C PO, 46, after serv in Fleet No 7, SPac, 45-46. Mem: NH Archaeol Asn; Am Legion; Mason; Bow Rotary (vpres, 69-70, pres, 71-72); Grange. Relig: Methodist. Mailing Add: 14 Grandview Concord NH 03301

HANSON, ROGER LEON (R)
Minn State Sen
b Pelican Rapids, Minn, Nov 26, 25; s Henry Jacob Hanson & Anna Larson H; m 1952 to Dona Marie Schermerhorn; c Charles, Cynthia, Timothy, Cheryl & Hans. Educ: Dakota Bus Col, 44-45. Polit & Govt Pos: Minn State Rep, Dist 55, Otter Tail Co, 69-72; Minn State Sen, Becker, Otter Tail & part of Wadena Co, 72- Bus & Prof Pos: Owner, Hanson's Hardware Inc, 49; spec dep sheriff, Otter Tail Co; fire chief, Vergas Fire Dept. Mem: Lions; Vergas-Frazee Sch Bd (dir); Otter Tail Empire Resort Asn (pres). Relig: Lutheran. Mailing Add: Box 86 Vergas MN 56587

HANSON, THOMAS S (D)
Wis State Rep
b Oshkosh, Wis, Sept 14, 39; s Norman P Hanson & Hazel Daniels H; m to Lois M Gille; c Kathryn, Kristeen, Karen & Karolyn. Educ: La Crosse State Univ, BS. Polit & Govt Pos: Vchmn, Dodge Co Dem Party, Wis, 68-70; Wis State Rep, Dodge Co, 71-72 & 75- Mailing Add: Rte 4 Box 207 Beaver Dam WI 53916

HANSON, WALTER RAYMOND (DFL)
Minn State Rep
b St Paul, Minn, Mary 26, 31; s Walter R Hanson, Sr & Elizabeth Hamper H; m 1955 to Shirley Strobel; c Barbara, Deborah, Stephen, David & Peter. Educ: Univ Minn, 50-51. Polit & Govt Pos: Minn State Rep, 71- Bus & Prof Pos: Pres Brotherhood Rwy Clerk, Burlington Northern RR, currently. Mil Serv: Entered as Pvt, Air Force, 51, released as Sgt, 55, after serv in Security Forces, Korea, 53-54; Good Conduct Medal, Korean Serv Ribbon. Mem: Lexington Hamline Community Coun (pres). Relig: Catholic. Legal Res: 1136 Hague St Paul MN 55104 Mailing Add: Legis Mail Box State Capitol St Paul MN 55103

HANSON, WARREN EUGENE (R)
Chmn, Harvey Co Rep Cent Comt, Kans
b Osage City, Kans, Jan 13, 12; s Peter Nelson Hanson & Grace M Walthall H; m 1936 to Vera Louise Bennett; c Patricia Louise (Mrs Harper). Educ: Wichita Univ, Pre-Med, 29-32; Carver Col, DC, 36, PhD, 38; Phi Sigma Epsilon. Polit & Govt Pos: Chmn, Wichita Univ Collegiate Rep Club, Kans, 31, Harvey Co Young Rep, 46, Harvey Co Rep Vet, 58, & Harvey Co Rep Cent Comt, 60-69 & 73-; pres, Kans State Bd Chiropractic Exam, 40; presidential elector, Fourth Cong Dist, Kans, 68. Mil Serv: Entered as Pvt, Army, 42, released as Capt, 46, after serv in ETO, 43-46; Europe-Africa-Middle East Theater Ribbon with Two Bronze Stars; Am Theater Ribbon; Victory Medal. Mem: Kans Chiropractic Soc; Mason; Am Legion; 40 et 8; VFW. Relig: Methodist. Mailing Add: 416 N Pine Newton KS 67114

HANZALEK, ASTRID T (R)
Conn State Rep
b New York, NY, Jan 6, 28; d Arthur A Teicher & Luise Funke T; m 1955 to Frederick J Hanzalek. Educ: Concordia Col (NY), 45-47; Univ Pa, BS, 49; Alpha Chi Omega. Polit & Govt Pos: Pres, Suffield Rep Women's Club, formerly; regional vpres, Sixth East Cong Dist Rep Women's Orgn, currently; mem bd, Gtr Hartford Community Coun, currently; Conn State Rep, 61st Dist, 71-, Asst Majority Leader, currently. Mem: Nat Order Women Legislators; Nat Soc State Legislators; Traveler's Aid Asn (former vpres & dir pub rels); Hartford Symphony Fund Drives (local chmn); Suffield Country Club (bd gov). Honors & Awards: Man of the Year Award, Suffield Jaycees, 72. Relig: Lutheran. Mailing Add: 155 S Main St Suffield CT 06078

HAPKE, RICHARD DWAIN (D)
b Merna, Nebr, Sept 16, 35; s Alfred E Hapke & Nellie Madge Smith H; m 1964 to L Carolyn Brake. Educ: Eastern NMex Univ, BA, 68. Polit & Govt Pos: Mgr, Harold Runnels Cong Campaign, NMex, 70; admin asst, US Rep Harold Runnels, NMex, 71- Bus & Prof Pos: Ed, State Line Tribune, Farwell, Tex, 56-58; ed & gen mgr, Lovington Daily Leader, Lovington, NMex, 60-65; managing ed, NMex Farm & Ranch Mag, 65-70. Mil Serv: Entered as Pvt, Army, 58, released as SP-4, 60, after serv in Pac Stars & Stripes, Japan, 58-60. Mem: NMex Press Asn; Elks. Legal Res: Box 693 Lovington NM 88260 Mailing Add: 12619 Yardarm Pl Woodbridge VA 22191

HAPNER, JON CLARK (R)
b Hillsboro, Ohio, Nov 10, 34; s William Ralph Hapner & Kathryn Hendrickson H; m 1965 to Suzanne Evans; c Priscilla, Jonda & Jon. Educ: Ohio State Univ, BA, 56, JD, 58; Mexico City Col, 53; Univ Cincinnati, 64. Polit & Govt Pos: Pres, Young Rep of Highland Co, Ohio, 60-65; secy, Highland Co Rep Cent Comt, 65-70, chmn, formerly; city solicitor, Hillsboro, 65 & 68-69. Mil Serv: 2nd Lt, Army Artil, RFA, Capt, Army Res, 67. Mem: Am & Ohio Bar Asns; Hillsboro Rotary; Elks (Exalted Ruler, 64-65); Jaycees. Relig: Protestant. Legal Res: 130 Willow St Hillsboro OH 45133 Mailing Add: 100 S High St Hillsboro OH 45133

HARA, STANLEY IKUO (D)
Hawaii State Sen
b Honolulu, Hawaii, May 23, 23; s Kurazo Hara & Senyo Fujiwara H; m 1945 to Diane Hisako Yamashita; c Glenn Shoichi & Bradley Shoji. Educ: Honolulu Bus Col; Univ Hawaii. Polit & Govt Pos: Territory & Hawaii State Rep, 54-69, mem, All Standing Comt, 54-58, chmn, Agr & Forestry Comt, 54-57, Water Resources, Forestry, Reclamation & New Indust, 57-59, House Finance Comt, 59-65, vchmn, Govt Financing & Appropriations, 65-66, House Majority Floor Leader, 66-68; deleg, Hawaii Const Conv, 68-70; Hawaii State Sen, First Sen Dist, Hawaii, 69-, chmn, Comt on Educ, vchmn, Comt on Agr, Forestry & Conserv, mem, Comt on Econ Develop, Tourism & Transportation, Utilities Comt, Ways & Means Comt & Hawaii Select Comt, Hawaii State Senate, currently. Bus & Prof Pos: Owner, Hilo Factors & Kilauea Preserve Ctr; secy-treas, Akahi Painting Corp; trustee, Vacationland Assocs & Kaumana-Lani Assocs; mem, Nat Soc of State Legislators, 68-; mem, Educ Comn of The States, 68-; mem, Coun of State Govt, Legis Leaders, 68- Mem: Hawaii Farm Bur Fedn; Forester Court Mauna Kea; Native Sons & Daughters of Hawaii; Ment Health Asn of Hawaii; Japanese CofC. Honors & Awards: Grizzly Bear Award as Legis Conservationist of Year, Nat Wildlife Fedn & Sears-Roebuck Found, 66; Outstanding Serv Award, Distributive Educ Club of Am, 67; Outstanding Legis Sportsman Award; Hawaii Island Archery Club, 70. Relig: Buddhist. Mailing Add: 203 Kilauea Ave Hilo HI 96720

HARABEDIAN, MICHAEL THOMAS (D)
Mem, Steering Comt, 19th Cong Dist Dem Party, Calif
b Kars, Armenia, Sept 15, 14; s Thomas Harabedian & Noono Davidian H; m 1956 to Eleanore Burger; c Diana (Mrs Vanus Frederickson); David T, Dennis S, Dick M, Deborah & Michael Thomas, II. Educ: James A Garfield High Sch, 6 years. Polit & Govt Pos: Mem, Ways & Means Comt, 30th Sen Dist Dem Party, Calif, 67-; deleg, Dem Nat Conv, 68; mem, Steering Comt, 19th Cong Dist Dem Party, Calif, 68-; mem, Sen Exec Adv Comn, 28th Dist, 68- Bus & Prof Pos: Vpres, Operating Industs, Inc, 48-, Pomona Valley Reclamation, 54- & A & A Feeding, Inc, 56-; dir & organizer, Cerritos Valley Bank, 58- Mem: F&AM; Al Malaikah Temple; YMCA (bd dirs, 18 years); Shrine (past pres, Rio Hondo Club); Lions Inc (past pres & zone chmn, East Los Angeles Club, dep dist gov, Dist 4L2). Honors & Awards: Lion of the Year Award, 66. Relig: Armenian Apostolic; Dir, Relig Conf Bldg & chmn bd Saint Sarkis Church. Legal Res: 1800 Victoria Ave Montebello CA 90640 Mailing Add: 2425 S Garfield Ave Monterey Park CA 91754

HARCHENHORN, V LANNY (R)
Md State Deleg
Mailing Add: 307 Maple Ave New Windsor MD 21776

HARCOURT, H BAXTER (D)
Mem, Dem Party Ga
b Atlanta, Ga, Aug 27, 24; s Handley Harcourt & Ruby Mitchell H; m 1948 to Dorothy S Stephenson; c Raymond Baxter, Kevin M, Lauren & Christian. Educ: Atlanta Univ Law Sch, LLB. Polit & Govt Pos: Mem, Dem Party Ga, currently. Mil Serv: Seaman, Merchant Marine, 43-46, serv in Atlantic-Mediter & Pac. Mem: State Bar of Ga; Columbus Bar Asn. Relig: Episcopal. Legal Res: 1420 Eberhart Ave Columbus GA 31906 Mailing Add: 1711 Buena Vista Rd Columbus GA 31902

HARCOURT, J PALMER (R)
b Albany, NY, Jan 4, 07; s Samuel Charles Harcourt & Lois Palmer H; m 1935 to Anne Lee George; c John P, Jr. Educ: Union Col, 1 year 6 months; Alpha Delta Phi; Tiger's Eye. Polit & Govt Pos: Mem, NY State Rep Comt; committeeman, State & Town Rep Orgn; dep dir div safety, NY State, asst admin dir, Div Vet Affairs & asst admin dir, Civil Serv Dept; alt deleg, Rep Nat Conv, 68 & 72; chmn, Colonie Rep Orgn, currently. Bus & Prof Pos: Ins broker, Albany, NY; dir, Ten Eyck Insuring Agency, Inc. Mil Serv: Entered as 2nd Lt, Army, 42, released as Capt, 44, after serv in Qm Corps. Mem: Ft Orange Club; Univ Club; Elks; Am Legion. Relig: Episcopal. Mailing Add: 6 Cherry Tree Rd Loudonville NY 12211

HARDEN, BRUCE DONALD RICHARD (R)
Chmn, 15th Dist Rep Party, Alaska
b Bremerton, Wash, Oct 9, 40; s Richard Thomas Harden & Helen Eastmann H; m 1967 to Sandra Jean Cannon. Educ: Olympic Col, 58-60; Univ Alaska, 60-61. Polit & Govt Pos: Rep precinct chmn, Clear, Alaska, 68-70; treas, 15th Dist Rep Party, 68-70, chmn, 70- Bus & Prof Pos: Owner, Clear Sky Lodge, 66- Mil Serv: Entered as Pvt, Army, 63, released as Sp-4, 65, after serv in 1st Cavalry, Vietnam. Mem: Elks; Aircraft Owners & Pilots Asn; Nat Rifleman Asn; Clear Sky Sportsmans Club. Mailing Add: Clear Sky Lodge Clear AK 99704

HARDEN, CECIL MURRAY (R)
b Covington, Ind; d Timothy Murray & Jennie Clotfelter M; m 1914 to Frost R Harden; c Dr Murray Harden. Educ: Ind Univ. Polit & Govt Pos: US Rep, Ind, 48-56; Rep Nat Committeewoman, Ind, 64-72; deleg, Rep Nat Conv, 68. Mem: DAR; charter mem Bus & Prof Women's Club. Mailing Add: 302 Fifth St Covington IN 47932

HARDEN, ESTON A (D)
Ga State Rep
Mailing Add: 114 Cater St St Simons Island GA 31522

HARDEN, ROSS ULLMAN (D)
Chmn, Burke Co Dem Exec Comt, Ga
b Rockford, Ala, Apr 20, 09; s James Elzie Harden & Eunice Ward H; m 1938 to Ann Bates; c Sydney (Mrs Wynne) & Annette (Mrs Daniel). Educ: Mercer Univ, AB, LLB; Blue Key. Polit & Govt Pos: Law clerk, Ga Supreme Court, 36-43; asst attorney gen, Ga, 43-47; attorney, Burke Co, 52-65; chmn, Burke Co Dem Exec Comt, 60-; solicitor, State Court of Burke Co, 65- Mil Serv: Entered as 2nd Lt, Marine Corps, 44, released as 1st Lt, 45. Mem: Ga State Bar; Am Legion. Relig: Baptist. Legal Res: Waters St Waynesboro GA 30830 Mailing Add: 221 E Sixth St Waynesboro GA 30830

HARDER, JOSEPH C (R)
Kans State Sen
b Hillsboro, Kans, Feb 1, 16; s David E Harder & Margaret Flaming H; m 1939 to Maryan Lee Brooks; c Capt Brooks. Educ: Tabor Col & Bethel Col (Kans), 33-36. Polit & Govt Pos: City councilman, Moundridge, Kans, 54-58; precinct committeeman, McPherson Co Rep Party, 54-; bd mem, McPherson Co Hosp, 56-58; Kans State Sen, 61-, Majority Leader, Kans State Senate, 73-, chmn, Senate Educ Comt & Joint Comt Sch Finance, currently; state chmn, Rep Legis Campaign Comn, 64-66; mem, Nat Comt Sch Finance, currently. Bus & Prof Pos: Mgr, Harder Furniture Co, 50-60, secy-treas, Moundridge Tel Co, 55-, mgr, 60-; pres, Ami Inc, 59- Mem: Masons; Elks; Lions. Honors & Awards: Winner of Local Gold Club Tournaments on several occasions; Distinguished Serv Awards, Friends Univ. Relig: Protestant. Mailing Add: 109 N Christian Ave Moundridge KS 67107

HARDESTY, DORIS GIBSON (D)
b Louisville, Ky, Sept 1, 41; d Alva Paul Gibson & Mary Elizabeth Koenig G; m 1967 to Rex Hardesty; c Lawrence A & Elizabeth Willing. Educ: Loyola Univ (La), BSS, 63; Cardinal Key; Phi Phi Phi. Polit & Govt Pos: Polit asst to labor liaison, Humphrey Campaign, 68; labor liaison, Muskie Campaign, 72; staff, Deleg Selection Comn, Dem Nat Comt, 73; mem, Dem Nat Comt Charter Comn, 74; co-chmn, Precinct 4-17, Montgomery Co, Md, currently. Bus & Prof Pos: Admin asst, Dept Civil Rights, AFL-CIO, 65-70, polit consult, Comt on Polit Educ, 74; consult, Trends Mag, 75. Mem: Washington-Baltimore Newspaper Guild. Mailing Add: 11804 Greenleaf Ave Potomac MD 20854

HARDESTY, JIM W (D)
Okla State Sen
Mailing Add: State Capitol Oklahoma City OK 73105

HARDESTY, THOMAS FABIAN (R)
Chmn, Daviess Co Rep Party, Ky
b Whitesville, Ky, Jan 9, 28; s Samuel Alphonsus Hardesty & Della Boarman H; m 1954 to Delphine Marie Howard; c Anne Maureen & Alan Thomas. Educ: Evansville Col, 54-55; Univ Louisville, BSL, 59, LLB, 62; Chase Law Sch, 62; Univ Louisville Law Student Comt. Polit & Govt Pos: Chmn, Daviess Co Rep Party, Ky, 72- Mailing Add: 2936 Meadowland Dr Owensboro KY 42301

HARDIN, CLIFFORD MORRIS (R)
b Knightstown, Ind, Oct 9, 15; s James Alvin Hardin & Mabel Macy H; m 1939 to Martha Love Wood; c Susan Carol (Mrs Larry Wood), Clifford W, Cynthia Wood (Mrs Robert Milligan), Nancy Ann (Mrs Douglas L Rogers) & James Alvin. Educ: Purdue Univ, BS, 37, MS, 39, PhD, 41; Farm Found fel, Univ Chicago, 39-40; Sigma Xi; Alpha Zeta; Alpha Gamma Rho. Hon Degrees: DSc, Purdue Univ, 52 & NDak State Univ, 69; LLD, Creighton Univ, 56, Mich State Univ, 69 & Ill State Univ, 73; Doctorate, Nat Univ Colombia, 68. Polit & Govt Pos: Secy of Agr, 69-71. Bus & Prof Pos: Grad asst, Purdue Univ, 37-39 & 40-41; instr & asst prof, Univ Wis, Madison, 41-44; from assoc prof agr econ to prof & chmn dept, Mich State Col, 44-48, asst dir agr exp sta, 48, dir, 49-53, dean col agr, 53-54; dir Detroit br, Fed Reserve Bank Chicago, 53-54; chancellor, Univ Nebr, 54-69; mem bd, Asn State Univ & Land-Grant Col, 57-62, pres, 60, chmn exec comt, 61; mem bd trustees, Bankers Life Ins Co, Nebr, 58-69; mem educ comt, W K Kellogg Found, 60; mem nat adv coun on arthritis & metabolic diseases, US Pub Health Serv, 60-63; mem Africa liaison comt, Am Coun Educ, 60-64, dir coun, 62-66; dir Omaha br, Fed Reserve Bank Kansas City, 61-67, chmn, 62-67; trustee & mem, Rockefeller Found, 61-69 & 72-; mem, President's Comn Strengthen Security in the Free World, 63; trustee, Col Retirement Equities Fund, 63-65; dir, Behlen Mfg Co, Columbus, Nebr, 63-69; mem, Exec Comt Higher Educ Am Repub, 64-69; mem nat sci bd, Nat Sci Found, 66-70; vchmn bd, Ralston Purina Co, St Louis, Mo, 71-; dir, Overseas Develop Coun, 72-74; trustee, Farm Found, 73- Publ: Ed, Overcoming World Hunger, Prentice-Hall, 69; numerous articles & bulletins in the fields of agr & educ. Relig: Congregational. Mailing Add: Ralston Purina Co St Louis MO 63188

HARDIN, LUCIAN THOMAS (R)
Ky State Rep
b Inez, Ky, July 2, 30; s William H Hardin & Nollis Cassady H; m 1956 to Virginia Goble; c Joni Denise & Lucian Bartley. Educ: Georgetown Col, 49-51 & 56-57; Morehead Univ, AB, 58; Eastern Ky Univ, grad work. Polit & Govt Pos: Ky State Rep, Martin-Johnson-Lawrence Counties, 70- Bus & Prof Pos: Teacher, Inez High Sch, Ky, 58-69; banker, Inez Deposit Bank, 70-; social worker, Martin Co Bd Educ, 71- Mil Serv: Entered as Seaman, Navy, 50, released as RDSN, 59, after serv in Korea, 51-53. Mem: Ky & Nat Educ Asns; Jaycees; DAV. Relig: Protestant. Mailing Add: Box 202 Inez KY 41224

HARDING, EDWARD PERRY (NED) (R)
Mem, Maine State Rep Comt
b Boston, Mass, Feb 8, 23; s Francis A Harding & Dorothy Warner H; m 1946 to Suzanne Eckfeldt; c Anna Laurence, Edward P, Jr, Susan, Linda & Michael S. Educ: Harvard Univ, BS, 45; AD Club. Polit & Govt Pos: Asst nat dir, Nat Vol for Nixon-Lodge, 60; chmn, Portland Reed for Gov Comt, 66; nominee state chmn, Maine Rep State Comt, 67, mem, currently, chmn, Long Range Planning Comt, 70-; mem, South Freeport, Maine Rep Town Comt, 68; finance chmn, Cumberland Co Rep Comt, 68; deleg, Maine Rep State Conv, 68, 70 & 72; alt deleg, Rep Nat Conv, 68, deleg & chmn Maine deleg, 72; chmn, Maine Nixon for Pres Comt, 68; chmn, Maine United Citizens for Nixon-Agnew Comt, 68; chmn, GOP Action Comt, Maine, 69-70; Rep State Committeeman, Cumberland Co, 70-; chmn, co-chmn & finance chmn, Maine Comt for Reelection of the President, 72; pres, Maine Electoral Col, 72. Bus & Prof Pos: Pres & chmn bd, Harding-Glidden, Inc, Westwood, Mass, 46-60; pres & chmn bd, The Edson Corp, New Bedford, 56-61; pres & dir, Mastercolor of New Eng, Boston, 61-63; pres, Ft Hill Corp, 63-64; pres & chmn bd, Bicknell Photo Serv, Inc, Portland, Maine, 64-; pres, Maine Forum Corp, 68-70. Mem: Master Photo Dealers' & Finishers' Asn; Master Photo Finishers New Eng; Cumberland Club; CofC; Harraseeket Yacht Club. Relig:

Protestant. Legal Res: Box 4 South Freeport ME 04078 Mailing Add: Box 2011 Portland ME 04104

HARDING, G HOMER (R)
SDak State Sen
Mailing Add: 314 Mary Lane Pierre SD 57501

HARDING, KENNETH R (D)
Sgt at Arms, US House of Rep
b Medina, NY, Mar 28, 14; s Victor Hunt Harding & Edith Falk H; m 1938 to Jane S Wedderburn; c Kenneth Roberts, Richard Hunt, Bruce Addison & Victor Hunt. Educ: George Washington Univ, JD, 37. Polit & Govt Pos: Mem, Dem Nat Cong Comt, 46-54, exec dir, 54-72; Asst Sgt at Arms, US House of Rep, 54-72, Sgt at Arms, 72- Mil Serv: Col, Air Force Res (Ret). Mem: Nat Press Club. Relig: Protestant. Mailing Add: 3434 Greentree Dr Falls Church VA 22041

HARDING, MARGARET KATHERINE (MARTY) (D)
b Fredericksburg, Va, Oct 29, 36; d Irvin Thomas Harding & Octavia Coppage H; m 1956 to Trewitt DeLano Harding; c Trewdee Edwyna. Educ: Strayer Jr Col, Legal Secretarial Dipl, 55; George Washington Univ, BA with spec honors, 67; scholarship, class press & valedictorian, Strayer Jr Col. Polit & Govt Pos: Admin asst, US Rep George Grant, 56-64; admin asst, US Rep Frank A Stubblefield, Ky, 65-74. Mem: Cong Secy Club; North Va Art League. Honors & Awards: Valedictorian, Culpeper Co High Sch, Culpeper, Va, 55; honor student, George Washington Univ. Relig: Protestant. Mailing Add: 3822 12th St S Arlington VA 22204

HARDING, RALPH RAY (D)
b Malad City, Idaho, Sept 9, 29; s Ralph W Harding & Kathryn Olson H; m 1954 to Willa Conrad; c Ralph David, Cherie, Charlene, John Kennedy & Cozette. Educ: Brigham Young Univ, BS, polit sci, 55; studied acct, 55-56. Polit & Govt Pos: Idaho State Rep, 55-56; US Rep, Idaho, 61-64, mem, Agr Comt; deleg, Dem Nat Conv, 64, 68 & 72; spec asst for pub legis affairs to Secy of the Air Force, 65-66; Dem Nat Committeeman, Idaho, 70-72. Bus & Prof Pos: Staff auditor, Touche, Niven, Bailey & Smart, CPA's, San Francisco, Calif, 56-57; controller, Am Potato Co, Blackfoot, Idaho, 57-60, vpres, 67-70; pres, Harding Livestock & Land Co, 70- Mil Serv: Officer, Army, Korea, 51-53. Mem: Am Legion; Blackfoot CofC. Relig: Latter-day Saint: Mission to Cent States, 49-51. Mailing Add: Rte 4 Box 164 Blackfoot ID 83221

HARDISON, HAROLD WOODROW (D)
NC State Sen
b Lenoir Co, NC, Sept 8, 23; s Rutha Hardison & Annie Viola Stroud H; m 1944 to Arlene; c Pamela Jane. Educ: Atlantic Christian Col, 41-43. Polit & Govt Pos: Mem, Deep Run High Sch Adv Bd, NC, 49-, chmn, 55-; mem, Selective Serv Bd 55, 55-; vchmn, Lenoir Co Dem Exec Comt, 61-; NC State Rep, Ninth Dist, 71-72; NC State Sen, 72- Bus & Prof Pos: Pres, Humphrey-Hardison Oil Co. Mil Serv: Entered as Pvt, Air Force, 42, released as Cpl, 46, after serv in 7th Air Force, Pac Theatre, 44-46; Good Conduct Medal; Pac Theatre Award with one Battle Star. Mem: Mt Olive Col (bd trustees & exec bd); Mason; Scottish Rite; Shrine (Lt Comdr Legion of Honor); Lenoir Co Shrine Club. Relig: Baptist. Mailing Add: Box 128 Deep Run NC 28525

HARDT, A V (BILL) (D)
Ariz State Sen
Mailing Add: 112 North Broad St Globe AZ 85501

HARDY, FREDERICK WILLIAM (D)
Chmn, Monroe Dem Town Comt, Conn
b Bridgeport, Conn, Oct 27, 29; s Fred Hardy & Catherine Mitchell H; m 1956 to Joan DeMartino; c Lynn, Gail & Robert. Educ: Univ Bridgeport, 58-60. Polit & Govt Pos: Mem, Monroe Bd Tax Rev, Conn, 66-70; justice of the peace, Conn, 68-; mem, Monroe Planning & Zoning Comn, 70-74; chmn, Monroe Dem Town Comt, 74- Bus & Prof Pos: Eng asst, Sikorsky Aircraft, Stratford, Conn, 55- Mil Serv: Entered as Pvt, Army, 51, released as Cpl, 52, after serv in Inf, ETO; Army Occup Medal. Mem: Monroe Dem Club. Honors & Awards: Spark Plug Award, Monroe Jaycees, 65. Relig: Roman Catholic. Mailing Add: 99 Maplewood Dr Monroe CT 06468

HARDY, GEORGE (D)
Mem-At-Lg, Dem Nat Comt
Mailing Add: 1247 47th St Los Angeles CA 90017

HARDY, HELEN COLEMAN (D)
b Steelville, Mo, Oct 20, 04; d William C Coleman & Hettie Huitt C; m 1924 to W Clyde Hardy; c Marcy (Mrs Bowen) & Frances (Mrs Hoxworth). Polit & Govt Pos: Treas, Maries Co Dem Comt, Mo, 48-52, vchmn, 52-54, chmn, formerly; Mo State Rep, 55-66; vchmn, Maries Co Regional Planning Comn. Bus & Prof Pos: Mem bd, Belle State Bank, 70- Mem: Maries Co Hist Soc (mem bd); Cancer Soc (co-chmn); Eastern Star; White Shrine; Exten Club. Relig: Christian. Mailing Add: Belle MO 65013

HARDY, PAUL JUDE (D)
La State Sen
b Lafayette, La, Oct 18, 42; s Florent Hardy, Sr & Agnes Angelle H; m 1965 to Sandra Gatlin; c Gregory Paul & Yvette Rachelle. Educ: Univ Southwestern La, BA, 65; Loyola Univ, New Orleans, Law Sch, JD, 66; Delta Theta Phi; Phi Kappa Theta; Phi Lambda Beta; Newman Club; S Club. Polit & Govt Pos: La State Sen, Dist 22, 71-, mem, Judiciary A Comt, Natural Resources Comt, Legis Coun, Drug Abuse Comt, Comt Reorgn Levee Dists, chmn, Subcomt Pipeline Right of Way, La State Senate, 72-; mem, Atchafalaya Basin Comn, 72- Bus & Prof Pos: Attorney & law partner, Willis & Hardy, 66- Mem: Evangeline Area Guid Soc (vpres); KofC; Woodmen of the World Camp 134; Univ Southwestern La Alumni Asn; Pub Affairs Research Coun. Honors & Awards: Outstanding Sr Boy, Cecilia High Sch, 60; Track Letters, Univ Southwestern La, 62-64, Scholastic Award, 63; Student Coun Serv Award, Loyola Univ Law Sch, 66; Key Man Award, St Martinville Jaycees, 70; Outstanding Newcomer of Legis, Baton Rouge State Times, 72. Relig: Roman Catholic. Legal Res: 220 Resweber St St Martinville LA 70582 Mailing Add: 106 W Berard St St Martinville LA 70582

HARDY, PORTER, JR (D)
b Chesterfield Co, Va, June 1, 03; s Rev Porter Hardy & Jane Mahood H; m 1939 to Lynn Moore; c Lynn (Mrs Yeakel) & Porter, III. Educ: Randolph-Macon Col, AB, 22; Harvard Univ, 23-24; Tau Kappa Alpha; Kappa Alpha. Hon Degrees: LLD, Randolph-Macon Col, 55. Polit & Govt Pos: US Rep, Second Dist, Va, 47-69. Bus & Prof Pos: Dir, Portsmouth Terminals Inc, 65-, Atlantic Permanent S&L Asn, Norfolk, 69-, Dominion Bankshares Corp, 74- & Portsmouth Lumber Treating Inc, 74- Mem: Cedar Point Club; Harbor Club; Moose. Honors & Awards: First Citizen Award, Portsmouth, Va, 51; Mr Hampton Roads; Commerce Builder Award; Brotherhood Citation, Nat Conf Christians & Jews. Relig: Methodist. Legal Res: 3108 Laurel Lane Portsmouth VA 23703 Mailing Add: PO Box 6248 Portsmouth VA 23703

HARDY, ROBERT B (BOB) (D)
Miss State Sen
Mailing Add: 212 Court St West Point MS 39773

HARE, GEORGIA B (R)
Secy, Millard Co Rep Party, Utah
b Fillmore, Utah, Oct 12, 46; d Grant Brunson & Ethel Anderson B; m 1973 to Ronald Ray Hare; c Curtis Grant. Educ: Salt Lake Trade Tech Inst, Utah, PN, 65. Polit & Govt Pos: Secy, Millard Co Rep Party, Utah, 73- Bus & Prof Pos: LPN, Reading Hosp, Pa, 66-67; pub health nurse, Vis Nurses Asn, Reading & Berks Co, 67-72; charge nurse, Fillmore Latter-day Saint Hosp, Utah, 73; legal secy, Fillmore, 73- Mem: Old Capital JCW's; Fillmore Vol Fire Dept Auxiliary. Mailing Add: PO Box 328 Fillmore UT 84631

HARE, ROGER C (D)
Mem, Cumberland Co Dem Comt, Maine
b Houlton, Maine, July 27, 27; s Donald Hare & Hilda Porter H; m 1951 to Mary Margaret Thompson; c Stephan T, Maureen K, Mary Margaret (Mrs Maureen Perry), Roger C, II & Susan M. Educ: Houlton High Sch, grad, 51. Polit & Govt Pos: Mem, South Portland & Maine City Dem Comt, Maine, 59-; mem, Maine State Apprenticeship Coun, 66-69; mem, Cumberland Co Dem Comt, 69-; mem, Dem Nat Mid-Term Conf, 74. Bus & Prof Pos: Grand Lodge rep, Int Asn Machinists & Aerospace Workers, Washington, DC, 64- Mem: Columbia Athletic Club, YMCA (bd dirs). Relig: Roman Catholic. Mailing Add: 287 Lincoln St South Portland ME 04106

HARE, RONALD RAY (R)
Chmn, Millard Co Rep Party, Utah
b Fillmore, Utah, May 15, 47; s Kenneth Louis Hare & Doreen Coombs H; m 1973 to Georgia Brunson; c Curtis Grant. Educ: Univ Utah, JD, 71. Polit & Govt Pos: Chmn, Millard Co Rep Party, Utah, 73- Bus & Prof Pos: Attorney-at-law, Fillmore, Utah, 71- Mem: Utah State Bar; Old Capital Jaycees; Fillmore Vol Fire Dept. Mailing Add: PO Box 328 Fillmore UT 84631

HARELSON, JUANITA (R)
Ariz State Rep
b Stratford, Okla, July 4, 23; d Ivan Law & Callie Phillips L; m 1947 to James Earl Harelson; c Ted, Barry, Patrick & Rex. Educ: Ariz State Univ, BA, 45; Chi Omega. Polit & Govt Pos: Ariz State Rep, 72- Mailing Add: 1756 El Camino Tempe AZ 85281

HARENBERG, PAUL E (D)
NY State Assemblyman
b New York, NY; s Paul J Harenberg & Dorothy Miedema H; m 1953 to Sylvia Ann McArthur; c Paul Justin, Peter Stevenson, David Philip & Jennifer Rose. Educ: Columbia Col, AB, 53, MA, 54; Univ Tex, 59; Wesleyan Univ, 60-62; San Francisco State Col, 63; NY Univ, 65. Polit & Govt Pos: NY State Assemblyman, Fifth Assembly Dist, 75- Bus & Prof Pos: Teacher social studies, James Wilson Young High Sch, Bayport, NY, 55-75; Fulbright exchange teacher, Loughborough Col, Leics, Eng, 61-62. Publ: American Government, Monarch Press, Simon & Schuster, 65. Mem: Citizens for a Clean Environ; Steuben Soc; Nat Audubon Soc; Nat Geog Soc. Legal Res: 65 Harriet Rd Bayport NY 11705 Mailing Add: PO Box 80 Bayport NY 11705

HARFF, JAMES WARREN (R)
b Sheboygan, Wis, Dec 5, 40; s Ben Walter Harff & Helen Gruebner H; single. Educ: Northwestern Univ, BSJ, 63, MSJ, 65; Sigma Delta Chi; Chi Phi. Polit & Govt Pos: Chmn, Sheboygan Co Young Rep, Wis, 58-59; vpres, Northwestern Univ Young Rep, 59-60, pres, 61; co-chmn col activities, Rep Nat Conv, 60; mem nat steering comt, Youth for Nixon-Lodge, 60; campaign asst to Philip G Kuehn, Rep gubernatorial cand, Wis, 60 & 62; treas, Midwest Col Young Rep Fedn, 61; Rep deleg, NATO Nations Study Tour of Eng, France, Ger & Belgium, 61; chmn, Col Rep Nat Comt, 61-63; nat dir, Youth for Goldwater-Miller, 64; staffmem, Rep Nat Comt, 64; alt deleg, Rep Nat Conv, 68 & 72; chmn, Sheboygan Co Nixon for Pres, Comt, 68; state vchmn & research dir, Olson for Gov Campaign, Wis, 70; admin asst, US Rep Robert W Kasten, Jr, Wis, 75- Bus & Prof Pos: Reporter & ed writer, Radio Sta WHBL, Sheboygan, 63-68; reporter, Evanston Review, Evanston, Ill, 65; asst to the pres, Plastics Eng Co, Sheboygan, 65-72; dir pub affairs, Kohler Co, Wis, 72- Mil Serv: Entered as Pvt, Army Res, 65, released as SP-4, 68, after serv in Co C First Bn 334th Regt. Mem: Econ Club; Rotary Sheboygan Arts Found; Sheboygan Co Red Cross (bd dirs). Relig: Protestant. Mailing Add: 2606 Wilgus Rd Sheboygan WI 53081

HARGIS, GERROLL (D)
Mem Exec Bd, Tenn Fedn Dem Women
b Lafayette, Tenn, Nov 7, 11; d Joe Lee Carter & Jean Craighead C; m 1933 to Harold Wilson Hargis. Educ: Mid Tenn State Univ, 2 years; Cumberland Univ, 1 year. Polit & Govt Pos: Pres, Davidson Co Dem Women's Club, Tenn, 63, mem exec bd, currently; co-dir, Tenn Women's Div Presidential Campaign, 64; vpres, Tenn Fedn Dem Women, 64-66, pres, 66-68, mem bd dirs, 68-, mem exec bd, currently; deleg, Dem Nat Conv, 68; coordr women's div, primary elec, Stan Snodgrass for Gov Comt, 70; mem adv comt, Sen Albert Gore Campaign, 70; mem adv comt, regular elec, John Jay Hooker for Gov Campaign, 70; asst, reelect of US Rep Richard Fulton, Tenn, 72. Bus & Prof Pos: Teacher, Macon Co Sch Syst, 23 years, supvr, 53-55. Mem: Eastern Star; Past Matrons Asn; New Century Club (bd dirs); Colemere Country Club; Green Hills Civitan Auxiliary. Relig: Baptist; Mem bd dirs, Baptist Day Women, Belmont Heights Baptist Church. Mailing Add: 5041 Villa Crest Dr Nashville TN 37220

HARGRAVE, ROGER JAMES (DFL)
Chmn, 59th Sen Dist Dem-Farmer-Labor Party, Minn
b Clay Co, Iowa, Apr 22, 11; s Wallace Alexander Hargrave & Sarah Walters H; m 1960 to Anne Gerlovich. Educ: State Univ Iowa, BA, 36, MA, 42, PhD, 44; Nat Univ Law Sch, LLB, 54; valedictorian, Nat Univ Law Sch, 54, mem, Honor Soc; Delta Theta Phi (Scholar Key). Polit & Govt Pos: Legis asst, US Rep John A Blatnik, 47-54; chmn, 59th Sen Dist

Dem-Farmer-Labor Party, Minn, 70- Bus & Prof Pos: Instr polit sci, Duluth State Teachers Col, 44-46; asst prof, Bucknell Univ, 46-47; practicing attorney, Duluth, Minn, 54- Mil Serv: Mem, Int Brigades, George Washington Bn, Spain, 37-38; Cited for Bravery, Battle Brunette, 37. Publ: The Iowa State Comptroller, Iowa J Hist & Polit, 46. Mem: Minn State Bar Asn; AF&AM (Master, Euclid Masonic Lodge, 69); Scottish Rite (32 degree); Shrine; Moose. Honors & Awards: Amateur Boxer, Univ Featherweight Boxing Champion, 31; Man of Year, Euclid Masonic Lodge, 70. Relig: Methodist. Mailing Add: 1076 84th Ave W Duluth MN 55808

HARGRAVE, WILLIAM J (D)
Iowa State Rep
Mailing Add: 1103 Rochester Ave Iowa City IA 52240

HARGREAVES, JOHN R (D)
Md State Deleg
Mailing Add: Rte 2 Box 44L Pealiquor Landing Rd Denton MD 21629

HARGRETT, ANDREW JOSHUA (D)
b Savannah, Ga, Sept 19, 52; s Andrew Joshua Hargrett & Drucilla Williams H; single. Educ: Univ Chicago, currently. Polit & Govt Pos: Mem, Ill Youth Adv Comt, 71-; deleg, Dem Nat Conv, 72. Relig: Baptist. Mailing Add: 9438 S Prairie Ave Chicago IL 60619

HARGROVE, WILLIAM NICHOLAS (D)
Ark State Sen
b DeWitt, Ark, May 4, 13; s William Layton Hargrove & Dora Polstra H; m 1931 to Elsie Marie Frownfelter; c Nicky Edward. Educ: Ark A&M Col, 30-31. Polit & Govt Pos: Justice of the peace, Arkansas Co, Ark, 42-48; alderman, Stuttgart City Coun, 64-70; Ark State Sen, Dist 28, 75-, mem legis affairs & pub transportation comts, Ark State Senate, 75- Bus & Prof Pos: Farm owner & operator, Arkansas Co, Ark, 36-68; pres & co-owner, Southland Seeds, Chem & Fertilizer, 68- Mem: Stuttgart Rotary (pres, 75); Stuttgart CofC; Arkansas Co Farm Bur (dir); Arkansas Co Agr Mus Bd; War Mem Auditorium Bd. Relig: United Methodist. Mailing Add: 2001 S Prairie Stuttgart AR 72160

HARKER, JACQUELINE NUGENT (R)
Mem, Rep State Cent Comt Calif
b Tacoma, Wash, Oct 27, 24; d Robert W Nugent & Audrey Perry N; m 1945 to Richard Upson Harker; c Richard Upson, Jr, Edward William & Kenneth Nugent. Educ: Univ Calif, Los Angeles, AB, 45; Mortar Board, Zeta Phi Eta, Eta Sigma Phi; Kappa Kappa Gamma. Polit & Govt Pos: Mem, Nixon for Senate Comt, Los Angeles, Calif, 50; co-chmn, 22nd Cong Dist Citizens for Eisenhower, 56; co-chmn, Citizens for Nixon, San Fernando Valley, 60; chmn, Bell for Cong, 28th Cong Dist, 62; precinct chmn, 57th Assembly, 63-67; alt mem, Los Angeles Co Rep Cent Comt, 63-, mem exec comt, 73-; precinct chmn, Reagan for Gov, 57th Assembly Dist, 66; mem, Rep State Cent Comt Calif, 67-; chmn, Women for Nixon-Agnew, San Fernando Valley, 68; pres, Encino Rep Women's Club, Federated, 69 & 70; mem bd dirs, Los Angeles Co Fedn Rep Women, 71, pres, 73-; mem bd dirs, Calif Fedn Rep Women, 71-, Southern Div, 71-; bd mem, Calif State Dept Soc Welfare, 71-; deleg, Rep Nat Conv, 72; mem presch adv comt, Calif State Dept Educ, 72- Bus & Prof Pos: Vchmn, United Way, Inc, San Fernando Valley, 63-67; pres, San Fernando Valley Welfare Planning Coun, 64-65. Mem: Vol League San Fernando Valley (pres, 60-62). Honors & Awards: Merit Leadership Award, Los Angeles Co Rep Cent Comt; Ann Schlarb Award, Women's Div, United Way, Inc; San Fernando Valley Citizen of the Year, 70. Relig: Protestant. Mailing Add: 4500 Densmore Ave Encino CA 91316

HARKESS, NANCY ROBYN (D)
Nat Committeewoman, Young Dem Nev
b Altadena, Calif, May 14, 44; d Cecil Murray & Dorothy Spriggs M; m 1966 to George Robert Harkess; c Deanna & Craig. Educ: Univ Nev. Polit & Govt Pos: Nat committeewoman, Young Dem Nev, 71-; pres, Clark Co Young Dem, 71-; mem exec bd, Nev State Cent Comt, 71-; secy-treas, Clark Co Dem Cent Comt, 72-74; deleg, Dem Nat Conv, 72. Bus & Prof Pos: Local pres, Am Postal Workers Union, 69- Mem: League Women Voters; Am Cancer Soc; Nat Orgn Women; Ky Colonels. Mailing Add: 808 Sweeney Ave Las Vegas NV 89104

HARKIN, TOM (D)
US Rep, Iowa
b Cumming, Iowa, Nov 19, 39; m to Ruth Raduenz. Educ: Iowa State Univ, BS, 62; Cath Univ Am Law Sch, grad, 72. Polit & Govt Pos: Staff aide to Congressman Neal Smith, 69-70; staff mem, House Select Comt on US Involvement in SE Asia, 70; mem bd dirs, Iowa Consumers' League, 73; deleg, Dem Nat Mid-Term Conf, 74; US Rep, Fifth Dist, Iowa, 74-, mem agr comts & sci & technol comts, US House Rep, 74- Bus & Prof Pos: Attorney, Polk Co Legal Aid Soc, Iowa, 73-74. Mil Serv: Navy, 62-67; Lt Comdr, Naval Air Res, currently. Honors & Awards: Outstanding Young Alumnus, Iowa State Univ Alumni Asn, 74. Legal Res: 3412 Ontario Ames IA 50010 Mailing Add: US House of Rep Washington DC 20515

HARKINS, BERNARD JOSEPH (D)
Pres, Erie City Coun, Pa
b Erie, Pa, Oct 5, 15; s John P Harkins & Jennie Dunne H; m 1948 to Rita A Dill; c Rita Jane, John C, Nora, Ann & Patrick J. Educ: Findlay Col, BA; St Bonaventure Univ, MA; grad study, Univ Pa, Syracuse Univ, Allegheny Col, Univ of Pittsburgh & Edinboro State Col; courses taken at Inst for Training in Munic Admin of Int City Mgr Asn. Polit & Govt Pos: Pres bd trustees, Pa Soldiers' & Sailors' Home, 56-63; Dem coordr, WCity, Erie, 59-60 pres, SErie Dem Club, 60-63; councilman, Erie City Coun, Pa, 63-, pres, currently; vchmn, Northwestern Pa Region, Pa League Cities, 69-70, chmn, 70-71 & 73- Bus & Prof Pos: Head dept of health instrs & athletic coach, Erie Tech Mem High, Pa, 48-66; prin, John C Diehl Sch, 66- Mil Serv: CPO, Navy, 42-46. Mem: Pa State Educ Asn; Erie Teachers' Asn; Erie Sch Dist Adminr Asn; Erie Fedn Teachers Local 337, AFL-CIO; Am Legion Post 11, Erie, Pa (past Comdr). Relig: Catholic. Mailing Add: 2639 Schley St Erie PA 16508

HARKINS, MICHAEL EUGENE (R)
b Wilmington, Del, Apr 23, 41; s Eugene Francis Harkins & Aline Harrison H; m 1964 to Helen White; c Christine, Kelly Ann & Amy Michelle. Educ: Holy Cross, BS in Hist, 63; St John's Univ Law Sch, 64-65. Polit & Govt Pos: Campaign coordr, US Rep William Roth, Del, 66; research dir, Rep State Comt, Del, 66-68; campaign mgr, Hal Haskell For Mayor, Wilmington, Del, 68; spec asst to mayor Harry G Haskell, Jr, Wilmington, 69-70; vchmn, Mid-Atlantic Region II, Nat Fedn Young Rep Clubs, 69-; campaign mgr, W Laird Stabler, Jr for Attorney Gen, Del, 70; Del State Rep, 16th Dist, 70-72; admin asst to US Rep William S Cohen, Maine, 73- Bus & Prof Pos: Partner, The Agency Inc, Pub Rels & Campaign Consult Firm, 70- Relig: Catholic. Legal Res: 1105 Woodlawn Ave Wilmington DE 19805 Mailing Add: 1206 Market St Wilmington DE 19801

HARLLEE, JOHN (D)
b Washington, DC, Jan 2, 14; s William Curry Harllee & Ella Fullmore H; m 1937 to Jo Beth Carden; c John. Educ: US Naval Acad, BS, 34; Naval War Col, grad, 50. Polit & Govt Pos: Chmn, Citizens for Kennedy & Johnson, Northern Calif, 60; consult, Under Secy of Com for Transportation, 61; mem, Fed Maritime Comn, 61-63, chmn, 63-69; maritime mgt consult, currently. Bus & Prof Pos: Dir & past vpres, Peter Tare, Inc; prod planner, AMPEX Corp, 60; vpres, Edward I Farley & Co, Inc, New York, 60-61. Mil Serv: Ens to Rear Adm, Navy, 34-59; Comdr, Motor Torpedo Squadron 12, 43-44; mem, Naval Cong Liaison Unit, 48-49; Comdr, USS Dyess, 49-50 & USS Rankin, 58; Silver Star; Legion of Merit, Commendation Ribbon. Publ: Practical leadership aboard ship, 9/59, Patrol guerilla motor boats, 4/64 & The federal Maritime Commission and the American Merchant Marine, 9/70, US Naval Inst. Mem: Am Merchant Marine Libr Asn (trustee); Sons of Repub of Tex; Tex Soc of Wash; Tex Breakfast Club; Chevy Chase Club. Honors & Awards: Selected Man of the Year, NY Foreign Freight Forwarders Asn, 64; Golden Quill Award, Rudder Club; Brooklyn NY Hon Port Pilot Award, Port Long Beach, Calif, 68; Commendation, Fed Bar Asn, 69. Relig: Presbyterian. Mailing Add: Oakley Front Royal VA 22630

HARLOW, HAROLD G (R)
Conn State Rep
Mailing Add: Prospect St Litchfield CT 06759

HARLOW, PAUL KIDDER (D)
b Okobojo, SDak, Aug 25, 04; s Arthur I Harlow & Martha Bunch H; m 1929 to Margaret Barto; c Arthur Allen & Ruth Marie. Educ: Stanford Univ, BA, 30. Polit & Govt Pos: Mem sch bd, Thompson Falls, Mont, 40-43 & 52-55; Mont State Rep, Dist 27, 45-50 & 67-71; chmn, Green Mt Soil & Water Conserv Dist, 50-65; committeeman, Dem Party, 52-65; chmn, Sanders Co Dem Cent Comt, 54-64; crew leader, Agr Census, 64; vchmn, Western Interstate Comt Human Resources, Coun State Govt, 69-; deleg, Mont Const Conv, 72. Bus & Prof Pos: Sch teacher, 30-36, 43-44 & 49-50. Mem: Mont Citizens Comt for Pub Schs; Nat Comt for Pub Schs; Nat Comt for the Support of Pub Schs; charter mem Thompson Falls Lions. Relig: Protestant. Mailing Add: Box 277 Thompson Falls MT 59873

HARLOW, RONALD V (D)
Idaho State Rep
Mailing Add: 604 Burrell Dr Lewiston ID 83501

HARMAN, CHARLES WILLIAM (D)
Mem, Nebr Dem State Exec Bd
b Granum, Alta, Can, Feb 25, 03; s James Robert Harman & Emma Summer H; m 1938 to Eunice Pauline Rood. Educ: York Bus Col, York, Nebr, 2 years. Polit & Govt Pos: Chmn, Furnas Co Dem Party, Nebr, 59-; mem, Nebr Dem State Cent Comt, 60-; mem, Nebr Dem State Exec Bd, 67-; mem Judicial Nomination Comn, State of Nebr, currently. Bus & Prof Pos: Farmer & livestock producer, 18- Mem: Mason (Worshipful Master); Eastern Star (Worthy Patron); Nat Grange; Odd Fellows; Shrine. Honors & Awards: Champion & received plaque, DeKalb Corn Nat Growing, off yield 101.09 bushels per acre. Relig: Protestant. Mailing Add: 820 Tenth St Beaver City NE 68926

HARMAN, CHARLTON NEWTON (R)
WVa State Sen
b Davis, WVa, Aug 16, 15; s Charlie Newton Harman & Stella May Kimble H; m 1947 to Harriet Jane Dempsey; c James Kyle, John Duglas & Charlene Jane. Educ: Packard Merlin Sch, Warrington, Eng, 2 years; New Eng Aircraft Sch; Bell Aircraft Sch; completed drawing & design course, Col Eng, 42 and state and local govt course, 69, WVa Univ. Polit & Govt Pos: WVa State Deleg, 69-71; WVa State Sen, 15th Dist, 71- Bus & Prof Pos: Gen mgr, Harman Construction, 46- Mil Serv: Entered as Pvt, Air Force, released as T/Sgt, 46, after serv in 479th Fighter Group, 8th Air Force, ETO, 42-46; 5 Bronze Stars; Good Conduct Medal; Europe-Africa-Mid East Serv Ribbon; Am Theater Serv Ribbon; World War II Victory Ribbon; Air Medal. Mem: Mason; Grand Chap RAM; DeMolay (Commandery Noll); KT; Elks; VFW. Relig: Methodist; Sunday sch supt, United Methodist Blueville Church. Mailing Add: 4 Harman Ave Grafton WV 26354

HARMAN, ROBERT DALE (R)
WVa State Deleg
b Keyser, WVa, Oct 7, 37; s Herbert Roscoe Harman & Lillian Miller H; m 1958 to Phyllis Ann Sanders; c Kelley Ann, Robert Craig, Tracy Dawn, Stephen Kirk & Kami Beth. Educ: Potomac State Col, AA, 57; Shepherd Col, BA, 59; Frostburg State Col, 64; WVa Univ, MA, 69; La State Univ, summer 70; Theta Sigma Chi; Shepherd Col 4-H Club; Potomac State Newspaper & Yearbook; Shepherd Newspaper; Col Thespians. Polit & Govt Pos: WVa State Deleg, Mineral Co, 64-, minority chmn, House Educ Comt & mem, Rep coord comt, WVa Legis, 67-69; chmn, Mineral Co Rep Exec Comt, 65-; state adult adv, Fedn WVa TAR, 66-72; mem bd dirs, GOP Youth Camp, Inc, 68-; pres, WVa Young Rep, 69-71. Bus & Prof Pos: Counr, WVa Exten Serv, 54-59; teacher hist & govt, Mineral Co Schs, 59-70, dir fed & spec projs, 70-; retail merchant, Harman's WEnd Grocery, 61-63; radio sportscaster, Sta WKLP, 64-65 & Sta WKYR, 68-69. Mil Serv: ROTC, Potomac State Col. Publ: Column, Capitol Views, Mineral Daily News Tribune, 65- & Piedmont Herald, 67- Mem: Coun Exceptional Children; Jaycees; Kiwanis; Nat Found for Polio & Birth Defects (chmn Mineral Co chap); DeMolay (Chevalier). Honors & Awards: 4-H All-Star; Outstanding Freshman Legislator, Charleston Daily Mail, 65; WVa Outstanding 4-H Alumni Award, 72. Relig: Methodist. Mailing Add: 1090 Carolina Ave Keyser WV 26726

HARMAN, ROBERT WOODSON (D)
Chmn, Platte Co Dem Cent Comt, Wyo
b Granum, Alta, Jan 28, 10; s James Robert Harman & Emma Sommer H; m 1930 to Kate Linda Hill; c Randall Walton, Tommy Wade & Kathleen Anne (Mrs Lebsack). Educ: Kearney State Teachers Col, BS, 30, AB, 32; Univ Colo, ME, 39; Phi Tau Gamma. Polit & Govt Pos: Vchmn, Platte Co Dem Cent Comt, Wyo, 66-68, chmn, 68-; alt deleg, Dem Nat Conv, 72; alt deleg, Dem Nat Mid-Term Conf, 74. Bus & Prof Pos: Sci teacher & athletic coach, Miller Pub High Sch, Nebr, 31-35; supt schs, Lakeside Pub Schs, 35-37; supt, Sunflower Consol Schs, Mitchell, 37-42, 47-50; sta clerk, US Scotts Bluff Field Sta, Mitchell 42-47; teacher phys sci, Wheatland Pub Schs, Wyo, 50- Mem: Am Asn Phys Teachers; Nat Sci Teachers Asn; Nat & Wyo Educ Asns; AF&AM. Relig: Protestant. Mailing Add: Box 646 Wheatland WY 82201

392 / HARMER

HARMER, JOHN L (R)
b 1934; m to Carolyn J; c seven. Educ: Univ Utah, grad; George Washington Univ, law degree. Polit & Govt Pos: Spec aide to US Sen Wallace Bennett, Utah, formerly; mem, Calif Rep State Cent Comt, formerly; Calif State Sen, 67-75, chmn, Senate Rep Caucus, 71-75; deleg, Rep Nat Conv, 72. Publ: We Dare Not Fail, Southwest Publ, 68; auth, Among the Living are the Dead, Calif Ed Publ Co, 71. Mem: Nat Asn Mfrs (former pub affairs dir); San Fernando Valley Bus & Prof Asn (founder & former dir). Relig: Latter-day Saint. Legal Res: 7835 Morningside Loomis CA 95650 Mailing Add: 411 N Central Ave Glendale CA 91203

HARMER, SHERMAN D, JR (R)
Utah State Rep
Mailing Add: 1177 Matthew Ave Salt Lake City UT 84121

HARMODY, RICHARD M (D)
City Councilman, Cleveland, Ohio
b Cleveland, Ohio, Apr 8, 30; s Michael L Harmody & Mary A Gasper H; m 1958 to Elsie J Smith; c Matthew R, Ellen M & Mark R. Educ: Fenn Col, BBA, 57; Western Reserve Univ Sch Law, LLB, 60; Phi Alpha Delta. Polit & Govt Pos: Ward leader & precinct committeeman, Cleveland Dem Party, Ohio, 63-; city councilman, Cleveland, 64- Bus & Prof Pos: Attorney-at-law, 60- Mil Serv: Entered as Pvt, Army, 51, released as Sgt, 53; Combat Infantryman's Award; Korean Serv Unit Citations. Mem: Cleveland & Ohio Bar Asns; Polish Legion of Am Vet; Slovenian Nat Benefit Soc. Relig: Roman Catholic. Mailing Add: 4824 W 14th St Cleveland OH 44109

HARMON, AUGUSTUS CONAWAY (D)
b June 10, 36; s Walter Kermit Harmon, Sr & Lucille Johnson H; m 1965 to Bernita Vaughn; c Cassandra Dee & Augustus C, II. Educ: St Paul's Col (Va), BS, 57; teachers col, Columbia Univ, 58-59; Glassboro State Col, MA, 73; Alpha Phi Alpha. Polit & Govt Pos: Councilman, Pleasantville Dem, NJ, 70-; deleg, Dem Nat Conv, 72. Bus & Prof Pos: Teacher, Atlantic City Sch, NJ, 63-70; supvr, Oakcrest High Sch, 70-; co-owner, Harmon's Motel, Pleasantville, 67-72. Mil Serv: Entered as Pvt, Army, 60, released as 1st Lt, 63, after serv in Engrs Unit, US Army Europe, Karlsruhe, Ger, 61-62; Sharpshooter; Good Conduct Medal. Mem: Nat & NJ Educ Asns; NJ State League of Municipalities; Masons (Worshipful Master, Peninsula Lodge 127, 59-60). Honors & Awards: One of 50 Most Eligible Bachelors, Ebony Mag, United Press Int, 65; Distinguished Serv Award, Mainland Jaycees, 68; Outstanding Young Man of Am, US Jaycees, 69. Relig: Methodist. Mailing Add: 300 S Chester Ave Pleasantville NJ 08232

HARMON, DAN (R)
Mo State Rep
Mailing Add: PO Box 465 Noel MO 64854

HARMON, HARLEY LOUIS (D)
Nev State Assemblyman
b Las Vegas, Nev, Jan 5, 48; s Harley Emett Harmon & Cleo Katsaros H; m 1971 to Barbara Jeanne McBride. Educ: Univ Nev, Reno, 66-68. Polit & Govt Pos: Nev State Assemblyman, 75- Bus & Prof Pos: Corp secy, Harley E Harmon Ins, Las Vegas, Nev, 70- Mil Serv: Entered as Airman Basic, Air Force, 68, released as Sgt, 71, after serv in 58th Supply Squadron, Tactical Air Command, 68-72. Mem: Las Vegas Rotary; Elks Club; Big Bros Southern Nev (vpres); Salvation Army (mem adv bd). Relig: Catholic. Legal Res: 4069 Monthill Ave Las Vegas NV 89121 Mailing Add: PO Box 2748 Las Vegas NV 89104

HARMON, PAM JENKINS (R)
Chairwoman, Washington Co Rep Party, Ky
b Marion Co, Ky, Nov 13, 50; d Gardner Jenkins & Emogene Armstrong J; m 1969 to Joe Norris Harmon; c Jeanna Jo. Educ: Eastern Ky Univ, 1 year; Fuazzi Bus Col, med secretarial degree grad, 69. Polit & Govt Pos: Chairwoman, Washington Co Rep Party, Ky, 72- Bus & Prof Pos: Bookkeeper-acct, Jenkins Truck Co, Inc, 73-75. Relig: Christian. Legal Res: 106 Fair Dr Springfield KY 40069 Mailing Add: PO Box 388 Springfield KY 40069

HARMS, KARL HEINZ (R)
Chmn, Phillips Co Rep Comt, Mont
b Nienburg, Ger, Feb 1, 38; s Karl Harms & Sophie Barm H; m 1964 to Janice Evva Rausch; c Onnalee & Ranota. Educ: Jr Col in Calif, 57-58. Polit & Govt Pos: Precinct committeeman, Malta, Mont, 68-; chmn, Phillips Co Rep Comt, 70- Bus & Prof Pos: Apiarist, 59-; greenhouse owner, 70- Mil Serv: Entered as Pvt, Mont Nat Guard, 59, released as E-5, 65. Mem: 1200 Club of Mont. Relig: Lutheran. Legal Res: 419 N First St E Malta MT 59538 Mailing Add: PO Box 236 Malta MT 59538

HARMS, LINDA KAY (R)
VChmn, Vernon Co Rep Party, Mo
b Ash Grove, Mo, Apr 20, 39; d James Duncan Nicholson & Marie Arnhart N; m 1962 to James Fredric Harms, MD; c James David & Lori Jean. Educ: Burge Sch Nursing, grad, 61. Polit & Govt Pos: Vpres, Vernon Co Rep Women's Club, 73-; vchmn, Vernon Co Rep Party, Mo, 74- Mem: Community Coun for Performing Arts; Laurels, Federated Women's Club; Nevada Country Club (bd dirs); PEO. Relig: Methodist. Mailing Add: RR 3 Vallee Hi Country Estates Nevada MO 64772

HARMS, WENDELL G (R)
Chmn, Young Rep of Iowa
b Waterloo, Iowa, Jan 10, 49; s Wendell G Harms & Roesetta Davis H; single. Educ: Morningside Col, BA, 71; Univ Northern Iowa, currently. Polit & Govt Pos: Chmn, Young Rep of Iowa, 74- Mil Serv: Entered as Pvt, Marine Corps, 71, released as 1st Lt, 74, after serv in 6th Marines, Mediter, 73-74. Relig: Methodist. Mailing Add: 2712 Cedar Heights Dr Cedar Falls IA 50613

HARNED, HORACE HAMMERTON, JR (D)
Miss State Rep
b State College, Miss, July 27, 20; s Horace Hammerton Harned & Harriet Rice H; m 1949 to Nellie Howell; c Margaret Ann, Helen, Alice & Horace H, III. Educ: Miss State Univ, BS, 42; Blue Key; Kappa Sigma. Polit & Govt Pos: Miss State Sen, 52-56; Miss State Rep, 60-; Presidential Elector, Am Independent Party, 68. Bus & Prof Pos: Dairy & livestock farmer, 46- Mil Serv: Entered as Aviation Cadet, Air Force, 42, released as Capt, 46, after serv in 311th Photo Mapping Group, Am Theater, 43-44, 45-46 & China-Burma-India Theater, 44-45; Asiatic Combat Ribbon with 2 Battle Stars; Am Theater of Opers Ribbon. Mem: Dist Law Enforcement Coun; Rotary; Mason; Am Legion; 40 et 8. Relig: Baptist. Mailing Add: Rte 1 Box 27 Starkville MS 39759

HARNER, DORIS WILHIDE (R)
Chairperson, Carroll Co Rep Cent Comt, Md
b Frederick, Md, Dec 30, 27; d Lloyd Baxter Wilhide & Bernice Ritter W; m 1948 to John Smith Harner; c John Steven & Brenda Nadine. Educ: Baltimore Bus Col, Md, 45-46. Polit & Govt Pos: Mem bd, Taneytown Rep Town Cent Comt, Md, 48-52; chmn Northern region, Md State Fedn Rep Women, 74-; chairperson, Carroll Co Rep Cent Comt, 74- Mem: Taneytown Rep Women's Club (pres, 74-75). Relig: Lutheran. Mailing Add: RD 2 Box 21 Taneytown MD 21787

HARNETTY, CHARLES SAMUEL (D)
Chmn, Perry Co Dem Exec & Cent Comts, Ohio
b Junction City, Ohio, May 18, 37; s William A Harnetty & Florence G Paxton H; m 1965 to Barbara Elaine Eckard. Educ: US Navy Hosp Corps Sch, grad; Ohio Univ, Lancaster Br, 2 years. Polit & Govt Pos: Chmn Perry Co Dem Exec & Cent Comts, Ohio, 68-; vchmn, Dem Co Chmn Ohio, 69-, treas, 70-; exam-auditor, State of Ohio, currently; alt deleg, Dem Nat Conv, 72. Bus & Prof Pos: Foreman, Ludowici-Celadon Co, New Lexington, Ohio, 61- Mil Serv: Entered as Airman 3/C, Air Force, 55, released as Airman 1/C, 59, after serv in 36th Tactical Wing, Ger; Good Conduct Medal; Unit Citation Award. Mem: Elks; KofC (3 degree); Tenth Dist Dem Action Club; Perry Co Dem Action Club (chmn); Father Flanagan's Boys Town, Nebr. Relig: Catholic. Mailing Add: Box 234 Logan St Junction City OH 43748

HARNEY, JOHN THOMAS (D)
Chmn, Medfield Dem Town Comt, Mass
b Peabody, Mass, May 13, 33; s Thomas Francis Harney & Margaret O'Brien H; m 1964 to Mary Wynn; c Jeanne Marie & Christine Marie. Educ: Boston Col, AB, 56, MA, 60, MEd, 63. Polit & Govt Pos: Vchmn, Medfield Dem Town Comt, Mass, 71-72, chmn, 72-; deleg, Dem Nat Conv, 72. Bus & Prof Pos: Mkt dir, DC Heath & Co, 69-71, ed-in-chief, 71-73, gen mgr, 73- Mem: Am Asn Publ. Relig: Roman Catholic. Mailing Add: 5 Laurel Dr Medfield MA 02052

HARNEY, MICHAEL P (R)
NH State Rep
Mailing Add: 15 Walnut Ave North Hampton NH 03862

HARNISCH, THOMAS WILLIAM (D)
Wis State Men
b Galesville, Wis, Jan 16, 47; s LeRoy Wesley Harnisch (deceased) & Margaret Jane Schleifer H; single. Educ: Univ Wis, Madison, BA, 69; Univ Minn Law Sch, JD, 72; Alpha Chi Rho. Polit & Govt Pos: Wis State Sen, 75- Bus & Prof Pos: Auctioneer, Neillsville, Wis, 68-; attorney, Johnson, Harnisch & Sautebin Attorneys-at-law, 72- Mem: Wis State & Clark Co Bar Asns; Salvation Army; Wisconsin Jaycees; Mason. Relig: Presbyterian. Legal Res: 118 W Tenth St Neillsville WI 54456 Mailing Add: 410 S State Capitol Madison WI 53702

HAROLD, PAUL DENNIS (D)
Nat Committeeman, Mass Young Dem
b Boston, Mass, Sept 5, 48; s Joseph Robert Harold & Marguerite Burke H; single. Educ: John Hopkins European Ctr, Bologna, Italy, summer 69; Univ Mass, Amherst, BA, 70; Suffolk Univ Law Sch, JD, 73; Phi Alpha Delta; Dean's List, Univ Mass, 70. Polit & Govt Pos: Campaign coordr, US Sen Edward Kennedy, Ward 19, Boston, Mass, 70; aide, Mayor White's Off Pub Serv, 70-71; intern, US Rep James A Burke, Mass, 71; legis aide, Mass Senate Counsel's Off, 72; alt deleg, Mass Dem State Conv, 72; deleg, Young Dem City Comt, 72; pres, Mass Young Dem, 72-74; nat committeeman, 74-; mem, Dem Planning Comt, 74; alt deleg, Dem Nat Mid Term Conf, 74. Bus & Prof Pos: Columnist, Quincy Sun, 70- Mem: Quincy Good Govt Forum (chmn, 75-); New Eng Press Asn; Am Asn Polit Scientists; Quincy Hist Soc (curator, 68-); Am Civil Liberties Union. Honors & Awards: Key to Worcester, Mass, Mayor, 72; Ky Col, 73; Nat Young Dem Award, 73. Relig: Roman Catholic. Mailing Add: 31 Riverside Ave Quincy MA 02169

HARPER, BOB E (D)
Okla State Sen
Mailing Add: State Capitol Oklahoma City OK 73105

HARPER, EDWIN LELAND (R)
b Belleville, Ill, Nov 13, 41; s H Edwin Harper, Jr & Evelyn Wright H; m 1965 to Lucy Davis; c Elizabeth Allen. Educ: Principia Col, BA with honors, 63; Univ Va, PhD, 68; Raven Soc; Omicron Delta Kappa. Polit & Govt Pos: Spec asst to dir resources planning staff, Bur Budget, 68-69; spec asst to the President, 69-73; asst dir, Domestic Coun, 69-73. Bus & Prof Pos: Vpres, INA Properties Inc; guest scholar, Brookings Inst, 65-66; lectr, Rutgers Univ, 66-68; sr consult, Arthur D Little, Inc, Washington, DC, 69; pres, Air Balance, Inc; vpres, INA Corp, 73-75. Publ: Virginia, In: Presidential nominating procedures in 1964 (w Paul T David), Nat Munic League, 65; The implementation and use of PPB in sixteen federal agencies, Pub Admin Rev, 12/69; co-auth, Personnel limitations of instant analysis, In: Current practices in program budgeting (ed D Novick), Crane, Russak & Co, 73. Mem: Am Polit Sci Asn; fel Am Soc Pub Admin; South Polit Sci Asn. Honors & Awards: Nat Defense Fel; Ford Found Travel-Study Grant; Louis Brownlow Award, 69; Citation, Outstanding Young Men in Am, 72. Legal Res: 9200 Litzsinger Rd St Louis MO 63144 Mailing Add: 807 Chestnut St Wilmette IL 60091

HARPER, HAROLD DONALD (R)
Assoc Mem, Rep State Cent Comt Calif
b Los Angeles, Calif, June 17, 35; s Harold Allen Harper & Doris Virginia Bates H; m 1964 to Sharon Lee O'Brien; c Kristin Shawn & Michael Scott. Educ: Am Univ, 57; Claremont Men's Col, BA, 58; Claremont Grad Sch, 59-60; night div, Southwestern Univ Sch Law, 70- Polit & Govt Pos: Legis asst, US Rep John J Rousselot, Calif, 61-62; admin asst, 70-; prog comt chmn, United Rep Finance Comt Los Angeles Co, 67; mem, Rep State Cent Comt Calif, 69-70, assoc mem, 71-; first vpres, Pasadena Rep Club, 71- Bus & Prof Pos: Pub rels exec, Pac Outdoor Advert Co, Los Angeles, Calif, 65-70. Mem: Cong Secretaries Club. Honors & Awards: Nominee, J CofC Distinguished Serv Award. Relig: Catholic. Legal Res: 326 Alta Pine Dr Altadena CA 91001 Mailing Add: Off of Hon John H Rousselot US House of Rep Washington DC 20515

HARPER, KENNETH FRANKLIN (R)
Chmn, Kenton Co Rep Exec Comt, Ky
b Covington, Ky, Jan 15, 31; s Kenneth Wellington Harper & Elizabeth Brickler H; m 1953 to Eileen Ann Kathman; c Gregory, Scott, Glenn, Bryan & Lesley Ann. Educ: Univ Ky, 49-51; Pi Kappa Alpha. Bus & Prof Pos: Mem, Kenton Co Rep Exec Comt, Ky, 61-, chmn, 73-; Ky State Rep, 63rd Dist, 64-68, Asst Minority Floor Leader, Ky House Rep, 66; vchmn, Comt Hwy Policy Probs, SRegion, Coun State Govt, 66-67; asst comnr, Ky Dept Child Welfare, 68-69; mem exec comt, Ky Crime Comn & chmn, Juvenile Delinquency Subcomt, 68-; mem, Ment Health Manpower Comn, 68-72; mem, Lincoln Heritage Trail Found & Historic Events Celebration Comn, 70-71; comnr, Ky Dept Pub Info, 70-71; Secy of State, Ky, 71-72; deleg, Rep Nat Conv, 72. Bus & Prof Pos: Pres & treas, Prof Bus Serv Ky, Inc, 66-70; dir, First Nat Bank & Trust Co, 68-; assoc, F Krumpelman Realty, 72- Mil Serv: Entered as Pvt, Air Force, 51, released as Airman 1/C, 53, after serv in 5th Commun Group, 5th Air Force, Korean Theater; Korean & UN Serv Medals; Good Conduct Medal. Mem: Kenton-Boone Bd Realtors; Ky CofC; VFW; Northern Ky Heritage League; North Ky CofC. Honors & Awards: Outstanding Young Man of Ky, 63; Boss of the Year, Capitol Chap, Nat Secretaries Asn, 70. Relig: Roman Catholic. Mailing Add: 33 Arcadia Lakeside Park Ft Mitchell KY 41017

HARPER, MATTIE (D)
Iowa State Rep
Mailing Add: Box 22 West Grove IA 52538

HARPER, RICHARD L (R)
Kans State Rep
Mailing Add: RR 3 Fort Scott KS 66701

HARPER, ROBERT JOSEPH (D)
Mont State Rep
b Butte, Mont, Sept 21, 39; s Francis Vincent Harper (deceased) & Stella Marie Driscoll H; single. Educ: Carroll Col (Mont), 60-61; St Peter Chanel Col, San Rafael, Calif, 61-62; Pre-Buck Club. Polit & Govt Pos: Mont State Rep, Dist 20, 69- Bus & Prof Pos: Dir, Consumer Protection Div, Silver Bow Co Attorneys Off, 71- Mem: Butte Consumer Protection Coun, Inc (chmn & bd dirs, 68-); Mont Consumer Affairs Coun, Inc (dir, 69-73 & second vpres, 73-); Consumer Fedn of Am; Butte Youth Serv Ctr, Inc (bd dirs, 71-); Community Health Serv for Alcoholism, Inc (bd dirs, 71-); Serra Club Int (charter mem, Columbia Chap, 73). Relig: Catholic. Mailing Add: 68 Missoula Ave Butte MT 59701

HARPER, ROY W (D)
b Gibson, Mo, July 26, 05; s Marvin H Harper & Minnie Brooks H; m 1941 to Ruth Butt; c Katherine Brooks & Arthur Murray. Educ: Univ Mo, AB & LLB, 29; Delta Theta Phi. Polit & Govt Pos: Chmn, Mo Dem State Comt, 46-47; US Dist Judge, Eastern & Western Dist, Mo, 47-59, Sr Judge, 70-, Chief Judge, Eastern Dist, 59-70; mem, US Judicial Conf currently, chmn intercircuit assignment comt. Bus & Prof Pos: Pvt law practice, 31-34; mem, Law Firm of Ward, Reeves & Western, 34-47. Mil Serv: Entered as Pvt, Army Air Force, 42, released as Maj, 45, after serv in Southwest Pac; Col, Air Corps Res; Bronze Star Medal. Mem: Pemiscot Co Bar Asn; Grand Lodge of Mo (Grand Orator, 65); AF&AM, Steele, Mo; Scottish Rite; Shrine. Honors & Awards: Citation of Merit, Univ Mo Law Sch, 63. Relig: Presbyterian. Legal Res: 3 Woodcliffe Rd Ladue MO 63124 Mailing Add: 420 US Court House & Custom House St Louis MO 63101

HARPER, RUTH FLORES (R)
b Camarillo, Calif, Dec 21, 33; d William C Flores & Josephine DeSoto F; m 1961 to Howard T Harper; c Delisa R, Labrina R & David H F. Educ: San Diego City Col, AA; Calif State Univ, San Diego, AB. Polit & Govt Pos: Chmn, San Diego area, Spanish Speaking Rep Conf, 66-69; chmn ethnic affairs, Fedn Rep Women of San Diego Co, 71-72; mem bd dirs, Mex-Am Comt to Reelect the President, 72; mem bd adv, Hispanic Finance Comt, 72; alt deleg, Rep Nat Conv, 72. Bus & Prof Pos: Mem bd dirs, Chula Vista Fed Savings & Loan Asn, currently & Calif Alliance of Spanish Speaking Businessmen, currently. Mem: United Way (bd dirs); Human Rels Agency, San Diego Co (comnr, 70-); Mex-Am Educ Guidance Found (bd dirs); LaJolla Lutheran Church Womens Auxiliary. Mailing Add: PO Box 649 Solana Beach CA 92075

HARPER, THOMAS (D)
b Greenwood, Ark, Nov 23, 08; s Robert Atlas Harper & Merton Harrell H; wid; c Thomas, Jr, Granville, Blake & Kay. Educ: Univ Ill, 27-28; Delta Upsilon; Phi Eta Sigma. Polit & Govt Pos: Chmn, Sebastian Co Dem Cent Comt, Ark, 42-44; chmn, Ark Dem State Comt, 54-63; deleg, Dem Nat Conv, 56, 60, 64 & 68; Dem Nat Committeeman, Ark, 63-72. Bus & Prof Pos: Attorney-at-law, 30- Mil Serv: Entered as Seaman 1/C, Naval Res, 44, released as Lt(jg), 46, after serv at Norfolk Navy Yard & Treasure Island, Calif, 44-46; Am Theater Ribbon. Mem: Am, Ark & Sebastian Co Bar Asns; Motor Carrier Lawyers Asn; Am Legion. Relig: Methodist. Legal Res: 5001 S Cliff Dr Ft Smith AR 72901 Mailing Add: PO Box 43 Ft Smith AR 72901

HARPER, VIRGINIA MAUGHAN (D)
b Wood River, Nebr; d John Patrick Maughan & Florence Maus M; c Carl Brian. Polit & Govt Pos: Mem, Yolo Co Dem Cent Comt, Calif, 60, 62, 64 & 66, mem, Calif Dem State Cent Comt, 62-70; dir, Fourth Cong Dist, Calif, Dem Coun, 63-66; deleg, Dem Nat Conv, 64; dist aide, US Rep Robert L Leggett, Calif, 68- Mem: Am Civil Liberties Union; NAACP. Mailing Add: 2217 Woodside Lane 1 Sacramento CA 95825

HARPOOTIAN, JACOB (R)
RI State Rep
Mailing Add: 84 Cushman Ave East Providence RI 02914

HARRELL, BEVERLY (D)
Nev State Assemblyman
b Brooklyn, NY, June 2, 29; d Max Katz & Gertrude Zubkoff K; single. Educ: Rhodes Prep Sch; Acad Dramatic Art. Polit & Govt Pos: Nev State Assemblyman, 75- Bus & Prof Pos: Madame, authoress, lectr, film producer & pres mail order corp, currently. Publ: Co-auth, An Orderly House, Dell Publ, 75. Mailing Add: Cottontail Ranch Star Rte Box 15 Goldfield NV 89013

HARRELL, JAMES H (D)
Chmn, Pope Co Dem Comt, Ark
b Bearden, Ark, July 3, 37; s L V Harrell & Audrey Means H; m 1958 to Zella Keener; c William Bradford & Timothy Douglas. Educ: Ark Tech Univ, BA, 62. Polit & Govt Pos: Pres, Pope Co Young Dem, 58; Ark State Rep, Fourth Dist, 67-70; mayor, Norristown, 71-72; chief dep secy, State Ark, 72-73; co-organizer first uniform elec laws, Conf States, 73; chmn, Pope Co Dem Comt, 75- Bus & Prof Pos: Pres, Harrell & Co, currently. Mem: Lions; CofC; Russellville Jaycees. Relig: Protestant. Mailing Add: Skyline Dr Russellville AR 72801

HARRELSON, JAMES P (D)
SC State Sen
b Mullins, SC, June 28, 19; s Carson A Harrelson & Bertha Mae H; m 1943 to Hazel H Richardson. Polit & Govt Pos: Nat committeeman, SC Young Dem, 52-57; SC State Rep, 57-60; SC State Sen, 63-; deleg, Dem Nat Conv, 64, 68 & 72. Bus & Prof Pos: Lawyer, practicing in State, Fed & US Supreme Courts. Mil Serv: Army Air Corps, 40; disabled. Mem: Mason; York Rite; Shrine; Elks; VFW. Relig: Baptist; mem gen bd, SC Baptist Conv, 48-53. Mailing Add: PO Drawer 732 Walterboro SC 29488

HARRELSON, JOHN WILLIAM (D)
Youth VChmn, SC Dem Party
b Baltimore, Md, June 1, 45; s Herbert Aiken Harrelson & Catherine Donnelly H; m 1974 to Susan Hamilton Norvell. Educ: The Citadel, 64-65; Baptist Col Charleston; Tau Kappa Alpha. Polit & Govt Pos: Pres, Baptist Col Young Dem, 68-69; chmn, Charleston Co Young Dem, 69-70; vchmn, Charleston Co Dem Party, 71-73; youth vchmn, SC Dem Party, 74-; cong aide to US Rep John W Jenrette, SC, 75- Bus & Prof Pos: Secy, Estherville & Assocs, 75-; mem adv bd, Peoples Savings & Loan. Mil Serv: Entered as Pvt, Army, 66, released as Cpl, 67, after serv in Inf Training Unit, 5th Army. Mem: Georgetown Propeller Club; SC Young Dem Club; Georgetown Jaycees; SC Farm Bur; Georgetown Co Drainage Comn. Relig: Baptist. Legal Res: Belle Isle Club Georgetown SC 29440 Mailing Add: Rte 1 Box 389 Georgetown SC 29440

HARRELSON, WILLIAM L (D)
State Comnr of Agr, SC
b Mullins, SC, July 25, 13; s Maxey C Harrelson & Dora Page H; m 1956 to Grace Hough; c Cynthia Page & William Louis, Jr. Educ: The Citadel; Univ SC, LLB, 37. Polit & Govt Pos: Mem, SC Dairy Comn & Mkt Comn; SC State Rep, 41-42; SC State Sen, 53-55; State Comnr of Agr, SC, 56- Bus & Prof Pos: Former attorney. Mil Serv: Coast Guard, World War II. Legal Res: Mullins SC Mailing Add: PO Box 11280 Wade Hampton Off Bldg Columbia SC 29211

HARRIGAN, ALICE ANNA (D)
b Orwigsburg, Pa, Dec 2, 09; d Clarence Brown & Myrtle Newhard B; m 1933 to James F Harrison; c Alice Ann (Mrs Charles Stedman), Patricia (Mrs James Gallian) & James Joseph. Educ: Beckley Commercial Teachers Col, 29; Pa State Col, BA, 31. Polit & Govt Pos: Mem Gov adv comt, Alaska Centennial; mem exec comt, Alaska Centennial Comt; mem, Active Dem Party, 33-; Dem Nat Committeewoman, Alaska, 39-72; deleg, Dem Nat Conv, 72. Bus & Prof Pos: Commercial teacher, West Hazelton, Pa, 29-33; teacher, Mt Edgecumbe Voc Sch, Sitka, Alaska, 39-41. Mem: Alaska Day Festival Comt Club, Sitka (exec secy); Emblem. Mailing Add: PO Box 196 Sitka AK 99835

HARRIGAN, LUCILLE FRASCA (D)
Mem, Montgomery Co Dem Cent Comt, Md
b Tarrytown, NY, Aug 3, 30; d Vincent Frasca & Lucia Fastiggi F; m 1952 to Robert Evans Harrigan; c Reed Vincent & Eautha Emily. Educ: Barnard Col, AB, 51; Georgetown Univ, MA, 56; Am Univ, PhD, 75; Pi Sigma Alpha. Polit & Govt Pos: Jr mgt asst, US Dept of State, 52-53, acting asst chief pub correspondence br, 54-55, chief speaking arrangements br, 55-57, speech writer, 57-59; press secy, Hanson for Cong, Md, 62 & issues chmn, 64; nat exec dir, Conservationists for Humphrey-Muskie, 68; campaign mgr, William Willcox for Co Coun, 70; mem steering comt, Montgomery Co Udall for President Comt; precinct chmn, Montgomery Co Dem Cent Comt, 71-74, mem, 74- Bus & Prof Pos: Adj lectr polit sci, Am Univ, 72 & Montgomery Col, 72- Publ: Auth, Opportunities in Foreign Service, Universal Publ & Distributing, 63. Mem: Am Polit Sci Asn; Montgomery Co Citizens Planning Asn (bd gov, 70-); Canoe Cruisers Asn. Honors & Awards: Scholar, Barnard Col, 49-51; Outstanding Performance Award, US Dept of State, 54; fels, Am Univ, 71-73. Mailing Add: 5113 Wehawken Rd Bethesda MD 20016

HARRILL, FRED FALLS (D)
Chmn, Cleveland Co Dem Party, NC
b Cleveland Co, NC, Mar 2, 48; s Edwin Yates Harrill & Beulah Falls H; m 1969 to Carole Ann; c Leslie, Leigh & Fred, Jr. Educ: Western Carolina Univ, 66-68; Gaston Col, 68-69. Polit & Govt Pos: Mem, Lattimore Dem Precinct Comt, NC, 70-71, vchmn, 71-72, chmn, 72-74; chmn, Cleveland Co Dem Party, 74- Bus & Prof Pos: Sales rep, W R Grace & Co-Agr Chem Div, 69-73; self-employed farmer, Cleveland Co, 73- Mem: Mason; Elks; Scottish Rite; Shrine; Lions. Honors & Awards: Lions Pres Award; Serv Award, Dem Party. Relig: Baptist. Legal Res: Rural Rd 1333 Lattimore NC 28089 Mailing Add: PO Box 6 Shelby NC 28150

HARRIMAN, KATHERINE JORDAN (D)
NH State Rep
b Stratford, NH, Oct 17, 15; d Harry B Jordan & Mae McFadden J; m to James L Harriman; c Shirley (Mrs William J White), Elaine (Mrs Raymond Brunelle), Sara (Mrs Howard J Everett) & Arthur J. Educ: Concord Bus Col & Lee Inst of Brookline, Mass. Polit & Govt Pos: NH State Rep, 73-, mem resources comt & enrolled bills, NH House Rep, 73-; mem, Merrimack Co Dem Exec Comt, 73-; chmn, Winona Lake Legis Comt, 74- Mem: Gtr Concord Dem Woman's Club; Cath Daughters; Nat Order of Women Legislators. Relig: Catholic. Mailing Add: 69 Thorndike Concord NH 03301

HARRIMAN, W AVERELL
Ambassador at Large
b New York, NY, Nov 15, 91; m to Kitty Lanier Lawrence; m to Marie Norton Whitney; m to Pamela Digby Churchill Hayward; c Mrs Shirley C Fisk & Mrs Stanley G Mortimer, Jr. Educ: Yale Univ, BA, 13. Polit & Govt Pos: Mem Bus Adv Coun, Dept of Com, 33-39, chmn, 37-39; adminr, Nat Recovery Admin, 34-35; mem, Off of Prod Mgt, 40-41; spec rep of the President, Gt Brit, 41; US Ambassador, Russia, 43-46; US Ambassador, Gt Brit, 46; Secy of Com, 46-49; US Rep in Europe, 48-50; Spec Asst to the President, 50-51; dir, Mutual Security Admin, 51-53; Gov, NY, 55-58; US Ambassador-at-lg, 61 & 65-; Asst Secy of State for Far Eastern Affairs, 61-63; Under Secy of State for Polit Affairs, 63-65; Rep of the President to Peace Talks in Paris, 68-69. Bus & Prof Pos: Dir, Ill Cent RR, 15-31, chmn, exec comt, 31-46; vpres, Union Pac RR, 15-32, chmn bd, 32-46; founder, W A Harriman & Co, 20-31; Ltd partner, Brown Bros, Harriman & Co, 31- Legal Res: Harriman NY Mailing Add: 3038 N St NW Washington DC 20007

HARRINGTON, D ROY (D)
Tex State Sen
Mailing Add: 4620 Griffing Dr Port Arthur TX 77640

HARRINGTON, DANIEL WILLIAM (D)
Chmn, Silver Bow Co Dem Cent Comt, Mont
b Butte, Mont, Feb 12, 38; s Bernard J Harrington & Nova M Maddock H; m 1962 to Patricia E Gallagher; c Kathleen E & Daniel G. Educ: Mont Tech Univ, 57-58; Western Mont Univ, BS, 60. Polit & Govt Pos: Pres, Silver Bow Young Dem, Mont, 60-62; deleg, Mont Const Conv, 71-72; chmn, Silver Bow Co Dem Cent Comt, 72- Bus & Prof Pos: Teacher, Sch Dist 1, Butte, Mont, 61- Mem: Am Fedn Teachers, AFL-CIO; Mont Fedn Teachers (exec bd). Relig: Catholic. Mailing Add: 1201 N Excelsior Butte MT 59701

HARRINGTON, DONALD SZANTHO (LIBERAL PARTY, NY)
State Chmn, Liberal Party, NY
b Newton, Mass, July 11, 14; s Charles Elliot Marshall Harrington & Leita Hersey H; m 1939 to Rev Vilma Szantho; c Ilona Vilma (Mrs Joseph G Hancock, Jr) & Francis David. Educ: Antioch Col; Univ Chicago, AB, 36; Meadville Theol Sch, Chicago, BD, 38; Starr King Sch for the Ministry, Berkeley, Calif, STD, 59; Meadville Theol Sch, DD, 64. Polit & Govt Pos: Cand, Lt Gov, NY, 66; state chmn, Liberal Party, NY, 66- Bus & Prof Pos: Sr Minister of the Community Church, NY, 44- Mem: Mason; Sigma Pi Phi. Relig: Unitarian Universalist. Mailing Add: 1560 Broadway New York NY 10036

HARRINGTON, EDWARD DENNIS, JR (R)
Mass State Rep
b Worcester, Mass, Aug 11, 21; s Edward Dennis Harrington & Alice Beeso H; m 1943 to Jean Thomas; c Janet Elisabeth, James Thomas, Edward Dennis, III & Alison Jean. Educ: Holden High Sch. Polit & Govt Pos: Tax assessor, Holden, Mass, 49-59; Mass State Rep, 57- Bus & Prof Pos: Material expediter, Heald Machine Co, 40-42 & 46-50; foreman, security dept, Wyman Gordon Co, Mass, 50- Mil Serv: Entered as Pvt, Marine Corps, 42, released as Sgt, 46, after serv in 4th Marine Div, Pac; Letter of Commendation. Mem: Holden Dist Hosp (dir); Am Legion; VFW. Relig: Catholic. Mailing Add: 170 South Rd Holden MA 01520

HARRINGTON, JOSEPH JULIAN (D)
NC State Sen
b Lewiston, NC, Feb 18, 19; s Julian Picott Harrington & Ethel Barnes H; m 1948 to Lettie Early; c Robert E, Julian Picott & Victoria Leigh. Educ: Lewiston-Woodville High Sch. Polit & Govt Pos: Town comnr, Lewiston, NC, 52-56; mem sch bd, Lewiston, 56-60; NC State Sen, 62- Bus & Prof Pos: Pres, Harrington Mfg Co, Inc, 50-; trustee, Elizabeth City State Univ, 68-; Chowan Col, 69- Mil Serv: Entered as Pvt, Air Force, 42, released as T/Sgt, 46. Mem: Mason, David Lodge No 39; hon mem NC Bar Asn; Alpha Epsilon Agr Eng; Shrine. Honors & Awards: Hon attorney, NC Senate. Relig: Baptist; deacon, Sunday sch supt. Mailing Add: Lewiston NC 27849

HARRINGTON, KEVIN B (D)
Mass State Sen
Mailing Add: State Capitol Boston MA 02133

HARRINGTON, LEWIS B (D)
Del State Rep
Mailing Add: 307 Haven Lake Ave Milford DE 19963

HARRINGTON, MICHAEL JOSEPH (D)
US Rep, Mass
b Salem, Mass, Sept 2, 36; s Joseph B Harrington & Elizabeth Kenneally H; m 1959 to Dorothy M Leahy; c Leslie, Mark, Keith, Alison & Michael Justin. Educ: St John's Prep Sch, Danvers, Mass, 50-54; Harvard Col, BA, with honors in hist, 58; Harvard Law Sch, LLB, 61, Harvard Grad Sch Pub Admin, 62-63; Carnegie Inst internship in state govt. Polit & Govt Pos: Councilman, Salem City Coun, Mass, 60-63; Mass State Rep, 64-69; Dem State Committeeman, 68; US Rep, Mass, 69- Mem: Corporator Salem Hosp & Salem Savings Asn; Historic Salem. Relig: Roman Catholic. Legal Res: Bayview Ave Beverly MA 01915 Mailing Add: 405 Cannon Bldg Washington DC 20515

HARRINGTON, NANCY O (D)
Fla State Rep
Mailing Add: 1517 Delgado Ave Coral Gables FL 33146

HARRINGTON, PETER F (D)
Mass State Rep
b Washington, DC, Feb 12, 36; s Dr Peter F Harrington & Mary G McNulty H; m to Joan E Kelly; c John G, James P, Maura J & Matthew P. Educ: Providence Col, AB, 57; Boston Col Law Sch, 57-59; New Eng Sch Law, JD, 60; student coun. Polit & Govt Pos: Mem charter comt, City of Newton, 69-71, mem bd aldermen, 70-, vpres, 72-73; Mass State Rep, 73- Bus & Prof Pos: Attorney, Nicolazzo & Harrington, 65- Mil Serv: Sgt, E-6, Mass Army Nat Guard, released 66. Relig: Roman Catholic. Legal Res: 157 Lowell Ave Newtonville MA 02160 Mailing Add: 1357 Washington St West Newton MA 02165

HARRIS, A DEON (R)
First VChmn, Bannock Co Rep Cent Comt, Idaho
b Lewisville, Idaho, Jan 29, 34; s Alfred H Harris & Idola Empey H; m 1956 to Bonnie Rhoton; c Kelly Deon, Lance K, Gary Byron & Brian Kent. Polit & Govt Pos: First vchmn, Bannock Co Rep Cent Comt, Idaho, 74- Bus & Prof Pos: Gen contractor, Pocatello, Idaho, 68-72; salesman & realtor, 70- Mem: Idaho State Real Estate Bd Realtors; Pocatello Bd Realtors. Relig: Latter-day Saint. Mailing Add: 524 W Eldredge Pocatello ID 83201

HARRIS, B B, SR (D)
Ga State Rep
Mailing Add: Highway 120 Duluth GA 30136

HARRIS, BRIAN L (R)
b Hutchinson, Kans, Sept 11, 50; s Lloyd F Harris & Elizabeth Laughlin H; single. Educ: Friends Univ, 68-69; Kans State Univ, 69-72. Polit & Govt Pos: Chmn, Kans State Univ Col Rep, 70-71; vchmn, State of Kans Col Rep, 70-71, chmn, 71-72; field coordr, Owen for Lt Gov, 72; alt deleg, Rep Nat Conv, 72; chmn, Fourth Dist Kans Young Rep, 72-73; admin asst, Lt Gov David C Owen, Kans, 73- Publ: The modern techniques of campaigning, Wichita State Univ Polit Sci Dept, 71. Mem: Nat Educ Asn; Kans Young Rep Fedn. Honors & Awards: Citizenship Award, Friends Univ, 68; Outstanding Col Rep, Kans Col Rep, 71 & 72; Outstanding Young Man of Am, Jaycees of Am, 72. Relig: Congregational. Mailing Add: RR 1 Haven KS 67543

HARRIS, CHARLES ANTHONY (D)
SC State Sen
Mailing Add: Cheraw SC 29520

HARRIS, DANIEL SHERMAN, JR (R)
Chmn, Walla Walla Co Rep Cent Comt, Wash
b Takoma Park, Md; s Daniel Sherman Harris & Gwendolyn Somers H; m 1967 to Harri Joan Hohensee; c Troy Daniel. Educ: La Sierra Col, BA, 65; Loma Linda Univ, MA, 66; Univ Southern Calif, EdD, 74; Phi Delta Kappa; pres, Judicature Club; Young Rep Club. Polit & Govt Pos: Chmn, Riverside Co Young Rep, Calif, 62-63; vpres, Calif State Young Rep, 64-65; mem, Riverside Co Rep Cent Comt, 64-67; mem, State Rep Cent Comt Calif, 64-67; mem, College Place Rep Sch Bd, Wash, 69-, chmn, 73-; precinct committeeman, Walla Walla Co Rep Cent Comt, 71-, chmn, 74-; deleg, White House Conf, 71; cong aide, US House Rep, 71-72. Mem: Nat Asn Parliamentarians; Acad Criminal Justice Sci; Nat Coun Social Studies (mem exec bd, Wash State Coun, 75-); Coun on Social Work Educ; Am Sociol Asn. Relig: Seventh Day Adventist. Legal Res: Campbell Rd Walla Walla WA 99362 Mailing Add: Rte 2 Box 142 Walla Walla WA 99362

HARRIS, ED JEROME J (D)
Tex State Rep
b Trinity, Tex, May 19, 20; s Rev Ed J Harris, Sr & Alva Maxine Kuykendall; m 1945 to June Brickson; c Edward J, III & Ann Edna. Educ: Southwestern Univ, BA, 41; Univ Wis Sch Law, LLB, JD, 48; Southern Methodist Univ Sch Law, grad sch, 49-51. Polit & Govt Pos: Dem precinct chmn, Galveston Co, Tex, 58-61; councilman, Galveston, Tex, 61-63; Tex State Rep, Dist 19, Place 1, 63-, serves on various comts, Tex House of Rep, currently. Bus & Prof Pos: Attorney-at-law, 48-; sr partner, Galveston, Tex, law firm, Harris, Martin, Carmona, Cruse, Micks & Dunten, Attorneys-at-law. Mil Serv: Entered as A/S, Navy, 41, released as Comdr, Naval Aviator, after serv in NAtlantic & Pac Theater; Aviator flying PB 4Y-2 Patrol Bombers, 43-46. Publ: Weekly columnist, Legislative Report, by-lined, Tex City Daily Sun, Texas City, Tex. Mem: Tex Trial Lawyers; Navy League; Kiwanis Int Club; VFW. Honors & Awards: Charter mem Dirty Thirty reform coalition, 62nd session, State Tex Legislature; Outstanding House Mem of the 62nd Session, Texas Lawmen's Asn. Relig: Methodist. Legal Res: 18 Cedar Lawn South Dr Galveston TX 77550 Mailing Add: 600 US Nat Bank Bldg Galveston TX 77550

HARRIS, FLETCHER (D)
b Madison Co, Fla, Sept 24, 26; s Dela Fletcher Harris, Jr & Ruby Gibbs H; m 1955 to Florence Buckner; c Holly Lee, Gibbs Buckner, Bonny Lou & Dela Fletcher, IV. Educ: Duke Univ, 44; Univ NC, Chapel Hill, BS Com, 50; Sigma Chi. Polit & Govt Pos: Chmn, Lee Co Dem Exec Comt, NC, formerly. Mil Serv: Entered as Pvt, Army, 45, released as Sgt, 46, after serv in Seventh Air Force, Pac. Mem: Independent Ins Agents NC, Inc; Nat Asn Ins Agents; Carolinas Asn Mutual Ins Agents; Nat Asn Mutual Ins Agents; Am Legion. Relig: Methodist. Legal Res: 1314 Hermitage Rd Sanford NC 27330 Mailing Add: PO Box 990 Sanford NC 27330

HARRIS, FORREST JOSEPH (DFL)
Dir, Minn State Dem-Farmer-Labor Party
b Trent, SDak, May 7, 16; s Edward Michael Harris & Marion MacDonald H; m 1940 to Helen Virginia Cox; c Alan Joseph. Educ: Augustana Col, BA, 48; Univ SDak, MA, 49; Univ Minn, Minneapolis, 49-53. Polit & Govt Pos: Chmn, 11th Ward, Minneapolis Dem-Farmer-Labor Party, 59-60, chmn, Fifth Dist, 60-66; deleg, Minn State, Fifth Dist & Hennepin Co Dem-Farmer-Labor Conv, 60-; mem, Minn Dem-Farmer-Labor Exec & Cent Comts, 60-; co-chmn, Naftalin Campaign Comt, 61; secy, Mayor, Minneapolis, 61-62; alt deleg, Dem Nat Conv, 64, deleg, 68 & 72; first vchmn, Minn State Dem-Farmer-Labor Party, 66-74, dir, 74-; co-chmn, Minn McCarthy for President Campaign, 68 & 72. Bus & Prof Pos: Head soc studies, Univ Minn, Minneapolis, 55-74, dir, HELP Ctr, 67-72. Mil Serv: Entered as Pvt, Army, 43, released as T/4, 46, after serv in GHQ, USAFE, 44-46. Publ: The Social Studies Program in General College, Wm C Brown & Co, 60. Honors & Awards: Outstanding Teacher Award, Minn Sch Asn, 68; Teacher of Year, Alumni Asn, 69; Horace T Morse Award for Outstanding Contribution, Undergrad Educ, 74. Relig: Lutheran. Mailing Add: 6113 Second Ave S Minneapolis MN 55419

HARRIS, FRANK CARLETON (D)
Chief Justice, Ark Supreme Court
b Pine Bluff, Ark, Dec 31, 09; s Frank Alexander Harris & Johnnie Ada Rodgers H; m 1934 to Marjorie Allison Wilson; c Eugene Starke. Educ: Union Univ, 29-31; Cumberland Univ, LLB, 32; Alpha Phi Epsilon; Phi Alpha Delta; Alpha Tau Omega. Hon Degrees: LLD, Ouachita Baptist Univ, 60. Polit & Govt Pos: Ark State Rep, 33-38; prosecuting attorney, 11th Judicial Dist, 47-48; chancery & probate judge, Fourth Chancery Dist, 49-57; chief justice, Ark Supreme Court, 57- Bus & Prof Pos: Nat chmn, Conf Chief Justices, 66-67; mem nat coun, Boy Scouts. Mil Serv: Entered as Pvt, Marines, 44, released as Pfc, 45, after serv in Hq Co, Recruit Depot, San Diego, 44, & overseas duty, 45; Pac Theatre Ribbon; Sharpshooter. Mem: Soc Crippled Children; Mason; F&AM (Past Grand Orator); Shrine (Past Potentate); Cent State Shrine Asn (past pres). Honors & Awards: Outstanding Lawyer Award, Ark Bar Asn & Bar Found, 74. Relig: Baptist; Mem Exec Comt, Southern Baptist Conv, 67- Mailing Add: 2005 Laurel St Pine Bluff AR 71601

HARRIS, FRANK W (R)
Dist Chmn, Alaska Rep Party
b Seattle, Wash, Mar 13, 20; s Samuel Rhodes Harris & Judith Marie Eeckhoudt H; m to Mona M Ward; c Judith Marie, Catherine Ann, Gerald Jay, Matthew Joseph & Mary Beth. Educ: High Sch, grad. Polit & Govt Pos: Dist chmn, Alaska Rep Party, 63-64 & currently, state chmn, 65-66; alt delg, Rep Nat Conv, 68; Alaska State Sen, formerly; mem parole bd mem, State of Alaska, 68-70. Mil Serv: Entered as Pvt, Army Signal Corps, 42, released as T/Sgt, 46, after serv in Alaskan Theater. Mem: Elks; Lions; Am Legion. Relig: Catholic. Mailing Add: 610 Fireweed Lane Anchorage AK 99503

HARRIS, FRED M (R)
Kans State Rep
Mailing Add: 1202 W Second Chanute KS 66720

HARRIS, FRED R (D)
b Walters, Okla, Nov 13, 30; m to LaDonna; c Kathryn, Byron & Laura. Educ: Univ Okla, BA in govt & hist, LLB, 54; Future Farmers Am; Phi Beta Kappa. Polit & Govt Pos: Okla State Sen, 56-64, chmn, Dem Caucus, Okla State Sen, formerly; US Sen, Okla, 64-72, chmn, Okla Cong Deleg mem, Govt Opers Comt & Permanent Subcomt on Investigations, Subcomts on Exec Reorgn & Nat Security & Int Opers, chmn, Govt Research Subcomt, mem, Finance Comt, Select Comt on Small Bus & subcomts on Retail Distribution & Mkt Practices & Taxation, US Senate, formerly; mem, President's Nat Adv Comn Civil Disorders, 67-68; deleg, Dem Nat Conv, 68; chmn, Dem Nat Comt, 69-70. Bus & Prof Pos: Founder & sr partner, law firm, Lawton, Okla, until 64. Publ: Alarms and hopes, Harper & Row, 68; Now is the time: a new populist call to action, McGraw-Hill, 71. Honors & Awards: Outstanding Young Man in Okla, Okla Jr CofC, 59; One of Ten Outstanding Young Men in US, US Jr CofC, 65. Mailing Add: 1104 Waverly Way McLean VA 22101

HARRIS, GENEVIEVE IRENE (R)
Chmn, 23rd Dist Rep Party, NDak
b Walnut Grove, Minn, July 18, 36; d George Anderson & Gladys Purvis A; m 1965 to Robert A Harris; c Pauline Marie, Denise Rene, Daniel James & Robert Emerson. Educ: Windom High Sch, Minn, grad, 54. Polit & Govt Pos: Conv recording secy, NDak Young Rep, 63-67, vchairwoman, 64-67, nat committeewoman, 67-70, state chmn, 68-69; mem, 23rd Dist Women's Fedn, 66-; mem exec comt, NDak Rep Party, 67-; mem exec comt, Young Rep Nat Fedn, 67-70, speaker & grad, Leadership Training Sch, 68; chmn, Young Rep for Doherty Campaign, 68; chmn, NDak Absentee Voter Campaign, 68; mem, NDak Rep Campaign, Comt, 68; deleg, NDak State Rep Conv, 68 & 70; deleg, Rep Nat Conv & mem platform comt, 68; vchairwoman, NDak Rep Orgn Sub-Comt, 68-69; chmn, 23rd Dist Rep Party, NDak, 69-; secy, Daryl Thompson for Labor Comnr Comt, 70. Bus & Prof Pos: Exec secy, Neuropsychiatric Inst, Fargo, NDak, 59-60, Harold E Flint & Assocs, 60-65, Melroe Co, Cooperstown, 66-72 & Steiger Tractor, Inc, 72- Publ: North Dakota Young Republican Organizational Manual, privately publ, 67; contrib, Young Republican National Federation Club Extension Handbook, 68. Mem: Nat Secretaries Asn; Griggs Co 4-H Coun (secy coun & 4-H leader); Cooperstown Homemaker's Club. Honors & Awards: Secy of the Year, Red River Chap, Nat Secretaries Asn, 63; Outstanding Young Rep in NDak, 67-68; Distinguished Serv Award, Leadership Training Sch, Nat Young Rep Fedn, 68, Bronze, Silver & Gold Hardcharger Awards, 69. Relig: Lutheran. Mailing Add: RR 2 Fargo ND 58102

HARRIS, GEORGE F (D)
Ky State Rep
Mailing Add: Box 168 Salem KY 42078

HARRIS, GLENN H (R)
NY State Assemblyman
b Gloversville, NY, Dec 31, 19; m to Norah Larkins Avery; c Linda Michele (Mrs Ronald Reynolds) & Glynn Kelli; two grandchildren. Educ: Univ Miami, Fla; Utica Col. Polit & Govt Pos: Councilman, Arietta, NY, 11 years; NY State Assemblyman, 64-, chmn, Joint Legis Comt on Environ Mgt & Natural Resources, 68-73, Assembly Majority Whip, currently; mem, Interstate Legis Comt Lake Erie, currently; adv comt, Atmospheric Sci Research Ctr, currently; Comt Eval Effectiveness of Assembly Sci Staff, currently. Bus & Prof Pos: Owner, operator, Christmas Tree Lodge (hotel & restaurant). Mil Serv: Navy Air Corps, 43-46. Mem: Int Narcotic Enforcement Officers Asn; F&AM; Am Legion; VFW; Gloversville Elks. Honors & Awards: Adirondack Legislator, Adirondack Conserv Coun; Legis Conservationist of the Year, NY State Conserv Coun, 72; Distinguished Serv Award, Environ Planning Lobby, 72; Snowmobile Legislator of the Year, Northeast Snowmobiler, 72; Man of the Year for Legis Leadership, Snowgoer Mag, 73. Relig: Lutheran. Legal Res: Rte 10 Arietta Can Lake PO NY 12030 Mailing Add: Rm 521 Legis Off Bldg Albany NY 12224

HARRIS, HERBERT E, II (D)
US Rep, Va
b Kansas City, Mo, Apr 14, 26; m to Nancy F Harris; c Herbert III, Frank, Susan, Sean & Kevin. Educ: Mo Valley Col; Univ Notre Dame; Rockhurst Col, BA; Georgetown Univ Law Sch, JD. Polit & Govt Pos: Mem, Fairfax Co Bd Supvrs, 68-74, vchmn, 71-74, chmn, 72; comnr, Northern Va Transportation Comn, 68-74; mem bd dirs, Washington Metrop Area Transit Authority, 70-74, first vchmn, 71 & 74, second vchmn, 73; pres, Fairfax Co Fedn Citizens Asns; US Rep, Va, 75- Mem: DC & Mo Bar Asns; KofC. Relig: Catholic; former chmn Parish Adv Coun, Good Shepherd Cath Church. Legal Res: 9106 Old Mt Vernon Rd Alexandria VA 22309 Mailing Add: US House Rep Washington DC 20515

HARRIS, IDA LEWIS (D)
VChmn, St Louis Co Dem Cent Comt
b Electric Mills, Miss, Jan 31, 11; d Tom McCoy & Mary Bell M; wid; c Robert Shaw. Educ: LeMoyne Col, 1 year; Nat Coun Negro Women. Polit & Govt Pos: Committeewoman, St Louis City Dem Party, Mo, 64-; vchmn, St Louis Co Dem Cent Comt, 64- Bus & Prof Pos: Chief clerk, Recorder of Deeds, St Louis, Mo, 65- Publ: Who's Who in Democratic Politics in St Louis, 65; Shoes for Children, St Louis Argus. Mem: Homer G Phillips Hosp Auxiliary; 26th Ward Regular Dem Orgn. Honors & Awards: Most Outstanding Humanitarian in Community, 70. Relig: Baptist; Pres, Dist 4, St Louis, Mo. Mailing Add: 4818 Cote Brilliante St Louis MO 63113

HARRIS, J G (SONNY) (D)
Ga State Rep
Mailing Add: Rte 1 Box 32 Screven GA 31560

HARRIS, J MERVYN (R)
Committeeman, Pa State Rep Party
b Johnstown, Pa, Oct 28, 33; s Joseph Harris & Mae Williams H; m 1963 to Margaret Horn; c J Lloyd. Educ: Pa Mil Col, BS, 57; pres, student body. Polit & Govt Pos: Chmn, Rep Finance Comt, formerly; mem co bd, Young Rep, formerly; Pa State Rep, 65-67; Rep committeeman, Second Ward, Nether Providence Twp, Pa, 58-68; chmn, Nether Providence Rep Twp Exec Comt, 67-; mem, Del Co Campaign Comt, 67-; deleg, Rep Nat Conv, 68; committeeman, Pa State Rep Party, 70- Bus & Prof Pos: Assoc dir admissions, PMC Cols, 60- Mil Serv: Entered as Pvt, Army Res, 54, released as Capt, 65. Mem: ROA; Mil Govt Asn; Nat Gymanfa Ganu Asn; Am Acad Polit & Soc Sci; Welsh Soc Philadelphia. Relig: Episcopal. Mailing Add: 300 Copples Lane Wallingford PA 19086

HARRIS, J OLLIE (D)
NC State Sen
b Anderson, SC, Sept 2, 13; s John Frank Harris & Jessie Mae Hambright H; m 1934 to Abbie Wall; c J Ollie, Jr & Jane Wall Hambright. Educ: Gupton-Jones Col Embalming, Nashville, Tenn, 35. Polit & Govt Pos: Coroner, Cleveland Co, NC, 46-70; NC State Sen, 71-72 & 75- Bus & Prof Pos: Pres, Harris Funeral Home, Inc. Mil Serv: Entered as Pvt, Army, 44, released as S/Sgt, after serv in 65th Field Hosp, 3rd Army, ETO, 44-45; Three Campaign Ribbons; Bronze Star. Mem: NC Embalming Bd; NC Coroner's Asn; Mason; Lions; Shrine. Relig: Baptist. Mailing Add: 921 Sharon Dr Kings Mountain NC 28086

HARRIS, JAMES D, JR (D)
Ala State Rep
b Tallassee, Ala, Feb 12, 43; s James Douglas Harris & Edna Flournoy H; m 1966 to Jean Brooks; c Jennifer Brooks, James Douglas, III & Stewart Katherine. Educ: Univ Ala, AB, 65, JD, 67; Sigma Chi; Phi Alpha Delta. Polit & Govt Pos: Ala State Rep, 71- Bus & Prof Pos: Attorney & partner, Harris & Harris, 67- Mil Serv: Entered as 2nd Lt, Army, 67, released as 1st Lt, 69, after serv in 173rd Airborne Brigade, Vietnam, 67-68; Capt, Ala Army Nat Guard, 70-; Bronze Star Medal; Army Commendation Medal; Parachutist Badge. Mem: Am Judicature Soc; Am Legion; Jaycees; VFW; Ala Youth Legis, YMCA (bd dirs). Relig: Baptist. Mailing Add: 1254 Westmoreland Ave Montgomery AL 36106

HARRIS, JAMES MONROE (R)
Committeeman, Bronx Co Rep Party, NY
b New York, NY, Aug 2, 22; s Robert Eugene Harris & Annie Hall H; div. Educ: NY Univ, 46-48; Col Ins, New York, 60. Polit & Govt Pos: Committeeman, Bronx Co Rep Party, 78th assembly dist, NY, 67-; Rep nominee for US Rep, NY, 68. Bus & Prof Pos: Compensation claims supvr, State of NY Workmen's Compensation Bd, 46-59, Markoff, Gottlieb & Harkins, Esq, 59-60, Consolidated Mutual Ins Co, Brooklyn, 60-64, General Fire & Casualty Ins Co, New York, 64-65, Hartford Accident & Indust Ins Co, Jamaica, 65-66 & Mich Mutual Liability Ins Co, New York, 66-69; foreign claims supvr, Aetna Casualty & Surety, 69- Mil Serv: Entered as Pvt, Army, 42, released as Cpl, 45, after serv in qm, ETO, 44-45; Good Conduct Medal; European-Middle East Medal; four battle stars. Mem: De Witt Clinton Alumni Asn (mem bd gov); NAACP; 369th Vet Asn, Inc; Am Legion (Comdr, Post 1782, NY Co). Honors & Awards: Meritorious Serv Award, Am Legion. Relig: Methodist. Mailing Add: 865 E 167th St Bronx NY 10459

HARRIS, JANET LOUISE (D)
b Indianapolis, Ind, June 1, 42; d John G Harris & Helen M H; single. Educ: Ind Univ. Polit & Govt Pos: Staff asst to US Sen Vance Hartke, 64-67; proj asst, US Rep William Hungate, 70-72; caseworker, John V Tunney, 72-74; staff asst, US Rep Bob Traxler, formerly; admin asst to US Rep Floyd James Fithian, Ind, 75- Bus & Prof Pos: Washington rep, W S Dickey Clay Mfg Co, 68-70. Mem: Admin Assts Asn; US Capitol Hist Soc; Cong Staff Club of US Cong. Relig: Catholic. Mailing Add: 532 Ninth St SE Washington DC 20003

HARRIS, JEWELL G (D)
Ind State Rep
Mailing Add: 600 Cleveland Gary IN 46404

HARRIS, JIM (D)
Ark State Rep
Mailing Add: Box R Judsonia AR 72081

HARRIS, JOE FRANK (D)
Ga State Rep
Mailing Add: 1 Valley Dr Cartersville GA 30120

HARRIS, JOHN MATHEW WADE (R)
Committeeman, Md State Rep Cent Comt, Harford Co
b Covington, Va, July 21, 09; s Joseph Benjamin Harris & Marianna Crockett Harper H; m 1931 to Florence Dorothy Johnson; c John M, Jr, Thomas G, James R, Marianna J (Mrs Cooper) & Gloria R (Mrs Terlouw). Educ: Urbana Col. Polit & Govt Pos: Mem personnel, Dept of Army, 42-43 & 48-50; housing mgr, Fed Pub Housing Authority, 44-47; committeeman, Md State Rep Cent Comt, Harford Co, 59-; campaign mgr, Harford Co Rep Party, 60, 62, 64 & 68; alt deleg, Rep Nat Conv, 60, deleg, 64; mem, Harford Co Property Tax Appeal Court, 73- Bus & Prof Pos: Serv supvr, Minn Power & Light Co, Cloquet Div, Minn, 36-42; coast acct & acct, Consolidated Eng Co, Bainbridge, 50-51; acct, Zimmerman & Zimmerman, Indian Head, 52-53; mgr, Aberdeen Oil Co, 55-57; off mgr, Thomas Blackson, Contractor, Md, 57-; polit lectr, 60- Mem: Eagles; Moose; life mem Young Rep Club, Harford Co; Md Blood Bank, Inc (chmn steering comt, 69-). Relig: Christian Church of NAm. Mailing Add: 114 Anderson Ave Havre de Grace MD 21078

HARRIS, JOHN MYRON (D)
Mayor, Dearborn Heights, Mich
b Detroit, Mich, Aug 26, 26; s John Harris & Elizabeth C Grimmer H; m 1950 to Audrey Louise Saville; c Nancy Louise, Michael John, Mark Leonard & Paul Victor. Educ: Univ Detroit, 45-47; Wayne State Univ, 56; Univ Detroit Flying Club. Polit & Govt Pos: Trustee, Dearborn Twp, 59-63; supvr, Wayne Co, Mich, 63-66 & 67-68; councilman, Dearborn Heights, 63-75, city clerk, 64-67, mayor protem, 74-75, mayor, 75- Bus & Prof Pos: Parts merchandiser, Ford Motor Co, 50-65, parts merchandiser analyst, 65-68, sales promotion rep, 68-73, spec studies analyst, 73, financial analyst - A, 73-74. Mem: Int Asn Fire Chiefs; Mich Fire Chiefs Asn; Am Pub Works Asn; 15th Cong Dist Club. Honors & Awards: Distinguished Serv Award, US Jaycees, 56; Ford Motor Co Community Serv Award, 59, 60, 65, 67, 68 & 69. Relig: Catholic. Legal Res: 8225 Glengary Dearborn Heights MI 48127 Mailing Add: 6045 Fenton Dearborn Heights MI 48127

HARRIS, JOSEPH P (D)
Ind State Rep
b Kokomo, Ind, Oct 15, 38; s F Joseph Harris & Constance Phillips H; m 1959 to Emily R Pasquali; c Bridgette, Susan & Joseph M. Educ: Ivy Tech Col, 68-70. Polit & Govt Pos: Ind State Rep, Dist 27, 74- Mil Serv: Entered as Pvt, Marine Corps, 57, released as Cpl, 58. Mem: UAW Local 292; Indianapolis Press Club; KofC; Ind Firefighters Asn. Honors & Awards: Most Valuable Dem Award, Tipton Co Young Dem, 74. Relig: Catholic. Mailing Add: 3500 Cedar Ct Kokomo IN 46901

HARRIS, K DAVID
Justice, Iowa Supreme Court
b Jefferson, Iowa, July 29, 27; s Orville Williams Harris & Jessie Heloise Smart H; m 1948 to Madonna Coyne; c Jane (Mrs Martine), Julia Heloise & Frederick Thomas. Educ: Univ Iowa, BA, 49, JD, 51. Polit & Govt Pos: Greene Co attorney, Jefferson, Iowa, 58-62; dist court

judge, 16th Judicial Dist, 62-73, chief judge, 68-72; Supreme Court Justice, 72- Bus & Prof Pos: Attorney, pvt practice, Jefferson, Iowa, 51-62. Mil Serv: Entered as Pvt, Army, 44, released as Cpl, 46, after serv in 7th Inf Div; Pac, 45-46. Publ: Two Articles In: The Judges J, 65 & 66. Relig: Catholic. Legal Res: 507 W Harrison Jefferson IA 50129 Mailing Add: State House Des Moines IA 50319

HARRIS, KATHIE JEAN **(D)**
b Huntington Beach, Calif, Oct 24, 44; d Bob Lee Welty & Mary Jane Bartly W; m 1966 to John Lee Harris; c Elizabeth Jann & Donna Jill. Educ: Long Beach City Col, AA; Calif State Univ, Long Beach, BA, 75; Hist Students Asn. Polit & Govt Pos: Field dir, Four Assembly Dists McGovern-Shriver Camp, Southern Calif, 72; dir, Long Beach Staff of Jerome Waldie for Gov, 73-74; deleg, Dem Nat Mid-Term Conf, 74; dir, Jo Ann Richard's City Coun Camp, Long Beach, 75. Publ: Auth, Democratics in 1976, Orange Coast Daily Pilot Newspaper, 5/75. Mem: Long Beach Woman's Dem Club; Long Beach Area Citizens Involved. Mailing Add: 5114 Hanbury St Long Beach CA 90808

HARRIS, MARSHALL S **(D)**
b Detroit, Mich, Feb 2, 32; s David Harris & Dorothy Karol H; m 1958 to Harriet I Lipton; c Steven Matthew, Jennifer Lisa & Andrew David. Educ: Harvard Col, BS, 53; Law Sch, LLB, 56. Polit & Govt Pos: Fla State Rep, until 74; deleg, Dem Nat Mid-Term Conf, 74. Bus & Prof Pos: Attorney & partner, Harris & Robinson, 60; attorney & partner, Harris & Sirkin, 66- Mil Serv: Entered as Pvt, Army, 56, released as SP-3, 58, after serv in Korean Mil Adv Group, Korea, 57-58. Mem: Am Bar Asn; Jewish Occup Coun (vpres); Gtr Miami Jewish Fedn; Jewish Voc Serv; Anti-Defamation League of B'nai B'rith. Relig: Jewish. Legal Res: 4725 Pine Dr Miami FL 33143 Mailing Add: 4215 Ribault River Lane Jackson FL 32208

HARRIS, MARY ANGELA **(R)**
b Owensboro, Ky, June 21, 43; d Roy Edward Harris (deceased) & Dortha Bowles Buente H; single. Educ: Murray State Univ, BS, 66; Am Univ, grad cert in pub rels, 71; Kappa Pi. Polit & Govt Pos: Press secy, US Rep Roger H Zion, 67-72; pub rels dir, Young Voters for the President, 72; pub rels acct exec, Comt for Reelec of the President, 72; spec asst to dir of pub affairs, ACTION, 72- Bus & Prof Pos: Teacher, New Orleans, La, 66. Mem: House Rep Commun Asn; Cong Staff Club; Young Rep; Rep Women Capitol Hill; Nat Conf State Soc (pub rels dir). Mailing Add: 2213 Adams Ave Evansville IN 47714

HARRIS, NORRIS WILLIAM **(R)**
Mass State Rep
b Marblehead, Mass, Mar 16, 15; s Willard Roy Harris & Anne Doherty H; m 1942 to Phyllis Kathleen Gover; c Deborah (Mrs John Alford) & Martha (Mrs Paul Caradonna). Educ: Univ Fla, 33-34; Northeastern Univ, BBA, 52; Sigma Epsilon Rho. Polit & Govt Pos: Health comnr, Marblehead Bd Health, Mass, 41-45; selectman, Marblehead Bd Selectmen, 45-47, 54-66 & 67-70; Mass State Rep, Eighth Essex Dist, 73- Bus & Prof Pos: Cost clerk, Compo Shoe Machinery Corp, Boston, 40-43; wage, admin & labor rels specialist, Gen Elec Co, Lynn, 43-73. Mem: KofC; Marblehead Yacht Club (secy-treas, 40-); Gerry Five Vet Firemen's Asn. Relig: Roman Catholic. Mailing Add: 66 Overlook Rd Marblehead MA 01945

HARRIS, ORLAND HAROLD (IKE) **(R)**
Tex State Sen
b Denton, Tex, June 5, 32; s Orland Harris & Rebecca Yarbrough H; m 1955 to Ann Landrum; c Wynne & Gillian. Educ: NTex Univ, BS, 54; Southern Methodist Univ, LLB, 60, pres, Law Sch & Student Body; Cycen Fjodr. Polit & Govt Pos: Asst dist attorney, Dallas Co, Dallas, Tex, 60-62; Tex State Rep, 62-64; Tex State Sen, 67- Bus & Prof Pos: Attorney & assoc, Burt Barr, Dallas, Tex, 62-66, Harris & Miller, 66-68, Braecklein & Mitchell, 68-70, Braecklein, Mitchell, Harris & Timmins, 70-72 & Mitchell & Harris, 72- Mil Serv: Entered as Lt, Air Force, 54, released as Lt, 57, after serv in Air Training Command; Capt, Inactive Res. Mem: Dallas & Tex Bar Asns; Admitted to Practice before US Dist Court, US Court of Appeals & US Supreme Court; CofC. Relig: Methodist. Legal Res: 3425 Amherst Dallas TX 75225 Mailing Add: 2 Turtle Creek Village 919 Dallas TX 75219

HARRIS, PATRICIA ROBERTS **(D)**
Mem-at-lg, Dem Nat Comt
b Mattoon, Ill, May 31, 24; m to William Beasley Harris. Educ: Howard Univ, AB summa cum laude, 45; Univ Chicago; Am Univ; George Washington Univ Sch of Law, JD, John Bell Larner Prize as First in Class, 60; assoc ed, George Washington Univ Law Rev. Hon Degrees: LLD, Lindenwood Col, 67, Morgan State Col, 67, Russell Sage Col, 70, Tufts Univ, 70, Dartmouth Col, 70, Johns Hopkins Univ, 71, MacMurray Col, 71, Univ Md, Baltimore, 71, Williams Col, 71, Ripon Col, 72 & Brown Univ, 72; DHL, Miami Univ, 67 & Newton Col of the Sacred Heart, 72; DCL, Beaver Col, 68. Polit & Govt Pos: Mem staff, Dem Nat Comt, 56; attorney, criminal div, US Dept of Justice, 60-61; deleg, Dem Nat Conv, 64, seconded nomination of President Johnson; presidential elector, DC, 64; mem, PR Study Comn, 64-65; US Ambassador, Luxembourg, 65-67; US alt deleg, 21st & 22nd Gen Assemblies, UN, 66 & 67; US alt deleg, 20th Plenary Meeting, Econ Comn, Europe, 67; mem, Nat Adv Comt Reform Fed Criminal Laws; mem, Admin Conf US; mem, Nat Comn Causes & Prev Violence; co-chmn comt on govt & democracy, Dem Policy Coun, 69-; mem comt on admissions & grievances, US Dist Court for DC, 70-; chmn, Credentials Comt, Dem Nat Conv, 72; mem-at-lg, Dem Nat Comt, 73- Bus & Prof Pos: Prog dir for work with indust women, YWCA, Chicago, 46-49; asst dir, Am Coun on Human Rights, 49-53; exec dir, Delta Sigma Theta Inc, 53-59; assoc dean students & lectr law, Howard Univ, 61-63, asst prof law, 63-65, assoc prof, 65-67, prof, 67-69, dean sch of law, 69; partner, Fried, Frank, Harris, Shriver & Kampelman, Attorneys, Washington, DC, 70-; mem bd dirs, Georgetown Univ, 70-, Chase Manhattan Bank IBM Corp & Scott Paper Co, 71- Mem: Kappa Beta Pi; Am Asn Univ Prof; Delta Sigma Theta; Carnegie Comn Future Higher Educ; Comn Found & Private Philanthropy. Honors & Awards: Woman of the Year, Women's Auxiliary Jewish War Vet, 68; Emma V Kelley Award, Daughter Elks, 68; Centennial Citation, Wilson Col, 69; Aquinas Award, Aquinas Col, 72; One Nation Award, Philadelphia Action Br, NAACP, 72. Legal Res: 1742 Holly St NW Washington DC 20012 Mailing Add: 600 New Hampshire Ave NW Washington DC 20037

HARRIS, PATRICK B **(D)**
SC State Rep
Mailing Add: Box 655 Anderson SC 29621

HARRIS, RAYMOND ALEXANDER **(R)**
Mem Steering Comt, SC State Rep Party
b Wake Forest, NC, Feb 3, 27; m 1951 to Vi Barringer; c Belva John, Vi Haynsworth, Raymond A, Jr, Laurence Barringer, Mary Barringer & James Gill. Educ: Wake Forest Col, BA, 50. Polit & Govt Pos: Spec agent, Fed Bur Invest, 51-52; spec invest work, US Defense Dept, 56-61 & 62-63; mem, Workman for Senate Campaign Comt, 61; organizer, Darlington Co Rep Party, SC, 63, chmn, formerly; exec dir, SC State Rep Party, 65-68, chmn, 68-71, mem steering comt, 71-; campaign dir, Ed Young for Cong Comt, 72; mem, SC Reelect Nixon State Steering Comt, 72; mem, SC State Comt for Reelect of Thurmond, 72. Bus & Prof Pos: Supvr, Atlantic Coast Line RR, 53-54; partner, Barringer-McKeel Hardware Co, Darlington, SC, 55-; real estate broker, 68-69; pres, Dwelling Enterprises Ltd Inc, 71-; owner, Ray Harris Real Estate Co, 71- Mil Serv: Naval Air Corps, 44-46, serv in Far Eastern Theater. Mem: Darlington Realtors Asn (bd dirs, 71-); Nat Realtors Asn; Pee Dee Area Boy Scout Coun (exec bd & finance chmn, 71-); Darlington CofC (past pres); Kiwanis. Relig: Presbyterian; Mem, Darlington Presby Bd Deacons. Legal Res: 108 Oakview Dr Darlington SC 29532 Mailing Add: PO Box 61 Darlington SC 29532

HARRIS, ROBERT E **(R)**
Va State Deleg
Mailing Add: 4440 Glenn Rose St Fairfax VA 22030

HARRIS, ROBERT OBERNDOERFER **(D)**
b New York, NY, Nov 11, 29; s Samuel Doran Harris & Miriam Sonneborn H; m 1958 to Ritalou Rogow; c Peter Oberndoerfer & Gail. Educ: Columbia Col, AB, 51; Yale Law Sch, LLB, 54; Georgetown Univ, LLM, 61. Polit & Govt Pos: Mem staff, Off of the Gen Counsel, Dept of Health, Educ & Welfare, 57-59; mem staff, Off of the Solicitor, Dept of Labor, 59-61; spec asst to the chmn, Nat Labor Rels Bd, 61-67; counsel & staff dir, Comt on Labor & Pub Welfare, US Senate, 67-71, staff dir, Comt on DC, 71- Mil Serv: Entered as Cpl, Army, 54, released as SP-5, 56, after serv in 4447th Army Unit, Ger, 55-56. Publ: Several law rev articles. Relig: Jewish. Mailing Add: 3665 Upton NW Washington DC 20008

HARRIS, STANLEY EMERSON **(R)**
Chmn, Luzerne Co Rep Party, Pa
b Pittston, Pa, Sept 24, 14; s Merle Harris & Harriet Matilda Drew H; single. Educ: West Pittston High Sch, grad, 33. Polit & Govt Pos: Legis Chmn, Luzerne Co Rep Party, Pa, 53-74, chmn, 75-; admin asst to Pa State Sen T N Wood, 74-75. Bus & Prof Pos: In restaurant bus, West Pittston, Pa, 46-63 & laundromat bus, West Pittston, Forty Fort & Pittston, 63-75. Mil Serv: Entered as Pvt, Army, 42, released as S/Sgt, 45, after serv in Signal Corps, Cent Europe, 44-45; Good Conduct Medal; Am Campaign Medal; European African Mid Eastern Campaign Medal with 4 Bronze Stars; Victory Medal. Mem: Am Legion; VFW. Relig: Protestant. Mailing Add: 227 Linden St West Pittston PA 18643

HARRIS, VIVIAN FAYE **(R)**
Secy, Whitley Co Rep Cent Comt, Ind
b Columbia Twp, Ind, Apr 14, 09; d Walter Hiram Mosher & Mary Killian M; m 1932 to Gale Reiling Harris; c Donald Keith & Harvey Lee. Educ: Ind Cent Col, Indianapolis, 27-28; Ind Univ, Bloomington, AB, 31; St Francis Col (Ind), MA, 63; Alpha Delta Pi; Philalethea Lit Soc. Polit & Govt Pos: Vprecinct committeeman, West Col Twp, Whitley Co, Ind, 35-; secy, Whitley Co Rep Cent Comt, 59- Bus Prof Pos: Sec sch teacher, Whitley Co, Ind, 44-70; retired. Publ: Auth, My Prayer (poem), 70 & Thanks (poem), 72, Nat Poetry Press. Mem: Neighborhood Exten Orgn; Whitley Co Rep Women's Club. Relig: United Methodist. Mailing Add: RR 1 Wolf Rd Columbia City IN 46725

HARRIS, W S, JR **(D)**
NC State Rep
Mailing Add: Hanford Rd Graham NC 27253

HARRIS, WADE **(D)**
b Guntersville, Ala, Sept 23, 38; s Elihue Harris & Florence Montgomery H; m 1966 to Geraldine Williams. Educ: Morehouse Col, BA, 72; Atlanta Univ, MA, 73; Afro-Am Hall of Fame; bd, Frederick Douglas Inst; pres, Student Body. Polit & Govt Pos: Deleg, Dem Nat Conv, 72; mem, Atlanta Crusade Against Crime, Ga, currently. Mil Serv: Entered as Pvt, Army, 56, released as SP-4, 59, after serv in Med Corps, Japan & Korea, 57-58. Mem: Mason; NAACP. Relig: Protestant. Legal Res: 653 Beckwith St Atlanta GA 30314 Mailing Add: 519 Noble Ave Akron OH 44320

HARRIS, WILLIAM CULLEN **(R)**
Pres, Ill State Senate
b Pontiac, Ill, May 7, 21; s Raleigh J Harris & Bernadine Cullen H; m 1947 to Jeanne Kathryn Turck; c Charles Matthew & Barbara Ann. Educ: Mich State Univ, 2 years. Polit & Govt Pos: Ill State Rep, 55-61; Ill State Sen, 61-, Asst Majority Leader, Ill State Senate, 67 & 69, Pres, 73-; deleg, Rep Nat Conv, 68; chmn, Ill Budgetary Comn, 69-72, Ill Econ & Fiscal Comn, 72- Bus & Prof Pos: Dist agt, State Mutual of Am, 58- Mil Serv: Entered as A/S, Navy, 42, released as Aviation Chief Ordnanceman, 45, after serv in the Solomons, Asiatic-Pac; Asiatic-Pac Campaign Ribbon. Mem: Elks; Moose; Am Legion; VFW. Relig: Episcopal. Mailing Add: 706 S Walnut St Pontiac IL 61764

HARRIS, WILLIAM LEE **(D)**
VChmn, 24th Cong Dist Dem Party, Ill
b Marion, Ill, Aug 30, 23; s Oscar R Harris & Estelle Murphy H; m 1941 to Anna Lou Simpson; c William Michael. Educ: Univ Chicago, 56. Polit & Govt Pos: City comnr pub health & safety, Marion, Ill, 63-67; vchmn, Williamson Co Dem Party, 68-70, chmn, formerly; vchmn, 24th Cong Dist Dem Party, 70-; 59th Dist Sen chmn, 12 counties, 72- Bus & Prof Pos: Pub adminr, conservator & guardian, Circuit Court, First Dist, Ill, 61-69. Mem: Mason; Odd Fellows; Ill Police Asn; Hickory Hill Trust (pres, 73-). Relig: Presbyterian. Mailing Add: 512 S Market St Marion IL 62959

HARRISON, A L (TONY) **(D)**
Ala State Rep
Mailing Add: 1214-Fourth Pl N Birmingham AL 35204

HARRISON, ALBERTIS SYDNEY, JR **(D)**
Justice, Va Supreme Court
b Brunswick Co, Va, Jan 11, 07; s Albertis Sydney Harrison & Lizzie Goodrich H; m 1930 to Lacey Virginia Barkley; c Albertis Sydney, III & Antoinette (Mrs Jamison). Educ: Univ Va, LLB, 28; Omicron Delta Kappa; Delta Sigma Phi; Phi Delta Phi; Order of the Coif; Va Law Rev. Hon Degrees: LLD, Col William & Mary, 63. Polit & Govt Pos: Town attorney, Lawrenceville, Va, 29-31; commonwealth's attorney, Brunswick Co, 31-48; Va State Sen, 48-58; Attorney Gen, Va, 58-62; Gov, Va, 62-66; Justice Supreme Court of Va, 67- Mil Serv:

Lt(jg), Navy. Mem: Am & Va State Bar Asns; Va State Bar; Am Inst of Trial Lawyers. Relig: Episcopal. Mailing Add: Box 108 Lawrenceville VA 23868

HARRISON, CARL (R)
Ga State Rep
Mailing Add: PO Box 1374 Marietta GA 30060

HARRISON, CHARLIE JAMES, JR (D)
Mich State Rep
b West Palm Beach, Fla, May 16, 32; s Charlie James Harrison, Sr & Mariah Russell H; m 1955 to Marquita Jones; c Cheryl, Charlie, III, Marcella, Cynthia & Mark. Educ: Wayne State Univ, 50-51; Detroit Inst Dry Cleaning, grad, 65. Polit & Govt Pos: Comnr, Co of Oakland, Mich, 71-72; deleg, Dem Nat Conv, 72; Mich State Rep, Dist 62, 73- Bus & Prof Pos: Dry cleaning; real estate salesman; exec dir, Harambee, Inc, Pontiac, Mich. Mem: Pontiac Urban Coalition (bd gov, 71-73); NAACP; Chequemates Sportsman Club; Gibraltar Lodge 19. Honors & Awards: Most Promising Young Man of the Year, NAACP, 71. Relig: Methodist. Legal Res: 85 Carr Rd Pontiac MI 48058 Mailing Add: State Capitol Lansing MI 48901

HARRISON, DAVID ELDRIDGE (D)
Mem, Mass Dem State Comt
b Gloucester, Mass, June 19, 33; s Lester W Harrison & Hazel Eldridge H; m 1970 to Michele Holovak. Educ: Tufts Col, BA, 55; New Eng Sch Law, JD, 68; pres, Tower Cross. Polit & Govt Pos: Mass State Rep, 62-70; alt deleg, Dem Nat Conv, 64, deleg-at-lg & co-chmn deleg for Sen George McGovern for President, 68 & deleg, 72; mem, Mass State Dem Comt, 64-66, 68-72 & 72-, chmn, 68-70, vchmn Legis Comt, Pub Welfare, 65; chmn, Legis Comt Harbors & Pub Lands, 65-66; chmn Legis Comt, Natural Resources, 68; mem, Tufts Alumni Coun, 68-; mem Dem Nat Comt Rules, 69-72; chmn, Mass McGovern for President Comt, 72; coordr, New Eng McGovern for President Comt, 72. Bus & Prof Pos: Owner, D E Harrison Ins & Real Estate Agency, 61- Mil Serv: Entered as Pvt, Army, 55, released as Specialist 4/C, 57, after serv in Third Armored Div, Ger, 56-57. Mem: Am Red Cross (dir); Gilbert Home for Aged & Indigent Persons (trustee); New Eng Lacrosse Off Asn (chief referee); Eastern Intercollegiate Football Off Asn; Univ Boat Club, Boston. Honors & Awards: All-New Eng Lacrosse Player, 55; One of Ten Outstanding Young Men, Boston Jr CofC, 67. Relig: Episcopal. Mailing Add: PO Box 16 Gloucester MA 01930

HARRISON, DONALD C (D)
Chmn, Dem Town Comt, Roxbury, Conn
b New York, NY, Oct 13, 07; s Richard C Harrison & Florence Burtis H; m 1931 to Mary Adams; c Margaret (Mrs Case) & John A. Educ: Yale Univ, BS, 29; Mass Inst Technol, MS, 31; Fordham Univ Sch Law, LLB, 34; Sigma Xi; Alpha Chi Sigma. Polit & Govt Pos: Chmn, Dem Town Comt, Roxbury, Conn, 72- Bus & Prof Pos: Engr, Union Carbide Corp, New York, 31-35, patent lawyer, 35-44, mgr patent dept, 44-45, gen patent counsel, 55-68; retired. Relig: Episcopal. Mailing Add: Botsford Hill Rd Roxbury CT 06783

HARRISON, HATTIE N (D)
Md State Deleg
b Lancaster, SC, Feb 11, 28; d Albert Stewart & Ester Cunningham S; m 1943 to Robert Harrison; c Robert & Philip. Educ: J C Smith Univ, 67; Community Educ Develop, Richmond, Va, 69; Antioch Col. Polit & Govt Pos: Mem, Md State Dem Cent Comt, 70-; chairperson, Second Dist Dem Cent Comt Deleg, currently; panelist, Md Conf Social Welfare & Md Comn Higher Educ, 73; Md State Deleg, 73-; app, Md Comn on Status of Women, 74. Bus & Prof Pos: Dir, Dunbar Neighborhood Facil, Baltimore City Schs; chairperson, Community Sch Adv Coun, 72. Mem: Women's Comt for United Fund; Citizens for Fair Housing; Dunbar Community Sch Coun; Md 4-C Comt on Day Care; Nat Lab for Advan of Educ. Honors & Awards: Alpha Zeta's Woman of the Year, 74. Legal Res: 2721 Mura St Baltimore MD 21213 Mailing Add: 2503 E Preston St Baltimore MD 21213

HARRISON, JAMES EDWARD, III (R)
b Thomson, Ga, Feb 25, 40; s James Edward Harrison, Jr & Sara Bryant H; m 1966 to Ellen Reynolds Tipton; c James Edward, IV. Educ: Univ of Ga, BBA, 62; Kappa Alpha; Gridiron Secret Soc. Polit & Govt Pos: Mem, Ga State Rep Exec Comt, 64-66; chmn, McDuffie Co Rep Party, formerly. Bus & Prof Pos: Vpres, Harrison Farms, Inc, 62- Mem: Rotary; Farm Bur; Belle Beade Country Club; Plantation Club, Hilton Head Island, SC. Relig: Methodist. Mailing Add: Rte 2 Thomson GA 30824

HARRISON, JAMES THOMAS
Chief Justice, Mont Supreme Court
b Hankinson, NDak, Apr 4, 03; s Edward Charles Harrison & Karen Marie Anderson H; m 1926 to Leah Lambert; c Barbara Louise (Mrs R J Losleben, Jr), Beverly Ann (Mrs Stanley J Hould) & James T, Jr. Educ: St Paul Col of Law. Hon Degrees: LLD, Mont Sch Mines, 61; LLD, William Mitchell Col Law, 64. Polit & Govt Pos: Court reporter, 17th Judicial Dist, Mont, 29-38; city attorney, Malta, intermittently, 39-56; co attorney, Phillips Co, 49-52; chmn, State Bd of Pardons, 55-56; Chief Justice, Mont Supreme Court, 57- Bus & Prof Pos: Attorney-at-law, 26-29 & 38-56. Mem: AF&AM (past Grand Master Mont, Masons, 58-59, past Potentate, Algeria Shrine, 60); Elks; Moose; Eagles; Scottish Rite (sovereign grand inspector gen, 71-). Honors & Awards: Silver Beaver & Silver Antelope Award, Boy Scouts; occasional mem Awards Jury, Freedoms Found, Valley Forge. Relig: Methodist. Mailing Add: 1616 Highland Helena MT 59601

HARRISON, JAMES WILLIAM (BILL) (D)
b Piedmont, Okla, June 22, 22; s William Barney Harrison & Imogene Edmison H; m 1947 to Marjorie Elaine Eads; c Elaine (Mrs Allen R Snyder), James Roger & Elizabeth Ann (Mrs William Marek). Educ: Southwestern Univ (Tex), 43-45; Univ Tex, Austin, 45; Univ Okla Law Sch, 45-47; Okla City Col Law, LLB, 49; Kappa Sigma, Iota Chap, Southwestern Univ; Kappa Sigma, Tau Chap, Univ Tex. Polit & Govt Pos: Justice of the Peace, Oklahoma City, Okla, 50-51; dir hearings div, Comptroller Pub Acct, State of Tex, 60-62, tech adv, 58-60; asst city mgr, Georgetown, Tex, 51-53, Edinburg, Tex, 53-55, Lovington, NMex, 55-57, Omkulgee, Okla, 57-58, Baytown, Tex, 58, Seward, Alaska, 62-64, Cuero, Tex, 64-65, Kenai, Alaska, 65-69 & Silver City, NMex, 69-71; deleg, Dem Nat Conv, 72; chmn Dem ward, Silver City, NMex, 72-; exec dir, SW NMex Coun of Govt, Silver City, NMex, 72- Mil Serv: Entered as Y3/C, Naval Res, 41, released as Y1/C, 45, after serv in USS Kaskaskia, VF-36, CinCPac Staff, Navy V-12 Prog in Tex, Pac Theatre; Good Conduct Medal. Mem: Int City Mgrs Asn; Grant Soil & Water Conserv Dist (supvr, 71); Silver City Elks; Silver City-Grant Co CofC (secy-treas & mem indust comt, 69-). Honors & Awards: Cert of Appreciation for outstanding work in relation to Good Friday Earthquake Disaster, Town of Seward, Alaska, 64; Outstanding Cert for excellence in govt, Kenai CofC, 66 & 68; Spec Commendation, State of Alaska, Civil Defense Dept, 67; Hon Mem, Civil Air Patrol, 69. Relig: Episcopal. Legal Res: 2620 Panorama Dr Silver City NM 88061 Mailing Add: PO Box 1211 Silver City NM 88061

HARRISON, JOHN CONWAY (D)
Assoc Justice, Mont Supreme Court
b Grand Rapids, Minn, Apr 28, 13; s Francis Randall Harrison & Ethelyn Conway H; m 1941 to Virginia Flanagan; c N Nina Lyn, Robert Charles, Molly McKinley, John Conway, Frank Randall & Virginia Lee. Educ: Mont State Col, 31-34; Univ Mont Law Sch, 35-37; George Washington Univ, LLB, 40; Sigma Chi. Polit & Govt Pos: Asst co attorney, Lewis & Clark Co, 47-50, co attorney, 54-60; city attorney, East Helena, 51-60, Assoc Justice, Mont Supreme Court, 61- Mil Serv: Entered as 1st Lt, Army, 40, released as Lt Col, 45, after serv in Seventh Corps Hq, ETO; Five Battle Stars; Bronze Star; Croix de Guerre with Star. Mem: Mont Tuberc Asn; Am Lung Asn; Am Legion (comdr, 53); VFW; Kiwanis. Relig: Protestant Eipscopal. Mailing Add: State Capitol Helena MT 59601

HARRISON, JOSEPH WILLIAM (R)
Ind State Sen
b Chicago, Ill, Sept 10, 31; s Roy Joseph Harrison & Gladys Greenman H; m 1956 to Ann Hovey Gillespie; c Holly Ann, Tracy Jeanne, Thomas Joseph, Amy Beth, Kitty Lynne & Christy Jayne. Educ: Purdue Univ, 49-52; US Naval Acad, BS, 56; Ind Univ Law Sch, 67-69; Sigma Chi. Polit & Govt Pos: Pres, Attica Consolidated Sch Bd, Attica, Ind, 64-67; Ind State Sen, 66-, chmn Senate Finance Comt, Ind State Senate, 69-70, Pub Health & Welfare Comt, 71- Bus & Prof Pos: Asst to pres, Harrison Steel Castings Co, Attica, Ind, 60-64, sales research engr, 64-66, asst secy, 66-69, secy, 69-70, vpres, 71- Mil Serv: Entered as Midn, Navy, 52, released as Lt(jg), 60, after serv in Naval Intel, Washington, DC, 56-60; Naval Res, Lt(jg), 69. Mem: Am Legion; CofC; Wabash Valley Asn. Relig: Methodist. Legal Res: 504 E Pike St Attica IN 47918 Mailing Add: PO Box 60 Attica IN 47918

HARRISON, JOSEPH WYLIE (R)
Conf Asst Admin Legal Affairs, Food & Nutrit Serv, US Dept Agr
b Pasadena, Calif, Nov 9, 37; s Joseph Wylie Harrison (deceased) & Myra Sumption H; m 1973 to Marlene K Tillberg. Educ: Univ Notre Dame, AB, 59; Univ Tenn, Knoxville, MA, 61; Pi Sigma Alpha; Student Govt. Polit & Govt Pos: Research assoc, Rep Nat Comt, Washington, DC, 63-64, research specialist, campaign, 66; legis asst to US Rep Ed Reinecke, Calif, 65-66; admin asst to US Rep Garry Brown, Mich, 67-68; field rep, Nixon Presidential Campaign, Washington, DC, 68; spec asst to the Asst Postmaster Gen, 69-72; spec asst to comnr, Property Mgt & Disposal Serv, Gen Serv Admin, 72-74; conf asst to adminr legal affairs, Food & Nutrit Serv, US Dept Agr, 75- Bus & Prof Pos: Instr polit sci, Univ Tenn, Knoxville, 60-61; research dir, Nat Employ Asn, Washington, DC, 62-63. Mil Serv: Army Res, 61-67. Publ: The Bible, The Constitution & Public Education, Tenn Law Rev, spring 62. Mem: Am & Southern Polit Sci Asns; life mem, Calif Scholarship Fedn. Relig: Roman Catholic. Mailing Add: 4924 Sentinel Dr Bethesda MD 20016

HARRISON, MARK I (D)
b Pittsburgh, Pa, Oct 17, 34; s Coleman Harrison & Myrtle Seidenman H; m 1958 to Ellen R Gier; c Lisa & Jill. Educ: Antioch Col, AB, 57; Harvard Law Sch, LLB, 60. Polit & Govt Pos: Vchmn, Maricopa Co Dem Cent Comt, Ariz, 67-68; deleg, Dem Nat Conv, 68; vchmn, Ariz Dem Party, 68-70, gen legal counsel, 70-72. Bus & Prof Pos: Law clerk, Justices Lorna E Lockwood & Charles C Bernstein, Ariz Supreme Court, 60-61; partner, Harrison, Myers & Singer, Attorneys, 66- Publ: Arizona appellate briefs, 62 & Arizona appellate practice, 66, Ariz Weekly Gazette. Mem: Phoenix Asn Defense Counsel (bd dirs, 72-); Am Trial Lawyers Asn (bd dirs, Phoenix chap, 65-); State Bar Ariz (bd govs, 70-; pres, 75-); Am Judicature Soc; Phoenix Exec Club. Relig: Jewish. Legal Res: 326 E Kaler Dr Phoenix AZ 85020 Mailing Add: 1200 Ariz Title Bldg 111 W Monroe Phoenix AZ 85003

HARRISON, ROBERT DINSMORE (R)
b Panama, Nebr, Jan 26, 97; s Herbert Harrison & Jennie Dinsmore H; m 1921 to Mary Arra Sutton; c Nancibelle (Mrs Lingenfelter). Educ: Peru State Teachers Col, AB, 26; Univ Calif, summer 28; Univ Nebr, MA, 34. Polit & Govt Pos: Chmn, Madison Co Rep Party, Nebr, 47-50 & 68-74; US Rep, Nebr, 51-59; Civilian Conserv Corps consult, US Dept Agr, 59-60; state dir Fed Crop Ins, Lincoln, 60-62; deleg, Rep Nat Conv, 68 & 72. Bus & Prof Pos: Supt pub schs, Bradshaw, 3 years; supt pub schs, Dewitt, 26-35; marketer, Sinclair Refining Co, Norfolk, 35-60. Mil Serv: Entered as Pvt, Army, 18, released as Sgt, 19, after serv in 22nd Engrs, St Mihiel & Muese Argonne, 18. Mem: Elks; Mason; Kiwanis; Am Legion; Vet World War I. Honors & Awards: Aksarben Good Neighbor Award; Man of the Year Award, Jr CofC; Man of the Year, Norfolk CofC, 66; Man of the Year, Class of 1926, Peru State Teachers Col. Relig: Methodist. Mailing Add: 408 N 11th St Norfolk NE 68701

HARRISON, WILLIAM HENRY (R)
b Terre Haute, Ind, Aug 10, 96; s Russell Benjamin Harrison & Mary Saunders H; m 1920 to Mary Elizabeth Newton; c Maribeth Brewer & William Henry, Jr. Educ: Univ Nebr; Sigma Chi; Sigma Delta Kappa. Hon Degrees: LLD, Vincennes Univ. Polit & Govt Pos: Wyo State Rep, 45-51; US Rep at Large, Wyo, 51-54, 61-64 & 67-69; regional adminstr, Atlanta, 55-56; liaison officer, Housing & Home Finance Agency, Washington, DC, 57-58, mem, Renegotiation Bd, currently. Bus & Prof Pos: Attorney, 25- Mil Serv: Pvt, Signal Enlisted Res Corps, Army World War I, serv in US. Mem: Mason (33 degree); Scottish Rite; Shrine; Elks; Moose. Relig: Presbyterian. Mailing Add: Box 6046 Sheridan WY 82801

HARRISON, WILLIAM HENRY, JR (R)
Exec Committeeman, SC Rep Party
b Greenwood, SC, May 17, 50; s William Henry Harrison & Mary Hodges H; single. Educ: The Citadel, BS in Physics; Roundtable. Polit & Govt Pos: Exec committeeman, SC Rep Party, 73- Bus & Prof Pos: Proj mgr, Town & Country Real Estate, 73-74, gen mgr construction, 74, gen mgr, 74- Mil Serv: Entered as 2nd Lt, Army, 71, released as 2nd Lt, 73, after serv in Air Defense Sch, Ft Bliss, Tex; 1st Lt, Army Res; Distinguished Mil Grad. Mem: Kiwanis; Greenwood Area Citadel Club (pres); YMCA. Honors & Awards: Valedictorian, The Citadel, 72; Rhodes Scholar Nominee, 72; Am Legion Col Award, 72. Legal Res: Green Pastures Bradley SC 29819 Mailing Add: PO Box 187 Greenwood SC 29646

HARROD, M MERLE (R)
Dir, Ohio Rep Finance Comt
b Wapakoneta, Ohio, Dec 30, 06; s Walter L Harrod & Carrie L Wagstaff H; m to Doris Marie Fischer; c Mahlon M, Jr & Barbara (Mrs Olds); two grandchildren. Educ: Ohio State Univ, BS in Econ; pres, sr class & Sigma Chi; Alpha Kappa Psi; charter mem, Frontliners, Athletic

Dept. Polit & Govt Pos: Alt deleg, Rep Nat Conv, 56, 60 & 64, deleg, 68 & 72; mem finance, cent & exec comts, Auglaize Co Rep Comt, Ohio; regional chmn & dir, Ohio Rep Finance Comt, currently. Bus & Prof Pos: Chmn bd, chief exec off & dir, Wapakoneta Machine Co & Calif Saw Knife & Grinding, Inc, San Francisco; trustee, Ohio Info Comt; dir, First Nat Bank, Wapakoneta; trustee, Bowling Green State Univ, 67-69, Ohio State Univ, 69-, Ohio Far East Trade Mission, 67 & 70, Ohio SAm Trade Mission, 67 & Ohio European Trade Mission, 69; chmn, Ohio Int Trade Ctr; dir, Nat Right to Work Comt, currently. Mem: Machine Knife Trade Asn; Ohio Mfrs Asn (dir & first vpres); Metal Cutting Knife Trade Asn; Nat Asn Mfrs (indust probs comt, dir); Ohio CofC (dir). Honors & Awards: Exec Order of Ohio Commodores. Relig: United Church of Christ. Mailing Add: Glynwood Rd Wapakoneta OH 45895

HARROP, WILLIAM CALDWELL **(INDEPENDENT)**
US Ambassador to Guinea
b Baltimore, Md, Feb 19, 29; s George Argale Harrop & Esther Caldwell H; m 1953 to Ann Delavan; c Mark D, Caldwell, Scott N & George H. Educ: Harvard Col, AB, 50; Univ Mo, 51-52; Princeton Univ, 68-69; Fly Club. Polit & Govt Pos: Visa officer, vconsul, US Consulate Gen, Palermo, 54-55; second secy, US Embassy, Rome, 55-58; foreign affairs officer, Dept of State, 58-62; first secy, US Embassy, Brussels, 63-66; consul, US Consulate, Lubumbashi, Zaire, 66-68; dir research, Africa, Dept of State, 69-71, mem, Policy Planning Staff, 72-73; minister, US Embassy, Canberra, 73-75; US Ambassador to Guinea, 75- Mil Serv: Entered as Pvt, Marine Corps, 51, released as Cpl, 52. Mem: Am Foreign Serv Asn; UN Asn; Metrop Club of Washington. Honors & Awards: Merit Honor Award, Dept of State, 66. Legal Res: Princeton NJ Mailing Add: Conakry Dept of State Washington DC 20520

HARROUN, HAROLD FRANKLIN **(R)**
b Nebraska City, Nebr, Dec 26, 33; s C Howard Harroun & Ruth Russell H; m 1960 to Barbara Jo Wiltse; c John H, David F, Sharol R & Marcia J. Educ: Univ Nebr, 51-52; Univ Md Overseas Prog, 1 semester. Polit & Govt Pos: Councilman, Falls City, Nebr, 63-64, mem, park bd, 64-67, mem sch bd, Dist 56, 68-; chmn, Richardson Co Rep Party, formerly. Bus & Prof Pos: Mgr, Norman's IGA, Nebraska City, Nebr, 60; asst mgr, Falls City Fed Savings & Loan, 60-67, mgr & treas, 67- Mil Serv: Entered as Pvt, Army, 56, released as Sgt, 60, after serv in Inf, Ger, 56-58. Mem: US Savings & Loan Inst; Elks; CofC; VFW; Am Legion. Honors & Awards: Named Jaycee of the Year, 64. Relig: Methodist. Mailing Add: 923 St Mary's Ave Falls City NE 68355

HARRY, JAMES F, JR **(R)**
Dir Pub Rel, Ill Rep State Cent Comt
b Quincy, Ill, Dec 30, 39; s James F Harry & Helen I Cook H; m 1963 to Barbara M Hergenroeder; c Michael Scott & Michelle Marie. Educ: Ill Col, Jacksonville, Ill, AB, 63; Gamma Nu; Alpha Psi Omega; Hilltoppers; Letterman's Club. Polit & Govt Pos: Dir Pub Rel, Ill Rep State Cent Comt, 69- Bus & Prof Pos: Newsman, WTAX Radio, Springfield, Ill, 63-66; news dir, WMAY Radio, Springfield, Ill, 66-67; polit reporter, WBBM-CBS Radio, Chicago, Ill, 67-69. Mil Serv: Entered as Pvt, Army Res, 57-, released as Sp 4, 53. Mem: Ill News Broadcasters Asn; Ill Legis Correspondents Asn; Ill Press Club, Springfield; Am Fedn of Radio & TV Artist; Young Rep. Relig: Roman Catholic. Legal Res: 2301 Noble Ave Springfield IL 62704 Mailing Add: Ill Rep State Cent Comt 200 S Second St Springfield IL 62701

HARSHA, WILLIAM H **(R)**
US Rep, Ohio
b Portsmouth, Ohio, Jan 1, 21; m to Rosemary Spellerberg; c Bill, Mark, Bruce & Brian. Educ: Kenyon Col, AB; Western Reserve Univ, LLB. Polit & Govt Pos: Asst city solicitor, Portsmouth, Ohio, 47-51; Scioto Co prosecutor, 51-55; US Rep, Ohio, 60-, ranking minority mem, Pub Works Comt, US House Rep, currently, mem, House Comt on the DC, currently; mem & vpres, Rep Cong Comt. Bus & Prof Pos: Attorney-at-law. Mil Serv: Marine Corps, World War II. Publ: Numerous articles on water pollution & highway safety. Mem: Exchange Club; Elks (past Exalted Ruler); Mason (33 degree); YMCA; Bus & Prof Men's Club. Honors & Awards: Distinguished Serv Award, Nat Limestone Inst; Distinguished Serv Awards, Am for Const Action; Awards of Honor, Freedom Found; First Int Rd Safety Award, Eng Minister of Transportation in London, Eng; numerous awards for outstanding work in Cong. Relig: Presbyterian. Legal Res: Portsmouth OH 45662 Mailing Add: US House of Rep Washington DC 20515

HART, ADELAIDE JULIA **(D)**
Dep Chmn, Wayne Co Dem Comt, Mich
b Saginaw, Mich, Apr 24, 00; d Malachi Patrick Hart & Margaret Hogan H; single. Educ: Western Mich Col, Teachers Cert, 23; Marygrove Col, PhB, 30, MA, 37. Polit & Govt Pos: Mem bd of supvrs, Wayne Co, Mich, 48-50, mem rent adv bd, 48-51; mem exec bd, 17th Cong Dist Dem Party & precinct deleg, 48-; vchmn, Mich Dem State Cent Comt, 51-61 & 63-67; deleg, Dem Nat Conv, 52-64, alt deleg, 68, mem platform comt, 52 & 64; mem, State Ment Health Comn, 60-63; deleg & Dem caucus chmn, Const Conv, Mich, 61-62; chmn, Mich Fedn Dem Women, 63-67; co-chmn, Wayne Co Fedn Dem Women, 69-; chmn, registr of voters, Wayne Co Dem Comt, currently, dep chmn, 70- Bus & Prof Pos: Music teacher & head of fine arts dept, Detroit Bd of Educ, Mich, 23-63. Mem: Detroit Fedn of Teachers; Marygrove Col Alumnae Asn; Synod Implementation Comt, Archdiocese of Detroit Co. Relig: Catholic. Mailing Add: 801 W Long Lake Rd E-4 Bloomfield Hills MI 48013

HART, FLOYD HENRY **(R)**
b Medford, Ore, Dec 30, 31; s Floyd H Hart, Sr & Leah C Walther H; m 1952 to Jo Ann Barbara Larsen; c Pamela, Andrea & Margretha. Educ: Univ Colo, 49-50; Ore State Univ, 54; Southern Ore Col, 55-56; Sigma Nu. Polit & Govt Pos: Pres & comnr, City Planning Comn, Medford, Ore, 62-66; Ore State Rep, 19th Dist, 67-71; alt deleg, Rep Nat Conv, 68, deleg, 72; chmn, Ore State Rep Party, 71-73. Bus & Prof Pos: Partner, Security Ins Agency, 59-; dir, Crater Nat Bank & Rogue Valley Mem Hosp, 64- Mil Serv: Entered as Pvt, Air Force, 51, released as S/Sgt, 54, after serv in 307th Air Refueling Squadron, Hydrogen Bomb Tests, Marshall Islands, MidPac, 52; Airman of the Year Award, 53; Good Conduct Medal. Mem: Ore Asn of Ins Agents; Medford CofC; Rogue River Valley Univ Club; Rogue Valley Country Club; Air Force Asn. Relig: Episcopal. Mailing Add: 48 Hawthorne Ave Medford OR 97501

HART, GARY **(D)**
US Sen, Colo
b Ottawa, Kans, Nov 28, 37; m 1958 to Lee Ludwig; c Andrea & John. Educ: Bethany Col; Yale Univ Law Sch, LLB, 64. Polit & Govt Pos: Student vol, John F Kennedy Presidential Campaign, 60; attorney, Dept Justice; spec asst to Stewart Udall, Secy Interior; vol organizer, Robert Kennedy Presidential Campaign, 68; nat campaign dir, US Sen George McGovern, 70; US Sen, Colo, 75- Bus & Prof Pos: RR laborer; lectr, natural resources law, Univ Colo Sch Law. Publ: Right from the start, Quadrangle, 72. Mem: Denver Urban Renewal Authority (bd comnrs); Park Hill Action Comt (bd comnrs). Legal Res: CO Mailing Add: US Senate Washington DC 20510

HART, GARY K **(D)**
Calif State Assemblyman
b San Diego, Calif, Aug 13, 43; s Newman Lane Hart & Ruth Kersey H; m 1969 to Cary Smith. Educ: Stanford Univ, BA, 65; Harvard Univ, MAT, 66; Zeta Psi. Polit & Govt Pos: Comnr, Calif Coastal Zone Conserv Comn, 73-75; Calif State Assemblyman, 35th Dist, 74- Relig: Protestant. Legal Res: 2708 Montrose Pl Santa Barbara CA 93105 Mailing Add: State Capitol Sacramento CA 95814

HART, ILA JO **(R)**
Committeewoman, Dist Rep Party, Tex
b Gruver, Tex, Mar 11, 28; d Vic Ogle & Gertrude Van Zant O; m 1948 to Jack Hart; c Jerry & Ginger. Educ: Tex Woman's Univ, 45-46; WTex State Col, 46-47. Polit & Govt Pos: Committeewoman, Dist Rep Party, Tex, 70-; alt deleg, Rep Nat Conv, 72. Mem: Hansford Co Rep Women. Relig: Christian. Mailing Add: Box 566 Gruver TX 79040

HART, JEROME THOMAS **(D)**
Mich State Sen
b Saginaw, Mich, July 23, 32; s Bernard V Hart & Florence D Stevens H; single. Polit & Govt Pos: Treas, Saginaw Co Dem Comt, 54-58; exec asst to Treas, Mich, 62-64; chmn, Eighth Cong Dist Dem Party, 62-64; Mich State Sen, 34th Dist, 65-; deleg, Dem Nat Conv, 68. Bus & Prof Pos: Secy-treas, Qual Seal Oil Co, Saginaw, Mich, 54-58 & Saginaw Catholic Cemetery Comt, 59-62; owner-mgr, Tiny Town Clothing, 58-61. Mem: KofC. Relig: Roman Catholic. Legal Res: 2244 Woodbridge Saginaw MI 48602 Mailing Add: Box 240 Capitol Bldg Lansing MI 48902

HART, JOHN C **(R)**
Rep Nat Committeeman, Ind
b Indianapolis, Ind, Apr 26, 21; s Edgar Hart (deceased) & Elma Logsdon H; m 1950 to Mary Haselmire; c Barbara (Mrs Wolkhoff), Susan, John C, Jr, Victoria, James, Molly, Amy, Peggy & Joseph. Educ: Butler Univ, 40-42. Polit & Govt Pos: Ind State Rep, 69-74; Rep Nat Committeeman, Ind, 75- Bus & Prof Pos: Chmn legis comt, Local-State Builders, 63-69; pres, Marion Co Residence Builders, 66; pres, Ind State Home Builders, 70. Mem: IAC; CYO (bd dirs); Hoosier Motor Club (bd dirs); Jr Baseball Inc. Honors & Awards: Builder of Year, 68; CYO, John Bosco Award, Presby-Dawson Award. Relig: Presbyterian. Mailing Add: RR 1 Nollesville IN 46060

HART, KENNETH LEE **(D)**
Chmn, Madera Co Dem Cent Comt, Calif
b South San Francisco, Calif, Sept 8, 39; s Henry Hart & Mary Schmall H; m 1966 to Sherry Ann Russell. Educ: Fresno State Col, BA, 61, MA, 67; Delta Sigma Phi. Polit & Govt Pos: Mem, Fresno Co Dem Cent Comt, Calif, 68-69; mem, Madera Co Dem Cent Comt, 69-72, chmn, 72-; chmn, John Tunney Madera Co Campaign, 70; mem, Calif State Dem Cent Comt, 70-72; chmn, George McGovern Madera Co Campaign, 72; alt deleg, Dem Nat Conv, 72. Bus & Prof Pos: Teacher, Reedley High Sch, Calif, 64-68; instr, Merced Community Col, 68-71, chmn social sci div & pres, Col Faculty Asn, 72- Mil Serv: Entered as Pvt, Army 62, released as SP/4, 64, after serv in 232nd Signal Bn, Vietnam, 63-64. Publ: Democratic Party: founded for the common man, 10/9/70 & The Democratic National Convention, 10/72, Madera Daily Tribune. Mem: Calif Teachers Asn; Am Asn Community & Jr Cols. Honors & Awards: Outstanding Teacher, Mex-Am Adult Educ Asn, 68. Relig: Presbyterian. Legal Res: 124 N L St Madera CA 93637 Mailing Add: 6067 Nantucket Fresno CA 93704

HART, PARKER THOMPSON
b Medford, Mass, Sept 28, 10; s William Parker Hart & Ella Louisa Thompson H; m 1949 to Jane Constance Smiley; c Margaret Alice & Judith Ella. Educ: Dartmouth Col, BA, 33; Harvard Univ, MA, 35; L'Inst de Hautes Etudes Int, Geneva, 36; Georgetown Univ Sch Foreign Serv; Phi Kappa Sigma. Polit & Govt Pos: Career officer, US Dept of State Foreign Serv, 38-69, interpreter French, State Dept, 37-38, overseas serv in Vienna, Para, Rio de Janeiro, Cairo, Jidda, Dhahran & Damascus, with Div of Foreign Serv Planning, 47-49, attended Nat War Col, 51-52, dir Off Near Eastern Affairs, 52-53, dep asst secy of state for Near Eastern & SAsian Affairs, 58-61, minister to Yemen, 61-62; US Ambassador, Saudia Arabia, 61-65, Ambassador, Kuwait, 62-63, US Ambassador, Turkey, 65-68, Asst Secy of State for Near Eastern & SAsian Affairs, 68-69, dir, Foreign Serv Inst, Dept of State, 69. Bus & Prof Pos: Pres, Middle East Inst, Washington, DC, 69-73; Middle East Rep, Bechtel Corp, 73- Publ: Hanbalite and decree law in Saudi Arabia, Washington Foreign Law Soc, 53; An American policy toward the Middle East, The Annals, Am Acad Polit & Soc Sci, 7/70. Mem: Coun on Foreign Rels, Inc, NY; Am Turkish Soc NY (co-pres); Am Foreign Serv Asn, Washington, DC; Royal Geog Soc; Royal Cent Asian Soc. Honors & Awards: Nat Civil Serv League Citation, 57. Relig: Protestant. Legal Res: 4705 Berkeley Terr NW Washington DC 20007 Mailing Add: Bechtel Corp 1620 I St NW Washington DC 20006

HART, PHILIP A **(D)**
US Sen, Mich
b Bryn Mawr, Pa, Dec 10, 12; m 1943 to Jane C Briggs; c 4 sons & 4 daughters. Educ: Georgetown Univ, AB, cum laude, 34; Univ Mich Law Sch, JD, 37; Phi Delta Phi. Polit & Govt Pos: Comnr, Mich Corp & Securities Comn, 49-50; dir, Off Price Stabilization, 51; US Attorney, Eastern Mich, 52; legal adv to Gov Williams, Mich, 53-54; Lt Gov, Mich, 54-58; US Sen, Mich, 58-; deleg, Dem Nat Conv, 68. Mil Serv: Army, 41-46. Mem: Mich Bar Found; Lansing World Affairs Coun; Am Judicature Soc; Am Soc Inst Law. Legal Res: Mackinac Island MI 49757 Mailing Add: 253 Senate Off Bldg Washington DC 20510

HART, RICHARD ODUM **(D)**
Ill State Rep
b Benton, Ill, Dec 13, 27; s Marion Murphy Hart & Constance Skinner H; m 1951 to Carolyn Margaret Coddington; c Murphy Coddington & Paul Richard. Educ: Univ Ill, AB, 51; Washington Univ, JD, 54; Theta Chi. Polit & Govt Pos: Ill State Rep, 58th Dist, 69-72 & 59th Dist, 73- Mil Serv: Entered as Seaman 3/C, Navy, 45, released as Seaman 1/C, 46, after serv in Pac. Mem: Fel Am Col of Probate Counsel; VFW; Am Legion; Mason; Farm Bur. Relig: Protestant. Mailing Add: 301 W Reed Benton IL 62812

HART, RICHARD T, JR (R)
Chmn, Carlton Co Rep Comt, Minn
b Moose Lake, Minn; s Richard T Hart & Mabel Anderson H; single. Educ: Univ of Minn, BA, 42, LLB, 48; Phi Kappa Psi; Phi Delta Theta; M Club. Polit & Govt Pos: Munic judge, Moose Lake, Minn, 56-72; chmn, Carlton Co Rep Comt, currently. Mil Serv: Entered as 2nd Lt, Army, 42, released as Capt, 45, after serv in ETO, reentered serv as Capt, 51, released as Capt, 53, after serv in 504th Anti-Aircraft Artil, Combat Infantryman's Badge; Bronze Star; ETO Ribbon with Five Campaign Stars. Mem: AF&AM; Scottish Rite; Shrine; Moose; Am Legion. Relig: Episcopal. Legal Res: 333 Lakeshore Dr Moose Lake MN 55767 Mailing Add: Box 396 Moose Lake MN 55767

HART, THOMAS DANIEL (D)
b Morgantown, WVa, May 24, 39; s Walter Lawrence Hart II (deceased) & Mary Cox H; m 1974 to Louise Garland. Educ: WVa Univ, BA, 62; Am Univ, Washington Col Law, JD, 66; Phi Delta Phi; ed bd, Am Univ Law Rev, 65-66. Polit & Govt Pos: Elevator operator, US Capitol, 62-63; doorman, Members Gallery, US House Rep, 63-66; legis asst & staff attorney, Interstate & Foreign Com Comt, US House Rep, 66-68, consult, 70; regional campaign coordr, Dem Nat Comt, 68; spec asst to dir, Int Develop Div, COMSAT, 69-70; exec dir, Donahue for Senate Comt, 70; consult, Labor & Pub Welfare Comt, US Senate, 70-71; consult, House Admin Comt, US House Rep, 71; prof staff mem, Comt Judiciary, US Senate, 71-, counsel, subcomt on FBI Oversight, 73- Publ: Constitutional law: obscenity, Am Univ Law Rev, 64. Mem: US Supreme Court; Md Bar; Fed & Am Bar Asns. Relig: Catholic. Legal Res: 16 Wilson Ave Morgantown WV 26505 Mailing Add: 25 Turnham Ct Gaithersburg MD 20760

HARTDEGEN, JAMES ALAN (R)
Chmn, Pinal Co Rep Comt, Ariz
b Florence, Ariz, Oct 26, 45; s Arthur Hartdegen & Anna Nelson H; m to Dorothy Victoria Mirick. Educ: Mesa Community Col, 69-71; Ariz State Univ, 71-73. Polit & Govt Pos: Page, Ariz State Senate, 70-73; chmn, Pinal Co Rep Comt, 74- Bus & Prof Pos: Safety instr, Hecla Mining Co, 73. Mil Serv: Entered as Pvt, Army, 66, released as Sgt, 68, after serv in Third Brigade Fourth Inf Div, Vietnam; Nat Defense Serv Medal; Vietnam Commendation Medal; Vietnam Serv Medal; Good Conduct Medal; Combat Infantryman Badge. Mem: VFW. Mailing Add: PO Box 54 Casa Grande AZ 85222

HARTIGAN, MARGARET ANN (D)
Dem Nat Committeewoman, Vt
b Colchester, Vt, Nov 17, 26. Educ: High sch grad. Polit & Govt Pos: Dem Nat Committeewoman, Vt, currently; deleg, Dem Nat Conv, 72. Bus & Prof Pos: Mgr, Vt Transit Travel Bur; mem Vt Develop Bd. Relig: Roman Catholic. Mailing Add: 23 Hickok Pl Burlington VT 05401

HARTIGAN, NEIL F (D)
Lt Gov, Ill
Mailing Add: State House Springfield IL 62706

HARTKE, VANCE (D)
US Sen, Ind
b Stendal, Ind, May 31, 19; s Hugo Hartke & Ida Egbert H; m 1943 to Martha Tiernan; c Sandra, Jan, Wayne, Keith, Paul, Anita & Nadine. Educ: Evansville Col, AB; Ind Univ Law Sch, JD; ed, Ind Law J; Lambda Chi Alpha; Phi Delta Phi; Tau Kappa Alpha. Polit & Govt Pos: Attorney, Evansville, Ind, 48-58, Mayor, 56-58; dep prosecuting attorney, Vanderburg Co, 50-51; US Sen, Ind, 58-, chmn, Senate Comt Vet Affairs, mem, Senate Comt Finance & Comt Com, currently; deleg, Dem Nat Conv, 68 & 72; ex officio, Dem Nat Mid-Term Conf, 74. Bus & Prof Pos: Dir, Evansville's Future, Inc. Mil Serv: Navy & Coast Guard, World War II. Publ: Inside the new frontier, 63; The American crisis in Vietnam, 68; You and your senator, 70. Mem: Am & Ind Bar Asns; Wabash Valley Asn; Ohio Valley Improv Asn; Exchange Club. Relig: Lutheran. Legal Res: Evansville IN Mailing Add: 6500 Kerns Ct Falls Church VA 22044

HARTLE, PRISCILLA MORGAN (D)
Pres, Young Dem NC
b Newport News, Va, Dec 20, 42; d Volney Bennett Morgan, Jr (deceased) & Jean Martin Morgan Eller; div; c Anthony Larry. Educ: Wake Forest Univ, BA, 65. Polit & Govt Pos: Vpres, Young Dem NC, 71-72, nat committeewoman, 72-74, pres, 75-, Young Dem liaison, Dem Women NC, 75-; nat committeewoman, Young Dem Am, 75- Bus & Prof Pos: Mem, Coun Drug Abuse, Winston-Salem, NC, 70-; mem, Mayor's Coun Status Women, Winston-Salem, 75- Honors & Awards: J Albert House Award, NC Most Outstanding Young Dem, 71. Relig: Latter-day Saint. Mailing Add: 140 I Broadmoor Lane Winston-Salem NC 27104

HARTLEY, DAVID (D)
Ohio State Rep
Mailing Add: 211 N Belmont Ave Springfield OH 45503

HARTMAN, ARTHUR A
Asst Secy State European Affairs
b New York, NY, Mar 12, 26; m to Donna Ford. Educ: Harvard Univ, BA, 47. Polit & Govt Pos: Economist, Agency Int Develop, Paris, 48-52, asst econ comnr, 52-53; US deleg, EDC Conf, 53-54; foreign serv officer, Dept State, 54-, polit officer, US Mission NATO & European Regional Orgns, Paris, 54-56; econ officer, Saigon, 56-58, int rels officer, 58, foreign affairs officer, 58-59, staff asst to Under Secy State Econ Affairs, 61-63, spec asst to Under Secy State, 62-63; chief, Econ Sect, London, 63-67; spec asst to Under Secy State & staff dir, Sr Interdept Group, 67-69; spec asst staff dir, Under Secy Dept Com, 69, dep dir coord, 69-74; Asst Secy State European Affairs, 74- Bus & Prof Pos: Research asst, Univ Mich, 48. Mil Serv: Army, 44-46. Mailing Add: Dept of State Washington DC 20520

HARTMAN, BETTE RAE (R)
Chmn, Young Rep WVa
b Romney, WVa, Sept 1, 39; d J Wesley Knisley & Love Vanscoy K; m 1957 to Thomas E Hartman; c Thomas Paul, Robert Elwood, C Joseph & Cynthia Sue. Educ: Romney High Sch, WVa, grad, 57. Polit & Govt Pos: Chmn, Young Rep WVa, 73-; mem exec comt, Nat Fedn Young Rep, 73-; mem Berkeley Co Exec Comt, 74- Bus & Prof Pos: Advert rep, Martinsburg J, WVa, 69-, nat advert mgr, 72- Mem: State Press Asn; Muscular Dystrophy Asn (state bd dirs, 74-); Women of Moose (publicity dir). Honors & Awards: Outstanding Co Young Rep Chmn & Outstanding Young Rep Chmn, WVa Fedn Young Rep, 73, Outstanding Young Rep WVa, 74; Nat Hardcharger Award, Nat Fedn Young Rep, 74. Relig: United Methodist. Legal Res: Ahwenasa Inwood WV 25428 Mailing Add: Box A Inwood WV 25428

HARTMAN, JOSEPH ADOLPH (D)
Chmn, Greenwich Dem Town Comt, Conn
b Hartford, Conn, Feb 8, 20; s Emanuel M Hartman & Estelle Stein H; m 1964 to Ruth Lindsley; c Thomas Harris & Hattie Higginbotham. Educ: Harvard Col, BS, 41. Polit & Govt Pos: Mem, Hartford Bd Educ, Conn, 49-53; mem, Greenwich Dem Town Comt, 69-, chmn, 74-; mem, Greenwich Representative Town Comt, 72-; chmn, Greenwich Caucus Conn Dem, 72-74. Bus & Prof Pos: Dir, Hartman Tobacco Co, 48-; dir, TFH Corp, 57-63; pres, J A Hartman Corp, Greenwich, Conn, 66-; dir, Contact Systs Inc, 69-; chmn bd, Gordon's Gateway to Sports, 69- Mil Serv: Entered as A/S, Naval Res, 40, released as Lt Comdr, after serv in Atlantic, Pac & Mediter Theaters, 41-46; Eight Battle Stars. Mem: Harvard Club New York; Greenwich Club. Honors & Awards: Distinguished Serv Award, US CofC, 54. Relig: Jewish. Legal Res: 10 W Crossway Old Greenwich CT 06870 Mailing Add: 410 Greenwich Ave Greenwich CT 06830

HARTMAN, RALPH D (D)
NMex State Rep
b Berino, NMex, Mar 16, 30; s Carl G T Hartman & Thelma Avalos H; m to Peggy Herring; c Richard Frank, Yvonne Marie, Michael Ralph & James Duke. Educ: NMex State Univ, 49; NMex Highlands Univ, 50-51; Univ Colo Sch of Banking, grad, 61; Alpha Chap of Kappa Theta. Polit & Govt Pos: NMex State Rep, Dist 34, Dona Ana Co, NMex, 65-, vchmn, Agr Comt, 73- Bus & Prof Pos: Petroleum mgr, Farmer's Supply Coop, 54-55; asst vpres, First Nat Bank, Las Cruces, NMex, 55-; agt, Great Am Reserve Ins Co, 68-; pres, Anthony Waterworks, Inc, 71- Mil Serv: Entered as Pvt, Army, 52, released as Sgt, 54, after serv in 246th Field Artil, Missile Bn, Ft Bliss, Tex; Good Conduct Medal. Mem: Mason; Optimist Club; CofC; AF&AM (Anthony Lodge 48). Honors & Awards: Football Scholarship, Highlands Univ; Outstanding Serv Award, Anthony, NMex & Anthony, Tex. Relig: Methodist. Legal Res: 400 Main St Berino NM 88024 Mailing Add: Box 73 Berino NM 88024

HARTMAN, ROGER L (R)
Chmn, Buffalo Co Rep Party, Wis
b Manchester, Iowa, Jan 28, 29; s Carl Edward Hartman & Lucille Ann Nordurft H; m 1954 to Dolores Elaine Palmiter; c Kevin Lee. Educ: Univ Idaho, BS in Bus Admin, 54; Univ Wis, Madison, JD, 59; Scabbard & Blade; Phi Delta Phi. Polit & Govt Pos: City attorney, Alma, Wis, 60-; secy, Buffalo Co Rep Party, 62-66, chmn, 66-; village attorney, Pepin, Wis, 63-65; dist attorney, Buffalo Co, 65-; vchmn, Minn-Wis Boundary Comn, 67- Mil Serv: Entered as Pvt, Air Force, 51, released as 1st Lt, 55, after serv in 433rd Fighter Interceptor Squadron, Am Defense Command, 52-55; Maj & Gen Area Rep, Judge Adv Gen Corps, Air Force Res, 69; Am Defense Medal. Mem: Wis & Am Bar Asns; Nat Dist Attorney's Asn; Lions Int (secy); Am Legion (chaplain). Relig: Lutheran. Legal Res: 1301 River View Dr Alma WI 54610 Mailing Add: PO Box 337 Alma WI 54610

HARTMANN, ROBERT TROWBRIDGE (R)
b Rapid City, SDak, Apr 8, 17; s Miner Louis Hartmann & Elizabeth Trowbridge H; m 1943 to Roberta Edith Sankey; c Roberta (Mrs Charles Frederick Brake) & Robert Sankey. Educ: Stanford Univ BA, 38; Delta Chi; Delta Sigma Rho; Hammer & Coffin; Sigma Delta Chi. Polit & Govt Pos: Ed, Rep Conf, US House of Rep, 66-69, sgt at arms to minority & legis asst to Minority Leader Gerald R Ford, Mich, 69-73; asst to permanent chmn, Rep Nat Conv, 68 & 72; staff, US House of Rep Deleg to People's Repub of China, summer 72; chief of staff to the Vice President, 73-74; Counr to the President, 74- Bus & Prof Pos: Mem ed staff, Los Angeles Times, Calif, 39-64, chief, Wash Bur, 54-63, Mediterranean & MidE Bur, Rome, 63-64; NAm Regional Info Adv, Food & Agr Orgn, 64-65. Mil Serv: Entered as Ens, Naval Res, 41, released as Lt Comdr, 45, after serv in 11th Naval Dist & Pac Fleet; Capt, Naval Res (ret). Mem: Nat Press Club; Navy League of US; Int Club of Wash; Capitol Hill Club; Mil Order of the Carabao. Honors & Awards: Sigma Delta Chi Nat Distinguished Serv Award for Wash Correspondence, 58; Overseas Press Club Citation, 61; Vigilant Patriot Award, 60; English Speaking Union Better Understanding Award, 59; Freedoms Found Citation, 62. Relig: Protestant. Legal Res: 5001 Baltimore Ave Westgate MD 20016 Mailing Add: The White House Off Washington DC 20500

HARTNETT, ROBERT C (D)
Mem, Dade Co Dem Exec Comt, Fla
b Coral Gables, Fla, Sept 3, 38; s Fred B Hartnett & Elizabeth Grace Hartnett H; m 1972 to Elizabeth Rich. Educ: Univ Miami, BBS, 61; Alpha Kappa Psi; Iota Nu Sigma; Phi Delta Theta. Polit & Govt Pos: Admin asst to Secy of Fla State Senate, 61; mem, Dade Co Dem Exec Comt, Fla, currently; vchmn, Banks & Loans Comt, currently; Fla State Rep, 66-74, Dem Majority Whip & chmn, Select Comt on Equal Rights, Fla House Rep, 72-74. Bus & Prof Pos: Vpres & dir, Cove Inn Hotel, Naples, Fla, currently, US Truck Leasing Corp, currently; exec vpres, Commercial Div, Hartnett Realty, Inc, currently; chmn bd, Mid-Fla Equities, Securities & Real Estate Investment Trust, currently. Mem: Fla Asn of Realtors; Nat Soc of Legislators; United Fund Speakers Bur; Coral Gables Jr CofC. Relig: Roman Catholic. Legal Res: 1721 S Bayshore Lane Miami FL 33131 Mailing Add: 4551 Ponce de Leon Blvd Coral Gables FL 33146

HARTNETT, THOMAS FORBES (D)
SC State Sen
b Charleston, SC, Aug 7, 41; s Thomas C Hartnett & Catherine Forbes H; m 1965 to Bonnie Lee Kennedy. Educ: Charleston Col, 60-61. Polit & Govt Pos: SC State Rep, 65-73; SC State Sen, currently. Bus & Prof Pos: Realtor, vpres, Hartnett Realty Co. Mil Serv: Air Force, active duty; Air Force Res, currently. Mem: Charleston Optimist Club; KofC; Boy Scouts (scoutmaster, Troop 7); Bishop England Alumni Asn (pres); Hibernian Soc. Mailing Add: 908 Calvary Circle Mt Pleasant SC 29464

HARTRICK, GORDON DEAN (R)
b Stettler, Alta, Can, May 13, 15; s Maver Steven Hartrick & Lila M Dean H; m 1940 to Alma L Seely; c Holly (Mrs Ves Childs), Susan (Mrs Jerry MacDonald), Alice (Mrs Mike McBee), Heather (Mrs Dave Bevil), Nancy (Mrs Ken Stafford), Frank Dean, Fred Gordon, Jean Margaret, Robin Edmund & Betsy. Educ: Univ Mich, BS, 40, MSF, 41. Polit & Govt Pos: Chmn, Ashley Co Rep Party, Ark, 65-74. Bus & Prof Pos: Area forester, Ga Pac Corp, Crossett, Ark. Mem: Soc Am Foresters (chmn, Ozark sect); Ashley Co Develop Coun (chmn); Southeast Ark Resource & Conserv Develop Coun. Relig: Methodist. Mailing Add: Rte 3 Box 194 Hamburg AR 71646

HARTUNG, FRANK EDWIN (R)
Tex State Rep
b Cincinnati, Ohio, Feb 4, 40; s Raymond H Hartung & Anna Wagner H; m 1974 to Christin Stephens. Educ: Harvard Univ, AB, 63; Stanford Univ, MBA, 65. Polit & Govt Pos: Tex State Rep, Dist 92, 75- Bus & Prof Pos: Pres, Data Adv Inc, 69-; pres, South Tex Securities, Inc, 71- Legal Res: 2311 Fountain View Houston TX 77027 Mailing Add: PO Box 61429 Houston TX 77208

HARTVIGSEN, LESTER A (D)
Idaho State Sen
b Downey, Idaho, May 8, 11; s Joakim F Hartvigsen & Ellen Amelia Eilertsen H; m 1942 to Evelyn Jardine Williams (deceased); c James L, Rulon Eric & Kim Ray. Educ: Utah State Univ, BS in Econ, 36; Pi Gamma Mu. Polit & Govt Pos: Supvr, Bannock Co Agr Conserv Asn, Idaho, 38-41; asst, Power Co War Bd, 41-44; secy, Power Co Agr Conserv Asn, 41-44; Idaho State Rep, Dist 33, 67-74; Idaho State Sen, Dist 33, 74-; mem adv comt, Multistate Tax Compact, 75- Bus & Prof Pos: Owner-operator, Wheat Farms, 36-75. Mem: Lions Int. Relig: Latter-day Saint. Mailing Add: 255 E 155 S Malad ID 83252

HARTWELL, RAY VINTON, JR (D)
Chmn, Calhoun Co Dem Exec Comt, Ala
b Atlanta, Ga, June 23, 09; s Ray Vinton Hartwell, Sr & Leola Massengale H (deceased); m 1946 to Marguiritte Fryar; c Ray Vinton, III & Ellen Brinn (deceased). Educ: Ga State Col, 3 years; Jacksonville State Univ, BS with honors, 73. Polit & Govt Pos: Chmn, Calhoun Co Dem Exec Comt, Ala, 66-; deleg to Nat Dem Conv, 68; mem, Ala State Dem Exec Comt, Dist 16, 70- Bus & Prof Pos: With Citizens & Southern Bank, Atlanta, Ga, 26-36; head teller, Commercial Nat Bank, 47, 1st vpres, 47-73, sr vpres, 73-, on leave one year as exec vpres to help orgn Jacksonville State Bank, 70. Mil Serv: Entered as Pvt, Army, 41, released as Capt, 45, after serv in 121st Inf 8th Div & 143rd Inf 36th Div, NAfrican & ETO, 43-44; Capt, Army Res, 54; Silver Star; Purple Heart; Combat Inf Badge; Two Theatre Ribbons with Combat Cluster. Mem: Bank Mkt Asn; Am Legion; Alpha Kappa Psi; Kiwanis (past pres, Anniston Club); VFW. Honors & Awards: Awards, Anniston Gr Area CofC, 71-73. Relig: Methodist; Lay speaker, NAla Conf. Legal Res: 1006 Eighth Ave Jacksonville AL 36265 Mailing Add: PO Box 169 Jacksonville AL 36265

HARVEY, DANIEL (D)
Miss State Rep
b Smith Co, Miss, Sept 16, 27; s Lavelle Harvey & Thelma Stringer H; m 1954 to Mary Nell Williams; c Deborah A, Michael D & Larry L. Educ: Jones Jr Col, 45-46; Univ Southern Miss, BS, 51. Polit & Govt Pos: Miss State Rep, 60-; deleg to local, state & nat conv. Bus & Prof Pos: Supt, White Oak High Sch, 20 years. Mil Serv: Served during Korean War, 51-52; Merit Commendation Award with five Bronze Stars. Mem: Scottish Rite; Mason (32 degree); Shrine; Am Legion; VFW. Relig: Baptist. Mailing Add: Box 191 Mize MS 39116

HARVEY, DAVID CHRISTENSEN (D)
Utah State Rep
b Pleasant Grove, Utah, Sept 2, 34; s Leo Paul Harvey & Arvilla Christensen H; m 1959 to Dixie Renee Timons; c Craig David, Julie Ann, Mark Thomas, Stanley William, Carol Ann & Jeffrey Christopher. Educ: Brigham Young Univ, 1 year; Athenians. Polit & Govt Pos: Chmn, Fourth Dist Dem Party, Pleasant Grove, Utah, 60, secy, Peoples Party, 62; mem, Utah Co Dem Cent Comt, 62; Utah State Rep, 38th Dist, Utah Co, 65-66 & 69-; mem, Legis Coun, Utah House Rep, 69-71, chmn, Econ Develop Comt & mem, Const Rev Comt, 69-, mem, Higher Educ Comt, 71-, Interstate Pact comt, representing State of Utah in Agr, 59; deleg, Utah State Dem Conv, 67 & 69. Bus & Prof Pos: Self-employed farmer, currently. Mil Serv: S/Sgt, Army Res, 60-66, serv in Inf. Mem: Farm Bur Orgn; Farmers Union. Honors & Awards: Distinguished Serv Award, City of Pleasant Grove, 67. Relig: Latter-day Saint; Bishop, formerly, Stake Pres, currently. Mailing Add: Box 417 RD 1 Pleasant Grove UT 84062

HARVEY, J BATE (D)
SC State Rep
Mailing Add: Clover SC 29710

HARVEY, JAMES (R)
b Iron Mountain, Mich, July 4, 22; s Martin Harvey, Sr & Agnes Thomas H; m 1948 to June Elizabeth Collins; c Diane Elizabeth & Thomas Martin. Educ: Univ Mich, 40-43; Univ Mich Law Sch, LLB, 46-49. Polit & Govt Pos: Asst city attorney, Saginaw, Mich, 49-53, mem, city coun, 55-57, mayor, 57-59; US Rep, Mich, 61-75. Bus & Prof Pos: Attorney, Bauer & Williams, 53-56; partner, Nash, Nash & Harvey, 56-59; partner, Smith, Brooker, Harvey & Cook, 59-61. Mil Serv: Entered ROTC, Army Air Corps, 43, released as 2nd Lt, 45. Mem: Am & Mich Bar Asns; Germania Club; Congressional Country Club; Capitol Hill Club. Relig: Presbyterian. Mailing Add: 2746 W Genesee Ave Saginaw MI 48602

HARVEY, JAMES FERGUSON, JR (R)
Mem, Jackson Co Rep Exec Comt, Miss
b Simon, WVa, June 21, 16; s James Ferguson Harvey & Viola Morgan H; m 1946 to Mary Lyons; c James F, III, Chester Lyons & Patricia Lynn. Educ: Bowling Green Col Commerce, BS in commerce, 40; Pi Tau Nu. Polit & Govt Pos: Alt deleg, Rep Nat Conv, 68, deleg, 72; chmn, Jackson Co Rep Exec Comt, Miss, 68-73, mem, currently. Bus & Prof Pos: Dist chmn, Singing River Dist, Boy Scouts, 64-66 & camping & activities chmn, Pine Burr Coun, 67-69. Mil Serv: Entered as Pvt, Army, 41, released as Maj, 46, after serv in Continental Advance Sect, ETO, 43-45. Mem: Shrine; F&AM; Scottish Rite; Mason; Rotary. Honors & Awards: Silver Beaver, Boy Scouts. Relig: Methodist. Mailing Add: 1500 Dantzler St Moss Point MS 39563

HARVEY, LAVERN R (R)
Iowa State Rep
Mailing Add: 2307 Queens Court Bettendorf IA 52722

HARVEY, RALPH (R)
b New Castle, Ind, Aug 9, 01; s Eli M Harvey & Bessie Bouslog H; m 1925 to Charline Bowers. Educ: Purdue Univ, BSA, 23; Alpha Zeta; Tau Kappa Alpha; Alpha Gamma Rho. Hon Degrees: Dr, Purdue Univ, 67. Polit & Govt Pos: Mem, Co Coun, Ind, 32-42; Ind State Rep, 43-47; US Rep, Ind, 47-59 & 61-66; mem bd forest appeals, US Dept Agr, 70- Mem: Mason. Relig: Disciples of Christ. Mailing Add: Rte 5 New Castle IN 47632

HARVEY, ROBERT (D)
Ark State Sen
Mailing Add: Box 98 Swifton AR 72471

HARVEY, WILLIAM BRANTLEY, JR (D)
Lt Gov, SC
b Walterboro, SC, Aug 14, 30; s W Brantley Harvey & Thelma Lightsey H; m 1952 to Helen Coggeshall; c Eileen, William B, III, Helen, Margaret & Warren. Educ: The Citadel, AB in Polit Sci, 51; Univ SC Law Sch, LLB, 55; Phi Beta Kappa; Wig & Robe; Kappa Alpha Order; Phi Delta Phi. Polit & Govt Pos: SC State Rep, Beaufort Co, 59-74, chmn rules comt, SC House Rep, 67-74; Lt Gov, SC, 75- Bus & Prof Pos: Partner, Harvey, Battey, Macloskie & Bethea, 55-; dir & secy, Tidewater Investment & Develop Co, 58-; dir, Peoples Bank, Beaufort, 66- Mil Serv: Entered as 2nd Lt, Army, 52, released as 1st Lt, 54, after serv in Staff & Faculty AA&GM Br, Artil Sch, Ft Bliss, Tex. Mem: Am Bar Asn; Am Trial Lawyers Asn; Am Legion; Sertoma; CofC. Relig: Presbyterian; elder, teacher adult, Sunday sch class. Legal Res: 501 Pinckney St Beaufort SC 29902 Mailing Add: PO Box 1107 Beaufort SC 29902

HARVEYCUTTER, ROBERT CAREY, JR (D)
Chmn, Salem Dem Town Comt, Va
b Roanoke, Va, Jan 4, 52; s Robert Carey Harveycutter, Sr & Virginia Pitzer H; single. Educ: Va Western Community Col, 71-73. Polit & Govt Pos: Chmn, Salem Dem Town Comt, Va, 74- Bus & Prof Pos: Asst mgr, Salem Civic Ctr, 72- Mem: Salem Rescue Squad (secy, 75); CofC. Relig: Episcopal. Legal Res: 110 Broad St Salem VA 24153 Mailing Add: PO Box 35 Salem VA 24153

HARVILL, HALBERT (D)
Tenn State Sen
Mailing Add: 136 N Meadow Circle Clarksville TN 37040

HARWARD, ROYAL THOMAS (R)
Chmn, Wayne Co Rep Party, Utah
b Aurora, Utah, Nov 15, 10; s Thomas Franklin Harward & Sarah Jeanette Harding H; m 1934 to Donna Pauline Bagley; c Donna Carol (Mrs Dwight Williams), Carvel Royal, Ronald Vermont, Newell Edward, Thomas Kendall & Layne Bagley. Educ: Snow Col, 31-32. Polit & Govt Pos: Mem, Local Sch Bd, 40-, mem, 47-49; pres, Utah Sch Bd Asn, 56; Utah State Sen, 57-61; regional dir, Nat Sch Bd Asn, 59-63; Utah State Rep, 61-65 & 67-72; mem, Utah Legis Coun, 63-65 & 67-69; chmn, Wayne Co Rep Party, 75- Bus & Prof Pos: Self-employed rancher & merchant, currently. Mem: Lions; Southern & Eastern Utah Assoc Civic Clubs; Farm Bur. Honors & Awards: Utah Sch Bd Asn Distinguished Serv Award, 63 & 67 & Award for Long & Distinguished Serv, 72; Phi Delta Kappa Man of the Year Award, 68; Robert L Campbell Award, Utah Educ Asn & Utah Chap Nat Sch Pub Rels Asn, 72. Relig: Latter-day Saint. Mailing Add: Loa UT 84747

HARWOOD, EMMA G (D)
Chmn, Bennington Co Dem Comt, Vt
b Pownal, Vt, July 19, 35; d William Strohmaier & Blanche E Dunican S; m 1954 to Alden E Harwood. Educ: Bennington High Sch, grad, 53. Polit & Govt Pos: Secy, Vt Adv Comn, US Comt Civil Rights, 72; chmn, Bennington Co Dem Comt, Vt, 73-; state bd mem, Vt Human Servs Comn, 73-; mem, Gov Comn Status Women, 74-; mem, Regional Bd Manpower Comn, 74; deleg, Dem Nat Mid-Term Conf, 74. Bus & Prof Pos: Mem adv comt, Catamount Bank, Bennington, 74- Mem: Eastern Star; Grange; ILGWU, AFL-CIO; Am Civil Liberties Union. Relig: Congregational. Mailing Add: RFD 2 Middle Pownal Rd Bennington VT 05201

HARWOOD, MADELINE BAILEY (R)
Rep Nat Committeewoman, Vt
b Newbury, Vt, July 7, 14; d George Allen Bailey & Maud Smith B; m 1936 to Dr Clifford Burr Harwood; c Clifford B, Jr, Catherine A, Richard D & Roger B. Educ: Mary Fletcher Hosp Sch of Nursing, RN, 36. Polit & Govt Pos: Secy, Vt State Rep Comt, 61-63 & 64-67, vchmn, 67-69; mem drafting bd, Vt State Rep Platform Comt, 64, 66, 68 & 70, chmn, 72, chmn, Vt State Rep Conv, 72; deleg, Rep Nat Conv, 64, 68 & 72, mem, Drafting Comt, 64, secy, Platform Comt, 68 & mem exec comt, Platform Comt, 72; pres, Vt Fedn Rep Women, 65-67; Vt State Sen, 68-75, chmn, Senate Health & Welfare Comt, Vt State Senate, 73-75; mem, Gov Coun Civil Defense, 69-; mem, Vt Bicentennial Comt, 71-; Rep Nat Committeewoman, Vt, 73- Mem: Eastern Star (Past Matron); Champlain Col (trustee, 69-); Univ Vt (trustee, 71-); Ormsby Chap, DAR (state nat defense chmn, mem nat resolutions comt, 70); Manchester Bus & Prof Women's Club. Relig: Congregational. Mailing Add: Village View Rd Manchester Center VT 05255

HARWOOD, STANLEY (D)
Chmn, Nassau Co Dem Comt, NY
b Brooklyn, NY, June 23, 26; s Benjamin Harwood & Hannah Schwartz H; m 1950 to Deborah Weinerman; c Richard B, Ellen S, Michael C & Jonathan R. Educ: Columbia Col, New York, BA, 49; Columbia Univ Law Sch, LLB, 52. Polit & Govt Pos: Co committeeman, Dem Party, NY, 55-65; law secy to Justice NY State Supreme Court, 61-65; deleg, Dem State Conv, 62 & 66; NY State Assemblyman, 11th Assembly Dist, Nassau Co, 66-72; counsel, Minority, NY State Assembly, 73-; chmn, Nassau Co Dem Comt, NY, 73- Bus & Prof Pos: Attorney-at-law, pvt practice, Levittown, NY, 56-65; Mishkin, Miner, Harwood & Semel, Mineola, 65-69; Shayne, Dachs, Weiss, Kolbrener & Levy, 69-73; partner, Shayne, Dachs, Weiss, Kolbrener, Stanisci, Harwood & Levine, 73- Mil Serv: Entered as Cadet-Midn, Merchant Marine Acad, 44, released, 47, after serv in Acad & Merchant Vessels, Eng, Africa, India & Belgium, 45-46. Mem: Nassau Co Bar Asn (chmn courts comt, 72-); Kiwanis; Lions; KofP; Jewish War Vet. Relig: Jewish. Legal Res: 711 Birchwood Dr Westbury NY 11590 Mailing Add: 240 Mineola Blvd Mineola NY 11501

HASAY, GEORGE C (R)
Pa State Rep
Mailing Add: Capitol Bldg Harrisburg PA 17120

HASBROOK, THOMAS CHARLES (R)
Pres, City-Co Coun, Indianapolis, Ind
b Ft Wayne, Ind, July 29, 20; s Harold L Hasbrook (deceased) & Charlotte Hensel H (deceased); m 1943 to Mary Jane Thompson; c Carol (Mrs Jack Holmes), Dan, Bill, Charles, Nancy & David. Educ: Ind Univ, BS, 42; Kappa Sigma; Riviera Club. Polit & Govt Pos: Ind State Rep, 50-54; Ind State Sen, 54-58; councilman, City Coun, Indianapolis, Ind, 59-71, pres 68-71; City-Co Councilman, 71-, pres, 72- Bus & Prof Pos: Clerk, Eli Lilly & Co, 45-46; writer, 46-56, head employee commun dept, 56-66, head employee benefit dept, 66- Mil Serv:

Entered as Pfc, Marine Corps Res, 42, released as 2nd Lt, 44. Mem: Ind Soc Crippled Children & Adults; Nat Soc Prev Blindness; Blinded Vet Asn; Health & Rehabilitation Sect, Coun Soc Agencies; Cath Youth Orgn (adv). Honors & Awards: Outstanding Young Man & Good Govt Awards, US Jaycees; Grand Prize in Oper Comeback, Am Legion; Blind Father of Year, Nat Fathers' Day Comt; Sagamore of the Wabash from Gov. Relig: Catholic. Mailing Add: 5541 Central Ave Indianapolis IN 46220

HASEBROOCK, WILLIAM H
Nebr State Sen
Mailing Add: 544 N Lincoln West Point NE 68788

HASENKAMP, BRUCE HENRY (R)
b Brooklyn, NY, May 12, 38; s Henry Ernst Hasenkamp & Ruth Hoyer H; m to Inta Macs. Educ: Dartmouth Col, AB, 60; Stanford Univ, JD, 63; Phi Delta Phi; Sigma Phi Epsilon. Polit & Govt Pos: Mem staff, US Rep William B Widnall, NJ, 61-62; state pres, Calif Rep League, 71-73, dir, 71-74; mem exec comt, Calif Rep State Cent Comt, 71-74; first asst secy & mem finance comt, 73-74; deleg, Rep Nat Conv, 72; mem, Calif Steering Comt for Reelec of the President, 72; speakers bur chmn, Bay Area Citizens Comt for Reelec of the President, 72; mem exec comt, San Mateo Co Rep Cent Comt, 73-74; dir, President's Comn on White House Fels, currently. Bus & Prof Pos: Assoc, Simpson, Thacher & Bartlett, New York, 63-68; asst dean, Stanford Law Sch, Calif, 68-73; assoc gen secy, Stanford Univ, 70-73; educ & mgr consult, 73-74. Mil Serv: Entered as 1st Lt, Army, 64, released as 1st Lt, 66, after serv in Eighth Army, Korea, 64-66. Mem: World Affairs Coun of Northern Calif; Commonwealth Club Calif; Rotary Int. Honors & Awards: Outstanding High Sch Journalist, Scholastic Press Asn of NJ, 56. Relig: Episcopal. Legal Res: 24 Linaria Way Ladera Menlo Park CA 94025 Mailing Add: 5508 16th St N Arlington VA 22205

HASENOHRL, DONALD W (D)
Wis State Rep
Mailing Add: RR 1 Box 122 Pittsville WI 54466

HASHIM, ELINOR MARIE (R)
Mem, Conn Rep State Cent Comt
b Pittsfield, Mass, Dec 13, 33; d Michael David Hashim & Alice Simon H; single. Educ: Univ Vt, BA, 55; Southern Conn State Col, MS, 70; Gamma Phi Beta. Polit & Govt Pos: Pres, Manchester Rep Women's Club, Conn, 65-67; dist leader, Manchester Rep Town Comt, 63-73; secy, Manchester Charter Revision Comt, 67-68; mem, Conn Rep State Cent Comt, 72-; mem, Manchester Bd Educ, 73-; mem, Conn State Libr Comt, 74- Mem: Manchester Scholarship Found (bd dirs & chmn scholarship & loan comt, 74-); Conn Libr Asn (exec bd); New Eng Libr Asn (Conn rep, 73-); Am Libr Asn. Relig: Protestant. Mailing Add: 17 Goslee Dr Manchester CT 06040

HASKELL, FLOYD KIRK (D)
US Sen, Colo
b Morristown, NJ, Feb 7, 16; s E Kirk Haskell & Gladys C H; m to Eileen Nicoll; c Ione, Evelyn (Mrs Frank DiSante) & Pamela. Educ: Harvard Univ, AB, 37, Law Sch, LLB, 41. Polit & Govt Pos: Colo State Rep, 65-68; US Sen, Colo, 73- Bus & Prof Pos: Lawyer, Denver, Colo, 46-72. Mil Serv: Entered as Pvt, Army, 41, released as Maj, 45. Relig: Episcopal. Legal Res: 2707 Willamette Lane Littleton CO 80120 Mailing Add: 4104 New Senate Off Bldg Washington DC 20510

HASKELL, H HARRISON (JAY), II (R)
Pa State Rep
b Titusville, Pa, Dec 4, 39; s John Sargent & Charlotte McKinney S; single. Educ: Stetson Univ, AB, 62, masters cand, 65-66; Pi Kappa Alpha; Omicron Delta Kappa; Phi Alpha Theta. Polit & Govt Pos: Admin asst to Congressman James G Fulton, 63-64; staff aide to Congressman James A Weaver, 64; mem campaign staff, Raymond P Shafer for Gov, Pa, 66, asst to Gov Shafer, 68-69; asst secy for legis, 69-70; asst to Pa Rep State Chmn, 66-68; Pa State Rep, 71-; mem, Pa Pub TV Comn, currently; deleg, Rep Nat Conv, 72. Mem: Univ Pittsburgh (adv bd); Pa Young Rep; Tri-Co United Cerebral Palsy (bd dirs); Capitol Hill Club; Western Pa Conservancy. Relig: Episcopal. Legal Res: 215 W Main St Titusville PA 16354 Mailing Add: House of Rep Harrisburg PA 17120

HASKINS, STURGIS (D)
Chmn, Hancock Co Dem Comt, Maine
Educ: Univ Maine, Orono; Tuskegee Inst; New Sch for Soc Research. Polit & Govt Pos: Chmn, Hancock Co Dem Comt, Maine, 71-; mem, Hancock Co Planning Comn, currently. Publ: Numerous publ articles. Mem: Charles St Unitarian Church Boston (bd dirs); Hancock Co Hist Soc (mem bd); Sorrento-Sullivan Hist Soc (pres); Wilde-Stein Club. Honors & Awards: Maine State Jr Sailing Champion, 59; Maine State Men's Sailing Champion, 61, 71 & 72. Mailing Add: Sorrento ME 04677

HASLEY, DARRELL (SAM) (D)
Ark State Rep
Mailing Add: 1804 Sylvia Arkadelphia AR 71923

HASPER, GERRIT C (D)
Mich State Sen
Mailing Add: 1476 Beardsley Muskegon MI 49441

HASTE, JAMES FRANCIS (R)
Committeeman, Ill Rep State Cent Comt
b Rockford, Ill, Aug 7, 07; s Richard Haste & Sarah Kelley H; m 1939 to Marion Worden. Educ: High sch, grad; 1 year of col. Polit & Govt Pos: Alderman, Third Ward, Rockford, Ill, 29-45; secy, Winnebago Co Rep Cent Comt, 36 years, precinct committeeman, 31-67; chmn, Police & Fire Comn of Rockford, 55-59; committeeman, Ill Rep State Cent Comt, 60-; trustee, Sust Dist of Rockford, currently. Bus & Prof Pos: Sales rep, Smith Oil Corp, 39 years, in charge fuel oil sales, currently. Mil Serv: Pvt, Army, 43-45. Mem: Am Legion; Elks; 40 et 8; KofC; CofC. Relig: Roman Catholic. Mailing Add: 1919 Hillside Dr Rockford IL 61107

HASTINGS, JAMES FRED (R)
US Rep, NY
b Olean, NY, Apr 10, 26; s Glenn Tracy Hastings & Ruth Elizabeth Trail H; m 1947 to Barbara Louise Gaylor; c Linda Ann, Karen Diane, James Robert, David Michael & Tracy Eileen. Educ: High sch. Polit & Govt Pos: Mem, Town Bd, Allegany, NY, 53-62; police justice, Allegany, 56-62; NY State Assemblyman, 63-65; NY State Sen, 66-68; alt delg, Rep Nat Conv, 68; US Rep, NY, 39th Dist, 69- Bus & Prof Pos: Advert & sales, Procter & Gamble Distributing Co, 48-51; mgr & vpres, Radio Sta WHDL, 52-67; nat advert mgr & secy, Olean Times Herald Corp, 57-67. Mil Serv: Entered as A/S, Navy, 43, released as PO 2/C, 46. Mem: Am Legion; Amvets; Mason; Boy Scouts & Camp Fire Girls (mem exec bd); Georgetown Univ Health Policy Ctr. Relig: Methodist. Legal Res: Rushford Lake Caneadea NY 14717 Mailing Add: 113 Cannon House Off Bldg Washington DC 20515

HASTINGS, JOAN KING (R)
Okla State Sen
Mailing Add: State Capitol Oklahoma City OK 73105

HASTINGS, JOSEPH HENRY (R)
Chmn, Lake Co Rep Party, Mich
b Luther, Mich, June 3, 24; s John Percy Hastings, Sr & Irene Sibary H; m 1943 to Mary Ellen Foster; c Sharon Kay (Mrs Floyd Coon), Joseph H, Jr & Mark S. Educ: Luther Agr Sch, grad, 44. Polit & Govt Pos: Village councilman, Luther, Mich, 46-47 & 50-60, village marshal & fire chief, 47-49; mem, Luther Community Sch Bd, 56-62, pres, 2 years; chmn, Lake Co Rep Comt, 67-72 & 75-; mem, Lake Co Draft Bd 45, 70-72. Mem: Mason; F&AM; Luther Boy Scouts (committeeman); Luther Cub Scouts. Honors & Awards: Originator & dir recreational prog for Luther area, 20 years; organized benefits for crippled children; numerous other civic activities. Relig: Protestant. Mailing Add: 310 State St Luther MI 49656

HASTINGS, WILMOT REED (R)
Gen Counsel, Dept Health, Educ & Welfare
b Salem, Mass, May 29, 35; s Abner Horace Hastings & Florence Leslie Hylan H; m 1958 to Joan Amory Loomis; c W Reed, Jr, Melissa Hylan & Claire Amory. Educ: Harvard Col, AB, magna cum laude, 57; Univ Paris, 57-58; Harvard Law Sch, LLB magna cum laude, 61; ed, Harvard Law Rev. Polit & Govt Pos: Law clerk to Chief Justice Raymond S Wilkins, Mass, 61-62; first asst & dep attorney gen, Mass, 68-69; spec asst & exec asst to Under Secy of State, 69-70; gen counsel, Dept Health, Educ & Welfare, 70- Bus & Prof Pos: Assoc lawyer, Bingham, Dana & Gould, Boston, Mass, 62-68, partner, 73- Publ: Book rev, Harvard Law Rev, 62. Relig: Protestant. Mailing Add: 660 Concord Ave Belmont MA 02178

HASWELL, FRANK I
Assoc Justice, Montana Supreme Court
b Great Falls, Mont, Apr 6, 18; s Irvin A Haswell & Laura Cool H; m 1951 to June Arnold; c Frank Warren, Bruce Douglas & John Richard. Educ: Univ Mont, 37-39, LLB, 47; Univ Wash, BA, 41; Phi Sigma Kappa. Polit & Govt Pos: City Attorney, Whitefish, Mont, 48-51; Dist Judge 11th Judicial Dist, Mont, 58-67; Assoc Justice, Mont Supreme Court, 67-; chmn, Mont Probate Comn, 72-; chmn, Gov Jury Justice Adv Coun, 72- Mil Serv: Entered as Pvt, Marines, 43, released as Cpl, 46, after serv in various units in Pacific, 43-46. Mem: Mont Judges Asn (pres, 69-); Am Judicature Soc; Elks; Eagles; Rotary. Relig: Protestant. Mailing Add: 1370 Mill Rd Helena MT 59601

HATCH, FRANCIS WHITING, JR (R)
Mass State Rep
b Cambridge, Mass, May 6, 25; s Francis W Hatch & Marjorie H; m 1952 to Serena Merck; c Timothy, Serena, Francis W, III, George & Olivia. Educ: Harvard Col, BA, 44. Polit & Govt Pos: Alderman, Beverly, Mass, 57-62; committeeman, Mass Rep State Comt, 60-64; Mass State Rep, Third Essex Dist, 62-, Rep Floor Leader, Mass House Rep, 71-; deleg, Rep Nat Conv, 68. Bus & Prof Pos: Reporter, Minneapolis Star & Tribune, 46-48, nat advert salesman, 48-50; vpres, Suburban Ctr Trust, 51-54; dir advert & pub rels, New Eng Mutual Life Ins, 54-62. Mil Serv: Navy, 44-46, Ens, serv in USS Pensacola, Pac; two Campaign Stars; Purple Heart. Honors & Awards: Sears Roebuck Found, Regional Conserv Award, 66; New Eng Wildflower Soc Conserv Medal. Relig: Protestant. Mailing Add: Preston Pl Beverly Farms MA 01915

HATCH, ROBIN PAIGE (D)
Committeewoman, Mont Dem State Cent Comt
b Rio de Janeiro, Brazil, Aug 25, 47; d Robert Perry Zentner & Sharon Brezee Z; m 1968 to Bryant Donald Hatch; c Kimberly. Educ: Univ Calif, Santa Cruz; Univ Calif Berkeley. Polit & Govt Pos: Committeewoman, Mont Dem State Cent Comt, 74-; deleg, Dem Nat Mid-Term Conf, 74. Mem: Mont Equal Rights Amendment Ratification Coun (chmn, 73-); Mont Common Cause (co-chmn, 71-72); Mont Women's Polit Caucus. Mailing Add: 633 N Rodney Helena MT 59601

HATCHER, CHARLES (D)
Ga State Rep
Mailing Add: PO Box 750 Albany GA 31702

HATCHER, ELMER WARD, JR (R)
b Augusta, Ga, Apr 27, 50; s Elmer Ward Hatcher & Ola Booth H; single. Educ: Presby Col, BA, 72; Univ SC Law Sch, 73- Polit & Govt Pos: Vchmn, SC Rep Party, 72-74. Mil Serv: Entered as 2nd Lt, Army, 72, released as 2nd Lt, 73, after serv in Signal Corps; 2nd Lt, Army Reserve, 2 years. Relig: Baptist. Mailing Add: Rte 3 Box 370 Aiken SC 29801

HATCHER, LILLIAN (D)
VChairperson, First Cong Dist Dem Party Orgn, Mich
b Greenville, Ala, May 30, 15; d Robert Cook & Jimmie McTyeire C; m 1942 to John Hatcher; c Carlene (Mrs Polite), John L & Gloria M (Mrs Williams). Educ: Univ Mich, labor mgt, 46-48. Polit & Govt Pos: Precinct deleg, 13th Dist Dem Party Orgn, Mich, 48, secy, 50; deleg, Dem Nat Conv, 58, 68 & 72; deleg, Sen Dist 214, Mich Const Conv, 60-61; vchairperson, First Cong Dist Dem Orgn, 60-; deleg, Mich Legis Apportionment Comn, 71-72; mem, State Cent Rules & Procedure Comt, Mich Dem Party, 73. Bus & Prof Pos: Int rep, Fair Practices & Anti-Discrimination Dept, UAW, 46-58, Citizenship-Educ Dept, Union Coun, 61-65 & Women's Dept, UAW, currently. Publ: Ed, Women's Auxiliary News. Mem: Current Topic Study Club; GEMS (vpres); Dem Women's Caucus; NAACP (life mem); Nat Coun of Negro Women (life mem). Honors & Awards: Awards, Prince Hall Mason, 49, Current Topic, 57, Trade Union Leadership Conf, 58, Motor City Block Clubs, 60 & Black Trade Unionist, 73. Relig: Protestant. Mailing Add: 1694 W Boston Blvd Detroit MI 48206

HATCHER, MARTIN (D)
Colo State Sen
Mailing Add: 108 Roundtree Gunnison CO 81230

HATCHER, RICHARD G (D)
Mayor, Gary, Ind
b Michigan City, Ind, July 10, 33; s Carlton Hatcher & Catherine H; single. Educ: Ind Univ, BA; Valparaiso Univ, LLB. Hon Degrees: Dr, Duquesne, Fisk & Valparaiso Univs & Coppin State Col. Polit & Govt Pos: Former dep prosecutor, Lake Co, Ind; councilman-at-lg, City Coun, Gary, Ind, 63-66, mayor, 67-; chmn, Nat Comt on Inquiry & mem, Nat Steering Comt, Urban Coalition; co-convenor, Nat Black Polit Conv, 72; deleg, Dem Nat Conv, 72; chmn, First Cong Dist Dem Party, Ind, 72-; mem, Ind Dem State Cent Comt, 72-; co-chmn & host chmn, Gary Dem Precinct Orgn, 72-; pres, Nat Black Polit Coun, 73-; chmn, Ind State Black Caucus, 73-; mem deleg selection, Nat Dem Comt, 73-; spec deleg, Dem Nat Mid-Term Conf, 74. Bus & Prof Pos: Admitted to Ind bar & practiced in East Chicago, Ind. Mem: US Conf Mayors (mem legis action & human resources comt); Nat League of Cities (bd dirs); Rotary; NAACP (legal adv Gary chap, mem state exec bd); Int State Adv Comt, US Comn Civil Rights. Honors & Awards: Outstanding Young Man of the Year, Gary Jaycees, 68; One of Five Outstanding Men in Ind; Loren Henry Award, Ind State NAACP, 65; Outstanding Man of the Year, Nat Fel Comn. Mailing Add: City Hall 401 Broadway Gary IN 46402

HATFIELD, GUY, III (R)
Chmn, Estill Co Rep Party, Ky
b Gary, Ind, Apr 19, 50; s Guy Hatfield, Sr & Lucy Baker H; m 1974 to Sherry Witt, wid. Educ: Eastern Ky Univ, AB, 72, study toward MPA, 74-75; Sigma Alpha Epsilon, Eminent Archon, 3 times. Polit & Govt Pos: Chmn, Estill Co Rep Party, Ky, 72-; first vchmn, Ky Young Rep Fedn, 74- Bus & Prof Pos: Pres, Citizen Voice Publ, Inc, 73-; chmn bd, Sr Citizen Opportunity Ctr, 75-; awards chmn, Ky Press Asn, 75- Publ: Auth, Small county politics, 6/74 & Precinct methods of rural voters, 6/75, Ky Young Rep. Mem: Oleika Shrine; Estill Co Jaycees (vpres); Kiwanis; Bd Regents Eastern Ky Univ. Honors & Awards: Youngest Rep Co Chmn at age 21 when elected in 72; Man of Year, Ky Col Rep, 72-73; Man of Year, Ky Young Rep, 73-74. Relig: Methodist. Legal Res: 303 Main Irvine KY 40336 Mailing Add: 712 Main Ravenna KY 40472

HATFIELD, MARK ODOM (R)
US Sen, Ore
b Dallas, Ore, July 12, 22; s Charles Dolan Hatfield & Dovie Odom H; m 1958 to Antoinette Kuzmanich; c Elizabeth, Mark O, Jr, Charles Vincent & Theresa. Educ: Willamette Univ, BA, 43; Stanford Univ, AM, 48. Polit & Govt Pos: Ore State Rep, 51-55; deleg, Rep Nat Conv, 52, 56, 60, 64 & 68, mem, Conv Resolutions Comt, 52 & 56, chmn, Ore Deleg, 60, 64 & 68, keynoter & temporary chmn, 64, nominator for Richard M Nixon, 60 & seconded Nixon's nomination, 68; Ore State Sen, 55-57; Secy of State, Ore, 57-59, Gov, 59-67; US Sen, Ore, 67- Bus & Prof Pos: Assoc prof polit sci, Willamette Univ, 49-56, dean of students, 50-56. Mil Serv: Navy, World War II. Publ: Not Quite So Simple, Harper & Row, 68; Conflict and Conscience, World Books, 72. Relig: Baptist. Legal Res: PO Box 630 Newport OR 97365 Mailing Add: Rm 463 Senate Off Bldg Washington DC 20510

HATFIELD, MARSHAL JOE (R)
Chmn, McLean Co Rep Comt, Ky
b Livermore, Ky, Mar 8, 38; s J B Hatfield & Josephine Porter H; m 1957 to Elizabeth Sue Nantz; c Steven Lynn & David Allan. Educ: Livermore High Sch. Polit & Govt Pos: Chmn, McLean Co Rep Comt, Ky, 64-73 & 75- Bus & Prof Pos: Cashier, Farmers & Merchants Bank, 68- Mem: CofC; Livermore Lions Club. Relig: Baptist. Mailing Add: PO Box 61 Livermore KY 42352

HATFIELD, ROBERT F (D)
WVa State Sen
Mailing Add: State Capitol Charleston WV 25305

HATFIELD, ROLLAND F (R)
Auditor, State of Minn
b Chicago, Ill, Feb 5, 10; s Rolland F Hatfield & Ann Clark H; m 1967 to Charlotte Louise Tragnitz; c Gerald. Educ: Univ Chicago, BA & MA, 35; William Mitchell Col Law, LLB, 52; Phi Beta Kappa; Alpha Sigma Phi; Delta Theta Phi. Polit & Govt Pos: Tech adv, Minn Income Study, St Paul, 38-39; adv bus develop dept, State of Minn, 39-40, dir tax research, Minn Dept Taxation, 40-52, comnr taxation, 61-67, comnr admin, 67-70, auditor, 71-; dir, Minn Property Tax Study, 70. Bus & Prof Pos: Mgr pension & tax dept, Northwestern Nat Life Ins Co Minneapolis, Minn, 52-61. Mil Serv: Entered as 2nd Lt, Air Force, 42, released as Maj, 46, after serv in GHQ, Japan, Japanese Theatre, 45-46; Commendation from Gen MacArthur. Publ: Minnesota Property Tax, State of Minn, 70. Mem: Nat Asn Tax Adminrs (pres); Fedn Tax Adminrs (chmn bd trustees); Midwestern States Asn Tax Adminrs (pres). Relig: Protestant. Mailing Add: 2730 N Dale St Paul MN 55113

HATFIELD, WANDA HELENA (R)
b Buffalo, NY, July 22, 30; d Claude Steeves & Florence Rasinski S; m 1950 to James Marvin Hatfield Sr; c James Marvin, Jr, Cynthia Helena & Deborah Ann. Educ: Erie Commun Col, AAS, 50; State Univ NY Buffalo, part-time, 60-64; Cornell Univ, 64; State Univ NY Col Buffalo, BS, 71. Polit & Govt Pos: Secy, North Collins Rep Comt, 69-; pres & founder, North Collins Womens Rep Club, 70-; town coordr, co exec, Edward Regan Campaign, 71; town coordr, Housewives for Nixon, 71; committeewoman, Town of North Collins, 71; mem speakers bur, Erie Co Fedn of Women Rep Clubs, 71-, mem bd dirs, 72-; mem exec women, Erie Co, 71-; alt deleg, Rep Nat Conv, 72; town coordr, Jack Kemp for Cong Campaign, 72. Bus & Prof Pos: Teacher, Cheektowaga Sch Dist Nine, 60-66 & Bd of Coop Educ Serv, 66-68; pub health educator, Erie Co, 71- Publ: Ed, Republican Womens Newsletter, Erie Co, 71-73. Mem: Eastern Star. Relig: Methodist. Legal Res: 10142 Clarksburg Rd North Collins NY 14057 Mailing Add: PO Box Eden North Collins NY 14057

HATHAWAY, DONALD H (R)
VChmn, 39th Legis Dist, NDak
b Kingsley, Iowa, Dec 18, 14; s Ray Hathaway & Anna Brewster H; m 1946 to Helen Wyman; c Thomas & Richard. Educ: Beach High Sch. Polit & Govt Pos: Co-chmn, Rep Comt, 59-60; mem, NDak Rep State Cent Comt, 60-66; chmn, Twp Bd, 61-67 & Bd of Educ, 62-68; mem, NDak Rep State Exec Comt, 63-66; alt deleg, Rep Nat Conv, 64; vchmn, 39th Legis Dist, NDak, 66-; mem, NDak Sch Bds, Legis Comt, 68-69. Bus & Prof Pos: Farmer, 36- Mil Serv: Entered as Pvt, Army, 42, released as Capt, 46, after in 42nd Rainbow Inf; ETO; Combat Inf Badge; ETO Ribbon with Two Clusters; Good Conduct Medal; Army Occupational Medal; Letter of Commendation. Mem: Mason; Am Legion; NDak Stockmans Asn. Relig: Congregational. Mailing Add: Beach ND 58621

HATHAWAY, MICHAEL DAVID (R)
Mem, Rep State Cent Comt Md
b Washington, DC, Jan 5, 37; s George Edward Hathaway & Jeannette Forsythe H; m 1957 to Ellen Louise Hagedorn; c Michael Stuart, David Brian & Edward John. Educ: Univ Md, BS in Aeronaut Eng, 59; Scabbard & Blade. Polit & Govt Pos: Mem, Prince Georges Co Rep Cent Comt, Md, 66-70, chmn, 68-70; dir task force on energy & resources, House Republican Conf, 71-73; spec asst energy & environ to US Sen James A McClure, Idaho, 73-; mem, Rep State Cent Comt Md, 75- Bus & Prof Pos: Engr, Douglas Aircraft Co, Santa Monica, Calif, 59-60; sr engr, Space Div, Chrysler Corp, New Orleans, La, 62-65; pres, United Int Corp, Washington, DC, 65-; staff engr, Nat Rural Elec Coop Asn, 69-71. Mem: Opers Research Soc Am; Inst Elec & Electronic Engrs; Am Ord Asn; PTA (pres, 72-). Relig: Protestant. Mailing Add: Box 542 Rte 1 Accokeek MD 20607

HATHAWAY, ROBERT RICHARD (D)
Assessor, Santa Cruz Co, Ariz
b Nogales, Ariz, July 31, 30; s William Harrison Hathaway & Mary McIntyre H; m 1950 to Laura Ellen Hill; c Diane Susan, Mary Ellen, Evangeline Anne, Rosalie Lorraine & Robert William. Educ: Univ Ariz, 1 year. Polit & Govt Pos: Former mem sch bd, Dist 28, Santa Cruz Co, Ariz; Ariz State Rep, 55-64; Ariz State Sen, 65-67; assessor, Santa Cruz Co, 68-; asst dir dept revenue, Div Property & Spec Taxes, 75- Bus & Prof Pos: Former dir, Security Savings & Loan Asn, Nogales, Ariz. Mil Serv: Entered Nat Guard, 48, released as Capt, Army Res. Mem: Southern Ariz Cattle Protective Asn. Relig: Protestant. Legal Res: Duquesne Rd Nogales AZ 85621 Mailing Add: Unit 13 6533 N Seventh Ave Phoenix AZ 85013

HATHAWAY, STANLEY K (R)
b Osceola, Nebr, July 19, 24; s Franklin E Hathaway & Velma Holbrook H; m 1948 to Roberta Harley; c Susan & Sandra. Educ: Univ Wyo, 42-43; Univ Nebr, AB, 48, LLB, 50; Delta Theta Phi; Sigma Chi. Polit & Govt Pos: Prosecuting attorney, Goshen Co, Wyo, 54-62; nat committeeman, Young Rep Fedn, 58-60; committeeman, Wyo State Rep Party, 60-62, chmn & secy, 62-64, chmn, Goshen Co Rep Party, 62-64; Gov, Wyo, 67-75; deleg, Rep Nat Conv, 68 & 72; Secy, Dept of Interior, 75. Mil Serv: Entered as Pvt, Air Force, 43, released as T/Sgt, 45, after serv in 8th Air Force, ETO, 44-45; Five Air Medals & ETO Campaign Ribbon. Mem: Am Legion; VFW; Lions Int; AF&AM; Elks. Honors & Awards: Only person to ever serve through more than two legis sessions in Wyo. Relig: Episcopal. Mailing Add: 219 Linda Vista Torrington WY 82240

HATHAWAY, WILLIAM DODD (D)
US Sen, Maine
b Cambridge, Mass, Feb 21, 24; m 1945 to Mary Lee Bird; c Susan Louise & Fred William. Educ: Harvard Col, grad, 49, Harvard Law Sch, grad, 53. Polit & Govt Pos: Asst co attorney, Androscoggin Co, Maine, 55-57; hearing examr for State Liquor Comn, 57-61; deleg, Dem Nat Conv, 64, 68 & 72; US Rep, Maine, 65-72; US Sen, Maine, 75- Mil Serv: Army Air Force, 42-46. Mem: Am Bar Asn; Maine Med-Legal Soc; Lewiston-Auburn Chap of Am Red Cross & Lewiston-Auburn Asn for Retarded Children (mem bd dirs); Lewiston-Auburn United Fund (div chmn). Relig: Episcopal. Mailing Add: 40 Pine St Lewiston ME 04240

HATTAWAY, BOB (D)
Fla State Rep
Mailing Add: 143 Hattaway Dr Altamonte Springs FL 32701

HAUGEBERG, CARL (D)
b Minot, NDak, Jan 8, 35; s Art Haugeberg & Mabel Nicolaison H; m 1955 to Marlys Schmidt; c Bradley, Jarvis & Ross. Educ: NDak State Univ, 54. Polit & Govt Pos: Chmn, Dist Eight Dem Party, NDak, formerly; mem, State Dem Planning Comt, 66-; mem, State Dem Finance Comt, 68-; deleg & chmn, NDak Humphrey Deleg, Dem Nat Conv, 72. Mem: Farmers Union; Max Civic Club (pres, 68-69); Eagles; Toastmasters. Honors & Awards: Am Farmer Degree, Future Farmers Am, 55. Relig: Lutheran. Mailing Add: Max ND 58759

HAUGEN, ERNIE (R)
Alaska State Rep
Mailing Add: PO Box 248 Petersburg AK 99833

HAUGERUD, NEIL SHERMAN (DFL)
Minn State Rep
b Canton Twp, Fillmore Co, Minn, July 3, 30; s Allen Sherman Haugerud & Anna Armstrong H; m 1954 to Helen Arlene Anderson; c Renee Lynn, Susan Kay, Thomas Neil & Karen Marie. Educ: Winona State Teachers Col; Univ Minn, Minneapolis. Polit & Govt Pos: Co sheriff, Fillmore Co, Minn, 58-66; Minn State Rep, Dist 1A, Preston, 68-, Asst Majority Leader, Minn House Rep, 73- Bus & Prof Pos: Ins agt, Haugerud Ins Agency, 56-58; investment broker, John G Kinnard & Co, Minneapolis, 66-; pres, Headway Industs, Preston, 72- Mil Serv: Entered as Pvt, Marines, 48, released as Sgt, 52, after serv in Ord Div, 2nd Marines, 51-52. Mem: Hon life mem Minn State Sheriffs Asn; Am Legion; Lions; Toastmasters. Relig: Lutheran. Mailing Add: Rte 3 Preston MN 55965

HAUGH, JOHN H (R)
Rep Nat Committeeman, Ariz
b Clinton, Iowa, Nov 1, 10; s John Aloyisus Haugh & Paula Harms H; m 1939 to Emilie Loucille Johnson; c William & Emilie & stepsons Clyde & Carl Skinner. Educ: Lake Forest Col, 27-29; Univ Calif, Los Angeles, 31; Univ Ariz; Nat Forensic League; Kappa Sigma. Polit & Govt Pos: Precinct committeeman, Rep Party, Ariz, 50-; deleg, Rep Nat Conv, 56, 60 & 64, participant, 68 & 72, mem platform comt, 60; Ariz State Rep, 52-66 & 69-70, Rep Floor Leader, Ariz House Rep, 56-62, Asst Majority Floor Leader, 63-64, Majority Leader, 65-66, Speaker of the House, 69-70; Rep Nat Committeeman, Ariz, currently; mem, Rep Nat Comt Task Force Const Rev at State Level, 67-68 & Exec & Rule 29 Comts, 72- Bus & Prof Pos: Dir, Fats & Protein Research Inc, 62-; dir, Tucson Gas & Elec Co; pres, Tucson Tallow Co, Inc; trustee, Lake Forest Col; dir, Am Savings & Loan Asn, Tucson; chmn Ariz adv comt, Robert A Taft Inst Govt. Mem: Nat Renderers Asn (pres, 62-63); Rotary. Honors & Awards: Lake Forest Col Alumni Distinguished Serv Award. Relig: Episcopal. Mailing Add: 5705 N Campbell Ave Tucson AZ 85718

HAUGHT, ROBERT L (R)
b Lawton, Okla, May 20, 30; s Pete Haught (deceased) & Josie Mae Brandon H (deceased); div; c Robert Steven, Gary Wayne & Randall Keith. Educ: Univ Okla, BA in Jour, 54, MA Pub Admin, 72; Am Univ, 72-; Sigma Delta Chi. Polit & Govt Pos: Admin asst, Okla Nat Guard, Marlow, 48-49; info staff officer, Gov Henry Bellmon, Oklahoma City, Okla, 63-65; econ opportunity coordr, State Okla, 65-68; publicity dir, Bellmon for Senate Campaign, 68;

spec asst, US Sen Henry Bellmon, Washington, DC, 69-73, exec asst, 73-74, admin asst, 75- Bus & Prof Pos: Staff correspondent, bur & state news mgr, United Press Int, Oklahoma City, Okla, 54-63; exten specialist, Univ Okla, Norman, 68. Mil Serv: Entered as Sgt 1/C, Army, 50, released as Sgt 1/C, 51, after serv in Co G, 179th Inf, 45th Div, Japan. Relig: Protestant. Legal Res: 930 S Boulevard Edmond OK 73034 Mailing Add: 1311 Delaware Ave SW Apt S-127 Washington DC 20024

HAUGLAND, BRYNHILD (R)
NDak State Rep
b Minot, NDak, July 28, 05; d Nels Haugland & Sigurda Ringoen H; single. Educ: Minot State Col, BA; Delta Kappa Gamma. Polit & Govt Pos: NDak State Rep, 39-, chmn, Comt on Social Welfare, mem, Legis Research Comt; mem, Ward Co Zoning Comn, 3 years; vchmn, State Adv Coun for Hosp & Related Construction; chmn Adv Coun to State Unemployment Compensation Div & State Employ Serv Div, Workmen's Compensation Bur. Mem: Quota Club; Bus & Prof Women's Club; Int Peace Garden (first vpres, bd mem 20 years); Minot State Col Alumni Asn (bd dirs); Adv Coun to Minot Area Soc Serv Cent. Honors & Awards: Named Minot Woman of Year, 56 & 71. Relig: Lutheran. Legal Res: Farm Harrison Twp Ward Co Minot ND 58701 Mailing Add: PO Box 1684 Minot ND 58701

HAUGLAND, JEAN (D)
Mem, Dem Nat Comt, Iowa
Mailing Add: 301 N Grant Lake Mills IA 50450

HAUGO, ROGER ERLING (R)
Mem, SDak State Rep Cent Comt
b Sioux Falls, SDak, Oct 11, 33; s Erling Haugo & Clara Thompson H; single. Educ: Augustana Col (SDak), BA, 58; Univ Chicago, 58-60; Univ Oslo, summer 57; Univ SDak, JD, 64; Phi Delta Phi. Polit & Govt Pos: SDak State Rep, Minnehaha Co, 71-72; mem, SDak State Rep Cent Comt, 75- Bus & Prof Pos: Bank employee, Sioux Valley Bank, Sioux Falls, SDak, 56-58, 60-64; attorney-at-law, 64- Mil Serv: Entered as SKSN, Navy, 54, released as SKSN, 56, after serv in Destroyer Base, San Diego, Calif, 54-56. Mem: Minnehaha Co Bar Asn; Elks; Sioux Falls CofC; Sons of Norway; Nat Hist Soc. Relig: Lutheran. Legal Res: 312 W 27th St Sioux Falls SD 57105 Mailing Add: 1101 E Eighth St Sioux Falls SD 57103

HAUKE, THOMAS A (D)
Wis State Rep
Mailing Add: 10235 W Grant St West Allis WI 53214

HAUSAUER, ALVIN (R)
NDak State Rep
Mailing Add: State Capitol Bismarck ND 58501

HAUSAUER, LEROY (R)
NDak State Rep
Mailing Add: State Capitol Bismarck ND 58501

HAUSCHILD, WAYNE ARTHUR (D)
SDak State Rep
b Davenport, Iowa, June 20, 25; s Walter John Hauschild & Edna Tarket H; m 1949 to Rosemary Monier; c Patricia, Donna, Barbara & Melissa. Educ: St Ambrose Col, BA, 50; Univ SDak, ME, 52. Polit & Govt Pos: SDak State Rep, 71- Mil Serv: Entered as Seaman, Navy, 43, released as PO 2/C, 46, after serv in Pac, 44-45; Six Major Battle Stars. Mem: Nat & SDak Educ Asns; Brookings Educ Asn; Mason; Elks. Relig: Methodist. Mailing Add: 1028 Seventh Ave Brookings SD 57006

HAUSMANN, C STEWART (R)
Freeholder, Essex Co, NJ
b Orange, NJ, Oct 18, 22; s Charles F Hausmann & Christina Becker H; m 1944 to Lillian D'Addario; c Charles S, Steven C & Christine C. Educ: Upsala Col, AB; Montclair State Col, MA. Polit & Govt Pos: Mem, Bd of Educ, Irvington, NJ, 58-64; freeholder, Essex Co, 67-72; dir, Bd of Freeholders, 68; deleg, Rep Nat Conv, 68, alt deleg, 72. Bus & Prof Pos: Teacher, Irvington Pub Schs, 47-53; self-employed mortician, 53-; exec dir, NJ State Funeral Dirs Asn, 72- Mil Serv: Entered as Aviation Cadet, Air Force as Pilot, 42, released as Lt, 45, after serv in Air Transport Command, European & Am Theatres, 44-45. Mem: Am Legion; Lions; Elks; Mason; Shrine. Honors & Awards: Civic Award, Irvington CofC; Churchman of Year Award, Irvington Coun Churches; Citizen of Year, B'nai B'rith; Layman's Award for Contributions to Educ, Essex Co Educ Asn; Jewish War Vet Citizenship Award. Relig: Reformed Church. Mailing Add: 816 Rathjen Rd Brielle NJ 08730

HAUSSAMEN, CAROL W (D)
b New York, NY; d L Victor Weil & Beatrice Schwab W; m to Monroe Hemmerdinger, div; m Crane Haussamen; c Dale & Lyn Hemmerdinger. Polit & Govt Pos: Alt deleg, Dem Nat Conv, 72; mem bd dirs, Community Bd Five & Urban Design Coun; mem adv coun, NY State Dem Comt; committeewoman, Manhattan Co Dem Comt; hon comnr, Dept Civic Affairs & Pub Events, 74- Bus & Prof Pos: Mem bd dirs, Citizens Housing & Planning Coun & Parks Coun. Mem: City Club New York; Lexington Dem Club. Mailing Add: 40 Central Park S New York NY 10019

HAUSSLER, JOE D (D)
Wash State Rep
Mailing Add: Box 949 Omak WA 98841

HAUSWEDELL, ESTHER H (DFL)
Chmn, Lincoln Co Dem-Farmer-Labor Party, Minn
b Lyons, Nebr, June 27, 13; d Robert Mehling & Elsie Meyer M; m 1933 to Paul J Hauswedell; c Curtis, Melva (Mrs Bennett) & Connie (Mrs Robert Miller). Educ: Arco High Sch, Minn, 4 years. Polit & Govt Pos: Secy, Lincoln Co Dem-Farmer-Labor Party, Minn, 60-66, chmn, 66-72 & 74-; vchmn, Sixth Dist Dem-Farmer-Labor Party, 63-65, chmn, 66. Mem: Farmers Union; Nat Farm Orgn. Honors & Awards: 4-H Leader Awards; Award for managing campaign, Lincoln Co March of Dimes; Rural Community Leadership Award, 65-70. Relig: Lutheran. Mailing Add: Arco MN 56113

HAVENS, MARVIN LYNN (D)
Miss State Rep
Mailing Add: Rte 2 Box 49 Gulfport MS 39501

HAVILL, EDWARD ERNEST (R)
Chmn, Fla Fedn Young Rep
b New York, NY, June 6, 41; s Ernest Havill & Evelyn Weiner H; m 1960 to Jane Kenney Smith; c Kyle Lee, Leah Anne & Jennifer Lynn. Educ: WCoast Univ, BSME & BSEE, 68; Rollins Col, MCS, 71. Polit & Govt Pos: Precinct chmn, Lake Co Rep Party, Fla, 72-; pres, Lake Co Young Rep, 73-74; treas, Fla Fedn Young Rep, 73-74, chmn, 74-; co-chmn, Lake Co Lincoln Day Dinner, 74; dir, Lake Co Young Rep, 74- Bus & Prof Pos: Sr research technician, Spectrol Electronics, Industry, Calif, 62-66; systs engr, Aerojet-Gen, Azusa, 66-68; asst proj engr, Autonetics, Anaheim, 68-69; sr systs engr, Martin Marietta Corp, Orlando, 69-73; citrus grower & real estate broker, Eustis, Fla, 73- Mil Serv: Entered as Pvt, Army, 60, released as SP-4, 62, after serv in SigC; Marksman Badge; Good Conduct Medal. Mem: PTA. Honors & Awards: Best Club Chmn Fla Young Rep, Fla Fedn Young Rep, 73; Outstanding Young Man of Am, 74. Relig: Methodist; mem admin bd & Sunday sch teacher, First United Methodist Church Eustis, 73- Mailing Add: 1021 Fahnstock Ave Eustis FL 32726

HAWES, AARON EDWARD (D)
b Larned, Kans, Apr 21, 18; s Aaron Edward Hawes & Anna Bell Booker H; m 1951 to Mary Alice Crawford; c Deborah Kay & Donald Aaron. Educ: Kans State Teachers Col, BS in admin bus & teaching credential, 41; Army Officers Sch, Ft Benning, Ga, 42; Kappa Sigma. Polit & Govt Pos: Committeeman, Pawnee Co Dem Comt, Kans, 48-, chmn, 54-60; crew chief, Gov Census, 50; co chmn, Docking for Gov Campaign, 66; former deleg, Dem Nat Conv; chmn, Pawnee Co Dem Party, formerly. Bus & Prof Pos: Committeeman, Kans Livestock Asn, 48-; mem adv staff, Centennial Life Ins Co, Pittsburg, 64- Mil Serv: Entered as Pvt, Army, 40, released as Capt, 46, after serv in 475th Composite Burma, 43-45; Silver Star & Unit Citation, Frank Merrills Marauders, Mars Task Force; China-Burma-India Campaign Ribbons; Hon Capt, Army Res, 46-56. Mem: Am Legion; Shrine; Mason; Elks; Kans Wheat Comn. Relig: Presbyterian. Mailing Add: 308 Martin Larned KS 67550

HAWES, BRYAN (D)
Chmn, Edwards Co Dem Party, Kans
b Davis Co, Ind, May 26, 96; s Aaron Edward Hawes & Anna Belle Booker H; m 1922 to Ona Muriel McCandless; c Betty Jean (Mrs Thomas L Dittman) & Bryana Muriel (Mrs Calvin Hefner, Jr). Educ: Salt City Bus Col, Kans. Polit & Govt Pos: Clerk of Bd, Belpre, Kans, 28-34, trustee, 42-45 & mayor, 63-; dist supvr, Nat Farm Census, 34-35; dist supvr, Nat Farm & Population Census, Dodge City, Kans, 50; deleg, Dem Nat Conv, 52 & 68; mem, Kans Real Estate Bd, 57-60; bd mem & trustee, Laird Libr Fund, 61-; adv mem, Farmers Home Admin, 62-65; chmn, Edwards Co Dem Party, currently. Bus & Prof Pos: Farmer & stockman, Edwards, Haskell & Greeley Co, Kans. Mem: Mason (32 degree); Kiwanis. Relig: Baptist; deacon & moderator. Mailing Add: PO Box 82 Belpre KS 67519

HAWES, PEYTON SAMUEL, JR (D)
Mem Exec Comt, Ga State Dem Party
b Elberton, Ga, June 27, 37; s Peyton Samuel Hawes & Virginia Smith H; m 1961 to Mary Gregory; c David Cooper, Gregory Battle, Elizabeth Claiborne & Peyton Samuel, III (deceased). Educ: Univ NC, Chapel Hill, BA, 60; Univ Va, Charlottesville, LLB, 63; Sigma Alpha Epsilon; Order of Old Well; Order of Gimghoul; Phi Alpha Delta. Polit & Govt Pos: Asst attorney gen, Dept Law, Atlanta, Ga, 63-66; mem reorgn comt, Ga State Dem Party, 69, mem exec comt, 71-; Ga State Rep, 69-74, chmn, Fulton Co Deleg, Ga House of Rep, 70-74. Bus & Prof Pos: Attorney, Jones, Bird & Howell, Atlanta, Ga, 66-71; attorney, Cofer, Beauchamp & Hawes, 71- Mem: Am, Ga & Atlanta Bar Asns; Lawyers Club of Atlanta. Relig: Episcopal. Mailing Add: 78 Broad St NW Fourth Floor Atlanta GA 30303

HAWKE, ROBERT DOUGLAS (R)
Chmn, Gardner Rep City Comt, Mass
b Gardner, Mass, July 20, 32; s Arthur Eugene Hawke & Gladys Waite H; m 1958 to Nancy Moschetti; c Linda, Cynthia, Heather, Dean & Mark. Educ: Northeastern Univ, AB, 54; Boston Univ, LLB, 56; Fitchburg State Col, MEd, 71; Gamma Phi Kappa. Polit & Govt Pos: Chmn, Gardner Rep City Comt, Mass, 67-; chmn adv bd, Mt Wachusett Commun Col, 69- Bus & Prof Pos: Chmn soc studies dept, Murdock High Sch, 56-66; teacher, Gardner High Sch, 66- Mem: Mass Teacher's Asn; Polish-Am Citizens Club. Relig: Baptist; Deacon, First Baptist Church. Mailing Add: 12 Winslow St Gardner MA 01440

HAWKES, ELIZABETH (D)
b Washburn, Wis, Nov 22, 06; d Richard Hawkes & Maria Louisa Von Frank H; single. Educ: Boston Univ; Nat Univ. Polit & Govt Pos: Vchmn, Wis Dem State Cent Comt, 41-50, Co Statutory Chmn, formerly; alt deleg, Dem Nat Conv, 52 & 56, del, 60, 64 & 72. Bus & Prof Pos: Practicing attorney, Wis, 37- Mem: Wis State Bar Asn. Relig: Catholic. Mailing Add: Washburn WI 54891

HAWKES, JOHN DOUGLAS (R)
b Ogden, Utah, Dec 18, 38; s John B Hawkes & Laura McEntire H; m to Kae; c Ann. Educ: Brigham Young Univ, BS, 63, MA, 65; Delta Phi. Polit & Govt Pos: Voting dist chmn, Murray, Utah; deleg, Rep State Conv, 72; alt deleg, Rep Nat Conv, 72. Bus & Prof Pos: Owner-pres, Hawkes Publ, printing & publ co. Mil Serv: Entered Army Res, 57, released as SP-4, 64. Publ: New Testament Digest, Keys to dating success, Art of achieving success, Hawkes Publ. Relig: Latter-day Saint. Mailing Add: 156 W 2170 South Salt Lake City UT 84107

HAWKINS, AUGUSTUS F (D)
US Rep, Calif
b Shreveport, La, Aug 31, 07; s Nyanza Hawkins & Hattie H Freeman H; m 1945 to Pegga A Smith. Educ: Univ Calif, Los Angeles, BA; Univ Southern Calif, Inst of Govt. Polit & Govt Pos: Calif State Assemblyman, 34-62; US Rep, Calif, 62- Bus & Prof Pos: Real estate and retail bus, Los Angeles, 45- Mem: Mason. Relig: Methodist. Legal Res: 4251 1/2 Avalon Blvd Los Angeles CA 90011 Mailing Add: 125 North Carolina Ave SE Washington DC 20003

HAWKINS, CLARENCE MILEY (D)
Chmn, Alfalfa Co Dem Party, Okla
b Helena, Okla, Mar 24, 05; s John W Hawkins & Lola Cummings H; m 1930 to Ruth Hiebert; c Arlene (Mrs Wayman Calavan), Merrilyn (Mrs Wiley H Moseley), Benita (Mrs William Pierce) & Lon GaWayne & John G Miller. Educ: McPherson Col, BS, 28; Pittsburg State Univ, 28; Northwestern State Col, 33-34; Phillips Univ, 36-37; Okla State Univ, 53-54; Athletic M Club; College Glee Club. Polit & Govt Pos: Coordr, Gary for Gov, Alfalfa Co, Okla, 64 & 68; Hubert Humphrey for Pres, 68; chmn, Alfalfa Co Dem Party, 69- Bus & Prof Pos: From prin to supt, Driftwood High Sch, 33-35; Waukomis High Sch, 35-37; supvt,

Okarche High Sch, Okla, 37-53; supt schs, Carmen High Sch, 53-62; prin, Cleo Springs High Sch, 62-66. Mem: Mason; Scottish Rite; Masonic Hosp Asn (dir); Retired Sch Adminr; Farmers Coop Asn. Relig: Methodist. Mailing Add: 1307 S Penn Cherokee OK 73728

HAWKINS, DAVID OLIVER (D)
SC State Rep
b Spartanburg, SC, Aug 8, 45; s Esley Marion Hawkins & Ethel Turner H; m 1967 to Doretha O'Shields; c John David & Pamela Lane. Educ: Chapman High Sch, Inman, SC, grad, 64. Polit & Govt Pos: Magistrate, Spartanburg, SC, 71-75; mem comt, Civil & Criminal Court, Spartanburg Co, 74-75; SC State Rep, 75- Bus & Prof Pos: Homebuilder, Roebuck, SC, 70- Mil Serv: Entered as Pvt, Army Res, 64, released as S/Sgt, 72, after serv in Co C 391 Eng; S/Sgt, SC Nat Guard, currently. Mem: Roebuck Jaycees; Nat Asn of Homebuilders; Univ SC Spartan Rifles. Relig: Baptist. Mailing Add: 23 Independence Dr Roebuck SC 29376

HAWKINS, DONNA BLACK (D)
Nat Committeewoman, Ala Young Dem
b Birmingham, Ala, Sept 3, 44; d N F Black & Polly Strickland B; m 1963 to Don L Hawkins; c Jennifer Renee. Educ: Univ Ala. Polit & Govt Pos: Deleg, Dem Nat Conv, 68; nat committeewoman, Ala Young Dem, 68-; vpres, Jefferson Co Young Dem, 69- Mem: Jr Womens League; Birmingham Symphony Asn; Birmingham Festival of Arts Bd; Birmingham Music Club. Relig: Methodist. Mailing Add: 4008 Hunters Lane Birmingham AL 35215

HAWKINS, ELDRIDGE THOMAS ENOCH (D)
NJ State Assemblyman
b East Orange, NJ, Sept 4, 40; s Eldridge Hawkins & Agnes Goode H; single. Educ: Rutgers Univ, New Brunswick, BA, 62; Seton Hall Univ Law Sch, JD, 66; Zeta Beta Tau; Phi Sigma Delta. Polit & Govt Pos: Prosecutor, City of East Orange, NJ, 70-72; NJ State Assemblyman, 72- Mem: Am, Nat & NJ Bar Asns; Concerned Legal Assocs (dir); Nat Asn Black Legislators (trustee); Nat Conf Christians & Jews (nat bd, 72-). Honors & Awards: Jaycee of the Year, East Orange Jaycees, 72. Legal Res: 275 Elmwood Ave East Orange NJ 07018 Mailing Add: 586 Central Ave East Orange NJ 07018

HAWKINS, JAMES ROBERT (R)
Mayor, Durham, NC
b Mebane, NC, Apr 12, 25; s William A Hawkins (deceased) & Eva Pittard H (deceased); m 1950 to Helen Turissa Wright; c William Allen, III, Richard Wright, James Robert, Jr, Rebecca Elizabeth & Cora Turissa. Educ: Duke Univ, AB, 50, LLB, 51. Polit & Govt Pos: Mayor, Durham, NC, 71-; mem, State Local Govt Comn, 74- Bus & Prof Pos: Legal officer, Off Ord Research, Duke Univ, 51-56; secy-treas, Allenton Realty & Ins Co, Durham, NC, 56-; pres, Durham Ins Exchange, 60-61; pres, Durham Bd Realtors, 63-64; vpres, NC Asn Realtors, 70-71. Mil Serv: Entered as Pvt, Marine Corps, 43, released as Pfc, 45, after serv in Commun Detachment, Pac Theatre, 44-45. Mem: Rotary Club; Durham CofC; NC Manpower Serv Coun; Duke Univ Hosp Bd Adv; NC League Munic. Honors & Awards: Distinguished Serv Award, Jaycees, 60; Realtor Regional Serv Award, NC Asn Realtors, 73. Relig: Presbyterian. Legal Res: 2409 Wrightwood Ave Durham NC 27705 Mailing Add: PO Box 629 Durham NC 27702

HAWKINS, JOHN MORGAN (D)
Ga State Rep
b Winfield, Ala, June 22, 35; s John Morgan Hawkins & Bertie Beasley H; wid; c Roland Bernard. Educ: Univ Ala, AB, 57; Emory Univ Sch Law, 60-63; Ga Inst Technol, MSIM, 74; Phi Sigma Kappa. Polit & Govt Pos: Ga State Rep, 75- Bus & Prof Pos: Mem staff, US Pub Health Serv, 57-63; mem staff, Ga Power Co, 63-65; indust & labor rels, Lockheed-Ga Co, 65-72; personnel dir, Haverty Furniture Co, Inc, 72-74. Mil Serv: Entered as 2nd Lt, Army Res, 57, released as Capt, 65. Mem: Kiwanis; Am Soc Personnel Admin; Future Soc. Relig: Presbyterian; elder. Mailing Add: 1211 Kingsley Circle NE Atlanta GA 30324

HAWKINS, JOHN P (D)
RI State Sen
Mailing Add: 22 Woonasquatucket Ave Providence RI 02911

HAWKINS, JOHN RICHARD (D)
Wash State Rep
b Seattle, Wash, Jan 23, 42; s Victor Richard Hawkins & Betty Edmonds H; m 1972 to Patricia Hall; c Lisa. Educ: Everett Jr Col, 60-61; Highline Col, 64-66; Univ Wash, BA, 68. Polit & Govt Pos: Mem, Pierce Co Dem Exec Bd, Wash, currently; Wash State Rep, 26th Dist, 74- Bus & Prof Pos: Housing coordr, Chelan Co, Wash, 70; assoc planner, Pierce Co Planning Dept, 70- Mil Serv: Entered as Pvt, Marine Corps Res, 62, released as Sgt E-5, 68; Aerial Navigator Wings. Mem: Co-City Employees Union (trustee, Local 120); Optimists; South Kitsap Dem Action Group. Mailing Add: 3102 N Monroe Tacoma WA 98407

HAWKINS, MARY ELLEN HIGGINS (R)
Fla State Rep
b Birmingham, Ala; d Guy Higgins & Mary Davis H; m 1960 to James Hixon Hawkins, div, 71; c Andrew Higgins, Elizabeth & Peter Hixon. Educ: Univ Ala, Tuscaloosa, 45-47. Polit & Govt Pos: Cong aide to several mem US House Rep, 45-59; chmn, Sumter Co Rep Party, Ga, 70-72; vchmn, Third Dist Rep Comt, 70-72; Small Bus Admin, Community Adv Coun, Atlanta, 70-72; Fla State Rep, 74- Bus & Prof Pos: Art instr, Sumter Co Schs, Americus, Ga, 71-72; staff writer polit, Naples Daily News, Fla, 72- Mem: Int Platform Asn. Relig: Roman Catholic. Mailing Add: Collier Co Courthouse Complex Naples FL 33940

HAWKINS, PAULA F (R)
VChmn, Rep Nat Comt
b Salt Lake City, Utah; m 1947 to Walter Eugene Hawkins; c Genean, Kevin Brent & Kelley Ann. Educ: Schs in Atlanta, Ga; Utah State Univ. Polit & Govt Pos: Precinct committeewoman, Orange Co Rep Exec Comt, 64-, mem, Finance Comt, 66-; coordr, E J Gurney for Cong Campaign, 66; chmn speakers bur, Fla Rep State Exec Comt, 67-; deleg, Rep Nat Conv, 68 & 72, chmn, host comt, 72; co-chmn, Fla Nixon Campaign Activities, 68; mem, Comn on Status of Women, 68-; Inaugural Coordr for Fla, 69; Rep Nat Committeewoman, Fla, currently, vchmn & mem exec comt, Rep Nat Comt, 72-; co-chmn, Fla Comt to Reelect the President, 72; Fla Pub Serv Comnr, 72-; dir, Rural Tel Bank Bd, 73- Bus & Prof Pos: Dir, First Nat Bank of Maitland, Fla; pres, Something Great, Inc. Mem: Maitland Civic Ctr; Cent Fla Mus; Maitland Woman's Club; CofC; Am for Const Action Comt of 100, Fla (charter mem & secy-treas, 66-). Honors & Awards: Received State Chmn Award for Serv, 66-67; Outstanding Woman in GOP Polit Chmn Award, 68; first woman & first Rep elected to Fla Pub Serv Comn since its creation in 1887; Woman of Year, KofC. Relig: Latter-day Saint. Legal Res: 241 Dommevich Dr Maitland FL 32751 Mailing Add: 700 S Adams St Tallahassee FL 32304

HAWKINSON, JOHN W (R)
Chmn, Knox Co Rep Party, Ill
b Galesburg, Ill, Apr 30, 14; s Carl O Hawkinson & Francis Elizabeth H; m 1946 to Marilyn J Peterson; c Carl E & Judy E. Educ: Command & Gen Staff Col, grad, 53; Officer Cand Sch, Ft Lee, Va, grad, 42; Army Br Career Courses, completed. Polit & Govt Pos: Precinct committeeman, Galesburg, Ill, 62-; chmn, Knox Co Rep Party, 68-72 & 74- Bus & Prof Pos: Mgr, Peoria Off, Pittsburgh & Midway Coal Co, Subsidiary of Gulf Oil Corp, 64-; admission rep, North Park Col, Chicago, 65- Mil Serv: Entered as Pvt, Army, 41, released as Maj, 46, after serv in 14th Armored Div & others, Asiatic-Pac Theater, 44-46; Col, Army Res, 65; Asiatic-Pac Theaters, Carolines & Okinawa Campaigns with Battle Stars; Victory Medal; Res Medal; Am Defense Medal. Mem: Key mem Lions Int (pres, Galesburg Club, zone chmn & dept dist gov); John Erickson Rep League; Lake Bracken Country Club; Am Legion; Creve Coeur Club, Peoria. Relig: Evangelical Covenant; mem bd trustees. Mailing Add: RR 3 Galesburg IL 61401

HAWKS, WILLIAM HARRY, JR (D)
b Lebanon, Tenn, May 12, 45; s William H Hawks, Sr & Ellen Frances McPherson H; single. Educ: Univ Tenn, Knoxville, BA, 73; Quill & Scroll. Polit & Govt Pos: Mgr, Wilson Co Young Citizens for Sen Ross Bass, 66; chmn, Wilson Co Young Citizens for Sen Albert Gore; chmn, Wilson Co Young Citizens McGovern for Pres, 72; alt deleg, Dem Nat Conv, 72; mem, Univ Tenn Young Dem; mem, Tenn Young Dem; treas, Wilson Co Young Dem, 72-; mem staff, US Rep Joe L Evins, Tenn, 74- Mil Serv: Entered as Seaman Recruit, Navy, 66, released as PO 2/C, 70, after serv in Naval Security Group, Philippines, 66-68 & Panama, 68-70; Unit Citation. Relig: Church of Christ. Mailing Add: Rte 2 Springcreek Lebanon TN 37087

HAWKSLEY, RAYMOND H (D)
Gen Treas of RI
b East Providence, RI, Aug 13, 09; m to Helen B. Educ: Bryant Col, BA, 29; Brown Univ, RI Col of Educ, exten courses; Am Inst of Banking, pre-standard, standard, grad cert; Beta Sigma Chi. Hon Degrees: MSc in Bus Admin, Bryant Col, 57. Polit & Govt Pos: Gen Treas of RI, 49-; chmn, East Providence Dem City Comt, 56-73; deleg, Dem Nat Conv, 68. Bus & Prof Pos: Banker, Providence Inst for Savings, RI. Mil Serv: Navy, Pac Theatre, World War II; Navy Cross. Mem: Muscular Dystrophy Asn of Am (bd of dirs); Rising Sun Lodge (dir); Am Legion; VFW; RAM. Relig: Methodist; Pres & Financial Secy, Bd of Trustees, Providence Haven Methodist Church. Mailing Add: 102 State House Providence RI 02903

HAWKSLEY, WILLIAM J (R)
Chmn, Wasco Co Rep Cent Comt, Ore
b Portland, Ore, Nov 2, 19; s Mathew Marvin Hawksley & Clare Krimbel H; m 1943 to Dorothy E Davis; c Kim D. Educ: Washington High Sch, grad, 37. Polit & Govt Pos: Chmn, McCall for Secy of State, Clackamas Co, Ore, 63; Hatfield for Senator, Wasco Co, 68; committeeman, Precinct No 19, 68; chmn, Wasco Co Rep Cent Comt, 70-; mem budget & finance comt, Ore State Rep Cent Comt, 71- Bus & Prof Pos: Spec agt, Loyalty Group Ins, Portland, Ore, 37-47; partner & vpres, Walter J Pearson & Co, 47-48; asst vpres, Ore Auto Ins Co, 48-64; dir & owner corp, Kargl, Elwood & Geiger, The Dalles, 64-71; dir, Ore Asn Ins Agents, Portland, 68- Mem: Mason; AF&AM; Scottish Rite; Order of Blue Goose (past pres); Elks. Relig: Episcopal. Legal Res: 415 E 15th Pl The Dalles OR 97058 Mailing Add: PO Box 376 The Dalles OR 97058

HAWLEY, B JEANNE (D)
Mem Exec Comt, Ionia Co Dem, Mich
b Ionia, Mich, Nov 18, 27; d Wm Robert McKendry & Esther J Cook M; m 1950 to Darl R Hawley; c L Robert, Walter D, Martha (Mrs Larry Johnson), Sara, George, Homer, Jerri, Tina, Dan, Darlene & Alvin. Educ: Ferris State Col, 47. Polit & Govt Pos: Secy, Ionia Co Dem, Mich, 52-56, exec comt, 56-, vchmn, 75-; co-chmn, Dem Agr Comt & Exec Comt, 50-; vchmn, Fifth Dist Dem Party, 50- Bus & Prof Pos: Secy, Nat Farmer Orgn, 60-66, publicity chmn, 60-, pres fifth dist state bd, 75-, employed by Field Staff Dept, Nat Farmer Orgn, 75- Relig: Episcopal. Mailing Add: R 2 Goodenough Rd Lake Odessa MI 48849

HAWLEY, R STEPHEN (R)
NY State Assemblyman
Mailing Add: 8249 Bank St Rd Batavia NY 14020

HAWORTH, ROGER LEE (R)
Chmn, Jay Co Rep Cent Comt, Ind
b Portland, Ind, Feb 17, 16; s Laurence Haworth & Delcie Sackett H; m 1940 to Mabel M Tharp; c David P & Cathy L (Mrs Layman). Polit & Govt Pos: Twp trustee, Pike Twp, Jay Co, Ind, 59-67; chmn, Jay Co Rep Cent Comt, 66-; commodity auditor, Sch Lunch Div, Ind Dept Pub Instr, 67-69; dist supvr, License Br, Ind Bur Motor Vehicles, 69-73, investr, 73- Mil Serv: Entered as Pvt, Army, 44, released as Sgt, 46, after serv in Co K, 260th Inf, 65th Div, ETO; Combat Inf Medal with Two Battle Stars. Mem: Farm Bur; UAW; Am Security Coun. Relig: United Church of Christ. Mailing Add: RR 1 Portland OR 47371

HAY, JESS (D)
Dem Nat Committeeman, Tex
b Forney, Tex, Jan 22, 31; m 1951 to Betty Jo Peacock; c Deborah Anne & Patricia Lynn. Educ: Southern Methodist Univ, BA, 53, Sch of Law, JD magna cum laude, 55. Polit & Govt Pos: Dem Nat Committeeman, Tex, 72- Bus & Prof Pos: Assoc, Law Firm of Locke, Purnell, Boren, Laney & Neely, 55-61, partner, 61-65; pres, Lomas & Nettleton Financial Corp, 65-69, chief exec officer, 65-, chmn bd, 69-; chmn bd & chief exec officer, Lomas & Nettleton Mortgage Investors, 69-; bd dirs, Lomas & Nettleton Financial Corp, Lomas & Nettleton Mortgage Investors, Lomas & Nettleton Co, Trinity Industs, Inc, Mercantile Nat Bank Dallas, CMI Investment Corp, Continental Mortgage Ins, Inc, Republic Financial Serv & Allied Finance Co. Mem: Bd trustees & bd gov, South Methodist Univ. Relig: Methodist. Mailing Add: PO Box 5644 Dallas TX 75222

HAY, SAM M (R)
b Milwaukee, Wis, Apr 7, 26; s Samuel M Hay & Elizabeth Ottele H; m 1951 to Mary Davies; c Susan (Mrs Jeffrey Gullickson), David, Donald & Douglas. Educ: Univ Wis-Madison, BBA, 49; Phi Kappa Phi. Polit & Govt Pos: Chmn, Milwaukee Co Rep Party, 61-64; regional dir, Rep Nat Comt, 64 & Reagan for President Comt, 67-68; chmn, Warren for Attorney Gen Comt, 69-70; vchmn, Wis State Rep Party, 71-73; alt deleg, Rep Nat Conv, 72. Bus & Prof Pos: Supvr placement, A E Staley Co, Decatur, Ill, 49-51; asst personnel dir, Allen-Bradley

Co, Milwaukee, Wis, 51-67, dir labor rels & pub affairs, 67- Mil Serv: Lt Comdr, Naval Res. Mem: Personnel & Indust Rels Asn; Pub Affairs Coun; F&AM; Metro Flying Club. Relig: Protestant. Mailing Add: 1675 Berkshire Dr Elm Grove MI 53122

HAYDEN, H THOMAS (TOM) (R)
b Louisville, Ky, July 14, 41; s Quentin Joseph Hayden & Evelyn Buckner H; m 1967 to Gay Little. Educ: Calif State Univ, Long Beach, BA, 63; Pepperdine Univ, MBA, 75; Phi Lambda Chi (pres, 62-63). Polit & Govt Pos: Area develop officer, Agency Int Develop, South Vietnam, 66-69; Rep nominee US Rep, 70; pres, 41st Assembly Dist Coord Coun, 70-71; Sgt at Arms, Calif Rep State Cent Comt, 71-73, chmn youth standing comt, 71-73, chmn polit educ comt, 73-74; Calif chmn, Young Voters for the President, 72; alt deleg, Rep Nat Conv, 72. Bus & Prof Pos: Mgt consult, Missile Div, Hughes Air Craft & Space Div, NAm Aviation, 63-66; pres, Stanley-Hayden Prod Inc, 71-74; vpres, Coast Fed Savings, 74- Mil Serv: Marine Corps, 60-61; Marine Corps Res, Maj, 75- Most decorated US Civilian to have served in Vietnam; South Vietnam Cross of Gallantry, Medal of Merit, Ministry of Revolutionary Develop Honor Medal; Ministry of Social Welfare Honor Medal & Ministry of Public Health Honor Medal; Dept of State Superior Honor Award & Vietnam Serv Medal; Bronze Star with V; Purple Heart with Oak Leaf Cluster. Honors & Awards: Calif Jaycees Freedom Guard Award; NCAA All-Am, 63. Relig: Catholic. Mailing Add: 3334 W 152nd St Gardena CA 90249

HAYDEN, MIKE (R)
Kans State Rep
Mailing Add: 609 S Third Atwood KS 67730

HAYDEN, RICHARD D (R)
Calif State Assemblyman
Mailing Add: 21060 Homestead Rd Cupertino CA 95014

HAYDON, JOHN M (R)
b Billings, Mont, 1920; m to Jean Parker; c Four. Educ: Univ Wash. Polit & Govt Pos: Chmn, Oceanographic Comn, Wash, pres, Oceanographic Inst & mem, Gov Adv Comts, Dept of Com & Econ Develop & State Dept of Fisheries, currently; mem, Port of Seattle Comn, 60-, pres, currently; Gov, Am Samoa, 69-74. Bus & Prof Pos: Mem staff, Port of Seattle & Bardahl Int of Seattle, Wash, formerly; owner, Marine Digest, 56- Mil Serv: Air Force, World War II. Mem: Seattle Traffic Asn (mem bd); Pac Coast Asn Port Authorities (mem bd); Seattle Mayor's Maritime Adv Bd; Shoreline Commun Col & Seattle Commun Col (mem curriculum adv bd). Mailing Add: 1450 Palm Ave SW Seattle WA 98116

HAYDUK, ALBERT T (R)
Mem Exec Comt, Westchester Rep Co Comt, NY
b Yonkers, NY, Feb 26, 07; m to Margaret Pasuch; c Albert T, Jr, Robert, Richard & Deborah. Educ: Columbia Univ; Alexander Hamilton Inst. Polit & Govt Pos: Rep Co committeeman, Tenth Ward, Yonkers, NY, 33-; former ward leader, Tenth Ward Rep Co Comt; deleg, Rep State Gubernatorial & Rep Nat Convs; pres, Yonkers Rep Orgn, 40-44, former vpres; mem, Rep Club Tenth Ward; mem & hon pres, Slavonian-Am Rep Club Yonkers; co-chmn, Yonkers Rep City Comt, 58, chmn, 59-; dir, New York Off, NY State Dept Com, until 59; mem, Rep Coun Leaders, Westchester Co & mem exec comt, Westchester Rep Co Comt, currently; mem, NY State Pure Waters Authority, 67-69; deleg, Rep Nat Conv, 68; comnr, Westchester Co Bd Elec, 69- Bus & Prof Pos: Secy-treas, White City Linen Supply Co, Inc, 37-54; pres, White City Laundry Co, Inc, New York, 50-54; consult, Cascade Linen Supply Co Inc & Gen Linen Supply Co, Inc, 54-58; pres, Hayduk Linen Supply, Inc, currently. Mil Serv: Marine Corps, 43-45, serv in Aviation Supply; NY State Guard, Capt. Mem: Rotary Int; Salvation Army (mem adv bd); Boy Scouts Am (finance chmn, Yonkers Div); charter mem Am Inst Mgt (mem adv bd); Am Legion; KofC (4 degree). Relig: Roman Catholic. Mailing Add: 377 N Broadway Yonkers NY 10701

HAYES, DAVID SAYRE (R)
Pa State Rep
b Erie, Pa, Dec 31, 41; s A J Hayes, Sr (deceased) & Pauline F Hennen H; single. Educ: Gannon Col, BS in Finance, 63; Univ Miami, JD, 67; finance chmn, Blue Key; treas, Tau Kappa Epsilon, sr class & inter-fraternity coun; Phi Delta Phi; Int Law Club; Student Bar Asn; Am Inst Taxation & Law; Bar & Gavel. Polit & Govt Pos: Pres, Young Rep Gannon Col & Students for Scranton, 62; mem, Erie Co Exec Comt Young Rep, 62-63; staff aide to Gov Scranton, 63; deleg, Young Rep Leadership Conf, 64; page, Rep Nat Conv, 64; co-chmn, West Co Rep Campaign, 68; Pa State Rep, Fifth Dist, 69-, mem, Joint State Govt Comt on Water Pollution & mem, Real Property & Tax Collection Task Force, Pa House of Rep, 69, mem comts, Law & Order, Labor Rels, Agr & Dairy Industs & Northwestern Pa Med Sch, Northwestern Pa Fish Hatchery, formerly, mem, Consumer Protection, Bus & Com & Prof Licensure, 73-; mem, Congressman H John Heinz, III Campaign, 71; mem, Pa Rep State Finance Comt & Erie Co Rep Finance Comt, currently; chmn state speakers bur, Lewis-Lee Campaign, 74. Bus & Prof Pos: Pres, Gannon Col Student Investment Trust, 62-63; treas, Delta Chi Housing Corp, 62-63; dir, Jackburn Mfg Co, 63-, Hayes Corp, 67-, Girard Tool Co & Hayes Found; US rep, Am-Zurich Corp; plus others. Mem: Northwest Jaycees; Gannon Alumni Asn; Erie Co Sportsmen's League; Endowment Comt of Univ Miami; Pa Soc. Honors & Awards: Outstanding Young Man of the Year Award, 72; Spec Lt Dep Sheriff, Erie Co. Relig: Methodist. Legal Res: 140 W Main St Fairview PA 16415 Mailing Add: Box 33 Fairview PA 16415

HAYES, E E (D)
Colo State Rep
Mailing Add: 5350 E 66th Way Commerce City CO 80022

HAYES, FLORENCE M (R)
Chmn, Custer Co Rep Comt, Okla
b Pretty Prairie, Kans, Sept 12, 13; d Peter G Stucky & Elizabeth Kaufman S; m 1935 to Ernest James Hayes, wid; c Jeanine Ann (Mrs Zenge) & Sherry Elizabeth. Educ: Hutchinson, Kans Jr Col, grad; McPherson Col, Kans; Southwestern State Col, Okla. Polit & Govt Pos: Campaign coordr for Clyde Wheeler, Cong Cand, 60; task force chmn, Okla Rep State Comt, 61-62; vchmn, Sixth Dist Rep Cong Comt, Okla, 61-66; mem exec comt, Custer Co Rep Comt, 61-63 & 65-, chmn, currently; mem, Okla State Rep Exec Comt, formerly; deleg, Rep Nat Conv, 64; mem, Gov Comn on Status of Women, 68-, state committeewoman, Custer Co. Bus & Prof Pos: Tax acct. Mem: Miss Okla Pageant Corp (bd mem, 64-); Bus & Prof Women's Club; Wesleyan Serv Guild. Relig: Methodist; bd trustees, First Methodist Church. Legal Res: 708 Santa Fe Clinton OK 73601 Mailing Add: Box 141 Clinton OK 73601

HAYES, JAMES A (R)
Los Angeles Co Supvr, Calif
m to Claudia Lynch. Educ: Univ Calif Hastings Col Law, JD. Polit & Govt Pos: Vmayor of Long Beach, Calif, formerly; Calif State Assemblyman, 39th Dist, 66-72; Los Angeles Co Supvr, 72-, chmn, Dept Sheriff, Fire, Air Pollution, Assessor, Civil Serv, Sanit, Beaches & Parks, Beaches, Purchasing, Weights & Measures, currently; comnr, Calif Coastal Zone Comn, SCoast Region Coastal Comn & Local Agency Formation Comn, 72-; mem, Gov Earthquake Coun, 72- Publ: California divorce reform—parting is sweeter sorrow, Am Bar Asn J, 7/70. Honors & Awards: Described by the press in 1968 as The Calif Legis most adamant smog fighter; Assemblyman of the Year, Calif Trial Lawyers Asn, 70; Legislator of the Year, Los Angeles Trial Lawyers Asn, 72; Leading Legislator in Environ Law, Planning & Conserv League, 72; Man of the Year, Calif Pub Health League, 72. Mailing Add: 822 Hall of Admin Los Angeles CA 90012

HAYES, JANET GRAY (D)
Mayor, San Jose, Calif
b Rushville, Ind, 1926; d John P Frazee, Jr & Lucile Charman Gray F; m 1950 to Kenneth Hayes; c Lindy, John, Katherine & Megan. Educ: Ind Univ, AB; Univ Chicago Sch Social Serv Admin, MA; Phi Beta Kappa; Mortar Bd; Kappa Alpha Theta. Polit & Govt Pos: Councilwoman, San Jose, Calif, 71-73, vmayor, 73-75, mayor, 75-; mem nominating comt, Nat League Cities, 74; mem, Fed Environ Protection Agency Aircraft/Airport Noise Task Group & Nat League of Cities Environ Qual Policy Comt, currently; co-chmn, US Conf Mayors Task Force on Aging, mem, Asn Bay Area Govt, mem, Bicentennial Comn, City Selection Comt, Sanitation Dist 2 & 3, Santa Clara Valley Manpower Bd, Treatment Plant Adv Bd, Inter-City Coun, Legis Comt, Santa Clara Co Oper Area Coord Coun, South Bay Dischargers, currently; chairperson, Parking Authority City San Jose & Redevelop Agency, currently. Honors & Awards: Conservationist of Year for Santa Clara Co, United New Conservationists, 71. Relig: Methodist. Legal Res: Emory St San Jose CA 95126 Mailing Add: Mayor Off City Hall N First & Mission San Jose CA 95110

HAYES, JESSE C (D)
Ark State Rep
b Ingram, Ark, Oct 16, 14; s Agustus Hayes & Melvia Estell Tiner H; m 1935 to Jewel Dean Shaver; c Jesse Dean, Doris Jeanne (Mrs Johnson) & L A. Educ: Col of the Ozarks, Polit Sci, 57. Polit & Govt Pos: Ark State Rep, Dist Six, 63- Mil Serv: Entered as Pvt, Army Res, 38, released as Maj, 60, after serv in Inf & Artil in ETO, Far East & Korea; Combat Inf Badge; Bronze Star; Commendation Medal; ETO Ribbon with Three Battle Stars; Korean Campaign Ribbon with Three Battle Stars. Mem: Elks (Past Exalted Ruler, Lodge 1871); VFW (past post comdr, Post 2036 & Post 4556, past dist comdr, Dist Three, 62 & 65, comdr, currently); Farm Bur; CofC; Am Legion. Relig: Protestant. Mailing Add: RR 5 Box 90 Pocahontas AR 72455

HAYES, JOHN FRANCIS (R)
Kans State Rep
b Salina, Kans, Dec 11, 19; s John Francis Hayes & Helen Dye H; m 1950 to Elizabeth Ann Ireton; c Carl Ireton & Ann Chandler. Educ: Washburn Col, AB, 41, Law Sch, LLB, 46; Phi Delta Theta. Polit & Govt Pos: Deleg, Rep Nat Conv, 52; Kans State Rep, 53-55 & 67- Bus & Prof Pos: Partner, Gilliland, Hayes, Goering & Mills, Attorneys, Hutchinson, Kans; dir, Cent State Bank. Mil Serv: Entered as Pvt, Army, 42, released as Capt, 46, after serv in Qm Corps, US & Pac Theatre. Publ: Kansas marriage laws, 46 & Kansas automobile insurance laws, 53, Kans Bar J. Mem: Delta Theta Phi; Kans & Am Bar Asns; Int Asn of Ins Counsel; fel Am Col Trial Lawyers. Relig: Roman Catholic. Mailing Add: 106 Crescent Blvd Hutchinson KS 67501

HAYES, JOHN S (D)
b Philadelphia, Pa, Aug 21, 10; m to Donna Gough; c Jonathan, Peter O, Rhea & Laurie. Educ: Univ of Pa, AB, 31. Polit & Govt Pos: US Ambassador to Switz, 66-69; mem, US Deleg Int Conf Satellite Commun, 69- Bus & Prof Pos: Mem, NY Times Co, 45-48; mem, Wash Post Co, 48-66, vpres, 53-61, exec vpres, 61-66; pres, Post-Newsweek Sta; mem, Comn Educ TV, Carnegie Corp, NY, 65- Mil Serv: Commanding Officer, Am Forces Radio Network, ETO; Order of British Empire; French Croix de Guerre; Am Bronze Star. Publ: Co-auth, Both Sides of the Microphone. Mem: Nat Asn Broadcasters (mem bd); Am Acad Polit & Social Sci; Am Maximum Serv Telecasters (mem bd dirs); Nat Urban League (trustee); Radio Liberty (chmn). Mailing Add: 945 Ponte Vedra Blvd Ponte Vedra Beach FL 32082

HAYES, KAREN WOOD (D)
Nev State Assemblyman
b Cedar City, Utah, Oct 16, 35; d Lalif Wood & Roma Pollock W; m 1955 to Keith Casper Hayes; c Garry, Leslie, Bryan, Lisa, Kristen & Heidi. Educ: Brigham Young Univ, BS, 59; Univ Utah, 57-59. Polit & Govt Pos: Nev State Assemblyman, 75- Mem: City of Hope (secy); Paradise Dem Club; Multiple Sclerosis Soc. Relig: Latter-day Saint. Mailing Add: 6010 Euclid Las Vegas NV 89120

HAYES, PHILIP HAROLD (D)
US Rep, Ind
b Battle Creek, Mich, Sept 1, 40; s Robert Harold Hayes & Maurine Page H (deceased); m 1962 to Nancy Kollker; c Elizabeth & Courtney. Educ: Ind Univ, BA in Govt, 63, JD, 67. Polit & Govt Pos: Ind State Sen, 70-74; US Rep, Ind, 75- Bus & Prof Pos: Attorney-at-law, Evansville, Ind, 67-74. Relig: Roman Catholic. Legal Res: 6400 Newburgh Rd Evansville IN 47715 Mailing Add: 1132 Longworth House Off Bldg Washington DC 20515

HAYES, ROBERT E (D)
Ind State Rep
Mailing Add: 4024 Monterey Plaza Columbus IN 47201

HAYES, ROGER W (R)
Secy, DeKalb Co Rep Cent Comt, Ill
b Farmington, Minn, Apr 28, 16; s Marion Cleveland Hayes & Hattie Belle Rodgers H; m 1968 to Carolyn Eulass; c Carol Sue (Mrs Larry Cadle) & Roger W, Jr. Educ: Univ Ill, Urbana, BA, 39, Univ Ill, Urbana, Law Sch, LLB, 46; Phi Delta Phi. Polit & Govt Pos: State's attorney, McDonough Co, Ill, 48-56; Rep committeeman, Precinct 14B, DeKalb Co, 62-; secy, DeKalb Co Rep Cent Comt, 62-; spec attorney for People of State of Ill, Fulton Co, 67-; spec asst to Attorney Gen of Ill, 69- Bus & Prof Pos: Self employed lawyer, 46- Mil Serv: Entered as Aviation Cadet, Navy, 41, released as Lt Comdr, 45, after serv in Composite Squadron 97 as Carrier Fighter Pilot in Pac Theatre, 43-45, Comdr, Naval Res, 54-; Distinguished Flying

Cross; Air Medal with Five Stars. Mem: Am Trial Lawyers Asn; Am Legion; VFW; Elks; Moose. Relig: Protestant. Mailing Add: 1105 Garden Rd DeKalb IL 60115

HAYES, SAMUEL E, JR (R)
Pa State Rep
b Johnstown, Pa, Sept 3, 40; s Samuel E Hayes & Helen Fisher H; m 1963 to Elizabeth Orilee Keister; c Samuel E, III & Lee Hamilton. Educ: Pa State Univ, BS, 64, MEd, 65. Polit & Govt Pos: Pa State Rep, 71-, mem comts educ, state govt & ethics, Pa House of Rep, currently. Mil Serv: Army, 5 years active serv; Army Res, 7 years, serv in 149th Mil Intel Group, Vietnam, 66-67; final rank of Capt; Bronze Star Medal. Mem: Am Legion; VFW; Kiwanis Int. Relig: Protestant. Mailing Add: RD 3 Box 365A Tyrone PA 16686

HAYES, THOMAS A (R)
b Milwaukee, Wis, Jan 5, 43; m to Katherine V. Educ: Xavier Univ (Ohio), BS; Univ Mich Law Sch, JD. Polit & Govt Pos: Admin asst to US Rep William J Keating, Ohio, 71-75. Bus & Prof Pos: Attorney, Keating, Muething & Klekamp, Cincinnati, Ohio, 68-71. Mem: Am Bar Asn; Phi Delta Phi; Bull Elephants; House Rep Commun Asn; Cong Staff Asn. Honors & Awards: Hist Merit Scholar; Campbell Club Award. Legal Res: Cincinnati OH Mailing Add: 3820 Garfield St NW Washington DC 20007

HAYNE, JACK MCVICAR (R)
Committeeman, Mont Rep State Cent Comt
b Great Falls, Mont, Nov 22, 20; s George Roy Hayne & Effie McVicar H; m 1946 to Harriet Ann Danielsen; c Mary Joan, John David, Alice Sue & Nancy Ann. Educ: Grays Harbor Jr Col, 2 years; Wash State Univ, BA, 42; Lambda Chi Alpha. Polit & Govt Pos: Precinct committeeman, Pondera Co Rep Cent Comt, 60-69, chmn, 66-72; committeeman, Mont Rep State Cent Comt, Pondera Co, 62-66 & 72- Bus & Prof Pos: Owner, cattle ranch, Pondera Co, Mont, 53- Mil Serv: Entered as A/S, Navy, 42, released as Lt, 46, after serv Navy Amphibious Force, Pac Theatre. Mem: Am Legion; Mont Farm Bur Fedn. Relig: Presbyterian. Mailing Add: Box 285 Dupuyer MT 59432

HAYNER, JEANNETTE C (R)
Wash State Rep
Mailing Add: 850 E Chestnut Walla Walla WA 99362

HAYNES, ALTON MYLES (D)
b Cliffside, NC, May 17, 27; s Alton Myles Haynes, Sr & May Hines Watkins H; m 1956 to Christine Boger; c Alton Myles, III, Mary Beth Boger & Robert Cameron. Educ: Univ NC, AB, 49; George Washington Univ, JD, 52; Delta Psi. Polit & Govt Pos: NC State Rep, 60-61; mem, Mecklenburg Co Welfare Bd, 61-62, chmn, 62-63; chmn, Mecklenburg Co Dem Party, formerly. Bus & Prof Pos: Partner, Haynes, Baucom & Chandler, 63- Mil Serv: Seaman 1/C, Navy, 45-46, serv in Naval Air Force as Aviation Radioman. Mem: Am Judicature Soc; 26th Judicial, NC & Am Bar Asns; Charlotte CofC (bd mem, 72-73). Relig: Methodist. Legal Res: 3900 Stoney Ridge Trail Charlotte NC 28210 Mailing Add: 1512 E Fourth St Charlotte NC 28204

HAYNES, DAVID SCOTT (D)
b Brooklyn, NY, June 25, 47; s Hugh Marvin Haynes, Jr & Marianna Malovius H; m 1969 to Janet Ann Soderberg; c Erin. Educ: North Mich Univ, BA. Polit & Govt Pos: Coordr, Students for US Sen Philip Hart, Mich, 70-71; staff mem, McGovern for President, 71-72; deleg, Dem Nat Conv, 72. Bus & Prof Pos: Dir community rels, Bethlehem Lutheran Church, 73- Mil Serv: Entered as Airman, Air Force, 65, released as Sgt, 69, after serv in Europe, 65-69; Outstanding Airman, 601st Transportation Wing. Mem: Newspaper Guild, AFL-CIO. Legal Res: 242 W Ohio St Marquette MI 49855 Mailing Add: 450 Ovington Ave Brooklyn NY 11209

HAYNES, GLENN JOHNSON (R)
b Burnsville, Miss, Jan 14, 10; s Robin Alexander Haynes & Ollie Johnson H; m 1947 to Marcelle Loague. Educ: Miss State Univ, BS in bus, 42, BS in eng, 47; Marine Club; Latin Am Club; Itawamba Co Club. Polit & Govt Pos: Chmn, Itawamba Co Selective Serv Bd, 48-53; deleg, Rep Nat Conv, 50; mem, Miss State Rep Exec Comt, 50-51; chmn, Itawamba Co Rep Party, Miss, 50-52, 64-69 & 73-75. Bus & Prof Pos: Dir, Itawamba Co Develop Coun, 60-67; dir, Itawamba Co Fair Asn, 60-, vpres, 62-66. Mil Serv: Entered as Pvt, Marine Corps, 42, released as Cpl, 46, after serv in 4th Marine Div, Cent Pac; Marshal Islands, Saipan-Tinian & Iwo-Jima Campaign Ribbons; Presidential Unit Citation. Mem: Nat Fedn of Independent Bus (dist chmn); Lions; 40 & 8; Am Legion (state exec comt); VFW. Honors & Awards: Int Lions Exten Award. Relig: Methodist. Mailing Add: 101 Adams St Fulton MS 38843

HAYNES, LEE A (D)
b Madison, Fla; s Charlie Haynes & Carrie Robinson H; m 1961 to Hazel Espadron; c Victor Charles, Theron Lee, Kirk Leonce & Leandra Anastia. Educ: Southern Univ, Baton Rouge, MEd, 67; Univ Southwestern La, 30 hours, 67-73. Polit & Govt Pos: Chmn, Abbeville Dem Caucus, La, 72; deleg, Dem Nat Conv, 72; mem, Blacks in Polit, currently. Mem: NAACP (exec comt, 72-73). Relig: Catholic. Mailing Add: Rte 2 Box 53 Abbeville LA 70510

HAYNES, LONNIE RAY (D)
b Shreveport, La, July 15, 44; s Joseph Haynes & Mary Cooper H; m 1961 to Myrtle Tyson; c Carlys & Carmella. Educ: Centenary Col; La State Univ, Shreveport; Southern Univ. Polit & Govt Pos: Alt deleg, Dem Nat Conv, 72. Mem: Oil, Chem & Atomic Workers Int Union, A Philip Randolph Inst (vpres, La, currently); Caddo Coun on Minority Affairs (pres, currently); La Black Assembly (congr dist coordr). Relig: Baptist. Mailing Add: 2743 Milam St Shreveport LA 71103

HAYNES, ROLLIE ALBERT (R)
Chmn, Seventh Dist Rep Party, Wis
b Marshall, Minn, Oct 19, 34; s Rolla Albert Haynes & Mona Wilkins H; m 1957 to Karen Rae Turnquist; c Douglas & Allyson. Educ: Univ Minn, 54-58; Sigma Phi Epsilon. Polit & Govt Pos: Precinct chmn, Bloomington, Minn, 64-65, city chmn, 65-67; precinct chmn, Edina, Minn, 71-72; co chmn, Portage Co, Wis, 73-75; chmn, Seventh Dist Rep Party, Wis, 75- Bus & Prof Pos: Pres, Decker-Haynes Corp, Minneapolis, 62-66; vpres, Equity Securities Corp, Detroit, 66-70; dir mkt, Wall Street Growth Fund, St Paul, 70-72; financial planning develop mgr, Sentry Ins Co, Stevens Point, Wis, 72- Mil Serv: Entered as Seaman Recruit, Navy, 51, released as Hosp Corpsman 3/C, 54, after serv in Oakland Naval Hosp, Calif, 53-54. Publ: Another arrow for your quiver, Financial Planner, 71. Mem: Int Asn Financial Planners (Minn state chmn); Area Community Theatre (publicity chmn). Relig: Lutheran. Mailing Add: 101 Union Stevens Point WI 54481

HAYNES, WILLIAM G, JR (R)
Mem, Rep State Cent Comt La
b Chatham, La, Feb 14, 12; s William G Haynes & Eva Pilkinton H; m 1939 to Erlene Honeycutt; c Alice A & Kathleen J. Educ: Sch of Banking of the South, La State Univ, grad, 55. Polit & Govt Pos: Chmn, Ouachita Parish Rep Party, La, formerly; chmn, Fifth Dist Rep Party, formerly; mem bd dirs, Rep Polit Action Coun of La, 64-; mem, Rep State Cent Comt La, 65- Mil Serv: Entered as Pvt, Air Force, 42, released as T/Sgt, 46, after serv in Training Command. Mem: Am Legion. Relig: Christian Science. Legal Res: 200 Slack St West Monroe LA 71291 Mailing Add: PO Box 1215 West Monroe LA 71291

HAYNIE, MARY DONALDSON (D)
Committeewoman, NJ State Dem Comt
b Atlantic City, NJ, Dec 14, 23; d Edwin N Donaldson & Mary R Dolan D; m 1944 to John Francis Haynie; c Paul S & Mark C; one grandchild. Educ: Atlantic City High Sch, NJ, 41. Polit & Govt Pos: Committeewoman, NJ State Dem Comt, 69-; freeholder, Atlantic Co, 71-74. Bus & Prof Pos: Mem staff, Toll Off, NJ Bell Tel Co, Atlantic City, NJ, 42-65; mem staff, Proj Headstart, Atlantic City Pub Schs, 65; dir vol serv, Children's Seashore House, Atlantic City, 65- Mem: PTA; Am Soc Dirs Vol Servs; Am Mothers Comt Inc (pres, NJ Comt); Atlantic Co Coun Except Children (pres); Opportunity Ctr for Handicapped, Inc. Honors & Awards: B'nai B'rith Woman of Influence, 63; Mother of Year, Am Mothers Comt, Inc, NJ, 71; Silver Deer 1, Atlantic Area Boy Scout Coun; Thanks Badge, Girl Scouts. Relig: Roman Catholic. Mailing Add: 211 N Washington Ave Ventnor NJ 08406

HAYNSWORTH, CLEMENT FURMAN, JR
b Greenville, SC, Oct 30, 12; s Clement Furman Haynsworth & Elsie Hall H; m 1946 to Dorothy Merry Barkley; c Rufus C Barkley, Jr & Joseph G Barkley. Educ: Furman Univ, AB summa cum laude, 33 & hon LLD, 64; Harvard Law Sch, LLB, 36; Kappa Alpha Order; Lincoln's Inn, Harvard; Phi Alpha Delta. Polit & Govt Pos: Alt mem, Regional Wage Stabilization Bd, 51-52; mem, Judicial Coun State of SC, 56-57; judge, US Court of Appeals, Fourth Circuit, 57-64, chief judge, 64-; nominated Assoc Justice, US Supreme Court by the President, 69. Bus & Prof Pos: Former dir, SC Nat Bank, Liberty Life Ins Co, Southeastern Broadcasting Co, Greenville Hotel Co, Greenville COmmunity Hotel Co, South Weaving Co & Pickens RR Co; assoc, Haynsworth & Haynsworth, 36-40, partner, 40-46; exec partner, Haynsworth, Perry, Bryant, Marion & Johnstone, 46-57. Mil Serv: Entered as Ens, Navy, 42, released as Lt, 45, after serv in Amphibious Forces, Pac, 45. Publ: Numerous opinions, Fed Reporter, 2d, 57 & opinions in Fed Suppl, 57. Mem: Judicial Conf US; Am Law Inst; Am Judicature Soc; Am, & Fed Bar Asns. Relig: Episcopal. Legal Res: 415 Crescent Ave Greenville SC 29605 Mailing Add: Federal Bldg Greenville SC 29603

HAYS, FOREST, JR (D)
Ga State Rep
Mailing Add: St Elmo Rte 3 Chattanooga TN 37409

HAYS, J JEFFERSON (D)
Ind State Rep
b Archer City, Tex, Dec 27, 29; s Joseph Collins Hays & Vera Pruett H; m 1956 to Mary Louise Hoffman; c Lisa, Laura, Lynn, Christine & John. Educ: Univ Evansville, BS in Mkt, 55; Pi Epsilon Phi. Polit & Govt Pos: Ind State Rep, 71-72 & 75- Mil Serv: Entered as Pvt, Army, 51, released as Sgt, 53, after serv in Korean Theatre, 52-53; Bronze Star. Mem: Evansville Press Club (dir); Vandenburgh Co, Hope of Evansville (dir). Relig: Catholic. Mailing Add: 1113 Taylor Evansville IN 47714

HAYS, JACK D H (R)
Justice, Ariz Supreme Court
b Lund, Nev, Feb 17, 17; s Charles Hays (deceased) & Thelma Savage H; m 1971 to Dorothy M Taylor; c Eugene Harrington, Rory Cochrane, Bruce Harvey & Victoria Wakeling. Educ: Southern Methodist Univ, BS, 39, LLB, 41; Lambda Chi Alpha; Pi Alpha Delta. Polit & Govt Pos: Asst city attorney, Phoenix, Ariz, 49-52; Ariz State Rep, 52; state chmn, Eisenhower for Pres, 52; US Attorney, Phoenix, Ariz, 53-60; superior court judge, Maricopa Co, 60-69; Justice, Ariz Supreme Court, 69-72 & 74-, chief justice, 72-74. Bus & Prof Pos: Attorney, Hays & Webster, 46-, Myers, Whitlow & Hays, 52- Mil Serv: Entered as Pvt, Army, 41, released as Maj, 46, after serv in Field Artil, Ital Theatre, 44-45; Bronze Star. Mem: Ariz Acad; Ariz Inst (Phoenix comt); Rotary 100; Boy Scouts (adv bd, Roosevelt Coun); Valley Big Brothers (adv bd). Honors & Awards: Big Brother of the Year Award, 66; Awards Juror, Freedoms Found, Valley Forge, 73; Herbert Lincoln Harley Award, Am Judicature Soc, 74. Legal Res: 2302 E Lincoln Dr Phoenix AZ 85016 Mailing Add: Rm 221 Capitol Bldg West Wing Phoenix AZ 85007

HAYS, JOHN (R)
Ariz State Rep
Mailing Add: Hays Ranch Box 395 Yarnell AZ 85362

HAYS, JOHN (D)
NMex State Rep
Mailing Add: Box 1876 Clovis NM 88101

HAYS, KENNETH SHARP, JR (D)
b Chattanooga, Tenn, Nov 2, 54; s Kenneth Sharp Hays & Bobbie Gambrel H; single. Educ: George Washington Univ, 73-; Phi Delta Theta. Polit & Govt Pos: Deleg, Dem Nat Conv, 72; deleg, Tenn Dem State Conv, 74; clerical, House Judiciary Impeachment Inquiry Staff, 74; secy, DC Col Dem, 74-75; clerical, Dem Nat Comt, 75- Publ: Auth, Youth at the 1972 Democratic National Convention, Youth Mag, 12/72. Relig: Episcopal. Legal Res: 110 Wilder Dr Signal Mountain TN 37377 Mailing Add: PO Box 1976 Atlanta GA 30309

HAYS, MARILYN A (R)
Chmn, Christian Co Rep Party, Ky
b Bedford, Ind, July 12, 29; d Frank Foster Asbell & Doris Pitman A; m 1951 to Herbert Gene Hays; c Jack Paul, Peg J & Lee Ann. Educ: Ind State Teachers Col, 2 years; Sigma Kappa. Polit & Govt Pos: Chmn, Christian Co Rep Party, Ky, 68-72 & 75-; mem, Ky Women's Comn, 69-; chmn, Ky Fedn Rep Women State Annual Meeting, 71. Mem: Christian Co Rep Women's Club; Rotary Ann; United Cerebral Palsy Local Orgn. Relig: Church of Christ. Mailing Add: 616 Deepwood Dr Hopkinsville KY 42240

HAYS, PAUL M (R)
Secy, DC Rep Comt
b Washington, DC, Feb 23, 46; s Freeman Cornelius Hays, MD & Doris Baker H; single.

Educ: Georgetown Univ Sch For Serv, 3 years. Polit & Govt Pos: Page, US Supreme Court, 60-64; minority bill clerk, US House Rep, 68-; precinct chmn, DC Rep Comt, 67-, mem, 69-, secy, 72-; nat committeeman, DC, Young Rep Nat Fedn, 69-70; pres, DC Young Rep Club, 71-73. Mil Serv: Entered as Pvt, DC Army Nat Guard, 69, S/Sgt, 276th MP Co, 74- Mem: Kiwanis. Relig: Presbyterian. Legal Res: 310 S Carolina Ave SE Washington DC 20003 Mailing Add: H-324 US Capitol Washington DC 20515

HAYS, WAYNE L (D)
US Rep, Ohio
b Bannock, Ohio, May 13, 11; s Walter Lee Hays & Bertha Mae Taylor H; m 1937 to Martha Judkins; c Martha Brigitta. Educ: Ohio State Univ, BS, 33; Duke Univ, 35, grad work. Hon Degrees: LLD, Ohio Univ, 66 & Col Steubenville, 68. Polit & Govt Pos: Mayor, Flushing, Ohio, 39-45; Ohio State Sen, 41-42; comnr, Belmont Co, Ohio, 45-49; US Rep, Ohio, 48-, mem, House Foreign Affairs Comt, chmn, House Admin Comt & Subcomt on Int Opers, US House Rep, chmn, Dem Cong Comt, 73-; chmn, House Rep deleg, NAtlantic Assembly Conf, 55-, pres conf, 56-57, 69-70 & 74-75 & US rep, NAtlantic Assembly Standing Comt, currently. Bus & Prof Pos: Chmn bd dir, Citizens Nat Bank, Flushing; owner, Red Gate Farms, Belmont, Ohio; Cattle & Horse Breeder. Honors & Awards: Caritas Medal, 69. Relig: Presbyterian. Legal Res: OH Mailing Add: Rayburn House Off Bldg Washington DC 20515

HAYWARD, WILLIAM (R)
Mich State Rep
b Detroit, Mich, July 5, 06; s William Wellington Hayward & Dolly E Wixom H; m 1938 to Madelon Bernice Land; c Mary Helen (Mrs Thomas Kaser), Kaser), Susan (Mrs Leonard Siudara), Nancy (Mrs Raymond Howard) & William Hayward. Educ: Rutger's Univ, Grad Sch Banking, 40-42. Polit & Govt Pos: City Comnr, Royal Oak, Mich, 39-45 & 51-59, Mayor, 45-49 & 59-63; Mich State Rep, 59- Bus & Prof Pos: Exec positions in financial & banking insts, 42-59. Mailing Add: 1839 Sycamore Royal Oak MI 48073

HAYWORTH, DON (D)
b Toledo, Iowa, Jan 13, 98; s Charles LeRoy Hayworth & Mae Wilkinson H; m 1934 to Frances Knight; c Donna Lou, Francene & Barbara. Educ: Grinnell Col, AB, 18; Univ Chicago, AM, 21; Univ Wis, PhD, 29. Polit & Govt Pos: Dir, Victory Speakers Prog, Off of Civilian Defense, 42-43; info specialist, Dept of Interior, 43-45; US Rep, Mich, 55-56; consult, Dept of Agr, 63-64; consult, Soc Security Admin, 65-67. Bus & Prof Pos: Prof, Penn Col, Iowa, 23-27, Univ Akron, 28-37, Mich State Univ, 37-63; established Plastics Mfg Co, Lansing, Mich, 52-63. Mil Serv: Pvt, Army, 18. Publ: Several books & articles in prof speech jour; mag articles. Mem: Kiwanis; Torch Club; NAACP. Relig: Protestant. Mailing Add: 1311 Delaware Ave SW Washington DC 20024

HAZARD, WALTER ROBINSON (D)
RI State Rep
b Providence, RI, Sept 29, 11; s Ellsworth Joseph Hazard & Martha Elizabeth Dows H; m 1936 to Marian Elizabeth; c Robert E, Walter R, Jr, John E & Carolyn E. Educ: Wentworth Inst, 29-30. Polit & Govt Pos: Chmn, EGreenwich Town Dem Comt, RI, 42-52; councilman, EGreenwich, 50-52; chmn, NKingstown Town Comt, 55-62; RI State Sen, 21st Dist, 75- Bus & Prof Pos: Town mgr, Pittsford, Vt, Manchester, Vt & Wellfleet, Mass, 71; sales & promotion, Keyes Assocs, Providence, RI, 72-; land surveyor, M H Good Roads, RI Hwy Asn. Publ: A happy memorable time, Yankee Magazine, 2/64; Once upon a time in Wickford, Standard Times Tricentennial. Mem: Int City & Town Mgrs Asn. Mailing Add: 130 Congdon Hill Rd North Kingstown RI 02874

HAZELBAKER, FRANK W (R)
Mont State Sen
Mailing Add: PO Box 430 Dillion MT 59725

HAZELTON, DON F (R)
Fla State Rep
Mailing Add: PO Box 8306 West Palm Beach FL 33407

HAZOURI, THOMAS L (TOMMY) (D)
Fla State Rep
Mailing Add: 932 Cedar St Apt 4 Jacksonville FL 32207

HEAD, FRED (D)
Tex State Rep
Mailing Add: 109 N Wofford St Athens TX 75751

HEAD, JOE (D)
Ky State Rep
Mailing Add: Rte 2 Providence KY 42450

HEAD, PEGGY CAROL (D)
b Commerce, Tex, Dec 26, 43; d Roy Babbitt Hodges, Jr & Wilma Loyce Bell H; m 1963 to Charles Leon Head; c Jeffrey Grant, Christopher Marcus, Tara Brynn & Justin Gareth. Educ: ETex State Univ, BS, 71; El Centro Commun Col, 71; Polit Sci Honors Club. Polit & Govt Pos: Precinct secy, Precinct 253, Dem Party, Dallas, Tex, formerly, precinct chmn, currently. deleg Tex Dem State Conv, 16th Dist, 70 & 72; alt deleg, Dem Nat Conv, 72. Bus & Prof Pos: Teacher, Dallas Pub Sch, Tex, 71- Mem: Dallas Substitute Teachers Asn; Samuel-Grand Park & Recreation Ctr Coun. Relig: Baptist. Mailing Add: 610 Brookside Dr Dallas TX 75214

HEADLEY, DAVID L (D)
Ohio State Sen
Mailing Add: 3571 Greenwich Rd Barberton OH 44203

HEADY, MARION BENJAMIN (R)
Chmn, 54th Representative Dist Rep Party, Ill
b Newton, Ill, Dec 5, 08; s Joe Heady & Nora Pulliam H; m 1931 to Iva F Staley; c Duane & Nora (Mrs Mansur). Polit & Govt Pos: State oil well inspector, Ill, 53-59; Justice of the Peace, Newton, 54-58; treas, Jasper Co Rep Comt, 54-64; chmn, Jasper Co Rep Orgn, formerly; mem, Ill Rep State Cent Comt, 68-; chmn, 54th Representative Dist Rep Party, currently. Mem: Jasper Co Farm Bur; Moose. Mailing Add: PO Box 1 Newton IL 62448

HEALD, CLEON E (R)
NH State Rep
Mailing Add: 234 Washington St Keene NH 03431

HEALD, PHILIP C, JR (R)
NH State Rep
Mailing Add: RFD 1 Wilton NH 03086

HEALEY, E J (ED) (D)
Fla State Rep
Mailing Add: 5663 Middlecoff Dr West Palm Beach FL 33406

HEALEY, JAMES THOMAS (D)
Conn State Rep
b Waterbury, Conn, Oct 15, 18; s Patrick Healey & Kathleen Coughlan H; m 1946 to Marie D Tedeschi; c Patrick. Educ: Yale Univ, BA, 40 & LLB, 47. Polit & Govt Pos: Conn State Rep, 72nd Dist, 67- Bus & Prof Pos: Assoc, Healey & Healey, 47-52, partner, 52- Mil Serv: Entered as 2nd Lt, Army, 41, released as Capt, 45, after serv in 25th Field Artil Bn, Caribbean & Europe; Bronze Star; Am Serv Ribbon with Overseas Clasp; ETO Serv Ribbon; Victory Medal. Mem: Am Bar Asn; Waterbury Club; Country Club of Waterbury; Univ Club of Waterbury; Waterbury Br, Salvation Army (mem adv bd). Relig: Roman Catholic. Legal Res: 165 Hillside Ave Waterbury CT 06710 Mailing Add: c/o Healey & Healey Box 2299 Waterbury CT 06720

HEALEY, PHILIP B (R)
NY State Assemblyman
Mailing Add: 32 Frankel Rd Massapequa NY 11758

HEALEY, SKIP (R)
Rep Nat Committeeman, Okla
b Phoenix, Ariz, Feb 7, 34; m 1955 to Sue; c Colt, Clay & Casey Susan. Educ: Davis High Sch, Okla, grad, 54. Polit & Govt Pos: Vchmn, Third Cong Dist Rep Party, Okla, 62-66, chmn, 66-72; mem, Rep State Comt Okla, 62-; deleg, Rep Nat Conv, 64, alt deleg, 68; Rep Nat Committeeman, Okla, 72- Bus & Prof Pos: Cattle rancher, 50- Mem: Boy Scouts (dir, Arbuckle Area Coun); Cub Master; Okla Cattleman's Asn (dir, 63-); Hereford Heaven Asn; Tex-Okla Hereford Asn. Relig: Methodist; Supt Sunday Sch, Davis Methodist Church. Mailing Add: Flying L Ranch Davis OK 73030

HEALY, DANIEL J (D)
NH State Rep
Mailing Add: 366 Lake Ave Manchester NH 03103

HEALY, ELLEN (D)
b Coeur d'Alene, Idaho; single. Educ: Univ Idaho. Polit & Govt Pos: Former state vchmn, Idaho Dem State Cent Comt; deleg, five Dem Nat Conv, mem, Platform & Resolutions Comts, 64 & 68; Dem Nat Committeewoman, Idaho, 60-72; mem, City Planning Comn, Coeur d'Alene, 63-69; mem, Western State Dem Conf. Bus & Prof Pos: Pres & gen mgr, Graham Investment Co Inc, Real Estate & Ins. Mem: Univ Idaho Alumni Asn; Nat Asn of Ins Women; Cath Daughters of Am; Gonzaga Univ (bd regents). Mailing Add: 1221 E Lakeshore Dr Coeur d'Alene ID 83814

HEALY, GEORGE T (D)
NH State Rep
Mailing Add: 278 S Taylor St Manchester NH 03103

HEALY, JOHN EDWARD (JACK) (D)
Mont State Sen
b Butte, Mont, Sept 23, 07; s Dennis Healy & Julia McCarthy H; m 1938 to Irene Leary; c John E, Jr. Educ: Mont Tech, 2 years; Univ Wash, grad. Polit & Govt Pos: Engr, Mont State Hwy, 32-33 & 34-35; engr, Forest Serv, 33-34; co surveyor & engr, Silver Bow Co, Mont, 35-51; Mont State Rep, 61-74; Mont State Sen, 75-, mem many comts, Mont State Senate, currently. Bus & Prof Pos: Engr, Anaconda Co, 51-72. Mem: KofC; Elks; Mont Soc Engrs. Relig: Catholic. Mailing Add: 624 W Granite St Butte MT 59701

HEALY, JONATHAN LEE (R)
Mass State Rep
b Greenfield, Mass, Oct 10, 45; s Winston Healy & Margaret Lee H; single. Educ: Punahou Sch, Honolulu, Hawaii, 62-64; Williams Col, 64-68. Polit & Govt Pos: Mass State Rep, First Franklin Dist, 71-; alt deleg, Rep Nat Conv, 72. Bus & Prof Pos: Teacher, Doane Acad, 68-69; teacher & coach, Williams Col, 69-74. Legal Res: Mohawk Trail Shelburne Falls MA 01370 Mailing Add: State House Boston MA 02133

HEALY, WILLIAM JAMES (D)
Ohio State Rep
b Canton, Ohio, Mar 4, 39; s Charles Wilson Healy & Margaret Higgens H; m 1959 to Mary Ann Zugcic; c Joyce Renee, Jacqueline Ann & William J, II. Educ: Kent State Univ, Stark Br, 60-63. Polit & Govt Pos: Councilman, Ward Six & 12, Canton, Ohio, 70-75; mem, Stark Co Dem Exec & Cent Comts, 70-; Ohio State Rep, 50th Dist, 75- Bus & Prof Pos: Employee, Corrigated Box Div, St Regis Paper Co, Canton, Ohio, 60-73; admin dir, Goodwill Urban League Treatment Ctr, 73-74; employee, Culligan Soft Water, Canton, 74. Mil Serv: Entered as Airman 3/C, Air Force, 56, released as Airman 2/C, 60, after serv in Airborne Div. Mem: Jefferson Jackson Dem Mens Club. Relig: Catholic. Mailing Add: 1915 Morris Ave NE Canton OH 44705

HEANEY, ROBERT A (D)
RI State Rep
Mailing Add: 124 Terrace Ave Pawtucket RI 02860

HEANEY, ROBERT ELLIOTT (D)
Nev State Assemblyman
b Los Angeles, Calif, Feb 7, 40; s George A Heaney & Bettie Horowitz H; m 1965 to Patricia Lee Martin; c Pamela Ann & Susan Michelle. Educ: Univ Nev, Reno, BA, 62; Univ Calif, Davis, JD, 71; Phi Delta Phi; Blue Key; Sigma Alpha Epsilon. Polit & Govt Pos: Dep dist attorney, Washoe Co, Nev, 71-75; Nev State Assemblyman, Dist 26, 74- Bus & Prof Pos: Pvt law practice, Reno, Nev, 75- Mil Serv: Entered as 2nd Lt, Army, 63, released as 1st Lt, 65, after serv in 4th Bn, 23rd Inf, Alaska; Parachutist Badge. Mem: Elks; Rotary; Am Bar Asn;

Univ Nev Alumni Asn (admin bd, 74-). Honors & Awards: SAR Award, 59. Mailing Add: 6850 Prestwick Circle Reno NV 89502

HEARD, FRED W (D)
Ore State Sen
b Prineville, Ore, Sept 9, 40; s Darrell L Heard & Wilma E Straube H; m 1966 to Adair E Flann; c Frederick Marshall, Robin Adair & Heather Alice. Educ: Univ Ore, 58-60; Southern Ore Col, BS, 63, MS, 68; Pi Kappa Phi. Polit & Govt Pos: Chmn, Klamath Co Dem Cent Comt, Ore, 66-69; Ore State Rep, 69-73; Ore State Sen, 73- Bus & Prof Pos: Teacher, Klamath Union High Sch, Klamath Falls, Ore, 63-70; asst prof, Ore Inst Technol, 71- Mem: Ore State Employees' Asn; Grange (co officer, formerly, state exec officer, 70-74); Kiwanis. Relig: Congregational. Legal Res: 212 High St Klamath Falls OR 97601 Mailing Add: PO Box 337 Klamath Falls OR 97601

HEARD, ROLAND SHAEFER (D)
b Lanett, Ala, Oct 07, 95; s George Heard & Mary Shaefer H; m 1925 to Janie Lovelace. Educ: Bus Col in Atlanta, course in bookkeeping & acct, 16. Polit & Govt Pos: Lt Col, Staff of Gov Carl E Sanders, Gov S Ernest Vandiver & Gov Eugene Talmadge, 40-41; mem city coun, West Point, Ga, 56-62; Ga State Sen, 29th Dist, 63-64; staff, Gov Jimmy Carter, Ga, 70- Bus & Prof Pos: Cashier & off mgr, Gen Off, West Point Mfg Co; Heard-Williams Co; vpres, Valley Nat Bank, Lanett, Ala, retired; pres, Mid Chattahoochee River Develop Asn, 58-; dir & chmn, West Point Dam & Reservoir Comt, Valley Chamber of Commerce, West Point, 67-; mem bd registr, Troup Co, Ga; sales rep, Superior Match Co, Chicago, Ill. Mil Serv: Naval Res, 18-21; active duty, Charleston, SC, Yeoman 3/C; Victory Medal. Mem: West Point Lodge, F&AM (Past Master, 19-); Chap, Commandery, Shrine; Valley CofC (chmn dedication comt, 75-); Chattahoochee Valley Hist Soc (dir, 52-); Am Legion. Honors & Awards: Silver Beaver Award, Boy Scouts, 44; Achievement Award, West Point Lions Club, 51; Outstanding Civilian Serv Award, US Corps of Army Engrs, 68; Citation of Merit, Valley CofC, West Point; Presented Scroll, West Point Lions Club, 71. Relig: Baptist; lifetime deacon. Legal Res: 2011 Highway 29 West Point GA 31833 Mailing Add: PO Box 246 West Point GA 31833

HEARN, GEORGE HENRY (D)
Mem, NY State Dem Comt
b Brooklyn, NY, July 4, 27; s Henry G Hearn & Grace A Flaherty H; m 1952 to Cecelia Anne Philbin; c Annemarie Jude, Margaret Mary & George Henry. Educ: Fordham Univ Sch of Bus Admin, 48; St Francis Col, BA, 50; St John's Univ, LLB, 54. Polit & Govt Pos: New York Coun, 58-61; chmn, Kings Co Speakers Comt for Pres Elec, 60; vchmn comt nationalists & intergroup rels, NY State Dem Comt, 60-; comnr, Fed Maritime Comn, 64-75. Bus & Prof Pos: Lawyer, Haight, Gardner, Poor & Havens, New York, 54-61. Mil Serv: Naval Res, World War II, Pac Theater; Distinguished Serv Award. Publ: Limitations on liability of international carriers, NY Law Forum, fall 67; Administrative due process hearing requirements & the Federal Maritime Commission, Duke Law J, 2/70. Mem: Boy Scouts (dist comnr, 58-); US Jr CofC; St Patrick's Soc, Brooklyn; Am Comt Ital Migration (recording secy, Brooklyn Div); KofC. Mailing Add: 423 Bay Ridge Pkwy Brooklyn NY 11209

HEARN, IRENE FINNERTY (R)
Mem, Rep State Cent Comt Calif
b Glendale, Calif, Oct 21, 32; d Robert Emmet Finnerty & Margaret Flautt F; m 1965 to Frederick William Hearn. Educ: Immaculate Heart Col, BA, 54. Polit & Govt Pos: Campaign staff, Sen Thomas H Kuchel, 56; admin asst to US Rep H Allen Smith, Calif, 57-66, field rep, 66-; mem, Los Angeles Co Rep Cent Comt, 43rd Assembly Dist Rep Cent Comt & Rep State Cent Comt Calif, currently. Mem: Rep Buck & Ballot Brigade; Jr Auxiliary of Flower Guild Charities for Children; 43rd Rep Assembly; Glendale Rep Women's Workshop. Relig: Catholic. Mailing Add: 1245 Imperial Dr Glendale CA 91207

HEARNES, WARREN EASTMAN (D)
Dem Nat Committeeman, Mo
b Moline, Ill, July 24, 23; s Earle B Hearnes & Edna Eastman H; m 1948 to Betty Sue Cooper; c Lynn, Leigh & Julia B. Educ: US Mil Acad, BS, 46; Univ Mo Sch Law, AB & LLB, 52; Phi Delta Theta; Phi Delta Phi. Polit & Govt Pos: Mo State Rep, 51-61, Majority Floor Leader, Mo House Rep, 57-61; Secy of State, Mo, 61-65; Gov, Mo, 65-73; chmn, Nat Gov Conf; pres, Coun State Govt; mem, Adv Comn Intergovt Rels; deleg, Dem Nat Conv, 72; Dem Nat Committeeman, Mo, 72- Mil Serv: Enlisted in Army & serv in Hq Co, 140th Inf, 35th Div, 777th Antiaircraft, released as 1st Lt (vet), 49. Mem: Scottish Rite; York Rite; Shrine; Mason; Am Legion. Relig: Baptist. Mailing Add: 1015 Locust St Suite 800 St Louis MO 63101

HEATER, ELLIOTT VERMONT, JR (R)
b Grandview, Wash, May 22, 25; s Elliott Vermont Heater & Bernice Wilson H; m 1947 to Winifred Gemmell; c Monica, Stephen, Robert & Gregg. Educ: Spokane Community Col, 67-69. Polit & Govt Pos: Chmn, Stevens Co Rep Club, Wash, 67-; chmn, Stevens Co Rep Party, formerly. Bus & Prof Pos: Farming, 43-52; custom contract farming, 52-54; heavy duty mech, 54-66; retired, 66. Relig: Protestant. Mailing Add: Rte 2 Box 56A Colville WA 99114

HEATLY, WILLIAM STANFORD, JR (D)
Tex State Rep
b Mart, Tex, Sept 3, 12; s William Stanford Heatly & Byrta Rogers H; m 1946 to Jonnie Green Hawkins; c Eugene Newcomb, William Hawkins & William Stanford, III. Educ: Decatur Baptist Col, 31-33; Baylor Univ, AB & LLB, 36; law sch foreman, Baylor. Hon Degrees: LLD, Howard Payne Col, Tex & Dallas Baptist Col. Polit & Govt Pos: City attorney, Paducah, Tex, 50-52; Tex State Rep, 54-, chmn, Appropriations Comt, Tex House Rep, 59-60 & 63-73. Bus & Prof Pos: Farmer; rancher; oil & banking interests; attorney-at-law, Paducah, Tex, 47-; owner, Jones & Renfrow, Abstractors, 50- Publ: Alcohol-Public Enemy Number 1, Baptist Standard, 58. Mem: Am Bar Asn; Tex State Bar Asn (mem legis comt); Distributive Educ in Tex; State Bar of Tex; Comn on Alcoholism. Honors & Awards: All State Jr Col Quarterback, Decatur Baptist Col, 32 & 33; Clarendon Jr Col Award; Second in seniority in Tex House of Rep; Longest Time for Any Mem to Serve as Chmn, Appropriations Comt. Relig: Christian Church; former chmn bd of deacons & elders, First Christian Church of Paducah. Mailing Add: Drawer 1 Paducah TX 79248

HEAVEY, THOMAS RANDAL (D)
Mem, King Co Dem Party, Wash
b Bremerton, Wash, Aug 23, 51; s Bernard J Heavey, Jr & Thelma Peterson H; single. Educ: Pac Lutheran Univ, BA, 74; pres, Off Campus Students Asn; dir, Mil Serv Info Ctr, 70-74; asst to pres, Assoc Students, 72; chmn, Faculty-Student Publ Comt, 72-74; ed, Mooring Mast, 74. Polit & Govt Pos: Co-founder & treas, Seattle City Youth Coun, 68-69; alt deleg, Dem Nat Conv, 72; intern, Wash State Legis, 72; exec vpres, Young Dem, Pac Lutheran Univ, 72-74; mem, Pierce Co Dem Party, 72-74; mem, King Co Dem Party, 74-; vchmn, Wash Asn Independent Student Govt. Publ: Deferably speaking (column on Selective Serv), 70-72, co-auth, An interview with Curtis Tarr, 4/71 & auth, The blue jean machine wore suspenders, McGovern & Jackson, a comparison of styles, 10/72, Mooring Mast. Mem: Int Platform Asn. Relig: Lutheran; deleg, Am Lutheran Church Conv, 74. Mailing Add: 2015 N 75th Seattle WA 98103

HEBARD, EMORY (R)
Vt State Rep
b Carmel, Maine, Sept 28, 17; m to Irma M Mills; c Sammy M (Mrs Hedger). Educ: Middlebury Col, AB, 38. Polit & Govt Pos: State Rep Comt; chmn, Rep Co Comt, dir indust develop, Vt Develop Dept; town moderator, Glover & asst mgr, twice; dir, Orleans Co Fair & Vt Fairs Asn; trustee, Glover Fire Dept; Vt State Rep, 61-67 & 75- Mil Serv: World War II & Korea, Lt Comdr, US Coast Guard Res. Mem: Grange; Mason; Eastern Star; Odd Fellows; Am Legion. Relig: Congregational. Mailing Add: Box 143 Glover VT 05839

HEBARD, IRMA MAGINNIS (R)
Pres, Vt Fedn of Rep Women
b Mo; d Chelius Dugal Mills & Sarah Freeman M; m to Emory Amos Hebard; c Sammy (Mrs Hedger). Educ: Southwest Mo State Univ; George Washington Univ. Polit & Govt Pos: Pres, Vt Fedn of Rep Women, 73- Bus & Prof Pos: Budget analyst, Off War Info & Cent Intel Agency, Washington, DC, during World War III. Relig: Southern Baptist. Mailing Add: PO Box 143 Shadow Lake Rd Glover VT 05839

HEBERT, DENNIS P (D)
La State Rep
Mailing Add: 385 W Chestnut St Ponchatoula LA 70454

HEBERT, F EDWARD (D)
US Rep, La
b New Orleans, La, Oct 21, 01; s Felix Joseph Hebert & Lea Naquin H; m to Gladys F Bofill; c Dawn M (Mrs John M Duhe, Jr). Educ: Tulane Univ, 20-24; Delta Sigma Phi (nat vpres, 37-49); Sigma Alpha Kappa. Hon Degrees: LLD, Loyola Univ (La), 72. Polit & Govt Pos: US Rep, La, 41-, chmn, Armed Serv Comt, US House Rep, 70-75, chmn armed servs invests subcomt, 71- Bus & Prof Pos: Asst sports ed, New Orleans Times-Picayune, 18-23; asst sports ed, New Orleans States, 23-25, reporter & columnist, 28-37, city ed, 37-41; publicity dir, Loyola Univ of the South, 25-28. Publ: I went, I saw, I heard. Mem: Metairie Country Club; Young Mens Bus Club. Honors & Awards: George Wash Great Am Award, Am Legion; Minuteman Hall of Fame, Man of the Year & Purple Heart Award, Reserve Off Asn; Nat Preparedness Award, Nat Inst for Disaster Mobilization. Relig: Catholic. Legal Res: 5367 Canal Blvd New Orleans LA 70124 Mailing Add: 2340 Rayburn House Off Bldg Washington DC 20515

HEBERT, ROLAND N (D)
NH State Rep
Mailing Add: 340 High St Somersworth NH 03878

HEBNER, CHARLES L (R)
Del State Rep
Mailing Add: 913 Darley Rd Wilmington DE 19810

HECHINGER, JOHN W (D)
Dem Nat Committeeman, DC
Mailing Add: 2838 Chain Bridge Rd Washington DC 20016

HECHLER, KEN (D)
US Rep, WVa
b Roslyn, NY, Sept 20, 14; s Charles Henry Hechler (deceased) & Catherine Elizabeth Hauhart H; single. Educ: Swarthmore Col, AB, 35; Columbia, AM, 36, PhD, 40. Polit & Govt Pos: Research asst to Judge Sam I Rosenman on President Roosevelt's Pub Papers, 39-50; sect chief, Bur of Census, 40; personnel technologist, Off for Emergency Mgt, 41; admin analyst, Budget Bur, 41-42 & 46-47; spec asst to President Truman, 49-53; research dir, Adlai Stevenson Campaign, 56; US Rep, WVa, 59-; deleg, Dem Nat Conv, 64, 68 & 72. Bus & Prof Pos: Govt lectr, Barnard Col, Columbia Univ, 37-41; asst prof polit sci, Princeton Univ, 47-49; assoc prof polit sci, Marshall Univ, 57; radio-TV commentator, 57-58. Mil Serv: Maj, Army, 42-46; Col, Army Res, currently. Publ: Insurgency; Personalities & Policies of Taft Era, 40; The Remagen, 57; West Virginia Memories of President Kennedy, 65. Mem: Am Legion; VFW; DAV; Elks; Am Polit Sci Asn. Honors & Awards: WVa Speaker of the Year, 73. Relig: Episcopal. Legal Res: 917 Fifth Ave Huntington WV 25701 Mailing Add: US House Off Bldg Washington DC 20515

HECHT, BURTON (D)
NY State Assemblyman
b New York, NY, Dec 30, 27; m to Isabel H; c Mindy, Audrey & Allen. Educ: NY Univ & Law Sch. Polit & Govt Pos: Asst dist attorney, Bronx Co, NY; NY State Assemblyman, 62-, chmn ways & means comt, NY State Assembly. Bus & Prof Pos: Lawyer. Mem: Decatur Dem Club; Kingsbridge Heights Jewish Ctr (bd trustees); Bedford Park Neighborhood Civic Asn; United Jewish Appeal (speakers comt); Multiple Sclerosis Soc (bd trustees, Bronx Chap). Relig: Jewish. Mailing Add: 2715 Grand Concourse Bronx NY 10468

HECHT, CHIC (R)
b Cape Girardeau, Mo, Nov 30, 28; s Louis Hecht & Anna Sigiloff H (deceased); m 1959 to Gail Sharon Kahn; c Lori Ann & Leslie Lyn. Educ: Univ Mo, 45-46; St Louis Univ, 46-47; Wash Univ, BS in Bus Admin, 49; Sigma Alpha Mu. Polit & Govt Pos: Nev State Sen, 67-74, minority leader, Nev State Senate, 69-74; alt deleg, Rep Nat Conv, 68, deleg, 72. Mil Serv: Entered as Pvt, Army, 51, released as Cpl, 53, after serv as Spec Agent, Counter Intel, Berlin, Ger, 51-53; Army Occupation Medal. Mem: Retail Merchants Asn, Las Vegas; Nat Counter Intel Corp Asn (vpres, 71, pres, 72); CofC; Elks; Am Legion. Relig: Jewish. Mailing Add: 47 Country Club Lane Las Vegas NV 89109

HECHT, CHRISTINE SIGRID (D)
Mem, Fairfax Co Dem Comt, Va
b Chicago, Ill, Jan 22, 43; d Lothar H Schroeder & Theresa Wailand S; m 1961 to Stephen J Hecht; c Victoria Lynn & Lisa Katherine. Educ: Chicago City col, 1 year. Polit & Govt Pos:

Precinct chmn, Fairfax Co Dem Comt, Va, 65-, mem, currently; deleg, Fairfax Co Dem Conv & Dem Nat Conv, 68. Mem: League of Women Voters. Relig: Unitarian. Mailing Add: 6611 E Wakefield Dr Alexandria VA 22307

HECHT, HENRY DEL BANCO, JR (R)

b New Orleans, La, Nov 9, 01; s Henry Del Banco Hecht & Sarah Rohrbacher H; m 1923 to Harriet Jay; c Harriett (Mrs Rousseau) & Henry D, III. Educ: Warren Easton Sch, New Orleans, 4 years; Soule Bus Col, 3 years. Polit & Govt Pos: Asst campaign mgr, Rep Party, La, 48-54; mem, La State Rep Cent Comt, 60-68; secy-treas, Jefferson Parish Rep Exec Comt, 60-68, chmn, formerly; asst campaign mgr for Hugh Exnicious for Dist Attorney's Off, 67. Bus & Prof Pos: Gen ins, retired, 60. Mem: F&AM (dist Dep Grand Master, 68); Mason. Relig: Methodist. Mailing Add: 123 Midway Dr New Orleans LA 70123

HECHT, W ARTHUR (R)
Mem, Rep State Cent Comt Calif

b Bielefeld, Ger, Dec 13, 23; s Leo Hecht & Herta Lewinski H; m 1951 to Doris Ida Goldstein; c Stephen Thomas. Educ: Columbia Univ, BS, 48; Tau Beta Pi; Alpha Phi Omega. Polit & Govt Pos: Campaign worker, various local & state campaigns, Calif, 66-70; pres, EBay Div, Bay Area Rep Alliance, 67, vchmn alliance, 69-; mem, Rep State Cent Comt Calif, 67-; mem, Alameda Co Rep Finance Comt, 67-; co-chmn, Flournoy for State Controller, Calif, 70; mem, Piedmont Bd Educ, 70-, pres, 72-73. Bus & Prof Pos: Indust engr, various companies, 48-53; plant chief indust engr, Continental Can Co, Oakland, Calif, 53-60; vpres, Allwork Mfg Co, 60-66; chartered life underwriter, New York Life Ins Co, 67- Mil Serv: Entered as Pvt, Army, 42, released as Sgt, 46, after serv in 656th Engr Topographic Bn, European Theatre, 45-46; Capt, Army Intel Res, 46-49. Mem: Soc Chartered Life Underwriters (dir); Nat Asn Life Underwriters; Boy Scouts (Piedmont Coun exec bd); Piedmont Swim Club; Am Jewish Comt (dir, Oakland Chap). Honors & Awards: Silver Beaver, Boy Scouts. Relig: Jewish. Mailing Add: 71 Wildwood Ave Piedmont CA 94610

HECK, L DOUGLAS
US Ambassador, Niger

b Bern, Switz, Dec 14, 18; s Lewis Heck & Dorothy Tompkins H; m 1972 to Ernestine H Sherman; c Elizabeth Tompkins & Judith Kingsbury. Educ: Yale Univ, BA, 41; Zeta Psi. Polit & Govt Pos: Polit officer, Am Consulate Gen, Calcutta, India, 53-55 & Am Embassy, New Delhi, India, 56-59; charge d'Affaires, Am Embassy, Kathmandu, Nepal, 59; dep chief mission, Am Embassy, Nicosia, Cyprus, 59-62; polit counr, New Delhi, India, 62-65; country dir India, State Dept, Washington, 66-68; consul gen, Am Consulate Gen, Istanbul, Turkey, 68-70; minister, counr & dep chief mission, Am Embassy, Tehran, Iran, 70-74, US Ambassador, Niamey, Niger, 74- Mem: Himalaya Club; Delhi Golf Club; Diplomatic & Consular Officers, Retired. Honors & Awards: Mem of off deleg from US to the coronation of HM King Birendra of Nepal, 2/75. Legal Res: 3421 Northampton St NW Washington DC 20015 Mailing Add: Niamey-Via Air Pouch Dept of State Washington DC 20520

HECK, LORETTA JO (D)

b Spearfish, SDak, Sept 22, 48; d Clyde Lloyd Cooley & Carmen Septka C; m 1967 to John George Heck; c Jared & Jacqueline. Educ: Black Hills State Col, SDak, 66-69. Polit & Govt Pos: Vchmn, Campbell Co Dem Party, SDak, formerly. Mem: Jaycettes (secy, Herreid, SDak, 72-73). Honors & Awards: Scholarship, First Nat Bank of Black Hills, SDak, 67; Spokette Award, Herreid Jaycettes, 73. Relig: Methodist. Mailing Add: Box 321 Herreid SD 57632

HECK, WILFRED HENRY (D)

b Union, Conn, Feb 10, 27; s Albert Monroe Heck & Leila Willis H; m 1958 to Shirley Elaine Newton; c Elaine Irene & David Monroe. Educ: Windham Tech, 4 years. Polit & Govt Pos: Chmn, Union Dem Town Domt, Conn, formerly. Legal Res: Wales Rd Union CT 06076 Mailing Add: 86 Stickney Rd-Union Stafford Springs CT 06076

HECKARD, DONALD HARVEY (R)
Chmn, Cass Co Rep Party, Ind

b Logansport, Ind, June 19, 24; s John Harvey Heckard & Ruth Mae Grauel H; m 1974 to Bonnie Lou Raver; c Stephen Donald, Nancy Lynn & Thomas Nelson. Educ: Logansport High Sch, grad, 42. Polit & Govt Pos: Chmn, Second Dist Rep Party, Ind, 72-; chmn, Cass Co Rep Party, 74- Bus & Prof Pos: Farmer, Cass Co, Ind, 42-; salesman, Investors Diversified Serv, 66-; pres & owner, Logan City Ice, Inc, 74- Mem: Ind Voc Tech Col (bd trustees); Elks; Mason; Farm Bur; Pioneer Regional Sch Holding Corp (treas). Honors & Awards: Nat Honor Soc, 42; Sagamore of the Wabash, 74. Relig: Presbyterian. Legal Res: RR 1 Box 140B Logansport IN 46947 Mailing Add: PO Box 43 Logansport IN 46947

HECKARD, WILLIAM NORMAN (R)
Chmn, Martin Co Rep Party, Ind

b Bicknell, Ind, Feb 17, 22; s Darwin Manuel Heckard & Grace M McClure H; m 1947 to Delphia Doris; c Norman Wayne, William Malcolm, Grace Diane, Cathy Lynn, Ricky Lee & Darwin Ivan. Educ: Shoals High Sch, Ind, grad, 40. Polit & Govt Pos: Mem, Martin Co Selective Bd, Ind, 58-65; chmn, Halbert Twp Agr Stabilization & Conserv Comt, 65-66; chmn, Martin Co Rep Party, 68- Bus & Prof Pos: Timber dealer & farmer, 47- Mil Serv: Entered as A/S, Navy, 42, released as SSM-2/C, 45, after serving in Pac Seventh Fleet, 42-45. Mem: Mason; Shrine; Eastern Star; Moose; Elks. Relig: Methodist. Mailing Add: PO Box 36 Shoals IN 47581

HECKLER, MARGARET M (R)
US Rep, Mass

m 1953 to John M Heckler. Educ: Boston Col Law Sch; Albertus Magnus Col; US student rep, Univ Leiden, Holland. Hon Degrees: DHL, Northeastern Univ & Emmanuel Col; LLD, Stonehill Col, Regis Col & Albertus Magnus Col, 72. Polit & Govt Pos: Mem, Mass Gov Coun, 4 years; US Rep, Mass, 67-; deleg, Rep Nat Conv, 68 & 72. Bus & Prof Pos: Attorney-at-law. Mem: Women's Rep Club of Mass; Boston Bar Asn; Mass Trial Lawyers Asn; Am Bar Asn (comt govt legis & pub interest, Food, Drug & Cosmetic Law Div). Honors & Awards: Named an Outstanding Young Woman of Am, 65. Relig: Roman Catholic. Legal Res: 30 Colburn Rd Wellesley MA 02181 Mailing Add: 343 House Off Bldg Washington DC 20515

HECKMAN, CAREY EUGENE (R)

b Washington, DC, Mar 17, 54; s Jerome H Heckman & Margot Resh H; single. Educ: Dartmouth Col, 72-; Dartmouth Col Rep. Polit & Govt Pos: Intern, House Rep Conf, Research Comt, 71; chmn, Precinct 7-23, Montgomery Co, 71-72; alt deleg, Rep Nat Conv, 72; vpres, Dartmouth Young Rep, 73-74, comptroller, 74-75, pres, Dartmouth Col Rep, 75-; acting state chmn, NH Col Rep, 75- Bus & Prof Pos: Dir develop & legal affairs, WDCR, Hanover, NH, 74-75. Mem: Am Radio Relay League; Richard III Soc; assoc Nat Archives; BMW Car Club Am. Mailing Add: Hinman Box 2096 Hanover NH 03755

HECTOR, ROBERT C (D)
Fla State Rep

b Ft Lauderdale, Fla, Apr 16, 18; s Harry H Hector & Grace Kellerstrass H; m 1942 to Alice Guyton; c Elizabeth Bryan, Alice Guyton (Mrs Word), Robert C, Jr & Emily C. Educ: Princeton Univ, AB cum laude in Econ, 40; Charter Club; Triangle Club. Polit & Govt Pos: Fla State Rep, 104th Dist, 66-72, 114th Dist, 72- Bus & Prof Pos: Employee, Hector Supply Co, 40-42, vpres, 46-55, pres, 55-66, chmn bd, 66- Mil Serv: Entered as 2nd Lt, Army Res Artil, 42, released as Capt, 46, after serv in 415th Field Artil Group; Lt Col (Ret), Army Res, 62. Mem: Chief Exec Forum; Rotary; Orange Bowl Comt; Crippled Children's Soc. Honors & Awards: US Jr CofC Distinguished Serv Award, 52-53; Voted One of Five Outstanding Young Men in Fla, 53. Relig: Episcopal. Legal Res: 7830 Erwin Rd South Miami FL 33143 Mailing Add: 404 House Off Bldg Tallahassee FL 32304

HEDGES, GEORGANNE COMBS (R)

b Kansas City, Mo, Mar 14, 21; d Victor Rice Combs & Harriet Mahon C; m 1949 to Horace Smith Hedges; c Thomas Smith & Christopher Combs. Educ: Univ Mo-Columbia, 38-41; Delta Gamma. Polit & Govt Pos: Mem, Rep Nat Comt, Mo, 56-60; deleg & mem comt on arrangements, Rep Nat Conv, 60, alt deleg, 72; mem exec comt, Citizens Asn of Kansas City, Mo, 68-; co-chmn, Reelect the President Comt of Jackson Co, 72; mem bd, Elec Comnr of Kansas City, 73- Bus & Prof Pos: Secy & mem bd dirs, Benco Co, Cole Camp, Mo, currently. Publ: Ed, Young Rep Nat Fedn News, 52. Mem: Independence Jr Serv League; St Lukes Hosp Auxiliary. Relig: Episcopal. Mailing Add: 621 W 61st St Kansas City MO 64113

HEDLUND, EMERY E (D)
Idaho State Rep

Mailing Add: 1746 Main Ave St Maries ID 83861

HEDLUND, MARILOU (D)
Mem, Dem Nat Comt, Ill

Mailing Add: 930 W Castlewood Terr Chicago IL 60640

HEDRICK, CLAY E (R)

m to Florence L Greenway; c Clay E, John E & Georgianne (Mrs Robert A Mercer). Educ: Fairmont Col. Polit & Govt Pos: Mem bd educ, Newton, Kans, 45-46; mem, State Munic Acct Bd, 3 years; clerk, Harvey Co, 3 terms; Kans State Auditor, formerly. Bus & Prof Pos: Secy treas, Gen Distributing Co, Newton; Union Nat Bank. Mem: Lions; Mason; Kans Co Clerks Asn; Elks (past dist dep & past state treas). Relig: Episcopal; lay reader. Mailing Add: PO Box 205 Newton KS 67114

HEDRICK, RALPH (D)
Mo State Rep

Mailing Add: 308 E Olive Rich Hill MO 64779

HEEKE, DENNIS HENRY (D)
Ind State Rep

b Dubois, Ind, Sept 9, 27; s Theodore C Heeke & Clara Theising H; m 1950 to Leola Mae Schuler; c Terrence, Garret, Bruce & Brian. Educ: Dubois High Sch, 4 years. Polit & Govt Pos: Rep, Wabash Valley Interstate Compact, Ind; Ind State Rep, 65-, minority caucus chmn, Ind House of Rep, 73- Bus & Prof Pos: Farmer; poultryman. Mem: KofC; Dubois Community Club; Dubois Co Soil Conserv; Wabash Valley Asn; Ind State Poultry Asn. Relig: Catholic. Mailing Add: RR 2 Dubois IN 47527

HEER, LEO (D)
NC State Rep

Mailing Add: 718 W Farriss Ave High Point NC 27252

HEFFELFINGER, WILLIAM STEWART
Asst Secy Admin, Dept of Transportation

b Effingham, Kans, Jan 31, 25; s William Stewart Heffelfinger & Nora Estell H; m 1944 to Dorothy M Shockley; c William Stewart, III, Sharon A & Lee S. Polit & Govt Pos: Dir, Olney Facil, Fed Civil Defense Agency, 53-54, dir admin opers off, 55-56, asst adminr for gen admin, Exec Off of President, 58-62; reviewing off, Bd of Surv, 56-62; chmn bd, US Civil Serv Examr, 55-62; spec asst to asst secy water & power develop, Dept of Interior, 69; dep asst secy admin, Dept of Transportation, 69-70, asst secy admin, 70- Bus & Prof Pos: Secy & trustee, A J Rice Estates, 48-; dir prog rev, Martin-Marietta Corp, 62-69. Mil Serv: Army, 43-46. Mem: Am Soc Pub Admin; Am Legion; Mason. Honors & Awards: William A Jump Mem Found Meritorious Award, 60. Legal Res: 1708 Wolfram Ct McLean VA 22101 Mailing Add: Dept of Transportation 400 Seventh St SW Washington DC 20591

HEFFERNAN, GERALD JAMES (D)

b Derby, Conn, Apr 9, 39; s Harold James Heffernan & Marion Hogan H; m 1961 to Carol Ann Wailonis; c Kathleen, Marguerite & Laura. Educ: Fairfield Univ, BSS, 61. Polit & Govt Pos: Mem, Bd of Apportionement & Taxation, Ansonia, Conn, 65-; chmn, Ansonia Town Dem Comt, formerly. Bus & Prof Pos: Teacher, Ansonia Bd of Educ, Conn, 61-62; systs analyst, Avco Corp, Stratford, 62-63; field supvr, Travelers Ins Co, 63-67; vpres, Wm F Connelly, Jr Inc, 68- Mem: Elks. Relig: Roman Catholic. Mailing Add: 5 Byron Ave Ansonia CT 06401

HEFFERNAN, NATHAN STEWART (D)
Justice, Wis Supreme Court

b Frederic, Wis, Aug 6, 20; s Jesse Eugene Heffernan & Pearl Kaump H; m 1946 to Dorothy Hillemann; c Katie, Michael & Thomas. Educ: Univ Wis, BA, 42; Harvard Grad Sch Bus Admin, 43; Univ Wis Law Sch, LLB, 48; Phi Eta Sigma; Order of the Coif; Phi Delta Phi. Polit & Govt Pos: Admin asst to Gov of Wis, 48-49; asst dist attorney, Sheboygan Co, 51-53; city attorney, Sheboygan, 53-59; Dep Attorney Gen, Wis, 59-62; parliamentarian, Wis State Dem Conv, 60, chmn, 61 & 62; US Attorney, Dept of Justice, 62-64; justice, Wis Supreme Court, 64- Bus & Prof Pos: Assoc Schubring, Ryan, Peterson & Sutherland, Madison, Wis, 48-49; partner, Law Firm of Buchen & Heffernan, 50-62; lectr, Univ Wis Law Faculty, 60-64 & 70- Mil Serv: Entered as A/S, Navy, 42, released as Lt(sg), 46, after serv in ETO & Pac Theaters; Lt(Ret), Naval Res; ETO, Pac & Am Theater Ribbons; Naval Reserve & Victory Medals. Mem: Am Law Inst; Appellate Judges Seminar; Mil Order of World Wars; Am Legion; VFW. Relig: Congregational. Legal Res: 17 Veblen Place Madison WI 53705 Mailing Add: Wisconsin Supreme Court Madison WI 53702

HEFFNER, GEORGE E (D)
Md State Deleg
Mailing Add: 7921 Belair Rd Baltimore MD 21236

HEFLIN, CLARENCE H (D)
Mo State Rep
Mailing Add: 2311 Queen Ridge Dr Independence MO 64055

HEFLIN, HOWELL THOMAS (D)
Chief Justice, Ala Supreme Court
b Poulan, Ga, June 19, 21; s Marvin R Heflin & Louise Strudwick H; m 1952 to Elizabeth Ann Carmichael; c Tom. Educ: Birmingham Southern Col, BA; Univ Ala, JD. Polit & Govt Pos: Chmn, Ala Ethics Comn, formerly; chmn, Tuscumbia City Bd Educ, 10 years; pres, Ala Comt for Better Schs, formerly; chmn, Ala Teacher Tenure Comn, 5 years; chief justice, Ala Supreme Court, 71- Bus & Prof Pos: Law practice; mem faculty, Univ Ala & Florence State Univ. Mil Serv: Marine Corps, Pac, World War II, off-in-charge, Marine V-12 Unit, Purdue Univ; Silver Star Medal. Mem: Fel Int Acad Trial Lawyers; fel Am Col Trial Lawyers; fel Int Soc Barristers; fel Int Acad Law & Sci; Ala Bar Asn (past pres). Honors & Awards: First recipient of Daniel J Meador Award, Univ Ala Law Sch; Ala Citizen of the Year, Ala Cable TV Asn, 73. Relig: Methodist; Teacher, Men's Bible Class, First United Methodist Church, Tuscumbia, 15 years; former lay leader, Florence Dist. Mailing Add: Supreme Court of Alabama Montgomery AL 36101

HEFNER, W G (BILL) (D)
US Rep, NC
b Elora, Tenn, Apr 11, 30; s Emory J Hefner & Icie Holderfield H; m 1952 to Nancy Hill; c Stacye & Shelly. Educ: Univ Ala, Gadsden, 48. Polit & Govt Pos: Deleg, Dem Nat Mid-Term Conf, 74; US Rep, NC, 75-, mem, Interstate & Foreign Com Comt, subcomt on Health & Environ, Transportation & Com, mem, Vet Affairs Comt, subcomt on Hosp, Cemeteries & Burial Benefits, Compensation & Pension & Ins, 75- Bus & Prof Pos: Broadcast exec, Radio Sta WRKB, Kannapolis, NC; entertainer with Harvesters Quartet, 20 years. Mem: Cabarrus Co United Appeal (mem publicity comt); Odell PTA (pres); Cabarrus Co Humane Soc (bd dirs); Cabarrus Co Boys Club (bd dirs); Am Cancer Soc (bd, Cabarrus Co Chap). Relig: Baptist. Mailing Add: Rte 1 Concord NC 28025

HEHL, LAMBERT LAWRENCE, JR (D)
Mem Policy Comt, Ky State Dem Cent Exec Comt
b Newport, Ky, July 22, 24; s Lambert Lawrence Hehl, Sr & Martha Daly H; m 1946 to Helyn Mae Bathiany H; c Barbara Lynn & Susan Helyn. Educ: Salmon P Chase Col Com, 46-48, Col Law, 48-52; Kappa Xi Delta. Polit & Govt Pos: Dep tax comnr, Campbell Co, Ky, 53-56; city attorney, Crestview, 56-59; Ky State Sen, 59-63; deleg, Southern Regional Educ Bd, 61-63; comnr, Campbell Co Fiscal Court, 63-73; trustee & pres, NKy Area Planning Coun, 63-, deleg, 66-, pres, 70-71; dir, NKy Community Action Comt, 66; trustee & dir, Ohio-Ky-Ind Regional Auth, 66-; Fourth Cong Dist Committeeman, Ky State Dem Cent Comt, 68-, mem policy comt, 69-; Campbell Co Judge, 74- Bus & Prof Pos: Lawyer, 52- Mil Serv: Entered as Pvt, Marine Corps, 43, released as Sgt, 46, after serv in 3rd Island Command, FMF Pac; Asiatic Theater Ribbon. Mem: Campbell Co Jaycees; Am Legion; VFW; Newport Elks (presiding justice); KofC. Relig: Catholic. Mailing Add: 46 Madonna Dr Thomas KY 41075

HEIDE, RICHARD THOMAS (D)
Chmn, Tippecanoe Co Dem Party, Ind
b Lafayette, Ind, Feb 2, 31; s Richard Jacob Heide & Virginia Wells H; m 1958 to Evelyn Mae Thomas; c Richard Wayne. Educ: Purdue Univ, BS, 57; Indiana Univ Sch Law, DJ, 60. Polit & Govt Pos: Pres, Old Hickory Dem Club, Ind, 65-; city chmn, Lafayette, Ind, 66, corp counsel, currently; chmn, Tippecanoe Co Dem Party, Ind, 70- Bus & Prof Pos: Attorney-at-law, Lafayette, Ind, 60- Mil Serv: Navy, 51-55. Mem: Phi Delta Phi; Elks; Mason; Am Legion; Eagles. Relig: Church of Christ. Legal Res: 728 Cherokee Lafayette IN 47905 Mailing Add: 214 First Fed Bldg Lafayette IN 47902

HEIDE, WALTER JOHN (R)
Chmn, Smith Co Rep Cent Comt, Kans
b Harlan, Kans, Oct 31, 11; s Fredrick John Heide & Sallie DuVall H; m to Opal Pearl Grimes; c Robert Kay. Educ: Harlan High Sch, grad, 30. Polit & Govt Pos: Trustee, Harlan Twp, Kans, 41-47; dir, Harlan Sch Bd, 40-46; councilman, Smith Center City Coun, 57-63; chmn, Smith Co Rep Cent Comt, 67- Bus & Prof Pos: Pres, Heide-Christolear Inc, 59- Mem: Mason; Elks; Shrine; Smith Center Develop Asn. Relig: Methodist. Mailing Add: 114 W Third Smith Center KS 66967

HEIKENS, WARREN HENRY (D)
b Spencer, Iowa, Sept 27, 21; s William George Heikens & Martha Thompson H; m 1945 to Marjorie M Sommers; c Elsie Ellen (Mrs Philip Nelson), Martha Lea; Steven George & Alan Harry. Educ: Okoboji Consol High Sch, grad, 38. Polit & Govt Pos: Chmn, Clay Co Dem Party, Iowa, 57-63 & 70-74; dist storage supvr, US Dept of Agr, 63-69. Bus & Prof Pos: Farmer, 38-; crop-hail ins salesman, Nat Farmers Union, 62-; Sq Deal, 64-; Midwest Casualty & Surety Co, 69-; salesman & dealer, Heikens Bin Sales, 69- Mem: Moose; New Frontier Dem Party; Nat Farmers Union; Nat Farmers Orgn. Relig: United Methodist. Mailing Add: Rte 3 Box 72 Spencer IA 51301

HEIL, WALLACE LEE (D)
Mem Finance Comt & Exec Bd, Christian Co Dem Cent Comt, Ill
b Mt Vernon, Ill, June 6, 20; s Samuel Edward Heil & Ruby Louise Wallace H; m 1939 to Guinevere Barret Spillman; c Wallace Lee, Jr & Pamela. Polit & Govt Pos: Mem finance comt & exec bd, Christian Co Dem Cent Comt, Ill, currently. Bus & Prof Pos: Pres & mem bd dirs, Asn of Com, 62; past vpres, St Vincent Hosp Lay Bd, pres, 69-; area chmn, Ill Retail Merchants, currently. Mil Serv: Entered as Pvt, Army, 44, released as Pfc, 44, after serv in Co B, 23rd Armored Inf Bn, ETO; Victory Medal; European-African-MidETheater Ribbon with Three Bronze Battle Stars, Two Overseas Serv Bars; Good Conduct Medal; Purple Heart; Combat Inf Badge. Mem: Christian Co Shrine Club; Elks; VFW; Am Legion; Taylorville Jaycees. Relig: Methodist. Mailing Add: Lincoln Trail Taylorville IL 62568

HEILIG, GEORGE H, JR (D)
Va State Deleg
Mailing Add: Suite 15 Stoney Point 700 Newtown Rd Norfolk VA 23502

HEIN, RONALD REED (R)
Kans State Rep
b Seneca, Kans, Nov 7, 49; s H Allan Hein & Evelyn K Price H; m 1975 to Catherine Lee Fischer. Educ: Washburn Univ, AB, 71, JD, 74; Phi Alpha Delta; Phi Kappa Phi; Phi Delta Theta, mem alumni bd. Polit & Govt Pos: Kans State Rep, 75- Bus & Prof Pos: Exec dir, Assoc Students Kans, 73-74; asst city attorney, Topeka, 74- Mem: Am & Kans Bar Asns; Kans Trial Lawyers Asn. Mailing Add: 5230 W 20th Terr Apt 304 Topeka KS 66604

HEIN, SIDNEY S (R)
Mem, NY Rep State Comt
b New York, NY, Apr 16, 07; s Hugo Hein & Regina Pulitzer H; m 1937 to Frederica Elizabeth Clark; c Orrin M C & Holly Clark. Educ: St John's Univ, LLB, 28, LLM, 29. Polit & Govt Pos: Co-committeeman, Queens Co Rep Comt, NY, 28-; deleg, Rep State Conv, 32-; deleg, Judicial Conv, 32-; Rel chmn, 12th Assembly Dist, 48-51; deleg, Rep Nat Convs, 48-68; state committeeman, 19th & 12th Assembly Dist, 51-; mem, NY Rep State Comt, 62-; chmn, Queens Co Rep Comt, 68-72. Bus & Prof Pos: Partner, Hein, Bradie, Waters & Klein, Attorneys, 37-; dir, First Nat Bank of Inwood, 43-54; dir, Franklin Nat Bank, 61-; comnr, Port of NY Auth; dir, Am-Swiss Credit Corp. Mem: French Univ NY; Montauk Club; F&AM; Elks; Am Soc Legion Honor. Honors & Awards: Chevalier, French Legion Honor. Legal Res: 2518 Deerfield Rd Far Rockaway NY 11691 Mailing Add: 1600 Central Ave Far Rockaway NY 11691

HEINEMANN, DAVID JOHN (R)
Kans State Rep
b West Point, Nebr, July 18, 45; s Lester Otto Heinemann & Rita Charlotte LaNoue H; m 1972 to Kristine Stroberg. Educ: Augustana Col, BA in Polit Sci & German, cum laude, 67; Univ Kans, 67-68; Washburn Univ Law Sch, JD, 73. Polit & Govt Pos: Kans State Rep, 123rd Dist, 69-; alt deleg, Rep Nat Conv, 72; dep co attorney, Finney Co, 75- Bus & Prof Pos: Attorney-at-law. Mem: Phi Alpha Delta; Garden City Community Day Care Ctr (bd dirs, 69-72, vpres, 74-). Honors & Awards: Selected to participate in Eagleton Inst of Polit, Fifth Annual State Legislator Seminar for Outstanding State Legislators, 70. Relig: Lutheran. Mailing Add: PO Box 1346 Garden City KS 67846

HEINEMANN, JOHN G (D)
SC State Rep
Mailing Add: Georgetown SC 29440

HEINITZ, O J (LON) (R)
Minn State Rep
b Mountain Lake, Minn, Aug 27. 21; s Jacob D Hienitz & Mary Mieir H; m 1948 to Donna M Peterson; c Nancy, Barbara Ann & Thomas Jay. Educ: Univ Minn, BA. Polit & Govt Pos: Minn State Rep, 69- Bus & Prof Pos: Northwest CofC, Plymouth, Minn, 68- Mil Serv: Entered as Pvt, Army, 42, released as Maj, 65; after serv in ETO; Maj (Ret) Army Nat Guard; Bronze Star; Combat Infantry Badge. Mem: Golden Valley Health Ctr (vchmn bd gov); Health Central, Inc (bd gov); Lutheran Student Found Minn (treas); Lutheran Bd Missions Minn (secy). Relig: Lutheran. Mailing Add: 2555 Queensland Lane Wayzata MN 55391

HEINZ, HENRY JOHN, III (R)
US Rep, Pa
b Pittsburgh, Pa, Oct 23, 38; s Henry John Heinz & Joan Diehl H; m 1966 to Maria Teresa Thierstein Simoes-Ferreira; c Henry John, IV, Andre & Christopher. Educ: Yale Univ, BA, 60; Harvard Grad Sch Bus Admin, MBA, 63; Chi Psi. Polit & Govt Pos: Spec asst to US Sen Hugh Scott, Pa, 64; deleg, Rep Nat Conv, 68 & 72; chmn, Pa Rep Platform Comt, 70; US Rep, Pa, 71- Bus & Prof Pos: Mgt consult, pvt practice, 64-65; asst mgr profit planning, H J Heinz Co, 65, assoc mgr grocery prod mkt, 65-66, mgr, 66-68, gen prod mgr grocery mkt, 68-; lectr, Grad Sch Indust Admin, Carnegie-Mellon Univ, 70-71. Mil Serv: Entered as Airman Basic, Air Force, 63, released as Sgt, Air Force Res, 69, after serv in 911th Troop Carrier Group. Mem: Am Mgt Asn; Am Mkt Asn; Univ Pittsburgh (bd trustees); Childrens Hosp Pittsburgh (bd trustees). Relig: Episcopal. Legal Res: 1950 Squaw Run Rd Pittsburgh PA 15238 Mailing Add: 324 Cannon House Off Bldg Washington DC 20515

HEISKELL, EDGAR FRANK, III (R)
Secy of State, WVa
b Morgantown, WVa, Oct 10, 40; s Edgar Frank Heiskell, Jr & Barbara Baker H; m 1966 to Jerri Frances Deegan; c Christopher Neil & Edgar F, IV. Educ: WVa Univ, AB, 63; Univ Va Law Sch, LLB, 66; Phi Alpha Delta; Student Legal Forum. Polit & Govt Pos: Comnr in Chancery, 17th Judicial Circuit, 68-69; asst prosecuting attorney, Monongalia Co, WVa, 70-71; State Compensation Comnr, WVa, 71-73, Secy of State, 73- Bus & Prof Pos: Attorney, Morgantown, WVa, 66-67. Mil Serv: Entered as 2nd Lt, Air Force Res, 67, released as 1st Lt (Ret), 70, after serv in 146th Fighter Sq, Air Defense Command; Nat Defense Medal; Small Arms Expert. Mem: WVa State Bar; WVa Bar Asn; Nat Asn Secy of State; Am Fighter Pilots Asn. Relig: Presbyterian. Legal Res: 32 Lakeview Dr Morgantown WV 26505 Mailing Add: State Capitol Charleston WV 25305

HEISLER, LESLIE (D)
Chmn, Campbell Co Dem Party, SDak
b Mound City, SDak, Nov 27, 28; s Siegs Heisler & Maggie Schott H; m 1949 to Donna Seiler; c Pamela, Joe & John. Educ: Mound City Pub Schs, 9 years; Herreid Independent Schs, 3 years. Polit & Govt Pos: Committeeman, Fremont Dist Rep Party, SDak, 58-64; mem, Herreid Sch Bd, 64-70; chmn, Pollock-Herreid Irrigation Dist, 63-; adv, Campbell Co Neighborhood Youth Corps, 65; chmn, Campbell Co Dem Party, 65-; adv, Gov Comt Water & Irrigation, 67-; vchmn, Campbell Co Exten Bd, 68-; mem, Gov Comt on Children & Youth, 71. Bus & Prof Pos: Checker, Black Hills Depot, SDak, 50, foreman & supvr, 51; proj dir, Herreid Independent Sch Dist Neighborhood Youth Corps, 69-71. Mem: Moose; Jaycees (pres, 57); Herreid Community Club; Nat Farmers Orgn. Honors & Awards: Distinguished Serv Award, Herreid Jaycees. Relig: Baptist. Mailing Add: Herreid SD 57632

HEITMAN, BETTY GREEN (R)
Treas, Nat Fedn Rep Women
b Malvern, Ark, Nov 29, 29; d George Anderson Green & Inell Cooper G; m 1951 to Henry Schrader Heitman; c Donna Inell, Thomas Haile, Perry Schrader & Paul Anderson. Educ: Tex State Col for Women, BS in foods & nutrition, 49; Dietetic Internship, Charity Hosp, New Orleans, 49-50. Polit & Govt Pos: Vchmn, Sixth Cong Dist Rep Action Coun, 64-66; membership chmn, La Fedn Rep Women, 65-66, pres, 67-71; deleg, Rep Nat Conv, 68; vchmn campaigns, Nat Fedn Rep Women, 71, treas, 71-; mem, Rep State Cent Comt La, 72-; Rep Nat Committeewoman, La, currently. Bus & Prof Pos: Admin dietitian, Clarkson Hosp,

Omaha, Nebr, 51; pediatric dietitian, Charity Hosp, La, 53- Relig: Episcopal. Mailing Add: 655 Waverly Dr Baton Rouge LA 70806

HEITMAN, KATHRYN J (R)
Committeewoman, Vt Rep State Comt
b Weybridge, Vt, May 28, 02; m to Henry G Heitman, wid; c one son, two daughters. Educ: Plattsburg State Teachers Col. Polit & Govt Pos: Addison Co deleg chmn to Vt House of Rep; secy, Addison Co Exten Serv Adv Bd, Vt; mem, Addison Co Rep Comt; mem, Shoreham Town Rep Comt; clerk & dir, Shoreham Sch Bd; Vt State Rep, 63-74; committeewoman, Vt Rep State Comt, 74- Bus & Prof Pos: Teacher; secy; libr trustee. Mem: Homemakers Club; Women's Club; Eastern Star (Grand Warden, Vt chap); Addison Co Homemaker's Coun; Vt Homemaker's Coun (pres). Relig: Congregational. Mailing Add: Shoreham VT 05770

HELD, GERALD S (R)
Justice, State Supreme Court, NY
b New York, Dec 9, 32; s Albert Held & Rose Korman H; m 1958 to Carol E; c Jonathan Lawton, Rhonda Meryl & Lindsay Mason. Educ: Brooklyn Col, BA, Law Sch, LLB. Polit & Govt Pos: Alt deleg, Rep Nat Conv, 68, deleg, 72; leader, 45th Assembly Dist Rep Party, NY, currently; Justice, Supreme Court, Second Dist, NY, currently. Mil Serv: Entered as Pvt, Army, 54, released as Post Legal Adv, 55, after serv in 52nd AAA Brigade. Mem: VFW; Jewish War Vet; B'nai B'rith; Mason; KofP. Relig: Jewish. Legal Res: 2080 Ocean Ave Brooklyn NY 11230 Mailing Add: Supreme Court Bldg Brooklyn NY 11201

HELGENS, CHAR (R)
Committeeperson, Rep State Cent Comt Iowa
b Jones Co, Iowa, Aug 31, 34; d James Charles Alyea & Fern Leggett A; m 1955 to Galen John Helgens; c Katherine Jo & Lisa Jane. Educ: Anamosa High Sch, Iowa, grad, 51. Polit & Govt Pos: Committeewoman, Jones Co Rep Comt, Iowa, 68-70, co-chmn, 70-72; committeeperson, Rep State Cent Comt Iowa, 72- Mem: Iowa Womens Polit Caucus; Nat Appaloosa Horse Club; League Women Voters. Relig: Lutheran. Mailing Add: RR 2 Monticello IA 52310

HELGESON, DONALD KEITH (R)
Chmn, Manitowoc Co Rep Party, Wis
b Manitowoc, Wis, May 30, 32; s Gordon T Helgeson & Olivia Thompson H; m 1953 to Della Hansen; c Karin, Katherine & Constance. Educ: Univ Wis, BA; Alpha Gamma Rho. Polit & Govt Pos: Wis State Assemblyman, 69-72; chmn, Manitowoc Co Rep Party, 75- Mil Serv: Entered as Ens, Navy, 54, released as Lt(jg), 57, after serv in Pac Theatre, Lt Comdr, Res, 57-69. Mem: Elks. Relig: Protestant. Mailing Add: 937 N Fifth St Manitowoc WI 54220

HELGESON, KATHY PAULINE (D)
Chairperson, Winnebago Co Dem Comt, Iowa
b Garner, Iowa, May 27, 46; d Walter Garth Greiman & Dorothy Hartwig G; m 1966 to Robert Lon Helgeson; c Jason Harry. Educ: Univ Iowa, 64-66; Alpha Gamma Delta. Polit & Govt Pos: Dem precinct committeeperson, Lake Mills, Iowa, 72-; treas cent comt, Winnebago Co Dem Party, Iowa, 72-74, chairperson, 74- & chmn, Voter Identification Prog, 74- Bus & Prof Pos: Owner-mgr, Helgeson Furniture, Inc, Lake Mills, Iowa, 72- Mem: Nat & Iowa Women's Polit Caucus (treas, local orgn); Lake Mills CofC (mem & secy retail comt). Relig: Lutheran. Legal Res: 106 N Franklin Lake Mills IA 50450 Mailing Add: 113 N Mill Lake Mills IA 50450

HELLARD, VICTOR, JR (D)
Ky State Rep
b Versailles, Ky, Aug 16, 39; s Victor Hellard, Sr & Leona Tilghman H; m 1965 to Ellen Grayce Carpenter. Educ: Eastern Ky Univ, BA with distinction, 66; Univ Ky Col Law, JD, 68. Polit & Govt Pos: Pres, Woodford Co Young Dem, Versailles, Ky, 59-60; chmn, Sixth Cong Dist Young Dem, 60-61; secy, Eastern Ky Univ Young Dem, Richmond, 62-63; mem exec comt, Ky Young Dem, 64-71; mem, Ky Dem State Cent Comt, 68-72; chmn, Woodford Co Dem Party, 70-; Ky State Rep, 72-, mem, Appropriations & Revenue Comn, Elections & Const Amendments Comn, 71-, vchmn, Budget Rev Subcomt, 72-, chmn, Recreational Facilities Rev Comn, 73-, Ky Gen Assembly. Bus & Prof Pos: Partner, Law Firm of McCauley, Wilhoit & Elam, 69-70; partner, Law Firm of Rouse, Rouse & Hellard, 70- Mil Serv: Entered as E-1, Army Res, 57, released as E-5, 65, after serv in H/H 400th Regt, 100th Div, 57-65; Army Commendation Medal. Mem: Woodford Bar Asn (vpres, 72-73); Am Judicature Soc; Acad Polit Sci; Int Platform Asn; Woodford Co Fair Bd (pres, 73). Honors & Awards: One of the Ten Outstanding Young Dem, Ky Young Dem, 66; Outstanding Young Dem, Sixth Cong Dist Young Dem, 71; Outstanding Young Man, Woodford Co Jaycees, 72 & 73. Relig: Baptist. Mailing Add: 109 Woodford Village Dr Versailles KY 40383

HELLBAUM, HAROLD (R)
Wyo State Rep
b Wheatland, Wyo, Sept 26, 26; s Herman Hellbaum & Lydia Lust H; m 1950 to Margaret L Otis; c Rebecca, Holly, Robert & Bruce. Educ: Univ Wyo, 46-47; Sigma Nu. Polit & Govt Pos: Wyo State Rep, 62-, mem, Gov Agr Adv Comt, Med Assistance & Serv Adv Comt, Educ Comn State, Wyo Educ Coun, Gov Motor Pool Coun, Wyo State House of Rep; alt deleg, Rep Nat Conv, 64, deleg, 68; treas, Platte Co Rep Party, 66-; state chmn, Nixon Campaign, Wyo, 68. Bus & Prof Pos: Farmer, rancher & investments. Mem: Wyo Grain Feed-Seed Dealers Asn; Wyo Wheat Growers Asn; Lions; Farm Bur; State Stock Growers Asn. Relig: Protestant. Mailing Add: Box 55 Rte 1 Chugwater WY 82210

HELLER, JAN K (D)
Chairwoman, Mich Young Dem
b Mt Clemens, Mich, July 4, 51; d Walter J Pingel & Harriett Brown P; m 1972 to Roger L Heller. Educ: Macomb Co Community Col, 70-75. Polit & Govt Pos: Chairwoman, Macomb Co Young Dem, Mich, currently; chairwoman, Mich Young Dem, currently; exec secy, Macomb Co Dem Comt, currently; deleg, Dem Nat Mid-Term Conf, 74. Mem: Am Fedn State, Co & Munic Employees; Social Dem USA; Youth Comt Peace & Democracy in Mid East. Mailing Add: 38562 Capetown Ct Mt Clemens MI 48043

HELLER, MAX M (D)
Mayor, Greenville, SC
b Vienna, Austria, May 28, 19; s Israel Heller & Lea Hirsch H; m 1942 to Trude Schonthal; c Francie (Mrs Hurvitz), Susan (Mrs Moses) & Steven N. Educ: Real Gymnasium, Vienna, 4 years; Handels Bus Sch, 3 years. Polit & Govt Pos: Treas & finance chmn, Greenville Co Dem Party, SC, 66-68; deleg, Dem Nat Conv, 68, alt deleg, 72; city councilman, Greenville, SC, 69-71, mayor, 71- Bus & Prof Pos: Pres, Williamston Shirt Co, 45-48, Maxon Shirt Co, Greenville, SC, 48-68, Helco Inc, 57-68 & Trumax Inc, 57-; dir & co-founder, First Piedmont Bank & Trust, 68- Mem: CofC (chmn housing comt); Mason; City Club; Elks; Federated Jewish Charities. Relig: Jewish. Mailing Add: 36 Pinehurst Dr Greenville SC 29609

HELLER, WALTER WOLFGANG (D)
b Buffalo, NY, Aug 27, 15; s Ernst Heller & Gertrude Warmburg H; m 1938 to Emily Karen Johnson; c Walter P, Eric J & Kaaren Louise. Educ: Oberlin Col, BA, 35; Univ Wis, MA, 38, PhD, 41; Phi Beta Kappa; Beta Gamma Sigma; Alpha Kappa Psi. Hon Degrees: LLD, Oberlin Col, 64, Ripon Col, 67, Long Island Univ, 68, & Univ Wis, 69; LittD, Kenyon Col, 65; LHD, Coe Col, 67 & Loyola Univ, 70. Polit & Govt Pos: Fiscal economist & consult, Treas Dept, 42-53; chief internal finance, US Mil Govt, Ger, 47-48; consult, Comt for Econ Develop, 48-49, 54-57 & 66-; consult, UN, 52-60; consult, Minn Dept of Taxation, 55-60; tax adv, Gov, Minn, 55-60; consult, Nat Educ Asn, 58; chmn, Coun Econ Adv, 61-64; consult to Exec Off of the President, 65-69 & 74- Bus & Prof Pos: Assoc prof econ, Univ Minn, Minneapolis, 46-50, prof, 50-67, regents' prof, 67-, chmn dept, 57-61; mem bd dirs, Nat City Bank Minneapolis & Northwestern Nat Life Ins; commercial credit corporator, Int Multifoods; mem bd trustees, Oberlin Col. Publ: Co-auth, Monetary vs fiscal policy, W W Norton & Co, 69; auth, New Dimensions of Political Economy, Harvard Univ, 66; Economic growth & environmental quality: collision or co-existence?, Gen Learning Press, 73; plus others. Mem: Am Econ Asn (pres-elect, 73, pres, 74); Am Acad Arts & Sci; Nat Bur Econ Res; Fed City Club, DC; Joint Coun Econ Educ (dir, 71-). Honors & Awards: US Treas Distinguished Serv Award, 68; Outstanding Minnesotan, 73. Legal Res: 2203 Folwell St St Paul MN 55108 Mailing Add: Dept of Econ Univ of Minn Minneapolis MN 55455

HELLMAN, RUSSELL (D)
Mich State Rep
b Dollar Bay, Mich; m 1938 to Edith Kaarlela; c Kathleen, Gene & Nancy. Educ: High sch grad. Polit & Govt Pos: Former twp supvr, Mich; Mich State Rep, 60- Bus & Prof Pos: Mgr, Copper Country Fruit Growers, Inc. Mem: Mason. Relig: Lutheran. Mailing Add: Box 369 Dollar Bay MI 49922

HELLMUTH, JAMES GRANT (R)
Treas, NY Rep State Comt
b Washington, DC, July 31, 25; s William Frederick Hellmuth & Sybil Grant H; m to Daphne Preece; c James G, Jr & Timothy P. Educ: Yale, BS, 48; George Washington Univ Law Sch, LLB, 53. Polit & Govt Pos: Treas, Lefkowitz for Mayor, NY, 61, Lindsay for Mayor, 65, Rockefeller for Gov, 66 & 70 & Rockefeller for President, 68; treas, NY Rep State Comt, 66- Bus & Prof Pos: Vpres, Empire Trust Co, 60-67, Morgan Guaranty Trust Co of New York, 67-71 & Bankers Trust New York Corp, 71- Mil Serv: Entered as Pvt, Army, 43, released as 1st Lt, 46, after serv in Pac Theatre. Publ: Ed, Atomic Energy Law J, 60; auth, Modern Trust Forms, 65. Mem: Yale Club; Rockaway Hunt Club; Lawrence Beach Club. Legal Res: 1105 Park Ave New York NY 10028 Mailing Add: 280 Park Ave New York NY 10017

HELM, LEWIS MARSHALL (R)
Asst Secy Pub Affairs, Dept Health, Educ & Welfare
b Riverdale, Md, Sept 9, 31; s William Pickett Helm & Selma White Snider H; m 1953 to Alice Longworth Kupferman. Educ: Am Univ, AA, 56. Polit & Govt Pos: Nat information dir, Citizens for Nixon-Agnew, 68; asst to secy, Dept Interior, 69, dep asst secy for mineral resources, 69-72; asst secy pub affairs, Dept Health, Educ & Welfare, 73- Mil Serv: Entered as Pvt, Army, 50; Lt Col, Army Res, 74. Relig: Presbyterian. Mailing Add: 1110 Fidler Lane Silver Spring MD 20910

HELM, MARY ALNITA (R)
Okla State Sen
b Oklahoma City, Okla, Oct 27, 43; d Alvin R Bryan & Juanita Barnett B; div. Educ: Cent State Col, 61-64; Univ Ark, Fayetteville, BS, 66; Univ Ga, MS, 69. Polit & Govt Pos: Okla State Sen, Dist 46, 74- Bus & Prof Pos: Research asst, Dept Food Sci, Univ Ga, 67-69, electron microscopist, Dept Bot, 69-70; electron microscopist, Okla Med Research Found, 71-74. Mem: Electron Microscope Soc Am; Support Your Local Police Comt, Okla; John Birch Soc. Relig: Church of Christ. Mailing Add: 3201 NW 16 Oklahoma City OK 73107

HELMBRECHT, STEVEN H (D)
Mont State Rep
Mailing Add: Box 630 Havre MT 59501

HELMLY, ROBERT L (D)
SC State Rep
Mailing Add: Drawer 1194 Moncks Corner SC 29461

HELMS, JAMES MARVIN, JR (R)
Mem, Va State Rep Cent Comt
b Rock Hill, SC, Sept 4, 27; s James Marvin Helms & Almetta Moss H; m 1946 to Josephine Alice Goodman; c James Marvin, III & Kelly Elizabeth. Educ: Emory Univ, 44-45; Clemson Col, BS, 48; Univ Va, MA, 55, PhD, 62; Delta Tau Delta. Polit & Govt Pos: Organizer, Prince Edward Co Rep Party, Va, 64, co-committeeman, 64-; secy, Fourth Dist Rep Party, 64-70; organizer & adv, Longwood Col Young Rep Club, 64-; Va dir, Arts & Sci Div, Rep Nat Comt, 64-68; legis research, writing & pub rels work, US House of Rep, 66-68; campaign coordr for five counties, Nixon Campaign, 68; alt deleg, Rep Nat Conv, 68; mem, Va State Rep Cent Comt, 68-; Fourth Dist campaign coordr, Gubernatorial Campaign, Va, 69; Rep Cand for US Rep, Fourth Dist, Va, 70. Bus & Prof Pos: Mgr retail jewelry store with branches, 48-52; asst archivist, Alderman Libr Manuscripts Div, Univ Va, 53-54; prof hist, Longwood Col, 54-; mgr resort motel, summers 55-60; educ adv, Humphries Assocs, 66- Mem: Orgn of Am Historians; Va Soc Sci Asn; Asn for Preservation of Va Antiq. Relig: Methodist. Mailing Add: 412 Fourth Ave Farmville VA 23901

HELMS, JESSE (R)
US Sen, NC
b Monroe, NC, Oct 18, 21; m 1942 to Dorothy Jane Coble; c Jane (Mrs Charles R Knox), Nancy (Mrs John C Stuart) & Charles. Educ: Wingate Col; Wake Forest Col. Polit & Govt Pos: Admin asst, US Sen Willis Smith, 51-53; admin asst, US Sen Alton Lennon, 53; mem, Raleigh City Coun & chmn law & finance comt, 57-61; US Sen, NC, 72-, mem banking, housing & urban develop comt, mem agr & forestry comt & joint comt Cong opers, US Senate, 75- Bus & Prof Pos: Former city ed, Raleigh Times; exec vpres, WRAL-TV & Tobacco Radio Network, 60-72. Mil Serv: Navy, 42-45. Mem: NC Bankers Asn (exec dir, 53-60); Rotary (pres, Raleigh Club, 69-70); Mason (Grand Orator, Grand Lodge of Masons of NC, 64); NC Cerebral Palsy Hosp (bd dirs); Camp Willow Run (bd dirs). Honors & Awards: Two Freedoms

Found Awards; Annual Citizenship Awards, NC Am Legion, VFW & Raleigh Exchange Club. Relig: Baptist; Deacon & Sunday Sch Teacher, Hayes Barton Baptist Church, Raleigh. Legal Res: NC Mailing Add: Rm 5107 Senate Off Bldg Washington DC 20510

HELMS, WILLIAM J, JR (D)
Md State Deleg
b Anne Arundel Co, Md, Sept 3, 29; s William J Helms & Mary A Donnelly H; m 1952 to Marilyn Pinocher; c William, Karen, Lisa & LeRoy. Educ: Univ Va; Baltimore Inst. Polit & Govt Pos: Mem, Zoning Bd of Appeals, Md, 59-62; Md State Deleg, 62-; deleg, Dem Nat Conv, 68. Bus & Prof Pos: Ins broker, William Helms, Ins, 53- Mil Serv: Entered as Pvt, Air Force, 50, released as Cpl, 53. Mem: KofC; Elks. Relig: Roman Catholic. Mailing Add: 293 McKinsey Rd Severna Park MD 21146

HELSTOSKI, HENRY (D)
US Rep, NJ
b Wallington, NJ, Mar 21, 25; s Heronim Helstoski & Margaret Spiek H; m to Victoria Ubaldo; c Henry, Andrea & Renata. Educ: Paterson State Col; Montclair State Col, MA, 49. Polit & Govt Pos: Councilman, East Rutherford, NJ, 56, Mayor, 57-64; US Rep, NJ, 64-, mem ways & means comt, US House Rep, 74- Bus & Prof Pos: Teacher & high sch prin; supt of schs, 49-62; mgt consult, advert, 62-64. Mil Serv: Army Air Force, Control Nets Syst, 43-45. Mem: NJ Teachers Asn; Nat Educ Asn; NJ Teachers Vets Asn; active in many civic, fraternal, vet & prof orgn. Legal Res: 84 Cottage Pl East Rutherford NJ 07073 Mailing Add: 2331 Rayburn Bldg Washington DC 20515

HELTON, ARTHUR HENRY, JR (D)
Md State Sen
b Sword Creek, Va, Dec 18, 37; s Arthur Henry Helton, Sr & Alma Patrick H; m 1956 to Phyllis Brewer; c Connie, Kelly, Tracy & Art, III. Educ: Univ Baltimore, BS, 60; Harford Community Col; Butler Sch Mgt. Polit & Govt Pos: Treas, Harford Charter Home Rule, Md, 71-72; councilman, Second Dist, Harford Co Coun, 72-74; Md State Sen, Dist Six, 75- Bus & Prof Pos: Mgr, Western Auto Supply Co, 60-61; owner & mgr, Western Auto Stores, Perry Hall, Md, 61- & Aberdeen, 72- Mem: Md Jaycees; CofC; Moose; Elks; Harford Dem Club. Honors & Awards: Keyman Award, Md Jaycees, 70; Outstanding Young Men of Am, Jaycees, 70; Distinguished Serv Award, Jaycees, 71; Five Outstanding Young Men of Md Award, Md Jaycees, 72; Jaycee Int Sen, Md Jaycees, 74. Relig: Protestant. Mailing Add: 2003 Helton Ave Bel Air MD 21014

HELTON, JAMES CARTER (R)
Chmn, Bell Co Rep Exec Comt, Ky
b Pineville, Ky, May 16, 27; s James Skidmore Helton & Frances Kinningham H; m 1953 to Mary Cathern Napier; c Jimmy & Jeffery. Educ: Univ Ky, LLB, 50; Kappa Sigma; Phi Delta. Polit & Govt Pos: Chmn, Bell Co Rep Exec Comt, Ky, 64- Bus & Prof Pos: Chmn, Ky Mountain Theatre, Inc, 62-64. Mil Serv: Entered as A/S, Navy, 45, released as Pharmacist Mate 3/C, 46. Mem: Bell Co, Ky & Am Bar Asns; Middlesboro Country Club. Relig: Baptist. Legal Res: Sycamore St Pineville KY 40977 Mailing Add: Asher Bldg Pineville KY 40977

HEMBREE, GEORGE RAY (D)
Mem, Cherokee Co Exec Comt, Ga
b Dawsonville, Ga, Oct 17, 17; s William Alford Hembree (deceased) & Dorothy Irene Fouts H (deceased); m 1937 to Dicie Louise Pinyan; c Betty Louise (Mrs Roy Van Camp) & Shirley Catherine (Mrs Joseph Edwin Dowda). Polit & Govt Pos: Mem, Cherokee Co Exec Comt, Ga, 71-; mem, Ninth Dist Exec Comt, 71-; mem, Ga State Dem Exec Comt, formerly. Bus & Prof Pos: Owner, Hembredge Hills Subdiv & Rock Creek Estates Subdiv, currently; builder & developer; licensed real estate salesman. Mil Serv: World War II, Army & Air Force. Mem: Canton Masonic Lodge (Commandry); Mason (32 degree); Shrine; Atlanta Shrine Temple; Atlanta Ga Masonic Temple. Relig: Baptist. Mailing Add: Rte 6 Rock Creek Estates Canton GA 30114

HEMBREE, MARVIN H (D)
Chmn, Cedar Co Dem Comt, Mo
b Stockton, Mo, May 1, 20; s John A Hembree & Ethyl C Cheek H; m 1938 to Mary Lois Lean; c Ruth Ann (Mrs Billy J Frieze) & Ronald E. Educ: Stockton High Sch, Mo, grad, 37. Polit & Govt Pos: Auditor, Mo Dept Revenue, 65-72; chmn, Cedar Co Dem Comt, 74- Bus & Prof Pos: Farmer, Stockton, Mo, 37-; owner & operator drive-in theatres, 62- Mem: Mason; Nat Asn Theatre Owners; Mo Farmers Asn. Relig: Protestant. Legal Res: RFD 3 Stockton MO 65785 Mailing Add: PO Box V Stockton MO 65785

HEMENWAY, ROBERT BRUCE (R)
Chmn, Rep 16th House Dist of Alaska
b South Weymouth, Mass, Jan 28, 40; s William Andrew Mitchell & Constance Duncan Mitchell H (adopted by Floyd Norman Hemenway; m 1960 to Shirley Lorraine McFadden; c Robert Bruce, Jr, Ronald John, Sheri Lynn & Debbie Sue. Educ: Mass Radio & Tel Sch, Boston, Dipl, 57; various electronics sch & Rep Campaign Schs. Polit & Govt Pos: Rep campaign chmn, Tok Precinct, 16th House Dist, Alaska, 65-67, Delta Area chmn, Dr McKinley for US Sen, 66; Rep committeeman, Seventh Precinct, 16th House Dist, 67-; orgn chmn, Rep 16th House Dist, 67-68, chmn, 68-; alt deleg, Rep Nat Conv, 68. Bus & Prof Pos: Electronics field engr, RCA Serv Co, Cherry Hill, NJ, 61-62, electronics site rep, Murphy Dome, Alaska, 62-71, Pedro Dome, 71- Mil Serv: Entered as Airman, Air Force, 57, released as Airman 2/C, 61, after serv in Hq Bangor Air Defense Sector, Air Defense Command, 57-61; Res, 61-63; Good Conduct Medal. Mem: Tok Businessman's Asn (secy-treas); Jr CofC; Tok Rod & Gun Club (pres); IBEW; Golden Heart Toastmasters. Relig: Episcopal. Mailing Add: 128 Kantishna Way Fairbanks AK 99701

HEMENWAY, RUSSELL DOUGLAS (D)
Nat Dir, Nat Comt for an Effective Cong
b Leominster, Mass, Mar 24, 25; s Alan E Hemenway & Bessie Picard H; div; c Anne. Educ: Dartmouth Col, AB, 49; Inst d'Etudes Politiques, Paris, France, 49-50; Chi Phi. Polit & Govt Pos: Mem, US Foreign Serv, Paris, France & Athens, Greece, 50-53; dir, NY State Dept of Com for New York, 57-58; Dem campaign mgr, state & local off, 56-66; dep nat campaign mgr, Adlai E Stevenson, 60; deleg, Dem State & Nat Conv, 60-68; pres, Lexington Dem Club, New York, NY, 63-64; exec dir, NY Comt for Dem Voters, 64-66; nat dir, Nat Comt for an Effective Cong, 66- Bus & Prof Pos: Pres, Russell D Hemenway & Co, New York, NY 58-61, St Martins Develop Co, Inc, 61- & Mt Vernon Co Ltd, 69; trustee, Fleming Sch. Mil Serv: Entered as Seaman, Navy, 43, released as Qm 1/C, 46, after serv in USS Pittsburg, Pac Theatre. Publ: Cong Report, Nat Comt for an Effective Cong, four times yearly. Mem: Munic Arts Soc; Comt on Housing & Urban Develop, Commun Serv; Sierra Club; Wilderness Soc; Nat Capital Dem Club. Relig: Episcopal. Legal Res: 871 First Ave New York NY 10017 Mailing Add: 10 E 39th St New York NY 10016

HENDEL, PATRICIA THALL (D)
Conn State Rep
b New London, Conn, Jan 16, 32; d Morris Thall & Phyllis Cohen T; m 1951 to Seymour Loren Hendel; c Douglas, Clifford & Caroline. Educ: Barnard Col, AB, 53; Conn Col, MA, 68. Polit & Govt Pos: Conn State Rep, 75- Bus & Prof Pos: Dir summer & eve sessions, Conn Col, 71-75; vpres, Conn Asn Continuing Educ, 74-75, pres, 75-76. Mem: League Women Voters; Women's Polit Caucus; NOW; United Fund; Pub Libr (bd dirs). Relig: Hebrew. Mailing Add: 127 Parkway S New London CT 06320

HENDERSON, BILLY G (D)
b Spartenburg Co, SC, Apr 25, 34; s Gresham Henderson & Irene Crawley H; m 1952 to Mary Frances Long; c Daniel Elmer & Joseph Gresham. Educ: Equivalent to high sch & labor schs for eight years. Polit & Govt Pos: Deleg, Dem Nat Conv, 72. Bus & Prof Pos: Bus agent, United Brotherhood of Carpenters & Joiners of Am, 63-73. Relig: Baptist. Legal Res: 202 Pine St Varnville SC 29944 Mailing Add: PO Box 22 Varnville SC 29944

HENDERSON, CHARLES D (R)
NY State Assemblyman
b Beloit, Wis, Jan 1, 11; m 1939 to Carolyne Brown (deceased). Educ: Alfred Univ, BA, 36; Hon Degrees: LLD, Alfred Univ, 70. Polit & Govt Pos: NY State Assemblyman, 54-; chmn, Steuben Co Rep Party, NY, 68- Mil Serv: Nat Guard, 4 years. Mem: Grange; F&AM; Moose; Elks; Eagles. Relig: Episcopal. Mailing Add: 39 Church St Hornell NY 14843

HENDERSON, DANIEL J (D)
Mass State Rep
Mailing Add: State Capitol Boston MA 02133

HENDERSON, DAVID NEWTON (D)
US Rep, NC
b Hubert, NC, Apr 16, 21; s I N Henderson & Virginia Boney H; m to Mary Knowles; c David Bruce, Wiley Bryant & Wimbric Boney. Educ: Davidson Col, 3 years; Univ NC Law Sch, LLB, 49. Polit & Govt Pos: Asst gen counsel, Comt on Educ & Labor, US House Rep, 51-52; solicitor, Duplin Co Gen Court, NC, 54-58, judge, 58-60; US Rep, NC, 60-, mem, Pub Works Comt, Post Off & Civil Serv Comt & chmn, Subcomt Manpower & Civil Serv; ex officio, Dem Nat Mid-Term Conf, 74. Bus & Prof Pos: Attorney-at-law. Mil Serv: Entered as 2nd Lt, Air Corps, released as Maj, 46, after serv in India, China & Okinawa. Mem: Mason; Am Legion; VFW; Duplin Co Bar Asn; Lions. Relig: Presbyterian. Legal Res: Wallace NC 28466 Mailing Add: 235 Cannon House Off Bldg Washington DC 20515

HENDERSON, DONALD BLANTON (R)
Tex State Rep
b Houston, Tex, Aug 25, 49; s Donald Veitch Henderson & Marjorie Blanton H; single. Educ: Tulane Univ, 67-68; Univ Houston, BA in Polit Sci; Kappa Alpha Order. Polit & Govt Pos: Tex State Rep, 73- Bus & Prof Pos: Vpres, Cent Iron Works, Houston, Tex, 71-75. Relig: Episcopal. Legal Res: 4407 Langtry Houston TX 77041 Mailing Add: 6111 FM 1960 W Houston TX 77069

HENDERSON, DOUGLAS
US Rep to Inter-Am Comt for Alliance for Progress
b Newton, Mass, Oct 15, 14; s William Joseph Henderson & Nellie Kalloch H; m 1942 to Dorothy Frances Henderson (deceased); m 1970 to Marion Markle; c Peter, Bruce, Lee, Jennifer, Karen & Mark. Educ: Boston Univ Col Lib Arts, BS, 40; Fletcher Sch Law & Diplomacy, MA, 41; Phi Beta Kappa. Hon Degrees: DHL, Boston Univ, 69. Polit & Govt Pos: Career officer, US Dept of State Foreign Serv, 42-, vconsul, Nogales, Mex, Arica, Chile & Cochabamba, Bolivia, 42-47, Dept of Com, 47-50, consul, Bern, 50-56, asst chief, Econ Defense Div, 56-58, Sr Seminar in Foreign Policy, 59-60, counsr consul, Lima, 60-63, US Ambassador, Bolivia, 63-68, consult policy planning staff, 68-69, US Rep to Inter-Am Comt for Alliance for Progress, 69- Relig: Episcopal. Mailing Add: 2329 Nebraska Ave NW Washington DC 20016

HENDERSON, FRANCES (R)
b New York, NY; d Charles F Henderson & Mary Parker H; single. Educ: Barnard Col, BA, 37; George Washington Univ; Rutgers Law Sch, JD, 55. Polit & Govt Pos: Asst to chmn, Atomic Energy Comn, 47-49; mem, tech assistance staff, Int Bank for Reconstruction & Develop, 51-53; exec asst to US Sen Clifford P Case, NJ, 53-65, admin asst, 65- Bus & Prof Pos: Field secy, NY League of Women Voters, 38-40; research & assoc ed, Time Mag, New York, 41-45 & Washington correspondent, Washington, DC, 45-47; asst to pres, Fund for the Repub, New York, 53-54. Mem: Washington, DC Bar; Am & Fed Bar Asns; Am Newspaper Women's Club; Admin Asst & Secy Asn of US Senate. Mailing Add: Henderson Lane Indian Head MD 20640

HENDERSON, JAMES MARVIN (R)
b Atlanta, Ga, Mar 28, 21; s Isaac Harmon Henderson (deceased) & Ruth Ashley H (deceased); m 1945 to Donna Fern Baade; c Linda Dee, James Marvin, Jr & Deborah Fanchon. Educ: Furman Univ, 39-40; Clemson Col, 40-42; Univ NY Univ, 44; Univ Denver, BSC, 46; Harvard Univ, AMP, 56; Omicron Delta Kappa; Alpha Kappa. Polit & Govt Pos: Chmn, Eisenhower Campaign, Greenville Co, SC, 52; Spec Asst to the Postmaster Gen, 69-70; Rep Cand for Lt Gov, SC, 70; SC State chmn, comt for reelection of the President, 72; deleg, Rep Nat Conv, 72. Bus & Prof Pos: Sales supvr, Gen Foods Corp, NY, 42-44; acct exec, Curt Frieberger Advert Agency, Denver, Colo, 44-46; pres, Henderson Advert Agency, Greenville, SC, 46-69. Mil Serv: Entered as Pvt, Army, 42, released as Sgt, 43. Mem: Greenville Advert Coun; Am Asn Advert Agencies (chmn southeastern chap); Greenville Heart Asn (pres); Greenville Youth Comn; Chief Exec Forum. Honors & Awards: Young Man of the Year, 54; Silver Medal Award, Advert Fedn Am, 61; Salesman of the Year, 69. Relig: Methodist. Legal Res: Rte 7 Hickory Lane Greenville SC 29609 Mailing Add: PO Box 5308 Greenville SC 29696

HENDERSON, JAMES S (D)
Maine State Rep
Mailing Add: 323 Essex St Bangor ME 04401

HENDERSON, JOHN EARL (R)
b Crafton, Pa, Jan 4, 17; s William Clinton Henderson & Edna Vessels H; m 1943 to Wilma Maxine Gill; c James Clinton & Nancy Gill. Educ: Ohio Wesleyan Univ, AB, 39; Univ Mich, LLB, 42; Pi Sigma Alpha; Phi Mu Alpha; Phi Gamma Delta. Polit & Govt Pos: Ohio State Rep, 51-54; US Rep, Ohio, 55-60. Bus & Prof Pos: Attorney-at-law, 46- Mil Serv: Entered as Pvt, Army, 42, released as Capt, 46, after serv in 29th Div, 9th Army, ETO; Bronze Star; Army Commendation Medal; Combat Infantry Ribbon. Mem: Elks; Mason, Scottish Rite; Am Legion; Lions. Relig: Methodist. Legal Res: 1301 Foster Ave Cambridge OH 43725 Mailing Add: 126 N Ninth St Cambridge OH 43725

HENDERSON, MARY WARNER (R)
Councilwoman, Redwood City, Calif
b Fresno, Calif, Mar 26, 27; d Conrad Maupin Warner & Merle Allen W; m 1950 to Howard Randall Henderson; c Laura & Bruce Warner. Educ: Univ Calif, Berkeley, AB, 48; Delta Gamma. Polit & Govt Pos: Assoc mem, San Mateo Co Rep Cent Comt, Calif, 56-70, mem, 71-72; assoc mem, Calif Rep State Cent Comt, 62-68, mem 69-72; charter mem, Redwood City Rep Women Federated, 66-; city councilman, Redwood City, Calif, 66-, vmayor, 72-74, chmn legis comt, vchmn, Housing Concerns Comt & deleg, Asn Bay Area Govt, 66-, mem, Regional Govt Comt, 69-, mem adv group on govt orgn & performance, Calif State Legis Joint Comt on Seismic Safety, 69-74; community adv, Mid Peninsula Citizens for Fair Housing, 69-74; mem community adv comt, Jr League of Palo Alto, 69-74; mem bd dirs, San Mateo Co Rep Alliance, 69-74; mem adv bd, Calif Strong Seismic Motion Instrumentation Prog, 71-; mem, Gov Earthquake Coun, 71-; comnr, Bay Conserv & Develop Comn, 73-; mem, Attorney Gen Housing Task Force, 74- Mem: Nat League Cities (bd dirs & various comts); League Calif Cities (bd dirs & various comts); Calif Asn Women Hwy Safety Leaders; Calif Elected Women's Asn Educ & Research; Sierra Club. Relig: Episcopal. Mailing Add: 3098 Muller Ct Redwood City CA 94061

HENDERSON, OPAL MAE (D)
b Neosho Falls, Kans, Dec 2, 33; d Alex B McCullough & Neva Opal Stephens M; m 1953 to Clarence Wesley Henderson, Jr; c Terri L. Educ: Neosho Falls High Sch, Kans, grad, 51. Polit & Govt Pos: City clerk, Neosho Falls, Kans, 60-64; Dem committeewoman, Second Ward, Yates Ctr, 68-; vchmn, Woodson Co Dem Party, formerly. Bus & Prof Pos: Secy, J M Powell Ins Agency, Iola, Kans, 51-52; ins agent, Opal M Henderson Ins Agency, Neosho Falls, 63-68. Mem: Eastern Star; Womens Christian Soc. Relig: Methodist. Mailing Add: 305 E Madison Yates Center KS 66783

HENDERSON, PAUL (D)
b Sevierville, Tenn, Feb 15, 22; s Arthur Henderson & Josie Bryan H; m 1943 to Bonnie Parton; c Pauletta (Mrs Edwin Wey, Jr) & Carolyn Sue (Mrs David R Reed). Educ: Sevier Co High Sch, Sevierville, Tenn, 4 years. Polit & Govt Pos: Chmn, Sevier Co Elec Comn, Tenn, formerly; chmn, Sevier Co Dem Party, formerly; dir, Sevier Co Soil Conserv Serv, 73- Bus & Prof Pos: Farmer & real estate dealer, 43-61; dir, Sevierville Mutual Fire Ins, currently. Mem: Lions Club; Boosters Club; Farmers Livestock Asn; Farm Bur. Relig: Baptist. Mailing Add: Walnut Grove Rd Sevierville TN 37862

HENDERSON, RICHARD (R)
Hawaii State Sen
b Hilo, Hawaii, Dec 20, 28; s Walter Irving Henderson & Jean Park H; m 1950 to Eleanor Jones; c Richard, II, Catherine, Sandra & David. Educ: Wharton Sch Finance & Com, Univ Pa, BS in Econ, 50. Polit & Govt Pos: Hawaii State Sen, First Sen Dist, 70- Bus & Prof Pos: Dir, Hilo Elec Light Co, Ltd, Hawaii, 58-; CPA, Henderson, Henderson & Dobbins, Hilo, until 58; treas, The Realty Invest Co, Ltd, 58-63, exec vpres & treas, 63-68, pres & gen mgr, 68-; dir, Hawaiian Elec Co, Inc, Honolulu, 70-: pres & dir, Excelsior Dairy, Ltd, Realty Finance, Inc, Leilani Estates, Inc, Comtec, Inc & dir, Kapoho Land & Develop Co, currently. Mem: Am Inst Cert Pub Accts; Hawaii Soc Cert Pub Accts; YMCA (bd dirs); Kilauea Coun, Boy Scouts Am (bd dirs); Big Island Housing Found (pres & bd dirs). Relig: Protestant. Legal Res: 1101 Waianeunue Ave Hilo HI 96720 Mailing Add: PO Box 655 Hilo HI 96720

HENDERSON, ROBERT G (R)
Chmn, Cheboygan Co Rep Comt, Mich
b Detroit, Mich, Aug 5, 18; s Robert Henderson & Elizabeth Ambrose H; m 1938 to Patricia Haylor; c Barbara (Mrs Deeter) & Robert G, II. Educ: Univ Detroit, 48-50. Polit & Govt Pos: Training specialist, Vet Admin, 46-49; secy-treas, Cheboygan Recreation Comt, Mich, 57-68; chmn, Cheboygan Co Rep Comt, 64-; supvr, Cheboygan Co, 69-70; deleg, Rep Nat Conv, 72. Bus & Prof Pos: Owner-mgr, Royal Linen of Cheboygan Inc, 57- Mil Serv: Entered as Pvt, Army Air Force, 40, released as Chief Warrant Officer, 46, after serv in Flying Training Command, San Marcos, Tex. Mem: F&AM; Mason; Kiwanis; Am Legion; CofC (Mil Affairs Comt). Relig: Methodist. Mailing Add: 304 Riverside Dr Cheboygan MI 49721

HENDERSON, WALTER J (D)
Conn State Rep
Mailing Add: 43 Elm St Trumbull CT 06611

HENDERSON, WARREN S (R)
Fla State Sen
b Exeter, NH, Nov 14, 27; m to Polly Ann Schurr; c Warren C, Susan D & Wendy L. Educ: Denison Univ, BA, 51; Phi Delta Theta. Polit & Govt Pos: Mem, Sarasota Co Planning & Zoning Comn, Fla, 57-58; chmn, Sarasota Co Comn, 61-63; chmn, Manatee/Sarasota Airport Authority, 61-63; chmn, West Coast Inland Navig Dist, 62-63; Fla State Sen, currently, minority leader, Fla State Senate, 70-; deleg, Rep Nat Conv, 68 & 72; Rep State Committeeman, Fla, 70-73; mem, Fla Bicentennial Comn, 70- Bus & Prof Pos: Investments. Mil Serv: Navy, World War II. Mem: CofC (past pres); Elks (past Exalted Ruler); Mason. Relig: Presbyterian. Mailing Add: PO Box 1358 Venice FL 33595

HENDERSON, WILLIAM H (D)
b Salt Lake City, Utah, Nov 13, 08; s Evan B Henderson & Florence Jarman H; m to Dorothy M Hollberg; c W Ben & Robin G. Educ: Univ Utah, BS; Stanford Univ, LLB. Polit & Govt Pos: Law clerk, Sr Circuit Judge, US Circuit Court of Appeals, 35; chief, Claims & Leasing Secy, Div of Eng, Pac Div, War Dept, 44; chief, WCoast Antitrust Div, US Dept of Justice, 46; dep adminstr, Philippine Alliance Property Admin, 48-49; Dem cand for Attorney Gen of Utah, 60 & 62; deleg, Dem Nat Conv, 64; cand for US House Rep, 72; attorney, Fed Trade Comn, currently. Publ: Articles on antitrust law in Nebr Law Rev, Calif Law Rev & Fed Bar J; The race to Oligopoly, Duke Law J, 68. Mem: Fed Bar Asn; Businessmen's Alliance; Nat Lawyers Club; CofC. Relig: Latter-day Saint. Legal Res: 1837 Harvard Ave Salt Lake City UT 84108 Mailing Add: Suite 104 John Hancock Bldg 455 S Third East St Salt Lake City UT 84111

HENDREN, JAMES E (CHICK) (R)
Tenn State Rep
Mailing Add: 99th Rep Dist 4568 Parkwood Rd Memphis TN 38128

HENDREN, WILLIAM FOSTER (D)
b Indianapolis, Ind, Jan 14, 29; s William Foster Hendren & Fannie Williams H; m 1951 to Sue Ellen Flater; c William Mark & Tammy Ann. Educ: Ind Univ, Bloomington, BS, 51; Ind Univ Law Sch, JD, 61; Phi Kappa Psi; Phi Delta Phi. Polit & Govt Pos: Dep Ind Securities Comnr, 58-59, Ind Securities Comnr, 60; Chief Dep Ins Comnr, Ind, 61-64; precinct committeeman, Precinct Two, Bloomfield, 62-; chmn, Greene Co Dem Comt, formerly; dep presecuting attorney, 63rd Judicial Dist of Ind, 65-67, prosecuting attorney, 67-; city attorney, Linton & Jasonville, 66- Bus & Prof Pos: Vpres, H & H Motors, Inc, Ford dealership, Bloomfield, Ind, 51-58; secy-dir & counsel, United Presidential Life Ins Co, Kokomo, 64-; trustee & counsel, Founder Real Estate Investment Trust, Bloomfield, 67- Mil Serv: Entered as 2nd Lt, Army, 51, released as 1st Lt, 53, after serv in Inf, Korea; Lt Col, Ind Nat Guard, JAG, 60-; Combat Inf Badge; Korean Serv Badge. Publ: Municipal Cooperation, Ind Univ & Ind Dept of Com, 59; History of Bail & the Bondsman, Ind Univ & United Bonding Ins Co, 62. Mem: Am Legion; Elks; VFW; Mason; Shrine. Relig: Protestant. Mailing Add: 202 W Main Bloomfield IN 47424

HENDRICKS, B L, JR (D)
SC State Rep
Mailing Add: Box 612 Easley SC 29640

HENDRICKS, GARY LESTER (R)
Chmn, Perkins Co Rep Comt, SDak
b Hettinger, NDak, Mar 23, 38; s George Hendricks & Gladys Nelson H; m 1959 to Laureen Yvonne Murphy; c Jeffrey Alan, Lynette Yvonne & Michael Gary. Polit & Govt Pos: Chmn, Adams Co Young Rep, Hettinger, NDak, 62-63, state secy, NDak Young Rep, 62-63, Rep state fieldman, NDak Rep Party, 66, campaign coordr, 68, dir commun & research asst, 70-72, exec dir, formerly; chmn, Perkins Co Rep Comt, SDak, currently. Bus & Prof Pos: Co-ed, Adams Co Record, Hettinger, NDak, 56-64; secy, Hettinger Broadcasting Co, 58-68, news dir & advert mgr, KNDC Radio, 64, 65 & 67-, opers mgr, KBHB Radio, Sturgis, SDak, 69. Mem: Elks; Eagles; Toastmasters; Jaycees. Honors & Awards: Named Outstanding Young Man, Hettinger Jaycees, 64; Regional winner, Jaycee Speak-Up, 64 & 65. Mailing Add: RFD Hettinger ND 58639

HENDRICKS, JOHN HERBERT (D)
b Woodstock, Ill, Nov 19, 42; s Frank Douglas Hendricks, Sr & Elaine Jones H; single. Educ: San Jose State Univ, BA, 65, MA, 67; Delta Sigma Phi; Blue Key. Polit & Govt Pos: Asst admin analyst, Calif Legis, 69-70; admin asst, Calif State Sen A E Alquist, 70-73; campaign mgr, Camacho for Cong, 74; deleg, Dem Nat Mid-Term Conf, 74; field rep, US Sen John V Tunney, Calif, 75- Mil Serv: Entered as Ens, Naval Res, 67, released as Lt(jg), 69. Relig: Protestant. Legal Res: 324 Rio Del Mar Blvd Aptos CA 95003 Mailing Add: 1803 Laguna St San Francisco CA 94115

HENDRICKS, JOHN LYLE (R)
Wash State Rep
b Tacoma, Wash, Mar 3, 13; s John Lyle Hendricks & Maude Kershner H; m 1945 to Martha Virginia Kennemur; c Mary Virginia, Susan Kay (Mrs Brian Roesch), Carole Anne, Judith Lynn, Evelyne Lee, John Lyle, III, & James Raleigh. Educ: Univ Wash, BS in Pharm, 34. Polit & Govt Pos: Mem bd dirs, Olympia Sch Dist, 59-; Wash State Rep, currently. Bus & Prof Pos: Past pres, SW Wash Pharmaceutical Asn, Olympia Kiwanis Club & Wash Chap, Asn US Army. Mil Serv: Entered as Pharmacist Mate, Navy Res, 42, released as Chief Pharmacist Mate, 45, after serv in Pac Theatre of Opers; Pac Campaign Ribbons. Mem: Wash State Pharmaceutical Asn; F&AM (Past Master, Olympia Lodge 1, 64); Elks; Shrine. Relig: Episcopal; licensed lay reader. Mailing Add: 1923 Water St Olympia WA 98501

HENDRICKS, LEWIS S (R)
b New Salisbury, Ind, Sept 30, 19; s Solomon Charles Hendricks & Flora Temple H; m 1949 to Marguerite Macke; c Steven & John. Educ: Univ Iowa, BA, 41; Col Law, JD, 42; Beta Theta Pi; Phi Delta Phi. Polit & Govt Pos: Govt appeal agent, Calhoun Co Selective Serv, Iowa, 47-; co attorney, Calhoun Co, 49-55; mem, numerous dist & state conv comt & deleg, 49-; mem & attorney, Calhoun Co Hosp Comt, 58-; chmn, Calhoun Co Rep Cent Comt, 59-72; committeeman, Rockwell City Precinct, 62-66; mem, Rockwell City Zoning & Planning Comn, 67-; mem, State Platform Comt, 68-72, Presidential Elector, 72; alt deleg-at-lg, Nat Rep Conv, 68. Bus & Prof Pos: Attorney-at-law, L S Hendricks, 46-; dir & gen counsel, Nat Bank of Rockwell City, 52-; mem, 16th Dist Judicial Nominating Comn, 63-70; dir, North Cent Iowa Ment Health Asn, 64- Mil Serv: Entered as Aviation Cadet, Naval Air Corps, 42, released as Lt(jg), 46, after serv in Patrol Bombers, Atlantic & Pac, 43-46. Mem: Iowa State Bar Asn (bd gov, 72-); Rotary; Am Col & Probate Coun (fel); Iowa Acad Trial Lawyers; Am Legion. Relig: Methodist. Mailing Add: 110 E Main St Rockwell City IA 50579

HENDRICKS, MALVIN LEON, SR (R)
Committeeman, Pulaski Co Rep Party, Ark
b Magnolia, Ark, Jan 28, 21; s Clayton Hendricks & Maggie Easter H; m 1946 to Della Mae Graham; c Geneice H (Mrs Center), Barbara Ann, Malvin Leon, II & Michael Eugene. Educ: AM&N Col, BA, 60; Jackson Theol Sem, BD, 65; Sociol Club; Vet Club; Alumni Club. Polit & Govt Pos: Field coordr & asst mgr for Congressman Brock, Chattanooga, Tenn, 62; field coordr for Gov Rockefeller, Little Rock, Ark, 64; committeeman, Pulaski Co Rep Party, 65-; asst campaign mgr, State of Ark Minority Group, 66; originator of plans used by minority group, 66-; gov, Ark Coun Human Rels, 66-; mem, Ark State Screening Comt, 66-; gov, Ark Coun Human Resources, 66-; field coordr for Mr Ed Allison in a spec elec, 67; field coordr in voter's registr, nine co, 67-68; field coordr, Pulaski, Saline, Garland & Hot Spring Co, 68; Rep cand, Ark State Rep, Pulaski & Perry Co, Pos One, 68; deleg, Rep Nat Conv, 68, alt deleg, 72; mem, Ark State Rep Platform Comt, 68-; mem, Ark State Police Comn, 69- Bus & Prof Pos: Minister, Christian Methodist Episcopal Church, Little Rock, 47-, dist supt, 47- Mil Serv: Entered as Pvt, Air Force, 42, released as Sgt, 46, after serv in 805th Air Force Base; World War II Victory Ribbon; Good Conduct Medal; Am Theater Ribbon. Publ: TRI, Intercollegiate Press, 53. Mem: NAACP; Urban League; YMCA; F&AM (32 degree); Am League. Honors & Awards: Pastor of the Year, 62. Relig: Protestant. Mailing Add: 1311 W 15th St Little Rock AR 72202

HENDRICKS, ROBERT RYAN (BOB) (D)
Tex State Rep
b Farmersville, Tex, Oct 2, 25; s Roger Q Hendricks & Alma Moyers H; m 1946 to Oma Ruth Smith; c Stephen, Robert, Jr, Lisa & Lauri. Educ: Southern Methodist Univ, LLB, 51; Delta Theta Phi. Polit & Govt Pos: City attorney, Farmersville, Tex, 51-52; dist attorney, Collin Co, 53-55; Tex State Rep, Dist 24, 67- Mil Serv: Entered as Pvt, Air Force, 43, released as Cpl, after serv in Air Force, ATO, 43-46; S/Sgt, Army Res, Counter Intel, 50-52. Mem: Mason; Odd Fellows; Am Legion; CofC; Farm Bur. Relig: Methodist. Legal Res: 1706 N Waddill McKinney TX 75069 Mailing Add: 118 S Tennessee McKinney TX 75069

HENDRICKS, VIRGINIA ELLEN (R)
Mem, Mo Rep State Comt
b Stockton, Mo, June 1, 24; d Vernon Lee Lean & Alba Hornbeck L; m 1941 to Thomas Eugene Hendricks; c Larry Eugene & Stephen Lee. Educ: Stockton High Sch, Mo, grad, 41. Polit & Govt Pos: Mem, Mo Rep State Comt, 70-; mem, Bootheel Econ Develop Coun, 71-; bd mem, Status of Women for Mo, 74-; cong cand, Tenth Dist, 75. Bus & Prof Pos: Co-owner & operator, Stoddard Co Abstr Co, Mo, 53-73; co-owner & operator, Weber Abstr Land & Title Co, Bloomfield, 71-73. Mem: Monday Club Dexter; Am Legion Auxiliary; Soroptimist (secy). Relig: Christian. Mailing Add: 709 Fannetta St Dexter MO 63841

HENDRIX, B G (D)
Ark State Rep
b Jenny Lind, Ark, Dec 16, 22; s Bert Garrett Hendrix & Thelma H Dodson H; m 1945 to Janis Evans Williams; c William Daniel & Robin. Educ: Univ Tulsa, 1 year; Cent Col (Ark), 2 years. Polit & Govt Pos: Justice of Peace, Ft Smith, Ark, 4 years, Co Coroner, 4 years; Ark State Rep, 63- Mil Serv: Entered as Seaman 1/C, Coast Guard, 42, released as Seaman 1/C, 46, after serv in ETO & Asiatic Theatre, 42-46; several mil awards. Mem: Amvets (comdr, 47); Grotto Masonic Lodge (monarch, 60); Ft Smith CofC; VFW; United Commercial Travelers. Honors & Awards: Superior Citizens, Ft Smith, Ark. Relig: Methodist. Mailing Add: 2215 S 40th Ft Smith AR 72901

HENDRIX, OLEN (D)
Ark State Sen
Mailing Add: 841 E Main Prescott AR 71857

HENINGTON, C DAYLE (D)
b Bartlett, Tex, Mar 2, 31; s C W Henington & Ora Robbins H; single. Educ: Univ Nebr Omaha, BS, 63. Polit & Govt Pos: Admin asst to US Rep W R Poage, Tex, Washington, DC, 71- Mil Serv: Entered as Pvt, Air Force, 51, released as Maj, 71, after serv in 23rd Tactical Support Squadron, Southeast Asia, 66-67; Distinguished Flying Cross; Air Medal with Eight Oak Leaf Clusters; Vietnam Serv Medal. Mem: Mason; Shrine. Relig: Universalist. Legal Res: 1909 Forest Hills Dr Harker Heights TX 76541 Mailing Add: 2107 Rayburn House Off Bldg Washington DC 20515

HENKEL, LEE H, JR (R)
b Charleston, WVa, Sept 16, 28; s Lee H Henkel & Naomi Kathryn Neil H; m 1951 to Barbara Davidson; c Lee H, III, Barbara Lynette & Cathryn Carter. Educ: Duke Univ, AB, 49, Sch Law, LLB, JD, cum laude, 52; Order of the Coif; Phi Delta Phi; Sigma Chi. Polit & Govt Pos: Dep Chief Coun, Internal Revenue Serv, Washington, DC, 71, Chief Counsel, 72-73; Asst Gen Coun, Treas Dept, 72-73. Bus & Prof Pos: Sr mem, Swift, Page, Henkel & Chapman, Attorneys-at-law, Columbus, Ga, 52-71 & Henkel & Lamon, Atlanta, 73- Mem: Southern Fed Tax Inst (founder & first pres, 73-); Atlanta Lawyers Club; Columbus Lawyers Club, Ga; Columbus Rotary; Washington, DC Rotary. Honors & Awards: Comnr Award, Internal Revenue Serv, 73; Gen Coun Award, Treas Dept, 73, Secy of Treas Exceptional Serv Award, 73. Mailing Add: 3521 Northside Dr Atlanta GA 30305

HENKIN, DANIEL Z (D)
b Washington, DC, May 10, 23; m to Hannah Ronen; c Doron, Leora & Tamar. Educ: Univ Calif, grad. Polit & Govt Pos: Dir opers, Off of the Asst Secy of Defense for Pub Affairs, Dept of Defense, 65-67, Dep Asst Secy of Defense for Pub Affairs, 67-69, Acting Asst Secy of Defense for Pub Affairs, 69, Asst Secy of Defense for Pub Affairs, 69-73; vpres pub rels, Air Transport Asn, Washington, DC, 73- Bus & Prof Pos: Former staff mem, Buffalo Eve News, Washington, DC; mem staff, J of the Armed Forces, then the Army-Navy J, 41, asst ed & ed, 48-65. Mil Serv: Enlisted and serv as Coast Guard Combat Correspondent covering amphibious opers in the Pac Theatre, including D-Day landings at Saipan & the Philippines, World War II; released as Chief PO. Honors & Awards: Awarded Secy of Defense Meritorious Civilian Serv Medal, 65-69 & Exceptionally Meritorious Serv Award, 69-73. Mailing Add: 2306 Washington Ave Chevy Chase MD 20015

HENLEY, JOHN TANNERY (D)
NC State Sen
b Wadesboro, NC, Aug 10, 21; s Frank C Henley & Melissa Hamilton H; m 1943 to Rebecca Beddingfield; c John T, Jr, Robert Ray & Douglas Eugene. Educ: Univ NC, BS in Pharm, 43; Kappa Psi. Polit & Govt Pos: NC State Rep, 57-63; State Purchasing Officer, NC, 63-65; NC State Sen, 66- Mil Serv: Entered as Pvt, Army, 43, released as S/Sgt, 45, after serv in Europe; Bronze Star; Purple Heart. Mem: Bd of Sci & Technol, NC; NC Pharmaceut Asn; Mason; Kiwanis; Am Legion. Relig: Methodist. Mailing Add: 216 Lakeshore Dr Hope Mills NC 28348

HENLEY, LELAND (R)
b Marshall, Ark, July 10, 02; s Jackson Franklin Henley & Emma McBride H; m 1946 to Mary Ellen Ratchford. Educ: Little Rock Col, 1 year. Polit & Govt Pos: Chmn, Searcy Co Rep Cent Comt, Ark, 52-60 & 68-74; committeeman, Ark State Rep Party, 72-74. Bus & Prof Pos: Farmer & stockman, to 52; grocery owner, 52-57; owner & mgr, Searcy Co Creosoting Co, 57-68; retired. Mil Serv: Entered as Pfc, Army, released as Pfc, 18, after serv in Mil Police Hq Troops, Camp Pike, Little Rock, Ark, 4 months. Mem: Am Wood Preservers Asn; Farm Bur. Relig: Protestant. Mailing Add: St Joe AR 72675

HENNESSEY, J MARTIN (D)
Conn State Sen
Mailing Add: 40 Concord Circle Wethersfield CT 06109

HENNESSEY, MAURICE VINCENT (D)
Iowa State Rep
b Winthrop, Iowa, May 22, 27; s Maurice Hennessey & Ann Killeas H; single. Educ: High sch & some col through Col Level Exam Prog. Polit & Govt Pos: Mayor, Ryan, Iowa, 70-72; vchmn, Del Co Dem, Iowa, 72-73; Iowa State Rep, 73-, ranking mem com, mem ways & means, law enforcement & judiciary comts, Iowa House of Rep. Mil Serv: Entered as Pvt, Army, 52, released as Pfc, 53, after serv in 33rd Antiaircraft Artil Gun Bn. Mem: Ryan Lions (pres, 69-71); Am Legion. Relig: Roman Catholic. Legal Res: Box 116 Ryan IA 52330 Mailing Add: Box 116 Ryan IA 52330

HENNESSEY, WILLIAM J (D)
Maine State Rep
Mailing Add: Bath West Bath ME 04530

HENNESSY, FRANCIS XAVIER (D)
Chmn, Windsor Dem Town Comt, Conn
b New York, NY, Sept 11, 30; s Gervais Hennessy & Margaret O'Connor; m 1957 to Mary Frances Callery; c Maura, Mark, Matthew & Margaret Mary. Educ: Fordham Col, BSSS, 57; Univ Conn Sch Law, JD, 61; Student Govt Vet Club; French Club. Polit & Govt Pos: Chmn, Windsor Dem Town Comt, Conn, 66-; pres, Seventh Sen Dist Dem Orgn, currently; state comnr, Spec Revenue, Conn, currently. Bus & Prof Pos: Partner, Platt & Hennessy, Attorneys-at-law. Mil Serv: Entered as Pvt, Army, 51, released as Cpl, 53, after serv in 32nd Inf Regt, Seventh Div, Korea, 52; Purple Heart, Combat Infantrymans Badge; Good Conduct Medal; UN Medal; Korean Medal with two Battle Stars. Mem: Windsor Bar Asn (pres); KofC; Gtr Hartford Heart Asn; Conn Heart Asn (bd dirs); CofC. Relig: Roman Catholic. Legal Res: 37 Maple Ave Windsor CT 06095 Mailing Add: 45 Darwyn Dr Windsor CT 06095

HENRICKSON, GEORGE (R)
Chmn, Rep Party Hawaii
Mailing Add: Merchandise Mart Bldg Rm 438 Honolulu HI 96813

HENRIOD, FREDERIC HENRI (R)
Justice, Utah Supreme Court
b American Fork, Utah, Jan 26, 05; s Frederic Augustus Henriod & Melissa Greenwood H; m 1933 to Wilma Ellen Savage; c Richard Henri. Educ: Univ Utah, AB; Georgetown Univ, 1 year; Harvard Law Sch, LLB, 32; Sigma Nu Phi. Polit & Govt Pos: Pres, Young Rep Club, 38; chmn, Salt Lake Co Rep Party, Utah, 41-42; campaign mgr for Gov J Bracken Lee, 48; Justice, Utah Supreme Court, 51- Bus & Prof Pos: Utah State Bar Comnr, 8 years. Mil Serv: Entered as 2nd Lt, Air Corps, Intel Officer, 42, released as Capt, 45, after serv in Air Corps & Judge Adv Gen Dept, Africa, Sicily, Italy & Corsica, 43-45. Mem: Am Legion; VFW; DAV; Elks; Ft Douglas Club. Relig: Latter-day Saint. Mailing Add: State Capitol Salt Lake City UT 84114

HENRY, AARON EDD (D)
Chmn, Miss Dem Party
b Coahoma Co, Miss, July 2, 22; s Edd Henry & Mattie Logan H; m 1950 to Noelle Michael; c Rebecca. Educ: Xavier Univ La, BS, 50; Omega Psi Phi; pres student body, Xavier Univ, 50. Polit & Govt Pos: Deleg Dem Nat Conv, 68 & 72; chmn, Miss Dem Party, 68-; mem comt party reform, Nat Dem Party, 69; mem, Dem Nat Conv, currently; deleg, Dem Nat Mid-Term Conf, 74. Bus & Prof Pos: Secy, Miss State Pharmaceutical Soc, 54- Mil Serv: Entered as Pvt, Army, 43, released as S/Sgt, 46, after serv in Pac Theater, 45-46; Good Conduct Medal; pluses several Co & Bn awards. Mem: Nat Pharmaceutical Asn (pres, 63); Am Pharmaceutical Asn; Am Legion; Am Vet Comt; VFW. Honors & Awards: Rosa Parks Award, Southern Christian Leadership Conf; Outstanding Citizens Award, Office Econ Opportunity. Relig: Methodist. Legal Res: 636 Page St Clarksdale MS 38614 Mailing Add: 213 Fourth St Clarksdale MS 38614

HENRY, AILEE M (R)
Chmn, Jefferson Co Rep Cent Comt, Kans
b Oskaloosa, Kans, Sept 26, 03; d Charles E Decker & Monica Lowman D; m 1926 to R Glenn Henry; c Jane (Mrs Michner). Educ: Kans Univ; Gamma Phi Beta. Polit & Govt Pos: VChmn, Jefferson Co Rep Cent Comt, Kans, 45-66, chmn, 66-; state vchmn, Kans Rep State Comt, 55-59; mem, Kans Rep State Exec Comt, 55-65; vchmn, Rep Cong Dist, 59-65; deleg, Rep Nat Conv, 60, alt deleg, 64; dist dir, Women's Rep Clubs, 60-62; sponsor, Jefferson Co TAR Group, 68-; chaplain, Kans State Fedn Rep Women, 69-71; mem nat adv comt, White House Conf on Aging, currently. Bus & Prof Pos: Teacher, Jefferson Co Schs, 24-25; part-time asst to husband, R Glenn Henry, DDS, 28-33, 38- Mem: Am Legion Auxiliary; Eastern Star; Dent Auxiliary; Native Daughters of Kans; Kans Coun of Women. Honors & Awards: Award from Great Navy of Nebr, 62; Distinguished Jayhawker Award, 64; Outstanding Community Leader, 68; Estab First Hist Mus in Co. Relig: Presbyterian; Elder & Clerk of Session. Mailing Add: Oskaloosa KS 66066

HENRY, AL (D)
Wash State Sen
b Ness Co, Kans, Apr 12, 11; s Bert A Henry & Ethel Strobel H; m 1965 to Anne Boss Karr. Educ: Bus educ. Polit & Govt Pos: Wash State Rep, 41-57; mayor, White Salmon, Wash, 53-67; Wash State Sen, 57-, pres pro-tem, Wash State Senate, currently. Bus & Prof Pos: Admin asst, United Tel Syst, Hood River, Ore, 54- Mil Serv: World War II. Mem: Elks; Eagles. Mailing Add: Rio Vista White Salmon WA 98672

HENRY, CHARLES T (D)
Okla State Rep
b Norman, Okla, Apr 21, 36; s Thomas Henry & Alma Boully H; m 1960 to Audre L Garrett; c Charles Bradford, Thomas Dirk & Julie Gene't. Educ: ECent State Col, BA, 58; Univ Okla Law Sch, LLB & JD, 61; Phi Alpha Delta; Tau Kappa Epsilon. Polit & Govt Pos: Okla State Rep, 61-62, Okla State Rep, Dist 26, 72-; co judge, Pottawatomie Co, 62-66. Bus & Prof Pos: Sr partner, Henry, West & Sill, Attorneys-at-Law, 66- Mem: Okla Trial Lawyers Asn Legis Comt; Okla Bar Asn; Kiwanis; Jr CofC; March of Dimes. Honors & Awards: Distinguished Serv Award, Jr CofC, 63; Outstanding Young Man in Okla, 64. Relig: Baptist. Legal Res: 12 Turkey Knob Rd Shawnee OK 74801 Mailing Add: 232 N Broadway Shawnee OK 74801

HENRY, CLIFFORD, JR (R)
Tenn State Rep
Mailing Add: 20th Rep Dist 1202 S Heritage Dr Maryville TN 37801

HENRY, CONSTANCE FOSTER (R)
Chmn, Harvard Rep Town Comt, Mass
b Worcester, Mass, Aug 7, 26; d Howard S Foster & Mary Louise Forbes F; m 1947 to Malcolm C Henry; c Stephen M, Mark F & Susan F. Educ: Colby Jr Col, New London, NH, AA. Polit & Govt Pos: Vchmn, Harvard Rep Town Comt, Mass, 62-64, chmn, 64-; fel, 11th

Worcester Representative Rep Comt, 62-66 & 23rd Worcester Rep Representative Dist Comt; deleg, Mass State Rep Conv, 64, 66 & 70. Relig: Congregational. Mailing Add: Old Littleton Rd Harvard MA 01451

HENRY, DOUGLAS SELPH, JR (D)
Tenn State Sen
b Nashville, Tenn, May 18, 26; s Douglas Selph Henry & Kathryn Craig H; m 1950 to Loiette Hampton Hume; c Emily Olympe, Kathryn Craig, Loiette Hampton, Robert Selph, II, Mary Leland & Douglas Cornelius Hume. Educ: Vanderbilt Univ, AB, 49, LLB, 51; Eta Sigma Phi; Phi Sigma Iota; Phi Delta Theta. Polit & Govt Pos: Tenn State Rep, 79th Gen Assembly, 55-56; mem, Davidson Co Dem Primary Bd, Nashville, 57-58; Tenn State Sen, Davidson Co, 70- Bus & Prof Pos: Attorney-at-law, Hume, Howard, Davis & Boult, Nashville, Tenn, 51-55; asst counsel, Nat Life & Acct Ins Co, 56-70; attorney-at-law, Pvt Practice, 71- Mil Serv: Entered as Pvt, Army, 44, released as 1st Lt, 46, after serv in Armed Forces, Western Pac, 45-46. Publ: Legal problems in connection with the use of electronic equipment, Asn of Life Ins Counsel, 57. Mem: Tenn & Am Bar Asns; Asn Life Ins Counsel; Nat Soc State Legislators; Am Legion. Relig: Presbyterian. Legal Res: 408 Wilsonia Dr Nashville TN 37205 Mailing Add: 120 Capitol Hill Bldg Nashville TN 37219

HENRY, EDGERTON L (D)
La State Rep
b Jonesboro, La, Feb 10, 36; s Dallas E Henry & Ruby Lewis H; m 1958 to Frances Turner; c Patrick E & Lori Martiel. Educ: Baylor Univ, BA, 58; La State Univ, Baton Rouge, LLB, 61; Gamma Eta Gamma; Alpha Tau Omega; Circle K. Polit & Govt Pos: La State Rep, 68-, speaker, La House of Rep, 72-; alt deleg, Dem Nat Conv, 72; chmn, La Const Conv, 73. Bus & Prof Pos: Partner, Emmons & Henry Law Firm, Jonesboro, La, 61- Mem: Lions; Jaycees. Relig: Baptist. Mailing Add: Cecilia St Jonesboro LA 71521

HENRY, JOHN HUGH (D)
b El Dorado, Ark, Apr 29, 37; s John Marion Henry & Lois Thompson H; m 1967 to Mae Elizabeth Thompson; c Alexander & Katherine Louisa. Educ: Col William & Mary, 55-57; George Washington Univ, AB, 59; Columbia Univ, MA, 60. Polit & Govt Pos: Legis asst to US Rep David Pryor, Miss, 66-70, admin asst, 70-73; admin asst to US Rep David Bowen, Miss, 74- Relig: Episcopal. Legal Res: 6927 Southridge Dr McLean VA 22101 Mailing Add: 116 Cannon House Off Bldg Washington DC 20515

HENRY, JOHN RILEY (D)
Mem, Ark State Dem Party
b Black Oak, Ark, Nov 14, 41; s H S Henry & Mary Ellen Sealy H; m 1967 to Peggy Owens; c Gregory O & Laura Ann. Educ: Ark State Univ, BSE, 63; Univ Ark, JD, 67; Phi Alpha Delta. Polit & Govt Pos: Campaign coord, Bumpers for Gov, Poinsett Co, Ark, 70; mem, Ark State Dem Party, currently. Bus & Prof Pos: Supt, Jim Walter Corp, 63-65; partner, Tiner & Henry, 67-71; self employed, John R Henry, 71- Mil Serv: Entered as E-1, Army Nat Guard, 62, released as E-4, 69, after serv in 875th Engr Bn. Mem: Ark & Poinsett Co Bar Asns; Ark Cattlemans Asn; Mason. Relig: Church of Christ. Mailing Add: 214 Elm Harrisburg AR 72432

HENRY, MERTON GOODELL (R)
Mem, Maine Rep State Comt
b Hampden, Maine, Feb 4, 26; s Donald Merton Henry & Alda K Goodell H; m 1955 to Harriet Russell Putnam; c Donald P, Douglas M & Martha S. Educ: Bowdoin Col, AB, 50; George Washington Univ Law Sch, LLB, 55; Phi Beta Kappa; Alpha Delta Phi. Polit & Govt Pos: Asst to US Sen, Wash, DC, 53-58; mem, Sch Comt, Portland, Maine, 66-69; mem, Maine State, Cumberland Co, First Dist & Portland Rep Comts, currently. Bus & Prof Pos: Partner, Jensen, Baird, Chapman & Gardner, 59- Mil Serv: Entered as Pvt, Army, 44, released as M/Sgt, 46, after serv in 38th & 86th Div, Pac Theatre; entered as Lt, Army, 50, released as Lt, 53, after serv in Pentagon, Washington, DC, 50-53. Publ: History of Military Mobilization in the US Army 1775-1945, US Army, 53. Mem: Cumberland Co & Maine State, Bar Asns; Portland Club; Cumberland Club; Woodfords Club. Relig: Episcopal; Sr warden, Trinity Church, Portland, Maine; mem, standing comt & Diocesan Coun, Diocese of Maine. Mailing Add: 174 Prospect St Portland ME 04103

HENRY, MORRISS M (D)
Ark State Sen
Mailing Add: 1418 Hope St Fayetteville AR 72701

HENRY, PAUL BRENTWOOD (R)
Chmn, Kent Co Rep Party, Mich
b Chicago, Ill, July 9, 42; s Carl F H Henry & Helga Bender H; m 1965 to Karen Anne Borthistle; c Kara Elizabeth, Jordan Mark & Megan Anne. Educ: Wheaton Col (Ill), BA, 63; Duke Univ, MA, 68; PhD, 70. Polit & Govt Pos: Legis asst, Rep John B Anderson, 68-69; chmn, Kent Co Rep Party, Mich, 74- Bus & Prof Pos: Vol, US Peace Corps, 63-65; instr polit sci, Duke Univ, 69-70; assoc prof polit sci, Calvin Col, 70- Publ: Co-auth, The Dynamics of the American Political System, Dryden, 72; auth, Politics for Evangelicals, Judson, 74; auth, Evangelical Christianity & the radical left, In: The Cross & the Flag, Creation House Press, 73. Mem: Am & Midwest Polit Sci Asns. Mailing Add: 932 Joslin St SE Grand Rapids MI 49507

HENRY, ROSALIE E (D)
Committeewoman, Bottineau Co Dem Comt, NDak
b Westhope, NDak, June 12, 15; d Casper Jensen & Thora Sorenson J, III 1935 to Lyman D Henry; c Bette J (Mrs Leonard Lodoen); Robert D, Robyn L (Mrs Clyde Kerston) & Patricia L (Mrs Myron Lodoen). Educ: Westhope High Sch, grad. Polit & Govt Pos: Alt deleg, Dem Nat Conv, 72; committeewoman, Bottineau Co Dem Comt, NDak, currently. Mem: Homemaker's (pres, currently); Woman's Club (secy, 71-73); Women's Church Orgn. Honors & Awards: Hon membership to PTA Orgn, Newburg, NDak. Relig: Presbyterian. Mailing Add: 604 E Third St Westhope ND 58793

HENRY, WILLIAM KEITH (D)
Chmn, Scott Co Dem Party, Ky
b Georgetown, Ky, Sept 15, 17; s Dudley Davis Henry & Alice Sublett H; m 1963 to Sarah Tabb; c Mary Keith. Educ: Georgetown Col, AB, 41; Pi Kappa Alpha. Polit & Govt Pos: Ky State Rep, 62nd Dist, 50-68; chmn, Scott Co Young Dem Club, Ky, 52; alt deleg, Dem Nat Conf, 52 & 60; dist chmn, Sixth Cong Dist Young Dem, Ky, 54; deleg, Young Dem Nat Conv, 54, 56 & 58; asst & sgt at arms, Ky State Senate, 54 & 64; chmn, Scott Co Dem Party, 68- Bus & Prof Pos: Real estate bus & farmer, currently. Mil Serv: Serv in Army during World War II, 3 years. Mem: Rotary Int; Am Legion (comdr, Scott Co Post, 71-72); Scott Co Farm Bur (vpres, 71-73); 40 et 8; Int Order Odd Fellows (Noble Grand Knight, Golden Rule Lodge, 68-). Relig: Presbyterian; Deacon & Elder. Mailing Add: Rte 2 Georgetown KY 40324

HENSHAW, EDMUND LEE, JR (D)
Exec Dir, Dem Nat Cong Comt
b Bowling Green, Va, Dec 11, 25; s Edmund Lee Henshaw & Edna Earle Carter H; m 1950 to Barbara Louise Hanby; c Carol Lynne, Richard Edmund & Scott Frederick. Educ: Univ Md, BS, 54; George Washington Univ Law Sch, 55-56; Sigma Chi. Polit & Govt Pos: Research dir, Dem Nat Cong Comt, 55-72, Exec Dir, 72- Mil Serv: Army Air Force, 43-46. Publ: Co-ed, Who's Who in American Politics, Bowker Assocs, 67, 69, 71 & 73. Relig: Episcopal. Mailing Add: 9343 Sibelius Dr Vienna VA 22180

HENSLEE, FRANK BROOKS (D)
Ark State Rep
b Little Rock, Ark, Oct 7, 40; s F Brooks Henslee & Elsie Glover H; m 1965 to Hazel Ann Hardy. Educ: Pine Bluff High Sch, 54-58; Ark A&M Col, BSE, 61; Kappa Sigma Kappa; Theta Xi. Polit & Govt Pos: Jefferson Co deleg, Dem State Conv, 70-71; Ark State Rep, Dist 52, Grant & part of Jefferson Co, 71- Bus & Prof Pos: Part owner, Henslee Heights Furniture Co, 58-71; pres, Ark River Enterprises, Inc, 71. Publ: History of Cotton Belt Railroad, Pine Bluff News, 12/68. Mem: Coun of State Govt; Mason; Jaycees; Lions; Freshman Legislators Orgn of 68th Ark Gen Assembly (Farm Bur chmn). Relig: Baptist. Mailing Add: 6718 Dollarway Rd Pine Bluff AR 71601

HENSLER, CHARLES MORRIS (R)
Chmn, Jefferson Co Rep Party, Ind
b Jefferson Co, Ind, Dec 22, 24; s Joseph Morris Hensler & Clara Belle Davis H; m 1946 to Pauline Sams; c Robert Joseph & Deborah Anne. Educ: Hanover High Sch, grad, 42. Polit & Govt Pos: Deleg, Ind State Rep Conv, 60, 62, 64, 66 & 68; chmn, Jefferson Co Rep Party, Ind, 65-; deleg, Rep Nat Conv, 68. Bus & Prof Pos: Pres, Kreeger-Hensler, Inc, Hanover, Ind, 60- Mil Serv: Entered as Pvt, Army Air Force, 43, released as Pfc, 46, after serv in 806th Aviation Eng Bn, Pac Theatre, 44-46; Asiatic-Pac Theatre Ribbon with 2 Bronze Stars; Good Conduct Medal; Victory Medal. Mem: Mason; Scottish Rite; Shrine; Am Legion; Moose. Relig: Methodist. Mailing Add: Box 85 Hanover IN 47243

HENSLER, JANE ANN (R)
Secy, Saginaw Co Rep Comt, Mich
b Saginaw, Mich, June 7, 50; d Harold William Hensler & Geraldine Anna Bluhm H; single. Educ: Delta Col, Mich, AA, 70; Saginaw Valley Col, currently. Polit & Govt Pos: GOP girl, Saginaw Co Rep, Mich, 66-70; chmn, Delta Col Students for Milliken, 70; youth vchmn, Saginaw Co Rep Comt, 71-74, secy, 74-, app, Mich Rep Bicentennial Comt, mem exec comt, 71-; youth vchmn, Eighth Dist Rep Comt, 71-73; mem youth coun, Mich Rep, 71-; precinct deleg, Mich Rep Party, 71-; mem, Friend of Richard Nixon, 72-; deleg, Rep Youth Leadership Conv, 72; deleg, Rep Nat Conv, 72. Bus & Prof Pos: Ward Clerk, St Mary's Hosp, 70-; polit news reporter, The Valley Star, 72-73. Mem: Saginaw Co Rep Women's Club; Marv Herzog Polka Boosters; Save the Children Fedn. Relig: Lutheran. Mailing Add: Apt 4 506 N Webster Saginaw MI 48602

HENSLEY, HAL DARRELL (R)
Chmn, McMinn Co Rep Party, Tenn
b Monroe Co, Tenn, June 13, 34; s Dewey Hensley & Stella Elizabeth Ivens H; m 1953 to Mary Anne Studdard; c Kevin, Keith & Kelly. Educ: Hiwassee Col, 52-53. Polit & Govt Pos: Property assessor, McMinn Co, Tenn, 68-; chmn, Winfield Dunn Co Adv Comt, 70-74; chmn, McMinn Co Rep Party, 70- Mem: Meridan Sun Lodge 50; Tenn Asn Property Assessors. Relig: Presbyterian. Mailing Add: Rte 4 Athens TN 37303

HENSLEY, WILLIAM L IGAGRUK (D)
Alaska State Sen
b Kotzebue, Alaska, June 17, 41; s John Hensley, Sr & Priscilla H; m 1968 to April L Quisenberry; c Baker Quisenberry Kingukituk. Educ: Univ Alaska, 60-62 & grad work, 66; George Washington Univ, BA, 66; Univ NMex Sch Law, 67; Univ Calif, Los Angeles Sch Law, 69; Alpha Kappa Psi. Polit & Govt Pos: Alaska State Rep, 66-71, chmn, Health, Educ & Welfare Comt, Alaska House Rep, 68-71; mem bd for state land use, Bur Land Mgt, 67-; deleg, Dem Nat Conv, 68; mem, Nat Coun Indian Opportunity, 69-70; mem, Proj Necessities, Bur Indian Affairs, 69-70; chmn, Alaska Dem Party, 70; Alaska State Sen, 71- Bus & Prof Pos: Chmn bd, Alaska Village Elec Coop, 68- Mem: Am for Indian Opportunity; Alaska Fedn Natives; Northwest Alaska Native Asn (exec dir, currently). Honors & Awards: John F Kennedy Mem Award, Experiment in Int Living for trip to Russia & Poland. Mailing Add: 1053 W 20th Anchorage AK 99501

HENSON, GERALD L (R)
b Anna, Ill, Jan 21, 26; s Claude Ray Henson & Lorene Orrell H; m 1953 to Nina Jane Westburg; c Gerald L, Jr, Craig W & Mark R. Polit & Govt Pos: Press aide & admin asst, US Rep Durward G Hall, 69-73; admin asst, US Rep Gene Taylor, Mo, 73- Bus & Prof Pos: Announcer, WMAY, Paducah, Ky, 47-49, WSIV, Pekin, Ill, 49-51 & WMAY, Springfield, Ill, 51-52; production mgr, KRES, St Joseph, Mo, 52-53; studio supvr & promotion dir, KODE TV, Joplin, Mo, 53-69. Mil Serv: Entered as Pvt, Army, 44, released as Pfc, 45, after serv in 79th Inf Div, ETO, 45-46. Mailing Add: 4422 Medford Dr Annandale VA 22003

HENSON, JOHN L (D)
SC State Rep
Mailing Add: Box 760 Charleston SC 29401

HENSRUD, NEIL (R)
NDak State Rep
Mailing Add: State Capitol Bismarck ND 58501

HENTGES, RICHARD ANTHONY (R)
Mayor, Fargo, NDak
b Petersburg, NDak, July 22, 34; s Anthony Joseph Hentges & Lillian Lucille Phalen H; m 1959 to Lynn Graham; c David, Kathryn & Robert. Educ: Univ NDak, BS Bus Admin, 58; Alpha Tau Omega. Polit & Govt Pos: NDak State Rep, 68-74, mayor, Fargo, NDak, 74- Bus & Prof Pos: Pharmaceutical Sales, Roche Labs, Fargo, NDak, 58-66; real estate broker, Reed Investment, Fargo, NDak, 66- Mil Serv: Entered as Pvt, Army, 54, released as Pfc, 58, after serv in 2nd Army. Mem: Nat Asn Realtors; Nat Inst Real Estate Brokers; NCent Educ TV

(bd dirs); Elks; Am Legion; Eagles. Relig: Catholic. Mailing Add: 1601 S Tenth St Fargo ND 58702

HENTZEN, WILLIAM ROBERT (R)
b Milwaukee, Wis, Dec 5, 32; s Herbert D Hentzen, Sr & Marie Barry H; m 1957 to Nancy Anne Griffin; c William Robert, Jr, Elizabeth Anne & Susan Marie. Educ: Univ Wis, BBA, 54; Chi Psi. Polit & Govt Pos: Zone leader, North Shore Rep Club, Wis, formerly, precinct leader, 65, village chmn, 66, chmn, 67-68; chmn, Ninth Cong Dist Rep Party, Wis, formerly. Bus & Prof Pos: Salesman & secy, Wis Paint Mfg Co, 54-66; secy & vpres, Hentzen Chem Coatings, 66- Mem: Nat Paint & Coatings Asn; Wis Paint, Varnish & Lacquer Asn; Milwaukee & Nat 'W' Clubs; Univ Wis Alumni Asn. Relig: Roman Catholic. Mailing Add: 5235 N Diversey Blvd Milwaukee WI 53217

HEPFORD, H JOSEPH (R)
Pa State Rep
b Harrisburg, Pa, July 1, 24; s Ross Earl Hepford & Hilda Elizabeth Hassler H; m 1952 to Grace E Miller; c Diane Elizabeth & Marcia Elaine. Educ: Dickinson Col, 42-46, Sch Law, JD, 48; Phi Delta Theta. Polit & Govt Pos: Dir, Dauphin Co Young Rep, Pa, 49-51; Pa State Rep, 63-, Rep caucus secy, Pa House of Rep, 71-74. Bus & Prof Pos: Attorney-at-law. Mil Serv: Entered as Pvt, Air Corps, 42, released as 2nd Lt, 45. Mem: Am & Pa Bar Asns; Am Trial Lawyers Asn; Lions Int; Cent Pa Multiple Sclerosis Soc. Relig: Protestant. Mailing Add: Capitol Bldg Harrisburg PA 17120

HEPHNER, GERVASE A (D)
Wis State Rep
Mailing Add: RR 4 Box 287 Chilton WI 53014

HERBERT, DOROTHY FESS (R)
Committeewoman, Ohio Rep State Cent & Exec Comt
b Springfield, Ohio, June 12, 17; d Lehr Fess & Dorothy Davis F; m 1941 to Josiah T Herbert (deceased); c Jane Hall, Hannah Davis & Nancy Belle. Educ: Conn Col for Women, 34-35; Denison Univ, 35-36; Toledo Univ, BA, 38; Kappa Alpha Theta. Polit & Govt Pos: Pres, Maumee Women's Rep Club, 52-53; chairwoman, Lucas Co Rep Party, Ohio, 66-; vchmn, Lucas Co Rep Exec Comt, formerly, mem, currently; councilman, Maumee, 66-68; alt deleg, Rep Nat Conv, 68 & 72; mem, Bd of Elec Lucas Co, Ohio, 68-; committeewoman, Ohio Rep State Cent & Exec Comt, 68- Mem: Jr League, Toledo; Int Inst Gtr Toledo (bd of trustees); Maumee Valley Hist Soc; Toledo Bar Auxiliary; Zonta Club of Toledo (bd dirs, 71-73). Mailing Add: 228 E Broadway Maumee OH 43537

HERBST, LAWRENCE (R)
NY State Assemblyman
Mailing Add: 9 Leicht Pl Newburgh NY 12550

HERCHEK, JAMES CLAYTON (D)
Pres, NH Young Dem
b Malden, Mo, Jan 3, 54; s Robert Andrew Herchek & Geraldine Greiner H; single. Educ: Univ NH, currently; sen, Student Govt & trustee observer, Bd Trustees, 75- Polit & Govt Pos: Pres, NH Young Dem, 75-; vchmn, NH Dem State Exec Comt, 75- Mem: Nat Hist Soc; Friends of Theatre-by-the-Sea. Mailing Add: Split Rock Rd Exeter NH 03833

HERGENROEDER, HENRY ROBERT, JR (D)
Md State Deleg
b Baltimore, Md, Oct 26, 43; s Henry R Hergenroeder, Sr & Anna Reymann H; single. Educ: Univ Baltimore, BS, 67. Polit & Govt Pos: Md State Deleg, 69- Bus & Prof Pos: Commercial loan officer, Equitable Trust Co, Baltimore, 70- Mem: Am Red Cross; Boy Scouts; YMCA. Honors & Awards: McCormick Unsung Hero Award, Lacrosse & Earnest B Marx Mem Award in swimming. Relig: Roman Catholic. Mailing Add: Munsey Bldg Baltimore MD 21202

HERING, GEORGE C, III (R)
b 1930. Educ: Dickinson Col, 53; Dickinson Law Sch, 59. Polit & Govt Pos: Del State Rep, 67-72, Speaker, Del House of Rep, 67-70; alt deleg, Rep Nat Conv, 64, 68 & 72. Bus & Prof Pos: Attorney, Morris, James, Hitchens & Williams, 59-; dir & secy, Old Brandywine Village, Inc. Mil Serv: Army. Mem: Pres, Del Chap, UN Asn, 63; YMCA Camp Tockwogh (dir); Alumni Coun, Dickinson Col. Honors & Awards: Wilmington Jaycee Young Man of the Year, 65. Relig: Episcopal. Mailing Add: 1905 Field Rd Wilmington DE 19806

HERLEVI, MARTHA (D)
Mont State Rep
Mailing Add: Box 974 Red Lodge MT 59068

HERLONG, ALBERT SYDNEY, JR (D)
Mem, Securities & Exchange Comn
b Manistee, Ala, Feb 14, 09; s Albert Sydney Herlong & Cora Knight H; m 1930 to Mary Alice Youmans; c Mary Alice (Mrs Pattillo), Margaret (Mrs Mayfied), Dorothy (Mrs Hay) & Sydney (Mrs Johnson). Educ: Univ Fla, LLB, 30; Fla Blue Key; Omicron Delta Kappa; Phi Delta Phi; Pi Kappa Phi. Polit & Govt Pos: Acting postmaster, Leesburg, Fla, 35-36, city attorney, 47-48; Judge, Lake Co, Fla, 37-48; US Rep, Fla, 49-69; mem, Securities & Exchange Comn, 69- Bus & Prof Pos: Consult, Asn Southeast RR. Mil Serv: Capt, Army, 41. Mem: Mason (33 degree); Elks; Kiwanis; Moose; Odd Fellows. Relig: Methodist. Mailing Add: 1009 Shore Acres Dr Leesburg FL 32748

HERMAN, MARK B (D)
State VChmn, NY New Dem Coalition
b Brooklyn, NY, Mar 5, 33; s Nathan W Herman & Rebecca Rosenberg H; m 1957 to Ann Sara Presky; c Robert, Naomi, Michael & Lisa. Educ: Univ Conn, BA, 55; City Col New York, MBA, 60; founder, Beta Sigma Gamma. Polit & Govt Pos: Founder, Staten Island Dem Asn, NY, 61, mem exec comt, 64-, pres, 68; mem, Richmond Co Dem Comt, 61-; founding mem, Coalition for Dem Alternative, 67-; founding mem, New Dem Coalition, 69-; state vchmn, NY New Dem Coalition, 69-; alt deleg, Dem Nat Conv, 72. Bus & Prof Pos: Stock broker, Walston & Co, New York, NY; syst analyst, New York Off-Track Betting Corp, 71- Mil Serv: Entered as Cpl, Army, 55, released as Sgt, 57, after serv in Corps of Engrs, United Kingdom. Mem: Track & Field Comt, Metrop Amateur Athletic Union (various off, 63-). Honors & Awards: Official at track & field meets for past 15 years. Relig: Jewish. Mailing Add: 142 Oxford Pl Staten Island NY 10301

HERMAN, MARTIN A (D)
NJ State Assemblyman
Mailing Add: State House Trenton NJ 08625

HERMAN, RICHARD L (DICK) (R)
Rep Nat Committeeman, Nebr
b Fremont, Nebr, Aug 6, 20; s Mabel Williams Herman & father deceased; m 1941 to Margaret Martin; c Mary Catherine (Mrs Carl Bates), Richard Martin, Michael David & Anne Elizabeth. Educ: Univ Wash; Univ Nebr; Phi Delta Theta. Polit & Govt Pos: Chmn Douglas Co & metrop areas & asst to state chmn, Sen Carl T Curtis Campaign, 60; with sen campaign comts, Utah, Colo, SDak, Kans, Mo & Nebr, 60 & 62; co-chmn, Hruska Appreciation Dinner, 62; regional dir, Goldwater for President Comt, 64; deleg, Rep Nat Conv, 64 & vchmn comt on arrangements, 72; gen asst to campaign dir, Rep Nat Comt, 64, Rep Nat Committeeman, Nebr, 71-, mem exec comt, 73-; regional dir, Nixon for President, 68; mem staff, President-Elect Richard Nixon, 68-69; US comnr, Int Boundary Comn, US & Can, 69- Bus & Prof Pos: Chmn bd & treas, Herman Bros, Inc, Omaha, Nebr, currently. Mil Serv: Entered as 2nd Lt, Army, 42, released as Capt, 45, after serv in Western Task Force, Africa & 5th Army Hq, Africa & Italy. Mem: Nebr Motor Carriers Asn; Nebr State CofC; Nebr State Cancer Crusade. Relig: Catholic. Legal Res: 10324 Rockbrook Rd Omaha NE 68124 Mailing Add: PO Box 189 Omaha NE 68101

HERMANIES, JOHN HANS (R)
Chmn, Hamilton Co Rep Exec Comt, Ohio
b Cincinnati, Ohio, Aug 19, 22; s John Hermanies & Lucia Eckstein H; m 1953 to Dorothy Steinbrecher. Educ: Univ Cincinnati, 40-43; Pa State Univ, BA, 44; Univ Cincinnati Col Law, JD, 48; Phi Alpha Delta; Theta Chi. Polit & Govt Pos: Pres, Hamilton Co Young Rep Club, Ohio, 50-52; Asst Attorney Gen, Ohio, 51-57; chmn, Ohio League of Young Rep, 52; admin asst to Gov of Ohio, 57-58; pres, Hamilton Co Rep Club, 63-65; mem, Ohio State Bd of Bar Examr, 63-68; secy, Hamilton Co Rep Cent & Exec Comts, 65-74; vchmn, Hamilton Co Rep Policy Comt, 72-74; chmn, Hamilton Co Rep Exec Comt, 74- Bus & Prof Pos: Law firm partner, Beall, Hermanies & Bortz, 59-; trustee, Southwestern Ohio Regional Transit Authority, 73- Mil Serv: Entered as PFC, Marines, 43, released as Pvt 1/C, 45. Mem: Am Judicature Soc; Ohio State Bar Found; Am Trial Lawyers Asn; Cincinnati Lawyers Club; Ohio Acad Trial Lawyers. Relig: Protestant. Legal Res: 2110 Columbia Pkwy Cincinnati OH 45202 Mailing Add: 200 Dixie Terminal Bldg Cincinnati OH 45202

HERMANN, ALBERT BARTHOLOMEW (R)
b Milltown, NJ, Mar 28, 07; s Charles Joseph Hermann & Ida Jeanette Bosse H; m 1937 to Sylvia B Bernstein; c Ellen Barbara & Jo Ann. Educ: Colgate Univ, BS, 29; NY Univ Sch of Ins, 32; Skull & Scroll; Delta Upsilon; pres, graduating class. Polit & Govt Pos: Rep munic chmn, Milltown, NJ, 34-37; state pres, NJ Young Rep Fedn, 34-37; exec secy to Gov Harold G Hoffman & Clerk of NJ Court of Pardons, 35-38; admin asst to US Sen W Warren Barbour, NJ, 38-44; admin asst to US Sen H Alexander Smith, NJ, 44-49 & 52-55; exec dir, Polit Orgn, Rep Nat Comt, 49-52 & 57-61, campaign dir, 55-57, spec asst to chmn, 61-64, vchmn, 64-70, exec asst to chmn, 70-73. Bus & Prof Pos: Prof baseball in major & minor league for 9 years; pres, Berkshire Life Ins Co, 29-39 & Herman Baking Co, Milltown, NH, 31-35. Mem: JOUAM; Order of Redmen Lodge; Grange; Capitol Hill Club. Honors & Awards: Colgate Univ, All Am in Baseball & Basketball, won 11 letters in 3 sports; Lawrence Scholarship Prize for best student-athlete. Relig: Protestant. Mailing Add: 6900 Barrett Lane Bethesda MD 20014

HERMANN, ROBERT LAMBERT (R)
b Melrose, Mass, Oct 21, 25; s Frederick Hunt Hermann & Ida Lambert H; m 1946 to Kathleen McMullen; c Robert L, Jr & Karen Sue. Educ: Harvard Univ, ASTP, 43; Suffolk Univ, 46-49 & Law Sch, JDr, 53. Polit & Govt Pos: Pres & organizer, Gtr Lawrence Young Rep, Mass, 60-62; deleg, Rep State Conv, 62, 64, 66, 68 & 70; dir, Essex Club; county chmn for several statewide cand & officeholders; Asst Attorney Gen, formerly; chmn, North Andover Rep Town Comt, formerly. Bus & Prof Pos: Claim rep, Aetna Casualty & Surety Ins Co, 51-63; chmn & organizer, Gtr Lawrence Hwy Safety Comn, Mass, 60-; attorney-at-law, Lawrence, 53- Mil Serv: Entered as Pvt, Combat Intel Sch, Army Air Force, 43, released as Sgt, 46, after serv in India-China Theater; Asiatic-Pac Ribbon with 3 Stars; Presidential Unit Citation; China & Am Theater Ribbons; Victory & Good Conduct Ribbons. Mem: VFW; Lions; Grange; PTA; Boy Scouts. Honors & Awards: Chmn of Year Award, Jaycees, 60-61. Relig: Congregational. Mailing Add: 124 Hillside Rd North Andover MA 01845

HERMANN, SYLVIA (R)
Pres, Md Fedn Rep Women
b Newark, NJ; m 1937 to Ab Hermann; c Ellen (Mrs William Warfield) & Jo Ann. Educ: Barringer High Sch, Newark, NJ. Polit & Govt Pos: Pres, Rock Creek Women's Rep Club, Montgomery Co, Md, 51-53; campaign chmn, Nat Fedn Rep Women, 53-60, second vpres, 60-62; campaign chmn, Md Fedn Rep Women, 56-59, Washington Liaison, 59-63, state pres, 64-; polit educ chmn, Montgomery Co Fedn Rep Women, 62-64; vchmn, Md Rep State Cent Comt, formerly; deleg-at-lg, Rep Nat Conv, 68; dir vol, Md Comt Reelect of the President, 72; co-chmn vol comt, 1973 Inaugural Comt. Publ: (Campaign Manuals), Plan of Action for Precinct Womanpower, Operation Coffee Cup & Republican Roundtables. Mem: Am Newspaper Women's Club. Relig: Unitarian. Mailing Add: 6900 Barrett Lane Bethesda MD 20014

HERMANOWSKI, LEON F (D)
Conn State Rep
Mailing Add: 121 Smith St New Britain CT 06053

HERMELIN, WILLIAM MICHAEL (INDEPENDENT)
b New York, NY, July 28, 43; s Alfred Hermelin & Mildred Levine H. Educ: Colgate Univ, BA, 65; Univ Chicago Law Sch, 65-67; Washington Col Law, Am Univ, JD, 71; Pi Sigma Alpha; Tau Kappa Epsilon. Polit & Govt Pos: Legal asst, Off for Civil Rights, Dept Health, Educ & Welfare, Washington, DC, 67; legal asst, Off of Comnr of Educ, 68, admin dir, Reviewing Authority for Civil Rights, Off Secy of Health Educ, 68-71; admin asst, US Rep Tom Railsback, 19th Dist, Ill, 71- Mem: Ill State Soc; Nat Capitol Hill Club. Mailing Add: 309 Fourth St SE Washington DC 20003

HERNANDEZ, FRANK PATRICK (D)
b Galveston, Tex, June 18, 39; s Herculano Hernandez & Elida Vidaurri H; m 1960 to Jeanine Dishman; c Elida-Marie, Jeanine & J Frank. Educ: Tex A&M Univ, BA, 61; Southern Methodist Univ, LLB, 64; Phi Delta Phi. Polit & Govt Pos: Deleg, Dem Nat Mid-Term Conf,

74. Bus & Prof Pos: Pres, Hernandez, Inc, currently. Mem: State Bar Tex; Dallas Bar Asn; plus others. Relig: Unitarian. Mailing Add: 5318 Breakwood Dallas TX 75227

HERNANDEZ, JOE LUIS (D)
Tex State Rep
b Galveston, Tex, Nov 3, 33; s Jose Angel Hernandez & Preciliana Medina H; m to Clelia; c Deirdre Annette, Geraldine Holly, Joseph Anthony & Desiree Lorraine. Educ: Tulane Univ, 52-53; Univ Tex, Austin, BA, 56; St Mary's Law Sch, LLB, 63. Polit & Govt Pos: Tex State Rep, Dist 57-J, 73- Bus & Prof Pos: Attorney, Garcia, Hernandez & Campos, San Antonio, Tex, currently. Relig: Catholic. Legal Res: 2819 Depla San Antonio TX 78207 Mailing Add: 2400 Tower Life Bldg San Antonio TX 78205

HERNANDEZ, MARGARET MARIE (D)
b Pueblo, Colo, Mar 6, 31; d Augustine Munoz & Guadalupe Maciel M; m 1952 to Robert Lucas Hernandez; c Robert Michael, Randy Tomas, Roger Lucas, Russell Carlos & Rachelle Judene. Educ: Pueblo Jr Col, 63-64; Midwest Bus Col, Pueblo, 50-51; Epsilon Sigma Alpha. Polit & Govt Pos: Supvr, John Rosales for City Coun Hq, Pueblo, Colo, 64; coordr women's activities, State Rep Leo Locero, Dist 36 & 70; coordr women's activities, Amos Rivera for Co Coroner; elec judge, Dem Registr & Primary Elec, 72; alt deleg, Dem Nat Conv, 72; elected precinct committeewoman, Dist 5-B, Denver Dem Cent Comt, 72-, app finance chairwoman, 72-, exec mem, 73-, Dist 5-B Co-Capt, 73-; secy to state legis, Rep Dist Five, Denver, 73. Bus & Prof Pos: Licensed practical nurse, St Mary Corwin Hosp, Pueblo, Colo, 58-64; dep clerk, Co Assessor's Off, 64-68. Publ: December 1972 book review, El Conquistador, 12/72. Mem: Cameo Club (pres, secy, vchmn, treas & historian); Cheltenham Lay Adv Bd. Honors & Awards: Salutatorian, St Mary's High Sch, 49; Vol Serv, Adams Co Headstart, 72; Outstanding & Dedicated Serv, Adams Co Sch Dist 14, 72; Outstanding Parent Participation, Cheltenham Elem Sch, 72. Relig: Catholic. Mailing Add: 1586 Meade St Denver CO 80204

HERNANDEZ-COLON, RAFAEL (POPULAR DEM, PR)
Gov, PR
b Ponce, PR, Oct 24, 36; s Rafael Hernandez Matos & Dorinda Colon; m 1959 to Lila Mayoral; c Rafael, Jose Alfredo, Dora Mercedes & Juan Eugenio. Educ: Johns Hopkins Univ, AB, 56; Univ PR, LLB; Phi Beta Kappa; Phi Eta Mu. Hon Degrees: Johns Hopkins Univ & Cath Univ PR. Polit & Govt Pos: Assoc comnr pub serv, PR Pub Serv Comn, 60-62; attorney gen, PR Dept of Justice, 65-67; mem presidential comn, Popular Dem Party of PR, 68-; Dem Nat Committeeman, PR, 68-; sen & pres, PR Senate, 69-73; deleg, Dem Nat Conv, 72; Gov, PR, 73- Bus & Prof Pos: Partner, Hernandez Colon & Bauza, Law Off, 67-69. Publ: Manual of Civil Procedure, Equity, 69; The Commonwealth of Puerto Rico: territory or state, PR Bar Asn Law Rev, 59; plus others. Relig: Catholic. Legal Res: Calle Sol Ponce PR 00731 Mailing Add: La Fortaleza San Juan PR 00901

HERNANDEZ GONZALEZ, NEFTALI (POPULAR DEMOCRAT, PR)
Sen, PR Senate
Mailing Add: State Capitol San Juan PR 00901

HERNANDEZ SANCHEZ, JESUS MANUEL (NEW PROGRESSIVE, PR)
Sen, PR Senate
b Vega Baja, PR; s Santiago Hernandez & Delores Sanchez H; m to Laura Esther Santana; c Claribel, Amibal & Ariel. Educ: Univ PR, BSC, LLB & BBA; honor student; Phi Delta Gamma. Polit & Govt Pos: Vpres, New Progressive Party, PR, 68; Sen, PR Senate, 69- Bus & Prof Pos: Attorney-at-law. Mil Serv: Entered as 1st Lt, Army, 52, released, 55, after serv in 24th Inf Div, Korea; UN, Nat Defense & Korean Serv Medals; Repub of Korea Presidential Unit Citation; Commendation Ribbon with Pendant. Publ: Campus (poetry), Rumbos, Barcelona, 58. Mem: PR, Am & Interam Bar Asns; Int Platform Asn; San Juan Bd Realtors. Relig: Catholic. Mailing Add: St Ten 864 Montecarlo Rio Piedras PR 00924

HERNDON, JUDITH A (R)
WVa State Deleg
b Wheeling, WVa, July 5, 41; d Richard G Herndon & Virginia Holler H; single. Educ: Mary Washington Col, Univ Va, 59-61; Duke Univ, AB, 63; Northwestern Univ Sch Law, 64-65; WVa Univ Sch Law, JD, 67; Delta Delta Delta. Polit & Govt Pos: Price economist, US Dept Labor, 63-64; committeewoman, Ohio Co Rep Exec Comt, WVa, 68; WVa State Deleg, 70- Bus & Prof Pos: Partner, Herndon, Morton & Herndon Law Firm, 67- Mem: Ohio Co Bar Asn (bd dirs); WVa Bar Asn; WVa State Bar; Russell Nesbitt Sch Crippled Children (bd dirs); Legal Serv Ctr, Inc. Honors & Awards: Distinguished WVa Award. Relig: Roman Catholic. Mailing Add: 27 Elmwood Pl Wheeling WV 26003

HERNETT, GAIL H (R)
b Herman, Minn, Jan 9, 09; s Charles Hernett & Jennie Schram H; m 1936 to Juanita Junge; c Charles. Educ: Univ NDak, 28. Polit & Govt Pos: Alderman, Ashley, NDak, 46-50, mayor, 50-64; mem bd, NDak State Banking Bd, 51-58; NDak State Sen, 30th Dist, 55-72; mem, NDak State Budget Bd, 64; Rep dist chmn, 67-72; alt deleg, Rep Nat Conv, 68 & deleg, 72. Mem: Am Bankers Asn; NDak State CofC; Elks; Mason; Shrine. Relig: Lutheran. Mailing Add: Ashley ND 58413

HERR, GORDON (D)
Wash State Sen
b Seattle, Wash, 1926; m to Patricia; c five. Educ: Univ Wash. Polit & Govt Pos: Former Wash State Rep; Wash State Sen, currently. Bus & Prof Pos: Mfg & retail lumber bus. Mil Serv: Air Force, World War II. Mem: Elks; KofC; Am Legion. Relig: Catholic. Mailing Add: Suite 112 1818 Westlake N Seattle WA 98109

HERR, HELEN E (D)
Nev State Sen
Educ: NDak State Teacher's Col. Polit & Govt Pos: Secy, State Hwy Adv Bd, Nev; pres, Boulder Hwy Asn; chmn, Town Bd of Whitney; Nev State Assemblywoman, 4 terms; Nev State Sen, 67- Bus & Prof Pos: Real estate agent. Mem: Soroptimists. Mailing Add: 846 E Sahara Las Vegas NV 89104

HERREMA, LAVONNE JUNE (D)
Mem, Calif Dem State Cent Comt
b Chandler, Minn, June 3, 33; d Henry J Westerhof & Henrietta L Moret W; m 1952 to Gordon G Herrema; c Deborah Kay. Educ: Long Beach City Col, 1 semester; Cerritos Jr Col, 1 semester. Polit & Govt Pos: Mem, Calif Dem State Cent Comt, 68- Mem: Artesia Cerritos Lady Lions Club. Relig: Protestant. Mailing Add: 17910 Summer Ave Artesia CA 90701

HERREMA, ROBERT LOUIS (R)
b Rochester, NY, July 18, 39; s John Raymond Herrema & Helen Gara H; m 1966 to Joan Frances McKeever; c Jennifer & Amy. Educ: Rochester Inst Technol, AAS, 59; Marshall Univ, BA, psychol, 63; Univ Richmond, 64; George Washington Univ, 64-69; pres col fraternity & interfraternity coun. Polit & Govt Pos: Admin asst, US Rep Lowell P Weicker, Jr, Conn, 69-71. US Sen Lowell P Weicker, Jr, 71- Bus & Prof Pos: Draftsman, Satellite Prog, Naval Ord Div, Eastman Kodak Co, 57-58; research & develop technician, Kordite Corp, NY, 59-60; staff rep, Nat Hq, Sigma Phi Epsilon Richmond, Va, 63-64, asst dir chap serv, 64; personnel asst, George Washington Univ, 64-65, asst dir personnel, 65-69. Honors & Awards: Achievement medals for intercollegiate & amateur wrestling tournaments. Relig: Roman Catholic. Mailing Add: 10318 Democracy Lane Potomac MD 20854

HERRING, JAMES HAROLD, JR (R)
b Kinston, NC, Jan 4, 48; s James Harold Herring, Sr & Annie Sutton H; m 1972 to Beverly Susan Classon; c James Harold, III. Educ: Atlantic Christian Col, AB, 70; Sigma Pi. Polit & Govt Pos: Southern rep, Charles Edison Mem, 70; campaign dir, Bauman for NC State Senate, 70; Southern regional rep, Young Am for Freedom, 70-72; campaign dir, Helms for US Senate, NC, 72; admin asst, US Sen Jesse Helms, NC, 73-74. Bus & Prof Pos: Dir develop, Mt Olive Col, currently. Mem: Mt Olive Jaycees (secy, 75-); Kiwanis; Exchange Club; Rotary. Honors & Awards: Torch of Freedom Award, Young Am for Freedom, 70; Outstanding Sr Award, Sigma Pi, 70. Relig: Free Will Baptist. Legal Res: Rte 4 Box 205 LaGrange NC 28551 Mailing Add: Mt Olive Col PO Box 151 Mt Olive NC 28365

HERRING, ROBERT F (D)
Mem, Coweta Co Dem Exec Comt, Ga
b Newman, Ga, June 11, 11; s Robert Freeman Herring & Christine Arnold H; m to Hazel Lipscomb; c Robert F, III. Educ: Univ of the South; Kappa Alpha Order. Polit & Govt Pos: Registr, Coweta Co, Ga; mem, Coweta Co Dem Exec Comt, currently, chmn, formerly. Mil Serv: Pvt, Army. Mem: Civitan Club; Vet Club. Relig: Methodist Episcopal. Legal Res: 48 W Washington St Newnan GA 30263 Mailing Add: PO Box 792 Newnan GA 30263

HERRINGER, FRANK CASPER (R)
Adminr, Urban Mass Transportation Admin, Dept of Transportation
b New York, NY Nov 12, 42; s Casper F Herringer & Alice McMullen H; m 1968 to Nancy Lynn Blair; c William Laurence. Educ: Dartmouth Col, AB, 64, Amos Tuck Sch Bus Admin, MBA, 65; Phi Beta Kappa. Polit & Govt Pos: Staff asst to President, White House, 71-73; adminr, Urban Mass Transportation Admin, Dept of Transportation, 73- Bus & Prof Pos: Prin, Cresap, McCormick & Paget, Inc, New York, 65-71. Legal Res: 3333 Highland Lane Fairfax VA 22030 Mailing Add: 400 Seventh St SW Washington DC 20590

HERRMANN, KARL (D)
State Ins Comnr, Wash
b Granite Falls, Wash, Aug 24, 15; m to Beatrice; c four. Educ: Univ of Puget Sound; Wash State Univ; Gonzaga Univ, JD. Polit & Govt Pos: Former Wash State Sen; State Ins Comnr, Wash, 69 & 73- Mem: Wash State Bar Asn. Mailing Add: Box 195 Rte 2 Olympia WA 98503

HERRMANN, ROLAND ARTHUR (R)
b Carroll, Iowa, July 6, 30; s Rudolph Henry Herrmann & Louise Ida Paul H; m 1954 to Frances Mary Stoxen; c Mark Paul, Karen Jean & Paul John. Educ: Valparaiso Univ, BA & JD, 57; Phi Alpha Delta; Lambda Chi Alpha. Polit & Govt Pos: Asst state's attorney, McHenry Co, Ill, 59-66; city attorney, Harvard, 61-65; village attorney, McCullom Lake & Lakemoor, 63-66; attorney, McHenry Co Ment Health Bd, 68-; alt deleg, Rep Nat Conv, 72; asst pub defender, McHenry Co, 72- Mil Serv: Entered as Pvt, Army, 52, released as Cpl, 54, after serv in Hq Bn, Artil Div, US, 52-54; Cpl, Army Reserve; Nat Defense Serv Medal; Good Conduct Medal. Mem: Am Judicature Soc; Ill Defense Coun; McHenry Kiwanis Club; McHenry Jaycees; Am Legion. Relig: Lutheran. Mailing Add: 405 N Green St McHenry IL 60050

HERROLD, JOHN C (R)
Chmn, Fulton Co Rep Party, Ind
b Logansport, Inc, Apr 4, 34; s Carl M Herrold & Olive M Apt H; m 1954 to Nada C Willy; c Mick, Mark, Mindy & Michelle. Educ: Grass Creek High Sch, Ind, grad, 52. Polit & Govt Pos: Rep precinct committeeman, Wayne Twp, Ind, 12 years; chmn, Fulton Co Rep Party, currently. Bus & Prof Pos: Farmer. Mem: Eastern Star; Mason; Farm Bur. Relig: Methodist. Mailing Add: RR 2 Kewanna IN 46939

HERRON, JAMES HENRY (R)
b Junction, Tex, Dec 12, 41; s Jim Herron, Jr & Stella May Grobe H; m 1970 to Carroll Annette Harrell. Educ: Abilene Christian Col, BSE, 65. Polit & Govt Pos: Chmn, Frio Co Rep Party, Tex, 68-69 & 73-74. Bus & Prof Pos: Teacher, Pearsall Independent Sch Dist, 65-69 & 70-; Galveston Independent Sch Dist, 69-70; distributor, Amway Corp, Ada, Mich, 70. Mem: Tex State Teachers Asn; Tex Classroom Teachers Asn; Frio Co Hist Surv Comt. Relig: Church of Christ. Mailing Add: Box 754 Pearsall TX 78061

HERSCHLER, ED (D)
Gov, Wyo
b Kemmerer, Wyo, Oct 27, 18; s Edgar F Herschler & Charlotte Jenkins H; m 1944 to Kathleen Colter; c Kathleen (Mrs Hunt) & James C. Educ: Colo Univ, 36-41; Univ Wyo, LLB, 49; Sigma Phi Epsilon. Polit & Govt Pos: Co & prosecuting attorney, Lincoln Co, Wyo, 51-59; Wyo State Rep, 61-71; mem, State Parole Bd, 72-74; Gov, Wyo, 75- Mil Serv: Entered as Pvt, Marine Corps, 42, released as Platoon Sgt, 45, after serv in 3rd Raider Bn, SPac Theatre, 42-44; Purple Heart; Silver Star. Mem: Wyo State Bar Asn; Am Bar Asn; Int Soc Barristers; Am Judicature Soc; Am Legion. Relig: Episcopal. Legal Res: 823 Third W Ave Kemmerer WY 83101 Mailing Add: 300 E 21st St Cheyenne WY 82001

HERSETH, LORNA B (D)
Secy of State, SDak
b Columbia, SDak; m to Ralph Herseth; c Karen H (Mrs Wee), Constance (Mrs Stenseth) & Ralph Lars; seven grandchildren. Educ: Northern State Col. Polit & Govt Pos: Dep Co Supt Schs, 32-36, Co Supt Schs, 36-38; Secy of State, SDak, 72- Bus & Prof Pos: Former treas, Shelby Sch Bd. Mem: Easter Seal Soc Crippled Children & Adults (state dir, currently). Relig: Lutheran; Sunday Sch Supt, Trinity Lutheran Church. Mailing Add: Secy of State State Capitol Pierre SD 57501

HERSETH, RALPH LARS (D)
SDak State Rep
Mailing Add: Houghton SD 57449

HERSHBERGER, H M (MIKE) (R)
Alaska State Rep
Mailing Add: 2906 Will Rogers Pl Anchorage AK 99503

HERSHEY, LEWIS BLAINE
b Jamestown Twp, Ind, Sept 12, 93; s Latta Freleigh Hershey & Rosetta Richardson H; m 1917 to Ellen Dygert; c Kathryn Elizabeth (Mrs A Alvis Layne, Jr), Gilbert Richardson, George Frederick & Ellen Margaret (Mrs Sam Lewis Barth). Educ: Tri-State Col, BS, 12, BPD & AB, 14; Ind Univ, 17; Field Artil Sch of Fire, war course, 18 & 23; Command & Gen Staff Col, 33; Army War Col, grad, 34; Univ Hawaii, 35; Omicron Delta Kappa; Phi Beta Kappa. Polit & Govt Pos: Dep sheriff, Steuben Co, Ind, 13-17; secy & exec officer, Army-Navy Selective Serv Comt, 36-40; dep dir, Selective Serv Syst, 40-41, dir, 41-47 & 48-70, dir, Off of Selective Serv Records, 47-48; Adv to the President on Manpower Mobilization, 70-73. Bus & Prof Pos: Teacher country sch, Jamestown Twp, Steuben Co, Ind, 10-11; prin, Flint Pub Sch, 14-16; asst prof mil sci & tactics, Ohio State Univ, 23-27. Mil Serv: Serv successively as Pvt, Cpl, Sgt, 2nd Lt & 1st Lt, Ind Nat Guard, 11-16, Platoon Comdr, Co B, Third Ind Inf, 11-16; Entered as 1st Lt, Army, 16, serv as Bn Adj, Battery Exec Regt Adj, Third Ind Inf & 137th Field Artil, 16-18, Troop Movement Officer, Brest, France, 18-19, Battery Comdr, Regt Supply Officer, Tenth Field Artil, 19-22, Battery Comdr, Bn Exec & Bn Commanding Officer, 82nd Field Artil, 27-31; asst chief of staff, Hawaiian Dept, 34-36, & mem, War Dept Gen Staff, 27-31; Distinguished Serv Medals from Army, Navy & Dept of Defense; Mex Border Medal; World War I Victory Medal with Serv Clasp (France); Am Defense Serv Medal; Am Campaign Medal; World War II Victory Medal; Nat Defense Serv Medal with Oak Leaf Cluster; app Gen, 69- Gen (Ret), 73. Publ: Off to College, Huntington Col, 69; Selective Service, 69 & Military Draft, 69, World Publ Co. Mem: Life mem, Am Legion; VFW; Mason; Army, Navy & Air Force Vet in Can (pres, US Unit, 53-); ROA (hon pres, 69-). Honors & Awards: Spec Award, Freedoms Found; Scouter of the Year Award, Nat Capital Area Coun, Boy Scouts Am, 68; Presidential Gold Medal for outstanding serv to the Army, Asn US Army; Caleb B Smith Masonic Award, Ind & Gold Medal for 50 years as a Mason; Serv to Mankind Award, Sertoma Club of Washington, 68; plus numerous other awards. Legal Res: Angola IN Mailing Add: 5500 Lambeth Rd Bethesda MD 20014

HERSOM, LYLE E (R)
b Groveton, NH, Aug 9, 28; s Edwin W Hersom & Ethel Thompkins H; m 1949 to Ruth L McFarland. Educ: Groveton High Sch, grad, 48. Polit & Govt Pos: NH State Rep, Groveton, 57-59; sch moderator, Groveton, 57-73, town moderator, 57-73, sch bd mem, 69-70; Rep comnr & secy, NH State Racing Comn, 60-64; alt deleg, Rep Nat Conv, 72. Bus & Prof Pos: Salesman, Mainco Sch Supply, 60- Mil Serv: Entered as Pvt, Army, 52, released as Sgt, 54, after serv in Ord Corps. Mem: F&AM; North Star Lodge of Perfection; Wash Coun, Princes of Jerusalem (16 degree); Rose Croix (18 degree); NH Consistory (32 degree). Relig: Methodist. Mailing Add: 1 Preble Groveton NH 13582

HERTEL, DENNIS M (D)
Mich State Rep
Mailing Add: 5951 Whittier Detroit MI 48224

HERTEL, JOHN C (D)
US Sen, Mich
Mailing Add: 20705 Woodside Harper Woods MI 48225

HERTZ, KARL H (D)
Chmn, Clark Co Dem Exec & Cent Comt, Ohio
b Medicine Hat, Alta, Apr 9, 17; s Ernst Gottlieb Hertz & Adele Fischer H; m 1947 to Barbara M Shephard; c Paul Richard & Judith Ann. Educ: Capital Univ, BA, 37; Brown Univ, MA, 38; Lutheran Theol Sem Columbus, cert, 42; Univ Chicago, PhD, 48. Polit & Govt Pos: Mem, Clark Co Dem Exec & Cent Comt, Ohio 62-, chmn, 71-; mem city comn & mem regional planning comn, Model Cities Task Force, Springfield, 64-67. Bus & Prof Pos: Instr, Capital Univ, 38-42, assoc prof sociol, 48-53; from assoc prof to prof sociol, Wittenberg Univ, 53-67, prof church & society, Hanna Sch Theol, 67- Mil Serv: Entered as Pvt, Army, 42, released as Tech 3, 45, after serv in 120th Evacuation Hosp, ETO, 44-45; Two Battle Stars. Publ: Everyman a Priest, Fortress, 60; auth, The nature of voluntary association, In: Voluntary Association, Knox, 66; auth, Politics is a Way of Helping People, Augsburg, 74. Mem: Am Sociol Asn; Soc Sci Study Relig; Inst Relig in Age of Sci; Asn Voluntary Action Scholars. Relig: Lutheran. Mailing Add: 619 Faculty Court Springfield OH 45504

HERTZBERG, STUART E (D)
Dem Nat Committeeman, Mich
b Detroit, Mich, Nov 24, 26; s Barney Hertzberg & Rae Horowitz H; m 1950 to Marilyn Jean Cohen; c Cathy Lee, Robert Steven & John David. Educ: Univ Mich, BA, 50, JD with distinction, 51. Polit & Govt Pos: Deleg-at-lg, Dem Nat Conv, 60, 64, 68 & 72; finance dir, Mich State Dem Cent Comt, 63-66, treas, 66-75; Dem Nat Committeeman, Mich, 75- Bus & Prof Pos: Mem bd gov, Commercial Law League Am, 69-75, pres, 73-74; vpres, Narcotics Addiction Rehabilitation Coord Orgn (NARCO), 69-72, mem bd, 69-; chmn, Attorneys Sect Allied Jewish Campaign, 72 & 73; mem bd, Jewish Voc Serv, 69-, vpres, 73- Mil Serv: Entered as Pvt, Army, 45, released as Sgt, 46, after serv in Hq Detachment, Western Pac Theater, 45-46; Good Conduct Award; Expert Infantryman Badge; Philippine Independence Ribbon; Asiatic Pac Campaign Medal; World War II Victory Medal. Mem: Mason; VFW; NAACP (life mem); Founders Soc & Friends of Modern Art, Detroit Inst of Arts; Temple Emanu-El (bd trustees). Relig: Hebrew. Legal Res: 10100 Burton Ave Oak Park MI 48237 Mailing Add: 1530 Buhl Bldg Detroit MI 48226

HERZ, MARTIN F
US Ambassador, Bulgaria
b New York, NY; s Gustave L Herz & Edith Flammerschein H; m 1957 to Dr Elisabeth Kremenak. Educ: Franz Josef Realgymnasium, Vienna, Austria, 35; Oxford Univ, summer 35; Columbia Univ, BS, 37. Polit & Govt Pos: Third secy, Embassy, Vienna, 46-48, second secy, Paris, 50-54, Phnom Penh, 55-57, first secy, Tokyo, 57-59, staff mem, Bur of African Affairs, Dept State, 60-63, counr embassy for polit affairs, Teheran, Iran, 63-67, dir, Laos & Cambodia Affairs, 67-68, minister & counr for polit affairs, Saigon, 68-70, dep asst secy state for Int Orgn Affairs, Washington, DC, 70-74; US Ambassador, Sofia, Bulgaria, 74- Mil Serv: Entered as Pvt, Army, 41, released as Maj, 46, after serv in Psychol Warfare Br, Mil Intel, Africa & Europe, 43-45; Bronze Star; Purple Heart. Publ: Co-auth, The Golden Ladle, Ziff-Davis, 44; auth, A Short History of Cambodia, Praeger, 58; Beginnings of the Cold War, Indiana & McGraw-Hill, 65. Mem: Am Foreign Serv Asn. Honors & Awards: Commendable Award, Dept State, 60; Superior Honor Award, Dept State, 70; Medal of Honor with Silver Star, Republic Austria, 73. Mailing Add: Dept of State (Sofia) Washington DC 20520

HERZBERGER, ARTHUR CONRAD (R)
Colo State Rep
b Peyton, Colo, Jan 29, 17; s Karl Herzberger & Emma Barbara Prottengeier H; m 1942 to Adele (Lucky) Knowles; c Adele Barbara. Educ: Colo State Univ, DVM, 39; Sigma Alpha Epsilon. Polit & Govt Pos: Colo State Rep, Dist 21, 73- Bus & Prof Pos: Practice of vet med, Alamosa, Colo, 39-40; practice of vet med, Colorado Springs, 46-58; pres & gen mgr, Santa's Workshop, North Pole, Colo, 58-69; pres & mem bd, Park State Bank, Woodland Park, Colo, 66-68; real estate salesman & subdivider, Colorado Springs, 69-72. Mil Serv: Entered as 1st Lt, Army, Vet Corps, 40, released as Maj, 46, after serv in Remount Serv, US, 40-46. Mem: Am Vet Med Asn; Colo Vet Med State Bd Examr (pres, 58-, chmn); Pikes Peak Range Riders; Am Legion; Rotary Int (dir, 60-61 & 72-). Honors & Awards: Thanks Award, Girl Scouts, Wagon Wheel Coun, 70; Outstanding Serv Award, Colo Vet Med Asn, 71; Honor Alumnus Award, Colo State Univ, 72. Relig: Protestant. Mailing Add: 1700 Mesa Ave Colorado Springs CO 80906

HERZOG, V DARLENE (DFL)
VChairwoman, Lincoln Co Dem-Farmer-Labor Party, Minn
b Springfield, Minn, Feb 16, 34; d David H Johnson & Loretta Berbrich J; m to Robert C Herzog; c Vicki (Mrs Craig Pederson), David, Charles, Kevin & Denice. Educ: Sleepy Eye High Sch, Minn. Polit & Govt Pos: Chairwoman, Lincoln Co Dem-Farmer-Labor Party, Minn, 61-65, vchairwoman, 65-; third vchairwoman, Minn State Dem-Farmer-Labor Party, 70-74, dir, formerly; deleg, Dem Nat Conv, 72. Bus & Prof Pos: Secy, Marshall Deanery, New Ulm Diocese, Minn, 59-61; publ, Ivanhoe Times, Minn, 60- Mem: Am Legion; Ladies Guild; Rosary Soc; Divine Providence Hosp Auxiliary; Southwest Womens Asn of Fine Arts (local publicity chmn). Relig: Catholic. Mailing Add: 213 N Harold Ivanhoe MN 56142

HESLER, HARRY RAY (R)
Chmn, Parke Co Rep Cent Orgn, Ind
b Montezuma, Ind, Mar 17, 23; s Harry Roscoe Hesler & Elanor Susan Pruett H; m 1961 to Marjorie Jane Walsh; c Kendall W, Elizabeth A & Charles M. Educ: Ind State Teacher's Col. Polit & Govt Pos: Chmn, Parke Co Rep Cent Orgn, Ind, 61-; deleg, Rep Nat Conv, 68. Mil Serv: S/Sgt, Army, 46, ETO. Mem: VFW; Mason; Scottish Rite, Zorah Shrine; Elks. Relig: Presbyterian. Mailing Add: RR 1 Montezuma IN 47862

HESLIN, HELEN ELAINE (D)
b Wallingford, Conn; d James F Heslin & Helen Sutton H; single. Educ: Larson Jr Col, grad, 42. Polit & Govt Pos: Secy to US Rep John McGuire, Conn, 49-52; admin asst to US Rep Wayne Hays, Ohio, 54- Bus & Prof Pos: Employee, Fed Bur Invest, 42-46, Vet Admin, 46-48. Relig: Catholic. Legal Res: CT Mailing Add: 620 S 2111 Jefferson Davis Hwy Arlington VA 22202

HESS, ARTHUR EMIL
Dep Comnr, Soc Security Admin
b Reading, Pa, June 18, 16; s Emil Hess & Rose Brunner H; m 1942 to Ann McKeown Davis; c Jean Elizabeth, Ann McMaster & Elizabeth Carol. Educ: Univ Munich, summer 38; Princeton Univ, AB, 39; Univ Md Sch Law, LLB, 48, JD, 69; Phi Beta Kappa; Order of the Coif. Polit & Govt Pos: Field rep & mgr, Soc Security Admin, Pa & NJ, 39-44, admin pos, Baltimore, Md, 44-50, dep asst dir, 50-54, dir disability opers, 54-65; dir health ins, 65-67, dep comnr, 67- Mem: Admin Conf of US; Am Pub Welfare Asn; Nat Rehabilitation Asn; Int Soc for Disabled; Princeton Alumni Asn of Md. Honors & Awards: Recipient of Arthur S Flemming Award for Outstanding Fed Serv, Washington, DC Jr CofC, 55; Nat Civil Serv League Award, 67; President's Award for Distinguished Fed Civilian Serv, 67; Rockefeller Pub Serv Award, 69. Relig: Presbyterian. Mailing Add: 4805 Woodside Rd Baltimore MD 21229

HESS, DANIEL BARTLETT (R)
Mem, Kent Co Rep Exec Comt, Mich
b Oak Park, Ill, Aug 26, 40; s Dr Bartlett Leonard Hess & Margaret Johnston H; m 1966 to Marlene Alice Miller; c Daniel Bartlett, Jr & Laurie Elizabeth. Educ: Wheaton Col, BA, 62; Univ Vienna, Austria, 61; Univ Mich Law Sch, JD, 65; Pi Kappa Delta; Pi Gamma Mu. Polit & Govt Pos: Campaign chmn & mem exec bd, Univ Mich Col Young Rep, 63-64; precinct deleg, Grand Rapids, 66 & East Grand Rapids, 67-72; pres, Kent Co Young Rep, 67-69; co-chmn, Mich Fedn Young Rep, 67-70, chmn, 70-72; mem, Kent Co Rep Exec Comt, 71-; Rep nominee for state rep, 93rd Dist, Grand Rapids, 72; mem exec comt, Young Rep Nat Fedn, 73; mem, Mich Construction Code Comn, currently; Rep nominee, Kent Co Comnr, 74. Bus & Prof Pos: Law intern, Off of Attorney Gen, Mich, 64; with Law Off of Otis W Myers, Albion, summer 65; law clerk, Judge Lester Cecil, Sixth Circuit Court, 65-66; assoc, Law, Fallon, Weathers, Richardson & Dutcher, Grand Rapids, 66-67 & Azkoul & Krupp, 67-71; self-employed, 71- Mem: Christian Legal Soc; Legal Aid Soc of Grand Rapids & Kent Co (pres bd dirs); Mel Trotter Mission (mem bd dirs & secy); Grand Rapids Right to Life Comt (mem bd dirs & treas); Christian Guid Ctr (mem bd dirs). Honors & Awards: Hon Sgt at arms, Rep Nat Conv, 68. Relig: Christian Reformed. Mailing Add: 858 Giddings SE Grand Rapids MI 49506

HESS, JUDITH ANN (R)
NH State Rep
b Winchester, Va, Dec 16, 43; d Donald F Noord & Beverly F Brownell N; m 1966 to David W Hess; c Scott David. Educ: Simmons Col, BA, 64. Polit & Govt Pos: Deleg, NH Const Conv, 74-; NH State Rep, 75- Mem: League Women Voters; Hooksett Rep Comt (secy, 73-); Hooksett Woman's Club (corresponding secy, 74-); NH Comn Laws Affecting Ment Health; NH Women's Detention Facility Study Comt. Mailing Add: 9 Heather Dr Hooksett NH 03106

HESS, LYNDLE WILLIAM (R)
Chmn, Calhoun Co Rep Cent Comt, Ill
b Milton, Ill, Oct 6, 08; s Lee R Hess & Sallye Smith H; m 1931 to Mary Louise Martin; c Anne (Mrs Hudnall), Nancy (Mrs Gouran) & William B. Educ: Ill Col, AB, 30; Northwestern Univ Law Sch, JD, 33. Polit & Govt Pos: Chmn, Calhoun Co Rep Cent Comt, Ill, 74- Bus & Prof Pos: Attorney, Libby, McNeill & Libby, Chicago, Ill, 33-48, gen attorney, 48-56, dir, 56-, vpres, 56-62, sr vpres, 62-63, exec vpres, 63-67, pres, 67-68, chmn bd, 68-71. Mem: Am,

NY State, Ill State & Chicago Bar Asns; Ill Col (trustee); Univ Club Chicago. Mailing Add: Hamburg IL 62045

HESS, PAUL ROBERT (R)
Kans State Sen
b Albany, NY, Aug 29, 48; s Robert B Hess & Evelyn W Wortham H; m 1969 to Sharon Rose McFall. Educ: Wheaton Col, 66-68; Univ Wash, BA, 70; Univ Kans Law Sch, JD, 74. Polit & Govt Pos: Rep precinct committeeman, Wichita, Kans, 70-; Kans State Rep, 71-73; Kans State Sen, 73- Relig: Protestant. Legal Res: Box 18512 512 S Christine Wichita KS 67218 Mailing Add: Senate Chamber Topeka KS 66612

HESS, SHARON ROSE (R)
Kans State Rep
b St Louis, Mo, Mar 5, 48; d Ernest Allison McFall (deceased) & Virginia Rose Vickery M; m 1969 to Paul Robert Hess. Educ: Univ Kans BGS in Speech Communication & Human Rels, 75. Polit & Govt Pos: Kans State Rep, 75- Bus & Prof Pos: Dir pre-sch, YWCA, Topeka, Kans, 74. Mem: SSedgwick Co Ment Health Ctr (mem adv bd, 75-); Comn for the Status of Women (mem legis adv comt). Relig: Christian. Mailing Add: 816 S Estelle Wichita KS 67211

HESS, STEPHEN (R)
b New York, NY, Apr 20, 33; s Charles Hess & Florence Morse H; m 1959 to Elena Shayne; c Charles & James. Educ: Johns Hopkins Univ, BA, 53; assoc fel, Inst for Policy Studies, Wash, 64-65; fel, Inst of Polit, Harvard Univ, 67-68; sr fel, Brookings Inst, 72-; Phi Beta Kappa. Polit & Govt Pos: Admin asst to field dir, Rep Cong Comt, Washington, DC, 56; mem pub rels staff, Rep Nat Comt, fall 58; staff asst to the President, 59-61; asst to minority whip, US Senate, winter 61; speechwriter, Richard M Nixon Gubernatorial Campaign, Calif, 62; speechwriter, Spiro T Agnew Vice Presidential Campaign, 68; Dep Asst to the President for Urban Affairs, 69; nat chmn, White House Conf on Children & Youth, 69-71. Mil Serv: Entered as Pvt, Army, 56, released as Pfc, 58, after serv in Third Armored Div, Germany, 57-58. Publ: Nixon (with E Mazo), Harper & Row, 68; The Ungentlemanly Art (with M Kaplan), Macmillan, 68; The Presidential Campaign, 74; plus others. Mailing Add: 3705 Porter St NW Washington DC 20016

HESS, WILLIAM E (R)
Mem Exec Comt, Hamilton Co Rep Party, Ohio
b Cincinnati, Ohio, Feb 13, 98; s William F Hess & Rose Youngman H; m 1927 to Stella Ostendorf; wid. Educ: Univ of Cincinnati; Cincinnati Law Sch; Phi Delta Phi. Polit & Govt Pos: Mem, Cincinnati City Coun, Ohio, 21-25; US Rep, Ohio, 29-61; mem exec comt, Hamilton Co Rep Party, currently; alt deleg, Rep Nat Conv, 68. Mil Serv: Pvt, Army, 18. Mem: Mason; Shrine; Elks; Am Legion. Relig: Protestant. Mailing Add: 5751 Pine Hill Lane Cincinnati OH 45238

HESSER, WOODROW CLEVELAND (D)
Committeeman, Ariz Dem State Cent Comt
b Stillwater, Okla, Apr 1, 18; s Peter Cleveland Hesser & Lucy Adeline Mathews H; m 1939 to Rosemary Mahanay; c William Andrew, Peter Mac, Sharon Kay (Mrs Peters) & Neal Patrick. Educ: Okla State Univ, 3 years. Polit & Govt Pos: Precinct committeeman, Dem Party, Benson, Ariz, 56-, precinct area chmn, 58-70; Benson recreation chmn, 57-, city councilman, 69-; vchmn, Cochise Co Dem Party, 64-66, chmn, 67-68, exec committeeman, 67-; committeeman, Ariz Dem State Cent Comt, 64-, state exec committeeman, 67-; deleg, Dem Nat Conv, 68. Bus & Prof Pos: Self-employed, 39-56; chem supvr, Apache Powder Co, Benson, 56- Mem: Mason (officer); Benson Lions Club (pres, 70-71). Relig: Presbyterian. Legal Res: 100 Bonita St Benson AZ 85602 Mailing Add: Box 215 Benson AZ 85602

HESTER, EVA B (D)
Mem, Dem Nat Comt, Mass
Mailing Add: 14 Park St Clinton MA 01510

HESTER, PAUL FINLEY (D)
Mem, Hudson Dem Town Comt, Mass
b Worcester, Mass, Feb 9, 35; s John Joseph Hester (deceased) & Shirley Finley H; m 1957 to Jacqueline Roberts; c Patricia, Paula, Mary Ellen, Margaret, Brian, Colleen & Christine. Educ: Worcester Jr Col, AA, 54; Univ Maine, Orono, BA, 57; Tufts Univ, 60; Worcester Polytech Inst, MS, 64; Phi Gamma Delta. Polit & Govt Pos: Vchmn sch comt, Assabet Valley Regional Voc Sch, Mass, 67-; mem, Hudson Dem Town Comt, 68-; deleg, Dem Mid-Term Conf, 74; pres, Middlesex Co Teachers Asn, 74-75; elected to Hudson Bd Selectman, 75- Bus & Prof Pos: Life underwriter, State Mutual Am, 57-59; teacher math & sci, baseball & basketball coach, Hudson Cath High Sch, Mass, 59-65; teacher sci, baseball & basketball coach, Framingham South High Sch, 65- Mil Serv: Entered as Pvt E-1, Army Nat Guard, 57, released as Sgt E-5, 63, after serv in 1st Army & 181st Inf, 26th Yankee Div, Mass Nat Guard; Selected Outstanding Soldier, Training Cycle, Ft Dix, NJ, 57 & Outstanding Soldier 181st Inf, 58. Mem: Nat Educ Asn; Mass Teachers Asn; Middlesex Co Teachers Asn; Int Asn Approved Basketball Off; Mass Asn Sch Comn. Honors & Awards: Nat Sci Found grants, 60, 62, 63, 64 & 72; Marlboro Kiwanis Serv Award, 68 & 70. Relig: Roman Catholic. Mailing Add: 32 Wilkins St Hudson MA 01749

HESTER, ROBERT JAMES, JR (D)
b Elizabethtown, NC, Feb 5, 04; s Robert James Hester & Rena Gaston Melvin H; m 1927 to Mary Pitkin Thomas; c Robert James, III & Herbert Thomas. Educ: Wake Forest Col, 23-26. Polit & Govt Pos: Mayor, Elizabethtown, NC, 27-29; judge, Gen Court, Bladen Co, 29-33, solicitor, 37-39; co attorney, 55-; chmn, Bladen Co Dem Exec Comt, formerly; NC State Sen, 15th Sen Dist, 45-47 & 49-51; NC State Rep, Bladen Co, 47-49; trustee, Fayetteville State Col, 53-65; deleg, Dem Nat Conv, 60. Mem: Bladen Co Bar Asn (pres); NC Bar Asn; NC State Bar; Dist Bar Asn (pres); Mason. Relig: Presbyterian. Mailing Add: PO Box 176 Elizabethtown NC 28337

HESTER, WILLIAM H (R)
b Cairo, Ga, June 18, 36; s W B Hester & Evelyn Gainous H; m 1960 to Betty Jeanette Nowell; c William H, II, Hannah Eliseabeth & Joseph Mathew. Educ: Cairo High Sch, grad, 54. Polit & Govt Pos: Chmn, Grady Co Rep Party, Ga, formerly. Bus & Prof Pos: Ins agt, State Farm Ins Co, 61- Mil Serv: Entered as Pvt, Army, 56, released as Pfc, 59, after serving in Army Security Agency, Europe & Middle E Theatre, 56-58. Mem: Life Underwriter Asn; Jaycees; Cairo Country Club. Relig: Methodist. Mailing Add: 1173 Sixth St SE Cairo GA 31723

HESTERBERG, ALEXANDER GEORGE (D)
State Committeeman, NY State Dem Cent Comt
b Brooklyn, NY, June 11, 11; s Henry Hesterberg & Wilhelmina Schimpf H; m 1940 to Ruth Tooley; c Ann H (Mrs Derby), Frances, Henry, Alex G, Jr, Winifred & Gregory. Educ: Georgetown Univ, AB, 33; St John's Law Sch, LLB, 36. Polit & Govt Pos: Secy to Judge John J Fitzgerald, 39-42; secy to Nathan Sobel, 42-56; state committeeman, 44th Assembly Dist, Kings Co Dem Party, NY State Dem Cent Comt, 50-; comnr, Tax Comn, City of NY, 56-60; alt deleg, Dem Nat Conv, 68. Bus & Prof Pos: Practicing attorney, 38-; counsel to Pub Adminstr, Kings Co, 60- Mem: Brooklyn Bar Asn; Catholic Lawyers' Guild; Flatbush Boys Club; dir & counsel, Anthonian Hall, Inc. Relig: Catholic. Legal Res: 478 Argyle Rd Brooklyn NY 11218 Mailing Add: 32 Court St Brooklyn NY 11201

HETERICK, ROBERT CARY, JR (R)
Committeeman, Montgomery Co Rep Comt, Va
b Washington, DC, Apr 9, 36; s Robert Cary Heterick & Barbara Harrison H; m 1960 to Mollie Elizabeth Miller; c Robert Bruce, Dawn Elizabeth, Catherine Paige & Rebecca Leigh. Educ: Va Polytech Inst, BS in Civil Eng, 59, MS instruct eng, 61, PhD in Civil Eng, 68. Polit & Govt Pos: Chmn, Montgomery Co Rep Comt, Va, 65-68, committeeman, 70-, finance chmn, 72-73; chmn, Sixth Rep Legis Dist, 68-70 & 73- Bus & Prof Pos: Consult engr, 61-; assoc prof struct eng, Va Polytech Inst, 61- & dir comput ctr, 69-; pres, Commonwealth Comput Consult, 70-; mem bd dirs, Crime Prev Syst Corp, 70-73. Publ: An Introduction to Computers & Elementary FORTRAN, W C Brown Co, 68. Mem: Am Soc Civil Engrs (mem bd dirs, Va Sect); Nat Soc Prof Engrs; Va Soc Prof Eng (pres, Southwest Chap); Sigma Xi; Va Adv Coun on Educ Data Processing. Relig: Episcopal. Mailing Add: Va Polytech Inst & State Univ Blackburg VA 24061

HEUER, WILLIAM C F (D)
Mem, Todd Co Dem-Farmer-Labor Exec Comt, Minn
b Bertha, Minn, Nov 19, 05; s William Heuer & Anna Sonnenberg H; m 1927 to Selma C Rosenberg; c Donald, Gerald, Maxine (Mrs Lawrence Truax), Ramona (Mrs Warren Truax), James, Waldemar, Charles & Carolyn (Mrs Jim Tonneson). Educ: Co elem dist 85, eight years. Polit & Govt Pos: Town clerk, Bertha, Minn, 32-54, sch clerk, Dist 85, 33-46; sch treas, Bertha Consol, 47-54; chmn, PMA, Todd Co, 41-54; Minn State Sen, Todd-Wadena Co, 55-67; mem, Todd Co Dem-Farmer-Labor Exec Comt, 67- Bus & Prof Pos: Proj supvr, Green View Inc, 69- Mem: Farmers Union; Lions. Honors & Awards: Named Conservation Farmer of the Year, Todd Co Soil Conserv Serv. Relig: Lutheran. Mailing Add: Rte 1 Bertha MN 56437

HEVESI, ALAN G (D)
NY State Assemblyman
Mailing Add: 6764 Selfridge St Forest Hills NY 11375

HEWES, RICHARD DAVID (R)
Maine State Rep
b Biddeford, Maine, Aug 16, 26; s Judge Clyfton Hewes & May Frances Libbey H; m 1954 to Betsey Shaw; c Nancy D, Richard N, James S, Anne K & Carolyn C. Educ: Univ Maine, BA, 50; Boston Univ Sch Law, LLB, 53; vpres, Intra Fraternity Counsel; Beta Theta Pi. Polit & Govt Pos: Mem, Ord Rev Comt, Cape Elizabeth, Maine, 61-65, Sch Study Comt, 64-67 & Superintending Sch Comt, 65-67; Maine State Rep, 67-, speaker, Maine House of Rep, 73-74. Bus & Prof Pos: Attorney, Saco, Maine, 53-54, Portland, Maine, 60- & Liberty Mutual Ins Co, Boston, 54-60; partner, Hewes & Culley, Attorneys, currently. Mil Serv: Entered as Pvt, Army, 45, released as Capt, 60, after serv in 32nd Pt Bn, Korea Base Command, Asiatic Pac Theatre, 45-46. Publ: The evolution of contribution among joint tort-feasors in Maine, Boston Univ Law Rev, winter 64. Mem: Northern New Eng Defense Counsel Asn; Am Bar Asn; Maine State Bar Asn (mem comt gen liability law & miscellaneous casualty ins law); Odd Fellows; Morrill Am Legion Post, South Portland. Relig: Episcopal. Mailing Add: 897 Shore Rd Cape Elizabeth ME 04107

HEWITT, MERRITT S, JR (R)
Vt State Sen
Mailing Add: North Bennington VT 05257

HEYING, HILARIUS L (D)
Iowa State Sen
b Wineshiek Co, Iowa, Aug 19, 14; s John Heying & Elizabeth H; m to Josephine M Langreck; c Terry Ames, Sondra, Charles & Tresa. Educ: Columbia Acad, 36. Polit & Govt Pos: Iowa State Sen, formerly & 75- Bus & Prof Pos: Businessman; farmer; dir, Holy Name Cath Church, 20 years. Mem: Rotary; KofC; Holy Name Soc; Nat Hatchery Fedn. Relig: Catholic. Mailing Add: 115 Jefferson St West Union IA 52175

HEYMAN, HARRY CLINTON (D)
Chmn, Sandusky Co Dem Exec Comt, Ohio
b Detroit, Mich, Feb 28, 24; s William Heyman & Helen H; m 1947 to Jeanne Louise Wurzel; c James William, Richard Allen & Michael Scott. Educ: Bellevue High Sch. Polit & Govt Pos: Committeeman, Sandusky Co Dem Cent Comt, 61-73; chmn, Sandusky Co Dem Young Democrats, 62-67; pres & founder, Sandusky Co Dem Club, 67-73; bd elections, Sandusky Co, 72-; chmn, Sandusky Co Dem Exec Comt, 72- Mil Serv: Entered as Pvt, Marines, 43, released as Cpl after serv in 1st Marine Div, Pac Area, Marine Intel, 43-45; Purple Heart; Asia Theater Ribbon; Pac Theater Ribbon; Presidential Unit Citation. Mem: KofC (3 degree & 4 degree); Marine Corps League; Am Legion; Toastmasters Int (vpres, No 1402, 71). Honors & Awards: Founders Award, Sandusky Co Dem Club, 71. Relig: Roman Catholic. Mailing Add: 1604 Bark Lane Dr Fremont OH 43420

HIBBERD, LUCY REED (D)
Dist Chmn, Denver Co Dem Party, Colo
b Austin, Tex, Jan 2, 41; d Malcom Hiram Reed & Roberta Farish Purvis R; m 1961 to Frederick Hyde Hibberd, Jr; c Frederick Hyde, III. Educ: Finch Col, 1 year; Univ Tex, Austin, BA, 61. Polit & Govt Pos: Dist chmn, Denver Co Dem Party, Colo, currently. Bus & Prof Pos: Dir, Dickson Properties, Austin, Tex, 62-; dir, Colo River Develop Co, Austin, 62- Relig: Protestant. Mailing Add: 1937 E Alameda Ave Denver CO 80209

HIBDON, MINA (R)
Okla State Rep
b McAlester, Okla, June 18, 26; d Joseph Gilreath & Corabelle Bryant G; m 1944 to Dr James E Hibdon; c Mary Ann & Jennifer. Educ: McAlester High Sch, grad, 44. Polit & Govt Pos: Okla State Rep, 75- Mem: Norman Assistance League; Bus & Prof Women; CofC; Am Asn

Univ Women. Honors & Awards: League of Women Voters Meritorious Serv in Local Govt Award, 73. Relig: Baptist. Legal Res: 1501 Leslie Lane Norman OK 73069 Mailing Add: Rm 548 State Capitol Oklahoma City OK 73105

HIBNER, JANET LOUISE (R)
VChairperson, Wayne Co Rep Party, Ind
b Tippecanoe Co, Ind, July 26, 35; d Harvey Delbert Nelson & Alta Pearle Lucas; m 1957 to Dan W Hibner, MD; c Kevin Charles & Jill Anne. Educ: Ind Univ, AB, 57; Delta Zeta. Polit & Govt Pos: Secy, Wayne Co Rep Party, Ind, 72-74, vchairperson, 74- Bus & Prof Pos: Assoc microbiologist, Eli Lilly & Co, 57-61. Mailing Add: 50 S 24th St Richmond IN 47374

HICHENS, WALTER WILSON (R)
Maine State Sen
b Lynn, Mass, Mar 8, 17; s Walter G Hichens & Mary Norton H; m 1941 to Elmira A Ballard; c Walter W, Jr, Mary E, Jared C, Janice E, Judith I, Kathy A, Bethany L, Myra C (deceased) & Laurie J (deceased). Educ: Essex Agr & Tech Inst, Hathorne, Mass, 37. Polit & Govt Pos: Selectman, Eliot, Maine, 52-55, water dist dir, 56-59; Maine State Rep, 67-70; committeeman, York Co, 67-; Maine State Sen, 71-, chmn, Health & Instnl Comt & chmn, Agr Comt, currently; mem, State Comt Probs Ment Retarded, 71-; mem, Gov Comt Probs of the Blind, 72-; mem, State Comt on Deaf & Planning Comt NC Can-Am Regional Health Conf, 72- Publ: Holy Land Reflections (poetry), 70 & Footsteps of Jesus (poetry), 73, Chronicle Publ. Mem: Maine Farm Bur; Maine Baptist Men's Asn (vpres, 73-); Maine Christian Civic League (chmn legis comt, 71-). Honors & Awards: State Legislator Contrib Most for People of Maine, State Nursing Home Asn. Relig: Baptist. Mailing Add: 424 State Rd Eliot ME 03903

HICKEL, WALTER JOSEPH (R)
b Claflin, Kans, Aug 18, 19; s Robert A Hickel & Emma Zecha H; m 1945 to Ermalee Strutz; c Ted, Bob, Wally, Jack, Joe & Karl. Educ: Claflin High Sch, Kans, grad, 36. Honors & Awards: DE, Stevens Inst Technol, 70; LLD, St Mary of the Plains Col, 70, St Martin's Col, Univ Md & Adelphi Univ, 71, Univ San Diego, 72 & Rensselaer Polytech Inst, 73; DPA, Willamette Univ, 71; DEng, Mich Technol Univ, 73. Polit & Govt Pos: Rep Nat Committeeman, Alaska, 54-64; Gov of Alaska, 66-69; deleg, Rep Nat Conv, 68 & 72; Secy, US Dept of Interior, 69-70. Bus & Prof Pos: Former pres, Hickel Investment Co, chmn bd, 62-; mem bd, Western Airlines & Salk Inst Biol Studies, 72- Publ: Auth, Who Owns America?, Prentice-Hall, 71. Mem: Am Asn for Advan of Sci (mem comt on sci freedom & responsibility, 71-); Boys Club of Alaska (bd dirs, 69-); Elks; Navy League of US; KofC. Honors & Awards: Alaskan of the Year, 69; DeSmet Medal, Gonzaga Univ, 69; Man of the Year, Ripon Soc, 70; Horatio Alger Award, Am Schs & Cols Asn, 72. Relig: Catholic. Legal Res: 1905 Loussac Dr Anchorage AK 99503 Mailing Add: 935 W Third Ave Anchorage AK 99501

HICKEY, JAMES CLYDE (D)
Mem, Jefferson Co Dem Exec Comt, Ky
b Big Sandy, Tenn, Sept 25, 36; s R G Hickey & Clara York H; m 1970 to Ann Ewing. Educ: Vanderbilt Univ, BA, 59; Duke Univ, LLB, 65; Phi Kappa Psi; Phi Alpha Delta. Polit & Govt Pos: Deleg, Dem Nat Conv, 68 & 72; chmn, 32nd Legis Dist Dem Party, Ky, 68-71; mem, Jefferson Co Dem Exec Comt, 68- Bus & Prof Pos: Asst dir, Ky Comn Human Rights, Frankfort, 65-66; assoc, Erwin A Sherman, Attorney, Louisville, 66-68; assoc, Ewen, Mackenzie & Peden, Attorneys, 68- Mil Serv: Entered as Ens, Navy, 59, released as Lt(jg), 62, after serv in USS Lexington, CVA-16, Western Pac, 59-62; Lt, Res. Mem: Louisville, Ky, & Am Bar Asns. Relig: Presbyterian. Mailing Add: 724 Circle Hill Rd Louisville KY 40207

HICKEY, THEODORE M (D)
La State Sen
Mailing Add: 4756 Arts St New Orleans LA 70122

HICKEY, THOMAS J (D)
Nev State Assemblyman
Mailing Add: 805 Glendale Ave North Las Vegas NV 89030

HICKEY, VIVIAN VEACH (D)
Ill State Sen
b Clayton, Ill, Mar 25, 16; d Hamilton Erven Veach & Rilla M Cain V; m 1940 to Francis Emmett Hickey; c Charles D, Conn B & Martin E. Educ: Bradley Polytech Inst, Peoria, Ill, 33-34; Rockford Col, BA, 37; Univ NC, MA, 38; Univ Wis, Madison, 70-74. Polit & Govt Pos: Rock Valley Col Bd, Ill, 64-70; mem, Ill Bd Higher Educ, 71-74; Ill State Sen, 34th Dist, 74- Bus & Prof Pos: Teacher, Rockford Col, 38-40, Keith Country Day Sch, 39-40 & Winnebago High Sch, 64-65. Mem: League Women Voters, Am Asn Univ Women. Relig: Roman Catholic. Legal Res: 1234 National Ave Rockford IL 61103 Mailing Add: 825 N Main St Rockford IL 61103

HICKLE, RALPH (R)
NDak State Rep
b Sanger, NDak, Feb 18, 04; s Sherman Hickle & Nellie Lamb H; m 1946 to Doris Christenson; c Rodney, Janice, Arlene, Crystal, Carmen & Robert. Educ: Night col classes. Polit & Govt Pos: Committeeman, Co Agr Stabilization & Conserv Serv, NDak, 36-45; chmn, Co Soil Conserv Serv, 46-; NDak State Rep, 33rd Dist, 64-; chmn, 33rd Dist Rep Party, 66-, mem exec comt, currently. Mem: Co Livestock & Crops Asn; Farm Bur; Am Sheep Producers. Relig: Lutheran; mem church coun, until 64. Mailing Add: Center ND 58530

HICKMAN, CARTER MALCOLM (D)
Md State Deleg
b Felton, Del, Aug 25, 10; s Willard Hickman & Annie Killen H; m 1937 to Marion Elizabeth Hardesty; c David Hardesty & Marion Suzanne (Mrs John DeWitt Pratt). Educ: Wash Col, BS, 31; Columbia Univ, MA, 34; Univ Del & Univ Md, additional courses; Lambda Chi Alpha. Polit & Govt Pos: Md State Deleg, Queen Anne's Co, 63-, chmn, Joint Comt on Admin, Exec & Legis Rev, 72-, vchmn, House Judiciary Comt, 73-; mem, Md Rep Agr Comt, Coun of State Govt, 64-; mem, Md Gov Comt to Study Drug Addiction, 65- Bus & Prof Pos: High sch supvr, teacher & prin, Queen Anne's Co Bd Educ, 31-54; owner & mgr, Greensboro Supply Co, Inc, 54-65; real estate broker, Anthony & Co, 60-70; real estate broker, Queen Anne's Realty, Church Hill, Md, 71- Mem: Mason; Lions; Farm Bur. Relig: Methodist; bd trustees & lay deleg, Church Hill Methodist Church. Mailing Add: Walnut Hill Farm Church Hill MD 21623

HICKMAN, FREDERICK (R)
Asst Secy Tax Policy, Dept of the Treas
Legal Res: IL Mailing Add: Dept of the Treas 15th St & Pennsylvania Ave Washington DC 20220

HICKMAN, RUSSELL ORLANDO (D)
Md State Deleg
b Showell, Md, Feb 5, 08; s Charles H Hickman & Eva Floyd H; m 1931 to Sadie Katherine Donaway; c Herman William. Educ: High sch. Polit & Govt Pos: Md State Deleg, Worcester Co, 54-; deleg, Dem Nat Conv, 68 & 72. Bus & Prof Pos: Collection mgr, Mardelvia Finance Corp, Salisbury, Md, 25-29; field rep, Universal Credit Co, Philadelphia, Pa, 29-31; farmer, assoc with father, 31-40; mgr, US Finance Co, Berlin, Md, 40- Mem: Lions; Farm Bur; Worcester Co Hist Soc; hon mem Worcester Co Chap, Am Red Cross. Relig: Methodist; chmn finance comt, Whaleysville Methodist Church. Mailing Add: Whaleysville MD 21872

HICKMAN, THOMAS WILLIAM, JR (BILLY) (D)
Miss State Sen
Mailing Add: PO Box 702 Brookhaven MS 39601

HICKMAN, TIMOTHY RICKTOR (D)
Md State Deleg
b Arbutus, Md, Mar 6, 46; s Howard Joseph Hickman, Sr & Grace Mary Ricktor H; m 1973 to Jane Knobbe. Educ: Catonsville Community Col; Univ Md, Baltimore Co, BA, 71. Polit & Govt Pos: Legis aide to Sen M Steinberg, Md, 72; state legis liaison, Md Dept Employ & Social Servs, 73; dep dir, Community Leadership & Info Serv, 74; Md State Deleg, 75- Mil Serv: Entered as Pvt, Md Nat Guard, 65, released as Sgt, 71, after serv in 1st 115 Inf, 28th Div. Mem: Catonsville Recreation & Parks Coun (secy); New Dem Club First Dist; Citizens Opposed to Metrop Blvd (bd mem); Catonsville Short Line Bicycle Trail Comt (chmn); Patapsco River Basin Asn. Legal Res: 16 Montrose Manor Ct Catonsville MD 21228 Mailing Add: 754 Frederick Rd Catonsville MD 21228

HICKS, CARLTON TURNER (D)
Dem Nat Committeeman, Ga
b Perry, Ga, Dec 13, 39; s Carlton Hicks, Sr & Billie Robinette H; m 1962 to Jenny Hunt; c Molly Michelle & Holly Browyn. Educ: Mercer Univ, 2 years; Southern Col Optometry, OD & BS; Kappa Sigma. Polit & Govt Pos: Mem, Ga State Dem Exec Comt, 71-; Dem Nat Committeeman, Ga, 74-; deleg, Dem Nat Mid-Term Conf, 74. Mem: Phi Theta Upsilon; Ga Optometric Asn (pres elect, 70-71); Rotary. Honors & Awards: Optometrist of the Year, 71. Relig: Methodist. Legal Res: 63 Sunset Blvd Brunswick GA 31520 Mailing Add: PO Box 1623 Brunswick GA 31520

HICKS, DAVID L (R)
b Alma, Mich, Oct 4, 39; s Mervin L Hicks & Charlotte Vernon H; m 1961 to Sally J Severson; c Jane & Jynell. Educ: Ferris State Col. Polit & Govt Pos: Finance chmn, Eaton Co Rep Party, Mich, 65, chmn, formerly; deleg, Rep Nat Conv, 68. Bus & Prof Pos: Mgr, Radio Stas WCER & WCER-FM, Charlotte, Mich, 64- Mem: Kiwanis (past pres, Charlotte Club). Honors & Awards: Man of the Year Award, 65. Relig: Protestant. Mailing Add: Radio Sta WCER Charlotte MI 48813

HICKS, FLOYD V (D)
US Rep, Wash
b Prosser, Wash, May 29, 15; s J Otis Hicks & Ruth I Crofutt; m 1942 to Norma Jeanne Zintheo; c Tracie & Betsie. Educ: Cent Wash State Col, BEd, 38; Univ Wash Law Sch, LLB, 48. Polit & Govt Pos: Judge, Pierce Co Superior Court, Wash, 61-63; US Rep, Wash, 64-; ex officio deleg, Dem Nat Mid-Term Conf, 74. Bus & Prof Pos: Teacher, 35-42; lawyer, 48- Mil Serv: Maj, Army Air Force, 42-46. Mem: Wash Bar Asn; Kiwanis. Mailing Add: 3301 N 30th St Tacoma WA 98407

HICKS, HERVEY OWINGS (D)
Miss State Rep
b Benton, Miss, Aug 9, 1900; married. Polit & Govt Pos: Miss State Rep, 32-36, 48-64 & currently. Bus & Prof Pos: Planter; livestock dealer. Mem: Mason; Yazoo City Farm Bur (dir); Methodist Men's Club; Benton Farmers' Club. Relig: Methodist. Mailing Add: Rte 1 Box 64 Yazoo Co Benton MS 39039

HICKS, JAMES A (R)
Chmn, Clinton Co Rep Comt, Ky
b Rolan, Ky, Oct 8, 17; s Robert Phillip Hicks & Lula Flowers H; m 1940 to Lucille Cross; m 1960 to Doris Lewis; m 1975 to Shirley Ann Riddle; c Don R, Mary Carolyn (Mrs Warner), James A, Jr, Brett L & Rachel Annette. Educ: Cumberland Univ, 38-39; Jefferson Sch Law, 39-40. Polit & Govt Pos: Co attorney, Clinton Co, Ky, 46-51; commonwealth attorney, 40th Judicial Dist, Ky, 52-69; Ky State Sen, 16th Sen Dist, 70-75; chmn, Clinton Co Rep Comt, 75- Bus & Prof Pos: Attorney, gen civil practice, Albany, Ky, 40- Mil Serv: Entered as Pvt, Army, 42, released as S/Sgt, 45, after serv in Army Air Force, Caribbean Theatre. Mem: Ky Bar Asn; Lions; Nat Farmers Orgn. Relig: Protestant. Legal Res: Rte 4 Albany KY 42602 Mailing Add: PO Box 221 Albany KY 42602

HICKS, JOHN THOMAS, SR (D)
Tenn State Rep
b Nashville, Tenn, Aug 5, 25; s John George Hicks & Rhoda Briley H; m 1948 to Peggy Tomlin; c Donna Joyce & John Thomas, Jr. Educ: Univ Tenn, advan acct cert. Polit & Govt Pos: Tenn State Rep, 11th Legis Dist, 67- Mil Serv: Navy, 42-46, Machinist Mate 2/C. Mem: Nat Soc Pub Acct; Tenn Asn Pub Acct; Al Menah Temple; McWhirtersville Lodge; Lions. Honors & Awards: Outstanding Pub Acct of Year, 67-68. Relig: Methodist. Legal Res: 2820 Windemere Dr Nashville TN 37214 Mailing Add: 2517 Lebanon Rd Nashville TN 37214

HICKS, LOUISE DAY (D)
b South Boston, Mass, Oct 16, 23; wid; c two. Educ: Boston Univ Sch Educ, BS, 55, Sch Law, JD, 58. Polit & Govt Pos: Land court examr; counsel, Boston Juv Court; cand mayor, Boston, 67; mem, Boston City Coun, 69, chmn, Comt Urban Affairs, Comt Pub Serv & Comt Health & Hosps; US Rep, Mass, 71-72. Bus & Prof Pos: Treas, Boston Sch Comt, 62-67, chmn, 63-65. Mem: Mass Asn Women Lawyers; Mass Trial Lawyers Asn. Honors & Awards: Woman of Year Award, 64; Outstanding Citizen Award, 65. Mailing Add: 1780 Columbia Rd Boston MA 02127

HICKS, MARK C, JR (R)
b Sevierville, Tenn, Apr 18, 27; s Mark Clyde Hicks & Alice Trotter H; m 1953 to Lois Dillow; c Mark C, III & Ellen Lynn. Educ: Eastern Tenn State Univ, 46-48; Vanderbilt Univ Sch Law, JD, 51; Delta Theta Phi. Polit & Govt Pos: Chmn, Washington Co Rep Party, Tenn, 56-57; mem, First Cong Dist Rep Exec Comt, 66-70; past chmn, Washington Co Young Rep Club; past chmn, Washington Co Rep Exec Comt; mem & secy, Tenn Rep Exec Comt, formerly. Bus & Prof Pos: Mem bd, Tri-City Airport, Mem Hosp & Johnson City Power Bd; partner, Hicks, Arnold & Haynes, Johnson City & Jonesboro, Tenn, 71- Mil Serv: Entered as Vol, Navy, 45, released as Seaman 2/C, 46. Mem: Tenn & Am Bar Asns; Mason; Am Legion; SAR. Relig: Presbyterian. Legal Res: Scott Lane Jonesboro TN 37659 Mailing Add: PO Box 206 Jonesboro TN 37659

HICKS, WILLIAM H (D)
NJ State Assemblyman
Mailing Add: State House Trenton NJ 08625

HIDALGO DIAZ, ANTONIO (NEW PROGRESSIVE, PR)
Rep, PR House of Rep
Mailing Add: State Capitol San Juan PR 00901

HIEBER, GEORGE FREDERICK, II (R)
Fla State Rep
b Pittsburgh, Pa, Dec 28, 42; s Dr G Frederick Hieber & Cornelia McAuley H; single. Educ: Fla State Univ, BS Finance, 64; Univ SFla, MBA, 75. Polit & Govt Pos: Fla State Rep, 75-; mem, St Petersburg Budget Review Comt; Rep precinct committeeman; mem, Rep Exec Coun. Mil Serv: Entered as E-1, Army Res, 66, released as SP-4, after serv in 231st Transportation Unit, Vietnam, 68-69. Mem: Am Legion; Jaycees. Honors & Awards: Outstanding Young Man of St Petersburg, 75. Relig: Presbyterian; past Deacon. Mailing Add: 1139 Cordova Blvd NE St Petersburg FL 33704

HIGGINBOTHAM, G J (DUTCH) (D)
Ala State Rep
Mailing Add: PO Box 585 Opelika AL 36801

HIGGINS, ALOYCE HUBEL (R)
Chmn, Carver Co Rep Party, Minn
b Maynard, Minn; d Albert A Hubel & De Lella Holian H; m to Peter J Higgins; c Charles & Paul. Educ: St Olaf Col, BA, 50. Polit & Govt Pos: Treas, Fay Child Vol Comt, 48; chmn Eisenhower campaign, Granite Falls Carver Co Rep Party, Minn, 50, precinct chmn, 50-51; precinct chmn, Carver Co Rep Party, 60, dist chmn, 63-, vchmn, 65, chmn, 67-; nominee for Lt Gov, Minn, 70; mem, Minn Rep State Const Comt, 71. Mem: Minnetonka YWCA (bd mem, 66-); Minn Lutheran Church Women; Laketown Twp Planning Comn, (secy, 68-); Minn Div, Am Cancer Soc. Relig: Lutheran; Coun mem, Holy Cross Lutheran Church, 67-68. Mailing Add: Rte 1 Box 573-B Excelsior MN 55331

HIGGINS, DONALD GEORGE (D)
Asst Chmn, Brown Co Dem Party, Nebr
b Fairbury, Nebr, Dec 1, 14; s George Higgins & Agnes Hagerty H; m 1939 to Roberta June Gass; c Diane Kay (Mrs Shelbourn) & Kent David. Educ: St Agnes Acad High Sch, Alliance, Nebr, grad, 31. Polit & Govt Pos: Chmn, Brown Co Dem Party, Nebr, 67-70 & 72-73, asst chmn, 73- Bus & Prof Pos: Pres, Ainsworth Air Serv, 47-65 & Higgins Ins Agency, 65- Mil Serv: Entered as Flight Off, Air Force, 44, released, 46, after serv in Air Transport Command, China-Burma-India, 45-46; Air Medal; Distinguished Serv Award. Mem: Elks; Am Legion; VFW; CofC; Quiet Birdmen. Honors & Awards: Flying Cornhusker Award, Nebr Dept Aviation, 55; Distinguished Salesman Award, 65; Three Quarter Million Club, Investors Life Ins of Nebr, 65 & 66, Rookie of the Year, 66 & Salesman of the Year, 67. Relig: Catholic. Mailing Add: 732 E Third Ainsworth NE 69210

HIGGINS, LINWOOD MCINTIRE (R)
Maine State Rep
b Portland, Maine, Jan 11, 48; s Linwood Royal Higgins & Rachel Burnham McIntire H; m 1968 to Kathleen Callahan; c Eric Michael & Stephen Mathew. Educ: Univ NH, BA, 70; Tau Kappa Epsilon. Polit & Govt Pos: Town counr, Scarborough, Maine, 73-; Maine State Rep, Dist 33, 75- Bus & Prof Pos: Pres & mgr, L R Higgins, Inc, 70- Mem: Rotary; Mason. Mailing Add: 10 Church St Scarborough ME 04074

HIGGINS, MICHAEL A (D)
RI State Rep
Mailing Add: 292 Washington Ave Providence RI 02905

HIGGINS, NED PRESTON (R)
Mem, Morrow Co Rep Cent Comt, Ohio
b Mt Gilead, Ohio, Aug 11, 23; s Clark Higgins & Josie Fogle H; m 1949 to Roberta Geyer; c Robert, Dale, John & Nancy. Educ: Mt Gilead High Sch, Ohio, grad, 43. Polit & Govt Pos: Mem, Morrow Co Rep Cent Comt, Ohio, 58-; mem, Morrow Co Elec Bd, 68- Bus & Prof Pos: Farmer, 49; milk tester, Ohio State Univ, 43. Mil Serv: Entered as Pvt, Air Force, 43, released as Sgt, 45, after serv in Ninth Air Force, ETO, 44-46. Mem: Farm Bur; Morrow Co Bd for the Retarded. Honors & Awards: Efficient Prod Award, State of Ohio, 65. Relig: Protestant. Mailing Add: Rte 3 Fredericktown OH 43019

HIGGINS, RICHARD A (R)
b Salt Lake City, Utah, Dec 4, 47; s Richard Ambrose Higgins & Agnes Hales H; m 1971 to Marin Sweet; c Marshall Hales. Educ: Univ Utah, BA in polit sci, 73; Delta Phi Kappa; Student Body Officer, 70-71 & 72-73. Polit & Govt Pos: Deleg, Utah State Rep Conv, 70; deleg, Rep Nat Conv, 72; legis intern, Utah State Legis, 73; legis asst, US Rep Carlos J Moorhead, Calif, 73- Mem: Young Rep. Relig: Latter-day Saint. Legal Res: 2266 Downington Ave Salt Lake City UT 84108 Mailing Add: 9436 Horizon Run Rd Gaithersburg MD 20760

HIGGINS, THOMAS JAMES (D)
Iowa State Rep
b Springfield, Ill, July 20, 45; s Thomas A Higgins & Ruth Quinlan H; single. Educ: St Ambrose Col, BA, 67; Iowa State Univ, 67-69. Polit & Govt Pos: Iowa State Rep, Dist 82, 73-, chmn human resources comt, Iowa House Rep, 75-, mem appropriations & judiciary comts, currently; alt deleg, Dem Nat Mid-Term Conf, 74. Bus & Prof Pos: Exec dir, Quad-Cities Drug Abuse Coun. 70-72; commun consult, John Deere & Co, 74. Honors & Awards: Man of the Year Award, St Ambrose Col, 66. Relig: Catholic. Mailing Add: 2410 Kelling St Davenport IA 52804

HIGGINSON, JERRY CASSIM (R)
Mem, Utah Rep State Cent Comt
b Caldwell, Idaho, May 13, 38; s Elmo Cassim Higginson & Lelia Hatch H; m 1973 to Judith Ellen Waters. Educ: Univ Denver, BSBA, 62, MBA, 69; Brigham Young Univ, MA, 63; Alpha Kappa Psi; Intercollegiate Knights; Student Senate. Polit & Govt Pos: Chmn, Denver Co Young Rep, Colo, 70-71; chmn, Salt Lake Co Young Rep, Utah, 72-73; alt deleg, Rep Nat Conv, 72; chmn, State Young Rep, 73-75; mem, Utah Rep State Cent Comt, 75- Bus & Prof Pos: Acct exec, Bosworth Sullivan & Co, Salt Lake City, Utah, 70-74; acct exec, A G Edwards & Sons, Inc, Salt Lake City, 74- Mem: Am Cancer Soc (Salt Lake crusade chmn, 75); Salt Lake Bond Club. Honors & Awards: Outstanding Sr Award, Alpha Kappa Psi, 62. Relig: Latter-day Saint. Mailing Add: 3391 Crestwood Dr Salt Lake City UT 84109

HIGH, BEVERLY FRANCES (D)
b Washington, DC, Dec 3, 44; d Edward High & Edna Salter H; single. Educ: DC Teachers Col, BS, 67; Howard Univ, MA, 70; Chixs & Chatter Social Club. Polit & Govt Pos: Deleg, Dem Nat Conv, 72. Bus & Prof Pos: Teacher, Washington, DC Pub Sch Syst, 67-71; counr, 72- Mem: Urban League; Howard Univ Alumni Asn; DC Teachers Alumni Asn; Nat Capital Counrs Asn; Washington, DC Teachers Union. Honors & Awards: Outstanding Teacher, Research Club, 71; fel, George Washington Univ, 71. Relig: Presbyterian. Mailing Add: 1006 Crittendon St NE Washington DC 20017

HIGH, RICHARD S (R)
Idaho State Sen
Mailing Add: 802 Sunrise Blvd N Twin Falls ID 83301

HIGHAM, JUSTUS CHARLES (D)
b Trenton, NJ, Oct 26, 08; s Charles Higham & Mary Gribbin H; wid; c Mary Lou (Mrs Sheppard), Carol Elizabeth (Mrs White), Gerald William, Justus C, Jr, William Yard, Michael Edward, Eleanor Ann, Kathleen T (Mrs Iavarone), Timothy Patrick, Anthony Peter, Jane Ellen, Stephen Kevin, Susan Patricia, Dennis Sean & Terrance Brian. Educ: Seton Hall Univ, BA, 53. Polit & Govt Pos: Secy, NJ Dem State Comt, 54-69; chmn, Mercer Co Dem Party, formerly. Mem: Elks; Ancient Order of Hibernians. Relig: Roman Catholic. Mailing Add: 871 Revere Ave Trenton NJ 08608

HIGHTOWER, FOYLE ROBERT, JR (D)
NC State Rep
b Wadesboro, NC, Jan 21, 41; s Foyle Robert Hightower, Sr & Mildred Brigman H; m 1967 to Elizabeth Gore. Educ: Elon Col; Univ NC, Chapel Hill. Polit & Govt Pos: NC State Rep, 33rd Dist, 71-73, NC State Rep, 26th Dist, 73- Bus & Prof Pos: Vpres, Hightower Ice & Fuel Co, Inc, currently. Mil Serv: Entered Army Res, 63, released as Cpl, 69. Mem: Mason (32 degree); WOW; Jaycees; Civitan; Shrine. Relig: Presbyterian; pres, Men of the Church. Mailing Add: 715 E Wade St Wadesboro NC 28170

HIGHTOWER, JACK ENGLISH (D)
US Rep, Tex
b Memphis, Tex, Sept 6, 26; s Walter Thomas Hightower & Floy English H; m 1950 to Colleen Ward; c Ann, Amy & Alison. Educ: Baylor Univ, BA, 49, LLB, 51; Phi Alpha Delta. Hon Degrees: LLD, Howard Payne Col, 71. Polit & Govt Pos: Tex State Rep, 53-54; dist attorney, 46th Judicial Dist, Tex, 55-61; mem & vchmn bd regents, Midwestern Univ, 62-64; Tex State Sen, 65-74, pres pro tempore, Tex State Senate, 71; deleg, Dem Nat Conv, 68; mem bd trustees, Baylor Univ, 72-; US Rep, Tex, 75- Mil Serv: Entered as A/S, Naval Res, 44, released as Yeoman 2/C, 46. Mem: Mason (Grand Master, Tex, 72); Lions. Relig: Baptist. Legal Res: PO Box 1720 Vernon TX 76384 Mailing Add: US House of Rep Washington DC 20515

HILBRECHT, NORMAN TY (D)
Nev State Sen
b San Diego, Calif, Feb 11, 33; s Norman Titus Hilbrecht & Elizabeth Lair H; div; c Bonnie Jean. Educ: Northwestern Univ, BA, 56; Yale Law Sch, LLB, 59; Phi Beta Kappa; Phi Delta Phi; Delta Phi Epsilon; past pres, Theta Chi. Polit & Govt Pos: Chmn trustees, Clark Co Law Libr, Nev, 63-; vchmn, Clark Co Dem Cent Comt, 66-68; Nev State Assemblyman, 66-72, minority leader, Nev State Assembly, 71-72; deleg, Western Conf on Ombudsman, 68; deleg, First Nat Conf on Abortion Reform, 69; deleg, Rutgers State Legislator Seminar, 69; Nev State Sen, 75- Mil Serv: Entered as 2nd Lt, Army, 58, released as Capt, 66, after serv in various Judge Adv Gen & Mil Govt Units; Capt, Army Res, 66- Publ: The Colby case & full faith & credit, 7/63 & Farnham vs Farnham-variations on a theme, 1/65, Nev Bar J; Nevada public defender act, 1/64. Mem: Am Bar Asn (chmn, Comt on Legal Aid & Indigent Defense, 63-); Nev & Clark Co Bar Asns; Am Trial Lawyers Asn; Clark Co Legal Aid Soc. Relig: Unitarian. Mailing Add: 8601 Mohawk Las Vegas NV 89118

HILDEBRAND, DEAN (R)
NDak State Rep
Mailing Add: State Capitol Bismarck ND 58501

HILDEBRAND, GEORGE H (R)
b Oakland, Calif, July 7, 13; m to Margaret Boardman; c George, Stephen & Richard. Educ: Univ Calif, Berkeley, BA, 35; Harvard Univ, MA, 41; Cornell Univ, PhD, 42; Phi Beta Kappa. Polit & Govt Pos: Prin economist, Nat War Labor Bd & tech adv, President's Cost of Living Comn, World War II; labor arbitrator, 51-; consult & mem comt to guide the Secy of Labor's study of the basic steel indust, Dept of Labor, 59-60, Dep Under Secy for Int Affairs, 69-72; pub mem, Minimum Wage Bd for restaurant indust, NY & consult, Dept of Health, Educ & Welfare, 61-62; former chmn adv comt on research, Soc Security Admin. Bus & Prof Pos: Asst prof econ, Univ Tex, 41-43; instr, Univ Calif, Berkeley, 45-47, vis prof, 59-60; from asst prof to prof, Univ Calif, Los Angeles, 47-60, dir, Inst of Indust Rels, 56-60; Fulbright fel, 52-53; Guggenheim fel, 52-53 & 57-58; prof econ & indust labor rels, Cornell Univ, 60-, named Maxell M Upson Prof of Econ & Indust Rels. Publ: Co-auth, Pacific Coast Maritime Shipping Industry, 1930-1948, 52 & Manufacturing Production Functions in the United States, 57 & 65; auth, Growth & Structure in the Economy of Modern Italy, 65. Mem: Soc Sci Research Coun (mem bd dirs); Comitato per le Scienze Politiche e Sociali; Am Econ Asn; Indust Rels Research Asn (pres, 71); Nat Acad of Arbitrators. Mailing Add: 914 Highland Rd Ithaca NY 14850

HILDRETH, PETER C (D)
NH State Rep
Mailing Add: 28 Lakeview Ave Laconia NH 03246

HILL, ALBERT ALAN (R)
b Palo Alto, Calif, Feb 1, 38; s Albert Andrew Hill & Margaret Silver H; m 1961 to Mary Jeanette Smith; c Andrew Alan, Timothy Brewster & Michael Ralph. Educ: Col of the Pac, AB, 60; Univ Calif, Berkeley, 60-61; Golden Gate Col, 63-64 & 67-68; Blue Key; Alpha Kappa Phi. Polit & Govt Pos: Asst to Minority Leader, Calif State Senate, 62-64; state info officer, Calif Rep State Cent Comt, 65-69; asst to Secy for Resources, State of Calif, 69-70, comnr, San Francisco Bay Conserv & Develop Comn, 69-72, alt mem, Tahoe Regional Planning Agency, 70-72, dep dir, Dept of Conserv, State of Calif, 71-72, Dep Secy Agr & Serv Agency, 72- Bus & Prof Pos: Consult in pub affairs, 72- Relig: Episcopal; Vestryman, St Paul's Episcopal Church, San Rafael, Calif, 67-70, Sr Warden, 70- Mailing Add: 102 Coleman Dr San Rafael CA 94901

HILL, BOBBY L (D)
Ga State Rep
b Athens, Ga, July 24, 41; s Birl Hill & Fannie Hubbard H; m 1966 to Dolores Clarke. Educ: Savannah State Col, BS, 63; Howard Univ Sch Law, LLB, 66; Alpha Phi Alpha; Sigma Delta Tau; Thespian Dramatics Club. Polit & Govt Pos: Ga State Rep, 94th Dist, 69- Publ: Low income & poor educational status of one party is basis for holding a contract unconscionable, Howard Law J, Vol 1, No 12. Mem: Am Bar Asn; Nat Assembly for Social Policy & Develop (bd dirs); Nat Voter Educ Proj, US Youth Coun; NAACP Legal Defense & Educ Fund, Inc (coop counsel). Honors & Awards: Man of the Year Award, Savannah State Col & Alpha Phi Alpha; Achievement Award, Omega Psi; Alumnus Award, Howard Univ Sch Law Student Bar Asn. Relig: Baptist. Legal Res: 923 W 37th St Savannah GA 31401 Mailing Add: 208 E 34th St Savannah GA 31401

HILL, CECIL (D)
NC State Sen
Mailing Add: Brevard NC 28712

HILL, CHARLES ELLIOTT (D)
b Blairsville, Ga, May 13, 37; s Frank McDonald Hill & Pearl Elliott H; m 1962 to Jacquelyn Jaynelle Lance; c Gina, Elliott & Stacy. Educ: Young Harris Jr Col, 55-57; Western Carolina Col, 58; Univ Ga, BS Pharmacy, 60; Rho Chi; Phi Beta Kappa; Kappa Delta Sigma; Kappa Sigma; Phi Delta Chi; Phi Chi. Polit & Govt Pos: Co registr, Union Co, Ga, 65-69; mem, Ga State Dem Exec Comt, formerly. Bus & Prof Pos: Mem bd, Blairsville Industs, 62; chmn, Blairsville Family & Children's Serv, 64-; pres, Lanhill Inc, Blairsville, Ga, 64- Mil Serv: Entered as Airman Basic, Air Force, 61, released as T/Sgt, 67, after serv in 116th Air Nat Guard. Mem: Nat Asn Retail Druggists; Mason; Lions; Quarterback Club; Blue Ridge Soil & Water Conserv Asn. Relig: Baptist. Mailing Add: Blue Ridge Rd Blairsville GA 30512

HILL, EDWARD POLK, III (D)
b Bonanza, Ky, Sept 2, 04; s Edward Polk Hill, Jr & Adda Davis; m 1929 to Marie Doss; c Carolyn Doss (Mrs Coleman), Edward Polk, IV, John Josiah & Sarah Noel (Mrs Stumbo). Educ: Berea Col, 21-22; Bowling Green Bus Univ, 23; Jefferson Law Sch, 25-27. Polit & Govt Pos: Judge, Floyd Co Court, Ky, 38-45; Circuit Judge, 31st Dist, 45-63; Appellate Judge, Seventh Appellate Dist, Commonwealth of Ky, 65-69; Judge, Court of Appeals, Ky, 69-74, Chief Justice, 70-72. Bus & Prof Pos: Bank teller, 24; attorney, 28-38. Mem: Am Judicature Soc; Ky Bar Asn; Kiwanis; Odd Fellows; Mason. Relig: Baptist. Mailing Add: Prestonsburg KY 41653

HILL, EUGENE MARSHALL (D)
Iowa State Sen
b Newton, Iowa, Oct 24, 13; s George R Hill & Minnie Rees H; m 1946 to Ruth Ryburn; c David, Robert, Patricia, Kathleen & John. Educ: Iowa State Univ, BS, 37; Univ Ill, post grad work, 41; Alpha Zeta; Sigma Upsilon. Polit & Govt Pos: Supvr, Farm Security Admin, Dept of Agr; Iowa State Sen, currently. Bus & Prof Pos: Instr voc agr, Col Springs & Coin, Iowa High Schs, 46-49; farmer, Newton, Iowa, 50- Mil Serv: Marine Corps, World War II; 4th Tank Bn, Battles of Roi Namur, Saipan, Tinian & Iwo Jima; Maj, Marine Corps Res, currently; Letter of Commendation with Ribbon, Secy of Navy, 45; Presidential Unit Citation, Saipan, 44; Navy Unit Commendation, Iwo Jima, 45. Mailing Add: Rte 3 Newton IA 50208

HILL, GEORGE BARKER (D)
Chmn, Coal Co Cent Comt, Okla
b Sulphur Springs, Tex, July 9, 15; s John B Hill & Grace Martha Summers H; m 1943 to Margaret Ellen Culbertson; c John Carl, Judith Ann (deceased) & Mary Lynn (deceased). Educ: Ardmore Bus Col, 31-33; Okla Baptist Univ, 33-34; Sigma Delta Chi. Polit & Govt Pos: Secy, Johnston Co Cent Comt, Okla, 40-41 & 46-49; mem credentials comt, Okla State Dem Conv, 52, platform comt, 64, 66 & 68; chmn, Coal Co Cent Comt, Okla, 52-53 & 67-; deleg, Dem Nat Conv, 64; mem, state & dist resolutions & spec studies comts; mem, State Constitution Rev Comt, Okla State Dem Cent Comt, 64 & 66, party rev comt, 69; mem, Task Force Comt, Okla Dem Party, 70; mem, Judicial Nomination Comn, 71- Bus & Prof Pos: Publ, Coalgate Record Register, 49-; secy-treas, Okla Water Users Asn, 70- Mil Serv: Entered as Pvt, Army, 41, released as T-3, 45, after serv in Panama Mobile Force, Caribbean Defense Command, 42-44. Mem: AF&AM (Past Master, Past Dist Dep Grand Master, Grand Lodge, Okla); Odd Fellows; Lions; Am Legion; VFW. Honors & Awards: 50 Awards in State Press Contests: Nat Ed of the Week, 54; Spec Presentations, 4-H, Soil Conserv Serv, Mason, CofC, Okla Press Asn, Secy of Navy & Prime Minister of Ont. Relig: Baptist. Legal Res: 530 S Byrd Coalgate OK 74538 Mailing Add: Box 327 Coalgate OK 74538

HILL, GUY F (R)
Ga State Rep
Mailing Add: 1074 Boatrock Rd SW Atlanta GA 30331

HILL, JAMES DEAN (R)
b Ucon, Idaho, Feb 19, 23; s Robert E Hill & Fanny M Monsen H; m 1945 to Virginia Mae Burtenshaw; c Carolyn, Michelle, Sharyl, Janene & Von. Educ: Ricks Jr Col, AA, 46; Univ Utah, BS in Civil Eng, 48, MS, 49; Tau Beta Pi. Polit & Govt Pos: Hydraulic engr, US Geol Surv, 49-56; dist chmn, Rep Party, Utah, 63; deleg, State Rep Conv, 63 & 65; Utah State Rep, Davis Co, 65-72; chief clerk, Utah House of Rep, 73- Bus & Prof Pos: Pres, Great Basin Eng & Surv, Inc, 61-68; rep, Utah Eng Coun, 63, legis chmn, 70-; consult engr, Eng Assocs, Inc, 68-71; sr design engr, Terracor, Salt Lake City, 71- Mil Serv: Entered Army Air Corps, 43, released as 2nd Lt, 45, after serv in 398th Bomb Group, 8th Air Force, ETO, 45; Maj, Air Force Res, 45-73, (Ret); Air Medal with Three Oak Leaf Clusters; ETO Ribbon with Two Battle Stars; Victory Medal; Am Defense Medal; Res Ribbon with Hour Glass; Air Force Commendation Medal, 73. Mem: Am Soc Civil Engrs (secy Utah Chap, 60-62, pres, 62); Utah Coun Land Surveyors. Honors & Awards: Registered Civil Engr, Idaho, Utah & Ariz; Licensed Civil Engr, Mont; Outstanding Prof Engr for Community Serv, Utah Eng Coun, 71. Relig: Latter-day Saint; mem, Salt Lake Tabernacle Choir, 56-64 & 69- Mailing Add: 274 West 1350 North Bountiful UT 84010

HILL, JOHN ALLEN (D)
Fla State Rep
b Miami, Fla, May 20, 31; s Eugene Prentice Hill & Frances Allen H; m to Vivian Carlson; c John Alfred, Richard Allen & Kathy Ann. Educ: Miami Dade Jr Col, 68-69. Polit & Govt Pos: Fla State Rep, 74- Bus & Prof Pos: Pres, IBEW 359, Miami, 61-62, asst bus mgr, U-4, 63-64. Mil Serv: Entered as Sgt, Marine Corps Res, 50, released as M/Sgt, 63. Mem: Optimist Club; AAONMS, Scottish Rite; Eastern Star; Tree of Italy; Nat Asn Life Underwriters. Honors & Awards: Top Club Centurion Award, NY Life; Nat Sales Achievement Award, Nat Asn Life Underwriters. Relig: Presbyterian. Legal Res: 7440 Sabal Dr Miami Lakes FL 33014 Mailing Add: Suite 203 1140 W 50th St Hialeah FL 33012

HILL, JOHN JEROME (JACK) (D)
Ill State Rep
b Aurora, Ill, Oct 27, 18; m to Belva Mae Satterlee; c Patti Anne. Educ: St Ambrose Col. Polit & Govt Pos: Former mem, Aurora Civil Serv Bd; alderman, Aurora, Ill; Ill State Rep, currently. Bus & Prof Pos: Grievance committeeman & vpres, United Steel Workers, Local 3672. Mil Serv: Army, 2nd Armored Div, 4 years; Am Defense Serv Ribbon; European-African-Mid Eastern Theatre Ribbon with One Silver Star & Two Bronze Stars; Bronze Serv Arrowhead for Beach Head Landing in Sicily; Bronze Star Medal with Oak Leaf Cluster; Cert of Merit; Distinguished Unit Badge; Presidential Citation; Belgium Croix de Guerre. Mem: DAV; VFW; St Joseph Holy Name Soc. Relig: Catholic. Mailing Add: 741 Sheridan Aurora IL 60505

HILL, JOHN L (D)
Attorney Gen, Tex
b Breckenridge, Tex, Oct 9, 23; s John Luke Hill; m 1946 to Elizabeth Ann Graham; c Melinda (Mrs Mike Perrin), Graham & Martha. Educ: Univ Tex Sch Law, Austin, LLB, 47; Sigma Alpha Epsilon; Abbott of Friar Soc; Foreman of Cowboys; Phi Delta Phi; Chancellor's Legal Order. Polit & Govt Pos: Secy State, Tex, 66-68, Attorney Gen, 73-; deleg, Dem Nat Mid-Term Conf, 74. Bus & Prof Pos: Attorney-at-law, Houston, Tex, 47-73. Mil Serv: Entered Navy, 43, released as Lt(jg), 45 after serv as Commanding Off of LCI 572, Pac Theatre. Mem: Tex Bar Found (charter mem); VFW; Am Legion; Houston Heart Asn; Houston Methodist Bd Missions. Honors & Awards: Gold Medal, Law Sci Acad of Am, 60; cited four successive years by Tex State Bar for Outstanding Work in Continuing Legal Educ. Relig: Methodist; past chmn bd stewards, Chapelwood Methodist Church, Houston. Mailing Add: State Supreme Court Bldg Austin TX 78711

HILL, JOHN WILLIAM (D)
b Decherd, Tenn, Aug 20, 33; s James B Hill & Bertha Mooney H; m 1956 to Ina Maddux; c Cynthia & Donald. Educ: Mid Tenn State Univ, BS, 57; Univ Ark, Fayetteville, PhD, 61; Phi Beta Kappa. Polit & Govt Pos: Secy, St Croix Co Dem Party, Wis, 67-68, prog chmn, 69-, chmn, 70-72, mem exec bd, 71-74; deleg, Wis State Dem Conv, 67 & 71. Bus & Prof Pos: Asst prof chem, Northeast La State Col, 60-63; asst prof chem, Wis State Univ, River Falls, 63-65, assoc prof, 65-69, prof, 69-, chmn dept, 70-; vis prof chem, Univ Ariz, 71; tech adv, Minn-Wis Boundary Area Comn, 73- Mil Serv: Entered as Seaman Recruit, Navy, 50, released as PO 2/C, 54, after serv in USS Kearsarge, 7th Fleet, Korean Theatre, 52-53; UN Medal; Korean Serv Medal; China Serv Medal; Good Conduct Medal. Publ: Chemistry for Changing Times, Burgess Publ Co, 72 & 75. Mem: Am Chem Soc; River Falls CofC. Honors & Awards: Nat Sci Found Fel, 58-60; Shell Merit Fel, 70. Relig: Unitarian. Mailing Add: 532 N Seventh St River Falls WI 54022

HILL, LISTER (D)
b Montgomery, Ala, Dec 29, 94; s Luther Leonidas Hill & Lilly Lyons H; m 1928 to Henrietta Fontaine McCormick; c Henrietta (Mrs Charles C Hubbard) & Luther Lister. Educ: Univ Ala, BA, 14, LLB, 15; Columbia Univ, LLB, 16; Phi Beta Kappa; Delta Kappa Epsilon. Hon Degrees: LLD, Univ Ala, 39, Auburn Univ, 39, Nat Univ, 41, Woman's Med Col Pa, 56, Columbia Univ, 60, Wash Univ, 61, Univ Pa, 65, NY Univ, 66 & Gallaudet Col, 66; DSc, Hahnemann Med Col Pa, 58, New York Med Col, 61 & Jefferson Med Col, 66. Polit & Govt Pos: Pres, Montgomery Co Bd Educ, Ala, 17-22; US Rep, Ala, 23-38; US Sen, Ala, 38-69, sponsor, Hill-Burton Act, 46 & Hill-Harris Act, 63, chmn, Labor & Pub Welfare Comt, US Senate, 55-69. Mil Serv: Entered as 2nd Lt, Army, 17, released as 1st Lt, 19, after serv in 17th & 21st US Inf Regts. Mem: Lister Hill Nat Ctr Biomed Commun; Mason; Am Legion; Nat Conf Christians & Jews; Am Asn Pub Health. Honors & Awards: Albert Lasker Award, 59; Pub Welfare Medal, Nat Acad Sci, 69; City of Hope Salute to Med Prog Award; Airlie Found Award Statesman in Med & Health Award; Dean's Award, Univ Ala Sch Law, Annual Lister Hill Lectr, Univ Ala Sch Dent & Dent Alumni Asn. Mailing Add: 1618 Gilmer Ave Montgomery AL 36104

HILL, MARGARET C (R)
Rep Nat Committeewoman, Ind
b Indianapolis, Ind, Feb 23, 24; d Marvin E Curle & Florence Rilling C; m 1946 to Nat U Hill; c Dr Nat U, Jr & Philip C. Educ: Skidmore Col, 2 years; Ind Univ, Bloomington, AB in Econ, 44; Kappa Kappa Gamma; Psi Iota Xi. Polit & Govt Pos: Precinct vcommitteeman & organizer of block syst, Ind; vchmn, Monroe Co Rep Cent Comt, Ind, 63-68; vchmn, Seventh Dist Rep Cent Comt, 64-; mem, Ind State Rep Cent Comt, 64-; vpres, Monroe Co Woman's Club; dir, Women's Rep Workshops; deleg-at-lg & mem platform comt, Rep Nat Conv, 72; Rep Nat Committeewoman, Ind, 72- Bus & Prof Pos: Personnel dept, Electronic Labs, Indianapolis, 45-46. Mem: Woman's Dept Club; Boys' Club Bd; founder, Boys' Club Auxiliary; 19th Century Club; Navajo Club. Honors & Awards: Woman & Boy Award, Boy's Club Bloomington, 71. Relig: Christian Church; trustee, First Christian Church, Bloomington. Mailing Add: RR 11 Box 36 Kinser Pike Bloomington IN 47401

HILL, NANCY HALLMAN (R)
Secy, Vt Rep State Comt
b Philadelphia, Pa, July 6, 40; d Abrahm Lincoln Hallman & Elizabeth Nelson H; m 1963 to David Lorenz Hill; c Kimberly Elizabeth & Eric Lorenz. Educ: Beaver Col, BA in Eng, 62; Nat Honor Soc; Hist Honor Soc. Polit & Govt Pos: Secy, Lyndon Rep Town Comt, Vt,

67-; chmn, Caledonia Co Women's Rep Club, 69-; mem & secy exec bd, Vt Rep State Comt, 69-, secy, 71-; committeewoman, Caledonia Co Rep Comt, 70-; deleg, Rep Nat Conv, 72; publicity chmn for Vt, A Day for the President, 72; mem, Vt Rep State Conv Comt, 72. Relig: Protestant. Mailing Add: Box 367 Lyndonville VT 05851

HILL, PHILIP B (R)
Iowa State Sen
Mailing Add: 5403 Waterbury Rd Des Moines IA 50312

HILL, RENDER (D)
Ga State Sen
Mailing Add: PO Box 246 Greenville GA 30222

HILL, ROBERT CHARLES (R)
US Ambassador, Argentina
b Littleton, NH, Sept 30, 17; s Allen Frank Hill (deceased) & Katherine Lyle Morse; m 1945 to Cecelia Gordon Bowdoin; c W Graham Bowdoin & James Bowdoin. Educ: Dartmouth Col, 42; Alpha Delta Phi. Hon Degrees: LLD, Dartmouth Col, St Mary's Univ, San Antonio, Tex, Univ of Dallas, New Eng Col & Mex Acad of Int Law. Polit & Govt Pos: Vice consul, Foreign Serv, India, China & Burma, 43-45; clerk, Senate Banking & Currency Comt, 47-48; US Ambassador, Costa Rica, 53-54, El Salvador, 54-55, Mex, 57-61 & Spain, 69-71, spec asst to Under Secy of State for Mutual Security Affairs, 55-56, spec ambassador, El Salvador Inauguration, 56, 150th Anniversary Independence Ceremonies, Mex, 60 & Costa Rica Inauguration, 61; Asst Secy of State for Cong Rels, 56-57; NH State Rep, 61-62; chmn task force on foreign policy, Rep Nat Comt; mem task force on nat security, Rep Coord Comt, 67-68; Ambassador to Argentina, 74- Bus & Prof Pos: Asst vpres, W R Grace & Co, 49-53; dir, Todd Shipyards Corp, NY, 66. Publ: Contrib, Orbis, Reader's Digest & Wash Report. Mem: Newcomen Soc; Pan Am Socs of New Eng & US; Metrop Clubs of Washington, DC & New York, NY; Chevy Chase Club; Univ Club, Washington, DC. Honors & Awards: Aztec Eagle, First Class, Repub of Mex; Peruvian Grand Order of Merit, Repub of Peru; Cuerpo de Defensores de la Republica, Mex; La Orden Mexicana del Derecho y la Cultura, Mex; Gran Cruz de la Orden Isabella la Catolico, Spain. Relig: Episcopal. Mailing Add: The Boulders PO Box 350 Littleton NH 03561

HILL, ROBERT MCCLELLAN, JR (D)
Ala State Rep
b Florence, Ala, Apr 16, 32; s Judge Robert M Hill & Ratchel Fitzgerald H; m 1962 to Patsy Lynne Graydon; c Alicia Michelle. Educ: Florence State Col; Univ Ala, BS, 57, LLB, 59; Sigma Gamma Epsilon; Phi Alpha Delta; Phi Gamma Delta. Polit & Govt Pos: Law clerk, Ala Supreme Court, 59-60; Asst Attorney Gen, Ala, 60-63; Munic Judge, Florence, 63-66; Ala State Rep, Lauderdale Co, 66-; mem, Ala State Bldg Comn, 67-71, Ala Youth Authority, 69- & Ala Legis Coun, 72- Bus & Prof Pos: Partner, Keller & Hill, Attorneys, 66- Mil Serv: Entered as Seaman, Navy, 51, released as Seaman 1/C, 53. Publ: Bail & recognizance in Alabama: some suggested reforms, Ala Law Rev, summer 69. Mem: Am & Ala Bar Asns; Am Judicature Soc; Ala Munic Judges Asn; Ala Citizen's Judicial Cong. Relig: Methodist. Legal Res: 119 Mobile St Plaza Florence AL 35630 Mailing Add: PO Box 687 Florence AL 35630

HILL, ROBERT MICHAEL (R)
Committeeman, Bay Co Rep Exec Comt, Fla
b Corpus Christi, Tex, Nov 17, 43; s Gordon Scott Hill & Mary Miller H; m 1968 to Janice Carol Wilkes. Educ: Gulf Coast Jr Col, AS, 71. Polit & Govt Pos: Chmn, Bay Co Young Rep, Panama City, Fla, 66-68; committeeman, Bay Co Rep Exec Comt, 66-, chmn, 71-72; committeeman & co chmn rep, First Cong Dist, Fla Rep State Comt, 72-73; Bay Co area committeeman, Farmers Home Admin, US Dept Agr, 74- Bus & Prof Pos: Mortgage broker, Vet Admin, 72-, compliance inspector, 72-; partner, Hanson Y Lewis, Architect & R Michael Hill, Prod Mgt, currently; vpres, Dictograph Tel Co of WFla, Inc, currently. Mem: Bay Co Coun on Aging (dir, 72-); Lions; CofC (mil affairs comt, Bay Co, mem legis action comt, 75-); Jaycees; Boys Club (dir, Bay Co, 73). Honors & Awards: One of Top Ten Young Rep, Fla, 73. Relig: Presbyterian. Legal Res: 1415 Baker Court Panama City FL 32401 Mailing Add: PO Box 1757 Panama City FL 32401

HILL, ROGER C
Sen, VI Legis
Mailing Add: PO Box 712 Charlotte Amalie St Thomas VI 00801

HILL, SHERMAN L (R)
Pa State Rep
b Lancaster Co, Pa, Dec 4, 11; s Ellsworth J Hill & Mabel Lehman H; m to Kathryn Bender; c J Douglas & foster son, Stanley K Bowers. Educ: Millersville State Col, 35-36. Polit & Govt Pos: Organizational mem, Lancaster Co Jr Rep Comt, Pa; dist chmn, Lancaster Co Rep Finance Comt; committeeman, Millersville Borough; sustaining mem, Nat Rep Party; mem, Pa Rep Action Comt; Boys' Clubs of Am rep, Gov Comt on Children & Youth & Gov Comt on Fitness, 59-60; mem, Gov Adv Comt for Children & Youth, 63-69, vchmn, 67-68; Pa State Rep, 65-, mem, Comts on Pub Health & Welfare, Agr & Dairy Industs, Boroughs, Third Class Cities, Liquor Control, Motor Vehicles & Hwy Safety, Spec Comts on Capitol Cafeteria Opers, Invest State Insts & House-Senate Task Force to Study Quarries, Pa House of Rep, currently; mem, Nat Emergency Comt on Crime & Delinquency; mem, Pa Bicentennial Comn & rep to Regional Coop Task Force. Bus & Prof Pos: Playground supvr, Lancaster, Pa, 27-34; basketball official, 31-44; partner, restaurant & confectionary bus, 33-54; exec dir, Boys' Club of Lancaster, 44-68, dir community rels, 68- Mem: Boys' Clubs of Am Prof Asn; Lancaster Co Br, Am Asn Health, Phys Educ & Recreation; Millersville Recreation Asn (organizer); State Coun Civil Defense; F&AM. Honors & Awards: Commendation for Serv to Youth, Pa House of Rep Resolution, 68; Serv to Youth Award, Lancaster YMCA, 68; Youth Work Appreciation, Lancaster City Resolution, 68; Serv Citation, Urban League Lancaster Co, 68; Outstanding Citizenship Award, Millersville Jr CofC, 69. Relig: United Church of Christ; mem, Consistory, Zion United Church of Christ, 53-65 & 66-69, past pres; taught young adult & men's class, 8 years. Mailing Add: Capital Bldg Harrisburg PA 17120

HILL, STUART C (R)
NMex State Rep
Mailing Add: 11201 Morocco NE Albuquerque NM 87111

HILL, SUSIE H (D)
Mem, Dem Exec Comt Fla
b Madison Co, Fla, Feb 24, 13; d John Henry Hicks & Mary Rodgers H; m 1930 to William Rufus Hill; c John William. Educ: Univ Fla, MEd, 49; Phi Kappa Phi; Delta Pi Epsilon. Polit & Govt Pos: Branford town clerk, 42-46; mem, Dem Exec Comt Fla, 75- Bus & Prof Pos: Teacher, Suwannee Co, 32-72. Mem: Nat Educ Asn; Nat Retired Teachers Asn; Branford Woman's Club. Honors & Awards: Grad of Univ Fla with Honors; Teacher of the Year, Branford Woman's Club, 67. Relig: Methodist. Legal Res: Drane & White Branford FL 32008 Mailing Add: PO Box 65 Branford FL 32008

HILLEBOE, PETER STUART (R)
NDak State Rep
b Minneapolis, Minn, Sept 24, 21; s Christian Hilleboe & Mabell Johnson M H; m 1946 to Sarah A Fleck; c Laura, Stuart, Kristina & Amy. Educ: NDak State Univ, BS, 43; Univ NDak, MS, 46; Delta Sigma Pi; Sigma Chi. Polit & Govt Pos: Precinct committeeman, Rep Party, NDak, 49-, mem co exec comt, 58-64; deleg, NDak Rep Conv, 58-72; mem, Dist 21 Rep Finance Comt, 59-; state chmn for Nixon, 60; alt deleg, Rep Nat Conv, 64; NDak State Rep, 21st Dist, 64-, chmn, State & Fed Govt Comt & vchmn, State Fiscal Audit & Rev Comt, NDak State House of Rep, 69-; NDak state chmn for Rockefeller, 68. Bus & Prof Pos: Financial consult, currently; pres, Hilleo Supply Co, Lamp Lite & Stuart & Co, currently. Mil Serv: Entered as Aviation Cadet, Navy, 43, released as Airman 3/C, 46; Lt(jg), Naval Res. Mem: Nat Asn Securities Dealers; NDak Bus Found (dir); Am Legion; VFW; CofC. Relig: Protestant. Mailing Add: 216 Seventh St N Fargo ND 58102

HILLEGONDS, PAUL CHRISTIE (R)
b Holland, Mich, Mar 4, 49; s William C Hillegonds & Elizabeth Romaine H; m 1971 to Judith Schutt. Educ: Univ Mich, Ann Arbor, BA, 71; Phi Beta Kappa. Polit & Govt Pos: Legis asst to US Rep Philip Ruppe, Mich, 71-74, admin asst, 74- Mem: Univ Mich Alumni Club (second vpres). Relig: Presbyterian. Mailing Add: 4600 Connecticut Ave Apt 831 Washington DC 20008

HILLELSON, JEFFREY P (R)
b Springfield, Ohio, Mar 9, 19; s Henry Hillelson & Ann Morrison H; m 1952 to Alice Moore Goetz; c Debra Ann & Jan. Educ: Univ Mo, Kansas City, BA; Univ Mo Law Sch, 2 years. Polit & Govt Pos: US Rep, Mo, 53-55; exec asst Postmaster Gen of US, 55; deleg-at-lg, Rep Nat Conv, 56; acting postmaster, Kansas City, Mo, 57-61; mem, City Coun, Kansas City, 63-69; regional adminr, Gen Serv Admin for Mo, Kans, Iowa & Nebr, 69- Bus & Prof Pos: Contract sales mgr, Vendo Co, 61-68. Mil Serv: Entered as Pvt, Army, 42, released as Capt 46, after serv in Transportation Corps, Alaskan Dept; ETO, Am Theater & Pac Theater Ribbons; Victory Medal. Mem: Mil Order World War I & II; Am Legion; Shrine; Carriage Club, Kansas City, Mo; De Molay Legion of Honor. Relig: Episcopal. Mailing Add: 6711 Rainbow Mission Hills KS 66208

HILLENBRAND, JOHN A, II (D)
b Batesville, Ind, Oct 31, 31; s John W Hillenbrand & Mildred Johnson H; 1955 to Joan Lally; c John A, III, Amy M, Anne G, Peter L, Holly M & Daniel C. Educ: Georgetown Univ, BS in Foreign Serv, 57; Delta Phi Epsilon. Polit & Govt Pos: Mem comn, Ind State Conserv Dept, 61-65; chmn comn, Ind State Natural Resource Dept, 65-; mem, Ind Dem Platform Comt, 66-; mem comn, Dunes Nat Seashore, Dept of Interior, 67-; deleg, Dem Nat Conv, 72; mem adv comn, Ohio River Basin Comn, 72-; deleg, Dem Nat Mid-Term Conf, 74; mem, Dem Charter Comn, 74- Bus & Prof Pos: Vpres, Hill-Rom Co, Inc, Batesville, Ind, 56-71 & Hillenbrand Industs, 56-; pres, Heritage Acceptance Corp, Batesville, 71- Mil Serv: Entered as 2nd Lt, Air Force, 54, released as 1st Lt, 56, after serv in Air Defense Command, 54-56. Honors & Awards: Frank Fadner Citation, Georgetown Univ, 54; Outstanding Serv Award, Health Industs Asn, 67; Charles S Osborn Wildlife Conserv Award, Purdue Univ, 73. Relig: Catholic. Legal Res: Box 5 RR 3 Batesville IN 47006 Mailing Add: Hillenbrand Industs Rte 46 Batesville IN 47006

HILLENBRAND, MARTIN
US Ambassador to Germany
b Asst Secy European Affairs, Dept State, 70-73; US Ambassador, Germany, 73- Legal Res: IL Mailing Add: Dept of State Washington DC 20520

HILLIARD, BILL (D)
Tex State Rep
Mailing Add: 6400 Warrington Pl Ft Worth TX 76112

HILLIARD, EARL FREDERICK (D)
Ala State Rep
b Birmingham, Ala, Apr 9, 42; s William N Hilliard & Iola Frazier H; m to Mary Franklin; c Alesia & Earl F, Jr. Educ: Atlanta Univ, MBA; Morehouse Col, BA; Howard Univ, JD; Sigma Delta Tau; Alpha Phi Alpha. Polit & Govt Pos: Ala State Rep, 74- Bus & Prof Pos: Pres, Astro Realty Co, Inc, 71-; vpres, Metrop Bus Asn, 73-; sr partner, Hilliard, Jackson & Barnes, 74-; pres, Alpine Develop Co Inc, 74- Mem: Jefferson Co Community Action Prog (bd dirs); Nat Bar Asn (Ala regional dir, 74-); NAACP; Am Civil Liberties Union; Ala Bar Asn. Honors & Awards: Businessman of Year, Omega Psi Phi, 74; Distinguished Serv & Achievement Award, Birmingham Alumnae Chap, Delta Sigma Theta, 75. Relig: Baptist. Mailing Add: 1605 Eighth Ave N Birmingham AL 35203

HILLINGS, PATRICK J (R)
Mem, Los Angeles Co Rep Cent Comt, Calif
b Hobart Mills, Calif, Feb 19, 23; s Edward John Hillings & Evangeline Murphy H; m 1947 to Phyllis K Reinbrecht; c Pamela Jane, David Michael & Jennifer Ann. Educ: Univ of Southern Calif, BA, 47, JD, 49; Delta Theta Phi; Blue Key; Trogan Knights; Skull & Dagger. Polit & Govt Pos: Pres, Los Angeles Co Young Rep, 49; field asst to US Rep Richard Nixon, Calif, 49-50, personal rep, Vice Presidential Campaign, 52; US Rep, 25th Dist, Calif, 51-59; deleg, Rep Nat Conv, 52, 56, 60 & 64; chmn, Los Angeles Co Rep Cent Comt, 60, mem, currently; spec asst to John Mitchell, Nixon Campaign Mgr, 68; mem bd trustees, Rep Assocs, Los Angeles; mem, Calif State Rep Cent Comt, formerly; mem adv comt on the educ of Spanish & Mex Am, Dept Health, Educ & Welfare; mem, RN Assocs, currently. Bus & Prof Pos: Attorney-at-law, 49-; owner & pres, Pat Hillings Travel Agency, 62-; civic & govt affairs mgr, Ford Motor Co, Western US, currently; counsel, Reeves & Harrison, Washington, DC, currently. Mil Serv: Entered as Pvt, Army, 43, released as Sgt, 46, after serv in Signal Intel Serv, SPac; SPac Campaign Ribbons & Three Battle Stars; Presidential Unit Citation. Publ: Series of articles on Tour of Russia, Hearst Press, 55; California Federal Judicial Districts, State Bar J of Calif, 57. Mem: Los Angeles CofC; Am Legion; VFW; Kiwanis; KofC. Relig: Catholic. Mailing Add: Arcadia CA 91006

HILLIS, ELWOOD HAYNES (R)
US Rep, Ind
b Kokomo, Ind, Mar 6, 26; s Glen R Hillis & Bernice Haynes H; m 1949 to Carol Hoyne; c Jeffrey H, Gary L & Bradley R. Educ: Ind Univ, BS, 49, JD, 52; Sigma Nu; Phi Delta Phi; Alpha Kappa Psi. Polit & Govt Pos: Mem, Kokomo Housing Auth, Ind, 58-66, chmn, 62-66; Ind State Rep, Tipton & Howard Co, 66-69; US Rep, Ind, Fifth Dist, 71- Bus & Prof Pos: Dir, Union Bank & Trust Co, 56-; pres, Hillis Enterprises, Inc. Mil Serv: Entered as Pvt, Air Force, 44, released as 2nd Lt, 46, after serv in 9th Inf Div, 39th Regt, ETO, 46; Capt, Inf Res, until 54; Am Theater & Army of Occup Ribbons; Victory & Good Conduct Medals. Mem: Elks; Am Legion; VFW; Mason; Shrine. Relig: Presbyterian. Legal Res: 2331 S Wabash Ave Kokomo IN 46901 Mailing Add: PO Box 1205 Kokomo IN 46901

HILLIS, I V, JR (D)
Tenn State Rep
b Campaign, Tenn, June 30, 30; s I V Hillis, Sr & Iris Novella Bain H; m 1951 to Oma Lee Fults; c Donald H, Hugh S, Mickey Lynn, I V, III & James Randel (Randy). Educ: Tenn Sch of Broadcasting, 1 year. Polit & Govt Pos: Tenn State Rep, 13th Floterial Dist, 70- Bus & Prof Pos: Announcer, WSMT AM&FM Radio, 55. Mil Serv: Entered as Pvt, Air Force, 47, released as S/Sgt, 53, after serv in AACS. Mem: Am Legion; York Rite Mason; Lions Club; Cee-Bee Club. Relig: Church of Christ. Mailing Add: Rte 4 Sparta TN 38583

HILLMAN, ELSIE HILLIARD (R)
Rep Nat Committeewoman, Pa
b Pittsburgh, Pa, Dec 9, 25; d Thomas Jones Hilliard & Mariana Talbott H; m 1945 to Henry L Hillman; c Juliet Lea, Audrey Hilliard, Henry L, Jr & William Talbott. Educ: Westminster Choir Col. Polit & Govt Pos: Chmn, vchmn & mem many comts for campaigns & cand, 52-; secy, Allegheny Co Rep Exec Comt, 62-67, chmn, 67-70; mem, State Rep Women's Adv Comt, 62-; chmn, 14th Ward Rep Comt, Pittsburgh, 64-; mem, Pa State Rep Finance Comt, 63-70; alt deleg, Rep Nat Conv, 64, deleg, 68; co-chmn, Scott for Pa, 70; Rep Nat Committeewoman, 75- Bus & Prof Pos: Bd dirs, WQED Pub TV, 73- Mem: Health & Welfare Asn, Allegheny Co; Hill House Asn (bd dirs); Carlow Col (bd trustees); Pittsburgh Symphony Soc (bd dirs, 54-); Urban League of Pittsburgh (vpres, 71-). Honors & Awards: Women in Polit Award, Nat League of Woman Voters; Top Hat Award, Pittsburgh Courier; Humanitarian Award, Guardians of Gtr Pittsburgh; co-honoree with husband, Nat Conf Christians & Jews, 73. Relig: Episcopal. Mailing Add: Morewood Heights Pittsburgh PA 15213

HILLS, CARLA ANDERSON (R)
Secy, Dept Housing & Urban Develop
b Los Angeles, Calif, Jan 3, 34; d Carl Anderson & Edith Hume Anderson Wagner, m 1958 to Roderick Maltman Hills; c Laura Hume, Roderick M, Jr, Megan Elizabeth & Alison Macbeth. Educ: Oxford Univ, St Hilda's Col, 54; Stanford Univ, AB cum laude, 55; Yale Univ, LLB, 58. Hon Degrees: LLD, Pepperdine Univ, 75. Polit & Govt Pos: Asst US Attorney, Civil Div, Dept Justice, Los Angeles, Calif, 58-61; asst attorney gen, Civil Div, Dept Justice, Washington, DC, 74-75; mem coun, Admin Conf of US, Washington, DC, 75-; secy, Dept Housing & Urban Develop, 75- Bus & Prof Pos: Partner, Munger, Tolles, Hills & Rickershauser, Los Angeles, Calif, 62-74; adj prof law, Univ Calif, Los Angeles, spring 72. Publ: Co-auth, Federal Civil Practice, Calif Continuing Educ of Bar, 61; ed & co-auth, Antitrust Adviser, McGraw-Hill, 71. Mem: Yale Univ Law Sch Exec Comt; Pomona Col Bd Trustees; Am Bar Found (fel); Am Law Inst. Legal Res: Apt 9-D 10375 Wilshire Blvd Los Angeles CA 90024 Mailing Add: 3125 Chain Bridge Rd Washington DC 20016

HILLS, DAVE (D)
VChmn, Waldo Co Dem Comt, Maine
b Belfast, Maine, Aug 30, 33; s Silas C Hills & Doris Hodgdon H; m 1962 to Rebecca Pearl Andrews; c Darlene Rae & David Scott. Educ: Univ Conn, MA, 64. Polit & Govt Pos: Secy, Belfast Dem City Comt, 66-68, treas, 66-; vchmn, Waldo Co Dem Comt, Maine, 66-; cand, Maine House Rep, 66; cand, Maine Sen, 70. Bus & Prof Pos: Teacher hist & govt, Mount View High Sch, Thorndike, Maine, 62- Mil Serv: Entered as SR, Navy, 51, released as RM3, 54, after serv in USS Albany, CA-123, ETO; Good Conduct Medal; Korean Conflict Medal. Mem: Maine Teachers Asn; Nat Educ Asn; Maine Sch Adminr Dist Three Teachers Asn; Belfast Lions (pres, 72-73). Relig: Unitarian Universalist. Mailing Add: Main St Monroe ME 04951

HILLS, RODERICK M (R)
b Seattle, Wash, Mar 9, 31; s Kenneth M Hills & Sarah Love H; m 1958 to Carla Anderson; c Laura H, Roderick M, Jr, Megan E & Alison M. Educ: Stanford Univ, BA, 52, Law Sch, LLB, 55; Phi Delta Phi; Zeta Psi; Order of the Coif. Polit & Govt Pos: Co-chmn, Comt to elect H Flournoy, Controller, 64 & 68; chmn, Comt to Reelect Sen Kuechel, Southern Calif, 68; co-chmn, Southern Calif Comt to Reelect the President, 72; Counsel to the President, White House, Washington, DC, 75- Bus & Prof Pos: Law clerk, Justice Stanley F Reed, Supreme Court, 55-57; partner, Munger, Tolles, Hills & Rickershauser, Attorneys-at-law, 62-75; vis prof, Harvard Law Sch, 69-70; chmn bd, Republic Corp, 71-75. Publ: Auth, A close look at labor relations in the Kennedy years, Indust Rels J, 63; co-auth, The Antitrust Adviser, McGraw-Hill, 72. Mem: Chancery Club; State Bar Calif; Am Bar Asn; Am Bar Found (chmn, Research Comt); Claremont Col (bd trustees & chmn, Finance & Audit Comt). Relig: Episcopal. Mailing Add: 3125 Chain Bridge Rd NW Washington DC 20016

HILLYARD, LYLE WILLIAM (R)
Chmn, Cache Co Rep Exec Comt, Utah
b Logan, Utah, Sept 25, 40; s A Lowell Hillyard & Lucille Rosenbaum H; m 1964 to Allice Thorpe; c Carrie, Lisa, Holly, Todd Lyle & Matthew David. Educ: Utah State Univ, BS, 65; Univ Utah Law Sch, JD, 67; Pi Kappa Alpha; Phi Kappa Phi. Polit & Govt Pos: Mem, First Dist Juv Court Adv Bd, Utah, 70-; chmn, Cache Co Rep Exec Comt, 72- Bus & Prof Pos: Partner, Hillyard & Gunnell Law Firm, 67- Mem: Am Trial Lawyers Asn (Utah state rep, young lawyer's sect, 70-72); Utah State Bar; Cache Valley Coun Boy Scouts (mem exec bd, 69-); Kiwanis; Cache CofC (vpres, 74-). Honors & Awards: One of Ten Outstanding Young Men, Utah Jaycees, 72; Distinguished Serv Award, Logan Jaycees, 72. Relig: Latter-day Saint. Legal Res: 1584 E 1140 N Logan UT 84321 Mailing Add: 140 E Second N Logan UT 84321

HILLYER, WILLIAM HUDSON (R)
Chmn, Tuscarawas Co Rep Exec Comt, Ohio
b Uhrichsville, Ohio, July 28, 28; s Edgar Evans Hillyer & Louise Coldren H; m 1950 to Marie Cowan; c Blair, Brad, Beth & Becky. Educ: Ohio State Univ, BS, 50, JD, 52; Phi Delta Phi; Phi Kappa Tau. Polit & Govt Pos: Mem, Ohio Dept Develop, 56-58; mem, Civil Serv Comn, Uhrichsville, 64-; mem, Bd Elec, New Philadelphia, 66-; chmn, Tuscarawas Co Rep Exec Comt, 66-; bar examr, State of Ohio, 72- Bus & Prof Pos: Dir, Clay City Pipe Co, Uhrichsville, Ohio, 56-, Bowerston Shale Co, Bowerston, 56-, Union Country Club, New Philadelphia, 62-66; United Clay Pipe Co, Seminole, Okla, 63- & Ross Clay Prod Co, Gnadenhutten, Ohio, 64- Mil Serv: Entered as Ens, Naval Res, 46, released as Lt(sg), 59, after serv in Supply Corps, US. Mem: Ohio State Alumni Asn; Eagles; Elks; Mason. Relig: Methodist. Legal Res: 405 Park Dr Uhrichsville OH 44683 Mailing Add: 201 N Main St Uhrichsville OH 44683

HILSMEIER, BILL (R)
Colo State Rep
Mailing Add: 39 James Circle Longmont CO 80501

HILTON, LESTER ELLIOT (R)
Mem, Rep State Cent Exec Comt RI
b Pawtucket, RI, Oct 9, 23; s Charles Sawyer Hilton & Annie Lester Crofts H; m 1946 to Arlene Alden Newton. Educ: Am Col Life Underwriters, CLU, 68. Polit & Govt Pos: Chmn, Cumberland Rep Town Comt, RI, 68-72; pres, Asn Blackstone Valley Rep Chmn, 71-72; mem, Rep State Cent Exec Comt RI, 73- Bus & Prof Pos: Cost acct, Textron, Manville, RI, 41-48; off mgr, various RI textile mills & vending co, 48-59; registered rep, Metrop Life Ins Co, RI, 59- Mil Serv: Entered as Pvt, Marine Corps, 42, released as Sgt, 46, Paymaster Div, Hq Air FMF, Pac Theatre, 43-45. Mem: RI Badminton Asn; Am Badminton Asn (pres, 73-). Relig: Episcopal. Mailing Add: 15 Tanglewood Dr Cumberland RI 02864

HIMSL, MATHIAS A (R)
Mont State Sen
b Bethune, Sask, Sept 17, 12; s Victor S Himsl & Clara Engels H; m 1940 to Lois L Wohlwend; c Allen, Marilyn, Louise, Kathleen & Judith. Educ: St John's Univ (Minn), BA, 34; Univ Mont, MA, 40. Polit & Govt Pos: Rep Co Chmn, Mont, 52-64; Rep nominee for Mont State Rep, 64; deleg, Rep Nat Conv, 64; Mont State Rep, Flathead Co, 66-72; Mont State Sen, 72- Bus & Prof Pos: Secy-mgr, Himsl-Wohlwend Motors, Inc, 45-; dir, Conrad Nat Bank, 48; pres, Skyline Broadcasters, Inc, 58-; pres, Mont Auto Dealers' Asn, 68; instr polit sci, Flathead Valley Community Col, 69-72; ed writer, KGEZ Radio Prog. Mem: Elks; Kiwanis; CofC. Relig: Roman Catholic. Legal Res: 305 Fourth Ave E Kalispell MT 59901 Mailing Add: PO Box 838 Kalispell MT 59901

HINCHEY, JOSEPH FRANCIS (D)
Mem, Nat Credit Union Bd
b Philadelphia, Pa, Feb 16, 23; s Edward Hinchey & Ann Kelley H; m 1949 to Margaret Wade; c Christina, Joseph, Robert, Marguarite, Gerardette, Edward & Brian. Educ: LaSalle Col, BS, 49; Temple Univ, 49-50. Polit & Govt Pos: Examr, Nat Credit Union Admin, 52-60; mem, Nat Credit Union Bd, 71- Bus & Prof Pos: Mgr, Philadelphia Tel Fed Credit Union, 60-66; mgr, Philadelphia City Employees Fed Credit Union, 66- Mil Serv: Entered as Pvt, Army, 43, released as S/Sgt, 46, European & Pac, 44-46. Mem: Credit Union Nat Asn, Inc (dir, 68-); Industrial Valley Bank (dir, 70-); Third Fed Reserve Dist Automatic Clearing House (dir, 75-); Pa Credit Union League (dir, 65-). Relig: Catholic. Mailing Add: 407 Magee Ave Philadelphia PA 19111

HINCHEY, JUDY ELENA (R)
Mem, Ark Rep State Comt
b Jackson, Calif, Aug 20, 54; d John William Hinchey & Joyce Bell Hinchey Sanders; single. Educ: NArk Community Col, 74-75. Polit & Govt Pos: Mem, Ark Rep State Comt, Van Buren Co, 74- Relig: Protestant. Mailing Add: Rte 2 Box 33 Leslie AR 72645

HINDS, SAMUEL ARTHUR (R)
Maine State Rep
b Portland, Maine, Dec 20, 33; s Samuel Clinton Hinds & Mildred Maloy H; m 1963 to Marilyn Agnes Huffaker; c David Keith, Linda Agnes & Mark Samuel. Educ: Northeastern Univ Sch Bus, AA, 54. Polit & Govt Pos: Mem bd educ, South Portland, Maine, 54-60; Maine State Rep, 58-60, 63-64 & 75-; Maine State Sen, 61-62, chmn health & instnl servs, Maine State Senate, 61-62; asst legis finance officer, Augusta, 68-70. Mem: Nat, State & Portland Bd Realtors; FM&AM (32 degree); South Portland Bd Indust. Honors & Awards: Outstanding Community Serv Award, South Portland-Cape Elizabeth Jaycees, 64. Relig: Congregational. Mailing Add: 232 Walnut St South Portland ME 04106

HINE, ROBERT WALTER (R)
Chmn Audit Comt, Adams Co Rep Cent Comt, Colo
b New Milford, Conn, Dec 6, 24; s Raymond Arthur Hine & Cora Ferriss H; m 1948 to Vera Mae Rogers; c Linda Jean & Mary Alice. Educ: Western State Col, BA, 62. Polit & Govt Pos: Committeeman, Precinct 3004, Colo Rep Party, 63-, Precinct 3004, 64-; mem, Colo State Rep Cent Comt, 66-68; chmn, Sen Dist 31 Rep Party, 66-69; deleg, Rep Nat Conv, 68; chmn, audit comt, Adams Co Rep Cent Comt, 68-; campaign chmn, Colo State 32nd Representative Dist, 70- Bus & Prof Pos: Teacher, Aurora Schs, 63- Mil Serv: Entered as Pvt, Air Force, 43, released as SM Sgt, 63, after serv in Guam, 48-49, & Ger, 52-56. Mem: Nat & Colo Educ Asns; Am Asn Physics Teachers; Nat Asn Uniformed Serv; VFW. Relig: Baptist. Mailing Add: 1741 Havana St Aurora CO 80010

HINEMAN, KALO A (R)
Kans State Rep
b Dighton, Kans, Mar 4, 22; s George E Hineman & Nancy Esther Hutchins; m 1942 to Geneva Lois Durr; c Judy (Mrs Sjoberg), Don, Tom & Linda. Educ: Kans State Univ, DVM, 43; Sigma Phi Epsilon. Polit & Govt Pos: Sch bd mem, 56-70; Kans State Rep, 75- Bus & Prof Pos: Farmer & rancher, 47- Mil Serv: Entered as 1st Lt, Army Vet Corps, 43, released as Capt, 46, after serv in Remount Serv in US & OSS in CBI Theatre. Mem: Kans Livestock Asn; Am Nat Cattlemen's Asn; Kans Vet Med Asn. Relig: Methodist. Mailing Add: RR Dighton KS 67839

HINES, ARTHUR SNOW (R)
Chmn, Templeton Co Rep Party, Mass
b Baldwinville, Mass, Nov 14, 32; s Ronald Hines & Elizabeth Snow Hines Thompson; m 1956 to Kathleen Lilleen Hunter; c Cynthia May, Debra Ann, Michael Arthur & James Arthur. Educ: Worcester Trade Sch, Machine Trade Cert; Worcester Jr Col, AIE. Polit & Govt Pos: Vchmn, Templeton Co Rep Party, Mass, 66, chmn, 68- Bus & Prof Pos: Methods engr, Heald Machine Co, 56-63; sales engr, Lindco Inc, 63-70; abrasive sales engr, Rudel Machinery Co, Inc, 70- Mil Serv: Entered as Pvt, Army, 53, released as Cpl, 54, after serv in 623 FAB, Korea; Korean Medal. Mem: Am Soc Tool & Mech Engrs; Am Legion; Mason. Relig: Episcopal. Mailing Add: 6 Athol Rd Baldwinville MA 01436

HINES, LEON BROOKS (D)
Ala State Rep
b Ala, May 13, 47; s Jack W Hines, Sr & Elinor Brooks H; m to Betty Jean Low; c Ashley Elinor & Robert Brooks. Educ: Washington & Lee Univ, BA, 69; Vanderbilt Univ, 70-71; Beta Theta Pi. Polit & Govt Pos: Ala State Rep, 75- Bus & Prof Pos: Instr, Northern Va Community Col, 70-71; real estate broker, Hines Realty Co, Brewton, Ala, currently. Mem: Rotary. Relig: United Methodist. Legal Res: 805 Evergreen Ave Brewton AL 36426 Mailing Add: PO Box 345 Brewton AL 36426

HINES, LEON C (D)
Chmn, Dundy Co Dem Orgn, Nebr
b Benkelman, Nebr, June 10, 22; s Leon L Hines & Keturah E Sipe H; m 1946 to Anne E Rosser; c Elizabeth Susan, Patricia Ann & Barbara Ellen. Educ: Univ Nebr, BSc, 43, JD, 48; Phi Delta Phi; Kappa Sigma. Polit & Govt Pos: Mem, Nebr State Dem Cent Comt, 54-56; co attorney, Dundy Co, Nebr, 54-58; pres, Nebr Asn Housing & Renewal Authorities, 65-67; dir, Nat Asn Housing & Renewal Off, 66-68; chmn, Dundy Co Dem Orgn, 66- Mil Serv: Entered as Pfc, Army, 42, released as 1st Lt, 46, after serving in 106th Inf Div, ETO. Mem: Mason; Elks; Am Legion; CofC. Relig: Methodist. Mailing Add: 631 First Ave W Benkelman NE 69021

HINES, NEAL (D)
Iowa State Rep
Mailing Add: 225 J Ave Nevada IA 50201

HINES, PAULENA LININGER (R)
VChmn, Teller Co Rep Party, Colo
b Savannah, Mo, Sept 3, 09; d Atlee Burpee Lininger & Ollie Howard L; m 1931 to Ralph Everette Hines; c Marvin Eugene & Victor Burpee. Educ: Platt Bus Col, 29. Polit & Govt Pos: Vchmn, Teller Co Rep Party, Colo, 60- Bus & Prof Pos: Secy & bookkeeper, Mo Livestock Comn Co, 29-32. Mem: Ladies Auxiliary, VFW; Parent-Teacher Orgn; Lioness Club; Teller Co Rep Womens Club. Relig: Baptist. Mailing Add: Box 502 Woodland Park CO 80863

HINES, RICHARD TOWILL (R)
SC State Rep
Mailing Add: Box 6236 Spartanburg SC 29303

HINIG, WILLIAM E (D)
Ohio State Rep
b New Philadelphia, Ohio, May 24, 19; s Floyd W Hinig & Florence M Stilgenbauer H; m 1946 to Clara M Aldergate; c Judith L, Richard W & Jill. Educ: LaSalle Exten Univ. Polit & Govt Pos: Councilman-at-lg, New Philadelphia, Ohio, 62-63, pres, City Coun, 64; Ohio State Rep, Tuscarawas Co, currently. Bus & Prof Pos: Registered pub acct, Hinig & Miller Co, 53-66. Mil Serv: Entered as Pvt, Army, 41, released as Sgt, 46, after serv in Inf, ETO, 45; Purple Heart; ETO Ribbon. Mem: Nat Soc Pub Accts; Elks; DAV; VFW; Am Legion. Relig: Protestant. Mailing Add: 835 Hardesty Ave NW New Philadelphia OH 44663

HINKHOUSE, HERBERT CLARENCE (D)
Iowa State Rep
b West Liberty, Iowa, May 11, 17; s Fred W Hinkhouse & Clara L Pearson H; m 1941 to Doris Lenore Guthrie; c Richard W, H Clifford, Glenn A, Stanley Dean & Hilda Marie. Educ: Iowa State Univ, 37 & 38. Polit & Govt Pos: Iowa State Rep, 24th Dist, 75- Bus & Prof Pos: Pres, Hilhurst Farms Inc, Family Farm Corp, currently. Mil Serv: Entered as Pvt, Army, 42, released as Sgt, 46, after serv in ETO, 42-46; Bronze Star of Merit. Mem: Iowa Master Farmers Club; Cedar Co Farm Bur Bd; Fed Land Bank Asn of Iowa City; West Br CofC. Mailing Add: RR 2 Box 243 West Branch IA 52358

HINKLE, BERGIT EMMALINE (D)
Committeewoman, SDak State Dem Cent Comt
b Hyde Co, SDak, Dec 11, 12; d John Lamb Maginnis & Zoe E Hemphill M; m 1931 to Emory Evert Hinkle; c Mavis (Mrs George Kennedy), Harold & Joyce (Mrs Kenneth Ferris). Polit & Govt Pos: Secy, Dem Womens Club, Hyde Co, SDak, 63-; committeewoman, SDak State Dem Cent Comt, 66-; app, Abstractors Bd Examr, 73- Mem: Exten Homemaker's Club (chmn, Val-Loo Club, 60-68, 70-, state proj leader, Hyde Co, 66-68, 69-75, attended Nat Conv, 64, 66 & 68); Hyde Co Farmers Union (educ leader, Local 360, 54-); Hyde Co Hist & Genealogy Soc. Honors & Awards: Dedicated Serv Plaque, SDak Dem Party, 74. Relig: Methodist. Mailing Add: RR Holabird SD 57540

HINKLE, BEULAH FERN (D)
Secy-Treas, Holt Co Dem Cent Comt, Mo
b Bigelow, Mo, Apr 21, 13; d Roy Howe (stepfather) & Katherine Smith H; m 1931 to Alton B Hinkle; c Winona (Mrs Christensen), Wendell L & Anthony B. Educ: Mound City High Sch, Mo, grad. Polit & Govt Pos: Committeeman, Holt Co Dem Cent Comt, Mo, currently, secy-treas, currently. Mem: Holt Co Red Cross (chmn); Fortescue Garden Club; Womens Soc Christian Serv (admin chmn); Women's Dem Club (pres). Relig: Methodist. Mailing Add: Fortescue MO 64452

HINKLE, J D, JR (R)
WVa State Sen
Mailing Add: State Capitol Charleston WV 25305

HINMAN, GEORGE L (R)
Rep Nat Committeeman, NY
b Binghamton, NY, Sept 25, 05; s Harvey D Hinman & Phebe Brown H; m 1929 to Barbara Davidge; c Constance (Mrs Getz), Martha (Mrs Vaughn), Virginia (Mrs Robinson) & Harvey D, II. Educ: Princeton Univ, AB, 27; Harvard Univ, LLB, 30; Quadrangle Club. Hon Degrees: DHL, Elmira Col, 50; LLD, Union Univ, 62; LCD, Colgate Univ, 68. Polit & Govt Pos: Regent, State Univ NY, 48-50; mem, Lt Gov Comt on Teachers Salaries, 51; mem, NY Attorney Gen Comt on Ethical Standards in Govt, 55-59; counsel, NY State Temporary Comn on Const Conv & Spec Legis Comt on Rev & Simplification of Const, 56-58; exec asst to Gov Nelson A Rockefeller, NY, 58-59; Rep Nat Committeeman, NY, 59-, mem, Exec Comt, Rep Nat Comt, 74- deleg-at-lg, Rep Nat Conv, 60 & 64. Bus & Prof Pos: Partner, Hinman, Howard & Kattell, Binghamton, NY; spec counsel, Rockefeller Family & Assocs, New York, NY; dir, Int Bus Mach Corp, NY Tel Co, Security Mutual Life Ins Co of NY, First-City Nat Bank of Binghamton, Arlington Hotel, Inc & Lincoln First Banks, Inc. Mem: State Univ NY (trustee); Colgate Univ (trustee); Salvation Army NY State Adv Conf (exec comt); The Pilgrams; Harvard Club. Relig: Presbyterian. Legal Res: Hawleyton Rd Binghamton NY 13901 Mailing Add: Rm 5600 30 Rockefeller Plaza New York NY 10020

HINMAN, WALLACE PORTER (R)
Colo State Rep
b Nelson, Nev, June 16, 14; s Mark Merrit Hinman & Pearl Menhennett H; m 1940 to Ione Virginia Trantham; c Marian (Mrs Walton) & Jeanne. Educ: Kremmling High Sch, grad. Polit & Govt Pos: Colo State Rep, 69- Mem: Colo Hereford Asn; Routt Co Stock Growers; Colo Cattlemen's Asn; Elks, Idaho Springs, Colo; Aviation Club, Denver. Honors & Awards: Livestock Judging Awards; Serv Awards, State Fair Comn & Colo Cattlemen's Asn. Relig: Protestant. Mailing Add: PO Box 48 Yampa CO 80483

HINNERS, CHARLES CARSON (R)
Chmn, Dane Co Rep Party, Wis
b Wisconsin Rapids, Wis, May 11, 47; s Clark C Hinners & Edna Ferber H; m 1970 to Carol Mahoney; c Charles C, III & Catherine C. Educ: Univ Wis Sch Bus, BBA, 69, Law Sch, JD, 73; Phi Delta Phi; Delta Upsilon. Polit & Govt Pos: Chmn, Dane Co Rep Party, Wis, 75- Bus & Prof Pos: Lawyer, DeWitt, McAndrews & Porter, SC, 74; life underwriter, Conn Mutual Life Ins Co, 74- Mil Serv: Entered as Pvt, Army, 70, released as SP-4, 75, after serv in Co B, 1st Bn, 1st AIT Bde, Ft Leonard Wood, Mo, 70-71; Army Commendation Medal. Mem: Am Bar Asn; Dane Co Bar Asn (mem real property & probate comt); Madison Asn Life Underwriters (mem polit action comt); West Madison Jaycees; Wis Pub Links Golf Asn (mem exec comt). Honors & Awards: Grad of the Year, Phi Delta Phi, 73. Legal Res: 2244 Commonwealth Ave Madison WI 53705 Mailing Add: PO Box 1732 Madison WI 53701

HINSHAW, ANDREW J (R)
US Rep Calif
b Dexter, Mo, Aug 4, 23; s Ilene Hinshaw; c Andrew H. Educ: Univ Southern Calif, BS, acct & econ, Law Sch, 53-54, Appraisal Inst, 61. Polit & Govt Pos: Assessor, Orange Co, Calif, 65-73; US Rep, 39th Dist, Calif, 73-74, 40th Dist, 75- Mil Serv: Navy, 42-45. Legal Res: CA Mailing Add: 1128 Longworth House Off Bldg Washington DC 20515

HINSHAW, THOMAS MOORE (D)
b Muncie, Ind, Apr 8, 54; s Frederick Moore Hinshaw & Elizabeth Waite H; single. Educ: Northwestern Univ, Evanston, BA, 75; Ind Univ, Indianapolis Law Sch, currently. Polit & Govt Pos: Deleg, Ind Dem State Conv, 72 & 74; alt deleg, Dem Nat Conv, 72; alt deleg, Dem Nat Mid-Term Conf, 74; mem platform comt, Ind Dem Party, 72, mem deleg selection & affirmative action comt, 74; staff asst, Secy State, Ind, currently. Mem: Ind Friends Comt on Legis (exec secy, 72). Relig: Society of Friends. Mailing Add: 3625 Riverside Ave Muncie IN 47304

HINSON, CALDWELL THOMAS (D)
SC State Rep
b Lancaster, SC, Aug 1, 20; s Alexander M Hinson & Lula Barker H; m 1943 to Myrtle Louise Moore, c Caldwell T, Jr, Sarah, Donald M, Wanda E & Angela L. Educ: Buford High Sch, grad, 40. Polit & Govt Pos: SC State Rep, 69- Bus & Prof Pos: Grocery & meat market owner, 46-51; owner, Hinson Motors, 51-69. Mil Serv: Entered as Pvt, Army, serv as Rifleman & Machine Gunner, 10th Mt Inf, Italy, 44-45; Combat Inf Medal; Good Conduct Medal; Bronze Star with One Cluster; Purple Heart with Two Clusters. Mem: A&FM (Past Master, Jackson Lodge 53); RAM (Past High Priest, Keystone Chap 19); RSM (Past Illustrious Master, Witherspoon Coun 33 & Past Comdr, Rock Hill Commandary 15); Shrine (past pres, Jackson Club, charter mem Hejaz Temple Color Guard); AAONMS. Honors & Awards: York Cross of Honor, York Rite Masonry. Relig: Baptist. Mailing Add: 1115 Chesterfield Ave Lancaster SC 29720

HINSON, JON CLIFTON (D)
b Tylertown, Miss, Mar 16, 42; s Clifton Ford Hinson & Lyndell Newman H; single. Educ: Univ Southern Miss, 60-62; Univ Miss, BA, 64, Law Sch, 65-66; Cath Univ Law Sch, 67-68; Pi Kappa Alpha. Polit & Govt Pos: Doorman, US House of Rep, 67-68; legis asst to US Rep Charles H Griffin, Miss, 68-69, admin asst, 69-73; admin asst, US Rep Thad Cochran, Miss, 73- Mil Serv: Entered as Pvt, Marine Corps Res, 64, released as Cpl, 70. Legal Res: 509 Tyler Ave Tylertown MS 39667 Mailing Add: 502 Second St SE Washington DC 20003

HINTON, NELDA RUTH (D)
Mem, Cape Girardeau Co Dem Cent Comt, Mo
b Millersville, Mo, Sept 27, 37; d Roy Marshall Hahn & Berniece Rose M Jenkins H; m 1957 to Bob Clark Morton (deceased); m 1973 to Benny Ray Hinton; c Mark Anthony; stepsons, Anthony Gary Russell & Scott Andrew Ray Hinton. Educ: Oak Ridge High Sch, Mo, grad. Polit & Govt Pos: Dep circuit clerk, Cape Girardeau Co Court, 59-65; second vpres, Cape Co Young Dem Club, 63; secy, Byrd Twp Dem Club, 63-66; license bur agt, Jackson, 65-; mem, Cape Girardeau Co Dem Cent Comt, 70- Bus & Prof Pos: Dep magistrate clerk, Cape Girardeau Co, 73-74. Mem: Am Legion Auxiliary; Eastern Star; Beta Sigma Phi; Cape Girardeau Co Dem Women's Club; Suburban Garden Club (pres). Relig: Methodist. Mailing Add: Rte 2 Hwy 72 W Jackson MO 63755

HINTON, WAYNE KENDALL (D)
Chmn, Iron Co Dem Cent Comt, Utah
b St George, Utah, Aug 19, 40; s Wayne H Hinton & Jean Kendall H; m 1960 to Carolyn Spendlove; c Deborah, Julie Ann, Shawn & Kyle. Educ: Utah State Univ, BA, 62, MA, 64; Brigham Young Univ, PhD, 73; Phi Alpha Theta; Phi Kappa Phi; X Club; Utah State Lettermen's Club. Polit & Govt Pos: Voting dist chmn, Cedar City precinct, Utah, 64-66, precinct chmn, 70-71; deleg, Utah Dem State Conv, 64-73; mem & chmn, Iron Co Dem Cent Comt, 71-; chmn, Wayne Owens Campaign, Iron Co, 72. Bus & Prof Pos: Asst prof hist, Southern Utah State Col, currently, sen exec comt, Faculty Senate, 71- Publ: Co-auth, The Horn Silver Bonanza, Am West, A Reorientation, 66; auth, Civil rights controversy, 1948, Thetian, 4/67 & Mahonri Young & the Church: a view of Mormonism and art, Dialogue, winter 72; plus others. Mem: Orgn of Am Historians; Utah Hist Soc; Utah Educators Asn. Relig: Latter-day Saint. Mailing Add: 308 E 200 South Cedar City UT 84720

HIPPS, JUDY MATTHEW (D)
Second VChmn, NC State Dem Exec Comt
b Buncombe Co, June 6, 40; d Rev Grover S Matthew & Rhoda Irilla McCall M; m 1958 to Lenoir Wesley Hipps; c Kevin & Gaylyn. Educ: Enka High Sch, 58. Polit & Govt Pos: Mem, Beaver Dam No 4 Precinct Comt, 74-; mem, Haywood Co Dem Exec Comt, 74-, mem exec finance comt, 74-; second vchmn, NC State Dem Exec Comt, 75-, mem affirmative action study comt, 75- Bus & Prof Pos: Secy & off mgr, Nationwide Ins Agency, 68- Mem:

Pisgah Coun Girl Scouts Am; Boy Scouts Am (mother-asst, 75-); Canton YMCA Midget Majorettes (mothers auxiliary worker, 75-). Relig: Southern Baptist. Mailing Add: Rte 1 Woodland Circle Canton NC 28716

HIRABARA, MINORU (D)
Chmn, Hawaii Dem State Cent Comt
Mailing Add: PO Box 25 Kunia HI 96759

HIRKALA, JOSEPH (D)
NJ State Sen
Mailing Add: State House Trenton NJ 08625

HIRSCH, LOUIS RAPHAEL JOSEPH (D)
b Chicago, Ill, May 26, 51; s Irwin Hirsch & Edith H; single. Educ: Kendall Col, Evanston, Ill, 69-72; Univ Ill, Chicago Circle, 74- Polit & Govt Pos: State materials coordr, Ill McGovern for President, 72; research asst, Mass McGovern for President, 72; troubleshooter, Cleveland, Ohio McGovern for President, 72; canvass dir, Wayne & Westland, Mich, McGovern for President, 72; alt deleg, Dem Nat Conv, 72; polit action dir, Eighth Ward, Chicago, Ill McGovern for President, 72. Bus & Prof Pos: Mutual inspector, State Racing Bd, Ill, currently. Mem: Independent Precinct Orgn; Triangle Neighbors Asn. Relig: Jewish. Mailing Add: 3541 N Reta Chicago IL 60657

HIRSCHFELD, JOHN CHARLES (R)
Ill State Rep
b Urbana, Ill, Aug 5, 36; s Julius James Hirschfeld & Mary Hannagan H; m 1960 to Rita Porteous; c Laura Louise, John Sterling, Christopher Clark, Jennifer Elizabeth, Adam Benedict & Catherine Porteous. Educ: Univ Notre Dame, BA, 58, Law Sch, JD, 61; Blue Circle. Polit & Govt Pos: Ill State Rep, 48th Dist, 71-73, Ill State Rep, 52nd Dist, 73-, mem, Higher Educ Comt & Judiciary Comt, Ill House of Rep, currently. Bus & Prof Pos: Past asst pub defender, Champaign Co, Ill; partner, Meyer, Capel, Hirschfeld, Muncy, Jahn & Aldeen Law Firm. Mil Serv: Entered as 2nd Lt, Army, 58, released as 1st Lt, 64, after serv in Mil Intel, 58-64. Mem: Am Bar Asn; Ill Bar Asn (lectr, Inst on Continuing Educ); Am Judicature Soc; Am Arbit Asn; assoc League of Women Voters. Honors & Awards: Best Freshman Rep in 77th Gen Assembly, Readers of Newsletter, Ill Polit Reporter; Outstanding Freshman Mem House of Rep, 77th Gen Assembly, Ill State Med Soc; One of 50 Outstanding Legislators in US; Eagleton Inst Polit, Rutgers Univ; Outstanding Mem Rep Party in Ill, 72-73, Ill Col Rep Fedn, 73. Relig: Roman Catholic. Mailing Add: 1106 Country Lane Champaign IL 61820

HIRST, NANCY MELROSE (D)
b Los Angeles, Calif; d Dewey Franklin Hand & Margaret Jane Button H; m 1972 to Omer Lee Hirst; c Winifred Button & Christopher Llewelly Henderson. Educ: Stanford Univ, BA, 47; Pi Sigma Alpha; Phi Beta Kappa. Polit & Govt Pos: Legis aide, Sen Wm F Knowland, 47-51; writer, Rep Kenneth A Roberts, 53-57; writer & legis aide, Rep John C Watts, Ky, 54-71; staff dir, Spec Subcomt on Traffic Safety House Interstate & Foreign Com, 57-58; legis aide, Rep Curlin, 71-72; admin asst, Rep Carroll Hubbard, 75- Publ: Auth, Working Mothers, New York Herald Tribune, 54; photographer, Rio Rimac, Children's Book, 65. Honors & Awards: Phi Beta Kappa. Relig: Episcopal. Mailing Add: 5008 Philip Rd Annandale VA 22003

HIRST, OMER LEE (D)
Va State Sen
b Annandale, Va, Aug 30, 13; m to Nancy Melrose Hand. Educ: Washington & Lee Univ, BS; Phi Beta Kappa. Polit & Govt Pos: Mem adv comt, George Mason Col; Va State Deleg, 54-59; Va State Sen, 64-, chmn, Privileges & Elec Comt, currently. Bus & Prof Pos: Realtor; bd of trustees, Va Found for Independent Col; dir, Arlington Trust Co, Arlington, Va; dir, Northern Va Transportation Comn. Mil Serv: Lt, Marines. Mem: Hist Soc of Fairfax Co; Northern Va Bd of Realtors, Inc; North Va Bldrs Asn; City Tavern Club; Farmington Country Club. Honors & Awards: Evening Star Trophy, 62. Relig: Methodist. Mailing Add: PO Box 331 Annandale VA 22003

HISE, JOHN ANDREW, JR (R)
Vt State Rep
Mailing Add: Pilgrim Farms Bristol VT 05443

HISLOPE, LEONARD RUSSELL (R)
Ky State Rep
b Somerset, Ky, Mar 21, 13; s Russ Hislope & Stella Floyd H; m 1936 to Stella Mae Morgon Griffin. Educ: Western Ky State Univ, BS, 36; Eastern Ky Univ, grad work; Univ Chicago, law courses; Col Debating Club. Polit & Govt Pos: Ky State Rep, 56-59, caucus chmn, Ky House of Rep, 58, minority leader, 60 & 64, mem, Legis Research Comn, Ky Gen Assembly, 60-64; dir, Sites & Shrines Div & curator & regional dir, Ky Hist Soc, currently; Ky State Rep, 75- Bus & Prof Pos: Instr, Pulaski Co Bd Educ, 32-41; instr, Air Corps, 41-45; indust promotion, Ky Utility Co, 61- Publ: Tribute to a lady from Spain; Criticism of US Supreme Court & fiscal policies of US, 63 & Comments on Daniel Boone Show, various newspapers. Mem: Pulaski Co Hist Soc; Odd Fellows; CofC; Pulaski Co Farm Bur; Am Security Coun. Honors & Awards: One of Five Most Outstanding Mem, Ky House of Rep, 62, Hon Poet Laureate, 64, Orator of House for always writing own resolutions, 64. Mailing Add: 107 Church St Somerset KY 42501

HITCHCOCK, CAROLYN SPARK (R)
Mem, Minn Rep State Cent Comt
b McKees Rocks, Pa, Nov 27, 35; d Walter Spark & Frances Majewski S; m 1958 to Peter R Hitchcock; c Leslie, Nancy & Thomas. Educ: Chatham Col, BS, 57; Univ Pittsburgh, 1 year. Polit & Govt Pos: Chmn, 63rd Legis Rep Dist, Minn, 62-65; mem, Minn Rep State Cent Comt, 65-; chmn, St Louis Co Rep Party, 69-72; mem, Minn Rep State Adv Coun, 69- Bus & Prof Pos: Qual control anal, H J Heinz Co, Pittsburgh, Pa, summers 55 & 56; research chemist, Hagan Chemicals & Controls, 57-59; travel agt, Hitchcock Travel Agency, Hibbing, Minn, 65- Mem: Am Chem Soc; Am Asn Univ Women; League Women Voters; Coun Cath Women. Honors & Awards: Gov Citation for passage of Const Amendment. Relig: Catholic. Mailing Add: 333 Highland Dr Hibbing MN 55746

HITCHCOCK, DAVID N (D)
Wyo State Sen
Mailing Add: 1422 Sublette St Laramie WY 82070

HITCHCOX, FORREST L (D)
Treas, Anderson Co Dem Exec Comt, Tenn
b Pikeville, Tenn, Sept 10, 24; s John Marion Hitchcox & Elizabeth Tate H; m 1945 to Gwendolyn England; c Michael Forrest. Educ: Am Univ DC, nine months. Polit & Govt Pos: Secy, Oak Ridge Young Dem Club, Tenn, 52-54; Second Dist chmn, Young Dem Club Tenn, 52-54; treas, Anderson Co Dem Exec Comt, 62-; deleg, Dem Nat Conv, 68. Bus & Prof Pos: Mgr, Powell Clinch Utility Dist, 67- Mil Serv: Entered as A/S, Navy, 43, released as PhoM 2C, 45, after serv in Bomb & Mine Disposal Unit, SPac Theatre, 44-45; Navy & Presidential Unit Citations. Mem: Am Legion; Optimist Club. Relig: Protestant. Mailing Add: 114 Kingfisher Lane Oak Ridge TN 37830

HITE, F RICHARD (R)
b Lafayette, Colo, June 22, 14; s Arleigh Dempster Hite & Mae Daniels H; m 1946 to Alice Marjorie Brennan; c Richard Garth & Janis Ruthellen. Educ: Univ Colo, BA, 38, Law Sch, LLB, 41; Phi Delta Theta. Polit & Govt Pos: Dep dist attorney, Denver, Colo, 46-48; asst attorney gen, Colo, 50-52; mem, Colo Racing Comn, 53-60 & 67-70; mem, Jefferson Co Rep Exec Comt, 56-60; chmn, Jefferson Co Rep Finance Comt, 56-60; precinct committeeman, Jefferson Co Rep Party, 60-69; asst dist attorney, Jefferson Co, 61-67; secy, United Rep Fund, 62-64; chmn, Jefferson Co Rep Conv, 64; deleg, Rep Nat Conv, 64; chmn, Jefferson Co Rep Cent Comt, formerly. Mil Serv: Entered as Pvt, Army, 42, released as Capt, 46, after serv in 7th Div, Asiatic Theatre, 42-45. Mem: Colo & Jefferson Co Bar Asns; Lions; Mason. Relig: Protestant. Mailing Add: 3705 Garland Wheatridge CO 80033

HITT, MARY BARTON (D)
Dem Nat Committeewoman, Ga
b Augusta, Ga, Aug 20, 36; d Samuel Ashton Barton & Irene Widener B; m 1955 to William Alexander Hitt, MD; c William A, Jr, Mark Christopher, Matthew David, Melody Ann & Michael Barton. Educ: Waycross Ga Ctr, Univ Ga, currently. Polit & Govt Pos: Mem, Ga State Dem Exec Comt, 71-; mayor, Jesup, Ga, 71-72; mem, Dem Nat Comt, 72- Bus & Prof Pos: News ed, Jesup Sentinel, Ga, 68-70. Publ: Column Putting Around with Mary, Jesup Sentinel, 65 & many feature stories about Wayne Co. Mem: Ga Comt for the Humanities; Altamaha Woman's Club (proj chmn); Tecoma Garden Club; Augusta Pharmaceutical Auxiliary; Akk Med Wives Club. Relig: Methodist; past Sunday Sch Teacher; past pres, Koinonia Circle; mem choir. Mailing Add: 245 Williamson Dr Jesup GA 31545

HITT, PATRICIA REILLY (R)
Mem Exec Comt, Rep State Cent Comt Calif
b Taft, Calif, Jan 24, 18; d John B Reilly & Vera Hearle R (deceased); m 1947 to Robert J Hitt; c John & Patrick Hamilton. Educ: Univ Southern Calif, BS in Educ, 39; Delta Gamma. Hon Degrees: LHD, Chapman Col; LLD, Whittier Col, 72. Polit & Govt Pos: Mem & vchmn, Orange Co Rep Cent Comt, Calif, 55-62; mem bd, Calif Fedn Rep Women, Southern Div, 55-65; pres, Orange Co Fedn Women's Clubs, 56-60; mem exec comt, Rep State Cent Comt Calif, 58-; Rep Nat Committeewoman, Calif, 60-64; chmn women's activities, George Murphy Campaign, 64 & Robert Finch Campaign, 66; co-chmn, Nixon-Agnew Campaign, 68; Asst Secy for Commun & Field Serv, Dept Health, Educ & Welfare, 69-73; comnr, US Comn for US-Mex Border Develop & Friendship, 69-72; mem, President's Comn White House Fels, currently. Bus & Prof Pos: Partner, Miller-Hitt; part owner, Reilly Holdings; mem bd trustees, Los Angeles Orthop Hosp, 74- Mem: Whittier Col (bd trustees); Assistance League; Villa Park Property Owners Asn; CofC; Chapman Col (bd gov). Honors & Awards: Los Angeles Times Woman of the Year, 68; Alumni Merit Award, Univ Southern Calif, 72. Relig: Methodist. Legal Res: 178 Emerald Bay Laguna Beach CA 92651 Mailing Add: 730 Temple Pl Laguna Beach CA 92651

HLAVIN, LYNNE E (R)
Co-Dir Region V, Nat Young Rep Fedn
b Chicago, Ill, Aug 3, 41; d Merl Webster McCoy & Cornelia Jacobsen M; m 1971 to Richard John Hlavin; c stepchildren, Christine & Geoffrey. Educ: High Sch. Polit & Govt Pos: Secy, Ohio League Young Rep, 64-65, co-chmn, 65-66; deleg, Young Rep Nat Fedn Conv, 65 & 71; nat committeewoman, Nat Young Rep Fedn, 66-67, co-dir, Region V, 71- Bus & Prof Pos: Regional leasing mgr, Klingbeil Co, Columbus, Ohio, 67-70; property mgr, Columbia Properties, 70-71, property management dir, Sisson-Stern Cos, 71- Mem: Columbus Bd Realtors; Inst Real Estate Mgt; Gtr Cleveland Young Rep Club; Heart of Ohio Sighthound Club (secy, 73-74); Midwest Borzoi Club. Mailing Add: 7677 Riverside Dr Dublin OH 43017

HO, RICHARD CHUNG SING (D)
Hawaii State Rep
b Honolulu, Hawaii, Sept 10, 41; s Richard K W Ho (deceased) & Ethel K Keola H; m 1961 to Esmeralda Ventula Castanares; c Rita-Ann D H, Richard Chung Sing, II, Raymond Kong Wai, Russell Cres & Regina-Marie Mililani. Educ: Leeward Community Col, AA, 74. Polit & Govt Pos: Hawaii State Rep, 21st Dist, 75- Bus & Prof Pos: Cryptographic operator, US Naval Commun Sta, 69-74. Mil Serv: Entered as Pvt, Air Force, 60, released as Sgt, 68, after serv in 1864th Commun Grp-VN, 67-68; Nat Defense Ribbon; Vietnam Campaign; Vietnam Serv Longevity; Good Conduct; Marksmanship. Mem: Ewa Estate Community Asn (pres, 74-); Ewa Beach Community Asn (pres, Area Adv Coun, Parks & Recreation); VFW; Puuloa Hawaiian Civic Club; Jaycees. Honors & Awards: Cert of Appreciation, City & Co Honolulu, 74. Relig: Catholic. Mailing Add: 91-813 Kauwili St Ewa Beach HI 96706

HOAGLAND, JOSEPH JULIAN (R)
Kans State Rep
b Kansas City, Mo, Dec 14, 47; s Virgil L Hoagland & Estella Ruth Reed H; married. Educ: Tulane Univ, BA, 70; Univ Kans, JD, 74; Phi Kappa Sigma. Polit & Govt Pos: Kans State Rep, 22nd Dist, 73- Bus & Prof Pos: Vpres, Racket Merchandise Co, 70-71; partner law firm, Ross, Wells, Fagerberg & Hoagland, Overland Park, currently. Mem: Kans State Bar; Kansas City Jaycees. Relig: Lutheran. Mailing Add: 6921 W 79th St Overland Park KS 66204

HOAR, JOHN, JR (R)
NH State Rep
Mailing Add: Box 51 Epping NH 03042

HOBART, ANNE MOORE (R)
Mem, Oakland Co Rep Comt & Exec Comt, Mich
b Lansing, Mich, Dec 3, 29; d John Potts Hobart & Bertha V Robinson H; single. Educ: Alma Col, BA, 51; Wayne State Univ, sec teaching cert, 58-59; Instituto Technologico, Monterrey, Mex, summer 60; Univ Mich, MA, 69; Alpha Psi Omega; Sigma Phi; Drama Club. Polit & Govt Pos: Precinct deleg, Rep Party, Waterford Twp, Mich, 68-, twp dir, 72-; mem, 19th Cong Dist Rep Party, 69-; treas, Waterford Twp Rep Women, 72-; mem, Oakland Co Rep

Comt & Exec Comt, 72-; alt deleg, Rep Nat Conv, 72; comnr, Oakland Co, 73- Bus & Prof Pos: Med artist & photographer, Univ of Buffalo Chronic Disease Research Inst, 51-53; med photographer, Henry Ford Hosp, Detroit, Mich, 53-56; dent asst, Dr John McColl, Birmingham, 56-57; commercial artist, Gen Motors Photog, Detroit, 57-58; teacher speech & drama, Waterford Twp High Sch, Pontiac, 59-61; teacher Eng & art, Jr High Sch, Brooklyn, NY, 61-63; teacher speech & drama, Waterford Twp Sch, Pontiac, Mich, 63-72. Mem: People & Rep; Lincoln Club (bd dirs, 72-); Avon Players, Rochester, Mich; Elizabeth Lake Estates Improv Asn, Pontiac. Honors & Awards: Best Actress, Detroit-Windsor Theatre Coun, 61. Mailing Add: 4081 Arcadia Park Dr Pontiac MI 48054

HOBBINS, BARRY JOHN (D)
Maine State Rep
b Biddeford, Maine, May 17, 51; s J Raymond Hobbins & Harriet McDonough H; single. Educ: St Michael's Col, 69-71; Univ Maine, BA, 73; Sigma Phi Epsilon. Polit & Govt Pos: Pres-founder, Saco Young Dem, Maine, 72; Maine State Rep, 73- Honors & Awards: Youngest Rep in Maine State Legis. Relig: Catholic. Mailing Add: 14 Promenade Ave Saco ME 04072

HOBBS, CORNELIUS F (D)
NH State Rep
Mailing Add: 31 Dennett St Portsmouth NH 03801

HOBBS, LARRY F (R)
Colo State Rep
Mailing Add: Star Rte Box 122 Morrison CO 80465

HOBBS, MICHAEL DICKINSON (R)
Chmn, New Canaan Rep Town Party, Conn
b San Juan, PR, Sept 14, 41; s Theodore deFreyne Hobbs & Elizabeth Paddock H; m 1963 to Hazel Rich; c Michael, Scott & Ian. Educ: Johns Hopkins Univ, BS, 63; Beta Theta Pi. Polit & Govt Pos: Chmn, New Canaan Rep Town Party, Conn, 73- Bus & Prof Pos: Construction foreman, T deF Hobbs, Inc, 68-69, prod mgr & vpres, 69-75, pres, 75-; incorporator & founder, New Canaan Bank & Trust, 74-75. Mil Serv: Entered as Lt, Air Force, 63, released as Capt, 68; Jr Officer of Year, Norton AFB, 67. Mem: Rotary (bd dirs); Assoc Builders & Contractors Fairfield Co (vpres, 75-). Mailing Add: 255 Main St New Canaan CT 06840

HOBBS, RUTH JOSEPHINE (R)
b Wilmette, Ill, Jan 24, 13; d Samuel Cohen & Ronald Hilmer C; m 1932 to Wendell Wilson Hobbs; c Robert S & William S. Educ: Rockford Col, 30-32; Univ Mich, 40-43. Polit & Govt Pos: Pres, Ann Arbor Women's Rep Club, Mich, 54; mem, State Rep Cent Comt, 55-72, vchmn, women's activities, 64-65 & dir, 65-66; alt deleg, Rep Nat Conv, 56 & 64, alt deleg-at-lg, 68 & chmn, Transportation to Nat Conv, State Rep Cent Comt, 64 & chmn, Transportation to Nat Conv, 68; asst campaign coord, Second Cong Rep Comt, 60-63; co-chmn, Gov Inauguration, 64-65; pres, Rep Women's Fedn, 66-69; treas, Nat Fedn Rep Women, 68-72; comnr, Ann Arbor Human Rels Comn, 68-72; chmn, Housing Div, 69-72. Bus & Prof Pos: Vpres, Hobbs-Schmidt & Co, 58; pres, Ann Arbor Bd of Realtors, 62; dir, Mich Real Estate Asn, 62; corp secy, Hobbs, Caldwell Spaly & Co, 62-68, sales mgr, 68- Mem: Women's City Club; Ann Arbor's Workable Prog (secy); League of Women Voters; Ann Arbor Golf & Outing Club. Relig: Protestant. Mailing Add: 17 Westbury Ct Ann Arbor MI 48105

HOBBY, OVETA CULP (R)
b Killeen, Tex, Jan 19, 05; d I W Culp & Emma Hoover C; m 1931 to William P Hobby (deceased); c William & Jessica (Mrs Henry E Catto, Jr). Educ: Mary Hardin-Baylor Col. Hon Degrees: LLD, LHD, LittD & HHD from various cols & univs, 43-56. Polit & Govt Pos: Parliamentarian, Tex House of Rep, 26-31, 39 & 41; chief, Women's Interest Sect, Bur Pub Rels, War Dept, 41-42, appt dir WAAC, 42, WAC, 43-45; consult, Alt UN Freedom of Info Conf, Geneva, Switz, 48; consult, Comt on Orgn of Exec Br of Govt, 48; Fed Security Adminr, 53; Secy, Dept Health, Educ & Welfare, 53-55; mem, President's Comt on Employ of Physically Handicapped & President's Comt on Civilian Nat Honors; mem, Comt for White House Conf on Educ, 54-55; mem, Nat Adv Comt, Citizens for Eisenhower, 56; trustee, Am Assembly, 57-66 & Eisenhower Exchange Fels, 57-; mem, Carnegie Comn on Educ TV, 65-67, Vietnam Health Educ Task Force, Dept Health, Educ & Welfare, 66 & Nat Adv Comn on Selective Serv, 66-67. Bus & Prof Pos: Research ed, Houston Post, 31, lit ed, asst ed, vpres, exec vpres, ed & publisher, 31-53, pres, 55-65, ed, 55-; chmn bd, Houston Post Co, 65-; dir, Sta KPRC & KPRC-TV, 45-53, 55-, chmn, 72-; mem bd dirs, Gen Food Corp, 65-67 & Corp for Pub Broadcasting, 68-72. Mil Serv: Col, WAC, 42-45; Distinguished Serv Medal, 44; Philippine Mil Merit Medal, 47. Publ: Mr Chairman, parliamentary law textbook; syndicated column, Mr Chairman. Mem: Adv Comt on Econ Develop (bd, 56-); Southern Regional Comt for Marshall Scholarships (bd, 57-); Crusade for Freedom, Inc (bd, 58-); Rice Univ (trustee, 67-); Bus Comt for the Arts, Inc (trustee, 67-). Honors & Awards: Publisher of the Year Award, Headliners Club, 60; Living Hist Award, Research Inst of Am, 60; Honor Award, Nat Jewish Hosp, 62; Carnegie Corp Award for the Advan & Diffusion of Knowledge & Understanding, 67. Relig: Episcopal. Mailing Add: 4747 Southwest Freeway Houston TX 77001

HOBBY, WILBUR (D)
Mem, NC Dem State Exec Comt
b Durham, NC, Nov 8, 25; s W Curtiss Hobby & Carrie Holsclaw H; m 1968 to Jean Hogan; c Phyllis (Mrs Lasater), James Lester, Steven Rex, Russell Franklin, Michael Timothy & Susan Jane. Educ: Duke Univ, 52-55; Labor Studies Ctr, Washington, DC. Polit & Govt Pos: Secy, Durham Co Dem Party, NC, 55-58; mem, Durham Young Dem Clubs, 55-75; area dir, Comt on Polit Educ, AFL-CIO, 59-69; mem, NC Dem State Exec Comt, 70-; cand for Gov of NC, 72; deleg, Dem Nat Conv, 72. Bus & Prof Pos: Pres, Durham Cent Labor Union, NC, 54-58; polit dir, Textile Workers Union, SEastern States, 58; pres, NC State AFL-CIO, 69-75. Mil Serv: Entered as Seaman, Navy, 42, released as Gunners Mate 2/C, 46, after serv on USS Manlove Destroyer, Pac, 44-46; Good Conduct Medal; Am, Pac Theatre, 5 Stars, Philippines, Victory Medal. Publ: Ed, Durham Labor J, Progressive Party & Publ Co, 55-58, Carolina Labor Views, 69-73 & Carolina Labor News, 73-74, NC State AFL-CIO. Mem: Am Vet World War II; Tri-State Labor Sch (pres); NC Econ Educ Asn (vpres); NC Consumer Coun (exec bd); Appalachian Labor Coun (exec bd). Honors & Awards: Man of Year, Amvets, 58; Labor Man of Year, Histradrut, 72; Hon Membership, Meatcutters Union, 72. Relig: Baptist. Legal Res: 714 W Johnson St Raleigh NC 27605 Mailing Add: PO Box 10805 Raleigh NC 27605

HOBBY, WILLIAM PETTUS (D)
Lt Gov, Tex
b Houston, Tex, Jan 19, 32; s William Pettus Hobby, Sr & Oveta Culp H; m 1954 to Diana Poteat Stallings; c Laura, Paul, Andrew & Katherine. Educ: Rice Univ, BA in Am Hist, 53. Polit & Govt Pos: Parliamentarian, Tex State Senate, 59, pres, 73-; Lt Gov, Tex, 73- Bus & Prof Pos: Asst secy-treas, Houston Post, 57-59, assoc ed, 59-60, managing ed, 60-63, exec ed, 63- & pres, 65-. Mil Serv: Entered as Ens, Navy, 53, released as Lt (jg), 57, after serv in Naval Intel; Inactive Res, 57-59; Nat Defense Serv Medal. Mem: Better Bus Bur (bd dirs, 71-74); Tex Med Ctr (bd dirs, 73); Am Soc Newspaper Ed; Houston CofC (dir); Rotary. Honors & Awards: One of Five Outstanding Young Texans, Tex Jr CofC, 65. Relig: Episcopal. Legal Res: PO Box 326 Houston TX 77001 Mailing Add: Capitol Bldg Austin TX 78711

HOBDY, CLARENCE CHESTER (R)
Mem, Rep State Cent Comt Calif
b Alvord, Tex, Nov 28, 02; s Herbert Hobdy & Mainna Cornelia Sossaman H; m 1939 to Dorothy Dee Book; c Clarence Jr, Vida Delorez, Robert Raymond & David Darryll. Educ: Chillicothe Bus Col, Mo, 22; Tenor Soloist, College Male Quartet & Glee Club. Polit & Govt Pos: Dir, Vol for Eisenhower-Nixon, 52; mem & alt, Los Angeles Co Rep Cent Comt, 52-, mem, Rules Comt & chmn, Subcomt on Personnel Develop, 58-61, mem, Exec Comt, 69-74, treas, 71-74, chmn, Sr Citizens Comt, 72, mem exec bd, 73-74; precinct chmn, 40th Assembly Dist Rep Cent Comt, 52-54, chmn, 55-61; capt, home precinct, 52-72; chmn, Comt to Elect Norris Poulsen Mayor, 53; mem, Rep State Cent Comt Calif, 54-60 & 73-, assoc mem, 61-62; mem, US Sen Kuchel's Comt, 56; vchmn, 19th Cong Dist Rep Cent Comt, 56-61, polit educ chmn, 62-64 & chmn, 64 & 69-72; mem host comt, Rep Nat Conv, 56, asst sgt at arms, 60 & 64 & hon deleg-alt, 72; co-chmn, Mex-Am Serv Ctr, East Los Angeles, 60-61; Presidential Elector, 64; chmn, Norwalk Rep Hq, 64; polit hobbyist & adv to cand for many years. Bus & Prof Pos: Various assignments, Atchison, Topeka & Santa Fe Rwy Co, 22-39, personnel asst, 39-43, chief clerk to div supt, 43-49; asst supvr wage agreements, Santa Fe Rwy Syst, 49-50; supvr wage agreements, Los Angeles Junction Rwy Co, 50-69, retired; counr, Rose Hills Mem Park, Whittier, Calif, 69- Mil Serv: Entered as Pvt, Tex Nat Guard, 33, released as S/Sgt, 35; Sharpshooter. Mem: Mason (Master); Eastern Star (past Patron). Relig: Baptist. Mailing Add: 14513 Dumont Ave Norwalk CA 90650

HOBELMAN, MARGARET ELLEN (D)
Pres, Kans Fedn Women's Dem Clubs
b Kansas City, Mo, Mar 4, 26; d James Roy Morgan & Margaret Warner M; m 1946 to Delburt Joseph Hobelman; c David Joseph & Rita Marie. Educ: St Joseph's Col, 61. Polit & Govt Pos: Precinct committeewoman, Wilson Co Dem Cent Comt, Kans, 58-, secy, 61-63, treas, 63-65, vchmn, 65-67, chmn, 67-71, vchmn, 71-73, chmn, 73-; pres, Kans Fedn Women's Dem Clubs, 73-; deleg, Dem Nat Mid-Term Conf, 74. Publ: Co-ed, Home & Community Gov Comn 1968 report on the status of women, State Kans, 1/69. Mem: Nat Coun Cath Women; Women In Community Serv; Jaycee Jaynes; St Margaret's Hosp Auxiliary; Gov Comn Status Women (chmn, Home & Community, 67-73). Honors & Awards: Women In Community Serv Awards, 66-71, Wichita, Kans; Dem Woman of the Year, Wilson Co Dem Club, 68. Relig: Catholic. Mailing Add: 403 N 15th Fredonia KS 66736

HOBLITZELLE, GEORGE KNAPP (R)
Mo State Rep
b St Louis, Mo, Sept 28, 21; s Harrison Hoblitzelle & Mary D Jones H; m 1950 to Katharine L Wells; c Katharine, Trimble & Lucy. Educ: St Paul's Sch, Concord, NH, 36-39; Princeton Univ, AB, 43; Harvard Univ Bus Sch, Advan Mgt Prog, 62. Polit & Govt Pos: Mo State Rep, 73- Bus & Prof Pos: Trainee, Gen Steel Industs, Inc, 46-48, asst to vpres & treas, 48-51, secy, 53-56, vpres & secy, 56-72. Mil Serv: Entered as Officer Cand, Army, 43, released as Capt, 46, after serv in various units, ETO, 44-45; recalled to active duty, Asst Chief of Staff, G-2, Hq US Army, The Pentagon, 51-53; Bronze Star for Valor; various campaign ribbons. Mem: Life mem Nat Defense Transportation Asn; Sigma Xi; Arts & Educ Coun of Gtr St Louis (dir). Relig: Episcopal. Mailing Add: 42 Glen Eagles Ladue MO 63124

HOBSON, PHILLIP MAURICE (R)
NMex State Rep
b Alamogordo, NMex, Sept 11, 42; s Phillip Jack Hobson & Mabel Champion H; div; c Karen Louise. Educ: Univ Ariz, 60-61; NMex State Univ, BBA, 65; Sigma Alpha Epsilon. Polit & Govt Pos: NMex State Rep, Dist Two, 71-72, NMex State Rep, Dist 52, 72-, minority caucus leader & mem judicial coun, NMex House of Rep, 71- Bus & Prof Pos: Asst cashier, Security Bank & Trust, Holloman AFB, NMex, 65-67, asst cashier & br mgr, Security Ctr, Alamogordo, 67-68, bd dirs, Security Bank & Trust, Alamogordo, 66-, asst vpres, 68, exec vpres, 70-; bd dirs, Bank Securities, Inc of Alamogordo, 69-, vpres & secy, 72-; dir, Security Bank of Ruidoso, 70-, Am Bank of Carlsbad, Citizens State Bank, Vaughn, First Nat Bank of Portales & First State Bank, Rio Rancho Estates, 72- Mem: Rotary; Zia Sch for Retarded Children (bd dirs); Red Cross (bd dirs); Boys' Club of Alamogordo (bd dirs); Am Field Serv (bd dirs). Honors & Awards: Participant, Exchange Study Group to Visit Southern Australia, Rotary, 67. Relig: Methodist. Mailing Add: 515 16th St Alamogordo NM 88310

HOBSTETTER, ELIZABETH ALICE (R)
Secy, Meigs Co Rep Cent & Exec Comts, Ohio
b Gallipolis, Ohio, Feb 15, 19; d Rufus Andrew Pitchford & Callie Lee Johnston P; m 1940 to William Jacob Hobstetter; c James William. Educ: Gallia Acad High Sch, Gallipolis, Ohio, dipl, 37. Polit & Govt Pos: Committeewoman, Rutland Village, Meigs Co Rep Party, Ohio, 65-; secy, Meigs Co Rep Cent & Exec Comts, 68- Bus & Prof Pos: Clerk, Meigs Co Court, Pomeroy, Ohio, 55- Relig: Methodist. Legal Res: Salem St Rutland OH 45775 Mailing Add: Box 22 Rutland OH 45775

HOCHBERG, ALAN (D)
NY State Assemblyman
Mailing Add: 2040 Bronxdale Ave Bronx NY 10462

HOCHBRUECKNER, GEORGE JOSEPH (D)
NY State Assemblyman
b Queens, NY, Sept 20, 38; s Bertram Hochbrueckner & Alice Rogers H; m 1961 to Carol Ann Seifert; c George, Jr, Michael, Elizabeth & Matthew. Educ: NY State Univ, Oyster Bay, 59-60; Hofstra Univ, 60; Pierce Col (Calif), 62-64; San Fernando Valley State Col, 65. Polit & Govt Pos: NY State Assemblyman, 75- Bus & Prof Pos: Electronics technician, Grumman Aerospace Corp, 60-61; comput engr, Litton Industs, 61-64 & Teledyne Systs Co, 65-74. Mil Serv: Entered as Airman Apprentice, Navy, 56, released as Aviation Electronics Technician 2/C, 59, after serv in Heavy Attack Squadron 1, ECoast & Aboard Aircraft Carriers, 57-59.

Mem: Tanglewood Dem Club (pres). Relig: Roman Catholic. Legal Res: 1 Wycomb Pl Coram NY 11727 Mailing Add: Rm 723 Legis Off Bldg Albany NY 12224

HOCHMAN, NANCY RUTH (D)

b Norwalk, Ohio, Oct 23, 44; d Arthur Desire Henry & Ruth Linkenbach H; m 1972 to William R Hochman; c Timothy Arthur. Educ: Univ of the Pac, AB in Hist, 66; Univ Calif, Berkeley, grad work; Kappa Alpha Theta. Polit & Govt Pos: Mem, Lafayette Dem Exec Comt, Calif, 70-71; deleg, Colo Dem State Conv & Dem Nat Conv, 72. Bus & Prof Pos: Elem sch teacher, Holbrook Elem Sch, Concord, Calif, 66-71 & Colorado Springs Commun Sch, Colo, 71-73; math instr, El Paso Community Col, spring 72. Publ: The potential danger in comparative culture units, Calif Coun for Soc Studies, spring 70. Mem: Mortar Bd. Relig: Episcopal. Mailing Add: 1237 Terrace Rd Colorado Springs CO 80904

HOCHMAN, WILLIAM RUSSELL (D)

b New York, NY, Aug 28, 21; s Julius C Hochman & Ruth H H; m 1941 to Margaret D Schloss; c Abby (Mrs Odam), Dean (Mrs Kolstad), Meg & John; div; m 1972 to Nancy Henry; c Timothy. Educ: Lincoln Sch Teachers Col, dipl, 38; Columbia Col, AB, 42; Columbia Univ, MA, 48, PhD(hist), 55. Polit & Govt Pos: Mem, El Paso Co Dem Cent Comt, Colo, 58-75; alt deleg, Dem Nat Conv, 60 & 72, deleg & mem platform comt, Dem Nat Conv, 64, deleg & mem credentials comt, Dem Nat Conv, 68; secy, Dem Party Colo, 61-65. Bus & Prof Pos: Historian, Air Defense Command, US Air Force, 49-50, 52-53; instr hist, Univ Colo Exten Ctr, Colorado Springs, Colo, 53-55; from instr to prof hist, Colo Col, 55-, chmn dept hist, 70- Mil Serv: Entered as Ens, Navy, 42, released as Lt(jg), 45, after serv in Amphibious Force, ETO; Four Battle Stars. Mem: Nat Humanities Faculty; Am Hist Asn; Orgn Am Historians. Mailing Add: 1237 Terrace Rd Colorado Springs CO 80904

HODEL, DONALD PAUL (R)

b Portland, Ore, May 23, 35; s Philip E Hodel & Theresia Rose Brodt H; m 1956 to Barbara Beecher Stockman; c Philip Stockman (deceased) & David Beecher. Educ: Harvard Col, BA, 57; Univ Ore Law Sch, JD, 60; Phi Delta Phi. Polit & Govt Pos: Treas, Harvard Young Rep Club, 55-56, pres, 56-57; precinct orgn, Clackamas Co Rep Cent Comt, Ore, 64, secy, 64-65 & chmn, 65-66; chmn, Ore Rep State Cent Comt, 66-67; alt deleg, Rep Nat Conv, 68; dep adminr, Bonneville Power Admin, 69-72, adminr, 72- Bus & Prof Pos: Attorney, Davies, Biggs, Strayer, Stoel & Boley, 60-63; Georgia-Pacific Corp, 63-69. Publ: The Doctrine of exemplary damages in Oregon, Ore Law Rev, 4/65. Mem: Am, Ore & Multnomah Bar Asns. Relig: Lutheran. Mailing Add: 2825 Dellwood Dr Lake Oswego OR 97034

HODES, RICHARD S (D)

Fla State Rep

b New York, NY, Apr 24, 24; s Stanley Hodes & Rosabel Palley H; m 1946 to Marjorie Cohen; c Marilyn. Educ: Tulane Univ, BS, 44, MD, 46; Univ Minn, fel, 51; Phi Delta Epsilon; Sigma Alpha Mu. Polit & Govt Pos: Fla State Rep, currently, chmn comt on health & rehabilitative serv, Fla House of Rep, 70- Bus & Prof Pos: Dir, Dept of Anesthesia, Tampa Gen Hosp & clin asst prof, Univ Fla Sch Med, currently. Mil Serv: Entered as Pfc, Army, 43, released as Capt, 49, after serv in Med Dept, Tech Training Command Air Force, 49. Publ: Auxiliary myocardial revascularization, Surg, Gynecology & Obstetrics, 3/60. Mem: Hillsborough Co & Fla Med Asns; Am Med Asn (deleg); Am Soc Anesthesiologists (deleg); Fla Soc Anesthesiologists (deleg). Honors & Awards: Good Govt Award, Tampa Jaycees, 70 & Fla State Jaycees, 70. Relig: Jewish. Mailing Add: 238 E Davis Blvd Suite H Tampa FL 33606

HODGDON, SHIRLEY LAMSON (R)

Mem, NH Rep State Comt

b New Haven, Conn, Sept 24, 21; d Everett Carr Lamson & Bessie Rowena L; m 1942 to Richard Wyman Hodgdon; c Marilynn (Mrs Levinson), William & Clifton. Educ: Forsyth Sch Dent Hyg, RDH, 40. Polit & Govt Pos: Selectman, Ward II Rep Party, Portsmouth, NH, 68-74, moderator, 74-; area vchmn, Rockingham & Strafford Co Rep Party, 72-74; mem, Nat Fedn Rep Women, currently; asst chmn, NH Rep State Comt, 74, chmn, 74-75, mem, 74-; mem, Nat Rep Comt, 74-75. Bus & Prof Pos: Dent hygienist, Portsmouth, NH, 40- Mem: Eastern Star (Past Matron); DAR; Small Bus Admin (mem adv coun). Honors & Awards: Grand Cross Color, Rainbow Girls, 69. Relig: Congregational. Mailing Add: 10 Kent St Portsmouth NH 03801

HODGES, CHARLES EDWARD (D)

SC State Rep

b Tabor City, NC, Apr 2, 31; s Joseph Judson Hodges & Mada Lee Cox H; m 1951 to Patty Macon Nobles; c Charles Joseph & Charissa Dean. Educ: Tabor City High Sch, grad, 49; Kings Bus Sch, 1 year, Bus Admin. Polit & Govt Pos: SC State Rep, Horry Co, 68- Bus & Prof Pos: Pres, Hodges, Inc, 59-; farmer, 64-; comt chmn, Indust Developers, 66-67; treas, United Investors, Inc, currently. Mil Serv: Pfc, Air Force, 51. Mem: Nat Asn Accredited Talent & Beauty Pageant Judges; SC Retail Grocerymen Asn; Loris Libr Bldg Comt; Loris Merchants Asn; Carolina Country Club. Honors & Awards: Jaycee of the Year, 65 & 66, Sparkplug Award, Jaycees, 66 & 67; Loris Distinguished Serv Award, 67. Relig: Baptist. Mailing Add: 4307 Broad St Loris SC 29569

HODGES, GENE (D)

Fla State Rep

Mailing Add: PO Box 1022 Cedar Key FL 32625

HODGES, HAROLD YOUNG (R)

Chmn, Surry Co Rep Party, NC

b Surry, NC, July 14, 19; s Delmar Decauter Hodges & Lelia Dickens H; m 1948 to Dorothy June Klutz; c Harold Y, Jr, Richard Dale & Gene Daywalt. Educ: Wake Forest Col, 44-46; Appalachian State Col, 47; Sigma Pi. Polit & Govt Pos: Chmn, Surry Co Rep Party, NC, 55- Bus & Prof Pos: Partner, WKSP Radio, Kingstree, SC & Dixie Tobacco Warehouse, Mt Airy, 47-62, owner & operator, 62-; partner, Farmers Tobacco Warehouse, Kingstree, 53-63; farmer, Tobacco, Grain & Cattle. Mil Serv: 45-46. Publ: Farm News Prog, WPAQ Radio, 62-69. Mem: Mason (Past Master); Shrine; Moose (Past Gov); Elks (Past Exalted Ruler); Ruritan (Dist Gov); Am Legion. Relig: Baptist; deacon & Sunday Sch Supt. Legal Res: RFD 6 Box 267 Mt Airy NC 27030 Mailing Add: PO Box 547 Mt Airy NC 27030

HODGES, J ALEX (R)

Chmn Rules Comt, Rep Party of Ga

b Decatur, Ga, Mar 5, 41; s Thomas Lumpkin Hodges & Lillian Powell H; div. Educ: Mercer Univ, BA, 63; Walter F George Sch Law, 1 year; Phi Delta Theta; Scabbard & Blade. Polit & Govt Pos: Field rep, Ga Draft Goldwater Comt, 64; orgn dir, Bibb Co Rep Party, Ga, 64; field rep, Rep Nat Comt, 64; exec dir, Rep Party of Ga, 64-65 & 68-70, chmn rules comt, 70-; mem campaign mgr comt, Thompson for Mayor, Macon, 67; mem, Human Rels Comt, Macon, 67-68. Bus & Prof Pos: Bus & personnel mgr, Phil Walden Artists & Promotions, Macon, Ga, 67-68, pres, Paragon Agency of Walden Artists & Promotions, 70-; secy & mem bd dirs, Glendora Develop Corp, Atlanta, 67-; licensed real estate salesman, 68- Mil Serv: Entered as 2nd Lt, Army, 65, released as 1st Lt, 67, after serv in Finance Corp, SASCOM, 65-66 & Sixth Army, 66-67, Army Res, 66-69; Cert of Achievement, Ft Irwin, Calif. Publ: Author, County Chairmen's Manual, 65, Prospectus, Republican Party of Georgia, 1960-70, 68 & ed, The Candidate and the Press, Manual, 68, Rep Party of Ga. Mem: Licensed agt, Am Guild Variety Artists; Am Fedn Musicians; Atlanta Jaycees; first charter mem, Ga Rep Party 120 Club; Ga Sheriffs Asn. Relig: Methodist. Legal Res: 1237 S Jackson Springs Rd Macon GA 31201 Mailing Add: 1019 Walnut St Macon GA 31201

HODGES, PAUL V, JR (R)

Justice, Colo Supreme Court

b Monroe, Wis, Feb 4, 13; s Paul V Hodges & Grace Haren H; m 1967 to Carol Lee Maxey; c Paul V, III & Richard M. Educ: Regis Col, 32-36; Univ Colo Sch Law, LLB, 39; Phi Delta Phi. Polit & Govt Pos: Spec agt, Fed Bur Invest, 39-46; pres, Elec Comn, Denver, Colo, 47-51; Colo State Rep, 52-55; Munic Judge, Denver, 55-59; mgr, Denver Welfare Dept, 59-60; judge, Superior Court, 60-65; examr & counsr, Pub Utilities Comn, 65-66; justice, Colo Supreme Court, 67- Bus & Prof Pos: Partner, Kay & Hodges Law Firm, 46-56. Mem: Denver & Colo Bar Asns; Am Judicature Soc; Elks. Legal Res: 2688 S Wadsworth Way Lakewood CO 80227 Mailing Add: 308 State Capitol Bldg Denver CO 80203

HODGES, RALPH BYRON (NON-PARTISAN)

VChief Justice, Okla Supreme Court

b Anadarko, Okla, Aug 4, 30; s Dewey E Hodges & Pearl Emenhiser H; m 1951 to LaVerne Crain; c Shari, Mark & Randall. Educ: Okla Baptist Univ, AB, 52; Univ Okla Law Sch, LLB, 54. Polit & Govt Pos: Dist attorney, Bryan Co, Okla, 56-58; Dist judge, 59-65; Justice, Okla Supreme Court, 65-75, VChief Justice, 75- Relig: Baptist. Legal Res: Durant OK 74701 Mailing Add: State Capitol Bldg Oklahoma City OK 73105

HODGES, WILLIAM HOWARD (D)

Mem Exec Comt, Va Dem Cent Comt

b Hickory, Va, Apr 18, 29; m to Ann Turnbull Harding H. Educ: Randolph-Macon Col, BA; Washington & Lee Univ, LLB; Phi Kappa Sigma; Phi Delta Phi. Polit & Govt Pos: Former mem, Young Dem Club, Chesapeake, Va; Va State Deleg, 62-66; Va State Sen, 66-72; vchmn, Va Crime Comn, 66-72; mem exec comt, Va Dem Cent Comt, 66-, mem, Fourth Dist Comt, 68-; vchmn, Va Code Comn, 68-72; judge, First Judicial Circuit of Va, 72- Bus & Prof Pos: Chmn bd dirs, People's Bank, Chesapeake, Va, 67-73. Mil Serv: Coast Guard, 51-53. Mem: Portsmouth-Norfolk Co Bar Asn; Norfolk-Portsmouth Bar Asn; Am Legion; Cedar Point Club; Farm Bur. Relig: Methodist; trustee, Centenary Methodist Church. Mailing Add: PO Box 15205 Chesapeake VA 23320

HODGKIN, DOUGLAS IRVING (R)

Chmn, Maine Second Cong Dist Rep Comt

b Lewiston, Maine, May 11, 39; s Clayton Pierce Hodgkin & Laura Marion Meade H; m 1962 to Phyllis June Sherman; c Andrew Clayton, Deanna Louise & Valerie Ruth. Educ: Yale Univ, BA, 61; Duke Univ, MA, 63, PhD, 66; Phi Beta Kappa; Pi Sigma Alpha. Polit & Govt Pos: Mem, Maine State Govt Internship Adv Comt, 68-73; secy, Lewiston Rep City Comt, 68-72, chmn, 72-; finance chmn, Androscoggin Co Rep Comt, 68-70, chmn, 70-71; mem, Maine Second Cong Dist Rep Comt, 68-72, chmn, 72-; mem, Lewiston Bd Educ, 69-73, chmn, 73; mem, Maine House Apportionment Comn, 72 & 73; staff asst to the Majority Leader, Maine House of Rep, 73; mem, Maine Rep State Comt, 74- Bus & Prof Pos: Instr govt, Bowdoin Col, 64-66; vis lectr govt, Bates Col, 66-68, asst prof, 68-73, assoc prof, 73- Publ: Congress & the president, 1968 style, Polity, winter 68; The Maine Executive Council: representative of whom?, Juncture, 10/71. Mem: Am & New Eng Polit Sci Asns; Wales Grange; Androscoggin Pomona Grange; Auburn-Lewiston United Fund (budget comt). Relig: Congregational. Mailing Add: 9 Sutton Pl Lewiston ME 04240

HODGSON, JAMES DAY (R)

Ambassador to Japan

b Dawson, Minn, Dec 3, 15; s Fred Arthur Hodgson & Casaraha Day H; m 1943 to Maria Denend; c Nancy (Mrs Richard J Nachman) & Fredric. Educ: Univ Minn, Minneapolis, AB, 38, 40; Univ Calif, Los Angeles, 47-48; Phi Sigma Kappa. Hon Degrees: LLD, Temple Univ, 71 & Univ Cincinnati, 72. Polit & Govt Pos: Supvr youth employ, State of Minn Dept Employ, 40-41; mem exec comt, Los Angeles Mayor's Labor-Mgt Comt, Calif, 62-69; consult, State of Calif Comt Automation & Manpower, 65-67; under secy of labor, US Dept of Labor, 69-70, Secy of Labor, 70-72; Ambassador to Japan, 74- Bus & Prof Pos: Jr exec trainee, Dayton Co, Minneapolis, Minn, 38-40; personnel clerk, Lockheed Aircraft Corp, Burbank, Calif, 41-43, numerous indust rels positions including corporate dir indust rels, 46-68, corp vpres indust rels, 68-69, sr vpres, 73-; dir, Repub Corp, Los Angeles, 73-; dir, Calvin Bullock Inc, New York, NY, 73- Mil Serv: Entered as Ens, Navy, 43, released as Lt, 46, after serv in Naval Air Corps, Pac, 42-46. Publ: Automation, Univ Mich Quart, 63; Employing the unemployables, Harvard Bus Rev, 9/68. Mem: Am Mgt Asn; Town Hall Indust Rels Planning Comt Los Angeles; George Town Club, DC; Burning Tree Club, DC; Capitol Hill Club. Honors & Awards: Distinguished Serv Award, Univ Minn, 70. Relig: Presbyterian. Legal Res: 10132 Hillgrove Dr Beverly Hills CA 90210 Mailing Add: Dept of State Washington DC 20521

HOE, HARRY MORGAN (R)

Mem, Ky Rep State Cent Comt

b Middlesboro, Ky, May 25, 25; s Harry Allen Hoe & Ethel Morgan H; m 1948 to Mary Bob Hale; c Priscilla Hale, Harry Hale & Marilyn Morgan. Educ: Univ Tenn, BS, 49; Phi Gamma Delta. Polit & Govt Pos: Mem, Ky Rep State Cent Comt, 64-; mem, Ky Legis Research Comn, 66-67; Ky State Rep, 87th Dist & minority whip, Ky House of Rep, formerly, asst minority floor leader, 68. Bus & Prof Pos: Vpres, J R Hoe & Sons, Inc; past pres, Assoc Industs of Ky; dir, Nat Bank, Middlesboro. Mil Serv: Entered as Pvt, Army, 43, released after serv in 4th Inf Div, ETO, 44-45; Silver Star; Bronze Star with Oak Leaf Cluster; ETO Campaign Ribbon with Four Battle Stars. Mem: Kiwanis; Little League; Am Foundry Soc; Ky Crime Comn; Clear Creek Baptist Sch (chmn bd trustees). Honors & Awards: Gen chmn, Cumberland Gap Nat Hist Park Dedication, 59; One of Three Outstanding Young Men in Ky, 53. Relig: Baptist. Mailing Add: 413 Dorchester Ave Middlesboro KY 40965

HOEFS, RUDOLPH HERMAN (R)
Chmn, Richland Co Rep Party, NDak
b Hankinson, NDak, Apr 17, 96; s August Hoefs & Emilia Tews H; m 1930 to Marjorie E Scribner; c Lloyd A, Kenneth W & Ronald A. Educ: Hankinson High Sch, 4 years. Polit & Govt Pos: Chmn, Richland Co Rep Party, 42-67 & 73-; mayor, Hankinson, NDak, 44-56; mem, 26th Dist Rep Party Exec Comt, 68-71; deleg, Rep Nat Conv, 68; chmn, 1200 Club, 26th Dist for 1970; finance chmn, 25th & 26th Dist Rep Party, NDak, 68-70; precinct committeeman, Rep Party, 42- Bus & Prof Pos: Hardware clerk & truck driver, Wipperman Mercantile Co, Hankinson, NDak, 10-18; farm mgr, collector & livestock buyer, John R Jones Co, 27-42; Int Harvester Dealer, Hankinson, 42-63; owner, Hoefs Farm Store, 47-64. Mil Serv: Entered as Pvt, Army, 18, released as Musician 2/C, 20, after serv in 345 Field Art Band, 90th Div, 18-19 & Argonne Forest & Meuse Sect, 19-20; Good Conduct Medal. Mem: VFW; Elks; Am Legion; World War I Barracks 2719, Alexandria, Minn & World War I Barracks 1153, Seattle, Wash; Int War Vet Alliance, US & Can. Honors & Awards: Loyalty & Serv Award, NDak State Band, 62; Richland Co Rep Appreciation Award for 20 years serv as Rep Co Chmn, 64; Golden Cert & Am Citation Award, Am Legion, 73; Appreciation Award, Am Legion Auxiliary, 73. Relig: Lutheran. Mailing Add: 510 First Ave SW Hankinson ND 58041

HOEGH, LEO ARTHUR (R)
b Audubon Co, Iowa, Mar 30, 08; s William Hoegh & Annie K Johnson H; m 1936 to Mary Louise Foster; c Kristin F & Janis. Educ: Univ Iowa, BA, 29 & JD, 32; Omicron Delta Kappa; Pi Kappa Alpha; Delta Theta Phi. Polit & Govt Pos: Iowa State Rep, 37-42; city attorney, Chariton, Iowa, 41-42; chmn, Co Rep Finance Comt, 48-50; chmn, Iowa Rep Comt, 50-53; mem, Iowa for Eisenhower Comt, 51-52; Attorney Gen, Iowa, 53-55; Gov, 55-57; nat dir, Off of Civil & Defense Mobilization, 57-61. Bus & Prof Pos: Attorney-at-law, self-employed, 32-66; dir, Iowa Fund, Inc, 61-66; dir & gen counsel, Soypro, Int, 63-66; dir, Bank of Manitou, 70-, Total Pole, Inc, 70- & continent Resources, 70- Mil Serv: Entered as 1st Lt, Army, 42; released as Lt Col, 46, after serv in 104th Inf Div, ETO, 44-45; Col (Ret), Army, Res, 59; Legion of Honor; Croix de Guerre; Bronze Medal; Three Campaign Ribbons. Publ: Timberwolf Tracks, Infantry J, 46. Mem: Am Bar Asn; Am Legion; Amvets; Rotary; VFW. Relig: Methodist. Mailing Add: Chipita Park CO 80811

HOEH, SANDRA U (D)
b Baltimore, Md, Oct 8, 41; d Milton Unterman & Semah Zinsher U; m 1963 to David Charles Hoeh; c Christopher D, Jeffrey D & Jonathan Robert. Educ: Univ NH, BA, 63; Phi Beta Kappa; Phi Kappa Phi; Pi Sigma Alpha; Pi Gamma Nu; Alpha Chi Omega. Polit & Govt Pos: Chmn, Concord Dem Women Club, NH, 65-67; chmn, Concord McIntyre for Senate Comt, 66; mem platform comt, NH Dem State Conv, 66; chmn, Second Cong Dist Dem Party, 66-68; treas, Hanover Dem Town Comt, 67-72, vchmn, 70-72; alt deleg & mem credentials comt, Dem Nat Conv, 68; mem, NH Dem State Comt, 70-72; co-chmn, McGovern for President Campaign, NH, 72; mem, Milwaukee Co Dem Comt, 73-74; membership chmn, 25th Assembly Dist, Wis, 73-75; deleg, Dem Mid-Term Conf, 74. Mem: League of Women Voters; Am Civil Liberties Union. Mailing Add: 2422 E Newberry Blvd Milwaukee WI 53211

HOELLEN, JOHN JAMES (R)
Mem, Cook Co Rep Cent Comt, Ill
b Chicago, Ill, Sept 24, 14; s John James Hoellen, Sr & Mame Skellinger H; m 1948 to Mary Jane McMeans; c Elizabeth & Robert. Educ: Northwestern Univ, BA, 35, JD, 38; Phi Beta Kappa; Eta Sigma Phi; Delta Theta Phi. Polit & Govt Pos: Alderman, 47th Ward, Chicago, Ill, 47-75; mem, Cook Co Rep Cent Comt, 64-; Rep nominee, US House Rep, 68; deleg, Rep Nat Conv, 72; Rep nominee, Mayor, Chicago, 75. Bus & Prof Pos: Lawyer, Chicago; dir, Lincoln Sq Savings & Loan Asn, 59-; dir, Bank of Ravenswood, Chicago, 62-; pres, Sulzer Family Found, 63- Mil Serv: Entered as Ens, Naval Res, 41, released as Lt, 46, after serv in Naval Intel Serv & on USS Chester T O'Brien, Atlantic, Mediter & Pac; Theatre Ribbons; Philippine Liberation Medal. Publ: Various newspaper articles. Mem: Kiwanis; YMCA (Ravenswood chmn); VFW; Am Legion; Germania. Honors & Awards: Awards from Trinity Col & Chicago Col Indust Eng; VFW & Amvets awards for sponsoring vet legis; Man of the Year, Lions. Relig: Methodist. Legal Res: 1842 W Larchmont Ave Chicago IL 60613 Mailing Add: 1940 W Irving Park Rd Chicago IL 60613

HOENE, PAULETTE LOUISE (R)
Nat Committeewoman, Idaho Young Rep
b Sioux City, Iowa, June 10, 46; d Paul Bouvia & Evelyn Smith B; div; c Kateri Ann, Kraig James, Karyn & Kerry. Educ: Am Med Record Asn, grad, 73. Polit & Govt Pos: Staff asst to US Rep Steve Symms, Idaho, 73-; nat committeewoman, Idaho Young Rep, 75- Bus & Prof Pos: Med rec secy, St Mary's Hosp, Cottonwood, Idaho, 63-68, Idaho Co Nursing Home, Grangeville, 68-72 & St Joseph's Hosp, Lewiston, 73. Mem: Young Rep. Relig: Catholic. Mailing Add: 3732-16th St Lewiston ID 83501

HOEPPEL, JOHN HENRY (D)
b Tell City, Ind, Feb 10, 81; s John M Hoeppel & Barbara Zoll H; m 1907 to Anna Seitz; c Raymond, Charles & Mildred (Mrs Ruddick). Educ: Grade Sch, 93. Polit & Govt Pos: Postmaster, Arcadia, Calif, 23-31; US Rep, Calif, 32-36. Mil Serv: Entered as Pvt, 1st Artil, Army, 98, retired as M/Sgt, Signal Corps, 21; served 10 years in Alaska between 1900 & 1917 & with 1st Div, France, 17-18; many letters of commendation; 1st Lt (Ret), Air Force. Publ: Initiator & vol publisher, National Defense, 28-63. Mem: Organizer & 1st comdr, Post of Am Legion, also comdr, Arcadia Post 247; organizer & 1st comdr, Post of VFW & Camp of United Spanish War Vets. Honors & Awards: Was operator in charge of US Tel Off, Ft Egbert, Eagle, Alaska who reported success of Roald Amundsen's Sailing of the Northwest Passage, 03-05; obtained transfer of World War I Balloon Sch to Co of Los Angeles & funds for develop of the sch, plaque honoring this achievement erected in Los Angeles Co Park, Arcadia. Mailing Add: 35 E Floral Ave Arcadia CA 91006

HOESTENBACH, JOHN (D)
Tex State Rep
Mailing Add: 3701 E 30th St Odessa TX 79760

HOEVEN, CHARLES BERNARD (R)
b Hospers, Iowa, Mar 30, 95; s Gerrit Hoeven & Lena Weiland H; m 1919 to Velma Ruth Pike; c Pauline Ruth (Mrs Stanley J Marshall) & Charles Pike. Educ: State Univ Iowa, BA, 20, Col Law, LLB, 22; Phi Alpha Delta. Hon Degrees: LLD, Westmar Col, 56, Morningside Col, 65 & Buena Vista Col, 68. Polit & Govt Pos: Attorney, Sioux Co, Iowa, 25-37; Iowa State Sen, 37-41, pres pro-tem, Iowa State Senate, 39-41; permanent chmn, Iowa State Rep Conv, 40; permanent chmn, Iowa State Judicial Conv, 42; US Rep, Sixth & Eighth Cong Dists, Iowa, 43-65, chmn, Rep Conf, US House of Rep, 57-62, Dep Rep Whip, 57-65; cong deleg, Food & Agr Orgn, Rome, 57; US Deleg, Interparliamentary Union, London, 57, Brussels, 61, Belgrade, 63 & Copenhagen, 64; app mem, Spec Adv Comt on Pub Opinion, Dept State, 70- Bus & Prof Pos: Dir & vpres, Alton Savings Bank, Iowa, 32- Mil Serv: Entered as Pvt, Army, 17, released as Sgt, 19, after serv in 350th Inf, 88th Div, US, Eng & France; Victory Medal; Meuse-Argonne Medal. Mem: Masonic Blue Lodge; Shrine; Am Legion; VFW; Rotary. Honors & Awards: Cert of Accomplishment, State Univ Iowa, 47; Cert of Merit, Northwestern Col, 64; Honor Iowans Award, Buena Vista Col, 66. Relig: Presbyterian; moderator, Presbytery of Northwest Iowa, 67. Mailing Add: Box 290 Alton IA 51003

HOFF, PHILIP HENDERSON (D)
b Greenfield, Mass, June 29, 24; s Olaf Hoff, II & Agnes E Henderson H; m 1948 to Joan P Brower; c Susan Brower, Dagny Elizabeth, Andrea Clark & Gretchen Henderson. Educ: Williams Col, AB, 48; Cornell Law Sch, LLB, 51. Hon Degrees: Hon degrees from Am Int Col, Middlebury Col, Norwich Univ, Williams Col, Windham Col, Univ Vt. Polit & Govt Pos: Precinct worker, Dem Party, Vt, 51; Vt State Rep, Burlington, 61-62; Gov of Vt, 62-69; comnr, Pub Land Law Rev Comn, 65-71; deleg, Dem Nat Conv, 68 & 72; cand for US Sen, Vt, 70; chmn, Vt Dem State Party, 74-75. Bus & Prof Pos: Former partner, Black, Wilson & Hoff; attorney, Philip H Hoff; teaching fel, Dartmouth Col. Mil Serv: Entered Navy, 43, released as Seaman 1/C, 46, after serv in Submarine Serv. Mem: Nat Resources Coun (chmn); KT; Grange; YMCA; United Serv Orgn (hon mem). Honors & Awards: First Dem Gov in 109 years. Relig: Episcopal. Legal Res: 214 Prospect Pkwy Burlington VT 05401 Mailing Add: 192 College St Burlington VT 05401

HOFFMAN, A ALTON (R)
Utah State Rep
Mailing Add: RFD 1 Smithfield UT 84335

HOFFMAN, GARY ELLSWORTH (D)
Mem, San Diego Co Dem Cent Comt, Calif
b San Diego, Calif, Jan 18, 53; s Howard Ellsworth Hoffman & Margaret Denison H; single. Educ: San Diego Mesa Col, 71- Polit & Govt Pos: Campaign mgr, Virginia Taylor for Mayor, Calif, 71; staffer, McGovern for President, 71-72; deleg, Calif Dem Coun, 72; deleg, Dem Nat Conv, 72; mem, San Diego Co Dem Cent Comt, 73- Relig: Jewish. Mailing Add: 5664 Del Cerro Blvd San Diego CA 92120

HOFFMAN, GENE LOUIS (R)
Ill State Rep
b Canton, Ill, Sept 26, 32; s Wilbur Merle Hoffman & Helen Randolph H; m 1954 to Diane Wilma Thorton; c Mark, Lynn, Susan & Gregory. Educ: Ill State Univ, BS, 54; Northern Ill Univ, MS, 62; Pi Gamma Mu; capt, Football Team, 53 & Wrestling Team, 54. Polit & Govt Pos: Secy, Elmhurst Young Rep, Ill, 65-66, vpres, 66-67; Ill State Rep, currently, chmn Ill sch probs comt, Ill House of Rep, currently. Bus & Prof Pos: Chmn, Social Studies Dept, Fenton High Sch, Bensenville, Ill, 59- Mil Serv: Entered as Pvt, Army, 54, released as Cpl, 56, after serv in 130th Sta Hosp, Europe; Good Conduct & European Occup Medals. Mem: Nat & Ill Educ Asns; Elmhurst Jaycees. Relig: Protestant. Mailing Add: 111 E York Rd Elmhurst IL 60126

HOFFMAN, IRWIN F (D)
Md State Deleg
b Cumberland, Md, Jan 10, 27; married. Educ: Hagerstown Pub Schs. Polit & Govt Pos: Md State Deleg, 63- Bus & Prof Pos: Gen ins agent. Mil Serv: Navy, 45. Mem: Elks (Past Exalted Ruler, Lodge 378); Halfway Lions Club. Legal Res: Rte 3 Box 169A Hagerstown MD 21740 Mailing Add: 232 S Potomac St Hagerstown MD 21740

HOFFMAN, JOHN (D)
Ark State Rep
Mailing Add: PO Box 107 Royal AR 71968

HOFFMAN, JOHN R (R)
Mo State Rep
Mailing Add: Rte 2 Box 250 Willard MO 65781

HOFFMAN, JUDITH LINDA (D)
Chmn, Doniphan Co Dem Party, Kans
b Jackson, Mich, Feb 6, 39; d Lawrence Meidinger & Winneta Brady M; m 1961 to Wallace Gene Hoffman; c Catherine Sue & Scott Brady. Educ: Highland Jr Col, 2 years; Northwest Mo State Univ, BD in Educ & MS in Counseling; Student Nat Educ Asn; Kans Nat Educ Asn; Am Home Econ Asn. Polit & Govt Pos: Dem committeewoman, Wathena, Kans, 64-; vchmn, Doniphan Co Dem Party, 64-70, chmn, 70-; co-chmn, Bob Swan for Cong Comt, 68; chmn, Robert Kennedy for President Campaign, 68. Mem: PTA; Am Legion Auxiliary. Relig: Catholic. Legal Res: 410 Fremont Wathena KS 66090 Mailing Add: Box 66 Wathena KS 66090

HOFFMAN, LEROY GEORGE (R)
SDak State Sen
b McPherson Co, SDak, July 5, 32; s Edward R Hoffman & Rosa Thurn H; m 1954 to Claudia Boettcher; c E Thurn & Charles Boettcher. Educ: Univ Colo, Boulder, BMuEd; Phi Mu Alpha; Sigma Alpha Epsilon. Hon Degrees: Dr Music, Yankton Col, 74. Polit & Govt Pos: SDak State Sen, 20th Legis Dist, 75- Bus & Prof Pos: Bass soloist, Philadelphia Orchestra, Boston Symphony, Berlin Symphony, Montreal Symphony & Vienna Acad Choir; solo mem, Salzburg Opera; owner & operator, O Ranch, Inc & Bar HH Farms, Inc. Mil Serv: Entered as Pvt, Army, 54, released as SP-3, 56, after serv in Corps of Engr, Europe, 55-56. Mem: Yankton Col (bd trustees). Relig: United Church of Christ; state bd trustees & state moderator. Mailing Add: Rte 2 Box 109 Eureka SD 57437

HOFFMAN, PHILIP R (R)
Mo State Rep
Mailing Add: 9845 Wild Deer Rd Ladue MO 63124

HOFFMAN, QUINCY (R)
Mich State Rep
b Applegate, Mich, Apr 30, 13; married; c Howard, Janice. Educ: Col, 2 years. Polit & Govt Pos: Mich State Rep, 64-; sheriff, Sanilac Co, 5 terms; former village & sch bd pres. Bus & Prof Pos: Purebred beef farm owner & operator, Sanilac Co, Mich. Mem: Lions; F&AM; RAM; Am Cancer Soc (pres, Sanilac Unit); Boy Scouts (comnr). Relig: Methodist. Mailing Add: 2596 Clare St Applegate MI 48401

HOFFMAN, RONALD KENNETH (R)
Ill State Rep
b Chicago, Ill, Apr 5, 32; s Arthur Hoffman & Lillian Popa H; m 1953 to Marilyn Ella Roth; c Donna Lynn & Sharon Lee. Educ: Morton Col, 2 years. Polit & Govt Pos: Pres, Westchester Park Dist, Ill, 65-69; Ill State Rep, 69- Bus & Prof Pos: Mgr consult, Sunbeam Appliance Serv Corp, 55-; pres, R K Hoffman Mgt Consult, 70-; pres, Crest Conv Mgt & Travel Ltd, 72- Mil Serv: Entered as A/S, Navy, 51, released as PO, 55, after serv in Amphibious Unit, Korean Conflict; Good Conduct Medal; China Serv Medal; Nat Defense Medal; Korean Serv Medal; UN Serv Medal Letter of Commendation. Mem: German Am Rep Asn (vpres, 72-). Honors & Awards: Man of the Year Award, Italian Cath Fedn, 69; State Legis Awards, Ill Asn Park Dist, 71 & Fraternal Order of Police, 71; Meritorious Award, DAV, 72. Relig: Protestant. Legal Res: 10838 W Windsor Dr Westchester IL 60163 Mailing Add: 10353 W Roosevelt Rd Westchester IL 60163

HOFFMAN, THOMAS JOSEPH (D)
b Louisville, Ky, Nov 22, 50; s Richard Royale Hoffman, Sr & Catherine Ethella Michaelree H; single. Educ: St Louis Univ, 68-69; St Mary's Univ, BA summa cum laude, 73; pres, Students for McGovern/Shriver, 72. Polit & Govt Pos: Chmn, Precinct 226 Dem Conv, 72; deleg & parliamentarian, Sen Dist 26 Dem Conv, 72; deleg, Two Tex State Dem Conv, 72; alt deleg, Dem Nat Conv, 72. Bus & Prof Pos: Bro, Soc of Mary, 69-; teacher social studies & chmn dept, St Michael's High Sch, 73-; moderator, Nat Honor Soc, 74- Publ: Poems, On Afro-lit, Cascabel, spring 71, Thanatos/Eros, fall, 71 & Austin House, spring 72; The Thing Itself. Mem: Polit Sci Majors Asn (pres, 73); Polit Sci Honors Soc; San Antonio Intercollegiate Student Asn (bd trustees, 72-); Tri-Col Student Asn; Ill Coun Social Studies. Relig: Catholic. Mailing Add: 1640 N Hudson Ave Chicago IL 60614

HOFFMANN, MARTIN R
Gen Counsel, Dept Defense
Mailing Add: Dept of Defense Pentagon Washington DC 20310

HOFFMANN, MARY ANN (D)
Mem, Tenn State Dem Exec Comt
b Kossuth, Miss; d John Barry Jones & Mary Lee Gammel J; m 1970 to Frank Joseph Hoffmann; c Carole Ann (Mrs James D Redheffer) & Frederick Daniel Lansford. Educ: Hinds Jr Col, grad, 41; Lambuth Col, 50-53; Music Club. Polit & Govt Pos: Mem, Tenn State Dem Exec Comt, 74- Mem: Nashville & Davidson Co Dem Women's Club; Nashville League Women Voters; Hist Nashville, Inc; Nashville Bd Realtors. Relig: Baptist. Mailing Add: 213 Cliffdale Rd Nashville TN 37214

HOFFMANN, RICKI JO (D)
b Evansville, Ind, Sept 23, 47; d John E Hoffmann & Rose Henke H; single. Educ: Butler Univ, BA, 69; Delta Upsilon; Phi Kappa Phi; Alpha Lambda Delta; Mortar Bd; Kappa Alpha Theta. Polit & Govt Pos: Mem nat field staff, McCarthy for President, 68; admin aide to Sen Birch Bayh, Ind, 69-71; asst regional coordr, Bayh for President, 71; dep dir scheduling, Muskie for President, 72; press asst, McGovern for President, 72; campaign coordr, Hayes for Cong, 74; admin asst to US Rep Phil Hayes, Ind, 75- Honors & Awards: Sr Honor Scholar, Butler Univ, 68, Theta Sigma Phi Spoke Award, 67. Legal Res: 3500 Bexley Ct Evansville IN 47711 Mailing Add: 205 C St SE Washington DC 20003

HOFFNER, S F (BUCKSHOT) (D)
NDak State Sen
m to Pat. Polit & Govt Pos: NDak State Rep, 62-72, asst majority floor leader, NDak House of Rep, 65; Dem cand for US Rep, NDak; deleg, Dem Nat Conv, 68; mem, NDak Dem Non-Partisan League State Exec Comt, currently; NDak State Sen, currently. Bus & Prof Pos: Farmer. Mil Serv: Inf, France & Ger, World War II. Mem: VFW. Legal Res: Esmond ND 58332 Mailing Add: State Capitol Bismarck ND 43215

HOFHEINZ, JAMES FRED (D)
Mayor, Houston, Tex
b Houston, Tex, Mar 15, 38; s Roy Mark Hofheinz & Irene Cafcalas H; m 1961 to Elizabeth Winfrey; c Paul Winfrey & Tracey Virginia. Educ: Univ Tex, Austin, 60, MA, 63, PhD, 64; Univ Houston, JD, 64; Phi Beta Kappa; Phi Delta Phi; Delta Kappa Epsilon; Silver Spurs; Friar's Club. Polit & Govt Pos: Spec deleg, Dem Nat Mid-Term Conf, 74; mayor, Houston, Tex, 74-; bd dirs, Nat League of Cities, 74-; first vpres & bd dirs, Tex Munic League, 74-; mem legis action comt, US Conf Mayors, 74- Bus & Prof Pos: Mem, Houston Sports Asn, Astrodomain Corp, 64-69; attorney-at-law, Houston, Tex, 69-73. Mem: Tex Adv Comn Intergovt Rels; Tex Dept Community Affairs (adv comt); Tex & Houston Bar Asns; Am Econ Asn. Honors & Awards: 200 Rising Leaders, Time Mag, 74; Honor Award, Nat Jewish Hosp & Research Ctr, 75; Outstanding Alumnus Award, Univ Houston Law Sch, 75. Relig: Methodist. Mailing Add: Mayor's Off PO Box 1569 Houston TX 77001

HOFSTEDE, ALBERT JOHN (DFL)
Mayor, Minneapolis, Minn
b Minneapolis, Minn, Sept 25, 40; s Albert Hofstede & Florence Zebro H; single. Educ: Univ Minn, 58-60; Col St Thomas, BS, 64. Polit & Govt Pos: City councilman, Minneapolis, Minn, 67-71; chmn metrop coun, 71-73; mayor, 74-; deleg, Dem Nat Mid-Term Conf, 74. Mem: Minneapolis Soc Fine Arts; Minn Orchestra Asn; Col St Thomas Mgt Ctr (adv bd); Urban Affairs Comn. Honors & Awards: Jaycee Man of Year, 72; Time Mag Leader of Future, 74; 66-69; Nat Jaycee Top Ten Young Men, 75. Relig: Catholic. Legal Res: 2430 California St NE Minneapolis MN 55418 Mailing Add: 127 City Hall Minneapolis MN 55415

HOGAN, JOHN EDWARD
b Janesville, Minn; s J J Hogan & Ellen Ford H; m 1961 to Edith Burnside Howard; c Edith Chrystal & Terrence Howard. Educ: Univ Minn, AB; George Washington Univ, LLB; Georgetown Univ, LLM; John Marshall, Am Univ, MBA; Univ Md, PhD prog, currently. Polit & Govt Pos: Legal asst, Fed Reserve Bd, 57-59; law clerk, US Dist Court, Judge Leonard Walsh, 59-61; asst US Attorney for DC, 62-66; sr trial attorney & dep asst gen counsel for legis, Small Bus Admin, 66-69; exec asst & dir, Comn on Orgn Govt of DC, 71-72; minority counsel, DC Comt, US House of Rep, 69-74, counsel, Agr Comt, currently. Mil Serv: Entered as Lt(jg), Navy; Capt, Naval Res. Publ: Exec asst & dir, Report of the Commission on the Organization of the Government of the District of Columbia (3 vols), 72. Mem: Va & Minn Bars; Capitol Hill & Mt Carmel Restoration Socs; DC Bar Asn. Mailing Add: 213 Eleventh St SE Washington DC 20003

HOGAN, JOHN J (D)
b Cumberland, RI, Jan 29, 35. Educ: LaSalle Acad, 52; Providence Col, 62. Polit & Govt Pos: RI State Rep, 63-72; chmn, RI State Dem Party, until 72. Bus & Prof Pos: Pres-treas, Three-R Corp, Pawtucket, RI. Mil Serv: Navy Electrician, 52-56 in USS Gilbert Islands. Mem: KofC; Friendly Sons of St Patrick; Lions; Pawtucket Bd of Realtors. Relig: Catholic. Mailing Add: 200 Curran Rd Cumberland RI 02864

HOGAN, LAWRENCE JOSEPH (R)
b Boston, Mass, Sept 30, 28; c Mary Theresa (Mrs Wm Robert Lazarus) & Lawrence J, Jr. Educ: Georgetown Univ Col, AB, 49, Georgetown Univ Law Sch, JD, 54; Am Univ, MA, 66. Polit & Govt Pos: Alt deleg, Rep Nat Conv, 64, deleg, 68 & 72; US Rep, Fifth Dist, Md, 69-74. Bus & Prof Pos: Spec agent, Fed Bur Invest, 48-58; asst dept mgr, US CofC, 58-59; pres, Larry Hogan Assocs, Inc, 58-69; part-time prof, Univ Md, 60-68. Publ: Weekly article, In the Nation's capital, Telephony Mag, 61-69. Mem: Former Spec Agents of Fed Bur Invest. Honors & Awards: Admitted to practice before US Supreme Court. Mailing Add: Box 1231 Landover MD 20785

HOGAN, MARK ANTHONY (D)
Mem, Dem Nat Policy Coun
b Chicago, Ill, Jan 27, 31; s Mark Anthony Hogan (deceased) & Alice Glavin H (deceased); m 1954 to Nancy Stevenson; c Cary Lucile, Mark A, Jr, Lisa Ann, Matthew J & Michael J. Educ: Georgetown Univ, AB, 52. Polit & Govt Pos: Colo State Rep, 63-66, Asst Majority leader, Colo House of Rep, 65-66; Lt Gov, Colo, 66-70; mem, Dem Nat Policy Coun, 68-; Dem cand gov, 70. Bus & Prof Pos: Pres, Hogan-Stevenson Real Estate Co. Mil Serv: Entered as Ens, Naval Res, 52, released as Lt(jg), 54. Honors & Awards: Denver & Colo Young Man of the Year, Jr CofC, 58. Relig: Catholic. Mailing Add: 1861 S Niagara Way Denver CO 80222

HOGAN, MORRIS BERNARD (R)
Chmn, Burlington Rep Town Comt, Conn
b Harwinton, Conn, Feb 22, 02; s Patrick James Hogan & Marion Martha Morris H; m 1932 to Mabel M Casson. Polit & Govt Pos: Chmn, Rep Town Comt, Burlington, Conn, 32-, selectman, 49-57, mem bd finance, 57-; Conn State Rep, 177th Dist, 55-72. Bus & Prof Pos: Farm owner & mgr, 19- Mem: Grange; Farm Bur. Relig: Catholic. Mailing Add: Rte 4 Burlington CT 06085

HOGAN, ROSEMARIE (D)
VChmn, Ulster Co Dem Comt, NY
b East Kingston, NY, Apr 22, 24; d Santo F Amato & Mary Fuscardo A; m 1946 to John J Hogan; c Jay F. Educ: Kingston High Sch, grad, 42; Moran's Sch of Bus; High Sch Secy of Manning Chap, Nat Honor Soc. Polit & Govt Pos: Secy, Ulster Co Dem Women's Club, NY, 52-54, vpres, 54-56; committeeman, First Dist, 11th Ward, Kingston, 53-; mem, Civil Serv Comn, Kingston, 58-63, pres, 61-63; vchmn, Ulster Co Dem Comt, 63-; Dep City Clerk, Kingston, 71- Bus & Prof Pos: Office Mgr, Zwick & Schwartz, Kingston, 43-55, Washington Growers & Distributors, Poughkeepsie, NY, 59- Mem: Ulster Co Business & Prof Women's Club; Ulster Co Dem Women's Club; Ulster Co Dem Women's Div State of NY; Rapid Hose Ladies Auxiliary. Relig: Roman Catholic. Mailing Add: 47 German St Kingston NY 12401

HOGAN, STEPHEN DOUGLAS (D)
Colo State Rep
b Lincoln, Nebr, May 31, 48; s Howard Bruce Hogan & Alice Marie Williams H; m 1971 to Kathleen Elizabeth Warren; c Timothy Warren. Educ: Univ Denver, BA, 70; Univ Nebr Sch Law, 70-71; Order of Omega; Lambda Chi Alpha. Polit & Govt Pos: Colo State Rep, 75- Bus & Prof Pos: Advert mgr, Union Supply Co, Denver, 71- Mem: City Club of Denver. Relig: Presbyterian. Mailing Add: 12556 E Bates Circle Denver CO 80232

HOGAN, THOMAS SHERIDAN, JR (R)
b Gainesville, Fla, Jan 18, 54; s Thomas Sheridan Hogan & Mary Lanier H; single. Educ: Univ SFla, Tampa, 72. Polit & Govt Pos: Deleg, Rep Nat Conv, 72. Bus & Prof Pos: Owner, H & H Cattle Co, 72- Mem: Rotary (interacting dist gov). Honors & Awards: Boys State, 71. Relig: Methodist. Mailing Add: 1039 S Mildred Ave Brooksville FL 33512

HOGAN, WILLIAM F (D)
Mass State Rep
Mailing Add: State Capitol Boston MA 02133

HOGEN, MARVIS THOMAS (R)
SDak State Rep
b Kadoka, SDak, Nov 6, 23; s Thomas N Hogen & Marie Vangorgan H; m 1943 to Florence L Brown; c Philip N, Randi (Mrs Don Oyan), Baxter & Cash. Educ: Dakota Wesleyan Univ, 43. Polit & Govt Pos: SDak State Rep, 23rd Dist, 73- Mailing Add: Kadoka SD 57543

HOGEN, PHILIP N (R)
Chmn, Jackson Co Rep Cent Comt, SDak
b Kadoka, SDak, Nov 15, 44; s Marvis T Hogen & Florence Brown H; m 1967 to Marilyn Teupel; c Vanya Sue & Herbert Hoover. Educ: Augustana Col, BS, 67; Univ SDak, JD, 70; Websterian Soc; Phi Delta Phi. Polit & Govt Pos: Deleg, Jackson Co Rep Cent Comt, SDak, 70, chmn, 75-; chmn, Lyman Co Rep Cent Comt, 72, deleg to state conv, 72; admin asst, Congressman James Abdnor, SDak, 73-75; states attorney, Jackson Co, 75- Mil Serv: SDak Nat Guard, 64-70. Mailing Add: PO Box 237 Kadoka SD 57543

HOGUE, GRADY CLAUDE (D)
Chmn, Bee Co Dem Party, Tex
b Poynor, Tex, Nov 14, 25; s Claude Hogue & Bessie Stringfield H; m to Mable Delphine Harrison; c Mary (Mrs Tom Aman), Deborah, Grady, Jr & John. Educ: ETex State Univ, BS & MS. Hon Degrees: LLD, Univ Corpus Christi, 72. Polit & Govt Pos: Tex State Rep, 52-56; chmn, Bee Co Dem Party, 72- Bus & Prof Pos: Pres, Cisco Jr Col, 56-66; pres, Bee Co Col, Tex, 66- Mil Serv: Cpl, Marines, 43-46, serv in 1st Marine div, Pac Theatre, 43-45; Purple Heart. Mem: Rotary. Legal Res: 1400 Wren Lane Beeville TX 78102 Mailing Add: Bee County College Rte 1 Beeville TX 78102

HOGUE, JAMES
Dep Under Secy Legis Affairs, Dept Labor
Mailing Add: US Dept of Labor Off of the Secy Washington DC 20210

HOHMAN, GEORGE H, JR (D)
Alaska State Sen
b St Louis, Mo, June 2, 32; s George Harold Hohman, Sr & Margaret Church H; m 1953 to Nancy Lou Mead; c Margaret Carrie, Laura Marie, Sally Anne, Catherine Ann & George H, III. Educ: Mich State Univ, BA, 59. Polit & Govt Pos: Alaska State Rep, formerly; deleg, Dem Nat Conv, 72; Alaska State Sen, 73- Mil Serv: Entered as Pvt, Army, 52, released as Cpl, 55. Mem: Kuskokwim Native Asn; Alaska Educ Asn. Relig: Protestant. Mailing Add: Box 233 Bethel AK 99559

HOHMAN, LOREN H, II (D)
Kans State Rep
b Clay Center, Kans, Feb 6, 45; s Loren H Hohman, Sr & Betty Lou Schurr H; m 1967 to Cheryll Kay Fitts; c Audrey J & Loren, III. Educ: US Mil Acad, West Point, BS Eng, 67; Washburn Law Sch, JD, 73; Phi Alpha Delta. Polit & Govt Pos: Mem, Kans Young Dem, Topeka, 71-; Kans State Rep, 55th Dist, 75- Bus & Prof Pos: Vpres, Hohman Ins, Topeka, Kans, 71-; attorney-at-law, 73- Mil Serv: Entered as 2nd Lt, Army, 67, released as Capt, 71, after serv in 196th Brigade, Vietnam, 69-70; Capt, Army Res; Silver Star; Bronze Star; Air Medal; Cross of Gallantry with Silver Star. Mem: Kans & Topeka Bar Asns. Relig: Presbyterian. Legal Res: 1626 Plass Topeka KS 66604 Mailing Add: 5205 Southwest Dr Topeka KS 66614

HOILES, WILLIAM MCHENRY (R)
b Alliance, Ohio, June 19, 36; s Arthur Jones Hoiles & Martha McHenry H; m 1959 to Susan Fralich; c William McHenry, Melissa Lawson & Peter Beakley. Educ: Culver Mil Acad, 51-55; Mt Union Col, 55-57; Univ Pa, BS Econ, 59; Univ Pittsburgh, LLB, 65; Sigma Alpha Epsilon. Polit & Govt Pos: Asst attorney gen to Attorney Gen William B Saxbe, Ohio, 65-66, admin asst, 67-68; admin asst, US Sen William B Saxbe, Ohio, 69-74. Legal Res: 4347 Mumford Dr Columbus OH 43220 Mailing Add: 1107 Flor Lane McLean VA 22101

HOKANSON, ELGIN S (D)
Utah State Rep
Mailing Add: 201 Nicolette Dr Midvale UT 84047

HOKANSON, SHIRLEY ANN (D)
Minn State Rep
b Morris, Minn, Feb 8, 36; d Clarence Irvin Fogle & Gunda Irene Hagen F; m 1959 to Robert Carl Hokanson; c Gregory Reed & Thomas Blake. Educ: Univ Minn, BA, 58; Mankato State Col, currently. Polit & Govt Pos: Mem, Dem-Farmer-Labor Cent Comt, 68-72; mem, Metrop Health Bd, 73-74; Minn State Rep, 75- Mem: League Women Voters; Minn Hist Soc; CofC; Minn Social Serv Asn; PTA. Mailing Add: 7345 Russell Ave S Richfield MN 55423

HOLADAY, T W (BILL) (R)
Okla State Rep
b Oklahoma City, Okla, Apr 16, 21; s Noble Austin Holaday & Mary Agnes Walker H; m 1947 to Mary Adeline MaGuire; c Holly Diane. Educ: Univ Okla, 41. Polit & Govt Pos: Mem state reapportionment comt, Okla Co Rep Comt, Okla, 62, precinct chmn, 63-64; organizer & pres, Northwest Rep Club, 62-64; Okla State Rep, 82nd Dist, 64-, mem, Bus & Indust, Elec & Privileges, Prof & Occupational Regulations, Pub Safety & Roads & Hwys Comts, Okla House of Rep; mem adv comt, Young Rep Action Comt, 65-66; mem, Okla State Rep Comt, 65-66. Bus & Prof Pos: Owner, T W Holaday & Assocs, Designers, 55- Mil Serv: Entered as Pvt, Air Force, 42, released as Sgt, 45, after serv in 62nd Troop Carrier Squadron, 314th Group, ETO, 43-45; recalled as S/Sgt, 50-51, Tinker AFB; Distinguished Unit Badge with One Bronze Oak Leaf Cluster; Europe-Africa-Mid East Serv Ribbon with One Silver Serv Star & Two Bronze Serv Stars. Mem: Lions; Oklahoma City CofC; Northwest CofC; Nat Fedn Independent Bus, Inc. Relig: Episcopal. Mailing Add: 3844 NW 64th St Oklahoma City OK 73116

HOLAND, PAMELA KRISIDA (D)
NDak State Sen
b Dallas, Tex, Jan 22, 40; d John Lowery Vines & Mary Elizabeth Matthews V; m 1967 to Dr Roy Wilder Holand; c David Lee, Deborah Lynn, DiAnn Elizabeth, Brian Roy & Michael Wilder. Educ: High sch, Dallas, Tex, GED. Polit & Govt Pos: NDak State Sen, 74- Bus & Prof Pos: Mem, Educ TV Auxiliary, currently; mem bd dirs, State Med Auxiliary, Community Coord Child Care & Adv Bd to State Social Serv Dept, currently. Mem: Many civic & cult orgns. Relig: Protestant. Mailing Add: 543 Fourth Ave W West Fargo ND 58078

HOLBERT, SALIN (R)
b Owenton, Ky, Apr 10, 98; s Farmer Reese Holbert & Nannie Belle Wilburn H; div. Educ: Univ Ky, AB. Polit & Govt Pos: Teacher, Owen Co Bd Educ, 26-27; teacher, Ky House of Reform, 28-31, receiver, 44; chmn, Owen Co Rep Comt, Ky, 40-58, 60-66 & 73-75; auditor, Ky Dept Revenue, 45-48; acting postmaster, Owenton, Ky, 58-60. Bus & Prof Pos: Farmer; asst shipping clerk, Belknap Hardware, 41; timekeeper, Mengel Co, Louisville, 43-44; self-employed tax consult. Mem: Mason; Odd Fellow. Honors & Awards: 50 Year Membership Pin, Odd Fellows. Relig: Christian Church; Deacon & teacher Bible class, El Bethel Christian Church. Mailing Add: RR 3 Owenton KY 40359

HOLBROOK, CHARLES R, III (R)
Ky State Rep
b Ashland, Ky, Sept 1, 38; s Charles R Holbrook, Jr & Margaret Peters H; m 1962 to Sonia Ann Ward; c Russell W. Educ: Univ Cincinnati, 59-60; Morehead State Univ; Univ Ky, AB, 68, JD, 70. Polit & Govt Pos: Campaign chmn, Boyd Co Rep Party, Ky, 72; chmn, Comt to Welcome the President, Ashland, 72; Ky State Rep, 100th Dist, 72- Bus & Prof Pos: Attorney, Ashland, Ky, 70- Mil Serv: Entered as E-1, Army, 62, released as E-4, 65, after serv in Cincinnati Air Defense Command, 5th Missile Bn, 62-65; Bn Citation; Good Conduct Medal. Mem: Am & Ky State Bar Asns; Ashland Area Jaycees (dir, 72-73); Ashland Optimist Club; Am Legion. Relig: Presbyterian. Mailing Add: 2735 E Grove Ashland KY 41101

HOLBROOK, STEPHEN (D)
Utah State Rep
Mailing Add: 235 Elizabeth St Salt Lake City UT 84102

HOLCOMB, JOHN LAWRENCE (R)
Nat Committeeman, Ind Young Rep
b Reynolds, Ind, Dec 14, 39; s Francis Joseph Holcomb & Helen Safford H; single. Educ: St Bede Acad, High Sch grad. Polit & Govt Pos: State treas, Ind Young Rep, 72-73, nat committeeman, 73- Bus & Prof Pos: Vpres, Holcomb Construction Inc, 70-; pres, Holcomb Ready Mixed Concrete, 75; dir, White Co Home Builders, 75- Mem: United Fund (co chmn), Bicentennial Comn (chmn, 74). Mailing Add: PO Box 33 Reynolds IN 47980

HOLCOMB, ROBERT H (R)
Mem, Ky State Rep Cent Comt
b Toledo, Ohio, May 25, 16; s Howard H Holcomb & Carrie Ryan H; m 1965 to Juanita Lowe; c Robert Howard & stepchildren, Phillip, Linda (Mrs Cline) & James. Educ: Univ Ky, 34-35; WVa Univ, 35-36. Polit & Govt Pos: Mem, Small Coal Mines Adv Comt, Ky, 63-68; mem, Tech Adv Comn on Reclamation of Strip Mining, 68-; mem, Ky State Rep Cent Comt, 69- Bus & Prof Pos: Pres, Roberts & Holcomb Enterprises, 54-; Dixie Mining Co of Ky, Inc, 55-; Consumers Natural Gas Co of Ky, 59-; Ky Shale Gas Co, 60-; Queen Coal Corp, 61- Mem: Coal Operators Assoc (pres, 58-); Nat Independent Coal Operators Asn; Pikeville CofC. Relig: Baptist. Legal Res: Ratliff Creek Rd Pikeville KY 41501 Mailing Add: PO Box 2728 Pikeville KY 41501

HOLCOMB, THOMAS M (D)
Mich State Rep
Mailing Add: 2931 Hemlock Pl Lansing MI 48910

HOLCOMB, WILLIAM ROBERT (R)
Mayor, San Bernardino, Calif
b San Bernardino, Calif, Mar 1, 22; parents deceased; m 1945 to Pearl Pennington; c John Stewart, Terri Lee, William Winfield & Robert Grant. Educ: Univ Calif, Berkeley, BA, Hastings Sch Law, JD. Polit & Govt Pos: Chmn, Bd Water Comnr, Calif, 64-71; pres, Upper Santa Ana Water Coord Coun, formerly; chmn, Manpower Area Planning Coun, 71-74; mayor, San Bernardino, 71-; vchmn, Tri Co Coun on Criminal Justice, 74-; chmn, San Bernardino Transit Syst, 74- Mil Serv: 1st Lt, Air Force, 42-45. Mem: League of Calif Cities (pres, citrus belt div, 73-74, mem human resources comt, currently); US Conf Mayors (mem environ comt); Southern Calif Asn Govt (mem exec bd, 72-); Native Sons of Golden W; Eagles. Honors & Awards: Citizen of Year, San Bernardino Bd Realtors, 69; Hon Life Membership, PTA, 70. Relig: Baptist. Mailing Add: 3702 Hemlock Dr San Bernardino CA 92404

HOLDEN, A C (D)
Okla State Sen
Mailing Add: State Capitol Oklahoma City OK 73105

HOLDEN, CREIGHTON DAVIDSON (R)
Rep Nat Committeeman, Mich
b Detroit, Mich, Jan 19, 17; s Creighton Holden & Belinda Davidson H; m 1941 to Rebecca Jean Harshbarger; c Holly, Creighton, Jr, Belinda, Becky & Heather. Educ: Dartmouth Col, BA, 40; Dragon Sr Soc; Phi Gamma Delta. Polit & Govt Pos: Dir, Citizens for Mich, 61-64; chmn, Goldwater for Pres, Great Lakes Area, 64; mem, Gov Comt on Higher Educ, 64-65; chmn, Mich Campaigns, 68; Rep Nat Committeeman, Mich, 72- Bus & Prof Pos: Pres, Am Hotel & Motel Asn, formerly; pres, Mich Hotel Asn, 58. Mil Serv: Entered as Pvt, Army, 43, released as Pfc, 46, after serv in Inf, ETO; Combat Inf Award; ETO Ribbon with Three Battle Stars; Purple Heart. Mem: Mich State CofC; Detroit Athletic Club; Rotary; VFW; DAV. Relig: Protestant. Mailing Add: 500 N Riverside St Clair MI 48079

HOLDEN, GEORGE GORDON (D)
Chmn, Lander Co Dem Cent Comt, Nev
b Broken Bow, Okla, Jan 17, 17; s Dan Holden & Laura Henryetta Heald H; m 1965 to Margaret June Cunningham; c Patsy Ann (Mrs David Barnet) & Margaret Lynne (Mrs Michael Stewart). Educ: Univ Nev, 47-50; Univ Denver, BS, 52; Univ SDak, LLB, 53; Phi Alpha Delta. Polit & Govt Pos: Dist Attorney, Lander Co, Nev, 53-66; chmn, Lander Co Dem Cent Comt, 57-; Dep Attorney Gen, Nev, 66-68; mem, Nev State Dem Cent Comt, 66 & 70-; attorney, Fair & Recreation Bd, Lander Co, 72- Bus & Prof Pos: Practicing lawyer, 53-55 & 68-; Lander Co dist attorney, 75- Mil Serv: Entered as Pvt, Air Force, 43, released as T/Sgt, 45, after serv in 100th Bomb Group, 349 Bomb Squadron Hq 8th Air Force, ETO; Air Medal with Three Oak Leaf Clusters. Mem: Nev Bar Asn; Lions; Am Legion; Battle Mountain CofC (pres, 72); Nev Mines & Prospectors Asn (chmn, 72). Honors & Awards: Appreciation Award, Nev State Dem Cent Comt, 68. Relig: Protestant. Legal Res: 102 E Second St Battle Mountain NV 89820 Mailing Add: PO Box 448 Battle Mountain NV 89820

HOLDEN, NATE (D)
Calif State Sen
Mailing Add: 4401 Crenshaw Blvd Los Angeles CA 90043

HOLDEN, ROBERT WARREN (D)
Mem, San Diego Dem Co Cent Comt, Calif
b Quincy, Mass, Sept 17, 34; s Carl Mason Holden & Helen Klinger H; m 1961 to Eileen Loraine Ginter; c Erich John & Wayne Douglas. Educ: Worcester Polytech Inst, BS, 55, MS, 59; San Diego State Univ, BA, 70. Polit & Govt Pos: Alt deleg, Dem Nat Conv, 72; mem, San Diego Dem Co Cent Comt, Calif, 74- Bus & Prof Pos: Engr, Eastman Kodak Co, Rochester, NY, 55-56; instr mech eng, NMex State Univ, 56-58; research engr, Shell Oil Co, Martinez, Calif, 60-61; teacher eng & math, Grossmont Col, 61- Mil Serv: Entered as Pvt, Army, 57, released, 57. Mem: Am Fedn Teachers Local 1934 (research dir, 63-); Sierra Club; Common Cause. Relig: Unitarian. Mailing Add: 6733 Sunny Brae Dr San Diego CA 92119

HOLDEN, WAYNE M (D)
Okla State Sen
Mailing Add: State Capitol Oklahoma City OK 73105

HOLDERMAN, JAMES (D)
Kans State Rep
Mailing Add: 212 S Market Wichita KS 67202

HOLDERMAN, SAMUEL JAMES (R)
b Morris, Ill, Dec 21, 01; s Samuel D Holderman (deceased) & Mae E Wilcox; wid; c Gordon B, Helen (Mrs Schmult) & James B. Educ: Univ Ill Col Law, LLB, 25; Phi Alpha Delta; Square & Compass. Polit & Govt Pos: State's attorney, Grundy Co, Ill, 32-48; chmn, Grundy Co Rep Cent Comt, Ill, 52-74; chmn, Indust Comn, Ill, 53-63; judge, Ill Court of Claims, 70- Bus & Prof Pos: Lawyer, Morris, Ill, 25- Mem: Cedar Lodge AF&AM; Mohammed Temple; Morris Shrine Club; Eagles; Elks. Relig: Presbyterian. Legal Res: Rte 3 Morris IL 60450 Mailing Add: 302 1/2 Liberty St Morris IL 60450

HOLDSTOCK, RICHARD S (D)
Mem, Calif Dem State Cent Comt
b Southampton, Eng, June 30, 34; s John E Holdstock & Lilian Jury H; m 1953 to Jacqueline May; c Kenneth A, Daniel A & Marcia D. Educ: John Muir Col, AA, 54; Univ Calif, Los Angeles, BSc, 58, MSc, 60; Bruin Pub Health Asn. Polit & Govt Pos: Mem, Econ Opportunity Comn, Yolo Co, Calif, 67; mem, Calif Dem State Cent Comt, 68-; mem, Yolo Co Dem Cent Comt, 68-; mem adv bd of sanitation standards, Calif State Health Dept, 69; councilman, City of Davis, Calif, 72-; deleg, Dem Nat Conv, 72. Bus & Prof Pos: Pub health sanitarian, Los Angeles Co Health Dept, 58; pub health sanitarian, Placer Co Health Dept, 59; environ health & safety officer, Univ Calif, Davis, 62. Mil Serv: Entered as Pvt, Army, 54, released as SP-3, 56, after serv in Med Corps, Army Optical Activity, St Louis, Mo; Good Conduct Medal. Publ: Public health effects on microwave radiation, J Environ Health, 59. Mem: Health Physics Soc; Nat Asn of Sanitarians; Am Conf of Govt Indust Hygienists; Calif Asn of Sanitarians (pres); Davis Human Rels Coun. Honors & Awards: Named Humanitarian of the Year by Davis Human Rels Coun, 68. Relig: Protestant. Mailing Add: 933 K St Davis CA 95616

HOLE, RICHARD EUGENE, II (R)
Exec Secy, Darke Co Rep Party, Ohio
b Greenville, Ohio, Apr 26, 37; s Richard Eugene Hole & Harriett Watson H; m 1965 to Barbara Davenport; c Elizabeth Jane & Amy Lynn. Educ: Ohio Northern Univ, BA, 59, JD, 65; Alpha Sigma Phi; Delta Theta Phi. Polit & Govt Pos: Exec secy, Darke Co Rep Party, Ohio, 67-; safety dir, Greenville, 68- Bus & Prof Pos: Attorney-at-law, Spidel, Staley, Hole & Hanes, Greenville, 66- Mil Serv: Entered as Pvt, Army, 61, released as Specialist, 4/C, 63, after serv in Garrison, Ft Sam Houston, Tex, 61-63. Mem: Am, Ohio & Parke Co Bar Asns; Elks; Rotary. Relig: United Church of Christ. Mailing Add: 622 Chestnut St Greenville OH 45331

HOLEWINSKI, MICHAEL S (D)
Ill State Rep
b Chicago, Ill, Apr 30, 47; s Stanley Holewinski & Genevieve Gorzela H; m 1972 to Mary Plaza. Educ: Univ Ill, Chicago, BA, Polit Sci, 69; John Marshall Law Sch, 72-; Alpha Phi Omega. Polit & Govt Pos: Cand, City Coun, Chicago, 71; ward coordr, Walker for Gov, 72; deleg, Dem Nat Conv, 72; Ill State Rep, 75- Bus & Prof Pos: Assoc buyer, Montgomery Ward, 69-73; asst exec secy, Ill Racing Bd, 73-74. Mil Serv: SP-4, Army Res, Mil Police, 69-; Cert Achievement Outstanding Performance, 71. Mem: Comt Ill Govt (bd mem); Independent Precinct Orgn (ward commun action chmn, 72-73). Honors & Awards: Cert Proficiency, Civil Air Patrol, 63. Relig: Roman Catholic. Mailing Add: 4164 W Nelson St Chicago IL 60641

HOLIFIELD, CHET (D)
b Mayfield, Ky, Dec 3, 03; s Ercie V Holifield & Bessie Brady H; m to Vernice Caneer; c Lois Anita (Mrs William Mulholland), Betty Lee (Mrs Robert H Feldmann), Willa Mae (Mrs Donald Lee Douglas) & Jo Ann (Mrs Robert Ward); grandchildren, 15. Educ: Ark Pub Schs. Hon Degrees: AA, ELos Angeles Col, 62; LLD, Lynchburg Col, 64 & Whittier Col, 66. Polit & Govt Pos: Chmn, Los Angeles Co Dem Cent Comt, 34-38; chmn, Calif State Cent Comt, 12th Cong Dist, 38-40; deleg, Dem Nat Conv, 40, 44, 48, 52, 56, 60, 64 & 68; US Rep, 19th Cong Dist, Calif, 42-74, chmn joint comt on atomic energy, govt opers comt & mil opers subcomt, US House of Reps; mem, President's Spec Eval Comn on Atomic Bomb Tests at Bikini Atoll, 46; mem, Comn on Orgn of Exec Br of Govt; cong adv US deleg, Int Conf on Peaceful Uses of Atomic Energy, Geneva, 55 & 71; rep first orgn meeting, Int Atomic Energy Agency, Vienna, 57, cong adv US delegs to gen confs, 59, 63, 68, 69 & 70 & Tokyo, 65; cong adv US deleg, First Int Symp on Water Desalinization, 65; cong adv Am delegs, Confs on Discontinuance of Nuclear Weapons Tests, Geneva, 59 & 61; cong adv US delegs, Eighteen-Nation Disarmament Confs, Geneva, 67-70; vchmn, President's Comn on Govt Procurement, 70-72; deleg, Dem Nat Mid-Term Conf, 74. Bus & Prof Pos: Mfg & selling of men's Apparel, 20- Honors & Awards: Cong Distinguished Serv Award, Am Polit Sci Asn, 67; First Nat Security Award, US Civil Defense Coun, 69. Relig: Christian Church. Mailing Add: 2001 Lincoln Ave Montebello CA 90640

HOLLADAY, HUGH EDWIN (D)
Mem, St Clair Co Dem Exec Comt, Ala
b Ashville, Ala, Jan 6, 23; s Roy Harris Holladay & Mary Louella Jenkins H; m 1945 to Patty Nell Stine; c Hugh Edwin, Jr, Patricia Lynn, Carl Gibson & Ethel Ann. Educ: Univ Ala, Tuscaloosa, BS, 47, LLB, 50; Phi Alpha Delta; Chi Phi. Polit & Govt Pos: Past pres, St Clair Co Young Dem Club, Ala; Ala State Rep, 62-70; mem, St Clair Co Dem Exec Comt, 68-; app judge, 30th Judicial Circuit, Ala, 73, elec judge, 74- Bus & Prof Pos: Lawyer; past pres, Pell City Jr CofC & Pell City CofC. Mil Serv: Entered as Cadet, Air Force, 42, released as 1st Lt, 45, after serv in 8th Air Force, ETO, 42-45; Purple Heart. Mem: Ben M Jacobs Masonic Lodge; VFW; Am Legion; Ala Farm Bur; St Clair Co Cattleman's Asn. Relig: Baptist. Legal Res: 818 Cogswell Ave Pell City AL 35125 Mailing Add: PO Box 646 Pell City AL 35125

HOLLAND, ARTHUR JOHN (D)
Mayor, Trenton, NJ
b Trenton, NJ, Oct 24, 18; s Joseph F Holland & Helen Groh H; m 1962 to Elizabeth Anne Jackson; c Cynthia, Elise, Christopher, Timothy & Matthew. Educ: St Francis Col, NY Rutgers Univ, AB in soc studies, MA, in pub admin. Polit & Govt Pos: Dep dir, Dept of Pub Affairs, Trenton, NJ, 51-52, dir, 55-62; dep dir, Dept of Parks & Pub Property, 52-55; mayor, Trenton, NJ, 59-66 & 70-; deleg, White House Conf to Fulfill These Rights, 66; past mem bd dirs, Young Dem of Mercer Co; mem, Gov Welfare Study Comn, 70- Bus & Prof Pos: Res analyst, Opinion Res Corp, 45-49; assoc dir, Princeton Research Serv, 49-51; adj research specialist, Urban Studies Ctr & Bur Community Serv, Rutgers, The State Univ, 66-69, adj research prof, Urban Studies Ctr, 69-70, lectr polit sci, Univ Col, 67-; consult, Dept of Housing & Urban Develop, 66; consult, Nat Inst of Pub Affairs, 66- Publ: The Study of the Metropolitan Desk Concept from the Viewpoint of the Mayor, Dept of Housing & Urban Develop, 66; The Changing Functions of Urban Government, Wash Exec Conf held at Brookings Inst, sponsored by Am Univ, 67; proj dir, The Roles of the States in Solving Urban Problems, Rutgers Urban Studies Ctr. Mem: KofC; Nat Munic League (mem adv coun); Kiwanis (hon mem); NAACP; Torch Club. Honors & Awards: Young Man of the Year, Trenton Jr CofC, 54; Cath Interracial Coun of NY Award for Interracial Justice, 64; NJ Americanization Conv Citizenship Award, 64; commendation for meritorious achievement in furthering the cause of int understanding through the town affiliation prog of the President's People to People Prog. Relig: Roman Catholic. Mailing Add: 138 Mercer St Trenton NJ 08611

HOLLAND, CECIL FLETCHER (R)
b Falling Water, Tenn, Dec 10, 07; s Fletcher Holland & Matilda Lewis H; m 1933 to Alice Carden; c Mrs Robert L Hughes, Cecil F Jr, Alice Carden & Martha Stewart. Educ: Univ Tenn, Chattanooga, AB, 29; Blue Key; Pi Gamma Mu; Sigma Tau Delta. Polit & Govt Pos: Admin asst to US Sen Robert P Griffin, Mich, 68-72; admin asst to Asst Minority Leader, US Senate, 73- Bus & Prof Pos: Reporter & ed, Chattanooga News, Tenn & Washington Star; reporter, Washington Bur, Chicago Sun & Sun-Times; correspondent, NY Herald-Tribune. Mil Serv: Entered as Capt, Army Air Force, 42, released, 45, after serv in Air Transport Command & Air Staff, ETO. Publ: Morgan & his raiders, MacMillan, 42. Mem: Sigma Delta Chi. Mailing Add: 14 W Lenox St Chevy Chase MD 20015

HOLLAND, CHARLES FRANK (D)
Mem, Tenn Dem State Exec Comt
b Eupora, Miss, Oct 9, 27; s Ocre M Holland & Pauline Estes H; m 1958 to Mary Lou Jett; c Randy. Educ: Univ Tenn. Polit & Govt Pos: Mem, Tenn Dem State Exec Comt, currently. Bus & Prof Pos: Owner & ed, North Shelby Advertiser, Tenn, currently; pres, Betty Rose Corp, currently; partner, Norman Ricci Realty & Molton Ins Agency, currently. Mil Serv: Ens, Navy, 44-48. Mailing Add: 2987 Mountain Terr Memphis TN 38127

HOLLAND, DONALD HARRY (D)
SC State Sen
Mailing Add: 1710 Fair St Kershaw SC 29067

HOLLAND, EDWARD MCHARG (D)
Va State Sen
b Washington, DC, Nov 28, 39; s Edwin Trammell Holland & Elizabeth McHarg H; m 1966 to JoAnn Dotson; c David Ames, Allan Taylor & Lee McHarg. Educ: Princeton Univ, AB, 62; Univ Va Law Sch, LLB, 65; Georgetown Univ Law Ctr, LLM in Tax, 67; Princeton Quadrangle Club. Polit & Govt Pos: Va State Sen, 31st Sen Dist, 71- Bus & Prof Pos: Tax law specialist, Internal Revenue Serv, Washington, DC, 65-66; assoc, Tolbert, Lewis & Fitzgerald, Arlington, Va, 66-70; partner, Wilson & Holland, 70-74, sole practitioner, 74-; trustee, First Va Mortgage, Real Estate, Investment & Trust, 72-; dir, Vet Mem YMCA, Arlington. Mem: Explorers Club, New York; Arlington Kiwanis; Arlington Jaycees. Honors & Awards: W Kuhn Barnett Spec Award, Va Fedn of Coun for Exceptional Children, 73. Relig: United Methodist. Legal Res: 3168 N 21st St Arlington VA 22201 Mailing Add: 2054 N 14th St Arlington VA 22201

HOLLAND, EVELYN FAUCETTE (D)
Treas, Dade Co Dem Exec Comt, Fla
b Lillington, NC, Sept 11, 27; d Henry Bethune Faucette, Sr & Virginia Stegall F; m 1946 to Sherman William Holland, Jr; c Karen (Mrs Charles Wilfred Shaffer), Sherman William, III & Michael Edward. Educ: Charron-Williams Commercial College, 45-46; Univ Miami Ins Prog, 48. Polit & Govt Pos: Vpres, Miami Int Allied Printing Trades, 65-68; pres, local 11, Int Brotherhood Bookbinders, 66-68; Comt on Polit Educ deleg, Dade Co Fedn Labor, 66-68; mem alcoholism comt, Dade Co Welfare Coun, 67-68; co coun mem, Dade Co Dem Women's Club, 67-68; comnr, Hialeah Housing Authority, 67-, vchmn, 70; mem & vchmn, Dade Co Personnel Adv Bd, 67-; alt deleg, Dem Nat Conv, 68; mem, Brotherhood Comt, 68-; Dem Committeewoman, 70; treas, Dade Co Dem Exec Comt, Fla, 71-; mem, State Fla Comt Status of Women, 73-; admin asst to Fla State Rep John A Hill, currently. Bus & Prof Pos: Owner, ATSCO Tractor Co, Miami, 54-; pres, Videon Corp, Hialeah, 60; secy-treas, Falco Printing, Inc, 62 & pres, Falco Printing, Inc, 69; pres, Falco & Assoc, Inc, 69- Publ: The Student, Falco & Assocs, Inc, 69; Operation Rescue, Southeast Publ, 72. Mem: Dade Co Dem Women's Club; Dade Co Allied Trades Coun; Dade Fedn of Labor, AFL-CIO; Gtr Miami Dem Woman's Club; Young Dem of Dade Co. Honors & Awards: Service Award, Dept of Veteran's Affairs, 64; Appreciation Award, Lions Club, 65; Serv Award, Hialeah Sr Citizens; Serv Award in Pub Housing, Housing Corp Am. Relig: Catholic. Legal Res: 330 W 54th St Hialeah FL 33012 Mailing Add: 675 NW 90th St Miami FL 33150

HOLLAND, IRIS K (R)
Mass State Rep
b Springfield, Mass, Sept 30, 20; d Leo Kaufman & Sadie Stahl K; m 1941 to Gilbert Strom Holland; c Judith (Mrs David Borden), Richard & Donald. Educ: Rider Col, BS; Alpha Epsilon Pi; Class Pres. Polit & Govt Pos: Mass State Rep, 73-74 & 75- Bus & Prof Pos: Teacher, formerly; businesswoman, currently. Publ: Your state ombudsman, newspaper column, 73- Mem: Zonta Int; Goodwill Indust (dir); Girls Clubs (dir, Carew Hill Club). Honors & Awards: Mass Woman of Year; Outstanding Legislator, Joint Urban Affairs, Harvard Univ & Mass Inst Technol; First Person in Hist Mass Polit to Win as Sticker Cand; Only Woman Ever Elected from Western Mass to Mass House Rep; Ment Health Appreciation Award Honoree. Mailing Add: 38 Hazelwood Ave Longmeadow MA 01106

HOLLAND, JAMES FRANCIS (R)
NH State Rep
b Nashua, NH, Sept 24, 38; s Frank Theodore Holland & Margaret Cummings H; m 1963 to Linda Helen Fair; c James Michael, Johanna Lee & Timothy J. Educ: Northeastern Univ, 61-66. Polit & Govt Pos: NH State Rep, 75- Bus & Prof Pos: Police officer, Nashua Police Dept, NH, 60-68; realtor, Tamposi Assoc Inc, Nashua, 69-74; self-employed realtor, Nashua, 74- Mil Serv: Entered as Pvt, Army, 57, released as SP-3, 59, after serv in First Army Band; Marksman Rifle Award. Mem: Nashua Bd Realtors; Nat Inst Real Estate Brokers; Farm & Land Inst of Nat Asn Realtors. Relig: Catholic. Mailing Add: 62 New Searles Rd Nashua NH 03060

HOLLAND, JOE S (D)
SC State Rep
Mailing Add: Box 264 Clinton SC 29325

HOLLAND, JOHN (D)
Polit & Govt Pos: Former Dem Nat Committeeman, NH; deleg, Dem Nat Conv, 72. Mailing Add: 5 Glenn Rd Bedford NH 03102

HOLLAND, KENNETH L (D)
US Rep, SC
b Hickory, NC, Nov 24, 34; m to Jean Carroll; c Lamar, Amy & Beth. Educ: Univ SC, BA, 60, LLB, 63, JD, 70; Blue Key. Polit & Govt Pos: Mem, State Hwy Comn, SC, 72-74; mem exec comt & legal counsel, SC Dem Party, currently; US Rep, SC, 75- Bus & Prof Pos: With, State Hwy Dept, 53-55; instrumentman, Daniel Construction Co, 56; sr partner, Holland, Furman, Tetterton & Groom, Camden, 70-74. Mem: SC & Am Bar Asns; Am Trial Lawyers

Asn; Kiwanis; Jaycees (former state vpres). Relig: Methodist; teacher Sunday Sch; mem admin bd. Legal Res: PO Drawer 100 Camden SC 29020 Mailing Add: US House Rep Washington DC 20515

HOLLAND, WILLIAM C (INDEPENDENT)
Wyo State Rep
Mailing Add: 312 N Main St Buffalo WY 82834

HOLLANDER, SANFORD LLOYD (D)
Mem, NJ Dem Policy Coun
b Paterson, NJ, Apr 1, 32; s Edward Hollander & Fay Dobinsky H; m 1958 to Roslyn Theresa Turkin; c Joseph E, Andrew B, David A & Elizabeth A. Educ: Brown Univ, AB, 54; Columbia Univ Law Sch, LLB, 57. Polit & Govt Pos: Staff mem, NJ Attorney Gen Off, 57-58; asst to Hon Vito A Concilio, 58-59; chmn, Dem Munic Orgn, Newton, NJ, 60-67; munic counsel for Town of Newton, 63-; mem, Newton Bd Educ, 63-, pres, 64-69; deleg, Dem Nat Conv, 64; deleg, NJ Const Conv, 66; mem, NJ Dem Policy Coun, 69-; mem, Sussex Co Voc Tech Bd Educ, 71- Bus & Prof Pos: Attorney, self-employed, 59-64; partner, Trapasso, Dolan & Hollander, 64- Mil Serv: Entered as Pvt, NJ Army Nat Guard, 58, released as Specialist, 64. Mem: Anti-defamation League, B'nai B'rith (chmn, NJ Regional Bd); Bd Turstees, Sch of Arts (chmn); United Jewish Appeal (Sussex Co annual chmn); mem young leadership cabinet. Relig: Jewish. Mailing Add: 5 Dogwood Dr Newton NJ 07860

HOLLANDER, THOMAS (D)
b Monessen, Pa, Mar 9, 36; s Edward Hollander & Edith Bergstein H; m 1960 to Barbara Ann Stone; c Scott Michael, Leslie Rachel & David Louis. Educ: Pa State Univ, BA, 58; Univ Pittsburgh, JD, 61; Omicron Delta Kappa; Phi Epsilon Pi. Polit & Govt Pos: Committeeman, Mt Lebanon Twp Dem Comt, Pa, 66-; deleg, Dem Nat Conv, 68; chmn, Allegheny Co Dist Orgn Comt to Reelect Sen Joseph S Clark, 68; mem bd & off, Neighborhood Legal Serv Asn, 70-; pres, Pittsburgh chap, Am for Dem Action, 71-; mem bd, Western Pa Youth Develop Ctr, 73- Bus & Prof Pos: Partner, Evans, Ivory & Evans, Attorneys, Pittsburgh, 69- Mem: Am Arbit Asn (arbitrator); South Hills Asn Racial Equality; Am Civil Liberties Union; Acad Trial Lawyers of Allegheny Co; YMCA. Honors & Awards: Undergrad of the Year, Phi Epsilon Pi, 57; Blackburn Mem Award; Samuel Wagner Prize, 61. Relig: Jewish. Legal Res: 272 Vee Lynn Dr Pittsburgh PA 15228 Mailing Add: 711 Frick Bldg Pittsburgh PA 15219

HOLLANDER, WALTER G (R)
Wis State Sen
b Fond du Lac, Wis, Sept 8, 96. Educ: Omro High Sch. Polit & Govt Pos: Local elective off, Rosendale, Wis, 29-; mem, Fond du Lac Co Bd, 38-53, chmn, 53-; Wis State Sen, 56- Bus & Prof Pos: Ins agt & farmer, Springvale, Wis; retired. Mailing Add: Rte 1 Rosendale WI 54974

HOLLAR, CHARLES HAYS (R)
Co-chmn, Dyer Co Rep Exec Comt, Tenn
b Custer, Okla, Dec 3, 97; s Charles Rush Hollar & Lura Viola Pierce; m 1921 to Orbyn Ruth Craddock; c Orbyn Sunshine (Mrs Davis). Educ: High Sch, Bus Col & Govt Tax Course. Polit & Govt Pos: Dir, Population Census, Eighth Dist, Tenn, 60; former chmn, Dyer Co Rep Exec Comt, co-chmn, currently. Bus & Prof Pos: Owner, C Hays Hollar Seed Co, Newbern, Tenn, 31- Mem: Rotary; Farm Bur; Mason; Commandery; Shrine. Relig: Methodist; Dist trustee, Methodist Church properties. Legal Res: 503 W Main Newbern TN 38059 Mailing Add: PO Box 279 Newbern TN 38059

HOLLEY, JIMMY W (D)
Ala State Rep
Mailing Add: Rte 3 Box 191E Elba AL 36323

HOLLEY, RUDOLPH EUGENE (D)
Majority Leader, Ga State Senate
b Aiken, SC, Feb 15, 26; s Norton Hansford Holley & Harriett Holley H; m 1953 to Louise Brittingham; c Robert Eugene, Phillip Gerard, Stephen Thomas, Anna Louise & Eugene Norton. Educ: Univ Ga, BBA, 49, Sch Law, LLB magna cum laude, 58; Phi Beta Kappa; Chi Psi; Phi Kappa Phi. Polit & Govt Pos: Dept Asst Attorney Gen, Atlanta, Ga, 64-65; Ga State Sen, 65-, majority leader, Ga State Senate, 71- Bus & Prof Pos: Attorney, Congdon & Leonard, Augusta, Ga, 58, Congdon & Holley, 59-66 & Sanders, Hester, Holley, Askin & Dye, 67- Mil Serv: World War II, 43-45; reentered as Lt, Air Force, 49, released as Capt, 55, after serv as F-86 Jet Fighter Pilot, Korea, 50-52; Air Medal with Oak Leaf Cluster; Distinguished Flying Cross. Mem: YMCA; Augusta CofC; Am Legion; Com Club, Atlanta; Augusta Country Club. Relig: Baptist. Legal Res: Flowing Wells Rd Rte 2 Box 364 Augusta GA 30904 Mailing Add: Suite 1500 Southern Finance Bldg Augusta GA 30904

HOLLIDAY, HAROLD L (D)
Mo State Rep
b Muskogee, Okla, June 28, 18; m 1942 to Margaret Louise Garrett; c Harold L, Jr & Bertha G. Educ: Lincoln Univ; Univ Mich; Univ Mo, AB, MA & LLB; Omega Psi Phi. Polit & Govt Pos: Case worker, Mo State Dept of Welfare, formerly; with US Employ Serv, formerly; former Vet Employ Rep; contact rep, US Vet Admin, formerly; economist, Off of Price Stabilization, formerly; Mo State Rep, 64- Bus & Prof Pos: Attorney-at-law. Mil Serv: Army, 2nd Lt, 42-45, ETO. Mem: Mo State Conf of NAACP Br (pres); Freedom Inc (bd dirs). Relig: Presbyterian. Mailing Add: 2907 Cleveland Kansas City MO 64128

HOLLIDAY, JOSEPH R (D)
WVa State Deleg
Mailing Add: State Capitol Charleston WV 25305

HOLLIFIELD, GORDON R (R)
Idaho State Rep
Mailing Add: Rte 3 Box 115 Jerome ID 83338

HOLLIMAN, MARGARET CLOUD (R)
Pres, Ga Fedn Rep Women
b Bainbridge, Ga, Apr 4, 30; d Edward Albert Cloud & Avo Boles C; m 1960 to Albert Louis Holliman; c Gary Wendell & Michael Glenn Bryan. Educ: Ga Southwestern Col, dipl, 48. Polit & Govt Pos: Pres, North Fulton Co Rep Womens Club, 67; secy, Fifth Dist Rep Party, 68-71; membership chmn, Ga Fedn Rep Women, 69-71, pres, 71-; deleg, Rep Nat Conv, 72. Bus & Prof Pos: Secy, Westinghouse Elec Corp, Atlanta, Ga, 48-50 & Ga Inst Technol, 56-60. Relig: Church of Christ. Mailing Add: 450 Forest Hills Dr NE Atlanta GA 30342

HOLLINGS, ERNEST FREDERICK (D)
Asst Majority Whip, US Senate
b Charleston, SC, Jan 1, 22; s Adolph G Hollings & Wilhelmine D Meyer H; m 1971 to Rita Louise Liddy; c Michael Milhous, Helen Hayne, Patricia Salley & Ernest Frederick, III. Educ: The Citadel, BA, 42; Univ SC, LLB, 47. Polit & Govt Pos: SC State Rep, 48-54, Speaker-Pro Tem, SC State House of Rep, 50-54; mem, Hoover Comn on Intel Activities, 54-55; mem, Presidential Adv Comn on Intergovt Rels, 59-63; Lt Gov, SC, 55-59, Gov, 59-63; US Sen, SC, 66-, mem, Budget, Commerce, Appropriations, Post Off & Civil Serv Subcomts, US Senate, chmn, Comts on Legis Appropriations, Postal Opers & Oceans & Atmosphere, mem, Senate Dem Policy Comt, chmn, Senate Dem Campaign Comt, 71-73, Asst Majority Whip, currently; deleg, Dem Nat Conv, 72; mem, Technol Assessment Bd, 73- Bus & Prof Pos: Attorney-at-law. Mem: Asn Citadel Men; Hibernian Soc; Phi Delta Phi; Sertoma Club. Honors & Awards: One of Ten Outstanding Young Men, US Jr CofC, 54. Relig: Lutheran; Mem Exec Coun; Bd Adjudication, Lutheran Church of Am. Legal Res: 141 E Bay St Charleston SC 29401 Mailing Add: 437 Senate Off Bldg Washington DC 20510

HOLLINGSWORTH, DAVID JEFFREY (R)
Chmn, Waldo Co Rep Comt, Maine
b Boston, Mass, July 1, 52; s George Frederick Hollingsworth & Beatrice Sweeney H; single. Educ: Univ Maine, Orono, BA; Nat Honor Soc; Beta Eta of Beta Theta Pi; Sr Skull Soc. Polit & Govt Pos: State chmn, Maine Young Am for Freedom, 70-75; mem, Gov Youth Task Force, 70-71; vchmn, Waldo Co Rep Comt, 72-73, chmn, 73-; New Eng field rep, Young Am for Freedom, Inc, 74-75; co-founder & dir, Main Conservative Union, 74. Bus & Prof Pos: Admin asst, City of Portland, Maine, 71; research aide dept hist, Univ Maine, Orono, 72; sec sch instr, Belfast, 74-75; dir commun, Med Liability Comn, Chicago, Ill, 75- Publ: Auth, The lady from Maine, New Guard Mag, 12/72; auth, Mainely right (weekly column), Maine Campus, 73-74; auth & ed, MLC Commentary (monthly nat newsletter), Med Liability Comn, 75- Honors & Awards: Outstanding TAR of US, Young Rep Nat Fedn, 69; Outstanding Col Chap in US, Young Am for Freedom, 71, Award of Freedom, 73; Personal Letter of Appreciation & Commendation by President of US, Nov, 72. Relig: Episcopal. Legal Res: 20 Miller St Belfast ME 04915 Mailing Add: 1004 1244 N Dearborn Chicago IL 60610

HOLLINGTON, RICHARD R, JR (R)
Mem Exec Comt, Ohio Rep Orgn
b Findlay, Ohio, Nov 12, 32; s Richard R Hollington & Annett Kirk H; m 1959 to Sally Stecher; c Lorie, Julie, Richard, III & Peter. Educ: Williams Col, BA, 54; Harvard Univ, LLB, 57. Polit & Govt Pos: Spec counsel, Ohio Attorney Gen, 63-70; mem exec comt, Cuyahoga Co Rep Orgn, 64-; Ohio State Rep, 56th Dist, 67-70; law dir, City of Cleveland, 71-73; mem, Ohio Comn on Local Govt Serv, 72-; trustee, Regional Sewer Dist, 72-; mem exec comt, Ohio Rep Orgn, currently. Bus & Prof Pos: Dir, Ohio Bank & Savings Co, 57-; partner, Law Firm of Baker, Hostetler & Patterson; trustee, Cleveland State Univ; dir, Cleveland Conv & Visitors Bur, 73- Mil Serv: Entered as Pvt, Ohio Nat Guard, 57, released as 1st Lt, 63. Mem: Citizens League; Cleveland Grays; Newcomer Soc; Ripon Club; Bluecoats, Inc. Relig: Episcopal. Mailing Add: 2950 Attleboro Rd Shaker Heights OH 44120

HOLLINS, HARRY M (D)
La State Rep
b Lake Charles, La, Aug 25, 32; s Arthur Hollins, Jr & Mary Muth H; m 1957 to Caroline Skipper; c Kelly McCullough & Virginia. Educ: Washington & Lee Univ, BA in Polit Sci, 55; Sigma Alpha Epsilon. Polit & Govt Pos: Mem, Lake Charles Dem Exec Comt, La, 56-60; La State Rep, Dist 35, 64-, chmn com comt & vchmn environ comt, La House of Rep; mem bd, La Sabine River Authority, 68. Bus & Prof Pos: Bd mem, Lake Charles Better Bus Bur, 64, Lake Charles Downtown Develop, 66, La Ment Health, 68, La Econ Educ, 69, Calcasieu-Cameron Red Cross, 69 & First Nat Bank of Lake Charles. Mil Serv: Entered as 2nd Lt, Army, 56, released as 1st Lt, 57, after serv in Transportation Coop. Mem: Calcasieu Kiwanis; Lake Charles Country Club; Pioneer Club. Relig: Episcopal. Legal Res: 1605 Enterprise Blvd Lake Charles LA 70601 Mailing Add: PO Box 1889 Lake Charles LA 70601

HOLLIS, LUCILLE JEWELL (D)
b Maries Co, Mo, July 17, 27; d Rainey Clarence Woody & Dulcy Mae Burnham W; m 1947 to Eugene Alvin Hollis; c Judy Carol (Mrs Dale Edward Logan); Randy Eugene & Rex Woody, one grandchild. Educ: Cent Mo State Teachers Col, 46; Southwest Baptist Col, 48. Polit & Govt Pos: Secy, Maries Co Dem Comt, Mo, 54-56, treas, 56-70, vchmn, formerly; asst treas, Maries Co, 63- Bus & Prof Pos: Grade sch teacher, Maries Co Sch Syst, 46-50. Mem: Am Legion Auxiliary. Honors & Awards: Awards for parade floats, Am Legion Auxiliary. Relig: Protestant. Mailing Add: Star Rte 1 Box 29 Vienna MO 65582

HOLLISTER, DAVID CLINTON (D)
Mich State Rep
b Kalamazoo, Mich, Apr 3, 42; s Russell Corwin Hollister & Julia Harrison H; m 1962 to Judith Ann Artz; c Jerry, Todd & Robert. Educ: Kellogg Community Col, AA, 62; Mich State Univ, BA, 64, MA, 67. Polit & Govt Pos: Comnr, Ingham Co Bd Comnr, 69-75, bd chairperson, 73-75; chairperson, Tri-Co Regional Manpower Consortium, 74-75; Mich State Rep, 57th Dist, 75- Bus & Prof Pos: Mem, Bus-Indust Comt to Prevent Dropouts, 67-68; chairperson, Gtr Lansing Community Orgn, 70-71; bd mem, Martin DePorres Credit Union, 72-74; mem, Boys' Training Sch Feasibility Rev Comt, 73-74 & Lansing Comt on Aging, Subcomt on Spanish-Speaking, 73-74; bd dirs, Big Bros-Big Sisters, 74- Mem: NAACP; Northside Neighborhood Asn; Am Civil Liberties Union; Sol de Aztlan; Nat Asn of Counties (mem welfare steering comt, 72-74). Honors & Awards: Outstanding Young Educator of the Month, Lansing Jaycees, 67; Named Nat Outstanding Citizen of the Year, Nat Asn of Social Workers, 74 & Outstanding Citizen of the Year, Lansing-Jackson Chap, 74. Relig: Protestant. Legal Res: 1501 Vermont Ave Lansing MI 48906 Mailing Add: House of Rep Lansing MI 48901

HOLLISTER, JOHN BAKER (R)
b Cincinnati, Ohio, Nov 7, 90; s Howard Clark Hollister & Alice Keys H; m 1917 to Ellen W Rollins (deceased), remarried 1962 to Florence B Wigglesworth; c Mrs Anne H Stevenson; Alice (Mrs D Scott) & John B, Jr. Educ: St Paul's Sch, Concord; Yale, AB, 11; Univ Munich, 11-12; Harvard, LLB, 15. Hon Degrees: LLD, Univ Cincinnati, 61. Polit & Govt Pos: In charge of relief in Lithuania; Am Relief in Poland, 19; US Rep, Ohio, 31-36; deleg, Rep Nat Conv, 40-52; chmn, Mission to Netherlands, UNNRA, 45; pres, Little Miami RR Gov Nat Annual Report Coun, 47-51; exec dir, Hoover Comn, 53; consult, Secy of State, 54-; dir, Int Coop Admin, 55-57. Bus & Prof Pos: Dir of several corp; partner, Taft, Stettenius & Hollister, 24-55, 57-67, sr partner, 41-67. Mil Serv: Capt, 46th Artil, CAC, 17-19. Mem: Am, Ohio & Cincinnati Bar Asns; Psi Upsilon; Metrop Club, Washington. Relig: Presbyterian. Mailing Add: 603 Dixie Terminal Bldg Cincinnati OH 45202

HOLLISTER, WILLIAM HILLMAN (D)
Mem, Chittenden Co Dem Comt, Vt
b Washington, DC, July 8, 29; s Joseph Hillman Hollister & Katharine Lauder H; m to Joan Schaaff; c Jody, Mark, Hillman, Kristen Kay, Kip Elizabeth & Chad Joseph. Educ: Williams Col, BA. 51; Union Theol Sem, NY, BD, 54; Beta Theta Pi. Polit & Govt Pos: Vt State Rep, 66-68; mem, Legis Coun Penal Study Comt, 66-67; mem, Burlington Dem City Comt, 67-; deleg, Dem Nat Conv, 68; mem, Chittenden Co Dem Comt, 68-; mem, Vt State Bd Corrections, 69- Bus & Prof Pos: Pastor, Presby Church, Burlington 54-; dir, Burlington Ecumenical Action Ministry, 68- Mil Serv: Marine Corps Res, 48-50, Sgt, Serv in Platoon Leader's Class Prog, Quantico, Va. Publ: Recovery in suburbia, Union Sem Quart Rev, 4/61. Relig: Presbyterian. Mailing Add: 909 North Ave Burlington VT 05401

HOLLOMAN, JOHN HOLLIDAY, III (D)
b Columbus, Miss, Mar 5, 37; s John Holliday Holloman, Jr & Rosa Tate H; m to Ann Scales Klaus; c Edith Ann & Rosa Haley. Educ: Univ Miss, BA, 59, LLB, 61; Phi Alpha Delta; Phi Delta Theta. Polit & Govt Pos: Deleg, Dem Nat Conv, 60; Miss State Rep, 60-64; mem bd dirs, Tombigbee Water Mgt Dist, Miss, 63-69; prof staff mem, US Senate Judiciary Comt, 64-66, chief counsel & staff dir, 67- Bus & Prof Pos: Partner, Holloman & Holloman, Columbus, Miss, 61-64; instr, Miss State Col for Women, 61-64. Mem: Miss & Am Bar Asns; Kiwanis; US Senate Staff Club. Honors & Awards: Outstanding Young Man of the Year, Columbus, Miss Jr CofC, 63. Relig: Episcopal. Legal Res: Ridge Rd Columbus MS 39701 Mailing Add: Rm 2226 New Senate Off Bldg Washington DC 20510

HOLLOWAY, ALBERT WESTON (D)
Admin Floor Leader, Ga State Senate
b Poquoson, Va, Nov 4, 18; s John P Holloway & Octavia Weston H; m 1950 to Ethel Hilsman Edmondson; c Judith Warren. Educ: William & Mary Col, Norfolk, Va. Polit & Govt Pos: Ga State Rep, 57-58; Ga State Sen, 63-, majority leader, Ga State Senate, 69-71, admin floor leader, 71-, pres pro-tem, 75- Bus & Prof Pos: Pres & gen mgr, Eng & Equip Co; pres & dir, Albany First Fed Savings & Loan; pres, Ga State CofC, currently. Mil Serv: Air Force, Officers' Candidate Sch, Capt, 42-45; Air Medal with Five Clusters; Distinguished Flying Cross with One Cluster; Presidential Unit Citation. Mem: Elks; Rotary; Am Legion; CofC; Southern Wholesalers Asn. Relig: Episcopal; vestryman, St Paul's Episcopal Church. Mailing Add: Box 588 Albany GA 31702

HOLLOWAY, HERMAN MONWELL, SR (D)
Del State Sen
b Wilmington, Del, Feb 4, 22; s William Holloway & Hennie Hawk H; m 1941 to Ethel Mae Johnson; c Marlene, Sandra, Herman, John & Mercedes. Educ: Hampton Inst, 40-41. Hon Degrees: LLD, Del State Col, 68. Polit & Govt Pos: Fifth dist committeeman, Second Ward Dem Party, Del, 58-66; Del State Sen, 64-; alt deleg, Dem Nat Conv, 68; mem, Govt Merit Syst Study Comn, Wilmington Urban Renewal Comt & Del Citizens for Open Housing Legis. Bus & Prof Pos: Co-owner with sons, Convenient Janitorial Serv, 62-66; mem staff, Real Estate Dept, Wilmington Savings Fund Soc, currently. Publ: He Cried, They Cried. Mem: Am Judicature Soc; Paul Lawrence Dunbar Lodge; Del Citizens for Clean Air; Union Lodge No 21, AF&AM; Elks. Honors & Awards: Legion of Honor, Chapel of the Four Chaplains, Mt Joy Church. Relig: Methodist. Mailing Add: 2008 Washington St Wilmington DE 19802

HOLLOWAY, JAMES D (D)
b Granite City, Ill, Sept 8, 31; s Donald R Holloway & Elvira Massmann H; m to Doris Cundiff. Educ: Wash Univ. Polit & Govt Pos: Assessor & treas, Randolph Co, Ill, 54; Ill State Rep, 58-74; deleg, Dem Nat Mid-Term Conf, 74. Bus & Prof Pos: Admin asst to mgr, Egyptian Elec Coop Asn, 58- Mem: Mason, Miss Valley Consistory, Ainad Temple. Relig: Presbyterian. Mailing Add: Grant Pl Sparta IL 62286

HOLLOWAY, SUE LOCKE (R)
b Ogden, Utah, Mar 2, 28; d Madison Ernst Locke & Charlene Sims L; m 1949 to Halsey (Jack) Holloway; c Jacque (Mrs Dale Lowery), Patricia (Mrs James Baker), Deborah Lea & John Madison. Educ: Weber Jr Col, Ogden, Utah, 2 years; Univ Nev, Las Vegas, currently; Iota Tau Kappa. Polit & Govt Pos: Local & co chmn for several polit cand, 64-; vchmn, Nye Co Rep Cent Comt, Nev, 66-70, chmn, formerly. Bus & Prof Pos: Farming; sch bus driver, 63-; substitute teacher, 67- Mem: Beatty PTA; Beatty Bus & Prof Women's Club (secy, currently); Nev Fedn Bus & Prof Women's Clubs (dist secy, state proj chmn). Relig: Christian Science. Mailing Add: Box 45 Beatty NV 89003

HOLLOWAY, VERNON CARLYLE (D)
Fla State Sen
b Richmond, Va, Sept 5, 19; s Samuel Lee Holloway & Maude Estelle Powell H; m 1960 to Roberta Mae Galbraith; c Jean Estelle, Vernon C, Jr & Lee Anthony. Educ: Va Mech Inst; Univ Miami. Polit & Govt Pos: Chmn, Metrop Dade Co Elec Exam Bd, Fla, 54-66; mem, Dade Co Mediation Bd, 57-66; mem, Dade Co Bd Rules & Appeals, 64; Fla State Rep, Dade Co, formerly; Fla State Sen, currently. Bus & Prof Pos: Pres & founder, Interstate Elec Co, Miami, Fla, 49- Mem: Nat Elec Contractors Asn (mem code making panel); Fla State Elec Masters Asn; Fla Asn Elec Contractors; Fla Elec Coun; Inst Elec & Electronics Engrs, Inc. Relig: Lutheran. Mailing Add: 6444 NE Fourth Ave Miami FL 33138

HOLLOWAY, WENDELL MONDOZA (D)
b Washington, DC, Feb 25, 33; s John Henry Holloway & Fannie Simpson H; m 1957 to Kay Gwendolyn Trent; c Brian D, Karen J & Jonathan S. Educ: Ohio Wesleyan Univ, BA, 54; Univ Southern Calif, Los Angeles, MSSM, 67, MPA, 72; PhD, 75; Beta Sigma Tau; Theta Alpha Phi. Polit & Govt Pos: Admin asst to US Rep Yvonne B Burke, Calif, 74- Bus & Prof Pos: Adj asst prof, Auburn Univ, 73-74. Mil Serv: Entered as 2nd Lt, Air Force, 54, released as Lt Col, 74, after serv in Strategic Air Command, Syst Command, Air Univ; Bronze Star; Meritorious Serv Medals; Air Medals; Commendation Medal; Vietnam Serv Medal; Longevity Medals. Mem: Am Soc Pub Admin; Coun Minority Pub Adminr; Scapa Praetors; Admin Asst Asn. Legal Res: 11805 Canfield Rd Potomac MD 20854 Mailing Add: 336 Cannon House Off Bldg Washington DC 20515

HOLLOWELL, BILL (D)
Tex State Rep
Mailing Add: 618 High St Grand Saline TX 75140

HOLM, CHARLES R, JR (D)
b Savannah, Ga, Dec 24, 31; s Charles R Holm, Sr & Ruth Carr H; m 1952 to Lavenia Alice Clarke; c Charles R, III & James Douglas. Educ: Armstrong Jr Col, 51; Univ Ga, 52. Polit & Govt Pos: Aide to US Rep G Elliott Hagan, 61-62; cong liaison off, US Dept Agr, 62-66; spec asst to asst dir cong rels, Off Econ Opportunity, 66-68; admin asst to US Rep Ronald (Bo) Ginn, Ga, 73- Bus & Prof Pos: Secy-treas, Empire Lumber Co Inc, Oliver, Ga, 52-61 & Publicom Inc, Washington, DC, 68-71; private consult, 71-73. Legal Res: Oliver GA Mailing Add: 8700 Bridle Wood Dr Springfield VA 22152

HOLM, EDITH MURIEL (R)
Rep Nat Committeewoman, Alaska
b Takoma Park, Md, Jan 30, 21; d Henry LeRoy Transtrom & Hannah Howarth T; m 1941 to John Holm; c Stuart & James. Educ: La Sierra Col, Arlington, Calif, 38-40. Polit & Govt Pos: Secy, Fairbanks Rep Women's Club, Alaska, 57-58, vpres, 60-61 & pres, 65-66; precinct committeewoman, 60-61, 67 & 71-; Alaska deleg, Nat Fedn of Rep Women Conv, 64; state chmn, Rep Women's Conf, 66; campaign chmn, Rep Cent Dist of Alaska, 66; deleg, Cent Dist Rep Conv, 68, 70 & 72; deleg, State Rep Conv, 68, 70 & 72; deleg & mem platform comt, Rep Nat Conv, 68; mem, Alaska Rep State Cent Comt, 68-; pres, Alaska Fedn of Rep Women, 68-70; pres, Alaska Legis Wives Club, 68-70; mem, Fairbanks Urban Beautification Comn, 70-; Rep Nat Committeewoman, Alaska, 71-; secy, Western States Rep Conf, 71-73. Bus & Prof Pos: Secy, Tanana Valley Fair Asn, 50; admin asst to the comnr, Alaska Dept of Agr & ed, The Alaska Farmer, 51-52; secy to the mgr & advert mgr, Northern Commercial Co, Fairbanks, 58-60; mgr & co-owner, Garden Store & Nursery, Fairbanks, 60- Mem: Fairbanks Garden Club; Alaska Fedn of Garden Clubs; Fairbanks-Univ Symphony Orchestra Asn; Fairbanks Drama Asn; Quota Club. Relig: Protestant. Legal Res: 1600 College Rd Fairbanks AK 99701 Mailing Add: Box 682 Fairbanks AK 99707

HOLMAN, BENJAMIN
Dir Community Rels Serv, Dept Justice
b Columbia, SC, Dec 18, 30; s Benjamin F Holman & Joanna Hardy H; single. Educ: Lincoln Univ (Pa), 48-50; Univ Kans, BS, 52; Univ Chicago, 53-55; Sigma Delta Chi; Kappa Alpha Psi. Polit & Govt Pos: Asst dir, Community Rels Serv, Dept Justice, 65-68, dir, 69- Bus & Prof Pos: Reporter, Chicago Daily News, Ill, 52-62; reporter & ed, CBS News, Chicago, Ill & New York, 62-65; producer, NBC News, Washington, DC, 68-69. Mil Serv: Entered as Pvt, Army Res, 52, released as 1st Lt, 65, after serv in Europe & US. Publ: Auth, Assisting communities in conflicts, J Intergroup Rels, summer 74; auth, Agencies which can help: The federal government's role, Bus Lawyer, 4/74; auth, Desegregation and the Community Relations Service, Integrateducation, 2/75. Relig: Baptist. Legal Res: 2922 W St SE Washington DC 20020 Mailing Add: Community Rels Serv Dept of Justice Washington DC 20530

HOLMAN, CALVIN MORNS (R)
Ariz State Rep
b Topeka, Kans, Mar 30, 31; s Charles Edward Holman & Margaret Morns H; m 1956 to Margaret Elizabeth Jordan; c Calvin Mark & Mary Morns. Educ: Harvard Col, AB, 52; Stanford Grad Sch Bus, MBA, 56. Polit & Govt Pos: Committeeman, Century-Turquoise Precinct Rep Party, Maricopa Co, Ariz, 66-; dep registr, Maricopa Co, 66-74; chmn, Dists 17 & 24 Rep Party, 70-74; Ariz State Rep, Dist 24, 75- Bus & Prof Pos: Div asst, Northern Trust Co, Chicago, Ill, 56-59; mgr data processing, Home Fed Saving & Loan, Chicago, 59-61; asst controller, Valley Nat Bank, Phoenix, Ariz, 61-66; pres, A VIP Consults, Inc, Phoenix, 66- Mil Serv: US Army, 54, medically discharged 56, after serv in Construction Engrs. Publ: The systems approach in schools, Ariz AV J, 66. Mem: Harvard Club Phoenix; Stanford Club Phoenix; Foothills Tennis & Swim Club. Relig: Presbyterian. Mailing Add: 9225 N 53rd Pl Paradise Valley AZ 85253

HOLMAN, JOSEPH FREDERICK (R)
b Farmington, Maine, Aug 15, 25; s Currier C Holman & Rosa S Skillings H; single. Educ: Bowdoin Col, AB, 47; Boston Univ Law Sch, LLB, 50. Polit & Govt Pos: Assessor, Farmington Village Corp, Maine, 52-; co attorney, Franklin Co, 53-58; pub adminr, Maine, 57-; mem, Gov Adv Coun Fish & Game; Maine State Sen, 70-71; mem, Maine Rep State Comt, 71-74; alt deleg, Rep Nat Conv, 72. Mil Serv: Entered as A/S, Naval Res, released as Lt, 45, after serv in Am Theater. Mem: Maine Bar Asn (pres, 71-72); Am Bar Asn; Delta Upsilon; Mason; Shrine. Relig: Protestant. Mailing Add: 95 Main St Farmington ME 04938

HOLMAN, KINGSLEY DAVID (DFL)
Treas, Minn State Dem-Farmer-Labor Party
b Chicago, Ill, Mar 13, 22; s Hans J Holman & Leona Hookland H; m 1949 to Elaine Teresa Fischer; c David Lowell, Craig Byron & Dirk Whittier. Educ: Univ Minn, BSL, 49, LLB, 49. Polit & Govt Pos: Spec munic judge, Bloomington, Minn, 52-58; state finance dir, Dem-Farmer-Labor Party & rural Hennepin Co chmn, 54-58; chmn, Gov Adv Comn on Suburban Probs, 54-60; chmn, Minn Third Dist Dem-Farmer-Labor Party, 56-62; deleg, Dem Nat Conv, 64, alt deleg, 68; treas, Minn State Dem-Farmer-Labor Party, currently. Bus & Prof Pos: Moderator, Radio Prog, Politics & You, KANO, 69- Mil Serv: Entered as Pvt, Army, 42, released as S/Sgt, 46, after serv in 13th Armored Div, 3rd Army, ETO; Overseas Serv Bar; Am Campaign Medal; European-African-MidE Medal with Two Bronze Stars; Good Conduct & Victory Medals. Publ: Columnist, Political patter, Chicago Lerner Newspapers, 63 & Partisan patter, Minn Dem-Farmer-Labor News, 63-; weekly newspaper column, Lets get involved. Mem: Minn & Hennepin Co Bar Asns; Bloomington CofC; Mason. Legal Res: 10009 Drew Ave S Bloomington MN 55431 Mailing Add: 220 W 98th St Bloomington MN 55420

HOLMDAHL, JOHN W (D)
Calif State Sen
b San Francisco, Calif, 1924; married; c four. Educ: Univ Calif, 48, Sch Law, 51. Polit & Govt Pos: Oakland City Councilman, 55-58; Calif State Sen, 58-66 & 71- Bus & Prof Pos: Attorney. Mil Serv: World War II, Combat Inf, 99th Inf Div. Mem: Alameda Co Bar Asn; State Bar of Calif. Mailing Add: Civic Ctr Bldg Hayward CA 94546

HOLME, BARBARA SHAW (D)
Colo State Sen
b Long Beach, Calif, May 24, 46; d Harry Shaw (deceased) & Lillian Walton S; m 1968 to Howard Kelley Holme. Educ: Univ Calif Los Angeles, 62-63; Stanford Univ, BA, 67; Coro Found Intern Pub Affairs, Calif, grad, 68. Polit & Govt Pos: Student intern, US Congressman Ed Roybal, summer 66; mem, Mayors Adv Comn Youth, Denver, 69-70; co-pres, Colo Young Dem, 73-74; Colo State Sen, 75- Bus & Prof Pos: Student intern, Agency Int Develop, Washington, DC, summer 67; asst dir, Metro Denver Urban Coalition, Colo, 69-71; researcher, Conn Conf Mayors, 71-72; urban consult, Cogen Holt & Assoc, New Haven, Conn, 71-72; urban consult, Denver Housing Admin, Colo, 72-74. Mem: Capitol Hill United Neighborhoods (mem bd); Nat Coun Jewish Women; League Women Voters; Bicycles Now. Relig: Jewish. Mailing Add: 1232 Gaylord Denver CO 80206

HOLMER, ALAN F (R)
b New York, NY, July 24, 49; s Freeman Holmer & Marcia Wright H; m 1973 to Joan Ozark. Educ: Princeton Univ, AB, 71. Polit & Govt Pos: Admin asst to US Sen Bob Packwood, Ore, 72- Legal Res: 996 Lariat Dr Eugene OR 97401 Mailing Add: 1600 S Eads 1238-S Arlington VA 22202

HOLMES, ALVIN A (D)
Ala State Rep
Mailing Add: PO Box 6064 Montgomery AL 36106

HOLMES, DARRELL E (D)
WVa State Deleg
Mailing Add: State Capitol Charleston WV 25305

HOLMES, DAVID H (R)
b Omaha, Nebr, Jan 3, 28; s Allen W Holmes & Mary Wigton H; m 1951 to Beverly Ann Kaiser; c David Allen & Thomas Dwight. Educ: Iowa State Univ, BS, 51; Phi Delta Theta. Polit & Govt Pos: Pres, Woodbury Co Young Rep Club, Iowa, 65; chmn, Wiley Mayne for Cong Campaign Comt, 66, 68 & 70; chmn, Woodbury Co Rep Cent Comt, formerly. Bus & Prof Pos: Pres, Holmes Co, Food Brokers, Sioux City, Iowa, 69-71. Mem: Lions. Relig: Presbyterian. Mailing Add: 4542 Manor Circle Sioux City IA 51104

HOLMES, DAVID S, JR (D)
Mich State Rep
b Covington, Ky, Aug 11, 14; s Sanford Holmes & Elizabeth Cain H; m 1962 to Avis Ernestine Greene. Educ: Va State Col, BS; Univ Mich; Alpha Phi Alpha. Polit & Govt Pos: Mich State Rep, 58-; chmn, Mich Black Caucus, 66-; deleg, Dem Nat Conv, 68. Bus & Prof Pos: Sch teacher, Va, formerly; social worker & union organizer, Mich, formerly. Mem: Mason; Bus & Prof Men's Club; Trade Union Leadership Coun. Relig: Protestant. Mailing Add: 517 E Kirby Detroit MI 48202

HOLMES, DAVID WILLIAM (R)
Mem, Rep State Cent Comt Calif
b Woonsocket, SDak, Nov 24, 25; s David Lyle Holmes & Marie Smith H; m 1950 to Maxine Arnold; c Sheila, Hilary, Leslie & David William, Jr. Educ: San Francisco City Col, AA, 47; Univ San Francisco, BS, 49; Alpha Beta Tau; Mu Iota Epsilon. Polit & Govt Pos: Mem, Calif Rep State Cent Comt, 66-; mem, Rep State Finance Comt, Calif, 66-; chmn, Madera Co Rep Finance Comt, 66-; chmn, Comn on Calif State Govt Orgn & Econ, 67-; mem, Madera Co Rep Cent Comt, 69- Bus & Prof Pos: Proprietor, D W Holmes & Co, 54- Mil Serv: Entered as Pvt, Marines, 43, released as Cpl, 46, after serv in Corps Artil, Fifth Amphibious Corps, Pac Theatre, 43-45; Unit Citation. Mem: Nat Asn Securities Dealers; Elks (past exalted ruler, Madera Lodge 1918); Boy Scouts, 20-30 Club (past active); Commonwealth Club of Calif. Relig: Episcopal. Legal Res: 29181 Rd 26 Madera CA 93637 Mailing Add: 110 S A St Madera CA 93637

HOLMES, EDWARD S (D)
NC State Rep
Mailing Add: Pittsboro NC 27312

HOLMES, GEORGE M (R)
NC State Rep
Mailing Add: Rte 1 Hamptonville NC 27020

HOLMES, KIRBY GARRETT (R)
Mich State Rep
b San Diego, Calif, Mar 9, 33; s Harold Dorr Holmes & Shirley May Francis Frazeur H; m 1958 to Mary Elizabeth Strickland; c Kirby G, Jr, Kerry E, Harold Dorr, III & Tracy. Educ: Mich State Univ, BA, 59, MA, 62; Detroit Col Law, 72- Polit & Govt Pos: Mem, Region Seven Planning Comn, State of Mich, 66-67; comnr, Macomb Co, Mich, 66-68; supvr, Shelby Twp, Mich, 66-70; Mich State Rep, 73- Mil Serv: Entered as Pvt, Army, 52, released as Sgt, 55, after serv in Alaska; Nat Defense Medal; Korean Conflict; Good Conduct Medal. Mem: Am Legion (chaplain, Post 351, 72-73); F&AM; Washington Twp Lions; Kiwanis; Farm Bur. Mailing Add: 8430 Pamela Utica MI 48087

HOLMES, POLLY MUDGE (D)
Mont State Rep
b Cincinnati, Ohio, May 10, 23; d E Leigh Mudge & Olive Paul M; m 1951 to Robert M Holmes; c Steven Merrill, Timothy Edmund & Krystin Leigh. Educ: State Univ Iowa, BA, 46; Phi Beta Kappa. Polit & Govt Pos: Precinct committeewoman, Billings, Mont, 66-72; Mont State Rep, Billings, 73- Bus & Prof Pos: Instr link instrument flight, War Training Serv, Erie, 43-44; teacher, Scarritt Col, Nashville, 47-48; staff writer, Methodist Radio & Film Comn, 48-51; free lance writer, 51-; part-time teacher, Rocky Mt Col, 67-70. Publ: The Lakota Trail (play), 53; In lonely exile here (plays), Int J Relig Educ, 10-12/64; The Pigeon Roost (play), 69. Mem: League of Women Voters; Common Cause; Am Civil Liberties Union; Billings Am Indian Coalition; Latino Club. Relig: Methodist. Mailing Add: 1620 Ave F Billings MT 59102

HOLMES, ROBERT A (D)
Ga State Rep
b Shepherdstown, WVa, July 13, 43; s Clarence Arthur Holmes & Priscilla Lee Washington H; m 1963 to Jean Ann Patterson; c Donna Lee, Darlene Marie & Robert A, Jr. Educ: Shepherd Col, BS, 64; Columbia Univ, Woodrow Wilson Found fel, 65-66, MA, 66, Int fel Prog Award, 66-67, John Hay Whitney Found fel, 67-69 & Woodrow Wilson Found Dissertation fel, 68-69, PhD, 69. Polit & Govt Pos: Ga State Rep, Dist 39, 75- Bus & Prof Pos: Lectr, Hunter Col, 67-68; coordr Harvard-Yale-Columbia intensive summer studies prog, Columbia Univ, 69; assoc prof, Southern Univ, Baton Rouge, 69-70; dir, Search for Elevation Educ Knowledge, Baruch Col City Univ NY, 70-71; assoc prof, Atlanta Univ, 71- Publ: Auth, China-Burma relations since the rift, Asian Survey, 8/72; auth, Afro-American in the urban age, J Black Studies, 6/74; co-auth, Black Politics & Public Policy, Emerson Hall, 75; numerous other articles. Mem: Nat Conf Black Polit Scientists (pres, 73-74); Asn Social & Behav Scientists (pres-elect, 75-); Adams Park Residents Asn (pres, 73 & 74); Atlanta Southwest Community Groups (vpres, 73 & 74); Cascade PTA (pres, 73-74). Honors & Awards: Five Outstanding Young Men of the Year Award, Atlanta Jaycees, 74; Outstanding Young Man of the Year Award in Educ, YMCA Omega Y's Men, 74; Danforth Found Assocs Prog, 75- Relig: Baptist. Mailing Add: 2421 Poole Rd SW Atlanta GA 30311

HOLMES, ROBERT DEE (D)
Chmn, Bradley Co Dem Party, Tenn
b Cleveland, Tenn, May 3, 32; s Herbert Dee Holmes & Lydia McKnight H; m 1953 to Sylvia Jean Riden; c Micheal, Cheryl & Lydia. Educ: Tenn Tech Univ, BS in Indust Eng, 58. Polit & Govt Pos: VChmn, Bradley Co Dem Party, Tenn, 70-72, chmn, 74- Bus & Prof Pos: Mgt planning, Magic Chef, Cleveland, Tenn, 57-74; data processing supvr, Roper Corp, Lafayette, Ga, 74. Mil Serv: Entered as Pvt, Army, 50, released as Sgt, 52, after serv in 1st Cavalry Div, 8th Army, Korea, 51-52; Combat Inf Badge; Korea Campaign Ribbon with Two Battle Stars; Dist Unit Citation. Mem: Am Legion; VFW; Tenn Farmer Coop; Nat Hog Asn. Relig: Baptist. Mailing Add: 1716 McDonald Lane Cleveland TN 37311

HOLSHOUSER, JAMES EUBERT, JR (R)
Gov, NC
b Boone, NC, Oct 8, 34; s James Eubert Holshouser & Virginia Dayvault H; m 1961 to Patricia Hollingsworth; c Virginia Walker. Educ: Davidson Col, BS, 56; Univ NC Law Sch, LLB, 60; Phi Delta Theta; Phi Alpha Delta. Polit & Govt Pos: NC State Rep, 62-66 & 68-72; chmn, NC Rep Party, 66-71; deleg, Rep Nat Conv, 68; mem, Rep Nat Comt, 66-71; Gov, NC, 73- Bus & Prof Pos: Lawyer. Relig: Presbyterian. Mailing Add: Executive Mansion 200 N Blount St Raleigh NC 27601

HOLSTEAD, GEORGE B (D)
La State Rep
b Ruston, La, July 31, 24; s George B Holstead & Lois Oliver H; m 1947 to Mary Ellen Cochran; c Nancy Ellen, Helen Lois, Mary Kate & George B, III. Educ: La Polytech Inst, BA in Econ; La State Univ, LLB; Gamma Eta Gamma. Polit & Govt Pos: La State Rep, Lincoln Parish, 64- Mil Serv: Entered as Pvt, Army Air Force, 43, released as Sgt, 46, after serv in 43rd Bomb Group, 5th Air Force; Asiatic Pac Campaign Medal with Five Bronze Stars; Philippine Liberation Medal with Two Bronze Stars; World War II Victory Medal; Air Medal. Mem: Am Legion; VFW; Lincoln Parish & La State Bar Asns. Relig: Methodist. Legal Res: Woodlawn Dr Ruston LA 71270 Mailing Add: PO Box 609 Ruston LA 71270

HOLT, CHARLES (D)
NC State Rep
Mailing Add: 150 Ellerslie Dr Fayetteville NC 28303

HOLT, D N, JR (D)
SC State Rep
Mailing Add: 132 Banyon St North Charleston SC 29406

HOLT, ELEANOR LOUISE (R)
VChmn, Delaware Co Rep Party, Ind
b Lafayette, Ind, Oct 17, 28; d Roscoe Henry George & Rosa Smith G; m 1950 to Robert Alden Holt; c Gregory Alden & Randolph George. Educ: Purdue Univ, West Lafayette, BSHE, 50; Chi Omega. Polit & Govt Pos: Pres, Delaware Co Women's Rep Comt, Ind, 64-67; first vpres, Ind Fedn Rep Women, 69-73, dir, Tenth Dist, 73-75; membership chmn, Nat Fedn Rep Women, 74-; vchmn, Delaware Co Rep Party, Ind, 74- Bus & Prof Pos: Vpres, Perkins & Holt, Inc, 64-72. Mem: Ball Mem Hosp Auxiliary; Purdue Club of Muncie; University Club; Beverly Hills Home Demonstration Club. Honors & Awards: Outstanding Jayshee Award, 60. Relig: United Methodist. Mailing Add: 1007 Bougainvillea Terr Muncie IN 47302

HOLT, JAMES D (R)
Okla State Sen
Mailing Add: State Capitol Oklahoma City OK 73105

HOLT, JOE D (D)
Mo State Rep
b Mexico, Mo, Aug 25, 40; s Joe P Holt; m 1966 to Molly Deiter; c Ned, Dan & Phil. Educ: Westminster Col (Mo), BA, 62; Univ Mo-Columbia, JD, 67; Phi Kappa Delta; Zeta Tau Delta; Omicron Delta Kappa. Polit & Govt Pos: Mo State Rep, 67-, chmn, Reorganization Comt, mem, Judiciary, Appropriation & Joint Comt on Fiscal Affairs, Mo Gen Assembly, currently; mem, Mid-Mo Regional Law Enforcement Assistance Coun, Jefferson City, 69- Bus & Prof Pos: Sr partner in law firm, Holt, Krumm & Hamilton, Fulton, Mo, 72- Mil Serv: Entered as Cadet, Army, 58, released as Capt, after serv in Caribbean, 62-64. Mem: Mo Bar Asn (mem county & judiciary comt, 70-); AF&AM (Master, 72); Fulton Breakfast Optimist Club (pres, 70-71); Moolah Shrine, St Louis. Relig: Presbyterian. Legal Res: 808 Court St Fulton MO 65251 Mailing Add: 413 Court St Fulton MO 65251

HOLT, JOSEPH FRANK (D)
Assoc Justice, Ark Supreme Court
b Harrison, Ark, Oct 22, 10; s Noah Bud Holt & Melissa Adeline Moore H; m 1942 to Mary Reid Phillips; c Lyda Frances & Melissa Jeanne. Educ: Univ Ark, Fayetteville, LLD, 37; Inst of Int Studies, Geneva, Switz, 37-38; Phi Alpha Delta; Pi Kappa Alpha; Blue Key. Polit & Govt Pos: Dep prosecuting attorney, Sixth Judicial Dist, Ark, 47-54, prosecuting attorney, 54-60; Attorney Gen, State of Ark, 60-62; assoc justice, Ark Supreme Court, 62-66 & 69- Bus & Prof Pos: Pres, Ark Prosecuting Attorney Asn, 58-59; dir, Nat Asn of Prosecuting Attorneys, 58-60; Ark deleg, White House Conf on Children & Youth, 60; chmn, Ark Comt on Spec Serv for Juv, 60-61. Mil Serv: Entered as Pvt, Army, 42, released as S/Sgt, 43, after serv in Mil Intel, US, 42-43. Mem: Pulaski Co, Ark & Am Bar Asns; Am Legion; Red Cross. Honors & Awards: Freedoms Found, 70; Americanism Award, Ark Dept, Am Legion, 71. Relig: Baptist. Mailing Add: 3100 Reservoir Rd Little Rock AR 72207

HOLT, MARJORIE SEWELL (R)
US Rep, Md
b Birmingham, Ala, Sept 17, 20; d Edward R Sewell & Juanita Felts S; m 1940 to Duncan McKay Holt; c Rachel (Mrs Kenneth Tschantre), Edward Sewell & Victoria. Educ: Jacksonville Univ, 40-41; Univ Fla, 43-47; Univ Fla Col Law, JD, 49; Phi Kappa Delta; Phi Delta Delta. Polit & Govt Pos: Precinct leader, Anne Arundel Co Rep Party, Md, 61; supvr elections, Anne Arundel Co, 63-65; clerk, Circuit Court, 66-72; deleg, Rep Nat Conv, 68; US Rep, Fourth Dist, 73-; mem, House Armed Serv Comt, 73- Bus & Prof Pos: Attorney at law, Severna Park, Md. Publ: When is doctrine of comparative rectitude applied in Florida?, spring 49 & Spendthrift trusts, fall 49, Univ Fla Law Rev. Mem: Anne Arundel Co, Md & Am Bar Asns; Md Court Clerks Asn. Relig: Presbyterian; Elder. Legal Res: MD Mailing Add: 1510 Longworth House Off Bldg Washington DC 20515

HOLT, WILLIAM S (R)
Utah State Rep
Mailing Add: 1379 W 1700 S Syracuse UT 84041

HOLTER, W L (BILL) (R)
Finance Chmn, Mont State Rep Party
m 1948 to Nancy A Stolpe; c Lynn, Todd, Jan & Ross. Educ: Hibbing Jr Col, 47-48; Univ Minn, BA, jour, 50. Polit & Govt Pos: Mayor, Glasgow, Mont, 65-67; Comnr Planning & Econ Develop, State of Mont, 67-71; chmn, Mont State Rep Party, formerly, finance chmn, 74- Bus & Prof Pos: Prin owner, KLTZ Glasgow & KYLT Missoula. Mem: Big Sky-Holter Radio Stations (pres, 15 years); Shrine. Honors & Awards: Young Man of the Year, Williston, NDak Jaycees, 57; Boss of the Year, 64. Relig: Presbyterian. Legal Res: 1804 Beech Dr Great Falls MT 59404 Mailing Add: PO Box 3068 Great Falls MT 59403

HOLTON, A LINWOOD, JR (R)
b Big Stone Gap, Va, Sept 21, 23; s Abner Linwood Holton & Edith Van Gorder H; m 1953 to Virginia Harrison Rogers; c Virginia Tayloe, Anne Bright, A Linwood, III & Dwight Carter. Educ: Washington & Lee Univ, BA, 44; Harvard Law Sch, LLB, 49; Omicron Delta Kappa. Hon Degrees: LLD, Washington & Lee Univ, 71, Va State Col, 71 & Col William & Mary, 72. Polit & Govt Pos: Chmn, Roanoke City Rep Comt, 55; Rep cand, Va House of Deleg, 55 & 57; deleg, Rep Nat Conv, 60, 68 & 72; vchmn, Va Rep State Cent Comt, 60-69; state campaign mgr, H Clyde Pearson, cand for gov, Va, 61; Rep cand for Gov, 65; regional coordr, Nixon for President Comt, 67-68; mem exec comt, Nat Gov Conf, 70; Gov, Va, 70-74; chmn, Southern Regional Educ Bd, 72-73, Southern Growth Policies Bd, 72-73 & Rep Governors' Asn, 73; Asst Secy for Cong Rels, Dept of State, 74-75. Bus & Prof Pos: Attorney, Hunter, Fox & Holton, 49-53; attorney, Eggleston, Holton, Butler & Glenn, 54-69; mem, Hogan & Hartson, Attorneys, Washington, DC, 75- Mil Serv: Entered as A/S, Navy, 43, released as Lt(jg), 46, after serv in Submarine Force, Atlantic & Pac, 44-46; Capt, Naval Res; Am-Pac Theatre Medals; World War II Victory Medal; Naval Res Medal. Mem: Am, Va State & Roanoke Bar Asns; Shenandoah Club. Relig: Presbyterian. Legal Res: McLean VA Mailing Add: 815 Connecticut Ave NW Suite 600 Washington DC 20006

HOLTZ, LORRAINE (D)
b Apr 24, 35; d Emanuel Gelman (deceased) & Rita Rudd G (deceased); m 1955 to Sherman Leonard Holtz, div; c H Mark, Stephen L & Neil E. Educ: Col City New York, 52-55; Baruch Col, AAS, 70. Polit & Govt Pos: Mem, Bronx Co Dem Comt, NY, 74-; deleg, Dem Mid-Term Conf, 74. Bus & Prof Pos: Teacher, Soc Children with Emotional Disturbances, New York, 64-71; mem comnrs staff, Dept Purchase, New York, 72-; chmn ed bd, Coop City Times, 72-74; exec bd mem, Coop City Adv Coun, 72-74. Mem: Soc Children with Emotional Disturbances; Dist Coun 37 Local 1407; United Dem Club Coop City; Pelham Parkway Tenants Coun (organizer & past pres). Mailing Add: 5B Cooper Pl Bronx NY 10475

HOLTZ, PAUL ROSCOE (R)
b Lander, Wyo, June 25, 33; s Dr Paul R Holtz & Velma Clark H; m 1954 to Averill Joan Bishop; c Jeffrey, Bradley, Clifford & John. Educ: Univ Wyo, BS, 55; Iron Skull; Pi Delta Epsilon; Sigma Nu. Polit & Govt Pos: Legis asst to US Rep Keith Thomson, Wyo, 57-60; admin asst, Gov Cliff Hansen, Wyo, 62-66; admin asst to US Sen Cliff Hansen, 67- Bus & Prof Pos: Ed, New Era, Sweet Home, Ore, 55-56; ed, Independent Rec, Thermopolis, Wyo, 56-57 & 60-62. Mem: Wyo Press Asn; Kiwanis. Honors & Awards: First Place, Cold War Educ, Gubernatorial Aides Sch, Miami Beach, 64. Relig: Presbyterian. Legal Res: 3621 Capitol Cheyenne WY 82001 Mailing Add: 8234 Toll House Rd Annandale VA 22003

HOLTZMAN, ELIZABETH (D)
US Rep, NY
b Brooklyn, NY, Aug 11, 41; d Sidney Holtzman & Filia Ravitz H; single. Educ: Radcliffe Col, BA magna cum laude, 62; Harvard Univ Law Sch, JD, 65. Polit & Govt Pos: Asst, Mayor John V Lindsay, New York, NY, 67-70; committeewoman, NY State Dem Party, 70-72; deleg-at-lg, Dem Nat Conv, 72; US Rep, 16th Cong Dist, NY, 73-, mem budget comt, US House Rep, 75-, mem house comn on info & facilities, 75- & chairwoman task force on facilities & space, 75; deleg, Dem Mid-Term Conf, 74. Bus & Prof Pos: Assoc attorney, Wachtell, Lipton, Rosen, Katz & Kern Law Firm, 65-67 & Paul Weiss, Rifkind, Wharton & Garrison, 70-72. Mem: Bar Asn, New York, NY; Coun of NY Law Assocs; Brooklyn Women's Polit Caucus (founder, 71); Hadassah. Honors & Awards: Outstanding Achievement Award, Ed of Mademoiselle Mag, 73; Youngest Woman Elected to Cong, 73; Recognition Award, Radcliffe Col Alumnae, 73; Woman of Year, United HIAS Serv Women's Div, 74; Brooklyn Hadassah's Myrtle Wreath Award, 74. Mailing Add: 1452 Flatbush Ave Brooklyn NY 11210

HOMMRICH, DENIS E (D)
Chmn, 34th Dist Dem Comt, Ky
b Anniston, Ala, July 18, 45; s Edwin J Hommrich & Ethel Shanahan H. Educ: Bellarmine Col, BA, 67; Delta Sigma Rho-Tau Kappa Alpha; Debate Team; Student Senate. Polit & Govt Pos: Precinct capt, Dem Party, Ky, 69-; admin asst, Dept Bldg & Housing City Louisville; vet specialist, Commonwealth Ky, 72; deleg, Ky Dem Conv, 72; chmn, 34th Dist Dem Comt, 73- Mem: Louisville Area Coun Race & Relig. Relig: Catholic. Mailing Add: 1708 Eastern Pkwy Louisville KY 40204

HOMUTH, DONALD JAMES (D)
NDak State Sen
b Ft William, Ont, Can, May 22, 44; s Donald Carl Homuth & Lois Thelma Brigham H; m 1971 to Renee Jeanette Selig. Educ: NDak State Univ, BA, 70, MA Prog, 73-74; Pi Kappa Delta; Blue Key. Polit & Govt Pos: NDak State Sen, 21st Dist, 74- Bus & Prof Pos: Spec assignments reporter, KXJB TV, 70-72; exec secy, NDak Comt for Humanities, 72-73; continuing TV studies coordr, NDak State Univ, 74- Mil Serv: Entered as Pvt E-1, Army, 66, released as Sgt E-5, after serv in 11th Combat Aviation Bn, Vietnam, 67-68; Bronze Star With V; Army Commendation Medal. Mem: Nat Univ Exten Asn; Am Commun Asn; Nat Ski Patrol; Corvair Soc Am. Mailing Add: 601 Sixth St E West Fargo ND 58078

HONAMAN, JUNE N (R)
VChmn, Rep State Comt, Pa
b Lancaster, Pa, May 24, 20; d Lester W Newcomer & Maud Stauffer N; m 1948 to Peter K Honaman. Educ: Beaver Col, BFA, 41. Polit & Govt Pos: Committeewoman, 13th Dist, Pa, 60-64; vchmn, Rep State Comt, Pa, 63-; deleg-at-lg, Rep Nat Conv, 64, 68 & 72, mem platform comt, 68 & 72. Bus & Prof Pos: Teacher, Lancaster City Sch Dist, 48-54. Mem: Am Asn Univ Women; Disaster Comt & Home Serv, Am Red Cross; Bus & Prof Women; Pa Gov Comn on Status of Women. Relig: Episcopal. Mailing Add: 400-15 Main St Landisville PA 17538

HONNOLD, JOHN OTIS, JR (D)
b Kansas, Ill, Dec 5, 15; s John Otis & Louretta Wright H; m 1939 to Annamarie Kunz; c Carol (Mrs Vinton Deming), Heidi (Mrs David Spencer) & Edward. Educ: Univ Ill, BA, 36; Harvard, JD, 39; Phi Beta Kappa; Phi Kappa Phi; Guggenheim fel, 58; Fulbright sr research scholar, Univ of Paris, 58. Polit & Govt Pos: Adv, US deleg, Diplomatic Conf on Unification of Int Sales Law, The Hague, Holland, 64; deleg, Dem Nat Conv, 68; US deleg, UN Comn on Int Trade Law, Geneva, Switz, 69-, secy comn, 70-; chief, Int Trade Law Br, UN, 70- Bus & Prof Pos: Attorney-at-law, Wright, Gordon, Zachry & Parlin, New York, NY, 39-41; attorney, Security Exchange Comn, 41; chief court rev br, Off Price Admin, 42-46; mem of faculty, Univ Pa Law Sch, 46-52 & prof law, 52-; mem bd ed, Am J Comp Law, 59-; mem faculty law session, Salzburg Seminar Am Studies, Austria, 60 & chmn, 63 & 66. Publ: Life of the Law, 64; Commercial Law (with E Allen Farnsworth), second ed, 68; Unification of the Law Governing International Sales of Goods, 66; plus others. Mem: Am & Philadelphia Bar Asns; Sor de Legis Comparee; Gr Philadelphia Br, Am Civil Liberties Union (mem bd, 65-); SE Pa Br, Am for Dem Action (mem bd, 65-). Honors & Awards: Admitted to practice before US Supreme Court. Relig: Society of Friends. Legal Res: Braxmar Dr S Harrison NY 10528 Mailing Add: Secretariat 3464 A United Nations NY 10017

HOOD, DAVID CRAIG (D)
Okla State Rep
b Oklahoma City, Okla, Apr 4, 46; s Paul Clayton Hood & Bette Jayne Staats H; div. Educ: George Washington Univ, BA, 68; DePauw Univ, 64-66; Okla Univ, JD, 74; Sigma Delta Chi; Sigma Chi; Gate & Key. Polit & Govt Pos: Okla State Rep, 74- Bus & Prof Pos: Attorney, 74- Mil Serv: Entered as Pvt, Army, 68, released as 1st Lt, 71, after serv in 5th Spec Forces Group, Vietnam, 69-70; Bronze Star; Army Commendation Medal; Air Medal; Vietnamese Staff Serv Medal. Publ: Auth, The identity of an offense, 2/74 & Disclosure of informants, 3/74, Advocate; auth, Why judges should sentence, Okla Observer, 3/75. Mem: Common Cause; Am & Okla Bar Asns; Am & Okla Trial Lawyers Asns. Honors & Awards: Deans List, Univ Okla Law Sch, 71-73. Relig: Unitarian. Mailing Add: 1001 NW 39th St Oklahoma City OK 73118

HOOD, GEORGE HAY (R)
Mem, Exec Bd, Rep State Cent Comt Wash
b Seattle, Wash, Oct 23, 20 to George Thomas Hood & Neva Hay H; m 1947 to Louise Walker; c Deborah & Diane. Educ: Univ Wash, BA, 47. Polit & Govt Pos: Rep precinct committeeman, Mercer Island, Wash, 63-, regional chmn, 67-; dist chmn, Rep 41st Dis- Dist, 69-71; deleg, Rep Nat Conv, 72; mem exec bd, Rep State Cent Comt Wash, 73- Bus & Prof Pos: Traffic mgr, Pac NW Bell Tel, 47-64, personnel magr, 64- Mem: Pac Northwest Personnel Mgt Asn (bd dirs, 68-70); Mercerwood Shore Club; Elks. Relig: Protestant. Mailing Add: 4205 93rd SE Mercer Island WA 98040

HOOD, MORRIS, JR (D)
Mich State Rep
Mailing Add: 8872 Cloverlawn Detroit MI 48204

HOOD, RAYMOND WALTER (D)
Mich State Rep
b Detroit, Mich, Jan 1, 36; s Morris Wardelle Hood & Ruth Elizabeth Stevenson H; m 1962 to Helen Blackwell; c Raymond W, Jr & Roger S. Educ: Fullerton Jr Col. Polit & Govt Pos: Mich State Rep, 65-; mem, New Detroit Comt on Housing & New Detroit Comt on Health, currently. Bus & Prof Pos: Exec bd, Harlem Gallery Square, currently. Mem: Soc of State Legislators; Am Civil Liberties Union; Century Club, Mich Dem Party; Trade Union Leadership Coun, Metrop Detroit Labor Commun Asn; First Cong Dist Dem Orgn. Relig: Catholic. Legal Res: 20522 Picadilly Detroit MI 48221 Mailing Add: State Capitol Lansing MI 48901

HOOFMAN, CLIFF (D)
Ark State Rep
Mailing Add: 4012 Hillside Dr North Little Rock AR 72118

HOOG, THOMAS WILLIAM (D)
b Ste Genevieve, Mo, Sept 21, 39; s Leo J Hoog & Edna M Basler H; m 1962 to Sandra Gray Garrett; c Michael, Mark & Michele. Educ: Univ Ill, AeroE, 60; Student Senator; Intramural Football; Newman Club; Univ Ill Assoc Students. Polit & Govt Pos: Vol, John Kennedy for President; Bobby Kennedy for President & George McGovern for President; state polit dir, Gary Hart for Senate; admin asst to US Sen Gary Hart, 75- Bus & Prof Pos: Airline capt, Continental Airlines, 67-74. Mil Serv: Entered as Cadet, Navy, 60, released as Lt, 66, after serv in VR21 & VT29, Vietnam; Vietnam Air Medal. Relig: Catholic. Legal Res: 8850 Morton Rd Longmont CO 80501 Mailing Add: Dirksen Senate Bldg Suite 6327 Washington DC 20510

HOOGLAND, JACOB JOHN, JR (JAKE) (D)
b Ogden, Utah, Apr 30, 52; s Jake Hoogland & Evelyn VanLeeuwen H; single. Educ: Weber State Col, BA, 74; Univ Utah Col Law, 74-; Phi Kappa Phi; Student Bar Asn; Anthropos. Polit & Govt Pos: Co-chmn, Weber Co Citizens for McGovern/Shriver, Utah, 72; chmn subcommittee, Utah State Dem Platform Comt, 72; deleg, Utah State Dem Conv, 72; deleg, Dem Nat Conv, 72; legis staff intern, Sen Frank E Moss; coordr, Owens for Sen, 74. Bus & Prof Pos: Mem ombudsman comt, Weber State Col, 71-72, Acad Coun, 72-73, Fine Arts Lect Series Comt, 72-73. Publ: From killing to living, Probe, spring 72. Honors & Awards: Most valuable contrib, Probe Literary Arts Mag, 72; Cert of Appreciation, Weber Co Dem Party, 73; Utah & Western Hist Award, Utah State Hist Soc, 74; Outstanding Achievement Award, Weber State Col. Relig: Society of Friends. Mailing Add: 1135 38th St Ogden UT 84403

HOOKER, ROGER WOLCOTT, JR (R)
b Niagara Falls, NY, May 14, 41; s Roger Wolcott Hooker & Grace Garden H; m 1975 to Joan Wiggins. Educ: Princeton Univ, AB, 63; Columbia Law Sch, LLB, 67; Ivy Club. Polit & Govt Pos: Dep secy to Gov & dir Washington off, NY, 72-74; Asst to Vpres for Cong Affairs, 75- Bus & Prof Pos: Assoc, Webster Sheffield, Fleischman, Hitchcock & Brookfield, 67-70; assoc dir & counsel, Fleischmann Comn on Educ in NY, 70-72; dep dir for panels & dir domestic studies, Comn on Critical Choices for Am, New York, 74- Publ: Co-auth & co-ed, Fleischmann Report on Quality Cost & Financing of Elem & Secondary Educ in NY State, Viking Press, 73. Mem: Asn Bar New York; Univ Club, New York; Int Club, Washington, DC. Mailing Add: 414 Fourth St SE Washington DC 20003

Geary Co Dem Party, 56-60 & 66-72; chmn, Second Cong Dist Dem Party, Kans, formerly. Mailing Add: 102 Bunker Hill Dr Junction City KS 66441

HORNE, CHARLES J (D)
Treas, Dem Party Va
b Oakwood, Va, Apr 27, 34; s Charles W Horne & Etha Matney H; m 1957 to Nerissa P Villaneuva; c Valerie, Jessica, Candice & Stephanie. Educ: Univ Philippines, BS Polit Sci; Roosevelt Univ, grad; Harvard Advan Mgt Prog, grad. Polit & Govt Pos: Mem steering comt & state cent comt & treas, Dem Party Va, 73-; Dem cand for Cong, Ninth Dist, 74; mem finance coun, Dem Nat Comt, 75- Bus & Prof Pos: Vpres, Gen Tel & Electronics Indust, 64-67; exec vpres & chief oper officer, Philippine Commun Satellite Corp, 67-73; exec vpres, Philippine Overseas Telecom Corp, 67-73; pres, Pioneer Gen Corp, 73- & Gen Energy Corp, 75- Mil Serv: Entered as Pvt, Army, 54, released as E-5, 57, after serv in Security Agency, Pac Theatre. Mem: Rotary (vpres); Elks. Relig: Catholic. Mailing Add: Altamont Abingdon VA 24210

HORNE, EDWARD F (D)
Chmn, Riley Co Dem Party, Kans
b Alma, Kans, Jan 30, 36; s Millard Jennings Horne & Ruth Brabb H; m 1961 to Connie Marie Metzger; c Angela. Educ: Kans State Univ, BS, 61; Univ Kans, JD, 67; Chancery Club; Young Dem. Polit & Govt Pos: Chmn, Riley Co Dem Party, Kans, 73- Bus & Prof Pos: Lobbyist, Kans Farm Bur, Manhattan, 63-64, staff attorney, Kans Farm Bur Ins Co, 67-72; city attorney, Manhattan, 72-; partner, Fick, Myers & Horne, Attorneys, 74- Mil Serv: Entered as 2nd Lt, Army, 61, released as 1st Lt, 63, after serv in III Corps & Ft Hood, 4th Army. Mem: Kans Bar Asn; Riley Co Bar Asn (pres, 74-); Elks; Mason; CofC. Legal Res: 3405 Sioux Circle Manhattan KS 66502 Mailing Add: Suite 302 Union Nat Bank Tower Manhattan KS 66502

HORNE, TOMMY ARTHUR (D)
Miss State Rep
b Bonita, Miss, Sept 12, 36; s Arthur Major Horne & Irma Lee Mazingo H; m 1957 to Eveline Regina Kremin; c Stephen & Jeffrey. Educ: Univ Miami, 54-55; Univ Southern Miss, BS; Jackson Sch Law, JD; Sigma Delta Kappa. Polit & Govt Pos: Miss State Rep, 72- Mil Serv: Entered as Pvt, Army, 55, released as Cpl, 57, after serv in 13th Inf Regt, Berlin Command, 56-57; European Occup Medal; Good Conduct Medal; Expert Marksman Badge. Mem: Miss State Bar Asn; Miss Trial Lawyers Asn; VFW; Mason; Shrine. Relig: Methodist. Mailing Add: 1210 N Lake Dr Meridian MS 39301

HORNE, WILLIAM S (D)
Md State Deleg
Mailing Add: PO Box 204 Easton MD 21601

HORNIG, DONALD FREDERICK (D)
b Milwaukee, Wis, Mar 17, 20; s Chester Arthur Hornig & Emma Knuth H; m 1943 to Lilli Schwenk; c Joanna Gail (Mrs Ronald Fox), Ellen Constance (Mrs J Douglas Deal, III), Christopher Wayne & Leslie Elizabeth. Educ: Harvard Univ, BS, 40, PhD, 43. Hon Degrees: LLD, Temple Univ, 64, Univ Notre Dame, 65, Boston Col, 66 & Dartmouth Col, 74; DHL, Yeshiva Univ, 65; ScD, Rensselaer Polytech Inst, 65, Univ Md, 65, Ripon Col, 66, Widener Col, 67, Univ Wis, 67, Univ Puget Sound, 68, Syracuse Univ, 68, Princeton Univ, 69, Seoul Univ, 73 & Univ Pa, 75; DE, Worcester Polytech Inst, 67. Polit & Govt Pos: Mem, President's Sci Adv Comt, 60-69, chmn, 64-69; chmn, Fed Coun Sci & Technol, 64-69; dir, Off Sci & Technol & spec asst to the President for sci & technol, Exec Off of President, 64-69. Bus & Prof Pos: Research assoc, Woods Hole Oceanographic Inst, 43-44; group leader, Los Alamos Lab, Univ Calif, 44-46; prof chem & dir, Metcalf Research Lab, Brown Univ, 46-57; Donner prof sci & chmn dept chem, Princeton Univ, 57-64; prof chem, Univ Rochester, 69-70; vpres, Eastman Kodak Co, 69-70; pres, Brown Univ, 70-; dir, Upjohn Co, 71-; Westinghouse Elec Corp, 72- Publ: Over 80 sci papers publ. Mem: Nat Acad Sci; Am Asn Advan Sci; Am Phys Soc; Am Chem Soc; Faraday Div, The Chem Soc. Honors & Awards: Eng Centennial Award, Widener Col, 67; Charles Lathrop Parsons Award, Am Chem Soc, 67; the first Mellon Inst Award, 68; Order of Civil Merit, Korean Govt, 68. Relig: Lutheran. Legal Res: 55 Power St Providence RI 02906 Mailing Add: Box 1860 Brown University Providence RI 02912

HORNSBY, BEN F (D)
SC State Rep
Mailing Add: Rte 3 Box 75 Winnsboro SC 29180

HOROWITZ, BETTY (D)
b Lakewood, NJ, Feb 20, 26; d Harry Sherman & Sarah Levine S; m 1945 to Leonard Horowitz; c Don & Richard. Educ: City Col New York, BBA, cum laude, 49; Adelphi Univ, MA, 65; Beta Gamma Sigma; Lampert House Plan. Polit & Govt Pos: Vchmn, Am for Dem Action, 71-73; deleg, Dem Nat Conv, 72. Bus & Prof Pos: Nursery sch dir, Parkway Sch, Levittown, NY, 59-61; elem sch teacher, Cinnaminson, NJ, 61-; col instr, Trenton State Col, 68-71. Mem: NJ & Nat Educ Asns; Am Civil Liberties Union (bd dirs, 71-); NJ League of Women Voters. Relig: Jewish. Mailing Add: R230 Tenbytowne Apts Delran NJ 08075

HORRIGAN, JAMES OWEN (D)
NH State Rep
b Joliet, Ill, Dec 27, 30; s Owen Peter Horrigan & Eleanor Hurley H; m 1955 to Mary Clifton Griswold; c Timothy, Eleanor & Katherine. Educ: Univ Notre Dame, BS, 52; Univ Chicago, MBA, 56, PhD, 67; Beta Gamma Sigma. Polit & Govt Pos: Chmn, Parks & Recreation Comt, Durham, NH, 71-72; deleg, NH Dem State Conv, 74; NH State Rep, 75- Bus & Prof Pos: Asst prof, Univ Notre Dame, 56-66; prof, Univ NH, 66-; vis prof, Univ Kent, Eng, 72-73. Mil Serv: Entered as Ens, Navy, 52, released as Lt(jg), 55, after serv in USS Peterson (DE-152), Destroyer Fleet, Atlantic. Publ: Auth, Some empirical bases of ratio analysis, 65, A short history of financial ratio analysis, 68, Acct Rev; Some hypotheses on the valuation of stock warrants, J Bus Finance & Acct, 74. Mem: Am Acct Asn (ed bd); Am Econ Asn; Am Finance Asn; Save Our Shores. Legal Res: Bennett Rd Durham NH 03824 Mailing Add: 422 McConnell Univ NH Durham NH 03824

HORTON, FRANK (R)
US Rep, NY
b Cuero, Tex, Dec 12, 19; m to Marjorie Wilcox; c Frank & Steven. Educ: La State Univ, BA, 41; Cornell Univ Law Sch, LLB, 47; Phi Kappa Phi. Polit & Govt Pos: Councilman-at-lg, Rochester, NY, 55-61; US Rep, NY, 63-, ranking minority mem, Comt Govt Opers & mem, Joint Comt on Atomic Energy, US House Rep; deleg from US Cong to dedication of Israeli Parliament, Israel, 66; deleg to Ditchley Conf on Anglo-Am Affairs, Eng, 72; participant, US-Can Interparliamentary Conf, Ottawa, 67- & Washington, DC, 73; comnr, Comn Govt, Procurement, 69-; comnr, Comn of Fed Paperwork. Bus & Prof Pos: Former exec vpres, Int Baseball League; Rochester attorney; past pres, Rochester Commun Baseball. Mil Serv: Entered as 2nd Lt, Army, 41, released as Maj, 45, after serv in NAfrica & Italy, 42-45; Lt Col, Army Res; Legion of Merit; Bronze Star. Publ: How to end the draft, Nat Press, Inc, 67; Election reform & The public's right to know, Case & Comment; plus others. Mem: Order of the Coif; F&AM (master, Seneca Lodge 920); RSM (Doric Coun 19); KT (Monroe Commandery 12); Mason (33 degree). Relig: Presbyterian. Legal Res: 2123 East Ave Rochester NY 14610 Mailing Add: 2229 Rayburn House Off Bldg Washington DC 20515

HORTON, GERALD TALMADGE (D)
Ga State Rep
b Tupelo, Miss, July 5, 34; s Osborne T Horton & Lorene Shook H; m 1959 to Jane Winston Carpenter; c Elizabeth Carlton, Gerald Talmadge, Jr & William Henry Dannehl. Educ: Murphy High Sch, Atlanta, Ga; Harvard Univ, AB cum laude, 56; publ, Harvard Advocate; Harvard Southerners' Club. Polit & Govt Pos: Admin asst to Rep Charles L Weltner, 63-64; Ga State Rep, 95th Dist, Post Five, 68-72, Ga State Rep, 43rd Dist, Post Two, 73- Bus & Prof Pos: Coordr, Forward Atlanta Prog, Atlanta CofC, 61-62; pres, Research Group, Inc, Atlanta, 65- Mil Serv: Entered as Seaman Recruit, Navy, 59, released as Lt(jg), 61, after serv in staff, US Comdr 2nd Fleet & NATO Comdr Striking Fleet Atlantic, 59-61. Publ: Auth, The Mayor & Federal Aid, 67 & co-auth, The Cities, the States, & HEW, 73, US Conf Mayors; co-auth, Local Capacities for Policy Planning, US Dept Housing & Urban Develop, 72. Mem: Nat Legis Conf (co-chmn community develop comt, 72-); Am Soc Planning Officials (bd, 73-75). Honors & Awards: Harvard Southern Regional scholar, 56; Outstanding Young Man of Year in Community Serv, Atlanta, Ga, 66. Relig: Protestant. Legal Res: 212 Bolling Rd NE Atlanta GA 30305 Mailing Add: 1230 Healey Bldg Atlanta GA 30303

HORTON, JACK OGILVIE (R)
Asst Secy Land & Water Resources, Dept Interior
b Saddlestring, Wyo, Jan 28, 38; s Jack O Horton & Josephine Jahn H; single. Educ: Princeton Univ, BA, with honors, 60; Oxford Univ, Rhodes Scholar, MA, 66. Polit & Govt Pos: Asst to Under Secy, Russell Train, Dept Interior, 69-70, asst to Secy, Walter Hickel, 70-71, dep asst secy, Policy & Planning, 71, dep under secy, 71-72 & asst secy, Land & Water Resources, 73-; co-chmn, Joint Fed-State Land Use Planning Comn for Alaska, 72-73. Mil Serv: Lt, Navy, 60-65; 5 Air Medals; 165 Combat & Reconnaissance Missions in Southeast Asia. Publ: Great Circle Route, J Navigation. Honors & Awards: All-Am Lacrosse Player, 59 & 60, All South, Eng, 66. Legal Res: HF Bar Ranch Saddlestring WY 82840 Mailing Add: 3421 N St NW Washington DC 20007

HORTON, LYNN C (R)
NH State Rep
Mailing Add: 51 High St Lancaster NH 03584

HORTON, MARION (EBB) (D)
Miss State Sen
Mailing Add: RFD 6 Box 328 Louisville MS 39339

HORTON, SEAB SANFORD, JR (R)
Mem, Rep State Cent Comt Ga
b Rome, Ga, May 14, 32; s Seab Sanford Horton, Sr & Martha McKinney H; m 1959 to Jane Adelia Reeves; c Martha Adelia, Lydia Reeves & Mary Jane. Educ: Univ Ga, BBA, 54; Univ Munich, 56; Phi Delta Theta. Polit & Govt Pos: Secy, Polk Co Rep Party, Ga, 60-63, chmn, 64-70; mem, Seventh Cong Dist Rep Exec Comt, 64-; mem, Rep State Cent Comt Ga, 70- Bus & Prof Pos: Vpres, Spar Oil Co, 56-61; owner & pres, Ideal Oil Co, 61- Mil Serv: Entered as 2nd Lt, Army, 54, released as 1st Lt, 56, after serv in Comptroller Div, Southern Area Army Command, Ger, 55-56; Occup Ribbon. Mem: Jr CofC; Lions (pres, 72-73). Relig: Episcopal. Mailing Add: 829 College Dr Cedartown GA 30125

HOSACK, ROBERT E (D)
Idaho State Rep
Mailing Add: 820 West C St Moscow ID 83843

HOSKINS, ROBERT GERALD (D)
b Milwaukee, Wis, Oct 29, 35; s Gerald Hoskins & Isabel Johann H; m 1954 to Janet Ruth Strike; c Robert, Elizabeth, Pamela, Rebecca, Gerald & James. Educ: Carroll Col, Wis, BS, 57; Univ Iowa, 57-58; Univ Wis-Milwaukee, MS, 69; Sigma Tau Delta; Kappa Delta Pi; Beta Pi Epsilon. Polit & Govt Pos: Precinct committeeman, Waukesha Co Dem Statutory Comt, Wis, 62-74; vchmn, Ninth Cong Dist Dem Party, 64; bd mem, Waukesha Co Dem Admin Comt, 67-74; chmn, Waukesha Co Dem Party, 67; treas, Waukesha Co McCarthy for Pres Comt, 68; alt deleg, Dem Nat Conv, 68; exec-secy, Wis State Bingo Control Bd, 74- Bus & Prof Pos: Caseworker, Waukesha Co Welfare Dept, 58-60; Eng teacher, Oconomowoc High Sch, 61-74. Mil Serv: Sgt, Marine Corps Res. Mem: Wis Educ Asn; Wis Coun Teachers of Eng; IBT. Honors & Awards: Sigma Tau Delta Award. Relig: Catholic. Legal Res: Delafield WI 53018 Mailing Add: Rte 1 Box 402 Nashotah WI 53058

HOSMER, CRAIG (R)
b Brea, Calif, May 6, 15; s Chester Cleveland Hosmer & Mary Jane Craig H; m to Marian Caroline Swanson; c Susan Jane & Craig Larkin. Educ: Univ Calif, AB, 37; Univ Southern Calif, JD, 40; Phi Kappa Psi; Phi Alpha Delta. Polit & Govt Pos: Spec asst, US Dist Attorney for Atomic Energy Comn, Los Alamos, NMex, 48, adv, Int Atomic Energy Agency Deleg, 59-; US Rep, Calif, 52-74; adv, US Atoms for Peace Deleg, Geneva, 58, 63, 71; adv, US Deleg to 18 Nation Disarmament & UN Conf of Comn on Disarmament Conferences, 65-74; cand, US House of Rep, 74. Bus & Prof Pos: Ed, Univ Southern Calif Rev, 39-40; writer & lawyer, Long Beach, Calif, 46- Mil Serv: Navy, 41-46, Rear Adm, Naval Res. Mem: Am Nuclear Soc. Mailing Add: 1635 E Ocean Blvd Long Beach CA 90802

HOSPERS, JOHN (LIBERTARIAN)
b Pella, Iowa, June 9, 18; s John De Gelder Hospers & Dena Verhey H; div. Educ: Central Col, BA, 39; State Univ Iowa, MA, 41; Columbia Univ, PhD, 44. Hon Degrees: LLD, Central Col, 62. Polit & Govt Pos: Cand, President of US, Libertarian Party, 72; cand, Gov Calif, Libertarian, 74. Bus & Prof Pos: Mem staff, Univ Minn, 48-66, City Univ New York, 56-66 & Univ Southern Calif, Los Angeles, 66- Publ: Human Conduct, Harcourt Brace, 61; Introduction to Philosophical Analysis, Prentice-Hall, 67; Libertarianism, Nash Publ Co, 71. Mem: Am Philosophical Asn; Am Soc Aesthetics; Mind Asn; Aristotelian Soc. Honors & Awards: Fulbright research scholar, Univ London, Eng, 54-55. Mailing Add: 8229 Lookout Mt Ave Los Angeles CA 90046

HOSTETLER, H RICHARD (D)
Mem, Pa Dem State Comt
b Mifflintown, Pa, May 15, 39; s John Blair Hostetler & Klara Parnell H; m 1971 to H Roxie Notestine. Educ: Lycoming Col, ABA, 62. Polit & Govt Pos: Pres, Juniata Co Young Dem Club, Pa, 58-64; state dir, Young Dem Clubs Pa, 60-62, vpres, 62-64; regist chmn, Juniata Co Dem Party, 63-65, mem exec comt, 63-; dept state chmn, Pa Dem State Comt, 65-72, mem, 72-; deleg, Const Conv, 67-68; state regist chmn, Pa Dem Party, 68, state committeeman, 68-, state dir spec projs, 70; alt deleg, Dem Nat Conv, 68; cand, US Rep, Pa, 68; state campaign chmn, Manderino for Supreme Court, 69; dir, Bur Rural Affairs & Consumer Serv, Pa Dept Agr, Commonwealth of Pa. Bus & Prof Pos: Owner-operator, Hostetler Eggs & dealer, De Kalb Agr Asn, 62-; owner, Juniata Tribune, Mifflintown, 71-; owner, H&G Gun Shop, Mifflintown. Mem: Nat Rural Housing Coalition; Rural Develop Coun of Am; Concerned Consumers of the Alleghenies; Rural Transportation Task Force for Pa; Pa Rail Task Force. Relig: Lutheran. Mailing Add: RD 2 Mifflintown PA 17059

HOSTETTLER, DORIE MCFETRIDGE (R)
Rep State Committeewoman, Lake Co, Fla
b Creighton, Pa, Sept 4, 10; d George Edwin McFetridge & Ida Stacy Smith M; m to Donald Cook Hostettler (deceased); div; c Donna (Mrs J H Dickson). Educ: Marjorie Webster Sch Speech, BE, 33; Rollins Col, AB, 49; Univ Fla, MA, 53; Sigma Alpha Eta; Comus; Delta Delta Delta. Polit & Govt Pos: Pres, Golden Triangle Rep Womens Club, Fla, 60-62, 67-69 & 74-75, secy, 63, prog chmn, 69-72; Fla deleg, White House Conf on Children & Youth, 60; deleg, Rep Nat Conv, 64 & 68; precinct committeewoman; Rep State Committeewoman, Lake Co, currently; vchmn, Fifth Cong Dist Rep Party, currently. Bus & Prof Pos: Teacher speech & drama, Eustis High Sch, Fla, 49-55; teacher, Howey Acad, 56-59; chmn speech & drama dept, Brenau Col, 55-56. Mem: PEO. Relig: Christian Scientist. Legal Res: Waycross & Sunset Eustis FL 32726 Mailing Add: PO Box 775 Eustis FL 32726

HOUCK, MARIE (R)
Chairwoman, Montgomery Co Rep Exec Comt, Ohio
b Columbus, Ohio, Feb 19, 34; d Andrew Rozum & Anna Mikula R; m 1954 to Fred C Houck, Jr; c Jeffrey, Stephen, Gregory & Michael. Educ: Ohio State Univ, 51-53; Kappa Kappa Gamma. Polit & Govt Pos: Leader, Kettering Third Ward Rep Party, Ohio, 66-73; chairwoman, Montgomery Co Rep Exec Comt, 73- Bus & Prof Pos: Bd mem, Stillwater Health Ctr, 69-75. Mem: Kappa Kappa Gamma Alumnae; Kettering Rep Club. Relig: Roman Catholic. Legal Res: 4816 James Hill Rd Kettering OH 45429 Mailing Add: 131 N Jefferson St Dayton OH 45402

HOUFF, MARY FRANCES (D)
Chmn, Augusta Co Dem Comt
b Boston, Mass, Feb 4, 18; d Joseph Mayo & Amelia Jones M; m 1943 to Francis Harvey Houff; c Dennis Francis. Educ: Univ Maine, 36-37. Polit & Govt Pos: Vchmn, Augusta Co Dem Comt, Va, 69-73, chmn, 73- Bus & Prof Pos: Mem staff, Fed Bur Invest, Washington, DC, 41-43; cashier, Statler Hotel, Washington, DC, 45-55. Mem: Va Farm Bur Fedn (women's chmn cent dist, 74-); Augusta Co Farm Bur (women's chmn & bd dirs, 68-); Staunton-West Augusta Cancer Soc (bd dirs & info chmn, 74-); Mid-Valley Health Forum (chmn, 70-). Honors & Awards: Represented Va Farm Bur Fedn, Assoc Country Women of World Triennial Conf, Oslo, Norway, 71 & Perth, Australia, 74; Outstanding Women's Comt, Va Farm Bur, 73 & 74. Mailing Add: Rte 1 Box 70 Weyers Cave VA 24486

HOUGH, JOHN E (R)
b Janesville, Wis, July 5, 16; s Azel Clarence Hough & Dorothy Whitehead H; m 1940 to Vivian Swensson; c Gordon Richard & Lawrence A. Educ: Cornell Univ, BA, 37. Polit & Govt Pos: Rep city chmn, Janesville, Wis, 48-52; chmn, Rock Co Rep Orgn, 53-55; chmn, First Dist Rep Orgn, 58-61; treas, Wis Rep Party, 61-68, chmn, until 73; alt deleg, Rep Nat Conv, 68, deleg, 72; Rep Nat Committeeman, Wis, formerly. Bus & Prof Pos: Pres, Hough Mfg Corp, 37- Mem: Wis CofC (dir); Chief Execs Forum; Rotary; Cornell Club of New York, NY. Relig: Episcopal. Legal Res: 1901 Ruger Ave Janesville WI 53545 Mailing Add: PO Box 591 Janesville WI 53545

HOUGH, RALPH DEGNAN (R)
NH State Rep
b Hanover, NH, May 21, 43; s Frank Fisher Hough & Renna Degnan H; m 1971 to Susan Elizabeth Rector; c Anna Elizabeth. Educ: St Michael's Col (Vt), AB in Govt, 67. Polit & Govt Pos: NH State Rep, 73-, mem appropriations comt, NH House of Rep, 73- Bus & Prof Pos: Ins broker, Degnan Ins Agency & Dewey, Peck & Co, Lebanon, NH, 69- Mil Serv: Entered as E-1, Army, 67, released as Sgt, after serv in Signal Corps, Vietnam, 68-69; Army Commendation Medal; Good Conduct Medal. Mem: NH Asn Independent Ins Agents; VFW; Am Legion; Elks; Lions. Relig: Roman Catholic. Mailing Add: Poverty Lane West Lebanon NH 03784

HOUGHTON, CHARLES G, III (D)
b Glens Falls, NY, Aug 17, 44; s Charles G Houghton, Jr & Stella Bixby H; single. Educ: Harvard Univ, BA cum laude in Econ, 67; Spee Club; Hasty Pudding-Inst of 1776, pres, 66-67. Polit & Govt Pos: Admin asst to US Rep James W Symington, Mo, 70- Bus & Prof Pos: Exec, Anchorfilm Co, St Louis, Mo, 64-67. Mil Serv: Entered as Ens, Navy, 67, released as Lt(jg), after serv in USS Navasota, Vietnam; Nat Defense Serv Medal; Vietnam Serv Medal. Mem: Mo Hist Soc; Friends of City Art Mus; Nat Mus of Transport. Relig: Episcopal. Legal Res: 750 Cella Rd St Louis MO 63124 Mailing Add: c/o James W Symington US House of Rep Washington DC 20515

HOULEY, ROBERT D (D)
Conn State Sen
b Berlin, NH, Nov 20, 27; s James Feeney Houley & Val Marquis H; m 1957 to Helen M Daly; c James Feeney, Kathleen Anne & Elizabeth Ruth. Educ: Univ NH, BS, 53; Theta Kappa Phi; Newman Club; NH Club; Senior Skulls. Polit & Govt Pos: Secy, Zoning Comn, Vernon, Conn, 65-66, chmn, Econ Develop Comt, 65-67, mem, Vernon Dem Town Comt, 65-, bd of rep, 67-69; Conn State Sen, 69-73 & 75-, chmn, Comt on Appropriations, Conn State Senate, 71-73 & 75-76; mem, Vernon Town Coun, 72- Bus & Prof Pos: Sales rep, L G Balfour Co, Mass, 53-59, sales mgr, 59-61, dist commercial sales mgr, 61- Mil Serv: Entered as Pvt, Marine Corps, 46, released as Cpl, 48, after serv in 8th Marines, 2nd Div. Mem: Nat Soc State Legislators. Relig: Roman Catholic. Legal Res: 75 Merline Rd Vernon CT 06086 Mailing Add: PO Box 0035 Vernon CT 06066

HOULIHAN, JOSEPH T (D)
RI State Rep
Mailing Add: 41 Parker Ave Newport RI 02840

HOUSE, DALE WIESNER (R)
Single. Educ: Centenary Col for Women, AA, 60; Univ NC Chapel Hill, AB, 62; Delta Delta Delta; Gamma Beta Epsilon. Polit & Govt Pos: Exec Secy to US Rep Alphonzo Bell, Calif, 65- Mem: Woodley Rd Tennis Club; Capitol Hill Tennis Club (bd dirs); Ripon Soc. Honors & Awards: Cheerleader, University Park, Univ NC, Chapel Hill. Relig: Episcopal. Legal Res: 2205 California St Washington DC 20008 Mailing Add: 2329 Rayburn House Off Bldg Washington DC 20515

HOUSE, ERNEST JONES (D)
Chmn, McDowell Co Dem Exec Comt, NC
b Marion, NC, Jan 4, 26; s Ernest Jones House & Annie Kate Burgin H; m to Margaret Honeycutt; c Kay Burgin, Margaret Ellen & Elizabeth Hedley. Educ: Univ NC, Chapel Hill, BS, 49; Phi Beta Kappa; Sigma Alpha Epsilon; Philanthropic Lit Soc. Polit & Govt Pos: Deleg, Dem Nat Conv, 56; mem, NC Med Care Comn, 62-67; chmn, McDowell Co Bd Elections, 67-68; mem, NC State Bd Elections, 68-72; chmn, McDowell Co Dem Exec Comt, 74- Mil Serv: Entered as Pvt, Air Force, 44, released as Cpl, 45, after serv in Harlingen AFB, Tex. Mem: Marion Kiwanis; Mystic Tie Masonic Lodge (Past Master, 53); McDowell CofC. Honors & Awards: Jaycees Young Man of Year, 58. Relig: Presbyterian; deacon. Legal Res: 105 Rutherford Rd Marion NC 28752 Mailing Add: Box 548 Marion NC 28752

HOUSE, JAMES EVAN, II (D)
b Sullivan, Ind, Mar 19, 50; s James Evan House & Mary Shonk H; m 1970 to Linda Diane Brown. Educ: Ind State Univ, Terre Haute, BS in Polit Sci, 72. Polit & Govt Pos: Pres, Clay Co Teen Dem, Ind, 66; coordr, Robert F Kennedy for President, 68; aide, US Sen Birch Bayh, 70; aide, Roach for Cong, 70; chmn, Brazil Dem Cent Comt, 71; chmn, Clay Co Youth Registr, 72; deleg, Ind Dem State Conv, 72 & 74; precinct committeeman, Clay Co, 72; deleg, Dem Nat Conv, 72. Mem: Clay Co Ment Health Asn (fund drive chmn, 73); Jaycees. Honors & Awards: Elks Youth Leadership Award, 68. Relig: Methodist. Mailing Add: 512 S Depot St Brazil IN 47834

HOUSE, MARY CORBIN (D)
Mem Exec Comt, Ark State Dem Comt
b Clay, Ky, Apr 7, 25; d Lonnie James Corbin & Georgia Alma Clark C; m 1948 to Howard Leland House; c Dianne Lee. Educ: St Anthony's Sch Nursing, Louisville, Ky; Nazareth Col, Ky. Polit & Govt Pos: Committeewoman, Ark State Dem Comt, 66-, mem exec comt, 72-; third vpres, Dem Women's Club Ark, 67-68; deleg, Dem Nat Conv, 68 & 72; mem, Gov Comn on Status of Women, Ark, 70- Mem: Nat Asn Jr. Auxiliaries, Inc; Dem Women's Club of Independence Co (treas); Batesville Jr Auxiliary (pres). Relig: Methodist. Mailing Add: 1775 Highland Rd Batesville AR 72501

HOUSE, VAL A, JR (D)
b Scottsville, Ky, June 22, 29; s Val A House & Elsie Siegrist H; single. Educ: Centre Col, BA, 50; Univ Louisville, LLB, 54; Phi Delta Theta; Phi Alpha Delta. Polit & Govt Pos: Master Comnr, Circuit Court, Allen Co, Ky, 58-65; chmn, Allen Co Dem Exec Comt, formerly; attorney, City of Scottsville, 72- Bus & Prof Pos: Smith & Smith, Attorneys, Louisville, Ky, 57-58; attorney-at-law, Scottsville, 58- Mil Serv: Entered as E-2, Army, 54, released as Specialist 3/C, 56, after serv in US Army Terminal Command, Atlantic Theatre, Ft Knox, Ky. Mem: Pres, Allen Co Jaycees, 65; chmn, Allen Co United Givers Fund, 65. Relig: Methodist. Legal Res: 510 E Cherry St Scottsville KY 42164 Mailing Add: Box 454 Scottsville KY 42164

HOUSE, VINCENT F (R)
Mem, Rep State Cent Comt Calif
b Salt Lake City, Utah, Jan 5, 38; s Vincent H House & Bernadine Marron H; m 1958 to Thekla Lamberty; c Liana, Kevin & Leslie. Educ: Rosemead High Sch, Calif, two years. Polit & Govt Pos: Secy, 50th Assembly Dist & 25th Cong Dist, Los Angeles Co Rep Cent Comt, 68-70, mem, 70-; mem, 35th Sen Dist Rep Cent Comt, currently; mem, Rep State Cent Comt Calif, 71- Bus & Prof Pos: Field rep, Hycon Mfg, Monrovia, Calif, 62-66, acting proj engr, 66-68; pres V & T Enterprises, La Puente, Calif, 68- Mil Serv: Entered as Pvt, Air Force, 55, released as A 2/C, 59, after serv in 405th Tactical Air Command Missile Wing, ETO, 56-59; Good Conduct Medal; Outstanding Unit Citation; Presidential Unit Citation; Guided Missile Insignia. Mem: US Jaycees; La Puente Valley Jaycees; Boy Scouts of Am; La Puente Indust Rotary Club. Honors & Awards: Jaycee of the Month; Key Man Award. Relig: Methodist. Mailing Add: 358 Dalesford Dr La Puente CA 91744

HOUSEL, JERRY WINTERS (D)
Mem, Dem Nat Comt, Wyo
b Cripple Creek, Colo, Aug 9, 12; s James Robert Housel & Emma Winters H; m 1941 to Mary Elaine Bever; c James Robert, Jerry Laine, John Ora & Peter Elliott. Educ: Univ Wyo, BA, 35, JD, 36; Am Univ, PhD, 41. Polit & Govt Pos: Asst to Sen Harry H Schwartz, Wyo, 37-40; mem, Cody City Coun, 50; chmn & state committeeman, Park Co Dem Comt, formerly; mem, Wyo Dem State Exec Comt, formerly; pres, Wyo Dem Club, formerly; mem, Dem Nat Comt, 72-, mem, Charter Comn, 74. Bus & Prof Pos: Attorney-at-law, Laramie, Wyo, 36-37, Cody, 46-; teaching asst, Am Univ Grad Sch, 37; attorney, Fed Trade Comn, Washington, DC, 41-42, War Relocation Authority, 42; chmn, First State Bank, Cody; dir, First Nat Bank, Meeteetse; mem, Wyo Bd Law Examr, 56-70, pres, 66-70. Mil Serv: Naval Res, 43-46. Mem: Wyo State, Am & Park Co Bar Asns; Am Judicature Soc; Cody CofC; Am Legion (past Comdr). Legal Res: 1500 11th St Cody WY 82414 Mailing Add: Box 69 Cody WY 82414

HOUSER, THOMAS JAMES (R)
Comnr, Fed Commun Comn
b Chicago, Ill, June 28, 29; s Tom Houser & Mayme Mikulecky H; m 1954 to Jo-Ann Ochsenhirt; c Deborah Ann, Deneen Jo & David Gerad. Educ: Hanover Col, BA, 51; Advan Sch of Int Studies, Washington, DC, 52; Northwestern Univ Law Sch, JD, 59; Gamma Sigma Phi; Beta Theta Phi. Polit & Govt Pos: Rep committeeman, Wheeling Twp, Ill, 62-66; campaign mgr, Percy for Gov, 64; campaign mgr, Percy for Sen Comt, 66; chmn exec comt, Cook Co Rep Cent Comt, 64-; dep dir, Peace Corps, 69-71; comnr, Fed Commun Comn, 71-; campaign chmn, Ill Comt for the Reelec of the President, 71-72; alt deleg, Rep Nat Conv, 72. Bus & Prof Pos: Com attorney, Asn of Western RR, 59-62; partner, Sidley & Austin Law Firm, Chicago, 73- Mil Serv: Entered as Pvt, Army, 54, released as Sgt, 56, after serv in Counter-Intel Corps, Ger. Mem: Am, Ill & Chicago Bar Asns; Union League Club of Chicago;

Tavern Club of Chicago. Honors & Awards: All conf col halfback, Hanover Col, 50; all city high sch football, Chicago, 46. Relig: Christian Church. Legal Res: 15214 Kishwaukee Valley Rd Woodstock IL 60098 Mailing Add: One First Nat Plaza Chicago IL 60670

HOUSLEY, GRADY EUGENE (D)
b Copperhill, Tenn, Dec 19, 37; s Grady Melvin Housley & Charlotte Stymus H; m 1960 to Mary Dupree; c Julie Desiree & Zachary Eugene. Educ: John Marshall Univ, LLB, 59. Polit & Govt Pos: Pres, Young Dem Cobb Co, Ga, 58-60; mem, Cobb Co Bd of Educ, 64-68, pres, 67-68; mem, Ga State Dem Exec Comt, formerly; mem & Lt Col, Aide-de-Camp, Gov Staff, Ga, 67-; Ga State Rep, Dist 117, Post 1, 69-72. Bus & Prof Pos: Mem, City of Marietta Employees Retirement Bd, Ga, 63-64; referee, Juv Court, Cobb Co, 64-69; pub rels dir, Housley Riding Equip, Marietta, 69- Publ: Juvenile delinquency: a national problem, 64 & Your child's future depends on you, Communities Newspapers Inc, 68. Mem: Lions; Marietta-Cobb Boys Club; Ga Sheriff's Boys Ranch; Jaycees; Ga Peace Officers Asn. Honors & Awards: Distinguished Citizen Award, Marietta Jaycees, 68; Outstanding Serv Award, Cobb Co Bd of Educ, 69. Relig: Baptist. Mailing Add: 1011 Housley Rd Marietta GA 30060

HOUSTON, HOWARD EDWIN (R)
b Ryan, Iowa, Nov 2, 10; s Frederick Lincoln Houston & Ida Woodard H; m 1939 to Frances Gregory Crawford; c Frederick Woodard & Molly Crawford. Educ: Columbia Univ, AB, 32; Psi Upsilon (pres). Polit & Govt Pos: Mayor, Meriden, Conn, 47-51 & 62-63; chmn, Gov Comt on Med Schs, 52; chmn, Rep Town Comt, Meriden, 52; comnr, State Welfare Dept, 53-54; dep dir, US Aid Mission to India, 55-57, dir & minister, 57-59; mem, Mutual Security Prog Eval Team to Peru; chmn, Rep State Comt, Health & Welfare; mem, Rep State Cent Comt, Conn, 60-66; deleg, Conn Const Conv, Fifth Cong Dist, 65; dir econ affairs & US Agency Int Develop, Korea, US Embassy, Seoul, Korea, 70-71, minister-dir, Agency, New Delhi, India, 71- Bus & Prof Pos: Dir, Meriden Savings Bank, Meriden Trust & Safe Dep Co & Morningside House of NY; dir, Bradley Home for Aged, Meriden, 35-54; chmn, Meriden-Wallinford Region Health Coun, 54; chmn, India Comt of Asia Soc of NY, 61; mem assoc bd, Conn Bank & Trust Co, 68-71; trustee, Colby Jr Col, New London, NH, 68-; mem coun, SCent Community Col, Conn, 68-70; corporator, Marine Biol Lab, Woods Hole, Mass, 68- Mil Serv: Entered as Pvt, Army, 43, released as 1st Lt, 46, after serv in Med Serv Corps, SW Pac, 44-46. Mem: Am Legion; Elks; Mason; Eagles; Rotary. Relig: Episcopal. Legal Res: 691 Preston Ave Meriden CT 06450 Mailing Add: New Delhi ID c/o Dept of State Washington DC 20521

HOUSTON, NEAL J (R)
b Barre, Vt, Aug 22, 26; s Ira Nathaniel Houston & Alice Clyde Quinn H; m 1949 to Marilyn Mills; c Deborah Ann, Neal J, Jr, Rebecca Hadley, Virginia Gale, Laura Lee & Alison Joan. Educ: Univ Vt, 46-49; Kappa Sigma. Polit & Govt Pos: Asst to Gov, Vt, 55-58; State Dir Budget, Vt, 59; admin asst to US Rep Stafford, Vt, 60- Bus & Prof Pos: Reporter, 48-55. Mil Serv: Army Air Corps, World War II, 43-45. Mem: Plainfield Village Trustees; Montpelier Rotary Club; Windsor Jr CofC. Relig: Episcopal; St Luke's Vestry & treas, St Luke's Episcopalian Church. Legal Res: Plainfield VT 05667 Mailing Add: 5219 Dirksen Sen Off Bldg Washington DC 20510

HOUSTON, PATRICK LEO (D)
Chairperson, Crawford Co Dem Comt, Iowa
b Dow City, Iowa, Apr 11, 27; s John Thomas Houston & Susie Kelly H; m 1945 to Lois Anne Lenz; c Colette (Mrs Koenck), Barbara (Mrs Staller), Sally (Mrs Quandt), Tim, Jane & Anne. Educ: Dow City Consol High Sch, Iowa, grad, 44. Polit & Govt Pos: Third Ward chmn, Denison City Dem Party, Iowa, 66-72, second ward chmn, 72-74; chairperson, Crawford Co Dem Comt, 74- Bus & Prof Pos: Self-employed agr, Denison, Iowa, 47- Mil Serv: Entered as A/S, Navy, 45, released as Fireman 2/C, 46. Mem: Am Legion; KofC; Crawford Co Indust Develop Corp; Iowa Farm Adv Bd (sixth dist secy). Relig: Catholic. Mailing Add: RR 3 Crestview Dr Denison IA 51442

HOUSTON, PAUL DENNIS (D)
Chmn, Warrick Co Dem Cent Comt, Ind
b Warrick Co, Ind, Apr 16, 21; s Gurney Earl Houston & Leonora Evelyn Spain H; m 1943 to Mary Jean Tevault; c Donna Jean (Mrs John Purdue), Jay B & Kent E. Educ: Boonville High Sch, grad, 40. Polit & Govt Pos: Chief of Police, Boonville, Ind, 56-63; sheriff, Warrick Co, 63-71; chmn, Warrick Co Dem Cent Comt, 68-; assessor, Warrick Co, 71- Bus & Prof Pos: Eng dept, Northern Coal Co, 42-53. Mil Serv: Entered as Pvt, Army, 42, released as Sgt, after serv in 100 Inf Div, Ger, 44-46. Mem: Am Legion; VFW; Boonville Lions; Stranger Rest Lodge 240, F&AM; Hadi Temple Shrine, Evansville. Relig: Protestant. Legal Res: 1016 E Monroe St Boonville IN 47601 Mailing Add: PO Box 562 Boonville IN 47601

HOUTCHENS, DELTON LOUIS (D)
b Deepwater, Mo, Jan 14, 18; s Emmet Houtchens & Bessie Lowderman H; m 1938 to Betty Jo Kirkwood; c Richard K & Joyce Sue. Educ: Westminster Col, 36-38; Univ Mo, LLB, 41. Polit & Govt Pos: Prosecuting attorney, Henry Co, Mo, 43-44; Mo State Rep, 48-52, Majority Floor Leader, Mo House of Rep, 50-52; mem, Personnel Adv Bd of Mo, 59-64; state wide campaign mgr for Gov Warren E Hearnes, 64; chmn, Mo State Dem Party, 65-73; deleg, Dem Nat Conv, 68 & 72. Mil Serv: Entered as Pvt, Army, 43, released as 1st Lt, 45, after serv in Med Admin Corps. Mem: Shrine; Scottish Rite; Mason; Elks; Am Legion. Relig: Baptist. Legal Res: 406 S Eighth St Clinton MO 64735 Mailing Add: Box 231 Carney Bldg Clinton MO 64735

HOUTON, KATHLEEN KILGORE (D)
b Washington, DC, July 11, 46; d Lowell Berry Kilgore & Helen Lorilla Ford K; m 1969 to Daniel Joseph Houton; c Maria Gifford. Educ: Oberlin Col, AB, 68; Fletcher Sch Law, MA, 69. Polit & Govt Pos: Alt deleg, Dem Nat Conv, 72. Bus & Prof Pos: Mkt analyst, Herman B Direeter Assocs, Washington, DC, 67-68; ed, Harbridge House, Boston, 69-70; contrib ed, Metro-Boston Mag, 71-72; contrib ed, Boston Mag, 72- Publ: The Boston Harbor tangle, Metro-Boston Mag, 10/71; Women in prison, The Phoenix, 5/17/72; New slums for old-rehabilitation for profit and squalor, Boston Mag, 7/72. Mem: State Club; Nat Women's Polit Caucus; Irish Soc Club of Boston; Am Cancer Soc (vpres, Dorchester Br, 70-73); Columbia Savin Hill Civic Asn. Honors & Awards: Serv Award, Am Cancer Soc, 72. Relig: Congregational. Mailing Add: 5 Bayside St Dorchester MA 02125

HOVIS, RAYMOND LEADER (D)
b Phoenixville, Pa, Jan 13, 34; s Raymond S Hovis & Mary Leader H; m 1961 to Lorraine Catherine Baugher; c Michelle P, Michael D & Steven M. Educ: Wharton Sch Finance & Com, Univ Pa, BS in Econ, 55, Law Sch, JD, 58; Pi Kappa Alpha. Polit & Govt Pos: Mem, York Co Dem Comt, Pa, 64-74; vpres, York-Adams Co Ment Health-Ment Retardation Bd, 68-69; Pa State Rep, 93rd Legis Dist, 69-72; chmn, York Co Govt Study Comn, 73-74. Bus & Prof Pos: Assoc, Stock & Leader, Attorneys, 59-66, partner, 66- Mil Serv: Entered as Enlistee, Army Nat Guard, 58, released as 1st Lt, 65, after serv in 104th Armored Cavalry. Mem: York Co Bar Asn (chmn legis liaison comt, 70-73); Pa Bar Asn (mem statutory law comt, 71-); Izaak Walton League; YMCA. Honors & Awards: Charles C Rohlfing Citizenship Award, 55. Relig: Lutheran. Mailing Add: RD 1 Box 499 Wrightsville PA 17368

HOWARD, ASBURY (D)
Ala State Rep
Mailing Add: 1930 Exeter Ave Bessemer AL 35020

HOWARD, CHARLES ALLEN, JR (R)
b Aberdeen, SDak, Aug 11, 04; s Charles A Howard & Grace Brown H; single. Educ: Princeton Univ, AB, 27; Harvard Law Sch, LLB, 30; Phi Beta Kappa; Pi Kappa Delta; Delta Sigma Rho; Terrace Club. Polit & Govt Pos: Mem, SDak State Rep Cent Comt, 50-64, chmn, 64-70; mem, Rep Nat Comt, 64-70. Bus & Prof Pos: Pres, Howard & Hedger Co, 33- Mil Serv: Entered as 1st Lt, Army Air Force, 42, released as Maj, 46, after serv in ETO; Lt Col(Ret), Army Air Force Res; Bronze Star; Presidential Unit Citation; ETO Ribbon with six Battle Stars; Ger Occup Ribbon. Mem: Scottish Rite (33 degree); AF&AM (Past Master Grand Lodge); Am Legion; Rotary. Relig: Episcopal. Legal Res: 1201 N Main St Aberdeen SD 57401 Mailing Add: Box 248 Aberdeen SD 57401

HOWARD, DONALDA K (R)
NH State Rep
Mailing Add: Box 5 Glen NH 03838

HOWARD, ELOISE KATHLEEN (R)
Exec Secy, NC Fedn Young Rep
b Marshalltown, Iowa, June 13, 43; d Robert Paul McGinty & Ella Louise Sawyer M; m 1964 to Malcolm Jones Howard (Mack); c Shannon Lea. Educ: Coker Col, 61-62; Univ Philippines, 62-63; Univ Hawaii, 63-64; Univ Va, 70. Polit & Govt Pos: Deleg & vchmn NC deleg, Rep Nat Conv, 72; off dir, Eastern NC Comt to Reelect the President, 72; panel speaker, NC Rep Womens Ballot Sem, 72; charter mem & officer, Pitt Co Rep Womens Club, 72; mem, Pitt Co Rep Party, 72; sustaining mem, NC Rep Party, 72-; mem, NC Fedn Rep Women, 72; mem, Wake Co Young Rep, 73; NC Rep Party Conv coordr, 73; mem exec comt, NC Fedn Young Rep, 73-, exec secy, 73-, dir conv banquet, 73; fel cand, NC Inst Polit, 73. Mem: Cedar Hills Garden Club; Greenville Art Ctr; Lenoir Hist Soc; Cadette Girl Scout Troop 2061 (co-leader, 71). Honors & Awards: Mgr, Miss NC Young Rep, 73; attended Inaugural Balls, President Nixon & Gov Holshouser, 73. Relig: Baptist. Legal Res: Greenville NC Mailing Add: 417 Rose Haven Dr Raleigh NC 27609

HOWARD, G ROBERT (D)
Ga State Rep
Mailing Add: 723 Iroquois Dr Marietta GA 30060

HOWARD, GENE C (D)
Pres Pro Tempore, Okla State Senate
b Perry, Okla, Sept 26, 26; s Joe W Howard & Nell Lillian Brown; m 1951 to Marian Ruth Berg; c Jean Ann & Joe Ted. Educ: Univ Okla, LLB, 51; Phi Delta Phi. Polit & Govt Pos: Pres, Young Dem Okla, 54; secy, Tulsa Co Elec Bd, 54; Okla State Rep, 58-62; deleg, Dem Nat Conv, 64; Okla State Sen, 64-, pres pro tempore, Okla State Senate, 75- Mil Serv: Entered as Pvt, Army, 44, released as Sgt, 46, after serv in Gen Hq, Army, Pac, World War II, Asiatic-Pac Theatre, 45-46; reentered as Capt, Air Force during Berlin Crises, 61-62; Lt Col, Air Force Res, 69; Asiatic-Pac Ribbon with Two Battle Stars; Philippine Liberation with One Battle Star. Mem: Okla Bar Asn; Mason (32 degree); Tulsa Consistory; Tulsa Club. Honors & Awards: Named Outstanding Young Attorney, Tulsa Co Bar Asn, 53. Relig: Christian Church. Legal Res: 1738 S Erie Pl Tulsa OK 74112 Mailing Add: 520 Center Bldg 630 W Seventh St Tulsa OK 74127

HOWARD, J T (JERRY) (D)
Mo State Rep
b Oak Ridge, Mo, Mar 28, 36; s John Thomas Howard; m 1973; c Erin Diane, Michael Rathjen, John Trevor, Eliza Jane & William Perry. Educ: Southeast Mo State Univ, BS, 60; Delta Tau Alpha. Polit & Govt Pos: Mo State Rep, 157th Dist, 72- Mil Serv: Entered as Cpl, Army, 54, released as Sgt E-5, 56, after serv in Tank Co, 21st Inf Regt, Korea, 55-56; 1st Lt, Army Nat Guard, 61-68; Good Conduct Medal. Mem: AAONMS; AF&AM; Scottish Rite; Elks. Mailing Add: Rte 2 Dexter MO 63841

HOWARD, JAMES J (D)
US Rep, NJ
b Irvington, NJ, July 24, 27; s George P Howard & Bernice M H; m to Marlene Vetrano; c Kathleen (Mrs Lowther), Lenore & Marie. Educ: St Bonaventure Univ, BA, 52; Rutgers Univ, MEd, 58. Polit & Govt Pos: US Rep, NJ, 64-, chmn, Subcomt on Energy of Pub Works Comt, US House of Rep, 73-; deleg, Dem Nat Conv, 68; ex officio, Dem Nat Mid-Term Conf, 74. Bus & Prof Pos: Teacher & prin in Wall Twp Sch Syst, 52-64. Mil Serv: Navy; SPac Theatre. Mem: Monmouth Co Educ Asn (pres); NJ Educ Asn (deleg assembly); Nat Educ Asn. Legal Res: 562 Wall Rd Spring Lake Heights NJ 07762 Mailing Add: 131 Cannon House Off Bldg Washington DC 20515

HOWARD, MELVIN (R)
Nev State Assemblyman
Mailing Add: 1225 Bridge St Winnemucca NV 89445

HOWARD, NORMAN R (D)
Ore State Sen
Mailing Add: 5230 SE 37th Ave Portland OR 97202

HOWARD, PIERRE, JR (D)
Ga State Sen
Mailing Add: 600 First Nat Bank Bldg Decatur GA 30030

HOWARD, RAYMOND (D)
Mo State Sen
b St Louis, Mo, Mar 13, 35; s Raymond Howard & Geneva Howard H; m 1969 to Sharon Cecile Enoex; c Raymond Howard, III. Educ: Univ Wis, BS, 56; St Louis Univ Law Sch, JD, 61; Kappa Alpha Psi; Student Senate, pres, Debate Team & Young Dem, Univ Wis; Student

Senate & secy, Sr Class, St Louis Univ Law Sch. Polit & Govt Pos: Mo State Rep, 65-69; Mo State Sen, 69-; alt deleg, Dem Nat Conv, 72; deleg, Dem Nat Mid-Term Conf, 74. Bus & Prof Pos: Attorney, St Louis, Mo. Mil Serv: Entered as 2nd Lt, Army, 56, released as 1st Lt, 58, after serv in 82nd Air Borne Inf Div; Parachute Wings. Publ: Abolition of capital punishment, 65 & Racial protests, 66, St Louis Bar J. Mem: Am & Nat Bar Asns; Am Trial Lawyers Asn; Nat Asn Defense Law in Criminal Cases. Honors & Awards: Distinguished Award as Mem of Mo Legis & Award in Recognition of Outstanding Serv to Legal Profession, St Louis Bar Asn; chosen as First Black Mayor of St Louis in poll conducted by St Louis Sentinel. Relig: Protestant. Mailing Add: 5022 Aubert St St Louis MO 63115

HOWARD, RHEA (D)
b Wichita Falls, Tex, July 25, 92; s Ed Howard & Jettie Lee Maloney H; m 1913 to Kathleen Benson; c Anna Katherine (Mrs Barnett). Educ: Trinity Univ, Waxahachie, Tex; Eastman Col, Poughkeepsie, NY; Sigma Delta Chi. Polit & Govt Pos: Mem, Wichita Falls Sch Bd, 14 years; deleg, Dem Nat Conv, 52, 56, 60, 64 & 68; committeeman, 30th Senatorial Dist, 66. Bus & Prof Pos: Pres, publisher & ed, Wichita Falls Times & Wichita Falls Record News. Mil Serv: 1st Lt, Army Nat Guard, Adjutant on Col's Staff, World War I. Mem: Am Newspapers Publishers Asn; YMCA (adv bd); Mason (33 degree); Shrine; CofC. Honors & Awards: Elected Publisher of Year by Headliners Club, Austin, Tex, 60; Salesman of the Year, Wichita Falls, 70. Relig: Presbyterian. Legal Res: 2105 Berkeley Dr Wichita Falls TX 76308 Mailing Add: PO Box 120 Wichita Falls TX 76307

HOWARD, SAMUEL HUNTER, JR (D)
SC State Rep
b Greer, SC, Aug 13, 53; s Samuel Hunter Howard, Sr & Jean Garrison H; m 1974 to Martha Susan Baldwin. Educ: Univ SC, BS, 74; Kappa Alpha; Deans List, 73. Polit & Govt Pos: Page, SC Senate, 72-74; SC State Rep, 75- Bus & Prof Pos: Acct, Howard Acct Serv, 74- Mem: SC Asn Acct Practitioners; Lions; YMCA (bd dirs). Relig: Baptist. Mailing Add: 404 N Main St Fountain Inn SC 29644

HOWARD, SHARON JANEENE (D)
b Ardmore, Okla, July 31, 54; d Eugene Francis Howard & Wilma Smith H; single. Educ: Cent State Univ, 72-75; Univ Okla, 75-; pres, Young Dem, 73-74. Polit & Govt Pos: Chmn, Dem Precinct R-13, Kay Co, Okla, 73; nat committeewoman, Okla Young Dem, 73-75; state pres, Okla Dem Youth Caucus, 75- Publ: Co-auth, Young Democrats answer, Okla Observer, 9/74. Mem: Young Dem Am. Legal Res: RR 1 Box 130 Kildare OK 74642 Mailing Add: 739 Chautauqua Norman OK 73069

HOWARD, W O (BOB) (D)
Mo State Rep
Mailing Add: Rte 2 Elsberry MO 63343

HOWARD, W RICHARD (R)
b Salt Lake City, Utah, Oct 6, 41; s William A Howard (deceased) & Winifred Langlois H; m 1964 to Marcia Anne Northrop; c William Kent & Erik Northrop. Educ: Univ Southern Calif, BS in Mgt, 63, MBA, 66; Blue Key; pres, Sigma Phi Epsilon. Polit & Govt Pos: Spec Asst to the Asst Secy of Com for Domestic & Int Bus, US Dep Com, 69-70; asst to dir of commun, The White House, 70-71, staff asst to the President, 71-73, Spec Asst to the President, formerly. Bus & Prof Pos: Sales exec, IBM, Los Angeles, Calif, 63-69; exec vpres, Concentric Tool Corp, Pasadena, San Marino, 66-69. Relig: Latter-day Saint. Legal Res: CA Mailing Add: 9210 Crosby Rd Silver Spring MD 20910

HOWARD, WALTER BOIVIN (D)
Pub Rels Dir, Hamilton Co Dem Party, Ohio
b Carbondale, Pa, Dec 20, 27; s Frank Walter Howard & Philomena Donato H; m 1953 to Jeanne E Thomas; c Marc Walter, Melissa Jean, George Gregory, Paul Francis, Marybeth & Patricia Lorraine. Educ: Hobart Col, BA cum laude with honors in Econ, 53; Columbia Univ, 53-54; Maxwell Sch of Citizenship & Pub Affairs, Syracuse Univ, MA with honors, 55; Phi Beta Kappa; Chi Eta Sigma; Sigma Chi; Baccia. Polit & Govt Pos: Precinct exec Clermont Co Dem Party Ohio, 58-62; chmn speakers bur Hamilton Co Dem Party, 58-62, pub rels dir, 62- & mem steering comt, currently; mem, Dem State Platform Comt, 62, 64 & 66; chmn election comt, Young Dem for Ohio, 66, Citizens for Reams Campaign Comt, 66 & Hamilton Co Citizens for Humphrey, 68; deleg-at-lg, Young Dem of Ohio, 66-68; deleg, Dem Nat Conv, 68; co-chmn, Businessmen for Humphrey, 68; mem, Hamilton Co Young Dem, currently; chmn, Springer for Cong, 70. Bus & Prof Pos: Gen commercial supvr, Cincinnati & Suburban Bell Tel Co, 66-67, gen pub rels supvr, 67-68; pres, B H W, Inc, 66-; exec vpres, Wabash Consol Corp, 68; vpres, Sauter, Gilligan & Assocs, 69-; econ consult, Ohio-Ky-Ind Regional Planning Authority, 71-; dir revenue requirements, Mid-Continent Tel Corp, Hudson, Ohio, 71-72, dir gen servs, 72- Mil Serv: Entered as Pvt, Air Force, 45, released as Sgt, 48, after serv in Air Transport Command, ETO, 45-48. Publ: The image of Cincinnati, Images, 69; Economic and demographic analysis for regional planning area; Financial analysis for Hamilton County; plus others. Mem: Am Mkt Asn; Univ of Cincinnati Tech Adv Coun; CofC (chmn econ research comt, bus indust dir comt); Jr Achievement (bd mem); Sigma Chi Alumni Chap. Honors & Awards: Recipient of Distinguished Serv Award, Gtr Cincinnati CofC; Outstanding Citizen of the Year Nominee, Cincinnati, Ohio. Relig: Catholic. Mailing Add: 8021 Valley View Rd Hudson OH 44236

HOWE, ALBERT BERRY, JR (R)
Chmn, Campbell Co Rep Exec Comt, Ky
b Dayton, Ky, June 28, 17; s Albert B Howe & Marie Kaufman H; m 1942 to Margaret M Rune; c Berry, Candy & Tom. Educ: Xavier Univ, BS, 39. Polit & Govt Pos: Chmn, Campbell Co Rep Exec Comt, Ky, 74- Bus & Prof Pos: Pub rels, Snodgrass Distributing Co, 75- Mil Serv: Entered as Pvt, Air Force, 42, released as Capt, 46, after serv in China-Burma-India Theatre, 43-45. Mailing Add: 118 Hartweb Ft Thomas KY 41075

HOWE, ALLAN TURNER (D)
US Rep, Utah
b South Cottonwood, Utah, Sept 6, 27; s Edward E Howe & Mildred Cuddy H; m 1952 to Marlene Dee; c Cynthia (Mrs Keith Tarver), Lyndon, Kenneth, David & Christopher. Educ: Univ Utah, BS, LLB & LLD. Polit & Govt Pos: Nat pres, Young Dem Clubs Am; pres, Atlantic Asn Young Polit Leaders; field rep & admin asst to US Sen Frank E Moss, Utah, 59-64; legal counsel & admin asst to Gov Calvin L Rampton, Utah, 65-68; exec dir, Four Corners Regional Develop Comt, 68-72; dep attorney, Salt Lake City; city attorney, City of South Salt Lake; Asst Attorney Gen, Utah; US Rep, Utah, 75- Mil Serv: US Coast Guard. Relig: Latter-day Saint. Legal Res: 4143 Parkview Dr Salt Lake City UT 84117 Mailing Add: 1525 Longworth House Off Bldg Washington DC 20515

HOWE, ANITA GONZALEZ (D)
b San Antonio, Tex, June 22, 48; d Ruperto Trevino Gonzalez & Esther Cortez G; m 1968 to Jay Edwin Howe. Polit & Govt Pos: Dem precinct committeewoman, 68-; deleg, Iowa Dem State Statutory Conv, 70 & Dist, Adair Co, Iowa State & Dem Nat Conv, 72. Mem: Girl Scouts (troop leader, 70-). Mailing Add: 401 SW Second Greenfield IA 50849

HOWE, CHARLES BRYAN (D)
Colo State Rep
b Ft Lupton, Colo, Nov 16, 35; s Charles Daniel Howe & Elizabeth Bryan H; m 1961 to Joan Merle Satter; c Charles Scott & Mary Elizabeth. Educ: Univ Denver, BS, 58, LLB, 60, MS in Pub Admin, 60. Polit & Govt Pos: Attorney & govt consult, Gov Local Affairs Comt, State of Colo, 63-65; precinct coordr, Boulder Co Dem Party, 66, committeeman, Precinct 22, 67; munic judge, City of Boulder, 67-; deleg, Dem Nat Conv, 68; mem, Boulder Co Dem Cent Comt, Colo, 69-; Dem cand for Colo State Rep, 70; Colo State Rep, Dist 53, 73- Bus & Prof Pos: Gen counsel, Colo Munic League, 65-68; attorney, Boulder, 68- Mil Serv: Entered as 1st Lt, Army, 60, released as Capt, 62, after serv in Judge Adv Gen Corps, Ft Monmouth, NJ, 60-62; Distinguished Mil Grad, Univ Denver, 59. Mem: Toastmasters. Relig: Unitarian. Legal Res: 4605 Talbot Boulder CO 80303 Mailing Add: 2040 14th St Suite 140 Boulder CO 80302

HOWE, DENNIS (R)
b Belleville, Kans, Nov 11, 40; s Louis Taft Howe & Alice Francis H; m 1965 to Mary Belden; c Elizabeth & Janice. Educ: Univ NMex, BA in Govt, 67. Polit & Govt Pos: Pres, Univ NMex Young Rep, 63-64 & Bernalillo Co Young Rep, 65-66; NMex State Rep, Dist 11, 67-68; NMex State Rep, Dist 14, 69-70; admin asst to US Sen Pete Domenici, NMex, 73- Mil Serv: Entered as Airman Basic, Air Force, 58, released as Airman 1/C, 62; Good Conduct Medal. Relig: Methodist. Legal Res: Albuquerque NM Mailing Add: 3 Bunker Court Rockville MD 20854

HOWE, ELIZABETH PROUT (D)
Chairwoman, Oakland Co Dem Party, Mich
b Chicago, Ill, July 12, 36; d William John Prout & Aili Tormala P; m 1958 to Franklin Edward Howe; c Aili Elizabeth. Educ: Mich State Univ, BA, 58; Mortar Bd; Theta Sigma Phi; Phi Kappa Phi. Polit & Govt Pos: Chairwoman, Oakland Co Dem Party, Mich, 71-; mem, Oakland Co Planning Comn, 72-74; deleg, Dem Nat Mid-Term Conf, 74. Bus & Prof Pos: Advert copy chief, J L Hudson, Detroit, Mich, 58-60; ed, Rochester News & Tri-City Messenger, 65; educ writer, Birmingham Eccentric, 65-68; with Jerry Lynch & Assoc, Pub Rels, Detroit, 68; partner, Winnermakers, Inc Pub Rels, Southfield, currently. Legal Res: 206 Charles Rochester MI 48063 Mailing Add: 1383 N Woodward Bloomfield Hills MI 48013

HOWE, EUNICE P (R)
Rep Nat Committeewoman, Mass
b Belmont, Mass, Apr 24, 18; m 1947 to Henry Dunster Howe; c Eunice Dunster & Mary Alice Boardman. Educ: Geneva Col, Switz, 36-37; Mount Holyoke Col, AB, 38; Boston Univ Sch Law, LLB, 41. Polit & Govt Pos: Mem, Mass Bar, 41-; Asst Attorney Gen, Mass, 41, 44 & 46; counsel, Div of Employ Security, 46-47; pres, Brookline Women's Rep Club, 63-65; mem, Mass Consumers Coun, 65-; vpres, New Eng Citizens Crime Comn, 66-; chmn, Brookline Rep Town Comt, 67-69; mem, Mass Coun on Crime & Correction & chmn, Comt on Consumer Educ, 68-; hon pres, Mass Fedn of Rep Women, 68-; Rep Nat Committeewoman, Mass, currently. Bus & Prof Pos: Attorney-at-law. Mil Serv: Lt(jg), Naval Res, World War II. Mem: Mount Holyoke Col (chmn, Bequest & Annuities Comt, 60-). Relig: Episcopal; mem of vestry, Church of Our Saviour, Brookline. Mailing Add: 6 Woodbine Rd Belmont MA 02178

HOWE, GORDON A (R)
b Rochester, NY, Jan 19, 04; s Frank Ballou Howe & Agnes Morrow H; m 1937 to Lois Speares; c Gordon, II, Gretchen & David S. Polit & Govt Pos: Justice of the Peace, 29-34; town supvr, Greece, NY, 33-60; deleg, NY State Rep Conv, 34-; chmn bd supvr, Monroe Co, NY, 48-60, co mgr, 60-71; founding dir, Ken Keating Rep League, 60; deleg, Rep Nat Conv, 60, 64, 68 & 72; chmn, Monroe Co Rep Comt, 60-62; committeeman, NY State Rep Comt; cand for Presidential Elector, 68. Bus & Prof Pos: Gov appointee, NY State Fire Adv Bd; chmn adv bd, Monroe Co Mutual Aid Plan for Fire Protection, 44; mem, Joint City-Co Comt on Elimination of Overlapping Functions of Govt in Rochester & Monroe Co, 55, chmn, Joint City-Co Civic Ctr Comn, NY, 55- Mem: Masons; Damascus Temple, Shrine; Elks; Red Jacket Coun, Boy Scouts (former dist comnr). Honors & Awards: Speaker, Urban Co Cong of Nat Asn of Co Officers, 59; Outstanding Rep of Year, Lincoln Rep League, 61; Civic Awards, Rotary, Kiwanis & CofC; Mgt Award, Rochester Inst Technol; Excellence Award, Monroe Co Legis. Relig: Presbyterian; elder. Mailing Add: 402 Beach Ave Rochester NY 14612

HOWE, JOHN ABIJAH (R)
Vt State Rep
b Tunbridge, Vt, Sept 9, 13; s James K Howe & Marion Whitney H; m 1939 to Shirley Frances Ainsworth; c David John, Dale Ainsworth, Karen Shirley (Mrs Davies), Dean Raymond & Timothy James. Educ: Vt Sch Agr, grad, 31. Polit & Govt Pos: Selectman, Tunbridge, Vt, 45-54 & 71-74, lister, 56-71; Vt State Rep, 75- Bus & Prof Pos: Owner-operator, Dairy Farm, 40- Mem: Rising Sun Lodge, F&AM; Mt Sinai Temple, Shrine; Worlds Fair (pres, Tunbridge, Vt); Northern Farms Coop (pres). Relig: Methodist. Mailing Add: Tunbridge VT 05077

HOWE, MARIE ELIZABETH (D)
Mass State Rep
b Somerville, Mass, June 13, 39; d William Andrew Howe & Amelia Gertrude McCauley H; single. Educ: Brooks Jr Col, dipl, 60; Suffolk Univ; New Eng Sch Law, Boston, JD, 69. Polit & Govt Pos: Mem, Somerville Sch Comt, Mass, 62-65, vchairlady, 63, chairlady, 64; mem, Ward & City Dem Comts, 62-; staff, Dist Attorney's Off, Middlesex Co, 63-64; Mass State Rep, 65-, asst majority leader, Mass House of Rep, currently. Bus & Prof Pos: Exec secy, Tech Research Group, Inc, 60-63. Publ: Administrators forum, Sch Mgt, 3/66. Mem: Mass Legislator's Asn; Nat Cong Parents & Teachers; Nat & Mass Asns of Sch Comts; Somerville Community Coun. Honors & Awards: Woman Doer of Mass in 65, Mass Fedn Women's Dem Clubs, Inc. Relig: Roman Catholic. Mailing Add: 19 Pembroke St Somerville MA 02145

HOWE, RICHARD C (D)
Utah State Rep
Mailing Add: 830 E 5600 S Murray UT 84107

HOWE, RICHARD RAY (R)
Chmn, Lewis Co Rep Cent Comt, Mo
b Decatur, Ill, Aug 23, 32; s Elbert D Howe & Marie Harris H; m 1954 to Elaine Bondurant; c Richard, Jr, Scott William, Dale Alan & John Tracy. Educ: Univ Mo, Columbia, AB, 54 & JD, 59; Phi Alpha Delta; Alpha Tau Omega. Polit & Govt Pos: Prosecuting attorney, Lewis Co, Mo, 68-73; chmn, Comn for Reapportionment of Mo Legis, 71; chmn, Lewis Co Rep Cent Comt, 71-; comnr, Mo Comn on Human Rights, 74-; chmn, Ninth Cong Dist Rep Comt, 74- Bus & Prof Pos: Attorney, gen practice, Canton, Mo, 59- Mil Serv: Entered as 2nd Lt, Air Force, 55, released as 1st Lt, 57, after serv in Strategic Air Command, 55-57. Mem: Am Bar Asn; Am Trial Lawyers Asn; Am Judicature Soc; Kiwanis; Mason. Relig: Baptist. Legal Res: Rte 2 Canton MO 63435 Mailing Add: 436 Lewis St Canton MO 63435

HOWELL, ALBERT S (D)
Mem, Greene Co Dem Exec Comt, Ga
b Waite Plains, Ga, Nov 14, 98; s Albert Sidney Howell, Sr & Cora Moore H; m 1928 to Edna Perrin Jenkins. Educ: Ga Sch Technol, BS Chem Eng, 21. Polit & Govt Pos: Mem, City Coun, Waite Plains, Ga, 28-48, mayor, 48-53; mem, Greene Co Dem Exec Comt, Ga, 30-, chmn, 52-56, 64-70. Mil Serv: Entered as 2nd Lt, Army, 21, 11th Inf, 21-23; 62nd CAAA, 23-25, ret phys disability, 25. Mem: Am Legion. Mailing Add: PO Box 13 Waite Plains GA 30678

HOWELL, HENRY EVANS, JR (INDEPENDENT)
Lt Gov, Va
b Norfolk, Va, Sept 5, 20; m to Elizabeth McCarty; c Mary, Henry III & Susan. Educ: Col William & Mary, 2 years; Univ Va, LLB. Polit & Govt Pos: Va State Rep, 60-66; Va State Sen, 66-71; cand for Gov, Va, 69; Lt Gov, Va, 71- Bus & Prof Pos: Attorney-at-law. Mem: Va Trial Lawyers Asn; Norfolk CofC; Hampton Rds Foreign Com Club; Hampton Rds Maritime Asn; Ocean View Dem Club. Relig: Episcopal. Mailing Add: 808 Maritime Tower Norfolk VA 23510

HOWELL, JAMES F (D)
Okla State Sen
b Wewoka, Okla, July 14, 34; s Forrest Felton Howell (deceased) & Lena Hand H; m 1956 to Diann Lea Harris; c Cheryl Beth, David F & Mark J. Educ: Eastern A&M Jr Col, 54-56; Okla Baptist Univ, BS, 56; Okla Univ Sch Law, JD, 63; Delta Theta Phi (pres, 63). Polit & Govt Pos: Munic judge, Midwest City, Okla, 64-70; Okla State Sen, 70-, vchmn educ comt, mem judiciary, munic govt, pub safety & penal affairs & wildlife comts, Okla State Senate, currently, chmn common educ comt & mem banks & banking, judiciary & social welfare comts, 73- Bus & Prof Pos: Speech teacher & basketball coach, Wetumka High Sch, 56-57; attorney, Smith, Johns & Neuffer, Oklahoma City, 63-65; partner, Johns, Howell & Webber, Law Firm, 66-; dir, Baptist Mem Hosp; bd trustees, Okla Baptist Univ, 73. Mem: Okla Bar Asn; Okla Co Bar Asn (dir); Am & Okla Trial Lawyers Asns; NAm Judges Asn. Honors & Awards: Outstanding Citizen of Midwest City Award & Distinguished Serv Award, Jr CofC, 70 & 71; nominated, Outstanding Young Man of Okla, 70; Most Promising Young Senator, Okla State Senate, 72; Selected One of Top Five Senators, 73. Relig: Baptist; youth dir, First Baptist Church, Midwest City, 57-61, chmn deacons, 64-67, trustee, supt, Sunday Sch & teacher, 62-70. Mailing Add: 3101 Glenoaks Midwest City OK 73110

HOWELL, MAX (D)
Ark State Sen
b Lonoke, Ark, Dec 22, 15; s Flavius Josephus Howell & Margaret Anthony H; m 1967 to Inez Donham; c Max, Jr, Patricia (Mrs Tate), Rachel, William, Katrina & Don. Educ: Ark Law Sch, 37-40. Polit & Govt Pos: Ark State Rep, 46-50; Ark State Sen, First Dist, 50- Mil Serv: Entered as Pvt, Air Force, 42, released as Maj, 46; Col, Army Res, currently. Mem: Ark & Am Bar Asns; Am Legion; Mason; Consistory. Relig: Presbyterian. Legal Res: 1200 Oakhurst Jacksonville AR 72076 Mailing Add: 211 Spring St Little Rock AR 72201

HOWELL, PINKNEY ALBERT (D)
Md State Deleg
b Chesterfield, SC, Feb 10, 16; s Pinkney Howell & Rebecca Hillen H; m 1938 to Sarah Elizabeth Paige; c Rosemary (Mrs George Douglas), Sara (Mrs Eugene Smalley), Olivia (Mrs David Alexander) & Pinkie (Mrs James Drayton). Educ: Univ Md, 62-69; Loyola Col, 69-71. Polit & Govt Pos: Md State Deleg, 41st Dist, 73-, mem environ matters comt & spec joint comt on corrections, Md House Deleg, 74- Bus & Prof Pos: Teacher, Baltimore Pub Sch 181, 62-; businessman, Hilton Court Liquors, 74-, vpres, 75. Mem: Mason; Falcon Rod & Gun Club; Craftsmen Club; Md State & Nat Educ Asns; Md State & DC Barber Asn, AFL-CIO (vpres). Honors & Awards: Cert of Achievement for Outstanding Leadership in Field of Educ, Polit & Community Action, Douglass Adult High Sch, 73. Relig: Methodist; Layleaders, 70-73. Mailing Add: 2815 Mohawk Ave Baltimore MD 21207

HOWELL, RICHARD S (R)
Chmn, Cowlitz Co Rep Party, Wash
b Longview, Wash, Oct 27, 35; s Gen Sherman Howell & Corderlia Gabriel H; m 1959 to Caroline Jean McCoy; c Richard Keith, Michael Sherman & Amy Lynn. Educ: Centralia Jr Col, AA, 59; Wash State Univ, BA & MS; Alpha Tau Alpha. Polit & Govt Pos: Committeeman, Wash State Rep Party, 71-73; chmn, Cowlitz Co Rep Party, currently, committeeman, Dungan Precinct, currently. Bus & Prof Pos: Pres, Agr Teachers Dist, SW Wash, 70-72; pres, Kelso Educ Asn, 71-73, negotiator, 8 years; prof negotiator, Wash Educ Asn, 72-74, budget consult, 74-75. Mil Serv: Entered as Pvt, Army, 54, released as Pfc, 56, after serv in Mil Intel SigC, Orient, 55-56; Normal Awards & Decorations. Mem: Nat, Wash & Kelso Educ Asns; Elks; Voc Agr Teachers. Honors & Awards: Hon State Farmer, Future Farmers Am, 70, Hon Am Farmer, 75. Relig: Methodist. Mailing Add: 2910 Allen St Kelso WA 98626

HOWELL, ROLLIN KNIGHT (D)
Iowa State Rep
b Rockford, Iowa, Mar 24, 29; s Floyd Knight Howell & Ella M Roehr H; m 1950 to Joyce Elaine Stiles; c Barbara J (Mrs James D Hoff), Steven K & David M. Polit & Govt Pos: Precinct committeeman, Scott Twp, Iowa, several years; chmn, Floyd Co Dem Party, 69-; Iowa State Rep, 13th Dist, 73- Mil Serv: Entered as Pvt, Army, 50, released as Cpl, 53, after serv in Eng Corps, Far East, 52-53. Mem: Nat Farmers Orgn; Nat Farmers Union; Butler Co Rural Elec Coop; Am Legion. Relig: Methodist; chmn social concerns, United Methodist Church. Mailing Add: RFD 2 Box 144 Rockford IA 50468

HOWELL, WARREN LOMAX (INDEPENDENT)
b Montgomery, Ala, May 4, 40; s Warren Howell & Elna Miller H; m 1962 to Martha Wilson; c Jayna Elizabeth & Christopher Lomax. Educ: Troy State Univ, BS in Educ, 62, MS in Educ, 65; Auburn Univ; Kappa Delta Pi; Phi Delta Kappa; Lambda Chi Alpha. Polit & Govt Pos: Deleg, Rep Nat Conv, 72. Bus & Prof Pos: Coach & teacher, Pub Schs, Prattville, Ala, Ozark, Ala & Panama City, Fla, 62-65; coach & instr, Troy State Univ, 66-70; headmaster, SMontgomery Acad, 70-71; first exec dir, Ala Private Sch Asn, 71- Mem: Ala Comn on Higher Educ; Southern Independent Sch Asn (bd dirs); Citizen Adv Bd on State & Local Govt; Int Platform Asn; Youth Adv Coun, Ala. Mailing Add: 3340 Montezuma Rd Montgomery AL 36106

HOWELL, WILLIAM MOBLEY (D)
Ga State Rep
b Blakely, Ga, Aug 18, 20; s William Omar Howell & Lottye Smith H; m 1972 to Joanne Turner; c William Omar & Charlotte Frances. Educ: S Ga Col. Polit & Govt Pos: Ga State Sen, Ninth Dist, 57-58; Ga State Rep, 86th Dist, 65- Mil Serv: Navy, World War II. Mem: Blakely-Early Co CofC (exec dir); Mason; Rotary; Am Legion; VFW. Relig: Methodist. Mailing Add: PO Box 348 Blakely GA 31723

HOWER, WARD (D)
Mem, Idaho Dem State Cent Comt
b Cowley, Wyo, June 18, 21; s Oliver Hower & Mabel Kinnison H; m 1955 to Phyllis Phillips; c Philip & Mark. Educ: Stanford Univ, AB, 47, JD, 49; Phi Alpha Delta. Polit & Govt Pos: Legis asst, US Sen Frank Church, Idaho, 57-61, admin asst, 61-64; dep dir, Peace Corps, Brazil, 64-66, dir, Guyana, 66-68, dep dir, Off of Eval, 68-70; prosecuting attorney, Valley Co, Idaho, 70-72; deleg, Dem Nat Conv, 72; mem, Idaho Dem State Cent Comt, 74- Bus & Prof Pos: Practicing lawyer, Cascade, Idaho, 70- Mil Serv: Entered as Seaman 2/C, Navy, 41, released as Capt, Marine Corps Res, 45, after serv in 2nd Marine Air Wing, Southwest Pac, 42-45; Air Medal. Mem: Idaho State Bar. Mailing Add: PO Box 799 Cascade ID 83611

HOWLAND, JOHN HUDSON, SR (R)
Vt State Sen
b Windsor, Vt, Nov 14, 15; s Glenn C Howland & Flora Hudson H; m 1941 to Mary Kiernan; c Mary Ann (Mrs Francis McFaun), John H, Jr, William G, Margaret M & Glenn C. Educ: Phillips Exeter Acad, 35; Harvard Univ, BS, 39. Polit & Govt Pos: Vt State Sen, 74- Bus & Prof Pos: Founder & pres, Windsor Mach Prod, 50-65; founder & mgr, Mt Ascutney Ski Area, 56-65; exec secy, Vt Asn Ins Agents, 66. Mil Serv: Entered as Ens, Navy, 43, released as Lt(jg), 45, after serv as Exec Officer LSM 213, Pac Theatre. Publ: Ed, Green Mountain Agent, Vt Asn Ins Agents. Mem: Rotary; Vt Farm Bur; Am Legion; Hist Windsor Inc (dir); CofC (dir). Honors & Awards: Citation from Am Legion for employing handicapped vets, 54; Award of Merit, President Eisenhower Comt on Employ of Handicapped, 74. Relig: Catholic. Legal Res: West Windsor VT Mailing Add: PO Box 44 Windsor VT 05089

HOWLETT, MICHAEL J (D)
Secy of State, Ill
b Chicago, Ill, Aug 30, 14; m to Helen Geary; c Michael, Robert, Edward, Catherine, Mary Christine & Helen Marie. Educ: DePaul Univ, 34. Polit & Govt Pos: Chicago Area dir of Nat Youth Admin, 40-42; Ill State Bank Examr; exec dir, Off Orgn & Admin, Chicago Park Dist; regional dir, Off of Price Stabilization, 51; State Auditor of Pub Acct, Ill, 60-72; deleg, Dem Nat Conv, 68 & 72; Secy of State, Ill, 73- Bus & Prof Pos: Ins bus, 37-40; vpres, Sun Steel Co, Chicago, 52-60. Mil Serv: Navy, 42-45. Honors & Awards: Winner many Amateur Athletic Union gold medals & Inter-Ocean Swimming championships. Legal Res: 9630 S Winchester Chicago IL 60643 Mailing Add: 213 State House Springfield IL 62706

HOWSDEN, ARLEY LEVERN (D)
b Huntley, Nebr, Oct 17, 26; s Harry Ray Howsden & Hattie K Donley H; m 1947 to Vivian May McCready; c Jo Ann (Mrs Alsey), Jean (Mrs House), Harry Scott, Karen, Kathie & Jan. Educ: Univ Nebr, BS, 48, MA, 52 & EdD, 58. Polit & Govt Pos: Pres, Chico Dem Club, Calif, 63; mem, Butte Co Dem Cent Comt, 64-65, vchmn, 71-73, chmn, 73-75; co supvr, Butte Co, 65-71; Butte Co chmn for McCarthy Comt, 68; alt deleg, Dem Nat Conv, 68; mem, Calif State Dem Cent Comt, 72-75. Bus & Prof Pos: Supt & coach, Axtell, Nebr, 48-51; high sch coach & teacher, North Platte, 51-53; dir of educ, Am Samoa, 53-54; supt of schs, Oxford, Nebr, 55-56; commun educ coordr, Univ Nebr, 56-58; prof educ, Calif State Univ, Chico, 58-, dean sch educ, 70- Mil Serv: Pvt, Army Specialized Training Prog, Army, 44-45. Mem: Life mem Nat Educ Asn; Far Western Philos of Educ; Rotary; Mason; Toastmasters. Relig: Unitarian. Mailing Add: Rte 2 Box 263 Chico CA 95926

HOY, REX BRUCE (R)
Kans State Rep
b Lincoln, Nebr, July 27, 28; s Les B Hoy & Mabel Gilliland H; m 1948 to Lillian Kathryn Roth; c Sharon Rae. Educ: Univ Nebr, Lincoln, BS, 52; Purdue Univ Life Ins Mkt Inst, 62-63. Polit & Govt Pos: Mem, City of Mission Planning Coun, Kans, 65-66; Kans State Rep, 24th Dist, 69- Bus & Prof Pos: Vpres, Metrop Aviation, 68-69. Mil Serv: Entered as Pfc, Army Engrs, 45, released as T-5, 46, after serv in Hq Co 123 Eng Surv Bn, Ft Belvoir & Japan; World War II Victory Medal; Army of Occup Medal, Japan. Mem: Life Underwriters Asn; Mission CofC; Optimists; Mason; Univ Nebr Alumni Asn. Relig: Methodist. Mailing Add: 3801 Johnson Dr Shawnee Mission KS 66205

HOYER, STENY HAMILTON (D)
Md State Sen
b New York, NY, June 14, 39; s Steen Hamilton Hoyer & Jean Baldwin H; m 1961 to Judith Elaine Pickett; c Susan, Stefany & Anne. Educ: Univ Md, BS, 63; Georgetown Univ Law Sch, LLB, 66; Omicron Delta Kappa; Pi Sigma Alpha; Kalegethos; Sigma Chi. Polit & Govt Pos: Exec asst to US Sen Daniel B Brewster, 62-66; pres, Young Dem Clubs of Md, 64-65; Md State Sen, 67-, pres, Md State Senate, 75-; deleg, Dem Nat Conv, 68; first vpres, Young Dem Clubs Am, 69- Bus & Prof Pos: Attorney, Haislip & Yewell, 66-68; attorney, gen practice, 68-69; partner, Hoyer & Fannon, 69- Mem: Am & Md Bar Asns; Am Trial Lawyers Asn; Am Judicature Soc; Crescent Cities Jaycees. Honors & Awards: Outstanding Male Grad, Univ Md, 63. Relig: Baptist. Legal Res: 6621 Lacona St Berkshire MD 20028 Mailing Add: 6108 Old Silver Hill Rd District Heights MD 20028

HOYT, NORRIS (D)
Vt State Rep
b Chicago, Ill, July 23, 35; s Norris Hulbert Hoyt & Jean Archibald H; m 1974 to Kathleen Conner Clark. Educ: Amherst Col, AB, 57; Harvard Law Sch, JD, 61; Boston Univ Law Sch, LLM, 69. Polit & Govt Pos: Asst gen counsel, Nat Sci Found, 62-68; gen counsel & dep comnr, Vt Dept of Taxes, 69-71; legal counsel to Gov Vt, 73-74; Vt State Rep, 75-, mem ways & means comt, Vt House Rep, 75- Bus & Prof Pos: Lawyer, Norwich, Vt, 71- Mem: Vt Bar

Asn. Legal Res: Upper Turnpike Rd Norwich VT 05055 Mailing Add: PO Box L Norwich VT 05055

HOYT, WILLIAM B (D)
NY State Assemblyman
Mailing Add: 16 Irving Pl Buffalo NY 14201

HRIC, PAUL J (D)
Ind State Rep
Mailing Add: 7039 Northcote Ave Hammond IN 46324

HRUSKA, ROMAN LEE (R)
US Sen, Nebr
b David City, Nebr, Aug 16, 04; s Joseph C Hruska & Caroline L H; m 1930 to Victoria E Kuncl; c Roman L, Jr, Quentin J & Jana L. Educ: Univ Omaha; Univ Chicago Law Sch, 28; Creighton Univ Col of Law, LLB, 29. Hon Degrees: LLD, Creighton Univ & Doane Col; HHD, Coe Col. Polit & Govt Pos: Chmn bd of co comnr, Douglas Co, Nebr, 45-52; mem adv comt, Nebr Bd of Control, 47-52; pres, Nebr Asn of Co Officers, 50-51; mem bd of regents, Univ Omaha, 50-57; vpres, Nat Asn of Co Officers, 51-52; US Sen, Nebr, 54-; deleg, Rep Nat Conv, 68 & 72. Bus & Prof Pos: Attorney-at-law. Mem: Nebr State & Am Bar Asns; Kiwanis; Shrine; Nebr Fraternal Cong. Relig: Unitarian. Legal Res: 2139 S 38th St Omaha NE 68105 Mailing Add: Senate Off Bldg Washington DC 20510

HUBBARD, ARTHUR J, SR (D)
Ariz State Sen
Mailing Add: Box 451 Ganado AZ 86505

HUBBARD, CARROLL, JR (D)
US Rep, Ky
b Murray, Ky, July 7, 37; s Dr Carroll Hubbard, Sr & Addie Beth Shelton H; m 1966 to Joyce Lynn Hall. Educ: Georgetown Col, BA, 59; Univ Louisville, LLB, 62; Delta Omicron Kappa; Kappa Alpha. Polit & Govt Pos: Vpres, Young Dem Ky, 60, state col chmn, 60 & 62; Ky State Sen, First Dist, 68-75; US Rep, First Dist, Ky, 75- Mil Serv: Entered as Airman Basic, Air Force Nat Guard, 62, Capt, 69-71; Army Nat Guard Selective Serv Hq, Legal Adv for Ky Selective Serv, 67-71; Mem: Ky & Am Bar Asns; Phi Alpha Delta; Rotary; Jaycees. Honors & Awards: Selected as Outstanding Young Man of Graves Co, Ky, 3 years; One of Three Outstanding Young Men of Ky, Ky Jaycees, 68. Relig: Southern Baptist. Legal Res: 410 Macedonia Rd Mayfield KY 42066 Mailing Add: 423 Cannon House Off Bldg Washington DC 20515

HUBBARD, DORTHY STUART (DOTTY) (D)
Mem, Mo State Dem Comt
b Hannibal, Mo, Aug 14, 28; d Grover Cleveland Stuart & Hattie Garver S; m 1947 to Richard Glenn Hubbard; c Kyle Jean. Educ: Center Pub Schs, Center, Mo, 12 years. Polit & Govt Pos: Secy, Marion Co Young Dem, Mo, 58-59; admin vpres, Mo Young Dem, 61, nat committeewoman, 64-66; chmn, Ninth Dist Mo Young Dem, 62; pres, Marion Co Womens Dem Club, 69-, corresponding secy, 72-73; fourth vpres, Ninth Dist Womens Dem Clubs, 70-71, second vpres, 71-73; mem, Mo Dem State Comt, 70-; secy treas, Mo Dem Days Exec Bd, 71- Mem: Eastern Star (Worthy Matron, 72-73); Abilities Develop Orgn (adv bd); Hannibal Study Club; Hannibal Assembly, Rainbow Girls (mother adv); Hannibal Parliamentary Law Club Federated. Honors & Awards: Hon Lt Col on staff, former Gov Sanders, Ga. Relig: United Methodist; secy, Comt Archives & Hist, Mo E Conf United Methodists, asst supt, Oakwood Methodist Sunday Sch; lay speaker; mem, pastoral rels comt, deleg, annual Conf Sunday Sch Teachers. Mailing Add: 1406 Viley Hannibal MO 63401

HUBBARD, EULA PEARL (R)
Committeewoman, Russell Co Rep Party, Ky
b Jamestown, Ky, May 4, 97; d Christopher Colombus Holt & Gertrude Lawless H; m 1921 to Zelmer Ray Hill, div 1937; c Jean (Mrs Schlehuber) & Jack Owsley; m 1939 to Sam R Hubbard. Educ: Lindsley Wilson Col, teachers cert, 16. Polit & Govt Pos: Postmistress, Montpelier, Ky, 17; toured Ky during state & nat campaigns to organize Rep party from precinct level; organizer & mem, Russell Co Rep Womens Club; committeewoman, Russell Co Rep Party, 45- Bus & Prof Pos: Owner & operator, appliance & furniture store, Russell Springs, Ky, 20 years. Mem: Eastern Star (Past Worthy Matron); Bus & Prof Women Club; Lincoln Club. Honors & Awards: Ky Col; Eisenhower Award, presented by President & Mrs Nixon; plaque from fifth dist congressman. Relig: Christian Church. Mailing Add: Jamestown St Russell Springs KY 42642

HUBBARD, KEITH W (R)
Ariz State Rep
Mailing Add: 1717 W Flower Phoenix AZ 85015

HUBBARD, ORVILLE LISCUM (R)
Mayor, Dearborn, Mich
b Union City, Mich, Apr 2, 03; s Ralph Star Hubbard (deceased) & Sylvia Elizabeth Hart H (deceased); m 1927 to Fay Cameron; c four sons, one daughter. Educ: Marine Corps Inst; Int Correspondence Schs; US Army exten courses; Detroit Inst Technol; Ferris Inst; Detroit Col Law, LLB, 32; Univ Mich & Henry Ford Community Col, exten courses. Polit & Govt Pos: Cand, Mich State Senate, 32; Rep precinct deleg, Dearborn, Mich, 32; Asst Attorney Gen, Mich, 39-40; alt deleg, Rep Nat Conv, 40, deleg, 52; mem, Wayne Co Bd Supvr, 42-68 & former mem airport & ways & means comts; mayor, Dearborn, 42- Bus & Prof Pos: Farm hand, factory worker, cement factory, Union City, Mich; employee serv dept, Dodge Bros, Hamtramck, Mich, 20; laborer, clerk & stenographer purchasing dept, Ford Motor Co, Detroit, Mich, 25; secy to dir purchasing, Chrysler Corp, Highland Park; reporter, Wall St J, Detroit Bur, 29-34; Mich State Trooper, 42-45. Mil Serv: Marine Corps, Sgt, 22-25; Army Res, officer, 30-37. Publ: Government-In-Exile, 50. Mem: Dearborn Bar Asn; Marine Corps League (first state commandant). Honors & Awards: Recipient of Distinguished Citizen Award, Dearborn CofC, 62; defeated every year for ten years for pub off until first elected mayor in 1941; holds nat longevity record for serv as full-time mayor; honored by US Marine Corps on 50th anniversary of joining the Marines, Parris Island, 72. Legal Res: 7055 Mead Dearborn MI 48126 Mailing Add: Off of the Mayor City Hall Dearborn MI 48126

HUBENAK, JOE ADOLPH (D)
Tex State Rep
b Frenstat, Tex, July 2, 37; s John Joe Hubenak & Rosemary Polansky H; single. Educ: Alvin Jr Col, AA, 63; Univ Houston, BBA in Acct, 65; Phi Beta Kappa (pres, 62). Polit & Govt Pos: Tex State Rep, Dist 20, 69- Bus & Prof Pos: Partner, Hubenak & Webb, 63- Mil Serv: Entered as Pvt, Army, 55, released as Sgt 1/C, 62, after serv in Tex Nat Guard, 36th Div. Mem: Lions; CofC (Rosenberg-Richmond Br); Jr CofC (Rosenberg-Richmond Br); Farm Bur; KofC. Relig: Catholic. Legal Res: 1214 Austin St Rosenberg TX 77471 Mailing Add: 2635 Sequoia Rosenberg TX 77471

HUBER, DAVID G (R)
Maine State Sen
Mailing Add: 430 Blackstrap Rd Falmouth ME 04105

HUBER, JOHN (D)
Alaska State Sen
Mailing Add: PO Box 2591 Fairbanks AK 99701

HUBER, LEROY JAMES (D)
Secy, Perry Co Dem Comt, Mo
b Perryville, Mo, July 5, 27; s Edwin F Huber & Inice Colin H; m 1948 to Velma Lee Gibbar. Educ: Univ Mo, 1 year; Rubicam Bus Sch, grad. Polit & Govt Pos: Comnr spec rd dist 1, Perry Co, Mo, 15 years, pres, 7 years; committeeman, Perry Co Dem Party, 63-; chmn, Perry Co Dem Comt, formerly, secy, currently. Bus & Prof Pos: Real estate broker, Huber & Beeson Real Estate, 48-50; farmer, Perry Co, Mo, 50-60; salesman, Perryville Steel, Butler Bldgs, 60-62; owner & operator, Hubers House of Color, 60- Mil Serv: Entered as A/S, Navy, 45, released as Yeoman 3/C, 46, after serv on USS Ellyson DMS 19. Publ: Ed, Voice, Dem Quart, Perry Co Dem Comt, 69. Mem: Farmer Elected Committeeman Orgn; Mo Construction Orgn; Am Legion; VFW; KofC. Relig: Catholic. Mailing Add: Rte 3 Box 263A Perryville MO 63775

HUBER, OSCAR EDWIN (R)
Chmn, Edmunds Co Rep Party, SDak
b Bowdle, SDak, Aug 22, 17; s Richard F Huber & Rosina Schlaht H; m 1974 to Judith Sheppard. Educ: Northern State Col, Aberdeen, SDak, BS, 41; Univ Minn, grad study, 52-53; Northern State Col, grad study, 59-60; Sigma Delta Epsilon; Kappa Delta Pi. Polit & Govt Pos: SDak State Rep, 60-72, chmn, Munic & Mil Affairs Comt, SDak House Rep, 67-68, chmn, Comt on Educ, 69-72; mem, Local Govt Study Comn, 66-67; chmn, Edmunds Co Rep Party, 75- Bus & Prof Pos: Prin & teacher, Roscoe High Sch, 46-57; teacher, Hosmer High Sch, 57-58. Mem: Elks. Relig: Lutheran. Mailing Add: Bowdle SD 57428

HUBER, RAY ARLEN (D)
b Quakertown, Pa, June 23, 33; s Percy Dubbs Huber & Pearl Fluck H; m 1957 to Karin Margaret Mathiesen; c Ray Alan, Jr, Kent Brian, Scott Kevin, Dirk Michael & Cindy Michelle. Educ: Moravian Col, 3 years; Pi Delta Epsilon. Polit & Govt Pos: Fed proj coordr, Mayor's Off, Bethlehem, Pa, 66; admin asst to US Rep Fred B Rooney, Pa, 66- Bus & Prof Pos: Ed, Moravian Col Student Newspaper, 54-55; staff writer & columnist, Bethlehem, Pa Globe-Times Newspaper, 58-66. Mil Serv: Entered as Pvt, Army, released as SP-3, after serv in Army Security Agency, Europe, 55-58. Honors & Awards: Four Keystone Press Awards for News Writing, Pa Newspaper Publishers Asn. Relig: United Church of Christ. Legal Res: Bethlehem PA 18017 Mailing Add: 9424 Wallingford Dr Burke VA 22015

HUBER, ROBERT DANIEL (R)
Mem, Marin Co Rep Cent Comt, Calif
b Charlotte, Mich, Dec 20, 22; s Charles Huber & Maybel Holden H; m 1946 to Jean Murray; c David, Jane, Timothy & Mary. Educ: Univ Mich, AB, 47; Univ San Francisco, JD, 50; Tau Kappa Epsilon. Polit & Govt Pos: City councilman, Mill Valley, Calif, 54-62, mayor, 56-62; mem, Marin Co Rep Cent Comt, 61-; mem, State Rep Cent Comt, Calif, 64- Bus & Prof Pos: Partner, Hassard, Bonnington, Rogers & Huber, San Francisco, 50- Mil Serv: Entered as A/S, Navy, 42, released as Ens, 46, after serv on Tanker, Pac Theatre, 42-44. Mem: Calif, Am & San Francisco Bar Asns. Relig: Protestant. Mailing Add: 245 Tamalpais Mill Valley CA 94941

HUBER, ROBERT J (R)
b Detroit, Mich, Aug 29, 22; m to Mary Pauline Tolleson. Educ: Ford Sch in Detroit; Culver Mil Acad; Sheffield Sci Sch, Yale Univ, BS, 43. Polit & Govt Pos: Mem, Oakland Co Bd Supvr, Mich, 59-63; mayor, Troy, 59-64; Mich State Sen, 16th Dist, 64-70; US Rep, 18th Dist, formerly. Bus & Prof Pos: Dir, Alloy Steels, Inc, Detroit & Troy Nat Bank; pres, Tolber Corp, Hope, Ark & Mich Chrome & Chem Co, Detroit. Mil Serv: Entered as Pvt, Army, 43, released as 1st Lt, 46. Mem: Nat Asn Metal Finishers; Elks; Am Legion; City Club Lansing; Am Ord Asn. Relig: Catholic. Mailing Add: 4909 Beach Rd Troy MI 48084

HUBER, ROBERT T (D)
b Eckelson, NDak, Aug 29, 20; s Theodore J Huber & Rose Ziebert H; m 1944 to Beatrice Bartlein; c John Michael & Robert Thomas. Educ: West Allis High Sch, Wis, grad, 38. Polit & Govt Pos: Mem, Gov Comt on Wis Water Resources; Wis State Rep, 22nd Dist, 48-72; Minority Floor Leader, Wis State Assembly, 55, 57, 61, 63, 67 & 69, Speaker Pro Tem, 59, Speaker, 65; deleg, Dem Nat Conv, 68; Dem Nat Committeeman, Wis, 68-72. Bus & Prof Pos: Former contractor, 44-48; auto parts & serv salesman; merchandising salesman. Mem: Holy Name Soc; Local 9, Brewery Workers' Union; KofC. Relig: Catholic. Mailing Add: 2228 S 78th St West Allis WI 53219

HUBERT, RICHARD NORMAN (D)
Mem, Ga State Dem Exec Comt
b Decatur, Ga, Mar 24, 34; s Otis C Hubert & Ruth Swann H; m 1957 to Claire Marcom; c Richard Gregory, Rebecca Swann, May Kendall & Mary Ruth. Educ: Stetson Univ, 1 year; Duke Univ, AB, 57; Emory Univ Law Sch, LLB, 60; Alpha Tau Omega. Polit & Govt Pos: Judge, Atlanta Munic Court, Ga, 64-; mem, DeKalb Co Dem Exec Comt, 66-; mem, Ga State Dem Exec Comt, 71- Bus & Prof Pos: Law partner, Haas, Holland, Levison & Gilbert, 60- Mem: Am, Ga & Atlanta Bar Asns; Active Voters, Inc; Lawyers Club Atlanta. Relig: Unitarian. Mailing Add: 1155 Lullwater Rd NE Atlanta GA 30307

HUBING, LEE (R)
Mont State Rep
Mailing Add: Terry MT 59349

HUCKABA, FRANK J (D)
Mem, Ark State Dem Comt
b Oil Trough, Ark, Aug 1, 34; s Sylvester F Huckaba & Mabel French H; m 1959 to Joy M Sanders; c Parker Sanders, Marisa Ann & Melanie Lee. Educ: Ark State Univ, BS & BA,

52-58; Memphis State Univ, 57; Univ Ark, Fayetteville, LLB, 61; Pi Kappa Alpha. Polit & Govt Pos: Law clerk to Justice George Rose Smith, Ark Supreme Court, Little Rock, 61-62; spec agent, Fed Bur of Invest, Washington, DC, 62-65; chmn, Baxter Co Arkansans for Const of 70, Mountain Home, 70; dep prosecuting attorney, Baxter Co, 71-72; mem, Ark State Dem Comt, 71-; mem, Ark Pub Bldg Authority, 71- Mil Serv: Entered as Pvt, Army, 54, released as Sp-4, 56, after serv in Signal Bn, Far East Hq, Tokyo, Japan, 65-66; Foreign Serv Medal; Good Conduct Medal; Soldier of the Month. Publ: Auth of feature articles in Newport Daily & Weekly Independent, Ark, 59. Mem: Baxter-Marion Co Bar Asn; Ark & Am Bar Asns; Rotary Club. Relig: Baptist. Mailing Add: 200 W High St Mountain Home AR 72653

HUDDLESTON, WALTER (DEE) (D)
US Sen, Ky

b 1926; m 1947 to Martha Jean Pearce; c Stephen & Philip Dee. Educ: Univ Ky, BA. Polit & Govt Pos: Ky State Sen, 66-72; US Sen, Ky, 73-; deleg, Dem Nat Mid-Term Conf, 74; mem exec comt, Dem Nat Comt, currently. Bus & Prof Pos: Gen mgr, Radio Sta WIEL, 52-72. Mil Serv: Army, World War II. Mem: Ky Broadcasters Asn; CofC; Rotary. Relig: Methodist. Legal Res: KY Mailing Add: US Senate Washington DC 20510

HUDGINS, FLOYD (D)
Ga State Sen

b Gadsden, Ala, Mar 11, 30; s William L Hudgins & Ollie Hudgins H; m 1950 to Margie Louise Hand; c Floyd Wayne, Wanda Lynne & Sharon Janelle. Educ: St Clair Co High Sch, Odenville, Ala. Polit & Govt Pos: Ga State Rep, 64-66; Ga State Sen, currently. Bus & Prof Pos: Operating engrs, Columbus, Ga, 50- Mil Serv: Ga Nat Guard, 52-60. Mem: Mason. Relig: Methodist. Mailing Add: 1221 14th Ave Columbus GA 31906

HUDNUT, WILLIAM HERBERT, III (R)

b Cincinnati, Ohio, Oct 17, 32; s William Herbert Hudnut, Jr & Elizabeth Kilborne H; m 1974 to Susan Greer Rice; c Michael C, Laura Ann, Timothy N, William H, IV & Theodore B. Educ: Princeton Univ, BA, 54; Union Theol Sem, New York, BD summa cum laude, 57; Phi Beta Kappa; Charter Club. Hon Degrees: DD, Hanover Col, 67 & Wabash Col, 69. Polit & Govt Pos: Mem, Bd of Pub Safety, Ind, 70-72, acting dir, 72; US Rep, Ind, 73-75. Bus & Prof Pos: Asst minister, Westminster Presby Church, Buffalo, NY, 57-60; sr minister, First Presby Church, Annapolis, Md, 60-63 & Second Presby Church, Indianapolis, Ind, 63-72. Publ: Samuel Stanhope Smith, enlightened conservative, J of Hist of Ideas, 9/55; Art of love through management, Personnel Mgt Mag; plus several sermons in different issues of The Pulpit. Mem: Moose; Columbia Club; Scottish Rite; Indianapolis Antelope Club. Relig: Presbyterian. Mailing Add: 722 Pine Dr Indianapolis IN 46260

HUDSON, BETTY (D)
Conn State Sen

b Port Chester, NY, Mar 5, 31; d Ernest Bagi & Mary Mihalo B; m 1952 to Donald E Hudson; c Leigh & Todd. Educ: Mich State Univ, 50-52. Polit & Govt Pos: Mem, Madison Dem Town Comt, Conn, 70-; selectwoman, Madison Bd Selectmen, 72-75; mem, Madison Conserv Comn, 72-75; comnr, Permanent Comn on Status of Women, 75-; Conn State Sen, 33rd Dist, 75-, mem, Appropriations Comt, Senate chairperson, Human Rights & Opportunities Comt, Human Serv Comt & Subcomt on Welfare, Conn Gen Assembly, 75- Mem: Conn & Madison League of Women Voters; Order of Women Legislators; Nat & Conn Women's Polit Caucus. Mailing Add: 155 Bishop Lane Madison CT 06443

HUDSON, CALE (R)
Kans State Sen

Mailing Add: 933 S Evergreen Chanute KS 66720

HUDSON, COLA H (R)
Vt State Rep

Mailing Add: Box 511 Lyndonville VT 05851

HUDSON, DOUGLAS (R)
NY State Sen

m to Mildred Purdy; c one son. Educ: Albany Bus Col. Polit & Govt Pos: App Co Welfare Comnr, NY, 42, elected 3 terms; sheriff, Rensselaer Co, 2 terms; former NY State Assemblyman; NY State Sen, 67-; deleg, Rep Nat Conv, 72. Mailing Add: 116 Green Ave Castleton-on-Hudson NY 12033

HUDSON, EUGENE TALMADGE (TED) (D)
Ga State Rep

b Ocilla, Ga, Feb 8, 23; s Dee Dugley Hudson & Ella F Williams H; m 1957 to Anne Bass, c Julianne & Mike Harris. Educ: Univ Ga, BSA in Agronomy, BSA in Animal Husbandry & BSA in Agr Econ. Polit & Govt Pos: Ga State Rep, Post Two, 48th Dist, 69-73, Ga State Rep, 115th Dist, 73- Bus & Prof Pos: Registered prof sanitarian, Ga State Health Dept, 63- Mil Serv: Entered as Pvt, Army, 43, released as Lt, 46, after serv in Armor Cavalry, Southwest Pac Theatre, 44-46; Combat Inf Badge; Battle Stars; Comn Ribbon. Mem: Elks; Mason; RAM; Shrine; Farm Bur. Honors & Awards: Gov Staff, Congressman Stuckey's Staff. Relig: Methodist. Mailing Add: 301 Glynn Ave Fitzgerald GA 31750

HUDSON, GEORGE (RAY) (R)
Ill State Rep

Mailing Add: 520 Walter Rd Hinsdale IL 60521

HUDSON, JAMES WEISSINGER (R)

b Des Moines, Iowa, Aug 31, 25; s Fred M Hudson & Anne E Weissinger H; m 1949 to Frances Leone Whisler; c James C, Carol Ann, David Carl & Thomas Edwin. Educ: Univ Iowa, BA, 48, LLB, 50; Sigma Nu; Phi Delta Phi. Polit & Govt Pos: Co Attorney, Pocahontas Co Iowa, 55-60; city attorney, Pocahontas, currently; chmn, Pocahontas Co Rep Party, 60-74; dir, Bd Educ, Pocahontas Community Sch, 71-74. Bus & Prof Pos: Pres, Pocahontas CofC; mem bd, Pocahontas Community Found. Mil Serv: Entered as Pvt, Army Air Corps, 44, released as 2nd Lt, 46. Mem: Iowa State & Am Bar Asns; Mason; Am Legion; Rotary. Relig: Methodist. Mailing Add: 1000 Sunset Dr Pocahontas IA 50574

HUDSON, MORLEY ALVIN (R)
VChmn NW Region, Rep Party, La

b San Antonio, Tex, Mar 31, 17; s Oscar Alvin Hudson & Ruth Morley H; m 1944 to Lucy Worthington North; c Nancy, Lucy & Courtney. Educ: Ga Tech, BS in Mech Eng, 38; Tau Beta Pi; Omicron Delta Kappa; Phi Kappa Phi. Polit & Govt Pos: La State Rep, 64-68, Minority Leader, La House of Rep, 64-68; deleg, Rep Nat Conv, 64 & 68; campaign mgr, Nixon-Agnew Campaign, 68; state vchmn NW Region, Rep Party, La, 68-; Rep cand for Lt Gov, La, 72; La State dep chmn, Comt to Reelect the President, 72. Bus & Prof Pos: Pres & gen mgr, Hudson-Rush Co, 52-; vpres, McElroy Metal Mills, Inc, 62-74; dir, United Servs Fund, Inc, 74- Mil Serv: Entered as Lt, Army, 38, released as Capt, 42, after serv in Inf. Mem: Am Soc Mech Engrs; Shreveport Power Squadron. Relig: Presbyterian. Mailing Add: 4609 Gilbert Dr Shreveport LA 71106

HUDSON, PERRY J (D)
Ga State Sen

Mailing Add: 3380 Old Jonesboro Rd Hapeville GA 30354

HUDSON, SAMUEL W, III (D)
Tex State Rep

Mailing Add: 5220 Fleetwood Oaks 110 Dallas TX 75235

HUDSON, WINSON (D)
Chmn, Leake Co Dem Party, Miss

b Carthage, Miss, Nov 17, 16; s John Wesley Gates & Emma Gates Kirkland; wid. Educ: Mary Holmes Col, 72; Southern Legal Rights Asn, lay advocate, 75. Polit & Govt Pos: Chmn, Leake Co Dem Party, Miss, 72-; Social Serv specialist, Head Start Prog, 73-; Justice of the Peace, 75- Publ: Soul Sister, Grace Halsell, 71. Mem: Leake Branch NAACP (pres, 61-); Am Civil Liberties Union (mem bd). Honors & Awards: Testimonious Day, 74. Mailing Add: Rt 3 Box 287 Carthage MS 39051

HUEBNER, LEE WILLIAM (R)

b Sheboygan, Wis, Oct 23, 40; s Carl W Huebner & Doris Hultgren H; single. Educ: Northwestern Univ, BA, 62; Harvard Univ, MA, 63, PhD, 68; Phi Beta Kappa. Polit & Govt Pos: Pres, Ripon Soc, Inc, 67-69; staff asst, White House, Washington, DC, 69-71, Dep Spec Asst, 71-73, spec asst to the President & assoc dir, Ed Dept, 73- Bus & Prof Pos: Teaching fel in hist, Harvard Univ, 64-68, dir debate, 67-68; instr, Nat High Sch Inst in Speech, Northwestern Univ, 63-68. Publ: Co-ed, The Ripon Papers, 1963-1968, Nat Press, 68; contrib, History of US Political Parties, Chelsea House, 73. Relig: Lutheran. Legal Res: 738 N 28th St Sheboygan WI 53081 Mailing Add: Apt 221 2475 Virginia Ave NW Washington DC 20037

HUENEFELD, FRED, JR (D)
Mem, Dem Nat Comt, La

Mailing Add: 2100 Pargoud Blvd Monroe LA 71201

HUENNEKENS, HERBERT F (D)
Mont State Rep

b Milwaukee, Wis, June 26, 12; s Alfred R Huennekens & Clara Frank H; m 1937 to Helen M Little; c Robert J & Holly D. Educ: Univ Wis-Milwaukee, 30-35; Univ Wis-Madison, PhB, 40; US Dept Agr Grad Sch; Pa State Univ. Polit & Govt Pos: Bd mem, Dept Natural Resources & Conserv, State of Mont, 72; Mont State Rep, Dist 68, 73-, chmn judiciary comt, Mont House Rep, 75- Bus & Prof Pos: Meteorologist, Nat Weather Serv, 36-72; cattle ranch operator, 54- Mil Serv: Entered as Pvt, Army Air Corps, 42, released as S/Sgt, 45, after serv in 451st Bomb Group, Mediter, 44-45; Air Medal with Three Palms; Distinguished Unit Citation with Two Palms; Mediter Theater with Eight Battle Stars. Mem: Wilderness Asn; Sierra Club; Southern Mont Am Civil Liberties Union (dir); Northern Rocky Mt Ctr on Environ; Rod & Gun Club (bd dirs, 68-75, vpres, 72). Honors & Awards: First non-attorney to be chmn judiciary comt, Mont House Rep, in over two decades. Relig: Unitarian-Universalist. Legal Res: 3216 Rimrock Rd Billings MT 59102 Mailing Add: Mont House of Rep Helena MT 59601

HUFF, BEATTIE EUGENE (D)
SC State Rep

b Greenville, SC, May 21, 11; s Beattie Gustavis Huff & Lora Edwards H; m 1942 to Gladys L Rainey; c Glenda (Mrs Eddie West), Eugenia (Mrs H Miles), Beattie Greg, Lora Victoria & Gladys Elizabeth. Educ: Lincoln Mem Univ. Polit & Govt Pos: SC State Rep, 61- Bus & Prof Pos: Contractor; real estate. Mem: Lions; WOW; Farm Bur; CofC; Mason. Relig: Baptist. Mailing Add: White Horse Rd Rte 1 Greenville SC 29611

HUFF, DANIEL EMRA (R)
Ind State Rep

b Galesburg, Ill, June 24, 21; s Emra Orville Huff & Faye Meeks H; m 1943 to Barbara Jean Roe; c Carolyn Sue (Mrs Robert Ross) & Daniel Mark. Educ: Browns Bus Col, 46-48; Butler Univ, BA, 59; Christian Theol Sem, MDiv, 63, DDiv, 75. Polit & Govt Pos: Ind State Rep, 71- Bus & Prof Pos: Off mgr, Franseen Acct Serv, Galesburg, Ill, 46-48; chief acct & asst to bus mgr, Knox Col, 48-53; asst minister, First Christian Church, Galesburg, 53-55; minister, Augusta Christian Church & Linwood Christian Church, Indianapolis, 61-; vpres, Christian Church Orgn of Marion Co, 60-62, pres, 62-64; pres, Tuxedo Coun Churches, 63; prog chmn, World Conv Christian Churches, PR, 65; serv on numerous comts & bd of Ind Coun Churches, dist, state & nat levels of Christian Church & Church Fedn of Gtr Indianapolis; chmn, Marion Co Conf Local Govt, Church Fedn, 67; mem exec comt, Christian Church Union. Mil Serv: Entered as Pvt, Air Force, 42, released as Sgt, 45, after serv in US. Mem: Prof Activities for Prof Educ, Pendleton Prison Prog; Pub Action in Correctional Effort (bd dirs); Local Draft Bd; Christian Theol Sem Alumni Asn (pres); Northwest Marion Co Ministerial Asn. Relig: Christian Church. Mailing Add: 838 Ellenberger Pkwy W Dr Indianapolis IN 46219

HUFF, DOUGLAS, JR (D)
Ill State Sen

Mailing Add: 2834 W Warren Blvd Chicago IL 60612

HUFF, GENE (R)
Ky State Sen

b Franklin, Ohio, Oct 6, 29; s Adam Huff & Maud H; m 1952 to Ethel Delores Dayberry; c Georgia Arlene, Martin Blaine, Marsha Gail, Anna Marie & Roberta Jean. Educ: Union Col, AB, 60; Miami Univ, 61-62. Polit & Govt Pos: Pres, Young Rep, 66-67; Ky State Rep, 85th Dist, 68-72, Ky State Sen, Dist 21, 72-; alt deleg, Rep Nat Conv, 72. Bus & Prof Pos: Minister, Pentecostal Churches, 44- Mem: Rotary (pres). Relig: Protestant. Mailing Add: 231 E Fourth St London KY 40741

HUFF, IRA LU (R)
Chmn, Morgan Co Rep Cent Comt, Mo
b Gravois Mills, Mo, Oct 23, 19; d Ira B Williams & Mary Lucetta Holst W; m 1939 to Elmer Gregory Huff; c Robert G, Rebecca Ann (Mrs Claude Joy) & Rachel Lynn (Mrs Michael McDorman). Polit & Govt Pos: Treas, Morgan Co Rep Club, Mo, 56-60; mem, Morgan Co Rep Cent Comt, 56-, treas, 58-62, vchmn, 62-68 & chmn, 68-; mem, State Comt, Mo, 67-; circuit clerk & ex officio recorder of deeds, 75- Mem: Eastern Star (Past Matron); Eve Sorosis Federated Club; Gravois Mills Bus & Prof Womens Club; Westminister Presby Women's Asn. Relig: Presbyterian. Mailing Add: Rte 3 Versailles MO 65084

HUFF, LEROY CHRISTOPHER, JR (R)
Mem, DC Rep Comt
b Charlotte, NC, Dec 14, 31; s Leroy Christopher Huff, Sr & Estelle Lewis H; m 1958 to Ruby Juanita Ragins; c LaRoya A & Leroy Christopher, Jr. Educ: Benedict Col, BS, 54; Ind Univ, Bloomington, 58; George Washington Univ, MA, 70; Phi Delta Kappa. Polit & Govt Pos: Co-chmn & precinct capt, Precinct Organizing Task Force, Washington, DC, 68-; mem, DC Rep Comt, currently. Bus & Prof Pos: Teacher, DC Pub Schs, 65-74, actg asst principal, 75- Mem: Capital City Rep Club; Washington Teachers Union; BALCO Club. Relig: Methodist. Mailing Add: 524 Nicholson St NE Washington DC 20011

HUFF, LILLIAN (D)
Dem Nat Committeewoman, DC
Mailing Add: 5124 12th St NE Washington DC 20011

HUFF, MARK EMLY, JR (R)
b Wichita Falls, Tex, Oct 24, 34; s Mark Emly Huff, Sr & Opal Marley H; m 1956 to Lucy Ann Meissner; c Cheryl Lynn, Mark Emly, III, Joseph Edgar, Melinda Lee & Jennifer Ann. Educ: Univ Tex, Austin, 51-54, Univ Tex Southwestern Med Sch, MD, 58; intern, Dallas Methodist Hosp, 58-59; gen surgery residency, Dallas Vet Admin Hosp, 59-61; orthopedic surgery residency, Parkland Mem Hosp, 61-62 & 65-66, Baylor Univ Med Ctr, 66-67 & Tex Scottish Rite Crippled Children's Hosp, 67; Alpha Epsilon Delta; Phi Delta Theta; Kappa Psi. Polit & Govt Pos: Chmn, Wichita Co Rep Party, Tex, formerly; mem, US Dist Court Appointed Bi-Racial Comt, Wichita Falls, 70- Bus & Prof Pos: Orthopedic consult & acting chmn med adv comn, NTex Rehabilitation Ctr, 67-; med adv, Am Phys Therapy Asn, 67; chief orthopedics, Bethania Hosp, 72-73. Mil Serv: Entered as Capt, Air Force, 62, released as Capt, 65, after serv in Orthopedic Surgery, Sch Aerospace Med, Brooks AFB, Tex & Sheppard AFB, Tex, 62-65; Capt, Air Force Res, currently. Mem: Am Med Asn; Am Acad Orthopedic Surgeons; Phi Beta Pi; Rotary; Tex Archaeol Soc. Honors & Awards: Dipl, Am Bd Orthopedic Surgery. Relig: Christian Church. Mailing Add: 3000 Hamilton Wichita Falls TX 76308

HUFF, SARA ELLEN (D)
b Warren, Pa, Nov 14, 07; d Forrest Albert Huff & Mary Rebecca McAdoo H; single. Educ: Clarion State Col, 27-36; Wharton State Col Exten & Pa State Col Exten, 37-39; pvt lessons in pub speaking. Polit & Govt Pos: Supvr of bonds & ins, Pa State Liquor Control Bd, Harrisburg, 36-42; br supvr, Naval Supply Depot, Mechanicsburg, Pa, 42-55; mem & vchmn, Forest Co Dem Comt, 55; Dem cand for Pa State Rep, Forest Co, 56; Forest Co Dem State Comt, mem exec bd & policy comt, Pa Dem State Comt, 58-72, mem, State Comt, currently; mem, Gov Comt on Children & Youth, 59; deleg & secy Pa deleg, Dem Nat Conv, 68; regional dir, Pa Fedn Dem Women, 4 years; coordr for Forest Co Campaign of Auditor Gen of Pa, 72. Bus & Prof Pos: Elem sch teacher, Forest & Jefferson Co, Pa, 27-36; pres, Clarington Sand & Gravel Co, Clarington, Pa, 55-56; mem & secy bd, Polk State Sch, Pa, 58-63; auditor, Auditor Gen Dept of Pa, 61- Mem: Bethlehem State Chap, Eastern Star, Harrisburg, Pa; Joppa Shrine, New Bethlehem; Clarion Co Women's Club; trustee, Polk State Sch; Clarion Co Dem Women's Club (chaplain, 55-56). Honors & Awards: Meritorious Awards for Serv at Naval Supply Depot, Mechanicsburg, Pa during World War II. Relig: Presbyterian. Legal Res: Clarington PA 15828 Mailing Add: 738 Hillcrest Rd Hershey PA 17033

HUFFMAN, BILL S (D)
Mich State Rep
b Estelle, Ga, Dec 27, 24; married; c Sherry, Marvin, Krisaundra & Beth. Educ: Lawrence Inst Technol, spec courses. Polit & Govt Pos: Mem city coun, Madison Heights, Mich, 2 terms & mayor, 1 term; Mich State Rep, 62- Mil Serv: Navy, 42-47; participated in Navy V-12 prog. Mem: Kiwanis Club. Relig: Protestant. Mailing Add: 30151 Dequindre Madison Heights MI 48071

HUFFMAN, DONALD WISE (R)
Chmn, Roanoke City Rep Party, Va
b Staunton, Va, Dec 5, 27; s Thomas Elmer Huffman & Virginia Wise H; m 1950 to Colleen James; c Teresa Lynn & Kelly Virginia. Educ: Va Polytech Inst, BS, 50; Washington & Lee Univ, LLB, 66; Phi Beta Kappa; Omicron Delta Kappa; Scabbard & Blade; Alpha Pi Mu; Order of the Coif; Sigma Phi Epsilon. Polit & Govt Pos: Vchmn, Lexington-Rockbridge-Buena Vista Rep Party, Va, 64-65, former chmn; mem, Roanoke City Rep Party, 68-, chmn, 72-; mem, Va Rep State Cent Comt, 73- Mil Serv: Entered as Pvt, Army, 46, released as Pfc, 47; Army Res, 49-60. Mem: Lexington CofC (pres); Lexington Merchant's Comt (chmn); Jaycees; Rotary; Downtown Roanoke, Inc. Relig: Presbyterian. Mailing Add: 3002 Burnleigh Rd SW Roanoke VA 24014

HUFFMAN, JAMES WYLIE (D)
b Chandlersville, Ohio, Sept 13, 94; s John Alexander Huffman & Tacy Careins H; c Margaret (Mrs Graff) & James W, Jr. Educ: Ohio Wesleyan Univ; Ohio State Univ; Univ Chicago, LLB; Phi Gamma Delta; Delta Phi. Polit & Govt Pos: Secy to Gov Vic Donahey, 24-26; mem, Pub Utilities Comn, 26-30; State Dir of Com, 45; US Sen, Ohio, 45-47. Bus & Prof Pos: Attorney-at-law, Columbus, Ohio, 30-65; vpres, Logan Clay Prod, Logan, 50-; chmn bd, Motorists Mutual Ins Co, 58-; chmn bd, Motorists Life Ins Co, Columbus, 65- Mil Serv: Entered as 2nd Lt, Army, 17, released as 1st Lt, 19, after serv in 329th Inf, 83rd Div, Ohio, 17 & 120th Machine Gun Bn, 32nd Div, France, 18-19; Vesle Aisne, Soissons, Argonne & Dun-sur Meuse Campaign Ribbons; Army of Occup Medal. Publ: The Legend of Duncan Falls. Mem: Am Legion; VFW; Mason; Scottish Rite; Shrine. Honors & Awards: Trustee emer, Ohio State Univ, Distinguished Serv Award, 57. Relig: Presbyterian. Mailing Add: Motorists Life Ins Co 471 E Broad Columbus OH 43215

HUFFMAN, MILDRED P (R)
Mo State Rep
Mailing Add: 14600 Laketrails Ct Chesterfield MO 63017

HUFFMAN, ODELL HAMPTON (D)
WVa State Sen
b Wyco, WVa, Feb 18, 23; s Mitchell Odell Huffman & Callie Whittington H; m 1950 to Anna Geraldine Cline; c Katherine Ann, David Hampton, William Odell & John Bruce. Educ: Concord Col, 40-43 & 46-47; WVa Univ Col Law, JD, 50; Phi Delta Phi. Polit & Govt Pos: Mem, Princeton City Coun, WVa, 63-67; Mayor, Princeton, 65-66; WVa State Deleg, 69-72; WVa State Sen, 73- Mil Serv: Entered as Pvt, Air Force, 43, released as Sgt, 46, after serv in 3rd Air Force. Mem: WVa State Bar; WVa Trial Lawyers Asn; WVa & Am Bar Asns. Relig: Methodist. Mailing Add: 1604 W Main St Princeton WV 24740

HUGGINS, HARRY F (R)
NH State Rep
b Pittsburg, NH, Aug 13, 02; married; c three. Educ: Plymouth Teachers Col. Polit & Govt Pos: Sexton, auditor, supvr, selectman & mem sch bd, formerly; NH State Rep, 65- Mem: Guides Asn (dir); Patrons of Husbandry; Odd Fellows. Relig: Protestant. Mailing Add: Pittsburg NH 03592

HUGGINS, JAMES BERNARD (D)
Committeeman, Nat Young Dem, WVa
b Parkersburg, WVa, June 5, 50; s Bernard A Huggins & Evelyn Wiblin H; single. Educ: Parkersburg Community Col, AA, 70; George Washington Univ, 74; WVa Univ, BA, 75; Student Legis. Polit & Govt Pos: Asst to dir, Dem Youth Camp, 70; deleg & caucus chmn, Dem State Conv, WVa, 72; co organizer, John D Rockefeller IV Gubernatorial Campaign, 72; state co-chmn, Youth for Randolph, US Senate, 72; asst to Majority Whip, US Senate, 73-; committeeman, Nat Young Dem, WVa, 74- Bus & Prof Pos: Sr partner, Georgetowne Assocs, Inc, Washington, DC, 75- Mem: WVa Univ Alumni Asn; WVa Soc Washington, DC. Legal Res: 3010 Hemlock Ave Parkersburg WV 26101 Mailing Add: 3306 Gunston Rd Alexandria VA 22302

HUGGINS, ROBERT GENE (D)
Miss State Rep
Mailing Add: Box 223 Greenwood MS 38930

HUGHES, CHARLES E (R)
Del State Sen
Mailing Add: 1406 Lincoln Ave Silverside Hts Wilmington DE 19809

HUGHES, CHARLES E (D)
b Sherman, Tex, Apr 30, 27; s Roy E Hughes & Mary Fowler H; m 1954 to Wilma Haralson. Educ: Univ Tex, BA & LLB; Phi Delta Phi. Polit & Govt Pos: Tex State Rep, 51-62; chmn, Grayson Co Dem Party, 64-71; US Magistrate, Eastern Dist, Tex, 71- Bus & Prof Pos: Attorney-at-law, Sherman, Tex, 51- Mil Serv: Entered as Recruit, Merchant Marine, released as Commun Officer, after serv in Pac & Atlantic. Mem: Am, Tex State & Grayson Co Bar Asns; Elks. Relig: Baptist. Legal Res: Rte 2 Box 64 J Denison TX 75020 Mailing Add: 104 S Crockett St Sherman TX 75090

HUGHES, EDWARD R, JR (D)
RI State Rep
b Cumberland, RI, Sept 3, 38; s Edward R Hughes, Sr & Margaret Meehan H; single. Educ: Boston Col, BA, 60; Georgetown Univ Law Sch, 60-61, Grad Sch, 61; New Eng Sch Law, JD, 65; Delta Theta Phi. Polit & Govt Pos: Pres, Cumberland Young Dem, RI, 61-63; deleg, Cumberland Dem Town Comt, 62-63; deleg, RI Dem State Comt, 66-74; secy, Comn to Study Dem Party Reform, 70-; RI State Rep, Dist 69, Cumberland, 71-; deleg, RI Dem State Exec Comt, 72-74. Mem: Am Bar Asn; St Thomas Coun, KofC; Sons of Irish Kings; Blackstone Valley Am Cancer Soc (bd dirs, 72-); St Patrick's Parish Coun (pres, 71-73). Relig: Roman Catholic. Mailing Add: 11 Elizabeth St Cumberland RI 02864

HUGHES, HAROLD EVERETT (D)
b Ida Grove, Iowa, Feb 10, 22; s Lewis C Hughes & Etta Kelly H; m 1941 to Eva Mercer; c Connie (Mrs Dennis Otto), Carol & Phyllis. Educ: Univ Iowa, 40-41. Hon Degrees: DSc Govt, Col of Osteopathic Med & Surgery, 65; LLD, Cornell Col, 66, Buena Vista Col, 67, Graceland Col, 67, Loras Col, 68, Lehigh Univ, 69 & Grinnell Col, 69; DHL, Marycrest Col, 67; DCL, Simpson Col, 69. Polit & Govt Pos: Mem, Interstate Com Comn Joint Bd, 59-62; mem, Iowa State Com Comn, 59-63, chmn, 59-60 & 61-62; Gov, Iowa, 63-69; deleg, Dem Nat Conv, 64, 68 & 72; comts on state planning, fed-state rels, state & local revenue, health & welfare & transportation, Nat Gov Conf, mem exec comt, 65-67; chmn, Dem Gov Conf, 66-68; mem pub officer adv coun, US Off Econ Opportunity, 66-68; trustee, States Urban Action Ctr, 67-68; chmn, Comn on Dem Selection of Presidential Nominees, 68; vchmn, Spec Dem Comn on Party Structure & Deleg Selection, 69-; US Sen, Iowa, 69-75, Asst Majority Whip, US Senate, 69-75, chmn, Subcomts on Alcoholism & Narcotics, 69-75, chmn, Subcomt Vet Housing & Ins, 71-75 & Subcomt Drug Abuse in the Mil, 71-75; chmn, Midwest Dem Conf of Senators, 72-75; mem, Nat Comn Marijuana & Drug Abuse, 70-; pres, Int Coun Alcohol & Addictions, 72-; cong rep, Dem Nat Comt, 72-75. Bus & Prof Pos: With motor transportation industry, 46-58; mgr, Hinrich's Truck Line, Ida Grove, Iowa, 50-53; field rep, Iowa Motor Truck Asn, 53-55; founder & mgr, Iowa Better Trucking Bur, 55-58. Mil Serv: Pvt, Army, 42-45, with serv in 83rd Chem Bn, North Africa, Sicily & Italy, 43-45. Mem: Am Legion; KofP; Mason; RAM; Shrine. Relig: Methodist. Mailing Add: Ida Grove IA 51445

HUGHES, HARRY ROE (D)
b Easton, Md, Nov 13, 26; s Jonathan Longfellow Hughes & Helen Roe H; m 1951 to Patricia Ann Donoho; c Ann D & Elizabeth R. Educ: Mt St Mary's Col, 44-45; Univ of Md, BS, 49; George Washington Univ Sch Law, LLB, 52. Bus & Prof Pos: Md State Deleg, 55-59; Md State Sen, 59-71, mem, Gov Comn on City-Co Fiscal Rels, Md State Senate, 59, Gov Reapportionment Comn, 62, chmn, Standing Comt on Taxation & Fiscal Matters, 62-64, chmn, Exec Nominations Comt, 62-64, Comn Revised Condemnation Laws of Md, 63-64, spec legis comt, State-Local Fiscal Rels, 65, Legis Coun Md, 65-70, chmn, Gov Comt on Taxation & Fiscal Reform, 67 & chmn, Joint Budget & Audit Comt, Md Gen Assembly, 68-70; alt deleg, Dem Nat Conv, 68; chmn, Md State Dem Party, 70-71; Secy, Md Dept Transportation, 71- Mil Serv: Entered as A/S, Naval Air Corps Training Prog, 44, released as Aviation Cadet, 45. Mem: Md State Bar Asn; Am & Caroline Co Bar Asns; Am Legion; Rotary. Mailing Add: 20 Bouton Green Baltimore MD 21210

HUGHES, JAMES A (D)
VChmn, Barkhamsted Dem Town Comt, Conn
b Bangor, Maine, Aug 15, 35; s James A Hughes & Mary Godin H; m 1962 to Carroll Coughlin. Educ: Univ Maine, BA, 58, MA, 63; St Joseph Col, 69- Polit & Govt Pos: Mem,

Charter Revision Comt, Winsted, Conn, 63; deleg, Conn State Dem Conv, 64; mem, Barkhamsted Dem Town Comt, 64-, chmn, formerly, vchmn, currently; secy, Zoning & Planning Comn, 69- Bus & Prof Pos: Teacher, Northwestern Regional Sch, 58-; chmn social studies dept, 67- Mem: Phi Delta Kappa; Nat & Conn Educ Asns; Nat Coun Social Studies; Barkhamsted Lions Club. Relig: Roman Catholic. Legal Res: East West Hill Rd Barkhamsted CT Mailing Add: Box 7 Pleasant Valley CT 06063

HUGHES, JEROME MICHAEL (D)
Minn State Sen
b St Paul, Minn, Oct 1, 29; s Michael Joseph Hughes & Mary Malloy H; m 1951 to Audrey Magdalene Lackner; c Bernadine, Timothy, Kathleen, Rosemarie, Margaret Mary & John. Educ: Col St Thomas, Minn, BA, 51; Univ Minn, Minneapolis, MA, 58; Wayne State Univ, PhD, 70; Phi Delta Kappa. Polit & Govt Pos: Precinct chmn, Dem Party, Maplewood, Minn, 59-65; legis dist coordr, 50th Dist, 64-66; chmn, Village Maplewood Police Comn, 64-66; Minn State Sen, 50th Dist, 67-; chmn, State Community Sch Adv Coun, 71-; mem, Minn Educ Coun, 71- Bus & Prof Pos: Pres, St Paul Counr Asn, 63-64; bd dirs, Minn Counr Asn, 63-66. Mem: Minn & Am Personnel & Guid Asns; Twin City Voc Guid Asn; Minn Educ Asn; Boy Scouts (dist vchmn). Relig: Catholic. Mailing Add: 1978 Payne Ave Maplewood Village St Paul MN 55117

HUGHES, JOHN WILLIAM (R)
Mem, Stratford Town Rep Comt, Conn
b Stratford, Conn, July 9, 26; s James Henry Hughes & Irene Lucey H; m 1948 to Mary Louise Madigan; c James Prescott, Alexandria Mary, Jeffrey Clarke & John Britton. Educ: Southern Conn State Col, BS in Educ, 50; Univ Bridgeport, MS in Educ, 56. Polit & Govt Pos: Mem, Stratford Town Rep Comt, Conn, 55-; mem, Stratford Bd Educ, 56-61; comnr, Stratford Housing Authority, 64-69; Conn State Rep, 67-72. Bus & Prof Pos: Teacher, Stratford, Conn, 50-54; compensation coordr, United Aircraft Corp, 54- Mil Serv: Entered as Seaman, Navy, 43, released as Qm, PO, 45, after serv in Motor Torpedo Boat Sq, Mediter; ETO & Atlantic Theatre Ribbons. Relig: Roman Catholic. Mailing Add: 415 Housatonic Ave Stratford CT 06497

HUGHES, LAWRENCE EDWARD (R)
Ohio State Rep
b Columbus, Ohio, Apr 13, 22; s Frank S Hughes & Florence Powell H; m 1950 to Ruth Eileen Keller; c Lawrence E, Jr, John Bradford, David James & James Michael. Educ: Ohio State Univ, BS, 48; Sigma Alpha Epsilon (past pres). Polit & Govt Pos: Ohio State Rep, 69- Bus & Prof Pos: Rep, Ohio Bell Tel Co, 56-60, coordr, Southwest Area, 60-64, nat acct exec, 64-69, asst directory supvr, 69- Mil Serv: Entered as Naval Air Cadet, Navy, 42, released as Pilot, 45, after serv in Naval Air Corps & Naval Intel. Mem: Aladdin Shrine; F&AM (Past Master, Goodale Lodge); KT (Mt Vernon Commandry Off); AASR; Mason (32 degree). Relig: Lutheran. Mailing Add: 4319 Fairoaks Dr Columbus OH 43214

HUGHES, MARTIN (D)
Mem-at-Lg, Dem Nat Comt, Ohio
Mailing Add: 20525 Center Ridge Cleveland OH 44116

HUGHES, MARY ANN (D)
Mem Exec Comt, El Paso Co Dem Party, Tex
b Chicago, Ill, Mar 16, 44; d Hubert A Schneider & Mary Plum S, div; c David M, D Clark, Jr & Mary Elizabeth. Educ: Univ Tex, El Paso, BA, 73. Polit & Govt Pos: Precinct chmn, Dem Party El Paso, Tex, 70-; mem exec comt, El Paso Co Dem Party, 70-; deleg, Dem Nat Conv, 72. Bus & Prof Pos: Bus agt, Retail Clerks Int Asn, 70-72; travel consult, Whitmore Travel Serv, El Paso, 72- Mem: Tex Asn for Ment Health; El Paso Co Ment Health Asn (dir, 70-); Woman's Nat Dem Club El Paso (vpres, 68-); Am Civil Liberties Union. Relig: Episcopal. Mailing Add: 483 Castile Ave El Paso TX 79912

HUGHES, MAXWELL VERNON (D)
b Hazlehurst, Ga, Feb 4, 29; s Oscar Vernon Hughes & Lillian Summerlin H; m 1950 to Jeanette Harrell; c Nancy & Sharon. Educ: Hazlehurst High Sch, Ga, grad. Polit & Govt Pos: Chmn, McIntosh Co Dem Exec Comt, Ga, formerly. Bus & Prof Pos: Comnr, Coastal Area Planning & Develop Comt, three years; Coastal Hwy Dist, one year; chmn, Darien Housing Authority, Ga, two years; owner & mgr, Darien Tax Serv, 12 years. Mem: Mason (past Master, Live Oak Lodge); Darien-McIntosh Co CofC (mem bd dirs, five years); Darien-McIntosh Co Vol Fire Dept (charter mem, ten years). Relig: Baptist; pres, Mens Sunday Sch Class, First Baptist Church, chmn, Bldg Fund. Legal Res: Fort King George Dr Darien GA 31305 Mailing Add: PO Box 615 Darien GA 31305

HUGHES, OLIVER H (R)
b Chanute, Kans, Jan 19, 21; s John Francis Hughes & Ione White H; m 1948 to Melba V; c Marilyn S, Stephen R & Melinda Ann. Educ: Kans Univ Sch Bus, BSBA; Kans Univ Sch Law, LLB; Phi Delta Phi; Sigma Alpha Epsilon. Polit & Govt Pos: Former Rep precinct committeeman & former mem various polit comts; chmn, Kans State Rep Comt, 64-66. Bus & Prof Pos: Dir, Educators Investment Co Kans, Inc, 60-; chmn bd, Wichita State Bank, 65-; pres, Citizens Nat Bank, Emporia, 66-; dir, The Key Co, 69- Mil Serv: Entered as Pvt, Army, 43, released as Capt, 46, after serv in ETO. Publ: Co-auth, Thornton on the Law of Oil & Gas, 48. Mem: Rotary; Wichita Estate Planning Coun; Kans Chap, Nat Conf Christians & Jews. Relig: Presbyterian. Legal Res: 1966 Morningside Dr Emporia KS 66801 Mailing Add: PO Box 459 Emporia KS 66801

HUGHES, PEASTER LEO (D)
Miss State Rep
b West, Miss, Aug 28, 10; married. Educ: Univ Miss. Polit & Govt Pos: Comnr, Madison Co Soil Conserv Dist; Miss State Rep, 60- Bus & Prof Pos: Farmer; cattleman. Mem: Elks; Optimist Club; Lions; Citizens Coun; Miss Cattlemens' Asn. Relig: Baptist. Mailing Add: Box 188 Madison MS 39110

HUGHES, PHYLLIS JOSEPHINE (D)
Pres, Iowa Fedn of Dem Women's Clubs
b The Dalles, Ore, Mar 7, 15; d Edward M Hughes & Elizabeth Rowe H; single. Educ: Marquette Univ, PhB, 33, JD, 35; Theta Rho; Delta Sigma Rho; Kappa Beta Pi. Polit & Govt Pos: Unemployment compensation examr, Indust Comn of Wis, 36-37; secy, Milwaukee Co Young Dem, 36-40 & Young Dem of Wis, 40-42; mem, Bd of Appeals, Milwaukee, 40-44; pres, Jane Jefferson Club of Del Co, Iowa, 49-51, 67-; advisor Second Dist, Iowa Fedn of Dem Women's Club, 54-64, secy, 62-64, pres, 64-; vchmn, Del Co Dem Cent Comt, 60-64 & 70-74, chmn, 64-68 & 70-74, proj dir, 68-70. Bus & Prof Pos: Pvt practice of corporation law, 35-; pres, E M Hughes Dept Store, Manchester, Iowa. Publ: Poetry, Lyrical Iowa, 63. Mem: Wis State Bar Asn; Bus & Prof Women's Club; CofC; Federated Women's Club; Rotary Anns. Relig: Catholic. Legal Res: 501 E Main Manchester IA 52057 Mailing Add: 112 S Franklin Manchester IA 52057

HUGHES, RICHARD J (D)
Chief Justice, NJ Supreme Court
b Florence, NJ, Aug 10, 09; m 1954 to Betty Murphy; c Ten. Educ: St Joseph's Col; NJ Law Sch; Rutgers Univ, LLB. Polit & Govt Pos: Dem cand for Cong from Fourth Dist, NJ, 38; Asst US Attorney for NJ, 39-45; judge, Mercer Co, 48-52; chmn, Supreme Court's Comt on Juv & Domestic Rels Courts; judge, Superior Court of NJ, 52-61, Appellate Div, 57-61; Gov NJ, 62-70; deleg, Dem Nat Conv, 68 & 72; Dem Nat Committeeman, NJ, formerly; chief justice, NJ Supreme Court, currently. Bus & Prof Pos: Partner, Hughes, McElroy, Connell, Foley & Geiser, currently; chmn, Comn on Correctional Facilities & Serv, Am Bar Asn, currently. Mem: Citizens Adv Comt to Investigate Welfare Practices in Trenton; Who's Who in Am Politics (mem adv comt, 69); Elks (Past Exalted Ruler); KofC (Past Grand Knight). Relig: Catholic. Mailing Add: State House Trenton NJ 08625

HUGHES, ROBERT FELIX (D)
Ky State Rep
b St Marys, Ky, Dec 7, 18; s Joseph B Hughes & Alpha Sutton H; m 1946 to Elloise Ferry; c Robert Felix, Jr, Mary Ann, Michael Alan, Marie Elaine & Helen Jane (Mrs Tillman). Educ: Male High Sch, 35-39. Polit & Govt Pos: Ky State Rep, 46th Dist, Jefferson Co, 70-; vchmn, Ky Drug Formulary Coun, 72- Bus & Prof Pos: Owner, Hughes Super Key Mkt, Louisville, Ky, 45- Mil Serv: Entered as Pvt, Army, 41, released as Sgt, 45, after serv in 9th Inf Div, 39th Inf Regt, African, Mediter & European Theatres, 42-45; Purple Heart; Bronze Star with Oak Leaf Cluster; Silver Star; Presidential Unit Citation; Combat Med Badge; Pre-Pearl Harbor Medal; Good Conduct Medals, African, Mediter & European Theatres. Mem: Okolona Optimist Club; Black Mudd Optimists; Ky Hist Soc; Order Ky Cols; Amvets. Relig: Catholic. Legal Res: 7900 Gayeway Dr Louisville KY 40219 Mailing Add: 8002 Old Shepherdsville Rd Louisville KY 40219

HUGHES, RODNEY H (R)
Ohio State Rep
Mailing Add: 1169 Erie Bellefontaine OH 43311

HUGHES, ROYSTON CHARLES (R)
Asst Secy Prog Develop & Budget, Dept Interior
b Rochester, NY, Sept 8, 38; s John Henry Hughes & Winifred Evans H; m 1961 to Joan Rosswork; c Jennifer, Evan Gerard & Amy Elizabeth. Educ: US Naval Acad, BS, 60; Am Univ, MA, 67. Polit & Govt Pos: Legis asst to Congressman Rogers C B Morton, Washington, DC & Md, 69-71; asst to Secy, Dept Interior, Washington, DC, 71-74; Asst Secy Prog Develop & Budget, 74- Mil Serv: Entered as Midn, Navy, 60, released as Lt, after serv in Bur Naval Personnel, Washington, DC, 68-69; Joint Serv Commendation Medal; Navy Expeditiary Medal; Vietnam Serv Medal; Nat Defense Medal. Mem: Anne Arundel Co YMCA (bd dirs); Gingerville Community Asn (pres). Honors & Awards: Outstanding Alumnus, Sch Int Serv, Am Univ, 75. Relig: Roman Catholic. Mailing Add: 91 Tarragon Lane Edgewater MD 21037

HUGHES, SHELBY BOND (D)
b Clinton, Mo, June 4, 03; s Robert Lee Hughes & Alice Frances Bond H; m 1928 to Aetna Mary Jeude; c Robert Shelby, William Bond & James Lawrence. Educ: Univ Mo, AB, 26, BS in Med, 27; St Louis Univ, MD, 29; Alpha Kappa Kappa. Polit & Govt Pos: Coroner, Henry Co, Mo, 36-40; chmn, Henry Co Dem Cent Comt, 38-42 & 60-74; mayor, Clinton, Mo, 46-52; dep state health comnr, Henry Co, 56-; mem, Mo State Bd Registr for Healing Arts, 65- Bus & Prof Pos: Gen practice of med, 30-; mem staff, Clinton Gen Hosp, Mo, 40- Mil Serv: Entered as 1st Lt, Army, 42, released as Capt, 45, after serv, in Med Corps, World War II, Continental US. Mem: Am, Southern & Mo State Med Asns; Am Astron Asn; Mo Archaeol Soc (trustee). Relig: Methodist. Legal Res: 210 E Wilson Clinton MO 64735 Mailing Add: 106 S Third Clinton MO 64735

HUGHES, STEPHEN THOMAS (D)
Maine State Rep
b Portland, Maine, July 26, 43; s Albert Wellwood Hughes, Sr & Edith Bivins Hughes; single. Educ: Duke Univ, 61-64; Univ Maine at Orono, BA, 70, Sch Law, 71-; Phi Kappa Sigma; Sr Skulls. Polit & Govt Pos: Mem, Auburn Dem City Comt, Maine, 70-; mem, Androscoggin Co Dem Comt, 70-; mem, Maine Dem State Comt, 72-74; Maine State Rep, 75-; mem, NE Bd Higher Educ, 75- Bus & Prof Pos: Trustee, Univ Maine, 69-74. Mil Serv: Entered as Pvt, Army, 64, released as SP-4, 66; after serv in several units, Conarc, 64-66; Nat Defense Serv Medal; Good Conduct Medal. Relig: Protestant. Mailing Add: Box 141A W Auburn Rd Auburn ME 04210

HUGHES, TERESA (D)
Calif State Assemblywoman
Mailing Add: State Capitol Sacramento CA 95814

HUGHES, WILLIAM JAMES (R)
Colo State Sen
b Kansas City, Kans, Feb 21, 35; s William E Hughes & Margret Davis H; m 1958 to Barbara June Beckham; c Kathy, Susan & Elizabeth. Educ: Emporia State Teachers Col, 59; Univ Kans, MA Social Work, 65. Polit & Govt Pos: Colo State Sen, 75- Bus & Prof Pos: Asst dir, Ozanam Home for Boys, Kansas City, Mo, 65-67; dir, Gillis Home for Children, Kansas City, 67-69; family counseling serv dir, Colorado Springs, Colo, 69-70; asst dir, Pikes Peak Mental Health Ctr, Colorado Springs, 70- Mil Serv: Entered as Air Pilot Cadet, Navy, 55, released as AT3 Res, 57. Mem: Mental Health Asn; Nat Coun Alcoholism; Asn For Retarded Children; Nat Asn Social Workers. Relig: Christian. Mailing Add: 2905 Highland Dr Colorado Springs CO 80909

HUGHES, WILLIAM JOHN (D)
US Rep, NJ
b Salem, NJ, Oct 17, 32; s William W Hughes (deceased) & Pauline Neicen Hughes Mehaffey; m 1956 to Nancy L Gibson; c Nancy Lynne, Barbara Ann, Tama Beth & William J, Jr. Educ: Rutgers Univ, AB, 55, JD, 58; Pi Sigma Alpha; Delta Sigma Phi. Polit & Govt Pos: US Rep, NJ, 75- Bus & Prof Pos: Gen law practice, Loveland, Hughes & Garrett, Ocean City, NJ, 59-; asst prosecutor, Cape May Co, 60-70. Mem: Exchange Club; CofC; F&AM; Shore Mem Hosp (bd gov); Ocean City Hist Soc. Honors & Awards: Big E Award, Nat Exchange Club, 65;

Book of Golden Deeds Award, 75. Legal Res: 1019 Wesley Rd Ocean City NJ 08226 Mailing Add: 327 Cannon House Off Bldg Washington DC 20515

HULEN, BERNICE (R)
Secy, Sullivan Co Rep Cent Comt, Ind
b Bicknell, Ind, Feb 1, 32; d Homer Irwin Christy (deceased) & Martha Chasteen C; m 1949 to John W Hulen; c Judy (Mrs Keith Sheffler) & Mitchell. Educ: Sullivan High Sch, 49. Polit & Govt Pos: VComnr, Precinct Two, Ind, 64-66, Precinct Six, 74-; secy, Sullivan Co Rep Cent Comt, 74- Bus & Prof Pos: Clerk, Sullivan Loan Co, 61-69; bookkeeper, Bob Brown Ford Sales, 69-71; license bur clerk, State Ind, 71- Mem: Beta Sigma Phi (secy); Town & Country Home Econ Club (treas, 73, pres, 75-); Rep Womens Club; VFW Auxiliary 2459. Relig: Methodist. Mailing Add: RR 4 Box 153A Sullivan IN 47882

HULETT, STANLEY WILLIAM (R)
b San Francisco, Calif, July 31, 38; s Leo Stanley Hulett & Isabelle Francis Walker H; m 1968 to Mary Ann Minenna; c Gregory Allen. Educ: Menlo Sch & Col, AA, 58; Stanford Univ, AB, 60; El Toro Club, Stanford Univ. Polit & Govt Pos: Chmn bd trustees, Willits Unified Sch Dist, Calif, 66-69; vchmn, Mendocino Co Rep Cent Comt, 69; legal asst to US Rep Don H Clausen, Calif, 69-71; assoc dir, Nat Park Serv, 71-74. Bus & Prof Pos: Vpres & dir govt affairs, Am Paper Inst, 74- Mem: Nat Asn Lumber Salesman; Willits CofC; Hoo-Hoo Int; Mendocino Co CofC, Ukiah; Calif Redwood Asn (research comt). Honors & Awards: Man of Year Award, Willits Jaycees. Relig: Protestant. Legal Res: 248 Pine St Willits CA 95490 Mailing Add: 1635 Maddox Lane McLean VA 22101

HULL, ANN REMINGTON (D)
Md State Deleg
b Seattle, Wash, Feb 24, 25; d Arthur Ernest Remington & Marian Knowlton R; m 1949 to Gordon Crittenden Hull; c Suzanne & Peter Crittenden. Educ: Univ Wash, BA, 45; Syracuse Univ, MA, 48; Phi Beta Kappa. Polit & Govt Pos: Md State Deleg, 67-, speaker pro tem, Md House Deleg, 75- Bus & Prof Pos: Geographer, US Govt, 48-54. Mem: Asn of Am Geographers; League of Women Voters. Relig: Protestant. Mailing Add: 1629 Drexel St Takoma Park MD 20012

HULL, DANIEL STREETER, III (D)
Nat Committeeman, Calif Fedn Young Dem
b Sacramento, Calif, Mar 2, 51; s Daniel Streeter Hull, II & Nellie Craven H; single. Educ: Cabrillo Col, 73. Polit & Govt Pos: Pres, Northern Calif Young Dem, 71-72; mem, Calif Dem State Cent Comt, 73-, mem comt on rules, 73-75, mem comt on resolutions, 75-; nat committeeman, Calif Fedn Young Dem, 74- Legal Res: 14936 Jerries Dr Saratoga CA 95070 Mailing Add: 1385 Prospect Ave Capitola CA 95010

HULL, FRANK ROTHWELL (D)
b Grover Twp, Mo, Apr 7, 99; s Jehu William Hull & Eula Rothwell H; m 1931 to Mary Elizabeth Farmer; c James William. Educ: Cent Mo State Col, 17-20. Polit & Govt Pos: Pres, Johnson Co Young Dem, Mo, 32-36; mem, Johnson Co Dem Comt, 48-52, treas, formerly; deleg, Dem Nat Conv, 60. Mil Serv: Army, 18. Mem: Elks; Farm Bur; Am Legion. Relig: Presbyterian. Legal Res: 811 S Maguire Warrensburg MO 64093 Mailing Add: 111 E Culton Warrensburg MO 64093

HULL, HADLAI A (R)
Asst Secy Financial Mgt, Dept Army
b New London, Conn, May 30, 14; s Charles Hadlai Hull & Grace Stoddard H; m 1939 to Anne Dalrymple; c Charles Hadlai, John Dalrymple & Thomas Stoddard. Educ: Yale Univ, BA, 36, LLB, 39; Alpha Delta Phi. Polit & Govt Pos: Asst secy financial mgt, Dept Army, 71- Bus & Prof Pos: Assoc, Sullivan & Cromwell, 39-41; secy-treas, Minn & Ontario Paper Co, 44-55; sr vpres, Dayton Hudson Corp, 55-71. Mil Serv: Entered as Ens, Navy, 41, released as Comdr, 45, after serv in Atlantic, European & Pac Theatres, 42-45. Relig: Protestant. Legal Res: MN Mailing Add: 5001 Rockwood Pkwy Washington DC 20016

HULL, T CLARK (R)
Lt Gov, Conn
m 1948 to Betty Jane Rosoff; c T Clark III, Jonathan C & Steven D. Educ: Yale Univ, AB, 42; Harvard Univ, LLB, 48. Polit & Govt Pos: Conn State Sen, 24th Dist, Danbury, 63-71; Lt Gov, Conn, 71- Bus & Prof Pos: Lawyer-partner, Pinney, Hull, Payne & Vanlenten, 48- Mem: Danbury, Am & Conn Bar Asns; Ridgewood Country Club; Am Legion. Relig: Protestant. Legal Res: 187 Kohanza St Danbury CT 06810 Mailing Add: State Capitol Bldg Hartford CT 06115

HULL, W R, JR (D)
b Weston, Mo, Apr 17, 06; wid; c W R Hull, III, Mrs Susan Hudson. Educ: Pub Schs. Polit & Govt Pos: US Rep, Mo, 54-72; former mayor, Weston, Mo. Bus & Prof Pos: Dir, First Nat Bank, Leavenworth, Kans; co-owner, Hull's Tobacco Warehouse, Weston, Mo. Mem: Kansas City Area Coun Boy Scouts; CofC. Relig: Christian Church; deacon. Mailing Add: Weston MO 64098

HULLINGER, ARLO (D)
Iowa State Rep
Mailing Add: RR 1 Leon IA 50144

HULLINGHORST, DICKEY LEE (D)
Chairwoman, Boulder Co Dem Cent Comt, Colo
b Maywood, Nebr, June 27, 43; d Richard L Shepard & Neva Sloan S; m 1965 to Robert Stanley Hullinghorst; c Lara Lee. Educ: Univ Wyo, grad, 65; Univ Colo, currently; Gamma Phi Beta. Polit & Govt Pos: Finance chairperson, Boulder Co Dem Cent Comt, Colo, 71-72, vchairperson, 73-75, chairperson, 75- Bus & Prof Pos: Comput programmer, Dept Housing & Urban Develop, Washington, DC, 65-67; comput programmer-analyst, Davis Bros, Inc, Denver, 68-70. Mem: Colo Women's Polit Caucus (vpres); Nat Women's Polit Caucus; Child Care Coalition; YWCA (pub affairs comt); Am Civil Liberties Union. Relig: Episcopal. Mailing Add: 7301 Mt Meeker Rd Longmont CO 80501

HULSE, JAMES WARREN (D)
Mem, Washoe Co Dem Cent Comt, Nev
b Pioche, Nev, June 4, 30; James Gordon Hulse & Berene Cutler H; m 1962 to Betty Kay Wynkoop; c Jane & James Charlton. Educ: Univ Nev, BA, 52, MA, 58; Stanford Univ, PhD, 62; Phi Alpha Theta; Phi Kappa Phi; Kappa Tau Alpha. Polit & Govt Pos: Mem, Washoe Co Dem Cent Comt, Nev, 64-; mem, Nev Equal Rights Comn, 63-66; deleg, Dem Nat Conv, 68; mem, Nev Dem Cent Comt, 70-72. Bus & Prof Pos: Polit reporter, Nev State Jour, Reno, 54-58; asst prof, Cent Wash Col, 61-62; asst prof, Univ Nev, 62-66, assoc prof, 66-69, prof, 70- Mil Serv: Entered as Pvt, Army, 52, released as Cpl, 54, after serv in 83rd Eng Bn, France, 53-54. Publ: The forming of the communist international, Stanford Univ Press, 64; The Nevada adventure: a history, Univ Nev Press, 65; Revolutionists in London, Oxford Univ Press, 70. Mem: Am Hist Asn; Am Civil Liberties Union; Am Asn for Advan Slavic Studies; Odd Fellows. Relig: Unitarian. Mailing Add: 940 Grandview Ave Reno NV 89503

HULSHIZER, R DALE (D)
b Parsons, Kans, Aug 23, 29; s L Stanford Hulshizer, Sr & Emily P Frazier H; m 1954 to Julia Ann Wendling; c Rebecca Jo, Ronald Dale, Jr, Daniel Joseph & Ann Marie. Educ: Drake Univ, BA, 53; Univ Southern Calif, 53; pres, Sigma Alpha Epsilon. Polit & Govt Pos: Chmn, El Paso Co Stewart for Cong Comt, Colo, 60; vpres, Colo Springs Young Dem, 62, pres, 63; staff dir, Dem Party of Colo, 63-65; asst to US Rep Frank E Evans, Colo, 65-67, admin asst, 67- Bus & Prof Pos: Admissions counsr, Drake Univ, Des Moines, Iowa, 53-56; rep, New Eng Life Ins, 56-58; rep, KRDO-TV, Colorado Springs, Colo, 58-60; res mgr, KOAA-TV, 60-61, KKTV, 61-63. Mil Serv: Entered as Pvt, Air Force, 48, released as Cpl, 49, after serv at Lackland, San Marcos & Randolph AFB, Tex, Res, 49-55. Relig: Protestant. Legal Res: Colorado Springs CO Mailing Add: 4321 Cedarlake Court Alexandria VA 22309

HULTEN, JOHN JAMES (D)
Hawaii State Sen
b San Francisco, Calif, Nov 2, 13; s Augustin Anthony Hulten & Margaret Trosak H; m 1937 to Helen Salopek; c John James, Jr, Stephen Paul, Virginia Marie & Thomas Anthony. Educ: Univ San Francisco, Eve Div, 3 years. Polit & Govt Pos: Tax adv, Pub Housing Admin, 45-46, regional tax adv, 46-47; chief appraisal sect, US Vet Admin, 48-51; precinct chmn, Dem Party, Hawaii, 57-58, dist chmn, 59; Hawaii State Sen, currently, sgt at arms, Hawaii State Senate, currently; deleg, Dem Nat Conv, 68. Publ: Land Reform in Hawaii, Land Econ, Univ Wis, 5/66; The Appraisal Report, In: Encycl on Appraising, Prentice-Hall, 57. Mem: Am Inst Real Estate Appraisers (Honolulu Chap); Soc Residential Appraisers (Honolulu Chap). Relig: Roman Catholic. Legal Res: 631 Paopua Loop Kailua Oahu HI 96734 Mailing Add: House of Senate Sgt at Arms State Capitol Honolulu HI 96813

HULTMAN, BERTHA (D)
Chmn, Klamath Co Dem Cent Comt, Ore
b South Bend, Wash; div. Educ: Univ Wash; Cent Wash Col Educ, BS; Alpha Delta Kappa. Polit & Govt Pos: Mem, Teachers Standards & Practices State Comn, 70-75; vchmn, Second Cong Dist Dem Party, 72-; mem, State Intergroup Human Rels Comn, 74-; chmn, Klamath Co Dem Cent Comt, 74- Bus & Prof Pos: Teacher, Klamath Falls Schs; coordr reading & subj matter, Klamath Falls Schs. Mem: Grange; Klamath Co Welfare Bd; Klamath Co Juv Bd. Mailing Add: 330 Pacific Terr Klamath Falls OR 97601

HULTMAN, CALVIN O (R)
Iowa State Sen
Mailing Add: 1501 Miller Ave Red Oak IA 51566

HUME, DONALD E (D)
Ind State Rep
Mailing Add: RR 1 Winslow IN 47598

HUME, LINDEL O (D)
Ind State Rep
Mailing Add: RR 1 Box 270 Oakland City IN 47660

HUMES, JOHN PORTNER (R)
b New York, NY, July 21, 21; m to Jean Cooper Schmidlapp; c six boys. Educ: Princeton Univ, Woodrow Wilson Sch Pub & Int Affairs, AB, 43; Fordham Univ Law Sch, JD, 48. Polit & Govt Pos: US Ambassador to Austria, 69-75. Bus & Prof Pos: Assoc, Shearman & Sterling, 48-55; partner, Humes, Andrews & Botzow, 56-69; founder & pres, Humes Found; secy bd trustees, Portledge Sch, Locust Valley, NY; trustee, St Luke's Hosp, Kips Bay Boys Club, Fay Sch, Southborough, Mass, Seaman's Church Inst NY, Soc of St Johnland, NShore Bird & Game Sanctuary, Episcopal Found for Educ, Diocese of LI & Nat Art Museum of Sport. Mem: Nassau Co Exec Coun, Boy Scouts; AF&AM; Alliance Franciase; Eng Speaking Union; Confrerie des Chavaliers de Tastevins (grand off). Honors & Awards: NY State Squash Racquet Champion, 51. Relig: Episcopal. Mailing Add: Oyster Bay Rd Locust Valley NY 11560

HUMES, THEODORE LEON (R)
b Pittsburgh, Pa, Feb 1, 22; m 1948 to Betty Jane Iams; c Linda (Mrs Bennett), Paul Michael, Robert G, Barbara Ann, Theresa Lynn & Theodore L, Jr. Educ: Univ Pittsburgh, AB in Econ, 48; George Washington Univ, JD, 52; Delta Tau Delta. Polit & Govt Pos: Coordr, Nationalities Comt Nixon for President, Pittsburgh, Pa, 60; deleg, Rep Nat Conv, 64; state chmn, Citizens for Goldwater-Miller, 64; field dir, Nixon for President Comt, Pa, 68; asst to Secy of Labor, 69-70; asst to chmn, Securities & Exchange Comn, 70, assoc secy, 70-72. Bus & Prof Pos: Bus analyst, Consol Coal Co, Pittsburgh, Pa, 55-61; dir pub affairs, Kennametal, Inc, Latrobe, 61-64; dir pub rels, Black & Decker Mfg Co, 66-68. Mil Serv: Entered as PO 3/C, Navy, 42, released as PO 1/C, 45, after serv in Amphibious Forces, Mediterranean, European, Cent & SPac Theaters; Appropriate Theater Ribbons. Publ: Various articles in jour of contemporary pub opinion. Mem: Bar of Dist of Columbia; Econ Club of Pittsburgh; Am Soc Pub Rels; Sigma Delta Chi; Kosciuscko Found. Relig: Roman Catholic. Legal Res: 30 Rocklyn Place Pittsburgh PA 15228 Mailing Add: 1428 Winding Waye Rd Silver Spring MD 20902

HUMMEL, ARTHUR W, JR (R)
b China, June 1, 20; s Arthur William Hummel & Ruth Bookwalter H; m 1951 to Betty Lou Firstenberger; c Timothy & William. Educ: Univ Chicago, MA, 49; Nat War Col, 60-61; Phi Beta Kappa. Polit & Govt Pos: Foreign affairs officer, State Dept, Washington, DC, 50-52; pub affairs officer, US Consulate, Hong Kong, 52-55; dep pub affairs officer, US Embassy, Tokyo, 55-57; pub affairs officer, US Embassy, Rangoon, 57-60; dep dir, Voice of Am, Washington, DC, 61-63; Dep Asst Secy State, 63-65; Dep Chief of Mission, US Embassy, Taipei, Taiwan, 65-68; US Ambassador to Burma, 68-72. Bus & Prof Pos: Teacher Eng, Chinese High Sch, Peking, 40-41; field surv off, UNRRA, Tientsin, 45-46; staff lectr, fund raising orgn, New York, 46-47. Mil Serv: Interned by Japanese, 12/8/41, escaped from internment camp, 44; joined Chinese guerrilla unit behind Japanese lines from 44-45. Mem: Asn for Asian Studies. Honors & Awards: Arthur S Flemming Award, 59; Superior Honor

Award, State Dept, 66. Relig: Protestant. Mailing Add: 4923 Essex Ave Chevy Chase MD 20015

HUMPHERY, EDDIE (D)
b Ft Worth, Tex, Mar 29, 25; s Eddie Humphery & Bessie William Gipson H; m 1954 to Gladys Hackney. Educ: High Sch, Ft Worth, Tex, grad, 43; bus col, 48-52. Polit & Govt Pos: Deleg, Dem Mid-Term Conf, 74. Mil Serv: Entered as Pvt, Air Force, 43, released as T-5 Sgt, after serv in ETO, 44-46. Mem: A Philip Randolph Inst (dist vpres); Local P54 AMCBW (Cope chmn). Mailing Add: 6013 Prothrow St Ft Worth TX 76112

HUMPHREY, HOWARD (D)
Polit & Govt Pos: Chmn, Idaho Dem State Party, formerly. Mailing Add: Dem State Hq Idaho Bldg Boise ID 83702

HUMPHREY, HOWARD S, SR (R)
NH State Rep
Mailing Add: Box 233 Antrim NH 03440

HUMPHREY, HUBERT HORATIO (D)
US Sen, Minn
b Wallace, SDak, May 27, 11; s Hubert Horatio Humphrey & Christina Sannes H; m 1936 to Muriel Fay Buck; c Nancy (Mrs C Bruce Solomonson), Hubert Horatio III, Robert Andrew & Douglas Sannes. Educ: Denver Col Pharm, 33; Univ Minn, BA, 39; La State Univ, MA, 40; Phi Beta Kappa. Polit & Govt Pos: State dir, War Prod Training & Employment, 42; asst dir, War Manpower Comn, 43; mayor, Minneapolis, Minn, 45-48; US Sen, Minn, 49-64 & 71-; Vice President, United States, 65-69; deleg, Dem Nat Conv, 68; Dem cand for President, United States, 68, nominee, 72. Bus & Prof Pos: Mem faculty, Macalester Col & Univ of Minnesota, Minneapolis, 69-. Publ: The war of poverty, McGraw-Hill, 64; School desegregation: document & commentary, Thomas Y Crowell, 64; The cause is mankind, Frederick Praeger Co, 64. Relig: United Church of Christ. Legal Res: Waverly MN 55390 Mailing Add: 232 Old Senate Office Bldg Washington DC 20510

HUMPHREY, HUBERT HORATIO, III (DFL)
Minn State Sen
b Minneapolis, Minn, June 26, 42; s Hubert H Humphrey, Jr & Muriel F Buck H; m 1963 to Nancy Lee Jeffery; c Florence Christine, Pamela Katherine & Hubert H, IV. Educ: Am Univ, BA, 65; Univ Minn Law Sch, JD, 69; Alpha Sigma Phi. Polit & Govt Pos: Dem-Farmer-Labor precinct chmn, Plymouth, Minn, 69-71; first vchmn, 33rd State Sen Dem-Farmer-Labor Dist, 69-71, deleg, State Conv, 70; Minn State Sen, 44th Dist, 73- Bus & Prof Pos: Attorney, O'Connor, Green, et al, 69-72; self-employed, 72- Mem: Am & Minn Bar Asns; Am Judicature Soc; Optimists Int; Northwest YMCA (dir, 72-73). Mailing Add: 8116 40th Ave N New Hope MN 55428

HUMPHREY, JAMES A (R)
NH State Rep
Mailing Add: Box 7 Andover NH 03216

HUMPHREY, LOUISE B (R)
b White Lake, SDak; d August Adolph Beutner & Louise Nihart B; m to Bert Humphrey, wid; c Mary Louise (Mrs R K Stanley); three grandchildren. Educ: Yankton Col, BA, 27; Aristonian. Polit & Govt Pos: Assessor, Mellette Co, SDak, 31-32; deleg, Rep Nat Conv, 48; Rep precinct committeewoman, Mellette Co, SDak, 50-54; vchmn, Mellette Co Rep Party, 50-54; mem, Gov Adv Comt, 52-56; State Cent Committeewoman, 54-64; supvr agr census, Westriver, 55; SDak State Rep, 42nd Dist, Bennett & Mellette Counties, 58-62; mem, State Court Study, Joseph Ward & SDak Centennial Comns, 61; Rep Nat Committeewoman, SDak, 64-71; mem, SDak State Fed Housing Admin Bd, currently. Bus & Prof Pos: Teacher, White River High Sch, SDak, 27-28, Rural Sch, White River, 34-35. Mem: Yankton Col (mem corp bd & bd trustees). Bus & Prof Pos: Women's Club; Am Legion Auxiliary; Federated Women's Club; Rep Federated Women's Club. Relig: Lutheran. Mailing Add: White River SD 57579

HUMPHREY, LUCIE KING (R)
Rep Nat Committeewoman, Nev
b Mokelumne Hill, Calif, Feb 23, 11; d Ralph Mower King & Mabel Plumb K; m 1932 to Marvin Bender Humphrey; c Joseph King, Barbara (Mrs Redman), Sara (Mrs White) & Ellen. Educ: Lassen Jr Col, 27-29; Univ Nev, AB, 31; Gamma Phi Beta. Polit & Govt Pos: Mem, Washoe Co Rep Cent Comt, Nev, 49-; mem, Rep Women's Club, Reno, 49-, bd pres, 63-67; pres, Nev Fedn Rep Women, 50-53, mem bd, 50-; mem, Nev Rep State Cent Comt, 63-; Rep Nat Committeewoman, 68-, mem exec comt, Rep Nat Comt, 74- Bus & Prof Pos: Teacher, 31. Relig: Episcopal. Mailing Add: 30 Suda Way Reno NV 89502

HUMPHREY, NELSON HINE (D)
Chmn, Ashtabula Co Dem Party, Ohio
b Ashtabula, Ohio, Aug 24, 19; s Russell Clark Humphrey, Jr & Zoe Hine H; m 1946 to Shirley Jean Kemmer; c Brian K, Kay A, Wendy S & Todd L. Educ: Ashtabula High Sch, Ohio, grad, 38. Polit & Govt Pos: VChmn, Ashtabula Co Dem Party, 56-58, secy, 58-60, chmn, 60-; mem, Ashtabula Co Elect Bd, 62-; deleg, Dem Nat Conv, 64 & 68; vchmn, Dem Co Chairmen of Ohio, 67-69. Bus & Prof Pos: Real estate salesman, All-Co Realty, Ashtabula, 70- Mem: Ashtabula Co Bd Realtors; Ohio Asn Elect Off; Ashtabula Co Dem Club; Elks. Relig: Protestant; trustee, First Congregational Church, 68- Mailing Add: 6413 Jefferson Rd Ashtabula OH 44004

HUMPHREYS, FREDERICK M (R)
Chmn, Clark Co Rep Comt, Kans
b Sterling, Kans, Feb 18, 22; s John Ephraim Humphreys & Vinette Hutchinson H; m 1946 to Carrie May Arnold; c Karen, Iras, John, Tom & Fred. Educ: Kans Univ, BS, 43; Phi Mu Alpha; Pi Kappa Delta; Sigma Alpha Epsilon. Polit & Govt Pos: Rep precinct committeeman, Kans, 56-60; city councilman, Ashland, 60-66; chmn, Clark Co Rep Comt, currently. Bus & Prof Pos: Gen mgr, Home Lumber & Supply Co, 64- Mil Serv: Entered as A/S, Navy, 43, released as Lt, 45, after serv in Motor Torpedo Boat Squadron 33, SPac, 44-45; Campaign Ribbons. Mem: Am Legion; VFW; AF&AM; CofC; Kiwanis. Relig: Presbyterian. Mailing Add: Ashland KS 67831

HUMPHREYS, PRISCILLA FAITH (R)
Rep Nat Committeewoman, WVa
b Huntington, WVa, Apr 28, 12; d James Edward Cobb & Bertie Esque C; m 1936 to Irvin Wendell Humphreys; c David Wendell, Bertie Anne & John Edward. Educ: Marshall Univ. Polit & Govt Pos: Pres, Huntington-Cabell Rep Womens Club, WVa, 61-63; vchmn, Cabell Co Rep Exec Comt, 63-66; Rep Nat Committeewoman, WVa, currently; deleg, Rep Nat Conv, 72. Mem: Huntington Mothers Club; Women's Club of Huntington; Alpha Delta Mothers Club. Relig: Baptist. Mailing Add: 1546 16th St Huntington WV 25701

HUMPHREYS, RAYMOND V (R)
b Huntington, WVa, s Edward Humphreys & Zelda Henson H; single. Educ: Marshall Univ, 31-34. Polit & Govt Pos: WVa State Deleg, 50-52; dir educ & training, Rep Cong Comt, 57-63, Rep Nat Comt, 63-69. Bus & Prof Pos: Pres, Assoc Underwriters, 38-42; pres, Raymond V Humphreys Assoc, Ins, 46-51; exec vpres, Nat Sales, 54-57; managing partner, Raymond V Humphreys Assocs Mgt Consult, 69- Mil Serv: Entered as Pvt, Army, 42, released as Maj, 52, after serv in Gen Staff, AA Command, Gen MacArthur Command; SW Pac Theater, 43-45. Relig: Baptist. Legal Res: Lonesome Cedar Farm Hurricane WV 25526 Mailing Add: PO Box 175 Haymarket VA 22069

HUMPHRIES, T W (D)
La State Rep
Mailing Add: 3401 Byers Dr Monroe LA 71201

HUMPLEBY, TWYLA JEAN (R)
b Creston, Iowa, Aug 14, 33; d Emmett H Worthington & Edna Anna Hocke W; m 1951 to Edwin Albert Humpleby; c Bobbie Lynn, Kim Denise & Nicole Jean. Educ: Mascatine High Sch, grad, 51. Polit & Govt Pos: Finance chmn, Johnson Co Rep Womans Club, Iowa, 63-65, pres, 66-67; committeewoman, Iowa Rep Party, formerly; vchmn, First Dist Young Rep, 64-; chmn campaign activities, First Dist Rep Women, 67-, first vpres, 68-70, pres, 70-71; alt deleg, Rep Nat Conv, 68; co-chmn, Iowa State Rep Rev Comt, 68- Mem: Univ Athletic Club; Iowa City Christian Women's Club; Iowa City Woman's Club; Johnson Co Rep Women. Honors & Awards: Outstanding Rep Women in Johnson Co, Johnson Co Rep Women's Club. Relig: Evangelical Free Church of Am. Mailing Add: 5 Highview Knoll Iowa City IA 52240

HUNCOCK, D HOWITT (INDEPENDENT)
b East Norwich, NY, Oct 31, 15; s Edward Erving Huncock & Dorothy Fanny H; m 1935 to Joanna Coulter Chambers; c John Dale Coulter & Rachel Christina; three grandchildren. Educ: Exeter Col, Oxford. Polit & Govt Pos: Spec asst to NY State Assemblyman, 3 years; former mem, Tax Study Comt; deleg, Dem Nat Conv, 72. Bus & Prof Pos: Lawyer, 25 years; dir, Bluecoat Life Ins Co; chmn bd, Bentinck Wool Corp. Mil Serv: Navy, 41-45. Relig: Episcopal. Mailing Add: 8554 E Mackenzie Dr Scottsdale AZ 85251

HUNGATE, WILLIAM LEONARD (D)
US Rep, Mo
b Benton, Ill, Dec 14, 22; s Leonard Wathen Hungate & Maude Irene Williams H; m 1944 to Dorothy Nell Wilson; c William David & Margie Kathryn (Mrs Branson L Wood, III). Educ: Univ Mo, AB, 43; Harvard Law Sch, LLB, 48. Hon Degrees: LLD, Culver-Stockton Col, 68. Polit & Govt Pos: Prosecuting attorney, Lincoln Co, Mo, 51-56; Asst Attorney Gen, Mo, 58-64; US Rep, Ninth Dist, Mo, currently. Bus & Prof Pos: Sr partner, Hungate & Grewach, Attorneys, 56-68. Mil Serv: Entered as Pvt, Army, 43, released as Pfc, 46, after serv in Co L, 377th Inf Regt, 95th Inf Div, ETO, 44-45; Bronze Star; 3 Battle Stars; Combat Inf Badge; Medal of Metz. Publ: Administration of criminal justice, Chieftain, 57; Rules are made to be, Mo Law Rev, 4/66. Mem: Am Bar Asn; Mason; VFW; Am Legion; Kiwanis. Relig: Disciples of Christ. Legal Res: 755 Cap-au-Gris St Troy MO 63379 Mailing Add: 2437 Rayburn House Office Bldg Washington DC 20515

HUNGERFORD, ROBERT LEON, JR (BOB) (R)
Ariz State Sen
b Oklahoma City, Okla, Dec 7, 38; s Robert Leon Hungerford & Geraldine Ruth Corrigan H; m 1958 to Sandra Jean Williams; c Lori Jean, Teresa Ann & Robert Leon, III. Educ: Ariz State Univ, BA, 67, JD, 70. Polit & Govt Pos: Ariz State Rep, Dist 26, 70-74; Ariz State Sen, Dist 28, 75- Mem: Optimists. Relig: Roman Catholic. Mailing Add: 11234 N Miller Rd Scottsdale AZ 85260

HUNKING, LOILA GRACE (D)
SDak State Rep
b Milwaukee, Wis, Aug 21, 39; d Harold Alvin Belcher & Lois Marie Bigler B; m 1961 to Floyd Raymond Hunking; c Jeffrey Scott. Educ: Jamestown Col, BA, 60; Univ Hawaii, 61; Augustana Col, 67. Polit & Govt Pos: Mem, SDak Comt on Status of Women, 73-; SDak State Rep, Dist 11, 73-; mem, State Comn on Indian Affairs, 75- Bus & Prof Pos: Teacher, Bowman, NDak, 60-62, Blue Earth, Minn, 62-63 & Brandon Valley High Sch, SDak, 67-; reporter & women's ed, Sioux Falls Argus Leader, 64-67. Mem: Nat Orgn for Women; Nat Women's Polit Caucus; Nat, SDak & Brandon Valley Educ Asns. Mailing Add: 2309 S Stephen Sioux Falls SD 57103

HUNNINGS, R H (R)
b Attica, Ind, Sept 9, 14; s Raymond Harrison Hunnings & Kate Henson H; m 1942 to Viola Isabell Shultz; c R H, II & Virginia Jo. Educ: Ind Univ, 33-35; Ind State Univ, BS, 48; Miami Univ, grad work, 50-51. Polit & Govt Pos: Young Rep chmn, Clinton Co, Ind, 30-33; Rep precinct committeeman, Fayette Co, 56-62; chmn, Fayette Co Rep Party, formerly. Bus & Prof Pos: Teacher, Connersville Pub Schs, Ind, 45-53; real estate broker, 51- Mil Serv: Entered as Pvt, Army, 41, released as Capt, 46, after serv in Second Armored Div, ETO, 44-45; Capt (Ret), Army Res; Purple Heart; Bronze Star. Mem: Elks; Mason; Shrine; Lions; Am Legion. Relig: Methodist. Mailing Add: RR 3 Connersville IN 47331

HUNSAKER, EDWIN STERLING, II (R)
b Glendale, Calif, Jan 3, 53; s Edwin Sterling Hunsaker & Karla Hill H; single. Educ: Univ Utah, 72-, mem, Rep steering comt, 72- Polit & Govt Pos: Committeeman, Voting Dist 524, 72, co deleg, 72; deleg, Utah State Rep Conv, 72 & Rep Nat Conv, 72; Young Voters for the President Comt, Utah, 72. Bus & Prof Pos: Lifeguard & swim instr, White Tower Swim Club, 69-71 & Meadow Brook Downs, 72-73. Mem: Kearns Youth Aquatic Club. Honors & Awards: Blue Chip Swimming Award, Kearns High Sch, 70, Most Outstanding Swimmer, 71. Relig: Latter-day Saint. Mailing Add: 4920 S 4135 West Kearns UT 84118

HUNSINGER, JOSEPHINE D (D)
Mich State Rep
b Acosta, Pa; d Joseph Drivinsky & Kathryn Moskal D; m 1930 to Raymond L Hunsinger; c Irene K (Mrs B Locher, Jr); three grandchildren. Educ: Mich State Univ. Polit & Govt Pos: Jury comnr, Wayne Co, Mich, 53-54; Mich State Rep, 54-; chmn, Wayne Co Deleg, 65- Mem:

17th Cong Dist Dem Party Orgn; Nat Order of Women Legislators; Int Platform Asn; Nat Fedn of Bus & Prof Women's Clubs, Inc; Athena Club & Women's City Club, Detroit. Honors & Awards: Only woman in Mich to receive the Mich Agr Conf Award in recognition of distinguished serv. Legal Res: 24414 Frisbee St Detroit MI 48219 Mailing Add: State Capitol Lansing MI 48901

HUNT, BILLY (R)
b Beckville, Tex, Jan 19, 25; s Arthur E Hunt & Pellie McLeroy; single. Educ: Univ of Tex, Austin, LLB, 48. Polit & Govt Pos: Tex State Rep, 55-56; chmn, Shelby Co Rep Exec Comt, formerly. Bus & Prof Pos: Partner, Fairchild & Hunt, Attorneys, Center, Tex, 56- Mem: Tex Bar Asn. Mailing Add: PO Box 666 Center TX 75935

HUNT, DOUGLAS I (D)
Utah State Rep
Mailing Add: 2875 W 5600 S Roy UT 84067

HUNT, HOWARD E (R)
Mem, Rep Nat Comt, Ind
Mailing Add: 322 S Harvey Dr Muncie IN 47304

HUNT, JAMES BAXTER, JR (D)
Lt Gov, NC
b Greensboro, NC, May 16, 37; s James Baxter Hunt & Elsie Brame H; m 1958 to Carolyn Joyce Leonard; c Rebecca Joyce, James Baxter, III, Rachel Henderson & Elizabeth Brame. Educ: NC State Univ, BS, 59, MS, 62; Univ NC, Chapel Hill, JD, 64; Phi Kappa Phi; Gamma Sigma Delta; Kappa Phi Kappa; Golden Chain; Blue Key; Thirty & Three; Alpha Zeta; Phi Alpha Delta; ed, The Agriculturist; two terms, student govt pres. Polit & Govt Pos: Vpres, NC Young Dem Clubs, deleg & mem rules comt, Dem Nat Conv, 68; asst to state Dem chmn, NC Dem Party, 68-70; chmn, State Jefferson-Jackson Dinner, 69; mem, Nat Dem Party Comn Rules, 69-70; chmn, NC Dem Party Study Comn, 69; Lt Gov, NC, 73- Bus & Prof Pos: Econ adv, His Majesty's Govt of Nepal, employed by Ford Found, 64-66; mem firm, Kirby, Webb & Hunt, Attorneys-at-law, 66-72; training consult to Peace Corps, 66-67. Publ: Acreage controls & poundage controls for flue cured tobacco, NC Agr Tech Bull, 62; numerous articles on land reform & agr develop, HMG Press, 64-66; Rally around the precinct, NC Dem Party Precinct Manual, 68. Mem: NC Bar Asn; Sertoma Club; Jaycees; Grange. Relig: Presbyterian; elder, First Presby Church, Wilson, NC. Legal Res: Route 1 Box 138 Lucama NC 27851 Mailing Add: State Legis Bldg Raleigh NC 27611

HUNT, JOHN E (R)
Mem, NJ Rep State Comt
b Lambertville, NJ, Nov 25, 08; m to Doris R Foster; c Deborah. Educ: Bus Sch, 3 years; US Army Air Force Intel Sch; Fed Bur of Invest Police Acad; Harvard Sch of Police Sci. Polit & Govt Pos: Sheriff, Gloucester Co NJ, 59 & 62; former NJ State Policeman & exec officer; NJ State Sen, formerly; US Rep, NJ, 69-74; deleg, Rep Nat Conv, 72; mem, NJ Rep State Comt, currently. Mil Serv: Entered as 2nd Lt, Army, World War II, released as Maj, 46, after serv as Combat Intel Officer, Africa, Sicily, Italy, France, Germany, Yugoslavia, Bulgaria & Roumania; Bronze Star Medal; Air Medal with 2 Oak Leaf Clusters; Purple Heart; Presidential Unit Citation with 1 Oak Leaf Cluster; EAME Campaign Medal with 8 Bronze Stars; Am Theatre, Victory & Army Res Medals. Mailing Add: 508 Pitman Ave Pitman NJ 08071

HUNT, JOHN JOSEPH, JR (D)
Mem, Olmsted Co Dem-Farmer-Labor Comt, Minn
b Arlington, Minn, May 21, 31; s John J Hunt & Kathryn Collins H; m 1955 to Rita Marie Zeck; c Thomas L, Nancy Jo, Susan Kay & John Joseph, III. Educ: St Johns Univ, 50; Univ Minn, BS in pharm, 53; Rho Chi; Phi Delta Theta; Phi Delta Chi. Polit & Govt Pos: Mem, Olmsted Co Dem-Farmer-Labor Comt, Minn, 64-, spec events officer, 66-68, sustaining fund chmn, 68-; mem, Rochester Jr Col Adv Comt & ACRE Educ Comt, 66-; chmn, mayors adv comt on urban renewal, 68-69. Bus & Prof Pos: Pres, Hunt Drugstore, Inc, 63- Mil Serv: Entered as Pvt, Army, 54, released as Cpl, 56, after serv in 98th Gen Hosp, ETO & Neubrucke, WGermany, 55-56; Army of Occupation Good Conduct Medal. Mem: Nat Asn Retail Pharmacists; Rochester CofC; KofC (Past Grand Knight); Sertoma Club; NAACP. Honors & Awards: Knight of the Year, KofC, 68. Relig: Catholic. Mailing Add: 2115 Eighth Ave NE Rochester MN 55901

HUNT, LLOYD EDWARD (D)
SC State Rep
b Pickens Co, SC, Nov 22, 02; s Luthes E Hunt & Mary Ella Bowen H; m 1930 to Mattie Lee Meares. Educ: N Greenville Acad. Polit & Govt Pos: Mayor, Greer, SC, 55-66; SC State Rep, formerly & 75- Bus & Prof Pos: Dir, SC Peach Festival Asn; dir, First Nat Bank of Greer, retired. Mem: Lions Club; Munic Asn of SC; Blue Ridge Coun, Boy Scouts (dir); Mason (32 degree); Shrine. Mailing Add: 110 Oakdale Ave Greer SC 29651

HUNT, MCPHERSON WILLISS (MACK) (R)
Dist Committeeman, Kay Co Rep Party, Okla
b Lincoln, Nebr, May 30, 33; s Burt Williss Hunt & Elizabeth Julia McPherson H; m 1953 to Audrey Fae Alexander; c Mark Alan, Scott Willis, Julia Fae, Kevin Roy & Eric Earl. Educ: Nebr Wesleyan Univ, AB, 55; Univ Nebr, MS, 57; Phi Lambda Upsilon; Sigma Xi; Crescent Fraternity. Polit & Govt Pos: Publicity chmn, Kay Co Young Rep, Okla, 58-59, co-chmn, 64-66; precinct vchmn, Kay Co Rep Party, 59-60, precinct chmn, 61-62, co chmn, 67-73, fund drive chmn, 73, dist committeeman, 73-; conv chmn, Okla Fedn Young Rep, 65, state vchmn, 69-73. Bus & Prof Pos: Assoc research chemist, Continental Oil Co, Ponca City, 57-60, research chemist, 60-63, sr research chemist, 63-67, research group leader, 67- Mil Serv: Electrician 3/C, Naval Res, 58- Publ: Benzene 3-nitro & 3-amino-cinnolines, 59 & Sulfonates as dye sites in polypropylene, 69, Am Chem Soc. Mem: Am Chem Soc; Am Soc Testing & Materials; Soc Automotive Engrs; YMCA (bd dirs); Boy Scouts (comnr, explorer adv & asst cubmaster). Honors & Awards: Young Alumni award, Nebr Wesleyan Univ, 68; plus local awards; fourteen US & several foreign patents in fields ranging from detergents to rocket fuels. Relig: Presbyterian. Mailing Add: 903 E Cleveland Ponca City OK 74601

HUNT, OCIE (D)
b Moro, Tex, Apr 22, 93; s Meno Hunt & Julia Brewer H; m 1917 to Nell Irvin; c Olivia (Mrs Bill Horn). Educ: Tex Tech, Correspondence course in Eng; Air War Col & Air Univ, grad, 66. Polit & Govt Pos: Chmn, Nolan Co Dem Party, Tex, formerly. Bus & Prof Pos: Owner & operator, local fire & casualty ins agency, 12-; dep collector, NTex div, Internal Revenue Serv, currently. Mem: Elks, Sweetwater, Tex; AF&AM, Ft Worth; Dallas Consistory; Suez Shrine, San Angelo; Odd Fellows, Big Springs. Relig: Methodist. Legal Res: 1708 Pease St Sweetwater TX 79556 Mailing Add: 105 W Third Sweetwater TX 79556

HUNT, PATRICIA STANFORD (D)
NC State Rep
b Dunn, NC, June 9, 28; d Lewis Knox Denning & Florence Cooper D; m 1949 to Donald M Stanford, Wid; m 1972 to Thomas Montague Hunt, Sr; c Donald McIver, Jr, Randolph Lewis, Charles Ashley & James Cooper Stanford. Educ: Sweet Briar Col, 46-48; Univ NC, Chapel Hill, AB & MA & further grad work, 68-72; Phi Beta Kappa; Valkyries; Order of the Old Well; Alpha Delta Pi. Polit & Govt Pos: Pres, Orange Co Dem Women, NC, 69-71; mem, Recreation Comn, Chapel Hill, 70-72; NC State Rep, 73-; mem, Gov Coun on Advocacy of Youth & Children, 73- Bus & Prof Pos: Pres, Chapel Hill Classroom Teachers Asn, 68-69; chmn citizenship comt, NC Asn Educators, 69-70; pres, Chapel Hill Asn Educators, 71-72. Publ: Co-auth, North Carolina History, Geography, & Government, Harcourt, Brace, Jovanovich, 72. Mem: Am & NC Hist Asns; Acad Polit & Social Scientists; Am & NC Asns Guid Personnel. Honors & Awards: Outstanding Woman Grad, Univ NC, 50. Relig: Presbyterian. Mailing Add: 1079 Burning Tree Dr Chapel Hill NC 27514

HUNT, ROBERT RICHARD, SR (R)
b Buffalo, NY, Feb 1, 28; s Albert H Hunt & Esther Richards H; m 1953 to Audrey Ann Carlson; c Andrea Louise & Robert Richard, Jr. Educ: Rensselaer Polytech Inst BSc in Eng, 52; Pi Delta Epsilon; Theta Chi; Scalp & Blade. Polit & Govt Pos: Comnr, Farmington Indust Develop Comn, Conn, 57-60; pres, Farmington Young Rep, 57-60; chmn, Farmington Rep Town Comt, formerly; comnr, Farmington Town Planning & Zoning Comn, 67- Bus & Prof Pos: Sales engr, United Aircraft Corp, 52-56, sr sales engr, 56-57; asst to pres, New Brit Tool & Mfg Co, Inc, 57-61, vpres, 61-66; secy, Winsted Container Co, Inc, 64-; chmn bd & treas, New Eng Cup Co, Inc, 68-73; pres, New Brit Tool & Mfg Co, Inc, 68- Mil Serv: Entered as Pvt, Army, 46, released as Technician, 47, after serv in 181st Signal Depot Co, Second Army, 47; Good Conduct Medal. Mem: Wyllys Lodge 99 AF&AM. Relig: Episcopal. Mailing Add: 4 Parish Rd Farmington CT 06032

HUNT, ROGER L (D)
NH State Rep
b Jan 23, 99; m 1928 to Pauline Alice Fuller; c three. Educ: Northumberland, NH. Polit & Govt Pos: Trustee of trust funds; former police chief; health officer; selectman, 3 years; mem, Planning Bd; NH State Rep, Concord, 65-, mem hwy safety comt, NH House of Rep; councilman, White Mountain Regional Asn. Mem: Weeks Mem Hosp (trustee); Upper Conn Valley Hosp (dir); KofP (Grand Master at Arms); Mason. Relig: Protestant. Mailing Add: North Stratford NH 03590

HUNT, STUART W, SR (R)
Vt State Rep
b Brattleboro, Vt, Apr 28, 27; s Dewey W Hunt & Ione Pearson H; m 1953 to Barbara Malcolm; c Stuart, II, Douglas, Thomas & Jane. Educ: Arnold Col, Bridgeport Univ. BS. Polit & Govt Pos: Selectman, Guilford, Vt, 60-70; Vt State Rep, 75- Mil Serv: Entered as Pvt, Air Force, 45, released as Cpl, 46, after serv in 2nd Air Force. Mem: Brattleboro Lodge 1499 Elks; Am Legion; Brattleboro Post 5. Relig: Protestant. Mailing Add: RFD 4 Box 300 West Brattleboro VT 05301

HUNT, WILLIAM ROBERT (R)
Comnr, Allegheny Co, Pa
b Duquesne, Pa, Oct 10, 13; s Robert Harry Hunt & Lillian Pearl Grumling H; m 1938 to Helen Mary Stewart; c Patricia (Mrs Fry). Educ: Univ Pittsburgh, BS, 35, Med Sch, MD, 38; McKeesport Hosp, Pa, Internship; St Vincent's Hosp, Pa, Surg Residence; Druids; Phi Kappa Sigma. Polit & Govt Pos: Coroner, Allegheny Co, 65-67, comnr, 67-; mem, Nat Adv Coun on Regional Med Prog, US Dept, Health, Educ & Welfare, 70-71; & Nat Adv Coun for Disease Control, 72-; deleg, Rep Nat Conv, 72. Bus & Prof Pos: Physician, McKeesport Hosp, Pa, 38-, sr staff surgeon, 51- Mil Serv: Entered as Lt(jg), Navy, 42, released as Lt Comdr, 46, after serv in Submarine Serv, Pac Theatre, 43-46; Pac Theatre Ribbon; SPac Theater Ribbon; Philippine Campaign Medal. Publ: The role of insurance abuse in hospital bed utilization, Am Med Asn J, 64. Mem: VFW Post 166; DAV; Mason; Fraternal Order of Police; Am Legion. Honors & Awards: Man of the Year in Med, Pittsburgh Acad of Med, 65; The Voice of Med for 1968, Pa Med Soc, 68. Relig: Presbyterian. Legal Res: 2412 James St McKeesport PA 15132 Mailing Add: 119 Court House Pittsburgh PA 15219

HUNTER, CONNIE MAUREEN (R)
b Shelley, Idaho, Mar 31, 27; d Arnfred John Christensen & Elizabeth Hyatt C; m 1944 to Commodore Hunter; c Clint Maurice, Cara Maureen & Chad Lynn. Educ: Firth High Sch, Idaho, grad, 45. Polit & Govt Pos: Co treas, Bingham Co, Idaho, 65-; secy-treas, Nat Asn Co Treas & Finance Officers, 70-72, vpres, 72-75, pres, 75-; secy, Bingham Co Rep Cent Comt, Idaho, 74- Bus & Prof Pos: Bookkeeper, teller & secy to mgr, Idaho First Nat Bank, 54-64. Mem: Women League Voters & Bus & Prof Women; Soroptomist (corresp secy). Relig: Latter-day Saint. Legal Res: 395 E Locust Shelley ID 83274 Mailing Add: Bingham Co Courthouse Blackfoot ID 83221

HUNTER, DONALD H (R)
Justice, Supreme Court Ind
b Anderson, Ind, Oct 21, 11; s Carl Edward Hunter & Mary Samuels H; m 1941 to Violet K Oemler; c Samuel E & Jean Ellen. Educ: Lincoln Univ Sch Law, LLB, 37; Phi Delta Phi. Polit & Govt Pos: Ind State Rep, Madison Co, 43; dep attorney gen, Indianapolis, 43 & 46-47; hearing examr, Ind Pub Serv Comn, 48; judge, LaGrange Circuit Court, 48-62; judicial mem, Statewide Comt Rev Adoption Laws, 50-52; judicial mem, Adv Comt Probation & Parole, Ind Citizens Coun, 53-55; judge, Appellate Court Ind, 63-66; chmn exec comt, Ind First Judicial Conf, 67; justice, Supreme Court Ind, 67-; mem, Const Rev Comt, 67- Mil Serv: Entered as Pvt, Army, 43, released as Cpl, 46, after serv in 47th Inf, Ninth Inf Div, ETO, 43-46; Five Campaign Stars; Combat Inf Badge; Combat Medic Badge; Bronze Star; Purple Heart; Belgique Fouragere; Four Presidential Unit Citations. Mem: Ind State Bar Asn; Mason; Am Legion; VFW; 40 et 8. Relig: Protestant. Mailing Add: State House Indianapolis IN 46204

HUNTER, ESTHER LENORE (R)
Chmn, Nuckolls Co Rep Party, Nebr
b Tobias, Nebr, May 12, 01; d Frank Marcellus Phillips & Josephine Bernice MacPherson P; m 1929 to Ray Lewis Hunter, wid; c Frank B (deceased) & Lewis Ray. Educ: Univ Nebr-Lincoln, 19-25; New Eng Conservatory, Boston, Mass, 25-29. Polit & Govt Pos: Vchmn, Webster Co Rep Party, Nebr, 36-49; sr vpres, Founder's Day State Orgn Lincoln,

49; vchmn, Nuckolls Co Rep Party, 54-68, chmn, 68-70 & 74- Bus & Prof Pos: Pub sch teacher, Nebr & Mass, 18-29; pvt music teacher, 29- Mem: DAR (State Regent Nebr, 72-74); Eastern Star (Worthy Matron, 59); Co Exten Club. Honors & Awards: Hon State Regent, DAR, 74. Relig: United Presbyterian; Platte Presbyterial Pres, 54-56. Mailing Add: 340 E Seventh St Superior NE 68978

HUNTER, GUY I (R)
Maine State Rep
Mailing Add: RFD 1 Clinton Benton ME 04927

HUNTER, HAL EDWARD, JR (D)
Mem, Mo State Dem Comt
b New Madrid, Mo, June 5, 21; s Hal Edward Hunter, Sr & Colleen Jackson H; m 1942 to Mary Virginia Crisler; c Hal Edward, III, Carolyn Ann (Mrs Lamanna), Mary Catherine, Lora Teresa, Stephen Craig & Lee Andrew. Educ: Univ Notre Dame, AB, 43, JD, 44. Polit & Govt Pos: Mem, New Madrid Co Dem Comt, Mo, 48-60; clerk, New Madrid Co Magistrate Court, 48-60; mem, Mo State Dem Comt, 60-; prosecuting attorney, New Madrid Co, 62-; deleg, Dem Nat Conv, 72. Bus & Prof Pos: Partner, Hunter & Hunter, 69- Mil Serv: Entered as Pvt, Army, 41, released as Pvt, 42. Mem: Mo & 34th Judicial Bar Asns; CofC; Jr CofC. Honors & Awards: Hon Colonel for three Gov. Relig: Catholic. Mailing Add: 1199 Scott New Madrid MO 63869

HUNTER, JACK CORBETT (R)
Mayor, Youngstown, Ohio
b Youngstown, Ohio, Mar 13, 30; s Charles E Hunter & Margaret Corbett H; m 1973 to Pauline Ann Pieton. Educ: Univ Denver, undergrad degree in econ; Youngstown State Univ, additional studies; Kent State Univ, grad degree in polit sci. Polit & Govt Pos: Mem exec comt, Ohio State Rep Party, currently; city councilman, Fifth Ward, Youngstown, Ohio, 65-69, mayor, 70- Bus & Prof Pos: Erie Lackawanna Tower operator, 48-58; asst trust off, Mahoning Nat Bank, 60-69; part-time instr econ & pub finance, Youngstown State Univ, 62-68. Mil Serv: Marine Corps, 50-54, Sgt. Mem: Smithsonian Inst; Orgn of Protestant Men; Phi Sigma Alpha; Navy League; Am Pub Works Asn. Honors & Awards: Frank Purnell Award. Relig: Presbyterian. Legal Res: 467 W Boston Ave Youngstown OH 44511 Mailing Add: City Hall Bldg Boardman at Phelps Youngstown OH 44503

HUNTER, LAWRENCE J (D)
Wyo State Rep
Mailing Add: 107 Sunset Dr Gillette WY 82716

HUNTER, LORA TERESA (D)
b Sikeston, Mo, Sept 13, 53; d Hal Edward Hunter, Jr & Mary Crisler H; single. Educ: Memphis State Univ, currently. Polit & Govt Pos: Deleg, Dem Nat Conv, 72. Honors & Awards: Citizenship Award, DAR, 71. Relig: Roman Catholic. Mailing Add: 1199 Scott St New Madrid MO 63869

HUNTER, MARGARET BLAKE (MAXINE) (R)
Pres, Mass Fedn Rep Women
b Vancouver, BC, Oct 30, 13; d Harry Melvin Urquhart & Jessie Boynton U; m to Donald Hunter; c Donald M, Stephen B, David L & Richard E. Educ: Hudson High Sch, Mass. Polit & Govt Pos: Vchmn, Leominster Rep City Comt, Mass, 58-70; mem, Mass Rep State Cent Comt, Third Dist, 69-; secy Mass deleg & deleg, Rep Nat Conv, 72; pres, Mass Fedn Rep Women, 73- Mem: Leominster Women's Rep Club; Worcester Co Rep Club; World Affairs Coun; Rep Club Mass; Middlesex Rep Club. Honors & Awards: Outstanding Serv Award, Leominster CofC, 71. Relig: Unitarian-Universalist. Legal Res: 96 Carriageway Dr Leominster MA 01453 Mailing Add: PO Box 803 Leominster MA 01453

HUNTER, ROBERT EDWARD (D)
b New Orleans, La, June 11, 12; s Joseph Cooper Hunter & Alice C Sporl H; m 1935 to Marie Le Blanc; c Rev Patrick Joseph, SJ. Educ: Loyola Univ of the South, Phb, 48; Alpha Pi; past pres, DC Chap, Loyola Alumni. Polit & Govt Pos: Admin asst to US Sen Russell B Long, La, 56-73; consult, currently. Mil Serv: Entered as Pvt, Army, 44, released as 2nd Lt, 45; Maj (Ret), Army Res. Mem: La Post, Soc Am Mil Engrs; Commercial Athletic Asn of New Orleans; Fed Bus Asn of New Orleans. Relig: Catholic. Legal Res: New Orleans LA Mailing Add: 2400 36th St SE Washington DC 20020

HUNTER, ROBERT THOMAS
Justice, Wash State Supreme Court
b Lawton, Okla, Sept 29, 07; s Alfred Lewis Hunter & Nancy Jane Fisher H; m 1938 to Helen Maureen Neary; c Janice (Mrs William Michael Murphy), Marilynn (Mrs Clyde Jan Garner), Patricia (Mrs James C McDonald) & Robert Thomas, Jr. Educ: Univ Wash, LLB, 34; Phi Alpha Delta; Alpha Sigma Phi. Polit & Govt Pos: City attorney, Grand Coulee, Wash, 36-46; superior court judge, Grant & Douglas Counties, 46-57; justice, Wash State Supreme Court, 57- Mem: Wash State Superior Court Judges; Odd Fellows (Past Grand Master); Lions. Relig: Presbyterian. Mailing Add: 1402 Rolling Hills Terr Olympia WA 98502

HUNTER, THOMAS B (D)
NC State Rep
Mailing Add: 618 Fayetteville Rd Rockingham NC 28379

HUNTER, WILLIAM ARMSTRONG (INDEPENDENT-D)
Vt State Rep
b Boston, Mass, Sept 27, 53; s Armstrong Hunter & Edith Fisher H; single. Educ: Princeton Univ, 73-75; Yale Univ, 74- Polit & Govt Pos: Auditor, Weathersfield, Vt, 72-73; Vt State Rep, 75- Bus & Prof Pos: Ed & publ, The Weathersfield Weekly, 71- Mem: Vt Farm Bur; Hawks Mountain Grange; Weathersfield Hist Soc; Weathersfield Serv. Mailing Add: RFD 2 Box 339A Weathersfield VT 05156

HUNTINGTON, JIMMY (R)
Alaska State Rep
Mailing Add: Galena AK 99741

HUNTLEY, MARGARET ELIZABETH (R)
Committeewoman, Ark Rep State Comt
b Mecklenburg Co, NC; d Samuel F Mullis & Flora Q Jones M; m 1945 to Patrick Ross Huntley; c Mikel. Educ: King's Col, 40-41. Polit & Govt Pos: Pres, Washington Co Rep Women's Club, Ark, 72-74; committeewoman, Ark Rep State Comt, 74- Mem: Women's Civic Asn (vpres, 73). Mailing Add: 1219 W Lakeridge Dr Fayetteville AR 72701

HUNTON, BENJAMIN LACY (R)
Asst Dir Educ & Training, Bur of Mines, Dept of Interior
b Washington, DC, Nov 25, 19; s Benjamin H Hunton & Evelyn Lacy H; m 1961 to Kelsy Jean Cooper; c Benjamin Lorimer. Educ: Howard Univ, AB, 40, MA, 42; Am Univ, PhD, 54; Gamma Tau. Polit & Govt Pos: Supv dir, Pub Schs, Washington, DC, 51-58, asst to asst supt jr sr high schs, 58-66; area dir, Equal Educ Opportunity Prog, Dept of Health, Educ & Welfare, 66-69; Job Corps Prog officer, Dept of Interior, 69-70, asst dir educ & training, Bur of Mines, 70- Bus & Prof Pos: Teacher, Washington, DC Pub Schs, 42-51. Mil Serv: Entered as Platoon Leader/Supply Off, Army, 42, released as asst prof of mil sci & tactics, Howard Univ, 49, after serv in US; Brigade Comdr, First Brigade, 80th Div, Army Res, 61, Col, Minority Affairs Off, CORC, DA, 70-; World War II Victory & Am Theater Medals; 20 Year Res Ribbon. Publ: Budget of the department of war 22-32, Am Univ, 54; Basic track in junior high schools, 62, & Study of selected school dropouts 63-66, 67, DC Pub Schs. Mem: Asn of US Army; ROA; Am Fedn of Govt Employees; Amvets. Relig: Catholic. Mailing Add: 7737 Ardmore-Ardwick Rd Hyattsville MD 20784

HUOT, J OLIVA (D)
b Laconia, NH, Aug 11, 17; s Amedee Huot & Marie Bibiane Decelles H; m 1938 to Irene R Fournier; c David O. Educ: High Sch. Polit & Govt Pos: Mem sch bd, Laconia, NH, 53-59, mayor, 59-63; nominee for NH House of Rep, First Dist, 62; deleg, Dem Nat Conv, 64; US Rep, First Dist, NH, 65-67. Bus & Prof Pos: Supvr, Tabulating Dept, Scott & Williams, Inc, 35-56; advert mgr, Laconia Eve Citizen, 56-64; gen mgr, Lakes Region Trader, 59-64; trustee, City Savings Bank, Laconia, 65- & Gustock Jr Col, 66- Mem: New Eng Daily Newspapers Asn; KofC; Elks; Kiwanis; Moose. Relig: Roman Catholic. Mailing Add: 32 Adams St Laconia NH 03246

HUPP, FRANCES JANE (D)
VChairperson, Shawnee Co Dem Party, Kans
b Frankfort, Kans, July 5, 23; d Thomas Charles Clark & Minnie Elizabeth Stevens C; m 1945 to Earl Wayne Hupp; c Linda (Mrs John Morse), Carol (Mrs Douglas Cook) & Thomas Allen. Educ: Frankfort High Sch, Kans, grad; Beauty Sch, Topeka. Polit & Govt Pos: Secy, Shawnee Co Dem Party, Kans, 8 years; vchairperson, 72-; deleg, Dem Nat Mid-Term Conf, 74. Mem: Nat & Local Hairdressers Asns; Am Legion Auxiliary. Relig: Catholic. Mailing Add: 916 SW 31st Terr Topeka KS 66611

HURD, EDWARD FLOYD (R)
b Knoxville, Tenn, Mar 29, 08; s Raymond Edward Hurd & Lillian Bankston H; m 1935 to Newell Sanders Hooper; c Jane (Mrs Alan Christner), Frances (Mrs Albert Mullen), Sandra (Mrs Russell Bowman) & Annabelle (Mrs Henry Buchanan). Educ: Univ Tenn, Knoxville, JD, 31; Phi Delta Phi; Alpha Tau Omega. Polit & Govt Pos: Co attorney, Cocke Co, Tenn, 38-62 & 68-; deleg, Rep Nat Conv, 48; chmn, Cocke Co Rep Exec Comt, formerly. Mem: Am, Tenn & Cocke Co Bar Asns; Mason; Elks. Relig: Baptist. Legal Res: Route 1 Carson Springs Rd Newport TN 37821 Mailing Add: PO Box 303 Newport TN 37821

HURD, JOHN GAVIN (R)
b Sacramento, Calif, July 2, 14; s Eugene Hurd & Nella Claire Wilson H; m 1957 to Nancy Smith; c Patricia (Mrs Harvey), Sally (Mrs Garcia), Victoria Louise, John Radcliffe; six grandchildren. Educ: Harvard, AB, 34, LLB, 37; Chancery Club; Pow Wow Club, Moot Court; Varsity Fencing Team, 32-34, Capt, 34; Intercollegiate Foil Champion, 34. Polit & Govt Pos: Chmn, Webb Co Rep Party, Tex, 48-64; mem, Tex Rep State Exec Comt, 21st Sen Dist, 64-65; alt deleg, Rep Nat Conv, 64, deleg, 68; dep state chmn, Tex Rep Party, Region III, 65-67; state chmn, Tex Nixon for President, 68; US Ambassador to Repub of SAfrica, 70-75. Bus & Prof Pos: Attorney, Pillsbury, Madison & Sutro, San Francisco, Calif, 37-39; Standard Oil Co Calif, Land & Legal Dept, Employee Personnel Dept, 39-41; independent oil producer, cattle rancher & investments in US & Mex, 46-; gen partner, corp officer & vpres, Killam & Hurd, Ltd & Killam Land & Cattle Co; gen partner, Killam & Hurd Investments, Ltd, Hurkil Corp, Laredo Offshore, Ltd, Rio Bravo Cattle Co, Mex; corp officer & vpres, Texpata Pipe Line Co; dir, Alamo Nat Bank, San Antonio, Tex, Union Nat Bank, Laredo, Laredo Savings & Loan Asn, Mid-Continent Oil & Gas Asn, Tex Mid-Continent Oil & Gas Asn, Independent Petroleum Asn of Am & Gulf Energy & Develop Corp, San Antonio, Tex. Mil Serv: Entered as Ens, Naval Res, 34, retired as Comdr, 54, after serv in Naval Intel, 12th Naval Dist & Sea Duty Anti-Submarine Warfare, Atlantic Fleet as Exec Off in USS Hayter DE212, 41-45; US Defense, Am & European Theatre decorations with Battle Stars; Bronze Star Medal 'V'; Naval Res Medal. Mem: Tex Bar Asn; Am Legion; Laredo CofC; Rotary Int; Masons. Honors & Awards: All Am Wildcatter for the Year, 69; Outstanding Texan, Jr CofC, 49; US Olympic Fencing Team, Berlin, Ger, 36. Relig: Episcopal. Legal Res: 2101 Gustavus St Laredo TX 78040 Mailing Add: PO Box 499 Laredo TX 78040

HURLEY, BRUCE WALLACE (R)
Tenn State Rep
b Sneedville, Tenn, Feb 16, 34; s Harvey Edgar Hurley & Cordia Gertrude Trent H; m 1965 to Doris Janett Edwards; c Pamela Jane. Educ: Monterey Tech Inst, Mex, 57; ETenn State Univ, BS, 59, post grad, 60-61; Delta Sigma Pi; Pi Kappa Alpha. Polit & Govt Pos: Vpres, Tenn Fedn Young Rep, 54 & 60, pres, 61; deleg, Tenn Ltd Const Conv, 65-66; Tenn State Rep, Hawkins & Hancock Co, 70- Bus & Prof Pos: Field rep, Census Bur, 22 ETenn Co, 59; breeder, Tenn Walking Horses & Charolais Cattle, Hawkins Co, Tenn, 59-; safety engr, Holston Army Ammunition Plant, 61-70, asst personnel mgr, 70- Mil Serv: Entered as Pvt, Army, 54, released as Pfc, 55, after serv in Field Artil; Good Conduct Award. Mem: Am Legion; Farm Bur; Hawkins Co Soil Conserv Dist Alumni; ETenn State Univ Doctors Comt. Honors & Awards: Outstanding Soil Conserv Award, 69; ETenn State Col Hall of Fame; hon mem bd dirs, Outdoor Drama, Sneedville, Tenn. Relig: Protestant. Mailing Add: Rte 1 Johnson Estates Surgoinsville TN 37873

HURLEY, CHARLES SULLIVAN (D)
b Selma, Ala, Feb 17, 23; s Charles Sloan Hurley & Harriet Sullivan H; m 1945 to Flora Ann Koelmel; c Harriet Roushey, Susan (Mrs Peter Fuhrman), Charles S, Jr & James Joseph. Educ: Univ Minn, BA, 47; Sacramento State Univ, grad work in polit sci, 69-71; Sigma Delta Chi. Polit & Govt Pos: Dep state controller, State Controller Alan Cranston, Calif, 61-65; admin asst, Rep Phillip Burton, 65-69; asst to assembly Dem caucus chmn, George Zenovich, 69-71; asst to assembly rules comt chmn, John L Burton, 71-73; asst to Dem majority leader, Jack Fenton, 73-74; admin asst, US Rep George Miller, Calif, 75- Bus & Prof Pos: Reporter, Albuquerque J, Albuquerque, NMex, 48-52 & The Glendale News Press, Glendale, Calif, 52-53; polit writer, The Fresno Bee, 53-58, city ed, 58-61. Mil Serv: Entered as Pvt, Marine

Corps, 41, released as Cpl, 45, after serv in 1st Marine Div, Guadalcanal, Cape Gloucester & Peleliu Landing; Presidential Unit Citations; Four Combat Stars. Mem: Calif Lung Asn (bd dirs, 69-); Marines Mem Asn, San Francisco; Contra Costa Press Club; Sierra Club; Sacramento/Emigrant Trails Lung Asn; House Rep Admin Asst Asn, Washington, DC. Relig: Episcopal. Legal Res: Port Costa CA 94569 Mailing Add: 1532 Longworth Bldg Washington DC 20515

HURLEY, DANIEL GERARD (D)
b Boston, Mass, Sept 10, 42; s Daniel Joseph Hurley & Mary McAuley H; m 1968 to Sharon Lee Dolan; c Melissa June. Educ: Northeastern Univ, BA; New Eng Sch Law, LLB. Polit & Govt Pos: Admin asst, Middlesex Co Comn, Mass, 65-72; deleg, Dem Nat Conv, 72. Bus & Prof Pos: Vpres, Harbor Mkt Group, Inc, 72- & Independent Distributors Exchange Asn, Inc, 73. Mil Serv: Mass Nat Guard, 69. Mem: Aiding Leukemia Stricken Am Children (bd dirs, Gtr Boston, 66-); Mass Jaycees (dir, 69-73); Barry Research Found for Emotionally Disturbed Children (dir, 65-73); Heart Fund Asn (Gtr Boston Bd, 72-73); Nat Munic League. Honors & Awards: Outstanding Serv, United Fund, 68-69 & Mass Heart Asn, 69. Relig: Catholic. Mailing Add: 170 Mystick St Exten Medford MA 02155

HURLEY, ELISABETH A (R)
b Cuyahoga Falls, Ohio, Oct 5, 21; d Walter Leroy Tucker & Florence Corwin T; m 1942 to Richard Louis Hurley; c Martha Lou. Educ: Kent State Univ, 39-41; Alpha Phi. Polit & Govt Pos: Precinct committeeman, Precinct D, Hudson, Ohio; area dir of vol, Summit Co, 64; deleg, Ohio Rep State Conv, 68 & 72; mem, Summit Co Rep Exec Comt, 68; chmn, Summit Co Neighbor to Neighbor & Ohio Rep Finance Comts, 68-73; regional dir of vol, Comt for Reelect of the President, 72; alt deleg, Rep Nat Conv, 72. Bus & Prof Pos: Secy-treas, W L Tucker Supply Co, 64- Mem: Womens Div, Akron Area CofC; Hudson CofC; Womens Auxiliary, Gtr Akron Builders Exchange. Relig: Protestant. Mailing Add: 940 Westhaven Dr Hudson OH 44236

HURLEY, GEORGE S (D)
Wash State Rep
Mailing Add: 10709 First Ave NW Seattle WA 98177

HURLEY, JAMES F (R)
NY State Assemblyman
Mailing Add: 28 High St Lyons NY 14489

HURLEY, JAMES RICHARDSON (R)
NJ State Assemblyman
b Seaford, Del, Jan 29, 32; s Victor Elzey Hurley & Annabel Jarman H; m 1956 to Walda Lou Reed; c Leslie, Jamie & Kerri Anna. Educ: Wesley Col, Dover, Del, AA, 53; Univ NC, Chapel Hill, AV, 55; Sigma Nu. Polit & Govt Pos: Freeholder, Cumberland Co, NJ, 66-67; NJ State Assemblyman, Dist 1, 67-, asst Rep leader, NJ Assembly, 72- Bus & Prof Pos: Broadcaster, WBOC, Salisbury, Md, 57-59; teacher, Millville Sr High Sch, NJ, 59-61; news dir, WMVB, Millville, 61-63; vpres, S Jersey Nat Bank, 63-71. Mil Serv: Entered as E-1, Army, 55, released as E-3, 57, after serv in Signal Corps. Mem: Bank Pub Rels & Mkt Asn; NJ Bankers Asn; Kiwanis; YMCA; United Fund. Honors & Awards: Distinguished Serv Award, Millville Jr CofC, 62. Relig: Presbyterian. Mailing Add: 2 Elizabeth Ave Millville NJ 08332

HURLEY, MRS JOSEPH E (D)
Wash State Rep
b Winnebago, Minn; m to Joseph E, wid; c four. Educ: Holy Names Col, BA. Polit & Govt Pos: Wash State Rep, currently. Bus & Prof Pos: Teacher; homemaker. Mem: Citizens Against Residential Freeways. Mailing Add: 730 E Boone Ave Spokane WA 99202

HURLEY, KIRK LAMAR (R)
b Cambridge, Md, Feb 8, 52; s Charles F Hurley & Mildred Hallsa H; single. Educ: Frostburg State Col, BS, 73; Pi Kappa Delta; Phi Alpha Theta. Polit & Govt Pos: Aide to Congressman William O Mills, Md, 71-73; deleg, Rep Nat Conv, 72; aide to State Sen Edward Mason, 73; mem excess property adv comn, Dorchester Co, 75- Bus & Prof Pos: Mem staff, Airpax Electronics, 75- Mem: East New Market Heritage Found; Dorchester Co Young Rep. Relig: United Methodist. Mailing Add: Box 236 East New Market MD 21631

HURLEY, PATRICK JOSEPH (D)
Kans State Rep
b Leavenworth, Kans, Apr 8, 41; s John Philip Hurley & Catherine Fitzgerald H; m 1968 to Patricia Sommer; c Mary Therese, Matthew, Philip & Mark. Educ: St Benedict Col, BA, 63; Washburn Univ Law Sch, JD, 67; Delta Theta Phi. Polit & Govt Pos: Kans State Rep, 75- Bus & Prof Pos: Attorney, Off Gen Counsel, Dept Agr, Kansas City, Mo, 67-71; attorney-at-law, Beall & Hurley, Leavenworth, Kans, 71- Mem: Am & Kans Bar Asns; Leavenworth CofC (dir); Leavenworth United Fund (dir); Leavenworth Red Cross (dir). Relig: Catholic. Legal Res: 228 Fourth Ave Leavenworth KS 66048 Mailing Add: PO Box 369 818 N Seventh St Leavenworth KS 66048

HURLEY, PAULA M (D)
Secy, Fitchburg City Dem Comt, Mass
b Fitchburg, Mass, Apr 14, 48; d William Patrick Hurley & Mary Clacoss H; single. Polit & Govt Pos: Mem campaign staffs, Robert F Kennedy, 68, Robert F Drinan for US Cong, Mass, 69-70 & US Sen Edward Kennedy, 69-70; mem cong staff, US Rep Robert F Drinan, Fourth Dist, 70-72; campaign mgr, Mayor Carleton E Blackwell, Fitchburg, 71; campaign mgr, Selectman Bob Newton, Ashby, 71; secy, Fitchburg City Dem Comt, 71-, chmn, Ward Three, 71-; campaign coordr, George McGovern for President, Mass, 72; deleg, Dem Nat Conv, 72; fed-state funding coordr, City of Fitchburg, 72-; deleg, Dem Nat Mid-Term Conf, 74. Mem: Common Cause; CP Pax; Mass Youth Caucus. Relig: Catholic. Mailing Add: 745 River St Fitchburg MA 01420

HURLEY, STERLIN (D)
Ark State Rep
Mailing Add: PO Box 288 Clarksville AR 72830

HURRELL, JAMES PHILIP (D)
Mass State Rep
b Methuen, Mass, Mar 1, 44; s Stanley Joseph Hurrell & Winifred Miller H; single. Educ: Suffolk Univ, 3 years; Alpha Phi Omega. Polit & Govt Pos: State senate aide, Boston, Mass, 64-67; Mass State Rep, 67- Bus & Prof Pos: Owner & broker, James P Hurrell Realty, currently. Mil Serv: Entered as Pvt, Nat Guard, 69. Mem: State Legislators Asn; Nat Legislators Asn; Nat Realtors Asn; Elks; KofC. Relig: Roman Catholic. Legal Res: 522 Chickering Rd North Andover MA 01845 Mailing Add: Box 205 North Andover MS 01845

HURSH, JOHN R (R)
Wyo State Rep
b Scottsbluff, Nebr, Feb 16, 43; s R Max Hursh & Virginia Adams H; m 1969 to Nancy Jane Watkins; c Bryan Watkins. Educ: Univ Wyo, BA, 65, JD, 68; Omicron Delta Kappa; Sigma Nu; pres, Assoc Students, Univ Wyo, 65. Polit & Govt Pos: Wyo State Rep, 75- Bus & Prof Pos: Attorney, Hamilton & Hursh, PC, 69-, secy-treas, 74-; pres, Hursh Agency, Inc, Riverton, Wyo, 72-; dir, First Guaranty Savings & Loan, Riverton, 72- Mil Serv: Entered as 2nd Lt, Marine Corps, 68, released as Capt, 71, after serv in Staff Judge Adv Corps, 69-71; Capt, Marine Corps Res, currently. Mem: Mason; Lions; Wyo Outdoor Coun; Wyo Stockgrowers Asn. Honors & Awards: Pres, Pac Student Pres Asn, 66; Emery S Land Award, Univ Wyo, 66. Relig: Episcopal; mem vestry. Legal Res: 318 N Second W Riverton WY 82501 Mailing Add: 105-107 S Sixth E Riverton WY 82501

HURST, EDDIE DURDEN (D)
Mem, Ga State Dem Exec Comt
b Metter, Ga, May 24, 31; d Eddie Durden & Estelle Waye D; m 1948 to Carl Lindy Hurst. Educ: Swainsboro Tech Sch, secy & bus courses, 69. Polit & Govt Pos: Campaign adv for various local & state elec; nat campaign worker, Kennedy for President; secy, Hagan for Cong, Jenkins Co, 60-; campaign adv, Lester Maddox, Jenkins Co, 65; campaign adv, Jay Cox for Senate, 65; mem, Comn on Status of Women, 67-; chmn, Jenkins Co Jimmy Carter's Gubernatorial Campaign, 70; mem, Ga State Dem Exec Comt, 71- Bus & Prof Pos: Operator, Southern Bell Tel & Tel Co, 48, serv rep, 60-65, secy, 65- Mem: Jaycettes; Green Thumb Garden Club; Garden Coun; VFW Auxiliary; Farm Bur. Honors & Awards: Orgn pres, Jenkins Co Jaycettes & Green Thumb Garden Club; Southern Bell of the Month, 10/67. Relig: Baptist. Mailing Add: Hillcrest Millen GA 30442

HURST, GLYNN J (D)
Treas, Ziebach Co Dem Party, SDak
b St Lawrence, SDak, Aug 19, 10; s Levi Charles Hurst & Julia Petersen H; m 1937 to Sybil Bird; c Phyllis Rose. Educ: Dupree High Sch. Polit & Govt Pos: Auditor, Ziebach Co Dem Party, SDak, 56-59, chmn, 58-62 & 64-70, treas, 62- Mil Serv: Entered as Pvt, Army, released as T/Sgt, 40, after serv in 975th Field Artil Bn, ETO; Four Major Campaign Ribbons. Mem: SDak Asn of Co Off (pres); Odd Fellows; Mason; Am Legion; VFW. Relig: Congregational. Mailing Add: DuPree SD 57623

HURST, JOHN (D)
Ky State Rep
Mailing Add: Rte 1 Bloomfield KY 40008

HURST, JULIUS (R)
b McNairy Co, Tenn, 1919; m 1947 to Mary Louis Nipp; c Suzanne & David. Educ: Univ Tenn, BA, 40, MA, 50. Polit & Govt Pos: Rep campaign chmn, McNairy Co, Tenn, 52, 56 & 60; mem, McNairy Co Rep Exec Comt, 54; supvr, McNairy Co Schs, 59-; Rep nominee for Cong, Seventh Cong Dist, 64 & 69; chmn, Tenn Rep State Exec Comt, 65. Bus & Prof Pos: Prin, Jr High Sch, 40; dir, Tenn Farm Bur, 52-53. Mil Serv: Army, World War II. Mem: Nat, Tenn & Co Educ Asns; Rotary. Honors & Awards: Outstanding Citizen, CofC, 65. Relig: Presbyterian. Mailing Add: 1252 E Poplar Selmer TN 38375

HURST, WILDA (D)
NC State Rep
Mailing Add: Box 290 Hubert NC 28539

HURTADO, RALPH FRANK (D)
b San Francisco, Calif, Feb 22, 42; s Tony Peria Hurtado & Helen Gonzales H; single. Educ: San Francisco State Univ, BA, 64; Univ Calif, Berkeley, MSW, 68; Alpha Phi Gamma. Polit & Govt Pos: Regional campaign coordr, Calif McGovern-Shriver Campaign, 72; co-chairperson, W San Gabriel Valley McGovern for President Comt, 71-72; deleg, Dem Nat Conv, 72; alt, Los Angeles Co Dem Cent Comt, Calif. 72-73; legis asst, US Rep George Brown, Jr, Calif, 73-75; legis asst, US Rep Herman Badillo, NY, 75- Bus & Prof Pos: Assoc dir, Community Planning Coun, Pasadena, Calif, 68-70, consult, 70-72; mem bd dirs, Foothill Free Clin, Pasadena, 68-71; asst clin prof, Sch Social Work, Univ Southern Calif, 70-73, preceptor, Dept of Community Med, Sch of Med, 71-72; mem bd dirs, Vol Action Ctr, Pasadena, 72-73, Los Amigos de Humanitad, Univ Southern Calif, 72-73 & Pasadena Planning Forum of United Way, 72-73; mem bd, Minority Legis Educ Prog, Washington, DC, currently. Mil Serv: Entered as Pvt, Army, 64, released as SP-4, 68, after serv in Letterman Gen Hosp, Presidio of San Francisco, 64-66. Publ: Pasadena area primary & secondary drug resources directory, Community Planning Coun, Pasadena, 70; A look at the District of Columbia schools, In: Viewpoints I!I: Contemporary Educational Issues, 74 & Soviet education & the 5 year plan, In: Viewpoints III: Education in the Soviet Union, 74, George Washington Univ. Mem: Pasadena Girls Club (adv bd, 70-); ACT; Nat Asn Soc Workers; Univ Senate, Univ Southern Calif. Honors & Awards: Newhouse grant, 66; scholar, San Francisco Jr CofC, 66; scholar, Eli Lilly & Co; Dem of the Year, Los Angeles Co Dem Cent Comt, 73. Legal Res: DC Mailing Add: 445 Fifth St NE Washington DC 20002

HURWITCH, ROBERT ARNOLD
US Ambassador to Dominican Repub
b Worcester, Mass, Oct 15, 20; s Frank Hurwitch & Sema Sorin H; m 1945 to Saralee Pilot; c Jan, Paula, Carol & Sally. Educ: Univ Wis, 43; Univ Chicago, AB, 49. Polit & Govt Pos: Vconsul, Am Embassy, Lima, Peru, 51-53, Am Consulate Gen, Hamburg, Germany, 53-55; labor attache, Am Embassy, Bonn, 55-56; labor attache, Am Embassy, Bogota, Colombia, 56-60; int rels officer, Dept State, 60-64; spec asst, Am Embassy, Santiago, Chile, 64; dep chief mission, Am Embassy, La Paz, Bolivia, 64-66; dep chief mission, Am Embassy, Vientiane, Laos, 67-69; Dep Asst Secy State, 69-73; US Ambassador to Dominican Repub, 73- Mil Serv: Entered as Pvt, Army, 43, released as Capt, 47, after serv in 63rd Inf Div, 7th Army, Europe, 45-46; Bronze Star with Oak Leaf Cluster; Combat Infantryman's Badge. Publ: Today's senior foreign service officers, 64 & Cuban missile crisis—three anecdotes, 72, Am For Serv J. Mem: Am Foreign Serv Asn. Honors & Awards: Commendable Serv Award, Dept State, 61, Distinguished Serv Award, 63 & President's Award for Mgt, 72. Relig: Jewish. Legal Res: 300 N State St Chicago IL 60610 Mailing Add: Am Embassy Santo Domingo Dominican Republic

HUSAK, EMIL J (D)
Iowa State Rep
Mailing Add: RR 2 Toledo IA 52342

HUSFLOEN, ABRAHAM (ABE) (D)
Mem State Cent Comt, NDak Dem Non-Partisan League
b Osterdalen, Norway, Dec 31, 93; s Ole Halvorson Husfloen & Johanna Moen H. Polit & Govt Pos: Mem State Cent Comt, NDak Dem No-Partisan League, currently, chmn, 4 years; precinct committeeman, 66-; co chmn, Rep Party, 4 yrs. Bus & Prof Pos: Rancher, Hereford Cattle, 25- Mil Serv: Pvt, Army, 18-19. Mem: Am Legion; Farmers Union; Vets World War I. Relig: Lutheran. Mailing Add: 505-2 Ave NW Mandan ND 58554

HUSKINS, JOSEPH PATTERSON (D)
NC State Rep
b Burnsville, NC, June 23, 08; s Joseph Erwin Huskins & Mary Etta Peterson H; m 1934 to Mildred Amburn; c Mrs William Power. Educ: Univ NC, Chapel Hill, AB, 30. Polit & Govt Pos: Mem, Area Rent Control Bd, NC, 47-51, Statesville Zoning Bd, 60-62 & NC Bd Higher Educ, 66-72; NC State Rep, 35th Dist, 71- Bus & Prof Pos: Pres & gen mgr, Statesville Daily Rec, Ind, 46-; pres, NC Asn Afternoon Dailies, 48-49; pres, Assoc Dailies of NC, 65-66; chmn bd trustees, Mitchell Col, 62-66 & 70-; bd gov, Univ NC, 72-73; bd gov, Legis Serv Comn, 72- Mil Serv: Entered as Lt(jg), Naval Res, 43, released as Lt(sg), 46, after serv in Air Navig Sect, Hydrographic Off, Washington, DC. Mem: Statesville CofC; Statesville Elks (Past Exalted Ruler); Statesville City Club (vpres); Am Legion; Statesville Arts & Sci Mus. Relig: Methodist. Legal Res: Our Dell Statesville NC 28677 Mailing Add: 220 E Broad St Statesville NC 28677

HUSS, JOHN FREDERICK (JACK) (R)
Mem, NDak State Rep Exec Comt
b Aberdeen, SDak, Sept 11, 24; s A W Huss & Irene Nelson H; m 1947 to Dorothy Nantz; c Stephanie (Mrs Borud), Laurie Ann, John M & Jeffrey N. Educ: Northern State Col, 42 & 46-47; Univ Minn BBA, 48. Polit & Govt Pos: Rep precinct committeeman, Williston, NDak, 60-; Campaign dir, Williams Co, 60, co chmn, 61-65; committeeman, NDak State Rep Cent Comt, 65-67, secy, 66-67, chmn, 69-72; mem, Rep Nat Comt, 70-72, mem co comt, 70-72; deleg & mem rules comt, Rep Nat Conv, 72; mem, NDak State Rep Exec Comt, 72- Bus & Prof Pos: Owner, J F Huss & Co, Ins, 53-68; spec agent, Northwestern Mutual Life Ins Co, 68- Mil Serv: Entered as Pvt, Air Force, 43, released as Sgt, 46. Relig: Presbyterian. Mailing Add: 504 E Interstate Bismarck ND 58501

HUSSEY, NORA W (R)
Rep Nat Committeewoman, SDak
b New York, NY, Mar 26, 15; m 1947 to Shirley B Hussey. Educ: NY Univ. Polit & Govt Pos: Organizer, Meade Co Federated Rep Women, SDak; Rep precinct committeewoman; vchmn, Meade Co Rep Party, formerly, chmn, 64-72; Rep Nat Committeewoman, SDak, 72- Bus & Prof Pos: Med records librn, formerly. Mem: Red Cross (home nursing chmn); PEO (chap treas); Toastmistress Club. Honors & Awards: First woman co chmn in SDak. Relig: Episcopal; Pres church women. Mailing Add: 1928 Arizona Ave Sturgis SD 57785

HUTAR, PATRICIA (R)
First VPres, Nat Fedn Rep Women
b Minneapolis, Minn; d George Hansom Miller & Selma Barge M; m 1953 to Laddie Frank Hutar. Educ: Univ Minn, 46-49; Memphis State Col, BS, 50. Polit & Govt Pos: Pub chmn group work & recreation div, Community Welfare Coun of San Diego, Calif, 52; Vol Young Rep, San Diego, 52; precinct capt, 39th Precinct, 43rd Ward, Ill, 55-; playground proj chmn & vpres, 43rd Ward Young Rep Orgn, Inc, 55-56, pres, 56-57, deleg, 57-; spec activities chmn, Young Rep Orgn of Cook Co, Inc, 56-57, vchmn-at-lg, 57-; co-dir Region V, Nat Fedn Young Rep, 57-, co-chmn publicity, 59-; co-chmn Cook Co membership drive, United Rep Fund, 59-; bd gov, 62-65; vpres, Rep Citizens League, Ill; asst chmn, Rep Nat Comt, formerly; fourth vpres, Nat Fedn Rep Women, 71-73, second vpres, 73-75, first vpres, 75- Bus & Prof Pos: Group social worker, Girl Scout Coun of San Diego Co, Inc, 51-52; recorder, First Annual Conf on Group Leadership, San Diego State Col, 52; fashion photographers model & fashion lectr, 54-58; with Beveridge Orgn, Inc, pub rels, 58-; partner, Investment Club Counsrs, 59-; dir, Nuscope Co, Inc, Chicago; free lance writer. Mem: Art Inst, Chicago; Metrop Opera Guild, Chicago; Chicago Arden Shore Asn (donations chmn, 56-); Metrop YMCA (recording secy, Women's bd). Honors & Awards: Named Most Outstanding Young Rep Woman of Ill, 55-57. Mailing Add: 3800 Lake Shore Dr Chicago IL 60613

HUTCHENS, JOHN GROVER (R)
Chmn, Sixth Cong Dist Rep Party, NC
b High Point, NC, Nov 28, 28; s George Elijah Hutchens & Elizabeth Lineback H; m 1950 to Jane Campbell Davis; c John G, Jr, Julia, James & Jane Campbell. Educ: Davidson Col, BS, 51; Univ NC, Chapel Hill, LLB, 54; Univ NC Law Review; Sigma Alpha Epsilon; Phi Delta Phi. Polit & Govt Pos: Chmn, High Point Rep Party, NC, 65; mem exec comt, Guilford Co Rep Party, 65-; deleg, Rep Nat Conv, 68; campaign chmn, James C Gardner for Gov, 68; mem, NC State Rep Cent Comt, 70-; mem, NC State Rep Exec Comt, 70-; chmn, Sixth Cong Dist Rep Party, 70- Bus & Prof Pos: Vpres & treas, Big Bear of NC, Inc, 56-; secy & treas, ORD Enterprises, Inc, 59-; dir, Wachovia Bank & Trust Co, 64-; dir, Life Assurance Co of Carolina, 65- Publ: Taxation of Trusts, Univ NC Law Review, 54. Mem: Am & High Point Bar Asns; Emerywood Country Club (pres, 68); Willow Creek Golf Club; String & Splinter Club. Relig: Presbyterian. Mailing Add: 803 Country Club Dr High Point NC 27262

HUTCHERSON, NATHAN B, JR (D)
Mem, Va State Dem Cent Comt
b Rocky Mt, Va, Aug 24, 18; s Nathan B Hutcherson, Sr & Sallie Divers H; m 1947 to Ellen E Lamberth; c Ellen Divers, Virginia Peyton & Sallie Elizabeth. Educ: Hampden-Sydney Col, 36-37; Col of William & Mary, AB, 40, Law Sch, 3 years; German Club; Varsity Club; Sigma Rho. Polit & Govt Pos: Asst Commonwealth Attorney, Franklin Co, Va, 47-48, Asst Co Court Judge, 48-59; secy, Franklin Co Electoral Bd, 48-59; chmn, Franklin Co Dem Comt, 48-72; chmn, Franklin Co Dept Pub Welfare, 48-; Va State Deleg, 59-66; mem, Va State Dem Cent Comt, 69- Bus & Prof Pos: Owner, Hutcherson & Rhodes, 47; dir, Bankers Trust Co, Rocky Mt, 52-; trustee, Franklin Mem Hosp, 59-63. Mil Serv: Entered as Pvt, Army, 42, released as Sgt, after serv in ETO; Purple Heart; Oakleaf with Cluster; ETO Ribbon with 5 Battle Stars; Combat Inf Badge; Paratrooper Badge. Mem: Va Bar Asn; Law Sci Acad; Rotary; VFW; Am Legion. Relig: Christian. Legal Res: 118 S Main St Rocky Mt VA 24151 Mailing Add: 284 Knollwood Dr Rocky Mt VA 24151

HUTCHESON, JOHN WILLIAMS (R)
b Bolivar, Mo, Dec 7, 15; s Zenas Willard Hutcheson & Sue Farmer H; m 1940 to Lillian Faye Hicks; c John Williams, Jr & Sue Ann (Mrs Cansler). Educ: Southwest Baptist Jr Col, AA, 35; Univ Mo, BS in Agr, 37; Alpha Gamma Rho. Polit & Govt Pos: Chmn, Polk Co Rep Cent Comt, Mo & Seventh Cong Comt, formerly; deleg, Rep Nat Conv, 68; chmn, Mo State Agr Stabilization & Conserv Serv, 69- Mem: Mason; Rotary; Mo Farmers Asn. Relig: Baptist. Mailing Add: Box 34 Rte 3 Bolivar MO 65613

HUTCHINGS, MARJORIE CLYDE (R)
Maine State Rep
b Meredith, NH, Nov 25, 22; d Harold P Felker & Corinne E Emerson F; m 1942 to Herbert Colby Hutchings, Sr; c Diane Terry & Michael Colby. Educ: Univ NH, 40-42; Bennett Private Secretarial Sch, Springfield, Mass, AA, 42. Polit & Govt Pos: Committeewoman, Maine State Rep Party, 69-; Maine State Rep, Dist 55, 75- Bus & Prof Pos: Assoc mem, Penobscot Bay Bd Realtors, 72- Mem: Lincolnville Beach Improv Asn (secy); Rockport Boat Club; Waldo Co Farm Bur. Relig: Protestant. Legal Res: Youngtown Rd Lincolnville ME 04849 Mailing Add: RD 1 Lincolnville ME 04849

HUTCHINS, C W (BILL) (D)
Iowa State Rep
Mailing Add: 902 Prairie Guthrie Center IA 50115

HUTCHINS, CHRISTINE BURBANK (R)
Mem, Washington Co Rep Comt, Vt
b Marshfield, Vt, Aug 3, 19; d Leo C Burbank & Marion Badger B; m to Alden M Ladeau (deceased); m 1966 to Earl J Hutchins. Educ: St Johnsbury Acad; Santa Ana Jr Col; Johnson Teachers Col; Univ Vt, BA, 70. Polit & Govt Pos: Sch dir, Marshfield-Plainfield, 54-66; Vt State Rep, 63-66, mem Legis Coun, Vt House Rep, 64-66, chmn Educ Comt, 66; auditor, Plainfield, Vt, 68-; mem, Washington Co Rep Comt, 72-; Justice of the Peace, 75- Bus & Prof Pos: Teacher, 37-66; asst supt, Washington Southern Sch Dist, Northfield, Vt, 66-69; prin, Berlin Elem Sch, Vt, 69- Mem: Vt Educ Asn; Nat Educ Asn; Delta Kappa Gamma. Mailing Add: Rte 1 Plainfield VT 05667

HUTCHINS, ELIZABETH DENNIS (R)
Mem, Columbia Rep Town Comt, Conn
b Cliffside Park, NJ, May 5, 14; d Edward LeRoy Dennis & Elizabeth Wilson D; m 1940 to Carlton Winslow Hutchins; c Lawrence Dennis & Sally (Mrs Grimmelman). Educ: Conn State Col, AB, 36, Univ Conn Law Sch, LLB, 39. Polit & Govt Pos: Justice of the Peace, Conn, 50-; trial justice, Columbia Justice Court, 53-61; mem, Columbia Rep Town Comt, 53-, vchmn, 53-58, chmn, 58-68; secy, Conn Trial Justice Assembly, 59; town counsel, Columbia, 66-68. Bus & Prof Pos: Attorney-at-law, 39-; with Dennis & Dennis, 39-46; secy, Multiple Listing Serv, Willimantic Bd of Realtors, 61-64; chmn legis comt, Conn Heart Asn, 74- Mem: Conn & Tolland Co Bar Asns; Eastern Chap Conn Heart Asn; Columbia Grange; Willimantic Woman's Club. Relig: Congregational. Mailing Add: Lake Rd Columbia CT 06237

HUTCHINS, FRED S, JR (R)
NC State Rep
b Winston-Salem, NC, Aug 31, 32; s Fred S Hutchins, Sr & Annie Laurie Wier H; m 1955 to Florence Jane Stone; c Laurie Louise & Fred S, III. Educ: Univ NC, Chapel Hill, BS, 54; Wake Forest Univ, JD cum laude, 59; Sigma Alpha Epsilon. Polit & Govt Pos: Local mgr & mem campaign staff, Mizell for Cong, 68, mem policy comt, 70; chmn, Forsyth Co Rep Party, NC, 69-; mem, NC Rep State Exec Comt, 69-; NC State Rep, 72- Bus & Prof Pos: Partner, Deal, Hutchins & Minor, Attorneys, 63- Mil Serv: Entered as Pvt, Army, 54, released as Cpl, 56, after serv in 111th CIC Detachment, Birmingham, Ala. Mem: Am & NC Bar Asns; NC State Bar; Mason (32 degree); Shrine. Honors & Awards: Jaycee Chmn of Year, 63. Relig: Presbyterian. Mailing Add: 200 Sherwood Forest Rd Winston-Salem NC 27104

HUTCHINS, ROBERT WENDEL (D)
Chmn, Washington Co Dem Party, NC
b Anderson Co, Tenn, June 19, 45; s Burns Wendel Hutchins & Nora Bunch H; m 1964 to Barbara Todd; c Rebecca Michelle & Erin Elizabeth. Educ: Univ Ind, 64-65; Univ Md, 65-66; Univ NC, BA & JD; Delta Theta Phi. Polit & Govt Pos: Chmn, Washington Co Dem Party, NC, 74-; mem, NC State Dem Exec Comt, currently. Bus & Prof Pos: Partner, Hutchins, Romanet, Hutchins & Thompson, 75- Mil Serv: Entered as E-1, Air Force, 64, released as E-4, 68, after serv in Security Serv; Vietnam Serv Ribbon. Mem: Am & NC Bar Asns; Washington Co Bicentennial Comn (chmn). Relig: Episcopal. Mailing Add: Quail Dr Plymouth NC 27962

HUTCHINSON, AMOS K (D)
Pa State Rep
Mailing Add: Capitol Bldg Harrisburg PA 17120

HUTCHINSON, DONALD PAUL (D)
Md State Sen
b Baltimore, Md, Dec 31, 45; s Preston Amidon Hutchinson & Evelyn Gartside H; m 1969 to Margaret Louise Hoffman. Educ: Frostburg State Col, BS, 67; Univ Md Grad Sch Govt & Polit, 68-69. Polit & Govt Pos: Deleg, Md Const Conv, 67-68; Md State Deleg, 69-74, chmn subcomt educ, Md House of Deleg, 71-74, mem comn on young offenders, 70; Md State Sen, 75- Bus & Prof Pos: Fidenity Union Life Ins Co, 68-69; div dir, United Fund of Cent Md, 69-70; assoc dir, Endowment & Gifts, Univ Md, 70-72; asst to vpres, Towson State Col, 72- Mem: Essex-Mid River CofC; Essex-Mid River Jr CofC; Essex Community Col (adv coun community serv off); Mid River Boys' Club (adv coun). Relig: Methodist. Mailing Add: 624 Dorsey Ave Baltimore MD 21221

HUTCHINSON, EDWARD (R)
US Rep, Mich
b Fennville, Mich, Oct 13, 14; m 1959 to Janice Eleanor Caton. Educ: Univ Mich, JD, 38. Polit & Govt Pos: Mich State Rep, 46-50; Mich State Sen, 51-60; deleg & vpres, Mich Const Conv, 61-62; US Rep, Fourth Dist, Mich, 63- Bus & Prof Pos: Attorney. Mil Serv: Army, 41-46, discharged as Capt. Legal Res: St Joseph MI 49085 Mailing Add: 2336 House Off Bldg Washington DC 20515

HUTCHINSON, FREDERICK W (R)
Vt State Rep
Mailing Add: 43 Brainerd St St Albans VT 05478

HUTCHINSON, JOHN GUIHER (D)
Mayor, Charleston, WVa
b Charleston, WVa, Feb 4, 35; s Edwin Berry Hutchinson & Mary Guiher H; m 1969 to Julia Roseberry Thomas; c John Guiher, Jr & William Lewis Owens & Andrew Allemong, III & James Kay Thomas Payne (stepchildren). Educ: WVa Univ, BS, 56; Sigma Nu. Polit & Govt Pos: Treas, Charleston, WVa, 67-71, mayor, 71- Bus & Prof Pos: Partner, Edwin B Hutchinson & Son Ins Agency, 59. Mil Serv: Entered as 2nd Lt, Air Force, 56, released as 1st Lt, after serv in 1254th Air Transport Group, 57-59; Distinguished Mil Grad, WVa Univ, 56. Mem: US Conf Mayors (chmn, Standing Comt on Environ & Solid Waste Task Force); Fed Energy Admin (mem, Coal Indust Adv Comt); Lions (past pres). Relig: Presbyterian. Mailing Add: 19 Norwood Rd Charleston WV 25314

HUTCHINSON, RICHARD SHIRLEY (D)
Ga State Rep
b Harris Co, Ga, Oct 19, 01; s Thomas Rolan Hutchinson & Annie Rebecca O'Neal H; m 1933 to Lula Voyles; c Sara Etta. Educ: Ga Inst Technol, grad, 22. Polit & Govt Pos: Ga State Rep, Dist 133, 65- Bus & Prof Pos: Life & gen ins, 47 years. Mem: Mason; Exchange Club Methodist Church. Relig: Methodist. Mailing Add: 915 Sixth Ave Albany GA 31705

HUTCHINSON, WILLIAM DAVID (R)
Pa State Rep
b Minersville, Pa, June 20, 32; s Elmer E Hutchinson & Elizabeth Price H; m 1957 to Louise Meloney; c Kathryn, William, Louise & Andrew. Educ: Moravian Col, BA magna cum laude, 54; Harvard Univ Law Sch, JD, 57; Drama Club; Polit Sci Club; ed, Col Newspaper. Polit & Govt Pos: Mem, Blue Mountain Sch Bd, Cressona, 63-66; asst dist attorney, Schuylkill Co, Pa, 63-69; solicitor, Blue Mountain Sch Dist, 68-; solicitor, Schuylkill Co, 69-71; Pa State Rep, 73- Bus & Prof Pos: Reporter, Pottsville Eve Rep, 57-58; attorney, Pottsville, Pa, 58-62; partner, Law Firm, Williamson, Friedberg & Jones, 62- Mem: Schuylkill Co Bar Asn; Comt on Continuing Legal Educ; Am & Pa Bar Asns; Am Judicature Soc. Honors & Awards: Sr ed, Harvard Law Rec, 56-57. Relig: Methodist. Legal Res: Seventh Floor Schuylkill Trust Bldg Pottsville PA 17901 Mailing Add: Capitol Bldg Harrisburg PA 17120

HUTCHISON, ERVIN A (R)
b Sioux City, Iowa, June 27, 07; s Arthur M Hutchison & Edna E Purcell H; m 1935 to Elizabeth A Popham; c Mrs Kurt Smith. Educ: State Univ Iowa, LLB, 39. Polit & Govt Pos: Precinct committeeman & co finance committeeman, Rep Party, 46-66; chmn, Woodbury Co Rep Cent Comt, Iowa, 60-68; chmn, Rules Comt, Iowa Rep State Conv, 64; alt deleg, Rep Nat Conv, 72. Mil Serv: Entered as Pvt, Army, 44, released as Sgt, 45, after serv in 749th Field Artil Bn, Hq Battery; Good Conduct Medal & others. Mem: SC Country Club; SC Boat Club; Farm Bur; Lions; SC Bus Leaders Club. Relig: Methodist; Trustee, First Methodist Church of Sioux City. Legal Res: 3927 Country Club Blvd Sioux City IA 51104 Mailing Add: 414 Security Bldg Sioux City IA 51101

HUTCHISON, RAY (R)
Tex State Rep
Mailing Add: 1313 Fidelity Union Life Bldg Dallas TX 75201

HUTHMACHER, MARILYN ANNE (D)
b Trenton, NJ, June 30, 30; d James C Catana & Anne Faggella C; m 1957 to Dr J Joseph Huthmacher; c David. Educ: Rider Col, 48-49. Polit & Govt Pos: Committeeperson, 27th Dist Dem Party, Del, 72-; deleg, Dem Nat Mid-Term Conf, 74; mem affirmative action comt, Del State Dem Comt, currently. Bus & Prof Pos: Bus mgr, Life Underwriter Training Coun, Washington, DC, 58-65; systs consult, 69-71; pres, Horseshoe Enterprises, 72-; partner, Amerind Artisans, 74- Mem: Nat Women's Polit Caucus (finance comt, 75-); Del Women Polit Caucus (co-chmn, 73-). Mailing Add: 47 the Horseshoe Newark DE 19711

HUTSON, H KEITH (R)
b Hereford, Tex, Mar 4, 31; s Rufus B Hutson & Beatrice Dennis H; m 1952 to Phyllis Buehler; c Leslie Brooke & Whiney Rae. Educ: Tex Tech Col, BS, 56; Phi Psi. Polit & Govt Pos: Asst chmn, Guadalupe Co Rep Party, Tex, 62-67, chmn, formerly. Bus & Prof Pos: Vpres, Seguin Jr CofC, 58-59; pres, Seguin & Guadalupe Co CofC, 63-64. Mil Serv: Entered as Airman Basic, Air Force, 51, released as Airman 1/C, 54 after serv in 20th Air Force Div, Far East & Okinawa, 53-54. Mem: Am Inst Indust Engrs; Lone Star Chap, Tex Mfrs Asn (vchmn, 69-); Am Legion; Kiwanis (pres, Seguin Club, 59-60). Relig: Lutheran. Mailing Add: 531 Berkeley Seguin TX 78155

HUTTO, EARL (D)
Fla State Rep
Mailing Add: PO Box 230 Panama City FL 32401

HUTTO, THOMAS AUGUSTUS (D)
b LaFayette, Ga, Aug 10, 32; s James Buist Hutto & Lila Cleghorn H; m to Elise Reed; div; remarried, 1965 to Lark Dixon Cowart; c (by first wife) David Allen, Daniel Carter, Douglas Eliot & Donald James. Educ: Truett-McConnell Col, Cleveland, Ga, AA, 51; Univ Ga, BSEd, 57, MEd, 61; Phi Sigma; Beta Kappa Chi. Polit & Govt Pos: Chmn, Southern WVa Comt for Sane Nuclear Policy, 67-69, mem bd dirs, Nat Comt for Sane Nuclear Policy World, 67-69; WVa State Chmn, McCarthy for President Orgn, 68; chmn WVa Chap, Am for Dem Action, 69-71, mem nat bd dirs, Washington, DC, 69-71, polit reporter, WVa ADA World, 73-74; Dem nominee, WVa House Deleg, 70; alt deleg, Dem Nat Conv, 72; secy-treas & mem bd dirs, WVa Youth Citizenship Fund, 72; pres, WVa Coalition for Clear Air, currently. Bus & Prof Pos: Head dept sci, Sandy Springs High Sch, Fulton Co, Ga, 57-60; asst prof biol, Eastern Ky Univ, Richmond, 61-63; asst prof biol, Sch of the Ozarks, Point Lookout, Mo, 63-64, head dept sci, Winston Churchill High Sch, Montgomery Co, Md, 64-65; asst prof sci educ, Wis State Univ-Oshkosh, 65-66; assoc prof biol, WVa State Col, Institute, 66- Mil Serv: Entered as Pvt E-1, Army, 52, released as Sgt E-5, 54, after serv in 101st Bn Inf Div, Ft Jackson, SC, 52-54; Personnelman Chief E-7, Navy Res, 63-67; Good Conduct Medal; Nat Defense Serv Medal. Publ: The status of the Junior Academy of Science in Kentucky, Trans Ky Acad Sci, 63; A need for direction in the college biology curriculum, Am Biol Teacher, 65; Some current problems & issues in the training of biology teachers, Sch Sci & Math, 67. Mem: Am Asn Advan Sci; Am Inst Biol Sci; Nat Sci Teachers Asn; Nat Asn Biol Teachers; Am Fern Soc. Honors & Awards: Teacher of the Year, Jr Womens Club, NFulton Co, Ga, 60; Danforth assoc, Danforth Found, 72. Relig: Unitarian. Mailing Add: 16 Carter Terr St Albans WV 25177

HUTTON, E M (TINY) (D)
b Hampton, Va, Sept 25, 20; s Elbert McKinley Hutton & Alva Price H; m 1943 to Margaret Paul Vestal; c Paul Scott & Kathryn. Educ: Univ NC, Chapel Hill, 37-42; Alpha Phi Omega; Chi Phi. Polit & Govt Pos: Admin asst, Rep Thomas N Downing, Va, 67-; deleg, Va State Dem Conv, 68. Bus & Prof Pos: News dir, WVEC, Hampton, Va, 62-67. Relig: Episcopal. Legal Res: 311 Columbia Ave Hampton VA 23669 Mailing Add: 2624 Ft Farnsworth Rd Alexandria VA 22303

HUTTON, RICHARD ARTHUR (D)
Chmn, Chippewa Co Dem Comt, Wis
b Great Falls, Mont, Feb 4, 30; s Roger Hutton & Mona Blanche Combs H; m 1956 to Geraldine T Meagher; c Teresa M, Catherine M, Michael S, Anne L, Mathew J, Wade F, Nancy K & Hugh R. Educ: Chippewa Falls Sr High Sch, Wis, grad. Polit & Govt Pos: Chmn, Chippewa Co Dem Comt, Wis, 75- Bus & Prof Pos: Proprietor, Hutton's Hydraulic Jack Repair Serv, 66- Mil Serv: Entered as Recruit, Marine Corps, 51, released as Cpl, 51, after serv in 1st Div, Korea, 52; Unit Citation. Mem: Chippewa Youth Hockey Asn; UAW; United Transportation Union (vchmn, 75-). Mailing Add: 621 E Grand Ave Chippewa Falls WI 54729

HYATT, JERRY HERBERT (D)
Md State Deleg
b Damascus, Md, Sept 29, 40; s Herbert Souder Hyatt & Ruby Williams H; m 1973 to Barbara Lutz; c Timothy Haskins, Stephen Williams, John Lutz & Jerry Williams. Educ: Washington & Lee Univ, BA, 62; Univ Md Sch Law, JD, 65; Delta Tau Delta, Phi Alpha Delta. Polit & Govt Pos: Asst states attorney, Baltimore City, Md, 70-72; mem, Property Tax Assessment Appeal Bd for Montgomery Co, Md, 73-74; Md State Deleg, Dist 15-A, 75- Bus & Prof Pos: Dir, Bank of Damascus, 68- Mil Serv: Entered as 2nd Lt, Army, 65, released as Capt, 67, after serv in Co D, First Bn (Abn), 12th, 1st Cav Div (AM), Vietnam, 66-67; Capt, Army Res; Bronze Star with valor device, First Oak Leaf Cluster; Army Commendation Medal with valor device; Air Medal. Mem: Am Legion Post 171; VFW Post 10076 (sr vcomdr, 75); Montgomery Co Farm Bur; Md Bankers Asn; Am Bar Asn. Relig: Episcopal. Legal Res: 27521 Mt Radnor Rd Damascus MD 20750 Mailing Add: 9900 Main St Damascus MD 20750

HYDE, ANTHONY (D)
b Windsor, Eng, July 20, 07; s Dorsey William Hyde, Jr & Sybil Cox H; m 1933 to Katherine Stringer, div; c Anthony Jr; m 1950 to Phyllis Elizabeth Reynolds, div; m 1962 to Pauline Patricia Selig; c Timothy Alexander David. Educ: Yale Univ, BA. Polit & Govt Pos: Dep dir, Off War Info, 41-42 & Off War Mobilization & Reconversion, 43-46; chmn, Dem Abroad, 64-; deleg, Dem Nat Mid-Term Conf & mem, Dem Nat Charter Comn, 74. Bus & Prof Pos: Managing dir & pres, Tea Coun of USA, NY, 48-56; vpres, McCann-Erickson Inc, NY, 57-58; exec vpres, Robert Durham Assoc, NY, 59-60; chmn, Smith-Warden Ltd, London, 61-67 & Tavener-Rutledge Ltd, Liverpool, 70- Relig: Episcopal. Mailing Add: 38 Lower Belgrave St London England

HYDE, DEWITT STEPHEN (R)
b Washington, DC, Mar 21, 09; s Burr Hamilton Hyde & Ethel Holland Larrick H; m 1935 to Mildred Sullivan. Educ: George Washington Univ, JD, 35; Kappa Sigma. Polit & Govt Pos: Law clerk, Farm Credit Admin, 33-38; Md State Del, 47-50; Md State Sen, 51-52; US Rep, Md, 53-58; assoc judge, DC Court of Gen Sessions, 59-71, Superior Court of the DC, 71- Bus & Prof Pos: Partner, Hilland & Hyde, 38-59; prof law, Benjamin Franklin Univ, 46-52 & 60-; chmn bd dirs, Christ Church Child Ctr, 61- Mil Serv: Entered as Lt(jg), Navy, 43, released as Lt Comdr, 46, after serv in SPac Command, Am Theater & SPac Theater; Lt Comdr, Naval Res, 46, Victory Ribbon; Am Area Campaign Ribbon; Asiatic-Pac Area Campaign Ribbon. Mem: Am & DC Bar Asns; The Barristers; Columbia Country Club; George Washington Univ Alumni Asn. Legal Res: 5606 McLean Dr Bethesda MD 20014 Mailing Add: Superior Court of the DC Fourth & E St NW Washington DC 20001

HYDE, FLOYD H
b Fresno, Calif, 1921. Educ: Fresno State Col, 42; Univ Southern Calif Law Sch, JD, 49. Polit & Govt Pos: Mayor, Fresno, Calif, 65-69; Asst Secy for Model Cities & Govt Rels, Dept of Housing & Urban Develop, 69-71, Asst Secy Community Develop, 71-73, Under Secy, Dept, 73-74. Bus & Prof Pos: Lawyer, 50-; vpres, Nat League Cities, 68; adv bd, US Conf Mayors, 68; mem, Nat Urban Coalition. Mil Serv: Capt, Marine Corps, World War II, Pac Theater. Legal Res: Fresno CA Mailing Add: 1435 Fourth St NW Washington DC 20410

HYDE, HENRY JOHN (R)
US Rep, Ill
b Chicago, Ill, Apr 18, 24; s Henry Clay Hyde & Monica Kelly H; m 1947 to Jeanne Marie Simpson; c Henry, Jr, Robert, Laura & Anthony. Educ: Georgetown Univ, 42-43, BSS, 47; Duke Univ, 43-44; Loyola Univ Sch Law, JD, 49; Sigma Chi; Phi Alpha Delta. Polit & Govt Pos: Ill State Rep, 67-74; US Rep, Ill, 75- Bus & Prof Pos: Pres, Trial Lawyers Club of Chicago, 62. Mil Serv: Entered as A/S, Navy, 42, released as Lt(jg), 46, after serv in 7th Fleet, SPac Theatre, 44-46; Comdr, Res, 61-69. Mem: Am, Ill State & Chicago Bar Asns; Ill Defense Counsel; KofC. Honors & Awards: Best Freshman Rep, 75th Gen Assembly, Ill Polit Reporters. Relig: Roman Catholic. Mailing Add: 1200 S Knight Ave Park Ridge IL 60068

HYDE, HENRY VAN ZILE, JR (R)
b Syracuse, NY, Sept 10, 36; s Henry Van Zile Hyde, MD & Ellen Tracy H; m 1965 to Eveline Zoppi. Educ: Hamilton Col, AB, 58; Cornell Law Sch, 61-63; Delta Kappa Epsilon. Polit & Govt Pos: Mem, Staff of US Rep Bray, Ind, 59; mem, Staff of Vice President Richard Nixon, 59-61; asst schedule dir, Nixon Campaign, 68; asst to the Secy, Dept of Health, Educ & Welfare, 69-71; exec dir, President's Adv Panel on Timber & the Environ, 71- Bus & Prof Pos: Mem staff, United Rep Fund, Chicago, Ill, 63-64; buyer & br supvr, Ill Power Transmission, Inc, 65-68. Mil Serv: Entered as Pvt, Army Res, 59, released as Cpl, 65, after serv in US; Spec Letter of Commendation. Mem: Phi Delta Phi. Relig: Protestant. Mailing Add: 5807 Aberdeen Rd Bethesda MD 20034

HYDE, HERBERT LEE (D)
NC State Rep
b Bryson City, NC, Dec 12, 25; s Ervin M Hyde & Alice Medlin H; m 1949 to Kathryn Long; c Deborah, Lynn, Karen & Benjamin. Educ: Western Carolina Teachers Col, AB, 51; NY Univ Sch Law, LLB, 54; Phi Delta Phi; Alpha Phi Sigma. Polit & Govt Pos: NC State Sen, 63-66; NC State Rep, 75- Bus & Prof Pos: Lawyer. Mil Serv: PO 3/C, Naval Res, 44-46. Mem: NC State Bar; NC & Am Bar Asns; Lions. Relig: Baptist. Mailing Add: 93 East View Circle Asheville NC 28806

HYDEN, JESSE L (JACK) (R)
b Prestonburg, Ky, Mar 29, 27; s Chauncey L Hyden & Clora Adams H; m 1951 to Doris Anne Clark; c Jack Clark & Judy Anne. Polit & Govt Pos: Chmn, Floyd Co Rep Party, Ky, formerly. Bus & Prof Pos: Mgr, Prestonburg Lincoln-Mercury, Ky, 51-53; owner, Jack Hyden Auto Sales, Prestonburg, 53- Mil Serv: Entered as A/S, Navy, 44, released as Seaman 1/C, 46, after serv in Pac Theatre. Mem: Mason; VFW; Am Legion. Relig: Baptist. Mailing Add: 202 Third Ave Prestonburg KY 41653

HYDRICK, BOB DURRETT (R)
b Sylacauga, Ala, Jan 6, 39; s Julius Cannon Hydrick, Sr & Esther Durrett H; m 1962 to Ruth Stephens; c Robert, Stephen, John & Susan. Educ: Mercer Univ, 2 years; Auburn Univ, BS, 61; Phi Delta Theta. Polit & Govt Pos: Various comt chairmanships & positions in local dist & Ga Rep Party; chmn subcomt, Columbus-Muscogee Co Charter Comn, 69-70; chmn, Muscogee Co Rep Party, 69-73; vchmn, Third Dist Rep Party, 70-73; mayor, Columbus, Ga, 73-75. Bus & Prof Pos: Asst to vpres mkt, Royal Crown Cola Co, 61-64, dir packaging dept, 64-67, dir manpower div, 67-70, venture mgr, 70-73; pres, Home Decorative Accessories, Inc, 70-73. Mem: Advert Club Columbus; Jaycees; Kiwanis. Honors & Awards: Outstanding Young Man of the Year, Columbus, Ga, 70; one of five Outstanding Young Men in Ga, Ga Jaycees, 70; Silver Medal, Am Advert Fedn; Award for contribution to the advert profession & to commun, 70; drafted charter for first successful city co merger in Ga. Relig: Baptist. Legal Res: 2848 Suemack Dr Columbus GA 31906 Mailing Add: Box 2651 Columbus GA 31902

HYLAND, BERNICE IRENE (R)
First VPres, Kans Fedn Rep Women
b Concordia, Kans, June 9, 18; d Charles Emery Bonebrake & Mabel Driscoll B; m 1938 to Herbert Neil Hyland; c Thomas Edwin & James Patrick. Educ: Mankato High Sch, Kans, grad, 36. Polit & Govt Pos: Committeewoman, Washington City, Kans, 62-; vchmn, Washington Co Rep Cent Comt, 62-64, 70-74, chmn, 66-68; pres, Washington Co Rep Women's Club, 63-64; secy, Fedn of Rep Women, Second Dist, 67, second dist dir, 68-69, dist dir, 70-71; secy, Kans Fedn Rep Women, 72-74, first vpres, 74- Bus & Prof Pos: Bookkeeper & cashier, Kans Power & Light Co, Mankato, Washington & Concordia, Kans, 37; secy, Hyland Abstract Co, Washington, 50-73. Mem: Eastern Star; Am Legion Auxiliary; 8 et 40 Marshall Co Salon; Washington Co Kans Hosp Auxiliary; Wesleyan Serv Guild. Honors & Awards: Methodist Family of Year Award, 58; Distinguished Jayhawker from Gov John Anderson, 64. Relig: Methodist. Mailing Add: 12 Sunset Lane Washington KS 66968

HYMAN, LESTER SAMUEL (D)
b Providence, RI, July 14, 31; s Carl Hyman & Alice Adelman H; m 1959 to Helen Sidman; c David Anthony, Andrew Theodore & Elizabeth Alice. Educ: Brown Univ, AB, 52; Columbia Univ, LLB, 55; Tower Club. Polit & Govt Pos: Asst to Gov, Commonwealth of Mass, 61-63, secy com, 64-65; deleg, Dem Nat Conv, 64 & 68; sr consult, US Dept Housing & Urban Develop, 66; chmn, Mass Dem State Comt, 67-69; mem, Dem Charter Reform Comt, 74-75. Bus & Prof Pos: Attorney, US Securities & Exchange Comn, 55-56; partner, Springer, Goldberg, Levenson & Hyman, Mass, 60-68; partner, Leva, Hawes, Symington, Martin & Oppenheimer, Washington, DC, 69- Mil Serv: Entered as Seaman Recruit, Navy, 56, released as Yeoman 3/C, 57, after serv in USS Calcaterra. Mem: Nat Exec Comt; Am Jewish Comt; Close-Up (bd adv). Honors & Awards: Outstanding Young Man of Year, Gtr Boston Jr CofC, 63. Relig: Jewish. Legal Res: Tyringham Rd Monterey MA 01250 Mailing Add: 3414 Lowell St NW Washington DC 20016

HYMEL, GARY GERARD (D)
b Apr 25, 33; s Andrew Joseph Hymel & Elise Carriere H; m 1954 to Alice Fox; c Amy Marie, Margaret Mary, Gregory Paul, Elizabeth Ann, Madeleine Teresa, Kevin Michael, Joy Odile & Judith Ann. Educ: Loyola Univ, 50-54; La State Univ, MA, 59; Blue Key; Thirty Club; Beggars Fraternity; ed, Loyola Maroon. Polit & Govt Pos: Exec asst to Majority Leader, US House of Rep, currently. Bus & Prof Pos: Sports; polit reporter. Mil Serv: Lt, Army, 54-56; Capt, Army Res. Mem: Press Club of New Orleans. Relig: Catholic. Mailing Add: 4111 Rosemary St Chevy Chase MD 20015

HYNES, EDWARD H (D)
NJ State Assemblyman
Mailing Add: State House Trenton NJ 08625

HYNES, THOMAS C (D)
Ill State Sen
Mailing Add: 10540 S Western Chicago IL 60643

I

ICE, THEODORE BRANINE (R)
Chmn, Harvey Co Rep Party, Kans
b Newton, Kans, June 30, 34; s C Fred Ice & Mildred Branine I; m 1957 to Rachel Sue Harper; c Laura Lynn, Nancy Ellen & Evan Harper. Educ: Univ Kans, AB, 56; Omicron Delta Kappa; Phi Delta Theta; Collegiate Rep; Student Coun. Polit & Govt Pos: Co attorney, Harvey Co, Kans, 65-69; chmn, Harvey Co Rep Party, Kans, 68-; alt deleg, Rep Nat Conv, 72. Bus & Prof Pos: Law partner, Branine, Ice, Turner & Ice, Newton, Kans, 61- Mil Serv: Entered as Ens, Navy, 56, released as Lt, 59, after serv in Western Pac, 56-59. Mem: Cent Kans Bar; Kans & Am Bar Asns; Rotary; Elks. Relig: Presbyterian. Mailing Add: 220 E First Newton KS 67114

ICHORD, RICHARD HOWARD (D)
US Rep, Mo
b Licking, Mo, June 27, 26; m to Millicent Murphy Koch; c Richard Howard III, Pamela & Kyle. Educ: Univ Mo, BS, 49, JD, 52; Phi Eta Sigma; Delta Sigma Pi; Alpha Pi Zeta; Beta Gamma Sigma; Phi Delta Phi. Hon Degrees: Dr Pub Serv, Southwest Baptist Col, 72. Polit & Govt Pos: Mo State Rep, 52-60, speaker pro tem, Mo House of Rep, 57-58, speaker, 59-60; comnr, Little Hoover Comn, Mo, 53-54; US Rep, Mo, 60-, mem armed serv comt & chmn subcomt M-16 rifle prog, US House Rep, 69-, chmn subcomt installations & facilities, currently; deleg, Dem Nat Mid-Term Conf, 74. Bus & Prof Pos: Attorney-at-Law. Mil Serv: Naval Air Corps, World War II, Pac Area, 2 years. Mem: Mo Asn Retarded Children (adv bd); Asn Am Dentists (bd Adv); Acad Mo Squires; VFW; Lions. Honors & Awards: Watchdog of the Treas Award, Nat Asn Businessman; Alumni Merit Award, Univ Mo-Rolla; Torch of Freedom Award, Mo State Young Am for Freedom; 21st Annual Americanism Award, Westchester Co Am Legion; Outstanding Citizen of the Year Award, Am Security Coun, 71. Relig: Baptist. Legal Res: 116 W Main St Houston MO 65483 Mailing Add: 2402 Rayburn House Off Bldg Washington DC 20515

IKEDA, DONNA RIKA (R)
Hawaii State Rep
b Honolulu, Hawaii, Aug 31, 39; d William G Yoshida & Lillian Kim Y; m to William M Ikeda; c Rika, Aaron & Julie. Educ: Univ Hawaii-Honolulu, BA in speech. Polit & Govt Pos: Legis researcher, House Rep Research Off, 71-74; Hawaii State Rep, Seventh Dist, 75- Bus & Prof Pos: Substitute teacher, Honolulu Dist, 69-71. Mailing Add: 918 Wainiha St Honolulu HI 96825

ILCHUK, PETER KENNETH (INDEPENDENT)
b Philadelphia, Pa, Jan 15, 47; s Eugene Peter Ilchuk & Erma Cardoni I; single. Educ: Georgetown Univ, BSFS, 69. Polit & Govt Pos: Legis & press asst to US Rep Jack Edwards, Ala, 69-70; press asst to US Rep Hastings Keith, Mass, 70; legis asst to US Rep Mario Biaggi, NY, 70-71, admin asst, 72- Relig: Roman Catholic. Mailing Add: 633 Maryland Ave NE Washington DC 20002

IMES, KENNETH CHURCHILL (D)
Ky State Rep
b Murray, Ky, Feb 13, 47; s John Richard Imes & Martha Churchill I; m 1966 to Mary Elizabeth Beale; c Molly & John Beale. Educ: Murray State Univ, 65-67; Ky Sch Mortuary Sci, Louisville, grad, 67; Class Pres, Sch Mortuary Sci, 67. Polit & Govt Pos: Ky State Rep, Fifth Dist, 72- Bus & Prof Pos: Funeral dir & embalmer, Murray, Ky, 69; co-owner, J H Churchill Funeral Home, 72; co-owner, Imes Farms, Almo, 72. Mem: Pi Sigma Eta; Nat & Ky Funeral Dirs Asns; Order of the Golden Rule; Mason. Honors & Awards: Young Man of the Year, Murray-Calloway Co Jaycees, 73. Relig: Baptist. Mailing Add: 201 S Third St Murray KY 42071

IMHOFF, LAWRENCE EDWARD
b Elkville, Ill, July 25, 08; s Wiley B Imhoff & Laura E Castelton I; m 1930 to Maybelle B Carroll; c Larry C & Maren E. Educ: Oberlin Col, AB, 30; Manchester Col, 34-35; Purdue Univ, MPE, 40. Polit & Govt Pos: Budget analyst, Dept of Com, 46-51; dir minerals & fuels div & staff asst to asst secy mineral resources, Dept of Interior, 51-60; dep dir off budget & mgt, Dept of Com, 60-62, dir off of budget & finance, 62-65, Dep Asst Secy of Com for Admin, 65-72. Bus & Prof Pos: Investment banker, 30-32; family bus, 32-35; teaching, 35-42. Mil Serv: Capt, Army Air Force, World War II; Pac Theater Opers Ribbon; Purple Heart; Bronze Star. Mem: Am Soc Pub Admin; Budget Off Conf; Conglist; Mason (32 degree); Nat Civil Serv League. Honors & Awards: Meritorious Serv Award, Dept of Interior, 60; Distinguished Serv Award, Dept of Com, 65. Mailing Add: 4540 Chesapeake St Washington DC 20016

IMMONEN, JACOB J (R)
Maine State Rep
Mailing Add: West Paris ME 04289

IMPERIALE, ANTHONY (INDEPENDENT)
NJ State Sen
Mailing Add: State House Trenton NJ 08625

INABA, MINORU (D)
Hawaii State Rep
b Holualoa, Hawaii, Feb 20, 04; s Jentaro Inaba & Hatsuyo Miyamoto I; m 1955 to Sumie Mizuno; c Jeannette (Mrs Tinnel), Mae (Mrs Karl Kawahara) & Annette (Mrs Tatsumi Sato). Educ: Univ Hawaii, BA, 29. Polit & Govt Pos: Hawaii State Rep, 68-72 & 75- Bus & Prof Pos: Vprin, Konawaena High & Intermediate Sch, Kealakekua, Hawaii, 56-66; vpres & Kona br mgr, General Hawaiian Financial Corp, Holualoa, 68- Mem: Nat, Hawaii & Kona Educ Asns; Kona Mauka Trollers; Holualoa Athletic Asn. Honors & Awards: Sportsman of the Year Award, Island of Hawaii. Legal Res: PO Box 233 Kealakekua HI 96750 Mailing Add: House of Rep State Capitol Honolulu HI 96813

INDERMUHLE, MARTHA A (D)
Chmn, Kittitas Co Dem Cent Comt, Wash
b Tonasket, Wash, Feb 12, 17; d Guy Vaughn Burge & Goldie Fisher B; m 1960 to James Merlin Indermuhle; c Delores Darlene (Mrs Tracey) & Colleen Fay (Mrs Pyatt). Educ: Tonasket High Sch, Wash, grad, 34. Polit & Govt Pos: Councilwoman, Kittitas City Coun, Wash, 68-75; committeeperson, Kittitas City Precinct, 68-; chmn, Kittitas Co Dem Cent Comt, 70- Mem: Women of the Moose; Pioneer Asn of Wash State; Okanogan Co Hist Soc; Kittitas Co Exten Homemakers Coun; Wash State Homemakers Exten Coun. Honors & Awards: Homemaker of Co Award, 70. Relig: Catholic. Legal Res: 303 King St Kittitas WA 98934 Mailing Add: Box 1004 Kittitas WA 98934

INFANGER, RAY E (R)
Idaho State Rep
Mailing Add: Rte 1 Box 174 Salmon ID 83467

INFELT, JIM (D)
Idaho State Rep
Mailing Add: 179 E 16th St Idaho Falls ID 83401

INGALLS, JAMES W (D)
b Aberdeen, SDak, Sept 3, 25; s James L Ingalls & Ila A Knott I; m 1951 to Beverly D Evans; c Jan V, David J & Jon W. Educ: Univ Idaho, LLB, 51; Phi Alpha Delta; Delta Tau Delta. Polit & Govt Pos: Committeeman, Idaho State Dem Cent Comt, formerly, mem exec comt, 65-70; prosecuting attorney, Kootenai Co, Idaho, 55-61; deleg, Dem Nat Conv, 60; chmn, Kootenai Co Dem Cent Comt, Idaho, 61-66. Mil Serv: Entered as Pvt, Air Force, 43, released as S/Sgt, 45, after serv in Eighth Air Force, ETO, 44-45; Air Medal with Three Clusters; Bronze Star; European-African-Mid East Ribbon with Three Bronze Stars. Mem: Idaho Prosecuting Attorneys Asn; Univ Idaho Col Law Alumni Asn; VFW; Elks; Eagles. Relig: Methodist. Legal Res: 108 Teresa Dr Fernan Lake Village ID Mailing Add: Box 427 Coeur d'Alene ID 83814

INGALLS, WALTER MONTE (D)
Calif State Assemblyman
b Hemet, Calif, Oct 17, 44; s Horace Monte Ingalls & Edith McKibben I; single. Educ: Univ Calif, Riverside, BA in Polit Sci, 66, Univ Calif, Berkeley, Boalt Hall Sch Law, JD, 69; Phi Delta Phi. Polit & Govt Pos: Dep dist attorney, Riverside Co Dist Attorney's Off, Calif, 69-72; Calif State Assemblyman, 73- Mem: Am & Calif State Bar Asns; Native Sons of the Golden West; Univ Calif Alumni Asn; Rotary. Relig: Protestant. Legal Res: 3386 Spring Garden St Riverside CA 92501 Mailing Add: PO Box 542 Riverside CA 92502

INGEGNERI, PHILIP ALFRED (D)
Maine State Rep
b New York, NY, Aug 22, 10; s Domenick Ingegneri & Mary Forgione I; m 1938 to Roslyn Isaacson; c Philip Lewis & Lois (Mrs David Bernstein). Educ: Fordham Univ, BA, 32; Columbia Univ, 34-36; City Col New York, 46-48; French Club; Ital Club. Polit & Govt Pos: Spec agt intel div, Internal Revenue Serv, Augusta, Maine, 55-72; mem, Bangor Sch Comt, 72-; mem, Regional Voc Educ Bd, South Penobscot Co, 73-; Maine State Rep, 75- Bus & Prof Pos: Tax consult, Bangor, Maine, 73- Mem: Nat Asn Retired Fed Employees; Univ Maine Women's Resource Ctr (bd mem). Honors & Awards: Albert Gallatin Award, US Treasury, 72. Mailing Add: 37 Fifth St Bangor ME 04401

INGERSOLL, ROBERT STEPHEN (R)
Dep Secy State
b Galesburg, Ill, Jan 28, 14; s Roy Claire Ingersoll & Lulu May Hinchliff I; m 1938 to Carolyn Eleanor Reid; c Carolyn Eleanor, Nancy, Joan (deceased), Gail & Elizabeth G. Educ: Phillips Acad, grad, 33; Yale Univ Sheffield Sci Sch, BS, 37; Phi Gamma Delta. Polit & Govt Pos: US Ambassador to Japan, 72-74; Dep Secy State, 74- Bus & Prof Pos: With Armco Steel Corp, 37-39; with Ingersoll Steel & Disc Div, Borg-Warner Corp, Chicago, 39-41, 42-54, pres, Ingersoll Prod Div, 50-54, admin vpres, Borg-Warner Corp, 53-56, pres, 56-61, chmn, 61-72, chief exec officer & dir, 58-72; trustee, Chicago Symphony, Univ Chicago, Calif Inst Technol & Aspen Inst Humanistic Studies, currently. Mem: Winnetka Sch Bd; US CofC; Chicago Asn Com & Indust; Indian Hill Club; Detroit Athletic Club. Legal Res: 10 Indian Hill Rd Winnetka IL 60093 Mailing Add: Dept of State 2201 C St NW Washington DC 20521

INGLE, JOHN R (D)
Mem Exec Comt, NC Dem Party
b Siler City, NC, Feb 13, 32; s Joseph B Ingle & Lillie Clark I; single. Educ: Univ NC, Chapel Hill, AB, 54, JD, 59; Phi Beta Kappa; Phi Alpha Theta; Delta Theta Phi; Richardson Found Fel, 59. Polit & Govt Pos: Pres, Mecklenburg Co Young Dem Club, NC, 62 & 63; mem, Mecklenburg Co Dem Precinct Comt, 65-67; chmn, Mecklenburg Co Dem Exec Comt, 66-72; mem exec comt, NC Dem Party, 70-; chmn, Mecklenburg Co Bicentennial Comt, 71- Mil Serv: Entered as 2nd Lt, Air Force, 54, released as 1st Lt, 56, after serv in Mil Air Transport Command, Capt Res. Mem: 26th Judicial Dist Bar Asn; NC Bar Asn; Am Bar Asn; Am Judicature Soc; Charlotte Civitan Club (vpres). Honors & Awards: Ted Williams Award for Outstanding Young Dem in Mecklenburg Co, 68. Relig: Methodist. Mailing Add: 208 Hillside Ave Charlotte NC 28209

INGRAM, CARROLL (D)
Miss State Sen
Mailing Add: 301 W Front St PO Box 24 Hattiesburg MS 39401

INGRAM, GARY JOHN (R)
Idaho State Rep
b St Paul, Minn, Nov 29, 33; s Raymond Walter Ingram & Evelyn Murphy I; m 1975 to Maureen Lundy; c Michelle, Theresa, Sonja & Gregory. Educ: Cretin High Sch, St Paul, Minn, grad, 52. Polit & Govt Pos: Dist chmn, Idaho Young Rep League, 64-65, vchmn, 66-68; state committeeman, Kootenai Co Rep Cent Comt, 66-68, precinct committeeman, 68-70, chmn, 70-72; Idaho State Rep, 72- Bus & Prof Pos: Sales rep, Pace Nat Co, Kirkland, Wash, 67- Mem: Small Bus Admin (adv coun, 72-73); Western States Forestry Task Force; Toastmasters Int (pres, 71). Honors & Awards: Area Four First Pl, Toastmasters Int, 70. Relig: Fundamental. Mailing Add: 3530 Highland Dr Coeur d'Alene ID 83814

INGRAM, JOHN RANDOLPH (D)
Comnr of Ins, NC
b Greensboro, NC, June 12, 29; s Henry Lewis Ingram & DeEtte Bennett I; m 1954 to Virginia Brown; c Gini Linn, John Randolph, II, Beverly Brown & Michelle Palmer. Educ: Univ NC, Chapel Hill, BS acct, 51; Law Sch, LLD, 54; Phi Beta Kappa; Beta Gamma Sigma; Phi Eta Sigma; NC Law Rev; pres, law sch grad class; Sigma Chi; Phi Delta Phi. Polit & Govt Pos: Treas, Randolph Co Dem Exec Comt, NC, 58-60, precinct chmn, 62-; NC State Rep, 27th Dist, 71-73; Comnr of Ins, NC, 73- Mil Serv: 1st Lt, Army, 55-58, serv in Judge Adv Gen Corps, Ft Benning, Ga; Letter of Commendation. Publ: Tort liability—mental anguish, 53 & Indicia of title, 54, NC Law Rev. Mem: Am Trial Lawyers Asn; Am Bar Asn; AF&AM (Master, dist dep, Grand Master, NC Grand Lodge); Scottish Rite; Shrine. Honors & Awards: Only Dem elected from 27th Dist. Relig: Methodist; Chmn off bd, 62 & 63. Legal Res: Asheboro NC 27203 Mailing Add: PO Box 26387 Raleigh NC 27611

INGRAM, JOHN WATSON (R)
b Cleveland, Ohio, Apr 6, 29; s John Hall Ingram & Dorothy Trombley I; m 1971 to Marian Redding. Educ: Syracuse Univ, BSBA, 52; Columbia Univ Grad Sch Bus, MS in Transportation Econ, 55. Polit & Govt Pos: Adminr, Fed RR Admin, 71-74. Bus & Prof Pos: Dir profit anal, NY Cent RR, 55-61; dir cost & price anal, Southern Rwy, 61-66; vpres mkt, Ill Cent RR, 66-71; pres & chief exec officer, Chicago, Rock Island & Pac RR, Chicago, 74- Mil Serv: Pvt, Army, 52-54, serv in Signal Corps. Mem: Transportation Research Forum (treas); Am Econ Asn; Nat Asn Bus Economists; Nat Freight Traffic Asn; Union League Club. Honors & Awards: Dept Officer of the Year, Mod RR Mag, 68-69; RR Man of the Year Award, St Louis Rwy Club, Mo, 73; Silver Medal for Outstanding Contributions, Secy of Transportation. Relig: Episcopal. Mailing Add: 1350 N State Parkway Chicago IL 60610

INGRAM, LOUIS WILSON, JR (R)
b Boston, Mass, Jan 30, 32; s Louis W Ingram & Muriel Ione Lauer I; single. Educ: Choate Sch, 50; Rollins Col, AB, 54; Univ SC, LLB, 62; Theta Alpha Phi. Polit & Govt Pos: Minority counsel, Comt on House Admin, US House of Rep, 75- Mil Serv: Entered as E-1, Army, 55, released as E-4, 57, after serv in Hq 7th Army as Pub Rels Dir, 7th Army Symphony, Europe, 55-57. Relig: Episcopal. Legal Res: 1054 McKean Circle Winter Park FL 32789 Mailing Add: 5850 Cameron Run Terr Alexandria VA 22303

INGRAM, MICHAEL B (R)
NH State Rep
Mailing Add: 24 Ministerial Rd Bedford NH 03102

INGRAM, ROBERT L (D)
b Mt Sterling, Ill, Dec 1, 30; s Owen R Ingram & Carlene Wemhoener I; m 1950 to Deloris Joan Dorsey; c Deborah Lynn, Bradford Byron & Deanna Denise. Educ: Pekin Community High Sch, 44-48. Polit & Govt Pos: Dem precinct committeeman, Tazewell Co, Ill, 62-; deleg, Dem Nat Conv, 68 & 72; mem exec bd, Tazewell Co Dem Cent Comt, 69; mem, Tazewell Co Bd, 72-; treas, Dem Cent Comt; deleg, Dem Nat Mid-Term Conf, 74. Bus & Prof Pos: Mem staff, Caterpillar Tractor Co, 48-, design engr, 64- Mem: Harry Truman Club (treas); Mason (32 degree). Relig: Christian Church of North America. Mailing Add: RR 1 Pekin IL 61554

INGRAM, W K (BILL) (D)
Ark State Sen
Mailing Add: Box 369 West Memphis AR 72301

INHOFE, JAMES MOUNTAIN (R)
Okla State Sen
b Des Moines, Iowa, Nov 17, 34; s Perry D Inhofe & Blanche Mountain I; m 1959 to Kay Kirkpatrick; c James Mountain, II, Perry Dyson, II, Molly Marie & Kay Kirkpatrick. Educ: Univ Tulsa, Lib Arts Degree, 57. Polit & Govt Pos: Okla State Rep, 66-68; Okla State Sen, 68-, minority floor leader, Okla State Senate, currently. Bus & Prof Pos: Pres, Quaker Life Ins Co, currently; vpres, Mid-Continent Casualty Co, currently; vpres, Okla Surety Co, currently. Mil Serv: Vet, Army. Mailing Add: 2139 E 32nd Tulsa OK 74105

INMAN, MARY LOU (TEDDI) (R)
Chairwoman, Ill Rep State Cent Comt
b Evanston, Ill, Nov 23, 25; s Glen Arnold Barrer & Wilhelmina Yocum B; m 1957 to Merle Truman Inman. Educ: Ripon Col, 42-43; Northwestern Univ, BS, 46; Southern Ill Univ, MS, 73; Delta Zeta. Polit & Govt Pos: Pres, Calhoun Rep Women, Ill, 64-66; chmn, Calhoun Co Rep Party, 64-72; dir to Congressman Paul Findley, Calhoun Co, 64-; mem exec bd, Ill Fedn Rep Women, 65-70 & 73-74; committeeman, 50th Dist Rep, 66-68 & 70-72; committeewoman, 20th Cong Dist, Ill Rep State Cent Comt, 66-74, chairwoman, 75- Bus & Prof Pos: Display dir, Mavrakos Candy Co, St Louis, Mo, 48-53; art dir, Victoria Printed Products, Inc, 53-56; free lance artist, Cassell & Paul Advert Art Studio, 56-57; secy-treas, Inman Marine, 60- Mem: People for the Preservation of Calhoun Co; Eastern Star (past Matron); Calhoun Homemaker's Exten Asn; Am Asn Univ Women. Relig: Protestant. Mailing Add: RR 1 Batchtown IL 62006

INNES, ALLAN C (R)
Mem, Thomaston Rep Town Comt, Conn
b Thomaston, Conn, Apr 13, 01; s Robert Innes & Elizabeth Anderson I; m 1925 to Agda Sandell; c Marion (Mrs DePecol), Helen (Mrs Titus) & Elaine A (Mrs Joseph Buckley). Educ: Eastman Bus Col. Polit & Govt Pos: Mem, Thomaston Rep Town Comt, 40-; mem, Finance Bd, Thomaston, 34-75, chmn, 40-58 & 73-75; Conn State Rep, 42-46 & 52-66, chmn appropriations comt, Conn House of Rep, 61-66. Bus & Prof Pos: Pres & treas, Innes Bros Inc, Gen Contractors, 28-66 & 75; dir, Thomaston Savings Bank, 48, chmn & dir, 73; vpres, Innes Realty Inc, 54. Mem: Union Lodge 96, F&AM; Rotary. Relig: Congregational. Mailing Add: 78 High St Thomaston CT 06787

INNES, GEORGE BARR (R)
Dir Finance Div, Rep Party Wis
b Ashland, Wis, Mar 15, 38; s Marvin A Innes & Barbara Barr I; m 1965 to Sheila Jane Giese; c Jennifer & Amy. Educ: Superior State Univ, Wis, BS, 66; Univ Wis Law Sch, Madison, 66-67. Polit & Govt Pos: Field rep, Rep Party Wis, 67, exec finance comt, 68-, dir finance div, currently, dep dir, currently. Mil Serv: Entered as Airman Basic, Air Force, 57, released as Airman, 2/C, 61. Mem: Elks; Big Bros of Dane Co, Wis. Relig: Lutheran. Mailing Add: Rte 1 Hensen Dr Sun Prairie WI 53590

INOUYE, DANIEL KEN (D)
US Sen, Hawaii
b Honolulu, Hawaii, Sept 7, 24; s Hyotaro Inouye & Kame Imanaga I; m 1949 to Margaret Shinobu Awamura; c Daniel Ken, Jr. Educ: Univ Hawaii, BA, 50; George Washington Univ Law Sch, JD, 52. Polit & Govt Pos: Hawaii Territorial Rep & Majority Leader, Hawaii Territorial House of Rep Asst Majority Whip, US Senate, 64-, mem, Senate Dem Policy Comt, 64-, mem Com Comt & vchmn Dem Sen Campaign Comt, 69-71; mem Comt on Appropriations & chmn Subcomt For Com & Tourism, 71-, chmn Appropriations Subcomt on Foreign Opers, 72-, mem Select Comt Presidential Activities, US Senate, 73-; temporary chmn & keynoter, Dem Nat Conv, 68, deleg, 72. Bus & Prof Pos: Attorney-at-law, 53- Mil Serv: Entered as Pvt, Army, 43, released as Capt, 47. Publ: Journey to Washington, Prentice-Hall, 67. Honors & Awards: Selected as One of the Ten Outstanding Young Men of the Year by the US Jr CofC, 60, One of the 100 Most Important Men & Women in the US by Life Mag, 62; Alumnus of the Year Award, George Washington Univ, 61; Splendid Am Award, Thomas A Dooley Found, 67. Legal Res: 2332 Coyne St Honolulu HI 96814 Mailing Add: 442 Russell Senate Off Bldg Washington DC 20510

IPPOLITO, ANDREW VINCENT (D)
b New York, NY, Mar 6, 30; s Andrew Vincent Ippolito & Antoinetta Emmanuele I; m 1954 to Constance Mary Di Mitrio; c Jenette, Andrew, Paul & Michael. Educ: Queens Col, NY, 2 years; Georgetown Univ, BSFS, 55; Pratt Inst, MLS, 59; founder, Student Vet Orgn. Polit & Govt Pos: Pres, North Queens Independent Dem, 67-68; deleg, Dem Nat Conv, 68- first vpres, Dem for New Politics, 70- Bus & Prof Pos: Law clerk, Berg, Mezansky & Mendes, NY City, 58; dir, Lindenhurst Pub Libr, LI, 59-60, N Babylon Pub Libr, 60-62 & Merrick Pub Libr, 62-65; mem bd, Sunnyside Progressive Nursery, 62; mem bd, Bayside Coop Nursery Sch, 65-67; dir libr & research, Newsday, Garden City, 65-; mem exec bd, Pub Sch 130, Bayside, 66-67; pres, Happy Time Nursery Sch, Bayside, 70-; mem bd, Queens Sch; lectr, Am Mgt Asn. Mil Serv: Hosp Corps, Navy, 50-52. Publ: Electronic frisk, Odds & Book Ends, fall 64; Library without books, Suffolk Co Libr Asn Data, winter 68; Special equipment, In: Planning the special library, Spec Libraries Asn, 72. Mem: Admin Mgr Soc; NY, Nassau Co Libr Asn (bd); Suffolk Co Libr Asn; hon mem, Nassau-Suffolk Sch Libr Asn; Nat Microfilm Asn. Mailing Add: 42-46 209 St Bayside NY 11361

IRICK, JOHN B (R)
NMex State Sen
Mailing Add: 6500 Rogers Ave NE Albuquerque NM 87110

IRVIN, JACK (D)
Ga State Rep
Mailing Add: Rte 1 Baldwin GA 30511

IRVIN, ROBERT ANDREW (R)
Ga State Rep
b Atlanta, Ga, Sept 9, 48; s Dr W Andrew Irvin & Irene Stephens I; single. Educ: Col William & Mary, AB, 70; Emory Univ, JD, 73. Polit & Govt Pos: Pres, Col William & Mary Young Rep Club, 68-69; orgn dir, Thompson for Cong, Ga, 70; state chmn, Ga Young Rep, 71-72; Ga State Rep, Dist 23, 73- Mem: Phi Beta Kappa; Omicron Delta Kappa; Pi Delta Epsilon; Optimist Club; Roswell Hist Soc. Relig: Presbyterian. Legal Res: 150 S Atlanta St Roswell GA 30075 Mailing Add: Box 325 Roswell GA 30075

IRVIN, THOMAS TELFORD (D)
Comnr Agr, Ga
b Lula, Ga, July 14, 29; s Clint Telford Irvin & Gladys Hogan I; m 1947 to Edna Bernice Frady; c James, Johnny, David, Londa & Lisa. Educ: Hall Co Pub Schs, Ga. Polit & Govt Pos: Mem, Habersham Co Bd Educ, 56-; Ga State Rep, Habersham Co, 57-61 & 65-69; mem, Ga Dem Exec Comt, 60-68; exec secy to Gov, Ga, 67-68; pres, Ninth Dist Legis Asn, 68; Comnr Agr Ga, 69-; mem, Soil & Water Conserv Comn, Ga Develop Authority State Bd Children & Youth, Ga Tobacco Adv Bd, Ga Livestock & Poultry Disease Bd & eight Ga Agr Commodity Comns. Mem: Ga Sch Bd Asn; Ga Forestry Asn; Ga PTA; Ga Educ Improv Coun; Stone Mt Mem Asn. Honors & Awards: Distinguished Leadership Award, Ga Sch Bd Asn; Distinguished Serv Award, Univ Ga Col Agr Alumni Asn; Doctor of Educ, Ga State House Rep Resolution; Outstanding Leadership Award, Ga Forestry Asn; Jaycee of Year, Habersham Co, 64. Relig: Baptist. Legal Res: Rte 1 Mt Airy GA 30563 Mailing Add: State Capitol Atlanta GA 30334

IRVINE, DAVID ROBERT (R)
Utah State Rep
b Salt Lake City, Utah, Aug 30, 43; s Robert George Irvine & Lucy Brown I; m 1969 to Linda Jean Hatch. Educ: Univ Utah, BS in Polit Sci, 68, Law Sch, JD, 71; Pi Sigma Alpha. Polit & Govt Pos: Deleg, David Co & Utah State Rep Conv, 66-; secy, Davis Co Rep Party, 67-69; chmn, 69-; mem, Utah State Rep Cent Comt, 67-; Hinckley intern, Utah Rep Gubernatorial Cand, 68; mem, Utah State Rep Exec Comt, 69-; asst attorney gen, State of Utah, 72; Utah State Rep, 73- Bus & Prof Pos: Mgr, Irvine Printing Co, Bountiful, Utah, 59-68, partner, Irvine, Smith & Murphy, 71-; mem assoc bd ed, Dialogue Mag, 69- Mil Serv: Pvt, Army, 62; serv in Hq, 96th Res Command; Capt, Army Res. Mem: Utah State Bar Asn; ROA. Honors & Awards: Freedom Found Honor Medal, 68. Relig: Latter-day Saint. Mailing Add: 886 S 850 East Bountiful UT 84010

IRVINE, WILLIAM A (R)
b Pittsburgh, Pa, May 24, 18; s William A Irvine & Olivia Bertram I; m 1947 to Elvera Siket; c Marsha (Mrs Burke) & Janice. Educ: Allegheny Col; Phi Delta Theta. Polit & Govt Pos: Admin asst to Rep Robert J Corbett, 39-40 & 47-61; chief dep sheriff, Allegheny Co, Pa, 42-43 & 45-47; asst staff dir, Post Off & Civil Serv Comt, US House Rep, 61-74; mem bd govs, US Postal Serv, 75- Mil Serv: Entered as Pvt, Army Air Corps, 43, released as 2nd Lt, 45, after serv as Pilot. Relig: Catholic. Legal Res: Hampton Twp PA Mailing Add: Turkey Point Edgewater MD 21037

IRVING, DON (D)
Mem, Ill Dem State Cent Comt
b Chambersburg, Ill, Sept 20, 98; s Wade Hampton Irving & Martha Hume I; m 1920 to Marjorie Lindsey; c Mary Frances (Mrs Christenson), Brice Lindsey & Roger Wade. Educ: James Millikin Univ, 18; Eureka Col, 19; Gem City Bus Col, 20. Polit & Govt Pos: Sch dir, local grade & high sch, 28-51; chmn, Pike Co Bd Supvrs, Ill, 37-52; chmn, Pike Co Defense Comt, 40-52; automobile investigator, 45-52; chmn, Pike Co Dem Comt, 49-65 & formerly; cattle quarantine inspector, 61-; mem, Ill Dem State Cent Comt, currently. Bus & Prof Pos: Farmer, 21-45; ins agency owner, Ill, 57- Mil Serv: Pvt, Army, 18, serv in Students Army Training Corps. Publ: Weekly column for five co newspapers, 50- Mem: Am Legion Post 152; Farm Bur; Farmers Union. Honors & Awards: Mem, Co All Star Basketball Second Team, 17; mgr, local baseball team, 41 years. Relig: Christian; Bd Mem. Mailing Add: Chambersburg IL 62323

IRVING, HELEN (D)
Dem Nat Committeewoman, Mich
Mailing Add: 4510 Kensington Detroit MI 48224

IRVING, TERRY KATHRYN (D)
NDak State Rep
b Little Rock, Ark, July 17, 44; d Terry C Rodgers & Kathryn Maxey Rodgers Gilbert; div. Educ: Univ Houston, BA, 68; Univ NDak, JD, 74; Order of the Coif. Polit & Govt Pos: Mem, NDak Comn on Status of Women, 73-; NDak State Rep, 73-, chmn Dem caucus, NDak House Rep, 75-; mem exec comt, 18th Dist Dem Non-Partisan League Party, NDak, 74- Bus & Prof Pos: Methods examr, Prudential Ins Co, 68-70; legis intern, NDak Legis Coun, 73; self-employed lawyer, Grand Forks, 75- Mem: Am & NDak State Bar Asns; Am Civil Liberties Union (mem exec bd, Red River Chap, 74-); NDak Women's Coalition; Common Cause. Mailing Add: 311 N Eighth St Apt 6 Grand Forks ND 58201

IRVIS, K LEROY (D)
Majority Leader, Pa House of Rep
b Saugerties, NY, Dec 27, 19; s Francis H Irvis & Harriet Cantine I; m to Cathryn L Irvis. Educ: NY State Teachers Col, AB summa cum laude; NY Univ, MA; Univ Pittsburgh Law Sch, JD; teaching fel, 39; Owens fel in law; ed student mag; Signum Laudis; varsity debating team; track team; Pi Gamma Mu; Order of the Coif; Phi Delta Phi; Phi Beta Kappa. Polit & Govt Pos: Civilian attache, War Dept, Aviation Training Div; asst dist attorney, Pa, 57-63; mem, NAACP Legal Redress Comt; Pa State Rep, 58-, minority caucus chmn, Pa House of Rep, 63-64, majority caucus chmn, 65-66, minority whip, 67-68, majority leader, 69-72 & currently, minority whip, 73-75; mem, Univ Pittsburgh Med Sch Adv Comt, Gen State Authority Exec Bd, Bicentennial Comn Pa, Neighborhood Assistance Adv Bd & Training Employ & Manpower Adv Bd; bd dirs, TRIAD; treas, Joint State Govt Comn & Criminal Justice Planning Bd; deleg, Dem Nat Conv, 68 & 72. Bus & Prof Pos: Attorney; mem, Fed, Dist & all Commonwealth Courts; law clerk to Judges Anne X Alpern & Lornan Lewis, 55-57; former ed, Pittsburgh Urban League Mag; auth; former sch teacher, Baltimore, Md; steel chipper, Crucible Steel, Pittsburgh; research asst to prof, Law Sch; newscaster, Pittsburgh Courier; secy pub rels & bd dirs, Urban League Pittsburgh; bd dirs, Port Authority Pittsburgh, United Black Front, Pittsburgh Coun for the Arts, Bidwell Cult Ctr, Negro Educ Emergency Drive, Community Action of Pittsburgh; bd trustees, Univ Pittsburgh; bd dirs & bd trustees, Pittsburgh Play House. Mem: Hon mem Pub Defender Asn. Mailing Add: 1420 Centre Ave Pittsburgh PA 15219

IRWIN, DONALD JAY (D)
b Rosario, Argentina, Sept 7, 26; s Montrose Wellington Irwin & Marion Reynolds I; m 1952 to Mary Stapleton; c Patrick, Marion, Lucile & Stephen. Educ: Yale Univ, BA in Am Hist, 51, LLB, 54. Polit & Govt Pos: Mem, Norwalk Bd of Educ, 55; US Rep, Fourth Dist, Conn, 58-60 & 64-68; gen counsel, US Info Agency, 61; Conn State Treas, 62. Bus & Prof Pos: Counsel, Tierney, Zullo, Flaherty & Cioffi, 69-. Mil Serv: Entered as Pvt, Army, 45, released as Pfc, 47. Mem: Rowayton Vol Hose Co; Norwalk Stamford Inter-Racial Coun; KofC. Honors & Awards: Yale Swimming Team; Soccer & Rugby; Distinguished Serv Award, Jr CofC. Relig: Catholic. Mailing Add: 3 Topsail Rd Norwalk CT 06853

IRWIN, JOEL (D)
Committeeman, Ark Dem State Comt
b Little Rock, Ark, Apr 19, 30; s Moody Miles Irwin & Irene Allison I; m 1958 to Mary Wade; c Lisa Allison, Jeffrey Wade & Matthew Miles. Educ: Ark State Teachers Col, BA, 54; Phi Sigma Epsilon; Royal Rooters. Polit & Govt Pos: Committeeman, Ark Dem State Comt, 72- Bus & Prof Pos: Ed, Cleburne Co Times, 58- Mil Serv: Entered as Recruit, Army, 50, released as Pfc, 51, after serv in AGC. Mem: Soc Prof Journalists; Sigma Delta Chi; Sugar Loaf Masonic Lodge; Little Rock Consistory (32 degree); Scimitar Shrine Temple. Relig: Baptist. Legal Res: Reservoir Rd Heber Springs AR 72543 Mailing Add: Rte 2 Box 135 Heber Springs AR 72543

IRWIN, JOHN N (R)
Polit & Govt Pos: Under Secy State, Dept State, 70-72; US Ambassador to France, formerly. Legal Res: NY Mailing Add: Dept of State Washington DC 20520

IRWIN, JOHN R (D)
Ga State Rep
Mailing Add: Dawson GA 31742

IRWIN, LEON, III (D)
Mem, Dem Nat Comt, La
Mailing Add: John Hancock Bldg New Orleans LA 70130

IRWIN, PAT (D)
Justice, Okla Supreme Court
b Leedey, Okla, June 12, 21; s Marvin J Irwin & Ollie D Newton I; m 1950 to Margaret L Boggs; c William Jackson & Margaret Ann. Educ: Southwestern State Col, 39-40; Okla Univ, 40-41, Col of Law, LLB, 49. Polit & Govt Pos: Co attorney, Dewey Co, Okla, 48-50; Okla State Sen, 51-54; secy of comnrs, Land Off Okla, 54-58; Assoc Justice, Okla State Sen, 51-54; secy of comnrs, Land Off Okla, 54-58; Assoc Justice, Okla Supreme Court, formerly, Justice, currently, chief justice, 69-70. Mil Serv: Entered as Aviation Cadet, Navy, 42, released as Capt Marine Corps, 45, after serv in Marine Corps, fighter pilot in Pac Theaters. Mailing Add: State Supreme Court Oklahoma City OK 73105

ISAACS, JOHN DONALD (R)
Del State Sen
b Milford, Del, Apr 8, 32; s Earle Lofland Isaacs & Sara Stayton I; m 1951 to Clydia Drucilla McGinnes; c Lisa Drucilla, Nicholas Waldon & Melissa Elaine. Educ: Milton High Sch, grad, 50. Polit & Govt Pos: Pres, Lower New Castle Co Asn Young Rep, Del, 59, vpres, Del State Asn Young Rep, 60, pres, 61; Del State Sen, 62-, chmn environ control & natural resources comt & mem joint finance comt, Del State Senate, chmn exec pub safety & finance comt, 73-, pres pro-tempore, 73- Bus & Prof Pos: Mem state bd, Del Farm Bur, 60; pres, New Castle Co Farm Bur, 60-62; chmn, Southern State Bd, 760-64. Mem: Mason; Farm Bur; Shrine; Grange; Lions. Honors & Awards: Outstanding Young Farmer Del, Jaycees; Nat Robert S Kerr Award. Relig: Methodist. Mailing Add: RD 2 Townsend DE 19734

ISAACSON, MAE DELORIS (DFL)
Mem, Minn State Dem-Farmer-Labor Cent Comt
b St Paul, Minn, May 21, 24; d Charles Jalmer Kulla & Amanda Hestenes K; m 1947 to Roy William Isaacson; c Janis Mae & Keith Allan. Educ: Moorhead State Col, BS Elem Ed, magna cum laude, 69; Bemidji State Col, SLBP Cert, 72, MS Elem Educ, 73; Alpha Eta Chap, Delta Kappa Gamma. Polit & Govt Pos: Vchairwoman, Otter Tail Co Dem-Farmer-Labor Party, Minn, 59-63, co chairwoman, 63-72; mem, Minn State Dem-Farmer-Labor Cent Comt, 69-70, 75-; chmn, resolutions comt, Minn Seventh Dist Dem-Farmer-Labor Conv, 66, 68, 70 & 72; vchairwoman, Minn Seventh Dist Dem-Farmer-Labor Party, 66-72; third vchairperson, Minn Senate Dist Ten, 72, secy, 75- Bus & Prof Pos: Elem teacher, Sch Dist 553, New York Mills, 65- Mem: Nat Educ Asn; Northwest Reading Coun; Minn Reading Asn; Farmers Union; Candlelight Study Club. Relig: Lutheran. Mailing Add: RR 3 New York Mills MN 56567

ISAACSON, ROBERT A (D)
Pub Rels Dir Region One, Young Dem Am
b Lewiston, Maine, July 18, 45; s Peter J Isaacson (deceased) & Frances Ruch I; single. Educ: Bowdoin Col, BA, 75; Zeta Psi; Young Dem; Polit Forum. Polit & Govt Pos: Pres, Bowdoin Col Young Dem, 73-75; publicity dir, Maine Young Dem, 73-74; deleg, Dem Nat Mid-Term Conf, 74; pub rels dir region one, Young Dem Am, 74- Relig: Jewish. Mailing Add: 5 Central Ave Lewiston ME 04240

ISCH, HELEN A (R)
Chairwoman, Wood Co Rep Exec Comt, Ohio
b Bowling Green, Ohio, Dec 2, 07; d Afton A Whipple & Martha J Lipsett W; wid; c Frances J (Mrs Mueller) & Mary Jo (Mrs Bagelmann). Educ: Bowling Green State Univ, BS in Ed, 27; Delta Gamma. Polit & Govt Pos: Chairwoman, Wood Co Rep Exec Comt, Ohio, 71-; mem bd elec, Wood Co, Ohio, 74- Bus & Prof Pos: Teacher, Mich & Colo, 28-31; med asst, Bowling Green, Ohio, 31-33. Mem: Eastern Star; Bicentennial Comt for Bowling Green; Wood Co Hist Soc. Relig: Protestant. Mailing Add: 854 Parker Ave Bowling Green OH 43402

ISENBARGER, JOHN P (R)
Chmn, Delaware Co Rep Party, Ind
b La Crosse, Ind, June 20, 23; s Paul M Isenbarger & Mazie M Palm I; m 1946 to Jean Phillips; c John Phillips, Thomas Paul & Philip Lee. Educ: DePauw Univ, AB, 47; Delta Upsilon. Polit & Govt Pos: Comnr, Delaware Co, Ind, 69-; chmn, Delaware Co Rep Party, 73- Bus & Prof Pos: Mfrs rep, Muncie, Ind, 47-50, Dayton, Ohio, 52-56 & Chicago, Ill, 56-62; gen sales mgr, Durham Mfg Corp, Muncie, Ind, 62-65. Mil Serv: Entered as Pvt, Army, released as 1st Lt, after serv in 104th Div, ETO, 44-45 & Korean Conflict, 50-52; Purple Heart; 3 Battle Stars; ETO Ribbon; Korean War Theatre Ribbon. Mem: Mason; Scottish Rite; Shrine; Rotary. Relig: Protestant. Mailing Add: 2106 Woodbridge Dr Muncie IN 47304

ISLER, JOHN J (D)
Ky State Rep
b 1908. Polit & Govt Pos: Secy & former pres, Dem Club; Ky State Rep, 56- Bus & Prof Pos: Rwy clerk; acct. Mem: Eagles; Cent Covington Civic Club; Crusaders East End Club; Peaselburg Liars Club; St Augustine Holy Name Soc. Relig: Catholic. Mailing Add: 1813 Jefferson Ave Covington KY 41014

ISON, DONALD (R)
Chmn, Breathitt Co Rep Comt, Ky
b Oscaloosa, Ky, June 22, 39; s Edgar Ison & Lona Hampton I; m 1962 to Marsha Allen; c Cheryl Anne, Kelly Chris & Melissa Carol. Educ: Morehead State Univ, BS, 61. Polit & Govt Pos: Chmn, Breathitt Co Rep Comt, Ky, 68- Mil Serv: Entered as Pvt, E-1, Army Nat Guard, 61, released as Sgt E-6, 68, after serving in 201st Engr Bn; Merit Award, 68. Mem: Breathitt-Jackson Airport Bd; Breathitt Co Indust Bd; Jaycees. Honors & Awards: Jaycee of the Year, 66; Outstanding Breathitt Countian, 69-70. Relig: Protestant; Deacon, Christian Church. Mailing Add: Panbowl Rd Jackson KY 41339

ISON, MARGARET A (R)
Chmn, Jefferson Co Rep Comt, Wash
b Cincinnati, Ohio, Sept 4, 33; d N J Ison & Eula Johnson I; m 1956 to Glenn W Ison; s Stuart D & John B. Educ: Denison Univ, BA, 55; Phi Alpha Theta; Alpha Phi; Young Rep Club; Women's Coun. Polit & Govt Pos: Vchmn, Jefferson Co Rep Party, Wash, 72-74, chmn, 74- Mem: Jefferson Co Rep Women's Club (membership chmn), George Welch Orthopedic Auxiliary (secy). Mailing Add: 830 Franklin St Port Townsend WA 98368

ISRAEL, LESLEY LOWE (D)
b Philadelphia, Pa, July 21, 38; d Herman Albert Lowe & Florence Segal L; m 1960 to Fred Israel; c Herman Allen & Sanford Lawrence. Educ: Smith Col, BA cum laude, 59. Polit & Govt Pos: Coordr media advan, Humphrey for Pres Comt, 68; dir scheduling, The Bayh Comt, 71; dir of polit intel, Humphrey for President Comt, 72; mem, Dem Nat Charter Comn, 73-74; deleg, Dem Nat Mid-Term Conf, 74. Publ: Co-auth, The Democratic Charter, Dem Rev, 74. Mem: Am Asn Polit Consult; Women's Nat Dem Club. Honors & Awards: Young Leadership Award, Jewish Welfare Bd; Outstanding Contribution, Womens Polit Caucus Montgomery Co. Relig: Jewish. Mailing Add: 8512 Burning Tree Rd Bethesda MD 20034

ISRAEL, RICHARD JEROME (R)
Attorney Gen, RI
b Woonsocket, RI, Dec 9, 30; s Fred Israel & Cecile Kantrowitz I; m 1955 to Harriet Gladstein; c Susan Emily, Eric Steven & Karen Esta. Educ: Brown Univ, AB, 51; Yale Univ Law Sch, JD, 54; Phi Beta Kappa; Delta Sigma Rho. Polit & Govt Pos: Chief, Div Workmen's Compensation, RI, 61; asst attorney gen, RI, 67-71, Attorney Gen, 71- Bus & Prof Pos: Attorney-at-law, Woonsocket, RI, 54-71. Mil Serv: Entered as 2nd Lt, Army, 55, released as 1st Lt, 57, after serv in 692nd Field Artil Bn, Fort Sill, Okla, 55-57; Lt Col, Army Res, 65. Mem: Am Judicature Soc; Nat Asn Attorneys Gen (exec comt, 72-); Nat Dist Attorneys Asn (dir, 71-); B'nai B'rith; Mt Vernon Lodge F&AM. Relig: Jewish. Legal Res: 194 Sixth St Providence RI 02903 Mailing Add: 250 Benefit St Providence RI 02903

ISTA, RICHARD GLEN (D)
Chmn, NDak Dem Party
b Walcott, NDak, Nov 12, 28; s George W Ista & Susie Towne I; m 1967 to Diane Overby; c Laurel (Mrs Aldrich), Robin & DeNae. Educ: Colfax High Sch, grad; salutatorian. Polit & Govt Pos: Precinct committeeman, Colfax, NDak, 52-58; mem, Colfax City Coun, 54-65; pres, Colfax Sch Dist, 58-65; chmn, Richland Co Dem Party, 60-65; deleg, Dem Nat Conv 64 & 72; comnr, NDak Workmen's Compensation Bur, 65-68; coordr, Sen Kennedy Campaign, 67; chmn, US Senate Campaign, 68; finance chmn, Kennedy Mem Bldg, 68; chmn, NDak Dem Party, 69-; mem, Dem Nat Comt, currently. Bus & Prof Pos: Farming, Colfax, NDak & Ada, Minn, 48-; pres & treas, Colfax Investment Co, 56-; pres, Black Angus, Inc & Black Angus Restaurant & Supper Club, 68-; mem exec bd, Fargo CofC, 70- Mem: Elks; Kiwanis; Farmers Union; Farm Bur; Jeffersonians. Honors & Awards: Speech Contest; 4-H Crop Award Trip to Chicago; many awards for showing livestock. Relig: Evangelical United Brethren. Mailing Add: 901 24th Ave S Fargo ND 58102

ISZLER, HARRY EUGENE (R)
NDak State Sen
b Streeter, NDak, Sept 11, 30; s Gottlieb M Iszler & Mary Wolt I; m 1953 to Leona Hoffer; c Bernadean (Mrs Keith Ketterling), Holly (Mrs Dennis Becker), Michael, Mary Jean & Timothy. Educ: State Sch Sci, 50-51. Polit & Govt Pos: Chmn, Dist 31, Rep Comt, NDak, 71-72; NDak State Sen, 74- Bus & Prof Pos: Farmer & rancher, 53- Mil Serv: Entered as Pvt, Army, 52, released as Cpl, 53, after serv in 3rd QM Co, Korean Theatre; Korean Serv Medal with 1 Bronze Star; UN Serv Medal. Mem: Elks; Lions (vpres); Am Legion; Farm Bur; Am Nat Cattlemens Asn. Relig: United Methodist. Mailing Add: Streeter ND 58483

ITKIN, IVAN (D)
Pa State Rep
b New York, NY, Mar 29, 36; s Abraham Aaron Itkin & Eda Kreger I. Educ: Polytech Inst Brooklyn, BChE, 56; NY Univ, MNucE, 57; Univ Pittsburgh, PhD(Math), 64. Polit & Govt Pos: Judge of elec, 19th Dist, 14th Ward, Pittsburgh, Pa, 66-68; chmn, 14th Ward Dem Comt, 70-72; Pa State Rep, 23rd Legis Dist, 73- Bus & Prof Pos: Assoc scientist, Bettis Atomic Power Lab, Westinghouse Elec Corp, 57-59, scientist, 59-64, sr scientist, 64-71, fel scientist, 71-73. Publ: Analysis of the neutron capture cross section & resonance integral of hafnium, 62, Approximate methods for solving linear & non-linear multidimensional integral equations & boundary value problems, 64 & co-auth, Evaluated cross sections for the hafnium isotopes, 67, US Atomic Energy Comn. Mem: Am Nuclear Soc; Am Civil Liberties Union; Am Jewish Cong; Group Against Smog & Pollution; New Dem Coalition. Relig: Jewish. Mailing Add: Capital Bldg Harrisburg PA 17120

ITTA, BRENDA T (D)
Alaska State Rep
Mailing Add: Box 264 Barrow AK 99723

IVERSEN, KIRK VICTOR (D)
Mem, Calif State Dem Cent Comt
b Chicago, Ill, Nov 15, 51; s Victor Iversen & Ann Pedersen I; single. Educ: Orange Coast Col, Degree, 71; Calif State Univ, Fullerton, Degree in Biol, 75. Polit & Govt Pos: Col coordr, McGovern for Pres, Calif, 72; Orange Co student coordr, Moscone for Gov, 73-74; student coordr & field dir, Farris for Cong, 39th Dist, 74; deleg, Dem Nat Mid-Term Conf, 74; mem, Calif State Dem Cent Comt, 75- Mem: Friends of the Earth; Sierra Club; Scientists' Inst Pub Information; Common Cause. Mailing Add: 719 E Hoover Ave Orange CA 92667

IVERSON, LOIS O (R)
Chmn, Washington Co Rep Party, Utah
b Toquerville, Utah, July 21, 22; d Arthur H Olds & Lottie Dodge O; m 1942 to Rulon (Rudy) Iverson; c Suzanne (Mrs Dewayne Nicholson), Norman R & Paul J. Educ: Hurricane High Sch, grad, 40; LDS Bus Col, 41-42; Alice Louise Reynolds Literary Book Club; Dixie Col Faculty Women. Polit & Govt Pos: Mem exec comts, Cedar City League Women Voters, 55-60; secy, St George City, 65-69; secy, Washington Co Rep Party, Utah, 67-69, vchmn, 69-71, chmn, 73-; vchmn, St George City Rep Party, 69-73; deleg, Rep Nat Conv, 72. Bus & Prof Pos: Mgr & asst mgr, Cafeteria & Inns, Utah Parks Comn, Zion & Grand Canyon Nat Parks, 47-50; postmaster, Grand Canyon Post Off, 50-51; receptionist & secy to pres, Dixie Col, St George, Utah, 61-65, bus mgr & registr, 61-65; acct technician, Dexter C Snow, CPA, Bradshaw, Snow & Mathis, CPA's & Elmer Fox & Co, CPA's, 65- Publ: Ed, Water resources of Iron Co, Senate Hearing on Dixie Proj, 57. Mem: League Women Voters; Mutual Improv Asn, LDS Church (Primary Presidency); Alice Louise Reynolds Literary Book Club (vpres, currently). Relig: Latter-day Saint. Legal Res: 276 S 600 E St George UT 84770 Mailing Add: PO Box 575 St George UT 84770

IVES, ALDEN ALLEN (R)
b Torrington, Conn, May 21, 25; s Sherman Kimberly Ives & Lida Skilton I; m 1951 to Janet Reed Stiles; c Richard Allen, Russell Reed & Tracey Jean. Educ: Univ Conn, BS in Bus Admin & Law Sch, 1 yr. Polit & Govt Pos: Treas, Morris, Conn, 52-58; Conn State Rep, Morris, 57-59; Conn State Sen, 32nd Dist, 61-73, Minority Leader, Conn State Senate, 71-73; deleg, Rep Nat Conv, 72; Treas, Conn, formerly. Bus & Prof Pos: Vpres & treas, Ives Ins, Inc, 60-64; exec vpres, Patrons Mutual Ins Co, 64- Mil Serv: Entered as Recruit Army, 43, released as S/Sgt, 46, after serv in Co L, 302nd Inf, 94th Inf Div, ETO; European Theater Ribbon with three Battle Stars; Silver Star; CW4 Army Res, 46- Mem: Am Legion; VFW; AF&AM; Grange; Vol Fire Dept. Relig: Congregational. Legal Res: Morris CT Mailing Add: 769 Hebron Ave Glastonbury CT 06033

IVES, GEORGE SKINNER (R)
b Brooklyn, NY, Jan 10, 22; s Irving McNeil Ives & Elizabeth Skinner I; m 1948 to Barbara K Turner; c Elizabeth & Nancy. Educ: Dartmouth Col, AB, 43; Cornell Univ Law Sch, LLB, 49. Polit & Govt Pos: Legal asst to chmn, Nat Labor Rels Bd, 49-50; admin asst & legal counsel to US Sen Irving M Ives, NY, 53-58; presidential appointee, Nat Mediation Bd, 69- Bus & Prof Pos: Assoc attorney, Simpson, Thatcher & Bartlett, New York, 50-53; pvt practice of law & labor arbitration, Washington, DC, 59-69. Mil Serv: Lt(sg), Naval Res, 43-46. Mem: Am, NY & DC Bar Asns; Nat Acad Arbitrators; Am Arbitration Asn. Legal Res: 5969 Searl Terr Bethesda MD 20016 Mailing Add: 1230 16th St Washington DC 20572

IVES, TIMOTHY READ (D)
b Chicago, Ill, Apr 9, 28; s Ernest L Ives & Elizabeth D Stevenson I; m 1954 to Adrienne A Osborne; c Alison A, Sandra R & Timothy O. Educ: Univ Va, 47-51; Phi Gamma Delta; V Club. Polit & Govt Pos: Precinct committeeman, Dem Party, Bloomington, Ill, 58-69; deleg, Ill State Conv, 64, 68, 70 & 72; secy, Ill Sch Bldg Comn, 65-72; deleg, Dem Nat Conv, 68 & 72. Bus & Prof Pos: Radio Sales, WBT, Charlotte, NC, 55-56, WJBC, WJBC-FM, Bloomington, Ill, 56-60; radio sta mgr, WJBC-WBNQ, 60-, pres, WJBC Commun Corp, 72-; pres, Bloomington Broadcasting Corp, 71; vpres, WROK, Inc, 71- Mil Serv: Entered as enlisted man, Air Force, 51, released as 1st Lt, 55, after serv in 5th Air Force, Korea, & Training Command in US, 53-55; Capt, Air Force Res, Retired; Air Medal. Mem: Nat Asn Broadcasters; Ill Broadcasters Asn; Nat Asn FM Broadcasters; Rotary; Am Legion. Mailing Add: Oak Hill RR 1 Bloomington IL 61701

IVES, WILLIAM CHARLES (R)
VChmn, Ill Rep State Cent Comt
b Aledo, Ill, Feb 5, 33; s Dale G Ives & Anna Grace Philleo I; div; c David William, Carol Elaine & Daniel Winston. Educ: Knox Col (Ill), BA, 55; Harvard Law Sch, JD, 60; Phi Beta Kappa; Pi Sigma Alpha; Delta Sigma Rho; Phi Gamma Delta; Lincoln's Inn. Polit & Govt Pos: Founder & first pres, Knox Col (Ill) Young Rep Club, 54; pres, Harvard Law & Grad Sch Rep, 60; co-chmn, Speakers Bur Midwest Vol for Nixon-Lodge, 60; representative committeeman, DuPage Co, Ill, 63-64; deleg, Young Rep Nat Conv, 61, 63 & 67; dist gov, Ill Young Rep, 62-65; mem, Ill State & DuPage Co Young Rep Bd, 62-70; precinct committeeman, Hinsdale, Ill, 62-; mem, Ill State Young Rep Bd Gov, 64-69; chmn, Hinsdale, Ill Regular Rep Orgn, 64-70; chmn, Speakers' Bur for Rep John N Erlenborn, Ill, 64-; mem, Ill Rep State Cent Comt, 66-, vchmn, 70-; mem, Nat Rep Cong Adv Comt, 68; Rep Presidential Elector, 68, chmn, Ill Col Presidential Electors, 72; dir, DuPage Co Workshops, 68-; chmn, Ill Fair Employ Practices Comn, 69-73; mem, Secy of State's Adv Panel Int Law, 71-74; Small Bus Admin Adv Coun, 71- Mil Serv: Entered as 2nd Lt, Army, 55, released as 1st Lt, 57, after serv in Counter Intel, Ger, 56-57. Mem: Ill State & Am Bar Asns; Bar Asn Seventh Fed Circuit; Chicago Coun on Foreign Rels; State Ill Hist Soc. Honors & Awards: Outstanding Ill Col Young Rep, 55; Outstanding Ill Young Rep, 66. Relig: Protestant. Legal Res: 5743 S Grant St Apt H Hinsdale IL 60521 Mailing Add: 8300 Sears Tower Chicago IL 60603

IVORY, ELLIS R (R)
Rep Nat Committeeman, Utah
Mailing Add: 151 S Main St Salt Lake City UT 84111

IVY, JOHN T (D)
Kans State Rep
Mailing Add: 1620 Montana El Dorado KS 67042

IZAC, EDOUARD VICTOR MICHEL (D)
b Cresco, Iowa, Dec 18, 91; s B Michel Izac & Mathilda Geuth I; m 1915 to Agnes Elmer Cabell; c Cabell, Edouard, Jr, Charles, Suzanne Forrest & Andre. Educ: Sch of the Assumption, Iowa; US Naval Acad. Polit & Govt Pos: US Rep, 20th & 23rd Dists, Calif, 37-47. Mil Serv: Entered as Midshipman, Navy 11, retired as Lt Comdr, 21; Cong Medal of Honor; Croce de Guerra, Italy; Cross of Montenegro. Publ: Prisoner of the U 90, Houghton Mifflin; The Holy Land Then & Now, Vantage Press. Relig: Catholic. Mailing Add: 5608 Chesterbrook Rd Bethesda MD 20016

IZARD, HAROLD HALE (D)
NY State Assemblyman
b Buffalo, NY, July 4, 39; s Emmette F Izard & Rhea Lucille Smith I; m 1961 to Linda May Quigley; c Arthur, Judy, Bruce, Kirk, Norman & Warren. Educ: Univ Buffalo, BA, 60; Canisius Col, MS, 64; State Univ NY at Buffalo, 64-67; Alpha Phi Omega. Polit & Govt Pos: Committeeman, Tonawanda Dem Comt, 73-; NY State Assemblyman, 75- Bus & Prof Pos: Biol teacher, Amherst & Tonawanda, NY, 62-74; biol instr, State Univ NY at Buffalo, 65-66; chmn sci dept, Sweet Home Cent Schs, 73-74. Mem: NY State United Teachers; Erie Co & Sweet Home Educ Asns; Am Fedn Teachers; Sci Teachers Asn of NY State; Phi Delta Kappa. Relig: Roman Catholic. Legal Res: 356 McKinley Ave Kenmore NY 14217 Mailing Add: State Capitol Albany NY 12224

IZQUIERDO MORA, JOSE G (POPULAR DEMOCRAT, PR)
Rep, PR House of Rep
Mailing Add: State Capitol San Juan PR 00901

IZQUIERDO-MORA, LUIS A (POPULAR DEMOCRAT, PR)
Sen, PR Senate
b Mayquez, PR, Mar 19, 31; s Luis A Izquierdo-Galo & Jenara Mora-Rios; m 1955 to Rita D Encarnacion-Fas; c Luis A, Jose M, Natalio J, Manuel E & Rita D. Educ: Univ PR, BSB, 50, MSSc, 51, MD, 56. Polit & Govt Pos: Mem bd gov, Popular Dem Party of PR, 69-; pres, Popular Dem Party of San Juan, 69-; mem, Dem Party, PR Chap, 72-; Sen, PR Senate, 73-; pres, Finance Comt, vpres, Socio-Econ Develop Comt, vpres, Housing & Urban Develop Comt, secy, Health & Welfare Comt & mem, Ways & Means Comt, PR Senate, 73- Bus & Prof Pos: Practicing physician, Rio Piedras, PR, 59-73; mem, Blue Shield Plan of PR, 60-73 & Blue Cross Plan of PR, 69-73; mem courtesy staff in eight hosps, San Juan, 60-73; med examr, Salvation Army, 70-73; mem bd trustees, St Joseph Sch, 71-73. Mil Serv: Capt, Med Corps, Army Res, 57-59, serv in Caribbean. Publ: Social Responsibility of the Puerto Rican Physician, Parejas, Spain, 69; Our goals, PR Med Asn J, 67; The right to be born, El Mundo, San Juan, PR, 73. Mem: Am Acad Family Physicians; PR State Med Asn; Right to be Born Comt (pres, 73-); House of Spain; Ateneo de PR. Honors & Awards: Plaque, Lions Club, Dist 51, PR, 67; Plaque Col Soc Workers, 68; Outstanding Young Man Plaque, Ment Retardation Inst, 69; Plaque, Salvation Army, 72. Relig: Roman Catholic. Legal Res: 1504 Rhin El Paraiso Rio Piedras PR 00926 Mailing Add: Box BJ Rio Piedras PR 00928

J

JABLONSKI, ROBERT J (D)
b Jersey City, NJ, Apr 15, 33; s Jess Jablonski & Helen Kowalski J; m 1958 to Anne J Frost; c Barbara & Susan. Educ: Jersey City State Col, BSEd, 58. Polit & Govt Pos: Secy to Senate Minority, NJ State Senate, 72-73; dep state coordr, Byrne Campaign, 74; treas, NJ Hwy Authority, 74-; deleg, Dem Nat Mid-Term Conf, 74. Bus & Prof Pos: Pres, Jablonski Assoc, 68-70; acct exec, Boland, Sarrin Gordon & Sutter, New York, 70- Mil Serv: Entered as Pfc, Air Force, 51, released as S/Sgt, 55, after serv in Korea. Legal Res: 6 Nash Ave Clifton NJ 07011 Mailing Add: 45 Wall St New York NY 10005

JACKAMONIS, EDWARD G (D)
Wis State Rep
b New Britain, Conn, Oct 19, 39; s Edward Jackamonis & Sophie Horosik J; m 1962 to Barbara Bastenbeck. Educ: Northeastern Univ, BA with high honors & honors in polit sci, 62; Univ Wis-Madison, MS, 64; Pi Sigma Alpha; Phi Alpha Theta; The Acad. Polit & Govt Pos: Tax enumerator, Conn State Tax Dept, 58, admin fiscal mgt aide, 61; adv, Univ Wis Young Dem, Waukesha, 66-71; chmn, Waukesha Co Citizens for LaFollette for Gov Comt, 68; secy, Waukesha Co Dem Party, 68-69; deleg, Wis Dem State Conv, 68-72; Wis State Rep, 71-; vchmn assembly state affairs comt, mem rules comt, nat resources comt, environ qual comt & speaker pro tempore, Wis State Assembly, currently; chmn, Ninth Cong Dist Lindsay for President Comt, 72; mem, Wis Legis Coun; mem, Natural Resources Coun State Agencies; mem intergovt rels comt, Nat Conf State Legislatures. Bus & Prof Pos: Libr asst, Hartford Pub Libr, Conn, 59-62; proj asst, Univ Wis-Madison, 62-64, teaching asst, 64-65; instr polit sci, Univ Wis-Waukesha, 66-71, chmn social sci div, 68-69, mem cent faculty comt, 68-69, chmn student life & interests comt, 69-70, mem exec comt, Univ Wis Ctr Syst Polit Sci Dept, 68-71. Mem: Am Polit Sci Asn; Waukesha Environ Coun; Waukesha Coun Human Rels; Waukesha Co Asn Retarded Children. Honors & Awards: Sears B Condit Award, Northeastern Univ; Third Prize, DAR Essay Contest, New Britain, Conn, 55. Legal Res: 622 Greenmeadow Dr Waukesha WI 53186 Mailing Add: State Capitol Madison WI 53702

JACKSON, ALPHONSE, JR (D)
La State Rep
Mailing Add: 108 Plano St Shreveport LA 71100

JACKSON, BARBARA RICHARDS (D)
b San Augustine, Tex, Oct 7, 35; d William Richards & Syble Irvin R; m 1953 to Harold Floyd Jackson; c Deborah Lynn, Sharon Kay & Judith Darlene. Educ: Thomas Jefferson High Sch, grad, 54. Polit & Govt Pos: Deleg, Tex Rep State Conv, 66 & 68; vchmn, Jefferson Co Rep Party, 66-70; pres, Jefferson Co Rep Women's Club, 67; deleg, Tex Dem State Conv, 72; deleg, Dem Nat Conv, 72; chmn, Jefferson Co Wallace for President in 1976, 73. Mem: Taxpayers Against Car Tax (co-chmn, 73-); Am In Action (secy-treas, 72-). Relig: Church of Christ. Mailing Add: 1412-18th St Nederland TX 77627

JACKSON, BARRY WENDELL (D)
b Long Branch, NJ, Jan 27, 30; s Rodney H Jackson & Marion Englebright J; m 1955 to Susan Braddy Shields; m 1972 to Karen Van Wallinga; c Stacy Ann, Sydney Elise, Leslie Barry, Morgan Susan & Bruce Edward. Educ: Stanford Univ, AB in Polit Sci, 52, JD, 58; Delta Theta Phi. Polit & Govt Pos: City attorney, Fairbanks, Alaska, 59-63; staff dir, Borough Study Group, 62-63; Alaska State Rep, 65-67 & 69-71, mem, Finance Comt, Alaska House Rep, 65-66, chmn, Judiciary Comt, 69-70; permanent chmn, Alaska Cent Dist Dem Conv, 72; chmn, Dem Legis Campaign Comt, 72; chmn comt on comt & parliamentarian, Alaska State Dem Conv, 72 & 73; mem, Unification Charter Comn, Fairbanks NStar Borough, 72- Bus & Prof Pos: Mem, Coun of Advice, Missionary Dist Alaska, 66-67, exec bd, 67-68; attorney, Jackson & Nordale, 72- Mil Serv: Entered as 2nd Lt, Marine Corps, 52, released as 1st Lt, 55; Maj (Ret), Marine Corps Res; commanding off, Composite Co, 17-3, Naval Res, 66-68; Korean & UN Serv & Am Defense Medals. Mem: Am Trial Lawyers Asn; Alaska Acad Trial Lawyers; Fairbanks Dem Club; Marine Corps Res Officer Asn; Alaska Conserv Soc. Relig: Episcopal. Legal Res: 500 Lincoln St Fairbanks AK 99701 Mailing Add: PO Box 348 Fairbanks AK 99707

JACKSON, CLEO B (D)
Ark State Rep
Mailing Add: 109 E Public Square Green Forest AR 72638

JACKSON, CLYDE WILSON (SONNY) (D)
VPres, Seventh Dist Dem Party, Ga
b Cartersville, Ga, Sept 6, 36; s Louis W Jackson & Beatrice McCamy J; m 1963 to Mary Sue Fagon; c Donald Fagon & Louise McCamy. Educ: Univ Ga, 55-56. Polit & Govt Pos: Vpres, Seventh Dist Dem Party, Ga, currently. Bus & Prof Pos: Owner, Jackson's Dairy, currently. Mil Serv: Entered as Airman Basic, Air Force, 53, released as Airman 1/C, 61, after serv in Air Nat Guard. Mem: Euharlee Farmers Club; Cartersville Country Club (pres, currently); Elks. Relig: Methodist. Mailing Add: Mission Rd Rte 5 Cartersville GA 30120

JACKSON, ELLEN M (D)
b Boston, Mass, Oct 29, 35; d David Swepson & Marguerite Booker S; m to Hugh L Jackson; c Ronica, Darryl, Sheryl, Troy & Stefani. Educ: State Teachers Col at Boston, 2 years; Kennedy fel, Kennedy Inst Polit, Harvard Univ, 69-70. Polit & Govt Pos: Alt deleg, Dem Nat Conv, 68, deleg, 72; deleg, Dem Nat Mid-Term Conf, 74. Bus & Prof Pos: Parent group coordr, Northern Student Movement, 63-64; social serv supvr, First Head Start Prog, 64-65; exec dir, Operation Exodus, Inc, 65-; exec dir, Black Women's Community Develop Found, 68- Publ: Co-auth, Family experiences in Operation Exodus, Community Health J, Columbia Univ Press, 67. Mem: Roxbury Fedn of Neighborhood Ctrs; Civil Liberties Union of Mass (adv bd); Legal Defense & Educ Fund, Inc (Mass adv bd); Mass State Cols (bd trustees); Nat Coun of Women of the US. Honors & Awards: Kiwanis Recognition Award, 65; Lambda Kappa Mu Award, 66; Nat Coun of Women of the US Award, 67; Sojourner Truth Awards, Nat Asn of Negro Bus Prof Women's Clubs, Inc, 68; Simon Gutman Found Award, 69. Relig: African Methodist. Mailing Add: 27 Brookledge St Roxbury MA 02121

JACKSON, EMIL A (R)
b Natchez, Miss, Feb 2, 11; s Ernest Jackson, Sr & Florence Mattie Ross J; m 1934 to Mildred Mayo McGrew; c Millicent Jeannie. Educ: Univ Buffalo, 48-50, Bryant & Stratton Bus Inst, 52-54. Polit & Govt Pos: Committeeman, Erie Co Rep Orgn, Buffalo, 50-, chmn, Nixon Minority Campaign, 60-, chmn, Nelson Rockefeller Minority Campaign, 62-; sgt at arms, NY Senate, 66-67, engrossing clerk, 67-68, gen clerk & aide to Majority Leader, 68-70; Equal Employ Opportunity field rep, State NY, 70-; deleg, Rep Nat Conv, 72- Bus & Prof Pos: Owner, Emil Jackson Real Estate & Ins Agency, Buffalo, 46-70; vpres, NAACP, Buffalo, 52-56; exec bd, mem, Buffalo Urban League, 52-62; mem legis comt, Buffalo CofC, 55-57; exec bd mem, Gtr Buffalo Bd Realtors, 55-57; pres, YMCA Bus & Prof Mens Club, 58-64; vpres, Am Negro Labor Coun, Buffalo Chap, 60-61. Mil Serv: Entered as Pvt, Army, 43, released as S/Sgt, 46, after serv in 696 Ord Ammunition Co, ETO, 45. Mem: YMCA Bus & Prof Mens Club; Civil Serv Employee Asn; Civil Serv Educ & Recreation Asn; Legis Counsel & Aide Asn; NY State Employees Retirement Asn. Honors & Awards: Bus Award, Iota Phi Lambda, 52; Cert of Merit, NAACP, 58; Polit Seminar Cert, Buffalo CofC, 60; Serv Award, Buffalo Urban League, 62; Merit Serv Award, YMCA Bus & Prof Mens Club, 64. Relig: Roman Catholic. Mailing Add: 195 Hamlin Rd Buffalo NY 14208

JACKSON, FRANCES HATCHER (D)
b Greeneville, Tenn, May 17, 45; d Vance Rutherford Hatcher, Jr & Frances Brabson H; m 1969 to George Moore Jackson. Educ: Univ NC, Greensboro, BA, 67; Samford Univ, MS, 71. Polit & Govt Pos: Alt deleg, NC State & Dist Dem Conv, 72; alt deleg, Dem Nat Conv, 72; adv, Lee Co Teen-Dem Club, 72-; third vchmn, Jonesboro Precinct, Sanford, 72- Bus & Prof Pos: Teacher, Kiser Jr High, Greensboro, NC, 67-69, Mountain Brook Jr High, Ala, 69-71 & Sanford Cent High Sch, NC, 71- Mem: NC Asn Educators. Relig: Baptist. Mailing Add: 2114 Lee Ave Sanford NC 27330

JACKSON, GEORGE WINFIELD (R)
Chmn, Second Cong Dist Rep Party, NC
b Belhaven, NC, Nov 17, 37; s Clarence Benjamin Jackson & Lillian Winfield J; m 1962 to Dorothy Ann Freeman; c Burton Winfield, Gregory & Jan Meredith. Educ: Univ NC, AB, 60; Univ NC Sch Law, JD, 66; Chi Psi; Delta Theta Phi. Polit & Govt Pos: Attorney, Second Cong Dist Person Co Selective Serv, NC, 67-71; mem bd dir, Second Cong Dist Rep Party, NC, 68-, chmn, 71-; chmn, Person Co Rep Party, 68-71; pres Person Co Young Rep, 68, dir, 68-71; city attorney, Roxboro, 69-71, mayor, 71-; mem resolutions comt, NC Rep Conv, 70, mem planning & orgn comt, 71, chmn platform comt, 75; mem, NC Rep Action Forum, 71; mem, NC Rep Party Cent Comt, 71-, mem NC Party Rep Exec Comt, 71-; bd dirs, Dist Bd Health, 71-; NC comnr, Nat Conf Comnrs on Uniform State Laws, 74-; mem Butner munic adv comt, NC Dept Human Resources, 74- Bus & Prof Pos: Assoc, Ramsey & Long, 66-67; partner, Ramsey, Long & Jackson, 67-70; partner, Ramsey, Jackson & Hubbard, 70-73; partner, Ramsey, Jackson, Hubbard & Galloway, 73- Mil Serv: Entered as Pvt, Army, 60, released as S/Sgt, 63, after serv in 112th Intel Corps Group, Fourth Army Area, 61-63. Mem: NC & Am Bar Asns; Ninth Judicial Dist Bar Asn of NC; Jaycees. Relig: Baptist. Legal Res: 612 Hillhaven Terr Roxboro NC 27701 Mailing Add: PO Box 601 Roxboro NC 27573

JACKSON, HENRY M (D)
US Sen, Wash
b Everett, Wash, May 31, 12; m 1961 to Helen Eugenia Hardin; c Anna Marie & Peter Hardin. Educ: Univ of Wash Law Sch, LLB, 35. Polit & Govt Pos: Prosecuting Attorney, Snohomish Co, Wash, 38; US Rep, 41-52; US Sen, 53-; chmn interior & insular affairs comt, US Senate, currently, mem govt opers comt, armed serv comt & joint comt atomic energy;

JACKSON, HENRY RALPH (D)
Mem, Tenn State Dem Exec Comt
b Birmingham, Ala, Aug 22, 15; s William M Jackson & Delia Bennings J; m 1944 to Hattie Elie; c Zita (Mrs Blankenship) & Cheri. Educ: Daniel Payne Col; Shorter Col, AB; Jackson Theol Sem, BD, 46. Hon Degrees: DD, Campbell Col, 50; LHD, Wilberforce Univ, 55 & Daniel Pay Col, 59; LHD, Allen Univ, 56. Polit & Govt Pos: Mem, Tenn Dem State Exec Comt, currently. Bus & Prof Pos: Dir dept minimum salary, African Methodist Episcopal Church, 60, minister, currently. Mem: Nat Coun Churches; Fraternal Coun Churches; F&AM; NAACP. Honors & Awards: Meritorious Serv Award, Brotherhood African Methodist Episcopal Church, Co-Citizens Award of Year, Women's Missionary Soc; Man of Year Award, Elks; Appreciation & Gratitude Award, Memphis Bus League. Relig: African Methodist Episcopal. Legal Res: 1443 S Parkway E Memphis TN 38106 Mailing Add: 280 Hernando St Memphis TN 38126

JACKSON, J ELVIN (D)
First VChmn, Moore Co Dem Party, NC
b West End, NC, Mar 17, 38; s William Elias Jackson & Helen Sullivan J; m 1971 to Patricia Wallace. Educ: Am Inst of Banking, 58-59; Carolina's Sch of Banking, Univ NC, summers, 64, 65. Polit & Govt Pos: Co mgr, Young Voter's Prog for Terry Sanford for Gov, NC, 60; vpres, Moore Co Young Dem Club, 61, pres, 62-63, dir, 64-66; chmn, Eighth Cong Dist Young Dem Club, 63; state organizer, Young Dem Club of NC, 63 & 64; state co-campaign mgr, H Clifton Blue for Lt Gov, 64; mem, Moore Co Agr Exten Adv Bd, 64-66; chmn, Moore Co Dem Exec Comt, 64-68; Finance Chmn, Moore Co Dem Party, 68-70, first vchmn, 70-; campaign mgr for H Clifton Blue, Eighth NC Cong Dist, 70. Bus & Prof Pos: Loan mgr, Carolina Bank, Pinehurst, NC, 58-62, asst cashier, Carthage, NC, 62-63, cashier, Vass, 63-66, asst vpres & cashier, 66-67, vpres & mgr, Carthage, 67-70; vpres financial affairs, Troy Lumber Co, NC, 70-71, exec vpres admin & finance, 71- Mil Serv: Sgt, Army Res, 61- Mem: Am & NC Bankers Asn; Vass Indust Develop Comt; Sandhills Area Develop Asn; Mason (Master, Carthage Lodge 181, 68). Honors & Awards: Named one of ten outstanding Young Dem in NC, 63; Distinguished Serv Award, Carthage Jaycees, 68; Rotary Found two month travel grant to represent NC in Israel, 69; politics & stock mkt. Relig: Presbyterian; chmn, Bd Deacons. Legal Res: Vass Rd Carthage NC 28327 Mailing Add: Box 372 Carthage NC 28327

JACKSON, J WELDON (D)
Treas, Cass Co Dem Cent Comt, Mo
b Belton, Mo, Sept 9, 08; s John H Jackson & Stella O'Dell J; m 1941 to Olive Herrick; c John H, Judith M (Mrs Dennis Moss), Linda Jo (Mrs Gary Lloyd), Jerald W, Janet L (Mrs Bernie Thurman), Jacquie S, Jeffrey A & James H. Educ: Mo Univ, 26-28; Warrenburg State Univ, 29. Polit & Govt Pos: City clerk, Belton, Mo, 47-61; mem sch bd, Belton Sch Dist, 48-66; committeeman, Cass Co Dem Comt, 52-; chmn, Cass Co Dem Cent Comt, two terms, treas, 68- Bus & Prof Pos: Trustee, Cass Co Mem Hosp, Mo, 61-; pres, Citizens Bank of Belton, 62-75; presiding judge, Cass Co Court, 75- Mil Serv: Entered as P/O 3rd Class, Navy, 42, released as P/O 1st class, 45, after serv in Naval Res; Good Conduct Medal. Mem: Cass Co Bankers Asn; Mo Bankers Asn; Belton Optimist Club; Belton Businessmen Asn; Am Legion. Honors & Awards: Hon Col, Gov Hearnes staff; pres of all above orgn. Relig: Methodist; past chmn bd, Belton United Methodist Church, cert lay speaker. Legal Res: 200 Mill Belton MO 64012 Mailing Add: PO Box 276 Belton MO 64012

JACKSON, JACK (D)
SDak State Sen
Mailing Add: 1325 Utah SE Huron SD 57350

JACKSON, JAMES WILLIAM (R)
Chmn, Gallatin Co Rep Cent Comt, Ill
b Ridgway, Ill, Sept 21, 19; s Will Jackson & Martha Downen J; m 1946 to Lorene Stoponi; c James W, Jr, Joseph M & John M. Educ: High Sch. Polit & Govt Pos: Chmn, Gallatin Co Rep Cent Comt, Ill & treas, Ill Rep Co Chmn Asn, currently; mem, Ill Rep Cent Comt, 69- Mil Serv: Entered as Pvt, Army Air Force, 42, released as S/Sgt, 45, after serv in 454th Bomb Group, Second Air Force; Am Theater Ribbon; European-African Middle East Theater Ribbon with One Silver Battle Star & Three Bronze Battle Stars; Four Overseas Serv Bars; Two Presidential Unit Citations. Mem: AF&AM; Scottish Rite; VFW; Am Legion. Relig: Methodist. Mailing Add: PO Box 66 Ridgway IL 62979

JACKSON, JERRY DONALD (D)
Nat Committeeman, Ark Young Dem
b Warren, Ark, Nov 18, 44; s Olin Jackson & Lurline Moore J; m 1966 to Sharon Ragan; c Michael Steel. Educ: Little Rock Univ, 62-65; Univ Ark, Fayetteville, LLB, 68; Phi Alpha Delta; Sigma Nu. Polit & Govt Pos: Deleg, Ark Dem State Conv, 66-70; pres, Ark Young Dem, 69-70, nat committeeman, 71-; mem exec comt, Pulaski Co Dem Comt, 70-71; mem, Ark Dem State Comt, 70- Bus & Prof Pos: Attorney, Ark State Dept Ins, 68- Mil Serv: Entered as Pvt, Army Res, 68, SP-4, currently. Mem: Ark & Am Bar Asns. Relig: Methodist. Mailing Add: 7120 Cloverdale Dr Little Rock AR 72209

JACKSON, JERRY DWAYNE (D)
Ga State Rep
b Jackson Co, Ga, Oct 7, 41; s Claude Isabelle Jackson & Allene Crowe J; m 1962 to Margie Elise Kent; c Kim & Ginger Elise. Educ: South Hall High Sch, grad, 59. Polit & Govt Pos: Vchmn, Hall Co Civil Serv Bd, 73-74; Ga State Rep, 75- Mem: Hall Co Farm Bur; Upper Chattachoochee Soil & Water Conserv; Kiwanis; Gainesville Jr Col (bd trustees, 75). Relig: Baptist. Legal Res: Rte 2 Box 347 Winder Hwy Flowery Branch GA 30542 Mailing Add: PO Box 7275 Chestnut Mountain GA 30502

JACKSON, JERRY LEE (R)
b Nashville, Tenn, Aug 9, 39; s Robert L Jackson (deceased) & Paulina Jones Traughber J; m 1967 to Aleece Wolfe Jackson; c Jerry Lee, Jr & Angela Michelle. Educ: Univ Tenn, BS Chem Eng, 62. Polit & Govt Pos: Charter chmn, Dyer Co Young Rep, Tenn, 66-68; chmn, Co Baker for Senate, 66; state young Rep coordr, Dunn for Gov, 70; chmn, Dyer Co Rep Party, 70-72; chmn, Tenn Young Rep Fedn, 71-73; presidential elector for Nixon-Agnew, 72; WTenn Chmn, Young Voters for the President, 72; mem state adv comt, Winston for Gov, 74. Bus & Prof Pos: Chief chemist, Colonial Rubber Works, Inc 62-68, vpres & tech serv dir, 68- Mem: Southern Rubber Group; Kiwanis; Dyersburg Country Club (dir, 73-); Am Chem Soc (dir rubber div, 74-); Dyer Co March of Dimes. Honors & Awards: Outstanding Local Chmn, Tenn Young Rep Fedn, 67; Man of Year, Southern Rubber Group, 72. Relig: Methodist. Mailing Add: 1836 William Cody Rd Dyersburg TN 38024

JACKSON, JOHN W (D)
b Griffin, Ga, Apr 24, 00; s Zachary Taylor Jackson & Alice Knowles J; m 1924 to Lois Hendry; c Lois Hendry (Mrs K M Brooks), Mary Nichols (Mrs James E Bleckley) & Eleanor Ann (Mrs Johnnie Howard Cooper). Educ: Univ Ga, BSA, 24, MEduc, 51; Sigma Alpha Epsilon. Polit & Govt Pos: Chmn, Long Co Dem Comt, Ga, formerly. Bus & Prof Pos: Prin, Braselton High Sch, Ga, 46-56; prin. Ludowici High Sch, 56-66; Title I Coordr, Long Co Bd Educ, Ludowici, Ga, 66-70. Mem: Lions. Relig: Southern Baptist. Mailing Add: PO Box 306 Ludowici GA 31316

JACKSON, JOHNNY, JR (D)
La State Rep
Mailing Add: 3922 Metropolitan New Orleans LA 70126

JACKSON, JONI BRADLEY (R)
First VChmn, Rep Party Wis
b Shaker Heights, Ohio, Apr 10, 32; d Sylvanus Law Bradley & Margaret Berryhill B; m 1953 to Lowell B Jackson; c Jessica Lynn, Steven Kimberly & Kevin Hale. Educ: Northwestern Univ, Evanston, BS, 54; Purdue Univ, Lafayette, teacher's license, 58; Univ Ill, 61-62; Kappa Kappa Gamma. Polit & Govt Pos: Rep precinct committeewoman, Tippecanoe Co, Ind, 62-65; vchmn, Tippecanoe Co Goldwater-Miller Comt, 64; vchmn, Dane Co Rep Party, Wis, 67-71; secy, Second Dist Rep Party, 69-71; campaign chmn, Wis Fedn Rep Women, 69-71; Rep precinct committeewoman, Dane Co, 70-; first vchmn, Rep Party Wis, 71-; deleg, Rep Nat Conv, 72. Bus & Prof Pos: Admin secy, Asst Minority Leader, Wis State Assembly, 73- Mem: Zeta Phi Eta; Kappa Delta Pi; Univ Exten League (vpres, 66-67). Relig: Christian Science. Mailing Add: 5321 Milward Dr Madison WI 53711

JACKSON, JULIA CAROLYN (R)
Chmn, Monroe Co Rep Exec Comt, Fla
b Greensboro, NC, July 25, 34; d Robert Lee Blanchard & Maude Ether Haire M; m 1973 to William H Jackson; c George Severin, Jr & Cheri Ann. Educ: Richmond Prof Inst, Col William & Mary, BFA, 56. Polit & Govt Pos: Mem, Young Rep Club, Monroe Co, Fla, 64-67; committeewoman, Monroe Co Rep Exec Comt, 70-, chmn, 71- Bus & Prof Pos: Advert, Pensacola News J, 56-57; artist, Todd-Borroughs, Greensboro, NC, 57-58; teacher, Key West, Fla, 58-59; advert, Key West Citizen, 59-60 & 63-65; teacher, Key West, 60-63 & 65- Publ: Co-auth, Curriculum Guide Elementary Art, Monroe Co Sch Bd, 73. Mem: Fla & Nat Educ Asns; Classroom Teachers' Asn. Relig: Presbyterian. Mailing Add: 212 Stadium Key West FL 33040

JACKSON, LARRY (D)
Idaho State Rep
Mailing Add: 3300 Bogus Basin Rd Boise ID 83702

JACKSON, LEO ALBERT (D)
Mem, Ohio State Dem Exec Comt
b Lake City, Fla, Mar 10, 20; s William Jackson & Hattie Howard J; m 1945 to Gilberta Jackson; c Linda Adelle & Leonard Alan. Educ: Morehouse Col, AB, 43; Atlanta Univ, MA, 46; Cleveland-Marshall Law Sch, LLB, 50; Kappa Alpha Psi. Polit & Govt Pos: Councilman, Ward 24, Cleveland, Ohio, 58-70; vchmn, Cuyahoga Co Dem Exec Comt, 63-70; mem policy comt, Cuyahoga Co Dem Orgn, 67-70; mem, Electoral Col, Ohio, 68; deleg, Dem Nat Conv, 68; Judge, 8th Dist Court of Appeals, 70-; mem from 21st dist, Ohio State Dem Exec Comt, 70- Bus & Prof Pos: Attorney-at-law; vis lectr, Western Res Univ, John Carroll Univ & Cleveland State Univ, formerly; mem bd trustees or exec bd, Forest City Hosp, Community Housing Corp, AIM Job, Cleveland Music Sch Settlement, Cleveland Legal Aid Soc, Glenville YMCA, Glenville Neighborhood Ctr, Consumers League of Ohio, Better Homes for Cleveland Found, Cleveland Coun on Soviet Anti-Semitism, Northern Ohio Children's Performing Music Found & Lions Eye Clin. Mil Serv: Pvt, Army, 42-43, serv at Ft Benning, Ga. Publ: Wartime Adjustment of Labor Disputes Involving Negro Workers in the Railway Express Industry of the Southeast, 46. Mem: Glenville Area Community Coun; NAACP; Gtr Cleveland YMCA (mem pub rels comt); Lions; Citizens League. Honors & Awards: Testimonial Dinner & Plaque, Citizens of Gtr Cleveland, 63; Outstanding Community Serv Plaque, Nat Coun Bus & Prof Women, 67; Outstanding Serv Plaque, Glenville Youth Athletic Asn, 67; Community Serv Award, Cleveland Diocesan Union of Holy Name Soc, 68; Cleveland Bus League Award of Honor; Brothers Keeper Award, Cleveland Jewish Community Fedn, 69. Relig: Baptist. Mailing Add: 3155 Ludlow Cleveland OH 44120

JACKSON, M MORRIS (D)
Ohio State Sen
b Ga, 1920; married; c two sons. Educ: Cleveland Col. Polit & Govt Pos: Ohio State Sen, 67-; deleg, Dem Nat Conv, 72; mem, Dem Nat Comt, 72-; deleg, Dem Nat Mid-Term Conf, 74. Bus & Prof Pos: Real estate broker. Mailing Add: 1723 E 70th St Cleveland OH 44103

JACKSON, MARY HILLARD (R)
b St Paul, Minn, Oct 13, 18; d Thomas Jones Hilliard & Marianna Talbott H; m 1938 to Donald Eldredge Jackson, Jr; c D Eldredge, III, Marianna Hilliard & Mary (Mrs Holiday). Educ: Sarah Lawrence Col, 40. Polit & Govt Pos: Pres, Red Bridge Coun Rep Women, RI, 53-55; finance chmn, RI Fedn Rep Women, 55-58; past mem exec comt, Rep State Cent Comt; Rep Nat Committeewoman, RI, 60-69; deleg, Rep Nat Conv, 68; mem exec comt, President's Adv Comt on the Arts, 70- Relig: Episcopal. Mailing Add: 99 President Ave Providence RI 02906

JACKSON, MAYNARD HOLBROOK (D)
Mayor, Atlanta, Ga
b Dallas, Tex, Mar 23, 38; s Maynard Holbrook Jackson; m to Bunnie Hayes Burke; c Elizabeth, Brooke & Maynard Holbrook, III. Educ: Morehouse Col, Ford Found scholar, 52-56, BA, Glancy fel, 54-56, BS, 56; NC Cent Univ, JD, cum laude, 64; Metrop Applied Research Ctr fel. Polit & Govt Pos: Vmayor, Atlanta, Ga, 70-74, mayor, 74- Bus & Prof Pos: Managing attorney & dir community rels, Emory Neighborhood Law Off, Atlanta, 68-69; sr partner, Jackson, Patterson & Parks, 70-73. Mailing Add: 68 Mitchell St SW Atlanta GA 30303

JACKSON, MILDRED IRENE (D)
Mem, Nebr Dem Party
b Burke, SDak, Aug 3, 21; d Juddson Stanley Darnall & Gertie Cornell D; m 1945 to Robert Charles Jackson. Educ: Nat Bus Inst, Lincoln, Nebr, grad, 41. Polit & Govt Pos: Committeewoman, Nebr State Cent Dem Party, 72-; chmn, Butler Co Dem Party, Nebr, 73- Mem: Eastern Star (Past Grand Rep, Nebr Order, 65-). Relig: United Methodist. Mailing Add: Rising City NE 68658

JACKSON, MILDRED KATE C (R)
b Sevierville, Tenn, Apr 23, 38; d Lee Anderson Cardwell & Lula Lamons C; m to Ernest W Jackson, Jr; c Mark Wesley, Ernest Wesley, III & Elaine Kate. Educ: Draughon's Bus Col, Knoxville, Tenn. Polit & Govt Pos: Exec secy to US Rep James H Quillen, First Dist, Tenn, 63-68; exec asst to US Rep James C Cleveland, NH, 69- Bus & Prof Pos: Secy, Cincinnati Cordage & Paper Co, 55-58; secy to pres, Cherokee Textile Mills, 58-63. Mem: Rep Women's Fed Forum; Cong Secy Club; Tenn State Soc. Relig: Southern Baptist. Legal Res: Rte 1 Seymour TN 37865 Mailing Add: 9720 Loudoun Ave Manassas VA 22110

JACKSON, MURRAY EARL (D)
Chmn, First Dist Dem Party, Mich
b Philadelphia, Pa, Dec 21, 26; s Murray Jacob Jackson & Mabel Steele J; m 1952 to Dauris Gwendolyn Smart; c Linda & Murray David. Educ: Adrian Col, 49; Wayne State Univ, BA, 54, MA, 59; Kappa Alpha Psi; Am Commoners Club; Letterman's Club. Hon Degrees: PH, Shaw Univ. Polit & Govt Pos: Chmn, Wayne State Univ Chap, Dem Acad Resources Comt, Mich, 66-69; chmn, First Dist Dem Party, Mich, 67-; deleg, Dem Nat Conv, 68. Bus & Prof Pos: Group leader, Wayne Co Youth Home, 51-55; acad adv, Wayne State Univ, 55-64, instr humanities, 58-60, exec asst to Dean Lib Arts, 65-67, asst to vpres student affairs, summer 67, asst dean student urban affairs, 69-70; instr social studies, Highland Park Jr Col, 57-58; coordr spec projs, Univ Mich, 64-65, asst prof higher educ & acting dir, Ctr Study Higher Educ, currently; exec secy, Wayne Co Community Col, 68-69, exec dir, 69, acting pres, 69-70, pres, 70-71, emer pres, 71- Mil Serv: Entered as Seaman, Navy, 45, released as Seaman 1/C, 46, after serv in Seabees. Publ: Helping to educate the disadvantaged, Kappa Alpha Psi J, 5/65. Mem: NAACP; Urban League; Comt 99; Mich Tuberc & Respiratory Disease Asn; Polit Reform Comt. Honors & Awards: Mackenzie Honor Soc & Phi Delta Kappa, Wayne State Univ; Commendation, Mich House Rep; Mayor, Detroit, Murray Jackson Day, 71; Wayne Co Resolution; Common Coun Resolutor. Relig: Episcopal. Mailing Add: 19398 Stratford Rd Detroit MI 48221

JACKSON, NYLE MERINGO (R)
b Bradleyville, Mo, Mar 27, 14; s James Richard Jackson & Emma Huntsman J; m 1938 to Ina Elaine Hutcheson. Educ: Westminster Col, BA, 35; Southwest Mo State Col, 35; Nat Univ Law Sch, 46. Polit & Govt Pos: Exec secy to US Rep Earl Wilson, Ind, 41-53; admin asst to US Sen William E Jenner, Ind, 53-59; spec staff mem, US Sen Homer E Capehart, Ind, 59; legis asst to US Sen Thruston B Morton, Ky, 59; exec asst to the Postmaster Gen, 59-61, asst to the Exec Asst Postmaster Gen, 61-63, asst dir, Customer Rels Div, US Post Off Dept, 62-69, exec asst to the Asst Postmaster Gen, Bur of Opers, 69; asst to Spec Counsel to the President, 69-70; managing dir, Interstate Com Comn, 70-73. Bus & Prof Pos: Advert mgr, daily & weekly newspaper, Seymour, Ind, 38-41. Mil Serv: Entered as Ens, Navy, 42, released as Lt(sg), 46, after serv in Armed Guard & Amphibious Forces, Am European & Asiatic Theatres; Naval Res. Mem: Am Legion; Senate Asst Asn; VFW; Order of the Carabao; Orgn of Cabinet Asst. Honors & Awards: Distinguished Serv Award, 60 & Meritorious Serv Award, 67 & 68, US Post Off Dept. Relig: Baptist. Legal Res: Seymour IN 47274 Mailing Add: 4429 35th St NW Washington DC 20008

JACKSON, OTHA DILL (R)
Chmn, Neshoba Co Rep Party, Miss
b Neshoba Co, Miss, Jan 11, 25; s Will J Jackson & Mary E J; m 1950 to Edna Earl Hillman; c Will James. Educ: Miss State Univ, BS, 49; Block & Bridle Club. Polit & Govt Pos: Chmn, Neshoba Co, Miss, 67-; committeeman, Miss State Exec Comt, 72- Bus & Prof Pos: Teacher, Neshoba Co, Miss, 49-53; mgr, Neshoba Co Gin Asn, Philadelphia, 53- Mil Serv: Entered as Pvt, Army, 43, released as Pfc, 45, after serv in 1st Calvary, Pacific Theatre, 44-45; Purple Heart. Mem: Neshoba Co Farm Bur; Am Legion Post 138 (past commander); Rotary; Am Red Cross. Relig: Presbyterian. Legal Res: 533 Peoples Ave Philadelphia MS 39350 Mailing Add: PO Box 326 Philadelphia MS 39350

JACKSON, PATRICK T, JR (R)
Maine State Rep
Mailing Add: 40 Main St Yarmouth ME 04096

JACKSON, PAULINA RUTH (D)
Mem, Union Co Dem Cent Comt, Iowa
b Adams Co, Iowa, June 1, 32; d Harold Leland Hayes & Helen Houchin H; m 1966 to Lyle Douglas Jackson; c Charles Michael, Stephen Paul, Anthony Carl & Teresa Angela. Educ: Creston Community Col, AA, 64. Polit & Govt Pos: Deleg, Dem Nat Conv, 72; chmn, Get Out the Vote Dem Comt, 72; chmn, Elec Day, 72; chmn, Tel Surv, 72; mem, Union Co Dem Cent Comt, 72-; pres, Union Co Dem Women, 72-; mem, Nat Abortion Rights Action League, currently. Mem: Nat Orgn Women; NAACP; Another Mother for Peace. Relig: Catholic. Mailing Add: 213 N Oak St Creston IA 50801

JACKSON, PHILIP C (R)
Maine State Sen
Mailing Add: Main St Harrison ME 04040

JACKSON, RANDY (D)
b Clovis, NMex, Oct 16, 44; s James Dorfus Jackson & Carmen Brown J; div; c Gail Lynn & Neil Allan. Educ: Artesia High Sch, NMex, grad, 62. Polit & Govt Pos: Deleg, NMex State Dem Conv, 68; chmn, Voting Dist 23, Cache Co, Utah, 72; deleg, Utah Dem Conv, 72; chmn-founder, Peoples Organizing Comt, Utah, 72; alt deleg, Dem Nat Conv, 72; co-chmn, Cache Co Citizens for McGovern, 72; chmn, Utah Title I Parents Comt, 72-73; organizer, Artesia Munic Employee Strike, NMex, 73-; organizer, United Steelworkers of Am Local 8035, 73- Bus & Prof Pos: Restaurant mgr, Jackson Restaurant, Artesia, 63-69; restaurant mgr, Walgreen Co, Logan Utah, 69-72. Mem: Nat Welfare Rights Orgn (organizer, 72). Legal Res: 770 E Ninth N Logan UT 84321 Mailing Add: 814 N Seventh St Artesia NM 88210

JACKSON, ROBERT WALTER (R)
Chmn, Dade Co Rep Party, Mo
b Drumright, Okla, Sept 6, 43; s Thomas Everett Jackson & Ruby Irene Hinson J; m 1966 to Alice Kaye Long; c Robert Charles, Kristina Diane & Bryan David. Educ: Okla State Univ, BSEd, 65, MSEd, 69; vpres, Phys Educ Majors & Minors Club. Polit & Govt Pos: City councilman, Greenfield, Mo, 72-74; committeeman, Dade Co Rep Party, 72-74, chmn, 74- Bus & Prof Pos: Asst dir of recreation, Stillwater, Okla, 63-65; teacher & coach, Waynesville R-4 Schs, Mo, 65-69; teacher & coach, Greenfield R-4 Schs, 69-; ins salesman, Franklin Life, Springfield, 75. Publ: Individual drills for man to man team defense, Coaching Clin, 1/75. Mem: Mo Basketball Coaches Asn; Greenfield Area Jaycees; Mason; Mo State Teachers Asn; Greenfield Community Teachers Asn. Honors & Awards: Selected as Outstanding Young Man by Greenfield Jaycees, 72; 73-74 Basketball Team finished second in Mo Class A play. Relig: Disciples of Christ. Mailing Add: 307 Hewitt Greenfield MO 65661

JACKSON, RONALD EDWARD (D)
Ala State Rep
b Birmingham, Ala, July 8, 48; s Daniel William Jackson & Gladys Young J; single. Educ: Univ Ala, JD, 72; Miles Col, BA, 75; Col of Wooster, exchange student; Alpha Phi Alpha. Polit & Govt Pos: Ala State Rep, 74- Bus & Prof Pos: Partner, Law Firm of Hilliard, Jackson, Barnes & Mixon. Mem: Am & Ala Bar Asns; Am Trial Lawyers Asn; Ala Black Lawyers Asn; Birmingham Human Rels Coun. Honors & Awards: Distinguished Serv Award, Delta Theta Sigma; Distinguished Alumnus Award, Miles Col; Outstanding Young Man, Jaycees, 75; Merit Award, Metrop CME Church, 75. Relig: Baptist. Mailing Add: Frazier Bldg 1605 N Eighth Ave Birmingham AL 35703

JACKSON, ROSELLA MILDRED (R)
Treas, Alpine Co, Calif
b Clinton Co, Ohio, Sept 10, 16; d Martin William Cole & Edith Meyers C; m 1948 to Robert Milton Jackson; c Jeanette Ann (Mrs Turnbeaugh), Judith K & John Robert. Educ: Millers Col of Bus, Cincinnati, Ohio, 2 years; Univ Nev, exten. Polit & Govt Pos: Mem & secy-treas, Alpine Co Rep Cent Comt, Calif 6 years, chmn, 1 year; chief dep, co clerk, auditor & recorder, Alpine Co, 9 years, treas, 68-; mem local adv comt, Grover Hot Springs State Park, 71-; mem, Rep State Cent Comt Calif, 73- Mem: Am Red Cross (secy-treas, Alpine Co Chap, 48-59, chmn, 59-); charter mem Alpine Mother's Club (past pres). Relig: Protestant. Legal Res: Laramie St Markleeville CA 96120 Mailing Add: PO Box 236 Markleeville CA 96120

JACKSON, SAMUEL CHARLES (R)
b Kansas City, Kans, May 8, 1929; s James C Jackson & Mattie Webber J; m 1952 to Judy Bradford; c Marcia Lyn & Brenda Sue. Educ: Washburn Univ, AB, 51, Law Sch, JD, 54; Sagamore; Kappa Alpha Psi; Arnold Air Soc; Press Club. Polit & Govt Pos: Vchmn, Kans Collegiate Rep, 50-54; vchmn, Kans Young Rep, 57-59; precinct committeeman, Shawnee Co Rep Comt, Kans, 60-63; mem, Shawnee Co Rep Exec Comt, 60-63; dep gen counsel, Kans Dept Soc Welfare, 62-65; comnr, Equal Employ Opportunity Comn, 65-68; asst secy for metrop develop, Dept of Housing & Urban Develop, 69-72. Bus & Prof Pos: Practicing attorney, Scott, Scott & Jackson, Topeka, Kans, 57-65; vpres & dir, Nat Ctr for Dispute Settlement, Am Arbit Asn, 68-69; attorney, Stroock & Stroock & Lavan, New York & Washington, DC, 72- Mil Serv: Capt, Air Force, 54-57, with serv in Judge Adv Dept, 8th Air Force Strategic Air Command. Publ: EEOC vs Discrimination, Inc, Crisis Mag, 1/68; Using the law to attack discrimination in employment, Washburn Law J, winter 69. Mem: Topeka Bar Asn; Nat Conf Black Lawyers; NAACP; Am Legion; Nat Lawyer's Club. Honors & Awards: Man of the Year, Topeka, 65; numerous honors & awards for civil rights activities. Relig: Protestant. Legal Res: KS Mailing Add: 1855 Upshur St NW Washington DC 20011

JACKSON, STEVEN GARY (R)
b Tulsa, Okla, Dec 14, 53; s Richard Clark Jackson & Gloria Joyce Lairmore J; single. Educ: Rice Univ, BA, 74; Univ Tex Law Sch, 74-; chmn, city lobby comt, Univ Tex Student Govt, 75- Polit & Govt Pos: Alt deleg, Rep Nat Conv, 72; Rep precinct chmn, Precinct 361, Houston, 72-74. Bus & Prof Pos: Ed, Rice Thresher, 72-74; ed, Tex Law Forum, 75-76. Publ: Auth & ed, A Short Collection of Comments Concerning the Place, Rice Univ, 74; ed, Alternatives for Austin 1975, Univ Tex City Lobby, 75. Honors & Awards: Eagle Scout. Mailing Add: 3301 Red River Austin TX 78705

JACKSON, THOMAS F (R)
Chmn, Hardeman Co Rep Party, Tenn
b Rockford, Ohio, Aug 5, 27; s Roy R Jackson & Beta L Snyder J; m 1948 to Miriam L Hays; c Thomas F, Jr & Pamela J. Educ: Bowling Green State Univ, BA in Chem. Polit & Govt Pos: Chmn, Hardeman Co Rep Party, Tenn, 73- Bus & Prof Pos: Works mgr, Kilgore Corp, Toone, Tenn, 51- Mil Serv: Entered as Pvt, Army, 45, released as S/Sgt, 47, after serv in ChemC, Pac Theatre, 45-47. Mem: Am Defense Preparedness Asn. Relig: Lutheran. Mailing Add: Rte 1 Box 445 Bolivar TN 38008

JACKSON, WALTER FRANK (D)
Ala State Rep
b Wilsonville, Ala, Mar 13, 15; s William Jones Jackson & Ida McEwen J; m 1940 to Mary Etta Brown; c Judy Lee (Mrs Scofield), Mary Frances (Mrs Bryan) & Martha Sue. Educ: Shelby Co High Sch, Columbiana, Ala, grad, 33. Polit & Govt Pos: Mem, Opp City Bd Educ, Ala, 51-52; mem, Opp City Coun, 52-60; Ala State Rep, Dist 40, 67- Bus & Prof Pos: Warehouse foreman-salesman, Int Harvester Co, Birmingham, 37-45, dealer, Opp, 45-61; vpres & gen mgr, Morgan Distributing Co, 61- Mem: Mason (Worshipful Master, Opp Lodge, 49-51); charter mem Opp Lions Club; CofC; McArthur Trade Sch Comt. Honors & Awards: Outstanding Young Man of Year, Opp Lions Club, 50. Relig: Baptist; deacon & past supt, Sunday Sch, First Baptist Church. Legal Res: Forest Park Opp AL 36467 Mailing Add: PO Box 209 Opp AL 36467

JACOB, J LAIRD, JR (D)
b Morganton, NC, Jan 31, 40; s John Laird Jacob, Sr & Jeanne Verreault J; single. Educ: Wake Forest Univ, BBA, 62, Law Sch, JD, 65; Pi Kappa Alpha; Alpha Kappa Psi; Phi Delta Phi. Polit & Govt Pos: Pres, Burke Co Young Dem, NC, 67-; alt deleg, Dem Nat Conv, 68; prosecutor, 25th Judicial Dist, 70-72; fourth vpres, Caldwell Co Young Dem Club, NC, 72- Bus & Prof Pos: Asst dist attorney, 25th Judicial Dist, NC, currently. Mem: NC & Burke Co Bar Asns; NC State Bar. Relig: Presbyterian. Mailing Add: PO Box 418 Rutherford College NC 28671

JACOBETTI, DOMINIC J (D)
Mich State Rep
b Negaunee, Mich, July 20, 20; m 1942 to Marie D Burnettee; c Judith K, Colin K, Dominic

J, Jr. Educ: High sch grad. Polit & Govt Pos: Mich State Rep, 54- Bus & Prof Pos: Rep, United Steelworkers of Am. Mem: Moose; Eagles; KofC; Elks; Rod & Gun Club. Honors & Awards: Presented Distinguished Serv Award by Mich Practical Nurses Asn, 61. Relig: Catholic. Mailing Add: 1017 Owaissa Negaunee MI 49866

JACOBS, ALMA RAU (R)
b Philadelphia, Pa, July 27, 24; d Harry Bernhardt Rau & Ruth Leidy R; m 1955 to J Alexander Jacobs. Educ: Bryn Mawr Col, 42-43; Univ Pa, 69-70. Polit & Govt Pos: Chmn, Whitpain Twp Rep Comt, 70-; mem, Bd Dirs, Pa Coun Rep Women, 70-72; vpres, 72-; alt deleg, Rep Nat Conv, 72. Bus & Prof Pos: Mem, Bd Mgrs, Montgomery Hall for Juvenile Delinquents, Montgomery Co, Pa, 68-; pub affairs supvr, Bell Tel Co of Pa, 71- Mem: Pub Affairs Coun (bd dirs, 72-); Bus & Prof Women (vpres, Ambler, Pa, 72); Pa Fedn of Bus & Prof Women (ed, Conv Manual, 73); Eastern Montgomery Co Coun of Rep Women (hon pres, 69-); Hannah Penn Career Group (vchmn, 69-72). Honors & Awards: Meritorious Award, Chapel of Four Chaplains Legion of Honor, in recognition of outstanding serv to all people regardless of race or faith, 70; Cert of Appreciation, Optimist Int, 72. Relig: Presbyterian. Mailing Add: 435 Holly Rd Blue Bell PA 19422

JACOBS, ANDREW, JR (D)
US Rep, Ind
b Indianapolis, Ind, Feb 24, 32; s Andrew Jacobs, Sr & Joyce Wellborn J; single. Educ: Ind Univ, BS, 55, LLB, 58; Phi Alpha Delta. Polit & Govt Pos: Safety dir, Marion Co Sheriff's Dept, Ind, 55-56; Ind State Rep, 59-61; US Rep, Ind, 65-72; deleg, Dem Nat Conv, 68; US Rep, Ind, 75-; mem Ways & Means Comt, US House Rep, 75- Bus & Prof Pos: Lawyer, Jacobs & Jacobs, 58- Mil Serv: Entered as Pvt, Marines, 50, released 52, after serv in First Marine Div, Korea, 51. Publ: The jury system, Am Co Govt, 3/66. Mem: Am Legion. Relig: Catholic; Parishioner of S S Peter & Paul Cathedral. Mailing Add: 7989 Evanston Rd Indianapolis IN 46240

JACOBS, CARROLL I (D)
b Hannibal, Mo, Mar 26, 25; d Thomas Austin Hawkins & Mildred Butcher H; m 1957 to Harold Corbyn Jacobs; c Julie C, Joseph C & John C. Educ: Hannibal La-Grange Col, 1 year 6 months. Polit & Govt Pos: Publicity chmn, Marion Co Dem Cent Comt, formerly, treas, formerly. Bus & Prof Pos: Cent off clerk, Southwestern Bell Tel Co, Hannibal, Mo, 45-57. Mem: Choral Soc, Quincy, Ill; Area Asn Girl Scouts, Palmyra, Mo (chmn); Palmyra Garden Club; Palmyra Saddle Club. Relig: Methodist. Mailing Add: 901 Sloan Palmyra MO 63461

JACOBS, EARL BRYAN (R)
Comnr, Greene Co, Pa
b Waynesburg, Pa, Oct 2, 08; s Joseph Warren Jacobs & Emma Dulany J; m 1934 to Blanche Louise Widdup. Polit & Govt Pos: Chmn, Greene Co Rep Comt, Pa, formerly; comnr, Greene Co, 64-67 & 72- Bus & Prof Pos: Owner-mgr, Jacobs Oil Prod, 36-; past vchmn, Greene Co Soil & Water Conserv Dist & Wheeling Creek Watershed. Mem: Pa Petroleum & Fuels Asn; Greene Co Mem Hosp; Greene Co Chap, Am Red Cross; Pa Motor Truck Asn; Pittsburgh Petroleum Club. Mailing Add: 424 S Washington St Waynesburg PA 15370

JACOBS, JOEL (DFL)
Minn State Rep
Mailing Add: 11932 Zion St Coon Rapids MN 55433

JACOBS, NATHAN L
Justice, NJ Supreme Court
Mailing Add: State House Trenton NJ 08625

JACOBS, ORAL (JAKE) (D)
Ill State Sen
Mailing Add: 309 19th St East Moline IL 61244

JACOBSEN, GLENN EUGENE (D)
Mont State Rep
b Phoenix, Ariz, Jan 22, 28; s Paul Jacobsen & Anne Pedersen J (deceased); m 1951 to Bernice Lorraine Brenteson; c Bruce Lind, Diane Rae, Brian Paul & Glenn Arne. Polit & Govt Pos: Committeeman, Sheridan Co Dem Cent Comt, Mont, 59-, chmn, 64-68; Mont State Rep, 75- Bus & Prof Pos: Vchmn, Community Oil Co, 64- Mil Serv: Entered as Pvt, Air Force, 46, released as Pfc, 49, after serv in 11th & 82nd Airborne Divs, Japan & Pac Areas, 46-48; Occup & World War II Victory Medals. Mem: Mont Grain Growers Asn; Mont Farmers Union; Sheridan Co Soil & Water Conserv; VFW; Century Invest Club. Relig: Lutheran. Mailing Add: Reserve MT 59258

JACOBSON, ALF EDGAR (R)
NH State Rep
b Spokane, Wash, Apr 4, 24; s Carl Magnus Jacobsson & Emmy Bjoresson J; m 1951 to Sonja Ruth Torstenson; c Kurt Torsten & Brent Burgess. Educ: Northwestern Univ, BS, 52; Tufts Univ, MA, 54; Harvard Univ, STB, 54, STM, 55, PhD, 63. Polit & Govt Pos: Libr trustee, New London, NH, 60-63, mem planning bd, 65-71, chmn, 67-69; moderator, Kearsarge Regional Sch Dist, 68-; NH State Sen, Seventh Dist, 69-, asst majority leader, NH State Senate, 69-70, pres, 75; town moderator, New London, 70-73, selectman, 73-, chmn bd selectmen, 75- Bus & Prof Pos: Prof, Colby Col Women, 58-; chmn social & behavioral sci, Colby-Sawyer Col. Mil Serv: Entered as Pvt, Marine Corps, 43, released as Sgt, 46, after serv in Joint Intel Ctr, Pac Ocean Area & 2nd Bn, 27th Marines, Japan & Pac Occup Force Japan, 44-46. Mem: Bibliog Soc Am; Am Econ Asn; Am Soc Church Hist; Am Philatelic Soc; Manuscript Soc. Honors & Awards: Brewer Prize, Am Soc Church Hist. Relig: Swedish Congregational. Legal Res: Burpee Hill Rd New London NH 03257 Mailing Add: Box 188 New London NH 03257

JACOBSON, IRVEN JULIAN (D)
NDak State Rep
b Corinth, NDak, July 29, 20; s Andrew James Jacobson & Karen Sateren J; m 1943 to Carol Leone Wilson; c Karen (Mrs Dale Lucas), Irven Julian, Jr, Marjorie (Mrs Steve Fossum), Jeanine (Mrs Steve Roavold), Marilyn, Laurie & Luann. Educ: Williston High Sch, NDak. Polit & Govt Pos: Dem precinct committeeman, 40th Legis Dist, NDak, 56-66; state cent committeeman, Divide Co Dem Party, 64-66; chmn, Redlin for Cong Club, West Dist, 64 & 66; chmn, Dist Two Dem Party, 66-68; vchmn, West Dist Dem Party, 67-; mem bd dirs, NDak Century Club, 69-73; NDak State Rep, Dist Two, 70- Mem: Crosby Country Club; Moose; Elks; Farmers' Union. Relig: Lutheran. Mailing Add: State Capitol Bismarck ND 43215

JACOBSON, J GARVIN (R)
NDak State Sen
Mailing Add: State Capitol Bismarck ND 58501

JACOBSON, JONATHAN G (D)
Exec Committeeman, Orange Co Dem Comt, NY
b New York, NY, June 20, 53; s Seymour A Jacobson (deceased) & Ruth Kraf J; single. Educ: Duke Univ, BA, cum laude, 74; NY Law Sch, 74- Polit & Govt Pos: Committeeman, Newburgh Dem Comt, NY, 72-; deleg, Dem Nat Mid-Term Conf, 74; exec committeeman, Orange Co Dem Comt, NY, 74- Relig: Jewish. Mailing Add: 77 Susan Dr W Newburgh NY 12550

JACOBSON, SUSAN G (D)
b Baltimore, Md, Mar 7, 42; d Edward A Gersuk & Stella Cohen G; m 1963 to Alan B Jacobson; c Jonas Adam & Meredith Alix. Educ: Univ Md, BS, 66; Alpha Sigma Lambda. Polit & Govt Pos: First vchmn, New Dem Coalition of Md, 70-71; vpres, Columbia Dem Club, 71-72, pres, 72-; campaign coordr, McGovern for President, Sixth Cong Dist, 72; campaign chmn, Howard Co Dem Presidential Campaign, 72; alt deleg, Dem Nat Conv, 72; second vpres, United Dem Clubs of Howard Co, 73- Bus & Prof Pos: Teacher, Arlington Elem Sch, Baltimore, 61-63; psychometrist, Johns Hopkins Hosp, 65-66. Mem: League Women Voters; Md Womens Polit Caucus (chairwoman, nominating comt, 73); Planned Parenthood of Md; Theatre Upstairs (bd dirs, 71-). Mailing Add: 5225 Eliot's Oak Rd Columbia MD 21044

JACOME, HERBERT ARTHUR (D)
Chmn, Deep River Dem Town Comt, Conn
b Boston, Mass, Dec 31, 22; s Arthur Jacome & Bertha Gonzales J; m 1946 to Barbara Pearson; c Deborah (Mrs Dean Zanardi), Gary Arthur, Jan L & Terri L. Educ: Univ Conn, 46-48; Nat Asn Life Underwriters. Polit & Govt Pos: Mem sch bd, Deep River, Conn, 60-69, justice of the peace, 60-; chmn, Deep River Dem Town Comt, 74- Mil Serv: Entered as Pvt, Air Force, 42, released as S/Sgt, after serv in ETO, 45; Air Medal with 3 Oak Leaf Clusters; Unit Citation with Clusters; Victory Medal; Theater Medal with Clusters. Mem: Lions (treas); AFL-CIO Ins Workers. Honors & Awards: Lions Advan Key Award, 66. Legal Res: 6 Jones Lane Deep River CT 06417 Mailing Add: 159 Main St Deep River CT 06417

JACQUES, EMILE (D)
Maine State Rep
Mailing Add: 31 Pleasant St Lewiston ME 04240

JACQUES, NORMAN JOSEPH (D)
b Pawtucket, RI, Aug 31, 43; s Domenique Jacques & Gilberte Guilbeault J; m 1970 to Christine Welch; div; c Michael E Henri-David. Educ: Emerson Col; Portia Law Sch, Boston, 66-67; Harvard Univ Law Sch, spec student, 66-67; Antioch Sch Law, 72-73; Boston Int Rels Soc (vpres); Class treas, Emerson Col. Polit & Govt Pos: Student intern, US Sen Pell, RI, summer 61; mem, President Kennedy's White House Seminar, 62 & 63; RI State Rep, 65-66; RI State Sen, 67-68; state committeeman, Pawtucket, 67-68; mem, Dem Adv Comt, 67-68; deleg, Dem Nat Conv, 72. Bus & Prof Pos: Dir develop corp, Urban Am, Washington, DC, 69; speech writer asst to Marlo Thomas, Beverly Hills, Calif, 72. Publ: Auth-dir, The Conversation (play), produced in RI, 4/63. Relig: Agnostic. Legal Res: 16 Comstock St Pawtucket RI 02860 Mailing Add: Great Rd Lincoln RI 02865

JACQUIN, WILLIAM C (R)
b Peoria, Ill, Sept 1, 35; s W C Jacquin & Kathryn Niehaus J; m 1959 to Deborah Young; c Susan, Gregg & Lisa. Educ: Wabash Col, AB, 57; Univ Ariz Law Sch; Sphinx Club; Beta Theta Pi. Polit & Govt Pos: Chmn, Ariz State Young Rep Conv, 62; deleg, Rep Nat Conv, 64 & 72; Ariz State Rep, formerly; Ariz State Sen, Pima Co, Dist 14, 67-74, majority whip, Ariz State Senate, 67 & 68, majority leader, 69-70, pres, 71-74; precinct & state committeeman; vpres, Pima Co Young Rep League, formerly; secy, Pima Co Rep Club, formerly; mem exec comt, chmn legis awards comt & mem comt on fed-state rels, Nat Conf State Legis Leaders, 70-; vchmn govt opers task force, intergovt rels comt & mem comt on legis training, Nat Legis Conf, formerly; western regional vchmn, Nat Conf Lt Gov, 72-73. Bus & Prof Pos: Retail mgr, Jacquin & Co, Peoria, Ill, 57-58; ins salesman, Conn Mutual Life, Peoria, Ill & Tucson, Ariz, 59-61; Aetna Life & Casualty, Tucson, 62 & Tucson Realty & Trust Co, 62-73; self-employed life & health ins, 73- Mem: Ariz State CofC (dir pub & govt affairs, 75-); Ariz Club; Tucson E Community Ment Health Ctr (citizens adv bd); Tucson Press Club; United Community Campaign (vol). Relig: Presbyterian. Legal Res: 5202 E Alhambra Pl Tucson AZ 85711 Mailing Add: c/o Ariz CofC 2210 Townehouse 1000 W Clarendon Phoenix AZ 85013

JAEGER, CLARENCE RICHARD (R)
NDak State Rep
b Beulah, NDak, Oct 22, 33; s August Jaeger & Rose Jacober J; m 1962 to Leah Lackman; c Kay, Kurt, Kip & Kent. Educ: Beulah High Sch, NDak, grad, 52. Polit & Govt Pos: NDak State Rep, 72- Bus & Prof Pos: Pres, Tri-Co Corp, Beulah, NDak, 72- Mil Serv: Entered as Pvt, Army, 53, released as Cpl, 55. Mem: Beulah CofC; Liberty Amendment Comt; life mem John Birch Soc (chap leader, 65-). Honors & Awards: Nat Mid-Winter Marksman Pistol Championship, 55. Relig: Independent Christian. Mailing Add: Beulah ND 58523

JAFFE, AARON (D)
Ill State Rep
b Chicago, Ill, May 15, 30; s Karl Jaffe & Dora Goldberg J; m 1951 to Charlotte Miriam Bender; c Alan Michael, Alisa Caryn & Lowell Seth. Educ: Univ Ill, 48-49; Univ Calif, Los Angeles, 49-50; DePaul Univ, JD, 53; Nu Beta Epsilon. Polit & Govt Pos: Committeeman, Niles Twp Dem Comt, Ill, 69-; Ill State Rep, 71-; deleg, Dem Nat Conv, 72. Bus & Prof Pos: Attorney-at-law, Pvt Practice, 54- Mem: Am, Ill & Chicago Bar Asns; Niles Twp Bar Asn; Am Judicature Soc; Decalogue Soc of Lawyers. Honors & Awards: Past chmn, Skokie March of Dimes. Relig: Jewish. Mailing Add: 4441 Wilson Terr Skokie IL 60076

JAFFE, IRVING (D)
Dep Asst Attorney Gen Civil Div, Dept of Justice
b New York, NY, Aug 20, 13; s Max Elias Jaffe & Annie Shill J; m 1936 to Alice Cardin Bein; c Matthew Ely & Daniel Paul. Educ: City Col New York, BS, 33; Fordham Univ, LLB, 35. Polit & Govt Pos: Staff attorney, Bd Immigration Appeals, Dept of Justice, Washington, DC, 42-44, trial attorney, chief trial attorney, 44-49, chief trial attorney, chief estates & trusts, chief spec litigation sect, Off Alien Property, 50-61, spec litigation counsel, civil div, 61-63, chief court claims sect, 63-67, dep asst attorney gen civil div, 67-, acting asst attorney gen

civil div, 73-74 & 75; legal consult, US Displaced Persons Comn, 50; mem legal remedies study group, Comn on Govt Procurement, 70. Bus & Prof Pos: Law practice, New York, 36-42; partner, Firm of Wasserman & Jaffe, Washington, DC, 49-50. Mem: Int, Am, DC & Fed Bar Asns; Asn Immigration & Nationality Lawyers (bd adv). Legal Res: 9105 LeVelle Dr Chevy Chase MD 20015 Mailing Add: Dept of Justice Ninth & Pennsylvania Ave NW Washington DC 20530

JALBERT, LOUIS (D)
Maine State Rep
b Lewiston, Maine, May 7, 12; s Arthur J Jalbert & Celina Simard J; m 1938 to Yvonne Sproul. Educ: Portland Jr Col, BA, 51; Portland Law Univ, 1 year. Polit & Govt Pos: Finance agt, Dem Party, 44; Maine State Rep, 45-, Dem leader, Maine House of Rep, 47-49; ranking mem, Legis Research Comt, 14 years, chmn, 65-67, mem, currently; deleg, Dem Nat Conv, 68; chmn, Androscoggin Co Dem Party, 71- Mailing Add: 39 Orestis Way Lewiston ME 04240

JAMBOR, LOUISE IRMA (R)
Chmn, Ford Co Rep Cent Comt, Kans
b San Francisco, Calif; d Jean Louis Hinterman & Fannie Schlesinger H; m 1947 to James John Jambor; c Christopher Noel, Ann & Jonathan Jean. Educ: San Francisco Jr Col, 2 years. Polit & Govt Pos: Pres, Ford Co Rep Women's Club, 64; precinct committeewoman, Dodge City, Kans, 64; treas, First Dist Rep Women's Clubs, 66; chmn, Ford Co Rep Cent Comt, 66-; bd mem, Rep Assocs, Western Kans, 66-69; vchmn, First Cong Dist, 68; alt deleg-at-lg, Rep Nat Conv, 68, deleg & mem platform comt, 72. Bus & Prof Pos: Bd Dirs, Dodge City Community Concert Asn, 68-70. Mem: PEO; Ford Co Med Auxiliary; Trinity Hosp Auxiliary; St Anthony Hosp Auxiliary; Ford Co Hist Soc. Honors & Awards: Community Leader Award, 69. Relig: Episcopal. Mailing Add: 1707 Ave A Dodge City KS 67801

JAMES, HILARIO FELIX (D)
Mem, St Thomas Dem Dist Orgn Comt, VI
b St Thomas, VI, July 15, 46; s Henry Chaffinch James & Frances Albertina Smith J; m 1968 to Laura Ethel Lanclos; c Denise, Laura & Hilario, Jr. Educ: Manhattan Community Col, 65-66; Col VI, 66-69; Black Cultural Asn. Polit & Govt Pos: Treas, Young Dem of St Thomas, VI, 67-69; state vchmn, Dem Party of VI, 70-72; deleg, Second Const, Conv, 71-73; alt deleg, Dem Nat Conv, 72; mem, St Thomas Dem Dist Orgn Comt, 72- Bus & Prof Pos: Acct, Mannassah Enterprises, Inc, 68-70; pres, Sunny Isles Athletics, Inc, 71; pres, Opota, Inc, 73. Mem: Nat Sporting Goods Asn; St Thomas CofC; VI Businessmen Asn; Int Traders; Community Action Policy Bd (vchmn, 71-). Relig: Episcopal. Legal Res: 16 Altona & Welgunst St Thomas VI 00801 Mailing Add: PO Box 3728 St Thomas VI 00801

JAMES, JOSEPH SHEPPARD (D)
Auditor of Pub Accounts, Va
b Gum Spring, Va, May 25, 02; s Richard Gregory James & Lillie Lee Sale J; m 1925 to Virginia Parker Lambeth; c Mary Beverly (Mrs Weeks), & Joseph Sheppard, Jr. Educ: Va Mech Inst, Cert in Acct, 25, CPA, 32. Polit & Govt Pos: Asst Auditor Public Accounts, Va, 44-67, Auditor of Public Accounts, 67- Relig: Methodist. Mailing Add: 3850 Brook Rd Richmond VA 23227

JAMES, L ELDON (D)
b Dendron, Va, Jan 1, 13; s Leonard Wallace James & Lillian Noyes J; m 1939 to Aurelia Mitchell; c Nancy J (Mrs Buhl); Quinby J (Mrs Amory), Sally L (Mrs Andrews) & L Eldon, Jr; six grandchildren. Educ: Col William & Mary, BS, 34, Law Sch, 34-35; George Washington Univ Law Sch, JD, 37; George Wythe Law Club; Sigma Phi Epsilon. Polit & Govt Pos: Mem, Va State Bar Coun, 61-67; mem, US Vet Adv Comn, 67-68; US observer, SVietnam Elec, 67; chmn, Hampton Dem Town Exec Comt, Va, 67-68, mem, 68-71; deleg, Dem Nat Conv, 68; nat chmn, Vet for Humphrey-Muskie, 68; nat vchmn, Dem for Nixon, 72. Mil Serv: Entered as Lt(jg), Naval Res, 44, released as Lt, 46, after serv in Assignments in Washington, DC & Portsmouth, NH. Publ: Articles in Nat Educ Asn J; Am Legion Mag & Parade. Mem: Va State Bar Asn; Hampton Bar Asn (pres, 68); Va Trial Lawyers Asn; Am Legion (nat comdr, 65-66); Lions Int. Honors & Awards: Distinguished Serv Award, Col William & Mary; Two Honor Cert Awards, Freedoms Found; Two Citations, President US; Distinguished Citizen Award, Hampton, Va; Alumni Achievement Award, George Washington Univ. Relig: Baptist. Legal Res: 9 Terrace Rd Hampton VA 23361 Mailing Add: PO Box 38 Hampton VA 23369

JAMES, MARY F (R)
Chairwoman, Madison Co Rep Party, Ky
b Rowan Co, Ky, May 12, 15; d James Fultz & Vesta Goodman F; m 1935 to Ival James; c Gregory & Shelia Katherene. Educ: Morehead High Sch, 2 years. Polit & Govt Pos: Vpres, Madison Co Woman's Rep Club, Ky, 64-66, pres, 67-69, secy, 69-70, treas, 70-; chmn, Madison Co Rep Party, 68- Relig: Baptist. Mailing Add: Four Mile Rd Rte 6 Richmond KY 40475

JAMES, MATTHEW EDWARD (D)
Committeeman, Mont State Dem Exec Comt
b Circle, Mont, Aug 15, 26; s David James & Anna Marie Pedersen J; m 1970 to Judith Ann Latimer. Educ: Mont State Col, 46; Dawson Co Jr Col, AA, with honors, 62. Polit & Govt Pos: Committeeman, Precinct 8, McCone Co, Mont, 60-64 & 70-; chmn, McCone Co Dem Cent Comt, 61-64; Dem nominee for Mont State Sen, 64; committeeman, Mont State Dem Exec Comt, 67-, exec committeeman-at-lg, 67-70, agr adv, 70-; presidential elector, 68. Bus & Prof Pos: Mem, McCone Co Fair Bd, Mont, 48-68; chmn adv bd, Eastern Br Mont Agr Exp Sta, Sidney, 61-4. Mil Serv: Entered as Recruit, Army, 53, released as Cpl, 55, after serv in 7734 Signal Serv Platoon, German Occup Forces, 54-55; Honor Grad, US Army Signal Corps; Powerman Training Course, Camp San Luis Obispo, Calif, 53. Publ: Winter Feeding with a Plan, Mont Farmer Stockman, 11/70. Mem: VFW Post 4813 (comdr, 61-62, chmn community serv, 61-62, chmn loyalty day, 61-65 & 67-). Honors & Awards: Am Legion Sch Award, Circle Pub Schs, 40. Relig: United Christian. Mailing Add: David James Ranch Circle MT 59215

JAMES, RONALD HARVEY (D)
Ohio State Rep
b Huntington, WVa, Apr 1, 48; s James Harvey James & Geraldine Smith J; m 1971 to Jacqueline Simpson. Educ: Marshall Univ, AB, 71; Tau Kappa Epsilon. Polit & Govt Pos: Ohio State Rep, 92nd Dist, 75- Bus & Prof Pos: Advert acct exec, Russell, Ky, 71; social worker, Ironton, Ohio, 71-74. Mem: Elks; Grange; Southern Hills Sportsmen Club; Lawrence Community Betterment Club. Relig: Protestant. Mailing Add: Rte 3 Box 485 Proctorville OH 45669

JAMES, SUSAN LOUISE (D)
Ariz State Rep
b Chicago, Ill, July 11, 46; d Allen Bernard Wachter & Alphild Louise Lundman W; m 1972 to Roland Wesley James. Educ: Univ Ariz, 64-66 & 70-71; Ariz State Univ, 72-73; Folklanders. Polit & Govt Pos: Ariz State Rep, Dist 20, 75- Bus & Prof Pos: Clerk, serv rep & supvr, Mountain Bell, Tucson & Phoenix, Ariz, 64-73; mgr self serv gas sta, Mobil Oil, Phoenix, 74. Mem: Human Rights; Ariz Women's Polit Caucus; Am Civil Liberties Union; Arizonans for Peace. Relig: Lutheran. Legal Res: Apt 7 5110 N 21st Ave Phoenix AZ 85015 Mailing Add: 1700 W Washington Phoenix AZ 85007

JAMES, TROY LEE (D)
Ohio State Rep
b Texarkana, Tex; s Samuel W James & Anniebell J; m to Betty Jean Winslow; c Laura M. Educ: Bethany Col, WVa, degree, Bldg Legis; Western Reserve Univ, 2 years; Fenn Col, 1 year. Polit & Govt Pos: Precinct committeeman, Ward 11 Dem Orgn, 8 years, pres, 7 years; Ohio State Rep, Dist Nine, 67-, Dem whip, Ohio House of Rep, 70-, chmn environ & natural resources, currently. Bus & Prof Pos: Businessman, self-employed, 23 years; employee, Ohio Crankshaft, 12 years. Mil Serv: World War II & Korean War. Mem: 11th Ward Dem Club (pres); 40th & 43rd St Neighborhood Block Club (pres); Ohio Soc State Legis; Dem Exec Coun; Mayor's Comt Housing. Relig: Baptist. Mailing Add: 4216 Cedar Ave Cleveland OH 44103

JAMES, VERNON G (D)
NC State Rep
Mailing Add: Rte 1 Elizabeth City NC 27909

JAMES, WILLIAM G (BILL) (R)
Fla State Rep
Mailing Add: 1725 Lake Dr Delray Beach FL 33444

JAMES, WILLIAM S (D)
b Aberdeen, Md, Feb 14, 14; married. Educ: Tome Sch, 28-32; Univ Del, 32-34; Univ Md Law Sch, LLB, 37. Polit & Govt Pos: Md State Rep, 47-55; Md State Sen, 55-74, pres of Senate & chmn rules comt & chmn legis coun, Md State Senate, 63-74; deleg, Dem Nat Conv, 68 & 72; chmn, Md State Dem Party, 72-75; mem, Dem Nat Comt, 72-75; deleg, Dem Nat Mid-Term Conf, 74. Mem: Harford Co (bd libr trustees, 45-53); Rotary. Mailing Add: 26 Office St Bel Air MD 21014

JAMIEL, MORPHIS ALBERT (D)
RI State Rep
b Warren, RI, Dec 19, 21; s Albert George Jamiel & Mary Falugo; single. Educ: Univ RI, BS, 43; Boston Univ Law Sch, JD, 48. Polit & Govt Pos: RI State Sen, 63-66; Probate Judge, 13 years; town solicitor, Warren, RI, 2 years, mem planning bd, 4 years, town councilman, 2 years, charter comn, 1 year; RI State Rep, 71- Bus & Prof Pos: Lawyer, self-employed, 20 years; auctioneer, Jamiel Realty Co, 8 years, real estate broker, 20 years, ins broker, 4 years, mortgage loans, 20 years; chem engr; judge. Mil Serv: Entered as Pvt, Army, 42, released as 1st Lt, 46, after serv in 7th Armored Div, ETO, 44-46 & 50-52; Col, RI Army Nat Guard; Purple Heart; Bronze Star with Three Oak Leaf Clusters. Mem: Nat Guard Asn; Bristol Lions Club; Warren Scholar Found; RI & Am Bar Asns. Mailing Add: 10 Market St Warren RI 02885

JAMIESON, NORMAN LESLIE (R)
VChmn, Sixth Cong Dist Rep Comt, Mich
b Howell, Mich, Aug 5, 34; s Norman Richard Jamieson & Mary Burns J; m 1969 to Lynne Marie Merrill; c Todd & Terri. Educ: Mich State Univ, BA, 56; Pre-law club; Off club. Polit & Govt Pos: Voter identification chmn, Livingston Co Rep Comt, Mich, 61-63, orgn chmn, 63-67, chmn, 67-74; vchmn, Livingston Co Young Rep, 62; justice of the peace, Marion Twp, 65-69; mem exec comt, Sixth Cong Dist Rep Comt, 67-75, vchmn, 75-; deleg, Rep Nat Conv, 68. Bus & Prof Pos: Casualty underwriter, Citizen's Mutual Ins Co, Howell, 59-63, sr commercial lines underwriter, 63-66; asst vpres & ins mgr, Howell Town & Country, Inc, 66-71; substitute teacher, Howell-Livingston Co Int Sch Dist, 69; pres, Jamieson-Milner Agency, Inc, 71- Mil Serv: Entered as Pvt, Army, 56, released as Sp-4, 58, after serv in Intel Sect, Hq, Second Missile Command, Fifth Army, 56-58. Mem: Nat Asn Mutual Ins Agts; Elks (Past Exalted Ruler); Howell Area CofC; Econ Club Detroit; Mich State Univ Livingston-Washtenaw Alumni Club. Relig: Presbyterian. Legal Res: 205 Mason Rd Howell MI 48843 Mailing Add: 1002 E Grand River Howell MI 48843

JAMISON, LESLIE D (R)
b Charleston, SC, Sept 23, 26; d Daniel William Dukes & Sarah Massenburg D; m 1946 to Dr Elmer Alvis Jamison (deceased); c William Robert & John Charles. Educ: Sch Nursing, Med Col SC; The Citadel, night sch, Charleston; Hall Inst Real Estate, grad. Polit & Govt Pos: Women's campaign chmn, Citizens for Nixon-Lodge, 60; Rep precinct secy, Pickens Co, SC, 62-64, 66 & 68; Rep campaign chmn, 62, 64, 66 & 68; precinct committeewoman, 68-, campaign coordr, 70-72; chmn, Pickens Co Rep Party, 64-67; SC Conv vchmn, Rep Women's Conf, Washington, DC, 66; SC State Publicity chmn, Rep Women's Conf, Little Rock, Ark, 67; SC State co-chmn, Women for Nixon-Agnew, 68; first vchmn, SC Rep Party, formerly; deleg, Rep Nat Conv, 72; mem, State Steering Comt to Reelect the President, 72. Bus & Prof Pos: Assoc, Charles D Wyatt & Co, Inc, Realtors, Charleston. Mem: Pickens Co Med Auxiliary; Pickens Co Friends of the Libr. Relig: Episcopal. Mailing Add: 122 Lakeview Dr Easley SC 29640

JANES, R KIPPEN (R)
Mem, New Hartford Rep Town Comt, Conn
b Hartford, Conn, Sept 27, 37; s Harold A L Janes & Susan Matheson J; m 1960 to Elaine L Meyers; c Sarah E & Robert K, Jr. Educ: Trinity Col, BA, 59; Delta Phi. Polit & Govt Pos: Justice of the Peace, New Hartford, Conn, 68-; mem, First Fire Dist Comn, 68-; mem, New Hartford Rep Town Comt, 68-, chmn, formerly; mem, Zoning & Planning Comn, 70-; asst clerk, Conn State Senate, 73- Mil Serv: Entered as Pvt, Marine Corps, 59, released as 1st Lt, 63. Mem: New Hartford Jaycees. Honors & Awards: New Hartford Jaycee of the Year, 69, Distinguished Serv Award, 71. Relig: Congregational. Mailing Add: PO Box 243 Main St New Hartford CT 06057

JANES, ROBERT JAMES (R)
RI State Sen
b Wethersfield, Conn, Nov 10, 25; s James Fox Janes & Eleanor McKee J; m 1952 to Julia Griffiths; c Elizabeth & Heidi. Educ: Brown Univ, AB, 47; Delta Tau Delta. Polit & Govt Pos: Chmn, Barrington, RI, Sch Comt, 62-74; RI State Sen, 75- Bus & Prof Pos: Vpres, Ins Underwriters, Inc, 70- Mil Serv: Entered as V-5, Navy, 44, released as Ens, 46, after serv in USS Buckthorn, 46. Mem: Am Field Serv, Barrington Chap (pres); St Andrews Sch (trustee); Univ Club, Providence (bd gov); Providence CofC (bd dirs). Relig: Episcopal. Mailing Add: 45 Meadowbrook Dr Barrington RI 02806

JANEWAY, EDWARD G (R)
Vt State Sen
b New Rochelle, NY, Aug 25, 01; s Dr Theodore Caldwell Janeway & Eleanor Alderson J; m 1925 to Elinor White; c five & 17 grandchildren. Educ: Yale Col, 22. Polit & Govt Pos: Chief conserv, Tin & Lead Div, War Prod Bd, 41-42; chmn, Vt for Eisenhower Comt, 51-52; Vt State Rep, 51-57; Rep Nat Committeeman, Vt, 52-72; mem, Vt Little Hoover Comn, 57-58; Vt State Sen, 59- Bus & Prof Pos: Investment bus, NY, 24-41; dairy farming & purebred cattle breeding, Vt, 45-; mem bd trustees, Experiment in Int Living, Putney, Vt; chmn, Conserv Soc Southern Vt; dir, Stratton Corp, Vt & Catamount Nat Bank. Mil Serv: Entered Navy, 42, released as Lt, 46, serv in Amphibious Forces, Africa & Eng, Lt Comdr, Naval Res; Bronze Star; Croix de Guerre. Mem: Grange; Am Legion; Links Club, NY; Tavern Club, Boston; Ekwanok Club, Vt. Relig: Congregational. Legal Res: Middletown Farm South Londonderry VT 05155 Mailing Add: PO Box 117 South Londonderry VT 05155

JANKLOW, WILLIAM JOHN (R)
Attorney Gen, SDak
b Chicago, Ill, Sept 13, 39; m to Mary Dean; c Russell, Pamela & Shawna. Educ: Univ SDak, BS & JDS. Polit & Govt Pos: Dir, SDak Legal Aid, 67-72; chief prosecutor, Off Attorney Gen, SDak, 73-74; Attorney Gen, 75- Bus & Prof Pos: Attorney-at-law, Pierre, SDak, 72-73. Mil Serv: Entered as Pvt, Marine Corps, released as Pfc, after serv in 3rd Marine Div, Southeast Asia, 56-59. Mem: Am & SDak Trial Lawyers Asns, Am Judicature Soc; Am & SDak Bar Asns. Honors & Awards: Nat Award for Legal Excellence & Skill, Off Equal Opportunity Legal Serv. Legal Res: 214 S Washington Pierre SD 57501 Mailing Add: State Capitol Pierre SD 57501

JANSEN, DONALD O (R)
Committeeman, Tex State Rep Exec Comt
b Odessa, Tex, Nov 17, 39; s Orville C Jansen (deceased) & Dolores Olps J; m 1964 to Lynn Friedman; c Donald Jr, Lauren, Christine & David. Educ: Loyola Univ (La), BBA, 61, LLB, 63; Georgetown Univ, LLM, 66; Alpha Sigma Nu; Beta Gamma Delta Theta Phi; Delta Sigma Pi; Upsilon Beta Lambda; Blue Key. Polit & Govt Pos: State chmn, Tex Young Adult Rep Comt, 69-70; chmn co clubs, Tex Young Rep Fedn, 69-70; campaign mgr, Congressman Bill Archer Campaign, 70; exec committeeman, Harris Co Rep Party, 69-; mem, Houston Mass Transit Comt, 72-73; committeeman, Tex State Rep Exec Comt, 72- Bus & Prof Pos: Lawyer-partner, Fulbright & Jaworski, Houston, Tex, 66- Mil Serv: Entered as 1st Lt, Army, 63, released as Capt, 66, after serv in JAGC, the Pentagon, 63-66; Army Commendation Medal. Publ: P L 85-804 & Extraordinary Contractual Relief, Georgetown Law J, 67. Mem: Am Cancer Soc (dir, Harris Co Unit); Fed Bar Asn (mem, Nat Coun); Tex Bill of Rights Found (dir); State Bar Tex; La State Bar Asn. Honors & Awards: Regional Finalist, White House Fellow Prog, 72; Outstanding Male Adult Leader, Tex Young Rep Fedn, 70; President's Award, Harris Co Young Rep Club, 68 & 72. Relig: Roman Catholic. Mailing Add: 2522 Pomeran Houston TX 77055

JANSSEN, JACK WESLEY (D)
Kans State Sen
b Lyons, Kans, July 6, 23; s Juanita Hughes J, (father deceased); m 1943 to Dorothy Link. Educ: Univ Okla, 2 years. Polit & Govt Pos: Co comnr, Rice Co, Kans, 59-65; Kans State Sen, 33rd Dist, 65-69, Kans State Sen, 23rd Dist, 69- Bus & Prof Pos: Pres, Rice Co Develop Corp, 64-68; bd mem, Gov Nuclear Energy Coun, 66-; bd mem, Alliance for Progress Comt, 68- Mil Serv: Entered as Cadet, Army Air Force, 42, released as 1st Lt, 45, after serv as Bomber Pilot, 8th Air Force, ETO, 44-45; Lt Col, Air Force Res, 69-, Liaison Officer for Air Force Acad, currently; Air Medal with Seven Oak Leaf Clusters; European-African-Mid Eastern Serv Medal; Northern France-Ger Serv Medal; Victory Medal Air Force Res Medal. Mem: Eagles; Odd Fellows; Optimists; CofC; Am Legion. Relig: Christian Church of NAm. Mailing Add: PO Box 626 Lyons KS 67554

JANZEN, JACOB JOHN (R)
Committeeman, SC Rep State Exec Comt,
b Ukraine, Europe, Mar 29, 19; s Cornelius Janzen & Anna Derksen J; m 1948 to Betty Lou Mathisen; c Mona (Mrs Michael Turner), Sherry & Robert. Educ: Univ Man, BSA, 44; Univ Wis-Madison, MS, 47, PhD, 52, post-doctorate study, 53. Polit & Govt Pos: Secy-treas, Precinct, Pickens Co, SC, 64-66; precinct pres, Clemson, 66-, committeeman, SC Rep State Exec Comt, Pickens Co, 68-; dist chmn, Third Cong Dist, 72-; deleg, Rep Nat Conv, 72; presidential elector, SC, 72. Bus & Prof Pos: Lectr, Univ Man, 47-49; research asst, Univ Wis, 49-50, research assoc, 51-52; research chemist, Research Dept, Continental Can Co, 53-58; prof dairy sci, Clemson Univ, 58- Publ: Over 30 papers in scientific & trade journals. Mem: Am Dairy Sci Asn; Inst of Food Technologists (coun, 70-); Sigma Xi; Gamma Sigma Delta; SC Dairy Technol Soc. Relig: Presbyterian. Mailing Add: 211 Highland Dr Clemson SC 29631

JAQUESS, JAMES (HARRY) (D)
Chmn, Putnam Co Dem Party, Tenn
b Cookeville, Tenn, Nov 29, 37; s Frazier Jaquess & Jimmie Hughes J; m 1960 to Marcia Ann Bartlett; c Jeffrey Charles. Educ: Tenn Tech Univ, 56-60; Sigma Iota Epsilon. Polit & Govt Pos: Chmn, Putnam Co Dem Party, Tenn, currently. Bus & Prof Pos: Charter appointee & secy, Putnam Co Airport Authority, Tenn, 71- Mem: Cookeville Jaycees; Putnam Co Band Booster Club; Putnam Co Jr High PTA. Honors & Awards: Cookeville Jaycee Outstanding Young Man, 64; Tenn Jaycee Outstanding Regional Vpres, 67; Tenn Jaycee Vol Corp, 69; US Jaycee Jr Chamber Int Senatorship, 69. Relig: Church of Christ. Legal Res: Hunter Cove Rd Rte 8 Cookeville TN 38501 Mailing Add: 118 N Cedar Ave Cookeville TN 38501

JARABO ALVAREZ, JOSE G (POPULAR DEMOCRAT, PR)
Rep, PR House of Rep
Mailing Add: State Capitol San Juan PR 00901

JARBOE, JOHN BRUCE (D)
Secy-Treas, First Dist, Okla Dem Party
b Tulsa, Okla, Mar 28, 40; s Joseph Ralph Jarboe & Mildred Maguire J; m to Sally; c John B, II. Educ: Univ Okla, BA, 62; Univ Tulsa, JD, 65; Sigma Chi; Phi Alpha Delta. Polit & Govt Pos: Nominee, US Rep, First Dist Okla, 68; Secy-treas, First Dist, Okla Dem Party, 69- Bus & Prof Pos: Research asst, US Dist Court, Tulsa, 63-65; trial attorney, US Dept Justice, Washington, DC, 65-66; pvt law practice & cattle bus, Tulsa, 68-; mem bd regents, Okla Col of Liberal Arts, 71- Mil Serv: Entered as Pvt, Army, 66, released as SP-5, 68, after serv in Staff Judge Adv Off, Ft Polk, La, 66-68; Nat Serv Medal; Army Commendation Medal. Publ: Taxation, Tulsa Law J, 64. Mem: Okla, Am & Fed Bar Asns; Nat Lawyers Club; Am Legion. Honors & Awards: Ed-in-chief, Tulsa Law J & Outstanding Law Grad, Univ Tulsa, 65. Relig: Catholic. Mailing Add: 2186 Owasso Tulsa OK 74114

JARDINE, SUSAN KIM (D)
Chairwoman, Butte Co Dem Party, Idaho
b Idaho Falls, Idaho, Oct 5, 55; d Jay L Jardine & Bette Jane Cooper J; single. Educ: Ricks Col, 74-75; Idaho State Univ, 75- Polit & Govt Pos: Chairwoman, Butte Co Dem Party, Idaho, 74- Mem: Donkey Club. Relig: Latter-day Saint. Mailing Add: Box 512 Arco ID 83213

JARMAN, BETH SMITH (D)
Utah State Rep
b Salt Lake City, Utah, Apr 6, 41; d Wayne David Smith & Jean Hathaway S; m 1962 to Michael Cooley Jarman; c Joseph Alexander & Michelle. Educ: Univ Utah, BS, 64, MS, 70, PhD cand; Phi Alpha Theta; Delta Kappa Gamma. Polit & Govt Pos: Legis chairwoman, Davis Co Dem Party, Utah, 72-, mem exec comt, 73-; mem, Utah Dem State Exec Comt, 73-; Utah State Rep, 75-, mem local state & fed comt, Utah House Rep, 75-, mem bus, consumer affairs & indust develop comt, 75-, mem natural resources appropriation subcomt, 75- Mem: Utah Women's Polit Caucus. Honors & Awards: Teaching fel, Univ Utah, 74; Special Honor for Sponsoring Equal Rights Amendment, YWCA, 75. Mailing Add: 360 E 400 North Bountiful UT 84010

JARMAN, JOHN (R)
US Rep, Okla
b Sallisaw, Okla, July 17, 15; s John H Jarman & Lou N Jones; m 1942 to Ruth Bewley, wid. 1964; m 1968 to Marylin Grant; c Jay, Susan & Steve. Educ: Yale Univ, BA, 37; Harvard Law Sch, LLB, 41; Westminster Col, Mo. Polit & Govt Pos: Okla State Rep; Okla State Sen; US Rep, Okla, 50-; deleg, Dem Nat Conv, 68. Bus & Prof Pos: Lawyer. Mil Serv: Army, 42-45. Legal Res: 1805 Huntington Oklahoma City OK 73112 Mailing Add: 2416 Rayburn House Off Bldg Washington DC 20515

JAROS, MIKE (DFL)
Minn State Rep
b Yugoslavia, Apr 12, 44; s Michael Jaros & Barbara Nojburger J; m 1968 to Annette Nordine; c Bani B & Adam P. Educ: Univ Minn, BA, 68. Polit & Govt Pos: Minn State Rep, 73- Relig: Humanistic. Legal Res: 162 W Palm St Duluth MN 55811 Mailing Add: State Capitol St Paul MN 55101

JARRATT, JOYCE HOWARD (R)
Committeewoman, Tex State Rep Exec Comt
b Port Arthur, Tex, May 3, 30; d Harry William Howard & Rose Strain H; m 1951 to Kenneth Lee Jarratt; c Judy & John. Educ: Kilgore Col, 48-49; Victoria Col, AA; Univ Houston, 73; Kilgore Rangerettes. Polit & Govt Pos: Committeewoman, Tex State Rep Exec Comt, 73- Relig: Baptist. Mailing Add: Rte 1 Box 8 Edna TX 77957

JARRETT, DONALD DUWAYNE (R)
b Britton, SDak, May 23, 29; s Ray S Jarrett & Lena B Jahnig; m 1964 to Jeannine C Wyun; c Jason P, Sarah D, Wayne A & Bryce N. Educ: SDak State Univ, winter quarter 49. Polit & Govt Pos: Deleg, Rep Nat Conv, 56, alt deleg, 72, gave seconding speech for President Eisenhower, 56; Young Rep Nat Committeeman, SDak, 60; committeeman, SDak Rep Cent Comt, Marshall Co, 66-72, mem adv bd, 71-72. Mil Serv: Entered as Pvt, Army, 53, released as Sgt, 55, after serv in 76th Eng Bn, Korea, 53-55. Mem: Am Farm Bur; Farmers Union; Masonic Lodge (Master, 62); VFW (Comdr, 62); Am Legion (Comdr, 66). Relig: Presbyterian. Mailing Add: Britton SD 57430

JARRETT, EVELYN L (D)
Vt State Rep
Mailing Add: 101 Spruce St Burlington VT 05401

JARVIS, BARBARA (D)
Polit & Govt Pos: Former mem, Dem Nat Comt, Ariz. Mailing Add: 1266 Skyline Dr Globe AZ 85501

JARVIS, NORMAN O (R)
Mem, DC Rep Comt
b Washington, DC, Nov 3, 08; s William Ernest Jarvis & Elva Catherine Minor J; m 1928 to Mary Hallie Jackson; c Norman W, W Ernest, Richard Wilson, Anne Elizabeth (Mrs Bennett), Sidney Jackson, Stephen Daniel, Mary Constance (Mrs Dixon) & Charlotte Marie (Mrs Allen). Educ: Denver Univ, 29-30; Howard Univ, 30-33; Frelinhysen COE, DSS, 36. Polit & Govt Pos: Asst to chmn, DC Forward Looking Rep; alt deleg, Rep Nat Conv, 64; mem bd dirs & spec asst to chmn, DC Rep Comt, formerly, mem exec adv comt, 68, mem, 74-; mem bd dirs & spec asst to chmn, New York City Rep Party, 64- Bus & Prof Pos: Pres, W Ernest Jarvis Co, 45-66. Mem: Int Elks; Mason; DePriest 15; Urban League NAACP; YMCA. Honors & Awards: Won Sr Championship, United Golf Asn, 62. Relig: Episcopal. Mailing Add: 3003 Van Ness St Washington DC 20008

JASKULSKI, ROBERT W (D)
Ohio State Rep
Mailing Add: 10109 Park Heights Blvd Garfield Heights OH 44125

JASPER, CLAUDE J (R)
b Alma, Iowa, Aug 23, 05; s John K Jasper & Julia Brost J; m 1946 to Shirley Tholen; c William, Thomas & Julia. Educ: St Thomas Col; Univ Wis Law Sch. Polit & Govt Pos: Treas, Taft for President Campaign, 52; treas, Wis Rep Party, 52-58, chmn, 58-62; alt deleg, Rep Nat Conv, 52, 56 & 60, deleg, 64; mem, Rep Nat Comt, 58-62. Bus & Prof Pos: Attorney, Jasper, Winner, McCallum & Sauthoff. Mem: Wis & Am Bar Asns; Elks. Relig: Catholic.

Legal Res: 122 E Gilman St Madison WI 53704 Mailing Add: 111 S Fairchild Madison WI 53703

JASTAD, ELMER (D)
Wash State Rep
b Chehalis, Wash, 1906; m to Edna Mae; c one son. Educ: Wash State Univ Sch of Pharm. Polit & Govt Pos: Wash State Rep, currently. Bus & Prof Pos: Pharmacist. Mem: Mason; Shrine; Scottish Rite; Eagles; Elks. Mailing Add: Box 67 Morton WA 98356

JAVITS, JACOB KOPPEL (R)
US Sen, NY
b New York, NY, May 18, 04; s Morris Javits & Ida J; m 1947 to Marion Ann Borris; c Joy, Joshua & Carla. Educ: NY Univ Law Sch, LLB, 27. Hon Degrees: Hon degrees from 21 cols & univs including NY Univ, Hartwick Col, Yeshiva Univ, Hebrew Union Col, Long Island Univ, Ithaca Col, Colgate Univ, Niagara Univ, Jewish Theol Sem, Lincoln Univ & Dartmouth Col. Polit & Govt Pos: Mem, Ivy Rep Club, 18th Cong Dist, 32; US Rep, 21st Dist, NY, 46-54, mem, Foreign Affairs Comt, US House Rep; attorney gen, NY, 54-56; chmn, NATO Parliamentarians' Conf Spec Comt on Econ Develop Less-Develop NATO Nations, Rapporteur, NATO Polit Comt; US Sen, NY, 56-, mem, Foreign Rels & Govt Opers Comts, Comt on Labor & Pub Welfare, Joint Econ Comt, Select Comt on Small Bus, US Senate; deleg, Rep Nat Conv, 68 & 72; US deleg, UN Gen Assembly, 70. Mil Serv: Entered as Maj, Army, 42, released as Lt Col, 45, after serv as Asst to Chief Opers Chem Warfare, ETO, 43, Pac Theatre, 44; Legion of Merit; Army Commendation Ribbon. Publ: Order of battle, a Republican's call to reason, Atheneum, 64, rev, 66; Discrimination, USA, 60, rev, 62; co-auth, Who Makes War (w Don Kellermann), 73. Mem: Am Legion; VFW; Jewish War Vets. Relig: Jewish. Legal Res: 110 E 45th St New York NY 10017 Mailing Add: Russell Senate Off Bldg Washington DC 20510

JAWORSKI, LEON
b Waco, Tex, Sept 19, 05; s Rev Joseph Jaworski & Marie Mira J; m 1931 to Jeannette Adam; c Joanie, Claire & Joseph, III. Educ: Baylor Univ, LLB, 25, LLD, 60; George Washington Univ, LLM, 26; Order of the Coif; Phi Delta Phi. Hon Degrees: Various hon degrees. Polit & Govt Pos: Spec asst US attorney gen, 62-65; spec counsel attorney gen, Tex, 63-65 & 72-73; mem, President's Comt Law Enforcement & Admin Justice; US mem, Permanent Int Arbitration, The Hague; mem, Comn Marine Sci, Eng & Resources; mem, President's Comn Causes & Prev of Violence; chmn, Gov Comn Pub Sch Educ Bd; dir, Off Watergate Spec Prosecution Force, 73- Bus & Prof Pos: Sr partner, Fullbright, Crooker & Jaworski, Houston, Tex, 51-; dir & chmn exec comt, Bank of Southwest; dir, Southwest Bankshares Inc, Houston Anderson Clayton & Co, Gulf Pub Co, Intercontinental Nat Bank, Coastal States Gas Producing Co & Village Nat Bank; regent, Nat Col Dist Attorney; trustee, United Fund, 58-; chmn trustees & mem exec comt, Southwestern Legal Found; trustee, Tex Med Ctr, Baylor Col Med; pres, Baylor Med Found & M D Anderson Found. Mil Serv: Col, Army, 42-46; chief war crimes trial sect Judge Adv Gen Dept, ETO. Publ: After Fifteen Years, 61; plus others. Mem: Am Col Trial Lawyers (fel); Rotary; Tex Bar Asn; CofC; Am Law Inst. Relig: Presbyterian. Legal Res: 3665 Ella Lee Lane Houston TX 77027 Mailing Add: Bank of Southwest Bldg Travis & Walker Houston TX 77002

JEBENS, JOHN HERMAN (R)
Supvr, Scott Co, Iowa
b Davenport, Iowa, June 6, 18; s John H Jebens & Mathilde Looges J; m 1948 to Marian I Blank; c John H Jebens, III. Educ: St Ambrose Col, BA, 39. Polit & Govt Pos: Alderman at lg, Davenport, Iowa, 57-66, mayor, 67-71; mem, Air Pollution Control Comn, State of Iowa, 69-72; supvr & mem bd, Scott Co, Iowa, 73- Bus & Prof Pos: Owner, Blackhawk Printing Co, Davenport, 40- Mil Serv: Entered as Ens Navy, 44, released as Lt(jg), 46, after serv in Mediterranean & Pacific. Mem: Elks; Eagles; Moose; Am Legion; VFW. Relig: Episcopal. Mailing Add: 3203 Arlington Ave Davenport IA 52803

JEFFE, DOUGLAS I (D)
b Los Angeles, Calif, Jan 17, 43; s Harry Jeffe & Mary Cornblith J; m 1968 to Sherry Bebitch. Educ: Harvey Mudd Col, 60-61; Univ Calif, Los Angeles, AB, 65; Pi Sigma Alpha; Sigma Delta Chi. Polit & Govt Pos: Dir pub affairs, Calif Dem State Cent Comt, 63-66; dir info, Comt for Proposition Eight, Calif Gen Elec, 66; research consult, Comt on Elec & Reapportionment, Calif State Assembly, 67, sr asst, Dem Caucus, 71-74; coordr, Kennedy for President Calif Campaign, 68; Southern Calif press secy, Humphrey for President Campaign, 68; admin asst, Calif State Assemblyman Kenneth Cory, 68-71; deleg, Dem Nat Conv, 72. Bus & Prof Pos: Partner, Pac Mgt Assocs, 67-69; gen mgr, Braun Campaigns Inc, 75- Mailing Add: 5019 W 63rd St Los Angeles CA 90056

JEFFERIS, D ALLEN (R)
Chmn, Randolph Co Rep Comt, Ind
b Union City, Ind, Oct 10, 37; s O Duane Jefferis & Pauline Schockney J; m 1958 to Elizabeth McKinley; c Amy, Scott & Brad. Educ: Univ Cincinnati, BBA, 60; Beta Theta Pi. Polit & Govt Pos: City Chmn, Union City, Ind, 64-74; jury comnr, Randolph Co, 68-75; chmn, Randolph Co Rep Comt, 74- Bus & Prof Pos: Gen mgr, Coca-Cola Bottling Co, Inc, Union City, Ind, 70- Mem: Rotary; CofC; Jaycees; United Fund Bd; Elks. Legal Res: 1060 DeBolt Ave Union City IN 47390 Mailing Add: PO Box 52 Union City IN 47390

JEFFERIS, EDWARD FOREST, III (R)
b Columbus, Ohio, Aug 12, 43; s Edward F Jefferis Jr & Julia Ann Gutman J; single. Educ: Ohio State Univ, BChE & MS, 66; Phi Eta Sigma; Tau Beta Pi; Chi Phi. Polit & Govt Pos: Co chmn, Door-Door Comt to Reelect the President, 72; alt deleg, Rep Nat Conv, 72. Bus & Prof Pos: Tech supt, E I Du Pont de Nemours & Co, Inc, 71- Mem: Am Inst Chem Engrs (local secy, 72-73). Relig: Catholic. Mailing Add: 1150 Vultee Blvd Nashville TN 37217

JEFFERS, MARY L (D)
Committeewoman, Calif Dem State Cent Comt
b Lebanon, Tenn; d Preston C Lloyd, MD & Lillie Officer L; m 1960 to Clifton R Jeffers. Educ: Spelman Col, 51-53; Tenn State Univ, AB, 56, MA, 57; Wayne State Univ & Univ Calif, Berkeley, grad work; Sigma Rho Sigma; Pi Sigma Alpha. Polit & Govt Pos: Committeewoman, Calif Dem State Cent Comt, 68- Bus & Prof Pos: Sec Eng & hist teacher, Detroit Unified Sch Dist, Mich, 57-59; polit sci instr, Col San Mateo, 63- Mem: Acad of Polit Sci; Northern Calif Polit Sci Asn; Am Fedn of Teachers; Am Asn Univ Prof; NAACP. Relig: Protestant. Mailing Add: 36 Thrift St San Francisco CA 94112

JEFFERSON, SHIRLEY ALMIRA (R)
VChmn, Onondaga Co Rep Comt, NY
b Mass, July 12, 29; d Harry Chester Williams & Delphine Kelland W; m 1952 to Dr Milton T Jefferson. Educ: Boston Univ, 46-48; NY Sch Interior Design, dipl, 65. Polit & Govt Pos: Coordr women's affairs, Onondaga Co Rep Comt, 66-70, vchmn, 70-; committeewoman, NY State Rep Comt, 70-; deleg, Rep Nat Conv, 72. Bus & Prof Pos: Admin asst, Beneficial Mgt, Boston, Mass, 49-52; admin asst develop, Cornell Univ, 56-58; dist mgr, US Bur Census, 70. Mem: Fedn Women's Rep Clubs NY (first vpres); Zonta Int (comt chmn, Syracuse Chap); Nat Fedn Rep Women (bd mem); Onondaga Co Hist Site Comt (adv). Relig: United Methodist. Mailing Add: 606 Oswego St Liverpool NY 13088

JEFFORDS, CLIFFORD HAROLD (D)
b Marmaduke, Ark, Feb 27, 29; s Roy E Jeffords & Sylvia Dickinson J; m 1955 to Lavina Joie Roose; c Janet Yvonne & Glenn Alan. Educ: Sec educ, Northeast Ark; various mil schs. Polit & Govt Pos: Admin asst to Congressman Bill Alexander, Ark, 68- Mil Serv: Entered as Pvt, Air Force, 48, released as SMS, 67, after serv as personnel supt & in various orgns, Korea, Japan, Okinawa, Iwo Jima & Turkey; various serv medals & campaign ribbons. Mem: Mason; Shrine; Eastern Star; Elks; life mem Jaycees. Honors & Awards: Outstanding Jaycee pres, State of Ark, 64-65. Relig: Church of Christ. Legal Res: Rte 1 Box 145B Mansfield AR 72944 Mailing Add: US Congressional Field Off Jonesboro AR 72401

JEFFORDS, JAMES MERRILL (R)
US Rep, Vt
b Rutland, Vt, May 11, 34; s Olin Merrill Jeffords & Marion Hausman J; m 1961 to Elizabeth C Daley; c Leonard Olin & Laura Louise. Educ: Yale Univ, BS, 56; Harvard Law Sch, LLB, 62. Polit & Govt Pos: Rep town chmn, Shrewsbury, Vt, 63-72, town agt, 64, town grand juror, 64; chmn, Vt Rep Fund Raising Dinner, 67; Vt State Sen, 67-68; Attorney Gen, Vt, 69-73; US Rep, Vt, 75- Bus & Prof Pos: Law clerk, Judge Ernest W Gibson, US Dist Court, 62; partner, Crowley, Bishop & Jeffords, 63-66; partner, Kinney, Carbine & Jeffords, 67-68. Mil Serv: Entered as Ens, Navy, 56, released as Lt(jg), 59, after serv in USS McNair DD 679; Comdr, Naval Res, 69; Naval Expeditionary Medal for Lebanon Crisis. Mem: Vt Bar Asn (mem bd trustees); Am Judicature Soc (mem bd dirs); Legal Aid; Lions; Elks. Relig: Congregational. Legal Res: VT Mailing Add: US House of Rep Washington DC 20515

JEFFREY, HARRY PALMER (R)
b Dayton, Ohio, Dec 26, 01; s Samuel E Jeffrey & Grace S Wilson J; m 1935 to Susan Virginia Gummer; c Harry P, Jr, Juliet L (Mrs Jacobs) & Susan J. Educ: Ohio State Univ, BA, 24, JD, 26; Phi Beta Kappa; Order of Coif; Phi Delta Phi. Polit & Govt Pos: Spec Asst Attorney Gen, Ohio, 33-36, US Rep, Third Cong Dist Ohio, 43-44. Bus & Prof Pos: Secy & gen counsel, Foremanship Found, 45-71; mem, bd dirs, of numerous corps; partner, Law Firm of Jeffrey, Donnelly, Snell, Rogers & Greenberg, currently. Mil Serv: 2nd Lt, Army Res, 27-31. Mem: Acad Polit Sci; Am Bar Asn (mem Labor sect); fel, Am Col Trial Lawyers; Mason (33 degree, Master, 36-37); CofC. Honors & Awards: Citizen Legion of Honor Award, Dayton Serv Clubs, 62. Relig: Presbyterian. Legal Res: Apt 48 2230 S Patterson Blvd Dayton OH 45409 Mailing Add: 2260 Winters Bank Tower Dayton OH 45402

JEFFREY, MILDRED (D)
b Alton, Iowa, Dec 29, 11; d Bert David McWilliams & Bertha Merritt M; m to 1936 to Homer Newman Jeffrey; c Sharon Rose & Daniel Balfour. Educ: Univ Minn, BA, 32; Bryn Mawr Col, 34. Polit & Govt Pos: Investr, Nat Recovery Admin, 35-36; deleg, White House Conf Children & Youth, 50 & 60; chmn platform comt, Mich Dem Party, 55-60; alt nat committeewoman, 57-; mem, Nat Platform Comt, 56-60; mem, Citizens Adv Comt Sch Needs, 57-59; vchmn, Mich Consumers Asn, 59; mem, Detroit Libr Comn, 59-; vchmn, Nat Comt Employ Youth, 59-; Dem Nat Committeewoman, Mich, 61-72, mem exec comt, Dem Nat Comt, 68-72, mem charter comn, currently; deleg & mem credentials comt, Dem Nat Conv, 68, deleg, 72; mem, Polit Reform Comn, Mich Dem Party, 69-70; co-chmn, Mich Comn for the Vote at 18, 70-; pres, Detroit Parks & Recreation Comn, 70-; secy, Consumer Alliance Mich, 71-; mem exec comt, Am for Dem Action, 72; mem, Mich Consumer Coun, 72- Bus & Prof Pos: Dir women's bur, Int Union United Automobile, Aircraft & Agr Implement Workers Am, 44-49, dir radio dept, 49-50 & dir commun rels dept, 51-; mgr, Sta WDET-FM, Detroit, 50-51; secy, Metrop Detroit Relig & Labor Conf, 54-59; labor rep chmn, Adult Educ Study United Commun Serv, 58-60. Honors & Awards: Distinguished Commun Serv Award, Workmen's Circle, 55; St Cyprian's Award, PE Church of Diocese, Mich, 59; Outstanding Layman of the Year Award, Detroit Coun Churches, 60; Human Rights Liberty Award, 68. Mailing Add: 8000 E Jefferson Detroit MI 48214

JEFFS, A DEAN (R)
Utah State Rep
Mailing Add: 220 E 1950 South Orem UT 84057

JELONEK, SUSAN JEAN (R)
b Oakland, Calif, Sept 9, 50; d Chester John Jelonek & Maryana Szczepanski J; single. Educ: Univ Santa Clara, 68-69, Univ Calif, Berkeley, BA, 72; Gamma Phi Beta. Polit & Govt Pos: Task force mem, White House Conf on Youth, Foreign Rels Task Force, 69-70; cong intern, US Rep Jerome Waldie, Calif, summer 71; deleg, Rep Nat Conv, 72. Bus & Prof Pos: Consult, MicroEar Sound Prod, Richmond, Calif, 72- Mem: Prytanean (bd dirs, 73). Relig: Catholic. Mailing Add: 2704 Glasgow Ct Richmond CA 94806

JENCKES, JOSEPH SHERBURNE, V (R)
b Phoenix, Ariz, Sept 24, 35; s Joseph Sherburne Jenckes, IV & Alexandra Karneva J; m 1972 to Linda Sue Leppa. Educ: Univ Ariz, JD, 61; Phi Delta Theta. Polit & Govt Pos: Asst US Attorney, Chief Criminal Div, Dist Ariz, Phoenix, 69-73; admin asst to US Sen Paul Fannin, Ariz, 73- Mem: State Bar Ariz. Honors & Awards: Spec Achievement Award, US Dept Justice, 72. Legal Res: 601 W Flynn Lane Phoenix AZ 85013 Mailing Add: Rm 3121 Dirksen Senate Off Bldg Washington DC 20510

JENEWEIN, JUDITH KAY (JUDY) (D)
Nat Committeewoman, Ohio Young Dem
b Bellaire, Ohio, Sept 8, 45; d Melvin Wayne Jenewein & Hazel Crum J; single. Educ: Ohio Univ, Belmont Co Branch, 69-70. Polit & Govt Pos: Pres, Belmont Co Young Dem, Ohio, 70-71; recording secy, Ohio Young Dem, 70-72, nat committeewoman, 72-; nat comt mem, Young Dem Am, 72- Bus & Prof Pos: Dep auditor, personal tax dept, Belmont Co Auditor's Off, Ohio, 64-70, dep auditor, personal tax dept, Belmont Co Auditor's Off. Ohio, 64-70, dep auditor in chg payroll dept, 70-75. Relig: Protestant. Legal Res: 409 S Main St Bethesda OH 43719 Mailing Add: Box 126 Bethesda OH 43719

JENISON, EDWARD HALSEY (R)
b Fond du Lac, Wis, July 27, 07; s Ernest Manley Jenison & Laura Hinsey J; m 1929 to Barbara Weinburgh; c Edward Hinsey. Educ: Univ Wis, 3 years. Polit & Govt Pos: US Rep, Ill, 47-52; Ill State Rep, 65-66; alt deleg, Rep Nat Conv, 68; deleg, Sixth Ill Const Conv, 69-70. Bus & Prof Pos: Ed & publ, Daily Beacon News, Paris, Ill, 31- Mil Serv: Entered as Lt(jg), Navy, 43, released as Lt Comdr, 46, after serv in Naval Aviation. Mem: Sigma Delta Chi. Relig: Protestant. Mailing Add: 711 Shaw Ave Paris IL 61944

JENKINS, EDGAR LANIER (D)
b Young Harris, Ga, Jan 4, 33; s Charlie S Jenkins & Evia Souther J; m 1960 to Jo Thomasson; c Janice & Amy. Educ: Young Harris Col, AA, 51; Univ Ga, LLB, 59. Polit & Govt Pos: Exec secy to US Rep Phil Landrum, Ga, Washington, DC, 59-61, rep for Ninth Dist, 63-; asst US Attorney, NDist, Atlanta, 61-63; mem, Ga State Dem Exec Comt, formerly, mem rules comt, Ga State Dem Party, formerly. Mil Serv: Entered as S/A, Coast Guard, 52, released as 2nd Petty Off, 55, after serv in Air/Sea Rescue Unit, Alaskan Command, 53-54. Mem: Ga Bar Asn; VFW; Lions; Am Legion; Jaycees. Relig: Baptist. Legal Res: Airport Rd Jasper GA 30143 Mailing Add: Box 400 Jasper GA 30143

JENKINS, JEFF WAYNE (D)
b Elizabethton, Tenn, Nov 22, 50; s Kenneth Paul Jenkins & Edna Earl Wilson J; single. Educ: ETenn State Univ, BS, 73. Polit & Govt Pos: Organizer & coord, ETenn State Univ Students for McGovern, 71-72, treas, Col Young Dem, 72-; alt deleg, Dem Nat Conv, 72. Bus & Prof Pos: Teacher social studies, currently. Mem: Elizabethton Educ Asn (vpres, 75-); Tenn Educ Asn (polit liaison individual). Relig: Baptist. Mailing Add: 377 Pine Hill Rd Elizabethton TN 37643

JENKINS, LOUIS (WOODY) (D)
La State Rep
b Baton Rouge, La, Jan 3, 47; s Louis Elwood Jenkins, Sr & Doris Laverne Rowlett J; m 1968 to Diane Carole Aker. Educ: La State Univ, BA in Jour, 69, Law Sch, JD, 72. Polit & Govt Pos: Mem, La Dem State Cent Comt, 71-; deleg, Dem Nat Conv, 72; La State Rep, 72-, chmn joint subcomt on health, 74-; deleg, La Const Conv, 73, co-auth, Declaration of Rights, La Const Conv, 74; deleg, Dem Nat Mid-Term Conf, 74; mem, Dem Adv Coun Elected Officials, 75- Bus & Prof Pos: Announcer, Radio Sta WLCS, Baton Rouge, La, 64-65; announcer, WAFB-TV, 65-66; ed & publ, North Baton Rouge J, 66-69; advert agency owner, 72- Publ: General practice section: what's in it for you?, Student Lawyer J, 5/71; Quotas hurt everyone, Human Events, 12/72; La Constitution: declaration of rights, Loyola Law Rev, spring 75. Mem: Am Bar Asn (asst ed, Docket Call, 72-); Nat Taxpayers Union (bd adv, 73-); Heritage Found; North Baton Rouge Lions (bd dirs, 71-73); Am Legis Exchange Coun (nat secy, 74-75). Relig: Methodist. Mailing Add: PO Box 52889 Baton Rouge LA 70805

JENKINS, MARY MAXINE (R)
Chairwoman, Lawrence Co Rep Cent Comt, Ohio
b Lawrence Co, Ohio, Sept 27, 26; d Salem Fuller & Eva Lee Farley F; m 1947 to Jesse A Jenkins; c Audrey, Cheyrl, Marsha, Robert, Ronald & T J. Educ: Rome High Sch, Proctorville, Ohio, grad, 44. Polit & Govt Pos: Pres, Fairland Rep Club, Ohio, 69-71; chairwoman, Lawrence Co Rep Cent Comt, 74- Mem: Proctorville Womans Club (corresponding secy, 74-); Fairland Womans Rep Club. Relig: United Methodist; pres, United Methodist Women, 65-67. Legal Res: State Rte 243 Proctorville OH 45669 Mailing Add: Box 160A Rte 2 Proctorville OH 45669

JENKINS, MERRILL (D)
Utah State Rep
Mailing Add: RFD 2 Box 192 Ogden UT 84404

JENKINS, WILLIAM CALVIN (D)
Mayor, Scottsdale, Ariz
b Kansas City, Kans, May 4, 29; s Albert Thomas Jenkins & Ruth Viola Keller J; m 1950 to Grace Susan Liebenow; c Debbie & Mark. Educ: Kansas City Jr Col, AA, 49; Ariz State Univ, BS, 52, MA, 63; Phi Delta Kappa; Phi Alpha Theta. Polit & Govt Pos: City councilman, Scottsdale, Ariz, 66-74, mayor, 74- Bus & Prof Pos: Teacher social studies, Scottsdale High Sch, Ariz, 58- Mil Serv: Entered as Ens, Navy, 53, released, 56, after serv in Off Naval Intel; Capt, Naval Res, 74; Meritorious Unit Commendation; Armed Forces Res Medal. Mem: Naval Reserve Asn; Nat Educ Asn; Nat Coun Social Studies; US Conf Mayors (task force on aging, 74-, vchmn mayor's comt bicentennial, 74-); Nat League Cities (comt pub safety, 75-). Relig: Protestant. Mailing Add: 7719 E Vernon Scottsdale AZ 85257

JENNESS, LINDA JANE (SOCIALIST WORKERS PARTY)
b El Reno, Okla, Jan 11, 41; d Wilson Marshal Osteen & Velma Dull O; m to Douglas Jenness. Educ: Antioch Col, 58-62. Polit & Govt Pos: Cand for President of US on Socialist Workers Party Ticket, 71-72; nat comt mem, Socialist Workers Party, 72- Publ: Co-auth, Women & the Cuban Revolution, 70, auth, Socialism & Democracy, 72 & ed, Feminism & Socialism, 72, Pathfinder Press. Mailing Add: 237 E Fifth St New York NY 10003

JENNINGS, GARY (R)
Wyo State Rep
Mailing Add: Rte 1 Box 434 Riverton WY 82501

JENNINGS, JAMES PATRICK THOMAS (R)
b Scranton, Pa, Nov 24, 18; s James Patrick Jennings & Helen Moran J; m 1951 to Dorothy Knight; c Patricia, Jacqueline & James P, Jr. Educ: Lackawanna Jr Col, 38-39; Univ Pa Wharton Sch of Bus, AA, 42. Polit & Govt Pos: Treas, Clarks Green Borough, Pa, 54-; co campaign chmn, Lackawanna Co Rep Party, 63, co vchmn, 64-72; deleg, Rep Nat Conv, 72. Bus & Prof Pos: Self employed pub acct, 47- Mem: Pa Soc Pub Acct; Nat Soc Pub Acct; KofC; Scranton Country Club; Pa Soc. Relig: Catholic. Mailing Add: 315 Gordon Dr Clarks Green PA 18411

JENNINGS, RENZ DIXON (D)
b Phoenix, Ariz, Aug 4, 41; s Renz L Jennings & Leola Lesueur J; single. Educ: Ariz State Univ, BA, 64. Polit & Govt Pos: Dem committeeman, Palmcroft Precinct, Ariz, 64-65; Ariz State Rep, 69-71; judge, East Phoenix Justice Court 1, 71-; deleg, Dem Nat Conv, 72. Mailing Add: 1311 E McKinley Phoenix AZ 85006

JENNINGS, RUDOLPH DILLON (D)
b Bluefield, WVa, Oct 28, 23; s William Webb Jennings & Vangie Francisco J; m 1949 to Maymie Jean Hubbard; c Nigel Lewis, Laura Lee, Maxine Elizabeth & James Webb. Educ: Morris Harvey Col, BS in Acct, 54; Blackfriers. Polit & Govt Pos: Deleg at lg, Dem Nat Conv, 64 & 68; cong candidate, Dem Primary Election, WVa, 66; mem, Mercer Co Dem Club, 66-; Dem cand for State Senate, Tenth Cong Dist WVa, 72; deleg, WVa Dem State Conv, 72. Bus & Prof Pos: Owner, R D Jennings, Acct, 55; secy, Kearns Ins Agency, Inc, 62-73; instr, WVa Bus Col, 64-65; pres, Acct Systs, Inc, 64-67. Mil Serv: Entered as Pvt, Army Air Force, 42, released as Sgt, 45, after serv in 405th Fighter Squadron, ETO, 44-45; Sharpshooter Medal; Distinguished Unit Badge; Normandy & Rhineland Campaign Stars; European-African-Mid East Theater Ribbons. Publ: News articles in Waverly News & Waverly Watchman, 59. Mem: Int Platform Asn; Am Legion; Waverly Toastmasters (former pres); Nat Coun United Presby Men (past pres, Waverly Chap); Air Force Asn. Honors & Awards: Award of Merit, Blackfriers; Personality of the South, 68. Relig: Presbyterian. Legal Res: 608 College Ave Bluefield WV 24701 Mailing Add: PO Box 647 Bluefield WV 24701

JENNINGS, SHIRLEY KIMBALL (D)
b West Peabody, Mass, Sept 11, 22; d Linwood Kimball & Carrie Sawyer K; m to Sam Jennings; c John Charles & Nancy Sawyer Merrill. Educ: Univ NH, BS, 44; Alpha Xi Delta. Polit & Govt Pos: NH State Rep, 67-74; alt deleg, Rep Nat Conv, 68 & 72; mem, Lebanon City Coun, formerly; mayor, Lebanon, NH, formerly; asst chmn, NH State Rep Comt, formerly; mem appeals tribunal & chmn adv coun, Dept Employ Security, formerly; comnr pub utilities, State of NH, 73-74. Mem: Lebanon Woman's Club; Alice Peck Day Hosp Auxiliary; Bus & Prof Women. Honors & Awards: Citizen of the Year, Lebanon, 73. Relig: Protestant. Mailing Add: Bartlesville OK 74003

JENNINGS, WILLIAM PAT (D)
Dem Nat Committeeman, Va
b Camp, Va, Aug 20, 19; m to Annabel Cox; c Grover C, Pat, Jr, Mary Ann & Richard Joel. Educ: Va Polytech Inst, BS in Agr, 41. Polit & Govt Pos: Sheriff, Smyth Co, Va, 48-54; US Rep, Va, 54-66, mem, Comts on Agr & Ways & Means, US House Rep, formerly, clerk, US House Rep, 67-; deleg, Dem Nat Conv, 68 & 72; Dem Nat Committeeman, Va, 72-; mem, Va Dem State Cent Comt, 73- Bus & Prof Pos: Bus & farm interests, Marion, Va, mem bd trustees, Va Col, Lynchburg, mem bd dirs, Bank of Marion & chmn bd, Jennings-Warren Motor Co, Marion, currently. Mil Serv: Maj, Army, 41-46, served in US & ETO; Col, Air Force Res, 70- Mem: Asn of Secretaries Gen of Parliaments; Kiwanis; Mason; Shriner; Am Legion. Relig: Methodist. Legal Res: Marion VA 24354 Mailing Add: H-105 The Capitol Washington DC 20515

JENNISON, HAROLD STEWART (R)
Chmn, Lane Co Rep Party, Kans
b Scott City, Kans, Nov 24, 22; s Herlan Stewart Jennison & Katharine Ehmke J; m 1949 to Yvonne Siegrist; c Pamela F & Lois D. Educ: Ft Hays Kans State Col, 3 semesters. Polit & Govt Pos: Precinct committeeman, Cheyenne Twp Rep Party, Kans, 52-; dir, Common Sch Dist, 56-65; chmn, Lane Co Rep Party, 56-; treas, Kans Rep Comt, 58-60; pres, Unified Sch Dist, 65-69. Bus & Prof Pos: Vpres, First State Bank, Healy, Kans, 46-49, cashier, 49-73, exec vpres & cashier, 73- Mil Serv: Entered as Pvt, Army & transferred to Air Force, 43, released as 2nd Lt, 45, after serv as B-24 navigator. Relig: Methodist. Mailing Add: Healy KS 67850

JENRETTE, JOHN WILSON, JR (D)
US Rep, SC
b Conway, SC, May 19, 36; s John Wilson Jenrette, Sr (deceased) & Mary Herring Jenrette Housand; m 1960 to Sara Louise Jordan; c Elizabeth & Harold. Educ: Wofford Col, AB, 58; Univ SC Sch Law, LLB, 62; Kappa Sigma. Polit & Govt Pos: City judge, Ocean Drive Beach, SC, 62-68, city attorney, 62-69; SC State Rep, Horry Co, 65-72; vchmn urban affairs comt, Coun State Govt; Dem nominee for US Rep, Sixth Cong Dist, 72; US Rep, SC, 75- Mil Serv: Entered as 2nd Lt, Army, 59, released as 1st Lt, 59, after serv in Co A, 18th Bn, 1st Training Regt; Capt, Cmndg Officer, A Co, 263rd Armored Div, SC Nat Guard, formerly; Capt, Judge Adv Gen Dept, Air Force Res, currently. Mem: Am Bar Asn; SC Munic Asn; Farm Bur; Lions; CofC. Honors & Awards: Distinguished Serv Award, SC Munic Asn; One of Outstanding Young Men of Am. Relig: Methodist. Mailing Add: 457 N Main St North Myrtle Beach SC 29582

JENSEN, CARL ARTHUR (R)
Minn State Sen
b Sleepy Eye, Minn, Dec 11, 20; s Jens Jensen & Hulda Hansen J; m 1948 to Lorraine Johnson; c Steven, Karen, Scott, Paul & Bruce. Educ: Univ Minn, BSL, 48, LLB, 49; Acacia. Polit & Govt Pos: Deleg, Minn State Rep Conv, 50-; deleg, Brown Co Rep Conv, Minn, 50-; Minn State Rep, Brown Co, 51-61; mem, Co Rep Comt, 60-66; attorney, Minn Asn of Twp Officers; city attorney, Sleepy Eye, 58-; Minn State Sen, 67- Bus & Prof Pos: Attorney, Sleepy Eye, Minn, 49- Mil Serv: Entered as Pvt, Army Air Force, 44, released as S/Sgt, 46. Mem: Minn & Am Bar Asns; Sleepy Eye Indust Develop Corp (bd dirs); Sleepy Eye United Fund (attorney); Lions. Relig: Lutheran. Mailing Add: 209 First Ave S Sleepy Eye MN 56085

JENSEN, DONALD HUGO (D)
b Denison, Iowa, Mar 26, 20; s Hugo P Jensen & Grace Mullen J; m 1950 to Ann Caryle; c Linda Ann, Mary Lisa & Andrea Kay. Educ: Denison High Sch, grad, 38. Polit & Govt Pos: Chmn, Third Ward Dem Comt, Iowa, 60; chmn, Crawford Co Dem Cent Comt, formerly. Bus & Prof Pos: Receiving mgr, Montgomery Ward, 39-69. Mem: KofC. Relig: Catholic. Mailing Add: 1339 Fifth Ave N Denison IA 51442

JENSEN, GERALDINE MARY (D)
b Chicago, Ill, May 9, 46; d Vernon Human Jensen & Kathryn King J; single. Polit & Govt Pos: Alt deleg, Dem Nat Conv, 72; alt deleg-at-lg, Dem Nat Mid-Term Conf, 74; chmn, Young Dem Cook Co, Ill, 74- Bus & Prof Pos: Supvr, Cook Co Sheriff's Off, 72- Mem: Ill Police Asn; Nat Fedn Bus & Prof Women; Concerned Citizens for a Better Community; Nat Alliance of Young Polit Leaders. Honors & Awards: Outstanding Woman, Young Dem of Ill, 71; Outstanding Woman, Young Dem of Cook Co, 72. Relig: Catholic. Mailing Add: 4157 N Paulina St Chicago IL 60613

JENSEN, H L (D)
Wyo State Rep
b Salt Lake City, Utah, Dec 26, 28; s Charles LeRoy Jensen & Lela Drissel J; m 1955 to Doloras Ann Lumley; c Mike & stepdaughter, Louise Leona Jacobs. Educ: Univ Utah, 46-48. Polit & Govt Pos: Wyo State Rep, 75- Bus & Prof Pos: Dir, Jackson CofC, Wyo, 57-59; dir, Wyo Liquor Dealers, Cheyenne, 61-68, vpres, 68- Mil Serv: Air Force. Mem: AF&AM; Wyo Consistory; AAONMS; Elks. Honors & Awards: Five Year Chmn Award, Teton Co Heart Fund; Retailer of Year, Wyo Liquor Dealers Asn, 72. Relig: Episcopal. Legal Res: 132 Moran St Jackson WY 83001 Mailing Add: Box 1165 Jackson WY 83001

JENSEN, INGEMAN (R)
SDak State Rep
Mailing Add: Stockholm SD 57264

JENSEN, JOHN W (D)
Maine State Rep
b Portland, Maine, Oct 9, 52; s Carl P Jensen & Emily Paulin J; single. Educ: Univ Maine, Portland-Gorham, 71- Polit & Govt Pos: Southern coordr, Maine Young Dem, 69-70; mem, Cumberland Co Dem Comt, 69-; chmn, Cumberland Co Young Dem, 71-72; chmn, Portland Dem City Comt, 72-; Maine State Rep, 75- Bus & Prof Pos: Develop dir, Maine Audubon Soc, 71- Mem: Nat & Mass Socs Prof Fund Raisers. Relig: Catholic. Legal Res: 9 Boynton St Portland ME 04102 Mailing Add: PO Box 943 Portland ME 04104

JENSEN, LINDA JANE STRNAD (D)
Mem, Nebr Dem State Cent Comt
b Omaha, Nebr, June 12, 40; d Frank J Strnad & Helen R Lierley; m 1962 to Denis Alan Jensen; c Mark Alan & Melinda Jane. Educ: Univ Nebr, Omaha, BS, cum laude, 62, MS in Educ, 71; Sigma Kappa; Kappa Delta Pi; Corinthions & Waokiya; charter pres, campus YWCA. Polit & Govt Pos: Mayor's Lit Study Comt, 61; neighborhood chmn, Nebr Cong Campaign, 68; charter pres, Douglas Co Dem Women, Nebr, 69-70; eighth ward chmn, Douglas Co Cent Comt, 70-72; deleg, Nebr State Dem Conv, 70 & 72; deleg, Douglas Co Dem Conv, 70 & 72; mem credentials comt, 70; mem Omaha steering comt, McGovern Campaign, 71-72; deleg, Dem Nat Conv, 72; mem, Nebr Dem State Cent Comt, 72-, legis chmn, 72- Mem: Nat Educ Asn; Nebr High Sch Press Asn; Dem Women Dist II (charter pres, 69-70); Mrs Jaycees (historian, 65-70); PTA. Honors & Awards: Outstanding Ward Co-chmn, Dem Co Cent Comt, 71. Mailing Add: 2213 S 84th St Omaha NE 68127

JENSEN, MAYNARD WAYNE (D)
Co-Chmn, Hamilton Co Dem Party, Nebr
b Marquette, Nebr, Dec 15, 24; s Hans O Jensen & Helen Christensen J; m 1946; c David, Andrew, Gay & Clinton. Educ: Univ Nebr, 42-43; Farmhouse Fraternity. Polit & Govt Pos: Mem, Nebr Dem State Cent Comt, 60-; co-chmn, Hamilton Co Dem Party, 65-; mem state exec comt, Nebr Dem Party, 72- Bus & Prof Pos: Pres, Jensen Farms Inc, 46- Mil Serv: Entered as Apprentice Seaman, Navy, 43, released as Motor Machinist 1/C, 46, after serv in Amphibious Force, ETO, 44-45. Mem: Am Legion (dept comdr, 71-72); Mason; Shrine (pres, Cent Nebr Club, 69); Elks; CofC. Honors & Awards: Map Maker, CofC, 60; Cert of Honor, Nebr Dept of Agr, 62; Hon Chap Farmer, Future Farmer of Am, 68; Action Time Comdr, Nat Am Legion, 72. Relig: Methodist. Mailing Add: Rte 2 Box 102 Aurora NE 68818

JENSEN, MORONI L (D)
Utah State Rep
Mailing Add: 2940 Filmore St Salt Lake City UT 84106

JENSEN, ROBERT C (DFL)
Minn State Rep
Mailing Add: 17837 Flagstaff Ave W Farmington MN 55024

JENSEN, THOMAS LEE (R)
Minority Leader, Tenn House of Rep
b Knoxville, Tenn, Oct 28, 34; s Irving Oscar Jensen & Christine Scarbrough J; m 1960 to Carolyn Frances Carter; c Lucinda Anne & Thomas Carter. Educ: Univ Tenn, 52-58. Polit & Govt Pos: Tenn State Rep, 66-, majority whip, Tenn House of Rep, 68-70, minority leader, 70-; chmn intergovt rels comt, Nat Legis Conf, 73- Bus & Prof Pos: Pres, Jensen Corp, 58-66; vpres, Delta Cleaning Contractors, 64-68; pres, Delta Develop Corp, 65- Mem: Nat Asn Independent Businessmen; Nat Conf State Legislatures (pres-elect); CofC; Better Bus Bur; Nat Soc State Legislators (pres, 73). Honors & Awards: Jaycee of the Year, 66; Tenn Jaycees Key Man, 67; Knoxville Outstanding Young Man, 70. Relig: Baptist. Legal Res: 2323 Juniper Dr Knoxville TN 37912 Mailing Add: PO Box 3310 Knoxville TN 37917

JENSEN, WILLIAM MARTIN (R)
SDak State Rep
b Omaha, Nebr, Oct 31, 03; s Martin Christian Jensen & Marie Nelsen J; m 1929 to Agnes Marie Stromer; c Clifford Wayne, Janet Jeanine (Mrs Krogman) & Barry Marlin. Polit & Govt Pos: SDak State Rep, 67- Bus & Prof Pos: Pres & dir, Fed Land Bank Asn, Winner, SDak, currently; pres & dir, Cherry Todd Elec, Mission, currently; dir, SDak Asn of Coop, currently. Mem: Farmers Coop Oil Asn, Winner, SDak; Mason; Oriental Consistory; Shrine; Eastern Star. Honors & Awards: Agr Conserv Plaque. Relig: Methodist. Mailing Add: Rte 1 White River SD 57579

JEPHSON, EVELYN S (D)
Mem State Comt, Maine Dem Party
b Bristol, Conn, Aug 16, 27; d Karl Scheschinski & Pauline Doplestein S; m 1950 to George Hastings Jephson; c Leslie Carla. Educ: Waterbury Sch Nursing, 46. Polit & Govt Pos: Mem, Waldoboro Sch Bd, Maine, 62-64; mem, Maine Dem State Platform Comt, 62, 64, 68, 70 & 72; deleg, Dem Nat Conv, 64, 68 & 72; mem, Platform Comt, 64 & 68; justice of the peace, Maine, 66; mem, Maine Dept of Environ Protection, 67-; mem, Gov Adv Comn on Status of Women, 67-; treas, Waldoboro Dem Women's Club, 68; dedimus justice, Maine, 68; mem, State Comt, Maine Dem Party, Lincoln Co, 68-; mem, Bd of Selectmen, Town of Waldoboro, 70-; secy, Waldoboro Dem Town Comt, 72- Bus & Prof Pos: Owner, Shop of Folly Farm, 68- Mem: Saco River Corridor. Relig: Lutheran. Legal Res: Bremen Rd Waldoboro ME 04572 Mailing Add: 5 Forest Lane Kennebunk ME 04043

JEPPSON, JEFFORD J (R)
b Granville, Ill, Oct 4, 30; s Jefford M Jeppson & Sadie Gately J; m 1953 to Lorreta Jeanne Buff; c Kim Marie. Educ: Hopkins High, dipl, 48; jr col, one year. Polit & Govt Pos: Alderman, Granville, Ill, 57-; precinct committeeman, Granville Rep Party, 60-; chmn, Putnam Co Rep Cent Comt, formerly. Mil Serv: Entered as Pvt, Army, 51, released as Sgt, 52, after serv in Co K, 14th Inf, 25th Div, Korean Theatre, 51-52; Combat Infantryman's Badge with Bronze Star; Korean Serv Medal. Mem: Mason; VFW; Am Legion. Relig: Protestant. Mailing Add: 518 W Main Granville IL 61326

JEPSEN, ROGER WILLIAM (R)
b Cedar Falls, Iowa, Dec 23, 28; s Ernest Emil Jepsen & Esther Sorensen J; m 1958 to Dee Ann Delaney; c Jeffrey, Anne Marie, Craig, Deborah, Linda & Coy. Educ: Ariz State Univ, BS in Psychol, 50, MA in Counseling & Guid, 53; Blue Key; Tau Kappa Epsilon; Psi Chi. Polit & Govt Pos: Chmn, Scott Co Young Rep, Iowa, 57-60; chmn, Scott Co Rep Party, 61; co supvr, Scott Co, 62-65; Iowa State Sen, 66-68; Lt Gov, Iowa, 68-72; deleg, Rep Nat Conv, 72. Bus & Prof Pos: Vet adv & asst registr, Ariz State Univ, 50-53; ins agent, Am United Life, 54-56; br mgr, Conn Gen Life Ins Co, 56-71; exec vpres, Agridustrial Electronics, Inc, 73- Mil Serv: Entered as Pvt, Army, 46, released as Sgt, 47, after serv in 82nd Airborne Div; Capt, Army Res, 48-60. Mem: Nat Asn Life Underwriters; Gen Agents & Mgrs Asn; Nat Lt Gov Conf (vchmn, 70-71); Kaaba Shrine; Jesters. Relig: Lutheran. Mailing Add: 2330 Harrison St Davenport IA 52801

JERGESON, GREG (D)
Mont State Sen
Mailing Add: Box 8 Star Rte 71 Chinook MT 59523

JERNIGAN, GLENN R (D)
NC State Sen
Mailing Add: 2414 Rollinghill Rd Fayetteville NC 28304

JERNIGAN, ROBERTS HARRELL, JR (D)
NC State Rep
b Ahoskie, NC, Nov 24, 15; s Roberts Harrell Jernigan & Jessie Garrett J; m 1949 to Linda Williams; c Roberts, III, Elizabeth & Clawson. Educ: Naval Acad Prep Sch, 32-33; Wake Forest Col, 33-36; Univ NC, AB, 37, Law Sch, 37-39. Polit & Govt Pos: Chmn, Hertford Co Dem Exec Comt, NC, 58; NC State Rep, 63- Bus & Prof Pos: Farmer; pres & treas, Ahoskie Meat & Provision Co, Inc; Standard Vacuum Oil Co mgr, Peiping Off, China, pre-World War II. Mil Serv: Prisoner of Japanese, 23 months, World War II; Ensign, USN, 43-46; Invasion of SFrance. Mem: Sigma Nu; Rotary; Hertford Co Young Dem Club. Relig: Episcopal; sr warden. Mailing Add: 401 N Curtis St Ahoskie NC 27910

JERNIGAN, WALLACE LAWSON (D)
b Jesup, Ga, June 23, 25; s Fred Wallace Jernigan & Sammie Bishop J; m 1951 to Carolyn Moore; c Nancy Elizabeth. Educ: Ga Inst Tech, BSCE, 46; Am Soc Civil Engrs; Sigma Phi Epsilon (treas); Interfraternity Coun. Polit & Govt Pos: Co surveyor, Clinch Co, Ga, 49-53; Ga State Sen, 59-60, chmn educ comt, Ga State Senate, 59-60; Ga State Rep, 61; admin asst to Gov S Ernest Vandiver, Ga, 61 & exec secy, 62; mem, Gov Carl Sanders' Comn to Improve Educ, 63; dist rep for US Rep W S Stuckey, Jr, Ga, 67- Mem: Ga Funeral Dirs (pres, Eighth Dist, 61); Ga Beekeepers Asn (past pres); Mason; Lions; Ga Sportsman Fedn. Relig: Baptist. Legal Res: 215 Peagler St Homerville GA 31634 Mailing Add: 401 Sweat St Homerville GA 31634

JERNSTEDT, KENNETH A (R)
Ore State Sen
Mailing Add: 911 Pine St Hood River OR 97031

JERREL, BETTYE LOU (R)
VChmn, Vanderburgh Co Rep Party, Ind
b Evansville, Ind, Oct 29, 30; d John Brill Baird & Georgia Howell B; m 1949 to Bryan Leigh Jerrel; c Cynthia Leigh & John Bryan. Educ: Univ Evansville, BS, 62, MA, 66; Phi Kappa Phi; Mortar Bd; Alpha Omicron Pi. Polit & Govt Pos: Vchmn, Vanderburgh Co Rep Party, Ind, 58-; State Textbk Comnr, 73-; park comnr, Evansville, 74- Mem: Ind State Teachers Asn; Evansville Teachers Asn; Nat Educ Asn; Nat Park Bd Asn. Relig: Presbyterian. Legal Res: 1529 Adams Ave Evansville IN 47714 Mailing Add: Box 2544 Sta D Evansville IN 47714

JERVIS, ELOISE KATHERINE (R)
b Venango, Nebr, Apr 25, 19; d Daniel Foster Van Voorhies & Hadie Schneider V; wid; c Judith Kay (Mrs Joe E Swain) & Daniel Robert. Educ: Chillicothe Bus Col, Mo, 37; Berea Col, Ky, 64-65; Hopkinsville Commun Col, 71-73. Polit & Govt Pos: Acct, Sioux Ord Depot, Dept of Army, Sidney, Nebr, 44-49; admin asst, Gallup Area Off, Bur Indian Affairs, NMex, 57-59; exec secy, Army & Air Force Exchange Serv, Ofuna, Japan, 61-63; exec secy, Tenth Med Lab, Landstuhl, Germany, 66-68; alt deleg, Rep Nat Conv, 72; chairperson, Hopkinsville-Christian Co Planning & Zoning Comn, 75- Bus & Prof Pos: Hosp admnr, Sidney Hosp, Nebr, 52-57; asst to dean of women, Berea Col, Ky, 63-66; exec secy, Pennyroyal Area Develop Dist, Inc, Hopkinsville, 68-70; equal employ opportunity counr, Med Dept Activity, Ft Campbell, Ky, 74-, fed women's coordr, 75- Publ: Co-auth, Initial overall economic development plan, Spindletop Research, Lexington, Ky, 70. Mem: Hopkinsville Art Guild; Hopkinsville Bus & Prof Club; Christian Co Rep Club; Eastern Star (secy, Chap 2, Yokohama, Japan, 62, treas 63). Honors & Awards: Sustained Superior Serv Awards, Gallup Area Off, Bur Indian Affairs, NMex, 59, Army & Air Force Exchange Serv, Ofuna, Japan, 63 & Tenth Med Lab, Landstuhl, Germany, 68; one-man art show, Hopkinsville Art Guild, 67. Relig: Presbyterian. Mailing Add: 2921 Cox Mill Rd Hopkinsville KY 42240

JESK, JAMES WILBERT (D)
Committeeman, Ill Dem Cent Comt
b Chicago, Ill, May 14, 07; s Michael Jesk & Bertha Bartels J; m 1929 to Mary Ruth Lyons; c James W, Jr, Mary (Mrs Rust), Dale Edward, Terrance, Sharon (Mrs Poe), John & Robin. Educ: Chicago Law Sch, LLB, 33. Polit & Govt Pos: US Postmaster, Oak Forest, Ill, 42-45; supvr, Bremen Twp, Ill, 49-; committeeman, Ill Dem Cent Comt, 64- Bus & Prof Pos: Dir, Interstate Bank of Oak Forest, 69- Mem: Lions; Twp Off Ill. Relig: Catholic. Mailing Add: 15146 Cicero Ave Oak Forest IL 60452

JESSE, NORMAN GALE (D)
Iowa State Rep
b Des Moines, Iowa, Nov 9, 37; s James Rollin Jesse & Helen Grace Mahan J; single. Educ: Iowa State Univ, BS, 61; Drake Univ Law Sch, Des Moines, Iowa, LLB, 64; Theta Xi Soc Fraternity; Phi Alpha Delta Legal Fraternity. Polit & Govt Pos: Iowa State Rep, Polk Co, 69- Bus & Prof Pos: Attorney-at-law, Phipps, Jesse & LeTourneau, Des Moines, Iowa, 73- Mem: Polk Co, Iowa State & Am Bar Asns; Iowa Dem Conf; Iowa Civil Liberties Union. Relig: Lutheran. Legal Res: 2016 Avalon Rd Des Moines IA 50314 Mailing Add: Suite J 3821 71st St Des Moines IA 50322

JESSON, BRAD (D)
Polit & Govt Pos: Former chmn, Ark State Dem Cent Comt Mailing Add: 1601 Rogers Ave Ft Smith AR 72901

JESSUP, BEN F, SR (D)
Ga State Rep
b Chester, Ga, Sept 7, 15; s Ben F Jessup & Lissie Mae Coley J; m 1936 to Lillie Mae Barrow;

c Ben F, Jr & Wayne. Educ: Eastman High Sch, 33-34. Polit & Govt Pos: Mem city coun, Cochran, Ga, 48-55; Ga State Rep, 48-60 & 65- Bus & Prof Pos: Auto dealer, 40- Mem: Moose; Elks. Relig: Baptist. Mailing Add: Box 468 Cochran GA 31014

JESSUP, ROGER L (R)
Ind State Sen
b Feb 23, 29; married; c four. Educ: Purdue Univ, BS; Ball State Univ, MA. Polit & Govt Pos: Ind State Rep, 67-72; Ind State Sen, 72- Bus & Prof Pos: Owner & operator of farm; high sch teacher. Mem: Fairmount Masonic Lodge; Am Legion. Mailing Add: 383 East Rd 1200 South Summitville IN 46370

JETT, LOVELL DWAYNE (D)
Chmn, Bracken Co Dem Cent Comt, Ky
b Germantown, Ky, July 11, 38; s Fay Lovell Jett & Elsie Keens J; m 1961 to Janice Marie Haitz; c Jennifer Dwayne. Educ: Bracken Co High Sch, grad, 56. Polit & Govt Pos: Sheriff, Bracken Co, Ky, 70-; chmn, Bracken Co Dem Cent Comt, 71- Mil Serv: Entered as Pvt, E-1, Army Res, 55, released as E-8, 63, after serv in Hq Co. Mem: Jaycees (state dir, Bracken Co, 71-72); Lions. Relig: Methodist. Mailing Add: Box 264 Miami St Brooksville KY 41004

JEVITZ, JOHN LOUIS (R)
Exec Secy, Will Co Rep Cent Comt, Ill
b Chicago, Ill, Apr 24, 01; s John J Jevitz & Cecelia Hren J (deceased); m 1925 to Lottie Marie Witczak; c Dorothy M (Mrs Reno Sartori), Geraldine A (Mrs Stuart Christensen), John D & Eugene J. Educ: St Joseph's Parochial, Seventh Grade; Farragut Pub Sch, Eighth grade grad. Polit & Govt Pos: Dep twp assessor, Joliet, Ill, 27-33; precinct committeeman, Rep Town & Co Cent Comts, Ill, 27-38 & 48-69; asst supvr, Will Co Bd Supvr, 29-33; dep sheriff, Will Co, 38-42, officer & chief dep sheriff, 48-52; exec secy, Will Co Rep Cent Comt, 50-; supt forest preserves, Will Co, 56-69; Slovenian adv nationalities div, Rep Nat Comt, 60-; town clerk, Joliet, 69-; campaign mgr, several successful Rep local off cand. Mem: Am Fraternal Union (past Supreme Vpres); Western Slavonic Asn; Men's Holy Name Soc (pres, St Joseph's Parish Chap, 60); Eagles; Am Cancer Soc (crusade chmn, Will Co Chap, 60). Honors & Awards: Recipient of the only Gold Life Time Presidency, Old Timers Baseball Asn, Joliet & Will Co, Ill, recipient of 5 keep-sake gavels in recognition of presidency in various Slovene & other groups. Relig: Catholic. Mailing Add: 810 Oakland Ave Joliet IL 60435

JEWELL, JERRY D (D)
Ark State Sen
Mailing Add: 1813 Pulaski Little Rock AR 72206

JEWETT, CLAYTON EDWIN (D)
Treas, Penobscot Co Dem Comt, Maine
b Ripley, Maine, June 3, 06; s James Gilman Jewett & Cora Knowles J; m 1934 to Susan Hanley Laughton; c Glorilea (Mrs Eugene Byers), Donalene (Mrs Colby Tapley), Joanne, Jeanette, Jacquelyn (Mrs Clifford Overlock), Lawrence & Laughton. Educ: NH Fay High Sch, Dexter, Maine, grad. Polit & Govt Pos: Selectman, assessor & overseer of poor, Ripley, Maine, 28, chmn bd, 29-36; mem, Ripley Sch Bd, 37; Maine State Rep, 37-41; chmn, Hermon Dem Town Comt, 68-72; treas, Penobscot Co Dem Comt, 71- Mem: Maine Teachers Asn; Hermon PTA (secy, 67-68, pres, 68-69); Grange (past master, Ripley 462, Dexter 128 & East Somerset Pomona 28). Relig: Protestant. Legal Res: Klatt Rd Hermon ME Mailing Add: RD 2 Carmel ME 04419

JILEK, RAY R (D)
Chmn, Dist 38 Dem Party, NDak
b Dickinson, NDak, Feb 15, 33; s Joe F Jilek & Hattie J; m 1952 to Kathryn Roshau; c Wanda, Randy, Raymond, Joyce & Ryan. Educ: Versippi High Sch. Polit & Govt Pos: Chmn, Dist 38 Dem Party, NDak, 74- Bus & Prof Pos: Dir, West Plains Elec Coop, Inc, 65-, pres, 72-; dir, Farmers Coop Elevator, 60- Mem: Farmers Union. Honors & Awards: Outstanding Young Farmer, Dickinson Jaycees, 67. Relig: Catholic. Mailing Add: Rte 2 Box 125 Dickinson ND 58601

JOB, EUGENE KEITH (R)
b Quincy, Ind, Oct 7, 27; s Tillman Ellis Job & Dorothy Sandy J; m 1951 to Alice Louise Fender; c Michael Keith, Marsha Louise & Monte Lee. Educ: Quincy Pub Schs, Ind, 12 years. Polit & Govt Pos: Owen Co Comnr, Ind, 61-63; chmn, Owen Co Rep Party, formerly; asst dir sch lunch div, Ind Dept Pub Instruct, 67-69; supt, McCormicks Creek State Park, Ind, Dept Natural Resources, 69- Mem: Conserv Club; Lions. Relig: Baptist. Mailing Add: Rte 1 Spencer IN 47460

JOCHUM, THOMAS J (D)
Iowa State Rep
Mailing Add: 2368 Jackson Dubuque IA 52001

JOH, ERIK EDWARD (R)
Committeeman, Young Rep Nat Fedn
b Binghamton, NY, Mar 28, 45; s John Adam Joh & Alma Gale J; m 1973 to Roberta Ann Schmidt. Educ: Dartmouth Col, AB, 67; Albany Law Sch, JD, 70; Psi Upsilon; Dartmouth Rowing Club. Polit & Govt Pos: Pres, Broome Co Young Rep Club, NY, 73; state chmn, Young Lawyers for Breitel, 73; asst legal counsel, Asn NY State Young Rep Clubs, 73-74, vpres, 75-; committeeman, Young Rep Nat Fedn, 74- Bus & Prof Pos: Freshman crew coach, Dartmouth Col, 66-67; asst football coach, Christian Bros Acad, Albany, NY, 68-69; attorney-at-law, Hinman, Howard & Kattell, Binghamton, 70- Publ: Auth, Franchise sales—Are they sales of securities?, Albany Law Rev, winter 70. Mem: Broome Co Chap Am Red Cross (vchmn, 73-); Am & NY State Bar Asns; Binghamton Club; Quaker Lake Yacht Club. Honors & Awards: Stewards' Award, Dartmouth Col, 67; Outstanding Young Rep, Asn NY State Young Rep Clubs, 74. Relig: Presbyterian. Legal Res: 7 Vine St Binghamton NY 13903 Mailing Add: 724 Security Mutual Bldg Binghamton NY 13901

JOHN, JOHN N, III (D)
La State Rep
Mailing Add: PO Box 921 Crowley LA 70526

JOHNICAN, MINERVA JANE (D)
b Memphis, Tenn, Nov 16, 39; d John Bruce Johnican Sr (deceased) & Annie Mae Rounsonville J; single. Educ: Cent State Col, Ohio, 56-57; Tenn A&I Univ, BS; Memphis State Univ, Librn Cert & currently attending; Alpha Kappa Alpha. Polit & Govt Pos: Chairperson, Inner-City Voter Educ Comt, Inc, 70-; bd mem, Shelby Co Dem Club, 71-72; alt deleg, Dem Nat Conv, 72. Bus & Prof Pos: Elem teacher, Memphis City Schs, Tenn, 60-65, elem librn, 65- Mem: Vol Women's Roundtable, Inc (chairperson, 71-); Am Civil Liberties Union (bd, WTenn, 72-); Proj First Offenders (mem bd, 73-); YWCA; Nat Women's Polit Caucus. Relig: Presbyterian. Mailing Add: 1265 Dunnavant St Memphis TN 38106

JOHNS, CHARLEY EUGENE (D)
b Starke, Fla, Feb 27, 05; s Everett Earnest Johns & Annie Johns Pettit; m 1927 to Thelma Brinson; c Charley Jerome & Markleyann (Mrs Cash). Educ: Univ Fla. Polit & Govt Pos: Fla State Rep, 35-37; Fla State Sen, 37-65; Acting Gov, Fla, 53-55. Bus & Prof Pos: Owner, Charley E Johns Ins Agency, DVC, Starke, Fla, 30-; pres, Commun State Bank of Starke, 57- Mem: Moose; Elks; Mason; Shrine; CofC. Relig: Baptist. Legal Res: 415 E South Starke FL 32091 Mailing Add: 131 S Walnut Starke FL 32091

JOHNS, GENE (D)
Ill State Sen
Mailing Add: 402 Bainbridge Rd Marion IL 62959

JOHNS, JOHN S (D)
Mem, Exec Comt, Ohio Dem Party
b Beaver Falls, Pa, Mar 4, 15; s George Johns & Rose Abraham J; m 1941 to Emma Dager; c Robert & Irene. Polit & Govt Pos: Mem, Canton Recreation Bd, 15 years; deleg, Dem Nat Conv, 64 & 68; mem, Ohio Dem Party, currently, exec comt mem, currently. Mil Serv: Entered as Pvt, Army, 42, released as Sgt, 45; Marksmanship & Good Conduct Medals; Pac Theater Ribbon & others. Mem: USW (staff rep, 41-52, dir, Dist 27, 52-, vpres, 73-); Kent State Univ (mem bd trustees, 71-); Ohio AFL-CIO (vpres, nine terms); Moose; Eagles. Relig: Syrian Orthodox. Legal Res: 2118 University Ave NW Canton OH 44709 Mailing Add: 5 Gateway Ctr Pittsburgh PA 15222

JOHNS, MERRILL BLAINE, JR (R)
b Chicago, Ill, Apr 9, 16; s Merrill Blaine Johns & Ellen Davis J; m 1940 to Claire Golden, div; m 1973 to Mary Greer Soldow; c Gail & Jennifer. Educ: Cornell Univ, 33-34; Univ Chicago, 34-35; Psi Upsilon. Polit & Govt Pos: NMex State Rep, 52-54; mem, NMex State Bd Finance, 52-54 & 56-58; Rep Nat Committeeman, 54-56 & 66-67; chmn, NMex Rep Party, 54-56 & 66-67; state treas, NMex, 68; mem, Pub Employees Retirement Bd, State Invest Coun, & Educ Retirement Bd, 68; mem, NMex State Bd Finance, 70-; mem, Santa Fe Mayor's Task Force, 71- Bus & Prof Pos: Rep, Leo Burnett, Inc, 37-40; rep, Time Mag, 40-46; owner, Santa Fe Real Estate & Invest Co, NMex, 46-; dir Storer Broadcasting Co; vpres, US Uranium Corp, 52-55; pres, Strata Corp; chmn bd, Santa Fe Cablevision, 69-; dir, Guadalupe Resources Inc, 70- Mil Serv: Entered as 2nd Lt, Army, 41, released as Maj, after serv in Adj Gen Dept, 41-46. Mem: Am Nat Cattlemen's Asn; Colo Cattlemen's Asn; Wyo Stock Growers Asn; Am Quarter Horse Asn; Denver Club. Relig: Protestant. Legal Res: 2313 Calle Halcon Santa Fe NM 87501 Mailing Add: Box 2425 Santa Fe NM 87501

JOHNS, MICHAEL E (R)
Chmn, Washington Co Rep Party, Pa
b Washington, Pa, Feb 27, 46; s Albert P Johns & Nevada Sorrels J; single. Educ: Univ Pittsburgh, BA, 69; Wake Forest Univ, 72; Sigma Chi. Polit & Govt Pos: City councilman, Washington, Pa, 72-; chmn, Washington Co Rep Party, Pa, 74-; mem, Rep State Platform Comt, 74. Bus & Prof Pos: Teacher, John F Kennedy Sch, 68-69 & Immaculate Conception High Sch, 69-74. Mem: Nat Forensic League; Am Acad Polit & Social Sci; Eagles; Elks; Am Fedn Teachers. Honors & Awards: Speech Coach of the Year, Taylor Alderdice High Sch, Pittsburgh, 71, T Wingate Andrews Chap, High Point, NC, 72, Catonsville Chap, Catonsville, Md, 73 & Univ Pa, 74, Nat Forensic League. Relig: Roman Catholic. Mailing Add: 99 Dunn Ave Washington PA 15301

JOHNS, WILLIAM CAMPBELL (R)
Mem, NMex Rep State Comt
b Ames, Iowa, Sept 4, 25; s Erwin William Johns & Maria Jongewaard J; m 1951 to Madge Hazlett; c Donald William, Janice Ruth, Lawrence Campbell & Maria Josephine. Educ: Univ NMex, 43 & 46-47; Wheaton Col, Ill, 47-48; Northwestern Univ Med Sch, BS in Med, 48, MD, 52; Phi Chi. Polit & Govt Pos: Chmn, Redman Comt for Cong Cand, NMex, 62 & 64; chmn, NMex Rep State Finance Comt, 66-67, co-chmn, 67-74, mem, currently; mem, NMex Rep State Comt, currently; deleg, Rep Nat Conv, 68. Bus & Prof Pos: Pres med staff, Presby Hosp Ctr, Albuquerque, NMex, 64-65; mem, NMex Bd of Med Examr, 67-73. Mil Serv: Entered as Pvt, Army, 43, released as S/Sgt, 46, after serv in 86th Inf Div, ETO. Mem: Fel Am Col of Obstetricians & Gynecologists; Am & NMex Med Asns. Honors & Awards: Civic Serv Award, Albuquerque Jr CofC, 64; A H Robins Award for Civic Serv, NMex Med Soc, 70. Relig: Presbyterian. Legal Res: 1726 Notre Dame NE Albuquerque NM 87106 Mailing Add: 717 Encino Pl NE Albuquerque NM 87106

JOHNS, WILLIAM GORDON (R)
Chmn, St Johns Co Rep Party, Fla
b Lacouchee, Fla, Feb 28, 28; s Felder Leon Johns & Blanche Mickler J; m 1950 to Jacqueline Surface; c William David, Holly Khristina & William Mark. Educ: Jacksonville Univ, BSBA, 61. Polit & Govt Pos: Chmn, St Johns Co Rep Party, Fla, 75- Mil Serv: Entered as Pfc, Air Force, 52, released as Sgt, 54, after serv in Dobbins AFB, Ga. Relig: Methodist. Mailing Add: 3025 Bishop E Rd Jacksonville FL 32223

JOHNSON, ALBERT W (R)
US Rep, Pa
b Smethport, Pa, Apr 17, 06; s John A Johnson & Edla Marie Ostrom J; m 1926 to Virginia Balsley; c Richmond, David, Ronald & Karen. Educ: Univ Pa Wharton Sch, 26-28; John B Stetson Univ, LLB; Alpha Tau Omega. Polit & Govt Pos: Pa State Rep, 46-63, Majority Whip, Pa House Rep, 51, Minority Whip, 55, Minority Leader, 59 & 61, Majority Leader, 53, 57 & 63, chmn, House Comt on Rules, mem, Legis Budget & Finance & Interstate Coop Comts; chmn, Pa Rep Platform Comt, 58 & 62; US Rep, 23rd Dist, 63-, asst to Rep Floor Leader & mem, Banking & Currency & Post Off & Civil Serv Comts, US House of Rep; East Div Regional Rep Whip, currently; mem-at-lg, Rep Policy Comt, formerly, mem, Joint State Govt Comn, Gen State Authority, State Pub Sch Bldg Authority, State Hwy & Bridge Authority & State Coun Civil Defense. Bus & Prof Pos: Dir & counsel, Smethport Nat Bank, Pa, 42-62. Mem: Pa & McKean Co Bar Asns; Moose. Honors & Awards: Silver Medal of Merit, Nat VFW, 68. Relig: Protestant. Legal Res: 409 Franklin St Smethport PA 16749 Mailing Add: US House of Rep Washington DC 20515

JOHNSON, ALVAN NATHANIAL (D)
b Plains, Ga, Apr 16, 16; s William Decker Johnson & Winifred Elmira Simmon J; m 1964 to Verla C Clardy; c Alana Sue, Beatrice Renee & Eunice Eileen. Educ: Gordon Theol Sem, Boston, Mass, 47; Tufts Univ, 48-50. Polit & Govt Pos: Chairperson, 208th Precinct Dem Party, Tulsa, Okla, 67-; alt deleg, Dem Nat Mid-Term Conf, 74. Mil Serv: Entered as Seaman, Navy, 42, released as Shipfitter II, 45, after serv in Atlantic & Pac Theaters. Relig: Methodist. Mailing Add: 1940 E 28th St N Tulsa OK 74110

JOHNSON, ANICE WISMER (R)
Ohio State Sen
b Lumber City, Ga, Feb 22, 19; d Adelbert J Wismer & Kathryn Harwell W; m 1943 to George Clark Johnson, Jr; c Michael Anne, George C, III, Anice J (Mrs Ervin), Doan Burgess & Wismer Adelbert. Educ: Brenau Col, AB; Tau Kappa Alpha; Alpha Delta Pi; pres, Int Rels Club. Polit & Govt Pos: Pres, Aurora Rep, Ohio, 64-65; pres, Portage Co Women's Rep Club, 65-67; Ohio State Rep, Portage Co, 68-70; Ohio State Sen, 18th Dist, 72- Bus & Prof Pos: Continuity dir, Radio WRBL, Columbus, Ga, 39-42; reporter, Kent-Ravenna Rec Courier, 64-66. Mem: Nat Soc State Legislators (secy, Ohio, 68-); Aurora Study Club (pres). Relig: Episcopal. Legal Res: 286 Eggleston Rd Aurora OH 44202 Mailing Add: Ohio Senate State House Broad & High St Columbus OH 43215

JOHNSON, ARTIS VISANIO (D)
Okla State Rep
b Chandler, Okla, Mar 10, 41; s Clarence Odell Johnson & Bernice Humphress Johnson Roper; m 1974 to Villetta Bobo; c Alicia Rochelle, Andrea Nicole, Angela Rene & Dawn Partridge. Educ: Lincoln Univ, Mo, 58-62; Okla Univ Sch Law, LLB, 65; Alpha Phi Alpha; Delta Theta Phi. Polit & Govt Pos: Okla State Rep, 98th Dist, 66-73, Okla State Rep, Dist 99, 73-, chmn pub health comt, Okla House of Rep, 70-, mem common educ comt, judiciary comt, pub safety & penal affairs comts, 75- Bus & Prof Pos: Attorney-at-law, Okla, 65-; mem legal assocs, Darrell, Bruce, Johnson & Sims. Mem: Nat & Okla State Bar Asns; Community Action Bd; NAACP; YMCA; Urban League. Relig: Baptist. Legal Res: 2308 Hardin Dr Oklahoma City OK 73111 Mailing Add: Suite 408 Investors Capitol Bldg Oklahoma City OK 73102

JOHNSON, AUGUSTUS CLARK (D)
Mem, Fairfax Co Dem Comt, Va
b Covington, Ky, Apr 12, 14; s Augustus Clark Johnson & Elizabeth Brown J; m 1948 to Constantia Hommann; c Muriel T. Educ: George Washington Univ, AB in Math, 46, AM in Math, 48; Sigma Xi; Omicron Delta Kappa; Pi Delta Epsilon; Sigma Chi. Polit & Govt Pos: Fed Civil Serv, Govt Printing Off, Tariff Comn, Selective Serv Systs, Dept of Defense, 31-43; mem, Fairfax Co Dem Comt, Va, 55-, chmn, 58-64; deleg, Va State Dem Conv, 56, 60, 64, 68 & 72; Dem cand for Cong, Tenth Dist, Va, 62 & 64, deleg, Dem Nat Conv, 64; mem, Dem State Cent Comt, Va, 66-72; chmn, Tenth Dist Dem Comt, 66-72. Bus & Prof Pos: Instr, George Washington Univ, 46-48, mem faculty & research staff, 51-57; asst prof, Robert Col, Istanbul, Turkey, 48-51; partner, Appl Math Serv, 57-59; research dir, Booz-Allen Appl Research, Inc, 59-67; mem tech staff, Mitre Corp, 67-69; mgr, comp urban studies, Doxiadis-Syst Develop Corp, 69-70; mem tech staff, Mitre Corp, 70- Mil Serv: Entered as Pvt, DC Nat Guard, 31, released as Capt, 41. Mem: Am Asn for the Adv of Sci; Nat Capital Dem Club; Gtr Washington Citizens for Clean Air (mem bd); Am Civil Liberties Union (mem bd, Va Br). Relig: Unitarian. Mailing Add: 7012 Woodland Dr Springfield VA 22151

JOHNSON, BARBARA YANOW (D)
b New York, NY, July 8, 40; d Joseph Yanow & Diana Soshnick Y; m 1970 to Earl Johnson, Jr. Educ: Wash Square Col, NY Univ, BA, 61; St John's Univ Sch Law, LLB, 64. Polit & Govt Pos: Fel, Nat Ctr for Educ in Politics, 64 & Mich Dem Gubernatorial Campaign, 64-65; legis asst, Congressman Billie S Farnum, Mich, 65-66; cong liaison officer, Dem Nat Comt, 66; dep chief research & demonstration, Off Econ Opportunity Legal Serv Prog, 66-68; deleg, Dem Nat Conv, 72; dir, scheduling & advance, Citizens for Sen Alan Cranston, 73- Bus & Prof Pos: Attorney, San Francisco Neighborhood Legal Assistance Found, 68-69 & Western Ctr on Law & Poverty, 69-71; assoc advocate, The Advocates, 71-72; reporter-researcher, NBC News, First Tuesday, 72-73. Mem: Am Bar Asn; Nat Legal Aid & Defender Asn; Action for Legal Rights. Honors & Awards: Reginald Heber Smith Commun Lawyer Fel, Univ Pa, Sch Law, 68. Relig: Jewish. Mailing Add: 4213 The Strand Manhattan Beach CA 90266

JOHNSON, BEATRICE MARIAN (D)
Chmn, Lyon Co Dem Party, Nev
b Sparks, Nev, July 30, 30; d James Jordan Askey & Beatrice Etchegoin A; m 1947 to Harold Banks Johnson. Educ: Fernley High Sch, Nev, grad, 47. Polit & Govt Pos: Senate attache, Nev State Legis, 57, 59-61 & 63-65; chmn, Lyon Co Dem Party, 72- Mem: VFW Auxiliary (state pres, 67). Relig: Catholic. Legal Res: 270 Center St Fernley NV 89408 Mailing Add: PO Box 271 Fernley NV 89408

JOHNSON, BOBBY WARE (D)
Comnr, Warren Co, Ga
b Warrenton, Ga, Jan 12, 30; s Mashburn Columbus Johnson & Josie Dye J; single. Educ: Warrenton High Sch, 47. Polit & Govt Pos: Ga State Rep, Dist 29, formerly; comnr, Warren Co, Ga, 73-, chmn bd health, currently. Bus & Prof Pos: In pub rels. Mil Serv: Nat Guard, Sgt, 6 years. Mem: Mason; Scottish Rite; Augusta Consistory (32 degree); Kiwanis; Moose. Honors & Awards: Chosen one of the outstanding men of Am by Jr CofC; Award for Man of the Year, Ga Mobile Home Asn, 64. Relig: Baptist. Mailing Add: PO Box 122 Warrenton GA 30828

JOHNSON, BYRON JERALD (D)
Chmn, Dem Legis Dist, Idaho
b Boise, Idaho, Aug 2, 37; s Arlie Johnson & V Bronell Dunten J; m 1960 to Marie Elizabeth Rauseo; c Matthew, Ethan, Elaine & Laura. Educ: Harvard Univ, AB, 59, LLB, 62. Polit & Govt Pos: Pres, Ada Co Young Dem, Idaho, 64-65; regional vpres, Col Young Dem, 65-66; nat committeeman, Idaho Young Dem, 66; registration chmn, Ada Co Dem Cent Comt, 67-68, vchmn, 68-70; deleg, Dem Nat Conv, 68; chmn, Dem Legis Dist, 15, Idaho, 70-; mem charter comn, Dem Nat Comt, 73-; mem, Dem Nat Charter Comn, 74; deleg, Dem Nat Mid-Term Conf, 74. Bus & Prof Pos: Prog Chmn, Gr Boise CofC, 69; vpres, Nat Asn Estate Planning Coun, 70-71, pres, 71-72. Mem: Idaho, Boise & Am Bar Asns; mem bd dirs, Red Cross, Boise Philharmonic & Salvation Army; Boise United Fund (campaign chmn). Honors & Awards: Distinguished Serv Award, Boise Jr CofC, 70. Mailing Add: 1021 Glen Haven Dr Boise ID 83705

JOHNSON, BYRON LINDBERG (D)
b Chicago, Ill, Oct 12, 17; s Theodore Johnson & Ruth Lindberg J; m 1938 to Catherine Elizabeth Teter; c Steven, Christine & Eric. Educ: Univ Wis, Madison, BA, 38, MA, 40, PhD, 47; Phi Kappa Phi; Artus; Delta Sigma Rho. Polit & Govt Pos: In-Serv training apprentice, Wis State Bd of Health, 38-39, statistician, 40-42; pub utility rate analyst, Pub Serv Comn, Wis, 39-40; fiscal analyst, US Bur of the Budget, Exec Off of the President, 42-44; economist, Soc Security Admin, 44-47; Colo State Rep, Arapahoe Co, 55-56; cand for Cong, Second Dist, Colo, 56 & 60, Fifth Dist, 72; admin asst to Gov Steve McNichols, Colo, 57-58; US Rep, Second Dist, 59-60; deleg, Dem Nat Conv & mem platform comt, 60; consult, Agency for Int Develop, 61-64; deleg, Co, Dist, State Dem Conv & Dem Nat Conv, 68; mem adv comt to state dem chmn, 69- Bus & Prof Pos: Prof econ, Univ Denver, 47-56; pres, Mile High Housing Asn, 48-51; exec secy, Sr Homes of Colo, 53-58; prof econ, Univ Colo, 65-, assoc chmn of dept econ & dir ctr for urban affairs, Denver Campus, 68-70; mem, Bd Regents, Univ Colo, 71- Publ: The Principle of Equalization Applied to the Allocation of Grants in Aid, Soc Security Admin, 47; Need is Our Neighbor, Friendship Press & United Church Press, 66; Chap in Christianity Among Rising Men & Nations, Asn Press, 66. Mem: Am Econ Asn; Nat Tax Asn; Rocky Mt Soc Sci Asn; Peace Research Asn; Am Fedn of Teachers. Honors & Awards: Herfurth Efficiency Award, 38; Ky Col, 60; Whitehead Award, Colo Chap, Am Civil Liberties Union, 60. Relig: United Church of Christ. Mailing Add: 2451 S Dahlia Lane Denver CO 80222

JOHNSON, CARL MARCUS (DFL)
Minn State Rep
b St Peter, Minn, Sept 12, 33; s Chester M Johnson & Lena Renneke J; m 1957 to Adele Elizabeth Ellen Johnson; c Cameron Matthew, Anita Elizabeth & Martha. Educ: Mankato State Col, BS. Polit & Govt Pos: Treas, Co Dem-Farmer-Labor Party, Minn, 64-66; Minn State Rep, 67- Bus & Prof Pos: Farmer, 56-; owner & operator, Home Improv Co, 58- Mil Serv: Entered as Pvt, Army, 54, released as SP-4, 56, after serv in Mil Police, Korea, 54-56. Mem: Am Legion; Farmers Union; Farm Bur. Relig: Lutheran. Mailing Add: Rte 3 St Peter MN 56082

JOHNSON, CECIL L (R)
Ore State Rep
Mailing Add: 3515 Upper River Rd Grants Pass OR 97525

JOHNSON, CHESTER ARTHUR (D)
Committeeman, Broome Co Dem Comt, NY
b Cambridge, Mass, Nov 20, 19; s Arthur T Johnson & Carrie Rich Knowles J; m 1943 to Claire von Auw; c Pamela (Mrs Allen Gilmore), Ivan, Paul, Peter, Emilie (Mrs Dennis Blabac) & Maria. Educ: St John's Col (Md), BA, 49; Johns Hopkins Univ, 49-50. Polit & Govt Pos: Co-chmn, Broome Co Peace Coord Comt, NY, 67-68; treas, Broome Co Citizens for McCarthy, 68; treas, Broome Co Citizens for O'Dwyer & Nichols, 68; chmn, Broome Co New Dem Coalition, 69; committeeman, Broome Co Dem Comt, 71-; deleg & leader of deleg, Dem Nat Conv, 72. Bus & Prof Pos: Computer programmer, John Hancock Mutual Life Ins Co, Boston, 50-62; staff planner, IBM Corp, Endicott, NY, 62- Mil Serv: Entered as Pvt, Army Air Force, 42, released as T/Sgt, 45, after serv in Eighth Air Force, ETO, 44-45; Air Medal with Five Oak Leaf Clusters; Seven Campaign Stars. Mem: Asn for Comput Machinery; Soc for Gen Syst Research. Relig: Catholic. Mailing Add: 5 Chestnut St Binghamton NY 13905

JOHNSON, CONSTANCE ADA (CONNIE) (R)
VChmn, Vt Rep State Comt
b South Fayston, Vt, Apr 16, 34; d Guy Boyce Folsom & Harriet Spooner; m 1952 to Larry West Johnson; c Russell Kendall, Lauren Jeanne (Mrs Kim Leavitt), Erika Leigh, Kerrick Lance, Robin Winona & Marilyn Margaret. Educ: Univ Vt, 51-52; Goddard Col, summer 66. Polit & Govt Pos: Committeewoman, Vt Rep State Comt, 69-, vchmn, 71-; Justice of the Peace, Barre, 73- Bus & Prof Pos: Caterer, Johnson's Inc, 70- Mem: Barre Bus & Prof Women's Club (pres); Washington Co Rep Women; Am Legion Auxiliary. Relig: Congregational. Mailing Add: 18 Bridgeman St Barre VT 05641

JOHNSON, CYRUS (R)
Mem, Rep State Cent Comt Calif
b Milledgeville, Ga, Nov 2, 23; s Jesse C Johnson & Jessie Tucker J; m 1946 to Edna P Hill; c Debbie, Cy Duane & Janet. Educ: Mid Ga Col, dipl, 41; Univ Mo, 43-44; Univ Hawaii, 63. Polit & Govt Pos: Mem, Ventura Co Rep Cent Comt, 69-70; mem, Rep State Cent Comt Calif, 69-; deleg, Rep Nat Conv, 72. Mil Serv: Entered as Pvt, Air Force, 42, released as Lt Col, 64, after serv in Hq, Pac Air Forces, ETO & Korea, 61-64; Distinguished Flying Cross; Air Medal with Four Oak Leaf Clusters. Mem: Calif Lutheran Col Community Leaders' Club, Thousand Oaks (exec bd, 66-); Ventura Co Life Underwriters Asn; Thousand Oaks High Sch Scholarship Found; CofC. Honors & Awards: Outstanding Serv to the Community Award, Conejo Valley CofC; Outstanding New Agent, 65 & Outstanding Career Agent, 67, Ventura Co Life Underwriters. Relig: Protestant. Mailing Add: 1595 Kirk Ave Thousand Oaks CA 91360

JOHNSON, DARYL BENJAMIN (DFL)
Secy, Sibley Co Dem-Farmer-Labor Party, Minn
b Winthrop, Minn, July 29, 24; s Bennie G Johnson & Ellen M Lindstrand J; m 1948 to Alma Selma Krosting; c Barbara, Steven & Larry. Educ: High sch. Polit & Govt Pos: Chmn, Sibley Co Dem-Farmer-Labor Party, Minn, 66-68, secy, 74-; alt deleg, Dem Nat Conv, 72. Bus & Prof Pos: Gen contractor, Winthrop, Minn, 48-68. Mil Serv: Entered as Pvt, Army, 43, released as Pfc, 46, after serv in 42nd Div Inf, ETO, 43-46; 3 Battle Stars; Good Conduct Medal; Sharpshooters Badge. Mem: VFW; Am Legion. Relig: Lutheran. Mailing Add: 411 N Brown Winthrop MN 55396

JOHNSON, DAVID W (R)
Ohio State Rep
Mailing Add: 514 Marquardt NE North Canton OH 44720

JOHNSON, DON (D)
Okla State Rep
b Pawnee, Okla, Aug 17, 25; s Ralph Waldo Johnson & Ollie M Colvin J; m 1968 to E Charlene Smith. Educ: Okla State Univ, summer 44; Univ Mo-Columbia, BA in Jour, 48, grad work; Delta Upsilon; Alpha Delta Sigma. Polit & Govt Pos: Bd mem & pres, United Community Action Prog, Pawnee, Osage & Creek Co, Okla, many years; dir, Pawnee Co Civil Defense, 63-; Justice of the Peace, Pawnee, 64-67; pres, Pawnee Co Planning Bd, 65-; pres, Pawnee Housing Authority, 66-67; Okla State Rep, Dist 35, 72- Bus & Prof Pos: Advert mgr,

Valley Eve Monitor, McAllen, Tex, 48-52; advert mgr, The Pawnee Chief, Okla, 52-58; mgr, Pawnee Community CofC, 58-72. Mil Serv: Entered as Pvt, Army, 44, released as Pfc, 45, after serv in ETO; ETO Ribbon with Five Battle Stars; Presidential Unit Citation. Mem: Am Legion (serv officer, Earl Maggart Post 26, 53-); Pawnee Co Cattlemen's Asn; Farmer's Union; Farm Bur. Honors & Awards: Citizen of the Year, The Pawnee Chief, 48; Hon 4-H Mem, Pawnee Co 4-H Clubs; Guardsman Award, 45th Nat Guard Div; Man of the Year, Pawnee Bus & Prof Women's Club, 72. Relig: Episcopal; pres, Bishop's Comt; licensed lay reader. Mailing Add: RR 3 Pawnee OK 74058

JOHNSON, DONALD EDWARD (R)
Dep Asst Secy Domestic & Int Bus, Dept Com
b Cedar Falls, Iowa, June 5, 24; s Chris E Hansen & E Jacolyn Hansen J; m 1947 to Mary Jean Suchomel; c Alan Donald, David James, Brian Edward, Kevin Laird, Julie Jean, Kurt Arthur, Joan Marie, Robert Conway, Beth Ann & Susan Carol. Educ: Iowa State Univ, 41-42 & 46-47; Eastern Ore Col Educ, 43. Hon Degrees: Univ Athletic Club Hon LLD, Iowa Wesleyan Col, 71. Polit & Govt Pos: Councilman, West Branch, Iowa, 48-49 & 66-67; chmn, US Civil Rights Comn, 58; mem, Iowa Adv Comn Civil Rights, 59-60; exec consult, Off Emergency Preparedness, Iowa, 65-69; adminr vet affairs, Vet Admin, 69-74; mem, Domestic Coun, 72-74; mem, Coun Human Resources, 73-; Dep Asst Secy Domestic & Int Bus, Dept Com, currently. Bus & Prof Pos: Secy-treas, Johnson Hatcheries, Inc, West Branch, Iowa, 47-61; bd chmn, Protein Blenders, Inc, Iowa City, 61-66; pres, West Branch Farm Supply, Inc, 61-69; vpres, ME-JON Fertilizers, Inc, Oxford, 56-65; secy-treas, S & J Poultry Co, Inc, West Branch & Waterloo, 56-69. Mil Serv: Entered as Pvt, Army, 42, released as Sgt, 46, after serv in 3rd Army, ETO; Bronze Star; Purple Heart; Croix d'Officer de la Reconnaissance, Belgium, Five Battle Stars. Mem: Boy Scouts (nat coun & nat capital area coun, 72-); Herbert Hoover Presidential Libr (bd trustees, 72-); PTA; CofC; Am Legion. Honors & Awards: Iowan of Year, Radio & TV Broadcasters, 65; Am Legion Past Dept Commanders Club Man of the Year Award, 70; Gold Plate Award, Am Acad Achievement, 71; Iron Mike Award, Marine Corps League, 72. Relig: Catholic. Legal Res: PO Box 577 West Branch IA 52358 Mailing Add: Rm 3850 US Dept of Com 14th & Constitution Ave NW Washington DC 20230

JOHNSON, DONALD L (R)
Ky State Sen
b 1931. Educ: Univ Cincinnati, BA & LLB; Phi Alpha Delta. Polit & Govt Pos: Ky State Sen, 64- Bus & Prof Pos: Attorney. Mil Serv: Air Force. Mem: Campbell Co Jaycees; VFW; Campbell Co Bar Asn; Campbell Co Boys' Club of Am (legal coun). Mailing Add: Suite 200 Lawyers Bldg Newport KY 41071

JOHNSON, DOUGLAS J (DOUG) (DFL)
Minn State Rep
Mailing Add: Box 14 Cook MN 55723

JOHNSON, DUANE (D)
Mont State Rep
Mailing Add: 224 Pattee Creek Dr Missoula MT 59801

JOHNSON, DURWARD ELTON (D)
b Houston, Tex, Jan 2, 32; s Ivy Milton Johnson & Lucille Price J; m 1951 to June Elizabeth Martin; c Durward Elton, Jr & Richard Everett. Educ: Houston Conservatory of Music, 54-55; Nat Tech Sch, grad; Air Traffic Controller Sch, grad, 55; Houston Community Col, 72- Polit & Govt Pos: Mem membership comt, Moderate Dem Harris Co, Tex, 72; deleg, Precinct, Dist & State Dem Conv, 72; deleg, Dem Nat Conv, 72. Bus & Prof Pos: Mem, Prof Air Traffic Controllers, 57-58. Mem: Sheet Metal Workers Union. Relig: Baptist. Mailing Add: 2006 Counter Point Houston TX 77055

JOHNSON, E G (TED) (R)
Chmn, Trumbull Co Rep Party, Ohio
b Cortland, Ohio, July 6, 25; s Fred G Johnson & Blanche Byrnes J; m 1947 to Ruth L Sipple; c Kathleen (Mrs Love) & Ted David. Educ: Youngstown Univ, LLB, 52, JD, 69; Gessner Law Club. Polit & Govt Pos: Twp solicitor, Howland Twp, Ohio, 60-64; Rep precinct committeeman, Howland Twp Precinct J, Trumbull Co, 62-; chmn, Trumbull Co Rep Party, 66-; vchmn, Trumbull Co Bd of Elec, 68-; city law dir, Newton Falls, Ohio, 68-; alt deleg, Rep Nat Conv, 72. Bus & Prof Pos: Attorney-at-law, Warren, Ohio, 52- Mil Serv: Entered as A/S, Navy, 43, released as Aviation Elec Technician 1/C, 46, after serv in Naval Air Corps in the Caribbean & Pac, 44-46; Theatre Ribbons. Mem: Trumbull Co & Ohio State Bar Asns; Ohio Asn Elec Officers; Sports Car Club of Am. Relig: Protestant. Legal Res: 5875 Mines Rd Warren OH 44484 Mailing Add: 501-2 Union Savings & Trust Bldg Warren OH 44481

JOHNSON, E M (D)
WVa State Deleg
Mailing Add: State Capitol Charleston WV 25305

JOHNSON, EDDIE BERNICE (D)
Tex State Rep
b Waco, Tex, Dec 3, 34; d Mr & Mrs Edward Johnson; div; c Dawrence Kirk. Educ: St Mary's Col, Univ Notre Dame, grad, 55; Tex Christian Univ, Nat Inst Ment Health grant, 67, BS; NTex State Univ; Tex Woman's Univ, 71. Polit & Govt Pos: Voter registrn vol worker, 12 years; vchmn, State Dem Conv, Tex, 72; mem, Nat Dem Credentials' Comt, 72; committeewoman, Tex State Dem Exec Comt, 72-; Tex State Rep, Dist 33-0, 72-, mem state affairs comt, calendar comt & human resources comt, Tex House of Rep, 72- Bus & Prof Pos: Chief psychiatric nurse psychotherapist in day hosp, Vet Admin Hosp, 15 years; psychiatric consult to student nurses, Baylor Univ & Tex Woman's Univ; mem staff, Larue D Carter Psychiatric Hosp, Ind Univ Med Ctr; elec to serv on original Equal Employ Opportunity Comt, 66; elec adv hosp, Under-35 Employee Comt, 66; exec asst, Personnel Div, Neiman-Marcus, Inc, Dallas, 72; consult with Drs Carl Rogers, Eric Berne & Haim Ginott. Mem: Dallas Group Psychotherapy Soc; Behav & Social Sci Asn; Am Group Psychotherapy Asn; Neighborhood Improv Rep, Urban Planning Dept, Dallas; Jack & Jill of Am (pres, Dallas Chap, secy-treas, SCent Region). Honors & Awards: Hosp Sustained Superior Performance Award, 71; Holmes Sch Outstanding Serv Award, 71; Woman of the Year Award, Greyhound Corp; First black woman to become cand for Tex legis; First black woman to Tex House of Rep from Dallas Co & first woman from Dallas Co since 1935. Relig: Baptist; mem, Christian Educ Bd; coordr, Unit Control Comt; mem, Woman's Fellowship Group. Mailing Add: PO Box 8551 Dallas TX 75216

JOHNSON, ELMER L (R)
NH State Rep
Mailing Add: Warwick Rd Winchester NH 03470

JOHNSON, ELMORE THOME (R)
Nebr State Sen
b Broken Bow, Nebr, Jan 4, 05; s Henry Albert Johnson & Ella Thome J; m 1930 to Jean Claney; c William & Howard. Educ: Univ Nebr, BS, 27; Alpha Gamma Rho. Polit & Govt Pos: Supvr, Dodge Co, Nebr, 67-69; Nebr State Sen, 15th Dist, 69- Bus & Prof Pos: Mem bd dirs, South Omaha Prod Credit Asn, 48-56, pres bd, 52-56; mem bd dirs, Fremont Nat Bank, 69-; mem bd dirs, Equitable Fed Savings & Loan, 69- Mem: Mason; Golf Club. Relig: United Methodist. Mailing Add: 2120 Parkview Dr Fremont NE 68025

JOHNSON, G GRIFFITH, JR (R)
b New York, NY, Aug 15, 12; s Gove Griffith Johnson & May Francelia Russell; m 1936 to Janet Clementson Young; c Carol Lynne & Gove Griffith, III. Educ: Harvard Univ, BA, 34, MA, 36, PhD, 38; Delta Upsilon. Polit & Govt Pos: With US Treas Dept, 36-39, Nat Defense Adv Comn, 40-41 & Off Price Admin, 41-46; dir econ stabilization div, Nat Security Resources Bd, 48-49; asst chief fiscal div & chief economist, US Bur of the Budget, 49-50; asst adminr econ policy, Econ Stabilization Agency, 50; asst secy econ affairs, Dept of State, 62-65. Bus & Prof Pos: Consult economist, Nathans Asn, 46-47; economist, Motion Picture Asn of Am, 52, vpres, 52-62, exec vpres, 65-. Publ: The Treasury and Monetary Policy, 39; co-auth, Economic Effects of Federal Public Works Expenditures (w J K Galbraith), 40. Mem: Vis Comt, Harvard Sch Pub Admin; Am Econ Asn; Exec Comt, Nat Planning Asn (mem bd trustees). Mailing Add: 5100 Dorset Ave Chevy Chase MD 20015

JOHNSON, GARDINER (R)
Mem, Rep State Cent Comt Calif
b San Jose, Calif, Aug 10, 05; s George W Johnson & Izora Carter J; m 1935 to Doris Louise Miller; c Jacqueline Ann & Stephen Miller. Educ: Univ Calif, AB, 26; Univ Calif Sch Jurisp, JD; 28; Phi Delta Phi; Phi Beta Kappa; Kappa Delta Rho. Polit & Govt Pos: Mem, Alameda Co Rep Cent Comt, Calif, 34-47 & 59-; mem, Rep State Cent Comt Calif, 34-; Calif State Assemblyman, 35-47, Speaker Pro-Tem, Calif State Assembly, 40; alt deleg, Rep Nat Conv, 40, deleg, 56, 60, 64 & 68; mem, Nat Drafting Comt, Coun of State Govts, 44-47; chmn Calif deleg to White House Conf on Educ, 55; chmn, Gov Conf on Educ, 55; pres, Calif Rep Assembly, 59-60; mem, Citizens Legis Adv Comt, 57-61; mem, Rep Nat Comt, 64-68. Bus & Prof Pos: Law practice, San Francisco, 28-; partner, Johnson & Stanton, Attorneys, 52- Mem: Am Col Trial Lawyers; Commonwealth Club of Calif; Calif Hist Soc; Florence Crittenton Asn of Am (bd dirs, 69-, vpres, 73-); San Francisco Unit, Am Cancer Soc (bd dirs, 71-). Relig: Episcopal. Legal Res: 329 Hampton Rd Piedmont CA 94611 Mailing Add: 221 Sansome San Francisco CA 94104

JOHNSON, GARY CHARLES (D)
Nat Committeeman, Ky Young Dem
b Pikeville, Ky, Nov 2, 46; s Tommy Johnson & Hannah Osborne J; m 1968 to Anna Lou Burke. Educ: Berea Col, BA, 69; Univ Ky Col Law, JD, 72; Delta Theta Phi. Polit & Govt Pos: Publicity dir, Ky Young Dem Col Coun, 70-71; pres, Fayette Co Young Dem Club, 71-72; mem exec comt, Ky Young Dem, 71-72, nat committeeman, 72- Bus & Prof Pos: Attorney, 73- Mil Serv: Entered as Pvt, E-1, Army Res, 69, serv as Sgt, E-6, currently. Mem: Am & Ky Bar Asns; Jaycees. Mailing Add: Box 231 Pikeville KY 41501

JOHNSON, GARY KENNETH (D)
Wis State Rep
b Grand Forks, NDak, Sept 14, 39; s Cecil Philip Johnson & Helen Pickard J; m 1961 to Heather Anne Gelston; c Steven Wade & Daren Richard. Educ: Beloit Col, BA, 63; Univ Wis-Whitewater, 68-69; Tau Kappa Epsilon. Polit & Govt Pos: Wis State Rep, 45th Dist, Rock Co, 71-, mem assembly educ & taxation comts, Wis House of Rep, 71-72, mem senate & assembly joint comt finance, 72- Bus & Prof Pos: Social studies teacher, Beloit Pub Schs, Wis, 63-70; patrolman, Beloit Police Force, 65-67; admin asst, Beloit Mem High Sch, 68-69. Mem: Kiwanis. Relig: Lutheran. Mailing Add: 1818 Fayette Beloit WI 53511

JOHNSON, GEORGE DEAN (R)
SC State Rep
Mailing Add: 220 North Church St Spartanburg SC 29301

JOHNSON, GERALD LYNN (D)
Mem, Ga Dem State Exec Comt
b Marietta, Ga, June 8, 50; s Jim Pat Johnson, Jr & Martha Hicks J; m 1970 to Faith Virginia Roper. Educ: Kennasaw Jr Col, 69; West Ga Col, 68-72. Polit & Govt Pos: Mem, Carroll Co Dem Exec Comt, Ga, 74-; mem, Ga Dem State Exec Comt, 74- Bus & Prof Pos: Construction worker, Southern Bell Tel, 69-70; sales assoc, Costley Realty Co, Carrollton, Ga, 70-72; sales assoc, Thomas H Mitchell & Assocs, Inc, Atlanta, 72-73; pres & real estate broker, Gerald L Johnson & Assocs, Inc, Carrollton, 73- Mem: Optimists; Jaycees; Ga Indust Developers Asn; Nat Inst Farm & Land Brokers; Nat Asn Realtors. Relig: Baptist. Legal Res: Rte 9 Box 73 Carrollton GA 30117 Mailing Add: PO Box 815 Carrollton GA 30117

JOHNSON, GRACE MANCHESTER (R)
b Lebanon, Mo, Mar 26, 07; d Solon Hayes Manchester & Nora Farris M; m 1934 to Arvil Monroe Johnson, wid; c Sarah Frances (deceased). Educ: Southwest Mo State Univ, BS, Music Educ, 28; Univ Mo-Columbia, 31-32 & 62; Univ Kansas City, 60-61; Glee Club; Band; Dramatic Club; Hist Club. Polit & Govt Pos: Deleg, Mo Rep State Conv, 72; alt deleg, Rep Nat Conv, 72; mem, Nat Fedn Rep Women, currently. Bus & Prof Pos: Teacher pvt music in piano, voice & organ, Lebanon, Mo, 30-72; radio singer, WAAW & WOW, Omaha, Nebr, 33-34; mem & singer, Omaha Choral Union, 33-34; radio progs, Lebanon, Mo, 50-51; choir dir, First Methodist Church, 25 years; teacher music, Mo Pub Schs, 30 years; retired. Publ: History of the Methodist Church, Lebanon Daily Record, 50; poems, Easter thoughts & Repentance, Springfield Daily News, 56; Our flag fraternal (song), 73. Mem: Retired Teachers Asn of Mo; Rebekah Lodge 680, Independent Order of Odd Fellows; Int Asn Rebekah Assemblies; Eastern Star; Int Platform Asn. Honors & Awards: Placque serv award, Sch Bd, Lebanon Schs, Mo, 70 & First Methodist Church, 70. Relig: Methodist. Mailing Add: 160 E Sixth St Lebanon MO 65536

JOHNSON, HAROLD T (BIZZ) (D)
US Rep, Calif
b Calif; m to Albra I Manuel; c One Son, One Daughter. Educ: Univ of Nev. Polit & Govt Pos: Calif State Sen, 48-58; US Rep, Calif, 58-; mayor, Roseville Calif, 7 years, sch trustee,

city councilman; dist chmn, Brotherhood of Rwy Clerks; mem, Calif Dem State Cent Comt, currently; deleg, Dem Nat Mid-Term Conf, 74. Bus & Prof Pos: Supvr, Pac Fruit Express Co. Mem: Lambda Chi Alpha; Eagles; Moose; Elks; Am River Develop League (pres). Legal Res: 423 Grove St Roseville CA 95678 Mailing Add: US House of Rep 2347 Rayburn Bldg Washington DC 20515

JOHNSON, HELEN CHAFFIN (R)
State Prog Chmn, Mont Rep Women's Club
b Corvallis, Mont, June 7, 05; d Balem Sigel Chaffin & Rilla Jane Walls C; m 1929 to Melvin A Johnson; c Carol (Mrs Norman Strong). Educ: Univ Mont, BA, 27; Mortar Board; Tanan; Alpha Chi Omega. Polit & Govt Pos: Precinct committeewoman, Gallatin Co Rep Cent Comt, Mont, 46-69 & 70-; pres, Rep Women of Gallatin Co, 51-53; state vchmn, Mont Cent Rep Comt, 57-60; Mont State Rep, 61-62; state co-chmn for Goldwater, 64; dist co-chmn for Dick-Smiley, 66; state campaign acct, Mont Rep Women's Club, state prog chmn, 66-; Rep can for Mont State Rep, 70; state campaign activities chmn for Rep women, currently; mem, State Realtor Bd Dirs, currently. Bus & Prof Pos: Teacher, 7 years; home econ supvr, Farm Security Admin, 34-41; mem bd, State Bd of Health, Iowa, 53-60 & Hosp Adv Bd, 66-69; realtor & broker, 60- Mem: Soroptomists; CofC; Eastern Star; Daughters of the Nile; White Shrine; Farm Bur. Honors & Awards: Woman of the Year, Jaycees, 66 & Bus & Prof Women's Found, 72. Relig: Presbyterian. Mailing Add: 619 S Willson Bozeman MT 59715

JOHNSON, HENRIETTA (D)
Del State Rep
Mailing Add: 1213 Lobdell St Wilmington DE 19801

JOHNSON, HOUSTON K (D)
b Lafayette, Tenn, Jan 11, 09; s George A Johnson & Mildta Weems J; m 1930 to Willie B Williams; c Kenneth, Judy (Mrs Thomas Ray) & Wilma (Mrs Harvey Jerry). Educ: Macon Co High Sch, Tenn, 3 years; Bus Col, 2 years. Polit & Govt Pos: Precinct committeeman, Owen Co Dem Comt, Ind, 52-60, chmn, formerly; deleg, Ind State Dem Conv, 58-60; deleg, Dem Nat Conv, 60. Bus & Prof Pos: Employee, DuPont Rayon, 28-38; grocery bus, 38-43; mgr, Govt Post Exchange, 43-46; restaurant bus, 46-50; tool & cutter grinder, Allison Div, Gen Motors Corp, 50-; farmer, 50- Mem: Mason; Eastern Star; AFL-CIO; Farm Bur. Relig: Methodist. Mailing Add: 563 E North St Spencer IN 47460

JOHNSON, HOWARD CONWELL (D)
NDak State Rep
b Fairdale, NDak, Feb 10, 15; s Hans O Johnson & Clara Nygard J; m 1940 to Lillian Evelyn Hanson; c Bonnie (Mrs A Ronald Loraas), Patricia (Mrs David Fix), Howard, Jr, Larry & Kerry (Mrs Dennis Sullivan). Educ: Fairdale High Sch, grad, 33. Polit & Govt Pos: Twp supvr, Kinloss Twp, NDak, 44-50, mem, Kinloss Dist 129 Sch Bd, 45-48; NDak State Rep, 69-, mem appropriations comt, NDak House of Rep, 73- Bus & Prof Pos: Secy-treas, Fairdale Farmers Union Oil Co, 49-; supvr, Walsh Co Soil Conserv Dist, 59-69; secy-treas, Walsh Co Farmers Union, 59- Mem: NDak Asn Soil Conserv Dists (dir, 66-, pres, 69); NDak Farmers Union; Fairdale Boosters; Elks. Relig: Lutheran. Legal Res: Fairdale ND 58229 Mailing Add: State Capitol Bismarck ND 58501

JOHNSON, I S LEEVY (D)
SC State Rep
b Columbia, SC, May 16, 42; s Ollie James Johnson & Ruby Leevy J; m 1968 to Doris Yvonne Wright; c George Craig. Educ: Univ Minn, Assoc Mortuary Sci, 62; Benedict Col, BS, 65; Univ SC, JD, 68; Alpha Phi Alpha; Phi Alpha Delta. Polit & Govt Pos: Vchmn, Ward Seven Dem Party, Columbia, SC, 70; deleg, SC Dem State Conv, 70; SC State Rep, 71-73 & 75- Bus & Prof Pos: Mgr, Leevy's Funeral Home, 65-67; instr, Benedict Col; practicing attorney, currently. Mem: Richland Co, SC State & Am Bar Asns; Community Rels Guid Coun (bd dirs); Gtr Columbia CofC. Relig: Baptist. Mailing Add: 1808 St Louis Ave Columbia SC 29203

JOHNSON, IRENE L (D)
Chmn, Coos Co Dem Cent Comt, Ore
b Ala, Apr 12, 18; d William Campbell Leach & Doan Traylor L; m James F Johnson; c Juli, Jacquie, Janet (Mrs Robb) & William Buren. Educ: Agnes Scott Col, 2 years; George Washington Univ, 2 years; LaSalle Exten Univ, LLB, 69. Polit & Govt Pos: Secy to Congressman Joe Starnes, 40-44; secy-clerk, Law Comt State Legis, until 56; secy, Gov Robert Holmes, 57-59; law clerk, Circuit Judge James A Norman, currently; chmn, Coos Co Dem Cent Comt, Ore, 72- Bus & Prof Pos: Owner with husband, KOOS Radio, Coos Bay, Ore, 71- Mem: Dem Women of Coos Co; Bus & Prof Womens Club; Coos-Curry Press Club. Relig: Catholic. Mailing Add: 1142 N Tenth St Coos Bay OR 97420

JOHNSON, J WALLACE (D)
b Jasper, Ala, Jan 25, 41; s Floyd Hardy Johnson, Sr & Elva Harper J; single. Educ: Jacksonville State Univ, 59-63; Univ Ala, 64; George Washington Univ, 67-68; Ala Dist Circle K Int (gov). Polit & Govt Pos: Admin asst to US Rep Tom Bevill, Washington, DC, 67; admin asst to US Sen Harrison A Williams, 70-74; admin asst to US Rep James J Florio, NJ, 75- Relig: Presbyterian. Mailing Add: 501 Slaters Lane 19 Alexandria VA 22314

JOHNSON, JAMES BROWN (D)
Wyo State Rep
b Evanston, Wyo, Nov 11, 08; s Newell Benjamin Johnson & Isabella Brown J; m 1937 to Evelyn Syme; c Janet Evelyn, James S & Margaret Ann. Educ: Univ Utah, 31-32; Univ Wyo, BA, 36, MA; Phi Delta Kappa; Sigma Nu. Polit & Govt Pos: Wyo State Rep, 55-57 & 75- Bus & Prof Pos: Teacher social studies, Shoshoni Schs, Wyo, 36-37; jr high sch teacher, Reliance Sch, 38-43; high sch prin, Lovell Schs, 43-44; supt schs, Cokeville, 44-51; warehouseman, Mountain Feed Supply, Rock Springs, 51-58; elem prin, Superior Schs, 59-62; jr high sch prin, Rock Springs, 62-74. Mem: Lions. Relig: Latter-day Saint. Mailing Add: 112 Cedar St Rock Springs WY 82901

JOHNSON, JAMES P (R)
US Rep, Colo
b Yankton, SDak, June 2, 30; s Fred Johnson & Evelyn S J; m 1952 to Nancy Brown; c Dea Lynn, Julie Conner & Drake Bartel. Educ: Northwestern Univ, Evanston, BA, 52; Univ Colo, Boulder, LLB, 59; Sigma Alpha Epsilon. Polit & Govt Pos: Munic judge, Ault & Ft Collins, Colo; mem, Sch Bd, Ft Collins, 69-71; US Rep, Fourth Dist, Colo, 73- Bus & Prof Pos: Attorney, 59-72. Mil Serv: Entered as 2nd Lt, Marines, 52, released as Capt, 56, after serv in Marine Corps Res. Mem: Am Legion; Elks. Relig: Presbyterian. Legal Res: 922 Gregory Rd Ft Collins CO 80521 Mailing Add: 129 Cannon House Off Bldg Washington DC 20515

JOHNSON, JAMES VERNOR (D)
b Statesville, NC, June 14, 23; s Frank Link Johnson & Ruby Fraley J; m 1948 to Mary Geitner Thurston; c Mary Geitner & Ann Vernor. Educ: Univ NC, BS in Com, 46. Polit & Govt Pos: Chmn, Ninth Cong Dist, Young Dem Club, NC, 52-53; chmn, Statewide Sch Bd Selection Study Comn, 61-62; NC State Sen, 61-66; adv, Budget Comn, 63-64; mem, State Bd of Ment Health, 64-69; deleg, Dem Nat Conv, 68; chmn, NC Dem Exec Comt, 68-70. Bus & Prof Pos: Pres, Consolidated Coin Caterers Corp, Charlotte, NC; pres, Coca-Cola Bottling Co Consolidated; bd mem, Integon Corp & Cato Corp. Mil Serv: Sgt, Army Armored Div, 43-45; Prisoner of War, Ger, 44-45; Purple Heart. Mem: Kappa Sigma; VFW; Elks (Leading Knight, 56, Loyal Knight 57); Rotary; Am Legion. Honors & Awards: Young Man of the Year, Jaycees, 51. Relig: Methodist; mem off bd, 58-60 & 62-64 & chmn, 64-65, finance chmn, 58-63, lay leader, 64-66; vchmn admin bd, 75. Mailing Add: 3200 Wickersham Rd Charlotte NC 28211

JOHNSON, JED, JR (D)
b Washington, DC, Dec 27, 39; s Jed Joseph Johnson & Beatrice Luginbyhl J; m 1965 to Sydney Herlong; c Alice Herlong & Sydney Carlin. Educ: Univ Okla, BA, 61; Phi Eta Sigma; Omicron Delta Kappa; Pi Sigma Alpha; Pe-et. Polit & Govt Pos: US Rep, Sixth Dist, Okla, 64-66; spec asst to Sargent Shriver, Dir, Off Econ Opportunity, 67-68; mem educ prog, Equal Employ Opportunity Comn, 68-72; cand for Dem nomination for US Sen, Okla, 72; consult, US Senate Select Comt on Presidential Campaign Activities, 73; consult, Former Mem of Congress; pres, Jed Johnson Assocs, currently. Relig: Protestant. Mailing Add: 6740 Selkirk Dr Bethesda MD 20034

JOHNSON, JEWELLE RICHARDSON (D)
Chmn, Hot Spring Co Dem Cent Comt, Ark
b Prescott, Ark, Jan 15, 12; d Sylvester Richardson & Mattie Clark R; wid; c Robert O Browning, Jr & Betty (Mrs Conover). Educ: High Sch & Bus Sch. Polit & Govt Pos: Chmn, Hot Spring Co Dem Cent Comt, Ark, currently; chmn, Co Elec Comn; bd drs & vmayor, Malvern, currently. Bus & Prof Pos: Publisher & ed, newspaper, 64-66; partner, cosmetic co; owner of off supply & off furniture bus, Malvern. Mem: Eastern Star; Bus & Prof Women's Club; Press Asn; Hot Spring Co Farm Bureau; Retarded Children's Asn Hot Spring Co (bd dirs). Relig: Presbyterian. Legal Res: 1415 McBee St Malvern AR 72104 Mailing Add: PO Box 68 Malvern AR 72104

JOHNSON, JOE ARLEY (D)
Okla State Rep
b Spiro, Okla, Nov 2, 30; s Oscar Arley Johnson & Sylvia Casey J; m to Martha Ellen Gentry; c David, Ann Mead, Lee, Bill & George. Educ: Univ Okla Sch Jour, BA, 51. Polit & Govt Pos: Okla State Rep, 72-, vchmn pub safety & penal affairs comt, Okla House Rep, 75- Mem: Kiwanis; Retired Vol Firemen; Mason; ITU. Relig: Christian Church. Legal Res: 413 E First Heavener OK 74937 Mailing Add: Box 237 Heavener OK 74937

JOHNSON, JOEL J (D)
Pa State Rep
Mailing Add: Capitol Bldg Harrisburg PA 17120

JOHNSON, JOHN DAVE (D)
Chmn, Beadle Co Dem Party, SDak
b Hetland, SDak, Aug 22, 19; s John David Johnson & Mary Austed J; m 1941 to Margaret Gilmore; c Gary Davis, Kimeron Jill & Pamela Jean. Educ: Dakota Wesleyan Univ, BA, 42. Polit & Govt Pos: Mem city recreation bd, Huron, SDak, 62-66; chmn, Beadle Co Dem Party, 67- Bus & Prof Pos: Prin, Highmore Sch Syst, SDak, 42-45. Mem: Sertoma; Elks; Mason. Mailing Add: 1701 McDonald Dr Huron SD 57350

JOHNSON, JOHN EDWARD (D)
Ohio State Rep
b Monroe, Ind, Oct 26, 37; s Floyd Franklin Johnson & Osie Lenora Striker J; m 1959 to Carolyn Joyce Seifried; c Coleen Jenet, John Edward, II, twins, Heidi Michelle & Jill Renet, James Eric & Mark Stanley. Educ: Heidelberg Col, BA, 59; Univ Heidelberg, Ger, 57; Western Mich Univ Grad Sch, 61-62; Ind Univ Grad Sch, 62; Kent State Univ, MEd, 63; Univ Akron Col Law, JD, 75; Phi Kappa Delta; Sigma Tau Nu. Polit & Govt Pos: Deleg, Dem State Conv, Mich Dem Party, 64; cand, Nomination to Cong, Ninth Dist Dem Primary, Mich, 64; publicity dir, Leelanau Co Dem Comt, Mich, 64, chmn, 65; exec comt mem, Ninth Cong Dist Comt, 65; Wayne Co campaign mgr for Bob Secrest for Cong, Ohio, 66; city councilman, Orrville City Coun, 68-69; pres, Wayne Co Dem Club, 69-70; Ohio State Rep, 71-, chmn agr & natural resources comt, Ohio House Rep. Bus & Prof Pos: Educator & commun consult. Honors & Awards: Intercollegiate Debate Champion of Ohio, 56-58. Relig: United Church of Christ. Mailing Add: RR 2 Orrville OH 44667

JOHNSON, JOHN WARREN (R)
b Minneapolis, Minn, Jan 29, 29; s Walter E Johnson & Eileen Hemphill J; m 1950 to Marion Louise Myrland; c Daniel, Karen & Nancy. Educ: Univ Minn, BA, 51 M Club. Polit & Govt Pos: 13th ward alderman, Minneapolis City Coun, 63-67; Minn State Rep, 67-74; Rep cand for Gov, Minn, 74. Bus & Prof Pos: Exec vpres, Am Collectors Asn, 55-; mem bd dirs, First Nat Bank Edina, currently. Mil Serv: Entered as Seaman Recruit, Naval Res, 48, released as Tradesman 3/C, after serv in Korean Conflict, 2 years. Mem: Minn & Am Soc Asn Execs; US CofC; Nat Insts Bd Regents (chmn); Minn Med Ctr (dir). Honors & Awards: Nat Key Man Award, Am Soc Asn Execs, 65. Relig: Lutheran. Mailing Add: 5101 Irving Ave S Minneapolis MN 55419

JOHNSON, JOSEPH A (D)
Va State Deleg
Mailing Add: 436 Court St Abingdon VA 24210

JOHNSON, JOSEPH E (D)
NC State Rep
Mailing Add: 4301 Yadkin Dr Raleigh NC 27609

JOHNSON, JOSEPH EARL (D)
Chmn, Custer Co Dem Party, Nebr
b Ann Arbor, Mich, Aug 14, 46; s Earl Cedric Johnson & Leila Micheel J; single. Educ: Kearney State Col, 64-65; Nebr Wesleyan Univ, BA, 71; Student Senate, Nebr Wesleyan Univ; Young Dem Nebr Wesleyan; Nat Honor Soc; Elks Scholarship. Polit & Govt Pos: Pres, Custer Co Teen Dem, Nebr, 63-64; co-chmn, Kearney State Col Young Dem, 64-65; state committeeman, Young Dem Nebr, 66-68, exec secy, 68, treas, 68-69; third dist

committeeman, 69-; pres, Young Dem Nebr Wesleyan Univ, 67-68; alt deleg, Dem Nat Conv, 68, deleg cand, 72; alt deleg, Nebr Dem State Conv, 68, deleg, 72; pres, Citizens for Debate, 68-; third dist chmn, Spec Comt Young Dem Affairs, 68-; campaign coordr, Thomas for Senate & Callan for Cong, 70; spec research, Exon for Gov, 70; mem, Gov Inaugural Comn, 70; probation counsr, Lancaster Co, 70-; chmn, Custer Co Dem Party, 72-; legis lobbyist, Mid-Nebr Wildlife Club, Nebr State Legis, 73- Bus & Prof Pos: Foreman, Johnson Ranch, Anselmo, Nebr, 64-; campus rep, Time, Inc, & Braniff Int Airlines, 66-67; pres, Quest Assocs, 69-; law clerk, Runyan & Johnson, Attorneys, 73- Publ: A Political Biography of William J Bryan, Nebr Wesleyan Univ, 72; A History of the Nebraska Democratic Party, Nebr Dem Party, 5/67; Shall Earth & Man Survive, Nebr Wesleyan Univ, 5/69. Mem: Lancaster Legal Aid Soc (legal asst); Am Astro Res Group; Common Cause (dir legis res, 73-); Broken Bow Community Playhouse (publicist, 73-). Relig: Episcopal. Mailing Add: Quest Assocs Box 16 Rte 1 Anselmo NE 68813

JOHNSON, JOY JOSEPH **(D)**
NC State Rep
b Laurel Hill, NC, Nov 2, 22; s William Joseph Johnson & Edith Bucchanan J; m 1945 to Omega Evangeline Foster; c Deborah Charita. Educ: Shaw Univ, AB; Alpha Phi Alpha; Shaw Players. Hon Degrees: DD, Friendship Jr Col; LLD, Shaw Univ. Polit & Govt Pos: Dem precinct chmn, Fairmont, NC, 66-69; town comnr, Fairmont, 66-70; vchmn, Seventh Cong Dist Dem Party, 67-69; vchmn, Robeson Co Dem Exec Comt, 68-70; NC State Rep 24th Dist, 71- Bus & Prof Pos: Pastor, First Baptist Church, Fairmont, NC, 51-; vpres, Gen Baptist State Conv, 67-; pres, Southern Regional Nat Progressive Baptist Conv, 68-70; pres, Lumber River Housing Corp, Inc, 68- Publ: The modern prodigal, Baptist Informer, 3/69; Preacher Practical Politician. Mem: Lumber River Baptist Asn; Mason; NAACP; United Order of Salem; Southern Christian Leadership Conf. Honors & Awards: Man of Year Award, Fairmont, 71; NC State Baptist Citizenship Award, 71; Ambassador of Good Will Award & Youth Leadership Award, State Baptist Dist, 71; Community Relig & Polit Achievement Award, 72; Distinguished Community Serv Award, 73. Relig: Christian. Legal Res: PO Box 455 Fairmont NC 28340 Mailing Add: Box 7209 State Legis Bldg Raleigh NC 27611

JOHNSON, KAREN ANN **(D)**
VChairwoman, Fall River Co Dem Party, SDak
b Sauk Centre, Minn, Feb 4, 41; d Albert George Eggers & Alvina Fuoss E; m 1969 to James C Johnson; c Brenda Kay. Educ: Black Hills State Col, BSEd, 63. Polit & Govt Pos: Deleg, SDak Dem Conv, 68; vchairwoman, Custer Co Dem Party, 68-73; adv, Custer Co Young Dem, 72; vchairwoman, Fall River Co Dem Party, 73- Bus & Prof Pos: Instr govt, Am hist & typing, Sturgis Pub Schs, SDak, 63-65; instr govt & typing, Stanley Co High Sch, Ft Pierre, 65-67; instr social studies & math, Hot Springs Pub Schs, 67-69; substitute teacher, Custer Pub Schs, 70-72; substitute teacher, Hot Springs Pub Schs, 73- Mem: Am Lutheran Church Women (stewardship secy, 69-73). Relig: American Lutheran. Legal Res: 900 Sherman Hot Springs SD 57747 Mailing Add: Box 511 Hot Springs SD 57747

JOHNSON, KARNES OTTO **(R)**
NDak State Rep
b New England, NDak, Aug 16, 12; s Otto C Johnson & Ida J; m 1941 to Ruth E Clariss; c William K & Gail (Mrs Wayne Weishoar). Polit & Govt Pos: NDak State Rep, 65-, chmn agr comt, NDak House Rep, 69- Mem: Elks; Mason; NDak Stockmans Asn. Honors & Awards: Top Hand Award, NDak Stockmans Asn, 73. Mailing Add: Sentinel Butte ND 58654

JOHNSON, KURT L **(R)**
Idaho State Rep
Mailing Add: Rte 6 Box 407 Idaho Falls ID 83401

JOHNSON, LANCE FRANKLIN **(R)**
Chmn, Dodge Co Rep Party, Nebr
b Topeka, Kans, Aug 5, 38; s Harry Franklin Johnson & Dorothea Anne Simons J; single. Educ: Univ Kans, AB, 60; Univ Denver, MBA, 63; Omicron Delta Kappa; Sigma Chi. Polit & Govt Pos: Chmn, Fremont City Rep Party, Nebr, 67; mem, Nebr Equal Employ Opportunities Comn, 68-71; chmn, Dodge Co Rep Party, 68-; committeeman, Nebr State Rep Party, 68- Mil Serv: Nebr Air Nat Guard, 63-69, S/Sgt; Am Spirit Honor Medal. Mem: Rotary; Jaycees. Relig: Methodist. Legal Res: 1974 E Military Ave Fremont NE 68025 Mailing Add: 325 S Main St Fremont NE 68025

JOHNSON, LARRY ALAN **(D)**
b Farmington, Ill, July 17, 35; s Kenneth C Johnson & Merle Record J; m 1956 to Phyllis Mohn; c Perry Alan, Lori Rae, Denis Lynn & Scott Fitzgerald. Educ: Bradley Univ, 57 & 58. Polit & Govt Pos: Dem precinct committeeman, Ill, 62-69, chmn, Peoria Co Dem Cent Comt, formerly; pres, Limestone Dem Club, Limestone Twp, 63, 68 & 69; alt deleg, Dem Nat Conv, 64 & 68, deleg, 72. Bus & Prof Pos: Vpres, Kenney Johnson Moving & Storage, 53- Mem: Limestone Human Rels Coun (vpres); Oak-Grove PTA (vpres). Relig: Presbyterian. Mailing Add: 4104 Baker Lane Bartonville IL 61607

JOHNSON, LAWRENCE H **(R)**
Mem, Rep State Cent Comt & Exec Comt NMex
b Cedar Rapids, Iowa, May 30, 26; s Harry S Johnson & Florence Wagner J; m 1962 to Joyce Howard; c Regina. Educ: Okla State Univ, 45; Coe Col, AB(econ), 49; Univ Mich Law Sch, LLB, 52; Tau Kappa Epsilon; Phi Kappa Phi; Pi Delta Epsilon; Delta Theta Phi. Polit & Govt Pos: Pres, Coe Col Young Rep, 48; treas, Lea Co Rep Party, NMex, 56-67, chmn, 67-71; mem, Rep State Cent Comt & Exec Comt NMex, 67-, treas, 71-75. Bus & Prof Pos: Assoc, U M Rose, Attorney, Hobbs, NMex, 53; partner, Rose & Johnson, Attorneys, 54- Mil Serv: Entered as Seaman 1/C, Navy, 44, released as Electronic Technician's Mate 3/C, 46. Mem: Am Legion; VFW; Hobbs Community Players; Hobbs CofC; Gtr Hobbs United Fund (bd dirs, 71-73). Honors & Awards: Tom Mason award for outstanding serv to Hobbs Community Players, 68. Relig: United Presbyterian; mem bd trustees, First Presbyterian Church, Hobbs, 68-71 & 72-74. Legal Res: 702 Seco Dr Hobbs NM 88240 Mailing Add: Box 159 Hobbs NM 88240

JOHNSON, LEROY REGINALD **(D)**
b Atlanta, Ga, July 28, 28; s Leroy Johnson & Elizabeth Heard J; m 1948 to Nydia Cleopatra Whittington; c Michael Vince. Educ: Morehouse Col, AB, 49; Atlanta Univ, MA, 51; NC Col Law Sch, LLB, 57; Phi Beta Sigma. Polit & Govt Pos: Criminal investr, Solicitor Gen Off, 57-61; vpres, Southern Conf Dem, 62; Ga State Sen, 38th Dist, 62-74, chmn judiciary comt, Ga State Senate, 69-74; spec ambassador, Independence Celebration of Zanzibar, 63; pres, Ga Asn Citizens Dem Clubs, 64-; pres, Fulton Co Citizens Dem Clubs, 66-; mem, Ga State Dem Comt, formerly; vpres from Ga, Southern Conf Dem, currently. Bus & Prof Pos: Attorney-at-law, 61- Publ: United States Foreign Policy Towards Germany Since the Potsdam Conference, 51. Mem: Gate City Bar Asn (vpres); Ga Bar Asn; West Side Br, YMCA (bd dirs); Atlanta Negro Voters League (exec comt); Atlanta Jr Voters League (one of three founders). Honors & Awards: Citizen of the Year, Omega Psi Phi, 63; Freedom Award, NAACP, 63; Scottish Rite Mason of the Year; Lovejoy Award, Int Elks, 63; Commended by Ga State Senate, 67. Relig: Baptist. Legal Res: 372 Larchmont Dr NW Atlanta GA 30318 Mailing Add: 1014 Gordon St SW Atlanta GA 30310

JOHNSON, LESTER R **(D)**
b Brandon, Wis, June 16, 01; s John E Johnson & Ella M Paine J; m to Violet F Graunke, wid 1953; m 1954 to Marjorie M Gray; c Mary Lynn (Mrs Lindow), Jane Laura (Mrs Siefert) & Jone Lee (Mrs Hoffman). Educ: Lawrence Col, 19-21; Univ Wis, PhB, 24, LLB, 41. Polit & Govt Pos: Chief clerk, Wis State Assembly, 35-39; Dist Attorney, Jackson Co, Wis, 43-47 & 53; US Rep, Ninth Dist, Wis, 53-65. Bus & Prof Pos: Part-owner, Johnson Lumber & Fuel Co, Brandon, 24-35; liquidated banks trusts, 41-45; licensed real estate broker, Wis, 42-54; law practice, Black River Falls, Wis, 43-53. Mem: Tri-County Bar & Wis Bar Asns; Masons. Relig: Lutheran. Mailing Add: RFD 1 Box 222 Augusta WI 54722

JOHNSON, LOUISE B **(D)**
La State Rep
b Dubach, La, Oct 6, 24; d Thomas Anderson Brazzel & Ethel Holley B; m 1942 to Sam Johnson; c Samuel. Educ: La Tech Univ, 42, 61, 67, 70 & 71. Polit & Govt Pos: Chmn, Union Parish Tourist Comn; mem, Comt for Union Parish Retarded Children's Asn, currently; La State Rep, Union & Claiborne Parishes, 72-, mem appropriations comt, com comt, no fault ins comt & malpractice study comt, La House of Rep, currently. Mem: La & Nat Asns Ins Agts; Garden Club; La Trail Coun (vpres); El Dorado Art League. Honors & Awards: Spec Oscar for Pub Rels & Advert, Hartford Ins Co, 69, Agency of Year for La, 69. Relig: Baptist; Bernice First Baptist Church Choir. Legal Res: Hwy 167 S Bernice LA 71222 Mailing Add: PO Box 206 Bernice LA 71222

JOHNSON, LUCY BLACK **(D)**
Committeewoman, Conn State Dem Cent Comt
b Philadelphia, Pa, Sept 25, 24; d MacKnight Black & Lucy Grey Black Stimson; m 1948 to Pyke Johnson, Jr; c MacKnight Black & Thomas Pyke. Educ: Wheaton Col (Mass), BA magna cum laude, 46. Polit & Govt Pos: Mem, Greenwich Dem Town Comt, Conn, 59-, dist leader, 63-; deleg, Conn Dem State Conv, 62-; committeewoman, Conn State Dem Cent Comt, 36th Dist, 68-; mem, Conn State Dem Platform Comt, 74. Bus & Prof Pos: Publicity dept, Farrar, Straus & Co, New York, 46-48 & Alfred A Knopf, Inc, 48-54; free lance book reviewer, various newspapers & mag, 54-67; first reader & reviewer, Book-of-the-Month Club, 57-62; instr aide in Eng, Greenwich High Sch, Conn, 73-; first reader, Readers Digest Condensed Book Club, 74- Publ: Auth book rev, NY Herald Tribune, Providence J, Milwaukee J, Chicago Sun-Times, Progressive, Book-of-the-Month Club News, Saturday Rev & NY Times, 54-67; co-ed, Cartoon Treasury (anthology of cartoons from all over the world), Doubleday & Co, Inc, New York, 55. Mem: Greenwich Dem Women's Club; Greenwich Caucus of Conn Dem; Conn Women's Polit Caucus; League of Women Voters; NAACP. Relig: Religious Society of Friends (Quaker). Mailing Add: 5 Old Club House Rd Old Greenwich CT 06870

JOHNSON, MARY CATHERINE **(D)**
b Dilworth, Minn, Sept 7, 20; d Charles W Coryell & Sarah Duffy C; wid; c Catherine (Mrs Larry Anderson). Educ: High Sch, grad, 37; Tel Sch & R R Acct, summer 45. Polit & Govt Pos: Treas, Stutsman Co Dem Women, 58-64, campaign dir, 64-66; secy & regional dir, Dist 29 Dem Women, 66-68; deleg, NDak State Dem Non-Partisan League Conv, 66, 68, 70 & 72; secy, Stutsman Co Dem Non-Partisan League Party, 68; deleg, Dem Nat Conv, 68, mem rules comt, 72; dir, NDak Comt on Polit Educ-WAD, 68; dir, NDak Comt on Polit Educ, AFL-CIO, 69-70; NDak mem, Nat Dem Charter Comn, 73-; NDak rules observer & alt deleg, Dem Nat Mid-Term Conf, 74. Bus & Prof Pos: Direct serv agent, B N Inc, NDak & Minn, 45-69. Mem: VFW Auxiliary; BRAC (T-C Div). Relig: Catholic. Mailing Add: 354 E Main St Valley City ND 58072

JOHNSON, MARY LORRAINE **(D)**
Utah State Rep
Mailing Add: 464 Harvard Ave Salt Lake City UT 84111

JOHNSON, MELVIN **(D)**
b Hudson, SDak, June 24, 02; s Olaf Johnson & Sinava J; m 1926 to Margrat Nelson; c Joseph, Clifford & Norman. Educ: Geddes High Sch. Polit & Govt Pos: Pres, Charles Mix Co Weed Bd, SDak, 62-69; committeeman, Agr Stabilization Conserv Comt, 63-64 & 65; chmn, Charles Mix Co Dem Party, 64-72; chmn, SDak Dem Party, 64-66; Dem nominee, SDak State Sen, 66. Mem: Dist One Farmers Union (vpres, 67-); Mason (master, 54, Dist Master, 54-59); RAM; Consistory; Shrine. Relig: Lutheran; Past pres, Luther League. Mailing Add: Geddes SD 57342

JOHNSON, MICHAEL **(D)**
Mem, Dem Nat Comt, Pa
Mailing Add: 101 Pine Harrisburg PA 17101

JOHNSON, MICHAEL GEORGE **(D)**
Kans State Rep
b El Paso, Tex, Jan 24, 37; s James Tobin Johnson & Katherine George J; m 1962 to Gwyn Ellen Hendricks; c Timothy Tobin, Ann Kathleen, Robert Hendricks, Mary Elizabeth & Emily Lynn. Educ: Kans State Col, 56-58; Univ Mo, Kansas City, DDS, 59-63. Polit & Govt Pos: Kans State Rep, 75- Bus & Prof Pos: Dentist, 63- Mem: Am & Kans Dent Asns; Elks; KofC. Relig: Roman Catholic. Mailing Add: RR 4 Abilene KS 67410

JOHNSON, NEAL SOX **(R)**
Mem, Ark Rep State Comt
b Murfreesboro, Ark, Feb 14, 33; s John Olvy Johnson & Elsie Faye Kelling J; m 1956 to Carmen Louise Webb; c Tena Elizabeth, Neal Steven & Olvy Lynn. Educ: Henderson State Teachers Col, BSE, 55; Hendrix Col; Univ Ark; Little Rock Univ; Lamar Tech Col; summers, Am Bridge Div, US Steel training course struct steel drafting, 55, Nat Soc Found stipend, Univ Ark, 60. Polit & Govt Pos: Chmn, Howard Co Goldwater for President Comt, Ark, 64; mem, Howard Co Elec Comn, 66, chmn, 67; chmn, Howard Co Rockefeller for Gov, 66; chmn, Howard Co Rep Comt, formerly; mem, Ark Rep State Comt, 66-; deleg, Nat Rep Campaign Mgr Seminar, 67; mem, Ark Game & Fish Comn, 67; chmn two political rallies

for Gov Winthrop Rockefeller Campaign, 68; exec dir, Ark Rep Party, formerly. Bus & Prof Pos: Owner, Johnson's Texaco Serv Sta, Ark, 46-51; hwy construction eng dept, Ark Hwy Dept, 52; archit drafting & estimating, Lollar Construction Co, 52-55; struct steel draftsman, Am Bridge Co, Gary, Ind & Orange, Tex, 55-56 & 56-57; design draftsman, Shipbuilding Div, Bethlehem Steel Corp, Tex, 57; gen drafting & surv, Stowers & Boyce, Architects, Ark, 58; gen drafting & supv of jr draftsmen, Swaim & Allen, Architects, 59; instr, Bryant High Sch, 57-60; supvr pub rels & sales construction supvr, Stanley Brown, Architect, 60-62; partner & mgr, Carroll Bldg & Appliance Co, 62-66; owner, Nashville Bldg Specialties, 66- Mil Serv: Army Res, 56-64, Capt, serv in Inf & Combat Engrs. Mem: F&AM (Master Mason); Sigma Phi Epsilon; Rotary (dir); CofC (pres); Nashville City Planning Comn. Relig: Baptist. Mailing Add: 6511 Cantrell Rd Little Rock AR 72207

JOHNSON, NINA SIDLER (D)
State Committeeman, NY Dem Comt
b North Rose, NY, Apr 13, 27; d Harry Eugene Sidler & Lena Belle Sears S; m 1952 to Robert S Johnson; c Susan Sidler. Educ: Rochester Inst of Tech Sch for Am Craftsmen, 1 year. Polit & Govt Pos: Secy, Wayne Co Dem Comt, NY, 60-; secy to chmn, Wayne Co Dem Party, 63-69; state committeeman, NY Dem Comt, 68-; town clerk, Rose, NY, 72- Bus & Prof Pos: Secy to pres, William C Moore & Co, Newark, NY, 51-63. Mem: Nat Rural Letter Carrier's Auxiliary, NY State Hist Asn; Wayne Co Hist Soc; Univ Rochester Art Gallery; Eng Setter Asn, Mid-Atlantic Region. Relig: United Methodist. Mailing Add: 482 Glenmark Rd North Rose NY 14516

JOHNSON, ODELL (D)
Chmn, 17th Assembly Dist Dem Unit
b Laurel, Miss, Aug 2, 36; s Ollie Johnson & Bernice Baker J; div. Educ: Univ Wis-Milwaukee, BA, 73. Polit & Govt Pos: Mem exec comt, Milwaukee Co Dem Unit, 71; chmn, Seventh Ward Dem Unit, 71-72; bd dirs, Milwaukee Ment Health Asn, 71-72; mem inner-city comts, Lindsay for President & McGovern for President, 72; bd dirs, Milwaukee Am Civil Liberties Union, 73; chmn, 17th Assembly Dist Dem Unit, 73- Bus & Prof Pos: Dist sales mgr, Milwaukee Jour, 61-65; co-mgr, Kroger Co, 65-68; mgr, Odell's Supermarket, 68-70; consult, Ill Migrant Coun, 70; training supvr, Concentrated Employment Prog, 71-72, dir, 72. Mil Serv: Entered as E-1, Army, 55, released as E-5, 58, after serv in Army Security Agency, Japan, 56-58; Letter Commendation. Honors & Awards: Civic & Leadership Award, YMCA, 55. Relig: Protestant. Mailing Add: 3300 N 11th St Milwaukee WI 53206

JOHNSON, OWEN H (R)
NY State Sen
Mailing Add: 6 Learner St West Babylon NY 11704

JOHNSON, PAUL BURNEY (D)
b Hattiesburg, Miss, Jan 23, 16; s Gov Paul B Johnson (deceased) & Corrine Venable J; m to Dorothy E Power; c Patricia, Paul B, III (Chipper) & Shelby Venable. Educ: Univ Miss, LLB, 40, pres, Student Body; Blue Key; Omicron Delta Kappa; Membership, Hall of Fame. Polit & Govt Pos: Asst US Attorney, Southern Dist, Miss, 48-51; Lt Gov, Miss & pres, Miss State Senate, 60-64; Gov, Miss, 64-69. Bus & Prof Pos: Lawyer. Mil Serv: Entered as Pvt, Marine Corps, 42, released as Capt, 46, after serv in SPac; Maj, Marine Corps Res. Mem: Sigma Alpha Epsilon; Moose; Mason (32 degree); Scottish Rite; Shrine. Honors & Awards: Distinguished Serv Award, Am Vet of World War II, 49. Relig: Methodist. Mailing Add: Memorial Dr Hattiesburg MS 39401

JOHNSON, PAUL EDWIN (R)
Chmn, Huntington Co Rep Cent Comt, Ind
b Huntington Co, Ind, Jan 2, 34; div; c Jeff, Jeni & Jamie. Educ: Ind Univ, 1 year. Polit & Govt Pos: Precinct committeeman, Huntington Co, Ind, 60-70; chmn, Huntington Co Young Rep, 60-66; deleg, Ind Rep State Conv, 62-68; chmn, Huntington City Comt, 67; chmn, Fourth Dist Ind Young Rep, 67-70; chmn, Ind Young Rep, 69-71; youth chmn, Ind State Platform Comt, 70; chmn, Huntington Co Rep Cent Comt, 70-; deleg, Rep Nat Conv, 72. Mil Serv: Entered as Pvt, Army, 58, released as Sgt 1st class, 59, after serv in 187th Brigade, Paratroopers, Europe. Mem: VFW; Elks; Am Legion. Mailing Add: 458 Agnes St Huntington IN 46750

JOHNSON, POMPIE LOUIS, JR (R)
Asst Treas, Rep State Cent Comt Calif
b Pocatello, Idaho, Dec 19, 26; s P L Johnson, Sr & Nellie Pittman J; m 1958 to Mary Lynn T Hughes; c Tamara & Karen. Educ: Idaho State Univ, BA; Boston Univ Sch Law, JD; Pi Kappa Delta; Alpha Phi Alpha. Polit & Govt Pos: Asst to dir of orgns, Citizens for Eisenhower-Nixon, Nat Hq, NY, 52; chmn, Negro Californians for Rockefeller, 64; mem, Adv Comt, Calif State Dept of Corrections, 65-68; secy-treas, Black Calif State Rep Caucus, 68-70; mem, Rep State Cent Comt Calif, 70-, asst treas, 75-; exec secy, Calif Progressive Rep Club, 71; deleg, Rep Nat Conv, 72, mem, Permanent Orgns Comt, 72; vpres, Cosmopolitan Rep Club, 73- Bus & Prof Pos: Practice of law, Boston, Mass, 53-60; vpres & managing off, Safety Savings & Loan, 60-66; asst vpres, Security Pacific Nat Bank, 66-73; vpres & mgr, Calif Fed Savings & Loan, 73- Mil Serv: Entered as Pvt, Air Force, 45, released as Cpl, 46, after serv in training command, 45-46; Am Theatre of Opers; Victory Medals. Honors & Awards: Community Serv Award, Calif Women's Polit Study Group, 65 & Los Angeles Co Bd Supvr, 66; Unsung Hero's Award, Los Angeles Sentinel, 72. Relig: Episcopal. Mailing Add: PO Box 18934 Los Angeles CA 90018

JOHNSON, RALEIGH WEST (R)
Mem Ariz Rep State Comt
b Phoenix, Ariz, Aug 11, 34; s Charles Edgton Johnson & Julia Gwendolyn West J; m 1961 to Margene Symons; c Grant, Shauna, Lori, Mark & Julie. Educ: Brigham Young Univ, BS, 60; Columbia Univ Sch Law, JD, 63; Columbia Univ Grad Sch Bus, MBA, 63; Blue Key; Nat Scholar. Polit & Govt Pos: Mem, Navajo Co Rep Exec Comt, Ariz, 64-, chmn, 68-70; Town attorney, Snowflake, Ariz, 65-70, Holbrook, 66-, Taylor, 67-; precinct committeeman, Navajo Co Rep Party, Ariz, 66-; mem, Ariz State Rep Exec Comt, 68-72; mem, Ariz Rep State Comt, 68-; bd educ, Holbrook, Ariz, 69- Bus & Prof Pos: Law partner, Axline & Johnson, Holbrook, Ariz, 64- Mem: Am Judicature Soc; Ariz & Am Bar Asns; Rotary. Relig: Latter-day Saint. Legal Res: 806 N Seventh St Holbrook AZ 86025 Mailing Add: PO Drawer 160 Holbrook AZ 86025

JOHNSON, RAYMOND ALLAN (R)
Chmn, Marlboro Rep City Comt, Mass
b Marlboro, Mass, July 18, 36; s Herbert Gottfrid Johnson & Theresa Pietras J; m 1966 to Carolyn Gates Whithed. Educ: Worcester Polytech Inst, Mass, BSME, 58; vpres, The Shield. Polit & Govt Pos: Vpres, Young Rep Club, Marlboro, Mass, 63-64, treas, 64-66, ed & founder, Newsletter, 64-66, pres, 66-68; ward one chmn, Marlboro Rep Ward Comt, 64-68; hq coordr, Frank Walker's Marlboro Mayorality Campaign, 65 & 67; deleg, Mass Rep State Conv, 66; chmn, City of Marlboro Inaugural Ball, 66; trustee, Marlboro Pub Libr, 66-68; chmn, Marlboro Rep City Comt, 68- Bus & Prof Pos: Indust engr, Johnson-Claflin Corp, Marlboro, Mass, 58-59 & 61-65, vpres & sales mgr, 69-; safety engr, Buckler, Irvin & Graf, Winchester, 65-69. Mil Serv: Entered as Pvt, Army, 59, released as SP-5, 61, after serv in Ord Missile Command, Redstone Arsenal, Huntsville, Ala, 59-61. Mem: Am Soc Mech Engr; Mason (Master); Friends of the Marlboro Pub Libr (vpres, 70-). Honors & Awards: Cyrus Felton Medal, Rensselaer Polytech Medal & Marlboro Rotary Club Scholarship, 54. Relig: Unitarian Universalist; Asst Dir Sr High, Unitarian-Universalist Rowe Camp, summer 59, incorporator, 64-68, Mem Parish Comt, Marlboro Unitarian-Universalist Church, 64-67 & 69-, finance chmn, 65 & 67. Mailing Add: 206 Bolton St Marlboro MA 01752

JOHNSON, RAYMOND BLAIR (R)
Mem, Cambria Co Rep Exec Comt, Pa
b Johnstown, Pa, Sept 17, 09; s Stewart William Johnson & Marcella Grace O'Neil J; m 1938 to Louise Amelia Thiele; c Stewart William & Raymond Blair, Jr. Educ: Lebanon Valley Col, AB, 34; grad study, Univ Md, 34 & Univ Pittsburgh, 37. Polit & Govt Pos: Chmn, Civil Serv Fire Dept, Johnstown, Pa, 55-56, publicity chmn, Cambria Co Rep Finance Comt, 56, mem, 58-; mem, Cambria Co Rep Exec Comt, 57-; deleg, 22nd Cong Dist, Rep Nat Conv, 56 & 64; mem, City Coun, Johnstown, 58-62; chmn, Cambria Co Rep Presidential Campaign, 64; mem, Bd Cambria Co Comnr, 64- Bus & Prof Pos: Teacher social sci, Cochranville High Sch, 36-41; pres, Johnson's Heating & Air Conditioning, Inc, 47- Mem: Asn of Blind (dir); Co Ment Health & Ment Retardation Asn (bd mem, currently); Mason; Shrine; Rotary. Relig: Lutheran. Mailing Add: 347 Elknud Lane Johnstown PA 15905

JOHNSON, ROBERT E (R)
Colo State Sen
Mailing Add: Box 572E Rte 1 Golden CO 80401

JOHNSON, ROBERT HENRY (D)
Wyo State Sen
b Denver, Colo, Aug 16, 16; s Henry Johnson & Ellen Haines J; m 1949 to Helen M Hamm; c Susan M, Glen R & Leslie Ellen. Educ: Univ Wyo, BA, 38, JD, 63; Univ Colo, 62; Alpha Tau Omega. Polit & Govt Pos: Precinct committeeman, Sweetwater Co Dem Comt, Wyo, 48-49 & 51-, chmn, currently; committeeman, Wyo State Dem Comt, 66-; chmn educ subcomt, Wyo Statute Rev Comn, 67-69; Wyo State Sen, 67-; alt deleg, Dem Nat Conv, 68, deleg, 72; mem libr bd, Sweetwater Co, 68-, chmn, 72-73; mem, State Comn Intergov Coop, 69-71; deleg, Dem Nat Mid-Term Conf, 74. Bus & Prof Pos: State ed, Wyo State Tribune, Cheyenne, 37-38; news ed, Northern Wyo Daily News, Worland, 38-41, gen mgr, 45-48; ed, Rock Springs Daily Rocket, 48-49, gen mgr, 51-61, state mgr, United Press Asns, Cheyenne, 49-51; attorney-at-law, Rock Springs, 63- Mil Serv: Entered as Pvt, Army, 41, released as Maj, 45, after serv in 8th Air Force, ETO, 44-45; Air Force Res, Lt Col; Distinguished Flying Cross; Air Medal with Four Oak Leaf Clusters; Good Conduct Medal; Am Defense Serv Medal; Am Campaign Medal; European Campaign Ribbon with Four Battle Stars; World War II Victory Medal; Air Force Res Medal. Mem: Wyo State Bar; Am Bar Asn; Wyo Press Asn; Elks; Am Legion. Relig: Protestant; chmn bd of trustees, First Congregational Church, 65-66. Mailing Add: 1515 Albany Circle Rock Springs WY 82901

JOHNSON, ROBERT MAURICE (R)
Fla State Rep
b Akron, Ohio, Sept 1, 34; s Maurice N Johnson & Mary Elizabeth Skinner J; m 1969 to Patricia Edenfield; c Jeannene Elizabeth, Cecilia Ann, Christopher Michael & Kathryn Rebecca. Educ: Fla State Univ, BS, 58; Duke Univ, 61-62; Univ Fla Col Law, JD, 64; Omicron Delta Kappa; Gold Key; Univ Hall of Fame; Sigma Chi; Phi Alpha Delta. Polit & Govt Pos: Fla State Rep, Dist 74, 70- Bus & Prof Pos: Attorney, Boylston, Johnson & Harnden, Sarasota, Fla, 64- Mil Serv: Entered as 2nd Lt, Air Force, 58, released as 1st Lt, 61, after serv in 92nd Bomb Wing, SAC, 58-61; Capt, Air Force Res, 64; Presidential Unit Citation, Presidents Eisenhower & Kennedy. Mem: Fla & Am Bar Asns; Federal Bar; Am Trial Lawyers Asn; Kiwanis. Honors & Awards: Sarasota Citizen of Year, 71; Outstanding First Year Legislator, 71; Pelican Award for Conserv, 73; Legis Friend of Arts & Cult Award, 73; Fla Sch Bd Asn Award for Excellence in Educ Legis, 73. Relig: Methodist. Mailing Add: 5042 Oxford Dr Sarasota FL 33581

JOHNSON, ROBERT T (BOB) (R)
Mo State Rep
Mailing Add: 201 Nolleen Lane Lee's Summit MO 64063

JOHNSON, ROBERTSON LEE (R)
Attorney Gen, Ore
b Portland, Ore, 1930; s Clarence Dean Johnson & Ruth Robertson J; m 1956 to Dorothy Marie Miller; c Theodore Robertson, Cynthia Ann, Charles Lee, Ruth Baker & Marie Ferrar. Educ: Princeton Univ, AB, 53; Stanford Univ Law Sch, JD, 59. Polit & Govt Pos: Trial attorney, Anti-trust Div, US Dept Justice, 59-61; Ore State Rep, 65-69; Attorney Gen, Ore, 69- Bus & Prof Pos: Attorney, King, Miller, Anderson & Yerke, Portland, Ore, 61-63, Hampton & Weiss, 63-65 & Mautz, Souther, Spaulding, Kinsey, Williamson, 65-69. Mil Serv: Entered as Ens, Navy, 56, released as Lt(jg), 59, after serv in USS Destroyer Shelton, Squadron 21; Two Letters of Commendation. Mem: Am, Fed & Ore Bar Asns. Mailing Add: State Capitol Salem OR 97310

JOHNSON, ROGER (D)
Ga State Rep
Mailing Add: PO Box 1034 Canton GA 30114

JOHNSON, ROGER (D)
b Grass Lake, Mich, Dec 3, 14; s Ira Lee Johnson & Ina Funk J; m 1968 to Maryann Wilcox; c Thomas, Robert, Laura, John & Sally (Mrs Holden) & stepchildren, Ronald Kreps, Rebecca (Mrs Smith), Lucinda (Mrs Craig) & Kenneth Kreps. Educ: Battle Creek Col, 33-34; Albion Col, AB, 37; Univ Mich Law Sch, 37-38; Western Mich Univ, 40-41, teaching cert; Delta Tau Delta. Polit & Govt Pos: Mich State Sen, 65-66; co comnr, Marshall, 69-70; admin asst to Secy of State, Mich, 71- Mil Serv: Flying cadet, Army Air Corps, 40. Relig: Protestant. Mailing Add: 632 Birch St Marshall MI 49068

JOHNSON, ROY MONRAD (D)
SDak State Rep
b Wentworth, SDak, Aug 26, 08; s Carl Johannes Johnson & Gubjor Halverson J; m 1932 to Lillie Stella Halverson; c Carvel Henry, Gertrude Royann, Roger Stanton & Karen Leann. Educ: Ruthland High Sch, grad, 28. Polit & Govt Pos: Mem, Ruthland Twp Bd; SDak State Rep, Lake & Moody Co, 57-61 & 65-67, SDak State Rep, Lake & Miner Co, 69- Bus & Prof Pos: Pres & dir, Sioux Valley Elec Bd, Colman, SDak; mem, Ruthland Farmers Elevator Bd, 9 years. Mem: SDak Farmers Union. Honors & Awards: Award for Outstanding Parliamentary Procedure at Nat Rural Elec Conv. Relig: Lutheran; pres, Madison Lutheran Church. Mailing Add: Wentworth SD 57075

JOHNSON, ROY W, JR (D)
Ala State Rep
Mailing Add: 4501 20th St NE Tuscaloosa AL 35401

JOHNSON, RUDOLPH (D)
Ga State Rep
Mailing Add: 6126 Navaho Trail Morrow GA 30260

JOHNSON, S ALBERT (D)
Idaho State Rep
Mailing Add: Rte 3 N Box 219 Pocatello ID 83201

JOHNSON, SAM (R)
Ore State Rep
Mailing Add: 415 S Canyon Dr Box 356 Redmond OR 97756

JOHNSON, SAM D (D)
Assoc Justice, Tex Supreme Court
b Hubbard, Tex, Nov 17, 20; s Sam D Johnson, Sr; m 1946 to June Page; c Susan Page (Mrs Harris); Janet Lynn (Mrs Beard) & Sam Jim. Educ: Baylor Univ, BBA, 46; Univ Tex, LLB, 49. Polit & Govt Pos: Co attorney, Hill Co, Tex, 53-54; dist attorney, 66th Judicial Dist, 55-58, dist judge, 59-65; with Houston Legal Found, 65-67; judge, 14th court of civil appeals, Houston, 67-72; assoc justice, Tex Supreme Court, Austin, 73- Mil Serv: Entered as Pvt, Army, 42, released, after serv in 95th Inf Div, Third Army, 45. Relig: Presbyterian. Legal Res: Houston TX Mailing Add: PO Box 12248 Capitol Station Austin TX 78711

JOHNSON, SEYMOUR BENNETT (R)
Mem Exec Comt, Miss Rep Party
b Quincy, Ill, June 4, 28; s Vivion Arvid Johnson & Emily Kay Seymour J; m 1951 to Joan Lee Dorsett; c Leslee Kay, Lynn Annette & Gay Dorsett. Educ: Iowa State Univ, BS, 50; Harvard Bus Sch, MBus, 52; Beta Theta Pi. Polit & Govt Pos: Chmn, Sunflower Co Rep Party, Miss, formerly; vchmn, Miss Deleg Rep Nat Conv, 64; mem exec comt, Miss Rep Party, currently. Mil Serv: Entered as 2nd Lt, Air Force, released as 1st Lt, after serv in Air Transport Command, 53-55. Mem: Miss Soybean Asn (dir, 69-); Miss Seed & Cattle Improv Asns & Farmer Grain Mkt Terminal (dir); Am Soybean Inst (bd dir, 69-); Miss Soybean Promotion Bd (chmn, 70-). Relig: Presbyterian. Legal Res: 8 Seymour Dr Indianola MS 38751 Mailing Add: PO Box 7 Indianola MS 38751

JOHNSON, SIDNEY ARTHUR (R)
VChmn, Steele Co Rep Cent Comt, Minn
b Litchfield, Minn, Oct 23, 39; s Clifford Charles Johnson & Pearl Ebba J; m 1959 to Maureen Kay Larson; c Bryce Kirby. Educ: Litchfield High Sch, 4 years; Humboldt Inst, 6 months. Polit & Govt Pos: Club vchmn, Minn State Young Rep, 68-69, club chmn, 69-70, dist chmn, 70-71, state chmn, 71-73; vchmn, Steele Co Rep Cent Comt, 73- Mil Serv: Entered as Pvt, Army Res, 62, released as E-4, 68, after serv in 47th Avn Bn. Mem: Southern Minn Data Processing Asn (secy-treas, 70-); Data Processing Mgt Asn (committeeman, 71-). Relig: Methodist. Mailing Add: Echo Heights Rte 3 Owatonna MN 55060

JOHNSON, STANLEY ARTHUR (R)
SDak State Rep
b Mitchell, SDak, Jan 13, 25; s S R Johnson & Erma Larson J; m 1950 to Marjorie E Barnhart; c Dale Allen, Cherie Louise, Leila Marie Carmen Lea, Debra Rena & Kimberly Kay (deceased). Educ: Dakota Wesleyan Univ, 43-44; SDak State Univ, 47-49; Alpha Zeta. Polit & Govt Pos: Supvr & treas, Davison Co Conserv Dist, SDak, 52-, pres, SDak Asn Conserv Dist, 57-59; comnr, SDak Water Resources Comn, 61-64; twp clerk, Mitchell Twp; SDak State Rep, Davison Co, 68- Mil Serv: Entered as Pvt, Army Engrs, 45, released as T/5, 47, after serv in 1151st Combat Engrs, ETO, 46; Victory Ribbon; Commendation Award. Mem: Davison-Hanson Co Farm Bur; CofC; Davison Co 4-H (leader). Relig: Presbyterian; elder. Mailing Add: RR 5 Mitchell SD 57301

JOHNSON, STEPHEN R (BART) (D)
b Cleveland, Miss, Mar 12, 47; s T R Johnson & Margret Lyons J; m 1969 to Doris Buchanan. Educ: Univ Fla, BSBA, 69; Alpha Tau Omega. Polit & Govt Pos: Admin asst to US Rep Charles E Bennett, Fla, 74- Bus & Prof Pos: Asst vpres, Barnett Bank, Jacksonville, Fla, 70-74. Mil Serv: PO-3, Coast Guard Res, 69. Mailing Add: 7308 Burroughs Lane Falls Church VA 22043

JOHNSON, SYLVIA TAYLOR (D)
b Chicago, Ill, Nov 27, 37; d Henry S Taylor & Katie Webster T; m 1966 to Howard N Johnson; c Stephen & JoAnne. Educ: Howard Univ, BA, 59; Southern Ill Univ, MS, 61; Mich State Univ, 63; Univ Iowa, PhD, 74; Alpha Kappa Alpha; pres, Alpha Chap, Nat Const Comt, 60, founder & adv to chap, Western Ill Univ, 70-71. Polit & Govt Pos: Mem, League Women Voters, 70-; mem steering comt, Citizens for Shirley Chisolm, Iowa City, Iowa, 72; deleg, Johnson Co Dem Conv, 72; deleg, State Dem Conv, 72; deleg, Nat Dem Conv, 72; mem local affairs comt, Chicago Chap Independent Voters Ill, 73-74. Bus & Prof Pos: Grad asst, Southern Ill Univ, 59-61; counr, Roosevelt Univ, 61-62; asst instr, Mich State Univ, 62-63; research spec, Encycl Brittannica, 63-64; asst prof, Trenton State Col, 64-66; counr, Bloom Twp High Sch, 66-68; lectr, Northeastern Ill State Col, 68-69; asst prof, Western Ill Univ, 69-71; lectr, Augustana Col, 71-72; spec research asst, Univ Iowa, 72-74; asst prof statistics & research methodology, Howard Univ, 74- Publ: Auth, Factor Analysis of a Self-Concept Instrument, Proc Mid-South Educ Research Asn, 73. Mem: Am Educ Research Asn; Nat Coun on Measurement Educ (mem 74 Task Force on Affective Measurement); Alpha Kappa Alpha. Honors & Awards: Scholar Group Rels Workshop, Am Jewish Comt, 54; Nat Competitive Scholar, Howard Univ, 55; Woman of the Year, Howard Univ Womens Club, 59. Relig: Protestant. Mailing Add: 301 Gilsan Ct Silver Spring MD 20902

JOHNSON, THATCHER (R)
Iowa State Dep Secy of Agr
b Gowrie, Iowa, Aug 3, 28; s Axel Emanuel Johnson & Laura Mollenhoff J; m 1956 to Sherrill Lynn McCarty; c Tyra Lynn, Kelly Lane, Shane Thatcher & Courtney McCarty. Educ: State Univ Iowa, 47-50; Drake Univ, BA, 73, Sigma Alpha Epsilon. Polit & Govt Pos: Mem, Webster Co Conserv Bd, Iowa, formerly; mem, Fifth Cong Dist Rep Cent Comt, 68-69; chmn, Webster Co Rep Cent Comt, 68-69; Iowa Dep Secy Agr, 73- Bus & Prof Pos: Owner & operator, Johnson Lumber Co, Gowrie, Iowa until 69; lobbyist, Iowa Nursing Home Asn, 70; proj work, Iowa Bankers Asn. Mil Serv: Entered as Pvt, Army, 46, released as Tech-5, 47, after serv in Hq Serv Record Detachment. Mem: Toastmasters; Gowrie Commercial Club; Kiwanis. Honors & Awards: Established a continuing prog of banking educ courses in all 16 Iowa regional commun cols. Relig: Lutheran; mem coun, St John's Lutheran Church, Madrid, Iowa. Mailing Add: RR 2 Madrid IA 50156

JOHNSON, THOMAS STEPHEN (D)
Mem Exec Comt, Dem Party of Ga
b Campbellsville, Ky, Sept 27, 49; s Thomas Harvey Johnson & Sybil Elliott J; m 1974 to Connie Holcomb. Educ: Ga Inst Technol, BS, 71; Ga State Univ, MBA, 73; Lambda Chi Alpha; Student Ctr Bd. Polit & Govt Pos: Comnr, City of Decatur, Ga, 74-; mem staff, Gov Ga, 75-; mem exec comt, Dem Party of Ga, currently. Mil Serv: 2nd Lt, Army Res, 73, 1st Lt, currently. Publ: Co-auth, A structural approach to job enrichment, Bank Admin, 6/73, Do away with on the job boredom, Mgt Rev, 10/73 & Successful job enrichment, Atlantic Econ Rev, 11-12/74. Mem: Admin Mgt Soc; Ga Munic Asn (community develop comt); DeKalb Munic Asn. Relig: Baptist. Mailing Add: 1225 Church St Apt B1 Decatur GA 30030

JOHNSON, U ALEXIS
US Ambassador-at-Large
b Falun, Kans, Oct 17, 08; s Carl Theodore Johnson & Ellen Forsse J; m 1932 to Patricia Ann Tillman; c Judith (Mrs Mason S Zerbe), Stephen Tillman, William & Jennifer (Mrs Lee Bishop). Educ: Occidental Col, AB, 31, LLD, 57; Georgetown Univ Sch of Foreign Serv, 31-32. Polit & Govt Pos: Career officer, US Dept of State Foreign Serv, 35-; lang attache, Am Embassy, Tokyo, Japan, 35-37; vconsul, Seoul, Korea, 37-39, Tientsin, China, 39 & Mukden, Manchuria, 40-42; second secy, Am Embassy, Rio de Janeiro, 42-44; US Army Civil Affairs Training Sch, Univ Chicago, 44; Am Consul, Manila, Philippines, 45; Gen Hq Supreme Comdr Allied Powers, Tokyo, Japan, Aug 45; Am Consul, Yokohama, 46, Am Consul Gen, 47-50; dir, Off of Northeast Asian Affairs, Dept of State, 50-51, Dep Asst Secy of State for Far Eastern Affairs, 51-53; US Ambassador, Czech, 53-58, Thailand, 58-61; Dep Under Secy of State for Polit Affairs, 61-64 & 65-66; Dep Ambassador, Vietnam, Saigon, 64-65; US Ambassador, Japan, 66-69; Under Secy of State for Polit Affairs, 69-73; Ambassador-at-Large & Chief of US Deleg to Strategic Arms Limitation Talks, 73- Mem: Japan-Am Soc; Phi Beta Kappa; Am Foreign Serv Asn; Chevy Chase Club. Honors & Awards: Nat Civil Serv League's Career Serv Award; Rockefeller Pub Serv Award; Presidential Award for Distinguished Fed Civilian Serv, 71; Appt Rank Career Ambassador; Medal of Freedom. Mailing Add: 3133 Connecticut Ave NW Washington DC 20008

JOHNSON, VANNETTE WILLIAM (D)
b Little Rock, Ark, May 27, 30; s Charlie Johnson & Laura Miller J; m 1959 to Delois Davis; c Juliette, Alberta, Melanie & Leontyne. Educ: Ark AM&N Col, AB, 52; Univ Ark, Fayetteville, MEd, 61, DEd, 70; Phi Delta Kappa; Alpha Kappa Mu; Alpha Phi Alpha. Polit & Govt Pos: Co deleg, Dem State Conv, 74; deleg, Dem Nat Mid-Term Conf, 74. Bus & Prof Pos: Asst coach & instr, Merrill High Sch, Pine Bluff, Ark, 52-57; asst coach, head track coach & instr, AM&N Col, 57-62, head football coach & athletic dir, 62-73; prof & dir athletics, Univ Ark, Pine Bluff, 73-74, prof health & phys educ, 74- Mem: Nat Athletic Steering Comt (exec secy, 75-); Am Football Coaches Asn; Am Alliance for Health, Phys Educ & Recreation; Pine Bluff CofC; Ark High Sch Coaches Asn. Honors & Awards: Coach of Year, Ark Elks, 67; head coach, Astrodome First Annual Black All-Star Football Classic, 71; Cert of Achievement, Army ROTC, 72. Relig: Methodist. Legal Res: 1905 Collegiate Dr Pine Bluff AR 71601 Mailing Add: PO Box 123 Univ Ark Pine Bluff Pine Bluff AR 71601

JOHNSON, VERNON LEE, JR (R)
b Williamsburg, Ky, Aug 13, 33; s Vernon Lee Johnson, Sr & Myrtle Haun J; m 1957 to Mattie Clay Cartmill. Educ: Univ Ky, 51; Pikeville Col, 52; Transylvania Col, 53; Ky State Univ, 72; Univ Ky & Transylvania Col Young Rep Clubs. Polit & Govt Pos: Pres, Pendleton Co Young Rep Club, Ky, 63; campaign chmn, Boyle Co Rep Comt, 67; chmn, 14th Sen Dist Rep Exec Comt, 50th Legis Dist Rep Exec Comt & 50th Judicial Dist Rep Exec Comt, 68-71; exec officer, Ky Dept of Ins, 68-71, analyst, 71-; chmn, Boyle Co Rep Exec Comt, 68-72; comnr, Ky Comn Human Rights, 71-75. Bus & Prof Pos: Owner, Johnson Floral Co, Falmouth, Ky, 57-63; supvr, Retail Credit Co, Danville, 63-68. Mil Serv: Entered as Pvt, Army, 54, released as Pfc, 56, after serv in Adj Gen Corps, Caribbean Theatre, 55-56. Publ: Newspaper features. Mem: Blue Grass Lincoln Club; Royal Bombay Bicycle Club; Ky Col; Ky Adm. Relig: Southern Baptist. Mailing Add: 610 Logan Ave Danville KY 40422

JOHNSON, VIRGIL JOEL (R)
Chmn, Houston Co Rep Party, Minn
b Caledonia, Minn, Apr 23, 32; s John Emannuel Johnson & Ethel Ann Mitchell J; m 1966 to Mary Ann Muenkel. Educ: Houston Pub High Sch, Minn, grad, 50; Air Training Command Sch & Air Traffic Control Radar Repairman Course. Polit & Govt Pos: Mem, Comt on Planning, Recreation & Natural Resources, Asn Minn Counties, 65-, bd dirs, 72-; mem, Houston Co Planning Comn, 65-, past chmn; mem, Houston Co Welfare Bd, 65-, past chmn; mem, Houston Co Bd Comnr, 65-, past chmn; mem, Minn Rep State Task Force Comt on Govt Opers, 69-70; mem, Minn Rep State Cent Comt, 69-; chmn, Houston Co Rep Party, 69- Bus & Prof Pos: Farmer, Houston Co, Minn, 50- Mil Serv: Entered as Airman Basic, Air Force, 54, released as S/Sgt, 58, after serv in 1951st Airways & Air Community Squadron, Mil Air Transport Serv, Far East, 55-57. Mem: Minn Welfare Asn; Caledonia CofC (pres, 73-); Caledonia Rod & Gun Club; Minn Asn Retarded Children; VFW. Relig: Methodist. Mailing Add: 104 E Grove St Caledonia MN 55921

JOHNSON, WALLACE HAROLD, JR (R)
Asst Attorney Gen, Land & Natural Resources Div, Dept Justice
b Cleveland, Ohio, Oct 7 39; s Wallace Harold Johnson & Esther Emma Miller J; m 1962 to Donna Mae Simpson; c Kimberley A, W Todd, Victoria & Eric William. Educ: Ohio Univ, BA, 61; Rutgers Sch Law, 61-62; Univ Toledo Sch Law, JD, 65; Sigma Nu. Polit & Govt Pos: Trial attorney, US Dept of Justice, 65-69; minority counsel, Subcomt on Criminal Practices & Procedures, US Senate Judiciary Comt, 69-70; assoc dep attorney gen, Dept of Justice, 70-72, asst attorney gen, Land & Natural Resources Div, 73-; spec asst to the President, 72-73. Mem: Am & DC Bar Asns; Phi Alpha Delta. Honors & Awards: Admitted to practice

before the Supreme Court of Ohio, Courts in the DC, and the Supreme Court of the US; Outstanding Alumni, Ohio Univ, 72. Relig: Lutheran. Mailing Add: 1858 Foxstone Dr Vienna VA 22180

JOHNSON, WILLIAM ARTHUR (R)
Chmn, Jennings Co Rep Party, Ind
b Harrisville, Mich, Nov 5, 24; s Milo Naper Johnson & Cora Teeple J; m 1946 to Janet Mary Nonenmacher; c Jill, Julia, Todd & Jennifer. Educ: Miami Univ, 43-45; Univ Mich, MD, 49; Sigma Chi; Phi Alpha Kappa. Polit & Govt Pos: City councilman, North Vernon, Ind, 60-68; chmn, Jennings Co Rep Party, 68- Bus & Prof Pos: Pvt practice of medicine, North Vernon, Ind, 52- Mil Serv: Entered as Seaman, Navy, 43, released as Midn, 46, after serv in V-12 Prog; entered as Lt(jg), Navy, 49, released as Lt, 51, after serv in Med Corps, Korea. Mem: Am Med Asn; Airplane Owners & Pilots Asn; Am Acad Gen Practice; Shrine; VFW. Relig: Methodist. Mailing Add: 318 Jennings St North Vernon IN 47265

JOHNSON, WILLIAM R (R)
b Oct 21, 30; married; c two daughters. Educ: Dartmouth Col; Harvard Law Sch. Polit & Govt Pos: Vchmn, Legis Coun, NH; chmn, NH Rep State Comt, formerly; NH State Sen & Majority Leaders, NH State Senate, formerly; NH State Rep, formerly; assoc justice, NH Superior Court, currently. Bus & Prof Pos: Attorney-at-law; instr of law, Tuck Sch, Dartmouth Col. Mil Serv: Army, 2 years. Mailing Add: 14 Rayton Rd Hanover NH 03755

JOHNSON, YOLANDE MARIE (R)
b New Orleans, La, Aug 27, 06; d Alvah Bell & Camille Marie Cohen B; m 1947 to Marshall N Cheatham. Educ: YMCA Bus Sch, 32-34; Northwestern Col Chiropody, DSC, 39. Polit & Govt Pos: Pub mem, Labor Dept, State of Ill, 69-75; alt deleg, Rep Nat Conv, 72. Bus & Prof Pos: Pres & owner, Landa Realty Co, 62-75; dir, South Cent Real Estate Bd, 73-75; exec secy, South Cent Med Bldg Corp, 73-75; comt on salesmen, Chicago Real Estate Bd, 75- Mem: Alpha Gamma Pi (exec secy, 69-71, pres, 71-73); Girl Friends, Inc (pres, 68-72); Independent Acct Asn (comt mem). Relig: Theosophist. Mailing Add: 2548 Murfreesboro Rd Nashville TN 37217

JOHNSRUD, JUNNE MARGARETTE (D)
Committeewoman, Mont Dem State Cent Comt
b Hinsdale, Mont, June 12, 20; d Hilmer Bert Lund & Anna Bertha Croxton L; m 1942 to Lyle Carter Johnsrud, Sr; c Lyle Carter, Jr & Mark Randall. Educ: Hinsdale High Sch, grad honors, 40. Polit & Govt Pos: Co cong committeewoman, 67-73; mem gov comt, Land & Water Resource Bd, 71-73; secy-treas to Sen McGowan, 73-75; committeewoman, Mont Dem State Cent Comt, 73- Bus & Prof Pos: Head off girl, Local 751 Area Machinists, Tacoma, Wash, 41-43; saleswoman for five large toy mfr, Pac Northwest, 43-44; chmn, State Home Demonstration Clubs, 55-60; pres, Mont Fedn Garden Clubs, 60-63; dir, Rocky Mountain Region, 65-67, nat chmn of Resolutions Policy Proj, 67-75, fourth vpres, Nat Coun State Garden Clubs, 75- Publ: Co-ed, Mont Gardens, 58-60 & 67-69, ed, 60-63. Mem: Mont Home Demonstrations (chmn); Mont Federated Garden Clubs; Nat Coun State Garden Clubs, Inc. Honors & Awards: Nat Conserv Award for Rocky Mountain Region; Nat Publ Award for Mont Gardens; Cited Hon Engr Award, Mont Hwy Dept by Gov Anderson, 72. Relig: Lutheran. Mailing Add: 1308 Front Ft Benton MT 59442

JOHNSTON, ANN F (D)
Chmn, Union Co Dem Party, Iowa
b Bedford, Iowa, Dec 18, 16; d Miles J Murphy & Fannie Patrick M; m 1954 to Bernard O Johnston; c George F Hayes. Educ: Clarenda Commun Col, 2 years. Polit & Govt Pos: Chmn, Union Co Dem Party, Iowa, 66- Bus & Prof Pos: Adminr & owner of two nursing homes, Creston, Iowa, 55- Mem: VFW Auxiliary; Am Legion Auxiliary; Creston CofC (chmn, 72); Rebecca Lodge; Elks Auxiliary. Relig: Protestant. Mailing Add: 610 Grand Ave Creston IA 50801

JOHNSTON, EDWARD ELLIOTT (R)
High Comnr, Trust Territory of the Pac Islands
b Jacksonville, Ill, Jan 3, 18; s Leonard Edward Johnston & Erma Lytle Elliott J; m 1950 to Clara Margaret Stacey; c Janice Linell (Mrs Louis J Regine, III) & Karen Elleen. Educ: Ill Col, Jacksonville, AB in Psychol & Econ, 39; CPCU, 64; Phi Beta Kappa. Hon Degrees: Hon LLD, Ill Col, 70. Polit & Govt Pos: Deleg, Hawaii State Rep, Conv, 53-68; chmn, Honolulu Co Rep Comt, Hawaii, 55-58; Lt Gov, Hawaii, 58-59; deleg & mem platform comt, Rep Nat Conv, 60, alt deleg, 64 & deleg, 68; chmn, Hawaii State Bd of Econ Develop, 60-63; state chmn, Rep Party of Hawaii, 65-69; high comnr, Trust Territory of the Pac Islands, 69- Bus & Prof Pos: Pres, 50th State Ins Assocs, Inc, 60-66; vpres, Hawaiian Ins & Guaranty Co, Ltd, 66-69. Mil Serv: Entered as Pvt, Army Air Corps, 42, released as Maj, 52, after serv in World War II & Korea, Continental US & Pac Area. Mem: YMCA; PTA; Kiwanis; Waikiki Athletic Club; Capitol Hill Club. Honors & Awards: Received many awards, debating, high sch & col, state high sch champion, Ill, finalist in 2 nat tourneys. Relig: Congregational. Legal Res: HI Mailing Add: PO Box 116 Capitol Hill Saipan Mariana Islands

JOHNSTON, ELTON ANDREW (R)
Chmn, Wayne Co Rep Cent Comt, Iowa
b Diagonal, Iowa, June 27, 08; s George Andrew Johnston & Sadie Fisher J; m 1939 to Beatrice Helena Bradley; c John Andrew, Mary Lynn (Mrs Dodds), Kathleen Ann, Mary Ellen (Mrs Talbot) & Paul Bradley. Educ: Creston Jr Col, 33-35; Drake Univ, LLB, 38; Delta Theta Phi. Polit & Govt Pos: Chmn, Drake Univ Young Rep, 36; Attorney, Wayne Co, Iowa, 47-51; chmn, Iowa Rep State Conv, 62; chmn, Wayne Co Rep Cent Comt, currently. Mil Serv: Marine Corps, 27-31; re-entered as Lt(jg), Navy, 44, released as Lt, 46, after serv in US Naval Armed Guard, 44-45; African-European, Am & SPac Ribbons; Second Nicaraguan Campaign Ribbon. Mem: Wayne Co Bar Asn (pres); Third Judicial Dist, Iowa State & Am Bar Asns; Am Legion. Relig: Protestant. Mailing Add: 107 W Jackson Corydon IA 50060

JOHNSTON, GEORGE R (D)
Mont State Rep
Mailing Add: 504 Third St SE Cut Bank MT 59427

JOHNSTON, HARRY A, II (D)
Fla State Sen
Mailing Add: 221 Monroe Dr West Palm Beach FL 33405

JOHNSRUD, IMOGENE BANE (R)
Exec Secy, Rep State Cent Comt Md
b Lundale, WVa, July 7, 22; d Augustus Fulweider Bane & Ellamae Rollins B; m 1948 to Drexel Marion Johnston. Educ: Marshall Col, 40-41; WVa Univ, 45-48; Alpha Sigma Alpha. Polit & Govt Pos: Rep precinct chmn, Harford Co, Md, 58-62, dist chmn, 62-66; chmn, Harford Co Rep Cent Comt, formerly; pres, Harford Fedn Rep Women, 68-70; exec secy, Rep State Cent Comt Md, 69-; Northern regional vchmn, Md Fedn Rep Women, 70-; deleg, Rep Nat Conv, 72. Bus & Prof Pos: Statistician, Army Air Forces, DC, 42-45; admin asst, sales dept, Sterling Faucet, Morgantown, WVa, 49-51; tea room mgr, Hutzler's, Baltimore, Md, 51-55; dent asst to Dr Drexel Johnston, Perry Hall, 55-60. Mem: Md State Dent Asn Women's Auxiliary; Baltimore Co Dent Asn; Federated Garden Clubs of Md; Baltimore Civic Opera Guild. Relig: Protestant. Mailing Add: 2600 Mountain Rd Rte 1 Joppa MD 21085

JOHNSTON, J BENNETT, JR (D)
US Sen, La
b Shreveport, La, June 10, 32; m 1956 to Mary Gunn; c Bennett, Hunter, Mary & Sally. Educ: Washington & Lee Univ; US Mil Acad; La State Univ Law Sch, LLB, 56. Polit & Govt Pos: La State Rep, 64-68, Floor Leader, La House Rep; La State Sen, 68-72; US Sen, La, 72-; deleg, Dem Nat Mid-Term Conf, 74. Bus & Prof Pos: Attorney, Johnston, Johnston & Thornton, until 72. Mil Serv: Judge Adv Gen Corps, Army, 56-59. Mem: Admitted to La Bar; Am, La & Shreveport Bar Asns. Legal Res: LA Mailing Add: Rm 254 432 Senate Off Bldg Washington DC 20510

JOHNSTON, JANET J (R)
Mem, Rep State Cent Comt Calif
b Woodland, Calif, Aug 25, 39; d Henry Harold Johnston & Margaret Chulick J; single. Educ: Am River Col, Sacramento, Calif, grad, 62. Polit & Govt Pos: Vpres, Women Rep Federated Club, Winters, Calif, 67-68; mem, Yolo Co Rep Cent Comt, 69-73, vchmn, 72-73; assoc mem, Calif Rep State Cent Comt, 70-72, mem, 72-; deleg, Rep Nat Conv, 72; elector, Calif State Electoral Col, 72; Rep Nat Committeewoman, 72-75, co-chmn, Rep Nat Comt, 73-74; mem, Calif Rep State Exec Comt, 72- Bus & Prof Pos: Dir, Winters Dist CofC, Calif, 64-70, vpres, 65-66 & pres, 66-67; dir, Yolo Co CofC, 65-70. Mem: Int Arabian Horse Asn; Order of Rainbow for Girls (life mem); Calif Farm Bur Fedn; Calif Arts Soc; Nat Fedn Rep Women. Relig: Presbyterian. Mailing Add: Box 201 Rte 1 Winters CA 95694

JOHNSTON, JEFFREY SMITH (D)
Okla State Rep
b Seminole, Okla, Jan 16, 51; s Charles W Johnston & Arlene Smith J; single. Educ: Univ Okla, BA, 73; Univ Okla Law Sch, 73-; Phi Beta Kappa; Phi Eta Sigma; Phi Delta Phi; Phi Delta Theta. Polit & Govt Pos: Okla State Rep, 75- Bus & Prof Pos: Mem bd eds, Okla Law Rev, 74- Mem: Seminole & Wenoka CofC; Seminole Rotary; Seminole Co Cattlemen's Asn; Seminole Co Dem Women's Club. Honors & Awards: Robert Bass Award in Polit Sci, Univ Okla, 72; Selected one of ten top graduates, Univ Okla, 74. Relig: Baptist. Legal Res: 640 Morningside Dr Seminole OK 74868 Mailing Add: Box 1724 Seminole OK 74868

JOHNSTON, KENNETH DARWIN, JR (D)
b Minneapolis, Minn, July 10, 29; s Kenneth Darwin Johnston & Irma Elizabeth Ardnt; m 1966 to Betty M Webb; c Karen, Kathy, Kris, Kim & Kenneth Darwin, III. Educ: Univ Wash; Metrop Bus Col, Seattle, grad. Polit & Govt Pos: Mem exec comt, Wash State Dem Cent Comt, 69-, treas, 71-72; deleg, State & Nat Dem Conv, 72; assessor, Pierce Co, Wash, 71- Bus & Prof Pos: Dept head, Fed Res Bank, Seattle, Wash, 51-56; sr bank examr, Wash Div Banking, Olympia, 56-62; exec mgr, CofC, Burien, 63; pres, dir & founder, Nat Bank, Puyallup, 63-66; treas & dir, Fed Old Line Ins Co, 66; orgn & legis rep, Wash State Credit Union League, 66-71. Mil Serv: Pfc, 47-50, Army. Mem: Eagles; Wash State Assessors Asn; Int Asn of Assessing Officers; AMVETS (mil liaison off); Local 461 Teamsters. Honors & Awards: Outstanding State Dir of Wash, Jaycees, 58; Selected Outstanding Young Man of Wash State & Puyallup, 64. Legal Res: Rte 2 Box 330 Eatonville WA 98328 Mailing Add: Rm 831 Co-City Bldg Tacoma WA 98402

JOHNSTON, KENNETH R (D)
Treas, Sierra Co Dem Cent Comt, NMex
b Los Angeles, Calif, July 7, 27; s Benjamin Bynum Johnston & Doshie May Hedrick J; m 1949 to Jacqueline McKinney; c Mark Kevin & Jana Rae. Educ: NMex State Univ, 1 year. Polit & Govt Pos: NMex State Sen, 57-60 & 65-66; treas, Sierra Co Dem Cent Comt, NMex, 69- Bus & Prof Pos: Pres, Elephant Butte Boat Co, Inc, NMex, 60-68; partner, Elephant Butte Lodge, 63-68; owner, Johnston Oil Co, Elephant Butte, 66-; co-owner, ProGas Serv, Elephant Butte, 72- Mil Serv: Entered Army, 50, released as Cpl, 52, after serv in 716th AAA. Relig: Protestant. Legal Res: Lots 7 & 8 Block J Hot Springs Landing Elephant Butte Lake NM 87935 Mailing Add: PO Box 110 Elephant Butte NM 87935

JOHNSTON, KEVIN P (D)
Conn State Rep
Mailing Add: Park St RR 1 Putnam CT 06260

JOHNSTON, MAUREEN (R)
b Murphysboro, Ill, Dec 24, 14; d Harold Worthen & Mabel Logan W; m 1932 to Charles Wayne Johnston, div; c Charles Thomas, Timothy Wayne, Robert Harold & John Allan. Educ: Marion Pub Schs, Ill. Polit & Govt Pos: Secy, Williamson Co Rep Women's Club, 59-63, pres, 63-67, parliamentarian, 67-; chmn, Williamson Co Rep Comt, formerly. Bus & Prof Pos: City clerk, Marion, Ill, 59- Mem: VFW Auxiliary; Eastern Star; Hosp Auxiliary. Relig: United Methodist. Legal Res: 100 Public Square Marion IL 62959 Mailing Add: 607 E Meridian Marion IL 62959

JOHNSTON, PETER W (D)
Maine State Sen
Mailing Add: W Linestone Rd Ft Fairfield ME 04742

JOHNSTON, PHILIP WILLIAM (D)
Mass State Rep
b Chelsea, Mass, July 21, 44; s Philip William Johnston & Elizabeth Foley J; m 1965 to Beverly Ruth Balestrier; c Ellen & Robert. Educ: Univ Mass, Amherst, BA, 67. Polit & Govt Pos: Mass State Rep, 75- Bus & Prof Pos: Social worker, Mass Dept Pub Welfare, 67-69; exec dir, Robert F Kennedy Action Corps, 69-75. Mem: New Eng Asn Child Care; Common Cause; Proj Friend (bd dirs); Coun Vol Child Care Agencies (bd dirs). Legal Res: 134 Tilden Rd Marshfield MA 02050 Mailing Add: State House Boston MA 02133

JOHNSTON, ROBERT EDWARD (D)
Ark State Rep
b Little Rock, Ark, Sept 11, 40; s Ezekiel Bennet Johnston & Kathleen Conley J. Educ: Rice Univ, BA, 62, BSME, 63; Oxford Univ, BA, 65, MA, 68; Columbia Univ, PhD, 73. Polit & Govt Pos: Ark State Rep, 73- Bus & Prof Pos: Assoc prof, Univ Ark, Little Rock, 70- Mil Serv: Entered as 2nd Lt, Army, 65, released as Capt; Capt, Res. Publ: Co-auth, Politics in Arkansas: the constitutional experience, Acad Press Ark, 72. Mailing Add: 2122 Broadway Little Rock AR 72206

JOHNSTON, RONALD VERNON (D)
Deleg, Los Angeles Co Dem Cent Comt
b Los Angeles, Calif, Dec 27, 42; s Arthur Vernon Johnston & Lillian K Nelson J; m 1963 to Patricia Joan Westerlind; c Michael A R. Educ: Pasadena City Col, AA, 63; LaSalle Univ, 4 years; Phi Kappa Tau. Polit & Govt Pos: Chmn, 43rd Assembly Dist, Dem Vol Comt, Calif, 64-65; nominee, 43rd Assembly Dist, Dem Party, 68; deleg, Los Angeles Co Dem Cent Comt, 54th Assembly Dist, 68-; deleg, Calif Dem State Cent Comt, 68-73. Bus & Prof Pos: Packaging engr, Owen-Illinois Inc, 63-67; mgt-consult, Boise-Cascade Corp, 67-68; resident mgr, Reynolds Securities Inc, San Diego, 74- Mem: Registered Rep, NY Stock Exchange; Am Stock Exchange; Nat Asn Securities Dealers. Relig: Methodist. Mailing Add: 1239 Berkeley Dr Glendale CA 91205

JOHNSTON, WILLIAM JAMES (R)
Chmn, Bannock Co Rep Cent Comt, Idaho
b Twin Falls, Idaho, Apr 18, 42; s Peter Barbour Johnston, Jr & Ruth Brown J; m 1965 to Karen Yvonne Sundrud; d Kristine Diane, Michael James, Russell William, Sherri Lynn & Suzanne Elizabeth. Educ: Univ Idaho, BSEd, 65; Brigham Young Univ, MRE, 68; Idaho State Univ, DA Govt, 75; Silver Lance; Farm House Fraternity; Delta Sigma Phi; Tau Kappa Epsilon; Phi Mu. Polit & Govt Pos: Chmn, Inkley for Utah State Rep, 64; chmn, George Hansen for US Rep Comt, 74; chmn, Bannock Co Rep Cent Comt, Idaho, 74- Bus & Prof Pos: Teacher, Ogden High Seminary, 65-67; chaplain, Univ Calgary, 67-71; instr, Inst Relig, Idaho State Univ, 71-; realtor, C Forsman Real Estate, 73- Honors & Awards: Student Body Pres, Univ Idaho, Distinguished-Outstanding Sr, Theopholius Sr Award; Outstanding Adv, Student Asn Univ Calgary; Serv Award United Campaign; March of Dimes Serv Award. Relig: Latter-Day Saint. Legal Res: 2126 Pole Line Rd Pocatello ID 83201 Mailing Add: Box 132 Idaho State Univ Pocatello ID 83201

JOHNSTONE, DOUGLAS INGE (D)
Ala State Rep
b Mobile, Ala, Nov 15, 41; s Harry Inge Johnstone & Kathleen Cawthorne Yerger J; m 1970 to Mary Frances Jayne; c Inge. Educ: Rice Univ, AB, 63; Tulane Univ Law Sch, JD, 66; Phi Delta Phi. Polit & Govt Pos: Ala State Rep, 75- Bus & Prof Pos: Attorney-at-law, Mobile, Ala, 66- Mil Serv: Entered as 2nd Lt, Army, Combat Engr Corps, 63, released as Capt, 72, after serv in 547th Engr Bn, 7th Army, ETO, 67-69. Publ: History of Equity in Alabama, Ala Lawyer, 7/66. Mem: Am & Ala Bar Asns; Mobile Bar Asn (mem legis comt, 75-); Mobile Cerebral Palsy Asn (trustee, 70-); Jaycees; Mobile Co Wildlife Asn. Honors & Awards: Meritorious Serv Award, Mobile Co Bd Health, 68; Humanitarian Serv Award, Mobile Cerebral Palsy Asn, 73; Second Place in Nation in Environ Improv, US Jaycees, 73. Relig: Episcopal. Legal Res: 2351 Venetia Rd Mobile AL 36605 Mailing Add: 3100 Cottage Hill Rd Suite 311 Mobile AL 36606

JOINER, FRED C (D)
Okla State Sen
Mailing Add: State Capitol Oklahoma City OK 73105

JOINER, WILLIAM STANLEY (R)
Chmn, Orange Co Rep Comt, Tex
s John D Joiner & Katherine Spencer J; m 1963 to Ann Levingston; c Glen, Susan, David & Lynn. Educ: Univ Tex, Austin, BBA, 59; Beta Gamma Sigma; Phi Delta Theta. Polit & Govt Pos: Chmn, Orange Co Rep Comt, Tex, 73- Bus & Prof Pos: Exec vpres, Joiner Assocs Inc, Orange, Tex, 62- Mem: Rotary; Tex Asn Ins Agts; Orange CofC. Honors & Awards: Chartered Property Casualty Underwriter, 62. Relig: Methodist. Legal Res: 4507 Meeks Dr Orange TX 77630 Mailing Add: PO Box 98 Orange TX 77630

JOLICOEUR, EDWARD THOMAS (D)
Chmn, Ventura Co Dem Cent Comt, Calif
b Waverly, Minn, Mar 15, 21; s Edward Jerome Jolicoeur & Cora Beauchamp J; m 1951 to Lorraine Elizabeth Daigle; 12 children. Educ: St Thomas Col, BA, 49; Loyola Univ, Los Angeles, 49-50. Polit & Govt Pos: Mem, Human Rels Comn, Ventura Co, Calif, 70-74; chmn, Ventura Co Dem Cent Comt, mem resolutions comt & exec bd, 73-; trustee, Community Col Bd, Ventura Co, 75- Mil Serv: Entered as Pvt, Air Corps, 42, released as Cpl, 46. Mem: IMAGE; NAACP; Lions; League of Women Voters; Common Cause. Legal Res: 1793 Calle Rocas Camarillo CA 93010 Mailing Add: PO Box 692 Camarillo CA 93010

JOLLY, CARL (D)
Ala State Rep
Mailing Add: PO Box 366 Gardendale AL 35071

JOLLY, DAN (D)
Wash State Sen
b Leahy, Wash, Apr 3, 07; s Willis Monroe Jolly & Abigail Campbell J; m 1931 to Harriet Vaughn; c Danell (Mrs Arnold Hudlow), Janis (Mrs James Pavel, deceased) & Sandra (Mrs Merlin Wallace). Educ: High sch. Polit & Govt Pos: Pub utility dist comnr, Franklin Co, 47-70; pub hosp dist comnr, Connell, 51-63; mayor, Connell, 56-69; Wash State Rep, 63-69; Wash State Sen, currently. Bus & Prof Pos: Farmer; pres, Connell CofC, 54; pres, Connell Parent Teachers Asn, 54-55. Mem: Grange (exec comt, Wash State Grange, 48-). Relig: Methodist. Mailing Add: Box 10 Connell WA 99326

JOLLY, EDWARD SIDNEY (D)
Miss State Rep
Mailing Add: Box 36 Collinsville MS 39325

JOLLY, HENRY LEVI (D)
Chmn, Cherokee Co Dem Comt, SC
b Gaffney, SC, May 17, 37; s Joe Dean Jolly & Winnie Anthony J; m 1966 to Mary Mason McConnell; c Mary Christian, Sarah Lisa & Henry L, Jr. Educ: Limestone Col, AB in Econ & Govt; Converse Col, grad work; Lambda Mu Sigma. Polit & Govt Pos: Chmn, Young Dem of Cherokee Co, SC, 61; SC State Rep, 62-68; chmn, Cherokee Co Dem Comt, 75- Bus & Prof Pos: Teacher, Gaffney Sr High Sch, SC, 65-66; realtor, Henry L Jolly Co, Gaffney. Mil Serv: Naval Res (Ret). Mem: Cherokee Co Asn Real Estate Bd; Civitan Club; Life Scout; RSM; Jr CofC. Relig: Baptist. Mailing Add: 104 Pinewood Dr Gaffney SC 29340

JOLOVITZ, HERBERT ALLEN (D)
b Canton, Ohio, Aug 28, 30; s Louis Jolovitz & Dora Shapiro J; m 1958 to Reva Feldman; c Paul Adam & Jennifer Susan. Educ: Ohio State Univ, BS, 48, LLB, 53. Polit & Govt Pos: Admin asst to Sen Young, Ohio, formerly; deleg, Dem Nat Conv, 64 & 68; spec asst for fed liaison to Gov John Gilligan, Ohio, Washington, DC, 71-74; chief legis asst to US Sen Patrick Leahy, Vt, currently. Mil Serv: Entered as 2nd Lt, Air Force, 54, released as 1st Lt, 56, after serv in Judge Advocate Gen Corp. Mem: Beta Gamma Sigma; Phi Eta Sigma. Legal Res: Canton OH Mailing Add: 7531 Sebago Rd Bethesda MD 20034

JOLY, CYRIL MATTHEW, JR (R)
Rep Nat Committeeman, Maine
b Waterville, Maine, May 22, 25; s Cyril M Joly & Lorette LaPointe J; single. Educ: Colby Col, BA, 48; Boston Univ Law Sch, LLB, 51; pres, Newman Club, Delta Upsilon & Interfraterbity Coun. Polit & Govt Pos: City chmn, Rep City Comt, Waterville, Maine, 52 & 66-; Cent Maine chmn, Eisenhower for President Campaign, 52; mem staff, Rep Nat Comt, Washington, DC, 54; spec asst to Secy Health, Educ & Welfare, 55-57; mem staff, Rep Cong Comt, fall 56; mem staff, Inaugural Comt, winter 56; mem, Manhattan Rep Comt, New York, 59; mayor, Waterville, Maine, 62-65; mem, Kennebec Co Rep Comt, 62-; chmn, Maine Goldwater for President Comt, 64; chmn, Maine State Rep Comt, 67-71; Maine State Sen, 72-74; Rep Nat Committeeman, Maine, currently. Bus & Prof Pos: Attorney-at-law, Waterville, Maine, 51-53 & 61-; pub affairs dir, Nat Asn Mfg, New York, 57-61. Mil Serv: Entered as Pvt, Army, 43, released as S/Sgt, 46, after serv in 66th Inf Div, ETO, 44-46. Mem: Local, co & state bar asns; Elks; Am Legion; Rotary Int; VFW. Relig: Roman Catholic. Mailing Add: 63 Mayflower Hill Dr Waterville ME 04901

JONAS, CHARLES RAPER (R)
b Lincolnton, NC, Dec 9, 04; s Charles Andrew Jonas & Rosa Petrie J; m 1928 to Annie Elliott Lee; c Charles Raper, Jr & Richard Elliott. Educ: Univ NC, AB, 24, Law Sch, JD, 28; Chi Phi; Phi Delta Phi; Order of the Coif. Honors & Awards: LLD, Elon Col. Polit & Govt Pos: US Rep, Ninth Dist, NC, 53-72; deleg, Rep Nat Conv, 72. Mil Serv: Entered as Capt, NC Nat Guard, 40, released as Lt Col, 46, after serv in Judge Adv Gen Dept; Commendation Medal. Mem: DC & NC Bar Asns; Am Legion. Relig: Methodist. Mailing Add: 302 Colville Rd Charlotte NC 28207

JONAS, MILTON (R)
NY State Assemblyman
b New York, NY, Dec 14, 26; s Jack Jonas & Miriam Sherman J; m 1953 to Zelda Coon; c Lisa Ann & Ilaina Ruth. Educ: Pace Col, BBA, 50; Brooklyn Law Sch, LLB, 53; Debating Soc; co-capt, Swimming Team. Polit & Govt Pos: Rep committeeman, Uniondale, NY, 55-56; Rep committeeman, North Bellmore, NY, 58-; mem bd dirs, North Bellmore Rep Club, 59-61, first vpres, 62-63; alt deleg, Rep Judicial Conv, 63; legis counsel to Assemblyman Francis P McCloskey, 63-64; counsel, Joint Legis Comt on Probs of the Aged, 64-65; NY State Assemblyman, 13th Dist, Nassau Co, currently; chmn, Joint Legis Comt for Higher Educ, 69-73 & 74-75, chmn, Standing Comt Com, Indust & Econ Develop, 73-74, ranking minority mem assembly codes comt, currently. Bus & Prof Pos: Attorney, pvt practice. Mil Serv: Entered as Enlisted Man, Air Force, released as Sgt, 46, after serv in 308th Bombardment Wing, Asian Theater. Mem: Am & Nassau Co Bar Asns; South Nassau Lawyers Asn; Fedn Lawyers Club of Nassau Co; Lions. Relig: Jewish. Mailing Add: 1854 Zana Ct North Merrick NY 11566

JONASSEN, TOR HEYDEN (D)
b Detroit, Mich, Sept 26, 43; s Sevgrin Lawrence Jonassen & Berte van der Heyden J; m 1965 to M Catherine Applegarth; c Tao, Tanya, Jonas & Sean. Educ: Temple Univ, BS, 66, MS, 70; ed, Stylus (lit mag). Polit & Govt Pos: Pa State Senate cand, Dem Primary, 70; committeeman, Springfield Dem Party, Pa, 70-; alt deleg, Dem Nat Conv, 72. Bus & Prof Pos: Teacher, Mardle-Newton High Sch, 67-68 & Swarthmore High Sch, 68-69; speech writer, William F Seslar, Dem cand for US Senate, 70-71; tax investr, Pa Dept of Revenue, Harrison, 71-72; teacher, Philadelphia Sch Dist, 72- Publ: Various articles, Stylus, 63-66; The Pete Seegar index, Orpheus, 70. Mem: Am Fedn Teachers; Am Civil Liberties Union; New Dem Coalition (mem exec bd, 70-); Young Dem of Delaware Co (state liaison info officer, 72-). Mailing Add: 330 Yale Ave Morton PA 19070

JONCAS, GRACE LUCILLE (D)
NH State Rep
b Rollinsford, NH, Dec 22, 23; d Hector L Senechal & Emelia B Bisson S; m 1946 to Richard J Joncas; c Richard J, Jr. Educ: St Joseph's Acad, South Berwick, Maine, bus course, 4 years. Polit & Govt Pos: Chmn bd supvrs, Rollinsford, NH, 56-; secy, Rollinsford Dem Town Comt, 58-; NH State Rep, 69- Bus & Prof Pos: Owned & operated dept store, Rollinsford, 59-61; operator catering bus, 61-68. Mem: Nat & State Owl Orgn; auxiliary mem Am Legion. Mailing Add: 15 Prospect St Rollinsford NH 03869

JONDAHL, H LYNN (D)
Mich State Rep
Mailing Add: 5166 Park Lake Rd East Lansing MI 48823

JONES, A CLIFFORD (R)
Mo State Sen
b St Louis, Mo, Feb 13, 21; c A Clifford, Jr, Irene C, Wesley McAfee & Janet. Educ: Princeton Univ, 42; Wash Univ, 48. Polit & Govt Pos: City clerk, Ladue, Mo, 48-50; Rep nominee for St Louis City Supvr, 58; Mo State Rep, 50-58, majority chmn, Mo House Rep; Mo State Sen, 64-, minority floor leader, Mo State Senate, currently. Bus & Prof Pos: Bus exec; lawyer; pres, Aluminum Truck Bodies, Inc & Mo Polaris Corp; secy-treas, Hewitt-Lucas Body Co, Inc, St Louis. Mil Serv: Navy, World War II, sea duty in Atlantic, Pac & Indian Oceans. Mem: Mo Bar Asn; Mo Asn for Social Welfare; AF&AM; Scottish Rite; Am Legion. Honors & Awards: Gold Key Award, for distinguished serv to city, state & nation, 52; Outstanding Young Man, Gtr St Louis, 52; St Louis Globe-Dem Award, Outstanding Mem of the Mo State House of Rep, 58 & Mo State Senate, 66 & 70. Mailing Add: 7 Willow Hill Ladue MO 63124

JONES, BEATRICE ELEANOR (D)
VChmn, Hancock Co Dem Comt, Maine
b Somerville, Mass, Dec 27, 04; d Arthur Murch Jones & Hattie Dolloff J; m 1926 to Harry

Sargent Jones, Jr; c Eleanor Louise, Harriet (Mrs George Mahon) & Harry Sargent, III. Educ: Farmington State Teachers Col, 23-25; Univ Maine, 44. Polit & Govt Pos: Secy & treas, Ellsworth Dem City Comt, Maine, 28-71; mem legis comt, Hancock Co Dem Comt, 64-66, vchmn, 66-, treas, 72-, charter mem, Hancock Co Dem Woman's Club, 65, vpres, 65-69, pres, 69-70; voting deleg, Maine Asn Dem Womens Clubs, 66-69; deleg, Maine Dem State Conv, 66-70, 72. Bus & Prof Pos: Teacher, Ellsworth Pub Schs, 23-27, substitute teacher, 39-47; bookkeeper, Jones Grain Store, 47-59, Hancock Co Creamery, 59- & Alice Fashions, 72- Mem: Nokomis Rebekah Lodge (past Noble Grand); Past Noble Grands Club Nokomis Rebekah Lodge (charter mem, pres, secy & treas); Ladies Auxiliary of Patriarch Militant; Eastern Star; Sr Citizens Club Ellsworth (treas). Honors & Awards: Decoration of chivalry & jewel, Rebekah Assembly, Maine, 53, 50 year cert pin, Bayside Grange & Hancock Co Pomona, 70; Award & Pin, Nokomis Rebekah Lodge, 75. Relig: Protestant; Sunday sch teacher & mem guild, First Congregational Church, Ellsworth. Mailing Add: Bayside Rd Rte 1 Ellsworth ME 04605

JONES, BENJAMIN F (D)

b Smithfield, Va, Apr 25, 19; s Ben Jones & Avrilla Parsons J; m 1951 to Wetona B. Educ: Va State Col, BS, 42; NY Univ, MS, 46; Omega Psi Phi. Polit & Govt Pos: Comnr, Orange, NJ, 63-; deleg, Dem Nat Conv, 72. Relig: Protestant. Mailing Add: 163 Central Pl Orange NJ 07050

JONES, BENNER, III (R)

Mem Exec Comt, Cumberland Co Rep Party, NC

b Jackson, Ohio, June 16, 39; s Benner Jones & Margaret Slavens J; m 1962 to Sabra Eubanks; c Benner, IV & Sarah Margaret. Educ: Kenyon Col, 57-58; Rio Grande Col, 58-59; Univ NC, Chapel Hill, AB, 61, Law Sch, LLB, 65; Lambda Chi Alpha; Archon. Polit & Govt Pos: Pres, Club 21, Ohio, 56-57; treas, Pitt Co Rep Party, NC, 65-66; treas, Cumberland Co Rep Party, 68-70, mem exec comt, 68-, chmn, 70-72. Bus & Prof Pos: Partner, Barrington, Smith & Jones Law Firm, 69- Mem: Am Bar Asn; Cumberland Co Bar Asn (treas, 70-, mem young lawyers sect); Fayetteville Jaycees; Cape Fear Optimist Club; Upper Cape Fear Young Rep. Relig: Methodist. Mailing Add: 109 Crescent Ave Fayetteville NC 28305

JONES, BILL (R)

Chmn, Fresno Co Rep Comt, Calif

b New York, NY, Jan 25, 29; s William E Jones & Carolyn E Pulici J; m 1960 to Anne L Butler; c Lawrence, Carolyn, Timothy & Daniel. Polit & Govt Pos: Finance chmn, 51st Assembly Dist Rep Cent Comt, Calif, 69-; chmn, Fresno Co Rep Comt, Calif, presently. Mem: Whittier chmn, Nat Fed of Independent Businessmen, 65-66; chmn, speakers bur, Whittier CofC, 67-68. Relig: Lutheran. Mailing Add: 213 Gregg Court S Mendota CA 93640 Pl Whittier CA 90601

JONES, CASEY C (D)

Ohio State Rep

b Paducah, Ky, June 15, 15; s Clarence Jones & Boydie Brandon J; m 1936 to Lovell Barber; c LaVerne (Mrs Zackary Redden), Casey, Jr, Clarence, Sarah, Marsha (Mrs Lamont Williams), Marylan, Curtis, Carlton & stepson, William Lester Harris. Educ: Toledo Univ, 37-39 & 64-65. Polit & Govt Pos: Inspector, Lucas Co Sanit Eng Dept, Ohio, 49-65; personnel dir, Lucas Co, 65-66; pupil personnel dir, Miami Children Ctr, 66-68; Ohio State Rep, Dist 78, 69-73, Ohio State Rep, Dist 45, 73- Bus & Prof Pos: Prof basketball player, Toledo Nat Basketball Asn, Globe Trotters & NY Komidy Kings. Mem: Pub Personnel Asn of Am; Ind YMCA (bd dirs); Nat Soc State Legislators; Community Planning Coun Northwestern Ohio, Inc; Frontiers Int. Relig: Methodist. Mailing Add: 1467 Avondale Ave Toledo OH 43607

JONES, CHARLES FRED (D)

Fla State Rep

b Auburndale, Fla, Apr 19, 30; s Paul J Jones & Lessie Smith J; m 1967 to Vivian Juanita Cannon; c James, Troy Ann & Vivian. Educ: Univ Fla, BS, 52; Phi Eta Sigma; Student Coun; Hon Court, Fla Blue Key. Polit & Govt Pos: Mayor, Auburndale, Fla, 62-64; Fla State Rep, 70-, chmn transportation comt, Fla House Rep, 75-; mem, Gov Hwy Safety Comn, 75- Bus & Prof Pos: Sales staff, & Gamble Distributing Co, Jacksonville, Fla, 54-56 & Nat Cylinder Gas Co, Tampa, 56-58; asst supt & supt harvesting operation, Adams Packing Asn, Auburndale, 58-65; supvr personnel, indust engr & territory mgr, Int Paper Co, Auburndale, 65-70. Mil Serv: Entered as 2nd Lt, Air Force, 52, released as 1st Lt, 54, after serv in 3rd Air Force Overseas Staff Auditor, Eng. Mem: Fla Farm Bur; Fla Citrus Mutual; Rotary; Children's Home Soc Fla (bd dirs, 75); F&AM. Honors & Awards: Legislator of the Year of the Fla House Rep, Fla Farm Bur Fedn, 72. Relig: Baptist. Legal Res: 504 Arneson Ave Auburndale FL 33823 Mailing Add: PO Box 1246 Auburndale FL 33823

JONES, CLEO SATTIS (R)

b Sissonville, WVa, Nov 17, 17; s William Marshall Jones & Estella J; m 1940 to Agatha Matilda Miller; c Dale C, Denise & Becky. Educ: Morris Harvey Col; WVa Univ, LLB, 50. Polit & Govt Pos: Dir of orgn, State Young Rep Club, WVa, 52-54, pres, 54-55; city prosecutor, Charleston, 55-71; deleg-at-lg, Rep Nat Conv, 60, deleg, 64; chmn, Kanawha Co Rep Exec Comt, 62-64; vchmn, Rep State Exec Comt WVa, 64-74; WVa State deleg, until 74. Mil Serv: Entered as Seaman, Navy, 43, released as PO 1/C, 45, after serv in Pac; Pac Theater Campaign Ribbon. Mem: Kanawha Co & WVa Bar Asns; WVa State Bar; WVa RR Asn (exec dir, 74-). Relig: Baptist. Mailing Add: Security Bldg Charleston WV 25301

JONES, CLIFFORD L (R)

b Sharon, Pa, Dec 31, 27; m 1951 to Jean; c Nancy, Martin & Bradley. Educ: Westminster Col (Pa), BA; Univ Pittsburgh. Polit & Govt Pos: Dep secy commerce, State of Pa, 63-67, secy of commerce, 67-69, secy of labor & indust, 69-; deleg, Rep Nat Conv, 72; chmn, Pa State Rep Cent Comt, formerly; mem, Rep Nat Comt, formerly. Honors & Awards: Outstanding Man of the Year, Hazleton & Pa Jaycees, 62. Relig: Methodist. Mailing Add: 2100 Milltown Rd Camp Hill PA 17011

JONES, CURTIS (D)

SDak State Sen

Mailing Add: Britton SD 57219

JONES, D LEE (R)

Ariz State Rep

b 1903. Polit & Govt Pos: Ariz State Rep, 67- Bus & Prof Pos: Semi-retired cattle & feed grain rancher. Mailing Add: 1201 E Windsor Ave Phoenix AZ 85006

JONES, DALE PASCHAL (R)

Committeeman, Rep State Comt Okla

b Gillham, Ark, Oct 19, 36; s Ray Elgin Jones & Alma Lee Wheeler J; m 1963 to Anita Ruth Collier; c Lee Anna & Leisa Raye. Educ: Univ Ark, Fayetteville, BS, 58; Univ Md, Agana, Guam, 59-60; Southern Methodist Univ, 66; Univ Okla, grad sch, 70; Beta Alpha Psi; Alpha Kappa Psi; Blue Key. Polit & Govt Pos: Precinct chmn, Duncan Rep Party, Okla, 71-73; chmn, Stephens Co Rep Party, 73-75; committeeman, Rep State Comt Okla, 75- Bus & Prof Pos: Auditor, Arthur Andersen & Co, St Louis, Mo, 58-59, sr auditor, Dallas, Tex, 62-65; corp auditor, Halliburton Co, Dallas, 65-67; financial coordr, Eastern Hemisphere, Halliburton Servs, London, Eng, 67-70; asst to controller, Halliburton Servs, Duncan, Okla, 70-71, vpres finance, 71- Mil Serv: Entered as 2nd Lt, Air Force, 59, released as 1st Lt, 62, after serv in Auditor Gen Dept. Mem: Am Inst CPA; Elks (chmn audit comt & budget comt, 75); Financial Execs Inst; CofC (2nd vpres, 75; mem bd dirs, 75-); Rotary Int (dir, 75-). Relig: Baptist. Mailing Add: 2721 Stagestand Rd Duncan OK 73533

JONES, DENZIL EUGENE (R)

Ore State Rep

b Ione, Ore, Sept 21, 10; s Eugene S Jones & Ruth Andrews J; m 1931 to Mildred Altnow Jones; c Karen (Mrs Dinsmore) & Eugene. Polit & Govt Pos: Juntura Sch Bd, Juntura, Ore, 40; mem, Malheur Co Budget Bd, 60 & Malheur Co Juv Coun, 60; Ore State Rep, 73- Bus & Prof Pos: Pres, D E Jones & Son, Inc, 58-; vpres, Ontario Livestock Mkt Develop Comn, 69-74, trustee, 74- Mem: Am Nat Cattlemens Asn; Ore Cattlemens Asn; Masons; Elks; Malheur Pioneer Asn. Honors & Awards: Malheur Co Cattleman of the Year, 55; Jaycees Citizenship Award, 68. Mailing Add: 1461 NW Third Ave Ontario OR 97914

JONES, DORIS HARDY (R)

Exec Committeewoman, SC Rep Party

b Augusta, Ga, June 26, 30; d John C Hardy & Mildred O'Neal H; div; c Lark W & W Lance. Educ: Augusta Jr Col, grad. Polit & Govt Pos: Pres, North Augusta Rep Women, 66-71; first vchmn, Aiken Co Rep Party, 70-72; ambulance comnr, Aiken Co, 71-74; secy, Third Cong Dist, currently; exec committeewoman, SC Rep Party, Aiken Co, currently; co campaign mgr for Gov James B Edwards, 74. Mem: SC Hist Soc. Honors & Awards: Irene Watts Award to Most Outstanding Clubwoman, Augusta Jr Woman's Club, 58. Relig: Methodist; mem admin bd, Grace United Methodist Church. Mailing Add: 1008 Fairwood Ave North Augusta SC 29841

JONES, EARL (D)

Ark State Rep

Mailing Add: 2318 Jefferson Texarkana AR 75501

JONES, ED (D)

US Rep, Tenn

b Yorkville, Tenn, Apr 20, 12; m to Llewellyn Wyatt; c Mary Llew & Jennifer. Educ: Univ Tenn, BS, Dairy Husbandry, 34. Hon Degrees: DLitt, Bethel Col, 63. Polit & Govt Pos: Inspector, Div Insect & Plant Diseases Control, Tenn Dept Agr, 34; mem staff, Tenn Dairy Prod Asn, 41-43; agr agt, Ill Cent RR, 44-69, leave of absence to serv as Tenn Comnr Agr, 49-52; US Rep, Seventh Dist, Tenn, 69- Bus & Prof Pos: Pres, Yorkville Tel Coop; assoc farm dir, Radio Sta WMC, Memphis; mem bd trustees, Bethel Col, 17 years, pres bd several years. Mem: WTenn Artificial Breeding Asn (organizer & former pres). Honors & Awards: Man of the Year in Agr, Memphis Agr Club, 57; Distinguished Pub Serv Awards, Univ Tenn Dairy Club, 66 & Am RR Asn, 70; Distinguished Nat Leadership Award, Future Farms Am, 70; Award, Univ Tenn Block & Bridle Club, 72. Relig: Cumberland Presbyterian. Legal Res: Yorkville TN 38389 Mailing Add: 407 Cannon House Off Bldg Washington DC 20515

JONES, EDMUND EUGENE (SONNY) (R)

Tex State Rep

b Houma, La, Oct 27, 37; s Edmund Eugene Jones, Sr & Nida Smith J; m 1958 to Judith Howell; c Melinda Holt & Michael Howell. Educ: Univ Houston, BS, 60. Polit & Govt Pos: Precinct chmn, Rep Party, Tex, 62-65, area chmn, 63; deleg, Rep Co & State Conv, 62, 64, 66, 68 & 70; mem, Goldwater Adv Comt, 63-64; dist chmn, Bush for Sen Campaign, 64; mem, Eighth Cong Dist Rep Credentials Comt, 64; dir, Harris Co Young Rep Club, 64, vpres, 65, pres, 66; vchmn, Northwest Texans for Tower, 66; deleg, Young Am for Freedom Nat Conv, 66; Tex State Rep, Harris Co, Dist 22, formerly & 75- Mil Serv: Entered as Airman Basic, Tex Air Nat Guard, 61, released as Airman 2/C, 64, after serv in 147th Fighter Group; Airman 2/C, Air Force Res, 64-67. Mem: Independent Ins Agts Asn; Nat Rifle Asn; Bill of Rights Found; Houston Asn Health Underwriters (dir, 68-); Jaycees. Honors & Awards: Guardian of Freedom, Tex Young Am for Freedom, 69. Relig: Episcopal. Legal Res: 5019 Forest Nook Ct Houston TX 77008 Mailing Add: 8102 Meadville Houston TX 77017

JONES, EMIL, JR (D)

Ill State Rep

b Chicago, Ill, Oct 18, 35; s Emil Jones & Marilla Mims J; m to Patricia A Sterling; c Debra Ann, Renee L & John M. Educ: Roosevelt Univ, 53-55; Loop Col, AA, 71; Deans List. Polit & Govt Pos: Precinct capt, 21st Ward Regular Dem Orgn, Ill, 62-70, secy, Young Dem, 63-67, mem exec bd, Orgn, 65-70; secy to alderman, Chicago City Coun, 67-73; precinct capt, 34th Ward Regular Dem Orgn, 71-, exec secy, 71-; Ill State Rep, 28th Dist, 73- Bus & Prof Pos: Chlorine engr, City of Chicago, 64-67; mem bd dirs, Racine Courts Coop, Chicago, 71-; pub rels, 72-; mem bd dirs, STEA, Inc, 73- Mem: Sheldon Heights Community Coun; Morgan Park Savings & Loan; Morgan Park Civic League; Mason (32 degree); Shrine. Relig: Baptist. Mailing Add: 11357 S Lowe Chicago IL 60628

JONES, EVELYN ROSE (D)

Secy, Holmes Co Dem Cent & Exec Comt, Ohio

b Loudonville, Ohio, July 12, 04; d William Herbert Mohler & Anna Maria Leidheiser M; m 1933 to Thomas Paul Jones. Educ: High sch grad. Polit & Govt Pos: Secy, Holmes Co Dem Cent & Exec Comt, currently. Bus & Prof Pos: Operator, chief operator tel, chief operator cashier & bookkeeper, Loudonville Tel Co, 24-39; mem eng dept, Flxible Co, Loudonville, Ohio, 41-45; surv work for Holmes Co Commun Action Comt. Mem: Am Red Cross; Grange; Womens Federated Dem Asn, Ohio; DAR; Pythian Sisters. Relig: Lutheran; Assoc mem Methodist Church, Nashville, Ohio. Legal Res: East Millersburg St Nashville OH 44661 Mailing Add: Box 2 Nashville OH 44661

JONES, EVERETT, JR (R)

Chmn, Campbell Co Rep Exec Comt, Tenn

b Caryville, Tenn, Aug 8, 27; s Everett Jones, Sr & Dora Cooper J; m 1950 to Lillian McCarty; c William Arnold & David Everett. Educ: Univ Tenn, BS, 50, MS, 54, 55-56 & 65. Polit &

Govt Pos: Chmn, Campbell Co Rep Exec Comt, Tenn, 74-; supt schs, Campbell Co, 74- Mil Serv: Entered as A/S, Navy, 45, released as Seaman 1/C, after serv in USS Alabama, Pac Theatre, 45-46. Relig: Baptist. Mailing Add: Rte 2 Jacksboro TN 37757

JONES, FRANCIS A, III (MIKE) (R)
Chmn, Fourth Cong Dist Rep Comt, Mich
b Iowa City, Iowa, Oct 9, 35; m 1958 to Judith Hartman; c Deborah Ann & Francis A, IV. Educ: Univ Colo, BA; Wayne State Univ, LLB; pres, Student Bar Asn; exec vpres, Am Law Student Asn; Gold Key Scholarship; McKenzie Honor Soc. Polit & Govt Pos: Chmn, Berrien Co Rep Party, Mich, 69-73 & Fourth Cong Dist Rep Comt, Mich, 73-; mem, Mich Rep State Comt, 75- Bus & Prof Pos: Partner, Hartwig, Crow, Jones & Postelli, Attorneys, currently. Mem: Humane Soc; Planned Parenthood (dir); Community Fund (div chmn); Delta Tau Delta; Mich State Bar (legis liaison). Relig: Episcopal; vestryman, 74- Legal Res: 227 N Sunnybank St Joseph MI 49085 Mailing Add: PO Box 456 Benton Harbor MI 49022

JONES, FRED REESE (D)
Ala State Rep
b Montgomery, Ala, Oct 18, 35; s Sam Jones & Abia Brophy J; m 1963 to Jean Troglen; c Connie, Jennifer & Julie. Educ: Auburn Univ, BS, 60; Jones Law Sch; Univ Ala; Alpha Tau Omega. Polit & Govt Pos: Asst dir, Ala Civil Defense Dept, 62-63; admin asst to Gov, Ala, 63-66; chmn, Montgomery Bd Equalization, 67-70; Ala State Rep, Montgomery Co, 71-, chmn, Montgomery House Deleg; chmn, Gov Comn on Drug Abuse. Bus & Prof Pos: Exec dir, Ala Mfg Housing Inst, currently; dir, past pres & first vpres, Ala Credit Union League; past pres, Montgomery Chap Credit Unions. Mil Serv: Maj, Ala Nat Guard. Mem: Elks; Am Legion; Exchange Club. Relig: Methodist. Mailing Add: 3513 Dresden Dr Montgomery AL 36111

JONES, G PAUL, JR (R)
b Florence, SC, June 28, 30; m 1965 to Dallis; c G Paul, III, Mary Sanford & Louise Hollis. Educ: Ga Inst Technol, BS in Mech Eng, 52. Polit & Govt Pos: Deleg-at-lg, Rep Nat Conv, 64, deleg, 68; first vchmn, Rep Party Ga, 64, state chmn, 65-69; Ga State Rep, 64-66; cand for US Rep, Sixth Dist Ga, 66. Bus & Prof Pos: Pres, Macon Prestressed Concrete Co. Mil Serv: Army, 52-54, Korea; Capt, Army Res, Corps of Engrs. Mem: Ga Soc of Prof Engrs; Assoc Indust of Ga. Relig: Presbyterian. Mailing Add: Old Forsyth Rd Macon GA 31201

JONES, GARY D (D)
Mass State Rep
Mailing Add: State Capitol Boston MA 02133

JONES, GEORGE WILSON (R)
Va State Deleg
b Huntington, Pa, Dec 21, 26; s P Rixey Jones & Donna Wilson J; m 1950 to Elvie Gallimore; c Susan, Anne & Sharon. Educ: Va Polytech Inst & State Univ, BS, 53; Delta Kappa Epsilon. Polit & Govt Pos: Vchmn, Chesterfield Co Rep Party, Va, 67-68; Va State Deleg, 69-, asst minority leader, Va House of Deleg, 72-; mem, Gov Budget Adv Comt, 72- Bus & Prof Pos: Prof rep, Upjohn Co, 54-66; life underwriter, Sun Life Assurance Co of Can, 66-71; assoc, Otto Sales Co, 71- Mil Serv: Entered as Pvt, Army, 45, released as Pfc, 46, after serv in Mil Police, 13th Air Force, Pac Theatre, 45-46; Campaign Medals. Mem: AF&AM; Scottish Rite; Shrine. Relig: Presbyterian. Mailing Add: 8821 Rockdale Rd Bon Air VA 23235

JONES, GERALDINE W (R)
Rep State Committeewoman, NY
b Jerusalem, NC, July 22, 29; d Henry Edward Woods & Mattie Wood W; m 1964 to Fred Jones; c stepson Fred A Jones. Educ: Brooklyn Col, 48; Drakes Bus Sch, Brooklyn, NY, 49. Polit & Govt Pos: Mem, Queens Co Rep Comt, NY, 67-; Rep State Committeewoman, 26th Assembly Dist, 70-72, 29th Assembly Dist, 72-; deleg, NY Rep State Conv, 72 & Rep Nat Conv, 72; dist leader, 29th Assembly Dist, 72- Bus & Prof Pos: Supvr & mgr, David Sarkin, Inc, New York, 55-65; asst dir & personnel off mgr, Aladdin House Ltd, 65-67; off mgr, Cameron C Haynes, City Marshal, New York, 67-70; off mgr, Proj Mgt Off, Mayor's Off, 70-71; city marshal, New York Marshal 79, 71- Mem: Nat Negro Bus & Prof Women, Inc; NAACP; Ebony Women for United Serv Orgn of New York (vchmn, 70-); Fedn of Rep Women (pres, local chap, 70-); Urban League, Inc. Honors & Awards: Achievement Award, Negro Bus & Prof Women, 71; First Black Woman City Marshal, Jamaica Polit Action League, Inc, 71. Relig: African Methodist Episcopal Zion Church. Mailing Add: 192-10 104th Ave Hollis NY 11412

JONES, GLEE CAROL (R)
Kans State Rep
b Fairview, Kans, Dec 10, 20; d Grover Cleveland Cyphers & Lena Nyfeler C; m 1941 to Harold R Jones; c Ronald Cleveland & Eddie Richard. Educ: Highland Jr Col. Polit & Govt Pos: Kans State Rep, 71- Bus & Prof Pos: Teacher vocal music, Hamlin Elem & High Schs, Kans. Mem: Kans Farm Bur Women (first dist chmn, 16 years, vchmn, 15 years); Kans Coun for Children & Youth; Kans Sch Health Adv Coun; Florence Cook Sch Practical Nursing, Kans Univ Med Ctr (adv coun); Native Sons & Daughters of Kans. Honors & Awards: Mem, Distinguished Group of Am Women to Visit Soviet Union, 72. Relig: Baptist; exec bd, Kans Baptist Women. Mailing Add: RR Hamlin KS 66430

JONES, GLENN ROBERT (R)
Treas, Arapahoe Co Rep Exec Comt, Colo
b Jackson Center, Pa, Mar 2, 30; s Alvin Robert Jones & Viola Jenkins J; m 1953 to Aldene Beagle; c Christine Elaine, Suzanne Meredith & Glenn Michael. Educ: Findlay Col, 48-49; Allegheny Col, BA in Econ, 52; Univ of Pa Law Sch, 56-57 & 58-59; Univ of Colo Law Sch, JD, 60; Phi Gamma Delta. Polit & Govt Pos: Rep cand, US Rep, First Cong Dist of Colo, 64; finance chmn, Arapahoe Co Rep Party, 68-69; mem, Arapahoe Co Rep Exec Comt, 68-69, treas, 71-; mem, Colo Rep State Cent Comt, 69- Bus & Prof Pos: Attorney-at-law, pvt practice, Denver, Colo, 61-66; pres, Silver King Cable Co, 66-; pres, Data Transmission, Inc & Silver King Co, 68-; pres, Silver King Commun TV, Inc, Jones Int, Ltd, 69- & Jones Intercable, Inc, 71- Mil Serv: Entered as A/S, Navy, 52, released as Lt(jg), 56, after serv in Amphibious Corps, Pac & frogman, Explosive Ord Disposal, Far East, 54-56; Naval Res, 56-66, 1st Lt; Am Spirit Hon Medal. Publ: Jones Dictionary of CATV Terminology, Johnson Publ Co, 71 & 73. Relig: Congregational. Mailing Add: 4555 Wagon Trail Littleton CO 80120

JONES, GLORIA LEE (R)
VPres Seventh Dist, Tenn Fedn of Rep Women
b Rochester, NY; Sept 22, 23; d Benjamin Court Lee & Florence Hutchinson L; m to Dr Chester Kawel Jones; c Lucinda Lee (Mrs James LauBach), Karen Kawel & Owen Chester, II. Educ: Geneseo State Teachers Col, 41-42; Jackson State Community Col & Lambuth Col, attend currently; Alpha Chi Omega. Polit & Govt Pos: Pres, Madison Co Fedn of Rep Women, Tenn, 62-64; chmn, Madison Co Rep Exec Comt, 62-72; vpres, Seventh Dist Tenn Fedn of Rep Women, 63-; state co-chmn, Goldwater for President Campaign, 64; deleg, Rep Nat Conv, 64; state chmn for women's conv, Nat Fedn of Rep Women, 64. Mem: Jackson Serv League; Jackson Symphony League; Jackson Art Asn. Relig: Episcopal. Mailing Add: Tinker Hill Rd Jackson TN 38301

JONES, GRANT (D)
Tex State Sen
b Abilene, Tex, Nov 11, 22; s Morgan Jones & Jessie Wilder J; m 1948 to Anne Smith; c Morgan Andrew & Janet Elizabeth. Educ: Southern Methodist Univ, BBA; Wharton Sch Finance & Com, Univ Pa, MBA. Polit & Govt Pos: Tex State Rep, 65-73; Tex State Sen, 73- Bus & Prof Pos: Casualty underwriter, Trezevant & Cochran, 50-54; partner, Abtex Ins, 54- Mil Serv: Entered as Aviation Cadet, Army Air Corps, 43, released as 1st Lt, after serv in Troop Carrier Command, Italy; ATC, SAm. Mem: Soc Chartered Property & Casualty Underwriters; Kiwanis; State Bar Tex. Relig: Methodist. Legal Res: 1509 Woodridge Abilene TX 79605 Mailing Add: PO Box 1320 Abilene TX 79604

JONES, HAROLD LEON (R)
Mem, Maine Rep State Comt
b Unity, Maine, May 23, 27; s Harold Frank Jones & Nancy Walton J; m 1948 to Winona Dow; c Karen & Alan. Educ: Augusta Sch Bus, Assoc Bus, 46; Stonier Grad Sch Banking, ABA, 68; Rutgers Univ. Polit & Govt Pos: Chmn, Augusta Rep City Comt, Maine, 66-70; treas, Maine Rep State Comt, 67-72, chmn, 73-74, mem, currently; mem, Rep Nat Comt, 73-74. Bus & Prof Pos: Sr vpres & cashier, Bank of Maine, Augusta, 64- Mem: Maine Soc Pub Accountants; Am Inst CPA's; Mason; Kiwanis. Relig: Congregational. Legal Res: 99 Purinton Ave Augusta ME 04330 Mailing Add: 187 State St Augusta ME 04330

JONES, HELEN GWENDOLYN (R)
NH State Rep
b Concord, NH, Jan 12, 03; d Joseph Goddard Jones & Helen McCurrach Duncan J; single. Educ: Univ NH, BA, 27, MA, 29; Univ Chicago Sch Social Serv Adminrs, 32-33; Chicago-Kent Col Law, 35-37; Phi Kappa Phi; Kappa Delta Pi; Delta Kappa; Masque & Dagger. Polit & Govt Pos: NH State Rep, 73- Bus & Prof Pos: Instr in sociology, Univ NH, 30-32; probation officer, Cook Co Juvenile Court, Chicago, Ill, 34-36; social worker, clerk & supvr, Chicago Municipal Court, 36-54; counr, Personal Servs YWCA Metrop Div, 54-55; supt, Scottish Old Peoples Homes, Riverside, Ill, 55-56; exec housekeeper, Home for Incurables, Chicago, 56-59; supt, Elizabeth Carleton House, Roxbury, Mass, 59-71. Mem: Odd Fellows (Noble Grand); Nat Asn Social Workers; League Women Voters; Central Eleanor Club; Womens Educ & Indust Union. Relig: Universalist. Mailing Add: 11 Maple St Concord NH 03301

JONES, HENRY LEE (D)
Miss State Rep
b Richton, Miss, Oct 28, 04; s Thomas Eugene Jones & Emma Williams J; m 1929 to Nina Barrett; c Thomas Henry, Frank Harold & Sue (Mrs Scott). Educ: Newton Co Agr High Sch, 4 years. Polit & Govt Pos: Co supvr, Perry Co, 52-68; Miss State Rep, Greene & Perry Co, 68-; first vpres, Southern Miss Econ Develop Dist, Inc, 71. Mem: Nat Soc State Legislators (vpres, Miss Chap, 71, pres, 72-73); Rotary; CofC; Farm Bur; Pine Burr Area Coun, Boy Scouts (bd rev, councilman & dist finance comt). Relig: Baptist; deacon, First Baptist Church. Mailing Add: PO Box 449 Richton MS 39476

JONES, HERBERT, JR (R)
Ga State Rep
b Toombs Co, Ga, Feb 20, 30; s Herbert Jones & Bessie L Alexander J; m 1955 to Kay B Peterson; c Sharon Kay, Cynthia Ann & Philip Todd. Educ: Univ Ga, BS, 56; Alpha Epsilon Delta; Kappa Sigma. Polit & Govt Pos: Univ Ga, BS, 56; Alpha Epsilon Delta; Kappa Sigma. Polit & Govt Pos: Vchmn, Chatham Co Rep Party, Ga, 67-68, chmn, 68-69; chmn, Chatham Co & Dist Platform & Nominating Comts; deleg, Chatham Co, Dist & Ga State Rep Conv; Ga State Rep, 69-; deleg, Rep Nat Conv, 72. Bus & Prof Pos: Pres, Savannah Terminal, Inc, currently. Mil Serv: Entered as Seaman Recruit, Navy, 48, released as HM-3, 52, after serv in USS Hector & Naval Hosps, Korean Conflict; UN, Korean & Good Conduct Medals. Mem: Mason; Scottish Rite; Shrine; Jaycees (local, state & nat off); Lions. Honors & Awards: Distinguished Serv Award, Jaycees; various commendations. Relig: Methodist. Mailing Add: 413 Arlington Rd Savannah GA 31406

JONES, J L (D)
Treas, Second Cong Dist Dem Coun, Wash
b Harris Co, Tex, July 4, 16; s Sean P Jones & Annie Laura Lester J; m 1948 to Anne Maxinchuk; c Elizabeth & Barbara. Educ: Univ Tenn, 33-35. Polit & Govt Pos: Deleg, Dem Nat Conv, 64; treas, Second Cong Dist Dem Coun, Wash, currently; state committeeman, Whatcom Co Dem Party & precinct committeeman, currently. Bus & Prof Pos: Br & div mgr, Norman G Jensen, Inc, 48- Mem: Elks; KofC (4 degree); CofC; Bd of Trade, Vancouver, Can. Relig: Roman Catholic. Legal Res: 540 Eighth St Blaine WA 98230 Mailing Add: Box 1268 Blaine WA 98230

JONES, JAMES FRED (D)
Assoc Justice, Ark Supreme Court
b Mount Ida, Ark, Jan 12, 07; s Ira Seward Jones & Ella Tyler J; m 1937 to Walta Lorea Hoback; c James Voland, Vanda (Mrs Crocker) & Lyn. Educ: Univ Ark, LLB, 37. Polit & Govt Pos: Ark State Rep, 35-39; asst prosecuting attorney, 18th Judicial Dist, 36-38; munic judge, Little Rock, 50-51; assoc justice, Ark Supreme Court, 67- Mem: Am Bar Asn; Am Judicature Soc; Inst Judicial Admin; Inter Am Bar Asn; Mason. Relig: Methodist. Legal Res: 1208 Silverwood Trail North Little Rock AR 72116 Mailing Add: State Capitol Little Rock AR 72201

JONES, JAMES LOCKE (D)
Mem, Miss Dem State Exec Comt
b West Point, Miss, Nov 1, 34; s William M Jones & Mabel Locke J; m 1959 to Ann Carolyn Stevens; c Sheri Lyn & Terri Ann. Educ: Millsaps Col, AB, 56; Emory Univ, MA, 57; Southern Methodist Univ, BD, 62; Kappa Sigma. Polit & Govt Pos: Co-chmn, Lafayette Co Dem Party, Miss, 68; deleg, Dem State Conv, 68; deleg, Dem Nat Conv, 68; mem, Miss Freedom Dem Exec Comt, 69-; mem, Miss Dem State Exec Comt, 69- Bus & Prof Pos: Methodist minister, Tupelo, Miss, Mobile, Ala, Southaven, Miss, Dallas, Tex, 57-69; campus minister, Univ Miss, 65-69; assoc exec secy, Comn on Relig & Race, United Methodist

Church, 69-71. Relig: United Methodist. Mailing Add: 10547 Tolling Clock Way Columbia MD 21044

JONES, JAMES PARKER (D)
Chmn, Ninth Cong Dist Dem Comt, Va
b Tampa, Fla, July 3, 40; s Edmund L Jones & Nellie Parker J; m to Mary Trent; c James Trent, Benjamin & Jonathan. Educ: Duke Univ, AB, 62; Univ Va Law Sch, LLB, 65. Polit & Govt Pos: Chmn, Washington Co Dem Comt, Va, 73-; chmn, Ninth Cong Dist Dem Comt, 75- Bus & Prof Pos: Partner, Penn, Stuart & Eshridge, Attorneys, 68- Mem: Washington Co United Fund (bd dirs); Barter Theatre Found (bd dirs); Smyth-Bland Legal Aid Soc (bd dirs); Washington Co Daycare Ctr (bd dirs). Honors & Awards: Outstanding Young Man of Washington Co, Jaycees, 74. Relig: Episcopal. Legal Res: 107 Hillside Dr Abingdon VA 24210 Mailing Add: PO Box 749 Abingdon VA 24210

JONES, JAMES PAUL (R)
b Slaton, Tex, Dec 13, 22; s Braxton B Jones & Nellie Heifner J; m 1946 to Patricia Groves; c Frederick Braxton & Paul Stanley. Educ: Tex Tech Col, BS, 50; Block & Bridle Club; Future Farmers of Am. Polit & Govt Pos: Commun chmn, Swisher Co Rep Party, Tex, 61-65, chmn, 65-69 & 73-74; chmn, Farmers & Ranchers for US Rep Bob Price, 68; chmn, Tex Farmers & Ranchers for Nixon-Agnew, 68; Southwest Area dir, Agr Stabilization & Conservation Serv, 69- Bus & Prof Pos: Teacher voc agr, Cotton Center High Sch, 50 & Kress High Sch, Tex, 52-53; farmer, cotton, grain, sorghum, wheat & livestock, 51-69. Mil Serv: Entered as Pvt, Marines, 43, released as Cpl, 46, after serv in Marine Air Group 14, SPac, Philippines & Okinawa, 44-46; Unit Citation. Mem: Lions Club; Am Legion; Am Farm Bur. Relig: Methodist. Mailing Add: Star Rte Kress TX 79052

JONES, JAMES ROBERT (D)
US Rep, Okla
b Muskogee, Okla, May 5, 39; s Robert Patrick Jones & Margaret Wich J; m 1968 to Olive Olivia; c Geoffrey Gardner & Adam Winston. Educ: Univ Okla, BA, 61; Georgetown Univ Law Ctr, LLB, 64; Lambda Chi Alpha; Delta Theta Phi. Polit & Govt Pos: Publicity writer & speaker, Howard Edmondson's Campaign for Gov, Okla, 58; info specialist, Dept Agr, Dallas, summer 60; legis asst, US Rep, Ed Edmondson, Okla, 61-64; White House staff asst, W Marvin Watson, 65-68; Spec Asst & Appointments Secy, President Lyndon B Johnson, 68-69; mem, President's Adv Comn on Youth Opportunities, 69; US Rep, Okla, 73-, mem, Ways & Means Comt, US House Reps, 74- Bus & Prof Pos: Attorney, Holliman, Langholz, Runnels & Dorwart, Tulsa, 69-73; pres, Media Assoc, Inc, 70-73. Mil Serv: Entered as Capt, Army, 64-65, serv in Counter-Intel Corps. Mem: Am & Okla Bar Asns; CofC; Univ Okla Bd Overseers. Honors & Awards: One of Ten Outstanding Young Men of Am, US Jaycees, 68. Relig: Catholic. Legal Res: 2101 S Madison Tulsa OK 74114 Mailing Add: 317 E Capitol Washington DC 20002

JONES, JAMES ROYDICE (R)
Chmn, Calhoun Co Rep Exec Comt, WVa
b Big Bend, WVa, Jan 11, 36; s Homer Jacob Jones & Icy Bell Kemp J; m 1964 to Brenda Lou Starcher. Educ: Glenville State Col, AB, 60; WVa Univ, grad work, 64-65; Int Rels Club; Polit Sci Club; Col 4-H Club. Polit & Govt Pos: Pres, Calhoun & Gilmer Young Rep Club, 58-60; dir col activities, Young Rep League, WVa, 58-60; dir first voters activities, 61-62 & dir, Rep Youth Camp, 64-66; dir region three, Col Young Rep Nat Fedn, 58-60; WVa State Deleg, 63-64; pres bd dirs, WVa Rep Youth Training Camp, Inc, 65-; chmn, Calhoun Co Rep Exec Comt, WVa, 65-; supvr, State Rd Comn, Calhoun Co, currently. Mil Serv: Entered as Pvt, Marine Corps, 61, released as Lt Col, 62, after serv in First Marine Div, Camp Pendleton, Calif. Publ: Youth in Politics, Young Rep League of WVa, 61. Mem: Nat Educ Asn; Odd Fellows; WVa 4-H All Stars; admiral of line, Cherry River Navy; Calhoun Co Young Rep Club. Relig: Church of Christ. Legal Res: Big Bend WV 26136 Mailing Add: PO Box 381 Grantsville WV 26147

JONES, JAMES SAMUEL (D)
State Land Comnr, Ark
b Lonoke, Ark, Mar 26, 13; s Samuel Allen Jones & Bertha Tygart J; m 1965 to Helen Beane Monroe; c Judith Ann (Mrs David Hopper). Educ: Ouachita Baptist Col, 31-32; Univ Ala, 33. Polit & Govt Pos: State Land Comnr, Ark, 57- Bus & Prof Pos: Comn agt, Standard Oil Co; contractor, Int Paper Co; contractor, Crossett Lumber & Paper Co; sales rep, Dierks Lumber & Coal Co. Mil Serv: ROTC, Ouachita Col. Mem: Small Bus Asn. Relig: Methodist. Legal Res: 34 Nob View Circle Little Rock AR 72205 Mailing Add: PO Box 1531 Little Rock AR 72203

JONES, JEAN BOSWELL (R)
Mem, Mo State Rep Comt
b Baxter Springs, Kans, June 27, 20; d Dr James Henry Boswell & Maud Cramer B; m 1941 to Dr Edward S Jones; c Stephen Edward, Pamela Jane & Bradley Boswell. Educ: Univ Kans, AB; Chi Omega. Polit & Govt Pos: Pres, Cass Co Rep Fedn Womens Clubs, Mo, 64-65 & 68-69; chmn, Cass Co Rep Party, formerly; mem, Mo State Rep Comt, 68-, vchmn, 68-70, acting chmn, summer 70 & secy, formerly; deleg, Rep Nat Conv, 72. Mem: DAR; Delvers Federated Club; PEO Sisterhood; PTA; Cass Co Hist Soc (founder & dir). Honors & Awards: Homemaker of the Year, Third Dist Federated Clubs, 72. Relig: Episcopal; Mem, Vestry Bd, 69. Mailing Add: 301 N Price Ave Harrisonville MO 64701

JONES, JERRY HOLTON (R)
b Lamesa, Tex, June 13, 39; s Frank Bedford Jones & Forrest Mary Wicker J; div. Educ: Harvard Col, AB, 61; Harvard Bus Sch, MBA, 64. Polit & Govt Pos: Staff asst to the President, White House. 71-72 & 72-73, spec asst to the President, 73-74, staff secy to the President, 74-; dep dir polit div, Comt to Reelect the President, 72. Legal Res: 910 N Sixth St Lamesa TX Mailing Add: 700 New Hampshire Ave NW Washington DC 20037

JONES, JIMMIE (RED) (D)
State Auditor, Ark
b Magnolia, Ark, Mar 14, 20; s Stephen Herbert Jones & Ethel May Stevens J; m 1957 to Bonnie Inez Smith. Educ: Southern State Col; Ark Law Sch. Polit & Govt Pos: Tax collector, Columbia Co, Ark, 50-55; State Land Comnr, 55-57; State Auditor, 57- Bus & Prof Pos: Commercial mgr, Radio Sta KVMA, Magnolia, Ark. Mil Serv: Entered as 1st Lt, Air Corps, 42, released as Maj, 45, after serv in Eighth Air Force; ETO Ribbon with Eight Battle Stars; Distinguished Flying Cross with Two Oak Leaf Clusters; Air Medal with Six Oak Leaf Clusters; Lt Col, Ark Nat Guard, 45- Relig: Methodist. Legal Res: Magnolia AR Mailing Add: State Capitol Bldg Little Rock AR 72201

JONES, JOAN S (D)
Va State Deleg
Mailing Add: 1928 Thomson Dr Lynchburg VA 24501

JONES, JOHN D (R)
Wash State Sen
Mailing Add: PO Box 867 Bellevue WA 98009

JONES, JOHN DAVID (R)
Ill State Rep
b Springfield, Ill, Jan 3, 12; s Oscar David Jones & Sally Boyd J; m 1934 to Marjorie Gale; c Gale (Mrs Jack P Fixmer) & David B; five grandchildren. Educ: Springfield High Sch; col exten courses. Polit & Govt Pos: Rep precinct committeeman, City Precinct 32, Springfield, Ill, 22 years; chmn, Sangamon Co Rep Cent Comt, currently; Ill State Cent committeeman, 20th Cong Dist Rep Party, 3 years; founder & vchmn or chmn, Springfield Airport Authority, 45-64; Ill State Rep, 50th Dist, 65-, chmn house affairs comt & vchmn higher educ comt, Ill House of Rep, currently, mem appropriations comt, legis info systs comt, legis space needs comn, Ill spec events comn & house leadership & secy & mem exec comt, Ill Bicentennial Comn, currently. Mem: Founder, Ill Pub Airport Asn; Springfield & Sangamon Co Regional Plan Comn; Springfield Jaycees (founder); YMCA (bd); Mason. Relig: Methodist; vchmn, Finance Comn of 700 United Methodist Church Conf, 12 years; dist lay leader; lay deleg, currently. Legal Res: 6 Walnut Ct Springfield IL 62704 Mailing Add: Rm 2004 State Off Bldg Springfield IL 62706

JONES, JOHN DOUGLAS (J D) (D)
Chmn, Chesterfield Co Dem Exec Comt, SC
b Chesterfield, SC, Sept 10, 16; s Neal Crawford Jones & Lana Melton J; m 1946 to Sarah Alliene Fields. Educ: Univ SC, BS, 39. Polit & Govt Pos: Mem, Co Bd of Pub Welfare, SC, 52-59; vpres, Chesterfield Dem Club, 58-60, pres, 60-; chmn, Chesterfield Co Dem Exec Comt, 62-; comnr, Chesterfield Co, 66-69. Mil Serv: Entered as Pvt, Army, 43, released as T/Sgt, 46, after serv in 42nd Gen Hosp, SW Pac, 43-46; Battle of Luzon Medal & Battle Star; Meritorious Occup of Japan Medal. Mem: Am Legion; VFW; 40 et 8. Relig: Southern Baptist; chmn bd deacons, Douglas Mill Church. Mailing Add: Jones Pharmacy 146 Main St Chesterfield SC 29709

JONES, JOHN ROBERT (R)
b Sampson Co, NC, Oct 25, 28; s Miles S Jones & Zelma Carter J; m 1956 to Etta B Locklear; c Sybil, Robert W & Tommie M. Educ: NC State Univ, grad, 51. Polit & Govt Pos: Rep precinct chmn, Pembroke, Robeson Co, NC, 67-71; mem, Robeson Co Rep Exec Comt, 67-72; NC State chmn, Am Indians Comt to Reelect the President, 72; deleg, Rep Nat Conv, 72. Bus & Prof Pos: Partner, Jones Cleaners, Pembroke, NC, 60-; pres bd, The Stable, 70-; bd mem, Advan Inc, Lumberton, 70-; bd mem, Lumbee Regional Develop Asn, Pembroke, 70-, chmn bd, 72-; vchmn bd, Lumbee Bank, Pembroke, 71- Mil Serv: Entered as E-1, Army 52, released as E-5, 53, after serv in 351st Regt Combat Team Trust, 52-53. Mem: Farm Bur. Relig: Baptist. Mailing Add: Rte 2 Pembroke NC 28372

JONES, JOHNNIE ANDERSON (D)
La State Rep
b Laurel Hill, La, Nov 30, 19; s Henry Edward Jones & Sarah Ann Coats J; m 1948 to Sebell Elizabeth Chase; c Johnnie Anderson, Jr, Adair Darnell, Adal Dalcho & Ann Sarah Bythelda. Educ: Southern Univ, Baton Rouge, BS in Psychol, Sch Law, JD; Alpha Phi Alpha. Polit & Govt Pos: Asst parish attorney, East Baton Rouge Parish, La, 69-72; La State Rep, Dist 67, 72- Bus & Prof Pos: Mem bd dirs, Ada Bullock-Blundon Asn, Inc; mem bd dirs, Baton Rouge Coun Human Rels; pres bd dirs, Community Advan, Inc; legal adv, Am Found Negro Affairs; attorney & counr, Supreme Court of US. Mil Serv: Entered as Pvt, Army, 42, released as Warrant Officer, 46, after serv in 494th Port Bn, ETO, 43-46. Mem: Boy Scouts (bd dirs); Legal Aid Soc (bd dirs & chmn original personnel comt); Oper Upgrade (bd dirs & treas); Baranco-Clark YMCA (comt mgt); Cancer Soc Gtr Baton Rouge. Honors & Awards: Plaque, YMCA Expansion Fund Campaign; Cert of Appreciation, Lyndon B Johnson & Hubert H Humphrey, 64; Plaque, Alpha Kappa Alpha; Plaque, Asn Sec Sch Prin of La Educ Asn; Most Outstanding Man of the Year, Mt Zion First Baptist Church, Baton Rouge, 70. Relig: Baptist. Legal Res: 1438 N 32nd St Baton Rouge LA 70802 Mailing Add: 1263 Government St Baton Rouge LA 70802

JONES, KENNETH B (R)
SDak State Sen
Mailing Add: 1701 Pine Yankton SD 57078

JONES, L W (JACK) (D)
Wyo State Rep
b Geneva, Nebr, Feb 12, 03; s Cornelous Walter Jones & Matilda Ann James J; m 1930 to Louise Winmill; c Richard Cornelous. Educ: Univ Wyo, 24-28; Kappa Sigma; W Club. Polit & Govt Pos: Mem exec bd, Young Dem Club Utah, 33-38; life mem, Summit Co Fair Bd, Utah, 36-; treas, Summit Co Dem Party, 40-46; mem, Utah Inheritance Tax Comn, 43-46; mem bd trustees & chmn phys plant comt, Univ Wyo, 51-69, pres, Univ Found, 69-; precinct committeeman, Rock Springs Dem Party, Wyo, 60-; mem, Gov Comt Med Educ, 63-66; chmn, Rock Springs Planning Comt, 71-; Wyo State Rep, 71-, mem ways & means comt, Wyo State House of Rep, 71- Bus & Prof Pos: Exec, various oil & gas industs, 33-68. Mem: Wyo Safety Found; Am Petroleum Inst; Independent Petroleum Asn, Rocky Mt Oil & Gas Asn; Wyo Trucking Asn. Honors & Awards: Silver Beaver Award, Boy Scouts Am; Outstanding Boss, 63; Wyo Distinguished Serv Award, 66. Relig: Protestant. Mailing Add: 1024 Lincoln Ave Rock Springs WY 82901

JONES, LARRY MALLORY (D)
Chmn, Brunswick Co Dem Party, Va
b Brunswick Co, Va, Dec 25, 39; s Sidney Rivers Jones, Jr & Virginia Spraggins J; m 1965 to Justine Stansbury; c Lori Elizabeth & Larry Mallory, Jr. Educ: Va Commonwealth Univ, BS, 61; Univ Richmond TC Williams Sch Law, JD, 64; Phi Alpha Delta. Polit & Govt Pos: Attorney for the Commonwealth, Brunswick Co, Va, 72-; chmn, Brunswick Co Dem Party, currently. Bus & Prof Pos: Attorney-at-law, Lawrenceville, Va, 64- Mem: Am Bar Asn; Nat Dist Attorneys Asn; Va Commonwealth Attorneys Asn; Lions; Ruritan. Relig: Baptist. Mailing Add: Box 138 Lawrenceville VA 23868

JONES, LAWRENCE F (D)
First VChmn, Fond du Lac Co Dem Party, Wis
b Belvidere, Ill, May 15, 99; s Frederic W Jones & Carrie Alfreda Longley J; m 1929 to Anna

Irene Russell; c Caroline Ekval (deceased). Educ: Wis Univ, BEd, 32; Ruralete Soc; Debate Squad. Polit & Govt Pos: City comnr, Fond du Lac, Wis, 36-53, city councilman, 73-; chmn, Fond du Lac Co Dem Party, 65-68, first vchmn, currently; treas, Wis Sixth Dist Dem Party, 69-; mem, Gov Mass Transit Study Comt, 72- Bus & Prof Pos: Instr, Fond du Lac Voc Sch, 29-35; pub rels dir, Wis Asn of Coop, 58-61, exec secy, 61-64. Mil Serv: Capt, Army, 43-47, serv in Mil Govt; Maj (Ret), Army Res, 54; ETO & Three Campaign Ribbons. Mem: Fond du Lac Hist Soc; Mason; United Commercial Travelers; Eastern Star (secy, 73); F&AM (past worshipful master, 73). Relig: Presbyterian; Elder & deacon. Mailing Add: 123 E Division Fond du Lac WI 54935

JONES, LEM T (R)
Mem, Mo State Rep Cent Comt
b Ebensburg, Pa, Jan 23, 96; s Thomas D Jones & Mary Ann Hughes J; m 1921 to Jessie E Stover; c Lem T, Jr, Russell S, Thomas D (deceased), Sally Jacquelyn, Mary Ann & John Paul. Educ: Univ Iowa, AB. Hon Degrees: LLD, Parsons Col; LHD, Tarkio Col. Polit & Govt Pos: Mem adv comt, Regional Health & Welfare Coun; mem, Rep Nat Finance Comt; mem, Kansas City Crime Comn, Mo, 51-; chmn finance comt, Mo State Rep Comt, 60-62, chmn, formerly; mem, Mo State Rep Cent Comt, currently. Bus & Prof Pos: Teacher rural elem schs, Iowa; instr & head dept com, Anamosa Reform Sch, Iowa; instr & bus mgr, J Sterling Morton High Sch & Jr Col, Cicero, Ill; instr principles of acct, Ottumwa High Sch, Iowa; exec & partner, Russell Stover Candies, Inc, 28-60, pres, 60-; vpres, Empire State Bank, Kansas City, Mo, 62-; sr vpres, Logistics Research Inc, 68-; sr vpres, Aviation Research Inc, 69- Mil Serv: Entered as Fireman 3/C, Navy, 17, released as Ens, 19, after serv in Pay Corps, First Naval Dist. Mem: Nat Coun Churches (mem gen bd); Nat Coun, United Negro Col Fund, Inc; Kansas City Conf Christians & Jews (founding mem & mem bd dirs); Relig in Am Life (mem laymen's comt); Mason. Honors & Awards: Nat Red Feather Award, Community Chests Am, 51; Silver Beaver Award, Boy Scouts. Relig: Presbyterian; Elder. Legal Res: 803 W 54th Terrace Kansas City MO 64112 Mailing Add: 700 Waltower Bldg Kansas City MO 64106

JONES, LUTHER (D)
Tex State Rep
b Corpus Christi, Tex, Aug 22, 46; s Luther Edward Jones, Jr & Helen Grant J; m 1970 to Carroll Shelton; c Caroline Melissa. Educ: Odessa Jr Col, Tex; Univ Tex, El Paso; St Mary's Univ Sch of Law; Tribune, Delta Theta Phi. Polit & Govt Pos: Asst dist attorney, El Paso, Tex; Tex State Rep, 73- Bus & Prof Pos: Pvt attorney, El Paso. Mem: Tex & El Paso Bar Asns; Jaycees; Kiwanis; Young Dem. Legal Res: 240 Crown Point El Paso TX 79912 Mailing Add: PO Box 5391 El Paso TX 79953

JONES, MARK PERRIN, III (D)
Secy, White Co Dem Comt, Ark
b Searcy, Ark, Jan 19, 32; s Mark Perrin Jones, Jr & Jamie Baugh J; m 1970 to Anna Lee McGill Duncan; c Mark Perrin, IV. Educ: Univ Ark, BS in Jour, 53, MA in Govt, 64; Omicron Delta Kappa; Alpha Phi Omega; Sigma Chi; Lambda Tau; ed, Traveler & Razorback; chmn, Bd of Student Publ. Polit & Govt Pos: Chmn, Searcy Civil Serv Comn, Ark, 58-74; mem, Ark State Bd Educ, 59-68; secy, White Co Dem Comt, Ark, 59-72 & 74-; mem, Ark State Dem Comt, 68-70; vpres, Ark Const Conv, 69. Bus & Prof Pos: Publ, Searcy Daily Citizen & White Co Citizen, 59- Mem: Sigma Delta Chi; Nat Asn State Bd Educ (dir, secy & treas, 68-); CofC; Rotary; Mason (32 degree). Honors & Awards: Americanism Ed Award, Continental Oil Co, 59; Ark Young Man of the Year, Jr CofC, 65. Relig: Presbyterian; vpres, Men of the Church of East Ark Presbytery, 65, moderator, Presbytery, 72. Legal Res: 708 W Academy Ave Searcy AR 72143 Mailing Add: 209 W Arch Ave Searcy AR 72143

JONES, MARSHALL WILLIAM, JR (R)
Treas, Rep State Cent Comt, Md
b Columbia, SC, Feb 3, 32; s Marshall William Jones & Viola Brown J; m 1954 to Gloria Delores Adams; c Iris Romaine, Sharon Anita & Marshell Delores. Educ: Temple Univ Community Col, Assoc in Tech, 52; Eckels Col Mortuary Sci. Polit & Govt Pos: Mem, Ninth Ward Civic Orgn, Md; mem, Baltimore Community Rels Comn, 63-64; mem, Bur Recreation & Parks, Baltimore, 64-65; mem, Bd of Supvrs of Elec, Baltimore, 65-67, secy, 69-; treas, Model Cities Community Coun-Area B, Eastern Terr Community Coun, Inc, 69-; treas, Rep State Cent Comt, currently; alt deleg, Rep Nat Conv, 72. Bus & Prof Pos: Owner, Marshall W Jones, Jr Funeral Home, 61- Mil Serv: Entered as Pvt, Air Force, 52, released as S/Sgt, 56; Nat Defense, UN & Korean Serv Medals; Good Conduct Medal. Mem: Nat Funeral Dirs & Morticians Asn (dist gov, dist 2 & mem bd dirs); Baltimore Urban League & Urban Guild; Citizens Planning & Housing Asn; Am Legion; F&AM. Relig: Baptist. Mailing Add: 1735 Harford Ave Baltimore MD 21213

JONES, MARVIN (D)
b Valley View, Tex, Feb 26, 86; s Horace King Jones & Docia Hawkins J; single. Educ: Southwestern Univ, BS, 05; Univ Tex, LLB, 07; Delta Chi. Hon Degrees: LLD, Tex A&M Univ, 52 & Southwestern Univ; hon Order of the Coif, George Washington Univ, 61. Polit & Govt Pos: Chmn, Bd Legal Exam, Seventh Judicial Dist, Tex, 12-15; US Rep, Tex, 17-40, chmn, Comt on Agr, US House Rep, 31-40; judge, US Court of Claims, Washington, DC, 40-47, chief judge, 47-64, sr US judge, 64-; asst to James F Byrnes, US War Mobilization, 43, mem, War Mobilization Comt, 43-45, US War Food Adminr, 43-45; pres, First Int Cong on Food & Agr, 43. Publ: How War Food Saved American Lives; War Food, in Encyclopaedia Britannica, 44; Should Uncle Sam Pay, When & Why?, 63. Relig: Methodist. Legal Res: 2807 Hughes St Amarillo TX 79109 Mailing Add: US Ct Claims 717 Madison Pl NW Washington DC 20005

JONES, MARVIN O (R)
Chmn, Douglas Co Rep Cent Comt, Ill
b Arthur, Ill, Aug 2, 23; s Alfred H Jones & Viola Halley J; m 1965 to Betty D; c Mark H. Educ: Univ Ill, Champaign, 41-43; Lambda Chi Alpha. Polit & Govt Pos: Chmn, Douglas Co Rep Cent Comt, Ill, 72- Bus & Prof Pos: Supvr, Douglas Co, Ill, 67- Mem: Mason; Moose. Mailing Add: RR 2 Arthur IL 61911

JONES, MARY GARDINER (R)
b New York, NY, Dec 10, 20; d Charles Herbert Jones & Anna Livingston Short; single. Educ: Wellesley Col, BA, 43; Yale Univ, JD, 48; Order of the Coif. Polit & Govt Pos: Research analyst, Off of Strategic Serv, 44-46; trial attorney, Dept of Justice, 53-61; comnr, Fed Trade Comn, 64-73. Bus & Prof Pos: Attorney & spec asst to Gen William J Donovan, Donovan, Leisure, Newton & Irvine, 48-53; attorney, Webster, Sheffield, Fleischmann, Hitchcock & Chrystie, 61-64; prof, Col Law & Col Com & Bus Admin, Univ Ill, Urbana-Champaign, 74-75; vpres consumer affairs, Western Union Tel Co, 75-; mem bd dirs, Coun Econ Priorities, Am Airlines Inc, Alcon Labs, Inc, John Wiley Publ Co, Nat Consumer Law Ctr, Boston, Nat Consumer League, Washington, DC & Nat Training Labs Inst; mem adv comt, Action for Children's TV, currently. Publ: Program for a Democratic counter-attack to Communist penetration of government service (w William J Donovan), Yale Law J, 49; National minorities: a case study in international protection, Law & Contemporary Probs, 49; Marketing strategy and government regulation in dual distribution practices, The George Washington Law Rev, 66. Mem: Fed Coun Sci & Technol (mem comt sci & tech info); Yale Law Sch Asn (vpres, DC, 72-, mem exec comt, 71-); Wellesley Col (mem bd trustees, 71-); Colgate Univ (mem bd trustees, 72-); Asn Consumer Res (mem adv coun). Relig: Episcopal. Mailing Add: 1631 Suter Lane NW Washington DC 20007

JONES, MARY L (R)
Chairwoman, Butler Co Rep Exec Comt, Ohio
b Middletown, Ohio, Dec 31, 34; d George Bethel Geary & Alice Hinkle G; m 1957 to Richard Heber Jones; c Geary, Richard, Kelly, Kerry & Suzanne. Polit & Govt Pos: Alt deleg, Rep Nat Conv, 72; chairwoman, Butler Co Rep Exec Comt, Ohio, 74- Mem: Butler Co Ment Hyg Asn (pres, 74-); Ohio Asn Ment Health (vpres, 74-); Middletown Area United Way (bd mem, 75-); Middletown City Planning Comn; League Women Voters. Mailing Add: 3701 Rosedale Rd Middletown OH 45042

JONES, MILTON (D)
b Columbus, Ga, Aug 13, 36; s Robert Vance Jones & Thea Gamble J; m 1955 to Jeanette Beaird; c Janice, Eleanor, Carolyn & Michael. Educ: Emory at Oxford, Emory Univ & Law Sch; Phi Alpha Delta; Alpha Tau Omega. Polit & Govt Pos: Ga State Rep, Muscogee Co, Dist 84, Post 2, 63-71; asst to the Gov Ga, 71-; deleg, Dem Nat Mid-Term Conf, 74. Bus & Prof Pos: Lawyer, self-employed, 59-61; partner, Grogan & Jones & Layfield, Attorneys, 61- Mil Serv: Army Res, 54-62. Mem: Ga Bar Asn; Scottish Rite; Mason; Kiwanis; Jaycees. Relig: Baptist. Mailing Add: 3438 Sue Mack Dr Columbus GA 31906

JONES, MORTON EDWARD (R)
Mem, State Rep Exec Comt, Tex
b Alhambra, Calif, Apr 12, 28; s Edward Palmer Jones & Bonnibel Sanford J; m 1951 to Patricia L Walker; c Shelley, Steven, Kent & Jay. Educ: Univ Calif, Berkeley, BS, 49; Calif Inst Tech, PhD, 53; Sigma Xi; Kappa Alpha. Polit & Govt Pos: Alt deleg, Rep Nat Conv, 68; mem, State Rep Exec Comt, Tex, 68- Bus & Prof Pos: Mem tech staff, Tex Instruments Inc, 53-61, sr scientist, 61-65, lab dir, 65- Publ: The Structure of Pentaborane, Proc Nat Acad Sci US, 52; Transistors Intermetaliques, L'Onde Eletrique 61; Treatise on solid state chemistry, In: Growth From the Vapor, 75. Mem: Sr mem, Inst Elec & Electronics Engrs; Tex Acad Sci; Electrochem Soc; Dallas Co Rep Men's Clubs. Relig: Episcopal. Mailing Add: 619 Northill Richardson TX 75080

JONES, ORTON ALAN (R)
WVa State Sen
b Spencer, WVa, Jan 24, 38; s French Smith Jones & Myrtle Ashley J; m 1961 to Mary Jo Chisler; c Rebecca Sue. Educ: Glenville State Col, 56-58; WVa Univ, JD, 61; Alpha Psi Omega; Phi Delta Phi; Kappa Sigma Kappa. Polit & Govt Pos: Prosecuting attorney, Roane Co, WVa, 65-68; WVa State Deleg, 68-72; WVa State Sen, 72- Bus & Prof Pos: Partner, Hedges & Jones, Law Firm, Spencer, WVa, 61- Mil Serv: Entered as 1st Lt, Air Force, 61, released as Capt, 64, after serv in Off of the Staff Judge Adv, Keesler Tech Training Ctr, Air Training Command, 61-64; Maj, Air Force Res. Publ: Immortality enough (w Dr C Trent Busch), Southern Speech J, spring 68. Mem: Am & WVa Bar Asns; Fifth Judicial Circuit Bar Asn; WVa State Bar; Rotary. Honors & Awards: Named One of WVa Five Outstanding Young Men, WVa Jaycees, 70. Relig: Protestant. Legal Res: Ridgemont Rd Spencer WV 25276 Mailing Add: First Nat Bank Bldg PO Box 16 Spencer WV 25276

JONES, PAUL C (D)
b Kennett, Mo, Mar 12, 01; m 1923 to Ethel Rockholt; c Betty Anne (Mrs Joe D Cash), Paul C, Jr & Nell (Mrs Tom B Mobley). Educ: Univ Mo, BJ, 23. Polit & Govt Pos: Mem, City Coun & Mayor, Kennett, Mo; pres & mem, Kennett Bd of Educ; Mo State Rep, 35-37; Mo State Sen, 37-44; chmn, State Hwy Comn, 45-48; US Rep, Mo, 48-68. Bus & Prof Pos: Co-publ, Dunklin Dem, 28-53; gen mgr, Radio Sta KBOA, 47-66. Mil Serv: Dir of orgn of Sixth Mo Inf, Mo State Guard, Comndg Officer, Vol Regt, 40-46. Mem: Miss Valley Flood Control Asn; Lions Int (past dist gov); Mason. Honors & Awards: Mo Squire, 67. Relig: Christian Church of NAm; mem off bd, 20 years; supt of Sunday sch. Legal Res: 444 W Washington Ave Kennett MO 63857 Mailing Add: PO Box 527 Kennett MO 63857

JONES, PHA L (R)
Secy, Seneca Co Rep Cent & Exec Comt, Ohio
b New Castle, Ind, Oct 1, 01; s Charles H Jones & Anna Huffman J; m 1927 to Mabel Wagner; c Barbara Ann (Mrs R G Ingerham). Educ: Earlham Col, BA, 24. Polit & Govt Pos: Precinct committeeman, Seneca Co Rep Cent Comt, Ohio, 50-, secy, 64-; mem, Seneca Co Rep Exec Comt & adv comt, Eighth Cong Dist, 64-; alt deleg, Rep Nat Conv, 64; mem, Seneca Co Bd of Elec, 64-72. Bus & Prof Pos: Mgr, Kresge Store, 28-41; prod mgr, Fostoria Corp, 42-69; retired, 70. Mem: Mason; Shrine; Kiwanis. Relig: Methodist. Mailing Add: 1398 N Union St Fostoria OH 44830

JONES, PLEAS E (R)
Chmn, Fifth Cong Dist Rep Party, Ky
b Williamsburg, Ky, Dec 23, 12; s Nathaniel B Jones & Rachel Lundy J; m 1942 to Nancy Marie White; c Pleas D & Gorman Stanley. Educ: Cumberland Col, AB, 34; Univ Ky Col Law, LLB, 52; Nat Col of State Trial Judges; Phi Delta Phi. Polit & Govt Pos: Circuit court clerk, Whitley Co, Ky, 40-51, judge, 54-57; commonwealth attorney, Whitley & McCreary Co, 59-63; circuit judge, Whitley & McCreary, 34th Judicial Dist, 64-; chmn, Fifth Cong Dist Rep Party, 64- Bus & Prof Pos: Teacher, Whitley Co, 32-36; teacher, Williamsburg Independent Sch Dist, 36-39. Mil Serv: Entered as Pvt, Army, 42, released as Pfc, 45, after serv in 113th Inf, Eastern Defense Command, 42-45. Mem: Lions (pres); Am Legion (Comdr); Mason; Shrine; Univ Ky Law Alumni (pres). Relig: Protestant. Mailing Add: Box 157 Williamsburg KY 40769

JONES, RALPH (D)
Mo State Rep
Mailing Add: 9030 Link Dr Overland MO 63114

JONES, RICHARD R (DICK) (R)
b Huntley, Mont, Sept 5, 10; m to Estes; c 3. Educ: Worden High Sch, Mont. Polit & Govt Pos: Town councilman, Powell, Wyo, 4 years, mayor, 4 years; Wyo State Rep, 2 years; Wyo

State Sen, until 74; cand for Gov, 74. Bus & Prof Pos: Trucker. Relig: Methodist. Mailing Add: 1614 Cedar View Dr Cody WY 82414

JONES, ROBERT ALDEN (D)
NC State Rep
b Forest City, NC, June 8, 31; s Basil Thomas Jones, Jr & Rosagray Chesson J; m 1954 to Nancy Hardwick; c Pamela, Robert A, Jr & John H. Educ: Wake Forest Col, 48-50; Wake Forest Univ, BA, 59, Law Sch, LLB cum laude, 60; Alpha Sigma Phi; Phi Alpha Delta. Polit & Govt Pos: Research asst to Justice Higgins, NC Supreme Court, 60-61; Rutherford Co Civil Defense Dir, NC, 67-; NC State Rep, 68- Bus & Prof Pos: Mem bd trustees, Florence Crittenton Home, Charlotte, NC, currently; bd dirs, The Biblical Recorder, currently. Mil Serv: Entered as Pvt, Air Force, 50, released as 1st Lt, 56, after serv in Newfoundland, 51-53 & France, 54-56, Maj, Res; usual theater awards. Mem: NC, Rutherford Co & 29th Judicial Dist Bar Asns; NC State Bar; VFW. Honors & Awards: Distinguished Award, Forest City Jaycees, 67. Relig: Baptist; Sunday Sch teacher & jr deacon, First Baptist Church. Mailing Add: 122 Woodland Ave Forest City NC 28043

JONES, ROBERT EMMETT, II (D)
US Rep, Ala
b Scottsboro, Ala, June 12, 12; s Robert Emmet Jones, Sr & Augusta Smith J; m 1938 to Christine Francis; c Robert E, III. Educ: Univ Ala, LLB, 35; Kappa Alpha. Polit & Govt Pos: Judge, Jackson Co, Ala, 41-43 & 46; US Rep, Ala, 47- Mil Serv: Entered as Ens, Navy, 43, released as Lt, 46. Relig: Methodist. Legal Res: Old Larkinsville Rd Scottsboro AL 35768 Mailing Add: 2426 Rayburn House Off Bldg Washington DC 20515

JONES, ROBERT G (D)
La State Sen
b Lake Charles, La, May 9, 39; s Sam H Jones & Louise Gambrell J; m 1961 to Sarah Quinn; c Sam Houston, II, Anna Gambrelle & Genin Quinn. Educ: La State Univ, 56-57; Tulane Univ, BS in Eng, 60; Harvard Bus Sch, MBA, 62; Tau Beta Pi; Omicron Delta Kappa; Phi Eta Sigma; Sigma Alpha Epsilon; Alpha Chi Sigma. Polit & Govt Pos: La State Rep, Calcasieu & Cameron Parishes, 68-72; La State Sen, 72- Bus & Prof Pos: Stock broker, Kohlmeyer & Co, 62-65, asst mgr, Lake Charles Off, 65-69, mgr, 69- Mem: Young Men's Bus Club. Honors & Awards: Chosen Outstanding Young Man of Lake Charles, Lake Charles Jaycees, 72. Relig: Methodist. Mailing Add: 301 Shell Beach Dr Lake Charles LA 70601

JONES, ROBERT H (D)
Dem Nat Committeeman, Pa
Mailing Add: 18th & Herr Sts Harrisburg PA 17120

JONES, ROBERT L, JR (R)
Ind State Rep
Mailing Add: 5210 N Park Ave Indianapolis IN 46226

JONES, S GARTH (R)
Utah State Rep
Mailing Add: Box 312 Cedar City UT 84720

JONES, SIDNEY (D)
Asst Secy Treas Econ Policy
Polit & Govt Pos: Former Asst Secy Econ Affairs, Dept Commerce; Counselor to Secy-Treas, William E Simon Mailing Add: Dept of Treasury Washington DC 20230

JONES, STANLEY GORDON, JR (D)
Ind State Rep
b Cincinnati, Ohio, Nov 22, 49; s Stanley Gordon Jones & Lois Weiland J; m 1973 to Linda Vaughan. Educ: Purdue Univ, West Lafayette, Eng, 73; Sigma Chi. Polit & Govt Pos: Ind State Rep, Dist 30, 75- Bus & Prof Pos: Recreation educ dir, Gtr Lafayette Community Ctr, 73-75. Mailing Add: 145 Andrew Pl West Lafayette IN 47906

JONES, TERRY T (R)
WVa State Deleg
b Morgantown, WVa, July 15, 37; s George F Jones, Jr & Mary Rose Taylor J; m 1958 to Barbara Kaye Giffen; c Stephen Scott & Deborah Lynn. Educ: WVa Univ, AB, 59; Cooper Sch Art, dipl, 62; Western Reserve Univ, grad work, 60-62; Beta Theta Pi. Polit & Govt Pos: Councilman, Morgantown, WVa, 67-71; mayor, 69-71; WVa State Deleg, 71- Bus & Prof Pos: Secy-treas, Valcraft, Inc, 64- Mil Serv: Entered as Pvt, Army, 62, released as SP-4, 64, after serv in Ord; Sgt 6/C, Army, 2 years. Mem: Morgantown Kiwanis (bd dirs, 71-). Relig: Presbyterian. Mailing Add: 617 Schubert Pl Morgantown WV 26505

JONES, THEODORE TANNER (R)
Mem, Ohio Rep State Exec Comt
b Cleveland, Ohio, June 23, 34; s Paul Vincent Jones & Winifred Lemmon J; m 1959 to Alison Trabue Corning; c Warren Tanner & Edith Trabue. Educ: Yale Univ, BA, 57; Phi Gamma Delta. Polit & Govt Pos: Pres, Young Rep Club, Geauga Co, Ohio, 62; deleg, Ohio State Rep Conv, 62, 64, 66, 68 & 70; precinct committeeman, Rep Cent Comt, 62-64; alt deleg, Rep Nat Conv, 64, deleg, 68; chmn, Geauga Co Rep Cent & Exec Comt, Ohio, formerly; mem, Ohio Rep State Exec Comt, currently; co-chmn, Geauga Co Reelect the President Comt, 72. Mil Serv: Entered as Pvt, Army, 57, released as 2nd Lt; 2nd Lt, Army Nat Guard, 66. Relig: Protestant. Mailing Add: RR 2 Kirtland-Chardon Rd Chardon OH 44024

JONES, THOMAS ROBERT (R)
b Utopia, Tex, Oct 24, 24; s Robert Newton Jones & Ada Lavalee J; m 1945 to Dorothy V Marshall; c Cindy & Marilyn. Educ: Rice Univ. Polit & Govt Pos: Chmn, Cameron Co Rep Party, Tex, formerly. Mil Serv: Entered Naval Res, 42, released as Comdr; Naval Res Medal; Am, Asiatic-Pac & Korean Areas Medals; Victory & UN Medals. Legal Res: 418 Retama Pl Harlingen TX 78550 Mailing Add: PO Box 1006 Harlingen TX 78550

JONES, WALTER BEAMAN (D)
US Rep, NC
b Fayetteville, NC, Aug 19, 13; s Walter G Jones & Fannie M Anderson J; m 1934 to Doris Long; c Mrs Bob Moye & Walter B, II. Educ: NC State Col, BS in Educ, 34. Polit & Govt Pos: Mem Bd of Comnrs, Farmville, NC, 47-49; Mayor pro tem, Farmville, 47-49; Mayor, Farmville & judge, Farmville Recorder's Court, 49-53; NC State Rep, 55-61; NC State Sen, 61-66; US Rep, NC, 66-; ex officio, Dem Nat Mid-Term Conf, 74. Bus & Prof Pos: Off equip dealer; dir, Farmville Savings & Loan Asn. Mem: Mason; Scottish Rite; Rotary (pres, 49); Moose; Elks. Relig: Baptist; Deacon, 45- Legal Res: Farmville NC Mailing Add: 130 Cannon House Off Bldg Washington DC 20515

JONES, WILFRED DENTON (R)
Chmn, Greene Co Rep Exec Comt, Ohio
b Xenia, Ohio, Nov 14, 22; s Clinton Arthur Jones & Amy Long J; m 1944 to Louise Faye Kendig; c Frank Arthur. Educ: Univ Dayton, 43; Miss State Col, 44. Polit & Govt Pos: Committeeman, Greene Co Rep Cent Comt, Ohio, 60-, chmn, 72-; vchmn, Greene Co Rep Exec Comt, 64, chmn, 64-; committeeman, Seventh Cong Dist Rep Party, 64-; mem bd elec, Greene Co, 66-; presidential elector from Ohio, 72. Bus & Prof Pos: Mgr, Jones Mgts, Xenia, Ohio, 46-60; salesman, Gen Motors Langs Inc, 60-61; bus mgr, Greene Co Automobile Club, Inc, 62-67, secy-mgr, 67-; pres, Western Conf of Ohio AAA Clubs, 67-71; exec vpres, Greene Co AAA, 72- Mil Serv: Entered as Aviation Cadet, Army Air Force, 42, released as Flight Off, 46, after serv in Third Combat Cargo Group, Tenth Air Force, China-Burma-India, 45; Air Medal with clusters; Am Campaign Serv Medal; Victory Medal; Asiatic-Pac Serv Medal. Mem: Charter mem, Young Rep Club; Scottish Rite; Kiwanis (dir); Am Legion (past adj & past comdr); Eastern Star (past patron). Relig: Protestant. Mailing Add: 1566 Red Fox Dr Dayton OH 45432

JONES, WILLIAM (D)
Alderman, New Haven, Conn
b Youngstown, Ohio, Sept 14, 34; s Harry Jones & Johnnie Mae White J; m to Eunice Louise Rogers; c Lowell Irving, Diana Marie & Sherri Lynn. Educ: St Phillips Col, AS, 59; Huston-Tillotson Col, BA, magna cum laude, 61; Trinity Univ; Southern Conn State Col, summer 69; Univ Mass, 72-; Alpha Kappa Mu; Alpha Phi Alpha. Polit & Govt Pos: Pres, Progressive Dem, 67-; deleg, Dem State Conv, 68 & 70; deleg, Dem Nat Conv, 68; mem, Conn Dem State Cent Comt, 68-70; exec vpres, Conn Dem Caucus, 68-; alderman, 22nd Ward, New Haven, Conn, 70-; chmn region I, Nat Black Caucus Local Elected Off, 71-; bd rep, Conn Asn Local Legislators, 72- Bus & Prof Pos: Off Prod Div, Int Bus Machines Corp, 65-67; vchmn, Opportunities Indust Ctr, 66-69; salesman, Xerox Corp, 67-68; exec dir, Community Anal & Develop, Conn, 68-; pres, Serv, Inc, New Haven, 68-; prof, SCent Conn Col, 69; dir health educ & community rels, New Haven Health Care, Inc, 72- Mil Serv: Entered as Airman, Air Force, 54, released as Airman 1/C, 58, after serv in AEC Command. Mem: Bus & Prof Men's Club; New Haven Midget Football League (pres); Tuberc & Respiratory Disease Asn; Gtr New Haven Black Coalition (vchmn, 71-); Boy Scouts. Honors & Awards: Gtr New Haven Human Rel Coun Man of Year, 70. Relig: Protestant. Legal Res: 60 Orchard Pl New Haven CT 06511 Mailing Add: Box 7215 Kilby Sta New Haven CT 06519

JONES, WILLIAM TOWNES (D)
b Ware Shoals, SC, Jan 29, 22; s William Townes Jones & Helen Sims J; m 1950 to Selma Singleton Gilland; c William Townes, Howard Gilland, Selma Thorne, Nelson Logan & Caroline Gibbes. Educ: Univ SC, Omicron Delta Kappa; Sr Superlative; pres, Student Body; Hon Bd. Polit & Govt Pos: SC State Rep, Greenwood Co, 49-52; solicitor, Eighth Judicial Circuit, SC, 52-; deleg, Dem Nat Conv, 56, 60, 64, 68 & 72. Bus & Prof Pos: Lawyer, SC, 49- Mil Serv: Entered as A/S, Naval Res, 42, released as Lt(jg), 46, after serv in Amphibious Unit, Atlantic Theater. Mem: Mason; Shrine; Lions; Am Legion; 40 et 8. Relig: Episcopal. Mailing Add: 302 Janeway Greenwood SC 29646

JONKIERT, CASIMIR S (D)
Del State Rep
Mailing Add: 403 South Broom St Wilmington DE 19805

JONSSON, JOHN ERIK (R)
b Brooklyn, NY, Sept 6, 01; s John Peter Jonsson & Charlotte Palmquist J; m 1923 to Margaret Elizabeth Fonde; c Philip R, Kenneth A & Margaret Ellen (Mrs George V Charlton). Educ: Rensselaer Polytech Inst, ME, 22; Phi Beta Kappa; Alpha Tau Omega. Hon Degrees: DE, Rensselaer Polytech Inst, 59; DSc, Hobart & William Smith Col, 61 & Austin Col, 63; LLD, Southern Methodist Univ, 64; DCL, Univ of Dallas, 68; LLD, Carnegie-Mellon Univ, 72 & Skidmore Col, 72; LHD, Okla Christian Col. Polit & Govt Pos: Mayor, Dallas, Tex, 64-71; mem, Urban Transportation Adv Coun, US Dept Transportation, 70-75; app by President, Am Revolution Bicentennial Comm, 70-73. Bus & Prof Pos: Managerial positions, Aluminum Co of Am, NJ & Dumont Motor Car Co, Inc, 23-30; officer, Geophys Serv, Inc, Dallas, 30-42; vpres, Tex Instruments Inc, 42-51, pres, 51-58, chmn, 58-66, hon chmn, 67-; dir, Equitable Life Assurance Soc of US, NY, 67-73; dir, Repub Tex Corp, 67- Publ: Of Time & the Cities, Gantt Medal Bd of Award, 69; Avalanche: the Cities and the Seventies, FBI Law Enforcement Bul, 3/69 & Mech Eng, 6/69; Days of Decision, Goals for Dallas, Vols I-IV. Mem: Nat Acad Eng; Soc of Exploration Geophysicists; life mem, Am Mgt Asn; Am Newcomen Soc; Philos Soc of Tex. Honors & Awards: Soc of Indust Realtors Industrialist of the Year Award, 65; Bene Merenti Medal, 66; Gantt Medal, 68; Horatio Alger Award, 69; Hoover Medal, 70. Relig: Methodist. Legal Res: 4831 Shadywood Lane Dallas TX 75209 Mailing Add: 3300 Republic Bank Tower Dallas TX 75201

JONTZ, JAMES (D)
Ind State Rep
Mailing Add: RR 1 Williamsport IN 47993

JOOS, VICTOR, SR (D)
NH State Rep
Mailing Add: Milton NH 03851

JOPP, RALPH P (CONSERVATIVE)
Minn State Rep
b Hollywood Twp, Minn, 1913; married; c three. Educ: Watertown Pub High Sch. Polit & Govt Pos: Mem, Twp Zoning & Planning Bd, Minn; Minn State Rep, 60- Mem: Carver Co Fair Asn (bd dirs). Relig: Lutheran; pres, St John Lutheran Congregation. Mailing Add: Mayer MN 55360

JORDAN, ANN (D)
Mem, Dem Nat Comt, Pa
Mailing Add: 5955 Upland Way Philadelphia PA 19131

JORDAN, BARBARA C (D)
US Rep, Tex
b Houston, Tex, Feb 21, 36. Educ: Tex Southern Univ, BA in Polit Sci & Hist magna cum laude, 56; Boston Univ, LLB, 59; Delta Sigma Theta. Polit & Govt Pos: Admin asst to co

judge, Harris Co, Tex; Tex State Sen, 67-72; US Rep, 18th Dist, Tex, 72-, mem steering & policy comt, US House Rep Dem Caucus, currently; mem, Dem Nat Comt, 72-; vchmn, Tex State Dem Comt, currently. Bus & Prof Pos: Attorney. Mem: Am, Tex & Houston Bar Asns; Tex Trial Lawyers Asn; NAACP. Honors & Awards: Dem Woman of Year, Woman's Nat Dem Club, 75. Relig: Baptist. Legal Res: TX Mailing Add: Rm 1725 House Off Bldg Washington DC 20515

JORDAN, DAVID MALCOLM (D)
b Philadelphia, Pa, Jan 5, 35; s Robert Norris Jordan & Mary McCulken J; m 1960 to Barbara Lee James; c Diana Megan, Laura Jane & Sarah Melissa. Educ: Princeton Univ, AB, 56; Univ Pa, JD, 59; Cloister Inn. Polit & Govt Pos: Chmn, Jenkintown Dem Comt, Pa, 64-72; councilman, Jenkintown Borough Coun, 66-; mem, Pa Dem State Comt, 68-70; mem, Pa Dem State Platform Comt, 70; chmn, Montgomery Co Dem Comt, 72-75. Bus & Prof Pos: Partner, Wisler, Pearlstine, Talone, Craig & Garrity, Norristown, Pa, currently. Mil Serv: Pvt, Army Res, 60. Publ: Roscoe Conkling of New York, Cornell Univ, 70. Mem: Pa & Montgomery Co Bar Asns; Am Judicature Soc; Sharswood Law Club; Abington Libr Soc (pres, 70-72, vpres, 72-). Honors & Awards: Outstanding Vol of Montgomery Co, Am Cancer Soc, 67. Relig: Presbyterian. Mailing Add: 410 Rodman Ave Jenkintown PA 19046

JORDAN, HUGH (D)
Ga State Rep
Mailing Add: 1284 Park Blvd Stone Mountain GA 30083

JORDAN, JAMES D (D)
Iowa State Rep
Mailing Add: RR 3 Marion IA 52302

JORDAN, KENNETH WAYNE (D)
Chmn, McLean Co Dem Party, Ky
b Calhoun, Ky, Oct 4, 26; s Arthur Clarence Jordan & Hilda Dixon J; m 1963 to Nell McCarley; c Beth Wayne. Polit & Govt Pos: Chmn, McLean Co Dem Party, Ky, 72- Mil Serv: Entered as Pvt, Army, 45, released Pfc, 46, after serv in Ceremonial Detachment. Mem: Farm Bur; Mason (tyler, Masonic Lodge, 60-61). Honors & Awards: Honor Guard at Tomb of Unknown Soldier and for President Truman, US Army, 46. Relig: Christian. Mailing Add: Box 124 Calhoun KY 42327

JORDAN, LEONARD BECK (R)
b Mt Pleasant, Utah, May 15, 99; s Leonard Eugene Jordan & Irene Beck J; m 1924 to Grace Edgington; c Joseph, Stephen & Patricia (Mrs Charles Story). Educ: Univ Ore, BA, 23; Phi Beta Kappa; Alpha Tau Omega. Polit & Govt Pos: Idaho State Rep, Idaho Co, 47-49; Gov, Idaho, 51-55; chmn, Int Joint Comn US-Can, 55-58; mem, US Develop Adv Bd, 58-59; US Sen, Idaho, 62-72; deleg, Rep Nat Conv, 68. Bus & Prof Pos: Self-employed, bus, livestock & farming. Mil Serv: Entered as Pvt, Army, 18, released as 2nd Lt, 19. Mem: Mason; Scottish Rite (33 degree); Shrine; Rotary; Am Legion. Relig: Methodist. Mailing Add: 3110 Crescent Rim Dr Boise ID 83704

JORDAN, LEWIS HENRY (D)
Chmn, Madison Co Dem Cent Comt, Iowa
b Spencer, Iowa, Apr 12, 30; s Lewis Stewart Jordan & Hannah Lorena Davis; m 1968 to Irma Kay Chastain; c Jill Renee. Educ: State Univ Iowa, BA, 57; State Univ Iowa Col Law, JD, 58. Polit & Govt Pos: Co attorney, Madison Co, Iowa, 63-67 & Winterset City Attorney, 73-75; chmn, Madison Co Dem Cent Comt, 72- Bus & Prof Pos: Lawyer, Webster & Frederick, 58-62, partner, Webster, Frederick & Jordan, 62-67; partner, Webster & Jordan, 67-70 & Webster, Jordan & Oliver, 70- Mil Serv: Entered as Seaman Recruit, Navy, 51, released as AT2, 54, after serv in FASRON 108, Air Force Atlantic Fleet, Air Wing 3, 51-54. Mem: Madison Co, Iowa State & Am Bar Asns; Iowa Acad Trial Lawyers; Am Trial Lawyers Asn. Relig: Episcopal. Legal Res: 605 W Jefferson Winterset IA 50273 Mailing Add: F&M Bank Bldg Winterset IA 50273

JORDAN, N PAULINE (R)
VChmn, Kosciusko Co Rep Cent Comt, Ind
b Rockford, Ohio, Mar 1, 11; d Charles Estel Jordan & Carrie Near J; single. Educ: Int Bus Col, Ft Wayne, 1930; Beta Sigma Phi. Polit & Govt Pos: Vchmn, Kosciusko Co Rep Cent Comt, Ind, 50-; clerk, Kosciusko Circuit Court, 52-60; secy, Ind Rep Fedn Women, 62-64; state legis chmn, Ind Bus & Prof Women, 64-65; worked for & chaired the orgn meetings, Kosciusko Co Hist Soc, 65. Bus & Prof Pos: Owner & mgr, Jordan Advert Co, 65- Mem: Warsaw Arts & Crafts Club (hon & charter mem); Warsaw Bus & Prof Women's Club. Honors & Awards: Woman of the Year, Warsaw Bus & Prof Women's Club, 57; Honored for work in the Rep Party by Congressman Earl Landgrebe & Kosciusko Co Rep Cent Comt, 72. Relig: Trinity United Methodist. Mailing Add: 218 Fort Wayne Ave Warsaw IN 46580

JORDAN, ORCHID IRENE (D)
Mo State Rep
b Clay Center, Kans, Aug 15, 10; d Maraman Harve Ramsey & Susan Maud Eyre R; m to Leon M Jordan, wid. Educ: Wilberforce Univ, 2 years; Gamma Kappa Phi; Alpha Kappa Alpha. Polit & Govt Pos: Mem, Freedom, Inc, 64-; vchmn, Local Citizens for Humphrey-Muskie Campaign, 68; Mo State Rep, 70-; mem, Mo State Dem Comt; mem-at-lg, Dem Nat Comt, 73-, mem adv planning comt; deleg, Dem Nat Mid-Term Conf, 74. Mem: Urban League (local bd mem); life mem NAACP; Links, Inc (pres, Kansas City Chap, 68-70, chmn cent area freedom & fine arts, 69-71). Honors & Awards: Miss Wilberforce, 31; Lady of Day, local radio sta; two award for serv rendered, Links, Inc. Relig: Episcopal. Mailing Add: 2745 Garfield Kansas City MO 64109

JORDAN, PAUL THOMAS (D)
Mayor, Jersey City, NJ
b Jersey City, NJ, Aug 8, 41; s William George Jordan & Rita McLaughlin J; m 1968 to Patricia Brennan; c Robert Francis & Brian Patrick. Educ: Georgetown Univ, BA Hist, 63; NJ Col Med, Newark, MD, 68. Polit & Govt Pos: Mayor, Jersey City, NJ, 71-; deleg, Dem Nat Conv, 72. Bus & Prof Pos: Med dir, Essex Co Drug Abuse-Narcotics Addiction Clin, 70-71; med dir, Patrick House, Jersey City, 71. Mil Serv: Capt, NJ Nat Guard, currently. Relig: Roman Catholic. Legal Res: 76 Bentley Ave Jersey City NJ 07304 Mailing Add: 280 Grove St Jersey City NJ 07302

JORDAN, RAYMOND A, JR (D)
Mass State Rep
Mailing Add: State Capitol Boston MA 02133

JORDAN, RUSSELL CLINGER, JR (D)
Committeeman, Sarasota Co Dem Comt, Fla
b Kansas City, Mo, Oct 28, 26; s Russell C Jordan & Lois Van Evera J; m 1973 to Judith Jester; c Robert Michael, Gregory, Suzanne, Jamie & Sherrill. Educ: Kans City Univ, 1 year; Rose Polytech Inst, 1 year; Ind Univ, 6 months; Command & Gen Staff Col, 70. Polit & Govt Pos: Committeeman, Sarasota Co Dem Comt, Fla, 60-; Fla State Rep, Sarasota Co, 62-64. Bus & Prof Pos: Pres, Russ Jordan Ins, Inc, Sarasota, Fla, 50-; pres, Russ Jordan Property, Inc, 55- Mil Serv: Entered as Pvt, 43, Air Corps, released as 2nd Lt, 48, after serv in 24th Inf Div, Far East Theatre, 47-48; Col, Army Res, 68- Mem: Sarasota Asn Independent Ins Agents (vpres); Fla Asn Independent Ins Agents; Am Legion; CofC; Power Squadron, SAR. Relig: Christian; Bd, First Christian Church. Mailing Add: 2101 Ringling Blvd Sarasota FL 33577

JORGENSEN, JACK J (DFL)
b Enderlin, NDak, July 25, 14; s Hans Jorgen Jorgensen & Anna Melin J; m 1940 to Florence V Kinrade; c Jack J, Jr, James Alan & Sandra Lee. Polit & Govt Pos: Fifth dist chmn, Dem Party, Minneapolis, Minn, 52; alderman, 13th Ward, Minneapolis, 55; deleg, Dem Nat Conv, 68 & 72; comnr, Metrop Airports Comn, Minneapolis-St Paul, currently. Bus & Prof Pos: Secy-treas, Teamsters Local 359; pres, Minn Teamsters Joint Coun 32; gen organizer, IBT, currently. Mem: Mason; Amicus. Relig: Lutheran. Mailing Add: 216 E 135th St Burnsville MN 55378

JORGENSEN, STEVEN LANG (R)
Nat Committeeman, SDak Young Rep
b Aberdeen, SDak, June 10, 41; s Berl Cook Jorgensen & Helen Lang J; m 1966 to Mary Lou Wieseler; c Erik & Brett. Educ: Drake Univ, 59-60; Univ SDak, Vermillion, BA, 63, JD, 70; Sigma Alpha Epsilon. Polit & Govt Pos: Chmn, Minnehaha Co Young Rep, 69-70; vchmn, SDak Young Rep, 70-71, Nat Committeeman, 71-; chmn, Ballot Security Comt for Reelection of the President, 72; mem, Minnehaha Co Rep Adv Bd, 73; deleg, Young Rep Nat Conv, 73. Bus & Prof Pos: Partner, Willy, Pruitt, Matthews & Jorgensen, 70- Mil Serv: Pfc, Army, 64-70, serv in 147th Field Artillery, SDak Nat Guard. Mem: SDak Bar Asn; SDak Trial Lawyers Asn; Minnehaha Co Bar Asn (secy & treas, 70-72); Elks; Sertoma. Relig: Catholic. Mailing Add: 4004 S Cliff Ave Sioux Falls SD 57103

JORNLIN, FRANCIS M (R)
Del State Rep
Mailing Add: 2314 Ridgeway Rd Wilmington DE 19805

JORNLIN, MARY DUGGAN (R)
State Treas, Del
b Minneapolis, Minn, Jan 15, 27; parents deceased; m to Francis M Jornlin; c Frank, Mary Ellen, John, Therese, Kevin & Len. Educ: McConnell Sch, Inc, Minneapolis. Polit & Govt Pos: Committeewoman, Wilmington Rep City Comt, Del, 65; campaign mgr for Off of City Coun, Wilmington, 68; State Treas, Del, 73- Bus & Prof Pos: Merchandiser, Neiman-Marcus, Dallas, Tex, 47; dir, Patricia Stevens Modeling & Finishing Sch, Minneapolis, 48-50. Mem: US Savings Bonds Adv Comt for State of Del (women's chmn); Nat Asn State Auditors, Comptrollers & Treas; Am Soc Distinguished Citizens; Tower Hill Sch (trustee); Del Women's Polit Caucus (participant). Relig: Catholic. Legal Res: 2314 Ridgeway Rd Wilmington DE 19805 Mailing Add: Thomas Collins Bldg Dover DE 19901

JOSEFSON, J A (R)
Minn State Sen
b Minneota, Minn, Mar 5, 15; s Johann A Josefson & Winnie Hoftieg J; m 1950 to Gladys O Coover; c Lois Eileen. Educ: Univ Minn, 38. Polit & Govt Pos: Chmn, Lyon Co Prod & Mkt Admin, Fed Farm Prog, 46-54; Minn State Sen, 54-, pres pro tem, Minn State Senate, 71-73. Bus & Prof Pos: Dir & chmn bd dirs, Farmers & Merchants Supply Co, 45-73. Mem: All York & Scottish Rite Masonic Orders; Am Farm Bur Fedn; Rotary Int. Relig: Lutheran. Mailing Add: Minneota MN 56264

JOSEPH, GERALDINE M (GERI) (D)
b St Paul, Minn, June 19, 23; d Samuel S Mack & Edith Berkovitz M; m 1953 to Burton M Joseph; c Shelley M, I Scott & Jonathan P. Educ: Univ Minn, BA, 45; Theta Sigma Phi; Delta Phi Lambda. Polit & Govt Pos: State women's chmn, Vol for Stevenson, Minn, 56; chairwoman, Minn Dem-Farmer-Labor Party, 58-60; Dem Nat Committeewoman, 60-72; mem, President's Comt on Youth Employ, 62-64; mem prog comt, Anti-Defamation League & Gov Coun on Youth Training, Inc; mem adv coun, Nat Inst Ment Health, 63-67; mem, President's Comn on Income Maintenance Progs, 68-70; vchmn, Dem Nat Comt, 68-70. Bus & Prof Pos: Contrib ed, Minneapolis Tribune; dir, Northwestern Nat Bank, 73-; mem bd dirs, Hormel Co, currently. Mem: Nat Asn for Ment Health (pres, 68-70); Citizens Coun Delinquency & Crime. Honors & Awards: First woman to win Sigma Delta Chi Award, 50; Outstanding Achievement Award, Univ Minn, 74. Relig: Jewish. Mailing Add: 5 Red Cedar Lane Minneapolis MN 55410

JOSEPH, MAURICE FRANKLIN (D)
b Freeburg, Ill, Sept 29, 05; s Frank Henry Joseph & Ruth Carr J; m 1925 to Viola Mae Sterling; c Robert F & Virginia (Mrs Gordon). Educ: High Sch. Polit & Govt Pos: Ill State Police, 33-41; precinct committeeman, Dem Party, Ill, 34-; supvr, New Athens Twp, 41-50; treas, St Clair Co, 50-54 & 66-, dep sheriff, 58-62 & sheriff, 62-66; chmn, St Clair Co Dem Cent Comt, 50-72; chmn, Ill State Dem Comt, 60-72, treas, 60-72; deleg, Dem Nat Conv, 68. Bus & Prof Pos: Appliance & furniture bus, 41-58. Mem: Mason; Shrine; Jesters; Eastern Star; Moose. Relig: Methodist. Mailing Add: Apt 2 46 Ben Louis Dr Belleville IL 62223

JOSEPHSON, JOSEPH PAUL (D)
b Trenton, NJ, June 3, 33; s David Samuel Josephson & Jenny Randelman J; m 1960 to Karla Z; c Peter Ben, Andrew Louis & Sara. Educ: Univ Chicago, BA, 50-53; Catholic Univ Am Sch of Law, JD, 60; Phi Kappa Psi; Iron Mask Soc. Polit & Govt Pos: Legis asst to US Sen E L Bartlett, Washington, DC, 57-60; Alaska State Rep, 63-66; councilman, Anchorage, 66-68, mayor pro tem, 67-68; assemblyman, Gtr Anchorage Area Borough, 67-68; Alaska State Sen, 69-72, Minority Leader, Alaska State Senate, 71-72; co-chmn, Joint Fed-State Land Use Planning Comn, 72- Bus & Prof Pos: Lectr Am govt & polit sci, Univ Alaska & Anchorage Community Col, 64-67; const law, Alaska Methodist Univ, 67-68 & 72. Mil Serv: Entered as Pvt, Army, 55, released as Lt, 58, after serv in Mil Police Corps; Soldier of the Month, Ft Monroe, Va, 57. Mem: Alaska, Am & Anchorage Bar Asns; Am Trial Lawyers Asn; SCent Alaska Red Cross. Honors & Awards: Nominated by US Sen E L Bartlett & Anchorage Jr CofC as One of Ten Outstanding Young Men. Relig: Jewish. Mailing Add: 1526 F St Anchorage AK 99501

JOSEY, CLAUDE KITCHIN (D)
NC State Rep
b Scotland Neck, NC, Sept 6, 23; s Robert Carey Josey, Jr & Anna Kitchin J; m 1948 to Roberta Linnell Bruce; c Roberta (Mrs Charles J Vaughan), Claude Kitchin, Jr & Robert Bruce. Educ: Wake Forest Univ, 41-42; US Mil Acad, BS, 45; Duke Univ, LLB, 56; Delta Theta Phi; Kappa Alpha. Polit & Govt Pos: Asst superior court solicitor, Guilford Co, NC, 58-59; chmn, Guilford Co Dem Exec Comt, 62-65; NC State Rep, Seventh Dist, 71- Mil Serv: Entered as 2nd Lt, Army, 45, released as Capt, 53, after serv in 187th Air-Borne Regt Combat Team, Far East & Korea, 50; Purple Heart; Distinguished Serv Cross. Mem: NC, Am & NC State Bar Asns; VFW; Kiwanis. Relig: Baptist. Legal Res: Rich Square Rd Scotland Neck NC 27874 Mailing Add: 110 E Tenth St Scotland Neck NC 27874

JOSLIN, ALFRED HAHN
Assoc Justice, RI Supreme Court
b Providence, RI, Jan 29, 14; s Philip C Joslin & Dorothy Aisenberg J; m 1941 to Roberta Gardner Grant; c Andrew J & Susan A (Mrs Jonathan Leader). Educ: Brown Univ, AB, 35; Harvard Univ, LLB, 38; Phi Beta Kappa; Pi Lambda Phi. Polit & Govt Pos: Mem comn to revise corp laws of RI, 49-50; mem comn to revise elec laws, 57-58; assoc justice, RI Supreme Court, 63- Mil Serv: Entered as Lt(jg), Navy, 42, released as Lt Comdr, 45, Eastern Sea Frontier; Area Ribbons. Mem: RI & Am Bar Asns; Am Judicature Soc; Univ Club; Bristol Yacht Club. Honors & Awards: Big Brother of Year, 58; Citation, Brown Univ, 57. Relig: Jewish. Legal Res: 4 Mulberry Rd Bristol RI 02809 Mailing Add: RI Supreme Court 250 Benefit St Providence RI 02903

JOSLIN, ROGER (R)
Chmn, McLean Co Rep Cent Comt
b Bloomington, Ill, June 21, 36; s James Clifford Joslin (deceased) & Doris McLaflin J; m 1958 to Stephany Moore; c Scott, Jill & James. Educ: Miami Univ, BS in Bus, 58; Univ Ill Col Law, Urbana, JD, 61; Phi Beta Kappa; Omicron Delta Kappa; Beta Alpha Psi; Beta Sigma Pi; Phi Eta Sigma; Phi Delta Phi; Sigma Phi Epsilon. Polit & Govt Pos: Pres, McLean Co Young Rep Club, Ill, 64-66; dir, Rep Workshops of Ill, 65-67; dist gov, Ill Young Rep, 65-67; chmn, McLean Co Rep Cent Comt, 66-; deleg, Rep Nat Conv, 68; vpres, Ill Rep Co Chmn Asn, 68-72, treas, 72- Bus & Prof Pos: Attorney, Davis, Morgan & Witherell, Peoria, Ill, 61-63; controller, Union Ins Group, Bloomington, 63-64; dir, Normal State Bank, 64-67; asst vpres, State Farm Mutual Automobile Ins Co, Bloomington, 64-69, vpres & controller, 69- Mem: Am, Ill State & McLean Co Bar Asns; Ill Soc CPA; Bloomington Asn Com. Relig: Presbyterian; bd trustees, Second Presby Church, 71-74, pres, 73-74. Mailing Add: 2001 E Cloud St Bloomington IL 61701

JOSLIN, WILLIAM RICHARD (R)
b Keene, NH, July 9, 45; s George Elias Joslin & Marie Elder J; m 1967 to Karen Seaver; c Sarah Elizabeth. Educ: Clark Univ, AB, 67; Georgetown Univ Law Ctr, JD, 73. Polit & Govt Pos: Deleg & mem platform comt, NH Rep State Conv, 66; legis asst, US Rep James C Cleveland, NH, 70-71, admin asst, 72- Bus & Prof Pos: Vol, Peace Corps, Bihar, India, 67-69. Legal Res: Spofford NH 03462 Mailing Add: c/o James C Cleveland 2236 Rayburn House Off Bldg Washington DC 20515

JOSSERAND, ROBERT WARREN (R)
Chmn, Pratt Co Rep Cent Comt, Kans
b Gray Co, Kans, Aug 31, 96; s John F Josserand & Anna Dulin J; m 1923 to Helen Douglas; c Robert Douglas & James Rolf. Educ: Cimmeron High Sch, Kans, grad. Polit & Govt Pos: Chmn, Pratt Co Rep Cent Comt, Kans, 59-; deleg, Rep Nat Conv, 60; mem-at-lg, Electoral Col, 68. Bus & Prof Pos: Sch teacher, 20-21 & 22; retail bus, 23-40; land owner & livestock, 40-69. Mil Serv: Entered as Pvt, 20th Inf, Army, 18-19. Mem: Mason; Shrine; Elks; Lions Int; Am Legion. Honors & Awards: Yearly State Awards for polit achievement in leadership & finances, past 12 years. Relig: Methodist. Mailing Add: 1001 Random Rd Pratt KS 67124

JOVA, JOSEPH JOHN
US Ambassador to Mexico
b Newburgh, NY, Nov 7, 16; s Joseph Luis Jova & Maria Josefa Gonzalez-Cavada; m 1949 to Pamela Johnson; c Henry Christopher, John Thomas & Margaret Ynes. Educ: Dartmouth Col, AB, 38; Sigma Phi Epsilon. Hon Degrees: PhD, Mt St Mary Col, 73; LLB, Dowling Col, 73. Polit & Govt Pos: Career Officer, US Dept of State Foreign Serv, 47-; vconsul, Basra, 47-49; second secy, vconsul, Tangier, 49-52; consul, Oporto, 52-54; first secy, Lisbon, 54-57; officer-in-charge, French-Iberian Affairs, 57-58; attended Sr Sem in Foreign Policy, Foreign Serv Inst, 58-59; asst chief, Personnel Opers Div, 59-60, chief, 60-61; counsr, Santiago, Chile, 61-65; US Ambassador to Honduras, 65-69; US Ambassador to the Orgn of Am States, 69-74; US Ambassador to Mexico, 74- Bus & Prof Pos: Asst overseer & div inspector, Fruit Co, Guatemala, 38-41; trustee Mt St Mary Col (NY), currently. Mil Serv: Entered as Ens, Naval Res, 42, released as Lt, 46, after serv in Am & European Theaters. Mem: US Foreign Serv Asn; Am Soc Pub Admin; Rotary; Knights of Malta; Order of Morazan, Honduras. Relig: Roman Catholic. Legal Res: c/o First Nat Bank Ft Lauderdale FL 33310 Mailing Add: Mexico City Dept of State Washington DC 20520

JOWETT, WILLIAM (R)
Mich State Rep
Mailing Add: 2430 Riverside Dr Port Huron MI 48060

JOY, MICHAEL BILL (D)
b Las Vegas, NMex, Mar 16, 44; s Minus Berg Joy & Mrs Earl Ludwig; m 1972 to Jerri Herath. Educ: Univ SC, 62-66, BA, Econ, 66. Polit & Govt Pos: Legis asst, US Sen Ernest F Hollings, SC, 66-68, admin asst, 69- Legal Res: 901 Sumter St Columbia SC 29201 Mailing Add: 437 Senate Off Bldg Washington DC 20510

JOYCE, ALBERT JOHN, JR (D)
b Ancon, CZ, Sept 19, 32; s Albert John Joyce & Mary Gertrude Mulrey J; m 1959 to Maria Victoria Faraudo; c Albert John, III & Richard Michael. Educ: The Citadel, Mil Col SC, BA, 54; Univ SC Sch Law, LLB, 60; Pi Sigma Alpha; Phi Alpha Delta; Int Rel Club, The Citadel. Polit & Govt Pos: Intel analyst, Dept of Army, US Army Caribbean, 56-57; vchmn, CZ Regional Dem Cent Comt, 60-62, chmn, 62-72; acting Pub Defender, CZ Govt, 66; deleg, Dem Nat Conv, 68; mem, Dem Nat Comt, formerly. Bus & Prof Pos: Attorney-at-law, CZ, 60- Mil Serv: Entered as 2nd Lt, Army, 54, released as 1st Lt, 56, after serv in Ft Amador, CZ, Far East Command, 55-56; Maj, Army Res, currently. Publ: Acting sports page ed, Star & Herald, 56-57; contrib sports writer, Panama Am, 60- Mem: ROA; Am, Fed & CZ Bar Asns. Mailing Add: PO Box 615 Balboa CZ

JOYCE, DANIEL L, JR (D)
Mass State Rep
b Woburn, Mass, May 14, 34; s Daniel L Joyce, Sr & Mary E Logan J; m 1960 to Beverly F Hubert; c Colleen, Daniel L, III, Patricia, Michael & Kathleen. Educ: Boston Col, BS & BA; Suffolk Law Sch, LLB. Polit & Govt Pos: Mass State Rep, 22nd Middlesex Dist, 69- Bus & Prof Pos: Claims adjuster, Gen Accident Co, Boston, 64; attorney, pvt practice, Woburn, 64- Mil Serv: Entered as Pvt, Army, 53, released as Cpl, 55, after serv in 8th Army. Mem: Am, Middlesex & Mass Bar Asns; Lions; KofC. Relig: Catholic. Mailing Add: 10 Revere Rd Woburn MA 01801

JOYCE, JEROME J (D)
Ill State Sen
Mailing Add: RR Reddick IL 60961

JOYCE, JOHN J (D)
Maine State Rep
Mailing Add: 67 Carter St Portland ME 04103

JOYCE, ROBERT H (D)
Chmn, Grant Co Dem Comt, Kans
b Ulysses, Kans, Apr 25, 18; s Richard H Joyce & Estell E Towler J; m 1930 to Myrna E Reeves; c Robert H, Jr, Richard M & Rebecca. Educ: Kans State Univ, BS in Eng, 40; Theta Chi. Polit & Govt Pos: Mem, Grant Co Dem Comt, Kans, 58-64, chmn, 64- Bus & Prof Pos: Draftsman, Navy, 40-41; engr, Soil Conserv Serv, 41-43; commun committeeman, Agr Stabilization & Conserv Serv, 54-64. Mil Serv: Entered as Pvt, Army Corps Eng, 43, released as T-4, 45, after serv in 1375th Eng Petrol Dist Co EAME, 44-45; EAME Theater Ribbon with Four Bronze Serv Stars; Victory & Good Conduct Medals. Mem: Am Soc Agr Engrs; Mason; Am Legion; VFW. Relig: Methodist. Mailing Add: Star Rte 2 Hugoton KS 67951

JOYNER, CONRAD FRANCIS (R)
Supvr, Pima Co, Ariz
b Connersville, Ind, Oct 21, 31; s Hubert Williams Joyner & Louise Ariens J; m 1955 to Arabella Ann Maxey; c Conrad Francis, Jr, Michael Joseph & Mark Maxey. Educ: Earlham Col, BA, 53; Univ Fla, MA, 54, PhD, 57; Univ Sydney, 55-56; Phi Beta Kappa; Phi Eta Sigma; Tau Kappa Alpha; Pi Sigma Alpha. Polit & Govt Pos: Rep precinct committeeman, Fayette Co, Ind, 52-54; chmn, Tenth Dist Young Rep, Ind, 52-54; mem, Gov & Sen Mark O Hatfield's Staff, Ore, 60-61, summers 64 & 68, mgr, Richard Burke's Cong Campaign, Ariz, 62; co-mgr, Lew Davis' Campaign for Mayor, Tucson, Ariz, 63; Rep ward committeeman, Tucson, 63-70; dir arts & sci div, Ariz Rep State Cent Comt, 63-68; mem Congressman Ogden Reid's staff, Washington, DC, summer 65; Rep precinct committeeman, Pima Co, Ariz, 66-; mem, Ariz Rep State Cent Comt, 66-74; city councilman, Tucson, 67-71, vmayor, 69-70; alt deleg, Rep Nat Conv, 68; mem, US Census Adv Comn, 72-; supvr, Pima Co, 73- Bus & Prof Pos: Instr WVa Univ, 56-57; from asst prof to assoc prof, Univ Southwestern La, 57-61; from assoc prof to prof, Univ Ariz, 61- Publ: The Republican Dilemma, 63 & The American Politician, 71, Univ Ariz; The Commonwealth and Monopolies, F W Cheshire, Melbourne & London, 63. Mem: Am Asn Univ Prof; Ariz League Cities & Towns; NAACP; Coun on Orgn Ariz State Govt; Tucson Coun Civic Unity. Honors & Awards: Fulbright Scholar, 55-56; John Henry Newman Honor Soc; Outstanding Young Men Am, Jr CofC, 64; Outstanding Male Faculty Mem, Univ Ariz, 65; E Harris Harbison Prize, Danforth Found, 67. Relig: Catholic. Mailing Add: 5322 E Second St Tucson AZ 85711

JUAREZ, OSCAR F (R)
b Guatemala City, Guatemala, June 28, 40; s Oscar A Juarez & Helen D J; m 1964 to Nancy Plapp; c Julia Elena. Educ: Stetson Univ, BA, 63; Univ Tenn, 64; Spanish Fraternity; Lambda Chi Alpha; Student Govt Asn; Newman Club. Polit & Govt Pos: Treas, Young Rep Club, Orange Co, Fla, 67-68; admin asst to US Rep Lou Frey, Jr, Fla, 69- Mil Serv: Entered Army, 57, released as SP-3, 65, after serv in Army Res. Mem: Civitan Club; Int Jaycees; Fla State Soc; Young Rep Club; Am for Constitutional Action. Honors & Awards: Ford Found Scholarship, Grad Assistantship. Relig: Roman Catholic. Legal Res: 2012 Merritt Park Dr Orlando FL 32803 Mailing Add: Off of Hon Lou Frey Jr 214 Cannon House Off Bldg Washington DC 20515

JUBELIRER, ROBERT CARL (R)
Pa State Sen
b Altoona, Pa, Feb 9, 37; s Samuel H Jubelirer & Darothy Brett J; m 1959 to Myra Millstein; c Laurie R, Andrew W & Jeffrey S. Educ: Pa State Univ, BA, 59; Dickinson Sch Law, JD, 62; Alpha Phi Omega; Delphi; Parmi Nous; Skull & Bones; Beta Sigma Rho. Polit & Govt Pos: Chmn, Young Rep Pa, 72-74; Pa State Sen, 30th Dist, 75- Bus & Prof Pos: Partner, Jubelirer, Carothers, Krier & Halpern, Attorney-at-law, Altoona, Pa, 62- Mem: Pa Bar Asn; Altoona Rotary; Mason; Blair Co Farmers Asn. Relig: Jewish. Legal Res: 4032 Ridge Ave Altoona PA 16602 Mailing Add: 217 Cent Trust Bldg Altoona PA 16601

JUDD, BURNHAM A (R)
NH State Rep
Mailing Add: Main St Pittsburg NH 03592

JUDD, C DEMONT, JR (D)
Utah State Rep
b Kanab, Utah, Aug 26, 28; s Clarence DeMont Judd, Sr & Elizabeth DeLong J; m 1955 to Ramona Fay Stoven Covey; c RoseMarie, Michelle, Jefferson DeMont, Jennifer Caye, Spencer Mark, Christopher Jourdan, C DeMont, III & Rodney Scott. Educ: Univ Utah, JD, 56. Polit & Govt Pos: Utah State Rep, 69- Mil Serv: Entered as Pvt, Army, 51, released as Pfc, 53, after serv in Med Corps. Mem: Am Bar Asn; Nat Asn Defense Counsel in Criminal Cases. Relig: Latter-day Saint. Mailing Add: Suite 102 2650 Washington Blvd Ogden UT 84401

JUDD, CLAUD R (D)
Idaho State Sen
Mailing Add: Rte 3 Orofino ID 83544

JUDD, HARLAN EKIN, JR (R)
Chmn, Cumberland Co Rep Party, Ky
b Glasgow, Ky, Apr 20, 43; s Harlan Ekin Judd & Helen Curtis J; m 1968 to Patsy Ann Huff; c Harlan Ekin, III. Educ: Am Univ, 64-65; Transylvania Univ, AB, 65; Univ Ky Col Law, JD, 68; Phi Kappa Tau; Lampas; Phi Delta Phi. Polit & Govt Pos: Attorney, Dept Revenue, Frankfort, Ky, 68-69 & Dept Econ Security, 69-72; attorney, Cumberland Co, 74-; chmn,

Cumberland Co Rep Party, Ky, currently. Bus & Prof Pos: Dir, Bank Marrowbone, 72- Mil Serv: Entered as Pvt, Army, released as 1st Lt; 1st Lt Army Res, 73-; Ky Serviceman's Ribbon. Mem: Mason; Scottish Rite; CofC; Jaycees; Am Legion. Honors & Awards: Mr Pioneer, Transylvania Univ, 65; Outstanding Young Man, Jaycees. Relig: Christian Church. Mailing Add: Burkesville KY 42717

JUDD, WALTER HENRY (R)
b Rising City, Nebr, Sept 25, 98; s Horace Hunter Judd & Mary Elizabeth Greenslit J; m 1932 to Miriam Louise Barber; c Mary Lou (Mrs Norman R Carpenter), Carolyn Ruth (Mrs J LaMont Johnson); & Eleanor Grace (Mrs Paul Quinn). Educ: Univ Nebr, BA, 20, MD, 23; Mayo Found, Univ Minn, fel in surg, 32-34; Phi Beta Kappa, Alpha Omega Alpha; Phi Rho Sigma; Omicron Delta Kappa. Hon Degrees: LLD, DS, DLitt, LHD, DCL, DSW, DHS & DD from 26 univs & cols. Polit & Govt Pos: US Rep, Fifth Dist, Minn, 43-62; US deleg to UN 12th Gen Assembly; founder of Rep Workshops. Bus & Prof Pos: Instr zool, Univ Omaha, 20-24, intern, Univ Omaha Hosp, 22-24; traveling secy, Student Vol Movement in cols & univs, 24-25; med missionary, Nanking, China, 25-26, Shaowu, Fukien, 26-31 & Fenchow, Shansi, 34-38; lectr in US, 39-40; physician & surgeon, Minneapolis, 41-42; contributing ed, Readers Digest, 63-; commentator, Washington Report of the Air, Am Security Coun, 64-70. Mil Serv: Entered as Pvt, Army, 18, released as 2nd Lt, 19, after serv in Field Artil. Mem: Am Med Asn (mem judicial coun); Minn Med Asn; Am Acad Family Physicians; hon fel Int Col Surgeons; China Soc. Honors & Awards: Distinguished Serv Awards, Univ Nebr, 45 & Am Med Asn, 61; George Washington Hon Medals, Freedom Found, 59, 61, 62, 64 & 67; CARE-MEDICO World Humanitarian Award, 62; Great Living Am Award, US CofC & Silver Buffalo Award, Boy Scouts, 63. Mailing Add: 3083 Ordway St NW Washington DC 20008

JUDE, THADDEUS VICTOR (DFL)
Minn State Rep
b St Cloud, Minn, Dec 13, 51; s Victor Nicholas Jude & Ruth Huisenruit J; single. Educ: Col St Thomas, BA, 72. Polit & Govt Pos: Chmn, Minn Sixth Dist Young Dem-Farmer-Labor, 70-71; exec vchmn, Minn Young Dem-Farmer-Labor, 71; Minn State Rep, Dist 42A, 73- Mil Serv: Entered as E-1, Army Res, 71, currently E-4, serv in 523rd Army Security Agency, Ft Snelling, Minn. Mem: Minn Citizens Concerned for Life; Jaycees. Relig: Catholic. Mailing Add: 5230 Sulgrove Rd Mound MN 55364

JUDGE, THOMAS LEE (D)
Gov, Mont
b Helena, Mont, Oct 12, 34; s Thomas Patrick Judge (deceased) & Blanche Guillot J; m 1966 to Carol Ann Anderson; c Thomas Warren & Patrick Lane. Educ: Univ Notre Dame, BA, 57; Univ Louisville, Advert Cert, 59. Polit & Govt Pos: Mont State Rep, Lewis & Clark Co, 61-67, Mont State Sen, 67-69; Lt Gov, 69-73, chmn, Nat Lt Gov Conf, formerly, vchmn rural & urban develop comt, currently; mem exec comt, Dem Gov Conf, currently; Gov, 73- Bus & Prof Pos: Pres, Judge Advert, 60-72. Mil Serv: 2nd Lt, Army, Adj Gen Corps, Ft Benjamin Harrison, Ind, 58, Capt Res. Mem: Pub Rels Soc Am; Elks; Eagles, KofC; Jaycees; CofC. Honors & Awards: Distinguished Serv Award, 63; Notre Dame Man of the Year, 66; Outstanding Young Man of Year, Mont Jaycees, 67. Relig: Catholic. Legal Res: 2 Carson Helena MT 59601 Mailing Add: State Capitol Bldg Helena MT 59601

JUELING, HELMUT L (R)
Wash State Rep
b Loup City, Nebr, 1913; m to Ruth; c two daughters. Educ: Univ Puget Sound, BA. Polit & Govt Pos: Wash State Rep, currently. Bus & Prof Pos: Owner laundry & linen supply bus. Mailing Add: 215 Contra Costa Tacoma WA 98466

JULIA, GILDA (R)
b San Juan, PR, Nov 18, 27; d Enrique Julia & Emilia Martinez J; div; c Maria Emilia, Luis Esteban, Jr, Mario Enrique, Maria Luisa, Andres Eduardo, Miguel Antonio & Maria Alexandra. Educ: Col of Sacred Heart, 44-46; Univ Va, 47-48. Polit & Govt Pos: Deleg, Rep Nat Conv, 68; Rep Nat Committeewoman, PR, 69-72. Bus & Prof Pos: Mem staff, Condominium Enterprises, Inc, Castle Enterprises, Inc, San Juan Realty Corp, City Enterprises, Inc, Ctr Enterprises Inc & Ceramic Enterprises, Inc. Mem: Sleepy Hollow Country Club, NY; Boulder Brook Club, NY. Relig: Catholic. Legal Res: 37 Mallorca St Hato Rey PR 00917 Mailing Add: Box 11605 Santurce PR 00910

JULIAN, CHESTER ROY (R)
b Poteet, Tex, Oct 16, 37; s William Robert Julian & Phoebe Adeline Patton J; m 1963 to Beverly Dale McClear; c Robert Dale, Melissa Dale & Patrick Donahue. Educ: Univ Alaska, Fairbanks, 56-57; Tex A&M Univ, BSCE, 61; Cath Univ Am, MCE, 64. Polit & Govt Pos: Hwy engr, DC Dept Hwy & Traffic, Washington, DC, 61-63, hwy planning engr, 63-65; opers research analyst, US Nat Bur Standards, 65-66; prog officer, US Dept Com, 66-67; spec asst, US Dept Transportation & Fed Hwy Admin, 67-70; Am Polit Sci Asn Cong fel, US Sen Montoya, NMex & US Rep Kuykendall, Tenn, 70-71; spec asst, Fed Hwy Admin, 71; admin asst, US Rep Dick Shoup, Mont, 71-75. Bus & Prof Pos: Univ lectr transportation, George Washington Univ, Southeastern Univ, Northern Va Ctr of Univ Va & Cath Univ Am, 64-68. Mil Serv: Entered as Pfc, Army Res, 61, released as Sgt 1/C, 67. Publ: An investigation of certain aspects of minibus operation in Washington, DC, Cath Univ Am, 64; Staggering work hours to improve highway transportation service, US Fed Hwy Admin, 71; Staggering work hours to ease existing street capacity problems, Inst Traffic Engs & Cong Record, 71. Mem: DC Capitol Area, Am Polit Sci Asn; Montgomery Co Rep Mens Club; Bull Elephants of US House of Rep; Conservative Luncheon Club Capitol Hill; Olney Village Citizens Asn (pres, 73). Relig: Presbyterian. Mailing Add: 3209 Gold Mine Rd Brookeville MD 20729

JULIAN, JOHN EDWARD (D)
Conn State Rep
b Stafford, Conn, Mar 22, 43; s Michael C Julian & Victoria Negro J; m 1965 to Hope MacFall; c Justin & Jennifer. Educ: Univ Conn, BA, 65. Polit & Govt Pos: Chmn, Stafford, Conn Bd Educ, 68-70; mem, Stafford Planning & Zoning Comt, 70-72; Conn State Rep, 75- Bus & Prof Pos: Owner, Julian Ins Agency, 65- Mil Serv: Entered as Pvt, Army, 65, released as Capt, 67, after serv in 1131 Inf Div, Camp Casey, Korea, 65-67; Capt, Army Res. Mailing Add: 45 Buckley Hwy Stafford Springs CT 06076

JULIANELLE, ROBERT LEWIS (D)
Conn State Sen
b New Haven, Conn, Feb 8, 40; s Lewis R Julianelle & Ida DeMartino J; m to Eleanor F O'Hara; c Mark L & Robert M. Educ: Fairfield Univ, BSS, 61; Georgetown Univ Law Ctr, JD, 64; Phi Delta Phi. Polit & Govt Pos: Mem, Milford Dem Town Comt, Conn, 70-, exec comt, 72-; mem re-voting dist comt, City of Milford, 74-; Conn State Sen, 14th Dist, 75- Bus & Prof Pos: Officer & dir, Schine, Julianelle, Kard & Bozelko, currently. Mem: Lions; Am & Conn Bar Asns; Am Asn Trial Lawyers; KofC. Mailing Add: 5 Jerome Lane Milford CT 06460

JUMONVILLE, J E (D)
La State Sen
Mailing Add: Ventress LA 70783

JUMP, HARRY V (R)
Mem, Huron Co Rep Exec Comt, Ohio
b Bellevue, Ohio, Nov 7, 14; s Otto V Jump & LuLa C Bell J; m 1937 to Leora Victoria Jacobs; c James R, Michael M, David A, Deborah V & Leora Ann. Educ: Bluffton Col, AB, 36. Polit & Govt Pos: Mem, Huron Co Rep Exec Comt, Ohio, 47-; co comnr, Huron Co, 49-56; Ohio State Rep, Huron Co, 57-66, Majority Whip, Ohio House of Rep, 61-66; Ohio State Sen, 13th Dist, 67-68; clerk of the Ohio Senate, 71-75. Bus & Prof Pos: Owner of gen ins agency, 46-75; dep dir, Ohio Dept of Ins, 69-70, dir, 75- Mem: Ohio Asn of Co Comnr; Ohio Asn of Ins Agents; Ohio Asn of Real Estate Bd; Rotary; Mason (32 degree). Relig: Methodist. Mailing Add: 221 E Howard St Willard OH 44890

JUNKER, WILLIS E (R)
Iowa State Rep
Mailing Add: 3415 Nebraska Sioux City IA 51104

JUNKIN, JOHN RICHARD (D)
Miss State Rep
b Natchez, Miss, Dec 16, 96; wid. Polit & Govt Pos: Mem, Bd of Supvr, Natchez, Miss, 28-36; Miss State Rep, 44-, speaker, Miss House Rep, 66- Bus & Prof Pos: Contractor; planter. Mem: Am Legion. Relig: Catholic. Mailing Add: Box 928 Natchez MS 39120

JUNKINS, LOWELL LEE (D)
Iowa State Sen
b Ft Madison, Iowa, Mar 9, 44; s Ralph Renaud Junkins & Selma J Kudebeh J; m 1963 to Linda Lee Decker; c Kristina Lynne & Kara Dyann. Educ: Iowa State Univ, 62-63. Polit & Govt Pos: Councilman, Montrose, Iowa, 69-70, mayor, 72-73; chmn, Montrose Planning & Zoning Comn, 70-71; committeeman, Dem Party, Iowa, 70-; chmn, North Lee Co Areawide Health Planning Coun, 71-72, vchmn, Lee Co Dem Party, 71-72; Iowa State Sen, 73- Bus & Prof Pos: Vpres & treas, Golden Acres, Inc; partner, Junkins, Hunold, Junkins Construction Co; mem, Nat Fedn Independent Businessmen; vpres, Lee Co Ambulance Serv, Inc, Iowa, 67- Mem: Eagles; Lions (first vpres, Montrose Club); Mason. Relig: Presbyterian; elder, Montrose Presby Church, currently. Mailing Add: PO Box 188 Montrose IA 52639

JURAM, WILLIAM CARL, JR (R)
Chmn, Roxbury Rep Town Comt, Conn
b Philadelphia, Pa, Feb 9, 11; s William Carl Juram & Bertha Ullmann J; m 1942 to Elloie Evans Jeter; c Brooke (Mrs Wheeler) & William C, III. Educ: Drexel Univ, BS in mech eng; Pi Tau Sigma. Polit & Govt Pos: Mem, Roxbury Rep Town Comt, Conn, 64-, chmn, 68-; exec dir, Power Facility Eval Coun, 72- Bus & Prof Pos: Various mkt pos; vpres mkt, Bristol Co, Waterbury, Conn, 35-70. Mil Serv: Entered as 2nd Lt, Army, 42, released as Capt, 45, after serv in US. Mem: Instrument Soc Am; Newcomen Soc NAm; F&AM. Relig: Episcopal. Mailing Add: Old Tophet Rd Roxbury CT 06783

JUSTICE, NORMAN E (D)
Kans State Rep
b Kansas City, Kans, Nov 1, 25; s Benjamin Samuel Justice & Willa Duckworth J; m 1954 to Kathryn Flanagan; c Patricia Ann (Mrs Roy Pierson). Educ: Fayetteville Teachers Col, NC, 47-48. Polit & Govt Pos: Dem precinct committeeman, Kansas City, Kans, 46-75; chmn, State Comn Civil Rights, 68-72; Kans State Rep, 34th Dist, 72-, mem adv comn children & youth, 74-75. Bus & Prof Pos: Sgt, Kansas City Police Dept, Kans, 54-57; rec secy, Construction Gen Laborers Local 1290, 65-67, vpres, 67-73, pres, 73- Mil Serv: Entered as A/S, Navy, 43, released as Stewards Mate 1/C, 45, after serv in USS NJ, Pac; Good Conduct Medal; Philippine Liberation Medal; Presidential Unit Citation. Publ: Legislative news, Kansas City Call Weekly News, 75; From the desk of your representative, Kansas City Globe Weekly News, 75. Mem: IB Blackburn Blue Lodge; Orient Consistory; Koran Temple. Honors & Awards: Certs of Award, Kansas City Proj Head Start, Econ Opportunity Found Bd Trustees, Community Action Progs & Optimist Int. Relig: African Methodist Episcopal. Mailing Add: 506 Washington Blvd Kansas City KS 66101

K

KAARDAL, ELMER ALFRED (D)
Chmn, Fourth Dist Dem-Farmer-Labor Comt, Minn
b Kosi, Africa, Jan 20, 27; s Rev Jetmund Iverson Kaardal & Sofia Riise K; m 1950 to Julia Martha Christensen, c Ivar, Loran, Thor, Jean, Bruce, Erick, Carol & Paul. Educ: Univ Minn, Minneapolis, BA, cum laude, 53; Augsburg Col, 1 year. Polit & Govt Pos: Chmn, Fourth Dist Dem-Farmer-Labor Comt, Redwood Falls, Minn, 63-; mem, Western Community Action Off Econ Opportunity Bd, Marshall, 65-; mem, Redwood Falls Police Comn, 67-; treas, Sixth Cong Dist Dem-Farmer-Labor Party, 70- Bus & Prof Pos: Agent, State Farm Ins Co, Redwood Falls, Minn, 58- Mil Serv: Army; Lt Col, Army Res, currently. Mem: Redwood Falls CofC (bd, 70, pres, currently); Redwood Falls Am Field Serv (pres, 70); VFW; Am Legion; Farmers Union. Relig: Lutheran. Mailing Add: 309 E Bridge St Redwood Falls MN 56283

KACH, ALBERT WADE (R)
Md State Deleg
b Baltimore, Md, July 19, 47; s Albert Jacob Kach, Jr & Josephine Bauer K; single. Educ: Towson State Col, 66-68; Western Md Col, BA, 70. Polit & Govt Pos: Chmn, Md Fedn Col Rep, 70; mem, Rep State Cent Comt Md, 70-73; Md State Deleg, 75- Bus & Prof Pos: Teacher, Baltimore Co Schs, Md, 70- Mem: Teachers Asn Baltimore Co; Md State Teachers Asn; Nat Educ Asn. Mailing Add: 1 E Queentree Ct Baltimore MD 21207

KADLECEK, JAMES M (D)
Colo State Sen
Mailing Add: 1127 16th St Greeley CO 80631

KADUK, FRANK J (D)
Chmn, Van Wert Co Dem Cent Comt, Ohio
b Van Wert, Ohio, Nov 14, 16; s Andrew Kaduk, Sr & Anna Hritz K; m 1938 to Betty Joe Huston; c Nancy Grayce, Paul Dean & Charles Lynn. Educ: Van Wert Pub Schs, 12 years. Polit & Govt Pos: Third Ward Dem councilman, Van Wert, Ohio, 58-60; city serv dir, 60-62; Dem precinct committeeman, Precinct 2-A, currently; chmn, Van Wert Co Dem Exec Comt, 67-; mem, Van Wert Co Bd of Elec, 68-, chmn, currently. Bus & Prof Pos: Sales mgr, Frederick Dodge, 63-69; truck sales mgr, Bruce Symons Chevrolet-Oldsmobile, 69; employed in sales dept, Kennedy Mfg Co, Van Wert, Ohio, 69-, sales serv mgr, currently. Mil Serv: Entered as Pvt, Ohio Nat Guard, 35, released as Sgt, 42, after serv in B Co, 112th Med Regt, 37th Div, Camp Shelby, Miss, 40-42. Mem: Van Wert Auto Dealers (chmn); CofC (mem bd trustees & legis action coun); Toastmasters Int (Area 8 Gov); Van Wert Hist Soc (pres); Boy Scouts (chmn orgn & exten comt, advan chmn, Holcolesquh Dist & exec comt, Shawnee Coun). Honors & Awards: Scouter of the Year Award; Silver Beaver Award, Shawnee Coun, Boy Scouts, 72. Mailing Add: 628 N Jefferson St Van Wert OH 45891

KAFOGLIS, NICHOLAS Z (D)
Ky State Rep
Mailing Add: 1008 Newman Dr Bowling Green KY 42101

KAFOURY, STEPHEN (D)
Ore State Rep
b Portland, Ore, Oct 4, 41; s David Ivan Kafoury & Eleanor Patten K; div; c Deborah & Katharine. Educ: Whitman Col, BA, 64; Reed Col, MAT, 68; Phi Delta Theta. Polit & Govt Pos: Ore State Rep, 73- Bus & Prof Pos: Vol, Peace Corps, Iran, 64-66; teacher, Portland Pub Schs, Ore, 67-69; asst dir, Fed Talent Search Prog, 69-72; vpres, Kafoury Bros, Inc, 72- Mil Serv: Entered as Pvt, Army Nat Guard, 59, released as Pfc, 63, after serv in Ore Nat Guard. Mem: Ore Environ Coun; Am Civil Liberties Union Ore (bd mem, 71); Ore Road Runners Club. Legal Res: 1905 NE 16th Portland OR 97212 Mailing Add: State Capitol Bldg Salem OR 97310

KAGAN, SAMUEL C (D)
RI State Rep
b Russia, Nov 11, 08; m to Ruth G, wid. Polit & Govt Pos: Mem, Spec Comt Study Ins Laws, RI; mem, Providence City Coun, 35-38; RI State Rep, 41-, dep majority leader, RI House of Rep, 62-; deleg, Dem Nat Conv, 60-64 & 68; mem, Nat Conf State Legis Leaders. Bus & Prof Pos: Chmn bd, Kagan & Shawcross, Inc, Ins & Real Estate. Mem: Order Hebraic Comradeship; life mem Hebrew Free Loan Asn; Congregation, Sons of Jacob (bd dirs); Zionist Orgn Am. Relig: Hebrew. Mailing Add: 161 Orms St Providence RI 02908

KAGEL, ALLEN DAVID (D)
Nat Committeeman, Young Dem Del
b Wilmington, Del, Aug 12, 45; s Samuel Kagel & Goldie Berkowitz K; m 1974 to Karen Ann Warach. Educ: Univ Del, 67-70, part-time, 72; founder & past pres, Univ Vet Asn. Polit & Govt Pos: Platform chmn, Young Dem Clubs of Am Nat Conv, Hot Springs, Ark, 71; founder & chmn, Legis Action Coun, Young Dem Del, 71-72; nat committeeman, 72-; mem rules comt, Dem Nat Conv, 72; assoc committeeman, 25th Representative Dist, 72-; exec dir, Del Dem State Comt, 73-74; founder & managing ed, The Del Dem, 73-; deleg, Dem Nat Mid-Term Conf, 74; exec asst to Co Exec New Castle Co, Del, 74-; dep sheriff, New Castle Co, 75- Mil Serv: Entered as A/S, Navy, 63, released as Commun Yeoman 3/C, 66, after serv in Commun Dept, USS Ranger CVA61, Vietnam, 64-66; Navy Unit Citation; Nat Defense Medal; Expeditionary Force Medal; Vietnam Medal; two letters of citation. Relig: Jewish. Mailing Add: 624 Lehigh Rd Apt Q-1 Newark DE 19711

KAHN, PHYLLIS (DFL)
Minn State Rep
Mailing Add: 100 Malcolm Ave SE Minneapolis MN 55414

KAIBEL, HOWARD LAWRENCE, JR (DFL)
Alt Deleg, Minn Dem-Farmer-Labor State Cent Comt
b Council Bluffs, Iowa, Sept 29, 44; s Howard Lawrence Kaibel, Sr & Wanda Varner K; m 1971 to Elizabeth Nussbaum; c Amanda Bayla & Maria Elizabeth. Educ: Univ Minn, BA, 67, Law Sch, JD, 71. Polit & Govt Pos: Chmn, Sixth Ward Dem-Farmer-Labor Party, Minn, 68-70; deleg, Dem Nat Conv, 68; chmn, 42nd Legis Dist Dem-Farmer-Labor Party, 70-72; asst adminr, Fed Emergency Employ Act, Minn, 71-72; exec secy, Minn Munic Comn, 72-; alt deleg, Minn Dem-Farmer-Labor State Cent Comt, 72- Mem: Am & Minn Bar Asns; Minn Civil Liberties Union (secy & dir, 67-); Citizens League of Minn; Am for Dem Action. Relig: Unitarian. Mailing Add: 3737 Colfax Ave S Minneapolis MN 55409

KAIRIT, ELEANOR JESSIE (R)
Chmn, Bridgewater Town Rep Comt, Mass
b North Abington, Mass, May 1, 24; d Elmer Edwin Colburn & Jean Alma Maclean C; m 1945 to John Walter Kairit; c Judith Elaine & William John. Educ: Abington High Sch, 38-42. Polit & Govt Pos: Chmn, Bridgewater Town Rep Comt, Mass, 66-; asst clerk, Town Hall, Bridgewater, 68-69. Mem: Womens Club; Garden Club; Red Cross; Church Groups (pres); Visiting Nurse Asn (pres). Relig: Congregational. Mailing Add: 1760 South St Bridgewater MA 02324

KAISER, GEORGE CHAPIN (R)
b Chicago, Ill, Jan 20, 33; s George Chapin Kaiser, Sr & Grace Betz K; div; c Mark Aurelius, Richard Alan & Charles Moore. Educ: Univ Ill, Urbana, BS, 54; Kappa Sigma. Polit & Govt Pos: Comnr, Wis Dept Admin, 65-67; mem, Wis Reorgn Comn, 65-67; mem, Mayor's Comt Reorgn Milwaukee City Govt, 68; treas, Rep Party, Wis, 68-73; mem adv comt, Dept Local Affairs & Develop, 68-71; mem, Milwaukee Co Planning Comn, 69-74; mem policy comt, Gov Comn Educ, 69-72; mem, Wis Metrop Study Comn, 71-73; alt deleg, Rep Nat Conv, 72; comnr, Delavan Lake Sanit Dist, 72-74; pres, Gtr Milwaukee Surv Social Welfare & Health Servs, Inc, 73-74. Bus & Prof Pos: Partner, Arthur Andersen & Co, Milwaukee, 57- Mil Serv: Entered as Ens, Naval Res, 54, released as Lt(jg), 56, after serv in Amphibious Fleet, Western Pac, 54-56. Mem: Am Inst CPA; Wis Soc CPA; Am Soc Pub Admin; Jr Achievement Southeastern Wis (adv). Relig: Congregational. Legal Res: 3379 S Shore Dr Delavan WI 53115 Mailing Add: Hotel Leningradskaya Moscow USSR

KALER, IRVING K (D)
Mem, Fulton Co Dem Exec Comt, Ga
b Pittsburgh, Pa, Oct 2, 18; s Sam Kaler & Dora Skigen K; m 1960 to Sylvia Kanter; c Jonathan, Dina, Amy, Matthew & Michael Jefferson. Educ: Washington & Lee Univ; Emory Univ Lamar Sch Law, LLB; Alpha Epsilon Pi. Hon Degrees: LLD, Emory Univ, 70. Polit & Govt Pos: Vchmn, Ga State Bd for Children & Youth, 63-; deleg, Dem Nat Conv, 64, mem, Credentials Comt, 64, mem, Rules Comt, 68; mem, Comt on Permanent Orgn of Dem Party of Ga, 64, chmn, steering comt, 64; mem, Atlanta Juvenile Coun, 66-; mem, bd dirs, Fulton Co Dem Party; chmn, Community Rels Comn, Atlanta, 67-; vchmn, Ga State Dem Exec Comt, formerly mem, Nat Rules Comn of Dem Party, 69-; mem young leadership coun, Nat Dem Party, 69; mem Dem Policy Coun Comt on Human Environ, 70; mem, Fulton Co Dem Exec Comt, 72-; mem, Fulton Co Housing Authority, 72-; deleg, Dem Nat Mid-Term Conf, 74. Mem: Atlanta CofC; Com Club; Lawyers Club of Atlanta; State Bar of Ga; B'nai B'rith Dist 5. Honors & Awards: Selected Outstanding Young Man of Year, Atlanta Jr CofC, 46; Distinguished Serv Award, Atlanta Gate City Lodge of B'nai B'rith, 67; Recipient of Outstanding Citizens Award of Jewish War Vet of US, Atlanta Post 112, 70; Abe Goldstein Human Rels Award, Anti-Defamation League of B'nai B'rith, 71. Relig: Jewish. Mailing Add: 960 W Kingston Dr NE Atlanta GA 30305

KALEY, J R (DICK) (R)
Minn State Rep
Mailing Add: 1409 29th St NW Rochester MN 55901

KALICH, HUGH EDWARD (D)
Wash State Rep
b Toledo, Wash, June 6, 21; s Joseph L Kalich & Annie Noble K; m 1943 to Mildred Norma Taylor; c Gary & Gordon. Polit & Govt Pos: Councilman, Toledo, Wash, 52-54; comnr, Lewis Co, 58-62; committeeman, Wash Dem State Comt, 58-64; Wash State Rep, 65-67 & currently. Bus & Prof Pos: Owner, Kalich Logging Co, 46-66. Mil Serv: Entered as Pvt, Army, 44, released as Pfc, 46; ETO Ribbons with 2 Battle Stars; Combat Infantryman's Badge. Mem: Elks; Moose; Lions; Am Legion; VFW. Relig: Catholic. Mailing Add: 2224 18th Ave Chehalis WA 98532

KALIS, HENRY J (DFL)
Minn State Rep
Mailing Add: Walters MN 56092

KALIVAS, DEAN SPIRO (D)
b Tacoma, Wash, Jan 5, 43; s Spiro John Kalivas & Maxine Manousos K; m 1964 to Diane G Belsvik; c Kristine & Paul. Educ: Univ Chicago, 61-63; Pac Lutheran Univ, BA, 66; Cath Univ Am Sch Law, JD, 74. Polit & Govt Pos: Counsel, House Govt Oper Comt, Subcomt on Manpower & Housing, 72-74; admin asst, US Rep Floyd V Hicks, Wash, 74- Bus & Prof Pos: Admin asst, Washington Savings & Loan League, 67-69; assoc prof law, Int Sch Law, Washington, DC, 74- Mem: Va Bar Asn. Legal Res: 3736 S D St Tacoma WA 98408 Mailing Add: 318 Second St SE Washington DC 20003

KAMAKA, HIRAM K (D)
Dir Finance, State of Hawaii
b Honolulu, Hawaii, Oct 13, 27; s William Keliiahonui Kamaka & Ana Tilton K; single. Educ: Creighton Univ Sch Law, Omaha, Nebr, JD, 52; Phi Alpha Delta. Polit & Govt Pos: Hawaii State Rep, 58-68; Dir Finance, State of Hawaii, 69- Mil Serv: Entered as Pvt, Army, 45, released as T-4, 47, after serv in Pac Area. Mem: Am, Nebr State & Hawaii Bar Asns. Relig: Roman Catholic. Mailing Add: State Capitol Honolulu HI 96813

KAMALII, KINAU BOYD (R)
Hawaii State Rep
b Honolulu, Hawaii, Oct 24, 30; c Rudolph Peter, Jr, Naunanikinau & Sissi. Educ: Univ Hawaii. Polit & Govt Pos: Mem, Young Rep; Rep precinct secy, Fourth Precinct, Eighth Representative Dist, 56-59, dist committeewoman; pres, Windward League Rep Women, 61; Rep precinct secy, Ninth Precinct, 17th Dist, 64, dist committeewoman, 66-67; Rep precinct secy, 15th Precinct, 68-69; vpres liaison, State Senate Oahu Co Comt, 69; mem, Oahu League Rep Women; deleg, Hawaii State Rep Conv, 61-71; deleg, Rep Nat Conv, 68; secy, Hawaii State Rep Cent Comt, 70; Rep Nat Committeewoman, Hawaii, 71-75; Hawaii State Rep, 75- Bus & Prof Pos: Secy, Dole Corp, 50-55; asst casting dir, Mirisch Corp, Los Angeles, Calif, 65-66; secy, State Rep, Joe Dwight, Hawaii, 61, Joe Garcia, 62 & Frank Judd, 63-64, Senate minority attorney's, 67; secy-researcher, Senate Rep Off, 68- Mem: Prince Kuhio Hawaiian Civic Club (pres, 71); Friends of Iolani Palace (dir, 70); Asn Hawan Civic Clubs (state secy, 64); Punahou Alumni Asn (pres, 63-64). Relig: Episcopal. Mailing Add: Sergeant at Arms State Capitol Honolulu HI 96813

KAMAS, LEWIS MELVIN (R)
Okla State Rep
b Knowles, Okla, Oct 24, 21; s Frank Munsor Kamas & Mabel Francis Shalloup K; m 1943 to Mary Darlien Cohlmia; c Leslie Allan & Carol Jeanne. Educ: Northwestern State Col, 39-40; Okla State Univ, 40-41; Farm House. Polit & Govt Pos: Supvr, Woods Co Soil & Water Conserv Dist 70, Okla, 48-66; Okla State Rep, Dist 58, currently, mem agr, bank & banking & road & hwys comts & vchmn tourism & recreation comt, Okla House of Rep, currently, minority caucus secy, 32nd Session, minority whip, 33rd & 34th Sessions, asst minority leader, currently. Bus & Prof Pos: Pres, Cimmaron Watershed Counsel of Soil & Water Dist of Okla, Kans, NMex & Colo, 50; mem, Red Carpet Co, Okla Northwest Inc, currently. Mil Serv: Entered as Pvt, Army Air Force, 42, released as 2nd Lt, 45, prisoner of war, 45, Stalagluft 1, Barth, Ger; Good Conduct & Air Medals; Purple Heart; Caterpillar Club; Europe-Africa-Mid East Theater Ribbon with Four Bronze Stars. Mem: Am Legion Hatch-Vincent Post; VFW (Black Wing Post 2847); Mason (32 degree); Shrine; Elks. Honors & Awards: Mem State Champion Livestock Judging Team, Okla, 37; Fourth Nat Livestock Judging Contest, Kansas City, Mo, Am Royal 1938. Relig: Orthodox. Mailing Add: Box 175 Freedom OK 73842

KAMBER, VICTOR SAMUEL (R)
b Chicago, Ill, May 7, 43; s Samuel J Kamber & Cordelia Awiz K; single. Educ: Univ Ill, AB, 65; Univ NM, MA, 66; Am Univ, JD, 69; George Washington Univ, LLM, 71; Omicron Delta Kappa; Phi Gamma Delta. Polit & Govt Pos: Campaign mgr, DC Rep Primary Elec, 68; dir of admin, United Citizens for Nixon-Agnew, 68; dir of admin, 1969 Inaugural Comt, 68-69; exec dir, Am Coun of Young Polit Leaders, 69-70; adminr asst to US Rep Seymour Halpern, NY, 70-75. Bus & Prof Pos: Prog dir, Univ NMex, 65-66; assoc prof, Prince George's Community Col, 66-69; asst prof, DC Teachers Col, 67; lectr, Am Univ, 67-68. Publ: Auth,

Need for a national standard for mental competency, NY Law J, 5/72; co-auth, Selecting federal judges, Am Bar Asn J, 6/72. Mem: Speech Asn of Am; Asn Col Unions; Am Acad of Polit Sci; Moose; Nat Rep Club of Capitol Hill. Honors & Awards: Phi Gamma Delta Washington Grad Chap Man of the Year Award, 68. Relig: Protestant. Mailing Add: 1511 W Thorndale Ave Chicago IL 60660

KAMINSKY, HARRY R **(D)**
b Birmingham, Ala, Apr 27, 05; s Harry W Kaminsky & Rosabell Hoarn K; m 1928 to Annie B Moore; c Harriett Ann (Mrs Bishop). Educ: Univ Ala, 2 years. Polit & Govt Pos: Chmn, Montgomery Co Dem Exec Comt, Ala, formerly. Bus & Prof Pos: Sales mgr, The Hub, Montgomery, Ala, 51- Mem: Optimist Club; Mason. Relig: Baptist. Mailing Add: 2012 E Fifth St Montgomery AL 36106

KAMMER, KERRY **(D)**
Mich State Sen
b Detroit, Mich, Aug 13, 48; s Kenneth W Kammer & Betty Lou Aebel K; m 1972 to Carole Busch. Educ: Wayne State Univ, BA, 70. Polit & Govt Pos: Mem, Oakland Co Dem Party, Mich, currently; mem, Mich Dem Party, currently; Mich State Sen, 75- Bus & Prof Pos: Claims examr, Zurich Ins Co, 66-70; spec aide to fisheries div, Mich Dept Natural Resources, 71; regional claims supvr, Mutual Benefit Life, Detroit, 71-73; city clerk, Pontiac, 73-74. Mem: Pontiac Jaycees; Pontiac Urban League; Oakland Co Sportsmen's Club. Mailing Add: 202 Cherokee Pontiac MI 48053

KAMMERER, MARVIN JULIUS **(D)**
Secy, Meade Co Dem Party, SDak
b Rapid City, SDak, Mar 3, 37; s Fredrick Ferdinand Kammerer & Susan Endres K; m 1958 to Joy Irene Bies; c Pam, Terry, Vonnie, Joe, Annie, Matt & Julie. Polit & Govt Pos: Co deleg, SDak Dem State Conv, 72; precinct committeeman, Meade Co Dem Party, SDak, 72, secy, 72- Bus & Prof Pos: Livestock rep, Rapid City Livestock Mkt Area; chmn, Nat Farmers Orgn, Meade Co, SDak, 71-73. Mem: Nat Farmers Orgn (co chmn & W River rep); Amalgamated Meat Cutters Union. Relig: Catholic. Mailing Add: Box 42 Rte 3 Rapid City SD 57701

KANBARA, BERTRAM T **(D)**
b Honolulu, Hawaii, Jan 7, 26; s Matsuichi Kanbara & Hama Hamamura K; single. Educ: Univ Hawaii, BA, 50; Harvard Univ Law Sch, JD, 53. Polit & Govt Pos: Dep corp counsel, City & Co of Honolulu, 54-62; Dep Attorney Gen, State of Hawaii, 63-68, Asst Attorney Gen, 68-69, Attorney Gen, 69-71; comnr, Hawaii Comn to Promote Uniform Legis, 72-; mem, Nat Conf of Comnrs on Uniform State Laws, 72- Mil Serv: Entered as Pvt, Army, 46, released as Staff Sgt, 47, after serv in Pacific. Mem: Am Bar Asn; Bar Asn of Hawaii (treas, 73-). Mailing Add: Suite 887 Kendall Bldg 888 Mililani St Honolulu HI 96813

KANDARAS, HOMER MICHAEL **(D)**
SDak State Sen
b Aberdeen, SDak, Aug 23, 29; s William D Kandaras & Hallie Ferguson K; m 1958 to Alice Johnson Ahrendt; c Brian & stepchildren Gwenythe (Mrs Roy Thompson) & Gregory Ahrendt. Educ: Univ SDak, JD, 54, grad study, 56-58; Pi Sigma Alpha. Polit & Govt Pos: Vpres, SDak Young Dem, 59-61; chmn, Pennington Co Dem Cent Comt, SDak, 59-70; deleg & mem platform comt, Dem Nat Conv, 60, deleg & mem rules comt, 64 & 68, deleg & chmn SDak deleg, 72; deleg & mem platform comt, Dem State Conv, 60, deleg, 68, 70 & 74; chmn, SDak State Adv Comt, Dem Party, 63-64; dist ten capt, SDak Dem Party, 69-70; SDak State Sen, Pennington Co, 70-, asst minority leader, SDak State Senate, 71-72, asst majority leader, 73-75, chmn judiciary comt, 73-, majority leader, 75-; chmn spec legis comt to study Probate Laws of SDak, 73-74; mem, SDak Code Comn, 73-; mem, State Elec Bd, 74- Bus & Prof Pos: Mem bd dir & secy, Black Hills Sports, Inc, 70-72; mem, Gov Comt Exec Reorgn, 71-72. Mil Serv: Entered as Pvt, Army, 54, released as Specialist 3/C, 56, after serv in 37th AAA Bn, Japan, 55-56. Mem: SDak Bar Asn; Black Hills Consumers League (mem bd dirs); Elks. Honors & Awards: Outstanding Young Dem for SDak, 61. Relig: Unitarian. Legal Res: Rte 1 Rapid City SD 57701 Mailing Add: Box 589 Rapid City SD 57701

KANDUCH, JOE F, SR **(D)**
Mont State Rep
Mailing Add: Barker Creek Anaconda MT 59711

KANE, ANGELINE BETTY **(D)**
VChmn, Chemung Co Dem Party, NY
b Virgil, NY, Jan 25, 26; d Arthur Raymond Hutchings & Pearl Maynard H; m 1946 to Thomas Francis Kane; c Mary Theresa & Thomas Francis. Educ: De Forest's Sch Electronics, Electronics Technician, 44; Elmira Col, 66. Polit & Govt Pos: Committeewoman, Big Flats Dem Party, NY, 57-68; secy, Young Dem Club, co-chmn, Big Flats Dem Club, vchmn, Big Flats Dem Comt, prog chmn, Chemung Co Dem Woman's Club, chmn, various Dem campaign hq, deleg or alt deleg, NY Dem State Conv & Dem nominee for Chemung Co Clerk, town clerk & justice of the peace, Big Flats, 57-69; secy, Chemung Co Dem Party, 62-66, vchmn, 69-, secy, Elmira Dem Party, 64-66; chmn, 19th Annual NY State Dem Women's Polit Conf, 69; mem, Citizen's Adv Comt, Elmira, 70; mem, City of Elmira Assessment Grievance Bd, 70. Bus & Prof Pos: Electronics technician, Eclipse Machinery, Elmira, 44-45; assembler, Remington Rand, 45-47; acct receivable off clerk, S F Iszards, 49-51; dining room hostess, Mark Twain Hotel, 51-53; bookkeeper & off mgr, Chem Co Fed Employ FCU, 63-70; real estate saleswoman, E E Wood, 65-68; bookkeeper, Telco Credit Union, Elmira, NY, 69- Publ: Quarterly article, From the President's Pen, NY State Postal Clerk, 64-70. Mem: Woman's Auxiliary to United Fedn of Postal Clerks; Chemung Co Dem Womans Club. Honors & Awards: Outstanding Woman Democrat, Chemung Co, 69. Relig: Catholic. Mailing Add: 107 Grove St Elmira NY 14905

KANE, CHARLES BAIRD, JR **(D)**
Chmn, Lemhi Co Dem Cent Comt, Utah
b Ogden, Utah, Mar 6, 27; s Charles Baird Kane, Sr & Vivian Buker K; m 1951 to Laura E Simpson; c Joy White, Walter B & Steven G. Educ: Univ Idaho, 3 years; Mens Independent Asn. Polit & Govt Pos: Chmn, Lemhi Co Dem Cent Comt, Utah, 59- Bus & Prof Pos: Foreman, Howe Sound Mining Co, Cobalt, Idaho, 46-51; salesman, Singer Sewing Machine, Mont, 51-58; mgr, Hidden Springs Fish Farm, Salmon, Idaho, 58-60; foreman, Lewis Food Co, 60-67; agent, Am Oil Co, 67- Mil Serv: Entered as Seaman, Navy, 45, released as Seaman 1/C, 46, after serv in Standard Landing Craft Unit 20, Pac. Mem: Am Legion; Elks; Grange. Relig: Episcopal. Legal Res: 315 S St Charles St Salmon ID 83467 Mailing Add: PO Box 1090 Salmon ID 83467

KANE, DAVID RONALD **(D)**
b Okmulgee, Okla, Feb 17, 34; s David William Kane & Clara Thionnet K; m 1957 to Judith Tiderman; c Kathy, Mark & Darby. Educ: Kans Univ, BS in Bus, 56, Phillips 66 scholarship; Phi Kappa Psi; Alpha Kappa Psi. Polit & Govt Pos: Ark State Rep, Pulaski-Perry Co, 69-70; Legis Aide to Dale Bumpers, Gov of Ark, formerly. Bus & Prof Pos: Sales trainee, sr sales rep & supplies & sch mgr, IBM Corp, Little Rock, Ark, 56-64; vpres & dir of agencies, Fifth Largest Ark Life Ins Co, 64-67; sr partner, Kane-Ferrill & Assocs, 67-; regional dir, Financial Serv Corp of Am, 68-; pres & bd chmn, Diversified Financial Serv Corp of Am, 69- Mem: Nat Asn Securities Dealers; Nat Asn Life Underwriters; CofC. Honors & Awards: Grateful Orgn Plaque, US Jaycees, 63. Relig: Episcopal; Vestryman, St Mark's Episcopal Church, 65-67. Legal Res: 321 Fairfax Little Rock AR 72205 Mailing Add: 121 E Fourth Suite 300 Little Rock AR 72201

KANE, GEORGE D **(D)**
Comnr Sch & Pub Lands, SDak
b Lemmon, SDak, Nov 7, 31; s Glen F Kane & Olive J Wenner K; m 1955 to LaVina M Weil; c LaDene I, Glen D & Lanette J. Educ: Lemmon High Sch, grad. Polit & Govt Pos: Treas sch bd, Lincoln Sch Dist, SDak, 56-65; community committeeman, Agr Stabilization & Conserv Serv, Perkins Co Dist Three, 58-66; chmn, Perkins Co Dem Party, 66-72; deleg & mem platform comt, Dem Nat Comt, 72; deleg, SDak State Dem Conv, 72, mem state platform comt, 72; Comnr Sch & Pub Lands, SDak, 72- Bus & Prof Pos: Chmn bd, Coop Food Ctr, Lemmon, SDak, 61-70; supvr Perkins Co, Nat Farmers Orgn, 69-72. Mem: SDak Weed Comn; adv mem, SDak Conserv Comn; Farmers Union (state vpres, chmn, Perkins Co); Lemon Country Club; Capitol Investment Club. Honors & Awards: Citizenship Award, Danforth Found, 49; Rural Leadership Award, SDak Farmers Union, 72. Relig: Presbyterian. Legal Res: Lemmon SD 57638 Mailing Add: 1006 S Garfield Pierre SD 57501

KANE, JAMES RICHARD **(R)**
b Salida, Colo, July 13, 38; s James Edward Kane & Lois Goddard K; m 1967 to Elizabeth Louise Kennedy; c Noel, Mikel John, Lois Anne & James Douglas. Educ: US Mil Acad, BS, 60. Polit & Govt Pos: Exec Dir, Rep Party of Tex, 71-72. Bus & Prof Pos: Mgr, safety & training, Campbell Soup Co, Sumter, SC, 66-67, asst personnel mgr, Paris, Tex, 67-69, personnel mgr, 69-71. Mil Serv: Entered as 2nd Lt, Army, 60, released as 1st Lt, 63, after serv in 3rd Inf, Ft Meyer, Va & 82nd Airborne Div, Ft Bragg, NC, 60-63. Mem: Elks. Relig: Episcopal. Legal Res: 1050 29th St SE Paris TX 75460 Mailing Add: 703 Dragon Austin TX 78746

KANE, RITA WILSON **(D)**
Dem Nat Committeewoman, Pa
Mailing Add: City County Bldg Pittsburgh PA 15219

KANE, ROBERT M **(R)**
Okla State Sen
Mailing Add: State Capitol Oklahoma City OK 73105

KANIN, DENNIS ROY **(D)**
b Boston, Mass, Feb 22, 46; s Irving Lynwood Kanin & Doris May Small K; single. Educ: Harvard Col, AB, 68; Harvard Law Sch, JD, 71. Polit & Govt Pos: Chmn, Mass Col Dem Clubs, 66-68; mem, Mass Dem Party Platform Comt, 72-73; mem, Dem Charter Comn, 73-74; legis asst to US Rep Frank Evans, Colo, 73-74; campaign mgr, Tsongas for Cong Campaign, 74; admin asst to US Rep Paul Tsongas, Mass, 75- Bus & Prof Pos: Attorney, Mahoney, Atwood & Goldings, 71-73. Mem: Am Bar Asn. Legal Res: 46 Fairmount St Lowell MA 01852 Mailing Add: 1101 New Hampshire Ave Suite 120 Washington DC 20036

KANIN, DORIS MAY **(D)**
Mem, Dem Nat Comt, Mass
b Somerville, Mass; d Sidney J Small & Ida Gelbsman S; m to Dr Irving Lynwood Kanin; c Dennis Roy, Erik Douglas & Lisa Julie. Educ: Boston Univ Col Lib Arts, BA in Govt, 66, Grad Sch Arts & Sci, MA in Polit Sci, 70, completed doctoral course work, Boston Univ Law Sch, 2 years. Polit & Govt Pos: Chairperson, McCarthy for President Campaign, Norwood, Mass, 67-68; coordr, Ninth Cong Dist McGovern for President Campaign, 71-72; deleg, Dem Nat Conv, 72; mem Mass McGovern Campaign Staff, coordr, Urban Ethnic Div & Concerned Clergy for McGovern Shriver, 72; Nat coordr, Inauguration of Conscience, Washington, DC, 72-73; mem, Dem Nat Comt, Mass, 72-; mem, steering comt, Dem Nat Committeewoman's Northeast Conf, 73; mem comt on legis, Nat Women's Polit Caucus, 73-; exec asst, US Rep Joe Moakley, Ninth Cong Dist, Mass, 73- Bus & Prof Pos: Pres, Lynwood Lab, Inc, Norwood, Mass, 58-73. Mem: Am Polit Sci Asn; Norwood League of Women Voters; Mass Citizens for Participation in Polit Action (mem-at-lg & exec bd, 73-); Citizens for Participation Politics; Mass Polit Action for Peace. Honors & Awards: Semi-finalist, Woodrow Wilson Scholar, 66. Relig: Jewish. Legal Res: 25 Buckingham Rd Norwood MA 02062 Mailing Add: Apt 410N 2111 Jefferson Davis Hwy Arlington VA 22202

KANTER, SAMUEL A **(R)**
Asst Attorney Gen, Ill
b Dubuque, Iowa, Sept 3, 05; s Louis Kanter & Celia Cohn K; m 1963 to Alma Dee Donohue. Educ: DePaul Univ, JD, 27. Polit & Govt Pos: Asst city prosecutor, Chicago, Ill, 29-31; referee, Dept of Revenue, 42-49; Rep committeeman, 23rd Ward, Chicago, 46-64; Asst Attorney Gen, Ill, 52- Relig: Jewish. Mailing Add: 5401 S Oak Park Chicago IL 60638

KANTOR, ISAAC NORRIS **(D)**
b Charleston, WVa, Aug 29, 29; s Israel Kantor & Rachael Cohen K; m 1956 to Doris Sue Katz; c Mark Bennett, Cynthia Faye & Beth Ellen. Educ: Va Mil Inst, BA, 53; WVa Univ, JD, 56; Sphinx Sr Men's Hon; Phi Delta Phi; Pi Lambda Phi. Polit & Govt Pos: Clerk judiciary comt, WVa House of Deleg, 60; pres, Mercer Co Dem Club, 61-62; mem, Mercer Co Dem Exec Comt, 64-68, chmn, 68-72; parliamentarian, WVa Dem Exec Comt, 68- Bus & Prof Pos: Partner, Katz, Katz & Kantor, Attorneys, Bluefield, WVa, 58-; attorney for town, Bramwell, 70-; attorney, Bluefield Sanit Bd, 70- Mil Serv: Entered as 1st Lt, Air Force, 56, released as 1st Lt, 58, after serv in Off of Staff Judge Adv, Hq Pac Air Forces, 57-58. Mem: WVa Trial Lawyers Asn; Elks; Rotary Club; Gtr Bluefield CofC; B'nai B'rith. Honors & Awards: Volunteer of Year, WVa Div Am Cancer Soc. Relig: Jewish. Legal Res: 131 Fincastle Lane Bluefield WV 24701 Mailing Add: PO Box 727 Bluefield WV 24701

KANY, JUDY C **(D)**
m 1958 to Robert H Kany; c Kristin, Geoffrey & Danny. Educ: Univ Mich, Ann Arbor, BBA, 59; Univ Maine, Orono, currently. Polit & Govt Pos: Maine State Rep, 75- Mem: Comn Maine's Future; Econ Resources Coun Exec Comt; Community Action Coun; Local

Homemakers Adv Comt; Am Civil Liberties Union. Mailing Add: 18 West St Waterville ME 04901

KAPILOFF, LAWRENCE (D)
Calif State Assemblyman
b Brooklyn, NY, Sept 22, 29; s Ben B Kapiloff & Florence Lanning K; m 1971 to Elizabeth Cowan; c Yvonne Elizabeth, Norman Emilio & Johanna Dianne Kapiloff & Tammie E, Heather M, Bonnie L & Kimberly C Manson. Educ: Monmouth Col (NJ), AA, 50; Univ Calif, Los Angeles, BA in Psychol, 57, JDS, 60; Lambda Sigma Tau; Phi Alpha Delta. Polit & Govt Pos: Dep counsel, San Diego Co, Calif, 61-73; Calif State Assemblyman, 78th Dist, 73-, mem revenue & taxation, energy & diminishing materials, resources & land use, select comt on revision of the corp code & permanent subcomt on coastal resources, Calif Legis, currently. Bus & Prof Pos: Attorney-at-law, Greer, Popko, Miller & Foerster, San Diego, Calif, 73- Mil Serv: Entered as Pvt E-1, Army, 51, released as Pvt E-2, 53, after serv in Mil Police Unit, Korea Far East Command, 52-53. Publ: Co-auth, How to sell your home in California without a broker, Greenleaf, 4/73. Mailing Add: 424 Pennsylvania Ave San Diego CA 92103

KAPLAN, BETSY BYRNS (R)
Chmn, St Lawrence Co Rep Comt, NY
b Ogdensburg, NY, Oct 2, 23; d Robert Hugh Byrns (deceased) & Mable Allen B (deceased); m 1955 to Samuel Kaplan; c John Allen. Educ: St Lawrence Univ, 2 years 6 months; Delta Delta Delta. Polit & Govt Pos: Mem, St Lawrence Co Rep Comt, 58-, chmn, 70-; mem, Potsdam Town Rep Comt, 60-66; mem, NY State Rep Comt, 68-; alt deleg, Rep Nat Conv, 72. Bus & Prof Pos: Mem staff, Bell Tel Labs, 44-45; secy, Drs William & Jennie Carson, Potsdam, NY, 46-55. Mem: St Lawrence Co Bd, Am Cancer Soc; Potsdam Hosp Guild; Potsdam Humane Soc (treas, 20 years). Relig: Episcopal. Mailing Add: 99 Market St Potsdam NY 13676

KAPLAN, JEROME (D)
b Jersey City, NJ, Mar 17, 26; s Julius Kaplan & Leah Levy K; m 1953 to Edith Jaffy; c Paul Louis. Educ: Temple Univ, BS; Univ Mich, JD; Tau Epsilon Rho. Polit & Govt Pos: Pres, Cent Philadelphia Reform Dem, Pa, 66; deleg, Dem Nat Conv, 68; chmn, Third Cong Dist McCarthy for President, 68; chmn exec comt, Am for Dem Action, Philadelphia, Pa & mem nat bd dirs, currently; pres, Third Dist New Dem Coalition, 68-72. Bus & Prof Pos: Internal revenue agt, US Treas Dept, 53-55; sr partner, Abrahams & Loewenstein, Attorneys, currently. Mil Serv: Pvt, Army, 44-45, with serv in Inf, ETO, 45; Combat Inf Badge. Publ: Buy, sell agreements, Ins Mag. Mem: Am & Philadelphia Bar Asns; Am Jewish Cong, Gtr Philadelphia (pres, 67-71); Am Civil Liberties Union; Nat Comt for Sane Nuclear Policy; Urban League. Legal Res: 2042 Pine St Philadelphia PA 19103 Mailing Add: Abrahams & Loewenstein Attys 1430 Land Title Bldg Philadelphia PA 19110

KAPLAN, MARK (DFL)
Chmn, 59th Dist Dem-Farmer-Labor Party, Minn
b Minneapolis, Minn, Apr 5, 49; s Sidney J Kaplan & Leonore Yaeger. Educ: Harvard Col, AB, 71; Col of St Thomas, MAT, 73; Univ Minn, 72-75. Polit & Govt Pos: Chmn, 59th Dist Dem-Farmer-Labor Party, Minn, currently. Bus & Prof Pos: Teacher, Henry Sibley High Sch, 73- Mem: Peavey Park Improv Asn; Dem-Farmer-Labor Sustaining Fund; Minn Fedn Teachers; Shadowfax Inc. Mailing Add: 2022 Oakland Minneapolis MN 55404

KAPLAN, MARK ALAN (D)
Vt State Rep
Mailing Add: 16 Prospect Hill Burlington VT 05401

KARCHER, ALAN (D)
NJ State Assemblyman
Mailing Add: State House Trenton NJ 08625

KARDOKUS, JAMES M (D)
Okla State Sen
Mailing Add: State Capitol Oklahoma City OK 73105

KAREM, DAVID KEVIN (D)
Ky State Rep
b Louisville, Ky, Aug 31, 43; s Judge Fred Joseph Karem (deceased) & Mary Jane Mansfield K; m 1967 to Anne Louise Schroeder; c Frederick Jeffrey. Educ: Univ Cincinnati, BS, 66; Univ Louisville, JD, 69; Pi Kappa Alpha. Polit & Govt Pos: Chmn, Cherokee Dem Club, 69-; mem adv comt, US Rep Romano L Mazzoli, Third Dist, Ky, 71-; Ky State Rep, 72-, chmn joint house-senate interim comt on judiciary, Ky Gen Assembly, 74-75; mem urban affairs & human resources comt, Southern Legis Conf, 73- Bus & Prof Pos: Partner, Karem & Karem, Attorneys, 70- Mem: Am & Ky Bar Asns; Am Trial Lawyers Asn; World Peace Through Law Ctr; Tavern Club. Relig: Roman Catholic. Legal Res: 2442 Ransdell Ave Louisville KY 40204 Mailing Add: Lincoln Fed Bldg Suite 564 Louisville KY 40202

KAREY, JOSEPH NORMAN (R)
Chmn, Baltimore Co Rep Cent Comt, Md
b Baltimore, Md, Apr 1, 32; s Joseph P Karcauskas & Margaret E Kraft K; m 1956 to Mary Patricia Fuchs; c Mary Abigail, J Alexander & Amy E. Educ: Loyolla Col, BS in Bus Admin; NY Univ, MBA; Univ Md Law Sch, BLL. Polit & Govt Pos: Mem, Baltimore Co Rep Cent Comt, 67-, chmn, 73-; alt deleg, Rep Nat Conv, 68; Rep mem bd supvrs, Elec, 69-73. Mil Serv: Entered as Seaman, Navy, 56, released as Seaman 3/C, 58. Mem: Baltimore City, Md & Am Bar Asns; Oriole Advocates, Inc; Sports Reporters Asn. Legal Res: 3624 Lochearn Baltimore MD 21207 Mailing Add: 1515 Washington Blvd Baltimore MD 21230

KARKUTT, A RICHARD, JR (D)
Chmn, Putnam Dem Town Comt, Conn
b Norwich, Conn, Nov 20, 31; s Albert Richard Karkutt, Sr & Marguerite Ensling K; m 1964 to Marilyn Norton; c Kathleen, A Richard, III, Mary Ellen, Patricia & Kenneth. Educ: Univ Conn, BA, 53; Boston Col Law Sch, LLB, 68; Tau Kappa Epsilon. Polit & Govt Pos: Corp counsel, City of Putnam, 61-, judge of probate court, 62-; chmn, Putnam Dem Town Comt, 68- Mil Serv: Entered as Pvt, Army, 53, released as Pfc, 55, after serv in 3rd Armored Cavalry Regt, Ft George G Meade, Md. Mem: Am, Conn & Windham Co Bar Asns; Putnam Rotary Club; Putnam Lodge of Elks. Relig: Roman Catholic. Mailing Add: Upper Walnut St RFD 2 Putnam CT 06260

KARMOL, IRMA HOTCHKISS (R)
Ohio State Rep
b Toledo, Ohio, Apr 13, 23; d Laurence H Hotchkiss & Leetha Hoover H; m 1952 to Walter Joseph Karmol; c David, Jeff, Beth & Jim. Educ: Miami Univ, BS, 45; Delta Delta Delta. Polit & Govt Pos: Precinct committeeman, Lucas Co Rep Exec Comt, Ohio, 64-74; Ohio State Rep, Dist 44, 75- Bus & Prof Pos: Substitute teacher, Sylvania Schs, Ohio, 67-69; caseworker, Lucas Co Children's Servs, 69-73. Mem: League Women Voters; Toledo Mus Art; Asn Women Legislators. Relig: Roman Catholic. Legal Res: 3730 Chesterton Dr Toledo OH 43615 Mailing Add: Statehouse Columbus OH 43215

KARMOL, WARREN HENRY, JR (D)
b Toledo, Ohio, May 31, 49; s Warren Henry Karmol, Sr & Ruth Clemens K; m 1971 to Jennifer Lynn Vigus; c Erikson. Educ: Univ Toledo, BA, 72. Polit & Govt Pos: Alt deleg, Dem Nat Conv, 72. Mem: Am Soc Pub Admin; Pi Gamma Mu; United Transportation Union; Lucas Co Young Dem; Univ Toledo Polit Sci Grad Student Asn. Relig: Catholic. Legal Res: Apt M-8 5055 Jamieson Dr Toledo OH 43613 Mailing Add: 714 Poinsettia St Toledo OH 43612

KARNIS, THEODORE HENRY (R)
NH State Rep
b Ft Bragg, Calif, Nov 9, 11; married. Educ: Univ Conn. Polit & Govt Pos: New Ipswich fire chief & dep warden, State of NH Forest Fire Serv; NH State Rep, 61-; deleg, Const Conv, 64. Bus & Prof Pos: Dir, Mason Village Savings Bank; gas sta owner. Mem: F&AM; NH Fire Chiefs; New Ipswich Athletic Asn; NH Farm Bur; Bethel Lodge No 24. Relig: Protestant. Mailing Add: Turnpike Rd Box 122 New Ipswich NH 03071

KARNS, JOHN M, JR (D)
PGFormer mem, Dem Nat Comt, Ill Mailing Add: 7705 W Main St Belleville IL 62223

KARP, GENE (D)
Chmn, Pima Co Dem Party, Ariz
b Philadelphia, Pa, July 16, 36; s Samuel Karp & Esther Bernstein K; m 1965 to Naomi Katherine Silver; c Gail Lauren. Educ: Univ Ariz, BS in Bus Admin, 58, JD, 61; Phi Eta Sigma; Tau Delta Phi. Polit & Govt Pos: Chmn, Pima Co Dem Party, Ariz, 70- Bus & Prof Pos: Pvt law practice, 61-65; partner, Silver, Ettinger & Karp, 65-72; partner, Silver & Karp, 73- Mil Serv: Ariz Nat Guard, 58-64. Mem: Pima Co, Ariz & Am Bar Asns; B'nai B'rith. Relig: Jewish. Mailing Add: 5855 E Wilshire Terr Tucson AZ 85711

KARP, GLORIA G (D)
b New York, NY, July 21, 25; d Louis Gendzier & Sally Koenig G; m 1948 to Gilbert T Karp; c Drina & Nicki. Educ: Hunter Col, BA, 44. Polit & Govt Pos: Chmn, Sane Nuclear Policy, Westchester, NY, 60, Women Strike for Peace, 62-, White Plains-Greenburgh Fair Housing Comn, 64-65 & Westchester Asn Fair Housing Comn, 66; exec dir, McCarthy for President & O'Dwyer for Sen, Westchester, NY, 68; vchmn, New Dem Coalition, Westchester-Putnam, 68-; vchmn, New Dem Coalition, NY, 70-72; deleg, Dem Nat Conv, 72; co-chmn, McGovern for President, Westchester, 72; Dem cand for Westchester Co Clerk, 73; dist leader, West Co Dem Party, currently; exec asst dir, West Co Community Ment Health Serv, currently. Bus & Prof Pos: Actuarial clerk, Equitable Life Assurance Soc, 45-46; textile converter, Hope Skillman Fabrics, 46-52. Mem: NY Civil Liberties Union; Am Jewish Cong; Day Care Coun (mem bd, 74-75); Consumer Action Coalition (chairperson). Relig: Jewish. Mailing Add: 21 Windmill Lane Scarsdale NY 10583

KARP, NAOMI KATHERINE (D)
b Tucson, Ariz, Mar 6, 42; d James J Silver & Rose Sosnowsky S; m 1965 to Gene Karp; c Gail Lauren. Educ: Mills Col, 60-62; Univ Ariz, BA in Psychol, 64, MEd in Spec Educ, 66. Polit & Govt Pos: Dem precinct committeewoman, Pima Co, Ariz, 66-; alt deleg, Dem Nat Conv, 72. Bus & Prof Pos: Teacher of emotionally disturbed, Tucson Sch Dist 1, 65- Mem: Tucson Educ Asn (bldg rep, 72-); Ariz & Nat Educ Asns; Pi Lambda Theta; Brandeis Nat Women's Comt. Relig: Jewish. Mailing Add: 5855 E Wilshire Terr Tucson AZ 85711

KARP, NATHAN (SOCIALIST LABOR PARTY)
Nat Secy, Socialist Labor Party
b Brooklyn, NY, Apr 25, 15; s Daniel Karp & Sarah Goldenzweig K; m 1937 to Anne Werthamer; c Diane, Alan & Stanley. Polit & Govt Pos: Nat secy, Socialist Labor Party, 69- Publ: Brinkmanship in Southeast Asia, Weekly People, 5/72; pamphlets, Unionism; Fraudulent or Genuine & Crises in America & others. Legal Res: 2330 California St Mountain View CA 94040 Mailing Add: PO Box 10018 Palo Alto CA 94304

KARPINSKI, HELEN BERNICE (D)
Mem, Ohio Dem State Exec Comt
b Cleveland, Ohio; d John Olszewski & Anna Grabowski O; m 1924 to John J Karpinski, wid; c Gloria Joy (Mrs Frank Battisti), Mercedes Helen (Mrs M Spotts) & Diane Joan. Polit & Govt Pos: Dem ward leader & precinct committeewoman, Ward 21, Ohio, 38-50; deleg, Dem Nat Conv, 40, 64 & 68; mem, Ohio Dem State Exec Comt, 42-; dep clerk, Jury Comn, Common Pleas Court, Cuyahoga Co, 45-49; pres, Women's Cosmopolitan Dem League, Ohio, 48-50; pres, Cleveland Civil Serv Comn, 59-68; mem, Bd Tax Rev, Cuyahoga Co, 69-; pres, Federated Dem Women of Ohio, formerly; mem, Cuyahoga Co Dem Exec Comt, currently. Mem: Polish Women's Alliance of Am; Alliance of Poles; Am Polish Women's Club of Gtr Cleveland; Cath Ladies of Columbia; Cleveland Cult Garden Fedn. Relig: Catholic. Mailing Add: 2897 Ludlow Rd Cleveland OH 44120

KARREL, OSCAR (D)
Chmn, Redding-Georgetown Dem Town Comt, Conn
b Boston, Mass, June 23, 05; m 1934 to Frances Whipple; c John Whipple. Educ: Northeastern Univ Law Sch, LLB, 31. Polit & Govt Pos: Chmn, Redding-Georgetown Dem Town Comt, Conn, 67- Bus & Prof Pos: Buyer, Lord & Taylor, NY, 34-68; mkt rep, Assoc Dry Goods, 68- Mil Serv: Entered as Pvt, Army, 43, released as Capt, 46, after serv in Off Qm Gen, Washington, DC. Relig: Jewish. Mailing Add: RFD 3 West Redding CT 06896

KARRH, RANDOLPH C (D)
Ga State Rep
Mailing Add: PO Drawer K Swainsboro GA 30401

KARTH, JOSEPH E (DFL)
US Rep, Minn
b New Brighton, Minn, Aug 26, 22; m to Charlotte Nordgren; c Kevin, Bradley & Brian.

Educ: Univ Nebr Sch Eng, 2 years. Polit & Govt Pos: Minn State Rep, 50-58; US Rep, Fourth Cong Dist, Minn, 58-; deleg, Dem Nat Conv, 68. Bus & Prof Pos: With Minn Mining & Mfg Co, formerly; int rep, OCAW-AFL-CIO, 10 years. Mil Serv: Army, serv in ETO, World War II. Mem: VFW; Am Legion. Honors & Awards: Outstanding Legislator, 58th Spec Session, Minn House Rep. Relig: Presbyterian. Legal Res: St Paul MN Mailing Add: 2408 Rayburn Bldg Washington DC 20515

KASH, J B **(R)**
Chmn, Henry Co Rep Party, Ky
b Hazel Green, Ky, Jan 26, 21; s Lindon Kash (deceased) & Bonnie Shockey K; m 1961 to June Carolyn McAlister; c Jon Farrell, Lana (Mrs Max Hurst) & Diane. Polit & Govt Pos: Exec officer, Hwy Dept, Ky, 67-; chmn, Henry Co Rep Party, 69-72 & 75- Mil Serv: Entered as Pvt, Army, 40, released as T/Sgt, 45, after serv in ETO; Combat Infantryman Award; ETO Ribbon. Relig: Methodist. Mailing Add: Port Royal KY 40058

KASHULINES, JUANITA E **(R)**
NH State Rep
Mailing Add: Rte 1 Box 570 Windham NH 03087

KASTEN, ROBERT W, JR **(R)**
US Rep, Wis
b Milwaukee, Wis, June 19, 42; s Robert W Kasten & Mary Ogden K; single. Educ: Univ Ariz, BA, 64; Columbia Univ Grad Sch of Bus, MBA, 66; vpres, Alpha Kappa Psi; pres, Sigma Nu. Polit & Govt Pos: deleg, Wis State Rep Conv, 70, 72 & 74; alt deleg, Rep Nat Conv, 72; mem, Wis Fedn of Young Rep; Wis State Sen, 73-74; US Rep, Wis, 75- Bus & Prof Pos: Mgr coord & asst to vpres, Genesco Inc, Nashville, Tenn, 66-68; dir, sales mgr & vpres mkt, Gilbert Shoe Co, Thiensville, Wis, 68- Mil Serv: Entered as Officer Trainee, Air Force, 67, released as 1st Lt, after serv in 128th Air Refueling Group, Wis Air Nat Guard, 67-72. Mem: Milwaukee Coun Alcoholism, Inc; Student Leadership Serv (bd adv); Wis Soc for Prev of Blindness (dir); Milwaukee Coalition Clean Water (regional dir); Mequon-Thiensville Jaycees. Honors & Awards: Jaycee of the Year Award, 72; Wis Conserv Legislator of the Year, 73; Deleg to Eagleton Inst Polit Legis Leadership Conf, Rutgers Univ, 73; Selected for JFK Sch Polit, Harvard Univ, 74. Relig: Episcopal. Legal Res: 125 E Freistadt Rd Thiensville WI 53092 Mailing Add: 1113 Longworth Off Bldg Washington DC 20515

KASTENMEIER, ROBERT WILLIAM **(D)**
US Rep, Wis
b Beaver Dam, Wis, Jan 24, 24; s Leo Henry Kastenmeier & Lucille Powers K; m 1952 to Dorothy Chambers; c William, Andrew & Edward. Educ: Carleton Col, Army Specialized Training Prog, 43-44; Univ Wis, LLB, 52; Phi Alpha Delta. Polit & Govt Pos: Br off dir, Claims Serv, War Dept, Philippine Islands, 46-48; chmn, Jefferson Co Dem Party, Wis, 53-56; mem, Dem Cent Comt, Wis, 55-56; justice of the peace, Dodge & Jefferson Co, 56-59; deleg, Dem Nat Conv, 56, 64, 68 & 72, mem credentials comt, 64; US Rep, Wis, 59- Mil Serv: Entered as Pvt, Army, 43, released as 1st Lt, 46, after serv in Hq Claims Serv, Armed Forces, Western Pac. Publ: Vietnam Hearings: Voices from the Grass Roots, Artcraft Press, 65; CBR: Pentagon boobytrap, The Progressive, 3/60; Pacem in terris, Continum, 63. Legal Res: 745 Pony Lane Sun Prairie WI 53590 Mailing Add: 2800 27th St N Arlington VA 22207

KASTER, JAMES J **(D)**
Tex State Rep
b El Paso, Tex, July 4, 33; s James J Kaster & Louize Beeman K; m 1958 to Helene Carol Vogelpohl; c James J, VI, Deborah Elaine, Laura Lee, Marian Kathleen & John Paul. Educ: Univ Tex, El Paso, BBA with honors, 58; Alpha Chi; Phi Kappa Tau. Polit & Govt Pos: Tex State Rep, 71-, chmn intergovt affairs comt, Tex House of Rep, 72- Bus & Prof Pos: Pres, El Paso Casket Co, El Paso, Tex, 58-66; funeral dir, Kaster & Maxon, 66-68; pilot, Southwest Air Rangers, 68-70; vpres, Evans Asn Indust, 70; pilot, Empire Club of El Paso, currently; pres, Tex State Travel Agency, Inc, 71- Mil Serv: Entered as Seaman, Navy, 52, released as Yeoman 3/C, 54, after serv in USS Heermann (DD-532), through the world; European Occup Ribbon; China Serv Ribbon; Korean Ribbon; UN Ribbon; Am Defense Medal; Presidential Unit Citation. Publ: Auth of articles in Lions Mag, 69 & Tangent Mag, 70. Mem: Lions Int. Honors & Awards: Conquistador Award, City of El Paso; Named Outstanding Young Man of the Year in El Paso, 64. Relig: Episcopal. Mailing Add: 3409 Nairn El Paso TN 79925

KATZ, ALAN STEWART **(D)**
Mem, Calif State Dem Cent Comt
b Niagara Falls, NY, Jan 27, 53; s Samuel Eaton Katz & Ethyl Nimelman K; single. Educ: Univ Calif, Los Angeles, AB, 75. Polit & Govt Pos: Mem, Calif State Dem Cent Comt, 75-; mem, Los Angeles Co Dem Cent Comt, 74-; deleg, Dem Nat Mid-Term Conf, 74. Bus & Prof Pos: Press secy, Cathy O'Neill for Secy State, Calif, 73-74; exec asst external affairs, Student Body Pres, Univ Calif, Los Angeles, 74-75, chmn univ policies comn, 74-75. Mem: 43rd Assembly Dist Dem Coun; Westwood Dem Club (bd dirs, 75-); Westwood CofC (legis action comt); Young Citizens for Open Govt (pres, 75-). Honors & Awards: Chancellor's Marshall, Univ Calif, Los Angeles, 75; Coro fel, 75. Relig: Jewish. Mailing Add: 219 N Glenroy Pl Los Angeles CA 90049

KATZ, ALVIN **(R)**
Pa State Rep
Mailing Add: Capitol Bldg Harrisburg PA 17120

KATZ, BENNETT DAVID **(R)**
Maine State Sen
b Springfield, Mass, Oct 7, 18; s Samuel J Katz & Frances Wolk K; m 1943 to Edith H Colmes; c Joyce E & Roger J. Educ: Tufts Col, AB, 40; Alpha Epsilon Pi. Polit & Govt Pos: Councilman, Augusta City Coun, Maine, 54-56; chmn, Maine Rep First Cong Dist Comt, 62-64, vchmn, 66-; mem, Gov Air Serv Adv Comt, 62-66; Maine State Rep, 63-66; chmn, Augusta Rep City Comt, Maine, 64-66; mem, Maine Transportation Comn, 65-67; mem, Kennebec Co Rep Comt, Maine, 66-; mem, Maine Comn on Rehabilitation Needs, 66-69, vchmn, 69-70; Maine State Sen, 67-, majority floor leader, Maine State Senate, 67-69, chmn interim legis comt on pub educ eval, 69-70; mem, Maine Sch Bldg Authority, 69-; Maine rep to Educ Comn of States, 69-71, treas, 71-; chmn, New Eng Bd Higher Educ, 72- Bus & Prof Pos: Treas, Dow & Stubling, Portland, Maine, 58-; pres, Nicolson & Ryan, Augusta, 66-; dir, Maine Retail Jewelers Asn, 66- Mil Serv: Entered as Flying Cadet, Army Air Corps, 40, released as Maj, 45, after serv in 1st Pursuit Group, Air Corps Ferry Command, 1st Troop Carrier Command, Mil Air Transport Serv; Air Medal; Pearl Harbor Ribbon; Am, Asiatic-Pac & ETO Ribbons. Mem: Shrine; Kiwanis; Am Legion; B'nai B'rith. Relig: Jewish. Mailing Add: 27 Westwood Rd Augusta ME 04330

KATZ, EDWARD A **(R)**
Chmn, Monroe Co Rep Comt, Pa
b New York, NY, Oct 4, 18; s David S Katz & Mary J Solomon K; wid & remarried 1968 to June H Heydt; c Ellen M & Michael J. Educ: City Col New York, 41; Princeton Univ, 68. Polit & Govt Pos: Mem, Pa Rep State Comt, 67-72; chmn, Monroe Co Rep Comt, Pa, 72- Bus & Prof Pos: Owner, D Katz & Sons, Inc Contractors, 46- Mil Serv: Entered as Pvt, Army, 41, released as 1st Lt, after serv in Chem Warfare Serv, China-Burma-India, 43-46. Mem: Stroudsburg Lions Club (pres); Rotary Int; Moose; Elks; Eagles. Relig: Jewish. Mailing Add: 1805 Laural St Stroudsburg PA 18360

KATZ, HAROLD A **(D)**
Ill State Rep
b Shelbyville, Tenn, Nov 2, 21; s Maurice W Katz & Evelyn Cohen K; m 1945 to Ethel Mae Lewison; c Alan M, Barbara R, Julia L & Joel A. Educ: Vanderbilt Univ, BA, 43; Univ Chicago, JD, 48, MA in Econ, 58; bd ed, Univ Chicago Law Rev. Polit & Govt Pos: Spec legal consult, Gov Ill, 61-63; master-in-chancery, Circuit Court, Cook Co, Ill, 63-67; Ill State Rep, 65-, chmn comn on the orgn of the gen assembly, Ill House of Rep, 65-, chmn house judiciary comt & vchmn house rules comt, currently; deleg, Dem Nat Conv, 72. Bus & Prof Pos: Attorney, Katz & Friedman, Chicago, Ill, 48-; lectr, Univ Chicago, Univ Col, 59-64. Publ: Liability of automobile manufacturers for unsafe design of passenger cars, Harvard Law Rev, 10/56; Make your opinion count, Reader's Digest, 12/68; Let the handicapped in our buildings, Today's Health, 5/72; plus others. Mem: Am Polit Sci Asn; Am Bar Asn; Int Soc Labor Law & Social Legis; Am Trial Lawyers' Asn. Honors & Awards: Recipient of Best Legislator Award, Independent Voters of Ill, 74th, 75th, 76th & 77th Gen Assembly; Citation for Meritorious Serv, President's Comt on Employ of the Handicapped, 67. Relig: Jewish. Legal Res: 1180 Terrace Ct Glencoe IL 60022 Mailing Add: 7 S Dearborn St Chicago IL 60603

KATZ, VERA **(D)**
Ore State Rep
b Ger, Aug 3, 33; d Lazar Pistrak & Raissa Goodman P; m 1954 to Melvin Katz; c Jesse. Educ: Brooklyn Col, BA, 54, MA, 56. Polit & Govt Pos: Ore State Rep, Dist Eight, 72- Honors & Awards: Serv to Mankind Award, Rose City Sertoma Club, 70. Mailing Add: 1214 NW 25th Ave Portland OR 97210

KATZENBACH, NICHOLAS DE BELLEVILLE **(D)**
b Philadelphia, Pa, Jan 17, 22; s Edward Lawrence Katzenbach & Marie L Hilson K; m to Lydia King Phelps Stokes; c Christopher Wolcott, John Strong Miner, Maria Louise Hilson & Anne de Belleville. Educ: Princeton Univ, BA; Yale Law Sch, LLB; Rhodes scholar, Balliol Col, Oxford Univ, 47-49. Polit & Govt Pos: With Off of Gen Counsel, Air Force, 50; Asst US Attorney Gen, 61-62; Dep US Attorney Gen, 62-64, US Attorney Gen, 65-66; Under Secy of State, 66-69. Bus & Prof Pos: Assoc prof, Yale Univ Law Sch; prof int law, Univ Chicago, 56-60; vpres & gen counsel, IBM Corp, 69- Mil Serv: Air Force, 1st Lt, 41-45; Air Medal with 3 clusters. Publ: Political Foundations of International Law (w Morton A Kaplan), 61. Mem: NJ, NY & Conn Bar Asns. Honors & Awards: Ford Found fel, 60-61. Relig: Episcopal. Mailing Add: IBM Corp Armonk NY 10504

KATZMAN, ARTHUR J **(D)**
City Councilman, New York, NY
b David Horodok, Russia, Sept 21, 03; s Henry Katzman & Anna Kunick K; m 1959 to Lillian Kleeper; c Marcia K Allen. Educ: Brooklyn Law Sch, LLB, 25. Polit & Govt Pos: City councilman, New York, NY, 62-; deleg, Dem Nat Conv, 72. Bus & Prof Pos: Attorney, Forest Hills, NY, 25- Mem: Am for Dem Action; Am & NY Civil Liberties Union; NY State New Dem Coalition; Queensboro Soc for Prev of Cruelty to Children (dir, 70-). Relig: Jewish. Legal Res: 110-45 Queens Blvd Forest Hills NY 11375 Mailing Add: 118-21 Queens Blvd Forest Hills NY 11375

KAUFFMAN, FRANK R **(R)**
Maine State Rep
Mailing Add: 830 Haley Rd Kittery ME 03904

KAUFMAN, GERALD **(D)**
b Pittsburgh, Pa, June 14, 32; s Samuel Kaufman & Sara Phillips K; div; c Ann Phillips & James Benjamin. Educ: Yale Univ, BA, 54; Columbia Univ Law Sch, LLB, 57. Polit & Govt Pos: Pa State Rep, formerly; mem, Pa Bd Welfare, currently; exec dir, Pa Legal Serv Ctr, currently; exec dir, Gov Task Force on Rehabilitation, 72-73; deleg, Dem Nat Conv, 72. Bus & Prof Pos: Lawyer, Kaufman & Kaufman, 58- Mil Serv: Entered as Pvt, Army, 57, released as SP-5, 63, after serv in Res. Publ: Towards a smaller house, Nat Munic League Reporter, 4/68. Mem: Am, Pa & Allegheny Co Bar Asns; Jewish Family & Children's Serv (vpres); Am Civil Liberties Union (mem state bd). Honors & Awards: Pa Asn Retarded Children Leadership Award; United Ment Health Serv of Allegheny Co Spec Award. Relig: Jewish. Mailing Add: 1108 Penn St Harrisburg PA 17102

KAUFMAN, IRENE MATHIAS **(R)**
b Augusta Co, Va, Jan 28, 42; d Ted Mathias & Mary Miller M. Educ: Mary Baldwin Col, BA, 63; Univ Va, MEduc, 68; Fine Arts Club. Polit & Govt Pos: Secy, Augusta Co Rep Comt, Va, 69-70; coordr, Women for Robinson for Cong, Augusta Co, 70; pres, Staunton-Augusta Rep Women's Club, 70-; coordr, Shafran for Lt Gov Va, Augusta Co, 71; reporter, Sixth Dist Rep News, 72-; Augusta Co Coordr, Scott for Senate, 72 & Butler for Cong, 72; mem, Educators for Butler, Sixth Dist, 72; adv, Young Rep Club of Augusta Co, 72-; deleg, Rep Nat Conv, 72. Bus & Prof Pos: Elem teacher, Waynesboro Pub Schs, 63-67, elem sch librn, 67-, elem sch prin, 72- Mem: Nat Educ Asn; Va Educ Asn; Waynesboro Educ Asn; Augusta Co Soc for Prev of Cruelty to Animals. Relig: Presbyterian. Mailing Add: Rte 3 Box 151 Staunton VA 24401

KAUFMAN, LEROY J **(R)**
SDak State Rep
Mailing Add: Freeman SD 57029

KAUFMAN, PAUL JOSEPH **(D)**
b Charleston, WVa, Mar 16, 20; s Sydney Joseph Kaufman & Sylvia Rose Miller K; m 1951 to Rose Jean Levinson; c Tod Joseph, Timothy Michael & Steven Miles. Educ: WVa Univ, AB, 42; Univ Va Law Sch, JD, 48; Pi Lambda Phi; Sphinx. Polit & Govt Pos: Mem, Charleston Police Civil Serv Comn, WVa, 54-56; pres, Young Dem Club, Kanawha Co, WVa, 56-60; Nat Legal Aid & Defender Assoc Cert of Pub Serv, 59; WVa State Sen, 60-68; mem, State Ment Health Dept Adv Comt, 62-; mem, Gov Comt on Admin Orgn of Exec Br, State

of WVa, 64-65; deleg, Dem Nat Conv, 68 & 72; dir, Appalachian Research & Defense Fund, Inc, 70-73; mem state adv comt, US Comn Civil Rights, 74-; mem adv panel on solar energy, Midwest Research Inst, 74- Bus & Prof Pos: Gen law practice, 48- Mil Serv: Entered as A/S, Coast Guard, 42, released as Lt, 46, after serv in Pac Theater & ETO. Publ: Fewer checks, more balance, Nat Civic Rev, 3/66; Wistfulginia, Mountain Life & Work, 5/69; Poor, rich West Virginia, New Repub, 12/72. Mem: Am, WVa State & Kanawha Co Bar Asns; Legal Aid Soc (founder & mem bd dirs, 51-70). Relig: Reform Jewish. Legal Res: 410 Sheridan Circle Charleston WV 25314 Mailing Add: 701 Nelson Bldg Charleston WV 25301

KAUPER, THOMAS EUGENE (R)
Asst Attorney Gen Antitrust Div, Dept of Justice
b Brooklyn, NY, Sept 25, 35; s Paul Gerhardt Kauper & Anna Marie Nicklas K; m 1958 to Shirley Yvonne Worrell; c Karen Yvonne & Krista Diane. Educ: Univ Mich, AB, 57, Law Sch, JD, 60; Phi Kappa Phi; Phi Beta Kappa. Polit & Govt Pos: Law clerk, Justice Potter Stewart, US Supreme Court, 60-62; dep asst attorney gen, Off Legal Counsel, Dept Justice, 69-71, Asst Attorney Gen Antitrust Div, 72- Bus & Prof Pos: Assoc, Sidley & Austin, Chicago, Ill, 62-64; prof law, Univ Mich, 64- Publ: Cease & desist, 67 & The Warren Court & the antitrust laws, 67, Mich Law Rev. Mem: Am & Ill State Bar Asns. Relig: Lutheran. Legal Res: 1125 Fair Oaks Pkwy Ann Arbor MI 48104 Mailing Add: 7803 Marion Lane Bethesda MD 20014

KAUPINEN, ALLAN GEORGE (R)
Mem, Alexandria Rep City Comt, Va
b Ravenna, Ohio, Dec 28, 35; s George Oscar Kaupinen & Gertrude Augusta Lange K; m 1971 to Miriam Noel Curth; c Lange Allan. Educ: Kent State Univ, BS, 57, Grad Sch Bus Admin, 57-59; Blue Key; Alpha Tau Omega; Varsity K; Soc for Advan Mgt. Polit & Govt Pos: Regional dir, Comt for Reelect of the President, 71-72; staff asst to the President, 72-73; mem, Alexandria Rep City Comt, Va, 72-; asst adminr, Gen Serv Admin, 73-74. Bus & Prof Pos: Mgr, East Cent Zone, Procter & Gamble Co, Philadelphia, 63-66, mgr, Eastern Area, 66-69; vpres, Inverness Capital Corp, 74- Mem: Young Rep; Heritage Groups Div, Rep Nat Comt. Honors & Awards: Va Young Rep of Year, 70. Relig: Lutheran. Mailing Add: 416 N St Asaph St Alexandria VA 22314

KAUTH, KENNETH (D)
SDak State Rep
Mailing Add: 215 Simmons SE Huron SD 57350

KAUTZ, MARY E (R)
Treas, Washington Co Rep Cent Comt, Idaho
b Weiser, Idaho, Oct 14, 28; d Pete March & Elizabeth Panike M; m 1947 to Reuben F Kautz; c Kathleen (Mrs Virgil Leedy), Larry & Edward. Polit & Govt Pos: Secy, Washington Co Rep Cent Comt, Idaho, 66-68, treas, 74-; clerk dist court, auditor & recorder, Washington Co, 67- Mem: Idaho State Asn Co Clerks & Recorders; Idaho State Asn Elected Co Off (secy-treas, 73-); Idaho State Asn Co Comnrs & Clerks (legis dist chmn, 75-); Weiser Lady Lions. Relig: Lutheran. Legal Res: 1211 W Fifth Weiser ID 83672 Mailing Add: 256 E Court Weiser ID 83672

KAUTZMANN, EMIL E (R)
NDak State Sen
Mailing Add: State Capitol Bismarck ND 58501

KAWAKAMI, RICHARD A (D)
Hawaii State Rep
Mailing Add: House Sgt at Arms State Capitol Honolulu HI 96813

KAWASAKI, DUKE (D)
Hawaii State Sen
Mailing Add: Senate Sgt at Arms State Capitol Honolulu HI 96813

KAY, PETER (R)
Ariz State Rep
b New York, NY, Feb 18, 24; s E M Kay & S V K; m 1949 to Miriam Spitalny; c Karen & Dianne. Educ: Univ NC, AB, 44; Stanford Univ, 43-44; Southwestern Univ, LLB, 49. Polit & Govt Pos: Mem & precinct capt, Ariz Rep State Cent Comt, 52-69; Ariz State Rep, 69- Bus & Prof Pos: Casualty claims adjuster, Ariz Adjust Agency, 52-69. Mil Serv: Entered as Pvt, Army, 43, released as T/5, 46, after serv in Signal Corps Cryptography, China-Burma-India Theatre, 45-46. Mem: Ariz Claimsmen's Asn. Mailing Add: 5002 E Calle Redonda Phoenix AZ 85018

KAY, THOMAS OLIVER (R)
b Anderson, SC, Sept 29, 29; s Thomas Crayton Kay & Gertrude Whitworth K; m 1966 to Bette Hutto Weathers; c Dallon H, Bruce T & George M. Educ: Furman Univ, AB, 50; Blue Key; Hand & Torch. Polit & Govt Pos: Admin asst to US Rep John H Buchanan, Ala, 66-73; admin asst, Off of Secy of Agr, 73- Bus & Prof Pos: Mem relig educ staff, First Baptist Churches, Cochran, Ga, 54-58 & Washington, Ga, 58-65; agt, New York Life Ins Agency, Atlanta, Ga, 65-66. Mem: Mason; Kiwanis; Capitol Hill Club; Poets; Bull Elephants. Relig: Methodist. Mailing Add: 12 S Abington Arlington VA 22204

KAYE, ROBERT (BOB) (R)
Mo State Rep
Mailing Add: 1587 Calhoun Chillicothe MO 64601

KAYLOR, OMER THOMAS, JR (R)
b Hagerstown, Md, July 14, 23; s Omer Thomas Kaylor & Mabel Slagen K; m 1947 to Jean Haskin Johnston; c Omer T, III, Laura H, Gwen S, Mark J & John M. Educ: Washington & Lee Univ, BS, 45, LLB, 49; Phi Beta Kappa; Phi Alpha Delta; Omicron Delta Kappa; Phi Kappa Psi. Polit & Govt Pos: Md State Deleg, 51-54; state's attorney, Washington Co, Md, 55-58; chmn, Rep State Cent Comt Md, formerly. Mil Serv: Entered as A/S, Navy, 43, released as Lt(jg), 46, after serv in Pac Theatre. Mem: Am Judicature Soc; Am Legion; Exchange Club; VFW; YMCA Bd. Relig: United Church of Christ. Mailing Add: 940 The Terrace Hagerstown MD 21740

KAZEN, ABRAHAM, JR (D)
US Rep, Tex
b 1919; married. Educ: Cumberland Univ, Tenn; Univ Tex. Polit & Govt Pos: Tex State Rep, 47-53; Tex State Sen, 53-66; US Rep, Tex, 67- Bus & Prof Pos: Attorney-at-law. Mil Serv: Army Air Corps. Mem: Am Legion; KofC. Relig: Catholic. Legal Res: 2301 Fremont Laredo TX 78040 Mailing Add: Rm 1514 Longworth House Off Bldg Washington DC 20515

KAZY, THEODORE JAMES (R)
b Providence, Ky, Feb 7, 29; s Joseph A Kazy (deceased) & Helen Bielecki K; m 1950 to Marjorie Belle Anderson; c Karen Anita & Joel Anderson. Educ: Univ Ariz, BA, 52; Bobcats; Pi Delta Epsilon. Polit & Govt Pos: Admin asst to Sen Barry Goldwater, 59-65; sr staff asst, Comt on Post Off & Civil Serv, US House Rep, formerly, assoc staff dir, currently. Bus & Prof Pos: Reporter, Ariz Repub, Phoenix, 53-59. Mil Serv: Entered as Seaman, Navy, 46, released as PO 2/C, 48. Relig: Catholic. Mailing Add: 101 Mel Mara Dr Oxon Hill MD 20022

KEACH, JOHN A, JR (R)
Pres, Easton Rep Town Comt, Mass
b Brockton, Mass, Oct 9, 38; s John A Keach & J Elizabeth Riis K; m 1967 to Arlene Marie Albert; c Andrew Albert. Educ: Northeastern Univ, BA, 61; Boston Univ Sch Law, JD, 64; Phi Alpha Theta; Pi Sigma Alpha. Polit & Govt Pos: Mem, Easton Rep Town Comt, Mass, 60-, pres, 69-; mem, Bristol Co Rep Club, 62-, auditor, 65-66, second vpres, 67-68, first vpres, 69-70, pres, 71-; assessor, Easton, 64-; mem, Middlesex Club, 64-; mem, Mass Rep Club, 64-; asst secy to Gov, Mass, 65-67; attorney, Mass Dept Pub Works, 67-69; chief counsel, Mass Dept Com & Develop, 69- Bus & Prof Pos: Private law practice, 65-; pres, Eastern Cable Relay Corp, 65-70; clerk, C&M Distributors, 68-; clerk, Empco Foods, Inc, 70- Mem: Mass Bar Asn; Easton Jaycees; Oakes Hall Develop Comt. Honors & Awards: Outstanding Young Man, Easton Jaycees, 69. Relig: Methodist. Mailing Add: 655 Foundry St Easton MA 02375

KEAN, THOMAS H (R)
NJ State Assemblyman
Mailing Add: State House Trenton NJ 08625

KEARNES, ELAINE (R)
Idaho State Rep
Mailing Add: 3040 Gustafson Circle Idaho Falls ID 83401

KEARNEY, DANIEL PATRICK (R)
Pres, Govt Nat Mortgage Asn, US Dept Housing & Urban Develop
b Chicago, Ill, May 11, 39; s Edward Patrick Kearney & Nora Clements K; m 1969 to Gloria Rose Kehl; c Daniel Patrick, Jr. Educ: Mich State Univ, BA, 61, MA, 62; Univ Chicago, JD, 65; Phi Kappa Phi; Beta Gamma Sigma. Polit & Govt Pos: Exec dir, Ill Housing Development Authority, Chicago, 69-73; managing dir, State Housing Bd, Chicago, 69-70; dep asst secy, Dept & asst comnr, Fed Housing Authority, US Dept Housing Authority, US Dept Housing & Urban Develop, 73-74, pres, Govt Nat Mortgage Asn, 74- Bus & Prof Pos: Attorney-at-law, Chicago, Ill, 65-69. Mem: Ill Bar Asn; Alumni Asn Univ Chicago; Chicago Coun Foreign & Domestic Affairs. Honors & Awards: Outstanding Sophomore, Mich State Univ, 59, Honors Col, 59-61; Outstanding Young Man, 73. Relig: Catholic. Mailing Add: 215 Green St Alexandria VA 22314

KEARNEY, DENNIS (D)
Mass State Rep
Mailing Add: State Capitol Boston MA 02133

KEARNEY, MARY PATRICIA (D)
Secy, Scott Co Dem-Farmer-Labor Party, Minn
b Prior Lake, Minn, Sept 20, 20; d Francis Lawrence Suel & Margaret Sweeney S; m 1944 to Eugene T Kearney; wid; c E Terrence, Mary, Margaret & Thomas. Educ: Univ Minn, 1 year. Polit & Govt Pos: Secy, Scott Co Dem-Farmer-Labor Party, Minn, 70- Bus & Prof Pos: Teacher, Scott & Dakota Co, 39-45; owner & operator, Kearney's V Store, Savage, Minn, 59- Mem: VFW Auxiliary; St John the Baptist Altar & Rosary Soc; Scott Co Human Serv Bd; Scott Co Library Bd (vchmn); Franciscan Retreat (coordr). Relig: Catholic. Mailing Add: 440 Ivy Lane Savage MN 55378

KEARNS, CARROLL D (R)
b Youngstown, Ohio, May 7, 00; s Patrick Henry Kearns & Ida May Carroll K; m 1933 to Nora Mary Lynch. Educ: Chicago Musical Col, BM, MM & DMus; Westminster Col, BS; Univ Pittsburgh, MEd; Phi Mu Alpha. Polit & Govt Pos: US Rep, 28th & 24th Dists, Pa, 47-63. Bus & Prof Pos: Asst dir spec schs, Chicago, Ill, 26-29; theater dir, 29-31; head dept music, Greenville Pub Schs, Pa, 31-38; head dept music, Slippery Rock State Teachers Col, 38-41; supt schs, Farrell, 41-45; vpres, Shenango Metalcraft Co, Pa, 63-67, pres, 67- Mil Serv: Student Army Training Corps, 18. Publ: Miscellaneous mag articles. Mem: Mason; Consistory; Shrine; Elks; Moose. Relig: Lutheran. Mailing Add: RD 1 Conneaut Lake PA 16316

KEARNS, FRANCIS J (D)
Del State Sen
Mailing Add: 23 E Edinburgh Dr Stratford New Castle DE 19720

KEARNS, HENRY (R)
b Salt Lake City, Utah, Apr 30, 11; s Henry A Kearns & Mary Orilla Robbins K; m 1938 to Marjorie Harriett Prescott; c Patricia (Mrs Clabaugh), Henry Timothy, Mary (Mrs David Rohe) & Michael Prescott. Educ: Univ Utah, 29-30. Hon Degrees: DBA, Woodbury Col, 60; Dr Econ, Chungang Univ, Korea, 71. Polit & Govt Pos: Mem, Hoover Comn Task Force on Intel Activities, 55-56; mem, Nat Coun of Consult, Small Bus Admin, 55-60; mem, Comt on Export Expansion, 57-60, US Govt rep, Gen Agreement on Tariffs & Trade, Int Union of Off Travel Orgn, Int Air Transport Asn & Pac Area Travel Asn; Asst Secy of Com for Int Affairs, 57-60; exec mem, Nat Exec Reserve Corps, 61-; mem, Los Angeles Dist Attorney's Adv Coun, 64-69; pres & chmn, Export-Import Bank of the US, 69-75. Publ: Various articles on int affairs. Mem: Am Soc Int Exec; Licensing Exec Soc, Inc; Scottish Rite; US Jr CofC. Honors & Awards: Grand Knight, Royal Order White Elephant, Thailand; Grand Officer, d'Order, Nat Rep Ivory Coast; Capt Robert Dollar Award, Nat Foreign Trade Coun, 72; Philadelphia Foreign Traders Award, 72. Relig: Episcopal. Mailing Add: 4903 Rockwood Pkwy NW Washington DC 20016

KEARNS, RICHARD P (D)
RI State Rep
Mailing Add: 83 Winter St Woonsocket RI 02895

KEARNS, VICTOR W, JR (R)
Kans State Rep
Mailing Add: 6555 Goodman Merriam KS 66202

KEATING, FRANCIS ANTHONY, II (R)
Okla State Sen
b St Louis, Mo, Feb 10, 44; s Anthony Francis Keating & Anne Martin K; m 1972 to Catherine Dunn Heller. Educ: Georgetown Univ, AB, 66; Univ Okla Col Law, JD, 69. Polit & Govt Pos: Asst chmn, Okla Rep State Finance Comt, 68; mem, Gov Comn on Boat & Water Safety, 68; asst to chmn, Nat Rep Gov Conf, 68; spec agt, Fed Bur Invest, 69-71; asst dist attorney, Tulsa Co, 71-72; mem, Tulsa Co Rep Exec Comt & Okla Rep State Exec Comt, 73; Okla State Sen, 73-74- Bus & Prof Pos: Assoc, Blackstock, Joyce, Pollard & McInerney, Attorneys-at-Law, 72- Mem: Phi Alpha Delta; Am & Okla Bar Asns; Tulsa Club. Relig: Roman Catholic. Legal Res: 2423 E 31st Tulsa OK 74114 Mailing Add: 300 Petroleum Club Bldg Tulsa OK 74103

KEATING, WILLIAM J (R)
b Cincinnati, Ohio, Mar 30, 27; s Charles H Keating & Adele Kipp K; m 1951 to Nancy Nenninger; c Nancy C, William J, Michael K, Daniel N, Susan M, Thomas J & John S. Educ: St Xavier High Sch; Univ Cincinnati, BBA & JD, 50. Polit & Govt Pos: Asst attorney gen, Ohio, 57-58; judge, Cincinnati Munic Court, 58-62;, presiding judge, 62-63; elected judge, Common Pleas, Hamilton Co, 67; majority leader & chmn finance comt, Cincinnati City Coun, 67-70; US Rep, Ohio, 71-74; deleg, Rep Nat Conv, 72. Bus & Prof Pos: Attorney, Keating, Muething & Klekamp. Mil Serv: US Navy, World War II; 1st Lt, US Air Force Res. Mem: Cincinnati & Ohio State Bar Asns; Mt Lookout Civic Club; Am Legion Post 744; KofC. Relig: Roman Catholic. Mailing Add: 2959 Alpine Terr Cincinnati OH 45208

KEATINGE, RICHARD HARTE (D)
b San Francisco, Calif, Dec 4, 19; m 1944 to Betty West; c Richard West, Daniel Wilson & Anne Elizabeth. Educ: Univ Calif, AB in Econ, 39; Harvard Univ, MA in Econ, 41; Georgetown Univ Law Sch, JD, 44; Phi Beta Kappa; mem bd ed, Georgetown Law J. Polit & Govt Pos: Deleg, Dem Nat Conv, 52 & 64; trustee, Dem Assocs, Inc, 58-, chmn, 67-70; mem, Calif Law Rev Comn, 61-68, chmn, 65-67; Spec Asst Attorney Gen, Calif, 64-68; pub mem, Admin Conf of the US, 68-74. Mem: Life fel Am Bar Found; Am Law Inst; Am Bar Asn (mem spec comt housing & urban develop law, 68-73, mem adv comn Housing & Urban Growth, 74-); State Bar of Calif; Los Angeles Co Bar Asn. Relig: Episcopal. Legal Res: 1160 Virginia Rd San Marino CA 91108 Mailing Add: Sixth Floor Broadway Plaza 700 S Flower Los Angeles CA 90017

KEATON, HARRY JOSEPH (R)
b Prague, Czech, June 8, 25; s Fred G Keaton & Nina Ordner K; m 1952 to Minto E Hannus; c Elizabeth, Deborah, Janette & Juliana. Educ: San Francisco City Col, 47-48; Univ Calif, Berkeley, BA in Econ, summa cum laude, 50, Univ Calif, JD, 53; Phi Beta Kappa; revising ed, Calif Law Rev, 52-53; Order of the Coif; Phi Alpha Delta. Polit & Govt Pos: Participant, Rep Polit Campaigns, including those for Eisenhower & Nixon, 60, 62, 68 & 72 & Reagan, 70; gen counsel, Young Rep of Calif, 60-61; nat committeeman, 61-62, pres, 62-63; mem, Calif Rep State Cent Comt, 61-74; mem exec comt & chmn labor comt, 61-64, co-chmn lawyer's comt, 73-74; founding mem, Calif Rep League, past exec vpres, Southern Calif & vpres for legal affairs, 68; vpres, Los Angeles Co Rep Assembly, 64; treas, Calif Lawyers for Nixon-Agnew, 68 & 72. Bus & Prof Pos: Partner, Mitchell, Silberberg & Knupp, Attorneys, Los Angeles, Calif, currently; lectr labor law, Univ Southern Calif, 62-66. Publ: Auth, articles on labor law & other legal subjects, 62-66. Mem: Atlantic Coun of the US, Inc (sponsor); Los Angeles World Affairs Coun; Atlantic Asn of Young Polit Leaders; Anti-Defamation League Western Regional Adv Bd (chmn exec comt, 73-). Relig: Jewish. Mailing Add: 1800 Century Park E Los Angeles CA 90067

KEDROFF, LEW (R)
Vt State Rep
Mailing Add: 119 Fairground Rd Springfield VT 05156

KEDROWSKI, DAVID RAY (D)
Wis State Rep
b Wisconsin Rapids, Wis, Mar 15, 42; s Raymond Barney Kedrowski & Esther Davies K; m 1964 to Carla Jean Gerard; c Michelle Lynn & Mark Anthony. Educ: Univ Wis, 60-62; Wis State Univ-Stevens Point, BS, 66; Alpha Gamma; Siasefi. Polit & Govt Pos: Treas, Vol Citizens for Kopela, 68-71; deleg, Wis State Dem Conv, 69-73; chmn, Bayfield Co Dem Party, 70-72; Wis State Rep, 74th Dist, 73- Mem: Wis Educ Asn (pres, 69-72, deleg, state conv, 69); Washburn Educ Asn; Nat Hist Soc; NCent Law Enforcement Asn; Washburn Men's Club. Relig: Lutheran. Mailing Add: 417 E Third St Washburn WI 54891

KEE, ELIZABETH (D)
m to John Kee (deceased); c James & Frances. Polit & Govt Pos: US Rep, WVa, 72nd-88th Cong, formerly. Bus & Prof Pos: Auth weekly column, WVa papers & weekly radio & TV progs; auth, articles on real estate. Mem: Am Newspaper Women's Club; Cong Club; Bluefield Country Club; DAR. Relig: Catholic. Mailing Add: 105 Oakhurst Ave Bluefield WV 24701

KEE, JAMES (D)
b Bluefield, WVa, Apr 15, 17; s John Kee & Elizabeth K; m to Helen Lee Chapman; c three daughters. Educ: Southeastern Univ Law Sch; Sch Foreign Serv, Georgetown Univ. Hon Degrees: LLD, WVa Inst Technol, 66. Polit & Govt Pos: Career foreign serv staff officer, US State Dept; asst to clerk of US House of Rep, 4 years; housing adv, US Housing Authority; admin asst to US Rep Elizabeth Kee, 53-65; chmn, State Soc Participation Comt, Kennedy-Johnson Inaugural Comt, WVa, 61; US Rep, WVa, 65-72. Mil Serv: Army Air Force. Mem: Wash Coal Club; Elks; Dem Club of DC; Greenbriar Mil Sch Alumni Asn; Am Legion. Honors & Awards: WVa Son of the Year, 62; West Virginian of the Year, 64. Relig: Episcopal. Mailing Add: 105 Oakhurst Bluefield WV 24701

KEEFE, ALEXANDER FRANCIS (BUD) (D)
Vt State Rep
Mailing Add: 43 Morse Pl Rutland VT 05701

KEEFE, EDMUND M (R)
NH State Rep
Mailing Add: 10 Keats St Nashua NH 03060

KEEFE, JAMES A, JR (D)
Mass State Rep
Mailing Add: State Capitol Boston MA 01233

KEEFE, JAMES EDWARD (D)
Wash State Sen
b New York, NY, 1908; m to Eileen; c two. Educ: Gonzaga High Sch. Polit & Govt Pos: Wash State Sen, currently. Bus & Prof Pos: Sales mgr. Mem: Elks. Mailing Add: 412 N Glass Ave Spokane WA 99205

KEEFE, JOHN B (R)
Minn State Sen
b Chicago, Ill, May 28, 28; s John L Keefe & Aurlia Gagnon K; m 1953 to Rosemary A Campion; c John, Jr, Lynn, Stephen & Lisa. Educ: Macalester Col, 49-51; Univ Minn, BA, 53; William Mitchell Col Law, LLB, 58; Alpha Tau Omega. Polit & Govt Pos: Munic judge, Hopkins, Minn, 62-63, mem park & recreation comn, 64-66; Minn State Rep, Dist 29 B, 67-72; Minn State Sen, 73- Mil Serv: Pfc, Army, 46-47, serv in 7th Cavalry, Japan. Mem: Lions Club; Elks; KofC; Citizens' League; Am Judiciary Soc. Relig: Catholic. Mailing Add: 201 Oakwood Rd Hopkins MN 55343

KEEFE, ROBERT JOSEPH (D)
Exec Dir, Dem Nat Comt
b Huntington, Ind, May 29, 34; s Francis J Keefe & Helen Teusch K; m to Sheila M; c Scot T, Michael J, Erin M, Kevin S, Dirk P & Christopher F. Educ: Marquette Univ, BS, 56; Sigma Delta Chi; Alpha Phi Omega. Polit & Govt Pos: Admin asst to US Rep J Edward Roush, 60-62; admin asst to US Sen Birch Bayh, Ind, 63-71; exec dir, Dem Nat Comt, 73- Bus & Prof Pos: Copywriter, Louis E Wade Advert, 56; sales & prom mgr, WANE-TV, 57-60; consult, AFL-CIO Comt on Polit Educ, 71-72 & Dem Gov Campaign Comt, 71-72; pres, PACA, Ltd, Polit Consult, 71- Relig: Catholic. Mailing Add: 100 W Linden St Alexandria VA 22301

KEEFE, RUTH ELEANOR (D)
b Cincinnati, Ohio, July 17, 24; d William A A Castellini & Ruth McGregor C; m 1947 to Judge John W Keefe; c John M, Thomas W, Daniel McGregor, Kevin Lausche, Ruth S & Lelia M. Educ: Univ Cincinnati, BA with high honors, 46; Alpha Lambda Delta; Guidon; Mortar Bd; Theta Phi Alpha. Polit & Govt Pos: Mem bd, Hamilton Co Women's Dem Club, Ohio, 57-59, 73-; deleg, Dem Nat Conv, 64; campaign mgr for Dem Judicial Cand, 63, 65, 66, 72 & 74; chmn women's div, Hamilton Co Dem Party, 64-66, precinct exec, 66-; mem, Hamilton Co Dem Exec & Steering Comts, Ohio, 66-70; vchmn, Fourth Ward, Cincinnati, Hamilton Co Dem Orgn, 68-69. Bus & Prof Pos: Chmn gov bd, Youth Employ Serv, 61-63, chmn pub rels, 61-70. Mem: Citizens' Comt on Youth (vpres exec comt & treas, 64-74); St Mary Hosp Guild; Our Lady of Mercy Hosp Guild; Mothers of Twins Club. Honors & Awards: Woman of the Year, 74. Relig: Roman Catholic. Mailing Add: 3662 Kendall Ave Cincinnati OH 45208

KEEFE, STEPHEN (DFL)
Minn State Sen
Mailing Add: 4217 Garfield Ave S Minneapolis MN 55409

KEEFE, WILLIAM F (D)
NH State Rep
b Portsmouth, NH, Apr 16, 11; married; c one; three grandchildren. Polit & Govt Pos: Clerk, Portsmouth deleg, NH; registr, Voters-at-lg; ward clerk; mem city coun, Portsmouth; NH State Rep, 59-69 & 75- Bus & Prof Pos: Real estate broker. Mem: KofC; Moose; Holy Name Soc. Relig: Catholic. Mailing Add: 155 Farm Lane Portsmouth NH 03801

KEEFER, SCOTT KING (R)
Chmn, North Smithfield Rep Town Comt, RI
b Woonsocket, RI, May 16, 27; s Jackson M Keefer & Dorothy King K; m 1951 to Betty Jane Geldart; c Patricia, Jeffrey, Kimberley, Jackson & Peter. Educ: Miami Univ, 46-48; Univ Southern Calif, 48; Univ Calif, Los Angeles, BA, 51; Delta Tau Delta. Polit & Govt Pos: Solicitor, Glocester, RI, 58-67; judge, 12th Dist Court, 67-68; chmn, North Smithfield Rep Town Comt, 68-; moderator, North Smithfield, 69-; spec asst attorney gen, State of RI, 70-71. Bus & Prof Pos: Partner, Macktaz, Keefer & Kirby Law Firm, Woonsocket, RI, currently. Mil Serv: Entered as S1/C, Navy, 45, released as STK 3/C, 46. Mem: Am Bar Asn; Lions; YMCA (pres); AF&AM (past Master). Relig: Episcopal. Legal Res: Edward Ave Slatersville RI 02876 Mailing Add: 52 Hamlet Ave Woonsocket RI 02895

KEEGAN, PHILIP MYLES (D)
b Newark, NJ, Apr 20, 42; s Frank X Keegan & Margaret Curran K; single. Educ: Villanova Univ, BS in Econ, 64; Delta Pi Epsilon; Student Coun Rep; chmn, Sr Activities. Polit & Govt Pos: Pres, NJ Young Dem, 68-70; chmn bd regional dirs, Young Dem Am, 69-; freeholder, Essex Co, NJ, 71-, bd dir, 73-; deleg, Dem Nat Conv, 72; mem exec comt, Dem Nat Charter Comn, currently; bd dirs, Am Coun Young Polit Leaders, currently. Bus & Prof Pos: Pres, Newark Testing Lab, Inc. Mil Serv: Entered as Pvt, Marines, 60; released as Sgt, 63, after serv in Platoon Leaders Class. Mem: Am Concrete Inst; Am Soc Testing & Mat; Elks. Honors & Awards: Outstanding Young Dem NJ, 67-69; One of Ten Young Dem, Nat Dem Comt, 67-69. Relig: Catholic. Mailing Add: 321 Sanford Ave Newark NJ 07106

KEEL, JOHN PEYTON (D)
Chmn, Jackson Co Dem Cent Comt, Ark
b Pine Bluff, Ark, Jan 11, 05; s John Hardee Keel & Gertrude Tucker K; m 1930 to Gladys Spencer; c Mary Katherine, Gertrude, Patsy, Joan, John Edward & Franklin. Educ: Newport High Sch, grad. Polit & Govt Pos: Mem, Jackson Co Dem Cent Comt, Ark, 28-, chmn, currently. Relig: Methodist. Mailing Add: Rte 4 Newport AR 72112

KEEL, WILLIAM ARNOLD, JR (D)
b Louisville, Ky, Oct 10, 24; s William Arnold Keel & Birdie Viola Durham K; m 1949 to Jean Harmon; c William Baker (deceased). Educ: Carson-Newman Col, 1 year; Univ Tenn, BS in Bus Admin; Phi Beta Phi; Jour Club; Orange & White. Polit & Govt Pos: Asst to dep chmn for pub affairs, Dem Nat Comt, 62-63, White House liaison for dept pub affairs, 63, research dir & ed of The Dem, 63-64; spec asst to adminr, US Small Bus Admin, 64-65; admin asst to US Rep Joe L Evins, Tenn, 65- Bus & Prof Pos: Govt & polit writer, Nashville Tennessean, 52-62. Mil Serv: Entered as A/S, Navy, 43, released as Pharm Mate 2/C, 46, after serv in 6th Marine Corps, Naval Hosp, US & Pac Theatre, 45-46; Victory Medal, Asiatic-Pac Medal, Am Theatre Medal. Mem: Cong Staff Club; Admin Asst Asn; Tenn State

Soc (pres); Univ Tenn Alumni Asn. Relig: Baptist. Legal Res: Smithville TN 37116 Mailing Add: 2300 Rayburn House Off Bldg Washington DC 20515

KEELER, VIRGINIA LEE (D)
VChmn, Dutchess Co Dem Comt, NY
b White Plains, NY, Oct 17, 30; d Wilbur Elwood Miles, Jr & Elizabeth Mary Woods M; m 1949 to Howard Stewart Keeler; c Scott Howard, Robin Elizabeth, Michael William, J Stuart & twins, Kerry Michael & Kelly Ann. Educ: Dutchess Community Col, various courses. Polit & Govt Pos: Town committeewoman, Wappingers Falls, NY, 65-69; vchmn, Wappingers Dem Club, 66-68; vchmn, Wappingers Dem Comt, 68-69; recording secy, Dutchess Co Women's Dem Club, 67-69, chmn nominating comt, 69-; vchmn, Citizens for Robert Kennedy, 68; vchmn, Dutchess Co Dem Comt, 68- Relig: Unitarian; chmn denominational affairs, Unitarian Church. Mailing Add: Spook Hill Rd Wappingers Falls NY 12590

KEELING, JOHN MICHAEL (D)
b Kilgore, Tex, Feb 24, 47; s Frank Marion Keeling (deceased) & Eva Mae Buse K; m 1969 to Michaela Elenora Halik. Educ: Yale Univ, BA, 69; Univ Tex at Austin Law Sch, JD, 71; Phi Delta Phi; Delta Kappa Epsilon. Polit & Govt Pos: Staff aide, Sen Ralph Yarborough Re-Elec Comt, Austin, Tex, 70; research dir, Interim Comt to Study Rural Land Assessments, Tex State Legis, 71; research assoc, Legis Research, Inc, 71; independent consult, Tex Farmers Union, Tex AFL-CIO, 71; research dir, Francis Farenthold for Gov Comt, 72; admin asst to US Rep J J Pickle, Tex, 72- Bus & Prof Pos: Attorney-at-law, 72. Mem: Am & Tex Bar Asns; House Admin Asst Asn. Legal Res: 3107 Skylark Austin TX 78753 Mailing Add: 2126 Connecticut Ave Washington DC 20008

KEENAN, FRANCIS JOYCE (R)
b Dover, NH, Jan 19, 24; s Thomas H Keenan & Mary E Winslow K; m 1956 to Joan M Swenson; c Thomas Winslow & Alan Joyce Christopher. Educ: Univ Notre Dame; Harvard Univ Grad Sch Arts & Sci; Econ Round Table, Notre Dame. Polit & Govt Pos: Asst campaign mgr for Sen Charles W Tobey, NH, 50; staff mem, Select Comt on Small Bus, US Senate, 50, asst chief clerk, Comt on Interstate & Foreign Com, 51-53; campaign coordr for US Rep Perkins Bass, NH, 54; legis asst to US Sen John Sherman Cooper, Ky, 56-57; admin asst to US Rep Florence P Dwyer, 12th Dist, NJ, 58-73; admin asst to US Rep Matthew J Rinaldo, NJ, 73- Bus & Prof Pos: Correspondent, Commonweal Mag, Wash, 53-55; rep, Louis de Rochemont-Cinerama, 53-56; legis ed, Am Aviation Publ, 55-56. Mil Serv: Entered as A/S, Navy, 43, released as Lt(jg), 46, after serv in Pac Area; Atlantic Campaign, Asiatic-Pac Campaign, Philippines & China Occup Ribbons. Mem: Am Polit Sci Asn; Notre Dame Club of Wash. Relig: Roman Catholic. Legal Res: 39 Hough St Dover NH 03820 Mailing Add: 115 Sixth St SE Washington DC 20003

KEENAN, THOMAS LE ROY (D)
Committeeman-at-Lg, Richmond City Dem Comt, Va
b Buffalo, NY, July 7, 28; s William Stephen Keenan, Sr & Catherine Lang K; m 1966 to Marilyn T Mahoney; c Carolyn Mary, Joseph Thomas & William Stephen. Educ: Univ Buffalo Law Sch, 51-52; Univ Buffalo, Millard Fillmore Col, 52-53; Univ Mich, AB, 54; Univ Mich Sch Social Work, MSW, 64; NY Vet scholar, 52; NY Dept Social Serv scholar, 62. Polit & Govt Pos: Mem, Human Rels Comn, Battle Creek, Mich, 66-68; deleg, Mich State Dem Conv, 68 & Spec Mich State Dem Conv on Party Reform, 70; Dem nominee for US Rep, Third Cong Dist, Mich, 68; rep of poor, Calhoun Community Action Agency, 68-69; chmn, Third Cong Dist Dem Conv, 69; co-chmn, Richmond McGovern for President Comt, 71-72; committeeman-at-lg, Richmond City Dem Comt, 71-; alt deleg, Dem Nat Conv, 72; work with McGovern campaign, Mich & NY Primaries, 72, state finance coordr, Va McGovern-Shriver Campaign Comt, 72. Bus & Prof Pos: Pub welfare, NY State, 59-66; dir, Calhoun Co Dept Social Serv, Battle Creek, Mich, 66-68; dir, Pub Housing Social Serv Prog, Neighborhood Serv Orgn, Detroit, 69-70; asst prof social work, Va Commonwealth Univ, 70- Mil Serv: Entered as Pvt, Army, 46, released as Cpl, 48, after serv in 702nd Counter Intel Corps Detachment, US Air Forces in Europe, 47-48. Mem: Coun Social Work Educ; Am Asn Univ Prof; Nat Asn Social Workers; Am Pub Welfare Asn; Nat Asn Housing & Redevelop Off. Relig: Roman Catholic. Mailing Add: 4502 Patterson Ave Richmond VA 23221

KEENE, BARRY (D)
Calif State Assemblyman
Mailing Add: 533 G St Eureka CA 95501

KEENEY, JOHN C
Acting Asst Attorney Gen, Criminal Div, Dept Justice
Mailing Add: Dept of Justice Washington DC 20530

KEENEY, PHYLLIS MOTTRAM (R)
Secy, Hillsborough Co Rep Comt, NH
b Hartford, Conn, Dec 10, 25; d Frank Edward Mottram & Gracie Burroughs M; m 1946 to Dr Norwood Henry Keeney, Jr; c Norwood Henry, III. Educ: Pa State Univ, BA, 46; Columbia Univ Sch Libr Serv, MS, 52; Phi Sigma Iota. Polit & Govt Pos: Libr messenger, NH Const Conv, 64; mem, Hudson Rep Town Comt, NH, 64-; NH State Rep, 67-72, mem, Interim Comt on Medicaid, NH House Rep, 67-68, vchmn, Legis Rev Comt, 69-70, vchmn, Enrolled Bills Comt, 71-72; clerk, Towns's Del, Hillsborough Co & mem, Hillsborough Co Rep Exec Comt, 71-72; defeated for NH State Sen, 72; selectman, Hudson, NH, 74-; secy, Hillsborough Co Rep Comt, 75- Bus & Prof Pos: Asst in acquisitions, Trinity Col Libr, Conn, 47-48; reference asst, Publ Libr, Bangor, Maine, 48-50; cataloguer, Brown Univ, 50-51; foreign law cataloguer & asst to dept head, Harvard Univ Law Libr, 52-57; cataloguer, Regina Libr, Rivier Col, Nashua, NH, 67-; instr, Univ RI Grad Libr Prog, 75- Publ: Individual poems. Mem: Hudson VFW Auxiliary; Hudson Fortnightly Club; Hudson Hist Soc; Nashua Bus & Prof Womens Club; Zonta Int. Relig: Episcopal. Mailing Add: Wason Rd Hudson NH 03051

KEESEE, MARGARET POLLARD (R)
VChmn, Guilford Co Rep Party, NC
b Greensboro, NC, Jan 6, 45; d Charles Rogers Keesee & Margaret Kersey K; single. Educ: Guilford Col, BA in Educ, 67. Polit & Govt Pos: Vchmn, Guilford Co Rep Party, NC, 72-; NC State Rep, 72-74; mem, Gov Adv Comt on Youth Develop, currently. Mem: NC Asn Educators; Asn Classroom Teachers; NC League Women Voters; Am Asn Univ Women; NC Polit Action Comt for Educ. Relig: Society of Friends. Mailing Add: 1013 W Friendly Ave Greensboro NC 27403

KEHRES, RAYMOND C (D)
Mich State Rep
b Monroe, Mich, June 2, 15; m 1941 to Eleanor M Payment; c Judith Ann & Robert W. Educ: High sch grad. Polit & Govt Pos: Chmn, Dem Co Comt, Mich, formerly; Mich State Rep, 64- Bus & Prof Pos: Welding foreman. Mil Serv: Army, S/Sgt, 41-45. Mem: KofC; Moose; DAV; Detroit Beach Boat Club; ESide Bus Men's Asn. Relig: Catholic. Mailing Add: 536 St Marys St Monroe MI 48161

KEIER, RICHARD FREDERICK (R)
Mem, Oakland Co Rep Exec Comt, Mich
b Toledo, Ohio, Nov 5, 39; s Frederick Henry Keier & Lazetta Meister K; m 1968 to Karen Sue Rowland; c Kathryn Ann & Gregory Richard. Educ: Wittenberg Univ, BS, 61; Am Col Life Underwriters, CLU, 69; Phi Gamma Delta. Polit & Govt Pos: Rep precinct deleg, Mich, 62-64 & 70-; deleg, Nat Young Rep Conv, 67 & 69; treas, Oakland Co Young Rep, Mich, 66, chmn, 67; treas, Mich Fedn Young Rep, 68-70, regional vchmn, 70-72; mem, 18th Cong Dist Rep Exec Comt, Mich, 69; mem campaign staff, Lenore Romney for US Senate, 70; mem, Oakland Co Rep Exec Comt, Mich, 71-; Southfield City chmn, Comt to Reelect President Nixon, 72. Bus & Prof Pos: Ins agt, Prudential Ins Co of Am, 62- Mem: South Oakland Life Underwriters Asn; Detroit Grad Chap, Phi Gamma Delta; Wittenberg Univ Alumni for Southeastern Mich. Honors & Awards: Sen Robert P Griffin Award for Outstanding Young Rep Man in Mich, 67-68. Relig: Lutheran; deacon & finance secy, Calvary Lutheran Church. Mailing Add: 17285 Redwood Blvd Southfield MI 48076

KEIL, ARMIN THEODORE (R)
Mem, NMex Rep State Cent Comt
b New York, NY, May 14, 30; s Ernest A Keil & Gertrude Novich K; m 1959 to Lois Moses; c Rebecca Susan, David Seth & Jonathen Matthew. Educ: Univ Conn, 48-50; George Washington Univ, AA, 50, BS, 52; Northwestern Univ, MD, 56; Tau Epsilon Phi; Gate & Key Soc. Polit & Govt Pos: Chmn, Colfax Co Rep Party, NMex, 66-69; mem, NMex Rep State Cent Comt, 66-; mem, State Adv Hosp Coun, 68- Bus & Prof Pos: Self-employed physician, 62- Mil Serv: Lt, Med Corps, Naval Res, 57-59, serv in Naval Air Sta, South Weymouth, Mass, Res, 59-68. Mem: Am Med Asn; NMex Med Soc; Am Col Physicians; Am Soc Internal Med; Rotary. Mailing Add: McFarland Rd Raton NM 87740

KEIL, NORMA FERN (D)
Committeewoman, Mont Dem State Cent Comt
b Speed, Kans, Sept 27, 06; d Edgar A Elliott & Mary Etta George E; m 1929 to John Keil, wid; c Edgar R, Daniel D & Stephen M. Educ: Kans State Teachers Col, 27. Polit & Govt Pos: Dem precinct committeewoman, Mont, 50-64; vchmn, Mont State Dem Women, 55-58, pres, 58-61; state committeewoman, Pondera Co, Mont Dem State Cent Comt, 62-65 & 71-, vchmn, 62-65; chmn, Dem Women's Conf, 66; deleg, Dem Nat Conv, 60, 64, 68 & 72; Dem Nat Committeewoman, Mont, formerly; mem, Charter Comn, Mont, 72-; co-chmn, Mont McGovern Campaign, 72. Bus & Prof Pos: Sch teacher, 24-28; pres, Pondera Action Coun, 68-; pres, Horizon Lodge, Inc, 72-; chmn, Pondera Co Coun on Aging, 74-; vchmn, NCent Area Agency on Aging, 74- Mem: Eastern Star; Farmers Educ & Coop Union (vchmn); Pondera Ment Health Asn (pres). Relig: Protestant. Mailing Add: 701 S Illinois Conrad MT 59425

KEILBAR, MONA MARY (R)
Mem, Alameda Co Rep Cent Comt, Calif
b Honaker, Va, May 10, 15; d John Randolph Hubbard & Amanda Ellen Hess H; m 1945 to Leland C Keilbar, Jr. Polit & Govt Pos: Vpres & auditor, Rep Womens Club of Alameda, Calif, 65, pres, 66, vpres & prog chmn, 67, mem bd dirs, 69, parliamentarian, 72, mem ways & means comt, 72, legis chmn, 73-74; chmn ways & means comt, Northern Div, Calif Fedn Rep Women, 68-69, sargeant at arms, 70-73, chmn of pages, 70-73, vpres Region V, 74-75; spec events chmn, State Bd, Calif Fedn Rep Women, 70-73; unit dir, Alameda Co Coord Rep Assembly, 69; assoc mem, Rep State Cent Comt Calif, 68-69, mem, 69-70 & 73-74; chmn, Nixon Phone Ctr, Oakland, 72; mem, Alameda Co Rep Cent Comt, 73-; treas, Alameda Co Rep Coord Coun, 73-, women's chmn, 75-; mem, Nat Fedn Rep Women, currently. Mem: Home Owners Asn; Alameda Welfare Coun; Calif Hist Soc. Adelphian Club. Relig: Protestant. Mailing Add: 629 Pond Isle Alameda CA 94501

KEIR, ROBERT MACARTHUR (R)
Chmn, Clay Co Rep Cent Comt, Iowa
b Sac Co, Iowa, June 6, 05; s Roy E Keir & Zada Corsaut K; m 1962 to Eileen Claer; c Richard, Wendell, Kendall & Heidi Galer. Educ: Iowa State Univ, BS, 27. Polit & Govt Pos: Iowa State Sen, 41-49; comnr, Iowa State Hwy Comn, 49-55 & 61-63; supvr, Clay Co, Iowa, 63-65 & 73-74, clerk dist court, 65-73; chmn, Clay Co Rep Cent Comt, 74- Bus & Prof Pos: Self-employed farmer, 33-74. Honors & Awards: Iowa State Univ Serv Alumni Award, 50; Iowa State Hwy Comn Award, 55 & 63; Iowa Good Roads Award of Merit, 58. Relig: Methodist. Mailing Add: 2001 W Tenth Spencer IA 51301

KEITH, CHARLES MICHAEL (D)
Chmn, Henry Co Dem Comt, Mo
b Clinton, Mo, Dec 13, 43; s James Milton Keith & Ruth Elizabeth Jones K; m to Joyce Sue Houtchens; c Brad Allen, Aaron Christopher & Ryan Patrick. Educ: Cent Mo State Col, BS in Educ, 65. Polit & Govt Pos: Secy-treas, Dem Cent Comt, Clinton, Mo, 68-73; Dem committeeman, Clinton Twp, 74-; chmn, Henry Co Dem Comt, 74-; deleg, Fourth Dist Dem Conv, 75; mem, Dem State Comt Mo, 74- Bus & Prof Pos: Mem, Asn of Independent Ins Agts of Mo, 66-; mem & treas bd dirs, Security Loan & Finance, Clinton, 68-; mem, Clinton Planning & Zoning Comt, 69-74, chmn, 71-74. Mem: Jaycees; CofC; Optimist; Elks; Duck's Unlimited. Honors & Awards: Col, Hon Staff of Gov Warren E Hearnes, 68; Freedom Guard Ward, US Jaycees, 73; Outstanding Young Man, Epsilon Nu Chap of Beta Sigma Phi; Distinguished Serv Award, Clinton Jaycees. Relig: Christian Church NAm. Legal Res: 803 E Clinton Clinton MO 64735 Mailing Add: PO Box 402 Clinton MO 64735

KEITH, DONALD MERLE (DFL)
Mem, Minn State Dem-Farmer-Labor Cent Comt
b Ellendale, NDak, Feb 11, 28; s Archie Keith & Eunice Ruth K; m 1948 to Donna Paulson; c Brenda, Todd, Tim, Kris Ann, Brett, Jennifer & Heather. Educ: Univ Minn, Minneapolis, BS, 54. Polit & Govt Pos: Councilman, Village of Braham, Minn, 66-; chmn, 21st Sen Dist & vchmn, Isanti Co Dem-Farmer-Labor Party, Minn, formerly; mem, Minn State Dem-Farmer-Labor Cent Comt & Polk Co Dem-Farmer-Labor Comt, currently. Bus & Prof Pos: Instr voc agr, Caledonia High Sch, Minn, 54-55 & Braham High Sch, 55- Mil Serv: Entered as Pvt, Army, 46, released as T/5, 48, after serv in 11th Medium Port Co, Korean Theatre, 47-48. Mem: Nat Educ Asn; Minn Voc Agr Instr Asn; Am Voc Asn; Nat Voc Agr

Teachers Asn; Braham Area Civic & Com Asn (pres). Relig: Lutheran. Mailing Add: 313 S Nelson Crookston MN 56716

KEITH, FREDERICK R (R)
Mem, Robeson Co Rep Exec Comt, NC
b Wilmington, NC, Dec 25, 00; s Benjamin Franklin Keith & Lillie Rulfs K; m 1927 to Grace Butler; c Fred R, Jr, Mary A & Thomas J. Educ: Campbell Col, 17-18; NC State Col, 19-20; Auburn Univ, BS, 22; exec prog, Univ NC, 54; Tau Kappa Epsilon. Polit & Govt Pos: Chmn, Robeson Co Rep Exec Comt, NC, 24-54, mem, currently; mayor & comnr, St Pauls, formerly; Rep cand for NC State Rep, 40, cand for NC State Sen, 44; cand for US Rep, 48; deleg, Rep Nat Conv, 48 & 60; mem, State Munic Rels Comt, 51-53; chmn, NC Agr Stabilization Comt & NC Drought Comt, US Dept Agr, 54; chmn, Seventh Cong Dist Rep Orgn, 56; state dir, Rep Exec Comt, formerly: Rep cand for NC Comnr Agr, 56; mem, NC Comt of Farmers Home Adm, 58-60, vpres advan, currently; Rep cand for NC State Treas, 60. Bus & Prof Pos: Chmn, St Pauls Guaranty Savings & Loan, 63-; dir, Guaranty Savings & Loan Co; dir & chmn loan bd, St Pauls First Union Nat Bank; pres, Keith Hardware & Furniture Co, Inc, St Pauls Drug Co, Inc, St Pauls Bldg & Loans Asn, Keith Farm & Land Co & Keith Realty Co, Inc. Mil Serv: Pvt, Army, 18-19. Mem: Lumberton Bd Realtors; Nat Asn Real Estate Bd, Inc; Am Inst Banking; Robeson Co Rural Fire Asn; Mason. Relig: Baptist. Legal Res: 2100 N Elm St Lumberton NC 28358 Mailing Add: Keith Realty Co Inc St Pauls NC 28384

KEITH, HASTINGS (R)
b Brockton, Mass, Nov 22, 15; s Roger Keith (deceased) & Carolyn Hastings K; m 1943 to Louise Harriman (deceased 1973); m 1974 to F Bland Jackson; c Helen H (Mrs A M Brink, Jr) & Carolyn L. Educ: Univ Vt, BS, 38; Harvard Univ, grad study; Command & Gen Staff Sch, grad; Sigma Phi. Polit & Govt Pos: Mass State Sen, 52-56; US Rep, Mass, 59-72; alt deleg, Rep Nat Conv, 68 & 72; spec asst, Northwest Atlantic Fisheries, Dept Com, 73; mem, Defense Manpower Comn, 74-75. Bus & Prof Pos: CLU mgt training course, Equitable Life of US, 38, agt, 38-40, asst mgr, Boston Agency, 46-52; incorporator, People's Savings Bank; partner, Roger Keith & Sons, gen ins, Brockton, Mass. Mil Serv: Mass Nat Guard, 40-42; Army, Lt Col, G-3, 42-45, Col, Res. Mem: Aircraft Owners & Pilots Asn; Am Legion; VFW; Elks; Mason. Relig: Congregational. Mailing Add: 5047 Glenbrook Terr NW Washington DC 20016

KEITH, JOHN RAY (D)
b Hillsboro, Ill, June 24, 48; s Clarence Robinson Keith & Audrey Settle K; single. Educ: Eastern Ill Univ, BA, 69, MA, 74; Baylor Univ, JD, 74; Pi Sigma Alpha; Delta Theta Phi; mem bd gov, Baylor Law Sch, 74. Polit & Govt Pos: Deleg, Dem Nat Mid-Term Conf, 74. Bus & Prof Pos: Legis staff intern, Ill State Senate, 70-71, staff asst, 71-72, legal asst, 74-75; attorney, Giffin, Winning, Lindner, Newkirk, Cohen, Bodewes & Narmont, 74- Mem: Am Bar Asn; Ill State Bar Asn; Sangamon Co Bar Asn; Moose; Eagles. Legal Res: Box 14 Hillsboro IL 62049 Mailing Add: 525 W Jefferson Box 2117 Springfield IL 62705

KEITH, THOMAS JOSEPH (R)
Chmn, Robeson Co Rep Party, NC
b Lumberton, NC, May 31, 41; s Frederick Rulfs Keith & Grace Butler K; single. Educ: NC State Univ, 59-61; Campbell Col, BS, 64. Polit & Govt Pos: Secy-treas, NC State Col Rep Party, 60, vchmn, 61; organizer & vchmn, Campbell Col Rep Party, 63; alt deleg, Rep Nat Conv, 64; finance chmn, Robeson Co Rep Party, NC, 64, mem exec comt, 64-, chmn, 68-; secy-treas, Seventh Cong Dist Rep Party, 66-; mem credentials comt, NC Rep Party, 68. Bus & Prof Pos: Asst mgr, Keith Farm Co, 64-; secy-treas, Keith Realty Co, Inc, 65- Mem: Lumberton Bd Realtors; Robeson Co Farm Bur (dir); Elks (Exalted Ruler, Lumberton Lodge, 70); New River Grape Growers Asn; Lumberton Jaycees. Relig: Baptist. Mailing Add: 2100 N Elm St Lumberton NC 28358

KEITH, WILLIAM RAYMOND (D)
Mich State Rep
b Jackson, Mich, Oct 24, 29; s Raymond J Keith & Ruth Young K; m 1954 to Ruth M; c Brian, David, Betty & April. Educ: Univ Mich Sch Banking, grad; Am Inst Banking, grad. Polit & Govt Pos: Mem, Garden City Bd Educ, Mich, 66-73, Northwestern Child Guid Clin, 7 years, Garden City Hosp Corp Bd, 4 years, Garden City Housing Comn, 2 years, Garden City Econ Comn, Charter Study Comt & Schoolcraft Community Col Found; chmn, Sr Citizens' Housing Comn; Mich State Rep, 73- Bus & Prof Pos: With Mfrs Nat Bank, 53-72. Mil Serv: Army. Mem: Jaycees; Rotary; Westland CofC. Honors & Awards: Civic Award, Garden City, 61; Outstanding Young Man of the Year, Garden City Jaycees, 63; Walter Scott McLucas Mem Award for Pub Speaking, 64-66. Relig: Presbyterian. Legal Res: 5684 Henry Ruff Rd Garden City MI 48135 Mailing Add: House of Rep Capitol Bldg Lansing MI 48901

KELLAR, CHARLES L (D)
Mem, Clark Co Dem Cent Comt, Nev
b Barbados, WI, June 11, 09; s James Kellar & Lowrencha Smith K; m 1960 to Cornelia Street; c Charles L, Jr & Michael. Educ: City Col New York, Bus & MS, 33; St John's Univ, LLB, 41; Omega Psi Phi. Polit & Govt Pos: Social investr, Dept Welfare, NY, 34-36; probation officer, Domestic Rels Court, 37-40; probation officer, Kings Co Court, 40-42; comn, US Draft Bd 205, NY, 46; deleg, Dem Nat Conv, 68; mem, Clark Co Dem Cent Comt, Nev, 68-; cand for Judge Eighth Judicial Dist, Fourth Dept, 70. Bus & Prof Pos: Practicing attorney, NY, 42-; mem, Dept Immigration & Appeals, Dept of Justice, 45; practicing attorney, Nev, 65-; mem, US Court of Appeals for various circuits, 66, US Tax Court & US Supreme Court, 68. Mem: Am Bar Asn; Am Trial Lawyers Asn; Boys Club of Clark Co; NAACP; Int Elks. Honors & Awards: Legal Achievement Award, 67, Award of Merit, 60-65, Outstanding Achievement Award, 69, Thalheimer Award & Noah Griffin Award awarded to Las Vegas Br, NAACP, 68. Relig: Episcopal. Legal Res: 1133 Comstock Dr Las Vegas NV 89106 Mailing Add: 623 Carson Ave Las Vegas NV 89101

KELLEHER, EDWARD C (D)
Maine State Rep
Mailing Add: 29 Vine St Bangor ME 04401

KELLEHER, JOHN G (D)
Mass State Rep
Mailing Add: State Capitol Boston MA 02133

KELLEHER, NEIL WILLIAM (R)
NY State Assemblyman
b Troy, NY, May 9, 23; s Cornelius James Kelleher & Helen Fleming K; m 1946 to June Elizabeth Frank; c Timothy, Neil & Tracy. Educ: Lansingburgh High Sch, 4 years. Polit & Govt Pos: City alderman, Troy, NY, 53-59, mayor, 60-63; NY State Assemblyman, 67-; mem adv bd, Young Am for Freedom, currently. Mil Serv: Entered as Seaman, Navy, 42, released as PO, 45, after serv in Destroyer Unit, Pac, 42-45. Mem: DAV; Am Legion; VFW; Navy Petty Officers. Relig: Catholic. Mailing Add: 406 Sixth Ave Troy NY 12182

KELLEHER, THOMAS (D)
Judge, RI Supreme Court
b Providence, RI, Jan 4, 23; m to Mary Frances. Educ: Providence Col; Boston Univ Law Sch, 48. Polit & Govt Pos: RI State Rep, 55-66, Dep Majority Leader, RI House Rep, 65; probate judge solicitor, Smithfield; chmn, Comt on Juvenile Delinquency, 61; mem, Govt Task Force Ment Health, 63; judge, RI Supreme Court, 70- Bus & Prof Pos: Lawyer. Mil Serv: World War II, Navy, Capt. Mem: ROA. Mailing Add: RI Supreme Court State Capitol Providence RI 02903

KELLER, CHARLES F (D)
Ill State Rep
b Effingham, Ill, Jan 22, 39; s Lolami Keller & Thelma Bushue K; m 1962 to Nome Hardiek; c Charles & Kiedrah. Educ: Univ Tulsa, 61; Tau Kappa Epsilon. Polit & Govt Pos: Ill State Rep, 69- Bus & Prof Pos: Pres, Keller Develop Corp, 62; mgr, Ramada Inn, Effingham, Ill, 63- Mem: Elks; KofC; Kiwanis; CofC; Moose. Relig: Catholic. Mailing Add: Rte 2 Effingham IL 62401

KELLER, DAVID W, JR (D)
SC State Rep
Mailing Add: Box 109 Florence SC 29501

KELLER, E W (R)
Okla State Sen
b Bonners Ferry, Okla, Sept 25, 36; m 1954 to Marsha Huffman; c Trent & Rachel. Educ: Univ Okla, BA & LLB. Polit & Govt Pos: Okla State Sen, 73- Mem: Okla Co, Okla & Am Bar Asns; Am & Okla Trial Lawyers Asns. Relig: Methodist. Legal Res: 2009 Briarcliff Bethany OK 73008 Mailing Add: 2101 First Nat Ctr Oklahoma City OK 73102

KELLER, FRANK L (D)
b Mitchell, SDak, May 1, 24; s Edmund C Keller & Lillian Brunner K; m 1969 to Joanne C Smith; c Patricia Lee, Cindy Lou, Francine Lynn, Mary Lisa, Robert Lance; Carolann Theresa Smith & James Milend Smith. Educ: Seattle Univ, BS, 57. Polit & Govt Pos: Vchmn, Kitsap Co Dem Cent Comt, Wash, 59-64, Sixth Dist Cong Dem Orgn, 59-64 & Western States Dem Conf; chmn, Wash State Dem Comt, 62-67; state campaign coordr, Robert F Kennedy Orgn, 68; aide, Sen Warren G Magnuson Campaign, 68; state chmn, Anti 256 Campaign, 70; mem, Comt Reelect Albert Rosellini Gov, Wash, 72. Bus & Prof Pos: Trustee, Teamsters Local 672, 59-; sales mgr, Glaser Beverage Co, 68- Mil Serv: Entered Navy, 42, released as Shipfitter 3/C, 44, after serv in Pac & European Theatres. Mem: Elks; Eagles; VFW; Am Legion; Sales & Mkt Execs. Relig: Catholic. Mailing Add: 5427 37th Ave SW Seattle WA 98126

KELLER, MILLETT FREDERICK
b Libby, Mont, Dec 31, 15; s Frederick Herbert Keller & Maude Millett K; m 1938 to Mary A Robischon; c Millett F, Jr, Judith Ann, Jeanne Marie & Janet F. Educ: Univ Calif, Berkeley, AB, 36; Omega Delta. Polit & Govt Pos: Rep precinct committeeman, Mont, 52-56; chmn, State Welfare Bd, 52-60; co chmn, Rep Party, 56-58; Mont State Rep, 61-64 & 70-72; chmn, Mont State Rep Comt, 66-69; mem, Medicaid Adv Bd, State Welfare, 66-; mem, Rep Nat Comt, Mont, 66-69. Mem: Am Optom Asn; Great Falls Kiwanis Club; Elks; Kiwanis; Farm Bur. Relig: Catholic. Mailing Add: 3101 Fourth Ave N Great Falls MT 59401

KELLER, RONALD L (D)
Committeeman, Wash Dem State Cent Comt
b Olympia, Wash, May 20, 37; s Roy L Keller & Flora E Davis K; m 1968 to Susan Ione McKinley; c Ronda, Renee & Renita. Educ: Wash State Col, 55-56; Univ Wash, 57-59; Delta Tau Delta. Polit & Govt Pos: Deleg, Dem Nat Mid-Term Conf, 74; committeeman, Wash Dem State Cent Comt, 75- Bus & Prof Pos: Admin asst, Comnr Pub Lands, Wash, 67-; mgr, Burien CofC, 67. Mem: Burien Jaycees. Honors & Awards: Outstanding First Year Jaycee & Outstanding State Vpres, Washington State Jaycees. Mailing Add: 1319 Dickinson Olympia WA 98502

KELLEY, CLARENCE MARION
Dir, Fed Bur Invest
b Kansas City, Mo, Oct 24, 11; s Clarence Bond Kelley & Minnie Brown K; m 1937 to Ruby Dyeantha Pickett; c Mary (Mrs Edward R Dobbins, Jr) & Kent C. Educ: Univ Kans, AB, 36; Univ Mo-Kansas City Sch Law, LLB, 40; Phi Alpha Delta; Sigma Nu. Polit & Govt Pos: Spec agt in charg Birmingham off, Fed Bur Invest, 57-60, Memphis off, 60-61; chief police, Kansas City, Mo, 61-73; Dir, Fed Bur Invest, 73- Mil Serv: Navy, 44-46. Mem: Int Asn Chiefs Police; Mo Chiefs Police Asn; Mo Peace Officers Asn; Rotary; CofC Gtr Kansas City. Honors & Awards: J Edgar Hoover Gold Medal for Outstanding Job, VFW, 70. Relig: Christian Church. Mailing Add: Fed Bur Invest Ninth & Pennsylvania Ave NW Washington DC 20535

KELLEY, CLARENCE R (R)
Ind State Sen
Mailing Add: 61551 Bremen Hwy Mishawaka IN 46544

KELLEY, DONALD E (R)
Justice, Colo Supreme Court
b McCook, Nebr, Jan 29, 08; s Charles W Kelley & Elsie Aston K; m 1930 to Georgia Pyne; c John Michael & Donald Pyne. Educ: Kearney Mil Acad; Univ Nebr Col Law, LLB, 30; Phi Delta Phi; Delta Upsilon. Polit & Govt Pos: Asst attorney gen, Nebr, 39-41; attorney, Red Willow Co, 42-44; US Dist Attorney, Colo, 53-59; attorney, Denver City & Co, 59-61; Colo State Sen, 63-67; Justice, Colo Supreme Court, 67- Bus & Prof Pos: Gen practice of law, McCook, Nebr, 30-38 & 42-45; mem law firm of Kelley, Inman, Flynn & Coffee, Denver, Colo, 62-67. Mem: Am Cancer Soc; Colo Bar Asn (bd gov); Nebr & Am Bar Asns; Am Law Inst. Relig: Episcopal. Mailing Add: 3144 S Columbine St Denver CO 80210

KELLEY, DOROTHY B (R)
Maine State Rep
Mailing Add: Machias ME 04654

KELLEY, FRANK (R)
Ariz State Rep
b 1923. Polit & Govt Pos: Aide to former US Sen Frank Carlson, Kans, formerly; Ariz State Rep, 65- Bus & Prof Pos: Former newspaper ed; pub rels dir, Good Samaritan Hosp, Phoenix. Mailing Add: Box 2989 Phoenix AZ 85006

KELLEY, FRANK J (D)
Attorney Gen, Mich.
b Detroit, Mich, Dec 31, 24; s Frank E Kelley & Grace Spears K; m 1945 to Josephine Palmisano; c Karen Anne, Frank E, II & Jane Frances. Educ: Univ Detroit Sch Com & Finance, 48, Law Sch, JD, 51; vpres, Student Body; Moot Court; Law Jour; Alpha Kappa Psi; Gamma Eta Gamma. Polit & Govt Pos: Pub adminr, Alpena Co, Mich, 56, mem bd supvr, 58-61; city attorney, Alpena, 58-61; Attorney Gen, Mich, 62-; chmn, Mich Munic Finance Comn, chmn, Corp Tax Appeal Bd, mem, State Admin Bd, Judges & State Employees Retirement Systs & Judicial Conf of Mich, currently; deleg, Dem Nat Conv, 68. Bus & Prof Pos: Attorney, Detroit, until 54; attorney, Alpena, 54-61; instr real estate law, Univ Mich Exten Serv; instr econ, Alpena Community Col. Mem: Nat Asn Attorneys Gen (pres, 67-); Midwest Regional Conf of Attorneys Gen (chmn); Northeast Mich Child Guid Clin (dir & pres); Northeast Mich Cath Family Serv; KofC (Advocate of Coun 529). Relig: Roman Catholic. Legal Res: 4267 Mar-Moor Dr Lansing MI 48917 Mailing Add: The Law Bldg Lansing MI 48913

KELLEY, JAMES (D)
Mem, Dem Nat Comt, Pa
Mailing Add: 231 Westmoreland Ave Greensburg PA 15601

KELLEY, JAMES R (D)
Pa State Sen
Mailing Add: 104 W Otterman St Greensburg PA 15601

KELLEY, JANE POLLARD (D)
NH State Rep
b Northampton, Mass, Feb 7, 26; d John Kingsley Pollard & Madeline Sullivan P; m 1953 to Frank Manton Kelley; c David, John, Melissa & Peggy. Educ: Skidmore Col, 43-46; Univ Md Overseas Prog, Alconbury, Eng, 66-67; Northeastern Univ, 67-68. Polit & Govt Pos: Committeewoman, Rockingham Co Dem Party, 72-74, chmn, 74-; deleg, NH Const Conv, 74-; mem exec comt, NH Dem State Comt, 74-; NH State Rep, Dist 12, 75- Bus & Prof Pos: Exec dir, NH Seacoast Regional Develop Asn, 72-74. Publ: Auth & ed, Seacoast Region Guide, NH Seacoast Regional Develop Asn, 74; auth, Churchamericard, United Church Herald, 11/68; auth, The only living heart donor, Boston Globe Sunday Mag, 11/68; plus weekly newspaper column. Mem: Daughters of Potato Famine, Inc (Supreme High Spud); Great Bay Sch & Training Ctr (trustee); Seacoast Vis Nurse Asn (dir, 72-); Am Legion Auxiliary; Am Red Cross (dir vols, Spangdahlem AFB, Ger). Relig: Independent. Legal Res: 179 N Shore Rd Hampton NH 03842 Mailing Add: PO Box 1 Hampton NH 03842

KELLEY, PETER STEPHEN (D)
b Houlton, Maine, Dec 3, 40; s Carroll E Kelley & Carolyn M Wilder K; m 1964 to Gail Jean MacAllister; c Jason. Educ: Phillips Exeter Acad, grad, 59; Harvard Col, BA, 63; Am Univ Law Sch, JD, 66; Hasty Pudding Inst; Varsity Club; DU Club. Polit & Govt Pos: Legis & press asst to Congressman Will Hathaway, 65-66; advance man for Sen Edmund Muskie Vice Presidential Campaign, 68; mem, Caribou City Coun, 68-70; chmn, Maine Mining Comn, formerly; complaint justice; disclosure comnr, Maine State Rep, 71-73; alt deleg, Dem Nat Conv, 72; Maine State Sen, 73-74. Bus & Prof Pos: Bd dirs, Washburn Trust Co. Mil Serv: Entered as Pvt, Maine Army Nat Guard, 66, released as 2nd Lt, 70, after serv in Caribou Guard Unit. Mem: Am Bar Asn; Citizens' Adv Comt to Bur of Rehabilitation; Kiwanis (vpres); Caribou CofC (bd dirs). Honors & Awards: Nominated Outstanding Young Man, 69; Selected as One of Two Outstanding Legislators in 105th Legis, Eagleton Inst Polit. Relig: Universalist. Mailing Add: 16 Teague St Caribou ME 04736

KELLEY, PHILLIP BARRY (D)
Ala State Rep
b Guntersville, Ala, Jan 5, 47; s Robert Milford Kelley & Beatrice Smith K; m 1966 to Betty Louise Pearce; c Phillip Brandon & Warren Christopher. Educ: Univ Ala, BSAE, 69; Lambda Chi Alpha. Polit & Govt Pos: Mem city coun, Guntersville, Ala, 72-74; Ala State Rep, Dist 26, 74- Bus & Prof Pos: Assoc engr, Northrop Corp, Huntsville, Ala, 69-74; sr engr, Northrop Servs, Inc, 74- Publ: Auth & co-auth, Various tech documents, Northrop Corp & NASA. Mem: Am Inst Aeronaut & Astronaut; Northrop Mgt Club; Ala Environ Qual Asn. Relig: Baptist. Mailing Add: Mountain Crest Dr Rte 2 Box 486 Guntersville AL 35976

KELLEY, RAMONA M (D)
Alaska State Rep
Mailing Add: 5214 East 24th Ave Anchorage AK 99504

KELLEY, RICHARD CHARLES (D)
VChairperson, King Co Dem Cent Comt, Wash
b Salt Lake City, Utah, July 8, 50; s Dr Vincent C Kelley & Dorothy McArthur K; m 1971 to Susan E Richmond. Educ: Harvard Univ, BA cum laude, 70; Univ Wash, MPA, 75. Polit & Govt Pos: Staff aide, Congressman Brock Adams, Wash, 70; chief dep auditor, Clark Co, 71-72; vchairperson, King Co Dem Cent Comt, 72-; deleg, Dem Nat Mid-Term Conf, 74; drug comnr, Seattle-King Co, 74-75; ed, King Co Democrat, 74-75. Bus & Prof Pos: Research dir, Soren Northwest, Inc, 73; asst producer, Pub Affairs I-9, KCTS-TV, 74; manpower planning prog coordr, Seattle, Wash, 75. Publ: Auth, Open government and open politics, Seattle Post-Intelligencer, 3/75; auth, Polls apart, monthly column, King Co Democrat, 74-75. Mem: Am Soc Pub Admin; Wash Environ Coun; Cent Seattle Community Coun Fedn. Honors & Awards: Harvard Nat Scholarship, 67; J Allen Smith Fel, Univ Wash, 74. Relig: Catholic. Mailing Add: 2524 Boyer Ave E Seattle WA 98102

KELLEY, THOMAS PAUL (D)
Dem Nat Committeeman, Nebr
b Omaha, Nebr, Nov 6, 19; s Paul Kelley & Ann Maher K; m 1944 to Maxene Clausen; wid; c Michael A. Educ: Creighton Univ, BSC, 42; Creighton Law Sch, LLD, 50; Mil Fraternity. Polit & Govt Pos: Dep Co Attorney, Douglas Co, Nebr, 53-56; Dem Nat Committeeman, Nebr, 69-; deleg, Dem Nat Conv, 72. Bus & Prof Pos: Sr partner, Kelley, Grant, Costello & Dugan, 50-71; sr partner, Kelley & Kelley, 71- Mil Serv: Entered as Lt, Army, 42, released as Maj, 46, after serv in Armoured Div, ETO, 45-46; Silver Star; Bronze Star. Mem: Am Bar Asn; Nat Asn Trial Attorneys; Am Legion; Eagles; KofC. Relig: Catholic. Legal Res: 8728 Broadmoor Dr Omaha NE 68124 Mailing Add: 7134 Pacific St Omaha NE 68106

KELLEY, YING LEE (D)
Councilmember, Berkeley, Calif
b Shanghai, China, Jan 21, 32; d Tsung-Chi Lee & Da-Tsien Tsu L; m 1963 to John L Kelley; c Max Lee & Sara Ying. Educ: Univ Calif, Berkeley, BA, 53, teaching credential, 64. Polit & Govt Pos: Deleg, Dem Nat Conv, 72; councilmember, Berkeley, Calif, 73- Mem: Am Fedn Teachers; Women for Peace; Asian-Am Community Alliance; Asian Polit Caucus. Legal Res: 862 Euclid Berkeley CA 94708 Mailing Add: 1711 University Berkeley CA 94703

KELLIHER, WALTER JAMES (D)
Mayor, Malden, Mass
b Malden, Mass, Feb 9, 13; s Hugh Cornelius Kelliher & Catherine Meaney K; m 1942 to Agnes Mary Lynch; c Nancy Kathleen. Educ: Northeastern Univ, LLB, 40. Polit & Govt Pos: Mem, Malden Sch Comt, Mass, 52-55, chmn, 54; mayor, Malden, 58-59 & 62-; deleg-at-lg, Dem Nat Conv, 64; mem, Malden City Dem Comt, 64-, chmn, 71-72; State Dem Committeeman, Fourth Middlesex Dist, 64- Mil Serv: Entered as Yeoman 3/C, Navy, 42, released as Lt(jg), 46, after serv in Staff, Comdr Naval Forces, ETO, 43-45; Victory Medal; Am Theater & ETO Ribbons; Lt(sg) (Ret), Naval Res. Mem: Mass Trial Lawyers Asn; KofC; Eagles; Kiwanis; Am Legion. Relig: Roman Catholic. Mailing Add: 99 Woodland Rd Malden MA 02148

KELLIS, JAMES GEORGE (D)
Chmn, Fairfield Dem Town Comt, Conn
b Greece, July 6, 17; s George John Kellis & Marina Loizos K; m 1942 to Sophie John Mourges; c John George & Michael J. Educ: Georgetown Univ, BA, 47, MA, 53, PhD, 63. Polit & Govt Pos: Comnr, Redevelop Comn, Fairfield, Conn, 63-66; vchmn, Housatonic Community Col Coun, 65-; chmn, Fairfield Improv Comn, 66-67; chmn, Fairfield Dem Town Comt, 67-; cand, US Rep, Fourth Cong Dist, 74. Bus & Prof Pos: Adj prof polit sci, Univ Detroit, 56-61; mgr opers res, Sikorsky Aircraft, United Aircraft Corp, 61-; lectr polit sci, Fairfield Univ, 62- Mil Serv: Entered as Pvt, Army, 36, released as Col, Air Force, 60, after serv in Third Air Force, Off Strategic Serv, Cent Intel Agency, NATO, Joint Chief Staff & Dept Air Force; Legion of Merit with Cluster; Bronze Star; Purple Heart. Mem: Am Polit Sci Asn; Am Econ Asn; Air Force Asn. Relig: Eastern Orthodox. Mailing Add: 175 Godfrey Rd Fairfield CT 06430

KELLOFF, GEORGE (D)
Mem, Dem State Exec Comt, Colo
b Segundo, Colo, Feb 22, 21; s Najib Kelloff & Susan Bacash K; m 1950 to Edna Mae Cunico; c Susan Renee & George Karl. Educ: Trinidad Jr Col, AA; Adams State Col, BA; Phi Beta Kappa. Polit & Govt Pos: City councilman, Aguilar, Colo, 47-49; committeeman, Rio Grande Co, 65-68; chmn, Rio Grande Co Dem Party, 69-72; mem, Dem State Exec Comt, Fourth Cong Dist, currently. Bus & Prof Pos: Pres, Kelloff Enterprises, Inc, 64- Mil Serv: Entered as A/S, Navy, 42, released as Chief Yeoman, 46, after serv in Asiatic & Pac Theatres, 42-46. Mem: VFW; Am Legion; Ment Health Clin; Ment Health Ctr Bd; CofC. Relig: Catholic. Mailing Add: RR 3 Two Miles West Monte Vista CO 81144

KELLOGG, JEANNINE GEORGE (D)
Chairperson, Antelope Co Dem Party, Nebr
b Orchard, Nebr, Dec 31, 28; d Joseph George & Jennie Saloum G; m 1948 to Bernard Kellogg; c Georgann (Mrs Ray Arp), Sue (Mrs Greg Wettlaufer), Annette, Patrick, Michael & Katherine. Educ: Orchard Pub High Sch, grad, 47. Polit & Govt Pos: Chairwoman, Antelope Co Dem Party, Nebr, 59-70, chairperson, 70- Bus & Prof Pos: Dairy sanitarian, Orchard Dairy Prod, Nebr, 68- Mem: Antelope Co Bi-Centennial (chmn, 73-); Am Legion Auxiliary; Orchard Libr Bd (secy-treas, 57-); Antelope Co Hist Soc. Honors & Awards: Number One Club, Nebr Gov, 71. Relig: Catholic. Mailing Add: RR 2 Orchard NE 68764

KELLOGG, MARY JOAN (D)
b East St Louis, Ill, Feb 12, 25; d Benjamin Frank Beller & Catherine Connors B; m 1947 to Robert Ray Kellogg; c Robert R, Jr, Marian, Kevin, Melanie & John. Educ: Linn High Sch, Mo, grad, 43. Polit & Govt Pos: Committeewoman & secy, Osage Co Dem Cent Comt, Mo, formerly. Relig: Catholic. Mailing Add: Box 168 Linn MO 65051

KELLY, ANITA PALERMO (D)
Pa State Rep
b Ozone Park, Long Island, NY; d Peter Palermo & Beatrice Valenti P; m to William J Kelly (deceased). Educ: Parochial & pub schs, Long Island, NY & studied abroad. Polit & Govt Pos: Currency counter, Fed Reserve Bank, 13 years; Dem committeewoman, 34th Ward & mem, 34th Ward Dem Exec Comt, Pa, 26 years; mem bd dirs & trustee, Ctr for Child Guid; Pa State Rep, 63-, Dem chmn comt health & welfare & mem prof licensure comt & ethics comt, Pa State Senate, currently, mem joint state govt comt task force on state licensing of professions & occup & human serv, mem state adv coun for comprehensive health planning & mem develop disabilities planning & adv coun, currently. Honors & Awards: Humanitarian Award for Outstanding Contrib & Dedication to People of Philadelphia, 68; First Woman Recipient of Man of the Year Award, Max Slepin Am Legion Post 896, 69; decorated by Ital Consul Gen with Star of Solidarity & Title of Cavaliere, 70. Mailing Add: Capitol Bldg Harrisburg PA 17120

KELLY, ANNE CATHERINE (D)
Committeewoman, NY State Dem Comt Buffalo, NY, Mar 6, 16; d John Patrick Donohue & Elizabeth Edwards D; m to Thomas E Kelly; c Maureen Anne, Michael Thomas, Edward John, Kevin Joseph & Theresa Elizabeth. Educ: State Univ NY, 34-37. Polit & Govt Pos: Alt deleg, NY State Dem Conv, 66; deleg, Eighth Judicial Dist Conv, 66-74; Erie Co committeewoman, 27th Dist, 67-74; committeewoman, NY State Dem Comt, 70-, mem exec bd, 74-75. Bus & Prof Pos: Teacher, Sisters of Mercy Schs, Buffalo, NY, 58-64; clerk, City Hall, Buffalo, 64-67, secy to Comptroller George D O'Connell, 67-69, coun clerk, 69-75. Mem: Ladies Guild of Monsignor Nash Coun; South Side Women's Dem Club (bd dirs); Mercy League of Mercy Hosp (bd dirs). Honors & Awards: Woman of Year Award, South Side Women's Dem Club, 69. Relig: Catholic.
Legal Res: 45 Weyand St Buffalo NY 14210 Mailing Add: 47 Marine Dr Buffalo NY 14202

KELLY, ARTHUR JOHN (D)
Treas, West Haven Dem Town Comt, Conn
b West Haven, Conn, Sept 9, 22; s Joseph F Kelly & Catherine McDermott K; m 1948 to Mary Jane Mansfield; c Michael John, Mary Jane, Marcella Jean & Arthur John, Jr. Educ:

West Haven High Sch, Conn, grad. Polit & Govt Pos: Mem, Develop Comn, West Haven, Conn, 52-54, chmn, Bd of Park Comn, 54-60, second selectman, 58-59, Redevelop Comnr, 59-61 & Police Comnr, 68-; mem, West Haven Dem Town Comt, 53-, dist chmn, 53-59, treas, 65-; deleg, Conn State Dem Conv, 58-68; alt deleg, Dem Nat Conv, 68. Bus & Prof Pos: Pres, Joseph F Kelly Co, Inc, Gen Contractors, 52- Mil Serv: Pvt, Army, 44-45, serv in 102nd Inf Unit. Mem: Asn Gen Contractors; New Haven Gen Contractors Asn; KofC; Elks; Knights of St Patrick. Honors & Awards: Elk of the Year Award for Community Serv, 58; Boy Scouts Award for Youth Serv, 58; Gold Bat Award, West Haven Twi-Light Baseball League, 64; Jimmy Fund Award for Youth Serv, 68; Knights of St Patrick Community Serv Award, 68. Relig: Catholic. Mailing Add: 137 Main St West Haven CT 06516

KELLY, ASA, JR (R)
Mem, Grant Co Rep Party, NMex
b Coopersville, Mich, June 10, 22; s Asa Kelly, Sr & Hazel Easterly K; m 1945 to Frances Goodall; c Dianne (Mrs Hennessy), Bruce, Michael, Dale & Lynn. Educ: Mich State Univ, BA, 47; Univ Mich Law Sch, LLB, 51; Pi Mu Epsilon. Polit & Govt Pos: Asst prosecutor, Ottawa Co, Grand Haven, Mich, 55-66; chmn, Grant Co Rep Party, Silver City, NMex, 69-71, vchmn, 71-72, mem, currently. Mil Serv: Entered as Sgt, Air Force, 42, released as Sgt, 46, after serv in 4th Air Force, US, 42-46. Mem: Mich & NMex Bar Asns; Am Legion. Relig: Methodist. Legal Res: 510 W Yankee Silver City NM 88061 Mailing Add: Box 1036 Silver City NM 88061

KELLY, BILL (DFL)
Minn State Rep
Mailing Add: 430 Tenth Ave N East Grand Forks MN 56721

KELLY, DANIEL A (D)
Del State Rep
Mailing Add: 101 Brookside Ave Wilmington DE 19805

KELLY, E KEVIN (R)
Iowa State Sen
b Sioux City, Iowa, Jan 22, 43; s John C Kelly & Dorothy Hagan K; m 1966 to Judith Ann Gurney; c Timory Lynn & Tracy Ann. Educ: Gonzaga Univ, BA, 65; Univ SDak Law Sch, JD, 68. Polit & Govt Pos: Nat committeeman, Young Rep Iowa, 68-70, state chmn, 70-; Iowa State Rep, 71-73; Iowa State Sen, 73- Bus & Prof Pos: Asst co-attorney, Woodbury Co, Iowa, 68-71; assoc attorney, Davis, Jacobs & Gaul, 68- Mem: Am & Iowa Bar Asns; Sioux City Young Lawyers Club; Sioux City Exchange Club; Sioux City Press Club. Relig: Catholic. Mailing Add: 2816 Sunset Circle Sioux City IA 51104

KELLY, EDNA FLANNERY (D)
b East Hampton, NY, Aug 20, 06; d Patrick J Flannery & Mary Ellen F; m to Edward L Kelly, wid; c William E, II & Maura Patricia; eight grandchildren. Educ: Hunter Col, BA, 28. Hon Degrees: LHD, Russell Sage Col, 63. Polit & Govt Pos: Assoc research dir, Dem Party, in NY State Legis, 43, chief research dir, 44-49; deleg, 18th Gen Assembly, UN; mem exec comt, Kings Co Dem Party, 44-66; Dem Nat Committeewoman, 56-68; US Rep, NY, 49-68; deleg, Dem Nat Conv, 52-68. Honors & Awards: President's Centennial Award, Hunter Col for role as legislator, work in int coop & help for econ disadvantaged; Mother Gerard Pilan Award for Model Christian Leadership in Home, Career & Pub Life, 62. Honors & Awards: Hunter Col Hall of Fame, Alumni Asn Hunter Col, 73. Relig: Roman Catholic. Mailing Add: 134 Meadow Rd Briarcliff Manor NY 10510

KELLY, EUGENE (D)
Chmn, Tioga Co Dem Comt, Pa
b Philadelphia, Pa, Aug 21, 31; s Eugene Kelly & Theresa Gallagher K; m 1951 to Mary Charlene Bebble; c Eugene, III, Colleen Anne, Patrick Michael & John Charles. Polit & Govt Pos: Campaign mgr, Citizens for Shapp for Gov, 66; Dem committeeman, South Union Twp, Tioga Co, Pa, 66-68; campaign mgr, State Senate, 23rd Sen Dist, formerly; coordr, Shapp for Gov Comt, 70; campaign mgr, State Sen, 72; chmn, Tioga Co Dem Comt, 72- Bus & Prof Pos: Sales rep, Can Dry Bottling, Williamsport, Pa & Lemmon Pharmaceutical Col, Sellersville; supvr, Pa Dept Labor & Indust. Mil Serv: Entered as Pvt, Army, 49, released as Sgt, 52, after serv in 2nd Inf Div, Korea, 49-51; Combat Inf Badge; Purple Heart, Bronze Star; Good Conduct Medal; Presidential Citation. Mem: VFW. Relig: Catholic. Mailing Add: Bur Occup & Indust Safety 416 Pine St Williamsport PA 17701

KELLY, FLOYD EUGENE (D)
Chmn, Logan Co Dem Party, Ill
b Carrollton, Ill, July 23, 14; s Fred E Kelly & Lillie Cunningham K; m 1941 to Lucile M Grant; c James, Joseph & John. Educ: St John High Sch, Carrollton, Ill, grad. Polit & Govt Pos: Precinct committeeman, Logan Co Dem Party, Ill, 72-, chmn, 74- Bus & Prof Pos: Bus mgr, Dept Corrections, Ill, 74-75. Mem: Lions; KofC; Ancient Hibernian. Relig: Catholic. Mailing Add: 107 N Vine Mt Pulaski IL 62548

KELLY, GARNETT A (R)
Mo State Rep
Mailing Add: Rte 2 Norwood MO 65717

KELLY, JAMES ANTHONY, JR (D)
Mass State Sen
b Worcester, Mass, May 11, 26; s James Anthony Kelly & Florence Adams K; m 1948 to Elisabeth M Allen; c James, Thomas, Michael, Robert, Paul, Jean & Maureen. Educ: Becker Jr Col, Worcester, Mass, 46-47; Clark Univ, BBA, 50. Polit & Govt Pos: Mem sch comt, Leicester, Mass, 48-51; Mass State Rep, 58-64; Mass State Sen, Fourth Dist, 64-, chmn ways & means comt, Mass State Senate, 70- Bus & Prof Pos: Owner, James A Kelly, Inc, CPA, currently. Mil Serv: Entered as A/S, Navy, 44, released as Aer M 2/C, 46, after serv in Weather Dept, Asiatic-Pac Theatre, 45-46; Good Conduct Medal; Am Theatre Medal; World War II Victory Medal; Asiatic-Pac Theatre Medal. Publ: Home rule, Selectman's Mag, 67; Computer law, Boston Bar, 68. Mem: Am Inst of CPA; Mass Asn of CPA; Am Acct Asn; VFW; Am Legion. Honors & Awards: Citation, Mass Dept of Polish Am Vet. Relig: Catholic. Legal Res: 1186 Stafford St Oxford MA 01540 Mailing Add: State House Boston MA 02133

KELLY, JAMES BENNETT, III (R)
Pa State Rep
b Pittsburgh, Pa, May 28, 41; s James Bennett Kelly, Jr & Margaret Yates K; m 1968 to Jeanne Denise Cooley; c James B, IV. Educ: Va Polytech Inst, BS, 63; Am Inst Foreign Trade, BFT, 64; Tau Kappa Alpha; various social clubs. Polit & Govt Pos: Spec asst to US Sen Richard Schweiker, 68-70; Pa State Rep, 70- Bus & Prof Pos: Int contracting engr, Chicago Bridge & Iron Co, Chicago & Europe, 64-68. Mailing Add: Capitol Bldg Harrisburg PA 17120

KELLY, JOHN BARNES (R)
Chmn, Logan Co Rep Cent Comt, Ohio
b West Liberty, Ohio, Aug 29, 25; s John Davis Kelly & Ruth Barnes K; m 1953 to Joan Louise Pearson; c John Pearson, Patricia Joan, Mary Margaret & Kathryn Ann. Educ: Ohio State Univ, 46-51, BS & LLB; Phi Alpha Delta; Sigma Nu. Polit & Govt Pos: Prosecuting attorney, Logan Co, Ohio, 53-56; chmn, Logan Co Rep Cent Comt, 56- Mil Serv: Entered as Cadet, Air Force, 43, released as 2nd Lt, 46. Mem: Mason; Shrine. Relig: Episcopal. Mailing Add: 121 E Columbus Ave Bellefontaine OH 43311

KELLY, JOHN BRENDEN, JR (D)
Councilman-At-Lg, Philadelphia, Pa
b Philadelphia, Pa, May 24, 27; s John B Kelly & Margaret Major K; m 1954 to Mary Freeman; c Ann F, Susan E, Maura G, Elizabeth B, John B, III & Margaret C. Educ: Univ Pa, AB in Econ, 50; Kappa Sigma; Varsity Club. Polit & Govt Pos: Councilman-at-lg, Philadelphia, Pa, currently; chmn, Nonpartisan Register & Vote Comt of Philadelphia. Bus & Prof Pos: Pres, John B Kelly, Inc, 60-; mem bd dirs, Lincoln Nat Bank. Mil Serv: Seaman, Naval Res, 45-46; Ens, Naval Res, 51-53. Mem: Bricklayers Union; Employing Bricklayers Asn of Deleware Co; Police Athletic League (chmn); US Olympic Comt; Nat Asn Amateur Oarsmen. Honors & Awards: Young Man of Achievement Award, Golden Slipper Square Club, 57; Outstanding Young Man of Year Award, Pa Jr CofC, 60 & 61; Am Heritage Found Award, 60 & 64; Philadelphia Zionist Award, 64; Brotherhood Award, Jewish War Vet, 66. Relig: Roman Catholic. Legal Res: 28G Plaza Apts 18th & Parkway Philadelphia PA 19103 Mailing Add: 1720 Cherry St Philadelphia PA 19103

KELLY, JOHN HENRY (D)
State Treas, WVa
b Kanawha Co, WVa, Feb 5, 22; s Lewis H Kelly & Rebecca Morrow K (both deceased); m 1949 to Theodocia Romaine Hardin; c Karen. Educ: Morris Harvey Col, BS, 49; Int Acct Soc of Chicago. Polit & Govt Pos: Dir finance, WVa Dept Agr, 48-60; State Treas, WVa, 61-; alt deleg, Dem Nat Conv, 68; alt deleg, Dem Nat Mid-Term Conf, 74. Mil Serv: Entered as Seaman 1/C, 45. Mem: Nat Asn State Auditors, Comptrollers & Treas (vpres, currently); Charleston Optimists; Charleston Jr CofC; Odd Fellows. Relig: Baptist. Mailing Add: State Capitol Charleston WV 25305

KELLY, JOHN MARTIN (D)
b Chelsea, Mass, Oct 1, 14; s James B A Kelly & Elizabeth B A Ford K; m 1938 to Esther Elizabeth Ladenburg; c Joseph James, Patricia Elizabeth, Mary Ann & John Michael. Educ: NMex Sch Mines, BS in Mining Eng, 36, Degree Petroleum Engr, 39. Hon Degrees: DSc, NMex Inst Mining & Technol, 63. Polit & Govt Pos: Mem & exec dir, NMex Oil Conserv Comn, 41-45; dir, NMex Bur Mines & Mineral Resources, 41-45; State Geologist, NMex, 41-45; coordr mines in NMex, War Prod Bd, 41-45; mem, Nat Coun Petroleum Regulatory Authorities under Petroleum Admin for War, 41-45; consult & mineral adv, NMex State Land Off, 45-61; Asst Secy of Interior for Mineral Resources, US Dept Interior, 61-65; US deleg, Energy & Petroleum Comts, Orgn Econ Coop & Develop, Paris, France, 61-65, mem adv comt to US deleg, Petroleum Comt, 65-; US deleg, NATO Petroleum Planning Comt, Paris, France, 61-65; chmn, US deleg, Second Petroleum Conf on Asia & the Far East, Econ Comn for Asia & the Far East, UN, Teheran, Iran, 62 & Third Petroleum Conf on Asia & the Far East, Tokyo, Japan, 65; mem, Nat Petroleum Coun, 65-; consult to Secy of Interior, 65- Bus & Prof Pos: Mining engr, Rosedale Gold Mines, 36; mine chemist, Am Metal Co, 36-37; petroleum engr, Lea Co Operators Co, 37-41; petroleum consult, 45-61 & 65-; pres, Elk Oil Co, 45-61; dir, Yucca Water Co, 45-61. Mem: Small Bus Admin (adv bd); Am Inst Mining Engrs; Am Asn Petroleum Geologists; Geol Soc Am (fel). Relig: Roman Catholic; Knight Grand Comdr, Holy Sepulchre; Knight of St Gregory. Mailing Add: Box 310 Roswell NM 88201

KELLY, LELONA KAY (LEE) (D)
Chmn, Ford Co Dem Party, Kans
b Beloit, Kans, Oct 9, 45; d M F Baker & Nadine Smith B; m 1965 to Michael Donald Kelly; c Sean R & Craig M. Educ: Col of Emporia, 63-66; Alpha Psi Omega. Polit & Govt Pos: Chmn, Ford Co Dem Party, Kans, 72-; mem state comt, Kans Dem Party, 72-; deleg, Dem Nat Mid-Term Conf, 74; staff mem, Bill Roy for Senate Campaign, 74. Bus & Prof Pos: Real estate salesperson, Dodge City, Kans, 73- Mailing Add: 1400 Ave C Dodge City KS 67801

KELLY, MARGARET BOYER (R)
Pres, Wyo Fedn Rep Women
b Torrington, Wyo, Nov 27, 29; d Gerald Deloss Boyer & Violet Bristol B; m 1951 to Sam Kelly, Jr; c Kurt. Educ: Univ Wyo, BS; Delta Delta Delta. Polit & Govt Pos: Pres, Rawlins Rep Women, Wyo, 62-64; mem, Carbon Co Rep Cent Comt, 62-72; committeewoman, Carbon Co Rep Party, 67-72; deleg, Rep Nat Conv, 72; mem, Wyo State Rep Cent Comt, 72-, vchmn, 73-, acting chmn, 75; pres, Wyo Fedn Rep Women, 72-; bd mem, Nat Fedn Rep Women, 72- Bus & Prof Pos: Secy-treas, Kelly Oil Co & Kelly Realty Co, 60- Mem: Soroptimists; PEO; Cath Womens Orgn-Deanery. Relig: Catholic. Legal Res: 213 E Brooks Rawlins WY 82301 Mailing Add: Box 1016 Rawlins WY 82301

KELLY, PATRICIA (TISH) (D)
NDak State Rep
Mailing Add: State Capitol Bismarck ND 58501

KELLY, PETER DILLON, III (D)
Exec Dir, Calif Dem State Cent Comt
b Pasadena, Calif, July 30, 48; s Peter D Kelly, Jr & Constance Purkiss K; single. Educ: Calif State Univ, Fullerton, BA, 72; Southwestern Univ Sch Law, 72-, mem & articles ed, Law Review, 74-; Phi Sigma Kappa. Polit & Govt Pos: Field dep, US Rep Charles Wilson, Calif, 71; finance dir, Calif State Cent Comt, 71-73 & exec dir, 75-; exec dir, Southern Calif Dem Party, Los Angeles, 73-75. Publ: Co-auth, Reform of the delegate selection process to Democratic National Conventions: 1964 to the present, Southwestern Univ Law Rev, Vol 7, 74-75. Relig: Roman Catholic. Legal Res: 269 S Lafayette Park Pl 436 Los Angeles CA 90057 Mailing Add: 6022 Wilshire Blvd Suite 201 Los Angeles CA 90036

KELLY, PHYLLIS MATHEIS (R)
Pres, NY Fedn Rep Women
b Buffalo, NY, May 7, 21; d Charles William Matheis & Florence Schlegen M; m 1946 to James Edward Kelly; c James E, III, Maureen, Colleen & Kathleen. Educ: Univ Buffalo, BA,

42; Phi Beta Kappa; Cap & Gown; Theta Chi; pres, Panhellenic Council. Polit & Govt Pos: Exec secy, Citizens for Eisenhower, Erie Co, NY, 51-52; co-chmn, Erie Co Citizens for Rockefeller, 58; founder, 20 Rep Women's Clubs, Erie Co, 61-; asst chmn, Erie Co Rep Comt, 61-; mem, NY State Rep Platform Comt, 66; coordr, Eighth Judicial Dist Women for Nixon-Agnew, 68; chmn, Erie Co Women for Nixon-Agnew, 68; vchmn, NY State Citizens for Javits, 68; campaign chmn, Nat Fedn Rep Women's Clubs, 70-71; pres, NY Fedn Rep Women, currently. Bus & Prof Pos: Ed, Bell Aircraft News, Bell Aircraft Corp, NY, 43-45. Mem: Women's Exec (pres); Buffalo Philharmonic; Zonta Club Amherst; Erie Co Fedn Women's Rep Clubs (pres); NY State Fedn Women's Rep Clubs. Honors & Awards: Erie Co Rep Woman of Year, 65. Relig: Roman Catholic. Mailing Add: 38 Raycroft Blvd Snyder NY 14226

KELLY, RALPH D (R)
Nebr State Sen
b Grand Island, Nebr, Dec 6, 20; s Martin J Kelly & Elva M Howard K; m 1941 to Patricia J Stone; c Michael R, Erin C & Michele A. Educ: Univ Nebr Col Eng, 39-40; Utah State Col, 43. Polit & Govt Pos: Mem, Grand Island Civil Serv Comn, 70-72; Nebr State Sen, 73- Bus & Prof Pos: Salesman, Kelly Supply Co, Grand Island, Nebr, 47-55, sales mgr, 55-60, vpres sales, 60-65, exec vpres, 65-; dir finance, Warden Mfg Co, 62-65; secy-treas, Philips Homes, Inc, Grand Island, 63; vpres sales, W & F Machine Works, 69. Mil Serv: Entered as Pvt, Army Air Corps, 42, released as 1st Lt, 45, after serv in Air Transport Command, China-Burma-India, 44-45; Two Air Medals; Distinguished Flying Cross; Battle Stars, Burma & China. Mem: Am Legion; VFW; Jaycees; CofC; Nebr Wholesale Plumbing & Heating Supply Asn. Honors & Awards: Boss of the Year Award, Grand Island Jr CofC, 58. Relig: Roman Catholic. Legal Res: 2015 W John St Grand Island NE 68801 Mailing Add: State Capitol Lincoln NE 68509

KELLY, RICHARD (R)
US Rep, Fla
b Atlanta, Ga, July 31, 24; s Frank W Kelly & Bertha Doner K; m 1960 to Loraine Miller; c Sherri & John. Educ: Colo State Col Educ, AB, 49; Vanderbilt Col Law, 49; Univ Fla, JD, 52; Col State Trial Judges, Reno, Nev, cert of grad, 71. Polit & Govt Pos: City attorney, Zephyrhills, Fla, formerly; sr asst to US Dist Attorney, Southern Dist Fla, 56-59; circuit judge, Sixth Judicial Dist, 60-74; US Rep, Fla, 75- Mil Serv: Entered as Pvt, Marine Corps, 42, released as Cpl, 46, after serv in 2nd Div, Cent Pac. Publ: Auth, A judge sees prison from the inside, St Petersburg Times, 1/71. Mem: Eagles; VFW; Am Legion; Lions Int. Relig: Presbyterian. Legal Res: 1712 Pine Tree Rd Holiday FL 33589 Mailing Add: 1130 Longworth Bldg Washington DC 20515

KELLY, RICHARD F, JR (D)
Ill State Rep
b Chicago, Ill, Oct 12, 36; s Richard F Kelly, Sr & Ruth Trunk K; m 1969 to Ethel Turanek. Educ: Wilson Jr Col, AA, 58; Am Inst Banking, grad, 65. Polit & Govt Pos: Ill State Rep, Ninth Dist, 73- Bus & Prof Pos: Bank officer, Mid-Am Nat Bank of Chicago, formerly. Mil Serv: Entered as Pvt, Nat Guard, 59, released as SP-4, 65, after serv in Missile Corps. Mem: Chicago Financial Advert; KofC; Tinley Park Sertoma Club (pres & chmn bd, 70-). Honors & Awards: Cert of Merit, VFW, 54; Environ Golden Legislator Award, 72-73; Educ Best Legislator Award, Ill Educ Asn, 72-73. Relig: Catholic. Mailing Add: 3203 Oak Ct Hazel Crest IL 60429

KELLY, ROBERT F (D)
Mont State Rep
b Butte, Mont, Nov 18, 32; s Frank Kelly & Minnie Florence Carter K; m 1964 to Virginia Perkins. Educ: Western Mont Col, BS, 58, MS, 66. Polit & Govt Pos: Mont State Rep, Dist 86, 75- Bus & Prof Pos: Sci teacher, Butte, Mont, 58- Mil Serv: Cpl, Army, 53-55, serv in 1st Armored Div. Mem: Nat Sci Teachers Asn; Elks; United Commercial Travelers; Am Fedn Teachers. Mailing Add: 1737 Florence Butte MT 59701

KELLY, ROBERT W (D)
SDak State Sen
b Rapid City, SDak, Mar 8, 35; s Patrick J Kelly & Mildred D K; m 1954 to Jeanne L Rolland; c Randy, Robert & Richard. Educ: SDak State Univ & Chadron State Col, BS & BA; Univ Nebr, summers 61-63; C-Club (pres); class pres. Polit & Govt Pos: SDak State Rep, 71-75; mem, Midwest Conf Com, 73-75; mem exec bd, LUDAC, 74-75; SDak State Sen, 75-, mem educ comt & state affairs comt, SDak State Senate, 75-, asst chmn com comt, 75-; deleg, Nat Malpractice Conf, 75. Mem: Elks; KofC; Country Club. Relig: Catholic. Legal Res: 1803 Palo Verde Rapid City SD 57701 Mailing Add: Suite 107 919 Main Rapid City SD 57706

KELLY, STUART STACY (D)
Chmn, Spencer Co Dem Party, Ky
b Mar 4, 13; s George Washington Kelly & Harriett Stacy K; m 1947 to Marguerite Sampson; c Vicky Mariena & Maurice Stacy. Polit & Govt Pos: Chmn, Spencer Co Dem Party, Ky, currently; Ky State Rep, 73-74. Mailing Add: Rte 3 Taylorsville KY 40071

KELLY, WILLIAM THOMAS (R)
Committeeman, Ark State Rep Party
b Little Rock, Ark, Nov 6, 19; s W J Kelly & Bertha Dehmer K; m 1941 to Lucille Elizabeth Metrailer; c W T, Jr, Carolyn Jane (Mrs O'Connor), Cornelia Marie, Paul Dehmer, Lucille Elizabeth, Kathleen Rose, Margaret Mary, Christine Louise, Marie Patrice, Francis Matthew, John Kevin, Joseph Lee, Brian Anthony & Michael Edward. Educ: St Louis Univ; Ark Law Sch, LLB; Phi Sigma Eta. Polit & Govt Pos: Chmn, Pulaski Co Rep Comt, Ark, formerly; committeeman, Ark State Rep Party, currently; vchmn, Ark Coun on Human Resources, currently; treas, Coun on Econ & Social Develop, currently; secy-treas, Cent Estate Planning Coun, currently. Bus & Prof Pos: Secy-treas, Employee Benefit Consult, Inc, currently. Mil Serv: Entered as Pvt, Army, 43, released as S/Sgt, 46, after serv in Signal Intel, China-Burma-India Theatre. Mem: Little Rock Life Underwriters Asn (vpres); Am Col Life Underwriters (secy- treas, Cent Ark Chap); Am Bar Asn; Million Dollar Round Table. Relig: Catholic. Legal Res: 5423 Maryland Little Rock AR 72204 Mailing Add: 401 Commercial National Bank Little Rock AR 72201

KELLY, WINFIELD MAURICE, JR (D)
Co Exec, Prince George's Co, Md
b Washington, DC, Sept 2, 35; s Winfield Maurice Kelly, Sr & Margaret Gwinn K; m 1953 to Barbara Fay Doolittle; c Kathleen Fay, Karen Mae, Barbara Kay, Winfield Maurice, III, Christopher David, Patrick Joseph, & Margaret Elizabeth. Educ: Prince George's Community Col, AA, 74; Univ Md, currently. Polit & Govt Pos: Councilman, Prince George's Co, Md, 70-74, co exec, currently. Bus & Prof Pos: Pres, Winnie's Corp, Brentwood, Md, 56-68; vpres Automatic Retailers Am Serv, Inc, 68-70. Mem: Lions; Md Asn Co; KofC; Mobile Indust Caterers Asn. Relig: Catholic. Legal Res: 7113 Bridle Path Lane Hyattsville MD 20782 Mailing Add: Courthouse Upper Marlboro MD 20870

KELM, MARILYNN (D)
SDak State Sen
Mailing Add: 3030 Donahue Dr Sioux Falls SD 57105

KELM, THOMAS ARTHUR (DFL)
Budget Dir, Minn State Dem-Farmer-Labor Cent Comt
b Chanhassen, Minn, Nov 12, 30; s Elmer Fred Kelm & Loretta Weller K; m 1951 to Mary Ann Lano; c Lisa Anne, Christine Mary, Michele Jean & Margaret Mary. Educ: St John's Univ (Minn), 4 years. Polit & Govt Pos: Former Dem Co chmn & Second Dist Dem chmn; state chmn, Citizens for Anderson Campaign; Minn Dem-Farmer-Labor deleg, Dem Nat Conv, 56-72; budget dir, Minn State Dem-Farmer-Labor Cent Comt, currently. Bus & Prof Pos: Pres, Polar Panel Co, 55- Mem: VFW; Am Legion; KofC. Relig: Catholic. Mailing Add: 1530 Nightingale Chaska MN 55318

KELSCH, SARAH JANE (R)
Chairperson, Leelanau Co Rep Party, Mich
b Boston, Mass, Aug 29, 49; d W Joseph Gallagher & Allene Herschline G; m 1972 to Gregory Kelsch; c Christopher. Educ: Aquinas Col, grad in speech & drama, 71. Polit & Govt Pos: Chairperson, Leelanau Co Rep Party, Mich, 74- Relig: Catholic. Mailing Add: Lake Leelanau MI 49653

KELSEY, JOHN T (D)
Mich State Rep
b Hamtramck, Mich, Dec 22, 21; m 1945 to Anne Ambrowski; c John Charles, Christine & Mark Anthony. Educ: Detroit Col Law, 1 year. Polit & Govt Pos: Twp trustee, Mich, 51-53; justice of the peace, Warren Twp, 53-58; munic judge, Warren, 58-61; deleg, Const Conv, 61-62; Mich State Rep, 64- Bus & Prof Pos: Real estate salesman. Mil Serv: Army, 42-45. Mem: United Dem of Warren; KofC; DAV; Polish Century Club; Exchange Club. Relig: Roman Catholic. Mailing Add: 8435 Westminster Warren MI 48089

KEMLER, JOAN R (D)
Conn State Rep
Mailing Add: 65 Norwood Rd West Hartford CT 06117

KEMMIS, DANIEL ORRA (D)
Mont State Rep
b Fairview, Mont, Dec 5, 45; s Orra Raymond Kemmis & Lilly Shidler K; m 1967 to Elaine Dorothy Dugas; c Deva Fall & John Orra. Educ: Harvard Col, AB magna cum laude, 68; Univ Mont Grad Sch, 72-74, Sch Law, 75- Polit & Govt Pos: Mont State Rep, Dist 100, 75- Honors & Awards: Nat Merit Scholar, 64. Mailing Add: 1025 Briar Missoula MT 59801

KEMNITZ, RALPH ALLEN (R)
Chmn, Haakon Co Rep Cent Comt, SDak
b Aberdeen, SDak, Sept 2, 42; s Ralph L Kemnitz & Delphia Benscoter K; m 1965 to Julianne K Ufen; c Ralph L & Candice R. Educ: Northern State Col, BS, 66; Univ SDak, JD, 69; Delta Theta Phi. Polit & Govt Pos: States attorney, Haakon Co, SDak, 71-; deleg, SDak Rep Conv, 72; chmn, Haakon Co Rep Cent Comt, 73- Bus & Prof Pos: Pres, Philip CofC, 73. Mil Serv: Capt, Army Nat Guard, 59. Mailing Add: PO Box 498 Philip SD 57567

KEMP, JACK (R)
US Rep, NY
b Los Angeles, Calif, July 13, 35; s Paul R Kemp; m to Joanne Main; c Jeffrey, Jennifer, Judith & James. Educ: Occidental Col, Los Angeles, BA, 57. Polit & Govt Pos: Spec asst to Gov, Calif, 67; spec asst chmn, Rep Nat Comt, 69; US Rep, NY, 71-, mem appropriations comt, defense subcom & NY state bipartisan cong steering comt, US House Rep, currently. Bus & Prof Pos: Pro football quarterback with Nat & Am League teams, 13 years; capt, San Diego Chargers & Buffalo Bills; pub rels officer, Marine Midland Bank of Buffalo. Mil Serv: Active duty, Army, 58-62. Mem: Nat Asn Broadcasters, Engrs & Technicians; Am Football League Players Asn (co-founder & pres); Nat Football League Players Asn (mem exec comt); Sierra Club; President's Coun on Phys Fitness. Honors & Awards: Am Football League Player of the Year in 65 while leading Buffalo Bills to second consecutive AFL championship, twice All-AFL Quarterback; Young Man of Year, Buffalo Jr CofC; Distinguished Serv Award, US Jr CofC; Outstanding Citizens Award, Buffalo Eve News; Nat Football Found & Hall of Fame Award. Relig: Presbyterian. Legal Res: 50 Idlewood Ave Hamburg NY 14075 Mailing Add: 132 Cannon House Off Bldg Washington DC 20515

KEMP, JAMES LAMAR (D)
Miss State Rep
Mailing Add: 667 Forest Ave Jackson MS 39206

KEMP, RAMEY FLOYD, SR (D)
Chmn, Davie Co Dem Party, NC
b High Point, NC, Sept 29, 19; s William Thomas Kemp & Etta Dailey K; m 1939 to Emily Lucille Betts; c Ramey Floyd, Jr & Gregg Dailey. Educ: Logan Col Chiropractic, DC, 50. Hon Degrees: FICC, Int Col Chiropractors, 74. Polit & Govt Pos: Chmn, Davie Co Bd Elections, NC, 58-74; chmn, Davie Co Dem Party, 74- Bus & Prof Pos: Chmn, vchmn & secy-treas, NC Bd Chiropractic Examr, 60-72. Mil Serv: Entered as Pvt, Army, 44, released as T/5, 46, after serv in 77th Inf & 1st Cavalry, Pac Theatre; All Hand Weapons Expert; 3 Battle Stars. Mem: Am & NC Chiropractic Asns; Moose; Jaycees. Honors & Awards: Distinguished Serv Award, Jaycees, 54; Chiropractic Dr of Year, NC Chiropractic Asn, 61, Distinguished Serv Award, 73 & 74; Pilgrim Degree of Merit, Moose, 68. Relig: Methodist. Legal Res: 842 Halander Dr Mocksville NC 27028 Mailing Add: PO Box 361 Mocksville NC 27028

KEMPE, ARNOLD EMIL (DFL)
Minn State Rep
b St Paul, Minn, Jan 23, 27; s Carl Eloy Kempe & Alice Polzer K; m 1953 to Elizabeth Sankovitz; c William Carl, Mary Lisa & Annette Michele. Educ: Univ Minn, BA, 50, JD, 56. Polit & Govt Pos: Mayor, West St Paul, Minn, 58-63, city attorney, 64-74; Minn State Rep, Dist 67-A, 75- Bus & Prof Pos: Law firm assoc, Hoffmann, Donahue, Graff, Schultz & Springer, 56-63; partner, Kempe & Murphy, 63- Mil Serv: Entered as Pvt, Marine Corps, 44,

released as Pfc, 46, after serv in Pac Theatre, 45-46. Mem: Jaycees; Northern Dakota Co CofC; Minn State Bar Asn. Honors & Awards: Distinguished Serv Award, US Jr CofC, 63. Relig: Catholic. Mailing Add: 28 Amelia Ave West St Paul MN 55118

KEMPE, RAY (DFL)
Minn State Rep
Mailing Add: 17837 Flagstaff Ave W Farmington MN 55024

KEMPEN, PAUL D (D)
Mem, Rep State Cent Comt Iowa
b Ft Dodge, Iowa, Nov 14, 42; s Fred Dee Kampen & Edna Leist K; m 1962 to Marcia Kay Hart; c Brett, Jeffery & Joel. Educ: Twin Rivers High Sch, Bode, Iowa, 4 years; bus col, Quincy, Ill, 63. Polit & Govt Pos: Served on comts for US Rep Stanley Greigg, Iowa State Paul Franzenburg & former Gov Harold E Hughes; Dem precinct chmn, Wacousta Twp, 62-69; co treas, Humboldt Co, Iowa, 64-66; co chmn, Humboldt Co Dem Party, 66-74; mem, Rep State Cent Comt Iowa, 74- Bus & Prof Pos: Farmer, 61-; mgr several houses, Humboldt & Ottosen, Iowa, 62-; salesman, Moormans Feed Co, 63-66; owner of hotel, Humboldt, 69- Mem: 4-H Leader; Ottosen Commercial Club; Livermore Lakes Region Bd; Farm Bur; Jaycees. Honors & Awards: Nominated Outstanding Young Farmer in Humboldt Co, 66 & 68; Outstanding Feed Salesman Plaque, 67; President Plaque, 68; Key Man Award, 68; Outstanding Jaycee, 68. Relig: Catholic. Mailing Add: RR 1 Ottosen IA 50570

KEMPINERS, WILLIAM LEE (R)
Ill State Rep
b Oak Park, Ill, Jan 26, 42; s Wilbur Henry Kempiners & Margaret Hardesty K; single. Educ: Augustana Col (Ill), BA, 64; Univ Iowa, 64-66; Phi Alpha Theta. Polit & Govt Pos: Ill State Rep, 73- Mil Serv: Entered as Pvt, Army, 66, released as SP-5, 68, after serv in Mil Intel Unit, Washington, DC, 67-68; Army Commendation Medal. Honors & Awards: Best Freshman Rep, Ill Polit Reporter, 73; Outstanding Freshman Legislator, Ill Educ Asn, 73; Best Legislator Award, Independent Voters of Ill, 74. Relig: Lutheran. Legal Res: 1209-D Cedarwood Joliet IL 60435 Mailing Add: 32 W Van Buren St Joliet IL 60431

KENAN, RICHARD MAXWELL (D)
SC State Rep
b Greensboro, NC, Mar 10, 40; s Judson Glenn Kenan & Archel Clifton K; m 1962 to Lillian Sinclair Kemper; c Clifton MacLaine & Richard Kemper. Educ: Univ NC, BS, 62; Univ SC, JD, 69; Chi Phi. Polit & Govt Pos: SC State Rep, 74- Bus & Prof Pos: Attorney-at-law, 69- Mil Serv: Entered as Ens, Navy, 62, released as Lt Comdr, 74, after serv in USS Neosho & Armed Forces Courier Serv, 62-65. Mem: Kiwanis; Am & SC Bar Asns; Nat Conf Ins Legislators; Newberry Bar Asn (pres, 75-). Relig: Presbyterian. Legal Res: 1910 Nance St Newberry SC 29108 Mailing Add: Drawer 639 Newberry SC 29108

KENCHELIAN, KARNEY K (R)
Mem, Rep State Cent Comt Calif
b Fresno, Calif, June 22, 17; s Leon Kenchelian & Helen Choagian K; m 1946 to Geraldine E Earp; c Helene E, Christine A, Mary L & Mark L. Educ: Stanford Univ, BA, 40; El Chadro Club. Polit & Govt Pos: Mem, Rep State Cent Comt Calif, 65-; mem bd educ, Napa Unified Sch Dist, 67- Bus & Prof Pos: Div mgr, Northern Div, Pac Tel, 62- Mil Serv: Entered as Pvt, Army, 42, released as 1st Lt, 46. Mem: Native Sons Golden West; Elks; Rotary; Silverado Country Club. Relig: Catholic. Legal Res: 1196 Ross Circle Napa CA 94558 Mailing Add: 2438 Jefferson St Napa CA 94558

KENDALL, BARBARA BERRY (R)
b Boston, Mass, Sept 19, 28; d Harold Hubbard Berry & Helen Scherer B; m 1951 to Don Robert Kendall; c Kathryne Ann, William Wayne, Don Robert, Jr & Geoffrey Grigsby. Educ: Burdette Col, Boston, 45-47; Theta Alpha Chi. Polit & Govt Pos: Secy, Joint Comt Rep Principles, 62; exec secy, platform comt, Rep Nat Conv, 64, alt deleg, Conv, 72; pres, Bd Elec Supvrs, Montgomery Co, Md, 67-68; nat coordr, Rep Women's Conf, Rep Nat Comt, 67-69; chmn, Montgomery Co Rep Cent Comt, 68-70; consult, Inaugural Comt, 69 & 73; confidential asst, Dir US Mint, Dept Treas, 70-72; spec asst to Anne Armstrong, co-chmn, Rep Nat Comt, 72; dir exec secretariat, Off Secy, Dept Housing & Urban Development, 73-; co-chairperson, Montgomery Co Charter Rev Comt, 73-74. Bus & Prof Pos: Notary pub, currently. Publ: Political columnist, Chevy Chase Tribune, Bethesda, 61-63 & Montgomery Co Sentinel, 68-70. Mem: Md Fedn Rep Women (campaign chmn, 72-); Rock Creek Women's Rep Club; DAR; Toastmistress. Honors & Awards: Spec Merit Award, US Dept Treas, 72. Relig: Congregational. Mailing Add: 7506 Maple Ave Chevy Chase MD 20015

KENDALL, DON ROBERT (R)
b Seymour, Ind, Apr 21, 26; s Will Marion Kendall & Kathryne Holman K; m 1951 to Barbara Marion Berry; c Kathryn Ann, William Wayne, Don Robert, Jr & Geoffrey Grisby. Educ: Harvard Col, AB, 49; Am Univ, 53-55. Polit & Govt Pos: Admin asst to US Rep William G Bray, Ind, 51-66; pres, Montgomery Co Young Rep Club, Md, 60; asst chief sgt at arms for radio & TV, Rep Nat Conv, 60; pres, Md Fedn Young Rep, 61-63; temporary chmn, Md Rep Conv, 62 & 66; chmn, Montgomery Co Rep Cent Comt, 62-66; US deleg, Conf Young Polit Leaders of NATO Nations, Bonn, 63; vchmn, Rep State Cent Comt Md, 66-69; exec dir, Rep Nat Comt, 66-69; dep chief of staff, Platform Comt, Rep Nat Conv, 68; chmn, Rep State Comt, Md, 69-70; dep dir cong rels, Dept Transportation, 70-72. Mil Serv: Entered Army Air Force, 44, released as Pfc, 46, after serv in Air Transport Command. Mem: Am Polit Sci Asn; Capitol Hill Club; Am Legion; Columbia Country Club. Honors & Awards: Cong Staff Fel, 66. Relig: United Church of Christ. Mailing Add: 7506 Maple Ave Chevy Chase MD 20015

KENDALL, ORIN PARKER (D)
Mont State Rep
b Williams, Iowa, Apr 30, 04; s Oliver Perry Kendall & Nellie Parker K; m 1927 to Ivy Agnes Reeder; c Willene (Mrs William Smith), JoAnne (Mrs Johnson), Patricia (Mrs Melvine Eldridge), Glenda (Mrs James Farlan) & Orin G. Educ: Eastern Wash Col Educ, 2 years; Univ Mont, 1 year. Polit & Govt Pos: Treas, Sanders Co, Mont, 43-47, sch supt, 47-49; mayor, Thompson Falls, 61-; Mont State Rep, Mineral-Sanders Co, 69- Mem: Mason; Order of Eastern Star; Grange (present Mont State master, Patrons of Husbandry). Relig: Protestant. Legal Res: 205 Gallatin Thompson Falls MT 59873 Mailing Add: PO Box 563 Thompson Falls MT 59873

KENDALL, RICHARD E (D)
Mass State Rep
Mailing Add: State Capitol Boston MA 02133

KENDALL, WILLIAM T (R)
b Newark, NJ, May 8, 21; s Harry W Kendall & Jane Bell K; m 1945 to Doris M Czernicki; c Paul W & Jonathan P. Educ: Rutgers Univ, AB, 49; Columbia Univ, MA, 51; Harvard Univ; Cong Staff fel, 65-66; Phi Beta Kappa; Sigma Xi; Phi Lambda Upsilon. Polit & Govt Pos: Pres, Morris Co Young Rep, NJ, 53-54; campaign mgr, US Rep Frelinghuysen, 54, 56 & 58; co Rep committeeman & precinct leader, Florham Park, 56-59; chmn southeast dist, Morris Co Rep Comt, 58-59; spec asst to chmn, Rep Cong Campaign Comt, 62-64; admin asst to US Rep Peter H B Frelinghuysen, NJ, until 74; mem staff platform comt, Rep Nat Conv, 68 & 72; mgr, Mathias Campaign, 74; admin asst, Sen Charles McC Mathias, 74-75; dep asst to the President for Legis Affairs, 75- Bus & Prof Pos: Research chemist, Allied Chem Corp, 50-59. Mil Serv: Entered as Pvt, Army, 43, released as S/Sgt, 46, after serv in Fourth Army of US; Am Theater Ribbon; Victory & Good Conduct Medals. Mem: Am Chem Soc; Am Legion; Capitol Hill Club; Harvard Faculty Club; Ripon Soc. Relig: Episcopal. Mailing Add: 7606 Geranium St Bethesda MD 20034

KENDIG, A EDWARD (D)
Wyo State Sen
b Burns, Wyo, June 28, 25; single. Educ: Univ Colo, BS; Harvard Law Sch, LLB; Beta Gamma Sigma; Beta Theta Pi. Polit & Govt Pos: Sch trustee, Sch Dist Nine, Wheatland, Wyo, 59-67; Wyo State Sen, Goshen-Platte Dist, 63-; mem, Platte Co Dem Comt, Wyo, 73- Bus & Prof Pos: Banker-lawyer; bd dirs, Wyo Taxpayers' Asn, 67-; Wyo dir & mem exec coun, Independent Bankers' Asn of Am, 71- Mil Serv: Entered as Pvt, Army, 43, released as Sgt 1/C, 46, after serv in 506th Mil Police Bn, ETO, 44-45. Mem: Wyo Bankers' Asn; Lions; Am Legion; VFW. Relig: Presbyterian. Mailing Add: 301 Tenth St Wheatland WY 82201

KENISON, LINDA B (R)
NH State Rep
b Rutland, Vt, Apr 8, 43; d Nathaniel W Bucklin & Evelyn I King B; m to Leon S Kenison; c Kelly Lynn, Kristine Francis, Karlee Ann, Leon S, Jr & Michael James. Educ: Univ NH, currently. Polit & Govt Pos: Secy, Concord Rep Comt, NH, Ward 6, 74-; mem exec bd, Concord Rep City Comt, 75-; mem, Rep State Comt, 75- Mem: Concord Jr Woman's Club; Concord Hosp Asn; NH Hosp Asn. Mailing Add: 82 West Concord NH 03301

KENKEL, GERHARD H (R)
Committeeman, Ark State Rep Party
b Chicago, Ill, Nov 3, 93; s Fredick P Kenkel & Elenor Von Kamptz K; m 1917 to Rose H Scholl; c Elizabet K, Robert, Mary Bell & Kitty Lou. Educ: Univ Mo, Columbia. Polit & Govt Pos: Committeeman, Ark State Rep Party, currently; chmn, Monroe Co Rep Party, 36-66, committeeman, 66-; chmn, Monroe Co Agr Soil Conserv Comt, 40-46; chmn, Marquette Centennial Comn Ark, 70- Bus & Prof Pos: Dir Ark Cotton Growers Asn, 24-30; dir, Mid-South Cotton Growers, 30-32. Mem: Farm Bur (dir, currently); Cath Knight of Am Fraternal Asn; Elks Lodge 1252 (Past Exalted Ruler, 51-52). Honors & Awards: Received letter of congratulations from President Nixon on 50 years participation in Rep party in Ark. Relig: Catholic. Mailing Add: RR 1 Box 125 Brinkley AR 72021

KENNAN, THOMAS CLYDE (D)
Ark State Rep
b Wesley, Ark, Nov 19, 03; s Walter Alexander Kennan & Margaret Parker K; m 1974 to Opal Warren; c Thomas Clyde, Jr; Carolyn (Mrs John L Wallis) & Nancy (Mrs Benton R Vernon, Jr). Educ: Springfield Bus Col, 22. Polit & Govt Pos: Ark State Rep, 75- Bus & Prof Pos: Dist mgr, Metrop Life Ins, 27-69, pres, SW Territory, 60. Mem: Mason; Shrine; CofC (bd mem). Honors & Awards: Plaque, Springdale CofC, 73, Trophy, 74 & Cert Lifetime Mem, 75. Relig: Methodist. Mailing Add: 402 Eastgate St Springdale AR 72764

KENNEDY, BELA ELLIS (R)
Mich State Rep
b Bangor, Mich, July 8, 18; s Bela George Kennedy & Ada Pearl Briggs K; m 1941 to Ermina Eleene Price; c Cindra (Mrs Dean Bishop) & Dawne (Mrs John Speeter). Educ: Mich State Univ, BS, 41; Lambdi Chi Alpha. Polit & Govt Pos: Mich State Rep, 45th Dist, 73- Mem: Mason; Eastern Star; Consistory; Van Buren Co Farm Bur Bd; Mich State Hort Soc. Relig: Protestant. Mailing Add: RR 2 Box 123 Bangor MI 49013

KENNEDY, BILLY F (D)
Okla State Rep
b Pawhuska, Okla, May 27, 18; s Sam S Kennedy & Amy A Freas K; m 1940 to Dorothy M Severns; c Billy Jo & Cheryl Ann. Educ: Univ Okla, specialized law enforcement, 68-69. Polit & Govt Pos: Dep sheriff, Pawhuska, Okla, 64-70; Okla State Rep, Dist 36, 71- Bus & Prof Pos: Rancher, 35-64. Mem: Okla Sher] iffs & Peace Officers Asns; Lions. Relig: Methodist. Mailing Add: PO Box 1235 Pawhuska OK 74056

KENNEDY, CAIN JAMES (D)
Ala State Rep
b Thomaston, Ala, Apr 2, 37; s Marcus Kennedy & Carrie Richardson K; single. Educ: Los Angeles City Col, AA, 64; Calif State Univ, Los Angeles, BA, 66; George Washington Univ, JD, 71. Polit & Govt Pos: Ala State Rep, Dist 98, 74- Bus & Prof Pos: Reginald Smith fel, Swafca, Selma, Ala, 71-73. Mil Serv: Entered as Seaman, Navy, 55, released as PO 1/C, 71, after serv in USS Colohan & USS Remey; China Serv Medal; Good Conduct Medal. Mem: Nat Bar Asn; Am Judicature Soc; Nat Lawyers Guild; Ala Black Lawyers Asn; Mason. Relig: Baptist. Legal Res: 317 Montgomery Ave Prichard AL 36610 Mailing Add: 1407 Davis Ave Mobile AL 36603

KENNEDY, CARROLL HENRY (D)
Miss State Rep
b Puckett, Miss, June 2, 02; married. Polit & Govt Pos: Miss State Rep, 56-60 & 68-; Brandon bd alderman, 8 years. Bus & Prof Pos: Farmer; motor truck & hardware dealer. Mem: Mason; Farm Bur. Relig: Baptist. Mailing Add: PO Box 82 Brandon MS 39042

KENNEDY, DAVID BOYD (R)
Attorney Gen, Wyo
b Ann Arbor, Mich, Sept 2, 33; s James Alexander Kennedy & Elizabeth Earhart K; m 1964 to Sally Martin Pyne; c Jane Elizabeth & Douglas Earhart. Educ: McGill Univ, 51-52; Univ Mich, 52-54; Univ Mich, AB, 58; Yale Univ, 61-62; Univ Mich, LLB, 63. Polit & Govt Pos: Wyo State Rep, 67-72; chmn, Wyo Rep State Cent Comt, 71-73; mem, Rep Nat Comt, 71-73; Attorney Gen Wyo, 74- Bus & Prof Pos: Partner, Burgess, Kennedy & Davis, Sheridan, Wyo, 63-73; partner, Kennedy & Healy, 75- Mil Serv: Entered as Pvt, E-1, Army, 54, released as

as SP-5, E-5, 57. Mem: Am Bar Asn; Farm Bur; Wyo Stock Growers Asn; CofC; Elks. Mailing Add: 510 S Jefferson Sheridan WY 82801

KENNEDY, DAVID MATTHEW (R)
b Randolph, Utah, July 21, 05; s George Kennedy & Katherine Johnson K (deceased); m Lenora Bingham; c Marilyn (Mrs Verl L Taylor), Barbara (Mrs Carol Law), Carol Joyce (Mrs Jack Whittle) & Patricia Lenore (Mrs Lewis Campbell). Educ: Weber Col, BA, 28; George Washington Univ, MA, 35, LLB, 37; Rutgers Univ Stonier Grad Sch Banking, grad, 39. Hon Degrees: LLD, Brigham Young Univ, Roosevelt Univ & George Washington Univ; LHD, Lake Forest Col. Polit & Govt Pos: Tech asst, Div Bank Opers, asst chief of govt security sect, Div of Research & Statist & asst to chmn bd, Bd of Gov, Fed Reserve Syst, 30-46; spec asst to Secy of Treas George M Humphrey, 53-54; Secy of Treas, 69-71; Ambassador at Large, 71-73, US Ambassador, US Mission to NATO, 72-73. Bus & Prof Pos: Bond Dept, Continental Ill Nat Bank & Trust Co, Chicago, 46-51, vpres, 51 & 54-56, dir & pres, 56-59, chmn bd dirs & chief exec officer, 59-69; publ, Chicago Mag. Mem: Chicago Found for Cult Develop (dir); Fed Adv Comt on Financial Assets; Nat Pub Adv Comt on Regional Econ Develop; Fed Adv Coun of Fed Reserve Syst; Brigham Young Univ (chmn exec comt, develop coun). Relig: Latter-day Saint; first counr, Chicago Stake presidency; bishop, Washington, DC. Mailing Add: 33 Meadow View Dr Northfield IL 60093

KENNEDY, DAVID T (D)
Mayor, Miami, Fla
b Baltimore, Md, May 7, 34; s Howard N Kennedy & Nancy Davies K; m 1970 to Lynda de Gibaja; c David T, Jr. Educ: Fla State Univ, MS Pub Admin, 55; Univ Miami, JD, 58; Gold Key; Fla State Univ Hall of Fame; Wig & Robe; Omicron Delta Kappa. Polit & Govt Pos: City comnr, Miami, Fla, 61-70, Mayor, 70- Bus & Prof Pos: Pres, Research & Develop Corp, currently. Mil Serv: US Air Force Res. Mem: Fla State Univ Found (bd adv); Nat Multiple Sclerosis Soc (chmn, Dade Co Chap); Am Cancer Soc (chmn, Speaker's Bur, Dade Co Unit); Mentally Retarded Children in State Insts (chmn, Christmas toy fund); Big Bros Gtr Miami. Honors & Awards: Nat Alumnus of Year, Fla State Univ Student Govt Asn, 66; Outstanding Young Man in Miami, Miami Jaycees; One of Five Outstanding Young Men in Fla, Fla Jaycees; One of the Outstanding Young Men in Am, US Jaycees; Legion of Hon, Int Coun DeMolay. Relig: Baptist. Mailing Add: 8510 NE Tenth Ave Miami FL 33138

KENNEDY, DONALD PATRICK (R)
Committeeman, Erie Co Rep Party, Pa
b Erie, Pa, Nov 29, 11; s John C Kennedy & Helen Kitzer K; m 1933 to Treva J Kenyon; c Patrick K, Robert T, Susan M, John D, James E & Dennis M. Educ: Correspondence courses in eng. Polit & Govt Pos: Committeeman, Erie Co Rep Party, Pa, 56-; deleg, Rep Nat Conv, 64. Bus & Prof Pos: Consult engr, pvt practice, 50- Mem: Nat Soc Prof Engrs; Univ Club; Maennerchor Club. Relig: Christian. Mailing Add: 441 W 31st St Erie PA 16508

KENNEDY, EARL (R)
b Jersey City, NJ, Mar 16, 17; m to Jessie M. Educ: Morehouse Col, BS; Wayne State Univ; Univ Mich Exten Sch. Polit & Govt Pos: Cand, US House of Rep, Mich, 58; nominee, Mich State Legis; chmn, Citizens for Eisenhower, First Cong Dist; mem, Mich Rep State Cent Comt, second vchmn, formerly. Bus & Prof Pos: Real estate broker, Torch Realty Co; dir, Kennedy Travel Agency; dir, Bahamas Develop Co. Mil Serv: Air Force, World War II. Mem: NAACP; Amvets; Mason (32 degree); Shrine; Am Fedn State, Co & Munic Employees. Relig: Episcopal. Legal Res: 1336 Nicolet Detroit MI 48207 Mailing Add: 5744 Woodward Ave Detroit MI 48202

KENNEDY, EDWARD MOORE (D)
US Sen, Mass
b Boston, Mass, Feb 22, 32; s Joseph Patrick Kennedy & Rose Fitzgerald K; m 1958 to Virginia Joan Bennett; c Kara Ann, Edward Moore & Patrick Joseph. Educ: Harvard Univ, BA, 54; Univ Va, LLB, 59. Polit & Govt Pos: Asst dist attorney, Suffolk Co, Mass, 61-62; US Sen, Mass, 62-, Asst Majority Leader, US Senate, 69-71; deleg, Dem Nat Conv, 68; ex officio deleg, Dem Nat Mid-Term Conf, 74. Bus & Prof Pos: Lawyer. Mil Serv: Enlisted as Pvt-1, Army, 51, released as Pfc, 53, after serv in France, 52-53; Decorated Order of Merit, Italy. Publ: Decisions for a Decade, Doubleday, 68; In Critical Condition, Simon & Schuster, 72. Mem: Joseph P Kennedy, Jr Found (pres, 61-); Emmanuel Col (adv bd); bd trustees, Boston Univ, Lahey Clin, Boston, Boston Symphony, John F Kennedy Ctr for Performing Arts, Washington, DC, Children's Hosp Med Ctr, Boston, Mus of Sci, Boston & John F Kennedy Libr. Honors & Awards: Selected as One of Ten Outstanding Young Men of 67 by US Jr CofC; Humanitarian Award from United Hebrew Immigrant Aid Social Serv; Citations for Meritorious Serv from US Comt for Refugees & Am Immigration & Citizenship Coun. Relig: Catholic. Legal Res: Hyannisport MA 02647 Mailing Add: Senate Off Bldg Washington DC 20510

KENNEDY, FRANCIS J (D)
Vt State Rep
Mailing Add: 30 Cross Parkway Burlington VT 05401

KENNEDY, GENE ALLEN (D)
b Lakeville, Mass, Nov 22, 28; s Edwin Allen Kennedy & Cynthia Washburn K; single. Educ: State Col, Bridgewater, Mass, BS Educ, 56, MEd, 59. Polit & Govt Pos: Campaign mgr, all Nick Begich Campaigns, 60-72; admin asst, Alaska State Senate Minority, 69-70 & US Rep Nick Begich, Alaska, 71-73; spec asst, US Sen Dick Clark, Iowa, 73; admin asst, US Rep William L Hungate, Mo, 73-74; admin asst, US Rep Gladys N Spellman, Md, 75- Bus & Prof Pos: Govt & hist teacher, Jr & Sr High Sch, Calif, Mass & Alaska, 56-64; part-time instr govt & hist, Univ Alaska Exten, Anchorage, 6 years; prin, Arcturus Jr High Sch, Ft Richardson, 64-68. Mil Serv: Entered as E-1, Army, 50, released as E-6, after serv in 78th AFA Bn, 2nd Armored Div, ETO, 50-52; Good Conduct Medal; European Theatre Ribbon. Mem: Mayflower Lodge, AF&AM; Old Colony Royal Arch Lodge; Bay State Commandery; Bartlett Dem Club. Relig: Episcopal. Legal Res: 5232 E 24th Ave Anchorage AK 99504 Mailing Add: Apt N521 800 Fourth St SW Washington DC 20024

KENNEDY, GOLDIE L (D)
Mem, Calif Dem State Cent Comt
b Novinger, Mo, Feb 18, 05; d William Burris Lilly & Edna May Harris L; m 1927 to Eugene V Kennedy, wid; c Neil E. Educ: Kirksville State Teachers Col, 21-24; Univ Southern Calif, 24. Polit & Govt Pos: Secy, Calif Dem State Cent Comt, 50-54, vchmn, 54-56, state chmn women's div, 56-58, mem, currently, mem woman's adv comt, 73-, US Senator John Tunney's proxy, currently; asst secy, Dem Nat Conv, 52, mem fund raising comt & credential comt, 56, chmn, Nat Deleg Hostess Comt, 60, originator of Golden Girls, 60; state women's chmn, Stevenson for President Campaign, 56; nat chmn & originator, hole in the sole, pin campaign for Adlai Stevenson, 56; state women's chmn, Lt Gov Glenn N Anderson Campaign, 58; creator of slogan & silver broom, Sweep the state in 58, for State Dem Party Campaigns, 58; asst coordr, Calif Disaster Off, 59-62; mem, Lyndon Johnson Deleg, 68; Ventura Co campaign coordr, Hubert Humphrey, 68; mem, Ventura Co Dem Cent Comt, formerly; Ventura Co coordr for John Tunney, 70; mem, Dem State Platform Comn, 70-72; mem, Calif Deleg on Humphrey for President, 72; Los Angeles coordr, Nat Telethon, 73; mem steering comt, Calif Dem Conf on Party Orgn & Policy, 74. Bus & Prof Pos: Prin, Bardadale Elem Sch, Fillmore, Calif, 43-53; exec dir, Fiesta de la Marina, City of Ventura, Calif, 67 & 68. Mem: Nat Retired Teachers Asn. Relig: Protestant. Mailing Add: 3220 Peninsula Rd Oxnard CA 93030

KENNEDY, J C (D)
Polit & Govt Pos: Former chmn, Okla Dem Party Mailing Add: Security Bank Bldg Lawton OK 73501

KENNEDY, JOHN LLOYD (D)
b Holly Springs, Miss, Mar 24, 31; s John Lee Kennedy & Elizabeth Rittelmeyer K; m 1953 to Alma McAlexander (deceased); c Helen Elizabeth, Sylvia Ann, John Marshall & Patricia Mosal; m 1971 to Jane M Haines. Educ: Miss State Univ, 49-50; US Naval Acad, 50-53; Univ Miss, 53, Sch Com, BA, 56, Sch Law, LLB, 59, JD, 68; US Army Eng Sch, Ft Belvoir, Va, with honors, 54; San Francisco State Col, 54-55; Marina Adult Speech Sch, with honors, 54-55; Phi Delta Phi; Phi Kappa Theta. Polit & Govt Pos: Miss State Rep, Marshall Co, 56-60; deleg, Dem Nat Conv, 68 & 72. Mil Serv: Entered as Pvt, Army, 54, released as Cpl, 55, after serv in Sixth Army, 54-55. Mem: Miss Educ Asn; Miss Bar Asn; Citizens Conf for Stronger Marriage Laws (founder & dir); Am Legion; Phi Delta Phi. Honors & Awards: Runnerup, Miss Man of Year, 57; nominee, Miss Outstanding Serv Award in Field of Govt, 58. Relig: Catholic. Legal Res: 320 Chulahoma Ave Holly Springs MS 38635 Mailing Add: PO Box 688 Holly Springs MS 38635

KENNEDY, JOSEPH EVERETT (D)
Ga State Sen
b Claxton, Ga, Oct 8, 30; s Jesse Gordon Kennedy & Nannie Byrd DuPree K; m 1953 to Lalah Jane; c Debra, Cliff & Adam. Educ: Claxton High Sch, Ga, grad, 47; Ga Mil Col, Bus, 49. Polit & Govt Pos: Ga State Sen, 67- Bus & Prof Pos: Self-employed acct, currently. Mil Serv: Entered as Pvt, Army, 50, released as Capt, 53, after serv in 8th US Army, Korea, 52-53; Bronze Star Medal; UN Ribbon; Korean Serv Medal with Two Battle Stars. Mem: Rotary; Am Legion; VFW; Scottish Rite; Mason (32 degree). Honors & Awards: Outstanding Young Man of Year, Claxton Jaycees, 62. Relig: Baptist; chmn bd deacons, First Baptist Church. Legal Res: 206 New Dr Claxton GA 30417 Mailing Add: Box 246 Claxton GA 30417

KENNEDY, LELAND J (D)
b Alton, Ill, Dec 3, 08; m to Mary E Cain; c Patrick & Maureen. Educ: Alton pub & parochial schs. Polit & Govt Pos: Mem, Alton City Coun, Ill, 41; Ill State Rep, until 74; deleg, Dem Nat Conv, 68; deleg, Dem Nat Mid-Term Conf, 74. Bus & Prof Pos: Operating engr. Mil Serv: World War II. Mem: KofC (4 degree). Relig: Catholic. Mailing Add: 4408 Terrace Lane Godfrey IL 62035

KENNEDY, MARTIN P (D)
Chmn, Benton Co Dem Party, Ind
b Oxford, Ind, May 28, 31; s Paul J Kennedy & Theone Hilsabeck K; m 1954 to Beverly Joan Smith; c Terrance, Mary, Kevin, Kim, Sheila, Paul & Jacqueline. Educ: St Joseph's Col (Ind), 2 years. Polit & Govt Pos: Chmn, Benton Co Dem Party, Ind, 70-; alt deleg, Dem Nat Conv, 72. Honors & Awards: Citizenship Award, Oxford High Sch, 50. Relig: Catholic. Mailing Add: RR 1 Oxford IN 47971

KENNEDY, NELSON D (D)
Ind State Rep
Polit & Govt Pos: Ind State Rep, currently. Bus & Prof Pos: Ins agt. Mil Serv: Army. Mem: Eagles; Young Dem. Relig: Methodist. Mailing Add: PO Box 275 Palmyra IN 47164

KENNEDY, ROBERT B (D)
Mass State Rep
Mailing Add: State Capitol Boston MA 02133

KENNEDY, STEPHEN WILLIAM (R)
NMex State Rep
b Gallup, NMex, Sept 5, 49; s John William Kennedy & Georgiana Monaco K; single. Educ: Univ NMex, BA, 73; Alpha Tau Omega. Polit & Govt Pos: NMex State Rep, Dist 5, 75- Bus & Prof Pos: Treas, Gallup Indian Trading Co Inc, 74- Mem: Sunrise Kiwanis; CofC; NMex Young Rep; Am Inst CPA. Honors & Awards: High Sch Sr of Month, Rotary Club, Gallup, NMex, Oct, 67, High Sch Sr of Year, 67-68; Outstanding Serv Award, NMex Eta Kappa Chap, Alpha Tau Omega, 73. Relig: Episcopal. Mailing Add: 1320 Country Club Dr Gallup NM 87301

KENNEDY, THOMAS C
Nebr State Sen
Mailing Add: PO Box 326 Newman Grove NE 68758

KENNEDY, WALTER LAWRENCE (R)
Chmn, Vt Rep State Comt
b Chelsea, Vt, May 10, 20; m to Phyllis I Playful; c two sons, one daughter. Educ: High sch, Chelsea. Polit & Govt Pos: Chmn, Town Selectmen; overseer of the poor; Vt State Rep, 61-71 & 73-74, vchmn, Bank & Corp Comt, Vt State House Rep, 63, chmn, Hwy Traffic Comt, 65, chmn, Hwy Comt, 66-67 & 69-71, Majority Leader, 69-71; Vt State Sen, 71-73; cand for Gov, 74; chmn, Vt Rep State Comt, 75- Bus & Prof Pos: Auto dealer. Mil Serv: Cpl, Army Air Force, World War II, 43-46. Mem: Mason; Am Legion; AAONMS; RAM; St Aldemar Commandery. Relig: Congregational. Mailing Add: Box 158 Chelsea VT 05038

KENNEDY, WALTER P (R)
Minority Sgt At Arms, US House of Rep
s Thomas Kennedy & Mary McElvogue K; m to Ana Louise Bou; c Walter P, Jr, Ana Louise, Thomas Francis, Dennis Michael, Stella Marie, Kevin & Kathleen. Educ: Seton Hall Univ, BS, 46; John Marshall Col Law, LLB, 48; Columbia Univ; Georgetown Univ. Polit & Govt Pos: Admin asst to US Rep Canfield, 48-60; spec asst to chmn, Nat Rep Cong Comt, 64-; minority pair clerk, US House Rep, 61-73, minority sgt at arms, 73- Mil Serv: Entered as Pvt, Army, 43, released as S/Sgt, 45, after serv in 44th Inf Div, ETO, 44-45; ETO Medal with

KENNEDY, WAYNE L (D)
Maine State Rep
Mailing Add: Box 47 Gray NE 04039

KENNELLY, JAMES J (D)
Conn State Rep
Mailing Add: 132 Cumberland St Hartford CT 06106

KENNER, PATRICIA E (D)
SDak State Rep
Mailing Add: 109 San Marco Rapid City SD 57701

KENNETT, ROSEMARY (R)
Chmn, NH Young Rep Fedn
b Boston, Mass, Apr 6, 36; d Russell Blaisdell Kennett & Hazel Lillian Prince K; single. Educ: RI Sch Design, Providence, BFA, 58; Brown Univ. Polit & Govt Pos: Vchmn, Nashua Young Rep Club, NH, 63-65, secy, 72-; treas, NH Young Rep Fedn, 65-67, secy, 67-69, nat committeewoman, 72, chmn, 72-; deleg, New Eng Young Rep Coun, 65-69, third vchmn, 67- Bus & Prof Pos: Owner, Kennett Interior Archit, 59-; owner, KIA Architectural Photography, 70- Mem: Prof Photographers of Am; Nashua Regional Planning Comn; Nashua Planning Bd. Mailing Add: 453 Main St Nashua NH 03060

KENNEVICK, JACK C (R)
Idaho State Rep
Mailing Add: 1 Mesa Vista Dr Boise ID 83705

KENNEY, BURTON (R)
Chmn, Provincetown Town Rep Comt, Mass
b Sanford, Maine, Apr 3, 10; s Reginald Cleveland Kenney & Mary Lydia Kaye K; m 1932 to Florence Volton; c Joan M (Mrs Tremblay). Educ: Sanford High Sch, grad. Polit & Govt Pos: Chmn, Provincetown Town Rep Comt, Mass, 62- Bus & Prof Pos: Acct, Metrop Life Ins Co, Plymouth, Mass, 50- Mem: King Hiram's Lodge AF&AM, Provincetown (Past Master); Cape Cod Shrine Club; Mass Consistory, Boston; AAONMS. Relig: Protestant. Mailing Add: 8 Pleasant St Provincetown MA 02657

KENNEY, DANIEL JOSEPH (R)
Chmn, Belmont Rep Town Comt, Mass
b Boston, Mass, Nov 29, 19; s George Thomas Kenney & Grace Gibbons K; m 1945 to E Mary Guthrie; c Daniel J, Mary E, Stephen M, Robert E, William F & Nancy L. Educ: Boston Col, 37-38; Millikin Univ, 39-40; Boston Col Law Sch, JD, 49. Polit & Govt Pos: Chmn, Belmont Rep Town Comt, Mass, 64-; chmn, Belmont Housing Authority, Mass, 65-66; assessor, Belmont, 72- Bus & Prof Pos: Lawyer, 49- Mil Serv: Entered as Pvt, Army, 42, released as Maj, 46, after serv in 412th Fighter Squadron, 373rd Fighter Group, Ninth Air Force, ETO, 44-45; Distinguished Flying Cross; Air Medal with 12 Oak Leaf Clusters; Army Commendation Ribbon; Air Force Commendation Ribbon; European-African-Mid Eastern Campaign Medal with 5 Battle Stars; Belgian Fourragere; World War II Victory Medal; Air Force Res Medal; Col, Air Force Res, 61- Mem: Fed Bar Asn; Am Mus of Nat Hist; Int Asn Assessing Officers; KofC; ROA. Relig: Catholic. Mailing Add: 29 Myrtle St Belmont MA 02178

KENNEY, EDWARD BECKHAM (R)
b Augusta, Ga, Dec 1, 29; s Robert Edward Kenney & Betty Beckham K; m 1958 to Eric Grete Grossman; c Robert E, II, Susan Lynn & twins, Alison Leigh & Beth Marie. Educ: Presby Col, AB, 50; Blue Key; Int Rels Club. Polit & Govt Pos: Exec asst to US Sen Strom Thurmond, SC, 61-67, admin asst, 67-69; prof staff mem, Senate Preparedness Investigating Subcomt, 69-72; prof staff mem, Senate Armed Serv Comt, 73- Bus & Prof Pos: City ed, Aiken Standard & Rev, Aiken, SC, 50-52, news ed, 54-61; bur chief, Sims News Bur, Washington, DC, 61. Mil Serv: Entered as 2nd Lt, Army, 51, released as 1st Lt, 54, after serv as Platoon Leader, Bn S-2, Regt Asst S-3, Korea, 52-53; Lt Col, Army Res, currently; Bronze Star for Valor with Oak Leaf Cluster; Purple Heart; Combat Infantryman Badge; UN & Korean Serv Medals; Three Battle Stars. Mem: Jaycees; Am Legion; Senate Staff Club; Cong Secretaries Club; Senate Press Asn. Honors & Awards: Distinguished Community Serv Awards from Jaycees, Am Legion; VFW & Non Commissioned Officers Asn; Gold P Award, Presby Col. Relig: Episcopal. Mailing Add: 733 Tantallon Dr Oxon Hill MD 20022

KENNEY, ERICA G (R)
Resolutions Chmn, Md Fedn Rep Women
b Czech, Apr 30, 33; d Joseph R Grossman & Leonore L Brunner G; m 1958 to Edward B Kenney; c Susan Lynn, Robert Edward & twins, Alison Leigh & Beth Marie. Polit & Govt Pos: Rep precinct chmn, Md, 68-71; mem, Prince George's Co Fedn Rep Cent Comt, 70-74; dir of precinct orgn for Congressman Larry Hogan, 70 & 72; mem, Hogan for Cong Comt, 71-73; alt deleg, Rep Nat Conv, 72; dir precinct orgn, Burcham for Cong Comt, 74; resolutions chmn, Md Fedn Rep Women, 74-; prog chmn, Prince George's Co Fedn Rep Women, 75. Bus & Prof Pos: Dist mgr, Census for Prince George's Co, 70. Mem: Good Luck Rep Women's Club; Tantallon Citizens Asn; PTA (pres, Burroughs Jr High, 73-74). Relig: Episcopal. Mailing Add: 733 Tantallon Dr Oxon Hill MD 20022

KENNEY, VIRGINIA BANNING (R)
b Evanston, Ill, Dec 6, 22; d Thomas Allan Banning & Margery Ames B; m 1944 to Frank D Kenney; c Claudia Anne, Pamela Jane (Mrs Voetberg), Sarah Deming & Stuart Deming. Educ: Univ Chicago, PhB, 45; Wyvern Club. Polit & Govt Pos: Co-chmn, Citizens for Eisenhower, Chicago, Ill, 52 & 56; co-chmn, Cook Co Young Rep Orgn, 56-57; secy, Ill Rep Citizens League, 60-62; first vpres, Ill Fedn Rep Women, 62-64, pres, 64-68; mem-at-lg exec comt, Nat Fedn Rep Women, 68-74, finance chmn, 69-71, community serv chmn, 71-73; alt deleg-at-lg, Rep Nat Conv, 68; mem, Defense Adv Comt on Women in the Services, 70-; dist admin asst to US Rep Robert McClory, 13th Dist, Ill, 71- Mem: Nat Conf Christians & Jews. Honors & Awards: Award for Serv with the Atomic Energy Comn, Manhattan Proj. Relig: Unitarian. Legal Res: PO Box 581 Barrington IL 60010 Mailing Add: 150 Dexter Ct Elgin IL 60120

KENNICK, JOSEPH M (D)
Calif State Sen
b Saginaw, Mich, Sept 25, 05; m 1927 to Ruth Wood; c Joan Ruth (Mrs Scott) & David Michael. Educ: Southwestern Univ Law Sch; Univ Southern Calif Sch Govt. Polit & Govt Pos: Pres, Nat Conf Juv Agencies, formerly; supvr, Dept Social Welfare & Juv Bur, Long Beach, Calif, 34-58; attorney gen, Citizen Crime Comn; Calif State Assemblyman, 58-66; Calif State Sen, 67- Bus & Prof Pos: Social worker. Mem: Mason; Elks; Moose; Long Beach Optimist (hon mem); PTA (life mem). Legal Res: 2375 Eucalyptus Ave Long Beach CA 90806 Mailing Add: 110 Pine Ave Suite 606 Long Beach CA 90802

KENNINGTON, BETTY HAGAN (R)
VChmn, Tenth Dist Rep Party, NC
b Nashville, Tenn, Mar 30, 32; d Louie Vernon Hagan & Eva Wilson H; m 1953 to Grady Shelton Kennington; c Grady Vernon, Dana Louise & Shelton Lee. Educ: Univ NC, Greensboro, BA, 54; Converse Col, 54. Polit & Govt Pos: Gaston Co vchmn, Jim Gardner for Gov Campaign, NC, 68; comnr, Regional Planning Bd, Gaston Co, 70-; vchmn, Tenth Dist Rep Party, 70-; Gaston Co mgr, Jim Broyhill for US Rep, NC, 72. Mem: Gaston Co Ment Health Asn (secy bd, 72-); Am Red Cross (bd mem, 72-); Gaston Co Coun of Garden Clubs (pres); YMCA (secy bd dirs); CofC (civic affairs comt). Relig: Baptist. Mailing Add: 1220 Crescent Ave Gastonia NC 28052

KENOYER, KENNETH DALE (D)
Committeeman, Calif Dem State Cent Comt
b Kimball, Nebr, Sept 18, 25; s Asa Vern Kenoyer & Jennie O'Neal K; m 1974 to Julie M Lima; c Kent B & stepdaughters Kellie & Desiree Payton. Educ: San Jose State Col, 48-50; Am Col Life Underwriters, 58-63; Studies in European Polit, Cabrillo Col, 65; Kappa Xi. Polit & Govt Pos: Committeeman, Calif Dem State Cent Comt, 64-; committeeman, Santa Cruz Co Dem Cent Comt, 64-, vchmn, 70-; chmn Santa Cruz Co, Jess Unruh for Gov Campaign, 70; dir, Santa Cruz Co Indust Planning Comn, 70-71; dir, Santa Cruz Co Indust Comn, 72-73; chmn Santa Cruz Co, Alioto for Gov Campaign, 74. Bus & Prof Pos: Pres, Santa Cruz Co Life Underwriters, 65-67, legis chmn, 67-69, pres-elect & dir, Miss Santa Cruz Co Pageant, 67-69, nat committeeman, currently. Mil Serv: Entered as Seaman 2/C, Navy, 44, released as PO 3/C, 46, after serv in SPac Task Force 58, 44-46; SPac Ribbon; Am Theater Ribbon; Philippine Liberation Medal, Okinawa with 1 star. Mem: Nat, Calif & Santa Cruz Life Underwriters Asns. Honors & Awards: Charter Pres Award, Nat Life Underwriters Asn; Miss Calif Pageant Dir Award; various sales achievement awards. Relig: Protestant. Mailing Add: PO Box 4267 Fresno CA 93744

KENT, JONATHAN HENRY (D)
b Coniston, Lancaster, Eng, July 22, 45; s Dr Geoffrey Kent & Katharine Mary Ruscoe K; m 1968 to Elaine Culley; c James Geoffrey & Katharine Greer. Educ: Yale Col, BA, 67; Univ Iowa Col Law, JD, 70; Delta Kappa Epsilon. Polit & Govt Pos: Press aid-researcher, Mezvinsky for Cong Campaign, 69-70, co-mgr-treas, 72; admin asst, US Rep Edward Mezvinsky, Iowa, 73- Bus & Prof Pos: Assoc attorney, Thomas F Bell, Mt Pleasant, Iowa, 70-72. Mil Serv: Entered as 2nd Lt, Army, 71, released as 2nd Lt, 71, after serv in TSB, 10BC, Ft Benning, Ga; 1st Lt, Army Res, 2 years. Mem: Iowa Bar Asn. Relig: Protestant. Mailing Add: 620 River St Iowa City IA 52240

KENT, MARY LOU (R)
Ill State Rep
b Quincy, Ill, Oct 3, 21; d Frank M McFarland & Myrtie Booth M; m 1941 to Laurence S Kent; c Curtis Booth, Roger Hathaway & Laura (Mrs James H Auckley). Educ: Nat Col Educ, Evanston, Ill, 39-41. Polit & Govt Pos: Ill State Rep, 48th Dist, 73-, mem house appropriations comt, Ill House of Rep, 73- Bus & Prof Pos: Admin asst, Quincy CofC, 60-73. Mem: Altrusa Int (pres, Quincy Chap, 71-72); PEO. Honors & Awards: First woman to serv on Ill House Appropriations Comt. Relig: United Methodist. Mailing Add: 22 Spring Lake Quincy IL 62301

KENT, ROGER (D)
b Chicago, Ill, June 8, 06; s William Kent & Elizabeth Thacher K; m 1930 to Alice Cooke; c Clarence C, Mary (Mrs Schardt) & Alice (Mrs Stephens). Educ: Thacher Sch; Yale Col & Law Sch. Polit & Govt Pos: Dem Nat Conv, 48, deleg, 56, 60 & 64, vchmn, 60; gen counsel, Dept Defense, 52-53; vchmn & chmn, Calif Dem State Cent Comt, 54-65, mem, Postmaster Gen Stamp Adv Comt, 61-68; mem, Int NPac Fisheries Comt, 64-68; co-chmn, Tunney for Sen Campaign, Northern Calif, 70. Mil Serv: Entered as Lt, Naval Res, 42, released as Lt Comdr, 45; Silver Star; Two Presidential Unit Citations; Pac Area Campaign Ribbons. Mem: Am, Calif & San Francisco Bar Asns; Yale Law Sch Asn. Relig: Protestant. Legal Res: 200 Woodland Rd Kentfield CA 94904 Mailing Add: 155 Montgomery St San Francisco CA 94104

KENTON, JOSEPH S (D)
Mo State Rep
Mailing Add: 8553 Holmes Kansas City MO 64131

KENTON, WILLIAM G (D)
Ky State Rep
Mailing Add: 109 North Mill St Lexington KY 40508

KENYON, ROBERT CURTIS (D)
Mem, Kane Co Dem Exec Comt, Ill
b Geneva, Ill, Feb 10, 38; s Harry Franklin Kenyon & Marie McIntosh K; m 1956 to Judith Lee Risch; c Curtis Alan, Laura Jo & Timothy Lee. Educ: Eastern NMex Univ, 58. Polit & Govt Pos: Mem, Kane Co Dem Exec Comt, Ill, 70-; Geneva Twp chmn, 70-; deleg, Dem Nat Mid-Term Conf, 74. Bus & Prof Pos: Phototypesetting consult, Miles Kimball Co, 67; sales mgr, Keyline Printing Co, 72-73; dir photocomposition, Progressive Typographers Inc, 73- Mil Serv: Entered as Airman Basic, Air Force, 55, released as Airman 2/C, 59, after serv in Strategic Air Command, 56-59. Mem: Int Typographical Union; Am Civil Liberties Union. Relig: Unitarian. Mailing Add: 717 Edison St Geneva IL 60134

KEOGH, BROOKS JAMES (R)
Chmn, McKenzie Co Rep Comt, NDak
b Williston, NDak, Aug 4, 14; s Frank Patrick Keogh & Elizabeth Carney K; m 1944 to Kathleen Hyland; c Frank P, Kathleen & Mary Elizabeth. Educ: St John's Univ, Minn, 33-35; Univ NDak, 35-37; Col St Thomas, Minn, BA, 38; Neuman Club; Kappa Sigma. Polit & Govt Pos: Rep precinct committeeman, Berg Twp, NDak, 54-; deleg, Rep Nat Conv, 60; chmn, Goldwater for President Club, NDak, 60 & committeeman, 64- chmn, McKenzie Co Rep

Comt, NDak, 63-70 & 73- Bus & Prof Pos: Dir, Nodak Mutual Ins Co, 58-64; dir, Northwest Bell Tel Co, 64-; mem bd regents, Mary Col, currently. Mil Serv: Pfc, Marine Corps, 43. Mem: Am Nat Cattlemen's Asn; NDak Farm Bur; Elks; KofC; Newcomen Soc. Relig: Catholic. Mailing Add: Keene ND 58847

KEOGH, EUGENE JAMES (D)
b Brooklyn, NY, Aug 30, 07; s James Preston Keogh & Elizabeth Kehoe K; m 1949 to Virginia Fitzgerald; c Susan (Mrs Louis Benedict Clarke) & E Preston. Educ: NY Univ Sch Com, BCS, 27; Fordham Univ Sch Law, LLB, 30. Polit & Govt Pos: NY State Assemblyman, 35-36; US Rep, NY, 37-67; chmn, Franklin Delano Roosevelt Mem Comn, currently. Bus & Prof Pos: Dir, City Title Ins Co, trustee, East NY Saving Bank & dir, Athlone Industs, Inc, currently; dir, Am Chemosol Corp; mem, NY State Racing & Wagering Bd, 73-; chmn, Franklin Delano Roosevelt Mem Comn. Mem: New York City, NY State & Am Bar Asns; Am Irish Hist Asn. Relig: Catholic. Legal Res: 333 E 57th St New York NY 10022 Mailing Add: 521 Fifth Ave New York NY 10017

KEPPLER, ERNEST C (R)
VPres, Wis State Senate
b Sheboygan, Wis, Apr 5, 18; s Ernst J Keppler & Meta Ruge K; m 1939 to Bertha L Zurheide; c E Michael & Mary Elizabeth (Mrs Steven C Schmidt); six grandchildren. Educ: Univ Wis-Madison, BA, 49, Law Sch, JD, 50. Polit & Govt Pos: Alderman, Sheboygan, Wis, 41-45 & 51-53; Wis State Assemblyman, 43-44; asst dist attorney, Sheboygan, 53-54; City of Sheboygan & Co Civil Defense Dir, 56-61; Wis State Sen, 61-, majority leader, Wis State Senate, 69-73, vpres, 73-75, chmn comt on senate orgn & comn on interstate coop, vchmn comt on hwy, joint comt on transportation & Am revolution bicentennial comn, currently. Bus & Prof Pos: Factory worker, 5 years; machinist helper, 1 year; truck driver, 1 year; bookkeeper, 1 year; attorney, 25 years. Mil Serv: Enlisted as Pvt, Army, 45, released as Acting 1st Sgt, 46, after serv in Philippines; Korean Conflict, 50-51. Mem: Boy Scouts (scoutmaster & Explorer adv, asst dir, Boy Scout Bugle & Drum Corps); Am Legion; VFW; Amvets; Eagles. Honors & Awards: Distinguished Eagle Scout Award & Silver Beaver Award, Boy Scouts. Relig: United Church of Christ. Mailing Add: 909 New York Ave Sheboygan WI 53081

KERANS, GRATTAN (D)
Ore State Rep
Mailing Add: 165 N Polk St 14 Eugene OR 97402

KERMOTT, MARJORIE LOUISE (R)
NDak State Rep
b New Lebanon, Ind, Apr 4, 13; d John Spears McNaughton & Lucile Coulson M; m 1934 to Dr L Henry Kermott, wid; c L Henry & John Bruce (deceased). Educ: Presby Hosp Sch Nursing, Chicago, Ill, RN, 34. Polit & Govt Pos: Vchairwoman, NDak Rep Party, 66-68; mem bd dirs, Minot City Libr, 69-; mem, Munic Parking Authority, Minot, 72-; deleg, Rep Nat Conv, 72; NDak State Rep, 72- Bus & Prof Pos: Dir, First Nat Bank, Minot, NDak, 72- Mem: PEO; NDak Med Soc Auxiliary; St Joseph Hosp Auxiliary; Minot Symphony Asn; Minot CofC. Relig: Presbyterian. Mailing Add: 200 Seventh Ave SE Minot ND 58701

KERN, HELMUTH F (D)
Mem Affirmative Action Coun, Ill Dem Party
b Magdeburg, Ger, June 3, 05; m to Eva O. Educ: Univ Halle, PhD, 26-29; Am Univ, 44-45. Polit & Govt Pos: Labor adv, US High comnr, West Ger, 49-51; mem operating comt, Comt on Polit Educ, AFL-CIO, currently; mem charter comn, Dem Party; mem affirmative action coun, Ill Dem Party, currently. Publ: Numerous. Mem: Meatcutters Union; Coun Nat Planning Asn. Legal Res: 9112 Samoset Trail Skokie IL 60076 Mailing Add: 2800 Sheridan Rd Chicago IL 60657

KERN, JOSEPHINE ANN (R)
Nat Committeewoman, NJ Young Rep Orgn, Inc
b Hackensack, NJ, July 17, 38; d Frank Cicardo & Jennie Pasquale C; m 1970 to Walter M D Kern, Jr; two children. Educ: Upsala Col, BBA, 60; Alpha Phi Delta. Polit & Govt Pos: Rep Co Committeewoman, Hackensack, NJ, 66-70; vchmn, Bergen Co Young Rep Club, Inc, 67-69; Bergen Co Coordr, Nixon/Agnew Girls, 68; legis aide, 68-69; asst secy, Bergen Co Rep Comt, 69-70; Young Rep Nat Committeewoman, NJ Young Rep Orgn, Inc, 70-; alt deleg, Rep Nat Conv, 72. Bus & Prof Pos: Personnel recruiter, Fed Elec Corp, Int Tel & Tel, 63- Relig: Episcopal. Mailing Add: 17 S Monroe St Ridgewood NJ 07450

KERNAN, THOMAS B (D)
Md State Deleg
Mailing Add: 1811 Aberdeen Rd Apt C Baltimore MD 21234

KERNELL, MICHAEL LYNN (MIKE) (D)
Tenn State Rep
b Memphis, Tenn, Dec 20, 51; s Sam Houston Kernell & Ima Irene Park K; single. Educ: Memphis State Univ, 69- Polit & Govt Pos: Pres, Shelby Co Young Dem, Tenn, 70-72; Tenn State Rep, 74-, mem comts com, labor & consumer affairs, Tenn House Rep, currently. Mailing Add: 1052 Railton Memphis TN 38111

KERNICK, PHYLLIS T (D)
Pa State Rep
b Allegheny Co, Pa, Dec 14, 24; d Chester A Taylor, Sr & Nell G Wilkinson T; m 1944 to William A Kernick, VMD; c William A, Jr, Sally Ann, Thomas W, Cynthia E, Phyllis J & Richard O'Leary. Educ: Point Park Col, 64-65; Univ Pittsburgh Inst Local Govt, 65-66; Duquesne Univ, 69. Polit & Govt Pos: Auditor, Penn Hills, Pa, 66, treas, 70-; mem, Allegheny Co Hosp Develop Authority, 71-; mem, Allegheny Regional Coun, Gov Justice Comt, 74-; mem Comn to Study Fiscal Needs of State Cult Insts, State of Pa, 75; Pa State Rep, 32nd Dist, Allegheny Co, 75- Mem: Nat Order Women Legislators; Penn Hills CofC; Penn Hills Serv Asn; League of Women Voters; Allegheny East Ment Health & Ment Retardation. Legal Res: 10753 Frankstown Rd Pittsburgh PA 15235 Mailing Add: Box 99 The Capitol Harrisburg PA 17120

KERR, BAILEY FURMAN (R)
Alt, Los Angeles Co Rep Cent Comt, Calif
b Okla, July 16, 06; s Charles Randolph Kerr & Mary Pybas K; m 1925 to Darline Craig; c Bailey F, Jr. Educ: Manzanola High Sch, Colo, 12 years. Polit & Govt Pos: Mem, Calif Rep State Cent Comt, 69-72; alt, Los Angeles Co Rep Cent Comt, Calif, 72-; chmn, Whittier City Planning Comn, 74- Bus & Prof Pos: Pvt secy, Colo Fuel & Iron Co, Pueblo, Colo, 27-33; prin clerk, asst regional acct, regional fiscal inspector & dep regional fiscal agt, US Forest Serv, Atlanta, Ga & Albuquerque, NMex, 33-47; off mgr, F R Yates Construction Co, South Gate, Calif, 48-54; controller, John D Lusk & Son, Whittier, Calif, 55-60; dir pub rels, Suburban Water Syst, La Puente, Calif, 61-74; Retired. Mem: Calif Water Asn; Southland Water Comt; Whittier Area Rose Float Asn (pres); CofC (dir, La Puente & West Covina chap & mem, Whittier & La Mirada chap). Honors & Awards: Comt Chmn of Year Award, La Puente CofC, twice. Relig: Episcopal. Mailing Add: 16203 E Honnington Whittier CA 90603

KERR, GORDON CHARLES (D)
b Alexandria, Va, June 1, 45; s Peyton Armstrong Kerr & Margaret Wilson K; m 1968 to Suzanne Schlaff; c Sarah Alexander & Gordon Charles, Jr. Educ: Yale Univ, BA, 67. Polit & Govt Pos: Admin asst to US Rep Jonathan Bingham, NY, 73- Mil Serv: Entered as Ens, Navy, 67, released as Lt(jg), 70, after serv in Atlantic Amphibians Unit & Navy Intel, Pentagon. Mailing Add: 912 E Capitol St NE Washington DC 20003

KERR, JOHN H, JR (R)
b Lexington, Ky, Oct 9, 21; s J Hervey Kerr & Elizabeth Latham K; m 1947 to Mary LaBach; c John H, III, Mary Shepherd & Bettie LaBach. Educ: Univ Ky, BS, 43; Omicron Delta Kappa; Beta Gamma Sigma; Phi Mu Alpha; Pershing Rifles; Scabbard & Blade. Polit & Govt Pos: Mem, State Police Merit Bd, Ky, 50-52; precinct committeeman, Fayette Co Rep Party, 52-; co comnr, Fayette Co, 53-57; co chmn, Fayette Co Rep Campaign, 54, 56 & 60; asst state chmn, Ky Rep Campaign, 62, 64, 66 & 67, chmn, 68; city comnr, Lexington, 63-65; deleg, Rep Nat Conv, 68 & 72; chmn, Ky State Rep Cent Comt, formerly; mem, Rep Nat Comt, formerly. Bus & Prof Pos: State secy-treas, Funeral Dir Asn of Ky, Inc, 50-; partner, Kerr Bros Funeral Home, 60- Mil Serv: Entered as Pvt, Army, 43, released as 1st Lt, 45, after serv in 28th Inf Div, ETO, 44-45; Purple Heart. Mem: Am Legion; Mason. Honors & Awards: Named Outstanding Young Man by Lexington Jaycees, 53; One of Three Outstanding Young Men of Ky, Jaycees, 54. Relig: Christian Church. Legal Res: 124 S Ashland Ave Lexington KY 40502 Mailing Add: 463 E Main St Lexington KY 40507

KERR, VERNON NORMAN (R)
NMex State Rep
b Gallup, NMex, Mar 11, 28; s Norman Alexander Kerr & Elizabeth Katherine Watkins K; m 1954 to Bettie Lorraine Poe; c David Vernon, Leslie Maureen & Stuart Brian. Educ: NMex Highlands Univ, BA, 49, MS, 54; Kappa Theta. Polit & Govt Pos: Finance chmn, Los Alamos Co Rep Cent Comt, NMex, 65-66, vchmn, 67-68; committeeman, NMex Rep State Cent Comt, 68-70; NMex State Rep, 71- Bus & Prof Pos: Staff chemist, Los Alamos Sci Lab, 54- Mil Serv: Entered as Recruit, Army, 50, released as Cpl, 52, after serv in 28th Gen Hosp, Supreme Hq, Allied Forces, Europe, 51-52. Publ: Co-auth, Quaternary salt formation of substituted oxazoles & thiazoles, J Am Chem Soc, 60, Parameters affecting the performance of large liquid scintillation counters, Rev Sci Instruments, 62 & Radiocarbon in plant products: geography, species, & time, Zeitschrift fur Physik, 62. Mem: Regional Environ Educ, Research & Improvement Orgn; Am Legion; Nat Rifle Asn; Nat Asn State Legislators; Los Alamos Sportsmens' Club. Relig: Presbyterian; ruling elder. Mailing Add: 113 Sherwood Blvd Los Alamos NM 87544

KERR, W EDWARD (R)
Utah State Rep
Mailing Add: RFD 1 Tremonton UT 84337

KERR, WILLIAM GRAYCEN (D)
b Oklahoma Co, Okla, Oct 18, 37; s Robert Samuel Kerr & Grayce Brenne K; m 1956 to Joffa Gemar; c David Kenworthy, Joffa, Kavar & Mara. Educ: Univ Okla, BA, 59, LLB, 62; Phi Delta Theta; Phi Alpha Delta. Polit & Govt Pos: Chmn, Dem State Cent Comt Okla, 67-69; deleg & chmn Okla deleg, Dem Nat Conv, 68; chmn, Youth Adv Coun, Dem Nat Comt, 68. Bus & Prof Pos: Dir, Farmers & Merchants Bank & Trust Co of Tulsa, Okla, 63-; dir, Penn Sq Nat Bank, Oklahoma City, 65-; chmn bd, Citizens Bank of Ada, 66-; attorney, Kerr, Davis, Irvine & Burbage, 67- Mem: YMCA (bd mgt, Oklahoma City Cent Br); Nat Cystic Fibrosis Research Found (trustee); Kerr Found (trustee); Nat Cowboy Hall of Fame & Western Heritage Ctr (trustee). Relig: Methodist. Legal Res: 2414 Smoking Oak Norman OK 73069 Mailing Add: 1510 Kermac Bldg Oklahoma City OK 73102

KERRY, RETA CHRISTINA (D)
Chmn, Columbia Co Dem Cent Comt, Ore
b Hood River, Ore, Nov 25, 23; d Burton Roy Andrus & Mary Carolina MacKinzie A; m 1961 to Harold William Kerry; c Timothy William, Michael Alexander Ridenour, Janis Ferrara & Janine Barr. Polit & Govt Pos: Chmn, Columbia Co Dem Cent Comt, Ore, 70-; bd mem, Rep State Exec Comt Ore, 74-; city councilperson, Scappoose, 75-; asst to State Rep Dick Magruder, currently. Mem: Am Legion Auxiliary; 40 et 8; Columbia Women's Club; Union CWA 9255; Willamette Dem Club (bd mem). Honors & Awards: Gold Heart Award, Ore Heart Asn, 70; Women of Achievement, Columbia Womens Club, 72. Legal Res: 405 SE Third Scappoose OR 97056 Mailing Add: PO Box 435 Scappoose OR 97056

KERSHAW, JOSEPH LANG (D)
Fla State Rep
b Live Oak, Fla, June 27, 11; s Albert Julius Kershaw & Theresa Lang K; m 1941 to Mamie Newton; c Joseph L, Jr. Educ: Fla Agr & Mech Univ, AB, 35, MEd, 55; Col Holy Cross, Xavier Univ, Fisk Univ & Univ Miami, post grad study; Kappa Alpha Psi. Polit & Govt Pos: Mem, Mayor's Comt on Civil Disobediences; Fla State Rep, 68-, mem comt on gen legis & comt on com, vchmn elec comt, Fla House of Rep, currently. Bus & Prof Pos: Sch teachen Dade Co, currently. Mem: Classroom Teachers Dade Co; Nat & Fla Educ Asns; Southern Polit Sci Asn; KofC (4 degree). Honors & Awards: First black to hold state elective off since reconstruction. Relig: Catholic. Legal Res: 2539 NW 46th St Miami FL 33142 Mailing Add: House Chambers Tallahassee FL 32304

KERTZ, HAROLD ALLAN (R)
Mem, DC Rep Comt
b Allentown, Pa, Dec 2, 06; s Christian John Kertz & Elizabeth Rudy K; m 1944 to Genevieve Hastings; c Robert Allan. Educ: Georgetown Col; Georgetown Univ Law Ctr, LLB, 28; Columbus Univ, LLM, 32; Sigma Nu Phi. Polit & Govt Pos: Precinct chmn, Rep Party, Washington, DC, 48, 52, 56 & 60; vchmn, DC Pub Serv Comn, 57-62; mem, DC Rep Comt, 60-, mem finance comt, 62-, mem exec adv comt, 64-; chmn, Oper Legal Eagle, 64; vchmn, DC deleg, Rep Nat Conv, 68. Bus & Prof Pos: Asst trust officer, Nat Metrop Bank, Washington, DC, 31-40; partner, Roberts & McInnis, 40-54; partner, Mercier, Kertz & Sanders, 54-57; legal contrib ed, Trusts & Estates & dir, Henlopen Hotel Corp, Chem-Met Co, O'Donnell's Sea Grill, Inc, R E Darling, Inc, Nat Litho Co, James R Dunlop, Inc & D&P

Prod, Inc, currently. Mem: Interstate Com Comn Practitioners Asn; Fed Commun Bar Asn; DC Bar Asn; Kiwanis; Capitol Hill Club. Relig: Episcopal. Legal Res: 2500 Virginia Ave NW Washington DC 20037 Mailing Add: 1906 Sunderland Pl NW Washington DC 20036

KESLING, JAMES WILLIAM **(R)**
SDak State Rep
b Timber Lake, SDak, Dec 13, 39; s J D Kesling & Mabel Moore K; m 1964 to Suzie Lipp; c Kandi K, Staci Lee & Jamie D. Educ: Dakota Wesleyan Univ, 60-61; Univ Kans, 57-60; Dallas Inst: MS, 63; Sigma Alpha Epsilon. Polit & Govt Pos: Finance chmn, Dewey Co Rep Party, 69; SDak State Rep, 71-, asst minority leader, SDak House of Rep, 71- Bus & Prof Pos: Partner, Kesling's Hardware, Kesling Lumber, Kesling Construction, Kesling Funeral Homes, Kesling Golden Carriage Dress Shop & Kesling Air Charter Serv; pres, Timber Lake Develop Corp. Mem: Shrine; Civil Air Patrol; Timber Lake Masonic Lodge (Past Master). Honors & Awards: Commercial pilot; cert first aid instr. Relig: Methodist. Mailing Add: Main St Timber Lake SD 57656

KESSELRING, LEO JOHN **(CONSERVATIVE PARTY, NY)**
Regional VChmn, Conservative Party, NY
b Rochester, NY, May 13, 33; s Clarence Charles Kesselring & Mary Mahoney K; m 1960 to Patricia Jean Dyer; c Susan Elizabeth & Stephen Lee. Educ: St John Fisher Col, BA in Acct cum laude, 55; St John's Univ Sch Law, LLB, 58; Phi Delta Phi; mem ed staff, St John's Law Rev & Cath Lawyer Mag, 56-58. Polit & Govt Pos: Research asst, US Attorney's Off, US Dept Justice, 56-57; mem legal staff, Joint Comt Legis Practices & Procedures, NY State Legis, 58-59; Monroe Co committeeman, Conservative Party, NY, 62-, mem exec comt, 62 & chmn, 65-; regional vchmn & mem, State Exec Comt, Conservative Party, NY, 68-; spec asst, Staff US Sen James L Buckley, 71- Bus & Prof Pos: Lectr real estate law, Rochester Inst Technol, 59-65; lectr bus law, Rochester Bus Inst, 60-61; attorney, Burns, Suter & Doyle, Rochester, 61- Mil Serv: Entered as Recruit E-1, Army, 59, released as SP-4/C, 65, after serv in 727th Ord Bn, 27th Armored Div, NY Nat Guard. Publ: The attorneys duties of disclosure, St John's Law Rev, 57, The supreme court, The Smith Act, & The clear & present danger test, 57. Mem: Monroe Co & NY State Bar Asns. Relig: Roman Catholic. Mailing Add: 333 Thayer Rd Fairport NY 14450

KESSLER, ANN ELIZABETH **(D)**
b Aberdeen, SDak, Jan 28, 28; d George William Kessler & Elizabeth Sahli K; single. Educ: Mt Marty Col, BA, 53; Creighton Univ, MA, 57; Univ Notre Dame, PhD, 63. Polit & Govt Pos: Deleg, SDak Dem Conv, 72-75; cand, SDak State Rep, 72 & 74; chairperson, Yankton Co Dem Party, 73-74; deleg, Dem Nat Mid-Term Conf, 74; mem, Citizen's Comn Correctional Policies & Prog, SDak, 75- Bus & Prof Pos: Retail clerk, Kessler's Dept Store, Aberdeen, SDak, 41-45; elem sch instr, Lincoln, Nebr, 47-49; instr hist & social studies, Mt Marty High Sch, Yankton, SDak, 52-56; elem sch teacher, Webster & Yankton, 57-59; prof hist & polit sci, Mt Marty Col, 62-, mem faculty senate, currently; vis prof hist, Marquette Univ, 69-70. Publ: Auth, The Effects of the Laic Laws of 1901 & 1904 on the Benedictines in France, Univ Microfilms, 63; auth, French Benedictines under stress, 66 & Political legacy to the religious in France, 69, Am Benedictine Rev. Mem: League Women Voters; Am Asn Univ Women; SDak Hist Asn; Asn Asian Studies. Honors & Awards: Three Scholarships to Hamline Univ, 66-72; James Award, Mt Marty Col, 67. Relig: Catholic. Legal Res: 1101 W Fifth St Yankton SD 57078 Mailing Add: Mt Marty Col Yankton SD 57078

KESTER, JOHN BARTON **(R)**
Secy, Darke Co Rep Cent Comt, Ohio
b Greenville, Ohio, Apr 29, 24; s John Barton Kester & Ella Mae Stoner K; m 1952 to Joan May Forward; c Rebbecca Joan & Cheryl Lynn. Educ: Ohio Northern Univ. Polit & Govt Pos: Secy, Darke Co Rep Cent Comt, Ohio, 64-, committeeman, 68- Bus & Prof Pos: Pres, Kesco Prod Co, 48- Mil Serv: Entered as Pvt, Army, 43, released as Sgt, 45, after serv in 9th Div, ETO, 45. Mailing Add: Park Ave Greenville OH 45331

KETCHAM, CHESTER SAWYER **(R)**
Vt State Rep
b Salisbury, Vt, Dec 6, 27; s Olin George Ketcham & Ruth Sawyer K; m 1971 to Catherine Marotti; c Tamara Lynn. Educ: Univ Vt, BA, 51; Yale Law Sch, LLB, 54; Sigma Alpha Epsilon. Polit & Govt Pos: Dep Attorney Gen, 63-65; Vt State Rep, 75- Bus & Prof Pos: Attorney-at-law, 54- Mil Serv: Entered as A/S, Navy, 45, released as Seaman 1/C, 47, after serv in 14th Naval Dist. Mem: Am & Vt Bar Asns; Am Trial Lawyers Asn; Mason; Lions. Relig: Roman Catholic. Legal Res: Painter Hill Rd Middlebury VT 05753 Mailing Add: Box 569 Middlebury VT 05753

KETCHUM, WILLIAM MATTHEW **(R)**
US Rep, Calif
b Los Angeles, Calif, Sept 2, 21; s Robert Milton Ketchum & Charmian Richards K; m 1942 to Lola Marie Heegaard; c Robert Milton & Margaret Kathleen (Mrs Charles Cole); 2 grandchildren. Educ: Colo Sch Mines, 39-40; Univ Southern Calif, 40-42; Alpha Kappa Psi; Kappa Alpha. Polit & Govt Pos: Mem, Calif Rep State Cent Comt, 64-66; Calif State Assemblyman, 29th Dist, 67-72; alt deleg, Rep Nat Conv, 68; US Rep, 36th Dist, Calif, 73- Bus & Prof Pos: Cattle raising & farming. Mil Serv: Army, serv in 77th Inf Div, Pac Theatre, 43-45, recalled, serv in 441st Counter Intel Corps, Korean War & Japan; Bronze Star; Purple Heart; Am Theater Ribbon; Asiatic Pac Medal with 3 Battle Stars; Combat Inf Badge; Philippine Liberation & Korean Serv Medals. Mem: Farm Bur; Calif Farm Bur Fedn. Relig: Episcopal. Legal Res: PO Box 1905 Paso Robles CA 93446 Mailing Add: 413 Cannon House Off Bldg Washington DC 20515

KETOLA, MARVIN EDWIN **(DFL)**
Minn State Rep
Mailing Add: 616 14th St Cloquet MN 55720

KEVE, KIRTLAND J **(D)**
Vt State Rep
Mailing Add: 30 Colonial Dr Montpelier VT 05602

KEVERIAN, GEORGE **(D)**
Mass State Rep
Mailing Add: State Capitol Boston MA 02133

KEVILLE, DOROTHY ANN **(D)**
Mem, Franklin Dem Town Comt, Mass
b Lowell, Mass, July 11, 38; d William Joseph LeRiche & Gertrude Lillian Brun L; m 1959 to Thomas Michael Keville, Jr; c Kathleen Ann, Karen Ellen, Patricia Marie, Thomas Michael, III & William Anthony. Educ: Cornell Univ, 70-71. Polit & Govt Pos: Deleg, Dem Nat Conv, 72; coordr six towns, McGovern for President Comt, 72; mem, Franklin Dem Town Comt, Mass, 72-; senatorial coordr, Dukakis for Gov Comt; alt deleg-at-lg, Dem Nat Mid Term Conf, 74. Bus & Prof Pos: Title XIX coordr, Wrentham State Sch, Dept Ment Health, currently. Mem: League of Women Voters; Common Cause; Am Civil Liberties Union; Citizens for Participation in Polit Action; Nat Women's Polit Caucus. Honors & Awards: Distinguished Serv Award, Jaycees, 75. Relig: Catholic. Mailing Add: 411 Partridge St Franklin MA 02038

KEYES, ORVAL ANDREW **(R)**
Nebr State Sen
b Springfield, Nebr, Nov 31, 13; s Robert H Keyes & Mary E Martenson K; m 1939 to Lois E Gottsch; c Gloria (Mrs Sass), Jodine (Mrs Osborn), Jerry, Mary Jean, Cheryl (Mrs Smith), Kimberly K, Clenda G & Brenda B. Educ: Springfield High Sch, Nebr, 26-30. Polit & Govt Pos: Nebr State Sen, 69- Bus & Prof Pos: Operating engr, packing house indust, 15 years; journeyman machinist, Douglas Aircraft Co, Inc; dir, Sch Bd Dist Eight, 46-48; dir, Sch Bd Dist 24, 50-54; farmer, currently. Mem: AFL-CIO; Eagles; Farm Bur; United Packinghouse Food & Allied Workers. Relig: Methodist. Mailing Add: 240 N Eighth St Springfield NE 68059

KEYES, THOMAS J, JR **(D)**
b Waterbury, Conn, Sept 2, 26; s Thomas J Keyes, Sr (deceased) & Anna Valaitis K; single. Educ: Post Jr Col Com, 44; St Lawrence Univ, 46-47; Sigma Pi. Polit & Govt Pos: Secy, Vet Admin, US Dept Labor, Wage Stabilization Bd & Fed Communication Comn, 46-54; exec secy to US Rep Arnold Olsen, Mont, 61-62; admin asst to US Rep John C Mackie, Mont, 65-66; legis asst to US Rep Joshua Eilberg, Pa, 67-68; admin asst to US Rep Mario Biaggi, NY, 69-70; admin asst to US Rep Charles J Carney, Ohio, 71-75; admin asst to US Rep Robert S Cornell, Wis, 75- Bus & Prof Pos: Legis secy, AFGE, AFL-CIO, Washington, DC, 58-59 & IAFF, AFL-CIO, 59-60; legis asst, Bldg & Construction Trades Dept, AFL-CIO, 63-65 & UAW, Washington, DC, 65-66. Mil Serv: Naval Res, Active, World War II. Mem: Officers & Prof Employees Int Union, AFL-CIO; Cong Secy Club; Nat Capitol Dem Club. Relig: Catholic. Legal Res: Waterbury CT 06702 Mailing Add: 1512 Longworth House Off Bldg Washington DC 20515

KEYS, JOHN GRANT **(D)**
VChmn, Ohio State Dem Cent & Exec Comt
b Barnesville, Ohio, June 15, 17; s James Ambrose Keys & Bertha Kathryn Glasow K; m 1944 to Mary Catherine Meany; c Corinne (Mrs Kent Dawson), Mary Michele (Mrs David Roe), Michael Brian, Patrick Grant, John Robert, Kelly Ellen, Thomas James, Timothy Grant, Anthony Regan, Kathleen Mary, James Gerald & Colleen Margaret. Educ: Ohio Univ, AB, cum laude, 60; Omicron Delta Kappa. Polit & Govt Pos: Mayor, Elyria, Ohio, 54-59; Dem precinct committeeman, Elyria, 54-; deleg, Dem Nat Conv, 56, 64 & 68; Ohio Dist Dem Committeeman, 13th Cong Dist, 56-; vchmn, Lorain Co Dem Exec Comt, 56-; mem, Lorain Co Bd Elec, 57-59; Ohio Dir Hwy Safety, 59-63; treas, Lorain Co, 63-; vchmn, Ohio State Dem Cent & Exec Comt, 68-; chmn, Gov Traffic Safety Comt, Ohio, 72- Bus & Prof Pos: Vpres, Elyria Bldg Co, Inc, 60-; mem exec comt, Pioneer Fed Savings & Loan, 62- Mil Serv: Entered as Pvt, Air Force, 42, released as 1st Lt, 46, after serv as pilot, ETO; Victory Medal. Mem: Ohio Archaeol Soc; Ohio State Asn Co Treas (pres, 75-); Ohio Comt Co Off (vpres, 72-); DAV; Ohio Univ (bd trustees, 74-). Honors & Awards: Cath Man of Year, Holy Name Soc; Distinguished Serv Award, Eagles; Distinguished Leadership Award, State & Prov Safety Coordr; Distinguished Leadership, Heart Asn; Distinguished Serv Award, Gov Traffic Safety Comt, 73. Relig: Catholic. Mailing Add: 409 Washington Ave Elyria OH 44035

KEYS, MARTHA **(D)**
US Rep, Kans
b Hutchinson, Kans, Aug 10, 30; d Rev S T Ludwig & Clara Krey L; m 1949 to Dr Samuel R Keys; c Carol, Bryan, Dana & Scott. Educ: Olivet Col, 46-48; Univ Mo-Kansas City, BA in Music, 52. Polit & Govt Pos: Alt deleg, Dem Nat Conv, 72; state coordr, McGovern for President Campaign, Kans, 72; chmn, Riley Co Dem Club, 72-73; mem, Spec Comn to Study Manhattan Recreational Needs, 73; US Rep, Kans, 75-, mem ways & means comt, US House Rep, 75- Bus & Prof Pos: Co-chairperson, United Way Drive, Manhattan & Riley Co, Kans, 73. Mem: Manhattan Arts Coun; Am Asn Univ Women; Sigma Alpha Iota; Kans State Univ Faculty Wives; Common Cause. Legal Res: 2339 Chris Dr Manhattan KS 66502 Mailing Add: 1207 Longworth House Off Bldg Washington DC 20515

KEYS, RUFUS B, JR **(R)**
Chmn, Anderson Co Rep Party, SC
b Belton, SC, June 8, 22; s Rufus B Keys, Sr & Selma Gambrell K; m 1946 to Elizabeth Marshall; c John Harrison & Brooks Marshall. Educ: Furman Univ, BA, 43; Sigma Alpha Epsilon. Polit & Govt Pos: Exec committeeman, Belton Rep Comt, SC, 70-74; chmn, Anderson Co Rep Party, 74- Bus & Prof Pos: Asst purchasing agt, Abney Mills, 50-60; owner, R B Keys Agency, 60- Mil Serv: Entered as Midn, Navy, 43, released as Lt(jg), after serv in Amphibious Forces, Atlantic & Pac Theaters. Mem: Lions; Belton Recreation Asn; Am Legion; SC Asn Ins Agts. Relig: Baptist. Legal Res: 117 Blair Rd Belton SC 29627 Mailing Add: Box 614 Belton SC 29627

KEYSOR, JIM **(D)**
Calif State Assemblyman
b Salt Lake City, Utah, Dec 10, 27; s James B Keysor & Bernice Brain K; m 1956 to Patricia Williams; c Bill, Susan, Karen & Julie. Educ: Univ Calif, Los Angeles, BS, 51; San Fernando Valley State Col, MBA. Polit & Govt Pos: Calif State Assemblyman, 71- Bus & Prof Pos: Pres, Keysor/Century Corp, until 70. Mil Serv: Entered as Pvt, Army, 46, released as Cpl, 48, after serv in Transportation Corps, US. Mem: Rotary Club. Relig: Latter-day Saint. Legal Res: 10139 Woodley Ave Apt 107 Sepulveda CA 91343 Mailing Add: 309 S Maclay Ave San Fernando CA 91340

KEYSTON, DAVID HILL **(R)**
Mem, San Mateo Co Rep Cent Comt, Calif
b San Mateo, Calif, Aug 2, 25; s George Noel Keyston & Hazel Elander K; m 1951 to Dolly Dee Janisch; c David Lawson, Douglas Arthur & Dee Ann. Educ: Univ Minn, BS, 45; Stanford Univ, MBA, 48; Phi Kappa Sigma. Polit & Govt Pos: Mem, San Mateo Co Rep Cent Comt, Calif, currently; assoc mem, State Rep Cent Comt Calif, currently; founding mem, Citizens for Constructive Action. Bus & Prof Pos: Exec vpres, Anza Pac Corp; partner, Keyston & Co; dir & treas, Keyston Bros. Mil Serv: Lt, Naval Res, World War II & Korean War. Mem: Govt Research Coun San Mateo Co (exec comt); San Mateo Co Develop Asn;

Rotary. Relig: Christian Science. Legal Res: 1452 Floribunda Ave Burlingame CA 94010 Mailing Add: Suite 25 1310 Bayshore Hwy Burlingame CA 94010

KEYTON, JAMES W (D)
Ga State Rep
Mailing Add: 137 Woodland Dr Thomasville GA 31792

KHARE, CAROL FICK (D)
Exec Dir, Richland Co Dem Party, SC
b Walterboro, SC, Mar 20, 45; d William Way Fick & Harriot Pearcy F; m 1965 to Frank Cornelius Khare, Jr; c Christopher Wescoat & Laura Noel. Educ: Columbia Col (SC), BA, 65. Polit & Govt Pos: Mem staff, Richland Co Dem Hq, SC, 74; exec dir, Richland Co Dem Party, 75- Bus & Prof Pos: Teacher, Walterboro, SC, 66-68. Mem: Nat Women's Polit Caucus; Richland-Lexington Women's Polit Caucus (vpres, 74-75); League of Women Voters. Relig: Episcopal. Legal Res: 7315 Venus Rd Columbia SC 29209 Mailing Add: PO Box 11506 Columbia SC 29211

KHOSROVI, CAROL MAYER (R)
b Cincinnati, Ohio, Aug 27, 35; d Albert J Mayer, Jr & Angela B M; m 1955 to Hamid Khosrove, div; c Parri Ann. Educ: George Washington Univ, BA, 60; Mt Holyoke Col, Mass, 2 years; Univ Calif, Berkeley, cand for JD. Polit & Govt Pos: Research asst, Rep Nat Comt, 60; legis asst, US Rep Richard S Schweiker, Pa, 62-63; legis asst, US Rep Robert Taft, Jr, Ohio, 63-65; legis & press asst, US Rep William Stanton, Ohio, 65-66; legis asst, US Sen Robert Griffin, Mich, 66-67; legis asst, US Sen Charles Percy, Ill, 67-69; mem, President Nixon's Transition Task Force on Pub Welfare, 68-69; dir, Off Cong & Govt Rels, Off Econ Opportunity, 69-70, dir, Vista, 70-71; dir, Off Prog Develop, 71-72; mem adv coun, Comt to Reelect the President, 72. Bus & Prof Pos: Prin, Planning Research Consult, Inc, Berkeley, Calif, 73- Mem: Action for Legal Rights (bd mem, 73-); Opportunity Funding Corp; Mt Holyoke Col Alumnae. Honors & Awards: Exceptional Serv Award, Off Econ Opportunity, 72. Mailing Add: 1771 Highland Pl Berkeley CA 94709

KHOURY, ARTHUR M (D)
Mass State Rep
Mailing Add: State Capitol Boston MA 02133

KIBBEY, JACK ROBINSON (R)
b Grayson, Ky, Dec 29, 18; s Delbert Valley Kibbey & Susie Helen Robinson K; m 1939 to Ruby Perry; c Mary Sue (Mrs Robert Stovall) & Linda Faye. Educ: Morehead State Univ Teaching Cert, 39; Jefferson Sch Law, Louisville, Ky, LLB, 49. Polit & Govt Pos: City attorney, Vanceburg, Ky, 53-57; commonwealth attorney, 20th Judicial Dist of Ky, 58-; chmn, Lewis Co Rep Party, Ky, 66-74. Mil Serv: Entered as Pvt, Army, 44, released as 1st Sgt, 46. Mem: Lions; Farm Bur; Am Bar Asn; Commonwealth Attorneys Asn. Relig: Protestant. Mailing Add: PO Box 36 Vanceburg KY 41179

KIBLER, MINIFRED ELIZABETH BURROW (R)
VChmn, Logan Co Rep Party, Okla
b Batesville, Ark, Dec 22, 11; d Frederick Douglass Waugh & Laura Bullard W; m 1946 to Rev O C Burrow; wid; m 1974 to Rev L R Kibler. Educ: Philander Smith Col, AB, 34; Northwestern Univ, MA, 53; Okla Univ, MLS, 63; Sigma Beta. Polit & Govt Pos: Rep precinct chmn, 63-65, secy-treas, 66-70; mem, Okla State Rep Party, 68-; vchmn, Logan Co Rep Party, 68-; mem, Okla Educ TV Authority, 67-72; co co-chmn, Bartlett for Senate-Nixon for President. Mem: Phi Delta Kappa; Am Libr Asn; YWCA (bd, North Tulsa); WCTU (social serv dir); Okla Fedn Colored Women's Clubs (chmn exec bd). Honors & Awards: Loyal Lady Rule of Year, Golden Circle Eastern Star, 68; Hon Loyal Lady Ruler of Dallas, Tex, 69; Hon Citation for Party Loyalty, US Sen, 71. Relig: Christian Methodist Episcopal. Mailing Add: 1828 N Boston Pl Tulsa OK 74106

KICKLIGHTER, HARRIS WILBUR (D)
b Glennville, Ga, July 27, 26; s Leaston Bryant Kicklighter & Nancy Bacon K; m 1947 to Nancy Hatten; c Harris Dale. Educ: Glennville Elem & High Schs, Ga, 11 years. Polit & Govt Pos: Mem, Co Bd Educ, Tattnall Co, Ga, 69-; mem adv bd, Ga State Mkt, Atlanta, 71-; mem, Finance Comt, State of Ga, 71-; mem, Ga State Dem Exec Comt, formerly; deleg, Dem Nat Conv, 72. Bus & Prof Pos: Owner & operator, TKF Farms, Inc, Glennville, Ga, currently. Mil Serv: Entered as Pvt, Army, 45, released as Pfc, 47, after serv in 732nd Mil Police Ban, Pac Theatre, 46-47; Expert Rifleman; Good Conduct Badge; Pac Theatre Campaign Badge. Mem: Am Legion; Lions Club; Farm Bur; CofC; Jaycees. Honors & Awards: Outstanding Young Farmer of Year, State of Ga; Citizen of Year, Glennville, Ga; Man of Year in Soil Conserv. Relig: Disciples of Christ. Mailing Add: Rte 2 Glennville GA 30427

KIDD, EDWARDS CULVER (D)
Ga State Sen
b Milledgeville, Ga, July 17, 14; s Edwards Culver Kidd & Tillie Smith K; m 1941 to Katie Rogers; c Tillie Anne (Mrs Fowler), Kathy (Mrs Walker), Edwards Culver, III & Margaret Harriett. Educ: Ga Mil Col, 32; Ga Inst Technol, BS, 36; Sigma Chi; Omicron Delta Kappa; Anals. Polit & Govt Pos: Mem, Baldwin Co Dem Comt, Ga, 53-65; Ga State Rep, 47-52; Ga State Sen, 63- Bus & Prof Pos: Salesman, Wyatt, Neal, Wagoner, 36-37; owner, Culver & Kidd Drug Co, 38-69; pres, Middle Ga Mgr Servs Inc, 59- Mil Serv: Entered as 2nd Lt, Army, 42, released as Maj, 45, after serv in 27th Inf Div, Pac, 43-45; Purple Heart. Mem: DAV; VFW; Am Legion; Eagles; CofC. Honors & Awards: Voc Rehabilitation Award, 70; Cystic Fibrosis State Award, 72; Outstanding Legis Serv to Retarded Children, 72; Cert Reorgn Viva, 74; Citation of Meritorious Servs, President's Comn Employ Handicapped, 75. Relig: Methodist. Legal Res: 101 E Handwiks St Milledgeville GA 31061 Mailing Add: Box 370 Milledgeville GA 31061

KIDD, MAE STREET (D)
Ky State Rep
Mailing Add: 2308 West Chestnut St Louisville KY 40211

KIDDER, BARBARA ANN (R)
NH State Rep
Mailing Add: 149 McGrath St Laconia NH 03245

KIDDER, ROLLAND ELLIOT (D)
NY State Assemblyman
b Jamestown, NY, Sept 14, 40; s Elliot Hall Kidder & Frances Swanson K; m 1972 to Jane Dawson; c Bartlett & Christopher. Educ: Houghton Col, BA, 62; Evangel Theol Sem, BD, 66; State Univ NY Buffalo, JD, 74. Polit & Govt Pos: Legislator, Chautauqua Co, NY, 72-74; NY State Assemblyman, 150th Dist, 75- Bus & Prof Pos: Attorney, Jamestown, NY, 75- Mil Serv: Entered as Ens, Navy, 67, released as Lt(jg), 70, after serv in Vietnam, 69-70; Lt, Naval Res, 70-74; Army & Navy Commendation Medals; Combat Action Ribbon. Relig: Presbyterian. Mailing Add: 33 Chestnut St Jamestown NY 14701

KIDDER, VICTOR LORAN (R)
NH State Rep
b Berlin, NH, Mar 25, 05; s Frank Loran Kidder & Effie Mae Mercier K; m 1935 to Ruth Arline Hammond; c Nancy Ann (Mrs Maynard T Bruns) & Robert Victor. Educ: Agr Col, 27; Cornell Univ, 31; Boston Sch Floral Art, 42. Polit & Govt Pos: Selectman, Shelburne, NH, 45-48 & 56-68; dep fire warden, Shelburne, 46-; NH State Rep, 56-57 & 71-; Coos Co deleg, 56-62. Bus & Prof Pos: Owner, Kidder's Greenhouses, 29-; landscape engr, NH State Hwy Dept, 31-42; part-time, NH Recreation Dept, 58-62; owner, White Birches Camping Area, 58- Mem: Dep Fire Wardens' Asn; NH Plant Growers' Asn (dir); Campground Owners' Asn; Mason; Odd Fellows (Past Noble Grand). Honors & Awards: Man of Year Award, Berlin-Gorham CofC. Legal Res: Shelburne NH 03594 Mailing Add: Star Rte 77 Gorham NH 03581

KIDDER, WILLIAM F (D)
NH State Rep
Mailing Add: Box 99 New London NH 03257

KIDWELL, WAYNE LE ROY (R)
Attorney Gen, Idaho
b Council, Idaho, June 15, 38; s John A Kidwell & Estelle Irene Konkle K; m 1962 to Shari Lynn; c Dale E & Vaughn W. Educ: Univ Idaho, BS, 60, LLB, 64; Sigma Chi; Delta Sigma Rho; Phi Alpha Delta; Bench & Bar; Sr Honor Court. Polit & Govt Pos: Chmn, Univ Idaho Young Rep, 63; research asst to US Sen Len Jordan, 63; prosecuting attorney, Ada Co, 66-68; Idaho State Sen, 69-74, chmn local govt & taxation comt, Idaho State Senate, 69-74, majority leader, 71-74; deleg, Rep Nat Conv, 72; Attorney Gen, Idaho, 75- Bus & Prof Pos: Lawyer, 64-66. Mil Serv: Entered as 2nd Lt, Army, 60, released as 1st Lt, 61, after serv in Mil Police Corps, Korea, 13 months. Publ: Prosecuting Attorney's Form Book, 67. Mem: Am Bar Asn; Idaho Peace Officers' Asn; Am Trial Lawyers Asn; Univ Idaho Exten Prog (mem faculty); Idaho Prosecuting Attorney's Asn. Honors & Awards: Outstanding Young Man, Jr CofC, Award, 67. Relig: Methodist. Mailing Add: 2201 W Boise Ave Boise ID 83706

KIEBERT, KERMIT V (D)
Idaho State Sen
Mailing Add: Box 187 Hope ID 83836

KIEFER, EDGAR L (R)
State Committeeman, Fla Rep Party
b Newark, NJ, May 25, 92; s Carl J J Kiefer & Lina Ziegler K; m 1946 to Carolyn Isabella Fletcher. Educ: Clason Point Mil Acad. Polit & Govt Pos: Asst to chmn, Pinellas Co Rep Party, Fla, 58-61; chmn, Pinellas Co Rep Exec Comt, 61-; deleg, Rep Nat Conv, 68 & 72; state committeeman, Fla Rep Party, 68- Bus & Prof Pos: Actor & singer, shows & vaudeville, 20-30; mgr, theatrical co, 30-41; regional rep, Pepsi-Cola Co, New York, 42-58. Honors & Awards: Cited as Mr Republican by elected off for work during 1968 Rep Campaign. Relig: Presbyterian. Legal Res: 4525 Hyacinth Way South St Petersburg FL 33705 Mailing Add: Pinellas Co Rep Exec Comt PO Box 7384 St Petersburg FL 33734

KIEFER, NAT GERARD (D)
La State Sen
b New Orleans, La, Feb 26, 39; s Ignatz Kiefer & Thelma Daivs K; m to Carol Ann Hazard; c Ignatz Gerard, Jr, Karen Ann, Kent & Kristopher. Educ: Tulane Univ, BBA, 62, Sch Law, LLB, 64; Order of the Coif; ed, Tulane Law Rev, 63-64. Polit & Govt Pos: La State Rep, 68-70; La State Sen, 70- Bus & Prof Pos: Partner, Jones, Walker, et al, Attorneys-at-Law, 69- Mem: Am, La & New Orleans Bar Asns; New Orleans CofC; Young Men's Bus Club. Relig: Catholic. Legal Res: 4801 Eunice Dr New Orleans LA 70127 Mailing Add: 225 Baronne St New Orleans LA 70112

KIEFFER, JAROLD A (R)
Asst Adminr for Pop & Humanitarian Assistance, Agency Int Develop
b Minneapolis, Minn, May 5, 23; m 1949 to Frances Rosalia Clarfield; c Edith Charlotte, Charles Edward & Philip William. Educ: Univ Minn, BA, 47, PhD, 50. Polit & Govt Pos: Staff asst to exec secy, Off Defense Mobilization, 51-52, exec secy, Defense Mobilization Manpower Comts, 51-52, staff secy, 52, asst to exec officer & exec secy borrowing authority rev bd, 53, spec asst to dir, 55-56, dep asst to dir, 56-58, consult, 58; exec secy, Personnel Adv Comt & exec asst to dir, Orgn & Personnel, Atomic Energy Comn, 52-53; liaison off, Task Force on Personnel & Civil Serv, 53-54; asst to Comnr Arthur S Flemming, Comn on Orgn of Exec Br, 53-55, President's Adv Comt Govt Orgn, 53-58, consult to comt, 58 & asst to chmn comt, 59-61; asst to Meyer Kestnbaum, Spec Asst to President, 55-56 & adv, Hoover Comn Matters, 56-58; Off Defense Mobilization alt mem, Planning Bd, Nat Security Coun, 56-58; adv, President's Adv Comt Career Exec Prog, 57; asst to Nelson A Rockefeller, 57-58; consult, Dept Health, Educ & Welfare, 58, asst to secy, 58-59, asst to secy prog anal, 59-61 & chief of prog anal activities, 59-61; secy bd trustees, Nat Cult Ctr, 59-63, exec dir, 61-63; mem adv coun & steering comt, Conf Pub Serv, Brookings Inst, 60-63; mem exec comt & bd dirs, Lane Co Auditorium Asn, 63-60; bd gov, Friends of Mus, Univ Ore, 64-69; vchmn, Gov Planning Coun Arts & Humanities, State Ore, 65-67; consult, Ore Arts Comn, 67-69; chmn, Proj 70's Task Force on State Reorgn for the 1970's, State Ore, 68-69; consult, Off High Speed Ground Transportation, US Dept Transportation, 68-69; mem, Twin Cities Citizens League Comt Urban Transportation Facilities, 69-71; mem, Task Force Advan Transportation Systs, Ctr Urban & Regional Affairs, Univ Minn, 70-71, consult, 71; consult, US Off Educ, 71; dir, Off Int Training, Agency Int Develop, 71-72, asst adminr for Pop & Humanitarian Assistance, 72- Bus & Prof Pos: Teaching asst polit sci, Univ Minn, 49, social sci prog, 50-51; research asst, Minneapolis Star, 49-50; lectr govt, Am Univ, 59-61, prof lectr, 61-63, adj prof int rels, 75-; assoc prof polit sci, Univ Ore, 63-67, acting head dept, 64, prof pub affairs & & admin, 67-69, chmn interdisciplinary master's degree prog pub affairs, Grad Sch, 65-69, chmn div pub affairs & admin, Lila Acheson Wallace Sch Community Serv & Pub Affairs, 67-69, adj prof, 69-70; adj prof polit sci, Macalester Col, 69-71, dir, Macalester Found on Higher Educ, 69-71. Mil Serv: Army, 42-46, serv in SPac & Philippines. Publ: Toward a system of individually taught courses, Lib Educ, 10/70; Comparison Between Fixed Guidway Transit Concepts for Medium Density Metropolitan Areas (w J Edward Anderson), Am Inst Aeronaut & Astronaut, 71; The Success of the Auto Should Be a lesson to Us, Am Soc Civil

& Mech Engr, 71; plus many others. Legal Res: 9019 Hamilton Dr Fairfax VA 22030 Mailing Add: Bur for Pop & Human Assistance AID US Dept of State Washington DC 20523

KIEFFER, REX H, JR (R)
Ohio State Rep
Mailing Add: 2201 Dresden Rd Zanesville OH 43701

KIHANO, DANIEL JAMES (D)
Hawaii State Rep
b Waipahu, Hawaii, Mar 16, 33; s Martin Kihano, Sr & Isabel Riley K; m 1952 to Elsie Kuulei Mokiao; c Debra Kaehuokalani, Joslyn Luana, Gwyneth Melani, Danette Uilani & Janine Leilani. Educ: Waipahu High Sch, dipl, 51; Cannon Sch Bus, 51-52; Leeward Community Col, 69-70. Polit & Govt Pos: Hawaii State Rep, 71- Bus & Prof Pos: Agt, Mid-Pac Ins Co, 54- Mem: Leeward YMCA (prog dir); Leeward Lions; Waipahu Filipino Community Asn; Leeward Jr CofC; Waipahu Community Asn. Relig: Protestant. Mailing Add: House of Rep State Capitol Honolulu HI 96813

KILADIS, NICHOLAS JAMES (D)
b Boston, Mass, June 18, 34; s James Nicholas Kiladis & Vaselia Makrokanis K; m 1962 to Mary Bahadouris; c James, Kira & Lia. Educ: Mass Inst Technol, SB, 56; Univ Baltimore Law Sch, JD, 64. Polit & Govt Pos: Admin asst, US Rep Paul S Sarbanes, Md, 71- Bus & Prof Pos: Proj engr, Caltech Jet Propulsion Lab, Pasadena, Calif, 56-59, contracts adminr, Martin Marietta Corp, Baltimore, Md, 59-70. Mem: Am & Md Bar Asns; Am Inst Aeronaut & Astronaut; Boys' Town Homes of Md (dir). Relig: Greek Orthodox. Legal Res: 9924 Richlyn Dr Perry Hall MD 21128 Mailing Add: 317 Cannon House Off Bldg Washington DC 20515

KILBERG, WILLIAM JEFFREY (R)
Solicitor, US Dept of Labor
b Brooklyn, NY, June 12, 46; s Jack Kilberg & Jeanette Beck K; m 1970 to Barbara Greene. Educ: Brooklyn Col, 63-64; NY State scholar, 63-66; William J Kelley scholar, 64; Cornell Univ, BS, 66; Harvard Law Sch, JD, 69; Pi Delta Epsilon; Alpha Epsilon Pi. Polit & Govt Pos: Research asst, Nixon for President Comt, 68; White House fel & spec asst to Secy Labor, US Dept of Labor, 69-70, assoc solicitor, 71-73, solicitor, 73-; gen counsel, Fed Mediation & Conciliation Serv, 70-71. Bus & Prof Pos: Apprentice electrician, IBEW, Local 3, New York, 63-67; assoc, Mudge, Rose, Guthrie & Alexander, 68. Publ: Labor relations in the municipal service, Harvard J Legis, 11/69; Appropriate subjects for bargaining in local government labor relations, Univ Md Law Rev, summer 70; Making realistic the arbitration alternative, J Urban Law, 8/72. Mem: Am Bar Asn (mem labor law sect, 69-); Harvard Law Sch Alumni Asn (class rep, 72-); Am Judicature Soc; Anti-Defamation League of B'nai B'rith (mem local bd, 72-, mem nat bd, 72-, mem comn on civil rights); IBEW. Honors & Awards: White House Fel, President of the US, 69; Man of Year, Lafayette High Sch, 70; Outstanding Young Man, Outstanding Young Men of Am, 72. Relig: Jewish. Legal Res: 30 Bay 28th St Brooklyn NY 11214 Mailing Add: 821 Clinton Pl McLean VA 22101

KILBURN, CLARENCE EVANS (R)
b Malone, NY, Apr 13, 93; s Frederick Douglas Kilburn & Clara Barry K; m 1917 to Anne Elizabeth Crooks; c James Crooks, Katharine (Mrs Bullard) & William Barry. Educ: Cornell Univ, BA, 16; Psi Upsilon. Hon Degrees: LLB, St Lawrence Univ, 58. Polit & Govt Pos: US Rep, NY, 40-65. Bus & Prof Pos: Pres, Kirk-Maher Ice Cream Co, Malone, NY, 21-26; managing dir, Gen Ice Cream Corp, 26-30; pres, Peoples Trust Co, Malone, 30-55; vpres, Northern NY Trust Co, 55-58. Mil Serv: Entered as 1st Lt, Army, 17, released as Capt, 18. Mem: Mason; Elks; Am Legion; VFW. Relig: Methodist. Mailing Add: 59 Milwaukee St Malone NY 12953

KILBURY, CHARLES DEBRIEL (D)
Wash State Rep
b Yakima, Wash, Feb 2, 19; s George William Kilbury & Rosa Hawthorne K; m 1944 to Florence delGrosso; c Brian Michael, Kathleen & Dennis Patrick. Educ: Yakima Valley Jr Col. Polit & Govt Pos: Mem, Planning Comn, Pasco, Wash, 56-60; Dem precinct committeeman, Precinct Five, 56-; mem, Gov Bd for Employ of Offenders, 58-62; councilman, Pasco, 60-64; chmn, Franklin Co Dem Cent Comt, 62-68, exec secy, 68-72; Presidential Elector, 64; chmn, Fourth Cong Dist Dem Coun, 64-69, exec secy, 69-72; chmn, Franklin Co Dem Club, 68-69; state committeeman, Wash State Dem Party, 68-72; Wash State Rep, 16th Dist, 71-, chmn agr comt, Wash House of Rep, 73- Bus & Prof Pos: Yardmaster, Northern Pac Rwy Co, 51-65; ins agt, Farmers Ins, 54-65; ins broker, Kilbury Ins, 66- Mil Serv: Entered as Seaman, 40, released as Master Merchant Marine, 46; Lt Comdr, Merchant Marine, 46- Mem: BRT (legis rep, Lodge 667); charter mem Pasco Exchange Club; United Transportation Union (chmn consol comt, 69, pres, Local 977, 69-); Rwy Labor Coun (founder, pres & emer pres); Benton-Franklin Counties Cent Labor Coun (secy-treas). Legal Res: 1840 W Margaret Pasco WA 99301 Mailing Add: Box 2482 Pasco WA 99302

KILDEE, DALE E (D)
Mich State Sen
b Flint, Mich, Sept 16, 29; m 1965 to Gayle Heyn. Educ: Sacred Heart Sem, BA; Univ Detroit, Teacher's Cert; Univ Mich, MA; Univ Peshawar, Pakistan, grad studies in hist & polit sci under a Rotary Found fel; Phi Delta Kappa. Polit & Govt Pos: Mich State Rep, 64-74; deleg, Dem Nat Conv, 68; Mich State Sen, 74-, mem appropriations comt, chmn subcomt on educ & vice & chmn joint capital outlay subcomt, Mich State Senate, currently. Bus & Prof Pos: Teacher. Mem: Educ Comn of the States; Optimists; Urban League; KofC; Am Fedn Teachers. Relig: Catholic. Mailing Add: 1214 Blanchard Flint MI 48503

KILEY, ANN SUE (D)
Mem, Ga Dem Exec Comt
b Kite, Ga, June 27, 36; d Loranza Dow Powell & Susie Beasley P; m 1958 to Donald J Kiley; c Lea Ann, Kevin James, Karen Sue & Lisa Fleur. Educ: SGa Col, 54-55. Polit & Govt Pos: Mem, Ga Women's Polit Caucus, 73-; mem, Dem Women DeKalb Co, 73-, chmn ways & means comt, 74-75; mem, Ga State Dem Exec Comt, 74-; mem, DeKalb Co Dem Exec Comt, 74- Bus & Prof Pos: Gen off work, Auto Driveaway Co, 73- Mem: Gainsborough 500. Honors & Awards: Dem Women DeKalb Co Annual Serv Award, 75. Relig: Protestant. Mailing Add: 4335 Chamblee Dunwoody Rd Atlanta GA 30341

KILEY, DANIEL PATRICK, JR (D)
b Lawrence, Mass, Mar 8, 24; s Daniel Patrick Kiley & Margaret Monahan K; m 1943 to Marcia Elizabeth Peterson; c Daniel Patrick, III, Thomas M, Ellen, Marcia E, Marp P & Robert P. Educ: Univ NH, 42-43 & 46-47; Boston Col Law Sch, LLB, 49; Sigma Beta. Polit & Govt Pos: Asst Attorney Gen, Mass, 59-63; mayor, Lawrence, formerly; deleg, Dem Nat Conv, 68; mem adv bd, US Conf Mayors. Mil Serv: Entered as Pvt, Army, 43, released, 46, after serv in Combat Engrs 78th Div, European Theatre, 44-46. Mem: Mass & Fed Bar Asns; Boston Col Law Club; Am Legion; VFW. Relig: Catholic. Mailing Add: 635 Haverhill St Lawrence MA 01840

KILEY, RICHARD B (D)
RI State Rep
b Pawtucket, RI; m to Ann T. Educ: Providence Col, 59. Polit & Govt Pos: RI State Rep, 64- Bus & Prof Pos: Vpres, Daniel P Kiley Inc. Mil Serv: Army Res, 6 years CID. Legal Res: 517 Pleasant St Pawtucket RI 02860 Mailing Add: State House Providence RI 02903

KILGORE, JAMES VEAZEY (D)
Mem, Ark State Dem Comt
b El Dorado, Ark, Aug 6, 51; s Earl Casper Kilgore & Mabel Veazey K; single. Educ: State Col Ark, 69-70; Univ Ark, Monticello, 72-76; Pi Kappa Delta; Sigma Tau Gamma; pres, Univ Ark Student Govt Asn, 75-76. Polit & Govt Pos: Vpres, Univ Ark Young Dem, 74-75; exec committeeman, Ark Young Dem, 74-75; mem, Ark State Dem Comt, 74- Relig: Baptist. Mailing Add: Rte 1 Box 173 Hampton AR 71744

KILGORE, JOE MADISON (D)
b Brown Co, Tex, Dec 10, 18; s William H Kilgore & Myrtle Armstrong K; m 1945 to Jane Redman; c Mark, Shannon, Dean & William. Educ: Westmoorland Col, San Antonio, Tex, 35-36; Univ Tex, 36-37, 38-41 & 45-46; Delta Theta Phi. Polit & Govt Pos: Tex State Rep, 47-55; deleg, Tex Dem State Conv, 47-66; US Rep, 15th Dist, Tex, 55-65; deleg, Dem Nat Conv, 56, 60 & 68; chmn, Water Adv Panel, Tex Water Develop Bd, 65-66; vchmn, Tex State Bar Legis Comt, 67- Bus & Prof Pos: Partner, McGinnis, Lochridge & Kilgore, 65-; chmn bd dirs, Tex State Bank, Austin, 66-; mem, Nat Pollution Control Found, Inc; mem bd regents, Univ Tex Syst, 66-73; mem, Coun Admin Conf, US, 68-73; mem bd, Wesley Found, 69-; mem bd, Austin Drug Ctr, 72- Mil Serv: Entered as Aviation Cadet, Army Air Corps, 41, released as Maj, 45, after serv in Ninth Bomber Command, Mediter Theater, 42-43; Silver Star, Legion of Merit, Distinguished Flying Cross, Air Medal with 2 Oak Leaf Clusters; Commendation Medal with Oak Leaf Cluster; Am Defense Serv Medal; Am Theater Campaign Medal with 4 Bronze Serv Stars; World War II Victory Medal; Maj Gen, Air Force Res (Ret). Mem: Am, Tex & Travis Co Bar Asns; CofC (vpres, Austin, 72-). Relig: Methodist; mem bd, Univ Methodist Church, 70- Legal Res: 331 River Rd Austin TX 78703 Mailing Add: Fifth Floor Tex State Bank Bldg 900 Congress Austin TX 78701

KILGORE, THOMAS M (D)
Ga State Rep
b Douglas Co, Ga, Jan 20, 35; s Steve Edward Kilgore & Lois Harper K; m 1961 to Carol McLendon; c Pamela Kay & Teresa Ann. Educ: Berry Col, BA, 56. Polit & Govt Pos: Ga State Rep, Dist 65, 75- Bus & Prof Pos: Sales rep, Seaboard Coast Line RR, 67- Mil Serv: Entered as Pvt, Army, 57, released as SP-4, 59, after serv in 18th Airborne Corps. Mem: Transportation Club Atlanta; Northwest Ga Traffic Club; Nat Defense Transportation Asn; Rwy Execs Atlanta; Rotary. Relig: Baptist. Mailing Add: 1992 Tara Circle Douglasville GA 30134

KILLAM, ANNE LORETTA (D)
Committeewoman, Colo State Dem Cent Comt
b Columbus, Ohio, Aug 10, 28; d Walter James Schirtzinger & Loretta Stine S; m 1949 to John George Killam; c Mary, John Richard, Robert G & Annette Marie. Educ: Ohio State Univ, 1 year. Polit & Govt Pos: Committeewoman, Adams Co Dem Comt, Colo, 62-; dist capt, Westminster area, 64-66; committeewoman, Colo State Dem Cent Comt, 64-; dist capt, Sherrelwood area, 66-68; asst mgr, Westminster Dem Hq Orgn, 67; treas, Jane Jefferson Dem Club, 69- Bus & Prof Pos: Supvr, Nationwide Ins Co, 47-50. Mem: PTA; Beta Sigma Phi. Relig: Catholic. Mailing Add: 7538 S Quay Ct Littleton CO 80123

KILLEN, ERNEST E (D)
Chmn, Del Dem State Comt
Mailing Add: 1014 Washington Wilmington DE 19801

KILLEY, RALPH ALLEN (R)
b Ill, Mar 7, 08; s Phillip Isaac Killey & Alice Winebright K; m 1932 to Frances Brent; c Barbara, Lester, William & Frank. Educ: High Sch & Brown's Bus Col. Polit & Govt Pos: Farmer coordr, Goldwater Campaign, Ill, 64; mem platform comt, Ill Rep Conv, 66; deleg, Rep Nat Conv, 68; chmn, Warren Co Rep Party, formerly. Bus & Prof Pos: Farmer; dir, Monmouth Trust & Savings Bank, currently. Mem: Farm Bur; Shrine; Monmouth Col Asn. Relig: Methodist. Mailing Add: Rte 4 Monmouth IL 61462

KILLIAN, ROBERT KENNETH (D)
Lt Gov, Conn
b Hartford, Conn, Sept 15, 19; s Edward Francis Killian & Annie Nemser K; m 1942 to Mildred Evelyn Farnan; c Robert Kenneth, Jr & Cynthia Elaine. Educ: Union Col, NY, BA, 42; Univ Conn, LLB, 48; Pres, Student Coun & Student Body; Beta Theta Pi. Polit & Govt Pos: Asst corp counsel, Hartford, Conn, 51-54; chmn, Hartford Dem Town Comt, 63-67; Attorney Gen, Conn, 67-74, Lt Gov, 74- deleg, Dem Nat Conv, 72. Bus & Prof Pos: Law partner, Gould, Killian & Krechevsky, Hartford, 48- Mil Serv: Entered as Pvt, Army, 42, released as 1st Lt, 46, after serv in Inf, Pac Theatre, 43-46; Purple Heart. Mem: Am Judicature Soc; Am Trial Lawyers Soc; Am Bar Asn; Hartford Div, Conn Cancer Soc (trustee, 59-); Hartford Legal Aid Soc (mem bd dir, 67-). Honors & Awards: Man of Year, Columbus Day Comt, 67. Relig: Roman Catholic. Legal Res: 234 Terry Rd Hartford CT 06105 Mailing Add: State Capitol Hartford CT 06115

KILLIAN, ROGER (D)
Ala State Rep
Mailing Add: PO Box 4 Ft Payne AL 35967

KILLION, DEAN (D)
b Poteau, Okla, May 3, 33; s Everett Lee Killion & Elva Thompson K; m 1963 to Barbara Eleanor Johnson; c Deena & Gary. Educ: Ore State Univ, 58-59; Univ Calif, 72. Polit & Govt Pos: Mem, Indust Accident Adv Bd, Ore Workmen's Compensation Bd, 72-, chmn, 75-; pres, Ore AFL-CIO, 73-; mem bd dirs, Tri-Met, 74-; deleg, Dem Nat Mid-Term Conf, 74. Bus & Prof Pos: Second vpres, Western Environ Trade Asn, 73-; mem bd dirs, Found for Ore Research & Educ, 74- Mil Serv: Entered as Pvt, Army, 53, released as Sgt, after serv in 8th Army, Korea, 54-55; Nat Defense Serv Medal. Mem: Elks; Int Woodworkers Am; Int Asn

Machinists & Aerospace Workers. Legal Res: 16572 S Heidi St Oregon City OR 97045 Mailing Add: c/o Ore AFL-CIO 411 Portland Labor Ctr Portland OR 97201

KILMARX, MARY NEIDLINGER (D)
RI State Rep
b Glen Ridge, NJ, Dec 12, 27; d Lloyd Kellock Neidlinger & Marion Walker N; m 1951 to Robert Dudley Kilmarx; c John, Peter & Elizabeth. Educ: Mt Holyoke Col, AB, 49; Phi Beta Kappa. Polit & Govt Pos: Deleg, RI Const Conv, 73; mem, Adv Bd Libr Comnrs, RI, 75-; RI State Rep, 75- Mem: League Women Voters; RI Women's Polit Caucus; Save the Bay (exec bd, 75-); Ecol Action; RI Audubon Soc. Mailing Add: 56 Elm Lane Barrington RI 02806

KILPATRICK, DON (D)
Okla State Rep
b Sayre, Okla, Sept 2, 39; s Wayne Kilpatrick & Mary Gesell K; div; c Kent. Educ: Oklahoma City Univ, LLB, 63; Phi Alpha Delta. Polit & Govt Pos: Okla State Rep, 71- Bus & Prof Pos: Attorney, Oklahoma City, Okla, 63- Mem: Okla Bar Asn; CofC; Lions. Relig: Protestant. Mailing Add: 2800 SE 46th Oklahoma City OK 73129

KILPATRICK, F JACK (R)
Committeeman, Tenn State Rep Exec Comt
b Etowah, Tenn, Feb 19, 20; s W F Kilpatrick; m 1948 to Guinn Ellen Kimsey; c Keith & Kent. Educ: McKenzie Bus Col, Chattanooga, Tenn, 39; Coyne Elec Sch, Chicago, Ill, grad, 40; Tenn Wesleyan Col, grad, 48; Univ Tenn, Knoxville, 49. Polit & Govt Pos: Mem, Polk Co Bd Educ, Tenn, 59-66, chmn, 60-61; secy-treas, Polk Co Rep Party, 66-; committeeman, Tenn State Rep Exec Comt, 74- Bus & Prof Pos: Mem staff, Tenn Valley Authority, Hiwassee Dam, NC, 39-41; Knoxville, Tenn, 46, jr acct, Turtletown, 49-52, acct, 52-62, off mgr, 62-; Mil Serv: Entered Army Air Force, 42, released as S/Sgt, 45, after serv in Eng & Sweden; Good Conduct Medal; 2 Battle Stars. Mem: Ruritan; Tenn Sch Bd Asn. Relig: Baptist; deacon & Sunday sch supt, Turtletown Baptist Church. Mailing Add: Rte 1 Turtletown TN 37391

KILPATRICK, JOHNNY MAX (D)
Miss State Rep
Mailing Add: 223 Myrtle St Philadelphia MS 39350

KILPATRICK, KENNETH DALE (D)
La State Sen
b Farmerville, La, June 14, 28; s Edgar Noel Kilpatrick & Effie Hicks K; m 1960 to Anne Burford; c Melanie, K D, Jr, Paula Sue & Richard. Educ: La Tech Univ, BA; Landig Col Mortuary Sci; Southern Methodist Univ. Polit & Govt Pos: La State Sen, 35th Dist, 72- Bus & Prof Pos: Pres, Kilpatrick Funeral Homes, Inc, 54- Mem: Lions; Kiwanis; CofC; Rotary. Relig: Baptist. Legal Res: Tech Farm Rd Ruston LA 71270 Mailing Add: PO Box 1038 Ruston LA 71270

KILVER, WAYNE M (D)
b Winchester, Ill, Apr 14, 28; s Clifford R Kilver & Helen L Massey K; m 1966 to Phyllis G Strawn. Educ: Winchester High Sch, 46. Polit & Govt Pos: Chmn, Scott Co Dem Orgn, Ill, formerly. Mil Serv: Entered as Pvt, Army, 51, released as Sgt, 53, after serv in Signal Corps, Korea; Good Conduct Medal; Korean Medal. Mem: Odd Fellows; Mason; Shrine; Consistory; Am Legion. Relig: Methodist. Mailing Add: 2 Broadway Winchester IL 62694

KIM, KENAM (D)
State Comptroller, Hawaii
b Honolulu, Hawaii, June 27, 27; s Duk You Kim & Pong Hee K; m 1971 to Vickie Sasano; c Dwight. Educ: Univ Hawaii, BA, 51; Syracuse Univ, fel, 52, MPA, 52; Sigma Lambda. Polit & Govt Pos: Budget analyst, Bur Ships, Navy Dept, Washington, DC, 52-54, budget admin, 54-55, supv budget off, 55-57, supv fiscal mgr, 57-58; budget officer, Pub Works Ctr, Pearl Harbor, Honolulu, 58-63; dep dir finance, State of Hawaii, 63-67, dir finance, 66; State Comptroller, Hawaii, 67- Mil Serv: Entered as Pvt, Army, 45, released as Tech 4, 47, after serv in 494th Depot Co, SPac Base Command, 45-46. Mem: Am Soc Pub Adminr; Nat Asn State Auditors, Comptrollers & Treas; Western States Treas Asn; Korean Community Coun; Univ Hawaii Alumni Asn. Honors & Awards: Consult Engrs Spec Award, 72; Pub Works Man of Year, State of Hawaii, 72; Citizen of the Day, Radio Sta KGU, 6/20/72. Legal Res: 2333 Kapiolani Blvd 1010 Honolulu HI 96814 Mailing Add: PO Box 119 Honolulu HI 96810

KIMBALL, BOB (R)
Wyo State Sen
Mailing Add: 1801 Brookview Casper WY 82601

KIMBALL, RALPH W (R)
NH State Rep
Mailing Add: 1 Hillcrest Dr Dover NH 03820

KIMBALL, ROBERT A (DFL)
Mem, Third Cong Dist Dem-Farmer-Labor Exec Comt, Minn
b Omaha, Nebr, Jan 20, 30; s James O Kimball (deceased) & Lillian Stimpson K; m 1958 to Shirley A Salmon. Educ: Univ Nebr, Lincoln, 47-48; Univ Minn, Minneapolis, BA, 70. Polit & Govt Pos: Mem adv comn on human rights, Crystal, Minn, 67-71, city councilman, 71-; mem, 31st Sen Dist Cent Comt, Dem-Farmer-Labor Party, Minn, 70-; mem, Third Cong Dist Dem-Farmer-Labor Exec Comt, 70- Bus & Prof Pos: Dist field off mgr, Peter Kiewit Sons Co, Omaha, Nebr, 52-57; bus mgr, Lindsay Co, Lincoln, 57-58; rehabilitation counr, Dept Serv for Blind, State of Nebr, 58-63; dir, Regional Rehabilitation Ctr, Minneapolis, Minn, 63-68. Mil Serv: Entered as Pvt E-1, Army, 53, released as Pvt E-1, 53, after serv in SigC, RTC, 53. Mem: League Minn Munic; Minn Environ Control Citizens Asn; North Suburban Human Rels Coun; Gtr Metrop Fedn, Minneapolis. Mailing Add: 5617 Adair Ave N Crystal MN 55429

KIMBALL, SHIRLEY A (DFL)
b Lincoln, Nebr, June 20, 36; d Maxwell W Salmon & Leola Wells S; m 1958 to Robert A Kimball. Educ: Lynchburg Col, BA, 57; Univ Minn, Minneapolis, 64-65; Kappa Delta Phi. Polit & Govt Pos: Vchairwoman, 27th Ward Dem-Farmer-Labor Club, Crystal, Minn, 68-70, trustee, 70-72; chairwoman, 31st Sen Dist Dem-Farmer-Labor Party, 70-74. Bus & Prof Pos: Elem teacher, Nebr Sch for Blind, Nebraska City, 57-58; nursery sch teacher, Dept Serv for Blind, State of Nebr, 58-59; homebound teacher, 59-63; instr, Regional Rehabilitation Ctr, Minneapolis, Minn, 63-64; elem teacher, Minneapolis Pub Schs, 65-71. Mem: Minn Environ Control Citizens Asn; Minn Epilepsy League; Am Acad Cerebral Palsy; North Suburban Human Rels Coun. Mailing Add: 5617 Adair Ave N Crystal MN 55429

KIMBERLIN, JO RAINEY (R)
Nat Committeewoman, NC Young Rep Club
b Caldwell, NC, Dec 12, 40; d Lee Nelson Rainey & Ruth Crews R; m 1960 to James Gareth Kimberlin. Educ: Am Inst Banking, 67; Caldwell Community Col, 70-72. Polit & Govt Pos: Treas, Caldwell Co Rep Party, 62; pres, Caldwell Rep Women's Club, 64-66; secy, NC Young Rep Club, 72-73. Bus & Prof Pos: Info chmn, Caldwell Co Heart Fund, 73- Mem: Lenoir Woman's Club; Cong Secys Club; Lenoir Bus & Prof Women's Club. Mailing Add: Rte 2 Box 426-A Granite Falls NC 28630

KIMBLE, GARY NILES (D)
Mont State Rep
b Ft Belknap, Mont, Jan 3, 42; s (father deceased) & Cecelia Stiffarm K Panick. Educ: Univ Mont, BA, 66, JD, 73. Polit & Govt Pos: Mont State Rep, 73- Bus & Prof Pos: Attorney-at-law, Kimble & Smith, 72- Mil Serv: Entered as Pvt, Army, 66, released as SP-4, 68, after serv in 4th Inf Div, Pleiku, Viet Nam, 67-68; Army Commendation Medal. Mem: Mont Bar Asn. Relig: Catholic. Legal Res: 640 S Sixth E Missoula MT 59801 Mailing Add: 211 W Front St Missoula MT 59801

KIME, OTHO G
Nebr State Sen
Mailing Add: Valentine NE 69201

KIMMELL, CURTIS VOLLMER (D)
Mem Finance Comt, Ind State Dem Cent Comt
b Vincennes, Ind, Dec 20, 15; s Joseph Woodman Kimmell & Cora Vollmer K; m 1939 to Dorothy Jane Funk; c Kathryn Jane (Mrs Jay Garrett), Joseph W, II & Deborah Vance (Mrs Terry Gray). Educ: Va Mil Inst, 33-34; Ind Univ, LLB, 34-39; Delta Upsilon. Polit & Govt Pos: Precinct committeeman, Dem Party, 39-53; mem finance comt, Knox Co Dem Party, Ind, 40-; dep prosecuting attorney, Knox Co, 46-47; chmn, Seventh Dist Young Dem, 46-48, state treas, 47-48; city attorney, Vincennes, 48-52 & 60-64; chmn, Seventh Cong Dist Dem Party, 49-52; mem finance comt, Ind State Dem Cent Comt, 60-64 & 70-; deleg, Dem Nat Conv, 72. Bus & Prof Pos: Partner, Law Firm of Kimmell, Kimmell & Funk, Vincennes, Ind, 39- Mil Serv: Entered as A/S, Navy, 42, released as Lt(sg), 45, after serv in Am & Pac Theaters. Mem: Jr CofC; Knox Co Bar Asn; Elks (Exalted Ruler, 50-51); Shrine; Moose. Relig: Methodist. Legal Res: 1403 Old Orchard Rd Vincennes IN 47591 Mailing Add: 112 N Seventh St Vincennes IN 47591

KIMMITT, JOSEPH STANLEY (D)
Secy for Majority, US Senate
b Lewistown, Mont, Apr 5, 18; m 1947 to Eunice L Wegener; c Robert M, Kathleen A, Joseph H, Thomas P, Mark T, Mary P & Judy J. Educ: Utah State Univ, BS, 60; George Washington Univ; Phi Sigma Kappa. Polit & Govt Pos: Admin asst to Majority Leader, US Senate, Secy for Majority, US Senate, 66- Mil Serv: Entered as Pvt, Army, 41, released as Col, 66; Silver Star; Legion of Merit; Bronze Star V with 3 Oak Leaf Clusters. Mem: Elks; KofC. Honors & Awards: Awarded Order of Mennelik II for Valor, Ethiopia. Relig: Catholic. Legal Res: Great Falls MT 59401 Mailing Add: 6004 Copley Lane McLean VA 22101

KIMURA, ROBERT YUTAKA (D)
Hawaii State Rep
b Honolulu, Hawaii, Aug 12, 24; s Toraki Kimura & Shitsu Matsumori K; m 1957 to Elsie Kim; c Robert, Jr, Kimberly, Arnold & Pamela. Educ: Univ Hawaii, BA, 48; Northwestern Univ Sch Law, JD, 51. Polit & Govt Pos: Milk comnr, State Dept Agr, Hawaii, 67-68; Hawaii State Rep, 68-, chmn agr comt & mem judiciary, health, tourism & fed-state-co comn, Hawaii House of Rep, 68-70, chmn comt on higher educ & vchmn judiciary comt, 71-, mem educ comt, consumer protection comt, environ protection comt & pub employ comt, 73- Bus & Prof Pos: Instr bus law, Univ Hawaii, 53-60; attorney-at-law, 53- Mil Serv: Entered as Pvt, Army, 43, released as S/Sgt, 45, after serv in Hq, 10th Army, Asiatic-Pac Theater, 44-45; Res, 45-67, Maj; Dept Army Commendation Medal. Mem: Hawaii Bar Asn; Mil Intel Vet Club Hawaii; Pauoa Community Asn; Punchbowl Youth Orgn (pres, 72-); Roosevelt High Sch Booster Club (pres, 72-). Relig: Protestant. Mailing Add: 1333 River St Honolulu HI 96817

KINCAID, DIANE DIVERS (D)
Mem Exec Comt, Ark State Dem Comt
b Washington, DC, Oct 25, 38; d William Keeveny Divers & Minna Rosenbaum D; m 1961 to Hugh Reid Kincaid; c William Reid & Kathryn Lea. Educ: Miami Univ, 55-56; Cornell Univ, BA, 59; Univ Ark, Fayetteville, MA, 67; Phi Beta Kappa; Pi Beta Phi. Polit & Govt Pos: Contract analyst, President's Comt on Govt Contracts, 59-60; research asst, US Senate Spec Comt on Unemploy, 60; legis secy, Sen Stuart Symington, 60-63; committeeman, Washington Co Cent Dem Comt, 68-; chmn, Gov Comn on Status of Women, 71-; deleg, Dem Nat Conv, 72, vchmn, Ark Deleg, 72; mem exec comt, Ark State Dem Comt, 72- Bus & Prof Pos: Instr, Dept Polit Sci, Univ Ark, Fayetteville, 68- Mem: Am Polit Sci Asn; Women's Polit Caucus; Mod Lit Club. Honors & Awards: Outstanding Faculty Woman Panhellenic Coun, Univ Ark, 71. Relig: Methodist. Mailing Add: 520 Lakeridge Dr Fayetteville AR 72701

KINCAID, DONALD R (R)
NC State Sen
b Lenoir, NC, June 2, 36; s Hugh Theodore Kincaid & Myrtle McCall K; m 1956 to Syretha Weatherford; c Donald, Jr & Lisa Anette. Educ: Appalachian State Teachers Col, BS, 59. Polit & Govt Pos: NC State Rep, 67-72; NC State Sen, 73- Mil Serv: Entered as Pvt, NC Nat Guard, 53, released as E-5, 62. Mem: Lenoir Lions Club; Gamewell Ruritan Club. Mailing Add: 227 Main St NW Lenoir NC 28645

KINCAID, H THOMAS (TAM) (R)
Committeeman, Pima Co Rep Party, Ariz
b San Antonio, Tex, Nov 27, 32; s Joseph Madison Kincaid, Jr & Marjory Nan Thomas K; m 1957 to Barbara Anne Colt; c H Thomas, Jr, Gail Eaton & Christopher Evan. Educ: Univ Ariz, BA, 61. Polit & Govt Pos: Committeeman, Pima Co Rep Party, Ariz, 67-; pub rels & speech writer, Pierce for Cong Comt, 68; ad writer, Pima Co Williams for Gov Comt, 68; mem, Tucson Trunk 'n Tusk Comt, 68-; mem, Pima Co ABC Fiesta Comt, 68-; pub rels, Pima Co Rep Exec Comt, 69-70; Ariz State Rep, Dist 13, 70-74; chmn, Citizens Adv Comt to Ariz Corp Comn, currently; mem, City of Tucson Comn on Improved Govt Mgt, currently. Bus

& Prof Pos: Staff writer, Ariz Daily Star, Tucson, 61-66; pres, Kincaid Enterprises, Inc, 66- Mil Serv: Entered as Pvt, Army, 52, released as SP-3, 55, after serv in 74th Regt Combat Team, 2nd Bn, Korean Conflict, 52-55; Good Conduct Medal; Nat Defense Serv Medal. Mem: Life mem Tucson Downtown Sertoma Club; Tucson Press Club; United Way (chmn, Pima Coun for Develop Disabilities, mem exec comt, Community Serv Div, mem, Health Educ Coun & Planning & Allocations Comt); Tucson CofC (mem comt on govt consolidation); Tucson Trade Bur (mem, Cent City Comt). Relig: Presbyterian. Mailing Add: 4821 E Winged Foot Pl Tucson AZ 85718

KINCAID, HUGH ARTHUR (D)
WVa State Deleg
b Point Pleasant, WVa, Feb 2, 11; s Arthur O Kincaid & Anna Jane Hunter K; m 1941 to Emma Lou Kittle; c Hugh A, Jr, Catherine Ann (Mrs Jack R Blacka), Carroll Barte (Mrs Charles F Twiss), Charles M & Jefferson C. Educ: Marshall Univ; Cincinnati Col Embalming. Polit & Govt Pos: Mem, Cabell Co Dem Exec Comt, WVa, formerly; WVa State Deleg, 54-56, 58-60 & 64- Bus & Prof Pos: Mortician. Mem: Mason; Odd Fellows; Elks; Big Green Club; YMCA (exec comt). Relig: Methodist. Mailing Add: 1544 Fifth Ave Huntington WV 25701

KINCAID, LLOYD H (R)
Wis State Rep
Mailing Add: 101 N Crandon Ave Crandon WI 54520

KINCAID, WILLIAM K (R)
NH State Rep
Mailing Add: 16 Union St Dover NH 03820

KINCANNON, PHYLLIS ANNE (R)
Secy, Pulaski Co Rep Comt, Ark
b Indianola, Iowa, Sept 9, 27; d Tandy VanNuys Allen & Thelma McGee A; m 1947 to John Absolum Kincannon; c John Allen, James Thomas & Jay Michael. Educ: State Col Ark, Conway, BSE, 49; Univ Southern Calif, 52-53; Nat Jr Honor Soc. Polit & Govt Pos: Precinct chmn, Pulaski Co Rep Comt, Ark, 66-, secy, 71-; pres, Little Rock Rep Women, 72-; chmn, Pulaski Co E Region, 72-; deleg, Rep Nat Conv, 72; campaign mgr, Cand for Secy of State, 72; chmn legis comt, Ark Fedn Rep Women, 72- Mem: Alpha Delta Kappa; Ark Home Builders Auxiliary of Gtr Little Rock. Relig: United Methodist; pres, United Methodist Women, 73. Mailing Add: 3 Belair Ct North Little Rock AR 72116

KINDNESS, THOMAS NORMAN (R)
US Rep, Ohio
b Knoxville, Tenn, Aug 26, 29; s Norman Garden Kindness & Christine Gunn K; m 1951 to Ann Gifford Hosman; c Sharon Lee, David Todd, Glen Jeff & Adam Bruce. Educ: Univ Md, AB, 51; George Washington Univ Law Sch, LLB, 53; Alpha Tau Omega. Polit & Govt Pos: Mayor, Hamilton, Ohio, 64-67; city councilman, 68-69; Ohio State Rep, 40th Dist, 71-72; Ohio State Rep, 58th Dist, 73-74; US Rep, Ohio, 75- Bus & Prof Pos: Attorney, Hilland, Hyde & Kindness, Washington, DC, 54-57; asst counsel, Champion Int Corp, Hamilton, Ohio, 57-73. Mem: Gamma Eta Gamma. Honors & Awards: Distinguished Serv Award, Hamilton Jaycees, 64. Relig: Presbyterian. Mailing Add: 328 South D St Hamilton OH 45013

KINDT, LOIS JEANNETTE (R)
Chmn, Waynesboro Rep Comt, Va
b Milwaukee, Wis, Feb 22, 27; d Roy Herman Woelffer & Rubie Ann Shekey W; m 1949 to Warren Frederick Kindt; c John Warren & June Ann. Educ: Univ Wis-Madison, BA, 48. Polit & Govt Pos: Ward coordr, Waynesboro Rep Comt, Va, 63-69, vchmn, 69-71, chmn, 71-; mem, Citizen's Adv Comt, Waynesboro, 69-71. Bus & Prof Pos: Crew leader, US Census Bur, Waynesboro, 70. Mem: Am Asn Univ Women; Waynesboro Community Hosp Auxiliary. Relig: Lutheran. Mailing Add: 1709 Lyndhurst Rd Waynesboro VA 22980

KING, ALVIN M (D)
Tenn State Rep
Mailing Add: 1874 Southern Memphis TN 38114

KING, BILL B (R)
Chmn, Lipscomb Co Rep Party, Tex
b Canadian, Tex, Sept 5, 42; s Jack Richard King & Lois Carol Bryant K; m 1962 to Denny Eldridge; c Jan. Educ: Tex Tech Univ, BS in Agr, 66; Block & Bridle Club; Tex Tech Rodeo Club; Future Farmers of Am. Polit & Govt Pos: Chmn, Lipscomb Co Rep Party, Tex, 68- Bus & Prof Pos: Self employed breeder of Hereford cattle & registered quarter horses. Relig: Baptist. Mailing Add: Rte 3 Canadian TX 79014

KING, BILL GENE (D)
Ala State Sen
b Huntsville, Ala, Oct 27, 34; s Benjimin Wilford King & Hattye Wallace King Moore; m Frances Anderson; c Pamela Lynn, Susan Malissa & Chrystopher Martin. Educ: Bowling Green State Univ, 52-53; Florence State Col, 58-59; Tenn Technol Univ, BS, 61. Polit & Govt Pos: Dir, Downtown Develop Housing Authority, Huntsville, Ala, 65-66; dir, Model City, 67-70; Ala State Rep, 70-74; Ala State Sen, 75- Bus & Prof Pos: Exec vpres, Medcare of Am, Inc, 65-67; chmn bd, Int Fiber Glass Inc; pres & chmn bd, Pub Systs Inc, formerly; pres, King Mgt Co; pres & chmn bd, Bus Properties, Inc, 72- Mil Serv: Entered as Airman Basic, Air Force, 51, released as S/Sgt, 55, after serv in Commun Squadron, Europe, 52-55. Publ: A new dimension in urban planning, Ala League of Cities, 69. Mem: Jaycees. Honors & Awards: Young Man of Year, Huntsville, 65; Outstanding Young Man of Ala, 66. Relig: Methodist. Legal Res: 704 Eustis Ave SE Huntsville AL 35801 Mailing Add: PO Box 382 Huntsville AL 35804

KING, BRUCE (D)
b Stanley, NMex; s William King & Molly Schooler K; m 1947; c William & Gary. Educ: Univ NMex, 43-44. Polit & Govt Pos: Co comnr, NMex, 54-58; NMex State Rep, 59-68, Speaker, NMex House of Rep, 62-68; legis mem, Bd Finance, NMex, 61-62; chmn, NMex Dem Party, 66-67; pres, NMex Const Conv, currently; Gov, NMex, 71-74; chmn, Nat Oil & Gas Compact Comn, 73; vchmn, Western States Gov Conf, 73-74; mem adv comt, Nat Dem Party; deleg, Dem Nat Mid-Term Conf, 74. Bus & Prof Pos: Rancher; livestock feeder. Mil Serv: World War II. Mem: NMex Farm & Livestock Bur (bd dirs); NMex Cattle Growers Asn; NMex Soil & Water Conserv (vpres); Northern NMex Fair Asn (chmn); NMex LPG Asn (bd mem). Relig: Protestant. Mailing Add: State Capitol Santa Fe NM 87501

KING, CARL LEANDER (D)
Chmn, Castro Co Dem Party, Tex
b Hale Center, Tex, Oct 26, 24; s Leander King & Nana White K; m 1953 to Frances Lee Vogelsang; c Janet, Carla & Steve. Educ: Tex Tech Univ, 1 year. Polit & Govt Pos: Chmn, Castro Co Dem Party, Tex, 68-; deleg, Dem Nat Mid-Term Conf, 74. Bus & Prof Pos: Dir, Dimmitt Agr Indust, 8 years; chmn, Boy Scouts Fund Dr, 2 years; dir, Castro Co Bldg Comt, 3 years; farmer & rancher, currently. Mil Serv: Entered as A/S, Navy, 43, released as Coxswain, 46, after serv in 7th Spec & 36th Spec Bn, Aleutian Islands, Asiatic & Pac Theatres; 2 Battle Stars. Mem: Am Legion; VFW; Farmers Union; Boy Scouts; Camp Fire Girls (dir). Relig: Church of Christ. Mailing Add: 707 W Grant St Dimmitt TX 79027

KING, CARLETON JAMES (R)
b Saratoga Springs, NY, June 15, 04; m to Constance M Roddy; c Comdr Carleton J, Jr & Mrs James A Murphy, Jr. Educ: Union Univ, LLB, 26. Polit & Govt Pos: Acting city judge, Saratoga Springs, NY, 36-41; Asst Dist Attorney, Saratoga Co, 42-50, Dist Attorney, 50-60; US Rep, NY, 60-74; NY Cand, US House of Rep, 74. Bus & Prof Pos: Lawyer, King, Duval & Murphy. Mem: NY State Bar Asn; Saratoga Co Bar Asn; NY State Dist Attorney's Asn. Legal Res: 444 Broadway Saratoga Springs NY 12866 Mailing Add: 8 Victoria Lane Saratoga Springs NY 12866

KING, CLARENCE LEROY, JR (D)
b Salina, Kans, Apr 5, 32; s Clarence Leroy King & Margaret Swift K; m 1951 to Doris I Altman; c Jeff & Joni. Educ: Kans Wesleyan Univ, AB, 54; Washburn Univ, LLB, 57; Beta Tau Omega; Phi Alpha Delta. Polit & Govt Pos: Dem precinct committeeman, Kans; pres, Saline Co Young Dem; mem, Leadership Conf, Denver, Colo, 60; chmn, Saline Co Dem Party, 66-74; mem, Century Club; deleg, Dem Nat Conv, 68; mem, Gov Comn Criminal Admin, 69; Kans State Hwy Comnr, 74- Bus & Prof Pos: Partner, Law Firm of King, Stokes, Knudson & Nitz, Chartered, Salina. Mem: Am Bar Asn; Am Trial Lawyers Asn; Defense Research Inst; CofC; Kans Wesleyan Univ Alumni Asn. Honors & Awards: Outstanding Young Man of Salina, 61; Outstanding Young Alumnus, Kans Wesleyan Univ, 65. Relig: Methodist; past teacher, mem off bd & mem Christian social concerns, finance & long range planning comns. Mailing Add: 840 Pentwood Dr Salina KS 67401

KING, CYRIL E
Gov, VI
Mailing Add: Govt House Charlotte Amalie St Thomas VI 00801

KING, DAVID S (D)
b Salt Lake City, Utah, June 20, 17; s Sen William H King (deceased); m to Rosalie L; c eight (two deceased). Educ: Univ Utah, BA, 37; Georgetown Univ Col Law, JD, 42; Phi Beta Kappa; Phi Kappa Phi. Polit & Govt Pos: Law clerk to Justice James M Proctor, US Dist Court, DC, 42-43; law clerk to Justice Harold M Stephens, US Court of Appeals, DC, 43-44; attorney, Off Price Admin, 44-45; attorney, Utah State Tax Comn, 45-47; US Rep, Utah, 59-62 & 66-67; US Ambassador to Malagasy Repub & to Mauritius, 67-69. Bus & Prof Pos: Practiced law, Salt Lake City, Utah, 47-59, 63-65 & 69-72; lectr bus law, Henager Sch Bus, 9 years. Publ: Lectures in pamphlet form & articles in Foreign Serv J. Mem: Boy Scouts; Salt Lake Jr CofC; Rotary; Foreign Serv Asn; US CofC. Honors & Awards: Spec Award, Utah Educ Asn; Spec Rep of the President to Mauritian Independence Day Ceremonies. Relig: Latter-day Saint; missionary to Gt Brit, 37-39; gen supt, Mutual Improv Asn, 47-59; seminary teacher, 44-51; bishop, Kensington Ward, Washington Stake, currently. Legal Res: Salt Lake City UT Mailing Add: 9614 Dewmar Lane Kensington MD 20795

KING, DAVID WILL (D)
b Albuquerque, NMex, June 28, 46; s Sam King & Margaret Lacy K; m 1966 to Veda Lorene Wilson; c David W, II. Educ: NMex State Univ, BS, 69; MS, 70; Omicron Delta Epsilon; Tau Kappa Epsilon; Baptist Student Union; Block & Bridle. Polit & Govt Pos: Pres, NMex State Univ Young Dem, 69-70; pres, Student Supreme Court, NMex State Univ, 69-70; nat committeeman, NMex Young Dem, 70-71; State Planning Dir, 71-74; State Border Comnr, 72-; deleg, Dem Nat Mid-Term Conf, 74; mem budget comt, Dem Party NMex, 74-75. Bus & Prof Pos: Research & teaching asst, NMex State Univ, 69-70; owner & operator, King Bros Ranches, Stanley, NMex, 60-; owner & operator, Pine Canyon, Inc, Stanley, 71-; mem exec bd, Resource Conserv & Develop Coun, 74- Publ: Co-auth, State Outdoor Recreation Plan, 71 & co-auth, 1973 & 1974 Annual Reports, NMex State Planning Off. Mem: Elks; NMex Amigos; Rotary Int; Am Soc Planners; NMex Cattle Growers. Honors & Awards: Citizen Appreciation Award, NMex Am Revolution Bicentennial Comn. Relig: Baptist; deacon, First Baptist Church Albuquerque; mem state mission bd. Mailing Add: 1716 Chacoma Pl SW Albuquerque NM 87104

KING, ERNEST P (D)
Lt Gov, Pa
Mailing Add: State Capitol Harrisburg PA 17120

KING, ETHYL BELL (R)
Chmn, Rep Comt Worth Co, Mo
b Oxford, Mo, July 13, 03; d Oliver Roberts & Eva Miller R; m 1923 to Harlan F King; c Oliver Fredrick & Keith Samuel. Educ: Worth High Sch, 2 years; Grant City High Sch, grad, 22. Polit & Govt Pos: Mem, Worth Co Rep Comt, Mo, 44-, chmn, currently. Bus & Prof Pos: Nurse aide, Mo Methodist Hosp, St Joseph, Mo, 10 years. Mem: Eastern Star. Relig: Christian. Mailing Add: Parnell MO 64475

KING, FRANK W (D)
Mem-At-Lg, Dem Nat Comt
Mailing Add: 271 E State St Columbus OH 43215

KING, FREDERICK JENKS (R)
Chmn, West Feliciana Parish Rep Exec Comt, La
b East Cleveland, Ohio, Feb 18, 11; s Herbert Doan King & Lillian Jenks K; m 1942 to Augusta Walmsley; c Semmes W, Frederick J, Carolyn D & Katharine H. Educ: Yale Univ, 33; Delta Kappa Epsilon. Polit & Govt Pos: Mem, West Feliciana Parish Rep State Cent Comt, La, 52-68; chmn, West Feliciana Parish Rep Exec Comt, 66- Bus & Prof Pos: Auditor, Cent Nat Bank, Cleveland, Ohio, 33-35; broker, Prescott Co, Cleveland, Ohio, 35-49; asst vpres, La Nat Bank, Baton Rouge, La, 53-73; retired. Mil Serv: Entered as 2nd Lt, Army Res, 33, released as Lt Col, 46, after serv as Dep A-1, Hq Western Tech Training Command, Denver, Colo, 42-46; Col (Ret), Air Force Res, 42-73. Mem: Nat Rifle Asn; Am Legion; Air Force Asn. Relig: Episcopal. Mailing Add: PO Box 2 Bains LA 70713

KING, GLENDON N (R)
Vt State Rep
Mailing Add: 3 Hill St Northfield VT 05663

KING, GORMAN H (D)
Dem Nat Committeeman, NDak
Mailing Add: 605 Eighth Ave Valley City ND 58702

KING, HAROLD LLOYD (D)
Ark State Sen
b Redlands, Calif, Apr 13, 26; s Samuel Martin King & Cordelia Francis K; m 1951 to Orlen Lydia Lemke; c Harold Lloyd, Jr, John Martin, James Robert, Sandra Kay & Dianna Marie. Educ: Ouachita Univ, 3 years; Ark Law Sch, LLB. Polit & Govt Pos: Ark State Sen, Dist Six, 71- Bus & Prof Pos: Partner, Acchione & King, 59- Mil Serv: Entered as Pvt, Army, 44, released as First Lt, 47, after serv in Eighth Army, Pac. Mem: Mason; Am Legion; Lions; Ark State Horse Show Asn (gen chmn); Mid-State Horse Show Asn (pres). Relig: Baptist. Mailing Add: Rte 1 Box 192-1 Sheridan AR 72150

KING, JASON WILLIAM
b Seattle, Wash, May 2, 49; s James W King & Marie Sampson K; single. Educ: Spring Hill Col, BS, 71; pres, Portier Debate Soc. Polit & Govt Pos: Wash state coordr, US Senate staff of Sen Henry M Jackson, 71-72, spec asst for state, 73-; mgr, First Cong Dist campaign of John W Hempelmann, 72; deleg, Dem Nat Conv, 72; legis asst, August P Mardesich, Majority Floor Leader, Wash State Senate, 73- Bus & Prof Pos: Asst mgr, Sea Use Coun, 73- Honors & Awards: Eagle Scout, Boy Scouts, 64; Officer of the Year, Jr Achievement, 66, Exec Award, 67. Mailing Add: 713 Laurel St Edmonds WA 98020

KING, JEAN SADAKO (D)
Hawaii State Sen
Mailing Add: Senate Sgt-at Arms State Capitol Honolulu HI 96813

KING, JOHN ALLEN (JACK) (D)
Ga State Rep
b Cusseta, Ga, Apr 13, 19; s B J King & Marie Allen K; m 1959 to Carolyn Hall; c John Stephen. Educ: Young Harris Jr Col, 38-40; Univ Ga, BBA, 42; Woodrow Wilson Col Law, JD, 69. Polit & Govt Pos: Airport mgr, Columbus Munic Airport, Ga, 52-65; Ga State Rep, Dist 85, Post 2, 71-, mem, Univ Syst, State of Repub & Judiciary Comts, Ga House of Rep, currently. Bus & Prof Pos: Vpres, secy & treas, King's Sch of Aviation, Inc, Columbus, Ga, 46-65; attorney, Columbus, 69- Mil Serv: Entered as Pvt, Army, 42, released as T/Sgt, 46, after serv in Security & Intel Div; Good Conduct Medal; Am Theatre Ribbon. Mem: Columbus Lawyers Club; Am Legion; Bulldog Club (pres); Ga Aviation Trades Asn (vpres); Civil Mil Air Safety Coun (chmn). Relig: Methodist. Mailing Add: 3110 Hooper Ave Columbus GA 31907

KING, JOHN GERARD (D)
Mass State Rep
b Beverly, Mass, Nov 30, 42; s James Gerard King & Evelyn M Curley K; single. Educ: Boston Univ, BA, 64; Suffolk Univ Law Sch, JD, 69. Polit & Govt Pos: Mem town coun, Danvers, Mass, 65-68, 69; Mass State Rep, Sixth Essex Dist, 71- Bus & Prof Pos: Attorney-at-law, currently. Mem: Essex & Mass Bar Asns. Relig: Roman Catholic. Mailing Add: 17 School St Danvers MA 01923

KING, JOHN W (D)
b Manchester, NH, Oct 10, 18; s Michael J King & Anna Lydon K; m to Anna McLaughlin. Educ: Harvard Col, BA; Columbia Oniv, MA in Pub Law; Columbia Univ Law Sch, LLB; Phi Delta Phi. Honors & Awards: LLD, Columbia Univ, St Anselm's Col & Univ NH; MA, Dartmouth Col; Dr Civil Laws, New Eng Col; Dr Pub Admin, Franklin Pierce Col & Suffolk Univ. Polit & Govt Pos: NH State Rep, 56-62, former mem, Ballot Law Comn, Manchester Charter Revision Comn & House Appropriations & Rules Comts & Minority Leader, 59-62, NH State House of Rep; Gov, NH, 62-68; deleg, Dem Nat Conv, 68; Justice of NH Superior Court, currently. Bus & Prof Pos: Sr partner, King, Nixon, Christy & Tessier, Manchester, NH, formerly; trustee, St Anselm's Col, formerly. Mem: Am Judicature Soc (dir); KofC; Elks; Eagles; Moose. Relig: Roman Catholic. Mailing Add: Connemara Farm Kennedy Hill Rd RD 1 Goffstown NH 03045

KING, LESLIE HENRY (R)
Mem, Tenn Rep State Exec Comt
b Los Angeles, Calif, Mar 28, 23; s Leslie Lynch King & Margaret Atwood K; m 1943 to Virginia Hester Hodges; c Pamela Virginia (Mrs A Hubert Smith, Jr), Kyra Leslie (Mrs Gary Patton Wyatt), Leslie Henry, Jr & Craig Hodges; two grandchildren. Educ: Lincoln High Sch, Nebr, 36-39; Kemper Mil Acad, Booneville, Mo, 39-40 & 41. Polit & Govt Pos: Chmn, Putnam Co Rep Party, Tenn, 64-68; alt deleg, Nat Rep Conv, 68; Putnam Co finance chmn, Brock for Sen, 70; Fourth Dist rep, Gov Dunn, 70-71; chmn, Putnam Co Finance Comt, 70-74; Fourth Dist chmn, Relect the President, 72; mem, Tenn Rep State Exec Comt, 74- Bus & Prof Pos: Owner & operator, King Auto Parts, Cookeville, Tenn, 46-68; owner, Goodyear Tire Ctr, 68-; bd dirs, Putnam Co CofC, 69- Mem: Mason; Shrine; Cookeville Optimist Club; Co Voting Comn; CofC. Relig: United Methodist. Mailing Add: 1256 E Eighth St Cookeville TN 38501

KING, LUCILLE (D)
Mem, Dem Nat Comt, NY
Mailing Add: 369 Rockingham St Rochester NY 14620

KING, MARJORIE PITTER (D)
b Seattle, Wash, Mar 8, 21; d Edward Alexander Pitter & Marjorie Allen P; m 1945 to John Thomas King; c Walter Joseph & Edward Allen. Educ: Univ Wash, Seattle; Howard Univ, Washington, DC; City Col New York; Alpha Omicron; Delta Sigma Theta. Polit & Govt Pos: Pres, Metrop Dem Womens Club, Wash, 59-63; vchmn, 37th Dist Dem Precinct Orgn, 58-60, chmn, 60-64; vchmn, King Co Dem Cent Comt, 60-67; nominating chmn & state finance chmn, State Fedn Dem Womens Clubs, 61-62, state treas, 63-64, orgn chmn, 66-68; organizer, State Teenage Dem, Wash State Cent Comt, 66; mem credentials comt, Dem Nat Conv, 64, deleg, 68; Wash State Rep, 65-67; state chmn operation support, Wash State Dem Comt, 67-; pres, Ann T O'Donnell Metrop Dem Women, 68-; pres, Seventh Cong Dist Fedn Dem Womens Clubs, 69- Bus & Prof Pos: Clerk, Adj Gen Off, War Dept, 42-43; indust engr, Univ Labs, 44; accts receivable clerk in chg-clerk, IV Seattle Eng Dept, 51-56; self employed tax consult, letter shop, M & M Serv Shop, 47- Mem: YMCA (bd mem); Urban League (bd mem); NAACP; EMadison Commercial Club; 3 M Urban Renewal. Relig: Lutheran. Mailing Add: 1627 25th Ave Seattle WA 98122

KING, MARY LOIS (R)
Dep Pres, Tex Fedn Rep Women
b Breckenridge, Tex, July 6, 24; d John C Ward & Mabel Daniel W; m 1948 to Gordon R King; c Gordon R, III, John C & David M. Educ: Hockaday Jr Col, 42-43; Southern Methodist Univ, BM, 45; Univ Colo, Boulder, 45; Delta Delta Delta. Polit & Govt Pos: Rep campaign hq chmn, McLennan Co, Tex, 62, 63 & 64, get-out-the-vote chmn, 64; deleg, Rep State Conv, 64, 66 & 68; deleg, Rep Nat Conv, 68; vchmn, McLennan Co Rep Party, 66; key Rep, Tex, 66; pres, McLennan Co Rep Women, 67; dep pres, Tex Fedn Rep Women, 68-; dep state chmn for Paul Egger's Campaign for Gov, Region One, 70; vchmn & treas, Congressman James Collins Fund Raising Dinner, 72; Tex Regional Subchmn, Comt to Reelect the President, 72. Mem: Serv League; Am Asn Univ Women; PTA. Honors & Awards: One of Ten Outstanding Rep Women of Tex, 67. Relig: Methodist. Mailing Add: 4206 Larchmont Dallas TX 75205

KING, MELVIN H (D)
Mass State Rep
Mailing Add: State Capitol Boston MA 02133

KING, PETER COTTERILL (R)
Adminr, Southwestern Power Admin, Dept of Interior
b White Plains, NY, Aug 23, 30; s Robert Cotterill King & Ruth McKeown K; m 1958 to Nancy English; c Margot E, Philip M & Sabrina P. Educ: US Mil Acad, West Point, NY, BS, 52; Univ Pa, MBA, 58; Harvard Univ, Mgt Sem Cert, 68. Polit & Govt Pos: Councilman, Lawton, Okla, 68-69; adminr, Southwestern Power Admin, Dept of Interior, 69- Bus & Prof Pos: Systs engr, Research Ctr, IBM Corp, Yorktown Heights, NY, 58-62; vpres, Security Bank & Trust Co, Lawton, Okla, 62-69; pres, Security Broadcasting Corp, Lawton, 64-69. Mil Serv: Entered as 2nd Lt, Army, 52, released as 1st Lt, 56, after serv in 350th Inf Regt, Austrian Theatre, 52-55; Maj, Army Res, 66; Nat Defense & Reserve Officers Serv Medal; Army of Occup Medal; Expert Inf Badge; Parachutist Badge. Mem: US CofC; Nat Asn Mfrs; Okla Bankers Asn. Relig: Episcopal. Mailing Add: 1120 E 24th Pl Tulsa OK 74114

KING, PHILLIP E (D)
Ky State Rep
b 1929. Educ: Georgetow Col; Univ Ky; Univ Cincinnati Col Law, LLB. Polit & Govt Pos: Ky State Rep, currently. Bus & Prof Pos: Attorney-at-law. Mil Serv: Army. Mem: Kenton Co & Ky Bar Asns; Taylor Mill Lions Club; Brotherhood of RR Trainmen. Relig: Baptist. Mailing Add: 15 W Southern Ave Covington KY 41015

KING, RAYMOND E, JR (D)
Mem, NC Dem Exec Comt
b Monticello, Fla, Dec 30, 23; s Raymond E King & Viola Clark K; m 1944 to Sara Jean Agnew; c Sara Anne & Raymond E, III. Educ: Abraham Baldwin Col, grad; Univ Ga, BS; Demothenian Lit Soc; Univ Ga Debate Team & Club. Polit & Govt Pos: Precinct chmn, Mecklenburg Co Dem Party, NC & chmn, 61-64; mem, Charlotte-Mecklenburg Intergovt Task Force Comt & Charlotte Redevelop Comn, 65-; mem, NC Dem Exec Comt, currently. Mil Serv: Entered as Pvt, Army, 44, released as Sgt, 46, after serv in Austria; 3 ETO Campaign Ribbons. Mem: Nat Asn Life Underwriters (pres); Chartered Life Underwriters Soc; NC Health Underwriters Asn (mem bd dirs); Ala Health Underwriters Asn; Gen Agts & Mgrs Conf. Relig: Presbyterian. Legal Res: 4015 Arbor Way Charlotte NC 28211 Mailing Add: 1373 E Morehead St Charlotte NC 28204

KING, RAYMOND LAMPREY (R)
Finance Chmn, Ogemaw Co Rep Party, Mich
b Braintree, Mass, Sept 1, 29; s Samuel Winslow King & Doris Lamprey K; m 1951 to Jean Ellen Peters; c Deborah Rae, David Winslow & Kathryn Mae. Educ: Univ Maine, BA, 52; Boston Univ Sch Law, LLB, 57; class pres, Boston Univ Sch Law, 57; Theta Chi; Univ Maine Men's Senate. Polit & Govt Pos: Rep precinct deleg, Pontiac, Mich, 58-60; statutory mem, Oakland Co Rep Comt, Mich, 59-60; mem finance staff, Oakland Co Rep Comt, 60; deleg, Mich Const Conv, 60-61; prosecuting attorney, Ogemaw Co, Mich, 62-68; finance chmn, Ogemaw Co Rep Party, 62-; mem, Mich Rep State Cent Comt, Tenth Dist, 63-64; chmn, Tenth Cong Dist Rep Comt, 64-68; city attorney, West Branch, Mich, 64-68; deleg, Rep Nat Conv, 68; probate judge, Ogemaw Co, Mich, 68- Bus & Prof Pos: Mgt trainee & merchandising mgr, Sears Roebuck & Co, Bangor, Maine, 52-54; supvr purchasing admin, Ford Motor Co, Dearborn, Mich, 57-60. Mil Serv: Entered as Sgt, Air Force, 51, released as S/Sgt, 52, after serv in 132nd Fighter-Interceptor Squadron, Eastern Air Defense Command; Air Force Res, inactive, 1st Lt. Mem: Am Bar Asn; Am Judicature Soc; Mich Bar Asn (chmn, Tenth Dist Character & Fitness Comt); Kiwanis; West Branch Country Club. Honors & Awards: Recipient of Ford Motor Co Award for Outstanding Community Serv, 59. Relig: Protestant. Legal Res: 321 Sidney St West Branch MI 48661 Mailing Add: PO Box 165 West Branch MI 48661

KING, RICHARD ALLEN (R)
Mayor, Independence, Mo
b St Joseph, Mo, July 4, 44; s Allen Weldon King & Lola Donelson K; m 1964 to Charlotte Helen Proett; c Mary, Suzanne & Allen. Educ: Univ Mo, Columbia, BA, 66, JD cum laude, 68; student ed, Mo Law Rev, 67-68; Phi Delta Phi; Order of the Coif; Scabbard & Blade; Beta Theta Phi. Polit & Govt Pos: Asst city counr, Independence, Mo, 68-69, mayor, 74-; mem, Mo Comn Human Rights, 73-74. Bus & Prof Pos: Assoc, Reese, Constance, Slayton, Stewart & Stewart, Independence, Mo, 68-73; partner, Constance, Slayton, Stewart & King, 73- Mil Serv: Entered as 2nd Lt, Army, 69, released as Capt, 71, after serv in 8th Inf Div, Europe, 69-71; Capt, Army Res; Nat Defense Serv Medal; Army Commendation Medal. Mem: Am Legion Boys State of Mo, Inc (bd dirs, 73-); Independence Sanitarium & Hosp (dir, 74-); Kiwanis Int; Independence Rep Club; Am Bar Asn. Honors & Awards: Mo Outstanding Young Man Award, Mo Jaycees, 75; Distinguished Serv Award, Independence Jaycees, 75; Hon Comnr, Mo Bicentennial Comn, 74- Relig: Methodist. Legal Res: 18403 Hanthorn Dr Independence MO 64057 Mailing Add: 103 N Main Independence MO 64050

KING, RICHARD ARTHUR (D)
Wash State Rep
b Ritzville, Wash, Aug 30, 34; s George Stanford King & Elsie O'Donnell K; m 1955 to Mary Evelyn Butler; c Douglas Ritchie, Diana Marie, Shawn O'Donnell & Sherry Elaine. Educ: Univ Wash, BA, 56, MA, 58; Delta Sigma Rho; Acacia. Polit & Govt Pos: Vpres, Young Dem of Wash, 59-61, pres, 61-63; chmn, Snohomish Co Young Citizens for Kennedy-Johnson, 60;

chmn, Snohomish Co Cent Dem Club, 60-62; vpres, Second Cong Dist Dem Coun, 64; Wash State Rep, 65- Mem: Phi Rho Pi; Am Asn of Univ Profs; Speech Asn of Am; Am Fedn of Teachers; Eagles. Relig: Unitarian. Mailing Add: 309 77th Place SW Everett WA 98203

KING, ROGER C (R)
NH State Rep
Mailing Add: RFD 1 Deerfield NH 03037

KING, SEMMES WALMSLEY (R)
Mem, La Rep State Cent Comt
b New Orleans, La, Nov 6, 43; s Frederick Jenks King & Augusta Walmsley K; m 1970 to Elizabeth Hanna Hood. Polit & Govt Pos: Mem-at-lg, West Feliciana Parish Rep Exec Comt, La, 66-, chmn, 66-68, secy, 68-; constable, West Feliciana Parish, 68-; mem, La Rep State Cent Comt, 68-, sgt-at-arms, 72-; mil mem, La Gov Staff, 72- Bus & Prof Pos: Pres, King Agency, 73-; notary pub, West Feliciana Parish, 72- Publ: Justice of the Peace Training Course Textbook & Guide, La State Univ Law Sch, 71. Mem: Nat Sheriffs' Asn; La Constables Asn (pres, 72-); Am Soc Notaries; Am Judges Asn. Legal Res: Cedars Plantation Bains LA 70713 Mailing Add: PO Box 2 Bains LA 70713

KING, SHIRLEY MCVEIGH (D)
Committeewoman, Dem Exec Comt, Fla
b Jacksonville, Fla, Feb 13, 27; d Neal Tennert McVeigh & Essie Thomas M; m 1947 to John Pyram King; c Mary (Mrs Carl Henderson), Kathleen (Mrs Joseph Lissandrello), Joni Pearl & John Pyram, Jr. Educ: Andrew Jackson High Sch, Jacksonville, Fla, grad, 44. Polit & Govt Pos: Precinct committeewoman, Duval Co Dem Exec Comt, Fla, 57-, vchmn, 67-; committeewoman, Dem Exec Comt, Fla, 74-; co-chmn, Get Out the Vote Campaign, 74-; mem rules comt & cent comt, Fla Dem Party, 74- Bus & Prof Pos: Mem, Local Draft Bd, 72-75. Mem: Donkey Club (bd mem); Southside Woman's Club. Mailing Add: 111 Florida Blvd Neptune Beach FL 32233

KING, SPENCER M
b San Juan, PR, Aug 11, 17; s Amos J King & Cora S Morison K; m 1966 to Josephine Montes Smith. Educ: Yale Univ, BA, 40; Sch Foreign Serv, Georgetown Univ, summer 40; Civil Affairs Training Sch, Univ Mich, 44-45; Univ Chicago, 51; Nat War Col, grad, 58. Polit & Govt Pos: Mem, Foreign Serv, 45-74; third secy & vconsul, La Paz, Bolivia, 46-48; assigned to Dept of State, 48-51; first secy & consul, Prague, Czechoslovakia, 51-54; chief, E European Br, Voice of Am, 54-55; spec asst to the Asst Secy of State for Inter-Am Affairs, 55-57; foreign serv inspector, 58-62; dep chief of mission & consul gen, Quito, Ecuador, 62; dep chief of mission & consul gen, Santo Domingo, Dominican Repub, 62-64; dep inspector gen, Dept of State, 64-69; US Ambassador, Guyana, 69-74; consult, Dept State, 74- Mil Serv: Entered Army, 41, released as Maj, 46, after serv in Pac Theatre of Opers. Mem: Alpha Sigma Phi; Cum Laude Soc; Canon & Castle; Yale Club, New York & Washington; Manor Country Club, Rockville, Md. Legal Res: Belfast ME 04915 Mailing Add: 2855 Arizona Terr NW Washington DC 20016

KING, TOM COBB, JR (R)
Mem Exec Comt, Calhoun Co Rep Comt, Ala
b Gadsden, Ala, Nov 30, 15; s Tom Cobb King & Sadie Belle Cox K; m 1942 to Joan Taylor; c Thomas, Wendy, Clifton, Joanne & Nancy. Educ: Univ Va, BS, 38, MD, 41; Phi Beta Kappa; Alpha Tau Omega; Tilka; German Club; Calconon Club. Polit & Govt Pos: Mem exec comt, Calhoun Co Rep Comt, Ala, 52-, chmn, 66-67. Bus & Prof Pos: Pvt med practice, 49-; pres, S G & O, Inc, 65-66; pres, Anniston Obstetricians-Gynecologists P A, 70- Mil Serv: Entered as 1st Lt, Army, 42, released as Maj, 45, after serv in 559th F A Bn, ETO; ETO Medal with Five Battle Stars; Bronze Star. Mem: Fel Am Col Surgeons; fel Am Col Obstetricians & Gynecologists; Ala Med Asn; Co Med Soc; Ala Asn Obstetricians & Gynecologists. Relig: Episcopal. Mailing Add: 543 Hillyer High Rd Anniston AL 36201

KING, VERNON C (D)
Mo State Rep
b Lawson, Mo, Oct 20, 23; s Clarence E King & Anna G Clevenger K; m 1952 to Ruth E Marriott; c Cordell J, Collette R & Kevin V. Educ: Cent Mo State Col, BS in bus admin, 50; Sigma Tau Gamma; Student Govt, three years. Polit & Govt Pos: Mem staff, Gov Hearnes, Mo, 65-72; pres, Clay Co Dem Club, 69-71; mem, Mo Dem State Cent Comt, 69-71; Mo State Rep, 71-; deleg, Dem Nat Mid-Term Conf, 74. Bus & Prof Pos: Pres, Vernon King Inc, 63- Mil Serv: Entered as Pvt, 43, released as Sgt, 46, after serv in Third Army, ETO, 44-45; Two Purple Hearts; Good Conduct; Rifleman Sharpshooter. Mem: Rotary. Honors & Awards: Hon Col, State of Mo, 65. Relig: Protestant. Mailing Add: 2007 E Ridge Dr Excelsior Springs MO 64024

KING, WILLIAM HAMPTON (D)
State Auditor Pub Accts, Miss
b Heidelberg, Miss, Oct 1, 09; s William Elisha King & Sarah Covington K; m 1934 to Eldridge Douglas Banks; c Carolyn (Mrs Andrew) & Sarah Kay (Mrs Miklas). Educ: Hinds Jr Col, 25-28; YMCA Grad Sch, 30-34; Univ Miss, BA, 39. Polit & Govt Pos: Field staff auditor, State Dept of Audit, Jackson, Miss, 53-56, asst dir, 56-62, dir, 62-63, State Auditor Pub Accts, 64- Bus & Prof Pos: Cannery mgr, Cumberland Coop, Crossville, Tenn, 37-39; faculty mem, Clarke Jr Col, Newton, Miss, 39-40; chief transportation sect, Ord Training Ctr & Plant, Flora, Miss, 41-44; acct, Woods Builders Supply Co, Jackson, Miss, 45-47; acct-in-charge, Scott Bldg Supply Corp, Cleveland, Miss, 47-52; CPA, self-employed, Cleveland, 52-53. Mem: Am Inst CPA; Munic Finance Officers' Asn of US & Can; Nat Asn State Auditors, Comptrollers & Treas; F&AM; Optimists. Relig: United Methodist. Legal Res: 404 Colonial Circle Jackson MS 39211 Mailing Add: PO Box 1060 Jackson MS 39205

KING, WILLIAM THEODORE (R)
Mem, Calif Rep State Cent Comt
b Detroit, Mich, Feb 3, 33; s Erle E Wright & Helen Louise Colvin W; m 1954 to Joan C Hutchon; c Jonatha Helen, Patrice Marie & William Theodore II. Educ: Principia Col, BA cum laude, 54; Harvard Univ, LLB, 57. Polit & Govt Pos: Chmn, Californians for Reagan, 66; state speakers chmn, Kuchel for Sen, 68; Southern Calif chmn, Citizens for Nixon, 68; spec gifts chmn, United Rep Finance Comt, Los Angeles Co, 68; campaign chmn, Alphonzo Bell for Mayor Comt, 69; co-chmn, Thomas Bradley for Mayor Comt, 69; field rep for Congressman Alphonzo Bell, currently; mem, Los Angeles Forward Exec Comt for Charter Revision, 69-70; mem, Calif Rep State Cent Comt, currently, Southern Calif finance chmn, 70-; attorney's chmn, United Rep Finance Dinner Comt, 70; Southern Calif vchmn, Murphy for Senate Comt, 70; mem Calif adv comt, US Comn on Civil Rights, currently. Bus & Prof Pos: Partner, Law Off Lindstrom, Robison, Lovell & King, currently; res assoc, Inst Govt & Pub Affairs, Univ Calif, Los Angeles, 69-70. Mem: Am Bar Asn (real property, probate & trust sect); Calif State Bar Asn; Los Angeles Co Bar Asn (mem exec comt, Los Angeles Probate & Trust Comt & Steering Comt to Support Admission of Minority Students to Law Schs); Am Judicature Soc; Const Rights Found (bd dirs). Relig: Christian Science. Legal Res: 306 Old Ranch Rd Bradbury CA 91010 Mailing Add: 550 S Flower St Los Angeles CA 90017

KINGHORN, ROBERT C (D)
Idaho State Sen
Mailing Add: 552 Cottage Ave Pocatello ID 83201

KINGSBURY, HARLEY RALPH (R)
Chmn, Walsh Co Rep Party, NDak
b Grafton, NDak, Mar 9, 13; s Charles Henry Kingsbury & Gertrude Johnston K; m 1936 to Noela Roxey Glenn; c C William, Patricia Ann (Mrs Duane Ganyo), Ralph Douglas, Linda Rae (Mrs Don Carlson) & Joyce Coleen (Mrs Leo Staskivige). Educ: High sch. Polit & Govt Pos: Twp treas, 23 years; mem sch bd, 22 years; NDak State Rep, 66-74; chmn, Walsh Co Rep Party, Dist 16, currently. Bus & Prof Pos: Dir, Grafton Nat Bank; dir, Deaconess Hosp, 15 years, past pres; dir, Unity Hosp, currently. Mem: Mason; KT (Past Grand Comdr); RSM (Past Grand Illustrious Master); Kem Temple Shrine; Eagles; Farm Bur; Nodak Rural Elec Asn (dir). Relig: Methodist. Mailing Add: 143 Eastwood Grafton ND 58237

KINGSFORD, LEONARD O (R)
Mem, Caribou Co Rep Cent Comt, Idaho
b Grace, Idaho, May 22, 18; s Robert Kingsford & Martha Mildred Ormond K; m 1942 to Helen Bernice Erickson; c Eric L & Edward. Educ: Univ Idaho, BS in Bus, 41, LLB, 48; Phi Alpha Delta. Polit & Govt Pos: Prosecuting attorney, Madison Co, Idaho, 49-50; precinct committeeman, Madison Co, 52-56, Bannock Co, 58-59 & Caribou Co, 62-; chmn, Caribou Co Rep Cent Comt, 66-72, mem, currently. Mil Serv: Entered as 2nd Lt, Army, 41, released as 1st Lt, 46, after serv in various units, Am & European Theaters, 41-46; Maj, Fin Dept, Army (Hon Res), 65- Mem: Am & Idaho Bar Asns; Am Judicature Soc; Am Land Title Asn; Idaho Land Title Asn. Relig: Latter-day Saint. Legal Res: 110 MacArthur Ave Soda Springs ID 83276 Mailing Add: PO Box 915 Soda Springs ID 83276

KINGSMORE, GERALD LEMOYNE (R)
Chmn, Union Co Rep Party, Ohio
b Toledo, Ohio, Aug 9, 01; s Donald James Kingsmore & Winifred Woodside K; m 1926 to Mary Rosina Hoffman; c Judith (Mrs William Grannis), Gerald L, Jr & Anne (Mrs Charles Cliffe). Educ: Heidelberg Col, AB, 23. Polit & Govt Pos: Councilman, Marysville, Ohio, 44-48, mayor, 48-54; chmn, Union Co Rep Party, 60-; mem, Seventh Dist, Ohio State Rep Cent Comt, 66- Mem: Mason (32 Degree). Relig: Protestant. Mailing Add: 210 N Maple Marysville OH 43040

KINKEAD, CECIL CALVERT (D)
b Waycross, Tenn, Oct 21, 11; s Robert David Kinkead & Winnie Alice Wilson K; m 1947 to Betty Alice Lane; c Lane Cecile, Emily Alice & Lizbeth Sue. Educ: High Sch. Polit & Govt Pos: Chmn, Unicoi Co Dem Party, Tenn, formerly. Mil Serv: Entered as Pvt, Army, 42, released as 1st Lt, 43, after serv in Artil Bn, Am Theater; Am Theater Ribbon; Victory Medal. Mem: Am Legion; VFW; Elks. Relig: Protestant. Legal Res: Jonesboro Rd Erwin TN 37650 Mailing Add: PO Box 147 Erwin TN 37650

KINKEAD, SHELBY C (D)
b Lexington, Ky, 1913. Educ: Univ Ky, BS. Polit & Govt Pos: City comnr, Lexington, Ky, 54-56, mayor, 56-60; Ky State Sen, 64-68; chmn, Ky State Dem Party, 70-72. Bus & Prof Pos: Businessman; farmer. Mil Serv: Navy. Relig: Episcopal. Mailing Add: 254 S Ashland Ave Lexington KY 40502

KINLER, GLADYS VERONICA (R)
Committeewoman, Rep State Cent Comt La
Polit & Govt Pos: Committeewoman, Rep State Cent Comt La, currently; chmn, St Tammany Parish Rep Party, La, formerly. Mailing Add: Rte 1 Box 118 Lacombe LA 70445

KINLEY, GEORGE RAYMOND (D)
Iowa State Sen
b Akron, Ohio, June 4, 37; s Raymond Frank Kinley & Marie McCormick K; m 1958 to Carolyn Ann Pritchard; c Raymond, Kathryn, Frank & Elizabeth. Educ: Drake Univ, BA, 60. Polit & Govt Pos: Iowa State Rep, 71-72; Iowa State Sen, 73- Bus & Prof Pos: Owner, Airport Golf Range, 55- Mem: Izaak Walton League; Dowling Club. Relig: Roman Catholic. Mailing Add: 5006 SW 18th Des Moines IA 50315

KINNAMAN, DANIEL L (D)
Wyo State Rep
Mailing Add: 320 Eighth St Rawlins WY 82301

KINNAMAN, THEODORE DWIGHT (D)
b Evanston, Ill, Nov 19, 28; s Theodore James Kinnaman & Mamie Robinson K; m 1953 to Janice Marilyn Herrington; c Jacqueline Ann, Kathleen Joyce & Theodore James. Educ: Northwestern Univ, BMusEd, 50 & MMus, 57; Univ Iowa, summers 62, 64, 66 & 69; Pi Kappa Lambda. Polit & Govt Pos: Co-chmn, Jamesville Citizens for McCarthy, Wis, 68; alt deleg, Dem Nat Conv, 68 & 72; mem nat steering comt, New Dem Coalition, 69-70; chmn, Wis New Dem Coalition, 69-70; mem, Wis Dem Party Develop Comn, 70-73; Wis correspondent, The New Democrat, 70-; mem-at-lg, Wis State Steering Comt, McGovern for President, 71-72. Bus & Prof Pos: Chmn, Humanities Div, Univ Wis Ctr-Rock Co, 73- Mem: Am Musicological Soc; Am Choral Dir Soc; Nat Comt for Sane Nuclear Policy; Am Civil Liberties Union. Relig: Protestant. Mailing Add: 1213 Columbus Circle Janesville WI 53545

KINNEY, CLARKE (D)
b Memphis, Tenn, July 22, 24; s Kenneth Hays Kinney & Ruby Baird K; m 1968 to Fonda Lou Baker; c Katherine K (Mrs Smith), Karen Jane, Clarke Kenneth & Allison Ann. Educ: Memphis State Univ, BS in Econ, 62; Northwestern Univ, Financial Pub Rels, 63-64. Polit & Govt Pos: Mem, City Coun, Hughes, Ark, 57-59; Ark State Rep, 59-66, mem, Ark Legis Coun, 63-64; info officer, Int Bank for Reconstruction & Develop, 66- Bus & Prof Pos: Mgr, K H Kinney & Sons, 46-60; zone mgr, Investors Diversified Serv, 60-62; dir pub rels, Planters Bank & Trust Co, 62-65; vpres, Union Mgt Corp, 65-66; agency supvr, Union Life Ins Co, Little Rock, Ark, 69-; vpres, Powell & Satterfield, Inc, 72- Mil Serv: Entered as Pvt, Army, 43, released as 1st Lt, 46, after serv in 539th Engr Pontoon Bridge Co, Corps of Engrs, Far East Command, Okinawa Engr Dist, 51; Good Conduct Medal. Mem: AAONMS; Little

Rock Racquet Club; Red Gum Lodge 696; Razorback Club; Am Legion. Relig: Methodist. Legal Res: 4903 E Crestwood Little Rock AR 72207 Mailing Add: 303 First Nat Bank Bldg Little Rock AR 72207

KINNEY, HARRY EDWIN (R)
Mayor, Albuquerque, NM
b Trinidad, Colo, June 7, 24; s Oliver Earl Kinney & Opal Sanger K; m 1970 to Carol Naus; c Charlotte & Donald Bruce. Educ: Univ NMex; Kappa Sigma. Polit & Govt Pos: Comnr, Bernalillio Co, NMex, 56-59 & 61-65; city comnr, Albuquerque, 66-73, mayor, 74- Bus & Prof Pos: Develop engr, Sandia Labs, 56-73. Mil Serv: Entered as A/S, Naval Res, 42, released as Lt, 52, after serv in Atlantic & Pac Fleet; Lt Comdr (Ret), Naval Res, 68. Mem: Am Soc Mech Engrs; Am Legion; Keep NMex Beautiful (exec bd). Relig: Episcopal. Mailing Add: 3006 Vista Grande NW Albuquerque NM 87120

KINNIE, KENNETH IVAN (R)
Colo State Sen
b Julesburg, Colo, Apr 28, 23; s Ernest H Kinnie & Ruth Smith K; m 1942 to Lucille H Fox; c Kenneth Joe, Dennis Craig & Ernest LeRoy. Educ: Colo Univ, 1 year. Polit & Govt Pos: Chmn, Sedgwick Co Rep Cent Comt, Colo, 65-; Colo State Sen, Dist 29, 71-74, Dist 35, 75- Bus & Prof Pos: Farmer & rancher, 46-; vpres, Hodges-Kinnie Grain Co, 58- Mil Serv: Entered as A/S, Navy, 42, released as PO 3/C, 44. Mem: Jaycees; Farm Bur; Wheat Growers Asn. Relig: Methodist. Mailing Add: Box 25 RR Julesburg CO 80737

KINSEY, DANIEL L (D)
Ala State Rep
Mailing Add: PO Box 246 Foley AL 36535

KINSEY, LLOYD (R)
Ore State Rep
Mailing Add: 2122 N E Alameda Portland OR 97212

KINSEY, ROBERT EVERETT (R)
Vt State Rep
b Barton, Vt, Aug 10, 27; s Frederick Cornelius Kinsey & Geneva Eva Whitcher K; m 1948 to Eunice Helen Rowell; c Jennie Ellen (Mrs John Stanger), Everett James, Erwin Carl, Earl George, Emily Joyce, Jeffrey Arthur & Valerie Eunice. Educ: Lyndon State Col, BS, 71. Polit & Govt Pos: Secy, Craftsbury Town Rep Comt, Vt, 65-68, chmn, 68-73; Vt State Rep, 71-, mem, Ways & Means Comt, Vt House Rep, 71-, mem, Natural Resources Comt & Spec Land Capabilities Comt, 73- Bus & Prof Pos: Farmer, 48- Mem: Farm Bur; Cabot Farmers Coop; Maple Valley Grange; Meridian Sun Lodge. Relig: Presbyterian. Mailing Add: Craftsbury Common VT 05827

KINSEY, ROBERT WAYNE (D)
Chmn, Dist Two Dem Non-Partisan League Party, NDak
b Washington, DC, Sept 13, 43; s Raymond McKinley Kinsey & Dorothy Lorraine Hazel K; single. Educ: Am Univ Sch Int Serv, BA, 65; Univ NDak Sch Law, JD with distinction, 68; Order of the Coif; Blue Key; Omicron Delta Kappa; Pi Gamma Mu; Pi Sigma Alpha; Alpha Phi Omega. Polit & Govt Pos: Co justice, Divide Co, NDak, 69-71; chmn, Dist Two Dem Non-Partisan League Party, 72-; State's attorney, Divide Co, 74- Publ: Auth, Ownership of banks in North Dakota, 67, Alternatives to increasing the maximum rate of interest in North Dakota, 68 & A contrast of trends in administrative costs in decedents estates between a uniform probate code jurisdiction (Idaho) & a non-uniform probate code jurisdiction (North Dakota), 74, NDak Law Rev. Mem: Kiwanis; Toastmasters; NDak, DC & Am Bar Asns. Relig: Episcopal. Legal Res: 110 N Main St Crosby ND 58730 Mailing Add: PO Box 30 Crosby ND 58730

KINSOLVING, CHARLES MCILVAINE, JR (D)
b New York, NY, Jan 27, 27; s Charles McIlvaine Kinsolving & Florence Natalie Hogg K; m 1963 to Coral May Eaton. Educ: Univ Pa, AB, 49; Harvard Univ, Columbia Univ, NY Univ & the Sorbonne, grad work; Phi Beta Kappa; Delta Psi. Polit & Govt Pos: Mem exec comt, secy & treas, Lexington Dem Club, 52-58; mem city & state bd, Am for Dem Action, 54-72; pres, Murray Hill Dem Club, 58-61; mem & secy, Comt for a Better NY, 60-64; dist leader, 65th Assembly Dist, Part D, 61-73; secy & mem exec comt, Comt for Dem Voters, 59-66; vchmn, New York Co Dem Exec Comt, 62-67, first vchmn, 67-71; co-chmn, Comt to Keep NY Habitable, 63-66; mem, Direct Primary Comt, 65-67; deleg, Dem Nat Conv, 68; campaign mgr, East Side of Manhattan, McCarthy for President, 68, Greitzer for Coun, 69, Paul O'Dwyer for US Senate, 70, Millard L Midonick for Surrogate, 71, Nanette Dembitz for Court of Appeals, 72 & Herman Badillo for Mayor, 73; mem, Planning Bd 6, 69-, mem exec comt, 72-, chmn health & hosps comt, 72-, co-chmn capital budget comt, 74; media adv, Kuh for Dist Attorney & Kretchmer for Cong, 74. Bus & Prof Pos: Stockholder rels rep, Am Tel & Tel Co, New York, NY, 51; research analyst, Young & Rubicam Advert Agency, 51-53; assoc mgr media research, McCann-Erickson Advert Agency, 53-58; mgr plans develop, Nat Broadcasting Co, 58-60; vpres mkt planning, Bur of Advert, Am Newspaper Publ Asn, 60- Mil Serv: Entered as Pvt, Army, 45, released as S/Sgt, 46, after serv in Army Ground Forces, Continental US, 45-46. Publ: The little old lady from Keokuk (& other traveler types), ASTA Travel News, 10/11/66; What is your image & who cares? (Savings Banks Forum), US Investor, 2/3/69. Mem: Am Asn Pub Opinion Research; Am Mkt Asn; Union Club; Metrop Squash Racquets Asn; Am Legion. Relig: Episcopal. Mailing Add: 441 Park Ave S New York NY 10016

KIPP, PHYLLIS T (R)
Conn State Rep
Mailing Add: 58 Nantucket Dr Mystic CT 06355

KIPPING, ROBERT KIRTLEY (R)
Chmn, Carroll Co Rep Exec Comt, Ky
b Carrollton, Ky, Mar 11, 09; s Oscar Gier Kipping & Mabel Kirtley K; m 1945 to Bulah Baker Butler; c Karlene Kirtley. Educ: Wis State Univ, Superior, summer sch; Univ Ky, AB; Sigma Chi; K Club. Polit & Govt Pos: Dep Ky State Fire Marshal, 47-49; elec comnr, Carroll Co, 49-55; chmn, Carroll Co Rep Exec Comt, 56- Bus & Prof Pos: Licensed funeral dir, Ky, 38-; pres, Scenic Rwys, Inc, 56-; pres, Park Lanes, Inc, 63- Mil Serv: Entered as Pvt, Army, 42, released as Capt, 46, after serv in Mil Police Corps, Am Theater; Am Theater Ribbon; Victory Medal; Expert Marksmanship Badge. Mem: F&AM; Kiwanis. Honors & Awards: Right tackle, Univ Ky Football Team, 29-32. Relig: Baptist. Legal Res: 716 Highland Ave Carrollton KY 41008 Mailing Add: Box 55 Carrollton KY 41008

KIRBO, CHARLES (D)
Polit & Govt Pos: Former chmn, Ga State Dem Party Mailing Add: 2500 Trust Company Bldg Atlanta GA 30303

KIRBY, EDWARD PAUL (R)
Chmn, Whitman Rep Town Comt, Mass
b Whitman, Mass, Jan 10, 28; s Frank A Kirby & Mabel K Linn; m 1957 to Mary Alice Mraz; c Matthew Paul, Jane DeChantal & Thomas More. Educ: Holy Cross Col, AB, 49; Boston Col Law Sch, MD, 52. Polit & Govt Pos: Mass State Rep, 61-66; comnr, Plymouth Co, Mass, 69-; chmn, Whitman Rep Town Comt, 73- Bus & Prof Pos: Pvt practice law, 56- Mil Serv: Entered as Pvt, Army, 52, released as 1st Lt, 55, after serv in Judge Adv Gen Corps, 53-55; Capt (Ret). Mem: Mass Bar Asn. Relig: Roman Catholic. Mailing Add: 379 Harvard St Whitman MA 02382

KIRBY, GEORGE ALBERT, III (R)
Chmn, Rep State Cent Comt, Md
b Cumberland, Md, Nov 8, 44; s George Albert Kirby, Jr & Juanita Elizabeth Shafer K; m 1970 to Kathleen Regina Figiel; c Christina Leigh. Educ: Frostburg State Col, BS, 66; George Washington Univ, MA, 73. Polit & Govt Pos: Chmn, Rep State Cent Comt, Md, 74- Bus & Prof Pos: Teacher, St Mary's Co, Md, 66-70, asst prin, 70- Mem: Nat Educ Asn; Md State Teachers Asn; Educ Asn of St Mary's Co. Relig: Christian. Mailing Add: PO Box 113 California MD 20619

KIRBY, JAMES RUSSELL (D)
NC State Sen
b Wilson Co, NC, Feb 17, 22; s Sanford Kirby & Cora Scott K; m 1946 to Rebekah Fulghum; c James Russell II, David Fulghum & Jane Darden. Educ: Univ NC, BS, 43; Univ NC Law Sch, JD, 48. Polit & Govt Pos: Deleg, Dem Nat Conv, 68; chmn, Traffic Code Comn, formerly; NC State Sen, 63-, speaker, Ban Comn, 65, chmn, Comt on Higher Educ, NC State Senate, 69-, mem, Health Sub-Comt & Legis Research Comn, 69-, chmn, Finance Comt, 72-; trustee, State Educ Assistance Authority, 66-69, chmn, 71-73; mem, NC Bd Higher Educ, 69-; mem, Gen Statutes Comn, 70-74 & NC Courts Comn, 72-; mem, Adv Budget Comn, 73- Bus & Prof Pos: Lawyer. Mil Serv: Sgt, Army, 43-45. Mem: Mason; Elks; Rotary. Relig: Methodist. Mailing Add: 1711 Brentwood Circle Wilson NC 27893

KIRBY, MICHAEL C (D)
Wis State Rep
Mailing Add: 10631 W Hampton Ave Milwaukee WI 53225

KIRBY, PETER (R)
Mem, Rep State Cent Comt Calif
b Washington, DC, Nov 7, 28; s Thomas Kirby & Marguerite McKinley K; m 1970 to Marie Duhring. Educ: Univ Pa, BArchit, 51; Univ Calif, Berkeley, MA, 55; Tau Sigma Delta; Delta Kappa Epsilon. Polit & Govt Pos: Mem bd dirs, San Francisco Young Rep, 57-64, vpres, 60, pres, 61; mem, San Francisco Rep Cent Comt, 60-68; mem, Rep State Cent Comt Calif, 64- Bus & Prof Pos: Draftsman, Corlett & Spockman, 55-57; job capt, Leo A Daly & Assocs, 58-62; proj mgr, John Carl Warnecke & Assocs, 62-64; exec architect, Kump, Masten & Hurd, 64-66; proj mgr, Wurster, Bernardi & Emmons, 67-68; dir San Francisco off & vpres, Wm L Pereira & Assocs, 68- Mil Serv: Entered as Ens, Navy, 51, released as Lt(jg), 54, after serv in Mobile Construction Bn 6, Atlantic; Comdr, Naval Res, 66; Nat Defense Ribbon; Armed Forces Res Ribbon. Mem: Am Inst Architects; Commonwealth Club of Calif; Naval Order of the US; Navy League. Relig: Episcopal. Mailing Add: 3952 19th St San Francisco CA 94114

KIRCHNER, WILLIAM G (R)
Minn State Sen
b Iowa, 1916; married; c Four. Educ: Morningside Col, BA; Harvard Grad Sch of Bus, MBA; Psi Chi; Pi Gamma Mu. Polit & Govt Pos: Minn State Rep, 63-67; Minn State Sen, 67- Bus & Prof Pos: Pres, Richfield Bank & Trust Co, 63-, chmn, currently. Mil Serv: Navy, 44-46, Pac. Mem: Morningside Col (trustee); Am Bankers Asn (area vpres); Minn Bankers Asn; Boy Scouts; Girl Scouts; Minn Hist Soc (dir). Relig: Methodist. Mailing Add: 6830 Newton Ave S Richfield MN 55423

KIRK, CLAUDE ROY, JR (R)
b San Bernardino, Calif, Jan 7, 26; s Claude Roy Kirk & Sarah McLure K; m 1967 to Erika Mattfeld; c Sarah Stokes, Katherine Gilmer, Franklin, William, Adriana, Claudia & Erik Henry. Educ: Emory Univ; Duke Univ, BS, 45; Univ Ala, Law, 49; Sigma Alpha Epsilon. Polit & Govt Pos: Gov, Fla, 67-70; deleg, Rep Nat Conv, 68. Bus & Prof Pos: Salesman, ins & bldg supplies, 49; vchmn, Am Heritage Life Ins Co, 54; partner, Hayden, Stone, Inc, 60; founder, Kirk Investment Co, 64. Mil Serv: Entered as 2nd Lt, Marine Corps, 43, released as 1st Lt, 46, reentered, 50 and released, 52, after serv in Korean Conflict; Air Medal. Mem: Financial Analysts Soc; Episcopal Church Found (trustee); Saints & Sinners; 21 Club, New York. Relig: Episcopal. Mailing Add: PO Box 668 Palm Beach FL 33480

KIRK, JOHN FRANCIS, JR (R)
Mem, New Castle Co Rep Exec Comt, Del
b Wilmington, Del, June 15, 31; s John Francis Kirk & Mary I Moody K; m 1953 to Margaret F Nickle; c John F, III, David Keith & Cynthia Sue. Educ: Goldey Col, 49-50. Polit & Govt Pos: Bd mem, Gunning Bedford Sch Dist, Del, 65-66, pres, sch bd, 66-69; vpres, interim sch bd, Gunning Bedford-New Castle Dist, 69-, bd mem, 69-70; Del State Rep, 69-74, speaker, Del House Rep, 73-74; mem, New Castle Co Rep Exec Comt, Del, 69- Bus & Prof Pos: Partner, Kirks Hardware, Delaware City, Del, currently. Mil Serv: Entered as Pvt, Army, 51, released as Cpl, 53, after serv in 7774th Signal Bn, ETO, 52-53; European Occup Medal. Mem: Del Sch Bd Asn; Lions Int; Grange. Relig: Catholic. Legal Res: 522 St Georges Rd Delaware City DE 19706 Mailing Add: State House of Reps Dover DE 19901

KIRK, LEWIS ROGER, JR (R)
b Baltimore, Md, May 23, 21; s Lewis Roger Kirk & Lucy White K; m 1948 to Edith Gagnell Blackstone; c Lewis Roger, III. Educ: Univ SC, AB, 43, MD, 49, doctoral prog, currently. Polit & Govt Pos: SC State Rep, Richland Co, 73-74; exec asst to Gov SC for Educ & Manpower, 75- Bus & Prof Pos: Prin & coach, Swansea schs, SC, 47-48 & Lower Richland High Sch, 48-49; asst prin, Hand Jr High, Columbia, 49-56; prin, Crayton Jr High Sch, 56-58 & Columbia High Sch, 58-72. Mil Serv: Entered as Pvt, Army, 43, released as Capt, 47, after serv in 43rd Div, 8th Army Hq, Southwest Pac & Japanese Occup Gen Hq, 44-47; Col(Ret), Res, 47-71; Combat Inf Badge; Army Commendation Ribbon; Asiatic-Pac-Am Theater; Res Medal; Occup Ribbon; Good Conduct Medal. Mem: SC Educ Asn; SC High Sch League;

Wardlaw Club; Nat Asn Sec Sch Prin; Southern Asn Cols & Schs (chmn, SC Sec Comt, 71, mem, Cent Rev Comt, 71-). Mailing Add: 4000 Yale Ave Columbia SC 29205

KIRK, PHILLIP JAMES, JR (R)
State Chmn, NC Young Rep
b Salisbury, NC, Nov 24, 44; s Phillip James Kirk & Geneva Bostian K; m 1966 to Carolyn Viola Parks; c Angela Carole & Wendi Rochelle. Educ: Catawba Col, AB, Eng & sec educ, 67. Polit & Govt Pos: Pres, East Rowan TAR, 63; state pres, NC TAR, 64, adv, 65; publicity chmn, NC Young GOP Exec Comt, 66, publ chmn, 66-68 & ed, Tarheel YR, 66-68; adv, East Rowan Teen Age GOP, 67-; pub rels dir, Earl Ruth for Cong, 68; sr party chmn, Rowan Co Rep, 68-; treas, NC Young Rep, 69, state chmn, 69-; NC State Sen, 70-74. Bus & Prof Pos: Reporter, Salisbury Eve Post, NC, 63-67; teacher, Knox Jr High Sch, Salisbury, 67-69, Boyden High Sch, 69- Mem: NC Educ Asn; Nat Educ Asn; Salisbury Classroom Teachers; Nat Asn of Sportswriters & Sportscasters; Optimists. Honors & Awards: NC Teen Age Rep of Year, 63; NC Young Rep of Year, 67; First Runner-up, Nat Male Young Rep of Year, 67; Rookie of Year, Salisbury Optimist Club; Youngest mem NC Gen Assembly, currently; Distinguished Serv Award, NC Young GOP, 71. Relig: First United Church of Christ. Mailing Add: Rte 5 Box 238 Salisbury NC 28144

KIRK, POLLY (R)
Mem, Kans Rep State Comt
b Sumner, Mo, Dec 17, 19; d John L Brown (deceased) & May Leathem B (deceased); m 1941 to Orlin H Kirk, Jr; c Linda A & Kevin D. Educ: Cent Bus Col, Kansas City, Mo, grad, 39. Polit & Govt Pos: Secy, Mo State Social Security Comn, 39-43; vchmn, Overland Park Rep City Comt, Kans, 60-68; precinct committeewoman, Johnson Co Rep Cent Comt, 60-73, secy, 61-64; mem, Rep Gubernatorial Campaign Comts for John Anderson, 62, Paul Wunsch, 64, William Avery, 66 & Richard Harman, 68; vpres, Overland Park Women's Rep Club, 63-64, pres, 64-65; chmn, Kans State Bd of Rev, 63-66; women's campaign chmn, US Sen James B Pearson, Kans, 66, asst to US Sen James B Pearson, Kans, 67-73; Johnson Co chmn, Kans Day Club, 68-; sustaining mem, Rep Nat Comt; secy, Kans Rep State Comt, 68-70, mem, 73-; mem, Frizzell for Gov Comt, 70; co chmn, Shultz for Lt Gov Comt, 70; mem, Reelect the President Comt, 72; state treas, Kans Fedn Rep Women, 72-73; regional fed women's prog coordr, Gen Servs Admin, Kansas City, 73-; mem fed exec bd, Fed Women's Prog Comt, 74-75, gen chairperson, Conf, 75; mem, Gtr Kansas City Int Women's Year Steering Comt, 74- Bus & Prof Pos: Secy, Lord Mfg Co, Burbank, Calif, 43-45. Mem: Overland Park PTA (libr chmn); Kans State Univ Alpha Chi Omega Mother's Club (pres); Kans Fedn of Rep Women; CofC; Federally Employed Women. Honors & Awards: Distinguished Jayhawker Award, 64. Relig: Methodist. Mailing Add: 8710 Eby Dr Overland Park KS 66212

KIRK, ROGER
Dep Dir, Bur Intel & Research, Dept State
b Newport, RI, Sept 2, 30; s Alan Goodrich Kirk & Lydia Chapin K; m 1954 to Madeleine Yaw; c Marian Elizabeth, Sarah Couzens, Julia & Alan Couzens. Educ: Princeton Univ, BA, 52; Johns Hopkins Sch Advan Int Studies, 53; Phi Beta Kappa. Polit & Govt Pos: Mem exec secretariat, Dept State, 55-57, polit officer, Am Embassy, Rome, 57-59, mem staff, Off Secy, 59-60, mem, Off Soviet Union Affairs, 60-61, Russian area training, Oberammergau, 62-63, polit officer, Am Embassy, Moscow, 63-65, Am Embassy, New Delhi, 65-67 & Am Embassy, Saigon, 67-69, mem staff, Bur EAsian Affairs, 69-71, mem, Sr Seminar, 71-72, dep asst dir, Int Rels Bur, Arms Control & Disarmament Agency, 72-73, Ambassador to Somalia, 73-75, dep dir, Bur Intel & Research, 75- Mil Serv: Entered as Airman, Air Force, 52, released as 1st Lt, 55, after serv in US. Mailing Add: 3230 Woodley Rd NW Washington DC 20008

KIRKENDALL, MARY M (R)
Secy-Treas, Jackson Co Rep Cent Comt, Ohio
b Oak Hill, Ohio, July 5, 17; d D Newton Davis & Annette Evans D; m 1945 to Rothbe H Kirkendall; c LeAnne (Mrs Steve Kamber) & R Gerald. Educ: Ohio State Univ, summers 38-42; Rio Grande Col, BS in Ed, 60; Alpha Sigma Tau; Women's Athletic Asn; Dramatic Club; Col Christian Asn. Polit & Govt Pos: Committeeman, Madison Twp, Jackson Co Rep Cent Comt, Ohio, 56-, secy-treas, 60- Bus & Prof Pos: Teacher, Moriah Grade Sch, Jackson Co, 37-38, Highby Sch, Ross Co, 38-41 & Oak Hill Elem, 41-45 & 55-; clerk-typist, Ordnance Off, Camp Hood, Tex, 45-46. Mem: Ohio Educ Asn. Relig: Protestant. Mailing Add: Rte 4 Box 216 Oak Hill OH 45656

KIRKPATRICK, EVRON MAURICE (D)
b Benton Co, Ind, Aug 15, 11; m to Jeane Jordan; c Douglas, John & Stuart. Educ: Univ Ill, BA, 32 & AM, 33; Yale Univ, PhD, 39; Phi Beta Kappa; Pi Sigma Alpha. Polit & Govt Pos: Asst research dir, research & anal br, Off of Strategic Serv, 45; with Dept of State, 46-54; exec dir, Am Polit Sci Asn, 54-; mem, President's Comn on Registr & Voting Participation, 63-64; mem, Comn on Presidential Campaign Debates, 63-64; mem, President's Task Force on Career Advan in Fed Serv, 66. Bus & Prof Pos: Instr, Univ Minn, 35-39, asst prof, 39-43, assoc prof, 43-48, prof, 48; prof lectr, Howard Univ, 57-61; prof lectr, Georgetown Univ, 59-; ed adv polit sci, Henry Holt & Co, 52-60; ed adv polit sci, Holt, Rinehart & Winston, 60-68; mem, Ed Adv Bd, Who's Who in Am Politics, 67, 69, 71, 73 & 75. Mem: Inst for Am Univs (chmn bd trustees, 58-); Opers & Policy Research, Inc (chmn bd trustees, 56-); Citizenship Clearing House; Helen Dwight Reid Found (pres); Int Polit Sci Asn. Legal Res: 6812 Granby St Bethesda MD 20034 Mailing Add: 1527 New Hampshire Ave NW Washington DC 20036

KIRKPATRICK, JAMES C (D)
Secy of State, Mo
b Braymer, Mo, June 15, 05; s Ray N Kirkpatrick & Lena L Rea K; m 1927 to Jessamine Elizabeth Young; c Don; three grandchildren. Educ: Cent Mo State Univ, Warrensburg, Mo; Sch Jour, Univ Mo. Polit & Govt Pos: Formerly admin asst to Gov, Mo; mem, Gov Comt on Com & Indust Develop; dir, Missourians for Progress, 62; Secy of State, Mo, 64- Bus & Prof Pos: Former publ, Windsor Rev; former ed, Warrensburg Daily Star J, Jefferson City Post-Tribune & Capital News; publ, Lamar Daily Dem, Mo, formerly; mem pres coun, Sch of the Ozarks, currently; mem bd trustees, Mo 4-H Found, currently. Mem: Nat Asn Secretaries of State; Mo Press Asn; Cent Mo Press Asn; Dem Ed of Mo; CofC. Honors & Awards: Mo Acad Squires, 68; Mo Good Rd & St Honor Award, 68; Medal for distinguished serv to jour, Univ Mo Sch Jour, 69; One of 50 Top Taus, Sigma Tau Gamma, 70; Univ Mo Faculty-Alumni Award, 72. Relig: Methodist. Mailing Add: Secy of State's Off Jefferson City MO 65101

KIRKWOOD, ROBERT CARTER (R)
Chmn, San Francisco Co Rep Cent Comt, Calif
b San Francisco, Calif, June, 1939; s Robert Carter Kirkwood & Jean Gerlinger K; m 1965 to Mary Frances Brooks; c R Carter, B Brooks & Corey S. Educ: Pomona Col, BA, 62; Harvard Law Sch, LLB, 65. Polit & Govt Pos: Chmn, San Francisco Co Rep Cent Comt, Calif, 75-; vchmn, United San Francisco Rep Finance Comt, 75-; mem exec comt, Rep State Cent Comt Calif, 75- Bus & Prof Pos: Eng clerk, Anderson, Mori & Rabinowitz, law firm, Tokyo, Japan, 67-68; attorney, Brobeck, Phleger & Harrison, San Francisco, Calif, 69- Mem: San Francisco Planning & Urban Renewal Asn (pres); Planning & Conserv League; San Francisco Art Inst; San Francisco Bar Area Coun. Legal Res: 2710 Filbert St San Francisco CA 94123 Mailing Add: 111 Sutter St San Francisco CA 94104

KIRSCHT, ROBERT LEON (BOB) (D)
Colo State Rep
b Pueblo, Colo, Apr 23, 42; s Peter H Kirscht & Erma Stockton K; m 1966 to Francine Lerma; c Shawna & Roberta. Educ: Southern Colo State, Polit Sci, 4 years. Polit & Govt Pos: Colo State Rep, 71- Bus & Prof Pos: News dir, KDZA, Pueblo, Colo, 64-70. Mil Serv: Entered as Pvt, Army Nat Guard, 63, released as SP-5, 69. Mailing Add: 1516 Zuni Rd Pueblo CO 81001

KISER, SAMUEL CURTIS (R)
Fla State Rep
b Oskaloosa, Iowa, June 17, 44; s Ira Manley Kiser & Emma Jean Raley K; m 1966 to Sara Margaret Hess; c Jennifer Lynn & Kevin Curtis. Educ: Univ Iowa, BA, 67; Fla State Univ, JD, 70. Polit & Govt Pos: Asst legal counsel to Gov, State of Fla, 70; mem, Fla State Dept of Community Affairs Adv Coun, 71-72; assoc, Munic Judge, City of Dunedin, 72; Fla State Rep, Pinellas Co, 72- Bus & Prof Pos: Attorney & partner, Dunbar, Kiser, Dunbar, 71- Mem: Dunedin Jaycees (dir, 71-72, legal counsel, 71-); Dunedin CofC; Gtr Pinellas Co Young Rep; Gtr Tarpon Springs Rep Club; Indian Bluff Island Civic Asn. Honors & Awards: Outstanding Young Man of the Year, Dunedin CofC, 72; Nominated to Outstanding Young Men of Am, Dunedin Jaycees, 72. Relig: Presbyterian. Mailing Add: 14 Peterson Lane Palm Harbor FL 33563

KISIELIS, BERNARD S (D)
Chmn, Montgomery Co Dem Comt, NY
b Amsterdam, NY, Apr 14, 29; s Stanley Kisielis & Victoria Shatas K; m 1959 to Lorraine A Winkle; c Paul, Kevin & John. Educ: Wilbur H Lynch High Sch, grad, 47. Polit & Govt Pos: Comnr, Pub Safety, Amsterdam, NY, 68-75; chmn, Montgomery Co Dem Comt, 73-; dir of purchasing, NY State Assembly, 75- Mem: JFK Dem Club; ALC. Relig: Roman Catholic. Legal Res: 358 Division St Amsterdam NY 12010 Mailing Add: PO Box 12 Amsterdam NY 12010

KISNER, IGNATIUS (ICKIE), (D)
Chmn, Stafford Co Dem Party, Kans
b Hays, Kans, Aug 18, 25; s Ignatz Kisner & Kathrine Gabel K; m 1948 to Jo Ann Dobbs; c Bobby Duane, Karla Rea & Kristi Lynn. Educ: Dodge City High Sch, Kans. Polit & Govt Pos: Vchmn, Stafford Co Dem Party, Kans, 69-72, chmn, 72- Bus & Prof Pos: Purchasing agent, Truck-Trailer Supply Co, Inc, 54-61; owner, Ickie Kisner & Assocs, Stafford, 61- Mil Serv: Entered as Seaman, Navy, 43, released as CSG 2, 46 & Korea, 50-52. Mem: Independent Agents Asn; Life Underwriters Asn; CofC; Optimists; Wheat Growers Asn. Legal Res: 328 N Keystone Stafford KS 67578 Mailing Add: PO Box 27 Stafford KS 67578

KISS, LOUISE (D)
b Seattle, Wash, Jan 24, 41; d Albert B Angel & Susan Azose A; m 1964 to Charles Kiss; c Renee Elizabeth & Sharon Lisa. Educ: Univ Wash, BS in Nursing, 64; Student Nurses Asn; Hillel. Polit & Govt Pos: Precinct deleg, 44-93 Wash, 72, precinct committeeman, currently; alt deleg, Wash Dem State Conv, 72, deleg, 74; alt deleg, Dem Nat Conv, 72. Mem: Am Nursing Asn; PTA (legis chmn & first vpres); 44th Dist Club; Nat Coun of Jewish Women. Relig: Jewish. Mailing Add: 12038 Tenth NW Seattle WA 98177

KISSINGER, HENRY ALFRED
Secy of State
b Fuerth, Ger, May 27, 23; s Louis Kissinger & Paula Stern K; div; m 1974 to Nancy McGinnis; c Elizabeth & David. Educ: City Col New York, 41-43; Harvard Univ, AB, 50, MA, 52, PhD, 54. Polit & Govt Pos: Consult to various govt agencies including, Weapons Syst Eval Group of the Joint Chiefs of Staff, Nat Security Coun, US Arms Control & Disarmament Agency & State Dept, 59-68; Asst to the President for Nat Security Affairs, 69-73; Secy of State, 73-; Asst to the President, 74- Bus & Prof Pos: Dir study on nuclear weapons & foreign policy, Coun on Foreign Rels, NY, 55-56; dir spec study proj, Rockefeller Bros Fund, 56-58; assoc dir, Ctr for Int Affairs, dir, Harvard Int Seminar, dir, Nat Security Studies Prog & assoc prof, Harvard Univ, 58-68. Mil Serv: Army, 84th Inf Div, 970th Counter Intel Corp, 43-46, Capt, Mil Intel, Res, 46-59. Publ: Nuclear Weapons & Foreign Policy, 57 & The Necessity for Choice: Prospects of American Foreign Policy, 61, Harper & Bros; The Troubled Partnership: a Reappraisal of the Atlantic Alliance, McGraw Hill, 65. Mem: Phi Beta Kappa; Century Club, New York, NY; Fed City Club; Asn of US Army; Am Acad Arts & Sci, Boston. Honors & Awards: Nobel Peace Prize, 73; Harvard Nat Scholar; Harvard Fel; Harvard Dettur; Rockefeller Found Fel for Polit Theory. Mailing Add: Dept of State Washington DC 20520

KISSLING, GILBERT JAMES (D)
b San Antonio, Tex, Feb 1, 31; s John T Kissling & Mary F Wrzeciono K; m 1957 to Irene Mary Mechler; c Tom, John, Mary Carol (deceased), James, Michael & Daniel. Educ: St Mary's Univ, 49-50; San Antonio Col, 51; Univ Tex, 52; Rho Beta Gamma. Polit & Govt Pos: Deleg, Dem Nat Conv, 72. Mem: San Antonio AFL-CIO Coun (treas, 66-); Plumbers & Pipe Fitters Union 142 (secy treas, 64-); Tex Code Adv Comt. Relig: Catholic. Mailing Add: 418 E Huisache San Antonio TX 78212

KISTLER, GUY A (R)
Pa State Rep
b Nanticoke, Pa, Nov 15, 10; s Wilbur A Kistler & Blance Nash K; m to Beatrice Davis Jenkins; c three. Educ: Plymouth Twp High Sch; Newberry-Murphy Schs of Merchandising, Mgt & Investment Control. Polit & Govt Pos: Former vchmn finance comt, Cumberland Co Rep Orgn, Pa; past pres, Coun of Borough, Camp Hill; Pa State Rep, 61-, chmn, State Govt Comt, mem, Educ & Appropriations Comts, Joint State Govt Comn Task Force on Conserv, Historic Sites & Optimum Use of State Col Facilities & mem bd, Pa Higher Educ Asst Agency & chmn, Comt on Appeals, Pa State House of Rep. Bus & Prof Pos: Former mgr dept stores; former exec vpres, Securitext, Inc; owner, Puritan Brookwood Co & Puritan Sales Co. Mem: Engrs Soc Pa; F&AM; Harrisburg Consistory; AAONMS; Harrisburg Hunters & Anglers. Relig: Methodist; bd mem, Grace Methodist Church. Mailing Add: 2327 Harvard Ave Camp Hill PA 17011

KISTLER, MARGARET KOY (D)
b Bellville, Tex, Aug 14, 44; d Ernest A Koy & Jane Cameron K, m 1971 to Allison Clay Kistler, II. Educ: Univ Tex, Austin, BS, 67; Tex Tech Univ, MA, 75. Polit & Govt Pos: Deleg, Bell Co Dem Conv, Tex, 72; deleg, Tex Dem State Conv, 72 & 74; alt deleg, Nat Dem Conv, 72; deleg, Lubbock Co Dem Conv, 74. Bus & Prof Pos: Sports writer, Abilene Reporter-News, Tex, 67-68; press aide, Speaker, Tex House of Rep, 68-69 & 70-71; capitol bur reporter, Dallas Morning News, Austin Bur, 69-70; bur chief, Temple Daily Telegram, Ft Hood Bur, 72- Relig: Episcopal. Mailing Add: 5530 First St Lubbock TX 79416

KITCHENER, RUTH MAE (R)
Chmn, Wilmington Rep Town Comt, Mass
b Orr's Island, Maine, Dec 13, 07; d Charles Agustus Coffin & Ella MacKeil C; m 1931 to Albert Edward Kitchener; c Loraine Ruth (Mrs James Martin Jones) & Albert Edward, Jr. Educ: Morse High Sch. Polit & Govt Pos: Secy, Wilmington Rep Town Comt, Mass, 50-64, finance chmn, 59-64, chmn, 64-; deleg, Mass Rep State Conv, 50-, mem platform comt, 64; coordr for President Eisenhower, 52 & 56, Gov John A Volpe, 60, US Rep F Bradford Morse, 62, Mass Attorney Gen Edward W Brooke, 63, US Sen Edward W Brooke, 67, President Nixon, 68 & 72 & Gov Francis W Sargent, 70; deleg, Nat Fedn Rep Women, 67. Mem: Mass Rep Club; Mass Fedn Rep Women; Wilmington Women's Club (legis comt); Wilmington PTA; Wilmington Water Exten. Relig: Methodist. Mailing Add: 116 Aldrich Rd Wilmington MA 01887

KITCHIN, ALVIN PAUL (D)
b Scotland Neck, NC, Sept 13, 08; s Alvin Paul Kitchin & Carrie Lawrence K; m 1934 to Dora Bennett Little; c A Paul, Jr & Henry Little. Educ: Oak Ridge Mil Inst; Wake Forest Col. Polit & Govt Pos: Mem, Fed Bur of Invest, 33-45; US Rep, NC, 57-63; counsel, US Sen Judiciary Subcomt, 63 & 64. Bus & Prof Pos: Attorney-at-law, 30-33 & 65- Mem: Scottish Rite; Mason (32 Degree); Rotary. Relig: Southern Baptist. Legal Res: Country Club Rd Wadesboro NC 28170 Mailing Add: Box 394 Wadesboro NC 28170

KITE, CONSTANCE LOUISE (D)
b Lynn, Mass, Oct 17, 36; d Earle Wentzel Dolphin & Elizabeth Atwood D; m 1958 to Henry Kite; c Kirsten Bradford, Kim Atwood & Kenric Adams. Educ: Earlham Col, AB, 57; Univ Vt, 69-73. Polit & Govt Pos: Mem, Chittenden Co Dem Women, Vt, 70-; cand, Vt Secy of State, 72; deleg, Dem Nat Credentials Comt, 72; deleg, Dem Nat Conv, 72; coordr, Chittenden Co Citizens for McGovern, Vt, 72; chmn, Ward Five Dem Comt, City of Burlington, 72- Bus & Prof Pos: Mus preparator, Harvard Univ, 57-59; expediter, Springfield Times-Reporter, Vt, 65-66; research asst, Univ Vt Med Sch, 67-68; bd trustees, Crossroads Rehabilitation Ctr, 73- Mem: League of Women Voters (Burlington bd, 66-); Vt Women's Polit Caucus; Am Civil Liberties Union. Relig: Unitarian-Universalist. Mailing Add: 161 Home Ave Burlington VT 05401

KITTERMAN, WILLIAM I (D)
Mass State Sen
Mailing Add: State Capitol Boston MA 02133

KITTRELL, RICHARD LINCOLN (R)
b Pueblo, Colo, July 30, 20; s Eugene Jefferson Kittrell & Rosa Bowers K; m 1941 to Louise Hollis. Educ: Cent High Sch, Pueblo, Colo, grad, 38. Polit & Govt Pos: Dist capt, Denver Co Rep Comt, Colo, 7 years; alt deleg, Rep Nat Conv, 72. Mil Serv: Entered as Pvt, Army, 42, released as S/Sgt, 46, after serv in US; Good Conduct Medal. Mem: Mason. Relig: Protestant. Mailing Add: 2926 St Paul St Denver CO 80205

KITZES, CONSUELO J (D)
Mem, Dem Nat Comt, NMex
Polit & Govt Pos: NMex State Sen, 75-; state chairwoman, NMex Dem State Cent Comt, 75- Mailing Add: Box 418 Santa Fe NM 87501

KIYABU, KEN S (D)
Hawaii State Rep
b Honolulu, Hawaii, Jan 25, 37; s Wallace S Kiyabu & Anne U Nakasone K; m 1958 to Blanche S Taira; c Blake & Bliss. Educ: Univ Hawaii. Polit & Govt Pos: Hawaii State Rep, 74- Bus & Prof Pos: Realtor, Kiy Realty, 66-; consult, Travel House, Inc, currently; secy-dir, Time Factors, currently. Mil Serv: Sr M/Sgt, Hawaii Air Nat Guard, 54- Mem: Hawaii Asn of Realtors; Kapahulu Community Asn; Kaimuki Bus & Prof Asn; Hawaii Nat Guard Enlisted Men's Asn. Honors & Awards: Outstanding Airman, Hawaii Air Nat Guard. Mailing Add: 3443 McCorriston St Honolulu HI 96815

KIZER, CHARLENE CRAIG (D)
Chairperson, Fifth Dist Dem Party, Okla
b Oklahoma City, Okla, Sept 6, 45; d Earl Samuel Craig (deceased) & Catherine Mary Ryan; div; c Jeffery Craig & Amy Elizabeth. Educ: Cent State Univ, 73-74; Sigma Kappa. Polit & Govt Pos: Mem bd dirs, Fedn Dem Womens Clubs, 73-; co-chairperson, Fifth Dist Dem Party, Okla, 73-75, chairperson, 75-; state coordr, McGovern for Pres, Okla, 72; chairperson legis task force, Okla Women's Polit Caucus, 74-; Dem nominee, State House Rep, Dist 85, 74; deleg, Dem Nat Mid-Term Conf, 74. Bus & Prof Pos: Partner & media dir, Ad Central USA, 69-71; polit consult, Ron Platt Assocs, 74; dir pub rels, Okla Heart Asn, 75- Publ: Auth, The people won in Kansas City, The Oklahoma Observer, 12/74; Womenpower & politics, The Okla New Woman, 5/75. Mem: Community of John XXIII. Relig: Catholic. Mailing Add: 2928 NW 47th St Oklahoma City OK 73112

KJAR, ROLLAND WILLIAM (R)
Chmn, St Charles Co Rep Cent Comt, Mo
b Lexington, Nebr, July 21, 32; s William Carl Kjar & Esther Alice Mitchell K; single. Educ: Gonzaga Univ, BA, 51; Univ Kans, MA, 54; Mont State Col, sec cert, 56. Polit & Govt Pos: Founder & pres of Grand Order of Pachyderms, Rep Mens Club of St Charles Co, Mo, 67-70; committeeman, Third Ward Rep Party, 68-; vchmn, St Charles Co Rep Cent Comt, 68-70, chmn, 72-; mem, Mo Rep State Comt, 72- Bus & Prof Pos: Chmn dept social studies, Duchesne High Sch, St Charles, Mo, 64- Publ: Auth of weekly hist articles, St Charles J, 68. Mem: Kiwanis; Duchesne Key Club (moderator); KofC; St Charles Co Jr Hist Soc (dir, 68-). Honors & Awards: Outstanding Young Educator Award, St Charles Jr CofC, 65; Outstanding Faculty Adv for Mo-Ark Key Clubs, 70; mem, Gov Adv Comn for Mo Sesquicentennial, 72. Relig: Roman Catholic. Legal Res: 1865 W Clark St Charles MO 63301 Mailing Add: PO Box 53 St Charles MO 63301

KLAPMAN, JARVIS RANDOLPH (R)
SC State Rep
b Columbia, SC, Mar 20, 16; s Ollie Furman Klapman & Bertha Moore K; m 1944 to Arlene McLellan; c Linda (Mrs Vallejo), Janet (Mrs Smith) & Brett Randolph. Educ: Brookland Cayce High Sch, grad, 34; Ft Benning Inf Motor Sch, 42; Gen Motors Inst Serv Mgr Sch, 51 & Prof Salesmaster Sch, 63. Polit & Govt Pos: Pres, Hookstore Precinct Dem Party, SC, 54-62 & Hookstore Precinct Rep Party, 62-70; mem, Brookland Cayce Sch Bd, 63-66; SC State Rep, 67-68 & 71-, mem, Hwy Safety Study Comt, Pub Hwy & Educ Comts & Med & Mil Affairs Comt, SC House Rep, currently, mem, Ways & Means Comt & vchmn, Joint House-Senate Comt on Internal Security, 73-; scholarship chmn, Lexington Co Rep Party, 67-, vchmn, 69- Bus & Prof Pos: Serv mgr, Hancock Buick Co, 51-60, prof salesman, 60- Mil Serv: Entered as Pvt, Army, 41, released as S/Sgt, 45, after serv in Airborne 88th, 326th, 13th AB Div, ETO, 45; Lt, SC Nat Guard, formerly; Pre-Pearl Harbor Ribbon; Combat Inf Badge; Am Theatre Ribbon; ETO Ribbon; Battle Star; Expert Marksman Ribbon; Good Conduct Medal. Mem: Nat Asn Legislators; Cayce-West Columbia Lions; Ruritan; Am Legion; 40 et 8. Relig: Lutheran; Life mem & past pres, Lutheran Churchmen. Mailing Add: 125 Hendrix St West Columbia SC 29169

KLAS, JOHN HALL (D)
Chmn, Utah State Dem Comt
b Beaver Dam, Wis, Sept 24, 17; s John Charles Klas & Helen Hall K; m to Carol L Thalman; c Mary Lynn (Mrs H F Nelson, Jr), Caroline J & Jacqueline Ann. Educ: State Univ of Iowa, BS; Alpha Gamma Rho. Polit & Govt Pos: Chmn, Voting Dist 43 & Legis Dist Five, Salt Lake Co Dem Party, Utah; chmn, Utah State Dem Comt, 68-; mem, Dem Nat Comt, 68- Bus & Prof Pos: Vpres, Continental Bank & Trust Co. Mil Serv: Col (Ret), Army, 40-45, ETO; Bronze Star for Valor; Purple Heart with Cluster. Relig: Unitarian. Mailing Add: 2718 Wilshire Blvd Salt Lake City UT 84111

KLATT, DANIEL OTTO (D)
Chmn, Winnebago Co Dem Party, Wis
b Underhill, Wis, Jan 18, 47; s Henry August Klatt & Anna Filipiak K; m 1971 to Jeanne Ann Tubesing. Educ: Univ Wis, Oshkosh, BA in Math, 69; Delta Chi. Polit & Govt Pos: Chmn, Winnebago Co Dem Party, Wis, 74- Bus & Prof Pos: Production mgr, OEC Graphics, Oshkosh, Wis, 69-72; owner, Aristro-Craft Press, Oshkosh, 72- Mem: Oshkosh Area CofC. Honors & Awards: One of Ten Outstanding Srs, Univ Wis, Oshkosh, 69. Relig: Lutheran. Mailing Add: 429 Linde Oshkosh WI 54901

KLAUS, WILLIAM J (R)
Chmn, Sharkey Co Rep Party, Miss
b Vicksburg, Miss, Feb 1, 07; s Edward Klaus & Gussie Haas K; m 1932 to Sadye Grundfest. Educ: Wash Univ 2 years; Zeta Beta Tau. Polit & Govt Pos: Mem bd aldermen, Cary, Miss, 45-69; chmn, Sharkey Co Soil Conserv Comt, to 69; mem co & dist bd, Sharkey Co Elected Rep committeeman; chmn, Sharkey Co Rep Party, 69- Bus & Prof Pos: Secy, Grundfest & Klaus Gin Co, 35-63; pres, Evanna Plantation, 46-; pres, Sabill Plantation Inc, 47- Mil Serv: Entered as Pvt, Army Air Force, 42, released as Sgt, 45, after serv in 27th Bn Unit, 8th Air Force & 853rd Bomber Squadron, 491st Bomber Group, ETO, 43-45; Unit Citation; Bronze Star; EMATO Medal. Mem: Miss Econ Coun; 4-H; Rotary; Boy Scouts (Andrew Jackson Coun); Delta Coun. Honors & Awards: Various farm awards. Relig: Jewish. Mailing Add: Cary MS 39054

KLAZURA, DENNIS JOSEPH (D)
Chmn, Fourth Cong Dist Dem Party, Wis
b Milwaukee, Wis, June 4, 40; s Joseph John Klazura & Mary Frelka J; single. Educ: Marquette Univ, 58-61; Univ Wis-Milwaukee, BA Econ, 70; treas, Delta Tau Delta; treas, Student Govt. Polit & Govt Pos: Dem ward committeeman, 17th Ward, City of Milwaukee, Wis, 62-64; chmn, Milwaukee Co Young Dem, 62-65; vchmn, Young Dem Clubs of Wis, 63-66, pres, 66-68; vchmn, Milwaukee Co Dem Party, 63-64, mem, Exec Bd, 72-; home dist staff aid, Congressman Henry S Reuss, Fifth Cong Dist, 68; alt deleg, Dem Nat Conv, 72; chmn, 19th Assembly Dist Dem Unit, 72-73; chmn, Fourth Cong Dist Dem Party, 73-; deleg, Dem Nat Mid-Term Conf, 74. Bus & Prof Pos: Dept supvr, Louis Allis Co, Milwaukee, Wis, 61-63; financial adv, Univ Wis-Milwaukee, 68-72; asst to dir, Auxiliary Enterprises of Univ Wis-Milwaukee, currently. Mil Serv: Entered as Pvt, Wis Army Nat Guard, 63, released as Sgt, 69, after serv in 257th Artil Group Hq; Unit Awards; expert in field. Mem: Int Asn Col Unions; Midwest Student Activities Dirs Conf; 4th of July Asn of Humboldt Park; S Suburban Milwaukee Kiwanis (youth & community serv chmn, currently). Honors & Awards: Serv Citation, Young Dem Clubs of Am, 69; hon lifetime mem, Young Dem Clubs of Wis, 68; serv citations, Student Govt, Univ Wis-Milwaukee, 66-69. Relig: Catholic. Legal Res: 3069 S Kinnickinnic Ave Milwaukee WI 53207 Mailing Add: PO Box 4508 Milwaukee WI 53207

KLEBANOFF, HOWARD MICHAEL (D)
Conn State Rep
b New Haven, Conn, May 17, 37; s Max Edward Klebanoff & Sayre Witten K; m 1959 to Sandra Fleischner; c Marcie Lynne, Amy Beth & Betsy Jill. Educ: Yale Univ, BA, 59; Univ Conn, LLB, 62; Phi Gamma Delta. Polit & Govt Pos: Dem Comt Mem, 24th Dist, Conn, 63-64 & Dem Co-Capt, 64-68; Justice of the Peace, 67-69 & 69-71; comnr, Human Rels Comt, Hartford, Conn, 67-70; Conn State Rep, Ninth Assembly Dist, 69-73, Eighth Assembly Dist, 73-, mem elec, human rights & educ comts, Conn Gen Assembly, 71-, house chmn, joint educ comt, 71-73, ranking minority mem, educ comt & mem, judiciary, banks & educ comts, 73-, chmn educ comt, 75; Comn to Study procedures for Nomination of Presidential Cands, 69-71; Legis Comn Human Rights & Opportunities, 69-71; comnr, Educ Comn of States; mem spec comt sch finance, Nat Legis Conf, 73-; mem adv bd, Inst Educ Leadership, Washington, DC; mem adv bd, Conn Educ Seminar; mem bd dirs, New Eng Bd Higher Educ, 75- Bus & Prof Pos: Attorney, US Dept Labor, Washington, DC, 62-63; attorney, Ritter & Berman, Conn, 63-67 & partner, 67-69; attorney & partner, Novick, Klebanoff & Ellis, 69-; dir & asst secy, Conn Housing Investment Fund, Inc, 67-69; attorney & partner, Kennelly, Klebanoff & Ellis, Hartford, 73- Mem: Nat Soc State Legislators (bd gov, 73-); Blue Hills Civic Asn; Hartford Chap, NAACP (dir); Conn Asn Retarded Children (adv bd); Conn Asn Children with Perceptual Learning Disabilities, Inc (adv bd, 73-). Honors & Awards: Outstanding Legislator in Conn House of Rep, Eagleton Inst Polit, 71-73; Conn Educ Asn Friend of Educ Award, 75. Relig: Jewish. Legal Res: 127 Ridgefield St Hartford CT 06112 Mailing Add: 410 Asylum St Hartford CT 06103

KLECKLEY, ALBERT LLOYD (D)
SC State Rep
b Ridgeland, SC, Sept 26, 43; s Leamon Daniel Kleckley, Sr & Isabelle Beach K; div. Educ: Univ SC, AB, 65, Sch Law, JD, 69; Phi Alpha Delta. Polit & Govt Pos: SC State Rep, 72-

Mem: Am, SC & Jasper Co Bar Asns; SC State Bar Asn; Jaycees. Relig: Baptist. Legal Res: Woodlawn St Ridgeland SC 29936 Mailing Add: Drawer X Ridgeland SC 29936

KLECKNER, ROGER EUGENE (R)
Mem Exec Comt, Young Rep Nat Fedn
b Sandusky, Ohio, Mar 19, 47; s Max L Kleckner & Beatrice F Wagner K; single. Educ: Bowling Green Univ, BSEd, 69; Kappa Delta Pi; Sigma Nu. Polit & Govt Pos: Pres, Erie Co Young Rep, Ohio, 69-71; mem exec bd, Erie Co Rep Party, 69-71, cent committeeman, 71-72, legis chmn, 72-73; mem chmn, Ohio League Young Rep, 70-71, treas, 71-72, vchmn, 72-73, exec secy, 73-74; mem exec comt, Young Rep Nat Fedn, 74- Bus & Prof Pos: Teacher, Huron City Schs, Ohio, 69-72; restaurant mgr, Cedar Point, 70; teacher, Margaretta Local Schs, 73- Mem: Nat & Ohio Educ Asns; Margaretta Teachers Asn; Great Lakes Hist Soc. Honors & Awards: Ray C Bliss Award, Ohio League Young Rep, 70, Robert A Taft Outstanding Young Rep Award, 73; Commendation, Ohio Gen Assembly, 71. Mailing Add: 106 W Boalt St Sandusky OH 44870

KLECZKA, GERALD DANIEL (D)
Wis State Sen
b Milwaukee, Wis, Nov 26, 43; s Harry J Kleczka & Agnes P Dusza K; single. Educ: Univ Wis-Milwaukee. Polit & Govt Pos: Deleg, Dem Nat Conv, 14th Ward Dem Unit, 64, 65 & 68; co coun rep, Milwaukee Co, 65-68; Wis State Rep, 14th Dist, 68-75; Wis State Sen, 75- Bus & Prof Pos: Acct, Northwestern Nat Ins Co, currently. Mil Serv: Entered as Airman Basic, Wis Air Nat Guard, 62, released as Sgt, 68, after serv in 128th Tactical Dispensary, 128th Air Refueling Squadron; Sgt, Wis Air Nat Guard Res. Mem: SSide Bus Club; St Joseph's Athletic Asn; Elks; Polish Nat Alliance; St Helen's Holy Name Soc (pres). Relig: Catholic. Mailing Add: 3427 S Ninth Place Milwaukee WI 53215

KLEIER, M J (JERRY) (D)
Ky State Rep
Mailing Add: 335 West Southside Court Louisville KY 40214

KLEIN, ANN (D)
b New York, NY, July 23, 23; d Mack Rosensweig & Hilda Barnett R; m 1943 to Robert Lawrence Klein; c Mara (Mrs Miller) & David Laurence. Educ: Barnard Col, BA; Columbia Univ Sch Social Work, MS. Polit & Govt Pos: NJ State Assemblywoman, 72-74; secy NJ deleg, Dem Nat Conv, 72; comnr, Insts & Agencies, NJ, 74- Bus & Prof Pos: Psychiat social worker, Worcester Child Guid Clin, 45-47; psychiat case worker, Family Serv of Morris Co, 53-55. Mem: League of Women Voters; Nat Orgn of Women; Women's Polit Caucus; Nat Asn Social Workers. Honors & Awards: Hannah Solomon Award, Nat Coun Jewish Women, 74; Woman of the Year, Women's Polit Caucus, 74; State Serv Award, NJ Asn Children with Learning Disabilities, 74. Relig: Jewish. Legal Res: 9 Woodlawn Dr Morristown NJ 07960 Mailing Add: State House Trenton NJ 08625

KLEIN, EDITH MILLER (R)
Idaho State Sen
b Wallace, Idaho, Aug 4, 15; d Fred L B Miller & Edith Gallup M; m 1949 to Sandor S Klein, wid. Educ: Univ Idaho, BS in Bus, 35; Wash State Univ, grad teaching fel, 35-36; George Washington Univ, JD, 46, LLM, 54; Kappa Beta Pi. Polit & Govt Pos: Interviewer, Idaho State Employ Serv, 40-41; personnel specialist, War Dept, DC, 43-46; judge, Munic Court, Boise, Idaho, 47-49; Idaho State Rep, 49-50 & 65-68; attorney, Fed Commun Comn, DC, 53-54 & Fed Housing Admin, New York, 55-56; chmn, Idaho Gov Comn on Status of Women, 65-71; Idaho State Sen, 68-, chmn Judiciary Comt, Idaho State Senate, 70- Bus & Prof Pos: Teacher, Grangeville High Sch, 36-37; pvt practice of law, 47-53; Lawyer, Langroise, Sullivan & Smylie, Boise, Idaho, 57- Mem: Ada Co Rep Women's Club; DAR; Bus & Prof Women's Club; Boise Toastmistress Club; Boise Art Asn. Honors & Awards: Woman of the Year, Boise Altrusa Club, 66 & Gtr Boise CofC, 70. Relig: Congregational. Legal Res: 1732 Warm Springs Ave Boise ID 83702 Mailing Add: PO Box 475 Boise ID 83701

KLEIN, HERBERT CHARLES (D)
NJ State Assemblyman
b Newark, NJ, June 24, 30; s Alfred Klein & Fae Sackin K; m 1952 to Jacqueline Krieger; c Roger M & Cynthia N. Educ: Rutgers Univ, BA, 50; Harvard Univ Law Sch, LLB, 53; NY Univ, LLB, 59; Tau Kappa Alpha; Tau Delta Phi. Polit & Govt Pos: Mem, Passaic Co Dem Comt, NJ, 58-63, vchmn, 71-; pres, Clifton Dem Club, 60-67; counsel, Passaic Co Park Comn, 62-68; cand for freeholder, Passaic Co, 67; alt deleg, Dem Nat Conv, 68; Passaic Co campaign mgr, Gov Robert Meyner, 69; NJ State Assemblyman, Dist 14A, 72-, Asst Dem Whip, NJ State Assembly, 72- Bus & Prof Pos: Assoc, Budd, Larner & Kent, Law Firm, Newark, 56-60; partner, Krieger & Klein, Passaic, 61-; trustee, First Real Estate Investment Trust of NJ, Hackensack, 61- Mil Serv: Entered as 2nd Lt, Air Force, 54, released as 1st Lt, 56, after serv in Air Material Command, Los Angeles Air Procurement Dist, 54-56. Mem: B'nai B'rith; Am Jewish Comt; Jewish War Vet; YMHA; Beth Israel Hosp, Passaic, NJ (bd trustees). Relig: Jewish. Mailing Add: 34 Lenox Ave Clifton NJ 07012

KLEINBAUM, JACK (DFL)
Minn State Sen
b 1917; married; c John, Richard, James & Jeff. Educ: N High Sch, Minneapolis. Polit & Govt Pos: Mem, Citizens Adv Comt; with Housing & Redevelop Authority; mem, City Coun, 60-64; Minn State Rep, 67-73; Minn State Sen, Dist 17, 73- Bus & Prof Pos: Owner & mgr, Jack's Outlet. Mil Serv: Navy, Foreman in Tacoma Shipyards. Mem: Elks; Eagles; Moose; Mason; Sertoma. Honors & Awards: Sertoman of the Year, 64. Relig: Jewish. Mailing Add: 1100 N 23rd Ave St Cloud MN 56301

KLEINDIENST, RICHARD GORDON (R)
b Winslow, Ariz, Aug 5, 23; s Alfred R Kleindienst & Gladys Love K (deceased); m 1948 to Margaret Dunbar; c Alfred Dunbar, Wallace Heath, Anne Lucile & Carolyn Love. Educ: Univ Ariz, 41-42; Harvard Univ, AB magna cum laude, 47, Law Sch, LLB, 50; Phi Beta Kappa; Sigma Alpha Epsilon. Polit & Govt Pos: Ariz State Rep, 53-54; chmn, Ariz Young Rep League, 55; chmn, Rep State Comt, Ariz, 56-63; mem, Rep Nat Comt, 56-63, gen counsel, 68; deleg, Rep Nat Conv, 60 & 64; nominee for Gov of Ariz, 64; nat dir field opers, Goldwater for President Comt, 64; nat dir field opers, Nixon for President Comt, 68; Dep Attorney Gen, Dept of Justice, 69-72, Attorney Gen of US, 72-73. Bus & Prof Pos: Law clerk, Ropes & Grey, Boston, Mass, 49-50; assoc & partner, Jennings, Strouss, Salmon & Trask, Phoenix, Ariz, 50-57; sr partner, Shimmell, Hill, Kleindienst & Bishop, 58-69. Mil Serv: Entered as Pvt, Army, 43, released as 1st Lt, 45, after serv as Navigator, 15th Air Force, Italy; ETO Ribbon. Mem: State Bar of Ariz; Am Bar Asn; Fed Bar Asn (vpres, formerly, pres, 72-); Am Legion; VFW. Relig: Episcopal; Lay Reader, Past Warden & Vestryman, Trinity Episcopal Cathedral & All Saints Episcopal Church; former mem exec coun, Ariz Diocese, Episcopal Church. Legal Res: Phoenix AZ Mailing Add: 8464 Portland Pl McLean VA 22106

KLEINER, A ROBERT (D)
Chmn, Fifth Cong Dist Dem Comt, Mich
b Grand Rapids, Mich, Dec 2, 16; s Anthony Kleiner & Lillian Lubetsky K; m 1943 to Dorothy Jane Kettring; c Nancy Elizabeth (Mrs Paul De Young). Educ: Univ Mich, AB, 38, Law Sch, JD, 41. Polit & Govt Pos: Secy, Fifth Cong Dist Dem Orgn, Mich, 59-61, elected chmn, Fifth Cong Dist Dem Comt at Dem State Conv, 73 & 75; mem exec comt, Kent Co Dem Comt, 60-, secy, 60-68, chmn, 68-70; mem, Comn on Legis Apportionment, 63-66 & 71-72; deleg, Dem Nat Conv, 64 & 68. Bus & Prof Pos: Attorney, pvt practice. Mil Serv: Entered as Pvt, Army Ord Dept, 43, released as 1st Lt, 46, after serv in Off Chief of Ord, Detroit, 44-46. Mem: Am, Mich & Grand Rapids Bar Asns. Mailing Add: 1134 Idema Dr SE Grand Rapids MI 49506

KLEPPE, THOMAS SAVIG (R)
Adminr, Small Bus Admin
b Kintyre, NDak, July 1, 19; s Lars O Kleppe & Hannah Savig K; m 1958 to Glendora Loew; c Janis (Mrs Jerry G Cunningham), Thomas Stewart, Jane & Jill. Educ: Valley City State Teachers Col, 37. Polit & Govt Pos: Mem subcomt on local govt, Intergovt Rels Comn; mayor, Bismarck, NDak, 50-54; nat security forum, Army War Col, 62; treas, NDak Rep Party, 63; US Rep, NDak, 66-70; adminr, Small Bus Admin, 71- Bus & Prof Pos: Asst mgr & helper, Farmers Co, Kintyre, 37-41; clerk & asst cashier, Dakota Nat Bank, Bismarck & Stock Growers Bank, Napoleon, 41-42; vpres & treas, Gold Seal Co, Bismarck, 48-58, pres & treas, 58-64; vpres & dir, J M Dain & Co, Inc, Minneapolis, Minn, 65-66. Mil Serv: Army, WO(jg), Finance Dept attached to Air Corps, 42-46. Mem: Slope Lutheran Homes, Inc (pres & chmn). Honors & Awards: Outstanding Young Man Award, Jaycees, 50. Relig: Lutheran; Chmn comts, Trinity Lutheran Church. Legal Res: MD Mailing Add: Small Bus Admin 1441 L St NW Washington DC 20416

KLEVANA, LEIGHTON Q J (R)
Mem, Windsor Co Rep Comt, Vt
b Prague, Czech; s Josef V Klvana & Bellina Louise Karlovsky K; m 1962 to Nancy Elizabeth Van Brunt; c Leighton Alexis Christian. Educ: Cornell Univ, BA, 57; Univ of Paris, Sorbonne, 57-58; Univ Va, JD, 61; Alpha Tau Omega. Polit & Govt Pos: Asst attorney gen, Vt, 70-; chmn, Hartland Rep Town Comt, 71-; mem, Windsor Co Rep Comt, 71-; alt deleg, Rep Nat Conv, 72. Bus & Prof Pos: Assoc, Olwine, Connelly, Chase, O'Donnell & Weyher, NY, 64-67; vpres & secy, Transit Air Freight, Inc, Jamaica, NY, 66-; secy & gen coun, Helme Prod, Inc, 67-70. Mem: Am & Vt Bar Asns; Asn of Bar of New York City; Hartland Citizens Asn (trustee & secy, 71-72); Woodstock Country Club. Relig: Protestant. Mailing Add: Box 101 Hartland VT 05048

KLEVEN, LESLIE J (R)
SDak State Rep
Mailing Add: 1325 Nellie St Sturgis SD 57785

KLICKA, GEORGE H (R)
Wis State Rep
Mailing Add: 8442 Kenyon Ave Wauwatosa WI 53213

KLINCK, MARY ELLEN (D)
Chmn, East Haddam Dem Town Comt, Conn
b New York, NY, Dec 29, 34; s Paul Sweeney & Mary Ellen Brett S; m 1955 to Donald R Klinck; c Kathleen, Elizabeth & Philip. Educ: St John's & Columbia Univs, 53-54. Polit & Govt Pos: Pres, East Haddam Dem Women's Club, 62-65; chmn, East Haddam Dem Town Comt, 70-; second electman, East Haddam, 71-73; mem, Conn Dem State Cent Comt, 74- Bus & Prof Pos: Vpres & secy, W C Rout Agency, Real Estate & Ins, 60- Mem: Realtor Bd of Gtr Middletown; East Haddam Garden Club. Mailing Add: Broom Rd East Haddam CT 06423

KLINE, ERNEST PAUL (D)
Lt Gov, Pa
b Allentown, Pa, June 20, 29; s Allen J Kline & Elna Natali K; m to Josephine Recupero; c Patricia, Samuel, Vincent, Michael, John, Myra & Monica. Educ: Rostraver High Sch. Polit & Govt Pos: Mem, Beaver Falls City Coun, Pa, 56-59; Workman's Compensation Referee, 61-63; Pa State Sen, 64-70, Minority Leader, Pa State Senate, 67-70; deleg, Dem Nat Conv, 68 & 72; Lt Gov, Pa, 71- Bus & Prof Pos: Radio newsman, Sta WVBP, Beaver Falls, 50-67. Relig: Roman Catholic. Legal Res: 2209 Seventh Ave Beaver Falls PA 15010 Mailing Add: Capitol Bldg Harrisburg PA 17120

KLINE, GWEN WEEKS (R)
Mem Exec Comt, Ohio Rep State Cent Comt
b Dayton, Ohio, Apr 22, 03; d Samuel Burt Weeks & Helen Lindsley W; m 1929 to Robert E Kline. Educ: Dayton Normal Sch, 21-23. Polit & Govt Pos: Chmn, Montgomery Co Rep Party, Ohio, 51-72; sales tax auditor, Dayton, 53-55; mem, Bd Elec, 62-72; mem exec comt, Ohio Rep State Cent Comt, 75- Bus & Prof Pos: Teacher, Northridge Sch Dist, 23-35. Mem: YWCA; YMCA; Kiwanis Women's Club; Ment Retarded Children's Coun; Rep Bus Women's Club. Relig: Protestant. Mailing Add: 700 Kenilworth Ave Dayton OH 45405

KLINE, PAUL ARTHUR (R)
b Mahanoy City, Pa, Oct 29, 19; s William Kline & Ellen Eckler K; m 1956 to Freeda M Swartz; c Richard A, Betsy J (Mrs Husson) & Gretchen Ellen. Educ: Univ Maine, 46-49; George Washington Univ, BA, 51. Polit & Govt Pos: Clerk, US Rep Frank Fellows, Maine, 49-52; legis asst to US Rep Clifford G McIntire, Maine, 53-64; research specialist, House Republican Conf, 65-66; legis asst to US Rep Catherine May, Washington, 66-67; admin asst to US Rep George A Goodling, 19th Dist, Pa, formerly. Mil Serv: Entered as Pfc, Army Air Force, 42, released as Cpl, 45, after serv in 589th Air Force Bn, ETO, 45; Good Conduct Medal; ETO Medal. Relig: Protestant. Mailing Add: 1505 Vivian Pl Silver Spring MD 20902

KLING, WILLIAM HOLT (R)
b York, Pa, Oct 14, 32; s Joseph Amon Kling & Mary Nellye Holt K; m 1967 to Barbara Glyn Cook; c Susan Carole, Kathy Nell, Barbara Louise, Elizabeth Harper & William Holt, Jr. Educ: York Jr Col, Pa, 50-52; Pa State Univ, University Park, BA Jour, 58; Medill Sch Jour, Northwestern Univ, Evanston, 58-59; Sigma Delta Chi; Delta Upsilon. Polit & Govt Pos: Admin asst to US Rep Samuel H Young, Tenth Dist, Ill, 73- Bus & Prof Pos: Reporter, The

Gazette & Daily, York, 50-58; reporter, City News Bur of Chicago, 59; reporter, Chicago Tribune, 59-62, asst polit ed, 62-67, Washington correspondent, 67-71; managing ed, Am Security Coun, Washington, DC, 71-73. Mil Serv: Entered as Pvt, Army, 52, released as Cpl, after serv in Signal Corps, Europe, 53-55. Mem: Chicago Headline Club; Nat & Chicago Press Clubs; Chicago Newspaper Reporters' Asn; Capitol Hill Club. Relig: Presbyterian. Mailing Add: 4510 Fidelity Ct Annandale VA 22003

KLINGAMAN, WILLIAM K, SR (R)
Pa State Rep
Mailing Add: Capitol Bldg Harrisburg PA 17120

KLOEPPEL, RICHARD J (D)
NMex State Rep
Mailing Add: Box 187 Bernalillo NM 87004

KLONOSKI, JAMES RICHARD (D)
Chmn, Dem Party Ore
b Virginia, Minn, Mar 24, 25; s James Phillip Klonoski & Jean Gerlach K; m 1960 to Mary Kay Haake; c Tom & Kathy. Educ: Univ Minn, BS, 47, MA, 48; Univ Mich, PhD, 58; Phi Beta Kappa; Phi Alpha Theta. Polit & Govt Pos: Chmn, Lane Co Dem Party, Ore, 70-74; chmn, Dem Party Ore, 74-; mem, Dem Nat Comt, 74- Bus & Prof Pos: Prof polit sci, St Olaf Col, 56-59; prof polit sci, Univ Ore, 61-68 & 69-; assoc provost, Fed City Col, 68-69. Mil Serv: Entered as Pvt, Army, 46, released as Cpl, 47, after serv in 1176 Engr Bn, Korea; reentered as Pvt, 50, released as Sgt, 51, after serv in 17th Army Airborne Corps, Ft Bragg, NC. Publ: Co-auth, The allocation of justice, J Pub Law, 65; co-auth, The Politics of Local Justice, Little, Brown & Co, 70; co-auth, Plea bargaining in Oregon, Ore Law Rev, 72. Mem: Northwest Polit Sci Asn (pres, 75-); Am Polit Sci Asn; Am Civil Liberties Union; Am Fedn Teachers. Honors & Awards: Cong Fel, Am Polit Sci Asn, 59; Nat Comt Fel, Dem Nat Comt, 62. Relig: Congregational. Mailing Add: 2795 Central Blvd Eugene OR 97403

KLOSAK, J HENRY (R)
Ill State Sen
Mailing Add: 3100 South 53rd Ct Cicero IL 60650

KLOTZ, FRANK P (R)
Chmn, El Paso Co Rep Comt, Colo
b Syracuse, NY, June 16, 21; s Frank A Klotz (deceased) & Minnie P K; m 1945 to Treva L Hardy; c Frank G & Bryan P. Educ: Syracuse Univ, 39-41; Univ Md, BS, 54; St Mary's Univ (Tex), MA, 59; Soc Old Crows (Electronic Warfare, pres); Sigma Nu. Polit & Govt Pos: Chmn, El Paso Co Rep Comt, Colo, 75- Bus & Prof Pos: Dir corp relocation, Wiedman & Co, 72-75; pres, Klotz, Mittello Shoe Corp, Syracuse, NY, 73-75. Mil Serv: Entered as 2nd Lt, Air Force, 42, released as Col, 72, after serv in Hq Air Defense Command, Aleutians, Ger, NAfrica, Eng & Southeast Asia; Distinguished Flying Cross; Air Medal with 3 Clusters; Meritorious Serv Medal; Commendation Ribbon with 5 Clusters; Humane Serv Award; European Theatre, Am Theatre & Southeast Asia Ribbons. Publ: Auth, The USAF as an Instrument of Foreign Policy, 58 & auth, An Alternative to Collective Bargaining, 60, St Mary's Univ (Tex); auth, The Problems of Igloo White, US Air Force, 69. Mem: Sertoma; Exchange Club. Relig: Episcopal. Mailing Add: Box 44 Monument CO 80132

KLUNK, FRED G (D)
Mem, Adams Co Dem Comt, Pa
b Centennial, Pa, July 30, 10; s Edward G Klunk (deceased) & Rose Gebhart K; m 1933 to Florence Elizabeth Rinehart; c Sylvia, James, Warren, Rosalie, Wayne, Fred R & Christine. Educ: Bus Col. Polit & Govt Pos: Mem, City Coun, New Oxford, Pa, 3 terms & pres, 2 terms; dir, Bur of Liquid Fuels Tax, Pa Dept Revenue; dep secy, Dept of Property & Supplies; exec secy, State Retirement Bd; mem, Adams Co Dem Comt, 33-, chmn, 43-72; mem, Pa State Dem Comt, 38-41; Pa State Rep, 91st Dist, Adams Co, 71-72. Bus & Prof Pos: Asst dir, Bur of Securities & Deposits, State Treas Dept; mfr of Bakery Prod. Mem: KofC (4 Degree); Elks; Moose; Eagles; Lions. Relig: Catholic. Mailing Add: 15 N Peter St New Oxford PA 17350

KNAPP, G EDWARD (R)
Mem, Bibb Co Rep Comt, Ga
b Ypsilanti, Mich, Mar 22, 16; s Jay (N) Knapp & Clara Norwood K; m 1945 to Mary Elizabeth Scott; c Nancy L, Henry Scott & Gregory Lee. Educ: Eastern Mich Univ, 34-36; Univ Mich, BSF, 40; Mich Forestry Club. Polit & Govt Pos: Ga State Rep, Dist 81, Post 2, 66-70; Bibb Co rep, Mid Ga Recreation Comn, 68-; chmn, Bibb Co Forestry Bd, Ga, 68-; mem, Bibb Co Rep Comt, 72- Mil Serv: Pilot instr & ATC Pilot, Air Force Res, 42-44. Mem: Soc of Am Foresters; Forest Farmers Asn; Am & Ga Forestry Asns; Macon Farmers Club. Relig: Baptist. Legal Res: 661 Forest Hill Rd Macon GA 31204 Mailing Add: 4435 Pio Nono Ave Macon GA 31206

KNAPP, JAMES IAN KEITH (R)
Pres, Calif Young Rep
b Brooklyn, NY, Apr 6, 43; s Rev Charles T Knapp & Christine Grange K; m 1975 to Marilyn Margaret Ewing; c Jennifer. Educ: Harvard Univ, AB cum laude, 64; Univ Colo, Boulder, JD, 67; Order of the Coif. Polit & Govt Pos: Pres, Los Angeles Co Young Rep, Calif, 71; secy, Lincoln Club Pasadena, 72-; nat vchmn, Young Rep Nat Fedn, 73-; chmn youth comt, Rep State Cent Comt Calif, 75- Bus & Prof Pos: Assoc, Swerdlow, Glikbarg & Shimer, 67-68; dep dist attorney, Los Angeles Co, Calif, 68-, exec dir uniform crime charging proj, 73-75, head pub fraud sect, 75- Publ: Ed, Harvard Conservative, 62; co-ed, University of Colorado Law Review, 66-67; ed & auth, Uniform Crime Charging Standards, Calif Dist Attorneys Asn, 75. Mem: Calif Bar Asn; Town Hall of Los Angeles; Los Angeles World Affairs Coun; Nat Dist Attorneys Asn (prosecution standards comt, 72-); Calif Dist Attorneys Asn (chmn crime charging standards supplementation comt, 75-). Relig: Episcopal. Mailing Add: 514 Orange Grove Blvd South Pasadena CA 91030

KNAUER, VIRGINIA HARRINGTON (R)
VChmn, Philadelphia Co Rep Comt, Pa
b Philadelphia, Pa, Mar 28, 15; d Herman Winfield Wright & Helen V Harrington W; m 1940 to Wilhelm F Knauer; c Wilhelm F, Jr & Valerie H (Mrs I Townsend Burden, III). Educ: Univ Pa, BFA, 37; Pa Acad Fine Arts, 33-38; Royal Acad Fine Arts, Florence, Italy, 38-39; Kappa Delta Epsilon; Zeta Tau Alpha. Hon Degrees: LLD, Univ Pa, Philadelphia Col Textiles & Sci, Allentown Col of St Francis de Sales & Russell Sage Col; LittD, Drexel Univ; LHD, Russell Sage Col & Pa Col Podiatric Med. Polit & Govt Pos: Vchmn, Philadelphia Co Rep Comt, Pa, 58-; councilman-at-lg, Philadelphia, 60-68; dir, Pa Bur Consumer Protection, 68-69; Spec Asst to President for Consumer Affairs, 69-; US rep & vchmn consumer policy comt, Orgn for Econ Coop & Develop, Paris, France; pres, Philadelphia Cong Rep Couns; dir, Pa Coun Rep Women, 58, dir, 63-; vpres, Rep Women of Pa, 71, dir, Off Consumer Affairs, 71- Bus & Prof Pos: Trustee, Pa Col Podiatric Med; bd dirs, Hannah Pa House, 56-, vpres, 71; vpres, Knauer Found for Hist Preservation; mem, Nat Trust Hist Preservation; trustee, Pa Col. Publ: Auth of numerous articles on consumer protection for nat mags. Mem: Doberman Pinscher Club. Honors & Awards: Distinguished Daughters of Pa, 69. Relig: Episcopal. Legal Res: 9601 Milnor Philadelphia PA 19114 Mailing Add: The White House 1600 Pennsylvania Ave Washington DC 20500

KNAUFT, MILFORD ROY, JR (R)
Mem, Rep State Cent Comt Calif
b St Paul, Minn, Aug 26, 18; s Milford Roy Knauft & Marie Simonet K; m 1946 to Doris Bovee; c Robert Lee, Nancy Louise & Sally Ann. Educ: Univ Calif, Los Angeles, 4 years; Sigma Nu; Scabbard & Blade. Polit & Govt Pos: Dir, Yorba Linda Co Water Dist, 65-; sch bd mem, Placentia Unified Sch Dist, 67-71; mem, Rep State Cent Comt Calif, currently; dist rep, Congressman Charles Wiggins, currently. Bus & Prof Pos: Off mgr, Hollywood Wholesale Paper Corp, Calif, 46-50, gen mgr & treas, 50-61; retired. Mil Serv: Entered as 2nd Lt, Army Air Force, 43, released as 1st Lt, 45, after serv in 96th Bomb Group, Eighth Air Force, ETO, 44-45; Air Medal; Three Oak Leaf Clusters; Distinguished Flying Cross. Mem: Rotary Club; life mem PTA. Relig: Presbyterian. Mailing Add: 5668 Kellogg Dr Yorba Linda CA 92686

KNAUSS, MARY ANN TINKLEPAUGH (R)
Dir Youth Activities, NY State Rep Comt
b Albany, NY, June 15, 30; d John Rossman Tinklepaugh, Sr & Myrtie Lasher T; m 1961 to Charles William Knauss, Jr; c Mary Susan, Seth Tinklepaugh & John Charles. Educ: Pine Manor Jr Col, 50; Barnard Col, BA, 52. Polit & Govt Pos: Organizer, Young Rep Club, Barnard Col & past pres; Rep committeeman, Livingston Rep Town Comt, 62-; mem exec comt, Columbia Co Rep Comt; nat committeeman, NY State Young Rep, 61-63, vpres, 64-65, pres, 66-67; dir, NY State TAR Sch, 65-67; alt deleg, State Nominating Conv, 62, deleg, 66; page, Rep Nat Conv, 64, asst chief page, 68; mem, NY Rep State Exec Comt, 66-68; corresponding secy, Fedn Women's Rep Clubs NY State, 66-67, mem-at-lg, Coun, 68-; mem, 28th Cong Dist Rep Comt, 68-; chmn, NY State Women for Nixon-Agnew, 68; dir youth activities, NY State Rep Comt, 69-, spec asst to chmn, 71-; coordr women's activities, Rockefeller Campaign Comt, 70; dep campaign dir, NY State Comt to Reelect the President, 72. Mem: DAR; Nat Grange; Old Chatham Hunt Club; Am Legion Auxiliary; Columbia Co Hosp Auxiliary. Honors & Awards: Outstanding Young Women of Am, 65. Relig: Lutheran. Mailing Add: Livingston NY 12541

KNEBEL, JOHN ALBERT (R)
b Tulsa, Okla, Oct 4, 36; s John A Knebel (deceased) & Florence Friend K; m 1959 to Zenia Marks; c Carrie A, John A, III & Clemens M. Educ: US Mil Acad, BS, 59; Creighton Univ, MA, 62; Wash Col Law, Am Univ, JD, 65; Omicron Delta Gamma (pres, Omaha Chap); Delta Theta Phi. Polit & Govt Pos: Admin asst to US Rep J E Wharton, NY, 63-65; asst counsel, Comt on Agr, US House of Rep, 69-71; gen counsel, Small Bus Admin, 71-73; gen counsel, US Dept of Agr, 73- Bus & Prof Pos: Assoc, Howrey, Simon, Baker & Murchison, Attorneys, 65-68. Mil Serv: Entered as 2nd Lt, Air Force, 59, released as 1st Lt, 63, after serv in Hq, Strategic Air Command, Omaha & Off of Secy of Air Force. Publ: Auth, Future interests in the District of Columbia, Am Univ Law Rev, 6/65; Legal basis for SBA's minority enterprise system, Fed Bar J, fall 71. Mem: AM & DC Bar Asns; Fed Bar Asn (chmn, Gen Counsels Comts, 72-73); Springfield Golf & Country Club, Va. Honors & Awards: Cert of the President, Fed Bar, 72; NASBIC, distinguished serv to small bus, 72. Relig: Catholic. Mailing Add: Dept of Agr Washington DC 20250

KNEECE, ROBERT EDWARD (D)
SC State Rep
b Columbia, SC, Dec 20, 33; s Otis Salter Kneece & Elise Blackmon K; m 1957 to Margaret Ann Medders; c Melanie Carol, Robert Edward, Jr, Richard Otis, Melinda Kyle, Rexford Patrick & Margaret Ann. Educ: Univ SC, LLB, 58; Sigma Chi. Polit & Govt Pos: Pres, Richland Co Young Dem, SC, 61; pres, SC Young Dem, 60-62; SC State Rep, 67-, second vchmn, Judiciary Comt, SC State House of Rep, formerly, first vchmn, formerly, chmn, currently; vchmn, State Crime Study Comt. Bus & Prof Pos: Attorney-at-law, 58- Mem: Mason, Shrine; CofC; Palmetto Sertoma. Relig: Lutheran. Mailing Add: 1338 Pickens St Columbia SC 29201

KNEELAND, GEORGE ROYAL (R)
Committeeman, Idaho Rep State Cent Comt
b Shelton, Wash, May 28, 18; s Allan Kneeland & Signe Anderson K; div; c Nancy (Mrs Hudson) & Georgina (Mrs Bottemiller). Educ: Cent Wash Col, BS, 40; Univ Wash, LLB, 49; Kappa Delta Pi; Delta Theta Phi. Polit & Govt Pos: Prosecuting attorney, Blaine Co, Idaho, 52-54; committeeman, Idaho Rep State Cent Comt, 71- Bus & Prof Pos: Lawyer, Kneeland, Laggis & Korb, Ketchum, Idaho, 50- Mil Serv: Entered as Cadet, Navy, 42, released as Lt, 46, after serv in Atlantic, Pac & Far East Theatres, 43-46. Legal Res: A-2 Bigwood Saddle Rd Ketchum ID 83340 Mailing Add: PO Box 258 Ketchum ID 83340

KNEIP, RICHARD FRANCIS (D)
Gov, SDak
b Tyler, Minn, Jan 7, 33; s Frank J Kneip & Bernice D Peterson K; m to Nancy Lou Pankey; c Kevin, Keith, Paul, Kent, Kurt, Philip, Patrick & Michael. Polit & Govt Pos: SDak State Sen, McCook, Hanson & Sanborn Co, 64-71, Minority Leader, SDak State Sen, 67-71; mem exec bd, Legis Research Coun & mem 13 Man Const Rev Comn, currently; Gov, SDak, 71-; mem exec comt, Nat Gov Conf, 72-; mem, Adv Comn on Intergovt Rels, 72- Bus & Prof Pos: Mem, Diocesan Sch Bd, Cath Diocese of Sioux Falls, SDak, 67- Mil Serv: Entered as Pvt, Air Force, 51, released as S/Sgt, 55; German Occup Medal. Mem: Am Legion. Relig: Catholic. Legal Res: 300 E Lincoln Salem SD 57058 Mailing Add: Governor's Residence Pierre SD 57501

KNELL, WILLIAM HENRY (R)
VChmn, San Miguel Co Rep Party, NMex
b Bronx, NY, May 3, 27; s William Charles Knell & Marie von Wernich K; div. Educ: Highlands Univ, BA, 52; Adelphi Univ, MA, 65; Alpha Psi Omega; Kappa Sigma Kappa; Int Rels Club; Social Sci Soc. Polit & Govt Pos: Mem, NMex State Cent Comt, 66-; mem, NMex State Exec Comt, 68-, chmn rules comt, 69-; chmn, San Miguel Co Rep Party, 71-75, vchmn, 75- Bus & Prof Pos: Ed-writer, New York Mirror, 53-60; teacher, Las Vegas City Schs, NMex, 60-65; writer, Santa Fe New Mexican, 60-62; asst prof Eng, speech & jour, Highlands Univ, 65- Mil Serv: Entered as A/S, Navy, 45, released as PO 3/C, 46, after serv in Pac Theatre, 45-46; Victory Medal; Asiatic Pac Medal; Am Theatre Medal. Publ: Auth, Double

exposure (prize poem), Manifold, London, Eng, 1/64; auth, Parade (prize poem), Quaderni di Poesia, Rome, 4/70; auth, Bird that sings no more (award poem), Masters of Modern Poetry, Rome, 75; plus others. Mem: Am Conservative Union; Carnegie Pub Libr (bd trustees); Centro Studi e Scambi Int. Relig: Lutheran; mem bd dirs, Immanual Lutheran Church. Mailing Add: 2200 B Collins Dr Las Vegas NM 87701

KNEPPER, JAMES W, JR (R)
Pa State Rep
Mailing Add: Capitol Bldg Harrisburg PA 17120

KNICKERBOCKER, JERRY (R)
Minn State Rep
Mailing Add: 10100 Minnetonka Blvd Minnetonka MN 55343

KNIGHT, DAVID L (R)
NH State Rep
Mailing Add: Box 42 Marlborough NH 03455

KNIGHT, EVELYN DELORIS (D)
Treas, Calif Dem State Cent Comt
b Mobile, Ala, Dec 19, 33; d Clarence Knight & Odell Deal K; single. Educ: St Louis Univ, BS, 55, MSW, 60; Univ Southern Calif, 65; Univ Calif, Berkeley, 66-67. Polit & Govt Pos: Secy, Eastside Dem Orgn, Calif, 64-65; treas, 32nd Cong Dist Coun, 63-65; mem bd, Citizens Urban Renewal Adv Bd, 66-67; mem & treas, Calif Dem State Cent Comt, 68- Bus & Prof Pos: Classroom teacher, Archdiocese of St Louis, 55-58; child welfare supvr, City of St Louis, 58-62; family agency supvr, Cath Welfare Bur, 62-66; community orgn prog develop dir, Contra Costa Co Community Serv, 66-67; sr social scientist, Westinghouse Elec Corp, 67-68, dir field serv, 68-; assoc dir, Protestant Community Serv, formerly, exec dir, 72-; part-time instr, Calif State Univ, Long Beach, currently. Mem: Nat Asn Social Workers; Acad Cert Social Worker-Nat Conf Social Welfare; Int Orgn Community Develop; Nat Asn Afro-Am Educators; Instr, Training & Prog Develop. Relig: Roman Catholic. Mailing Add: 2535 Cota Ave Long Beach CA 90810

KNIGHT, JAMES EDWARD (R)
b Electra, Tex, Dec 4, 20; s James Meadow Knight & Kathryn Love K; m 1951 to Elizabeth Stell Johnson; c J Barry. Educ: Tex A&M Univ, 38-39; Tarleton Col, 39-40 & 40-41; Univ Tex, 45-46; Delta Tau Delta. Polit & Govt Pos: Vchmn, Dallam Co Rep Exec Comt, Tex, 63, chmn, formerly. Mil Serv: Entered as Flying Cadet, Air Force, 41, released as Capt, 46; Lt Col, 9913th Air Res Squadron, Western Training Command, Air Force Res, retired, 69; Commendation, Air Res & Am Campaign Medals. Mem: Mason; Scottish Rite; Shrine; Farm Bur. Relig: Christian. Mailing Add: 1006 Keeler Ave Dalhart TX 79022

KNIGHT, MONROE OLNEY (R)
RI State Rep
b Foster, RI, July 16, 12; s Olney A Knight & Annie Card K; m 1942 to Lilla N Taudvin; c Theodore O & Randall M. Educ: Killingly High Sch, Danielson, Conn, dipl, 30. Polit & Govt Pos: Chmn, Canvassing Bd, Foster, RI; pres, town coun, 66-70; RI State Rep, 71- Bus & Prof Pos: Electrician, Am Tube & Controls, West Warwick, RI, currently. Mil Serv: Entered as Pvt, Army Signal Corps, 42, released as T/Sgt, 45, after serv in 914th Signal Corps Depot, Aviation, African & European Theatres. Mem: AF&AM; Moosup Valley Grange PofH. Relig: Protestant. Mailing Add: Moosup Valley Rd Foster RI 02825

KNIGHT, NATHAN G (D)
Ga State Rep
Mailing Add: PO Box 1175 Newnan GA 30263

KNIGHT, PETER SAGE (D)
b Medford, Mass, Feb 12, 51; s Richard B Knight & Janet Neill K; single. Educ: Cornell Univ, BA, 73; Red Key; Quill & Dagger; Psi Upsilon. Polit & Govt Pos: Admin asst, Fed Disaster Assistance Admin, Boston, Mass, 74; economist, Anti-Trust Div, Dept Justice, 74; admin asst, US Rep Torbert H Macdonald, Mass, 74- Mem: Mass State Soc; Admin Asst Asn. Legal Res: 15 Alden Lane Winchester MA 01890 Mailing Add: 5740 Drake Ct 273 Alexandria VA 22311

KNIGHT, RIDGWAY BREWSTER
b Paris, France, June 12, 11; m to Colette Lalier; c five. Educ: Univ Paris, BS, 28, PhB, 29; Harvard Bus Sch, MBA, 31. Polit & Govt Pos: Career officer, US Dept of State Foreign Serv, 41-43 & 45-73; vconsul, Casablanca, Algiers, 41-43; spec asst to Ambassador, Paris, 45-49, dep dir NATO Affairs, 50-51, dir Western European Affairs, 52-53, US asst, High Comnr for Ger, Berlin, 54-55; polit adv to Gen Gruenther & Norstad at SHAPE, Paris, 55-57, minister-counr, Karachi, 57-59, consul gen, Syria, 60-61, US Ambassador, Syria, 61-65, Belgium, 65-69 & Portugal, 69-73. Bus & Prof Pos: Bus exec, 31-41. Mil Serv: Maj, Army, 43-45; Salerno, Anzio & S France landings. Honors & Awards: State Dept Superior Serv Award for Serv in Syria, 65. Legal Res: c/o George W Knight 120 E 81st St New York NY 10028 Mailing Add: 32 rue de Varenne 75007 Paris France

KNIGHT, WILLIAM NOEL (R)
Mem, La State Rep Exec Comt
b Oakdale, Allen Parish, La, Aug 5, 35; s Norris Knight (deceased) & Jessie Watkins K; m 1961 to Donna Kay Bendily; c Nolan Roy, Stacey Lynn, Jodi Layne & Jill Watkins. Educ: La State Univ, BS, 59, LLB & JD, 59; Kappa Sigma; Gamma Eta Gamma. Polit & Govt Pos: Chmn, Jennings Munic Exec Rep Comt, La, 66-; Jefferson Davis Parish Exec Rep Comt, formerly; mem, Rep State Cent Comt, 66-; deleg, Rep Nat Conv, 68; chmn, Seventh Cong Dist Exec Rep Comt, formerly; secy, Jefferson Davis Parish Police Jury. Bus & Prof Pos: Secy-treas, Jefferson Davis Parish Bar Asn, 64- Mem: La & Am Trial Lawyers Asns; Am Judicature Soc; La State Univ Law Sch Alumni Asn; Lions. Relig: Methodist. Mailing Add: 610 Plaquemine St Jennings LA 70546

KNOBE, RICK W (R)
Mayor, Sioux Falls, SDak
b Barrington, Ill, Dec 6, 46; s Louis C Knobe & Nan V K; m 1967 to Marcia Maskevich; c Brian & Meghan. Educ: Morningside Col, Sioux City, Iowa, 64-66; Southern Ill Univ, Carbondale, 67-69; Career Acad Broadcasting, Kansas City, 69. Polit & Govt Pos: Mayor, Sioux Falls, SDak, 74- Bus & Prof Pos: Prog & news dir, KCHF Radio, Sioux Falls, SDak, 71-74. Mem: Sioux Falls Jaycees; Siouxland Lions; Nat Bicentennial Comt (vchmn). Legal Res: 4804 W 38th Sioux Falls SD 57106 Mailing Add: 224 W Ninth Sioux Falls SD 57102

KNOBLAUCH, REUBEN A (D)
Wash State Sen
b Sumner, Wash, 1914; single. Educ: Sumner High Sch. Polit & Govt Pos: Wash State Rep, 47-53; Wash State Sen, 53- Bus & Prof Pos: Retired farmer. Mil Serv: World War II. Mem: VFW; Am Legion; KofC; Grange. Mailing Add: Rte 1 Box 641 Sumner WA 98390

KNOLL, CATHERINE BAKER (D)
Mem, Pa State Dem Comt
b Pittsburgh, Pa; d Nicholas James Baker & Theresa Mary May B; m 1952 to Charles Albert Knoll, Sr; c Charles A, Jr, Mina Jane, Albert Baker & Kim Eric. Educ: Duquesne Univ, Educ, 52; MA in Counseling Psychol, 73. Polit & Govt Pos: Mem exec bd, Pa State Fedn Dem Women, currently; mem, Pa State Dem Comt, 72-; alt deleg, Dem Nat Mid-Term Conf, 74. Bus & Prof Pos: Inspector, Commonwealth of Pa, Dept Labor & Indust, 70; supvr, Traffic Safety Bur, Dept Transportation, 71- Mem: Duquesne Univ Alumni Bd Dirs (first vpres); Ohio Valley Col Club; Focus on Renewal-Civic Ctr; Jr Aide Soc-Ohio Valley Hosp; Allegheny Co Multiple Sclerosis Soc. Relig: Roman Catholic. Mailing Add: 1037 Chartiers Ave McKees Rocks PA 15136

KNOLL, CRAIG STEPHEN (P)
Md State Deleg
b Buffalo, NY, Nov 23, 44; s Carl John Knoll & Nancy Smith K; m 1967 to Susan Lombardo. Educ: Towson State Col, BA, 66; Hon Hist & Educ Socs. Polit & Govt Pos: Md State Deleg, 71- Bus & Prof Pos: Teacher, Prince George's Co Pub Schs, Md, 66- Mem: Md, Capitol Heights & Nat Educ Asns; Millwood Towne Civic Asn; Md Ment Health Asn; Prince George's Co Ment Health Asn (bd dirs). Relig: Catholic. Mailing Add: 4811 Riverdale Rd Riverdale MD 20840

KNOLL, FRANKLIN JUDE (DFL)
Minn State Rep
b St Cloud, Minn, Apr 30, 40; s Franklin Oker Knoll & Agnes Jude K; m 1965 to Margot Bussard; c Elizabeth Jude, Caroline Jean & Jonathan Mandeville. Educ: St John's Univ (Minn), BA, 62; Univ Minn, JD, 66. Polit & Govt Pos: Minn State Rep, Dist 61A, 73-, chmn govt structures div, comt govt opers, Minn House Rep, 75- Bus & Prof Pos: Patent attorney, 3M Co, St Paul, Minn, 66-70; gen counsel, Urban Coalition of Minneapolis, 70-74; defense attorney, Hennepin Co Pub Defender's Off, 74- Mil Serv: Entered as Airman Recruit, Naval Res, 66, released as Lt(sg), 73; Lt(sg), Reserve, currently. Mem: Minn State & Hennepin Co Bar Asns; Hennepin Co Pretrial Diversion Proj (bd mem). Relig: Roman Catholic. Mailing Add: 5316 First Ave S Minneapolis MN 55419

KNOPKE, RAY C (D)
Fla State Rep
b Chicago, Ill, Dec 13, 13; m to Virginia Lacy; c Susan, Keenan & Ray, Jr. Educ: Ohio State Univ; St Petersburg Jr Col. Polit & Govt Pos: Mayor, Temple Terrace, Fla, 14 years; city councilman; Fla State Rep, 63-66, 75-; Fla State Sen, formerly. Bus & Prof Pos: Pres, Garden of Memories, Inc. Mil Serv: Air Force, 3 years. Mem: Mason; Shrine; Elks; Lions; Temple Terrace CofC (dir). Relig: Presbyterian; Deacon. Mailing Add: 4207 E Lake Ave Tampa FL 33610

KNOREK, LEE J (D)
Chmn, Wood Co Dem Exec Comt, Ohio
b Rossford, Ohio, July 14, 21; s Michael Knorek & Katherine Paczyna K; m 1947 to Margaret B Hrabovsky; c Kristine Cuprys. Educ: Univ Detroit, 2 years; DeSales Col, 2 years; Sigma Alpha Epsilon; Ohio Mu. Polit & Govt Pos: Mem, Dem Precinct Comt, Rossford, Ohio, 55-; chmn, Wood Co Dem Exec Comt, 59-; pres, Rossford City Coun, 60-62; mem, Bd of Elec, Bowling Green, 62-; deleg, Dem Nat Conv, 68. Bus & Prof Pos: Mgr, New York Knicks, Madison Sq Garden, 46-50 & Tuck Tape, NY, 50-52; Ohio mgr, Schenley Distillers, 52-69. Mil Serv: Entered as Seaman, Navy, 43, released as Lt, Naval Res, 46, after serv in Underwater Demolition Team 12, Pac Theatre; Unit Citation. Mem: Ohio Distillers Asn; Election Officials Trustee, Ohio; Eagles; KofC; Am Legion (Comdr). Relig: Roman Catholic. Mailing Add: 1 Riverside Dr Rossford OH 43460

KNORR, JOHN PHILIP (D)
b Pittsburgh, Pa, Aug 27, 39; s A J Knorr & Florence Seaver K; m 1966 to Judith Lyn Gurekovich; c Stephanie Florence. Educ: St Mary's Area Sch Syst, 12 years. Polit & Govt Pos: Alt deleg, Dem Nat Conv, 72. Bus & Prof Pos: Mgr, WKBI AM/FM Elk Cameron Broadcasting Co, 53- Mem: Pa Asn of Broadcasters; Rotary; Elks. Honors & Awards: State Ed Award, Assoc Press, 70. Relig: Episcopal. Mailing Add: 209 N St Marys St St Mary's PA 15857

KNORR, MARTIN J (R)
NH State Sen
b Kings Co, NY, Jan 31, 06; s Martin G Knorr & Wilhelmine Rappold K; m 1938 to Pauline Richardson; c Clement Richardson, Constance Bradford & Prudence Ellis. Educ: Dartmouth Col, grad, 27; Brooklyn Law Sch of St Lawrence Univ, LLB; Phi Delta Phi. Polit & Govt Pos: Mem exec comt, Queens Co Rep Party, NY, 44-; asst attorney gen, NY Attorney General's Off, 45-47; law asst, Surrogate's Court, Queens Co, NY, 47-49; alt deleg, Rep Nat Conv, 52, 60, 68 & 72; NY State Assemblyman, Third Dist, 53-54; secy to munic court judge, Fourth Munic Court Dist, 55-59; Estates Tax attorney for Queens Co, NY State Dept of Taxation & Finance, 59-64; mem, NY Rep State Comt, 64-; law secy to Albert H Buschmann, NY State Supreme Court, Queens Co, 65; NY State Sen, 12th Dist, 66- Bus & Prof Pos: Attorney-at-law, 34- Mem: Queens Co Bar Asn; Blackstone Club of Ridgewood; pres, Assoc Civic Orgn of Ridgewood, Glendale, Maspeth & Middle Village, 42-; Yale Rep Club (past pres). Honors & Awards: Outstanding Community Serv Award, Am Legion Post 104, Queens Co, 64. Relig: Lutheran. Legal Res: 61-46 Palmetto St Brooklyn NY 11221 Mailing Add: 901 Seneca Ave Brooklyn NY 11227

KNOWLAN, W C (D)
Chmn, Clare Co Dem Comt, Mich
b Hudson, Mich, Sept 9, 07; m 1932 to Vila Mae Losey. Educ: High sch. Polit & Govt Pos: Chmn, Clare Co Dem Comt, Mich, 75- Bus & Prof Pos: Owner & operator truck freight line, 28-67; farmer, 51-63; owner grocery store, 67-71. Mailing Add: 2160 Bert Rd Harrison MI 48625

KNOWLES, JESSE M (D)
La State Sen
Mailing Add: 636 W La Grange St Lake Charles LA 70601

KNOWLES, ROBERT PIERCE (R)
Pres Pro Tempore, Wis State Senate
b River Falls, Wis, Feb 25, 16; s Warren P Knowles & Anna Deneen K; m 1941 to Madelyne Lucille Ullrich; c Barbara (Mrs Nelson), Robert P, Jr, Warren Patrick & Terrance C. Educ: Univ Wis-River Falls, BS, 38. Polit & Govt Pos: Wis State Sen, Tenth Dist, 55-; Majority Leader, Wis State Senate, 63-67, Pres Pro Tempore, currently; asst housing chmn, Rep Nat Conv, 60, exec secy arrangements comt, 64, 68 & 72; mem adv comn, Intergovt Rels, 69- Bus & Prof Pos: Dir, Bank of New Richmond, Bank of Clear Lake & Bank of Centuria, Wis, 64- Mil Serv: Entered as Aviation Cadet, Army Air Force, 41, released as Capt, 45, after serv in 44th Bomb Group, Eighth Air Force, ETO, 44-45; Air Medal with 4 Oak Leaf Clusters; Presidential Citation; Distinguished Flying Cross. Mem: Wis State Univ Found (bd trustee); Eagleton Inst of Polit, Rutgers Univ (adv comt); Elks; VFW; Am Legion. Mailing Add: 335 E First St New Richmond WI 54017

KNOWLES, WALT O (D)
Wash State Rep
Mailing Add: W 911 Sprague Spokane WA 99204

KNOWLES, WARREN P (R)
b River Falls, Wis, Aug 19, 08; s Warren P Knowles & Anna Deneen K; m 1943 to Dorothy Guidry; div. Educ: Carleton Col, BA, 30; Univ Wis Law Sch, LLB, 33. Hon Degrees: LLD, Northland Col, Marquette Univ, Ripon Col & Lakeland Col; LHD, Carroll Col; degree, St Norbert Col; Dr, Milton Col; LLD, Univ Wis, 73. Polit & Govt Pos: Mem, St Croix Co Bd, Wis, 35-40; Wis State Sen, Tenth Dist, 40-55, Rep Floor Leader, Wis State Sen, 43-53; deleg, Rep Nat Conv, 48-72, chmn, Wis Deleg, 68; Lt Gov, Wis, 55-59 & 61-63, Gov, 64-71. Bus & Prof Pos: Lawyer, Doar & Knowles, New Richmond, Wis, 33-; dir, Newton & Co & Heritage Bank-Mayfair, 71-; dir & vchmn bd, Heritage Bank of Milwaukee & Heritage Bank of Whitefish Bay, 71-; chmn bd, Inland Financial Corp, 71- Mil Serv: Entered as Lt(jg), Navy, 42, released as Lt, 46, after serv in USS Nevada in Aleutians, Normandy & Southern France; Aleutians, ETO & Mediter Campaign Ribbons. Mem: Am & St Croix-Pierce Co Bar Asns; Wis Acad Sci, Arts & Letters; Int Asn Ins Counsel; Upper Great Lakes Regional Planning Comn (co-chmn). Honors & Awards: Alumni Achievement Award, Wis Alumni Asn; Spec Citation for promotion of conserv, anti-pollution & ORAP legis, Wis Acad of Sci, Arts & Letters, 70; Nat Hwy Safety Coun Award for promotion of hwy safety progs in Wis, 70; numerous awards & citations from vet orgn for promotion of Americanism & patriotic progs, 70; Pro Urbe Award, Mt Mary Col, 71. Relig: Protestant. Legal Res: 3039 E Newport Ct Milwaukee WI 53211 Mailing Add: PO Box 339 Milwaukee WI 53201

KNOWLTON, DANIEL DAVID (R)
Chmn, Guernsey Co Rep Comt, Ohio
b Crooksville, Ohio, May 2, 24; s Daniel David Knowlton & Letha Langfried K; m 1948 to Barbara Pfaadt; c Karen & D David. Educ: Ohio State Univ, 45-48; Ohio Northern Univ, LLB, 51; Phi Kappa Psi; Phi Delta Theta. Polit & Govt Pos: Chmn, Guernsey Co Rep Comt, Ohio, currently; city solicitor, Cambridge, Ohio, 52-58; treas, Guernsey Co Rep Exec Comt, 54-66. Mil Serv: Entered as Pvt, Air Force, 42, released as 2nd Lt, Pilot, 45, after serv in ETO, 44-45; Air Medal; ETO Ribbon. Mem: Ohio State Bar Asn; Guernsey Co Bar Asn; Elks. Relig: Episcopal. Mailing Add: 1290 Edgeworth Cambridge OH 43725

KNOX, ANDREW GIBSON (R)
Del State Rep
b Philadelphia, Pa, Apr 26, 23; s Kerro Knox & Maude Gibson K; m 1947 to Sally Ann Johnson; c Andrew G, Jr, Karen B & Mark D. Educ: Williams Col, BA, 47; Univ Pa, MS & PhD, 50; Phi Beta Kappa; Alpha Delta Phi. Polit & Govt Pos: Del State Rep, currently. Bus & Prof Pos: Research supvr, E I duPont Co, 54- Mil Serv: Entered as Pvt, Army Air Force, 42, released as 1st Lt, 45, after serv in 99th Bomb Squadron, Italy; Air Medal; Combat Theatre Ribbons. Mem: Am Chem Soc. Relig: Episcopal. Mailing Add: Dupont Co Chestnut Run Wilmington DE 19899

KNOX, ARTHUR LLOYD (R)
Chmn, Lancaster Co Rep Cent Comt, Nebr
b Perkins, Okla, May 12, 32; s Myrl Frank Knox & Margaret Grant K; m 1955 to Earlene Lois Luff; c Angela Marie & Arthur Earl. Educ: Okla State Univ, BS, 55; Alpha Zeta; Farm House. Polit & Govt Pos: Chmn, Lancaster Co Young Rep, Nebr, 66-67; chmn, Nebr Fedn Young Rep, 68-69; chmn, First Dist Rep Party, 71-73; chmn, Lancaster Co Rep Cent Comt, 72-; dir, Natural Resources Dist, 75- Bus & Prof Pos: Shop asst, Lincoln Steel Corp, Nebr, 57-62, plant supt, 62-68, prod mgr, 68-71, vpres prod, 71-73, exec vpres, 73- Mil Serv: Entered as 2nd Lt, Army, released as 1st Lt, 57, after serv in 4th Armored Div, 55-57; Capt, Army Res, until 65. Mem: Rotary; Elks; Am Welding Soc; Nebr Asn Com & Indust. Honors & Awards: Gold Key Award, Jaycees, 65; Outstanding Young Rep, Lancaster Co Young Rep, 68; Outstanding State Young Rep, Nebr Fedn Young Rep, 68, Distinguished Serv Award, 69; Jr Pres, Founder's Day, 70- Relig: Presbyterian. Mailing Add: 920 Pine Tree Lane Lincoln NE 68521

KNOX, JOHN THERYLL (D)
Calif State Assemblyman
b Reno, Nev, Sept 30, 24; s Ernest B Knox & Jean Monat K; m 1949 to Margaret Jean Henderson; c John Henderson, Charlotte Marie & Mary Lucretia. Educ: Occidental Col, AB, 49; Hastings Col Law, JD, 52; Sigma Alpha Epsilon; Phi Delta Phi. Polit & Govt Pos: Mem, Contra Costa Co Dem Cent Comt, Calif, 55-69; mem exec bd, Calif State Dem Cent Comt, 60-; Calif State Assemblyman, 11th Dist, 60-, chmn, Calif State Assembly Local Govt Comt, 62-, chmn, Joint Legis Comt on Open Space, 67-; mem, Little Hoover Comt, Calif, 62-66; mem, President's Adv Comt on Real Estate, 64- Mil Serv: Entered as Pvt, Army, 43, released as Sgt, 45, after serv in 1469th Air Force Base Unit, Nome, Alaska; Asiatic-Pac Theatre Ribbon. Mem: F&AM; Eagles; Moose; Lions. Relig: Protestant. Legal Res: 229 Bishop Ave Richmond CA 94801 Mailing Add: 2566 Macdonald Ave Richmond CA 94804

KNOX, KATHARINE MCCOOK (R)
b Washington, DC; d Anson G McCook & Hettie Beatty McCook M; wid of Hugh Smith Knox; c Kathleen (Mrs Richard Austin Smith), Richard Austin, Jr & Roderick Sheldon; two grandchildren. Educ: Miss Spence's Sch, New York, dipl, 08. Polit & Govt Pos: Prog chmn, League of Rep Women, DC, 59-61; deleg, Nat Fedn Rep Women, 60; alt deleg, Rep Nat Conv, 60, deleg & mem credentials comt, 64; vchmn, DC Rep Comt; mem, President's Adv Comt on the Arts, 70- Publ: The Sharples: Their Portraits of George Washington & His Contemporaries, 30; Adams-Clement Portraits & Their Painters; Healy's Lincoln No I; plus others. Mem: Frick Art Reference Libr (reference worker & trustee); Frick Collection (fel); Corcoran Gallery of Art (donor); Colony Club NY (chmn art exhib, Washington, DC); Chevy Chase Club. Honors & Awards: Recipient Medal of Merit, Corcoran Gallery of Art, 66, Medal of Honor, Lincoln Sesquicentennial Comn, 60 & Meritorious Pub Serv Award, Rep Comt of Washington, DC, 60. Relig: Presbyterian. Mailing Add: 3259 N St NW Washington DC 20007

KNOX, RICK WILSON (R)
Committeeman, Tenn Rep State Exec Comt
b Nashville, Tenn, July 30, 49; s Sterling R Knox, Jr & Mary Cooksey K; m 1971 to Kimberly Harris; c Rachel Renee. Educ: David Lipscomb Col, BA; Cumberland Col, 69-71; LaSalle Exten Univ, LLB; Young Rep; Young Am for Freedom. Polit & Govt Pos: Youth dir, Davidson Co Rep Party, 70-; chmn, 16th Rep Dist Party, 74-; committeeman, Tenn Rep State Exec Comt, 74- Bus & Prof Pos: Pres, Metro Detective Agency, Nashville, 72-; pres, Knox & Assocs, 74- Mem: Nashville Rep Club (pres, 73-75); Young Am for Freedom; sustaining mem Rep Party; Tenn Rep Party. Relig: Church of Christ. Legal Res: 1214 Catina Nashville TN 37217 Mailing Add: PO Box 17179 Nashville TN 37217

KNOX, WAYNE N (D)
Colo State Rep
b Denver, Colo, June 30, 27. Polit & Govt Pos: Colo State Rep, 61-62, 65-72 & 75- Bus & Prof Pos: Sch teacher. Mem: Adams City Fedn Teachers (pres); Colo Fedn Teachers (pres, currently). Mailing Add: 1373 W Gill Pl Denver CO 80223

KNUCKLES, DENVER C (R)
Ky State Sen
b Beverly, Ky, Jan 1, 08; s George Matt Knuckles & Eliza Combs K; m 1949 to Julia Scoggins. Educ: Centre Col, grad, 33; Union Col(Ky), 31; Phi Kappa Tau; Freshman Football. Polit & Govt Pos: Ky State Sen, 56-59 & 72-; Ky State Rep, 70-72. Bus & Prof Pos: Crew caller, L&N RR, Hazard, Ky, 26-29; with Briggs Mfg Co, Detroit, Mich, 29; teacher, Pineville, 32-35; with Ky Utilities Co, 35-36; Old Dominion Power Co, Big Stone Gap, Va, 36-37; with Mutual Benefit Life Ins Co, 37- Mil Serv: Entered as Pvt, Marine Corps, 42, released as S/Sgt, 45, after serv in 5th Div, SPac, 45; SPac & Asiatic Theatre Medals; Two Bronze Stars; Presidential Unit Citation. Mem: Mason (Past Master); KT; Shriners Club; Am Legion; DAV. Honors & Awards: Most Outstanding Legislator in Ky, 70; Ambassador, Shriners Crippled Childrens Hosp, Lexington, Ky. Relig: Methodist. Mailing Add: 303 Englewood Rd Middlesboro KY 40965

KNUDSEN, D L (IKE) (D)
Mem, Valley Co Dem Cent Comt, Mont
b Malta, Mont, July 5, 30; s George Victor Knudsen & Mary Bibeau K; m 1952 to Mary Ann Shores; c Earline Maryann, Donald George, Vicki Rae & Lloyd Robert. Educ: Northern Mont Col, BS, 63; Tau Kappa; Circle K. Polit & Govt Pos: City councilman, Glasgow, Mont, 67-; Mont State Rep, Dist 5-B, Valley & Daniels Co, 69-72; mem, Valley Co Dem Cent Comt, currently. Bus & Prof Pos: Elem teacher, Prairie Union & South Wagner Schs, South Phillips Co, 50-54; rancher, 54-57; dept mgr, Sears, Lewiston, 58-60; math instr, Glasgow, Mont, 63- Mem: Glasgow Educ Asn; Mont Educ Asn (charter mem, Big Sky Legis Univ); life mem Nat Educ Asn; Nat Coun Math Teachers; Elks. Relig: Congregational. Mailing Add: 65 Aberdeen Glasgow MT 59230

KNUDSON, HARVEY BORNEMANN (R)
b Finley, NDak, June 26, 03; s Enoch Bornemann Knudson & Josephine Emelia Hanson K; m 1933 to Pearl Irene Pederson; c Harvey B, Jr, Duane A, Marion J (Mrs Rud) & Kay E (Mrs Jacobs). Educ: Univ NDak Law Sch; Phi Alpha Delta. Polit & Govt Pos: Sch treas, Finley, NDak, 34-38; NDak State Rep, 37-38; mem, Traill Co War Bd, 42-46; NDak State Sen, 51-58; alderman, City Coun, Mayville, 42-48, city attorney, 58-65; judge, NDak Supreme Court, formerly. Mem: Am & NDak State Bar Asns; First Dist Bar Asn; Mason; Shrine. Relig: Lutheran. Legal Res: Mayville ND 58257 Mailing Add: State Capitol Bismarck ND 58501

KNUDSON, KENNETH (R)
NDak State Rep
b Taylor, NDak, Nov 9, 27; s Knute Knudson & Evaline Hendrickson K; single. Educ: St Olaf Col, BA, 48. Polit & Govt Pos: Precinct committeeman, Stark Co & Dist 38 Rep Party, NDak, 62-; exec committeeman, Dist 38 Rep Party, 67-; NDak State Rep, Dist, 38, 67-, chmn, House Educ Comt, NDak House Rep, 71-, vchmn, LRC Comt on Educ, 71-; deleg, NDak Const Conv, 71. Bus & Prof Pos: Prin, Taylor High Sch, NDak, 64-69. Mil Serv: Entered as Pvt, E-1, Army, 50, released as Cpl, E-4, 52, after serv in 40th Inf Div, Korean Conflict; Army Occup Medal; UN Serv Medal; Korean Serv Medal. Mem: NDak Farm Bur; VFW; Am Legion. Relig: Lutheran. Mailing Add: Box 264 Taylor ND 58656

KNUPPEL, JOHN LINEBAUGH (D)
Ill State Sen
Mailing Add: 331 W Myrtle Virginia IL 62691

KNUPPEL, SHIRLEY LAVAUNE (R)
Mem, Rep State Cent Comt Calif
b Clinton, Iowa, Nov 3, 24; d Gerald Bertram Smith & Hazel Berger S; m 1944 to Wesley Franklin Knuppel; c Kay, Lee & Neil. Educ: James Millikin Univ; Indees. Polit & Govt Pos: Rep precinct capt, Lakewood, Calif, 64-66; Ways & Means Chmn, Long Beach G O P Jr Rep Women, 65; assoc mem, Rep State Cent Comt Calif, 66-68, mem, 69-; vpres, Fullerton Rep Women Fedn, 73-; field rep, Calif State Sen James E Whetmore, currently. Bus & Prof Pos: Secy-treas, Guild of Prof Musicians, Los Angeles, Calif, 59-68. Mem: Eastern Star, Rock Falls, Ill; Fullerton Federated Rep Women. Honors & Awards: Hon life mem, Calif Cong of Parents & Teachers Inc. Relig: Protestant. Mailing Add: 2763 Via Segovia Fullerton CA 92635

KNUTSON, HOWARD ARTHUR (R)
Minn State Sen
b Grand Forks, NDak, May 16, 29; s Arthur K Knutson & Ella Kamplin K; m 1958 to Jerroldine Margo Sundby; c David Lee, Douglas Arthur, Eric, Amy Lynn & Annette. Educ: Wabash Col, 47-49; Luther Col, AB, 51; William Mitchell Col Law, LLB, 59; Delta Theta Phi. Polit & Govt Pos: Chmn, Burnsville Indust Planning Comn, Minn, 64-66; Minn State Rep, Dist 12B, Northern Dak Co, 67-72; Minn State Sen, Dist 53, 73- Bus & Prof Pos: Partner, Bergman, Knutson, Street & Ulmen, Attorneys-at-law, Minneapolis, Minn. Mil Serv: Entered as Pvt, Army, 51, released as Cpl, 53, after serv in Signal Corps, ETO, 52-53. Mem: Hennepin Co, Minn State & Am Bar Asns; Open Door Soc. Honors & Awards: Distinguished

Serv Award, Minn Social Serv Asn, 74. Relig: Lutheran; Pres, Prince of Peace Lutheran Church, 73-74. Mailing Add: 1907 Woods Lane Burnsville MN 55337

KNUTSON, ROBERT JOHN, JR (D)
SDak State Rep
b Pipestone, Minn, Jan 27, 33; s Robert John Knutson, Sr & Imogene Duke K; m 1961 to Annie Elizabeth Simon; c Andrew Stewart, Nickolas Scott & Robert John, III. Educ: Pipestone Pub High Sch, Minn, grad; SDak State Univ, BS, MEd. Polit & Govt Pos: SDak State Rep, Pennington Co, 71- Mil Serv: Entered as Pvt, Army, 53, released as Pfc, 55, after serv in 32nd Engrs, Korea, 54-55. Mem: Rapid City Educ Asn; SDak Educ Asn; Nat Educ Asn; Elks. Relig: Lutheran. Mailing Add: 204 E Meade Rapid City SD 57701

KNUTSON, RONALD DALE (R)
Adminr, Farmer Coop Serv, Dept Agr
b Chippewa Co, Minn, July 12, 40; s Claus Knutson & Alice Petersen K; m 1961 to Sharron DeGree; c Scott, Ryan & Nicole. Educ: Univ Minn, St Paul, BS, 62, PhD, 67; Pa State Univ, MS, 63; Omicron Delta Epsilon; Gamma Sigma Delta. Polit & Govt Pos: Staff economist, Agr Mkt Serv, Dept Agr, 71-73, adminr, Farmer Coop Serv, 73- Bus & Prof Pos: Prof, Purdue Univ, 67-73. Publ: Economic analysis of the Minnesota dairy industry unfair trade practices act, J Law & Econ, 10/69; Cooperative strategies in imperfectly competitive market structures, Am J Agr Econ, 12/74; co-auth, Regulation of competition in food marketing, In: Economics of the Food Processing Industry, AVI Publ, 71. Mem: Am Econ Asn; Am Mkt Asn; Food Distrib Res Soc; Sigma Xi; Am Agr Econ Asn. Mailing Add: 4912 Andrea Ave Annandale VA 22003

KOBAYASHI, BERT TAKAAKI (D)
Assoc Justice, Supreme Court of Hawaii
b Honolulu, Hawaii, July 8, 16; s Zengoro Kobayashi & Kiyo Yamasaki K; m 1938 to Victoria Tsuchiya; c Bert Takaaki, Josephine Leilani, Victoria Puanani & Lincoln Kalani. Educ: Gettysburg Col, AB, 38; Harvard Univ, LLB, 43. Hon Degrees: LLD, Gettysburg Col, 66. Polit & Govt Pos: Law clerk to Attorney Gen, Hawaii, 45; dep city & co attorney, Honolulu, 46; dep pub prosecutor, Honolulu, 47-48; magistrate, Waialua Court, Oahu, 52-59; mem, Gov Comt on Sex Offenders, 59-60; Attorney Gen, Hawaii, 62-69; assoc justice, Supreme Court, Hawaii, 69- Bus & Prof Pos: Pvt practice law, Honolulu, 48-62; former dir, Island Venetian Blind Co, Aluminum Prod of Hawaii, Toma Contractor, Inc & Hardwood Furnishings, Ltd. Mem: Hawaii Subversive Activities Comt; Bar Asn of Hawaii; YMCA. Mailing Add: 4738 Analii St Honolulu HI 96821

KOBLE, ROSALIE ELIZABETH (R)
Chairwoman, Fairfield Co Rep Party, Ohio
b Philadelphia, Pa; d Charles Bartholomew & Sara Gilbert B; div; c Susan, Sandra, Sherri & Stuart. Educ: Germantown High Sch, Philadelphia, commercial dipl; Peirce Bus Sch, Philadelphia; Licking Co Voc Sch, Newark, Ohio, adult educ courses, 75. Polit & Govt Pos: Chairwoman, Fairfield Co Rep Party, Ohio, 74-; secy, Fairfield Co Rep Exec Comt, 74-; cent committeewoman, Walnut Twp, Fairfield Co, 74-; pres, Rep Women's Club, Millersport, 74-; TAR adv, Fairfield Co, 74- Bus & Prof Pos: File clerk-bookkeeping machine operator, Atlantic Refining Co, Philadelphia, formerly; control clerk, Eastern Mortgage Serv Co, Philadelphia, formerly; bookkeeper, Security Cent Nat Bank, Portsmouth, Ohio; sales rep, Field Enterprises Educ Corp, currently; clerk, Fairfield Co Courthouse, currently. Mem: Millersport & Fairfield Co Rep Women's Club; Nat & Ohio Fedn Rep Women; Creation Research Sci Educ Found, Inc. Relig: Protestant. Legal Res: 10081 Lancaster-Newark Rd Millersport OH 43046 Mailing Add: Rte 1 Box 289 Millersport OH 43046

KOCH, EDWARD HERMAN (D)
Secy, Clinton Co Dem Cent Comt, Ill
b Trenton, Ill, Oct 19, 36; s Herman Albert Koch & Frances Dressler K; m 1964 to Karen Patrica Kuhfuss; c Devin Edward & Caroline Suzanne. Educ: McKendree Col, 54-56; Ill State Univ, BS, 59, MS, 64. Polit & Govt Pos: Dem precinct committeeman, Trenton, Ill, 66-; secy, Clinton Co Dem Cent Comt, 68- Bus & Prof Pos: Teacher, Dept of Army, Frankfurt, Ger, 61-63; teacher, Dept of Defense, Upper Heyford, Eng, 64-65; partner, Koch Candy Co, Trenton, Ill, 65- Mem: Nat & Ill Asns of Tobacco Distributors; CofC. Relig: United Church of Christ. Mailing Add: 222 N Washington Trenton IL 62293

KOCH, EDWARD IRVING (D)
US Rep, NY
b New York, NY, Dec 12, 24; s Louis Koch & Joyce Silpe K (deceased); single. Educ: City Col New York, 41-43; NY Univ, LLB, 48; Omega Chi. Polit & Govt Pos: Dem dist leader, Greenwich Village, NY, 63-65; city councilman, New York, 67-68; US Rep, 18th Dist, NY, 69- Bus & Prof Pos: Partner, Koch, Lankenau, Schwartz & Kovner, 63-68. Mil Serv: Entered as Pvt, Army, 43, released as Sgt, 46, after serv in US Inf, ETO, 44-46; Two Battle Stars. Mem: NY Civil Liberties Union; Village Independent Dem; Mem Cong for Peace Through Law; Am for Dem Action; Dem Study Group. Legal Res: 14 Washington Pl New York NY 10003 Mailing Add: 1134 Longworth House Off Bldg Washington DC 20515

KOCH, GERALD D (JERRY) (R)
Nebr State Sen
b Campbell, Nebr, May 23, 24; s Frederick C Koch & Stella Brunke K; m 1947 to Joan McCashland; c Rick A & Scott T. Educ: Hastings Col, BA, 49; Univ Nebr, MA, 54; Phi Delta Kappa; Gamma Gamma Gamma. Polit & Govt Pos: Councilman, Ralston, Nebr, 66-74; Nebr State Sen, Dist 12, 75- Bus & Prof Pos: Teacher & coach, Franklin, Nebr, 49-54; teacher, coach, chmn dept & dir activities, Westside Community Schs, Omaha, 54-66; dir, Omaha Suburban Area Coun of Schs, Ralston, 67-; bd dirs, Lakeview Inc, Ralston, 68- Mil Serv: Entered as Pvt, Air Force, 43, released as S/Sgt, 45, after serv in 15th Air Force, Italy; Air Medal with 5 Stars; Unit Presidential Citation. Mem: Am Asn Sch Adminr; Ralston Area CofC (bd dirs); Am Legion (dist Americanism chmn); Ralston Boys Baseball Inc (bd dirs); Lions. Honors & Awards: Columbia Univ fel by Univ Nebr, 52; Educ & Youth Award, CofC, 68, Civic Leader of Decade, 70 & Man of Year, 73. Relig: Protestant. Mailing Add: 7610 Sunset Dr Ralston NE 68127

KOCH, HENRY FERD (R)
b Hammett, Idaho, Feb 27, 13; s Henry Ferdinand Koch & Amy S Krauth K; m 1935 to Marjorie Talboy; c Ronald, Roger, Cheryl (Mrs Zollman), Deanne M (Mrs Tawney) & Lynne E (Mrs Weathers). Educ: Univ Idaho, BSEE, 34; Sigma Tau; Scabbard & Blade; Blue Key; Silver Lance; Sigma Nu. Polit & Govt Pos: Chmn, Idaho State Elec Bd, 49-63; chmn, Idaho State Pub Works License Bd, 56-; mem, Boise City Coun, Idaho, 58-67, pres, 65-67; Idaho State Rep, 62-74, chmn, State Affairs Comt, Idaho House of Rep, 66-74, chmn, Local Govt Comt, 68-74, chmn, Interim Tax Study Comt, 68-74, chmn, Interim Comt on Recodification Workmen's Compensation, 69-70, Majority Leader, 73-74; pres, Idaho Asn of Cities, 66-67; alt deleg, Rep Nat Conv, 72. Bus & Prof Pos: Mem exec comt, Boise Indust Found, 66-71, pres, 71-; trustee, Boise State Col Found, 70-; mem, Airport Comn, 71- Mil Serv: Entered as 1st Lt, Army Res, 41, released as Lt Col, 46, after serv in 314th Inf, 79th Inf Div, ETO, 44-45, Lt Col, Inactive Res; Purple Heart; Silver Star; Combat Inf Badge; Croix de Guerre Unit Citation; two Presidential Unit Citations. Mem: CofC; Scottish Rite; Mason; Rotary; Elks; Am Legion. Honors & Awards: Distinguished Citizen, Idaho Daily Statesman. Relig: Methodist. Mailing Add: 257 Circleway Dr Boise ID 83702

KOCH, KARL E (D)
Idaho State Rep
Mailing Add: Hammett ID 83627

KOCH, LESTER DONALD (R)
Chmn, Tazewell Co Rep Cent Comt, Ill
b Tremont, Ill, Oct 20, 19; s Silas A Koch & Nora Luft K; m 1944 to Barbara Pfederer; c Joyce Kay & Michael Silas. Educ: High Sch. Polit & Govt Pos: Rep committeeman, Rep Party, Ill, 56-58, precinct committeeman, 56-66, sen committeeman, 66; trustee, Tremont, Ill, 57-63, mayor, 63; chmn, Tazewell Co Rep Cent Comt & Rep committeeman, 46th Dist, 66- Bus & Prof Pos: Agr fieldman, Libby McNeil & Libby, 61-66, agr supvr, 66-68, dist agr mgr, 68- Mil Serv: Entered as Pvt, Air Force, 41, released as Sgt, 45, after serv in ETO; European-African-Mid Eastern Theater Ribbon with One Silver & Two Bronze Battle Stars; Four Overseas Serv Bars; One Serv Stripe; Good Conduct Medal; 82nd Group Distinguished Unit Badge with Two Bronze Oak Leaf Clusters. Mem: Eagles; Am Legion; VFW; Tremont Community Men's Club; Tazewell Co Mayors Asn. Relig: Methodist. Mailing Add: 309 W South St Tremont IL 61568

KOCH, THOMAS F (R)
Mem, Vt Rep State Comt
b Hackensack, NJ, Nov 24, 42; s Elmer J Koch & Evelyn Zombeck K; m 1970 to Sally J Tucker; c Christine E & Donald T. Educ: Middlebury Col, AB, 64; Univ Chicago Law Sch, JD, 67. Polit & Govt Pos: Mem, Vt Rep State Comt, 73- Bus & Prof Pos: Partner, Bernasconi & Koch, Barre, Vt, 74- Mil Serv: Entered as 1st Lt, Army, 68, released as Capt, 70, after serv in 11th Armored Cavalry Regt, Vietnam, 69-70; Bronze Star Medal; Vietnam Serv Ribbon. Mem: Am Bar Asn; Vt Bar Asn (chmn comt unauthorized practice of law, 74-); Barre Lions Club. Relig: Lutheran. Mailing Add: RR 2 Lowery Rd Barre VT 05641

KOCHMAN, AL (D)
Chmn, San Mateo Co Dem Cent Comt, Calif
b Breslau, Ger, Jan 14, 26; s Siegfried Kochman & Edith Weissmann K; m 1957 to Alice Rabe. Educ: Peking Am Sch, 39-41. Polit & Govt Pos: Pres, San Mateo Dem Club, Calif, 65-66; dir, Calif Dem Coun, 66-68; chmn, United Dem Fund San Mateo, 69; vchmn, San Mateo Co Dem Cent Comt, 69-70, chmn, 70- Bus & Prof Pos: Off mgr, I Magnin Co, 47-62; treas, House of Karlson, 62- Mil Serv: Entered as Pvt, Army, 50, released as Pfc, 52. Mem: Common Cause; UN Asn; Am Civil Liberties Union. Relig: Jewish. Mailing Add: 502 S Grant St San Mateo CA 94402

KOEHLER, RICHARD NORMAN (D)
Mem, Butler Co Dem Exec Comt, Ohio
b Hamilton, Ohio, July 9, 26; s Harry J Koehler & Grace Heistermann K; m 1946 to Elva M Schell; c Paula, Richard N, II & Claudia. Educ: Oberlin Col, 1 year; Miami Univ, AB; Chase Col Law, LLB. Polit & Govt Pos: Chmn, Butler Co Dem Exec Comt, Ohio, 68-70, mem, currently; emeritus status, Gov Inaugural Comt, 71. Mil Serv: Naval Res, 44-45, A/S, serv in Naval aviation. Relig: Protestant. Mailing Add: 748 Main St Hamilton OH 45013

KOEHN, EMIL ALVIN (R)
Finance Chmn, Turner Co Rep Party, SDak
b Hillside, SDak, June 16, 16; s William A Koehn & Martha Wenzel K; m 1941 to Doris Louise Benning; c Stephen C, Thomas K & Margaret Ann. Educ: Univ SDak, BA, 38; Delta Sigma Phi. Polit & Govt Pos: Chmn, Parker Bd of Educ, SDak, 57-62; Rep state cent committeeman, 59-66; vchmn, SDak State Bd of Educ, 60-66, pres, 68-69; finance chmn, Turner Co Rep Party, 61-66 & 72-; chmn, Turner Co Rep Cent Comt, 66-68, mem, 68-; policy bd, Improving State Leadership in Educ, 70-73; President Nixon's Nat Reading Coun, 70-73. Bus & Prof Pos: Owner, Koehn's Dept Store, 38-66. Mil Serv: Entered as 2nd Lt, Army Air Force, 41, released as Maj, 46. Publ: State boards role in vocational education, AVA Mag, 10/70. Mem: Nat Asn State Bds of Educ; AF&AM (past master, Parker Lodge 30); Parker Shrine Club; Oriental Consistory; Mason (32 degree). Relig: Presbyterian. Mailing Add: PO Box 278 Parker SD 57053

KOEHNKE, MICHAEL (D)
Mem, Mont State Dem Cent Comt
b Scottsbluff, Nebr, Dec 30, 48; s Francis Koehnke & Betty Shafer K; single. Educ: Mont State Univ, BA in Govt, 72; Univ Mont, BS in Econ & Polit Sci, 72; Univ Ore, 73-75. Polit & Govt Pos: Page, Mont Deleg, Dem Nat Conv, 68; alt deleg, Dem Nat Conv, 72; mem, Mont State Dem Cent Comt, 73-; alt deleg, Dem Nat Mid-Term Conf, 74; campaign mgr, Max Baucus, Mont, 74. Legal Res: Helena MT 59601 Mailing Add: PO Box 692 Townsend MT 59644

KOELLA, CARL, JR (R)
Tenn State Sen
Mailing Add: PO Box 6 Maryville TN 37801

KOGA, GEORGE M (D)
Chmn City Coun, City & Co of Honolulu, Hawaii
b Honolulu, Hawaii, Mar 19, 28; s Kiuta Koga & Michie Eguchi K; m 1958 to Ruth Kiyoko Kamuri; c Suzanne. Educ: Univ Hawaii, BA, 50; Georgetown Univ, LLB, 56. Polit & Govt Pos: Hawaii State Rep, 59-64; councilman, City & Co of Honolulu, Hawaii, 65-, vchmn & floor leader, City Coun, 69-71, chmn, 71- Bus & Prof Pos: Gen counsel, Legal Aid Soc of Hawaii, 57-58; secy, Bar Asn of Hawaii, 58; instr bus law, Chaminade Col, 61-62. Mil Serv: Entered as 2nd Lt, Army, 51, released as 1st Lt, 53. Legal Res: 1254 Center St Honolulu HI 96816 Mailing Add: 1410 Amfac Bldg 700 Bishop St Honolulu HI 96813

KOGOVSEK, JOHN J (D)
Mem, Colo Dem State Cent Comt
b Pueblo, Colo, July 16, 46; s Frank L Kogovsek & Mary Blatnick K; single. Educ: Southern Colo State Col, BA, 68; Pi Delta Phi, Univ Paris, grad work, 70. Polit & Govt Pos: Mem,

Pueblo Co Dem Cent Comt, Colo, 68-; mem, Colo Dem State Cent Comt, 68- Bus & Prof Pos: Teacher hist & French, Seton High Sch, 68-, head social sci dept. Mem: Colo & Pueblo Educ Asns; Am Hist Soc; Am Fedn Teachers of French; St Francis Parish Coun (pres). Relig: Roman Catholic. Mailing Add: 2024 Pine St Pueblo CO 81004

KOGOVSEK, RAY P (D)
Minority Leader, Colo State Senate
b Pueblo, Colo, Aug 19, 41; s Frank L Kogovsek & Mary Blatnick K; m 1964 to Eulice A Korschel; c Lisa Marie & Toni Rae. Educ: Pueblo Jr Col, AA, 62; Adams State Col, BA in Bus, 64; Denver Univ, 73; Iota Xi. Polit & Govt Pos: Chief dep co clerk, Pueblo Co, Colo, 66-; Colo State Rep, 69-71; Colo State Sen, 71-, Minority Leader, Colo State Senate, currently. Bus & Prof Pos: Para-Legal. Mem: Am Fedn of Musicians, Local 69; Footprinters; Travelers Protective Asn. Relig: Catholic. Mailing Add: 1627 Horseshoe Dr Pueblo CO 81001

KOHL, HERBERT (D)
Mem, Dem Nat Comt, Wis
Mailing Add: 929 N Astor St Milwaukee WI 53202

KOHLER, FOY DAVID (INDEPENDENT)
Consult, Dept of State
b Oakwood, Ohio, Feb 15, 08; s Leander David Kohler & Myrtle McClure K; m 1935 to Phyllis Penn. Educ: Ohio State Univ, BS, 31; Phi Beta Kappa; Delta Upsilon; Beta Gamma Sigma. Hon Degrees: LHD, Ohio State Univ, 62; LLD, Univ Toledo, 64, Findlay Col, 67 & Univ Akron, 67. Polit & Govt Pos: Career officer, US Dept of State Foreign Serv, 31-67, consul, Windsor, Ont, Can, 32, Bucharest, 33-36 & Athens, 36-38; third secy, Cairo, 41; attended, Nat War Col, 46; counr, Moscow, 47-49; mem staff, Int Broadcasting Serv; dir, Voice of Am, 49-52; mem, Policy Planning Staff, Dept State, 52-53; counr, Ankara, 53-55; mem, ICA Eval Team, 56-58; Dep Asst Secy of State for European Affairs, 58-59, asst secy, 59-62; US Ambassador, USSR, 62-66; Dep Under Secy of State for Polit Affairs, 66-67; consult, Dept of State, 68- Bus & Prof Pos: Bank teller, 24-27; prof int studies, Cent Adv Inst Studies, Univ Miami, 68- Publ: Understanding the Russians: a Citizen's Primer, Harper, 70; Soviet Strategy for the Seventies—From Cold War to Peaceful Coexistence, 73 & The Role of Nuclear Forces in Current Soviet Strategy, 74, Univ Miami. Mem: Coun Foreign Rels; Am Acad Polit & Social Sci; Am Foreign Serv Asn; Tequesta Country Club. Honors & Awards: Superior Serv Award, Dept State, 52; Distinguished Honor Award, 66; Rockefeller Pub Serv Award, 67. Relig: Methodist. Legal Res: 215 Golf Club Circle Village of Tequesta Jupiter FL 33458 Mailing Add: PO Box 248123 Univ of Miami Coral Gables FL 33124

KOHLER, WALTER JODOK, JR (R)
b Sheboygan, Wis, Apr 4, 04; s Walter Jodok Kohler & Charlotte Schroeder K; m 1948 to Charlotte McAleer; c Terry Jodok & Charlotte Nicolette. Educ: Yale Univ, PhB, 25. Hon Degrees: LLD, Beloit Col & Northland Col; LittD, Ripon Col; LHD, Lakeland Col. Polit & Govt Pos: Chmn, Wis Deleg, Rep Nat Conv, 48 & 56; Gov, Wis, 50-57. Bus & Prof Pos: Secy, Kohler Co, 37-47; pres, The Vollrath Co, 47-68, chmn, 59- Mil Serv: Entered as Lt, Naval Res, 42, released as Lt Comdr, 45, after serv in Solomon Islands & Fast Carrier Task Force of 3rd & 5th Fleets, Western Pac Area, 43-45; Am Theater Medal; Pac Theater Medal with Five Stars; Philippine Liberation Medal with Two Stars; Bronze Star; Presidential Unit Citation; Victory Medal. Mem: Am Cancer Soc. Legal Res: Windway Kohler WI 53044 Mailing Add: Box 611 Sheboygan WI 53081

KOHLHOF, LAVERN LOUIS (D)
Treas, Nebr State Dem Party
b Norfolk, Nebr, Nov 24, 29; s Louis Kohlhof & Trudie Trussell K; m 1951 to Bonnie Sue Rhodes; c Sarah, Karl, Carolyn & Leigh. Educ: Wayne State Col, BA, 57; Kappa Mu Epsilon; Pi Omega Pi. Polit & Govt Pos: Dist chmn, Exon for Gov, 69-70; vchmn, Lancaster Co Dem, 70-72 & Nebr Dem Party, 73-74; mem, Nebr Judicial Nominating Comt, 72-; treas, Nebr State Dem Party, 72- & Dyas for Cong Comt, 73-74. Bus & Prof Pos: Teacher, Wisner High Sch, 57-58; claim mgr, Bankers Life, Nebr, 58-64; vpres admin, Lincoln Liberty Life Ins Co, 64- Mil Serv: Entered as Pvt, Air Force, 48, released as S/Sgt, 54, after serv in Strategic Air Command. Mem: Lincoln YMCA (bd mem); Lincoln Rotary (bd mem); Am Legion; Nebr Ins Inst; Lincoln CofC. Honors & Awards: Grad High Honors & Distinction, Wayne State Col; Man of the Year, Wayne Nat Guard; Keynote Speaker, Nebr State Dem Conv, 74. Relig: Lutheran. Mailing Add: 7321 Vine St Lincoln NE 68505

KOHLMEYER, MILDRED LUCILLE (R)
Secy, Posey Co Rep Cent Comt, Ind
b Posey Co, Ind, Mar 2, 22; d Walter H Seifert & Matilda Dickhaut S; m 1942 to Carl A Kohlmeyer; c Melody (Mrs Larry Schmitt) & James A. Educ: Mt Vernon High Sch, grad, 39. Polit & Govt Pos: Secy, Posey Co Rep Cent Comt, Ind, 65-; assessor, Posey Co, 69- Mem: Eastern Star; Bus & Prof Women's Club; Posey Co Rep Women's Club. Relig: Methodist. Mailing Add: RR 2 Wadesville IN 47638

KOHN, ROBERT ALFRED (R)
SC State Rep
b New York, NY, Oct 3, 44; s Alfred Gould Kohn & Dorothy Moller K; m 1967 to Jacqueline Tumbleston; c Julia Meredith. Educ: Univ SC, BA, 67. Polit & Govt Pos: Precinct exec committeeman, Charleston Co Rep Party, SC, 70-74; SC State Rep, 75- Mailing Add: 4326 Evanston Blvd Charleston Heights SC 29405

KOHN, SUSAN MARION (D)
Nat Committeewoman, Calif Fedn Young Dem
b Plymouth, Eng, Nov 10, 45; d Fritz Kohn & Blanka Fleischmann K; single. Educ: Santa Monica Col, 63-65; Univ Calif, Los Angeles, BA, 67; Southwestern Univ Sch Law, 73- Polit & Govt Pos: Deleg, Young Dem Clubs of Am Conv, 71 & 73 & Calif Dem Coun Conv, 71, 72 & 73; co-chmn, Southern Calif Cong Dist Youth Caucus, 72; mem & young Dem coordr, Platform Comn, Calif Dem Party, 72; mem, Calif Dem State Cent Comt, 72-, co-chmn youth caucus, 74-75; nat committeewoman, Calif Fedn Young Dem, 72-; pres, Beverly Hills Young Dem, 73. Bus & Prof Pos: Customs adminr & licensed custom house broker, Williams, Clarke Co, Inc, Los Angeles, currently. Mailing Add: 1524 S Amherst Ave Los Angeles CA 90025

KOHNEN, RALPH BERNARD, JR (R)
City Councilman, Cincinnati, Ohio
b Cincinnati, Ohio, Oct 22, 35; s Ralph Bernard Kohnen & Helen Rose Hillenbrand K; m 1960 to Nancy Marie Stone; c Ralph William, Allen Stone, Nancy Marie, Jr & Daniel. Educ: Georgetown Univ Col Arts & Sci, AB, 57, Univ Cincinnati Col Law, LLB, 60; Phi Alpha Delta. Polit & Govt Pos: Ohio State Rep, 63-67; city councilman, Cincinnati, 67-, vmayor, 71-; pres, Coun of Govt of Cincinnati, Hamilton Co Criminal Justice Regional Planning Unit, 72, mem, 72- Bus & Prof Pos: Assoc, Waite, Schindel, Bayless & Schneider, Law Firm, 61-65, partner, 66-; bd mem, Community Improv Corp, 68- Mil Serv: Pfc, Army, 60-61. Mem: Cincinnati, Ohio State & Am Bar Asns; Assoc for Blind (bd trustees). Relig: Catholic. Legal Res: 2959 Wold Ave Cincinnati OH 45206 Mailing Add: 1318 Central Trust Tower Cincinnati OH 45202

KOK, PETER (R)
Mich State Rep
b Grand Rapids, Mich, Oct 24, 19; married; c three. Educ: Calvin Col, AB. Polit & Govt Pos: Mich State Rep, 64-, vchmn & chmn, Comt on Ment Health, Mich House Rep, formerly. Bus & Prof Pos: Realtor. Mil Serv: Capt, Air Force, four years. Relig: Christian Reformed Church. Mailing Add: 1920 Philadelphia Ave SE Grand Rapids MI 49507

KOLBERG, WILLIAM HENRY (R)
Asst Secy Manpower, Dept of Labor
Legal Res: MD Mailing Add: Dept of Labor Labor Bldg Washington DC 20210

KOLSTAD, ALLEN C (R)
Mont State Sen
b Chester, Mont, Dec 24, 31; s Henry B Kolstad & Mabel Webb K; m 1951 to Iva Matteson; c Cedric A, Chris A, Cheryl D & Corrine F. Educ: Concordia Col, Moorhead, Minn, 2 years; Alpha Epsilon Sigma. Polit & Govt Pos: Precinct committeeman, 62-66; chmn, Liberty Co Rep Party, 67-68; deleg, Rep Nat Conv, 68; Mont State Rep, Dist 19, 69-75; Mont State Sen, 75- Mem: Lutheran Home of the Good Shepherd, Havre, Mont (pres bd dirs); Mason (past Master); Shrine; Chester Jaycees (mem bd dirs); Havre Conf of Am Lutheran Churchmen. Honors & Awards: Outstanding Young Farmer Award, 65; one of Outstanding Young Men of Am, 66. Relig: Lutheran; past pres, St Olaf Lutheran Church. Mailing Add: PO Box 648 Chester MT 59522

KOLTER, JOSEPH PAUL (D)
Pa State Rep
b McDonald, Ohio, Sept 3, 26; s Stephen Kolter & Frances Shuster K; m 1949 to Dorothy Marie Gray; c Joseph P, Jr, James S, David M & Julie Ann. Educ: Geneva Col, BSBA, 50. Polit & Govt Pos: Treas, Beaver Co Dem Comt, 54-56; committeeman, Dem Party, Beaver Co, 54-67; councilman, New Brighton, Pa, 62-66; mem, Civil Serv Comn, 63-67; Pa State Rep, 14th Legis Dist, 68- Bus & Prof Pos: Cashier, St Joseph Lead Co, Monaca, Pa, 64-67; owner & operator, New Brighton Roller Drome, 67-69. Mil Serv: Entered as Pvt, Air Force, 45, released as Cpl, 46. Mem: Nat Asn Acct; Am Legion; Eagles; Optimist Int Beaver Valley. Mailing Add: Capitol Bldg Harrisburg PA 17120

KOMER, JANE GLEICK (D)
Secy, Cumberland Co Dem Comt, Maine
b St Louis, Mo, Sept 9, 26; d Harry Samuel Gleick & Henrietta Donen G; m 1947 to Robert William Komer, div; c Douglas Robert, Richard Donen & Anne Elisabeth. Educ: Oniv Wis-Madison, 44-47; Wash Univ, 47; Wis Hoofers. Polit & Govt Pos: Clerk-typist, Off of Alien Property, Justice Dept, 48-49; elec clerk, Va, formerly, Maine, currently; deleg, Maine Dem State Conv, 70; vchmn, Bridgton Town Dem Comt, 70-; secy, Cumberland Co Dem Comt, 70-; justice of peace, Maine, 70- Bus & Prof Pos: Worker, Primate Lab, Dept of Psychol, Univ Wis, 44-47; asst to dean pub rels & head concert dept, Juilliard Sch Music, New York, 46-47. Mem: Bridgton Pub Libr Corp; South Bridgton Women's Club. Mailing Add: 62 S High St Bridgton ME 04009

KOMSON, LINDA DAVIDSON (D)
Committeeperson, NY Dem State Comt
b Brooklyn, NY, Sept 18, 42; d William Davidson & Dorothy Poplofsky D; m 1964 to Fred Hugh Komson; c Janice Robin & Michael Brett. Educ: Cedar Crest Col, 60-62; Hofstra Univ, BA, 64, MS, 67; Phi Alpha Theta; Deans List; Phi Epsilon. Polit & Govt Pos: Campaign coordr, Legislator Martin Feldman, NY, 71-; Huntington campaign coordr, Congressman Otis Pike, NY, 72-; mem exec bd, Suffolk Co Dem Party & Huntington Town Dem Party, 73-; committeeperson, NY Dem State Comt, 73-; deleg, Dem Nat Mid-Term Conf, 74. Bus & Prof Pos: Teacher, Hicksville High Sch, NY, 64-67. Mem: Women's Polit Caucus; Dix Hills Dem Club (exec bd, 71-); Children's Med Ctr-Long Island Jewish-Hillside Med Ctr. Mailing Add: 40 Randolph Dr Dix Hills NY 11746

KONDELIK, EVELYN MARGUERITE (D)
State Committeewoman, Mont Dem Cent Comt
b Helena, Mont, June 25, 37; d Basil Orin Gavin & Paulina Geiger G; m 1961 to Emil John Kondelik; c Douglas Orin, Joseph LeRoy, Andrew John, Maureen Ann & Jeanne Marie. Educ: High Sch. Polit & Govt Pos: Vchmn, McCone Co Dem Club, 64-66, secy, 69-73; precinct committeewoman, McCone Co Dem Cent Comt, 63-, chmn, 64-67; state committeewoman, Mont Dem Cent Comt, 69-; asst regional dir, Mont Dem Women's Club, 74- Bus & Prof Pos: Secy to Dawson Co Attorney, Glendive, Mont, 58-61. Mil Serv: Entered as Pvt, Women's Army Corps, 55, released as SP-4, 58, after serv in 5th Army Finance & Acct Off, 5th Army Hq, Chicago, Ill, 55-57 & Med Supply Control Agency, Maison Forte, Orleans Area Command, France, 57-58; Airman 2/C, Air Force Res, 58-61; Good Conduct Medal. Mem: Women of the Moose; Mont Farmers Union; McCone Co Home Demonstration Club; McCone Nat Farmers Orgn; Ladies Altar Soc, St Francis Xavier Church. Relig: Catholic. Mailing Add: RR Circle MT 59215

KONDO, RONALD YONEO (D)
Hawaii State Rep
b Lahaina, Maui, Hawaii, Feb 18, 32; s Sango Kondo & Etsu Takita K; m 1956 to Janice Takako Honda; c Diane, Ronald Jr & Janine. Educ: Univ Hawaii, BS, 57. Polit & Govt Pos: Mem, Hawaii State Bd of Paroles & Pardons, 66-68; dir, Maui Young Dem, 66-69; Hawaii State Rep, 68- Bus & Prof Pos: Pres, West Maui Bus & Prof Asn, 65-66 & 67-68, dir, 66-67 & 68- Mil Serv: Entered as Pvt, Army, 51, released as Sgt, 54, after serv in Far East Command, Korea & Japan, 52-54. Mem: Jaycees; West Maui Vet Club. Relig: Methodist. Mailing Add: c/o House of Rep Sgt at Arms State Capitol Honolulu HI 96813

KONISHI, ALAN S (D)
b Lihue, Hawaii, Nov 13, 52; s Itsuo Konishi & Takeyo Tokita K; single. Educ: Univ Hawaii, 70-74. Polit & Govt Pos: Clerk, Senate Comt Consumer Protection, Hawaii, 72-; alt deleg, Dem Nat Conv, 72; vchmn, Hawaii Dem Conv, 72, mem platform comt & mem steering comt youth caucus, 72. Bus & Prof Pos: Agt, Minn Mutual Life Ins, 73-74; asst athletic dept, Univ

Hawaii, 74, mem bd publs & mem student conduct comt, currently. Mem: ILH-OIA Football Coaches Appreciation Comt (pres). Relig: Catholic. Mailing Add: 1403 Hoohulu St Pearl City HI 96782

KOOGLER, FRED L, SR (D)
Iowa State Rep
Mailing Add: RR 1 Oskaloosa IA 52577

KOON, LARRY LABRUCE (R)
SC State Rep
b Leesville, SC, Feb 18, 44; s Rev Carl B Koon & Jennie Porth K; m 1966 to Kathy Mack; c Labruce & Travis. Educ: Univ SC, BS in Bus Admin, 68. Polit & Govt Pos: SC State Rep, 75- Mem: Batesburg Leesville Jaycees; Batesburg Leesville Lodge 138; SC Fox Hunters Asn (pres); Black Creek Coon Hunters Asn; SC Farm Bur. Relig: Southern Baptist; deacon; Sunday sch supt. Mailing Add: Rte 7 Box 72P Lexington SC 29072

KOON, WALTER HAROLD (R)
Youth VChmn, Third Cong Dist Rep Party, SC
b Newberry, SC, Apr 30, 48; s Jack Harold Koon & Sybil Drucillia Fountain K; single. Educ: Newberry Col, AB, 70. Polit & Govt Pos: Chmn, Newberry Col Rep, SC, 69-70; chmn, SC Col Rep, 70-71; chmn, Newberry Co Rep Party, SC, 70-72; youth vchmn, Third Cong Dist Rep Party, 72- Mil Serv: SP-4, Army Res, 70- Mem: SC Tuberc & Respiratory Disease Asn (prog dir, 71-); SC Tuberc & Respiratory Disease Conf (secy, 72-); Greenwood Jaycees (membership chmn, 72-); Greenwood Community Theatre. Honors & Awards: Chmn, Greenwood Jaycees Miss Greenwood & Miss Jr Miss Pageant, 73. Relig: Lutheran. Mailing Add: PO Box 805 Greenwood SC 29646

KOONS, JAMES L (D)
Chmn, Noble Co Dem Party, Ind
b Avilla, Ind, June 1, 15; s William E Koons & Cecilia Ley K; m 1956 to Dorothy Mae Finney; c James William & Ann Marie. Educ: Avilla High Sch. Polit & Govt Pos: Chmn, Noble Co Dem Party, Ind, 41-; chmn, Fourth Dist Dem Party, 48-65; alt deleg, Dem Nat Conv, 68. Bus & Prof Pos: Owner & operator of food mkt, 41- Mem: Ind Soc; Avilla CofC (pres, 69 & 70, secy, 72-73); March of Dimes (co chmn, currently); Elks (past Exalted Ruler); Moose. Honors & Awards: Young Dem of Ind. Relig: Catholic. Legal Res: 120 Baum St Avilla IN 46710 Mailing Add: Main St Avilla IN 46710

KOONTZ, ELIZABETH DUNCAN (D)
b Salisbury, NC, June 3, 19; d Samuel Edward Duncan & Lena Jordan D; m 1947 to Harry Lee Koontz. Educ: Livingstone Col, AB, 38; Atlanta Univ, MA, 41; Columbia Univ & Ind Univ, grad study. Hon Degrees: LHD, Livingstone Col, 67, Coppin State Col, 69, Women's Med Col, 70, Hobart & William Smith Cols, 70, Keuka Col, 71 & Ohio State Univ, 73; PdD, Pac Univ, 69 & Bryant Col, 69; LLD, Am Univ, 69, Ball State Univ, Duke Univ, 71 & Stonehill Col, 73; EdD, Howard Univ, 69; HHD, Eastern Mich Univ, 69 & Hofstra Univ, 70; ScD in Ed, Northeastern Univ, 69 & Cedar Crest Col, 71; LittD, Atlanta Univ, 69 & Windham Col, 70. Polit & Govt Pos: Mem, Gov Comn on the Status of Women, NC, 62; mem, President's Adv Coun on Educ of Disadvantaged Children, 65-68; US Deleg, UN Comn on the Status of Women, 69-; dir women's bur, US Dept of Labor, 69-73; co-chmn, US Dept Labor Task Force Vol Action, 71-; asst secy nutrit, NC Dept Human Resources, 73- Bus & Prof Pos: Pub sch teachers, NC, 38-68. Mem: Salisbury Teachers Asn; NC Asn of Classroom Teachers; NEA (nat pres, 68-69); hon mem Zeta Phi Beta; hon mem Altrusa Club. Honors & Awards: Distinguished Alumni Medallion for Achievement, Livingstone Col; Distinguished Teacher Award, Civitan Club of Salisbury; Distinguished Citizenship Award, NC Dist W of Civitan Int; Cert of Merit, Cheyney State Col. Relig: Episcopal. Legal Res: 418 S Caldwell St Salisbury NC 28144 Mailing Add: NC Dept of Human Resources Raleigh NC 27603

KOORY, EDWARD FREDRICK, JR (R)
Ariz State Sen
b El Paso, Tex, Mar 9, 40; s Edward Fredrick Koory & Mary Lee Abdou K; m 1961 to Jessica Dorothea Thomas; c Deborah Lee & Edward Fredrick, III. Educ: Ariz State Univ, BA, 61; Blue Key; Kappa Delta Pi. Polit & Govt Pos: Rep precinct committeeman, Ariz, 66-68; Ariz State Rep, Dist 8-0, 67-70; Ariz State Sen, 70-; alt deleg, Rep Nat Conv, 72. Mil Serv: Entered as 2nd Lt, Marine Corps, 61, released as 1st Lt, 64; 1st Lt, Marine Corps Res, 64- Mem: Rotary; CofC; United Fund (bd dirs). Relig: Conservative Baptist. Mailing Add: 5753 W Morten Glendale AZ 85301

KOPALD, S L, JR (KOPIE) (R)
Chmn, Tenn State Rep Party
b Memphis, Tenn, Sept 4, 21; s S L Kopald, Sr (deceased) & Ethel Goodman K; m 1946 to Mimi Daves; c Nancy, Stephen, Jack & David. Educ: Washington & Lee Univ, BS, 43; Harvard Grad Sch Bus Admin, IA, 43; Phi Eta Sigma. Polit & Govt Pos: Mem, Shelby Co Planning Comn, Tenn, 58-60; vchmn, Shelby Co Rep Party, mem steering comt; mem finance comt, Howard Baker, Dan Kuykendall & Winfield Dunn Campaigns; chmn, Tenn State Rep Party, 71-; mem, Rep Nat Comt, 71- Bus & Prof Pos: Purchasing, asst to pres, vpres & exec vpres, HumKo Prod, 46-; dir, Union Planters Nat Bank & Bus Music Corp, Memphis. Mil Serv: Entered as Pvt, Army, 42, released as Capt, 46, after serv in 3rd Army, ETO, 44-46; Battle Ribbons. Mem: Am Oil Chemists' Soc; Hebrew Union Col-Jewish Inst Relig (chmn bd gov, 65-72, mem bd gov, currently); Memphis Br, Fed Res Bank of St Louis; Memphis Rotary; Memphis & Shelby Co Community Chest. Relig: Judaism; Pres, Temple Israel, Memphis, 57-61 & 63-64. Mailing Add: 4880 Lake Dr Memphis TN 38117

KOPECKY, BERNIE D (D)
SDak State Rep
b Highmore, SDak; s Ernest Kopecky & Ida Berreth K; m 1954 to Helen Vetch; c Vicky, Sandra, Kathleen & Gregory. Educ: Westport High Sch, 4 years. Polit & Govt Pos: Dep sheriff, Brown Co, SDak, 54-60, sheriff, 60-66; deleg, Dem Nat Conv, 68; SDak State Rep, 69- Bus & Prof Pos: Salesman, Leisen Realty Co, 66-68; vpres, 69- Mil Serv: Entered as Pvt, Marine Corps, 51, released as Cpl, 53, after serv in First Marine Div, Korean Conflict, 51-52; Three Purple Hearts. Mem: Elks; Moose; Am Legion; 40 et 8; Nat Sheriff's Asn. Relig: Catholic. Mailing Add: 102 S Second Aberdeen SD 57401

KOPEL, GERALD H (D)
Colo State Rep
b Md, June 16, 28; married; c two. Polit & Govt Pos: Spec Asst Attorney Gen for Legis Drafting, Colo, 59-61; Colo State Rep, 65-67 & 71-, chmn judiciary comt, Colo House of Rep, 75-; mem, Nat Comn on Uniform State Laws, 75- Bus & Prof Pos: Lawyer; dir refresher course for graduating law students, 58-; ed & publ, Bankruptcy Newsletter, 61- Mem: Am Bar Asn (bd gov, 75-); Park Hill Action Comt. Mailing Add: 1755 Glencoe Denver CO 80220

KOPLAN, STEPHEN (D)
b Boston, Mass, Mar 24, 36; s Daniel Koplan & Sarah Cohen K (deceased); m 1963 to Harriet Elaine Lindenbaum; c Michael, Bruce, David & Adam. Educ: Brandeis Univ, AB, 57; Boston Univ, JD, 60; NY Univ Grad Sch Law, LLM in Tax, 62. Polit & Govt Pos: Trial attorney, Tax Div, US Dept Justice, 62-67, dep chief fed progs sect, Civil Rights Div, 71-74; sr trial attorney, Small Bus Admin, 67; staff attorney, US Sen Lee Metcalf, 67-70; chief counsel, Comt on Post Off & Civil Serv, US Senate, 74- Bus & Prof Pos: Partner, Law Firm Freedman, Levin & Koplan, 70-71. Relig: Jewish. Mailing Add: 4133 Lenox Dr Fairfax VA 22030

KOPP, DONALD LEE (D)
WVa State Deleg
b Clarksburg, WVa, May 23, 35; s Francis Kopp & Jenny Wilkinson K; m 1955 to Beverley Ann Wyckoff; c Donald Lee, II, Jenny Le & Tina Marie. Educ: Clarksburg Pub Schs. Polit & Govt Pos: WVa State Deleg, 64-, chmn, Comt on Indust & Labor, WVa House Deleg, 59th, 60th & 61st Legis, chmn, Judiciary Redistricting Comt & mem, Rules Comt, currently; deleg, Dem Nat Conv, 72; deleg. Dem Nat Mid-Term Conf, 74. Bus & Prof Pos: Indust glass worker. Mem: Elks; Moose; Rolland Local 6; deleg to Harrison Co Fedn of Labor. Honors & Awards: Distinguished Consumer Safety Award, 71. Relig: Methodist. Mailing Add: 1615 W Pike St Clarksburg WV 26301

KOPP, EUGENE PAUL (R)
Dep Dir, US Info Agency
b Charleston, WVa, Nov 20, 34; s Eugene Alexander Kopp & Virginia King K; m 1967 to Katherine Rogers; c Eugene Paul, Jr. Educ: Univ Notre Dame, BA, 57, MA, 58; WVa Univ, Col Law, JD, 61; Phi Delta Phi. Polit & Govt Pos: Law clerk, US Dist Court, Northern & Southern Dist, WVa, 61-62; trial attorney, Tax Div, US Dept of Justice, 62-69; dep gen counsel, US Info Agency, 69-72, acting gen counsel & cong liaison, 72, asst dir for admin, 72-73, dep dir, 73- Mem: Am Bar Asn; WVa State Bar. Relig: Catholic. Mailing Add: 452 Argyle Dr Alexandria VA 22305

KOPP, JOHN GLENWRIGHT (R)
Gen Counsel, Eighth Cong Rep Comt, Ga
b Augusta, Ga, Mar 18, 23; s Charles Heartter Kopp & Maurine Parks K (deceased); m 1967 to Jewell Mizell; c Joseph Harper. Educ: Norman Col, 40-42; Col William & Mary, 43; Mercer Univ, AB, 46, LLB, 49; Kappa Sigma. Polit & Govt Pos: Mem, Ware Co Rep Exec Comt, Ga, 58-67; chmn, Charlton Co Rep Exec Comt, formerly; gen counsel, Eighth Cong Rep Comt, 68- Bus & Prof Pos: Secy & dir, United Fed S&L Assoc, Ga, 63- Mil Serv: Entered as Pvt, Army, 43, released as Sgt, 45, after serv in 95th Inf Div, Europe-African-Mid East, 44-45; Bronze Star; Purple Heart; Combat Medics Badge; Good Conduct Ribbon; Europe-African-Mid East Ribbon with Three Stars. Mem: Am & Ga Bar Asns; Waycross Bar Asn; Elks; Lion. Relig: Baptist. Legal Res: 708 Martin St Folkston GA 31537 Mailing Add: Box 356 Folkston GA 31537

KOPP, W BREWSTER (R)
b Rochester, NY, Nov 4, 25; s Frederick J Kopp & Bernice C Woodworth K; m 1949 to Ruth S Philpotts; c Bradford B, Jeffrey B & Alexander B. Educ: Harvard Col, AB, 47, Harvard Bus Sch, MBA, 49. Polit & Govt Pos: Asst Secy of the Army for Financial Mgt, 65-67; consult, Dept Defense, 67-69. Bus & Prof Pos: Financial analyst, Fitch Investors Serv, 46-47, Wertheim & Co, 49-50 & Standard Oil Co of Ohio, 51-53; various financial positions, including div comptroller & corp mgr of financial planning & budgets, Am Can Co, 54-65; sr vpres, First Nat Bank of Boston, Mass, 67-69; vpres finance & admin, Digital Equip Corp, Maynard, 69-71; sr vpres & mem exec comt, Am Stock Exchange, 71-73; dir Adv Bd Dirs, Envirodyne, currently; vpres, Otis Elevator Co, NY, 73-; mem pres coun, Narramore Christian Found, currently. Mem: Financial Execs Inst; Harvard Club of NY; NY Bible Soc (dir & mem finance comt); Am Defense Preparedness Asn (dir NY chap); Gtr NY Coun, Boy Scouts; Asn of US Army. Relig: Protestant. Legal Res: Winchester Rd Norfolk CT 06058 Mailing Add: 149 E 73rd St New York NY 10021

KOPP, WILLIAM ALBERT (D)
Ohio State Rep
b Franklin Co, Ohio, Mar 24, 30; s Albert William Kopp & Reva Hopkins K; m 1951 to Margaret E Rath. Educ: Ohio State Univ, 59; Capital Univ, 60. Polit & Govt Pos: Dep treas, Columbus, Ohio, 71-72; Ohio State Rep, 73- Bus & Prof Pos: Asst vpres, Dollar Savings Asn, 73- Mil Serv: Entered as Pvt, Marine Corps, 47, released as Sgt, 51, after serv in VMF 244. Mem: Kiwanis; VFW; Rockwell Int Mgt Club; Columbus Navy League. Relig: Catholic. Legal Res: 331 S Virginia Lee Rd Columbus OH 43209 Mailing Add: State House Columbus OH 43215

KORIOTH, A J (R)
Tex State Rep
Mailing Add: 2772 Bay Meadow Court Dallas TX 75234

KORN, CHARLES AUSTIN (D)
VChmn, Harrison Co Dem Comt, Iowa
b Wapello, Iowa, May 4, 16; s John Austin Korn & Lula Kemper K; m 1948 to Dorothy C Clausen, wid. Polit & Govt Pos: Iowa State Rep, 65-66; vchmn, Harrison Co Dem Comt, presently. Bus & Prof Pos: Farmer, 48-52 & 60-; soil conservationist, US Soil Conserv Serv, 52-56, work unit conservationist, 56-60. Mil Serv: Entered as Aviation Cadet, Navy, 42, released as Lt(jg), 46, after serv in Amphibs, Pac. Mem: Kiwanis; Farmers Union; Farmers Orgn. Relig: Lutheran. Mailing Add: RR 1 Box 13 Logan IA 51546

KORNBLUH, EDWARD CALVIN (D)
Committeeman, Westchester Co Dem Comt, NY
b New York, NY, Sept 29, 26; s Herbert Kornbluh & Rose Leifer K; m 1954 to Therese Kronish; c Thomas, James & Jon. Educ: Col William & Mary, 43-44; NY Univ Col Dent, DDS, 48; Alpha Omega. Polit & Govt Pos: Treas, Concerned Dem of Westchester, 67-68, mem exec comt, 67-, vchmn, 73-; chmn, Greenburgh Coalition of Concerned Dem, 69-70; committeeman, Westchester Co Dem Comt, NY, 69-; vchmn, Greenburgh Dem Town Comt, 71-; deleg, Dem Nat Conv, 72. Bus & Prof Pos: Dent interne, Montefiore Hosp, New York, 48-49; practicing dentist, New York, 48-; instr, NY Univ Col Dent, 54-58, asst prof, 58-67, assoc prof, 67-; chief pediat dent, Polyclin Hosp, 62-66; attend oral surgeon, Univ Hosp. Mil Serv: Entered as Lt(jg), Navy, 49, released, 50, after serv in Dent Corps, Pensacola Naval

Air Sta, 49-50; Lt, Navy Res, 52-53, Norfolk, Va & Mediter Fleet, N Atlantic, 52-53. Publ: Operative dentistry in pedodontics, NY State Dent J, 56; Modern pedodontics, NY Univ Dent J, 68. Mem: Am Dent Asn; Am Asn Hosp Dentists; Am Soc Implant Dent. Relig: Jewish. Mailing Add: 17 Stoneleigh Close Scarsdale NY 10583

KORNEGAY, HORACE ROBINSON (D)
b Asheville, NC, Mar 12, 24; s Marvin Earl Kornegay & Blanche Person Robinson K; m to Anne Ben Beale; c Horace Robinson, Jr, Kathryn Elder & Martha Beale. Educ: Wake Forest Univ, BS, 47, Sch Law, JD, 49; Phi Delta Phi; Omicron Delta Kappa; Alpha Sigma Phi. Polit & Govt Pos: Prosecuting attorney, 12th Dist, NC, 54-60; US Rep, NC, 60-69. Bus & Prof Pos: Lawyer; vpres-counsel, Tobacco Inst, Inc, Washington, DC, 69-70, pres & exec dir, 70- Mil Serv: US Army, 43-46; Combat Inf Badge; Purple Heart; Bronze Star; Two Campaign Stars. Mem: Greensboro, NC & Am Bar Asns; Am Judicature Soc; Fed Bar Asn. Relig: Methodist. Mailing Add: 7709 Charleston Dr Bethesda MD 20034

KORNEGAY, JESSE DEXTER (D)
b Centreville, Ala, Sept 15, 17; s Jesse D Kornegay & Georgia Pierson K; m 1948 to Lucille B Walters; c Ronald, Christopher, Kathryn & Patricia. Educ: Hueytown High, Ala, 32-35. Polit & Govt Pos: Mem, Santa Fe Co Comn, NMex, 54-58; chief, State Tax Comn, 63-68; State Treas, NMex, 68-74. Mem: Nat Asn State Auditors, Comptrollers & Treas; Int Asn Assessing Officers; Mason. Relig: Episcopal. Legal Res: 907 Old Santa Fe Trail Santa Fe NM 87501 Mailing Add: Box 608 Santa Fe NM 87501

KORNICK, MICHAEL (D)
Secy, Mahoning Co Dem Party, Ohio
b Vanderbilt, Pa, May 8, 05; s John Kornick & Mary Olenick K; m 1954 to Margaret Leitch Gorby; stepchildren, Kathryn Corinne Gorby & Carolyn Joyce (Mrs William Little). Educ: Sherwin Cody Sch Eng, 25; Youngstown YMCA Col, 26-27. Polit & Govt Pos: Dem precinct committeeman, Mahoning Co Dem Party, Ohio, 34-69, secy, 50-; twp trustee, Coitsville, Ohio, 36-39, chmn, 37-38; mem, Mahoning Co Dem Cent & Exec Comt, 40-; dep clerk of courts, Mahoning Co, 43-69; mem, Campbell Sch Bd, 48-55, chmn, 53 & 55; campaign mgr, speaker & speech writer for various Dem cand, including, Joseph Vrabel, former Mayor of Campbell. Bus & Prof Pos: Bus mgr, Campbell Hillcrests Semi-Pro Football Club, 28; publicity dir, Struthers Semi-Pro Football Club, 29; pres, Depression Baseball League, Campbell, Ohio, 32-33 & 34; ins agent, Firemen's Ins Co, Newark, NJ, 36-68; real estate broker, 36-43; ed, Campbell News-J, 44; owner, Campbell Florists, 42-69. Publ: Short Sketch on Helen Gibson, Films in Rev, 1/68, Hollywood Trip thru Movieland, 2/69 & Biography on Charles Ray, Film Classic Collector, 69; plus others. Mem: Baseball Town USA Oldtimers. Honors & Awards: Known historian on early movies & baseball & as such speak at various banquets & meetings; Vaudeville performer, singer & character actor. Relig: Byzantine Catholic. Mailing Add: 241 Gordon Ave Campbell OH 44405

KORNICK, NICHOLAS (D)
Treas, Fayette Co Dem Cent Comt, Pa
b Vanderbilt, Pa, Dec 15, 12; s John Kornick & Katherine Bodnovich K; m to Margaret Duke; c two. Educ: Pa State Univ Exten. Polit & Govt Pos: Pa State Rep, 50-67; Justice of the Peace, Uniontown, Pa, formerly, committeeman, formerly; chmn, Uniontown Dem Party, formerly; treas, Fayette Co, 68-; treas, Fayette Co Dem Cent Comt, 72- Bus & Prof Pos: Safety engr; scale inspector, Pa. Mem: Fayette Co Crippled Children (publicity chmn); Am (Russky) Social Club; Big Ten Baseball League, Fayette, Washington & Green Co (pres, 46-); Uniontown Slovak Club; Connellsville Slovak Club. Relig: Catholic. Mailing Add: 37 S Pennsylvania Ave Uniontown PA 15401

KOROLOGOS, TOM CHRIS (R)
b Salt Lake City, Utah, Apr 6, 33; s Chris T Korologos & Irene Kolendrianos K; m 1960 to Carolyn Joy Goff; c Ann, Philip Chris & Paula. Educ: Univ Utah, BA, 55; Columbia Univ, Grantland Rice Mem fel, 57, Pulitzer traveling fel & MS, 58; Sigma Delta Chi; Kappa Tau Alpha. Polit & Govt Pos: Press secy to US Sen Wallace Bennett, Utah, 62-65, admin asst, 65-71, spec asst to the President, White House, 71- Bus & Prof Pos: Reporter, Salt Lake Tribune, 50-60; reporter, New York Herald Tribune, 58; acct exec, David W Evans & Assocs, Salt Lake City, Utah, 60-62. Mil Serv: Entered as 2nd Lt, Air Force. 56, released as 1st Lt, 57, after serv in 825th Air Div, Strategic Air Command, Little Rock AFB, Ark; Capt, Air Force Res. Mem: US Senate Press Secy Asn; Asn Admin Assts to US Sen; Ahepa. Relig: Greek Orthodox. Legal Res: 383 Downington Ave Salt Lake City UT 84115 Mailing Add: 8222 Smithfield Ave Springfield VA 22150

KOROPP, NORMA (D)
Mem, Dem Nat Comt, CZ
Mailing Add: Box 511 Panama City CZ

KORRELL, RITA MAY (R)
VChmn, Cheyenne Co Rep Cent Comt, Colo
b First View, Colo, May 3, 28; d William Sherman Alderson & Urtle Gay Webb A; m 1948 to Gordon LeRoy Korrell; c Charlotte Ann & Michael James. Educ: Kit Carson High Sch, grad. Polit & Govt Pos: Dep co clerk, Cheyenne Co, Cheyenne Wells, Colo, 65-71, co clerk & recorder, 71-; pres, Cheyenne Co Rep Women's Club, Colo, 66-68; vchmn, Cheyenne Co Rep Cent Comt, 69-; committeewoman, Cheyenne Wells Precinct Three Rep Party, 69- Mem: VFW Auxiliary (pres, William A Kimmel Post 9700, 51-); Eastern Star. Relig: Methodist. Legal Res: 50 W Fourth St N Cheyenne Wells CO 80810 Mailing Add: PO Box 67 Cheyenne Wells CO 80810

KORTH, FRED (D)
b Yorktown, Tex, Sept 9, 09; s Fritz R J Korth & Eleanor Marie Stark K; div; c Nina Marie, Fritz-Alan & Vera Sansom. Educ: Univ Tex, AB, 32; George Washington Univ, LLB, 35; Phi Delta Phi; Sigma Phi Epsilon. Hon Degrees: LLD, George Washington Univ, 60. Polit & Govt Pos: Dep counr, Dept of Army, 51-52, Asst Secy of Army, 52-53, consult to Secy Army, 53-60; Secy of Navy, 62-63. Bus & Prof Pos: Law practice, Ft Worth, Tex, 35-62; partner, Wallace & Korth, 48-51; exec vpres, Continental Nat Bank, Ft Worth, 53-59, pres, 59-61; treas, Ft Worth Air Terminal Corp, 53-60; mem bd dirs, Panama Canal Co, 61-64; lawyer, Korth & Korth, Washington, DC, 64-; mem bd dirs, Fischbach & Moore, Am Air Filter Co & Southwest Nat Bank, El Paso, Tex; dir OKC Corp, Dallas, 66- Mil Serv: Lt Col, Air Transport Command, Army, 42-46. Mem: Am & Tex Bar Asns; Am Law Inst; Am Judicature Soc; Am Bankers Asn. Honors & Awards: Exceptional Civilian Serv Award, Dept of Army, 53. Mailing Add: Barr Bldg Farragut Sq Washington DC 20006

KOSCO, JOHN C (R)
Chmn, Elk Co Rep Comt, Pa
b Dubois, Pa, Sept 20, 32; s Joseph B Kosco & Julia Reagle K; m 1956 to Mary Mullaney; c Thomas, Ellen, Mary Patricia, Maurus, Anne & Joseph. Educ: Univ of Notre Dame, BS, 54; Princeton Univ, MS, 56; Pa State Univ, PhD, 58; Sigma Xi. Polit & Govt Pos: Borough chmn, St Mary's Rep Party, Pa, 62-64; chmn, Elk Co Rep Comt, 64- Bus & Prof Pos: Research metallurgist, Stackpole Carbon Co, 58-65, dir metallurgical research, 65-66, chief engr, 66-71; dir metal research, Keystone Carbon Co, 71- Publ: Detergency during infiltration in powder metal, 15th Annual Metal Powder Indust Fedn Meeting, NY, 59; Development of composites by liquid phase techniques, Am Soc Metals, 65; Contact materials, Electrotechnology, 66. Mem: Am Soc Metals; Am Chem Soc; Am Inst Mining & Metall Engrs; Am Powder Metal Inst. Relig: Roman Catholic. Mailing Add: 571 Charles St St Marys PA 15857

KOSINSKI, ROMAN J (D)
Ill State Rep
b Chicago, Ill, Feb 28, 17; s Roman Kosinski & Lucille Czekala K; m 1939 to Isabel Bukowski; c Paul. Educ: Northwestern Univ, 3 years. Polit & Govt Pos: Rep of Mayor, Sch Bd Nominating Comt, 70; Ill State Rep, 16th Dist, 71- Bus & Prof Pos: Owner, Roman Kosinski Jewelers. Mil Serv: Entered as Pvt, Army, 43, released as Sgt, 46, after serv in 2nd Army Hq. Publ: Auth of several articles. Mem: Chicago Jewelers Asn; CofC; Chicago Soc; Lions Club; Boy Scouts of Am (dist chmn). Honors & Awards: Nat Honor Soc. Relig: Catholic. Legal Res: 5446 N Paris Chicago IL 60656 Mailing Add: 5754 W Belmont Chicago IL 60634

KOSS, HELEN LEVINE (D)
Md State Deleg
b New York, NY, June 3, 22; d Herman Joseph Levine & Pearl Trotsky L; m 1946 to Howard Koss; c Deborah (Mrs Handel) & Tamar Edith. Educ: Bennington Col, BA, 42. Polit & Govt Pos: Md State Deleg, 71-, mem, Legis Comt on Const & Admin Law, Md Gen Assembly, 71-, chmn, Joint Comt on Legis Ethics, 72-, chmn, Subcomt Const & Admin Law on Elec Law, 73- & mem rules comt, Md House of Deleg, 73- Bus & Prof Pos: Mem bd vis, Bowie State Col, 70-; mem, Comn to Study Oper of Sunday Blue Laws & Gov Task Force to Study Campaign Financing, 74- Publ: Ed, Stateside, Montgomery Co Dem Cent Comt Newsletter, 69 & 70. Mem: Kensington-Wheaton Dem Club; Women's Nat Dem Club; League Women Voters; Am Asn Univ Women; Orgn Women Legislators. Mailing Add: 3416 Highview Ct Wheaton MD 20902

KOSTELKA, ROBERT WILLIAM (R)
b Shreveport, La, Feb 18, 33; s William Fabian Kostelka & Lillian Luzenburg K; m 1957 to Bobbie Ann Morales; c Kathryn Ann, William Corbett, Robert Clifton & Carol Susan. Educ: Centenary Col, Shreveport, La, 51-53; La State Univ, Baton Rouge, 53-54, Law Sch, JD, 57; Phi Delta Phi; Kappa Alpha. Polit & Govt Pos: Asst dist attorney, Fourth Judicial Dist of La, 64-70, dist attorney, 70-71; alt deleg, Rep Nat Conv, 72. Bus & Prof Pos: Sr law partner, Law Firm of Kostelka & Blackwell, 71- Mil Serv: Entered as Pvt, Army Res, 51, released as Sgt, 57. Mem: Am Judicature Soc; La & Fourth Dist Bar Asns; Rotary (dir, Monroe, 70-); Salvation Army Adv Bd (chmn, 70-73). Honors & Awards: Citizen of Year, Salvation Army, 72. Relig: Presbyterian. Legal Res: 2111 Maywood Monroe LA 71201 Mailing Add: 2205 Liberty Monroe LA 71201

KOSTER, RICHARD M (D)
Dem Nat Committeeman, CZ
b Brooklyn, NY, Mar 1, 34; s Harry Koster & Lily Silverstein K; m 1959 to Otilia Tejeira; c Ricardo & Lily. Educ: Yale Col, BA, 55; NY Univ, MA, 62. Polit & Govt Pos: Deleg, Dem Nat Conv, 64, 68 & 72; Dem Nat Committeeman, CZ, 66-; mem, Dem Charter Comn, currently; deleg, Dem Nat Mid-Term Conf, 74. Bus & Prof Pos: Instr, Nat Univ Panama, 60-61; correspondent, Copley News Serv, San Diego, Calif, 64-66; assoc dir Eng, Fla State Univ, CZ Br, 64-, lectr, 64-72, asst prof, 72- Mil Serv: Army, Counter Intel Corps, Southern Command, 56-59. Publ: Contrib, The New Republic; The Prince, William Morrow & Co, 72. Legal Res: Calle 47 No 9 Panama Repub of Panama Mailing Add: Box 390 Albrook CZ 09825

KOSTOHRYZ, RICHARD JOSEPH (DFL)
Minn State Rep
b St Paul, Minn, Apr 30, 30; s William Fredrick Kostohryz & Mary Voss K; m 1954 to Rosemary Glischinski; c Victoria, Nancy, Richard, Mary & Paula. Educ: Monroe High Sch, Minn, 4 years. Polit & Govt Pos: Vchmn, 50th Dist Dem-Farmer-Labor Party, Minn, 68, chmn, formerly, state cent committeeman, 68 & 70; Minn State Rep, 75- Bus & Prof Pos: Develop technol, 3M Co, St Paul, Minn, 70. Mil Serv: Entered as Seaman Recruit, Navy, 48, released as SS 2nd class, 53, after serv in Atlantic & Pac Fleets; European Occupation, China Serv, Japanese Occupation & UN Ribbons; Korean Serv Three Stars. Mem: Am Asn Textile Chem & Colorists; Lions. Relig: Roman Catholic. Mailing Add: 2478 E Indian Way North St Paul MN 55109

KOSTOPULOS, NICHOLAS PETER, SR (D)
b Portsmouth, Va, Nov 12, 16; s Peter Nicholas Kostopulos & Lilly Dufexis K; m 1951 to Madeline Anagnos; c Nicholas P, Jr & Dianne. Educ: Woodrow Wilson High Sch, Portsmouth, Va, grad, 33. Polit & Govt Pos: Asst to US Sen Estes Kefauver in Kefauver for President Campaign, 52 & 56; asst to US Sen Hubert H Humphrey in Johnson-Humphrey Campaign, 64-65; consult, Off of Econ Opportunity, 65-68; asst to Vice President Hubert H Humphrey, 68; asst, Humphrey for President, Dem Nat Comt, 68; spec asst to US Sen Fred R Harris, Okla, former chmn, Dem Nat Comt, 69, Lawrence F O'Brien, Mass, chmn, Dem Nat Comt, 70-72, Jean Westwood, chmn, 72 & Robert S Strauss, chmn, 72- Bus & Prof Pos: Owner, Monroe Restaurant, Portsmouth, Va, 41-50; registered rep, Investors Diversified Serv, Norfolk, 50-53; sole proprietor, Consolidated Investment Serv, 53-; sole proprietor, Saxony Motel, Virginia Beach, 58- Mem: Mason; Ahepa. Relig: Greek Orthodox. Mailing Add: 2109 Atlantic Ave Virginia Beach VA 23451

KOSTRON, FRANK E (D)
Mo State Rep
b St Louis, Mo, Apr 6, 16; m 1942 to Margaret D Namentcavage; c One daughter. Educ: McKinley High Sch. Polit & Govt Pos: Mo State Rep, 50- Bus & Prof Pos: Brewery worker. Mil Serv: Navy, 34-38, 41-45, SPac. Mem: VFW; Am Legion. Relig: Protestant. Mailing Add: 2812 Texas St St Louis MO 63118

KOTHMANN, GLENN HAROLD (D)
Tex State Sen
b San Antonio, Tex, May 30, 28; s Wilkes John Kothmann & Lilly Mertz K. Educ: Tex A&M

Univ, BS, 50. Polit & Govt Pos: Tex State Rep, until 67; Tex State Sen, currently. Mil Serv: Col, Army Res. Relig: Methodist. Mailing Add: 4610 Sea Breeze San Antonio TX 78220

KOTTIS, JOHN GREGORY (R)
VChmn, Uxbridge Rep Town Comt, Mass
b Epirus, Greece, Aug 9, 25; s Angelo Gregory Kottis & Mary D Tashulas K; m 1956 to Mary George Patrinos; c Van J, Chrys A, George B & Carl J. Educ: Brown Univ; Boston Univ Sch Law; Delta Theta Phi; Brown Debating Club. Polit & Govt Pos: Field secy, Mass Rep State Comt, 52; selectman, Uxbridge, Mass, 53-59; vchmn, Uxbridge Rep Town Comt, currently. Mil Serv: Entered as Pvt, Army, 43, released as Sgt, 46, after serv in Combat Engrs; Am, European & German Theater Ribbons with Two Battle Stars. Publ: Articles publ on const law in Christian Econ, 63-64. Mem: Mass & Worcester Co Bar Asns; VFW; DAV; Am Legion. Relig: Greek Orthodox. Legal Res: 29 Henry St Uxbridge MA 01569 Mailing Add: 10 S Main St Uxbridge MA 01569

KOUGL, PATRICIA ANNE (D)
VChmn, Dewey Co Dem Party, SDak
b Vermillion, SDak, Nov 2, 19; d Patrick L O'Conner & Margaret Kyte O; m 1937 to William Alfred Kougl; c Dr Donald A, John W, Nancy (Mrs O'Leary), Albert P & Marcia A. Educ: Univ High Sch, Vermillion, grad, 37. Polit & Govt Pos: Vchmn, Dewey Co Dem Party, Timber Lake, SDak, 72- Mem: Eastern Star (worthy matron, 56); Farm Bur (woman's co chmn, 73). Relig: United Methodist. Mailing Add: Box 158 Timber Lake SD 57656

KOUPAL, CARL MATHIAS, JR (R)
b Bonne Terre, Mo, June 16, 53; s Carl Mathias Koupal, Sr & Lillian Nations K; single. Educ: Mineral Area Col, AA, 73; Univ Mo-Columbia, BA, 75; Phi Theta Kappa; Mo Students Asn. Polit & Govt Pos: Alt deleg, Rep Nat Conv, 72; committeeman, St Francois Co Rep Comt, 72-74; chmn, Mo Col Rep, 73-74. Mem: Mo Col Rep. Honors & Awards: Am Legion Speech Contest, St Francois Co; Awarded scholar to sem govt, Washington, DC, Nat Honor Soc Essay Contest, 72. Relig: Christian. Mailing Add: 502 W Main St Flat River MO 63601

KOVACH, ROBERT (D)
Ind State Sen
b South Bend, Ind, Sept 19, 41; s Rudolph Kovach, Sr & Barbara Norris K; m 1967 to Karen Baughman; c Kristi & Kathryn. Educ: Purdue Univ, 59-61; Ball State Univ, BS in Educ, 64, MA in Social Sci, 69. Polit & Govt Pos: Councilman-at-lg, Mishawaka, 68-74, pres of coun, 72-73; Ind State Sen, 75- Bus & Prof Pos: Teacher, South Bend Community Sch Corp, 64- Mailing Add: 1133 E Third St Mishawaka IN 46544

KOVNER, SARAH SCHOENKOPF (D)
b Elizabeth, NJ, May 3, 35; d Isidor Schoenkopf & Ceile Season S; m 1964 to Victor A Kovner. Educ: Vassar Col, BA, 57. Polit & Govt Pos: Committeewoman, Dem State Party, NY, 60-65; mem, Mikulski Comn, 73; deleg, Dem Nat Mid-Term Conf, 74; co-chairperson, NY State Affirmative Action Comt, 74- Bus & Prof Pos: Pres, Arts, Letters & Polit Inc, 73-; organizer & mem bd dirs, First Women's Bank of New York, 75- Legal Res: 27 W 67th St New York NY 10023 Mailing Add: 250 W 57th St New York NY 10019

KOWALCZYCK, AL (R)
Minn State Sen
Mailing Add: 6016 70th Ave N Brooklyn Park MN 55429

KOWALSKI, MARGE HELENE (D)
Mem, Solano Co Dem Cent Comt, Calif
b Gilman, Ill, Oct 19, 22; d William Ray Piatt & Estelle Mae Holland P; m 1953 to Henry Kowalski; c Denise Marie (Mrs Driver), Nicole Cecile, Mark John, Paul Jacques & Suzanne Estelle. Educ: Univ Wash Exten, 51-52; Solano Community Col, 75-; Women for Change. Polit & Govt Pos: Secy & deleg, Lakewood Plaza Dem Club, Long Beach, Calif, 56-61; secy, Fairfield-Suisun Dem Club, 67-73; secy & deleg, Fedn Solano Co Dem, 68-73; co-chmn, Solano Co Unruh for Gov Comt, 70; co-chmn, Solano Co McGovern for President Comt, 72; deleg, Dem Nat Conv, 72; mem, Solano Co Dem Cent Comt, 74- Mem: PTA. Relig: Catholic. Mailing Add: 2042 Falcon Ct Fairfield CA 94533

KOWALYSHYN, RUSSELL (D)
Pa State Rep
b Northampton, Pa, Sept 16, 18; s Steven Kowalyshyn & Anna Kuzyk K. Educ: Leigh Univ, BA; Columbia Univ, MA; Dickinson Sch Law, LLB; Phi Beta Kappa. Polit & Govt Pos: Asst district attorney, Northampton Co, Pa, 56-63; mem, Northampton Area Sch Bd, 60-65; solicitor, Moore Twp, Northampton Borough; Pa State Rep, 64- Bus & Prof Pos: Lawyer. Mil Serv: Entered Army, 42, released as Capt, 46. Mem: Northampton Co & Am Bar Asns. Relig: Catholic. Mailing Add: Capitol Bldg Harrisburg PA 17120

KOZA, GEORGIA LYNNE (R)
Nat Committeewoman, Calif Young Rep
b San Francisco, Calif, Jan 31, 49; d Adolph B Koza & Audrey Ann Dillard K; single. Educ: Col of the Holy Names, dean's list four semesters, 67-70; Univ Calif, San Francisco Med Ctr, BS, 72. Polit & Govt Pos: Staff mem, Berryhill for Calif State Assembly, 69; area 12 dir, Calif Col Rep, 69-70; staff mem, Harmer for Attorney Gen, Calif, 69-70; deleg, Calif Col Rep State Conv, 69-70; deleg, Calif Young Rep State Conv, 71, 72 & 73; deleg, Young Rep Nat Fedn Conv, 71-73; asst secy, Calif Young Rep, 71, secy, 71-73, Nat Committeewoman, 73-75; assoc mem, Rep State Cent Comt Calif, 72-73. Bus & Prof Pos: Secy, Judge Hal C Broaders, Legis Advocate for Bank of Am, 68, Calif State Sen, Robert S Stevens, 69 & Calif State Sen, John Nejedly, 70; staff mem, Cong Reapportionment, Rep Senate Caucus, 71; dent hygienist, Sacramento, 72- Mem: Am Dent Hygienists Asn; Samoyed Fanciers of Sacramento; life mem Calif Scholar Fedn. Relig: Catholic. Mailing Add: 904 Carson St Barstow CA 92311

KOZER, TED (R)
b Royalton, Ill, June 13, 22; s Joseph Kozer & Mary Servonski K; single. Educ: Southern Ill Univ, Carbondale, 41-42; Chillicothe Bus Col, grad, 46. Polit & Govt Pos: City clerk, Royalton, Ill, 51-71; Rep precinct committeeman, 52-; chmn, Franklin Co Rep Party, 67-69 & 73-75. Bus & Prof Pos: Owner, Kozer Grocery, currently. Mil Serv: Entered as Pvt, Army, 42, released as S/Sgt, 46, after serv in 104th Field Artillery Bn; numerous awards & decorations. Mem: Am Legion; VFW; Lions; Elks; Odd Fellows. Relig: Non-denominational. Legal Res: 106 S Fairdale Royalton IL 62983 Mailing Add: PO Box 106 Royalton IL 62983

KOZLOSKI, WALTER JOHN (D)
NJ State Assemblyman
b Plymouth, Pa; s Walter V Kozlowski; m 1963 to C Louise Zebroski; c Walter Vincent, II, Lea Louise, Laura Lynn & Lorraine Lee. Educ: Bloomsburg State Col, BS, 56; Seton Hall Univ, MA, 67. Polit & Govt Pos: Councilman, Borough of Freehold, 67-74; NJ State Assemblyman, Dist 11, 74- Mil Serv: Army, 2 years, serv in 1st & 8th Divs, Ger; Good Conduct Medal. Mem: KofC; Freehold Fire Dept; Elks; NJ Educ Asn. Honors & Awards: Outstanding NJ Jaycee, 65; Outstanding Young Citizen, Western Monmouth Co, 67; Distinguished Serv Award for Community Work, 68. Relig: Catholic. Legal Res: 19 Schiverea Ave Freehold NJ 07728 Mailing Add: 30 W Main St Freehold NJ 07728

KOZLOWSKI, WALT E (R)
Mem, Nev State Rep Exec Comt
b Cudahy, Wis, Feb 8, 37; s Walter Kozlowski & Anne Heun K; m 1959 to Mary Kupec; c Mary Ann, Terry Lee & Kim Lyn. Educ: Marquette Univ, BSEE, 59. Polit & Govt Pos: Secy & founder, Polit Assocs, 64-; mem, Clark Co Rep Cent Comt, Nev, 64-, vchmn, 64-70, chmn, 70-72; mem, Nev State Rep Cent Comt, 64-; deleg, Clark Co & Nev State Rep Conv, 64, 66, 68 & 70; mem, Nev State Rep Exec Comt, 70-; spec asst to Gov Paul Laxalt. Bus & Prof Pos: Electronic engr, Boeing Co, Seattle, Wash, 59-61; electronic engr, EG&G, Las Vegas, Nev, 61-67, consult & sales training, 67-69; environ & indust develop consult, Hughes, Nev Opers, 69-70; gen consult, 70- Mem: Archaed-Nev Soc; Nev Open Spaces Coun; NAACP; Sierra Club; Community PTA (community coun). Honors & Awards: Outstanding Young Man Nominee, 70. Relig: Roman Catholic. Mailing Add: 709 Mallard S Las Vegas NV 89107

KOZUBOWSKI, WALTER S (D)
Ill State Sen
Mailing Add: 4812 S Racine Ave Chicago IL 60609

KRAEMER, JAMES S (R)
b San Francisco, Calif, Feb 8, 19; s Sanford J Kraemer (deceased) & Cora Saroni K; m 1941 to Helen Bjork; c James Sanford, Allan Lage & Susan Jean. Educ: San Francisco Jr Col, AA, 38; Univ Calif Exten, Cert in Real Estate, 48. Polit & Govt Pos: Mem fund raising comt, Goldwater for President Campaign, 63-64; pres, Oakland Rep Assembly, 64 & 69; dir Seven Cong Dist, Calif Rep Assembly, 65-67, vpres, 67-68, pres, 69-70; mem finance comt, Alameda Co Reagan Campaign, 66; registr chmn, Don Mulford Campaign, 66-68; registr chmn, 16th Assembly Dist Rep Party, 66-72, chmn, 16th Assembly Dist Coord Coun, 73-; vpres, Alameda Co Coord Rep Assembly, 67; mem, Rep State Cent Comt Calif, 67-74, mem exec comt, 70-72; treas, Lincoln Club of Alameda Co, 67-74; mem, Alameda Co Rep Cent Comt, 67-74, vchmn, 70; Alameda Co chmn, Rafferty for US Senate Campaign, 68; comt mem, Ronald Reagan Campaign, 70; finance comt mem, Don Mulford Campaign, 70; pres, Oakland-Piedmont Rep Assembly, 70; Alameda Co vol chmn, George Murphy for US Senate Campaign, 70. Bus & Prof Pos: Realtor & ins broker; partner, Kraemer & Kraemer, currently. Mil Serv: Entered as Pvt, Army Air Force, 42, released as T/Sgt, 46, after serv in Army Airways Commun Syst, ETO, 44-46. Mem: Real Estate Cert Inst; Oakland Real Estate Bd; Calif Real Estate Asn; Nat Asn Real Estate Brokers; F&AM. Relig: Protestant; Trustee & mem bd, Piedmont Community Church, formerly. Legal Res: 124 Nova Dr Piedmont CA 94610 Mailing Add: 2914 Telegraph Ave Oakland CA 94609

KRAFT, MYRTLE MOYER WESTBROOK (R)
b Buffalo, NY, Nov 29, 17; d Myron Myrtle Moyer & Emma Langkans M; m 1962 to C Theodore Kraft; c Anne Westbrook, Emily (Mrs Kenneth Baker) & Paul Westbrook. Educ: MacMurray Col, AB, 38; Univ Kans, 38-40; NY State Col Teachers, educ courses. Polit & Govt Pos: Clerk, Sch Bd, Portal, Ariz, 66-67; secy, Ariz Fedn Rep Women, 66-68, fourth vpres, 68-69, second vpres, 69-71, pres, 71-73; deleg, Rep Nat Conv, 72. Bus & Prof Pos: Teaching fel, Univ Kans, 38-40; secy, Cathedral of All Saints, 58-59. Publ: The Hoover report, Altamont Enterprise, 3/9/51; Should we centralize?, Rural New Yorker, 2/20/54; A boy...and...his horse, Morgan Horse Mag, 3/54. Relig: Episcopal. Mailing Add: Box 187 Portal AZ 85632

KRAGTORP, NORMA MARIE (D)
b Seattle, Wash, May 30, 19; d William Nicholas Federspiel & Ruth Marie Gain F; m 1954 to Melvin James Kragtorp. Educ: Highline High Sch, grad, 37; pres, Delta Theta Tau, 67, nat deleg, 68, province chmn, 69. Polit & Govt Pos: Dem Committeeman, Orcas precinct, Seattle, 64-; deleg & mem credentials comt, King Co Dem Conv, Wash, 64-74, secy, 66-74; deleg & mem credentials comt, Wash State Dem Conv, 64-74; exec secy, Wash State Senate, Olympia, 65; pres, White Ctr Dem Club, Seattle, 67-68; deleg, Dem Nat Conv, 72; secy & committeeman, 31st Dist Precinct Orgn, King Co, 72-74. Bus & Prof Pos: Secy, Sears, Roebuck & Co, Seattle, 37-41; exec secy, Supt Schs, Highline Dist, 41-44, Alaska Steamship Co, 44-54 & Lear, Inc, 54-60; secy, Lutheran Church, 60-63; exec secy, Neighborhood Youth Corps, King Co, 65-68; exec secy, Boeing Commercial Airplane Co, 68- Mem: Nat Secy Asn. Honors & Awards: J F Kennedy Award, Kennedy for President Comt, 60; R F Kennedy Award, Kennedy for President Comt & Kennedy Family, 68; Curly Witherbee Award, White Ctr Dem Club, 70; H (Scoop) Jackson Award, Henry M Jackson Comt, 72. Relig: Lutheran. Mailing Add: 1802 SW 149th Seattle WA 98166

KRAMER, A LUDLOW, III (R)
b New York, NY, June 10, 32; s A Ludlow Kramer, II & Mary Delafield Bowes K; c Mary Delafield, William Ludlow, Ann Livingston & John Leighton. Educ: Univ Md, Overseas; Am Inst Banking. Polit & Govt Pos: City councilman, Seattle, Wash, 62-64; Secy of State, Wash, 64-74; chmn, Const Rev Comt, Wash, 66; chmn, Urban Affairs Coun, Wash, 68; chmn, Comn on Causes & Prev of Civil Disorder, 69; deleg, Rep Nat Conv, 68; chmn, Electoral Reform Coun, 70; chmn, Human Affairs Citizen Coun, 71-; co-chmn, Gov Task Force on Aging, 72-; Bus & Prof Pos: Investment officer, Seattle Trust & Savings, Wash, 55-61; acting dir spec events, Seattle World's Fair, 62; Am Mgt Asn guest lectr, Kennedy Inst of Polit & other univs & cols, Wash. Mil Serv: Entered as Pvt, Air Force, 52, released as Sgt, 55, after serv in 440th Fighter Interceptor Squadron, Europe-Africa. Mem: Nat Asn for Retarded Children (bd, 72-); Acad for Contemporary Probs; Mason-Thurston Co Campfire Girls; Olympia Campfire Girls (bd dirs); United Good Neighbors. Honors & Awards: Selected one of nation's outstanding young men of US Jaycees, 64; one of three outstanding young men, 65, Wash State Jaycees; Wash chief rep, Trade Fair, Tokyo, 65; initiator, Flags for Servicemen Prog. Relig: Episcopal. Legal Res: Seattle WA Mailing Add: c/o Legislative Bldg PO Box 1974 Olympia WA 98501

KRAMER, DOUGLAS DUANE (R)
Chmn, Twin Falls Co Rep Cent Comt, Idaho
b Fairfield, Idaho, Jan 15, 25; s Charles William Kramer & Gladys Von Krosigk K; m 1969

to Kathleen Mingo; c Susan, Nancy, Theresa & Samuel. Educ: Univ Idaho, BA, 49, Col Law, JD, 51; Phi Alpha Delta; Intercollegiate Knights. Polit & Govt Pos: Precinct committeeman, Twin Falls Co Rep Cent Comt, Idaho, 52-, chmn, 70-; Nixon-Lodge Campaign, Southern Idaho, 60; state chmn, Scranton Campaign, 64; state chmn, Vet for Goldwater, 64; mem, Idaho Const Rev Comn, 65-70; deleg, Rep Nat Conv, 72; State Dist Judge, 74- Bus & Prof Pos: State comdr & nat committeeman, Am Legion, Idaho, 59-60; pres, Bar Asn Dist Bar, Eight Counties, 62-63; pres, Twin Falls CofC, 65-66; mem exam comt, Idaho State Bar, 71- Mil Serv: Entered as A/S, Navy, 43, released as SM 3/C. 46, after serv in USS Makin Island, Pac Theatre, 44-46; Asiatic-Pac Campaign Medal with Four Stars; Am Area Campaign Medal; Philippine Liberation Medal with Two Stars; World War II Victory Medal; Presidential Unit Citation Medal. Mem: Am & Idaho Bar Asns; Am Trial Lawyers Asn; Masonic Lodge & Shrine; Am Legion. Relig: Episcopal. Mailing Add: Hailey ID 83333

KRAMER, KEN (R)
Colo State Rep
Mailing Add: 3530 Carousel Lane Colorado Springs CO 80917

KRAMER, LAWRENCE F (R)
Mayor, Paterson, NJ
b Paterson, NJ, Feb 24, 34; s Lawrence F Kramer & Anne Walker K; m 1962 to Mary Ellen Forbes; c Kimberly, Lawrence F, Jr & Patrick Kelly. Polit & Govt Pos: Mayor, Paterson, NJ, 67-72 & 74-; comnr, NJ State Dept of Community Affairs, Trenton, 72-74. Bus & Prof Pos: Owner, Lawrence F Kramer Co, currently. Mailing Add: 155 Market St City Hall Paterson NJ 07505

KRANS, HAMILTON RICHEY, JR (D)
b Middletown, NY, Feb 21, 44; s Hamilton R Krans, Sr & Eulalia Padgett K; m 1972 to Pamela Lilly; c Heather & Hamilton, III. Educ: Dartmouth Col, BA, 66; Univ Miami, JD, 69; Phi Delta Phi; Phi Delta Alpha. Polit & Govt Pos: Deleg, Dem Nat Conv, 72; Dist Attorney, 74- Bus & Prof Pos: Pvt law pract, currently. Mil Serv: NH & Strafford Co Bar Asns. Relig: Methodist. Legal Res: 16 Hamilton St Dover NH 03820 Mailing Add: 595 Central Ave Dover NH 03820

KRANZLER, RICHARD MARTIN (D)
b Farmingdale, NY, Mar 5, 51; s Charles Kranzler & Eva Pines K; m 1956 to Dorothy Ruth Finger; c David Ian, Jean Ann & Susan Jane. Educ: Hofstra Univ, BS, 54; Denver Univ Col Law, JD, 58; Delta Tau; Phi Delta Phi. Polit & Govt Pos: Dist capt, Jefferson Co Dem Party, 62-69; mem exec comt, Arvada Dem Club, 67-72; chmn, Jefferson Co Citizens for Humphrey, 68; mem, Colo State Dem Cent Comt, 69-72; pres, Cent Jefferson Co Dem Club, 70- Bus & Prof Pos: Attorney, 58-64; partner-attorney, Brenman, Ciancio, Rossman & Baum, 64-; bd dirs, Legal Aid Soc, Denver, 70-, pres, 73-; secy, Mile High Child Care Asn, 72- Mil Serv: Entered as Pvt, Army, released as SP-4, 56, after serv in Sch Troops. Mem: Colo, Denver & Adams Co Bar Asns; Am & Colo Trial Lawyers Asns. Relig: Jewish. Mailing Add: 4095 Dudley St Wheatridge CO 80033

KRASKER, ELAINE S (D)
NH State Rep
Mailing Add: Little Harbor Rd Portsmouth NH 03801

KRATZERT, ARTHUR WILLIAM (R)
Chmn, Southington Rep Town Comt, Conn
b Rochester, Pa, Sept 16, 25; s Dr Oscar A Kratzert & Henriette Coombs K; m 1952 to Norma Lanahan; c A Gregg, Eric Oscar, Anne M, Benjamin W & Lauren V. Educ: Oberlin Col, AB, 47; Univ Pittsburgh, BS, 50; Sigma Tau; Beta Theta Pi. Polit & Govt Pos: Councilman, Southington, Conn, 71-73; chmn, Southington Rep Town Comt, Conn, 74- Bus & Prof Pos: Pres, Kratzert, Jones & Assoc, Inc, 63- Mil Serv: Entered as A/S, Navy, 43, released as Lt(jg), 46, after serv in Atlantic & Pac Theatres. Mem: Am Cong Asn of Land Surveyors. Relig: Episcopal. Mailing Add: 121 Summitt Farms Rd Southington CT 06489

KRAUS, ELMER J (R)
Chmn, Hancock Co Rep Cent Comt, Ill
b Nauvoo, Ill, Nov 26, 17; s John A Kraus & Minnie M Bruegger K; m 1940 to Adeline Dorothy Kaiser; c Daniel, Cathy, David, Jon & Deborah. Educ: Local schs. Polit & Govt Pos: Chmn, Tourism Adv Comn, Dept of Bus & Econ Develop, State of Ill, 65-, mem, Gov Adv Coun, 69; Rep precinct committeeman, 66; chmn, Hancock Co Regional Planning Comn, 66-; chmn, Hancock Co Rep Cent Comt, 68- Mem: Ill Hotel & Motel Asn (pres, 64-65, chmn bd, 65-); Robert Morris Col (bd dirs, 70-); Elks; KofC. Relig: Catholic. Mailing Add: Nauvoo IL 62354

KRAUS, VIRGIL L (R)
Idaho State Rep
Mailing Add: 500 North 11th E Mountain Home ID 83647

KRAUSE, ROBERT ALLEN (D)
Iowa State Rep
b Algona, Iowa, Jan 15, 50; s Robert Julius Krause & Rachel Weisbrod K; single. Educ: Univ Iowa, BA, 72; Alpha Tau Omega; pres, Univ Dem. Polit & Govt Pos: Ed-in-chief, Iowa Young Dem, 69-70; field organizer, Fulton for Gov, Iowa, 70; state finance chmn, Doderer for Lt Gov, 70; chmn, Students for Hughes for President, 70-71; state dir, Dollars for Dem, 71; Iowa State Rep, Dist Seven, 73-, chmn transportation comt, Iowa House of Rep, 75-; mem, Iowa Interstate Coop Comn. Mil Serv: Cadet, Army ROTC; 2nd Lt, Res, 1 year; 2nd Lt, Iowa Nat Guard, 74- Mem: Omicron Delta Kappa; Palo Alto Co Hist Soc; Iowa Civil Liberties Union. Mailing Add: Rte 1 Fenton IA 50539

KRAUT, RALPH JOHN (R)
b Chicago, Ill, Nov 24, 08; s Hans Baptiste Kraut (deceased) & Rosa Buchs K (deceased); m 1963 to Virginia Rose Dunn Smith, c Diane (Mrs Edward Matson), Karen (Mrs Daryl Annis) & Hans B. Educ: Univ Wis-Madison, BS in Mech Eng, 30; Tau Beta Pi; Phi Eta Sigma; Pi Tau Sigma; Theta Chi; Scabbard & Blade. Polit & Govt Pos: Chmn, Area Six, Wis Comt for Reelec of the President, 71-72; deleg, Rep Nat Conv, 72. Bus & Prof Pos: Machinist apprentice, Giddings & Lewis, Inc, Fond du Lac, Wis & Cincinnati Milling Mach Co, Cincinnati, Ohio, 25-30; prod engr, A O Smith Corp, Milwaukee, Wis, 30-31; traveling auditor, Gen Elec Co, Schenectady, NY, 31-35; chmn bd, Giddings & Lewis, Inc, Fond du Lac, Wis, 35-, chief exec officer, 35-72, consult & dir, 72-; dir, Great Northern Nekoosa Corp, Twin Disc, Inc, Harnischfeger Corp, Employers of Wausau, M&I Marshall & Ilsley Bank, Goldberg-Emerman Corp & Giddings & Lewis-Fraser, Ltd, Scotland, 48- Mil Serv: Entered as 2nd Lt, Army Res, 30, released as Lt Col, 45, after serv in 6th Inf Div, Southwest Pac, 44-45; Bronze Arrow; Philippine Liberation, Asiatic Pacific Ribbons. Publ: Many trade paper & mag articles in Bus Week, Am Machinist, Metalworking News & others, 46- Mem: Nat Mach Tool Builders Asn; Soc of Mech Engrs; Am Mgt Asn; Chief Execs Forum; Tuscumbia Country Club. Honors & Awards: Eng Alumni Award, Univ Wis. Relig: Protestant. Mailing Add: 545 Illinois Ave Green Lake WI 54941

KREAMER, ROBERT MCDONALD (R)
Iowa State Rep
b Sioux City, Iowa, Jan 5, 41; s Floyd W Kreamer & Helen E McDonald K; m 1964 to Charlotte Anne Hooker; c Todd Allan, Bradley McDonald & Andrew Robert. Educ: Univ Iowa, BA, 63; Univ Iowa Law Sch, JD, 66; Phi Kappa Psi; Phi Delta Phi. Polit & Govt Pos: Iowa State Rep, 69-, asst majority floor leader, Iowa House of Rep, 71-72 & 75-, Pres Pro Tempore, 73- Bus & Prof Pos: Attorney, Gamble, Reipe, Martin & Webster, Des Moines, Iowa, 66-69; trust off, First Fed State Bank, 69-70; attorney, Whitfield, Musgrave, Selvy, Kelly & Eddy, Des Moines, Iowa, 70- Mem: Polk Co Bar Asn; YMCA; Big Bros Am; Young Rep of Iowa; Westminster United Presby Church Men's Club. Relig: Presbyterian; Elder, Westminster United Presby Church. Mailing Add: 4705 Beavercrest Dr Des Moines IA 50310

KREBS, CAROLINE WAGNER (D)
VChairperson, Jefferson Co Dem Exec Comt, Ky
b Indianapolis, Ind, Sept 25, 30; d Charles E Wagner & Eleanor Guerin W; m 1953 to Thomas G Krebs; c Marie, Dorothy, Thomas, Jr, Theresa & Charlotte. Educ: Trinity Col, BA, 52; Univ Ky, MA, 67. Polit & Govt Pos: Vchairperson, Jefferson Co Dem Exec Comt, 48th Legis Dist, Ky, 74- Bus & Prof Pos: Instr social sci, Eastern Ky Univ, 66-70; instr hist, Univ Louisville, 70-71; asst prof polit sci, Bellarmine Col, 71- Mem: New Directions, Inc (treas, 73-75); Ky Humanities Coun (vchairperson, 74-75); Peace & Justice Comn (chairperson, 74-75); Citizens Adv Group, Jefferson Co. Mailing Add: 19 Pawnee Trail Louisville KY 40207

KREBS, IRENE MORRIS (R)
Secy, Canyon Co Rep Cent Comt, Idaho
b Logan, Iowa, Sept 6, 17; d Arville Greenfield Morris & Dora Heim M; m 1941 to Carl T Krebs; c Sandra (Mrs Dulin), Larry C & Jerry M. Educ: Whitney Col Com, 37; Inst of Certifying Secy, cert, 61. Polit & Govt Pos: Attache, Idaho State Legis, 39; dep clerk, Third Judicial Dist, Caldwell, Idaho, 59-67; secy, Canyon Co Rep Cent Comt, 67- Bus & Prof Pos: Mem staff, Idaho Compensation Co, Coeur d'Alene & Boise, Idaho, 38-43; secy, First Christian Church, Caldwell, 51-59; cert prof secy, Alexanderson, Davis, Rainey & Whitney, 67- Mem: Nat Secy Asn; Nat Asn Legal Secy; Soroptimist Am (off rec secy, 75-). Relig: Christian. Mailing Add: 314 W Beech St Caldwell ID 83605

KREBS, JOHN HANS (D)
US Rep, Calif
b Berlin, Ger, Dec 17, 26; m 1956 to Hanna; c Daniel Scott & Karen Barbara. Educ: Univ Calif, Berkeley, AB, 50; Univ Calif Hastings Col Law, LLB, 57. Polit & Govt Pos: Chmn, Fresno Co Dem Cent Comt, Calif, formerly; mem, Fresno Co Planning Comn, 65-69; mem, Fresno Co Bd Supvrs, 70-74, chmn, 73; US Rep, Calif, 75- Bus & Prof Pos: Attorney. Mil Serv: Army, 52-54. Mem: Am Cancer Soc; Fresno Co Bar Asn. Legal Res: 1383 West Sample Fresno CA 03705 Mailing Add: US House Rep Washington DC 20515

KREEGER, GEORGE H (D)
Ga State Rep
b Atlanta, Ga, July 6, 41; s George W Kreeger; single. Educ: Univ Ga, BSEd, 63 & JD, 66; Sigma Pi; Phi Delta Phi. Polit & Govt Pos: Ga State Rep, 69- Bus & Prof Pos: Partner, Law Firm, Tate & Kreeger, Marietta, Ga. Mil Serv: S/Sgt, Ga Air Nat Guard. Mem: Optimist Int; Jaycees; Am Legion. Relig: Methodist. Mailing Add: 3500 Lee St Smyrna GA 30080

KREMER, ARTHUR JEROME (D)
NY State Assemblyman
b Bronx, NY, May 27, 35; s Charles Kremer & Dorothy Wender K; m 1960 to Barbara Schatz; c Nora & Robin. Educ: NY Univ, 3 years; Brooklyn Law Sch, LLB. Polit & Govt Pos: Corp counsel, City of Long Beach, NY, 60-65; NY State Assemblyman, 66-, chmn comt corps, authorities & comns, NY State Assembly, currently. Bus & Prof Pos: Attorney-at-law, 58- Mem: NY State Defenders Asn; Nassau Co Lawyers Asn; Kiwanis Club of Long Beach; Elks; Mason. Honors & Awards: Americanism Award, Am Legion; Man of the Year, Cancer Care; Torch of Freedom Award, B'nai B'rith. Relig: Hebrew. Mailing Add: 605 E State St Long Beach NY 11561

KREMER, MAURICE A (R)
Nebr State Sen
b Milford, Nebr, Aug 31, 07; m 1932 to Alice M Troyer; c Kenneth D, Robert M, Ardys Ann (Mrs Rozhart), Beth Lorraine. Educ: Farm Operators Col of Agr, Lincoln, Nebr. Polit & Govt Pos: Nebr State Sen, 62-; mem & pres, Aurora Sch Bd; Hamilton Co Exten Bd; chmn, Hamilton Co Irrigation Bd. Bus & Prof Pos: Farmer; partner, Farmade Inc, Aurora, Nebr. Mem: Chaplain, Gideons; bd of dir, State Dairymen's Asn; Aurora CofC; Gideons Int (state pres). Mailing Add: 1415 Seventh St Aurora NE 68818

KREMKOSKI, JOE E (R)
Nat Committeeman, Wis Fedn Young Rep
b Racine, Wis, Dec 28, 49; s Lewis E Kremkoski & Sue M Claussen K; m 1971 to Janet Margaret Matyas. Educ: Carroll Col, BS, 72; Marquette Univ Law Sch, 73-; Student Bar Asn; Phi Alpha Delta; Phi Alpha Theta. Polit & Govt Pos: Mem exec comt, Racine Co Rep Party, Wis, 71-; chmn, First Dist Young Rep, 72-74; mem exec bd, Wis Fedn Young Rep, 72-, nat committeeman, 74-; alderman, Common Coun, Racine, 73- Mailing Add: 1811 Clayton Ave Racine WI 53404

KRESS, STANLEY ROBERT (D)
Idaho State Sen
b American Falls, Idaho, Oct 25, 43; s Raymond Virgil Kress & Fawn Bean K; m 1962 to Carolyn Faye Roberts; c Maria, Robert, David & Mark. Educ: Brigham Young Univ, BS, 65; Idaho State Univ, MEd, 69. Polit & Govt Pos: Idaho State Sen, Dist 27, 74- Bus & Prof Pos: Teacher, Spanish Fork, Utah, 65-66; counr & coach, Firth High Sch, Idaho, 66-67; jr high prin, Soda Springs, 67-69; sch supt, Clark Co, 69-71 & Firth Sch Dist, 71- Mem: Supt Asn (pres, Sixth & Seventh Dist); Interscholastics Asn (pres, Sixth & Seventh Dist); Farm Bur. Relig: Latter-day Saint. Mailing Add: PO Box 5 Firth ID 83236

KRET, DONALD BRUCE (D)
Chairperson, Walworth Co Dem Party, Wis
b Cudahy, Wis, July 5, 36; s John Charles Kret & Dorothy Rose Beier K; m 1967 to Theda Mae Immega; c John Steven & Robert Joseph. Educ: St Thomas High Sch, Rockford, Ill, grad, 54. Polit & Govt Pos: Mem exec bd, Walworth Co Dem Party, Wis, 68-, chairperson, 74-; mem, State Dem Statutory Cent Comt, 68-70; deleg, Dem Nat Mid-Term Conf, 74; mem exec bd, Dem Party Wis, 74- Bus & Prof Pos: Clerk, Badger Paint Stores, Rockford Ill & Delavan, Wis, 54-55; stock clerk, Nat Food Store, Delavan, Wis, 56-61; machine operator, Borg Textiles, Delavan, 62-69; staff rep, Midwest Dept, ILGWU, 69- Mem: Walworth Co Labor Coun, AFL-CIO. Mailing Add: Rte 4 Box 354 Delavan WI 53115

KRETCHMER, JEROME (D)
b Bronx, NY, Sept 15, 34; s Charles Kretchmer & Mollie Denerstein K; m 1960 to Dorothy Steinfeld; c Stephanie Lisa, Andrea Gail & Laurence Adam. Educ: NY Univ, BA, 55; Columbia Univ, LLB, 58. Polit & Govt Pos: NY State Assemblyman, 63-70; adminr, Environ Protection Admin, New York, 70-73; alt deleg, Dem Nat Conv, 72; spec counsel to Minority Leader, NY State Senate, 75- Bus & Prof Pos: Partner, Olshan, Grundman, Frome & Kretchmer, New York, 64- Mem: NY State Bar Asn; Pub Works Asn. Legal Res: 262 Central Park W New York NY 10024 Mailing Add: 90 Park Ave New York NY 10016

KRETSCHMAR, WILLIAM EDWARD (R)
NDak State Rep
b St Paul, Minn, Aug 21, 33; s William Emanuel Kretschmar & Frances Peterson K; single. Educ: Col St Thomas, BS, 54; Univ Minn, Minneapolis, LLB, 61; Phi Delta Phi. Polit & Govt Pos: Rep precinct committeeman, Venturia Precinct Ten, NDak, 66-74; dist secy, 30th Dist Rep Party, 67-; deleg, NDak Const Conv, 71-72; NDak State Rep, 72- Bus & Prof Pos: Partner in law firm, Kretschmar & Kretschmar, Ashley, NDak, 62- Mem: Third Judicial Dist Bar Asn; State Bar Asn NDak; Am Bar Asn; Ashley Lions Club; Aberdeen Elks. Relig: Catholic. Mailing Add: Box A Venturia ND 58489

KREUTZ, JAMES KIRK (R)
Treas, Colo State Rep Party
b Racine, Wis, Jan 2, 40; s George Curry Kreutz & Ethel Irene Coy K; m 1963 to Martha Jean Hill; c Julie Kristine & Sara Elizabeth. Educ: Colo State Univ, BS, 63; S Tex Col Law, JD, 67; Phi Alpha Delta; Sigma Phi Epsilon. Polit & Govt Pos: Finance chmn, Denver Co Rep Party, Colo, 69-70; Asst Attorney Gen, State of Colo, 69-; co-chmn cong campaign, Congressman J D McKevitt, 70; secy, Colo State Rep Party, 71-74, treas, 72- Mem: Denver & Colo Bar Asns; 12000 Club; Rep Assocs of Colo (dir, 70-); Jaycees. Relig: Protestant. Mailing Add: 3200 S Holly Denver CO 80222

KRIEGER, GREGORY HAWTHORNE (R)
Chmn, Brookings Co Rep Party, SDak
b DeSmet, SDak, May 8, 54; s George Hawthorne Krieger & Evelyn Romundstad K; m 1973 to Karen Jo Ham. Educ: Augustana Col, 72-73; SDak State Univ, BS in Econ, 76; Econ Club. Polit & Govt Pos: Secy-treas, Augustana Col Young Rep, SDak, 72-73; chmn, SDak State Univ Young Rep, 74-75; secy-treas, SDak Young Rep, 74-; chmn, Brookings Co Rep Party, 75- Honors & Awards: Outstanding State Teen-age Rep Boy, SDak Young Rep, 72. Relig: Am Lutheran. Mailing Add: 1422 E Eighth St Brookings SD 57006

KRIEKARD, HAROLD EDWARD (R)
Chmn, Alger Co Rep Party, Mich
b Kalamazoo, Mich, Oct 31, 12; s Edward C Kriekard & Nellie Gideon K; m 1938 to Marjorie Frances Wilson; c Thomas E, John A & Daniel J. Educ: Kalamazoo Col, BA; Inst of Paper Chem, 1 year, Sigma Rho Sigma; K Club. Polit & Govt Pos: Chmn, Alger Co Rep Party, Mich, 69-73 & 75- Bus & Prof Pos: Planning & materials supt, Kimberly-Clark, Niagara, Wis, 53-63, mgr & packaging specialist, Neenah, 63-65 & mgr admin serv, Munising, Mich, 66- Mem: Rotary; Boy Scouts (coun pres, 64-65). Relig: Episcopal. Mailing Add: Sand Point Rd Munising MI 49862

KRISTENSEN, LUTHER M (D)
NDak State Rep
b Ryder, NDak, Mar 7, 32; s Rev Elias Kristensen & Inga Bjorngjeld K; m 1950 to Marilyn Peterson; c Suzan, Thomas, Terrance, Mark, Karen & Jane. Educ: Valley City State Col, BS, 54; NDak State Univ, 59-61; Pi Omega Pi. Polit & Govt Pos: NDak State Rep, 74-, mem, Transportation Comt & State & Fed Govt Comt, NDak Legis, currently. Bus & Prof Pos: Bus instr & coach, Campbell Pub Schs, 54-57; bus instr, Starbuck Pub Schs, 57-62; rep, Horace Mann Educators, 62-; owner & mgr, Tree Movers Inc, NDak, 66- Mem: Elks; Sertoma (bd dirs, 74-75); Campus Ministry of NDak (pres, 72-); Gideons; NDak Sch Serv Asn (exec secy, 70-). Relig: Lutheran. Mailing Add: 914 21st Ave S Fargo ND 58102

KRITES, VANCE RICHARD (D)
b Wooster, Ohio, Nov 18, 42; s Adrian Victor Krites (deceased) & Irene Kirkman K; single. Educ: Kent State Univ, BA, 64; Cent Mich Univ, MA, 69; Univ WVa, summers 71, 72 & 74. Polit & Govt Pos: Publicity dir, Armstrong Co Dem Party, Pa, 73-, regist chmn, 74-; committeeman, Applewold Borough, 74-; alt deleg, Dem Mid-Term Conf, 74. Bus & Prof Pos: Teacher & coach, Mansfield Madison Sr High Sch, Ohio, 66-70. Mem: Am Polit Sci Asn; Am Econ Asn; Eagles; F&AM (32 degree). Honors & Awards: Cenith Alliance Award, 64. Relig: United Church of Christ. Legal Res: 307 Ridge Ave Kittanning PA 16201 Mailing Add: PO Box 262 Kittanning PA 16201

KROEGER, NADINE CLARA (D)
b Hays, Kans, Apr 3, 24; d Pete A Burbach & Minnie Tilton B; m 1964 to Lawrence Kroeger; c Patricia (Mrs Gerald Schremner), Terry, Randall, Lonnie & Jacquelyn Claycamp, Douglas & Gary Kroeger. Educ: Ft Hays Kans State Col, 2 years; YWCA. Polit & Govt Pos: Co assessor, Trego Co, Kans, 62-69; vchmn, Trego Co Dem Party, formerly. Bus & Prof Pos: Owner retail gas bus, Kans, 44-64; nurse's aide, Trego Lake Mem Hosp, 64-69. Publ: Epsilon Sigma Alpha sorority, Wichita Eagle-Beacon Paper, Kans, 69; articles in Western Kans World. Mem: Rebekah (past Noble Grand); Epsilon Sigma Alpha; Girl Scouts; Trego Co Tuberc Asn (chmn); Cub Scouts. Relig: Lutheran; past pres ladies orgn, secy, currently. Mailing Add: 121 S Sixth WaKeeney KS 67672

KROENING, CARL (DFL)
Minn State Rep
Mailing Add: 3539 Vincent Ave N Minneapolis MN 55412

KROGH, LEE VINCENT (DFL)
b St Paul, Minn, Apr 15, 33; s Leo Hjalmer Krogh & Della Glomski K; m 1958 to Margaret Mary Anderson; c Mark Antony, Ross Gregory, Michael Lee & Steven Edward. Educ: Winona State Col, BS, 55; Mankato State Col, MS, 61; Kappa Delta Pi. Polit & Govt Pos: Chmn, Otter Tail Co Bergland for Cong, Otter Tail Co Dem-Farmer-Labor Party, Minn, fall 70, publicity officer, 70- Bus & Prof Pos: Instr Eng & theatre, Fergus Falls State Jr Col, Minn, 61- Mem: Minn State Jr Col Faculty Asn; Minn Educ Asn; Nat Faculty Orgn. Relig: Catholic. Mailing Add: 1217 Somerset Rd Fergus Falls MN 56537

KROGSENG, DAVID NEIL (R)
b Duluth, Minn, June 16, 36; s Peter Torlaf Krogseng & Esther Stormoen K; m 1958 to Joan Johnson; c Pamela Diane, Julianne Joan & Marisa Esther. Educ: Univ Minn, BA in Polit Sci & Hist, 58, grad sch; Phoenix Soc; Grey Friars Soc; Order of Gopher. Polit & Govt Pos: Dir research, Minn Rep Party, 58-64; dir research, William E Miller Vice Presidential Campaign, 64; asst dir research, Rep Nat Comt, 64-65; admin asst to US Rep Clark MacGregor, Minn, 65-71; admin asst to US Rep Bill Frenzel, Minn, 71-72; chmn, Minn Rep State Cent Comt, 71-72. Publ: State Political Research Manual, Rep Nat Comt, 65. Mem: US Capitol & Minn Hist Socs; Minn Alumni Asn; Rep Workshop Minn. Relig: Lutheran. Mailing Add: 4406 Sunnyside Rd Minneapolis MN 55424

KRONFELD, LEOPOLD JAMES (D)
b Hartford, Conn, Sept 5, 41; s Alexander Kronfeld & Mae Blumenthal K; single. Educ: Syracuse Univ, AB, 63; Univ Hartford, MEd, 67; Cornell Univ Law Sch, LLB, 68. Polit & Govt Pos: Legis asst to US Rep Robert Leggett, Calif, 68-69; admin asst to US Rep Jeffery Cohelan, Calif, 70-71; spec counsel, US House of Rep Foreign Opers & Govt Info Subcomt, 71- Relig: Jewish. Mailing Add: 58 Craigmoor Rd West Hartford CT 06107

KROPP, PAUL K (R)
Mont State Rep
Mailing Add: Box 520 Malta MT 59538

KROUT, HOMER LEE (R)
b Davis, WVa, Sept 2, 17; s Curtis H Krout & Nora Blanche Alderton K; m 1948 to Doris Langman; c John C, David A (deceased) & Robert K. Educ: Univ Ala, BS, 51; Phi Eta Sigma; Beta Gamma Sigma; Omicron Delta Kappa; Pi Kappa Phi. Polit & Govt Pos: Mem campaign comt for US Rep Joel T Broyhill, Va, 52-, admin asst, 54-; comt chmn & comt mem various positions, Arlington Co Rep Party & Tenth Dist Rep Party, 52-; mem campaign comt for various co bd cand; mem rules comt, Va Rep State Conv, 68 & 69, chmn, 70-71; app mem, Arlington Co Sch Bd, 70-, chmn, 71-72. Bus & Prof Pos: Purchasing agent, M T Broyhill & Sons, Realtors, Arlington, Va, 51, subcontracts asst, 52, personnel officer, 53, off mgr, 54. Mil Serv: Entered as Airman, Royal Can Air Force, 41, released as Cpl, 43, after serv in Royal Air Force Bomber Squadron, Eng; transferred to US Air Force, as Sgt, released as Warrant Officer, 45. Mem: Lyon Village Civic Asn; YMCA (bd dirs, adv bd); Boy Scouts Am (scout officer). Honors & Awards: Distinguished Serv Award, Tenth Dist Chap Va DAV, 64. Relig: Baptist. Mailing Add: 1605 N Johnson St Arlington VA 22201

KROUT, JOHN D (R)
Mayor, York, Pa
b Spring Grove, Pa, Nov 15, 37; s Russell S Krout & Bessie M Diehl K; m 1956 to Polly A Graybill; c Steven M, Stephanie L & Scott A. Educ: Dover Area High Sch, grad, 55. Polit & Govt Pos: Mem city coun, York, Pa, 71-74, mayor, 74- Bus & Prof Pos: Owner, Krout Ins, York, Pa, 65- Mem: Mason; Elks; York Toastmasters; CofC; Rotary. Relig: Lutheran. Mailing Add: 623 W Princess St York PA 17404

KRUCKENBURG, HOMER ANDREW (D)
Chmn, Barton Co Dem Comt, Kans
b Great Bend, Kans, Feb 7, 37; s Herman A Kruckenburg & Margaret Hill K; m 1957 to LaVon Graham; c Gretchen, Kaydene, Kyle & John. Educ: Kans State Univ, BA, 59, MA, 63; Kans Univ, summer fel, 65; DePauw Univ, summer fel, 64; Phi Alpha Theta; Young Dem; Polit Sci Club. Polit & Govt Pos: Deleg, Dem Nat Conv, 72; mem, Kans State Dem Comt, 72-; chmn, Barton Co Dem Comt, 72- Bus & Prof Pos: Mem, United Duroc Swine Registry, 70- Mil Serv: Entered as Pvt, Army, 55, released as Cpl, 56, after serv in Anti Air Craft, North Mich-Canada. Publ: Early development of Kansas co-op elevators, Co-op Consumers Asn, 63; Written expressions of a concerned Democrat, Hutchinson News Series, 64-74. Mem: Harry Truman Library Asn; Am Civil Liberties Union; Farmers Union; Penn Jones-Asn Inquiry Study Group (charter mem); Kans Hist Soc. Honors & Awards: Guest speaker on Warren Comn Whitewash to Kans chap, Nat Coun Teachers Eng, 75; Guest Speaker on Hogs & Politics, Kans Asn Sec Sch Prin, 73. Relig: Lutheran. Legal Res: 1604 Monroe Great Bend KS 67530 Mailing Add: Rte 4 Great Bend KS 67530

KRUEGER, CLIFFORD W (R)
Wis State Sen
b Madison, Wis, June 24, 18. Educ: Merrill Commercial Col. Polit & Govt Pos: Alderman, Merrill, Wis, formerly; Wis State Sen, 46-54 & 56-; mem exec comt, Wis Rep Party, currently. Bus & Prof Pos: Sales Mgr. Mailing Add: 122 N State St Merrill WI 54452

KRUEGER, CULP (D)
b Riesel, Tex, June 8, 13; s Louis Adolph Krueger & Minnie Lee Culp K; m 1936 to Evelyn Smidt; c Cay. Educ: Univ Tex; Houston Night Law Sch; Radio & Jour Clubs. Polit & Govt Pos: Mem, Tex State Dem Exec Comt, 52-56; Tex State Sen, 15th Dist, 56-67, Pres Pro-Tempore, Tex State Sen, 62; regional coordr for Johnson & adv man for Kennedy-Johnson, 60; Acting Lt Gov, Tex, 62, Acting Gov, 62; regional coordr for eight states, Johnson-Humphrey Campaign, 64; former chmn, Pollution, Multiple Use Study, Tex Waters. Bus & Prof Pos: Dist supvr, Tex Unemploy Comn, 37-41; partner, Smidt-Krueger Motors, 46-54; pres, Radio Sta KULP, 46-68; publ, El Campo Leader-Sooboda News, 55-68; pres, Culp Krueger Real Estate, Inc & partner, Black Jak Farms, currently; pres, Pot-Belly Realty Co, currently; pres, First State Bank, Louise, Tex, 71- Mil Serv: Entered as Pvt, Army, 43, released as 1st Lt, 46, after serv in Cavalry, Pac Theater; Four Battle Stars. Mem: Sigma Delta Chi; Am Legion; VFW; Elks; Boy Scouts. Honors & Awards: Eagle Scout, 32. Relig: Catholic. Mailing Add: 908 Georgia St El Campo TX 77437

KRUEGER, JOHN WILLIAM (R)
Mem, Oneida Co Rep Exec Comt, Wis
b Marinette, Wis, Feb 7, 30; s Jesse A Krueger & Beulah Elwood K; m 1957 to Phyllis Evancheck; c Jess W, Eric John & Susan Elizabeth. Educ: Univ Wis-Madison, BS, 52, Law Sch, JD, 55; Phi Delta Phi. Polit & Govt Pos: City attorney, Rhinelander, Wis, 58-68; mem,

Oneida Co Rep Exec Comt, 59-; chmn, Oneida Co Rep Party, 66-71. Bus & Prof Pos: Partner, Krueger & Krueger, Attorneys-at-Law, 57- Mem: Am & Wis State Bar Asns; Oneida Co Bar Asn; Seventh Judicial Circuit Bar Asn; Am Trial Lawyers Asn. Relig: Lutheran. Mailing Add: Rte 3 Rhinelander WI 54501

KRUEGER, PHILLIP H (D)
Treas, Wash State Dem Cent Comt
b Ottumwa, Iowa, Nov 29, 27; s Julius Phillip Krueger & Hazel Morehouse K; m 1949 to Karol Jean Hawver; c Robin Lee & Jeffrey Phillip. Educ: Ill & Iowa sch systs; attend, Bellevue Community Col. Polit & Govt Pos: Treas, Wash State Dem Cent Comt, 75- Bus & Prof Pos: Numerical control analyst, Boeing Airplane Co, 65-; pres local C, IAMAW, 72- Mem: Mason; Dist 751 Aeromechanics Union (pres local lodge C & chmn legis comt); Wash State Machinist Coun (secy legis comt). Relig: Protestant. Mailing Add: 1333 Sunset Ave SW Seattle WA 98116

KRUEGER, ROBERT CHARLES (D)
US Rep, Tex
b New Braunfels, Tex, Sept 19, 35; s Arlon E Krueger & Faye Leifeste K; single. Educ: Southern Methodist Univ, BA, 57; Duke Univ, MA, 58; Oxford Univ, Merton Col, BLitt & DPhil, 64; Phi Beta Kappa. Polit & Govt Pos: US Rep, 21st Dist, Tex, 75- Bus & Prof Pos: Assoc prof Eng & vprovost & dean arts & sci, Duke Univ, 61-73; chmn bd, Comal Hosiery Mills, New Braunfels, Tex, 73- Publ: The Poems of Sir John Davies, Oxford Univ, 75. Mem: Am Mkt Asn; Mod Lang Asn; Lions Int; Optimist; WTex CofC. Relig: Protestant. Legal Res: New Braunfels TX 78130 Mailing Add: 512 Cannon House Off Bldg Washington DC 20515

KRUEGER, ROBERT WILLIAM (R)
b Philadelphia, Pa, Nov 16, 16; s Robert Henry Krueger & Frieda Lehmann K; m 1941 to Marjorie Evelyn Jones; c Arlene R (Mrs Reher) & Diane L. Educ: Univ Calif, Los Angeles, AB, 37, MA, 38, PhD in Physics, 42; Phi Delta Kappa; Mason. Polit & Govt Pos: Head various Rep precinct orgn, Calif Rep Assemblies & cong campaign comts, 49-69; pres, 60th Dist Calif Rep Assembly, 50-52; area chmn, 59th Dist Rep Precinct Orgn, 51-61; mem, 59th Dist Rep Cent Comt, 56-61, chmn, 58-61; chmn, 59th Dist Rep Coord Coun, 58-61; pres, 59th Dist Calif Rep Assembly, 58-61; campaign chmn, Robert S Stevens for 60th Assembly, 62; mem, Rep State Cent Comt Calif, 62-72; campaign chmn, Paul Priolo for 60th Assembly, 66; mem, Rep Assocs & Rep Nat Assocs, 68- Bus & Prof Pos: Research physicist, Douglas Aircraft, 42-46; asst chief missiles div, Rand Corp, Los Angeles, 46-53; pres, Planning Research Corp, 54-73; pres, Prof Servs Int, 73- Mem: Am Phys Soc; Opers Research Soc Am; Inst Mgt Sci; Los Angeles & Calif State CofC. Relig: Protestant. Mailing Add: 1016 Moraga Dr Los Angeles CA 90049

KRUEGER, VERNON H (R)
b Blue Hill, Nebr, July 26, 23; s Hugo Krueger & Johanna Vanboening K; m 1945 to Marcylene A Rasser; c Janice (Mrs K Budde) & Tom R. Educ: Kearney State Col, 2 years; Washburn Univ, 1 semester; Okla State Univ, 1 semester. Polit & Govt Pos: Precinct committeeman, Webster Co Rep Orgn, Nebr, 52-58, secy, 58-66, chmn, formerly. Bus & Prof Pos: Dir & secy, Farmers Union Gas & Oil, 52-61; dir & chmn, Farmers Union Coop, 58-64, Agri-Serv Inc, 60-64; dir, Cent Voc Col, 67-69. Mil Serv: Entered as A/S, Navy, 42, released as AETM/2, 45, after serv in VB 7, Pac Theatre. Mem: VFW; Am Legion; Lions. Relig: Lutheran. Mailing Add: Box 346 Red Cloud NE 68970

KRUEGER, YVONNE (R)
Chmn, Osborne Co Rep Cent Comt, Kans
b Luray, Kans, June 24, 11; d Clyde S Paschal & Martha Blanche Robinson P; m 1929 to Harold Roy Krueger; c Roy Rand, Thomas Henry, Marilyn (Mrs Bob Chesney), Cynthia, Pamela (Mrs Gary Miller) & Sylvia (Mrs Ken Havner). Educ: Luray High Sch, grad, 29. Polit & Govt Pos: Committeewoman, Rep Party, 46-69; dir, Natoma Bd of Educ, 54-57, treas, 60-63; deleg, Rep Nat Conv, 60; Natoma rep, Co Sch Unification Bd, 64-65; vchmn, Osborne Co Rep Cent Comt, Kans, 52-68, chmn, 66- Mem: Eastern Star (Worthy Matron, 54); Order of Rainbow for Girls (Mother Adv, 64); Self Cult Club; Grand Cross of Colors; Harmony Study Club. Relig: United Methodist. Mailing Add: Natoma KS 67651

KRUGER, JOHN W (R)
Chmn, Pulaski Co Rep Party, Ind
b Winamac, Ind, Aug 6, 13; s Will K Kruger & Letitia K; m 1941 to Marceil F Owen; c Katherine (Mrs Kiesling). Educ: Winamac High Sch, grad, 31. Polit & Govt Pos: Bd trustees, Winamac, Ind, 55-63, co comnr, Pulaski Co, 63-; chmn, Pulaski Co Rep Party, 63- Mil Serv: S/Sgt, Army, 42, released, 45, after serv in 24th Air Serv Command, SPac, 43-45. Mem: Amvets; Shrine; Am Legion; Mason; VFW. Relig: Presbyterian. Mailing Add: 308 S Riverside Dr Winamac IN 46996

KRUGLICK, BURTON S (R)
Chmn, Ariz State Rep Finance Comt
b Chicago, Ill, May 23, 25; s Joseph Kruglick (deceased); wid; c Arthur, Janice & Jacqueline. Polit & Govt Pos: Chmn, Ariz State Rep Finance Comt, currently; mem, Rep Nat Finance Comt, currently; deleg, Rep Nat Conv, 72. Relig: Jewish. Legal Res: 6442 E Camelback Rd Scottsdale AZ 85251 Mailing Add: 3300 N Central Ave Suite 300 Phoenix AZ 85012

KRULL, JACOB EDWARD (D)
SDak State Sen
b Sibley, Iowa, Jan 13, 09; s Jacob Sebastin Krull & Lina Poppen K; m 1932 to Katherine DeBerg; c Darlene Jean (Mrs Norman Olson), Kay Irene, Mary Ann (Mrs William S Ricker), Darrell Lee & Jacob James. Educ: Munger Pub Sch, 8 years; Nat Rural Coop Mgr Inst, grad. Polit & Govt Pos: Mem, Munger Sch Bd, 32-36; mem, Foley Sch Bd, 38-56; SDak State Rep, Codington Co, 60-62; chmn, Codington Co Dem Party, 64-68; SDak State Sen, 75- Bus & Prof Pos: Agt, Farmers Union Ins, Watertown, SDak, 60-; mem & treas bd, East River Elec Asn, 68-70. Mem: Watertown Coop Elevator Bd; East River Elec Bd; Lions; Farmers Union. Relig: Congregational; mem church bd, 58-67. Mailing Add: Rte 3 Watertown SD 57201

KRUMBHAAR, GEORGE DOUGLAS, JR (R)
b Boston, Mass, Aug 17, 36; s George Douglas Krumbhaar & Catherine Cole K (deceased), stepmother, Ruth Sears Cheney K; m 1965 to Elizabeth Jane Pratt; c Ruth Stevens & Frederick William. Educ: Harvard Col, AB, 58; Johns Hopkins Univ Sch of Int Studies, Washington, DC & Bologna, Italy, MA, 63; Columbia Univ Law Sch, LLB, 66; Fly Club; Varsity Club. Polit & Govt Pos: Attorney-adv, Off Gen Counsel, Treas Dept, 66-69; minority counsel, Joint Econ Comt, US Cong, 69- Mil Serv: Entered as Pvt, E-1, Army, 58, released as 1st Lt, 61, after serv in 2nd Armored Cavalry, Europe, 59-61. Mem: Fed Bar Asn; Nat Economists Club; Children's Hosp (campaign comt); Friendship House Educ Prog. Relig: Episcopal. Mailing Add: 3743 Upton St NW Washington DC 20016

KRUP, WILLIAM HENRY (D)
b Washington, Ind, Sept 3, 07; s Henry John Krup & Eva Belle Hembree K; single. Educ: Ind Univ, 34; course diesel eng, Madison, Wis. Polit & Govt Pos: Mem, Elec Bd, Ind, 60-69; chmn, Daviess Co Dem Party, formerly; mem, Daviess Co Elec Bd, 70- Bus & Prof Pos: Owner, tire & super sta, 28; mem staff, Eng Dept, Baltimore & Ohio RR, 38-56; real estate broker, 55-; own & operate apt house & rentals. Mil Serv: Entered as M/Sgt, Army, 42-46, serv in 331 Med Regt & I R T C, Camp Forrest, Tenn. Relig: Catholic. Mailing Add: 105 E Walnut St Washington IN 47501

KRUPA, JOHN GEORGE (D)
b East Chicago, Ind, July 21, 16; s John Krupa & Edith Zuba K; m 1948 to Lee Ann Jacobs; c Kathleen Louise, Marilyn Ann & Sandra Lee. Educ: Ind Univ Exten. Polit & Govt Pos: Chief dep clerk, Lake Co, Ind, 48-63; chmn, Lake Co Dem Cent Comt, 62-72; clerk, Lake Co Circuit Court, Ind, 64-72; sustaining mem, Nat Dem Party; gen supt, Dept Water Works, East Chicago, 72-; chief aide to Mayor Robert A Pastrick, currently. Mil Serv: Entered as Pvt, Air Force, 44, released as Cpl, 46. Mem: Ind Asn Co Clerks (state pres, 67-); Elks; Am Legion; Kiwanis; Moose. Relig: Roman Catholic. Legal Res: 5611 Northcote Ave East Chicago IN 46312 Mailing Add: 400 E Chicago Ave East Chicago IN 46312

KRUPSAK, MARY ANNE (D)
Lt Gov, NY
b Schenectady, NY, Mar 26, 32; d Ambrose M Krupsak & Mary Regina Wytrwal K; m 1969 to Edwin Margolis. Educ: Univ Rochester, BA in hist; Boston Univ, MS in pub commun; Univ Chicago Law Sch, JD, 62; Theta Eta; Marsiens. Hon Degrees: LHD, Russell Sage Col, 73. Polit & Govt Pos: Prog & legis aide to former Gov W Averell Harriman, NY, 55-58; admin asst to Rep Samuel S Stratton, 59; asst counsel to Pres Pro Tempore of NY Senate, 65-66; asst counsel to Speaker of Assembly, 65-68; NY State Assemblyman, 104th Assembly Dist, 68-72; deleg, Dem Nat Conv, 72; NY State Sen, 72-74; Lt Gov, NY, 75- Mem: NY State Bar; Bar of the City of New York; Amsterdam Bus & Prof Women's Club; Montgomery Co chap, Am Asn Univ Women; Emblem Club. Relig: Roman Catholic. Mailing Add: Shaper Ave Extension Canajoharie NY 13317

KRUSE, DEAN VERL (R)
Chmn, DeKalb Co Rep Comt, Ind
b Auburn, Ind, Sept 21, 41; s Russell W Kruse & Luella Boger K; m 1960 to Carol Ann Yoder; c Mitchell Dean & Stuart Allan. Educ: LaSalle Law Sch. Polit & Govt Pos: Organizer, DeKalb Co TAR, Ind; deleg, Ind State Rep Conv, 60, 62 & 64; caucus chmn, Rep Nat Conv, 62 & 64 & deleg, 64; mem, Ind State Rep Policy Comt, 66-67; mem, Electoral Col, 68; Rep precinct committeeman, formerly; chmn, DeKalb Co Rep Comt, 62-; chmn, Fourth Dist Cong Rep Comt, formerly; mem, Ind State Rep Cent Comt, formerly; Ind State Sen, formerly. Bus & Prof Pos: Mem bd, Wabash Life Ins Co. Mem: Northeastern Ind Realtors Asn; Ind Auctioneers Asn; Ind Farm Bur; Ind Asn Elected Officers; Ind Soc Chicago. Relig: Church of God. Mailing Add: RR 2 Auburn IN 46706

KRUSE, EDWARD H
b Ft Wayne, Ind, Oct 22, 18; s Edward H Kruse & Geneva Maxwell K; m 1945 to Joan Ley; c seven. Educ: Ind Univ, LLB, 42; Butler Univ; Beta Theta Pi. Polit & Govt Pos: Judge, Allen Superior Court, Ft Wayne, Ind, 52; US Rep, 49-50. Bus & Prof Pos: Pres, Kruse, O'Connor & Ling, Inc, Consult Actuarial Firm. Mil Serv: Entered as A/S, Navy, 42, released as Lt, after serv in PT Boats, Solomon Islands; Secy of Navy Commendation; Bronze Star; Pac & Am Theater Ribbons. Mem: Am Bar Asn (comt on taxation); Nova Univ of Technol (trustee). Relig: Catholic. Legal Res: Rte 1 5700 Holatee Trail Ft Lauderdale FL 33314 Mailing Add: 1415 Sunrise Blvd Ft Lauderdale FL 33304

KRYPEL, ROBERT JOSEPH (D)
b Chicago, Ill, Apr 16, 52; s Henry Joseph Krypel & Betty K; single. Educ: Marquette Univ, currently; Pi Sigma Alpha; Honor Roll, 70-71. Polit & Govt Pos: Alt deleg, Dem Nat Conv, 72; cong dist chmn, Humphrey for President Orgn, 72; mem, Wis Young Dem & Wis Dem Party, 72-; mem, Common Cause, 72- Bus & Prof Pos: Serv technician, Gen Elec Co, Chicago, 68- Mem: Temporary mem IBEW. Relig: Catholic. Mailing Add: 404 Selborne Rd Riverside IL 60546

KUBESH, NELL (D)
Chmn, Dawson Co Dem Cent Comt, Mont
b Teigen, Mont, Apr 20, 24; d William F Archer & Ella Walker A; m 1944 to John E Kubesh; c Terry L, Juanita E (Mrs Robert Martin), Janette (Mrs Frank Legato), Barbara (Mrs Gene Jarussi), Nancy Jo (Mrs Tim Gross), Patricia K & Grant. Educ: Rocky Mt Col, 40-42; Univ Mont, 42-43. Polit & Govt Pos: Pres, Dem Women's Club, Mont, 65-68, regional dir, 70-74; chmn, Dawson Co Dem Cent Comt, 72- Mem: Auxiliary of VFW; Dawson Co Farmers Union (educ dir, 64-73); Makoshika Toastmistress Club (pres, 72-73). Relig: Unitarian-Universalist. Mailing Add: Bloomfield Rte Glendive MT 59330

KUBIAK, DAN (D)
Tex State Rep
b Reagan, Tex, Mar 19, 38; s John T Kubiak & Connie Snider K; m 1967 to Zana Bassler. Educ: Blinn Col, AA, 59; Univ Tex, Austin, BBA, 62; Midwestern Univ, MEd, 68; pres of 16 college organizations. Polit & Govt Pos: Dem precinct chmn, Milam Co, Tex, 65-67; secy, Milam Co Dem Party, 67-68; pres, Dem of Tex, 68-69; Tex State Rep, Dist 27, 69-72, Dist 36, 73-, chmn, House Educ Comt, Tex House Rep, currently. Publ: Ten Tall Texans, Naylor, 67; We, The Americans, Tex Educ Asn, 66. Mem: Tex State Teachers Asn; Nat Educ Asn; Authors of Tex Asn, Univ Tex Ex-Students Asn (Milam Co pres); Lions. Honors & Awards: Teacher of the year award, 66-67; Auth of the Year Award, 67; Outstanding Young Man, 67; Distinguished Individual Supporter of Tex, 4-H Club Youth, Tex 4-H Develop Found, 70; Distinguished Serv Award, Voc Agr Teachers Asn of Tex, 70. Relig: Catholic. Legal Res: 2004 Murray Rockdale TX 76567 Mailing Add: Box 272 Rockdale TX 76567

KUBISCH, JACK B (CONSERVATIVE)
US Ambassador to Greece
Polit & Govt Pos: Asst Secy State Inter-Am Affairs, formerly. Legal Res: MI Mailing Add: Am Embassy 91 Vasillissis Sophia's Blvd APO New York NY 09253

KUCHARSKI, EDMUND JAMES (R)
b Chicago, Ill, Jan 30, 16; s Felix Kucharski & Frances Derbas K; m to Martha Evans; c Tobin, Edmund F & Kathleen (Mrs Joe Vogrich). Educ: Univ Ill, 37; John Marshall Law Sch, LLB, 41. Polit & Govt Pos: Clerk, Cook Co Superior Court, Ill, 52; recorder of deeds, Cook Co, 56, trustee, Metrop Sanit Dist, 60; under sheriff, 62, treas, 66; asst secy, State of Ill, 71-73; deleg, Rep Nat Conv, 72; chmn, Cook Co Rep Party, formerly. Relig: Catholic. Mailing Add: 6801 S Pulaski Chicago IL 60629

KUCHEL, THOMAS H (R)
b Anaheim, Calif, Aug 15, 10; s Henry Kuchel (deceased) & Lutetia Bailey K (deceased); m to Betty Mellenthin; c Karen (Mrs Delman W Smith). Educ: Univ Southern Calif, LLB, 35; Phi Delta Phi; Phi Kappa Phi; Phi Kappa Psi. Hon Degrees: LLD, Univ Southern Calif, Univ Calif, Chapman Col, Univ of the Pac, Univ Santa Clara & Tufts Univ; LHD, Univ Judaism; Hoyt fel, Jonathan Edwards Col, Yale Univ. Polit & Govt Pos: Calif State Assemblyman, 36-39; chmn, Rep State Cent Comt Calif, 40; Calif State Sen, 40-43; state controller, Calif, 46-52; US Sen, Calif, 53-69, Asst Rep Leader, US Senate, 53-69; deleg, Judicial Conf Ninth Circuit Court of Appeals, 73 & 74; US rep, 29th Session Gen Assembly UN. Bus & Prof Pos: Partner, Wyman, Bautzer, Rothman & Kuchel, Beverly Hills, Calif & Washington, DC, 69- Mem: Calif State Bar; Native Sons of the Golden West; Am Legion; Mason; Elks. Relig: Episcopal. Mailing Add: 9601 Wilshire Blvd Beverly Hills CA 90210

KUEGEL, WILLIAM MARTIN (D)
Chmn, Daviess Co Dem Party, Ky
b Owensboro, Ky, July 16, 24; s Martin Kuegel & Cecil Crabtree K; m 1945 to Carrie Newman; c William M, Jr & Marcia Lee. Educ: Georgetown Col, 2 years; Kappa Alpha. Polit & Govt Pos: Chmn, Daviess Co Dem Party, Ky, 69- Bus & Prof Pos: Farmer, currently. Mil Serv: Entered as Pvt, Marines, 44, released as Cpl, 46, after serv in 1st Marine Div, SPac & China. Mem: Farm Bur; Kyana Milk Producers Asn; Mason. Honors & Awards: Outstanding Young Farmer Award. Relig: Baptist. Mailing Add: Haycraft Lane RR 5 Owensboro KY 42301

KUEHN, DUANE ARTHUR (R)
Chmn, Dist 34 Rep Party, NDak
b Elgin, NDak, July 4, 28; s Daniel J Kuehn (deceased) & Ottilie Weiss K; m 1951 to Dorothy Delores Tietz; c David, Douglas & Brian. Educ: Bismarck Jr Col, NDak, 48-49. Polit & Govt Pos: NDak State Rep, 67-72; chmn, Dist 34 Rep Party, 74- Bus & Prof Pos: Elec serviceman, Mont-Dakota Utilities, Bismarck, NDak, 46-52, elec serv foreman, Mandan, NDak, 54-63, elec & gas serv foreman, 63-68, asst safety dir, Bismarck, NDak, 68- Mil Serv: Entered as Pvt, Army, 52, released as Sgt 1/C, 54, after serv in 45th Div, Artil, Korea, 52-53; Commendation Ribbon with Medal Pendant. Mem: NDak Soc Safety Engrs; Lions; Am Legion. Honors & Awards: Jaycee Outstanding Young Man Award. Relig: Lutheran. Mailing Add: 708 First Ave NE Mandan ND 58554

KUEHNLE, JAMES PAUL (R)
Wash State Rep
b Dubuque, Iowa, Dec 2, 23; s Louis Frederick Kuehnle & Weltha Groom K; m 1945 to Georgia Micka; c Kristine Joyce & Jeanette Lee. Educ: Ore State Univ, BS, 46. Polit & Govt Pos: Mem, Spokane Co Rep Cent Comt, Wash, 66-68; precinct committeeman, Spokane Co, 66-69; Wash State Rep, Fourth Dist, 69-; mem, Wash State Pub Pension Comn, 69- & Wash State Legis Coun, 72- Bus & Prof Pos: Commercial real estate exec. Mil Serv: World War II. Mem: Kiwanis; CofC; Elks; Mason; Aircraft Owners & Pilots Asn. Honors & Awards: Hon Life Mem, PTA; Outstanding Rep of Year Award, Young Am for Freedom, 73. Relig: Protestant. Mailing Add: S 1122 Skyline Pl Spokane WA 99206

KUENZEL, VERA VENITA (D)
b Havre, Mont, Jan 15, 18; d Gideon R Johnson & Stella Gates J; m 1938; c Byron K & Darla (Mrs Dennis T Kuntz). Educ: Northern Mont Col, cert teaching, 64. Polit & Govt Pos: Vpres, Woman's Club, Hill Co, Mont; Dem precinct committeewoman & Cong committeewoman, Mont; alt deleg, Dem Nat Conv, 72; mem, Mont State Comt for McGovern for President, 72. Mem: Eagles Auxiliary 166 (various off); Daughters of Nile; DAR. Relig: Lutheran. Legal Res: 434 Second Ave Havre MT 59501 Mailing Add: Box 645 Havre MT 59501

KUHL, HENRY YOUNG (R)
b Flemington, NJ, May 4, 30; s Paul Hervey Kuhl & Mabel R Kline K; m 1951 to Elsa Schaadt; c Kevin H & Jeffrey B. Educ: Rider Col, 2 years. Polit & Govt Pos: Pres, Raritan Twp Rep Club, NJ, 67; pres, Hunterdon C Club, 67-70; chmn, Hunterdon Co Rep Comt, 70-72; deleg, Rep Nat Conv, 72; chmn, State of NJ Poultrymen for Nixon, 72. Bus & Prof Pos: Pres, Kuhl Egg Equip Corp, 63-; pres, Kuhl Int Corp, 66- Mem: Elks; Flemington Fair Asn (dir). Relig: Presbyterian. Mailing Add: RD 1 Kuhl Rd Flemington NJ 08822

KUHLE, DONALD LEWIS (D)
Secy, Christian Co Dem Party, Ill
b Assumption, Ill, July 24, 12; s Lewis Kuhle & Freda K; m 1934 to Edwina Kuhle; c Don Kent & Mark. Polit & Govt Pos: Precinct committeeman, Dem Party, Assumption, Ill; mem sch bd, 20 years; secy, Christian Co Dem Party, currently; chmn, Christian Co Dem Adv Comt. Bus & Prof Pos: Farmer; Int Harvester dealer, Assumption & Taylorville, Ill, Ford dealer, Assumption, Ill. Honors & Awards: Soybean Award; Agr Honor Award; Ill Soybean Award, 70; Honor Award as Soybean Champion Grower in Midwest. Relig: Presbyterian. Mailing Add: RR 1 Assumption IL 62510

KUHN, JANET LAMMERSEN (R)
b Los Angeles, Calif, Nov 15, 42; d Walter Robert Lammersen & Marguerite Walsh L; m 1968 to Ira Francis Kuhn, Jr. Educ: Loyola/Marymount Univ Los Angeles, BA cum laude, 64; Georgetown Univ Law Ctr, currently; Curian Honor Soc; Gold Medal Distinction; Calif State Scholar; Lake Arrowhead, Calif Community Scholar; Marymount Scholar; Nat Merit Commendation; ed, Georgetown Univ Law J. Polit & Govt Pos: Research asst, US Rep Alphonzo Bell, Calif, 65-67, legis asst, 67-69, admin asst, 69- Bus & Prof Pos: Tech writer, Pac Tel & Tel, Los Angeles, Calif, 64-65. Mem: Capitol Hill Club; Calif State Soc; Phi Delta Phi; Kappa Beta Pi. Relig: Catholic. Mailing Add: 1226 Potomac School Rd McLean VA 22101

KULONGOSKI, TED (D)
Ore State Rep
Mailing Add: 1960 Graham Eugene OR 97505

KUMMERFELDT, ERNEST L (D)
Mont State Rep
Mailing Add: Nashua MT 59248

KUNASEK, CARL J (R)
Ariz State Rep
Mailing Add: 8315 E Mawson Rd Mesa AZ 85207

KUNATH, LORMA ROBINSON (D)
Chmn, Clay Co Dem Party, Iowa
b Waterloo, Iowa, Oct 28, 26; d John Wallace Robinson & Martha Johanna Pierson R; m 1949 to Karlton Lane Kunath; c David Paul & Mark Alan. Educ: Readlyn High Sch, grad, 44. Polit & Govt Pos: Deleg, Dem Mid-Term Conf, 74; Chmn, Clay Co Dem Party, Iowa, 75- Bus & Prof Pos: Commun Worker, Northwestern Bell Tel Co, 20 years; pres, Commun Workers Am, Local 7104, 70-; secy, Spencer Entertainment Inc, currently; bd mem, Community Concert Series, 72- Relig: Episcopal. Legal Res: 428 W Fourth St Spencer IA 51301 Mailing Add: Box 1132 Spencer IA 51301

KUNDERT, ALICE E (R)
State Auditor, SDak
b Java, SDak, July 23, 20; d Otto J Kundert & Maria Rieger K; single. Educ: Northern State Teachers Col, Teacher's Cert, 39; NSC Col-Summer Sch, 48-51; correspondence & off-campus courses, 51-53 & 57-61. Polit & Govt Pos: Dep supt of schs, Campbell Co, SDak, 54, co clerk of courts, 55-60, co registr of deeds, 61-68; secy-treas, Campbell Co Rep Party, 62-64, finance chmn, 62-68, vchmn, 64-69; presidential elector, Rep Party, SDak, 64; mem, SDak State Rep Adv Comt, 65-67; town treas, Mound City, 65-68; adv, Campbell Co TAR, 66-71; mem, State Local Study Comn, 68-; mem, State & Local Govt Adv Comt, US Off Econ Opportunity Fed Region VII, 68-73; State Auditor, SDak, 69- Bus & Prof Pos: Teacher, Campbell Co, SDak, 39-43 & 49-54; from clerk to mgr & buyer, dept store & dress shop, Calif, 43-48. Publ: Compiler and ed, Mound City Anniversary History Book, 59 & Macra Na Tuaite Book, Int Leaders Training Lab, Ireland, 63; auth, History of the County of Campbell, 60. Mem: Nat Fedn Rep Women; Nat Asn State Auditors, Comptrollers & Treas; SDak Fedn Bus & Prof Women; 4-H (leader & co proj leader); Ground Observer Corp (chief supvr). Honors & Awards: Cert of Recognition for Outstanding Craft & Recreation Club, 60; awarded plaque as Outstanding TAR Adv in Nation, 70 & 71; adv to Outstanding TAR in Nation, 70; SDak State Serv Award to Rep Party, SDak Fedn Rep Women; Nat Leadership & Serv to Rep Award, Nat Young Rep, 71. Relig: Congregational. Legal Res: Mound City SD 57646 Mailing Add: 407 N Van Buren Pierre SD 57501

KUNIMURA, TONY T (D)
Hawaii State Rep
b Koloa, Kauai, Hawaii, Dec 4, 23; s Sadajiro Kunimura & Katsu Fukushima K; m 1945; c Keith Gordon, Jessica Toni, Jon Mark, Peter, Daniel & Patrice Sueko. Educ: Kauai High Sch, Hawaii, grad. Polit & Govt Pos: Comt chmn, Kauai Co, Hawaii, formerly, mem bd supvr, 54-62; Hawaii State Rep & Asst Majority Floor Leader, 63-, deleg, Const Conv, 68; alt deleg, Dem Nat Conv, 72. Mil Serv: Entered as Pvt, Army, 43, released as Pfc, after serv in 442nd Inf Bn. Mem: Lions; PTA; sustaining mem, Kauai YMCA; W Kauai Sports & Commercial Club; Kauai Hist Soc; DAV. Relig: Christian. Mailing Add: RR 1 Koloa Kauai HI 96756

KUNIN, MADELEINE MAY (D)
Vt State Rep
b Zurich, Switz, Sept 28, 33; d Ferdinand May & Renee Bloch M; m 1959 to Arthur S Kunin; c Peter, Julia, Adam & Daniel. Educ: Univ Mass, BA, 56; Columbia Univ Sch Jour, MS, 57; Univ Vt, MA, 67. Polit & Govt Pos: Mem, Gov Comn on the Status of Women, 66-68; Vt State Rep, 73- Bus & Prof Pos: Reporter, Burlington Free Press, 57-58; instr, Trinity Col, 71-72; writer, 72- Publ: Co-auth, Vermont guidebook, Barre Publ, 74; auth, several articles, Chittenden Mag, 72-73; Vermont suffragist: Clarina Howard Nichols, Vt Life, 73-74. Relig: Jewish. Mailing Add: 122 Dunder Rd Burlington VT 05401

KUNKEL, JOAN MAPLETON (D)
b McKeesport, Pa, July 14, 29; d Dr Felix Andrew Mapleton & Alice Marley M; m 1947 to R Earl Kunkel, Jr; c Ronald Earl, Paul Michael, Michael Lee, John Adam, Laura Mapleton & Claudia Ann. Educ: Stetson Univ, 47-49. Polit & Govt Pos: Admin asst to US Rep William Lehman, Fla, 73- Mem: House of Rep Admin Asst Asn; Nat Women's Polit Caucus; Stetson Univ Alumni Asn; Md Cong of PTA; Md Horsebreeders' Asn. Relig: Catholic. Mailing Add: 1913 Briggs Chaney Rd Silver Spring MD 20904

KUNZ, DONNA MAE (R)
b Minn, Sept 6, 29; d Chester LeRoy Berggren & Millie Holden B; m 1951 to Robert Louis Kunz, wid; c Melinda Ann, Gary Lee & Timothy Robert. Educ: Univ Minn, BA, 51. Polit & Govt Pos: Mem, Minn & Beltrami Co Rep Federated Women, 67-75; deleg, Beltrami Co, Seventh Dist & Minn State Rep Conv, 68-75; area I chairwoman, Seventh Cong Dist, Minn, 70-; alt deleg, Rep Nat Conv, 72. Bus & Prof Pos: Owner-mgr, Minn Woods Prod, 65- Mem: Sons of Norway; Am Asn Univ Women; T T T Soc (pres, Minn L Chap, 71-72, state historian, Minn State Chap, Nat Soc, 72-73). Relig: Methodist. Mailing Add: 1119 Beltrami Ave Bemidji MN 56601

KUNZE, ANNE ILENE (D)
b Newton, Kans, July 27, 36; d Robert Lafayette Bird & Véltae Ilene O'Neal B; m 1957 to Lawrence D Kunze; c Scott Lee. Educ: Dak Wesleyan Univ, BS, cum laude, 68; SDak State Univ; Pi Gamma Mu; Phi Kappa Phi; Women's Hon Soc. Polit & Govt Pos: Chmn, Farm & Rural Life Task Force, Dem Nat Platform Comt, 72; deleg-at-lg, Dem Nat Conv, 72. Bus & Prof Pos: Sec educ teacher, Miller, Wessington & Wessington Springs, SDak, 68-71; owner-operator, Prairie Arts & Crafts, 74-75; SDak Rep, Friends of the Earth, 75; legis info & commun coordr, We The People, 75. Mem: United Serv Citizen Coun, Inc (pres, 72-74, bd dirs & secy, 74-75); Am Asn Univ Women (state consumer coord coun, 74-75); League of Women Voters; Farmers Union. Relig: Methodist. Mailing Add: RR 1 Alpena SD 57312

KUPFERMAN, THEODORE R (R)
b New York, NY, May 12, 20; m to Dorothee Hering (deceased); c Theodore R, Jr & Stephanie. Educ: City Col New York, BS; Columbia Univ Law Sch, LLB, Kent scholar; ed, Law Rev; Phi Beta Kappa. Polit & Govt Pos: Law secy to presiding justice, Appellate Div, Supreme Court First Dept, 48-49; chmn bd, NY Young Rep Club, 49-50; counsel & legis asst to minority leader, New York City Coun, 58-62; councilman, New York, 62-66; US Rep, NY, 66-69; justice, Supreme Court of NY, 69-71, justice, Appellate Div, 71- Bus & Prof Pos: Mem legal dept, Warner Bros Pictures, Inc, 49-51; mem legal dept, Nat Broadcasting Co, 51-53;

gen counsel, Cinerama Prod Corp, 53-58; adj prof law, NY Law Sch, 59-64; partner, Kupferman & Price, 59-66; counsel, Battle, Fowler, Stokes & Kheel, 67-69. Mem: Am Bar Asn (former chmn, Patent, Copyright & Trademark Rels Comt, Sect of Int & Comp Law & former ed, Bull of Int & Comp Law); Family Legal Adv (ed); Consular Law Soc (bd trustees); Am Arbit Asn. Mailing Add: 140 E 72nd St New York NY 10021

KURFESS, CHARLES FREDERICK (R)
Ohio State Rep
b Wood Co, Ohio, Feb 1, 30; s John F Kurfess & Margaret Zingg K; m 1956 to Helyn T Rudolph; c Todd Frederick, Ann Libbe & Laura Helyn. Educ: Bowling Green State Univ, BA, 51; Ohio State Univ, LLB, 57; Voelker fel, Wayne Univ, 51-52; Omicron Delta Kappa; Pi Sigma Alpha; Phi Kappa Tau; Phi Delta Phi. Polit & Govt Pos: Ohio State Rep, Wood Co, 57-, Speaker, Ohio State House of Rep, 67-72, Minority Leader, 73-; mem, Wood Co Rep Cent & Exec Comts, 64-; deleg Nat Conv, 68 & 72. Bus & Prof Pos: Attorney-at-law, 58-Mil Serv: Entered as Pvt, Army, 52, released as Cpl, 54, after serv in Counter Intel Corps, Far East, 53-54. Mem: Northwest Ohio & Am Bar Asns; CofC; Wood Co Farm Bur Fedn; Bowling Green State Univ Alumni Asn. Honors & Awards: Outstanding Young Man of Bowling Green, Ohio & area, 65. Relig: Lutheran. Mailing Add: 9449 Reitz Rd RR 1 Perrysburg OH 43551

KURKE, ELEANOR BERGAN (R)
State Committeewoman, Fla State Rep Comt
b Williston, NDak, June 24, 21; d Thomas Alfred Bergan & Ada Claire Brownson B; div; c Susan (Mrs Larry G Heine), John Matthew, Jr, William Jeffrey, Lance Brownson & Benjamin Thomas. Educ: NDak State Univ, 2 years; Gamma Phi Beta. Polit & Govt Pos: Pres, Women's Rep Club of Gtr Naples, Fla, 66-71; alt deleg, Rep Nat Conv, 68 & 72; chmn, Nixon for President, Collier Co, Fla, 68; state committeewoman, Fla State Rep Comt, 68-; chmn, Cramer for Senate Campaign, Collier Co, 70. Bus & Prof Pos: Exec secy, Royal Poinciana Golf Club, Naples, 71- Mem: Soc of Mayflower Descendants; Daughters of Am Colonists; DAR; Nat & Fla Fedn of Rep Women. Mailing Add: 3930 Belair Lane Naples FL 33940

KURODA, JOSEPH TOSHIYUKI (D)
Hawaii State Sen
b Aiea, Hawaii, Mar 24, 27; s Toyoichi Kuroda; m 1953 to Betty Mieko Nakagawa; c Lori, Kevin & Keith. Educ: Univ Hawaii, BEd, 52, MEd Adm, 65; Phi Delta Kappa. Polit & Govt Pos: Councilman, Tenth Dist, Hawaii, 65; Hawaii State Rep, 70-71; Hawaii State Sen, Fourth Dist, 71- Bus & Prof Pos: Teacher, elem sch, Dept of Educ, Hawaii, 53-59, vprin, elem sch, 59-61, prin, 61-66, 69-70, sch dist personnel officer, 66-69. Mil Serv: Entered as Pvt, Army, 45, released as T/Sgt 4, 47, after serv in Hq 2nd Inf Div; Lt Col, Army Res; Aviators Badge; Sr Aviators Wing; World War II Victory Medal; Pac Theatre Campaign Ribbon. Mem: Nat & Hawaii Educ Asns; Asn of US Army; 442nd Vet Club; Pearl City Lions Club (charter mem). Relig: Protestant. Mailing Add: c/o Senate Sgt at Arms State Capitol Honolulu HI 96813

KURTZ, MYRA BERMAN (D)
b New York, NY, July 20, 45; d Milton Robert Berman & Shirley Letzter B; m 1970 to Stuart Jacob Kurtz. Educ: Goucher Col, AB, 66; Harvard Univ Grad Sch Arts & Sci, PhD in Microbiol, 71. Polit & Govt Pos: Deleg, Dem Nat Conv, 72. Bus & Prof Pos: Post-doctoral research assoc, Dept Biol, State Univ NY Albany, 71-72; assoc prof, Fed Univ Sao Carlos, Brazil, 72- Publ: Co-auth, Suppression of a pleiotropic mutant affecting glycerol dissimilation, Biochem & Biophys Research Commun, Vol 38, 70, Glycerol specific revertants of a pep phosphotransferase mutant, 1/71 & Promoter-like mutant of the glycerol kinase operon, 6/71, J Bact. Mem: Am Asn Advan Sci; Am Soc Microbiol; Phi Beta Kappa; Adirondack Mt Club. Honors & Awards: Jesse L King Award for Excellence in Biol, Goucher Col, 66. Legal Res: 748 Leslie Lane East Meadow NY 11554 Mailing Add: Fed Univ of Sao Carlos Sao Paulo Brazil

KURZMAN, STEPHEN (R)
Asst Secy Legis, Dept Health, Educ & Welfare
b New York, NY, Mar 25, 32; s Albert W Kurzman & Ceyl Taylor K, m 1955 to Ellen Goldberg; c Charles T & George M. Educ: Harvard Col, AB, 53; Harvard Law Sch, JD, 56. Polit & Govt Pos: Law clerk, US Attorney's Off, Criminal Div, Southern Dist NY, 56-57, Asst US Attorney, 59-61; legis asst & counsel, US Sen Jacob K Javits, NY, 61-65; minority counsel, Comt Labor & Pub Welfare, US Senate, 65-66; consult, Subcomt Employ Manpower & Poverty, 67; consult & dep dir opers, Nat Adv Comn Civil Disorders, 67-68; consult, Rep Task Force Urban Affairs, US House of Rep, 68; spec counsel, Urban Coalition Action Coun, 69-70; consult, US Dept Treas, 69-70, Senate Comt Labor & Pub Welfare, 69-70 & Comt Grants & Benefits, Admin Conf US, 69-71; consult & dir inter-agency affairs, White House Conf Children & Youth, 70-71; Asst Secy Legis, Dept Health, Educ & Welfare, 71- Bus & Prof Pos: Partner, Kurzman & Goldfarb, 66-71; prof lectr, George Washington Univ Law Sch, summer 69; mem bd trustees, Harvard Yearbook Publ Bldg Fund; mem bd dirs, DC Chap & mem nat exec comt & nat adv comt, Am Jewish Comt. Mil Serv: Sgt, Army, 57-59. Publ: Federal Consumer Safety Legislation (W H Heffron, R Medalie & M Pearlman), Nat Comn Prod Safety, 70; Gordon's Modern Annotated Forms of Agreement, Prentice-Hall, 70; Profiles of Children, White House Conf Children, 70; plus others. Mem: Am Bar Asn (chmn comt health, educ & welfare); DC & Fed Bar Asns; Phi Beta Kappa; Fed City Club. Relig: Jewish. Legal Res: 1523 28th St NW Washington DC 20007 Mailing Add: Rm 5238 North Bldg Dept Health Educ & Welfare Washington DC 20201

KUSHNIR, MARY CONSTANCE (D)
Mem, Colo Dem State Cent Comt
b Beaver Falls, Pa, June 16, 08; d Abraam Isaac Fistell & Ella Pitler F; m 1943 to Jacob J Kushnir; c Deborah Lee. Educ: Univ Denver, 25-28; Pueblo Jr Col, 1 year; Southern Colo State Col, spec course; Western State Col, spec courses; Adams State Col, spec courses. Polit & Govt Pos: Secy, Young Dem, Pueblo, Colo, 59-60; deleg, Young Dem Conv, 4 times; Dem precinct vchmn, 12 years; mem, Colo Dem State Cent Comt, currently. Bus & Prof Pos: Field secy, Am Med Ctr, Denver, Colo, 35-61; field secy, Children's Asthmatic Research Inst, 61-62. Mem: Muscular Dystrophy Asn of Am; Prairie Belle Baton Corp of Pueblo; Pueblo Prairie Belles & Beaux (sponsor); Pueblo Trooperettes (sponsor); Am Field Serv (publicity chmn, 71). Honors & Awards: Cert of Merit, Muscular Dystrophy Asn; Cert of Merit, Am Cancer Soc. Relig: Jewish. Mailing Add: 818 Albany Pueblo CO 81003

KUSIC, SAMUEL N (R)
WVa State Sen
Mailing Add: State Capitol Charleston WV 25305

KUSS, MATTHEW J (D)
Mass State Rep
Mailing Add: State Capitol Boston MA 02133

KUSSE, ROBERT J (R)
Pa State Rep
Mailing Add: Capitol Bldg Harrisburg PA 17120

KUTHY, EUGENE WENDEL (D)
Chmn, 19th Cong Dist Dem Comt, Mich
b Dearborn, Mich, Dec 17, 30; s Wendell Kuthy & Elizabeth R Silagyi K; m 1952 to Jacqueline Ruth Getoor; c Douglas Eugene, James Alan, Thomas Jay & Robin Jacqueline. Educ: Univ Mich, AB, 54; Detroit Col Law, JD, 64; Druids; Delta Theta Phi. Polit & Govt Pos: Precinct deleg, Royal Oak Dem Party, Mich, 62-68; registr dir, Oakland Co Dem Comt, 64, finance dir, 65-66 & 68-70; deleg, Dem Nat Conv, 64 & 68; vchmn, 18th Cong Dist Dem Comt, Mich, 64-65, chmn, 65-69; mem, West Bloomfield Dem Club, 69-; mem finance Comt, Sen Phillip A Hart, 70; mem, Mich Dem State Cent Comt, 70-72; chmn, 19th Cong Dist Dem Comt, Mich, 73- Bus & Prof Pos: Mem faculty, Bus Admin Col, Univ Mich-Dearborn, 61-66; partner, Renfrew & Edberg, 64-72; vpres, Am Acad Transportation, 66-72; mgr govt serv, Ernst & Ernst, 72- Mil Serv: Entered as A/S, Navy, 54, released as Lt(jg), 58, after serv in Off Chief Naval Opers, DC, 55-58; Comdr, Naval Res Security Group Div 9-6, Detroit, formerly, Div 9-12, Southfield, 71-74, Nat Naval Security Group 314, Southfield, currently. Mem: Naval Reserve Asn; Navy League; Common Cause; Am Civil Liberties Union; Am Judicature Soc. Relig: Protestant. Mailing Add: 4595 Valleyview Dr Orchard Lake MI 48033

KUTUN, BARRY (D)
Fla State Rep
b Bronx, NY, Aug 30, 41; s Rubin Kutun & Pearl Kranz K; m 1962 to Judith Ann Notowitz; c Sheryl Lynn & Lawrence Berton. Educ: Univ Fla, BSBA, 62; Univ Miami Sch Law, JD, 66; Omicron Delta Kappa; Fla Blue Key; Iron Arrow; Wig & Robe Legal Honor Soc; Tau Epsilon Phi. Polit & Govt Pos: Mem, Miami Beach Minimum Housing Appeals Bd, Fla, 70-72; Fla State Rep, 72- Bus & Prof Pos: Attorney, Law Off-Barry Kutun, 66- Publ: Insurance against the assessment of punitive damages, 66 & co-auth, The equitable lien in Florida, 66, Univ Miami Law Rev. Mem: Am Arbit Asn; Mason; Elks; Jewish Voc Serv (dir, 71-); B'nai B'rith (lodge pres, 69). Honors & Awards: Roger Sorino Mem Award, Univ Miami Sch Law, 65. Relig: Jewish. Legal Res: 838 W 47th St Miami Beach FL 33140 Mailing Add: PO Box 40-2039 Miami Beach FL 33140

KUYKENDALL, DAN HEFLIN (R)
b Cherokee, Tex, July 9, 24; s Tom Groves Kuykendall & Sarah Johnson K; m 1951 to Jacqueline Meyer; c Dan Heflin, Jr, John Meyer, Kathleen Virginia & Jacqueline Kay. Educ: Tex A&M Col, BS, 47. Polit & Govt Pos: US Rep, Tenn, 67-74; deleg, Rep Nat Conv, 68, alt deleg, 72; consult, US Dept Transportation, currently. Bus & Prof Pos: Mgt, Procter & Gamble Co, 47-64; agent, Equitable Life Assurance Soc, 64- Mil Serv: Lt, Air Force, 42-45, serv as B-29 Pilot. Mem: Mil Order World Wars. Relig: Methodist. Legal Res: 2 1898 Poplar Woods Circle E Memphis TN 38138 Mailing Add: PO Box 40534 Washington DC 20016

KUYKENDALL, JEROME KENNETH (R)
Chmn, Indian Claims Comn
b Pomeroy, Wash, Dec 8, 07; s Elgin Victor Kuykendall & Margaret Scully K; m 1936 to Jane Brehm; c Gretchen Anne (Mrs Jones) & Penny Jane (Mrs Engel); m second time to Helen Douglas Dickinson. Educ: Univ Wash, Seattle, JD, 32; Phi Delta Phi; Phi Delta Theta, Oval Club. Polit & Govt Pos: Asst Attorney Gen, Wash, 41-44 & 46; chmn, Pub Serv Comn, Wash, 51-53; chmn, Fed Power Comn, 53-61; mem, Indian Claims Comn, 67-, chmn, 69- Bus & Prof Pos: Lawyer, Seattle, Wash, 32-41, Pebbles & Kuykendall, Olympia, Wash, 47-51 & Shanley, Fisher & Kuykendall, Washington, DC, 62-67. Mil Serv: Entered as Lt(jg), Naval Res, released as Lt, 46. Mem: Wash State, DC, Am & Fed Bar Asns; Metrop Club. Relig: Unitarian. Mailing Add: 2700 N Oakland St Arlington VA 22207

KUYKENDALL, RUFUS CALVIN (R)
b Indianapolis, Ind, Sept 24, 03; s John H Kuykendall & Anna B Jackson K, m 1939 to Clemmie Ethel Ransom. Educ: Ind Univ, AB, 27, Sch Law, LLB, 42; Kappa Alpha Psi; Sigma Pi Phi. Polit & Govt Pos: Organizer, Young Negro Rep, Ind, 24; worker, Young Negro Marion Co Groups for Hoover, 28; organizer & asst dir, Young Negro Rep Clubs, 30; asst to state chmn, Rep State Cent Comt, 36 & 46; mem, State Platform Comt, 43-50; dep prosecutor, 43-52; co-chmn, Seventh Ward Marion Co Rep Comt, 52; asst city attorney, 52-55; mem, US Comn for UNESCO, 54-55; asst staff dir, Legal Staff, US Comt on Civil Rights, 59-60; city councilman; criminal court pub defender, 64; judge, Marion Superior Court, currently; mem, US Dept of State Adv Coun on African Affairs, 70-72. Bus & Prof Pos: Legal adv, Frederick Douglas Rep Club, 65. Publ: Negro at Indiana, The Vagabond, 27. Mem: Marion Co Bar Asn; Kappa Alpha Psi; Citizens Forum, Inc; Sigma Pi Psi (secy, currently); Am Bar Asn. Honors & Awards: Indianapolis Recorder Newspaper Honor Roll, 55; NAACP Man of the Year, 57; C Francis Stratford Award, Nat Bar Asn, 63; Outstanding Kappa of the Year, Kappa Alpha Psi, 63. Relig: African Methodist Episcopal. Legal Res: 2202 N Capitol Ave Indianapolis IN 46208 Mailing Add: Marion County Superior Court Rm 6 Rm W-542 City-County Bldg Indianapolis IN 46204

KUYL, SHEILA MARIE (D)
b East Keansburg, NJ, Mar 15, 50; d Willem Kuyl & Doris Sullivan (Mrs Allen Schaeffer); single. Educ: Brookdale Community Col, Lincroft, NJ, currently; Ecology Club; Polit Sci. Polit & Govt Pos: Chairwoman, Monmouth Co Chap, Voting Age Coalition, Inc, 69-71; deleg, NJ Young Dem Conv, Asbury Park, 70, Lavallette, 71 & Atlantic City, 72; pres, Monmouth Co Young Dem, 71-73, state committeewoman, 73-; coordr, McGovern for President, Hazlet Twp, 72; alt deleg, Dem Nat Conv, 72. Relig: Catholic. Mailing Add: 51 Third St West Keansburg NJ 07734

KVAALEN, OSCAR SEIGEL (R)
Mont State Rep
b Lambert, Mont, Jan 1, 21; s Ostien Sonderson Kvaalen & Esther Armston K; m 1960 to Ruth C Johnson; c Jon Seigel & Elizabeth Esther. Educ: Concordia Col, BA, 43. Polit & Govt Pos: Conservationist, US Soil Conserv Serv, 49-52; field agt, State Land Dept, Mont, 53-55; Mont State Rep, 59-64, 67-71 & 73-, House Minority Leader, 73-, chmn, Educ Comt, Mont State House of Rep, 61, 63, 69 & 71. Mil Serv: Entered as Midn, Naval Res, 43, released as Lt(jg), 46, after serv in Amphibious Forces, Pac Fleet; Am Theater & Pac Theater Ribbons with 2 stars. Mem: VFW; Farm Bur. Relig: Lutheran. Mailing Add: Lambert MT 59243

KVAM, ADOLPH (CONSERVATIVE)
Minn State Rep
b Willmar, Minn; s Andrew Kvam; m to Doris Holm; c David, Gregory, Kristin & Karen. Educ: Univ Minn, BBA. Polit & Govt Pos: Minn State Rep, 67-; mem, Gov Adv Comn on Sch Aids Formula; treas, Litchfield Sch Bd. Mil Serv: World War II; China & India. Mailing Add: 25 W Lockerbie Litchfield MN 55355

KWITOWSKI, WALTER ANTHONY (D)
Treas, Erie Co Dem Party, Pa
b Erie, Pa, Aug 13, 24; s Walter Kwitowski & Pearl Kinecki K; m 1952 to Jeannette Marie Gorny; c Walter Andrew, Mark Anthony & Christine Marie. Educ: Gannon Col, 3 years; Univ Miami, 1 year. Polit & Govt Pos: Second ward chmn, Erie Dem Party, Pa, 50-52; chmn, Erie Young Dem, 51; personnel dir, Erie, 66-; treas, Erie Co Dem Party, 69-; alt deleg, Dem Nat Conv, 68; deleg, Dem Nat Mid-Term Conf, 74. Bus & Prof Pos: Real estate agt, Hurle Real Estate, 51-54; mgr, Erie Press Club, 54-55; investr, Commonwealth Pa Dept Pub Instr, 55-61. Mil Serv: Entered as Pvt, Army, 43, released as Pfc, 46, after serv in 7th Div. Mem: Northwestern Pa Personnel Asn; Philadelphia Chap, Pub Personnel Asn. Relig: Roman Catholic. Mailing Add: 542 E 12th Erie PA 16503

KYER, HARRY FRANKLIN (R)
Chmn, Braxton Co Rep Party, WVa
b Gassaway, WVa, May 15, 24; s Henry Earl Kyer & Emma Lockard K; m 1948 to Mary Louise Brady; c Ben L. Educ: Bowling Green Bus Univ, BS in Acct, 53. Polit & Govt Pos: Mem town coun, Gassaway, WVa, 67-73; chmn, Braxton Co Rep Party, 67- Bus & Prof Pos: Owner & operator of independent ins agency. Mil Serv: Entered as Seaman, Navy, 43, released as PO 1/C, 46, after serv in USS Ranger, ETO & USS Wasp, Pac Theatre, 44-45; Unit Citation; Good Conduct Medal; ETO Award; Battle Stars. Mem: Lions; VFW. Relig: United Methodist. Mailing Add: 500 Braxton St Gassaway WV 26624

KYL, JOHN H (R)
Asst Secy of Interior for Cong & Legis Affairs
b Wisner, Nebr, May 9, 19; s John George Kyl & Johanna Boonstra K; m 1941 to Arlene Griffith; c Jon, Jannene, & Jayne. Educ: Nebr State Teachers Col, Wayne, AB; Univ Nebr, MA; Univ Nebr & Drake Univ, Des Moines, grad work. Polit & Govt Pos: US Rep, Iowa, 59-64 & 66-72; mem, Pub Land Law Rev Comn & Outdoor Recreation Resources Rev Comn; mem, Lewis & Clark Trail Comn; Asst Secy of Interior for Cong & Legis Affairs, 73- Bus & Prof Pos: Hist teacher; coach & faculty mem of col, Wayne, Nebr; CofC mgr; farmer; dir news & spec events, KTVO, Ottumwa, Iowa; TV newscaster, 57-59. Relig: Presbyterian. Legal Res: 208 W North St Bloomfield IA 52537 Mailing Add: Dept of the Interior Washington DC 20240

KYL, JON LLEWELLYN (R)
Gen Counsel, Ariz State Rep Cent Comt
b Oakland, Nebr, Apr 25, 42; s John H Kyl & Arlene Griffith K; m 1964 to Caryll Collins; c Kristine & John. Educ: Univ Ariz, BA, 64, LLB, 66; Phi Beta Kappa; Phi Kappa Phi; Pi Kappa Delta; Phi Sigma Alpha; Pi Kappa Alpha. Polit & Govt Pos: Chmn, Maricopa Co Young Rep League, 68-69; chmn, Ariz Young Rep League, 70-71; gen counsel, Ariz State Rep Cent Comt, 70-; alt deleg, Rep Nat Conv, 72. Bus & Prof Pos: Partner, Jennings, Strouss & Salmon, Phoenix, 71- Publ: Fifth Amendment privilege against self-incrimination, fall 65 & Pre-trial discovery of impeachment evidence, spring 66, Ariz Law Rev; Legal and practical aspects of pesticide spraying cases, Ins Counsel J, 10/70. Mem: Am, Ariz & Maricopa Co Bar Asns; Planning Asn Ariz; Phoenix Asn Defense Counsel. Honors & Awards: Outstanding Man of Year, Maricopa Young Rep League; One of Outstanding Men of Phoenix, Jaycees, 70. Relig: Presbyterian. Mailing Add: 111 W Monroe Phoenix AZ 85003

KYLE, CHARLES CLAYTON (CASEY) (R)
Mem, Rep State Cent Comt Calif
b Whitehall, Mont, Feb 27, 23; s Charles Larabee Kyle & Marguerite Pearl Stephens K; m 1953 to Carmen Marie Bahr; c Candy Ann, Colleen Denise & Casey Jon. Educ: Santa Barbara Bus Col, 48. Polit & Govt Pos: City councilman, Santa Maria, Calif, 56-64 & 69, mayor, 60-64; mem, Santa Barbara Co Cong Mayors, 60-64; chmn channel div, League of Calif Cities, 63; mem, LAFCO, Santa Barbara Co, 64; mem, Rep State Cent Comt Calif, 69- Bus & Prof Pos: Co-owner, secy & treas, Kyle Roofing Co, Inc, 55-68; life underwriter, NY Life Ins Co, 68- Mil Serv: Entered as A/S, Navy, 43, released as Gunners Mate 3/C, 46, after serv in Armed Guard, Pac Theatre, 43-46; Six Ribbons. Mem: Santa Maria Contractors Asn; Roofing Contractors Asn; Nat Asn Life Underwriters; Kiwanis; Mason. Honors & Awards: Jr CofC Distinguished Serv Award, 60. Relig: Christian Church of NAm. Mailing Add: 231 N Palisade Dr Santa Maria CA 93454

KYLE, MARCUS AURELIUS (R)
Parliamentarian, Dade Co Rep Exec Comt, Fla
b Bennington, Okla, Dec 13, 23; s Don Thomas Kyle & Irene Corbett K; m 1949 to Carmen Lucila Perez; c Alan Glenn. Educ: Univ Denver. Polit & Govt Pos: Treas, Dist 15 & chmn, Precinct 221, Harris Co, Tex, 56-58; membership chmn, Dade Co Rep Exec Comt, Fla, 60 & 62, chmn, 62 & 66, committeeman, from Dist 27, 71-74, parliamentarian, 74- Bus & Prof Pos: Part-time bus driver, Univ Denver, 47-48; mechanic's helper, Pan Am Airways, 46, traffic supvr, 48-52; asst dir sta, Trans-Tex Airways, 52-58; supvr tech publ, Nat Airlines, Inc, Miami, Fla, 58-68 & 72-, dir off serv, 68-72. Mil Serv: Entered as A/S, Coast Guard, 42, released as Radarman 2/C, 45, after serv in Amphibious Forces; Am & Asiatic-Pac Theater Campaign Ribbons; Philippine Liberation Medal with Two Battle Stars. Mem: VFW (past dist comdr, 12th Dist of La). Relig: Episcopal. Mailing Add: 925 Majorca Coral Gables FL 33134

KYLE, SAMUEL WILLIAM (BILL) (R)
b Redfield, SDak, Apr 12, 25; s William Cassidy Kyle & Frances Hewitt K; m 1964 to Norma Suzanne Lyons; c Tracey, Carrie & Christopher. Educ: Clark High Sch, 4 years. Polit & Govt Pos: Chmn, Clark Co Rep Comt, SDak, formerly; dir, SDak State Agency Surplus Property, 69. Bus & Prof Pos: Mgr, Kyles Hardware, Clark, 48- Mil Serv: Entered as A/S, Navy, 43, released as Pharmacist's Mate 3/C, 45, after serv in Naval Hosp, Fleet Air Wing 13, Pac Theater, 43-45. Mem: Mason; Shrine; Am Legion. Relig: Congregational. Mailing Add: 210 N Cloud Clark SD 57225

KYROS, PETER NICHOLAS (D)
b Portland, Maine, July 11, 1925; s Nicholas Kyros & Anna Poulos K; m 1947 to Alice Williams; c Peter N, Jr & Joanne Carol. Educ: Mass Inst Technol; US Naval Acad, BS, 47; Harvard Law Sch, LLB, 57. Hon Degrees: LLB, Unity Col & St Joseph's Col, Maine. Polit & Govt Pos: Attorney, Maine Pub Utilities Comn, 57-60; chmn, First Dist Dem Comt, Maine, 62-64; chmn, Maine State Dem Comt, 64-66; US Rep, Maine, 67-74; deleg, Dem Nat Conv, 68; Maine cand, US House of Rep, 74. Mil Serv: Entered as Midn, Navy, 45, released as Lt, 53, after serv in Naval Supply Corps. Mem: Am & Maine Bar Asns; Am & Maine Trial Lawyers Asn; Maine Hist Soc. Relig: Greek Orthodox. Mailing Add: 82 Frost St Portland ME 04102

L

LABERGE, WALTER B
Asst Secy of the Air Force Research & Develop
b Chicago, Ill, Mar 29, 24; m 1949 to Patricia Ann Sammon; c Peter R, Stephen M, Jeanne M, Phillip R & Jacqueline. Educ: Univ Notre Dame, BS in naval sci, 44, BS in physics, 47, PhD in physics, 50. Polit & Govt Pos: Mem, Defense Sci Bd Panel on Remotely Piloted Vehicles, 71-72; dep tech dir, Naval Weapons Ctr, 71-73 & tech dir, 73; mem, Chief of Naval Opers Indust Adv Comt on Telecommun, 72; Asst Secy of the Air Force Research & Develop, 73- Bus & Prof Pos: Prog engr, Sidewinder Missile, Naval Ord Test Sta, China Lake, Calif, 50-55 & prog mgr, Sidewinder Missile, 55-57; dir eng, Western Develop Labs, Philco-Ford Corp, Palo Alto, Calif, 57-63, dir, Philco Houston Opers, Tex, 63-65, vpres, Research & Develop Corp Staff, Philadelphia, Pa, 65-66, vpres, Western Develop Labs, Palo Alto, Calif, 66-67 & vpres, Electronics Group, 67-71. Mil Serv: Entered as Cadet, Navy ROTC, 41, released as Lt(jg), 46, after serv in USN/YMS 165 Comdr, SPac, 43-45. Honors & Awards: Calif Legis Resolution of Appreciation for Sidewinder Contrib, 57; One of Five Outstanding Young Men of Calif, Calif Jr CofC, 57; Centennial Award to 50 Outstanding Sci Grad, Univ Notre Dame, 67; Navy Superior Civilian Serv Award, 72. Mailing Add: 1300 Capulet Ct McLean VA 22101

LABINE, OLIVER JOSEPH (D)
VChmn, Marshall Co Dem Party, Minn
b Argyle, Minn, Oct 17, 21; s Phillip Labine & Elizabeth Proulx L; m 1945 to Doris Dascomb; c Barbara, Jeanne (Mrs Gene Durand), Noel, Karen, Mark, Myra & Charles. Educ: Northwest Sch of Agr, 2 years. Polit & Govt Pos: Vchmn, Marshall Co Dem Party, Minn, 70- Bus & Prof Pos: Farmer, currently. Mil Serv: Entered as Seaman, Navy, 42, released as EMT 1/C, 45, Naval Res. Mem: B Master Electrician; Am Legion; Lions; Nat Farmers Orgn; KofC. Relig: Catholic. Mailing Add: Rte 2 Argyle MN 56713

LABONTE, ARTHUR H (D)
NH State Rep
Mailing Add: 675 S Main St West Franklin NH 03235

LABORDE, M J (D)
La State Rep
Mailing Add: 1421 Loretto Ave Sulphur LA 70663

LABORDE, RAYMOND J (D)
La State Rep
Mailing Add: 310 N Main St Marksville LA 71351

LABOVITZ, DEBORAH R (D)
b Philadelphia, Pa, Oct 13, 42; d Samuel Rubin & Clara Blank R; m 1962 to Judah I Labovitz; c Gail Susan, Bruce Joel & Daniel Mark. Educ: Univ Pa, BSOT, 63, MA, 74. Polit & Govt Pos: Alt deleg, Dem Nat Conv, 72. Bus & Prof Pos: Dir occup therapy, Mercy Douglass Hosp, Philadelphia, Pa, 63-66; consult family therapy, Eastern Pa Psychiat Inst, 69-70; instr, Sch of Allied Med Profs, Univ Pa, 71- Mem: Eastern Pa Occupational Therapy Asn; Asn Schs Allied Health Professions; Am Asn Univ Prof; Am Asn Univ Women; Nat Orgn Women. Relig: Jewish. Mailing Add: 1027 Lakeside Ave Philadelphia PA 19126

LABSON, BETH ANN (D)
VChmn, San Mateo Co Dem Cent Comt, Calif
b Washington, DC, Nov 21, 53; d Arnold Labson & Dorothy Deskin L; single. Educ: Univ Calif, Berkeley, 73- Polit & Govt Pos: Dem nominee, Calif State Assembly, 26th Dist, 72; deleg, Dem Nat Conv, 72, mem, Nat Platform Comt, 72; vchmn, San Mateo Co Dem Cent Comt, 73-; co-chmn, 11th Cong Dist Dem Exec Comt, 73- Relig: Jewish. Legal Res: 2611 Barclay Way Belmont CA 94002 Mailing Add: 328 Stern Hall Campus Univ of Calif Berkeley CA 94720

LACEY, MICHAEL CHARLES (R)
Treas, Madison Co Rep Cent Comt, Ind
b Anderson, Ind, Sept 18, 48; s Charles Hoover Lacey & Treva Steves L; m 1972 to Diana Baum. Educ: Western Mich Univ, BA, 70; Ind Univ Sch Law, Bloomington, JD, 73; Phi Eta Sigma; Omicron Delta Kappa. Polit & Govt Pos: Treas, Madison Co Rep Cent Comt, Ind, 74- Mem: Am & Ind State Bar Asns; Kiwanis Int. Legal Res: 106 N Shore Blvd Anderson IN 46011 Mailing Add: PO Box 847 Anderson IN 46015

LACHANCE, CRAIG ROBERT (D)
Chmn, Dist 34 Dem Party, Idaho
b Pocatello, Idaho, Sept 16, 50; s Harry Lawerence LaChance & Vivian LeBlanc L; single. Educ: Idaho State Univ, BA, 72; Coun Int Rels & UN affairs. Polit & Govt Pos: Pres, Idaho State Univ Young Dem, 68-72; state vpres, Idaho Young Dem, 70-71, state pres, 71-73; mem, Idaho Dem Exec Comt, 71-73; chmn, Dist 34 Dem Party, 71-; mem, Idaho State Dem Cent Comt, 71-, mem rules comt, 72-; deleg, Idaho State Dem Conv, 72; cand, Dem Nomination for State Rep, Dist 34, Pocatello, 72; Presidential elector, 72. Mem: Retail Clerks Union. Relig: Roman Catholic. Mailing Add: 734 Birch St Pocatello ID 83201

LACHANCE, HENRY J (D)
NH State Rep
Mailing Add: 201 W Hollis St Nashua NH 03060

LACHARITE, BERTRAND M (D)
Mem, Cumberland Co Dem Comt, Maine
b Brunswick, Maine, Dec 19, 46; s Bertrand A LaCharite & Constance Levesque L; m 1969

to Stella D Sevigny; c Christopher & Jonathan. Educ: Northeast La State Col, 65-66; Tau Kappa Epsilon. Polit & Govt Pos: Maine State Rep, 72-74; mem, Cumberland Co Dem Comt, 72- Bus & Prof Pos: Salesman, Union Mutual Life Ins Co, Portland, Maine, 71- Mil Serv: Entered as Pvt, Nat Guard, 66, released as E-5, 72, after serv in South Portland, Maine, 1st Coast Guard Dist, 68-72. Mem: Southern Maine Asn of Life Underwriters; Brunswick Jaycees. Relig: Catholic. Legal Res: 172 Linnhaven Brunswick ME 04011 Mailing Add: PO Box 462 Brunswick ME 04011

LACKEY, BERNICE (BEE) CATHERINE (R)
Chmn, Van Buren Co Rep Comt, Mich
b Chicago, Ill, Nov 13, 15; d James Smetana & Anna Slack S; m 1946 to William Franklin Lackey; c Susan Ann. Educ: Carl Schurz High Sch, Chicago, grad, 32. Polit & Govt Pos: Deleg, Van Buren Co & Mich State Conv, 65-75; Fourth Dist Comt Mem, 66-70; pres, Van Buren Co Rep Women's Club, 66-72; co chairperson to reelect Sen Griffin Comt, Van Buren Co, 72; chairman, Van Buren Co Rep Comt, 73- Bus & Prof Pos: Vchmn population comt, Adv Coun, Bloomingdale High Sch, Mich, 69-71; chmn bd rev, Waverly Twp, Paw Paw, Mich, 71-75. Mem: Eastern Star; Van Buren Co Farm Bur; VFW Auxiliary; Co Cancer Soc; Tri-Co Child & Family Serv (bd mem, 71). Relig: Protestant. Mailing Add: RR 2 Glendale Paw Paw MI 49079

LACKEY, J M (D)
b Alexander Co, NC, Mar 29, 16; s Chalmers A Lackey & Pearl Price L; m 1942 to Hazel Elizabeth Barnes; c Lynne & Joy. Educ: NC State Col, Raleigh. Polit & Govt Pos: Chmn, Alexander Co Dem Exec Comt, NC, formerly; mem bd, Co Comnrs Alexander Co, currently. Mil Serv: Entered as Pvt, Army, 43, released as S/Sgt, 45, after serv in Inf, ETO. Mem: Mason; CofC; Grange; NC State Bd of Health; Am Legion. Relig: Presbyterian. Mailing Add: Rte 2 Hiddenite NC 28636

LACKEY, JOHN FARIS (D)
Ky State Sen
Mailing Add: 536 Lancaster Ave Richmond KY 40475

LACKEY, PLEAS (D)
NC State Sen
Mailing Add: PO Box 166 Hiddenite NC 28636

LACROSSE, GLADYCE MAE (DFL)
VChairwoman, Red Lake Co Dem-Farmer-Labor Party, Minn
b Thief River Falls, Minn, Nov 4, 38; d Clarence W Meyer & Bertha Weise M; m 1959 to John Fredrick LaCrosse; c Cynthia Jean, Keith Fredrick, Mark Allen & Anthony John. Educ: Thief River Falls Area Voc Sch, 57-58. Polit & Govt Pos: Vchairwoman, Red Lake Co Dem-Farmer-Labor Party, Minn, 70- Bus & Prof Pos: Practical nurse, Red Lake Falls Clin, 64-71; mem exec bd, Inter-Co Nursing Serv, 70- Mem: Am Legion Auxiliary. Relig: Catholic. Mailing Add: RR 1 Red Lake Falls MN 56750

LACY, BENJAMIN WATKINS, IV (D)
Chmn, Flagler Co Dem Comt, Fla
b Montgomery, Ala, Oct 22, 38; s Benjamin Watkins Lacy, III & Grace Scott L; m 1966 to Judy Ann Vacovich; c Judy Ann & Benjamin Watkins, V. Educ: Emory Univ, BA, 61; Emory Univ Col Dent, DDS, 65; Psi Omega; Delta Tau Delta. Polit & Govt Pos: Chmn, Flagler Co Dem Comt, 74-; trustee, Daytona Beach Community Col, 75- Bus & Prof Pos: Dir, Flagler Co CofC, 69-, vpres, 74. Mil Serv: Entered as Capt, Army, 66, released as Capt, 68, after serv in Dental Detach, Ft Monmouth, NJ, 66-68. Mem: Volusia Co Dent Soc (secy-treas, 75-); Cent Dist Dent Soc; Fla Dental Asn (deleg, 74-); Am Dent Asn. Relig: Episcopal. Mailing Add: PO Box 816 Bunnell FL 32010

LACY, JAMES REYNOLDS (R)
Chmn, Wolfe Co Rep Cent Comt, Ky
b Hazel Green, Ky, May 4, 44; s William Reynolds Lacy & Maxine Walter L; m 1968 to Phyllis Lee Pelfrey; c James Scott. Educ: Morehead State Univ, AB, 66; Polit Sci Club. Polit & Govt Pos: Secy, Wolfe Co Rep Cent Comt, 68-72, chmn, 72- Bus & Prof Pos: Teacher, Wolfe Co High Sch, Campton, 66-; farmer, Campton, currently. Mem: Wolfe Co Jaycees (state dir, 73-); Nat, Ky & Wolfe Co Educ Asns. Honors & Awards: Outstanding Young Man of Am, 72. Relig: Church of Christ. Mailing Add: Box 432 Campton KY 41301

LADD, ELIZABETH R (R)
NH State Rep
Mailing Add: Northfield Rd Winchester NH 03470

LADDEY, RICHARD VICTOR (D)
Chmn, Sussex Co Dem Comt, NJ
b Newark, NJ; s John V Laddey & Louise Stilwell L; m 1941 to Rita C Byrne, wid; c Richard S, Brian M, Victoria (Mrs Donald DeMuth) & Deborah F. Educ: Univ NC, Chapel Hill, AB, 38; Rutgers Univ Law Sch, JD, 47. Polit & Govt Pos: Pres, Sparta Dem Club, NJ, formerly; chmn, Sussex Co Bd of Elec & Sussex Co Dem Comt, NJ, 73- Bus & Prof Pos: Pres, PRE Assoc, Ins Auditors & Engrs, Morristown, NJ, 71-; pres, Marlad Inc, Realty Holding & Develop, 72- Mil Serv: Entered as Pvt, Army, released as Sgt, after serv in 102nd Cavalry. Mem: Elks (pres of trustees, past Exalted Ruler); Casualty Ins Auditors Asn. Legal Res: 71 W Shore Trail Mohawk Sparta NJ 07871 Mailing Add: PO Box 341 Sparta NJ 07871

LADNER, EARL E, JR (D)
Miss State Rep
Mailing Add: Box 134 Kiln MS 39556

LADNER, HEBER AUSTIN (D)
Secy of State, Miss
b Pearl River City, Miss, Oct 4, 02; m to Daisy Bowles; c two. Educ: Millsaps Col, BS, 29; Duke Univ, MA, 38. Polit & Govt Pos: Miss State Rep, 36-40; secy, State Budget Comn, 40-42; clerk, Miss House of Rep, 42-48; Secy of State, Miss, 48- Bus & Prof Pos: Farmer; teacher. Publ: James Kimball Vardaman in Mississippi Politics, 38. Relig: Baptist. Mailing Add: State Capitol Jackson MS 39205

LADY, FRANK (D)
Ark State Rep
Mailing Add: 1912 Brookhaven Jonesboro AR 72401

LADY, WENDELL (R)
Kans State Rep
Mailing Add: 8732 Mackey Overland Park KS 66212

LAESSIG, WALTER BRUCE (R)
b Englewood, NJ, Aug 11, 41; s George Bruce Laessig & Eileen Codling L; m 1964 to Susan Jane Lamme; c Katherine Anne, Sarah Eileen & Matthew Lamme. Educ: Cornell Univ, AB, 63, MBA & LLB, 66; Phi Kappa Phi; Sigma Pi. Polit & Govt Pos: Minority economist, Joint Econ Comn, US Congress, 71-72, minority counsel, 72-75, asst minority counsel, Ways & Means Comt, 75- Bus & Prof Pos: Attorney, Nixon, Hargrave, Devans & Doyle, Rochester, NY, 66-68 & Martin, Whitfield & Thaler, Washington, DC, 68-70. Mem: Am & DC Bar Asns. Relig: Presbyterian. Mailing Add: 3312 Wake Drive Kensington MD 20795

LAFALCE, JOHN J (D)
US Rep, NY
b Buffalo, NY, Oct 6, 39; s Dominic E LaFalce & Catherine Stasio L; single. Educ: Canisius Col, BS, 61; Villanova Univ Law Sch, JD, 64; Alpha Sigma Nu; Di Gamma Honor Soc. Polit & Govt Pos: NY State Sen, 71-72; NY State Assemblyman, 73-74; co-chmn, NY State People for Muskie, 72; mem, NY State Dem Adv Coun, currently; US Rep, NY, 75- Bus & Prof Pos: Attorney, 64- Mil Serv: Entered as 1st Lt, Army, 65, released as Capt, 67, after serv in Adj Gen Corps, Ft Belvoir, Va; Army Commendation Medal. Mem: NY State & Am Bar Asns; Am Judicature Soc; Justinian Legal Soc; Tonawanda Jr CofC. Honors & Awards: Legal counsel, NY State Jr CofC. Relig: Roman Catholic. Mailing Add: 800 Starin Ave Kenmore NY 14223

LAFAVE, REUBEN (R)
Wis State Sen
b Oconto, Wis. Educ: Wis Pub Schs; RR Auditors Sch. Polit & Govt Pos: Wis State Assemblyman, 37-51; mem, Co Bd, formerly; pres, Northeastern Wis Conserv Coun, formerly; chmn, Sportsmen's Conserv Cong, formerly; Wis State Sen, 57- Bus & Prof Pos: Real estate broker. Mil Serv: Coast Guard. Honors & Awards: Outstanding Achievement in Conservation Field Award, Mil Sen, 53; Mr Conservation, Wis Conserv Club 256, 60. Mailing Add: Rte 1 Box 89A Oconto WI 54153

LAFFIN, STANLEY E (R)
Maine State Rep
Mailing Add: 21 Fairfield Ave Westbrook ME 04092

LAFITTE, JOHN HANCOCK, JR (R)
SC State Rep
b Columbia, SC, June 25, 36; s John Hancock LaFitte & Lunette Madison Epes L; m 1959 to Dorothy Hucks; c John H, III & Robert M. Educ: Univ SC, BS bus admin, 63; Sigma Chi. Polit & Govt Pos: SC State Rep, 72- Mil Serv: Entered as Pvt 1/C, 56, after serv in 1st Marine Air Wing, Far East, 54-55. Mem: Prof Builders Asn Inc; Nat, SC & Columbia Asns of Homebuilders; Nat Audubon Soc; Sons of Confederate Vet. Relig: Episcopal. Mailing Add: 1711 Shady Lane Columbia SC 29206

LAFLEUR, LEO D (R)
Ill State Rep
b Callaway, Nebr, May 11, 21; s Harry Clay LaFleur & Ethyl Russell L; m to Lucille Roloff. Educ: High sch, Calif. Polit & Govt Pos: Police magistrate, Bloomingdale, Ill, 50-60; co auditor, DuPage Co, Ill, 60-72; Ill State Rep, Second Dist, 72- Mil Serv: Air Force, 42-43. Mem: Mason; Elks; Lions; Brittany Spaniel of Am. Honors & Awards: Pub Serv Award, Michael J Howlett, Auditor of Pub Accts, 68. Relig: Protestant. Mailing Add: 216 N Bloomingdale Rd Bloomingdale IL 60108

LAFOLLETTE, DOUGLAS J (D)
Secy of State, Wis
b Des Moines, Iowa, June 6, 40; s Joseph Henry LaFollette & Frances Van der Wilt L; single. Educ: Marietta Col, BS, 63; Stanford Univ, MS, 64; Columbia Univ, PhD, 67; Phi Beta Kappa; Kappa Mu Epsilon; Sigma Xi. Polit & Govt Pos: Deleg, Dem Nat Conv, 72; Wis State Sen, 22nd Dist, 73-74; Secy of State, Wis, 75- Bus & Prof Pos: Research assoc, Univ Wis, 68-69, asst prof chem & ecol, 69-72. Publ: Co-auth, Intramolecular solution, Am Chem Soc J, 69; auth, Survival Handbook, Wis Environ Decade, 71; A Million-Billion Dollar GNP—Insanity Or Growth? Boston Law Sch Environ Affairs, 72. Mem: Fedn of Am Scientists; Wis Fedn of Teachers; Wis Ecol Soc (bd, 69-); Wis Environ Decade (dir, 69-); Union of Concerned Scientists. Honors & Awards: Outstanding Young Man of Year, Wis Jaycees, 71. Legal Res: 705 Orton Ct Madison WI 53703 Mailing Add: Rm 112 W State Capitol Madison WI 53702

LA FOLLETTE, PATRICIA ANNE (D)
b Martinsville, Ind, July 4, 27; d Marvin L Barger & Juanita M Jacobs B; m to Charles E La Follette; c Diana Huntley, Kathy Traylor, twins, William & Robert, Charles, Jr, John L, Sammy L & Paul S. Educ: Arsenal Tech of Indianapolis High Sch, grad 46. Polit & Govt Pos: Tax examr, Ind Dept Revenue, 63-70; precinct committeewoman, Wayne Twp, 16th Precinct, 65-75; case investr, Center Twp Trustee, 70-71; alt deleg, Dem Nat Mid-Term Conf, 74; corresp secy, 19th Dist Dem Club, 75- Mem: Wayne & Decatur Twp Dem Clubs; 19th Dist Dem Club; Gtr Indianapolis Woman's Polit Caucus; Ind State Woman's Dem Club. Mailing Add: 2717 S Berwick St Indianapolis IN 46241

LA FONTAINE, RAYMOND M (D)
Mass State Rep
Mailing Add: State Capitol Boston MA 02133

LAFONTANT, JEWEL (R)
Dep Solicitor Gen, Dept of Justice
b Chicago, Ill, Apr 28, 22; d Cornelius Francis Stradford & Aida Carter S; m 1961 to H Ernest Lafontant; c John Rogers. Educ: Oberlin Col, AB, 43; Univ Chicago, JD, 46. Hon Degrees: Recipient six hon doctorates. Polit & Govt Pos: Mem-at-lg, Bd Gov, Ill Young Rep, 49; vchmn-at-lg, Cook Co Young Rep, 53; treas, Sixth Ward Young Rep, 53-55; bd dirs, Cook Co Rep Women, 53-55; asst US attorney, 55-58; alt deleg, Rep Nat Conv, 60, deleg, 72, seconded nomination of Richard Nixon for President of US, 60; chmn, Ill Vol for Nixon/Lodge, 60; civil rights adv to Henry Cabot Lodge, 60; adv State Treas, 62-64; chmn, Second Cong Dist, Ill Lawyers for Nixon/Agnew, 68; mem, US Adv Comn on Int Educ & Cultural Affairs, 69- & President's Coun on Minority Bus Enterprise, 70-; spec asst attorney gen, Ill, 70-73; bd dirs, Women's Nat Rep Club of Chicago, 70-73; comnr, Ill Family Study Comn & Ill Dept of Corrections, formerly; mem, Adv Comt to Cook Co Dept Pub Aid, Cook

Co Welfare Serv Comt & Ill Status of Women Comn, formerly; chmn, Ill Adv Comt to US Civil Rights Comn; village attorney, Robbins & East Chicago Heights, Ill, formerly; US deleg, UN, 72; Dep Solicitor Gen, Dept of Justice, 73- Bus & Prof Pos: Trial attorney, Legal Aid Bur, United Charities of Chicago, 47-53, chmn, Legal Aid Staff Comt, 52; partner, Stradford, Lafontant, Fisher & Malkin, Law Firm, currently; dir, Jewel Companies, Inc, 71-, Trans World Airlines, 72- & Foote, Cone & Belding 72- Publ: Auth, Restrictive covenants, Nat Bar J, 48; Status of women & race discrimination, Dept of State Bull. Mem: Admitted to US Supreme Court; Provident Hosp & Training Sch Asn (vpres bd trustees); Home for Destitute Crippled Children (mem bd dirs); Am Civil Liberties Union; Fed Bar Asn (mem bd mgrs). Honors & Awards: Woman of Distinction Achievement Award, Iota Phi Lambda; Woman of the Year, Ill Asn Colored Women, & Antioch Baptist Church, Lambda Kappa Mu, Church Women of Gtr Chicago & State St Coun; Achievement Award, Cook Co Bar Asn; Three Serv Awards, YMCA Metrop Chicago; Women of the Year Award, Women's Share in Pub Serv, 70. Relig: Methodist; trustee, St Mark Methodist Episcopal Church, past vpres, Bus & Prof Club. Legal Res: 4959 S Greenwood Chicago IL 60615 Mailing Add: 69 W Washington Chicago IL 60602

LAGESCHULTE, RAY (R)
Iowa State Rep
Mailing Add: RR 2 Waverly IA 50677

LAGOMARSINO, ROBERT JOHN (R)
US Rep, Calif
b Ventura, Calif, Sept 4, 26; s Emilio J Lagomarsino & Marjorie Gates L; m 1960 to Norma Jean Mabrey; c Karen, Dexter & Dana. Educ: Univ Calif, Santa Barbara, BA, 50; Univ Santa Clara, LLB, 53; Alpha Sigma Nu; Delta Sigma Phi. Polit & Govt Pos: Mayor & city councilman, Ojai, Calif, 58-61; Calif State Sen, 24th Sen Dist, Ventura Co, 61-74; deleg, Rep Nat Conv, 68; US Rep, Calif, 75- Mil Serv: Entered as A/S, Navy, 44, released as Pharmacist Mate 2/C, 46, after serv in US & Pac Theatre. Mem: Elks; Eagles; Moose; Am Legion; Rotary. Honors & Awards: One of Calif Five Outstanding Young Men, Calif Jr CofC, 61. Relig: Catholic. Legal Res: 1137 Gridley Rd Ojai CA Mailing Add: 1319 Longworth Bldg US House of Rep Washington DC 20515

LAGRONE, DONNA JOAN (D)
Mem Cent Comt, Colo Dem Party
b Pasadena, Calif, Mar 29, 31; d Harry Louk Wheeler & Ruth Elizabeth Minter W; wid, 61; c Michael Jerome, Timothy Kevin, Brien Thomas & Sean Patrick Irvin; m 1962 to Clyde Winfred LaGrone; c David Lee & Steven Laurance. Educ: Colo State Univ, 49-52. Polit & Govt Pos: Committeewoman, Precinct 220, Arapahoe Co, Colo, 68-70; deleg, Arapahoe Co Dem Conv, 68 & 72, chmn, Uncommitted Deleg, 72; deleg, Colo Dem State Conv, 68 & 72; vchmn, Rep Dist 38, Dem Party, 68-70; Arapahoe Co Dem Party rep, State Rules Comt, 72-; vchmn, Arapahoe Co Dem Party, formerly; mem, State Cent Comt, Colo Dem Party, 71-; rep on reapportionment from Arapahoe Co, Colo State Legis, 72; chmn, Muskie for President, Arapahoe Co, 72; mem, Haskell for Senate Comt, 72; deleg, Dem Nat Conv, 72; cand, Colo House of Rep, Dist 39, 72. Bus & Prof Pos: Gen distributor, Bestline Prods, 67-; lobbyist, Colo Open Space Coun, 70-71; pres, L & L Mfr & Distributing Co, 72-; bus mgr, Colo Dem, 72. Publ: A uniform for mom, Scouting Mag, 12/69; co-auth, Colorado election 1972, Dem Party Cand Assistance Comt, 5/72. Mem: Rocky Mt Writers Guild; Englewood Jane Jefferson Club (pres, 70-71, parliamentarian, 71-); State Jane Jefferson Fedn (rec secy, 71-72, vpres, 72-73); We Care, Women's Environ Coalition; Altar & Rosary Soc. Honors & Awards: Mem, Top Ten Nat Distributors, Bestline Prods, 68. Relig: Catholic. Mailing Add: 5941 S Pennsylvania Littleton CO 80121

LAHMAYER, ALBERT T (D)
b Milwaukee, Wis, May 10, 27; s Albert Lahmayer & Arleen Hanson L; m 1950 to Jeanette Isaacs; c Bruce, Mark & Ruth. Educ: Univ Wis, Whitewater; Northern Ill Col Optom, BS & OD; Phi Chi Epsilon. Polit & Govt Pos: Chmn, Jackson Co Dem Party, Wis, formerly; mem, Third Dist Dem Cabinet, 71-; dir, WWis Health Planning Orgn, 71-; mem, Gov Health Policy & Prog Coun, 73- Bus & Prof Pos: Optometrist. Mil Serv: Entered as Pvt, Army, 45, released as Sgt, after serv in Mil Invest, 47. Mem: Am Optom Asn; Wis Optom Asn (mem bd dirs, secy, 71-73); SCent Optom Soc (pres); Wis Pub Health Asn. Relig: Protestant. Legal Res: Rte 1 Black River Falls WI 54615 Mailing Add: Box 408 Black River Falls WI 54615

LAIDIG, GARY WAYNE (R)
Minn State Rep
b York, Pa, Aug 15, 48; s Rev Robert Vance Laidig & Daisy Harvey; m 1972 to Paula Jane Kinney. Educ: Morningside Col, 66-67; Univ Wis-River Falls, 70- Polit & Govt Pos: Minn State Rep, Dist 51A, 72- Mil Serv: Entered as Pvt E-1, Marine Corp, 68, released as Cpl E-4, 70, after serv in Force Logistics Command, Danang, SVietnam, 68-69; Nat Defense Medal; Two Vietnamese Serv Ribbons; Combat Action. Mem: VFW; Jaycees; Am Legion. Relig: United Methodist. Mailing Add: 114 N Fourth St Bayport MN 55003

LAIR, DANIEL HERLEY (D)
b St Paul, Minn, July 20, 45; s Herley Daniel Lair & Alice Marie Benson L; m 1971 to Peggy Jo Power; c Terri Jean. Educ: Southwestern Okla State Univ, BA, 68, MEd, 75; chief justice, Student Supreme Court, 74-; Pi Kappa Alpha. Polit & Govt Pos: Mem, Young Dem of Southwestern Okla State Univ; deleg, Dem Nat Mid-Term Conf, 74. Mil Serv: Entered as Pvt, Army, 69, released as 1st Lt, 73, after serv in Spec Ammunition Medal. Mem: Am Polit Sci Asn (adv mgr summer ed, Broadside Newspaper, 74). Relig: Catholic. Legal Res: 506 N Second St Weatherford OK 73096 Mailing Add: PO Box 537 Weatherford OK 73096

LAIRD, CHARLES F (D)
Kans State Rep
b Topeka, Kans, June 4, 41; s Donald L Laird, Sr (deceased) & Isabel Hoffman L; m 1964 to Sue Melton; c Timothy P, Daniel J & Michael C. Educ: St Thomas Sem, 59-60; Washburn Univ, BA, 64; Univ Md, College Park, MEd, 70. Polit & Govt Pos: Bd mem, US Dist 450, Dem Party, Kans, 71-; Kans State Rep, 59th Dist, 73- Bus & Prof Pos: Salesman, Mass Mutual Life Ins Co, 70- Mil Serv: Entered as 2nd Lt, Air Force, 64, released as Capt, 70, after serv in 4252 Strategic Wing, 8th Air Force, Kadena Air Base, Okinawa, 67-70; Air Force Commendation Medal; AF Longevity Award; Distinguished Unit Citation with two Oak Leaf Clusters. Mem: Nat Asn of Life Underwriters; Shawnee Heights Optimist Club. Relig: Catholic; Mem, St Matthew Cath Church Parish Coun. Mailing Add: Suite 800 1st Nat Bank Tower Topeka KS 66603

LAIRD, H V (R)
Mem, Walthall Co Rep Party, Miss
b Bassfield, Miss, May 26, 13; s Earl D Laird & Ether Broom L; m 1930 to Jessie Leu Hathorn; c Darroh H, Dalton, Kenneth D, Duel & Daphne. Educ: Bassfield High, Bassfield, Miss. Polit & Govt Pos: Chmn, Walthall Co Rep Party, Miss, formerly, mem, currently. Bus & Prof Pos: Owner & mgr, Laird Motor Co, 49- & Laird Garage & Serv Sta, formerly. Relig: Baptist. Legal Res: Rte 2 Tylertown MS 39667 Mailing Add: PO Box 287 Tylertown MS 39667

LAIRD, MELVIN ROBERT (R)
b Sept 1, 22; s Melvin Robert Laird & Helen Connor L; m 1945 to Barbara Masters; c John Osborne, Alison & David Malcolm. Educ: Carleton Col, BA. Hon Degrees: LHD & Dr Polit Sci degrees from various cols & univs. Polit & Govt Pos: Wis State Sen, 46-51, chmn, Senate Vet Affairs Comt, chmn, Wis Legis Coun; deleg, Rep Nat Conv, 48, 52, 56, 60, 64 & 68, mem platform comt, 52 & 56, vchmn, 60 & chmn, 64; chmn, Wis State Rep Conv, 54 & 60; US Rep, Seventh Dist, Wis, 53-69, chmn, Joint House-Senate Comt on Rep Policy, 60, chmn, House Rep Conf, US House of Rep, 65-69; mem US Deleg, WHO, 59, 63 & 65; mem, Rep Coord Comt, 64-; Secy of Defense, 69-73; Counr to The President for Domestic Affairs, 73-74. Bus & Prof Pos: Sr counr nat & int affairs, Readers Digest Asn, currently. Mil Serv: Entered Navy, 42-46, serv in Third Fleet, Pac Theater; Purple Heart. Publ: A House Divided: America's Strategy Gap, Henry Regnery Co, 62; ed, The Conservative Papers, 64 & Republican Papers, 68, Doubleday & Co. Mem: Am Legion; 40 et 8; VFW; DAV; F&AM. Honors & Awards: Cong Distinguished Serv Award, Am Polit Sci Asn, 67; Man of Year Award, US Pub Health Asn, 68; UPI Pub Serv Award, Fla Unipress Asn, 69; Citation for Legis Statesmanship, Coun Exceptional Children, 69; Minute Man Award, ROA, 70; plus numerous other awards & hon mem. Relig: Presbyterian; Ruling Elder. Mailing Add: 1730 Rhode Island Ave NW Washington DC 20036

LAISE, CAROL C
b Winchester, WVa, Nov 14, 17; m to Ellsworth Bunker. Educ: Am Univ, BA, 38 & MA, 40. Polit & Govt Pos: Mem, Civil Serv Comn, 41-46; UNRRA, London, 46-47; career officer, US Dept of State Foreign Serv, 48-, State Dept Officer on Int Orgn Affairs, 48-55, consul & first secy, New Delhi, 56-61, Sr Seminar on Foreign Affairs, 61-62, dep dir, Near Eastern & SAsian Affairs, 62-65, dir, Off of SAsian Affairs, 65-66, US Ambassador to Nepal, 66-73, nominated Asst Secy State for Pub Affairs, 73, dir gen, Foreign Serv, 74- Honors & Awards: Superior Accomplishment Award, 45; Commendable Serv Award, 60; Fed Woman's Award, 65. Mailing Add: Dept of State 2201 C St Washington DC 20520

LAITIN, JOSEPH (D)
Asst Secy Defense Pub Affairs
b Brooklyn, NY, Oct 2, 14; s Harry Laitin & Irene Lubetkin L; m 1961 to Christine Henriette Houdayer; c Sigrid & Peter. Polit & Govt Pos: Asst to dir, Bur of Budget, 63-64; asst press secy to President, 65-66; asst to dir for pub affairs, Off Mgt & Budget, 66-74; pub affairs consult, President's Comt on Selective Serv, 66-67; dir info, Nat Comn Causes & Prevention Violence, 68-70; pub affairs consult, President's Comn Campus Unrest, 70; Asst Secy Defense Pub Affairs, 74- Bus & Prof Pos: Correspondent, United Press Int, Washington, DC, 41-45; foreign correspondent, Reuters, Ltd, Far East, Europe & Latin Am, 45-50; chief correspondent, Research Inst Am, Washington, DC, 50-52; freelance writer, 52-63. Mem: Nat Press Club; Overseas Press Club. Honors & Awards: Calif State Fair Award for Best Radio Documentary, Changing Face of Hollywood, 57. Legal Res: 7204 Exfair Rd Bethesda MD 20014 Mailing Add: Dept of Defense Washington DC 20301

LAKE, JAMES HOWARD (R)
b Fresno, Calif, Aug 16, 37; s Howard Benton Lake & Maryetta McPherson L; div; c James Charles, Michael Benton & Garrett Douglas. Educ: Bakersfield Col, AA, 57; Univ Calif, Los Angeles, BS, 59; Pi Rho Phi; Alpha Gamma Sigma; William H Danforth Fel; Circle K Int. Polit & Govt Pos: Clerk & trustee, Delano Union Sch Dist, Calif, 64-66; dist rep to US Rep Bob Mathias, 18th Dist, Calif, 67-69, admin asst to US Rep Mathias, 70-73; dep asst secy, US Dept Agr, 73- Mem: Delano Businessmen's Asn; Delano Dist CofC; Kiwanis; Mason; Commonwealth Club Calif. Mailing Add: 1929 Cherry St Bakersfield CA 93304

LAKE, ROBERT CAMPBELL, JR (D)
SC State Sen
b Whitmire, SC, Dec 27, 25; s Robert Campbell Lake, Sr & Susan Howze L; m 1955 to Carolyn Young Gray; c Sarah Linda, Robert C, III & Samuel Young. Educ: Univ SC, 43-47, Law Sch, LLB, 49; Blue Key; Pi Kappa Phi. Polit & Govt Pos: Pres, Newberry Co Dem Conv, 52-64; deleg, SC Dem State Conv, 54-66; city attorney, Whitmire, SC, 55-: attorney, Newberry Co, 60-68; secy, Nursing Home Comn, SC, 63-; deleg, Dem Nat Conv, 64; mem SC Study Comn on Higher Educ, 65-66; SC State Sen, Laurens, Newberry, Union, Cherokee & Saluda Co, 69- Bus & Prof Pos: Pres, Whitmire Jr CofC, 52; attorney, State Bldg & Loan Asn, 55-; pres, Newberry Co Bar Asn, 62; vchmn, Whitmire United Fund, 66-67 & 68; dir, State Bank & Trust Co, Whitmire, 66-; chmn, Newberry Co Develop Bd, 67 & 68. Mil Serv: Entered as Pvt, Army, 44, released as Pfc, 45, after serv in Spec Serv; Good Conduct Medal. Mem: Hejaz Shrine Temple (High Priest & Prophet, Potentate, 72-73); Union Elks Lodge 1321; Newberry & Mid-Carolina Country Clubs; Greenville City & Palmetto Clubs. Relig: Presbyterian; Deacon, Presby Church of Whitmire. Legal Res: N Main St Whitmire SC 29178 Mailing Add: State House Columbia SC 29211

LAKNESS, MILTON A
SDak State Rep
b Watertown, SDak, Apr 22, 34; s Art Lakness & Johanna Grudt L; m 1954 to Benita Stormo; c Nathan, Stephanie, Naomi & Joe. Educ: Hazel High Sch, SDak, grad, 52. Polit & Govt Pos: SDak State Rep, 75- Bus & Prof Pos: Bd mem, Hamlin Co Crop Improv Asn, 67-75; pres, Hazel Farmers Elevator, 71-74; pres, SDak Young Men & Women, 73-; secy, SDak State Flax Comn, 74- Mem: Farm Bur (vpres). Honors & Awards: Outstanding Young Farmer Award, 67. Relig: Lutheran. Mailing Add: RR Hayti SD 57241

LAKRITZ, SIMON (D)
Chmn, Kings Co Dem Cent Comt, Calif
b Detroit, Mich, May 14, 30; s Max Lakritz & Anna Wayne L; m 1953 to Mary Elizabeth Lyon; c Andrew Morris, Jeffrey, Bradley William & Thomas Spencer. Educ: Univ Ariz, BA, 53, MEd, 57; Hillel. Polit & Govt Pos: Mem, Kings Co Dem Cent Comt, 68-, chmn, 70-; mem, Calif Dem Cent Comt, 70-; mem, San Joaguin Caucus, 74-; city councilman, Hanford, Calif, 74- Bus & Prof Pos: Pres, Hanford Teachers Asn, 63-64; dir fed projs, Hanford High Sch, 66-, dir spec educ, 74- Mil Serv: Entered as Pvt, Army, 53, released as Cpl, 55, after serv in Adj Gen Corp, Army Hq, Europe, 54-55; Good Conduct Medal. Mem: Calif Teachers Asn; Sec

Sch Adminrs; Kings Co Comn on Aging Coun (chmn); Kings Co Community Action Orgn. Relig: Jewish. Mailing Add: 175 E Birch Ave Hanford CA 93230

LAMARCA, RUSSELL J (D)
Pa State Rep
b Reading, Pa, Dec 17, 28; s Harry LaMarca & Mary Genova L; m to Elizabeth Keiper; c One. Educ: Univ Pittsburgh Col, BA; Univ Pittsburgh Sch of Law, LLB; Sigma Alpha Epsilon; phi Alpha Theta; Phi Alpha Delta. Polit & Govt Pos: Solicitor, Reading Redevelop Authority, Pa, 61-64; Pa State Rep, 64- Bus & Prof Pos: Attorney. Mil Serv: Sgt, Marine Corps, Korean Conflict. Mem: Amalgamated Clothing Workers. Mailing Add: Capitol Bldg Harrisburg PA 17120

LAMB, EDWARD (D)
Mem, State Dem Exec Comt, Ohio
b Toledo, Ohio, Apr 23, 02; s Clarence M Lamb & Mary Gross L; m 1931 to Prudence Hutchenson; c Edward Hutchinson & Prudence Priscilla (Mrs Guyton). Educ: Dartmouth Col, NH; Harvard Law Sch; Western Reserve Law Sch. Hon Degrees: LHD, Wilberforce Univ; LLD, Gannon Col. Polit & Govt Pos: Mem, State Dem Exec Comt, Ohio currently; deleg-at-lg, Dem Nat Conv, 64, 68 & 72. Publ: The planned economy of Soviet Russia, 34; No lamb for slaughter, 64. Mem: Overseas Press Club; Nat Press Club; Am Bar Asn; Ctr Study Dem Insts (mem bd trustees); UN Asn of the US (dir). Relig: Episcopal. Legal Res: 408 E Broadway Maumee OH 43537 Mailing Add: 600 Edward Lamb Bldg Toledo OH 43603

LAMB, GERALD (L) EDWARD (D)
b Alpena, Mich, July 21, 47; s Carl John Lamb & Dorothy Anne Kujawa L; single. Educ: Alpena Community Col, 66-67; Aquinas Col, 67-69; treas, Gamma Alpha Pi, 68, pres, 69. Polit & Govt Pos: Chmn, Alpena Cath Teen Dem, 60-64; chmn, Aquinas Col Young Am for Freedom, 68-71; state regional dir, Mich Young Am for Freedom, 69-71; state youth dir, Mich Am Independent Party, 69-70, mem, State Cent Comt, 69-70; campaign dir, Kent Co Wallace Campaign, 72; deleg, Dem Nat Conv, 72, mem exec comt, Mich Deleg, 72; state coordr, Fifth Cong Dist Wallace Action Movement, 73. Bus & Prof Pos: Teacher, Grand Rapids Dioscesan Schs, 68; salesman, Christian Music Ctr, 70-73. Mem: Mich Sch Band & Orchestra Asn. Relig: Catholic. Legal Res: 600 34th St SW Wyoming MI 49509 Mailing Add: PO Box 2504 Grand Rapids MI 49501

LAMB, JAMES L (D)
Chmn, 18th Dist Dem Party, NDak
b Grand Forks, NDak, Nov 1, 24; s James S Lamb & Johanna Londergan L; m 1949 to Mary Jean Bavendick; c J Lawrence, David S, Timothy C, Brian P, Steven S & Jean Marie. Educ: Univ Notre Dame, AB & BNS, 45, LLB, 50. Polit & Govt Pos: Precinct committeeman, Grand Forks, NDak, 54-; chmn, Grand Forks Co Dem Comt, 58-66; deleg, Dem Nat Conv, 60; mem exec comt, NDak State Dem Party, 60-66, mem state policy comt, 68- & liaison comt, 73; chmn, NE Dist Comn, 62-66; mem, Urban Renewal Comn, Grand Forks, 67-; chmn, 18th Dist Dem Party, 68- Mem: Am Bar Asn (mem fidelity & surety com, 63-); NDak State Bar Asn (mem procedure comt, 68-); Grand Forks Co Bar Asn (pres, 72-); Elks; VFW. Relig: Catholic. Mailing Add: 517 Reeves Dr Grand Forks ND 58201

LAMB, NORMAN (R)
Okla State Sen
Mailing Add: State Capitol Oklahoma City OK 73105

LAMB, THOMAS A (D)
RI State Rep
Mailing Add: 100 Woodside Ave West Warwick RI 02893

LAMB, THOMAS F (D)
b Pittsburgh, Pa, Oct 22, 22; s James J Lamb & Agnes B Dunne L; m 1957 to Barbara Joyce; c Thomas, Jr, James, Michael & Barbara. Educ: Duquesne Univ, BA, 48 & LLB, 52. Polit & Govt Pos: Pa State Rep, 58-66; Pa State Sen, 66-74, majority leader, Pa State Senate, 71-74; deleg, Dem Nat Conv, 72. Bus & Prof Pos: Attorney, Allegheny Co Bar Asn, 53- Mil Serv: Entered as A/S, Navy, 42, released as Lt(jg), 46, after serv in Pac Theater. Mem: Am Legion; VFW; KofC; Knights of Equity. Relig: Roman Catholic. Mailing Add: 905 Gladys Ave Pittsburgh PA 15216

LAMBERT, AARON COLUS (BUTCH) (D)
Miss State Rep
b Holcut, Miss, Feb 27, 23; s Alvin Grady Lambert & Gertrude Jourdan L; m 1942 to Ida Yvonne Gilliland; c Butch, Jr, Vicki, Scott & Amy. Educ: Univ Mo, BSPE. Polit & Govt Pos: Miss State Rep, 60-64 & 68- Bus & Prof Pos: Athletic dir, Itawamba Jr Col, 49-52; field agt, Miss State Tax Comn, 52-56; personnel mgr, Rockwell Mfg Co, 56- Mil Serv: Entered as A/S, Navy, 43, released as 1/C PO, 45, after serv in Great Lakes Naval Training Ctr. Mem: Mason; Shrine; Touchdowner; Southeastern Conf Football Referee; Southeastern Conf Basketball Referee. Honors & Awards: Officiate, Sugar Bowl Football Game, Gator Bowl Football Game, three NCAA Basketball Tournaments & Sugar Bowl Basketball Tourney. Relig: Church of Christ. Mailing Add: Box 1508 Tupelo MS 38801

LAMBERT, EZEKIEL ROY (D)
Ga State Rep
b Madison, Ga, June 18, 25; s Ezekiel R Lambert & Lula Bowers L; m 1954 to Christine Davis; c Leigh & Anne. Educ: Tulane Univ; Univ Ga, BBA, LLB; Phi Delta Theta. Polit & Govt Pos: Ga State Sen, 55-56 & 61-62; Ga State Rep, 63- Bus & Prof Pos: Attorney. Mil Serv: QM 3/C, Navy, 43-46. Mem: Kiwanis; Am Legion; VFW. Relig: Methodist. Mailing Add: Box 169 Madison GA 30650

LAMBERT, HENRY M (D)
Nat Committeeman, Young Dem
b New Orleans, La, Feb 8, 42; s John D Lambert & Dehlia Kennedy L; single. Educ: Loyola Univ (La), BBA, 63, JD, 65; Inst Polit, New Orleans, grad, 69; Metrop Area Comt Leadership Forum, Urban Studies Ctr, Tulane Univ; Delta Sigma Pi; Blue Key; pres, Loyola SAK Alumni Asn. Polit & Govt Pos: Dep dir safety & permits, City of New Orleans, 70-72, urban policy specialist III, Mayors Off, 72-; Nat Committeeman, Young Dem, currently. Bus & Prof Pos: Attorney-at-law, Lambert, Nowalsky & Lambert; admissions councellor, Loyola Univ, 68-69, instr bus law, 70-71. Mil Serv: Entered as 2nd Lt, Army, 66, released as Capt, 67, after serv in Fourth Inf Div, Cent Highlands, Vietnam; Capt, Army Res, 3 years; Bronze Star; Vietnam Campaign Medal with Two Oak Leaf Clusters; Vietnam Serv Medal; Nat Defense Serv Medal; Cert of Achievement from Commanding Gen, Ft Sam Houston, Tex. Mem: Nat Asn Housing & Redevelop Officials (vpres, New Orleans Chap); Alliance for Good Govt; Southern Regional Coun, Inc; KofC; Am Pub Works Asn. Relig: Catholic. Mailing Add: 3635 Gentilly Blvd New Orleans LA 70122

LAMBERT, LAWRENCE ARTHUR (DFL)
Mem Exec Comt, Sixth Cong Dist Dem-Farmer-Labor Party, Minn
b Green Valley, Minn, Sept 21, 21; s Arthur Lambert & Eva Suprenant L; m 1947 to Beverly Jean Pitha; c Brian, Carol Leigh, Luann & Susan. Educ: Palmer Col Chiropractic, DC, 50. Polit & Govt Pos: Chmn, Chippewa Co Dem-Farmer-Labor Party, Minn, 67-69, deleg, 70-; mem exec comt, Sixth Cong Dist Dem-Farmer-Labor Party, Minn, 70- Mil Serv: Entered as Seaman 2/C, Navy, 42, released as Pharmacists Mate 2/C, 45, after serv in Fleet Air Wing 17, Southwest Pac Theatre, 44-45. Mem: Am Chiropractic Asn; Minn Chiropractic Asn (chmn southwest dist, 62-); VFW; Lions; KofC. Honors & Awards: Distinguished Serv Award Community Serv, Marshall, Minn, 54. Relig: Roman Catholic. Mailing Add: 105 N Fourth St Montevideo MN 56265

LAMBERT, LUCIEN G (D)
NH State Rep
Mailing Add: 55 Amory St Manchester NH 03102

LAMBERT, PHILLIP E (D)
Okla State Sen
Mailing Add: State Capitol Oklahoma City OK 73105

LAMBERT, WILLIAM CHESLEY (R)
Chmn, Shenandoah Co Rep Comt, Va
b Edinburg, Va, Dec 28, 14; s William Franklin Lambert & Mary Lottie Painter L; m 1936 to Evelyn Pauline Eckard; c Jerry Franklin, Wayne Allen & Bonnie Jo. Educ: Nat Bus Col, Roanoke, Va, 32; Massanutten Mil Acad, Woodstock, 32-33. Polit & Govt Pos: Va State Deleg, 48-49; mem Woodstock Town Coun, Va, 54-58; finance chmn, Shenandoah Co Rep Comt, 67, chmn, 68- Bus & Prof Pos: Owner & operator, Lambert's Poultry Co, 39-50, Valley Alleys, 50-52 & pvt real estate & farm opers, 50- Mem: Lions; Shenandoah Co Mem Hosp (mem bd dirs); Shenandoah Co March of Dimes (chmn). Honors & Awards: Selected Citizen of the Week by Shenandoah Herald, Woodstock, Va. Relig: United Methodist. Mailing Add: Rte 1 Box 139-B Woodstock VA 22664

LAMBERTY, PATRICIA ANN (D)
Mem, Nebr Dem State Cent Comt
b Seward, Nebr, Oct 11, 42; d Mervin W Zillig & Myrna Marie Sieck Z; m 1960 to Louis Earlyon Lamberty; c Kim, Craig & Christopher. Educ: Rutgers Univ, 64-65; Univ Del, 66; Univ Nebr, Omaha, 69-70. Polit & Govt Pos: Mem, Nebr McGovern Reform Comt, 69-70; state coordr, McGovern Campaign, 72; alt deleg & mem platform comt, Dem Nat Conv, 72; mem, Nebr Dem State Cent Comt, 72-; chairwoman, Nebr Dem Legis Search Comt, 72- Bus & Prof Pos: Prog dir, YWCA, 73- Mem: Nebraskans for Peace (mem state steering comt, 72-73); League of Women Voters (unit leader, 69-70); Mayors Comn on Status of Women (mem social concerns comt, 73-); Gov Comn on Status of Women, 73- Relig: United Church of Christ. Mailing Add: 301 S 51 Ave Omaha NE 68132

LAMBETH, THOMAS WILLIS (D)
b Clayton, NC, Jan 8, 35; s Mark Thomas Lambeth & Ina Henrietta Willis L; m 1964 to Donna Brooks Irving; c Donna Catherine, Mark Hunter & Thomas Richard. Educ: Univ NC, AB in Hist, 57, grad work in hist, 57-58; Phi Alpha Theta; Order of the Golden Fleece; Order of the Grail; Order of the Old Well; Amphoterothen Soc. Polit & Govt Pos: Asst to the Chmn, NC Dem Exec Comt, Fall Campaign, 60; admin asst to the Gov NC, 61-65; mem bd dirs, Guilford Co Young Dem, 68-69; admin asst to US Rep Richardson Preyer, 69- Bus & Prof Pos: Dir, Univ NC, Chapel Hill Student Union, 57-58; reporter & copy ed, Winston-Salem Jour, 59; admin assoc, Smith Richardson Found, Greensboro, 65-69; trustee, Consolidated Univ NC, 69-72 & Univ NC Chapel Hill, 72- Mil Serv: Entered as Pvt, Army Reserve, 58, released as Sgt, 65, after serv in Military Police Corps. Mem: PATH Sch, Greensboro (mem bd dirs); Nat Repertory Theatre (bd dirs, NC Chap); Ruth Z Fleishman Found (mem bd trustees). Honors & Awards: Outstanding Young Dem in NC, 70. Relig: Methodist. Legal Res: 210 W Drewry Lane Raleigh NC 27609 Mailing Add: 7753 Patriot Dr Annandale VA 22003

LAMBOLEY, PAUL H (D)
Chmn, Dem Party Nev
b Milwaukee, Wis, July 17, 40; s F Earl Lamboley & Ada Zweiger L; m 1963 to Stephanie J West; c Nicole & Joelle. Educ: Univ Notre Dame, BS, 62; Univ Wis, JD, 67; Phi Alpha Delta. Polit & Govt Pos: Law clerk to Justice David Zenoff, Nev Supreme Court, 67-68; chmn, Washoe Co Dem Party, 70-72; mem, Dem Nat Comt, 74-; chmn, Dem Party Nev, 74- Bus & Prof Pos: Lawyer, Reno, Nev, 68- Mem: State Bars Wis & Nev; Am Bar Asn; Elks. Relig: Catholic. Legal Res: 108 Greenridge Reno NV 89502 Mailing Add: PO Box 169 Reno NV 89504

LAMBORN, CLIFTON C (R)
Iowa State Sen
b Bellevue, Iowa, Jan 17, 19; s Chas E Lamborn & Inez Montgomery L; m 1942 to Marshalline Davis; c Janet Anne. Polit & Govt Pos: Iowa State Sen, currently, chmn, Senate Transportation Comt, 69-; alt deleg, Dem Nat Conv, 72. Mil Serv: Entered as Pvt, Army, 41, released as M/Sgt, 46, after serv in 1023rd Engr Treadway Bridge Co, European & Pac Theaters; Victory Medal; Am Theatre Ribbon; European-African-Middle Eastern Theater Ribbon; Asiatic-Pac Theater Ribbon. Mem: Lions; Farm Bur. Relig: Methodist. Mailing Add: 207 S Vermont St Maquoketa IA 52060

LAMBRIGHT, BETTY LOUISE (R)
Secy, LaGrange Co Cent Comt
b Converse, Ind, Dec 17, 34; d Samuel G Aschliman & Anna Plank A; m 1953 to Freeman J Lambright (Fritz); c Brent Alan, Brenda Jean, Bradley James & Becky Renee. Educ: New Paris High Sch, grad, 53. Polit & Govt Pos: Secy, LaGrange Co Cent Comt, currently. Relig: Mennonite. Mailing Add: Rte 1 Box 38 Topeka IN 46571

LAMBROS, NICKOLAS (D)
Mass State Rep
Mailing Add: State Capitol Boston MA 02133

LAMKIN, EUGENE HENRY, JR (NED) (R)
Ind State Rep
b Owensboro, Ky, Feb 23, 35; s Eugene Henry Lamkin & Nancy Elizabeth Davidson L; m 1968 to Martha Savanah Dampf; c Melinda Magness & Matthew Davidson Educ: DePauw Univ, BA, 46; Ind Univ Sch Med, MD, 60; internship, Philadelphia Gen Hosp, 60-61; fel endocrinol & metab & residency in int med, Ind Univ Med Ctr, 61-62 & 64-66; Am Bd Internal Med, dipl, 67; Phi Eta Sigma; Phi Beta Kappa; Delta Omicron Chi; Alpha Omega Alpha; Beta Theta Pi; Nu Sigma Nu; nat vpres Student Am Med Asn, 59-60. Polit & Govt Pos: Vpres, Marion Co Young Rep, 66-67; Ind State Rep, Marion Co, 66-, chmn, Marion Co deleg, Ind House Rep, 69-72; chmn, Pub Safety Comt, formerly, chmn, Affairs of Marion Co Comt, 69-74, mem, Pub Health & Environ Affairs Comts, currently; chmn, Independent Sector Study Comt; mem, Gov Traffic Safety Comn, 69-70 & 73- & Gov Comn Med Educ, 69-70; mem steering comt, Mayor's Task Force on Drug Abuse, 69-70; chmn, Mayor's Task Force on Metrop Transportation, 70-; bd dirs, Gtr Indianapolis Progress Comt, 70-; mem steering comt, Manpower & Develop Task Force, Ind Comprehensive Health Planning Coun, 71; mem adv bd, Indianapolis Pub Transportation Corp, 73; mem, Indianapolis Amtrack Adv Bd. Bus & Prof Pos: Pvt practice, internal med & endocrinology, Scheidler, Gabovitch, Lamkin, Ross & Tavel, 66-; pres, Reference & Index Serv, Inc, 66-; instr med, Ind Univ Med Ctr, 66-; mem teaching faculty, Methodist Hosp of Indianapolis, 66-; mem, bd of dirs, Kennedy Mem Christian Home, 69- Mil Serv: Capt, Army, 62-64, serv in 1st Corps Artil, Korea, 62-63 & Ft Hamilton Dispensary, Brooklyn, NY, 63-64. Mem: Am Med Asn; Mason (32 degree); Scottish Rite; Indianapolis Ski Club; Indianapolis Jaycees. Honors & Awards: One of Outstanding Community Leaders of Am, 68; Distinguished Serv Award, Indianapolis Jaycees, 69; One of Five Outstanding Young Men in Ind, 70. Relig: Christian; elder & mem bd, Northwood Christian Church. Legal Res: 41 E 54th Indianapolis IN 46220 Mailing Add: 1935 N Capitol Ave Indianapolis IN 46202

LAMM, RICHARD D (D)
Gov, Colo
b Madison, Wis, Aug 3, 35; m; c Scott Hunter & Heather. Polit & Govt Pos: Pres, Denver Young Dem, formerly; vpres, Colo Young Dem; mem, Mayor's South Platte River Comt; Colo State Rep, until 74, asst minority leader, Colo House Rep, until 74; Gov, Colo, 75- Bus & Prof Pos: Attorney-at-law; CPA. Mil Serv: 1st Lt, Army Res. Legal Res: 400 E Eighth Ave Denver CO 80203 Mailing Add: State Capitol Denver CO 80203

LAMONICA, JAMES ANTHONY (D)
Committeeman, Ark State Dem Comt
b Rochester, Pa, Aug 4, 33; s Joseph LaMonica & Rose Simone L; m 1959 to Lura Joyce Plumley; c Michele & Timothy. Educ: Salem Tech Sch, grad, 60. Polit & Govt Pos: Committeeman, Benton Co Dem Comt, Ark, 68-; committeeman, Ark State Dem Comt, 70-; admin aide, Gov Staff, Ark, 71- Bus & Prof Pos: Mgr mfg & eng, Deming Div, Crane Co, 51- Mil Serv: Entered as Pvt, Air Force, 51, released as Airman 1/C, 55, after serv in Fighter Test Squad, Air Proving Grounds, 52-55; Good Conduct Medal. Relig: Catholic. Mailing Add: 46 Colony Rd Little Rock AR 72207

LAMONT, FRANCES STILES (PEG) (R)
SDak State Sen
b Rapid City, SDak, June 10, 14; d Frederick Bailey Stiles & Frances Kenny S; m 1937 to William Mather Lamont (deceased); c William Stiles, Nancy Brereton, Peggy (Mrs Greg Lauver) & Frederick Mather. Educ: Univ Wis-Madison, BA, 35, MA, 36; Northern State Col, 42-43; Phi Kappa Phi; Mortar Bd; Crucible; Theta Sigma Phi; Kappa Alpha Theta. Polit & Govt Pos: Mem, SDak Women's Comn on Civil Defense, 57-62; secy, SDak Comn on Aging, 59-61, gov rep, 61-67; mem, White House Conf on Aging, 61; mem, Gov Study Comn Elem & Sec Educ, 64-66; vchmn, Gov Comn on Status of Women, 64-73; mem, SDak Adv Coun on Aging, 63-; chmn, Gov Adv Coun on Aging, 67-73; SDak State Sen, Dist 2, 75-; mem appropriations comt & health & welfare comt, SDak State Senate, 75- Bus & Prof Pos: Mem staff, McCalls Mag, New York, 36-37; mem staff, Lamont Off, Aberdeen, SDak, 73- Publ: Funding small county museums, Preservation News, 3/74. Mem: Am Asn Univ Women (nat trustee educ found); Nat Trust for Hist Preservation (state adv, 71-); Brown Co Mus & Hist Soc. Honors & Awards: Named $3000 Fel Hon Serv to Educ, SDak Br, Am Asn Univ Women, 70; Sertoma Serv to Mankind Award, 72; SDak Mother of Year, 74 & Nat Citation for Civil Responsibility by Am Mothers Comt, New York; Dakota State Col Hist Preservation Award, 75; Univ Wis Distinguished Alumni Award, 75. Relig: Episcopal; mem vestry. Legal Res: Meadowlark Rte 1 Aberdeen SD 57401 Mailing Add: Lamont Off PO Box 1209 Aberdeen SD 57401

LAMONTAGNE, LAURIER (D)
NH State Sen
b Berlin, NH, Mar 6, 17; div; c six. Educ: St Patrick Sch. Polit & Govt Pos: Mem, City Coun, 46-55; NH State Sen, 55-, Minority Floor Leader & Dean, NH Senate; Mayor, Berlin, NH, 58-62. Bus & Prof Pos: Operator, Lamontagne's Express & Leasing. Mil Serv: Navy, World War II. Mem: VFW; Am Legion; Elks; Eagles; DAV (chmn nat finance comt, 59-). Honors & Awards: 21 years perfect attendance record, NH State Senate; Hon Membership, Tenth Spec Forces Group, Ft Devens, Mass, 73. Relig: Catholic. Mailing Add: Box 509 Berlin NH 03570

LAMORA, JUDY LYNNE (R)
Pres, Colo Fedn Rep Women
b San Antonio, Tex, Mar 23, 39; d Timothy E Gristy & Clovis Mooring Hills G; m 1960 to Donald E LaMora; c Leigh Suzanne, Grant Donald & Eric Jon. Educ: Tex Tech Univ, 56-60; Kappa Alpha Theta. Polit & Govt Pos: Mem publ comt, Dominick for Sen, El Paso Co, Colo, 62 & 68; Rep precinct committeewoman, Precinct 16, El Paso Co, 62; first vpres, Pikes Peak Rep Women's Roundtable, 64-68; pub rels chmn, Colo Fedn Rep Women, 65-67, mem exec comt, 67-69, ed Fedn publ, Tusk Talk, 69-71, second vpres, 69-72, first vpres, 72-74, pres, 74-; publicity chmn, El Paso Co Rep Cent Comt, 66; publicity for Colo Third Rep Cong Dist, 66; mem publicity comt, Bradley for Cong, 68; mem, Gov Comn on Status of Women, 68-72; mem, Colo State Rep Cent Comt, 69-71, mem exec comt, 74-; vchmn pub rels, Nat Fedn Rep Women, 74- Bus & Prof Pos: Proofreader, Lubbock, Tex Avalanche-J, 59-60; reporter, Colo Springs Gazette Tel, 60; lectr pub rels, 64-; mem, Buchanan for Regent Comt, 70. Publ: Co-auth & co-ed, See how she runs, a guide for the woman candidate, 72. Mem: Wagon Wheel Coun, Girl Scouts, US (field vpres, 70-72). Relig: Christian Church of NAm. Mailing Add: 8 Menary Way Colorado Springs CO 80906

LAMOTT, PAUL I (R)
NH State Rep
Mailing Add: Court St Ext Box 56 Haverhill NH 03765

LAMPE, HENRY OSCAR (R)
b Bremen, Ger, Apr 8, 27; s Henry D Lampe & Dorothea Gatje L; m 1953 to Virginia Harvey. Educ: Swarthmore Col, 45-46; Am Univ, BS, 52; Omicron Delta Kappa; Pi Delta Epsilon; Alpha Psi Omega; Delta Upsilon. Polit & Govt Pos: Vchmn, Arlington Co Rep Comt, Va, 62-66; mem, Pub Utilities Comn, Arlington, 64-66; mem, Va Rep State Cent Comt, 64-68 & 71-72; chmn Va Rep State Party Plan Comt, 68-71; mem, Northern Va Regional Planning Comn, 67-70; first vchmn, Tenth Dist Rep Comt, Va, 68-71; Va State Deleg, 70-71; vchmn, Va Metrop Areas Transportation Study Comn, 71-; deleg, Rep Nat Conv, 72. Bus & Prof Pos: Agent, US Info Agency, 53-56; budget examr, Bur of Budget, 56-59; vpres, Birely & Co, Washington, DC, 59-66; asst br mgr, Thomson & McKinnon Auchincloss, Inc, NY Stock Exchange, Arlington, Va, 67- Mil Serv: Entered as Seaman 2/C, Navy, 45, released as Seaman 1/C, 46, after serv in various stas; World War II Victory Medal. Mem: Lions; Am Legion; Arlington Comt of 100, Northern Va Fine Arts Asn; Arlington Health & Welfare Coun; Northern Va Ment Health Asn (treas, 71-73). Honors & Awards: Citation of Merit, US Mil Govt, Berlin Sector. Relig: Lutheran. Mailing Add: 2914 N Greencastle St Arlington VA 22207

LAMSON, FRED I (R)
Chmn, Malden City Rep Comt, Mass
b Stonington, Maine, Dec 11, 10; s Fred Irvin Lamson & Florence Noyes L; m 1931 to Glenys Davis L; c Fred I, Jr. Educ: Everett High Sch. Polit & Govt Pos: Councilman, Malden, Mass, 40-41, alderman, 42-43, mayor, 48-57; Mass State Rep, 45-48; pres, Mass Mayors Asn, 52; Mass State Sen, 53-72; chmn, Malden City Rep Comt, 65-; deleg, Rep Nat Conv, 68. Bus & Prof Pos: Pres, Lamson & Davis Inc, Malden, Mass, 48-58. Mem: Elks; Moose; Odd Fellows; B'nai B'rith; United Amvets. Relig: Protestant. Mailing Add: 36 Dodge St Malden MA 02148

LAMY, CATHERINE GLORIA (D)
NH State Rep
b Manchester, NH, Feb 15, 40; d Joseph Lajorie & Jennie Bolser L; m 1958 to Robert E Lamy; c Karen Ann, Patricia Ann, Lisa Ann & Shari Ann. Educ: Cent High Sch, 2 years. Polit & Govt Pos: NH State Rep, 71- Bus & Prof Pos: Child care bus, Cathy's Infant Nursery, 60-70. Mem: Manchester Dem Womens Club (pres, 73-). Relig: Catholic. Mailing Add: 607 Granite St Manchester NH 03102

LAN, DONALD PAUL (D)
Dem Nat Committeeman, NJ
b Newark, NJ, Dec 19, 30; s Samuel Lan & Mary Kufferman L; m 1951 to Hannah Paula Resnik; c Donald Paul, Jr, Richard Alan & Barbara Susan. Educ: Seton Hall Univ, 48-51. Polit & Govt Pos: Munic chmn, Springfield Dem Comt, NJ, 68-71; exec dir, Union Co Dem Comt, 72-73; committeeman, NJ State Dem Comt, Union Co, 73-; exec secy, Gov Brendan Byrne, 74-; Dem Nat Committeeman, NJ, 74-; deleg, Dem Mid-Term Conf, 74. Bus & Prof Pos: Pres, Dell Sales Co, Hillside, NJ, 52-73, vpres, Dell Prod Corp, 52-73; pres, Sunshine Fruit Juice Co, Hillside, 56-73. Mil Serv: Entered as Pvt, Air Force, 51, released as Pfc, after serv in Strategic Air Command, 51-52. Mem: B'nai B'rith. Relig: Jewish. Mailing Add: 34 Cypress Terr Springfield NJ 07081

LANCASTER, BILL (R)
Calif State Assemblyman
b Bakersfield, Calif, Apr 29, 31; m to Treece; c Cort, Dianne & Chris. Polit & Govt Pos: City councilman, Duarte, Calif, 58-65, mayor, three terms; field rep, Calif Taxpayers Asn, 65-67; dist rep, US Rep Charles E Wiggins, Calif, 67; Calif State Assemblyman, Los Angeles Co, 72-, mem educ, finance, ins & com, local govt comts & chmn subcomt on munic annexation reform, Calif State Assembly, currently. Mailing Add: 372 E Rowland St Covina CA 91723

LANCASTER, CHARLES DOERR, JR (R)
La State Rep
b New Orleans, La, Sept 22, 43; s Charles D Lancaster & Helen Stafford L; m 1969 to Edith Field Shannon; c Edith Helen. Educ: Univ Southwestern La, BA, 66; Loyola Univ Sch Law, JD, 68; Blue Key; Law Rev; Phi Alpha Theta; Pi Lambda Beta; Circle K; Kappa Sigma; Delta Theta Phi; Interfraternity Coun. Polit & Govt Pos: Attorney, Vet Admin, New Orleans, La, 71-72; La State Rep, 72- Bus & Prof Pos: Attorney-at-law, self employed, 68-71 & 72- Mil Serv: Entered as E-1, Army Nat Guard, 68, E-5, currently. Publ: The United Mine Workers, case note, Loyola Law Rev, 67-68. Mem: Jefferson Parish & La State Bar Asns; Jefferson Parish Young Rep. Relig: Catholic. Mailing Add: 2208 Division St Metairie LA 70001

LANCASTER, KAREN R (R)
VChmn, Allegany Co Rep Cent Comt, Md
b Cumberland, Md, Dec 16, 38; d Joseph Elmer Ridder & Elizabeth Dixon R; m 1960 to Ronald Lagora Lancaster; c Lisa Anita. Educ: Univ Md, College Park, BA, 60; Frostburg State Col, 67-74; Alpha Gamma Delta; pres, Univ Md Young Rep. Polit & Govt Pos: Co-dir, Region III Col Young Rep, Md, 59-60, dir, 60; pres & treas, Young Rep Club Allegany Co, 68-72; pres, Mt Savage Rep Club, 69-70; dir vol, Allegany Co for Sen J G Beall, 70; dir vol, Sixth Dist, Mason for Congress, 72; vchmn, Allegany Co Rep Cent Comt, 74- Bus & Prof Pos: Teacher, Allegany Co Elem Schs, Md, 67- Mem: Eastern Star; Mt Savage Beautification Comt, Inc (treas, 74-); Nat Educ Asn; PTA (vpres, Corriganville Sch, 75-); VFW Ladies' Auxiliary. Honors & Awards: Young Rep Outstanding Woman Award, Allegany Co Young Rep, 70; Young Rep Woman of Year Award, Md Fedn Young Rep, 70. Relig: Methodist. Mailing Add: 104 Church Hill St Mt Savage MD 21545

LANCASTER, RAY H (D)
b Concord, NC, July 10, 35; s J Lionel Lancaster & Lillie L; m 1962 to Anne Jewell; c Marianna, Elizabeth & Robert. Educ: NC State Univ, 53-56; Pfeiffer Col, AB, 60; Univ NC, MA, 65; Phi Kappa Phi; Woodrow Wilson fel; Sigma Chi. Polit & Govt Pos: Legis asst to US Rep Ed Jones, Tenn, 69-72, admin asst, 72- Bus & Prof Pos: Asst prof, Univ Tenn, Martin, 64-69. Mem: US House Rep Admin Asst Asn. Relig: Methodist. Legal Res: Martin TN 38237 Mailing Add: 7614 Clive Pl Springfield VA 22151

LANCE, WESLEY L (R)
Committeeman, NJ Rep State Comt
b Glen Gardner, NJ, Nov 21, 08; s Leonard A Lance & Florence Smith L; m 1951 to Anne Anderson, wid; c James W & Leonard A; m 1970 to Jeannette Bonnell Gill. Educ: Lafayette Col, BS, 28; Harvard Law Sch, LLD, 35. Polit & Govt Pos: NJ State Assemblyman, 38-41; NJ State Sen, 41-43 & 54-62, majority leader, NJ State Senate, 58, pres, 59; deleg, Const Conv, 47 & 66; acting gov, NJ, several occasions, 59; committeeman, NJ Rep State Comt, Hunterdon Co, 62-; mem & pres, NJ Electoral Col, 68. Mil Serv: A/S, Navy, 43; released

as QM 3/C, 46, after serv in aircraft carrier, Pac Theatre. Publ: Under the State House Dome, column in weekly newspaper, 54-62. Relig: Lutheran. Legal Res: 49 West St Annandale NJ 08801 Mailing Add: 36 Center St Clinton NJ 08809

LANCIONE, A G (D)
Ohio State Rep
b Cementon, Pa, Feb 12, 07; s John Baptist Lancione & Elizabeth Del Guzzo L; m 1931 to June Davies Morford; c John, Bernard & Richard. Educ: Ohio State Univ, AB, 27, JD, 29; Alpha Phi Delta. Polit & Govt Pos: Asst prosecuting attorney, Belmont Co, Ohio, 36-44; Ohio State Rep, 47-, Majority Leader, Ohio State House of Rep, 49-51, Speaker-Pro Tem, formerly, Minority Leader, 61-72, Speaker, 73-75, chmn, Rules Comt, currently; nat committeeman, Young Dem of Ohio, 48-49; chmn, Taxation Comn, 59-61; vchmn, Ohio Legis Serv Comn, 65-66 & 69-70; alt deleg, Dem Nat Conv, 68 & 72. Bus & Prof Pos: Dir & vpres, Farmers & Merchants Nat Bank. Mil Serv: Cand in Officers Training Sch. Mem: DAV; Am Legion (life mem); Sons of Italy (life mem); Press Club of Ohio; League of Ohio Sportsmen. Relig: Episcopal. Legal Res: 3765 Tallman Ave Bellaire OH 43906 Mailing Add: PO Box O Bellaire OH 43906

LANCIONE, BERNARD GABE (D)
b Bellaire, Ohio, Feb 3, 39; s A G Lancione & Phyllis June Morford L; m 1959 to Kathleen Ann Mountain; c Amy Jeanette, Caitin Mountain & Gillian Justin. Educ: Ohio Univ, BSc, 60; Franklin Law Sch, Capitol Univ, JD, 65. Polit & Govt Pos: Legal counsel & parliamentarian, Young Dem Clubs Ohio, 66-68, cand pres, 68, chmn const comt, 69, chmn, Const Conv, 69; mem, Ohio Comt Col Young Dem, 69, chmn membership comt, 70, pres, 70-72; city solicitor, Bellaire, Ohio, 68-72; asst co prosecutor, Belmont Co, Ohio, 69-72; mem, Ohio State Dem Exec Comt, 69-71; mem, Ohio Party Structure & Deleg Selection Comt, 69-70; legal counsel, Young Dem Clubs Am, 71-73; participating mem, Dem Nat Comt. Bus & Prof Pos: Attorney, Lancione, Lancione & Lancione, currently. Mem: Ohio Acad Trial Lawyers (trustee, 69-); Am Arbit Asn (mem panel, 70); Am Trial Lawyers Asn; Am Judicature Soc; Am Civil Liberties Union. Honors & Awards: Hon Attorney Gen, Ohio, 58-62; hon Lt Gov, 58-62. Legal Res: 4901 Jefferson St Bellaire OH 43906 Mailing Add: Prof Complex 38th & Jefferson St Bellaire OH 43906

LANCIONE, NELSON (D)
Chmn, Franklin Co Dem Party, Ohio
b Bellaire, Ohio, July 10, 21; s John B Lancione (deceased); m 1948 to Tillie L Lapitsky; c Nelson William, Robert Michael & David. Educ: Ohio State Univ, BS, 41, JD, 43; Alpha Phi Delta; Phi Delta Phi; Inter-Fraternity Pres Coun. Polit & Govt Pos: With Off Gen Counsel, US Treas Dept, 43-49, US Treas rep, 45-47, acting treas attache, Am Embassy, Manila, Philippines, 46-47, asst attorney gen, Ohio, 49-50; pres, Ohio League of Young Dem Clubs, 54-55; chmn, Speakers Bur, Ohio Dem Hq, 56; vpres, Young Dem Clubs of Am, 56-57, pres, 57-58; deleg, Dem Nat Conv, 56, 60, 64 & 68; deleg, Atlantic Conf Polit Youth Leaders, 58; spec counsel for Attorney Gen, Ohio, 58-62; deleg, Atlantic Cong, 59; mem & chmn finance comt, Franklin Co Dem Exec Comt, Ohio, 68-71; chmn, Gov Inaugural Comt, 70-71; mem, Ohio State Dem Exec Comt, 70-; chmn, Franklin Co Dem Party, 72- Bus & Prof Pos: Attorney-at-law, self-employed, 51-; secy & gen counsel, NAm Equitable Life Assurance Co, 59-68. Publ: Preliminary study of certain financial laws & institutions: Denmark, 9/44 & Albania, 11/44; The Ohio agents—General Motors fight on agents licensing, Rough Notes, 1/53. Mem: Am Judicature Soc; Am Trial Lawyers Asn; Am Soc Int Law; life mem, Moose; Franklin Co Ment Health Asn. Honors & Awards: Hon fel, Harry S Truman Libr Inst. Relig: Methodist. Legal Res: 3838 Walhaven Rd Columbus OH 43221 Mailing Add: 42 E Gay St Suite 1312 Columbus OH 43215

LAND, JOHN CALHOUN, III (D)
SC State Rep
b Manning, SC, Jan 25, 41; s John Calhoun Land, Jr & Anne Weisiger L; m 1965 to Marie Adell Mercogliano; c John Calhoun, IV, Frances Ricci & William Ceth. Educ: Univ Fla, 60; Univ SC, Columbia, BS, 65, JD, 68; Phi Delta Phi; Sigma Chi. Polit & Govt Pos: Comnr, SC Hwy Dept, Columbia, 71-75; SC State Rep, 75- Mem: Clarendon Co Ment Health Asn; Clarendon Co Farm Bur. Relig: Methodist. Legal Res: Pinestraw Lane Manning SC 29102 Mailing Add: PO Drawer G Manning SC 29102

LANDAU, GEORGE W
US Ambassador to Paraguay
b Austria, Mar 4, 20; s Dr J A Landau & Jeannette Klausner L; m 1947 to Maria Anna Jobst; c Robert W & Christopher T. Educ: George Washington Univ, AA. Polit & Govt Pos: Commercial attache, Am Embassy, Montevideo, Uruguay, 57-62; first secy & polit officer, Am Embassy, Madrid, Spain, 62-65; state dep rep, Can Nat Defence Col, Kingston, Ont, 65-66, dir, Off of Spanish & Portuguese Affairs, Dept State, Washington, DC, 66-72; US Ambassador, Paraguay, 72- Bus & Prof Pos: Asst vpres, Intra-Mar Shipping Corp, New York, NY, 47-55; gen mgr, Alejandro Garces Ltd, Cali, Colombia, 55-57. Mil Serv: Entered as Pvt, Army, 42, released as Capt, after serv in 6825 MIS Bn, Fifth Army, Fifteenth Army Group, US Forces in Austria, 44-47; Col, Mil Intel, Army Res, 47-; Army Commendation Medal; Campaign Ribbons. Mem: Am Foreign Serv Asn; Fed City Club Washington, DC. Honors & Awards: Superior Serv Award, Dept State, Washington, DC, 71. Relig: Roman Catholic. Legal Res: 5006 Nahant St Washington DC 20016 Mailing Add: Am Embassy APO New York NY 09881

LANDERS, H LACY (D)
Ark State Rep
Mailing Add: 522 River St Benton AR 72015

LANDERS, WILLIAM LYTLE (JUG) (D)
Mem, Bedford Co Dem Exec Comt
b Shelbyville, Tenn, Apr 9, 26; s W A Landers (deceased) & Elaine Taylor Ingle L; m 1952 to Jean Wiggs; c Ben & John. Educ: Mid Tenn State Univ, BS, 50; Vanderbilt Univ Law Sch, 50; Phi Delta Theta. Polit & Govt Pos: Secy & clerk, Off of US Sen K D McKellar, 51-52; deleg, Tenn Ltd Const Conv, 59 & 65; mem, State Libr & Arch Comn, Tenn, 63-; Bedford Co co-chmn Johnson-Humphrey Ticket, 64 & Humphrey-Muskie Ticket, 68; secy, Bedford Co Dem Primary Bd, Tenn, 66-; mem, Tenn State Dem Exec Comt, Fourth Cong Dist, 66-70; deleg, Dem Nat Conv, 68; mem & secy, Tenn State Elec Comn, 69-; mem, Bedford Co Dem Exec Comt, 70- Bus & Prof Pos: Civil Serv job, Washington, DC, 53-54; ins agent, Tullahoma, Tenn, 55-59; owner, Lytle Landers Agency, Shelbyville, 59- Mil Serv: Entered as Pvt, Marine Corps, 45, released as Pfc, 46, after serv in Sixth Marine Div, 15th Marines, Pac Theatre, China, 45-46. Mem: Bedford Co Insurers; Am Legion; VFW; Rotary; CofC. Honors & Awards: Our Stake in Better Govt Award, Shelbyville Jaycees, 65. Relig: Christian Church of NAm; deacon, First Christian Church. Legal Res: 114 Burrum Dr Shelbyville TN 37160 Mailing Add: PO Box 617 Shelbyville TN 37160

LANDES, IRWIN J (D)
NY State Assemblyman
b Brooklyn, NY, Mar 6, 26; s Harry Landes & Sylvia Silberman L; m to Alice Zigelbaum; c Steven & James. Educ: Harvard Col, BA, 50, Harvard Law Sch, LLB, 51. Polit & Govt Pos: Deleg, Dem Nat Conv, 68; NY State . Assemblyman, 16th Dist, Nassau, 71- Bus & Prof Pos: Partner, Landes, Wingate & Shamis, 53-73. Mil Serv: Entered as Pvt, Army, 44, released as Sgt, 46, after serv in 34th Inf Div, 5th Army, Italy, 44-46; Combat Infantryman Badge; Battle Stars. Mem: Fed Bar Asn; Am Comt for Rescue & Resettlement of Iraqi Jews (hon mem). Relig: Jewish. Legal Res: 8 Mirrielces Circle Great Neck NY 11021 Mailing Add: 25 Great Neck Rd Great Neck NY 11021

LANDES, JAMES (R)
Treas, Hancock Co Rep Cent Comt, Ind
b Philadelphia, Pa, Mar 31, 26; s Carl J Landes & Martha Graber L; m 1945 to Carol Hoilman; c James Lynn, Deborah Jean (Mrs J R Koch) & Reah Martha (Mrs J L Smolek). Educ: Bluffton Col, BS, 50; Miami Univ, MS, 51. Polit & Govt Pos: Treas, Hancock Co Rep Cent Comt, Ind, 63- Bus & Prof Pos: Instr bact, Univ Ariz, 51-53; proj engr, Waste Water, Infilco Inc, Tucson, Ariz, 53-56; bacteriologist, Eli Lilly & Co, Indianapolis, Ind, 56- Mailing Add: 1314 Sherwood Dr Greenfield IN 46140

LANDGRAF, VERNON H (R)
Mem, Mo State Rep Comt
b Cape Girardeau, Mo, Oct 4, 24; s L H Landgraf & Hilda Gerler L; m 1952 to Mary Victoria Williams; c Mark Thomas, Luke Turner, Jeffrey Franklin & John Paul. Educ: South East Mo State Col, 42 & 46-48; Los Angeles City Col, 44; Webster Society. Polit & Govt Pos: Mem, Mo State Finance Comt, 67-68; Rep nominee, US Rep, Mo, 68; finance chmn, Rust for Congress Campaign, 70; mem, Mo State Rep Comt, 70- Bus & Prof Pos: Vpres, L H Landgraf Lumber Co, Inc, 50-69; pres, Landgraf Real Estate & Develop Corp, 58-69; mem exec bd, Cape Supply Co, 62-68; pres, SLR Promotion Co, Inc, 63-69; treas, Rental Land, Inc, 66-69; vpres, West Side Improv Co, Inc, 66-69. Mil Serv: Entered as Pvt, Army, 43, released as S/Sgt, 46, after serv in 548th Field Artillery Bn, ETO, 44-46. Mem: VFW; Am Legion; CofC (pres); Lions (pres); Jaycees (pres). Honors & Awards: State Distinguished Serv Award, Jaycees. Relig: Lutheran, Mo Synod. Mailing Add: 444 Marie Cape Girardeau MO 63701

LANDGREBE, EARL FREDERICK (R)
b Valparaiso, Ind, Jan 21, 16; s Edward William Landgrebe & Benna Marie Broderman L; m 1936 to Helen Lucile Field; c Ronald & Roger. Educ: Wheeler High Sch, 4 years. Polit & Govt Pos: Ind State Sen, 59-68; US Rep, Ind, 69-74, cand, US House of Rep, 74; deleg, Rep Nat Conv, 72. Bus & Prof Pos: Pres, Landgrebe Motor Transport, Inc, 43-; pres, Landgrebe & Son, 67- Mem: Rotary; CofC. Relig: Lutheran. Mailing Add: 451 Lincolnway Valparaiso IN 46383

LANDIS, RANDALL ELDON (R)
Committeeman, Young Rep League Minn
b Jackson, Minn, Sept 4, 54; s L Eldon Landis & Alice Strom L; single. Educ: Worthington State Jr Col, currently; Student Senate. Polit & Govt Pos: Deleg, Nobles Co Rep Conv, Minn Sixth Dist Rep Conv, Minn State Rep Conv & Rep Nat Conv, 72; dir youth, Nobles Co Rep Bd Dirs, 72-; mem, Nat Student Adv Comt for Washington Workshops, Cong Seminars, 72-73; legis research consult, Minn State Legis, 73-; committeeman, Young Rep League Minn, 74- Bus & Prof Pos: Mgr, Trojan Drive-in Restaurant, 72-73; owner, Landis Enterprises, 73- Mem: Circle K; Ripon Soc. Relig: Baptist. Mailing Add: 333 Galena St Worthington MN 56187

LANDOLT, ALLAN FRANCIS (R)
b Litchfield, Ill, June 20, 25; s Harold F Landolt & Anna M Talley L; m 1949 to Joan Adel Burns; c Mary Theresa, Kathleen Ann, Allan Joseph, Maura Jane, Mark William, Renee Louise & Matthew Girard. Educ: Univ Notre Dame, BA in Bus Admin, 50. Polit & Govt Pos: Chmn, Cass Co Rep Cent Comt, Ill, formerly; dir of aeronaut, State of Ill, 71- Bus & Prof Pos: Mgr, Am Investment Co of Ill, 51-54; supvr, Liberty Loan Corp, St Louis, Mo, 54-58; vpres & loan officer, Northtown Bank, Decatur, Ill, 58-61; pres & owner, Cass Consumers Serv, Inc, Virginia, Ill, 61- Mil Serv: Entered as Aviation Cadet, Navy, 43, released as Lt (jg), 50, after serv in Naval Air Transport Serv, Hawaii & Aleutians, 45-46. Mem: KofC; Kiwanis; Am Legion; Elks. Relig: Roman Catholic. Mailing Add: S Side of Square Virginia IL 62691

LANDON, ALFRED M (R)
b West Middlesex, Pa, Sept 9, 87; s John M Landon & Anne Mossman L; m 1915 to Margaret Fleming (deceased); c Margaret Anne; m 1930 to Theo Cobb; c Nancy Josephine & John Cobb. Educ: Univ Kans, LLB, 08; Phi Gamma Delta; Phi Delta Phi. Hon Degrees: LLD from various cols & univs; LHD, Kans State Univ, 68. Polit & Govt Pos: Chmn, Kans Rep State Cent Comt, 28; Gov, Kans, 33-37; cand for President, 36; mem, Pan Am Conf, Lima, Peru, 38; deleg-at-lg, Rep Nat Conv, 40, 44 & 48. Bus & Prof Pos: Bookkeeper; oil producer, 12-; radio broadcasting stas, 50- Mem: Odd Fellows; Elks; Am Legion; Mason; hon mem, Blue Key, 69. Honors & Awards: Distinguished Citizenship Awards, Washburn Univ, 67 & Baker Univ, 75. Relig: Methodist. Legal Res: Prospect Hills Topeka KS 66606 Mailing Add: PO Box 1280 Topeka KS 66601

LANDRETH, JOSEPH FRANKLIN (R)
Treas, Dade Co Rep Cent Comt, Mo
b Aldrich, Mo, Dec 25, 07; s Lola Montez Landreth & Winnie Edge L; m 1938 to Mabel Dorothy Burros. Educ: Southwest Mo State Col, BS, 33; Country Life Club. Polit & Govt Pos: Chmn, Dade Co Rep Cent Comt, Mo, 64-70, treas, currently. Bus & Prof Pos: Soc sci, phys educ & sci instr, Pub Schs, Southwest Mo, 30-42; sr aircraft inspector, US Navy, 42-46; mgr & owner, Landreth Supermkt, Greenfield, Mo, 46-68; gen agent, Mod Security Life Ins Springfield, Mo, 69- Mem: CofC; Odd Fellows; Lions; Farm Bur Hon Chap Farmer, Future Farmers of Am. Relig: Baptist. Mailing Add: 728 Crestview Greenfield MO 65661

LANDRIEU, MOON EDWIN (D)
Mayor, New Orleans, La
b New Orleans, La, July 3, 30; s Joseph Landrieu & Loretta Bechtel L; m 1954 to Verna Satterlee; c Mary, Mark, Melanie, Michelle, Mitchell, Madeline, Martin, Melinda & Maurice. Educ: Loyola Univ, La, BBA, 52, LLB, 54. Polit & Govt Pos: La State Rep, 60-66, councilman-at-lg, New Orleans, 66-70, mayor, 70-; deleg, Dem Nat Conv, 72. Bus & Prof Pos: Attorney, Landrieu, Calogero & Kronlage Law Firm, 58-69. Mil Serv: 2nd Lt, Army,

54-57, serv in Judge Adv Gen Corps. Mem: Total Community Action Inc; Inter-Am Munic Orgn (first vpres); US Conf Mayors (pres); Nat League of Cities (mem human resources develop comt). Relig: Catholic. Legal Res: 4301 S Prieur St New Orleans LA 70125 Mailing Add: Mayor's Off City Hall New Orleans LA 70112

LANDRIEU, PHYLLIS (D)
Mem, Dem Nat Comt, La
Mailing Add: 4600 Venus St New Orleans LA 70122

LANDRUM, PHILLIP MITCHELL (D)
US Rep, Ga
b Martin, Ga, Sept 10, 07; s Phillip Davis Landrum & Blanche Mitchell L; m 1933 to Laura Brown; c Phillip Mitchell & Susan. Educ: Piedmont Col, 39; Atlanta Law Sch, LLB, 41; Mercer Univ; La State Univ. Polit & Govt Pos: Asst attorney gen, Ga, 46-47; exec secy to Gov, Ga, 47-48; US Rep, Ga, 53-, co-auth, Landrum-Griffith Bill, US Cong, 59, mem, House Ways & Means Comt, currently; deleg, Dem Nat Mid-Term Conf, 74. Bus & Prof Pos: High sch athletic dir & coach, Bowman, Ga, 32-35 & Nelson, Ga, 35-37; supt pub schs, Nelson, 37-41; attorney-at-law, Jasper, 49- Mil Serv: Army Air Force, 42-45. Mem: Ga Bar Asn; Am Legion; VFW; Mason; Elks. Relig: Baptist. Legal Res: Jasper GA Mailing Add: 2308 Rayburn House Off Bldg Washington DC 20515

LANDRY, JOHN JOSEPH, JR (D)
La State Rep
b New Orleans, La, Nov 10, 30; s John Joseph Landry, Sr & Zelma Lucas L; m 1956 to Diane A Betzer; c Lisa Gaye & Jay Bryan. Educ: Univ Southwestern La, BS, 53; Sigma Pi Alpha. Polit & Govt Pos: La State Rep, 72- Mem: KofC; Pharmaceutical Rep Asn New Orleans (pres). Relig: Catholic. Mailing Add: 4477 Franklin Ave New Orleans LA 70122

LANDRY, RICHARD EDWARD (D)
Mass State Rep
b Waltham, Mass, May 29, 36; s Francis Lawrence Landry & Alfreda Anne Ferguson L; m 1965 to Patience Monroe Deturk; c Richard Edward. Educ: Newton Jr Col, AA, 61; Boston Univ, BS, 62; Young Dem of Waltham. Polit & Govt Pos: Pres, Young Mens Civic League, Waltham, 52-54 & Waltham Dem City Comt, 57-; deleg, Mass Dem State Conv, 58, 60, 62, 64, 66, 68, 70 & 72 & Dem Nat Conv, 68; Mass State Rep, 63-, chmn, Bill in Third Reading, Mass House Rep, 73, chmn, Comt on Pub Serv, 74. Mil Serv: Entered as Pvt, Army, 54, released as Sgt, 57, after serv in Counter Intel, Europe, 55-57; ETO Medal. Mem: DAV; VFW. Relig: Catholic. Legal Res: 11 Crafts St Waltham MA 02154 Mailing Add: State House Boston MA 02133

LANDRY, WALTER J (D)
State Co-Chmn Affirmative Action, Dem State Cent Comt La
b Willswood, La, Jan 23, 31; s John T Landry & Lelia Peltier L; m 1962 to Carolyn K; c Celeste H, John T, Joseph C, Catherine G, Walter J, Jr & James W. Educ: Univ Notre Dame, BSME, 52; George Washington Univ Law Sch, 55-57; Tulane Univ Law Sch, JD, 58; Am Univ, MA Int Rels, 69. Polit & Govt Pos: Legis asst to US Sen Russell B Long, Washington, DC, 56-57; foreign serv officer, Dept State, 61-70; mem & action officer, US Deleg to Am Conv on Human Rights, San Jose, Costa Rica, 69; mem, Dem State Cent Comt La, 71-, state co-chmn affirmative action, 75-; counsel, Bill of Rights Comt, La Const Conv, 73-74; deleg, Dem Nat Mid-Term Conf, 74. Bus & Prof Pos: Attorney-at-law, New Orleans, La, 58-61, partner, Landry, Poteet & Landry, Lafayette, 74-; asst prof, Univ Southwestern, 70-74. Mil Serv: Maj, Marine Corp Res, 52-, serv in Korea, 52-54. Publ: Auth, French-Spanish Provision in 1974 Dem Charter of US. Mem: Int Rels Asn of Acadiana (pres, 74-75); Hamilton PTA (pres, 73-74); Am Bar Asn (chmn, Int Law Working Group, 71-); Rotary; Toastmasters. Legal Res: 501 Tulane Ave Lafayette LA 70501 Mailing Add: 215 W Main St Lafayette LA 70501

LANDSMAN, ALBERT MICHAEL (D)
Treas, Nev Dem Party
b Kiev, Russia, June 21, 07; s Phillip Landsman & Sarah Becker L; m 1952 to Mary E Karsh; c Sally R (Mrs Terman). Educ: Chicago & Harrison High Sch. Polit & Govt Pos: Trustee & receiver, Bankruptcy Court, 56-; treas, Nev Dem Party, 59-; chmn, Dem Exec Comt, 60-62; mem, Nev Constables Asn, 60-; mem adv comt, Small Bus Asn, 62-66; comnr, State of Nev Comt on Equal Rights, 63-65; deleg, Dem Nat Conv, 64 & 68; receiver & forclosurer, Fed Housing Admin Apt Forclosures, 64-, contracting agent, Fed Housing Admin, 65-; vchmn, Clark Co Housing Authority, 65- Bus & Prof Pos: Owner, Towne & Country Interiors, 53-; part owner, Craig Rd Speedway, 65- Mil Serv: CPO, Navy, 43-45 & 50-51, serv in Seabees, Pac Theatre & Korea, Seabees, Naval Res, 51-58; Expert Rifleman Medal; Overseas Duty Medal; Good Conduct Medal; One Star. Mem: Mason; Shrine. Relig: Jewish. Legal Res: 2112 Santa Ynez Las Vegas NV 89105 Mailing Add: 701 E Stewart Las Vegas NV 89101

LANE, CLARENCE D (R)
NY State Assemblyman
b Ashland, NY, Mar 17, 22; s Eli Lane & Nora Dolan L; m to Eleanor Thompson; c Jeffry, Claudia, Roger & Kenneth. Educ: Ithaca Col, BS, deans list, 3rd in class; Columbia Univ. Polit & Govt Pos: Organizer & first pres, Windham Rep Club; budget officer, Greene Co Bd Supvrs; supvr, Windham, formerly; co supvr, 57-62; NY State Assemblyman, 62- Bus & Prof Pos: Former sch teacher; resort owner & mgr; dir, Windham Water Co. Mil Serv: Lt, Marine Corps. Mem: Mason; Boy Scouts; Farm Bur. Relig: Methodist; trustee, Windham Methodist Church. Mailing Add: Windham NY 12496

LANE, DAVID CAMPBELL (R)
Fla State Sen
b Medford, Mass, June 17, 27; s Thomas Edward Lane & Jean Mathilda Campbell L; m 1958 to Benita Johnson; c Benjamin Johnson, Brett Mullikin, Helen Lucinda & David Campbell, Jr. Educ: Univ Tenn & Harvard Univ; Okla A&M Col, BS, 47; Univ Tenn Med Sch, MD, 51; Univ Wis Med Sch, DAB, 57; Phi Epsilon Psi; Omicron Delta Kappa; Alpha Omega Alpha; Sigma Chi; Phi Chi. Polit & Govt Pos: Fla State Sen, 67-, mem, Comts of Health & Welfare, Educ, Rules & Calendar, Select Comt on Gubernatorial Suspension, Select Comt on Tuberc Hosp & Spec Select Comt on Univ Fla Med Sch, chmn, Welfare Comt, Legis Coun, Fla State Senate, 67-69, Minority Leader, 72-; mem, Electoral Col, 68; mem, Hosp Serv for Indigent Adv Bd, State of Fla, 69-; app by President Nixon to Nat Adv Health Coun, Dept Health, Educ & Welfare, 70-; deleg, Rep Nat Conv, 72. Mil Serv: Entered as Seaman, 1/C, Naval Res, 44, released as Comdr, 64, after serv in Asiatic-Pac Theatre; Philippine Liberation Ribbon; Am Theatre; Victory Medal. Mem: Am Asn of Neurological Surgeons; Fla Neurosurg Soc; Lauderdale Yacht Club (bd gov); Ft Lauderdale CofC; Rep Citizen's Comt (bd dirs); Comt for Aid to Handicapped. Honors & Awards: One of Five Outstanding Young Men in Fla, Jaycees; Outstanding Sen in Comt, Fla Senate, 69. Relig: Episcopal. Mailing Add: 300 SE 17th St Ft Lauderdale FL 33316

LANE, DAVID JUDSON (R)
Mass State Rep
b Gloucester, Mass, July 6, 27; s Roy H Lane & Clara C Clark L; m 1951 to Claire A Beckmann; c Heather Lea & Judson Arthur. Educ: Harvard Col, AB, 48. Polit & Govt Pos: Dist coordr, Brooke for Attorney Gen, Mass, 64; chmn, Essex Rep Town Comt, 65-72; town moderator, Essex, 66-73; dist coordr, Brooke for Sen, 66; comnr, Spec Comn on Automobile Ins, 68-70; Mass State Rep, Second Essex Dist, 73- Bus & Prof Pos: Exec vpres, Hastings-Tapley Ins Agency, 66- Mil Serv: Entered as Seaman 1/C, Navy, 45, released as ETM 3/C, 46. Mem: Soc Chartered Property & Casualty Underwriters; Mass Asn Independent Ins Agents & Brokers. Mailing Add: John Wise Ave Essex MA 01929

LANE, DICK (R)
Ga State Rep
Mailing Add: 2704 Humphries St East Point GA 30344

LANE, EDWARD E (D)
Va State Deleg
b Richmond, Va, Jan 28, 24; m to Jean Wiltshire; c Edward E Jr & Gregory T. Educ: Va Polytech Inst; Univ Richmond Law Sch, LLB. Polit & Govt Pos: Va State Deleg. 54-, chmn, Comt on Corp, Ins & Banking & Adv Legis Coun, vchmn, Appropriations Comt, mem, Gov Budget Adv Comt & Rules Comt, Va State House of Deleg. Bus & Prof Pos: Lawyer; pres, Edward E Lane & Assoc, Law Offices; mem bd dirs, RF&P RR. Mil Serv: World War II Pilot. Mem: Cent Richmond Asn; Va Asn of Professions (pres); trustee, Jamestown Found; Country Club of Va; Commonwealth Club. Honors & Awards: Award for Distinguished Serv to Richmond & State of Va as Outstanding Young Man, Jr CofC, 52. Relig: Episcopal. Mailing Add: 6301 Ridgeway Rd Richmond VA 23226

LANE, J K, JR (D)
Chmn, Hill Co Dem Exec Comt, Tex
b Itasca, Tex, Feb 19, 30; s J K Lane, Sr & Ina Duckett L; m 1950 to Janette Rose; c Kirby & Jennifer. Educ: Hillsboro Jr Col, AA, 49; Baylor Univ, BA, 51. Polit & Govt Pos: Chmn, Hill Co Dem Exec Comt, Tex, 70- Bus & Prof Pos: Pres, Hillsboro Jaycees, 54-55; pres, Hillsboro CofC, 60-61. Mem: Tex & Nat Pres Asns; Tex Asn Broadcasters; Rotary; Hill Co Farm Bur. Honors & Awards: Key Man Award, Jaycees, 54, Distinguished Serv Award, 56. Relig: Methodist. Legal Res: 1003 E Franklin Hillsboro TX 76645 Mailing Add: Box 569 Hillsboro TX 76645

LANE, JANET ISABEL (R)
Secy, Logan Co Rep Exec Comt, Ohio
b Columbus, Ohio, Jan 12, 22; d Herbert Charles Bowers & Anna Laura Chambers B; m 1942 to Raymond Paul Lane; c Shirley Rae (Mrs Larry Alspaugh, Jr) & Dennis Ray. Educ: Columbus Comptometer Sch, grad, 40. Polit & Govt Pos: Dep, Clerk of Courts, Logan Co, 60-63, clerk, 69-; dep registr, Bellefontaine, Ohio, 66-69; secy, Logan Co Rep Exec Comt, currently. Bus & Prof Pos: Payroll clerk, Timken Roller Bearing, Columbus, Ohio, 40-42; secy, Union Implement Co, Marysville, Ohio, 63-64; off worker, John Deere Implement, West Mansfield, Ohio, 64-65. Mem: Rep Women's Orgn; Starlight Circle of Kings Daughters. Relig: Methodist. Mailing Add: E State St West Mansfield OH 43358

LANE, JIM E (D)
Okla State Sen
b Broken Bow, Okla, May 5, 34; s Clarence Henry Lane & Vivian Wood L; m 1954 to Nancy Griggs; c Steven Bradley, Clarence Thomas, James Edwin, Jr, Cynthia Joy & Joe Glenn. Educ: Eastern Okla A&M Col, 55. Polit & Govt Pos: Okla State Rep, First Dist; Okla State Sen, Dist 5, currently, chmn, Comt on Parks, Forestry & Indust Develop, Okla State Senate. Bus & Prof Pos: Serv mgr, Lane Motor Co, 56-57; real estate develop; partner, J&J Cattle Co & pres, McCurtain Leasing Co, currently; owner, Frontier Motors, Broken Bow, Okla, 68- Mem: Okla & Nat Auto Dealers Asn; Okla Cattlemen's Asn; Mason; Jaycees. Honors & Awards: Designated by Foreign Policy Asn as one of the 500 Men under 35 Most Likely to Effect the Future Foreign Policy of US, 68; Outstanding Dealer Award, Okla Auto Dealers Asn, 68. Relig: Presbyterian. Legal Res: Rte 3 Box 51C Idabel OK 74745 Mailing Add: 10 NE First Idabel OK 74745

LANE, JOHN JONES (R)
Chmn, North Brookfield Town Rep Comt, Mass
b North Brookfield, Mass, Apr 1, 31; s John C Lane & Susan Bryden L; m 1952 to Margaret Inez Ryan; c Stephen R, Jeffrey R & Pamela M. Educ: North Brookfield High Sch. Polit & Govt Pos: Chmn, North Brookfield Town Rep Comt, Mass, 69- Bus & Prof Pos: Pres, John C Lane & Sons, Inc, 69. Mil Serv: Entered as Pvt, Air Force, 48, released as S/Sgt, 52, after serv in Fifth Air Force, Japan & Korea, 50-52. Mem: Rotary Int; VFW; Am Legion. Relig: Protestant. Mailing Add: 2 Hillside Ave North Brookfield MA 01535

LANE, JULIAN B (D)
Fla State Sen
b Tampa, Fla, Oct 21, 14; s Thomas W Lane & Roberta Fisher L; m to Frances LaMotte; c Susan (Mrs Kent McCain), Julian, Jr, Virginia L & William L. Educ: Univ Fla, BS, 37; Fla Blue Key; Alpha Tau Omega; Hall of Fame. Polit & Govt Pos: Secy, Fla Racing Comn, 51-53; with Hillsborough Pilots Asn, 52-53; mayor, Tampa, Fla, 59-63; chmn, Hillsborough Co Hosp Coun, 68-69; mem, Tampa Housing Authority, 69-70; Fla State Rep, Dist 64, 70-72; Fla State Sen, Dist 23, 72- Bus & Prof Pos: Owner, Lane Cattle Co Dairy, currently; chmn bd, Pan Am Bank of Tampa, currently. Mil Serv: Entered as 1st Lt, Army, 41, released as Lt Col, 46, after serv in 23rd Corps Artil, ETO, 44-45; Bronze Star; Various Theatre Awards. Mem: Fla League Municipalities; Tampa Kiwanis Club; Mason; Scottish Rite; Shrine. Honors & Awards: Kiwanis Club Layman of the Year Award, Tampa, 72; Dairyman of the Year Award, Dairy Farmers, Inc, Fla, 72; Distinguished Am Award, Nat Football Found, 72. Relig: Presbyterian. Legal Res: 3001 Euclid Blvd Tampa FL 33609 Mailing Add: 402 N Howard Ave Tampa FL 33606

LANE, LAWRENCE EDWARD (D)
b Tulsa, Okla, Nov 29, 47; s Matthew M Lane & Estella Wright L; single. Educ: Northeastern State Col, BA, 71; Oral Roberts Univ, 72. Polit & Govt Pos: Legis asst, US Sen Fred R Harris, Okla, Washington, DC, summer 71; alt deleg, Dem Nat Conv, 72. Mem: Oral Roberts Univ Titan Club. Relig: Baptist. Mailing Add: 1531 N Cheyenne Tulsa OK 74106

LANE, THOMAS J (D)
b Lawrence, Mass, July 6, 98; m to Jane R Murphy. Educ: Suffolk Law Sch. Hon Degrees: BS in Pub Admin, Suffolk Univ. Polit & Govt Pos: Mass State Rep, 27-38; Mass State Sen, 39-41; US Rep, Mass, 41-61; mem, Gov Coun, Fifth Dist, 64-; mem, Mass Exec Coun, currently. Bus & Prof Pos: Attorney. Mil Serv: Vet of World War I. Mem: Am Legion; Elks; Hiberians; KofC; World War I Vets of US. Honors & Awards: Sponsor of GI Bill of Rights, US House of Rep; Hon, Ital-Am Vets. Relig: Catholic. Mailing Add: 92 Abbott St Lawrence MA 01843

LANE, TIMOTHY R (D)
Pres, Young Dem Clubs Ind
b LaPorte, Ind, Jan 6, 49; s Claude Edward Lane & Margaret Aikns; m 1969 to Lynette Kay Smith. Educ: Univ Ky, 70; Univ Ind, 71-73. Polit & Govt Pos: Pres, Marion Co Young Dem, Ind, 72-74; pres, Young Dem Clubs Ind, 74-; supt voting machines, 75- Bus & Prof Pos: Pres, Correlated Conv Servs, 74-; assoc, Robbins, Lane, Browning-Realtors, 74- Mil Serv: Entered as Pvt, Army, 69, released as Sgt, 71, after serv in Mil Police, Rep Vietnam, 70; Army Commendation Medal; Two Bronze Stars. Mem: Ind Bd Realtors; Serv Employees Union 551; Marion Co Cent Labor Coun (deleg & chmn manpower comt). Mailing Add: 8840 N Township Line Rd Indianapolis IN 46260

LANE, W JONES (D)
Ga State Rep
b Statesboro, Ga, June 23, 20; s Emory Spree Lane & Mary Jones L; m 1941 to Susie May Franklin; c William Jones Jr, Gloria Suzan, Robert Emory & Mary Ann. Educ: Univ Ga, 2 years. Polit & Govt Pos: Ga State Rep, 61- Bus & Prof Pos: Gen Mem: Rotary; Elks. Relig: Primitive Baptist. Mailing Add: Box 484 Statesboro GA 30458

LANEY, JAMES E (PETE) (D)
Tex State Rep
b Plainview, Tex, Mar 20, 43; s Wilber G Laney & Frances Wilson L; m 1963 to Nelda Kay McQuien; c Kalyn & Jamey Kay. Educ: Tex Tech Univ, BS, 65; Phi Delta Theta. Polit & Govt Pos: Chmn, Hale Co Dem Party, Tex, 70-; Tex State Rep, Dist 76, 73- Mem: Hale Co Soil & Water Conserv Bd (dir); SPlains Asn Soil & Water Conserv Bd(secy-treas); Mason (32 degree); Shrine; Hale Co Water Asn (vpres). Relig: Church of Christ. Mailing Add: 304 Skaggs Bldg Plainview TX 79072

LANG, BERNICE AGNES (DFL)
VChmn, Swift Co Dem-Farmer-Labor Party, Minn
b Murdock, Minn, Oct 14, 13; d Patrick C McGovern & Anne Bridget Cannon M; m 1939 to Chester L Lang; c James J, Mary Margaret (Mrs Koltes), Robert J & Anne Therese (Mrs Gorres). Educ: St Cloud State Col, 1 year; Minerva Club. Polit & Govt Pos: Chmn, Swift Co Dem-Farmer-Labor Party, Minn, 64-68; vchmn, 70-; mem, Swift Co Welfare Bd, 70- Bus & Prof Pos: From asst postmaster to postmaster, Murdock, Minn, 62-64. Mailing Add: Murdock MN 56271

LANG, GENE LEO (R)
Mo State Rep
b Boonville, Mo, Nov 19, 47; s Frank Leo Lang & Louise Marie Dueber L; m 1969 to Mary Jay Kay. Educ: Cent Mo State Univ, BS in Int Relat, 72; Phi Delta Theta; Acacia. Polit & Govt Pos: Mo State Rep, Dist 114, 73- Mil Serv: Entered as Pvt, Army, 68, released as SP-5, 70, after serv in Hq, 6th Bn, 44th Artil, 8th Army, Korea, 71-72. Mem: Am Legion (chmn, Sixth Dist Mo Oratorical, 72-); Sunrise Optimist; Elks; Johnson Co Hist Soc. Mailing Add: 902 Tyler Warrensburg MO 64093

LANG, GEORGE EDWARD (D)
Chmn, Hart Co Dem Party, Ky
b Peekskill, NY, Apr 7, 32; s George Louis Lang & Florence Sheehan L; m 1955 to Rose Marie Corrao; c G Vincent & Kathleen. Educ: Univ Notre Dame, BA, 54, Law Sch, JD, 55; Int Rels Club. Polit & Govt Pos: Attorney, Hart Co, Ky, 62-70; city attorney, Munfordville & Bonnieville, 70-; chmn, Hart Co Dem Party, 71-; hearing officer, Workmen's Compensation, Munfordville, 72- Bus & Prof Pos: Mem bd dirs, Radio Sta WLOC, Munfordville, Ky, 61-; mem bd dirs, Bonnieville Mfg Co, Inc, 64-70; exec secy, Thoroughbred Kampers, Inc, Hardyville, 69-; mem bd dirs, Cub Run Industs, Inc, 73- Mem: Ky Bar Asn; Lions; CofC; Munfordville Indust Found (pres). Relig: Roman Catholic. Mailing Add: Fourth & Hubbard Munfordville KY 42765

LANG, LOUISE MARY (D)
Committeewoman, Moniteau Co Dem Party, Mo
b Tipton, Mo, July 31, 17; d Joseph Deuber & Blanche Fischer D; m 1936 to Frank Leo Lang; c Mary Lou (Mrs Gene Reintjes), James (deceased), Eugene, Cathy, David & twins, Barbara (Mrs James Huhmann) & Blanche (Mrs Pat Franken) & Paul & Paulette. Educ: St Andrew's Cath Sch. Polit & Govt Pos: Committeewoman, Moniteau Co Dem Party, Mo, 68-, vchmn, formerly. Mem: Daughters of Isabella; Am Legion Auxiliary; Tipton Woman's Club; Grow & Glow Garden Club; Co Exten Bd. Honors & Awards: Merit Mother, Mo Mothers Asn, 71. Relig: Catholic. Legal Res: 460 W Cooper Tipton MO 65081 Mailing Add: Box 323 Tipton MO 65081

LANG, PHILIP DAVID (D)
Ore State Rep
b Portland, Ore, Dec 16, 29; s Henry W Lang & Vera M Kern L; m 1952 to Marcia Jean Smith; c Philip D, III. Educ: Lewis & Clark Col, Portland, Ore, 54; Northwestern Col Law, 56; Theta Chi. Polit & Govt Pos: Admin asst to mayor, Portland, Ore, 56-58; mem, Multnomah Co Dem Cent Comt, 56-; deleg, Ore Dem State Conv, 60; Ore State Rep, 61-, Speaker, Ore House Rep, currently. Bus & Prof Pos: State police officer, Ore, 53-55; adjuster, Glen Falls Ins Co, 55-56 & Ore Auto Ins Co, 59-61; asst mgr, NPac Ins Co, 61-63, mgr & asst vpres, 63- Mil Serv: Entered as Pvt, Air Force, 47, released as Sgt, 50, after serv in Air Force Intel, Far East & Japan; Occupation Medal. Mem: Mason; DeMolay Legion of Honor; VFW; Ins Underwriters Asn. Relig: Methodist. Mailing Add: 7330 SE 42nd Ave Portland OR 97206

LANG, SCOTT WESLEY (D)
Nat Committeeman, Wis Young Dem
b Oceanside, NY, Oct 25, 50; s Richard Lang & Norah Mclean Lang Pober; m to Marquerite Ann Sheehy. Educ: Marquette Univ, BA, 72; Georgetown Univ Law Sch, 73-; Phi Alpha Theta; Pi Sigma Alpha; Nat Student Register; Athleta; Avalanche Club. Polit & Govt Pos: Nat youth coordr, Humphrey for President, 72-; staff liaison, Hathaway for Senate, 72; staff, Coalition for Dem Majority, 73; asst to the exec officer, Dem Nat Conv, 73-75; staff dir, Compliance Review Comn, Dem Nat Comt, 75-; nat committeeman, Wis Young Dem, 74- Legal Res: 3057 N Gordon Place Milwaukee WI 53212 Mailing Add: 322 Fourth St NE Washington DC 20003

LANG, THEODORE A (TED) (R)
NDak State Rep
Mailing Add: State Capitol Bismarck ND 58501

LANGE, ERNEST J (D)
Chmn, Valley Co Dem Comt, Nebr
b Ord, Nebr, Jan 21, 00; s George H Lange & Augusta M Bremer L; m 1921 to Esther Marie Bredthauer; c Vesta L (Mrs Huffman), Eldon E, David G, Wilma J (Mrs Loseke), Geralding E (Mrs Don Uden) & Carol E (Mrs David Uden). Polit & Govt Pos: Chmn, Valley Co Dem Comt, Nebr, 66-; pres, Rural Fire Dist & Rural Sch Dist; alt deleg, Dem Nat Conv, 68. Bus & Prof Pos: Farmer, irrigator & livestock feeder. Mem: Nat Farmers Orgn; Lions. Relig: Lutheran. Mailing Add: RR 1 Ord NE 68862

LANGE, MARTHA LUND (R)
Mem Exec Bd, Wis Rep Party
b Hammond, Ind, Sept 24, 02; d Erick Lund & Belle Jenks L; m to Harold Kelso (deceased); m 1940 to Rudolph Fritsch Lange; c George Kelso & Louise Esther. Educ: Purdue Univ; Ind State Teachers Col, Muncie & Terra Haute. Polit & Govt Pos: Deleg, Wis State Rep Conv, 58-, chmn, Credentials Comt, 63 & mem, Resolutions Comt, twice; First Dist chmn & Walworth Co pres, Fedn of Rep Women, 60-64; vchmn, Walworth Co Rep Party, 60-64; participant, Annual Spring Conf Rep Women, DC, 60-66; state chmn, Pyramid Nat Fund Raising Proj, Women's Div, Rep Party, 61-62; pres, Wis Fedn Rep Women & mem, Nat Bd Dirs, Fedn Rep Women, 63-67, participant, Nat Bd Dirs Conf, Phoenix, Ariz, 63, Louisville, Ky, 64, New York, NY, 65 & Colorado Springs, 66; mem state exec bd, Wis Rep Party, 63- Mem: Daughters of Am Colonists (regent, Chief Big Foot Chap, nat Midwest chmn, nat awards comt, 70-); Women Descendents of the Ancient & Hon Field Artillery (state chaplain, 70-); DAR (regent, Samuel Phoenix Chap, 72-); Am Legion Auxiliary Unit 95; Friday Book Rev Club (pres, 72-). Honors & Awards: Four Gold Awards, John Melchert Vanderpool Chap, DAR, 59-63; Two Gold Awards, Samuel Phoenix DAR. Relig: Episcopal. Mailing Add: 115 Vine St Delavan WI 53115

LANGEN, ODIN (R)
b Minneapolis, Minn, Jan 5, 13; s Joe Langen & Selma Almquist L; m 1928 to Lillian Clauson; c Wayne, Lynden & Lois. Educ: Dunwoody Inst, 2 years. Polit & Govt Pos: Chmn & comt mem, Prod & Mkt Admin, Kittson Co, Minn, 46-50; chmn sch bd, Kennedy, Minn & mem, Red River Town Bd, 47-50; Minn State Rep, 50-58; US Rep, Minn, 58-70; deleg, Rep Nat Conv, 68; adminr packers & stockyards, Dept of Agr, 70- Bus & Prof Pos: Farmer, 35- Mem: Mason; Lions; Farm Bur; Lutheran Churchmen; 4-H Club. Relig: Lutheran. Mailing Add: Kennedy MN 56733

LANGFORD, ANNA RIGGS (D)
Alderman, Chicago City Coun, Ill
b Springfield, Ohio, Oct 27, 17; d Arthur J Riggs & Alice Reid R; div; c Lawrence W Langford, Jr. Educ: Roosevelt Univ, 46-48; John Marshall Law Sch, LLB, JD with Honors, 72; Order of John Marshall. Polit & Govt Pos: Alderman, Chicago City Coun, Ill, 71-; mem, Gov Comt for Sr Citizens, 71-73; deleg, President Nixon's Conf on Aging, 71; deleg-at-lg, Dem Nat Conv, 72. Mem: NAACP; Nat Bar Asn; Defense Lawyers Asn; Am Civil Liberties Union; People United to Save Humanity. Honors & Awards: Civil Rights Award, Cook Co Bar Asn, 68; Polit Achievement Award, Oper Breadbasket, Southern Christian Leadership Conf, 71; Achievement Award, Seventh Ward Independent Dem Orgn, 71; Community Serv Award, Radio Sta WBEE, 71; Boot Strap Award, Opportunity Ctrs, 71. Relig: Protestant. Legal Res: 6036 S Bishop St Chicago IL 60636 Mailing Add: 1249 W 63rd St Chicago IL 60636

LANGFORD, GEORGE ADAMS (D)
Mem, Ga State Dem Exec Comt
b Augusta, Ga, May 9, 48; s Vince Thomas Langford & Doris Elizabeth Adams L; m 1969 to Marilyn Ann Drury. Educ: Armstrong State Col, grad, 75; Sigma Nu; pres, Young Dem, 72-74; vpres, Student Govt Asn. Polit & Govt Pos: Mem, Ga State Dem Exec Comt, 74- Bus & Prof Pos: Salesman & writer, Glynn Reporter, Brunswick, Ga, 65-66. Mil Serv: Entered as E-1, Army, 69, released as E-4, 71, after serv in 360th QM Bn Hq Co, South Vietnam, 67. Relig: Baptist. Mailing Add: Rte 3 Box 500 Lot 28 Savannah GA 31406

LANGFORD, JAMES BEVERLY (D)
Ga State Sen
b Calhoun, Ga, Apr 11, 22; s Otto Charles Langford & Kathryn Brock L; m 1946 to Edna Mary Snyder; c Carol Juliette (Mrs Carter), James B, Jr & Mary Lucinda. Educ: Univ Ga, LLB, 47; Sigma Chi; Phi Delta Phi. Polit & Govt Pos: Ga State Sen, 51st Dist, 75- Bus & Prof Pos: Chmn, Ga Game & Fish Comn. Mil Serv: Entered as Pvt, Air Force, 43, released as 1st Lt, 46, after serv in 12th Air Force, ETO, 45. Mem: Rotary; VFW; Am Legion; Mason; Red Carpet Cattlemen's Asn. Relig: Protestant. Legal Res: 5 Sequoyah Terr Calhoun GA 30201 Mailing Add: PO Box 207 Calhoun GA 30701

LANGFORD, ROBERT DEAN (DFL)
Chmn, Winona Co Dem-Farmer-Labor Comt, Minn
b Bismarck, NDak, July 18, 36; s Dale E Langford & Julia Ostrom L; m 1960 to Annette Marie Jansonius; c Jennifer, Daniel, Nancy & David. Educ: Rutgers Univ, New Brunswick, BA, 58; Univ NDak Sch Law, JD, 71; Harvard Univ Law Sch, 71; Phi Delta Phi; Phi Gamma Delta. Polit & Govt Pos: Comnr, Winona Port Authority, Minn, 69-; mem, Minn Dem-Farmer-Labor State Cent Comt, 72-; chmn, Winona Co Dem-Farmer-Labor Comt, Minn, 72-; mem, South Minn River Basin Comn, 73- Bus & Prof Pos: Partner law firm, Streater, Murphy, Broshahan & Langford, Winona, Minn, 64- Mil Serv: Entered as 1st Lt, Air Force, 61, released as Capt, 64, after serv in Staff Judge Adv Air Material Command; Air Force Commendation Medal. Mem: Gustavus Adolphus Col (trustee, 73-). Honors & Awards: Bush Leadership Fel, 70; Outstanding Young Man, Winona, 70. Relig: Lutheran. Legal Res: 263 W Fifth St Winona MN 55987 Mailing Add: 64 E Fourth St Winona MN 55987

LANGILLE, PHILIP G (R)
NH State Rep
b Hinsdale, NH; s Charles H H Langille & Mary S Spencer L; m 1949. Educ: Asbury Col,

AB; Univ Ky, 1 year; New York Community Col, Brooklyn, 2 years. Polit & Govt Pos: NH State Rep, Dist 3, 75- Bus & Prof Pos: Mem clin tech lab staff, Brooklyn, NY, 3 years; mem staff, Employers Ins Co, New York, 14 years. Mil Serv: Entered as Pharm Mate, Navy, 42, released as Chief Pharm Mate, after serv in Amphibious Force, Mediter, Cent Europe & Atlantic Fleet; Naval Res; 3 Battle Stars; Unit Citation; Good Conduct Medal. Mem: Am Tech Soc; SAR; Nat Huguenot Soc. Relig: Protestant. Mailing Add: 41 Highland Ave Hinsdale NH 03451

LANGLEY, BYRON (D)
NDak State Rep
Mailing Add: State Capitol Bismarck ND 58501

LANGLEY, LAWRENCE DESALES (D)
Mem, Arlington Co Dem Exec Comt, Va
b Washington, DC, Nov 5, 05; s Andrew DeSales Langley & Pearl E L; m 1934 to Elise Foster; c Richard Lawrence. Educ: George Washington Univ, 24. Polit & Govt Pos: Mem, Arlington Co Dem Exec Comt, Va, 50-, treas, 57-61; deleg, Dem State Conv, 52, 56, 60, 64 & 68; deleg, Dem Nat Conv, 60, 64 & 68; co-chmn precinct orgn, Arlington Co, J Lindsey Almond Campaign for Gov, 57, Alburtis Harrison, Jr, 61 & Mills Godwin, 65; chmn precinct orgn, late Harry F Byrd, Sr Campaign for US Senate, 64 & Harry F Byrd, Jr, 66; mem adv comt, Tenth Cong Dist of Va for Kennedy-Johnson Presidential Campaign, 60, Johnson-Humphrey, 64 & Humphrey-Muskie, 68; mem, Comt Strip Mining & Hwy Construction Practices, Va Adv Legis Coun, 64-65, Comt Surface Mining other than Coal, 66-67; comt clerk, Va Gen Assembly, 67-69, senate clerk, 69-73; mem fiscal affairs comt, Arlington Co, Va, 69; chmn precinct orgn, Arlington Co, Va for reelection of Hon Mills E Godwin to off Gov, 73; precinct chmn, Arlington Co, Va for Hon Joel T Broyhill for US Rep, 74. Bus & Prof Pos: Time clerk, Chesapeake & Potomac Tel Co of Va, 25-26, stock clerk, 26-30, installer, 30-44; co repairman, 44-54, analyst, 54-66. Mem: Soc Va; Lyon Village Citizens Asn; CWA; Pioneers of Am; Cardinal Soc Va (chmn, 71-73). Relig: Episcopal. Mailing Add: 1612 N Edgewood St Arlington VA 22201

LANGLEY, STANLEY R (D)
Mem, Ark Dem State Comt
b Conway, Ark, Feb 15, 41; s Rayburn Langley & Eva Sevier L; m 1961 to Dianne Williams; c Laura & Michael. Educ: Univ Cent Ark, BSEd; Univ Ark, JD; Phi Alpha Delta; Theta Xi. Polit & Govt Pos: Mem, Ark Dem State Comt, 74- & mem rules comt, 74- Bus & Prof Pos: Attorney-at-law, Jonesboro, Ark, 72- Mil Serv: Entered as Lt, Air Force, 63, released as Capt, 67, after serv in Air Training Command, 64-67; Air Force Outstanding Unit Award, Publ: Venue laws of Arkansas, Ark Law Rev, 72. Mem: Am, Ark & Craighead Bar Asns. Relig: Episcopal. Legal Res: 2317 Redbud Jonesboro AR 72401 Mailing Add: PO Box 1346 Jonesboro AR 72401

LANGSETH, KEITH L (DFL)
Minn State Rep
b Moorhead, Minn, Jan 20, 38; s Norman Clifford Langseth & Ruth Rosenquist L; m 1957 to Lorraine Mae Ersland; c Danny, Gayle & Joy. Educ: Glyndon High Sch, grad, 56. Polit & Govt Pos: Chmn, Dist 9 Dem-Farmer-Labor Party, Minn, 73-74; chmn, Clay Co Dem-Farmer-Labor Party, 74; Minn State Rep, Dist 9B, 75- Mailing Add: Glyndon MN 56547

LANIER, DAVID WILLIAM (D)
Chmn, Dyer Co Dem Comt, Tenn
b Dyer Co, Tenn, Nov 16, 34; s James Parker Lanier & Robbye Sullivan L (deceased); m 1962 to Mary Joan Mills; c Leigh Anne & Robbye Claire. Educ: Memphis State Univ, 52-55; Univ Tenn, Knoxville, LLB, 58; Kappa Sigma. Polit & Govt Pos: Deleg, Tenn Limited Const Conv, 59; pres, Dyer Co Young Dem, Tenn, 60-61; vpres, Tenn Young Dem, 60-61; alderman, City of Dyersburg, 63-65, mayor, 65-; campaign mgr, Buford Ellington for Gov, 66; state chmn, Mayors for Hooker for Gov, 68; Dyer Co campaign mgr, Ray Blanton for Senate, 72; chmn, Dyer Co Dem Comt, Tenn, 74- Bus & Prof Pos: Attorney-at-law, 59- Mil Serv: Entered as Airman, Air Nat Guard, 59, released as S/Sgt, 65, after serv in Memphis Air Nat Guard. Mem: Dyer Co Bar Asn (pres, 71-72); Tenn Munic League (dir, 68, vpres, 71, pres, 72); Voc Rehabilitation Bd (dir, 68-72); Downtown Merchants Asn (dir, 66-); Dyersburg CofC (dir, 66-). Relig: Church of Christ. Legal Res: 2117 Starlight Dr Dyersburg TN 38024 Mailing Add: PO Box 822 Dyersburg TN 38024

LANIER, JAMES OLANDA (D)
Tenn State Rep
b Newbern, Tenn, Sept 8, 31; s James Parker Lanier & Robbye Sullivan L; m 1950 to Carolyn Holland; c James Elton, Donna Kay & Amy Claire. Educ: Memphis State Univ, BS, 55, JD, 69; Sigma Delta Kappa; Kappa Sigma. Polit & Govt Pos: Tenn State Rep, 59-61 & 71-, chmn, House State & Local Govt Comt, currently; co attorney, Dyer Co, 72- Bus & Prof Pos: Indust engr, Milan Arsenal, Milan, Tenn, 53-54; social worker, Dept Pub Welfare, Tenn, 55-57, sr social worker & appeals examr, 57-58; pres & gen mgr, Main Sporting Goods, Dyersburg, 59-61; adjuster, USF&G Ins Co, Memphis, 65-69; lawyer, Dyersburg, 69-; pres, Northwestern Tenn Coun for Promotion Tourism, 72- Mem: Am Trial Lawyers Asn; Moose; Dyer Co CofC; Dyersburg Country Club; Kiwanis. Honors & Awards: Man of the Year Award, Sigma Delta Kappa, 67-68. Relig: Church of Christ. Legal Res: 617 Sunset Blvd Dyersburg TN 38024 Mailing Add: 208 N Mill St Dyersburg TN 38024

LANIGAN, CHARLES THOMAS (R)
b Rome, NY, Feb 3, 25; s Charles T Lanigan; m 1949 to Barbara Gifford; c Charles T, III, Mary Kay, Valerie, Catherine & Julie. Educ: Colgate Univ, BA, 49; Delta Kappa Epsilon. Polit & Govt Pos: Mayor, Rome, NY, 60-62; mem exec comt, Oneida Co Rep Comt, 63-66; dir, NY State Off Planning Coord, 67-69; chmn, NY Rep State Comt, 69-72; mem, Rep Nat Comt, 69-72; chmn, Northeastern Rep State Chmn Asn, 70-72; deleg, Rep Nat Conv, 72. Bus & Prof Pos: Exec secy, Rome CofC, 53-55; sales prom mgr indust prod, Revere Copper & Brass, Rome Mfg Co Div, 55-59; treas, NY State Thruway Authority, 72-; vpres, Metrop Life Ins Co, NYC, 73- Mil Serv: Entered as A/S, Navy, 43, released as FC 3/C, 46, after serv in USS Aegir, Atlantic & Pac Theaters, 44-46. Mem: Nat Health Coun (mem bd); Pub Affairs Coun. Relig: Roman Catholic. Legal Res: 156 River Rd Box 312 Scarborough Briarcliff Manor NY 10510 Mailing Add: Metropolitan Life Insurance Co 1 Madison Ave New York NY 10010

LANKFORD, THOMAS J (R)
b Sandborn, Ind, Dec 5, 26; s Thomas Calvin Lankford & Susie E Berryman L; m 1956 to Patricia Ann Fulmer; c Thomas Todd & Patricia Kim. Educ: Vincennes Univ, AS in Eng, 46; Evansville Col, BS in Bus Admin, 50; Georgetown Law Sch, 53-54; life mem, Acacia. Polit & Govt Pos: Rep precinct committeeman & ward chmn, Ind, 48-52; Rep cand for auditor, Knox Co, 50; exec asst to US Rep William G Bray, 51-52; Majority Clerk, US House of Rep, 53, Minority Clerk, 54-; deleg, Rep Nat Conv, 56, alt deleg, 60, 64, 68 & 72. Bus & Prof Pos: Admin asst, William A Atkins Enterprises, 53; pres, Thomas J Lankford, Inc, 53- Mil Serv: Entered as A/S, Navy, 44, released as PO 2/C, 46, after serv in Supply, Ammunition Depot, Hawthorne, Nev. Mem: Cong Country Club; Capitol Hill Club (treas); Shrine; Am Legion; Congressional Secretaries Club. Relig: Methodist; pres Bd Trustees, Potomac United Methodist Church. Legal Res: Box 231 Sandborn IN 47578 Mailing Add: 9209 Farnsworth Dr Potomac MD 20854

LANKLER, ALEXANDER MACDONALD (R)
b Wilkes-Barre, Pa, June 30, 28; s Ralph Conover Lankler & Helen MacDonald L; m 1951 to Celeste Baldwin Skeen; c Melissa M & Lesley L. Educ: Hamilton Co, BA, 48; Cornell Law Sch, LLB, 51; Cornell Law Quart; Phi Kappa Phi; Sigma Phi. Polit & Govt Pos: Founder & pres, Younger Rep Clubs Am, 44; pres, Jr Rep NY State, 46; pres, Jr Rep Am, 48; dir youth activities, NY Rep State Comt, 49-50; dir, NY State Registr Vote, 60; law asst, Gov Thomas E Dewey, 54; asst to Sen Irving M Ives, 56; asst to asst Secy Treas, David Kendall, 57; admin spec asst, Gen Serv Admin, 57-59; dep mgr, Nelson A Rockefeller Reelect Campaign, 62 & Campaign for President, 63-64 & 68; finance chmn, Md Rep State Cent Comt, 67-68, counsel to state chmn, 69-70, chmn, 70-73; deleg, Rep Nat Conv, 72; chmn, Northeast Rep State Chmn Asn, 73- Bus & Prof Pos: Assoc, Chapman, Walsh & Bryson, Walsh & O'Connell, New York & Washington, DC, 53-56; partner, Chapman, Walsh & O'Connell; Hawkins, Delafield & Wood, 59-64; private practice of law, Washington, DC, 64-67; sr partner, Lankler & Crolius, 67-69; sr partner, Lankler & Parker, 69-72; attorney, Law Off of Alexander M Lankler, 73- Mil Serv: Entered as Ens, Coast Guard Res, 51, released as Lt(jg), 53, after serv at Hq, Washington, DC. Mem: NY State Bar Asn; Metrop Club; Montgomery Co Men's Rep Club; Nat Press Club; Fed City Club. Honors & Awards: Distinguished Serv Medal, Gen Serv Admin, 59; Am Heritage Found Award, 61. Relig: Presbyterian. Legal Res: Red Barn Lane Potomac MD 20854 Mailing Add: 3526 K St NW Washington DC 20007

LANNING, JUDITH A (JUDY) (R)
Chairwoman, Hocking Co Rep Party, Ohio
b Logan, Ohio, May 23, 28; d John Gottlieb Buntz & Ruth McCarty B; m 1949 to Wilbur W Lanning; c David W, John Philip & Sarah Ann. Educ: Logan High Sch, grad, 46. Polit & Govt Pos: Chairwoman, Hocking Co Rep Party, Ohio, 73-; secy, Tenth Dist Rep Comt, 74- Bus & Prof Pos: Clerk's asst, Logan City Schs, 69-72; auditor's asst, City of Logan, 73-75; med secy, 75- Mem: Hocking Hills Rep Women's Club; Hocking Co Hist Soc; Ohio Hist Asn; Ohio Rep Women's Asn. Relig: Presbyterian. Mailing Add: 172 Mound St Logan OH 43138

LANO, JOAN RITA (DFL)
Secy-Treas, Todd Co Dem-Farmer-Labor Party, Minn
b Milwaukee, Wis, Oct 13, 20; d Frederick J Schermerhorn & Lillian Harrison S; m 1946 to Frank J Lano; c Barbara, David, Mary & Diane. Educ: Washington High Sch, Milwaukee, Wis, 4 years. Polit & Govt Pos: Secy-treas, Todd Co Dem-Farmer-Labor Party, Minn, 68- Bus & Prof Pos: Stenographer, Northwestern Mutual Life Ins Co, 42; statistician, Vis Nurses Asn, 44-; receptionist-stenographer, Milwaukee Labor Press, 45-46. Mem: VFW; Long Prairie Firemen's Auxiliary; Minn State Women's Dem-Farmer-Labor Fedn; Todd Co Womens Dem-Farmer-Labor Orgn. Relig: Catholic. Mailing Add: 31 Ninth SE Long Prairie MN 56347

LANSING, MARY HUBBARD (D)
b Providence, RI, May 2, 49; d A Ten Eyck Lansing & Elizabeth Hubbard L; single. Educ: Fairfield Pub High Sch, Conn, grad, 67. Polit & Govt Pos: Off mgr, US Rep Toby Moffett, Conn, 75- Bus & Prof Pos: Admin asst, Rural Housing Alliance, 69-73. Mem: Frontier Nursing Serv (mem Washington Comt). Legal Res: 17 Hitchcock Rd Westport CT 06880 Mailing Add: 639 Massachusetts Ave NE Washington DC 20002

LANTERMAN, FRANK D (R)
Calif State Assemblyman
b Los Angeles, Calif, Nov 4, 01; single. Educ: Univ Southern Calif Col Music. Hon Degrees: LLD, Univ Southern Calif, 73. Polit & Govt Pos: Mem, Los Angeles Rep Cent Comt, Calif, 38-50; Calif State Assemblyman, 50-, chmn, Ways & Means Comt, Calif State Assembly, 69-70, vchmn, 71-; deleg, Rep Nat Conv, 64 & 68. Bus & Prof Pos: Land Developer. Mem: Kiwanis; CofC; Red Cross; Musicians Local 47, AFL (life mem). Relig: Congregational. Mailing Add: 106-A S Los Robles Pasadena CA 91101

LANTING, WILLIAM JOHN (R)
b Twin Falls, Idaho, Mar 18, 18; s John Lanting & Grace Visser L; m 1940 to Marguerite Lillian Caudle; c James William, Arthur John, Patricia Grace & Robert Joseph. Polit & Govt Pos: Trustee, Filer Sch Dist, Idaho, 52-61; Idaho State Rep, Twin Falls Co, 59-74, majority leader, Idaho House of Rep, 63-67, speaker, 67-74, mem exec bd, Western Conv of Coun State Govt, 62-74, chmn, Water Probs Comt, 64-65 & Human Resources Comt, 65-, vpres, 66-68, pres, 68-; mem, Idaho Legis Coun, 63-74, co-chmn, 65-74; mem bd mgrs, Coun State Govts, 66-74; vchmn, Nat Coun State Govt, 69-72, chmn, 73-74. Bus & Prof Pos: Farmer & stock raiser, 40- Mem: Farm Bur; Grange; Idaho Cattlemen's Asn; past dir, Twin Falls CofC. Relig: Presbyterian. Legal Res: Hollister ID Mailing Add: Rte 1 Twin Falls ID 83301

LANTIS, SARA JEAN (R)
Chmn, Young Rep NDak
b Portland, Ore, Mar 10, 48; d Donald Paul Vernier & Mary Patricia Clark V; m 1968 to Bernard Tipton Lantis; c twins Amy Rachelle & Julie Erika. Educ: Ore State Univ, 66-68; Univ Wash, BA, 70; Pi Beta Phi. Polit & Govt Pos: First vchmn, NDak Young Rep, 74-75, chmn, 75- Bus & Prof Pos: Freelance interior designer, Seattle, Wash, 70-71 & 73-74; interior designer, Eddy Furniture, Jamestown, NDak, 71-73. Mem: Fedn of Rep Women. Relig: Roman Catholic. Mailing Add: 1013 Thomas Ave NE Jamestown ND 58401

LANTZ, JERRY NEIL (D)
b Richmond, Ind, Aug 21, 40; s James C Lantz & Dorothy Lucille Dingle L; m 1963 to Kathleen Sue Mitchell; c Thomas Mitchell, Lee Ann & Paige Suzanne. Educ: Tri-State Col, Ind, 1 year. Polit & Govt Pos: Chmn, Steuben Co Dem Party, Ind, 70-74. Bus & Prof Pos: Mgr, Eckman's Dept Store, 61-64; buyer, Gilbert's Men's Store, 64-67; mgr, Jarrard's Toggery, 67- Mem: Elks; Moose; United Fund (publicity chmn). Relig: Methodist; Bd mem, Fremont United Methodist Church. Legal Res: 407 Toledo St Fremont IN 46737 Mailing Add: Box 201 Fremont IN 46737

LAPHAM, HARRY HOUSTON, JR (R)
b Ocala, Fla, Jan 6, 07; s Harry Houston Lapham & Ethel B Mark L; m 1951 to Grace Ellen Read. Educ: Univ of Fla, 24-28; Alpha Kappa Psi; Scabbard & Blade; Sigma Lambda Tau. Polit & Govt Pos: Treas, Thurston Co Rep Cent Comt, 64-65, chmn, formerly; asst sgt at arms, Washington House Rep, 67-71; deleg, Rep Nat Conv, 68. Mil Serv: Entered as Pvt, Army, 43, retired Maj, 63, after serv in Far East Command, Japan, 47-51, US Commun Zone, France, 54-57 & 8th Army-UNC Korea, 60-61; Bronze Star Medal; Army Commendation Medal. Mem: Olympia Lions Club (past pres); VFW; Salvation Army Advisory Bd (past chmn). Honors & Awards: Thurston Co Distinguished Serv Award, 68. Relig: United Church of Christ. Mailing Add: Rte 9 Box 458 Olympia WA 98501

LAPIDES, JULIAN LEE (D)
Md State Sen
b Baltimore, Md, Sept 17, 31; s Solomon M Lapides & Doris Racusin L; m 1964 to Linda Zeva Fishman. Educ: Towson State Col, BS, 54; Univ Md Sch Law, LLB, 61; Kappa Delta Pi, pres, Towson chap, 53-54. Polit & Govt Pos: Pres, Mt Royal Dem Club, formerly; Md State Deleg, Second Dist, Baltimore City, 63-67; Md State Sen, 67-, chmn, Joint Budget Comt on Pub Safety & Transportation, Md State Senate; mem, Legis Coun Md, 69-; mem, Nat Legis Conf, 73. Bus & Prof Pos: Teacher sci, High Sch, 56-60; attorney-at-law, 60- Mil Serv: Entered as Pvt, Army, 54, released as E-4 Spec 3rd, 56, after serv in 2nd Inf Bn Combat Team, Iceland Defense Force, 55-56; Good Conduct Medal. Mem: Citizens Adv Bd, Alcoholism Clin of Baltimore; Baltimore Beautification Comt (founder & chmn); Sierra Club; Victorian Soc of Am; Better Air Coalition. Honors & Awards: Participant, Eagleton Inst Polit Sem for Outstanding State Legislators, 70; Md Pub Health Asn Ann Achievement Award, 71; Nat Kidney Found Distinguished Serv Award, 71; Distinguished Alumnus Award, Towson State Col, 72; Young Dem of Md Outstanding State Official Award, 73. Mailing Add: 1528 Bolton St Baltimore MD 21217

LAPIDUS, I RICHARD (D)
b Brooklyn, NY, Apr 7, 35; s George Lapidus & May Goldstein L; m 1959 to Leah Kahan Blumberg; c Louise Diana & Lenora Michelle. Educ: Univ Chicago, AB, 55, BS, 56, MS, 57; Columbia Univ, PhD, 63. Polit & Govt Pos: Chmn, Teaneck Dem Coun, NJ, 66-67; chmn, Bergen Co Dem Coun, 67-68; mem exec bd, NJ Dem Coun, 67-68; mem exec bd, Bergen Co & NJ Vol for McCarthy, 68; deleg, Dem Nat Conv, 68 & 72; trustee, Teaneck Polit Assembly, 68-70; chmn, Dem Coalition of Bergen Co, 69-70; chmn, Bergen Co Citizens for McGovern, 72. Bus & Prof Pos: Teaching asst, NY Univ, 56, Univ Chicago, 56-57 & Columbia Univ, 57-59; lectr, City Col New York, 59-61; research asst, Columbia Univ, 61-63, research assoc, 63- asst prof, Stevens Inst Technol, 63-68, assoc prof, 68-; vis assoc prof, Columbia Univ, 69; vis fel, Princeton Univ, 70-71. Publ: Approximately 25 articles on physics & molecular biol in prof jour. Mem: Sigma Xi; Am Phys Soc; Am Asn Advan Sci; Sci Research Soc Am; Fedn Am Scientists. Honors & Awards: Ford Found scholar, 51-55; Univ Chicago scholar, 55-56; NASA faculty fel, 66; Stevens Inst Technol research grants, 65, 68 & 71. Mailing Add: 1273 W Laurelton Pkwy Teaneck NJ 07666

LAPLANTE, BRYAN FRANKLIN (R)
Assoc Comnr, Fed Water Qual Admin, Dept of Interior
b Mine LaMotte, Mo, Oct 20, 15; s Charles Marion LaPlante & Alma Rickman L; m 1941 to Helen Friedlinda Sonnleitner. Educ: Jefferson Col, 35-36; Washington Univ, 34-38; Indust Lenders Tech Inst, 40-42. Polit & Govt Pos: Dir security opers, asst gen mgr & legis liaison, US Atomic Energy Comn, DC, 47-58; dep staff dir, US Senate Rep Policy Comt, 61-69; assoc comnr, Fed Water Qual Admin, Dept of Interior, 69-; dir, Fed-State Coord, Environ Protection Agency, DC Hq, currently, dep dir, Off of Legis. Bus & Prof Pos: Client rep, Joyce & Fisher Assocs, 58-60; dir, Washington, DC, Mitre Corp Off, 60-61. Mil Serv: Entered as Pvt, Air Force, 43, released as Capt, 46, after serv as Intel Officer, Manhattan Eng Dist, DC & NY, 44-46; Res Officer, Mil Intel, 47-50. Mem: Am Soc for Indust Secys; Men of Holy Cross; Am Legion; John Carroll Soc. Relig: Catholic. Mailing Add: 4106 Orleans Pl Alexandria VA 22304

LAPLANTE, DONAT JOSEPH (D)
Mass State Rep
b Harrisville, RI, Aug 12, 13; s William F Laplante & Mary Ann Paul L; m 1939 to Jeannette G Pirani; c Gabrielle, William, Edouard, Julie (Mrs Lacroix), Jacqueline, Antoine, Albert, Joseph, Michel, Philippe & Catherine. Educ: Sch Commercial Sci, Woonsocket, RI, grad 36. Polit & Govt Pos: Town finance comt, Bellingham, Mass, formerly, town treas, formerly, tax assessor, 55-; Mass State Rep, 23rd Norfolk Dist, 75- Mem: Club Marquette-Woonsocket; Franco-Am Club, Bellingham. Relig: Roman Catholic. Mailing Add: 91 Paine St Bellingham MA 02019

LAPOINTE, AGNES R (R)
b Providence, RI, Oct 29, 29; d William Robidoux & Eugenie Dionne R (deceased); m 1948 to Charles William Lapointe, Jr; c William Charles, Shirley-Ann & Stephen Michael. Educ: Warwick & Providence Sch Syst. Polit & Govt Pos: Mem, Coventry Town Rep Comt, RI, 61-; mem, Housing Authority, Coventry, 67-; mem exec bd, Fedn Rep Women, 68; vchmn, RI Rep State Cent Comt, 69-73; deleg, Rep Nat Conv, 72. Mem: Rep Women's Club Coventry. Relig: Catholic. Mailing Add: 26 Grant Dr Coventry RI 02816

LAPOINTE, FRANCIS CHARLES (D)
Mass State Rep
b Chicopee, Mass, Jan 13, 39; s Francis Joseph Lapointe & Edna Vandal L; m 1964 to Adele Evelyn Ruel; c David Ruel & Audrie Caron. Educ: State Col Westfield, BS, 62; State Col Westfield & Univ Mass, 62-64, MEd, 64; fel, Col Holy Cross, Univ Calif, Los Angeles & NY Univ. Polit & Govt Pos: Mass State Rep, Third Hampden Dist, 69- Bus & Prof Pos: Instr, Chicopee High Sch, Mass, 62-64, Huntington Sch, San Marino, Calif, 64-65 & Van Sickle Sch, Springfield, Mass, 65-68. Publ: Monthly newspaper column for the Holyoke Daily Transcript, Holyoke, Mass. Mem: AFL-CIO; Am Fedn Teachers; Soc State Legislators; Jaycees; KofC. Honors & Awards: Distinguished Serv Award, US Jaycees, 66. Relig: Catholic. Mailing Add: 43 Mt Vernon Rd Chicopee MA 01013

LAPOINTE, THOMAS R (D)
Maine State Rep
Mailing Add: Box 244 DS Portland ME 04111

LAPPIN, PETER THOMAS HAYDEN (D)
Mass State Rep
b Portland, Maine, Sept 25, 38; s Thomas Joseph Lappin & Margaret Berry L; m 1971 to Linda Lee Klein. Educ: Cathedral Col, 57; Otero Jr Col, La Junta, Colo, 57-58; Am Int Col, 58-61; Columbia Univ, 65-66. Polit & Govt Pos: Mass State Rep, Eighth Hampden Dist, 73- Bus & Prof Pos: Asst supvr educ, Mass Rehabilitation Comn, 66-68; rehabilitation & placement coun, Goodwill Indust, 68-70; admin asst to mayor, City of Springfield, Mass, 70-73. Mil Serv: Entered as Pfc, Army, 61, released as SP-4, 63, after serv in 101st Airborne; Good Conduct Medal. Mem: SEnd Community Ctr; Elks; KofC; Springfield Civic Ctr, Conv & Visitors Bur (bd mem, 70-); Tuesday Club. Honors & Awards: Award for Placement of 138 Handicapped & Retarded Adults, Goodwill Industs, 69. Relig: Roman Catholic. Legal Res: 40 Belvidere St Springfield MA 01108 Mailing Add: Statehouse Boston MA 02133

LARK, HENRY W (R)
b Shamokin, Pa, May 16, 05; s H Wilson Lark & Grace Aucker L; m 1926 to Isabel Witmer; c Isabel. Educ: Franklin & Marshall Col, AB, 26; Phi Kappa Psi. Polit & Govt Pos: Chmn, Northumberland Co Rep Comt, 39-74; mem, Pa Rep State Exec Comt, 41-74; deleg, Rep Nat Conv, 48, 52, 56 & 64, secy of deleg, 56; chmn, Pa Rep State Primary Campaign Comt, 56. Bus & Prof Pos: Vpres, Ashland Coal & Coke, WVa & Ashland Mining Corp; vpres, Harmon Mining Corp, Grundy, Va; vpres, Sovereign Pocahontas Co, Bluefield, WVa, Filmore Construction Co, Edwardsville, Pa & Sovereign Coal Corp, Jamboree, Ky; pres, Gateway Apt Assocs, Wilkes Barre; vpres, Majestic Collieries Co, Majestic, Ky. Mem: Mason (32 degree); Shrine; Union League; Elks; Moose. Relig: United Church of Christ. Legal Res: Apple Hill Farm Dewart PA 17730 Mailing Add: 518 Market Sunbury PA 17801

LARK, ROBERT F (D)
b Sharon, Pa, Apr 12, 44; s Donald J Lark & Erma G Mitchell L; single. Educ: Slippery Rock State Col, BS Educ cum laude, 66 & grad study hist; Sigma Pi; Pi Gamma Mu; Kappa Delta Pi. Polit & Govt Pos: Deleg, Dem Nat Conv, 72; mem, Mercer Co Govt Study Comn, Pa, 72. Bus & Prof Pos: Teacher soc studies, Butler Area Schs, Pa, 66- Publ: A history of the underground railroad in Mercer & Butler Counties, Mercer Co Hist, 71. Mem: Nat & Pa State Educ Asns; Pa Farmer-Labor Fedn; Mercer Co Hist Soc. Relig: Methodist. Mailing Add: 339 Garfield St West Middlesex PA 16159

LARKIN, RAY THOMAS (R)
Chmn, Ramsey Co Rep Comt, Minn
b St Paul, Minn, Sept 25, 33; s Thomas John Larkin & Margaret Egan L; m 1953 to Carol Fern Jenney; c Pamela, David & Jody. Educ: Univ Minn, 65-66. Polit & Govt Pos: Chmn, Rep Dist Comt, Ramsey Co, 70-72, first vchmn, 72-73; chmn, Ramsey Co Rep Comt, 73- Bus & Prof Pos: Serv rep, Am Mach & Foundry Corp, 57-66; prod mgr, Sewall Gear Co, 66-75. Mil Serv: Entered as Pvt, Army, 53, released as Cpl, 55, after serv in 2nd Armored Div, Ger, 53-55. Relig: Lutheran. Mailing Add: 2658 Marion St Paul MN 55113

LARKINS, JOHN DAVIS, JR (D)
b Morristown, Tenn, June 8, 09; s John D Larkins & Emma Cooper L; m 1930 to Pauline Murrill; c Emma Sue (Mrs D H Loftin) & Polly (Mrs J H Bearden). Educ: Wake Forest Col, BA, 29; Belin Univ, LLD, 57; Phi Alpha Delta. Polit & Govt Pos: NC State Sen, 36-44 & 48-54; deleg-at-lg, Dem Nat Conv, 40, 44, 48, 56 & 60; chmn, Gov Adv Budget Comn, NC, 51-53; secy, NC Dem Exec Comt, 52-54, chmn, 54-59; mem, Dem Nat Comt, 58-60; US Dist Judge, Trenton, NC, 61- Bus & Prof Pos: Law practice; secy, Larkins Stores, Inc; dir, Life Ins Co of NC. Mil Serv: Pvt, Army, 45. Mem: Am Cancer Soc (dir, nat bd dirs & vchmn); Am Legion; Mason; Elk; Moose. Honors & Awards: Distinguished Serv Award, Am Cancer Soc. Relig: Baptist; Deacon. Legal Res: Trenton NC 28585 Mailing Add: c/o Federal Bldg Trenton NC 28585

LARO, DAVID (R)
Chmn, Genesee Co Rep Party, Mich
b Flint, Mich, Mar 3, 42; s Sam Laro & Florence Chereton L; m 1967 to Nancy Lynn Wolf; c Rachel Lynn & Marlene. Educ: Univ Mich, BA, 64; Univ Ill Col Law, JD, 67; NY Univ Law Sch, LLM in taxation, 70; Phi Delta Phi; Zeta Beta Tau (pres). Polit & Govt Pos: Chmn, Miliken for Gov, 70; chmn, Genesee Co Rep Party, Mich, 71-; chmn, Reelect the President Comt, Genesee Co, 72; deleg, Rep Nat Conv, 72; chmn, State Tenure Comn, currently & Mich Seventh Cong Dist, Rep Party, 73-; mem, Gov Rep Rev & Develop Comt, 73- Bus & Prof Pos: Partner, Winegarden, Booth, Ricker, Shedd & Laro, 71-; dir, Genova, Inc, 72- Publ: Elective one-month-liquidations, Am Bar Asn J, 5/71. Mem: Am & Genesee Co Bar Asns; State Bar of Mich; Univ Club of Flint. Honors & Awards: First Place Winner, Moot Court Competition, 67. Relig: Jewish. Legal Res: 1057 Briarcliffe Dr Flint MI 48504 Mailing Add: 501 Citizens Bank Bldg Flint MI 48502

LA ROCHE, DAVID (D)
Polit & Govt Pos: Chmn, NH Dem State Comt, formerly. Mailing Add: 323 Franklin Manchester NH 03101

LAROSA, PAUL A (D)
Conn State Rep
Mailing Add: 225 Hanmer St Hartford CT 06114

LARRABEE, LELAND EARL, JR (D)
Mem Exec Bd, Calif State Dem Cent Comt
b Alameda, Calif, Nov 1, 28; s Leland E Larrabee, Sr & Frances Elizabeth Scott L; m 1959 to Lorraine Barbara Giannoni; c Susan Katherine & Debra Ann. Educ: Fresno State Col, 6 months; Fresno City Col, 6 months; San Francisco State Col, BA, 56. Polit & Govt Pos: Mem, Commun Serv Orgn, Off Econ Opportunity, Fresno Co, Calif, 65; Citizens Adv Comt for Compensatory Educ, 66; bldg adv comn, Fresno City Unified Sch Dist, 66; trustee, Calaveras Unified Sch Bd, 70; membership chmn, Dem of Northern Calif, SLake Tahoe, 71; mem exec bd, Calif State Dem Cent Comt, 71-; chmn, Calaveras Co Dem Cent Comt, formerly. Bus & Prof Pos: Army, retired, 59. Publ: Article in Infantry J, 11/49; Valley Labor Citizen, 62-64. Mem: Calif Sch Bd Asn; West Point Lions Club; VFW; Hwy 26 Asn; West Point Rod & Gun Club. Honors & Awards: Hon life mem, Calif Congress Parent, Teachers Asn. Mailing Add: Box 339 West Point CA 95255

LARSEN, ALLAN F (R)
Idaho State Rep
Mailing Add: Rte 5 Box 33 Blackfoot ID 83221

LARSEN, GEORGE KEEFE (R)
Ga State Rep
b Jacksonville, Fla, Nov 8, 40; s George Keefe Larsen, Sr & Carol Mary L; m 1971 to Mary Julia Champion. Educ: Emory Univ, AB, 63; Harvard, 63-64. Polit & Govt Pos: Ga State Rep, 27th House Dist, 71-, minority whip, Ga House of Rep, 74- Bus & Prof Pos: Systs eng, Int

Bus Machines Corp, 64-68, mkt rep, 68- Mil Serv: Entered as Pvt, Army, 57, released as Cpl, 60, after serv in 101st Airborne Div, 57-60; Parachutists Wings. Honors & Awards: Conservationist of the Year, League of Conserv Voters, 72; Legis Conserv Award, Nat Wildlife Fedn, 73; Spec Award, Ga Lung Asn, 74. Relig: Methodist. Mailing Add: 405 State Capitol Atlanta GA 30334

LARSEN, JACK LUCAS (R)
Hawaii State Rep
b Honolulu, Hawaii, May 30, 24; s Nils Paul Larsen & Sara Lucas L; m 1971 to Chonita Gibbs; c Jennifer Sara & Nils Harold. Educ: Univ Hawaii, 46-48; Colgate Univ, BA, 50; Phi Kappa Psi. Polit & Govt Pos: Chmn, Dist Rep Party, Hawaii, 66-68; Hawaii State Rep, Eighth Dist, 75- Bus & Prof Pos: Consult agriculturalist, Hutchinson Sugar Co & Hawaiian Agr Co, 52-55; pineapple agriculturalist, corp staff mem & dir pineapple planning, Dole Corp, Lanai, Wahiawa & Honolulu, Hawaii, San Jose, Calif & Salem, Ore, 55-72; independent agro-indust consult, 72- Mil Serv: Entered as Pvt, Air Force, 43, released as Cpl, 46, after serv in Marianas Islands, 45-46. Mem: Hawaii CofC; Pacific Club; Sierra Club; Common Cause. Mailing Add: 3707 Diamond Head Rd Honolulu HI 96816

LARSEN, MELVIN L (R)
Mich State Rep
Mailing Add: 1383 Beemer Court Oxford MI 48051

LARSEN, RICHARD F (R)
Dep Asst Secy Developing Nations Finance, Dept Treas
Polit & Govt Pos: Former Lt Gov, NDak; Dep Asst Secy Developing Nations Finance, Dept Treas, 73- Legal Res: Bismarck ND Mailing Add: Dept of the Treasury 15th & Pennsylvania Ave Washington DC 20220

LARSEN, W W, JR (D)
Ga State Rep
Mailing Add: PO Box 2002 Dublin GA 31021

LARSON, ALMA (R)
VChmn, Gregory Co Rep Party, SDak
b Vivian, SDak, May 21, 32. Educ: Opportunities Inst of Denver. Polit & Govt Pos: Secy of State, SDak, 64-72; vchmn, Gregory Co Rep Party, 75- Mem: Am Legion Auxiliary; Bus & Prof Women's Club; SDak Young Rep League; LBH Asn. Relig: Lutheran. Mailing Add: Gregory SD 57533

LARSON, CLARENCE EDWARD (R)
Comnr, Atomic Energy Comn
b Cloquet, Minn, Sept 20, 09; s Louis L Larson & Caroline Ullman L; m 1957 to Jane R Warren; c Robert E, E Lawrence & Lance S. Educ: Univ Minn, BS, 32; Univ Calif, Berkeley, PhD, 37; Phi Lambda Epsilon; Sigma Xi; Tau Beta Pi. Polit & Govt Pos: Mem, Gov Comt on Sci & Technol, Tenn, 68-69; comnr, Atomic Energy Comn, 69- Bus & Prof Pos: Chmn chem dept, Col of the Pac, 38-42; dir research & develop, Electromagnetic Plant, Oak Ridge, Tenn, 43-47, supt, 47-49; dir, Oak Ridge Nat Lab, 50-55; vpres research, Union Carbide Corp, NY, 56-61, pres nuclear div, 61-69. Mem: Nat Acad Eng; annual mem, US-USSR Joint Comn Sci & Tech Coop, 73-74; Am Chem Soc; Am Nuclear Soc; Rotary. Honors & Awards: Distinguished Mgt Award, Soc for Advan of Mgt. Relig: Protestant. Legal Res: 6514 Bradley Ave Bethesda MD 20034 Mailing Add: Atomic Energy Commission Washington DC 20545

LARSON, CLIF (D)
Polit & Govt Pos: Chmn, Iowa State Dem Party, formerly. Mailing Add: 1120 Mulberry Des Moines IA 50309

LARSON, CURTIS DEY (R)
Chmn, Nez Perce Co Rep Cent Comt, Idaho
b Hazen, NDak, Mar 16, 31; s Joseph Larson & Rosalia Kittler L; m 1968 to Karmen Jewett; c Heather. Educ: Univ Idaho, 65-67. Polit & Govt Pos: Precinct committeeman, Nez Perce Co Rep Cent Comt, Idaho, 60-75, vchmn, 72-75, chmn, 75- Bus & Prof Pos: Sales mgr, H W Hulbert Co, 60-67; ins agt, Farmer Ins Group, 67-75. Mem: Gtr Lewiston CofC; Elks; Rotary. Relig: Unitarian. Legal Res: 3328 Bryden Ct Lewiston ID 83501 Mailing Add: 145 K Thain Rd Lewiston ID 83501

LARSON, ELDON C (D)
b Fargo, NDak, Aug 22, 30; s Clifford Larson & Isabel Tolstad L; m 1956 to Catherine Crogan; c Susan, Cheryl, Jean & Janice. Educ: State Sch of Sci, Wahpeton, NDak, 2 years. Polit & Govt Pos: Dwight Twp clerk, NDak, 57-69; NDak State Rep, 65-67; vchmn, 25th Dist Dem Party, NDak, 69-70, chmn, 70-74. Mem: Mason; Elks; PTA; Brotherhood; Toastmasters; 4-H Club (leader, 60-62). Honors & Awards: Richland Co Outstanding Young Farmer, 63. Relig: Lutheran. Mailing Add: Rte 1 Wahpeton ND 58075

LARSON, HARVEY CASPER (R)
Mem, NDak Rep State Comt
b Bismarck, NDak, May 26, 22; s Andrew Nels Larson & Helen Satter L; m 1943 to Roberta Jean Burman; c Bonnie Rae (Mrs John Warren Lee). Polit & Govt Pos: Precinct committeeman, Burleigh Co Rep Party, NDak, 61-, treas, 62-63, chmn, 63-72; chmn, 32nd Dist Rep Party, formerly; state campaign chmn, NDak Rep Party, 66-67, treas, 66-68, mem state exec comt, 67-68, mem state comt, 67-; deleg, Rep Nat Conv, 68. Bus & Prof Pos: Pressman, Commercial Printing Co, 46-55, mgr, 55-68, owner-mgr, 68- Mil Serv: Entered as Pvt, Army, 42, released as Cpl, 46, after serv in Med Corps, SPac Theater, 44-46. Mem: Am Legion (Past Comdr, Bismarck Post); Mason (Past Master, Bismarck Lodge); Rotary. Relig: Protestant. Mailing Add: 2217 Ave E East Bismarck ND 58501

LARSON, JOHN R (R)
Ind State Rep
Mailing Add: 161 Sheffield Ave Valparaiso IN 46383

LARSON, LESTER GEORGE (D)
NDak State Sen
b Nelson Co, NDak, Dec 26, 14; s Ole B Larson & Gunhild Shjervem L; m 1934 to Clara Knutson; c Janet Yvonne. Polit & Govt Pos: Mem bd, Brocket Twp, NDak, formerly; NDak State Rep, 56-63; NDak State Sen, 65-, asst minority floor leader, 73- Bus & Prof Pos: Former sch dir; mem, Farmers Union Oil Co; pres Equity Elevator & Trading Co. Mem: Crop Improv Asn. Relig: Lutheran; Clerk & Treas. Mailing Add: State Capitol Bismarck ND 58501

LARSON, LEW W (CONSERVATIVE)
Minn State Sen
b Preble Twp, Minn, 1911; married; c two sons & one daughter. Educ: Univ Minn. Polit & Govt Pos: Comnr, Fillmore Co, Minn, 53-59; Minn State Sen, 58- Bus & Prof Pos: Breeder registered livestock; farmer. Mem: Mason; State Asn Co Comnr. Mailing Add: Mabel MN 55954

LARSON, MARGARET BRUNSDALE (R)
b Minneapolis, Minn, Aug 27, 25; d Norman Brunsdale & Carrie Lajord B; m 1955 to Edson Germain Larson. Educ: Wellesley Col, BA, 47. Polit & Govt Pos: Secy to chmn, Rep Nat Finance Comt, 53-55; chmn, Traill Co Rep Party, NDak, 62-66; deleg & mem rules comt, Rep Nat Conv, 64; chmn, 20th Legis Dist Rep Party, NDak, formerly. Mem: Farm Bur. Relig: Lutheran. Mailing Add: Mayville ND 58257

LARSON, MILDRED (D)
m to Henry R Larson. Educ: LaSalle Exten Univ. Polit & Govt Pos: Superior Court reporter; asst supt of schs; secy to mgr of Navy Yard, Pearl Harbor; secy to US Sen & majority leader Ernest W McFarland; former secy, Western States Dem Conf & chmn, 67-69; mem, Defense Adv Comt on Women in Mil Serv; deleg & mem platform comt, Dem Nat Conv, 64 & 68, co-chmn rules comt, 64; Dem Nat Committeewoman, Ariz, 65-72. Bus & Prof Pos: Law librn; spec serv, KTVK-TV, Channel 3 currently. Mem: DAR (state regent); Phoenix Musical Theatre Guild; Phoenix Symphony Guild; Daughters of the Nile; Phoenix PTA; Ariz Mus (bd dirs). Mailing Add: 4701 N 24th St Phoenix AZ 85016

LARSON, ROSEMARY DUFFY (D)
b Corning, Ohio, May 5, 20; d Samuel S Sicilian & Rose A Powers S; wid; m 1971 to C E Larson, II; c R Scott. Educ: Ohio Univ, BA, 43; Cincinnati Conservatory Music, MA, 49. Polit & Govt Pos: Alt deleg, Dem Nat Conv, 56, deleg-at-lg, 72; worked on Presidential Campaigns of Adlai Stevenson, John F Kennedy, Lyndon B Johnson & Hubert H Humphrey, 68 & 72; vchairwoman, Ohio State Dem Exec Comt, 70-72; committeewoman, 15th Dist Dem Party, Ohio, 70 & 72; vchairwoman credentials comt, Ohio State Dem Conv, 71-72; state coordr, Hubert H Humphrey Campaign, 72; organized & past pres, Tri-Village Dem Women's Club, Franklin Co; organized & adv, Northwest Dem Women's Club; mem, Franklin Co Dem Women's Club, West Side Dem Women's Club, Eleanor Roosevelt Women's Club, Pickaway Co Dem Women's Club & Madison Co Dem Club; mem, Steering Comt for Elec of Gov Gilligan; worked on Platform & Const for State of Ohio; bd trustees, Franklin Co Veterans Mem, 69; mem, Ohio Arts Coun, 74; mem, Bd License Appeal, 74. Mem: Am Cancer Crusade (nat bd); Am Asn Univ Women; Federated Dem Women Ohio; Cent Ohio Women's Coun for Care, Inc (pres); Women in Communications, Inc. Honors & Awards: Invited by President Kennedy to White House Conf on Civil Rights, Women's Role in Polit & Civil Rights & Ment Retardation, 64; COTA Award, Outstanding Serv Award Nat Kidney Found. Relig: Roman Catholic. Mailing Add: 1400 Cambridge Blvd Columbus OH 43212

LARY, CAMM CARRINGTON, JR (D)
Tex State Rep
b Blanco, Tex, Nov 26, 41; s Camm Carrington Lary & Christian Hobbs L; m 1967 to Louise Knotts. Educ: Tex A&M Univ, BA, 64; Univ Tex Sch Law, LLB, 67. Polit & Govt Pos: Attorney, Tex Water Rights Comn, 68; Asst Attorney Gen, Tex, 68-71; Tex State Rep, Dist 43, 73- Bus & Prof Pos: Attorney, pvt practice, Burnet, Tex, 71-73. Mil Serv: Lt Naval Res, 6 years. Mem: Tex State Bar. Mailing Add: Box 456 Burnet TX 78611

LASEE, ALAN J (R)
Wis State Rep
Mailing Add: RR 2 DePere WI 54115

LASH, DONALD R (R)
Ind State Rep
b Bluffton, Ind, Aug 15, 14; s Brandon Lash & Pearl Landis L; m 1938 to Margaret May Mendenhall; c Russell, David & Marguerite. Educ: Ind Univ, BS & MS, 40; Delta Chi. Polit & Govt Pos: Ind State Rep, 73- Bus & Prof Pos: Spec agt, Fed Bur Invest. retired 62; Regional dir, Fellowship of Christian Athletes, 62-73; trustee, Ind Univ, 69-72; real estate broker, Rockville, Ind, presently. Honors & Awards: Mem US Olympic Team, 36; Former World Record Holder, 2 mile run; Nat Champion seven years, cross country; James E Sullivan Award, most outstanding athlete in US, Amateur Athletic Union, 38. Relig: Methodist. Mailing Add: RD 1 Marshall IN 47859

LASHER, HOWARD LOUIS (D)
NY State Assemblyman
b New York, NY May 7, 44; s Martin Lasher & Pearl Frankel L; m 1968 to Geraldine Deborah Goldman; c Lisa. Educ: Brooklyn Col, BS, 65; Brooklyn Law Sch, JD, 68; Town House; Acct Soc; Hillel. Polit & Govt Pos: NY State Assemblyman, 46th Dist, King's Co, 73- Bus & Prof Pos: Teacher, New York Pub Schs, 68-70; assoc attorney, Greenberg, Harris, Cantor, Reiss & Blasky, New York, 70-72; partner, Lasher & Wasserstein, 73- Mem: B'nai B'rith Ocean View Lodge; B'nai B'rith Brightwater Lodge; Mason; Beach Haven Jewish Ctr (mem bd dirs, 72-); Brighton Beach Jewish Ctr. Honors & Awards: Guest of Honor, United Jewish Appeal, 73. Relig: Jewish. Mailing Add: 2634 West St Brooklyn NY 11223

LASHKOWITZ, HERSCHEL (D)
NDak State Sen
Mailing Add: State Capitol Bismarck ND 58501

LASHLEE, FRANK P (D)
Tenn State Rep
Mailing Add: Box 504 Camden TN 38320

LASHUAY, KENNETH EDWARD (R)
Third VChmn, Rep Party Mich
b Midland, Mich, July 22, 55; s Francis Marion Lashuay & Rosemary Maloney L; single. Educ: Mich State Univ, 73- Polit & Govt Pos: Precinct deleg, Mt Haley Twp, Mich, 74; custodian, Mich House Rep, 74-75; asst tel campaign dir, Mich for Milliken Comt, 74; asst to constituent rels sect, Mich House Rep Staff, 75-; third vchmn, Rep Party Mich, 75- Bus & Prof Pos: Lab technologist, Dow Chem Co, Midland, Mich, 72-73. Mem: Mich Rep Bi-Centennial Comt; Midland Skin Divers Asn; Mich Asn of Psephologists. Honors & Awards: Selected by Nat Honor Soc to attend the Presidential Classroom for Young Americans, sec sch prog at Washington, DC, 73; Selected as Most Promising Jr in Social Sci,

Bullock Creek High Sch, 72. Relig: Roman Catholic. Legal Res: 556 E Gordonville Rd Midland MI 48640 Mailing Add: 404 E Michigan Ave Lansing MI 48933

LASKE, EUGENE C (GENE) (R)
NDak State Rep
b Leonard, NDak, Dec 23, 25; s Clarence H Laske & Ima Mary Bird L; m 1948 to Evelyn M Thurnau; c Jacqueline (Mrs Qualio), Mary Beth (Mrs Wells), Douglas & Karen. Educ: NDak State Col, 43-44; Dakota Bus Col, grad, 48; Sigma Chi. Polit & Govt Pos: NDak State Rep, currently. Bus & Prof Pos: Owner & mgr, Gene's Red Owl Food Store, Oakes, NDak, 54-73; owner & mgr, Oakes Skogmo Family Store, 68- Mil Serv: Entered as Seaman, Navy, 44, released as PO 1/C, 46, after serv in Pac. Mem: Mason; NDak Food Retailers Asn; Am Legion; Lions; Gtr NDak Asn (dir-at-lg, state CofC). Honors & Awards: Boss of Year, 65. Relig: Methodist. Mailing Add: 321 S Sixth Oakes ND 58474

LASKEY, NORMA JEAN (R)
Exec VChmn, Wayne Co Rep Comt, Mich
b Ludington, Mich, Sept 15, 30; d Walter Hutchison & Ida E Knaebe H; m 1952 to Stephen M Laskey. Educ: Wayne Univ, 49-50; Nat Young Rep Leadership Sch, Washington, DC, grad, 63. Polit & Govt Pos: Chmn, Wayne Co Young Rep Comt, Mich, 62-64; mem, Olympic Exec Comt, 63; committeewoman from Mich, Nat Young Rep, 63-65, mem exec bd, 65; mem, Orgn of Young Am for North-Atlantic Treaty, 66; coordr, Griffin for US Sen, 66; vchmn, Wayne Co Rep Comt, 66-68; exec vchmn, 68-; Rep nominee, Wayne Co Charter Comn, 68; deleg, eight Mich Rep Conv; chmn, Reelect the President & US Sen Robert Griffin Comt, 14th Cong Dist, Mich, 72; comnr, Wayne Co Jury Comn, 73- Bus & Prof Pos: Mem, speakers bur, Repub Steel Corp, 69. Publ: Mandatory Jail Sentences for Serious Crime Offenders, 11/68, Inauguration of President Nixon, 1/69 & The Argument for ABM, 5/69, East-Side Newspapers. Mem: Mich CofC (pub conduct comt); Muscular Dystrophy (area coordr); Int Platform Soc. Honors & Awards: Miss Young Rep of Mich, 62; Outstanding Young Rep Woman in the US, 63. Relig: Lutheran. Mailing Add: 6164 Guilford Ave Detroit MI 48224

LASKEY, THOMAS PENROSE (R)
Mem, Conn Rep State Cent Comt
b Old Town, Maine, Jan 4, 31; s Samuel Hudlow Laskey & Grace Wickette L; m 1959 to Jean Duncanson; c Thomas Penrose, Jr, Peter Duncanson, Katherine Jean & Gregory Earl. Educ: Univ Maine, BSME, 53; Phi Eta Kappa; M Club. Polit & Govt Pos: Deleg, Conn Rep Coun, 64-65; chmn, Conn Fedn Young Rep Clubs, 65-66; mgr, Cong Campaign, 66; mem & negotiation chmn, Woodstock Bd Educ, 67-71; mem, Conn Rep State Cent Comt, 70-; staff asst, US Sen Lowell Weicker, Conn, 71-; Presidential Elector, 72. Bus & Prof Pos: Exp engr, United Aircraft Corp, 53-58; field test engr, Chandler-Evans Corp, 58-61; sales engr, Pearse-Pearson Corp, 61-; pres, Key Builders, Inc, 73- Mil Serv: Naval Res, 49-53. Mem: Conn Rep Key Comt; Am Soc Mech Engrs. Mailing Add: Pulpit Rock Rd Woodstock CT 06281

LASSEN, ARNE F (R)
Treas, Bannock Co Rep Cent Comt, Idaho
b Hjørring, Denmark, Nov 7, 10; s Lars Christian Lassen & Anna Christine Nielsen L; m 1940 to Edith Smith; c Inge (Mrs David Miller) & Mary. Educ: Randers Sch, Denmark. Polit & Govt Pos: Treas, Bannock Co Rep Cent Comt, 69- Mailing Add: 350 Richland Pocatello ID 83201

LASSITER, JAMES HUGH (D)
Ark State Rep
b Fort Smith, Ark, June 18, 45; s Hugh Wells Lassiter & Margaret Collins L; single. Educ: Henderson State Col, BA, 68; Young Dem; Circle K. Polit & Govt Pos: Page, US Cong, 62; mem campaign staff, Congressman Trimble, Third Dist, 66; deleg, Nat Young Dem Conv, 67, mem bd dirs arrangement comt, 71; high sch coordr, Ark Young Dem, 68, secy, 69-70, first vpres, 71; mem, Frank Whitbeck Campaign Staff, 68; co coordr, Dale Bumpers Campaign Staff, 70; mem, Ark Dem State Cent Comt, 71-; Ark State Rep, Dist 16, 72- Bus & Prof Pos: Vpres, Bonanza Land, Inc. Mem: PTA; Jaycees; CofC; Scott Co Hosp Bd Dirs. Honors & Awards: President's Award, Ark Young Dem, 70. Relig: Methodist. Mailing Add: Box 56 Waldron AR 72958

LASTER, DONNA JEAN (D)
b Columbus, Ohio, May 9, 44; d Virgil Dow Corbin & May Williams C; m to Billy Bob Laster; c Casandra Cae & Penelope Lynnette. Educ: Olentangy High Sch. Polit & Govt Pos: Alt deleg, Dem Nat Conv, 72. Bus & Prof Pos: Assigner, Ohio Bell, 69- Mem: Commun Workers Am (committeeman, 62-). Mailing Add: 3955 Seldom Seen Rd Powell OH 43065

LASTINE, ADELLA EDITH (D)
b LeRoy, Minn, Apr 20, 17; d William H Errington & Synva Lillegraven E; m 1938 to Gordon Lastine; c William, James, Thomas, Kathryn & Daniel. Educ: LeRoy High Sch, grad, 34. Polit & Govt Pos: Chmn, Watonwan Co Dem Party, Minn, 68-72; recording secy, Second Dist Comt Polit Educ, 70- Bus & Prof Pos: Treas, Tony Downs Employees Fed Credit Union, 66- Mem: Amalgamated Meat Cutters & Butcher Workmen of NAm (pres, Local P-1153, 70-71); Am Legion Auxiliary. Relig: Methodist. Mailing Add: 820 Seventh Ave N St James MN 56081

LATHEROW, CLIFFORD BRANDON (R)
Ill State Sen
b La Harpe, Ill, Dec 4, 15; s George Alexander Latherow & Gail Miller L; m 1940 to Betty Jane Hungate; c Linda Lou, Donald Brice & Jerry Allen. Educ: Western Ill Univ, BEd, 37. Polit & Govt Pos: Supvr, Twp, Ill, 51-65; Ill State Sen, 47th Dist, 65- Bus & Prof Pos: Coach & teacher, High Sch, 37-43. Mil Serv: Entered as Ens, Navy, 43, released as Lt, 46, after serv in Am, Atlantic, Pac & Asiatic Theaters. Mem: Ill Police Asn; Elks; Mason (33 degree); Shrine; Farm Bur. Relig: Presbyterian. Mailing Add: Route 3 Carthage IL 62321

LATO, STANLEY J (D)
Wis State Rep
Mailing Add: Gilman WI 54433

LATONI RIVERA, RAUL (POPULAR DEMOCRAT, PR)
Sen, PR Senate
Mailing Add: State Capitol San Juan PR 00901

LATSHAW, ROBERT E, JR (R)
b Milwaukee, Wis, Dec 10, 44; s Robert E Latshaw & Jane Meyers L; m 1963 to Marian Wettern; c Karen, Robert III & Scott. Educ: Ga Inst Technol, 62-63; Johns Hopkins Univ, BS, 67; George Washington Univ Grad Sch, 67-68; Delta Sigma Pi. Polit & Govt Pos: Md State Deleg, 71-74; alt deleg, Rep Nat Conv, 72; legis adv, Citizen's Tax Comn, currently. Bus & Prof Pos: Purchasing agt, J Schoeneman, Ind, 63-67; asst treas, Johns Hopkins Hosp, 67-72; pres, Robert E Latshaw, Jr & Co Inc, Realtors, 72- Mem: Nat Inst Real Estate Brokers; Baltimore Co Young Rep; Ninth Dist Rep Club; Loch Raven Village Asn; Towson-Loch Raven Community Coun. Relig: Presbyterian. Mailing Add: 306 W Chesapeake Ave Towson MD 21204

LATTA, DELBERT L (R)
US Rep, Ohio
b Weston, Ohio, Mar 5, 20; m to Rose Mary Kiene; c Rose Ellen & Robert Edward. Educ: Ohio North Univ, AB & LLB. Polit & Govt Pos: Ohio State Sen, 3 terms; US Rep, Ohio, 59-; deleg, Rep Nat Conv, 68. Relig: Church of Christ. Legal Res: Bowling Green OH 43402 Mailing Add: 2309 Rayburn House Off Bldg Washington DC 20515

LAUB, WILLIAM MURRAY (R)
Rep Nat Committeeman, Nev
b Corregidor, Philippines, July 20, 24; both parents deceased; m 1947 to Mary McDonald; c William, Jr, Andrew, Mary, John & David. Educ: Univ Calif, Los Angeles; Univ Calif, Berkeley, BS, 47, LLB, 50. Polit & Govt Pos: Chmn, Clark Co Rep Cent Comt, Nev, 64-; Rep Nat Committeeman, Nev, currently; deleg, Rep Nat Conv, 68. Bus & Prof Pos: Exec vpres & various capacities, Southwest Gas Corp, 48-64, pres, 64-; law practice, Los Angeles, 51-55. Mil Serv: Lt(jg), Navy, 42-46, serv in Pac. Relig: Methodist. Mailing Add: 1000 Rancho Circle Las Vegas NV 89107

LAUCK, MARIE THERESA D (D)
Ind State Sen
b Indianapolis, Ind; d Anthony P Lauck & Marie E Habig L; single. Educ: St Mary-of-the-Woods Col, BA, 34; Butler Univ, MA, 47; Ind Univ Sch Law, JD, 55; Sigma Tau Delta; Kappa Gamma Pi. Polit & Govt Pos: Probation officer, Marion Co Munic Court, Ind, 35-48; civilian instr, The Adj Gen Sch, US Army, 51-55; secy to House Attorneys & Legislators, 51-59; cand for Ind State Rep, 56 & 62; Ind State Sen, 59-60; Ind State Sen, 64-69 & 72-, cand, 70; mem, Ind Legis Adv Coun, 67-68. Bus & Prof Pos: Attorney-at-law, Indianapolis, Ind. Publ: Free lance articles in such mag as Catholic Digest, Sch Jour & Extension Mag. Mem: Nat Asn of Women Lawyers (deleg from Ind, 65-, secy, 63-64, pres, 69-); Ind Asn of Women Lawyers St Thomas More Soc of Lawyers Int Fedn of Cath Alumnae; Ind Chap, Legion of Decency (chmn, 34-); Indianapolis Bar Asn. Relig: Catholic. Mailing Add: 323 Peoples Bank Bldg Indianapolis IN 46204

LAUDADIO, JOHN F (D)
Pa State Rep
b Penn, Pa, Dec 26, 16; s Frank Laudadio & Marie Dreistadt L; m 1940 to Pearl E Ferrara; c John F, Jr. Educ: Carnegie Inst Technol, cert, 44. Polit & Govt Pos: Mem, Westmoreland Co Recreation & Park Comn, formerly; chmn, Park Develop, formerly; Pa State Rep, 63-72, vchmn, House Fisheries Comt, Pa House of Rep, formerly; Pa State Rep, 75- Mem: Pa Fedn Sportsmen's Clubs (pres); Westmoreland Co Sportsmen's League; Penn Rod & Gun Club (officer, 38-); AFL-CIO (exec bd, Local 601, IUE). Honors & Awards: Cert of Merit, Isaac Walton League, 65; First State Award as Legis Conservationist of Year, 65; Nat Award as Legis Conservationist of Year, Nat Wildlife Fedn & Sears Roebuck Conserv Found, 65. Relig: Catholic. Mailing Add: Capitol Bldg Harrisburg PA 17120

LAUDONE, VINCENT A (R)
Chmn, Conn Rep State Cent Comt
Mailing Add: 10 Huntington Lane Norwich CT 06360

LAUER, JOHN R (R)
Ill State Rep
b Sept 25, 29; m 1951 to Jane Oechsle; c Karen, Lee Anne, Christie & John. Educ: Univ Ill Urbana-Champaign, BS in Agr, 51 & MS in Agr Econ, 52; Univ Mo, Columbia, grad work, 64; Sangamon State Univ, grad work, 70-71. Polit & Govt Pos: Cand, deleg to State Const Conv, 69; Ill State Rep, currently. Bus & Prof Pos: Farmer, Broadwell, Ill, 52-; assoc prof econ & chmn Dept Bus & Econ, Lincoln Col, 61-72; part time instr bus & econ, Lincoln Land Community Col, Springfield, 68-72. Mem: Cent Ill Rose Soc (founder & past pres); Toastmasters Int; Elks; Mason; Ansar Shrine. Legal Res: Broadwell IL 62623 Mailing Add: 12 Arcade Bldg Lincoln IL 62656

LAUFENBURGER, ROGER ALLYN (DFL)
Minn State Sen
b Stockton, Minn, Sept 5, 21; s Ray Morse Laufenburger & Rosa Marie Hoppe L; m 1947 to Selma Louise Nesbit; c Carolyn Jean, Bruce Allyn, Kay Ann & Dawn Marie. Educ: Winona Pub Schs, Minn. Polit & Govt Pos: Justice of the peace, Minn, 54-56; Lewiston Village councilman, 57-63; Minn State Sen, Winona Co, 63-, secy, Dem-Farmer-Labor Lib Caucus, Minn State Senate, 65-67. Mem: Lewiston Bus Asn; Lions Club; Mason, Winona Shrine Club, Osman Temple, St Paul; Winona Athletic Club; Elks; Eagles. Honors & Awards: Named Winona Co Centennial Sports Champion, 58 & Regional Baseball Comnr, 59-64. Relig: Presbyterian. Mailing Add: Box 428 Lewiston MN 55952

LAUGHLIN, BRUCE JAMES (D)
NDak State Rep
b Finley, NDak, Nov 25, 30; s Harold M Laughlin & Johanna Irene Schroeder L; m 1950 to Sue Nell Pladson; c Janice Arlene (Mrs Rayner) & Jody Ann. Educ: Pickert Sch, NDak, 6 years; Finley Pub Sch, 6 years. Polit & Govt Pos: NDak State Rep, Dist 23, 71- Mem: Commercial Club; Farmers Union; Nat Farmers Orgn. Relig: Lutheran. Mailing Add: Finley ND 58230

LAUGHLIN, CHARLES (D)
Pa State Rep
Mailing Add: Capitol Bldg Harrisburg PA 17120

LAUGHLIN, EUGENE L (D)
Wash State Rep
Mailing Add: 734 NW 23rd Casas WA 98607

LAUGHLIN, MICHAEL LUKENS (D)
SC State Sen

b Aiken, SC, Mar 20, 44; s Thomas I Laughlin & Louise Bailey L; single. Educ: Univ Va, BS, 66; Sigma Phi. Polit & Govt Pos: SC State Sen, 69- Bus & Prof Pos: Pres, Horizon Aviation, Inc, Charlottesville, Va, 65-; pres & chmn bd, Eagle Aviation, Inc, Aiken, SC, 67-; dir SC Nat Bank, 68-; pres & chmn bd, VIP Indust, Inc, Columbia, 68-; pres, Coosaw River Develop Co, Aiken; pres, Radio Sta WAKN, Aiken. Mem: Southeastern Transportation Conf; Rotary; Civil Air Patrol; Farm Bur; CofC (dir). Relig: Episcopal. Legal Res: 330 Kershaw St SE Aiken SC 29801 Mailing Add: State House Columbia SC 29211

LAUHOFF, HERMAN E (D)
Tex State Rep

b St Joe, Tex, Aug 8, 33; m; c Jill Ellen & Kurt Edward. Educ: STex Jr Col, 55-57; Univ Houston, 55. Polit & Govt Pos: Tex State Rep, 74- Bus & Prof Pos: Off & personnel adminr, Texasgulf, Inc, Houston, Tex. Mil Serv: Entered as Pvt, Army, 53, released as Pfc, 55, after serv in 95th AAA, 7th Army, Ger, 54-55. Mem: Houston Sports Officials (pres, 65-74); Parkway Civic Club; Federated Civic Club; Gtr Houston Civic Coun (vpres, 70-71, pres, 72-73); CofC (civic affairs comt, 72-74). Relig: Catholic. Mailing Add: 5430 Winding Way Houston TX 77088

LAURENTI, JEFFREY (D)
Mem Exec Comt, Mercer Co Dem Orgn, NJ

b Trenton, NJ, Jan 23, 50; s Mario John Laurenti & Doris Fauver L; single. Educ: Harvard Col, BA, 71; Princeton Univ, MPA, 74; Phi Beta Kappa. Polit & Govt Pos: Mem exec comt, Mercer Co Dem Orgn, NJ, 72-; asst to senate minority, NJ Senate, 72-74; asst to Senate majority leadership, 74-; deleg, Dem Mid-Term Conf, 74. Mil Serv: E-4, Army Res. Relig: Catholic. Mailing Add: 1010 Greenwood Ave Trenton NJ 08609

LAURICELLA, FRANCIS E (HANK) (D)
La State Sen

Mailing Add: 7300 Jefferson Hwy Harahan LA 70123

LAURINO, WILLIAM J (D)
Ill State Sen

Mailing Add: 4743 N Keeler Ave Chicago IL 60630

LAUSCHE, FRANK J (INDEPENDENT)
b Cleveland, Ohio, Nov 14, 95; m 1928 to Jane Sheal. Educ: John Marshall Law Sch, LLB; Delta Theta Phi; Phi Sigma Kappa; Omicron Delta Kappa. Hon Degrees: LLD, John Marshall Law Sch, Kenyon Col, Denison Univ, Ohio Wesleyan Univ, Miami Univ, Ashland Col, Defiance Col, Washington & Jefferson Col, Oberlin Col, Western Reserve Univ, Ohio Univ, Akron Univ, Marietta Col & Le Moyne Col; Dr of Pub Serv, Rio Grande Col; Dr of Commun Sci, Tiffin Bus Col. Polit & Govt Pos: Judge, Munic Court, Cleveland, Ohio, 32-37; judge, Common Pleas Court, 37-41; mayor, Cleveland, 41-44; Gov, Ohio, 45-46 & 49-56; US Sen, Ohio, 56-68. Honors & Awards: Centennial Award, Northwestern Univ; Vet Award, Joint Vet Comt of Cuyahoga, 58; Good Citizen Medal, SAR; Cert of Merit, Am Vet World War II. Legal Res: Gates Mills OH 44040 Mailing Add: 6916 Marbury Rd Bethesda MD 20034

LAUSI, ANTHONY THOMAS (R)
Chmn, Arlington Co Rep Comt, Va

b Keene, NH, Nov 22, 16; s Thomas Joseph Lausi & Evelyn Casillo L; m 1941 to Margaret Sutton; c Donna T (Mrs Kendall) & Anthony Thomas, Jr. Educ: Nat Univ Sch Law, LLB, 41. Polit & Govt Pos: Staff asst, US Sen Ernest W Gibson, Sr, Ernest W Gibson Jr & George D Aiken, 37-41, 46-53; dir territories, US Dept Interior, 53-61; admin asst, US Rep Silvio O Conte, Mass, 61-62; chmn, Arlington Co Rep Comt, Va, 70- Bus & Prof Pos: Sales rep, Bellante, Clauss, Miller & Nolan, Inc, Scranton, Pa, 61-; real estate salesman, Robertson & Heck, Inc, Arlington, Va, 66- Mil Serv: Entered as CPO, Coast Guard, 42, released as Lt(jg), 45, after serv in Coast Guard Hq, Washington, DC & three years at sea aboard transports, Asiatic Theatre, 42-45; Am & Pac Theatre Ribbons. Mem: Am Legion; Army-Navy Country Club; Arlington Forest Civic Asn; Arlington Hist Asn. Relig: Roman Catholic. Mailing Add: 122 North Park Dr Arlington VA 22203

LAVALLEE, GASTON HAROLD (R)
Chmn, Woonsocket Rep City Comt, RI

b Woonsocket, RI, Jan 13, 16; s Frank Lavallee & Palmyre Lamoureux L; m 1936 to Lillian Blais; c Claudette (Mrs La France), Jacqueline (Mrs Rogeski) & Therese (Mrs Tuttle). Educ: RI State Col Exten, Eng Sci & Mgt. Polit & Govt Pos: Chmn, Woonsocket Rep City Comt, RI, 32- Bus & Prof Pos: Employ mgr, Owens Corning Fiberglass, 40-46; gen contractor, 46- Mem: Club Marquette. Honors & Awards: Exceptional Serv Award, Civil Air Patrol; Award, Auxiliary of the US Air Force, 56. Relig: Catholic. Mailing Add: 580 Front St Woonsocket RI 02895

LAVELLE, WILLIAM A (D)
Mem, Dem Nat Comt

m 1954 to Marion H Yanity; c Francis, John, Lydia & Amy. Educ: Ohio Univ, BSC, 49; Ohio State Univ Col of Law, JD, 52. Polit & Govt Pos: Chmn, Athens Co Bd of Elec, Ohio, 67-; chmn, Ohio State Dem Party, 71-74; Mid-W Mem, Exec Comt, Dem Nat Comt, 72- Mem: Am Bar Asn; Rotary; Am Legion; VFW; Elks. Relig: Catholic. Legal Res: 39 Cable Lane Athens OH 45701 Mailing Add: 88 E Broad St Columbus OH 43201

LAVENDER, JOHN GOULD (R)
Chmn, Lyon Co Rep Cent Comt, Iowa

b Omaha, Nebr, Apr 8, 18; s Gould Frank Lavender & Helen Downing L; m 1942 to Maryanna Pearl Ray; c John, Mary & Louise. Educ: Univ Omaha, 36-39; Univ Nebr Col Med, MD, 43; Alpha Omega Alpha. Polit & Govt Pos: Pres, George Commun Sch Bd, 50-; dir, Iowa Asn Sch Bds, 66-; chmn, Lyon Co Rep Cent Comt, 70- Mil Serv: Entered as 1st Lt, Army, 44, released as Capt, 46, after serv in Med Corps, Am Theater, 44-46. Mem: Lyon Co & Iowa State Med Soc; Am Med Asn. Relig: Lutheran. Legal Res: 504 E Michigan George IA 51237 Mailing Add: 108 N Maine George IA 51237

LAVENDER, ROBERT EUGENE (R)
Justice, Okla Supreme Court

b Muskogee, Okla, July 19, 26; s Harold James Lavender & Vergene Martin L; m 1945 to Maxine Knight; c Linda (Mrs Dean Courter), Robert K, Debra Lucille & William J. Educ: Univ Tulsa, Pre-Law, 46-49; Univ Tulsa Sch of Law, LLB, 53. Polit & Govt Pos: Asst city attorney, Tulsa, Okla, 54-55; mem sch bd, Catoosa Independent Dist Two, Rogers Co, 58-65; city attorney, Catoosa, 62-65; Justice, Okla Supreme Court, 65- Bus & Prof Pos: Pvt practice law, Tulsa, Okla, 55-60 & Claremore, 61-65; mem law firm, Bassmann, Gordon, Mayberry & Lavender, 62-65; Mil Serv: Entered as A/S, Navy Res, 44, released as Seaman 1/C, 46, after serv in Armed Guard, Okinawa Campaign, SPac, 45; Battle Ribbons. Publ: Author, various opinions as mem of Okla Supreme Court, since 65. Mem: Am Bar Asn; Am Judicature Soc; AF&AM; Am Legion; hon mem, Phi Alpha Delta. Relig: Methodist. Legal Res: 1020 N Lynn Lane Rd Tulsa OK 74138 Mailing Add: 2910 Kerry Lane Oklahoma City OK 73120

LAVERTY, BETTY CLARK (D)
b Hailey, Idaho, Feb 19, 33; d Wayne Clark & Ann Browning C; m 1959 to Edward J Laverty; c Richard Wayne & Kent J. Educ: Univ Denver, 51-53. Polit & Govt Pos: Chmn, Blaine Co Econ Develop Comt, 64-68; pres, Blaine Co Young Dem, 65-69; dist chmn, Idaho Young Dem Clubs, 66-68; precinct committeeman, Blaine Co Dem Cent Comt, 68-70, chmn, 70-74; vchmn, Blaine Co Planning & Zoning Bd, 70-; chmn, Arrangements Comt, Idaho State Dem Conv, 72; chmn, Conv Comt, Idaho State Dem Cent Comt, 73- Bus & Prof Pos: Vpres & dir, Triumph Mineral Co, Inc. Mem: Nat Asn Real Estate Bd; Idaho Asn Realtors (dir, 72-); Blaine Soil & Conserv Dist (supvr, 72-); Idaho Asn of Soil Conserv Dists, (mem pub rels & info comt, 72-); Ketchum-Sun Valley CofC. Honors & Awards: Valedictorian Bellevue High Sch; deleg, Idaho Girls' State; Commun Leader of Am Award, 72. Legal Res: PO Box 116 Ketchum ID 83340 Mailing Add: PO Box 582 Sun Valley ID 83353

LAVERTY, DOROTHY (R)
Maine State Rep

Mailing Add: 206 Highland Ave Millinocket ME 04462

LAVIT, THEODORE HOWARD (R)
Chmn, Marion Co Rep Party, Ky

b Brooklyn, NY, Apr 9, 39; s Richard Phillips Lavit & Rose Convisar L; m 1961 to Marilyn Boston Allen; c Laura P & David A. Educ: Centre Col of Ky, BA, 61; Vanderbilt Univ Sch of Law, LLB, 64, JD, 69; Delta Theta Phi; Delta Kappa Epsilon. Polit & Govt Pos: Pres, Centre Col Young Rep Club, 57-61; campaign chmn, Sen John Sherman Cooper, Boyle Co, Ky, 60 & Marion Co, 66; rep cand, US House of Rep, Marion Co, 68; campaign chmn, Sen Marlow Cook, Marion Co, 68; deleg, Second Dist Rep Conv, 68 & 72, Marion Co Rep Conv, 68 & 72, Ky State Rep Conv, 68 & 72 & Rep Nat Conv, 72; chmn, Marion Co Rep Party, 73-; comnr, Marion Co Bd Elec, 73- Bus & Prof Pos: Assoc attorney, Gess, Mattingly, Saunier & Atchinson Legal Firm, Lexington, Ky, 64-65; attorney-at-law, Lebanon, 65-67; partner, Lavit & Blandford Legal Firm, 68- Publ: Southern regional strategy, Rep Nat Comt, 60. Mem: Am & Ky Bar Asns; Jaycees (bd dirs, 73-); Rotary; Farm Bur. Honors & Awards: Outstanding Serv, Am Legion, 67; Serv Award, Univ of Ky Bus for Youth, 67; Serv Award for Proj Headstart, Marion Co Action Comt, 67; Eisenhower Award for Outstanding Serv to Rep Party, 69. Relig: Jewish. Mailing Add: 509 Park Dr Lebanon KY 40033

LAVORANDO, JOSEPH, JR (D)
b Plattsburg, NY, Oct 22, 53; s Joseph Lavorando & Ellen LaPan L; single. Educ: Clinton Community Col, AA, 75, pres, Student Govt Asn, 74-75. Polit & Govt Pos: Pres, Clinton Co Young Dem, NY, 74-; deleg, Dem Mid-Term Conf, 74. Bus & Prof Pos: Advert salesman, WKDR Radio Sta, Plattsburg, NY, 75- Mil Serv: Entered as E-1, Army, 71, released as SP-4, 73, after serv in overseas command, Vietnam (MACV), 72-73; Nat Defense Ribbon, Vietnam Campaign Ribbon & Army Commendation Medal. Honors & Awards: Presidents Leadership Award, Clinton Community Col, 74. Relig: Catholic. Mailing Add: PO Box 85 West Chazy NY 12992

LAW, JAMES L (R)
Mem, Tenn State Rep Comt

b Westmoreland, Tenn, Jan 1, 26; s Henry Clay Law & Gracie Freeman L; m 1944 to Eunice Dorris; c Larry C & Dorris E (Mrs Mikeal Tully). Educ: High Sch. Polit & Govt Pos: Mem, Tenn State Rep Comt, 70- Bus & Prof Pos: Pres, L&B Lumber Co, Inc, 53- Relig: Methodist. Mailing Add: Box 443 Westmoreland TN 37186

LAWAETZ, FRITS EDUARD (D)
Sen, VI Legis

b Frederiksted, St Croix, VI, Oct 5, 07; s Carl Lawaetz & Marie Nyborg L; m 1935 to Bodil Tornoe; c Hans, Bent & Frits Tornoe. Educ: Stenhus, Hollack, Denmark, real estate exam, 25. Polit & Govt Pos: Sen, VI Legis, 55-, chmn comt pub works, 55-, vchmn finance comt, agr comt & recreation comt, 70- Bus & Prof Pos: Gen mgr & partner, Annaly Farms Cattle Ranch, 40- Mil Serv: Capt, Home Guard, 42. Mem: Frederiksted Boys Club (adv); Boy Scouts (exec coun); CofC. Relig: Lutheran; mem coun, Holy Trinity Lutheran Church. Mailing Add: Annaly Farms PO Box 366 Frederiksted St Croix VI 00840

LAWING, JIM (D)
Kans State Rep

Mailing Add: 211 S Chautauqua Wichita KS 67221

LAWLER, SANDRA MAE (R)
Chairwoman, Hart Co Rep Party, Ky

b La Rue Co, Ky, Aug 29, 44; d Clarence Oliver Vernon & Josie Barnes V; m 1961 to William J Lawler, RPh; c William J, Jr & Robert Keenan. Educ: Western Ky Univ, 74- Polit & Govt Pos: Campaign chairwoman, Hart Co Rep Party, Ky, 67-68, chairwoman, 71- Bus & Prof Pos: Secy & clerk, Lawler Pharmacy, Munfordville, Ky, 62- Mem: Munfordville Woman's Club (treas, 74-75). Relig: Baptist. Mailing Add: Second St Munfordville KY 42765

LAWLER, VIOLET M (D)
Vice Chairwoman, Laramie Co Dem Cent Comt, Wyo

b Lawrence, Kans, July 16, 97; d Wallace Edward Newman & Lou Arnette N; m 1946 to Joseph P Lawler. Educ: Stamford Col, 13-16; Univ Tex, Austin, 17-20. Polit & Govt Pos: Precinct committeewoman, Laramie Co Dem Cent Comt, Wyo, 58-64; dist capt, 62-64; co treas, 63-66; mem, State Finance Comt, 63-, vice chairwoman, 68-, ed, newsletter, 69; deleg & mem, Credentials Comt, Dem Nat Conv, 64 & 68; Wyo chmn, Women's Nat Dem Conf, 68. Bus & Prof Pos: Buyer, Nat Furs & Fashion, 50-60; owner & mgr, Holiday Motel, 51-73. Mem: Am Bus Women Asn (past pres, Cheyenne Chap & past regional dir); Laramie Co Chap, Nat Found on Polio (past secy); Cheyenne Drove (past pres); Benevolent Patriotic Order of Does. Honors & Awards: Certificate of Appreciation, March of Dimes; Nat Citation, Am Bus Women's Asn. Relig: Catholic. Mailing Add: 217 E Sixth Ave Cheyenne WY 82001

LAWLESS, KIRBY GORDON, JR (R)
Chmn, Fifth Cong Dist Rep Comt, Ala
b Birmingham, Ala, Aug 12, 24; s Kirby Gordon Lawless & Ethel May Black L; m 1951 to Dora May Busbee; c Kirby Gordon, III, Madelene & Marc. Educ: Auburn Univ, BA, 48; Emory Univ, LLB, 51; pres, Phi Alpha Delta; Legal Aide Soc of Atlanta; Kappa Sigma; Case Club. Polit & Govt Pos: Attorney, Gen Counsel, Civil Aeronaut Admin, 51-53; chmn, Young Rep Club, Tuscaloosa, Ala, 56-60; secy, Young Rep Fedn of Ala, 58-62; alt deleg, Rep Nat Conv, 60 & 64; vchmn, Co Rep Comt of Tuscaloosa, 60-64; mem, Ala State Rep Exec Comt, 62-, sr vchmn, 74-; mem, Zoning Bd of Adjustment, Tuscaloosa, 64-73, chmn, 73-; chmn, Rep finance comt, Fifth Cong Dist, Ala, 69-; chmn, Founders Club, Ala Rep Finance Comt, 70-; chmn, Tax Study Comn, Tuscaloosa, 70-; chmn, Fifth Cong Dist Rep Comt, 71-; chmn Ala-Miss Export Coun, US Dept Com, 74- Bus & Prof Pos: Credit mgr, Southeast Tool & Die Co, 53-55; vpres & gen mgr, Phifer Wire Prod, Inc, 55-66, vpres, 68-; dir, Aluminum Siding Asn, 68- & Archit Aluminum Mfrs Asn, 70-; chmn, Nail Mfrs, Aluminum Asn, 68-70 & Bar, Rod & Wire Comt, 70-71; vchmn, Ala Export Coun, 72- Mil Serv: Entered as Aviation Cadet, Navy, 42, released as Lt, 46, after serv in Naval Training Command, Corpus Christi, Tex; Lt, Naval Res, 46-66; Am Theater Ribbon; Reserve Medal. Publ: Commerce Clause, Emory Univ Law Rev, 51. Mem: Aircraft Owners & Pilots Asn; Tuscaloosa CofC (dir); Univ Ala AIESEC (adv); Tuscaloosa Appeals Review Bd (chmn); Kiwanis (first vpres, 65). Relig: Methodist; Mem, Bd of Stewards. Mailing Add: 1228 Claymont Dr Tuscaloosa AL 35401

LAWLESS, WILLIAM JOSSELYN, JR (D)
Conn State Rep
b Newton, Mass, Apr 13, 19; s William J Lawless & Anna Lemon L; m 1941 to Ruth Atwood Gammons; c Philip Gammons & William Josselyn, III. Educ: George Washington Univ, BA, 52; Phi Beta Kappa. Polit & Govt Pos: Chief, Off Machine Prod, Nat Security Agency, 50-53; mission dir, Agency Int Develop, Ghana, 62-64 & Nigeria, 64-65; Conn State Rep, 75-, asst majority leader, Conn House of Rep, 75- Bus & Prof Pos: Mgr research lab, IBM Corp, 58-59, corp dir systems eng, 60-61, corp dir corp planning, 66-68, gen mgr in Latin America, 68-74 & consultant, 74-; mem bd dirs & exec comt, Overseas Develop Coun. Mil Serv: Entered as Pvt, Army, 42, released as Capt, after serv in Army Signal Corps, Nat Security Agency, Washington, DC, 42-46; Legion of Merit. Publ: Auth, Computer logic, In: Encyclopedia of Electronics, 62; auth, Developments in computer logical orgn, In: Advances in Electronics, Academic Press, 58; co-auth, Developments in the logical organization of computer arithmetic & control units, Proceedings of Inst of Radio Engrs, 61. Mem: Inst Electrical & Electronics Engrs (sr mem); Am Asn Advan Sci; Inst Mgt Sci. Mailing Add: 6 Golden Court Rowayton CT 06853

LAWRENCE, GLORIA EDITH (D)
Committeewoman, New York Co Comt, NY
b New York, NY; d Victor Lawrence & Mamie Moss L; single. Educ: City Col, BS, 56; New Sch for Social Resarch & Columbia Univ Sch of Social Work, 58-59. Polit & Govt Pos: Staff assoc, Robert F Kennedy, 67, minority coordr, Robert Kennedy Presidential Campaign, 68; deleg, Dem Nat Conv, 72; committeewoman, New York Co Comt, NY, 73- Bus & Prof Pos: Dir pub rels, Southern Elec Fund, 68-69; dir develop, Harold Oram Inc, 70-71; minority coordr, McGovern-Shriver Campaign, 72; dir develop, Harlem-Dowling Childrens Serv, 73-74; polit coordr, Ramsey Clark Campaign, 74- Mem: Am for Dem Action (mem bd dirs, NY State); Morningside Community Ctr (bd dirs); Direct-Mail Fund Raisers Asn; George Faison Dance Co (mem bd dirs); Double Image Theatre, Lincoln Square Community Ctr (mem adv coun). Mailing Add: 165 West End Ave New York NY 10023

LAWRENCE, HARRY UPHAM (R)
Vt State Rep
Mailing Add: Lyndonville VT 05851

LAWRENCE, M LARRY (D)
b Chicago, Ill, Aug 16, 26; s Sidney A Lawrence & Tillie P Astor L; c Robert, Leslie & Andrea. Educ: Univ Ariz, BA, 47; Zeta Beta Tau. Polit & Govt Pos: Alt deleg, Dem Nat Conv, 60, deleg, 64, 68 & 72; chmn, Van Deerlin for Cong, 61-66; finance chmn, Brown for Gov, 62-66; vchmn, San Diego Co Dem Cent Comt, 62-66; mem, President's Club, 64-67; finance chmn & nat finance comt, McCarthy for President Campaign, 68; Southern Calif finance chmn, Unruh for Gov Campaign, 70; Southern Calif chmn, Calif Dem Party, 71-73; mem electoral col, Calif Dem Deleg, 72; finance chmn, Cranston for Senate Reelec, 74; state chmn, Dem for Flournoy for Gov, 74. Bus & Prof Pos: Chmn, Coronado Transient Occupancy Tax Adv Bd, 74- Mil Serv: Maritime Serv, 44-45. Mem: San Diego & Coronado CofC; Calif State Comn on Tourism & Visitor Serv; United Jewish Appeal (San Diego chmn, 58-61); United Commun Serv (San Diego campaign dir, 65-67). Mailing Add: 1500 Orange Ave Coronado CA 92118

LAWRENCE, MARGERY B (R)
Pres, Maine Fedn Rep Women
b Rockland, Maine, June 2, 18; d Russell Eustice Bartlett & Frances Merle Doe B; m 1957 to Frank A Lawrence, Jr; c Janet (Mrs Leo T Martel) & Martha (Mrs Bouchard). Educ: Rockland High Sch, grad, 36; Ballard Bus Sch, 36-37. Polit & Govt Pos: Pres, Knox Co Rep Women, 65-67; mem chmn, Maine Fedn Rep Women, 67-69, rec secy, 69-72, 2nd vpres, 72-74, pres, 75-; vchmn, Rockland City Comt, 68-72. Relig: Protestant. Mailing Add: Juniper Hill Rockland ME 04841

LAWRENCE, NORMAN B (D)
NH State Rep
Mailing Add: Pelham Center Pelham NH 03076

LAWSON, HUGH (D)
Mem, Dem Party Ga
b Hawkinsville, Ga, Sept 23, 41; s Roger Hugh Lawson & Barbara Daniel L; m 1963 to Sydney Davis; c Sabra, Nancy & Harley. Educ: Emory Univ, AB, 63, LLB, 64; Phi Delta Phi; Chi Phi. Polit & Govt Pos: Mem, Dem Party, Ga, currently; mem, State Bd Community Develop, currently. Bus & Prof Pos: Attorney, 65- Mem: Mason; KT; Shriner. Relig: Methodist. Mailing Add: 11 Pine Level Dr Hawkinsville GA 31036

LAWSON, THOMAS SEAY (D)
b Greensboro, Ala, May 3, 06; s Lewis Joshua Lawson & Amy Seay L; m 1932 to Rose Gunter (deceased), m 1970 to Kathleen McLean Crampton; c Thomas Seay, Jr & Jule (Mrs Lanier). Educ: Davidson Col, AB, 26; Univ Ala, LLB, 29; Omicron Delta Kappa; Sigma Alpha Epsilon; Phi Delta Phi. Hon Degrees: DHL, Univ Ala, 72. Polit & Govt Pos: Asst attorney gen, State of Ala, 31-39, attorney gen, 39-42; assoc justice, Ala Supreme Court, 42-74. Mil Serv: Entered as Lt(jg), Navy, 43, released as Lt, 45, after serv in Judge Advocate Gen Off, Washington, DC & USS Mass, Third & Fifth Fleets. Relig: Methodist. Legal Res: Greensboro AL Mailing Add: PO Box 218 Montgomery AL 36101

LAWSON, WALTER NESBIT (D)
Chmn, Florence Co Dem Party, SC
b Florence, SC, Sept 7, 35; s Walter N Lawson & Charlotte Davis L; m 1957 to Sarah Ella Stone; c Charlotte Croft, Walter Nesbitt & Eugene Theodore. Educ: Wofford Col, 53; Univ Ga, 58; Sigma Nu. Polit & Govt Pos: US Marshal, SC, 66-69; vchmn, SC Hwy Comn, chmn, 72-73; chmn, Florence Co Dem Party, 74- Bus & Prof Pos: Nat leaders corps, Equitable Life, 71-75. Mil Serv: Entered as Pvt, Marine Corps, 53, released as Sgt, 56, after serv in Fourth Marines Regimental Combat Team, Korea, Asian Theatre, 54-56; Sigman Rhee Presidential Unit Citation; Expert Rifleman. Mem: Am Legion; VFW; Nat Asn Life Underwriters; Million Dollar Round Table. Relig: Episcopal. Legal Res: 1015 Park Ave Florence SC 29501 Mailing Add: 1511 Florence SC 29501

LAWSON, WILLIAM VINTON, JR (R)
Chmn, Shelby Co Rep Party, Tenn
b Omaha, Nebr, Sept 3, 31; s William Vinton Lawson (deceased) & Elva Erickson L; m 1955 to Mary Carolyn Townes; c Mary Lucian, William Vinton, III & Carolyn Townes. Educ: Tex A&M Univ, 49-50; Southwest at Memphis, 50-54; Sigma Alpha Epsilon (chap pres, 54). Polit & Govt Pos: Tenn State Rep, Shelby Co, Dist 9, 68-72, asst minority whip, Tenn House Rep, 71-72; mem steering comt, Shelby Co Rep Party, 70-, chmn, 73-; chmn, Shelby Co Elec Comn, 73-74. Bus & Prof Pos: Field rep, Gen Motors Acceptance Corp, Tupelo, Miss & Memphis, Tenn, 54-56; agt, Nat Life Ins Co of Vt, Memphis, Tenn, 56-63; spec agt, Northwestern Mutual Life Ins Co, 63- Mil Serv: Entered as Pvt, Army Res, 51, released as Cpl, 57, after serv in various units of active Reserve. Mem: Memphis Asn of Nat Asn of Life Underwriters (secy, 66-67, treas & membership chmn, 67-68); Memphis Chap, Am Soc of Chartered Life Underwriters (received designation, 64); Univ Club of Memphis; Memphis-Shelby Co Ment Health Ctr. Honors & Awards: Received Nat Membership Award, Nat Asn Life Underwriters as Membership Chmn of Memphis Asn, 68. Relig: Episcopal. Legal Res: 19 S Ashlawn Rd Memphis TN 38112 Mailing Add: PO Box 4286 Memphis TN 38104

LAWTHER, ROBERT M (R)
Mem, Cuyahoga Co Rep Exec Comt, Ohio
b McKeesport, Pa, May 23, 27; s LeRoy Lawther & Martha Helen Morledge L; m 1953 to Jo Anne Evelyn Paxton. Educ: Col of Wooster, BA, 50; Western Reserve Univ Sch of Law, LLB, 53; Delta Sigma Rho; Pi Sigma Alpha; Phi Alpha Delta. Polit & Govt Pos: Precinct committeeman, Co Rep Orgn, Ohio, 55-59; mem, Lakewood City Planning Comn, 56-57; mem, Lakewood City Coun, 57-63, pres, 62-63; mem, Cuyahoga Co Rep Exec Comt, 64-; mayor, Lakewood, 64-; pres, Cuyahoga Co Mayors & City Mgrs Asn, 68- Bus & Prof Pos: Practice of law, 53- Mil Serv: Seaman 1/C, Navy, 44-46. Mem: Cleveland & Ohio Bar Asns. Relig: Protestant. Mailing Add: City Hall Lakewood OH 44107

LAWTON, MARION R (R)
Chmn, Hampton Co Rep Party, SC
b Garnett, SC, Mar 5, 18; s Brewton Sams Lawton & Marian Smith L; m 1947 to Margaret Dell Leech; c Marion R, Jr, Margaret Doris & Brewton Wallace. Educ: Clemson Univ, BS, 40; Blue Key; Tiger Brotherhood. Polit & Govt Pos: Precinct chmn, Estill Rep Party, SC, 64; chmn, Hampton Co Rep Party, 65-; deleg, Rep Nat Conv, 68. Bus & Prof Pos: Partner, Walker & Lawton Lumber Co, 50; owner, Estill Feed Milling Co, 50; owner, M R Lawton Poultry Farms, 65; pres, Patrick Henry Acad. Mil Serv: Entered as 2nd Lt, Army, 40, released as Maj, 46, after serv in Inf, Attached to Philippine Army, Bataan Bn Comdr, 42-43; prisoner of war, 42-45; Bronze Star; Purple Heart; Distinguished Unit Citation with Three Clusters. Mem: Lions; Am Legion; Clemson Univ Alumni Asn (nat dir, 54-55); Coastal Empire Coun, Boy Scouts (vpres, 60-62, mem exec bd, 62-64, mem-at-lg, 65-66). Honors & Awards: Silver Beaver Award, Boy Scouts, 57. Relig: Presbyterian; Elder; moderator, Charleston Presbytery. Mailing Add: Box 156 Estill SC 29918

LAWTON, MARK EDWARD (D)
Mass State Rep
b Boston, Mass, July 26, 49; s James Robert Lawton & Jeanne Gloria L; m 1975 to Patricia Ann O'Leary; c Sean Patrick. Educ: Stonehill Col, AB, 71; New Eng Sch Law, JD, 74. Polit & Govt Pos: Mass State Rep, 12th Plymouth Dist, 75-, mem pub serv comt, Mass House Rep, 75- Mem: Boston Irish Social Club; Brockton Land Trust (pres); University Club. Relig: Catholic. Mailing Add: 103 Belcher Ave Brockton MA 02401

LAWTON, ROBERT M (R)
NH State Rep
Mailing Add: RFD 2 Parade Rd Meredith NH 03253

LAXALT, PAUL (R)
US Sen, Nev
b Reno, Nev, Aug 2, 22; s Dominique Laxalt & Theresa Alpetche L; m 1946 to Jackalyn Ross, div; c Gail, Sheila, John, Michelle, Kevin & Kathleen. Educ: Santa Clara Univ, 40-43; Univ Denver, BS, LLB, 49. Polit & Govt Pos: Dist attorney, Ormsby Co, Nev, 51-54; city attorney, Carson City, 54-55; lt gov, Nev, 62-67, gov, 67-70; deleg, Rep Nat Conv, 68; US Senator, Nev, 75- Bus & Prof Pos: Lawyer, partner, Firm of Laxalt, Ross & Laxalt, 54-62; Laxalt, Berry & Allison, Carson City, Nev, currently; pres, Ormsby House & Casino, 72- Mem: Am Bar Asn; Am Legion; VFW; Eagles. Mailing Add: 412 N Division St Carson City NV 89701

LAXSON, JOHN H (R)
b Atascosa Co, Tex, July 13, 86; s John Laxson & Georgia Titsworth L; m 1930 to Dorothy McNallie; c Gaye (Mrs C W Turner), Kaye (Mrs C J Hall), June (Mrs Hubert Lynch), Bay Clifton, Wilma (Mrs Paul Hodge), Nellie V (Mrs Rowill Jones), Johnanna (Mrs E J Bowers) & J H. Polit & Govt Pos: Chmn, Dimmit Co Rep Party, Tex, formerly; sgt-at-arms, Rep Nat Conv, 68. Bus & Prof Pos: Travelling salesman, San Antonio Grocery; rancher, 10-60; citrus farmer, 64-69. Mem: Odd Fellows; Rotary; Lions; Farm Bur. Relig: Church of Christ. Mailing Add: Rte 1 Carrizo Springs TX 78834

LAY, CHRISTOPHER DAVID (R)
Mem Exec Comt, Young Rep Nat Fedn
b Houston, Tex, Nov 9, 46; s Carl Franklin Lay & Maurine Roberts L; single. Educ: Tex Christian Univ, BS, 69; Univ Calif San Diego, grad work, 69; Univ Colo, grad work, 70-71; Physics Soc (pres, 67-68), Tex Christian Univ. Polit & Govt Pos: Mem, Col Rep, Tex

Christian Univ, 64-69; mem bd dirs, Denver Young Rep, Colo, 70-71, pres, 71-72; mem, Am Conservative Union, 70-; state chmn, Colo Young Am for Freedom, 71-72; campaign coordr, McClure for Senate & Symms for Cong Idaho, 72; nat committeeman, Colo Young Rep, 72-73; mem exec comt, Young Rep Nat Fedn, 73-; legis asst, US Rep Steve Symms, 73- Bus & Prof Pos: Research asst, NASA Marshall Space Ctr, Huntsville, Ala, summer 68; physicist, Martin Marietta Corp, Denver, Colo, 70-72. Mem: Am Nuclear Soc; Am Inst Aeronaut & Astronaut. Relig: Methodist. Legal Res: 2607 Simondale Dr Ft Worth TX 76109 Mailing Add: 1410 Longworth House Off Bldg Washington DC 20515

LAYMAN, EARL ROBERT **(R)**
Committeeman, Tenn Rep State Exec Comt
b Knoxville, Tenn, Aug 5, 32; s William Earl Layman & Marie Frances Little L; div; c William Douglas, Marilyn Lee, Linda Ann & Sharon Gail. Educ: Univ Tenn, Knoxville, BS, 55, JD, 62; Phi Delta Phi. Polit & Govt Pos: Pres, Knox Co Young Rep Club, 63; mem, Knox Co Elec Comn, 67-71; committeeman, Tenn Rep State Exec Comt, 72- Bus & Prof Pos: Acct, East Tenn Packing Co, Knoxville, 57-59; assoc, Joyce & Wilson, Attorneys, Oak Ridge, 62-64; attorney, Key, Lee & Layman, Knoxville, 64-; part-time instr, Univ Tenn Col Law, 66-70. Mil Serv: Entered as 2nd Lt, Army, 55, released as 1st Lt, after serv in Inf. Mem: Am, Tenn & Knoxville Bar Asns; Elks Club; Sertoma. Mailing Add: Rte 1 Lakefront Lane Concord TN 37922

LAYNE, WILLIAM HENRY **(R)**
Rep VChmn, Seventh Cong Dist, Ky
b Paintsville, Ky; s James Trimble Layne & Flora May Wheatley L; m 1931 to Francis Elizabeth McKinney; c William Joseph. Educ: Univ Ky, 30-31; Morehead State Univ, 3 years; Delta Tau Delta. Polit & Govt Pos: Mem, Rowan Co Sch Bd, Ky, 34-44; mayor, Morehead, Ky, 46-; chmn, Rowan Co Rep Party, formerly; Rep vchmn, Seventh Cong Dist, 67- Bus & Prof Pos: Clothing merchant, 48- Mem: Pres, Morehead CofC, 69; past pres, Ky Munic League, 60-61; past comdr, Morehead F&AM, 68; Shrine. Honors & Awards: Distinguished faculty award, Morehead State Univ Alumni. Relig: Methodist. Legal Res: 112 Wilson Ave Morehead KY 40351 Mailing Add: 110 Main Morehead KY 40351

LAZARUS, STEVEN JAY **(D)**
b Brooklyn, NY, Aug 2, 51; s Hyman Lazarus (deceased) & Esther Feldman L; m 1974 to Denise Ross. Educ: Queens Col, NY, BA cum laude, 72, MA Urban Studies, 75; Pi Sigma Alpha. Polit & Govt Pos: Legis aide, Queens Councilman-at-lg, Alvin Frankenberg, 71-; deleg, Dem Nat Conv, 72; co-chmn, Comt for Reelec of Alan Hevesi, Assemblyman, 72; dist mgr, Mayor's Off Neighborhood Servs, 73-; co-chmn, Citizens for Strauss for Councilman, 74. Mem: New Frontier Regular Dem Club (exec secy & campaign chmn). Relig: Jewish. Mailing Add: 103-11 68th Dr Forest Hills NY 11375

LAZZIO, THOMAS **(R)**
b Paterson, NJ, July 29, 11; s Salvatore Lazzio & Caterina L; m 1938 to Theresa C Mandata. Educ: Rutgers Univ. Polit & Govt Pos: NJ State Assemblyman, 52-57; emmem, Vets Reemploy Rights Comt & Civil Rights Comt; comnr, Paterson Bd of Educ, NJ; one of thirty original mems, White House Conf on Educ, Eisenhower Admin; mem, Comt on Study of Pub Assistance, Dept of Health, Educ & Welfare, 70-71; chmn, Passaic Valley Sewerage Comn, State of NJ, 70-; alt deleg, Rep Nat Conv, 72. Bus & Prof Pos: Field serv rep, Wright Aero Div, Curtiss Wright Corp, civilian adv on engines attached to Air Force with 9th Bomb Group B-29, Tinian & Saipan, 2nd World War. Publ: Free trade Unions Method of Combating Communist unions in Italy, State Dept, 54; Labor & cooperative movement's influence of government of Scandinavian countries, State Dept, 54. Mem: UAW (treas, Local 300, 48-50, financial secy, 50-52, pres, 52-63). Relig: Catholic. Mailing Add: 25 Doremus St Paterson NJ 07522

LEACH, CHARLES PARMLEY, SR **(R)**
Chmn, Clarion Co Rep Orgn, Pa
b New Bethlehem, Pa, Sept 27, 11; s George Washington Leach & Ursula Dawes Parmley L; m 1936 to Clare Louise Skinner; c Charles Parmley, Jr, Cara L (Mrs Thornley) & Hamilton Skinner. Educ: Bucknell Univ, 29-31. Polit & Govt Pos: Councilman, New Bethlehem Borough, Pa, 42-58, pres, 48-58; mem, Pa State Rep Finance Comt, 54-; mem, Pa State Rep Exec Comt, 62-; sch dir, New Bethlehem, 62-; chmn, Clarion Co Rep Orgn, 64-70 & 74-; mem, Electoral Col, 72. Bus & Prof Pos: Secy, Joe F Sherman Co, 46-; dir, H E Brosius Co, Inc, 54-; pres, Bruin Drilling Corp, 60-; dir, Hawthorne Mfg Co; pres, Charles P Leach Agency, Inc, 67- Mem: Eagles; Moose; Elks: CofC (dir); Boy Scouts of Am (mem exec comt Region III). Relig: Presbyterian. Legal Res: 533 Penn New Bethlehem PA 16242 Mailing Add: PO Box 8 New Bethlehem PA 16242

LEACH, CLAUDE, JR **(D)**
La State Rep
Mailing Add: PO Box 1247 Leesville LA 71446

LEACH, MARJORIE M **(D)**
b Odessa, Wash, Nov 6, 34; d Herman John Uhrich & Anna Wraspir U; m 1955 to Richard Dean Leach; c Renaye Marie, Randall Dean, Michelle Anne & Melissa Sue. Educ: Dak Wesleyan Univ, BA, 56; Univ SDak, Vermillion, summer 66; Univ Marburg, WGermany, 60; Lakeland Col, 73. Polit & Govt Pos: Alt deleg, Dem Nat Conv, 72; ballot clerk, Town of Herman, Wis, 73- Bus & Prof Pos: Elem sch teacher, Denver Pub Schs, Colo, 56-58, Gregory Pub Schs, Gregory, SDak, 66-68 & Howards Grove Pub Schs, Sheboygan, Wis, 74- Relig: Methodist. Mailing Add: Box 164C Rte 1 Sheboygan Falls WI 53085

LEACH, RUSSELL **(R)**
Chmn, Franklin Co Rep Party, Ohio
b Columbus, Ohio, Aug 1, 22; s Charles A Leach & Hazel Thatcher L; m 1945 to Helen Sharpe; c Susan (Mrs Greg A Waggy), Terry D & Ann D. Educ: Univ Conn, 43; Ohio State Univ, BA, 47, JD, 49; Delta Theta Phi; Chi Phi. Polit & Govt Pos: Asst city attorney, Columbus, Ohio, 51 & 53-57, city attorney, 57-63; judge, Franklin Co Munic Court, 63-66; chmn, Franklin Co Rep Party, 74- Bus & Prof Pos: Partner, Bricker, Evatt, Barton & Eckler, Attorneys-at-law, 66- Mil Serv: Entered as Pvt, Army, 42, released as T/Sgt, 46, after serv in Asiatic Theatre, 45-46; 1st Lt, Judge Adv Gen Corp, Asst Staff Judge Adv, 37th Inf Div, 51-53. Publ: Co-auth, articles in Ohio State Law J, 50-51. Mem: Ohio Bar Asn (coun deleg, 70-75); Columbus Bar Asn (bd pres, 68-75); Am Legion; Agonis Club; Columbus CofC. Honors & Awards: Young Man of Year, Jaycees, 56 & 57. Relig: Methodist. Legal Res: 1232 Kenbrook Hills Dr Columbus OH 43220 Mailing Add: 100 E Broad St Columbus OH 43215

LEADER, GEORGE MICHAEL **(D)**
b York, Pa, Jan 17, 18; s Guy Alvin Leader & Beulah Boyer L; m 1939 to Mary Jane Strickler; c George Michael, Frederick, Jane Ellen & David. Educ: York Collegiate Inst, 34-35; Gettysburg Col, 36-38; Univ Pa, BS, 39. Polit & Govt Pos: Pa State Sen, 50-54; Gov, Pa, 55-59; deleg, Dem Nat Conv, 68 & 72. Bus & Prof Pos: Chmn of bd, Better Govt Assoc, Inc; pres, Commonwealth Indust, Inc. Mem: Bd, Lincoln Univ. Legal Res: 1010 Black Rock Rd Gladwyne PA 19035 Mailing Add: 17 Morris Ave Bryn Mawr PA 19010

LEAFE, JOSEPH A **(D)**
Va State Deleg
Mailing Add: 6162 Powhatan Ave Norfolk VA 23508

LEAHY, ELIZABETH CLARE **(D)**
Secy, Seneca Co Dem Exec & Cent Comts, Ohio
b Conneaut, Ohio, Apr 12, 11; d John Gilbert Kelley & Mary Shannon K; m 1937 to James Clarence Leahy; c James Patrick, Daniel Edward, Susan Elizabeth (Mrs Aller), Timothy Joseph, Colleen Marie, Shannon Rosanne, Theresa Louise (Mrs Kline) & Mary Catherine. Educ: St Mary's High Sch, Conneaut, Ohio, 4 years. Polit & Govt Pos: Dem precinct workers, Ashtabula Co, Ohio, 34-37, Seneca Co, various times from 40-69; committeeman, Dem Cent Comt, 57 & 58-69; vpres, Dem Women of Seneca Co, 57-59, pres, 59-63 & 71-, prog chmn, 60-69; secy, Seneca Co Dem Exec & Cent Comts, 59- Mem: Emblem Club; Federated Dem Women of Ohio; Daughters of Isabella; St Mary's Altar Soc; St Francis Guild. Honors & Awards: Nat Girl Scout Thank You Award. Relig: Roman Catholic. Mailing Add: 275 W Market St Tiffin OH 44883

LEAHY, PATRICK J **(D)**
US Sen, Vt
b Montpelier, Vt, Mar 31, 40; s Howard F Leahy & Alba Z L; m 1962 to Marcelle Pomerleau; c Kevin, Alicia & Mark. Educ: St Michael's Col, BA, 61; Georgetown Univ, JD, 64. Polit & Govt Pos: Drafter & provided legal background for Vt Legis, 3 years; mem several Gov Comns; states attorney, Chittenden Co, 66-74; US Sen, Vt, 75- Mem: Nat Dist Attorneys Asn (vpres). Honors & Awards: Received numerous community & orgn citations. Legal Res: VT Mailing Add: US Senate Washington DC 20510

LEAL, HARLAN RUSSELL **(D)**
b San Diego, Calif, July 24, 48; s Anthony Leal & Lucielle Bonbrake L; single. Educ: Southwestern Col, 67-71. Polit & Govt Pos: Alt deleg, Dem Nat Conv, 72. Bus & Prof Pos: Farm labor asst & rural manpower asst, Calif State Employ Develop Dept, San Ysidro, 69-73; social ins rep, Dept Health, Educ & Welfare, San Diego, 73- Publ: Authored & co-authored in Eng & Spanish, various leaflets & pamphlets in behalf of Sen George McGovern's campaign, 71-72, San Diego Dem Comt, 71-72. Mem: Asn Fed Govt Employees Union. Relig: Roman Catholic. Mailing Add: 220 E Park Ave San Ysidro CA 92073

LEAMOND, FREDERICK JULIAN **(D)**
SC State Rep
b Charleston, SC, Mar 5, 05; s Frederick Julian LeaMond & Marie Wing L; m 1926 to Catherine Frances Dowling; c Frederick Julian, Jr, Harold Joseph, Catherine Ann, John Eugene & Jean Marie. Polit & Govt Pos: SC State Rep, 54-; consult sea & airlift matters, House Comt on Armed Servs, US Congress, 61-64. Bus & Prof Pos: Pres & treas, Allied Paper Co, Charleston & Dangerous Materials Disposal Co, vpres, Regis Milk Co & dir, Cooper River Savings & Loan Asn, currently. Mil Serv: Entered as Fireman 3/C, Navy, 26, retired as Capt, 51, after serv as Comndg Officer of various types of Navy ships, all theaters; Bronze Star Medal with Combat V; Navy Commendation with Combat V; Naval Res Medal with Star; Am Defense Ribbon with Star; Am, ETO, African & Asiatic-Pac Ribbons; Victory Medal; Expert Pistol & Expert Rifle Medals; Command-at-Sea Insignia. Mem: Mason (Past Master); Shrine; Rotary; Country Club; Propeller Club. Honors & Awards: Legis Conserv Award, 68; Coach, US Navy Boxing Team. Relig: Episcopal. Mailing Add: 165 St Margaret St Charleston SC 29403

LEARNER, IDA **(D)**
Chmn, LaCrosse Co Dem Party, Wis
b Mason City, Iowa, May 18, 20; d James Learner & Sophie Cohen L; single. Educ: Mason City Jr Col, 38-39; Univ Minn, fall 39; Wright City Jr Col, Chicago, 40. Polit & Govt Pos: Chmn, LaCrosse Co Dem Party, Wis, 64-; vchmn, Third Dist Dem Party, 71- Mem: Women's Polit Caucus; Friends of LaCrosse Pub Libr. Relig: Hebrew. Mailing Add: 2936 Mesa Grande Pl LaCrosse WI 54601

LEARY, JUNE ELLIS **(D)**
Committeewoman, Ore State Dem Cent Comt
b Chickasha, Okla, Sept 7, 21; d Ellis Lee Moss & Miriam Quinby M; m 1947 to Daniel Francis Leary; c Daniel Francis, Jr, James Michael & Miriam Helen (Sue). Educ: Okla Col for Women, 6 months. Polit & Govt Pos: Precinct committeewoman, Jackson Co Dem Cent Comt, 63-, secy, 66-68, vchmn, 68-70, chmn, 70-72; committeewoman, Ore State Dem Cent Comt, 68- Bus & Prof Pos: Supvr, Southwestern Bell Tel Co, Chickasha, Okla, 46-47; Pac Northwest Bell, Portland, Ore, 52-53, cent off clerk, Medford, 60-64. Mem: Epsilon Sigma Alpha (Palla Athene Award); Eleanor Roosevelt League (treas, 67); Dem Social Club. Honors & Awards: App by state rep Al Densmore to act as an alt in case of emergency. Relig: Catholic. Mailing Add: 3235 Antelope Rd White City OR 97501

LEARY, THEODORE MOREAU, JR **(D)**
b Beverly, Mass, Feb 18, 45; s Theodore Moreau Leary & Mary Frances Horgan L; m 1967 to Eleanor Brownell Lockwood. Educ: Harvard Col, BA, 66; George Washington Univ Law Sch, JD, 69. Polit & Govt Pos: Attorney, Nat Labor Rels Bd, 69-70; legis asst, US Sen Tom McIntyre, 70; spec asst, US Sen Abe Ribicoff, Conn, 70-74, admin asst, 74- Relig: Roman Catholic. Legal Res: 846 Massachusetts Ave Arlington MA 02174 Mailing Add: 509 Third St SE Washington DC 20003

LEARY, WARREN W **(R)**
NH State Rep
Mailing Add: Alton NH 03809

LEASE, M HARRY, JR **(DFL)**
VPres 61st Legis Dist Dem-Farmer-Labor Party, Minn
b Plainfield, Ind, Aug 15, 27; s Martin Harry Lease & Beatrice Irene Krebs L; m 1969 to Jeanne Marie Lachance. Educ: Ind Univ, Bloomington, BA, 53, MA, 55, PhD, 61; Pi Sigma Alpha. Polit & Govt Pos: Deleg, Dem-Farmer-Labor Co, Cong Dist & State Conv, Minn, 62

& 68; Dem precinct chmn, Duluth, 62-69; chmn, 61st Legis Dist Dem-Farmer-Labor Party, 64-65, vpres, 70-; city chmn, Dem-Farmer-Labor Party, 65-67; deleg, Dem Nat Conv, 68; deleg, Dem-Farmer-Labor State, Cong Dist & Legis Dist Convs, 70; mem, Wendell Anderson for Gov Comt, 70; treas, 61B Legis Dist Campaign, 70; deleg, Eighth Sen Dist Conv, 72; northeastern coordr, Educators for Mondale, 72. Bus & Prof Pos: Instr, Univ Miami, 55-56; from assoc prof to prof, polit sci & asst dean grad sch, Univ Minn, Duluth, 57- Mem: Am Polit Sci Asn; Midwest Polit Sci Asn; Am Asn Univ Prof. Honors & Awards: Nat Ctr Educ in Polit fel, Western States Dem Conf, 62-63. Legal Res: 2320 Harvard Ave Duluth MN 55803 Mailing Add: Dept of Political Science Univ of Minn Grad Sch Duluth MN 55812

LEATHERBURY, DOUGLAS CLAY (D)
b Bennington, Ind, Aug 21, 41; s Clarence B Leatherbury & Pearl Davis L; single. Educ: Ind Univ, AB, 64, Law Sch, JD, 68. Polit & Govt Pos: Chmn, Switzerland Co Dem Party, Ind, formerly; prosecuting attorney, Fifth Judicial Circuit Court, Ind, 71-; mem, Dem Nat Charter Comn, currently. Mem: Am Bar Asn; Am Judicature Soc; F&AM; Kiwanis; Elks. Relig: Baptist. Mailing Add: 211 W Main St Vevay IN 47043

LEAVEL, WILLARD HAYDEN (D)
Mem, Denver Co Dem Cent Comt, Colo
b Columbia, Mo, July 28, 27; s Willard Hayden Leavel & Beatrice Temmen L; single. Educ: Univ Denver, 48-53; Univ Wash, Seattle, PhD, 53-60; Phi Beta Kappa; Omicron Delta Kappa; Phi Sigma Alpha; Acacia. Polit & Govt Pos: Campaign mgr, Wes Uhlman, Wash House Rep, 58 & 60; mem, King Co Dem Exec Comt, 59-60; campaign mgr, Mark Hogan for Colo House Rep, 64 & Lt Gov, 66; chmn, Dem Comt on Reapportionment, 65; mem, Denver Co Dem Cent Comt, 65-, capt-at-lg, 65-; mem, Colo Dem State Cent Comt, 67-75; chmn, Comt to Elect a Dem Legis, 68; campaign mgr, Craig Barnes, Dem Cand Cong, First Dist, Colo, 70; chmn, Colo Dem Party, 71-72; deleg, Dem Nat Conv, 72; mem, Dem Nat Comt, 72-74; chmn, Colo Udall for President Comt, currently. Bus & Prof Pos: Instr, Univ Wash, 58-60; asst prof, Wis State Col, Eau Claire, 60-62; assoc prof, Univ Denver, 62- Mil Serv: Entered as Pvt, Air Force, 46, released as Cpl, 47. Publ: Campaign, Prentice-Hall, 60. Mem: Am Asn Univ Prof; Western Polit Sci Asn. Mailing Add: 331 E Ellsworth Denver CO 80209

LEAVITT, DIXIE L (R)
Utah State Sen
b St George, Utah, Aug 27, 29; s Vincen E Leavitt & Erma Leavitt L; m 1949 to Anne Okerlund; c Michael O, Dane O, Mark O, Eric O, David O & Matthew O. Educ: Col Southern Utah, grad; Utah State Univ, grad. Polit & Govt Pos: Utah State Rep, 63-65; Utah State Sen, 65-, Majority Leader, Utah State Senate, 72-74. Bus & Prof Pos: Pres, Dixie Leavitt Ins Agency, 55- Mem: Kiwanis; Rotary Int. Relig: Latter-day Saint. Mailing Add: 393 S 700 West Cedar City UT 84720

LEAVITT, STANLEY A (D)
Utah State Rep
b Leavitt, Alta, May 17, 18; s Melvin Leavitt & Sarah Broadbent L; m 1944 to Edna Murl Holman; c Raymond, Betty (Mrs Tracy Eyre), Carey (Mrs Kurt Lloyd), Diane, Larry, Donna & JoAnn. Educ: Univ Alta, BS, 49; Brigham Young Univ, MEd, 54, EdD, 64. Polit & Govt Pos: Chmn, Orem Precinct, Utah, 63-65; councilman, Orem, 66-69; Utah State Rep, 71-, mem, State Audit Comt, Utah House Rep, 71-73, mem, Educ Appropriations Comt, 71- & Legis Coun, 73- Bus & Prof Pos: Prin, Barnwell Sch, Alta, 48-52; Lincoln Jr High Sch, Orem, Utah, 58-63 & Orem Jr High Sch, 63-64; supvr jr high schs, Alpine Sch Dist, 65- Mil Serv: Entered as Airman, Royal Can Air Force, 43, released as Flying Off, 45, after serv in Air Bomber, ETO, 44-45. Mem: Phi Delta Kappa; Nat, Utah & Alpine Educ Asns; Orem CofC. Relig: Latter-day Saint. Mailing Add: 940 S 100 East Orem UT 84057

LEBAMOFF, GEORGE (D)
Treas, Allen Co Dem Cent Comt, Ind
b Ft Wayne, Ind, July 18, 27; s Argire Vasil Lebamoff & Helen Kotchandonoff L; m 1955 to Rosemary G Tsiguloff; c Deborah, Andrew, John & Thomas. Educ: Ind Univ, Bloomington, 46-49; Huntington Col, BS Bus, 51. Polit & Govt Pos: Treas, Allen Co Dem Cent Comt, Ind, 72-; alt deleg, Dem Nat Conv, 72. Bus & Prof Pos: Dir, Ind Package Store Asn, 67- Mil Serv: Entered as Pvt, Army, 51, released as Pvt, after serv in Info & Educ, Salzburg, Austria, 51-53. Mem: Ft Wayne Press Club; Ft Wayne CofC; Ind Univ Alumni Asn; Ind Soc of Natural Hist (life mem); Am Legion. Honors & Awards: Retailer of the Year, Nat Retailers Asn, 59; Nat Brand Names Winner, Nat Brand Names Liquor Asn, 59-60. Relig: Eastern Orthodox. Mailing Add: 1438 Ardis Dr Ft Wayne IN 46819

LEBAMOFF, IVAN A (D)
Mayor, Fort Wayne, Ind
b Fort Wayne, Ind, July 20, 32; s Argire V Lebamoff & Helen Katsandonoff L; m 1963 to Katherine Stephanoff; c Damian I, Jordan I & Justin A. Educ: Ind Univ, AB, 54; Ind Univ Law Sch, JD, 57; Phi Alpha Theta; Phi Delta Phi. Polit & Govt Pos: US Comnr, North Dist of Ind, 62; deleg, Dem Nat Conv, 68-72; chmn, Allen Co Dem Party, Ind, 68-72, 74-; Mayor, Ft Wayne, 72- Bus & Prof Pos: Partner, Lebamoff, Ver Wiebe & Snow, Ft Wayne, Ind, 69-72. Mil Serv: Entered as Airman Basic, Air Force, 58, released as A/1C, 64, after serv in Air Guard, France, 62-63. Mem: Ind & Am Bar Asns; Mason. Relig: Eastern Orthodox. Legal Res: 205 E Packard Ft Wayne IN 46806 Mailing Add: City-County Bldg One Main St Fort Wayne IN 46802

LEBEDOFF, DAVID MICHAEL (DFL)
Mem, Minn State Dem-Farmer-Labor Cent Comt
b Minneapolis, Minn, Apr 29, 38; s Martin David Lebedoff & Mary Galanter L; single. Educ: Univ Minn, BA, 60; Harvard Law Sch, LLB, 63; Phi Beta Kappa, pres, Minn Chap, 75. Polit & Govt Pos: Chmn, Anderson for Gov Comt, 69-70; mem, Minn State Dem-Farmer-Labor Cent Comt, 72-; adv comt, Hofstede for Mayor, 73; mem, Dem Charter Comn, 74-75; deleg, Dem Nat Mid-Term Conf, 74; comnr, Higher Educ Coord Comn of Minn, 75- Bus & Prof Pos: Attorney, spec master, US Dist Court, 74- Publ: The 21st Ballot, Univ Minn, 69; Ward Number Six, Charles Scribners Sons, 72. Relig: Jewish. Mailing Add: 17 S First St Apt 1702A Minneapolis MN 55401

LEBEL, IRENEE REMI (R)
Chmn, Portsmouth City Rep Comt, NH
b Brunswick, Maine, Aug 13, 26; s Emile H Lebel & Nelida Dionne L; m 1956 to Frances Dowdell; c Cynthia, Patricia, Michael & Thomas. Educ: Boston Univ, BS in Bus Admin. Polit & Govt Pos: Chmn, Portsmouth City Rep Comt, NH, 74-; mem, State Bd Accountancy, 75- Mil Serv: Entered as A/S, Navy, 44, released as Radioman 3/C, 46, after serv in Pac Theatre, 45-46. Mem: Kiwanis Club Gtr Portsmouth (pres, 74-75); Am Inst CPA's; Great Bay Sch & Training Ctr (mem bd, 73-). Relig: Catholic. Mailing Add: 457 Broad St Portsmouth NH 03801

LEBEL, LORRAINE FRANCES (D)
NH State Rep
b Norwood, Mass, Feb 6, 45; d Lawrence A Landers & Corinne J Wood L; m 1963 to Roland George Lebel; c Laurie Ann, Lynn Ann & Mark Roland. Educ: Mt St Mary Sem, Nashua, NH, grad, 63; New Eng Col (NH). Polit & Govt Pos: Clerk, NH Dem Caucus, 72; mem, Comt to Reelect US Sen McIntyre, 72; deleg, NH Dem Conv, 73; NH State Rep, 73-, mem, House Transportation Comt & Sub-Comt, Co Probation, NH Gen Court, 73- Bus & Prof Pos: Tel operator, New Eng Tel Co, 63-64; typist, Nashua Motor Express, 70-71. Mem: Am Cancer Soc; PTA; Order Women Legislators; Forty Three Club; Sch Monitor Asn. Honors & Awards: Advan Studies in Biol Award, New Eng Col (NH), 63. Relig: Roman Catholic. Mailing Add: 4 Yarmouth Dr Nashua NH 03060

LEBLANC, ARMAND A (D)
Maine State Rep
Mailing Add: Van Buren ME 04785

LEBLANC, CHARLES JOHN (R)
Mem, Rep State Cent Comt, La
b Plattenville, La, July 15, 98; s Ernest T LeBlanc & Alice Fremin L; single. Educ: St James High Sch. Polit & Govt Pos: Mem, Rep State Cent Comt, La, 56-; W Baton Rouge Parish Dir, US Census, 60. Publ: Poetry, Am Poets & Songwriter, 49, Poetry, Talent, Songwriters & Poets, 47. Mem: Am Soc Composers, Authors, Publishers; Boy's Town. Relig: Pentacostal. Legal Res: 470 Michigan Ave Port Allen LA 70767 Mailing Add: Box 443 Port Allen LA 70767

LEBLANC, EDWARD FAISANS, JR (D)
Exec Dir, Young Dem Am
b Abbeville, La, Sept 17, 49; s Edward Faisans LeBlanc, Sr & Evelyn Hebert L; single. Educ: La State Univ, 67-71; La State Univ Sch Law, 70-71. Polit & Govt Pos: Committeeman, Dem Nat Platform Comt, 72-; pres, La Young Dem, 73-74; deleg, Dem Nat Charter Conf, 74; exec dir, Young Dem Am, 74- Bus & Prof Pos: Chmn, Social Studies Dept, Vermillion Cath High Sch, Abbeville, La, 71; correspondent, Daily Iberian, New Iberia, 72; fund raiser, Gtr New Orleans Tourist & Convention Comn, 73; solicitor, New Orleans Saints, 73-; commun consult, Jim Pertuit & Assocs, 74- Mem: Am Asn Polit Consult. Relig: Roman Catholic. Mailing Add: 209 Chevis St Abbeville LA 70510

LEBLANC, SAM A (D)
La State Rep
b Donaldsonville, La, Nov 12, 38; s Sam A LeBlanc, Jr (deceased) & Marcelle Reese L; m 1961 to Noelle Engler; c Sam, Raoul & Marcel. Educ: Georgetown Univ, 56, 58 & 60; Universite de Fribourg, Switz, 58-59; Tulane Univ Law Sch, LLB, 63; Order of the Coif; Phi Delta Phi; Delta Kappa Epsilon. Polit & Govt Pos: Mem, MHC Interparish/Intersyst Coop Task Force for Metrop Sch; mem, Consumer Adv Bd, Fed Trade Comn; mem, Ad Hoc Polit Support Comt; mem, Gov Property Tax Study Comt; mem, Gov Adv Comt, to Consumer Protection Div; secy-treas, Young Lawyers Sect. La State Bar Asn, 68, vchmn, 69, chmn, 70 & mem bd gov, 70; pres, Metrop Young Lawyers Asn, 70-71; mem, La House Deleg, 71-73, La State Rep, 72-, mem, Interpum Comt for North-South Expressway, mem, Comt on Judiciary B, mem, Ways & Means Comt, La House Rep, 72- Bus & Prof Pos: Assoc, Adams & Reese Law Firm, New Orleans, La, 63-69; partner, 66- Publ: Ed, The Memorandum, La Defense Counsel Asn, 66-69; auth, Reflections on Rodrique, Counsel Jour, 69; Ponca City (play), La Mise en Scene Theatre, 70. Mem: La Civil Serv League (vpres & chmn, Legal Comt); Alliance for Good Govt; Young Men's Bus Club; Aurora Civil Asn; Aircraft Owners & Pilots Asn. Honors & Awards: Class Agent, Tulane Law Class, 63; Alumni Interviewer, Georgetown Univ; Chmn First Law Day of New Orleans, 65. Relig: Catholic. Legal Res: 5425 Wimbledon Court New Orleans LA 70114 Mailing Add: Suite D 600 Terry Pkwy Gretna LA 70035

LEBLEU, CONWAY (D)
La State Rep
Mailing Add: PO Box 266 Cameron LA 70631

LEBOUTILLIER, PHILIP JR (R)
b New York, NY, Feb 24, 16; s Philip LeBoutillier & Gertrude H Tifft L; m 1940 to Felia Ford; c Philip Grandin, George Ford & Ford. Educ: Princeton Univ, AB cum laude, 38. Polit & Govt Pos: Dep Asst Secy of Defense for Supply & Logistics, 59-60; mem, Ohio Rep Finance Comt & co-chmn, Lucas Co Rep Finance Comt, formerly. Bus & Prof Pos: Pres, Ottawa River Paper Co, 48-58; vpres, Mead Containers, Inc, 58; chmn & pres, Hixon-Peterson Lumber Co, 58-60; gen partner, Collin, Norton & Co, 61-64; vpres, Clark Dodge & Co, Inc, 64- Mil Serv: Entered as Ens, Navy, 42, released as Comdr, 45, after serv in NAtlantic Patrol, Caribbean, Normandy, Philippines & Iwo Jima; Silver Star; Secy of Defense Meritorious Serv Award Medal. Mem: Dir, Boys' Clubs of Am; trustee, Boys' Clubs of Toledo. Relig: Episcopal. Legal Res: 29407 E River Rd Perrysburg OH 43551 Mailing Add: 221 Gardner Bldg Toledo OH 43604

LEBRETON, EDWARD FRANCIS, JR (D)
La State Rep
b New Orleans, La, Aug 16, 13; s Edward Francis LeBreton, Sr & Carmen Suarez L; m 1947 to Gladys Lodoiska Gay; c Edward Francis, III, Gladys Fenner Gay & Robert Aime. Educ: Tulane Univ, 33. Polit & Govt Pos: Mem, President of US Automobile Safety Comt, 52-64; La State Rep, 52-; treas, Audubon Park Comn, 54-61; mem, New Orleans Mosquito Control Comt, 63-71; deleg, Dem Nat Conv, 64; mem, Gov Joint Legis Comt on Econ, 64 & chmn, Comt on Off-Track Betting Feasibility, 73; mem, President of US Adv Comt on Studies of Natural Disaster, Dept of Housing & Urban Develop, 65; mem, Am Assembly of Columbia Univ in coord with the Southern Assembly, 67-70; mem by proxy of Speaker of House, La Stadium & Expos Dist, 67; pres, Nat Soc of State Legislators, 68-69; adv comt, 69; mem, Gov Joint Legis Comt on Hurricane & Ins & Joint Interim Legis Comt on State Air Transportation Needs, 69; deleg, La Const Conv; mem, Nat Legis Conf Intergovt Rels Comt, 73. Bus & Prof Pos: Partner, Martin-LeBreton Ins Agency, New Orleans, La, 38-; mem bd dirs, New Orleans Opera House Asn, 58; mem bd dirs & exec comt, Nat Asn of Casualty & Surety Agents, 64; mem bd dirs, Jackson Homestead Asn, 67 & Int House, 68, exec comt, 71 & 72; vpres & mem bd dirs, Adult Educ Ctr, 71-72. Mil Serv: Entered as Coxswain, Navy, 42, released as Chief Boatswain Mate, 45, after serv in N & SAtlantic & Gulf of Mex. Polit & Govt Pos: Legislative committee on economy report on fire & extended coverage insurance of State of Louisiana,

66 & Employee group insurance coverage for State of Louisiana, 67; State of Louisiana joint sex crime study committee report 1960, Nat Soc State Legis Dir, 70; plus one other. Mem: Metaire & New Orleans Country Clubs; Paul Morphy Chess Club; Press Club; New Orleans Lawn Tennis Club. Relig: Roman Catholic. Legal Res: 1420 First St New Orleans LA 70130 Mailing Add: 219 Carondelet St New Orleans LA 70130

LEBRUN, DONALD H (D)
NH State Rep
Mailing Add: 37 Pearl St Claremont NH 03743

LECARDO, FRANK A (D)
Chmn, Stratford Dem Town Comt, Conn
b Bridgeport, Conn, Aug 28, 30; s Angelo T LeCardo & Lorretta M Kiley L; m 1955 to Jeanette Fabrizio; c Frank A, Jr. Educ: Stratford High, Conn, grad, 49. Polit & Govt Pos: Councilman, Second Dist, Stratford, Conn, 65-69; chmn, Stratford Dem Town Comt, 69- Bus & Prof Pos: With John Hancock Ins Co, Bridgeport, Conn, 61- Mil Serv: Entered as A/S, Navy, 49, released as Gunner 3/C, 52, after serv in USS Mercury, Mediter, 50-52; Navy Occup Medal. Mem: Mt Carmel Soc; Stratford Oldtimers. Relig: Catholic. Mailing Add: 101 Academy Hill Terr Stratford CT 06497

LECHNER, IRA MARK (D)
Va State Deleg
b New York, NY, May 4, 34; s Joseph Lechner & Rae Gelfand L; m 1959 to Susan Schwartz; c Jack & Eve. Educ: Randolph-Macon Col, BA, 55; Yale Law Sch, LLB, 58; Phi Beta Kappa; Omicron Delta Kappa; Pi Gamma Mu; Phi Delta Chi; Theta Chi. Polit & Govt Pos: Chmn, Arlington Co Tenant-Landlord Comn, 71-74; Va State Deleg, 74-, chmn, legis sub-comt on Va State Lottery, 74-75. Bus & Prof Pos: Attorney, Nat Labor Rel Bd, 62-64; asst gen coun, Retail Clerks Int Asn, 64-66; partner, Spelman, Lechner & Wagner, 66-71; Pvt Practice, 71-74; partner, Roman, Davenport & Lechner, 74- Mil Serv: Entered as Pvt, Army, 59, released as 1st Lt, 62, after serv in JAG Corps, 60-62; Army Commendation Medal. Mem: Am Bar Asn; Arlington Co Hosp & Nursing Home Comn; B'nai B'rith; Cancer Soc (bd dirs); Dem Forum-Rev (Va correspondent). Honors & Awards: Fairfax Co Police Asn Award, 75. Relig: Jewish. Mailing Add: 2812 N Kensington St Arlington VA 22207

LECHOWICZ, THADDEUS STANLEY (D)
Ill State Rep
b Chicago, Ill, Dec 20, 38; s Frank Lechowicz & Rose Loboda L; m 1964 to Suzanne H Keiler; c Edward John & Laura Ann. Educ: Wright Jr Col, Chicago, Ill, AA, 58; N Park Col, BA, 60; De Paul Univ, 1 year; Delta Sigma Pi; Newman Club; bd dirs, WNPC; Kiwanis; Commerce Club, De Paul Univ. Polit & Govt Pos: 35th ward rep, Young Dem of Cook Co & Ill, 60-68; 35th ward bd dirs, Regular Dem Orgn, Ill, 60-69, 30th ward committeeman, currently; w area chmn, Young Dem of Cook Co, 62-63, Eighth Cong Dist chmn, 66; Cook Co regional dir, Young Dem of Ill, 65-67, second vpres, 68; Ill State Rep, 17th Dist, 69-, mem, Appropriations & Munic Comts, Ill House of Rep, 69- Bus & Prof Pos: Dir data processing, Ill, Toll Hwy Comn, 65, asst dir finance, 66-68; sr syst analyst, Cook Co, 69-; mem bd dirs, Capitol Bank of Chicago. Mil Serv: 1st Lt, Army Res, 68; Outstanding Trainee of the Cycle, Ft Leonard Wood, Mo. Mem: KofC; Holy Name Soc; Amvets; Polish Nat Alliance; Chicago Soc. Honors & Awards: Outstanding Young Dem, State of Ill, 69 & Legislator of the Year, 72. Relig: Catholic. Mailing Add: 5117 W Drummond Place Chicago IL 60639

LECKENBY, WILLIAM (R)
Wash State Rep
Mailing Add: 9105 Fauntleroy Way SW Seattle WA 98136

LECLAIR, CLARENCE GEORGE (D)
Vt State Rep
Mailing Add: 666 Riverside Ave Burlington VT 05401

LECRAW, JULIAN (R)
Mem, Fulton Co Rep Exec Comt, Ga
b Atlanta, Ga, May 21, 30; s Roy LeCraw & Julia Adams L; m 1952 to Joanne Sue DeLany; c Suzanne Alice, Ellen Elaine & Julian, Jr. Educ: Ga Inst Technol, BS in indust mgt, 52; Woodrow Wilson Col of Law, LLB, 58; Chi Phi. Polit & Govt Pos: Alt deleg, Rep Nat Conv, 64; first vchmn, Fulton Co Rep Party, Ga, 64-66, treas, 66-68; finance chmn, Congressman Fletcher Thompson, 68 & 70; mem, Fulton Co Rep Exec Comt, 68- Bus & Prof Pos: Owner, Julian LeCraw & Co. Mil Serv: Entered as Ens, Navy, 52, released as Lt(jg), 55, after serv in Amphibious Forces in Atlantic; Lt, Naval Res, 60-; Korean Serv Medal. Mem: Westminster Sch, Atlanta, Ga (trustee); Presby Col, Clinton, SC (trustee); Capital City Club; Commerce Club; Atlanta Country Club Estates. Relig: Presbyterian; elder, North Ave Presby Church. Mailing Add: 3445 Wood Valley Rd NW Atlanta GA 30327

LECY, RAYMOND OSCAR (R)
Mem, Wood Co Rep Exec Comt, Wis
b Chicago, Ill, June 25, 27; s Curtis M Lecy & Marie Vetrano L; m 1948 to Lorraine Kreuser; c Vicki, Teresa, Joni, Ray, Jr, Gary & Lori. Educ: Wis State Univ, BE, 52; Univ Wis, Madison, MS, 60. Polit & Govt Pos: Young Rep chmn, Wis State Univ, 51; co-chmn, State Young Rep for Taft, 51-52; state treas, Wis Fedn of Young Rep, 51-52, first vchmn, 53-54, publicity dir, 55; secy, Wood Co Rep Party, 54-59, vchmn, 60-66, chmn, 67-68; secy, Seventh Cong Sr Rep Dist, 56-60; Rep precinct committeeman, Grand Rapids, 60-69; mem, Wood Co Rep Exec Comt, 69- Bus & Prof Pos: Prin, Woodside Sch, Wis Rapids, Wis, 60-69; asst prin, West Jr High Sch, 70-71. Mil Serv: Entered as A/S, Navy, 45, released as Yeoman 3/C, 46, after serv at Naval Air Sta, Pac Sta Command, 45-46; Unit Commendation. Mem: Phi Delta Kappa; Wis Educ Asn; Wis Elem Prin Asn; Wood Co Educ Asn; Wis Rapids Prin Asn; Elks. Relig: Catholic. Mailing Add: 3751 Seventh St S Wisconsin Rapids WI 54494

LEDBETTER, CALVIN REVILLE, JR (D)
Ark State Rep
b Little Rock, Ark, Apr 29, 29; s Calvin Reville Ledbetter & Virginia Campbell L; m 1953 to Mary Brown Williams; c Grainger, Jeffrey & Snow. Educ: Princeton Univ, BA, 51; Univ Ark Law Sch, LLB, 54; Northwestern Univ, PhD, 60; Phi Alpha Theta; Blue Key; Phi Delta Theta; Sigma Alpha Epsilon; Student Sen, Univ Ark. Polit & Govt Pos: Chmn, Pulaski Co Community Action Prog, Ark, 65; mem exec comt, Young Dem of Ark, 65-66; Ark State Rep, 67-; deleg, Dem Nat Conv, 68 & 72; mem, Citizens Adv Comt to City Govt, Little Rock, Ark, 69-; mem, Criminal Justice Comt, Coun State Govt, 71-; Southern Regional Growth Policies Bd, 72-; Intergovt Rels Comt, Nat Leadership Conf, 73-; deleg & mem exec comt, Ark Const Conv, 75; mem, Ark Legis Coun; chmn law enforcement & criminal justice task force & mem exec comt, Nat Conf State Legislatures. Bus & Prof Pos: Mem bd trustees, Philander Smith Col, Ark, 63-68; bd dir, Health & Welfare Coun of Pulaski Co, 65-68; mem Ark Adv Coun of Pub Elem & Sec Educ, 69- Mil Serv: Entered as 1st Lt, Army, 55-57, after serv in Judge Adv Gen Corps, Hq US Army Europe, Heidelberg, Germany, 55-57, Capt, Army Res, 57-59. Publ: Co-auth, Politics in Arkansas: the constitutional experience, Acad Press of Ark, 72; auth, Annulment by parents minors above statutory marriage age, fall 53 & Property-recognition of rights in ideas, schemes & plans, spring 54, Ark Law Rev. Mem: Am Acad Polit & Soc Sci; Nat Soc of State Legislators; Ark Acad Sci; Ark Hist Asn; Rotary. Honors & Awards: Educator of the Year, 68. Relig: Presbyterian; Deacon, 63-66; Elder, 69- Mailing Add: 3230 Ozark Little Rock AR 72205

LEDBETTER, JESSE INGRAM (R)
Chmn, 11th Cong Dist Rep Party, NC
b Arden, NC, Dec 22, 22; s Richard Johnson Ledbetter & Etta Maria Ingram L; m 1943 to Sue Marie Ensley; c Patricia (Mrs Tom Haley) & Catherine. Educ: Brevard Col, 39-41; Univ Md, BS, 58. Polit & Govt Pos: Chmn, 11th Cong Dist Rep Party, NC, 68-; cand for US Cong, 72. Bus & Prof Pos: Pres, Ledbetter Realty Co, Asheville, 66-; bd dirs, Asheville Bd Realtors, 73- Mil Serv: Entered as Aviation Cadet, Army Air Force Commendation Medal; Air Medal with Five Oak Leaf Clusters. Mem: Civitan Club; NC Grange, Relig: Methodist. Mailing Add: 63 Imperial Court Asheville NC 28803

LEDBETTER, JOEL YOWELL (D)
Ark State Rep
b Little Rock, Ark, Feb 19, 11; s Calvin Reville Ledbetter & Snow Yowell L; m 1937 to Julia Katharine Bond; c Virginia, Joel, Jr & Julia. Educ: Washington Univ, BSBA, 33; Phi Delta Theta. Polit & Govt Pos: Ark State Rep, 49-, chmn, Legis Coun, Ark House of Rep, 63-65, Majority Leader, 69-70, chmn, Revenue & Taxation Comt, currently. Bus & Prof Pos: Asst mgr, Hewled Mfg Co, 33-35; salesman, Williams & Rosen Ins, 35-46; vpres, Boyle Realty Co, 46- Mil Serv: Entered as 1st Lt, Army Air Force, 40, released as Lt Col, 45, after serv in Air Transport Command, US, India-Burma-China, 41-45; Lt Col (Ret), Air Force Res, 55; Bronze Star, Am, Pac, Asian & ETO Ribbons; Presidential Citation; Chinese Medal of Serv. Mem: Rotary; CofC; Am Legion; VFW. Honors & Awards: Mo Valley Swimming Champion Freestyle Dash, 30-32. Relig: Presbyterian. Legal Res: 4610 Crestwood Dr Little Rock AR 72207 Mailing Add: Boyle Bldg Little Rock AR 72201

LEDDY, ARLO R (D)
SDak State Sen
Mailing Add: Stockholm SD 57264

LEDDY, JOHN M (INDEPENDENT)
b Chicago, Ill, June 29, 14; m to Louise Crawford; c Thomas Byron Crawford. Educ: Georgetown Univ, BS For Serv, 41. Polit & Govt Pos: Mem staff, Pan Am Union, 37-41; econ, financial & social policy adv, State Dept, 41-57; spec asst to Under Secy of State, 57-61; Asst Secy of the Treas for Int Affairs, 61-62; US Ambassador to Orgn for Econ Coop & Develop, Paris, 62-65; Asst Secy of State for European Affairs, 65-69. Mem: Coun Foreign Rels; Atlantic Coun US; Cosmos Club. Honors & Awards: Rockefeller Pub Serv Award, 66. Mailing Add: 1619 Brookside Rd McLean VA 22101

LEDDY, JOHN THOMAS (D)
Treas, Chittendon Co Dem Comt
b Burlington, Vt, Nov 29, 49; s Bernard Joseph Leddy & Johannah M Mahoney L; single. Educ: Univ Vt, BA, 72; Kappa Sigma. Polit & Govt Pos: Mem, Ward 1 Dem Comt, Burlington, Vt, 72-; deleg, Vt Dem State Conv, 72; deleg, Dem Nat Conv, 72; admin asst, Salmon for Gov Comt, Bellows Falls, 72; city alderman, City of Burlington, 73-; mem, City Dem Comt, 73-; mem & treas, Chittendon Co Dem Comt, 73- Bus & Prof Pos: Sales consult, Burlington Copy Ctr, Vt, 72- Honors & Awards: Youngest alderman ever elected in Burlington, Vt. Relig: Catholic. Mailing Add: 195 N Prospect St Burlington VT 05401

LEDERBERG, VICTORIA (D)
RI State Rep
b Providence, RI, July 7, 37; d Frank Santopietro & Victoria Marzilli S; m 1959 to Seymour Lederberg; c Tobias & Sarah. Educ: Pembroke Col, AB, 59; Brown Univ, AM, 61, PhD, 66; Sigma Xi. Polit & Govt Pos: RI State Rep & chmn subcomt on educ, House Finance Comt, 75- Bus & Prof Pos: Assoc prof psychol, RI Col, 68- Publ: Co-auth, Hybridization between bacterial ribosomes, Exp Cell Research, 61; auth, A brief look at biomedical research, Pembroke Alumna, 69 & Perception of colors during voluntary saccadic eye movements, J Optical Soc Am, 70. Mem: New Eng & RI Psychol Asns; Women Educators; New Eng Educ Research Orgn. Honors & Awards: US Pub Health Serv fel physiol psychol, 64-66. Legal Res: 190 Slater Ave Providence RI 02906 Mailing Add: 600 Mt Pleasant Ave Providence RI 02908

LEDERER, RAYMOND F (D)
Pa State Rep
Mailing Add: Capitol Bldg Harrisburg PA 17120

LEDESMA, MARY LOUISE (D)
Dem Nat Committeewoman, Calif
b Huntington Beach, Calif, Jan 24, 33; d Bardomino Contreras & Ponposa Ruiz C; m 1951 to Eliseo Ledesma; c Kristine & Vincent. Educ: ELos Angeles Col, currently. Polit & Govt Pos: Staff mem, 30th Dist Sen Race, 66 & 68; campaign mgr, 23rd Cong Race, 70-71; vol worker, McGovern-Shriver Campaign, 71-72; entertainment chmn, Comt of 1,000 to re-elect US Rep Edward R Roybal, Calif, 72; Dem Nat Committeewoman, Calif, 72-, mem exec comt, Dem Nat Comt, 72-; mem rules & amendments comt, Dem Nat Mid-Term Conf, 74; mem, Comt to Elect Kathy Brown Rice & Comt to Elect Jacinto, Moore & Reiner, 75; mem affirmative action task force, Dem Party Calif, 75; polit coordr sch issues, 75. Bus & Prof Pos: Commun rep, Area-B, Los Angeles Bd Educ, 70-73, adv mem, Multicult Educ, 71-72; self-employed polit consult & pub rels consult, currently. Mem: Dem Chicano Caucus; Hispanic Urban Ctr (adv mem); YWCA (teen chmn, Southeast Area, Los Angeles, 70-); Southeast Mex Am Cult & Educ Asn. Honors & Awards: Outstanding community involvement, Southeast Mex Am Cult & Educ Asn, 71. Relig: Baptist. Mailing Add: 7106-D Hood Ave Huntington Park CA 90255

LEDGIN, NORMAN MICHAEL (D)
Chmn, Johnson Co Dem Cent Comt, Kans
b Passaic, NJ, July 15, 28; s Cy George Ledgin & Ida Samburg L; m 1969 to Marsha M Montague; c Stephanie Paula, David Henry & Allison Grace. Educ: Rutgers Univ, BLit, 50,

MA, 52; Univ Mo-Kansas City, 63-69; Omega Psi Phi. Polit & Govt Pos: Chmn, Johnson Co Dem Cent Comt, Kans, 74- Bus & Prof Pos: Reporter & bus ed, Paterson Morning Call, NJ, 52-56; asst prof jour, McNeese State Col, La, 56-57; mgr, Calcasieu Area Safety Coun, Lake Charles, 57-62; mgr, Gtr Kansas City Area Safety Coun, 62- Publ: Auth, Are we spinning our wheels?, 8/63, What they don't know may kill them, 11/63 & How about a Bill of Rights for the responsible, belted motorist?, 1/74, Traffic Safety Mag, Nat Safety Coun. Mem: Pub Rels Soc Am; Asn Safety Coun Execs; Am Soc Safety Engrs; Nat Safety Coun (bd dirs); Am Civil Liberties Union. Honors & Awards: Outstanding Serv to Safety Award, Safety Engrs Soc Southwest La, 61; Distinguished Serv Award, Jr CofC, Lake Charles, 62; Distinguished Serv to Safety Award, Nat Safety Coun, 74; Award of Honor, Asn Safety Coun Execs, 74. Mailing Add: 6920 W 98th Terr Overland Park KS 66212

LEDMAN, ELDON DALE **(R)**
Chmn Finance Comt, Cass Co Rep Comt, Mich
b Viroqua, Wis, June 17, 12; m 1940 to Jean K Gwilt. Educ: Univ Wis, BA; Delta Kappa Epsilon. Polit & Govt Pos: Chmn, Cass Co Rep Comt, Mich, 67-70 & Cass Co Rep Finance Comt, currently; mem, Mich State Rep Cent Comt, 70-72; alt deleg, Rep Nat Conv, 72. Bus & Prof Pos: Mfg rep. Mem: Elks; Nat 'W' Club. Legal Res: Route 5 Box 262 Dowagiac MI 49047 Mailing Add: PO Box 141 Dowagiac MI 49047

LEE, BILL L **(D)**
NMex State Sen
Mailing Add: Box 1355 Lovington NM 88260

LEE, BLAIR III **(D)**
Lt Gov, Md
b Silver Spring, Md, May 19, 16; s E Brooke Lee & Elizabeth Wilson L; m 1944 to Mathilde Boal; c Blair, IV, Pierre B, Joseph W, Christopher G, Frederick B, Philip L, John F & Jeanne M. Educ: Princeton Univ, AB, 38. Polit & Govt Pos: Deleg, Dem Nat Conv, 48, 60, 64, 68 & 72; Md State Deleg & chmn, Montgomery Co deleg, Md House Deleg, 55-62; campaign mgr for John F Kennedy, Montgomery Co, 60; regional coord Mid-Atlantic States, Johnson-Humphrey, 64; Md State Sen, 67-69; Secy State, Md, 69-71, Lt Gov, 71- Bus & Prof Pos: Ed, Md News, 45-49; pres, Silver Spring Bd Trade, 48-49 & Md Press Asn, 49; vchmn & park comnr, Md-Nat Capital Park & Planning Comn, 49-51, mem, 65-66; private planning & zoning consult, Silver Spring, 54-59; property mgt, 59- Mil Serv: Entered as Ensign, Naval Res, 41, released as Lt Comdr, 45. Relig: Episcopal. Legal Res: 400 Warrenton Dr Silver Spring MD 20904 Mailing Add: State House Annapolis MD 21404

LEE, CATHERINE PATRICIA **(R)**
Polit & Govt Pos: Vchmn, Kent Co Rep Exec Comt, Mich, formerly; alt deleg, Rep Nat Conv, 72. Mailing Add: 2150 Robinson Rd SE East Grand Rapids MI 49506

LEE, EDWARD S **(D)**
b Philadelphia, Pa, May 12, 35; s Edward S Lee & Winona Spencer L; m 1969 to Fay E Jones; c Michael & Eric. Educ: Cheyney State Col, BS in Polit Sci, 68; Univ Pa Fels Inst State Govt, 69-70. Polit & Govt Pos: Clerk of quarter sessions, City of Philadelphia, 72-; deleg, Dem Nat Mid-Term Conf, 74. Mil Serv: Air Force, 52-56. Mem: Cheyney State Col (chmn bd trustees); Pa Gov Justice Comn; Nat Asn Court Adminr (bd mem); Urban League of Philadelphia. Honors & Awards: Outstanding Achievement Award, Inter Urban League of Pa; exec asst to chmn, Second World Conf Arts & Cult; bd dirs, Police Athletic League; bd dirs, Community Serv & Develop Corp. Relig: Baptist; bd of trustees, Canaan Baptist Church. Mailing Add: 6146 Morton St Philadelphia PA 19141

LEE, ELEANOR **(R)**
Wash State Rep
Mailing Add: 1431 SW 152nd Seattle WA 98166

LEE, FERN ELLINGSON **(R)**
NDak State Rep
b Towner, NDak, June 6, 09; d John Ellingson & Bessie Hanson E; m 1928 to Norman Lee; c John H, Dale R & Russell A. Educ: High sch grad, 24; Sigma Delta Chi. Polit & Govt Pos: Secy, Dist Seven, NDak, 46-60, vchmn, 60-66; precinct committeeman, Rep Ward II, Towner, 50-58; NDak State Rep, Dist Seven, 67- Bus & Prof Pos: Ed-mgr, weekly newspaper, 43-65; part-time ed asst & free lance writer, 65-73. Mem: NDak Newspaper Asn; NDak Press Women; Am Legion Auxiliary; Nat Order of Women Legislators; Nat Fedn Press Women; NDak Fedn Rep Women. Honors & Awards: Press Woman of Year, NDak Press Women, 56; Community Betterment Leadership Award, NDak Community Betterment Asn, 66. Relig: Lutheran. Mailing Add: State Capitol Bismarck ND 58501

LEE, FRANK ROBERT **(R)**
b N Andover, Mass, June 4, 32; s Frank R Lee & Marjorie I Glennie L; m 1954 to Jane E Macomber; c F Robert, Richard D, Stephen B, Alan S & David W. Educ: Tufts Col, BS, 58; Johns Hopkins Univ, 59-60. Polit & Govt Pos: Chmn, Arapahoe Co Young Rep, Colo, 61-63; press asst, US Sen Peter H Dominick, Colo, 63-67; exec dir research div, Rep Nat Comt, 64; consult, Nixon for President Comt, 67-68; co chmn, Dominick for Senate Comt, Colo, 68; campaign dir, Armstrong for Lt Gov, 70; mem, Littleton Bd Educ, 71-; admin asst to US Rep William L Armstrong, 73-74. Bus & Prof Pos: Partner, Lee-Hannah & Assocs, 74- Mil Serv: Entered as Recruit, Navy, 51, released as PO 3/C, 55. Relig: Protestant. Mailing Add: 2 Meadowbrook Place Littleton CO 80120

LEE, GARY A **(R)**
NY State Assemblyman
Mailing Add: 940 Dryden Rd Ithaca NY 14850

LEE, H REX **(D)**
b Rigby, Idaho, Apr 8, 10; s Hyrum Lee & Eliza Farnsworth L; m 1937 to Lillian Carlson; c Lillian Sherry, Dixie Joanne (Mrs Born), Linda Louise (Mrs Irvine), Duane Rex & Mark Carlson. Educ: Univ Idaho, BS in Agr Econ, 36. Hon Degrees: LLD, Univ Idaho, 64. Polit & Govt Pos: Economist, Dept of Agr, Moscow, Idaho, 36-37; exten agent, Univ Idaho, 37-38; economist, Bur of Agr Econ, Dept of Agr, Berkeley, Calif, 38-42; asst to dir & chief, Relocation Div & Evacuee Property Div, War Relocation Authority, Washington, DC, 42-46; asst dir, Off of Territories, Dept of Interior, 46-50, assoc & dept comnr, Bur of Indian Affairs, 50-61; Gov, Am Samoa, 61-67; asst admin, Agency Int Develop, 67-68; Comnr, Fed Commun Comn, 68-74. Bus & Prof Pos: Distinguished visiting lectr, San Diego State Univ, 74-75; chmn bd dirs, Pub Serv Satellite Consortium, 75. Mailing Add: 4900 Rose Hedge Manor La Mesa CA 92041

LEE, HOWARD NATHANIEL **(D)**
Mem, Dem Nat Comt, NC
b Lithonia, Ga, July 28, 34; s Howard Lee & Lou Tempie L; m to Lillian Wesley; c Angela, Ricky & Karin Alexis Lou Tempie. Educ: Ft Valley State Col, grad in sociol & social work, with honors, 59; Grad Sch Social Work, Univ NC, Chapel Hill, MSW, 66. Hon Degrees: LLD, Shaw Univ. Polit & Govt Pos: Mayor, Chapel Hill, NC, 69-; vchmn, NC Dem Party, 70-72; mem, Dem Nat Comt, currently; bd trustees, Wake Forest Univ, currently; deleg, Dem Nat Conv, 72. Bus & Prof Pos: Officer, Juvenile Domestic Rels Court, Savannah, Ga, three years; dir youth serv, Duke Univ, 66-68, dir employee rels, 68-69, dir, Off Human Develop, 69; asst prof sociol, NC Cent Univ, 68-69. Mil Serv: Army, 59-61; Korea, one year. Publ: Many articles on several subjects. Mem: Nat Asn Soc Workers; NC Heart Asn; NC Advan Sch. Relig: Baptist; Former deacon, Binkley Baptist Church, Chapel Hill. Legal Res: 504 Tinkerbell Rd Chapel Hill NC 27514 Mailing Add: Municipal Bldg Chapel Hill NC 27514

LEE, JACKSON FREDRICK **(R)**
Mayor, Fayetteville, NC
b Fremont, Nebr, Apr 8, 20; s Earl Jackson Lee & Rebecca Pierce L; m 1941 to Virginia Ann White; c Jackson Fredrick, Jr (Jeff), W Thomas, David Stewart & Virginia Ann. Educ: Midland Col; Univ Nebr, BS Bus Admin; Officers Cand Sch, Air Force; Phi Delta Theta. Polit & Govt Pos: Appointee, Land Policy Coun NC; mem, Nat Adv Coun on Equality of Educ Opportunity; mayor, Fayetteville, NC, 71- Bus & Prof Pos: Vpres & mgr, Radio Sta WILM, Wilmington, Del, 46-60; owner & gen mgr, Radio Sta WFAI, Fayetteville, NC, 60-71; vpres, Murchison & Bailey, Inc, Advert Agency, 71. Mil Serv: Capt, Army Air Corps, 43-46; Col(Ret), Air Force Res, 74. Mem: Mason (32 degree); Fayetteville CofC; Air Force Asn; Asn of US Army. Relig: Presbyterian. Legal Res: 114 Hale St Fayetteville NC 28301 Mailing Add: 234 Green St Fayetteville NC 28302

LEE, JAMES G **(D)**
Ala State Rep
Mailing Add: 19 Crestline Dr Tuscaloosa AL 35401

LEE, JOSEPH BRACKEN **(INDEPENDENT)**
b Price, Utah, Jan 7, 99; s Arthur J Lee & Ida May Leiter L; m 1928 to Margaret Draper; c Helen Virginia, James Bracken, Margaret Jon & Richard Lewis. Educ: High Sch grad. Polit & Govt Pos: Mayor, Price, Utah, 36-47; Gov of Utah, 49-57; Mayor, Salt Lake City, 59-72. Mil Serv: Entered as Sgt, Army, 17, released as 2nd Lt, 19; Officer, Reserve Corps, 19-29. Mem: Charter mem, Elks; Mason, Shrine (33 degree); Utah Munic League. Honors & Awards: Class B Trapshooting Title in State Amateur Trapshooting Asn single matches, 50; Tom McCoy Award for outstanding munic officer, Utah Munic League, 67. Mailing Add: 2031 Laird Dr Salt Lake City UT 84108

LEE, KENNETH B **(R)**
b Nauvoo, Pa, Jan 23, 22; s Edward Lee & Evelyn Evans L; m to Marjorie Cole; c Susanne, Scott, Cole, Laura & Kenneth. Polit & Govt Pos: Pa State Rep, 56-74, majority leader, Pa House of Rep, 63-65, minority leader, 65-74; alt deleg, Rep Nat Conv, 68, deleg, 72. Bus & Prof Pos: Attorney, Dushore, Pa; bd dirs, 1st Nat Bank of Dushore, Muncy Valley Hosp. Mailing Add: 1 Lakewood Ave Eagles Mere PA 17731

LEE, KENNETH K L **(D)**
Hawaii State Rep
b Honolulu, Hawaii, Mar 13, 27; m to Peggy Y M; c Marion K Y, Sandra K O, Kenyon H T, Kendall H C & Debra. Educ: Univ Hawaii, BBA; Pi Sigma Epsilon. Polit & Govt Pos: Hawaii State Rep, 68- Bus & Prof Pos: Insurance agt & acct. Mil Serv: Entered as Pvt, Army, 45, released as Sgt, 47. Relig: Protestant. Legal Res: 516-B Hiram Lane Honolulu HI 96817 Mailing Add: House of Reps State Capitol Honolulu HI 96813

LEE, LAWRENCE J **(D)**
Mo State Sen
b St Louis, Mo, Nov 4, 32; s Patrick W Lee & Ruth Rose Allaway L; m 1956 to Joan Margaret Steube; c Daniel, Karen, Lawrence, Jr, Mark & Joan. Educ: St Louis Univ Sch of Com & Finance, BSC, 54, Sch Law, LLB, 56. Polit & Govt Pos: Prosecuting attorney, St Louis, Mo, 64-66; Mo State Sen, Third Dist, 66- Bus & Prof Pos: Practicing attorney, 56- Mem: Bar Asn Metrop St Louis; Mo & Am Bar Asns; Lawyers Asn. Honors & Awards: Meritorious Pub Serv Award, St Louis Globe Dem, 68 & 74. Relig: Catholic. Legal Res: 9 Arundel Pl St Louis MO 63105 Mailing Add: 506 Olive St St Louis MO 63101

LEE, LENA KING **(D)**
Md State Deleg
b Creighton, Pa, July 14, 11; d Samuel S King & Lula Gully K; wid. Educ: Morgan State Col, BS, 39; NY Univ, MA, 47; Univ Md, JD, 51; Lambda Kappa Mu; Sigma Gamma Rho. Polit & Govt Pos: Mem, Mayor's Redevelop Comn, 55; mem, Mayor's Mfrs Tax Comt, 56; mem, Urban Renewal & Housing Comn, 56-62; pres, Womens Dem Auxiliary, Inc, 58-; mem, Adv Coun on Higher Educ, 64; mem, Mayor's Adv Comt on Housing & Zoning, 65; Md State Deleg, 66- Bus & Prof Pos: Teacher, Baltimore City Schs, 31-38, adminr & prin, 38-64; lawyer, 52-; owner & mgr, Biddle Theater, 59- Publ: Newspaper articles. Mem: Women's Bar Asn of Md; Eastern Star; Md League of Women's Clubs (pres); Independent Order of Elks; Bus & Prof Womens Club. Honors & Awards: Founder, Herbert M Frisby Hist Soc; Sojourner Truth Award, Cheney Alumni; Leslie Pinckney Hill Award; Woman of Year, Ladies Dem Guild; Woman of Year, Zeta Pi Beta; Tau Gamma Delta Award; Md League of Women's Clubs Award. Relig: Methodist. Mailing Add: 1818 Madison Ave Baltimore MD 21217

LEE, LILLIE MAE **(D)**
b Fayette, Miss, Apr 28, 53; d Cora B Harris; single. Educ: Alcorn State Univ, BS, 74. Polit & Govt Pos: Mem, Fayette Planning Comn, 71-74; alt deleg, Dem Nat Conv, 72; mem, Munic Dem Exec Comt, 73-; city elec comnr, Dist III, 73-; secy, Jefferson Co Jury Comn, 75- Relig: Baptist. Mailing Add: PO Box 321 Fayette MS 39069

LEE, REX E
Asst Attorney Gen, Civil Div, Dept of Justice
b Los Angeles, Calif, Feb 27, 35; s Rex E Lee & Mabel Whiting L; m 1959 to Janet Griffin; c Diana, Thomas Rex, Wendy, Michael & Stephanie. Educ: Brigham Young Univ, BA, 60; Univ Chicago, JD, 63. Polit & Govt Pos: Law clerk, Justice Byron R White, US Supreme Court, 63-64; Asst Attorney Gen, Civil Div, Dept of Justice, 75- Bus & Prof Pos: Attorney, Jennings, Strouss & Salmon, 64-73, partner, 67-72; founding dean, J Reuben Clark Law Sch, Brigham Young Univ, 72-; lectr, Am Inst Foreign Trade, 66-68 & Univ Ariz Sch Law, 68-72. Mem: Young Mens Mutual Improv Asn (gen bd); Boy Scouts (bd dirs, Theodore Roosevelt

Coun); Rotary. Relig: Latter-day Saint. Legal Res: 1371 Cherry Lane Provo UT 84601 Mailing Add: Dept of Justice Washington DC 20530

LEE, ROBERT E (BOB) **(D)**
Mont State Sen
Mailing Add: 1945 Florida Butte MT 59701

LEE, ROBERT EMMET **(R)**
Comnr, Fed Commun Comn
b Chicago, Ill, Mar 31, 12; s Patrick J Lee & Delia Ryan L; m 1936 to Wilma Rector; wid; c Robert E, Michael B & Patricia (Mrs Martin Fisher). Educ: De Paul Univ Col of Commerce & Law. Hon Degrees: LLD, St John's Univ. Polit & Govt Pos: Spec agent, Fed Bur Invest, 38-53; staff dir, Appropriations Comt, US House of Rep, 46-53; comnr, Fed Commun Comn, 53-, chmn, Comt for Full Develop of All-Channel Broadcasting & Comt for Full Develop of Instructional TV Fixed Serv, vchmn, FCC, alt to chmn Dean Burch as FCC Space Comnr, FCC mem, Radio Tech Comn for Aeronaut, FCC Rep, Interagency Group on Int Aviation, mem, FCC Telephone & Telegraph Comt, vchmn, World Admin Radio Conf for Space Telecommun & 1973 Plenipotentiary Conf, chmn, Interconnection Adv Comts, chmn, US Deleg, World Admin Telephone & Telegraph Conf, currently. Mem: Inst Elec & Electronics Engrs; Capital Hill Club; Cong Country Club; Bolling Air Force Base Officers Club. Relig: Roman Catholic. Mailing Add: 3147 Westover Dr SE Washington DC 20020

LEE, RONALD BARRY **(D)**
b New York, NY, May 26, 32; s Kermit James Lee & Lillian Bryant Jackson L; m 1960 to Joyce Juanita Thomas; c Dean Eric; stepson, Gregory Carter Anderson. Educ: Springfield Col, 49-50; US Mil Acad, BS, 54; Univ Md, Sukiran, Okinawa, 57-59; Defense Lang Inst, Monterey, Calif, Vietnamese, grad with distinction, 62; Syracuse Univ, MBA, 64; Am Univ, PhD, 75; Beta Gamma Sigma; Alpha Phi Alpha. Hon Degrees: LLD, Western New Eng Col, 69. Polit & Govt Pos: White House Fel, White House & Post Off Dept, 65-66; dir, Planning & Systs Anal, US Post Off Dept, 66-68, Asst Postmaster Gen, 69-72. Bus & Prof Pos: Prof, Asst Provost, Dir, Cent for Urban Affairs & Dir, Equal Opportunity Progs, Mich State Univ, 68-69; dir mkt anal, Xerox Corp, 72-; NE region mgr tech servs, Xerox Corp; app to Police Comn, Weston, Conn. Mil Serv: Entered as 2nd Lt, Army, 54, released as Maj, 67, after serv in Signal Corps, Armored & Inf Units throughout World including Adv Duty in Vietnam, 62-63; Maj, Army Res, 67-; Nat Defense Serv Medal with Oak Leaf Cluster; AEF Medal; Army Commendation Medal with Oak Leaf Cluster; Vietnam Campaign Medal; Parachutist Badge. Publ: Know ye what ye judge: realities of the postal service, Defense Mgt J, summer 70; Bees in the mail, Am Honey Producer, 9/70; Planning & the management information system, (w Jonathon Cunite), 9/70; plus ten others. Mem: White House Fels Asn (past pres); Am Acad of Polit & Soc Sci; fel, Nat Acad of Pub Admin; Western New Eng Col (bd trustees, 69-); Nat Acad Pub Admin. Honors & Awards: Arthur Flemming Award as one of the ten most outstanding young men in the fed serv, 67; Outstanding Civilian Serv Medal, Dept of the Army, 68. Relig: Protestant. Mailing Add: 15 High Meadow Rd Weston CT 06880

LEE, SHIRLEY WILLIAMS **(R)**
NDak State Sen
b Bismarck, NDak, Jan 8, 24; d John E Williams & Maude Edgerton W; m 1942 to Warren T Lee, DDS; c Suzan (Mrs John Fibelstad), John W, Judy (Mrs Leon Guenthner) & Steven. Educ: St Olaf Col, 41-43. Polit & Govt Pos: Vchmn, Burleigh Co Young Rep, NDak, 58-60; secy, Burleigh Co Rep Comt, 60-62; chmn, Burleigh Co Rep Orgn, 62-64; chmn, NDak State Rep Orgn, 64-66; vchairwoman, NDak State Rep Comt, 66-68; NDak State Sen, Dist 8, 73- Mem: Turtle Lake Study Club (pres); Mercer-McLenn Regional Libr (trustee); Turtle Lake Community Chest (bd mem); PEO; DAR. Relig: Lutheran. Mailing Add: Box I Turtle Lake ND 58575

LEE, SIDNEY PHILLIP **(D)**
Dem Nat Committeeman, VI
b Philadelphia, Pa, Apr 20, 20; s Samuel Lee & Mollie Heller L; div; c Sidney, Jr & Candy. Educ: Univ Pa, BS, 39; Cornell Univ, MS, 40, McMullin fel, 50; Tau Beta Pi; Sigma Tau Epsilon; Sigma Xi; Phi Epsilon Pi. Polit & Govt Pos: Elec judge, Dallas Co, Tex, 46-50; deleg, Dem Nat Conv, 60, 64, 68 & 72; vchmn, Gov Comn Zoning, 64-68; mem, VI Dem Exec Comt, 64-, exec vpres, 69-71; mem, State Bd Educ, VI, 68-; Dem Nat Committeeman, VI, 70-; vchmn, Comn Voc & Tech Educ, 69-; deleg, VI Const Conv, 71-73. Bus & Prof Pos: Prin chem engr, Atlantic Richfield Corp, Philadelphia, Pa, 39-41; sr chem engr, Atlantic Richfield Corp, Dallas, 41-44; dir & chmn, Assoc Dallas Labs, 44-; pres, W I Invest Co, VI, 57-; chmn exec comt, W I Bank & Trust Co, VI, 56-; mem bd & exec comt, Am Ship Bldg Co, Cleveland, 60-65. Publ: Present values of future dollars, Bookman, 46; Economics of cumene, Am Chem Soc, 47. Mem: Fel Am Inst Chem; sr mem, Am Inst Petroleum & Mining Eng; Am Pub Health Asn; Rotary (pres, St Croix, 72-73); Jr CofC. Honors & Awards: One of Ten Outstanding Young Men of US, Jaycees, 49; Ben Bayne Trophy, VI Bridge Asn, 72; Westinghouse Sci Award, Westinghouse Co. Mailing Add: Box 130 Christiansted St Croix VI 00820

LEE, THEODORE ROBERT (TED) **(R)**
VChmn, Albany Co Rep Cent Comt, Wyo
b Hilliard, Fla, Aug 29, 23; s Elmer E Lee & Carrie Franston L; m 1948 to Jacquelyn Anderson; c Wayne, Greg, Scott & Mark. Educ: Univ Wyo, grad, 64. Polit & Govt Pos: Rep precinct capt, Wyo, 55-67; vchmn, Albany Co Rep Cent Comt, 67-, chmn, Mission 70's; alt deleg, Rep Nat Conv, 68; coord, Wyo State Work Release Prog, Casper, 72- Bus & Prof Pos: Hwy patrolman, Wyo, 55-59, probation & parole officer, 59- Mil Serv: Entered as Pvt, Army, 45, released as Sgt, 47, after serv as paratrooper, 82nd Airborne Div, Germany, ETO; Army Res, 47-50; Paratrooper Wings; ETO Ribbon; Good Conduct Ribbon. Publ: Conditional release procedures, 66 & Work release rehabilitation in Wyoming State Penitentiary, 1/73, Wyo Law Enforcement Mag; Work release in Wyoming, Casper Star Tribune, 4/72. Mem: Wyo Law Enforcement & Peace Officer's Asn; Probation, Parole & Corrections Asn; Mason (Deacon, Lodge No 3, Laramie, Wyo); Toastmaster's Club (past area gov, Laramie, Wyo, pres, Casper Club 97, 72-73); Odd Fellows. Honors & Awards: Mem, Honor Guard for Gen Dwight D Eisenhower, Frankfurt, Germany, 46; Able Toastmaster's Award, Toastmaster's Int, 72. Relig: United Methodist. Mailing Add: 745 W 14th St Casper WY 82601

LEE, TOM **(R)**
NMex State Sen
b China Spring, Gallup, NMex, Feb 14, 20; s Tom Lee & Mary Brown L; m 1947 to Emma Rose Casuse; c Sylvia Ann, Willa-Ann (deceased), Clarence Claude, Randolph Juan, Cherie Ophelia, Wendell Winright & Erecka Elvina. Educ: Tohatchi Boarding Sch, NMex, 8 years. Polit & Govt Pos: Community leader, Navajo Land, NMex, currently; mem sch bd, Bur Indian Affairs Indian Sch, 60-66; NMex State Sen, Dist 3, McKinley Co, 66- Bus & Prof Pos: Owner & operator, Twin Lakes Trading Post, NMex, 52- Mil Serv: Entered as Pvt, Army, 41, released as Cpl, 46, after serv in 200th & 515th Coast Artil Antiaircraft, Am ex-prisoner of War, Japan, 42-45; Am Defense Medal with One Bronze Serv Star; Asiatic Pac Theater Medal with One Bronze Serv Star; Philippine Defense Ribbon with One Bronze Serv Star; Good Conduct Medal; Distinguished Unit Badge with Two Oak Leaf Clusters; Victory Medal; Philippine Liberation Ribbon. Mem: VFW; NMex Cattle Grower's Asn; Bataan Vet Orgn; Am Defenders of Bataan & Corregidor, Inc. Relig: Pentecostal Full Gospel. Mailing Add: Twin Lakes Trading Post Gallup NM 87301

LEE, WILLIAM J (BILL) **(D)**
Ga State Rep
b Forest Park, Ga, Dec 15, 25; s Colie Rufus Lee & Velma Haynie L; m 1949 to Mary Mathews; c Rex & Trixie. Educ: Atlanta Law Sch, LLB, 60. Polit & Govt Pos: Ga State Rep, 57- Bus & Prof Pos: Southern Rwy Co, 42- Mil Serv: Navy, 44-46. Mem: Kiwanis; Mason; CofC. Relig: Baptist. Mailing Add: 5325 Hillside Dr Forest Park GA 30050

LEE, WILLIAM SPENCER **(D)**
b Angelus, SC, July 8, 15; s John Emsley Lee & Mayme McDaniel L; m 1940 to Willie Bess Gassett; wid; c William Spencer, IV, Rebecca & David Carl. Educ: Mid Ga Jr Col, 34; Univ Ga, LLB, 38; Phi Delta Theta. Polit & Govt Pos: Spec agt, Fed Bur of Invest, 41-56; Chief of Police, 56-58; Ga State Rep, 63-74; vchmn, Ga Organized Crime Prevention Coun, currently; deleg, Dem Nat Mid-Term Conf, 74. Bus & Prof Pos: Attorney-at-law, Ft Valley, 38-42; attorney-at-law, Albany, Ga, 58- Mem: Am & Ga Bar Asns; Am Judicature Soc; Elks; Kiwanis. Relig: Baptist; Deacons Adv Bd, 63. Legal Res: 1215 Baker Ave Albany GA 31705 Mailing Add: 1140B Dawson Rd Albany GA 31707

LEE, WILLIAM SWAIN **(R)**
Chmn, Sussex Co Rep Exec Comt, Del
b Philadelphia, Pa, Dec 18, 35; s Walter Hutchison Lee & Virginia Swain L; m 1965 to Mary Louise McGrew; c Mary Caroline, William Swain, Jr & Virginia Hutchison. Educ: Duke Univ, AB, 57; Univ Pa, LLB, 60; Sigma Nu; Hare Law Club. Polit & Govt Pos: Dep attorney gen, Del, 65-70; chmn, Sussex Co Bd Adjust, 69-70; counsel, Sussex Co Rep Comt, 69-72; chmn, Sussex Co Rep Conv deleg, 70-; gen counsel, Del Rep State Comt, 70-73; mem, Del State Tax Appeal Bd, 70-72 & Sussex Co Rep Adv Comt, 70-; solicitor, Sussex Co Coun, 71-72; mem, Rep State Comt, 73-; chmn, Sussex Co Rep Exec Comt, currently. Bus & Prof Pos: Attorney, David P Buckson, Esq, Dover, Del, 64-65; partner, Betts & Lee, Georgetown, 69- Mil Serv: Entered as Pvt, Marine Corps, 61, released as 1st Lt, 64; Capt, Marine Res, 71. Mem: Del State, Sussex Co & Am Bar Asns; Am Judicature Soc. Relig: Methodist; trustee, Epworth Methodist Church, Rehoboth Beach, dir, Old Union Church Soc. Legal Res: 12 Park Ave Rehoboth Beach DE 19971 Mailing Add: 15 S Race St Georgetown DE 19947

LEEDS, ISABELLE R **(D)**
b New York, NY, Dec 6, 26; d Louis Russek & Rose Bauman R; m 1947 to Marshall P Leeds, div; c David Russek & Amy Beth. Educ: Wellesley Col, BA, 47. Polit & Govt Pos: Spec asst to US Sen Claiborne Pell, RI, 61-72; mem, RI Adv Comt to US Civil Rights Comn, 62-72; alt deleg, Dem Nat Conv, 64, deleg, 68 & 72; chmn, Dem Representative Dist Comt, 66-68; committeewoman, RI Dem State Comt, 68-70; Dem Nat Committeewoman, RI, 69-72; spec asst to Gov Hugh L Carey for Int & UN Affairs, 75- Relig: Jewish. Mailing Add: 485 Park Ave New York NY 10022

LEEDY, DICK **(R)**
Wyo State Rep
Mailing Add: 214 Masonic Temple Bldg Riverton WY 82501

LEENEY, PHILIP J **(D)**
Conn State Rep
Mailing Add: 271 Grovers Ave Bridgeport CT 06605

LEFANTE, JOSEPH A **(D)**
NJ State Assemblyman
Mailing Add: State House Trenton NJ 08625

LEFEBVRE, ROLAND J **(D)**
NH State Rep
Mailing Add: 19 Dane St Nashua NH 03060

LEFEVER, ROSE ISABEL **(R)**
VChmn, Ulster Co Rep Comt, NY
b Walton, NY, Aug 22, 23; d Cecil Edward Feltman & Mary Cordelia Budine F; m 1941 to Raymond Freer LeFever; c Mary Jane (Mrs John Thomas Welsek), Frederick Spencer; two grandchildren. Educ: Walton High Sch, grad, 41. Polit & Govt Pos: Sch tax collector, Creek Locks Dist, NY, 50-58; corresponding secy, Ulster Co Women's Rep Club, 57-58, first vpres, 59, pres, 59-61; vchmn, Ulster Co Rep Comt, 60-, receptionist, 69; dir, Third Judicial Dist, NY State Fedn of Rep Women, 61-62, treas, 64-65; Ulster Co rep, NY State Citizens Info Serv, 70- Bus & Prof Pos: Dept mgr, J J Newberry, 44; owner & mgr, Volocta Farm Gift Shoppe, 49-55; real estate salesman, Caunitz Realty, 70- Mem: 4-H (leader, Ulster Co Asn, 55-58, judge for dress rev, 60-69); NY State Fedn of Rep Women; Hist Asn; Nat Fedn of Rep Women; Boy Scouts (Rip Van Winkle Coun). Relig: Protestant. Mailing Add: Box 115 Bloomington NY 12411

LEFEVRE, CLIFFORD S **(D)**
Utah State Rep
Mailing Add: 482 Vine St Clearfield UT 84015

LEFKO, TODD JEFFERY **(DFL)**
b Flint, Mich, Nov 6, 40; s Oscar Myron Patrick Lefko & Sylvia Gorkin L; m to Margaret Elizabeth Geier; c Stefana. Educ: Univ Minn, BA, 63, MA in Pub Admin, 67; Alpha Epsilon Pi. Polit & Govt Pos: Deleg, Dem Nat Mid-Term Conf, 74; mem, Metropolitan Coun Twin Cities. Bus & Prof Pos: Instr, Univ Minn, 72- Publ: Citizen participation-myth of reality, Northwest Architect, 73; Community councils, Common Ground, winter 75. Mem: Am Dem Action (nat bd dirs); Asn St Paul Communities; Citizens League. Honors & Awards: US Dept of Housing & Urban Develop fels, 67; Wall Street Jour Scholar Award, 68; Bush Leadership fel, 73. Relig: Jewish. Mailing Add: 1528 Grantham St Paul MN 55108

LEFKOWITZ, LOUIS J (R)
State Attorney Gen, NY
b New York, NY, July 3, 04; m to Helen Schwimmer; c Joan (Mrs Harold Feinbloom) & Stephen; two grandchildren. Educ: Fordham Univ Sch of Law, LLB, 25. Hon Degrees: LLD, Yeshiva Univ, 67 & Syracuse Univ, 70. Polit & Govt Pos: Chmn, Law Comt, NY Rep Co Comt, NY; counsel, NY Rep State Comt; research counsel to Speaker of NY State Assembly; deleg, NY State Rep Conv; NY State Assemblyman, 28-30; judge, Munic Court of New York, 35; dep tax comnr, 43-44; counsel, Joint Legis Comt on Elec Laws, 53-54; justice, City Court of NY, 54; deleg, Rep Nat Conv, 56, 60, 64 & 68; State Attorney Gen, NY, 57- Bus & Prof Pos: Lawyer. Mem: City of Hope Nat Med Ctr (campaign chmn); KofP; B'nai B'rith; Fed Bar Asn; Salvation Army Asn. Legal Res: Bldg 2 2 World Trade Bldg New York NY 10047 Mailing Add: c/o State Capitol Albany NY 12224

LEFLORE, JOHN LUZINE (D)
Ala State Rep
b Mobile, Ala, May 17, 07; s Dock R LeFlore & Clara Barber L; m 1926 to Teah Jessie Beck; c John L, Jr, Ruth Yvonne (Mrs Horace T Ward), Walker B & Eleanor Clarice (Mrs Townsend). Educ: Ala State Jr Col Br, Mobile; Univ Chicago Exten Classes. Polit & Govt Pos: Clerk-carrier, US Postal Serv, 26-65; comnr, Mobile Housing Bd, Ala, 65-70; dir, Mobile Comt for Support of Pub Educ, 71-; bd mem, Ala Coun for Comprehensive Health Planning, currently; mem, Ala State Adv Comt to US Comn on Civil Rights, currently; Ala State Rep, 74- Bus & Prof Pos: Staff correspondent, Chicago Defender, 42-52; assoc ed, Mobile Beacon, currently. Publ: Auth, The South today, Crisis Mag, 38. Mem: AF&AM; Mobile United; Salvation Army Bd; Non-Partisan Voters League (dir case work); NAACP. Honors & Awards: NAACP Nat & Regional Awards, 41 & 53; Citation, Chicago Defender, 46. Legal Res: 1504 Chatague Ave Mobile AL 36603 Mailing Add: PO Box 1091 Mobile AL 36601

LEFTWICH, WILLIE LORENZO (R)
b Washington, DC, June 28, 37; s Willie Lorenzo Leftwich & Maude Ida Wilkins L; m to Paula Grace Phillips. Educ: Howard Univ, BS Elec Eng, 60; Univ Mich, Ann Arbor, 65; George Washington Univ Sch Law, JD, 67, LLM, 72; Univ Va, Army Advocate Gen Sch, 68. Polit & Govt Pos: Coord, Nevius Campaign, 70; mem & former asst gen coun, DC Rep Comt; deleg, Rep Nat Conv, 72; chmn, DC Comt for Reelec of the President, counsel, 72; comnr, DC Human Rels Comn, 72-74; mem bd dirs, Pennsylvania Ave Develop Corp; mem com tech adv bd, US Dept Com; vchmn bd dirs, DC Redevelop Land Agency, 72-; mem, Judicial Nomination Comn, 75- Bus & Prof Pos: Engr, NASA, 60, Navy-Marines, 63-66 & Dept of Navy, 66-68; patent attorney, Fed Aviation Admin, Dept of Transportation, 68; vpres & corp coun, Tech Media Systs, 68-70; owner/counsel, Urbanetics, Inc, 69-71; attorney-at-law, Hudson & Leftwich, 70-; prof clin law, George Washington Univ Sch of Law, 71-72, prof lectr, 72. Mil Serv: Entered as 2nd Lt, Army Ord Corps, 60, released as 1st Lt, 62, after serv in 1st Cavalry Div, Korea. Publ: Many legal & technical papers. Mem: Bar of Supreme Court; Am Bar Asn (pub contracts sect); Ripon Soc (nat bd dirs); Nat Asn of Patent Lawyers (trustee & founder); DC Inst Ment Hygiene (dir). Relig: Baptist. Mailing Add: 1732 Shepherd St NW Washington DC 20011

LEGATES, RICHARD BOLTON (D)
Del State Rep
b West Cape May, NJ, June 25, 42; s Rutherford Baker LeGates & Esther Hand Woolson L; m 1964 to Leigh Dorothy Mathis; c Richard Bryan & Ronald Bolton. Educ: Cape May High Sch, grad, 60. Polit & Govt Pos: Del State Rep, 24th Dist, 75-, mem, Labor & Commerce Comt, Del House Rep, 75-, mem, Community Affairs Comt, 75-, chmn, Environmental Control Comt, 75- Bus & Prof Pos: Off worker, Chrysler Corp, Newark, Del, 65- Mil Serv: Entered as Pvt, Marine Corps, 61, released as Cpl, 65, after serv in Second Marines, Second Marine Div, 61-65; Good Conduct Medal; Expert Pistol Medal; Marksman Rifle Medal. Mem: United Auto Workers Union; New Castle Co Parks & Recreation Adv Bd; Coalition for Natural Stream Valleys Inc; Chryco Newark Fed Credit Union; Del Wildlife Fedn. Mailing Add: 13 Merion Rd Chestnut Hill Estates Newark DE 19713

LEGEL, JACK EUGENE (D)
Mich State Rep
b Detroit, Mich, Aug 6, 36; s Walter Raymond Legel & Gertrude Krystek L; m 1957 to Marianne LaVier; c Carolyn, Timothy, Michael & Christine. Educ: Univ Detroit, BBA, 66; Blue Key; Alpha Kappa Psi. Polit & Govt Pos: Exec bd mem, 17th Dist Dem Party, 62-70; Dem precinct deleg, Detroit, 62-74; vchmn, 17th Cong Dist Dem Party, Detroit, 70-74; comnr, Bd Canvassers, Detroit, 74-; Mich State Rep, 75- Bus & Prof Pos: Data processing acct coordr, Fisher Body Div, Gen Motors, Livonia, Mich, 59-68, cost estimator, Warren, Mich, 68-74. Mem: Redford Civilian Radio Patrol; Crary Community Coun; St Mary's of Redford Parish Coun; St Mary's of Redford Parish Dad's Club. Honors & Awards: Dean's Award for Distinguished & Exceptional Performance, Univ Detroit, 66; Distinguished Serv Award, Alpha Kappa Psi, 66. Relig: Catholic. Mailing Add: 15329 Gilchrist Detroit MI 48227

LEGER, RAY (D)
NMex State Sen
b San Miguel Co, NMex, Jan 6, 25; s Francisco Leger & Isabel Lopez L; m 1948 to Mela Lucero; c Howard, Randolph, Steven, Nicolas, Martin, Teresa & Annette. Educ: NMex Highlands Univ, BA & MA; Pi Gamma Mu; Alpha Zeta (Iota chap). Polit & Govt Pos: Deleg, NMex Const Conv, 69; NMex State Sen, 73- Bus & Prof Pos: Supt schs, W Las Vegas Schs, Las Vegas, NMex, 63- Mil Serv: Army Chem Corps. Mem: Nat Educ Asn NMex; Elks; VFW. Legal Res: Porter St Las Vegas NM 87701 Mailing Add: Box 1866 Las Vegas NM 87701

LEGG, LOUIS E JR (R)
b Coldwater, Mich, Jan 21, 28; s Louis E Legg & Dorothy A Wood L; m 1953 to Joan Mary Touhy Donkin; c Louis, III & Thomas Charles. Educ: Mich State Univ, BS, 50; Blue Key; Pi Kappa Delta; Beta Theta Pi; Excalibur. Polit & Govt Pos: Chmn, Meridian Twp Rep Comt, Mich, 60-62; chmn, Ingham Co Rep Comt, 62-65; deleg, Rep Nat Conv, 64; chmn, Sixth Cong Dist Rep Comt, Mich, 64-68; mem, Mich State Bldg Comn, 67-, chmn, 70- Bus & Prof Pos: Home builder, Battle Creek, Mich, 50-52; pres, Lansing Lumber Co, 52-, Pageant Homes, Inc, 56-, Home Assistance Corp, & Marion Lumber & Supply, Inc, 69-; dir, Bank of Lansing, Mich, 68-; chmn, Manufactured Homes, Inc, Marshall, 70- Mil Serv: Entered as 2nd Lt, Army Res, 50, released as Capt, 60. Mem: Nat Retail Lumber Dealers Asn; Contractors & Suppliers Asn (vpres); CofC (dir, Gtr Lansing Chap & pres, 69-); YMCA (vpres Lansing Chap & pres, 68, dir, Parkwood Chap); City Club of Lansing. Relig: Protestant. Mailing Add: 4850 Arapaho Okemos MI 48864

LEGGAT, LOIS BURNETT (R)
Pres, Ohio Fedn Rep Women
b Warren, Pa, Aug 23, 17; d John Clyde Burnett & Hazel Filer B; m 1937 to John Alfred Alexander Leggat; c Nancy Lou. Educ: Kirtland High Sch, grad, 37. Polit & Govt Pos: Mem, Lake Co Young Rep, 32-39; recording secy, Lake Co Rep Women, 52-55, pres, 56-60; corresponding secy, Ohio Fedn Rep Women, 52-56, recording secy, 66-70, first vpres, 71-73; pres, 73-, mem, Lake Co Bd Elec, 56-74; chmn, Lake Co Rep Party, 66-72; adv to Lake Co TARs, 67-70; co-chmn campaign comt, Nat Fedn Rep Women. Mem: DAR; Mamie Eisenhower Rep Club. Relig: Baptist. Mailing Add: 4945 Waldamere Ave Willoughby OH 44094

LEGGETT, CARROLL HARDEN (D)
Dep Attorney Gen, NC
b Windsor, NC, Sept 3, 41; s Turner Carter Leggett, Sr & Ruby Inez Harden L; single. Educ: Campbell Col, BA, 63; Wake Forest Univ Sch Law, JD, 68; Omicron Delta Kappa; Epsilon Pi Eta; Phi Alpha Delta. Polit & Govt Pos: Mem, Co Dem Campaign Comt, Preyer for Gov, 64; secy, NC Young Dem Clubs, 66; vpres, Wake Forest Univ Young Dem Clubs, 66-67; precinct chmn, Harnett Co Dem Party, 67-; mem, Gov Comn Reorgn Dem Party, 69-; mem staff, Gov Comt Law & Order, 69; spec asst attorney gen, NC Dept Justice, 69-, dep attorney gen, 73-; co-chmn, banquet comt, NC Jefferson-Jackson Dinner, 70; mem, Gov Environ Educ Task Force, 71-; chmn, NC Criminal Justice Info Syst Comn, 72-; admin asst, Sen Robert Morgan, currently. Mem: Am Bar Asn; Campbell Col (bd trustees); Harnett Co Young Dem Club; NC State Univ Friends of the Col; Campbell Col Alumni Asn (vchmn, pres, 71-). Relig: Baptist. Legal Res: 4711-C Walden Pond Dr Raleigh NC 27604 Mailing Add: 1251 Dirksen Senate Off Bldg Washington DC 20510

LEGGETT, GENE (D)
Ga State Rep
Mailing Add: 2219 Tara Lane Brunswick GA 31520

LEGGETT, ROBERT LOUIS (D)
US Rep, Calif
b Richmond, Calif, July 26, 26; m to Barbara Burnett; c Diana, Jeanne & Rob. Educ: Univ Calif, BA in Polit Sci, 47 & Boalt Hall Sch Jurisp, LLB, 50. Polit & Govt Pos: Calif State Assemblyman, 61-62; US Rep, Calif, 62-, mem, Armed Serv Comt, US House of Rep, mem, Budget Comt & chmn, Subcomt on Fisheries & Wildlife Conservation & the Environ of the Comt on Merchant Marine & Fisheries. Bus & Prof Pos: Lawyer; partner, Leggett, Gianola, Dacey & Harrison. Mil Serv: Navy Air Corps, 2 years. Mem: Kiwanis; Sons of Italy; Am Legion. Legal Res: Vallejo CA 94590 Mailing Add: US House of Rep Washington DC 20515

LEGGITT, RICHARD BAUMGARDNER (R)
b Amarillo, Tex, Sept 21, 41; s Clifford B Leggitt & Olean Baumgardner L; m 1968 to Glenda Orrell. Educ: Oklahoma City Univ, 59-61; Lambda Chi Alpha. Polit & Govt Pos: Info asst to Gov Winfield Dunn, Tenn, 70-72; press asst to US Rep Stanford E Parris, Va, 72-74; admin asst to US Rep William F Goodling, Pa, 75- Bus & Prof Pos: Regional exec, bur mgr & news reporter, United Press Int, Atlanta, Ga, 64-69. Mil Serv: Pvt, Marine Corps Res, 60-66. Mem: Rep Commun Asn (mem exec comt, 73-). Relig: Methodist. Legal Res: 5905 Frederick St Springfield VA 22150 Mailing Add: 1713 Longworth House Off Bldg Washington DC 20515

LEGRANDE, RUTH E (R)
Secy, Warrick Co Rep Cent Comt, Ind
b Warrick Co, Ind, June 23, 21; d Samuel A Kapperman & Minnie Mueller K; m 1942 to Lemuel Clinton LeGrande; c Yvonne (Mrs Moore), Mary Jane (Mrs Barnett) & Linda (Mrs Raven). Educ: Boonville High Sch, Ind, 39. Polit & Govt Pos: Clerk, Elec Bd, Ind, 55-72; dep assessor, Ohio Twp, Warrick Co, 58-70; secy, Warrick Co Rep Cent Comt, 72-, precinct committeeman, 72-; dep auditor, Warrick Co, 73-74; mgr license br, Newburgh, 75- Bus & Prof Pos: Secy, Fed Land Bank Loans, 40-41; secy, Warrick Co Agr Agt, 41-43. Mem: Oak Grove Exten Homemakers Club; Warrick Co Ment Health Asn. Relig: Cumberland Presbyterian. Mailing Add: Rte 2 Boonville IN 47601

LEGRID, GLORIA JEAN (R)
Mem Exec Comt, NDak Rep Party
b Tappen, NDak, Sept 28, 29; d Fred William Buck & Jennie Montgomery B; m 1952 to Donald Allen Legrid; c Keith, Carol & Jennifer. Educ: Jamestown Col, 47-49; St Cloud Hosp Sch of Med Tech, Med Technician; Alpha Zeta. Polit & Govt Pos: Campaign chmn, Stutsman Co Rep Party, NDak, 56-66, party chmn, formerly; nat committeewoman, NDak Young Rep, 61-63; Rep precinct committeeman, Jamestown, 64-69; dist chmn & mem exec comt, NDak Rep Party, 66-; alt deleg, Rep Nat Conv, 72. Relig: Lutheran. Mailing Add: 224 15th Ave NE Jamestown ND 58401

LEHMAN, DAVID J (D)
Fla State Rep
b Newark, NJ, Oct 20, 15; s David J Lehman & May Stern L; m 1969 to Mary Ann Pennington; c Wendi Ann, Bonnie May & David J, III (deceased). Educ: Univ Va, 33-35, Med Sch, MD, 39; dipl, Am Bd Intern Med. Polit & Govt Pos: Fla State Rep, Dist 97, 75- Bus & Prof Pos: Staff, Mt Sinai Hosp, New York, NY, 46-47; pvt practice internal med, Newark, NJ, 47-54; pvt practice, Hollywood, Fla, 54-; mem sr staff, Memorial Hosp, Hollywood, currently. Mil Serv: Entered as 1st Lt, Army, 41, released as Maj, 46, after serv in Med Corps. Publ: The seed, Role of the county medical society in the community drug abuse problem & The starting place, 4/71, Jour Fla Med Asn. Mem: Am Col Phys; Fla, Broward Co & Am Med Asns. Honors & Awards: Citizen of the Year Award, Elks; Cert of Merit, Broward Co Med Asn, 67; Distinguished Serv Award, Kiwanis Club, 67; Distinguished Community Serv Award, Pilot Club, 69; Meritorious Citizenship Award from Fla Asn of Grand Juries, 69. Relig: Hebrew. Legal Res: 3206 Calle Largo Dr Hollywood FL 33021 Mailing Add: 2740 Hollywood Blvd Hollywood FL 33020

LEHMAN, HARRY J (D)
Ohio State Rep
b Dayton, Ohio, Aug 29, 35; s H Jacques Lehman & Mildred Benas L; m 1964 to Linda L Rocker; c Sarah Beth, Adam Henry & Matthew Daniel. Educ: Amherst Col, BA, cum laude, 57; Harvard Law Sch, JD, 60; Psi Upsilon. Polit & Govt Pos: Ohio State Rep, 71-, chmn judiciary comt, Ohio House of Rep, currently. Bus & Prof Pos: Attorney, Burke, Haber & Berick, Cleveland, Ohio, 61-62, Falsgraf, Reidy, Shoup & Ault, 62-70 & Benesch, Friedlander, Mendelson & Coplan, 71- Mil Serv: Entered as Pvt, Army Res, 60, released as SP-4, 66, after serv in 9th Judge Adv Gen Corps, 60-66. Publ: Reapportionment in Ohio, 65 & Reapportionment revisited, 66, Cleveland Bar J. Mem: Cleveland, Ohio & Am Bar Asns;

Citizens' League of Gtr Cleveland; Am Civil Liberties Union. Honors & Awards: Outstanding Ten Young Men Award, Cleveland Jr CofC, 68 & 70; Distinguished Serv Award, NAACP, 68; Outstanding Freshman Legislator of Ohio Gen Assembly, Ohio Newspaper Correspondents Asn, 71-72. Legal Res: 2956 West Park Blvd Shaker Heights OH 44120 Mailing Add: 1100 Citizens Bldg Cleveland OH 44114

LEHMAN, JOHN FRANCIS, JR
Dep Dir, US Arms Control & Disarmament Agency
s John Francis Lehman, Sr; m 1975 to Barbara Thornton Wieland. Educ: St Josephs' Col, BS, 64; Cambridge Univ, BA & MA, 67; Univ Pa, MA & PhD, 74. Polit & Govt Pos: Exec dir, Bendix Corp-Univ Pa Int Arms Control Symposium, 66; staff mem, Foreign Policy Research Inst, Pa, 67-69; staff mem, Nat Security Coun, 69-71, spec counsel & sr staff mem, 71-74; mem, US Deleg to Mutual Balanced Force Reductions Talks, Vienna, 74-75; dep dir, US Arms Control & Disarmament Agency, 75- Publ: Co-ed, The Prospects for Arms Control, MacFadden, 65; co-ed, Arms Control for the Late Sixties, Van Nostrand, 67. Legal Res: 349 Roslyn Ave Glenside PA 19038 Mailing Add: 3336 Prospect St NW Washington DC 20007

LEHMAN, WILLIAM **(D)**
US Rep, Fla
b Selma, Ala, Oct 5, 13; s Maurice M Lehman & Connie Leva L; m 1939 to Joan Feibelman; c William Jr, Kathy (Mrs Donald Weiner) & Thomas. Educ: Univ Ala, 34; Univ Miami, teaching cert, 63; study at various cols & univs. Polit & Govt Pos: Mem, Dade Co Sch Bd, Miami, Fla, 69-72, chmn, 71-72; US Rep, 13th Dist, Fla, 73-; mem adv coun elected officials, Dem Nat Comt. Bus & Prof Pos: Car dealer, Miami, Fla, 36-41 & 46-72; aircraft mech instr, J P Riddle Co, 43 & Brazilian Air Force, Sao Paulo, 44; car dealer, DeSoto Plymouth Dealership, 56-59; Lehman Pontiac, Buick Dealership, Selma, Ala, 60-66; Lehman Motors, SMiami, Fla, 60-73; Lehman Auto Sales, 62-73; Gen Elec dealer, 63-67; teacher, Miami Norland Jr High Sch, 63-64; teacher, Miami Dade Jr Col, 64-66; dealer, William Lehman Buick, N Miami Beach, 66-73. Mem: Distributive Educ Clubs Am; Bethune-Cookman Col (trustee); Miami Comt on Foreign Rels; B'nai B'rith. Honors & Awards: Man of the year US Jaycees & Jaycees of North Miami Beach, 71; Humanitarian of the year, Am Jewish Comt, 72; Juvenile Diabetes Found Award, 74; Serv to Educ Award, Fla Dept Educ, 72; Meritorious Serv Award, Nat Asn Retired Fed Employees, 74. Relig: Jewish. Legal Res: 200 NW 143rd St North Miami FL 33168 Mailing Add: Rm 424 Cannon House Office Bldg Washington DC 20515

LEHMANN, KAREN ELIZABETH **(R)**
Chmn, Alcona Co Rep Comt, Mich
b Bay City, Mich, May 17, 46; d Ray John Lehmann & Martha Gehres L; single. Educ: Alpena Community Col, AA, 69. Polit & Govt Pos: TAR adv, Alcona Co Rep Comt, 66-71, chmn, 71-; vchmn, 11th Cong Dist Rep Comt, 72- Bus & Prof Pos: Staff mem, Alcona Co Libr, 64-68. Mem: Mich Libr Asn; Keep Mich Comt of Alcona Co (chmn, 71-). Relig: Methodist. Mailing Add: Route 1 Box 254 Harrisville MI 48740

LEHNER, EDWARD H **(D)**
NY State Assemblyman
Mailing Add: 680 Ft Washington Ave New York NY 10040

LEHR, GEORGE WARWICK **(D)**
State Auditor, Mo
b Kirksville, Mo, Mar 10, 37; s Emil Lehr & Sarah L; m 1956 to Barbara Jean Higgins; c Lisa Lynn, George Warwick, Jr & Teresa Ann. Educ: Univ Iowa, BS Acct, 59; Beta Alpha Psi (pres); Collegiate CofC (pres). Polit & Govt Pos: Auditor, Jackson Co, Mo, 63-66, collector revenue, 67-71, presiding judge, 71-73 & co exec, 73-75; state auditor, Mo, 75-; mem, Adv Comt of Elected Officials & Young Leadership Coun, Dem Nat Comt, currently. Bus & Prof Pos: Staff auditor, Arthur Young & Co, Kansas City, 59-62. Mem: St Mary's Col (pres adv bd); Human Resources Corp, Kansas City (bd mem). Honors & Awards: Distinguished Serv Award, Kansas City Jaycees, 68; Leon Jordan Mem Award, Freedom Inc, 71; Golden Torch Award, City of Hope-A Pilot Med Ctr, 72. Legal Res: 2 E 109th Terr Kansas City MO 64114 Mailing Add: Box 869 Jefferson City MO 65101

LEHR, STANFORD BUD **(R)**
Pa State Rep
b York, Pa, May 13, 12; s John Alexander Lehr & Mable Meisenhelder L; m 1937 to Naomi Jane Huson; c Stanford Terry & John Frederich. Educ: North York High Sch, grad. Polit & Govt Pos: Pa State Rep, 95th Dist, 69- Bus & Prof Pos: Merchant, Lehr's Food Mkt, 47-67. Mem: Elks; Exchange Club; York Co Meat Dealers Asn; Am Fedn of Musicians. Relig: Lutheran. Mailing Add: Capitol Bldg Harrisburg PA 17120

LEIB, REGINA S **(D)**
Mem, Dem Nat Comt, Pa
Mailing Add: 3886 Dawn-Mar St Harrisburg PA 17111

LEIBHAN, JOE B **(R)**
NDak State Rep
b Berwick, NDak, July 26, 25; s Alex Leibhan & Lucy L; m 1951 to Berenice Ann Leier. Educ: Esmond Pub Sch Dist, 12 years. Polit & Govt Pos: City Alderman, Esmond, NDak, 51-; Qm, Benson Co VFW Post 4251, 51-71; NDak State Rep, 12th Dist, 67-, State & Fed Govt Comt, NDak House Rep, 67-, mem, Comt Educ, State Educ Research, Agr Comt & Vet Affairs Comt, 69- Bus & Prof Pos: Secy & treas, Community Recreational Center, Inc, 62- Mil Serv: Entered as Pvt, Army, 43, released as M/Sgt, 46, after serv in 204th Ord & 164th NDak Nat Guard, Asian-Pac Theatre, 44-46; Good Conduct Medal; Infantry Combat Badge; SPhilippine Liberation Medal with One Bronze Serv Star; Army Occupation Medal, Japan; Victory Medal. Mem: VFW (life mem); Am Legion; Eagles; Sportsmen Club; Nat Farmers. Relig: Catholic. Mailing Add: Esmond ND 58332

LEIBLUM, MARK DAVID **(D)**
b Brooklyn, NY, Dec 20, 38; s Joseph Leiblum & Lillian Schere; m 1961 to Janet Marilyn Nissenbaum; c Mara & Dion. Educ: Brooklyn Col, BS, 61; Univ Southern Calif, Los Angeles, MS, 68, PhD, 74; Phi Lambda Delta. Polit & Govt Pos: Alt deleg, Dem Nat Mid-Term Conf, 74. Bus & Prof Pos: Scientific programmer, Litton Systems, Canoga Park, Calif, 61-62; computer prog analyst, Douglas Aircraft Corp, Culver City, 62-63; sr analyst & educ technologist, Syst Develop Corp, Santa Monica, 63-70; assoc prof & dir computer based educ, Katholieke Universiteit, Nijmegen, Netherlands, 70- Publ: Computer based instruction, past, present, future, SEAS Europe Int Conf, 71; Educational technology-an Americans perspective on the Dutch university scene, Educ Technol, 72; An analytical & comparative study of computer assisted instruction programming languages, Univ Southern Calif, Univ Microfilms, 74. Mem: Am Educ Research Asn; Asn for the Develop of Computer Based Instructional Systems; Asn for Educational Commun & Technol; Nat Soc for Performance & Instruction; Asn for Computing Machinery. Legal Res: 1226 N Fuller Ave Los Angeles CA 90046 Mailing Add: Aldenhof 61-51 Nijmegen Netherlands

LEICHTER, FRANZ S **(D)**
NY State Sen
b Vienna, Austria, Aug 19, 30; s Otto Leichter & Katherine Pick L; m 1958 to Nina Williams. Educ: Swarthmore Col, BA, 52; Harvard Law Sch, LLB, 57. Polit & Govt Pos: Dem dist leader, 71st Assembly Dist, Manhattan, NY, 61-69; vchmn, NY Co Dem Exec Comt, 62-63; deleg, NY State Dem Conv, 62, 64 & 66 & Dem Nat Conv, 64; NY State Assemblyman, 69th Assembly Dist, 69-74; NY State Sen, 75- Bus & Prof Pos: Attorney, Robbins, Bondi & Leichter. Mil Serv: Entered as Pvt, Army, 53, released as Cpl, 55, after serv in Far East. Mem: New York Bar Asn; Harvard Law Sch Asn; Am Civil Liberties Union; NAACP. Relig: Jewish. Legal Res: 600 W 111th St New York NY 10025 Mailing Add: 21 E 40th St New York NY 10016

LEIMBACK, HARRY EDWARD **(D)**
Wyo State Sen
b Joliet, Mont, Oct 5, 25; s Claude Leimback & Bessie Duffy L; m 1948 to Melda L Christiansen; c Thomas, Patrick & Linda. Educ: Casper Col, AA, 48; Univ Wyo, JD, 51. Polit & Govt Pos: Munic judge, Casper, Wyo, 51-53; co & prosecuting attorney, Natrona Co, 58-66; Wyo State Sen, 66- Bus & Prof Pos: Practicing attorney, Casper, Wyo, 51- Mil Serv: Entered as A/S, Navy, 43, released as Radioman 3/C, 46, after serv aboard ship in SPac, 44-46. Mem: Am & Wyo Bar Asns; Rotary; Elks; Eagles. Relig: Lutheran. Mailing Add: 1108 W 25th Casper WY 82601

LEINENWEBER, HARRY DANIEL **(R)**
Ill State Rep
b Joliet, Ill, June 3, 37; s Harry Dean Leinenweber & Emily Lennon L; m 1961 to Geraldine Dunn; c Jane Dunn, John Dunn, Thomas More & Stephen Becket. Educ: Univ Notre Dame, AB, 59; Univ Chicago, JD, 62. Polit & Govt Pos: City attorney, Joliet, Ill, 63-67; Rep committeeman, Precinct 14, Joliet, 65-; spec prosecutor, Circuit Court, Will Co, 68-70; Ill State Rep, 73-, mem judiciary & energy, natural resources & environ comts, Ill House Rep, currently. Bus & Prof Pos: Partner, Dunn, Stefanica, McGarry & Kennedy, Attorneys, 62- Mem: Ill State & Will Co Bar Asns; Joliet Montessori Sch; Joliet Univ Club. Relig: Roman Catholic. Legal Res: 813 Sherwood Place Joliet IL 60435 Mailing Add: 81 N Chicago St Joliet IL 60434

LEINER, HENRY ROBERT **(R)**
b New York, NY, Feb 11, 16; s Leo Martin Leiner & Magadalena Reindel L; m 1938 to Grace Loretta Dobbs; c Grace Loretta (Mrs McKiernan), Sharon (Mrs Bianchi), Robert Henry & JoAnn Henrietta (Mrs Burgess); ten grandchildren. Educ: Camden Cath High Sch, NJ, grad; night sch, writing & jour, 2 years. Polit & Govt Pos: Pres, 11th Ward Rep Club, Camden, NJ, 51-52; Rep co committeeman, 64-73; chmn, Camden Co Rep Party, formerly; alt deleg, Rep Nat Conv, 68; pres, Camden Co Park Comn, 69; mem, NJ Civil Serv Comn, currently. Bus & Prof Pos: Vpres & dir book sales, Curtis Circulation Co, New York, retired; commercial & indust real estate sales, currently. Mem: 25 Year Club of Independent Distributors of Newspapers & Mag; League to Aid Retarded Children (former chmn, nursery sch bd, Camden Co, NJ); PTA; Cherry Hill Twp Assembly; Comt of 100, Cherry Hill Rep Club. Relig: Catholic. Mailing Add: 157 Valley Run Dr Cherry Hill NJ 08034

LEISCHNER, DALE EDWARD **(R)**
b Huron, SDak, Aug 26, 37; s Edward Albert Leischner & Esther Hoffman L; m 1957 to Anita Beth Stulken; c Kelly Suzanne, Kristy Colleen & Kirk Edward. Educ: Univ SDak, 55-56. Polit & Govt Pos: Rep precinct worker, 59; mem, City Coun, Wessington Springs, SDak, 61-63; finance chmn, Jerauld Co Rep Party, 65-69, chmn, 70-74; deleg, State Rep Conv, 66, 70 & 72; mem, Bur Outdoor Recreation, 69- Bus & Prof Pos: Vpres, Springs Implement Co, Inc, 57- & Crist Prod, Inc, 70- Mil Serv: Sgt E-5, Army, SDak Nat Guard, 56-63. Mem: Mason; Wessington Springs CofC; Fish & Game Club; Vol Fire Dept; Elks. Relig: United Church of Christ. Mailing Add: Box 241 Wessington Springs SD 57382

LEISETH, ROBERT VERNON **(R)**
Treas, Seventh Cong Dist Rep Exec Comt, Minn
b Peever, SDak, Apr 29, 28; s Soren Henry Leiseth & Bertha Jordahl L; m 1957 to Marilyn Kathleen Johnson; c Bruce Robert, Jon Robert & Kristi Kay. Educ: NDak State Univ, 53-54; Concordia Col, BA in Bus Admin, 56; Sch of Banking, Univ Wis, grad, 66. Polit & Govt Pos: Secy, Becker Co Rep Comt, Minn, 62-63, chmn, 63-66; Minn State Sen, 65th Dist, 67-70; mem, Minn Govt Citizens Coun on Aging, 69-72; treas, Seventh Cong Dist Rep Exec Comt, 73- Bus & Prof Pos: Pres, Norman Co State Bank, Hendrum, 67-; pres & dir, C K of Sioux Falls, Inc, SDak, 71- Mil Serv: Entered as Sgt, Army, 50, released as Sgt 1/C, 52, after serv in Heavy Mortar Co, 196th Regt, Alaskan Theater; Good Conduct Medal, Nat Defense Medal; 1st Lt (Ret), Army Res, 63. Mem: Minn-Dak Conf NABAC; Rotary (Paul Harris Fel); Sons of Norway; CofC; Am Legion. Relig: Lutheran. Mailing Add: RR 3 Detroit Lakes MN 56501

LEISURE, JOHN **(D)**
Mo State Rep
Mailing Add: 1223 Dolman St Louis MO 63104

LEITHMAN, JOHN KENNETH **(D)**
Speaker Pro Tem, La House Rep
b New Orleans, La, July 24, 30; s John William Leithman & Annabel Poche L; m 1954 to Joan Cynthia Tillotson; c Lauren Maria & J Kenneth, Jr. Educ: Loyola Univ of the South, BS & distinguished mil grad, 52; Sigma Alpha Kappa. Polit & Govt Pos: Mem, Sch Bd, Jefferson Parish, La, 64-68; La State Rep, 68-, speaker pro tem, currently. Bus & Prof Pos: Vpres, Hartwig Moss Ins Agency, New Orleans, 54-64; owner & pres, Leithman & Assoc Inc, Ins Agency, 64- Mil Serv: Entered as 2nd Lt, Army, 52, released as 1st Lt, 54, after serv in Mil Police, Korea, 53-54; Korean Theatre Decoration. Mem: New Orleans Ins Exchange; Lions; Knights of Columbus (4 degree); New Orleans Track & Field Off Asn; Rotary. Honors & Awards: Outstanding Citizenship Award, West Bank Rotary; Outstanding Citizens Award, West Bank Lions. Relig: Catholic. Mailing Add: 50 Smithway Dr Gretna LA 70053

LEJAMBRE, SUSAN E (D)
Committeewoman, NJ Dem State Comt
b Trenton, NJ, Aug 6, 42; d James A LeJambre & Elizabeth Riley L; single. Educ: Trenton State Col, 61-62. Polit & Govt Pos: Pres, Burlington Co Young Dem, NJ, 65-66; committeewoman, Burlington Co Dem Comt, 66-; committeewoman, NJ Dem State Comt, 69-; alt deleg, Dem Nat Conv, 72. Bus & Prof Pos: Secretarial asst, Div of Econ Develop, State of NJ, 63-73. Mem: Trenton Bus & Prof Women's Club (first vpres, 73-); Bordentown Hist Soc (secy, 72-); Burlington Co Heart Asn (bd dirs, 72-); NJ State Employees Asn. Honors & Awards: Woman Doer, Dem Nat Comt, Washington, DC, 68. Relig: Roman Catholic. Mailing Add: 510 Farnsworth Ave Bordentown NJ 08505

LEKANDER, GILBERT (R)
Chmn, Prince William Co Rep Party, Va
b Butte, Mont, June 1, 18; m 1943 to Carol Foster; c Adele Ann (deceased) & John Foster. Educ: Mont Univ, BA; Sigma Delta Chi; Sigma Alpha Epsilon. Polit & Govt Pos: Admin asst to US Rep Wesley A D'ewart, Mont, 46-54 & US Rep Frank T Bow, Ohio, 55-; chmn, Prince William Co Rep Party, Va, 61-64, 66-69 & 73- Bus & Prof Pos: Gen ed work, Assoc Press, 40-41. Mil Serv: Entered as Pvt, Army Air Force, released as Capt, after serv in NAfrica & China-Burma-India, 42-46; Distinguished Flying Cross; Air Medal. Mailing Add: 5310 Feathered Lane Manassas VA 22110

LELAND, GEORGE THOMAS (D)
Tex State Rep
b Lubbock, Tex, Nov 27, 44; s Alice W Lewis Rains; single. Educ: Tex South Univ Sch of Pharm, BS Pharm, 70. Polit & Govt Pos: Deleg, Dem Nat Conv, 72; Tex State Rep, Dist 88, 73- Bus & Prof Pos: Consult, Menil Found, 73- Mem: Houston Pharmaceutical Asn; Med Comt for Human Rights; Orgn for Community Health Serv. Honors & Awards: Citation, NAACP, 72. Relig: Catholic. Legal Res: 3701 Cavalcade Houston TX 77026 Mailing Add: PO Box 2910 Capitol Station Austin TX 78767

LELLENSACK, FRANCIS J (D)
Wis State Rep
Mailing Add: 1812 S 23rd Manitowoc WI 54220

LEMANN, ARTHUR ANTHONY III (D)
Nat Committeeman, Young Dem La
b Augusta, Ga, May 14, 42; s Arthur Anthony Lemann, Jr & Camille Ker L; m 1964 to Roberta Ann Acosta; c Rachel, Arthur & Aimee. Educ: Tulane Univ, BA, 64; Loyola Univ (La), LLB, 67; George Washington Univ, LLM, 68. Polit & Govt Pos: Pres, Young Dem New Orleans, 71 & Young Dem La, 71-73, nat committeeman, 73- Bus & Prof Pos: Teaching fel, George Washington Univ, 67-68; assoc, Polack, Rosenberg & Rittenberg, New Orleans, 68-69; staff lawyer, La Legis Coun, Baton Rouge, 70-71; asst prof, Loyola Univ Sch of Law, New Orleans, 70-73; dir, Loyola Law Sch Law Clinic, 71-73; research supvr, La Const Conv, 73. Publ: Ed, Loyola Law Rev, 66-67; auth, Law schools find their way to court—and sometimes win, La Bar J, 72. Mem: La State Bar Asn (bd gov, 73); Am & La Trial Lawyers Asns; Am & New Orleans Bar Asns. Relig: Catholic. Mailing Add: 1323 Fern St New Orleans LA 70118

LEMIEUX, WILLIAM F S (D)
b Fond Du Lac, Wis, Oct 19, 38; s Will Lemieux & Shirley Wing L; single. Educ: Wis State Univ, Oshkosh, BS, 63; Univ Wis, Milwaukee, 64-66; Alverno Col, Cert Educ, 73; Int Rels Club; chmn Sixth Dist Young Dem, 60-62. Polit & Govt Pos: Coordr col orgn, Kennedy for President Comt, Wis, 59-60; coordr for northern Ind, McCarthy for President Comt, 68, nat coordr proj signature & polit research, 68; mem-at-lg, Exec Bd, Milwaukee Co Dem Party, Wis, 73-; secy Wis deleg, Dem Nat Mid-Term Conf, 74. Bus & Prof Pos: Polit consult, Milwaukee, Wis, 64-65; manpower specialist, Wis State Employ Serv, 65-68; teacher, St Gerard Sch, Milwaukee, 68-69; coordr, St Mary Sch, Port Washington, 69-74; coordr, St Agnes Sch, Milwaukee, 74- Publ: Co-auth, Congressional District Organization Handbook, McCarthy for President Comt, Ind, 68. Mem: Am for New Am; Am Civil Liberties Union. Relig: Catholic. Mailing Add: 1860 Prospect Ave Milwaukee WI 53202

LEMIRE, ARMAND R (D)
NH State Rep
Mailing Add: 150 Cumberland St Manchester NH 03102

LEMKE, LEROY WALTER (D)
Ill State Sen
Mailing Add: 2849 S Kedvale Ave Chicago IL 60623

LEMKE, RICHARD (DFL)
Minn State Rep
Mailing Add: RR 1 Lake City MN 55041

LEMMON, WILLARD LINCOLN (D)
Va State Deleg
b Marion, Va, Sept 30, 24; s Frank Tremaine Lemmon & Alexina Lincoln L; m 1946 to Rosa Kevan Rogerson; c Alexina (Mrs Curtis Copenhaver) & Elizabeth (Mrs Lynn Sayers). Educ: Davidson Col, 1 year; Univ Va, 6 months; Beta Theta Pi. Polit & Govt Pos: Va State Deleg, 68- Bus & Prof Pos: Pres, Lemmon Investment Corp, 50 & Consolidated Real Estate Corp, 56; dir, Bank of Marion, 56. Mil Serv: Entered as Pvt, Army, 43, released as Sgt, 45, after serv in Co I, 309th Inf, ETO, 44-45; Purple Heart; Bronze Star; Combat Inf Medal; Theatre Ribbons. Mem: Mary Baldwin Col (chmn, bd of trustees); Smyth Co Community Hosp (vpres); Kiwanis; Am Legion; VFW. Honors & Awards: Chosen outstanding young man, State of Va, 56; Man of the Year, Marion Rotary, 70. Relig: Presbyterian. Legal Res: Ridgeway Rd Marion VA 24354 Mailing Add: 101 Johnston Rd Marion VA 24354

LEMON, CHARLES MYRON (R)
Chmn, Maricopa Co Rep Party, Ariz
b Pratt, Kans, May 6, 26; s Rodney Clyde Lemon & Myrtle Crocker L; m 1948 to Donna Elizabeth Franklin; c Patricia & Michael. Educ: Ariz State Univ, 67; Phoenix Col, 67 & 70; Maricopa Tech Inst, 69. Polit & Govt Pos: Griffith precinct committeeman, 66-; Dist 8F chmn, 67-71; vchmn, Maricopa Co Rep Party, 71-73, chmn, 73- Bus & Prof Pos: Plant design engr, Airesearch, 55- Mil Serv: Entered as Apprentice Seaman, Navy, 44, released as 1/C, 46, after serv in Asiatic Pac, 45-46. Mem: Am Inst Plant Engrs (treas). Honors & Awards: Cub Scout Pack 223 Award. Relig: Protestant. Mailing Add: 4417 E Palm Lane Phoenix AZ 85008

LEMONS, CHARLES FRED (R)
Mem, Dade Co Rep Cent Comt, Mo
b Birch Tree, Mo, Oct 8, 26; s C O Lemons & Willa King L; m 1948 to LaRue Keran; c Keran, Renee, Kelley & Deidre. Educ: Southwest Mo State Col, BS in Educ, 49; Univ Wis Grad Sch Banking, 3 years. Polit & Govt Pos: Chmn, Dade Co Rep Cent Comt, Mo, 52-62 & 68-74, mem, 52-; mem & treas, Lockwood Sch Dist Bd Educ, 58-70. Mil Serv: Entered as Pvt, Army, 44, released as 1st Sgt, 46, after serv in 774 Field Artil, ETO, 45-46. Mem: Ozark Bankers Asn; Bank Admin Inst; Mason, Am Legion; CofC. Relig: Methodist. Mailing Add: 311 E 12th Lockwood MO 65682

LENA, SAM (D)
Ariz State Sen
b Evergreen, La, Jan 23, 21; s Sam Lena & Mamie Dolce L; m 1951 to Gloria O Gabusi; c Sam, Jr, Kathrine & John. Educ: Thomas Jefferson High Sch, Pt Arthur, Tex, grad, 39. Polit & Govt Pos: Ariz State Rep, Dist 16, Pima Co, 65-66, Dist 7C, 67-68; Ariz State Sen, Dist 7C, 69- Bus & Prof Pos: Foreman, Sheet Metal Dept, Davis Monthan Air Force Base, 43-46; self-employed retailer, 47-52 & 55-; salesman, Coca Cola Bottling Co, 52-55. Mem: Retail Licensed Beverage Asn (bd dirs); Ariz Asn for Retarded Children (adv bd); Elks; KofC; S Tucson Lions. Relig: Roman Catholic. Mailing Add: 2331 E Beverly Dr Tucson AZ 85719

LENAMON, JAMES LEVI (D)
Chmn, Shackelford Co Dem Party, Tex
b Mexia, Tex, Oct 23, 46; s James Lenamon, Sr & Francis Clark L; m 1965 to Pamela Faye Adams; c James L, III, John Adam & Jeffrey Brandon. Educ: NTex State Univ, 68-69. Polit & Govt Pos: Chmn, Shackelford Co Dem Party, Tex, 74- Publ: Persimmon Hill; Watt Matthews & Texas Tradition (ed, Dean Krakel), 74. Mem: Albany Independent Sch Dist (bd of trustees, 73-74); Tex & West Tex Press Asns. Relig: Methodist. Mailing Add: Box 278 Albany TX 76430

LENDE, RUSSELL MELVIN (R)
Chmn, Clatsop Co Rep Cent Comt, Ore
b Sandstone, Minn, Nov 13, 37; s Melvin Oluf Lende & Myrtle Elizabeth Adams L; m 1959 to Patricia Kay Goldmund; c Russell Melvin, Jr & Johnny Adam. Educ: Pac Univ, BSc, 59, OD, 60; Omega Epsilon Phi. Polit & Govt Pos: From vchmn to chmn, Clatsop Co Young Rep, Ore, 62-63; mem, Exec Young Rep Ore; precinct committeeman, 64-; mem, Sch Bd, 67-72; chmn, Clatsop Co Rep Cent Comt, 68-; mem, Ore State Rep Cent Comt, 68-, mem exec comt, 70-, chmn rules, by-laws, credentials & resolutions comts; mem, Clatsop Co Budget Comt, 70-73; vchmn, First Cong Dist Rep Party, 70-72, chmn, 72-; co campaign chmn for Clay Myers, 72. Publ: Practice management article, J Am Optom Asn, 4/65. Mem: Ore Optom Asn (treas, 72-); Clatsop Tillamook Optom Soc (secy, chmn, legis chmn); Am Field Serv (chmn, 61-64); Rotary (area rep, 72-); Grange (chmn various comts). Honors & Awards: Awarded first place in driving competition & knowledge of driving laws in West Linn & Ore City High Sch student competition, 54 & 55. Legal Res: Hamlet Rte Seaside OR 97138 Mailing Add: 10-A N Holladay Dr Seaside OR 97138

LENGERICH, MADONNA ANDREA (R)
b Redlands, Calif, Nov 30, 51; d Roman Anthony Lengerich & Mary Rose Lucas L; single. Educ: Col of Idaho, BA; Am Univ, 73; Washington Semester Prog. Polit & Govt Pos: Pres, Col of Idaho Young Rep, 71-72; intern, Idaho Legis Coun, 72; deleg, Young Rep Nat Leadership Conv, 72; deleg, Rep Nat Leadership Conf, 72; rep, Idaho Youth Adv Coun Elec, 72; col rep, Idaho State Rep Conv, 72; deleg, Rep Nat Conv, 72; dir, Speakers Bur, Idaho Comt to Reelect the President, 72; state rep, Col of Idaho Col Rep Club, 72-73; youth committeeperson, Canyon Co Cent Comt, 72-; spec proj asst, US Rep Symms, Idaho, 73- Mem: Caldwell CofC (govt affairs comt, 71-73). Honors & Awards: Whitaker Award, Colo of Idaho, 71 & Relen Mackey Award, 71 & 72. Relig: Catholic. Legal Res: College of Idaho Caldwell ID 82605 Mailing Add: 1410 Longworth House Off Bldg Washington DC 20515

LENHART, THOMAS B (D)
Mem, Calif State Dem Cent Comt
b Vancouver, BC, Aug 26, 10; s Frank A Lenhart & Irene Clemens L; m 1934 to Rachel E. Educ: Grants Pass High Sch, Ore, grad, 27; US Naval Acad, 30-31; Naval Supply Sch, Harvard Grad Sch Bus Admin, 44. Polit & Govt Pos: Dem cand, US House Rep, 35th Dist, Calif, 66, 68 & 70; mem, Calif State Dem Cent Comt, 69-; chmn, Orange Co Dem Fedn, 70-71. Bus & Prof Pos: Owned & operated commercial laundry, 55-63. Mil Serv: Marine Corps, 28; enlistee in Marine Corps Res Bn, 39, entered active duty Marines, 40, commissioned 2nd Lt, 42, retired as Maj, 59, after serv as instr, Marine Corps Sch of Qm Admin, 42-43, SPac Theatre, 44 & Korea, 53-54; Bronze Star with Combat V; Navy Commendation Medal with Combat V; Presidential Unit Citation; Navy Unit Citation; Korean Presidential Unit Citation. Mem: Portland Chap, Retail Clerks Union. Mailing Add: 13881 Dall Lane Santa Ana CA 92705

LENIHAN, MICHAEL PHILLIP (R)
Chmn, Westerly Rep Town Comt, RI
b Westerly, RI, Nov 18, 47; s Russell A Lenihan & Anne Nardone L; m 1971 to Denise M Duhaime; c Corye. Educ: Stonehill Col, 69. Polit & Govt Pos: Chmn, Westerly Rep Town Comt, RI, 75- Bus & Prof Pos: Vpres, Ralco Realty Corp, 69-74, pres & treas, 74- Mil Serv: S/Sgt, Air Nat Guard, currently. Mem: Rotary; CofC; Elks; Washington Co Bd Realtors; KofC. Relig: Roman Catholic. Legal Res: Old Post Rd Westerly RI 02891 Mailing Add: PO Box 336 Westerly RI 02891

LENKER, WILLIAM FRED (R)
Rep Nat Committeeman, SDak
b Colome, SDak, Mar 22, 23; s Carle B Lenker & Madeline Flint L; m 1952 to Mary Ann Boyce; c Linda, Laura, Timothy, Arthur & William. Educ: Univ Minn, Bus Admin, 49; Sigma Alpha Epsilon. Polit & Govt Pos: Deleg, State Cent Conv, 64, 66, 68, 70 & 72; chmn, Minnehaha Co Rep Cent Comt, SDak, formerly; mem, Electoral Col, 73-; Rep Nat Committeeman, 73- Bus & Prof Pos: Pres, Lenker, Nugen & Williams Agency, 55; pres, Lenker Realty, 66. Mil Serv: Entered as Cadet, Army Air Corps, 42, released as 1st Lt, 46, after serv as B-17 pilot in 305 Bomb Group, Eighth Air Corps, ETO, 45-46; Air Medal; European Theatre Ribbon. Mem: Am Legion (nat comt vet affairs & rehabilitation, currently); Lions; Shrine; Elks; Mason. Honors & Awards: Distinguished Citizenship Award, Elks, 71-72. Relig: Episcopal. Mailing Add: 1408 S Kiwanis Sioux Falls SD 57105

LENNON, ALTON ASA (D)
b Wilmington, NC, Aug 17, 06; m to Karine Welch; c Mars Lewis R Frost, III & Alton Yates. Educ: Wake Forest Col. Polit & Govt Pos: NC State Sen, 47 & 51; judge, New Hanover Co

Recorders Court; US Sen, NC, 53-54; US Rep, NC, 57-72. Bus & Prof Pos: Lawyer. Mailing Add: 306 Colonial Dr Wilmington NC 28401

LENNON, ARTHUR THOMAS **(R)**
Committeeman, Ill Rep State Cent Comt
b Joliet, Ill, Aug 11, 23; s Arthur A Lennon & Irene Haughton L; m 1951 to Jean Canty; c Dinah J, Elizabeth A, Arthur C & John H. Educ: Univ Ill, BS, 48, JD, 49; Sachem; Sigma Alpha Epsilon; Phi Alpha Delta. Polit & Govt Pos: Attorney, Joliet Bd Local Improv, Ill, 55-67; Rep precinct committeeman, Joliet, 62-73; attorney, Joliet Plan Comn, 64-67; committeeman, Ill State Rep Comt, 66-; asst states attorney, Will Co, 68-69; mem, Ill Sixth Const Conv, 69-70, chmn statutory transition comt & mem bill of rights comt; Judicial Adv Poll Comt; chmn, Joliet Int Airport Comt, 69- Bus & Prof Pos: Attorney-partner, Murphy Timm & Lennon; mem faculty, Ill Inst Continuing Legal Educ, currently; hearing off, Farm Employ Practices Comt, currently. Mil Serv: Entered as Pvt, Army, 42, released as 1st Lt, 45, after serv in Air Corps, Europe; extended active duty, Korea, 44-45; Col, Air Force Res; mem phys eval bd, Walter Reed Army Med Ctr; grad, Indust Col Armed Forces; Distinguished Flying Cross; World War II Victory Medal; Nat Defense Medal; Res Medal; 7 Air Medals & 3 Battle Stars. Mem: Am Legion; Elks; Kiwanis; Air Force Asn; KofC. Honors & Awards: Outstanding Rep Precinct Committeeman, 62. Relig: Catholic. Legal Res: 1405 Mayfield Ave Joliet IL 60435 Mailing Add: 5 E Van Buren St Joliet IL 60431

LENT, NORMAN F **(R)**
US Rep, NY
b Oceanside, NY, 1931; s Norman F Lent; c Norman, III, Barbara Anne & Thomas Benjamin. Educ: Hofstra Col, grad, 52; Cornell Law Sch, grad, 57. Polit & Govt Pos: Former assoc police justice, East Rockaway, NY; pres, Lynbrook Chap, Nassau Co Rep Recruits, 60; confidential law secy to Supreme Court Justice Thomas P Farley, 61-63; NY State Sen, Nassau Co, 63-70, chmn, Joint Legis Comt on Pub Health & Senate Comt on Health; US Rep, Fourth Cong Dist, NY, 71-; deleg, Rep Nat Conv, 72. Bus & Prof Pos: Law partner, Hill, Lent & Troescher, NY, 57-; mem, East Rockaway Bd Trade. Mil Serv: Entered as Seaman Recruit, Naval Res, 50, graduated Officers Cand Sch, 52, 2 years active duty, Korean War; Lt, Naval Res, at present. Mem: Nassau Co Boy Scouts (mem-at-lg, S-Cent Dist); Elks; Am Legion; Hofstra Col & Cornell Law Sch Alumni Asns. Legal Res: 48 Plymouth Rd East Rockaway NY 11518 Mailing Add: US House of Rep Washington DC 20515

LENTOL, JOSEPH ROLAND **(D)**
NY State Assemblyman
b Brooklyn, NY, Jan 15, 43; s Edward S Lentol & Matilda A Postis L; m 1970 to Susan M Gregorek. Educ: Univ Dayton, BA, 65; St John's Univ Law Sch, 66; Univ Baltimore Law Sch, JD, 69. Polit & Govt Pos: NY State Assemblyman, 58th Assembly Dist, 73- Bus & Prof Pos: Asst Dist Attorney, Kings Co, 71-73; attorney-at-law, Lentol & Kronowitz, Brooklyn, NY, 73- Mem: Greenpoint Civic Coun; Winthrop Civic Asn; Pioneer Dem Club; John Smolenski Dem Club; Consolidated Dem Club. Relig: Catholic. Mailing Add: 229 Monitor St Brooklyn NY 11222

LENTZ, EARL LEROY, JR **(R)**
b Sunbury, Pa, Aug 31, 24; s Earl Leroy Lentz & Hilda Getz L; m 1948 to Dorothy Marie Schrock; c William David & Beth Ann. Educ: Pa State Univ, BS in Chem Eng, 47; Lincoln Chiropractic Col, DC, 50; Phi Lambda Upsilon; Tau Beta Pi; Delta Tau Alpha. Polit & Govt Pos: Pres, Lock Haven Sch Bd, Pa, 58-; vchmn, Clinton Co Rep Comt, Pa, 61-63, chmn, formerly; mem, State Bd Chiropractic Exams, 65. Mil Serv: Entered as A/S, Navy, 44, released as Electronics Technician 2/C, 46, after serv in Commun Unit 624, Pac Theater. Mem: Pa Chiropractic Soc; Am Chiropractic Asn; Masonic Bodies; Elks; Am Legion. Relig: United Methodist. Mailing Add: Freedom Hill Woolrich PA 17779

LENTZ, RUSSELL LYNN **(D)**
Chairperson, Adams Co Dem Party, Wis
b Portage, Wis, Feb 15, 52; s Arthur J Lentz & Dora Warren L; single. Educ: Univ Wis-Stevens Point, BS, 74; Polit Sci Asn. Polit & Govt Pos: Secy-treas, Portage Co Dem Youth Caucus, 73-74; chmn, Dell-Oxford Countryside Dem Youth Caucus, 74-; chairperson, Adams Co Dem Party, Wis, 74- Mailing Add: Rte 2 Oxford WI 53952

LENZ, DONALD **(R)**
Nat Committeeman, Conn Fedn of Young Rep
b Hartford, Conn, June 9, 50; s Richard Lenz & Joan Fortin L; single. Educ: Cent Conn State Col, currently. Polit & Govt Pos: Legis asst, Off Minority Senate Leaders, Conn Gen Assembly, State Capitol, 69; admin asst, Kilbourn for Cong Campaign, Sixth Dist, Conn, 70; press staff asst, Exec Off of the President, 71, release dept, White House, 71; campaign mgr, Povinelli for Cong Campaign, Third Dist, Conn, 72; nat committeeman, Conn Fedn of Young Rep, 73- Bus & Prof Pos: Analyst, Hartford Ins Group, 73- Publ: 1600 Pennsylvania Ave, Washington, DC, Hartford Courant, 72. Honors & Awards: Hardcharger Award, Young Rep Nat Fedn, 73. Relig: Roman Catholic. Mailing Add: 15 Ellen Dr Farmington CT 06032

LENZO, TONY SAMUEL **(D)**
b East Chicago, Ind, Jan 22, 25; s Carmelo Lenzo & Antonia Pullella L; m 1968 to Valeria Zawada; c Anthony Joseph. Educ: Ind Univ, BS, 49, MS, 61; Defense Info Sch, Ft Harrison, Ind, grad, 64; Command & Gen Staff Col, Ft Leavenworth, Kans, grad, 69; Assoc Logistics Mgt Course, Ft Lee, Va grad, 72; Alpha Phi Omega. Polit & Govt Pos: Deleg, Ind Dem State Conv, 72; alt deleg, Dem Nat Conv, 72. Bus & Prof Pos: Commun media consult, New York, & Chicago, 54-56; bus & advert mgr, Our Sunday Visitor Newspaper, Gary, Ind, 55-67; radio-TV producer, Kenyon & Eckhardt Advert Agency, Chicago, 56-57; asst advert promotion mgr, Edwards Valves, East Chicago, Ind, 57; coordr, Resource Learning Ctr, Gary Pub Schs, 57-72; dir instructional media, East Chicago Pub Schs, 72- Mil Serv: Entered as Pvt, Army Air Corps, 43, released as Cpl, after serv in Air Transport Command, ETO, 44-46; recalled as 2nd Lt, Army, 3 years; Col, Army Reserve, 30 years; Campaign Ribbons; Good Conduct Medal; Army Commendation Medal; Army Reserve Components Achievement Medal; Reserve Medal. Mem: Phi Delta Kappa (secy, 73-); Riley Cult & Arts Asn; East Chicago Community Coun; Lions; KofC. Honors & Awards: Nat Teacher's Medal, Freedom's Found, Valley Forge, Pa, 65; Freedom Award, Gary Exchange Club, 65. Relig: Catholic. Mailing Add: 4811 Olcott Ave East Chicago IN 46312

LEON, JOHN F **(D)**
Ill State Rep
b Chicago, Ill, Mar 9, 10; married; c John, Jr. Educ: Chicago Pub Schs. Polit & Govt Pos: Pres, 36th Ward Dem Orgn, Chicago, Ill, formerly, secy, currently; Ill State Rep, currently. Mem: St Philomena Holy Name Soc; KofC; City Club. Relig: Catholic. Mailing Add: 1811 N Tripp Ave Chicago IL 60639

LEONARD, GERALD **(D)**
Ga State Rep
Mailing Add: 123 Murray Plaza Chatsworth GA 30705

LEONARD, HERBERT LEE **(R)**
Chmn, Lafayette Parish Polit Comt
b Morgan City, La, June 20, 31; s Byron Peter Leonard & Jeanne Braud L; m 1955 to Audrey Gary; c Bannie Lynn, Keitha Ann, Byron Madison, Patrick Olivier, Peter Justin, Rachel & Aimee. Educ: Southwestern La Inst; La State Univ, BA, 53 & LLB, 55; Phi Delta Phi; Sigma Nu. Polit & Govt Pos: Past parish chmn, O'Hearne Senate Race, Lyons Gubernatorial Race & Goldwater Nat Race; chmn, Lafayette Parish Rep Exec Comt, La, formerly; chmn, Lafayette Parish Polit Comt, currently. Bus & Prof Pos: Voorhies, Labbe, Fontenot, Leonard & McGlasson. Mil Serv: Entered as 2nd Lt, Air Force, released as 1st Lt, 57; 1st Lt, Air Force Res. Mem: La State & Am Bar Asns; Maritime Law Asn; La Asn Defense Counsel; Acadiana Defense Counsel Asn. Relig: Catholic. Legal Res: 2020 E Pine St Lafayette LA 70501 Mailing Add: PO Box 3527 Lafayette LA 70501

LEONARD, J DAVID **(D)**
Maine State Rep
Mailing Add: River Rd Woolwich ME 04579

LEONARD, JERRIS **(R)**
Mem, Rep Party Wis
b Chicago, Ill, Jan 17, 31; s Jerris Gilbert Leonard & Jean Marie Reville L; m 1953 to Mariellen Catherine Mathie; c Mary Alice, John Edward, Francis Xavier, Jerris Gilbert, Kathleen Ann & Daniel Joseph. Educ: Marquette Univ, BS in Bus Admin, 52, JD, 55; Alpha Sigma Nu; Sigma Nu Phi; Delta Sigma Pi. Polit & Govt Pos: Mem, Wis Young Rep Party, 49-66 & Rep Party Wis, 49-; Wis State Assemblyman, 57-61; Wis State Sen, 61-69, majority leader, Wis State Senate, 67-69; Rep nominee for US Senator, Wis; Asst Attorney Gen for Civil Rights, Dept of Justice, 69-71, Adminr, Law Enforcement Assistance Admin, 71-73. Bus & Prof Pos: Attorney-at-law, 55-64; attorney, Michael, Best & Friedrich, 64-69; partner, Leonard & Cohen, 73- Mem: Am, Wis, Milwaukee, Fed & Nat Bar Asns. Relig: Roman Catholic. Legal Res: Milwaukee WI Mailing Add: Suite 1111 1747 Pennsylvania Ave Washington DC 20006

LEONARD, JOE ELDON **(R)**
Mem, Faulkner Co Rep Comt
b Damascus, Ark, Jan 31, 22; s Joe Sevier Leonard & Elizabeth Graham L; m 1946 to Wilma Douglas; c Beth (Mrs Parish); Joe D, Timmy & Bobby. Educ: State Col Ark, 41. Polit & Govt Pos: Mem, Faulkner Co Rep Comt, 52-, chmn, 62-70; mem, Dist Rep Comt, currently. Bus & Prof Pos: Owner, Leonard Construction Co. Mailing Add: Damascus AR 72039

LEONARD, LARRY ELMER **(D)**
NC State Rep
b Thomasville, NC, Nov 22, 41; s Elmer Elwood Leonard & May Nell Gallimore L; m 1967 to Brenda Sue Westmoreland; c Caroline Sue & Marcus Larry. Educ: Western Carolina Univ, BS, 64; Wake Forest Sch Law, JD, 72; Tau Kappa Epsilon; Phi Alpha Delta. Polit & Govt Pos: NC State Rep, 30th Dist, 74- Bus & Prof Pos: Field rep, Gen Elec Credit Corp, 64; indust engr, Klopman Mills, Asheboro, NC & Johnson City, Tenn, 64-68; trucking, US Furniture Industs, High Point, NC, 68-69; partner, Saintsing, Leonard & Green, Attorneys, Thomasville, NC, 72- Mem: Am & NC Bar Asns; Thomasville Jaycees. Relig: United Church of Christ. Mailing Add: 708 Diana Dr Thomasville NC 27360

LEONARD, LAWRENCE KIRKWOOD **(R)**
b Richmond Co, Ga, Aug 15, 30; s Joseph Frank Leonard & Nell Collum L; m 1957 to Teibelle Winfield; c Laurie Estelle & Clayton Winfield. Educ: Univ Miami, BS, 55; Sigma Nu. Polit & Govt Pos: Deleg, SC State Rep Conv, 64 & 68; pres, Fifth Precinct Rep Orgn, SC, 70; chmn, York Co Rep Party, formerly. Bus & Prof Pos: Chemist, 20th Century Lab, Miami, Fla, 55-56, E I du Pont de Nemours & Co, Richmond, Va, 56-58 & Celanese Corp, Rock Hill, SC, 58-62; chemist & partner, Rock Hill Chem Co, 62-64; pres, Leonard Chem Co, Inc, 64- Mem: Am Chem Soc; Jaycees; Elks. Mailing Add: 613 Charlotte Ave Rock Hill SC 29736

LEONARD, LOUISE **(R)**
b Washington, DC, Oct 7, 19; d Roy Leslie McVey (deceased) & Florence Alberta Bellows M (deceased); m 1948 to Robert Prescott Leonard. Educ: George Washington Univ, BA, 48; Alpha Delta Pi; Phi Pi Epsilon. Polit & Govt Pos: Past chmn, Jefferson Co Rep Exec Comt, WVa; pres, Jefferson Co Planning Comn, 67-72; mem, Task Force on Regional & Local Planning, WVa, 68; mem adv bd, Fed Reformatory for Women, Alderson, WVa, 69-73; bd mem & legis chmn, Nat Fedn Rep Women; vpres, WVa Fedn Rep Women; past pres, Jefferson Co Fedn Rep Women; WVa State Sen, 16th Dist, 70-74; cand for US Sen, WVa, 72; deleg & mem platform comt, Rep Nat Conv, 72. Bus & Prof Pos: Civilian employee, US Engrs Dept, Off Strategic Serv & State Dept, Washington, Can, Alaska & India, World War II. Mem: Nat Soc State Legislators; Nat Order Women Legislators; WVa East Panhandle Land & River Protective Asn; DAR, Bee Line Chap; Women's Club of Harpers Ferry Dist. Relig: Episcopal. Mailing Add: PO Box 5 Harpers Ferry WV 25425

LEONARD, PAUL ROGER **(D)**
Ohio State Rep
b Dayton, Ohio, July 3, 43; s Paul Russell Leonard & Ida Helen Miller L; single. Educ: Ohio Univ, BS; Salmon P Chase Col Law, Cincinnati, JD. Polit & Govt Pos: Dem precinct committeeman, Ohio, 70-72; Ohio State Rep, 73- Bus & Prof Pos: Labor rels rep, Frigidaire Div, Gen Motors, 66-69; asst prosecuting attorney, Montgomery Co Prosecutors Off, Ohio, 69-72; practicing attorney, Dayton, 69- Mem: Dayton, Ohio State & Am Bar Asns; Ohio Acad Trial Lawyers. Honors & Awards: One of Five Outstanding Young men of Year, Dayton Jr CofC, 73; Cert of Commendation, Dayton Police Dept, 72. Relig: Protestant. Mailing Add: 2815 Lake Shore Pl Dayton OH 45420

LEONARD, RICHARD JOHN NELSON **(D)**
Committeeman, Essex Co Dem Comt, NJ
b Newark, NJ, July 28, 49; s Everett Nelson Leonard & Theresa Hilgreen L; single. Educ: Boston Univ, BA, 71; Univ of St Andrews, Scotland, summer 71; Montclair State Col, NJ, 72- Polit & Govt Pos: Committeeman, Essex Co Dem Comt, NJ, 67-, mem, Exec Comt, 68-; chmn, Roseland Dem Comt, 68-; mem, Roseland Citizens' Adv Comt, 70-72; mem, Essex

Co Young Dem, 70-; pres, Roseland Dem Asn, 71-; deleg, Dem Nat Conv, 72; councilman, Roseland, 73-75, mayor, 75- Bus & Prof Pos: Teacher, West Essex Mid Sch, 72- Mem: Am Inst for Foreign Study; Am Soc of Notaries; Rotary; NJ & Nat Educ Asns. Mailing Add: 18 Westview Ave Roseland NJ 07068

LEONARD, RICHARD WILSON (D)
b Nashua, NH, Aug 6, 19; s Thomas J Leonard & Cecelia M Cone L; m 1950 to Andrea Desmond; c Janet E. Educ: Univ Va, BS, 41, LLB, 47. Polit & Govt Pos: Dem Cand to Cong, 48; deleg, Dem Nat Conv, 60, 64 & 72; mem sch bd, Nashua, NH, 63-69; NH State Rep, 65-67; NH State Sen, 67-72; Dem cand for gov, 74. Bus & Prof Pos: Sr partner, Leonard Prof Asn, 48-; pres, Colonial Trust Co, Nashua, NH, 69- Mil Serv: Entered serv as Cadet, Army Air Corps, 41, released as Capt, 45, after serv in 451st Bomb Squadron, ETO; reentered serv as Capt, Air Force, 50, released as Maj, 53, after serv in 136th Tactical Fighter Wing, Korea; reentered as Lt Col, Air Force, 61, released as Lt Col, 62, after serv in 102nd Tactical Fighter Wing, Europe; Distinguished Flying Cross; Air Medal with 15 Oak Leaf Clusters; Army & Air Force Commendation Medals; ETO Ribbon with Six Battle Stars; Korean Medal with Three Battle Stars; Japanese Occup Medal; Distinguished Unit Citation. Mem: NH & Am Bar Asns; Elks; Am Legion; US Air Force Res. Honors & Awards: US Air Force Command Pilot. Relig: Catholic. Legal Res: 7 Farmington Rd Nashau NH 03060 Mailing Add: Box 615 Nashua NH 03060

LEONARD, TOM (D)
Ala State Rep
Mailing Add: 1725 Windsor Blvd Homewood AL 35209

LEONARD, WILL ERNEST JR (D)
Comnr, US Tariff Comn
b Shreveport, La, Jan 18, 35; s Will Ernest Leonard & Nellie Kenner L; m to Maureen Laniak; c Will Ernest, III, Sherry Elizabeth, Robert Scott & Stephen Michael. Educ: Tulane Univ, BA, 56; Tulane Univ Law Sch, LLB, 58; Harvard Univ, LLM, 66; Phi Beta Kappa; Omicron Delta Kappa. Polit & Govt Pos: Legis asst to US Sen Russell B Long, La, 60-65; prof staff mem, Senate Finance Comt, 66-68; comnr, US Tariff Comn, 68- Mem: Bars of US Supreme Court, State of La & DC. Honors & Awards: Cong Staff Fel. Relig: Roman Catholic. Legal Res: 6012 Camphor St Metairie LA 70003 Mailing Add: 6109 Durbin Rd Bethesda MD 20034

LEONHART, WILLIAM (INDEPENDENT)
b Parkersburg, WVa, Aug 1, 19; s Harry Kempton Leonhart & Rae Corinne Kahn L; m 1944 to Florence Lydia Sloan; c Deborah & Victoria. Educ: WVa Univ, AB, 39; Princeton Univ, MA, 41, PhD, 43. Polit & Govt Pos: Economist, Off of Coordr, Inter-Am Affairs, 41-43; econ analyst, Foreign Serv Auxiliary, Am Embassy, Buenos Aires, Argentina, 43-46; third secy & vconsul, Belgrade, Yugoslavia, 46-49; second secy & vconsul, Rome, Italy, 49-50; second secy & consul, Saigon, Phnom Penh & Vientiane, Indo China, 50-51; first secy & consul, Tokyo, 52-54; mem, policy planning staff, Dept of State, 55-57; Dept of State alt rep, Planning Bd Nat Security Coun, 56-57; Dept of State rep, Imperial Defense Col, London, Eng, 58; counr with rank of minister, Am Embassy, Tokyo, Japan, 59-62; first US Ambassador to Tanganyika, 62-64; US Ambassador to United Repub of Tanganyika & Zanzibar, 64; US Ambassador to United Repub of Tanzania, 64-65; detailed White House, 66, spec asst to the President, 67-68; spec asst to the President-Elect's Foreign Policy Liaison Rep, 68-69; US Ambassador to Yugoslavia, 69-71; dep commandant for int affairs, Nat War Col, 71- Bus & Prof Pos: Mem faculty, Dept of Polit, Princeton Univ, 39-40. Mil Serv: Army. Mem: US Strategic Inst; Princeton Club Washington; Fed City Club; Phi Beta Kappa; Delta Sigma Rho. Legal Res: WV Mailing Add: Quarters 15 Ft McNair Washington DC 20024

LEOPOLD, JOHN ROBINSON (R)
Hawaii State Sen
b Philadelphia, Pa, Feb 4, 43; s Irving Henry Leopold & Eunice Robinson L; m 1969 to Maureen Lahey. Educ: Hamilton Col, BA, 64; Theta Delta Chi. Polit & Govt Pos: Research asst to US Sen Hugh Scott, 65; chmn, 16th Dist Rep Party, Hawaii, 67; Oahu mem-at-lg, Hawaii State Bd Educ, 68-70; Hawaii State Rep, formerly; Hawaii State Sen, currently. Bus & Prof Pos: Dir, John Howard Asn; dir, Hawaii Planned Parenthood, 69- Honors & Awards: Keynote Speaker, Hawaii PTA Conv, 69; deleg, Nat Sch Bd Asn Conv, 69. Mailing Add: 11B 240 Makee Rd Honolulu HI 96815

LEPESKA, RICHARD GEORGE (D)
b Minneapolis, Minn, Feb 4, 40; s George L Lepeska & Arlene Ewert L; single. Educ: Dartmouth Col, 58-61; Lake City Community Col, AA, 63; Fla Atlantic Univ, BS, 67; Atlantic Key. Polit & Govt Pos: Admin asst to US Rep Paul G Rogers, Fla, 73- Mil Serv: Entered as Pvt, Marine Corps, 63, released as Lance Cpl, 65. Relig: Catholic. Legal Res: 346 Glenn Rd West Palm Beach FL 33405 Mailing Add: 2407 Rayburn Bldg Washington DC 20515

LEPORE, ALBERT J (D)
RI State Rep
Mailing Add: 33 Devon St Providence RI 02904

LEPORE, RALPH FRANK (D)
Treas, Ohio Co, WVa
b Wheeling, WVa, Mar 2, 13; s Frank LePore & Katheryn Callandra L; m 1939 to Florence Becker Rockabrand; c Frank August & Stephen Ralph. Educ: Elliott's Bus Sch, 35-39; Inst Appl Sci, Chicago, Ill, 41; Fed Bur Invest Nat Acad, DC, 41. Polit & Govt Pos: Clerk, Recreation Dept, Wheeling, WVa, 33-36; clerk of police court, Wheeling Police Dept, 36-41; spec agent, Fed Bur Invest, 41-48; chief dep sheriff, Ohio Co, 49-53, spec investr, Sheriff's Off, 57-61; chmn, WVa Racing Comn, 53-57; compliance officer, US Dept of Labor, 61-64; alt deleg-at-lg, Dem Nat Conv, 64 & 68; chmn, Ital Div, WVa All Am Coun; sheriff & treas, Ohio Co, 69-, chief investr, Prosecuting Attorney's Off, 73- Bus & Prof Pos: Vpres, Int Research Consults, 56-60; owner & operator, Ralph F LePore Assocs, 64-66; vpres, Intel Serv, Inc, 64- Mem: Fed Bur Invest Nat Police Acad; Fraternal Order of Police; Crippled Children's Fund; Am Legion Golden Gloves Boxing Tournament; Amen Corner, Pittsburgh (pres). Honors & Awards: Hon Ky Col. Relig: Roman Catholic. Mailing Add: 22 Hamilton Ave Wheeling WV 26003

LEPPERT, CHARLES JR (R)
b Johnstown, Pa, Oct 31, 32; s Charles (Lipari) Leppert, Sr & Frances Christina Grillo L; m 1966 to Karen Ann Rowe; c Ann Harney Lipari & Charles Augustine Lipari. Educ: Univ Pa, BA, 54; Univ Richmond Law Sch, LLB, 61. Polit & Govt Pos: Chmn, Cambria Co Young Rep, 61-63; minority counsel, Comt on Interior & Insular Affairs, US House Rep, 65- Mil Serv: Entered as Pvt, off training, Marine Corps, 54, released as 1st Lt, 58; Capt, Marine Res, until 68. Mem: Am & Va Bar Asns; Va Trial Lawyers Asn. Relig: Catholic. Legal Res: 6904 Baylor Dr Alexandria VA 22307 Mailing Add: 1329 Longworth House Off Bldg Washington DC 20515

LEREW, THEODORE (D)
SDak State Sen
b Aug 10, 25; married; c Tamyra, Patricia, Nancy, Susan & Joell. Educ: High sch. Polit & Govt Pos: Co comnr, 4 years; twp clerk, 8 years; SDak State Rep, 64-66; SDak State Sen, 75- Mil Serv: Army. Mem: Am Legion. Relig: Methodist. Mailing Add: Faulkton SD 57438

LERNER, LOUIS A (D)
b Chicago, Ill, June 12, 35; s Leo A Lerner & Deana Duskin L; m 1957 to Susan Winchester; c Lucy & Jane. Educ: Univ Chicago, 54; Roskilde Col, Denmark, 58; Roosevelt Univ, BA, 60. Polit & Govt Pos: Exec dir, Students for Stevenson, 52; bd mem, Students for Dem Action, 53; organizer, Reelect Mayor Richard J Daley, Chicago, 67, organizer & pub rels chmn, 71, 75; dir, Chicago Pub Libr, Ill, 67-, vpres, 75-; alt deleg, Dem Nat Conv, 68; comnr, Nat Comn Libr & Info Sci, 72-; mem, Cook Co Sheriff's Adv Comt, 73-; mem, Spec Ill Secy of State Comt on Privacy, 74-; mem finance comt, Jimmy Carter for President, 75- Bus & Prof Pos: Correspondent, Accredited Home Newspapers Am, Copenhagen, Denmark, 56-58; exec vpres, Lerner Home Newspapers, Chicago, 61-69, publ, 69-; pres, Lerner Suburban Commun Cable TV, 72- Mil Serv: Sgt E-6, Army Res, 54-61. Publ: News & News Values in the Danish Press, Scandinavian Seminars, 57. Mem: Sigma Delta Chi; Headline Club; Comt for Free & Competitive Press; Chicago Comt Ill Sesquicentennial; Statewide Citizens Comt; Ill State Libr (mem adv bd, 73-). Legal Res: 442 W Wellington Chicago IL 60657 Mailing Add: 7519 N Ashland Ave Chicago IL 60626

LEROY, L DAVID (R)
Dir Pub Rels, Nat Rep Cong Comt
b Tignall, Ga, Jan 2, 20; s Lansing Burrows LeRoy & Glennie David L; m 1945 to Mary Margaret Pridgeon; c David Charles & Gregory Alan. Educ: Univ Ga, AB in jour, 41; Berlitz Sch Lang, 47; treas, Sigma Delta Chi; Desmosthenians. Polit & Govt Pos: Dir publ, Nat Rep Cong Comt, 70-74, dir pub rels, 74- Bus & Prof Pos: Reporter, Wilmington Post, NC, 46-47; writer, Nat Hq, VFW, 47-48; writer, Gardner Advert Co, Washington, DC, 48-49; managing ed, Air Force Times, 49-53; mem bd ed, US News & World Report, 53-70. Mil Serv: Entered as 2nd Lt, Army, 41, released as Capt, 46, after serv in 1st Armored Div & other units, UK, Africa & Europe, 42-44; Purple Heart; European-African-MidE Campaign Ribbon with four Battle Stars; Am Serv Medal. Publ: Auth, Gerald Ford—Untold Story, Beatty, 74; articles in Army Times, Air Force Times, US News & World Report & others. Mem: Nat Press Club; Fairfax Rod & Gun Club; Capitol Hill Club. Relig: Presbyterian. Mailing Add: 4404 N 36th St Arlington VA 22207

LEROY, STEVEN HARRY (D)
b Lewiston, Idaho, Oct 16, 49; s Harold David Leroy (deceased) & Fay Palmer L; single. Educ: Univ Idaho, BS. Polit & Govt Pos: Press secy, Ravenscroft for Gov, summer 70; spec asst & youth coordr, Andrus for Gov Comt, fall 70; fed-state rels intern, Idaho Gov Cecil D Andrus, 71-72; alt deleg, Dem Nat Conv, 72; pub rels specialist, State Idaho, 72-; pub rels coordr, Idaho Sunshine Initiative Comt, 74; campaign mgr, Primary Campaign Solberg for Lt Gov, 74; campaign mgr, J Ray Cox for Cong Gen Elec, 74; pub info officer, Idaho Dept Law Enforcement, 75- Bus & Prof Pos: Newsman, KLEW TV, 69-70 & KTVB TV, summer 71; spec polit affairs consult & election analyst, Cable Channel Seven, 73- Mem: Young Dem of Idaho (dist chmn, 72-); Community Schs Adult Media Prog (polit sci coordr, 73-). Relig: Presbyterian. Legal Res: 920 Tenth Ave Lewiston ID 83501 Mailing Add: 1316 1/2 W State St Boise ID 83702

LESHER, LOIS M (R)
Del State Rep
Mailing Add: 1120 Harvey Rd Claymont DE 19703

LESKIW, MYRON (R)
b Ukraine, Nov 17, 09; s Joseph Leskiw & Magdalene Debrin L; m 1946 to Mary E Rudicel; c Mary Magdalene, Margaret R (Mrs Pierce) & Donald M. Educ: Newark Col Eng, NJ, 41-42. Polit & Govt Pos: State chmn & mem adv bd, Rep Heritage Groups Fedn, Newark, NJ, 69-72, state campaign dir, 74-; mem, NJ Rep State Comt, 70-72; alt deleg, Rep Nat Conv, 72; mem adv coun, Small Bus Admin, Newark Dist, 72-; alt deleg, Rep Nat Conv, 72. Bus & Prof Pos: Publ & mgr, Rep Heritage Rev, NJ, 70-73, co-ed, 74-75; mem, Nat Confederation Am Ethnic Groups, Washington, DC, 73-75. Mil Serv: Entered as Pvt, Air Force, 42, released as Sgt, 45, after serv in US & China-Burma-India, 43-45; Am Serv Medal; Asiatic Pac Serv Medal; Good Conduct Medal. Mem: Ukrainian Nat Asn; Ukrainian Nat Rep Fedn; Tel Pioneer Am, AFL-CIO; NJ Ukrainian Rep Asn. Mailing Add: 728 Ridge St Newark NJ 07104

LESLEIN, BETTY JEAN SWAYNE (D)
b Leesburg, Ohio, Mar 18, 32; d John Franklin Swayne & Myrtle Eubanks S; m 1954 to Walter Irwin Leslein; c Mark Edward, Walter Peter, Jr & Kathy Marie. Educ: Ohio State Univ, BSc educ, 64, MA, 70; Emory Univ, 68-69; Ga State Univ, 69-70. Polit & Govt Pos: Precinct chmn, McCarthy for President, Columbus, Ohio, 68; mem steering comt & one of founders, Dem Women of De Kalb, Ga, 69, first vchmn & prog chmn, 69-71, pres, 72-73 & 74-75; co-chmn for women, Carter for Gov Campaign, De Kalb Co, 70; mem steering comt, George T Smith for Lt Gov Campaign, 70; mem, De Kalb Co Dem Exec Comt, 70-75; mem, Ga Dem Party Exec Comt, 71-75; alt deleg, Dem Nat Conv, 72; mem, Gov Drug Abuse Adv Coun, 73-, chairperson subcomt drug abuse educ & prev, currently. Bus & Prof Pos: Teacher adjudged delinquent girls, Scioto Village High Sch, Ohio Youth Comn, 64-66; teacher & work study coordr, Scioto Local Sch Dist, Hilliard High Sch, Educ Ment Retarded, 66-68; research asst sociol, Emory Univ, Grady Hosp, 68-69; caseworker, Fulton Co Family & Children's Serv, summer 69; teacher, Hamilton Ctr Exceptional Children, De Kalb Co, 69-72; teacher hist, Columbia High Sch, Ga, 72-73; teacher hist, Henderson High Sch, 73- Mem: Nat Educ Asn; Ga Asn Educators; Orgn DeKalb Educators; Polit Action Comt Educ (chmn, 75-); Fourth Dist Coun for Social Studies (secy). Honors & Awards: Sustained Superior Performance Award, Fed Aviation Agency, 61. Relig: Unitarian Universalist. Mailing Add: 4033 Barr Circle Tucker GA 30084

LESSARD, LEO E (R)
NH State Rep
Mailing Add: 61 Old Madbury Lane Apts Dover NH 03820

548 / LESTER

LESTER, DENNIS ALAN (D)
Mont State Rep
b Great Falls, Mont, Apr 2, 51; s Roy Price Lester & Charlene Joyce Goettel L; single. Educ: Univ Mont, BA, 73; Beta Psi Chap of Phi Alpha Theta. Polit & Govt Pos: Mont State Rep, 75- Mem: Int Brotherhood Elec Workers. Relig: Roman Catholic. Mailing Add: 1412 Fourth Ave S Great Falls MT 59405

LESTER, HORACE BAXTER (D)
Miss State Rep
b Quitman Co, Miss, Sept 5, 19; s Simon Edward Lester & Willie Reid L; m 1942 to Dora Essie Sanford; c Horace B, Jr & Thomas S. Educ: Int Correspondence Course in Eng; Scabbard & Blade. Polit & Govt Pos: Miss State Rep, Hinds Co, 64- Bus & Prof Pos: Engr, 46-48; field civil engr, 48-50; chief engr, supv construction of sewer & water systs, 50-51; pvt practice, 51-54; consult engr, 55- Mil Serv: Entered as Pvt, Army, 42, released as Capt, 46, after serv in Pac Theater; Col, Army Res, currently; Am & Pac Theater Ribbons; Philippine Liberation & Reserve Medals; Victory Medal with 2 Overseas Serv Bars. Mem: Fel, Am Soc Civil Engrs; Nat & Miss Soc Prof Engrs; ROA; Rotary; CofC. Relig: Baptist. Mailing Add: 1350 Eastover Dr Jackson MS 39211

LESTER, JAMES LUTHER (D)
Ga State Sen
b Augusta, Ga, Jan 12, 32; s William McMorris Lester & Elizabeth Miles L; m 1958 to Gwendolyn Gleason; c James L, Jr & Frank G. Educ: The Citadel, AB; Univ Ga, LLB; Sigma Chi. Polit & Govt Pos: Pres, Young Dem Richmond Co, Ga, 64-66; chmn, Richmond Co Dem Exec Comt, 66-70; Ga State Sen, 23rd Dist, 71- Mil Serv: Entered as 2nd Lt, Army, 52, released as Capt, 59, after serv in 81st Inf Div, Korea, 53-54. Mem: Am & Ga Bar Asns; Kiwanis; Am Legion. Honors & Awards: Outstanding Serv to Ment Retarded Award, 73. Relig: Methodist. Legal Res: 3205 Wheeler Rd Augusta GA 30904 Mailing Add: First Fed Savings Bldg 985 Broad St Augusta GA 30902

LETCHER, ISABELLE SCOTT (R)
VChmn, Ottawa Co Rep Party, Okla
b Wilkes-Barre, Pa, July 10, 08; d Frank L Scott & Jean Fraser Menzies S; m 1933 to Dr Charles Wesley Letcher; c Charles Scott, John Henry, Frank Scott & William Frederick. Educ: Wyo Sem, Pa, 2 years; Wilson Col, 1 year. Polit & Govt Pos: Precinct chmn, Miami, Okla, 50; pres, Rep Women's Club, 54-56 & 65-69; dist committeewoman, Ottawa Co, 67-68; alt deleg, Rep Nat Conv, 68 & 72; vchmn, Ottawa Co Rep Party, Okla, 68- Mem: Letters & Arts; Garden Club; Rep Women's Club; Lioness Club. Relig: Presbyterian; deaconess. Mailing Add: 1525 Lincoln Blvd Miami OK 74354

LETENDRE, RAYMOND C (D)
RI State Sen
Mailing Add: 407 Hunt St Central Falls RI 02863

LETTERMAN, RUSSELL PAUL (D)
Pa State Rep
b Milesburg, Pa, Mar 8, 33; s Russell Lee Letterman & Savillia E Heltman L; m 1963 to Janice Grace Mapes; c Tor Eric. Educ: Bellefonte Pub Schs, Pa, 12 years. Polit & Govt Pos: Committeeman, Centre Co Dem Party, Pa, 61-; area & registr chmn, 65-69; finance chmn, 69; Pa State Rep, 70- Bus & Prof Pos: Prof baseball, St Louis Browns, 51; barber, self-employed, 62- Mil Serv: Entered as Seaman Recruit, Navy, 52, released as Ship's Serviceman 2/C, 55, after serv in USA Andromeda, AKA-15, Pac Theatre, 52-55; Good Conduct Medal; Korean Ribbon with two Battle Stars; Nat Defense, UN & China Serv Ribbons. Mem: Bellefonte Elks Lodge 1094; Bellefonte VFW Post 1600; Grand Lodge of Pa Lodge 146; Southern Clinton Co Sportsmen's Asn, Inc; Clarence Dem Club. Relig: Methodist. Mailing Add: PO Box 285 Milesburg PA 16853

LEVANDER, HAROLD (R)
b Swede Home, Nebr, Oct 10, 10; s Peter Magni LeVander & Laura Lo Vene L; m 1938 to Iantha Powrie; c Harold, Jean (Mrs Thomas King) & Dyan (Mrs Paul R Hammarberg). Educ: Gustavus Adolphus Col, BA, 32; Univ Minn, LLB, 35; Pi Kappa Delta; Gamma Eta Gamma. Hon Degrees: LLD, Gustavus Adolphus Col. Polit & Govt Pos: Asst co attorney, Dakota Co, Minn, 35-39; Gov Minn, 67-71; deleg, Rep Nat Conv, 68 & 72. Bus & Prof Pos: Pres, United Fed Savings & Loan Asn; prof speech, Macalester Col; attorney-at-law, St Paul, 39-67; dir, Am Nat Bank, Ecumenical Inst, Billy Graham Evangelistic Asn, St Paul Securities Inc & Coalition for Rural Develop. Mem: Nat Lutheran Coun (secy); Am & Minn Bar Asns; Town & Country Club; Pool & Yacht Club. Honors & Awards: Distinguished Alumni Awards, Univ Minn & Gustavus Adolphus Col. Mailing Add: 2323 Thompson Ave South St Paul MN 55075

LEVANDER, IANTHA POWRIE (R)
Rep Nat Committeewoman, Minn
b Milwaukee, Wis, Jan 13, 13; d William Robert Powrie (deceased) & Kathleen Graham P (deceased); m 1938 to Harold LeVander; c Harold P, Jean (Mrs Thomas King) & Dyan (Mrs Paul R Hammarberg). Educ: Univ Minn, BS in speech educ, 35; pres, Alpha Gamma Delta; Zeta Phi Eta; Hon Cadet Colonette. Polit & Govt Pos: First Lady of Minn, LeVander Campaign for Gov, Minn, 66-70; deleg numerous co, dist & state Rep conv; alt deleg, Rep Nat Conv, 72; Rep Nat Committeewoman, Minn, 72- Bus & Prof Pos: Instr swimming, diving, canoe trips in girls' camps, Minn & Mich, 31-35; teacher speech & Eng, high sch, 35-38. Publ: Where your governors live, 69. Mem: Schubert Club (bd); Bethesda Hosp Vols; Divine Redeemer Hosp Bd; Univ Minn Alumni (bd dirs); Minn Children's Mus (bd dirs). Honors & Awards: Minn Mother of the Year, Minn Chap, Am Mother, 70. Relig: Lutheran. Mailing Add: 2323 Thompson Ave South St Paul MN 55075

LEVASSEUR, ALPHONSE (D)
NH State Rep
Mailing Add: 298 North Main St Manchester NH 03102

LEVERENZ, TED E (D)
Ill State Sen
Mailing Add: 1629 S 17th Ave Maywood IL 60153

LEVERETT, ULYSSES S GRANT (R)
b Lexington, NC, May 29, 26; s Otis Leverett (deceased) & Lizzie May Martin L; m 1941 to Sarah A Bohannon; c James Keith, Ulysses Bernard, Stanley Charles, Pamela Regius, Cheryl Auita, Gwendolyn Renee & William Kevin. Educ: Shaw Univ, AB; Johnson C Smith Univ, MDiv; Lab Applied Bio-Dynamics, Yale Univ, Cert; Epsilon Delta Chi. Polit & Govt Pos: Deleg, White House Conf on Aging, 71; mem, Chesterfield Co Citizens Comt, SC; committeeman for the reelection of the President; deleg, Rep Nat Conv, 72. Mil Serv: Army, 43-47, Capt. Mem: Am Legion; NAACP. Honors & Awards: Presidential Campaign Award; Off Econ Opportunity Award for Serv; Booker T Davis Award in Syst Theology. Relig: Presbyterian. Mailing Add: 317 Second St Cheraw SC 29520

LEVERETTE, GIGI (D)
Mem, Ga State Dem Exec Comt
b Spalding Co, Ga, Sept 20, 56; d William Otis Leverette & Mary Ann Norsworthy L; single. Educ: Indian Springs Acad, dipl, 73; Tift Col, 73- Polit & Govt Pos: Mem, Ga Young Dem, currently; mem, Ga State Dem Exec Comt, 17th Sen Dist, Butts Co, 74-; co-chmn, 17th Sen Dist Caucus, currently; vol worker for Lt Gov Zell Miller Campaign, 74. Relig: Presbyterian. Mailing Add: 671 McDonough Rd Jackson GA 30233

LEVI, EDWARD HIRSCH
Attorney Gen of US
b Chicago, Ill, June 26, 11; s Gerson B Levi & Elsa B Hirsch L; m 1946 to Kate Sulzberger; c John, David & Michael. Educ: Univ Chicago, PhB, 32, JD, 35; Yale Univ, Sterling fel, 35-36, JSD, 38; Phi Beta Kappa; Order of the Coif. Hon Degrees: LLD & LHD from various cols & univs. Polit & Govt Pos: Spec asst to Attorney Gen US, 40-45; first asst, War Div, Dept Justice, 43, first asst, Antitrust Div, 44-45, chmn interdept comt monopolies & cartels, 45; counsel, Fedn Atomic Scientist, Atomic Energy Act, 46; counsel, subcomt monopoly power, Judiciary Comt, US Senate, 50; mem research adv bd, Comt Econ Develop, 51-54; mem, President's Task Force Priorities Higher Educ, 69-70; Attorney Gen of US, 75- Bus & Prof Pos: Asst prof, Univ Chicago Law Sch, 36-40, prof, 45-, dean, 50-62, provost, 62-68, pres, 68-74, emer pres, 75-, Karl Llewellyn Distinguished Serv prof, 75; Thomas Guest prof, Univ Colo, summer 60; bd Social Sci Research Coun, 59-62; mem, Coun Legal Educ & Prof Responsibility; mem, Citizens Comt Grad Med Educ, 63-66, Comn Founds & Pvt Philanthropy, 69-70, Sloan Comn Cable Commun, 70 & Nat Comn Productivity, 70-; trustee, Univ Chicago Int Legal Ctr, Woodrow Wilson Nat Fel Found, Inst Psychoanal, Chicago, Urban Inst, Mus Sci & Indust, Russell Sage Found, Aspen Inst Humanistic Studies & Inst Int Educ. Publ: Elements of the Law (with R S Steffen), 50; auth, Point of View, 69; auth, The Crisis in the Nature of Law, 69; plus others. Mem: Am Acad Arts & Sci; Am Bar Found; Am Law Inst; Am Judicature Soc. Honors & Awards: Legion of Merit, France. Legal Res: 5855 University Ave Chicago IL 60637 Mailing Add: Dept of Justice Washington DC 20530

LEVI, JOSEPH, II (R)
Pa State Rep
Mailing Add: Capitol Bldg Harrisburg PA 17120

LEVIN, ABRAHAM (R)
b Philadelphia, Pa, Oct 22, 03; s Morris Levin & Anna Samson L; m to Roslyne Van Straaten; c Donald. Educ: Univ Pa, BS, 25, LLB, 28; Zeta Beta Tau. Polit & Govt Pos: Asst Attorney Gen, Pa, 68-69; ward leader, Rep City Comt, Philadelphia, 71-; alt deleg, Rep Nat Conv, 72. Mem: Lawyers Club; Univ Pa Alumni Asn; Brith Sholom; Brith Sholom Found (vchmn); Philadelphia Lodge 500. Relig: Hebrew. Mailing Add: 6852 Elmwood Ave Philadelphia PA 19142

LEVIN, CHARLES LEONARD
Justice, Mich Supreme Court
b Detroit, Mich, Apr 28, 26; s Theodore Levin & Rhoda Katzin L; m 1956 to Patricia Oppenheim; c Arthur D, Amy S & Fredrick S. Educ: Univ Mich, Ann Arbor, BA, Law Sch, LLB. Polit & Govt Pos: Justice, Mich Supreme Court, 73- Mem: Am Law Inst; trustee, Marygrove Col. Relig: Jewish. Legal Res: 18280 Fairway Dr Detroit MI 48221 Mailing Add: Travelers Tower Box 9 26555 Evergreen Rd Southfield MI 48076

LEVIN, E THEODORE (D)
Md State Deleg
b Baltimore, Md, Aug 29, 41; s Jerome Bernard Levin & Marian Etta Gottlieb L; single. Educ: Univ Md, BA, 66, Sch Law, JD, 69; Johns Hopkins Univ, MLA, 73; Omicron Delta Kappa; Tau Epsilon Phi. Polit & Govt Pos: Md State Deleg, 75- Bus & Prof Pos: Attorney. Mil Serv: Entered Army, 69, released as E-4, 75, after serv in 611th Repair Parts. Relig: Jewish. Mailing Add: 626 Ralston Ave Baltimore MD 21208

LEVIN, GEORGE DANIEL (D)
b Sturgis, SDak, July 4, 21; s Daniel Oscar Levin & Dorothy Frazee L; m 1943 to Laura K Butler; c Lauren, Dennis & Sheryl. Polit & Govt Pos: Deleg, Dem Nat Conv, 68, alt deleg, 72. Mem: Bd, SDak Farmers Union, 66-; chmn bd, SDak Div, Independent Stockgrowers of Am, 68- Relig: Protestant. Mailing Add: Hereford SD 57743

LEVIN, IRVING H (D)
RI State Rep
Mailing Add: 39 Lyndon Rd Cranston RI 02905

LEVIN, MARILYN LOIS (D)
Pres, Young Dem Clubs, Pa
b Philadelphia, Pa, June 13, 52; d Harry Levin & Edith Karp L; m 1975 to Charles Anthony Ottaviano. Educ: Community Col Philadelphia, 69-71; Pa State Univ, BSS, 73. Polit & Govt Pos: Exec dir women's div, Pa Dem State Comt, 73-; pres, Young Dem Pa, 74-, mem, Consumer Adv Comt to Ins Dept, 75- Mem: Am Jewish Cong; NAACP; Women's Polit Caucus; Am Civil Liberties Union. Relig: Jewish. Legal Res: 1421 Unruh Ave Philadelphia PA 19111 Mailing Add: 1082 Summerwood Dr Harrisburg PA 17111

LEVIN, MYRTILLA FONES (R)
Chmn, Jasper Co Rep Cent Comt, Iowa
b Des Moines, Iowa, Aug 30, 38; d Welzie Harte Fones & Myrtilla Daniels F; m 1960 to Jack Dueland Levin; c Jack D, Jr, Stacy Margaret & Ann Myrtilla. Educ: Monticello Col, Ill, 57; Drake Univ, BA, 60, grad study, 68-69; Kappa Beta Kappa; Kappa Alpha Theta. Polit & Govt Pos: Vpres, Jasper Co Rep Women, Iowa, 65-66; chmn, Jasper Co Rep Cent Comt, 72-; alt deleg, Rep Nat Conv, 72; app, State Confidential Rec Coun, 73-; mayor, Newton, 73- Bus & Prof Pos: Teacher, High Sch Eng, Des Moines Pub Schs, 60-62; homemaker, 62- Mem: YMCA (vpres bd dirs, Newton, Iowa, 71-); Skiff Hosp Auxiliary (bd dirs, 71-). Relig: Episcopal. Mailing Add: 726 W Ninth St S Newton IA 50208

LEVIN, ROBERT **(D)**
Mem, Pa Dem State Comt
b Philadelphia, Pa, Feb 25, 44; s Albert Levin & Claire Kristal L; single. Educ: Syracuse Univ, AB, 66. Polit & Govt Pos: Mem, Pa Dem State Comt, 70-, mem, Steering Comt of Rules & Rev Comt, 71-72; deleg, Dem Nat Conv, 72. Bus & Prof Pos: Produce jobber, M Levin & Co, Philadelphia, Pa, 66- Relig: Jewish. Mailing Add: 231 Matthew Rd Merion PA 19066

LEVINE, PHILIP MICHAEL **(R)**
Chmn, Putnam Co Rep Party, NY
b New York, NY, Aug 14, 06; s Julius Levine & Mary Wolk L; m 1948 to Hilda Koenigsberg; c Judith Irene. Educ: NY Univ, 2 years; St John's Law Sch, 2 years; basketball team. Polit & Govt Pos: Town chmn, Rep Party, 60, co-chmn, 64; alt deleg, Rep Nat Conv, 64; chmn, Putnam Co Rep Party, NY, 64- Bus & Prof Pos: Pres, Leesons Clothes, Inc & J Levine Sons Corp. Mil Serv: Entered as Pvt, Army, 42, released as Sgt, 45, after serv in Mil Police Command; Good Conduct Medal. Mem: Vets Asn; Zionist; Clothing Mfrs Asn; KofP; Mahopac Civic Asn. Relig: Jewish. Legal Res: N Lake Blvd Mahopac NY 10541 Mailing Add: Empire State Bldg Suite 2806A New York NY 10001

LEVINSON, BERNARD HIRSH **(D)**
b Austin, Tex, Sept 2, 07; s Samuel Levinson & Rebecca Lewin L; m 1940 to Carlyn Krupp; c Peter Joseph & Brent Lewin. Educ: Univ Cincinnati, AB with high honors, 29; Harvard Law Sch, JD, 32; Phi Beta Kappa. Polit & Govt Pos: Attorney, Dept of Justice, Washington, DC, 39-42; attorney, Off of the Solicitor, Dept of Interior, 42-45, attorney, surplus property off, Honolulu, Hawaii, 45-47; dep attorney gen, Territory of Hawaii, 47; judge, First Circuit Court, 66-67; assoc justice, Hawaii Supreme Court, 67-74. Bus & Prof Pos: Attorney, Seattle, Wash, 33-39; attorney, Honolulu, Hawaii, 47-65; pvt law practice, Honolulu, 74- Mem: Scottish Rite Mason (33 degree); Shriner; B'nai B'rith; Am Jewish Comt; Hawaii Jewish Welfare Fund. Honors & Awards: United Jewish Appeal Award of Merit; B'nai B'rith Award of Merit; Father of the year in the field of law, Honolulu CofC. Relig: Jewish. Legal Res: 2003 Kalia Rd Honolulu HI 96815 Mailing Add: 1126 Pac Trade Ctr 190 S King St Honolulu HI 96813

LEVITAN, LAURENCE **(D)**
Md State Sen
b Washington, DC, Oct 22, 33; s Maurice Levitan & Nathlie Rosenthal L; m 1957 to Barbara E Levin; c Jennifer, Michelle & Lisa. Educ: Washington & Lee Univ, BS, 55; George Washington Univ Sch Law, JD, 58; Zeta Beta Tau. Polit & Govt Pos: Mem, Montgomery Co Financial Adv Comt, Md, 66-70; Md State Deleg, 71-74; Md State Sen, 75-, mem budget & taxation comt & chmn joint comt on mgt of pub funds, Md State Senate, currently. Bus & Prof Pos: Partner, Levitan, Ezrin, Cramer, West & Weinstein, 60- Mem: DC, Md & Am Bar Asns. Relig: Jewish. Legal Res: 11426 Georgetown Dr Potomac MD 20854 Mailing Add: 5454 Wisconsin Ave Chevy Chase MD 20015

LEVITAS, ELLIOTT HARRIS **(D)**
US Rep, Ga
b Atlanta, Ga, Dec 26, 30; s Louis Joseph Levitas & Ida Goldstein L; m 1955 to Barbara Claire Hillman; c Karen Eve, Susan Debra & Kevin Noah. Educ: Emory Univ, BA, 52, Law Sch, LLB, 56; Oxford Univ, Rhodes scholar, 52, BA, 54, MA, 58; Phi Delta Phi; Phi Beta Kappa; Omicron Delta Kappa. Polit & Govt Pos: Chmn, Ga Gov Spec Comt on Legis Const Coord, 64; deleg, Dem Nat Conv, 64; Ga State Rep, DeKalb Co, 66-74; US Rep, Ga, 75- Bus & Prof Pos: Partner, Arnall, Golden & Gregory, 55-75. Mil Serv: Entered as Lt, Air Force, 55, released as Capt, 62, after serv as Judge Adv, Air Force, 56-58. Mem: Am Bar Asn; Lawyers Club of Atlanta; Com Club of Atlanta; Emory Univ Alumni Asn; Emory Law Alumni Asn. Honors & Awards: Ga Speaker of the Year Award. Relig: Jewish. Legal Res: 829 Castle Falls Dr NE Atlanta GA 30329 Mailing Add: US House of Rep Washington DC 20515

LEVITT, ARTHUR **(D)**
Comptroller, State of NY
b Brooklyn, NY, June 28, 00; s Israel A Levitt & Rose Daniels L; m 1929 to Dorothy M Wolff; c Arthur, Jr. Educ: Columbia Univ, AB, 21, LLB, 24; Phi Sigma Delta. Hon Degrees: LLD, Siena Col, 68, Union Col, 68, Yeshiva Univ, 68, Columbia Univ, 69, St John's Univ, 69, & Pace Col, 71; LLB, Jewish Theol Sem, 71. Polit & Govt Pos: Pres, bd of educ, NY, 52-55; Comptroller, NY, 55-; chmn, Dem State Conv, 65; deleg, Dem Nat Conv, 68. Mil Serv: Pvt, Inf, World War I, reentered as Capt, Judge Adv Gen Corps, Army, 46, released as Col, 46, after serv in Judge Adv Div, 1st Army, Transportation Corps; Legion of Merit; World War I & II Victory Medals; Army Commendation, ETO & African Theater Ribbons; Col, Army Res, 66- Mem: Mason (33 degree); Shrine; KofP; Odd Fellows; Am Legion. Relig: Hebrew.. Mailing Add: 203 E 72nd St New York NY 10021

LEVITT, ROBERT ELWOOD **(R)**
Chmn, Stark Co Rep Party, Ohio
b Los Angeles, Calif, Nov 1, 26; s George L Levitt & Clara Olston L; m 1948 to Barbara Ann Toot; c John, Thomas & Susan. Educ: St Ambrose Col, 44-45; Northwestern Univ, BS, 47; Western Reserve Univ, LLB, 53; Phi Gamma Delta; Phi Delta Phi. Polit & Govt Pos: Spec counsel to Ohio Attorney Gen, 56-58; asst solicitor, Canton, Ohio, 56-59, councilman, 60-63; Ohio State Rep, 63-74, majority floor leader, Ohio House Rep, 69-72; chmn, Stark Co Rep Party, 75- Bus & Prof Pos: Attorney, Day, Ketterer, Raley, Wright & Rybolt, 60- Mil Serv: Entered as A/S, Navy, 44, released as Ens, 46. Mem: Am Legion; Stark Co Bar Asn; Ment Health Asn; Congress Lake Club; Canton Club. Relig: Presbyterian. Legal Res: 13344 Congress Lake Ave Hartville OH 44632 Mailing Add: 800 Cleve-Tusc Bldg Canton OH 44702

LEVY, EUGENE **(R)**
NY State Assemblyman
b Brooklyn, NY, Dec 1, 26; s Jack Levy & Helen Gerber L; m 1950 to Geraldine Elaine Schack; c Felicia & William. Educ: NY Univ, 44. Polit & Govt Pos: Vpres, WRamapo Rep Club, Suffern, NY, 63; dep dir, Rockland Co Civil Defense, 63; Councilman, Ramapo, 64-68; NY State Assemblyman, 94th Assembly Dist, 69-, chmn, Joint Legis Comt Consumer Protection & Assembly Subcomt Educ of Handicapped, mem, Assembly Subcomts Drug Educ, Primary & Sec Educ, Dangerous Pesticides, Venereal Disease, & Assembly Educ & Health Comts, currently. Bus & Prof Pos: Pres, Plaza Restaurant Inc, Spring Valley, NY, until 72. Mil Serv: Entered as HA 2/C, Navy Med Corps, 44, released as PhM 3/C, 46. Mem: F&AM (past master, Athelstane Lodge); Rotary (bd dirs, Spring Valley Club); Masters & Wardens Asn; B'nai B'rith; KofP. Honors & Awards: Distinguished Serv Award, Spring Valley Jaycees, 69; Humanitarian Award, New City Lions; Friend of Educ Award, Ramapo Sch Dist No 2 Prin Asn, 72; Appreciation Award, Welfare League, Letchworth Village, 72; Outstanding Serv Award in Educ Professionalism, Sch Adminrs Asn of NY, 72. Relig: Jewish. Mailing Add: 2 East Pl Suffern NY 10901

LEVY, HARRY CHARLES **(D)**
Treas, Nev State Dem Cent Comt
b Batavia, NY, Sept 12, 10; s Max Levy & Esther Holtzer L; m 1928 to Jeanne Sklar; c Alvin M & Elaine L (Mrs Turk). Educ: Los Angeles High Sch, grad, 27. Polit & Govt Pos: Chmn, Clark Co Juv Bd, Nev, 51-67; chmn, Las Vegas Housing Authority, 51; mem bd dirs, Nat Housing Conf, 58-; mem, Clark Co Dem Cent Comt, 59-; comnr, Nev State Tax Comn, 59-61; comnr, Las Vegas, Nev, 61-65; mem, Small Bus Adv Comt, 63-65; treas, Nev State Dem Cent Comt, 66-; chmn, Civilian-Mil Coun, SNev, 67-; deleg, Dem Nat Conv, 68. Bus & Prof Pos: Treas, Transwestern Life Ins Co, Reno, 58-64; dir, Nev Title Ins Co, 60-65; treas, Nev Savings & Loan, 61-66; dir, Nev State Bank, Las Vegas, 61-65; dir, Nev Nat Bank, Reno, 66- Mem: Mason; Scottish Rite; Shrine; Elks; B'nai B'rith (pres, Las Vegas Lodge). Honors & Awards: Variety Club Humanitarian Heart Award, 55; City of Hope Man of Year Award, 62; Jewish War Vet Community Serv Award, 66; Anti-Defamation League Man of Year Award, 62; B'nai B'rith Man of Year, 58. Relig: Jewish; pres, Temple Beth Sholom, 54-55. Mailing Add: 1700 Rexford Dr Las Vegas NV 89105

LEVY, NORMAN J **(R)**
NY State Sen
b Rockville Centre, NY, Jan 24, 31; s Emanuel Levy & Rose Ferraro L; m 1968 to Joy Saslow. Educ: Bucknell Univ, BA, 52; Univ Pa Law Sch, 1 year; Brooklyn Law Sch, JD, 58; Phi Alpha Theta; Sigma Alpha Mu. Polit & Govt Pos: Asst dist attorney, Nassau Co, NY, 59-70; Rackets Bur Chief, 62-70; NY State Sen, Seventh Dist, 71-73, Eighth Dist, 73-, chmn, Standing Comt on Labor, NY Senate, currently. Bus & Prof Pos: Attorney, 58- Mil Serv: Entered as Pvt, Army, 54, released as Pfc, 56, after serv in Judge Adv Gen Corps, First Army, 54-56; 2nd Lt, Army Res, 57-60. Mem: Mason; B'nai B'rith; Elks; Jewish War Vets; Sons of Italy. Honors & Awards: Humanities Award, Anti-Defamation League; Law Enforcement Award, Jewish War Vets; Christopher Columbus Award, Nat Columbus Day Soc; Long Beach CofC Man of the Year, 72; Nassau Co Auxiliary Police Award. Relig: Jewish. Mailing Add: 299 Merrick Ave S Merrick NY 11566

LEWANDOWSKI, MICHAEL **(D)**
b Brooklyn, NY, July 8, 51; s Edward Lewandowski & Irene Moger L; m 1974 to Maria Romano. Educ: Baruch Col, BBA, 72; Syracuse Univ Maxwell Sch, MPA, 74. Polit & Govt Pos: Campaign mgr, Solarz for Cong, 74; admin asst to US Rep Stephen J Solarz, NY, 75- Mem: Am Soc Pub Admin; Mid-Bay Dem Club; Am Asn Polit Consult; Am Asn Polit Sci; Int City Mgt Asn. Legal Res: 2292 Coney Island Ave Brooklyn NY 11223 Mailing Add: 5733 Leverett Ct Alexandria VA 22311

LEWIN, THEODORE E **(R)**
Maine State Rep
Mailing Add: 129 Purinton Ave Augusta ME 04330

LEWIS, ALBERT B **(D)**
NY State Sen
b Brooklyn, NY, Oct 16, 25; s David Lewis & Lillie Levine L; m 1949 to Sara Anne Beresniakoff; c David, Eric & Jonathan. Educ: Brooklyn Col, AB, 48; City Col NY, 49; St John's Univ Sch Law, LLB, 54. Polit & Govt Pos: Secy, Supreme Court Judge King, 62-66; NY State Sen, 67- Bus & Prof Pos: CPA & attorney-at-law, 54- Mil Serv: Entered as Pvt, Army, 43, released as Cpl, 49. Relig: Hebrew. Mailing Add: 123 Bay 25th St Brooklyn NY 11214

LEWIS, ARTHUR JOSEPH, JR **(D)**
Mass State Sen
Mailing Add: State Capitol Boston MA 02133

LEWIS, AVIS IDA **(R)**
Chairwoman, Chippewa Co Rep Party, Minn
b Mitchell, Iowa, Oct 23, 18; d William Arthur Schmidt & Laura Amelia Duenow S; wid; c Craig Dean, Laurine Anne & Valerie Jean. Educ: Hamilton Bus Col, Mason City, Iowa, 37-38. Polit & Govt Pos: Clerk-secy, Dept Air Force, Washington, DC, 41-50; chairwoman, Chippewa Co Rep Party, Minn, 68- Mem: Minn Farm Bur Fedn. Relig: Presbyterian. Mailing Add: Rte 2 Murdock MN 56271

LEWIS, B E (BUD) **(R)**
Idaho State Rep
Mailing Add: Rte 3 St Maries ID 83861

LEWIS, B ROBERT **(DFL)**
Minn State Sen
Mailing Add: 1601 Hillsboro Ave S St Louis Park MN 55426

LEWIS, BARBARA HALSTED **(R)**
Pres, Tex Fedn Rep Women
b Julesburg, Colo, Dec 30, 38; d Harold Seaver Halsted & Elizabeth Watteyne H; wid; c Laura. Educ: Cottey Col, 56-57; Colo State Univ, 57-58; Tex Tech Univ, 58-59; Sam Houston State Univ, BS, 60; Delphian Lit Soc. Polit & Govt Pos: Chmn var Rep senate, cong & statewide campaign & orgn comts, Tex, 60-74; precinct chmn, Austin Rep Party, 68-75; Tex coordr, Nat Fedn Rep Women Conv, 69-71; dep pres, Tex Fedn Rep Women, 69-71, vpres, 71-73, pres, 73- Bus & Prof Pos: Secy, Tex Eng Exten Serv, 58-59; teacher, Bryan Independent Sch Dist, Tex, 60-62; teacher, Northeast Independent Sch Dist, San Antonio, 62-63; vpres, Yucca Verde Land Co, 68-74; real estate & oil investments, 74- Mem: Am Cancer Soc (officer & comt mem, 73-); Eastern Star; Kerrville Independent Sch Dist Bd Trustees (pres). Honors & Awards: Annual Awards, Am Cancer Soc, 63-, Outstanding Serv to Control Cancer Award, 71-72; Texas Outstanding Young Woman Award, 75. Relig: Episcopal. Mailing Add: 110 1500 Scenic Dr Austin TX 78703

LEWIS, CHARLES WILLIAM (BILL) **(R)**
Ariz State Rep
b Warwick, NY, Apr 7, 26; s Charles William Lewis & Oleta Fuller L; m 1947 to Pearl Louise Pomeroy; c Charles Alan, Gary Steven & Donn William. Educ: Tusculum Col, AB, 47. Polit & Govt Pos: Ariz State Rep, 69- Bus & Prof Pos: Free lance author & photographer, 47-; prog dir, KRIZ Radio, Phoenix, 51-53; assoc ed, Ariz Farmer/Ranchman mag, 53-55; chief of info & educ, Ariz Game & Fish Dept, 55-64; sports writer & announcer, KTAR AM & TV,

Phoenix, 64-68; registered rep, Financial Progs, Inc, 68-72; pub rels, 72- Mil Serv: Entered as A/S, Navy, 44, released as Sonarman 3/C, 45, after serv in Fleet Sonar Sch, US, 44-45. Publ: Over 300 articles published in Western Outdoors, Outdoor Life, Phoenix, Wildlife-Sportsman, Ariz; Ariz Hwys, Wildlife Views, Saturday Evening Post & others. Mem: Outdoor Writers Asn of Am; Ariz Outdoor Writers; Phoenix Press Box Asn; Am Legion; Ariz Sportsmasters Rod & Gun Club. Relig: Methodist; Mem Choir, Brooks United Methodist Church, Phoenix. Mailing Add: 4426 N 63rd Ave Phoenix AZ 85033

LEWIS, CLOATEE ARNOLD (D)
Secy, Fulton Co Dem Party, Ga
b Ellaville, Ga, Sept 25, 23; d Calton Arnold (deceased) & Mary Boddie A; m 1974 to Nathaniel Cameron Lewis. Educ: Morris Brown Col, 41-45; Iota Phi Lambda. Polit & Govt Pos: Various clerical jobs, US Govt, 48-67; dep registrar, Fulton Co, Ga, 62-64; field worker, Rep Charles Weltner, 67, Lt Gov George T Smith, 68-69, Rep John Greer, 69, Rep Andrew Young, 69-, Gov David Gambrell, 69 & 71, Lt Gov Zell Miller, 73-74 & Gov George Busbee, 75-; secy, Gov Carl Sanders Campaign, 69, Mayor Sam Massell Campaign, 71 & Humphrey-Muskie Campaign, 72; admin asst, Fulton Co Comnrs, 74-; secy, Fulton Co Dem Party, 74-, secy exec comt, 74-; secy, Fifth Cong Dist Dem Party, 75-; mem, Ga Dem State Exec Comt, currently; campaign asst, Harold E Williams for Fulton Co Comnr, 74; asst mgr, Elec Polls, 74 & 75. Bus & Prof Pos: Secy, Atlanta Branch, NAACP, 67-69, Atlanta Residential Manpower Ctr, 69-70, Ctr Dir, YWCA Cent Off, Atlanta, 70-71 & Family Serv Div, Dept Offender Rehabilitation, 71-75. Mem: Prof Secy Club; Lemvel Civic Club; Washington Park Community Club; League of Women Voters; United Methodist Women. Honors & Awards: Outstanding Performance Award, Atlanta Branch, NAACP, 67-68; Queen YWCA, Atlanta, 65- Relig: United Methodist Church. Mailing Add: 997 Westmoor Dr NW Atlanta GA 30314

LEWIS, E GREY (R)
Gen Counsel, Dept of the Navy
b Atlantic City, NJ; s John Connell Lewis & Ella Grey L; div; c Amy. Educ: Princeton Univ, AB, 59; Univ Pa Law Sch, LLB, 63. Polit & Govt Pos: Asst US attorney, DC, formerly; dep asst attorney gen, Civil Div, Dept Justice, formerly; gen counsel, Dept of the Navy, 73- Mil Serv: 2nd Lt, Army, 59-60; Capt, Army Res. Relig: Protestant. Mailing Add: 408 Duke St Alexandria VA 22314

LEWIS, ERNEST CROSBY (D)
b Winnsboro, SC, Mar 4, 34; s Ernest Vann Lewis & Nell Brooks L; m 1970 to Cleo B Dickerson; c Lisa LaVelle, Allyson Lee & E Crosby Jr. Educ: Univ SC, Columbia, 52-55; Univ SC Law Sch, LLB, 58; Phi Delta Phi; Block C Club. Polit & Govt Pos: SC State Rep, 61-64, chmn, Mil, Pub & Munic Affairs Comt, SC House Rep; mcm bd trustees, SC Med Col of Charleston, 62-64; mem bd visitors, The Citadel, 62-64; mem & vchmn, SC State Bd Educ, 65-69; deleg, Dem Nat Conv, 68; chmn, SC Dem Party, 68-69; vchmn, Nat Asn Dem State Chmn, 69. Bus & Prof Pos: Partner, Law Firm of Lewis, Lewis, Robinson & Arnold, 58-; chmn bd dirs, First Palmetto State Bank & Trust Co, Inc, currently. Mil Serv: Entered as Pvt, Army, 52, released as Capt, 64, after serv in 12th Judge Adv Gen Corp, Third Army, 58-64. Mem: SC & Am Bar Asns; Mason (32 degree); Sons of the Confederacy; Shrine. Honors & Awards: Eagle Scout; vpres & pres, SC Law Student Bd; vjustice & justice, Phi Alpha Delta. Relig: Methodist. Mailing Add: 1717 Gervais St Columbia SC 29201

LEWIS, FRANK
Nebr State Sen
Mailing Add: 307 Anna Ave Bellevue NE 68005

LEWIS, FRED COLE (D)
b Marblehead, Mass, Oct 23, 25; s Fred Cole Lewis & Blanche Marie Letourneau L; m 1958 to Mary Jo Nelson; c Kristi, Paul, Mark & Stephen. Educ: Hobart Col, 46-47; Boston Univ, AB, 49; Univ Conn, 51-52. Polit & Govt Pos: Chmn, Whitman Col Dem Party, Wash, formerly. Bus & Prof Pos: Vpres, Control Data Corp, Minneapolis, 63-71; owner, Royal Motor Inn, Pullman, Wash, 71- Mil Serv: Entered as Pvt, Air Force, 43, released as 2nd Lt, 45, after serv in Third Air Force. Relig: Lutheran. Mailing Add: 120 W Main St Pullman WA 99163

LEWIS, GEOFFREY W
b Brookline, Mass, May 20, 10; m to Elizabeth Locke; c Geoffrey W, Jr & Mrs Robin Herbert. Educ: Harvard Univ, BA, 32; Trinity Col; Cambridge Univ. Polit & Govt Pos: Staff mem, Cabinet Comt on Palestine & Related Probs, London, 46; career officer, US Dept of State Foreign Serv, 46-70, retired, foreign affairs specialist, 46-49, acting asst chief, Div of Ger Econ Affairs, 49-50, dep dir, Bur of Ger Affairs, 50-54, Nat War Col, 55-56, first secy & counr, Karachi, 56-58, first secy, US Mission to NATO & European Regional Orgn, Paris, 58-61, dep chief of mission, Amman, 61-65, US Ambassador to Mauritania, 65-67; US Ambassador, Cent African Repub, 67-70. Bus & Prof Pos: Asst dean & asst hist instr, Harvard Univ, 33-37; headmaster, pvt sch, 39-40. Mil Serv: Lt Col, Army, 41-46. Mem: Harvard Club of Boston. Mailing Add: Cushing ME 04563

LEWIS, GIBSON D (GIB) (D)
Tex State Rep
b Oletha, Tex, Aug 22, 36; s Jack Lewis & Marie Gibson Croft L; m to Sandra Majors; c Cammie & Cathy. Educ: Tex Christian Univ, 56-57; Sam Houston State Univ, BA, 63. Polit & Govt Pos: Councilman, City of River Oaks, Ft Worth, Tex, 68-; Tex State Rep, 71-, chmn, Natural Resources Comt, mem, State Affairs Comt & chmn, Subcomt State Affairs, Tex House Rep, currently; mem, Southwest Regional Energy Coun, currently. Bus & Prof Pos: Salesman, Olmsted-Kirk Paper Co, 63-67; pres, Lewis Label Prod Inc, 64- Mil Serv: Air Force, 57, released as A/2c, 61. Mem: Ft Worth Jaycees; Ft Worth Litho Club; Ft Worth Club of Printing Craftsmen; River Oaks Lions Club; Rotary Club; North West YMCA (mem bd dirs, 68-). Honors & Awards: Ft Worth Outstanding Jaycee of Month, 63; Outstanding Jaycee Dir of Year, 64; US, E Club Award, 63; 100 Mem Pin award, World Serv Life, 64; Nominated Ft Worth Outstanding Young Man, 68. Relig: Church of Christ. Legal Res: Box 651G Rte 10 Ft Worth TX 76114 Mailing Add: Capitol Sta Box 2910 Austin TX 78767

LEWIS, HAROLD CRAIG (D)
Pa State Sen
b Hazelton, Pa, July 22, 44; s Harold W Lewis & Dorothy Miller L; m 1967 to Nancy Haigh; c Janet & Craig Robert. Educ: Millersville State Col, BS, 66; Univ Nebr, Lincoln Grad Sch, 66-67; Temple Univ Sch Law, JD, 71; Tau Gamma Lambda. Polit & Govt Pos: Pa State Sen, Sixth Dist & vchmn comt on aging & youth, Pa State Senate, 75- Bus & Prof Pos: Attorney, Howland & Hess, Philadelphia, Pa, 71- Mem: Frankford Rotary (bd dirs); The Bridge (bd dirs); Benjamin Rush Community Ment Health Ctr (bd dirs); Frankford Hosp Adv Coun. Legal Res: 2062 Roselyn Dr Feasterville PA 19047 Mailing Add: Senate Post Off Main Capitol Harrisburg PA 17120

LEWIS, HARRY B (R)
Wash State Sen
b Pittsburgh, Pa, 1927; married; c three. Educ: Univ Wash. Polit & Govt Pos: Wash State Sen, currently; Wash State Rep, 2 terms. Bus & Prof Pos: Owner, Woodfabricators, Inc. Mil Serv: Army. Mem: Soc Am Foresters; Elks; Phi Delta Theta; Am Legion. Mailing Add: PO Box 325 Yelm WA 98597

LEWIS, JAMES A, JR (D)
Ind State Sen
Mailing Add: 774 Level St Charlestown IN 47111

LEWIS, JAMES R (R)
Wis State Rep
Mailing Add: 4043 Hwy D West Bend WI 53095

LEWIS, JAMES WOODROW (D)
Assoc Justice, SC Supreme Court
b Darlington, SC, Mar 8, 12; s William Joseph Lewis & Mary Aletha Bryant L; m 1936 to Alice Lee; c Barbara (Mrs Haynes). Educ: Univ SC, AB, 32; admitted to SC Bar, 35. Polit & Govt Pos: SC State Rep, 35-36 & 43-45; mem staff, SC State Hwy Comn, 36-40; Circuit Judge, 45-61; assoc justice, SC Supreme Court, 71- Mil Serv: Pvt, Army, 45. Relig: Baptist. Mailing Add: PO Box 53 Darlington SC 29532

LEWIS, JAN (D)
Dem Nat Committeewoman, Miss
Mailing Add: Box 533 Starkville MS 39759

LEWIS, JEFFREY S (D)
b Ft Wayne, Ind, Mar 11, 45; s Hubert Kenneth Lewis & Maxine Jack L; single. Educ: Ball State Univ, BA, 67; Ind Univ Sch of Law, Bloomington, 67-68; Delta Sigma Rho; Tau Kappa Alpha; Blue Key Men's Nat Hon; Sigma Chi. Polit & Govt Pos: Youth coordr, Sen Bayh for US Senate Comt, 68; staff asst, US Sen Birch Bayh, 69; state campaign coordr, Larry Conrad for Secy of State, Ind, 70; admin asst to Secy of State, 70-72; deleg, Dem Nat Conv, 72. Bus & Prof Pos: Advert exec, Lewis, Lamm, Swinford & Assocs, currently. Relig: Unitarian. Mailing Add: 5869 N Keystone Indianapolis IN 46220

LEWIS, JERRY (R)
Calif State Assemblyman
Mailing Add: 101 S Sixth St Redlands CA 92373

LEWIS, JOHN WASHINGTON (D)
Fla State Rep
b Marietta, Ga, Aug 5, 49; s Earl Roland Lewis & Elouise Allen L; m 1970 to Elaine Beal. Educ: Fla Jr Col at Jacksonville, AA, 69; Fla State Univ, BS, 71; Alpha Phi Omega; Phi Gamma Delta; Student Body President. Polit & Govt Pos: Admin asst, Fla State Rep John R Forbes, 70-72 & Fla State Rep Eric Smith, 72-73; Fla State Rep, 74- Bus & Prof Pos: Ed & publ, The North Jacksonville Record-News, currently. Mil Serv: Seaman, Navy Reserve; Nat Defense Medal. Mem: Civitan; Toastmasters (vpres); North Jacksonville Businessmens Club; Sertoma. Honors & Awards: Claude Pepper Leadership Award, 69; Fla Blue Key Leadership Award, 69. Relig: Baptist. Legal Res: 904 Saratoga Ave Jacksonville FL 32208 Mailing Add: PO Box 9028 Jacksonville FL 32208

LEWIS, JOYCE E (R)
Maine State Rep
Mailing Add: RR 3 Maple Hill Auburn ME 04210

LEWIS, JUDITH ANN (R)
Chairperson, Miss Young Rep Fedn
b Morton, Miss, Oct 18, 49; d Dwight Levaughn Lewis & Mary Lou Conn L; single. Educ: Clarke Mem Col, AA, 69; Miss Col, BSEd, 71, MEd, 74; Univ Southern Miss, summer 72; Alpha Psi Omega; Pi Kappa Delta; Laguna Social Club. Polit & Govt Pos: Dir TAR, Miss Young Rep Fedn, 71-73, vchairwoman, 73-75, chairperson, 75-; mem platform & resolutions comts, Miss Rep Conv, 72; mem, Scott Co Exec Comt, 72- Bus & Prof Pos: Teacher speech, Forest Separate Sch Dist, Miss, 71-73; grad asst, Miss Col, 73-74, instr, 74- Mem: Eastern Star; Miss Speech Asn; Miss Educ Asn; Southeastern Theatre Asn. Honors & Awards: Miss Outstanding Young Rep Woman, Miss Young Rep Fedn, 73; Nominee, Outstanding Speech Teacher, Miss Speech Asn, 73; Best Over-All Play Dir, Miss Col Drama Festival, 74, Most Versatile Actress, 74. Relig: Southern Baptist. Mailing Add: B-8 101 Mt Salus Clinton MS 39056

LEWIS, KERMIT E (D)
Mem, Dem Nat Comt, Mo
Mailing Add: Box 269 Rte 2 Neosho MO 64850

LEWIS, MARY DAVIS WOODWARD (D)
Mem, Ark State Dem Cent Comt
b Magnolia, Ark, July 15, 03; d Joe L Davis & Ella Arnold D; m 1925 to Walter Ashton Galloway Woodward, wid; m 1974 to J Keene Lewis; c Walter Ashton Galloway, Jr, Mary Ann (Mrs McLaughlin), Joe D & Mac B. Educ: Galloway Woman's Col, Searcy, Ark, AB, 24; Hendrix Col, AB, 36; pres, Laniers, Galloway Woman's Col. Polit & Govt Pos: Alderwoman, Magnolia City Coun, Ark, 44-46; mem, State Girl's Training Sch Bd, 53-56; Fourth Cong rep, Ark State Dem Comt, 65-69; mem, Ark State Dem Cent Comt, 65-, sen deleg, 67-68; vchmn, Columbia Co Dem Cent Comt, Ark, 66-68; mem, Ark Hist Comt, 70- Bus & Prof Pos: Partner, Woodward & Kinard, Attorneys at law, Magnolia, Ark, currently; operator real estate & oil bus; owner, Frog Level Antique Shop, currently; newspaper feature writer. Mem: Life mem, Ark Hist Asn (pres, 65); Southern State Col Archaeol Soc; UDC (recorder of Mil Crosses, Ark Div, 65, pres, Columbia Co Mem Chap, 67-68); PEO, Chap AN (corresponding secy, 62-64). Honors & Awards: Ark Mother of the Year, 54. Relig: Methodist; pres, Women's Soc Christian Serv, First Methodist Church, 51. Mailing Add: 1710 Dogwood Magnolia AR 71753

LEWIS, PHILIP D (D)
Fla State Sen
Mailing Add: 317 Edmor Rd West Palm Beach FL 33401

LEWIS, PRESTON BROOKS, JR (D)
Ga State Rep
b Augusta, Ga, May 2, 30; s Preston Brooks Lewis & Clifford McElmurray L; m 1953 to Katherine D Hill; c Preston B, III, Clifford Ellis, Julian Carlton & Katherine Virginia. Educ: Univ Ga, BBA, 55, LLB, 58; Phi Kappa Alpha; Phi Delta Phi. Polit & Govt Pos: Secy-treas, Burke Co Dem Exec Comt, Ga, 60-; Ga State Rep, 50th Dist, 61-; solicitor, City Court of Waynesboro, 63-64. Bus & Prof Pos: Attorney-at-law, Lewis & Lewis, 58- Mil Serv: Seaman, Navy, 48-49; entered Army, 51, released as 1st Lt, 53, after serv in 45th Inf Div, Korea; Capt, Army Res; Bronze Star. Mem: Mason; Shrine; Rotary; Am Legion; VFW. Relig: Methodist. Legal Res: Forrest Dr Waynesboro GA 30830 Mailing Add: Box 88 Waynesboro GA 30830

LEWIS, R H (BOB) (R)
Wash State Sen
Mailing Add: W 4329 Arrowhead Rd Spokane WA 99208

LEWIS, RANDOLPH BRADFORD (D)
b Jacksonville, NC, Feb 25, 56; s Randolph Wilson Lewis & Kathryn Oyler L; single. Educ: Oak Ridge High Sch, grad; Presidential Classroom for Young Am, grad, 74. Polit & Govt Pos: Secy, Orange Co Young Dem, Fla, 72-73; deleg, Dem Nat Mid-Term Conf, 74; precinct committeeman, Orange Co Dem Exec Comt, 74-; chmn affirmative action comt, 75- Mem: Nat Forensic League. Honors & Awards: Dem Polit Leadership Sch Grad, 74; Dist Three Debate Champion, 74-75. Relig: Christian. Mailing Add: 7205 Willowwood Dr Orlando FL 32808

LEWIS, RICHARD (D)
Nebr State Sen
Mailing Add: Holbrook NE 68948

LEWIS, RICHARD HAYES (D)
Ky State Rep
b Hopkinsville, Ky, Dec 3, 37; s Fred Theodore Lewis & Nola Angeline Hayes L; m 1961 to Martha Jane Cunningham; c Laura Elizabeth, Cynthia Jane & Katherine Hayes. Educ: Murray State Univ, BS, 60; Univ Ky, LLB, 65, JD, 70; Sigma Chi; Phi Alpha Delta. Polit & Govt Pos: Exec dir, Benton Munic Housing Comn, 67-68; city attorney, Benton, Ky, 68-70; Ky State Rep, Dist 6, 70-; chief exec officer, Gov Off, Commonwealth of Ky, 75- Bus & Prof Pos: City planner, Ky Dept Commerce, 63; legal aide, Ky Dept Labor, 64; attorney, John Lovett Law Off, 65-69, partner, Lovett & Lewis, 69- Mil Serv: Entered as 2nd Lt, Army, 60, released as 1st Lt, 62, after serv in Army Reception Ctr, Ft Knox, Ky, 61-62; Capt, Army Res, 66-; Airborne Award. Mem: Ky Hist Soc; Lions; Marshall Co CofC; Am Legion; Murray State Univ Alumni Asn (bd dirs, 70-74, vpres, 74-75, pres-elect, 75-). Honors & Awards: Outstanding Freshman Rep, 1970 Ky Gen Assembly; Vet of the Year Award, Marshall Co Chap 118, Disabled Vet. Relig: Baptist. Legal Res: Greenwood Place Benton KY 42025 Mailing Add: PO Box 165 Benton KY 42025

LEWIS, ROGER KEITH (D)
b New York, NY, Aug 17, 23; s Harry Clay Donecker & Kretchen D; m 1946 to Julia Louise Kobman; c Cheryl & Neal. Educ: Univ Ariz, BA, 52; Phi Beta Kappa. Polit & Govt Pos: Admin asst, US Rep Morris Udall, Ariz, 61- Bus & Prof Pos: Reporter, Ariz Repub, Phoenix, 52-60; copy desk, Tucson Daily Citizen, 60-61. Mil Serv: Entered as Pvt, Army, 43, released as S/Sgt, 46, after serv in Signal Corps, Iran. Relig: Protestant. Mailing Add: Rte 2 Box 127-E Lovettsville VA 22080

LEWIS, RUFUS A (D)
Ala State Rep
Mailing Add: 801 Bolivar St Montgomery AL 36104

LEWIS, STERLING T (D)
WVa State Deleg
Mailing Add: State Capitol Charleston WV 25305

LEWIS, THOMAS F (TOM) (R)
Fla State Rep
Mailing Add: 729 Waterway Dr North Palm Beach FL 33408

LEWIS, VIRGINIA BOWLAND (R)
Chmn, Somerset Co Rep Cent Comt, Md
b Kingston, Md, Nov 23, 14; d Edward Lee Carol Long & Ella Eva Brown L; m 1934 to Jay Bowland, wid; now div; c Jay Edward Bowland. Educ: Wash Col, Chestertown, 32. Polit & Govt Pos: Chmn, Women's Fedn of Rep Club, First Cong Dist, 58-60; chmn, Somerset Co Rep Cent Comt, Md, currently; pres, Md Rep State Cent Comt, currently. Mem: Am Legion Auxiliary Post (pres); Women's Farm Bur Somerset Co (pres); Jr Hosp Bd (pres); Co Coun, PTA, Somerset Co (pres). Honors & Awards: Reward in Polit by President Eisenhower, 56; PTA Reward of the Year, 67. Relig: Methodist. Mailing Add: Kingston MD 21834

LEWIS, WILLIAM EDWIN (D)
Mo State Rep
b DeSoto, Mo, Sept 3, 18; s Joseph Edwin Lewis & Mamie Rupple L; m 1943 to Virginia Louise Sapp; c William E, Jr, Julie Mae (Mrs Wagner), Fredrick Craig & Timothy Bruce. Educ: DeSoto High Sch, grad, 37. Polit & Govt Pos: Mo State Rep, 125 Dist, 75- Bus & Prof Pos: Distributor salesman, Phillips 66 Co, 47-54; salesman, Graham Linen Supplies, 54-74. Mil Serv: Entered as Pvt, Army, 40, released as S/Sgt, 45, after serv in 35th Div & 30th Inf Div, ETO, 44-45; Maj (Ret), Army, 65; Combat Inf Award; Five Battle Stars; Two Bronze Stars; Army Commendation Award; Good Conduct Medal. Mem: Elks; Am Legion; life mem VFW; life mem Amvets; (state comdr, Mo, 73-74); United Glass & Ceramic Workers of North Am, AFL-CIO. Honors & Awards: White Clover Award, Amvets of the Year, 73. Relig: Christian. Legal Res: 300 Boyde St DeSoto MO 63020 Mailing Add: Capitol Bldg Jefferson City MO 65101

LEWIS, WOODROW (D)
NY State Assemblyman
Mailing Add: 1293 Dean St Brooklyn NY 11216

LEWISON, BERNARD (R)
Wis State Rep
b Viroqua, Wis, Feb 7, 02. Educ: Lawrence Col, 21-22. Polit & Govt Pos: Mem bd, Vernon Co, Wis; city alderman, Viroqua, mayor, 43-48; Wis State Rep, 54- Bus & Prof Pos: Tobacco buyer; real estate broker, dir, savings & loan asn; operator, automobile agency & body shop. Mailing Add: 11 S Washington Heights Viroqua WI 54665

LEY, DOROTHY (D)
Mem, Dem Nat Comt, Nebr
Mailing Add: 518 Hillcrest Rd Wayne NE 68787

LIAS, THOMAS LEE (R)
b Akron, Iowa, Sept 27, 34; s Earl Lias & Bess Stoutenburg L; m 1958 to Sharon Garrison; c Lisa. Educ: State Univ Iowa, BA, 56. Polit & Govt Pos: Campaign dir, assoc ed newsletter & asst to exec dir, Nat Rep Cong Comt, 59-69; dep spec asst to President, 69-71; exec asst to US Ambassador to UN, 71-73; exec asst to Chmn George Bush, Rep Nat Comt, 73- Mem: Capitol Hill Club. Relig: Methodist. Legal Res: Akron IA 51005 Mailing Add: 530 F St Terr SE Washington DC 20003

LIBHART, BONNIE L (R)
b Paragould, Ark, Feb 11, 35; d William Moses Taylor & Gladys Gardner T; m 1958 to Anthony Carova Libhart; c Dee Anne, Emily Dawn & Anthony Carova. Educ: Crowleys Ridge Col, AA, 68; Ark State Univ, 73-; Sigma Delta Chi. Polit & Govt Pos: Vchmn, Regional Rep Party, Ark; secy, Dist Rep Party; del, Co, Dist & State Rep Conv; deleg, Rep Nat Conv, 72. Mem: Am Women in Radio & TV; Women in Broadcasting; Cerebral Palsy Asn (bd mem, 73-); Bus & Prof Club (publicity chmn). Honors & Awards: Recognition Plaque, Kiwanis Club, 70; Vol Outstanding Serv Award, DAV, 71; Women of the Year, Jaycees, 72; Vol Serv Award, United Cerebral Award, 72; Appreciation Award, Lions Club, 72. Relig: Church of Christ. Mailing Add: 1404 Linden Jonesboro AR 72401

LIBONATI, ROLAND VICTOR (D)
b Chicago, Ill, Dec 29, 00; s Ernest M Libonati & Fiore Pellitteri L; m 1942 to Jeannette K Van Hanxleden; c Michael E. Educ: Univ Mich; Northwestern Univ Law Sch. Polit & Govt Pos: Ill State Rep, 30-34 & 40-42; Ill State Sen, 42-57; US Rep, Ill, 57-64; mem, Nat Dem Club; mem, First Ward Dem Orgn, Chicago, currently; mem, Ill Legis Pension Comn representing recipient pensioners. Mil Serv: Lt, Army, 18, serv in Inf, 86th Div, 9th Machine Gun Group. Mem: Justinian Soc; Moose; Fed Post, Am Legion; Voiture 220, 40 et 8. Honors & Awards: Sponsor & builder, Past Boys Camp for Indigent Children, Coloma, Wis. Relig: Roman Catholic. Legal Res: 909 S Loomis St Chicago IL 60607 Mailing Add: Rm 1301 134 N La Salle St Chicago IL 60602

LIBOUS, ALFRED JOSEPH (R)
Mayor, Binghamton, NY
b Binghamton, NY, Sept 24, 28; s Abraham Joseph Libous & Nazha Barke L; m 1954 to Debra Vann; c Lynn, Michael, Nancy, Gary & Shelley. Educ: North High Sch, Binghamton, NY, 46; Ridley Bus Sch, Binghamton, 49. Polit & Govt Pos: Councilman, Binghamton, NY, 62-69, mayor, 70- Mil Serv: Entered as Seaman, Navy, 50, released as Yeoman 1/C, 54, after serv in Air Br, Com Air Lant, 50-54; Good Conduct Medal; Overseas Ribbons. Mem: Elks (Binghamton Lodge 852); YMCA; Am Legion (Binghamton Post 1645). Mailing Add: 10 Sturges St Binghamton NY 13901

LICHT, FRANK (D)
b Providence, RI, Mar 13, 16; s Jacob Licht & Rose Kassed L (deceased); m 1946 to Dorothy Shirlee Krauss; c Beth Ellen (Mrs John Laramee), Carol Ann & Judith Joan. Educ: Brown Univ, AB, 38; Harvard Law Sch, LLB, 41; Phi Beta Kappa. Hon Degrees: LLD, St Francis Col, 69, Yeshiva Univ, 70, RI Col, 71 & Univ RI, 71; DHL, Cincinnati Sch of Hebrew Union Col-Jewish Inst of Relig, 71. Polit & Govt Pos: RI State Sen, 49-56; assoc justice, RI Superior Court, 56-68; Gov, RI, 69-73. Bus & Prof Pos: Law partner, Letts & Quinn, Providence, RI, 43-46, Letts, Quinn & Licht, currently; fel, Inst of Polit, Harvard Univ, currently. Publ: Co-auth, Trial judges code, Mass Law Quart, 6/65; auth, Observations on some aspects of the discovery provisions of the new rules, RI Bar Annual, Vol III, 66; The trial judge and today's social issues, Jackson Lectr reprinted In: The Judges J, 1/73. Mem: Providence Human Rels Comn; RI Coun Conf Christians & Jews; Nat Multiple Sclerosis Soc; Am & RI Bar Asns. Honors & Awards: Lehman Award for RI, 65; Man of Year, RI Mag of Providence Sunday J, 69; Herbert H Lehman Ethics Award, Jewish Theol Sem of Am, 69; Herbert H Lehman Citation, Nat Info Bur for Jewish Life, Inc, 70; Ford Found Grant. Relig: Jewish. Legal Res: 640 Elmgrove Ave Providence RI 02906 Mailing Add: 830 Hosp Trust Bldg Providence RI 02903

LICHT, RICHARD A (D)
RI State Sen
Mailing Add: 40 Overhill Rd Providence RI 02906

LICKAR, JOHN IVAN (D)
Treas, Third Cong Dist Dem Party, Wash
b Krain, Yugoslavia, Nov 15, 01; s John Lickar, Sr & Mary Stular L m; 1943 to Antiona Ulcar; c John, Jr, Edward, Evelyn, Tonie, Kenneth, Joe, Bob, Wilima, Dorthy, Hildereth, Danny & Diane. Educ: Mich Col Mines, 26. Polit & Govt Pos: Precinct committeeman & mem exec bd, Clark Co Dem Party, Wash, 58-66; deleg, Wash Dem State Conv, 60-, mem resolutions & agr comts, Dem Platform Comt, 60; deleg, Dem Nat Conv, 64; treas, Clark Co Dem Club; treas & mem exec comt, Third Cong Dist Dem Party, currently; mem exec comt, Clark Co Dem Cent Comt; deleg, Wash Dem Cent Comt. Bus & Prof Pos: Master farmer, Ill, 1930's; dairy farmer, Wash, currently. Mem: Grange (7 degree, Overseer, 72-); CofC; La Ctr Wheel Club; Wash State Dairy Fedn (comt on rural area expansion & develop); Fifth Ave Dem Club (treas). Relig: Lutheran. Mailing Add: Rte 1 25510 NW Timm Rd Ridgefield WA 98642

LICKTEIG, DAN W (D)
b Richmond, Kans, Feb 20, 07; s Herman H Lickteig & Anna Steinbach L; m 1930 to Monica C Bowman; c Robert H, Collen (Mrs Laurence Chandler) & Joan (Mrs Mark Roeckers). Educ: Richmond High Sch, 22-26. Polit & Govt Pos: Mem, Dem precinct comt, Kans, 60-; chmn, Franklin Co Dem Party, formerly; alt deleg, Dem Nat Mid-Term Conf, 74. Bus & Prof Pos: Vchmn loan comt, Ottawa Prod Credit Asn, 64- Mem: KofC (grand knight, 62-64); Elks; Grange; Farm Coop (bd mem & pres, 71-72); Rural Elec Admin Coop. Relig: Catholic. Mailing Add: RR 1 Richmond KS 66080

LIEBERMAN, JOSEPH I (D)
Conn State Sen
b Stamford, Conn, Feb 24, 42; s Henry Lieberman & Marcia Manger L; m 1965 to Elizabeth Haas; c Matthew & Rebecca. Educ: Yale Univ, BA, 64, Law Sch, LLB, 67; Phi Beta Kappa. Polit & Govt Pos: Chmn, Conn Citizens for Robert Kennedy, 68; Conn State Sen, New Haven, 71-, majority leader, Conn State Senate, 75- Bus & Prof Pos: Attorney, Wiggin & Dana, New Haven, Conn, 67-69; dir, studies in city planning, Yale, 69-; partner, Baldwin, Lieberman & Segaloff, 72- Publ: The Power Broker, 66 & The Scorpion & the Tarantula, 70, Houghton-Mifflin. Relig: Jewish. Mailing Add: 69 Colony Rd New Haven CT 06511

LIEBERMAN, RONALD STEPHEN (D)
Committeeman, Dade Co Dem Exec Comt, Fla
b Miami Beach, Fla, Apr 14, 46; s Alvin H Lieberman & Edith Freeman L; single. Educ: Univ Miami, AB, 68; Univ Tulsa Col Law, JD, 71; Phi Alpha Delta; Young Dem; Circle K Collegiate Coun UN. Polit & Govt Pos: Asst state attorney, Dade Co, Fla, 72-74; deleg, Dem Nat Mid-Term Conf, 74; committeeman, Dade Co Dem Exec Comt, Fla, 74- Bus & Prof Pos: Attorney, Ader & Orr, Miami, Fla, 72; asst state attorney, 72-74; attorney-at-law, 74- Mil Serv: SP-4, Army Res, 69- Mem: Young Dem (pres, Dade Co, 73-74); Dade Co Bar Asn (prog chmn, Young Lawyers Sect); Gtr Miami Jaycees (bd dirs, 72-); Transition (bd dirs, 75-); Am Bar Asn (mem comt, Fla Young Lawyers Chmn, 73-75). Honors & Awards: Outstanding Alumnus, Phi Alpha Delta, Univ Miami Chap, 73. Relig: Jewish. Mailing Add: 66 W Flagler St Suite 800 Miami FL 33130

LIEBERMANN, SHIRLEY CORRELL (R)
b Easton, Pa, Oct 3, 17; d Paul Correll, MD & Bertha Ingham C; m 1953 to James Ward Liebermann. Educ: Hartridge Sch & Knox Sch. Polit & Govt Pos: Committeewoman, Pa Rep State Comt, 58-66; vchmn, Northampton Co Rep Comt, 66, chmn, formerly. Bus & Prof Pos: Saleswoman with several real estate agencies, 46-53; chief inheritance tax appraiser, Dept of Revenue, Pa, 63- Mem: Easton Children's Home (mem bd dirs, currently). Relig: Presbyterian. Mailing Add: 7 Lehn's Ct Easton PA 18042

LIEN, EDWARD (D)
Mont State Rep
Mailing Add: SR 231 Box A33 Wolf Point MT 59201

LIFE, RUBY JACQUELYN (R)
Chmn, St Bernard Parish Rep Party, La
b Dallas, Tex, May 10, 06; d James Humphrey Dickason Jones & Clarabelle Ritter J; m 1937 to Dr Jesse Harrison Life; c James R & William A Jackson. Educ: Switzer Sch Music, Dallas, Tex, grad. Polit & Govt Pos: Pres, Mo Fedn Rep Women, 68-70; chmn, St Bernard Parish Rep Party, La, 70-; pres, La Fedn Rep Women, 73-75, mem exec bd, currently. Mem: Eastern Star (past Worthy Matron); Am Legion Auxiliary; Comt on Aging in St Bernard Parish (mem adv bd); Am Asn Retired Persons (adv bd); St Bernard Parish Women's Rep Club (secy-treas). Honors & Awards: Red Cross Medal, 55; Awards for teaching polit at Am Legion Girl's State, Mo, 67, 68 & 69; United Fund Award, La, 73-74; Hon citizen & Key to City of New Orleans, 73. Relig: Christian. Mailing Add: Rte Box 513 St Bernard LA 70085

LIGHT, CATHERINE (D)
Mem Exec Bd, Mich Dem State Cent Comt
b Manhattan, NY, Nov 29, 06; d Joseph Arleo & Madeline La Rocca A; wid; c Rosanne & Richard Allan. Educ: NY Univ, 3 years. Polit & Govt Pos: Co-founder Detroit Chap, Vol for Stevenson, Mich, 52; mem policy & exec comt, 17th Cong Dist Dem Orgn, 54-; mgr, Secy of State Off, 55-; mem, Mich Dem State Cent Comt, 58-, mem exec bd, currently; deleg, Dem Nat Conv, 60, 64 & 68; mem, Rochester Area Dem Club, 69-; Oakland Co Dem Comt, 69- Bus & Prof Pos: Clerk, Abraham & Straus, Brooklyn, NY, 22-25, mgr childrens books, 30-36; bookstore mgr, 25-27; mgr bookstore, Lit Bros Dept Store, 27-30. Mem: Meadowbrook Hall Guild (exec comt, 71-); Crittenton Hosp Auxiliary. Relig: Catholic. Mailing Add: 718 Great Oaks Blvd 97B Rochester MI 48063

LIGHT, FRANCES H (R)
b Appalachia, Va, May 10, 23; d Joel C Haun (deceased) & Myrtle M Hurd H (deceased); wid; c Jennifer Kay & Gwendolyn Sue. Educ: Middletown Bus Col, 41-42. Polit & Govt Pos: Mem, Sullivan Co Rep Womens Orgn, Tenn, 60-; admin asst to US Rep James H Quillen, Tenn, 63-; mem, Rep Womens Club of Capitol Hill, 68- Mem: Kingsport Altrusa Club; VFW Auxiliary; Hire the Handicapped Tenn (mem bd). Relig: Baptist. Legal Res: 234 Hammond Ave Kingsport TN 37660 Mailing Add: 2501 Calvert St NW Washington DC 20008

LIGHTSEY, HUGH TUTEN (D)
Chmn, Hampton Co Dem Exec Comt, SC
b Brunson, SC, May 3, 25; s John Herman Lightsey & Addie T. Educ: Citadel, BS, 50. Polit & Govt Pos: Former SC State Rep; chmn, Hampton Co Dem Exec Comt, SC, currently. Bus & Prof Pos: Farmer & businessman. Mil Serv: Navy, World War II. Mem: Shrine; Mason; Eastern Star; 40 et 8; Elks. Relig: Baptist. Mailing Add: Box 8 Brunson SC 29911

LIKES, HENRY L (D)
b Sayre, Okla, Aug 29, 13; s William Ed Likes & Mary Ann Loveless L; m 1935 to Billie Geraldine Tackett; c Jerry, Buddy & David. Educ: High Sch, Grad. Polit & Govt Pos: Exec reservist, Okla Dept Labor, currently; deleg, Dem Nat Conv, 68 & 72. Bus & Prof Pos: Financial secy, Plumbers Local 351, 57-63; secy-treas, Okla State AFL-CIO, 64-68, pres, 68-; pres, State Pipetrades, 67-70. Mil Serv: Navy, World War II. Mem: Mason; VFW; Am Legion. Legal Res: 704 Edmond Muskogee OK 74401 Mailing Add: 501 NE 27th St Oklahoma City OK 73105

LILL, RAYMOND JOSEPH (D)
NY State Assemblyman
b Rochester, NY, July 26, 13; s Harry Peter Lill & Viola Kleisle L; m 1938 to Marion C Fichtner; c Donald Raymond. Educ: St Joseph's High Sch, 27-28; Eastman Kodak Courses, 45-49. Polit & Govt Pos: Mem, Dem Co Comt, 34-73; city councilman, Rochester, NY, 62-67; NY State Assemblyman, 67- Bus & Prof Pos: Prod foreman, Eastman Kodak, 43-71; retired. Mem: Rochester CofC; Community Baseball (dir & 1st vpres); Eastman Kodak Mgt Club; Moose; Rochester Turners. Relig: Catholic. Mailing Add: 31 Wolfert Terr Rochester NY 14621

LILLEHAUGEN, C ARNOLD (R)
Chmn, 17th Dist Rep Party, NDak
b Brocket, NDak, Nov 13, 21; s Michael T Lillehaugen & Marie Moe L; m 1946 to Lorayne T Keck; c Meredith June (Mrs Dale Washburn), Mark Arnold & Paige Marie. Educ: Park River Agr Sch, 1 year. Polit & Govt Pos: Rep precinct committeeman, Perth Twp, NDak, 57-66, twp clerk, 57-; NDak State Rep, 17th Dist, 67-72; chmn, 17th Dist Rep Party, NDak, 72- Mem: Farmers Union; Nat Farmers Orgn; Elks; Sons of Norway Lodge (vpres, 72). Relig: Am Lutheran. Mailing Add: Brocket ND 58321

LILLEY, DANIEL T (D)
NC State Rep
b Martin Co, NC, Aug 15, 20; s Alfred T Lilley (deceased) & Ethel G Gurkin L (deceased); m 1944 to Imojene P Hites; c Eileen Carol & Daniel T, Jr. Educ: Spartan Sch Aeronautics, Tulsa, Okla, dipl; CLU, Am Col Life Underwriters. Polit & Govt Pos: Comnr, Lenoir Co, NC, 64-68; NC State Rep, 68- Bus & Prof Pos: Airport mgr, Stallings Field, Kinston, NC, 49-50; salesman, The Penn Mutual Life Ins Co, 50- Mil Serv: Entered as Pvt, Army Air Corps, 39, released as M/Sgt, 45, after serv in 24th Fighter Squadron, Panama, 39-43; Lt Col, Air Force Res, 45-; group comdr, NC Wing, Civil Air Patrol, Lt Col. Mem: Eastern NC Chap Chartered Life Underwriters; Lenoir Co Life Underwriters Asn; Coun of Governments; Rotary Int; Am Legion. Honors & Awards: Distinguished Serv Awards, US CofC, 54 & Kinston CofC, 63. Relig: Disciples of Christ; Lay Minister, Cove City Christian Church & Silver Hill Christian Church, NC. Legal Res: 1805 Sedgefield Dr Kinston NC 28501 Mailing Add: PO Box 824 Kinston NC 28501

LILLEY, TOM (R)
b Bluefield, WVa, Aug 13, 12; s Charles Ellis Lilley & Minnie Holland L; m 1936 to Nancy Clegg; c Anne (Mrs Hammond), Cynthia (Mrs Mazer) & Susan (Mrs McAllister). Educ: Harvard Col, AB, 34, Bus Sch, MBA, 36; Phi Beta Kappa; Delta Upsilon. Polit & Govt Pos: Mem, Nat Export Expansion Coun, 61-64; dir, Export-Import Bank of the US, 65-72. Bus & Prof Pos: Mem indust dept, Lehman Bros, New York, 36-40; mem staff, Burlington Mills, Greensboro, NC, 41-42; assoc prof & asst dir of research, Harvard Bus Sch, 42-48; from mem controller's off, Ford Div to asst gen mgr, Int Div & vpres, Int Staff, Ford Motor Co, Dearborn, Mich, 48-65; dir, Continental Ill Ltd, London, Eng, 73-74; treas, Pop Crisis Comt, Washington, DC, currently. Relig: Presbyterian. Mailing Add: 1522 34th St NW Washington DC 20007

LILLIS, JOAN FRANCES (D)
b Buffalo, NY, Mar 9, 36; d Louis Klipfel & Marion Britton K; m to Bernard J Lillis, wid; c Margaret Mary, Richard Martin & Maura Ann. Educ: Mt Mercy Acad, 53; Canisius Col, 53-54; Mercy Hosp Sch Nursing, RN, 56. Polit & Govt Pos: Councilwoman, Town Bd, West Seneca, NY, 67-; deleg, Dem Nat Mid-Term Conf, 74. Bus & Prof Pos: Staff nurse, Mercy Hosp, 56-66. Mem: Our Lady of Mercy Parents Guild (pres, 74-); Dem Women's League; CofC. Honors & Awards: Gold Medal Award, Mercy Hosp Sch Nursing, 56. Relig: Catholic. Mailing Add: 25 Leocrest Ct West Seneca NY 14224

LILLYWHITE, FRANK S (R)
NMex State Sen
Mailing Add: 309 Mesa Dr Aztec NM 87410

LIMA, GEORGE CHARLES (D)
RI State Sen
b Bristol, RI, Oct 22, 21; s Joseph Pacheco Lima & Mary Pacheco L; m 1946 to Emily Furtado; c Oryann, Frances Mary & George C, Jr. Educ: Boston Sch Anat & Embalming, 51. Polit & Govt Pos: RI State Rep, 57-62; RI State Sen, 75- Bus & Prof Pos: Founder & owner funeral home, Bristol, RI, 51-; mem bd dirs, Indust Nat Bank, 59- Mil Serv: Entered as Pvt, Army Post Band, 40, released as Sgt, 46, after serv in US & Africa-Middle East, 40-46. Mem: Portuguese Independent Band (treas, vpres, 68-); RI Funeral Dirs (bd govs); Nat Funeral Dir Asn; New Eng Funeral Dirs Asn; VFW (life mem). Honors & Awards: Fireman of the Year, Town of Bristol, RI. Relig: Catholic. Mailing Add: 367 High St Bristol RI 02809

LIMMER, FRANCIS EDMUND
City Councilman, Flint, Mich
b Flint, Mich, June 12, 30; s Joseph Wilbur Limmer & Ida Mae Cook L; m 1950 to Beverly L Fiebernitz; c Thomas F, Nancy K, Karen S & Lisa A. Educ: Genesee Commun Col, 2 years; Detroit Col Law, 2 years. Polit & Govt Pos: City Councilman, Flint, Mich, 68-, Mayor, 70-75. Mil Serv: Seaman recruit, Navy, 48, released as chief storekeeper, 70, after serv in CB Div 9-54, Flint. Publ: Mayor's Corner, weekly column, Flint Jour. Mem: Flint Chap, Soc Residential Appraisers; Flint Bd Realtors; Genesee Valley Kiwanis. Relig: Catholic. Mailing Add: 2701 Brown Flint MI 48503

LINARD, SHARLYN (D)
NMex State Rep
Mailing Add: 2013 Princess Jeanne Las Cruces NM 88001

LINCOLN, EMMA ETHEL (R)
Committeewoman, Conn Rep State Cent Comt
b East Lyme, Conn, Jan 20, 14; d Daniel Higgins & Mary Emma Holmes Higgins Lincoln (both deceased); single. Educ: Northfield Sch for Girls, Mass; Williams Mem Inst, New London, Conn. Polit & Govt Pos: Pres, New London Rep Women's Club, Conn, 53-54, pres, First Ward, 57-58; secy, New London Rep City Comt, 55-66, chmn, 66-72; Justice of Peace, 60-; alt deleg, Rep Nat Conv, 68 & 72; committeewoman, Conn Rep State Cent Comt, Dist 20, 72- Bus & Prof Pos: Owner, Lincoln Auto Serv, 40-; pres & treas, Lincoln Ctr Inc, 63- Mem: Bus & Prof Women's Club; Dale Carnegie Alumnae Asn; Rebekah (Noble Grand); Lawrence Mem Hosp & Norwich State Hosp Women's Auxiliaries. Honors & Awards: First person & only woman to break ground for bldg in New London's Redevelop, 64. Relig: Christian Scientist. Legal Res: 16 Glenwood Pl New London CT 06320 Mailing Add: PO Box 869 New London CT 06320

LINCOLN, EVERITT FLOYD (R)
Chmn, Jackson Co Rep Party, Mich
b Parma, Mich, Nov 7, 18; s Floyd Frederick Lincoln & Kathryn Marlette L; m 1942 to Nancy Virginia Rhines; c Pamela Jean (Mrs Marsh). Educ: Parma High Sch, Mich, grad, 36. Polit & Govt Pos: Chmn, Jackson Co Rep Party, Mich, 74-; supvr, Concord Twp, 75- Bus & Prof Pos: Owner-operator, Lincoln Dairy Farm, 46- Mil Serv: Entered as Pvt, Army Field Artil, 41, released as Capt, 46, after serv in 555 Signal Corps AW Bn 9th Air Force, ETO, 43-45; Recalled as a Reservist, Korean War, 17 months; World War II-5 Battle Stars; Am Defense Medal & Victory Medal. Mem: Mich Farm Bur; Mich Milk Producers Asn (local pres, 70-); Mich Animal Breeders Asn (dist secy, 68-); Lions Int (pres local club, 74-75). Relig: Protestant. Mailing Add: 1763 Bath Mills Rd Albion MI 49224

LINCOLN, J WILLIAM (D)
Pa State Rep
Mailing Add: Capitol Bldg Harrisburg PA 17120

LIND, JAMES FRANCIS (D)
b York, Pa, Oct 17, 00; s William E Lind & Alice K Shanabrough L; m 1922 to Grace Elizabeth Stahl; c James R. Educ: Pa State Univ Exten, 25. Polit & Govt Pos: US Rep, Pa, 49-52; co controller, York Co, Pa, 54-57 & reelected 5 times, serv ending 73. Mil Serv: Sgt, Army, 17-20, World War I; Lt Col, World War II, 41-46 & Korea, 53; Col (Ret), Army Res, 60; Aisne, Champagne-Marne, Aisne-Marne & Meuse Argonne Medals; Army of Occup Medal; Rhineland, ETO & Africa-Middle East Serv Medals; Am Defense & Serv Medals; Victory Medal; Nat Defense Serv Medal. Mem: F&AM; Consistory (32 degree); Shrine; Am Legion (past comdr). Relig: Lutheran. Mailing Add: 141 N Keesey St York PA 17402

LINDAHL, TED (R)
Kans State Rep
Mailing Add: Plevna KS 67568

LINDBERG, GEORGE W (R)
Comptroller, State of Ill
b Crystal Lake, Ill, June 21, 32; s Dr Alger V Lindberg & Rilla Wakem L; m 1964 to Linda Merlo; c Karen Dawn & Kirsten Ann. Educ: Northwestern Univ, BS, 54; Northwestern Sch of Law, JD, 57; Phi Delta Phi. Polit & Govt Pos: Ill State Rep, 32nd Dist, 67-73, chmn, Spec House Comt to Investigate Ill Judiciary, 69-73; Comn on Judiciary II & Ethics in Govt Study Comn, 70-73; comptroller, State of Ill, 73- Bus & Prof Pos: Vpres, John E Reid & Assocs, Chicago, 55-68; assoc, Franz, Franz, Wardell & Lindberg, Crystal Lake, Ill, 68-; sole practice of law, 70- Mem: Ill Chiefs of Police Asn; Spec Agents Asn; Am Polygraph Asn; Am Acad Forensic Sci; Ill Crime Investigating Comn. Honors & Awards: Outstanding Legislator Award. Relig: Episcopal. Legal Res: 420 Country Club Rd Crystal Lake IL 60014 Mailing Add: 210 State House Springfield IL 62706

LINDBLOM, RITA (D)
First VPres, Mont Dem Women's Club
b Wahpeton, NDak, May 17, 29; d Arthur M Forman & Hazel Miller F; m 1949 to Chester W Lindblom; c Karen (Mrs Angvick) & Bradley. Educ: NDak State Sch Sci. Polit & Govt Pos: Secy, Sheridan Co Dem Cent Comt, Mont, 58-61, vchmn, 64-68, precinct committeewoman, 66-, state committeewoman, 67-73, mem-at-lg, State Exec Bd, 69-; treas, Mont Dem Women's Club, 67-73, first vpres, 73-; deleg, Dem Nat Conv, 68; employed, Mont State Senate, 69 & 71; secy-treas, Sheridan Co Const Revision Comt, 70. Bus & Prof Pos: State liquor store vendor, 69- Mem: VFW Ladies Auxiliary (officer, nat, state & local); Nat Farmers Union; co & state Mont Dem Women's Club (officer). Honors & Awards: Outstanding State Pres Award, Nat VFW Auxiliary, 63-64. Relig: Lutheran. Mailing Add: Outlook MT 59252

LINDE, HANS ARTHUR (D)
b Berlin, Ger, Apr 15, 24; s Bruno C Linde & Luise Rosenhain L; m 1945 to Helen Tucker; c Lisa & David Tucker. Educ: Reed Col, BA, 47; Univ Calif, Berkeley, JD, 50; Phi Beta Kappa; Order of the Coif. Polit & Govt Pos: Law clerk to assoc justice Wm O Douglas, US Supreme Court, 50-51; attorney, Off Legal Adv, State Dept & US Mission to UN Gen Assembly, 51-53; legis asst to US Sen Richard L Neuberger, 55-58; mem, Ore Constitutional Revision Comn, 61-62; consult, Arms Control & Disarmament Agency, 62-72; alt deleg, Dem Nat Conv, 64, hearing officer, Credentials Comt, 72; mem comn on vice presidential selection, Dem Nat Comt, 73. Bus & Prof Pos: Assoc prof law, Univ Ore, 59-64, prof, 64-; vis prof, Univ Calif, Berkeley, 64-65, Stanford Univ & Univ Calif, Los Angeles, 72-73; Fulbright lectr, Univ Freiburg, Ger, 67-68. Mil Serv: Entered as Pvt, Army, 43, released as Pfc, 46, after serv in 414th Armored Field Artil Bn, ETO, 45. Publ: Constitutional rights in the public sector, Wash Law Rev, 65; numerous articles in other law journals. Mailing Add: 1131 E 20th St Eugene OR 97403

LINDEEN, ARNOLD RUDOLPH (R)
Iowa State Rep
b Swedesburg, Iowa, May 9, 10; s Rudolph Lindeen & Anna Sandberg L; m 1936 to Marjorie Olson; c Jerry & Jane (Mrs Wickham). Polit & Govt Pos: Treas, Henry Co, 68-75; Iowa State Rep, 75- Bus & Prof Pos: Farmer, Swedesburg, 27-58; bookkeeper, 59-62; Iowa State Sales & Use Tax Auditor, 62-66; treas & mgr, Henry Co Credit Union, 66-68. Relig: Lutheran. Mailing Add: Swedesburg IA 52652

LINDEMAN, ANNE (R)
Ariz State Rep
Mailing Add: 6542 West Earll Dr Phoenix AZ 85033

LINDENMEYER, PAUL ANDREW (R)
b Pawnee City, Nebr, Feb 25, 05; s Theodore Andrew Lindenmeyer & Daisy Ware L; m 1931 to Marlene A Hawver; c D W & Patricia (Mrs John Benison). Educ: Univ Mo, MA & BJ, 27; Sigma Delta Chi; Kappa Tau Alpha; MDS. Polit & Govt Pos: Precinct committeeman, Arcola Twp, Ill, 50-66; Rep committeeman, 48th Dist; chmn, Douglas Co Rep Cent Comt, formerly. Bus & Prof Pos: Ed, Custer Co Chief, Broken Bow, Nebr, 28-29; ed, Regional News, Lake Geneva, Wis, 29-31; city ed, Record-Herald, 32-36, ed & publisher, 36-57; ed & publ, Broom & Broom Corn News, Arcola, 40; Mem: Mason; Elks; Moose; Arcola CofC; US CofC. Relig: Christian Church. Legal Res: 252 S Pine St Arcola IL 61910 Mailing Add: PO Box 523 Arcola IL 61910

LINDER, HAROLD FRANCIS (D)
b Brooklyn, NY, Sept 13, 00; s Dr William Linder & Florence Strauss L; 1930 to Bertha Rubin; c Prudence (Mrs Daniel Steiner) & Susan. Educ: Columbia Univ, 17-19. Hon Degrees: LLD, Univ Pa, 71. Polit & Govt Pos: Dep Asst Secy of State for Econ Affairs, 51, Asst Secy, 52-53; pres & chmn, Export-Import Bank, Washington, DC, 61-68; US Ambassador to Canada, 68-69. Bus & Prof Pos: Mfg bus, 19-25; partner, Cornell, Linder & Co, 25-33; partner, Carl M Loeb, Rhoades & Co, 33-38; pres, Gen Am Investors Co, Inc, 48-56; bd mem, Sch Advan Int Studies, Johns Hopkins Univ, 61; chmn bd & trustee, Inst Advan Study, Princeton, NJ, 69-; consult, Int Finance Corp, 70; mem finance comts, Smithsonian Inst & Am Asn Advan Sci, 71. Mil Serv: Comdr, Naval Res, 42-45. Mem: Inst Int Exec (hon trustee); Inst Philos Research (trustee); Foreign Policy Asn; Coun Foreign Rels; Cosmos. Legal Res: 139 E 63rd St New York NY 10021 Mailing Add: 1901 24th St NW Washington DC 20008

LINDER, JIM (D)
Ark State Rep
Mailing Add: 202 Richmond Hill West Helena AR 72390

LINDER, JOHN E (R)
Ga State Rep
b Deer River, Minn, Sept 9, 42; s Henry Linder & Vera Elizabeth Davis L; m 1963 to Lynne Leslee Peterson; c Kristine Kerry & Matthew John. Educ: Univ Minn, Duluth, 60-63, Dent Sch, BS, DDS, 67; Delta Sigma Delta; Beta Phi Kappa. Polit & Govt Pos: Ga State Rep, 75- Bus & Prof Pos: Dentist, Atlanta, Ga, 69- Mil Serv: Entered as Capt, Air Force, 67, released as Capt, 69, after serv in MedC. Mem: Northern Dist Dent Soc; Am & Ga Dent Asns; Rotary. Relig: Presbyterian. Mailing Add: 5039 Winding Branch Dr Dunwoody GA 30338

LINDERMAN, SARAH PACKER (R)
Pres, DC Young Rep Club
b Pittsburgh, Pa, Feb 24, 41; d Sidney Ely Linderman (deceased) & Eugenia Pleasonton L (deceased). Educ: Strayer Col, secretarial, 59-60; Univ Md, College Park, 67-70; Am Univ, 74-75. Polit & Govt Pos: Social chmn & social vpres, DC Young Rep Club, 71, admin vpres & nat committeewoman, 71-72, pres, 75-; treas, Metrop Coun Young Rep Clubs, 71-72; treas, Region III Young Rep, 73-75. Bus & Prof Pos: Secy, Nat Inst Health, 60-61; legal secy, Wenderoth, Lind & Ponack, 61-72; exec asst, Sutherland, Asbill & Brennan, 73- Mem: Smithsonian Assocs. Relig: Episcopal. Legal Res: 3427 Reservoir Rd Washington DC 20007 Mailing Add: Suite 800 1666 K St Washington DC 20006

LINDESMITH, RUTH MILDRED (R)
Committeewoman, Rep State Cent & Exec Comt, Ohio
b Huntington, WVa, June 23, 14; d William Charles McCord, MD & Clara Jane Numan M; m 1941 to Leroy J Lindesmith; c George R Kent & William C Lindesmith. Educ: Youngstown Co Secretarial Sch, grad, 39. Polit & Govt Pos: Pres, Poland Rep Women's Club, Ohio, 64-; chmn, Bow for Cong Comt, Mahoning Co, 66, 68 & 70; Rep precinct committeeman, Poland Precinct 2, 66-, dist chmn, 66-; committeewoman, Rep State Cent & Exec Comt Ohio 68-72 & 75-; chmn spec comt for sr citizens, Ohio Fedn Rep Women's Orgns, 70-; deleg, Rep Nat Conv, 72. Bus & Prof Pos: Various clerical positions, Sealtest Foods, Youngstown, Ohio, 39-41; clerk, US Post Off, Poland, 44-54. Mem: Ruth White Shrine; Minnie Rebekah Lodge; Ohio Hist Soc; Stark Wilderness Ctr; Western Stark Co Area Rep Club. Relig: Methodist. Legal Res: 20 Second St Poland OH 44514 Mailing Add: Box 5237 Poland OH 44514

LINDGREN, DONALD ARTHUR (D)
Mem, Calif Dem State Cent Comt
b Racine, Wis, Apr 17, 32; s Arthur Edmond Lindgren & Dorothy Palmer L; m 1958 to Vilma Lopour; c Leslie Ann & Allison Leigh. Educ: Univ Wis, Madison, BBA, 57, MBA, 59, PhD, 68, IBM fel, summer 59; Nat Asn of Purchasing Agents fel; Alpha Kappa Psi; Kappa Sigma. Polit & Govt Pos: Pres, Ariz Dem Coun, 64; Dem cand for US Rep, 36th Dist, Calif, 68; mem, Downtown Dem Calif, 68-; mem, Calif Dem State Cent Comt, 68-; mem, United Dem, 69- Bus & Prof Pos: Statist analyst, Gen Motors Cent Foundry Div, 57-58; asst prof mkt, Ariz State Univ, 62-65; prof mkt, Calif State Univ, San Diego, 65-; pres, Lindgren Research Assocs, 68- Mil Serv: Entered as Pvt, Army, 53, released as Pfc, 55, after serv in Army Intel, Seattle, Wash & Okinawa; Defense Medal. Mem: Am Mkt Asn; Mkt & Sale Execs; Am Asn of Univ Prof; Dem clubs & orgn. Honors & Awards: Outstanding Prof, Sch of Bus, San Diego State Col, 69. Relig: Methodist. Mailing Add: 11054 Dutton Dr La Mesa CA 92041

LINDH, OCIE H (D)
Dist Committeewoman, Wilmington Dem Party, Del
b Paris, Va, Feb 28, 31; d Kenton Taylor Holsinger & Pauline Shifflett H; m 1961 to Alfred John Lindh; c Amelia & Eric. Educ: Md State Teachers Col, BS, 54; George Washington Univ, 55 & 61; Johann von Gothe Univ, 61-62; UN Club; Intramural Athletics. Polit & Govt Pos: Dist committeewoman, Wilmington Dem Party, Del, 66-; deleg, Dem Nat Mid-Term Conf, 74. Bus & Prof Pos: Tech aide, Vitro Corp Am, Silver Spring, Md, 55-59; research asst exp psychol, Johns Hopkins Appl Physics Lab, Silver Spring, 59-61; research asst demography, Community Serv Coun, Wilmington, Del, 64-66; planner pub elections, Community Action Prog, Wilmington, spring 67. Mem: Women's Polit Caucus Del (policy coun, 72-); Sch Young Children Elem Workshop (bd dirs); Northwest Civic Asn; Ninth Ward Dem Club. Relig: Unitarian-Universalist. Mailing Add: 801 W 32nd St Wilmington DE 19802

LINDH, PATRICIA SULLIVAN (R)
Rep Nat Committeewoman, La
b Toledo, Ohio, Oct 2, 28; d Lawrence W Sullivan & Lillian Devlin S; m 1955 to H Robert Lindh, Jr; c Sheila, Deborah & Robert L. Educ: Trinity Col, Washington, DC, BA, 50. Polit & Govt Pos: Vpres, EBaton Rouge Parish Women's Rep Club, 66-67, pres, 67-69; revisions chmn, La Fedn Rep Women, 67-68, mem-at-lg exec comt, 69-; mem, EBaton Rouge Parish Polit Action Coun, 67-; secy-treas, EBaton Rouge Parish Rep Exec Comt, 67-; alt deleg, Rep Nat Conv, 68, deleg & mem platform comt, 72; vchmn, La Rep Party, 70-; first vpres, Women in Polit, 72-; Rep Nat Committeewoman, La, 74-; spec asst to President for Women, currently. Mem: Found for Hist La; Anglo Am Mus; Jr League of Baton Rouge; Goals for Baton Rouge Prog (mem govt comt); Baton Rouge Symphony Asn (mem bd). Relig: Roman Catholic. Mailing Add: 3731 S Lakeshore Dr Baton Rouge LA 70808

LINDHOLM, FRANCES MARION (R)
Mem, Rep State Cent Comt Calif
b Minneapolis, Minn, Oct 19, 18; d Jens M Svendsen & Marie Fladeland S; m 1938 to Edward Lindholm, Jr, wid; c George Edward, Rex Ruben, Mark James & Michael Thomas. Educ: Univ Minn, 2 years. Polit & Govt Pos: Mem ways & means comt, Reseda Rep Women's Club, Federated, Calif, 64-65, membership comt, 65-66, publicity comt, 67-69, pres, 69-70, precinct chmn, 72-73; secy, W Valley 64th Calif Rep Assembly, 65-67; campaign off mgr, Calif State Sen Lou Cusanovich, 23rd Sen Dist, 66, Calif Assemblyman Patrick McGee, 64th Assembly Dist, 68; mem, Rep State Cent Comt Calif, 66-68 & 69-; W San Fernando Valley chmn, Women for Murphy, George Murphy for US Senate Campaign, Calif, 70; in charge of spec comput surv for US Rep Barry Goldwater, Jr, Calif, 73. Bus & Prof Pos: Exec secy, Save Am Movies, Hollywood, Calif, 62-68; exec secy, Scenic & Title Artists, 62-69. Mem: Friends of Taxco; Sister City Div, Canoga Park CofC; Canoga Park Civic Asn; Am Nat Red Cross (vol, Valley Dist, 72-). Honors & Awards: Award for work on Project Find, Am Nat Red Cross, 72. Relig: Lutheran. Mailing Add: 20846 Runnymede St Canoga Park CA 91306

LINDHORST, AMBROSE H (R)
Mem, Rep State Cent & Exec Comt Ohio
b Cincinnati, Ohio, July 27, 13; s Harry Lindhorst & Elizabeth Evers L; m 1943 to Betty Bush; c Claudia. Educ: Xavier Univ; Univ of Cincinnati; Chase Col of Law. Polit & Govt Pos: Former chmn, Hamilton Co Rep Exec Comt, Ohio; mem, Rep State Cent & Exec Comt Ohio, currently; deleg, Rep Nat Conv, 68. Bus & Prof Pos: Law Partner, Lindhorst & Dreidame, Attorneys; dir, Southern Ohio Bank, Buckeye Savings Asn, First Ohio Savings Asn, Cincinnati Royals & Cincinnati Gardens; mem bd trustees, Good Samaritan Hospital & Victor Transit Corp. Mem: Cincinnati, Ohio & Am Bar Asns; Am Col Trial Lawyers; Am Judicature Soc. Relig: Catholic. Legal Res: 1044 Roodwood Dr Cincinnati OH 45208 Mailing Add: 1200 American Bldg Cincinnati OH 45202

LINDJORD, HAAKON
b Kristiansand, Norway, July 10, 15; s Jacob H Lindjord & Jorgine Haugland L; m 1945 to Nancy Lancaster; c Jon Douglas, Bonnie Williams, Leigh Jorgine & Richard Charles. Educ: Univ Wash, AB in Econ & Bus summa cum laude, 41; Princeton Univ, MA in Int Rels, 50, PhD in Polit Sci, 51; Naval War Col, 61-62; Phi Beta Kappa; Beta Gamma Sigma. Polit & Govt Pos: In charge of policy planning tasks for the MidE & Africa areas, Army Gen Staff, Pentagon, 58-61; mem staff, Off of the Dep Asst Secy for Politico-Mil Affairs, US Dept of State, 63-66; from div chief to dir, Policy Planning Staff, Off of the Asst Secy of Defense for Int Security Affairs, Pentagon, 66-68; prof staff mem, Senate Sub-Comt on Nat Security & Int Opers, 68-69; spec asst for planning, Off of Emergency Preparedness, 69, asst dir, 69-73; dep dir, Bur Politico-Mil Affairs, Dept State, 73-74; nat security policy consult, currently. Mil Serv: Entered as 2nd Lt, Army, 41, retired as Col, 68, after serv in Intel Div, Supreme Hq, Allied Expeditionary Forces, ETO, 44-45, Berlin, 45-47, NATO Hq, Norway, 51-54 & Korea, 57-58; Legion of Merit with Two Oak Leaf Clusters; Army Commendation Medal; French Croix de Guerre; Belgian Croix de Guerre. Mem: Asn of Princeton Grad Alumni; Asn of the US Army; Princeton Club of Wash. Honors & Awards: Procter fel for high scholarship, Princeton Univ, 50; Superior Honor Award, US Dept of State, 66; Distinguished Serv Award, Off Emergency Preparedness, 73. Relig: Protestant. Legal Res: 9740 Eighth Ave NW Seattle WA 98117 Mailing Add: 1643 Wrightson Dr McLean VA 22101

LINDLEY, JOHN WILLIAM (R)
b Paoli, Ind, Aug 25, 20; s Harry V Lindley & Dana F L; m 1947 to Sara E Tegarden; c John H, Candace Anne & Mike T. Educ: High Sch; Ind Univ Exten Courses. Polit & Govt Pos: Pres, bd trustees, Orleans, Ind, 54-58, mem, 58-62; finance chmn & treas, Orange Co Rep Cent Comt, 64-65, chmn, formerly. Bus & Prof Pos: Serv mgr, Dictaphone Corp, 42-46; grocery bus, 47- Mem: Mason; Elks; Kiwanis; CofC; Farm Bur. Honors & Awards: Sagamore of the Wabash. Relig: Christian. Mailing Add: 365 W Vincennes St Orleans IN 47452

LINDQUIST, EDWARD H (D)
Ore State Rep
b Portland, Ore, Feb 14, 38; s Harold Carl Lindquist & Lola Feller L; m 1957 to Janet Anderson; c Dina Rae, Eric Edward & Lisa Kay. Educ: Portland State Univ, 58-59; Portland Community Col, 60-71; Clackamas Community Col, 70. Polit & Govt Pos: Ore State Rep, 73- Bus & Prof Pos: Capt, Milwaukie Rural Fire Protection Dist, 63- Mem: Oregon City Jaycees; Clackamas Co Prof Firefighters; Northwest Steelheaders; Clackamas Co Cent Labor Coun (vpres, 72, pres, 73-). Honors & Awards: Proj of the Year, Jaycees, 71-72. Relig: Protestant. Mailing Add: 5187 SE Rinearson Milwaukie OR 97222

LINDQUIST, STEPHEN CHARLES (DFL)
Treas, 38th Dist Dem-Farmer-Labor Party, Minn
b Minneapolis, Minn, Feb 28, 41; s Arnold Richard Lindquist & Evelyn Berg L; m 1968 to Nancy Sue Lindberg; c Sarah Christine. Educ: Bethel Col, 59-62; Univ Minn, Minneapolis, BS, 64; Mankato State Col, 69-71. Polit & Govt Pos: Deleg, 38th Dist Dem-Farmer-Labor Conv, 70; alt deleg, Minn State Dem-Farmer-Labor Conv, 70; chmn, Eighth Ward, Third Precinct Dem-Farmer-Labor Party, 70-; treas, 38th Dist Dem-Farmer-Labor Party, 70- Bus & Prof Pos: Teacher, Denver, Colo, 64-65; Cent High Sch, Minneapolis, Minn, 65-67; participant, Nat Sci Found Acad Year Inst in Math, San Diego State Col, 67-68; teacher, SHigh Sch, Minneapolis, 68- Mem: Nat & Minn Coun Teachers of Math; Minneapolis Math Club; Am & Minn Fedn Teachers. Honors & Awards: Selected to participate in Int Teacher Exchange Prog, Eng, 71-72. Relig: Protestant. Mailing Add: 3418-43rd Ave S Minneapolis MN 55406

LINDSAY, GROSS C (D)
Ky State Rep
Mailing Add: Union Federal Bldg Henderson KY 42420

LINDSAY, JOHN CHARLES (D)
SC State Sen
b Bennettsville, SC, Apr 18, 27; s Roos Moore Lindsay, Sr & Louise Crosland Bair; m 1949 to Frances Maxine. Educ: Univ SC, LLB, 51. Polit & Govt Pos: SC State Rep, 53-62; SC State Sen, 62- Bus & Prof Pos: Lawyer; dir, McColl State Bank; vpres, McColl Investors, Inc. Mil Serv: Marine Corps, 44-46, serv in A Co, 1st Bn, 21st Regt, Third Marine Div. Mem: Jaycees (bd dirs); VFW; Am Legion; Mason; Alpha Tau Omega. Mailing Add: State House Columbia SC 29211

LINDSAY, JOHN VLIET (D)
b New York, NY, Nov 24, 21; s George Nelson Lindsay & Eleanor Vliet L; m 1949 to Mary Harrison; c Katherine (Mrs Richard Schaffer), Margaret, Anne & John Vliet, Jr. Educ: Yale Univ, BA, 44, LLB, 48. Hon Degrees: Hon degree from Pace Col, Oakland Col, Harvard Univ, Manhattanville Col & Williams Col. Polit & Govt Pos: Exec asst to US Attorney Gen, 55-57; US Rep, NY, 59-65; Mayor, New York, 65-73; vchmn, Nat Comn Civil Disorders, 67; deleg, Rep Nat Conv, 60-68; deleg, Dem Nat Conv, 72. Bus & Prof Pos: Assoc, law firm Webster, Sheffield, Fleischmann, Hitchcock & Brookfield, 49-53, partner, 53-55. Mil Serv: Lt, Naval Res, 43-46. Publ: Journey Into Politics, Dodd, Mead, 67; The City, W W Norton, 70. Mem: Asn of Bar of City of New York; Am & NY Bar Asns. Honors & Awards: Distinguished Serv Citation, Faculty Univ Calif, Berkeley; Family of Man Award, Coun Churches. Relig: Episcopal. Mailing Add: New York NY 10023

LINDSAY, RICHARD P (D)
Utah State Rep
Mailing Add: 1886 W 4805 S Salt Lake City UT 84118

LINDSAY, ROBERT GOODALL (D)
Mem, NY Dem State Comt
b Glasgow, Scotland, Oct 28, 97; s William Ross Lindsay & Mary Kane L; wid; c Robert Arthur. Educ: Bus Col. Polit & Govt Pos: Secy to Boro pres, Richmond, 33; US Marshal, 38; mem, Coun of New York, NY, currently; mem, NY Dem State Comt, 62-; chmn, Richmond Co Dem Comt, 69-72. Bus & Prof Pos: Pres, Giffords Seafood Inc, 40- Mem: KofC. Relig: Catholic. Mailing Add: 891 Forest Ave Staten Island NY 10310

LINDSETH, JON A (R)
Finance Chmn, 54th Legis Dist Rep Party, Ohio
b Cleveland, Ohio, June 20, 34; s Elmer L Lindseth & Anne Fluckey L; m 1955 to Virginia MacDonald; c Andrew, Steven, Karen & Peter. Educ: Cornell Univ, BME, 57; Beta Theta Pi. Polit & Govt Pos: Rep committeeman, Fourth Ward, Waynesboro, Va, 60-66; mem, Va State Rep Cent Comt & treas, Rep Party of Va, 61-66; mem, Seventh Cong Dist Rep Comt & chmn, Finance Comt, Va, 63-66; mem, Va Rep Finance Comt, 63-66; alt deleg, Rep Nat Conv, 64; vchmn bd trustees, Waynesboro Pub Libr, 64-66; finance chmn, 54th Legis Dist Rep Party, Ohio, 66-; finance chmn, Taft for Mayor of Cleveland Comt, 67. Bus & Prof Pos: Sales specialist, Gen Elec Co, 59-65; mgr of mkt, TRW, Inc, 66-69; pres, Hines Flask Co & chmn, Hines Investment, 69- Mil Serv: Entered as Ens, Navy, 57, released as Lt(jg), 59; Lt Comdr, Naval Res, 59-66. Mem: Union Club; Cleveland Country Club. Relig: Protestant. Mailing Add: 2827 Scarborough Rd Cleveland Heights OH 44118

LINDSEY, BERTHA MAE (R)
Secy, Orange Co Rep Cent Comt, Ind
b French Lick, Ind, Oct 2, 24; d Banks Arthur Condra & Gertrude Gillum C; m 1965 to John Harold Lindsey; c Loletta Crawford & Mona Hammons. Educ: French Lick High Sch, Ind, grad, 42. Polit & Govt Pos: Secy, Orange Co Rep Cent Comt, Ind, 74- Mailing Add: RR 2 French Lick IN 47432

LINDSEY, ROBERT EUGENE (R)
Mayor, Salem, Ore
b Bakersfield, Calif, Sept 16, 27; s Lloyd Aaron Lindsey & Ruth Haverlandt L; m 1955 to Charolette Patricia Jelinek; c Maureen, Gerald, Thomas, Michael, Dennis & Susie. Educ: Col Educ, 51-53; Creighton Univ, dent, 53-57. Polit & Govt Pos: Mayor, Salem, Ore, 73- Mailing Add: 510 Snow White Way Salem OR 97302

LINDSTEDT, NORMAN L (D)
b Portland, Ore, Nov 12, 31; s Gustav J Lindstedt & Edith M Erickson L; m 1951 to Merrinell Merrigan; c Norvella Koelling, Brad, Judith, Kristi Sally & Eric. Educ: Univ Ore, BS in Bus Admin; Northwestern Sch of Law, Portland, LLB; Phi Gamma Delta. Polit & Govt Pos: Dist leader, Multnomah Co Dem Cent Comt, Ore, 60-68; chmn, Lawyers for Kennedy, Ore, 68; chmn, Local Sch Bd, Multnomah Co, 68-; chmn, Multnomah Co McGovern for President, 71-72; deleg, Dem Nat Conv, 72. Bus & Prof Pos: Salesman, Mercer Steel Co, Inc, 53-58; lawyer, Buss, Leichner, Lindstedt & Barker, 58- Mem: Am Trial Lawyers Asn; Ore State & Multnomah Co Bar Asns; Multnomah Atheltic Club. Relig: Protestant. Mailing Add: 4081 N Overlook Blvd Portland OR 97227

LINDVALL, MARTHA REBBECCA (R)
Secy, Marshall Co Rep Comt, Ind
b Callao, Mo, Aug 4, 13; d William Alexander Welch, MD & Martha Mrytle Randall W; m 1941 to Lawrence Henry Lindvall; c Lawrence, Jr, Marsha (Mrs John Banning), Sharon (Mrs Norman Witt) & Douglas. Educ: Columbia Col, teaching degree, 33; Culver-Stockton Col, 33-34. Polit & Govt Pos: Vchmn, Union Twp Rep Party, 60-75; secy, Marshall Co Rep Comt, 72- Bus & Prof Pos: Head, Drivers Licenses Dept, Plymouth, Ind, 64- Mem: Marshall Co Home Econ; Home & Hobby Club; Marshall Co Hosp Auxiliary; Ladies Group Trinity Lutheran Church; Rep Ladies Group. Relig: Lutheran. Mailing Add: RR 1 Culver IN 46511

LINEBERGER, LAWRENCE M (D)
Chmn, Owyhee Co Dem Party, Idaho
b St Louis, Mo, Nov 16, 15; s Ira H Lineberger & Vera McCaul L; m 1960 to Menna Bruns; c Alfred. Educ: Univ Idaho, BS in Bus. Polit & Govt Pos: Dem precinct committeeman, Idaho, 51-56; chmn, Owyhee Co Dem Party, 56-72 & 74- Mem: Elks; AF&AM; Scottish Rite; Shrine. Mailing Add: Rte 1 Box 55 Homedale ID 83628

LING, ROGER D (R)
b Rupert, Idaho, Nov 5, 33; s Mervin V Ling & Delphia E Rogers L; m 1961 to Judy E Jones; c Dawn Catherine, Melissa Ann, Robert Clay & Timothy Darren. Educ: Idaho State Univ, BS in Acct, 61; Willamette Univ, LLB, 64; Phi Delta Phi. Polit & Govt Pos: Dep prosecuting attorney, Minidoka Co, Idaho, 64-66; chmn, Minidoka Co Rep Cent Comt, formerly. Bus & Prof Pos: Legal counsel, Minidoka Irrigation Dist, Rupert, Idaho, 64-, Minidoka Sch Dist 331 & A&B Irrigation Dist, Rupert, Idaho, 69- Mil Serv: Entered as Pvt, Army, 64, released as SP-4, 66, after serv in 496th AAA Bn, 20th Group, Fifth Army, 65-66; Good Conduct Medal. Mem: Idaho State & Fifth Judicial Bar Asns; Rotary; Rupert CofC (dir); Elks. Relig: Methodist. Legal Res: RR Rupert ID 83350 Mailing Add: PO Box 623 Rupert ID 83350

LINGREN, RONALD HAL (D)
Wis State Rep
b Gowrie, Iowa, June 26, 35; s Herbert George Lingren (deceased) & Zula Bolton L; m 1964 to Dorothy Kriebel; c Scott Allen & Kristin Lee. Educ: Iowa State Univ, BS, 60; Univ Iowa, MA, 61, PhD, 65; Phi Delta Kappa. Polit & Govt Pos: Wis State Rep, 97th Dist, 75- Bus & Prof Pos: Consult psychologist, Jefferson Co Schs, Iowa, 61-62; asst dir Pine Sch Research Proj, Univ Iowa, 62-64, consult, Child Psychiat Clin, 63-65; prof, Dept Educ Psychol, Univ Wis-Milwaukee, 65- Mil Serv: Entered as Pvt, Army, 53, released as Cpl, 55, after serv in 84th Engrs, 8th Army, Korea, 54-55; Maj (Ret), Air Force Res, 56-74; Korean Serv, UN Serv, Nat Defense, Ten-Year Reserve Serv, Expert Marksmanship, Iowa Nat Guard Serv & Good Conduct Medals. Publ: 13 Articles & research papers. Mem: Am Psychol Asn; Nat Asn Sch Psychologists; Wis Psychol Asn (bd dirs, 74-); Wis Sch Psychologists Asn; Wis Coun of Asns for Pupil Serv (pres, 74). Honors & Awards: Nat Leadership Award, Nat Asn Sch Psychologists, 70 & 71; Outstanding Leadership Award, Wis Sch Psychologists Asn, 71. Mailing Add: W140 N8162 Lilly Rd Menomonee Falls WI 53051

LININGTON, VICTOR A (R)
Chmn, Dist Five Rep Party, NDak
b Montreal, Can, Oct 13, 08; s Alfred William Linington & Zella Goodwin L; m 1956 to Geneva H Parke; c Barbara (Mrs Hamlet), Lynn (Mrs Haymaker), Patrick Linington & Vicki Linington. Educ: Moosejaw Col (Sask), 25-27; Northwestern Univ, Chicago, 29-30. Polit &

Govt Pos: Sch bd mem, Minot, NDak, 44-50; park bd mem, Minot Park System, 50-60; chmn, Dist Five Rep Party, NDak, 74- Bus & Prof Pos: Pres, NDak Lignite Coun, 74- Mem: Mason; Elks; Eagles; Kiwanis; Air Force Asn. Honors & Awards: Distinguished Service Award, Minot Jr CofC, 39. Relig: Presbyterian. Mailing Add: 818 Fourth Ave NW Minot ND 58701

LINK, ARTHUR A (D)
Gov, NDak
b Alexander, NDak, May 24, 14; m to Grace Johnson; c five sons & one daughter. Educ: NDak State Univ Agr & Applied Sci. Polit & Govt Pos: Mem, Randolph Twp Bd, 28 years; mem, McKenzie Co Welfare Bd, 21 years; mem, sch bd, 18 years; NDak State Rep, 47-71, speaker, NDak House Rep, 65; chmn, NDak State Adv Coun Voc Educ, 69-71, chmn second interim comt legis procedure & arrangements, Subcomt Educ; US Rep, 70-72; Gov, NDak, 73- Bus & Prof Pos: Farmer. Mem: Williston Univ Ctr Found (bd mem); Lions; PTA; Nat Cowboy Hall of Fame. Relig: Lutheran; Coun Pres & Sunday Sch Supt, Alexander Trinity Lutheran Church. Legal Res: Alexander ND 58830 Mailing Add: State Capitol Bismarck ND 58501

LINK, DONALD RICHARD (D)
b Denham, Ind, July 2, 45; s Raymond H Link & Myrtle Cole L; single. Educ: Francesville High Sch, 63. Polit & Govt Pos: Chmn, Pulaski Co Dem Cent Comt, Ind, formerly. Bus & Prof Pos: Assoc with family bus, Retail Groceries & Automotive Serv, Ind, currently. Mem: Winamac Jaycees; Ind Farm Bur; Pulaski Co Fair Bd (chmn). Relig: Baptist. Mailing Add: Rte 3 Box 80 Winamac IN 46996

LINKOUS, T CECIL (D)
Chmn, Warren Co Dem Exec Comt, Ohio
b Stillwater, Ky, Mar 12, 20; s Otis B Linkous & Margaret Cecil L; m 1942 to Dorothy Welch; c Diane R, Steven A, Jennifer & Jeffrey B. Educ: Lebanon High Sch, grad, 39. Polit & Govt Pos: Co comnr, Warren Co, Ohio, 59-62; precinct committeeman, Dem Party, Ohio; chmn, Warren Co Dem Exec Comt, Ohio, 61-62 & 68-; mem, Warren Co Bd Elec, 70-, chmn, 72-75. Bus & Prof Pos: Ins Agent, 50- Mil Serv: Entered as Pvt, Army, 42, released as Cpl, 43, after serv in 14th Armored Div. Mem: Am Legion Post 186 (life mem); Dem Club. Relig: Protestant. Mailing Add: 2545 Dayton Rd Lebanon OH 45036

LINNELL, JOHN R (R)
Chmn, Maine Rep State Comt
Mailing Add: 80 Shepley St Auburn ME 04210

LINOWITZ, SOL MYRON (D)
b Trenton, NJ, Dec 7, 13; s Joseph Linowitz & Rose Oglenskye L; m 1939 to Evelyn Zimmerman; c Anne, June, Jan & Ronni. Educ: Hamilton Col, AB, 35; Cornell Univ, LLB, 38; Phi Beta Kappa; Phi Kappa Phi; Order of the Coif. Hon Degrees: Over 20 hon doctorate degrees from Am cols & univs, 65- Polit & Govt Pos: Asst gen counsel, Off Price Admin, Washington, DC, 42-44; US Ambassador, Orgn Am States, formerly; US Rep, Inter-Am Comn of Alliance for Progress, 66-69; chmn, Nat Urban Coalition, 69- Bus & Prof Pos: Partner, Sutherland, Linowitz & Williams, 46-58; firm, Harris, Beach, Keating, Wilcox, Dale & Linowitz, 58-66; former chmn bd & exec comt, Xerox Corp; former chmn, State Dept Adv Comt on Int Orgn; sr partner, Coudert Bros law firm, 69-; trustee, Mutual Ins Co of NY, 69-; dir, Time, Inc, 69-, Marine Midland Banks Inc & Pan Am World Airways Inc, currently. Mil Serv: Lt(sg), Naval Res, 44-46. Mem: Foreign Policy Asn (chmn nat coun, 69-); Am Red Cross (bd gov); Am Asn for UN (pres, NY State); Rochester Asn for UN; Am Bar Asn. Relig: Jewish. Legal Res: 2563 East Ave Rochester NY Mailing Add: 2325 Wyoming Ave NW Washington DC 20008

LINSKY, MARTIN A (R)
Mem, Brookline Rep Town Comt, Mass
b Boston, Mass, Aug 28, 40; s Harold M Linsky & Ruth Doran L; m 1964 to Helen Strieder; c Alison Doran & Samuel Strieder. Educ: Williams Col, BA, 61; Harvard Law Sch, LLB, 64. Polit & Govt Pos: Mem research staff of Sen Leverett Saltonstall of Mass, 60; mem, Town Meeting, Brookline, 64-; mem, Brookline Rep Town Comt, 64-; legis & research asst to Lt Gov of Mass, 65-66; asst attorney gen, Commonwealth of Mass, 67; Mass State Rep, 13th Norfolk Dist, 67-72, asst minority leader, Mass House Rep, 71-72; alt deleg, Rep Nat Conv, 68. Bus & Prof Pos: Instr Fed-State Rels, Northeastern Univ, Boston, 66-69; sr social scientist, ABT Assocs Cambridge, Mass, 72-; fel, Kennedy Inst Polit, Harvard Univ, spring 73. Publ: Hi-how's it going - a day in the life of a state legislator, Ripon Forum & Boston Globe Sunday Mag, 10/69; Boston legal establishment, 1/70 & The Massachusetts legislature, 12/31/72, Boston Globe Sunday Mag. Mem: World Affairs Coun of Boston; Anti-Defamation League of B'nai B'rith (New Eng Regional Bd); Jewish Voc Serv of Gtr Boston; Mass Voc Rehabilitation Planning Comn; Brookline Ment Health Asn. Honors & Awards: Selected as one of the ten outstanding young men of the year, Gtr Boston Jr CofC, 68; Citation for Outstanding Achievement in Pub Serv, Bryant & Stratton Sch, Boston, 68. Relig: Jewish. Mailing Add: 25 Thatcher St Brookline MA 02146

LINTON, DWAYNE (D)
b Marion, Ill, Sept 29, 17; s William Earl Linton (deceased) & Mable Clara Hester L (deceased); m 1936 to Margaret Ruth Richmond; c William D, Richard B & Douglas R. Educ: Regina Univ, Can, 40-41. Polit & Govt Pos: Aeronaut inspector, Ill Dept of Aeronaut, 49-53; mem & chmn, Local Bd 213, Selective Serv Syst, Williamson Co, 50-71; gen assistance adminr, Williamson Co, 56-61; labor conciliator, Ill Dept of Labor, 61-69 & 72-; drivers license examr, Secy of State, Ill, 70-71; alt deleg, Dem Nat Conv, 72. Bus & Prof Pos: Owner, Linton Electronics, Herrin, Ill, 46-68; pres, Linton Inertiamatics, Inc, 70- Mil Serv: Entered as Airman, Royal Can Air Force, 40, released as Flight Comdr, 45, after serv in Fighter Command, ETO, 41-45, retired; Purple Heart; Distinguished Flying Cross European Theatre Campaign Ribbons. Publ: High Flight, Lindsey-Swab Publ, 48. Mem: Mason; Blue Lodge; Shrine (32 degree); Elks; Am Legion. Honors & Awards: 20 years serv to nation, Selective Serv, Presidential, 71. Relig: Unitarian. Legal Res: 631 Indian Hill Dr Herrin IL 62948 Mailing Add: PO Box 322 Herrin IL 62948

LINVILLE, ROBERT G, JR (R)
Chmn, Idaho Rep State Cent Comt
Mailing Add: PO Box 2267 Boise ID 83701

LINZEY, BOBBY LEE (D)
First VChmn, Fulton Co Dem Party, Ga
b Montgomery, Ala, Nov 20, 38; s Theo Webster Linzey & Katie Bell Hatchett L; m 1967 to Anna Bridget Brim; c Laura Kate. Educ: Woodrow Wilson Col Law, Atlanta, Ga, LLB,

LISK / 555

60; Sigma Delta Kappa. Polit & Govt Pos: Dist vchmn, Fulton Co Dem Party, Ga, 66, dist chmn, 67-68, vchmn, 69-70, first vchmn, 71-, mem, currently; mem, Ga State Dem Exec Comt, currently; Dem nominee for Ga State Rep, 70 & 72; mem, Fulton Co Dem Exec Comt, 72- Mil Serv: Entered as Airman 3/C, Ga Air Nat Guard, 56, released as Airman 1/C, 62, after serv in 116th Hq Squadron, Mil Air Transport Serv. Relig: Baptist. Mailing Add: 2799 Plantation Dr East Point GA 30344

LIONBERGER, ERLE TALBOT LUND (R)
Mem, Mo Rep State Comt
b St Louis, Mo, Apr 29, 33; d Joel Yowell Lund & Erle Hall Harsh L; m 1956 to John Shepley Lionberger, Jr; c Erle Talbot & Louise Shepley. Educ: Vassar Col, AB, 55. Polit & Govt Pos: Alt deleg, Rep Nat Conv, 68, deleg, 72; committeewoman, Hadley Twp Rep Party, Mo, 65-; mem, Mo Rep State Comt, 68- Mem: Jr League St Louis; Nat Soc Colonial Dames Am. Mailing Add: 21 Dartford St Louis MO 63105

LIONETT, DAVID JEROME (R)
Dep State Chmn, Mass Rep State Comt
b Boston, Mass, Oct 3, 43; s William F Lionett (deceased) & Pauline E Atkinson L; m 1971 to Gail L Granum. Educ: Tufts Col, AB in Econ, 65; Chartered Life Underwriter, 68; Theta Delta Chi; Debating Club. Polit & Govt Pos: Mem, Holden Rep Town Comt, Mass, 67-69; mem, Worcester Rep Ward One City Comt, 69-; Mass State Rep, 71-74; Rep cand for US Rep, Mass, 74; dep state chmn, Mass Rep State Comt, 75- Bus & Prof Pos: Life underwriter, Northwestern Mutual Life Ins, 67- Mem: Nat Asn Life Underwriters; life mem Million Dollar Round Table; Big Bros; Jaycees; Worcester Co Rep Club. Honors & Awards: One of Ten Outstanding Young Men, Worcester, Mass, 70. Relig: Protestant. Mailing Add: 17 Nottingham Rd Worcester MA 01609

LIPIN, ALFRED JEROME (D)
Md State Sen
b Anne Arundel Co, Md, Mar 16, 20; m to Irene Hein; c Mary Lou, Nancy Lee, Jack & Laura. Educ: Univ Baltimore. Polit & Govt Pos: Mem, Anne Arundel Co Zoning Appeals Bd, 56-57; Md State Deleg, Dist 6-A, Anne Arundel Co, 67-71, chmn, Legis Subcomt of Md Airport Study, 69-70; Md State Sen, 71- Bus & Prof Pos: Businessman & real estate agent. Mil Serv: Participated in five European campaigns during World War II; Silver Star; Comdr, Glen Burnie Nat Guard, 4 years. Mem: Glen Burnie CofC; Glen Burnie Civitan Club; Am Legion; VFW; Elks. Mailing Add: 502 Second Ave SW Glen Burnie MD 21061

LIPMAN, WYNONA M (D)
NJ State Sen
Mailing Add: 50 Park Pl Newark NJ 07102

LIPPIAN, CHARLES JOSEPH (D)
Miss State Rep
Mailing Add: Box 1015 Pascagoula MS 39567

LIPPITT, FREDERICK (R)
RI State Rep
b Washington, DC, Dec 29, 16. Educ: Yale Univ, BA, 39; Yale Law Sch, LLB, 46. Polit & Govt Pos: RI State Rep, 61-; deleg, Rep Nat Conv, 68; Rep Nat Committeeman, currently. Bus & Prof Pos: Lawyer. Mil Serv: Army World War II. Mailing Add: 1109 Hospital Trust Bldg Providence RI 02903

LIPS, EVAN EDWIN (R)
NDak State Sen
b Bismarck, NDak, Oct 17, 18; s William Edwin Lips & Margaret Griffith L; m 1946 to Elsa M Kavonius; c Evan William, Deborah Jane & Erik George. Educ: Univ NDak, BS, 41; Blue Key; Alpha Tau Omega. Polit & Govt Pos: Precinct committeeman, Rep Party, NDak, 50; dist chmn, Rep Party, 50-54; Mayor, Bismarck, 54-66; NDak State Sen, Dist 32, 60- Bus & Prof Pos: Pres, Murphy Ins, Inc, 52-; chmn bd, Dakota Fire Ins Co, 57-; dir, First Nat Bank, 61-, Bismarck Bldg & Loan Asn, 62 & Provident Life Ins Co, 67- Mil Serv: Entered as Pfc, Marine Corps, 41, released as Maj, 46, after serv in Third Marine Div, Pac Theater, Staff Officer, 43-45; Col (Ret), Marine Corps Res; Presidential Unit Citation; Legion of Merit; Bronze Star. Mem: Am Legion; VFW; Elks; Mason; Shrine. Honors & Awards: Boss-of-the-Year Award & Distinguished Serv Award, Jaycees; Distinguished Serv Award, Eagles. Relig: Lutheran. Mailing Add: 203 W Owens Ave Bismarck ND 58501

LIPSKY, JOAN (R)
Iowa State Rep
b 1919; m to Abbott Lipsky; c Ann, John & Abbott, Jr. Educ: Northwestern Univ, BSc, Univ Iowa Grad Sch, 1 year. Polit & Govt Pos: Iowa State Rep, 67-; chmn, Human Resources Comt, Midwest Conf State Govts, 72-; mem, Intergovt Legis Conf, 73- Mailing Add: 655 Cottage Grove Ave SE Cedar Rapids IA 52403

LIPTON, JOHN M (D)
Ark State Rep
Mailing Add: 108 South Walnut Warren AR 71671

LISA, JOSEPH F (D)
NY State Assemblyman
Mailing Add: 56-12 Van Doren St Corona NY 11368

LISK, DAVID KENNETH (R)
City Councilman, Roanoke, Va
b Rome, NY, Nov 26, 28; s Maynard Carlton Lisk & Rose Brooks L; m 1953 to Jean R Hebard; c Timothy David, Thomas Alan & Robert Kenneth. Educ: Univ Rochester. Polit & Govt Pos: Chmn, Roanoke Rep Party, 64-65; state finance chmn, Sixth Dist Rep Party, 63-64; pres & nat committeeman, Young Rep Club of Va, 54-60; mem City Coun, Roanoke, 66-, Vmayor, 72-, vchmn airport comn, mem develop & housing authority, civic ctr adv bd, regional landfill comt, regional courthouse comt, regional jail comt, city coun legis comt & chmn, city coun real estate comt; nat vpres, Sister City Orgn, currently; mem personnel comt, Va League of Cities, currently; mem pub safety comt, Nat League of Cities, currently; mem, Mayor's Comt for Handicapped, 69-; mem, Gov Comt for Need of Handicapped, 72- Bus & Prof Pos: Vpres, Roanoke Develop Corp, currently; vpres, Cent Roanoke Develop Found, currently; dir, Planned Parenthood Comt, 72-, Halfway House, NW, 72- & Youth Ctr, NW, 72- Mil Serv: Entered as Cadet, Air Force & released as 1st Lt, 50, also Res Capt, Air Force, 3565th Training Squadron Instr, 50; Good Conduct Medal; Purple Heart; Am Victory Award.

556 / LISKOV

Mem: Civitan Club (dir); Fraternal Order of Police (dir, 67-); Moose; Roanoke Valley Kiwanis Club (dir); Elks. Honors & Awards: Named Jaycee of Month three times & received Key Man Award, 63-64. Relig: Episcopal; Vestryman, Lay Leader & Dir Christian Educ, St Elizabeth Episcopal Church. Mailing Add: 909 Carrington Ave SW Roanoke VA 24015

LISKOV, SAMUEL (D)
Conn State Rep

b Bridgeport, Conn, Mar 18, 08; s Nathan Liskofsky & Esther Pomerance L; m to Helen Werner; c Judith (Mrs Zabin), Andrew Seth & Richard Grant. Educ: Jr Col Conn, Bridgeport, AA, 30; New York Univ, LLB, 36. Polit & Govt Pos: Conn State Rep, 67-, chmn comn intergovt coop, Conn House Rep, currently. Bus & Prof Pos: Attorney-at-law, Bridgeport, Conn, 37- Mem: Conn & Bridgeport Bar Asns; Mayor's Comn on the Arts; Housatonic Community Col (mem adv coun); Mason. Relig: Hebrew. Mailing Add: 97 Tesiny Ave Bridgeport CT 06606

LIST, ROBERT FRANK (R)
Attorney Gen, Nev

b Visalia, Calif, Sept 1, 36; s Frank W List & Alice Dove L; m 1962 to Kathryn Geary; c Suzanne Kathryn, Franklin Mark & Michelle Alice. Educ: Utah State Univ, BS, 59; Univ Calif Hastings Col Law, JD, 62; Sigma Alpha Epsilon. Polit & Govt Pos: Chmn, Young Rep Club, Carson City, Nev, 63-64; deleg, Young Rep Nat Conv, 63, 65, 67 & 69; chmn platform comt, 69; chmn, Young Nevadans for Laxalt Sen Campaign, 64, Gubernatorial Campaign, 66; deleg, Rep Co & State Conv, 64, 66 & 68; deleg, Young Rep State Conv, 64-69; chmn, Nev Young Rep, 65-66; vchmn, Young Rep Nat Fedn, 67; Young Rep deleg, Conf in Vietnam, 67; dist attorney, Carson City, 67-70; deleg, Rep Nat Conv, 68, deleg & chmn Nev deleg, 72; Young Rep deleg, NATO Conf, Brussels, Belgium, 68; deleg, Trip to USSR, Am Coun of Young Polit Leaders, 71, mem bd dirs, 72-; Attorney Gen, Nev, 71-; Presidential appointee, Comn for the Rev of Nat Policy Toward Gambling, 72- Bus & Prof Pos: Attorney-at-law, 62-66; mem exec comt, Nat Asn of Attorneys Gen, 72-; chmn, Western Conf of Attorneys Gen, 72- Mem: Nev & Am Bar Asns; Nat Dist Attorneys Asn; Rotary; Elks. Honors & Awards: Distinguished Alumni, Utah State Univ, 73. Relig: Protestant. Legal Res: 2 Crest Dr Carson City NV 89701 Mailing Add: PO Box 1057 Carson City NV 89701

LISTER, JOE U (D)
Chmn, Archuleta Co Dem Comt, Colo

b Pagosa Springs, Colo, Dec 26, 27; s Joe Ruben Lister & Frances A Maestas L; m 1950 to Delfina Rose Manzanares; c Rubin Larry, Peggy Lou, Joe U, Jr, Michael John, Leslie M, Donna Sue & Pamela R. Educ: Pagosa Springs Pub Schs, 12 years. Polit & Govt Pos: Dep marshall, Pagosa Springs, Colo, constable, formerly; precinct committeeman, Archuleta Co; chmn, Archuleta Co Dem Comt, Colo, 69-; mem, Town Bd Trustees, Pagosa Springs, Colo, 72- Bus & Prof Pos: Employee, sawmill, Colo, 3 years; ins agent, Great Eastern Mutual Ins Co, Denver; salesman, Gibson Chevrolet, Pagosa Springs; partner, furniture bus, 5 years; owner, furniture & appliance bus, 62- Mem: Lions (pres, 71-72, secy, 72-); Southwest Community Action Prog (dir). Relig: Catholic. Mailing Add: Box 711 Pagosa Springs CO 81147

LISTER, TONEY J (R)
SC State Rep
Mailing Add: New South Village Spartanburg SC 29301

LITTAU, FRED M (R)
SDak State Rep
Mailing Add: Millboro SD 57554

LITTLE, ASA REED (R)
Chmn, Menifee Co Rep Comt, Ky

b Pomeroyton, Ky, Mar 8, 96; s Robert Thomas Littles & Elizabeth Demir L; m to Myrtle Bates Amburgy. Polit & Govt Pos: Chmn, Menifee Co Rep Comt, Ky, 34- Mailing Add: Means KY 40346

LITTLE, BRADLEY JAY (R)
b Emmett, Idaho, Feb 15, 54; s David Little & Geraldine Laidlaw L; single. Educ: Univ Idaho, 72-; Phi Delta Theta. Polit & Govt Pos: Deleg, TAR Conv, 69; alt deleg, Idaho State Rep Conv, 72; deleg, Rep Nat Conv, 72. Bus & Prof Pos: Co-owner, Little Cattle Co, 72- Mem: Nat Adv Comt, Wash Workshops Found. Honors & Awards: Grad, Wash Workshops Cong Seminar I, 72. Relig: Episcopal. Mailing Add: Box 68 E Fourth St Emmett ID 83617

LITTLE, CLAYTON N (D)
Ark State Rep
Mailing Add: 307 NW Sixth St Bentonville AR 72712

LITTLE, DAVID (R)
Rep Nat Committeeman, Idaho

b Emmett, Idaho, Jan 31, 18; s Andrew Little & Agnes Sproat L; m 1941 to Geraldine Laidlaw; c James A, Judith Ann (Mrs Lee Judy) & Bradley Jay. Educ: Univ Idaho, BSEd, 41; Sigma Chi. Polit & Govt Pos: Finance chmn, Idaho Rep Party, 51-53, co chmn, 65-67; Rep Nat Committeeman, Idaho, 68-; Idaho State Rep, 73-74, Idaho State Sen, 75- Mem: Idaho Livestock Prod Credit Asn (vpres, 64-); Southern Idaho Timber Protective Asn (pres, 67-); Taxpayer of Idaho (assoc); Idaho Wool Growers Asn; Elks. Legal Res: E Fourth Emmett ID 83617 Mailing Add: 210 Main Box 68 Emmett ID 83617

LITTLE, DOROTHY LYNN (DOT) (D)
Mem, Dem Nat Comt, Ala

b Jasper, Ala, Dec 6, 28; d Cleveland Posey & Celestie Long P; m 1951 to Cecil Scott Little; c Scott, Chris & Davie. Educ: Judson Col, Marion, Ala, 48-49. Polit & Govt Pos: Treas, Madison Co Young Dem, Ala, 64-68; pub rels dir, Madison Co Dem Women, 66, pres, 67, adv, 68-73; deleg-at-lg, Dem Nat Conv, 68; nominee for elector, Dem Nat Party, 68; committeewoman, Madison Co Dem Exec Comt, 68-, vchmn, 71-; vchmn of women's affairs, Ala State Dem Exec Comt, 70-; mem, Dem Nat Comt, 72- Publ: Ed, A peep into Alabama politics, Ala State Dem Women, 72. Mem: Garden Clubs; Drake-Garth Women's Club; Valley Recreational Club; Harris Home for Children (bd dirs); Lamar Soc. Relig: Baptist. Mailing Add: 1013 Toney Dr SE Huntsville AL 35802

LITTLE, DUANE EWING (D)
State Committeeman, Shoshone Co Dem Cent Comt, Idaho

b Kellogg, Idaho, July 2, 37; s Ewing Henry Little & Elizabeth Sala L; single. Educ: Univ Idaho, BS in bus admin, 61. Polit & Govt Pos: Vpres, Univ Idaho Young Dem, 60-61; pres, Shoshone Co Young Dem, Idaho, 61-62 & 64-66; asst dir, Shoshone Co Civil Defense, 64-68; exec bd mem, Shoshone Co Dem Cent Comt, Idaho, 64-, state committeeman, 68-; treas, Young Dem Clubs of Idaho, 64-66, nat committeeman, 66-70; chmn, Western States Conf, Young Dem Clubs of Am, 68-69. Bus & Prof Pos: Secy-treas, Jackass Ski Bowl Asn, Inc, 64-69, pres, 69-; partner in charge, Turnbow, Maisel, Little & Assocs, 65-; treas, Silver Crown Mining Co, 66-; vpres, R-G Mining Co, 66-69, pres, 69-; partner, Silver Develop Co, 67-; secy, Silver Aurora Mining Co, Inc, 67-; vpres, Silver Ramona Mining Co, Inc, 67-; pres, Silver Horizon Mining Co, Inc, 67-; pres, Silver Chalice Mining Co, Inc, 67-; consult, McKim-Kiser Co, 68- Mem: Jaycees; Am Chem Soc; Toastmasters Int (pres, Club 245, 73-). Honors & Awards: Among the first 12 chosen for the Peace Corps' first project. Relig: Congregational. Mailing Add: 211 W Elder St Kellogg ID 83837

LITTLE, N CLAYTON (D)
Ky State Rep
Mailing Add: PO Box 404 Hartley KY 41532

LITTLE, T D (TED) (D)
Ala State Sen

b Andalusia, Ala, June 21, 42; s Grover Henry Little & Hesta Brogden L; m 1968 to Jonnie Dee Riley; c Mollie Dora & Terre Su. Educ: Univ Ala, BS, 64, Sch Law, JD, 67; Rho Alpha Tau; Phi Alpha Delta; Pi Kappa Alpha. Polit & Govt Pos: Mem, Lee Co Dem Exec Comt, Ala, 71-74; mem, City of Auburn Zone Adjustment Bd, 72-74; pub defender, Auburn, 73-74; Ala State Sen, 74- Bus & Prof Pos: Asst prof bus law, Auburn Univ, 68-74, legal adv to students, 71-73. Mem: Kiwanis Club of Gtr Auburn; Am Bar Asn; Ala Farm Bur; Omicron Delta Kappa; Phi Eta Sigma. Relig: Baptist. Legal Res: 544 Sherwood Dr Auburn AL 36830 Mailing Add: PO Box 342 Auburn AL 36830

LITTLE, WALTER E (R)
Idaho State Rep
Mailing Add: Rte 1 New Plymouth ID 83655

LITTLEFIELD, JOHN ALLAN (R)
Chmn, Kennebec Co Rep Comt, Maine

b Bangor, Maine, Aug 7, 35; s Sheldon Ellsworth Littlefield (deceased) & Helen L Shorey L; single. Educ: Univ Maine, Orono, BA in jour, 57; pres, Press Club; ed-in-chief, Maine Campus. Polit & Govt Pos: Mem, Second Cong Dist Rep Comt, Maine, 60-62; mem, Randolph Rep Town Comt, 60-; former publicity chmn & vchmn, treas, currently; deleg or alt, Maine & Dist Rep Convs, 60-; chmn, Randolph Town Nixon for President Comt, 68; publicity chmn & youth coordr, Kennebec Co Rep Comt, 68-70, mem exec comt, 70-, chmn, 70-; former exec comt, Maine Fedn Young Rep, 68-71; publicity chmn, Maine Fedn Young Rep & TAR, 68-71; adv, Gardiner TAR, 68-; counr, First Nat TAR Youth Leadership Conf, Trinity Col, Washington, DC, 69; chmn, Erwin for Gov, Randolph, 70; counr & speaker pub rels, Pa TAR Inst & Conv, Pa State Univ, 70; guest, NY State TAR Sch Polit, Siena Col, 70; counr, Nat TAR Camp East, Univ Bridgeport, 70; mem-at-lg, First Cong Dist Rep Comt, Maine, 70-72; mem, Maine Rep Co Chmn Asn, 70-, chmn, currently; guest, Rep Nat Conv, 72; counr, Pa TAR Inst & Conv, 73 & 74. Bus & Prof Pos: Reporter-photographer, Gardiner News Bur Chief, Maine; asst sports ed, Daily Kennebec J, 57-67; sports writer & ed, Bath-Brunswick Times-Record, 68; dir pub rels, Thomas Col, 68-; chmn, MSAD 11 Sch Bd, currently. Mil Serv: Entered as Pvt, Maine Army Nat Guard, 58, released as SP-4, 64, after serv in 142nd Ord Co, 121st Pub Info Detachment. Mem: Nat Asn Intercollegiate Athletics Sports Info Dirs Asn; Maine Col Pub Rels Dirs; Maine Asn Coaches & Sports Writers; Maine YMCA (chmn pub rels coun, mem world serv comt); South Cent Dist YMCA (dir, bd secy & chmn publicity & world serv comts, adv, Gardiner Hi-Y, 69-). Honors & Awards: One of Ten Outstanding Young Men of Maine, Maine Jaycees, 67; honored by Gardiner Rotary, Hi-Y, YMCA, Demolay, Boy Scouts, VFW & TAR for serv to youth & community. Relig: Methodist. Mailing Add: 12 Closson St Randolph ME 04345

LITTLEFIELD, LLOYD (R)
Maine State Rep
Mailing Add: MRC Box 161 Bangor Hermon ME 04401

LITTLEJOHN, CAMERON BRUCE (D)
Assoc Justice, Supreme Court of SC

b Pacolet, SC, July 22, 13; s Cameron Littlejohn & Lady Sara Warmoth L; wid; c Inell (Mrs Dan Lewis Allen, III) & Cameron Bruce, Jr. Educ: Wofford Col, AB, 35; Blue Key. Hon Degrees: LLD, Wofford Col, 68. Polit & Govt Pos: SC State Rep, 37-43, speaker, SC House Rep, 47-49; circuit judge, Seventh Judicial Circuit, 49-67; assoc justice, Supreme Court of SC, 67- Bus & Prof Pos: Deleg, Nat Conf State Trial Judges, 64-66; bd trustees, NGreenville Jr Col, 62-67; mem alumni bd dir, Wofford Col, 66-68; deleg, Nat Appellate Judges Conf, 67-70. Mil Serv: Entered as Pvt, Army, 43, released as 1st Lt, 46, after serv in Judge Adv Gen Corps, Pac, 45-46. Publ: Several articles in Trial Judges' J, 65-67. Mem: Am Bar Asn; Civitan; Am Legion; 40 et 8; VFW. Relig: Baptist. Legal Res: 450 Connecticut Ave Spartanburg SC 29302 Mailing Add: PO Drawer 2526 Spartanburg SC 29302

LITTLEJOHN, MARVIN LEROY (R)
Kans State Rep

b Palisade, Colo, Apr 6, 23; s Leroy Littlejohn & Eva Beatrice Gabbert L; m 1956 to Eugenie Hope Culbertson; c Timothy James. Educ: Univ Mo-Columbia, 45-48. Polit & Govt Pos: Municipal judge, Phillipsburg, Kans, 66-69; Kans State Rep, 75- Bus & Prof Pos: Auditor-analyst, Consumers Cooperative Asn, 48-51; self-employed, Phillipsburg, Kans, 51-53; acct, AKansas-Nebraska Nat Gas Co, 53-68 & Great Plains Lutheran Hosps, Inc, 68- Mil Serv: Entered as Pvt, Marine Corps, 42, released as Pfc, 45, after serv in Raider Bn Battalion, South Pac Area, 43-44; Two Purple Hearts. Mem: Hosp Financial Mgt Asn; Elks; VFW. Honors & Awards: Silver Beaver Award, Boy Scouts Am, 58; Follmer Award, Hosp Financial Mgt Asn. Relig: Episcopal. Mailing Add: 14 Southwest Second Phillipsburg KS 67661

LITTLER, RICHARD L (R)
Chmn, Chase Co Rep Party, Kans

b Cottonwood Falls, Kans, Oct 25, 30; s Clyde F Littler & Kathryn Tipton L; m 1951 to Ora Lou Drinkwater; c Kathryn Maree & David Eugene. Educ: Kans State Teachers Col, 49-50; Phi Delta Chi. Polit & Govt Pos: Chmn, Chase Co Rep Party, 68- Bus & Prof Pos: Vpres, Mark Cattle Co, Strong City, Kans, 66. Mil Serv: Entered as Pvt, Army, 51, released as Sgt 1/C, 53, after serv in 25th Inf Div, Artil, Korea, 52-53; Korean & UN Ribbons; Good Conduct

Medal. Mem: Am Legion; VFW. Relig: Presbyterian. Mailing Add: Rte 1 Cottonwood Falls KS 66845

LITTLETON, OBIE J (D)
Ala State Sen
Mailing Add: PO Box 1288 Clanton AL 35045

LITTON, JERRY (D)
US Rep, Mo
b Lock Springs, Mo, May 12, 37; s Charles Oscar Litton & Mildred Tomlinson L; m 1959 to Sharon Ann Summerville; c Linda Lorraine & Scott Stuart. Educ: Univ Mo-Columbia, BS in Agr Jour, 61; Alpha Zeta; Omicron Delta Kappa; Alpha Gamma Rho. Polit & Govt Pos: US Rep, Sixth Dist, Mo, 73-; mem agr comt & various subcomts, US House of Rep, 73- Bus & Prof Pos: Vpres, Litton Charolais Ranch, Inc, 60- Mil Serv: Army Nat Guard. Publ: Ed, Charolais bull-o-gram. Mem: Performance Registry Int (pres); Am Int Charolais Asn. Relig: Presbyterian. Legal Res: Rte 5 Chillicothe MO 64601 Mailing Add: 1502 Longworth House Off Bldg Washington DC 20515

LIVANOS, PETER E JR (R)
Mem, Rep State Cent Comt Calif
b Oakland, Calif, Oct 24, 37; s Peter E Livanos & Helen Beeson L; m 1961 to Gayle Laura Jones; c Peter E, III, Michael Thomas & Christopher Michael. Educ: Univ Calif, Berkeley, BA, 59; Hastings Col Law, JD, 62; Chi Psi; Phi Alpha Delta. Polit & Govt Pos: Dir, Castro Valley Rep Assembly, Calif, 67-69; mem, Rep State Cent Comt Calif, 69- Bus & Prof Pos: Dep dist attorney, Kern Co, Calif, 64-65; partner, Raymond, Keon & Livanos, Bakersfield, Calif, 65-66; attorney-at-law, Law Off of Peter Livanos, Castro Valley, Calif, 66- Mil Serv: Entered as Lt, Army, 59, released as Capt, 69, after serv in Seattle Indust Security Field Off, 62-64. Mem: Alameda Co Bar Asn; Barristers Club of Alameda Co; CofC (dir, Castro Valley Boys Club, 67-); Lions (pres, 70-71); F&AM. Honors & Awards: Cert of Excellence in Corp Law, Hastings Col of Law, 62; Citizen of the Day, Kabel, Bay Area, 67; Man of the Year, Castro Valley, 68. Relig: Protestant. Mailing Add: 5717 Coldwater Dr Castro Valley CA 94546

LIVERMORE, PUTNAM (R)
Mem Exec Comt, Rep State Cent Comt Calif
b San Francisco, Calif, May 29, 22; s Norman Banks Livermore & Caroline Sealy L; single. Educ: Univ Calif, AB, 46, Law Sch, LLB, 49. Polit & Govt Pos: Chmn, San Francisco Co Rep Cent Comt, 65-68; vchmn, Rep State Cent Comt Calif, 69-70, chmn, 71-72, mem exec comt, currently; mem, Rep Nat Comt, 71-72; deleg, Rep Nat Conv, 72. Mil Serv: Entered as Pvt, Marines, 42, released as Capt, after serv in Pac Theater, 44-45. Mem: State Bar of Calif; Am & San Francisco Bar Asns; Am Judicature Soc. Relig: Episcopal. Mailing Add: 1023 Vallejo St San Francisco CA 94133

LIVINGSTON, BARBARA ALLEN (R)
Committeewoman, Ark Rep State Comt
b Maynard, Ark, May 4, 01; d Amos L Allen & Annie Fenn A; m 1919 to Raymon Douglas Livingston; c Lowanda (Mrs Charles Roberts), Patricia (Mrs David Jewett), Blake, Richard & Barbara (Mrs Teddy McCoy). Educ: 12th grade, 16. Polit & Govt Pos: Pres, Rep Independent Club, Imboden, Ark, formerly, secy-treas, 74-75; deleg, Ark Rep Conv, 74; committeewoman, Ark Rep State Comt, currently. Bus & Prof Pos: Elem sch teacher, Southeast Mo, 17-18; bank clerk, Bank of Portia, Ark, 19-20; elem sch teacher, Truman, 20-21; sales lady, dept store, Dexter, Mo, 60-61; homemaker, Imboden, Ark, currently. Mem: Gen Fedn Women's Club; Home Demonstration Mem & Officer; PTA; Lawrence Co Rep Club; Women's Rep & Independent Women's Club of Imboden. Honors & Awards: Eight year award as 4-H Club Leader; Co Pres, Lawrence Co EH Club; Woman of Year, Gen Fed Women's Club, Imboden. Relig: Church of Christ. Legal Res: Fourth St Imboden AR 72434 Mailing Add: Box 67 Imboden AR 72434

LIVINGSTON, CLYDE BURNS (D)
Chmn, Orangeburg Co Dem Party, SC
b Orangeburg, SC, Aug 10, 47; s Atn Burns Livingston & Charlotte Valentine L; m 1973 to Nancy Ruth Ballard. Educ: Univ SC, BS in acct, 69; Omicron Delta Kappa; Beta Alpha Psi; Kappa Sigma Kappa. Polit & Govt Pos: Chmn, Orangeburg Co Dem Party, SC, 74- Bus & Prof Pos: Staff acct, Ernst & Ernst, Atlanta, Ga, 69-70; mgr, Wright & Bailey CPA's, PA, Orangeburg, 70-74; partner, Livingston & Scarborough, 74- Mil Serv: Entered as E-1, Army, 69, released as E-5, 75. Mem: Toastmasters Int; Orangeburg Area Cattlemens Asn. Relig: United Methodist. Legal Res: Rte 5 Box 312 Orangeburg SC 29115 Mailing Add: PO Box 1744 Orangeburg SC 29115

LIVINGSTON, JEAN WICKSMAN (D)
Dem Nat Committeewoman, Tenn
b New York, NY, Sept 11, 21; d Paul Wicksman & Fannie Max W; m 1942 to Philip Henry Livingston; c Richard Paul, Ann (Mrs William B Raines, Jr) & Dean Edward. Educ: Vanderbilt Univ, BA, 42; Phi Beta Kappa; Phi Sigma Iota; Mortar Bd. Polit & Govt Pos: Women's chmn, Hamilton Co Kefauver for Senate, 54; mem bd, Tenn Fedn of Dem Women, currently, vpres, ETenn, 58-59, state pres, 68-70; chmn, Tenn Strategy for Peace, Kennedy-Johnson Campaign, 60; women's chmn, Olgiati for Gov, 62; comnr & secy, Metrop Govt Charter Comn, 62-64; ETenn chmn, Ross Bass for Senate, 64, Tenn chmn, 66; co-chmn, 16th Precinct, Hamilton Co Exec Comt, 70; Third Dist committeewoman, Tenn State Dem Exec Comt, 70-; Dem Nat Committeewoman, Tenn, 72- Mem: Hamilton Co Dem Women's Club (parliamentarian); Citizens Comt for Better Schs, (bd & chmn, 72-); Chattanooga League of Women Voters; Tenn League of Women Voters; Tenn Citizens for Court Modernization (bd, 72-). Honors & Awards: Life mem, PTA, 68. Relig: Unitarian. Mailing Add: 1718 Minnekahda Rd Chattanooga TN 37405

LIVINGSTON, MARION G (R)
Mem, Franklin Co Rep Exec Comt, Ohio
b Philadelphia, Pa, d Joseph Franklin Gaskill & Marion E Cook G; m 1946 to Dr N B Livingston, Jr; c John Morrow, Peter Gaskill & William Cook. Educ: Bryn Mawr Hosp Sch of Nursing, 44-46. Polit & Govt Pos: Area chmn, Neighbor to Neighbor Prog, Ohio Rep Finance Comt, 67-71; alt deleg, Rep Nat Conv, 68 & 72; mem, Am Citizenship Comt, Ohio Fedn of Rep Women, 68-70; mem campaign staff, Chalmers P Wylie for Cong, 70 & 72; mem hq staff, Tom Moody for Mayor Comt, 71; mem, Franklin Co Rep Exec Comt, 72- Mem: Buckeye Rep Club (trustee, 73-); Six Pence Sch (sustaining bd); Navy League of US; Eastern Star; Wittenberg Guild (vpres, 71-72). Relig: Protestant. Mailing Add: 4444 Langport Rd Columbus OH 43220

LIVINGSTON, RICHARD LEE (D)
Miss State Rep
Mailing Add: Box 38 Pulaski MS 39152

LIVINGSTON, SCHUYLER WILLIAM, JR (D)
Chmn, Alexandria Dem City Comt, Va
b Washington, DC, Nov 10, 44; s Schuyler William Livingston & Mary Walton McCandlish L; m 1968 to Elizabeth Ann Marshall; c Philip Moore. Educ: Carleton Col, BA, 66; Harvard Law Sch, JD, 69. Polit & Govt Pos: Deleg, Dem State Conv, Va, 71 & 72; chmn, Alexandria Dem City Comt, 73- Bus & Prof Pos: Attorney, Covington & Burling, 70- Relig: Episcopalian. Mailing Add: 1105 Powhatan St Alexandria VA 22314

LIZOTTE, JEAN-PAUL MARCEL (D)
Maine State Rep
b Biddeford, Maine, June 5, 27; s Benjamin Lizotte & Florence Gaudette L; m 1948 to Fleurette Theresa Nadeau; c Diane (Mrs Loranger), Suzanne, Guy & Janice. Educ: St Louis High Sch, 4 years. Polit & Govt Pos: Maine State Rep, 71-72, 75- Bus & Prof Pos: Owner, Mike's Market, 51-; real estate broker, 62- Mil Serv: Entered as Seaman 3/C, Navy, 45, released as Seaman 1/C, 46, after serv in Pac Theatre. Mem: KofC; Rotary Club. Relig: Catholic. Mailing Add: 312 Elm Biddeford ME 04005

LLOYD, JAMES D (D)
Colo State Rep
Mailing Add: 1730 W Eighth St Loveland CO 80537

LLOYD, JAMES FREDRICK (D)
US Rep, Calif
b Helena, Mont, Sept 27, 22; s Robert E Lloyd & Maria Lunders L; m 1948 to Jacqueline Vaughan; c Brian. Educ: Univ Ore, 2 years; Stanford Univ, BA in Polit Sci, 58; US Naval Post Grad Sch, 58; Univ Southern Calif, MA, 66; Pi Sigma Alpha; Kappa Sigma. Polit & Govt Pos: Mem, Los Angeles Co Dem Cent Comt, 66-68; mem, Calif Dem State Cent Comt, 68-72; city councilman, West Covina, Calif, 68-, mayor, 73; mem, Southern Calif Aviation Comt; US Rep, Calif, 75- Bus & Prof Pos: Owner & exec dir, Lloyds Pub Rels, 66-; instr polit sci, Mt San Antonio Col. Mil Serv: Entered as Seaman 2/C, Navy, 42, released as Lt Comdr, 63, after serv in Naval Aviation, SPac, Korea & Guantanamo Bay, Cuba, 42-63; Asiatic Pac Theater, World War II, Occup, Philippine Liberation, Nat Defense, Cold War & Expert Pistol & Rifle Naval Unit Commendations. Mem: Friends of Ontario Int Airport (bd dirs). Relig: Protestant. Legal Res: 3204 Whitebirch Dr West Covina CA 91791 Mailing Add: Suite 505 100 S Vincent West Covina CA 91790

LLOYD, MARILYN LAIRD (D)
US Rep, Tenn
b Ft Smith, Ark, Jan 3, 29; d James E Laird & Iva L; wid; c Nancy (Mrs Smithson) & Debbie (Mrs Riley), Mari & Morty. Educ: Shorter Col. Polit & Govt Pos: US Rep, Tenn, 75-, mem comt pub works & transportation, comt sci & technol & select comt aging, US House Rep, 75- Mem: Tenn Fedn Bus & Prof Women's Club; Assoc Women for Boyd-Buchanan Sch; PTA (pres). Relig: Church of Christ. Legal Res: 1105 Vannoy Dr Chattanooga TN 37411 Mailing Add: 1017 House Off Bldg Washington DC 20515

LLOYD, RUSSELL G (R)
Mayor, Evansville, Ind
b Plymouth, Pa, Mar 29, 32; s Russell Lloyd & Margaret McCluskey L; m 1956 to Genevieve Anne Ragunas; c Russell G, Jr, Michael, Joel, Daniel, Mary & Julie. Educ: Kings Col, Pa, BA Hist, 49; Notre Dame Univ, LLB, 61. Polit & Govt Pos: Exec secy, Vanderburgh Co Rep Party, Ind, 65-66, treas, 66-68, campaign chmn, 68; co attorney, Vanderburgh Co, 69-71; Mayor, Evansville, 72-; chmn platform comt, Ind State Rep Conv, 72; alt deleg, Rep Nat Conv, 72; chmn, Ind Mayors & Munic Off Comt for Reelec of the President, 72. Bus & Prof Pos: Attorney, Legal Aid Soc of Evansville, Ind, 61-62; attorney, F Wendell Lensing, Attorney, 62-66, self employed, 66-68, Trockman, Lloyd, Flynn & Swain, 69-71 & Lloyd & Swain, 69. Mil Serv: Entered as Pvt, Army, 52, released as Cpl, 54, after serv in US & Korea, Army Reserve, 54-60. Mem: Ind Asn of Cities & Towns (2nd vpres, 72-); VFW; Evansville Chap, Am Red Cross (bd dirs, 64-); Legal Aid Soc of Evansville (bd dirs, 68-); Ind Civil Liberties Union. Honors & Awards: Man of Year, Notre Dame Univ, 72. Relig: Catholic. Legal Res: 3204 Washington Ave Evansville IN 47715 Mailing Add: 302 Civic Ctr Complex Evansville IN 47708

LLOYD, SAMUEL (D)
Vt State Rep
Mailing Add: Weston VT 05161

LLOYD, SHERMAN PARKINSON (R)
b St Anthony, Idaho, Jan 11, 14; s Charles Edward Lloyd & Lucy Parkinson L; m 1935 to Edith Ann Gunn; c Sherman G, Kathryn (Mrs Sharp), Diane (Mrs McMaster) & Elizabeth Ann (Mrs Smith). Educ: Utah State Univ, BS; George Washington Univ Law Sch, LLB. Polit & Govt Pos: Utah State Sen, 55-62, pres, Utah State Sen, 59-61, chmn, Legis Coun, 59-61, Rep Majority & Minority Leader; deleg, Rep Nat Conv & cand, US Rep, Utah, 60; US Rep, Utah, 63-64 & 67-72. Bus & Prof Pos: Exec mgr & gen counsel, Utah Retail Grocers Asn, 40-64; vis lectr polit sci, Univ Utah, 65; founder & mem exec comt, Beehive State Bank. Mem: Utah State Bar Asn; CofC (mem bd gov, Salt Lake Chap); March of Dimes (chmn); Kiwanis (dir, Salt Lake Club). Relig: Latter-day Saint. Mailing Add: 1467 Arlington Dr Salt Lake City UT 84103

LLOYD, THOMAS REESE (R)
Mem, Rep State Cent & Exec Comt Ohio
b Cambridge, Ohio, Jan 5, 20; s John Russell Lloyd & Margaret Patterson L; m 1962 to Doris Irene Alloway. Educ: Muskingum Col, AB, 44; Ohio State Univ Col of Eng, 41-44; Duke Univ Sch of Law, LLB, 47; Delta Tau Delta; Phi Delta Phi. Polit & Govt Pos: Deleg, Rep State Conv, Ohio, 48-64; chmn, Guernsey Co Rep Cent comt, 48-68, chmn, exec comt, 48-68 & currently; Asst Attorney Gen, Ohio, 51-55 & spec counsel to Attorney Gen, 55-58 & 63-; chmn, Ohio State Racing Comn, 55-60; mem, Guernsey Co Bd of Elec, 59-; deleg, Rep Nat Conv, 60; mem, Rep State Cent & Exec Comt Ohio, 60-64 & 68-; vpres, Guernsey Regional Planning Comn, 62- Bus & Prof Pos: Civil Engr, NY Cent RR, 43-44; attorney-at-law, Cambridge, Ohio, 47-; acting adminr, Cambridge Community Hosp, 63-64; secy & gen mgr, Ameritel Enterprises, Inc, Cambridge, Ohio, 67-; secy, Ameritel Corp, Cambridge, 67-; pres, Rumac Inc, Athens, 69- Mem: Guernsey Co, Ohio State & Am Bar Asns. Honors & Awards: Admitted to practice before Supreme Court of Ohio, Supreme Court of US, US Court of

Appeals & US Dist Court. Relig: Presbyterian. Legal Res: 1350 Edgeworth Ave Cambridge OH 43725 Mailing Add: PO Box 705 Cambridge OH 43725

LOCKAMY, JOHN NATHAN (D)
Mem, NC Dem Exec Comt
b Sampson Co, NC, Aug 31, 27; s William Lischer Lockamy & Dora Patience Pope L; m 1950 to Jean Evelyn Strickland; c John Nathan, Jr. Educ: High Sch, grad, 44. Polit & Govt Pos: Dem precinct chmn, Belvoir Precinct, Sampson Co, NC, 58-; community committeeman, US Dept Agr, Belvoir Prencinct, Sampson Co, 63-66, vchmn, 66-; mem, NC Agr Stabilization & Conserv Serv State Training Ctr, Raleigh, 68; mem bd dirs, NC Asn Farmer Elected Committeeman, 67-; southeast area dir, Nat Asn Farmer Elected Committeeman, 67-; deleg, Dem Nat Conv, 68; chmn, Sampson Co Dem Finance Comt, 68-; asst comnr, NC Dept Motor Vehicles, 69-; mem, NC Dem Exec Comt, 70- Bus & Prof Pos: Farmer, Clinton, NC, 44-; owner & operator, Farm Supplies, 46-; vchmn, Farmers' Dehydration, Inc, 67- Mil Serv: Merchant Marine, 45-46; NC Nat Guard, 50-52, Sgt. Mem: Mason; Shrine; Sudan Temple; Asn Shrine Oriental Bands; Nat Farmers' Orgn. Honors & Awards: Cert of Appreciation, NC Dem Exec Comt, 66. Relig: Methodist. Mailing Add: Rte 1 Clinton NC 28328

LOCKE, BARRY M (R)
b Boston, Mass, Dec 21, 30; s Arthur Leo Locke & Lillian Mahler L; m 1957 to Ann Boggio; c Vanessa, Valerie & Alison. Educ: Boston Univ, BS, 53. Polit & Govt Pos: Chief adminr & press secy to Gov Keyser, Vt, 61-63; New Eng pub info officer, US Internal Revenue Serv, Boston, Mass, 63-64; chief press secy to Gov John A Volpe, Mass, 64-68; spec asst to Secy of Transportation John A Volpe, Dept of Transportation, Washington, 69-73; dir of pub affairs, Off of Econ Opportunity, 73-; spec asst, White House Energy Policy Off, 73-; spec asst, Law Enforcement Assistance Admin, Dept Justice, 73-74. Bus & Prof Pos: Ed, Three Rivers, Mich, Daily Newspaper, 56-57; guest lectr, Boston Univ Sch of Pub Commun, currently; gen partner, Smith & Locke Assocs, 74- Mil Serv: Entered as Pvt, Army, 53, released as Sgt 1/C, 55. Mem: Govt Info Officers Asn; Emerson Col Develop Adv Coun; Publicity Club of Boston; Comt for Christian A Herter Endowment, Brandeis Univ. Honors & Awards: Cert of Merit for distinguished serv as staff correspondent, United Press Int News & Vt State Bur Mgr; Secretary's Award & Secretary's Medal for Outstanding Fed Serv, Dept of Transportation. Mailing Add: 11821 Milbern Dr Potomac MD 20854

LOCKE, DAVID HENRY (R)
Mass State Sen
b Boston, Mass, Aug 4, 27; s Allen W Locke & Florence Elizabeth Henry L; m 1952 to Barbara Blood; c David Byron, Jeffrey Allen, Jennifer, Amy Beth & John Adam. Educ: Harvard Univ, AB, 51; Harvard Law Sch, LLB, 54. Polit & Govt Pos: Mem, Wellesley Town Meeting, Mass, 49-; mem, Wellesley Rep Town Comt, 52-; selectman, Wellesley, 59-62; Mass State Rep, 60-68; Mass State Sen, Norfolk-Middlesex Dist, 69-, mem health care, human serv & elderly affairs, ins, judiciary & rules comts & asst floor leader, Mass State Senate, currently. Bus & Prof Pos: Spec asst dist attorney, Norfolk Co, Mass, 56-57; attorney, Jameson, Locke & Fullerton, Wellesley. Mil Serv: Entered as Pvt, Marines, 45, released as Pfc, 46. Mem: Am, Mass, & Boston Bar Asns; Norfolk Co Bar Asn; Trial Lawyer's Asn. Relig: Roman Catholic. Legal Res: 15 Ordway Rd Wellesley MA 02181 Mailing Add: 8 Grove St Wellesley MA 02181

LOCKE, GEORGE (BUTCH) (D)
Ark State Sen
Mailing Add: Box 30 Hamburg AR 71646

LOCKE, JUDSON CLEVELAND SR (D)
Chmn, Perry Co Dem Exec Comt, Ala
b Perry Co, Ala, Apr 1, 90; s Adoniran Judson Locke & Martha Elizabeth Heard L; m 1925 to Etoile Tucker; c Frances Lorraine (Mrs Rumley), Margaret Elizabeth (Mrs McCluney), Christa Jean (Mrs Hall), Gwendolyn L (Mrs Miller), Judson C, Jr & Jimmy (deceased). Educ: Marion Mil Inst, 11-13; Univ Ala, JD. Polit & Govt Pos: Ala State Rep, 35-57; Ala State Sen, 58-64; chmn, Perry Co Dem Exec Comt, currently. Bus & Prof Pos: Attorney-at-law, sr mem real estate firm, Locke & Crenshaw, 25-26; owner & operator, Forest Lands, mineral interest, beef cattle producer & real estate rentals, Fla. Mil Serv: Entered as Sgt, Army, 17-18, serv in Hq Co 123, Inf 31st Div. Mem: Am Legion; KofP; Odd Fellows. Honors & Awards: Bronze, Silver & Gold Medal for oratory in sch. Relig: Independent. Legal Res: 217 W LaFayette St Marion AL 36756 Mailing Add: PO Box 73 Marion AL 36756

LOCKE, NINA SPENCER (R)
Mem, Orange Co Rep Exec Comt, Fla
b New York, NY, Nov 13, 29; d Charles Burr Spencer & Marjorie Thorp S; m 1950 to James Locke; c Marjorie Vivian, Diana Stoddard & John. Polit & Govt Pos: Vol chmn, Young Rep, 62; precinct coordr, Gurney for Cong, 62 & 64; mem, Winter Park Draft Goldwater Comt, 63; mem, Orange Co Rep Exec Comt, Fla, 63-, precinct educ chmn, 64-65; mem exec comt, Winter Park Citizens for Goldwater & co-chmn, 11th Dist Citizens for Goldwater, 64; deleg, Rep Nat Conv, 64; chmn, Orange Co MORE Prog, 64; Fla State Rep committeewoman, Orange Co, 64-66; asst to chmn & precinct dir, Orange Co Kirk for Gov Comt, 66; precinct dir, Ken Plante for Sen, 66. Mem: Orlando Women's Rep Club; Cent Fla Rep Club; Youth Ctr; Women's Comt Fla Symphony; Gala Guild. Relig: Conservative Baptist. Mailing Add: 1300 Summerland Ave Winter Park FL 32789

LOCKE, PETER FREDRICK, JR (R)
Mem, Stafford Rep Town Comt, Conn
b Stafford, Conn, Jan 15, 37; s Peter Fredrick Locke, Sr & Charlotte Sopstyle L; m to Bette-Jean Beck; c Peter Fredrick, III & John Neil. Educ: Windham Regional Tech Sch, 51-55. Polit & Govt Pos: Mem, Stafford Rep Town Comt, Conn, 66-; mem, Stafford Housing Authority, 67-69; selectman, Stafford, Conn, 71-73; Conn State Rep, 49th Dist, 71-72, 52nd Dist, 72-74, asst majority leader, Conn House Rep, 73-74. Mil Serv: Entered as Recruit, Naval Res, 55, released as Electricians Mate 2/C, 63. Mem: Wolcott Lodge No 60; Stafford Fire Dept No 1; Staffordville PTA; Orient Chap 42, RAM; Italian Benefit Soc. Relig: Protestant. Mailing Add: 40 Prospect St Stafford Springs CT 06076

LOCKER, DALE LE ROY (D)
Ohio State Rep
b Sidney, Ohio, Nov 2, 29; s Claude Locker & Ida Allen L; m 1950 to LaDonna Mae Limbert; c LaDonna Kae, Dale LeRoy, II, Louis Randolph, Alan Jay, Eric Justin & Aaron Frazier. Educ: Bowling Green State Univ, BS in Educ, 53; Ohio Northern Univ, 60; Ohio Univ, 62. Polit & Govt Pos: Ohio State Rep, Shelby Co, 65-67 & 80th House Dist, 73-; mem, Am Revolution Bicentennial Comn, 73- Bus & Prof Pos: Music instr, Melmore Pub Sch, 54 & Huntsville Pub Sch, 55-58; guid dir, Jackson Ctr Pub Sch, 59-; instr guid & voc, Anna Pub Sch, 69- Mem: Ohio Educ Asn; Anna Local Educ Asn; Kiwanis; Eagles, Aerie 1304; Civic Asn. Honors & Awards: Outstanding High Sch Teacher of the Year, 72. Relig: Methodist; lay speaker, United Methodist Church. Mailing Add: Box 356 Anna OH 45302

LOCKETT, JOHN A, JR (D)
Ala State Rep
Mailing Add: PO Box 1354 Selma AL 36701

LOCKHART, RICHARD SPENCE (R)
NH State Rep
b Belmont, Mass, June 21, 27; s Hubert Winfield Lockhart & Emily Buckout L; m 1954 to Joan Heselton; c William Lawson (deceased) & R Spence. Educ: Univ Maine, BA, 50; Beta Theta Pi. Polit & Govt Pos: Sch bd mem, New Castle, NH, 63-; bd mem, New Castle Recreation & Conserv Comn, 65-; chmn, New Castle Rep Comt, 67-68; NH State Rep, 69- Bus & Prof Pos: Salesman, Von-Olker, Snell Paper Co, 50-52; Eastern supvr, Joseph Dixon Crucible Co, 53-56; publisher's rep, DC Heath & Co, 56-69; bus adminr, Portsmouth Ment Health Clin, 69-71; 2nd vpres, Strawbery Banke, Inc, 72-; admin dir, Seacoast Regional Coun Ctr, 72- Mil Serv: Entered as A/S, Coast Guard, 45, released as Fireman 1/C, 46, after serv in USS Charlotte & Potomac, Am & European Theaters, 45-46; seaman 1/C, Navy, 50-52, with serv in USS New Jersey, Korea, 50-52; Am & European Theater, Good Conduct & Japanese Occup Ribbons; Korea Campaign Ribbon With One Star. Mem: Prof Bookmen of Am; New Eng Educ Salesmen's Asn; Kittery Point Yacht Club (dir); Portsmouth Yacht Club. Relig: Congregational. Legal Res: Wild Rose Lane New Castle NH 03854 Mailing Add: Box 245 New Castle NH 03854

LOCKLIN, JACK G (D)
Mem, Ky State Dem Cent Exec Comt
b Monroe, Ga, Apr 15, 03; s William Clarence Locklin & Daisy Griffeth L; m 1926 to Reatha Webb. Educ: Ga Sch of Technol, 21-23; Sigma Alpha Epsilon. Polit & Govt Pos: Dist engr, Ky Dept Hwy, 23-36; mem, Ky State Dem Cent Exec Comt, 60-; chmn, Whitley Co Dem Comt, Ky, 60-72; city judge, Williamsburg, Ky, 63- Bus & Prof Pos: Consult, Eng Gen, Ky, 36-46; owner, Williamsburg Supply Co, 46-60; partner, Personal Finance Co, Whitley City, 60-64; mgr & partner, City Loan Co, Williamsburg, 60-; partner, Burnside Loan Co, 64- Mem: Prof Engrs of Ky; Mason; Shrine; Elks. Mailing Add: Box 383 Williamsburg KY 40769

LOCKLIN, ROBERT RIVES (D)
b Monroeville, Ala, May 20, 29; s Anderson J Locklin & Irene Elizabeth Moore L; m 1950 to Betty Jean Huffstutler; c Jeanie, Eleanor, Lawrence & Tracy. Educ: Univ Ala, BA, 50, LLB, 52; Phi Delta Phi; Delta Kappa Epsilon. Polit & Govt Pos: Mem, Ala State Bd of Educ, 55-61; vpres, Young Dem of Ala, 56; gen counsel, US Senate Select Comt on Small Bus, 61-67; admin asst to US Sen John Sparkman, Ala, 67-; deleg, Dem Nat Conv, 68. Bus & Prof Pos: Partner, Law Firm of Hamilton, Denniston, Butler & Riddick, Mobile, Ala, 55-61. Mil Serv: Entered as 2nd Lt, Air Force, 53, released as 1st Lt, 55, after serv in Judge Adv Gen Dept, 53-55. Mem: Ala & Am Bar Asns; Admin Asst Asn; Nat Capital Dem Club, Washington, DC; Ala State Soc of Washington, DC. Relig: Methodist. Legal Res: Mobile AL Mailing Add: 3203 Dirksen Senate Off Bldg Washington DC 20510

LOCKREM, LLOYD CLIFFORD, JR (R)
Mont State Rep
b Billings, Mont, Nov 10, 34; s Lloyd C Lockrem & Amy Frye L; m 1958 to Rose Lawrence; c Russell Scott & Michael Lee. Educ: Mont State Col, 2 years; Eastern Mont Col, 2 years. Polit & Govt Pos: Nominee, Mont State Rep, 66; Rep precinct man, 67-69; pres Rep Club, Yellowstone Co, 68; Mont State Rep, Dist Eight, 69-, asst minority leader, Mont House of Rep, 73-75, minority leader, 75- Bus & Prof Pos: Pres, Billings Contractors Coun, 70; pres, Lloyd C Lockrem, Inc, currently. Mil Serv: Entered as Pvt, Marines, 55, released as Cpl, 57, after serv in 11th Marines, Korean Theatre; Korean Theatre Ribbon; UN Ribbon; Nat Defense Ribbon. Mem: Rimrock Lodge No 149 AF&AM; York Rite; Al Bedoo Shrine Temple. Relig: Episcopal. Legal Res: 3109 Edmond St Billings MT 59102 Mailing Add: PO Box 1471 Billings MT 59103

LOCKWARD, WILLIAM HENRY (D)
Fla State Rep
b Ridgewood, NY, Oct 17, 18; s Harry Lockward & Clemitine Grote L; m 1945 to Doris Marie Raab; c Robert C & Gary M. Educ: Univ Miami, 52. Polit & Govt Pos: Councilman, City of Hialeah, Fla, 49-71, vpres coun, 53-55, pres, 55-57 & 59-63; pres, Dade League of Cities, 69-70; dir, Fla League of Cities, 69-71; Fla State Rep, 72- Bus & Prof Pos: Owner, Lockward Ins Agency, 52. Mil Serv: Entered as Pvt, Marines, 40, released as Cpl, 45, after serv in S & Cent Pac, 41-45; Purple Heart; Am Theatre Ribbon; Pac Unit Citation; Good Conduct. Mem: Gtr Miami Asn Ins Agents; DAV (state comdr, 70); Moose; Hialeah-Miami Springs Elks; Hialeah-Miami Springs CofC. Honors & Awards: Appreciation Award, Dade Co, 66; Good Govt Award, Hialeah Jaycees, 69; Outstanding Off, Fla DAV, 70; 20 Year Serv Award, City of Hialeah, 72; Citizens Award, Citizens Comt Hialeah, 72. Relig: Protestant. Legal Res: 290 W 50th St Hialeah FL 33012 Mailing Add: 1511 E Fourth Ave Hialeah FL 33010

LOCKWOOD, JANE BIGGERS (R)
Mem, Montgomery Co Rep Cent Comt, Md
b Toledo, Ohio, Aug 12, 20; d John David Biggers & Mary Kelsey B; m 1942 to Corwin Rees Lockwood, Jr; c Corwin Rees, III. Educ: Garland Jr Col, Boston, Mass, 39-41; King-Smith Studio Sch, Washington, DC, 41-42. Polit & Govt Pos: Mem, Rep Nat Finance Comt, 48-54, vol absentee voters bur, 48-59; mem & mem bd, DC League Rep Women's Club, 48-62; vol, Sen J Glenn Beall Sr Campaign, 52, Eisenhower-Nixon Campaign, 52 & 56, Rep DeWitt S Hyde Campaign, 54 & Sen John Marshall Butler Campaign, 56; asst Rep chmn, Precinct 7-7, Montgomery Co, Md, 58, chmn, 59-63; patron, Montgomery Co, 59-69; mem, Nixon-Lodge Campaign Comt, Montgomery Co, 60; committee mem, Rep Charles M Mathias Jr Campaign, 60 & 62; vol, Montgomery Co Rep Hq, 61-67; mem, Montgomery Co Rep Cent Comt, 63-, women's vchmn, 63-70 & 72-73; mem comt, Goldwater-Miller Campaign, 64; campaign mgr, Edward J Clarke for House Deleg, 66; mem, Const Conv Nominating Comt, 67; deleg, Rep Nat Conv, 68; co-chmn, Nixon-Agnew Comt, Montgomery Co, 68; chmn, Women for Nixon-Agnew Montgomery Co, 68; vchmn hospitality comt, Nixon-Agnew Inaugural, 68-69; co-chmn, Invitation Comt for the Reception for Vice President Elect & Mrs Agnew, Inaugural Comt, 68-69, chmn, 72-73; co-chmn finance comt, James P Gleason for Co Exec, 70; presidential elector for Md, 72; staff mem, Vol Comt, Nixon-Agnew Inaugural, 72-73. Mem: Rock Creek Women's Rep Club (former mem bd); Rockville Women's Rep Club

(pres, 71 & 72). Relig: Methodist. Mailing Add: 10500 Rockville Pike Apt 1702 Rockville MD 20852

LOCKWOOD, LORNA E (D)
Justice, Ariz Supreme Court
b Douglas, Ariz, Mar 24, 03; d Alfred Collins Lockwood & Maude Lincoln L; single. Educ: Univ Ariz, AB, 23, JD, 25; Pi Kappa Phi; Chi Omega. Polit & Govt Pos: Ariz State Rep, 39-42 & 47-48; price attorney, Dist of Ariz, US Off of Price Admin, 42-44; Asst Attorney Gen, Ariz, 48-50; judge, Maricopa Co, 51-60; Justice, Ariz Supreme Court, 61-75, VChief Justice, 64-65 & 69-70, Chief Justice, 65-66 & 70-71. Bus & Prof Pos: Mem firm, Lockwood & Savage, Phoenix, 39-41; mem firm, Cox, Lockwood & Lockwood, 44-48. Mem: Inst of Judicial Admin; Nat Asn Women Lawyers; Eastern Star; Ariz Judges Asn; Plus 60 Personnel. Honors & Awards: Judicial Award of Merit, Am Trial Lawyers Asn, 70; Builder of a Gtr Ariz, Law & Govt Award, 71; Nat Conf Christians & Jews, Brotherhood Award, 72; Univ Ariz Alumni Distinguished Citizen Award, 72; Ariz Fifth Dist of Am Legion Americanism Award, 72. Relig: Congregational. Mailing Add: Ariz Supreme Court State Capitol Bldg Phoenix AZ 85007

LOCKYEAR, RALPH ALAN (R)
b Longview, Wash, Jan 22, 53; s Ralph Lockyear & Virginia Martin L; single. Educ: Wake Forest Univ, currently. Polit & Govt Pos: Deleg, Cowlitz Co Rep Conv, Wash, 72; deleg, Wash State Rep Conv, 72; alt deleg, Rep Nat Conv, 72; chmn, Young Voters for the President, Wake Forest Univ, NC, 72; mem, NC Young Rep, 72-; pres, Wake Forest Col Rep, 73-74; mem, Rep Southern Conf, 73; mem, Rep Nat Leadership Conf, 75. Legal Res: 2746 Ocean Beach Hwy Longview WA 98632 Mailing Add: Box 8784 Reynolda Sta Winston-Salem NC 27109

LOCKYER, BILL (D)
Calif State Assemblyman
Mailing Add: 14895 E 14th St San Leandro CA 94578

LODGE, GEORGE CABOT (R)
b Boston, Mass, July 7, 27; s Henry Cabot Lodge & Emily Sears L; m 1949 to Nancy Kunhardt; c Nancy Kunhardt (Mrs Webbe), Emily Sears, Dorothy Merserve, Henry Cabot, George Cabot & David. Educ: Harvard Col, AB cum laude, 50. Polit & Govt Pos: Dir of info, Dept of Labor, 54-58; Asst Secy for Int Affairs, 58-61; vchmn, Inter-Am Social Develop Inst, 70- Bus & Prof Pos: Reporter, Boston Herald, 50-54; lectr, Harvard Bus Sch, 63-68, assoc prof, 68-71, prof, 71- Mil Serv: Seaman 3/C, Navy, 45, released as Seaman 1/C, 46. Publ: Spearheads of Democracy, Harper & Row, 62; Engines Change, A A Knopf, 70. Mem: Coun Foreign Rels. Relig: Protestant. Mailing Add: 275 Hale St Beverly MA 01915

LODGE, HENRY CABOT (R)
b Nahant, Mass, July 5, 02; s George Cabot Lodge & Elizabeth Davis L; m 1926 to Emily Sears; c George Cabot & Henry Sears. Educ: Harvard Col, AB, 24. Hon Degrees: Many hon degrees from various univs & cols. Polit & Govt Pos: Mass State Rep, 33-37; US Sen, Mass, 37-43 & 47-53; chmn resolutions comt, Rep Nat Conv, 48; campaign mgr, Effort to Secure Rep Presidential Nomination for Gen Eisenhower, 52; US rep, UN & mem, President Eisenhower's Cabinet, 53-60; Rep nominee for Vice President of US, 60; dir gen, Atlantic Inst, 61-63; US Ambassador, Vietnam, 63-64 & 65-67; Ambassador-at-lg, 67-68; Ambassador, Ger, 68-69; Personal Rep of the President of the US, Paris Meetings on Vietnam, 69-70; Spec Envoy to Visit Vatican, 70- Mil Serv: Entered as Pvt, Army Res, 25, released as Lt Col, 45, after serv in Second Armored Div, Fourth Corps, Sixth Army Group, World War II; Maj Gen, Army Res; ETO Ribbon with Five Battle Stars; Legion of Merit; Bronze Star; French Legion d'Honneur & Croix de Guerre with Palm; Brit MidE Citation; first US Sen since Civil War to resign from Senate for Army serv. Honors & Awards: Theodore Roosevelt Asn Medal; Chevalier, Order of Polonia Restituta; Humane Order of African Redemption, Liberia; Grand Cross of Merit, Sovereign Order of Malta; Grand Cross, Nat Order, Repub of Vietnam. Mailing Add: 275 Hale St Beverly MA 01915

LODGE, JOHN DAVIS (R)
US Ambassador to Argentina
b Washington, DC; s George Cabot Lodge & Matilda E F Davis L; m to Francesca Braggiotti; c Lily & Beatrice; six grandchildren. Educ: Harvard Univ, BA, 25 & JD, 29; Ecole de Droit, Paris; Phi Beta Kappa. Hon Degrees: LLD, Trinity Col, Middlebury Col & Hobart & William Smith Cols; DSc, Worcester Polytech Inst; LHD, Fairfield Univ. Polit & Govt Pos: US Rep, Fourth Dist, Conn, 47-51, mem, Foreign Affairs Comt, US House of Rep; Gov, Conn, 51-55; chmn, New Eng Gov Conf, 2 terms; chmn, New Eng Comt for Peaceful Uses of Atomic Energy; spec ambassador for President Eisenhower to Panama, Costa Rica & PR, 53; US Ambassador to Spain, 55-61; deleg & asst floor leader, Conn Const Conv, 65; US Ambassador to Argentina, 69- Bus & Prof Pos: Attorney, Cravath, de Gersdorff, Swaine & Wood, New York; actor, motion pictures & theatre; attorney-at-law. Mil Serv: Navy, World War II; Capt, Naval Res; Croix de Guerre with Palm; Chevalier, French Legion of Honor. Mem: Am Legion; VFW; ROA; Navy League; Conn State Grange (7 degree). Honors & Awards: Degree of Grand Officer of the Order of Merit of the Repub of Italy, 53; Grand Cross of the Noble Order of Charles III & Gold Medal of Madrid, Spain, 62; Order of Polonia Restituta, Polish Govt-in-Exile, 64. Legal Res: 129 Easton Rd Westport CT 06880 Mailing Add: Am Embassy Buenos Aires Argentina

LOEB, JOHN LANGELOTH JR (R)
b New York, NY, May 2, 30; s John Langeloth Loeb & Frances Lehman L; m 1974 to Meta Martindell Harrsen; c Alexandra. Educ: Harvard Col, BA cum laude, 52, Harvard Grad Sch Bus Admin, MBA, 54. Polit & Govt Pos: Alt deleg, Rep Nat Conv, 64, hon deleg, 72; mem, Joint Legis Comt on Matrimonial & Family Affairs, State of NY, 66-67; spec asst to Gov Nelson A Rockefeller on Environ Protection, 67-73; chmn, NY State Coun on Environ Adv, 70-; chmn, Keep NY State Clean Prog, 73- Bus & Prof Pos: Sr partner & mem mgt comt, Loeb, Rhoades & Co, 59-73, chmn bd, Loeb, Rhoades Inc, 71-73, ltd partner, currently; past dir, Denver & Rio Grande West RR, MGM, John Morrell & Co & Holly Sugar Corp, Colo, 69-71; chmn bd & mem exec comt, Holly Sugar Co, 69-71. Mil Serv: Entered as 2nd Lt, Air Force, 54, released as 1st Lt, 56. Mem: Century Country Club; Recess; St James Club, London, Eng; Royal Swedish Yacht Club. Relig: Jewish. Legal Res: Ridgeleigh Anderson Hill Rd Purchase NY Mailing Add: c/o Loeb Rhoades & Co 375 Park Ave New York NY 10022

LOEN, VERNON CARROLL (R)
b Howard, SDak, Oct 18, 31; s Lauris Loen & Selina Edith Langorgen L; m to Raemalee J Anderson; c Douglas Todd, Vance Stephen & Jeffrey Scott. Educ: SDak State Univ, BS, 53. Polit & Govt Pos: Asst to US Sen Francis Case, 58-61; admin asst to US Rep Reifel, SDak, 61-69; admin asst to US Rep Quie, Minn, 69-74; Special Asst to the President, 74-75; Dep Asst to the President, 75- Bus & Prof Pos: Writer, Sioux Falls Argus-Leader, 54-58. Mem: Past pres, SDak State Soc of Washington, Cong Secretaries Club; Bull Elephants (bd dirs). Relig: Lutheran. Legal Res: Sioux Falls SD Mailing Add: White House Off Washington DC 20500

LOESCH, HARRISON (R)
b Chicago, Ill, Mar 10, 16; s Constance Harrison L; m 1940 to Louise Mills; c Jeffrey. Educ: Colo Col, BA, 36; Denver Univ Law Sch, 36-37; Yale Univ Law Sch, LLB, 39. Polit & Govt Pos: Asst Secy for Pub Land Mgt, Dept of the Interior, 69-73; minority counsel, Senate Interior Comt, US Senate, 73-74, Senate Interior & Insular Comt, 75- Bus & Prof Pos: Attorney-at-law, Moynihan & Hughes, Montrose, Colo, 39-42, Strang & Loesch, 45-51, Strang, Loesch & Kreidler, 51-56, Loesch & Kreidler, 56-61 & Loesch, Kreidler & Durham, 61-69. Mil Serv: Entered as Pvt, Army, 42, released as Maj, 45, after serv in ETO. Mem: Colo Bar Asn. Legal Res: Montrose Co CO Mailing Add: 3106 Dirksen Senate Off Bldg Washington DC 20510

LOEVINGER, LEE (D)
b St Paul, Minn, Apr 24, 13; s Gustavus Loevinger & Millie Strouse L; m 1950 to Ruth E Howe; c Barbara Lee, Eric Howe & Peter Howe. Educ: Univ Minn, BA, summa cum laude, 33, Sch Law, JD, 36; Phi Beta Kappa; Sigma Xi; Delta Sigma Rho; Sigma Delta Chi; Phi Delta Gamma; Tau Kappa Alpha; Alpha Epsilon Rho. Polit & Govt Pos: Regional attorney & attorney, Nat Labor Rels Bd, 37-41; attorney, Antitrust Div, Dept of Justice, 41-46, asst attorney gen in charge of Antitrust Div, 61-63, spec asst to US Attorney Gen for Int Antitrust, 63-64; spec counsel, US Senate Small Bus Comt, 51-52; chmn, Minn Atomic Develop Probs Comt, 57-59; assoc justice, Supreme Court of Minn, 60-61; US rep to Orgn for Econ Coop & Develop Comt on Restrictive Bus Practices, Paris, 61-64; comnr, Fed Community Comn, 63-68; US rep to Int Telecommun Union Conf of Aeronaut Frequency Allocation, Geneva, Switz, 64 & 66. Bus & Prof Pos: Partner, Larson, Loevinger, Lindquist, Freeman & Fraser, Minneapolis, Minn, 46-60; partner, Hogan & Hartson, Washington, DC, 68-; vpres & dir, Craig-Hallum Corp, Minneapolis, Minn, 68- Mil Serv: Entered as Lt(jg), Navy, 42, released as Lt Comdr, 46, after serv in Amphibious Force, NY Port Dir Off & US Naval Transportation Corps, ETO & Am Theater; Lt Comdr (Ret), Naval Res; ETO Ribbon with One Battle Star; Am Theater Ribbon; Victory Ribbon. Publ: The Law of Free Enterprise, Funk & Wagnalls, 49; An introduction to legal logic, Ind Law J, 52; Regulation & competition as alternatives, Antitrust Bull, 65; plus more than 100 others. Mem: Am, Fed, DC, Minn & Fed Commun Bar Asns. Honors & Awards: Outstanding Achievement Medal, Univ Minn, 68. Relig: Unitarian. Mailing Add: 5669 Bent Branch Rd Tulip Hill MD 20016

LOFTON, JAMES SHEPHERD (R)
b Charlotte, NC, Mar 22, 43; s Thomas Stark Lofton, Sr & Helen Marie Carter L; m 1966 to Sarah Clarinda Knight; c Sarah Clarinda & Mary Melissa. Educ: Lees-McRae Col, NC. Polit & Govt Pos: Admin asst, US Rep James G Martin, NC, 73- Bus & Prof Pos: Buyer, Belk Bros Co, Charlotte, 63-66; dir civic affairs, Charlotte CofC, 66-69; mkt off, First Union Nat Bank, Charlotte, 69-72. Mil Serv: Entered as Airman 3/C, NC Air Nat Guard, 66, released as Sgt, 71, after serv in Supply Unit. Mem: Bull Elephants; Capital Hill Club. Relig: Episcopal. Legal Res: 1639 Beverly Dr Charlotte NC 28207 Mailing Add: 115 Cannon House Off Bldg Washington DC 20515

LOFTUS, JOSEPH ANTHONY (R)
b Scranton, Pa, June 1, 07; s George J Loftus & Bridget Duffy L; m 1956 to Mary Frances Schoeps Mann; c JoAnne (Mrs Thomas O Young) & Marianne (Mrs John B Cumming). Educ: Scranton Univ, AB, 28; Columbia Univ, MS, 31; Harvard Univ, Stark Fel, 60-61. Polit & Govt Pos: Spec asst to the Secy of Labor for Commun, Dept of Labor, 69-72; spec asst to the Secy of Treas for Pub Affairs, 73- Bus & Prof Pos: Correspondent, NY Times, Washington, DC, 44-69. Mem: Nat Press Club. Relig: Unitarian. Mailing Add: 3327 Legation St NW Washington DC 20015

LOFTUS, ROBERT A (D)
Chmn, Luzerne Co Dem Comt, Pa
b Pittston, Pa, July 10, 18; s John J Loftus & Margaret McNeely L; m 1945 to Rita M Shea; c Robert A, Jr & Mary Frances. Educ: Univ Scranton, 1 year; Wyo Seminary Bus Sch, 2 years. Polit & Govt Pos: Mayor, Pittston, Pa, 62-; chmn, Luzerne Co Dem Comt, 70- Bus & Prof Pos: Dir, First Nat Bank, Pittston, Pa, 59, Pittston Hosp, 62, Pittston CofC, 65, Wyo Valley March of Dimes, 70 & Wyo Valley Motor Club, 71. Mil Serv: Entered as Pvt, Army, 43, released as Sgt, 45, after serv in First US Army, ETO, 43-45; Five Battle Stars, ETO Ribbon. Mem: Am Legion (comdr, John D Stark Post 542); VFW Post 635; KofC. Relig: Catholic. Legal Res: 151 Broad St Pittston PA 18640 Mailing Add: Miners Bank Bldg Pittston PA 18640

LOGAN, BARD A (AMERICAN PARTY)
b Hancock Co, Ind, Apr 4, 12; s Ralph Gates Logan & Carrie Lucille Jackson L; m 1936 to Mary Ann Miller; c John Frederick, B Arnold & Andrew Brandt. Educ: Ind Univ, AB, 35; Phi Beta Pi; Kappa Delta Rho. Polit & Govt Pos: Co-founder, Constitution Party, 50, state chmn, 60-62; cand for US Senate, Constitution Party, 58-60; state chmn, Conservative Party of Tex, 63-68; state chmn, American Party of Tex, 68-70. Bus & Prof Pos: Bacteriologist, Eli Lilly & Co, 35-40; sales rep, Winthrop Chem Co, 40-49; owner & mgr, The Criss Cross Serv, 49- Mil Serv: Entered as 1st Lt, Army, 42, released as Capt, 46, after serv in Med Corps, 35th Gen Hosp, 33rd Gen Hosp, Hq, Camp Swift, Tex & 193rd Gen Hosp, ETO, 44-45; ETO Ribbon with One Battle Star; Am Defense Medal. Mem: VFW; Am Legion; DAV; SAR. Relig: Protestant. Mailing Add: 4519 Rimrock San Antonio TX 78228

LOGAN, BENJAMIN H JR (D)
b Dayton, Ohio, June 25, 43; s Ben H Logan, Sr & Jeanne Ross L; m 1969 to Creola Wiggins; c Fonda Jeanne & Benjamin Matthew. Educ: Ohio Northern Univ, BA, 68, Law Sch, JD, 72; Wayne State Law Sch, 72-73; Phi Alpha Delta; pres, Ohio Chap, Black Am Law Students Asn, 71-72. Polit & Govt Pos: Deleg, Dem Nat Conv, 72, co-chmn, Black Caucus & co-chmn youth, Ohio Deleg, 72; mem, Black Polit Conv, Gary, Ind, 72; mem, Grand Rapids Dem Exec Comt, Mich, 73- Bus & Prof Pos: Cost acct, Dayton Tire & Rubber Co, Ohio, 69-70; research asst, Model Cities Legal Serv, Dayton, 70; law clerk, Legal Aid Soc, Grand Rapids, Mich, 71, staff attorney, 72-73; legal intern, Legal Aid Soc, Lima, Ohio, 72; instr, Davenport Bus Col, 72-73; pvt attorney, Jackson & Logan, Attorneys & Counrs-at-law, 73- Mem: NAACP (bd dirs & chmn, Polit Action, 73-); Jaycees; Human Rels Comn (bd dirs); Black Am Law Students Asn (bd adv, Ohio, 72-73); Emerging Arts Forum (bd dirs, 72-73). Honors & Awards: Outstanding Mem, Black Am Law Students Asn, 72. Relig: Baptist. Legal Res: 744 Fuller SE Grand Rapids MI 49506 Mailing Add: 600 McKay Tower Grand Rapids MI 49503

LOGAN, HUGH (D)
Ga State Rep
Mailing Add: 1328 Prince Ave Athens GA 30601

LOGAN, IRENE ELIZABETH (R)
Mem Exec Comt, Mich Rep State Cent Comt
b Granite City, Ill, Oct 31, 12; d Harry Cole Rae & Jennie Hutton R; m 1952 to Kenneth John Logan. Educ: Bus sch in St Louis, Mo. Polit & Govt Pos: Mem exec comt, Mich Rep State Cent Comt, 64-, ways & means comt, 69-70; deleg, Rep Nat Conv, 68. Bus & Prof Pos: Legal secy, Logan & Huchla, 47- Mem: River Rouge Womens Club; Bus & Prof Womens Club (vpres). Relig: Presbyterian. Mailing Add: 74 Chestnut River Rouge MI 48218

LOGAN, JAMES L (D)
NH State Rep
Mailing Add: 26 Messenger St Lebanon NH 03766

LOGAN, ROBERT MAURICE (BOB) (D)
Miss State Sen
Mailing Add: PO Box 143 Lake MS 39092

LOGAN, ROGER V, JR (D)
Ark State Rep
b Springfield, Mo, Aug 28, 44; s Roger V Logan, Sr & Belle Raley L; m 1967 to Bonnie J Fox; c Sarah A. Educ: Univ Ark, BA & JD, 62-68; Pershing Rifles Hon Mil Fraternity. Polit & Govt Pos: Ark State Rep, 71-73, Dist 25, 73- Bus & Prof Pos: Attorney-at-law, Moore, Logan & Berryhill, 68- Publ: Mountain heritage, 69. Mem: Am & Ark Bar Asns; Boone-Newton Co Bar Asn; Lions Int; Odd Fellows. Relig: Christian. Legal Res: Rte 8 Harrison AR 72601 Mailing Add: Box 58 Harrison AR 72601

LOHR, CHARLES E (D)
WVa State Deleg
b Moundsville, WVa, Apr 30, 16; s Charles Lohr & Florence Guthrie L; m 1939 to Mary Elizabeth Crumpecker; c Charles E, II & Mary Elizabeth. Educ: WVa, BA, Bus Admin. Polit & Govt Pos: WVa State Deleg, 60- Bus & Prof Pos: Drug store owner. Mem: Elks; Moose; Red Men; Mercer Angler Club; Triangle Club. Relig: Methodist. Mailing Add: Rte 1 Princeton WV 24740

LOHSE, ROBERT CHARLES (D)
b Erie, Pa, Aug 15, 46; s Robert Louis Lohse & Mable Fickenworth L; single; c Michelle Lee (adopted). Educ: Gannon Col, BA, 72; Pi Kappa Alpha. Polit & Govt Pos: Deleg, Dem Nat Conv, 72; Dem nominee for Co Prothonotary, 73. Bus & Prof Pos: Detective, Erie Co, Pa, 73- Mil Serv: Entered as E-3, Navy, 69, released as E-5, 71, after serv in Pac Theatre. Mem: Nat & State Co Detectives Asn; Am, Fed, State, Co & Munic Employees Union; Farm-Labor Orgn. Relig: Catholic. Mailing Add: 320 E 34th Erie PA 16504

LOIZEAUX, M SUZANNE (R)
b Boston, Mass, Sept 3, 05; d J J Loizeaux & Margaret Sanderson L; single. Educ: Abbot Acad, Andover, Mass, 25-26; Simmons Col Grad Sch, 27. Polit & Govt Pos: NH State Rep, 49, 53, 55 & 59; NH State Sen, 51-52; vchmn, NH Rep State Comt, 67-68, secy, formerly. Bus & Prof Pos: Ed & publ, Plymouth Rec, newspaper, 30-43; realtor, NH Colonials, 45- Mem: Asquamchumauke Chap, DAR; Pemigewasset Women's Club; NH Hist Soc; Twin Valleys Women's Rep Club; NH Heart Asn. Relig: Congregational; Bd Trustees. Mailing Add: Dave Gibson Farm RFD 2 Plymouth NH 03264

LOKKEN, LESLIE FERRIS (D)
b Colfax, Wash, Apr 3, 26; d Robert Donald Ferris & Leslie Smith F; m 1953 to George Stanley Lokken; c Leslie & Wynne. Educ: Wash State Univ, BA, 48; Theta Sigma Phi; Nat Col Radio Guild; Sigma Kappa. Polit & Govt Pos: Co-chairperson, Mich Sixth Dist Citizens for McGovern, 71-72; precinct deleg, Dem Party, Okemos, 72-74; deleg, Dem Nat Conv, 72; mem, Exec Comt, Ingham Co Dem Party, 73; mem, Mich Dem State Cent Comt, 73. Bus & Prof Pos: Radio writer, Sta KBYR, Anchorage, Alaska, 48-50; Army spec serv recreation dir, Army Arctic Indoctrination Ctr, Alaska, 50-51; Eielson AFB, Alaska, 51-52, Camp Hale & Ft Carson, Colo, 52-53. Mem: Common Cause (lobbyist, Mich, 73-); Nat Orgn Women; Nat Women's Polit Caucus; Am Civil Liberties Union. Relig: Unitarian. Mailing Add: 2114 Tecumseh River Dr Lansing MI 48906

LOMBARD, BEN JR (R)
Chmn, Jackson Co Rep Cent Comt, Ore
b Seattle, Wash, Sept 2, 40; s Ben T Lombard & Jesse Craig Smith L; m 1970 to Bernadette Verschingel; c Christopher Hawkins & Ian Craig. Educ: Univ Ore, BA in econ, with honors, 62; Univ Mich Law Sch, LLB, 65; Phi Delta Phi; Phi Gamma Delta. Polit & Govt Pos: Legal Coun, Rep State Cent Comt Ore, 71-74, mem, 72-; mem, Jackson Co Rep Cent Comt, 72-, chmn, currently. Bus & Prof Pos: Assoc, Souther, Spaulding, Kinsey, Williamson & Schwabe, Portland, Ore, 67-72; partner, Hampton & Lombard, attorneys, Ashland, 72- Mem: Jackson Co, Ore State & Am Bar Asns; Elks; Kiwanis. Relig: Episcopal. Legal Res: 133 Manzanita St Ashland OR 97520 Mailing Add: PO Box 459 Ashland OR 97520

LOMBARD, GERALD P (D)
Mass State Rep
Mailing Add: State Capitol Boston MA 02133

LOMBARDI, ANGELA FUNAI (R)
Mem, Rep State Cent Comt Calif
b Barga, Tuscany, Italy, Mar 20, 98; d Alessandro Funai & Maria Cocchini F; m 1924 to Louis Lombardi; c Marta (Mrs Lawson M Brown), Sandra (Mrs Frederick Farrell), Nalda (Mrs Charles J Staff, Jr), Louis Lombardi, Jr & Adria (Mrs Gerald Griswold). Educ: Boston Univ, AB, 20, AM, 22; Harvard, 23; Gamma Phi Beta. Polit & Govt Pos: Mem, Calif Rep Women's Fedn, 46-, Los Angeles Co pres, 58-60, state vpres, 63-66, state chmn, 66, mem nat comt heritage, 73-; mem, Rep State Cent Comt Calif, 48-; assembly-precinct dir, Rep Party, Calif, 50-54; deleg, Rep Nat Conv, 68. Bus & Prof Pos: Teacher, Mass & Calif. Mem: Am Asn Univ Women; Women's Civic League of Glendale; Glendale Symphony Bd; Glendale Beautiful. Honors & Awards: Los Angeles Rep Assocs Serv Award; Press Woman of the Year, Glendale News, 68; Commendation from City of Pomona. Relig: Congregational. Mailing Add: 1945 W Mountain St Glendale CA 91201

LOMBARDI, MICHAEL J (D)
Mass State Rep
Mailing Add: State Capitol Boston MA 02133

LOMBARDI, TARKY JAMES, JR (R-CONSERVATIVE)
NY State Sen
b Syracuse, NY, Sept 2, 29; s Tarky Lombardi & Jenny Cerio L; m 1958 to Marianne Edgcomb; c Tarky, III, Jennine, Marianne & Michael. Educ: Syracuse Univ, BS, 51; Syracuse Univ Col Law, LLB, 54. Polit & Govt Pos: Rep dist councilman, Syracuse, NY, 60-63, councilman-at-lg, 64-65; NY State Sen, Onondaga-Madison Co, 66, 46th Dist, Onondaga-Cortland Co, 67- Mil Serv: Entered as Pvt, Army, 55, released as SP-3 (T), 57, after serv in Battery C, 505 AA Missile Bn. Mem: Am, NY State & Onondaga Co Bar Asns. Honors & Awards: NY State Jr CofC Distinguished Serv Award, 60. Relig: Catholic. Legal Res: 99 Burlingame Rd Syracuse NY 13203 Mailing Add: 723 Hiawatha Blvd W Syracuse NY 13201

LOMBARDINO, FRANK (D)
Tex State Sen
Mailing Add: 500 Gunter Bldg San Antonio TX 78205

LOMEN, MARY ELIZABETH (R)
Women's Chmn for Alaska, Rep Nat Finance Comt
b Seattle, Wash, July 20, 19; d Elmer G Shipman & Elizabeth Kirkham S; m 1942 to Alfred J Lomen; c Gilbert J, Julie Ann & James W. Educ: Stephens Col, 37-38; Univ Wash, BA, 41, 43-44; Pi Beta Phi. Polit & Govt Pos: Mem, Territorial Bd Libr Serv, Alaska; pres, Fairbanks Rep Women's Club, Alaska, 59; mem & chmn, Cent Dist Rep Comt, 60-66; secy, Alaska Rep State Cent Comt, 66-70, treas, 74-; comnr, Western Interstate Comn for Higher Educ, 67-71; mem, Community Action Coun, 71-; mem & women's chmn for Alaska, Rep Nat Finance Comt, currently. Mem: Girl Scouts Bd; Garden Clubs; United Good Neighbors. Relig: Protestant. Mailing Add: 202 Slater Dr Fairbanks AK 99701

LOMNICKY, KATHI (D)
Secy, Ore Dem State Cent Comt
b Portland, Ore, June 18, 47; d Claude N Patterson & June R Bishop P; div; c Darren B & Trista R. Educ: Bassist Fashion Inst, Portland, cert, 68. Polit & Govt Pos: Vchmn, Columbia Co Young Dem, Ore, currently; secy, Ore Dem State Cent Comt, 74- Mem: Willamette Dem Soc; Int Woodworkers Am. Relig: Protestant. Legal Res: Rte 1 Box 382A Scappoose OR 97056 Mailing Add: PO Box 381 Scappoose OR 97056

LOMPREY, MARGARET (D)
Mem, Clark Co Dem Cent Comt, Nev
b Whitelaw, Wis, July 23, 14; d Adolph E Brunner & Theresa Kohlbeck B; m 1935 to Ernest V Lomprey; c Marlene (Mrs George Buzzelli), Lorne, Ernest, Jr, James, Robert & Rebecca (Mrs Edward Plawski). Polit & Govt Pos: Dep registr, Clark Co, Nev, 58-; campaign worker, John F Kennedy, 60; coordr, Henderson campaign, Sen Alan Bible, 62, Gov Grant Sawyer, 62 & 66 & Sen Howard Cannon, 64; mem, Clark Co Dem Cent Comt, 63-, open mem, Exec Bd, 70 & 72; mem, Nev State Dem Cent Comt, 68-74, treas, 74-; worker, Humphrey-Muskie Ticket, 68; chmn, Vols for O'Callaghan, 70; app mem, Nev State Pre-Conv Comt for Credentials, 72, Nev State Credentials Comt; deleg, Dem Nat Conv, 72; polit adv, Las Vegas Women's Dem Club, 75; city councilwoman, Henderson, 75- Mem: City Solicitation Rev Bd; No Fault Ins Comt; Henderson Dem Club (pres, 74-); Southern Nev Dem Club; Clark Co Women's Dem Club (chmn, Polit Educ Comt, 72). Honors & Awards: Outstanding Woman Dem Trophy, Henderson Dem Club, 60; invitation to attend inauguration of John F Kennedy as President of US; Dem Worker of Month, 68; initiated successful movement to draft Donal 'Mike' O'Callaghan Gov, Nev, 70; selected by Nat Educ TV to show what a typical conv deleg experiences, 72. Relig: Catholic; secy-treas, Altar Soc, various terms, 56-71; pres, St Jude's Guild, 66; pres, St Peter's Altar Soc, 68. Mailing Add: 601 Federal St Henderson NV 89015

LONDRIGAN, JAMES T (D)
Ill State Rep
b Springfield, Ill, Feb 23, 25; s James Edward Londrigan & Sophia Albright L; m 1950 to Marilyn Jeanne Brust; c Linda, Janet, Timothy, Lisa & Mary Jeanne. Educ: Univ Ill, 43, 45-47; Kent Col Law, JD, 49. Polit & Govt Pos: Hearing officer, State Ill, 50-53; pres, Young Dem Ill, 60-62, nat committeeman, 63-65; city attorney, Springfield, 61-63; technical legal advisor, State of Ill, 63-69; Ill State Rep, 69- Mil Serv: Entered as Pvt, Army, 43, released as Pfc, 45, after serv in 75th Inf Div, ETO, 44-45; Two Purple Hearts. Mem: DAV; KofC; VFW; Am Legion; Am Bus Club. Relig: Catholic. Mailing Add: 2019 Briarcliff Springfield IL 62704

LONERGAN, JOYCE (D)
Iowa State Rep
b Benton Co, Iowa, Mar 5, 34; d Robert Jacobi & Fannie Duda J; m 1950 to Paul Joseph Lonergan; c Patrick Joseph, Peter Thomas, Kathleen Ann & Staci Marie. Educ: Boone Jr Col, 52 & 65. Polit & Govt Pos: Iowa State Rep, 44th Dist, 75- Relig: Catholic. Legal Res: 1215 Mamie Eisenhower Ave Boone IA 50036 Mailing Add: State Capitol Des Moines IA 50319

LONG, BETTY JANE (D)
Miss State Rep
b Electric Mills, Miss, May 5, 28; single. Polit & Govt Pos: Miss State Rep, 56- Bus & Prof Pos: Lawyer. Mem: Am Asn Univ Women; Miss Farm Bur; Pilot Club; Bus & Prof Womens Club; Salvation Army Bd. Relig: Presbyterian. Mailing Add: 2219 49th Ave Meridian MS 39301

LONG, BETTYE VIRGINIA (D)
b Bernice, La, July 13, 24; d Luther C Bolt & Bernice Lowry B; m 1946 to Henry Lawrence Long; c Larry Thomas, Charles Edward, Lawrence Allan & John Stephan. Educ: Kilgore Jr Col, BS, 43; Kilgore Co Rangerettes; Sans Souci. Polit & Govt Pos: Deleg, Dem Nat Conv, 72; state vchmn, Tex Dem for Wallace, 72-; deleg, Dem Nat Mid-Term Conf, 74; app, State Health Adv Comn, 74; regional coordr, First Lady's Vol Prog, Tex, currently. Mem: Evergreen Garden Club (vpres, 74-); Coun Kilgore Garden Clubs (secy, 72-73); Kilgore Jr High PTA (publ chmn, 72-73); Kilgore Improv & Beautification Asn. Relig: Baptist. Legal Res: 2902 Royal Dr Kilgore TX 75662 Mailing Add: PO Box 1336 Kilgore TX 75662

LONG, BLANCHE REVERE (D)
b Covington, La, Dec 17, 04; d Robert Harrison Revere & Beulah Talley R; m 1932 to Gov Earl Kemp Long; wid. Educ: Tulane Univ, 2 years. Polit & Govt Pos: Dem Nat Committeewoman, La, 56-60 & 64-72; mem, Ment Health Comn; La Tax Comn, 64-; deleg, Dem Nat Conv, 68. Mem: La Arts & Sci Bd (first vpres, 65-); La Coun for Music & Performing Arts (chmn bd). Relig: Methodist. Mailing Add: 7449 Boyce Dr Baton Rouge LA 70809

LONG, BOBBY (D)
Ga State Rep
Mailing Add: Sixth St NW Cairo GA 31728

LONG, CHARLES W (R)
Mass State Rep
Mailing Add: State Capitol Boston MA 02133

LONG, CLARENCE DICKINSON JR (D)
US Rep, Md
b South Bend, Ind; s Clarence Dickinson Long & Gertrude Cooper L; m 1937 to Susanna E Larter; c Clarence D, III & Susanna Elizabeth (Mrs Philip Moore). Educ: Washington & Jefferson Col, AB, 32, AM, 33; Princeton Univ, AM, 35, PhD, 38; Phi Beta Kappa; Alpha Tau Omega. Polit & Govt Pos: Mem research staff, Nat Bur of Econ Research, 46-56; assoc task force dir, First Hoover Comn, 49; sr staff mem, President's Coun of Econ Adv, 53-54 & 56-57; acting chmn, Md State Dem Cent Comt, 61-62; US Rep, Second Dist, Md, 63-; deleg, Dem Nat Conv, 68; ex officio, Dem Nat Mid-Term Conf, 74. Bus & Prof Pos: Instr, Wesleyan Univ, 36-40, assoc prof, 41-45; assoc prof, Johns Hopkins Univ, 46-47, prof, 47-62. Mil Serv: Entered as Lt(jg), Naval Res, 43, released as Lt, 46, after serv in Bur of Ships. Publ: Building Cycles & the Theory of Investment, 40, The Labor Force Under Changing Income & Employment, 58 & Wages & Earnings in the United States, 1860-1960, 60, Princeton Univ Press. Mem: Am Asn for Advan of Sci (fel); Am Legion; L'Hirondelle Club, Ruxton, Md; 14 W Hamilton St Club, Baltimore, Md. Relig: Presbyterian. Legal Res: 1015 Boyce Ave Towson MD 21204 Mailing Add: US House of Rep Washington DC 20515

LONG, EMMA (D)
b Pampa, Tex, Feb 29, 12; d Robert Rudd Jackson & Lillie Mae Saylor J; m 1936 to Stuart Morrison Long; c Jeb Jackson & Jefferson Paine. Educ: Univ Tex, Austin, BA, 36. Polit & Govt Pos: City councilman, City of Austin, Tex, 49-59 & 63-69, mayor pro Tem, 67-69; deleg, Dem Nat Conv, 72, chmn, Humphrey for President Deleg, 72. Bus & Prof Pos: Mgr, Long's Printing Shop, 47-52; news reporter, Long News Serv, 48-69. Mem: VFW Auxiliary; Am Legion Auxiliary; Women's Federated Clubs; Town Lake Beautification Prog; Typographical Auxiliary. Honors & Awards: Pub serv award, VFW Post 8787, 68; plaque, Metro Neighborhood Ctr Adv Comt, 69; plaque, United Church Welfare Serv, Caritas, 69; cert of award for patriotic serv, Tex State Guard, 69. Relig: Christian. Mailing Add: 1306 Bradwood Rd Austin TX 78722

LONG, GILLIS WILLIAM (D)
US Rep, La
b Winnfield, La, May 4, 23; s Floyd H Long Sr & Birdie Shumake L; m 1947 to Mary Catherine Small; c George Harrison & Janis Catherine. Educ: La State Univ, BA, 49, JD, 51; Omicron Delta Kappa; Delta Kappa Epsilon. Polit & Govt Pos: Legal counsel, Select Comt on Small Bus, US Sen, 51-53; chief legal counsel, Spec Comt on Campaign Expenditures (elecs), US House of Rep, 52, 56, 58 & 60; assoc counsel, Adv Comt on Rules, Dem Nat Comt, 54-55; US Rep, La, 63-65 & 73-, mem rules comt, US House Rep, 73-, co-founder, Cong Rural Caucus & vchmn, United Dem of Cong, 73-75, chmn, 75-, mem joint econ comt, 75-; deleg, Dem Nat Conv, 64; asst dir, Off Econ Opportunity, Exec Off of the President, 64-66; legis coun, Spec Comt on Hist Preservation, 65-66; legis coun, Nat Comt on Urban Growth Policy, 68-69. Bus & Prof Pos: Investment banker; soybean farmer; law practice, Long & Hamm, 70-72; chmn, La Superport Task Force, 73; pres & mem bd comnr, La Deep Draft Harbor & Terminal Authority, 72-73; pres, Lower Miss Valley Flood Control Asn, 73. Mil Serv: Capt, Army Inf, World War II, ETO; Five Campaign Ribbons; Bronze Star; Purple Heart. Mem: VFW; Am Legion; Lions; Sierra Club; La State Univ Alumni Asn. Relig: Baptist. Legal Res: Apt 244 4125 Jackson St Alexandria LA 71301 Mailing Add: 215 Cannon House Off Bldg Washington DC 20515

LONG, GREGORY F (R)
Chmn, Grand Co Rep Cent Comt, Colo
b Fraser, Colo, Oct 17, 45; s Morris M Long & Dorothy Gene Noonen L; m to Jan R Waldroop; c Kirsten Marie & Rachel Bennet. Educ: Regis Col, BA, 67; Denver Univ, JD, 71; Alpha Kappa Psi. Polit & Govt Pos: Dep dist attorney, 14th Judicial Dist, Colo, 72-74, asst dist attorney, 74-; chmn, Grand Co Rep Cent Comt, 72- Bus & Prof Pos: Admis counr, Regis Col, 67-68, asst dir admis, 68-69, asst to dean of students, 69-72; attorney-at-law, Granby, Colo, 72- Publ: Auth, A misinterpretation of facts: Wyman v James, Denver Law J, 72. Mem: Northwestern Colo & Colo Bar Asns; Colo Trial Lawyers Asn; Nat & Colo Dist Attorney's Asns. Legal Res: 349 Garnet Ave Granby CO 80446 Mailing Add: Box 755 Granby CO 80446

LONG, HILDA SHEETS (D)
m to Edward H Long (deceased); c Berridge (Mrs Noel Copen). Educ: Marshall Univ, 25. Polit & Govt Pos: Mem, Gov Adv Comt on Ment Health & Gov Adv Comt of Employ Security Coun; Dem Nat Committeewoman, WVa, until 72; deleg, Dem Nat Conv, 72. Bus & Prof Pos: Exec vpres & treas, Huntington Publ Co, 59-63, pres, 63-; publ, Huntington Advertiser, 60-; asst secy, Radio Sta WJR, Inc, 61-64. Mem: Colonial Dames of Am; DAR; Delta Zeta; Huntington Garden Club; Woman's Club. Legal Res: 2020 Wilshire Blvd Huntington WV 25701 Mailing Add: 946 Fifth Ave Huntington WV 25720

LONG, JAMES EUGENE (D)
NC State Rep
b Burlington, NC, Mar 19, 40; s George Attmore Long & Helen Long L; c James E, Jr & Rebecca Ann. Educ: NC State Univ, 58-62; Univ NC, Chapel Hill, AB, 63, Sch Law, JD, 66; Tau Kappa Epsilon; Phi Alpha Delta. Polit & Govt Pos: Treas, Alamance Co Young Dem Club, 67, pres, 68, mem exec comt, 69, second vpres, 70; secy, Sixth Dist, NC Young Dem Clubs, 71, North State Caucus Treas, 74-75; NC State Rep, 21st Dist, 70-72, 22nd Dist, 72-, chmn comt on pub utilities, NC House of Rep, 73-74, chmn joint legis comt on taxation of local units of govt, 74-75 & chmn legis comt on rights & responsibilities of state employees, 74-75. Bus & Prof Pos: Assoc. Long, Ridge, Harris & Walker, Attorneys, Burlington & Graham, NC, 66-67, partner, Long, Ridge & Long, 67- Mem: Nat Asn RR Trial Counsel; Burlington Jaycees; Am Bus Club; Burlington-Alamance Co CofC; Alamance Co Young Lawyers (pres, 72-). Relig: Episcopal. Mailing Add: PO Box 690 Burlington NC 27215

LONG, JAMES H (D)
Chmn, Lexington Co Dem Party, SC
b Greer, SC, Feb 2, 36; s Leonard James Long & Leila Hoytte L; m 1957 to Mary Anne Sizemore; c James H, Jr, Michael W & Elizabeth Anne. Educ: Greenville High Sch, SC, grad, 54. Polit & Govt Pos: Exec committeeman, Challedon Precinct Dem Party, SC, 72-; chmn, Lexington Co Dem Party, 74- Bus & Prof Pos: Rep, Thurow Electronics, Lakeland, Fla, 58-62; rep, Hammond Electronics, Daytona Beach, 62-64; mgr inside sales, Dixie Radio Supply Co, Greenville, SC, 64-67, indust sales mgr, 67- Mem: Mason. Mailing Add: 207 Garmony Rd Columbia SC 29210

LONG, JIMMY DALE (D)
La State Rep
b Winnfield, La, Oct 6, 31; s Ruben Ray Long & Ruby Smith L; m 1953 to Dorothy Griffin; c Jimmy D, Jr. Educ: Northwestern State Col, 1 year. Polit & Govt Pos: La State Rep, Dist 23, 68- Bus & Prof Pos: Owner, Dixie Food Store, Natchitoches, La, 59-, Dixie Creme, 66- & Zesto of Natchitoches, 68- Mil Serv: Entered as A/S, Navy, 48, released as CS-2, 54, after serv in Atlantic A or C, Pacific Fleet. Mem: Mason; VFW; Kiwanis; CofC. Honors & Awards: Outstanding Young Man, Natchitoches Parish, 64. Relig: Baptist. Legal Res: Rte 2 Natchitoches LA 71457 Mailing Add: 1232 Texas St Natchitoches LA 71457

LONG, JOHN D, III (D)
SC State Sen
b Union, SC, Feb 20, 30; s John D Long & Mary Baker L; m 1956 to Patricia Ann Willard; c Lou Ann, Mary Jane, John William & Stephen Willard. Educ: Univ SC, AB, 51, LLB, 53. Polit & Govt Pos: Chief Page, SC House of Rep, 53; co solicitor, Union Co, SC, 61-64; SC State Sen, Dist 5, Union Co, 66- Bus & Prof Pos: Lawyer, currently. Mil Serv: Enlisted man, 101st Airborne Div, Army, 2 years, Maj, Judge Adv Gen Corps, Army Res, currently. Mem: Elks; Shriner; Hejaz Temple; Mason (32 degree). Mailing Add: State House Columbia SC 29211

LONG, JOHN JOSEPH (D)
Mass State Rep
b Fall River, Mass, Dec 10, 27; s William F Long, Sr & Susanna G Daley L; m 1951 to Clare Patricia Coogan; c John Patrick, Susanne Marie, Terence, Stephen, James Joseph & Annemarie. Educ: BMC Durfee High Sch, grad; Boston Univ Col Bus Admin, 1 year. Polit & Govt Pos: Mass State Rep, Seventh Bristol Dist, 57-; deleg, Dem Nat Conv, 68. Bus & Prof Pos: Ins broker, Long & Parent Ins Agency Inc, 52-, real estate broker, Long & Parent Realty, 52- Mil Serv: Entered as Pvt, Army, 46, released as Sgt, 48, after serv in 63rd Inf Regt, Korea Mem: Fall River Realtors; Gtr Fall River Ins Agents Asn; DAV; Elks; KofC. Relig: Roman Catholic. Mailing Add: 109 Barre St Fall River MA 02723

LONG, JOSEPH J, SR (D)
Md State Deleg
b Delmar, Md, July, 1921; married. Educ: Paynter Bus Sch. Polit & Govt Pos: Pres, Young Dem Club of Wicomico Co, Md, 60-61; mem, Salisbury Dem Comt; mem, Salisbury City Coun; Md State Deleg, 63-, chmn, Wicomico Co Deleg, Md House Deleg, 66-, chmn Labor & Mgt Subcomt, 67- Bus & Prof Pos: Electrician. Mil Serv: Air Force, 42-46. Mem: Moose; Am Legion; E Side Men's Club; Farm Bur. Mailing Add: 730 S Park Dr Salisbury MD 21801

LONG, MELVIN THOMAS (D)
b New Almelo, Kans, Aug 7, 40; s Andrew Isadore Long & Regina Otter L; single. Educ: St Mary's Col, Minn, BA, 62; Univ Madrid, Spain, 64; Univ Barcelona, 65; Cath Univ Louvain, MA & PhD, 66; Eta Sigma Phi; Tau Omega Sigma. Polit & Govt Pos: Deleg, First Cong Dist & Kans State Dem Convs, 72; alt deleg, Dem Nat Conv, 72; chmn, McGovern for President Comt, First Cong Dist & Saline Co, 72. Bus & Prof Pos: Assoc pastor, Sacred Heart Cathedral, Salina, Kans, 66-68; assoc pastor, Perpetual Help Church, Concordia, 68-70; chmn, Liturgical Comt, Diocese of Salina, 68-, secy, Priests Senate, 71-72, pres, 72-; prof, Marymount Col, 70- Mem: Common Cause; Cath Campus Ministry Asn; Moose; Elks; KofC. Honors & Awards: Serv to Inner-Cities of Am, Mid-Continent Regional Educ Labs, 72; Achievements in Drug Abuse Educ, Kans Univ, 72. Relig: Catholic. Legal Res: 2001 E Iron Salina KS 67401 Mailing Add: Marymount Col E Iron Ave Salina KS 67401

LONG, MICHAEL THOMAS (D)
Chmn, Simsbury Dem Town Comt, Conn
b Hartford, Conn, Feb 22, 42; s Michael Joseph Long & Mary Maguire; m 1967 to Ann Marie O'Connell; c Michael Brendan, Maura Kathleen & Deirdre Ann. Educ: Univ Notre Dame, BBA, 64; Univ Conn, JD, 67; Student Bar Asn. Polit & Govt Pos: Chmn, Simsbury Dem Town Comt, Conn, 74- Bus & Prof Pos: Asst secy, E-B Industries, Inc, 72-; asst secy, Ensign-Bickford Co, 72-, controller aerospace div, 74-; secy, Ensign Bickford Realty Corp, 74-; secy, Forest Interiors Inc, 72-74. Mem: Conn & Hartford Co Bar Asns; Univ Notre Dame Conn Valley Alumni Asn (secy, 72-); Simsbury Farms Men's Club (founder, 72); Simsbury Jaycees (exec vpres, 73). Honors & Awards: Governor's Civic Leadership Award, Jaycees, 74. Relig: Roman Catholic. Mailing Add: 4 Maple Court Simsbury CT 06070

LONG, ROBERT C BIGGY (D)
Md State Deleg
b Westover, Md, May 15, 19; s William Broughton Long & Ethel Miles L; m 1946 to M Lorraine Wilson; c Daniel Miles, Robin Charleen, Ellen Broughton, Claudia Ann & Kelly Lorraine. Educ: Washington High, grad, 36; Valley Forge Mil Acad, 36-37; Beacom Bus Sch, grad, BA Bus Admin, 39. Polit & Govt Pos: Comnr, Somerset Co, Md, 54-58 & 66-74; Md State Deleg, 58-66 & 74- Bus & Prof Pos: Partner, Long Bros, Inc, 38-58, pres, 58- Mil Serv: Entered as Seaman, Navy, 45, released as SKV 3/C, 46, after serv in USS Omaha, SAtlantic, 45-46. Mem: Md Farm Bur; Princess Anne Lions (charter mem); Am Legion, O T Beauchamp Post 94; Elks; VFW. Relig: Protestant. Mailing Add: PO Box 216 Westover MD 21871

LONG, ROBERT WILLIAM (R)
Asst Secy Conserv, Research & Educ, Dept of Agr
b Ashland, Pa, Mar 23, 23; s Robert Raymond Long & Ethel Raisbeck L; m 1944 to Lorena S Kaufhold; c Robert S, Joan L & Elizabeth A. Educ: Dickinson Col, PhB, 44, LLB, 48. Polit & Govt Pos: Attorney, Bur of Mines, Washington, DC, 50-52; attorney, Off of Solicitor, Dept of Interior, 52-62, asst solicitor oil & gas, 62-70, assoc solicitor mine health & safety, 70-73; asst secy conserv, research & educ, Dept of Agr, 73- Bus & Prof Pos: Individual practice law,

Pa, 48-50. Mil Serv: Marine Corps Res, 43-46, PTO; Purple Heart. Mem: Fed Bar Asn; Am Legion; Phi Kappa Sigma. Relig: Episcopal. Legal Res: CA Mailing Add: Dept of Agr Conserv Res & Educ 14th & Independence Ave SW Washington DC 20250

LONG, RUSSELL B **(D)**
US Sen, La
b Shreveport, La, Nov 3, 18; s Huey P Long & Rose McConnell L; m to Carolyn Bason; c Rita Katherine (Mrs Dean Mosely) & Pamela Rust (Mrs Prescott McCardle). Educ: La State Univ, BA, 41 & LLB, 42; Delta Kappa Epsilon; Omicron Delta Kappa; Order of Coif; Tau Kappa Alpha; Phi Delta Phi. Polit & Govt Pos: US Sen, La, 48-, chmn mil construction subcomt, US Senate, 52, mem armed serv comt, banking & currency comt, foreign rels comt, govt opers comt, interior & insular affairs comt, rules & admin comt & post off & civil serv comt, formerly, mem, comt com & chmn subcomt merchant marine, mem select comt small bus, rotating chmn joint comt internal revenue taxation & mem joint comt reduction non-essential fed expenditures, currently, Asst Majority Leader, 65-68, chmn comt finance & alt chmn joint comt internal revenue, 66-, mem Dem Steering comt, 73-; deleg, Dem Nat Conv, 68. Bus & Prof Pos: Attorney; admitted to La Bar, 42. Mil Serv: Lt, Naval Res, 42-45. Mem: Lions; Elks; Am Legion. Legal Res: Baton Rouge LA Mailing Add: 217 Senate Off Bldg Washington DC 20510

LONG, SPEEDY O **(D)**
b Tullos, La, June 16, 28; s Felix F Long & Verda Pendarvis L; m 1955 to Florence Marie Theriot; c Felix Paul & David Theriot. Educ: Northeast Jr Col, 50; Northwestern State Col, BA, 51; La State Univ Law Sch, JD, 59. Polit & Govt Pos: La State Sen, 56-64; US Rep, La, 64-73; dist attorney, La Salle Parish & Caldwell Parish, La, 73- Bus & Prof Pos: Attorney-at-law, Long & Peters Law Firm, 69- Mil Serv: Navy, 46-48 & 51-53. Mem: Kiwanis; Am Legion; Mason (32 degree); Shrine; hon chap farmer, LaSalle Parish Future Farmers of Am. Relig: Baptist. Mailing Add: Drawer L Jena LA 71342

LONG, SUSANNA LARTER (SUSIE) **(D)**
b Newark, NJ; d Harry Clifton Larter & Susanna Ekings L; m to Clarence Dickinson Long; c Clarence Dickinson, III & Susanna (Mrs Philip L Moore). Educ: Wells Col, 2 years. Polit & Govt Pos: Deleg, Dem Nat Mid-Term Conf, 74. Mem: Junior League; Women's Polit Caucus; UN Asn of Md (bd dirs, 60-); Woman's Nat Dem Club; Cong Club. Relig: Protestant. Mailing Add: 1015 Boyce Ave Ruxton MD 21204

LONG, WILLIAM L **(R)**
Ind State Rep
Mailing Add: 720 S Ninth St Lafayette IN 47905

LONGBOTHAM, RALPH MAYNARD **(R)**
Committeeman, Ark Rep State Comt
b St Paul, Minn, July 20, 22; s Ralph M Longbotham & C Gloria Jones L; m 1952 to Elsie DeBonis; c Carol L & Lael G. Educ: Carleton Col, BA, 48; US Army Command & Gen Staff Col, grad, 60. Polit & Govt Pos: Vchmn, Lonoke Co Rep Comt, Ark, 68, chmn, 68-72; state campaign chmn, Jerry Climer for Secy of State Comt, 72; committeeman, Ark Rep State Comt, 72-; mem, Lonoke Co Elec Comn, currently. Bus & Prof Pos: Personnel dir, Goodwill Industs of Ark, Little Rock, 68- Mil Serv: Entered as Pvt, Army, 43, released as 1st Lt, 46, after serv in several units, Asian-Pac Theatre, Hq, Armed Forces, Western Pac, 45, recalled, 48-66, 1st Lt to Lt Col; Silver Star; Bronze Star with V & Oak Leaf Cluster; Purple Heart; Army Commendation Medal; Presidential Unit Citation with Cluster. Mem: Nat Rehabilitation Asn; Ret Off Asn; Eng Riding Club, Inc (pres, 71-). Relig: Methodist; Chmn Bd, United Methodist Church of Cabot, 70- Mailing Add: Rte 2 Box 346 Cabot AR 72023

LONGE, ROSAIRE J **(D)**
Vt State Rep
Mailing Add: 55 Tracy Dr Burlington VT 05401

LONGLEY, BENJAMIN LEHMANN **(R)**
Tenn State Rep
b La Grange, Ga, Aug 7, 30; s Julian McLauren Longley, Sr & Mary Bowen Robertson L; m 1957 to Anne Elizabeth Hayes; c Mary Elizabeth & Amy Lauren. Educ: Vanderbilt Univ, BA, 51; Pi Kappa Alpha. Polit & Govt Pos: Secy, Tenn Young Rep, 63-65; staff mem, US Rep, W E Brock, Tenn, 63-65; dist chmn, Third Cong Dist, Tenn Rep Party, 65-72; Tenn State Rep, 66-, asst minority leader, Tenn House of Rep, 71-; alt deleg, Rep Nat Conv, 68. Bus & Prof Pos: Credit mgr, Hardwick Stove Co, 54-61, controller, 62-66; agt, Mutual Benefit Life Ins Co, 61-62; agt, Provident Life Ins Co, 66- Mil Serv: Entered as Pvt, Army, 51, released as Sgt, 54. Mem: Million Dollar Round Table; Nat Asn of Life Underwriters; Am Legion; Elks; Civitan. Relig: Methodist. Legal Res: 3635 Westview Dr NE Cleveland TN 37311 Mailing Add: PO Box 211 Cleveland TN 37311

LONGLEY, JAMES BERNARD **(INDEPENDENT)**
Gov, Maine
b Apr 22, 24; s James Bernard Longley & Catherine Wade L; m to Helen Walsh Longley; c James B, Jr, Kathryn, Susan M, Stephen J & Nancy. Educ: Bowdoin Col, 47; Am Col Life Underwriters, CLU, 54; Univ Maine Law Sch, LLB, 57. Polit & Govt Pos: Gov, Maine, 75- Bus & Prof Pos: Gen agt, New England Mutual Life Ins Co, Boston, Mass; partner, Longley & Buckley, Lewiston; pres, Longley Assocs. Mem: Million Dollar Round Table; Androscoggin Co, Maine & Am Bar Asns; Andy Valley & Maine Life Underwriters Asns. Honors & Awards: Lucien Howe Prize, Bowdoin Col, 47; Three Time Winner of President's Trophy Award, New England Life. Relig: Catholic. Legal Res: 40 Robinson Gardens Lewiston ME 04240 Mailing Add: State House Augusta ME 04330

LONGLEY, LAWRENCE DOUGLAS **(D)**
Chmn, Outagamie Co Dem Party, Wis
b Bronxville, NY, Nov 12, 39; s Henry N Longley & Effie Devers L; div; c Rebecca. Educ: Oberlin Col, BA, 62; Vanderbilt Univ, MA, 64, PhD, 69; Delta Sigma Rho. Polit & Govt Pos: Area campaign mgr, US Sen Gaylord Nelson, Wis, 67-68; chmn, Outagamie Co Dem Party, 69-; vchmn, Eighth Dist Dem Party, 70-; mem-at-lg admin comt, Wis State Dem Party, 71-; Northeast Wis regional coordr, Muskie for President, 72; Wis Dem Presidential Elector, 72. Bus & Prof Pos: Instr govt, Lawrence Univ, 65-69, asst prof, 69- Publ: Co-auth, The Politics of Electoral College Reform, Yale Univ Press, 72 & 75, The Politics of Broadcast Regulation, St Martin's Press, 73 & The Biases of the Electoral College, Brookings Inst, 73; plus others. Mem: Wis Polit Sci Asn (exec comt, 66-); Am, Midwest & Southern Polit Sci Asns. Relig: Congregational. Legal Res: 35 Woodmere Ct Appleton WI 54911 Mailing Add: PO Box 498 Appleton WI 54911

LONGMIRE, GEORGE **(R)**
NDak State Sen
b LaFollette, Tenn, Aug 2, 15; married; c two. Educ: Lincoln Mem Univ; Univ NDak; George Washington Univ. Polit & Govt Pos: States attorney, Grand Forks Co, NDak, formerly; chmn, NDak Rep Party, formerly; NDak State Sen, 57- Bus & Prof Pos: Lawyer. Legal Res: 3733 Belmont Rd Grand Forks ND 58201 Mailing Add: 24 N Fourth St Grand Forks ND 58201

LONGO, FRANK J **(D)**
Mayor, Bristol, Conn
b New London, Conn, June 24, 18; s Peter Longo & Sebastiana Drago L; m 1945 to Viola Martin; c Frank J, Jr, Margaret, Ann, Patricia, Mary, Peter, Paul, Marie & Barbara. Educ: Bristol High Sch, GED. Polit & Govt Pos: Mayor, Bristol, Conn, 71-, chmn bd finance, park bd, police bd & fire bd, 71- Bus & Prof Pos: Mgr, Longo's Sports Mart, Bristol, Conn, 40- Relig: Roman Catholic. Legal Res: 12 Mossa Dr Bristol CT 06010 Mailing Add: City Hall N Main St Bristol CT 06010

LONGORIA, RAUL L **(D)**
Tex State Sen
b Grulla, Tex, Feb 22, 21; s Andres Longoria & Enriqueta L; m 1947 to Martha Earlene Moorman; c Samuel Glenn, Janiece Maxene, Roy Alan & twins, Martha Elaine & Cecilia Joyce. Educ: Univ Tex, BBA & LLB, 52. Polit & Govt Pos: Tex State Rep, Dist 38, Pl 1, 61-63, Dist 37-F, 65-67 & Dist 49, Pl 1, 67-73; Tex State Sen, Dist 27, 73- Bus & Prof Pos: Attorney-at-law, 52-53 & 64-; assoc, Hartley & Latimore, Attorneys, 53-55; asst dist attorney, Hidalgo Co, Tex, 55-57; assoc, Longoria & Evins, Attorneys, 57-64; Raul L Longoria Law Firm, 64- Mil Serv: Entered as Pvt, Air Force, 42, released as Sgt, 46, after serv in ETO. Mem: Lions Int; Am Legion; Tex & Hidalgo Co Bar Asns; Tex Asn of Plaintiff's Attorneys. Relig: Catholic. Legal Res: W Jackson St Pharr TX 78577 Mailing Add: PO Box 182 Edinburg TX 78539

LONGSTREET, VICTOR MENDELL **(D)**
b Louisville, Ky, Jan 1, 07; s Joseph Emens Longstreet & Allan McKinley L; m 1930 to Mary Margaret Landry; c Katherine Allan (Mrs H Goett). Educ: Harvard Col, BS, magna cum laude, 30; Phi Beta Kappa. Polit & Govt Pos: Sr economist, Fed Reserve, Bd, 40-43; assoc chief div of econ develop, State Dept, 45-48; dep US sr rep, NATO Finance Comt, 50-51; dep dir off of trade & finance, Econ Coop Admin, Paris, 51-52; Asst Secy, Dept of Navy, 62-65. Bus & Prof Pos: Vpres, Fed Reserve Bank of St Louis, 53-57; dir of mgt research, Schering Corp, 57-62; assoc dir, Int Mgt Group of Boston, Mass, 66-69; dir, NAm Fund Mgt Corp, 66-; dir, Baldt Corp, 69-; chmn, The Boston Group, Inc, 70- Mil Serv: Entered as Capt, Army Air Corps, 43, released as Lt Col, 45; Navy Meritorious Citation. Publ: Financial Control in Multi-National Companies, Financial Execs Research Found, New York, 71. Mem: Am Econ Asn; Coun Foreign Rels; Army Navy Club; Harvard Club of Boston & New York. Relig: Non-Denominational. Mailing Add: Depot Rd Truro MA 02666

LOOBY, JOSEPH LAWRENCE **(D)**
Wis State Rep
b Eau Claire, Wis, Nov 24, 17; s Thomas E Looby & Anna Sippel L; m 1942 to Myrtle Irene Brettingen; c Judith Ann (Mrs John Ruhe), Kathleen Jo, Cheyrl Marie, Kevin Thomas, Karen Lea, Brian Timothy & Constance Sue. Educ: St Patricks High Sch, Eau Claire, Wis, grad. Polit & Govt Pos: Mem, State Exec Bd, Wis AFL-CIO, Milwaukee, 62-; mem, Eau Claire City Coun, 64-68; mem, Eau Claire Co Bd, 64-; Wis State Rep, Eau Claire First Dist, 69- Bus & Prof Pos: Secy-treas, URW Lodge 19, 61-69. Mil Serv: Entered as Pvt, Army, 43, released as Pfc, 46, after serv in Tenth Mt Div, Europe & MidE, 44-46. Relig: Catholic. Mailing Add: 1529 Howard Ave Eau Claire WI 54701

LOOMIS, HENRY **(INDEPENDENT)**
Pres, Corp for Pub Broadcasting
b Tuxedo Park, NY, Apr 19, 19; s Alfred Lee Loomis & Ellen Holman Farnsworth L; m 1946 to Mary Paul Macleod; div; c Henry Stimson, Mary Paul, Lucy Farnsworth & Gordon Macleod; m 1974 to Jacqueline C Williams. Educ: Harvard, AB, 41; Univ Calif, Berkeley, 46-47. Polit & Govt Pos: Asst to chmn, Research & Develop Bd, Dept Defense, 50-51; consult, Psychol Strategy Bd, 51-52; staff asst, President's Comt on Info, 53; chief, Off of Research & Intel, US Info Agency, Washington, DC, 54-57, dir, Voice of Am, 58-65, dep dir, US Info Agency, 69-72; staff dir to spec asst to President for Sci & Technol, 57-58; dep US Comnr of Educ, Dept Health, Educ & Welfare, 65-66; pres, Corp for Pub Broadcasting, Washington, 72- Bus & Prof Pos: Mem, Staff, Radiation Lab, Univ Calif, 45-47; asst to pres, Mass Inst of Technol, 47-50; partner, St Vincents Island Co, 66-68. Mil Serv: Entered as Ens, Navy, 40, released as Lt Comdr, 45, after serv on Staff, Comdr-in-Chief, Pac Theatre; Bronze Star & Air Medal. Mem: Metrop Club; Middleburg Hunt Club; Cruising Club of Am. Honors & Awards: Rockefeller Pub Serv Award in Foreign Affairs & Distinguished Serv Award, US Info Agency, 63. Relig: Episcopal. Legal Res: Trough Hill Farm Middleburg VA 22117 Mailing Add: 888 16th St NW Washington DC 20006

LOORAM, MATTHEW
US Ambassador to Somali
b New York, NY, Mar 26, 21; s Matthew Looram & Constance Peabody L; m 1943 to Bettina de Rothschild; c Bettina & Peter. Educ: Harvard Col, BA, 43. Polit & Govt Pos: Foreign serv officer, US State Dept, 48-, third & second secy, Rome, 48-52, second secy, Paris, 52-55, European Bur, US State Dept, 55-59, US Consul, Ethiopia, 59-62, African Bur, US State Dept, 63-69, US Ambassador, Repub of Dahomey, 69-73; US Ambassador to Somali, 73- Mil Serv: Entered as Pvt, Army, 43, released as Capt, 46, after serv in 13th ABN Div & 88th Inf Div, ETO. Mem: Metrop Club, Washington, DC. Relig: Protestant. Legal Res: 1308 29th St NW Washington DC 20007 Mailing Add: Dept of State Washington DC 20521

LOPES, THOMAS DENNIS **(D)**
Mass State Rep
b New Bedford, Mass, Sept 7, 42; s Thomas Augustus Lopes & Catherine Marie Perry L; m 1970 to Maria de los Angeles Rosado; c Christine & Denise. Educ: Univ Bridgeport, BS, 68; Mass Inst Technol, 69; Bryant Col, MBA, 74; Newman Club; NAACP; Track; Indust Rels Club. Polit & Govt Pos: Airport comnr, New Bedford, Mass, 73-74; Mass State Rep, 75-, mem spec comn ment retarded, Mass House Rep, 75- Bus & Prof Pos: Employ specialist, CofC, Bridgeport, Conn, 68; dep dir, Onboard, Inc, New Bedford, Mass, 68-70; community coordr, Youth Resources Agency, 71-72; asst mgr, New Eng Tel & Tel, 72-74. Mil Serv: A/S, Naval Res, 68. Mem: Cape Verdeau Vet Asn; Comprehensive Health Planning Asn; New Bedford Area Ment Health & Retarded Bd; New Bedford NAACP. Honors & Awards: Rev Hubert

Award for Outstanding Achievement in Sch, Church & Community. Relig: Roman Catholic. Mailing Add: 453 Hillman St New Bedford MA 02740

LOPEZ, BETTY DAVILA (D)
VChairwoman, Ariz Dem Exec Comt
b Tucson, Ariz, Aug 29, 26; d Monte Davila & Mary Moreno D; m 1953 to Henry Sayre Lopez; c Henry D, III, Monica Anne & twins, Michael Anthony & Frederick Mark. Educ: Univ Southern Calif, BS, 49; Lambda Kappa Sigma; Rho Chi. Polit & Govt Pos: Committeewoman, Precinct 19 Dem Party, Ariz, 71-; secy, Dist 11 Dem Club, 72-73, chairperson, 74-; mem, Ariz Dem Exec Comt, Dist 11, 72-, vchairwoman, 74- Bus & Prof Pos: Pharmacist & owner, South Stone Pharm, 56-70; pharmacist, El Rio-Santa Cruz Neighborhood Health Ctr, Tucson, 71-74; retired. Mem: Mex Am Cult Ctr Comt; League Mex Am Women; Kino Community Hosp (exec mem bd gov, 73-); Comn Improved Govt Mgt; Ariz Mex Am Human Resources Coalition. Honors & Awards: League Mex Am Women's Award for Community Work, 75. Relig: Catholic. Mailing Add: 32 N Linda Ave Tucson AZ 85705

LOPEZ, EDWARD JOSEPH (D)
NMex State Rep
b Cincinnati, Ohio, May 3, 38; s Joseph Francis Lopez & Norma Brunton L; m 1958 to Rozella Melinda Lucero; c Melinda L, Edward J, Jr, Elizabeth A & Karen Jean. Educ: Univ NMex, 56 & 57. Polit & Govt Pos: Supvr traffic div, NMex State Police, 59-62; Dem precinct chmn, Precinct 17, Santa Fe Co, 62-64; mem, Santa Fe Co Dem Cent Comt, 62-64; admin off oil & gas units div, NMex State Land Off, 62-68; mem, Santa Fe Co Dem Exec Comt, 69; NMex State Rep, Santa Fe Co, Dist Two, 69-, chmn, Tax & Revenue Comt, NMex House of Rep, 71-, vchmn, Legis Finance Comt, 73- Bus & Prof Pos: Landman, Bokum Corp, 68-, asst to vpres, 70-, corp exec, Bokum Resources, 72- Mem: Elks; NMex State Employees Credit Union (chmn bd); Jr CofC; YMCA (bd dirs); Univ NMex Alumni Asn. Relig: Roman Catholic. Mailing Add: 303 Pinos Verdes Santa Fe NM 87501

LOPEZ, SOTO DANNY (NEW PROGRESSIVE, PR)
Rep, PR House of Rep
b Utuado, PR, Mar 13, 41; s Pablo Lopez Vera & Mariana Soto de L; m 1964 to Merilyn Pujals; c Danny & Merilyn. Educ: Univ PR, BBA, 65. Polit & Govt Pos: Pres, Third Precinct Young Rep, PR, 56-60; vpres, San Juan Young Rep, 60-64; vpres, PR Young Rep, 64-67; Rep, PR House Rep, Third Precinct, 69- Bus & Prof Pos: Loan rep, Chase Manhattan Bank, 64-65; owner, Bargain Center, Inc, 65-69. Honors & Awards: Citation for Meritorious Serv, Am Legion. Relig: Catholic. Mailing Add: Calle Trinitaria 1913 Urbanizacion Santa Maria Rio Piedras PR 00927

LOPEZ GARCIA, JOSE A (POPULAR DEMOCRATS, PR)
Rep, PR House Rep
Mailing Add: State Capitol San Juan PR 00901

LOPIANO, WILLIAM J (R)
Mayor, Tempe, Ariz
b Mass, Aug 2, 26; s Salvatore LoPiano & Nancy Maida L; m 1960 to Dorothy Jean Starr; c Lisa Starr & Marie Starr. Educ: Palmer Col Chiropractic, DC, 51, Phoenix Col & Ariz State Univ, 52-; Los Angeles Col Chiropractic, DC, 54. Polit & Govt Pos: Mem bd adjustment, Tempe, Ariz, 61-66, mem bd freeholders, 64, councilman, 66-74, vmayor, 68-72, mayor, 74- Bus & Prof Pos: Self employed chiropractor, Tempe, Ariz, 52-; treas, B & L Enterprises, Tempe, 64-; pres, JeLiMa Investments, Tempe, 69- Mil Serv: Entered as Pvt, Army, 44, released as T-5, 46, after serv in 182nd Inf, Asiatic Pac Theatre, 45-46; Philippine Liberation Medal; Bronze Star; Asiatic Pac Theatre Medal; Good Conduct Medal; Army of Occupation & WWII Victory Medal. Mem: US Conf Mayors; League Ariz Cities & Towns (bd dir); Rotary Int; VFW; Am Legion. Honors & Awards: Youth Welfare Award, US Jr CofC, 57; Outstanding Community & Distinguished Serv Award, Jaycees, 70; Ariz Serv to Mankind Award, Sertoma, 73; Nat Boy's Club Medallion Award, 74. Legal Res: 409 E Alameda Dr Tempe AZ 85282 Mailing Add: 196 E Fifth St Tempe AZ 85281

LOPRESTI, MICHAEL, JR (D)
Mass State Sen
b Boston, Mass, Apr 30, 47; s Michael LoPresti, Sr & Anna Katin L; m 1970 to AnnMarie Calabresi; c Anna Christine & Michael, III. Educ: Worcester Acad, Mass, grad, 66; Harvard Univ, BA, 70; Boston Univ Law Sch, JD, 73; Sigma Alpha Epsilon; Young Dem. Polit & Govt Pos: Mass State Sen, Suffolk & Middlesex Dist, 73- Bus & Prof Pos: Football coach, Harvard Univ, formerly; asst dist attorney, Suffolk Co, 74; attorney-at-law, Boston, Mass, currently; instr govt, Bunker Hill Community Col, 75-; bd dirs, Indust Credit Union, currently; bd dirs, Shared Exp Prog, Pub Affairs Action Comt, Western Elec, currently. Mem: KofC; Sons of Italy; Winthrop Lodge Elks; Harvard Club Boston; Hasty Pudding Club. Honors & Awards: Legislators Elderly Honor Roll, 73; United Cerebral Palsy Award, 75. Relig: Catholic. Mailing Add: 23 Waldemar Ave East Boston MA 02128

LOPRESTO, JOHN GEORGE (R)
NY State Assemblyman
b New York, NY, July 10, 40; s Charles S Lopresto & Frances Chiparo L; m 1966 to Carol Ann Maddi; c Francine, Margaret Ann & John, Jr. Educ: St John's Univ, BA, 62; NY Law Sch, LLB, 66; Lambda Epsilon Chi. Polit & Govt Pos: Confidential asst, Attorney Gen, NY, 63-64; law secy, Judge Civil Court, New York, 69-70; NY State Assemblyman, 71- Mem: Queens Bar Asn; Queens Jr CofC; Long Island Lawyers Asn; Columbian Lawyers Asn; Ital Legislators Club, Inc. Honors & Awards: United Sr Ctrs Gtr New York Hon Award, 71; Long Island RR Police & PBA Pub Serv Award, 72; Hanec-Wep Learning Ctr Man of Year Award, 72; Thomas Creegan Mem Award, 74; North Queens Homeowners & Civic Asn Jackson Heights Hon Award, 74. Legal Res: 138-01 15th Ave College Point NY 11357 Mailing Add: NY State Assembly Albany NY 12224

LORENTZ, C FRED (R)
Kans State Rep
b Kansas City, Kans, Sept 3, 44; s Calvin Frederick Lorentz & Mary Schweitzer L; m 1968 to Vicki Jean Moyer; c Ricky, Jay, Joel & Ryan. Educ: Baker Univ, 62-64; Kans State Teachers Col, BS in Bus, 66; Washburn Univ, JD, 69; Delta Tau Delta; Phi Alpha Delta. Polit & Govt Pos: Co attorney, Wilson Co, Kans, 70-74; Kans State Rep, 75- Mil Serv: SP-5, Army Nat Guard, 69- Mem: Am & Kans Bar Asns; Elks; Eagles; Rotary Int. Relig: Presbyterian. Mailing Add: 530 N Tenth Fredonia KS 66736

LORENZ, RAYMOND JOSEPH (R)
Chmn, 39th Dist Rep Comt, NDak
b Bowman, NDak, Apr 10, 25; s Rudolph J Lorenz & Johanna L; m 1950 to Irene Grenstiener; c John R & Patricia. Educ: Bowman Pub Sch, 12 years. Polit & Govt Pos: Pres, City Comnr, Bowman, NDak, 60-64, city comnr, 72; chmn, 39th Dist Rep Comt, 74- Bus & Prof Pos: Pres, Lorenz Motor, Inc, Bowman. Mem: Bowman Rotary Club; Elks Club; KofC. Relig: Catholic. Mailing Add: 8 W First St Bowman ND 58623

LORENZEN, DOROTHY WALKER (R)
Committeewoman, Conn Rep State Cent Comt
b Cape Elizabeth, Maine, Aug 13, 09; d Leon Valentine Walker & Maribel Holt W; m 1931 to Frederick William Paul Lorenzen; c Lucinda (Mrs Donald Kegans) & Gale (Mrs Stanley Flagg). Educ: Smith Col, Mass, BA, 30. Polit & Govt Pos: Mem, Stamford Rep Town Comt, 19th Dist, Conn, 54-64; mem, Conn Rep State Cent Comt, 27th Dist, 62-; mem, Conn Const Conv, 27th Dist, summer 66; alt deleg, Rep Nat Conv, 72. Mem: Fairfield Co Rep Women's Asn; Fourth Cong Dist Rep Women's Asn (bd, 72-); Stamford Rep Women's Club (parliamentarian, 72-). Relig: Protestant. Mailing Add: 242 Dogwood Lane Stamford CT 06903

LORGE, GERALD D (R)
Wis State Sen
b Bear Creek, Wis, July 9, 22; s Joseph J Lorge & Anna Marie Petersen L; m 1957 to Christina C Ziegler; c Four. Educ: Marquette Univ Law Sch, JD, 52. Polit & Govt Pos: Mem, Milwaukee Co Rep Precinct Comt, 4th Ward, formerly; Outagamie & Waupace Co Rep Units, formerly; Wis State Assemblyman, 50-54, educ comt & contingent expenditures, formerly; Wis State Sen, 54-, past chmn, Comt Commerce, Labor, Taxation, Ins & Banking, chmn, Comt on Comts, Comt Judiciary & Ins, mem, Comt Interstate Coop, Wis Legis Coun & Comt Legis Procedure, currently; Eighth Cong Dist Parliamentarian, 67; chmn, Justice & Law Enforcement Comt, Midwestern Coun State Govts, 70-72; vchmn, Conf Ins Legislators, formerly, dir, 71-73. Bus & Prof Pos: Attorney-at-law. Mil Serv: T/Sgt, Marine Corps, 42-46. Mem: Moose; KofC; Am Legion; VFW; DAV. Relig: Catholic. Legal Res: RR 1 Bear Creek WI 54922 Mailing Add: Rm 335 S State Capitol Madison WI 53702

LORING, MURRAY (D)
b New York, NY, Sept 1, 17; s Philip Murray & Rose M; m 1945 to Mildred Rogers; c Arthur S, Trudy & Sandra Ellen. Educ: Brooklyn Col, BA; Cornell Univ; Middlesex Univ, DVM; Marshall-Wythe Sch of Law, Col William & Mary, JD, 68. Polit & Govt Pos: Chmn, Johnson-Humphrey Campaign, 63, Gov Godwin Campaign, 64 & Sen William B Spong Campaign, 66; deleg, Dem Nat Conv, 64; chmn, Williamsburg-James City Co; supvr & mem, Planning Comt, James City Co, 64-; rep, Va State Dem Cent Comt, formerly. Bus & Prof Pos: Pres, CofC, 63; mem, Williamsburg-James City Merger Comt, 63; mem, Welfare Bd, 64-; Gen practice of law, Williamsburg, Va, currently. Mil Serv: Army Vet Corps, 44-46. Publ: Liability of cat scratch, Int Cat Fancy, 68; Liability Kennel Mgt, 68; The Risks & Rights of Animal Ownership, Arco, 73. Mem: Am & Va State Vet Med Asns; Am Bar Asn; Ruritan; AF&AM. Honors & Awards: Assoc ed, Kennel Mgt Mag. Relig: Hebrew. Legal Res: 104 Willow Dr Williamsburg VA 23185 Mailing Add: Drawer 280 Williamsburg VA 23185

LORY, EARL C (R)
Mont State Rep
Mailing Add: Rte 5 Miller Creek Rd Missoula MT 59801

LOSER, JOSEPH CARLTON (D)
b Nashville, Tenn, Oct 1, 92; s Henry J Loser & Willie May McConnico L; m 1915 to Pearl Dean Gupton; c Mrs Paul Storey, Mrs Don Gass & Judge Joe C, Jr. Educ: Cumberland Univ, LLB, 23; Sigma Alpha Epsilon; Colemere Club. Polit & Govt Pos: Secy to mayor, Nashville, Tenn, 17-20; asst city attorney, Nashville, 23-29; asst dist attorney, Tenth Judicial Dist, Tenn, 29-34, dist attorney, 34-56; deleg, Dem Nat Conv, 44, 52 & 60; US Rep, Tenn, 56-62; former Dem Presidential Elector, committeeman, Davidson Co Dem Comt & committeeman & secy, Tenn State Dem Comt. Mil Serv: Coast Guard Res, 44. Mem: Mason; KT; KCCH (32 degree); Shrine; Kiwanis. Relig: Baptist. Mailing Add: 92 Belle Meade Tower 105 Leake Ave Nashville TN 37205

LOSH, FREDDIE FRANKLIN (D)
Chmn, Reynolds Co Dem Comt, Mo
b Piedmont, Mo, Aug 14, 14; s Stephen Roten Losh & Mary Ann Rhoads L; m 1967 to Zelle Wood Conway. Educ: Pub sch, Reynolds Co, Mo. Polit & Govt Pos: Alderman, Ellington, Mo, 66-; chmn, Coun on Aging, Reynolds Co; pres, Reynolds Co Coun on Aging, Inc; mem, Area & Reynolds Co Off of Econ Opportunity Bd; committeeman, Logan Twp Dem Party, 70-72; treas, Reynolds Co Dem Comt, 70-75, chmn, 75- Bus & Prof Pos: Owner & operator, Losh Elec Serv, 54- Mil Serv: Entered as Pvt, Army, 41, released as T-4, 45, after serv in Coast Artil & Engrs, SPac Theatre, 44-45; Good Conduct Medal; Philippine Liberation Ribbon with Bronze Star; Bronze Serv Arrowhead. Mem: CofC; Am Legion (comdr, Daniel Cowin Post 346); Sr Citizens Housing, Inc (secy). Relig: Baptist; Mem, Baptist Men's Orgn, First Baptist Church, Ellington. Mailing Add: Rte 2 Box 191 Ellington MO 63638

LOSH, ZELLE (D)
Committeewoman, Reynolds Co Dem Party, Mo
b Shannon Co, Mo, Feb 18, 18; d Charles Conway & Stella Woolf C; m 1967 to Freddie Franklin Losh; c Rose (Mrs Williams), Joann (Mrs Hill), Glenda (Mrs Long) & Paul Wood. Educ: Shannon Co Pub Schs. Polit & Govt Pos: Committeewoman, Reynolds Co Dem Party, Mo, 70- Mem: Am Legion Auxiliary (chaplain, Daniel Cowin Unit 346). Relig: Baptist. Mailing Add: Ellington MO 63638

LOTT, CHESTER TRENT (R)
US Rep, Miss
b Grenada, Miss, Oct 9, 41; s Chester Paul Lott & Iona Watson L; m 1964 to Patricia Elizabeth Thompson; c Chester Trent, Jr & Tyler Elizabeth. Educ: Univ Miss, BPA & JD; Phi Alpha Delta; Sigma Nu. Polit & Govt Pos: Admin Asst to US Rep William M Colmer, Miss, 68-72; US Rep, Miss, 73- Bus & Prof Pos: Field rep, Univ Minn, 63-65, law alumni secy, 66-67; pvt practice, Bryan & Gordon, Attorneys, Pascagoula, Miss, 67-68. Mem: Jackson Co, Miss & Am Bar Asns; Jaycees. Relig: Baptist. Mailing Add: 907 Washington Ave Pascagoula MS 39567

LOTTINGER, MORRIS ALBERT, JR (D)
La State Rep
b Houma, La, Aug 12, 37; s Morris Albert Lottinger & Effie Hellier L; m 1960 to Yvonne

Use; c Morris A, III, Theresa Elizabeth & Stephanie Anne. Educ: Nicholls State Univ, BS, 62; La State Univ, JD, 65; Sigma Chi. Polit & Govt Pos: Mem, Terrebonne Parish Reapportionment Comn, La, 69-70, secy, 69; La State Rep, 70- Mem: Nat Soc State Legislators; KofC; Houma-Terrebonne CofC; Terrebonne Sportsman's League; Terrebonne Quarterback Club. Relig: Roman Catholic. Legal Res: 109 Burkwall Dr Houma LA 70360 Mailing Add: PO Box 828 Houma LA 70360

LOUDEN, SILAS (D)
Pres, Desoto Co Dem Party, Miss
b Lake Cormorant, Miss, Jan 26, 17; s Eliash Louden & Fannie Noah L; m 1952 to Solomia Dukes; c Gloria Ann, Enda Mae, Ester, Silas, Jr & Lucilla. Educ: Booker T Washington High Sch, Tenn, 4 years. Polit & Govt Pos: Pres, Desoto Co Dem Party, 68- Bus & Prof Pos: Ordained minister, 55-; social worker, North Miss Rural Legal Serv, 69-71. Mil Serv: Entered as Pvt, Army, 42, released as S/Sgt, 45, after serv in 3981st Om Trk Co, 42-44; Victory Medal; Am Theatre Ribbon; European-Africa-MidE Theatre Ribbon with four Bronze Battle Stars; Three Overseas Serv Bars; Victory Conduct Medal. Publ: Articles in World Book of Encyclopedias, Ebony Mag & Memphis Tri-State Defender. Mem: Mason; Men Club Am; NAACP (pres, Desoto). Honors & Awards: Desoto Co Citizen Award, 67; Afro-Am Leadership Award; Masonic Award in Humanities, State of Miss, 73. Relig: Baptist. Mailing Add: PO Box 206 Walls MS 38680

LOUGH, RAYMOND EVERETT (R)
Chmn, Pushmataha Co Rep Comt, Okla
b Tulsa, Okla, Aug 28, 35; s Raymond Sanford Lough & DeVerne Esbaugh L; m 1962 to Barbara Ann Trout; c Stuart Sanford & Gregory Keith. Educ: Tulsa Univ, 54-58. Polit & Govt Pos: Chmn, Pushmataha Co Rep Comt, Okla, 72- Bus & Prof Pos: Cashier, State Nat Bank, Weleetka, Okla, 63-68 & City Nat Bank, Lawton, Okla, 68-70; vpres, Farmers Exchange Bank, Antlers, 70-75. Mil Serv: Entered as E-1, Navy, 57, released as E-5, 61, after serv in VP-47, Whidbey Island Wash, 59-61; Good Conduct Medal. Mem: Lions (pres, 74-75); CofC; AF&AM. Relig: Methodist. Mailing Add: 901 NE Third St Antlers OK 74523

LOURIE, ISADORE E (D)
SC State Sen
b St George, SC, Aug 4, 32; s Louis Lourie & Ann Friedman L; m 1959 to Susan Reiner; c Lance, Joel & Neal. Educ: Univ SC, LLB, 56; pres student body, 53; Blue Key; Phi Epsilon Pi. Polit & Govt Pos: SC State Rep, 65-72; deleg, Dem Nat Conv, 72; SC State Sen, 73- Bus & Prof Pos: Attorney-at-law. Mem: Am & State Trial Lawyers Asn; SC Jaycees; Civitan Club; B'nai B'rith. Honors & Awards: Named Young Man of the Year, Columbia, SC, 60. Relig: Jewish. Mailing Add: State House Columbia SC 29211

LOUX, RICHARD CHARLES (PETE) (D)
Kans State Rep
b Ottawa, Kans, Apr 2, 29; s John Peter Loux & Zelma Sutherland L; m 1948 to Opal Lee Hill; c Chrysa Jeanne, Marilyn Lee, Joan Lorraine, Judy Janel, Mary Jane, Paula Jean & Richard Lawrence. Educ: Wichita State Univ, BA, 51. Polit & Govt Pos: Kans State Rep, 95th Dist, 65-, Dem Leader, Kans State House of Rep, 69- Bus & Prof Pos: Pres, Wichita Estate Planning Coun, 66-67 & Wichita CPA, 64-65. Mem: Kiwanis; Am Inst CPA; Nat Asn Acct; United Cerebral Palsy Asn Am (dir). Relig: Catholic. Mailing Add: 237 S Custer Wichita KS 67213

LOVE, CLARENCE CHESTER (D)
Kans State Rep
b Weir City, Kans, Feb 24, 22; s Arthur James Love & Frances Frey L; m 1941 to Travestine Myers; c Marva (Mrs John Roberson), Cheryl (Mrs Nelson Thompson), Travestine (Mrs Clarence Moore), Terri Lynn & Clarence Jr. Educ: Kans State Teachers Col, 2 years. Polit & Govt Pos: Kans State Rep, 67- Bus & Prof Pos: Owner, dry cleaners, 46-60. Mil Serv: Entered as Pvt, Army, 44, released as S/Sgt, 45, after serv in Qm, Pac, 44-45. Mem: Mason; Cleaners Union 12; Orient Consistory. Relig: Methodist. Mailing Add: 2853 Parkview Kansas City KS 66104

LOVE, CLYDE B (D)
Mem, Calif Dem State Cent Comt
b Tupelo, Miss, Nov 2, 21; s Thomas L Love & Mont Stockard L; m 1946 to Phyllis Jean Briney; c Jack D & Russell A. Polit & Govt Pos: Mem, Calif Dem State Cent Comt, 68- Bus & Prof Pos: Pres, Cent Calif Musicast, Pac Coin Machine Distributors & Safety Marker Co; vpres, Nickabob Sales Co & ABC Music Serv; secy-treas, Commercial Properties & Commercial Finance Co; partner, Mineral King Broadcasters, Rebfin of Calif & Mooney Develop Assoc. Mil Serv: Entered as SF 3/C, Navy, Seabees, 43, released as SF 2/C, 45, after serv in 105th Bn & PAD 3, Pac Theatre, 44-45. Mem: Mt Whitney Area Boy Scouts (bd dirs); Visalia Moose; CofC; Elks; Kiwanis. Relig: Protestant. Mailing Add: 933 W Iris St Visalia CA 93277

LOVE, HAROLD M (D)
Tenn State Rep
b Nashville, Tenn, Sept 8, 19; s Samuel D Love & Lillian C Adams L; m 1959 to Mary Alice Yancey; c Chrystal Faye, Candyce A, Cheryl L & Carolyn A. Educ: Tenn State Univ, BS, 39; Fisk Univ, MA, 49; Alpha Kappa Mu; Omega Psi Phi. Polit & Govt Pos: Councilman, Nashville, Tenn, 61-63; metrop councilman, Nashville & Davidson Co, 63-; Tenn State Rep, Fifth Dist, 68- Bus & Prof Pos: Agt, Atlanta Life Ins Co, 48-67; part-time instr, Fisk Univ, 57-66; agt, Prudential Ins Co, 67- Mil Serv: Entered as Pvt, Army, 42, released as First Sgt, 45, after serv in Inf & Qm, ETO, 44-45; ETO Ribbon; Good Conduct Medal with Three Battle Stars. Publ: Pilot Mag, Nat Negro Ins Asn. Mem: Nashville Life Underwriters Asn; North End Citizenship Asn; Better Educ Promoters of N Nashville; 100 Men Club of Lee Chapel. Relig: Methodist. Mailing Add: 4207 Drakes Hill Nashville TN 37218

LOVE, JIMMY LEWIS (D)
NC State Rep
b Sanford, NC, Dec 21, 34; s James Alonzo Love & Willie Brannon L; m 1957 to Etta Brown Howard; c Joni Brown, Jimmy L, Jr & Melody Campbell. Educ: Univ NC, AB, 53, LLB, 60. Polit & Govt Pos: Pres Lee Co Young Dem Club, NC, 58; solicitor, Lee Co Criminal Court, 61-66; NC State Rep, 66- Bus & Prof Pos: Law clerk to Chief Justice, NC Supreme Court, 60-61. Mil Serv: 2nd Lt, Air Force, 57-58; serv in 464th Combat Support Group, Pope Air Force Base, NC, Judge Advocate Gen, 61-; Capt, Air Force Res, 61- Mem: Am & NC Bar Asns; NC State Bar; Mason; Rotary. Honors & Awards: All-State baseball. Relig: Baptist. Legal Res: Rte 5 Box 953 Sanford NC 27237 Mailing Add: PO Box 309 Sanford NC 27330

LOVE, JOHN ARTHUR (R)
b Gibson City, Ill, Nov 29, 16; s Arthur C Love & Mildred Shaver L; m 1942 to Ann Daniels; c Dan, Andy & Becky. Educ: Univ Denver, BA, 38 & Law Sch, LLB, 41; Omicron Delta Kappa; Sigma Phi Epsilon. Hon Degrees: LLD, Colo Col, Colo Sch Mines & Univ Denver. Polit & Govt Pos: Pres, El Paso Co Young Rep, Colo, 47-48; former mem, Colo Rep Cent Comt & El Paso Co Rep Exec Comt; chmn, Nat Gov Comt State Planning; former mem, Rep Coord Coun; Gov, Colo, 62-73; chmn, Rep Gov Conf, 66; chmn, Nat Gov Conf, 69-70; dir, Off Energy & Natural Resources, 73. Bus & Prof Pos: Attorney, Love, Cole & Murphy, 42-62; pres, Ideal Basic Ind, Inc, 74- Mil Serv: Lt, Navy, 41-42, serv with Black Cat Squadron, SPac; Distinguished Flying Cross; Air Medal with clusters. Mem: Am Bar Asn; Coun of State Govt (exec comt); Mason; Rotary; Am Legion. Honors & Awards: Selected Colo Man of the Year, United Press Int for three years. Relig: Congregational. Mailing Add: 100 Lafayette Denver CO 80218

LOVE, LUCILLE A (R)
RI State Rep
b Fall River, Mass, June 28, 22; m to M Fred Love. Educ: J F Wilbur High Sch, 40. Polit & Govt Pos: Mem, RI Rep State Cent Comt; mem, Little Compton Rep Town Comt, currently, chmn, currently; RI State Rep, 63- Bus & Prof Pos: Housewife & tel operator. Mailing Add: Potterville Rd Little Compton RI 02837

LOVE, RODNEY MARVIN (D)
b Dayton, Ohio, July 18, 08; s Robert M Love & Sallie Ray Schenck L (both deceased); m 1934 to Margaret Sullivan; c Nancy (Mrs Tewksbury) & Robert S. Educ: Ohio State Univ, AB, 30; Univ Dayton, LLB, 33; Mich Law Sch, summer sch for lawyers, 61; Delta Chi. Polit & Govt Pos: Chief dep, Probate Court, Montgomery Co, Ohio, 41-45, probate judge, 45-59; US Rep, Third Dist, Ohio & mem, House Armed Serv Comt, 65-66; judge, Common Pleas Court of Montgomery Co, 69- Bus & Prof Pos: Former partner, Smith & Schnacke, Dayton. Publ: Hospitalized or committed, Pub Welfare Mag, 50; Transfer of decedents estates, Practising Law Inst of Ohio State Bar Asn, 50. Mem: Shriners; Dayton Bicycle Club; Miami Valley Lodge 660, Scottish Rite (32 degree); Sertoma Club; World Fixers. Relig: Presbyterian. Mailing Add: 209 E Dorothy Lane Dayton OH 45419

LOVE, SHIRLEY DEAN (D)
Mem, Fayette Co Dem Exec Comt, WVa
b Oak Hill, WVa, May 15, 33; s Earl Clinton Love & Winona Hall L; m 1952 to Eunice Audrey Painter; c James Chappell, IV, Crystal Lynn & Brian Stephen. Educ: Collins High Sch, Oak Hill, WVa. Polit & Govt Pos: Committeeman, Fayette Co Dem Exec Comt, WVa, 60-; dir, Fayette Co Civil Defense, 69-73; deleg, Dem Nat Conv, 72; secy, Fayette Co Dem Conv, 72. Bus & Prof Pos: Sports dir, WOAY TV, 74-76, news dir, 66-68, sales mgr, 68-73. Mem: Oak Hill Merchants Asn; Mason; RAM; Beni Kedem Temple Shrine; Civitan. Honors & Awards: Fayette Co Skeet Champion, Fayette Co Sportsman Asn, 66-67 & 69-72; Outstanding Young Man of the Year, Jr CofC, 70. Relig: Methodist. Legal Res: Salem Rd Oak Hill WV 25901 Mailing Add: Box 601 Oak Hill WV 25901

LOVELESS, HERSCHEL CELLEL (D)
b Hedrick, Iowa, May 5, 11; s Mace Loveless & Sophia Gearing L; m 1933 to Amelia Rebecca Howard; c Alan Kay & Sandi Ann (Mrs Yates). Educ: High Sch; hon, Phi Theta Pi; assoc mem, Eng Soc. Polit & Govt Pos: Supt, Street Dept, Ottumwa, Iowa, 47, Mayor, 49-53; mem legis comt, Iowa League of Munic, 51, chmn first class cities group, 52; deleg-at-lg, Dem Nat Conv, 52, 56, 60 & 64; Gov, Iowa, 57-61; chmn states comt, Mo Basin Inter-Agency Comn, 59; mem exec coun, Gov Conf, 59; chmn, Nat Adv Comt on Agr, Dem Nat Comt, 59-60; nat chmn, Farmers for Kennedy & Johnson & chmn, Iowa Deleg & rules comt, 60; mem, Renegotiation Bd, 61-69. Bus & Prof Pos: With Chicago, Milwaukee, St Paul & Pac RR, 27-39, 44-47 & 48; power plant operator, John Morrell & Co, 39-44; owner & operator, Gen Munic Supplies, 54-56; vpres, Chromalloy Am Corp, 69- Mem: Lions; Elks; Eagles; Boy Scouts (mem-at-lg). Honors & Awards: Silver Beaver Award, Boy Scouts. Relig: Methodist. Legal Res: 1952 Gladstone St Ottumwa IA 52501 Mailing Add: 7523 17th St NW Washington DC 20012

LOVELL, GORDON (D)
SDak State Rep
Mailing Add: 1817 South Hawthorne SD 57105

LOVELL, RALPH MARSTON (R)
Maine State Rep
b Waldoboro, Maine, Dec 19, 1910; s John Harvey Lovell & Lottie E Magune L; m 1935 to Rita M Ferron; c Marilyn, Maxine, Susan L, Marston D, Ross B, Dean R & Barbara A. Educ: Mass Col Pharm, PhG, 33; Kappa Psi. Polit & Govt Pos: Field adv, Small Bus Admin, Maine, 52-60; US Trade Mission to Africa, Dept of Com, 60; Maine State Sen, York Co, 60-65; Inspection of NASA Installations in US by US Sen Margaret Chase Smith, 63; Maine State Rep, 75-, mem comt on health & insts, Maine House Rep, 75- Bus & Prof Pos: Proprietor, Lovell's Pharmacy, Sanford, 40 years; state mgr, Rexair Div, Martin Parry Corp, 4 years; state distributor, Filter Queen, Health-Mor, Inc, 7 years; wholesale ice cream business, 20 years; owner, Lovell's Ambulance Serv, 15 years. Mem: Elks; Lions; Newcomen Soc NAm; Riverside Grange; Mason. Honors & Awards: Citizen of the Year, Sanford Kiwanis Club, 60; Cert for outstanding serv to the community, Sanford-Springvale Rotary Club, 62; Made mem Indian Tribe of State of Okla, 62; Hon Mem, Nat Cowboy Hall of Fame, Oklahoma City, 62; Special Presidential Award for outstanding serv in Lionism in the Free World, Lions Int, 64. Relig: Congregational. Mailing Add: 83 Main St Sanford ME 04073

LOVENHEIM, DAVID A (R)
b Hackensack, NJ, Oct 1, 42; s Earl P Lovenheim & Belle Yampolski L; m 1965 to Roberta Levine; c Helene & Greta. Educ: Brown Univ, BA, 64; George Washington Univ, JD, 67; Phi Delta Phi. Polit & Govt Pos: Legis aide to US Rep Frank Horton, NY, 65-67, admin asst, 67-, mem, Cong Staff Task Force, Human Investment Act, 66; investigative mission to Europe, Near East & SAsia for Cabinet Comt on Int Narcotics Control, 72. Bus & Prof Pos: Lectr, Washington Semester Prog, Am Univ, 69- Publ: Berlin: a tale of two cities, Brown Daily Herald Suppl, 63, Birmingham in crisis (series), Brown Daily Herald, Providence Eve Bull. Mem: Bull Elephants; Cong Staff Club; George Washington Law Asn; Am & Fed Bar Asns. Relig: Jewish. Legal Res: 90 Georgian Court Rd Rochester NY 14610 Mailing Add: 4140 N 27th St Arlington VA 22207

LOVETT, ROBERT ABERCROMBIE (D)
b Huntsville, Tex, Sept 14, 95; s Robert Scott Lovett & Lavinia Chilton L; m 1919 to Adele Quartley Brown; c Evelyn (deceased), Robert Scott, II. Educ: Yale Univ, BA, 18; Harvard

Grad Schs, 19-21. Hon Degrees: LLD, Amherst Col, Brown Univ, Columbia Univ, Harvard Univ, Long Island Univ, Princeton Univ, Sam Houston State Teachers Col & Williams Col; MA & LLD, Yale Univ. Polit & Govt Pos: Spec asst to Secy of War, 40-41, Asst Secy of War for Air, 41-45; Undersecy of State, 47-49; Dep Secy Defense, 50-51; Secy of Defense, 51-53; consult to President Kennedy, 61-63. Bus & Prof Pos: Clerk, Nat Bank of Com, New York, 21; gen partner, Brown Bros, Harriman & Co, 26-; dir & mem exec comt, Union Pac RR & subsidiary transportation companies & Union Pac Corp; mem NY Investment Comt, Royal Globe Ins Companies; dir & mem finance comt, CBS, Inc; life mem, Emeritus Corp, Mass Inst Technol. Mil Serv: Entered as A/S, Navy, 17, released as Lt Comdr, 18; Navy Cross; Distinguished Serv Medal; Grand Cross Order Leopold II, Belgium; Presidential Medal of Freedom. Mem: Century Asn; Yale, Creek, Metrop & Links Clubs. Legal Res: Locust Valley Long Island NY 11560 Mailing Add: 59 Wall St New York NY 10005

LOVITT, CRAIG EDWARD (D)
Chmn, Knox Co Dem Cent Comt, Ill
b Terre Haute, Ill, Feb 18, 32; s John Preston Lovitt & Mildred Pence L; single. Educ: Knox Col, BA, 54; Univ Va, MA, 59; Phi Beta Kappa; Delta Sigma Rho; Alpha Delta. Polit & Govt Pos: Chmn, Knox Col Students for Stevenson, Ill, 52; chmn, Knox Co Citizens for Sen Douglas, 54; precinct committeeman, Knox Co Dem Cent Comt, Ill, 60-, chmn, 64-; admin asst to US Rep Gale Schisler, Ill, 65-66; asst to Gov Otto Kerner, Ill, 67-68; committeeman, 19th Cong Dist, Ill State Dem Cent Comt, 67-70; asst to Gov Samuel Shapiro, Ill, 68-69; admin asst to Lt Gov Paul Simon, Ill, 69-72; legis asst to Ill State Senate President Cecil Partee, 72- Bus & Prof Pos: Admissions Counr, Knox Col, 56-57; admin asst to dir of Soviet bloc foreign econ rels proj, Univ Va, 57-59; assoc dir & dir of pub rels, Knox Col, 59-64. Publ: Yugoslavia and the Soviet Union, Pakistan Horizon, 59; State practices to coordinate applications for federal aid grants at the state level, Proc of 1968 Conf on State Aspects of Fed Aid Prog, Ill Comn on Intergovt Coop; Getting people and institutions to cooperate in the local community, Allerton Park Inst Series, No 15, Univ Ill, 69. Mem: Lions. Relig: Unitarian. Mailing Add: 364 Day St Galesburg IL 61401

LOVVORN, W A (D)
Chmn, Randolph Co Dem Exec Comt, Ala
b Woodland, Ala, Nov 28, 04; s Mark Damascus Lovvorn & Frances Traylor L; m 1934 to Lila M McCarley; c Anita (Mrs Ed Dark), Pat (Mrs T D Bivin) & Nance (Mrs Cecile White). Educ: Auburn Univ, BS in Ed, 46, MS in Admin, 57. Polit & Govt Pos: Chmn, Randolph Co Dem Exec Comt, Ala, 74- Bus & Prof Pos: Supt, Randolph Co Bd of Educ, 37-41; prin, Fayetteville High Sch, Sylacauga, Ala, 46-69. Mem: Nat Retired Teachers Asn. Relig: Baptist. Mailing Add: Box 95 Woodland AL 36280

LOW, DANIEL TIEN KEE (R)
b Honolulu, Oahu, Hawaii, Sept 19, 98; s Louis Sam Low (deceased) & Lucy Kyau Tai Fong Wong L; m 1929 to Katherine Hoon Seu Young; c Mildred H O (Mrs Dwight McGraw) & Donald H C. Educ: Univ Hawaii, BS. Polit & Govt Pos: Alt deleg, Rep Nat Conv, 68; Rep co committeeman, Dist 6, Precinct 17, 73- Bus & Prof Pos: Cadastral engr, Co of Maui, Hawaii, retired. Mil Serv: Cpl, Student Army Training Corps, 18; World War I Victory Medal. Mem: Maui Chinese Club; Maui Outdoor Circle; Am Asn Retired Persons; Am Legion; Hawaiian Govt Employees Asn. Relig: Protestant. Legal Res: 324 Oluloa Dr Wailuku HI 96793 Mailing Add: PO Box 962 Wailuku HI 96793

LOW, GEORGE MACK (D)
b Merced, Calif, Aug 2, 42; s George Bryant Low & Virginia McKim L; m 1960 to Madalyn Leigh; c Jeri, George Brian & Jessica. Educ: Univ Utah, BS, 68, 68-69. Polit & Govt Pos: Precinct secy, Blanding Dem, Utah, 70; deleg, Utah Dem State Conv, 70, 71 & 72; chmn, San Juan Co Dem Party, 71-73; justice of peace, Blanding City Court, 72; mem, Utah State Dem Cent Comt, 73-75. Bus & Prof Pos: Educator, San Juan Sch Dist, 69; polit action chmn, San Juan Educ Asn, 70-72. Mem: Utah Justice of Peace Asn; San Juan, Utah & Nat Educ Asns; Blanding Lions. Relig: Latter-day Saint. Mailing Add: PO Box 212 Blanding UT 84511

LOW, NORMAN C, JR (D)
b Talking Rock, Ga, Dec 16, 25; s Norman C Low, Sr & Jewell Bunch L; m 1956 to Helen Hobson; c Michael C, Holly Lynn & Joe C. Educ: NGa Col, 2 years. Polit & Govt Pos: Chmn, Pickens Co Dem Exec Comt, Ga, formerly. Bus & Prof Pos: Owner, NC Low Gen Merchandise, 50-; mgr, NC Low Pulpwood Co, 52- Mil Serv: Entered as Pvt, Marines, 44, released as Sgt, 46, after serv in Second Marine Air Wing, Pac Theater, 45-46. Mem: Mason; Farm Bur; Ga Forestry Asn; Am Pulpwood Asn. Relig: Baptist. Mailing Add: PO Box 5 Talking Rock GA 30175

LOW, STUART M (D)
Mem, Dem State Cent Comt, Conn
b Scarsdale, NY, Sept 3, 17; s Clarence H Low & Madeleine Mayer L; wid; David S & Barbara (Mrs McBride). Educ: Univ Mich, BA, 39. Polit & Govt Pos: Mem, Darien Dem Town Comt, Conn, 66-; mem, Darien Bd Educ, 56-66, vchmn, 64-66; mem, Dem State Cent Comt, Conn, 66-; mem, Conn Transportation Authority, Wethersfield, 75- Bus & Prof Pos: Dir pub rels, Crowell Collier Publ Co, 60-64; pres, Flents Prod Co, Inc, Norwalk, Conn, 64- Mil Serv: Entered as Pvt, Army, 41, released as Capt, 45, after serv in TranspC, ETO, 43-45; Maj, Army Res, 46-58. Mem: Darien Country Club; Indust Safety Equip Asn. Mailing Add: 19 Crooked Mile Rd Darien CT 06820

LOW, THEODORE F (R)
Mem, RI State Rep Cent Comt
b Providence, RI, Mar 31, 27; s Isador S Low & Cecile Siden L; m 1960 to D Kay Hohenthaner; c Sara Beth & Emily Lauren. Educ: Brown Univ, BA, 49; Ohio State Sch Bus, 54; Pi Lambda Phi; pres of class, 49. Polit & Govt Pos: RI State Rep, Fourth Dist, Providence, 65-74; mem, Rep Second Ward Comt, Providence, 65-; chmn, Rep Party of Providence, currently; mem, RI State Rep Cent Comt, currently; vchmn, RI Comn to Name All New Construction, currently. Bus & Prof Pos: Pres, Kinsley Burner & Machine Co, 58-62; pres & chmn bd, Sims Corp, 58- Mil Serv: Entered as Pvt, Army, 44, released as Capt, 52; serv in 43rd Inf & other divs, 8th Army, 44-47, Pac Theater, 47 & Korean Theater, 50-52; Pac & Am Theater & Victory Ribbons; Korean Conflict Ribbon with 3 Battle Stars; UN & Unit Commendation Medals. Mem: Providence Engr Soc; Appalachian Mt Club; Narragansett Boating Club; Swiss Alpine Club; Sierra Club. Honors & Awards: Community Leader of Am Award, 68 & 70; Outstanding Alumnus award, Moses Brown Sch, 69. Relig: Unitarian. Mailing Add: 95 Blackstone Blvd Providence RI 02906

LOWANCE, FRANKLIN E (R)
City Councilman, Santa Barbara, Calif
b Monroe Co, WVa, Dec 29, 07; s William Franklin Lowance & Dora Hill Gibson L; m 1930 to Thelma Duane Beckham; c William Franklin. Educ: Roanoke Col, BS, 27; Duke Univ, AM, 31 & PhD, 35; Sigma Xi. Polit & Govt Pos: City councilman, Santa Barbara, Calif, 65- Bus & Prof Pos: Prof physics, Ga Inst of Technol, 42-50; assoc tech dir, Naval Ord Test Sta, 53-55; vpres, Westinghouse Air Brake Corp, 55-58; vpres, Crosley Div, Avco Corp, 58-60; pres, Advan Technol Corp, 60-63. Publ: Magnetic effects in metals, Phys Rev, 35; Operations Research, Case Inst, 55; Engineering Organization, Riverside Press, 61. Mem: Nat Soc Prof Engrs; Am Soc Civil Engrs (fel); Railway Soc of Pittsburgh; Am Ord Asn; Am Phys Soc. Relig: Presbyterian. Mailing Add: 41 Tierra Cielo Santa Barbara CA 93105

LOWDEN, ELMER W (D)
Conn State Rep
Mailing Add: 60 Fairview Ave Stamford CT 06902

LOWE, A LYNN (R)
Chmn, Ark Rep State Comt
Mailing Add: 25 Arnold Dr Texarkana AR 75501

LOWE, JERE B (R)
Chmn, Poinsett Co Rep Party, Ark
b Fulton, Ky, June 30, 29; s Kellie R Lowe & Nelle Graves L; m 1958 to Gertrude Nidermaier; c Derek Bates & Brendon Slemp. Educ: Univ Louisville, 47-48; Okla Baptist Univ, 48-49; Univ Tenn, DDS, 60; Delta Sigma Delta. Polit & Govt Pos: Chmn, Poinsett Co Rep Party, Ark, 66-; chmn, Northeast Ark Co Rep Chmn, 69- Bus & Prof Pos: Dent health consult, Ark Pub Health Dept, 61- Mil Serv: Entered as Pvt, Air Force, 50, released as S/Sgt, 54, after serv at Laon-Couvron AFB Hosp, France, 52-54. Mem: Mason; Am Legion; Farm Bur; Rotary; Northeast Ark Coun, Boy Scouts (exec bd). Relig: Methodist; mem off bd, First Methodist Church, Harrisburg, Ark. Mailing Add: PO Box 587 Harrisburg AR 72432

LOWE, THOMAS HUNTER (D)
b McDaniel, Md, Jan 1928; s Denton Scott Lowe & Louise Price L; m 1953 to Jane Bradley; c John Vincent & James Monahan. Educ: Towson Jr Col, AA, 50; Washington Col, AB cum laude, 52; Univ Md Law Sch, LLB, 56; Omicron Delta Kappa; Kappa Alpha (pres). Polit & Govt Pos: Law clerk, Supreme Court, Baltimore City, 55-56; mem dept of legis reference, Md House of Deleg, 56-57; Md State Deleg, 59-73, chmn, House Judiciary Comt, 63-68, majority leader, 67-68, speaker, 69-73; gen counsel, Md Dem Party, 67-68; alt deleg, Dem Nat Conv, 68; assoc judge, Court of Spec Appeals, Md, 73- Bus & Prof Pos: Attorney-at-law, 56-73, St Michaels, 58-70, Penn Cent RR, 68-73. Mil Serv: Marine Corps, 45-46. Mem: Miles River Yacht Club; VFW; Talbot Rod & Gun Club; Easton CofC; Talbot Football, Inc. Relig: Protestant. Legal Res: Wittman MD 21676 Mailing Add: 225 Stewart Bldg Easton MD 21601

LOWE, W R, JR (D)
Tenn State Rep
Mailing Add: PO Box 406 Lewisburg TN 37091

LOWENSTEIN, ALLARD K (D)
Dem Nat Committeeman, NY
b Newark, NJ, Jan 16, 29; m 1966 to Jennifer Lyman; c Frank Graham, Thomas Kennedy & Katharine Eleanor. Educ: Univ NC, BA, 49; Yale Univ, LLB, 54. Polit & Govt Pos: Spec asst, Sen Frank Porter Graham, NC, 49; nat chmn, Students for Stevenson, 52; foreign policy asst, Sen Hubert H Humphrey, Minn, 59; alt deleg, Dem Nat Conv, 60, deleg, 68 & 72; US Rep, NY, 69-71; co-chmn, Conf Concerned Dem, 67; nat chmn, Am for Dem Action, 71-73; Dem Nat Committeeman, 72- Bus & Prof Pos: Mem faculty, Stanford Univ, NC State Univ & City Col New York; vis lectr, Harvard Univ, Yale Univ & others. Mil Serv: Enlisted man, Army, 54-56. Publ: Brutal mandate: a journey to southwest Africa, Macmillan, 62. Relig: Jewish. Mailing Add: 163 Lindell Blvd Long Beach NY 11561

LOWENSTEIN, HAROLD LOUIS (R)
Mo State Rep
b Kansas City, Mo, Aug 18, 39; s Herman J Lowenstein & Janice Saffran L; m 1964 to Linda Elaine Hipsh; c Marc Benjamin, Todd Bennett & Susan Beth. Educ: Univ Mo, BS bus admin, 61 & JD, 65; Phi Delta Phi; Zeta Beta Tau. Polit & Govt Pos: Asst attorney gen, Kansas City Off, 71-73; Mo State Rep, 73- Bus & Prof Pos: Assoc attorney, Rogers, Field & Gentry, 65-69; house coun, Am-Multi Cinema, 69-71. Publ: Weekly articles in area newspapers. Mem: Am Judicature Soc; Kansas City & Mo Bar Asns; Am Jewish Comt (bd mem, 71-). Honors & Awards: Vol Award, Joint Action in Community Serv, 72. Relig: Jewish. Mailing Add: 1 E 110 St Kansas City MO 64114

LOWERY, THOMAS JOHN, JR (D)
Chmn, Onondaga Co Dem Comt, NY
b Syracuse, NY, Sept 4, 29; s Thomas John Lowery & Gladys Helen Thurston L; m 1953 to Mary Frances Boynton; c Maureen, Deborah & Martha. Educ: Lemoyne Col, BS, 51; Syracuse Univ Col Law, LLB & JD, 53; Phi Beta Phi; Alpha Phi Omega. Polit & Govt Pos: Treas, Onondaga Co Dem Comt, NY, 66-68, chmn, 70-; comnr, NY State Lottery, 67-; NY coordr, Robert F Kennedy for Pres, 68; alt deleg, Dem Nat Conv, 68; mem exec comt, NY State Dem Comt, currently; Dem Nat Committeeman, NY, currently. Bus & Prof Pos: Partner, Lowery, Carrigan & Keough, Attorneys-at-law, Syracuse, NY, 53-; pres, Syracuse Sand & Gravel Co, 61-63; treas, Onondaga Ready Mix Inc & Consumer Ready Mix Inc, 62-63; dir, Metrop Bank of Syracuse, 65- Mil Serv: Entered as Pvt, Army Res, 52, released as Sgt 1/C, 60, after serv in 1209th ARASU, Syracuse, NY. Mem: Gtr Syracuse CofC; Am Cancer Soc (dir); Cavalry Club; Assocs Lemoyne Col (pres). Relig: Roman Catholic. Legal Res: 5092 Bradbury Dr Syracuse NY 13215 Mailing Add: 1509 Mony Plaza Syracuse NY 13202

LOWMAN, ZELVIN DON (R)
Nev State Assemblyman
b McCune, Kans, Sept 8, 21; s James Martin Lowman & Mary Bonner L; m 1943 to Mary Bethena Hemphill; c Freda (Mrs Douglas Farr), James Fredrick, William Martin & Elizabeth June (Mrs Joseph Herbst); two grandchildren. Educ: Western State Col, Colo, AB, 43; Univ Southern Calif, 46-47. Polit & Govt Pos: Personnel tech, San Diego, Calif, 46-47 & Los Angeles, Calif, 47-50; Nev State Assemblyman, Dist 4, 67-, Majority Floor Leader, 69, chmn, Transp Comt, mem, Bi-partisan Legis Comn, vchmn, Judiciary & Environ & Pub Resources Comts, mem & Chmn, Subcomt Illegal Use of Narcotics & Dangerous Drugs, & others; alt

deleg Rep Nat Conv, 72; mem, Cent Comt, Nev Rep Party. Bus & Prof Pos: Personnel dir, Southern Nev Power Co, 54-57; commercial mgr, Nev Power Co, 57-63, dir pub rels, 63- Mil Serv: Entered as A/S, Navy, 43, released as Lt(jg), 46, after serv in Asiatic-Pac Area & in Korea, 50-54; Capt, Naval Res, 64; Navy Unit Commendation; Armed Forces & Naval Res Ribbons; Asiatic-Pac Theater Ribbon with 4 Stars; Am Theater & Nat Serv Ribbons; Philippines Liberation Ribbon with 2 Stars; Victory Medal. Mem: Boulder Dam Area Boy Scouts (pres); Girl Scouts (comt chmn); Kiwanis of Uptown Las Vegas (pres); Las Vegas CofC; Las Vegas Press Club. Honors & Awards: Meritorious Serv Award, Clark Co Classroom Teachers Asn, Elem Prin Asn & Sec Prin Asn, 67; Service to Mankind Award, N Los Angeles Dist Sertoma Int, 69; 1970 Freedoms Found Honor Cert; Free Enterprise Award of Southern Nev; Thanks Badge, Frontier Girl Scout Coun. Relig: Methodist. Mailing Add: 1246 Cashman Dr La Vegas NV 89102

LOWRY, LEVI SMITH (R)
b Chicago, Ill, Apr 12, 02; s Nathan Arnold Lowry & Stella Kelly L; m 1942 to Cecil Faye Williams; c Julia (Mrs Dennis Lettington) & Jane Ann (Jann) (Mrs William Sutton). Educ: Princeton schs, Princeton, Mo, 12 years; Univ Mo-Columbia, 1 year. Polit & Govt Pos: Alderman, Unionville, Mo, 36-43; chmn, Mercer Co Rep Cent Comt, Mo, formerly; deleg, Rep Nat Comt, 60. Bus & Prof Pos: Yardman, Lowry-Miller Lumber Co, 22-, pres, 63- Mil Serv: Entered as Pvt, Army, 42, released as Pvt, 43, after serv in 321st Combat Engrs, 76th Div. Mem: Princeton Rotary Club; Mason; Shrine; Mercer Co Farm Bur; Am Legion. Relig: Baptist. Mailing Add: 304 S Ballew Princeton MO 64673

LOWRY, SAMUEL EARLE (D)
Chmn, Oconee Co Dem Party, SC
b Seneca, SC, Oct 10, 10; s Earle Westmoreland Lowry & Roxie Duncan L; m 1945 to Fayetta Alexander; c Brenda (Mrs Cromer), Sandra Lou & Lydia Kaye. Educ: Clemson Univ, BS in Elec Eng. Polit & Govt Pos: Mem, Oconee Co Sch Bd, SC, 60-68, chmn, 62-68; dir, SC Sch Bd Asn, 62-68; chmn, Oconee Co Centennial Comn, 68; alt deleg, Dem Nat Conv, 68 & 72; chmn, Oconee Co Dem Party, SC, 68- Bus & Prof Pos: Teacher, Oconee Schs, Seneca, SC, 33; clerk, Texaco Oil Dist Plant, 33-41; distributor, Texaco Oil, Loris, 46-53 & Seneca, 53-; dir, Oconee Savings & Loan Asn, 59-; dir, Oconee Mem Hosp, 71- Mil Serv: Entered as 2nd Lt, Army, 42, released as Maj, 46, after serv in 1447 Intel Corps Unit, Ft Benning, Ga, Lt Col, Army Res, Retired; Commendation Medal; Victory Medal; Meritorious Serv Unit Award; 4th Serv Command Cert of Commendation. Mem: Am Legion; Farm Bur. Relig: Baptist; deacon, Seneca Baptist Church. Mailing Add: Rte 5 Seneca SC 29678

LOWTHER, DALE CHARLES (D)
Chmn, Wood Co Dem Exec Comt, WVa
b Parkersburg, WVa; s Glen K Lowther & Sophia Dennis L; m 1970 to Donna Blake; c Craig Michael. Educ: Marshall Univ, AB, 66; Lambda Chi Alpha; Robe Men's Leadership; Student Govt; Athletic Bd, 1 year; Base Gold; One of Ten Best Dressed Men. Polit & Govt Pos: Chmn, TeenAge Dem, Pleasants Co, WVa, 60-61; dir, Fourth Cong Young Dem Club WVa, 65-67; cand WVa State Sen, Third Dist, 68; chmn, Wood Co Dem Exec Comt, 72-; mem, Parkersburg City Dem Exec Comt. Mem: Wood Co Classroom Teachers Asn; We Care, Inc (vpres, 72, pres, 73-74); St Marys Elks; Eagles; Jaycees (chaplain, Parkersburg area, 72, dir, 74). Honors & Awards: Transportation Award, WVa Young Dem, 66. Relig: Baptist; dir youth & Christian educ, First Baptist Church of Parkersburg. Mailing Add: 1621 Oak St Parkersburg WV 26101

LOWTHER, GERALD HALBERT (D)
b Slagle, La, Feb 18, 24; s Fred B Lowther & Beatrice Velma Halbert L; m 1946 to Patti Jean Byers; c Teresa, Craig, Natalie & Lisa. Educ: Pepperdine Col, AB, 48; Univ Mo, LLB, 51; Beachcombers; Phi Delta Phi. Polit & Govt Pos: Mem, Mo Savings & Loan Comt, 64-68; mem, Mo Sen Redistricting Comt, 65; deleg, Dem Nat Conv, 68 & 72, mem rules comt, 68; mem, Mo Indust Develop Comt, 68-72; treas, Mo State Dem Party, 68-72. Bus & Prof Pos: Sr partner, Miller, Fairman, Sanford, Carr & Lowther, 51-; bd dirs, Modern Am Life Ins Co, Am Investors Life Ins Co, Founders Am Investment Co, Founders Preferred Life Ins Co, Trans States Security Life Ins Co; vchmn bd dirs, Empire Bank; pres, Cox Med Ctr. Mil Serv: Entered as Pvt, Army, 46, released as Sgt, 47, after serv in Signal Corp. Publ: Pleading res ipsa loquitur, 63 & Defense of products liability cases, 67, Mo Bar J. Mem: Int Asn of Ins Counsel; Law-Sci Acad (lectr); Kiwanis; Ozark Christian Counseling Serv (dir); CofC (dir). Relig: Protestant. Mailing Add: 833 E Elm Springfield MO 65804

LUBNAU, THOMAS E (R)
Chmn, Campbell Co Rep Party, Wyo
b Grosse Pointe, Mich, Oct 23, 31; s Oscar E Lubnau & Mary Ruth Ryan L; m 1956 to Cynthia L'Vere Kirkland; c Thomas Edwin II, Kathryn Lee & Robert Douglas. Educ: Casper Col, AA, 52; Univ Wyo, BA, 57, JD, 60; Sigma Chi. Polit & Govt Pos: Police judge, Gillette, Wyo, 61-; chmn, Campbell Co Rep Party, 63-; dist bar comnr, Fourth Judicial Dist, 64-66; mem bd dirs, Campbell Co Grade Schs, 65-67; alt deleg, Rep Nat Conv, 68. Mil Serv: Entered as Pvt, Army, 54, released as Cpl, 56, after serv in 6th Inf; Nat Defense Serv Award; Good Conduct Medal. Publ: The spouse is a stranger to the deed, 59 & Incorporating non-testamentary documents into a will, 60, Wyo Law J. Mem: Wyo Mining Asn; Asn Petroleum Landmen; Rotary; Odd Fellows; Elks. Relig: Protestant. Mailing Add: PO Box 1028 Gillette WY 82716

LUCAS, BETTYE DANIEL (D)
Pres, Tenn Fedn Dem Women
b Covington, Tenn, Jan 13, 43; d Frank Troy Daniel & Mildred Bradshaw D; m 1967 to Louis Russell Lucas. Educ: Miller-Hawkins Bus Col, Memphis, Tenn, grad, 63. Polit & Govt Pos: Mem, Shelby Co Dem Exec Comt, Tenn, 66-; deleg, Dem Nat Mid-Term Conf, 74; mem, State Dem Exec Comt, Tenn, 73-; pres, Tenn Fedn Dem Women, 75- Bus & Prof Pos: Asst vpres, William B Tanner Co, Memphis, 70- Mailing Add: 2100 Fox Run Cove Memphis TN 38138

LUCAS, CHARLES C (D)
b Brackenridge, Pa, Apr 15, 27; s Robert Lee Lucas & Mattie Ellard L; m 1948 to Melverna M Dumas; c Cosetta (Mrs Earl J Pittman), Zorita (Mrs Morris Brown), Darenda (Mrs Gregory Garth), Ranotta (Mrs Eugene T Allensworth), Ricardo & Veleta. Educ: Community Bus Col, New Kensington, Pa, 9 months; AFL-CIO training course, accredited union counr, 67; Allegheny Steel Training Dept in Supv, 69; NAACP Leadership Develop Inst, 70. Polit & Govt Pos: Mem steering comt, Allegheny-Kiski Valley Citizens for Peace, 71-; mem, Umberall Drug Prog, 71-; consult to coordr, Off Econ Opportunity-Citizens Advocate Ctr Progs, 71-; deleg, Dem Nat Conv, 72. Bus & Prof Pos: Prod foreman, Allegheny Ludlum Steel Inc, 70- Mil Serv: Entered as Pvt, Army, 45, released as T/Sgt, 48, after serv in Inf, ETO, 46-47; Good Conduct Ribbon, Overseas Ribbon. Mem: Allegheny Valley YMCA (bd, 72-); Allegheny-Kiski Valley NAACP (pres, 69-); Am Legion; Int Platform Asn; Am for Dem Action. Honors & Awards: Plaque award, Community Leaders of Am, 70, Cert of Merit, 71 & 72; citation, Pa House of Rep, 70; Allegheny Valley CofC Award for community participation, 73; NAACP Spec Pin Award for soliciting over 100 memberships for the year, 74; Allegheny-Kiski Valley NAACP Plaque Award & Testimonial Dinner, 74; plus others. Relig: Methodist. Mailing Add: 836 Third Ave Brackenridge PA 15014

LUCAS, DAVID E (D)
Ga State Rep
Mailing Add: 950 Barney A Smith Motors Gray Hwy Macon GA 31201

LUCAS, ETHEL VIOLET (D)
Chmn, Fulton Co Dem Exec Comt, Ohio
b Linton, Ind, Oct 15, 13; d Desire Cuvelier & Minnie Barnett C; m 1931 to Robert Elmo Lucas; c Patricia Lee & Leslie Louise (Mrs Neumann). Educ: Linton High Sch. Polit & Govt Pos: Rural mail carrier, Ohio, 45-60; pres, Fulton Co Bd of Elec, 48-; precinct committeewoman, Dem Party, 50-; postmaster, Wauseon, 52-53; alt deleg, Dem Nat Conv, 60, 64 & 68; pres, Ohio State Elec Off, 66, secy, 70 & 73; former secy-treas, Dem Exec Comt, mem, 70-; Ohio State Cent Committeewoman, 70-; chmn, Fulton Co Dem Exec Comt, 71- Mem: Eastern Star; State Bd of Elec Officers, Bus & Prof Women's Club; Elks Ladies. Relig: Congregational; mem, Church Choir. Mailing Add: 311 S Fulton St Wauseon OH 43567

LUCAS, GEORGE BOND (D)
Chmn, Jefferson Co Dem Comt, Colo
b New Orleans, La, Dec 21, 24; s George Cook Lucas & Mabel Helen Bond L; m 1962 to Euphama Jane Van Tuyl; c Van Tuyl & Euphama Jane (Mrs Thomas De Mars, Jr). Educ: Tulane Univ, BS, 48; Iowa State Univ, PhD, 52; Alpha Chi Sigma; Phi Lambda Upsilon. Polit & Govt Pos: Precinct committeeman, Jefferson Co Dem Comt, 72-, chmn, 75- Bus & Prof Pos: Post doctoral fel, Northwestern Univ, Evanston, Ill, 52-53; sr research chemist, Rohm & Haas C, Huntsville, Ala, 53-56; asst prof of chem, Colo Sch Mines, Golden, Colo, 56, assoc prof, 61-66, prof, 67- Mil Serv: Entered as Pvt, Army, 43, released as Pfc, 46, after serv in Southwest Pac Theater, 44-45; Western New Guinea Campaign with Three Bronze Stars; Philippines Campaign Ribbon with Two Bronze Stars. Mem: Am Chem Soc; Geochemical Soc; Sigma Xi. Honors & Awards: Outstanding Teacher Award, Standard Oil Found, 67 & 74. Relig: Unitarian. Legal Res: 50 Loomis Way Rte 2 Golden CO 80401 Mailing Add: Dept Chem Colo Sch Mines Golden CO 80401

LUCAS, HENRY, JR (R)
Mem Exec Comt, Rep Nat Comt
b Rahway, NJ, Feb 27, 32; m to Cerella A, MD; c Karen, Kimberly & Kyle. Educ: Howard Univ, BS, 54; Meharry Med Col, DDS, 60. Polit & Govt Pos: Dentists for Reagan for Gov, 66 & 70; deleg, Rep Nat Conv, 68; chmn Region II, Citizens for Nixon/Agnew, 68; deleg, Calif Rep State Conv, 69 & 70; Rep Dentists for Reagan for Gov, 70; Black chmn, Northern Calif Comt for Reelec of the President, 72; mem exec comt, Rep Nat Comt, currently; chmn, Nat Black Rep Coun, currently. Bus & Prof Pos: Pvt practice dent, Franklin Hosp Med Ctr, San Francisco; pres & chmn bd, Enterplastics Inc, San Francisco; mem faculty, Div Preventive Dent & Community Health, Univ Calif Sch Dent, San Francisco. Mil Serv: Entered Air Force, 60, released as Capt, 62, after serv in Chanute AFB Hosp, Urbana, Ill. Mem: Am Acad Gen Dent; fel Am Acad Gen Dent; Am Dent Asn; Int Acad Orthodontics; Am Soc Dent for Children. Honors & Awards: Outstanding Young Man in Am, 66. Mailing Add: 34 Ora Way San Francisco CA 94131

LUCAS, JAY SCOTT (R)
NH State Rep
b Newport, NH, Oct 18, 54; s Harry F Lucas & Norma Murchie L; single. Educ: St Paul's Sch Advan Studies Prog, 71; Yale Univ, currently; Yale Polit Union. Polit & Govt Pos: Deleg, NH Const Conv, 74-; NH State Rep, 75-, mem house judiciary comt, NH House Rep, 75-76, mem house Rep caucus, 75-, mem young legis caucus, 75, clerk, Sullivan Co Deleg, 75. Mailing Add: 52 N Main St Newport NH 03773

LUCAS, MARY LOUISA (D)
b Marion, Va, Aug 2, 36; d Benjamin Lucas & Mary Rosa Gibson. Educ: Mary Washington Col; Pan-Am Sch. Polit & Govt Pos: Admin Asst to US Rep John J Flynt, Jr, Ga, currently. Bus & Prof Pos: Exec secy, Fulton Nat Bank of Atlanta, 57-62. Mem: Am Shetland Pony Club; Am Horse Show Asn; Midwest Hockney Soc. Relig: Methodist. Legal Res: Griffin GA Mailing Add: 9 Fifth St SE Washington DC 20003

LUCAS, SCOTT WIKE (D)
b Cass Co, Ill, Feb 19, 92; s William D Lucas & Sarah Catherine Underbrink L; m 1923 to Edith Biggs; c Scott W, Jr. Educ: Ill Wesleyan Univ, LLB, 14; Phi Alpha Delta. Hon Degrees: LLD, Ill Wesleyan Univ, John Marshall Law Sch & Western Md Col. Polit & Govt Pos: State attorney, Mason Co, Ill, 20-26; deleg, Dem Nat Conv, 32 & 40-64; chmn, Ill State Tax Comn, 33-35; US Rep, Ill, 35-39; US Sen, 39-50, majority leader, US Senate, 49-50; chmn Midwest Regional Hq, Dem Nat Comt for Campaign to Reelect Franklin D Roosevelt, 40. Bus & Prof Pos: Attorney-at-law, 14-; mem bd dirs, State Loan & Finance Corp & Washington Mutual Investors Fund, currently. Mil Serv: Entered as Pvt, Army, 18, released as Lt, 18, after serv at Fortress Monroe, Va; Officers' Res Corps, 18-34, then Judge Adv Gen with rank of Col, Ill Nat Guard. Mem: Am, Ill & DC Bar Asns; Burning Tree Club, Bethesda (pres); Am Legion. Honors & Awards: Played prof baseball, 3-I League, 3 years; won 3 letters, baseball, basketball & football, Ill Wesleyan Univ. Relig: Baptist. Legal Res: 314 W Main St Havana IL 62644 Mailing Add: 1028 Connecticut Ave NW Washington DC 20036

LUCCO, JOE ENRICO (D)
Ill State Rep
b Dawson, NMex, Apr 29, 12; s Lorenzo Lucco & Mary Marco L; m 1937 to Marina Tepatt; c Marina Louise (Mrs Eovaldi); Joseph William. Educ: Greenville Col, AB, 34; Univ Ill, Champaign, MA, 41. Polit & Govt Pos: Ill State Rep, 56th Dist, 75- Bus & Prof Pos: Teacher, athletic coach, high sch prin & asst supt for various schs in Pocahontas, Kincaid & Edwardsville, Ill, 34-73. Mem: Phi Delta Kappa; KofC; Rotary. Honors & Awards: Ill Basketball Coaches Hall of Fame. Relig: Catholic. Legal Res: 214 Banner Edwardsville IL 62025 Mailing Add: 109 Purcell Edwardsville IL 62025

LUCE, CLARE BOOTHE (R)
b New York, NY; d William F Boothe & Ann Snyder B; m 1935 to Henry R Luce. Educ: The Castle, Tarrytown, NY, 17-19. Hon Degrees: Numerous hon degrees from various cols

& univs. Polit & Govt Pos: US Rep, Conn, 43-47; US Ambassador to Italy, 53-57. Bus & Prof Pos: Assoc ed, Vogue, 30; managing ed, Vanity Fair, 33-34; newspaper columnist, 34; playwright, 35-; consult, Encycl Britannica. Publ: The Women (play), 37; Margin for Error (play), 39; ed column, Without Portfolio, McCall's Mag, 60-67; plus others. Honors & Awards: Grand Cross of the Order of Merit of the Ital Repub, 56; Dame of Malta, Rome, 56; plus numerous other awards. Relig: Roman Catholic. Mailing Add: 4559 Kahala Ave Honolulu HI 96816

LUCE, GORDON C (R)
b San Diego, Calif, Nov 21, 25; s Edgar A Luce & Carma C Coppard L; m 1955 to Karon Turnbow; c Randall, Kelly & Andrew. Educ: Stanford Univ, BA, 50 & MBA, 52; Am Savings & Loan Sch, grad; Chi Psi. Polit & Govt Pos: alt deleg, Rep Nat Conv, 64, deleg & whip, Calif Favorite Son Deleg, 68, deleg, 72; chmn, San Diego Co Rep Assocs, 64; chmn & trustee, Rep Assocs, 66-67; chmn, San Diego Co Reagan for Gov Comt, 66; mem exec comt, Calif Rep State Cent Comt, 69-76, vchmn, Comt, 71-72, chmn, 73-75; secy bus & transportation, State Calif. Bus & Prof Pos: Pres, Am Savings & Loan Inst, 59. Mil Serv: Entered as Pvt, Army, 44, released as Cpl, 46, after serv in 97th Inf Div, Europe & Japan, 44-46; Bronze Star; Combat Inf Badge; European Oper Medal with two Battle Stars. Mem: San Diego Downtown Asn; Univ Club; Stanford Club; San Diegans, Inc; Calif State CofC (dir); Scripps Hosp of La Jolla. Relig: Episcopal. Mailing Add: PO Box 2592 San Diego CA 92183

LUCENTI, MARGARET (D)
Mem, Dem Nat Comt, Vt
Mailing Add: 3 Jacques St Barre VT 05401

LUCENTO, JANE (D)
Polit & Govt Pos: Mem, Dem Nat Comt, WVa, formerly. Mailing Add: PO Box 308 Alpoca WV 24710

LUCERO, ANTHONY A (D)
b Albuquerque, NMex, Mar 5, 21; s Bart Lucero & Dolores Romero L; m 1946 to Flora Zamora; c Anthony Ely, Esther Marie, Marian Edissa, Judieth Elaine, Thaddeus Paul & Flora Therese. Educ: Univ NMex, BA; Am Univ, 1 year; Honors Degree; mem, Const Comt; vpres, Sr Class, 52. Polit & Govt Pos: Precinct committeeman, Bernalillo Co, NMex, 63-65; NMex State Rep, Dist Six, 64-66; NMex State Sen, formerly, mem, Finance Comt, Rules Comt & Legis Coun, NMex Senate, formerly. Bus & Prof Pos: Elem teacher, Fairfax Co Va, 52-54; Bernalillo Co, NMex, 54-55; ins broker, Lucero Agency, 55-60; state auditor, Bur of Revenue, 59-60; self employed, Tyra Construction Co, 60-65; ins & stock broker, NMex Securities & pub rels, Paisano Investments, 65- Mil Serv: Entered as Pvt, Army, 40, released as T/4, 45, after serv in ETO; ETO Ribbon; Peacetime Medal; Good Conduct Medal; Arrowheads for Invasions; Combat Stars. Mem: VFW; DAV; Am Legion; Lions Club; Toastmasters Club. Relig: Roman Catholic. Mailing Add: 2010 Rio Grande Blvd NW Albuquerque NM 87104

LUCERO, CHRIS M (D)
NMex State Rep
Mailing Add: Box 7012 Albuquerque NM 87104

LUCERO, LEO (D)
Colo State Rep
Mailing Add: 109 Sharon Place Pueblo CO 81006

LUCEY, PATRICK JOSEPH (D)
Gov, Wis
b LaCrosse, Wis, Mar 21, 18; s Gregory Charles Lucey & Ella Young McNamara L; m 1951 to Jean Vlasis; c Paul, Laurie & David. Educ: Univ Wis, 46. Polit & Govt Pos: Wis State Assemblyman, 49-50; state chmn, Proxmire Senate Campaign, 57; state chmn, Dem Party, 57-63; Lt Gov, Wis, 65-66, Gov, 71-; ex officio deleg, Dem Nat Mid-Term Conf, 74. Mil Serv: Entered as Pvt, 41, released as Capt, 45. Mailing Add: Governor's Off State Capitol Madison WI 53702

LUCHT, VIRGINIA LEA (R)
Committeewoman, Mont State Rep Exec Comt
b Great Falls, Mont, Apr 29, 21; d Riley Davis Robinson & Nina Larkin R; m 1941 to Archie H Lucht; c Linda Kay (Mrs Farrell) & Robin Douglas; 3 grandchildren. Educ: Northern Mont Col, dipl 41; Mont State Univ, 49; Univ Ariz, summer 72. Polit & Govt Pos: Precinct Rep committeewoman, Libby & Helena, Mont, 59-75; pres, Rep Women's Club, Libby & Helena, 65-71; committeewoman, Mont State Rep Exec Comt, 65-, mem state exec bd & Western Dist committeewoman, 73-; treas, Mont Fedn Rep Women, 59-71, publicity chmn, 71-73. Bus & Prof Pos: Adv bd mem, Small Bus Admin, 73- Mil Serv: Entered as Pvt, Marine Corps, 42, released as Pfc, 45, after serv in San Francisco, 43-45. Mem: Delta Kappa Gamma; Lewis & Clark Sch Employees (credit comt, 73-); Mont Educ Asn (state citizenship chmn, 71-). Honors & Awards: Outstanding Sec Teacher, Helena Pub Schs, 72 & 73. Relig: Presbyterian. Mailing Add: 1923 Broadway Helena MT 59601

LUCKHARDT, ESTHER DOUGHTY (R)
Wis State Rep
b Wis; married; c Thomas, Mary & Patricia Doughty. Educ: Horicon High Sch, grad. Polit & Govt Pos: Wis State Rep, 62- Bus & Prof Pos: Ins & real estate agt. Mem: Am Legion Auxiliary; Izaak Walton League; VFW Auxiliary; Ins Agts Adv Bd; Dodge Co Rep Women's Club. Mailing Add: 211 N Hubbard Horicon WI 53032

LUCKHART, ELTON WAGNER (R)
Chmn, Mahoning Co Rep Cent & Exec Comts, Ohio
b Tylersburg, Pa, Mar 26, 10; s John Webster Luckhart & Harriet Wagner; m 1964 to Elaine Cossler; c Leland Richard, Robert Allen & Shirley. Educ: Univ Ala, BS in Educ; Univ Colo, MA in Eng Lit; Youngstown State Univ, JD; Phi Delta Kappa; Kappa Delta Pi; Psi Chi; Athenian Club. Polit & Govt Pos: Asst city law dir, Youngstown, Ohio, 48-54; pres, Mahoning Co Young Rep Club, 48-50; official, Rep Nat Conv, 52, deleg, 64 & 68; pres, McKinley Club of Niles, 55; asst prosecutor, Mahoning Co, 56-58; mem, Mahoning Co Bd Elecs, 58-62 & 70-; chmn, Mahoning Co Rep Cent & Exec Comts, 59-70 & 74-; mem, Ohio State Cent & Exec Comts, 65-66. Bus & Prof Pos: Supv prin, West Middlesex Schs, 42-45; instr, Youngstown State Univ, 48-54; sr partner, Luckhart, Mumaw, Morrisroe, Zellers & Robinson, 58-; dir, Indust Engine Serv Co, 59-; dir, Falcon Foundry Corp, 65- Mem: Ohio State, Mahoning Co & Trumbull Co Bar Asns; Odd Fellows. Relig: Unitarian. Legal Res: 2705 Normandy Dr Youngstown OH 44511 Mailing Add: 305 Legal Arts Ctr Youngstown OH 44503

LUCY, JACQUELINE TILLMAN (D)
Committeewoman, Vt Dem State Comt
b Temple, Tex, Sept 25, 44; d Robert Tillman & Carmen Morales T; div; c Carmen Heather & Jennifer Dawn. Educ: Col Notre Dame (Md), BA, 66; Auburn Univ, 67. Polit & Govt Pos: Committeewoman, Vt Dem State Comt, 73-; treas, Orange Co Dem Comt, 73; chmn, Thetford Dem Town Comt, 73-; deleg, Dem Nat Mid-Term Conf, 74. Bus & Prof Pos: Dir & teacher, Hartford Day Care, 75- Legal Res: Post Mills VT 05058 Mailing Add: 6 Fairview Terrace White River Junction VT 05001

LUCY, WILLIAM (D)
Chmn, DC Dem Party
Mailing Add: 1625 L St NW Seventh Floor Washington DC 20005

LUDDEN, BARBARA ANN HARRISON (R)
b Washington, DC, Nov 6, 32; d William Henry Harrison & Lois Magee H; m 1957 to James Gregory Ludden. Educ: US Dept Agr Grad Sch, 50-51; Am Univ, 51-52. Polit & Govt Pos: Mem, US Atomic Energy Comn, Reactor Develop Div, 50-54; personal & polit secy to US Rep Marguerite Stitt Church, 54-63; mem, Citizens Comt on Fair Labor Standards, 57; mem, US Deleg to UN, 61; admin asst to US Rep Donald Rumsfeld, Ill, 63-69; conf asst to dir, Off Econ Opportunity, 69-70; admin asst to US Rep Robert McClory, Ill, 70-71; cong liaison officer, Gen Serv Admin, 71-72; dir of cong affairs, Pay Bd, Exec Off of the President, 72-73; assoc dir, Cost of Living Coun for Cong Affairs, 73; dir cong affairs, US Consumer Prod Safety Comn, 73-75, exec asst to chmn, 75- Mem: Cong Secretaries Club; Immaculate Conception Acad Alumnae; Nat Rep Sustaining Fund; Capitol Hill Club. Relig: Roman Catholic. Mailing Add: 8512 Stable Dr Alexandria VA 22308

LUDDY, WILLIAM F (D)
Committeeman, NY State Dem Party
b Cambridge, NY, Oct 23, 10; s Thomas W Luddy & Mary Kane L; m 1940 to Virginia M O'Neil; c Thomas W, Brian A, David F, James N & Jean M. Educ: Cambridge High Sch. Polit & Govt Pos: Committeeman, NY State Dem Party, 41-; deleg, Dem Nat Conv, 48, 54, 60, 64 & 68; chmn, Westchester Co Dem Party, NY, 15 years, mem exec comt, currently. Mailing Add: 58 Gedney Park Dr White Plains NY 10605

LUDERS, EDWARD T (D)
Wash State Rep
Mailing Add: N 5620 Moore Spokane WA 99208

LUDLAM, LILLIAN J (R)
Secy, Conn Rep State Cent Comt
b New York, NY, Nov 1, 18; m 1946 to Richard Price Ludlam. Educ: Rider Col; New Sch for Social Research. Polit & Govt Pos: Pres, New Hartford Women's Rep Club, Conn, 54; pres, Litchfield Co Women's Rep Club, 56-62; committeewoman, Conn State Rep Cent Comt, 60-64 & 66-, secy, 64-, secy & bd mem, Pub Rels Comt, 65-, mem, Planning Comt; chmn, Liaison Comt, Rep Coun, 63; vpres, Sixth Cong Dist W Rep Party, currently; alt deleg, Rep Nat Conv, 72; chmn, Gov Consumer Adv Coun, 72-; mem adv coun, Small Bus Admin, 73- Bus & Prof Pos: Asst bus mgr, Electronics Mag, McGraw-Hill Publ Co, NY, 38-44; admin asst, Lord & Taylor, 44-45; advert & publicity dir, Monitor Equip Corp, 45-48; morning radio prog, Sta WTOR, 53-55; acct exec, B R Martin Assocs, Ill, 57-; vpres, Village Lumber & Oil, Conn, 60-; publ, Foothills Trader, New Hartford, Conn, 64- Pub: Connecticut west, 8/70; feature writing. Mem: Gov Adv Coun; New Hartford Community Club (dir); Conn State Fedn Women's Clubs; Winsted Area Community Chest (vpres). Relig: Congregational; mem, Stewardship Comt. Mailing Add: Town Hill New Hartford CT 06057

LUEBECK, ALFRED S (D)
Mont State Rep
b Butte, Mont, Jan 6, 39; s Joseph Luebeck & Gertrude Masur L; m 1967 to Clare Ann Gannon; c Steven, Laura & Mark. Educ: Mont State Univ, BS. Polit & Govt Pos: Mont State Rep, 75- Bus & Prof Pos: Teacher, Butte High Sch, 61-75. Mem: Mont Fedn Teachers. Relig: Catholic. Mailing Add: 2710 Amherst Ave Butte MT 59701

LUECK, HENRY LONGLEY (D)
Chmn, Kans Dem State Comt
b Holton, Kans, Jan 18, 13; s Charles Daniel Lueck & Bertha Longley L; m 1945 to Alice Hess. Educ: Univ Kans, 30-32; Kappa Sigma. Polit & Govt Pos: Pres, Kans Young Dem, 40-41; chmn, Jackson Co Dem Party, 47-70; chmn, First Cong Dist Dem Party, 47-67; deleg, Dem Nat Conv, 56 & 60; chmn, Kans Dem State Comt, 75-; mem, Dem Nat Comt, 75- Bus & Prof Pos: Owner & mgr, Lueck Grain Co, Netawaka, Kans, 32-74; mem, Kans Grain Adv Comn, 58-61 & 69-, chmn, 71-; mem bd dirs, Kans Agr Labor Rels Bd, 72- Mil Serv: Entered as Pvt, Army, 41, released as T/Sgt, 45, after serv in Co B, 103rd Inf, 43rd Div, Pac, 42-45; 2 Purple Hearts; Combat Inf Badge. Mem: DAV; Am Legion; VFW; Mason; Rotary. Relig: United Methodist. Mailing Add: PO Box 108 Netawaka KS 66516

LUECK, LORAYNE E (DFL)
Secy, 27th Sen Dist Dem-Farmer-Labor Orgn, Minn
b Arlington, Minn, Apr 10, 18; d William Nolting & Jessie Rethwill N; m to Roy O Lueck, div; c Joleen (Mrs Fred Pearson), JesAnn, Janell, Jetabee, Jennifer & Jolette. Educ: Minneapolis Bus Col, 37. Polit & Govt Pos: Judge, Bloomington Elecs, Minn, 54-; pres, Bloomington Dem-Farmer-Labor Women's Club, 67-69; chmn, 11th Precinct Caucus, 69-70; secy, 27th Sen Dist Dem-Farmer-Labor Orgn, 70-; Dem-Farmer-Labor Party cand, S Sch Bd, Dist 271, Bloomington, 72. Mem: Bloomington Blood Donors Club (pres, 67-); Hennepin Co Nat Found (secy, 69-); SSuburban Toastmistress (secy, 72-73, pres, 73-75); Metro Unit Parliamentarians (secy, formerly, pres, 73-75); Bloomington Hist Asn. Honors & Awards: Nominated for Woman of Year, Bloomington. Relig: United Methodist; secy, Hillcrest Methodist Off Bd, 63-66 & 67-70. Mailing Add: 9000 Nicollet Ave Bloomington MN 55420

LUEDTKE, ROLAND ALFRED (R)
Nebr State Sen
b Lincoln, Nebr, Jan 4, 24; s Alfred C Luedtke & Caroline Senne L; m 1951 to Helen Dorothy Snyder; c Larry O & David A. Educ: Univ Nebr, BS, 49; Col Law, Univ Nebr, LLB, 51; Delta Theta Phi. Polit & Govt Pos: Treas, Lancaster Co Young Rep, Nebr, 46-47; treas, Nebr Young Rep, 53-54; dep secy of state, Nebr, 53-59; jr pres, Founders Day, Rep Orgn, 58; chmn, Lancaster Co Rep Party, 62-64; Nebr State Sen, 28th Legis Dist, 67-, chmn, Judiciary Comt, Nebr State Senate, 71-74. Bus & Prof Pos: Partner, Law Firm of Kier & Luedtke, 62-72, pvt

law practice, 73- Mil Serv: Entered as Pvt, Army, 43, released as Pfc, 45, after serv in 26th Inf Div & Ninth Air Force, ETO, 44-45; Bronze Star Medal; Purple Heart; Combat Inf Badge; France & Rhineland Campaign Ribbons. Publ: Nebraska corporation law, a statutory jungle, Nebr Law Rev, 5/57. Mem: Am Bar Asn; Am Legion; DAV; Gateway Sertoma Club; Lutheran Laymen's League. Relig: Lutheran, Missouri Synod. Legal Res: 327 Park Vista Lincoln NE 68510 Mailing Add: 303 Executive Bldg Lincoln NE 68508

LUFKIN, DAN WENDE **(R)**
Mem, Rep Nat Finance Comt
b New York, NY, Sept 17, 31; c Chauncey F Lufkin & Margaret Wende L; m 1961 to Elise Grace Blagden; c Elise Grace Blagden, Margaret Wende & Alison Wende. Educ: Yale Univ, BA, 53; MBA & CFA, Harvard Bus Sch, 57; Skull & Bones; Fence Club. Polit & Govt Pos: Conn key man, 68-; mem steering comt, Weicker for US Senate, 69-70; alt mem, Newtown Rep Comt, 69-; mem, White House Conf Children & Youth, 70-71; mem, Conn Rep Finance Comt, currently; mem Rep Nat Finance Comt, currently. Bus & Prof Pos: With firm of Jeremiah Milbank, 57-59; mem firm, Donaldson, Lufkin & Jenrette, Inc, 59-, pres, 59-65, chmn bd dirs, 65-70, chmn exec comt, 70-; mem bd gov, NY Stock Exchange; chmn bd dirs, Ariz-Colo Land & Cattle Co; chmn bd dirs, Ontario Motor Speedway, Inc, Calif; dir & mem exec comt, Overseas Nat Airways, Inc; dir, Pan Ocean Oil Corp; dir, Able Commun; mem exec coun, Harvard Bus Sch Asn; dir, Harvard Bus Sch of New York; trustee, Hotchkiss Sch, Pine Manor Jr Col, Danbury Hosp, Conn, Nat Conf Christians & Jews; dir, Opportunity Funding Corp; trustee & mem exec comt, Nat Coun on Crime & Delinquency; mem & dir nat steering comt, Earth Day, 70; chmn & pres, Conn Action Now, Inc; dir, Environ Defense Fund; proprietor & owner, Poverty Hollow Farm, breeder of purebred Holstein-Friesian cattle, Conn, currently. Mil Serv: Entered as Pvt, Marine Corp, 53, released as 1st Lt, 55, after serv in 3rd Marine Div, Far East, 53-55; Company Honor Man, Basic Training. Publ: The canary is dead, Vital Speeches of the Day, 11/70. Mem: Holstein-Friesian Asn Am; Links Club; Nat Golf Links Am; Madison Square Garden Club; City Midday Club. Honors & Awards: Presented speeches on the environment at the Harvard Bus Sch & Harvard Bus Sch Club of NY, 70. Relig: Presbyterian. Mailing Add: Poverty Hollow Farm RD 1 Poverty Hollow Rd Newtown CT 06470

LUFT, RICHARD N **(D)**
Ill State Sen
Mailing Add: 1412 W Shore Dr Pekin IL 61554

LUFTIG, RITA SHEILA **(D)**
Chairperson, San Diego Co Dem Cent Comt, Calif
b Union City, NJ, June 23, 27; d Samuel Stillman & Eleanor Sophie Drapkin S; m 1947 to Murry Luftig; c Vicki Ann Soper, Mitchell Louis, Andrea Gail & Laura Rae; one grandson. Educ: Univ Calif at Los Angeles, BA; Phrateres. Polit & Govt Pos: Mem, State Cent Comt Calif, 64-75; former vpres, Calif Dem Coun; former vpres, treas & secy, San Diego Co Dem Cent Comt, chairperson, currently. Bus & Prof Pos: Govt teacher, San Diego Community Col Adult Sch, 69- Mem: League of Women Voters; Hadassah. Relig: Jewish. Mailing Add: 5730 Bounty St San Diego CA 92120

LUGAR, RICHARD GREEN **(R)**
Mayor, Indianapolis, Ind
b Indianapolis, Ind, Apr 4, 32; s Marvin L Lugar & Bertha Green L; m 1956 to Charlene Smeltzer; c Mark, Robert, John & David. Educ: Denison Univ, BA, 54; Oxford Univ, BA & MA, 56; Phi Beta Kappa; Omicron Delta Kappa; Blue Key; Pi Delta Epsilon; Pi Sigma Alpha; Beta Theta Pi. Hon Degrees: Numerous hon degrees from various cols & univs. Polit & Govt Pos: Mem, Bd of Sch Comnr, Indianapolis, Ind, 64-67; deleg, Ind State Rep Conv, 64, 68 & 72, keynoter, 68; deleg & mem, Platform Comt, Rep Nat Conv, 68, deleg & keynoter, 72; surrogate spokesman for the President, 72; Mayor, Indianapolis, Ind, 68-; vchmn, Adv Comn on Intergovt Rels, 69-; vpres & mem exec comt, Nat League of Cities, 69-, pres, 70-71, mem adv bd, 71-; mem adv coun, US Conf of Mayors; mem bd dirs, Nat Asn of Counties; bd dirs, Nat Serv to Regional Coun, until 71; mem, President Nixon's Model Cities Adv Task Force, 69; mem State & Local Adv Comts, Off Econ Opportunity, 69-73; mem, US Dept of Com Regional Export Expansion Coun; app by Gov Whitcomb to Criminal Justice Planning Agency of Ind; mem steering comt, Urban Coalition, 71; Nat Adv Comn Criminal Justice Standards & Goals, currently. Bus & Prof Pos: Vpres & treas, Thomas L Green & Co Inc, 60-67, secy-treas, 68-; treas, Lugar Stock Farm, Inc, 60- Mil Serv: Entered as Seaman, 2/C, Navy, 57, released as Lt(jg), 60, after serv on staff of Chief of Naval Opers, Pentagon, 58-60. Mem: US Dept Com Regional Export Expansion Coun; Rotary; Indianapolis Urban League (bd dirs); Ind Farm Bur; Nat 4-H Serv Comt. Honors & Awards: Outstanding Young Man, Indianapolis, 66; One of Five Outstanding Young Men, Ind, Jr CofC, 66; Exceptional Serv Award, Off Econ Opportunity, 72; hon fel, Seattle Pac Col, 72. Relig: Methodist. Legal Res: 3200 Highwoods Ct Indianapolis IN 46222 Mailing Add: 2501 City-Co Bldg Indianapolis IN 46204

LUHRS, JANET ANNE **(R)**
Leader, 68th Assembly Dist, NY
b New York, NY, Dec 19, 42; d John Luhrs & Mathilde Bruning L; single. Educ: Valparaiso Univ, BA, 64; Alpha Phi Delta. Polit & Govt Pos: Mem bd dirs, Knickerbocker Rep Club, New York, 67-; committeeman, New York Co Rep Comt, 67-, exec mem, 69-; assoc leader, 68th Assembly Dist, 69-75, leader, 75-; alt deleg, Rep Nat Conv, 72. Bus & Prof Pos: Prom supvr, WPIX-TV, New York, 67-69, sr producer pub affairs prog, 69- Mem: Nat Acad TV Arts & Sci; Boys & Girls Serv League (mem jr comt, 75-); Colonial Dances, Ltd (bd gov, 74-). Honors & Awards: Emmy Award Nomination, NY Chap, Nat Acad TV Arts & Sci, 70. Relig: Lutheran. Mailing Add: 301 E 73rd St New York NY 10021

LUIS, JUAN
Lt Gov, VI
Mailing Add: Govt House Charlotte Amalie St Thomas VI 00801

LUJAN, B **(D)**
NMex State Rep
Mailing Add: Rte 1 Box 102 Santa Fe NM 87501

LUJAN, FRANCISCO GUERRERO **(D)**
Dem Nat Committeeman, Guam
b Agana, Guam, May 2, 04; s Jesus Santos Lujan & Dolores San Agustin Guerrero L; wid; m 1957 to Lydia Majnas Bernardo; c Frank, Doris (Mrs Antonio Balajadia), Rufo, Victor, James, David & Julia (Mrs Joseph Torres). Educ: Univ Hawaii, 46; LaSalle Exten Univ, 47-52. Polit & Govt Pos: Assemblyman, Guam Assembly, 35-36; judge, Police Court, 47-60; Sen, Guam Legis, 73-74, chmn judiciary comt, 65-74, vchmn, 69-74; deleg, Dem Nat Conv, 72; Dem Nat Committeeman, Guam, 75- Bus & Prof Pos: Sch prin, Agana, Guam, 24-46; notary pub, 30-40. Mem: Judicial Coun Guam; Guam Bar Asn. Relig: Roman Catholic. Mailing Add: Chalan Pago Agana GU 96910

LUJAN, MANUEL, JR **(R)**
US Rep, NMex
b San Ildefonso, NMex, May 12, 28; s Manuel Lujan & Lorenzita Romero L; m 1948 to Jean Couchman; c Terra, James, Barbara & Jeff. Educ: Col Santa Fe, BA, 50. Polit & Govt Pos: Former vchmn, NMex State Rep Party; US Rep, NMex, First Dist, 69-, mem joint comt on atomic energy & comt on interior & insular affairs, US House Rep, currently; deleg, Rep Nat Conv, 72. Bus & Prof Pos: Partner in ins bus, currently. Mem: Kiwanis; St Michael's Col Alumni Asn; KofC (past Grand Knight); Elks. Legal Res: 1209 California NE Albuquerque NM 87110 Mailing Add: 1323 Longworth House Off Bldg Washington DC 20515

LUKE, ROBERT KENNETH **(D)**
Chmn, Turner Co Dem Party, SDak
b Sioux Falls, SDak, Nov 28, 49; s Kenneth Luke & Joyce Zeman L; m 1970 to Lynn Hazel Styles; c Robert Kenneth, Jr. Educ: Univ SDak, 69-70. Polit & Govt Pos: Chmn, Turner Co Dem Party, SDak, 74- Mil Serv: Entered as E-1 Naval Res, 70, released as E-2, 71. Mem: Marion Area Jaycees (secy, 75-76); Marion Bowling Asn (bd dirs, 74-76). Honors & Awards: Local Speak Up Winner, Marion Area Jaycees; Personnel Dynamics Chmn. Relig: Roman Catholic. Mailing Add: 167 E First Marion SD 57043

LUKEN, JAMES T **(D)**
Ohio State Rep
Mailing Add: 2416 Central Parkway Cincinnati OH 45214

LUKENS, DONALD E **(R)**
Ohio State Sen
b Harveysburg, Ohio, Feb 11, 31; s William A Lukens & Edith Greene L; m 1973 to Toshiko Davis. Educ: Ohio State Univ, BSc in Criminology, 54; Delta Chi; Alpha Phi Omega; Arnold Air Soc; Scabbard & Blade; Student Coun on Relig Affairs; Student Coun, Mil Coun; Univ 4-H; Univ Grange; Ohio Union Bd; May Week; Homecoming Week; Greek Week. Polit & Govt Pos: Acting minority counsel, US House of Rep Rules Comt, 61-63; mem, DC Rep Cent Comt, 62-63; pres, DC Young Rep, 62-63; mem exec comt, Rep Nat Comt, 63-65; nat chmn, Young Rep Nat Fedn, 63-65; mem, Butler Co Rep Exec Comt, Ohio, 66-70; US Rep, Ohio, 66-72; Ohio State Sen, 70-, minority whip, Ohio State Senate, currently. Bus & Prof Pos: Mgt Consult, 66- Mil Serv: Entered as 2nd Lt, Air Force, 54, released as Capt, 60, after serv in Off of Spec Invest, 56-60; Maj, Air Force Res, 66- Mem: Mason; Shrine; Ohio Reserve Officers Asn (vpres); Kiwanis; Int Wine & Food Soc. Relig: Quaker. Mailing Add: 1066 E Parklane Middletown OH 45042

LUKOWSKY, ROBERT OWEN **(D)**
Assoc Justice, Court of Appeals Ky
b Covington, Ky, Aug 23, 27; s Robert Owen Lukowsky, Sr & Esther Cole L; m 1969 to Rosemary Domaschko. Educ: Univ Cincinnati, 44-46; Univ Cincinnati Col Law, JD, 49; Judge Advocate Gen's Staff Officer Course, Air Command & Staff Sch, Maxwell AFB, Ala, 52; Nat Col State Trial Judges, Univ Colo, 64; Alpha Psi Omega & Sigma Delta Pi. Polit & Govt Pos: Co judge pro tem, Kenton Co, Ky, 53-56; circuit judge, 16th Judicial Dist Ky, 62-75; mem, Ky Civil Rules Adv Comt, 64-74; mem, Ky Crime Comn, 64-; mem, Ky Adv Comt for Criminal Law Revision, 70-74; assoc justice, Court of Appeals of Ky, 75- Bus & Prof Pos: Trial lawyer, pvt practice, Covington, Ky, 49-62. Mil Serv: Entered as Pvt, Army Corps of Engrs, 46; Lt Col Air Force Res, currently. Publ: Auth, The constitutional right of litigants to have the state trial judge comment upon the evidence, Ky Law J, 66; auth, Post conviction relief: tribulation after trial, Ky Law J, 69; co-auth, Civil Proceedings Before Trial, Nat Col State Judiciary, 74. Mem: Ky State, Am & Fed Bar Asns; Judge Advocates' Asn; Mil Order World Wars. Honors & Awards: Outstanding Citizen Award, Alpha Kappa Tau, 69; Outstanding & Dedicated Serv Award, Chase Col Law, Northern Ky State Col, 74; Dedicated Serv Award, Nat Col State Judiciary, 74. Relig: Roman Catholic. Legal Res: 228 W Orchard Rd Ft Mitchell KY 41011 Mailing Add: 201 State Capitol Bldg Frankfort KY 40601

LUNA, FRED **(D)**
NMex State Rep
Mailing Add: Rte 1 Box 239 Los Lunas NM 87031

LUNASCO, OLIVER PATRICK **(D)**
Hawaii State Rep
b Waialua, Hawaii, May 13, 42; s Mariano Lunasco & Juanita Cassasos L; div; c Oliver Shane & Ted Allen. Educ: Waialua High Sch. Polit & Govt Pos: Hawaii State Rep, 70- Mil Serv: Entered as Pvt, Army, 62, released as E-4, 65, after serv in 320th Artil, 101st Airborne Div, Ft Campbell, Ky, 63-65. Mem: Wahiawa Jaycee; Wahiawa Filipino Asn; West Oahu Parent Teacher Student Asn Bd. Relig: Catholic. Legal Res: 67-668 Kea Pl Waialua HI 96791 Mailing Add: House of Reps Honolulu HI 98613

LUND, ART **(R)**
Mont State Rep
Mailing Add: Box 806 Scobey MT 59263

LUND, JANET CAMPBELL **(DFL)**
Mem, Minn State Dem-Farmer-Labor Cent Comt
b Minneapolis, Minn, June 10, 29; d Arthur William Thomas & Ethel Willis T; m 1958 to Dean Arthur Lund; c Julie Campbell, Margaret Ann & Erika Jean. Educ: Hamline Univ, BA cum laude; Univ Minn, MA; Nat Honor Soc, Hamline Univ. Polit & Govt Pos: Chairwoman, Second Ward, Dem-Farmer-Labor Party, Minn, 60-61, 41st Dist, 70-72; comt aide, Govt Opers Comt, Minn State Senate, 73-; mem, Minn State Dem-Farmer-Labor Cent Comt, currently; mem, 57th Dist Dem-Farmer-Labor Cent Comt, Minn, currently; mem, Fifth Cong Dem-Farmer-Labor Cent Comt, Minn, currently. Bus & Prof Pos: Mem staff acct dept, NATO Hq, Naples, Italy, 56-57; personnel dept, Minn Hwy Dept, St Paul, Minn, 58; counr, Housing Dept, Univ Minn, Minneapolis, 59-60; instr pub admin dept, Univ EAfrica, 65. Mem: Minneapolis Citizens Comt on Pub Educ; Minneapolis Citizens League; Southeast Minneapolis Planning & Coord Comt; Minneapolis Citizens Sch Facilities Comt; Am for Dem Action (bd mem, Minn Chap, 71-72). Relig: Unitarian. Mailing Add: 92 Orlin Ave SE Minneapolis MN 55414

LUND, RHODA S (R)
b Butternut Valley, Minn; d Andrew O Berge & Thalia Sunde B; m 1929 to Russell Thomas Lund; c Russell T, Jr & Mrs Robert Row. Educ: St Olaf Col, BA, 26. Polit & Govt Pos: Chairwoman, Third Dist Rep Party, Minn, 51-52; chairwoman, State Rep Party, 53-54; mem, Defense Adv Comt on Women in the Serv, 58-61; pres, Rep Workshop of Minn, 59-60; deleg, Rep Nat Conv, 56, 64, 68 & 72, alt deleg, 60, mem, Platform & Arrangements Comts, 64 & 68, chmn, Minn Deleg, 72; Rep Nat Committeewoman, Minn, 60-72; mem, Minn Adv Comt, US Comn on Civil Rights, 64- Mem: Kennedy Ctr Performing Arts (adv comt, 70-); Minn Coun Delinquency & Crime; Correctional Serv Minn & Minneapolis Boys Club Women's Auxiliary (bd mem); Nat City Bank of Minneapolis (bd mem); Ecumenical Inst on Research & Culture (bd). Relig: Lutheran. Mailing Add: 4814 Lakeview Dr Minneapolis MN 55424

LUNDBERG, LOIS ANN (R)
Mem, Rep State Cent Comt Calif
b Tulsa, Okla, Sept 21, 28; d John T McQuay & Anna M Patterson M; m 1954 to Ted W Lundberg; c Linda Ann & Sharon Lynn. Educ: Long Beach City Col, 1 year. Polit & Govt Pos: Mem bd dir, La Habra Rep Women, Calif, 61-62 & currently, secy, 63, pres, 64-65; area chmn, Orange Co Rep Precinct Orgn, 61-65, div chmn, 65, precinct chmn, 65-; 35th Assembly Dist chmn, Orange Co Rep Cent Comt, 65-, assoc mem, 68-, mem, 72-, mem, Rep State Cent Comt, Calif, 67-; exec dir, Sen George Murphy, 70; dir, Comt to Reelect the President, Orange Co, 72; deleg, Rep Nat Conv, 72; mem bd trustees, Nixon Law Off Preservation, Inc, 72-74. Bus & Prof Pos: Bus off rep, Pac Tel Co, 50-57, serv observer, 57-60, bus off supvr, 60-65. Mem: United Rep of Calif. Honors & Awards: Orange Co Rep Award for Outstanding Serv, 67; Gov Reagan Award as one of the top ten polit precinct chmn in Calif, 68. Relig: Lutheran. Mailing Add: 1341 Carmela Lane La Habra CA 90631

LUNDBERG, MELVIN EDWARD (R)
b Woods Cross, Utah, Apr 13, 04; s Alfred A Lundberg & Margaret Southworth L; m 1926 to Reva Rowe. Educ: Univ Utah, BS in Eng, 30. Polit & Govt Pos: Mem, Nev State Planning Bd, 47-56; mem, Columbia Interstate Compact Comt, 51-58; chmn, Gov Sch Surv Comt, 53-57; chmn, Nev Deleg to White House Conf on Educ, 55; chmn, Elko Co Rep Cent Comt, 56-64; mem, Nev State Parole Bd, 57-71; deleg, Rep Nat Conv, 60, alt deleg, 64 & 68; mem citizens adv coun, Univ Nev Col of Eng, 60-75; mem, Nev Civil Defense Comn, 62-75; finance chmn, Nev State Rep Party; Rep Nat Committeeman & mem, Rep Nat Finance Comt, Nev, 64-68; chmn, Nev State Coun on Educ & mem, Nat Citizens' Coun Better Schs; mem, Gov Comt on Educ, 65; mem, Citizens' Conf on Nev Courts, 68; mem, Gov Salary Study Comn for Elected State Officers, 69; mem regional adv group, Intermountain Regional Med Prog, 72- Bus & Prof Pos: Secy & gen mgr, Uintah Power & Light Co, 32-39; asst mgr & dir, Elko Lamoille Power Co, 40-53, vpres & gen mgr, 53-61, vpres & Elko div mgr, Nev Power Co, 61-73, dir, Nev Power Co, 61-; dir, Elko Broadcasting Co, 48-75; dir, Transwestern Life Ins Co, 58-67. Mem: Nev Soc Prof Engrs (pres, Elko Chap, 71-); Nev Cong of Parents & Teachers (hon life mem); Elks (past Exalted Ruler, hon life mem & Dist Dep Grand Exalted Ruler, 59-60); CofC (dir, Elko Chap); Lions. Relig: Latter-day Saint. Legal Res: Apt 10 720 Rahas Rd Elko NV 89801 Mailing Add: PO Box 776 Elko NV 89801

LUNDEEN, IONE I (R)
b Fargo, NDak, Dec 13, 28; d Peter Engaman Iverson & Dorothy Ormiston I; m 1950 to Willard Averell Pollard, III, wid, 1954; m 1959 to Edward Daniel Lundeen; c James Random, Olivia Ormiston & Edward Daniel, II. Educ: Northwestern Hosp Sch Nursing, RN, 49. Polit & Govt Pos: Staff nurse, US Dept Interior, Bur Indian Affairs, Consol Chippewa Agency, Cass Lake, Minn, duty sta, Cloquet, Minn, 49-50; precinct chairwoman, Ward II, Precinct I, Fergus Falls, Minn, 60-61; secy, Fergus Falls Area Women's Rep Club, 61-62, vpres, 63-64, pres, 65-66; coordr & chmn vol, Otter Tail Co Rep Hq, 66; vchairwoman, Seventh Cong Dist Rep Comt, Minn, 67-70; mem, Minn Rep Ethics in Govt Task Force, 68; mem, Minn State Rep Platform Comt & chmn, Govt Subcomt Ethics in Govt, 68; pres, Minn Fedn Rep Women, 70-74. Publ: Ed, Five Pointer (newspaper), Northwestern Sch Nursing, 47-49, Star (annual book), Jones Press, 49 & Minn Fedn Rep Women Report, 70 & 71. Mem: Northwestern Hosp Alumni Asn; Fergus Falls Lake Region Hosp Auxiliary; Fergus Falls Woman's Club; Fergus Falls Area Women's Rep Club; Exp in Int Living. Relig: Presbyterian. Mailing Add: Guttenberg Heights Fergus Falls MN 56537

LUNDENE, HENRY (D)
NDak State Rep
Mailing Add: State Capitol Bismarck ND 58501

LUNDERVILLE, HOWARD P (R)
Vt State Rep
b Williston, Vt, Aug 18, 23; single. Educ: Burlington High Sch. Polit & Govt Pos: High bailiff, Essex Junction, Vt, 51-53, acting chief of police, 56; acting chief of police, South Burlington, Vt, 59-60, first constable, tax collector & dep sheriff, 43-, fire chief, 49-, fire warden, 59- & cemetery comnr, 50-; Vt State Rep, 53-57 & 63- Bus & Prof Pos: Farmer, part-time. Mem: KofC; Grange; Holy Name Soc. Relig: Catholic. Mailing Add: Williston VT 05495

LUNDGREN, JAMES (R)
b Portland, Ore, May 24, 14; s John Lundgren & Marie Christensen L; m 1937 to Doris C Staley; c Gary J, Janice F (Mrs Chaffin), John S & Carol F (Mrs Shephard). Educ: Univ Wash, BS Forestry, 39. Polit & Govt Pos: App pres, Small Bus Develop Corp, Alaska, 69-; senate dist chmn, Rep Party, Alaska, 71-72; alt deleg, Rep Nat Conv, 72. Bus & Prof Pos: Chmn, Fairbanks Joint Apprenticeship Comt Carpenters, 52-; trustee, Joint Comt Carpenters Health & Welfare, 60-; trustee, Joint Comt Carpenters Pension Trust, 64- Mem: Alaska Chap, Assoc Gen Contractors; Alumni Asn, Col of Forestry, Univ Wash; Fairbanks CofC. Honors & Awards: Hard Hat Award, Alaska Chap, Assoc Gen Contractors, 70; Hammer & Saw Award, Carpenters, 71. Relig: Baptist. Mailing Add: 420 College Rd Fairbanks AK 99701

LUNDQUIST, CLARENCE THEODORE (D)
b Chicago, Ill, Jan 3, 09; s Frank Lundquist & Bessie Larson L; m 1938 to Edith Margaret Otte; c Donna Fey (Mrs Collins). Educ: Univ Ill, BS, 32; Northwestern Univ Grad Sch, 32-35; Georgetown Law Sch, LLB, 44; second prize High Scholarship, Sr Year Law Sch. Polit & Govt Pos: Various fed govt pos, 35-55; dep adminr, Wage & Hour & Pub Contracts Div, US Dept of Labor, 55-57, adminr, 58-69. Bus & Prof Pos: With Ill Bell Tel Co, Chicago, 29-30; attorney, 69-; adminr code of ethics, Direct Selling Asn, 71- Mil Serv: Entered as 2nd Lt, Army, 42, released as Lt Col, 46, after serv in Intel Activities; Army Commendation Ribbon; Lt Col (Ret), Army Res. Mem: DC Bar; Nat Press Club; Am Legion. Relig: Protestant. Legal Res: IL Mailing Add: 4822 Tilden St NW Washington DC 20016

LUNDQUIST, ELDON F (R)
Ind State Sen
b Elkhart, Ind, 1915; s August Frederick Lundquist & Nellie Peterson L; m 1939 to Helen; c John & Jane; two grandchildren. Educ: Univ Wis Grad Sch Banking. Polit & Govt Pos: Mem, Bd of Parks & Recreation, Elkhart, 51-55; secy, Sch Bd Trustees, 55-60; Ind State Rep, 61-64; Ind State Sen, 65-, incumbent mem, Legis Coun, 67-, asst majority leader, 69-, chmn, Voc Educ Study Comt, 70 & State Educ Comt, 71, Ind State Senate; mem, State of Ill Dept Pub Instr Reorgn Comt, currently. Bus & Prof Pos: Vpres & pub rels dir, St Joseph Valley Bank, Elkhart, 51-68; dir resources & develop, Elkhart Gen Hosp, 68-; partner, Miller-Lundquist Assocs, 66-68; first chmn, Bd Trustees, Ind Voc Tech Col; lectr, Grad Sch Banking, Univ Wis. Mem: Ind Bankers Asn; Elks; City Club; Elcona Country Club; Rotary. Honors & Awards: Active in broadcasting area high sch basketball games & various other sportcasting through the media, Elkhart Community, 35-68. Relig: Methodist. Legal Res: 227 Marine Ave Elkhart IN 46514 Mailing Add: PO Box 1329 Elkhart IN 46514

LUNDSTEN, JOHN MALCOLM (R)
Finance Chmn, Wright Co Rep Party, Minn
b Minneapolis, Minn, Aug 13, 39; s Malcolm Lester Lundsten & Ruth Kilstofte L; m 1967 to Mary Ellen Hurlbutt; c Andrew Hamilton. Educ: Carleton Col, BA with honors, 61; Univ Minn, Minneapolis, LLB cum laude, 64; article ed, Minn Law Rev. Polit & Govt Pos: Trial attorney, Antitrust Div, Justice Dept, Washington, DC, 64-67; chmn, Wright Co Rep Party, Minn, 69-72, finance chmn, 72-; mem, Buffalo Planning & Zoning Comn, 71- Bus & Prof Pos: Dir, Buffalo Nat Bank, Minn, 62-; pres, 69- Mem: Independent Banks Asn Am; Phi Delta Phi; Rotary; Jaycees; Buffalo Asn Com. Honors & Awards: Warren L Beson Award for athletic & scholastic excellence, Carleton Col. Relig: Unitarian. Mailing Add: 1311 Viking Dr Buffalo MN 55313

LUNDY, JAMES HARWOOD JR (R)
b Woodson, Tex, Feb 28, 27; s James Harwood Lundy & Marguerite Jones L; m 1948 to Jacqueline Eugenia Maddox; c James H, III, Margaret Ann & Eugenia Arlin. Educ: Tex Col Mines, BSME, 54; Alpha Phi Omega. Polit & Govt Pos: Sgt of arms, Ariz Rep State Comt, 60-64; mem adv comt, Ariz Rep Party, 60-70; vchmn, Gila Co Rep Party, 64-68, chmn, 68-74, finance chmn. Bus & Prof Pos: Asst chief engr, Inspiration Consol Copper Co, 66-68, chief mine engr, Christmas Mine Div, 69; drilling & blasting foreman, Inspiration, 70-71, gen foreman open pit, 71-72, pit supt, 73- Mil Serv: Entered as Pvt, Army, 45, released as Cpl, 46, after serv in 3rd Army, ETO, 45-46. Mem: Am Inst Mining & Metall Engrs (sr mem); Cobre Valley Country Club. Relig: Church of Christ. Legal Res: 80 Upper Circle Inspiration AZ 85537 Mailing Add: PO Box 166 Inspiration AZ 85537

LUNDY, JOSEPH RAYMOND (D)
Ill State Rep
b Chicago, Ill, Jan 21, 40; s Francis Lorain Lundy & Alice Whitcomb L; m 1966 to Marjorie Wagner. Educ: Princeton Univ, BA, 62; Harvard Univ Law Sch, 63-64; George Washington Univ Law Sch, LLB, 70. Polit & Govt Pos: Legis asst, US Rep Abner J Mikva, Ill, Washington, DC, 69-71; Ill State Rep, 11th Dist, 73- Bus & Prof Pos: Civilian adv to SVietnamese pacification prog, Saigon & SVietnam, 66-67; law clerk, Clifford & Miller, Washington, DC, 68. Mil Serv: Entered as 2nd Lt, Air Force, 63, released as 1st Lt, 65, after serv in 363rd Tactical Reconnaissance Wing, Shaw Air Force Base, SC, 64, Spec Serv Unit, Washington, DC, 65. Publ: Auth, Police undercover agents: new threat to First Amendment freedoms, George Washington Law Rev, 3/69; co-auth, The 91st Congress & the Constitution, Univ Chicago Law Rev, spring 71. Mem: Chicago, Ill State & Am Bar Asns; Chicago Coun Lawyers. Legal Res: 140 Custer Ave Evanston IL 60202 Mailing Add: 1791 Howard St Chicago IL 60626

LUNDY, RAYFIELD (R)
b Calif, July 30, 16; s John P Lundy & Martha Walker L; m 1942 to Maxene Lorena Thomas; c Rayfield, Jr, Keith Roger, Marsha Darlene, Laurel Theresa, William L (deceased) & Marnetta Lynette. Educ: Howard Univ, 34-39, Law Sch, 39-42; Southwestern Univ Law Sch, 46-48; Univ Southern Calif, 48-52, Law Sch, 52-56; pres frosh class; sports ed; letterman in basketball & track; mem & pres, Kappa Sigma Debating Soc; Kappa Alpha Psi. Polit & Govt Pos: Mem & pres bd trustees, Los Angeles Co Sch Bd, Calif, 51-54; mem, Los Angeles Co Rep Cent Comt, 52-74; mem, Calif Rep State Cent Comt, 54-74; mem exec comt, 69; Rep nominee, US Rep, Calif, 52, 54, 56, 62, 64, 68 & 72; mem, Calif State Bd Pharm, 69-72. Bus & Prof Pos: Faculty mem, Univ Southern Calif Sch Pharm, 70, 71 & 72. Mil Serv: Entered as Pvt, Army Transportation Corps, 42, Honorably Discharged as M/Sgt & Post Sgt Maj, 46, after serv in 1st Ave Cantonment, Seattle, Wash, Hq 8th Sv Comd, Officers' Cand Sch, New Orleans Army Air Base, Ft McArthur, Calif & Camp Lee, Va, 42-46; Good Conduct & Expert Rifleman Medals. Mem: Compton Lawyers, Langston Law Club; Boys Club (founder); Criminal Courts Bar Asn (founder); Boy Scouts; Centennial High Sch Boosters Club (founder). Honors & Awards: Compton Civic Merit Award, Club Ideal. Relig: Methodist. Legal Res: 1816 E 122nd St Los Angeles CA 90059 Mailing Add: 527 W Compton Blvd Compton CA 90220

LUNT, FREDERICK B (R)
Maine State Rep
Mailing Add: 51 Barton St Presque Isle ME 04769

LUPRO, CHARLES (D)
Mem, Dem Nat Comt, Alaska
Mailing Add: PO Box 438 Juneau AK 99801

LURVEY, MILDRED EDWINA (R)
Mem, Mass State Rep Comt
b Rochester, NH, July 6, 27; d Richard Edward Stebbins & Sarah Elizabeth Dopheny S; m 1950 to Robert Joseph Lurvey. Educ: Colby Jr Col, 43-45; Univ NH, AB, 47. Polit & Govt Pos: Finance chmn, Groton Rep Town Comt, Mass, 64-66, chmn, 66-; mem, Mass Rep State Comt, 68- Mem: Groton Womans Club; Mass State Federated Womens Clubs; Nat Early Am Glass Club; Int Platform Comt; Groton Hist Soc (dir). Relig: Protestant. Mailing Add: 24 Blossom Lane Groton MA 01450

LUSCHOW, JOHN TIMOTHY (D)
Mem, Wis Dem State Cent Comt
b Tomahawk, Wis, May 26, 03; s August Charles Luschow & Anna Coffey L; single. Educ: Marquette Univ, BS in Bus Admin, 33; Marquette Univ Glee Club; Al Smith Brown Derby Club. Polit & Govt Pos: Dep collector revenue agt & revenue officer, Bur of Internal Revenue, US Treas Dept, 42-66; enumerator bur census, US Dept of Com, 49; deleg, Eighth Dist &

Wis Dem State Conv, 69-72; chmn, Marinette Co Dem Party, Wis, 70-73; mem, Eighth Dist Dem Exec Comt, 70-; mem, Wis Dem State Cent Comt, 71-; campaign worker, Re-elections of US Sen Nelson & US Sen Proxmire, Wis, 72. Bus & Prof Pos: Tax consult, 66- Mem: KofC (3 degree, 50 years, 4 degree, 25 years & Faithful Navigator, 8 years); Elks; United Commercial Travelers. Relig: Roman Catholic. Mailing Add: 1527 Grant St Marinette WI 54143

LUSK, HALL S (D)
b Washington, DC, Sept 21, 83; s Charles Stoner Lusk & Florence Speake L; m 1914 to Sara Catherine Emmons; c Polly Carpenter (Mrs LLoyd Appleman); Catherine Holmead (Sister Elizabeth of the Trinity), Margaret Addison (Mrs Edgar Framm), Mary Emmons (Mrs Glenn Meade) & Jeanne Van Wyck (Mrs Donald Fox). Educ: Georgetown Univ, BA, 04, LLB, 07; Delta Chi; Delta Theta Phi. Hon Degrees: LLD, Univ Portland, 41, Georgetown Univ, 54. Polit & Govt Pos: Secy to Chief Justice Shepard, Court of Appeals, DC, 06-09; asst US attorney, Dist of Ore, 18-20; circuit judge, Multnomah Co, 30-37; app to Ore Supreme Court, 37, elected to court, 34, 44, 50 & 56, Chief Justice, 49-52, judge pro tem, 61-67; US Sen, Ore, 60. Bus & Prof Pos: Instr corp law, NW Col Law, Portland, formerly; attorney-at-law, Portland, 10-12; assoc, Dolph, Mallory, Simon & Gearin, 12-18; partner, Emmons, Lusk & Bynon, Attorneys, 20-30. Mem: Am & Ore State Bar Asns; Univ Club; Multnomah Athletic Club; Arlington Club. Relig: Catholic. Mailing Add: 1780 Fairmount Ave S Salem OR 97302

LUSTIG, WAYNE (R)
Chmn, Second Cong Dist Rep Comt, Va
b White Plains, NY, Dec 19, 34; s Joseph Lustig & Cecelia Blau L; m 1957 to Elaine Bohorad; c Tracy Allison, Charles Barnet & Heidi Anne. Educ: Univ Pa, BA, 56; Univ Va Sch Law, LLB, 59; Delta Sigma Rho; Sigma Alpha Mu; ed bd, Va Law Rev. Polit & Govt Pos: Mem, City of Norfolk Rep Comt, Va, 61-; mem, Va State Rep Cent Comt, 63-; chmn, Second Cong Dist Rep Comt, Va, 63-; Rep cand, US Rep, Second Dist, Va, 64; Rep cand, Va State Sen, Norfolk, 67; chmn, Whitehurst for Cong Campaign Comt, 68, 70, 72 & 74; deleg, Rep Nat Conv, 68; mem, Va State Rep Exec Comt, 68-; Second Cong Dist chmn, Holton for Gov Comt, 69; mem adv comt, Dir Pub Welfare, City of Norfolk, 69-73; mem bd visitors, Old Dom Univ & bd mem, Jewish Family Serv, 69, pres bd, 71. Mil Serv: Entered as Pvt, Army Res, 59, released as 1st Lt, 67, after serv in Judge Adv Gen Corps. Mem: Norfolk-Portsmouth Bar Asn (pres, 73); Am & Va State Bar Asns; Va Trial Lawyers Asn; AF&AM (Past Master). Honors & Awards: First Place, Va State Speak-Up Jaycee Award, 60. Relig: Jewish. Legal Res: 6813 Meadowlawn Dr Norfolk VA 23518 Mailing Add: 1340 Va Nat Bank Bldg Norfolk VA 23510

LUTHER, WILLIAM PAUL (DFL)
Minn State Rep
b Fergus Falls, Minn, June 27, 45; s Leonard Henry Luther & Eleanor Suenneby L; m 1967 to Darlene Joyce Dunphy. Educ: Univ Minn, BS, 67; Univ Minn Law Sch, JD, 70; Tau Beta Pi; Phi Delta Phi; Alpha Delta Phi. Polit & Govt Pos: Judicial clerkship, US Court of Appeals, Eighth Circuit, 70-71; mem, Gov Coun on Consumer Affairs, 74-; Minn State Rep, 75- Bus & Prof Pos: Attorney, 71- Mem: Jaycees; Minneapolis Citizens League; Hennepin Co Legal Advice Clinics. Relig: Catholic. Mailing Add: 6925 Dallas Rd Brooklyn Center MN 55430

LUTON, DANNY LEE (R)
b Jackson, Wyo, Dec 10, 52; s Everett Luton & Elaine Josephson L; m 1974 to Chaundelle Carpenter. Educ: Univ Wyo, 72-74; justice, Univ Wyo Residence Hall Judicial Coun, 72-73. Polit & Govt Pos: Deleg, Wyo State Rep Conv, 72 & 74; alt deleg, Rep Nat Conv, 72. Mem: Jackson Hole Outfitter & Guides Asn; assoc Wyo Outfitters Asn; life mem DeMolay. Honors & Awards: Polit Sci Scholar, Jackson, Wyo Chap, Am Legion, 72. Relig: Episcopal. Mailing Add: Turpin Meadow Ranch Box 48 Moran WY 83013

LUTON, JOHN D (D)
Okla State Sen
Mailing Add: State Capitol Oklahoma City OK 73105

LUTTS, ROBERT HAMILTON (R)
Nat Committeeman, Conn Fedn Young Rep
b Hackensack, NJ, July 20, 44; s Frederick A Lutts & Dorothy Weeks L; m 1964 to Christine Kimball; c Jennifer Victoria & Gregory Hamilton. Educ: Univ Mass, BA in Hist, 66. Polit & Govt Pos: Mem, Planning Comn, Vernon, Conn, 73-; mem, Vernon Rep Town Comt, 74-; chmn, Pension Bd, Vernon, 74-; second vpres, Vernon Young Rep, 74-75, exec vpres, 75-; nat committeeman, Conn Fedn Young Rep, 75- Mailing Add: 26 Wolcott Lane Vernon CT 06066

LUTZ, BARRY LAFEAN (D)
Committeeperson, Suffolk Co Dem Comt, NY
b Windsor, Pa, Jan 2, 44; s Ray Donald Lutz & Nina Capitola Bull L; m 1966 to Karen Lee Witman. Educ: Lebanon Valley Col, BS, 65; Princeton Univ, PhD, 68. Polit & Govt Pos: Committeeperson, Suffolk Co Dem Comt, 72-, mem legis adv comt, 73-; coordr, Brookhaven New Dem Coalition, 73-74 & 75-; deleg, NY State New Dem Coalition Conv, 73-74, mem exec comt, 75-; Suffolk Co coordr, Ramsey Clark for US Senate Comt, 74; deleg, Dem Nat Mid-Term Conf, 74; mem exec bd & zone leader, Brookhaven Dem Town Comt, 74- Publ: Co-auth, Probabilities for radiation & predissociation. The excited states of CH, CD, & CHplus & some astrophysical applications, Part I, 2/70, auth, Molecular hydrogen on Uranus. Observation of the 3-O quadrupole band, Part I 6/73 & Neutral Potassium in dusty clouds, Part II, 8/74, Astrophys J. Mem: Am Astronomical Soc; Int Astronomical Union; Sigma Xi. Mailing Add: 6 Acorn Lane Stony Brook NY 11790

LUTZ, CAROL RUTH (D)
Mem, Greenwich Dem Town Comt, Conn
b Fitchburg, Mass, Jan 28, 31; d Michael Francis Lombard & Ruth Laine L; m 1949 to George Joseph Lutz; c Mary Carol Fox (Mrs Paul Richard), Catherine Anne, Thomas Michael, Elizabeth Mary, Barbara Marie & Anne Elizabeth. Educ: St John's Univ (NY), BA cum laude, 50; Fordham Univ Law Sch, 73-; Squaws. Polit & Govt Pos: Mem, Greenwich Dem Town Comt, Conn, 69-, dist chmn, 70-72, chmn, 72-74. Mem: Old Greenwich Art Soc; Greenwich League of Women Voters; Greenwich Friends of the Libr. Honors & Awards: Biol Medal, St John's Univ, 50. Relig: Roman Catholic. Mailing Add: 112 Patterson Ave Greenwich CT 06830

LUTZ, HARTWELL BORDEN (D)
Ala State Rep
b Montgomery, Ala, July 28, 32; s James Penrose Lutz & Edna Gray Borden L; m 1955 to Nancy Elizabeth Martin; c John Hartwell, James Martin & Robert Gray. Educ: Univ Ala, JD, 56; Delta Tau Delta; Phi Delta Phi. Polit & Govt Pos: Ala State Rep, Madison Co, 70- Bus & Prof Pos: Attorney, Lutz, Faye & Foley, Huntsville, Ala, 60- Mil Serv: Entered as 1st Lt, Army, 57, released as 1st Lt, 60, after serv in Judge Adv Gen Corps, 57-60. Mem: Farrah Law Soc; Elks; Kiwanis; Ala Cattlemens Asn; Tenn Walking Horse Breeders Asn. Relig: Presbyterian. Legal Res: 1247 Blevins Gap Rd Huntsville AL 35802 Mailing Add: Suite 52 Cent Bank Bldg Huntsville AL 35801

LUTZ, IRI KARIST (R)
Chmn, Bethel Rep Town Comt, Conn
b Estonia, Nov 7, 34; d Heino Karist & Hilda Saar K; m 1960 to William Lutz; c Russell Karist & Gregory Steven. Educ: Western Conn Col, AS, 54; Univ Conn, BA, 57; Delta Zeta. Polit & Govt Pos: Vchmn, Bethel Rep Town Comt, Conn, 71-73, chmn, 73-; Bethel coordr, Congressman Ronald A Sarasin, 73- Mem: Delta Zeta Alumnae Chap Fairfield Co; Bethel Rep Club; GOP-5; Bethel Hist Soc. Relig: Lutheran. Mailing Add: Old Hawleyville Rd Bethel CT 06801

LUTZ, THEODORE C
Dep Under Secy Budget & Prog Rev, Dept Trans
Mailing Add: Dept of Transportation Washington DC 20590

LUUKINEN, JEANNE (R)
Secy, Rep State Cent Comt, Minn
b Webster City, Iowa, Mar 31, 26; d Roy Jesse Lee & Lila Weedman L; m 1947 to Rudolph Terho Luukinen; c Lynn & Kay. Educ: Stephens Col, AA, 46; Alpha Epsilon Rho; Delta Chi Delta. Polit & Govt Pos: Secy, Rep State Cent Comt, Minn, 69-, deleg, Rep Nat Conv, 72. Bus & Prof Pos: Continuity writer, KICD, Spencer, Iowa, 47; continuity writer, Heinrich Advert, Peoria, Ill, 52-54; continuity writer & women's dir, WIRL, Peoria, Ill, 56; traffic mgr, WDSM Radio/TV, Duluth, Minn, 60; pub affairs & pub rels, Westmoreland, Larson & Hill, Inc, Duluth, Minn, 66- Mem: Northstar Chap, Am Women in Radio & TV; Duluth Area CofC; Soc Mining Engrs; Women's Asn of the Duluth Symphony; Duluth Women's Rep Club. Relig: Presbyterian. Legal Res: Duluth MN 55811 Mailing Add: Westmoreland Larson & Hill Inc 325 Lake Ave S Duluth MN 55802

LUZZATI, RUTH ELWOOD (D)
Kans State Rep
b Omaha, Nebr, Oct 19, 22; d Harold Elwood & Pleasant Holyoke E; div; c Katharyn (Mrs Reiser). Educ: Univ Calif, Los Angeles, 40-43; Alpha Chi Omega. Polit & Govt Pos: Kans State Rep, 72- Mem: League of Women Voters; Nat Womens Polit Caucus; NAACP; YWCA (mem bd). Relig: Unitarian. Mailing Add: 5203 Plaza Lane Wichita KS 67208

LYDDY, RAYMOND C (D)
Conn State Rep
Mailing Add: 526 W McKinley Ave Bridgeport CT 06604

LYDMAN, JACK W
b New York, Feb 6, 14; (both parents deceased); m 1946 to Josefa Cummings. Educ: Bard Col, Columbia Univ, AB, 36; Columbia Univ, 37-40. Hon Degrees: LLD, Bard Col, 73. Polit & Govt Pos: Dep chief, Northeast Asia Research, Dept of State, 46-50, chief, Southeast Asia Research, 50-52, dep dir research, 52-54 & 55-56, Seconded to off of Nelson A Rockefellar, White House, 54-55; Seconded to SEATO as dep dir research, Bangkok, Thailand, 56-58, Am Consul, Surabaya, Indonesia, 58-60; econ counr, US Embassy, Djakarta, Indonesia, 60-62, minister & counr, 66-69; dep chief of mission, US Embassy, Canberra, Australia, 63-65, US Ambassador to Malaysia, 69-74. Bus & Prof Pos: Instr, Bard Col, Columbia Univ, 37-42; opers analyst, US War Dept, 42-46; chief, Urban Areas Div, US Strategic Bombing Survey/PACIFIC, 45-46. Relig: Christian. Legal Res: New York NY Mailing Add: US Embassy Kuala Lumpur Malaysia

LYMAN, CURTIS LEE (R)
Chmn, Orleans Co Rep Comt, NY
b Albion, NY, Apr 5, 26; s William Chester Lyman, Sr & Laura Lee L; m 1948 to Evelyn M Lake; c Curtis, Jr, Nathan M & James G. Educ: Hiram Col, AB, 48; Cornell Univ Law Sch, JD, 51; Pi Kappa Delta; Ball & Chain; Phi Alpha Delta. Polit & Govt Pos: Research asst, Joint Legis Comt Water Resources Planning, 58-61; trustee, Albion, NY, 62-66; vchmn, Orleans Co Rep Comt, 65-67, chmn, 67-; asst counsel, Joint Legis Comt Court Reorgn, 66-67; assoc counsel, Joint Legis Comt Prob Ment Handicapped, 68-; deleg & alt deleg, Eighth Judicial Dist Conv, various times. Bus & Prof Pos: Mem panel arbiters, Am Arbit Asn, 57-; attorney, Marine Midland Bank, Western Albion Off, 60- Mil Serv: Entered as E-1, Army, 43, released as Sgt, 46, after serv in Coast Artil Command, Panama Canal Defense, 45-46; recalled, 51-61, Capt, Artil, Am Theatre, 51-52; Good Conduct Medal; Am Theatre Ribbon; World War II Victory Medal; Korean Serv Medal. Publ: History of the Orleans County Courthouse, NY State Bar Asn, 59. Mem: Bar of the Supreme Court US; F&AM; Am Legion; Albion Sportsmen's Club; Cobblestone Soc. Honors & Awards: Leonard H Milliman Coop Award, 51. Relig: Presbyterian; Past Ruling Elder, First Presby Church Albion. Legal Res: 231 N Main St Albion NY 14411 Mailing Add: 51 N Main St Albion NY 14411

LYNAM, MARSHALL L (D)
b Bishop, Tex, Nov 27, 24; s Elbert L Lynam & May Pierson L; m 1949 to Eddie Ann Forrest; c Marsha Ann, Charles Lee & Sharon Kaye. Educ: Tex Col Arts & Indust. Polit & Govt Pos: Admin asst to US Rep Jim Wright, Tex, 62- Bus & Prof Pos: Reporter, Ft Worth Star-Telegram. Mil Serv: Entered as Pvt, Army Air Force, 43, released as S/Sgt, 45, after serv as Gunner on B-17 with 15th Air Force in Italy & 97th Bomb Group, 44-45. Relig: Protestant. Legal Res: 6117 Ten-Mile Bridge Rd Fort Worth TX 76135 Mailing Add: 6423 Lee Hwy Arlington VA 22205

LYNCH, ARTHUR P (D)
Maine State Rep
Mailing Add: Box 64 Livermore Falls ME 04254

LYNCH, DANIEL FRANCIS (D)
b Los Angeles, Calif, Dec 30, 30; s Frank Joseph Lynch, Jr & Grace Sutherland L; m 1958 to Suzanne Harvey; c Ann Sutherland, Daniel F, Jr, Eleanor Harvey & John Carroll. Educ: Univ Colo, BA, 52, Law Sch, 55-56; Georgetown Univ Law Ctr, LLB, 59. Polit & Govt Pos: Legis asst to Sen John A Carroll, 57-60; counsel, Colo Real Estate Comn, 60-61; regent, Univ Colo, 65-71; chmn, Colo Dem State Cent Comt, 69-71. Bus & Prof Pos: Lawyer, Denver, 61-; co-publ & ed, Rocky Mountain J, 73- Mil Serv: Entered as 2nd Lt, Marine Corps, 52, released

as 1st Lt, 55, after serv in 1st & 3rd Eng Bn, Korea, Japan, Camp Pendleton, Calif & Quantico, Va. Mem: Am, Colo & Denver Bar Asns. Relig: Roman Catholic. Legal Res: 1750 Ivy St Denver CO 80220 Mailing Add: 1465 S Holly St Denver CO 80222

LYNCH, DONALD J (D)
Del State Rep
Mailing Add: Gumboro Rd Selbyville DE 19975

LYNCH, DORIS THERESA (D)
NH State Rep
b Waterbury, Conn, Apr 4, 28; d William Joseph Desrosiers & Gladys Daley D; m 1945 to Albert William Lynch; c William Albert, Colleen (Mrs Audley) & Cathy. Educ: Hessers Bus Col, 44. Polit & Govt Pos: NH State Rep, 70-; vchmn, Hillsborough Co Deleg, 74-; vchmn, Hillsborough Exec Bd, 74-; mem, Dem Woman's Platform. Bus & Prof Pos: TV modeling, 47-65; prof modeling, 47-70; sportswear buyer, 57-61; mgr bridal shop, 67-70; saleswoman, Henry & Murphy Realtors, 70- Mem: Bradford Young House (bd dirs); Prof Bus Women's Club; NH League of Women Voters; Owls of NH; St Rapheal's Church Guild. Relig: Catholic. Mailing Add: 225 Boynton St Manchester NH 03102

LYNCH, FRANCIS J (D)
Pa State Sen
Mailing Add: 860 N Woodstock St Philadelphia PA 19130

LYNCH, FRANK J (R)
Pa State Rep
b Philadelphia, Pa, Nov 6, 22; s Daniel J Lynch & Elizabeth Fox L; m 1955 to Eleanor Marie King; c Daniel J, Edward A, James F & Dennis A. Educ: LaSalle Col; Temple Univ Law Sch, JD, 52. Polit & Govt Pos: Pa State Rep, 67- Bus & Prof Pos: Attorney. Mil Serv: Entered as Pvt, Army, 43, released as 1st Sgt, 46, after serv in 688th Ord Co, Asiatic-Pac Theater; Asiatic-Pac Campaign Medal; Good Conduct Medal; World War II Victory Medal; Am Campaign Medal. Mem: Delaware Co Bar Asn; KofC; St Thomas More Soc; Am Legion; Upper Darby Forum (dir). Relig: Roman Catholic. Legal Res: 620 Shadeland Ave Drexel Hill PA 19026 Mailing Add: Law Bldg Ludlow St & Copley Rd Upper Darby PA 19082

LYNCH, GARRETH J (D)
Mass State Rep
Mailing Add: State Capitol Boston MA 02133

LYNCH, JAMES H (D)
b Ridgely, Md, Nov 20, 19; s Calvin D Lynch & Lotela Golt L; m 1969 to Mary B Long; c Carol (Mrs Eugene Dempsey); James H, Jr & Robert T. Educ: Goldey Bus Col, 2 years. Polit & Govt Pos: Mayor, Ridgely, Md, 50-53; mem, Md State Dem Cent Comt, formerly; chmn, Caroline Co Dem Cent Comt, 64-72. Bus & Prof Pos: Pres, Lynch Oil Co, 55-; pres, Lynch Grain & Feed Inc, 60- Mil Serv: Entered as Pvt, Army, 43, released as S/Sgt, 46, after serv in 82nd Airborne Div, ETO, 44-46; Belgian Citation; Holland Citation; Good Conduct Medal. Mem: Lions (dep dist gov); VFW; Am Legion; Caroline Co Country Club (secy). Relig: Catholic. Mailing Add: 101 Sunrise Ave Ridgely MD 21660

LYNCH, JIM C (R)
Chmn, Lake Co Rep Cent Comt, Ore
b Lakeview, Ore, Feb 2, 36; s Con Lynch & Mary Barry L; single. Educ: Univ Ore; Ore Sch Law; Phi Beta Kappa; Alpha Tau Omega; Phi Delta Phi. Polit & Govt Pos: Chmn, Lake Co Rep Cent Comt, Ore, 66- Bus & Prof Pos: Partner, Conn & Lynch, Ore, 64- Mil Serv: Entered as 1st Lt, Army, 62, released as Capt, 63, after serv in Mil Dist of Wash. Mem: Elks; KofC; Lions; CofC; Am Bar Asn. Honors & Awards: Winner of Koyl Cup & Paul Patterson Mem Scholarship. Relig: Roman Catholic. Mailing Add: 620 First St N Lakeview OR 97630

LYNCH, JOHN A (D)
NJ State Sen
b New Brunswick, NJ, Mar 10, 08; s John T Lynch & Margaret Corrigan L; m to Evelyn Rooney; c Barbara, John, Bill, Mary-Lynn & Gerry. Educ: Fordham Univ, LLB. Polit & Govt Pos: Clerk to Late Supreme Court Justice Peter F Daly; mem, Middlesex Co Bd of Elec, NJ; Prosecutor of the Pleas of Middlesex Co; magistrate, New Brunswick, 6 years, dir of Parks & Pub Property, formerly; dir of Revenue & Finance, formerly; dir of Pub Affairs, formerly; acting dir of Pub Safety, formerly; mem Bd of City Comnrs & Mayor, 4 years; NJ State Sen, 55-, pres, NJ State Senate, 66. Bus & Prof Pos: Trial lawyer. Mem: Middlesex Co Bar Asn. Mailing Add: 75 Paterson St New Brunswick NJ 08901

LYNCH, JOHN D (D)
Mont State Rep
b Butte, Mont, Sept 17, 47; s Leo D Lynch & Queenie Veronica Lynch L; single. Educ: Western Mont Col, BS, 69; Circle K (gov, 69-70); student body pres, 68-69. Polit & Govt Pos: Mont State Rep, 71-73, 75- Bus & Prof Pos: Teacher, Eng, Butte High Sch, Mont, 70- Mem: Am Fedn of Teachers; KofC; Elks; Butte Teachers Union. Relig: Catholic. Mailing Add: 527 W Mercury Butte MT 59701

LYNCH, JOHN WILLIAM (D)
b Athens, Ohio, May 27, 98; s Edward Albert Lynch & Anna Call L; m to Maxine Sayres; c Patricia, Jean, JoAnn, Rosemary, John W, Jr, Edward M & Mrs Patricia King. Educ: Cambridge Col, Ohio, grad. Polit & Govt Pos: Mem, Tulare Co Dem Cent Comt, 56-58; mem, Second Dist, Calif State Bd of Equalization, 59-, vchmn, 59-65, chmn, 69- Bus & Prof Pos: Employee, major oil companies, 25 years; dep collector, internal revenue agt & mem racket squad, Bur Internal Revenue, 11 years; tax consult & pub acct, Tulare, Calif, 56- Mil Serv: Pvt, Army, 17-19, serv in Princess Patricia's Can Light Inf, France; British & Can Victory Medals; Mil Medal. Mem: Commonwealth Club; Am Legion; Moose; Elks; life mem DAV. Relig: Roman Catholic. Legal Res: 1724 Minnewawa No 132 Clovis CA 93612 Mailing Add: PO Box 2246 Fresno CA 93720

LYNCH, NEIL JOSEPH (D)
Majority Leader, Mont State Senate
b Butte, Mont, Sept 18, 34; s Mr & Mrs Earl J Lynch; m to F Charlotte; c Kimberly Elaine, Anne Marie, Neil Joseph, Marcella Florence & Kelly Elizabeth. Educ: Santa Clara Univ, 52-53; Mont State Univ, BSMechEng, 57; Columbus Law Sch, LLB, 60. Polit & Govt Pos: Patent examr, US Patent Off, 57-60; asst attorney gen, Mont, 63-64; committeeman, Silver Bow Co Dem Comt, 66-68; Mont State Sen, 69-, majority leader, Mont State Senate, currently. Bus & Prof Pos: Engr, Mont Power Co, 60-63; attorney-at-law, Genzberger,

Genzberger & Lynch, Butte, Mont, 64-70; attorney-at-law, Sullivan & Lynch, 70- Mem: Silver Bow Co Dem Club, Butte Exchange Club; dir, Butte Indust Develop Corp, 66-; secy, Park N Shop Inc, 66-; Butte CofC, Promote Active Commun Effort. Mailing Add: 3561 Hartford Butte MT 59701

LYNCH, THOMAS A (D)
RI State Sen
Mailing Add: 66 Gray St Warwick RI 02889

LYND, PRISCILLA ANN (R)
Nat Committeewoman, Young Rep Fedn, Ky
b Ironton, Ohio, Feb 4, 42; d Jacob E Lynd & Margaret Richards L; single. Educ: Univ Ky, AB, 64, MD, 68; Alpha Epsilon Delta. Polit & Govt Pos: Secy, Univ Ky Young Rep, 61-62, vpres, 62-63; precinct committeewoman, Fayette Co Rep Party, Ky, 72-; pres, Fayette Co Young Rep, 73-74; nat committeewoman, Young Rep Fedn, 74- Bus & Prof Pos: Asst prof pediatrics, Univ Ky Col Med, 73- Publ: Co-auth, Perinatal infection & vaginal flora, Am J OB-Gyn, in press; auth, Naroxone in the newborn, Am J Hosp Pharm, in press. Mem: Am & Ky Med Asns; Fayette Co Med Soc; Am Acad Pediatrics; Ky Acad Pediatrics. Relig: Methodist. Mailing Add: 697 Berry Lane Lexington KY 40502

LYNDE, ALLISON HOWARD (D)
b San Francisco, Calif, Dec 31, 47; s Charles Theodore Lynde & Eiko Yoshinaga L; single. Educ: Univ Hawaii, BA summa cum laude, 70. Polit & Govt Pos: Chmn, Hawaii Young Dem, 71-73; alt deleg, Dem Nat Conv, 72; chmn, Am Dem Action, Hawaii, 74-75. Bus & Prof Pos: Social work technician, Liliuokalani Trust, 71-74; research asst, Hawaii House Rep, 74; clerk, Hawaii Senate Health Comt, 75. Mem: Citizens for Hawaii. Mailing Add: 3121 Pualei Circle Apt 16 Honolulu HI 96815

LYNG, RICHARD (R)
b San Francisco, Calif, June 29, 18; s Ed J Lyng & Sarah McGrath L; m 1944 to Bethyl Ball; c Jeanette (Mrs Robinson) & Marilyn. Educ: Univ Notre Dame, PhB. Polit & Govt Pos: Dir, Calif Dept of Agr, 68-69; asst secy, US Dept Agr, 69-73. Bus & Prof Pos: Pres, Ed J Lyng Co, Inc, Modesto, Calif, 49-67; pres, Am Meat Inst, 73- Mil Serv: Entered as Pvt, Army, 42, released as 2nd Lt, 45, after serv in SPac Theater, 42-44. Relig: Roman Catholic. Mailing Add: 4058 41st St North Arlington VA 22207

LYNN, FRANK D (D)
Miss State Rep
Mailing Add: 113 McInnis Ave Moss Point MS 39563

LYNN, FRED L (D)
Mo State Rep
b Vera Cruz, Mo, Mar 8, 24; s Fred Leon & Edith Fern Roper L; m 1946 to Opal C Trantham; c Judith Ann (Mrs Richard Haver) & Melinda Jo. Educ: Draughon's Bus Univ, 42 & 43; Am Broadcasting Sch, 44 & 45; Baptist Bible Col, 59-61. Polit & Govt Pos: Mo State Rep, 148th Dist, 75- Bus & Prof Pos: Announcer & newscaster, KGBX, 46-52; announcer & newscaster, KWTO, 53-63 & 67-73; pastor, Glendale Baptist Church, 63-67; pastor, Corinth Church, Cassville, 67- Mem: CofC; Kiwanis Int. Relig: Southern Baptist. Mailing Add: 2215 N Robberson Springfield MO 65803

LYNN, JAMES THOMAS (R)
Dir, Off of Mgt & Budget
b Cleveland, Ohio, Feb 27, 27; s Fredrick Robert Lynn & Dorthea Estelle Petersen L; m 1954 to Joan Miller; c Marjorie, Peter & Sarah. Educ: Adelbert Col, Western Reserve Univ, AB, 48; Harvard Univ Law Sch, LLB, 51; Phi Beta Kappa. Polit & Govt Pos: Gen counsel, Dept of Com, 69-71, under secy, 71-73; secy, Dept of Housing & Urban Develop, 73-75; Counsellor to the President for Community Develop, formerly; Dir, Off of Mgt & Budget, 75- Bus & Prof Pos: Attorney, Jones, Day, Cockley & Reavis, Cleveland, Ohio, 51-69, partner, 60-69. Mil Serv: Entered Navy, 45, released as ETM 2/C, 46. Mem: Am, Fed, Ohio & Cleveland Bar Asns. Honors & Awards: First Jr Honors, Western Reserve Univ, 47; First Sr Honors, 48; Justice Rufus Ranney Scholar to Harvard Law Sch, 48-49; Harvard Law Rev, 49-51; Harvard Law Sch Acad Scholar, 49-50. Relig: Protestant. Legal Res: 2635 N Park Blvd Cleveland Heights OH 44118 Mailing Add: Off of Mgt & Budget Exec Off Bldg Washington DC 20503

LYNN, JOHN EDWARD (D)
b Bartlesville, Okla, Aug 5, 45; s Randolph Hardy Lynn & Maudie Clair Johnston L; m 1968 to Jane Sharon Abramson. Educ: Univ Okla, BA, 67; George Washington Univ Law Sch, 67-71. Polit & Govt Pos: Legis asst, US Rep John Jarman, Fifth Dist, Okla, 67-69; legis asst, US Rep Ed Edmondson, Second Dist, Okla, 69-72; admin asst, US Rep James R Jones, First Dist, Okla, 73- Relig: Jewish. Legal Res: 2101 Dewey Place Bartlesville OK 74003 Mailing Add: 225 Cannon House Off Bldg Washington DC 20515

LYNN, LAURENCE EDWIN JR (INDEPENDENT)
b Long Beach, Calif, June 10, 37; s Laurence Edwin Lynn & Marjorie Louise Hart L; m 1972 to Patricia C Ramsey; c Stephen Louis, Daniel Laurence, Diana Jane & Julia Suzanne. Educ: Univ Calif, Berkeley, AB, 59; Yale Univ, PhD, 66; Phi Beta Kappa; Sigma Chi. Polit & Govt Pos: Weapon syts analyst, Off of Asst Secy Defense, Washington, DC, 65-66, dir strategic mobility & transportation div, 66-68; dep asst secy for econ & resource anal, Dept Defense, 68-69; asst for prog anal, Nat Security Coun, 69-70; asst secy for planning & eval, Dept Health, Educ & Welfare, 71-73; asst secy for prog develop & budget, Dept of Interior, 73-74. Bus & Prof Pos: Assoc prof bus econ, Grad Sch Bus, Stanford Univ, 70-71; ed, Aldine Publ Co, Chicago, Ill, 73-; consult ed, Evaluation Mag, Minneapolis, Minn, 73-; sr fel, Brookings Inst, 74-75; prof pub policy, Harvard Univ, 75- Mil Serv: 1st Lt, Army, 63-65, after serv in Inf, Ft Benning, Gordon & Belvoir & Off of Asst Secy of Defense, 63-65. Publ: The analysis of strategic mobility problems, Transportation Res Forum Seventh Annual Meeting Papers, 11/66; Economic analysis of public investment decisions: interest rate policy and discounting analysis, In: Hearings before the subcommittee on economy in government of the joint economic committee, US Govt Printing Off, 68; Systems analysis-challenge to military management, In: Systems, organizations, analysis, management: a book of readings, McGraw, 69. Mem: Coun Foreign Rels; Univ Calif Alumni Asn. Honors & Awards: Meritorious civilian serv award, Secy of Defense, 69; cert of distinguished achievement, the President, 70. Relig: Protestant. Mailing Add: Witches Spring Rd RFD 2 Milford NH 03055

LYON, CECIL BURTON
b New York, 1903; m 1933 to Elizabeth S Grew; c Two. Educ: Nat War Col, 17; Harvard Univ, AB, 27. Polit & Govt Pos: Career officer, US Dept of State Foreign Serv, 30-, vconsul,

Havana, Cuba, 31, vconsul, Hong Kong, 32; third secy, Tokyo, 33, third secy, Peiping, China, 33-38, third & second secy, Santiago, Chile, 38-42, with Dept of State, 42-44, first secy, Cairo, 44-46, spec asst to Asst Secy of State for Polit Affairs, 47-48, counr, Warsaw, Poland, 48-50; counr, Nat War Col, 50-51, dir, Off of High Comnr for Ger, Berlin, 51-54, dir, Bur of German Affairs, 54-55, Dept Asst Secy of State for Inter-Am Affairs, 55-56, US Ambassador to Chile, 56-58, US Minister, France, 58-64, US Ambassador to Ceylon, 64-68. Bus & Prof Pos: Investment banking firm, NY, 27-30; dir, Int Rescue Comt & Harris Found; chmn bd, Henry St Settlement, New York, currently. Mailing Add: King's Hwy Hancock NH 03449

LYON, DANIEL F (D)
NMex State Rep
b New York, NY, July 4, 36; s Daniel R Lyon & Leta B Southworth L; m 1954 to Ida M Hanson; c Daniel F, Jr, Sherry M, Dennis R, Mary L & Thomas D. Educ: Beloit Col; Wis State Univ, Whitewater; Univ Wis, Madison; Milton Col, BA, 60; Western NMex Univ; Univ Utah; Blackstone Sch Law, LLB; Univ NMex Sch Law, JD, 68; Alpha Sigma Phi. Polit & Govt Pos: Deleg, NMex State Const Conv, 69; NMex State Rep, Bernalillo Co, 70-; mem, Nat Comnr Uniform Laws. Bus & Prof Pos: Employed in various indust positions, 55-58; dep sheriff, Rock Co, Wis, 58-60; owner, Beloit Laminating Serv, 56-62; teacher & coach fifth grade, South Beloit Pub Schs, Ill, 60-61; machinist, Gunite Foundries Div, Kelsey-Hayes Co, 61, first aid man, 61, safety dir, 62; teacher jr high dept, Powers Sch, Beloit, Wis, 62-63; molder, Beloit Foundry Co, Ill, summer 63; state probation & parole off, State NMex, 64-68; attorney, Legal Aid Soc Albuquerque, 68-70; distributive educ teacher-coordr, Del Norte High Sch, 70- Mem: Am & NMex Voc Asns; Distributive Educ Clubs Am; NMex Distributive Educ Asn (Del Norte High Sch Chap); Nat Asn Distributive Educ Teachers. Honors & Awards: Pearce C Rodney Mem Prize, 63. Relig: Catholic. Mailing Add: 808 Silver Ave SE Albuquerque NM 87102

LYON, STEPHEN ANDREWS (D)
Colo State Rep
b Fredonia, Kans, Dec 11, 40; s Jacob Andrews Lyon & Belle Crandall L; m 1970 to Peggy Hanska; c Dirck Andrews & Robert Stephen. Educ: Univ Kans, BA, 63, MPA, 66; Pi Sigma Alpha; Kappa Sigma. Polit & Govt Pos: Asst city mgr, Junction City, Kans, 64; asst dir public works, Independence, Mo, 64-66; dir finance, Englewood, Colo, 66-72; city mgr, Breckenridge, Colo, 72; Colo State Rep, 75- Bus & Prof Pos: Pres, Lyon, Collins & Co, Denver, Colo, 72- Mem: Int City Mgr Asn; Munic Finance Off Asn; Urban Regional Info Syst Asn. Legal Res: 5548 S Lowell Littleton CO 80123 Mailing Add: House of Rep State Capitol Denver CO 80203

LYONS, ELAINE TURNER (R)
Asst Majority Leader, NH House of Rep
b Boston, Mass, Sept 27, 28; d Maurice Steele Turner & Edna Grace T; m 1952 to John Edward Lyons; c Judith Ann & Stephen Turner. Educ: Sargent Col, Boston Univ, BS, 49, Sch Educ, grad courses; permanent treas, Sargent Col Class of 49- Polit & Govt Pos: Charter mem & vpres, Merrimack Federated Rep Womans Club, 66-; co-chmn, Peterson for Gov, Merrimack, 68-70; NH State Rep, 71-, mem legis educ comt & Order of Woman Legislators, NH House of Rep, 71-, asst majority leader, 75-; clerk, Hillsborough Co Exec Comt & Hillsborough Co Deleg, 73- Bus & Prof Pos: Supvr phys educ, Manchester, NH, 49-57; instr swimming, YWCA, 66, 67 & 70; teaching substitute, Merrimack Sch Dept, 66-70; vchmn, Explorer Scouts of NH, 72-74; NH bd dirs, Boy Scouts, 73-74. Publ: Curriculum guide to physical education in New Hampshire, written with team of eight phys educators, State of NH, 54. Mem: Asn Manchester Col Womens Club; Appalachian Mt Club; US Eastern Amateur Ski Asn; Merrimack Med Ctr; Reeds Ferry Womans Club. Honors & Awards: Am Red Cross Two & One Half Gallon Blood Donor. Relig: Episcopal. Mailing Add: Shore Dr Merrimack NH 03054

LYONS, ROBERT EMMET (D)
SDak State Rep
b Wagner, SDak, Dec 29, 09; s William F Lyons & Katherine Cosgrove L; m 1935; wid; m 1953 to C Alice Bickford; c John C. Educ: Wagner High Sch, grad, 1929. Polit & Govt Pos: Dem Twp Committeeman, SDak, 49-; deleg, Dem Nat Conv, 68; agr chmn, SDak Dem Party, 68; zone capt, various co, SDak, 69; SDak State Rep, 71-; regional chairperson, SDak Dem State Cent Comt, currently. Bus & Prof Pos: Farmer, 34- Mem: KofC; Rotary; Farmers Union; Nat Farmers Orgn. Relig: Catholic. Mailing Add: Rte 1 Wagner SD 57380

LYONS, THOMAS G (D)
b Chicago, Ill, May 24, 31; s Thomas Vincent Lyons & Marian Daniels L; m 1958 to Ruth Tobin; c Mary Alexandra, Francis Xavier, Thomas V & Rachel Ann. Educ: Xavier & Loyola Univs; Loyola Univ Law Sch; Blue Key; Alpha Sigma Nu. Polit & Govt Pos: Asst Attorney Gen, Ill, 61-64; Ill State Sen, 64 & 71-72, chmn, Comt on Appropriations, Ill State Senate, 71-72; vchmn, Ill Const Study Comn, 65, chmn, 67; committeeman, 45th Ward Regular Dem Orgn, 68-; deleg & vpres, Ill Const Conv, 69; deleg, Dem Nat Conv, 72; deleg, Dem Nat Mid-Term Conf, 74. Bus & Prof Pos: Attorney-at-law, 57, Cook Co Assessor's Off, 58 & O'Keefe, O'Brien, Hanson, Ashenden & Assocs, 64- Mil Serv: Entered as 2nd Lt, Army, 54, released as 1st Lt, 56, after serv in 3rd Inf Div, ZI; Capt, Army Res, 56-62. Publ: The Revenue Article, Ill Bar Rec, 66. Mem: Ill Police Asn; Chicago Patrolmen's Asn; KofC (4 degree); Amvets; Moose. Honors & Awards: Selected Best New Mem Ill Senate, 65; Chosen Outstanding Young Mem of Ill Legis, Rutgers Univ, 66. Relig: Catholic. Legal Res: 6457 N Hiawatha Ave Chicago IL 60646 Mailing Add: 38 S Dearborn St Chicago IL 60603

LYONS, WILLIAM WATSON
Dep Under Secy, Dept of the Interior
b Lansing, Mich, Jan 3, 35; s Edward T Lyons & Martha Watson L; m to Mary Elizabeth Long; c Lisa, Laura, Bridget & Sarah. Educ: Mich State Univ, BA, 59. Polit & Govt Pos: Prog liaison spec, Dep of the Interior, 66-68, regional planner, Appalachian Regional Comn, 68-70; asst to secy, 70-71, dept asst secy, 71-73, dep under secy, 73- Bus & Prof Pos: Asst off mgr, Oldsmobile Div, GMC, Portland, Ore, 59-60, dist mgr, Great Falls, Mont, 60-61, Seattle, Wash, 61-65 & Los Angeles, 65-66. Mil Serv: Army, 55-57. Mailing Add: 6805 Sorrel St McLean VA 22101

LYSEN, KING (D)
Wash State Rep
Mailing Add: 12844 Shorecrest Dr SW Seattle WA 98146

LYTAL, LAKE HENRY (D)
Comnr, Palm Beach Co, Fla
b St Martinville, La, Aug 26, 06; s James True Lytal & Pauline Fleming L; m 1934 to Ruth Best; c Lake Henry Jr & Lynn (Mrs Donald Fountain). Educ: Loyola Univ, 28-30; Univ Fla, 31; Cumberland Law Col, LLB, 32; Blue Key. Polit & Govt Pos: Comnr, Palm Beach Co, Fla, 42-66 & 71-; chmn, Palm Beach Co Dem Comt, formerly. Mem: Fla Asn of Co Comnr (pres); Jr CofC; Kiwanis; Elks. Honors & Awards: Good Govt Award, Jaycees, Exchange Club & Civitan. Relig: Catholic. Mailing Add: 7200 W Lake Dr West Palm Beach FL 33406

LYTEL, ELAINE (D)
b Baltimore, Md, Sept 10, 23; d Arnold Greenabaum (deceased) & Rose Berliner (deceased); m 1954 to Allan H Lytel; wid; c Laurie & David. Educ: Antioch Col, BA in psychol, 45; NY Univ, 48-49; Bank Street Col Educ, teacher cert, 50; Syracuse Univ, MA in Pub Admin, 65. Polit & Govt Pos: Committeewoman, Third Elec Dist, DeWitt, NY, 64-; chairperson, DeWitt Town Dem Party, 69; upstate coordr, Mary Anne Krupsak Campaign for Lt Gov, 74; alt deleg, Dem Nat Mid-Term Conf, 74; legislator, Onondaga Co Ninth Dist, 73- Bus & Prof Pos: Personnel interviewer, NY Herald Tribune, New York, 46-48; training counselor, Gimbel Brothers, Philadelphia, Pa, 53-55; teacher, Syracuse Bd Educ, 56-57; researcher, Syracuse Govt Bur, Syracuse, 67; research assoc, Syracuse Univ Research Corp, 68-71; coordr, Youth Theater, Salt City Playhouse, 71-73. Publ: County Comments, a weekly column in Suburban Life, DeWitt New Times & Eagle Bull, 75- Mem: Pub Broadcasting Coun Cent NY (mem bd trustees, 75-); Co Officers Asn NY; Nat Asn Co; Nat Orgn Women; Onondaga Co Women's Polit Caucus. Relig: Jewish. Mailing Add: 222 Ambergate Rd DeWitt NY 13214

M

MAAG, JAMES S (R)
Speaker Pro Tem, Kans House of Rep
b Ottawa, Kans, Nov 24, 39; s L W Maag & Mildred Scoville M; m 1964 to Kathleen Covert; c Laura Denise & Jared Scoville. Educ: Washburn Univ, BA, 61; Univ Kans, MA, 64; Sagamore; Alpha Delta. Polit & Govt Pos: Kans State Rep, 116th Dist, 69-, asst majority floor leader, Kans House Rep, 73-74, speaker pro tem, 75- Bus & Prof Pos: Instr, Dodge City Community Jr Col, 64- Mem: Washburn Univ Alumni Asn (bd dirs); Kans Hist Teachers Asn; Kans Asn of Pub Community Jr Cols. Relig: Methodist. Mailing Add: 14th & By Pass Dodge City KS 67801

MABRY, HERBERT H (D)
Mem, Dem Nat Comt, Ga
Mailing Add: 501 Pulliam St SW Atlanta GA 30312

MABRY, MALCOLM H, JR (R)
Miss State Rep
b Dublin, Miss, June 28, 33; single. Polit & Govt Pos: Miss State Rep, currently. Bus & Prof Pos: Farmer, currently. Mem: Farm Bur. Relig: Methodist. Mailing Add: Dublin MS 38739

MACARI, ADAM B (D)
RI State Rep
Mailing Add: 1310 Plainfield St Johnston RI 02919

MACARTHUR, DOUGLAS II
b Bryn Mawr, Pa, July 5, 09; s Capt Arthur MacArthur, USN & Mary Hendry McCalla M; m to Laura Barkley; c Laura (Mrs Goditiabois-Deacon). Educ: Yale Univ, BA, 32. Polit & Govt Pos: Am consulate, Vancouver, 35-36; Am consulate, Naples, 36-38; third & second secy, Am Embassy, Paris, 38-40 & 44-48; third & second secy, Am Embassy, Vichy, 40-42; intern, Dept of State, 42-44; first secy of embassy, Brussels, 48-49; chief, Div Western European Affairs & dep dir, Off European Regional Affairs, 49-51; polit adv to Gen Eisenhower at SHAPE, 51-52; counr, Dept of State, 53-56; US Ambassador to Japan, 56-61; US Ambassador to Belgium, 61-65; asst Secy for Cong Rels, 65-67; US Ambassador to Austria, 67-69; US Ambassador to Iran, 69-72. Bus & Prof Pos: Int bus consult & co dir, 72- Mil Serv: Lt, Army, 32-35. Mem: Metrop Club; Chevy Chase Club. Legal Res: DC Mailing Add: 65 Rue Langeveld 1180 Brussels Belgium

MACAULAY, ANGUS HAMILTON (D)
Chmn, Richmond City Dem Comt, Va
b Spartanburg, SC, Apr 1, 28; s Angus H Macaulay & Margaret White M; m 1962 to Amanda C Tevepaugh; c Angus, Jr, Alexander M & Katherine. Educ: The Citadel, AB, 50, scholar medal; Yale Univ Law Sch, LLB, 55; Phi Delta Phi. Polit & Govt Pos: Mem, Richmond Air Pollution Control Bd, Va, 65-; mem, Va Dem State Cent Comt, 68-; mem, Third Dist Cent Comt, 68-; mem, Richmond City Dem Comt, Va, 68-, chmn, 73- Bus & Prof Pos: Partner, Mays, Valentine, Davenport & Moore, Attorneys-at-law, Richmond, Va, 61-; mem bd dirs, Colonial Life & Accident Ins Co, Columbia, SC, 67- Mil Serv: Entered as Pvt, Army, 46, released as Cpl, 47, after serv in 9th Inf Div; Army Occup, Ger; 2nd Lt, Army, 51, released as 1st Lt, 53, after serv in 45th Inf Div, Combat, Korea, 52-53. Mem: Am, Va & Richmond Bar Asns; Richmond Kiwanis (bd dirs, 75-); Downtown Club of Richmond. Honors & Awards: Gold Feather Award for Outstanding Community Serv, Richmond Jaycees, 72; Award for Outstanding Serv, Richmond Community Action Prog, 74. Relig: Presbyterian. Legal Res: 502 Henri Rd Richmond VA 23226 Mailing Add: PO Box 1122 Richmond VA 23208

MACAULAY, JOSEPH HUGH (R)
b Desoto, Wis, May 28, 24; s Joseph A Macaulay & Ruth French M; m to Patsy Parkin; c Scott & Colin. Educ: George Washington Univ, BA, 62; Johns Hopkins Univ, 65; Am Univ, 65-66; Cong Staff fel, Am Polit Sci Asn, 65; Pi Sigma Alpha. Polit & Govt Pos: Mem staff, US Rep Henry J Latham, Third Dist, NY, 47; admin asst to US Rep Charles B Hoeven, 48-64; legis asst to US Rep Charlotte T Reid, 15th Dist, Ill, 66-69, admin asst to US Rep Charlotte T Reid, 69-71; spec asst to US Rep Leslie C Arends, 17th Dist, Ill, 72; admin asst to Minority Whip, US House of Rep, 73-75; admin asst to US Rep Virginia Smith, Nebr, 75- Mil Serv: Navy, 45-46. Mailing Add: 5712 Marengo Rd Bethesda MD 20016

MACCALLUM, DOUGLAS C (R)
Chmn, Westchester Co Rep Comt, NY
b New York, NY, July 10, 02; s Harry MacCallum & Agnes Curtis M; m 1925 to E Claire

Mersereau; c Douglas C. Educ: New York Univ Col, BS, 25; New York Univ Grad Col, 1 year; Psi Upsilon. Polit & Govt Pos: Pres, Westchester Co Young Rep, NY, 45-46; city councilman, White Plains, NY, 56-64; chmn, White Plains Rep City Comt, 62-69; mem, NY State Rep Comt, 64-69, mem exec comt, 69-; chmn, Westchester Co Rep Comt, 68-; trustee, Power Authority of State of NY, 70- Bus & Prof Pos: Account exec, Shields & Co, White Plains, NY, 70- Honors & Awards: Merit Award, White Plains CofC. Relig: Methodist. Mailing Add: 44 N Broadway White Plains NY 10603

MACDONALD, CLYDE JR (D)
Committeeman, Maine Dem State Comt
b Old Orchard Beach, Maine, Jan 25, 29; s Clyde MacDonald, Sr & Nellie Carroll M; m 1956 to Trudy MacKenzie. Educ: Bates Col, BA, 58; Univ Maine Grad Sch, Orono, MA, 66, PhD, hist, 73. Polit & Govt Pos: Chmn, Hampden Dem Town Comt, 68-; orgn chmn, Penobscot Co Dem Comt, 68-; chmn, Penobscot Co Get-Out-The-Vote Campaign, 70; committeeman, Maine Dem State Comt, Penobscot Co, 70-; chmn, Hampden Planning Bd, 71-; second cong dist coordr, Get-Out-The-Vote Campaign, 72; mem nat deleg selection comn, Dem Nat Comt, 73- Bus & Prof Pos: Teacher, Hermon High Sch, 58-61; instr, Univ Maine, Orono, 67-73, prof, 73- Mil Serv: Entered as Pvt, Army, 51, released as Cpl, 54, after serv in 43rd Div, Ger. Mailing Add: MRA Box 199 Bangor ME 04401

MACDONALD, DAVID R
Asst Secy Enforcement, Oper & Tariff Affairs, Dept Treas
Mailing Add: Off of Secy Treas Washington DC 20220

MACDONALD, DONALD GORDON (R)
b Chicago, Ill, Nov 18, 21; s Peter Gordon MacDonald & Jeanne Merle M; m 1942 to Barbara McCloskey; c Mark, Donald, Jr & Jean (Mrs William Mathers). Educ: Wesleyan Univ, BA, 43; Princeton Univ, MA, 48. Polit & Govt Pos: Mgt analyst, Mutual Security Agency/Foreign Opers Admin, Washington, DC, 50-52; dir off pub serv, Agency for Int Develop, Turkey, Int Coop Admin, 55-58, dir, SAsian Affairs Admin, Washington, DC, 58, exec secy, 59-60, detailed to White House, 60, dir, Japan-Korea Affairs, 61, dep coordr, Alliance for Progress, Agency, 61-62, dep dir, Pakistan, 62-63, dir, 63-65, dir, Nigeria, 66, dir, Vietnam, 66-70, asst adminr, Bur for Asia, Washington, DC, 70-74; pvt consult, currently. Bus & Prof Pos: Instr polit, Woodrow Wilson Sch, Princeton Univ, 47-50; research asst, research assoc & consult, US Off Educ, Conn Comn on State Govt Orgn & NJ Comn on Need for Med Sch, 47-50. Mil Serv: Entered as Midshipman, Naval Res, 43, released as Lt, after serv in Amphibious Serv Overseas, Atlantic, European, Mediter & Pac from 43 to 46; various awards. Mem: Am Polit Sci Asn; Am Soc Pub Admin. Honors & Awards: Meritorious Honor Award, Foreign Opers Admin, 53; Distinguished Pub Serv, Int Coop Admin, 55; Superior Honor Award, Agency for Int Develop, 65, Distinguished Honor Award, 70; Career Serv Award, Nat Civil Serv League, 67. Mailing Add: RFD 1 Williamstown VT 05679

MACDONALD, DONALD PAUL (D)
Treas, Denver Co Dem Cent Comt, Colo
b Newport, RI, Apr 19, 31; s Bertram I MacDonald & Pauline Toomey M; m 1959 to Diane Carroll; c Theresa Carroll, Sheila Joan & D Patrick. Educ: Providence Col, AB, 52; Georgetown Univ, LLB, 56, LLM, 63; Phi Alpha Delta. Polit & Govt Pos: State coordr, Sen Carroll Senate Campaign, 62; dist capt, Denver Co Dem Cent Comt, Colo, 66-71, chmn rules comt, 71-73, treas, 73-; mem, Colo Dem State Cent Comt, 66-71, publicity dir, 69-70; deleg-at-lg, Dem Nat Conv, 68; Denver chmn, Lynch Senate Campaign, 68; mem, Steering Comt for Humphrey, Colo, 68; chmn, Kennedy Campaign, Denver, 68. Bus & Prof Pos: Assoc, law firm, Smith & Pepper, Washington, DC, 58-62; asst US attorney, Denver, Colo, 63-66; vis lectr, Univ Colo Law Sch, 66-, dir, Legal Aid & Defender Prog, 67-69; partner, law firm, Carroll & MacDonald, 66-71; partner, MacDonald & Fattor, 71-74; partner, Hornbein, MacDonald & Fattor, 74- Mil Serv: Entered as Pvt, Army, 52, released as Cpl, 54, after serv in Spec Serv, Ft Dix, NJ, 52-54. Mem: Am Bar Asn; Georgetown Univ Alumni Asn (bd gov); Nat Legal Aid & Defender Asn; Denver Bar Asn (chmn defense of indigents comt); United Cerebral Palsy (dir, 72-). Relig: Catholic. Mailing Add: 740 Fillmore St Denver CO 80206

MACDONALD, ELMER (R)
Ind State Rep
Polit & Govt Pos: Ind State Rep, 65-66 & 71-; co councilman, Allen Co, 69-70. Bus & Prof Pos: Pres & gen mgr, W&W Concrete, Inc, Roanoke. Mil Serv: Corps of Engrs, Army. Mem: Scottish Rite; Home Lodge; Mizpah Temple; Elks; YMCA. Relig: Presbyterian. Mailing Add: 722 Pelham Dr Ft Wayne IN 46825

MACDONALD, JOHN LAWRENCE (D)
NH State Rep
b Boston, Mass, Nov 27, 24; s William Francis MacDonald & Mary Isabel MacIsaac M; m to Judith A Spiers; c Eileen Marie (Mrs Donahue), John Lawrence, II, Susanne Rita, Paul Thomas, William Martin, William Joseph Carey & Judith Elizabeth Carey. Educ: Univ Nebr, 43; St Norbert's Col, 43-44; Boston Univ, 46-52. Polit & Govt Pos: Sch committeeman, City of Manchester, NH, 57-61, chmn finance comn, 61-62; staff, US Senate, 62-63; NH State Rep, 71- Bus & Prof Pos: Pres, Mailway's of New Eng, 50-57; pres, Boston Distrib Serv, 57-66; pres, MacDonald Assocs, Advert, 62-; dir, Adman Sign & Display, Manchester, 71-; dir, New Eng Region, Miss Am Teenager Pageant, 74- Mil Serv: Entered as Pvt, Army, 43, released as Cpl, 45, after serv in 75th Inf Div, Africa, Italy, France, Ger & Austria, 44-45; Rome Arnc Campaign, Southern France, Cent Europe & Cassino Medals with Four Battle Stars; Two Presidential Unit Citations. Mem: Advert Specialty Asn; Advert Club of NH; NH Sign Asn (secy); Nat Plastic Sign Asn; United Commercial Travelers (past counr). Honors & Awards: Salesman of the Year, Advert Distrib of Am, 49. Relig: Catholic. Mailing Add: 2971 Brown Ave Manchester NH 03103

MACDONALD, KEN (D)
Calif State Assemblyman
Mailing Add: 3212 Loma Vista Rd Ventura CA 93003

MACDONALD, RAYMOND M (R)
RI State Rep
Mailing Add: 145 Coldbrook Rd Warwick RI 02888

MACDONALD, TORBERT H (D)
US Rep, Mass
b Boston, Mass, June 6, 17; s John G Macdonald & Harriet Hart M; m 1944 to Phyllis Brooks; c Torbert Hart, Laurie, Brian & Robin. Educ: Phillips Andover Acad; Harvard Univ, AB, 40; LLB, 46. Polit & Govt Pos: Trial attorney, New Eng Nat Labor Rels Bd, 48-52; US Rep, Mass, 55-; deleg, Dem Nat Conv, 68. Bus & Prof Pos: Legal asst to Eric Johnston, Motion Picture Producers Asn, 46-47. Mil Serv: Lt(jg), Naval Res, 42-44; Comdr, PT boat; decorated Silver Star; Presidential Citation. Mem: Fed, Mass & Middlesex Bar Asns. Legal Res: 63 Appleton St Malden MA 02148 Mailing Add: 2470 Rayburn Bldg Washington DC 20515

MACDONALD, VIRGINIA B (R)
Ill State Sen
Mailing Add: 515 S Belmont Ave Arlington Heights IL 60005

MACDONALD, WILLIAM (D)
Mem, Nev State Dem Cent Comt
b Los Angeles, Calif, Nov 23, 32; s Maxwell Macdonald & Helen Margaret Langner M; m 1963 to Blanche Jean Trounday; c Michael & Maureen. Educ: Univ of Nev, BS in Agr, 57; Washington Col of Law, LLB, 63; Lambda Chi Alpha; Delta Theta Phi. Polit & Govt Pos: Deleg, Nev State Dem Conv, 54-; chmn of alt deleg, Dem Nat Conv, 56, deleg & secy deleg, 68; ranching rep, Nev Indust Comt, 57-59; staff mem, US Sen Alan Bible, Washington, DC, 60-63; lawyer & Asst Dist Attorney, Humboldt Co, Nev, 63-66, Dist Attorney, 67-; Acting Dist Attorney, Lander Co, 64-66, chmn, Humboldt Co Dem Cent Comt, 64-66; mem, Nev State Dem Cent Comt, 64- Bus & Prof Pos: Sportswriter, Nev State J, Reno, 50-51 & 54-57; legal asst, Sierra Pac Power Co, 63. Mil Serv: Entered as Seaman 2/C, Navy, 52, released as PO 3/C, 53. Mem: Nat Dist Attorneys Asn (dir, 71-); Nev Dist Attorneys Asn; KofC; Elks; Nev Taxpayers Asn. Honors & Awards: Man of the Year, Humboldt Co, Nev, 70. Relig: Catholic. Legal Res: One Vista Ave Winnemucca NV 89445 Mailing Add: Humboldt County Court House Winnemucca NV 89445

MACE, HELENE G (R)
State Committeewoman, NJ State Rep Party
b Waltham, Mass, Apr 4, 18; d William John Trumble & Ellen Cronin T; m 1946 to Charles Mace, Jr. Educ: Our Lady Help of Christians High Sch, Mass, grad, 37. Polit & Govt Pos: Pres, Ladies' Rep Club, NWildwood, NJ, 55; pres, reorgn chmn & past pres Rep Club of Cape May Co, 58-60; pres, Cape May Co Women's Rep Club, 59; mem bd gov NJ Fedn Rep Women, 60-63, southeastern regional chmn, 64-66, second vpres, 71-; state committeewoman, NJ State Rep Party, 61-; chmn, Nixon-Lodge Campaign, Cape May Co, 60, Goldwater-Miller Campaign, 64 & Women for Nixon-Agnew, 68; mem, NJ Rep Gubernatorial Screening Comt, 65; mem, Cape May Co Bd Elec, 67-, chmn, 70; mem six mem comt, NJ Gubernatorial Ethics Comt, 69; campaign chmn, Cape May Co Rep Orgn, 71-72, chmn, Fund Raising Dinner, 71 & 72; Cape May Co chmn, Reelec of the President, 72. Mem: Cape May Co Heart Asn; Am Heart Asn; Cath Daughters Am (Court Ann Aloysius 1634, Wildwood, NJ). Honors & Awards: Bronze Medal, Community Serv Munic chmn, Cape May Co Heart Asn, 55-66, Silver Medallion secy, 56-66; Mahogany & Brass Plaque chmn, Heart Fund, 58 & 59. Relig: Catholic. Mailing Add: Four Weeks Ave Mace Tract North Wildwood NJ 08260

MACEACHERN, ROBERT A (D)
Maine State Rep
Mailing Add: 18 E Broadway Lincoln ME 04457

MACELWEE, HELEN (COLLINS) (R)
b Stevens Point, Wis; d Dr Joseph V Collins & Jeannette M Gasehe C; m to Irvin R MacElwee; wid; c Marilyn (Mrs Bruce Throckmorton) & Donald Beall. Educ: Univ Wis, Stevens Point, grad; Delta Zeta. Polit & Govt Pos: Pres, Rep Women Pa, Philadelphia, 55-60; pres, Pennsylvania Coun Rep Women, Harrisburg, 60-62, mem policy comt, currently; mem exec comt, Nat Fedn Rep Women, 61-64; alt deleg, Rep Nat Conv, 72. Publ: Co-auth, 4 Algebras, Am Bk Co, 16; co-auth, Hints for Reading Bible, Holman Bible Co, 32; Words from Greek & Latin Origin, Bukolt Publ Co, 40. Mem: Colonial Dames; DAR (regent, Philadelphia chap); Womens Soc Prevention Cruelty Animals (dir, Philadelphia). Honors & Awards: Alumni Achievement Award, Univ Wis, Stevens Point; Citizens Plaque, Lions. Relig: Presbyterian. Legal Res: 909 Mt Holyoke Pl Swarthmore PA 19081 Mailing Add: Box 143 Swarthmore PA 19081

MACFARLAND, CELIA COGHLAN (R)
b New York, NY, July 9, 45; d John Philip Coghlan & Barbara Blyth C. Educ: Stanford Univ, AB, 66. Polit & Govt Pos: Staff asst, McCloskey for President Campaign, Calif, 71-72; staff asst, US Rep Paul N McCloskey, Jr, 72-73, admin asst, 73- Bus & Prof Pos: Staff asst, Marsh & McLennan, Inc, Calif, 67-68; staff asst, Owens-Corning Fiberglas, 69-70; asst dir, Univ Mich Law Sch Fund, 70-71. Legal Res: 1800 Floribunda Ave Hillsborough CA 94010 Mailing Add: 1255 35th St NW Washington DC 20007

MACFARLANE, M JAMES (D)
Utah State Sen
b Hooper, Utah, July 7, 21; s John Menzies Macfarlane & Nora Parker M; m 1949 to Marilyn Petty; c Sheri Lynn, Geri Ann, John P, Janene & Jefferey J. Educ: Brigham Young Univ, BS, 47; Univ Utah, MS, 59; Phi Delta Kappa. Polit & Govt Pos: Utah State Rep, 59-63 & 65-67; mem, Utah Legis Coun & Western Interstate Coun State Govt Comt on Hwys, 65-67; State Bd Family Serv, Salt Lake City, 69-; Utah State Sen, 71- Bus & Prof Pos: Teacher health & phys educ, Jordan Sch Dist, Sandy, Utah, 47-56, co-dir, Jordan Merit Study, 56-59, elem sch prin, 59- Mil Serv: Entered as Pvt, Air Force, 42, released as 1st Lt, 45, after serv as pilot, 8th Air Force; Lt Col, Air Force Res, currently; Distinguished Flying Cross; Air Medal with Three Oak Leaf Clusters; ETO Campaign Ribbon with Two Battle Stars. Mem: Nat Educ Asn; Utah Educ Asn; Jordan Educ Asn; Midvale Kiwanis; Midvale Community Develop Coun. Relig: Latter-day Saint. Mailing Add: 567 Coolidge St Midvale UT 84047

MACGREGOR, CLARK (R)
b Minneapolis, Minn, July 12, 22; s William E MacGregor & Edith Clark M; m to Barbara Porter Spicer; c Susan, Laurie & Eleanor. Educ: Dartmouth Col on acad scholarship, AB, with honors, 44; Univ Minn, LLB, 48. Polit & Govt Pos: US Rep, Minn, 60-70; deleg, Rep Nat Conv, 64 & 68; Counsel to President, 71-72; campaign mgr, Comt to Reelect the President, 72. Bus & Prof Pos: Lawyer, practicing trial lawyer, 48-60, partner in King & MacGregor. Mil Serv: Army; commissioned directly in the field in Burma while serv with Off Strategic Serv. Mem: Am Legion; VFW. Relig: Presbyterian. Mailing Add: 2834 Foxhall Rd NW Washington DC 20007

MACGREGOR, HERBERT L (R)
NH State Rep
Mailing Add: 50 N Main St Derry NH 03038

MACHEN, HERVEY GILBERT, JR **(D)**
b Washington, DC, Oct 14, 16; s Hervey Gilbert Machen & Helen Middleton M; m 1941 to Marian Kathryn Davis; c William L, Hervey G, III, Susan H (Mrs Gill), Judith A & Theodore D. Educ: Southeastern Univ, Washington, DC, LLB, 39, LLM, 41; Sigma Delta Kappa; Delta Sigma Phi. Polit & Govt Pos: Asst state's attorney, Prince George's Co, Md, 47-51; city attorney, Cheverly, 47-57, Hyattsville, 50-57; Md State Deleg, 55-64; US Rep, Md, 65-69; deleg, Dem Nat Conv, 68. Bus & Prof Pos: Attorney-at-law, 40-64; dir, Md Home Title Co, 54-, Citizen's Bank of Md, 61-; partner, Machen & Brooks, Attorneys, 64-71 & Machen & Aldridge, 71- Mil Serv: Enlisted in Coast Artil, Army, 41, released as Capt, 46, after serv in Qm Gen Off, Washington, DC & Spec Detachment, European Theater, 44-45; European Campaign Ribbon with Two Battle Stars. Mem: Md & Am Bar Asns; Kiwanis Club; Am Legion; Almas Temple Shrine; Mt Hermon Lodge. Relig: Episcopal. Legal Res: 4107 Hamilton St Hyattsville MD 20781 Mailing Add: 4328 Farragut St Hyattsville MD 20781

MACHIDA, GERALD KIYOYUKU **(D)**
Hawaii State Rep
b Puunene, Maui, Hawaii, Sept 23, 37; s Seichi Machida & Mildred Hazama M; m 1959 to Eleanor Misuye Suzuki; c Roxanne Kimie & Keith Mikio. Educ: Univ Hawaii, Degree Mech Eng; Hui-o-Haumana. Polit & Govt Pos: Hawaii State Rep, 74- Bus & Prof Pos: Div chief, Hawaii Govt Employees' Asn, 67- Mem: Lions; PTA; Hawaii Heart Asn. Relig: Christian. Mailing Add: 508 Kamehameha Ave Kahului HI 96732

MACHIN, RAFAEL **(POPULAR DEMOCRAT, PR)**
Rep, PR House of Rep
Mailing Add: State Capitol San Juan PR 00901

MACINNES, GORDON A, JR **(D)**
NJ State Assemblyman
Mailing Add: State House Trenton NJ 08625

MACIVER, DALE **(D)**
Counsel, DC Comt, US House Rep
b Superior, Wis, Apr 13, 23; s Ernest D MacIver & Elsie Swanson M; single. Educ: Univ Minn Sch Bus Admin, BBA, 47, Law Sch, JD, 50; Phi Delta Phi. Polit & Govt Pos: Asst city attorney, Duluth, Minn, 51-54; Asst Attorney Gen, Minn, 55 & 62; Comnr of Aeronaut, State of Minn, 56-61; admin asst to US Rep Don Fraser, 63-73; counsel, DC Comt, US House Rep, 73- Mil Serv: Entered as A/S, Navy, 43, released as Lt(jg), 46; Atlantic & Pac Theatre Ribbons. Mem: Am & Fed Bar Asns. Relig: Presbyterian. Mailing Add: 1001 Third St SW Washington DC 20024

MACIVER, JOHN KENNETH **(R)**
b Milwaukee, Wis, Mar 22, 31; s Wallace MacIver & Elizabeth MacRae M; m 1954 to Margaret Jean Vail; c Douglas Bruce, Carolyn Vail, Kenneth Dunkin & Laura Elizabeth. Educ: Univ Wis, BS, 53, LLB, 55; Phi Kappa Psi; Phi Delta Theta; Phi Delta Phi. Polit & Govt Pos: Urban coordr, Knowles for Gov Comt, 64 & 66, vchmn, 68; chmn, Wis Nixon for President Comt, 68 & 72; vchmn, Leonard for US Sen Comt, 68; deleg, Rep Nat Conv, 68, alt deleg, 72; chmn, Olson for Gov Comt, 70. Mem: Wis Bar Asn; Nat Coun Alcoholism (chmn bd & mem exec comt); Milwaukee Symphony Orchestra (mem bd & exec comt); Wis Cardiovascular Found (mem bd); Gtr Milwaukee Surv of Soc Welfare & Health Serv, Inc (chmn health comt). Relig: Methodist. Mailing Add: 5486 N Lake Dr Milwaukee WI 53217

MACK, BARRON BAYLES **(D)**
Exec Committeeman, SC State Dem Party
b Ft Mill, SC, Sept 19, 34; s William Bayles Mack & Elizabeth Mills M; m 1957 to Joanne Arnold; c Barron Bayles, Jr & Frances Elizabeth. Educ: Davidson Col, BS, 56; Washington & Lee Univ, LLB, 60; Sigma Phi Epsilon; Phi Delta Phi. Polit & Govt Pos: Exec Committeeman, York Co Dem Party, SC, 60-72, vchmn, 72-73; admin asst to Congressman Tom S Gettys, 64-65; home secy, 65; deleg, Dem Nat Conv, 68 & 72; magistrate, Ft Mill, SC, 69-70; mem, SC Crime Comn, 70-75; mem, Nat Finance Coun, Nat Dem Party. Bus & Prof Pos: Partner, Mack & Mack, Attorneys-at-law, 60-; pres, Ft Mill Credit Bur Inc, 61-, Dollars & Sense Investment Co Inc, 65- & Key Investment Corp, 66-; city attorney, 70- Mil Serv: Entered as 2nd Lt, Army, 56, released as Capt, 68, after serv in Judge Adv Gen Corps. Mem: SC Trial Lawyers Asn; CofC; Elks; SC Munic Asn (bd dirs); Am Legion. Honors & Awards: Distinguished Serv Award & Outstanding Young Man of the Year, Ft Mill Jr CofC. Relig: Presbyterian; pres of men & deacon, Unity Presby Church. Legal Res: 217 Banks St Ft Mill SC 29715 Mailing Add: PO Box 128 Ft Mill SC 29715

MACK, DONALD CHARLES **(R)**
Chmn, Young Rep League of Minn
b Minneapolis, Minn, July 15, 48; s Charles A Mack, Jr & Lorraine Grabowski M; single. Educ: Col of St Thomas, BA, 70; Minn State Univ, Mankato Campus, MBA, 73; Alpha Phi Omega; Green Machine. Polit & Govt Pos: Mem, Young Rep League of Minn, 69-, club chmn, 70-71, dist chmn, 71-72, state treas, 72, state first vchmn, 73, chmn, 74-; campaign mgr, Pettijohn for State Auditor, 70; clerk, Comt Com & Ins, Minn State Senate, 71; city adminr, Forest Lake, 72-74. Bus & Prof Pos: Budget analyst, ITT Thorp Corp & ITT Financial Corp Subsidiaries, Int Tel & Tel Corp, 74- Mem: Asn Master Bus Admin Execs; Citizen's League Twin Cities. Relig: Roman Catholic. Mailing Add: 1457 Hartford Ave St Paul MN 55116

MACK, JAMES A **(R)**
Ariz State Sen
b Inglewood, Calif, July 26, 33; s Cecil W Mack & Dorothy Mae Ograin M; m 1957 to Juanita Sharon Haseman; c Renee Lynn, Cheryl Sue, Deborah Lee & James John. Educ: Phoenix Col, AA, 53; Ariz State Univ, BA, 58; Phi Delta Theta. Polit & Govt Pos: Rep precinct committeeman, Tempe, Ariz; Ariz State Sen, Maricopa Dist 27, 71-, chmn, Natural Resources & Environ Comt & mem, Transportation & Agr, Commerce & Labor Comts, Ariz State Senate, Senate rep, spec adv quart rev comt, Ariz Trade-Off Model Proj, mem, Gov Hwy Classification Study Comt & Gov Adv Comt on Ariz Environ, chmn, Joint House-Senate Interim Comt for Revision of Registr of Contractor's Code & mem, Joint Interim Comt Study on Water Rights, chmn, Spec Legis Study Interim Comt on Rio Salado Reclamation Proj, currently; chmn, Natural Resources & Land Use Planning Comt for Western Conf, Coun State Govt, 73- Bus & Prof Pos: Teacher & coach, Patagonia High Sch, 59; pres & gen mgr, J Mack & Co, 60-62; sales mgr, Power Tool & Machinery Sales, 63-65; pres & gen mgr, Ariz Indust Sales, 65- Mil Serv: Entered as Pvt, Army, 53, released as Pfc, 55, after serv in 7th Army, Europe, 53-55; Nat Defense, ETO & Good Conduct Medals. Mem: Phoenix Businessmens Asn; Am Soc Tool & Mfg Engrs; Ariz Mfr Asn; Toastmasters; Tempe Diablos. Relig: Congregational; Bd mem, Young Life, 73- Legal Res: 1101 Broadmor Tempe AZ 85282 Mailing Add: State Capitol Phoenix AZ 85007

MACK, PETER FRANCIS, JR **(D)**
b Carlinville, Ill, Nov 1, 16; s Peter F Mack & Catherine Kelly M; m to Romona North; c Mona Catherine & Romona Melaine. Educ: Blackburn Col; St Louis Univ; aviation courses at Springfield Jr Col, Springfield Aviation Sch. Polit & Govt Pos: US Rep, Ill, 49-63; deleg, Dem Nat Conv, 68; Ill cand, US House of Rep, 74. Bus & Prof Pos: Sponsor, Mack Educ Tours; commercial pilot; pilot, Friendship Flame, flight in interest of peace; asst to pres, Southern Rwy Syst, 63- Mil Serv: Aviator, Naval Air Force, 4 years; Comdr, Res; Air Trophy, 52. Relig: Catholic. Mailing Add: 1524 South Grand W Springfield IL 62703

MACK, THOMAS CORNELIUS **(D)**
Chmn, Orleans Co Dem Comt, NY
b Medina, NY, Sept 25, 39; s Cornelius James Mack & Hazel Gibbin M; m 1972 to Kathleen Driscoll; c Cornelius James, V & Sheila Maureen. Educ: Canisius Col, BA, 61; Georgetown Univ Law Ctr, 61-62; Buffalo Law Sch, JD, 64; Academia Debating Soc; Buffalo Law Rev. Polit & Govt Pos: Asst co attorney, Orleans Co, NY, 71-; mem, Orleans Co Indust Develop Agency, 73-; chmn, Orleans Co Dem Comt, 74- Bus & Prof Pos: Vpres & secy, Paper Welder Inc, Medina, NY, 67-; attorney & partner, Hart & Mack, Medina, 68- Mil Serv: Entered as 1st Lt, Air Force, 64, released as Capt, 67, after serv in Judge Adv Gen Dept, Strategic Air Command. Mem: Am & New York State Bar Asns; Orleans Co Bar Asn (pres, 72-); KofC; YMCA. Legal Res: 219 W Center St Medina NY 14103 Mailing Add: PO Box 248 Medina NY 14103

MACKAY, KENNETH H, JR **(D)**
Fla State Sen
Mailing Add: 214 Senate Off Bldg Tallahassee FL 32304

MACKAY, WILLIAM RAYNOR **(R)**
Rep Nat Committeeman, Mont
b Tenafly, NJ, Nov 12, 11; s Malcolm S Mackay & Helen Raynor M; m 1937 to Joyce Selleck Childs; c Julia Childs (Mrs Snell), Helen (Mrs Kampfe) & William R, Jr. Educ: Williams Col, 35; Kappa Alpha. Polit & Govt Pos: Mont State Rep, 51-53; Mont State Sen, Dist 13, 53-72; chmn, Mont Rep State Cent Comt, 54-56; mem, Mont Legis Coun, 57-63, chmn, 61-63, chmn, Mont Legis Audit Comt, 67-68, mem, 68-72; Rep Nat Committeeman, Mont, 72- Bus & Prof Pos: Pres, Lazy E L Ranch Corp, 34-; secy, Foothills Co, 55- Mem: Mason; Elks; Shrine; Mont Club; Mont Stockgrowers Asn. Relig: Congregational. Mailing Add: Box 1198 Helena MT 59601

MACKEL, EDWARD H **(R)**
Maine State Rep
b Danvers, Mass, Dec 17, 18; s Harry Mackel & Olympia Stellas M; m 1944 to Harriet Goodwin; c Andrew & Sarah. Educ: Univ NH, BS, 43; Northwestern Univ, MA, 49. Polit & Govt Pos: Maine State Rep, 75- Mil Serv: Entered as 2nd Lt, Marine Corps, 43, released as Col, 72. Mailing Add: RFD 2 Wells ME 04090

MACKENDRICK, DONALD ANTHONY **(D)**
Mem, Mesa Co Dem Exec Comt, Colo
b Hotchkiss, Colo, Nov 8, 25; s Richard P MacKendrick & Isabelle Johan Kuester M; single. Educ: Colo State Univ, BS, 50; Univ Colo, MA, 53; Lancers; Pacemaker; Pi Delta Epsilon; Ind Students Asn. Polit & Govt Pos: Secy, Mesa Co Dem Cent Comt, Colo, 61-67, chmn, 67-69; mem, Mesa Co Libr Bd, 67-73; mem, Mesa Co Dem Exec Comt, 69-; chmn, Mesa Co Centennial-Bicentennial Adv Comt, 72- Bus & Prof Pos: Teacher, Delta Co Pub Schs, 50-55; instr hist, Mesa Co Jr Col, 55- Mil Serv: Entered as Pvt, Army, 44, released as S/Sgt, 46, after serv in 90th Mil Govt Co, Army of Occupation, Japan, 45-46; Good Conduct Medal; Pac Theatre Ribbon. Mem: Am Asn Univ Prof; Grand Junction Hist Mus; Orgn Am Historians; Colo Hist Soc; VFW. Relig: Roman Catholic. Mailing Add: 117 Red Mesa Heights Grand Junction CO 81501

MACKENZIE, CHARLES A, JR **(R)**
Mass State Rep
Mailing Add: State Capitol Boston MA 02133

MACKENZIE, RONALD CONRAD **(R)**
Mass State Sen
b Waltham, Mass, May 3, 34; s Gordon Sidebotham (stepfather) & Area Freeman S; m 1958 to Janet Lee Proctor; c Jody & Scott. Educ: Dartmouth Col, AB, 56; Suffolk Univ Law Sch, currently; Phi Gamma Delta. Polit & Govt Pos: Mem, Burlington Rep Town Comt, 62-; Mass State Sen, 66-, minority whip, Mass State Sen, 66-; deleg, Rep Nat Conv, 68 & 72. Mil Serv: Entered as 2nd Lt, Army, 56, released as 1st Lt, 58, after serv in 325th AAA Bn, Air Defense Command, 56-58. Mem: Bd gov, Nat Soc of State Legis, 73-; Mass & Nat Legis Asns; Boston Life Underwriters Asn; Elks; Rotary. Honors & Awards: Named one of four outstanding young men in Mass & one of three outstanding young men in New Eng, 68. Relig: Protestant. Mailing Add: 18 Spruce Hill Rd Burlington MA 01803

MACKEY, MALCOLM H **(D)**
First VChmn, Los Angeles Co Dem Cent Comt, Calif
b Hoboken, NJ, July 20, 29; s William G Mackey & Winifred Walker Hamilton M; m 1962 to Sharon Scovill; c Michael M. Educ: NY Univ, AB, 51; Southwestern Law Sch, LLB & JD, 58; Univ Southern Calif, 58-59; Sigma Lambda Sigma. Polit & Govt Pos: Mem, Los Angeles Co Dem Cent Comt, Calif, 65-66, first vchmn, 69-; chmn, 54th Dist Dem Party, 66-68; pres, Glen Eagle Park Dem Club, 67-69; mem, Calif Dem State Cent Comt, 68- Bus & Prof Pos: Sales rep, Tidewater Oil Co, Calif, 51-54 & Richfield Oil Co, 54-55; ins adjuster, All State Ins Co, 55-56; attorney-at-law, 59- Mil Serv: Entered as Pvt, Marine Corps, 46, released as Cpl, 48, after serv in Tank Corps, ECoast & Mediterranean Areas, 46-48; Cpl, Marine Corps, 49-50; Navy Good Conduct & World War II Victory Medals; Navy Occup Medal, Mediterranean Area. Mem: Am & Los Angeles Co Bar Asns; Mason; Mex Am Polit Asns; Sons of Italy. Relig: Presbyterian. Legal Res: 5351 Vincent Ave Los Angeles CA 90041 Mailing Add: 215 W Fifth St Los Angeles CA 90043

MACKEY, RALPH EARLE **(R)**
b Everett, Wash, June 17, 30; s Earle M Mackey & Laura L Johnson M; m 1954 to Maurine Emily Gerards; c Kevin, David & Jeffrey. Educ: Univ of Puget Sound, BA in Bus, 54; Sigma Chi. Polit & Govt Pos: Rep precinct committeeman, Wash, 60-; chmn, Snohomish Co Rep Cent Comt, 62-66; comnr, Wash State Park & Recreation Comn, 67-; state committeeman,

Wash State Rep Party, 72-74. Bus & Prof Pos: Mem bd, Fireplace Asn of Am, 69-; pres, Wash Stove Works, 70- Mem: Everett Elks; Salvation Army; Boy Scouts; Am Alpine Club; Everett Mountain Rescue Unit. Honors & Awards: Snohomish Co Man of the Year Award in Sports, 63; Climbed Mt McKinley, Alaska, Mt Aconocaqua, Argentina & Mt Kilimanjaro, Africa; Civic Pride Award, 65. Relig: Presbyterian. Mailing Add: 4611 Westview Dr Everett WA 98201

MACKIE, RICHARD D (D)
Md State Deleg
Mailing Add: Little Elk Farms RD 5 Elkton MD 21921

MACKINNON, GEORGE EDWARD (R)
b St Paul, Minn, Apr 22, 06; s James Alexander MacKinnon & Cora Asselstine M; m 1938 to Elizabeth Valentine Davis; c Catharine A, James D & Leonard D. Educ: Univ Colo, 23-24; Univ Minn, 24-29; Phi Delta Phi; Delta Tau Delta; M Club. Polit & Govt Pos: Minn State Rep, 29th Dist, 35-42; US Rep, Third Dist, Minn, 47-48; US Attorney, Dist of Minn, 53-58; Rep nominee for Gov, Minn, 58; spec asst to US Attorney Gen, Dept of Justice, 60; judge, US Court of Appeals, DC Circuit, 69- Bus & Prof Pos: Asst to counsel, Investors Syndicate, 29-42; gen counsel & vpres, Investors Mutual, Inc, 61-69. Mil Serv: Entered as Lt(jg), Naval Res, 42, released as Comdr, 46, after serv in Eastern Sea Frontier; cited for meritorious serv by Comdr Air Force, US Atlantic Fleet. Publ: Author, Old Age Assistance Act, 36, Minn Reorganization Act & State Civil Service Act, 39. Mem: Am & Minn Bar Asns; Am Judicature Soc; Mason; Scottish Rite. Relig: Episcopal. Mailing Add: US Court of Appeals Washington DC 20001

MACLAUGHLIN, HARRY HUNTER (D)
Assoc Justice, Minn Supreme Court
b Breckenridge, Minn, Aug 9, 27; s Harry Hunter MacLaughlin & Grace Swank M; m 1958 to Mary Jean Shaffer; c David & Douglas. Educ: Univ Minn, BBA, with distinction, 49, JD, 56; Beta Gamma Sigma; Phi Delta Phi. Polit & Govt Pos: Mem bd ed, Univ Minn Law Rev; mem, Minn Charter comn, Minneapolis, 66-72; mem nat adv coun, Small Bus Admin, 67-69; mem, Minn State Col Bd, 71-72; mem Minn Judicial Coun, 72; assoc justice, Minn Supreme Court, 72- Bus & Prof Pos: Law secy, Justice Frank Gallagher, Minn Supreme Court, 55; Attorney, Larson, Loevinger, Lindquist, Freeman & Fraser, 56-58, MacLaughlin & Mondale, 58-61 & MacLaughlin & Harstad, 61-72. Mil Serv: Entered as Seaman 2/C, Navy, 45, released as Yeoman 2/C, after serv in UD, 45-46. Mem: Am & Minn Bar Asns; Am Trial Lawyers Asn; Am Judicature Soc; Am Legion. Relig: Methodist. Mailing Add: 2301 Oliver Ave S Minneapolis MN 55405

MACLEAN, WILLIAM Q, JR (D)
Mass State Rep
b New Bedford, Mass, Nov 4, 34; s William Q MacLean & Charlotte L Hillman M; m 1956 to Martha M George; c Douglas Louis, Kim Marie & Laureen Jean. Educ: Univ Mass. Polit & Govt Pos: Mem, Fairhaven Sch Comt, Mass, 59-60; Mass State Rep, currently. Bus & Prof Pos: MacLean's Seafood, 60-66; Cornish & Co, Gen Ins, 66- Mem: Moose; Lions. Relig: Episcopal. Mailing Add: 60 Lafayette St Fairhaven MA 02719

MACLEOD, JAMES C (R)
Maine State Rep
Mailing Add: Bar Harbor ME 04609

MACOMBER, WILLIAM BUTTS JR (R)
b Rochester, NY, Mar 28, 21; s William Butts Macomber & Elizabeth Currie Ranlet M; m 1963 to Phyllis D Bernau. Educ: Yale, AB, 43, MA, 47; Harvard, LLB, 49; Univ Chicago, MA, 51. Polit & Govt Pos: Rep committeeman, Rochester, NY, 46-51; spec asst to spec asst to secy for intel, US Dept State, 53-54; admin asst to Sen John S Cooper, 54; spec asst to Undersecy of State Herbert Hoover, Jr, 55, spec asst to Secy of State John F Dulles, 55-57, Asst Secy of State for Cong Rels, 57-62 & 67-69, ambassador to Jordan, 61-64, asst adminr, Agency for Int Develop, 64-67, Dep Undersecy of State for Admin, 70-73; US Ambassador to Turkey, 73-74. Bus & Prof Pos: Lectr govt, Boston Univ, 47-49. Mil Serv: Marine Corps, 43-46. Legal Res: 5 Buckingham St Rochester NY 14607 Mailing Add: Dept of State Washington DC 20521

MACY, JOHN WILLIAMS JR (D)
b Chicago, Ill, Apr 6, 17; s John Williams Macy & Juliette Shaw M; m 1944 to Joyce Hagen; c Thomas L, Mary D, Susan B & Richard H. Educ: Wesleyan Univ, BA, 38; Am Univ, 38-39; Phi Beta Kappa. Hon Degrees: LLD, Cornell Col, 63, Colgate Univ, 65, Allegheny Col, 65, Eastern Ky Col, 66, Dartmouth Col, 66, Univ of Del, 67, Wesleyan Univ, 67, Ind State Univ, 68, Ithaca Col, 69, St John's Univ, 69 & Austin Col, 72. Polit & Govt Pos: Asst dir, Civilian Personnel, War Dept, Washington, DC, 40-43 & 46-47; dir of personnel & orgn, Santa Fe Opers Off, Atomic Energy Comn, Los Alamos, NMex, 47-51; spec asst to Under Secy of Army, Washington, DC, 51-53; exec dir, US Civil Serv Comn, 53-58, chmn, 61-69. Bus & Prof Pos: Exec vpres, Wesleyan Univ, 58-61; pres, Corp for Pub Broadcasting, Washington, DC, 69-72; mem bd gov, Am Stock Exchange, 72-; co-chmn, Comn Acad Tenure, 71-72; mem, Comn Non-Traditional Study, 71-73; pres, Coun of Better Bus Bureaus, Inc, 73- Publ: Co-auth, Public Workers & Public Unions, Prentice Hall, 71; Faculty Tenure, Jossy-Bass, 73; To Irrigate a Wasteland, Univ Calif, 74; plus others. Mil Serv: Entered as Pvt, Air Force, 43, released as Capt, 47, after serv in US & Pac Theaters. Mem: Am Soc for Pub Admin; Soc for Adv of Mgt; Pub Personnel Asn; Soc for Personnel Admin. Honors & Awards: Presidential Medal of Freedom, 69. Relig: Protestant. Mailing Add: 1127 Langley Lane McLean VA 22101

MADAY, MICHAEL JEROME (DFL)
Mem, Minn Dem-Farmer-Labor State Cent Comt
b Fairmont, Minn, May 13, 54; s Philip Valentine Maday & Constance Hayes M; single. Educ: Univ Minn, Minneapolis, 72- Polit & Govt Pos: Mem, Wright Co Dem-Farmer-Labor Cent Comt, Minn, 72-; deleg, Dem Nat Mid Term Conf, 74; mem, Dem-Farmer-Labor State Cent Comt, 74- Bus & Prof Pos: Driver, Blue & White Cab Co, Minneapolis, Minn, 74. Mem: Teamsters Union Local 792; Am & Minn Civil Liberties Union; Am for Dem Action. Honors & Awards: Nat High Sch Hon Soc, 71-72; John Philip Sousa Award, Buffalo High Sch Music Dept, 72; Most Valuable Player, Buffalo High Sch Golf Team, 72; Advertising Award, Minnesota High Sch Press Asn, 73; Best Dancer, Buffalo High Sch, 72. Relig: Catholic. Legal Res: 209 NW Sixth St Buffalo MN 55313 Mailing Add: 3318 Centennial Hall Univ Minn Minneapolis MN 55455

MADDEN, RAY J (D)
US Rep, Ind
b Waseca, Minn. Educ: Creighton Univ, LLB. Polit & Govt Pos: Munic judge, Omaha, Nebr; city comptroller, Gary, Ind, 35-38; treas, Lake Co, 38-42; US Rep, Ind, currently, chmn, Rules Comt, US House Rep, currently; deleg, Dem Nat Conv, 68; ex-officio deleg, Dem Nat Mid-Term Conf, 74. Bus & Prof Pos: Attorney. Mil Serv: World War I. Mem: Am Legion. Legal Res: Gary IN Mailing Add: US House of Rep Washington DC 20515

MADDEN, ROBERT BRUCE (D)
Kans State Sen
b Norfolk, Va, Nov 22, 44; s Bruce B Madden & Helen Bradshaw M; m 1970 to Elizabeth Ann Lower; c Tracy, Robert, II & Randall Bradshaw. Educ: Ventura Jr Col, 63-64; Rockhurst Col, 64-65; Wichita State Univ, 69-70. Polit & Govt Pos: Dem precinct committeeman, Wichita, Kans, 66-70; Kans State Rep, Dist 85, 67-73; chmn, Fifth Ward Rep Orgn, 68-70; Kans State Sen, 73- Bus & Prof Pos: Pres, Prof Bus Serv; acct exec, E F Hutton, currently. Mil Serv: Entered as Pvt, Army, 67, released as 1st Lt, 70, after serv in 173rd Airborne Bde, 2/503rd Inf, Vietnam, 69-70; Bronze Star; Air Medal; Vietnamese Serv Medal; Vietnam Campaign Ribbon; Nat Defense Medal. Publ: The dangers of drug abuse, 70. Mem: VFW; Am Legion. Relig: Catholic. Mailing Add: 1976 Greenfield Wichita KS 67217

MADDOX, ALVA HUGH (D)
Assoc Justice, Ala Supreme Court
b Andalusia, Ala, Apr 17, 30; s Christopher Columbus Maddox & Audie Freeman M; m 1958 to Virginia Ann Roberts; c Robert Hugh & Patricia Jane. Educ: Univ Ala, AB, 52, LLB, 57; Omicron Delta Kappa; Sigma Delta Chi; Phi Alpha Delta; Arnold Air Soc; Pershing Rifles; Jasons; Quadrangle; Press Club. Polit & Govt Pos: Law clerk, Court of Appeals, Ala, 57; field examr, Vet Admin, 57-58; law clerk, US Dist Court, Montgomery, 58-60; circuit judge, 15 Judicial Circuit, 63, asst dist attorney, 63-64; legal adv, Gov George C Wallace, 65-67, Gov Lurlee B Wallace, 68 & Gov Albert P Brewer, 68-69; assoc justice, Ala Supreme Court, 69- Bus & Prof Pos: Assoc, Law Off of John P Kohn, 61-65. Mil Serv: Entered as 2nd Lt, Air Force, 52, released as 1st Lt, 54, after serv in Air Forces of Europe; Lt Col, Air Force Res, 72-; Nat Defense Serv Medal; Army of Occup of Europe. Mem: Am & Fed Bar Asns; Am Legion; Ala YMCA Youth Legis & Cent Br YMCA, Montgomery (bd dirs); Farrah Law Soc. Relig: Southern Baptist; Deacon, First Baptist Church, Montgomery, Ala. Mailing Add: 3406 LeBron Rd Montgomery AL 36111

MADDOX, LESTER G (D)
b Atlanta, Ga, Sept 30, 15; s Dean G Maddox & Flonnie M; m 1936 to Virginia Cox; c Linda, Lester, Jr, Virginia Louise & Larry. Educ: Col equivalent correspondence course. Polit & Govt Pos: Gov, Ga, 67-71, Lt Gov, 71-75. Bus & Prof Pos: Real estate, grocery, restaurant, furniture store, souvenir & novelty shop. Mem: Mason; Moose; hon mem, Ga Sheriffs' Asn, Peace Officers Asn & Justice of Peace & Constables' Asn. Relig: Baptist. Mailing Add: 100 Robin Rd SE Marietta GA 30060

MADDOX, LUTHER WARREN (D)
Mo State Rep
b Houston, Ark, Mar 25, 24; s Luther E Maddox & Orphie Jane Lawson M; m 1953 to Rebecca Irene James; c John Warren, James Kendall & Lu Ann. Educ: Gideon Pub Schs, 12 years. Polit & Govt Pos: Mo State Rep, 71- Bus & Prof Pos: Owner, Maco Construction Co, Clarkton, Mo & Farm Lands. Mem: Mason (32 degree); Consistory; Shrine; Kiwanis Club; Farm Bur. Relig: Presbyterian; chmn bd deacons. Mailing Add: Rte 1 Clarkton MO 63837

MADDOX, NEVA WILEY PEMBERTON (D)
VChmn, Seventh Cong Dist Dem Cent Comt, Mo
b Crane, Mo, Sept 5, 19; d W Lloyd Wiley & Jessie Thomas W; m 1940 to Neil S Pemberton, wid; remarried 1972 to Bill J Maddox; c Gail (Mrs R V Saunders) & L Steven. Educ: Southwest Mo State Univ, BS, 56; Univ Mo, MEd, 65; Okla State Univ, 69-70; Delta Pi Epsilon; Pi Omega Pi; Bus Club. Polit & Govt Pos: Committeewoman, Hurley Twp, Mo, 60-; secy, Stone Co Dem Cent Comt, formerly, chmn, formerly, vchmn, currently; publicity chmn, Seventh Dist, Women's Dem Club, 68-69; secy-treas, Stone Co Dem Club, 69-; secy, Seventh Cong Dist Dem Cent Comt, 70-72, vchmn, 72-74, chmn, 74-; deleg, Dem Nat Conv, 72. Bus & Prof Pos: Dept head, Off Admin & Bus Educ, Southwest Mo State Univ, 73- Mem: Delta Kappa Gamma; Nat Bus Educ Asn; Am Voc Asn; Admin Mgt Soc (vchmn, 75-); SW Mo Resource Conserv & Develop Proj (secy, 74-). Honors & Awards: Outstanding Farm Family, Stone Co, 62. Relig: Church of Christ. Mailing Add: Rte 2 Crane MO 65633

MADDOX, ODE (D)
Ark State Rep
Mailing Add: PO Box 598 Oden AR 71961

MADDUX, DON STEWART (D)
Ohio State Rep
b Lancaster, Ohio, Mar 23, 40; s Robert Wilson Maddux & Donna Louise Potter M; m 1970 to Vickie Elaine Smith; c Jason. Educ: Wittenberg Univ, BS, 62; Ohio Northern Univ Law Sch, 65-66; Ohio State Univ, 66-67; Pi Sigma Alpha. Polit & Govt Pos: Ohio State Rep, 25th Dist, 69-73, 90th Dist, 73- Bus & Prof Pos: Lifeguard, Miller Pool, Lancaster, Ohio, 56-59, mgr, 60; asst mgr & swimming & diving coach, Tiki Swim Club, 61; lifeguard, Glen Echo Swim Club, Md, 62; mem staff, YMCA, Springfield, Ohio, 62; teacher health & Am hist & softball coach, Alice Deal Jr High Sch, Washington, DC, 62-65; with recreation dept, Columbus, Ohio, 66; teacher Am hist & health, Lancaster Jr High Sch, 67-68. Mem: All Lancaster Masonic Bodies; United Commercial Travelers; Fairfield Grange. Honors & Awards: Nat High Sch Honor Soc, 58; Outstanding Young Man of Am, 70; recognized as Distinguished Mem of 108th Gen Assembly in Ohio by unanimous passage of House Resolution 215, 70; participant, Eagleton Inst Polit, 71. Relig: Presbyterian. Mailing Add: 135 Berkeley Dr Lancaster OH 43130

MADDY, KENNETH LEON (R)
Calif State Assemblyman
b Santa Monica, Calif, May 22, 34; s Russell T Maddy & Anna M Balzer M; m 1957 to Beverly Ann Chinello; c Deanna G, Donald P & Marilyn M. Educ: Fresno State Col, BS, 57; Univ Calif, Los Angeles Law Sch, JD, 63; Blue Key; Sigma Nu; Phi Delta Phi. Polit & Govt Pos: Calif State Assemblyman, Dist 32, 71- Bus & Prof Pos: Attorney at law, Chinello, Chinello, Maddy & Shelton, Fresno, Calif, 63- Mil Serv: Entered as 2nd Lt, Air Force, 57, released as 1st Lt, 60, after serv in Air Defense Command; Capt, Air Force Res. Mem: Calif State Bar Asn; Rotary; Jr CofC; CofC. Relig: Protestant. Legal Res: 1221 Van Ness Ave Fresno CA 93721 Mailing Add: State Capitol Sacramento CA 95814

MADEIRA, EUGENIA CASSATT (R)
VChmn, Chester Co Rep Finance Comt, Pa
b Ithan, Pa, Aug 11, 97; d Joseph Gardner Cassatt & Eugenia Carter C; m 1927 to Charles Davis, div, 39; m 1952 to Percy Childs Madeira, wid, 68; stepchildren, Percy C Madeira III, Francis K C, Madeira & Eleanor (Mrs Thomas N White). Educ: Presby Sch of Nursing, Philadelphia, 18-19; Westover Sch. Polit & Govt Pos: Chmn, Chester Co Comt for Repeal of Prohibition, Pa, 28-32; dir-at-lg, founder & first pres, Valley Forge Coun of Rep, 37-; mem bd, Willistown, Tredyffrin, Easttown Joint Sch Dist, 48-69; vchmn, Chester Co Rep Finance Comt, 70-; mem, Pa Rep Finance Comt, currently; alt deleg, Rep Nat Conv, 72; Pa Mem, Electoral Col, 72. Mil Serv: Nurse, Free French Forces, 42-43, serv in Africa, Brazzaville, Pointe Noire & Ft Lamay; Civil Affairs Med Dept, 43-44, Algiers; Off of Strategic Serv, Italy, France & London, 44-45. Mem: Gulph Mill Golf Club; Pohoqualine Fish Asn; Pa Farmer Asn. Relig: Episcopal; Vestry woman, Church of the Good Samaritan, Paoli, Pa. Mailing Add: Crumdale Farm 3424 Grubbs Mill Rd Berwyn PA 19312

MADEL, RAYMOND PETER JR (R)
Chmn, Waseca Co Rep Comt, Minn
b Evanston, Ill, Aug 29, 30; s Raymond Peter Madel & Alice Mathews M; m 1957 to Mary Ann Schumacher; c Mary Elizabeth, Raymond Peter, III, Barry John & Christopher William. Educ: Cornell Univ, BS, 52; Alpha Tau Omega. Polit & Govt Pos: Vchmn, Waseca Co Rep Comt, Minn, 65-71, chmn, 71- Bus & Prof Pos: Mgr, Sherman Hotel, Wolf Point, Mont, 52-56; mgr, Burke Hotel, Vermillion, SDak, 56-58; asst mgr, Westward Ho Country Club, Sioux Falls, 58-60; adminr, Lake Shore Nursing Home, Waseca, Minn, 60- Mil Serv: Entered as 2nd Lt, Army, 52, released as 1st Lt, 54, after serv in 8th Army Hq, Korea, 53-54; Army Commendation Medal; Hea-Rang with Silver Star; Korean Campaign Ribbon; UN Medal; Nat Defense Campaign Ribbons. Mem: Am Col Nursing Home Adminrs (fel, 70-); Rotary (treas & past pres, Waseca Club, 60-); Who's He, Inc (pres, 61-). Relig: Roman Catholic. Legal Res: 304 Sixth St NE Waseca MN 56093 Mailing Add: 108 Eighth St NW Waseca MN 56093

MADESON, MARVIN LOUIS (D)
Nat VChmn, New Dem Coalition
b New York, July 8, 25; s Morris Madeson & Ann Levine M; div; c Marianne, Frances & Julia. Educ: Brooklyn Col, BA, 47; NY Univ Sch of Law, JD cum laude, 50; Phi Delta Phi. Polit & Govt Pos: Deleg, Dem Nat Conv, 68, alt deleg, 72; chmn, McCarthy for Pres Campaign, Mo, 68; committeeman, Hadley Twp Dem Club, St Louis Co, 68-; chmn, New Dem Coalition of Metropolitan St Louis, 68-70; nat chmn, New Dem Coalition, 70-72, vchmn, 72-, Mo chmn; deleg, Dem Mid Term Conf, 74; mem, Mo Dem Party Planning & Policy Comt, 75. Bus & Prof Pos: Attorney, Office of Price Stabilization, Washington, DC, 51-53; supvr sales, First Investors Corp, New York, 53-56; divisional dir, Heritage Securities, 56-58; vpres, Empire Planning Corp, 58-60; treas, ITT Aetna Corp, St Louis, Mo, 60-72; polit consult, 72- Mil Serv: Entered as Pvt, Air Force, 43, released as Sgt, 46, after serv in Army Airways Communications Syst, SAtlantic Theatre, 44-46; Good Conduct Medal; SAtlantic Theatre Ribbon. Mem: NY State & District of Columbia Bar Asns; Univ City Civic Asn (former chmn); Univ City Plan Comn (former vchmn). Relig: Jewish. Mailing Add: 7829 Bentley Dr St Louis MO 63143

MADIGAN, EDWARD R (R)
US Rep, Ill
b Lincoln, Ill, Jan 13, 36; s Earl T Madigan & Theresa Loobey M; m 1955 to Evelyn George; c Kim, Kelly & Mary Beth. Educ: Lincoln Col, grad bus admin, 55. Hon Degrees: DHL, Lincoln Col. Polit & Govt Pos: Ill State Rep, 66-72; US Rep, 21st Dist, Ill, 73-, mem, Agr Comt, Interstate & Foreign Com Comt, US House of Rep, 73- Bus & Prof Pos: Owner, Yellow-Lincoln Cab Co & Car Leasing Firm, 55- Publ: Ill Jaycees (vpres, 65); Young Rep Fedn of Ill (dist gov, 64); Elks; Kiwanis; Lincoln Cof C. Honors & Awards: Outstanding Young Men of Am, Jaycees, 65; Outstanding Legis, Ill Asn of Sch Supt, 67; Excellent Record rating, Ill Agr Asn, 2 times. Relig: Catholic. Legal Res: 412 Broadway St Lincoln IL 62656 Mailing Add: 1728 Longworth House Office Bldg Washington DC 20515

MADIGAN, MICHAEL J (D)
Ill State Sen
Mailing Add: 6025 S Kenneth Ave Chicago IL 60629

MADISON, JESSE D (D)
Ill State Sen
Mailing Add: 4746 W Monroe Chicago IL 60644

MADLA, FRANK (D)
Tex State Rep
Mailing Add: PO Box 3288 San Antonio TX 78211

MADONNA, WILLIAM JOSEPH, JR (D)
Md State Deleg
b Baltimore, Md, Sept 30, 51; s William J Madonna, Sr & Phyllis Ann Stine M; single. Educ: Johns Hopkins Univ; Univ Baltimore, currently. Polit & Govt Pos: Admin asst to Sen Julian L Lapides, 73-74; Md State Deleg, 75- Bus & Prof Pos: Clerk, Files & Commun Div, Fed Bur Invest, formerly. Mem: Moose; Remington-Hampden Civic & Polit Asn (pres); Mt Royal Dem Club (bd dirs). Honors & Awards: Youngest legislator in Md Gen Assembly. Relig: Roman Catholic. Legal Res: 211 W 25th St Baltimore MD 21211 Mailing Add: 848 W 36th St Baltimore MD 21211

MADRON, THOMAS WM (D)
Mem, Warren Co Dem Exec Comt, Ky
b Salt Lake City, Utah, Oct 4, 37; s Thomas C Madron, Jr & Margaret A M; m 1960 to Beverly Brown. Educ: Westminster Col (Utah), BS, 59; Am Univ, MA, 64; Tulane Univ, PhD, 65. Polit & Govt Pos: Pres, Lycoming Co Dem Coun, 64-66; campaign aide, Milton Shapp, Pa, 66; mem, Warren Co Dem Exec Comt, 72-; deleg, Dem Nat Mid-Term Conf, 74. Bus & Prof Pos: Spec asst, Sen Frank E Moss, 59-60; instr in polit sci, Westminster Col (Utah), 60-61; asst prof polit sci, Lambuth Col, Jackson, Tenn, 63-64 & Lycoming Col, Williamsport, Pa, 64-66; prof govt & coordr for academic computerization, Western Ky Univ, Bowling Green, Ky, 67- Publ: Auth, Small Group Methods & The Study of Politics, Northwestern Univ Press, 69; co-auth, Political Parties In the US, Holbrook Press, 74 & Religion as a determinant of civil rights militancy & political participation, Am Behav Sci, 74. Mem: Am, Midwest & Western Polit Sci Asns; Southern Polit Sci Asn (coun mem). Honors & Awards: Researcher of the Year, Western Ky Univ, 74. Relig: Methodist. Legal Res: 1303 College St Bowling Green KY 42101 Mailing Add: PO Box U21 College Heights Sta Bowling Green KY 42101

MADSEN, PETER EDGAR (R)
Wyo State Sen
b Alta, Iowa, Sept 23, 05; s Christian Madsen & Christina Peterson M; m 1932 to Alice Fraser; c Barbara (Mrs Rogers) & Karen. Educ: Colo State Univ, DVM, 31; Alpha Tau Omega. Polit & Govt Pos: Wyo State Rep, 57-61; Wyo State Sen, 61-, VPres, Wyo State Senate, 66-69, Majority Floor Leader, 69-71, Pres, 71-72, chmn judiciary comt, 73-; deleg, Rep Nat Conv, 72. Bus & Prof Pos: Pres, Whitney Trust, 65-; bd dirs, First Fed Savings & Loan Asn. Mil Serv: Entered as 1st Lt, Army, 42, released as Maj, 46, after serv in Materiel Command with Air Corps. Mem: Am Vet Med Asn; Wyo Vet Med Asn; Wyo Taxpayers Asn (bd dirs, 68-); Mason; Shrine. Honors & Awards: Hon Alumnus, Colo State Univ, 72. Relig: First Baptist. Mailing Add: 1760 Martin Ave Sheridan WY 82801

MADSON, GARY KENT (R)
b Spring Valley, Wis, Oct 3, 37; s Clarence Arthur Madson & Alice Swenson M; m 1960 to Nancy Katherine Robert; c Sara Katherine & Peter Nils. Educ: Wis State Univ, River Falls, BS, 59. Polit & Govt Pos: Legis asst, US Rep Paul Findley, 70-72; dep dir for agr, Comt for the Re-Elect of the President, 72; admin asst, US Rep Edward Madigan, Ill, 73- Bus & Prof Pos: Farm ed, Daily Gazette, Sterling, Ill, 59-60; area fieldman, Wis Farm Bur Fedn, Madison, 60-63; info dir, Colo Farm Bur Fedn, Denver, 63-65; asst ed, Ill Agr Asn, Bloomington, 65-70. Mil Serv: Entered as Pvt, E-1, Army, 60, released as E-2, 60, after serv in Army Res. Mem: Aircraft Owners & Pilots Asn. Honors & Awards: Key Man, Jaycees, 68. Relig: Lutheran. Mailing Add: 7117 Devonshire Rd Alexandria VA 22307

MADURO, JOHN LAWRENCE (D)
Pres, VI Legis
b St Thomas, VI, July 1, 21; s Joseph L Maduro & Azalia Sille M; m 1949 to Claudia W Huyghue; c Juanito, Winthrop & Janice Mabel. Educ: Hampton Inst, 41-43; NY Univ, BS, 48; Nat Univ Sch Law, LLB, 54. Polit & Govt Pos: Sen, VI Legis, 58-, pres, 69-; deleg, Dem Nat Conv, 68. Bus & Prof Pos: Attorney-at-law, Birch, Maduro, PeJangh & Parrelly, 55- Mil Serv: Entered as Pvt, Army, 43, released as M/Sgt, 46, after serv in 13th Hu Pon Br, NAfrica, Italy, France & Ger, 43-46; Good Conduct Medals; Theatre Ribbons. Mem: VI, Supreme Court & Am Bar Asns; Am Legion. Relig: Roman Catholic. Mailing Add: Box 2033 Charlotte Amalie St Thomas VI 00801

MAGEE, DOUGLAS MACARTHUR (R)
b Magee, Miss, Jan 22, 42; s Walter Whaley Magee & Eva Ainsworth M; m 1964 to Jan Walker; c Deborah & Angela. Educ: Univ Southern Miss, BS in Eng, 63; George Washington Univ Sch Law, 65-66; Univ Miss Sch Law, JD, 67; basic, procurement & labor law courses, Judge Adv Gen Schs, Charlottesville, Va, 67, 69 & 70; defense small purchase course, Dept of Navy, Washington, DC, 69; Scabbard & Blade; Omicron Delta Kappa; Phi Kappa Tau. Polit & Govt Pos: Chmn, Univ Miss Young Rep, 63; campaign mgr, Prentiss Walker, 64, admin asst to US Rep Prentiss Walker, Fourth Dist, Miss, 65-66; deleg, Rep Nat Conv, 72; chmn, Mendenhall Rep Town Exec Comt, 73- Bus & Prof Pos: Private law practice, Mendenhall, Miss, 71- Mil Serv: Capt, Judge Adv Gen Corps, Army, 67-, Dep Staff Judge Adv, Ft Gordon Ga, 71-; Army Commendation Medal, 71. Mem: Am Bar Asn; Am Judicature Soc; Bar of Supreme Court of Miss; Jaycees (vpres, 73-74); Lions. Relig: Baptist. Mailing Add: 145 Maud St Mendenhall MS 39114

MAGGARD, JACK SAMUEL (D)
Chmn, Leslie Co Dem Exec Comt, Ky
b Hyden, Ky, July 9, 32; s Claude Maggard & Evelyn Morgan M; m 1959 to Eva Caldwell; c Roderick Claude, Bige Colin, Jack Samuel, II, Michele & Kevin Scott. Educ: Univ Ky, AB, 53; Comt of 240. Polit & Govt Pos: Co campaign chmn, Kennedy-Johnson, 60, Breathitt for Gov, 63, Johnson-Humphrey, 64; deleg, Ky Dem State Conv, 60, chmn co deleg, 64 & 68; mem, Leslie Co Bd Elec Comnr, Ky, 60-63; chmn, Leslie Co Dem Exec Comt, Ky, 60-; campaign chmn, Humphrey-Muskie, 68. Bus & Prof Pos: Teacher-coach, Leslie Co Schs, 53-61, dir pupil personnel, 61-63 & vis teacher, 63-; guid counr, Leslie Co Adult Educ, 65-; partner, Maggards Dept Store, Hyden, Ky, 65-; ed asst, Leslie Co Independent, 69- Mil Serv: Entered as Pvt, Army, 55, released as Specialist in Commun, 57, after serv in Hq Third Reconnaissance Bn, Third Inf Div, US. Mem: Leslie Co, Upper Ky River, Ky & Nat Educ Asns; Univ Ky Alumni Asn. Relig: Presbyterian. Mailing Add: PO Box 102 Hyden KY 41749

MAGGIACOMO, EDWARD LOUIS (D)
RI State Rep
b Providence, RI, July 2, 36; s Giuseppe Maggiacomo & Giulia Cicerone M; m 1961 to Ingeborg Leers; c Susanne E, Edward L, Jr, Michael A & Stephen F. Educ: Providence Col, BS, 58; Georgetown Univ Sch Law, LLB, 64. Polit & Govt Pos: Mem, Personnel Appeals Bd, Cranston, RI, 64-65; town solicitor, Smithfield, 66; trustee, Cranston Pub Libr, 67-; RI State Rep, Dist 24, 67- Mil Serv: Entered as 2nd Lt, Army, 59, released as 1st Lt, 61, after serv in Mil Intel, ETO. Mem: RI Bar Asn. Relig: Catholic. Legal Res: 32 Belcrest Rd Cranston RI 02920 Mailing Add: 1560 Cranston St Cranston RI 02920

MAGNUSON, ARVID WALTER (D)
b Pierre, SDak, Oct 1, 25; s Oscar A Magnuson & Ethel Borders M; m 1947 to Cecile Lintvedt; c Richard A, Elaine C & Denise K. Polit & Govt Pos: Mem, Sch Bd, 60-64; chmn, Jones Co Dem Comt, SDak, formerly; mem, Murdo City Coun, 71- Bus & Prof Pos: Owner & mgr, farm implement bus, 65-70; salesman, Ford & Mercury dealership, 71- Mem: Lions; Community Mem Hosp Bd (chmn, 71-). Relig: Lutheran Church-Missouri Synod; Pres, Lutheran Laymans League, 68-69. Mailing Add: 408 E Second St Murdo SD 57559

MAGNUSON, DONALD HAMMER (D)
b Freeman, Wash, Mar 7, 11; s Ellis William Magnuson & Ida Hammer M; div; c Craig, Terry Lynn (Mrs Cairns), Joel Ellis, Mary Elizabeth & Erik George. Educ: Spokane Univ, 26-28; Univ Wash, AB, 31; Theta Xi. Polit & Govt Pos: US Rep, Wash, 83rd-87th Cong; spec asst, US Dept Interior, 63-69; writer-ed, US Dept Labor, 69- Bus & Prof Pos: Reporter, Daily Olympian, Olympia, Wash, 34-41 & Seattle Times, 41-52. Mem: Am Newspaper Guild. Relig: Presbyterian. Mailing Add: Box 11 Dockton WA 98018

MAGNUSON, WARREN GRANT (D)
US Sen, Wash
b Moorhead, Minn, Apr 12, 05; s William G Magnuson & Emma Carolina Anderson M; m 1964 to Jermaine Elliott Peralta; c Juanita Peralta (Mrs Donald Garrison). Educ: Univ NDak, 23, NDak State Univ, 24; Univ Wash, JD, 29. Hon Degrees: LLD, Gonzaga Univ, 61; Dr of Polit Sci, Univ of the Pac, 70. Polit & Govt Pos: Wash State Rep, 33-34; prosecuting attorney, King Co, Wash, 34-36; US Rep, Wash, 37-44; US Sen, Wash, 44-, chmn, Commerce Comt, ranking Dem mem, Appropriations Comt, chmn, Appropriations Sub-Comt on Labor,

Health, Educ & Welfare, mem, Appropriations Subcomts of Dept of Defense, Dept of Transportation & Dept of Housing & Urban Develop Independent Offices, mem, Comt on Aeronaut & Space Sci & mem, Dem Policy Comt, US Senate; former chmn, Dem Sen Campaign Comt, currently; ex-officio, Dem Nat Mid-Term Conf, 74. Mil Serv: Lt Comdr, Navy, serv in USS Enterprise, SPac, World War II; received spec Presidential citation for participation in first raid on Tokyo. Publ: The Darkside of the Marketplace (with Jean Carper), Prentice Hall, 68. Mem: Adv comt, Who's Who in Am Polit, 67, 69 & 71; Elks; Eagles; Am Legion; VFW. Honors & Awards: Maritime Man of the Year, Maritime Press Asn, 55; Man of the Year, Nat Fisheries Inst, 64; World Trade Awards, Metrop Wash Bd Trade, 61; Chap Award, Nat Defense Transportation Asn, 60, Nat Bd Dirs Award, 61, Nat Man of the Year Award, 62; Award, Am Cancer Soc, 62. Relig: Lutheran. Legal Res: Seattle WA 98104 Mailing Add: 127 Senate Office Bldg Washington DC 20510

MAGNUSSON, KINGDON B (R)
Chmn, Ninth Rep Legis Dist, NDak
b Wolford, NDak, May 7, 05; s Walter L Magnusson & Hannah Burger M; m 1941 to Olga Lillian Erickson; c Keith C & James R. Educ: Univ NDak, BS in Com, 27. Polit & Govt Pos: Mayor, Rolette, NDak, 66-; chmn, Ninth Rep Legis Dist, 67-72 & 74-; co comnr, Rolette Co, 69-72. Bus & Prof Pos: Auditor, Red Owl Stores, Inc, Minneapolis, 29-42, store mgr, Rolla, NDak, 45-47; self-employed, Rolette, 47-66; rep, Hamilton Mgt Co, Denver, Colo, 66-70. Mil Serv: Entered as Pvt, Army, 42, released as Technician-5, 45, after serv in 163rd Engr Combat Bn, ETO, 43-45. Mem: Elks; Am Legion; VFW. Relig: Presbyterian. Mailing Add: Rolette ND 58366

MAGONE, JOSEPH M (D)
Mont State Rep
Mailing Add: Rte 1 Box 5 Superior MT 59872

MAGRUDER, DICK (D)
Ore State Rep
Mailing Add: Rte 2 Box 36 Clatskanie OR 97016

MAGUIRE, ANDREW (D)
US Rep, NJ
b Columbus, Ohio, Mar 11, 39; m 1968 to Margaret Green; c Jay. Educ: Oberlin Col, BA, 61; Harvard Univ, PhD, 66; Woodrow Wilson fel & Danforth Grad fel; London Univ Sch Oriental & African Studies, 63. Polit & Govt Pos: UN adv on Polit & Security Affairs, 66-69; dir, Multi-Develop Prog for Jamaica, NY, 69-72; nat campaign staff, Citizens for Goldberg/Patterson Gubernatorial Campaign, 70; consult, Ford Found, 72-74; campaign dir, Brendan Byrne for Gov, Bergen Co, 73; US Rep, NJ, 75- Mem: UN Asn; Common Cause; Ridgewood Tennis Asn; YMCA. Honors & Awards: Achievement Award, Jamaica CofC, 70. Relig: Community Church. Legal Res: 112 S Irving St Ridgewood NJ 07450 Mailing Add: US House Rep Washington DC 20515

MAGUIRE, RICHARD ROBLES (R)
b St Thomas, VI, Dec 29, 44; s Walter John Maguire, Jr & Thelma Watson M; m 1966 to Joanne Perkings Maguire; c Ruth & Laura. Educ: Paul Smith Col, 62-63; Univ Miami, 63-64. Polit & Govt Pos: Co-founder, Young Rep, VI, 69; mem, Rep Territorial Comt, 69-; vpres, St Thomas Rep Party, 70-71; field investr, Small Bus Develop Agency, 70-71; asst exec secy, Legis VI, 71-73; deleg, Second Const Conv, VI, 71-72; alt deleg, Rep Nat Conv, 72; mem, Elec Reform Comt, 72-; asst comnr, Dept Conserv & Cult Affairs, 73- Bus & Prof Pos: Reservations mgr, Hotel 1829, 60-62; mgr, Maguire Car Rental, 64-65, gen mgr, 68-70. Mil Serv: Entered as Pvt, Army, 65, released as 1st Lt, 68, after serv in S&MA, Europe, 67-68; Good Conduct Medal; Nat Defense Serv Medal; Commendation Cert Achievement. Mem: Rotary. Relig: Jewish. Legal Res: 108-A-16 Contant St Thomas VI 00801 Mailing Add: PO Box 1341 St Thomas VI 00801

MAGUIRE, ROBERT WYMAN JR (R)
Chmn, Windsor Co Rep Comt, Vt
b Springfield, Vt, Feb 26, 44; s Robert W Maguire, Sr & Rosamond Templeton M; single. Educ: Champlain Col, ABA, 64; Husson Col, BS, 67; Pro-Con Soc; Christian Youth Asn; Concert Comt. Polit & Govt Pos: Vchmn, Vt Citizens for Nixon-Agnew, 68; Justice of Peace, Springfield, Vt, 69-73; mem, Springfield Bd Civil Authority, 69-73; chmn, Windsor Co Rep Comt, 69-71 & 73-; mem, Vt State Rep Comt, 69-71; mem, Windsor Co Elec Bd, 69-71. Bus & Prof Pos: Rep, Investors Diversified Serv; mgr, Giant, Inc, Claremont, NH, 68-70. Mem: Vt Jaycees (past dir); Vt Epilepsy Asn (dir). Honors & Awards: Distinguished Citizen Award, 69. Relig: Protestant. Mailing Add: 30 White St Springfield VT 05156

MAHADY, FRANK G (R)
Mem Exec Comt, Vt Rep State Comt
b Taunton, Mass, Mar 31, 39; s Frank Doyle Mahady & Doris Potter M; m 1967 to Sherry Symmes; c Tara. Educ: Dartmouth Col, AB, 61; Georgetown Univ, LLB, 64. Polit & Govt Pos: Asst Attorney Gen, State of Vt, 67-68, Dep Attorney Gen, 68-69; State's Attorney, Windsor Co, 69-72; mem, Vt Rep State Comt, 70-, mem exec comt, 71-; deleg, Rep Nat Conv, 72; chmn rules comt, Vt Rep State Conv, 72-; comnr, Legis Apportionment Bd, 72-; Lebanon Reg Airport Authority, 74- Mem: Am Bar Asn; Vt Law Sch (trustee, 73-); Vt Heart Asn (dir, 69-); United Way of the Upper Valley (dir, 72-); Vt Inst of Natural Sci (dir, 72-). Relig: Methodist. Legal Res: Hartford Rd Hartford VT 05047 Mailing Add: 17 Main St White River Junction VT 05001

MAHADY, PAUL W (D)
Coun to the Pres Pro Tem, Pa State Senate
b Latrobe, Pa, Nov 19, 08; s James J Mahady & Katharine O'Neill M; m to Janet Matlock; c Two. Educ: Harvard Col, AB; Harvard Univ Law Sch, LLB; Ames Competition; Sayre Law Club; McReynolds Law Club. Hon Degrees: PhD, St Vincent Col, 73. Polit & Govt Pos: Pa State Sen, 58-73, coun to the Pres Pro Tem, Pa State Senate, 73-; mem, Gtr Lakes Comn, currently; chmn, Local Govt Comn, currently; chmn exec bd, Pa Higher Educ Assistance Agency, currently; mem, Pa Hist Mus Comn, currently; mem Pa State Planning Bd, currently. Bus & Prof Pos: Practiced law before the Westmoreland Co Courts, Pa Superior & Supreme Courts, Fed Dist Court & US Supreme Court; author & ed; dir-secy, Newcomer Prod Inc, Westmoreland Fed Savings & Loan Asn & Latrobe Broadcasters, Inc. Mil Serv: Lt Col, Army, 41-46; Brig Gen, Pa State Guard, 73; Legion of Merit; Army Commendation Ribbon with Oak Leaf Clusters. Mem: Salvation Army Int; Lions Int; Am Legion; Am Bar Asn; Am Acad Polit & Social Sci. Relig: Roman Catholic. Legal Res: 202 Main St Latrobe PA 15650 Mailing Add: 824 Walnut St Latrobe PA 15650

MAHALAK, EDWARD E (D)
Mich State Rep
b Wyandotte, Mich, Sept 25, 21; married; c Gregory & Denise. Educ: Wayne State Univ; Detroit Col Law. Polit & Govt Pos: Justice of the Peace, Mich, 55-67; Mich State Rep, 64- Mil Serv: Air Force, World War II. Mem: Ushers Club; VFW; Polish Legion of Am Vet Post 7. Relig: Catholic. Mailing Add: 9404 Chamberlain Ave Romulus MI 48174

MAHAN, EUGENE ROBERT (D)
SDak State Sen
b Union Co, SDak, Aug 14, 33; s Michael Frances Mahan & Helen M McCarthy M; m 1959 to Mary Louise Swedean; c Michael Eugene, Brian Patrick, Timothy James & Michelle Mary. Educ: SDak State Univ, BS, 63. Polit & Govt Pos: SDak State Rep, Union Co, 71-73; SDak State Sen, Dist 13, 73- Bus & Prof Pos: Farming-mgr, lifelong; salesman, Equitable of US, 64-67. Mil Serv: Entered as E-1, Army, 53, released as E-5, 55, after serv in Ft Riley, Kans, Korean Conflict & Walters AFB, Tex, 53-55. Relig: Catholic. Legal Res: SD Mailing Add: RR 2 Akron IA 51001

MAHANY, LUMAN P (D)
Maine State Rep
Mailing Add: Easton ME 04740

MAHAR, WILLIAM F (R)
Ill State Sen
Mailing Add: 1756 Cedar Rd Homewood IL 60430

MAHE, HENRY EDWARD JR (EDDIE) (R)
Exec Dir, Rep Nat Comt
b Pueblo, Colo, Aug 12, 36; s Henry Edward Mahe & Guernadine Boston M; m 1962 to Frances Ogden Harvey; c Sharon Kay, Theresa Ann, William, Kathy & Debra Lee. Educ: Univ Denver, BSBA, 58; Lambda Chi Alpha. Polit & Govt Pos: Chmn, NMex Young Rep State Conv, 65, vpres, NMex Young Rep, 65-66; mem, Cent, Exec & Finance Comts, Bernalillo Co Rep Party, NMex, 65-66; exec secy, 66; mem, NMex Rep Cent Comt, 65-67, exec dir, 67-69; field dir, Nat Rep Cong Comt, 69-70; campaign mgr, Eggers for Gov Comt, 70; campaign mgr, Domenici for US Senate, Albuquerque, NMex, 72; field dir, Nat Rep Sen Comt, 73; dir polit activities, Rep Nat Comt, 73-74, exec dir, 74- Bus & Prof Pos: Salesman, Weagley Real Estate Agency, Albuquerque, 63-66; pres, Citizen Newspapers, Austin, Tex, 71-; pres & gen mgr, Austin Publ Co, Tex, 71-72. Mil Serv: Army, 1 month. Mem: NMex Asn Real Estate Brokers. Honors & Awards: Young Rep Man of Year, Bernalillo Co & NMex, 66. Relig: Protestant. Mailing Add: 3312 Parkside Terr Fairfax VA 20030

MAHER, JAMES C (D)
RI State Sen
b Burrillville, RI, Apr 10, 13; m to Averill M. Educ: Burrillville Schs. Polit & Govt Pos: Mem, Dem Town Comt, RI, chief, Glendale Fire Dept, 39-; mem, Burrillville Bd of Estimate, 47-63; RI State Rep, 59-63; RI State Sen, 63- Bus & Prof Pos: Sales mgr. Mem: Lions; Fire Chiefs Club of RI; New Eng Asn Fire Chiefs; Wallum Lake Rod & Gun Club; North RI Firemen's League. Mailing Add: Main St Glendale RI 02826

MAHER, JOHN FRANCIS (D)
NDak State Sen
b Beresford, SDak, Apr 27, 21; s James J Maher & Florence McIlvenna M; m 1946 to Betty M Kenison; c Kenneth, Patricia Shannon (Mrs Schmit), Tim J & Dan G. Educ: NDak State Univ, BS in agr. Polit & Govt Pos: Sch dist recreation comnr, Bowman, NDak, 60-72; mem, City of Bowman Park Bd, 65-72; munic judge, Bowman, 71-74; NDak State Sen, 75- Mailing Add: 608 W Second Bowman ND 58623

MAHER, MARY BARBARA (D)
Vt State Rep
Mailing Add: Box 2331 660 Hinesburg Rd South Burlington VT 05401

MAHLING, BERNA JO (B J) (DFL)
Secy, Seventh Cong Dist Dem-Farmer-Labor Party, Minn
b Enid, Okla, Apr 12, 36; d Bernard Buchner (B B) Blakey & Josephine L Walker B; m 1958 to Henry W Pickett, Jr, wid; m 1968 to Albert C Mahling; c Keri Lyn Pickett & Kimberly Diane Pickett Mahling. Educ: Phillips Univ, BA, 59; Univ Minn, Minneapolis, MA, 68; Alpha Delta; Cardinal Key; Zonta Club, Phillips Univ. Polit & Govt Pos: App by Gov as Seventh Cong Dist Rep, Minn Coun Quality Educ, 71, elected vchairperson, 71-73, chairperson, 73-; app by Minn Secy of State, Pub Adv Bd, 75; Secy, Seventh Cong Dist Dem-Farmer-Labor Party, Minn, 72-; chmn, Dem-Farmer-Labor State Conv Const Comt, 74; deleg, Dem Nat Mid-Term Conf, 74. Bus & Prof Pos: Women's ed, Suburban Newspapers, Inc, Hopkins, Minn, 65-67; teaching asst, Sch Jour & Mass Commun & prod ed, Jour Quart, nat jour publ, Univ Minn, Minneapolis, 67-68; instr jour, North Hennepin State Jr Col, Brooklyn Park, 68-70. Mem: Am Asn Univ Women (Little Falls Chap); Farmers Union (non-farm mem). Relig: Protestant. Mailing Add: Rte 1 Box 316 Little Falls MN 56345

MAHON, GEORGE HERMAN (D)
US Rep, Tex
b near Haynesville, La, Sept 22, 00; s John Kirkpatrick Mahon & Lola Willis Brown M; m 1923 to Helen Stevenson; c Daphne (Mrs Duncan W Holt, Jr). Educ: Simmons Univ, Abilene, Tex, BA, 24; Univ Tex, Austin, LLB, 25; Univ Minn, summer 25; Phi Delta Phi; Delta Theta Phi. Polit & Govt Pos: Co attorney, Mitchell Co, Tex, 26; dist attorney, Thirty-Second Judicial Dist, 27-32; US Rep, Tex, 35-; chmn, House Appropriations Comt & Defense Appropriations Subcomt, currently. Bus & Prof Pos: Attorney-at-law, Colorado City, Tex, 25. Mem: Am Bar Asn; Regent, Smithsonian Inst; Mason; Lions; Kiwanis. Honors & Awards: Am Polit Good Govt Soc, 69; Distinguished Pub Serv Award, Am Legion, 73; VFW Cong Award, 74; Reserve Officers Asn Minute Man Award, 74; George & Helen Mahon Libr, Lubbock, Tex, 74. Relig: Methodist. Legal Res: 611 Federal Bldg Lubbock TX 79401 Mailing Add: 2314 Rayburn House Office Bldg Washington DC 20515

MAHONEY, DONNABELLE (D)
Ind State Rep
Mailing Add: 7107 State Line Ave Hammond IN 46324

MAHONEY, EUGENE T (R)
Nebr State Sen
b Chicago, Ill, Mar 27, 28; single. Educ: Univ Omaha. Polit & Govt Pos: Nebr State Sen, 61-;

Admin Asst to Congressman Glenn Cunningham, formerly. Bus & Prof Pos: Dir of Commercial Savings Asn; Pub Rels-Customer Rels. Mil Serv: Officer, US Army Res Corps. Mem: St Vincent de Paul Stores (bd dirs); Nat Conf Christians & Jews (bd dirs); KofC; Eagles; South Omaha Merchants & Professional Men's Asn. Relig: Catholic; St Stanislaus Parish & Holy Name Soc. Mailing Add: 4956 S 41st St Omaha NE 68107

MAHONEY, FRANCIS JAMES (D)
Conn State Rep
b Manchester, Conn, May 12, 14; s John Frank Mahoney & Ruth Stonebridge M; m 1940 to Lucille Murphey; c Nancy (Mrs Mark Mooney) & Susan (Mrs Robert Broniell). Educ: Manchester High Sch, Conn, 4 years. Polit & Govt Pos: Mem bd dirs, Manchester, Conn, 56-69, Mayor, 62-66; mem, Conn River Valley Flood Control Comn, 64-; incorporator, Manchester Mem Hosp, 69; Conn State Rep, 69-; co-chmn, Bi-centennial Comt of Manchester, currently. Mem: KofC; Elks. Honors & Awards: Plaques for contributions to KofC & Manchester, Conn. Relig: Catholic. Mailing Add: 19 Hamlin St Manchester CT 06040

MAHONEY, FRANCIS XAVIER (D)
Committeeman, Dem State Cent Comt, Ill
b Peabody, Mass, Mar 21, 22; s Joseph R Mahoney & Lucy H Hahesy M; m 1944 to Ruth Lambert; c Michael. Educ: Boston Col, AB, 43; Northwestern Univ Sch of Law, JD, 48; Phi Alpha. Polit & Govt Pos: Dem precinct committeeman, 17th Precinct, Stephenson Co, Ill & vchmn, Stephenson Co Dem Cent Comt, 64; Ill State Rep, Freeport, 65-66; former mem, Const Study Comn, Ill; mem, Platform Comt for Dem Conv, State of Ill, 70-; committeeman, Dem State Cent Comt, Ill, 70-; chmn, Stephenson Co Dem Cent Comt, formerly. Mil Serv: Entered Navy, 43, released as ETM 2/C, 46, after serv in Amphibious Forces, Atlantic; Victory Medal & Atlantic Theater Ribbon. Mem: Am Legion; VFW; Moose; Elks; KofC. Relig: Roman Catholic. Legal Res: 707 E Garden St Freeport IL 61032 Mailing Add: 214 W Stephenson St Freeport IL 61032

MAHONEY, HENRY ELMORE (D)
NH State Rep
b Newport, NH, Mar 29, 10; s William Henry Mahoney & Annie Austin M; m 1935 to Margaret Gertrude LeBrun; c Dennis Michael & Catherine A (Mrs Stillson). Educ: Keene State Col, 33; Alpha Pi Tau. Polit & Govt Pos: Mem & chmn, Newport Sch Bd, 57-62; sch dist moderator, 64-72; treas, NH Planning Bd, Newport, 73-; vpres planning & regional, Upper Valley-Lake Sunapee Coun, 74-; NH State Rep, 75- Bus & Prof Pos: Newspaper reporter, Manchester Union-Leader correspondent, Argus-Champion, 33-42, newspaper correspondent, 35-42; postal clerk, US Post Off, Newport, NH, 42-64, asst postmaster, 64-72. Mil Serv: Entered as A/S, Navy, 43, released as Photographers Mate 1/C, after serv in Atlantic Fleet Camera Party, Atlantic, 43-45. Publ: Ed, Newport BiCentennial Booklet, 61; ed & publ, Granite State Postal Notes (NH Post Office Clerks), privately publ, 63-68; article on Sarah Josepha Hale, Yankee Mag, 73. Mem: Am Legion Post 25; KofC; Newport CofC. Honors & Awards: NH Fedn of Postal Clerks Award of Merit, 70. Relig: Roman Catholic. Mailing Add: 7 Highland Ave Newport NH 03773

MAHONEY, J DANIEL (CONSERVATIVE, NY)
State Chmn, Conservative Party, NY
b Orange, NJ, Sept 7, 31; s Daniel Vincent Mahoney & Louisa Dunbar M; m 1955 to Kathleen Mary O'Doherty; c J Daniel, Jr, Kieran Vincent, Francis Kirk, Mary Louisa, Eileen Ann & Elizabeth. Educ: St Bonaventure Univ, BA, magna cum laude, 52; Columbia Univ Law Sch, Kent Scholar & LLB, 55; Phi Alpha Delta. Polit & Govt Pos: State vchmn, Conservative Party, NY, 62, state chmn, 62- Bus & Prof Pos: Assoc, Simpson, Thacher & Bartlett, 58-62; assoc, Wormser, Kiely, Alessandroni, Mahoney & McCann, 65-66, partner, 66-74; partner, Windels & Marx, 74- Mil Serv: Entered as A/S, Coast Guard, 55, released as Lt(jg), 58. Publ: Action Speaks Louder—The Story of the New York Conservative Party, Arlington House, 67; various articles & book reviews for BNA, Am Bar Asn Jour, Columbia Law Review, Nat Review & Modern Age. Mem: NY State Bar Asn. Relig: Roman Catholic. Legal Res: 82 Brookfield Rd Mt Vernon NY 10552 Mailing Add: 51 W 51st St New York NY 10019

MAHONEY, JAMES F (D)
RI State Rep
Mailing Add: 36 Norman St Newport RI 02840

MAHONEY, JOHN F JR (D)
b Gloversville, NY, Nov 2, 23; s John F Mahoney & Genevieve Hine M; m 1952 to Ann Van Arnam; c Elizabeth, Monica, John, III, Patrick, Paul, Stephen, Bridget & David. Educ: Georgetown Univ, BSS; NY Univ Grad Sch of Polit Sci, 1 year. Polit & Govt Pos: Chmn, Fulton Co Dem Comt, NY, 65-72; elec comnr, Fulton Co, 65- Bus & Prof Pos: Pres, Alma Leather Co, Inc, 58. Mil Serv: Entered as Pvt, Army, 43, released as Sgt, 45, after serv in 386th AAA Bn, ETO, 43-45. Mem: KofC; Eccentric Club; Cath War Vet; VFW; Concordia Club. Relig: Roman Catholic. Mailing Add: 133 First Ave Gloversville NY 12078

MAHONEY, THOMAS HENRY DONALD (D)
Mass State Rep
b Cambridge, Mass, Nov 4, 13; s Thomas Henry Mahoney, Jr & Frances Estelle Lucy M; m 1951 to Katharine Phyllis Norton; c Thomas H, IV, Linda Elizabeth, David Leonard, Peter James & Philip Andrew. Educ: Boston Col, AB, 36, AM, 37; George Washington Univ, PhD, 44; Harvard Law Sch, Carnegie fel in law & hist, 65-66; Harvard Univ, John F Kennedy Sch Govt, MPA, 67; Pi Gamma Mu. Polit & Govt Pos: Sch committeeman, Cambridge, Mass, 48-54, city councilor, 64-72; Mass State Rep, 71-; mem comt sci & technol, Nat Legis Conf, Washington, DC, 72- Bus & Prof Pos: Instr Latin, French & hist, Gonzaga Sch, Washington, DC, 37-39; instr hist, Dunbarton Col, 38-39; asst prof hist & govt, Boston Col, 39-44 & Holy Cross Col, 44-46; vis lectr hist & govt, Smith Col, 44-45; from asst prof to assoc prof hist & polit sci, Mass Inst Technol, 45-61, prof, 61-; vis lectr hist & govt, Wellesley Col, 47-48 & Univ Southern Calif, summer 50; lectr, Lowell Lect Ser, Boston, 57. Publ: Edmund Burke & Ireland, Harvard & Oxford Univ Presses, 60; China, Japan & the Powers, 2nd ed, Ronald Press, 60; The United States in World History, 3rd ed, McGraw-Hill, 64. Mem: Royal Hist Soc (fel); Am Hist Asn; Am Cath Hist Asn; Mass Hist Soc; Harvard Club of Boston. Honors & Awards: Guggenheim Fel; Am Coun Learned Soc Fel. Relig: Roman Catholic. Mailing Add: 86 Sparks St Cambridge MA 02138

MAHONEY, WILLIAM PATRICK JR (D)
b Prescott, Ariz, Nov 27, 16; s William Patrick Mahoney & Alice Fitzgerald M; m 1946 to Alice Doyle; c William Patrick, III, Gladys S, Richard D, Mary Alice, Eileen, Lawrence V, J Emmett, Noel F & Sheila P. Educ: Univ Notre Dame, AB, 39, LLB, 40, JD, St Norbert's Col, 64. Polit & Govt Pos: Asst attorney gen, Ariz, 46-48; Dist Attorney, Maricopa Co, 53-57; US Ambassador, Ghana, W Africa, 62-65; fed aid coordr, Maricopa Co, Ariz, 66-68; mem, Nat Adv Comt to Legal Serv Prog, Off of Econ Opportunity, 67-; deleg, Dem Nat Conv, 68. Bus & Prof Pos: Bd of dirs, GRAMCO Int, Nassau, Bahamas, 66 & Greater Ariz Savings & Loan Asn, Phoenix, Ariz, 67- Mil Serv: Entered as Ens, US Navy, 42, released as Lt(sg), 45, as Trial Judge Adv War Crimes Cases, Pac Ocean. Publ: Nkrumah in Retrospect, Rev Polit, 4/68; & numerous other articles in professional & scholarly publications. Mem: Am Soc Int Law; Am Judicature Soc; Am Arbit Asn; Supreme Court US Bar Asn; Nat Conf Christians & Jews. Relig: Catholic. Mailing Add: 6248 N Seventh Ave Phoenix AR 85013

MAHONY, JOSEPH KIRBY, II (D)
Ark State Rep
b El Dorado, Ark, Sept 12, 39; s Emon A Mahony & Mabel Farmer M; m 1969 to Bettie Anne Humphreys; c Joseph K, III & Michael Emon. Educ: Washington & Lee Univ, 56-58; Univ Ark, 58-60, LLB, 66; Southern State Univ, BA, 62; Sigma Nu. Polit & Govt Pos: Mem, Union Co Elec Comn, Ark, 69-70; deleg, Ark State Dem Conv, 70 & 72; committeeman, Ark State Dem Party, 70-73; Ark State Rep, 71-, mem comt legis reorgn, Ark House Rep, currently. Bus & Prof Pos: Mem, Mahony & Yocum Attorneys, El Dorado, Ark, currently. Mil Serv: Entered Marine Corps, released as Lance Cpl, 65. Mem: Ark Bar Asn; Am Judicature Soc; Am Civil Liberties Union; Ark Hist Asn; Union Co Humane Soc (treas). Relig: Presbyterian. Legal Res: 609 N Jackson El Dorado AR 71730 Mailing Add: 406 Armstrong Bldg El Dorado AR 71730

MAIER, EUGENE EDWARD J (D)
Mem, Dem Nat Comt
b Philadelphia, Pa, July 22, 37; s Louis J Maier & Elizabeth Corcoran M; m 1961 to Constance Mary Wombough; c Eugene Edward J, II, P Douglas, Elizabeth Anne & Catharine Regina. Educ: Temple Univ, BS, 68, Law Sch, JD, 71; Phi Alpha Delta, treas. Polit & Govt Pos: Div committeeman & mem rules reform comn, Pa Dem State Comt, 62-73, mem, 67-; chmn, 46th Ward Dem Exec Comt, Pa, 65-71; exec asst to Dem City Chmn Peter J Camiel, 71-; city comnr of Philadelphia, 73-; deleg, Dem Nat Mid-Term Conf, 74; mem, Dem Nat Comt, 75- Publ: Auth, The Presidential Franchise, Temple Law Quart, 71. Mem: Am, Pa & Philadelphia Bar Asns; KofC (4 degree); Am Cath Hist Soc. Honors & Awards: Honor Awards, Const Law, 69, Const Hist, 70 & Nursing Home Campaign Comt, Inc, 72. Relig: Roman Catholic. Legal Res: 1167 Bridge St Philadelphia PA 19124 Mailing Add: NWC Bridge & Horrocks Sts Philadelphia PA 19124

MAIER, HENRY W (D)
Mayor, Milwaukee, Wis
b Dayton, Ohio, Feb 7, 18; s Charles Maier, Jr & Marie L Kniseley M; m 1941 to Mary Ann Monaghan; c Melinda Ann (Mrs Carlisle) & Melanie Marie. Educ: Univ Wis, BA, 40 & MA, 64. Polit & Govt Pos: Wis State Sen, 50-60, Minority Leader, Wis State Senate, 53, 55, 57 & 59; Mayor, Milwaukee, 60-; past pres, US Conf Mayors; past pres, Nat League of Cities; chmn, Coalition for Human Needs & Budget Resources; pres, Nat Coalition Dem Mayors. Mil Serv: Naval Res, World War II, Lt(sg). Publ: Challenge to the cities. Mailing Add: City Hall Milwaukee WI 53202

MAIER, RICHARD FRANKLIN (R)
Ohio State Rep
b Massillon, Ohio, Oct 9, 25; s Franklin Leonidas Maier & Maude Pietzcker M; m 1952 to Marilyn Trumpour; c Richard F, Jr, Janice Lynn & Donald Robert. Educ: Yale Univ, BA, 48; Univ Mich, Ann Arbor, JD, 51. Polit & Govt Pos: Asst city solicitor, Massillon, Ohio, 54-55, city solicitor, 57-63; bd mem, Stark Co Metrop Housing Authority, 71-73; Ohio State Rep, 48th Dist, 73- Bus & Prof Pos: Partner, Maier & Maier, Massillon, Ohio, 51-71; attorney-at-law, 71- Mil Serv: Entered as Seaman 3/C, Navy, 44, released as Signalman 3/C, 45, after serv in 5th Fleet, Pac Theatre, 44-45. Mem: Boys Clubs of Am (bd mem, Massillon); Delta Theta Phi; Phi Beta Kappa. Honors & Awards: Bronze Medallion, Boys Clubs of Am, 72, Silver Medallion, 73. Relig: Methodist. Mailing Add: 1222 Providence NE Massillon OH 44646

MAIGRET, MAUREEN ELAINE (D)
RI State Rep
b Pawtucket, RI, Feb 11, 44; d Alfred Hallal & Aura Cheltra H; m 1964 to Robert Joseph Maigret; c Robert & Michael. Educ: Mem Hosp Sch Nursing, dipl, 61; RI Col, BS, 74. Polit & Govt Pos: RI State Rep, 75- Bus & Prof Pos: Staff nurse, Kent Co Mem Hosp, RI, 69- Mem: Am & RI Nurses Asns; Vol of Warwick Schs; RI & Warwick Women's Polit Caucus. Relig: Catholic. Mailing Add: 232 Vancouver Ave Warwick RI 02886

MAILE, FRANCIS A (D)
Mem Exec Comt, Summit Co Dem Party, Ohio
b Phoenixville, Pa, Nov 19, 19; s Joseph Maile & Ellen Lawlor M; m 1962 to Marguerite Rose Kappus; c Michael & Shawn. Educ: St Anne's Parochial Sch, 10 years. Polit & Govt Pos: Alt deleg, Dem Nat Conv, 68, mem exec comt, Summit Co Dem Party, Ohio, currently; mem planning comn, City of Barberton, Ohio. Bus & Prof Pos: Dir polit dept, URW, AFL-CIO, Akron, Ohio, 62-; mem, Nat Comt on Polit Educ Operating Comt, AFL-CIO, 12 years. Mil Serv: Entered as Pvt, Army, 40, released as Sgt, 45, after serv in US Ranger Dept & 80th Inf Div, ETO, 43-45; Bronze Star, Five Battle Stars; Good Conduct Medal. Mem: Am Legion; VFW; URW; AFL-CIO. Relig: Catholic. Legal Res: 476 E Hopocan Barberton OH 44203 Mailing Add: 87 S High Akron OH 44308

MAILLIARD, WILLIAM SOMERS (R)
b Belvedere, Calif, June 10, 17; s John Ward Mailliard, Jr (deceased) & Kate Peterson M; m 1957 to Millicent Fox; c William Somers, Jr, Antoinette, Henry Ward, Kristina, Julia Ward, Josephine Fox & Victoria Leigh. Educ: Yale Univ, BA, 39. Polit & Govt Pos: Asst to dir, Calif Youth Authority, 47; secy to Gov Earl Warren, 49-51; US Rep Sixth Dist, Calif, 53-74; ambassador & permanent rep of US to Orgn Am States, 74- Bus & Prof Pos: Am Trust Co, San Francisco, 40-41 & 46; asst to dir, Calif Acad Sci, 51-52. Mil Serv: Entered as Ens, Naval Res, 39, released as Lt Comdr, 46, after serv as Asst Naval Attache, US Embassy, London, Eng, 39-40; Bur of Naval Personnel, 41-42 & Flag Lt & Aide to Vice Adm D E Barbey, Seventh Amphibious Force, 43-46; Bronze & Silver Stars; Legion of Merit; Naval Res, Asiatic-Pac Campaign, China Serv, Am Defense Serv, Armed Forces Res, Am Campaign, Navy Occup Serv & Philippine Liberation Ribbons; Victory Medal; Order of Yun Hui; Rear Admiral, Naval Res, 65. Mem: Am Legion; Mil Order of Carabao; US Navy League; VFW; Capitol Hill Club of Washington, DC. Relig: Episcopal. Mailing Add: ARA/USOAS Dept of State Washington DC 20520

MAINEY, DONALD E (D)
Kans State Rep
Mailing Add: 430 Sumner Topeka KS 66616

MAINVILLE, RICHARD JOSEPH (R)
Chmn, Wyo League Young Rep
b Cohoes, NY, Oct 4, 47; s Joseph Raymond Mainville & Emeline Lemay M; m 1971 to Linda Lou Washburn; c Mark Christopher, Richard Joseph, II & Brandi Lynn. Educ: Montgomery Col, 71; Northeastern Col (Colo), 72-73; Univ Wyo, 73-; Phi Theta Kappa. Polit & Govt Pos: Nat chmn, Vietnam Vets for Just Peace, 71; chmn, Wyo League Young Rep, 74-; chmn, Wyo Young Am for Freedom, 74- Bus & Prof Pos: Mgr, Stop & Go Mkt, Las Vegas, Nev, 71-72. Mil Serv: Entered as Pvt, Marine Corps, 64, released as Sgt, 68, after serv in F Co, 2nd Bn, SVietnam, 66-67; 2nd Lt, Army Res, currently; Vietnamese Cross of Gallantry; 2 Purple Hearts; Good Conduct Medal. Publ: Wyoming Examiner, 74. Mem: VFW (univ liaison officer); Jaycees. Honors & Awards: Presidential Appreciation Award, Laramie Jaycees, 74-75, Jaycee of the Month & Jaycee of the Quarter, 75. Relig: Catholic. Mailing Add: 2311 Land 330 Laramie WY 82070

MAISH, FRANK ANTHONY (D)
Mem, Pima Co Dem Exec Comt, Ariz
b Tucson, Ariz, Apr 29, 53; s Frank Maish & Magdeline Dominguez M; single. Educ: Univ Ariz, currently. Polit & Govt Pos: Deleg, Ariz Dem State Conv, 72; alt deleg, Dem Nat Conv, 72; Dem precinct committeeman, Tucson, 72-; mem, Pima Co Dem Exec Comt, 72-; chmn, Pima Co Dem Voter Registration, 74; committeeman, Ariz Rep State Comt, 74- Mem: Young Dem Ariz; Univ Ariz Young Dem; Dem of Gtr Tucson (rep to exec comt, 72-); Dist 11 Dem Club; Metrop Youth Coun (bd dirs, 74-75). Relig: Catholic. Mailing Add: 772 W Missouri Tucson AZ 85714

MAITLAND, GUY EDISON CLAY (R)
Pres, NY State Young Rep Clubs
b London, Eng, Dec 28, 42; s Paul M Maitland (deceased) & Virginia F Carver M; single. Educ: Columbia Univ, BA, 64; New York Law Sch, JD, 68; Phi Delta Phi; Alpha Delta Phi. Polit & Govt Pos: Chmn, NY State Students for Rockefeller, 63-64; mem staff, US Rep John V Lindsay, NY, 64; mem, New York City Planning Bd, Number 8, 65-66; mem, NY State Rep Exec Comt, 74-; pres, NY State Young Rep Clubs, 74-; mem, New York Co Rep Exec Comt, 75- Bus & Prof Pos: Attorney, Burlingham Underwood & Lord, New York, 69-74 & Union Carbide Corp, 74- Mem: Maritime Law Asn US; Fed Bar Coun; Am Judicature Soc; Asn of Bar of New York City; Am Bar Asn. Relig: Episcopal. Mailing Add: 31 E 72nd St Apt 14B New York NY 10021

MAJAK, RALPH ROGER (D)
b Hammond, Ind, July 14, 41; s Ralph L Majak & Florence Flanigan M; m 1965 to Sally Ann Armentrout. Educ: Northwestern Univ, BS in jour, 64; Ohio State Univ, MA, 65, doctoral courses, 65-67; Sigma Delta Chi; Acacia. Polit & Govt Pos: Admin asst to US Rep Jonathan B Bingham, NY, 70-73; staff consult, Int Rels Comt, US House Rep, 75- Mem: Int Studies Asn; Am Polit Sci Asn; Am Soc Int Law; Nat Press Club. Mailing Add: 1011 E St SE Washington DC 20003

MAJHANOVICH, STEVE (D)
Wyo State Sen
b Rock Springs, Wyo, Jan 20, 26; s Bob Majhanovich & Mary Ivankovich M; m 1948 to Caroline Shipley Wilde; c Carole Ann. Educ: Col of St Thomas, 43-45. Polit & Govt Pos: City councilman, Rock Springs, Wyo, 50-58; Wyo State Rep, 65-72; Wyo State Sen, 73- Mil Serv: Entered as A/S, Navy, 43, released as Ens, 46, after serv in Amphibious Assault Group, Philippine Islands, 45-46; Philippine Campaign Ribbon. Mem: Elks; Southwestern Wyo Jr Col Adv Bd; Exchange Club; Sweetwater Co Conserv Asn; CofC. Relig: Catholic. Mailing Add: 1412 Clark St Rock Springs WY 82901

MAJOR, BEVERLY BRUHN (D)
Mem, Windham Co Dem Comt, Vt
b Burlington, Vt, Oct 6, 35; d Elmer Henry Bruhn & Marion Moore B; m 1958 to Randolph Thomas Major, Jr; c David Randolph, Stephen Campbell, Christina Karin & Seth Andrew. Educ: Swarthmore Col, BA, 57; Columbia Univ, 57-58; Windham Col Inst of Critical Lang, Putney, Vt, summers 61 & 62; Antioch Putney Grad Sch Educ, Vt, grad, 73. Polit & Govt Pos: Sch dir, Westminster, Vt, 70-; deleg, Dem Nat Conv, 72 & Vt Dem State Conv, 72; clerk, Westminster Dem Town Comt, 72-; mem, Windham Co Dem Comt, 72-; mem, Gov Blue Ribbon Comn on Higher Educ, 74. Bus & Prof Pos: Secy, Exp in Int Living, Paris, France & Putney, Vt, 58-61; secy, Vt Credit Union League, 62-; research asst, Mass Inst Technol Ctr of Int Studies, 63-64; kindergarten teacher, Westminster, Vt, 72- Publ: Ed World perspectives on international politics, Little, Brown & Co, 65. Mem: Phi Beta Kappa; Southeastern Vt Sch Dirs Asn (secy, 70-72, vchmn, 72-74, chmn, 74); Vt Women's Polit Caucus (bd dirs, 72-); Vt State Sch Dirs Asn (bd dirs, 74-); Community House, Brattleboro, Vt (bd dirs). Relig: Protestant. Legal Res: Patch Rd Westminster VT 05158 Mailing Add: RD 3 Putney VT 05346

MAJOR, CONLEY ROY (D)
Mem, San Diego Co Dem Cent Comt, Calif
b Elizabethton, Tenn, June 24, 46; s Nathaniel Major & Molly Ann McQueen M; m 1967 to Anna E Wilkerson; c Annette, Theresa, Shelia & Sandra. Educ: San Diego State Col Exten, 71; San Diego City Col, AA, 72; US Int Univ, San Diego, 72-; Alpha Phi Alpha; Alpha Sigma Gamma; Black Student Coun; Student Govt. Polit & Govt Pos: Deleg, Dem Nat Conv, 72; deleg, Nat Black Polit Conv, 72; mem, San Diego Co Dem Cent Comt, Calif, 72- Mil Serv: Entered Army, 65, released as E-4, 68, after serv in Army Res Unit, Nurenburg Germany, 20th Sta Hosp, 8 months; Nat Defense Serv Medal; Expert Riflemans Badge. Mem: NAACP; Urban League; San Diego Black Fedn; Educ Finance Reform Project; 79th Assembly Dist Citizens Adv Bd. Honors & Awards: Outstanding Youth in Polit, Calif State Assemblyman Peter S Chacon, 71; Outstanding Student Plaque, San Diego City Col, 72; Appreciation Award, San Diego Eve Col, 72. Mailing Add: Apt 2 382 S 46th St San Diego CA 92113

MAKELA, GLADYS (D)
Dem Nat Committeewoman, Mont
Mailing Add: Box 802 Helena MT 59601

MAKRIS, HARRY PETER (D)
b Nashua, NH, Dec 24, 25; s Nicholas D Makris & Fannie Tsintsiras M; div; c Alexis & Deborah. Educ: Univ NH, BS, 49; Kappa Sigma; Mask & Dagger Club; Interfraternity Coun. Polit & Govt Pos: NH State Rep, Ward 5, 65-66; alt deleg, Dem Nat Conv, 68 & 72; exec dir, NH Dem Party, 68-70, chmn, 71-73. Mil Serv: Entered as A/S, Navy, 43, released as QM 2/C, 46, after serv in Pac Fleet, Southwest Pac, 44-46. Mem: Int Kiwanis; Am Legion; Elks. Relig: Greek Orthodox. Mailing Add: 25 Vine St Nashua NH 03060

MALADY, REGIS ROWLAND (D)
b Elizabeth, Pa, Feb 9, 17; s James C Malady & Laura Kistler M; m 1941 to Virginia Sullivan; c Regis R, Jr, Linda M, James Kevin, Virginia Ann, John Francis, Mary Beth, Neil Patrick & Michael Roderick. Educ: Pa State Exten, 36-38; Allegheny Tech Inst, Electronic & Instrument Eng, 60-62. Polit & Govt Pos: Borough councilman, Elizabeth, Pa, 62-65, Mayor, Elizabeth, 66-71; exec committeeman, Asn Mayors of Boroughs of Pa, 66-68, fed legis rep, 67-71, vpres, 68-71; exec committeeman, Allegheny Co Borough Mayors, 68-71, vpres, 68-71; Pa State Rep, 39th Legis Dist, Allegheny Co, 69-74. Bus & Prof Pos: Shipping clerk, Miss Glass Co, Floreffe, 36-37; wire & cable inspector, Copperweld Steel Co, Glassport, 37-49, electronic instrument repairman, 49-53, instrument engr, 53-, supvr, 70- Mem: Instrument Soc Am; Inst Certification of Eng Technicians; Am Soc Cert Eng Technicians (sr cert); Moose; Owls. Relig: Catholic. Mailing Add: 709 Seventh Ave Elizabeth PA 15037

MALAVE-RIOS, MANUEL B (NEW PROGRESSIVE)
Chmn, Anasco Rep Munic Comt, PR
b Las Navias, PR, Dec 29, 12; s Manuel Malave-Rivera & Maria L Rios Lugo M; m 1942 to Cruz Maria Gomez; c David E, Gustavo E, Manuel A, Lydia, Antonio, Angel B, Pedro A & Maria A (Mrs Forte). Educ: Univ of PR, BEd cum laude. Polit & Govt Pos: Secy, San Sebastian Dist Court, PR, 33-40; pres, Rep Party Anasco, 52-64; social worker, PR Social Work Dept, 71-72; mem, Bd Educ, 72-; chmn, Anasco Rep Munic Comt, 72- Bus & Prof Pos: Teacher, Dept Educ, PR, 41-52; Pub Rels Officer Cent Igualdad, Inc, 52-69. Mem: PR Teachers Asn; Rotary (pres, Anasco Club, 60-62, secy, 63-64). Mailing Add: Box 522 Anasco PR 00610

MALDONADO, DANIEL CHRIS (D)
b Los Angeles, Calif, Oct 19, 42; s Chris Vargas Maldonado & Maria Saldana M; m 1966 to Irma Herlinda Cusick; c Eve & Jose. Educ: Loyola Univ, Los Angeles, BA in Polit Sci, magna cum laude, 65; Univ Calif, Los Angeles, MS in Jour, 66; Georgetown Univ, doctoral prog, Govt, currently; Pi Gamma Mu; Sigma Delta Chi. Polit & Govt Pos: Research analyst & spec sci consult, US Dept of Com, 67; writer & ed, White House Conf on Youth, 71; admin asst to US Rep Edward R Roybal, Calif, 71- Bus & Prof Pos: Asst to exec dir, Eastland Community Action Coun, Montebello, Calif, 68-69; research adminr, Extramural Support, Univ Calif, Los Angeles, 69-70. Publ: Co-auth, Federal scientific and technological research policies and programs on regional development, US Dept of Com, 12/67; Spanish speaking staff on the hill, The Bureaucrat, summer 73. Honors & Awards: Fel, John Hay Whitney Found, 70-71; Scholarship, Georgetown Univ, 70-71. Mailing Add: 1223 Massachusetts Ave SE Washington DC 20003

MALDONADO TORRES, JUAN (POPULAR DEMOCRAT, PR)
Sen, PR Senate
b Arecibo, PR, Aug 11, 36; s Jose Maldonado Marin & Basilisa Torres Pabon M; m 1956 to Alicia del Valle Colon; c Rose Marie, Jose & Liza. Educ: InterAm Univ, BA. Polit & Govt Pos: Sen, PR Senate, 73-, chmn comt indust & pub lands, 73-75. Relig: Catholic. Legal Res: 12 First St Radioville Arecibo PR 00612 Mailing Add: PR Senate San Juan PR 00901

MALEDY, CHARLES ROBERT (R)
Chmn, Dent Co Rep Party, Mo
b Salem, Mo, Feb 13, 50; s Robert F Maledy & Patricia A Putman M; m 1975 to Cindy Lou Rueter. Educ: Univ Mo-Columbia, BS in bus & pub admin, 72; Delta Sigma Pi. Polit & Govt Pos: Chmn, Dent Co Rep Party, Mo, 74- Bus & Prof Pos: Gen mgr, Maledy Motors, Salem, Mo, currently. Relig: Methodist. Mailing Add: Mildred Ave Salem MO 65560

MALEK, FREDERIC VINCENT (R)
b Oak Park, Ill, Dec 22, 36; s Frederic William Malek & Martha Smickilas M; m 1961 to Marlene McArthur; c Frederic & Michelle. Educ: US Mil Acad, BSE, 59; Harvard Grad Sch Bus Admin, MBA with honors, 64. Polit & Govt Pos: Mem, Calif Rep State Cent Comt, 66-67; former mem exec comt, Los Angeles Co Rep Precinct Orgn; dep undersecy, Dept Health, Educ & Welfare, 69-71; spec asst to President, 71-73; dep budget dir, Off Mgt & Budget, 73-74. Bus & Prof Pos: Mkt planner, Swissair, Zurich, Switz, 63; mgt consult, McKinsey & Co, Los Angeles, Calif, 64-67; chmn & co-chief exec off, Triangle Corp, Orangeburg, SC, 67-69; adj prof, Univ SC. Mil Serv: Entered as 2nd Lt, Army, 59, released as 1st Lt, 62, after serv as Counter Guerilla Warfare Adv, Vietnam, 60-61; Armed Forces Expeditionary Medal; Ranger Award; Airborne Grad. Publ: Building profits through facilities planning, Factory; Assessment of management quality, Bus Horizons; An analytical approach to merger negotiations, Harvard Bus Rev. Mem: Am Mgt Asn; first vpres & dir, Harvard Club of Southern Calif; Univ Club of Los Angeles; Los Angeles CofC. Relig: Episcopal. Mailing Add: 917 Windsor Dr Los Angeles CA 90039

MALIN, MARJORIE CLAIRE (D)
Mem, Ark State Dem Cent Comt
b Augusta, Ark, June 21, 28; d William E Malin, Sr & Lura Elizabeth Thomason M; single. Educ: Ward-Belmont Jr Col, Nashville, Tenn, grad, 46; Univ Ark, BS, 48; Ind Univ, Bloomington, MA in Zool, 51; Chi Alpha; Chem Club, Univ Ark; Sigma Sigma Sigma; Nat Sci Found grant, Desert Biol Inst for Col Prof, Ariz State Univ, summer 60. Polit & Govt Pos: Pres, Woodruff Co Young Dem Club, Ark, 65-66; vpres, Ark State Young Dem Club, 66, acting pres, 66-67; mem, Ark State Dem Cent Comt, 66-; deleg & mem platform comt, Dem Nat Conv, 68; deleg, Dem Mid Term Conf, 74. Bus & Prof Pos: Sci teacher, Augusta High Sch, Ark, 51-55 & 70-; mgr, Lura Theatre, Augusta, 51-; asst prof biol, State Col of Ark, Conway, 57-64; sci teacher, Cotton Plant High Sch, 68-70. Mem: Delta Kappa Gamma (secy, 72-74); Am Inst of Biol Sci; Bus & Prof Women's Club (pres, 66-67); Ark Educ Asn; Woodruff Co Teachers Asn. Honors & Awards: Showman of the Year, Nat Asn of Theatre Owners of Ark-Miss-Tenn Orgn, 65; Awarded Plaque, State Conv of Young Dem Club, 69; hon lifetime mem, Ark Young Dem Club; Ark Audubon Soc Ruth Thomas scholarship natural hist & conserv, 73. Relig: Methodist. Mailing Add: 109 N Third St Augusta AR 72006

MALINOU, MARTIN S (D)
b Providence, RI, Dec 5, 32; s Dr Nathaniel J Malinou & Etta E Rezepter M; single. Educ: Brown Univ, AB, 55; Boston Univ Law Sch, JD, 59. Polit & Govt Pos: Committeeman, Providence Dem City Comt, Ward 12, RI, 60-68; pub adminr, City of Providence, 61-63; treas, RI New Dem Coalition, 68-71; alt deleg, Dem Nat Conv, 72. Bus & Prof Pos: Lawyer, Providence, 60-; deleg, RI State Const Conv, 73. Publ: An appraisal of the Writ of Certiorari

as a means of controlling administrative agency action in Rhode Island, Boston Univ Law Rev, 60. Mem: Asn Trial Lawyers Am; RI & Am Bar Asns; Am Judicature Soc; AF&AM (Master, Redwood Lodge 35, 69-70). Relig: Jewish. Mailing Add: 334 Smith St Providence RI 02908

MALKIN, SUSAN ROBERTA (D)
b Pittsburgh, Pa, Feb 12, 45; d Morris Shane & Betty Fink S; m 1968 to Dr Stanley Lee Malkin; c Justin Ross & Keith Richard. Educ: Univ Pittsburgh, BS, 66. Polit & Govt Pos: Campaign worker, McCarthy for President, 68; campaign worker, Gerald Kaufman for Pa State Rep, 68; munic coord, Ft Lee, NJ, McGovern Presidential Campaign, 72, mem exec bd, NJ Citizens for McGovern, 72; alt deleg, Dem Nat Conv, 72. Bus & Prof Pos: School-teacher, Pittsburgh Pub Sch Syst, 66-69; schoolteacher & educator, Ft Lee Bd Educ, 69-71. Mem: Horizon Tenant's Asn, NJ (secy, 70-72). Relig: Jewish. Mailing Add: 555 North Ave Fort Lee NJ 07024

MALKUS, FREDERICK C, JR (D)
Md State Sen
b Baltimore, Md, July 1, 13; married. Educ: Western Md Col, AB, 34; Univ Md, LLB, 38. Polit & Govt Pos: Md State Deleg, 47-51; Md State Sen, 51- Mil Serv: Army. Mem: Md Bar. Mailing Add: 500 Spring St Cambridge MD 21613

MALLARY, RICHARD WALKER (D)
b Springfield, Mass, Feb 21, 29; s R De Witt Mallary & Gertrude Robinson M; m 1955 to Mary Harper Coxe; c Richard Walker, Jr, Anne Campbell, Elizabeth Harper & Sarah Roberts. Educ: Dartmouth Col, AB, 49; Phi Beta Kappa. Hon Degrees: LLD, Am Int Col, 73. Polit & Govt Pos: Selectman & chmn bd, Fairlee, Vt, 51-53; mem, Fairlee Rep Town Comt, 52-, chmn, 56-58; alt deleg, Rep Nat Conv, 56, deleg, 68; Vt State Rep, 61-69, chmn, Appropriations Comt, Vt House of Rep, 63-65, Speaker, 66-69; trustee & treas, Vt State Col, 62-65; chmn, Vt Legis Coun, 65-67; chmn, Vt Rep Platform Conv, 66 & 70; mem & vchmn, Vt Const Rev Comt, 68-; Vt State Sen, 69-70; Vt Comnr of Admin, 71; US Rep, Vt, 72-75. Bus & Prof Pos: Farmer, Bradford, Vt, 50-70; partner, Farrell & Mallary Sales, Woodstock, 51-52. Mem: Trustee, Eastern States Expos, 56-; Orange Co Farm Bur (vpres, 55-56); New Eng Holstein Friesian Asn (dir, 54-56); Vt Holstein Asn (pres, 54-56); Vt Farm Bur. Mailing Add: Mallary Farm Bradford VT 05033

MALLORY, WILLIAM L (D)
Ohio State Rep
Mailing Add: 907 Dayton St Cincinnati OH 45214

MALLOY, WILLIAM A (D)
Treas, Douglas Co Dem Comt, Mo
b Arno, Mo, Apr 7, 08; s John Malloy & Ida Turner M; m 1942 to Billie Sue James; c Patricia Ann (Mrs Bingman) & Carol Sue (Mrs Ginger). Educ: Bartlesville Jr Col, 1 year; Okla State Univ, 1 year. Polit & Govt Pos: Twp Rep committeeman, Douglas Co, Mo, 70-; treas, Douglas Co Dem Comt, 70- Mil Serv: Entered as Pvt, Army, 42, released as Sgt, 45, after serv in VI Corps, Field Artil, NAfrica & European Theatres, 43-45; Silver Star, Bronze Star Arrow Head; Good Conduct Medal. Mem: Geol Asn; Mason; Eastern Star; Am Legion; VFW. Relig: Methodist. Mailing Add: PO Box 415 Ava MO 65608

MALONE, HUGH (D)
Alaska State Rep
Mailing Add: PO Box 9 Kenai AK 99611

MALONE, J EDWARD (R)
Md State Deleg
b Baltimore, Md, Nov 25, 27; s William James Malone, Sr & Rosemary Sullivan M; m 1956 to Margaret Daniels; c James E, Jr, Peggy Ann, Daniel Sullivan & Patrick Shawn. Educ: St Charles' Col, 2 years; St Mary's Univ, 1 year. Polit & Govt Pos: Deleg, Md State Dem Conv, 64; Md State Deleg, 67- Bus & Prof Pos: Clerk, Western Md Railway Co, 47-55; eng inspector, 55-59, supvr track, 59-67, eng asst, 67-79; asst mgr, Indust Develop & Real Estate, 69- Mil Serv: Entered as Recruit, Army, 50, released as Sgt, 52, after serv in 70th AAA, Baltimore & Washington Areas, 50-52. Mem: Elks; Optimist Club; Am Legion; Eng Consul; Arbutus Community Asn. Relig: Roman Catholic. Mailing Add: 5536 Oakland Rd Baltimore MD 21227

MALONE, ROBERT (KEN) (D)
Ala State Rep
Mailing Add: PO Box 298 Saraland AL 36571

MALONEY, JAMES (CON) (D)
Miss State Sen
b Washington, DC, May 13, 39; s James C Maloney & Dolly Schimpf M; m 1960 to Betty Priske; c Chris, Steve & Mark. Educ: Hinds Jr Col, 58; Millsaps Col, 60; Kappa Sigma. Polit & Govt Pos: Miss State Sen, 71-, mem audit comt, Miss State Senate, currently. Bus & Prof Pos: Pres, Cowboy Maloney Supply, 69- Mem: Jackson Home Builders; Sertoma Club of Jackson; Jackson Touchdown Club (dir); Jackson Girls' Club (bd pres). Relig: Catholic. Legal Res: 5314 Suffolk Jackson MS 39211 Mailing Add: Box 9905 Jackson MS 39206

MALONEY, MARVIN L (D)
Mo State Rep
b Pleasant Hill, Mo, Mar 6, 42; s Walter J Maloney & Cleo Davidson M; m 1962 to Dorrine R Brening; c Sherilyn Renae & Erin Michelle. Educ: William Jewell Col, AB, 64; Univ Mo Sch Law, Kansas City, JD, 70; Delta Theta Phi (gtr Kansas City alumni pres, 75). Polit & Govt Pos: Mo State Rep, 45th Dist, 75- Bus & Prof Pos: Attorney-at-law, Independence, Mo, 71- Mem: Am & Mo Bar Asns; Ararat Shrine; Lions Int. Relig: Protestant. Mailing Add: RR 1 Box 42A Napoleon MO 64074

MALONEY, MICHAEL JOSEPH (R)
Minority Leader, Ohio State Senate
b Covington, Ky, Jan 31, 29; s Michael J Maloney & Sara E Fisher M; m 1957 to Mary Catherine Bollman; c Timothy M, Thomas N, Richard P, Patrick J & Brigid M. Educ: Xavier Univ, BS magna cum laude, 61. Polit & Govt Pos: Asst to chmn, Hamilton Co Rep Cent Comt, Ohio, 62-73; Ohio State Sen, 64-, Asst Pres Pro Tem, Ohio State Senate, formerly, Minority Leader, currently. Bus & Prof Pos: Gen assignment reporter, Cincinnati Enquirer, Columbus, Ohio, 48-56, polit reporter, 56-61, chief bur, 61-62; exec vpres, Adams, Gaffney & Assocs, Inc, Cincinnati, 73- Mil Serv: Entered as Pvt, Air Force, 50, released as T/Sgt, 54, after serv in Far East Air Logistic Forces; Korean Theater, 52-54; Korean Theater, UN Forces & Good Conduct Ribbons. Mem: Am Polit Sci Asn; Xavier Univ Alumni Asn; KofC. Honors & Awards: Cong fel, Am Polit Sci Asn, 86th Cong. Relig: Roman Catholic. Legal Res: 8560 Gwilada Dr Cincinnati OH 45236 Mailing Add: State Capitol Bldg Columbus OH 43215

MALONEY, ROBERT (BOB) (R)
Tex State Rep
Mailing Add: 3528 Bryn Mawr Dallas TX 75225

MALONEY, THOMAS J (R)
b Bethlehem, Pa, Aug 13, 39; s James P Maloney & Elmira McDonald M; m 1960 to Ann Louise Kervin; c Marybeth, Judith, Thomas & Patrice. Educ: St Joseph's Col, BS, 61; Temple Univ, LLB, 64; Nat Jesuit Honor Soc. Polit & Govt Pos: Deleg, Rep Nat Conv, 72; Pa State Rep, 135th Dist, 73-74. Bus & Prof Pos: Attorney, Butterfield, Joachim, Brodt & Maloney, 63-69; attorney, pvt practice, 69-70; attorney, Maloney & Goodman, 71-72; prof in const law, Moravian Col, 72-73; attorney, Maloney, Danyi, Goodman & Hensel, Bethlehem, Pa, 73- Mem: Am Bar Asn; Am Judicature Soc; Bethlehem Boys Club; Bethlehem Cath High Sch Alumni Asn; Kiwanis. Honors & Awards: Bethlehem's Outstanding Young Man of the Year, Jr CofC, 67. Relig: Catholic. Mailing Add: 2033 Sycamore St Bethlehem PA 18107

MALONEY, THOMAS M (D)
Mem Exec Comt, Whitman Co Dem Party, Wash
b Raymond, Wash, Feb 18, 31; s Peter Maloney & May Jacobson M; m 1960 to Donna J MacCallum; c William T, Carol D & Joseph R. Educ: Wash State Univ, BA, 56; Phi Delta Kappa; Epsilon Pi Tau. Polit & Govt Pos: Dem precinct committeeman, Whitman Co, Wash, 63-66; committeeman, Wash State Dem Party, 65-66; state chmn, Dollars for Dem, 65-66; chmn, Whitman Co Dem Party, Wash, 66-73, mem exec comt, 73- Bus & Prof Pos: Wood technologist, Wash State Univ, 56- Publ: Ed, Proc of Wash State Univ Particleboard Symp, Wash State Univ, 67-72; Effect of production variables on particleboards of planer shavings, Forest Prod J, 58. Mem: Forest Prod Research Soc (chmn particle & fiber processes div, 70); Soc Wood Sci & Technol; Elks; Kiwanis; Sigma Xi. Mailing Add: 830 Fountain SW Pullman WA 99163

MALOOMIAN, HELEN (D)
NH State Rep
b West Andover, Mass, July 24, 18; d Sarkis Kachanian & Catherine Anokian K; wid; c Ralph & Diane (Mrs Dunsford). Educ: Salem Schs, NH. Polit & Govt Pos: NH State Rep, 71- Relig: Protestant. Mailing Add: 8 Emery St Somersworth NH 03878

MALOTT, HARRY C (D)
Ohio State Rep
Mailing Add: RR 2 Mt Orab OH 45154

MALRY, LENTON (D)
NMex State Rep
Mailing Add: 3000 Santa Clara SE Albuquerque NM 87106

MANAHAN, JAMES HINCHON (R)
b Madelia, Minn, Aug 27, 36; s Cecil James Manahan & Ruth Hinchon M; div; c Theodore J, Corinne R, Matthew D & Anne J. Educ: Harvard Col, BA, 58, Law Sch, JD, 61. Polit & Govt Pos: Secy, Mankato Police Civil Serv Comn, Minn, 71-; alt deleg, Rep Nat Conv, 72. Publ: Lawyers should be audited, Am Bar Asn J, 4/73. Mem: Sixth Dist Bar Asn (pres, 74-75). Legal Res: 218 Iota Ave Mankato MN 56001 Mailing Add: PO Box 152 Mankato MN 56001

MANASCO, CARTER (D)
b Townley, Ala, Jan 3, 02; s John Claude Manasco & Dora Letitia Beaty M; m 1942 to Mae Emma Guyton (deceased); c two. Educ: Howard Col, 20-22; Univ of Ala, LLB, 27. Polit & Govt Pos: Ala State Rep, 30-34; mem, Hoover Comn; US Rep, Ala, 41-49. Bus & Prof Pos: Lawyer; pub rels. Mem: Ala Bar Asn; Mason; Lions. Mailing Add: 5932 Chesterbrook Rd McLean VA 22101

MANATT, CHARLES TAYLOR (D)
Chmn, Calif Dem Party
b Chicago, Ill, June 9, 36; s William Price Manatt & Lucille Taylor M; m 1957 to Kathleen Klinkefus; c Michele Anne, Timothy Taylor & Daniel Charles. Educ: Iowa State Univ, BS, 58; George Washington Univ Law Sch, JD, 62. Polit & Govt Pos: Nat committeeman, Iowa Young Dem, 58-59; chmn, Nat Col Young Dem, 59-61; Am deleg, NATO Young Polit Leaders Conf, 60; exec secy, Young Dem of Am, 61-62; chmn, Young Citizens for Johnson-Humphrey, Southern Calif, 64 & Cranston, Van Nuys, Calif, 68; finance co-chmn, Valley Brown for Gov Comt, 66; chmn, 22nd Cong Dist for Hubert Humphrey, 68; finance chmn, James C Corman, 68; mem, Calif Dem Adv Comt, 67-68; Dem Elector Nominee, 68; mem, Calif Dem State Cent Comt, 68-69; San Fernando Valley finance chmn, Bradley for Mayor, 69; dep campaign dir & Southern Calif chmn, John V Tunney for Senate, 70; chmn, Calif Dem Party 71-73 & 75-, Southern Calif chmn, 73-75; Southern chmn, Western Conf of Chmn of Dem Parties, 73-; mem, Dem Charter Comn, currently. Bus & Prof Pos: Lawyer, Manatt, Phelps & Rothenberg, Los Angeles, Calif, 64- Mil Serv: Lt, Army, 59; Capt, Judge Adv Gen Corps, Army Res. Mem: Am Bar Asn (mem banking comn, Admin Law Sect); Calif State Bar Asn (mem corp comt, 69-); Los Angeles Co Bar Asn (bd trustees, 72-); Boy Scouts (participating chmn, Scout Fair, 70); Van Nuys Jr CofC. Honors & Awards: Distinguished Serv Award, 70; Resolution of Commendation, City of Los Angeles, City Coun Los Angeles & Co Los Angeles. Relig: Methodist; Mem, Admin Bd. Legal Res: 10485 Charing Cross Rd Los Angeles CA 90024 Mailing Add: 1888 Century Park E 21st Floor Los Angeles CA 90067

MANCHESTER, PAUL C (R)
Conn State Rep
b New York, NY, July 11, 23; s Sherman A Manchester & Ilse Loescher M; m 1971 to Margaret Peirce; c Susan, Paul C, II, Vicky & Joan. Educ: High sch. Polit & Govt Pos: Mem, Representative Town Meeting, Westport, Conn, 52-56, treas, Rep Town Comt, 56-58, dir, Civil Defense, 57-61, pres, Young Rep, 59-60, Conn State Rep, 135th Dist, 75- Bus & Prof Pos: Pres, Weston-Westport Agencies, Inc, Weston, Conn, 50- Mem: Westport Bd Realtors; Soc Real Estate Appraisers, Conn Chap; Mid Fairfield Co Asn Independent Ins Agts. Honors & Awards: Sr Residential Appraiser, Soc Real Estate Appraisers, 63 & Sr Real Property Appraiser, 70. Relig: Protestant. Mailing Add: 19 Woodside Ave Westport CT 06880

MANCINI, JOSEPH A (R)
Committeeman, Fla State Rep Exec Comt
b New Britain, Conn, Apr 9, 18; s Anthony Mancini & Margarite Totire M; m 1950 to Marjorie Louise Howard; c Joseph A, Jr, John Daniel & Richard A. Educ: Edison Col; Miami Inst Food Technol. Polit & Govt Pos: Co-chmn, Kirk for Gov Comt, Fla; chmn, Hardee Co Rep Comt, formerly; committeeman, Fla State Rep Exec Comt, 70-, asst treas, formerly. Bus & Prof Pos: Pres, The Mancini Packing Co, 48-; organizer, 1st Nat Bank, Wauchula, Fla, 60, chmn bd dirs, 66-; pres, J & R Fruit Harvesters, 61- Mil Serv: Entered as Pfc, Marine Corps, 43, released as Capt, Marine Corps Res, 58, after serv in Fleet Marine Force, Pac. Mem: Inst Food Technologists; Elks. Legal Res: 705 W Main St Wauchula FL 33873 Mailing Add: PO Box 395 Wauchula FL 33873

MANDEL, MARVIN (D)
Gov, Md
b Baltimore, Md, Apr 19, 20; married. Educ: Univ of Md Law Sch, LLB, 42. Hon Degrees: LLD, Univ Md, 69, Towson State Col, 69 & Washington Col, 71; Dr, Morgan State Col, Yeshiva Univ & Xavier Univ, Ohio, 71. Polit & Govt Pos: Justice of the Peace, Baltimore, Md, 51; mem, Dem State Cent Comt, 51; mem, Gov Comn on Munic Court for Baltimore; Md State Deleg, 52-69, Acting Speaker, 63, Speaker, 64-69; deleg, Dem Nat Conv, 68; Gov Md, 69-; chmn, Mid Atlantic States Gov Conf, 70-71; chmn, Caucus of Dem Gov, 71-72; chmn, Nat Gov Conf, 72-73; deleg, Dem Nat Conv, 72; ex-officio, Dem Nat Mid-Term Conf, 74. Mil Serv: Army, 42-44. Mem: Am, Md & Baltimore Bar Asns; Am Legion; Jewish War Vet. Relig: Jewish. Mailing Add: Government House Annapolis MD 21404

MANDERINO, JAMES J (D)
Pa State Rep
Mailing Add: Capitol Bldg Harrisburg PA 17120

MANDIGO, MELVIN HARVEY (R)
Vt State Sen
b Moretown, Vt, July 16, 13; s Arthur A Mandigo & Louella Harvey M; m 1934 to Enid Wakeman. Educ: Dartmouth Col, 31-33; Univ Vt, BS, 37; Alpha Zeta; Kappa Phi Kappa. Polit & Govt Pos: Tax assessor, Glover, Vt, 52-60; Vt State Rep, Dist 28, 66 & 69-74; moderator, Glover Town Meeting, 66-; chmn, Orleans Co Rep Party, 68-69 & currently, vchmn, formerly; mem, Vt Rep State Comt, 68-71; sch dir, Glover Town Sch Dist, 69-; Vt State Sen, 75- Bus & Prof Pos: Instr in voc agr, Thayer High Sch, Winchester, NH, 37-41 & Barton Acad, Vt, 42-46; farm mgt & operation, 46-48; Instnl-on-Farm vet instr, Orleans High Sch, Vt, 48-60; distributor-inseminator, Curtiss Breeding Serv, 53- Mem: Orleans Co Farm Bur. Relig: Protestant. Mailing Add: Glover VT 05839

MANDINA, CONSTANCE MARGARET (D)
b New York, NY, Dec 30, 42; d Joseph A Mandina & Constance Bayors M; m 1974 to Sid Davidoff. Educ: Harpur Col; Univ Dayton, BA, 64; Univ Louisville Sch Law; Brooklyn Law Sch, LLB & JD, 67. Polit & Govt Pos: Law clerk, Caracciolo & Moringiello, Brooklyn, 67; research, Appeals Bur & Crime Prevention Prog, Off of Dist Attorney, Queens Co, 67, off asst, 68; admin asst to majority leader, Fla House of Rep, 68-69; trial attorney, Matthews, Mandina & Lipsky, Miami, Fla, 68-69; asst dist attorney, Queens Co, 69-70; law secy to Hon Ann B Dufficy, Civil Court of City of New York, 70-73 & Supreme Court of State of NY, 74-; deleg, Dem Nat Mid-Term Conf, 74. Mem: Fla Bar; Asst Dist Attorney's Asn of Queens Co (pres, 75); Queens Co Bar Asn (civil rights comt); Criminal Courts Bar Asn of Queens Co; Am Judicature Soc. Relig: Catholic. Legal Res: 222-41 93rd Ave Queens Village NY 11428 Mailing Add: Supreme Court 88-11 Sutphin Blvd Jamaica NY 11435

MANES, DONALD (D)
Mem, Dem Nat Comt, NY
Mailing Add: 72-50 Austin St Forest Hills NY 11375

MANESS, INA MAE (D)
Mem, Mo State Dem Comt
b Kansas City, Mo, Aug 16, 21; d Lewis Fry Alexander & Inez Barker A; m 1941 to Carl Christy Maness; c Carla (Mrs Zaine) & Maryla A. Educ: Northeast High Sch, 4 years. Polit & Govt Pos: Dep recorder deeds, Jackson Co, Mo, 57-67; mem, Mo State Dem Comt, 70-; committeewoman, Blue Twp Dem Comt, Jackson Co, Mo, 70-; mem, Jackson Co Charter Transition Comn, 71- Bus & Prof Pos: Corp secy, Shure-Way Motors, Independence, Mo, 69- Mem: Dem State Club Mo; Dem Forum, Inc; Sugar Creek Dem Club; Dem Good Govt Asn. Relig: Episcopal. Mailing Add: 801 Fairview Independence MO 64053

MANEY, MARILYN HICKS (D)
Mem Exec Bd, Mont State Dem Cent Comt
b Miles City, Mont, May 13, 49; d Harry Edwin Hicks & Florence Laird H; m 1970 to Richard Leo Maney; c Larisa Lynn & Skye Brienna. Polit & Govt Pos: Chmn, Silver Bow Co McGovern Campaign, 72; area coordr, Equal Rights Amendment Ratification Coun, 73-74; state committeewoman, Silver Bow Co Cent Comt, 73-; mem exec bd, Mont State Dem Cent Comt, 73- Bus & Prof Pos: Scriptwriter, Independent Film Bus, currently. Publ: Film, The Winddrinkers (documentary), 72 & Outside the Melting Pot (documentary), Mont TV Network, 74. Mem: Nat Women's Polit Caucus; Dem Women's Club. Honors & Awards: Program of the Year Award for TV, The Winddrinkers, Gtr Mont Found, 72; Mont Inst Arts Film Festival Winner, 72 & 73. Relig: Roman Catholic. Mailing Add: 110 S Crystal Butte MT 59701

MANFORD, DON (D)
Mo State Sen
Mailing Add: 9409 Oakland Kansas City MO 64138

MANGAN, TOM (DFL)
Minn State Rep
Mailing Add: 533 Bean St Anoka MN 55303

MANGANILLO, RONALD JOSEPH (D)
b Brooklyn, NY; married to Francine; c Gina & Jennifer. Educ: New York Schs & Univs. Polit & Govt Pos: Spec dep attorney gen, Bur Elec Frauds, NY Attorney Gen Off, 68; govt appeal agent, New York Selective Serv Syst, 69-; dir, Narcotic Task Force, 24th Cong Dist NY, currently; pres, Fedn Ital Am Dem Orgn State NY, currently; consult, NY State Joint Legis Comt Pub Health, Medicare & Compulsory Health Ins currently; mem, NY State Senate Comt on Health, currently; Marshall, City of New York, 72- Bus & Prof Pos: Assoc with J Richard Thomas & Partners, currently; Manganillo & Tomaselli, currently. Mil Serv: NY Army Nat Guard, 56-, Comdr, 42nd Inf Div Armed Forces Serv Medal; Long & Faithful Serv Medal State NY. Mem: Nat Dist Attorneys Asn; Nat Narcotic Enforcement Officers Asn; Nat Sheriff's Asn; hon mem Nat Detectives & Spec Police Asn; Am Legion. Legal Res: 75-26 Bell Blvd Bayside NY 11364 Mailing Add: 89-31 161st St Jamaica NY 11432

MANGANO, JAMES V (D)
Mem Exec Comt, NY Dem State Comt
b Brooklyn, NY, Nov 21, 05; s Gaetano Mangano & Virginia Verdoliva M; m 1928 to Rose Mancaruso; c Guy James. Educ: Syracuse Univ; NY Univ, currently. Hon Degrees: LLD, Shaw Univ, 75. Polit & Govt Pos: Admin dir & gen clerk, NY Supreme Court, Kings Co, 54-; mem exec comt, NY Dem State Comt, currently; mem, Kings Co Dem Exec Comt. Mil Serv: Capt, Army Nat Guard, 14th Regiment. Mem: Atlantic Liberty Savings Bank (dir); Swedish Hosp (dir); Arthritis Found Telethon, Kings Co (chmn); Gowanus Settlement (chmn bd dirs). Honors & Awards: Star of Solidarity, Repub of Italy; Freedom Found Award, Valley Forge, Pa, 63; Citation Baith Israel Anshei Emes-State Israel Bond Drive; Plaque from St Thomas More Law Soc, St Francis Col. Relig: Catholic. Mailing Add: 101 Clark St Brooklyn NY 11201

MANGUM, TOM GIBSON (D)
SC State Rep
b Chesterfield, SC, Jan 23, 16; s Inglis Parks Mangum & Sara Funderburk M; m to Louise Clyburn. Educ: Univ SC, 33-34; Wingate Jr Col, 34-35. Polit & Govt Pos: SC State Rep, 55-58 & 61- Bus & Prof Pos: Merchant; farmer; real estate. Mil Serv: Army Air Force, 45. Mailing Add: Main St Lancaster SC 29720

MANGUS, RICHARD W (R)
Ind State Rep
Mailing Add: 69391 U S 31 Lakeville IN 46536

MANIBOG, G MONTY (D)
Committeeman, Calif Dem State Cent Comt
b Manila, Philippines, Feb 14, 30; s Gonzalo Manibog & Adela Montilla M; m 1954 to Jean Gingerich; c G Monty, Jr, Adela Lisa, Ricardo Luis, Marina Lana, Dean Carlo & Darren Anthony. Educ: Univ of the Philippines, BA, 52; Loyola Univ Sch of Law, JD, 60; Van Norman Univ Col of Law, LLM & LLD, 69; Phi Alpha Delta. Polit & Govt Pos: Mem adv comt, Calif State Sen Alfred Song, 68-; committeeman, Calif Dem State Cent Comt, 68- Bus & Prof Pos: Sr partner, Manibog & Shalant, Attorneys, Los Angeles, Calif, 61-; prof law, Van Norman Univ, 67-69. Mil Serv: Entered as Pvt, Army, 54, released as Specialist 3/C, 56, after serv in Psychol Warfare Sect, Tokyo, Japan, 54-56; Capt, Judge Adv Corps, Army Res; Spec Commendation for Outstanding Serv, Psychol Warfare Sect, 56. Publ: Weekly series, Point of Law, Philippine News, San Francisco, Calif, 67-68. Mem: Am & Los Angeles Co Bar Asns; Monterey Park Beautiful, Inc (pres). Honors & Awards: Former World Olympian, Helsinki, Finland, 62. Relig: Catholic. Legal Res: 489 Van Buren Dr Monterey Park CA 92754 Mailing Add: Suite 14 Burlington Bldg 1725 W Beverly Blvd Los Angeles CA 90026

MANKIEWICZ, DON MARTIN (D)
b Berlin, Ger, Jan 20, 22; s Herman J Mankiewicz & Sara Aaronson M; m 1946 to Ilene Korsen, div, 1972; c Jane & John Herman; m 1972 to Carol Bell Guidi. Educ: Columbia Sch Law, 41-42; Columbia Col, BA, 42. Polit & Govt Pos: Deleg or alt, numerous NY State Dem Conv; mem campaign staff, Herbert Lehman for Sen, 50, Stevenson for President, 52 & 56 & Robert F Kennedy for Sen, 64; vchmn, Nassau Co Dem Comt, 53-73; campaign mgr, Nassau Co Dem Party, 58; alt deleg, Dem Nat Conv, 60, deleg, 68 & 72; deleg-at-lg, NY Const Conv, 67. Bus & Prof Pos: Reporter, New Yorker Mag, 46-48; freelance writer, novels, plays, mag articles, motion pictures, radio, TV & short stories, 47- Mil Serv: Entered as Pvt, Army, 42, released as S/Sgt, 46, after serv in Intel & Counter-Intel, ETO, 44-46; ETO Ribbon; Two Battle Stars. Publ: See How They Run, AA Knopf, 50; Trial, Harper Bros, 55; It Only Hurts a Minute, Putnam, 67. Mem: Nat Acad TV Arts & Sci (bd gov); Auth League; Dramatists Guild. Honors & Awards: Writers Guild of Am, E Harper Prize for novel Trial, 55; nominated for Motion Picture Acad Award for I Want To Live, 59; nominated for TV Acad Award for Ironside, 68 & Marcus Welby, MD, 70. Mailing Add: Prospect Ave Sea Cliff NY 11579

MANKINS, JAMES EARL (JIMMY) (D)
Tex State Rep
b Electra, Tex, Feb 9, 26; s Alma Earl Mankins & Thelma Inez Cooper; m 1948 to Virginia Lucille Henley; c Cherryl Jane (Mrs Jeff Mercer), James Earl, Jr, Virginia Inez & Elizabeth Jan. Educ: Tex A&M Univ, 43; Kilgore Col, AA, 48; NTex Univ, BBA, 50; Alpha Lambda Pi. Polit & Govt Pos: City comnr, Kilgore, Tex, 65-71; deleg, State Dem Conv, 74; Tex State Rep, 75- Bus & Prof Pos: Pres, Eagle Trucking Co, Kilgore, Tex, 67-; dir, Woodbine Savings & Loan Asn, 74- Mil Serv: Entered as Pfc, Army Air Force, 44, released as Cpl, 46. Mem: Rotary; Sharon Temple Shrine; Oilfield Haulers Asn; Tex Motor Transportation Asn. Honors & Awards: Zeus Award for Aid to Mankind, Epsilon Sigma Alpha Tex State Coun, 70; Serv Award, Oilfield Haulers, 71; Albert Gallatin Nat Award for Outstanding Small Businessman in Nation, 75. Relig: Presbyterian. Legal Res: 2211 Green Hills Dr Kilgore TX 75662 Mailing Add: Box 471 Kilgore TX 75662

MANLEY, ART (D)
Idaho State Sen
b Coeur d'Alene, Idaho, Jan 22, 16; s Roy A Manley & Gurie Braaten M; m 1941 to Margaret Swan; c Victor, Mary Carol & James. Educ: Univ Idaho, BA in Polit Sci, 38, MA in Polit Sci, 40. Polit & Govt Pos: Case worker & co supvr, Idaho Dept of Pub Assistance, 39-48; with US Civil Serv Comn, Washington, DC, 40-41; Idaho State Rep, Kootenai Co, 64-66; Idaho State Sen, Dist Two, 66-72; Idaho State Sen, 75- Bus & Prof Pos: Off mgr & acct, Boundary Farmers Supply, Inc, 48, Co-op Supply, Inc, 48-51 & Van's Creamery, Inc, 51-65; mgr real estate dept, Thomas Agency, 65- Mil Serv: Entered as Pvt, Army, 43, released as Tech 3/C, 45, after serv in Southwest Pac, 44-45; New Guinea, Southern Philippines & Luzon Campaign Ribbons; Good Conduct Medal with One Bronze Star; Bronze Star. Mem: Eagles; VFW; Idaho Wildlife Fedn. Relig: Baptist. Mailing Add: 1109 11th St Coeur d'Alene ID 83814

MANLEY, JOHN EMMETT (D)
Mont State Sen
b Deer Lodge, Mont, Aug 2, 28; s James Clifford Manley & Alma Christina Bissonnette M; m 1955 to Janet Anice Eccleston; c Peggy Ann, Tracy John, Kerry Anice & Nicky Clifford. Educ: Powell Co High Sch, mil dipl. Polit & Govt Pos: Mont State Sen, Dist 14, 75- Bus & Prof Pos: Rancher. Mil Serv: Entered as Pvt, Marine Corps, 44, released as Pfc, 46; Sgt,

Marine Corps Res, serv in Pac Korean Theatre, 50-53. Mem: Am Legion Post 125. Relig: Catholic. Mailing Add: Drummond MT 59832

MANLEY, RICHARD SHANNON (D)
Ala State Rep
b Birmingham, Ala, June 23, 32; s Richard Sabine Manley (deceased) & Alice Hughes M (deceased); m 1953 to Lillian Grace Cardwell; c Richard Shannon, Jr & Alyce Hughes. Educ: Univ Ala, BS, 53, LLB, 58; Phi Delta Phi; Delta Chi. Polit & Govt Pos: Secy, Demopolis City Planning Comn, Ala, 60-68; Ala State Rep, Dist 27, 67-, mem spec comt intergovt coop, Ala House Rep, 67-, chmn judiciary comt, 75-; mem, Demopolis City Bd Educ, 69-70; dir, Marengo Co Ment Health Asn, 68-; mem, Ala State Bd Bar Comnrs, 72- Bus & Prof Pos: Attorney-at-law, 58-; mem bd dirs, New Southland Nat Ins Co, 69- Mil Serv: Entered as Pvt, Marine Corps, 54, released as 1st Lt, 56, after serv in G-2 Sect, 2nd Marine Air Wing, Continental US, 54-56; Lt Col, Marine Corps Res; Nat Defense Serv Ribbon; Marine Res Medal; Armed Forces Res Medal. Mem: Am Bar Asn; Am Trial Lawyers Asn; Commercial Law League of Am; Am Judicature Soc; Rotary. Relig: Methodist. Legal Res: 1501 Country Club Dr SW Demopolis AL 36732 Mailing Add: PO Drawer U Demopolis AL 36732

MANLOVE, WILLIAM CLARK (D)
Mem, Md Dem State Cent Comt
b Cecilton, Md, Feb 1, 34; s Joseph Edgar Manlove & Isabel Thomas Clark M; m 1954 to Mary Williams; c William Clark, II & Jane Elizabeth. Educ: Cecilton High Sch, Md, grad, 52. Polit & Govt Pos: Mem, Md Dem State Cent Comt, 74- Bus & Prof Pos: Night shift supvr, Gen Cable, Elkton, Md, 62-67; line foreman, RMR Corp, Elkton, 67-70; self-employed dairy farmer, Earleville, 70- Mil Serv: Entered as E-2, Army, 55, released as E-5, 58, after serv in WASSA, White Sands, NMex, 56-58. Mem: AF&AM; Cecil Co Young Farmers. Relig: Protestant. Mailing Add: RD 1 Box 13A Earleville MD 21919

MANMILLER, JOSEPH C (R)
Pa State Rep
Mailing Add: Capitol Bldg Harrisburg PA 17120

MANN, CHARLES C (D)
Ga State Rep
Mailing Add: 238 Elbert St Elberton GA 30635

MANN, CHARLES W (R)
Chmn, Hanson Rep Town Comt, Mass
b Pittsfield, Mass, Apr 27, 35; s Howard Gorden Mann & Marion L Cummings M; m 1958 to Jacqueline E Storm; c Deborah, Karen & Jennifer. Educ: Northeastern Univ, 3 years. Polit & Govt Pos: Mem sch comt, Hanson, Mass, 63-67; Mass State Rep, 67-70; chmn, Hanson Rep Town Comt, 68-69 & 73- Bus & Prof Pos: Sales mgr & food broker, F N McClure of Mass, Inc, 58-66; real estate broker, 66- Mil Serv: Entered as Pvt, Army, 55, released as Cpl, 56. Mem: Mass Legislators Asn; Boston Press Club; Kiwanis; Elks; Whitman-Hanson Citizens Scholarship Found. Relig: Episcopal. Mailing Add: 801 Winter St Hanson MA 02341

MANN, EZRA B (R)
NH State Rep
Mailing Add: 16 Pine St Woodsville NH 03785

MANN, FLETCHER CULLEN (R)
Attorney, SC Rep Party
b Pittsboro, NC, Sept 21, 21; s Fletcher C Mann & Bertie Outlaw M; m 1944 to Blanche Poole; c Sharon (Mrs Joe Piper), Fletcher C, Jr & William P. Educ: Univ NC, Chapel Hill, AB, 42, LLB, 48; Phi Alpha Delta. Polit & Govt Pos: Deleg, SC Rep State Conv, 64, 66 & 68, deleg & parliamentarian, 72; chmn, Greenville Co Rep Conv, SC, 66, 68 & 72; attorney, SC Rep Party, 66-; chmn, SC Lawyers for Nixon-Agnew, 68; chmn, Greenville Co Rep Conv, SC, 69; vchmn, SC Comt of Lawyers to Reelect the President, 72; mem, SC Comt to Reelect the President, 72. Bus & Prof Pos: Partner, Leatherwood, Walker, Todd & Mann, Attorneys, Greenville, SC, 48-; chmn, Greenville Co Pub Defender Corp, 70- Mil Serv: Entered as Ens, Navy, 43, released as Lt, 45, after serv in ETO; ETO Theater Ribbon & Battle Star. Mem: Am Bar Asn; Int Asn Ins Counsel; US CofC (Govt Opers & Expenditures Comt); Am Red Cross (Southeastern Area Adv Coun); Pleasantburg Rotary. Relig: Episcopal. Legal Res: 110 Rock Creek Dr Greenville SC 29605 Mailing Add: PO Box 2248 Greenville SC 29602

MANN, FRANK E (D)
Va State Deleg
Mailing Add: Box 322 Alexandria VA 22313

MANN, FRANKLIN BALCH (D)
Fla State Rep
b Ft Myers, Fla, Aug 29, 41; s George Theodore Mann & Barbara Balch M; m 1961 to Mary Lee Ferguson; c Franklin Balch, Jr & Ian Ferguson. Educ: Vanderbilt Univ, BA, 64; Phi Kappa Psi. Polit & Govt Pos: Fla State Rep, 74- Bus & Prof Pos: Adjustor, Gen Adjustment Bur, 64-66; ins agt, Hyde & Dinkel Ins Agency, 66-67; pres & gen mgr, Mann-Webb Ins Agency, Inc, 67- Mem: Rotary; Mason; Scottish Rite; Shrine; Audubon Soc. Relig: Presbyterian. Legal Res: 1415 Sandra Dr Ft Myers FL 33901 Mailing Add: PO Box 1605 Ft Myers FL 33902

MANN, GEORGE (D)
Minn State Rep
b Heron Lake, Minn, Mar 26, 18; s Charles Mann & Carrie M; m 1939 to Alice May Benson. Educ: Jackson Co Pub Schs, 32. Polit & Govt Pos: Minn State Rep, 58-, chmn agr comt, Minn House Rep, 73-; mem, Nat Bd Rural Am for Johnson & Humphrey, 64; chmn, Dem-Farmer-Labor Rural Caucus, 72-73. Bus & Prof Pos: Farmer, 30 years; mem, US Dept Agr Nat Corn Comt, formerly; pres, Windom Coop Elevator; dir, Farmers Union GTA; leader, USA People to People Deleg to Europe & Soviet Union, 67. Mem: Mason; Shrine; Nat Farmers Orgn; Farmers Union. Relig: Methodist; trustee, Windom Methodist Church. Mailing Add: Rte 1 Windom MN 56101

MANN, HELEN LOUISE (D)
b Sanford, Fla, July 20, 43; d Clements John Southcate Hallett & Mary Anzy Seaver H; m 1963 to Fred Harold Mann; c Kenneth John Shannon & Kimberly. Educ: Trans-World Airline Sch, Tampa, Fla, grad, 62. Polit & Govt Pos: Secy coord, George Wallace Hq, Orlando, Fla, 72; fund raising secy, Orange Co Wallace Comt, 72; deleg, Dem Nat Conv, 72; mem, Dem Nat Rules Comt, 72-73; lobbyist against ERA, State of Fla, 75. Mem: PTA (membership chmn, 70-73); Fla Fedn Women for Responsible Legis; John Birch Soc; Orange Co Dem (pub rels, 71-72); Young Dem Soc (pub rels, 71-72). Relig: Episcopal. Mailing Add: Rte 3 Box 213B Bonifay FL 32425

MANN, JAMES ROBERT (D)
US Rep, SC
b Greenville, SC, Apr 27, 20; s Alfred Cleo Mann & Nina Mae Griffin M; m 1945 to Virginia Thomason Brunson; c James Robert, Jr, David Brunson, William Walker & Virginia Brunson. Educ: The Citadel, BA, 41; Univ of SC, LLB, 47; Phi Beta Kappa; Omicron Delta Kappa; The Citadel Hon Soc; Wig & Robe. Polit & Govt Pos: SC State Rep, Greenville Co, 49-52; solicitor, 13th judicial circuit, SC, 53-63; exec committeeman, SC State Dem Party, Greenville Co, 64-66; US Rep, Fourth Dist, SC, 69- Bus & Prof Pos: Sr partner, Mann & Mann Attorneys, 56-63, Mann, Foster, Johnston & Ashmore Attorneys, Greenville, SC, 63-68; dir, Palmetto State Life Ins Co Columbia, SC, 57-; pres, Gtr Greenville CofC, 65. Mil Serv: Entered as 2nd Lt, Army, 41, released as Lt Col, 46, after serv in 82nd AAA Group, Panama Canal Dept, 41-45; Col, Army Res. Publ: 'The Writ of Prohibition,' Selden Soc Yearbook, (Univ of SC Law Quart), 47. Mem: Am Bar Asn; Shrine; Kiwanis; Elks; VFW (SC Dept Comdr, 51-52). Relig: Baptist. Legal Res: 118 W Mountain View Ave Greenville SC 29609 Mailing Add: 1214 Longworth House Off Bldg Washington DC 20515

MANN, JANEAN LEE (R)
b Riverdale, Md, Sept 14, 43; d Francis Lee Mann & Jean Hughes M; single. Educ: Univ SC, BA, 66; Theta Sigma Phi; Delta Zeta. Polit & Govt Pos: Admin asst to US Rep, John Buchanan, Ala, 69- Bus & Prof Pos: Staff writer, Birmingham Post-Herald, Birmingham, Ala, 66-69. Mem: Rep Commun Asn; Admin Assts Asn; Birmingham Press Club. Honors & Awards: First Place, Spot Newswriting Award, Assoc Press, 68; Pub Serv Award, US Dept Treas, 69. Legal Res: 1005 55th St S Birmingham AL 35222 Mailing Add: 608 Sixth St NW Washington DC 20002

MANN, LLOYD W (D)
Nev State Assemblyman
Mailing Add: 717 Scholl Dr Las Vegas NV 89107

MANN, ROBERT E (D)
Ill State Rep
b Hyde Park-Kenwood, Ill; m to Sylvia Romagnoli; c Stephen, Stuart, Laurie & Elise. Educ: Univ Ill, grad, 50; Univ Chicago, MBA & JD. Polit & Govt Pos: Ill State Rep, currently, chmn comt higher educ, Ill Gen Assembly. Bus & Prof Pos: Taught in Sch Bus, Univ Chicago & Univ Ill, Chicago Circle; assoc, Chicago Jury Proj; partner, Law Firm of Mann & Kahn. Mil Serv: Army, 2 years. Mem: Chicago Lodge B'nai B'rith; Coun Community Rels (chmn); Century Club; YMCA; KAM Temple Men's Club (bd dirs). Honors & Awards: Voted best legislator 6 times, Independent Voters of Ill; Best Legislator Award, Am Civil Liberties Union, Ill Div. Mailing Add: 5539 S Harper Chicago IL 60637

MANN, TERRY LAWRENCE (D)
Ky State Rep
b Campbell Co, Ky, May 15, 48; s Thomas A Wald & Margaret Johnson W; m 1969 to JoAnna Louise Ficke; c Matthew Lawrence. Educ: Hanover Col, BA, 70; Lambda Chi Alpha. Polit & Govt Pos: Ky State Rep, 72-; chmn, State Subcomt on Professions, 74-; chmn, State Young Dem Conv, 75. Bus & Prof Pos: Voc coordr, Newport Sch Syst, 70- Mem: Ky Educ Asn; Campbell Co Jaycees; Educ Comn of States. Honors & Awards: R F Struck Mem Award, Hanover Col, 69; Jaycee Outstanding Young Man, Campbell Jaycees, 74. Relig: Catholic. Mailing Add: 19 Douglas Dr Newport KY 41071

MANN, THEODORE D (R)
Mayor, Newton, Mass
b Boston, Mass; m to Florence Ober; c five. Educ: Boston Univ; Boston Col. Polit & Govt Pos: Mass State Rep, formerly, mem, Ins, Mil Affairs & Low Income Housing Comts, Mass House of Rep, formerly; alderman, Newton, Mass, former chmn, Franchise & Licenses Comt, mem, Urban Renewal, Pub Bldg, Educ, Ward Lines & Munic Parking Comts; mem, Mass Bd of Elevator Regulations, 2 terms; mem, Adv Consumers Coun; mem, Spec Comt of Mass Legis to Investigate MDC, Local Airport & Solid Waste Disposal; Mayor, Newton, Mass, 72- Bus & Prof Pos: Licensed ins agent. Mil Serv: Navy, World War II; Seven Battle Stars; Unit Citation. Mem: Kiwanis Int (New Eng chmn, Boys & Girls Work Comt, pres, Roxbury Club); Am Legion; AF&AM; Big Brother Asn; VFW. Honors & Awards: Distinguished Serv Award, Kiwanis; Advocate Carnation; Award in Recognition of Dedicated Serv, Combined Jewish Philanthropies. Relig: Jewish. Mailing Add: 21 Littlefield Rd Newton Centre MA 02159

MANNA, MARIO JOSEPH (R)
Mem, Conn State Rep Cent Comt
b Middletown, Conn, Mar 23, 15; s Antonio Manna & Angelina Baraiola M; single. Educ: Bentley Col of Acct & Finance, Mass; Kappa Pi Alpha. Polit & Govt Pos: Dist chmn, Second Dist Rep Comt, Conn, 55-65; city treas, Bristol, 59-63; town chmn, Rep Town Comt, 65-66; 31st Sen Dist mem, Conn State Rep Cent Comt, currently. Bus & Prof Pos: Mfrs rep. Mil Serv: Entered as Pvt, Army, 42, released as Capt, 46, after serv in NAfrican Div, Air Transport Comn; reentered serv as Capt, Air Force, 51, released, 52, after serv with Auditor Gen in Europe; Good Conduct & Reserve Medals; ETO & Am Theater Ribbons; Bronze Medal. Mem: Life mem, Seicheprey Post 2, Am Legion (Past Comdr); Elks; KofC; Air Force Asn. Relig: Roman Catholic. Mailing Add: 377 Pine St Apt 1 Forestville CT 06010

MANNING, DAVE MARTIN (D)
Mont State Sen
b Chippewa Falls, Wis, Feb 28, 97; s David Jackson Manning & Amelia Hogan M; m 1920 to Ruth Ann Clark; c Shirley (Mrs Mouat), Vivian (Mrs Lasalle) & David (deceased). Educ: Univ Mont. Polit & Govt Pos: Mont State Rep, 33-41; Speaker, Mont House Rep, 39-40; Mont State Sen, 41-; deleg, Dem Nat Conv, 68, alt deleg, 72. Bus & Prof Pos: Gen contractor, Dave M Manning Construction Co, 29-69. Honors & Awards: Longest legis serv in hist of Mont. Relig: Catholic. Mailing Add: Hysham MT 59038

MANNING, DONALD J (D)
Mass State Rep
b Waltham, Mass, June 23, 29; s George Manning & Mary Roach M; m 1954 to Pauline Elizabeth Kondrup; c Cheryl Ann, Robbin Theresa & Donna Jeanne. Educ: Boston Col, BS in Econ, 58; Portia Law Sch, LLB, 66; Chess Club. Polit & Govt Pos: City coun, Waltham City Coun, Mass, 58-; Mass State Rep, 11th Middlesex Dist, 61- Bus & Prof Pos: Salesman,

Door & Window Co, Waltham, 58-61; attorney, 67- Mil Serv: Entered as Pvt, Army, 51, released as Acting Cpl, 53, after serv in Signal Corps. Mem: Moose. Relig: Catholic. Mailing Add: 16 Grant Pl Waltham MA 02154

MANNING, EDWARD P (D)
RI State Rep
Mailing Add: 711 Indust Bank Bldg Providence RI 02903

MANNING, JOE ROLATER, JR (R)
Okla State Rep
b Cushing, Okla, Dec 17, 46; s Joe Rolater Manning & Grace Madeline Callan M; single. Educ: Okla State Univ, BA, 69; Univ Okla Col Law, JD, 73. Polit & Govt Pos: Staff mem, US Sen Henry Ballmon, Washington, DC, 69; asst to state chmn, Okla Rep State Comt, 73-74; Okla State Rep, 75- Bus & Prof Pos: Attorney-at-law, Cushing, Okla, 74- Mil Serv: 2nd Lt, Army Res, 73- Mem: Scottish Rite; Akdar Shrine Temple; Lions; CofC; Okla State Univ Alumni Asn. Relig: Methodist. Mailing Add: PO Box 8 Cushing OK 74023

MANNING, L CLEAVES (D)
Va State Deleg
Mailing Add: 302 Citizens Trust Bldg Portsmouth VA 23704

MANNING, M JOSEPH (D)
Mass State Rep
b Milton, Mass, Sept 23, 24; s M Joseph Manning & Mary E Chisolm M; m 1965 to Audrey L Hawkins; c M Joseph, Jr. Educ: Milton High Sch, Mass, grad, 42; Bentley Col Acct & Finance, Boston, grad, 51. Polit & Govt Pos: Mem, Town Meeting, Milton, Mass, 46-; Bd Park Comnr, 50-59, Bd Assessors, 57-; mem, Milton Dem Town Comt, 50-, chmn, 66-; mem, Mass Dem State Comt, currently; Notary Pub, Commonwealth of Mass, 61-; Mass State Rep, 67- Bus & Prof Pos: Training adminr, Mass Dept Labor & Industs, 47-, currently on leave of absence. Mil Serv: Entered as Pvt, Marine Corps, 43, released as T/Sgt, 46, after serv in Marine Bombing Squadron 443-MAG 61, First Marine Air Wing, SPac Theatre, 44-45; Asiatic Pac Campaign Medal; World War II Medal; Presidential Unit Citation. Mem: Int Assessor's Asn; Asn Mass Assessors; Am Legion; KofC; Amvets. Relig: Catholic. Mailing Add: 583 Adams St Milton MA 02186

MANNING, MARGARET R (D)
Del State Sen
b 1918; m to Robert N. Educ: Conn Col, BA. Polit & Govt Pos: Del State Rep, 2 terms; Del State Sen, currently. Mailing Add: 605 Greenbank Rd Wilmington DE 19808

MANNING, SAM P (D)
SC State Rep
Mailing Add: Box 355 Spartanburg SC 29303

MANNION, JAMES MICHAEL (D)
Conn State Rep
b Bethel, Conn, Dec 2, 45; s Arthur James Mannion, Sr & Frances Mulochill M; m 1973 to Geraldine Clidester. Educ: Western Conn State Col, 63-65; Mt St Mary's Col, BA 68; St John's Univ, JD, 71; ed yearbook, 68; pres, Legal Soc; secy, Paradise Guild; Young Dem. Polit & Govt Pos: Mem, Bethel Dem Town Comt, Conn, 71-; Justice of the Peace, Bethel, 71-75; counsel, charter comn, 73; deleg, Conn Dem State Conv, 71-; Conn State Rep, 75- Mem: Am, Conn & Danbury Bar Asns; United Way; Bethel Lions (bd dirs). Legal Res: 2 Whitney Rd Bethel CT 06801 Mailing Add: PO Box 121 Bethel CT 06801

MANNIX, FRANCIS F (R)
Chmn, Powell Co Rep Cent Comt, Mont
b Avon, Mont, June 6, 20; s William H Mannix & Clara Sanford M; m 1950 to Dorothy Caswell; c Paula, William, John & Melany. Educ: Powell Co High Sch, grad; Am Inst Banking, 1 year. Polit & Govt Pos: Chmn, Powell Co Rep Cent Comt, Mont, 70- Mil Serv: Entered as Pvt, Air Force, 41, released as M/Sgt, 47, after serv in Air Transport Command, NAfrica. Mailing Add: Avon MT 59713

MANNIX, JOHN F (R)
Conn State Rep
Mailing Add: 166 Nod Hill Rd Wilton CT 06897

MANNIX, KEVIN LEESE (D)
b Queens, NY, Nov 26, 49; s John Warren Mannix, Sr & Editta Gorrell M; m 1974 to Susanna Chiocca. Educ: Univ Va, BA, 71, Law Sch, JD, 74; Phi Delta Phi; Phi Epsilon Pi. Polit & Govt Pos: Chmn, Seventh Dist Citizens for McGovern, Va, 71-72; deleg, Va Dem Conv, 72; deleg, Dem Nat Conv, 72; coordr, Seventh Cong Dist McGovern-Shriver Campaign, Va, 72; coordr, State Elec Day McGovern-Shriver Campaign, Va, 72. Bus & Prof Pos: Photographer, Charlottesville, Va, 68-74; law clerk, Ore Court of Appeals, 74- Mem: Am Civil Liberties Union; Ore State Bar Asn. Relig: Roman Catholic. Mailing Add: 375 18th St NE Salem OR 97301

MANNIX, RICHARD E (R)
NY State Assemblyman
Mailing Add: 111 Beach Ave Larchmont NY 10538

MANNS, PAUL W (D)
Va State Sen
b Traverse City, Mich, June 18, 10; m to Emma Nunnally. Educ: William & Mary Exten, Richmond, Va. Polit & Govt Pos: Va State Deleg, 52; Va State Sen, 66- Bus & Prof Pos: Newspaper ed & publ; funeral dir. Mem: Ruritans; Mason; Southern Regional Ed Bd; Va Press Asn. Relig: Methodist. Mailing Add: 107 S Main St Bowling Green VA 22427

MANRIQUEZ, CAROL HUANTE (D)
Mem, Calif Dem State Cent Comt
b Los Angeles, Calif, Mar 19, 30; d Joe O Huante & Jessie Vergara H; m 1949 to Gil Moreno Manriquez; c Gilbert Charles, Jr, Maria Lisa & Carlotta Joy. Educ: Univ High Sch, Westwood, Calif, grad, 48. Polit & Govt Pos: Mem, Calif Dem State Cent Comt, 68- Mem: Latin Am Civic Asn; Rotary (Women's Div); League United Latin Am Citizens Nat Orgn; CofC; San Fernando Valley Girl Scout Coun (leader, Troop 1217). Relig: Catholic. Mailing Add: 10012 Memory Park Ave Sepulveda CA 91343

MANSFIELD, DONALD WILLIAM (D)
b Akron, Ohio, Nov 22, 27; s Stanley Mansfield & Amy Jones M; m 1948 to Joy Lee Cassady; c Mark Stanley, Ruth Elaine & Virginia Dell. Educ: Univ Akron, BA, 50; Ohio Univ, MA, 57; Pi Kappa Delta; Pi Sigma Alpha; Phi Alpha Theta; Phi Delta Theta. Polit & Govt Pos: Admin asst, US Rep John F Seiberling, Ohio, 71- Mil Serv: Entered as 2nd Lt, Air Force, 50, retired as Lt Col, 70, after serv as B-25 instr pilot, 51-52, B-26 aircraft comdr, 3rd Bomb Wing, Korea, 53, asst prof air sci, Ohio Univ, 54-57, B-47 instr pilot, Strategic Air Command, 57-63, student, Air Command & Staff Col, 63-64 & Defense Lang Inst, 64-65, Air Attache, US Embassy, Repub China, 66-69, dep chief staff plans, 7th Air Force, Vietnam, 69-70; Distinguished Flying Cross; Bronze Star; Two Air Medals; Repub Korea Presidential Citation; UN Serv Medal; USAF Commendation Medal; Am Campaign Medal; World War II Victory Medal; Nat Defense Serv Medal; Vietnam Serv Medal; Korean Serv Medal; Repub China Distinguished Serv Medal; Repub Vietnam Serv Medal. Mem: Air Force Hist Found; Aircraft Owners & Pilots Asn; Ohio Soc of Wash; Order of Daedalians; Retired Off Asn. Relig: Episcopal. Mailing Add: 4426 Neptune Dr Alexandria VA 22309

MANSFIELD, MICHAEL J (D)
Majority Leader, US Senate
b New York, NY, Mar 16, 03; s Patrick J Mansfield & Josephine O'Brien M; m 1931 to Maureen Hayes; c Anne F (Mrs Robin Marris). Educ: Mont Sch Mines, 27-28; Univ Mont, AB, 33, MA, 34; Univ Calif, Los Angeles, 35-37; Alpha Tau Omega. Hon Degrees: LLD, Univ Mont, Mich State Univ, Gonzaga Univ, Col of Great Falls, Carroll Col, Stonehill Col, Clarke Col, Mont State Univ, St Mary's Col (Kans), Seton Hall Univ, Yeshiva Univ & Boston Col; DH Rocky Mt Col. Polit & Govt Pos: US Rep, Mont, 43-53; US Sen, Mont, 53-, Dem Whip, US Senate, 57, Asst Majority Leader, 57-61, Majority Leader, 61-; deleg, Dem Nat Conv, 68; mem, Dem Exec Comt. Bus & Prof Pos: Miner & mining engr, 22-30; prof Latin Am & Far Eastern Hist, Univ Mont, 33-42, on leave with permanent tenure. Mil Serv: Seaman 2/C, Navy, 18-19; Pvt, Army, 19-20; Pfc, Marine Corps, 20-22. Relig: Catholic. Legal Res: Missoula MT 59801 Mailing Add: 133 Senate Office Bldg Washington DC 20510

MANSFIELD, WILSON S (R)
NH State Rep
Mailing Add: Spring St Box 264 Belmont NH 03220

MANSI, NICHOLAS ANTHONY (D)
Chmn, 90th Rep Dist Dem Comt, RI
b Providence, RI, Dec 15, 30; s Louis Mansi & Felicia Petrucci M; m 1955 to Anna Cotoia; c Sheila Ann, Nicholas A, Deborah Joyce & Stephen John. Educ: Boston Univ, AB, 61; RI Col, MA, 67; Boston Univ Novice Debating Team; Newman Club. Polit & Govt Pos: Chmn, Warren Dem Party, RI, 67-70; mem, 47th Sen Dist Dem Comt, 67-; mem, Legis Comn Studying the Feasibility of Regulating Correspondence Schs in RI, RI Gen Assembly, 68-69; chmn, 90th Rep Dist Dem Comt, 70-; mem, Gov Adv Coun on Drug Abuse, 70-; mem 100 man adv bd, RI Bd Regents, 70- Bus & Prof Pos: Salesman, Bristol Co Bus Machines, RI, 57-61; Eng & Social Studies Teacher, Voc Tech Sch, RI, Providence, 61-67; guid counsr, Portsmouth High Sch, 67- Mil Serv: Entered as A/S, Navy, 50, released as Radarman 2/C, 54, after serv in USS Atka, USS Waccamaw & USS Allagash, Atlantic Serv Fleet Command; Good Conduct Ribbon; Korean Campaign Ribbon. Mem: Nat Educ Asn; Am Personnel & Guid Asn; Italian Am War Vet (post comdr); KofC; Warren Rod & Gun Club. Relig: Catholic. Mailing Add: 111 A Touisset Rd Warren RI 02885

MANTEY, CARL F (R)
b Fairgrove Twp, Tuscola Co, Mich, Sept 21, 02; s Rudolph R Mantey & Bertha Eckleman M; m 1925 to Bernice J Campbell; c Helen (Mrs Wm Young), Carol (Mrs Norbert Jankowski) & Gretchen (Mrs Alex Amstutz). Educ: Ferris Inst, 20-21. Polit & Govt Pos: Chmn, Tuscola Co Rep Comt, Mich, formerly; deleg, Rep Nat Conv, 68. Bus & Prof Pos: Operator, Laundry & Dry Cleaning Plant, currently. Mem: Pres & secy, Exchange Club & Rotary of Caro; secy, Caro Develop Corp. Relig: Protestant. Legal Res: 229 Quinn Ave Caro MI 48723 Mailing Add: 141 S Almer St Caro MI 48723

MANTHEY, CHARLES EDWIN (R)
b Akron, Ohio, Dec 24, 22; s Edwin Louis Manthey & Mary Gledhill M; m 1952 to Catherine Livingston McKeever; c Cheryl, Valarie, Mary, Robert, Catherine & Edward. Educ: Western Reserve Univ, 40-43; George Washington Univ Sch of Med, MD, 46; Delta Tau Delta. Polit & Govt Pos: Chmn, Broward Co Physicians for Goldwater, Fla, 64; sec, Rep Nat Conv, 64; health officer, City of Oakland Park, Fla, 65-69; finance chmn, Broward Co, Gurney for Sen, 68; treas, Rep Citizens Comt Broward Co, 68-; mayor, Sea Ranch Lakes, Fla, 74-75. Mil Serv: Entered as Pfc, Army, 43, released as Capt, 49, after serv in Armed Med Corps, ETO, 47-49; Good Conduct Medal. Mem: Iowa Soc Anesthesiologists (secy-treas, 57-58, pres, 59); Am, Fla & Broward Co Med Asns; Navy League of US. Relig: Catholic. Mailing Add: 23 Seneca Rd Ft Lauderdale FL 33308

MANTLE, C LEE (R)
Mem, Ohio Rep Cent Comt
b Painesville, Ohio, Nov 26, 11; s Hermon Lee Mantle & Elizabeth Herring M; m 1936 to Helen Curtiss; c Nancy (Mrs Glascoe) & Charles Curtiss. Educ: Oberlin Col, 30-32; Ohio State Univ, BA, 35; Alpha Gamma Sigma. Polit & Govt Pos: Mem, Painesville Twp Bd of Educ, Ohio, 48-56; mem, Lake Co Bd of Educ, 52-56 & 62-, pres, 65-; Ohio State Rep, Lake Co, Ohio, 55 & 56; Ohio State Sen, 24th-26th Dist, NE Ohio, 57 & 58; committeeman, Ohio State Rep Cent Comt, 11th Dist, 62-64 & mem, 69-, treas, 75; chmn, Lake Co Rep Exec Comt, Ohio, 62-70; deleg, Rep Nat Conv, 68; Presidential Elector, 68 & 72. Bus & Prof Pos: Instr, Lakeland Community Col, 68. Mem: Nat Asn of Real Estate Bd; Mason; Shrine; Elks; Kiwanis. Honors & Awards: Realtor of the Year, Lake Co Bd Realtors, 68. Relig: Congregational. Legal Res: 188 Mantle Rd Painesville OH 44077 Mailing Add: PO Box 699 Painesville OH 44077

MANUEL, REX (D)
Mont State Rep
Mailing Add: Fairfield MT 59436

MANUEL, ROBERT FRANK (D)
Pres, La Young Dem
b Ville Platte, La, Apr 15, 54; s Eugee Manuel & Nettie Mae Pitre M; single. Educ: La State Univ, 72-75. Polit & Govt Pos: Parish pres, Evangeline Parish Young Dem, 72-74; state vpres, La Young Dem, 73-74, state pres, 74-75, state expansion secy, 75- Mem: La Young Dem; Ville Platte Jaycees. Honors & Awards: Best External & Internal Proj Awards, Ville Platte Jaycees, 75. Relig: Catholic. Mailing Add: 218 N Thompson Ville Platte LA 70586

MANZELLI, ROBERT A (R)
Mass State Rep
Mailing Add: State Capitol Boston MA 02133

MAPLE, BARBARA D (R)
Mem, Rep State Cent Comt Calif
b San Diego, Calif, Sept 18, 15; d Hubert L Dawson & Lillian J Crutcher D; m 1939 to Earl Woods Maple; c Thomas Hadley, Earl Christopher, Robert C, Timothy J & Melanie E. Educ: Fullerton Jr Col, 33-35; Whittier Col, BA, 37; Athenian Soc. Polit & Govt Pos: Mem, Rep State Cent Comt Calif, 67-; first vpres, Whittier Area Rep Women's Club, 68-70; chmn, Whittier Area Women's Chmn for Nixon Campaign, 68 & Whittier Area Nixon Phone Bank, 72. Bus & Prof Pos: Teacher, El Monte Sch Dist, Calif, 37-41. Mem: Whittier Hist Comn; Whittier Bicentennial Comt; Whittier Heritage Asn; La Serna High Sch PTA (jr class rep, 72-73, historian, 73-74); Whittier Hist Soc. Honors & Awards: Whittier Area Rep Woman of the Year, 72. Relig: Protestant. Mailing Add: 15070 La Cuarta Whittier CA 90605

MAPLES, JUANITA E (R)
VChmn, Stone Co Rep Party, Mo
b Ponce-de-Leon, Mo, June 5, 20; d John Perry Steele & Callie B Norman S; m 1939 to Leonard L Maples; c Gena Lynn & Tammi Denise. Educ: Abesville High Sch, Mo, grad, 39. Polit & Govt Pos: Twp committeewoman, Stone Co Rep Party, Mo, 45-75, vchmn, currently. Bus & Prof Pos: Secy, family bus, 50-75; asst postmaster, Ponce-de-Leon, Mo, currently. Relig: Assembly of God. Mailing Add: Ponce-de-Leon MO 65728

MARAGOS, SAMUEL C (D)
Ill State Rep
b Sioux City, Iowa, Aug 19, 22; s Constantine T Maragos & Irene Maragos; m 1950 to Cleo Mavrick; c Dean, Thomas, James & George. Educ: Univ Chicago, AB, 43; John Marshall Law Sch, JD, 48; Delta Theta Pi. Polit & Govt Pos: Hearing officer, Bd Tax Appeals, Cook Co, Ill, 55-56; hearing referee, Dept Revenue, Ill, 61-66; Ill State Rep, 30th Dist, 69-, chmn revenue comt, Ill House of Rep, currently; chmn, Ill Comn Atomic Energy, currently. Bus & Prof Pos: Sr law partner, Maragos, Richter, Berman, Russell & White, Chtd, currently. Mil Serv: Entered as Pvt, Army, 43, released as 2nd Lt, 46, after serv in various dept of Army; hon Res, 53. Mem: Chicago Coun Foreign Rels; Nat Soc State Legis; Am Hellenic Dem Coun Ill; Am Legion; South Chicago CofC. Honors & Awards: Silver Beaver Award, Chicago Area Coun Boy Scouts. Relig: Greek Orthodox. Legal Res: 9207 S Yates Ave Chicago IL 61617 Mailing Add: 69 W Washington St Suite 1154 Chicago IL 60602

MARAZITI, JOSEPH J (R)
b Boonton, NJ, June 15, 12; m to Eileen Hopkins; c Joseph J, Jr, Charles, Eileen, Margaret, Mary Ellen (Mrs Baldwin), Katherine & Maria. Educ: Fordham Univ Pre-Law Sch; Fordham Univ Law Sch; NJ Law Sch, LLB. Polit & Govt Pos: Legis legal adv to Morris Co Bd of Chosen Freeholders, NJ, 52-55; chmn, Boonton Charter Comn Study Group; Town Police Judge, Boonton; first asst prosecutor, Morris Co NJ State Assemblyman, 58-69; alt deleg, Rep Nat conv, 68; NJ State Sen, 69-73; US Rep, NJ, 73-75. Bus & Prof Pos: Munic attorney. Mem: NJ Bar Asn; US Supreme Court; KofC. Honors & Awards: Selected Legislator of the Year, State Asn of Freeholders, 62; recipient of Educ Award, 66. Mailing Add: 414 Dixon Ave Boonton NJ 07005

MARBURY, CHARLES CLAGETT (D)
b Upper Marlboro, Md, Nov 2, 99; s Alexander Marshall Marbury & Lucy Clagett Berry M; m 1927 to Kathryn Worthington Lancaster; c Priscilla (Mrs William Fitts Ryan). Educ: Johns Hopkins Univ, AB, 22; Georgetown Univ, Law Sch, LLB, 25; Alpha Delta Phi. Polit & Govt Pos: Md State Deleg, 30-38; Md State Sen, 38-41; judge, Seventh Judicial Circuit of Md, 41-60; judge, Court of Appeals, Md, 60-69. Bus & Prof Pos: Attorney-at-law, Md & DC, 25-41. Mil Serv: Pvt, Md Nat Guard, 17-19, released after serv in Battery D, 110th Field Artil 29th Div, AEF, France. Mem: Md State & Am Bar Asns; Am Legion; VFW; AF&AM. Honors & Awards: Cert of 25 years of serv as Chmn, Selective Serv Bd No 56, Md. Relig: Episcopal. Mailing Add: PO Box 58 Upper Marlboro MD 20870

MARBUT, GARY RAYMOND (D)
b Denver, Colo, Feb 28, 27; s George C Marbut & Charlotte B Reed M; m 1953 to Edith Tupper True; c Michael, Stephen, Debra & Randall. Educ: Univ Denver, 45-50; Univ Mont, 51-53; Pi Gamma Mu. Polit & Govt Pos: Elem sch trustee, Missoula Co, Mont, 53-57; Mont State Rep, 64-74; mem comt human resources, Coun State Govt, 70-; mem, Secy Health, Educ & Welfare Adv Comt, Region VIII, 72-; chmn, Mont Ment Health Adv Coun, 74- Bus & Prof Pos: Pres, Grant Creek Ranch Corp, Missoula, Mont, 59- Mem: Mont State Coun Develop Disabilities; Nat Ctr Law & Handicapped, South Bend, Ind (pres, 72-); Nat Asn Retarded Children (bd dirs & vchmn nat comt govt affairs, 71-, chmn nat comt legal advocacy, 72-); Nat Legis Conf; Nat Soc State Legislators. Honors & Awards: Outstanding Serv to Handicapped Award, Mont Rehabilitation Asn, 72. Relig: Episcopal. Mailing Add: Grant Creek Missoula MT 59801

MARCANO, HIPOLITO (POPULAR DEM, PR)
Majority Leader, PR Senate
b Humacaco, PR, Aug 13, 13; s Miguel Marcano & Josefa Ortiz M; m 1968 to Sara Mercado; c David & Hipolito, Jr. Educ: Inter-Am Univ PR, AB, 37; Univ PR Law Sch, LLB, 40. Hon Degrees: LLD, Inter-Am Univ PR, 63. Polit & Govt Pos: Legal counsel, Dept Labor, PR, 42-43; mem cent comt, Popular Dem Party, 56-60 & 64-, mem gov bd, 69-; Sen, PR Senate, 56-, majority leader, 69-, chmn, Joint Legis Comt on Controller's Reports, 69- Bus & Prof Pos: Gen counsel, PR Fedn Labor, AFL-CIO, 43-; dean, Inter-Am Univ PR Law Sch, 60-; secy bd dirs, Labor Bank PR, 62- Mem: Am Acad Social Sci; Mason (33 degree); Eastern Star; Royal Order of Scotland; Elks. Relig: United Church of Christ. Legal Res: 1620 Calle Santa Ursula Urbanizacion Sagrado Corazon Rio Piedras PR 00926 Mailing Add: PO Box 1648 San Juan PR 00903

MARCHANG, THEODORE J (D)
La State Rep
Mailing Add: 5519 Urquhart New Orleans LA 70117

MARCHANT, THOMAS MOOD, III (R)
SC State Rep
b Greenville, SC, Oct 19, 40; s Thomas Mood Marchant, Jr & Elizabeth Lucas M; div; c Jessica Elizabeth & Thomas Mood, IV. Educ: Clemson Univ. Polit & Govt Pos: SC State Rep, 72-, Minority Whip & media coordr, SC House Rep, 75-, mem, Ways & Means Comt, 75- Bus & Prof Pos: Pres, Marchant Indust, Inc, 65- Mil Serv: US Marine Corp. Mem: Toastmasters Int (int dir, 72-74); Palmetto Toastmasters Club; Assoc Gen Contractors Am (dir & mem adv bd, 75-); SC CofC (mem legis policy comt, 75). Honors & Awards: Distinguished Toastmaster, Toastmasters Int; Greenville Chap Award, Women in Construction, 74. Relig: Episcopal. Mailing Add: Box 5656 Greenville SC 29606

MARCHI, JOHN JOSEPH (R)
NY State Sen
b Staten Island, NY, May 20, 21; s Louis B Marchi & Alina Girardello M; m 1948 to Maria Luisa Davini; c Joan Mary (Mrs Migliori) & Aline Grace. Educ: Manhattan Col, BA, 42; St John's Univ Sch Law, JD, 49; Brooklyn Law Sch, JSD, 52; Epsilon Sigma Pi. Hon Degrees: LLD, St Johns Univ, 71 & Manhattan Col, 73. Polit & Govt Pos: NY State Sen, 56-, chmn standing comt on City of New York, NY State Senate, currently, mem judiciary comt & chmn finance comt, currently, chmn joint legis comt on interstate coop, 66-; chmn exec comt & mem bd gov, Coun State Govts; alt deleg, Rep Nat Conv, 68; Rep & Conservative party cand for mayor, New York, 69 & 73; app to Nat Adv Coun Drug Abuse Prevention, 72- Bus & Prof Pos: Mem adv bd, St Vincent's Med Ctr, Richmond, currently. Mil Serv: Entered Coast Guard, 42, combat serv in Am, Pac & Asiatic Theaters; released to active res in 46, Comdr, currently. Mem: Am Bar Asn; Am Judicature Soc; Am Legion; VFW. Honors & Awards: Comdr of Order of Merit, Repub of Italy, 68; Mills G Skinner Award, Nat Urban League. Relig: Catholic. Mailing Add: 358 St Marks Pl Staten Island NY 10301

MARCHIORO, KAREN LOUISE (D)
Chairperson, King Co Dem Cent Comt, Wash
b Jacksonville, Ill, Sept 19, 33; d Morris Byus & Frances Hankins B; m 1956 to Thomas Marchioro; c Thomas, Kevin, Ann, Stephen, Joan, Katherine & Gregory. Educ: St Louis Univ, BS. Polit & Govt Pos: Chairperson, 48th Legis Dist Orgn, 71-74; deleg, Dem Nat Mid-Term Conf, 74; chairperson, King Co Dem Cent Comt, Wash, 74- Mem: League of Women Voters; United Nations Asn; Metrop Dem Club; Washington State Dem Women's Fedn. Relig: Catholic. Legal Res: 3408 116th NE Bellevue WA 98004 Mailing Add: 110 S Main Seattle WA 98104

MARCHISELLI, VINCENT ANDREW (D)
NY State Assemblyman
b Bronx, NY, Aug 18, 28; s Joseph M Marchiselli & Anna Raucci M; m 1967 to Eunice Pavia. Educ: Iona Col, BA, 51; NY Univ Sch Educ, MA, 53. Polit & Govt Pos: Mem, Mayor's Adv Comt on Handicapped, 71-72; legis asst to Councilman Mario Merola, 71-72; NY State Assemblyman, 75- Bus & Prof Pos: Pres, Marchiselli Funeral Homes, Inc, 52-; secy, Shawn Realty Co, 59- Mem: Acad Polit Sci; Catholic Men's Club, Williamsbridge; Wakefield Coun KofC; Catholic Interracial Coun of the Bronx; Williamsbridge Br NAACP. Relig: Roman Catholic. Legal Res: 4320 Van Cortlandt Park E Bronx NY 10470 Mailing Add: Dist Off-4309 A White Plains Rd Bronx NY 10466

MARCOTTE, GUY ALBERT (D)
Maine State Sen
b Biddeford, Maine, July 12, 37; s Andre H Marcotte & Lillian Gastonquay M; m 1961 to Barbara E Lloyd; c Christine Lloyd, Catherine Lillian & Carolyn A. Educ: Lawrence Acad, 55-56; Univ Maine, BS, 60; Phi Gamma Delta. Polit & Govt Pos: Maine State Sen, Dist 2, 71-, mem legis research comt, currently; alt deleg, Dem Nat Conv, 72. Bus & Prof Pos: Trainee, Gen Elec Co, 63-66, sales engr, 67-68; owner, Marcotte Oil, Neault & Marcotte Furniture Co & A & L Real Estate Co, Biddeford, Maine, 69- Mil Serv: Entered as 2nd Lt, Army, 50, released as 1st Lt, 63, after serv in QmC, Frankfurt, Ger, 61-63. Honors & Awards: Outstanding Sales Performer, Gen Elec Co, 68. Relig: Catholic. Mailing Add: 66 May St Biddeford ME 04005

MARCUS, MARK JAY (D)
Chmn, Westport Dem Town Comt, Conn
b New York, NY, Feb 3, 41; s Milton Marcus & Hilda Neuwerth M; m 1962 to Janice Pierce; c Jennifer H & Edward P. Educ: Univ Conn, Storrs, BA, 62 & Sch Law, Hartford, 63-64. Polit & Govt Pos: Mem, Bd Tax Rev, Westport, 65-69; secy, Mayor's Conf on Housing, Bridgeport, 66; mem, US Comn on Civil Rights, 67-74; selectman, Westport, Conn, 69-73, mem, Charter Revision Comt, 72-73; vchmn, Planning & Zoning Comn, 74-; chmn, Westport Dem Town Comt, Conn, 74- Bus & Prof Pos: Sr consult, Booz, Allen & Hamilton, New York, NY, 74- Mailing Add: 15 Oakwood Lane Westport CT 06880

MARCUS, SIDNEY J (D)
Ga State Rep
Mailing Add: 845 Canterbury Rd NE Atlanta GA 30324

MARCY, H TYLER
Asst Secy Navy Research & Develop
Mailing Add: Dept of the Navy Pentagon Washington DC 20350

MARDEN, DONALD HARLOW (R)
Mem, Maine State Rep Comt
b Waterville, Maine, Nov 19, 36; s Harold Chesterfield Marden & Dorothy Harlow M; m 1961 to Margaret Ann Bowzard; c Lee S, Donald Harlow, Jr, David B & Kenneth A. Educ: Univ Maine, 54-55; Cornell Univ, BS, 58; Boston Univ, JD, 64; Phi Gamma Delta. Polit & Govt Pos: Mem, Waterville City Rep Comt, Maine, 65-; mem city coun, Waterville, 65-67, mayor, 68-69; mem, Kennebec Co Rep Comt, 65-; mem, Maine State Rep Comt, 70-; asst co attorney, Kennebec Co, 71-72, co attorney, 73- Bus & Prof Pos: Mgt trainee, Kroger Co, Cleveland, Ohio, 58-59; attorney, Marden, Dubord, Bernier & Chandler, Waterville, Maine, 64- Mil Serv: Entered as 2nd Lt, Army, 59, released as 1st Lt, 61, after serv in 15th Qm Bn, ETO, 59-61; Capt, Army Nat Guard, 61-70, Maj, Staff Judge Adv Corps, Maine Army Nat Guard, 70-; Nat Defense Medal. Mem: Am Bar Asn; Nat Guard Asn; Medico Legal Soc; Am Judicature Soc; Mason. Honors & Awards: Outstanding Young Man, Jaycees, 69. Relig: Methodist. Legal Res: 85 Silver St Waterville ME 04901 Mailing Add: 44 Elm St Waterville ME 04901

MARDEN, ROBERT ALLEN (R)
b Waterville, Maine, Jan 4, 27; s Harold Chesterfield Marden & Dorothy Harlow M; m 1949 to Shirley Irene Marshall; c Sharon I, Robert M, Holly & Eric. Educ: Colby Col, 46-48; Boston Univ Sch Law, LLB, 51. Polit & Govt Pos: Mem city coun, Waterville, Maine, 51-52; Asst Co Attorney, Kennebec Co, 53-55, Co Attorney, 55-59; Maine State Sen, 60-62, Pres, Maine State Senate, 62-64; deleg, Rep Nat Conv, 64, alt deleg, 68; mem, Maine Const Comn, Gov Adv Bd on Ment Health & Air Transportation; Rep Nat Committeeman, Maine, formerly. Bus & Prof Pos: Admitted to Supreme Court of Maine, 51; assoc, Joly & Marden,

Attorneys, 51-63; partner, Marden, Dubord, Bernier, Chandler & Ayoob, Attorneys, 64. Mil Serv: Naval Air Force, 45-46; Lt Col, Civil Air Patrol. Mem: Am Bar Asn; Maine State Bar Asn (exec comt); Thayer Hosp (trustee); Waterville Savings Bank (trustee); Sugarloaf Mt Corp (dir). Relig: Methodist. Legal Res: 51 Roosevelt Ave Waterville ME 04901 Mailing Add: 44 Elm St Waterville ME 04901

MARDIAN, GOLDIE M (D)
Committeewoman, SDak State Dem Cent Comt
b Ipswich, SDak, Jan 26, 21; d William Brakhage & Daisy Menter B; m 1944 to Jacob Mardian; c Ronald & Donald. Educ: Northern State Col, BS, 72. Polit & Govt Pos: Committeewoman, SDak State Dem Cent Comt, 68- Bus & Prof Pos: Teacher, Leola Independent Sch, SDak, 64- Mem: Am Legion Auxiliary; Leola & SDak Teachers Asns. Relig: Catholic; mem, Altar Soc, Holy Cross Church, Ipswich, SDak. Mailing Add: Ipswich SD 57451

MARES, JOHN KIETH (R)
b Bear Creek, Wis, Oct 31, 24; s George P Mares & Hildegard Schindel M; m 1953 to Jean Lachelt; c Deborah. Polit & Govt Pos: Chmn, Waushara Co Rep Club, Wis, formerly; chmn, Waushara Co Rep Party, formerly. Mil Serv: Entered as Pvt, Army, 42, released as T/Sgt, 45, after serv in ETO; Purple Heart; ETO Medal with 4 Stars. Mem: Jaycees. Relig: Catholic. Mailing Add: Box 271 Wautoma WI 54982

MARESCHAL, GREGORY J (GREG) (D)
Mo State Rep
Mailing Add: 755 Tyson Dr Florissant MO 63031

MARESH, RICHARD (R)
Nebr State Sen
b Milligan, Nebr, Sept 8, 17; s Joseph F Maresh & Anna Betka M; m 1942 to Ruth Sweney; c Dixie (Mrs Gene Placek), Janet & Chere. Educ: Univ Nebr, night classes. Polit & Govt Pos: Mem, Fillmore Co Agr Stabilization & Conserv Comt, Nebr, 60-70; Nebr State Sen, 71- Mil Serv: Entered as Pvt, Air Force, 42, released as Flight Off, 45, after serv in 505th Bomb Group, 44-45; Distinguished Flying Cross; Air Medal with 4 Oak Leaf Clusters. Mem: Am Legion; VFW. Relig: Methodist. Mailing Add: Milligan NE 68406

MARGIOTTA, JOSEPH MICHAEL (R)
NY State Assemblyman
b Brooklyn, NY, June 6, 27; s Michael D Margiotta & Angela Lamanna M; m 1956 to Dorothy Crean; c Michael & Carol Lynn. Educ: Hofstra Univ, BA, 50; Brooklyn Law Sch, LLB, 53; Crown & Lance, Hofstra Univ. Polit & Govt Pos: Committeeman, 62nd Elec Dist, Uniondale, NY, 55; pres, Uniondale Rep Club, 58; legis counsel, NY State Sen Edward J Speno, 59; exec committeeman, Uniondale, 62; legis consult, Nassau Co Bd of Supvr, 65; NY State Assemblyman, 17th Dist, 65-, ranking minority mem, Assembly Educ Comt, former mem, Joint Legis Comt on Educ, mem, Assembly Ways & Means Comt, Comt on Local Govt & Real Estate, Mortgage & Penal Inst Comt, NY State Assembly; dep chmn, Hempstead Town Rep Comt, 66; chmn, 67; deleg, Rep Nat Conv, 68; chmn, Nassau Co Rep Comt, NY, 68-; deleg, Rep Nat Conv, 72. Bus & Prof Pos: Attorney, Margiotta, Levitt & Ricigliano, 53- Mil Serv: Entered as A/S, Navy, 45, released as Yeoman 3/C, 46, after serv aboard various ships; Asiatic-Pac Victory Medal. Mem: Nassau Co Bar Asn; Uniondale VFW Post (Past Comdr); Hempstead Elks; Uniondale Kiwanis; KofC. Honors & Awards: Grass Roots Award, Nassau Press Asn; Columbian of the Year, 69; Man of the Year, Long Island Indust Div, United Jewish Appeal & Marco Polo Lodge, 2214, Sons of Italy, Levittown; Pub Servant of Year Award, Hempstead Village CofC; C W Post Col Sch Bus Award. Relig: Catholic. Mailing Add: 844 Bedford Court Uniondale NY 11553

MARGOLIS, GWEN (D)
Fla State Rep
b Philadelphia, Pa, Oct 4, 34; d Joseph Liedman & Rose L; m to Allan B Margolis; c Edward, Ira, Karen & Robin. Polit & Govt Pos: Fla State Rep, 75-, mem, Finance & Taxation Comt, Community Affairs Comt & Growth & Energy Comt, Subcomt, Ad Valorem Taxes, Fla House Rep, 75- Bus & Prof Pos: Realtor & appraiser, currently; mem, Miami Bd Realtors, SFla Planning & Zoning Asn & Women's Coun of Realtors. Mem: CofC; Common Cause; Temple Emanu El; life mem City of Hope; Bus & Prof Women's Asn. Honors & Awards: Humanitarian of the Year, City of Hope. Legal Res: 13105 Biscayne Bay Dr Keystone Island Apt 5 North Miami FL 33161 Mailing Add: 1451 NE 163rd St North Miami Beach FL 33162

MARINO, MARY ELLEN (D)
b Newark, NJ, Oct 4, 39; d Lee J Marino & Eileen Burke M; m 1962 to John J Callahan; c Claire & Ruth. Educ: Rosemont Col, BA cum laude, 61; Boston Univ, MA, 63; Rutgers Univ, qualifying exams, 69-; Kistler Hon Soc. Polit & Govt Pos: Committeewoman, New Providence & Summit Dem Comt, 63-73; vchmn, Summit Dem Party, 69-73; deleg, Dem Nat Conv, 72; area coordr, Dietz Charman, Union Co, 72; landlord & tenant rels officer, NJ Dept of Community Affairs, 74- Bus & Prof Pos: Instr, Caldwell Col, 62-63 & Newark State Col, 64-68; instr & teaching asst, Douglass Col, 70-74. Mem: Am Polit Sci Asn; NJ Polit Sci Asn (mem coun, 73, 75-); Nat Asn Housing & Redevelop Officials. Honors & Awards: African Studies Prog Fel, 61; Panel Discussant, Northeastern Polit Sci Asn, 73. Legal Res: 86 Mountain Ave Summit NJ 07901 Mailing Add: 255 Mt Lucas Rd Princeton NJ 08540

MARINO, MICHAEL J (D)
NJ State Assemblyman
Mailing Add: State House Trenton NJ 08625

MARINO, RALPH JOHN (R)
NY State Sen
b Rochester, NY, Jan 2, 28; s James Marino & Antoinette Saraceno M; m 1955 to Ethel Bernstein; c Judith, James & Robert. Educ: Syracuse Univ, BA, 51; Fordham Univ Law Sch, LLB, 54. Polit & Govt Pos: Councilman, Oyster Bay Town Bd, NY, 66-68, majority leader, 67-68; Rep committeeman, East Norwich, 58-; exec leader, East Norwich-Brookville Rep Party, 67-; NY State Sen, Third Dist, 69- Bus & Prof Pos: Attorney, Zipper, Marino & Cronin, 55-59; attorney, Marino & Bernstein, 61- Mil Serv: Entered as Pvt, Army, 46, released as Tech 5/C, 47, after serv in MedC; Victory Medal. Mem: Nassau Bar Asn; Elks; Lions; CofC; Sons of Italy. Relig: Catholic. Mailing Add: 3 Lea Ct Muttontown Syosset NY 11791

MARION, GEORGE W, JR (D)
NC State Sen
Mailing Add: Forrest Oaks Dr Dobson NC 27017

MARIX, CARLYSLE JEROME (D)
Chmn, Iberville Parish Dem Party, La
b Plaquemine, La, Mar 25, 25; s Gervis Ernest Marix, Sr & Josephine Rills M; m 1930 to Lois Ruth Bourgeois; c Dwight, Darlene & Daryl. Educ: La State Univ, 47-48. Polit & Govt Pos: Mem, Iberville Parish Sch Bd, La, 63-; chmn, Iberville Parish Dem Party, currently. Bus & Prof Pos: Credit mgr & asst adminr, Rhodes J Spedale Gen Hosp, 72- Mil Serv: Entered as Seaman, Navy, 42, released as PO 1/C, 45, after serv in Atlantic & Pac; Purple Heart; Atlantic & Pac Medals. Mem: Am Legion; Elks; St John Fathers Club; Peace Officers Asn. Relig: Catholic. Mailing Add: 809 Robertson St Plaquemine LA 70764

MARKEL, J OGDEN (R)
b New Orleans, La, Aug 18, 98; s Jules W Markel & Ada Dillon M; m 1926 to Helena Lieberman; c Barbara Lee, Jules & twins, Louise & Joyce. Polit & Govt Pos: City councilman, Santa Ana, Calif, 54-58 & 65-75; retired. Bus & Prof Pos: Gen contractor, retired. Mem: Lions; KofC; Holy Name Soc; Toastmasters; S Main Improv Asn. Honors & Awards: Beni Morenti Gold Medal by Pope John 23rd; co & city plaques & testimonials for serv to community. Relig: Catholic. Legal Res: 1814 S Parton St Santa Ana CA 92707 Mailing Add: PO Box 2012 Santa Ana CA 92707

MARKERT, LOUIS A (D)
Secy, 20th Cong Dist Dem Orgn, Ill
b Mt Sterling, Ill, Dec 15, 27; s Louis F Markert & Corrinne Borden Kircher M; m 1949 to Barbara J Anderson; c Anne E, Daniel L, Jane L & Mary Kay. Educ: St Mary's Acad, 4 years. Polit & Govt Pos: Chmn, Brown Co Dem Comt, Ill, formerly; secy, 20th Cong Dist Dem Orgn, currently; Ill State Rep, 69-72. Bus & Prof Pos: Self-employed in Agr. Mem: Elks; KofC; Farm Bur. Relig: Catholic. Mailing Add: RR 1 Mt Sterling IL 62353

MARKES, JOHN F (D)
Mich State Rep
Mailing Add: Terri Dr W Westland MI 48185

MARKEY, DAVID JOHN, III (R)
b Frederick, Md; s David John Markey, Jr (deceased) & Mary Alice Moberly M; single. Educ: Western Maryland Col, BS, 63; Univ Maryland, Law Sch, LLB, 67; Delta Pi Alpha. Polit & Govt Pos: Law clerk, Judge Edward Northrop, Fed Dist Court, 65; law clerk, Judge Stewart Day, Third Judicial Circuit, Md, 65-67; asst legis officer, Gov Spiro T Agnew, 67-69; admin asst to US Sen J Glenn Beall, Jr, Md, 69- Mil Serv: Entered as Pvt, Army, 58, released as Pfc, 68, after serv in Signal Corp. Mem: Am & Md State Bar Asns. Relig: Protestant. Legal Res: 201 Grove Blvd Frederick MD 21701 Mailing Add: 1762 Dryden Way Crofton MD 21113

MARKEY, EDWARD J (D)
Mass State Rep
Mailing Add: State Capitol Boston MA 02133

MARKEY, JOHN ALLEN (D)
Mayor, New Bedford, Mass
b New Bedford, Mass, Dec 3, 34; s Stephen Allen Markey & Elizabeth M Allen M; m 1959 to Carol Ann Tweedie; c John Allen, Jr, Carol Ann, Christopher Matthew & Jennifer Mary. Educ: Stonehill Col, North Easton, Mass, BS, 58; Howard Univ Law Sch, JD, 65. Polit & Govt Pos: Mayor, New Bedford, Mass, 72- Bus & Prof Pos: Vpres & gen mgr, Cath Travel Off/Hodgson Travel Serv, Inc, 58-66; mgt specialist, Proj Create-Onboard, 66-67; mgt specialist, Dept Commun Affairs, 67-69; attorney, Mathieu & Markey, New Bedford, Mass, 69- Mil Serv: SP-5, Army Res. Mem: Washington, DC & Mass Bar Asns; US Supreme Court of Appeals, DC; US Court, DC; Supreme Judicial Court of Boston, Suffolk Co. Relig: Roman Catholic. Legal Res: 65 Cottage St New Bedford MA 02740 Mailing Add: 133 William St New Bedford MA 02740

MARKHAM, ALLAN WHITLOCK (D)
b Charlottesville, Va, Mar 5, 31; s Edwin Carlyle (Jerry) Markham & Janet Whitlock M; div; c Janet Leigh, Diane Carter, David Allan & Jerri Elizabeth. Educ: Univ of Colo, 49-51; Univ of NC, AB, 54, JD, 61; Order of the Coif; Sigma Chi; Phi Alpha Delta. Polit & Govt Pos: Asst dir, Inst of Govt, 61-66; dir, Div of Inst Eval & Accreditation, NC Dept of Community Cols, 66-68; admin asst to US Rep Nick Galifianakis, Fourth Dist, NC, 69-70; spec asst to adminr, Fed Aviation Admin, 70-71, chief legis counsel, 72- Mil Serv: Entered as Aviation Mid, Navy, 52, released as Comdr, 68, after serv in Korea, 52-53, Japan, 54-58; & Viet Nam, 68; Comdr, Naval Air Res; PTO; Korean Serv Medal; UN Medal; Nat Defense Serv Medal; China Serv Medal; Expert Rifle & Pistol; Three Air Medals. Publ: Public Education Organization in North Carolina, 65, County Government in North Carolina, 66 & Public School Transportation in North Carolina, 66, Univ of NC. Mem: Am Bar Asn; Nat Asn on Legal Probs in Educ; Nat Asn of Co Off; NC Dem Club of Wash; Cong Secy Club. Relig: Protestant. Legal Res: PO Box 341 Chapel Hill NC 27514 Mailing Add: 2733 36th St NW Washington DC 20007

MARKHAM, CHARLES BUCHANAN (R)
b Durham, NC, Sept 15, 26; s Charles Blackwell Markham & Sadie Hackney M; single. Educ: Duke Univ, AB, 45; Univ NC Law Sch, Chapel Hill, 45-46; George Washington Univ Law Sch, LLB, 51; Phi Beta Kappa; Omicron Delta Kappa; Phi Delta Theta. Polit & Govt Pos: Dir publicity & research, Young Dem Clubs of Am, 48-49, exec secy, 49-50; research analyst, Dem Sen Campaign Comt, 50-51; spec attorney, Internal Revenue Serv, Washington, DC & New York, 52-60; dir of research, Equal Employ Opportunity Comn, Washington, DC, 65-68; mem, Legal Research for Vote Fraud Task Force, Nat Lawyers Comt for Nixon-Agnew, 68; dep asst secy for community planning & mgt, Dept of Housing & Urban Develop, 69-72; mem, Durham Co Rep Exec Comt, 73-74. Bus & Prof Pos: Ed-in-chief, Duke Chronicle, Duke Univ, 44-45; reporter, Durham Sun, NC, 45; asst state ed & ed writer, Charlotte News, 47-48; assoc, Battle, Fowler, Stokes & Kheel, New York, 60-65; asst dean, Rutgers Univ Law Sch, Newark, NJ, 74-75. Publ: Ed, Jobs, Men & Machines; The Problems of Automation, Praeger, 64 & Equal Employment Opportunity Report No 1, Equal Employ Opportunity Comn, 3 vols, 69. Mem: Am Bar Asn; Asn of the Bar of the City of NY. Relig: Protestant Episcopal. Mailing Add: 204 N Dillard St Durham NC 27701

MARKHAM, JONNE PEARSON (R)
Second VChmn, Ariz Rep State Comt
b Iloilo, Philippine Islands, Sept 22 26; d George Edward Pearson & Margaret Blackinger P; m 1950 to Richard Glover Markham; c Fred Smith, Janet Blackinger, Charles Regan, Richard Glover, Jr & Marilyn Ann. Educ: Univ Idaho, 44-48; Prescott Col, 69-71, summer seminar,

71; Kappa Kappa Gamma. Polit & Govt Pos: Precinct committeeman, Yavapai Co Rep Comt, Ariz, 63-, vchairwoman, 64-66 & 68-72; committeeman, Ariz Rep State Comt, 63-, asst secy, 69-71, second vchmn, 72-; women's co chmn, Kleindienst for Gov, 64; dep registr, Yavapai Co Recorder's Off, 64-; co co-chmn, Women for Nixon, 68 & Fannin for Senate, 70; chmn, Yavapai Co Reelect the President, 72. Bus & Prof Pos: Journalist, The Paper, Prescott, Ariz, 71- Mem: Ariz Fedn Rep Women (sgt at arms, 66, campaign comt, 69-71, bd dirs, 72-74); Sharlot Hall Mus & Prescott Hist Soc (bd dirs, 68-73); Capitol Hill Club, Washington, DC; Prescott Rep Women (publicity chmn, 64-72). Honors & Awards: Golden Thumb Award, Ariz State Rep Comt, 67. Relig: Roman Catholic. Mailing Add: 945 Country Club Dr Prescott AZ 86301

MARKLAND, WILLIAM A (D)
Chmn, Howard Co Dem Comt, Mo
b Armstrong, Mo, Mar 22, 20; s Elvis H Markland & Ethel Collier M; m 1942 to Earline Howard; c Linda M (Mrs Frink), Susan (Mrs Donnelly), Mary E & John W. Educ: Cent Methodist Col, AB, 41; Univ Mo, Columbia, MEd, 44. Polit & Govt Pos: Secy, Howard Co Dem Comt, Mo, 48-60, chmn, 60- Bus & Prof Pos: High sch prin, Glasgow Schs, Mo, 48-65; elem sch prin, Fayette R-3 Schs, 65-; owner, Markland's Antique Shop, 63- Mem: Mo State Teachers Asn; Boonslick Hist Soc. Relig: Baptist; supt Sunday sch, Armstrong Baptist Church, 48- Mailing Add: 103 W Seminary Armstrong MO 65230

MARKLE, JOHN, JR (R)
Mem Finance Comt, Chester Co Rep Party, Pa
b Allentown, Pa, July 1931; s John Markle, II; m to Mary B McLean; c Ellen, John, III, Patricia, Stephen & Mary. Educ: Yale Univ, BA, 53; Harvard Law Sch, LLB, 58; Delta Psi. Polit & Govt Pos: Committeeman, Willistown Twp Rep Comt, Pa, 61-69; dist adminr, Pa Young Rep, 62-64, mem exec comt & gen counsel, 64-68; chmn, Chester Co Young Rep, 63-64; mem finance comt, Chester Co Rep Party, 66-; deleg, Rep Nat Conv, 68. Bus & Prof Pos: Assoc, Drinker, Biddle & Reath, 58-64, partner, 64- Mil Serv: Entered as 2nd Lt, Marine Corps, 53, released as 1st Lt, 55, after serv in Ninth & Fifth Regt, Japan & Korea, 54-55, Lt Col, Res, 55-; UN, Korean & Nat Defense Medals. Mem: Am Bar Asn; Indust Rels Asn; Indust Rels Research Asn; Am Arbit Asn (nat panel); Children's Aid Soc of Pa (pres, 69-72). Honors & Awards: Outstanding Young Rep in Pa, 66-68. Relig: Episcopal. Legal Res: 23 Andrews Rd Malvern PA 19355 Mailing Add: 1100 Philadelphia Nat Bank Bldg Philadelphia PA 19107

MARKOW, THEODORE JOSEPH (D)
Pres, Young Dem Clubs of Va
b Richmond, Va, June 9, 39; s Joseph J Markow & Marie Wagner M; m 1961 to Carol Bliley; c Theodore Joseph, Jr, Karen Lynn & Marie Taylor. Educ: Med Col Va; Sch Pharm, BS in Pharm, 61; Univ Richmond Sch Law, LLB, 68; Omicron Delta Kappa; McNeill Law Soc; Phi Delta Chi; Pharmaceutical Prof Fraternity; Phi Delta Phi. Polit & Govt Pos: Asst Attorney Gen, Commonwealth of Va, 70-; regional vpres, Young Dem Clubs of Va, 71-72, pres, 72- Bus & Prof Pos: Pharmacist, pvt practice pharm, Richmond & Petersburg, Va, 61-65; attorney, pvt practice law, 68-70. Mil Serv: Entered as Pvt, Va Nat Guard, 57, released as S/5, 62. Mem: Am, Richmond & Va Bar Asns; Jaycees. Honors & Awards: Spark Plug Award, Petersburg, Va Jaycees, 65 & Richmond, Va Jaycees, 70; Outstanding State Dir, Region III, Jaycees, 71. Mailing Add: 22 Lexington Rd Richmond VA 23226

MARKS, CHARLES HARDAWAY (D)
Va State Deleg
b Hopewell, Va, Jan 31, 21; m to Archie Davis Andrews H. Educ: Wake Forest Col, BA; Duke Univ; Univ Va Law Sch; Delta Sigma Phi; Delta Theta Phi. Polit & Govt Pos: Deleg, Dem Nat Conv, 60; Va State Deleg, 62- Bus & Prof Pos: Lawyer. Mil Serv: Capt, Marine Corps, 42-46, wounded on Iwo Jima. Mem: Farm Bur; Robert E Lee Boy Scouts (exec comt); VFW; Am Legion; Moose. Relig: Baptist. Mailing Add: Perry Bldg 1000 River Dr Hopewell VA 23860

MARKS, JEAN C (D)
Colo State Rep
b Forsyth, Mont, Mar 6, 34; d Jesse A Coate & Leah Tompkins; m 1956 to Floyd Marks; c Vicki, J David, Susan, Lynda J & Daniel J. Educ: Univ Colo; Metrop State Col, BA, 73. Polit & Govt Pos: Colo State Rep, 75- Relig: Jewish. Mailing Add: 11106 Elati St Northglenn CO 80234

MARKS, LEONARD HAROLD (D)
b Pittsburgh, Pa; s Samuel Marks & Ida Lewine M; m 1948 to Dorothy Ames; c Stephen Ames & Robert Evan. Educ: Univ Pittsburgh, BA, 35, LLB, 38; Omicron Delta Kappa; Sigma Delta Chi; Phi Beta Kappa; Order of Coif. Hon Degrees: LLD, Univ Pittsburgh, 67. Polit & Govt Pos: Asst to gen counsel, Fed Community Comn, 42-46; deleg, Int Broadcast Conf, Mexico City, 48; deleg, NAm Regional Broadcast Conf, Montreal, 49; State Dept lectr, adminr & consult law, India, 58 & Pakistan, Afghanistan-Iran, Turkey, 61; mem, US Deleg, Int Telecommun Conf, Geneva, 59 & 63; head, US Info Agency, 65-68; ambassador-chmn, Int Conf on Community Satellites, 68-69. Bus & Prof Pos: Prof law, Univ Pittsburgh Law Sch, 38-42; prof law, Nat Univ, 43-55; partner, Cohn & Marks, Attorney-at-law, 46-65 & 69- Mem: Am, DC & Int Bar Asns; Broadcasters Club (pres, 57-59); Metrop Int Club. Legal Res: 2833 McGill Terr NW Washington DC 20008 Mailing Add: 1920 L St NW Washington DC 20036

MARKS, MILTON (R)
Calif State Sen
b San Francisco, Calif, July 22, 20; m 1955 to Carolene Wachenheimer; c Carol, Milton & Edward David. Educ: Stanford Univ, AB; San Francisco Law Sch, LLB. Polit & Govt Pos: Calif State Assemblyman, 58-66; Calif State Sen, Ninth Dist, 67- Bus & Prof Pos: Judge, Munic Court, formerly. Mil Serv: Army; combat in Philippines; occup forces in Japan. Mem: VFW; Am Legion; Press & Union League Club of San Francisco; Lions; Nat Coun on Alcoholism. Legal Res: 55 Jordan Ave San Francisco CA 94118 Mailing Add: Rm 2070 State Capitol Sacramento CA 95814

MARKS, ROBERT HERMAN, JR (R)
Chmn, Howard Co Rep Party, Md
b Harrisburg, Pa, Aug 2, 22; s Robert Herman Marks & Mary Helen Shaffer M; m 1941 to Vera Mae Koontz; c Barbara Diane. Educ: Pa State Col, 41-43 & 46-47. Polit & Govt Pos: Mem, Howard Co Charter Writing Bd, Md, 64; liaison officer, Bd Co Comt to Develop New City of Columbia, 65-66; mem, Bd Zoning Appeals, Howard Co, 65-68; chmn, Howard Co Rep Party, 66-69 & 73-; mem, Charter Steering Comt, Howard Co, 68; alt deleg, Rep Nat Conv, 68; first vchmn, Rep State Cent Comt Md, 69-74; state dir, Md Conservative Union, 75- Bus & Prof Pos: Metallurgical analyst, Bethlehem Steel Corp, Johnstown, Pa, 41-53; marine surveyor, Am Bur Shipping, Baltimore, Md, 53- Mil Serv: Entered as Pvt, Army, released as Pfc, 45, after serv in 101st Airborne Div, ETO, 44-45; Purple Heart. Mem: Am Soc Testing & Mat; Am Welding Soc; F&AM. Relig: Lutheran. Mailing Add: 10705 Cardington Way Apt 101 Cockeysville MD 21030

MARKS, ROBERT L (R)
Mont State Rep
b Helena, Mont, Jan 11, 32; s Merle Milton Marks & Evelyn Rutherford M; m 1951 to Barbara Myles; c Robert David, Beverly Jean, Gary Douglas, Steven Michael, Richard Daniel & Christian Jay. Educ: Mont State Univ, 1 year; Univ Mont, 1 year. Polit & Govt Pos: Mem, Clancy Sch Bd, Mont, 53-61; mem, Jefferson Co High Sch Bd, 63-75; Mont State Rep, Dist 16, 69-73, Dist 12, 73-74 & Dist 80, 75-, mem educ comt, livestock & ranges comt & bills comt, Mont House Rep, 69, mem subcomt on Mont RR & pub serv comn, 69, chmn capitol complex planning comt, 71-73, Asst Minority Leader, 75-, chmn legis coun, 75- Bus & Prof Pos: Chmn, Helena Nat Forest Cattleman's Adv Bd, 62- Mem: Mont Stock Growers Asn; Mason; Scottish Rite; Am Nat Cattlemens Asn; Algeria Shrine. Relig: Methodist. Mailing Add: Clancy MT 59634

MARKS, STANLEY J (D)
Nat Committeeman Young Dem Ariz
b Milwaukee, Wis, June 7, 39; s Martin M Marks & Betty Volkoff; m 1968 to Sara Ann Gross; c Shelley & Carey. Educ: Cornell Univ, BA, 61; NY Univ, LLB, 65; Pi Lambda Phi. Polit & Govt Pos: Pres, Phoenix Young Dem, 69; Dem cand for Ariz State Legis, 70; precinct committeeman, Dem Party, 70-71; nat committeeman, Young Dem Ariz, 69- Bus & Prof Pos: Law clerk to Chief Justice Lorna E Lockwood, Ariz Supreme Court, 65-66; attorney, Langerman, Begam & Lewis, Phoenix, Ariz, 66- Mem: Ariz Trial Lawyers Asn (state committeeman & mem bd dirs, 70-, pres, 72-73); Phoenix Trial Lawyers Asn (bd dirs, 70-); Am Bar Asn (Ariz chmn, Automobile Reparations Comt, 71-); Am Trial Lawyers Asn; Am Arbitration Asn. Relig: Jewish. Mailing Add: 5909 E Solcito Lane Scottsdale AZ 85253

MARLER, FRED WILLIAM, JR (R)
b Auburn, Calif, Apr 6, 32; s Fred William Marler & Hazel Scott M; m 1955 to Irene Elaine Carlson; c Eric Scott & Aaron Mitchell. Educ: Univ Calif, Berkeley, AB, 54, Sch Law, 59; Phi Delta Phi. Polit & Govt Pos: Calif State Sen, Fifth Sen Dist, 65-66 & Second Sen Dist, 67-75; deleg, Rep Nat Conv, 72. Bus & Prof Pos: Attorney-at-law, 60- Mil Serv: Entered as 2nd Lt, Air Force, 54, released as 1st Lt, 56, after serv in Hq, 15th Air Force, Strategic Air Command. Mem: Elks; F&AM; Rotary; Calif State & Shasta-Trinity Co Bar Asns. Relig: Protestant. Legal Res: 1352 Norman Dr Redding CA 96001 Mailing Add: PO Box 2297 Redding CA 96001

MARLER, ROY LEE, SR (D)
b Howardville, Tenn, Aug 15, 19; s Walter Andrew Marler & Mabel Long M (deceased); m 1939 to Ruth Elizabeth Drake; c Lenda (Mrs Anthony Emanuele), Walter Herman, Roy Lee, Jr & Mary Ann. Polit & Govt Pos: Deleg, Dem Nat Conv, 72. Bus & Prof Pos: With Fla Glass & Mirror Co, Inc, Miami, 17 years, asst sales mgr, 68-; chmn, Friends of Turkey & Postal Evangel, Inc, 71- Publ: Verse and adverse (poetry column), North Miami Beach News Post, 68; items of poetry in other newspapers, such as, Miramar Mirror. Relig: Protestant. Mailing Add: 2601 W Arcadia Dr Miramar FL 33023

MAROOTIAN, SIMON (D)
Co-Chmn, Calif Dem State Cent Comt
b Fresno, Calif, Aug 31, 23; s Marginus Marootian & Anna Kalalian M; m 1952 to Irene DeVan; c Marcus & Robyn Ann. Educ: Fresno State Col, 41-43; Hastings Col of Law, Univ Calif, LLB & JD, 48; Sigma Nu Phi. Polit & Govt Pos: Mem, Fresno Co Dem Cent Comt, Calif, 60-62 & 66-68, chmn, 66-68; mem, Calif Dem State Cent Comt, 16th Cong Dist, 66-70, co-chmn, 72-; co-chmn, Humphrey for President, Fresno Co, Calif & Cranston for Senate, 68; co-chmn, Fresno Co Tunney for Senate Comt, 70; co-chmn, Fresno Co Brown for Gov, 74. Bus & Prof Pos: Attorney-at-law, 49- Mil Serv: Entered as Pvt, Air Force, 43, released as 2nd Lt, 45, after serv in Army Air Corps, Pac-Asiatic Theatre, 1 year; Asiatic-Pac Combat Medal; Philippine-Pac Combat Medal. Mem: Fresno Co Bar Asn; Elks; Am Legion; Fed Raisin Adv Bd. Relig: Armenian Apostolic. Legal Res: 6347 S Clovis Ave Fowler CA 93625 Mailing Add: 606 Del Webb Ctr Fresno CA 93721

MAROTTA, ANGELO (D)
Mass State Rep
Mailing Add: State Capitol Boston MA 02133

MAROVITZ, WILLIAM A (D)
Ill State Rep
b Chicago, Ill, Sept 29, 44; s Sydney Robert Marovitz & Jane Chulock M; single. Educ: Univ Ill, Urbana, BA, 66; DePaul Col Law, JD & LLB, 69; Tau Epsilon Phi. Polit & Govt Pos: Asst corp coun, Chicago, Ill, 73-74; Ill State Rep, 75- Bus & Prof Pos: Teacher, Chicago Bd Educ, 69-70; attorney, Marovitz, Powell, Pizer & Edelstein, 70-75. Mem: Ill State Bar Asn (assembly deleg, 72-); Chicago Bar Asn; Young Men's Jewish Coun; Decalogue Soc of Lawyers. Relig: Jewish. Legal Res: 3930 N Pine Grove Chicago IL 60613 Mailing Add: 134 N LaSalle St Chicago IL 60602

MARQUIS, NORMAN J F (D)
Mem, Maine State Dem Comt
b Lewiston, Maine, Oct 23, 30; s Norman H Marquis & Jeannette Poudrier M; m 1958 to Patricia Ann Hopkins; c Jacqueline Jeanne, David Dean & Peter Francis. Educ: Bradley Univ, Cert; Cavalier Towne & Country Club; Montagnard Soc Club. Polit & Govt Pos: Alderman, Lewiston, Maine, 66; Maine State Rep, 69-71; mem, Maine State Dem Comt, 70- Bus & Prof Pos: Self employed, retail & wholesale, 60- Mil Serv: Entered as Pvt, Air Force, 56, released as Airman 2/C, 60, after serv in 316th ADV, Africa, Morocco, 58-60; Good Conduct Medal. Mem: Nat Sporting Goods Asn; Jaycees. Honors & Awards: Outstanding Jaycee of the Year, 64. Relig: Roman Catholic. Mailing Add: Tall Pines Apt 8-4 Lewiston ME 04240

MARR, CARMEL CARRINGTON (R)
Third VChmn, Kings Co Rep Comt, NY
b Brooklyn, NY; d William Preston Carrington & Gertrude Lewis C; m 1948 to Warren Marr II; c Charles C & Warren Q, III. Educ: Hunter Col, BS, 45; Columbia Univ Law Sch, LLB, 48; Phi Beta Kappa; Alpha Chi Alpha; Alpha Kappa Alpha. Polit & Govt Pos: Adv on legal affairs, US Mission to UN, 53-67; mem, Gov Comt Educ & Employ Women, 64; bd vis, NY

State Training Sch at Hudson, 64-71; sr legal officer, UN Secretariat, 67-68; mem, NY State Human Rights Appeal Bd, 68-71; dir, UN Develop Corp, 69-72; third vchmn, Kings Co Rep Comt, 70-; comnr, Pub Serv Comn, 71-; deleg, Rep Nat Conv, 72; bd gov, John Crews Regular Rep Club, 72- Bus & Prof Pos: Pvt law practice, 49-53; law clerk, Dyer & Stevens, Esquires, 48-49. Publ: New York's Human Rights Court, Crisis, NAACP, 3/71; The price of peace, J United Church of Christ, Autumn 72; The consumer wants 'in', Nat Asn Water Co Quart, 12/72. Mem: Brooklyn Bar Asn; Nat Asn Regulatory Utility Comnrs (mem gas comt, 71-); Int Fedn Woman Lawyers; Brooklyn Women's Bar Asn; Nat Asn Women Lawyers. Honors & Awards: Outstanding young woman, Mademoiselle Mag, 54; outstanding achievement, Hunter Col, 55; Margaret Brown Award, TA-WA SES, Am Caribbean Scholarship Fund, 60; Sojourner Truth Award, Nat Asn Negro Bus & Prof Women; elected to Hunter Col Alumni Hall of Fame, 73. Relig: Episcopal. Legal Res: 333 New York Ave Brooklyn NY 11213 Mailing Add: Rm 2412 Two World Trade Ctr New York NY 10047

MARR, JOHN JOSEPH (D)
Mem, Fla Dem State Exec Comt
b Brooklyn, NY, May 21, 98; s John Marr & Anna White M; m 1923 to Lillian V Henningsen; c Phebe Ann & Dorothy (Mrs Villers). Educ: Mt Vernon Eve High Sch, Mt Vernon, NY, 44. Polit & Govt Pos: Court clerk, Darien City Court, Darien, Conn, 48-50; mem, Martin Co Dem Comt, Fla, 66-; mem, Fla Dem State Exec Comt, 75- Bus & Prof Pos: Gen chmn, Order RR Telegraphers, 50-64. Mem: Hiawatha Lodge F&AM; Brotherhood Rwy Clerks. Relig: Episcopal. Mailing Add: 64 Sunset Blvd Jensen Beach FL 33457

MARR, MARTHA CROSS (D)
Exec Dir, SC Dem Party
b Baltimore, Md, Nov 5, 43; d Malcolm A Cross & Marilyn C; div; c Elaine & Richard. Educ: Smith Col, BA, 65; Univ SC, MEd, 74. Polit & Govt Pos: Campaign coordr, Richland Co McGovern for President, SC, 72; dir spec proj, SC Dem Party, 73-74, exec dir, Party, 75-; campaign coordr, Columbia Dem City Coun, 74; vchmn, Richland Co Dem Party, 74-; exec dir, Richland Co Dem Party, 74-75. Bus & Prof Pos: Elem teacher, Spence Sch, New York, 65-66; admin asst, Community Develop Proj, New York, 66-67; Peace Corps vol & teacher, Ethiopia, 67; supvr student teachers, Univ SC, 73-74. Mem: League of Women Voters; Women's Polit Caucus; Columbia YWCA (bd dirs). Honors & Awards: Judge, Sertoma Int Serv Award, 75. Relig: Presbyterian. Mailing Add: 3119 Wilmot Ave Columbia SC 29205

MARRA, MARY ANN (R)
Committeewoman, Champlain Co Rep Comt, NY
b New York, NY, Jan 26, 18; d Peter Pepi & Penelope Cisco P; m 1944 to Robert Joseph Marra; c Richard Anthony, Margaret Penelope & Thomas Vincent. Educ: Wadleigh High Sch, New York, 3 years. Polit & Govt Pos: Committeewoman, Champlain Co Rep Comt, Dist Four, NY, 60-; vchmn, Clinton Co Rep Party, 66-70. Mem: Girl Scouts; Tri Co Coun for the Aged; Coun on the Arts; Coop Exten; YWCA; Red Cross (bd mem, 72-). Relig: Greek Orthodox. Mailing Add: 118 Maple St Rouses Point NY 12979

MARRIOTT, ALICE SHEETS (R)
VChmn, Rep Nat Comt
b Salt Lake City, Utah, Oct 19, 07; d Edwin Spencer Sheets & Alice Taylor S; m 1927 to John Willard Marriott; c John Willard, Jr & Richard Edwin. Educ: Univ Utah, BA, 27; Phi Kappa Phi; Chi Omega. Hon Degrees: DHL, Univ Utah, 75. Polit & Govt Pos: Asst treas, DC League of Rep Women, 55-57, vpres, 57-59, campaign activities, 59-66, chmn, Ways & Means, 65-; mem, Rep Nat Comt for DC, 59-; mem, DC Rep Comt, Exec Comt & Sub Exec Comt, 59; treas, Rep Nat Conv, 64, 68 & 72; mem, Rep Coord Comt, 65; vchmn & mem exec comt, Rep Nat Comt, 65-, vchmn, Inaugural Comt, 69, hon chmn, 73; chmn, Distinguished Ladies Reception Inaugural Comt, 69; chmn, Adv Comt on the Arts of The John F Kennedy Ctr for the Performing Arts, 70-, mem bd trustees, 72- Bus & Prof Pos: Partner & co-founder, A&W Root Beer Stores, Washington, DC, 27-29; vpres & mem bd dirs, Marriott Corp, 29- Mem: Nat Adv Coun for Children & Youth; Capital Speakers Club; Women's Nat Rep Club; Capitol Hill Club; Am Newspaper Womens Club. Relig: Latter-day Saint. Mailing Add: 4500 Garfield St NW Washington DC 20007

MARRIOTT, B GLADYS (D)
Mo State Rep
b Spearman, Tex, Jan 3, 22; d Lew Ewing Armstrong & Bessie Gladys Irons A; m 1941 to Lloyd Harold Marriott; c Marjorie Ann (Mrs Mike Fitterling) & Nancy Jane. Educ: High sch, Kansas City, Mo, grad. Polit & Govt Pos: Pres, North Blue Ridge Improv Asn, 52; committeewoman, Jackson Co Dem Party, 61-67; vchmn, Fourth Cong Dist Dem Party, 63-65; vpres, Jackson Co Dem Asn, 64; Mo State Rep, 37th Dist, 67-, Dem caucus secy, 75th Gen Assembly, 69, caucus chmn & chmn retirement & pensions comt, 77th Gen Assembly, Mo House Rep; co-chmn, Nat Order Women Legislator's Conv, 75; pres, Women's Eastern Dem Club, formerly. Mem: Eastern Star; Kansas City Women's CofC; Swope Park Women's Club. Relig: Christian. Mailing Add: 9001 Leeds Rd Kansas City MO 64129

MARRIOTT, GILBERT E (D)
Utah State Rep
Mailing Add: 948 W 26th St Ogden UT 84401

MARRIOTT, RICHARD HAROLD (D)
Mayor, Sacramento, Calif
b Ely, Nev, Feb 7, 18; s Joseph Edmund Marriott & Anna Bernard M; m 1943 to Geraldine Thane; c Richard, James, Anna Marie, Mary Beth, Martin & Christina. Educ: Univ San Francisco, BS, 40; Univ Calif Grad Sch. Polit & Govt Pos: City councilman, Sacramento, Calif, 60-68, Mayor, 68- Bus & Prof Pos: With bus dept, Oroville Mercury, 45-47, Alameda Times Star, 47-49, Sacramento Union, 49-50 & Cath Herald, 50-54; ed-mgr, Sacramento Valley Union Labor Bull, 54- Mil Serv: Marine Corps, OCS, 42. Mem: Int Labor Press Asn (bd mem); United Crusade (bd dirs); IBEW; Elks; Am Red Cross (pres, Sacramento Chap). Relig: Catholic. Mailing Add: 2716 Tenth Ave Sacramento CA 95818

MARRIOTT, VONCEILE JANIS (D)
b Stanberry, Mo, May 26, 20; d Charles Henry Myrick & Margot Scott M; m 1938 to Albert Reynold Marriott; c Reynold Scott. Educ: Platte Col of Com, 41-42; St Joseph Jr Col, 52-54; Univ of Minn, 58; Univ of Calif, 60; past pres, Epsilon Alpha; Beta Sigma Phi. Polit & Govt Pos: Supvr finance dept, US Govt, Ft Leavenworth, Kans, 44-46; chmn UN Day, UN Comt, St Joseph, Mo, 62; alt deleg-at-lg, Dem Nat Conv, 64, deleg, 72; supvr, Buchanan & Clinton Co, US Agr Census, 64-65. Bus & Prof Pos: Mgr retail sales, Anchor Serum Co, 46-57, sales conv secy, 57-60; owner & mgr, Career Placement & Vonceile's Agency, 60-; dir, Manpower, Inc, St Joseph, 63-; representative to Washington, DC, North Side Civic Club, 64; secy-treas, L&M Printing & Off Supply, Inc, 64-65; owner & mgr, Exec Exchange, 65-; real estate broker, 68-; mem col surv comt, Northwest Mo State Col, 68; mem adv comt, 69-; state chmn, Cert Employ Consult in charge of certification, 69-; operator, Kelly Serv Inc, St Joseph, 70-; mem comt comput sci, Mo Western Col, 70-71. Mem: Nat Personnel Assocs; Nat Employ Asn; Northwest Mo Press Asn; CofC; Dem State-Club of Mo. Honors & Awards: Nat Sales Award, Manpower, Inc, 65; Distinguished Serv Award, UN Comt, 62. Relig: Protestant. Legal Res: 5110 Eastcrest Ct St Joseph MO 64506 Mailing Add: East Hills Ctr St Joseph MO 64506

MARRS, THEODORE (R)
Spec Asst to President Human Resources
Polit & Govt Pos: Dep Asst Secy Manpower & Reserve Affairs, Dept Defense, formerly. Legal Res: AL Mailing Add: White House Off 1600 Pennsylvania Ave Washington DC 20500

MARSDEN, LAWRENCE DAVID (R)
NDak State Rep
b Bottineau, NDak, Mar 4, 24; s Sam Alex Marsden & Alice Mae Crowder M; m 1954 to Lila Lucille Krause; c Douglas, Candace (Mrs Steve Baune), Linda (Mrs Craig Nett), Kelly, Dana & Troy. Educ: Bottineau High Sch, grad, 41; Minot Bus Col, grad, 47. Polit & Govt Pos: Rep precinct committeeman, Minot, NDak, 62-66; comnr, Park Bd, Bottineau, 72-; NDak State Rep, Sixth Dist, 72- Bus & Prof Pos: Off mgr, Becwar-Cedarstrom Co, Minot, 47-55; gen mgr, TBA Wholesalers, 55-64; comptroller, Home Econ, 64-67; owner & operator, TBA Supply, Bottineau & Rugby, NDak, 67- Mil Serv: Entered as Pvt, Marine Corps, 42, released as Cpl, 46, after serv in Corps Hq, 1st & 3rd Amphibious Corps, Pac Theatre, 43-45. Mem: Elks; VFW; Am Legion; NDak Farm Bur; Toastmasters. Relig: Methodist. Mailing Add: State Capitol Bismarck ND 58501

MARSH, BENJAMIN FRANKLIN (R)
b Toledo, Ohio, Apr 30, 27; s Lester Randall Marsh & Alice Smith M; m 1952 to Martha Flowers Kirkpatrick; c Samuel Kirkpatrick & Elizabeth Randall. Educ: Ohio Wesleyan Univ, BA, 50; George Washington Univ, JD, 54; Omicron Delta Kappa; Delta Sigma Rho; Theta Alpha Phi; Phi Delta Phi; Kappa Sigma. Polit & Govt Pos: Personnel off, US Atomic Energy Comn, Washington, DC, 50-54; admin asst to Legis Serv Comn, Columbus, Ohio, 54-55; admin asst to Ray Bliss, Rep State Chmn Ohio, 54-55; cand, Ohio State Rep, 56; asst solicitor, Maumee, Ohio, 56-63, solicitor & prosecutor, 63-; pres, Lucas Co Young Rep Club, 57; mem, Lucas Co Charter Comn, Toledo, Ohio, 59-60; precinct committeeman, 59-73; pres, Rep Workshops of Ohio, Inc, 60-64; legal counsel & bd mem, Nat Coun Rep Workshops, 60-65; mem, Lucas Co Rep Exec Comt, chmn, 73-74; chmn, Maumee Rep Comt, Ohio, 60-71; chmn, Lincoln Day Banquet, 62; alt deleg, Rep Nat Conv, 64; vchmn, Salute to Ray Bliss Dinner, 65; cand for US Rep, Ninth Dist, Ohio, 68; mem, US Nat Comn for UNESCO, vchmn, currently, app deleg, UNESCO Gen Conf, Paris, 72; Asst Attorney Gen, Ohio, 69-71; pres, Citizens for Metroparks, 72-74; mem, bd elec, Lucas Co, 73- Bus & Prof Pos: Partner, Law Firm of Doyle, Lewis & Warner, 55-71; Law Firm of Ritter, Boesel, Robinson & Marsh, 71- Mil Serv: Seaman 1/C, Navy, 45-46, serv in Am Theater. Mem: Alumni Asn, Ohio Wesleyan Univ (mem bd dirs, 72-); Ohio Land Title Asn; Toledo Country Club; Press Club of Toledo; Capitol Hill Club, Washington, DC. Honors & Awards: Selected Outstanding Young Man of Toledo, 62. Relig: Presbyterian. Legal Res: 124 W Harrison Maumee OH 43537 Mailing Add: 610 United Savings Bank Toledo OH 43604

MARSH, DANIEL G (D)
Wash State Sen
b Salem, Ore, May 14, 37; s Gabriel J Marsh & Anne Dooper M; m 1964 to Diane K Spoklie; c Douglas James, Damon John & Dixon Joseph. Educ: Willamette Univ, BA, 59; Univ Ore Law Sch, JD, 62; Tau Kappa Alpha; Pi Gamma Mu; Phi Alpha Delta; Sigma Alpha Epsilon. Polit & Govt Pos: Wash State Rep, 65-73; Wash State Sen, 73- Bus & Prof Pos: Attorney, 63- Mil Serv: Nat Guard, 8 years. Mem: Am Bar Asn; Am Trial Lawyers Asn; Nat Soc State Legislators; Grange; Kiwanis. Legal Res: 207 Phoenix Way Vancouver WA 98661 Mailing Add: PO Box 1086 1111 Broadway Vancouver WA 98660

MARSH, FRANK (R)
State Treas, Nebr
b Norfolk, Nebr, Apr 27, 24; s Frank Marsh & Delia Andrews M; m 1943 to Shirley Mac McVicker; c Sherry Anne (Mrs Philip Tupper), Corwin Frank, Stephen Alan, Mitchell Edward, Dory Michael & Melissa Lou. Educ: Univ Nebr, BSEd, 50; Nat Parole Insts, grad, 63 & 64; Alpha Phi Omega. Polit & Govt Pos: State govt adv, Mayor's Comt for Int Friendship; Secy of State, Nebr, 53-70, Lt Gov, 70-74; mem, Nebr State Claims Bd; State Treas, 75- Bus & Prof Pos: Builder, businessman & part-time instr, 46-52. Mil Serv: Army, 43-46. Mem: Nat Coun for Community Serv to Int Visitors (pres); Nat Asn State Auditors, Comptrollers & Treas; US Nat Comn for UNESCO; Hon Consul Gen for Guatemala; VFW. Relig: Methodist. Legal Res: 2701 S 34th St Lincoln NE 68506 Mailing Add: Capitol Bldg Lincoln NE 68509

MARSH, JOHN O, JR (D)
Counsellor to the President
b Winchester, Va, Aug 7, 26; m to Glenn Ann Patterson M; c John O, III, Rebecca Patterson & Scot Wayland. Educ: Washington & Lee Univ, LLB; Phi Kappa Psi; Phi Delta Phi; Omicron Delta Kappa. Polit & Govt Pos: Former US Rep, Va; former mem, Shenandoah Co Sch Bd, Va; town attorney of New Market; town judge, Strasburg; Asst Secy of Defense for Cong Rels, 73-74; Asst to the Vice President, 74; Counsellor to the President, 74- Bus & Prof Pos: Lawyer; mem adv comt, The Papers of George Washington. Mil Serv: Army, World War II, grad, Inf Officers Cand Sch; currently, Lt Col, Va Nat Guard; Parachute Sch, 64 & Jumpmaster Sch, Ft Benning, Ga, 69. Honors & Awards: Designated Outstanding Young Man in Va, Va Jaycees, 59; Awarded Distinguished Serv Medal, Dept of Va, Am Legion; Dept of Defense Medal for Distinguished Pub Serv, 74. Relig: Presbyterian. Legal Res: Strasburg VA 22657 Mailing Add: The White House Off Washington DC 20500

MARSH, NORMAN CLAFFLIN (R)
NH State Rep
b Lexington, Mass, Aug 13, 36; s Norman A Marsh & Mary M O'Fallon M; m 1958 to Kathleen G Hansen; c James M, Lori A, Norma L & Michael P. Educ: New Eng Col, 56-57; Univ NH, 57-58; Sigma Phi Delta. Polit & Govt Pos: NH State Rep, 73-; vchmn, Belknap Co Deleg, 75-; chmn, Belknap Co Inst Comt, 75- Bus & Prof Pos: Gen mgr, E W Littlefield & Sons, 63-66; pres, NAtlantic Rental, Inc, 64-69; owner, Union Ave Serv Ctr, 68-75. Mil Serv: Entered as Recruit, Navy, 54, released as E-3, 56, after serv in HospC; EM2, Naval Res, 62. Mem: St Jean Soc (trustee). Honors & Awards: Blue Chip Pres, NH Jaycees, 71; Key Man Award, 71-72. Relig: Catholic. Legal Res: Upland Dr Gilford NH 03246 Mailing Add: RFD 4 Laconia NH 03246

MARSH, SHIRLEY MAC (R)
Nebr State Sen

b Benton, Ill, June 22, 25; d Dwight S McVicker & Margaret Hager M; m 1943 to Frank Marsh; c Sherry (Mrs Philip Tupper), Stephen Alan, Dory Michael, Corwin Frank, Mitchell Edward & Melissa Lou. Educ: Univ Nebr, BA, 72; Alpha Chi Omega. Polit & Govt Pos: Nebr State Sen, 73- Mem: Nebr Welfare Asn; Human Resources Comt of Midwest; Conf of Coun of State Govts; Gateway LaSertoma; YWCA. Relig: Methodist; Mem admin bd, Trinity United Methodist Church. Mailing Add: 2701 S 34th St Lincoln NE 68506

MARSH, THOMAS PARKER, JR (TOM) (D)
Ore State Rep

b Lafayette, Ind, Dec 7, 39; s Thomas Parker Marsh, Sr & Elizabeth Schermerhorn M; m 1963 to Judith Ann Mosher; c Megan & Meredith. Educ: Univ Ore, BS, 62, MS, 69; Univ Northern Iowa, summer 66; Pi Kappa Phi. Polit & Govt Pos: Precinct committeeman, Washington Co Dem Party, Ore, 71-; Ore State Rep, 75- Bus & Prof Pos: Pres, Beaverton Educ Asn, 72-73. Mem: Beaverton, Nat & Ore Educ Asns; Common Cause Ore. Honors & Awards: Nat Teacher Leader, US Off Educ, Nat Educ Asn & Am Fedn Teachers, 73; comnr, Gov Comn on Youth, State of Ore, 75-76. Mailing Add: 12060 SW Butner Rd Portland OR 97225

MARSHA, HOWARD CLARENCE (R)
Chmn, Clinton Co Rep Comt, NY

b Tupper Lake, NY, Nov 17, 93; s Charles Marsha & Dora Payee M; m 1917 to Grace D Sutton; c Constance B (Mrs Grant). Educ: Univ Buffalo, PhG, 17; Beta Phi Sigma. Polit & Govt Pos: Chmn, Clinton Co Rep Comt, NY, 50-; elec comnr, Clinton Co, 50-; deleg, Rep Nat Conv, 60 & 72, alt deleg, 64 & 68; pub rels staff of US Rep Carlton King, 61-64. Bus & Prof Pos: Pharmacist, 17-65; Pres, Elmore SPCA Inc, Peru, NY, 69- Mem: Pharm Alumni Asn, Buffalo; Prof Officers Soc, New York; Mason; Elks. Mailing Add: 8 Union St Peru NY 12972

MARSHALA, AUGUSTINE J (R)
NH State Rep
Mailing Add: RFD 1 Box 62 Keene NH 03431

MARSHALL, ANTHONY DRYDEN (R)
US Ambassador to Kenya

b New York, NY, May 30, 24; s Dryden Kuser & Brooke Russell K; m 1962 to Thelma Hoegnell; c Alexander & Philip. Educ: Brown Univ, BA, 50; Phi Delta Theta. Polit & Govt Pos: Consul, Istanbul, Turkey, formerly; US Ambassador, Malagasy Repub, 69-72; US Ambassador to Trinidad & Tobago, 72-74; US Ambassador to Kenya, 75- Bus & Prof Pos: Pres, African Research & Develop Co, New York, 59-69; pres, NIDOCO Ltd, Lagos, Nigeria, 61-69; limited partner, Tucker, Anthony & R L Day, 62- Mil Serv: Entered as Pvt, Marines, 42, released as Capt, 46, after serv in 3rd Marine Div, Pac, 44-45; Purple Heart; Presidential Unit Citation; Area Campaign Awards. Publ: Africa's living arts, 70, The Malagasy Republic, 72 & Trinidad & Tobago, 75, Franklin Watts, New York. Mem: Nigerian Am CofC (vpres, 60-69); NY Zool Soc (trustee, 64-); Vincent Astor Found (trustee); African Med Research Found (mem bd, 60-); fel African Studies Asn. Relig: Episcopal. Mailing Add: Am Embassy Nairobi Dept of State Washington DC 20520

MARSHALL, CLIFFORD HOLMES (D)
City Councilman, Quincy, Mass

b Quincy, Mass, Dec 14, 37; s Clifford Holmes Marshall (deceased) & Kathryn R Engel M (deceased); m 1961 to Louise Marie Caporale; c Clifford Holmes, III, Michael Joseph, Paul Stephen & Christopher James. Educ: Quincy High Sch, dipl, 56; Suffolk Univ, 69- Polit & Govt Pos: City councilman, Quincy, Mass, 66-; Mass State Rep, 69-74; mem, Mass Dem State Comt, 72- Mil Serv: Entered as Pvt, Marine Corps, 58, released as Cpl, 62, after serv in Naval Security Group; Good Conduct Medal; Outstanding Man Award, Parris Island, SC; Awarded 3 Meritorious Masts for Outstanding Leadership & Performance. Mem: Norfolk Co Sheriffs Assocs (nat legis conf comt on law enforcement & criminal justice); KofC; Elks; US Marine Corps League; Amvets. Relig: Catholic. Mailing Add: 64 Edison St Quincy MA 02169

MARSHALL, FRED VERN (DFL)
Treas, Itasca Co Dem-Farmer-Labor Party, Minn

b Pengilly, Minn, June 21, 18; s Fred Vern Marshall & Mary Elizabeth McQuillan M; m 1944 to Shirley Marguerite Simpson; c Mary, Michael, Timothy, Kathleen, Colleen, Daniel & Susan. Educ: Greenway High Sch, Minn. Polit & Govt Pos: Clerk, Greenway Twp, Minn, 44-56; dir sch dist 316, Coleraine; treas, Itasca Co Dem-Farmer-Labor Party, 69- Mil Serv: Entered as Pvt, Army, 40, released as Pfc, 43, after serv in 151st Field Artil, NAfrica; Tunisian Campaign Ribbon; Good Conduct Medal; Purple Heart. Relig: Catholic. Mailing Add: PO Box 134 Pengilly MN 55775

MARSHALL, HARRIS ANDREW (D)
b Chesterfield, SC, Jan 17, 35; s Harris A Marshall Sr & Mary Hurst M; m 1967 to Theresa Ann Weathers. Educ: Duke Univ, BA, 57; Univ SC, JD, 67; Phi Kappa Sigma. Polit & Govt Pos: Chmn, Orangeburg Co Dem Party, SC, formerly. Mil Serv: Entered as Ens, Navy, 57, released as Lt, 64, after serv in VF 14 & VF 41, ECoast; Lt Comdr, Naval Res, 66- Mem: Kiwanis. Relig: Baptist. Legal Res: Reddick St Bowman SC 29018 Mailing Add: Box 606 Orangeburg SC 29115

MARSHALL, HOWARD W (R)
Treas, Beaver Co Rep Party, Pa

b New Galilee, Pa, Mar 8; s Samuel John Marshall & Nancy McKim M; m 1924 to Mary McMillen; c James Hugh, Charles McMillen & John Curtis. Polit & Govt Pos: Committeeman, Beaver Co Rep Party, Pa, 63-, treas, 69-; mayor, Beaver Falls, Pa, 66-; deleg, Rep Nat Conv, 68; chmn, Beaver Falls, Rep Orgn, 69- Bus & Prof Pos: Supt, Babcock & Wilcox Tubular Prod, Beaver Falls, 55-57 & supt cold drawn div, Wis, 57-61; consult, Works Mgr Staff, Beaver Falls, 61-67; plant engr, United Hosp, New Brighton, 67-; tipstave, Beaver Co Court House, 70- Mem: Rotary; Beaver Falls Turners; Salvation Army (adv bd); Friends of Scouting; Mason. Relig: Presbyterian; elder, Trinity United Presby Church, Beaver Falls. Mailing Add: 915 11th St Beaver Falls PA 15010

MARSHALL, HUGH TALBOTT (D)
Chmn, Hardeman Co Dem Party, Tex

b Quanah, Tex, Jan 11, 05; s John Calvin Marshall & Emma Talbott M; m 1937 to Mary Lee Hampton; c Mary Talbott (Mrs Donald Clinton Bishop) & John Hampton. Educ: Univ Tex, 3 years. Polit & Govt Pos: Chmn, Hardeman Co Dem Party, Tex, 10 years; mem bd regents, Midwest Univ, Wichita Falls, currently. Bus & Prof Pos: Gen mgr, Quanah Cotton Oil Co, Tex, 56- Mem: Farm Bur; Farmers Coop Soc. Relig: Methodist. Mailing Add: 908 W Third St Quanah TX 79252

MARSHALL, LARRY R (R)
Mo State Sen
Mailing Add: 1009 Bob-O-Link Columbia MO 65201

MARSHALL, MARY AYDELOTTE (D)
Va State Deleg

b Cook Co, Ill, June 14, 21; d John Andrew Rice & Nell Aydelotte R; m 1944 to Roger Duryea Marshall; c Nell, Jenny & Alice. Educ: Swarthmore Col, BA with highest honors, 42; Phi Beta Kappa. Polit & Govt Pos: Economist, Dept Justice, 42-47; chmn, Arlington Co Dem Comt, 61-63; deleg, Dem Nat Conv, 64; Va State Deleg, 66-70 & 72- Mem: Va Ment Health Asn; United Church Women; State Libr Bd (vchmn); Nat Asn Ment Health (bd). Relig: Congregational. Mailing Add: 2256 N Wakefield St Arlington VA 22207

MARSHALL, OLEN H (R)
Tenn State Rep
Mailing Add: PO Box 1593 Morristown TN 37814

MARSHALL, RICHARD L (R)
NY State Assemblyman

b Horseheads, NY, Aug 21, 17; s Levi Marshall; m to Jean Meiswinkel. Educ: Elmira Bus Inst. Polit & Govt Pos: NY State Assemblyman, 62-, chmn agr comt, NY State Assembly, currently; trustee, acting mayor & budget officer, Village of Horseheads; mem, Horseheads Planning Comn. Bus & Prof Pos: Owner of Marshalls Feed Mill, formerly, dir, Chemung Canal Trust Co, Elmira. Mem: Horseheads Free Libr Asn (trustee); Chemund Co Comt Alcoholism (dir); Horseheads CofC (vpres); Mason (32 degree). Relig: Presbyterian; chmn bd trustees. Mailing Add: 7 Strathmont Park Elmira NY 14905

MARSHALL, ROBERT IGNATIUS (D)
Regional Dir, Young Dem of Am

b Wilmington, Del, Oct 16, 46; s Ignatius A Marchlewicz (Marshall) & Helen Dudziec M; m 1973 to Carol Ann Gillespie. Educ: Salesianum High Sch, grad, 64; Lincoln Univ, 4 years. Polit & Govt Pos: Pres, Young Dem, Wilmington, Del, 67-; nat committeeman, Young Dem of Del, 68-71; regional dir, Young Dem of Am, 69-; dir, Div Bus & Occup Regulation, State of Del, 73-; bd dirs, Nat Coun Occupational Licensing, 74- Mil Serv: Del Army Nat Guard, currently. Mem: Ment Health Asn Del (mem legis coun); Dem Forum of Del. Relig: Catholic. Mailing Add: 715 S Broom St Wilmington DE 19805

MARSHALL, THURGOOD
Assoc Justice, US Supreme Court

b Baltimore, Md, July 2, 08; s William Marshall & Norma A Williams M; m 1955 to Cecilia S Suyat; c Thurgood & John. Educ: Lincoln Univ, AB, 30, LLD, 47; Howard Univ, LLB, 33, LLD, 54; Alpha Phi Alpha. Hon Degrees: LLD from numerous Insts. Polit & Govt Pos: Civil rights cases argued include Tex Primary Case, 44, Restrictive Covenant Cases, 48, Univ Tex & Okla Cases, 50, visited Japan & Korea to investigate court martial cases involving Negro soldiers, 51 & sch segregation cases, 52-53; rep, White House Conf Youth & Children; consult, Constitutional Conf on Kenya London, 60; US Circuit Judge, 61-65; US Solicitor Gen, 65-67; Assoc Justice, US Supreme Court, 67- Bus & Prof Pos: Attorney-at-law, Baltimore, 33-37; asst spec counsel, NAACP, 36-38, spec counsel, 38-50, dir, Counsel Legal Defense & Educ Fund, 40-61; mem, NY State Comn, Worlds Fair; mem bd, John F Kennedy Mem Libr. Mem: Col electors, Hall of Fame, NY Univ; Nat & Am Bar Asns; New York Co Lawyers Asn; Mason (33 degree). Honors & Awards: Recipient, Spingarn Medal, 46; Living Hist Award from Research Inst. Relig: Episcopal. Legal Res: VA Mailing Add: US Supreme Court One First St NE Washington DC 20543

MARSHALL, WILLIAM C (D)
Mem-at-Lg, Dem Nat Comt
Mailing Add: 1034 N Washington Ave Lansing MI 48906

MARSHALL, WILLIAM HUSTON (D)
Treas, Dem Exec Comt Fla

b Pensacola, Fla, Dec 11, 26; s Willie Anthony Marshall & Martha Anderson M (both deceased); div; c Marilyn, Alvin & Carol. Educ: Lemoyne Col, BS, 51; Ala State Univ, MEd, 57; Tuskegee Inst; Kappa Alpha Psi. Polit & Govt Pos: Treas, Dem Exec Comt Fla, 75- Bus & Prof Pos: Teacher, Senatobia, Miss, 51-53, Bullock Co, Ala, 55-56 & Clark Co, Ala, 56-58; high sch teacher, Pensacola, Fla, 58-64; prin, DeVaughn Elem Sch, Pensacola, 64-65 & Spencer Bibbs Elem Sch, 65- Mil Serv: Entered as Pvt, Marine Corps, 46, released as Cpl, 47, after serv in 2nd Replacement Div, Asiatic-Pac Theatres; Pac Theatre Medal. Mem: Am Legion; Fla & Nat Educ Asns; United Teaching Profession. Honors & Awards: Pace Setter Award, Nat Educ Asn. Relig: Baptist. Mailing Add: 1803 E Scott St Pensacola FL 32503

MARSHALL, WILLIAM K (KEN) (D)
Kans State Rep
Mailing Add: 2301 Massachusetts Topeka KS 66605

MARTEL, ALBERT A (D)
NH State Rep
Mailing Add: 191A Maple St Manchester NH 03103

MARTELL, ARTHUR J (D)
Vt State Rep
Mailing Add: 40 Church St Swanton VT 05488

MARTENSON, DAVID LOUIS (R)
Secy, Ill Rep State Cent Comt

b Rockford, Ill, Nov 20, 34; s Louis L Martenson & Loretta L Lind M; m to Judith Ann Ehnen; c Scott, Brian & Kari. Educ: Millikin Univ, BA, 56; Univ Chicago Law Sch, LLD, 59; Tau Kappa Epsilon. Polit & Govt Pos: Pres, Millikin Univ Young Rep Club, 55; vpres, Col Orgn, Ill State Young Rep, 56, pres, 58, mem bd dirs, 58-63; chmn, Winnebago Co Rep Cent Comt, Ill, 64-71; committeeman, Ill Rep State Cent Comt, 16th Dist, 71-74, secy, currently; mem adv comt, Small Bus Admin, formerly. Bus & Prof Pos: Attorney, Martenson & Donohue. Mem: Winnebago Co, Ill & Am Bar Asns; Am Trial Lawyers Asn; CofC. Legal

Res: 5720 Coachman Court Rockford IL 61107 Mailing Add: 204 Rock River Savings & Loan Bldg Rockford IL 61101

MARTI, DOUGLAS (R)
Chmn, Bond Co Rep Cent Comt, Ill
b Mattoon, Ill, Feb 21, 34; s Freeman R Marti & Norma Suess M; m 1956 to Doris C Crist; c Kevin D & Lydia S. Educ: Univ Ill, BS, 54, JD, 68; Phi Kappa Phi; Phi Eta Sigma; Delta Theta Phi; Alpha Zeta. Polit & Govt Pos: Grad asst, Agr Law, 54-55; vpres, Ill Young Rep Club, 56, pres, 56-57; bill drafter, Legis Reference Bur, 57; asst state's attorney, Bond Co, Ill, 58, state's attorney, 64-68 & 72-; attorney, Off of the Gen Counsel, Dept Health, Educ & Welfare, 58-61; asst court adminr, Ill Supreme Court, 61-64; mem bd gov, Sangamon Co Young Rep Club, 64; chmn, Bond Co Rep Cent Comt, 66-68 & 74-; Rep precinct committeeman, Bond Co, 66-; alt deleg, Rep Nat Conv, 68; mem, Parole & Pardon Bd, 69; spec asst to Attorney Gen, St Louis Metrop Airport Authority, Ill, 70-; asst state's attorney, Madison Co, 69-72. Bus & Prof Pos: Asst prof, Greenville Col, 71-73. Mil Serv: 2nd Lt, Army, 57. Publ: Illinois inheritance laws, wills & joint tenancy, Univ Ill Col Agr, 6/55. Mem: Ill State & Bond Bar Asns. Relig: Baptist. Mailing Add: R 1 Greenville IL 62246

MARTIN, A W (R)
Chmn, Fayette Co Rep Comt, Iowa
b Aug 17, 26; s Albert W Martin & Ida Nielson M; m 1949 to Mary Jean Quinn; c Douglas N, Dennis R, Vicki K, Debra J & Duane J. Educ: Alburne Il Community High Sch, grad, 43. Polit & Govt Pos: Sch bd mem, Fayette Community Sch, 62-69; Rep precinct chmn, Smithfield Twp, 70-73; chmn, Fayette Co Rep Comt, 73- Bus & Prof Pos: Farmer, 47- Mil Serv: Entered as Pvt, Army, 45, released as Sgt, 46, after serv in Base M Hq, AFWESPAC, Philippines, 45-46; Good Conduct Medal; Victory, Asiatic & Pac Ribbons. Mem: Farm Bur; Am Legion. Relig: Methodist. Mailing Add: 92 Box 128 Fayette IA 52142

MARTIN, ANTOINETTE C (D)
Maine State Rep
Mailing Add: 24 Hawthorne St Brunswick ME 04011

MARTIN, BLANCHE RUTH (R)
Committeewoman, First Sen Dist Rep Party, Tex
b St Louis, Mo, Aug 17, 07; d Richard E Wachter & Blanche Reader W; m 1929 to Jack C W Martin, wid; c Joan (Mrs McIntosh), Jacqueline (Mrs Fojtasek) & Richard W. Educ: Soldan High Sch, Mo, grad. Polit & Govt Pos: Vchmn, Grayson Co Rep Party, Tex, 53-60, chmn, 60-66; committeewoman, Ninth Sen Dist Rep Party, 66-72; First Sen Dist Rep Party, 72- Relig: Presbyterian. Mailing Add: 228 W Hanna Denison TX 75020

MARTIN, BRAD (R)
Tenn State Rep
Mailing Add: 249 Conlee Pl Memphis TN 38111

MARTIN, CAROL LAHMAN (R)
Secy, Carroll Co Rep Party, Ga
b Oklahoma City, Okla, Nov 20, 26; d Wilbur Leroy Lahman & Marguerette Neerman L; m 1951 to Talmage McKinley Martin, Jr, MD; c Katherine Elizabeth, Anne Marie & Scott William. Educ: Okla State Univ, BA, 46; Stanford Univ, MA, 48; Theta Sigma Phi; Mortar Bd; Kappa Alpha Theta. Polit & Govt Pos: VChmn, Carroll Co Rep Party, Ga, 70-74, secy, 75-; deleg, 714B Precinct, Carroll Co, Ga Sixth Dist & Nat Rep Conv, 72. Mem: Carroll-Douglas-Haralson Med Auxiliary (legis chmn, 72-, prog chmn, 74-75). Relig: Methodist. Legal Res: Chapel Heights Rte 9 Carrollton GA 30117 Mailing Add: Rte 9 Box 175 Carrollton GA 30117

MARTIN, CELIA HARE (D)
b Ishpeming, Mich, Oct 4, 14; d Jeremiah Hare & Mary Ellen Sheridan H; wid; c Rebecca Ellen. Educ: Col of St Scholastica, 2 years; Col of St Teresa, BA, 32. Polit & Govt Pos: Admin asst to US Rep Lloyd M Bentsen, Jr, 48-55, US Rep Joe M Kilgore, 55-65 & US Rep E de la Garza, Tex, 65- Relig: Roman Catholic. Legal Res: McAllen TX 78501 Mailing Add: 2500 Que NW Washington DC 20007

MARTIN, CHARLES BEE (D)
Ala State Rep
b Corona, Ala, July 12, 31; s Claud Jasper Martin & Annie Jones M; m 1949 to Daphyne Kimbrell; c Patsy Ann (Mrs Joe Duncan), Joe Bearl, Scarlett (Mrs Carl Guyse), Charles Lee & Treva Jo (Mrs Gregg Standridge). Educ: Univ Ala, Huntsville, 60-63. Polit & Govt Pos: Mem, Park & Recreation Bd, Decatur, Ala, 67-72, city councilman, 68-74, mem, Boat Harbor Bd, 69-74; Ala State Rep, Dist Eight, 74- Bus & Prof Pos: Sr research engr, Monsanto Textile Co, Decatur, 52- Mem: Morgan Co Dem Party; Austin High Sch Booster Club. Relig: Methodist. Mailing Add: 1716 Camellia Dr SW Decatur AL 35601

MARTIN, CLARENCE (R)
NDak State Rep
Mailing Add: State Capitol Bismarck ND 58501

MARTIN, CLARENCE DANIEL, JR (D)
b Spokane, Wash, Oct 23, 16; s Clarence Daniel Martin & Margaret H Mulligan M; m 1944 to Charlotte Mary Yeoman; c Diana, Cary & Bradley. Educ: Harvard Univ, BS, 38; Univ Wash Law Sch, 39. Polit & Govt Pos: Past pres, Calif & Santa Monica Bay Coun; dep chmn, Dem Nat Comt, 60; Under Secy Com for Transportation, 61-65; mem, Alaska Rail & Hwy Comn, 61-72. Bus & Prof Pos: F M Martin Grain & Milling Co, Inc, Cheney, Wash, 39-41; wholesale hardware & raw materials bus, Seattle, 46-50; retail auto & real estate bus, Calif & Ariz, 50-; Panama Canal Corp, 61- Mil Serv: Navy, Lt Comdr, 41-46. Mem: Navy League; Rotary. Mailing Add: 25 Oakmont Dr Los Angeles CA 90049

MARTIN, DAVID THOMAS (R)
b Kearney, Nebr, July 9, 07; m to Margaret Taylor; c David K, Patricia Maloney & John L. Educ: Dartmouth Col. Polit & Govt Pos: Chmn, Nebr State Rep Comt, 49-54; mem, Rep Nat Comt, 52-54; US Rep, 60-75, ranking mem, Rules Comt & vchmn, Select Comt on Comts, US House Rep. Bus & Prof Pos: Retail lumber bus in Kearney. Mem: Elks; Shriner. Relig: Presbyterian. Mailing Add: Kearney NE 68847

MARTIN, EDWIN MCCAMMON (D)
b Dayton, Ohio, May 21, 08; s Harry Judson Martin & Clara McCammon M; m 1936 to Margaret Milburn; c Patricia Ann (Mrs Pedro Sanjuan) & Edwin M, Jr. Educ: Northwestern Univ, BA, 29; Phi Beta Kappa; Delta Sigma Rho; Phi Delta Theta; Deru. Polit & Govt Pos: Economist, Cent Statist Bd, 35-38; temporary nat econ comt staff, Bur Labor Statist, 38-40; exec, War Prod Bd, 40-44; dep dir far eastern research & anal, Off Strategic Serv, 44-45; career officer, US Dept of State, Foreign Serv, 45-, chief, Div of Japanese & Korean Econ Affairs, 45-47, acting chief, Div Occupied Areas Econ Affairs, 47-48, dep dir, Off Int Trade Policy, 48-49, dir, Off European Regional Affairs, 49-52, spec asst to Secy of State for Mutual Security Affairs, 52-53, dep chief, US Mission to NATO & European Orgn, Paris, 53-57, minister-counr econ affairs, London, 57-59, Asst Secy of State for Econ Affairs, 60-62, Asst Secy of State for Inter-Am Affairs, 62-64, US Ambassador, Argentina, 64-68, chmn, Develop Assistance Comt, Orgn Econ Coop & Develop, 68- Publ: Allied Occupation of Japan, Stanford Press, 48; Development Assistance, 68-72, Orgn Econ Coop & Develop. Mem: Coun for Foreign Rels; Ctr for Inter-Am Rels; Soc for Int Develop; Am Mus Natural Hist; Kenwood Country Club, Washington, DC. Relig: Methodist. Legal Res: 911 Caldwell St Piqua OH 45356 Mailing Add: 16 Villa Said Paris 16 France

MARTIN, ELMER (D)
Tex State Rep
Mailing Add: 725 Elm St Colorado City TX 79512

MARTIN, ERNEST D (D)
Okla State Sen
b Hugo, Okla, Apr 13, 22; s James E Martin & Maude Estes M; m 1946 to Helton Ineta Hegwood; c Larry Lynn, Anita Susan & Terry Lee. Educ: Am Acad Art, Chicago, Ill, 40-42; Univ Okla Sch Pharmacy, BS, 50; Oupha. Polit & Govt Pos: Okla State Sen, 64- Bus & Prof Pos: Pres, 5th Dist, Okla Pharm Asn, 58- Mil Serv: Entered as Pvt, 42, Air Force, released as S/Sgt, 46; Good Conduct & Am Theater Medals. Mem: Am Legion; Mason (32 degree); Scottish Rite; Rotary. Relig: Baptist. Mailing Add: Box 51 Hoxbar Rte Ardmore OK 73401

MARTIN, GENE STEPHEN DARRYL (D)
b White Plains, NY, Feb 5, 49; s Earl O'Dell Martin & Mary Jones M; div; c Gene, Jr & Zorah. Educ: Rutgers Univ, 72- Polit & Govt Pos: Chairperson, Fairview Dem Comt, NY, 73-; deleg, Dem Nat Mid-Term Conf, 74; mem affirmative action comt, NY State Dem Party, 74- Mailing Add: 20 Madison Pl White Plains NY 10603

MARTIN, GRAHAM ANDERSON
US Ambassador to Repub of Vietnam
b Mars Hill, NC, Sept 22, 12; s Gustav Alexander Martin & H Hildreth Marshbanks M; m to Dorothy May Wallace, 1934; c Janet, Nancy (Mrs Hugh Charles Lane, Jr) & David. Educ: Wake Forest Univ, AB, 32. Hon Degrees: DHL, Campbell Col (NC), 68; LLB, Wake Forest Univ, 69. Polit & Govt Pos: Aide to dep adminr, Nat Recovery Admin, 33-36; asst to chmn, Soc Security Bd, 36-37, dist mgr, 37-41; regional dir, Fed Security Agency, 41-42, chief of field opers, 46; branch chief, War Assets Admin, 46-47; career officer, US Foreign Serv, 47-; attache, Am Embassy, Paris, 47-50, coordr European regional admin affairs, 50, counr, 51, asst chief of mission, 53-55; Dept State adv, Air War Col, 55-57; spec asst to Under Secy of State for Econ Affairs, 57-59; spec asst to Under Secy of State, 59-60; consul gen, Geneva, 60-61, US rep, UN European Off & other Int Orgns, 60-62; dep asst adminr for Latin Am & dep US coordr, Alliance for Progress, 62-63; US Ambassador to Thailand & US rep, SEATO & ECAFE, 63-67; spec asst to Secy of State for Refugee-Migration Affairs, 67-69; US Ambassador to Italy, 69-73; US Ambassador to Repub of Vietnam, 73- Bus & Prof Pos: Newspaper correspondent, Washington, DC, 32-33. Mil Serv: Entered as 2nd Lt, Army Air Force, 42, released as Col, 46; Legion of Merit, Bronze Star. Publ: Toward a modern diplomacy, report to Am Foreign Serv Asn, 68. Mem: Am Acad Polit & Soc Sci; Am Foreign Serv Asn (vpres, 62-63); Univ Club, Washington, DC. Honors & Awards: Distinguished Honor Award, Dept of State, 67; Plaque for Humanitarian Serv, Nat Conf on World Refugee Problems, 69. Legal Res: Thomasville NC Mailing Add: c/o US Dept of State Washington DC 20521

MARTIN, HAROLD (D)
NJ State Assemblyman
b West New York, NJ, Feb 25, 18; s Harry Martin & Tillie M (both deceased); m 1956 to Reba Lerner; c Gary, Terry, Susan & Peter. Educ: Rutgers Univ, New Brunswick, BA in polit sci, 40, scholar, 41, MA in polit sci, 47; Tau Kappa Alpha. Polit & Govt Pos: Mem planning bd, Cresskill, NJ, 63-64; freeholder, Bd Freeholders, Bergen Co, 65-67; mem planning bd, Bergen Co, 66-67; NJ State Assemblyman, Dist 39, 73- Bus & Prof Pos: Economist foreign & domestic research, Fed Reserve Bank of New York, 47-49; sales rep in electronics, Harold Martin, Inc, 49-63; stocks & bonds acct exec, Shearson-Hammill & Co, 63-65; econ consult, self-employed, 68-73. Mil Serv: Entered as Pvt, Army, 43, released as 2nd Lt, 46, after serv in Am Theatre of Opers, 45-46; Good Conduct Medal. Mailing Add: 165 Palisade Ave Cresskill NJ 07626

MARTIN, JAMES DOUGLAS (R)
b Tarrant, Ala, Sept 1, 18; s Richard Edward Martin & Mary Graham M; m 1959 to Patricia Byrd Huddleston; c James Douglas, Jr, Annette Graham & Richard Eugene. Polit & Govt Pos: Cand, US Senate, 62; US Rep, Seventh Dist, Ala, until 66; cand, Gov Ala, 66; deleg, Rep Nat Conv, 68; Rep Nat Committeeman, Ala, 68-72. Bus & Prof Pos: Pres, Assoc Industs of Ala & Am Oil Jobbers. Mil Serv: Entered as Pvt, Army, released as Maj, after serv as battery comdr, artil, with Gen Patton's Third Army, Europe & intel officer with Army of Occup. Mem: Gadsden-Etowah CofC (pres); Kiwanis (pres & lt gov); Am Red Cross. Relig: Methodist. Mailing Add: PO Box 407 Gadsden AL 35902

MARTIN, JAMES GRUBBS (R)
US Rep, NC
b Savannah, Ga, Dec 11, 35; s Arthur M Martin & Mary Grubbs M; m 1957 to Dorothy McAulay; c James, Jr, Emily & Benson. Educ: Davidson Col, BS in chem, 57; Princeton Univ, PhD, chem, 60; Beta Theta Pi. Polit & Govt Pos: Mem, Mecklenburg Co Comnrs, Charlotte, 66-72, chmn, 66-68 & 70-72; chmn, Centralina Coun Govt, 68-70; US Rep, NC, 73-, mem, Ways & Means Comt, US House Rep. currently, mem subcomts on Health, Taxation & Oversight. Bus & Prof Pos: Asst prof chem, Davidson Col, 60-64, assoc prof, 64-72. Mem: Mason. Relig: Presbyterian. Legal Res: Greenway St Davidson NC 28036 Mailing Add: 115 Cannon House Office Bldg Washington DC 20515

MARTIN, JAMES PAUL (D)
b Lake Charles, La, Mar 10, 29; s Dr Claude A Martin & Ruth McLees M; m 1955 to Bernardine Fontenot; c Claude A, III, Paul M, Andree M & John S. Educ: Univ Southwest La, 48; Springhill Col, BS, 50. Polit & Govt Pos: Mem exec comt, Jefferson Davis Parish Dem Comt, 56-71; mayor, Welsh, La, 67-72; mem adv bd, Urban Studies Inst, La State Univ, New

Orleans, 68-72; bd mem, Southwest Dist Law Enforcement Planning Coun, 70-72; comn mem, La Law Enforcement & Admin of Criminal Justice, 71; La State Rep, 72- Bus & Prof Pos: Cattlemen, Welsh, La, 53-67; field underwriter, NY Life Ins Co, 53-; estate mgr, Welsh, La, 56- Mil Serv: Entered as Pvt, Army, 51, released as Cpl, 53, after serv in 585 Ord Main Co, ETO, 52-53. Mem: PAR (trustee); Nat Asn Life Underwriters; Welsh Rotary Club; Welsh CofC; KofC. Honors & Awards: Welsh Citizen Newspaper Citizen of Year, 64; Boy Scouts Silver Beaver Award, 67. Relig: Catholic. Legal Res: 401 S Elm St Welsh LA 70591 Mailing Add: 115 S Adams St Welsh LA 70591

MARTIN, JAMES R, JR **(D)**
Secy, Anne Arundel Co Dem Cent Comt, Md
b Annapolis, Md, Nov 3, 48; s James Risto Martin, MD (deceased) & Mabel Yutzy M; single. Educ: Anne Arundel Community Col, Arnold, Md, 67-68; Univ Md, College Park, BA, 72. Polit & Govt Pos: Nonvoting youth mem, Md Dept Social Serv Adv Bd, 71-74; mem, Young Dem of Anne Arundel Co, Md, currently; legis asst, Baltimore City Deleg, Md Gen Assembly, 72 & 74; secy, Anne Arundel Co Dem Cent Comt, 74-; mem affirmative action comt, Md Dem Party, 74-, mem comn to study young Dem, 75- Bus & Prof Pos: Proprietor, Annapolis Electro-Print, 73- Mem: Harundale Youth Ctr, Inc (pres bd dirs, 74-75); New Dem Coalition of Md, Inc (rec secy, 73-76); Anne Arundel Co Bicentennial Comn. Honors & Awards: Cert in Afro-Am Studies, Univ Md, College Park, 72. Relig: Episcopal. Mailing Add: 180 Main St Annapolis MD 21401

MARTIN, JEROME ALBERT **(D)**
Wis State Sen
b Rockland, Wis, Sept 24, 08; s Michael James Martin & Elizabeth Antoinette M; m 1964 to Lillian Emilly Feit. Educ: St Norberts Col, Depere, Wis, 28 & 29. Polit & Govt Pos: Mem, Manitowoc Co Bd, Wis, 58-70, chmn, 62-70; pres, Village Whitelaw, 69-71; mem Wis adv comt, Co Bd Asn, 64-70; mem, Task Force on Welfare Payments, 70-71; Wis State Sen, First Dist, 71- Bus & Prof Pos: Dir, Manitowoc Co Bank, currently; pres, Oil Jobbing Agency, 37- Mem: Lions; Eagles; Elks; Izaak Walton League; KofC. Relig: Roman Catholic. Legal Res: Box 6 Whitelaw WI 54247 Mailing Add: State Capitol 409 South Madison WI 53702

MARTIN, JIMMY LEEWOOD **(D)**
SC State Sen
b Aynor, SC, Aug 24, 34; s Marvin Pettaway Martin, Sr & Eva Hucks M; m 1955 to Betty Jones; c Melony, Jimmy L, Jr & Tanner Shay. Educ: Univ SC, BS, 61. Polit & Govt Pos: SC State Rep, 68-70; SC State Sen, Dist Eight, 72- Bus & Prof Pos: Pres, Jimmy Martin Realty, 64- & Martin & Assoc, 66- Mil Serv: Entered as Seaman, Navy, 53, released as Airman, 55. Mem: Bd Realtors; Home Builders Asn; Boy Scouts (bd); CofC; WOW. Honors & Awards: Boss of Year, Cayce-West Columbia Jaycees, 73. Relig: United Methodist. Legal Res: 953 Riverview Dr West Columbia SC 29169 Mailing Add: 1611 Augusta Rd West Columbia SC 29169

MARTIN, JOHN ALFRED **(D)**
SC State Sen
b Shellman, Ga, Apr 11, 21; s James A Martin & Ada Bass M; m to Mary M Boulware; c Linda, John, Jr, Marianne & Dubose Rivers. Educ: Univ SC, LLB, 47. Polit & Govt Pos: SC State Rep, 51-52; SC State Sen, 53- Bus & Prof Pos: Lawyer. Mil Serv: Navy, 43-46; Lt(jg), Naval Res. Mailing Add: State House Columbia SC 29211

MARTIN, JOHN ALLEN **(R)**
Dir Research, SC Rep Party
b Anderson, SC, June 19, 47; s James Roy Martin, Jr & Alma Murray M; m 1967 to Ellen Margaret Jervis; c John Allen, Jr. Educ: Clemson Univ, BA, cum laude, 69; Univ SC, 69-; Gamma Beta Phi; Col Rep; Campus Crusade for Christ; Baptist Student Union. Polit & Govt Pos: Dir research, SC Rep Party, 72- Bus & Prof Pos: Computer programmer, SC Elec & Gas, 71-72. Relig: Baptist. Legal Res: 101 Harden St Columbia SC 29205 Mailing Add: PO Box 5247 Columbia SC 29250

MARTIN, JOHN BUTLIN **(R)**
b Grand Rapids, Mich, Oct 3, 09; s John B Martin & Althea Winchester M; m 1934 to Helen Hickam; c Richard H, Judith Hartig & Gillian Sorensen. Educ: Dartmouth Col, AB, 31; Oxford Univ, Rhodes scholar & BLitt, 33; Univ Mich Law Sch, JD, 36; Delta Kappa Epsilon; Phi Delta Phi. Polit & Govt Pos: Legal secy to chmn, Securities & Exchange Comn, 36-38; first asst, State Div Securities, Ohio, 39-41; dep dir, Nat Off Civil Defense, 42-44; Mich State Sen, 17th Dist, 48-50; Auditor Gen, Mich, 50-54; chmn, Mich Comn on Aging, 57-67; Rep Nat Coord Comt Task Force on Aging; Rep Nat Committeeman, Mich, 57-68; deleg, Mich State Const Conv, 62-63; chmn, Gov Spec Comn Crime, Delinquency & Admin of Criminal Justice, 67-68; deleg, Rep Nat Conv, 68; Comnr on Aging, Dept of Health, Educ & Welfare, 69-73; spec asst to the President for the Aging, 69-73. Bus & Prof Pos: Partner, Bidwell, Schmidt & Martin, 46-51 & Harrington, Waer, Cary & Martin, 58-68; consult, Am Asn of Retired Persons, 73- Mil Serv: Entered as Lt(jg), Naval Res, 44, released as Lt Comdr, 46, after Serv in Off Strategic Serv, ETO, 44-46. Mem: Grand Rapids, Mich State, DC & Am Bar Asns. Relig: Unitarian. Legal Res: 6011 Grand River Dr SE Ada MI 49301 Mailing Add: 7607 Glendale Rd Chevy Chase MD 20015

MARTIN, JOHN L **(D)**
Speaker, Maine House of Rep
b Eagle Lake, Maine, June 5, 41; s Frank Martin, Jr & Edwidge Raymond M; single. Educ: Ft Kent State Teachers Col, 59-61; Univ Maine, BA, 63; grad work in polit sci, 63-64; Young Dem; treas, Pub Mgt Club. Polit & Govt Pos: Mem platform comt, Maine Dem Conv, 64-66; mem Allagash-St John Study Comt, 64-68; pres, Maine Young Dem, 64-68; mem & clerk, Intergovt Rels Comn, 64-; mem, Aroostook Co Dem Comt, 64-, treas, 69-70; chmn, Eagle Lake Dem Town Comt, 64-72; Maine State Rep, 65-, Minority Leader, Maine House Rep, 71-74, Speaker, 75-; mgr & campaign coordr, Elmer H Violette Campaign for US Senate, 66; mem, Gov Task Force Govt Reorgn, 67-; chmn, Gov Task Force Dickey-Lincoln, 67-68; comptroller & adv, Edmund S Muskie Vice Presidential Campaign, 68; mem, Maine Comn Party Struct & Deleg Selection, 69; treas & coordr, Maine for Muskie Comt, 70; alt deleg, Dem Nat Conv, 72; chmn, Land Use Regulation Comn, 72-73. Bus & Prof Pos: Instr, Ft Kent Community High Sch, 65-72; agt, Union Mutual Life Ins Co, 69-; part-time instr, Univ Maine, Ft Kent, 72- Mem: Nat Educ Asn; Northern Maine Gen Hosp, Inc (treas); Peoples' Benevolent Hosp (trustee); Eagle Lake Water & Sewer Dist (trustee); CofC; KofC. Honors & Awards: Ft Kent, Maine Jaycees Outstanding Young Man of 67. Relig: Roman Catholic; past pres, St Mary's Church Adv Parish Bd. Legal Res: Church St Eagle Lake ME 04739 Mailing Add: PO Box 276 Eagle Lake ME 04739

MARTIN, JOHN MARSHALL, JR **(D)**
b Martin, Tenn, Jan 4, 18; s John Marshall Martin & Luella Hefley M; m 1952 to Dorothy Shands; c John Marshall, III & Mary Luella. Educ: Univ Tenn, BA, 39, JD, 48; Johns Hopkins Univ, MA, 50; Sigma Chi; Sigma Nu Phi. Polit & Govt Pos: Chief legis sect, US War Claims Comn, 51-54; prof staff mem, Comt on Ways & Means, US House of Rep, 56-57, asst chief counsel, 58-67, chief counsel, 68- Mil Serv: Entered as Ens, Naval Res, 41, released as Lt, 46, after serv in Amphibious Forces, Atlantic & Pac, 42-46. Relig: Methodist. Mailing Add: 6909 Ft Hunt Rd Alexandria VA 22307

MARTIN, JOSEPHINE C **(R)**
NH State Rep
Mailing Add: Chestnut Hill Rd Amherst NH 03031

MARTIN, LOUIS EMANUEL **(D)**
b Shelbyville, Tenn, Nov 18, 12; s Louis Emanuel Martin & Willa Hill M; m 1937 to Gertrude E Scott; c Trudy, Anita, Toni, Linda & Lisa. Educ: Univ of Mich, AB, 34. Hon Degrees: LLD, Harvard, 70. Polit & Govt Pos: Mem bd supvrs, Wayne Co, Mich, 2 terms in 40's; dep chmn, Dem Nat Comt, 60-, mem, McGovern Comn, currently. Bus & Prof Pos: Ed & publ, Mich Chronicle, 36-59; ed-in-chief, Chicago Daily Defender, 47-59; vpres & ed, Sengstacke Newspapers, 69- Mem: Nat Urban League (vpres, 65-); Overseas Press Club; Nat Press Club; Fed Club. Relig: Catholic. Mailing Add: 5555 S Everett Ave Chicago IL 60637

MARTIN, MARILYN SUE **(D)**
b Old Glory, Tex, Jan 8, 35; d Willie Lee Hatch & Cleo Trice H; m 1955 to Lloyd C Martin; c Larry Alvin, David Scott & Bruce Allan. Educ: Univ Tex, 64-65; Sam Houston State Univ, 69-71; Alpha Delta Pi Sorority Alumni, Delta Mu Chap. Polit & Govt Pos: Deleg, Dem Mid-Term Conf, 74; deleg, Tex State Dem Conv, 74. Bus & Prof Pos: Mgr, San Jacinto Co Div, Walker Co Title Co, 72- Mem: Huntsville Study Club (pres, 73-74); Huntsville PTA (pres, 74-75); March of Dimes (chmn mothers' march, 73). Relig: Baptist. Mailing Add: 237 Royal Oaks Huntsville TX 77340

MARTIN, MARION E **(R)**
b Kingman, Maine, Jan 14, 00; d William H Martin & Florence MacLaughlin M; single. Educ: Bradford Acad, 17; Univ Maine, BA, 35; Wellesley Col, 2 years; Yale Law Sch, 36-37; Northwestern Univ Law Sch, summer 37. Hon Degrees: MA, Bates Col, 38; LLD, Nasson Col, 53 & Univ Maine, 72; Phi Beta Kappa; Sigma Mu Sigma; Alpha Omicron Pi. Polit & Govt Pos: Maine State Rep, 31-35; Maine State Sen, 35-39; Rep Nat Committeewoman, Maine, 36-47, asst chmn, 37-47; chmn, Bd of Boiler Rules & Regulations, Maine, 47-72; Comnr Labor & Indust, 47-72; mem, Indust Accident Comn, 47-72; chmn, Bd of Elevator Rules & Regulations, 49-72; chmn, Construction Safety Bd, 55-72; govt adv, Int Labor Orgn, 58 & 59; mem, Nat Comn on State Workmen's Compensation Laws, 71-72. Mem: Maine Lung Asn (bd dirs, 48-); Nat Safety Coun (bd dirs, 50-, exec bd, 52-, vchmn bd dirs, 74-); Maine Apprenticeship Coun; Vocational Educ (mem adv coun, 74-); Am Arbit Asn (panel mem, 72-). Honors & Awards: Distinguished Serv Award, Am Asn Univ Women, 50; Soroptomist Award of Achievement, New Eng Region, 52; Deborah Morton Award, Westbrook Jr Col, 64; Roselle W Huddilston Award, Maine Tuberc Asn, 66; Distinguished Serv Award to Safety, Indust Conf of Nat Safety Coun, 71; Award of Merit, Secy of Labor, 72; hon mem, Asn Labor Mediation Agencies, 72. Relig: Episcopal. Mailing Add: Westview Ave Hallowell ME 04347

MARTIN, MARY AGNES **(D)**
Conn State Sen
b Baltimore, Md, July 18, 25; d John Kukon & Helen Jones K; wid; c John Thomas, Howard Wright & Kathleen Helen. Polit & Govt Pos: Representative, Town Meeting, Groton, Conn, 64-68, mem, Bd Selectmen, 69-71, mem, Town Coun, 73-74; Conn State Rep, 71-73; Conn State Sen, 18th Dist, 75- Bus & Prof Pos: With Automatic Retailers Am, Chas Pfizer, Groton, Conn, 64-66; Conn Bank & Trust Co, Groton, 67-68; Outlet Co, New London, 68-70. Relig: Catholic. Mailing Add: 34 Pegasus Dr Groton CT 06340

MARTIN, MARY ELIZABETH **(D)**
b Wellsville, Mo, Sept 23, 02; d William Frank Williams & Mary Elizabeth Reiper W; div; c William Herbert & Kenneth Leon Martin. Educ: Wellsville High Sch, Mo, 16-20. Polit & Govt Pos: Cosmetology inspector, 56-; committeewoman, Wellsville uppe Loutre, Mo, 60-; chmn, Montgomery Co Dem Cent Comt, formerly. Mem: VFW; Methodist Guild; Eagles; Nat Hairdressers Cosmetology Asn; Dem State Club Mo. Relig: Methodist. Mailing Add: 217 Bates Wellsville MO 63384

MARTIN, MARY K **(R)**
VChmn, Parke Co Rep Party, Ind
b Rockville, Ind, July 6, 14; d Lyman Thompson & Eliza Bain T; m 1934 to Robert E Martin; c Cynthia A, Kathleen J (Mrs Bruce H Marshall), John J, Robert W & James E. Educ: Union Twp High Sch, 28-32. Polit & Govt Pos: Precinct vcommitteewoman, Parke Co Rep Party, Ind, 52-, co vchmn, 64-; mgr, Rockville License Br, 69- Relig: Protestant. Mailing Add: RR 1 Box 179 Rockville IN 47872

MARTIN, PEGGY SMITH **(D)**
b Corinth, Miss, May 22, 31; d Douglas Morris & Hattie Aycox M (deceased); div; c Genedrick & Sandra Smith. Educ: Univ Chicago, 52-54; Kennedy-King Col, 66-70. Polit & Govt Pos: Pres, Young Dem Club, Fourth Ward & precinct capt, 26th Precinct, Chicago, 49-55; off deleg, Young Dem Am Conv, 51; exec vpres, Young Dem Cook Co, 51-53; vchmn, Young Dem Hospitality Comn, Dem Nat Conv, 52; vchmn, Reelection of Martin H Kennelly Comt, 55; chmn, Univ & Col Drive for Stevenson-Kefauver, 56; deleg, Dem Nat Conv, 72; Ill State Rep, 26th Dist, 73-74; chairperson, 26th Dist Citizens Comt, currently. Mem: Proj Reach (bd mem); Concern Women-War on Crime; Ill Acad Criminology; Chicago Urban League; People United to Save Humanity. Honors & Awards: Outstanding Woman of Year, League of Black Women, 72; First Black Woman to ever serve as Temporary Speaker of the House, 73; Legislative Award, Ill Optometric Asn, 73. Relig: Roman Catholic. Mailing Add: 6810 S Loomis Blvd Chicago IL 60636

MARTIN, RICHARD E (DICK) **(D)**
Mo State Rep
Mailing Add: 1814 Lovers Lane Terr St Joseph MO 64505

MARTIN, RICHARD R **(D)**
Conn State Rep
Mailing Add: 18 Raymond St New London CT 06320

MARTIN, ROGER ALLEN (D)
Del State Sen
b Delmar, Md, Feb 27, 34; s Oscar Palmer Martin & Ruth Taylor M; m 1960 to Adelaide Naylor; c Lisa & Susan. Educ: Univ Del, BA, 61, MA, 72. Polit & Govt Pos: Del State Sen, 73- Bus & Prof Pos: Teacher Ger lang. Mil Serv: Entered as Pvt, Army, 54, released as Sgt SP-2, 57, after serv in Intel Corps, Ger, 55-57. Relig: Methodist. Mailing Add: 13 Pinedale Rd Newark DE 19711

MARTIN, ROGER EDWARD (R)
Ore State Rep
b Portland, Ore, Mar 10, 35; s Ray Lynn Martin & Georgianna Fay Benson M; m 1958 to Janet Joan; c Christopher D, David J & Kathleen E. Educ: Univ Ore, BS, 57; Phi Delta Theta. Polit & Govt Pos: Ore State Rep, 67- Bus & Prof Pos: Vpres, Martin Electric Co, 65; vpres, Western Utility Supply, currently. Mil Serv: 2nd Lt, Army, 57-58; Capt, Army Res, 64. Mem: Rotary; Elks. Relig: Catholic. Mailing Add: 13750 SW Kraus Rd Lake Oswego OR 97034

MARTIN, ROLAND DANNY (D)
Maine State Rep
b Sinclair, Maine, Jan 11, 49; s Roland L (Val) Martin (deceased) & Theresa Chamberland M; m 1970 to Laurette Mazerolle; c Shannon & Jason Val. Educ: Wisdom High Sch, grad, 67. Polit & Govt Pos: Chmn, Dem Party, Sinclair, Maine, 72-; mem, State & Co Dem Comt, 72-; Maine State Rep, 75- Bus & Prof Pos: Mgr, Martin Sporting Camps, Sinclair, Maine, 67- Mil Serv: Entered as Pvt, Army Nat Guard, 67, currently 1st Lt, commanding officer, C-Battery, 152nd Artillery; Fort Kent Maine. Mem: KofC; Am Legion; Madawaska CofC (hon dir); Sinclair Sanitary Dist (chmn). Relig: Catholic. Mailing Add: Box 131 St Agatha ME 04772

MARTIN, ROY BUTLER, JR (D)
b Norfolk, Va, May 13, 21; s Roy Butler Martin & Anne Holman M; m 1948 to Louise Freeman Eggleston; c Roy Butler, III & Anne Beverly. Educ: William & Mary Norfolk Div, 39-40; Univ of Va, BS in com, 43; Chi Phi; Alpha Kappa Psi. Polit & Govt Pos: Former chmn, Mayor's Youth Comn, Norfolk, Va, formerly; mem, Gov Comt on Youth, formerly; Mayor, Norfolk, 62-74; mem adv bd, Nat League of Cities; vpres & mem comt commun develop, US Conf Mayors, formerly; mem Southeastern Va Planning Dist Comn, formerly; VALC Zoning Procedures Comt, currently. Bus & Prof Pos: Pres, Foote Bros & Co, currently; bd dirs, First Nat Bank of Norfolk, Dominion Bank Shares & Atlantic Permanent Savings & Loan, currently. Mil Serv: Entered as Ens, Navy, 43, released as Lt, 46, after serv in Pac; Lt, Intel Unit, Naval Res, 48-52. Mem: Va Munic League (past vpres, pres & mem exec comt); Tidewater Va Develop Coun (trustee); Norfolk Boys Club (bd dirs); Old Dominion Col Educ Found (bd dirs); Harbor Club. Relig: Episcopal. Legal Res: 1519 Commonwealth Ave Norfolk VA 23505 Mailing Add: City Hall Norfolk VA 23510

MARTIN, SIDNEY (D)
Fla State Rep
Mailing Add: PO Box 51 Hawthorne FL 32640

MARTIN, TALMAGE MCKINLEY, JR (R)
Chmn, Carroll Co Rep Party, Ga
b Bowdon, Ga, July 12, 23; s Talmage McKinley Martin, Sr & Myrtice Johnson M; m 1951 to Carol Lahman; c Katherine Elizabeth, Anne Marie & Scott William. Educ: Univ Calif, San Francisco, AB & MD; Am Bd Surg, dipl; Nu Sigma Nu. Polit & Govt Pos: Chmn, Carroll Co Rep Party, Ga, 75- Bus & Prof Pos: Chief Surg, Tanner Hosp, Carrollton, Ga, 73- Mil Serv: Entered as 1st Lt, Air Force, 51, released as Capt, 53, after serv in Keesler AFB, Miss. Mem: Am Col Surg. Relig: Methodist. Mailing Add: Rte 9 Box 175 Carrollton GA 30117

MARTIN, WADE OMER, JR (D)
Secy of State, La
b Arnaudville, La, Apr 18, 11; s Wade O Martin & Alice Mills M; m 1938 to Juliette Bonnette; c Merle Mary, Marcelle, Wade O, III, David, Wallace & Gregory. Educ: Southwestern La Inst, BA, 32; La State Univ, LLB, 35; Gamma Eta Gamma; Kappa Sigma. Polit & Govt Pos: Asst attorney gen, Baton Rouge, La, 35-40; Secy of State, La, 44- Bus & Prof Pos: Attorney-at-law, 40-44. Mem: Am & La Bar Asns; Nat Asn of Secretaries of State; KofC. Mailing Add: 210 LSU Ave Baton Rouge LA 70808

MARTIN, WILLIAM ROY (D)
Chmn, Fayette Co Dem Exec Comt, Ala
b Millerville, Ala, May 29, 03; s John Simeon Martin (Methodist Minister) & Lelia Ophelia Strong M; m 1931 to Frankie A Nuckols; c John Arthur; grandchildren, Mary Frances, John A, Jr & Teresa Ann. Educ: High Sch, Elkmont, Ala, 24; Bus Courses, Birmingham & Montgomery, Ala & Nashville, Tenn. Polit & Govt Pos: Chmn, Fayette Co Dem Exec Comt, Ala, 44- Bus & Prof Pos: Stockman, various companies, 24-36; bookkeeper, Fayette Co Comnr Court, 43-48; gen mgr, Bagwell Coal Co, Carbon Hill, 49-50; bookkeeper, Newton Lumber Co, Bankston & Tuscaloosa, 50- Mem: Lions (held all offices, info chmn, Dist 34D, Int, 72-73); Mason (dist lectr, 14th dist Lodge of Ala), Charles Baskerville Lodge, Fayette (Worshipful Master, 5 times); F&AM (Sr Grand Steward, 67-68, Jr Grand Deacon, 69-70 & all offices, including Master 5 times). Honors & Awards: Col, Gov Staff; Citation from F D Roosevelt for bond sales during World War II; Cert of Appreciation for serv & 26 year Perfect Attendance Award, Int Lions. Relig: Methodist; steward & former trustee & supt, Sunday Sch, First Methodist Church, Fayette. Mailing Add: 205 Second Ave NW Fayette AL 35555

MARTINDELL, ANNE (D)
NJ State Sen
Polit & Govt Pos: NJ State Sen, currently; mem, Dem Nat Comt, NJ, currently. Mailing Add: 31-33 N Willow St Trenton NJ 08608

MARTINELLI, ANGELO R (R)
Mayor, Yonkers, NY
b Bronx, NY, Sept 13, 27; s Ralph Martinelli & Rose Patti M; m to Carol Medatto; c Michael, Paul, Robert, Richard, Thomas & Ralph. Educ: Syracuse Univ, 44; Rutgers Univ, 45. Polit & Govt Pos: Mayor, Yonkers, NY, 74- Bus & Prof Pos: Pres, Gazette Press Inc, 45-; Wall St Pub Inst, 65- & Surburban Publ Co Inc, 70-; owner, Radio Sta WWLE, 68- Mil Serv: Entered as Pvt, Army, 44, released as T-4, 45, after serv in 1st Army. Publ: Ed, Stock Market Mag & Hudson Valley Mag, monthly, currently. Mem: Westchester Employing Printers Asn (pres); Yonkers CofC (vpres); Enrico Fermi Educ Fund (bd trustees); Yonkers Heart Fund (co-chmn); St Eugene's Parish Coun. Honors & Awards: Man of the Year, Jewish Community Ctr, 74. Relig: Roman Catholic. Legal Res: 40 Harvard Ave Yonkers NY 10710 Mailing Add: Mayor's Off City Hall Yonkers NY 10701

MARTINEZ, ALEX G (D)
NMex State Sen
b 1926. Educ: St Michael's Col; Col Santa Fe. Polit & Govt Pos: NMex State Rep, 63-66; NMex State Sen, 67- Bus & Prof Pos: Agt for AT&SF Rwy. Mil Serv: Army, Pac Theater, 43-45; Purple Heart with 2 Clusters. Mem: Am Legion; VFW; Kiwanis; Order of Purple Heart; YMCA (bd dir). Relig: Catholic. Mailing Add: 1949 Hopi Rd Santa Fe NM 87501

MARTINEZ, CHARLES WILLIAM (D)
Northern Div Treas, Calif Dem State Cent Comt
b North Platte, Nebr, Feb 1, 43; s Joseph J Martinez & Sarah Ann Stout M; m 1967 to Dolores Estrada Duran; c Laura Jean & Shawn Lee. Educ: Sierra Jr Col, AA; Calif State Univ, Sacramento, BA Bus Admin; Delta Sigma Phi. Polit & Govt Pos: Alt deleg, Dem Nat Mid-Term Conf, 74; chmn, Placer Co Cent Comt, Calif, 74-; Northern Div Treas, Calif Dem State Cent Comt, 75- Mil Serv: Entered as E-1 Air Force, 61, released as E-4, 65, after serv in Nuclear Weapons Unit; Good Conduct Medal. Mem: Kiwanis; KofC; Econ Develop Comt, Placer Co; Roseville Community Hosp Assoc; Roseville Cult Comt. Relig: Catholic. Mailing Add: 3970 Annabelle Ave Roseville CA 95678

MARTINEZ, JESSE (D)
b Lovell, Wyo, Aug 19, 43; s Frank R Martinez & Juana Velasquez M; m 1965 to Reyes Juanita Florez; c Jennifer Rachel. Educ: Lovell High Sch, grad, 62. Polit & Govt Pos: Alt deleg, Dem Nat Conv, 72. Bus & Prof Pos: Leadman-warehouse, Ga Pac Corp. Mem: United Cement, Lime & Gypsum (pres, local 495, 68). Relig: Catholic. Mailing Add: Box 822 252 E Third St Lovell WY 82431

MARTINEZ, JOSEPH L (D)
Justice, NMex Supreme Court
b Revuelto, NMex; s Florenzio Martinez & Versabe Medina M; m to Carmen Baca; c Dr Inez, Dr Joseph L, Jr, Joanne & Damon Paul. Educ: Univ NMex, BS, 39; George Washington Univ, JD, 42. Polit & Govt Pos: Attorney Gen, NMex, 48-52, justice, NMex Supreme Court, 73- Relig: Catholic. Legal Res: 928 Avenida Manana NE Albuquerque NM 87110 Mailing Add: Box 848 Supreme Court Santa Fe NM 87501

MARTINEZ, THEODORA (D)
Mem, Dem Nat Comt, NY
Mailing Add: New York NY

MARTINEZ, WALTER K (D)
NMex State Rep
Mailing Add: Box 10 Grants NM 87020

MARTINIS, JOHN ANTHONY (D)
Wash State Rep
b Everett, Wash, June 4, 30; s Paul Martinis & Pearl Marincovich M; m 1950 to Virginia Olich; c Paulett, John, Tracy, Christie & Marty. Educ: Everett Jr Col, 48-49. Polit & Govt Pos: Port Comnr, Everett, Wash, 68-; Wash State Rep, 38th Dist, 69- Bus & Prof Pos: Owner, Bob's Sporting Goods, currently. Mem: Elks; Wash State Sportsmans Coun; Eagles; Wash State Environmental Coun. Relig: Catholic. Mailing Add: 1917 Broadway Everett WA 98201

MARTINSON, ROBERT WILLIAM (R)
NDak State Rep
b Bismarck, NDak, Dec 28, 46; s Edward L Martinson & Josephine Saldin M; single. Educ: Bismarck Jr Col, AA, 67; Mary Col (NDak), BS, 72; Alpha Tau Omega. Polit & Govt Pos: NDak State Rep, 72- Bus & Prof Pos: Pres, Martinson Assocs, 70- Mil Serv: Entered as Pvt, Army Nat Guard, released as Pvt, 69; Lt, NDak Nat Guard, currently; Virgil R Kottsick Award for Outstanding & Unselfish Serv; Army Leadership Award. Mem: Am Legion; Elks. Mailing Add: 1015 N Fourth St PO Box 178 Bismarck ND 58501

MARTINSON, RONALD LEE (R)
b Eveleth, Minn, Aug 19, 43; s Theodore Edwin Martinson & Marjorie Duame M; single. Educ: Univ Minn, BS, 66, MA, 68. Polit & Govt Pos: Admin asst to US Rep Bob Price, Tex, 71-74; admin asst to the Sgt-at-Arms US Senate, 75- Bus & Prof Pos: Instr, Elgin Community Col, Ill, 68-69; prof musician, organist & pianist, currently. Mem: Pi Gamma Mu. Mailing Add: 1347 S Carolina Ave SE Washington DC 20003

MARTI-NUNEZ, RAFAEL (POPULAR PARTY, PR)
Sen, PR Legis
b Caguas, PR, Jan 28, 32; s Jose Marti & Rosario Nunez; m 1974 to Marina Flores; c Rosalines, Maria Pilar, Margarita, Maria Socorro & Rafael. Educ: Notre Dame Univ, 49-51; Univ Zaragoza, MD, 60. Polit & Govt Pos: Pres, Munic City Bd, Popular Party, 68-; Sen, Popular Party, Humacao Dist, 72- Bus & Prof Pos: Pvt practice, Internal Med, 64- Mil Serv: Capt, Nat Guard, 64-67, PR. Mem: Am Asn Med; Asoc Medica de PR; Rotary Club; Mason (32 degree); Casa Espana. Legal Res: Verde Sur Caguas PR 00625 Mailing Add: Box 1205 Caguas PR 00625

MARTSCHINK, SHERRY SHEALY (R)
b Columbia, SC, Oct 26, 49; d Ryan Carthron Shealy & Elsie Elizabeth Porth S; m 1973 to Gustave Charles Martschink, Jr; c Tiffany Lynn. Educ: Columbia Col, 67; Univ SC, 69- Polit & Govt Pos: Deleg, co-chmn, SC Deleg & mem rules comt, Rep Nat Conv, 72; SC State Rep, 70-74, mem joint comt ment health, SC House Rep, 72-74, mem educ comt, 71-74; mem rule 29 comt, Rep Nat Comt, 73-75. Bus & Prof Pos: Dancing teacher, Columbia, SC, 67-73; organist-entertainer, 69-73; sch teacher, 70-71; pub rels, Martschink Beer Distributors, 74- Mem: Defense Adv Comt Women Serv; Charleston Co Am Cancer Soc (bd mem, 74-); Nat Order Women Legislators; Nat Asn Accredited Talent & Beauty Pageant Judges. Honors & Awards: SC Outstanding Young Woman of the Year, 73; One of Ten Outstanding Young Women in Nation, 73; Freedoms Found Valley Forge Medal, 74; One of Ten Am at 1973 NATO Conf, Brussels. Relig: Lutheran. Mailing Add: 1855 Ashley Hall Rd Charleston SC 29407

MARTY, JAMES FRANK (D)
b Monroe, Wis, Jan 21, 46; s Jack L Marty & Jeanette M Broege M; m 1968 to Marjorie E Perry. Educ: Univ Wis-Madison, BBA, 68; Univ Wis-Milwaukee, summers & eve, 69-71; Univ Okla, 72-74. Polit & Govt Pos: Chmn, Third Assembly Dist Dem Club, Waukesha Co,

70-72; vchmn, Waukesha Co Dem Party, 71-72, chmn, 72-73. Bus & Prof Pos: Instr math, Waukesha Pub Schs, 68-; exec secy, Educ Asn Waukesha, 68- Mem: Nat Coun Teachers of Math; UN Asn; Nat Educ Asn; Wis Educ Asn Coun. Mailing Add: 247 N Racine Ave Waukesha WI 53186

MARTY, LAWRENCE A (R)
Rep State Committeeman, Sweetwater Co, Wyo
b Platte Co, Nebr, June 17, 26; s Herman L Marty & Frances J Harvey M; m 1965 to Nellie M Moerke; c Karen L. Educ: Wayne State Teachers Col, 44-46; Creighton Sch of Law, 46-47 & 51-52; Univ Wyo, LLB, 54; Delta Theta Phi. Polit & Govt Pos: Munic judge, Green River, Wyo, 58-60; US Comnr, Sweetwater Co, Wyo, 58-70; chmn, Sweetwater Co Rep Cent Comt, 60-64 & 68-70; alt deleg, Rep Nat Conv, 64; Rep State Committeeman, Sweetwater Co, 64-66 & 70-; US Magistrate, 71- Bus & Prof Pos: Attorney-at-law, 54- Mem: Am & Wyo Bar Asns; Lions (past pres & zone chmn). Relig: Lutheran. Legal Res: 391 Hilcrest Way Green River WY 82935 Mailing Add: PO Box 231 Green River WY 82935

MARTZ, W WILSON (D)
Chmn, Bedford Co Dem Comt, Pa
b Dormont, Pittsburgh, Pa, Aug 28, 14; s John D Martz & Carolyn Hanson M; m 1938 to F LaRue Mensch; c W Wilson, Jr, Sandra (Mrs James Zembower), Gary L & Ned W. Educ: Pa State Col, 35. Polit & Govt Pos: Committeeman, Cumberland Village Twp Dem Comt, 54-62; vchmn, Bedford Co Dem Comt, 56-62, 71-73, chmn, 74-; supt hwys, Bedford Co, 71- Bus & Prof Pos: Mgr, Water Brooks Farm, Schellsburg, Pa, 38-45 & Louden Hill Farm, So Montrose, 45-46; adv for vets, Bedford Co Sch Bd, 45-55; supt dist II, Pa Turnpike Comn, 56-63. Mem: Bedford Artificial Breeding Coop (secy, 48-); Bedford Sch Dist Authority (secy, 55-). Mailing Add: 809 Preston St Bedford PA 15522

MARVEL, BILLY BRYAN (D)
b Bloomfield, Mo, Apr 6, 13; s Lewis W Marvel & Maude Mitchell M; m 1936 to Clarabelle Davis; c Louise (Mrs Essary), Emily (Mrs Penn) & David Roosevelt. Educ: Southeast Mo State Univ, 1 year. Polit & Govt Pos: Alderman, Poplar Bluff City Coun, Mo, 59-69; chmn, Butler Co Dem Comt, 63-72; deleg, Dem Nat Conv, 68; deleg, Dem Nat Mid-Term Conf, 74. Bus & Prof Pos: Owner & operator, Marvel Music Co, Mo, 47- Mem: Mason; Scottish Rite; Shrine. Relig: Protestant. Mailing Add: 406 North C St Poplar Bluff MO 63901

MARVEL, DOUGLAS JAMES (R)
Chmn, Grand Traverse Co Rep Comt, Mich
b Grand Island, Nebr, Feb 7, 44; s Richard Douglas Marvel & Oline Lindemann M; m 1967 to Mary Margaret Bradley. Educ: Mich State Univ, BS, 67. Polit & Govt Pos: Mem, Tenth Dist Rep Exec Comt, Mich, 73-; chmn, Grand Traverse Co Rep Comt, 75- Bus & Prof Pos: Plant mgr, RC Warren & Co, Inc, Traverse City, Mich, 67- Mailing Add: 14961 Shipman Rd Traverse City MI 49684

MARVEL, RICHARD DOUGLAS (R)
Nebr State Sen
b Hastings, Nebr, Dec 8, 17; s Archie Douglas Marvel & Ruth Capps M; m 1941 to Oline Ida Lindemann; c Douglas James & Anne Elizabeth. Educ: Univ Leipzig, Ger, 39; Hastings Col, BA, 40; Univ Nebr, MA, 60, PhD, 66; Eta Phi Lambda; Pi Gamma Mu. Polit & Govt Pos: Deleg, Nat Rep Conv, 48; co chmn, Rep Party, Nebr, 54-58; Nebr State Sen, 51-55 & 59-, chmn legis budget comt, 59- Mil Serv: Entered as Pvt, Army, 42, released as T/Sgt, 45, after serv in 119th AAA Group Hq, SPac, 43-45. Publ: The nonpartisan Nebraska unicameral, Midwest Legis Polit, 67; A member looks at the Nebraska unicameral, State Govt, summer 69. Mem: Educ Comn of the States (steering comt); AF&AM; VFW; Rotary; YMCA. Relig: Presbyterian. Mailing Add: 1249 N Lexington Hastings NE 68901

MARX, ROBERT PHILLIP (D)
Ore State Rep
b Oregon City, Ore, Jan 23, 49; s Joseph Wesley Marx & Louise Belen M; m 1968 to Paula Jayne Fisher; c Rachel Elizabeth & Justin Robert. Educ: Ore State Univ, BS in Polit Sci, 71; Pi Kappa Phi. Polit & Govt Pos: Campaign coordr, Students for McCarthy for President, 68; campaign dir, Cliff Trow for Sen, 69-70; Ore State Rep, Dist 34, 72- Bus & Prof Pos: Property appraiser, Marion Co. Honors & Awards: Star & Lamp Key Academic Award, Pi Kappa Phi, 69. Relig: Catholic. Legal Res: Rte 1 Box 64C Monmouth OR 97361 Mailing Add: State Capitol Salem OR 97310

MARYE, MADISON ELLIS (D)
Va State Sen
b Richmond, Va, Dec 3, 25; s Ambrose Madison Marye & Lelia Ellis M; m 1950 to Charlotte Urbas; c Charlotte Madison & James Madison. Educ: Univ Ga, Columbus Ctr, 57-59. Polit & Govt Pos: Va State Sen, 74-, mem, Com & Labor Comt, Gen Laws Comt, Local Govt Comt, Rehabilitation & Social Serv Comt, currently. Mil Serv: Entered as Pvt, Army, 44, released as Maj, 65, after serv in Europe, Korea, Vietnam, Panama & Hawaii; Combat Inf Badge; Bronze Star; Army Commendation Ribbon. Mem: Shawsville Ruritan Club (vpres); VFW; Am Legion; Am Nat Cattleman Asn. Relig: Presbyterian. Mailing Add: Shawsville VA 24162

MASANIAI, TEE ALOFAITULI
Assoc Judge, High Court, Am Samoa
b Am Samoa, Dec 1, 11; s Alofaituli Sanitoa Masaniai & Maria S Alofaituli M; m 1934; c Maria Pau, Iva Peters, Larry, Danny, Sanitoa, Tee Jr, Tagaimamao, Luisa, Eveline, Pili & Maotaotumua. Polit & Govt Pos: Assoc judge, High Court, Am Samoa, currently; high talking chief, Co of Vaifanua, East Dist, Am Samoa, currently. Mil Serv: Entered as A/S, Navy, 31, released as Boatswains Mate, 51. Mem: Am Samoa Bar Asn; Vet Asn. Relig: Latter-day Saint; pres, Tulao Br. Legal Res: Vatia American Samoa Mailing Add: PO Box 205 Pago Pago American Samoa

MASANZ, HUGO EDWARD (DFL)
Chmn, 45th Sen Dist Dem-Farmer-Labor Party, Minn
b St Paul, Minn, Aug 25, 25; s Joseph Carl Masanz & Hallie Thompson M; m 1951 to Dorothy Ann Hoffman; c Michael Robert & Mark Andrew. Educ: Mechanic Arts High Sch, 39-43. Polit & Govt Pos: Deleg, Ramsey Co Dem-Farmer-Labor Cent Comt, 62-70; chmn, 45th Sen Dist Dem-Farmer-Labor Cent Comt, 70-; deleg, Fourth Cong Dist Dem-Farmer-Labor Cent Comt, 70-; deleg, Minn State Dem-Farmer-Labor Cent Comt, 70- Bus & Prof Pos: Machine operator, US Bedding Co, St Paul, Minn, 48- Mil Serv: Entered as A/S, Navy, 43, released as Electricians Mate, 2/C, 46, recalled, 50-52, served in USS LST 686, SPac, 43-46 & Pac Res Fleet, 50-52; Am Theatre Ribbon; Asiatic Pac Ribbon with Three Stars; Philippine Liberation Ribbon with Two Stars. Mem: N End Improv Club; Upholsterers Union Local 61. Relig: Catholic. Mailing Add: 1306 N Dale St St Paul MN 55117

MASCO, DOROTHY BERYL (R)
Secy, Archuleta Co Rep Cent Comt, Colo
b Adelaide, S Australia, Mar 16, 18; d Albert Edward Hersey & Ida Tisher H; m 1944 to Charles Frederick Masco. Educ: Adelaide High Sch, S Australia, 4 years. Polit & Govt Pos: Secy, Archuleta Co Rep Cent Comt, Colo, 65- Bus & Prof Pos: Sales Counr, Fuller Brush Co, Salt Lake City, Utah, 65, PD dealer, Kansas City, Kans. Mem: Woman's Civic Club; Dr Mary Fisher Med Ctr Pagosa Springs (dir); Boy Scouts Am (counr); Bi-Centennial Fed Women's Clubs Plate (chmn). Relig: Methodist. Mailing Add: Box 412 Pagosa Springs CO 81147

MASCOLO, FREDERIC EDWARD (D)
Mem, Waterbury Dem Town Comt, Conn
b Waterbury, Conn, July 24, 29; s Edward Mascolo & Clelia Menichino M; m 1955 to Irene J Zoli; c Frederic D & Edward D. Educ: Seton Hall Univ, BS, 51; Georgetown Univ Law Sch, LLB, 53; Phi Alpha Delta. Polit & Govt Pos: Mem, Conn Dem State Comt, 62-64; city comptroller, Waterbury, 63-65; mem, Waterbury Dem Town Comt, 63-; alt deleg, Dem Nat Conv, 68 & 72; Judge of Probate, Waterbury, Wolcott & Middlebury Dist, Conn, 71- Bus & Prof Pos: Attorney-at-law, 54-; instr bus law, Mattatuck Community Col, 67-; owner & pres, Waterbury Dodgers, (Class AA Eastern League); dir, St Mary's Hosp, Waterbury, Conn; dir, Mattatuck Bank & Trust Co, Conn. Mil Serv: Entered as Pvt, Army, 55, released as SP-4, 57, after serv in Tenth Inf Div, Europe, 55-57. Mem: Am Bar Asn; Ital Am Dem Club; Conn Heart Asn; YMCA; Elks. Relig: Catholic. Mailing Add: 107 Eastfield Rd Waterbury CT 06708

MASLOFF, SOPHIE (D)
Secy, Pa Fedn Dem Women
b Pittsburgh, Pa, Dec 23, 17; d Louis Friedman & Jennie F; m 1939 to Jack Masloff; c Linda. Educ: Fifth Ave High Sch, grad, 36. Polit & Govt Pos: Secy, Allegheny Co Dem Women's Guild, Pittsburgh, Pa, 40-; Secy, Pa Fedn Dem Women, 67-; alt deleg, Dem Nat Conv, 68. Bus & Prof Pos: Chief Investr, Allegheny Co Court of Common Pleas, Pittsburgh, Pa, 40- Mem: B'nai B'rith; Hadassah. Relig: Jewish. Mailing Add: 3566 Beechwood Blvd Pittsburgh PA 15217

MASON, BRUCE BONNER (D)
Dem State Committeeman, Ariz
b Cleburne, Tex, Dec 19, 23; s Joseph Lee Mason & Daisy Bonner M; m 1946 to Jacqueline Tenery; c Douglas Lee. Educ: NTex State Col, BS, with highest degree, 47; Tex Christian Univ, MA, 49; Univ Tex, Austin, PhD, 52; Pi Sigma Alpha; Men's Independent Campus Asn. Polit & Govt Pos: Field surv off, Tex State Approval Agency, 48; consult, Ill Co Probs Comt, 58-60; pres, Champaign Co Dem Fedn of Ill Chap, 59; Dem precinct committeeman, Tempe, Ariz, 64-68; state co-chmn, Ariz McCarthy for Pres, 68; deleg, Dem Nat Conv, 68; Dem State Committeeman, Ariz, 70-, mem by-laws comt, Ariz State Dem Party, 72-; presidential elector, Ariz Dem Party, 72. Bus & Prof Pos: Asst prof, Northwestern State Col, La, 52-53, Memphis State Col, 53-54, & Univ Fla, 54-58; resident asst prof, Univ Ill, Urbana, 58-60; prof, Ariz State Univ, 60-; elec analyst, Am Broadcasting Co, 64, 68, 70 & 72. Mil Serv: Entered as Cadet, Army Air Corps, 42, released as Sgt, 45, after serv in Fourth Air Force, Nev, 43-45. Publ: Extra-Party Organizations in Illinois Politics, Univ Ill, 60; Arizona General Election Results, 1911-60, 61 & co-auth, Constitutional Government in Arizona, 4th ed, Ariz State Univ, 72. Mem: Am Polit Sci Asn; Am Soc for Pub Admin, Western Govt Research Asn; Am Civil Liberties Union; Ariz Dem Coun. Relig: Unitarian. Mailing Add: 320 E Fairmont Dr Tempe AZ 85282

MASON, CLARENCE EDWARD (R)
Chmn, Bailey Co Rep Comt, Tex
b Paint Rock, Tex, Nov 21, 24; s William Harry Mason & Maggie Williams M; m 1951 to Sondra Vannette Wagnon; c Clarence Edward, II, Linda Gail & Lisa Jane. Polit & Govt Pos: Pres, Parmer-Bailey Co Young Rep, Tex, 62-64; chmn, Parmer Bailey Co Rep Comt, 64-66 & 68- Mil Serv: Entered as Pvt, Army, 44, released as Pfc, 45, after serv in ETO, 44; Good Conduct Medal; Purple Heart. Mem: VFW; DAV. Relig: Church of Christ. Mailing Add: RFD 2 Box 240 Muleshoe TX 79347

MASON, DAVID GRAY (D)
Ky State Rep
Mailing Add: Hi-View St Eminence KY 40019

MASON, EDWARD JOSEPH (R)
Md State Sen
b Cumberland, Md, June 12, 30; s Bertrand Alphonsus Mason & Cora Gunning M; m 1952 to Sara Jane Dickerhoff; c Michael, Kathy & Patrick Scott. Educ: Strayer's Bus Col, Washington, DC. Polit & Govt Pos: Chmn, Allegany Co Rep State Cent Comt, Md, 69-70; Md State Sen, Dist 1-B, 71- Bus & Prof Pos: Restaurant proprietor, Mason's Barn, Cumberland, Md, 54- Mil Serv: Entered as Pfc, Air Force, 49, released as Pfc, 50. Mem: Rte 40 Asn (dir); Western Md CofC; Econ Develop Co. Honors & Awards: Young Rep of Year, Allegany Co, 67; Young Rep of Year, Md, 67 & 68. Relig: Roman Catholic. Legal Res: 1904 Bedford St Cumberland MD 21502 Mailing Add: Rte 2 Box 102-A Cumberland MD 21502

MASON, EDWYN E (R)
NY State Sen
b De Peyster, NY; m 1941 to Melva Bettinger; c Martha Anne & Richard Eric. Educ: Oswego State Teacher's Col, BS, 38; Syracuse Univ; Tex A&M Col; Univ Minn; Albany Law Sch, LLB. Polit & Govt Pos: Mem, Selective Serv Bd, town bd & justice of peace, Stamford, NY, formerly; NY State Assemblyman, 52-72, chmn assembly agr comt & vchmn joint legis comt on interstate affairs, formerly; NY State Sen, 72- Bus & Prof Pos: Instr shop courses; attorney, Rushmore, Mason, Marcus & Crocker, 41- Mil Serv: Army Mil Police. Mem: Am Legion; Am Bar Asn; Delaware Co Hist Soc; Odd Fellows; Mason. Honors & Awards: Award for Outstanding Contrib to Am Legion Boys State, NY State Am Legion, 68; Citation of Merit & Plaque by Rabbi Jacob Joseph Sch, Mother Yeshiva of Am, 69; Named Conserv Legislator of Year, NY State Conserv Coun, 70. Relig: Presbyterian. Mailing Add: Main St Hobart NY 13788

MASON, LOUIS, JR (D)
City Councilman, Pittsburgh, Pa
b Minneapolis, Minn, Mar 9, 15; s Louis Mason & Blanche Yancey M; m 1941 to Dorothea

Scott Harris. Educ: Univ Minn, BS, 40; Duquesne Univ, 45; Univ Pittsburgh, MA, 52; Omega Psi Phi; Loendi Club. Polit & Govt Pos: Asst dir, Mayor's Comn Fair Employ Practices, Pittsburgh, 53-55; dep dir, Mayor's Comn Human Rels, 55-63, exec dir, 63-67; city councilman, Pittsburgh, 67-, pres, City Coun, 70-; deleg, Dem Nat Conv, 68. Bus & Prof Pos: Asst dir indust rels, Urban League, Pittsburgh, 45-47, dir, 47-53. Mil Serv: Pvt, Army Inf, 43. Publ: The Extent of Membership and Participation of a Minority Group in Selected Trade Unions in Allegheny Co, 50; The Role of a Public Agency in Breaking Through Barriers to Open Occupancy, 56; Controlled Occupancy or Free Choice?, Comn on Human Rels, 63. Mem: Nat Asn Social Workers; Nat Asn Intergroup Rels Off; Soc Pub Admin; Hod Carriers Union; Dining Car Employees Union & Hotel & Restaurant Works Union. Relig: Episcopal; mem, Brain Trust Comt. Legal Res: 931 Clarissa St Pittsburgh PA 15219 Mailing Add: 510 City County Bldg Pittsburgh PA 15219

MASON, MARCELLA JUNE (D)
Chmn, Porter Co Dem Cent Comt, Ind
b Cannelton, Ind, Jan 19, 34; d Maurice Mason & Catherine Brunner M; single. Educ: Ind Univ, AB, 56; Alpha Xi Delta. Polit & Govt Pos: Secy, Second Dist Young Dem, Ind, 55-57, vpres, 57-65; secy, Porter Co Young Dem, 56-58, vpres, 58-59, pres, 59-60; vprecinct committeeman, Boone Twp, Porter Co, 60-62; vpres, Ind Young Dem, 61-63, conv chmn, 63, state conv chmn, 65; spec asst to pres, Young Dem Clubs of Am, 63-65; vchmn, Porter Co Dem Cent Comt, formerly, chmn, currently; clerk-treas, Town of Hebron, 72- Bus & Prof Pos: Reporter-photographer, Porter Co Herald, 56-61, free lance reporter, currently; asst mgr, Valparaiso License Bur, 61-69; legal secy, Petry & Fitzgerald, Attorneys-at-law, Hebron, 69- Mem: Ind Dem Ed Asn (treas, 70-71, secy, 71-72, vpres, 72-73, pres, 73-); Porter Co Chap, Nat Asn of Legal Secretaries (charter mem, int legal asst sect); Ind League of Clerks & Clerk-Treas; Eastern Star; Red Cross Grey Ladies. Relig: Methodist. Legal Res: 111 Sigler St Hebron IN 46341 Mailing Add: PO Box 7 Hebron IN 46341

MASON, MAURICE (D)
Dem Nat Committeeman
b Cannelton, Ind, Nov 9, 14; s Bert E Mason & Elsie Richey M; m 1932 to Catherine M Brunner; c Marcella June, Robert Dow & Cynthia Kay. Educ: High Sch. Polit & Govt Pos: Chmn, Porter Co Dem Cent Comt, Ind, 60-70 & 73-74; chmn, Second Dist Dem Comt, currently; Dem Nat Committeeman, currently. Bus & Prof Pos: Printer, Cannelton Newspaper, 32-40; make-up foreman, Vidette Messenger, 40-48; publ & owner, Porter Co Herald, 48- & Kouts Times, 51- Mem: CofC; Mason; Shrine; Moose; Elks. Relig: Methodist. Mailing Add: 111 Sigler St Hebron IN 46341

MASON, NORMAN CHRISTY (D)
Chmn, Somerset Co Dem Party, Md
b Crisfield, Md, Jan 9, 16; s Leonard Fillmore Mason, Sr & Catherine Christy M; m 1937 to Eloise Ida Redden; c Norman C, Jr & Catherine Jane. Educ: High sch grad. Polit & Govt Pos: Mem, Eastern Shore State Hosp Bd, Md, 4 years; mem, Somerset Co Welfare Bd, 4 years; chmn, Md Dem State Cent Comt, 50-72; chmn, Md Motion Picture Bd, 56-66 & Md Motion Picture Censor Bd, 58-66; alt deleg, Dem Nat Conv, 64; judge, Md Tax Court, 67-69; judge, Lower Somerset Co, 69-; chmn, Somerset Co Dem Party, currently. Bus & Prof Pos: Coal & concrete bus, Crisfield, Md, 35- Mem: Rotary; Elks; Crisfield Country Club. Relig: Methodist. Mailing Add: 321 Broadway Crisfield MD 21817

MASON, RONALD E (D)
NC State Rep
Mailing Add: Beaufort NC 28516

MASON, SAMUEL F (D)
NH State Rep
Mailing Add: 15 Harvard St Nashua NH 03060

MASON, WILLIE C (R)
Mem Exec Comt, DC Rep Party
b Washington, DC, June 3, 18; s Conder Mason & Mattie Robinson M; m 1961 to Clarice Walden; c Crystal Shirlee. Educ: Am Col Life Underwriters, Chartered Life Underwriter, 63. Polit & Govt Pos: Sgt, US Park Police, Dept Interior, 54-59; mem exec comt, DC Rep Party, 67- Bus & Prof Pos: Branch mgr, J E Jones Ins Agency, 59-63; ins consultant, NY Life Ins Co, 63- Mil Serv: SPA 2/C, Navy, 44-46. Mem: Life Underwriters Asn; Am Col Chartered Life Underwriters; F&AM; Consistory (32 degree); AAONMS. Relig: Methodist. Mailing Add: 1770 Verbena St NW Washington DC 20012

MASOVERO, JOHN (R)
Kans State Rep
Mailing Add: Box 583 Arma KS 66712

MASSA, SALVATORE (D)
RI State Rep
b Bristol, RI, Apr 5, 10; m to Marcelle Collins. Educ: Bristol Schs. Polit & Govt Pos: RI State Rep, 64-67 & 75-; councilman, Bristol Town Comt, 70- Bus & Prof Pos: Mechanic & operator of garage & used car lot. Mem: Credit Comn, Bristol Credit Union; Eagles; Bristol Co Lions; Swanee River Fishing Club. Mailing Add: 337 State St Bristol RI 02809

MASSAD, ERNEST LOUIS (D)
b Brinkman, Okla, Dec 25, 08; s Namey Massad & Shafiga Kouri M; m 1939 to Mozelle Sockwell; c Michael Louis & Elaine Mozelle. Educ: Okla Univ, maj in psychol, 28-35; vpres, Student Coun. Polit & Govt Pos: Mem sch bd, Ardmore, Okla, 56-66 & pres, 60-66; mem, Okla State Voters Comt, 66-; Dep Asst Secy of Defense Reserve Affairs, 68-69. Bus & Prof Pos: Chmn bd, United Life Ins Co, Ardmore, Okla, 61-68 & pres, 62-68. Mil Serv: Entered as 1st Lt, Army, 42, released as Col, 46, after serv in First Cavalry Div, 82nd Airborne & 11th Airborne Div, Pac Theatre, 44-45; Maj Gen (Ret), Army Res, 68; Distinguished Serv Medal; Silver Star; Legion of Merit; Bronze Star with Oak Leaf Cluster; Purple Heart; Okla Distinguished Serv Medal; Reserve Off of US Distinguished Serv Award. Publ: Are the Reserve Forces receiving a fair shake?, Armed Forces Mgt Mag, 6/69. Mem: Am Legion; VFW (comdr, Ardmore Chap); Mil Order of World Wars; Mason (32 degree); Lions. Honors & Awards: State Americanism Award, 57; Lebanese Man of Year, Western Fedn, 63; Distinguished Serv Citation, State of Okla, 68; selected to Okla Hall of Fame, 72; app by Gov David Hall to Carl Albert Mem Comn, 73. Relig: Methodist. Legal Res: 816 Rosewood Ardmore OK 73401 Mailing Add: 107 Hinkle St Ardmore OK 73401

MASSARI, PHILLIP (D)
Colo State Rep
b Segundo, Colo, Apr 12, 13; s Domenic Massari (deceased) & Angelina Pecorelli M (deceased); m 1936 to Mary Margaret Spota; c Phyllis Jean. Educ: Trinidad State Jr Col. Polit & Govt Pos: Vpres, Young Dem, Colo, 34-36; social worker, Las Animas Co Dept Pub Welfare, 36-48; probation officer, Third Judicial Dist, 48-; Colo State Rep, 52-, chmn fish & park comt, Colo House Rep; deleg, Dem Nat Conv, 60 & 68. Mil Serv: Pvt, Army, 43-44. Mem: Columbian Fedn; Izaak Walton League; Colo Parole & Probation Asn; DAV. Honors & Awards: Received Legis Conservationist Award by Colo Wildlife, Nat Wildlife Fedn & Sears-Roebuck Found, 66. Relig: Catholic. Mailing Add: 407 Goddard Ave Trinidad CO 81082

MASSARI, VINCENT (D)
Colo State Sen
b Luco nei Marsi, Italy; s Domenico Massari & Angela Pecorelli M; m 1917 to Amalia Perasso; c Angelina (Mrs Martella). Educ: Sem, Penne, Italy. Hon Degrees: LLD, Southern Colo State Col; DJour, Univ Toronto. Polit & Govt Pos: Colo State Rep, 54-64; Colo State Sen, 64-, mem legis coun, Colo State Senate, currently. Bus & Prof Pos: Asst ed, L'Unione, 17-21, ed & publisher, 21-47; owner & asst mgr, Massari Travel Agency, 21-; dir, First Fed Savings & Loan Asn, Pueblo, Colo, 34- Publ: Contrib ed, Colorado, Denver, Il Progresso Italo-Americano, NY & La Parola del Popolo, Chicago. Mem: Fidelity Lodge (pres, 32-); Protective & Beneficient Lodge; Columbian Fedn (nat pres, 37-); United Socs of Pueblo (treas, 38-); Kiwanis. Honors & Awards: Received Star of Solidarity from President of Italy for cementing good rels between US & Italy; Cert of Appreciation, Sertoma Club, Pueblo, Colo State Am Legion & Colo Dent Asn; Serv Award, Kiwanis Club; hon life membership, Civil Serv Asn of Colo; Superior Serv Award, Southern Colo State Col Alumni Asn, 70. Legal Res: 216 Lincoln St Pueblo CO 81005 Mailing Add: 322 S Victoria Ave Pueblo CO 81003

MASSELL, SAM (D)
b Atlanta, Ga, Aug 26, 27; s Sam Massell & Florence Rubin M; m 1952 to Doris M Middlebrooks; c Cynthia Diane, Steven Alan & Melanie Denise. Educ: Emory Univ, 44-45; Univ Ga, 47-48; Atlanta Law Sch, LLB, 49; Ga State Univ, BCS, 51, cert in selling 52, dipl in real estate, 53. Polit & Govt Pos: Councilman, Mountain Park, Ga, 50-52; secy, Atlanta City Exec Comt, 53-61; pres bd aldermen & vmayor, Atlanta, 62-69, mayor, 70-74; dir, US Conf Mayors, 71-74; vpres, Inter-Am Munic Orgn, 72-; pres, Nat League of Cities, 72, chmn adv coun, 73. Bus & Prof Pos: Chief of publ, Nat Asn Women's & Children's Apparel Salesmen, Inc, 49-51; with Allan-Grayson Realty Co, 51-69, vpres, 55-69, pres develop div, 74-; instr real estate, Smith-Hughes Atlanta Voc Sch, 56; vpres, Mallin Developers, Inc, 56-65; dir, Security Fed Savings & Loan Asn of Atlanta, 61-67 & United Trust Life Ins Co, 64-68. Mil Serv: Admin sch instr, Army Air Force, 46-47. Mem: Dem Party; Com Club; Standard Club. Relig: Jewish. Mailing Add: 2750 Wyngate NW Atlanta GA 30305

MASSENBURG, KATHERINE BLACK (R)
b Baltimore, Md, July 1, 21; d Walter Evan Black & Margaret Rice B; div; c George Yellott, III & Walter Black. Educ: Randolph-Macon Woman's Col, AB, 43; Johns Hopkins Univ; Phi Beta Kappa; Tau Kappa Alpha; Pi Beta Phi. Polit & Govt Pos: Secy, Md Fedn Young Rep, 51-53, co-chmn, 57-59; first vpres, Md Fedn Rep Women, 59-63, pres, 63-64; tech dir, Decennial Census, Seventh Cong Dist, 60; mem, State Rep Cent Comt & chmn, Third Legis Dist, 62-66; mem, Baltimore Commun Rels Comn, 63-66; Rep Nat Committeewoman, 64-72; admin asst to Mayor T R McKeldin, Baltimore, 65-67; chmn, Md Comn on Status of Women, 68-70; mem, Presidential Task Force on Women's Rights & Responsibilities, 69; confidential asst to mem, Renegotiation Bd, 69- Bus & Prof Pos: Teacher jr high sch, 44-45; law clerk & librn, Marshall, All, Carey & Doub, 45-47. Mem: Pi Beta Phi Alumnae; League Women Voters; Md Ment Health Asn; NAACP; Bus & Prof Women. Relig: Baptist. Mailing Add: 5608 Purlington Way Baltimore MD 21212

MASSEY, JAMES CLEMENTS (D)
Chmn, Blount Co Dem Exec Comt, Ala
b Locust Fork, Ala, Dec 11, 27; s Clements Morgan Massey & Rosseye Wilder M; m 1947 to Betty Joyce Sargent; c Deborah Joyce (Mrs Gary F Cornelius), James Michael & Rebekah Michele. Educ: High sch grad. Polit & Govt Pos: Chmn, Blount Co Dem Exec Comt, Ala, currently. Bus & Prof Pos: Owner, Massey Auto Parts, 11 years. Mem: Nat Star Route Mail Carriers Asn; Mason (past Master, Locust Fork Lodge); Shrine; Cumberland Lake Country Club. Honors & Awards: Hon Lt Col Aide-de-Camp, Ala State Militia, 68. Relig: Baptist. Mailing Add: PO Box 41 Locust Fork AL 35097

MASSEY, TOM C (D)
Tex State Rep
b San Angelo, Tex, Mar 5, 31; s Guilford Marion Cade & Nora Villa Ault M; m 1957 to Mary Anna Byrom; c Julie, Alyson, Byrom Cade & Will Truett. Educ: Tex A&M Univ, 54-55; Univ Tex, Austin, BA in Govt, 59, Univ Tex Law Sch, JD, 60; Phi Eta Sigma. Polit & Govt Pos: Chmn, Tom Green Co Dem Party, Tex, 70-71; Tex State Rep, 72-; mem, Southern Regional Educ Bd, 74- Bus & Prof Pos: Attorney-at-law, 60-; secy-treas & co-founder, Char-Swiss Breeders Asn, 70- Mil Serv: Entered as Pvt, Army, 51, released as Sgt, 53, after serv in Korea, 52-53; Bronze Star. Mem: State Bar of Tex; Tom Green Co Bar Asn; Rotary. Relig: Methodist. Legal Res: 1909 Douglas Dr San Angelo TX 76901 Mailing Add: PO Box 1663 San Angelo TX 76901

MASSIWER, MAUREEN ELIZABETH (D)
Nat Committeewoman, RI Young Dem
b Pawtucket, RI, May 28, 53; s John Anthony Massiwer & Mary Matook M; single. Educ: Brown Univ, currently; Pre-Law Soc; Col Young Dem. Polit & Govt Pos: Mem, Pawtucket Sch Comt, 72-, dep chmn, 73-75; mem, Gov Coun Voc Educ, 74-; nat committeewoman, RI Young Dem, 74-; campaign coordr, Michaelson for Attorney Gen, 74. Bus & Prof Pos: Legis asst, RI Asn Sch Comts, 73-, chmn legis comt, 75-; mem, Fed Rels Network, Nat Sch Bds Asn, 73- Publ: Auth, Art in RIASC Newsletter, RI Asn Sch Comts, 74 & 75. Mem: Jenks Jr High Sch Bldg Comt (secy, 75); Pawtucket & RI League of Women Voters; Handgun Alert. Honors & Awards: Scholastic-Citizenship Award, Housewares Club New Eng, 71; Nat Merit Scholar Award, Rotary Club RI, 71; Gavel for Youngest Elected Official, Mass Gen Court, 71. Relig: Eastern Orthodox. Mailing Add: 479 Newport Ave Pawtucket RI 02861

MASTANDREA, FRANK J (R)
State Committeeman, NY Rep Comt
b Bronx, NY, July 4, 20; s Angelo Mastandrea & Angelia Petrone M; m 1947 to Isabela Guadagno; c Frank, Jr, Robert & Michelle. Educ: New York Schs. Polit & Govt Pos: Leader, 95th Assembly Dist Rep Party, NY, 63; exec leader, 86th Assembly Dist Rep Party, 65, exec

mem, currently; state committeeman, NY Rep Comt, 66-; sr deleg, NY State Const Conv, 67; mem exec bd govt comt, mem comt on labor, civil serv & pensions, vchmn subcomt vet affairs & auth of 25 proposition, Rep Nat Conv, 68; spec asst to NY State Narcotic Comn, 68- Bus & Prof Pos: Pres, SMS Parts & Serv, Inc, 49-66. Mil Serv: Entered as Pvt, Air Force, 42, released as T/Sgt, after serv in Ninth Air Force, ETO, 44-45; Three ETO Citations. Mem: CWV (Comdr, Post 390); VFW (dist Comdr, NY State Chap, nat dep chief of staff); 47th Precinct (chmn); Police Athletic League (exec dir); Exec N Bronx Businessman's Asn. Honors & Awards: Citation of Merit, Police Athletic League, 63; Citation, Nation's Bus Week, 65; Citation, Future Mag, 66; Outstanding Bronx Businessman, Bronx Jaycees, 67; Nat Commun Leader Award, 68. Relig: Catholic. Mailing Add: 11 Oak Lane Pelham Manor Bronx NY 10803

MASTERMAN, HAROLD (R)
Chmn, Hull Rep Town Comt, Mass
b Boston, Mass, July 26, 23; s Jacob Masterman & Anne Roffman M; m 1945 to Esther Dores; c Wayne Mark, Linda Joy & Susan Jane. Polit & Govt Pos: Mem, Hull Planning Bd, Mass, 58; vchmn, Hull Housing Authority, 67; chmn, Hull Rep Town Comt, 68-; deleg, Mass Rep State Conv, 70 & 72. Bus & Prof Pos: Salesman, Boston Edison Co, Boston, Mass, 49, mgr, 53, supvr, 55, div head, 59, pub rels dist mgr, 68- Mil Serv: Entered as Pvt, Marine Corps, 43, released as Sgt, 45, after serv in Third Div, SPac, Theatre, 43-45; Presidential Unit Citation; Asiatic-Pac Theatre Citation. Mem: Mason (32 degree); Consistory; Aleppo Temple Shrine; United Fund Campaign (Boston Chmn, 63); hon life mem Gtr Boston CofC. Mailing Add: 90 Kingsley Rd Hull MA 02045

MASTERS, HAROLD WILLIAM (R)
Mem, Jackson Co Rep Comt, Mo
b Kansas City, Mo, Oct 30, 17; s Bert Hale Masters & S Ellen Fortner M; m to Peggy Jean Payne. Educ: Univ Kansas City, BA, 56. Polit & Govt Pos: Precinct Capt, Kansas City Rep Party, Mo, 38-42 & 46-60; ed, A Republican Report, 58-66; Rep cand Jackson Co Assessor, 66; Rep cand, US Rep, Fifth Dist, Mo, 68; mem, Jackson Co Rep Comt, Sixth Ward, 72- Bus & Prof Pos: Merchandiser, Masters Grain Co, Kansas City, 58- Mil Serv: Army, Ord Dept, serv in Theatre Overhead, Southwest Pac Theatre, 42-45. Mem: Kansas City Bd of Trade; Am Legion; Mo Hist Soc; Civil War Round Table; Nat Rifle Asn. Relig: Baptist. Mailing Add: 5300 Brookside Blvd Kansas City MO 64112

MASTERS, KENNETH HALLS (D)
Mem, Md Dem State Cent Comt
b Washington, DC, Aug 16, 43; s Kenneth Hubert Masters & Kathleen Maloney M; m 1967 to Patricia Pound; c Maura Patricia & Kathleen St John. Educ: Towson State Col, BA, 65; Univ Md Sch Law, Baltimore, JD, 72; Phi Alpha Delta. Polit & Govt Pos: Mem & second vchmn, Md Dem State Cent Comt, Baltimore Co, 74- Bus & Prof Pos: Social studies teacher, Baltimore Co, Md, 65-66; practicing attorney, Baltimore Co, 72- Mil Serv: Entered as Pvt, Army, 66, released as 1st Lt, 69, after serv in 196th Light Inf Brigade, Vietnam, 68-69; Bronze Star for Valor; Air Medal; Vietnam Serv Medal; Combat Infantryman's Badge; Aircraft Crewman's Badge; Distinguished Mil Grad, OCS. Mem: Am, Md State & Baltimore Co Bar Asns; Hibernian Soc Baltimore; Local Dem Clubs. Legal Res: 18-A Montrose Manor Ct Catonsville MD 21228 Mailing Add: 204 W Pennsylvania Ave Towson MD 21204

MASTERS, RICHARD STEARNS (R)
Chmn, Susquehanna Co Rep Comt, Pa
b Kingsley, Pa, June 14, 14; s Alva J Masters & Clara Stearns M; m 1932 to Eloise Williams; c Joyce (Mrs Richard Berish), Marcia (Mrs Gary Housel), Betsy (Mrs Jonathan Blattmachr), Richard W & Jacqueline (Mrs William Staples). Educ: Harford Voc High Sch; Univ Scranton, eve course in pub speaking. Polit & Govt Pos: Dir, Mt View Joint Schs, Pa, 45-55; chmn, Susquehanna Co Rep Comt, 52-; deleg, Rep Nat Conv, 68. Bus & Prof Pos: Pres, Masters Contracting Corp, 44. Mem: F&AM; Shrine. Relig: Congregational. Mailing Add: Kingsley PA 18826

MASTERSON, MICHAEL JON (R)
b DeKalb, Ill, Jan 1, 46; s Theodore J Masterson & Phyllis Rowe M; single. Educ: Trinity Col (Conn), BA, 68. Polit & Govt Pos: Deleg, US Youth Coun, 67-68; nat treas, Col Young Dem Clubs of Am, 67-69; state coordr, Humphrey for President, 72; press asst to US Rep John B Anderson, Ill, 72-73, admin asst, 74- Mil Serv: Entered as Pvt, Army, 69, released as SP-5, 71, after serv in 502 MI, 2nd Armored Div, III Corps, 5th Army, 70-71; Bronze Star; Am Spirit Honor Medal. Mem: Admin Asst Asn; Bull Elephants; Ill State Soc. Relig: Roman Catholic. Legal Res: New Landing RR4 Dixon IL 61021 Mailing Add: 2727 29th St NW Washington DC 20008

MASTICS, GEORGE E (R)
b Cleveland, Ohio, 1931; m; c five. Educ: Western Reserve Univ, BA, 53, Law Sch, LLB, 56. Polit & Govt Pos: Ohio State Rep, 67-74; Rep cand for US Rep, Ohio, 74; Chief Asst State Attorney Gen. Bus & Prof Pos: Lawyer. Mem: Fairview Park Rep Club. Mailing Add: 4587 Concord Dr Fairview Park OH 44126

MASTIN, PHILIP OLIN, JR (D)
Mich State Rep
b Wayne, Mich, May 27, 30; s Philip Olin Mastin & Gracia Ruth Hayward M; m 1947 to Donna June Keck; c Dawn (Mrs Michael Massong), Cheryl (Mrs Warren Pennington) & Philip, III. Educ: SMacomb Community Col, 3 years. Polit & Govt Pos: Alt dem deleg, Precinct Six, Hazel Park, Mich, 62-64; city councilman, Hazel Park, 62-68, mayor pro tem, 62, 66 & 68; treas, Oakland Co Dem Comt, 65, dep chmn, 65-70; co comnr, Oakland Co, 65-70; ed, Oakland Dem Newsletter, 65-68; alt deleg, Southeast Mich Coun Govt, 66-68; alt deleg, Dem Nat Conv, 68; Dem supvr caucus chmn, Oakland Co, 69-70; Mich State Rep, 69th Dist, 71- Bus & Prof Pos: Automotive chassis designer, Ford Motor Co, Mich, 55-57; sr automotive chassis designer, Chevrolet Div, Gen Motors Corp, 57-65. Mem: Soc Automotive Engrs; Am Soc Tool Engrs; Am Pub Works Soc; Hazel Park Jr CofC; UAW. Honors & Awards: Outstanding Young Man of Year, Hazel Park; Distinguished Serv Award, Hazel Park Jaycees, 65. Relig: Methodist. Mailing Add: 526 E Harry Hazel Park MI 48030

MASTRACCIO, ARMAND JOHN (D)
b Rome, NY, Aug 8, 48; s Armand Anthony Mastraccio & Louise Zeppieni M; single. Educ: Assumption Col, BA, 70; Crown & Shield Honor Soc. Polit & Govt Pos: Campaign coordr, Simmons for Cong, 31st Cong Dist NY, 70; Rome coordr, Bryant for Co Exec, Oneida Co, 71; 31st Cong Dist coordr, McGovern for President Comt, 72; deleg, Dem Nat Conv, 72; research analyst & admin aide, Oneida Co Exec, 72- Bus & Prof Pos: Teacher, St Mary's Sch, Rome, NY, 71. Mem: Oneida Co Adv Comt (coordr, 72-); Rome Area Cath Youth Orgn Exec Bd (treas, 72-). Relig: Catholic. Mailing Add: 203 Kossuth St Rome NY 13440

MASTRANGELO, EVELINO WILLIAM (D)
Chmn, Lake Co Cent & Exec Dem Comts, Ohio
b Cleveland, Ohio, Oct 20, 23; s Dominic Anthony Mastrangelo & Filomena Fatica M; m 1951 to Elizabeth Benedict; c Mark, Lisa, Susan & Ellen. Educ: Ohio State Univ, Univ, BS in educ, Ohio State Col of Law, JD; Alpha Phi Delta; Delta Theta Phi. Polit & Govt Pos: Spec counsel, Off of Attorney Gen, State of Ohio, 58-62; mem, Bd of Elecs, 58-, chmn, currently; dir of law, City of Wickliffe, Ohio, 62-; treas, Lake Co Dem Cent & Exec Comts, 58-68, chmn, 68-; deleg, Dem Nat Conv, 68. Bus & Prof Pos: Attorney, 53- Mil Serv: Entered as Pvt, Army, 43, released as Sgt, 46, after serv in 310th Ord Bn, ETO, 44-46; Am Theater Ribbon; Europe-Africa-Mid East Theater Ribbon with One Bronze Star; Good Conduct & World War II Victory Medals. Mem: Am Legion; Elks; Lake Co Bar (pres); Nat Inst of Munic Law Officers Asn; Am Bar Asn. Relig: Roman Catholic. Mailing Add: 36629 Ridge Rd Willoughby OH 44094

MASTRANGELO, RICHARD EDWARD (R)
Secy, US Coun on Environ Quality
b Watertown, Mass, May 14, 38; s Louis Mastrangelo, MD & Helen G Decost M; m 1973 to Lois Jean Ficker. Educ: Boston Univ Col of Gen Educ, AA, 57, Sch of Pub Rels & Commun, BS in Pub Rels, 59, Sch of Law, JD, 62; Tau Mu Epsilon; Scarlet Key; Chi Gamma Epsilon; Media; vpres, Boston Univ Student Govt; New Eng Sectional chmn, Alpha Phi Omega. Polit & Govt Pos: Chmn, Mass Col Rep Caucus, 57-58; campaign staff asst to US Sen Laverett Saltonstall, 60; town meeting mem, Watertown, Mass, 61-71, clerk, adv bd of rev, 60-61 & clerk, personnel bd, 62-64; campaign mgr, Quinlan for State Sen Comt, 62; mem credentials comt, Mass State Rep Conv, 62; chmn Mass deleg, Young Rep Nat Conv, 63 & 65; mem exec comt, Mass Rep State Comt, 63-65, exec dir, 69; chmn, Mass Coun of Young Rep Clubs, 63-65; alt deleg-at-lg, Rep Nat Conv, 64; asst dir of orgn, Richardson for Lt Gov Comt, Mass, 64; pres, Mass Young Rep Asn, 65; Young Rep Nat Committeeman, Mass, 65-67; spec asst to Lt Gov, Mass, 65-67; asst attorney gen, Chief Vet Div, Mass, 67-69; chmn, Watertown Rep Town Comt, 68-70; selectman, Watertown, 68-71, chmn, 70; asst to Secy, US Dept of Health, Educ & Welfare, 70-73; asst to Secy of Defense, US Dept Defense, 73; assoc dep attorney gen, US Dept Justice, 73; secy, US Coun on Environ Quality, 75- Bus & Prof Pos: Attorney-at-law, 62- Publ: The anatomy of a state senate campaign, 66. Mem: Mass & Boston Bar Asns; Boston Univ Gen Alumni Asn (dir); Mass Bay Chap, Nat Found (dir); Lions. Honors & Awards: Named Brother of Year, Zeta Upsilon Chap, Alpha Phi Omega, 58, Distinguished Serv Key, 59; Named Man of Year, Boston Univ, 59. Relig: Roman Catholic. Legal Res: 267 School St Watertown MA 02172 Mailing Add: 101 G St SW Washington DC 20024

MASTRIANNI, SILVIO A (D)
Conn State Rep
Mailing Add: 64 Emmett Ave Derby CT 06418

MASTROPIERI, EUGENE F (D)
Councilman-at-lg, New York City Coun
b Queens, NY, Sept 13, 37; s Frank Mastropieri & Frances DeNicola M; div; c Eugene & Diane. Educ: St John's Univ (NY), BBA, 59, Law Sch, JD, 60; Delta Psi Upsilon; Delta Theta Phi. Polit & Govt Pos: Asst dist attorney, NY; councilman-at-lg, New York City Coun, 71-; deleg, Dem Nat Mid-Term Conf, 74. Bus & Prof Pos: Trial attorney, Queens, NY, 61- Mem: NY State & Am Bar Asns; Dist Attorney's Asn Queens Co; Regular Dem Club (exec leader); CofC. Relig: Catholic. Mailing Add: 67-40 Myrtle Ave Glendale NY 11227

MATHENY, GORDON (R)
NDak State Rep
b Blackwater, NDak, Aug 29, 14; s James Ira Matheny & Martha Spillers M; m 1950 to Wylma Wolters; c Gary Edward, Bruce Allen, Nancy Kay & Jo Ann. Educ: Garrison High Sch, 4 years. Polit & Govt Pos: NDak State Rep, McLean Co, 69-71 & 72-; dist chmn, McLean Co Rep Party, NDak, currently; dir, White Shield Sch Bd, 72- Mem: NDak Stockmen's Asn; McLean Co Farm Bur. Relig: Protestant. Mailing Add: State Capitol Bismarck ND 58501

MATHERS, WILLIAM L (R)
Mont State Sen
Mailing Add: Box 267 Miles City MT 59301

MATHESON, FRANKLYN BOYD (R)
Utah State Rep
b Salt Lake City, Utah, Oct 30, 28; s Francis Brown Matheson & Naomi Tingey M; m 1951 to Mary Francis Maack; c Marjorie (Mrs King), Susan, Franklyn Brent, David Eugene, Richard Maack, Michael Kent & Bonnie Gae. Educ: Univ Utah, BS, 51, LLB, 55, JD, 67; Delta Phi; Pi Kappa Alpha. Polit & Govt Pos: Asst Attorney Gen, Utah, 58-64; dep recorder, Salt Lake Co, 53-56; chmn, Utah State Juv Court Adv Comt, 68-74; Utah State Rep, 68- Bus & Prof Pos: Attorney, 55-; pres, Am Western Life Ins Co, 66- Mil Serv: Entered as Pvt, Army, 51, released as Spec Agt, 53, after serv in Counter Intel Corps. Mem: Utah State Bar; Am Legion. Honors & Awards: Utah State Jaycee Young Man of the Year, 61; Salt Lake City Outstanding Young Man, 61. Relig: Latter-day Saint. Mailing Add: 2666 E 3120 South Salt Lake City UT 84109

MATHESON, GORDON CAMERON (R)
Mem, Rep State Cent Comt RI
b North Smithfield, RI, Mar 27, 30; s Col Guy Peter MacLean Matheson & Flora MacDonald M; m Margaret Mary Dwyer; c Christine Lynn, Gordon Cameron, Jr & Kimberly Ann. Educ: Univ of RI, 3 years, Sales Anal Inst, 1 year; Sigma Alpha Epsilon. Polit & Govt Pos: Mem, Chafee for Gov & O'Donnel for Lt Gov Campaign Comt, RI, 62; mem, North Smithfield Zoning Bd of Rev, 63-64; mem, North Smithfield Rep Town Comt, 64-, campaign mgr, 66 & chmn, 68-69; adv staff & coord, O'Donnel for Lt Gov Comt, 64-68; coordr, DiPrete For Cong Comt, North Smithfield, 67; cand, RI State Senate, 30th Dist, 68; mem, RI Real Estate Comn, 69-; mem, Small Bus Admin Adv Coun, 70-; mem, Rep State Cent Comt RI, 71-; mem, North Smithfield Water-Sewer Comn, 71-; mem, Chafee '72 Comt, 72; mem, De Simone for Gov Comt, 72. Bus & Prof Pos: Sales rep, Sun Oil Co, Providence, RI, 54-68 & land dept rep, 68- Mil Serv: Entered as Pvt, Army, 51, released as Cpl, 53, after serv in 306th Field Hosp, Europe, 52-53. Mem: RI Petroleum Asn; F&AM; Cumberland Civic Ctr; Woonsocket Hosp Corp (corp mem, 71-). Relig: Episcopal; mem vestry, St James Episcopal Church, 71,

chmn, RI Episcopal Charities Drive, 72- Legal Res: North Smithfield RI Mailing Add: 70 Bellevue Ave Union Village Woonsocket RI 02895

MATHESON, MANDELL L (D)
Okla State Sen
Mailing Add: State Capitol Oklahoma City OK 73105

MATHEWS, FORREST DAVID (D)
Secy, Health, Educ & Welfare
b Grove Hill, Ala, Dec 6, 35; m 1960; c 2. Educ: Univ Ala, AB, 58, MA, 59; Columbia Univ, PhD, 65; Phi Beta Kappa; Omicron Delta Kappa. Hon Degrees: LLB, Univ Ala, 70. Polit & Govt Pos: Secy, Health, Educ & Welfare, 75- Bus & Prof Pos: Counselor, dir men's activities & asst dean men, Univ Ala, 60-62; instr hist & philos educ, cols in NY area, 62-65; interim dean men, Univ Ala, 65-66, lectr hist, 65-; exec asst off pres, 66-68, exec vpres, 68-69, pres, 69; mem bd trustees, Am Univs Field Staff, 69-; mem exec comt & inst higher educ opportunity policy comn, Southern Regional Educ Bd, 70-; mem adv comt acad admin internship prog, Am Coun Educ, 70-; mem, Nat Prog Coun Educ TV, 70- Mem: Newcomen Soc. Legal Res: AL Mailing Add: Dept Health Educ & Welfare Washington DC 20201

MATHEWSON, JAMES L (R)
Mo State Rep
Mailing Add: 806 W Broadway Sedalia MO 65301

MATHIAS, CHARLES MCC, JR (R)
US Sen, Md
b Frederick, Md, July 24, 22; s Charles McCurdy Mathias & Theresa McElfresh Trail M; m to Ann Hickling Bradford; c Charles Bradford & Robert Fiske. Educ: Yale Univ, 43-44; Haverford Col, BA, 44; Univ Md, LLB, 49. Polit & Govt Pos: Asst Attorney Gen, Md, 53-54; city attorney, Frederick, 54-59; Md State Deleg, 59-60; US Rep, Md, 60-69; US Sen, Md, 69-; deleg, Rep Nat conv, 72. Mil Serv: Naval Res, Capt (Ret). Mem: Hist Soc Frederick Co; Hood Col (bd trustees); Episcopal Free Sch & Orphan House (trustee). Relig: Episcopal. Legal Res: Frederick MD 21701 Mailing Add: US Senate Washington DC 20510

MATHIAS, ROBERT BRUCE (R)
b Tulare, Calif, Nov 17, 30; m to Melba Wiser; c Romel, Megan & Marissa. Educ: Stanford Univ, AB, 53. Polit & Govt Pos: US Rep, Calif, 67-75. Bus & Prof Pos: Freelance TV, 56-62; owner, Bob Mathias Sierra Boys Camp, 62- Mil Serv: Marine Corps, 54-56; Capt, Res. Mem: Elks; Amateur Athletic Union; US Olympians. Honors & Awards: Olympic Decathlon Champion, 48 & 52; Sullivan Award; Outstanding Young Man Award, Jr CofC. Relig: Methodist. Mailing Add: 3235 Valley Lane Falls Church VA 22044

MATHIEU, THOMAS C (D)
Mich State Sen
Mailing Add: 1118 Sibley NW Grand Rapids MI 49504

MATHIS, ENOCH DOUGLAS (D)
b Waynesday, Ga, Dec 26, 35; s Warren Mathis & Mamie Davis M; 1959 to Yvonne O Hooks; c Milton Douglas & Deirdre Cerese. Educ: Savannah State Col, 3 years; Weaver Col Realty, 1 year; Mutual Benevolent Soc; Savannah State Alumni Asn. Polit & Govt Pos: Committeeman, Ga State Dem Exec Comt, formerly. Bus & Prof Pos: Superior cleaning & painting contractor, 68- Mem: Savannah Area Minority Contractors Asn; Black Bus & Prof Asn. Honors & Awards: Award, Boy Scout Am. Relig: African Methodist Episcopal. Legal Res: 511 W 42nd St Savannah GA 31401 Mailing Add: PO Box 3134 Savannah GA 31403

MATHIS, M DAWSON (D)
US Rep, Ga
b Nashville, Ga, Nov 30, 40; s Rev Marvin W Mathis & Nell Abel M; m 1959 to Patricia Ann Connell; c Anthony Dawson, Craig Steven, Jason Everett & Russell Dean. Polit & Govt Pos: US Rep, Ga, 71-; alt deleg, Dem Nat Conv, 72. Relig: Baptist. Legal Res: 1003 Forest Glen Rd Albany GA 31705 Mailing Add: 236 Cannon House Off Bldg Washington DC 20515

MATHIS, MARK JAY (D)
b New York, NY, Aug 25, 47; s Meyer Mathis & Beulah Nechemias M; m 1971 to Marylin Gail Goodman. Educ: Mass Inst Technol, BS, 69; Univ Pa, JD, 72; Pi Lambda Phi. Polit & Govt Pos: Minority counsel, Comt on DC, US House Rep, 75- Bus & Prof Pos: Assoc, Avent, Fox, Kintner, Plotkin & Kahan, Washington, DC, 72-75. Mailing Add: 4601 N Park Ave Chevy Chase MD 20015

MATHIS, THOMAS W (D)
WVa State Deleg
Mailing Add: State Capitol Charleston WV 25305

MATHISEN, CHRIS
m to Mary Calhoun; c Chris Tyler. Polit & Govt Pos: Admin asst to US Rep Harrison, Va, 50-63, US Rep Marsh, Va, 63-71 & US Rep Robinson, Va, 71- Bus & Prof Pos: Ed Dept, Washington Evening Star, 34-42, 46-50. Mil Serv: Navy, serv in Off of Chief Cable Censor; USS John C Butler (DE 339); Navy News Correspondent, Asiatic-Pac Theater. Mem: Nat Press Club; Audubon Naturalist Soc of Cent Atlantic States (former dir); Wash Newspaper Guild (former vpres); Am Soc Pub Admin; Fed Ed Asn. Mailing Add: 4019 N Randolph St Arlington VA 22207

MATHNA, WOODROW WILSON (R)
Mem, Ohio State Rep Comt
b Gibsonburg, Ohio, Mar 27, 13; s Clarence Mathna & Effie Rosenberry M; m 1938 to Kathleen Dillon; c Patrick Allen & Margaret Rose (Mrs Zgonic). Educ: Gibsonburgh High Sch & part-time courses. Polit & Govt Pos: Rep precinct committeeman, Lorain, Ohio, 50-; mem, Ohio State Rep Exec Comt, 50-; councilman, Lorain, Ohio, 56-61, mayor, 61-71, councilman-at-lg, 74- mem, Nat Adv Comt on Econ Opportunity, 70- Bus & Prof Pos: Owner, Mathna For Stamps, 30 years. Mil Serv: Ohio Nat Guard, Co D, 40-41. Mem: Life mem Ohio PTA; Elks; Kiwanis; KofP; IBEW, Local 509. Relig: Methodist; Sunday Sch teacher, Evangel United Brethren Church. Mailing Add: 507 W 32nd St Lorain OH 44055

MATLACK, ARDENA LAVONNE (D)
Kans State Rep
b Carlton, Kans, Dec 20, 30; d Walter Carl Williams & Bessie Major W; m 1951 to Donald Clyde Matlack; c Lucinda (Mrs Michael Manley), Roxanne, Terry Clyde, Rex William & Timothy Alan. Educ: Kans Wesleyan Univ, summer 48; Kans State Univ, 49-51; Washburn Univ, summer 55; Wichita State Univ, BA, 69; Mu Phi Epsilon; Gold Key; Alpha Xi Delta. Polit & Govt Pos: Dem precinct committeewoman, 4 years; Kans State Rep, 75- Bus & Prof Pos: Elem teacher, Carlton, Kans, 48-49; substitute teacher, Clearwater, 69-74, choir dir, 72-74. Mem: Clearwater United Methodist Women (dist social involvement coordr); Bus & Prof Women's Club (legis chmn); Clearwater Fed Women's Study Club; PTA; Dem orgns. Relig: United Methodist. Mailing Add: 615 Elaine Ave Clearwater KS 67026

MATRANGO, FRANK J (D)
Mass State Rep
Mailing Add: State Capitol Boston MA 02133

MATSON, JIM (R)
Wash State Sen
Mailing Add: Rte 2 Box 2311 Selah WA 98942

MATSUNAGA, SPARK MASAYUKI (D)
US Rep, Hawaii
b Kauai, Hawaii, Oct 8, 16; s Kingoro Matsunaga & Chiyono Fukushima M (both deceased); m 1948 to Helene Hatsumi Tokunaga; c Karen (Mrs George R Hardman), Keene Goro, Diane Yukie, Merle Masae & Matthew Masao. Educ: Univ Hawaii, BEd, 41; Harvard Law Sch, JD, 51; Soochow Univ, LLD, 73; Phi Kappa Phi; Pi Sigma Alpha; Pi Sigma Lambda; Saber & Chain; Varsity Debate. Polit & Govt Pos: Vet counr, Surplus Property Off, Dept of Interior, 45-47; chief priority claimants div, War Assets Admin, 47-48; mem, Territorial War Mem Found, 47-48 & Gov Comt on Housing, 47-48; mem, Hawaii Statehood deleg to Cong, 50-54; chmn rescue serv, Civil Defense Agency, 51-52; asst pub prosecutor, City & Co of Honolulu, 52-54; Oahu Co committeeman & exec bd mem, Dem Party of Hawaii, 52-54; deleg co & state Dem conv, 52-62, serv on Resolutions, Rules & Platform Comts; mem relocation adv comt, Honolulu Redevelop Agency, 53-54; pres, Dem Precinct Club, First Precinct, Fourth Dist, 53-55; Hawaii Territorial Rep, 54-59, Majority Leader, 59, chmn, Judiciary Comt & Juvenile Court, Recreation & Welfare Comt; vchmn, Citizens for Kennedy & Johnson, Hawaii, 60; pres, Dem Precinct Club, 59-64; mem, Pac War Mem Comn, Hawaii, 60-63; US Rep, Hawaii, 63-, mem rules comt, US House of Rep, 67-, comt on Aging & House Dem steering comt, currently, dep majority whip, 73-, deleg, Dem Nat Conv, 68 & 72. Bus & Prof Pos: Stevedore & warehouseman, 31-34; bookkeeper & sales clerk, gen merchandise store, 34-37; attorney-at-law, 54-63. Mil Serv: Entered as 2nd Lt, Army, 41, released as Capt, 46, after serv in 100th Inf Bn, 442nd Inf Regt & Mil Intel Serv, African-European-Asiatic Theatres, 41-46; Lt Col, Judge Adv Gen Corps, Army Res, 63-69; Bronze Star Medal with V; Purple Heart Medal with Oak Leaf Cluster; Army Commendation Medal; Asiatic Pac Campaign Ribbons; African-European Campaign Ribbons; Five Battle Stars; Am Theater Ribbon; Combat & Expert Inf Badges. Publ: An experiment in speech correction, Hawaii Educ Rev, 51. Mem: Am Bar Asn; Hawaii Chap, Muscular Dystrophy Asn & Soc for Crippled Children & Adults; DAV (Comdr & Judge Adv); life mem VFW; United Vet Legis Comt (chmn). Honors & Awards: Received YMCA Serv to Youth Award, Boy Scouts Meritorious Serv Award, DAV Nat Merit Award, Univ Hawaii Alumnus of the Year Award, Japanese-Am Citizens League Nat Nisei of the Biennium Award. Relig: Episcopal. Legal Res: 1717 Ala Wai Blvd Honolulu HI 96813 Mailing Add: Rm 218 Fed Off Bldg Honolulu HI 96813

MATTHEWS, CHARLES DAWSON (D)
b Little Rock, Ark, Feb 12, 39; s John Pope Matthews & Martha Dawson M; m 1961 to Susan Ann Scully; c Michael Dawson, James Patrick, Martha Ann & William Scully. Educ: Georgetown Univ, BS in Eng, 61; Univ Ark, LLB, 64; pres, Sr Class, 60-61; Georgetown Univ Varsity Swimming Team (capt); Univ Ark Student Bar Asn (pres); assoc ed, Univ Ark Law Rev; Blue Key. Polit & Govt Pos: Ark State Rep, Pos One, Dist 22, 66-68; chmn, Ark State Dem Comt, 68-72. Bus & Prof Pos: Vpres & mem bd dirs, Matthews Co & Crestwood Develop Co, North Little Rock. Mem: Am Bar Asn; CofC (bd dirs, North Little Rock Chap); YMCA (bd dirs); Ark Asn for the Crippled (pres); Ark Kidney Found (pres). Honors & Awards: Outstanding Freshman Mem, 66th Gen Assembly; Outstanding Cath, Bishop Fletcher Award, 64; Outstanding Young Man Award, North Little Rock Jaycees, 67. Relig: Catholic. Legal Res: 3604 North Hills Blvd North Little Rock AR 72116 Mailing Add: 1200 Warthen Bank Bldg Little Rock AR 72201

MATTHEWS, DONALD RAY (D)
b Micanopy, Fla, Oct 3, 07; s D H Matthews & Flora A M; m 1941 to Sara Lewis M; c Carolyn, Ann & Donald Ray, Jr. Educ: Univ Fla, BA, MA; Alpha Phi Epsilon; Pi Gamma Mu; Tau Kappa Alpha; Fla Blue Key; Scabbard & Blade; Sigma Phi Epsilon. Polit & Govt Pos: Fla State Rep, 35; US Rep, Fla, 52-67. Bus & Prof Pos: Sch teacher, high sch prin; admin staff, Univ Fla, 16 years; serv as dir, Fla Union, Student Activity Ctr & dir alumni affairs; instr Am Inst, Santa Fe Jr Col, Gainesville, Fla, 67- Mil Serv: Inf, 4 years; discharged as Capt. Mem: Am Legion; KofP; CofC; Elks; Moose. Relig: Presbyterian; elder, First Presbyterian Church, Gainesville. Mailing Add: 2611 SW Eighth Dr Gainesville FL 32601

MATTHEWS, DORSEY RUDOLPH (D)
Ga State Rep
b Emma, Ga, Aug 26, 13; s John Bailey Matthews & Carrie Johnson M; m 1938 to Elizabeth Taylor; c Melanie Sue, Lawton Virgil, Judith Elizabeth & Hugh Dorsey. Educ: Moultrie High Sch, 31. Polit & Govt Pos: Ga State Sen, 47th Dist, 55-56; Ga State Rep, 59- Bus & Prof Pos: Farmer; dir, Flue-Cured Tobacco Stabilization Coop of US. Mem: Farm Bur. Honors & Awards: Named Ga Master Farmer, 54. Relig: Methodist. Mailing Add: Rte 1 Moultrie GA 31768

MATTHEWS, GARY LEE (R)
Wash State Rep
Mailing Add: 14157 123rd Ave NE Kirkland WA 98033

MATTHEWS, HARVEY W (R)
Fla State Rep
Mailing Add: 751 Overspin Ave Winter Park FL 32789

MATTHEWS, HERBERT SPENCER (D)
b Clarksville, Ark, May 5, 21; s Herbert Spencer Matthews, Sr & Flora Lee M; m 1971 to Jacquelyn Barber; c Kathryn Ann (Mrs Davies), Patricia Floye & Patti Anne Matthews & Debbie Sidwell, Pamela & Grady Weeks. Educ: Tulane Univ, BS, 51; Naval War Col, 57-58; Oxford Univ, 65; Phi Beta Kappa. Polit & Govt Pos: Exec & admin asst to US Rep Bill

Chappell, Jr, Fla, 73- Mil Serv: Entered as Seaman, Navy, 40, released as Rear Adm, 73, after serv in various units, European & Pac Theatres; Distinguished Serv Medal; Legion of Merit; Bronze Star (Combat V); 11 Air Medals; SViet Order of Knight; 2 SViet Navy Crosses & 11 other medals; Cambodian Medal of Honor. Mem: Nat Dem Club; US Naval Inst; NY Yacht Club; Capitol Yacht Club; Md Hog Growers Asn. Honors & Awards: 38 US & Foreign Mil Awards. Relig: Presbyterian. Mailing Add: Birch Hanger Mechanicsville MD 20659

MATTHEWS, JOHN, JR (D)
SC State Rep
Mailing Add: Bowman SC 29018

MATTHEWS, JOHN G (R)
Conn State Rep
Mailing Add: 92 Rosebrook Rd New Canaan CT 06840

MATTHEWS, MARTIN, JR (BUD) (D)
Mem, Dallas Co Dem Exec Comt, Tex
b Shelbyville, Ky, Oct 14, 26; s Martin Charles Matthews & Vera Valentine M; m 1948 to Alyce Corrine Hessel; c Marsha Wilson, Andrew Gene & Marilyn Gaye. Educ: Univ Calif, Los Angeles; Univ of Wash; Southern Methodist Univ, BBA, 50; Okla Univ; Univ Tex, BME, 52. Polit & Govt Pos: Area chmn, Reelect L B Johnson, US Sen, 56; mem, Dem Comt for Responsible Govt, 66-; chmn trustees, Richardson Taxpayers Asn, 66-; area chmn, John Connally for Gov, 68; chmn, Tex Dem for Wallace, Ninth Sen Dist, 68-; precinct chmn, Dallas Co, 71-; mem, Dallas Co Dem Exec Comt, 71-; chmn rules comt, Am in Action, 72-; deleg, Dem Nat Conv, 72. Mil Serv: Entered as A/S, Navy, 41, released as Boatswains Mate 2/C, 49, after serv in Amphibious, SPac, Mediter, Atlantic, European & Asian Theatres, 41-45; recalled as Boatswains Mate 2/C, Navy, 50; Chief Boatswains Mate (Ret), Naval Res, 20 years; eight Campaign Stars; Navy Unit Citation; Presidential Unit Citation; Purple Heart; Navy Commendation Award; Survivors Medal; China Serv Ribbon; Capture & Defense of Guadalcanal Defense Ribbon. Mem: Built-in Cleaning Syst Inst (pres, 67-); Tex Mfg Asn; Mason; Richardson CofC; VFW. Relig: Baptist. Mailing Add: 533 Fairview Dr Richardson TX 75080

MATTHEWS, MORTIMER JOSEPH (D)
Mayor, Pasadena, Calif
b Cincinnati, Ohio, Apr 11, 33; s Stanley Matthews & Cecelia Prior M; m 1953 to Lydia Jane Simpson; c Lisa, Polly & Amy. Educ: Princeton Univ, AB in archit, 54; Princeton Key & Seal Club. Polit & Govt Pos: Planning comnr, Pasadena, Calif, 67-71, councilman, 71-, mayor, 74- Bus & Prof Pos: Dir planning, Welton Becket & Assocs, Los Angeles, 54-61; prin, Pulliam, Matthews & Assocs, 61- Mem: Am Inst Architects; Valley Hunt Club; Cal Tech YMCA (dir, 74-); Southern Calif Asn Govt (mem transportation & exec comts). Relig: Episcopal. Legal Res: 1435 Linda Ridge Rd Pasadena CA 91103 Mailing Add: 672 S Lafayette Park Pl Los Angeles CA 90057

MATTHEWS, RICHARD CARROLL (R)
Md State Deleg
b Hampstead, Md, July 11, 26; s Arthur Jennings Matthews & Gladys Bishop M; m 1945 to Dorothy Ann Hale. Polit & Govt Pos: Mem, Carroll Co Rep Cent Comt, Md, 62-66; Md State Deleg, currently. Bus & Prof Pos: Owner, Matthews Tire Co, 46- Mem: Lions; CofC. Relig: Methodist. Mailing Add: 111 Taylor Ave Hampstead MD 21074

MATTHEWS, ROBERT CHAPPELLE (D)
Ga State Rep
b Athens, Ga, Nov 1, 08; s Vincent Matthews & Susan Dorsey M; m 1965 to Dorothy Harris. Educ: Univ Ga, 33; Southern Law Sch, LLB, 34; Sigma Alpha Epsilon. Polit & Govt Pos: Ga State Rep, 49-72 & 75-; mem, Southern Regional Educ Bd, 50-, secy-treas, 58-60, mem legis adv comt; mem, Ga Sci & Tech Comt, 65; mem, Ga Coun to Improve Educ, 68. Bus & Prof Pos: Attorney-at-law; mem bd gov, Ga Bar Asn, 56-68 & chmn legis comt, 69- Mil Serv: US Cavalry, (Ret). Mem: Ga Nuclear Comn; Am Bar Asn; Am Judiciary Soc; Elks; Ga Farm Bur. Honors & Awards: Outstanding Alumni Award, 64 & Blue Key Award, 70, Univ Ga. Relig: Methodist. Legal Res: 190 Rutherford Lane Athens GA 30601 Mailing Add: 306 Southern Mutual Bldg Athens GA 30601

MATTHEWS, VIRGIL EDISON, JR (D)
Councilman-at-Lg, Charleston, WVa
b LaFayette, Ala, Oct 5, 28; s Virgil Edison Matthews (deceased) & Izetta Ware M (deceased); m 1960 to Shirley Elizabeth McFatridge; c Brian Keith, Michael Andre & Deborah Michele. Educ: Univ Ill, Urbana, BS, 51; Univ Chicago, SM, 52, PhD, 55; Sigma Xi; Phi Lambda Upsilon; Alpha Phi Alpha; Cosmopolitan Club. Polit & Govt Pos: Councilman-at-lg, Charleston, WVa, 67-; deleg, Dem Nat Conv, 68; Dem cand for WVa State Sen, Eighth Dist, 70; mem, Planning Comn, Charleston, WVa, 71- Bus & Prof Pos: Clerk, registr off, Univ Chicago, 51 & teaching asst chem, 51-52; part-time instr & prof chem, WVa State Col, 55-64, part-time prof, 64-70; research chemist, research & develop dept, Union Carbide Corp, WVa, 54-67, proj scientist, 67- Publ: Improved synthesis of salts & esters of nitroacetic acid, 60 & Synthesis of 1,1'-Bis (tri-n-dodecylsilyl) ferrocene, 62, J Organic Chem. Mem: Fel Am Asn Advan Sci; Am Chem Soc; Optimist Int; life mem, NAACP; Charleston Bus & Prof Men's Club. Honors & Awards: Fel, Am Inst Chemists, 68. Relig: Baptist. Mailing Add: 835 Carroll Rd Charleston WV 25314

MATTHEWS, WILLIAM JOSEPH (R)
b Middleburg, Tenn, Nov 15, 92; s William Morrow Matthews & Martha Ann Burrus M; m 1916 to Lillian Long; c Mary Louise (Mrs Pulliam); two granddaughters. Educ: Cent High Sch, Bolivar, Tenn, grad. Polit & Govt Pos: Asst postmaster, Tenn, 18-30; chmn, Hardeman Co Rep Exec Comt & mem Elec Comn, formerly. Bus & Prof Pos: Formerly operator, chain of silent movies & supermarket, ticket agent, Greyhound Bus Co & Ill Cent RR, & cotton buyer for numerous firms; night supvr, State Hosp, Bolivar, Tenn, 31-32; asst chief patrolman, Naval Air Sta, Millington, 43-44, chief patrolman, 45; cotton buyer & bookkeeper, Bolivar Gin Co, 45- Relig: Baptist. Mailing Add: 729 N Jones Bolivar TN 38008

MATTIES, CHARLES R (R)
Conn State Rep
Mailing Add: 84 Overbrook Rd West Hartford CT 06107

MATTINGLY, JOSEPH ALOYSIUS, JR (D)
b Leonardtown, Md, Mar 29, 48; s Joseph Aloysius Mattingly & Mary O'Connell M; single. Educ: Univ Md, College Park, BS, 75. Polit & Govt Pos: Deleg, Conf of Dem Orgn & Policy & Dem Nat Mid-Term Conf, 74; legis aide to Gov Educ Officer, 75- Mem: St Mary's Co Jaycees (dir); Md Jaycees (state dir); US Jaycees. Legal Res: Box 40 Leonardtown MD 20650 Mailing Add: 5708 Ager Rd Apt 204 Hyattsville MD 20782

MATTINGLY, MACK FRANCIS (R)
Chmn, Ga Rep Party
b Anderson, Ind, Jan 7, 31; s Joseph Hilbert Mattingly & Beatrice Wayts M; m 1957 to Carolyn Longcamp; c Jane & Anne. Educ: Ind Univ, Bloomington, BS, 57. Polit & Govt Pos: Rep cand US Rep, 66; mem exec comt, Ga Rep Party, 66-, vchmn, 72-75, chmn, 75-; chmn, Eighth Dist Rep Party, 66-72. Bus & Prof Pos: Prod scheduler, Arvin Indust, Columbus, Ind, 57-59; mkt rep, IBM Corp, 59- Mil Serv: Entered as Pvt, Air Force, 51, released as S/Sgt, 55, after serv in Strategic Air Command; Good Conduct Medal; Am Theater Medal. Mem: Mason; Brunswick-Golden Isles CofC; Am Legion; Glynco Steering Comt; Boy Scouts. Relig: United Methodist; mem admin bd, St Simons United Methodist Church. Mailing Add: 4315 Tenth St East Beach St Simons Island GA 31522

MATTINGLY, MICHAEL WILLIAM (R)
VChmn, Young Rep Nat Fedn
b Tacoma, Wash, Jan 3, 44; s William Hancock Mattingly & Virginia Mae Hall M; single. Educ: Univ Puget Sound, 63-64; Highline Community Col, 69-71, exec dir student govt, 71; chmn, Wash Collegiate Vets Asn. Polit & Govt Pos: Asst campaign mgr, Eberle for Cong, 68-69; treas, Wash Young Rep Fedn, 69-71; regional dir, Young Rep Nat Fedn, 71-73; Wash State Sen, 73-74; bd mem, Wash Conservative Union, 73-; vchmn, Young Rep Nat Fedn, 73- Bus & Prof Pos: Equip control & driver supvr, Time-DC Inc, Seattle, Wash, 71-74, terminal supvr, 74- Mil Serv: Entered as Seaman Recruit, Naval Res, 64, released as STS3(SS), 70, after serv in Submarine Serv, USS Spinax (SS-489), 66-68; Dolphins; Nat Defense Medal; Vietnam Combat Medal; two Battle Stars; Vietnamese Serv Medal. Mem: Young Americans for Freedom (state adv bd, 73-); Nat Right to Keep & Bear Arms Comt (nat adv bd, 74-); Cystic Fibrosis Found (state adv bd, 73-); Moose; Am Legion. Honors & Awards: Man of the Year, Highline Col Student Govt, 71; Liberty Award, Congress for Freedom, 72; Young Rep of the Year, Wash Young Rep Fedn, 72. Relig: Protestant. Mailing Add: 3818 SW Dash Pt Rd Federal Way WA 98002

MATTINGLY, REX MAX (R)
b Lucy, NMex, May 25, 19; s Eugene Aloysus Mattingly & Linnie Beard M; m 1941 to Laura Elizabeth Treat; c Sharon Gay, Sally Ann & Lloyd Eugene. Educ: Univ NMex. Polit & Govt Pos: Chmn, Bernalillo Co Rep Cent Comt, NMex, 65-67; chmn, NMex Rep State Cent Comt, 67-68; mem, Rep Nat Comt, 67-68; del, Rep Nat Conv, 68; bd mem, Renegotiation Bd, 69- Bus & Prof Pos: Brakeman, Southern Pac RR, 41-42; partner, Mattingly Oil Co, 46- Mil Serv: Entered as Aviation Cadet, Air Force, 42, released as 1st Lt, 45, after serv in Cent Flying Command. Mem: Mason; Scottish Rite; Shrine; Elks; NMex Club. Relig: Protestant. Legal Res: 291 Placitas Rd NW Albuquerque NM 87107 Mailing Add: 4116 Whispering Lane Annandale VA 22003

MATTISON, DOROTHY LOVE (DOT) (D)
Committeewoman, Tenn State Dem Exec Comt
b Itta Bena, Miss, Oct 11, 27; d David Nash Love & Mildred Campbell L; m 1949 to Louis Emil Mattison; c Lynn Rankin, Diana & Louis, Jr. Educ: La State Univ, BMus; Univ Ariz, 62-63; Phi Mu. Polit & Govt Pos: Treas, Sullivan Co Dem Women, Tenn, 69-70; vchmn, Sullivan Co Dem Party, 70-73; councilwoman, Bristol, Tenn, 73-; mem adv bd, Bristol Regional Speech & Hearing Clin, 73- & Bristol Ment Health Asn, 74-; committeewoman, Tenn State Dem Exec Comt, 74- Bus & Prof Pos: Music specialist, Sullivan Co Sch Syst, 63- Mem: Alpha Delta Kappa; Bristol Bus & Prof Womens Club. Relig: Protestant. Mailing Add: 323 Poplar St Bristol TN 37620

MATTLAGE, KARL P (D)
Chmn, Routt Co Dem Party, Colo
b Waco, Tex, Dec 8, 40; s Marvin William Mattlage & Ruth Hintze M; m 1962 to Ann Hunt; c Lara Annette, Karl Gregory & Amy Kathleen. Educ: Baylor Univ, BBA, 63, JD, 65; Phi Alpha Delta; Alpha Kappa Psi. Polit & Govt Pos: Dep dist attorney, Routt Co, Colo, 74-75; chmn, Routt Co Dem Party, 75- Bus & Prof Pos: Attorney, Law Firm of Yegge, Hall & Evans, 74- Mil Serv: Entered as 2nd Lt, Air Force, 66, released as Capt, 70, after serv in Judge Adv Gen Dept, Hq Air Force Commun Serv; Capt, Res, US Air Force Acad. Mem: Colo, Tex & Am Bar Asns. Mailing Add: 50030 Moon Hill Dr Steamboat Springs CO 80477

MATTOX, JAMES ALBON (D)
Tex State Rep
b Dallas, Tex, Aug 29, 43; single. Educ: Baylor Univ, Jackson Hughes scholar, 62-63, Humble Oil & Refining Co scholar, 63-64; Sr Bus Sch scholar, 64-65, BBA magna cum laude, 65; Southern Methodist Univ Sch Law, Dallas Airmotive Inc scholar, 66-67, JD, 68; Phi Delta Phi; Order of the Coif; Dean's Honor List; Int Law Soc; Alpha Chi; Beta Gamma Sigma; Omicron Delta Epsilon; Omicron Delta Kappa; Sch Bus Student Body, Baylor Univ (pres, 65, chmn, Bus Sch Honor Coun, 65). Polit & Govt Pos: Dem precinct chmn, Precinct 215, Dallas, Tex, 65, elec judge, 65-66; membership & prog chmn, Southern Methodist Univ Young Dem, 65-67; deleg, Dallas Co Dem Conv, 66 & 68; cong intern to US Rep Earle Cabell, Tex, summer 67; criminal prosecutor, Dallas Co, 68-70, asst dist attorney, formerly; campaign mgr, Judge Robert Hughes for Third Cong Dist, 68; precinct chmn, Dem Precinct 254, Dallas, 68-70; deleg, 16th Sen Dist Dem Conv, 72; deleg, Tex Dem State Conv, 72; Tex State Rep, 73-, mem criminal jurisprudence comt, mem state affairs comt, mem calendars comt, Tex House Rep, 73- Bus & Prof Pos: Bible salesman, Goodwill Publ, Gastonia, NC, summer 61; sheet metal helper, Matthews Eng Co, summer 62; dock worker, Southwestern Transportation Co, Dallas, 64-66; attorney, Firm of Crowder & Mattox, 70- Publ: Workmen's compensation—extra territorial injury provision-status of a Texas employee, Southwestern Law J 428. Honors & Awards: Alpha Kappa Psi Scholarship Key, 65; Am Jurisprudence Award for Excellence in Property II, 65, in Commercial Trans, 67; Wall St J Award, 65; Outstanding Freshman Legislator, Tex Intercollegiate Student Asn, 73. Relig: Baptist; pres, Sunday sch class, currently. Legal Res: 1110 Valencia Dallas TX 75223 Mailing Add: 2017 Cedar Springs Dallas TX 75201

MATTOX, RAY (D)
Fla State Rep
b Jessup, Ga, Mar 10, 27; c Marie Ann & Susanne. Educ: Fla Southern Col, BS; Univ Fla, LLB. Polit & Govt Pos: Fla State Rep, 56-68 & 70- Bus & Prof Pos: Attorney-at-law. Mil Serv: Lt, Army Res; War Serv, Navy. Mem: Jr CofC; Am Legion; Lions; Elks; Moose. Relig: Lutheran. Mailing Add: PO Box 917 Winter Haven FL 33880

MATTOX, VERNA D (R)
Mem, Rep State Cent Comt Calif
b Washington, Nebr, July 14, 16; d Fred C H Dalgas & Jacobina Madsen D; m 1941 to Tilden Mattox, wid, 69; c Frederick & Judy Ann. Polit & Govt Pos: Secy, Manhattan Beach Recreation Comn, Calif, 50-51; pres, SBay Club of Fed Rep Women, 62-63; co-chmn, SBay Citizens for Goldwater, 64; alt deleg, Rep Nat Conv, 64; mem, Rep State Cent Comt Calif, 63-, asst treas, 73-, first asst secy, 75-; current events chmn, Los Angeles Co Bd, Calif Fedn Rep Women, 64-, chmn, Speaker's Bur, Southern Div Bd, 66-, prog chmn, 72-73, resolutions chmn, Calif Statewide, 72-73 & res chmn, Nat, 72-73, corresponding secy, 74-75; alt, 46th Assembly Dist Rep Cent Comt, 65-70, mem, 70-73; second vpres, Los Angeles Co Fedn Rep Women, 67-69; pres, 69-71; secy, Los Angeles Co Rep Cent Comt, 71-73; Presidential Elector, 72. Bus & Prof Pos: Exec secy to vpres, Pac Finance Corp, 40-42; co-owner & operator, Tilden's Sport Shop, 43- Mem: Freedoms Found Women's Div; Citizens Legal Defense Alliance (adv bd). Relig: Presbyterian. Mailing Add: 22647 B Nadine Circle Torrance CA 90505

MATTSON, CATHERINE MARIE (R)
Chairwoman, Schuyler Co Rep Party, Ill
b Aledo, Ill, Feb 20, 35; d John James Elas & Mary Laktas E; m 1958 to Robert Leo Mattson; c Douglas Robert, Bradley Robert & Kristin Kay. Educ: Marquette Univ, BS, 69. Polit & Govt Pos: Chairwoman, Schuyler Co Rep Party, Ill, 64- Mem: Local Homemakers Exten Unit; Schuyler Co Rep Women's Club; Local Church Women United; St Rose Altar Soc; Schuyler Co Audubon Soc (charter mem). Relig: Catholic. Mailing Add: 325 W Lafayette St Rushville IL 62681

MATTSON, MARY-ALICE (D)
Mem, Butte Co Dem Cent Comt, Calif
b Ft Benning, Ga, June 17, 52; d Col(Ret) Robert S Coleman & Bette Liddell C; m 1972 to Charles Alexander Mattson. Educ: Mary Washington Col, 70-71; Riverside City Col, 71-72; Calif State Univ, Chico, BA with honors, 74; Sigma Alpha Gamma; pres, Polit Sci Students Union, 73-74. Polit & Govt Pos: Deleg, Dem Nat Mid-Term Conf, 74; campus coordr, Jerry Brown for Gov Campaign, 74 & Students for Dymally for Lt Gov, 74; consult, Bill Murphy for Supvr Butte Co, 74-; mem, Butte Co Dem Cent Comt, 75- Bus & Prof Pos: Manpower counr, Butte Co Manpower Admin, 74; coordr, Chico Women's Outreach Prog, 74; Chico rep, Northeastern Calif Higher Educ Coun, 74; asst, Dept Polit Sci, Calif State Univ, Chico, 75-; exec bd mem, Northeastern Calif Health Manpower Coun, 75- Publ: Contrib auth, Superior Calif Admin Newsletter, Calif State Univ, Chico. Mem: United Prof Calif; Am Soc Pub Adminr (conf fel, 73); Chico Area Comn on Status Women (treas); League of Women Voters. Mailing Add: 472 E Eighth Ave Chico CA 95926

MATTY, RICHARD PAUL (R)
Wis State Rep
b Menominee, Mich, Sept 16, 32; s Paul Frank Matykowski & Veronica Wrukus M; m 1953 to Sandra Alma Borman; c Richard Paul, Jr, David Joseph, Rochelle, Rhonda Jo, Michael Harvey, Scott Anthony & Kerry Lynn. Educ: US Serv Tech Schs, Parks AFB, San Francisco, Calif, 53. Polit & Govt Pos: Coroner, Marinette Co, Wis, 66-70; Wis State Rep, 73- Bus & Prof Pos: Owner, Matty's Supper Club, Crivitz, Wis, 55- & Matty's Foods, 60- Mil Serv: Entered as Pvt, US Army Band Serv, 49-50; Air Force, 50, released as S/Sgt, 54, after serv in 28th Strategic Reconnaissance Wing, 8th Air Force Strategic Air Command, 50-54; Good Conduct Medal; Nat Defense Medal; Korean Conflict Medal. Mem: Amvets; Am Legion; Crivitz Lions; Boy Scouts; Nat Soc Hiring of Handicapped. Relig: Catholic. Legal Res: 615 Henriette Crivitz WI 54114 Mailing Add: 335A N State Capitol Madison WI 53702

MATUSHEFSKE, JOHN (D)
Del State Rep
Mailing Add: 106 W Franklin Ave New Castle DE 19720

MAUGHAN, RICHARD JOHNSON (D)
Justice, Utah State Supreme Court
b Logan, Utah, Nov 13, 17; s Heber Chase Maughan & Ragna Johnson M; m 1946 to Laura Dell Torgeson; c Margith Christine, Joyce, Eloise, Richard & Mary Francis. Educ: Utah State Univ, BS, 48; Univ Utah, Salt Lake City, JD, 51; Pi Sigma Alpha; Phi Alpha Delta. Polit & Govt Pos: Asst Attorney Gen, State of Utah, 51-53; chmn, Salt Lake Co Young Dem, 53-55; secy, Utah State Dem Finance Comt, 53-55; Dem cand, Utah State Legis, 66; chmn, Davis Co Dem Cent Comt, 66-70; Dem cand, US House Rep, First Cong Dist, 68; mem, Utah State Bd Higher Educ, 69-; mem exec comt, Western Interstate Comn Higher Educ, 69-; mem, Utah State Comt for Polit Reform, 69; justice, Utah State Supreme Court, 75- Bus & Prof Pos: Chmn, Continuing Legal Educ Comt, Utah State Bar Asn, 62-69; mem & chmn bd trustees, Utah State Univ, 65-69. Mil Serv: Entered as Pvt, Air Force, 42, released as Sgt, 45. Mem: Utah, Davis Co & Salt Lake Co Bar Asns; Salt Lake Exchange Club. Relig: Latter-day Saint. Legal Res: 500 East Tenth N Bountiful UT 84010 Mailing Add: 615 Kearns Bldg Salt Lake City UT 84101

MAUGHMER, KARROL JUNE (R)
Committeewoman, Rep State Cent Comt Calif
b Hart Co, Ga, Apr 7, 32; d Oren Bowers & Clara Cleveland B; m 1952 to Robert Willis Maughmer; c Patricia Elizabeth, Phillip Robert & Susan Karrol. Educ: High sch grad. Polit & Govt Pos: Pres, Thousand Oaks Rep Women, Calif, 64-65, leadership training chmn, 71; assoc mem, Rep State Cent Comt Calif, 65, committeewoman, 65-; Ventura Co co-chmn, Finch for Lt Gov Calif, 66; founder & adv, Calif Lutheran Col Rep Youth, 66-; pres, Ventura Co Fedn Rep Women, Calif, 67-69; co women's chmn, Nixon for President, 68; co co-chmn to reelect Controller Houston Flournoy, 70; mem, Gov Reagan Campaign Adv Comt, 70; co chmn, Citizens Comt for Welfare Reform, 71; mem, Attorney Gen Vol Adv Comt, 71-; comnr, Community Action Comn, Ventura Co, 72-; mem, Assemblyman Paul Priolo Exec Comt, 74-; co chmn, Veneman for Lt Gov. Mem: Cultural Ctr Task Force; Thousand Oaks Rep Women's Club; Thousand Oaks Art Asn; NAACP; Arts Coun Conejo Valley (pres, 72-75, founder, Arts Coun Cult Ctr). Honors & Awards: Commendation from City of Thousand Oaks for initiating Green Power Found Day in the Valley; commendations from Ventura Co Bd Supvrs & City of Thousand Oaks for serv on community action comn. Relig: Nonsectarian. Mailing Add: 4707 Park Olivo Calabasas Park CA 91302

MAUNEY, W K (D)
NC State Sen
Mailing Add: 200 E Gold St Kings Mountain NC 28086

MAURER, FRIEDRICH C (R)
Treas, Milford Town Rep Comt, Conn
b Hartford, Conn, June 23, 36; s Friedrich Christian Maurer, Sr & Edna Wopschall M; m 1960 to Bonnie Susan Pride; c Friedrich C, III, Pamella Jean, Erich Christian, Sharon Lee & Beth Ann. Educ: Boston Univ, BS in Aero Eng, 59; New Haven Univ Grad Sch, 69- Polit & Govt Pos: Campaign mgr, Maine State Rep, Milford, Conn; finance chmn, Milford Town Rep Comt, 67-68, treas, 67-, vchmn, first dist, 68-70, chmn, 70-72. Mem: Germania-Schwaben Singing Soc, Inc; Boston Univ Varsity Club. Relig: Baptist. Mailing Add: 33 Tall Pine Rd Milford CT 06460

MAURER, LUCILLE SHIRLEY DARVIN (D)
Md State Deleg
b New York, NY, Nov 21, 22; d Joseph Jay Darvin & Evelyn Levine D; m 1945 to Ely Maurer; c Stephen Bennett, Russell Alexander & Edward Nestor. Educ: Univ NC, Greensboro, 38-40, Chapel Hill, AB, 42; Yale Univ, MA, 45. Polit & Govt Pos: Mem, Montgomery Co Bd Educ, Md, 60-68; deleg, Md Const Conv, 67-68; Md State Deleg, 69-, vchmn Montgomery co deleg to Gen Assembly, 72-, mem legis coun, 72-; mem, Gov Comn to Study Negotiations, 70-72, Gov Task Force on Sch Finance, 72, Educ Comn of States Task Force on Coord, Governance & Structure of Post-sec Educ, 72 & Gov Comn on Structure of Educ, 73-; mem educ task force & bd of coun on postsecondary accreditation, Nat Conf State Legis, 74- Bus & Prof Pos: Economist, US Tariff Comn, 42-43, pvt firms, 57-60; consult, Nat Ctr for Educ Statist, 69. Mem: Order of Women Legislators; League of Women Voters; Am Asn Univ Women; Nat Trust for Hist Preservation; Montgomery Co Child Day Care Asn (bd, 74-). Honors & Awards: Legislator of the Year, Md Asn for Retarded Children, 72; John Dewey Award, Montgomery Co Fedn Teachers, 72; Hornbook Award, Montgomery Co Educ Asn, 72; Outstanding Serv to Educ Award, Md Dept Elem Sch Principals, 74. Relig: Jewish. Mailing Add: 1023 Forest Glen Rd Silver Spring MD 20901

MAURO, GUY J (D)
VChmn, Columbiana Co Dem Exec Comt, Ohio
b Alliance, Ohio, Sept 19, 11; s Anthony T Mauro & Mary Ungaro M; m 1944 to Catherine E Morrow; c Eileen, James & Mary Kay. Educ: Ohio Northern Univ, 29-30; Ohio State Univ, BA, 33 & LLB, 36; Theta Kappa Phi. Polit & Govt Pos: Asst prosecuting attorney, Columbiana Co, Ohio, 38-40; deleg, Dem Nat Conv, 52 & 68, alt deleg, 60 & 64; chmn, Columbiana Co Welfare Adv Bd, Ohio, 63-65; vchmn, Columbiana Co Dem Exec Comt, currently; chmn, Salem Area Dem Comt, 70-; judge, Columbiana Co Court, 71-; mem, Columbiana Co Ment Health & Retardation Bd, 72- Mil Serv: Entered as Pvt, Army, 42, released as 1st Lt, 46, after serv in 13th Armored Div, ETO, 45; Bronze Medal. Mem: Am Legion; KofC (4 degree, Faithful Navigator, 69); Salem Kiwanis; Columbiana Co Cath Serv Bur; Elks. Honors & Awards: Award of Merit, Am Legion, 49. Relig: Catholic. Mailing Add: 544 E State St Salem OH 44460

MAURY, JOHN MINOR
Asst Secy Defense Legis Affairs
b Charlottesville, Va, Apr 24, 12; s John Minor Maury & Jane Bell Moon M; m 1939 to Mary Frances Stuart. Educ: Univ Va, 31-33, Law Sch, LLB, 36; Cornell Russian Inst, 43; Nat War Col, 52-53; Delta Tau Delta; Red Land Club, Charlottesville, Va; City Tavern Club, Washington, DC. Polit & Govt Pos: Asst commonwealth attorney, Charlottesville, Va, 36-40; intel officer, Cent Intel Agency, 46-74, mem, Nat Security Coun Task Force to review US Foreign Policy, 53, mem, US Disarmament Deleg, Geneva, 58, legis counsel, 68-74; Asst Secy Defense Legis Affairs, 74- Mil Serv: Entered as 2nd Lt, Marine Corps, 41, released as Lt Col, 46, after serv as Chief, US Mil Mission, Murmansk, Union of Soviet Socialist Republic, 44-46; Res, Col (Ret); Secy of Navy Commendation. Relig: Episcopal. Mailing Add: 3022 Dumbarton Ave NW Washington DC 20007

MAUTINO, RICHARD A (D)
Ill State Sen
Mailing Add: Webster Park Pl Spring Valley IL 61362

MAUZY, OSCAR HOLCOMBE (D)
Tex State Sen
b Houston, Tex, Nov 9, 26; s Harry Lincoln Mauzy & Mildred Kincaid M; c Catherine Anne, Charles Fred & James Stephen. Educ: Univ Tex, BBA, 50, LLB, 52; Delta Theta Phi. Polit & Govt Pos: Pres, Young Dem Club Dallas Co, Tex, 53-55; nat committeeman, Young Dem Clubs Tex, 54-56; Dem precinct chmn, 62-66; Tex State Sen, 23rd Dist, 67-, pres pro tem, Tex State Senate, 73- Mil Serv: Entered as A/S, Navy, 44, released as Radarman 3/C, 46; Pac Theater Oper with 12 Stars. Mem: Am Bar Asn; State Bar of Tex; Dallas Asn Trial Attorneys; Am Trial Lawyers Asn; VFW. Relig: Unitarian. Mailing Add: Mullinax Wells Mauzy & Baab Suite 200 8204 Elmbrook Dr Dallas TX 75247

MAUZY, THAMES L (R)
Ind State Rep
b Warsaw, Ind, Nov 13, 08; s Charles A Mauzy & Mae Harmon M; m 1933 to Helen K Nelson; c T Landon & Sharon Kay. Educ: Anthony Wayne Col, Bus Admin, 29; Alpha Gamma Upsilon. Polit & Govt Pos: Mem town bd, Winona Lake, Ind, 48-56; Ind State Rep, 67-; mem adv comn, Dept Nat Resources, currently. Bus & Prof Pos: Spec sales rep, Hibbard Spencer Bartlett, 30-35; sales & promotion, Sears Roebuck & Co, 35-39; sales mgr, Mellencamp Furniture, 39-42; personnel & labor rels, Arnolt Motors Corp, 42-45; owner-mgr, Home Furniture Mart, 46-71. Mem: Nat Asn Soc State Legislators; Elks; Mason; Scottish Rite; Shrine. Honors & Awards: Recipient ACI Award for Retail Excellence, 62; Skeet Champion, Kosko Club, 47. Relig: Presbyterian. Mailing Add: 1025 Country Club Lane Warsaw IN 46580

MAUZY, WHIT YANCEY, JR (D)
b Harrisonburg, Va, July 21, 26; s Whit Y Mauzy & Eunice Lambert M; m 1972 to Nancy Beggs; c Eleanor Ann & Grace Elizabeth. Educ: Mass Inst Technol, BS, 48; Sigma Alpha Epsilon. Polit & Govt Pos: Alt deleg, Dem Nat Conv, 72; chmn, Tulsa Co Dem Party, Okla, formerly. Bus & Prof Pos: Sr economist, Amoco Petroleum Corp, 66-69; design engr, Crest Eng, 69-71; pres, Mauzy Eng, 71- Mem: Soc Petroleum Engrs; Nat Soc Prof Engrs. Mailing Add: 1532 S Gillette Tulsa OK 74104

MAVAR, VICTOR V (R)
Rep Nat Committeeman, Miss
b Biloxi, Miss, July 27, 26; m 1958 to Gayle; c Victor, Jr, Claire, Geoffrey, Mary, Mark & Elizabeth. Educ: US Merchant Marine Acad, BS in Marine Eng, 47. Polit & Govt Pos: Active in Rep Affairs, Miss, 59-; Rep Presidential Elector, 64; deleg, Rep Nat Conv, 68 & 72; mem,

Regional Export Expansion Coun, 68-; chmn, Harrison Co Rep Party, currently; Rep Nat Committeeman, Miss, 72- Bus & Prof Pos: Partner, Mavar Shrimp & Oyster Co, Biloxi, Miss, 47-; bd dirs & secy-treas, Pet Food Inst, 63- Mem: Am Shrimp Canners Asn; Nat Canners Asn; Biloxi CofC; Biloxi Jaycees (mem bd dirs). Relig: Catholic; Bd dirs, Biloxi Cent Cath Sch Bd. Mailing Add: 427 E Beach Blvd Biloxi MS 39530

MAW, CARLYLE E
Under Secy Security Assistance, Dept State
Mailing Add: Dept of State 2201 C St Washington DC 20520

MAWBY, NANCY B (D)
b New York, July 6, 40; d Frank Mawby & Virginia McDonald; m 1964 to Howard T Mawby; c Andrea Britt & Michael Benton. Educ: Pierce Jr Col, 60-62; Univ Ctr, 71-72. Polit & Govt Pos: Dept chairperson, Dem State Comt, Pa, 72-73; mem, Dem Nat Charter Comn, 73-74; treas, Pa for Shapp-Kline, 73-75. Mem: Nat Fedn Bus & Prof Women's Clubs, Inc. Mailing Add: 25 N 26th St Camp Hill PA 17011

MAXCY, DANNY JOE, SR (JOE) (D)
Miss State Sen
Mailing Add: Box 227 Aberdeen MS 39730

MAXIE, PEGGY JOAN (D)
Wash State Rep
b Amarillo, Tex, Aug 18, 36; d Cleveland Maxie & Reba Harris M; single. Educ: Seattle Univ, BA in Psychol, 70; Univ Wash, MSW, 72. Hon Degrees: LLD, St Martin's Col. Polit & Govt Pos: Wash State Rep, 37th Dist, 71-, chairwoman higher educ comt, Wash House of Rep, currently. Bus & Prof Pos: Consult/exec dir, Cent Area Coun on Alcoholism. Publ: Epistle to the Black Christian, Cath Northwest Progress, 4/26/68. Mem: Totem Bus & Prof Women's Club; League of Women Voters; NAACP; Puget Sound Big Sisters; Nat Asn Social Workers. Relig: Catholic. Legal Res: 3302 E Pine St Seattle WA 98122 Mailing Add: House Off Bldg Olympia WA 98501

MAXWELL, ANITA MARIE (D)
b Yorkville, NY, Aug 4, 32; d Dominick Jiampietro & Josephine Mammone J; m 1949 to Edward D Maxwell; c Kathleen, Richard, Maria (Mrs John Johnson), Michael, Patrick, Josephine, Thomas, Colleen, Edward J, Daniel & Christopher. Educ: Whitesboro Cent High Sch, grad with honors, 49. Polit & Govt Pos: Herkimer Co secy, 71-73; alt deleg, Dem Nat Mid-Term Conf, 74. Bus & Prof Pos: Ed & auth, Farmers Freedom Press, monthly, 73- Mem: Nat Farmers Orgn (deleg to nat conv, 72, 73 & 74, secy-treas & publ dir, 72-). Relig: Roman Catholic. Mailing Add: RD 1 Newport NY 13416

MAXWELL, CLARK, JR (R)
Fla State Rep
Mailing Add: 1205 Sun Circle W Melbourne FL 32935

MAXWELL, DAVID OGDEN (R)
b Philadelphia, Pa, May 16, 30; s David Farrow Maxwell & Emily Nelson M; m 1968 to Joan Clark Paddock. Educ: Yale Univ, AB, 52; Harvard Law Sch, LLB, 55. Polit & Govt Pos: Exec vchmn, Pa Citizens for Shafer, 66; ins comnr, State of Pa, 67-69, secy of admin & budget secy, 69-70; dir, Nixon-Agnew Campaign, Pa, 68; gen counsel, Dept Housing & Urban Develop, 70-73. Bus & Prof Pos: Lawyer, Obermayer, Rebmann, Maxwell & Hippel, 59-63, partner, 63-67. Mil Serv: Entered as A/S, Navy, 55, released as Lt, 59, after serv in Judge Adv Gen. Mem: Am, Pa & Fed Bar Asns; fel Am Bar Found; Am Judicature Soc. Relig: Episcopal. Legal Res: PA Mailing Add: 451 Seventh St SW Washington DC 20410

MAXWELL, ROBERT LEE (D)
Del State Rep
b Wilmington, Del, June 4, 37; s William Heatherton Maxwell & Rebecca Graham M; m 1966 to Catherine Hull; c Wm H. Educ: Univ Del, BA, 70, working toward MA in Commun. Polit & Govt Pos: Dem committeeman, 14th Rep Dist, 74; Del State Rep, 75- Bus & Prof Pos: Social studies teacher, Alexis I du Pont High Sch, Del, 70. Mem: Del Chap, Am Cancer Soc; Hist Soc Del. Relig: Presbyterian. Mailing Add: 311 Village Rd Lancaster Village Wilmington DE 19805

MAXWELL, SIDNEY D (D)
Maine State Rep
Mailing Add: RFD Wilton Jay ME 04294

MAY, ALFRED A (R)
Chmn, First Cong Dist Rep Party, Mich
Polit & Govt Pos: Chmn, First Cong Dist Rep Party, Mich, currently; deleg, Rep Nat Conv, 72. Mailing Add: 17610 Fairway Dr Detroit MI 48221

MAY, CLARENCE EDWARD (D)
Committeeman, Rockingham Co Dem Party, Va
b Weyers Cave, Va, Apr 12, 03; s William Henry May & Eliza Jane Rankin M; m 1928 to Frances Zoll; c Clarence Edward, Jr. Educ: Bridgewater Col, BA, 24; Univ Va, MA, 31; Tau Kappa Alpha; Pi Delta Epsilon; Lambda; Valedictorian of both high sch & col classes. Polit & Govt Pos: Councilman, Bridgewater Town Coun, Va, 56-58; Mayor, Bridgewater, 58-68; deleg, Nat & State Dem Conv, 64; precinct chmn, Bridgewater Dem Party; committeeman, Rockingham Co Dem Party, currently, chmn, 69-72. Bus & Prof Pos: Teacher Eng, Cristobal High Sch, 41-42; asst commandant, Fork Union Mil Acad, 42-44; prin, Copeland Park Sch, 44-45 & Culpeper High Sch, 45-46; prof Eng & dir pub rels, Bridgewater Col, 46-48. Mem: SAtlantic Mod Lang Asn; Mason. Relig: Protestant Episcopal. Mailing Add: 421 E College Bridgewater VA 22812

MAY, DENNIS JAMES (D)
Chmn, Worth Co Dem Comt, Iowa
b Aug 21, 47; s Clifford Alvin May & Caroline Walk M; single. Educ: NIowa Area Community Col, 70. Polit & Govt Pos: Chmn, Worth Co Dem Comt, Iowa, 71- Bus & Prof Pos: Farmer, Worth Co, Iowa, 65- Honors & Awards: Salutorian, NIowa Col, 70. Relig: Lutheran. Mailing Add: RR 1 Kensett IA 50448

MAY, EDGAR
Vt State Rep
b Zurich, Switz, June 27, 29, naturalized US citizen, 54; s Ferdinand May & Renee Bloch M; m 1973 to Judith A Hill. Educ: Northwestern Univ, BS with highest distinction, 57; Kappa Tau Alpha. Polit & Govt Pos: Mem, President's Task Force War Against Poverty, 64; asst dir, Off Econ Opportunity, 64-68; spec adv to US Ambassador to France, 68-70; Vt State Rep, 75- Bus & Prof Pos: Reporter, ed, Bellows Falls, Vt Times, 51-53; reporter, Chicago Tribune, 55-57; free lance writer, Europe, 57; reporter, Buffalo Eve News, 58-61; dir, Pub Welfare Projs, State Charities Aid Asn, 62-64; consult, Ford Found, 72- Mil Serv: Cpl, Army, 53-55. Publ: The Wasted Americans, 64. Honors & Awards: Page One Award, Buffalo Newspaper Guild, 58; Walter O Bingham Award, 59; Pulitzer Prize for local reporting, 61; Merit Award, Northwestern Univ Alumni Asn, 62. Mailing Add: Muckross Springfield VT 05156

MAY, EDWIN HYLAND, JR (R)
b Hartford, Conn, May 28, 24; s Edwin Hyland May & Dorothy Wells Hannum M; m 1947 to Jean Blease; c Edwin H, III, Laura Wells & Lisa Barrie. Educ: Wesleyan Univ; Olin Scholar; Mystical Seven; Chi Psi. Polit & Govt Pos: US Rep, Conn, 57-58; chmn, Conn State Rep Party, 58-62; chmn, Northeastern State Rep Chmn Asn, 59-62; Cand for Gov, Conn, 62; cand, US Sen, Conn, 68; alt deleg, Rep Nat Conv, 68; mem, Health Ins Benefits Adv Coun, Dept of Health, Educ & Welfare, 71- Bus & Prof Pos: Partner, R C Knox & Co, 48-56; pres, May, Potter & Murphy Inc, 56- Mil Serv: Entered as Pvt, Army Air Force, 42, released as 2nd Lt, 45, after serv in Fourth Air Force; Pilot's Wings. Mem: US Jaycees; Gtr Hartford CofC (dir); Conn CofC; Wethersfield Country Club; Originator of Prof Golfers Asn Ins City Open Golf Tourney. Relig: Protestant. Legal Res: 802 Prospect St Wethersfield CT 06109 Mailing Add: 1 American Row Hartford CT 06103

MAY, JOHN AMASA (D)
b Graniteville, SC, Oct 30, 08; s John Amasa May, Sr & Martha Randall M; m 1937 to Louise McCreary Ariail; c Pamela Amasa. Educ: Wofford Col, AB, 31; Harvard Univ Law Sch, 31-32; Univ SC Law Sch, LLB, 34; Phi Delta Phi; Sigma Alpha Epsilon. Hon Degrees: LittD, Lander Col, 73. Polit & Govt Pos: Judge of City Court, Aiken, SC, 34-35; SC State Rep, Aiken Co, 35-66; Col on Staff of Gov Olin D Johnston & Ransome J Williams; mil secy, Gov, SC; chief, Div Outdoor Recreation, SC, 66-; app by President Johnson, mem, Nat Adv Coun on Historic Preservation, currently. Bus & Prof Pos: Sr mem law firm, May, Rich & Grant, 53-60; pres, Fidelity Home, Finance Co; 53-60; adv to SC Bicentennial Comn; dir, Southeast Region, Bur Outdoor Recreation Liaison Officers. Mil Serv: Entered as 2nd Lt, Army, 41, released as Maj, 46, after serv in Inf, ETO & War Crime Trials, 43-46; Maj, Army Res, 45; Bronze Star; Pre-Pearl Harbor, Ger Occup & Good Conduct Medals. Publ: South Carolina Secedes, Univ SC Press, 60; History of St Johns Methodist Church, Book Shop Press, 62; Tall Pines, Tidwell Press, 64. Mem: Southern Heritage Found (bd dirs); Am Legion (nat historian, 69-); Mason; Sons of Confederate Vet (nat comdr in chief); SAR. Honors & Awards: Nat Award of Distinction, US Civil War Centennial Comn. Relig: Methodist. Mailing Add: Mayfields Aiken SC 29801

MAY, PAUL W (D)
Nev State Assemblyman
Mailing Add: 3309 Wright Ave North Las Vegas NV 89030

MAY, STEPHANIE MIDDLETON (D)
Treas, Caucus of Conn Dem
b New York, NY, Apr 16, 28; d Thomas Hazelhurst Middleton & Ruth Stephens M; m 1949 to John Middleton May; c Elizabeth & Geoffrey. Educ: Stephens Col, 46-48; Columbia Univ, 49. Polit & Govt Pos: Bd mem, Nat Comt for Sane Nuclear Policy, 58-68; chmn, Conn Dissenting Dem, 67; secy-treas, McCarthy for Pres, Conn, 67-68; deleg, Dem Nat Conv, 68; treas, Caucus of Conn Dem, 69-; chmn finance comt, Duffey for Senate, 70; treas, Conn McGovern for President Comt, 72. Bus & Prof Pos: Prof portrait sculptor, currently. Mem: Fel, Royal Soc Arts; Conn Acad Fine Arts; Jr League of Hartford; United World Federalists; Another Mother for Peace. Honors & Awards: Sculptor of the Eleanor Roosevelt Peace Award. Relig: Episcopal. Mailing Add: 113 Duncaster Rd Bloomfield CT 06002

MAY, STEPHEN (R)
b Rochester, NY, July 30, 31; s Arthur J May & Hilda Jones M; single. Educ: Wesleyan Univ, BA, 53; Georgetown Law Sch, LLB, 61; Phi Beta Kappa. Polit & Govt Pos: Exec asst, US Rep & US Sen Kenneth B Keating, Washington, DC, 55-64; spec asst, Rep Vice-Presidential Cand Henry Cabot Lodge, 60; councilman-at-large, Rochester, NY, 66-73, mayor, 70-73; vchmn, Temporary State Comn Powers of Local Govt, 70-73; deleg, Rep Nat Conv, 72; cand for NY State Comptroller, 74. Bus & Prof Pos: Counsel, Branch, VanVoorhis, Turner & Wise, Rochester, NY, 65- Mil Serv: Entered as Pvt E-2, Army, 53, released as Pfc, 55, after serv in Ord, 53-55. Mem: Bd dirs, Police Found; Empire State Report Comt NY Drug Law Evaluation. Relig: Protestant. Legal Res: 9A Prince St Rochester NY 14607 Mailing Add: 65 Broad St Rochester NY 14614

MAY, TIMOTHY JAMES (D)
b Denver, Colo, Aug 3, 32; s Thomas H May (deceased) & Helen O'Conner M; m 1957 to Monica Anita Gross; c Stephanie, Maureen, Cynthia, Timothy, Jr & Anthony. Educ: Cath Univ Am, BA, 54; Georgetown Law Ctr, LLB, 57 & LLM, 60; Blue Key; Phi Kappa; Phi Delta Phi. Polit & Govt Pos: Acting chief counsel, Senate Subcomt on Stockpiling & consult, Exec Off of the President, 61-63; managing dir, Fed Maritime Comn, 63-66; gen counsel, Post Off Dept, 66-69. Bus & Prof Pos: Law clerk, Judge Danaher, US Court of Appeals, DC, 57-58; assoc mem, Covington & Burling, 58-61; partner, Patton, Blow & Boggs, 69- Publ: The Status of Federal Maritime Commission Shipping Regulation Under Principles of International Law, Georgetown Law J, 3/66. Mem: Am, Fed & Inter-Am Bar Asns; Jr CofC; Washington Bd of Trade. Relig: Roman Catholic. Legal Res: Denver CO Mailing Add: 3828 52nd NW Washington DC 20016

MAY, WILLIAM J S (D)
Wash State Rep
b England, 1902; m to Pearl M; c Three. Educ: High Sch; Spec courses in advert & elec. Polit & Govt Pos: Wash State Rep, currently; exec secy, Spokane Labor Coun. Mem: Elks. Mailing Add: Sans Souci W 3231 Boone Ave Space 711 Spokane WA 99201

MAY, WOODFORD F (D)
Ky State Rep
Mailing Add: Woodsbend KY 41476

MAYASICH, LORRAINE ELEANOR (D)
b Buyck, Minn, Oct 22, 33; d Alois Adam Claus & Mary Povroznik C; m 1954 to Joseph Frank Mayasich; c Joseph Michael, Denise Marie, Debra Jean, Mark Steven, Timothy Alan, Gregory Louis, Paul Kennedy & Christin Ann. Educ: Col Med Technol & Com, Minneapolis,

51-52, grad Med Secy, 52. Polit & Govt Pos: Chairwoman, Rudy Perpich for Lt Gov Vol Comt, Minn, 69-; chairwoman, 62nd Legis Dist Dem-Farmer-Labor Party, 70-74; assoc chairperson, Sen Tony Perpich for State Legis, 72 & Sixth Sen Dist Dem-Farmer-Labor Party, 72-74. Bus & Prof Pos: Med secy, Mayo Clin, Rochester, Minn, 52-53, Va Munic Hosp, Va, 53-55 & E Range Clin, Ltd, 70. Mem: Nat Cath Foresters; Another Mother for Peace; Save Lake Superior. Relig: Roman Catholic. Mailing Add: Rte 1 Box 251 Eveleth MN 55734

MAYBANK, BURNET R (D)
b Charleston, SC, May 2, 24; s Burnet R Maybank & Elizabeth Myers M; m 1948 to Marion Mitchell; c Burnet R & Marion M. Educ: The Citadel, BS, 47; Univ SC Law Sch, LLB, 50; Phi Alpha Delta; Sigma Alpha Epsilon. Polit & Govt Pos: SC State Rep, 52-58; Lt Gov, SC, 58-62; chmn, Charleston Co Dem Party, SC, formerly. Bus & Prof Pos: Attorney-at-law, Greenville, SC, 50-62, Maybank & Manucy, Charleston, 62-; chmn legis comt, Charleston CofC, currently. Mil Serv: Entered as Cadet, Army, 42, released as 1st Lt, 45; after serv in 394th Heavy Bomb Group, Eighth Air Force; ETO Air Medal; Distinguished Flying Cross. Mem: Am Trial Lawyers Asn; SC Muscular Dystrophy Asn (pres); SC Cerebral Palsy Asn (pres); SC Ment Health Asn (pres); Mason. Honors & Awards: SC nominee outstanding young man of year, Jr CofC, 58. Relig: Episcopal, Bd of Vestry. Legal Res: 2 Water St Charleston SC 29401 Mailing Add: PO Box 126 Charleston SC 29402

MAYER, ANITA ENGELKING (D)
Chmn, Austin Co Dem Party, Tex
b Wallis, Tex, Nov 20, 14; d William George John Engelking & Mattie Louise Sprain E; m 1935 to Bruno Martin Mayer; c William Martin. Educ: SW Tex Col, 33-35. Polit & Govt Pos: Dem chmn, Precinct 15, Tex, 64-66; chmn, Austin Co Dem Party, 66-; alt deleg, Dem Nat Conv, 72. Bus & Prof Pos: Bank teller, River Oaks Bank, Houston, Tex, 52-69. Relig: Lutheran. Mailing Add: Box 236 Wallis TX 77485

MAYER, HENRY MELVIN (D)
b Walla Walla, Wash, Aug 4, 44; s Junior Doze Mayer & Roberta Lois Cargill M; m 1966 to Laurie Ann Hamada; c Kimberly. Educ: Columbia Basin Col, 63-64. Polit & Govt Pos: Alt deleg, Dem Nat Mid-Term Conf, 74. Mil Serv: Entered as Seaman, Navy, 62, released as Seaman II, 63, after serv in NAAS Kingsville. Mem: United Transportation Union; Elks; Am Legion (Second VComdr). Relig: Protestant. Mailing Add: Box 196 Skagway AK 99840

MAYER, JEAN (INDEPENDENT)
b Paris, France, Feb 19, 20; s Andre Mayer & Jeanne Eugenie M; US citizen; m 1942 to Elizabeth Van Huysen; c Andre, Laura, John-Paul, Theodore & Pierre. Educ: Univ Paris, BLitt, summa cum laude, 37, BSc, magna cum laude, 38, MSc, 39; PhD, Yale, 48; DSc, summa cum laude, Sorbonne, 50. Hon Degrees: AM, Harvard Univ, 65; MD, J E Purkyne Col Med, Prague, 68. Hon Degrees: SD, Wittenberg Univ, 75. Polit & Govt Pos: Adv nutrit, Div Soc Affairs, UN, 48; mem nutrit div, Food & Agr Orgn, World Health Orgn, 48-49, first vchmn & acting chmn, Food & Agr Orgn Staff Asn, 48-49, tech secy int comt calorie requirements, 49 & 56, mem int comt protein requirements, 56; consult, Adv Mission, Ghana, 59 & Ivory Coast & West Africa, 60, mem joint expert comt nutrit, 61-, consult nutrit terminology, 68; spec consult to President, 69-70; chmn, White House Conf Food, Nutrit & Health, 69, conf follow-up, 70; chmn nutrition div, White House Conf on Aging, 71; mem, President's Consumer Adv Coun, 70- Bus & Prof Pos: Fel, Ecole Normal Superieure, Paris, 39; Rockefeller Found fel, Yale, 46-48, univ demonstrator, physiol chem, 47-48; res assoc pharmacol, George Washington Univ Med Sch, 48-49; from asst prof to prof nutrit, Harvard Univ, 50-, participant, Harvard Univ Mission to India, 55 & Ghana, 61, lectr hist pub health, 61-, mem ctr pop studies, 68-, fel, Eliot House, 71-73, Master, Dudley House, 73-, mem clin research ctr adv comt & consult, Children's Hosp, 57-; assoc ed, Nutrit Rev, 51-54; mem adv bd, Sargent Col, Boston Univ, 57-71; nutrition ed, Postgrad Mem, 59-70; mem bd ed, Am J Physiol & J Appl Physiol, 60-66; mem comt rev, US Pharmacopeia, 60-70; consult, US Army Research Inst Environ Med, Nat Acad Sci-Nat Research Coun, 64-66, mem subcomt human adaptability, Int Biol Prog, 66-67, subcomt acceptability & palatability, Space Sci Bd, 67-, subcomt calories, carbohydrates, fats, alcohol, Food & Nutrit Bd, 66-, Nat Res Coun, 73-, exec comt, 74- & comt nutrit, Adv Bd, Mil Personnel Supplies, 65-69, chmn, 69; mem subcomt med serv, US Olympic Comt, 66-70; fel, Am Acad Arts & Scis, 63, councillor, 68-71; mem bd ed, Family Health; chmn, Food & Nutrition Sect, Am Pub Health Asn, 72-73; pres, Soc Nutrition Educ, 74- lectr various soc, cong & univs; chmn various symposiums. Mil Serv: Field Artillery Off, French Army & Free French Forces, 39-45; fourteen decorations including Croix de Guerre with two Palms, Gold & Bronze Stars, Resistance Medal & Knight of the Legion of Honor. Mem: Fel Am Asn Advan Sci; Am Bd Nutrit; Hood Found (mem child health adv comt, 64-); Action Boston Community Develop (dir, 65-66, 68-); Planned Parenthood League Mass (dir, 67-); plus numerous others. Honors & Awards: Gold Medal, City of Paris, 36; Calvert Smith Prize, Harvard Univ Alumni Asn, 61; Alvarenga Prize, Col Physicians Philadelphia, 68; Atwater Prize US Govt, 71; Bradford Washington Prize, 75. Relig: Unitarian-Universalist; Mem Bd Trustees, First Parish, Sudbury, 58-61, chmn, 60-61, moderator, 61-66; vestryman, Kings Chapel, 71-74, sr warden, 74- Mailing Add: Dept of Nutrit Harvard Sch of Pub Health 665 Huntington Ave Boston MA 02115

MAYER, JEROME J (D)
SDak State Sen
Mailing Add: 1615 S Fifth Ave Sioux Falls SD 57105

MAYER, WILLIAM SNYDER (R)
Mem, East Granby Rep Town Comt, Conn
b West Haven, Conn, Nov 7, 24; s Stanley B Mayer & Aldenia Snyder M; m 1945 to Florence Scranton; c Wendy R, Alan S & Robin E. Educ: St Louis Univ, BS, 48. Polit & Govt Pos: Chmn, East Granby Planning & Zoning Comn, Conn, 54-62; mem, East Granby Rep Town Comt, 54-; East Granby rep, Capitol Regional Planning Agency, 57-59; Conn State Rep, 63-70; first selectman, East Granby, 70-74; Judge of Probate, 75- Mil Serv: Entered as Pvt, Army Air Force, 43, released as 1st Lt, 45, after serv as Pilot, Italy, 44-45; Air Medal with five Clusters. Mem: CofC; Grange. Relig: Congregational. Mailing Add: One Rainbow Rd East Granby CT 06026

MAYES, ED (D)
Tex State Rep
Mailing Add: Rte 2 Granbury TX 76048

MAYFIELD, FRANK HENDERSON, JR (R)
Ohio State Rep
b Cincinnati, Ohio, July 20, 39; s Frank Henderson Mayfield & Queenee Jones M; m 1958 to Judith Radabaugh; c Deborah Francis, David Glen, Diana Lee & Frank Henderson, III. Educ: Univ NC, Chapel Hill, AB; Univ Cincinnati Law Sch, 2 years; Chase Law Sch, LLB; Phi Alpha Delta. Polit & Govt Pos: Mem, City Planning Comn, Cincinnati, Ohio, 66-67; Ohio State Rep, 65th Dist, 68- Relig: Methodist. Legal Res: 6740 Hiddenhills Dr Cincinnati OH 45230 Mailing Add: 120 E Fourth St Suite 520 Cincinnati OH 45202

MAYHALL, JAMES ELWIN (R)
b Cumberland Co, Ill, Dec 25, 23; s William Mayhall & Myrtle Borror M; m 1946 to Marilyn L Claybaugh; c James David & Teri Lynn. Educ: Neoga Twp High Sch, Ill. Polit & Govt Pos: City clerk, Neoga, Ill, 48-50; co chmn, Citizens for Nixon, 60; chmn, Cumberland Co Rep Cent Comt, formerly; mem regional adv coun, Small Bus Admin, 69-; pub adminr, pub guardian & conservator, Cumberland Co, Ill, 70- Bus & Prof Pos: Agt, Metrop Life Ins Co, 53-55; asst mgr, Frank Kern Mfg Co, Neoga, Ill, 55- Mil Serv: Entered as Pvt, Army, 42, released as Cpl, 46, after serv in ETO; Am Campaign Medal; European-African-Mid Eastern Theater Ribbon with Three Bronze Battle Stars; Good Conduct & Victory Medals. Mem: Rep Co Chmn Asn of Ill; Am Legion; Odd Fellows. Relig: Presbyterian. Mailing Add: 736 Pine Ave Neoga IL 62447

MAYL, ESTHER (D)
Mem, Dem Nat Comt, Ohio
Mailing Add: 201 Westhaven Dr Kettering OH 45429

MAYNARD, DON (D)
Idaho State Rep
Mailing Add: Clark Fork ID 83811

MAYNARD, JOHN M (D)
Mich State Rep
Mailing Add: 22824 Ridgeway St Clair Shores MI 48080

MAYNARD, LAWRENCE RAY (D)
Ky State Rep
Mailing Add: 1340 S Sixth St Louisville KY 40208

MAYNARD, OLIVIA BENEDICT (LIBBY) (D)
VChmn, Mich Dem State Cent Comt
b Cincinnati, Ohio, June 24, 36; d Samuel Benedict & Elizabeth Carruthers B; div; c Elizabeth, Benjamin & John. Educ: Sweet Briar Col, 54-57; George Washington Univ, BA, 58; Univ Mich, MSW, 71; Student Govt Exec Bd; Bum Chums; Choir; World Affairs Club. Polit & Govt Pos: Recording secy, Mich Dem State Cent Comt, 67-71, vchmn, 71-; alt deleg, Dem Nat Conv, 68 & 72; mem, Mich Polit Reform Comn, 69; mem, Genesee Co Dem Exec Comt, 68-72; co-chmn, Mich Dem Policy Comt, 73 & 75; deleg, Dem Nat Mid-Term Conf, 74. Mem: Am Civil Liberties Union; Am for Dem Action; Flint Urban League; Flint League Women Voters; NAACP. Relig: Episcopal. Legal Res: 2026 Calumet Flint MI 48503 Mailing Add: 1535 E Lafayette Detroit MI 48207

MAYNARD, RALPH C (D)
NH State Rep
Mailing Add: 590 Kearsarge Way Portsmouth NH 03801

MAYNARD, RICHARD EDWARDS (D)
Committeeman, Ill Dem Party
b Monmouth, Ill, Jan 15, 33; s Clayton Dale Maynard & Sydnie Edwards M; m 1953 to Jennievee Ola Blackman; c Richard Edwards, Jr, Ronald Eugene, Roger Eric, Robert Eldon & Jane Elisabeth. Educ: Western Ill Univ, 1 year. Polit & Govt Pos: Sheriff, Mercer Co, Ill, 58-62; precinct committeeman, Mercer Precinct 2, 62-; supt of Veterans Assistance, Mercer Co, 67-; committeeman, Ill Dem Comt, 44th Dist, 68- Bus & Prof Pos: Ins & real estate broker, Ford & Maynard Agency, Aledo, Ill, 63- Mil Serv: Entered as Pfc, Army, 52, released as Cpl, 53, after serv in 44th FA Bn, Fourth Inf Div, Europe. Mem: AF&AM; VFW; Am Legion; Mason (32 degree); 40 et 8. Relig: Methodist. Mailing Add: 407 SE Fifth Ave Aledo IL 61231

MAYNE, WILEY (R)
b Sanborn, Iowa, Jan 19, 17; m 1942 to Elizabeth Dodson M; c Martha Elizabeth, Wiley, Jr & John. Educ: Harvard Col, BS, cum laude, 38; Harvard Law Sch, 38-39; Univ Iowa Law Sch, JD, 41. Polit & Govt Pos: Spec agt, Fed Bur Invest, 41-43; Nat Committeeman Young Rep, 48-52; nat vchmn, Young Rep, 49-51; Eisenhower Chmn for Woodbury Co, Iowa, 52; comnr, Uniform State Laws, 56-60; US Rep, Iowa, 67-74; Iowa cand, US House of Rep, 74. Bus & Prof Pos: Partner, law firm, Shull, Marshall, Mayne, Marks & Vizentos, 46-66; pres, Sioux City Symphony Asn, Iowa, 47-53 & Sioux City Symphony Found, 54-66; exec committeeman, Int Asn Ins Counsel, 61-64; pres, Iowa State Bar Asn, 63-64; chmn, Midwest Region Rhodes Scholar Selection Comt, 64-66; mem house of deleg, Am Bar Asn, 66-68. Mil Serv: Entered Navy, 43, released as Lt(jg), 46, after serv in Pac, Atlantic & European Theaters; Naval Res. Mem: Iowa State & Am Bar Asns; Am Col Trial Lawyers; Scottish Rite (33 degree); Mason. Honors & Awards: Sioux City Bar Award of Merit, 60. Relig: Presbyterian. Legal Res: IA Mailing Add: 107 Cannon House Off Bldg Washington DC 20515

MAYS, RICHARD L (D)
Ark State Rep
Mailing Add: 1022 Cross St Little Rock AR 72202

MAYS, ROBERT ALAN (R)
b Quincy, Ill, Oct 16, 21; s Howard L Mays & Edna Best M; m 1946 to Alice Morrison, div, 1968, m 1969 to Anne Markley Frank; c Richard Howard, Alan Morrison, Jeffrey Douglas & Elise. Educ: Northwestern Univ, BS in Indust Mgt, 43; Phi Gamma Delta. Polit & Govt Pos: Comnr, Quincy Park Dist, Ill, 47-; Adams Co chmn, United Rep Fund of Ill, 60-, mem bd gov, 63- Bus & Prof Pos: Sales mgr, Flava Mfg Co, 49-; pres, Miss Valley Canteen Serv Co, 55- Mil Serv: Entered as Ens, Navy, 42, released 46, after serv in Supply Corps, re-entered as Lt Comdr, 51-52, serv in 4th Fleet, Korea. Mem: Kiwanis; Am Legion; Quincy Consistory, Lambert Lodge AF&AM. Relig: Congregational. Mailing Add: 1682 Hampshire St Quincy IL 62301

MAYS, TROY A (R)
b Atlanta, Ga, Feb 25, 29; s Troy E Mays & Mary Knight M; m 1947 to Dorothy Ponder; c Deborah, Sherry & Terri. Educ: Ga Inst Technol, BTE. Polit & Govt Pos: Treas, Sixth Dist

Rep Party, Ga, 64-66; vchmn, Spalding Co Rep Party, 66-68, chmn, formerly. Relig: Baptist. Mailing Add: PO Box 97 Griffin GA 30223

MAZAN, WALTER L (R)
b Center Rutland, Vt, June 5, 21; s Lawrence W Mazan & Henrietta Mazur M; m 1956 to Lee Duffy; c Walter Lawrence, II, Lorilee, Michelle & Michael. Educ: Middlebury Col, 42; Univ Vt, BS, 49. Hon Degrees: LLD, Southern Colo State Col, 70. Polit & Govt Pos: Acting dir, Civil Defense, Vt, 51-57; mem staff state & local defense planning, Off of Emergency Planning, Washington, DC, 57-63; spec asst for fed-state rels, Off of Emergency Preparedness, 63-67, dep dir of liaison, 67-69, acting dir of liaison, 69; asst secy for pub affairs, Dept of Transportation, 69-70, spec prog adv to Secy Transportation, 72-; White House Dir of Inter-govt Rels, White House Conf Children & Youth, 70-71, exec dir, 71-72. Bus & Prof Pos: Polit campaign consult, Montpelier, Vt, 49; ins adjuster, Gen Adjust Bur, Inc, 49-51. Mil Serv: Entered as Sgt, Army Air Corps, 42, released as Pilot, 46, after serv in various units; various mil awards & decorations. Publ: Numerous articles with regard to position. Mem: Exec Off Pres Toastmasters' Club; Nat Conf of State Socs; Vt State Soc. Honors & Awards: Fed Outstanding Performance Award; Outstanding Serv Award, Presidential Classroom for Young Am, 72. Relig: Catholic. Mailing Add: 4856 N 35th Rd Arlington VA 22207

MAZANDER, CHARLES A, JR (R)
Chmn, Second Cong Dist Rep Party, Ark
b Washington Co, Ill, Nov 21, 27; s Charles A Mazander, Sr & Mildred Huff M; m 1948 to Bettie Jean Reed; c Rebecca & Charles A, III (Alex). Educ: Henderson State Col, BS, 55; Little Rock Univ, 56-57; Univ Ark, MS, 63; Alpha Chi. Polit & Govt Pos: Alderman, Benton, Ark, 64-66; secy-treas, Saline Co Rep Comt, 66-69; committeeman, Ark Rep Party, 68-, treas, 70-73; alt deleg, Rep Nat Conv, 72; chmn, Second Cong Dist Rep Party, currently. Bus & Prof Pos: Chemist, Alcoa, Bauxite, Ark, 55-58, tech engr, 58-60, prod engr, 60-63, supt planning & serv, 63-69, purchasing agt, 69-72; mem bd trustees, Henderson State Col. Mil Serv: Entered as Seaman, Navy, 45, released as PO 3/C, 47. Mem: Am Chem Soc; Benton-Bauxite Rotary; Ouachita Area Coun, Boy Scouts; Saline Co Community Fund & City Beautification Comt. Honors & Awards: Silver Beaver Award, Boy Scouts. Relig: Protestant. Mailing Add: 1302 Crystal Dr Benton AR 72015

MAZEWSKI, ALOYSIUS ALEX (R)
Mem Exec Comt, Cook Co Rep Cent Comt
b North Chicago, Ill, Jan 5, 16; s Felix Mazewski & Harriet Konieczny M; m 1948 to Florence W Heider; c Aloysius A, Jr & Marilyn. Educ: DePaul Univ Col Law, LLB, 40. Polit & Govt Pos: Former committeeman, 45th Ward Rep Orgn, Chicago, Ill; Master in Chancery, Superior Court, Cook Co, 63-64; alt deleg, Rep Nat Conv, 64; dir, Nationalities Div, Ill, 64-; mem, exec comt, Cook Co Rep Cent Comt, 64-, attorney, 65-; chmn, Nationalities Comt, Cook Co, 65-; alt US deleg, UN, 25th Gen Assembly. Bus & Prof Pos: Practicing Attorney-at-law, 40- Mil Serv: Entered as Pvt, Army, 42, released as Capt, 46, after serv in Med Admin Corps; Maj, Off Res Corps; Army Commendation Medal. Mem: Polish Nat Alliance (pres); Lions; Moose; Am Legion; Elks. Relig: Roman Catholic. Legal Res: 3813 Medford Circle Northbrook IL 60061 Mailing Add: 1520 W Division St Chicago IL 60622

MAZUR, JOHN (D)
Chmn, Northumberland Co Dem Comt, Pa
b Sagon, Pa, July 7, 26; s George Mazur & Theresa Povelchak M; m 1948 to Lorraine Ann Nebroski; c Paula, John, Jr, Karen & Seth. Educ: Pa Mil Col. Polit & Govt Pos: Cent vpres, Pa Young Dem, 58-60, dir, 60-64; city chmn, Mt Carmel, Pa, 59-64; chmn, Northumberland Co Dem Comt, Pa, currently; alt deleg, Dem Nat Conv, 68 & 72; chmn, 17th Cong Dem Asn. Bus & Prof Pos: Dept engr, Ford Motor Co, 52-56; chief automobile engr, Bur of Traffic Safety, 56-61; pres, Licoma Coal Co, 62-64; mfr rep, 64- Mil Serv: Entered as Seaman 2/C, Naval Res, 44, released as Seaman 1/C RM, 45; Victory Medal & Atlantic Theater Ribbon. Mem: Rotary Int; VFW; Am Legion; Moose; Elks. Honors & Awards: Hon Mention, All Am Wrestling Team, 48. Relig: Greek Catholic. Legal Res: 338 E Ave Mt Carmel PA 17851 Mailing Add: PO Box O Mt Carmel PA 17851

MAZZA, RICHARD THOMAS (D)
Vt State Rep
Mailing Add: Lake Shore Dr RD 3 Winooski VT 05405

MAZZA, VITO MICHAEL (D)
Conn State Rep
b New Haven, Conn, Aug 10, 35; s Vito Mazza & Frances Battista M; m 1960 to Mary Panagrosso; c Vito, Frances Ann, Mary & Diane. Educ: Quinnipiac Col, AS in Bus Admin, 73. Polit & Govt Pos: Mem, West Haven Dem Town Comt, Conn, 74-; Conn State Rep, 115th Dist, 75- Bus & Prof Pos: Asst mgr, Second New Haven Bank, 59-66; investment adv, Gruntal & Co, New York, NY, 66-74; new bus consult, Union Trust Co, New Haven, Conn, 74- Mil Serv: Entered as Pfc, Army, 56, released as SP-3, 68, after serv in Cent Intel Agency. Mem: Ital Am Civic Asn; New Haven Gridiron Club. Honors & Awards: Cub Scout Leadership Award. Relig: Catholic. Legal Res: 416 Third Ave West Haven CT 06516 Mailing Add: House of Rep State Capitol Hartford CT 06115

MAZZANTI, GENO M, JR (D)
Ark State Rep
b Lake Village, Ark, Apr 1, 29; s Geno Mazzanti, Sr & Frankie Carnavaletti M; m 1961 to Patricia Verdine Robertson; c Gina & Vincent. Educ: Univ Ark, Fayetteville, BSEE, 51; Pi Kappa Alpha. Polit & Govt Pos: Ark State Rep, 75- Bus & Prof Pos: Owner-mgr, Lakeside Oil Co, 53- & Lakeside Realty Co, 73- Mil Serv: Pvt, Army, 50; 2nd Lt, Air Force, 58-60. Relig: Catholic. Mailing Add: Rt 1 Box 225 Lake Village AR 71653

MAZZEI, FRANK (D)
Pa State Sen
Mailing Add: 14 Mt Oliver St Pittsburgh PA 15210

MAZZEO, DORINDA COUGHLIN (D)
Chairwoman, Knox Co Dem Comt, Maine
b Rockland, Maine, Aug 5, 39; d John Donald Coughlin & Dorinda Ann Adams C; m 1971 to John Bernard Mazzeo. Educ: St Joseph's Col (Maine), BA, 61; Univ Maine, Orono, MA, 70. Polit & Govt Pos: Chairwoman, Knox Co Dem Comt, Maine, 72- Bus & Prof Pos: Alumnae exec secy, Dean of Admissions, St Joseph's Col (Maine), 62-68; teacher hist & Eng, New Milford High Sch, Conn, 68-70. Mem: Rockland Seafoods Corp; St Bernard's Parish Coun; Daughters of St Bernard (pres, 72-73); St Bernard's Parish Bldg Fund (treas, 72-). Relig: Roman Catholic. Mailing Add: 235 Rankin St Rockland ME 04841

MAZZOLA, ALAN JOSEPH (R)
Conn State Rep.
b Willimantic, Conn, Oct 22, 46; s Joseph W Mazzola & Mary Carchidi M; single. Educ: Roger Williams Col, Providence, RI, BS, 71. Polit & Govt Pos: Mem, Windham-Willimantic Rep Town Comt, Conn, 72-; Conn State Rep, 49th Assembly Dist, 73- Mil Serv: Entered as Pvt, Army, 65, released as Cpl, 67, after serv in 4th Inf Div, Repub SVietnam, 66-67; Army Commendation Medal; Vietnam Campaign Medal; Vietnam Serv Medal; Good Conduct Medal. Mem: Am Mkt Asn; Kiwanis of Willimantic; Franco-Am Civic & Social Club; VFW (nat legis committeeman, Post 1724, 73); Order Sons of Italy. Relig: Roman Catholic. Mailing Add: 82 Foster Dr Willimantic CT 06224

MAZZOLI, ROMANO LOUIS (D)
US Rep, Ky
b Louisville, Ky, Nov 2, 32; s Romano Mazzoli & Mary Ioppolo M; m 1959 to Helen Dillon; c Michael Romano & Andrea Marie. Educ: Univ Notre Dame, BSc, 54; Univ Louisville, LLB, 60; Omicron Delta Kappa; Phi Kappa Phi. Polit & Govt Pos: Deleg, Dem Nat Conv, 68; Ky State Sen, 68-70; US Rep, Third Dist, Ky, 70-; chmn educ comt, Ky Gen Assembly, 70; mem, Dem Nat Comt Comn on Deleg, Selection for 1976 Nat Conv, currently. Mil Serv: Entered as Pvt, Army, 54, released as Cpl, 56, after serv in Alaska, 55-56. Mem: Am, Ky & Louisville Bar Asns. Honors & Awards: Outstanding Freshman Sen, Ky Gen Assembly, 68 & Outstanding Sen from the Pub Standpoint, 70. Relig: Roman Catholic. Mailing Add: 939 Ardmore Dr Louisville KY 40217

MCABEE, JENNINGS (D)
SC State Rep
Mailing Add: RFD McCormick SC 29835

MCADAMS, HARRY MAYHEW (D)
NMex State Sen
b Lorena, Tex, Aug 12, 16; s William Rufus McAdams & Violet Hutchinson M; m 1942 to Gladys Crume; c James M & Diane L (Mrs Gladow). Educ: NTex State Univ, BS, 38. Polit & Govt Pos: Mem, Hobbs Bd Educ, NMex, 61-; NMex State Sen, Dist 41, currently. Bus & Prof Pos: Pres, K-W-E-W, Inc, 45-; pres, Triple M Mining, Inc, 54-57; vpres, Plaza Develop, Inc, 60- Mil Serv: Entered as Pvt, Army, 41, released 45, after serv in ETO, African, Mid East & Am Theatres, 42-45; Lt Col, Air Force Res (Ret); Distinguished Flying Cross; Air Medal with nine Oak Leaf Clusters; Purple Heart; Presidential Unit Citation; Campaign Medals. Mem: RAM; Shrine; Air Force Asn; Soc Commissioned Off; Retired Officers Asn. Relig: Baptist. Mailing Add: 2112 N Fowler Hobbs NM 88240

MCAFEE, LILIAN FOOTE (R)
First VPres, Ga State Fedn of Rep Women
b Chicago, Ill, Aug 28, 11; d Lyle Milton Foote & Mae Speitel F; m 1934 to William Fort McAfee, Jr, wid; c Linda (Mrs William F Halford) & William Fort McAfee, III. Educ: Ward-Belmont Col, Nashville, Tenn, 1 year. Polit & Govt Pos: Pres, Albany Rep Women, Ga, 66-68; vchmn, Dougherty Co Rep Party, 66-73; mem, Ga State Rep Cent Comt, 66 & 68-73; deleg, Rep Nat Conv & mem platform comt, 68 & 72; dir, Second Dist Rep Women, Ga, 68; Third vpres, Ga State Fedn of Rep Women, 68-73, first vpres, 73- Honors & Awards: Albany Woman of the Year, 52; Albany Rep Woman of the Year, 68; Ga State Rep Woman of the Year, 69. Relig: Methodist. Mailing Add: 2103 Nottingham Way Albany GA 31705

MCALISTER, ALISTER DAVIDSON (D)
Calif State Assemblyman
b Highland, Ill, Nov 10, 29; s Deane J McAlister & Genevieve Davidson M; m 1952 to Evelyn Aileen Young; c Diane, Alister, II, Malcolm, Gwenevere & Courtney Lee. Educ: Greenville Col, AB, 51; Univ Ill Col Law, LLB, 57; Phi Delta Phi; ed-in-chief, Univ Ill Law Forum. Polit & Govt Pos: Bd trustees, ESide Union High Sch, Santa Clara Co, Calif, 65-71, pres, 68-69; mem, Santa Clara Co Dem Cent Comt, 66-; Calif State Assemblyman, 25th Assembly Dist, 71- Bus & Prof Pos: Instr, Univ Calif, Los Angeles Sch Law, 57-58; dep co counsel, Los Angeles Co Counsel, 58-60; asst prof law, Willamette Univ Sch Law, 60-62; asst prof bus admin, Portland State Col, 62-63; gen law practice, Johnson, Speed & Bamford, San Jose, Calif, 63-66 & Boccardo, Blum, Lull, Niland, Teerlink & Bell, 66-71. Mil Serv: Entered as Pvt, Army, 51, released as Pfc, 53, after serv in Mil Police. Publ: Labor, liberalism & majoritarian democracy, Fordham Law Rev, 4/63. Mem: Calif Bar Asn; Santa Clara Co Confedn Home Owners Asns; Santa Clara Co Ment Health Asn. Relig: Latter-day Saint. Legal Res: 1595 E Santa Clara San Jose CA 95127 Mailing Add: State Capitol Sacramento CA 95814

MCALISTER, R B (D)
Tex State Rep
Mailing Add: PO Box 2805 Lubbock TX 79408

MCALISTER, ROBERT BEATON (D)
Mem, Dem Nat Comt, Ohio
b New York, NY, Oct 5, 32; s Richard Charles McAlister & Martha Weisenbarger M; m 1957 to Sonya Douglas; c Michael Richard, Peter Douglas & Betsy Anne. Educ: Kenyon Col, AB, 54; Univ Mich, JD, 57; Beta Theta Pi; Phi Delta Phi. Polit & Govt Pos: Alt deleg-at-lg, Dem Nat Conv, 68; chmn, Ohio Elec Day Legal Serv Comt, Ohio Dem Party & Dem Nat Comt, 68; chmn, Ohio Party Struct & deleg, Selection Comt, 69; chmn, Ohio Elec Reform Comt, Ohio Dem Party, 68-69, mem affirmative action comt & deleg selection planning comt, 75-; mem, Ohio Dem Exec Comt, 70-; mem, Dem Nat Comt, 72- Bus & Prof Pos: Attorney, Alexander, Ebinger, Holschuh, Fisher & McAlister, Columbus, Ohio, 57-71. Mil Serv: Entered as Airman Basic, Air Nat Guard, 57, released as A/2C, 63, after serv in Ohio Air Nat Guard. Mem: Columbus, Ohio State & Am Bar Asns; Downtown Coun of Churches; Metrop Area Church Bd (bd dirs). Relig: Episcopal. Legal Res: 137 S Virginia Lee Rd Columbus OH 43209 Mailing Add: 17 S High St Columbus OH 43215

MCALISTER, THOMAS BUELL (R)
Mem, Ala State Rep Exec Comt
b Russellville, Ala, Dec 10, 22; s Charlie Edward McAlister & Gertrude Steele M; m 1947 to Dorothy Jackson; c Thomas E. Educ: High Sch. Polit & Govt Pos: Chmn, Russellville City Coun, Ala, 56-60; Rep cand, Ala State Rep, 66; chmn, Franklin Co Rep Comt, formerly; mem, Ala State Rep Exec Comt, currently. Bus & Prof Pos: Owner, Mac's Mkt, 46- Mil Serv: Entered as Pvt, Army, 44, released as T-5, 46, after serv in 2nd Div, ETO; two Battle Stars. Mem: VFW; Am Legion. Honors & Awards: Jaycees Young Man of the Year Award, 56. Relig: Methodist. Mailing Add: 1901 Circle Dr Hester Heights Russellville AL 35653

MCALLISTER, LERAY L (R)
Utah State Rep
b Anaconda, Mont, Apr 10, 30; s Leland G McAllister & Mary LuElla Gray M; m 1954 to LuJean Roper; c Ann, Douglas, Bruce, Marla & Eric. Educ: Brigham Young Univ, BS, 57; Ariz State Univ, MS, 59, DBusA, 71; Beta Gamma Sigma. Polit & Govt Pos: Utah State Rep, Dist 36, 75- Bus & Prof Pos: Asst prof acct, South Utah State Col, 59-63; assoc prof acct, Brigham Young Univ, 63- Mil Serv: Entered as E-1, Army, 53, released as Pfc, 55, after serv in Counter Intel Corp, Ft Holabird, Baltimore, Md. Mem: Am Acct Asn. Relig: Latter-day Saint. Mailing Add: 296 E 1864 S Orem UT 84057

MCALLISTER, RICHARD (D)
RI State Sen
Mailing Add: 1 Calaman Rd Cranston RI 02910

MCALLISTER, WILLIAM MENZIES
Assoc Justice, Supreme Court of Ore
b Portland, Ore, Nov 2, 05; s William James McAllister & Mary Menzies M; m 1932 to Jean Middleton; c William Middleton & Kathryn Jean. Educ: Willamette Univ, LLB, 28; Phi Delta Theta; Delta Theta Phi. Hon Degrees: LLD, Willamette Univ, 63. Polit & Govt Pos: Ore State Rep, 37-44, speaker, Ore House of Rep, 43-44; deleg, Rep Nat Conv, 48 & 52; Ore State Sen, 49-50; Assoc Justice, Supreme Court of Ore, 56-, Chief Justice, 59-66. Bus & Prof Pos: Attorney-at-law, Medford, Ore, 31-56. Mil Serv: Maj, Army, 43-45. Mem: Nat Col State Trial Judges; Ore State Bar; Mason; Shrine; Arlington Club, Portland. Relig: Presbyterian. Legal Res: 3403 Country Club Dr S Salem OR 97302 Mailing Add: Supreme Court Bldg Salem OR 97310

MCANERNEY, LEE (R)
Mem, Rep State Cent Comt, Alaska
b San Francisco, Calif, July 14, 20; d Sol (Solly) Urie & Hilma Hihnala U; wid; c Jane (Mrs Fournier), Ann (Mrs Oksoktaruk) & Peter. Educ: Univ Wash, 39-41; Kappa Delta. Polit & Govt Pos: Mem, Dartmouth Col Librs, Hanover, NH, 63-69; coun mem, Seward, Alaska, 71-73, mayor, 73-74; alt deleg, Rep Nat Conv, 72; comnr, Dept Community & Regional Affairs, Alaska, 74-; mem, Rep State Cent Comt, currently. Bus & Prof Pos: Family business, formerly. Mem: Pioneers of Alaska; CofC. Legal Res: Stanton Apts 3 Seward AK 99664 Mailing Add: 1003 326 Fourth St Juneau AK 99801

MCAULIFFE, EUGENE VINCENT
US Ambassador to Hungary
b Forest Hills, Mass, Oct 25, 18; s Thomas Joseph McAuliffe & Charlotte Metzger M; m 1946 to Winifred Marie; c Eugene, Jr, Paul, Marie, Lawrence, Stephen, Terence, Patricia & John. Educ: Boston Col, AB cum laude, 40; Boston Univ, 40-42; Nat War Col, 62-63. Polit & Govt Pos: Vconsul & polit officer, High Comnr for Germany, Berlin, 48-54; chief reports & opers, Exec Secretariat, Dept of State, Washington, DC, 54-58, first secy of embassy & polit officer, Am Embassy, Mexico City, Mex, 58-62; dir off pub serv, Bur Pub Affairs, Dept of State, Washington, DC, 63-64; exec secy, Policy Planning Coun, 64-66; dir, Off of NATO & Atlantic Polit-Mil Affairs, 66-68; minister & dep chief mission, Am Embassy Spain, Madrid, 68-70; polit adv, Supreme Allied Comdr Europe, Hq SHAPE, Mons, Belgium, 70-72; minister counr & dep chief of mission, US Mission to NATO, Brussels, 72-75; US Ambassador to Hungary, 75- Mil Serv: Entered as Pvt, Army, 42, released as Capt, 47, after serv in Hq Third US Army, ETO, 44-46; European Theatre Ribbon with 5 Battle Stars; Bronze Star Medal; Croix de Guerre, Belgium. Mem: Am Foreign Serv Asn; Boston Latin Sch Alumni Asn; Boston Col Alumni Asn; Nat War Col Alumni Asn; SHAPE Officers Asn. Honors & Awards: Meritorious Serv Award, Dept of State, 58. Relig: Roman Catholic. Legal Res: MA Mailing Add: Budapest c/o Dept of State Washington DC 20521

MCAULIFFE, ROGER P (R)
Ill State Sen
Mailing Add: 3228 N Newland Ave Chicago IL 60634

MCAVOY, RITA CLOUTIER (R)
Pres, NH Fedn Rep Women
b Lewiston, Maine, June 9, 17; d Gideon Cloutier & Eva Lambert C; m 1948 to George E McAvoy; c Richard Dixon & Suzanne Bette (Mrs Richard Hopgood). Educ: Lewiston High Sch, grad, 34. Polit & Govt Pos: Mem, NH State Rep Exec Comt, 74-75; mem, Natural Resources Conserv Awards Comt, Dept Defense, 74-; mem, NH State Probation Comn, 74-; pres, NH Fedn Rep Women, 74-; mem resolutions comt, Nat Fedn Rep Women, 75- Bus & Prof Pos: Asst mgr, Theyers Hotel, Littleton, NH, 49-69, asst mgr in charge of purchasing, housekeeping supvr & food & beverage supvr, 69-72; mem, US Assay Comn, Philadelphia, 70. Mem: Women's Auxiliary of Littleton Hosp; NH Asn Hosp Auxiliary (legis chmn, 74-75); Littleton Hosp (bd trustees, mem finance, develop funds & capital improv comt, capt, expansion fund drive); Profile Rep Women's Club; Littleton Area Dollars for Scholars Chap (secy, 63-75). Honors & Awards: Personal Award for Outstanding Serv, NH Tuberc & Health Asn, 66; Outstanding Serv Award, Littleton Area Chap Dollars for Scholars, 68; Woman of Year Award, Littleton Colonial Club, 72; Tribute to accomplishments given at Rep Women's Club Appreciation Night, Gov Meldrim Thomson, Jr, 74. Relig: Episcopal. Mailing Add: Bethlehem Rd Littleton NH 03561

MCAVOY, WALTER (BABE) (R)
Ill State Rep
b Chicago, Ill, Sept 10, 04; m 1932 to Mary E Egan; c Patricia & Thomas J. Educ: St Ritas Col, 21-24. Polit & Govt Pos: Mem, 15th Ward Rep Orgn, Ill, 32-73; Ill State Rep, currently, chmn, Banks & Savings Loan Comt, Ill Gen Assembly, 70-73. Bus & Prof Pos: Real estate broker, 57-73. Mem: Moose; KofC; Holy Name Soc; Marquette Manor CofC; Clearing Civic League. Honors & Awards: Tony Pieti Community Serv Award; Individual Freedom Award; Am Legion Award. Relig: Catholic. Mailing Add: 6033 S Richmond St Chicago IL 60629

MCBANE, ROBERT B (R)
Mem, Ind Rep Citizens Finance Comt
b Fortville, Ind, July 17, 18; s G B McBane & Margaret Kinnaman M (deceased); m 1941 to Virginia Richards; c Ben D, R Bruce & Bonnie (Mrs Hayes). Educ: DePauw Univ, BA, 40; Univ NC, Chapel Hill, MA, 57; Am Univ, MA, 65; Sigma Delta Chi; Sigma Chi. Polit & Govt Pos: Mem, Ind Rep Citizens Finance Comt, currently. Bus & Prof Pos: Vpres, SerVaas, Inc, Indianapolis, Ind, 68; exec dir & treas, Greater Indianapolis Rep Finance Comt, 69- Mil Serv: Entered as Pvt, Army, 41, released as Col, 68, after serv in Major Hq, South Pacific, Southwest Pacific; Korea & Southeast Asia, 43-64; Legion of Merit Awards; Bronze Star Medal. Mem: VFW (life mem); Am Legion; Nat Rifle Asn; Retired Officers Asn; Asn US Army. Mailing Add: 4848 Laurel Circle Indianapolis IN 46226

MCBEE, SUSAN GURLEY (D)
Tex State Rep
Mailing Add: PO Box 954 Del Rio TX 78840

MCBEE, WILLIAM K (D)
Ky State Rep
Mailing Add: 500 Florence Park Burlington KY 41005

MCBETH, GERALD DAVID (R)
Chmn, Vernon Co Rep Cent Comt, Mo
b Macon, Mo, Oct 28, 41; s James Lowell McBeth & Olwen Peterson M; m 1967 to Sara L Grimes; c Susan Stark & David Andrew. Educ: William Jewell Col, BA, 63; Univ Mo Sch Law, Columbia, JD, 71; Phi Delta Phi; Order of the Coif; Sigma Nu. Polit & Govt Pos: Chmn, Vernon Co Rep Cent Comt, 74- Mem: Mo Bar (mem, Young Lawyers Coun, 71-, treas, 74-); Vernon Co Bar Asn (pres, 74-). Honors & Awards: Missouri's Outstanding Young Men, Mo Jaycees; Distinguished Serv Award, Nevada Jaycees. Relig: Methodist. Legal Res: 320 S Lynn Nevada MO 64772 Mailing Add: Box 287 Nevada MO 64772

MCBLAIN, DAVID ALEXANDER (R)
Chmn, Grayson Co Rep Party, Tex
b Iowa City, Iowa, Sept 28, 40; s Robert Alexander McBlain & Stella Larsen M; m 1968 to Virginia Hoover; c Evan Alexander. Educ: Phillips Exeter Acad, NH, 58; Grinnell Col, BA, 62; Univ Iowa, MS, 64. Polit & Govt Pos: Rec chmn, Grayson Co Rep Party, Tex, 70-71, chmn, 71-; deleg, Tex Rep Conv, 70-74; mem platform & resolutions comt, 72; presidential elector, 72. Bus & Prof Pos: Grad asst, Comput Ctr, Univ Iowa, 63-64; instr math, Grinnell Col, 64-65; dir comput servs, Austin Col, 68- Mil Serv: Entered as Pvt, Army, 65, released as 1st Lt, 68, after serv in Vietnam, 66-67; Capt, Army Res, currently; Bronze Star. Mem: Asn Comput Machinery; Math Asn Am. Relig: United Methodist. Mailing Add: 653 Kessler Blvd Sherman TX 75090

MCBRAYER, W TERRY (D)
b Greenup, Ky, Sept 1, 37; s Ward McBrayer & Ethel Brown M; m 1964 to Mary Ware; c Sarah Randolph. Educ: Morehead State Univ, BS; Univ Louisville Sch Law, LLB. Polit & Govt Pos: Nat committeeman, past secy-treas & vpres, Young Dem of Ky Club; mem, Ky Port & River Develop Comm; mem, Gov Comn on Educ, 66; Ky State Rep, 76th Dist, formerly, speaker pro tempore, Ky House of Rep, 68-69, majority leader, formerly; mem, Gov Youth Adv Comn, 67; chmn rules comt, Ky Dem Conv, 68; deleg, Dem Nat Conv, 68. Bus & Prof Pos: Attorney-at-law. Mil Serv: Army; Ky Nat Guard. Mem: Greenup Lions; Greenup Jaycees; secy, Greenup Vol Fire Dept; Greenup Co Boy Scouts (counsel & area adv); CofC. Honors & Awards: Presented Key to City, New Orleans, 62; Omicron Delta Kappa Award, Univ Louisville, 62; Award of Merit, Dept Natural Resources, 66; Duke of Paducah, 66; Outstanding Ky Young Dem, 69. Relig: Christian Church; Deacon, Greenup Christian Church; Past Pres Sunday Sch Class; Teacher, Young Adults Class. Legal Res: 1208 Riverside Dr Greenup KY 41144 Mailing Add: Braden Bldg Greenup KY 41144

MCBREAIRTY, JAMES (R)
Maine State Rep
Mailing Add: R 1 Caribou Perham ME 04736

MCBRIDE, ABEL ERNEST (D)
NMex State Rep
b Belen, NMex, May 27, 33; s Max B McBride & Leonore Chavez M; m 1954 to Elsie Griego; c Sharon A, Sandra A; Sharman A & Stuart A. Educ: Univ NMex, BA, 63; Stillman Col, summer 63; Cent Univ Quito, Ecuador, summer 65; NMex Highlands Univ, MA, 73. Polit & Govt Pos: NMex State Rep, 73-, mem, Legis Sch Study Interim Comt, NMex House Reps, majority whip, 75-; NMex Rep comnr to the Educ Comn of the States, 75- Bus & Prof Pos: Asst prin, West Mesa High Sch, Albuquerque, NMex, 72-75; teacher-coach, Albuquerque Pub Schs, 63-72. Mil Serv: Entered as Seaman Recruit, Navy, 52, released as Aviation Electronics Tech 2/C, 56, after serv in VC-35, Far East Theatre, 53-56; Korean Campaign Ribbon, Nat Defense Ribbon & Air Crewman Wings. Mem: Nat Educ Asn. Relig: Presbyterian. Mailing Add: 5212 Ironwood Dr NW Albuquerque NM 87114

MCBRIDE, ANTHONY P (D)
Mass State Rep
b Adams, Mass, Aug 28, 32; s Frank B McBride & Geraldine Witt M; m 1957 to Ruth E McLaughlin; c Brian A, Peter F, Terrance K, Julie A & J Shamus. Educ: Manhattan Col, BS, 56; New Eng Inst, 56-57. Polit & Govt Pos: Mem, North Berkshire Region Sch Comt, North Adams, Mass, 60-65; selectman, Adams, 65-68; Mass State Rep, 69- Bus & Prof Pos: Partner, McBride Funeral Serv, 57-68. Mil Serv: Entered as Pvt, Marines, 53, released as Cpl, 55, after serv in FMF. Relig: Roman Catholic. Mailing Add: 10 Orchard St Adams MA 01220

MCBRIDE, DONALD OPIE (D)
Dir, Tenn Valley Authority
b Cowles, Nebr, June 1, 03; s James Monroe McBride & Lottie Belle Doyle M; m 1935 to Mary Lou Patterson; c Donald Keith, Betty Carolyn (Mrs Robert G Brown) & Roberta Sue (Mrs William Damon). Educ: Univ Nebr, 21-23; Tau Beta Pi. Polit & Govt Pos: Secy & mgr, Nat Reclamation Asn, Washington, DC, 46-49; mgr, Okla Water Develop Asn, Washington, DC, 49-50; spec asst to Sen Robert S Kerr, 50-63; spec asst to US Sen Mike Monroney, Okla, 63-66; dir, Tenn Valley Authority, Knoxville, 66- Bus & Prof Pos: Proj mgr, Grant, Fulton & Letton, Lincoln, Nebr, 24-27; worked with transmission lines & irrigation proj, pvt co & state agencies, 27-39; chief engr & dir, Okla Planning & Resources Bd, Oklahoma City, 39-44, chmn, 44-46. Publ: Auth of numerous publ on the subject of water resource develop. Mem: Prof Engr, Okla; Nat & Okla Soc of Prof Engrs; life mem Ark Basin Develop Asn. Honors & Awards: Eng Hall of Fame, Okla State Univ, 62; Recipient of Robert S Kerr Cong Award, 63. Relig: Baptist. Mailing Add: 8208 Chesterfield Dr Knoxville TN 37919

MCBRIDE, JERRY E (D)
Mo State Rep
Mailing Add: Edgar Springs MO 65462

MCBRIDE, JOSEPH H (D)
Ky State Rep
Mailing Add: Rte 1 Waverly KY 42462

MCBRIDE, ROBERT H (D)
NMex State Sen
b Grants, NMex, Jan 1, 37; s Max B McBride & Leonore Chavez M; m 1958 to Betty Vigil; c Robert, Jr & Maya. Educ: Univ NMex, BA, 59; Oklahoma City Univ, JD, 66; Delta Sigma Phi; Phi Alpha Delta. Polit & Govt Pos: NMex State Sen, 71-; mem, NMex Judicial Coun, currently. Mil Serv: Entered as 2nd Lt, Air Force, 59, released as Capt, after serv in 5th Air Force Hq; Outstanding Unit Award; Korean Campaign Ribbon; recalled to mil status during Pueblo conflict, 68. Mem: CofC; Optimist. Relig: Protestant. Mailing Add: 412 Alvarado NE Albuquerque NM 87108

MCBROOM, EDWARD (R)
Chmn, Kankakee Co Rep Cent Comt, Ill
b Kankakee, Ill; s Victor McBroom; m to Eleanor Bowman; c Victor. Educ: Univ Ill. Polit & Govt Pos: Chmn, Kankakee Co Rep Cent Comt, Ill, until 62 & 75-; Ill State Rep, 62-64; Ill State Sen, 43rd Legis Dist, 66-74. Bus & Prof Pos: Automobile dealer. Mil Serv: Navy. Mem: Am Legion; Elks; Moose; Rotary; Medinah Temple. Relig: Methodist. Mailing Add: 1190 S Eighth Ave Kankakee IL 60901

MCBRYDE, CHARLES MARION (R)
Chmn, Lee Co Rep Party, NC
b Sanford, NC, Aug 26, 18; s Napoleon Douglas McBryde & Estella Spivey M; m 1944 to Lois Harrington; c Martha M (Mrs Monroe), Frances Marion (Mann), Vicky Jane & Sarah Elizabeth. Educ: George Washington Univ. Polit & Govt Pos: Chmn, Selective Serv Bd, NC, 48-; chmn, Lee Co Rep Party, NC, currently. Mil Serv: Entered as Pvt, Army, 36, released as 1st Lt, 44, after serv in Inf, 1st Ranger Bn, Mediter Theater, Anzio, Italy, 44; Bronze Star; Purple Heart; ETO, Asiatic Pac Theater Oper & Am Theater Oper Medals; Good Conduct Medal; Combat Infantryman's Badge. Mem: Sanford Traffic Club; Am Legion (past post comdr); VFW; 40 et 8; Kiwanis. Relig: Protestant. Mailing Add: 633 Spring Lane Sanford NC 27330

MCBURNEY, JOHN FRANCIS, JR (D)
RI State Sen
b Pawtucket, RI, Feb 26, 25; m to Ann Rivello. Educ: Providence Col, 48; Boston Col Law Sch, 51. Polit & Govt Pos: RI State Sen, 59- Bus & Prof Pos: Attorney-at-law; elec contractor. Mil Serv: Army, World War II. Mailing Add: 15 Arlington St Pawtucket RI 02860

MCCABE, JAMES L (D)
b Chicago, Ill, July 11, 31; s LeRoy J McCabe & Mary Fleming M; m 1958 to Mary Kathryn Sullivan; c James, Ann, Carol, Robert, John, Jeanne & Marilyn. Educ: DePaul Univ, LLB, 54; Phi Alpha Delta. Polit & Govt Pos: Asst states attorney, Cook Co, Ill, 56 & 57; precinct capt, 37th Ward, Chicago Dem Orgn, 56-64; pres, 37th Ward Young Dem 58-60, mem exec bd, 58-62; mem, Young Dem Exec Comt, 58-62; precinct capt, Wheeling Twp Dem Orgn, 62-67, committeeman, 67-; Dem cand for US Rep, 13th Dist, Ill, 66; chief attorney, Dept of Registr & Educ, Ill, 67-69; deleg, Dem Nat Conv, 68 & 72. Bus & Prof Pos: Partner, law firm of McCabe & Venit, Chicago, Ill, 57- Mil Serv: Entered as Pfc, Army, 54, released as SP-3, 56, after serv in Hq Detachment, 35th Qm Bn, Ger, 55-56; Good Conduct Medal; Marksmanship Medal; Occup Forces Medal. Mem: Chicago & Northwest Suburban Bar Asns; Amvets; Elks; various church orgn. Relig: Roman Catholic. Mailing Add: 312 S Ridge Ave Arlington Heights IL 60005

MCCABE, JAMES WALTER, SR (D)
NY State Assemblyman
b Johnson City, NY, Apr 17, 17; s Robert Francis McCabe, Sr & Kathryn Murphy; m 1943 to Margaret Louise Flynn; c James Walter, Jr, Patricia Anne, Thomas Francis, Robert Francis, Dennis Charles, Gerard Patrick & Kevin Joseph. Educ: Univ Notre Dame, AB, 40; State Univ Albany, MA, 49; Syracuse Univ & Colgate Univ, grad work, summers 50-59. Polit & Govt Pos: Mayor, Johnson City, NY, 63-73; NY State Assemblyman, 73- Bus & Prof Pos: Teacher of Latin & English, Johnson City High Sch, 46-68; counr, 68-73. Mil Serv: Entered as Pvt, aviation student, Army Air Force, 43, released as T/Sgt, 45, after serv in Fifth Air Force, South Pacific, 45; Air Medal with Oak Leaf Cluster. Relig: Roman Catholic. Mailing Add: 127 Massachusetts Ave Johnson City NY 13790

MCCABE, THOMAS BAYARD (R)
Rep Nat Committeeman, Pa
b Whaleyville, Md, July 11, 93; m 1924 to Jeannette L; c Thomas B, Jr, Richard & James. Educ: Swarthmore Col, BS, 15. Polit & Govt Pos: Dep, Lend-Lease Admin, 40-41; chmn bd gov, Fed Reserve Syst, 49-51; Rep Nat Committeeman, Pa, currently; mem, Rep Nat Finance Comt, currently. Bus & Prof Pos: Dir, Scott Paper Co, currently. Relig: Presbyterian. Mailing Add: Scott Paper Co Scott Plaza Philadelphia PA 19113

MCCAFFERY, DOROTHY KANE (D)
b New York, NY, Aug 1, 16; d Thomas F Kane & Genevieve McCue K; m to John K M McCaffery; c Richard K M, Peter G, Sean M & Padraic. Educ: St Joseph's Col for Women, BA. Bus & Prof Pos: Secy bd of dirs, Regional Educ Concept Through United Effort, Conn; secy, Washington Planning Comn, 55-59; chmn, Washington Town Dem Party, 55-65; comnr, Conn State Bd of Labor Rels, 55-; deleg, Dem Nat Conv, 56 & 60; dir, Conn Fedn of Dem Women's Clubs, 58-62; 32nd Sen Dist Committeewoman, Conn State Dem Cent Comt, 58-70; secy, Abraham Ribicoff Campaign Comt for US Senate, 62; mem, Gov Dempsey's Clean Water Task Force, 65-66; circulation mgr, Ctr for Info on Am, Washington, Conn, 68-; mgr, Ella Grasso Campaign Comt, 70, admin asst environ matters, US Rep Ella Grasso, Conn, 71-75; mem bd dirs, Environ Protection Research Inst, 71-; comnr, Washington Conserv Comn Coun, 72-; app exec asst to State Labor Comnr Frank Santiguida, 75- Mem: League of Women Voters; Garden Club of Am. Relig: Catholic. Mailing Add: Kirby Corner Washington CT 06793

MCCAFFERY, JOHN K M (D)
Chmn, Washington Dem Town Comt, Conn
b Moscow, Idaho, Nov 30, 13; s Richard Stanislaus McCaffery & Kathleen Kirwan M; m 1940 to Dorothy Kane; c Richard, Peter, Sean & Padraic. Educ: Univ Wis-Madison, BA, 36; Columbia Univ, MA, 38; Chi Psi. Polit & Govt Pos: Chmn, Washington Dem Town Comt, Conn, 71-; in charge of radio & TV for Reelec Campaign of US Rep Ella Grasso, 71-72 & primary campaign of Stanley Poe for Congress, 74. Bus & Prof Pos: Ed, Doubleday & Co, 40-42; fiction ed, American Mag, 42-46; Eastern story ed, MGM, 48-50; newscaster, Eleventh Hour News, NBC TV, New York, 50-65; newscaster, WPIX-TV, New York, 64-66; Teleradio Corp, Educ Tapes, New York, 66. Publ: Ed, Ernest Hemingway-The Man & His Work, World Publ Co, 50; ed, The American Dream: a Half-Century View of the American Magazine, Doubleday & Co, 64; ed, Adventures for Americans (textbook), Harcourt Brace & World, 69. Mem: Am Fedn TV & Radio Artists; Am Screen Writers Guild; Washington Art Asn; Dem Town Comt. Honors & Awards: Emmy for Best Newscaster, 56; Award, Nat Conf Christians & Jews; Award, Anti Defamation League. Mailing Add: Kirby Corner Washington CT 06793

MCCAFFREY, WILLIAM R (D)
Md State Deleg
Mailing Add: 12405 Lytton Ave Brandywine MD 20613

MCCAIN, DAVID L
Justice, Fla Supreme Court
b Sebastian, Fla, July 23, 31; m to Helen Champion; c seven daughters & one son. Educ: Univ Fla, undergrad hist, Col Law, LLB, 55; Fla Blue Key; Hall of Fame; Kappa Sigma (pres); Alpha Phi Omega (vpres); Phi Delta Phi; Blue Key Speaker Bur. Polit & Govt Pos: Judge, Fourth Dist Court of Appeal, Fla, 67-70; Justice, Fla Supreme Court, 70- Bus & Prof Pos: Attorney, Ft Pierce Police Benevolent Asn; city attorney, City of Ft Pierce, Fla; attorney, Carlton, McCain, Brennan & McAliley, 55-67. Mil Serv: Entered as Capt, Air Force, 55-57, serv as Judge Adv for Hq, 30th Air Div, active in Mil Court Martials, 55-57; Air Force Commendation. Mem: Fla Acad Trial Lawyers; Am Trial Lawyers Asn; Nat Asn Munic Law Officers; YMCA (dir); Am Legion (judge advocate). Honors & Awards: Good Govt Award, Jaycees; Eagle Scout with Palm Award. Relig: First Baptist. Mailing Add: 2317 Killearney Way Tallahassee FL 32303

MCCAIN, WILBUR TEAL (D)
Chmn, Grant Parish Dem Comt, La
b Colfax, La, Oct 19, 13; s Clair Henry McCain & Minnie Gray M; m 1937 to Erin Purifoy Sandlin; c Linnie (Mrs Robert A Lee), Emily (Mrs Lynwood L Vallee), Erin (Mrs Charles E Andrews), Laura (Mrs Ken Moody), W T, Jr, John Thomas, Catherine (Mrs Gerald L Turner, Jr), Wilmot Sandlin, Cora Elizabeth & Joseph Lemee, II. Educ: Northwestern State Col, BA, 38; La State Univ Law Sch, LLB, 43, JD, 68; Lambda Zeta. Polit & Govt Pos: La State Rep, Grant Parish, 40-48; spec asst, Attorney Gen, 62-; mem eighth dist, La State Hwy Bd, 65-; chmn, Grant Parish Dem Comt, Ward One, currently; mem, La State Dem Cent Comt, 73- Bus & Prof Pos: Attorney, Bank of Montgomery, 59-; attorney, Colfax Banking Co, 68-; city attorney, Town of Montgomery, 59. Mem: Charter mem La State Bar Asn; charter mem La Trial Lawyers Asn; Am Trial Lawyers Asn; Am Judicature Soc; Munic Attorneys Asn. Honors & Awards: Outstanding Civic Leader of Am, 67; Scroll from Cent La Mayor's Asn, Outstanding Hwy Bd Mem, 67; Outstanding Southern Civic Leader, 67. Relig: Catholic. Legal Res: 401 Second St Colfax LA 71417 Mailing Add: PO Box 595 403 Second St Colfax LA 71417

MCCALEB, NEAL A (R)
Okla State Rep
b Oklahoma City, Okla, June 30, 35; s Jesse Burt McCaleb & Zelma Bridges M; m 1955 to Georgann Whatoff; c Kevin B, Kathleen R, Caleb G & Adam H. Educ: Okla State Univ, BS in Civil Eng, 57; Phi Kappa Phi; Sigma Tau; Chi Epsilon. Polit & Govt Pos: App by Gov Dewey Bartlett to Okla Ind Affairs Comn, 67-70; app by President Nixon to Nat Coun Indian Opportunity, 72-74; Okla State Rep, 74- Bus & Prof Pos: Pres, McCaleb Eng Co, Edmond, 61-74; pres, McCaleb-Musbaum-Tuovers, Edmond, 74- Mem: Am Soc Civil Eng; Okla Soc Prof Eng; Edmond CofC; Okla State Homebuilders (bd dirs, 72, 74 & 75). Honors & Awards: Outstanding Sr Civil Eng Scholarship, Assoc Gen Contractors, 57; Jaycees Outstanding Young Man Award, 68. Relig: Disciple of Christ. Legal Res: 2107 Vance Dr Edmond OK 73034 Mailing Add: PO Box 111 Edmond OK 73034

MCCALEB, SAMMIE LEE (R)
Chmn, Hickman Co Rep Exec Comt, Tenn
b Pinewood, Tenn, July 4, 11; s John McCaleb & Mattie Haubson M; m 1930 to Mattie Myatt; c Rannic, Billy, Robert, Polly & Wayne. Educ: High sch. Polit & Govt Pos: Chmn, Tenn Agr Soil Conserv Comt, 57-61; chmn, Hickman Co Rep Exec Comt, 66-67, 71-72 & 75- Bus & Prof Pos: Farmer, 40 years & cross tie & lumber bus, 25 years. Mem: Nat Farm Bur. Relig: Church of Christ. Mailing Add: Bon Aqua TN 37025

MCCALL, CARL H (D)
NY State Sen
Mailing Add: 180 Riverside Dr New York NY 10024

MCCALL, DANIEL THOMPSON, JR (D)
b Butler, Ala, Mar 12, 09; s Dr Daniel Thompson McCall & Caroline Winston Bush M; m 1937 to Mary Edna Montgomery; c Mary Winston (Mrs Laseter), Dr Daniel T, III & Nancy McCall (Mrs Poynor). Educ: Univ Ala, AB, 31, LLB, 33; Omicron Delta Kappa, Phi Delta Phi, Sigma Nu. Polit & Govt Pos: Mem, Bd Sch Comnr, Mobile, Ala, 50-56 & 58-60; Circuit Judge, Mobile, 60-69; chmn, Circuit Judges Comt on Continuing Legal Educ, 68; Assoc Justice, Ala Supreme Court, 69-75; Retired. Bus & Prof Pos: Partner, Johnston, McCall & Johnston, Attorneys, 43-60; mem bd trustees, Julius T Wright Sch for Girls, 53-63; mem bd trustees, Univ Ala, 65- Mil Serv: Entered as Lt(jg), Naval Res, 43, released as Lt, 45, after serv in Commun, 43-44 & Legal & Intel COCO SOLO, Naval Operating Base, Canal Zone, 44-45. Mem: Ala Asn Circuit Judges; Nat Conf State Trial Judges; Am Legion; 40 et 8; Navy League US. Relig: Episcopal; former vestryman. Mailing Add: 2253 Ashland Pl Ave Mobile AL 36607

MCCALL, THOMAS J (D)
Pa State Rep
Mailing Add: Capitol Bldg Harrisburg PA 17120

MCCALL, TOM LAWSON (R)
b Egypt, Mass, Mar 22, 13; s Henry McCall (deceased) & Dorothy Lawson M; m 1939 to Audrey Owen; c Thomas, Jr & Samuel. Educ: Univ Ore, BA, 36; Phi Delta Theta; Alpha Delta Sigma. Hon Degrees: LLD, Linfield Col, 65. Polit & Govt Pos: Exec asst to Gov McKay, Ore, 49-52; mem, Gov Blue Ribbon Comt on Govt Reorgn, 60; Secy of State, Ore, 65-67; Gov of Ore, 67-75; mem policy comt, Rep Gov Asn; nat chmn, Educ Comn of the States, 69-70, mem steering comt, 70-, chmn, Task Force on Consumer Educ, currently; mem, Citizens Adv Comt on Environ Qual, 70-; exec secy, Legis Interim Comts on Welfare, Pub Employees Retirement, Indian Affairs, Sex Offenses, Legis Procedures; chmn, City of Portland Youth Comn; mem, Gov Comts on Indian Affairs, Air Pollution Abatement, Govt Reorgn; pub info officer, Ore Civil Defense Agency; mem, Comt on Race & Educ; Portland Sch Dist 1 & adv comt, Ore Coun on Crime & Delinquency; vchmn, Ore Coun on Econ Educ;

chmn natural resources comt, Western Gov Conf, formerly, chmn conf, 73; deleg, Rep Nat Conv, 72; mem exec comt, Nat Gov Conf, 72-75. Bus & Prof Pos: Polit analyst, KGW Radio & TV, Portland; founding partner, Goodrich, McCall & Snyder. Mil Serv: Entered as Navy Combat Correspondent, 44, released as Specialist X 3/C, 46, after serv in Pac. Mem: Nat Conf Christians & Jews; Portland Urban League; Ore Crusade for Freedom; Nat Coun for Support of Pub Schs; Ore Hist Soc (mem bd). Honors & Awards: Golden Beaver Award, Izaak Walton League, 59; Award for Outstanding Documentary in US, Sigma Delta Chi, 62; Brotherhood Award, Ore Regional Conf Christians & Jews, 64; Freedom's Found Award for Weekly Radio Prog Report to the People; Medal of the Soc Award, Am Scenic & Hist Preservation Soc, 71. Relig: Episcopal. Mailing Add: 796 Winter NE Salem OR 97301

MCCALL, WAYNE C (D)
Fla State Rep
Mailing Add: 407 House Off Bldg Tallahassee FL 32304

MCCALLEN, ROBERT RAY (D)
b Effingham, Ill, Nov 15, 26; s Ray R McCallen & Fairy Byers M; m 1948 to Peggy Van Borssum; c Peggy (Mrs Alan Grossnickle), Page (Mrs Samuel Story), Bryan Todd, Paula Erin & Robert Ray III. Educ: Eastern Ill Univ, 46-48; Ind State Univ, Terre Haute, BS, 50; MS, 51; Ind Univ Sch Law, Bloomington, JD, 56. Polit & Govt Pos: City attorney, Wabash, Ind, 56-60 & 72-; city campaign chmn, Wabash, 71-72; nat rules comt, Dem Nat Comt, 72; alt deleg, Dem Nat Conv, 72; spec comt for election of Gov, Indianapolis, Ind, 72; comt for selection of Dem Vice Presidential Candidate, Washington, DC, 72; treas, Fourth Dist Dem Party, Ind, 73-74. Bus & Prof Pos: Teacher spec educ, Springfield, Ill, 50-52; actg state dir, SC Crippled Children's Soc, SC, 52-53; sr law partner, McCallen, Mattern & Downs, Wabash, 56-; develop & co-owner, Wabash Village Shopping Ctr & Lakes Village Shopping Ctr, Warsaw, 64-; developer, co-owner & operator, Friendly Nursing Homes, Wabash, Huntington & Peru, 64-74. Mil Serv: Entered as Seaman, Navy, 44, released as SoM 3/C, 46, after serv in Destroyer Escorts, Atlantic & Pacific Theatres, 44-46. Publ: Weekly column relating to speech & hearing therapy, Darlington, SC newspaper, 52-53. Mem: Wabash Co United Fund (co-founder); VFW (judge advocate, currently); Am Legion (judge advocate, currently); Wabash Co Bar Asn; Am Trial Lawyers Asn (pres, currently). Honors & Awards: Outstanding Dem of the Year, Wabash Co, 74. Relig: Presbyterian. Legal Res: Crestwood Dr Wabash IN 46992 Mailing Add: 40 West Hill PO Box 333 Wabash IN 46992

MCCALLUM, GEORGE WALTER (R)
Mont State Sen
b Conrad, Mont, July 8, 19; s Warren McCallum & Gwen Blackshaw M; m 1943 to Verdie Nadine Armstrong; c Janice (Mrs Johnson), Anita (Mrs Delong), Glenda (Mrs Ueland) & Debra. Educ: Hot Springs High Sch, 33-37. Polit & Govt Pos: Chmn, Sanders Co Rep Cent Comt, Mont, 63-69; Mont State Sen, 27th Dist, 71- Bus & Prof Pos: Area Supvr, J Hofert Co, 60-70. Mem: Mason; Scottish Rite; bd trustees, Hot Springs High Sch; East Sanders Co Hosp Bd; Sanders Co Fair Bd; Grange. Relig: Presbyterian. Mailing Add: Niarada MT 59852

MCCANLESS, GEORGE FOLSOM (D)
b Morristown, Tenn, June 8, 04; s Michael C McCanless & Nannie Louise Folsom M; m 1929 to Sarah Gaut Hardcastle; c Sarah McCanless Howell & George Folsom. Educ: Vanderbilt Univ, AB, 26, LLB, 28; Phi Kappa Sigma; Phi Delta Phi. Polit & Govt Pos: Chancellor, 13th Chancery Div of Tenn, 37-38; comnr, Finance & Taxation, 39-46; attorney gen, 54-69; mem, Tenn Hist Comn, 61-; Assoc Justice, Tenn Supreme Court, 69-74. Bus & Prof Pos: Pvt practice, Morristown, Tenn, 28-37 & 46-54. Mem: Tenn Hist Soc. Relig: Presbyterian. Mailing Add: Supreme Court Bldg 401 Seventh Ave Nashville TN 37219

MCCANN, DOROTHY H (D)
Idaho State Rep
Mailing Add: Box 618 Wallace ID 83873

MCCANN, FRANCIS X (D)
Mass State Sen
m to Jacquelyn Doyle; c Francis X, Jr, Susan Ellen, James Jude, Gregory & Gerald. Polit & Govt Pos: Mass State Sen, 54- Mil Serv: World War II. Mem: Am Legion; VFW. Mailing Add: 19 Hutchinson St Cambridge MA 02138

MCCANN, JAMES A (D)
Comptroller, City of Milwaukee, Wis
b Appleton, Wis, Mar 7, 24; s John McCann & Mary Garvey M; m 1954 to Shirley A Gerlach; c Brian J, Timothy J, Maureen T, Kathleen M, Sharon L & Michael J (deceased). Educ: Univ Wis, BBA, 59. Polit & Govt Pos: Wis State Assemblyman, 15th Dist, formerly; alderman, City of Milwaukee, Wis, 68-72, comptroller, 72- Bus & Prof Pos: Cost acct, Marathon Paper Corp, 49-55; owner & mgr, Real Estate & Ins Agency, 60-65; CPA Off, 65- Mil Serv: Entered as Pvt, Army, 42, released as M/Sgt, 46, reentered, 50, released, 52, after serv in 99th Inf Div, 887th FA Bn, ETO; Three Battle Stars; Ardennes-Rhineland-Cent Europe Campaign Ribbons; Presidential Unit Citation. Publ: Milwaukee's sewer service charge, Gavel, 6/69; City council involvement in determining the effectiveness of urban programs, Nation's Cities, 11/70; CPA's and political activity, Wis CPA, fall 70. Mem: Wis Soc of CPA's; KofC (4 degree, state treas, 66-70, state dep, 70-72, Master, 72-). Relig: Roman Catholic. Mailing Add: 3537 N 95th St Milwaukee WI 53222

MCCARRON, PAUL (DFL)
Minn State Rep
Mailing Add: 732 82nd Ave NE Spring Lake Park MN 55432

MCCARTER, JOE T (D)
Mem Exec Comt, Idaho State Dem Party
b Gooding, Idaho, May 30, 30; s William S McCarter & Mattie Thorpe M; m 1958 to Mercedes A Lolley; c Kathleen L, William L & Joan L. Educ: Univ Idaho, 48-49. Polit & Govt Pos: Dem precinct committeeman, Camas Co, Idaho, 58-64; chmn, Camas Co Dem Party, 64-66; chmn, Legis Dist 22 Dem Party, 66-, SCent Idaho regional chmn, 67-; deleg, Dem Nat Conv, 68; coordr for Hubert Humphrey, Second Cong Dist, 68; mgr, Ravenscroft Campaign for Gov, 70; chmn, Idaho State Dem Party, 70-73, mem exec comt, currently; chmn reelec comt, Gov Cecil D Andrus, 74. Bus & Prof Pos: Secy-treas, McCarter Cattle Co Inc, Corral, Idaho, 60- Mil Serv: Entered as Pvt, E-1, Army, 53, released as Cpl, E-4, 55, after serv in MP Detachment, Ft Lesley J McNair, Mil Dist of Wash, 54-55; Good Conduct Medal. Mem: Idaho Cattlemen's Asn; Nat Farmer's Orgn. Relig: Protestant. Mailing Add: Corral ID 83322

MCCARTHY, CHARLES E (R)
b Lusk, Wyo, Dec 6, 20; s Leslie P McCarthy & Carrie Gunther M; m 1951 to Wanna Herring; c Jack G, Julie Anne & Sharon Mary. Educ: Univ Wyo, 2 years; Univ Denver, BA & LLB, 49. Polit & Govt Pos: City attorney, Limon, Colo, 58-; chmn, Lincoln Co Rep Cent Comt, formerly. Mil Serv: Entered as Pvt, Army, 43, released as Cpl, 45, after serv in 15th Air Force, ETO, Italy, 44-45. Relig: Episcopal. Legal Res: 1500 Seventh St Limon CO 80828 Mailing Add: 183 East Ave Limon CO 80828

MCCARTHY, DIANE B (R)
Ariz State Rep
Mailing Add: 5041 W Kaler Dr Glendale AZ 85301

MCCARTHY, EDWARD PAUL (D)
Wyo State Rep
b Cherokee, Iowa, Mar 3, 45; s Edward Leroy McCarthy & Cleo Cantine M; m 1967 to Patricia Ann Dona; c Kathleen Ann & David Paul. Educ: Univ Wyo, 63-65 & 66; Tau Kappa Epsilon. Polit & Govt Pos: Precinct committeeman, Natrona Co, Dem Comt, Wyo, 66-67 & 68-74; state pres, Wyo Young Dem, 66-67; precinct committeeman, Albany Co, 67-68; Wyo State Rep, 75- Bus & Prof Pos: Speaker, Western Ins Info Serv, 74- Mil Serv: Entered as 1st Lt, Army Res, 65. Mem: KofC; Exchange Club (treas, 74-); Nat Guard Asn. Relig: Roman Catholic. Mailing Add: 537 E 11th St Casper WY 82601

MCCARTHY, EUGENE JOSEPH (INDEPENDENT)
b Watkins, Minn, Mar 29, 16; s Michael J McCarthy & Anna Baden M; m 1945 to Abigail Quigley; c Ellen Anne, Mary Abigail, Michael Benet & Margaret Alice. Educ: St John's Univ, Minn, AB, 35; Univ Minn, MA, 38. Hon Degrees: LLD, St Louis Univ, Univ Notre Dame & Col of St Thomas. Polit & Govt Pos: Civilian tech asst in mil intel, US War Dept, 44-45; US Rep, Minn, 49-59; cong deleg to int conf, WHO, 58; deleg, NATO Parliamentarian's Conf, Paris, 56, 57 & 62; off observer at Gen Agreement on Trade & Tariffs, Geneva, 57 & 62; US Sen, Minn, 59-70, chmn, Sen Spec Comt on Unemploy Probs, 59-60, mem, Dem Steering Comt; deleg, Dem Nat Conv, 68. Bus & Prof Pos: Teacher in pub high schs & pvt cols, 15 years; acting head sociol dept, Col St Thomas until 48; Adlai E Stevenson Prof Polit Sci, New Sch for Social Research, 73-; ed, Simon & Schuster, 73. Publ: A liberal answer to the conservative challenge, Macfadden-Bartell, 64; Year of the people, 69 & Other things and the aardvark (poetry), 70, Doubleday; plus others. Mem: Coun on Relig Freedom & Pub Affairs, Nat Conf Christians & Jews. Relig: Roman Catholic. Legal Res: St Paul MN Mailing Add: McCarthy '76 1223 Connecticut Ave NW Washington DC 20036

MCCARTHY, JOHN FRANCIS (D)
Mem, Bridgeport Dem Town Comt, Conn
b Bridgeport, Conn, Nov 23, 11; s Timothy McCarthy & Julia Driscoll M; m 1940 to Florence Reilly; c John F, Jr. Educ: Bridgeport Engr Inst, 41-43, Eve Sch, 44-48. Polit & Govt Pos: Mem & dist chmn, Bridgeport Dem Town Comt, Conn, 37-; pres, Bridgeport Young Dem, 38-39; pres, Conn State Young Dem, 40-46, nat committeeman, 47-51; deleg, Dem Nat Conv, 44 & 72, alt deleg, 48, 52, 56, 60, 64 & 68; dep registr voters, Bridgeport, 49-61, registr voters, 61-69, tax collector, 69-; nat treas, Young Dem Clubs Am, 51-53. Mem: Fed Bldg & Loan Asn; Home Savings & Loan Asn (dir, 69-); Neighborhood Orgn Ment Ill Children (dir, 66-); William Penn Fraternal Asn (secy, 61-); Hibernians. Relig: Catholic; Trustee, St George Roman Catholic Church. Mailing Add: 664 Atlantic St Bridgeport CT 06604

MCCARTHY, JOHN JOSEPH (D)
NJ Assemblyman
b Jersey City, NJ, July 19, 27; s James Aloysius McCarthy & Beatrice Logan M; m 1948 to Doris Engert; c Barbara (Mrs Michael Musanti), Dennis & Michael. Educ: John Marshall Law Sch, 46-48. Polit & Govt Pos: Councilman, Garwood, NJ, 64-68, mayor, 68-74; State Assemblyman, Dist 20, 74- Bus & Prof Pos: Pres, Garwood Auto Parts Co, Garwood, NJ, 70- Mil Serv: Entered as Seaman, Navy, 44, released as PO 3/C, 46, after serv in 16th Fleet, ETO, Asiatic & Am Theatres, 45-46; also served Korean Conflict, Navy, 50-52. Mem: KofC (treas, 64-); Lions; Garwood Dem Club (pres, 65-); VFW Post 6807; Cath War Vet. Honors & Awards: Distinguished Serv Award, 15 years serv, Getty Oil Co; Merit Award, Civil Disaster Control Dept, Union Co, NJ; Cancer Crusade Award, Am Cancer Soc, 74. Legal Res: 401 Brookside Pl Garwood NJ 07027 Mailing Add: 570 South Ave Garwood NJ 07027

MCCARTHY, KEVIN D (R)
RI State Rep
Mailing Add: 84 Main Ave Warwick RI 02886

MCCARTHY, LEO T (D)
Speaker, Calif State Assembly
b Auckland, NZ, Aug 15, 30; s Daniel J McCarthy & Nora Roche M; m 1955 to Jacqueline Burke; c Sharon, Conna, Adam & Niall. Educ: Univ San Francisco, BS, 55; San Francisco Law Sch, LLB, 61. Polit & Govt Pos: Admin asst to Calif State Sen McAteer, 59-63; mem, San Francisco Bd of Supvrs, 63-68; Calif State Assemblyman, 68-, chmn, Labor Rels & Aging Comts, Calif State Assembly, 71-74, speaker, 74- Honors & Awards: Legislator of the Year, Planning & Conserv League, 71; Outstanding State Legislator, Nat Coun Sr Citizens, 72. Legal Res: 400 Magellan St San Francisco CA 94116 Mailing Add: State Capitol Rm 3164 Sacramento CA 95814

MCCARTHY, PETER CHARLES (D)
Mass State Rep
b Peabody, Mass, Sept 8, 41; s Charles James McCarthy & Mary Leonard M; m 1966 to Mary Anne Joyce. Educ: Suffolk Univ, AB in Hist & Govt, 64. Polit & Govt Pos: Ward committeeman, Peabody Dem City Comt, Mass, 64-, mem, Home Rule Comn, 68-, chmn, 72-; committeeman, Peabody Sch Comt, 65-69, secy, 66-67, vchmn, 68; mem bd, Peabody Inst Libr & Lyceum, 66-; mem, North Shore Regional Voc Sch Planning Bd, 68-69; Mass State Rep, Fifth Essex Dist, 69- Bus & Prof Pos: Teacher, Essex A&T Inst, 65-70. Mil Serv: Entered as Pvt, Marine Corps, 64, released as L/Cpl, 65, after serv in 5th Marine Engrs; Res, 65-71. Mem: Mass State Legislators Asn; Am Judicature Soc; Ancient Order of Hibernians; KofC; Nat Hist Soc. Relig: Roman Catholic. Mailing Add: 16 Lenox Rd Peabody MA 01960

MCCARTHY, RICHARD DEAN (D)
b Buffalo, NY, Sept 24, 27; m 1957 to Gail E Coughlin; c Maura, Brendan, Dierdre, Dean & Barry. Educ: Canisius Col, BA; Univ Buffalo; Cornell Univ; Harvard Univ; Chubb Fellowship, Yale Univ, 69. Hon Degrees: JD, Brandeis Univ, 70. Polit & Govt Pos: US Rep, NY, 64-70. Bus & Prof Pos: Former newsman, pub rels exec; dir, pub rels, Nat Gypsum Co, 56-64. Mil Serv: Navy, 45-46; Army, 50-52. Publ: The ultimate folly, Alfred A Knopf, Inc,

69. Mem: Cent Park Asn; Buffalo Philharmonic Orch Soc; Buffalo Area CofC; Frontier Press Club; Buffalo & Erie Co Hist Soc. Relig: Catholic. Mailing Add: 193 Depew Ave Buffalo NY 14214

MCCARTHY, ROBERT EMMETT (D)
Mass State Sen
b Brockton, Mass, Jan 12, 40; s Robert Emmett McCarthy & Helen T O'Brian M; m 1964 to Roberta Ann Carpineti; c Robert E, III, Patricia A & Allen J. Educ: US Mil Acad, BS, 61; Boston Col Law Sch, JD, 67. Polit & Govt Pos: Selectman, East Bridgewater, Mass, 69-; Mass State Rep, Eighth Plymouth Dist, 71-74; Mass State Sen, 75- Bus & Prof Pos: Lawyer, Feeney & Malone, Boston, Mass, 67-70; Malone, McCarthy & Boluch, 71- Mil Serv: Entered as 2nd Lt, Army, 61, released as 1st Lt, 64, after serv in 82nd Airborne Div, 18th Airborne Corps, 62-64; Sr Parachutist Badge. Mem: Plymouth Co Bar Asn; Asn of New Eng Football Off; Eastern Asn of Intercollegiate Football Off; Kiwanis; East Bridgewater Commercial Club. Relig: Roman Catholic. Mailing Add: 353 Summer St East Bridgewater MA 02333

MCCARTHY, ROBERT W (D)
Ill State Sen
b May 28, 24; married; c Douglas & Diane. Educ: Univ Ill Col Law. Polit & Govt Pos: Ill State Rep & vchmn, Judiciary Comt, Ill House of Rep, formerly; Ill State Sen, 60-, mem, Judiciary, Revenue, Elec Exec & Judicial Rev Comts; mem, Intergovt Coop, Elec Laws & Tort Liability Laws. Bus & Prof Pos: Attorney-at-law. Mil Serv: World War II. Mem: Am Bar Asn. Mailing Add: 260 N Woodlawn Ave Decatur IL 62522

MCCARTHY, TERRENCE P (INDEPENDENT)
Mass State Rep
Mailing Add: State Capitol Boston MA 02133

MCCARTHY, THOMAS CARRELL (D)
b Ames, Iowa, Apr 7, 25; s Carrell Cox McCarthy & Mary Gribbon M; m 1947 to Margaret Beall; c Melissa & Becky. Educ: Northwest Mo State Teachers Col, Maryville, 1 year; Iowa State Univ, BS, 48; Univ Iowa, JD, 50; Phi Kappa Psi. Polit & Govt Pos: Dem precinct committeeman, Wash, 54-59 & 68-72; deleg, Dem Co & Wash State Dem Conv, 56, 68, 70 & 72; alt deleg, Dem Nat Conv, 68; dist coordr, Wash Dem Coun, 68-69; mem exec bd, King Co Dem Cent Comt, 69-70; mem, Wash Dem State Comt, 73-75. Bus & Prof Pos: Title examr, Wash Title Ins Co, Seattle, 50-53; asst counsel, Fed Nat Mortgage Asn, 53; lawyer, Bellevue, 53-; comnr, Bellevue Dist Justice Court, 63- Mil Serv: Entered as A/S, Navy, 43, released as Aviation Cadet, 45, after serv in numerous training units in US. Mem: Wash State & East King Co Bar Asns. Mailing Add: 3111 98th NE Bellevue WA 98004

MCCARTHY, WILLIAM AUGUSTUS (R)
State Committeeman, Mass Rep State Comt
b Gloucester, Mass, Nov 12, 11; s William Francis McCarthy & Lillian Astrom M; m 1953 to Mildred Nadeau; c William J & Janice M. Educ: Wentworth Inst. Polit & Govt Pos: Chmn, Ward 8 Rep City Comt, Mass, 56-58; chmn, Gloucester Rep City Comt, 58-64; pres, Essex Club, 66-69; deleg, Rep Nat Conv, 68; dir, Mass Rep Club, 71-; state committeeman, Mass Rep State Comt, 72- Bus & Prof Pos: Pres & treas, McCarthy Contracting Co, Inc, 46-; mem adv bd, First Nat Bank of Ipswich, 73-; incorporator, Cape Ann Savings Bank, 73- Mil Serv: Entered as Pvt, Army, 42, released as Maj, 1st Armored Div, ETO, 44-46; European-African-Mid Eastern Serv Medal; World War II Victory & Am Serv Medals; Bronze Star Medal; Meritorious Serv Plaque. Mem: Lions; Am Legion; VFW; Elks; Friends of the NShore Community Col. Relig: Catholic. Legal Res: 95 Hesperus Ave Gloucester MA 01930 Mailing Add: PO Box 42 Magnolia MA 01930

MCCARTHY, WILLIAM FRANCIS (D)
RI State Rep
b Central Falls, RI, May 13, 25; s Michael McCarthy & Mary Keough M; m 1944 to Mary Jardin; c William Francis, Michael Patrick, Timothy Dennis, Maureen, Robert Emmett & Kevin Shawn. Polit & Govt Pos: RI State Rep, 80th Dist, 73- Bus & Prof Pos: Caterer, 51-70; real estate broker, 70- Mil Serv: Entered as Seaman, Navy, 43, released as Storekeeper 2/C, 46, after serv in Pac Theatre. Mem: Am Legion; VFW; Elks; CofC. Relig: Catholic. Mailing Add: 921 Cottage St Pawtucket RI 02861

MCCARTY, VIRGINIA DILL (D)
b Plainfield, Ind, Dec 15, 24; d E Millard Dill & Gertrude Paddack D; m 1946 to Mendel O McCarty, wid 1973; c Michael B & Janet M. Educ: Ind Univ, Bloomington, AB, 46, Sch Law, LLB, 50; Alpha Lambda Delta; Phi Beta Kappa; Order of Coif; Mortar Board; Pi Beta Phi; Pleiades. Polit & Govt Pos: Attorney, Off Price Stabilization, Indianapolis, Ind, 51-53; Asst Attorney Gen, Ind, 65-69; from mem & secy to treas, Ind Bd Law Examr, 71-; co-chmn platform comt, Ind Dem State Cent Comt, 72 & 74; deleg, Dem Nat Mid-Term Conf, 74; chief coun, Marion Co Prosecuting Attorney, 75-; mem, Gov Comn on Privacy, 75- Bus & Prof Pos: Pres, Dill-Fields Implement Co, Greenfield, Ind, 68-; attorney-at-law, Dillon, McCarty, Hardamon & Cohen, Indianapolis, 69- Mem: Gtr Indianapolis Women's Polit Caucus (pres, 71-); Ind Women's Polit Caucus (pres, 71-72, policy coun, 72-); Nat Women's Polit Caucus (chmn orgn comt, Admin Bd, 73-75); Indianapolis Bar Asn (chmn, court liaison comt, 75); Ind Bar Asn. Honors & Awards: Woman of Year, Indianapolis B'nai B'rith, 73; Award, Theta Sigma Phi, 73; Human Rights Award, Polit Action, Indianapolis Educ Asn, 74. Legal Res: 5809 Washington Blvd Indianapolis IN 46220 Mailing Add: 120 E Market No 511 Indianapolis IN 46204

MCCAULEY, JOHN E (D)
Mich State Sen
b Delaware, Ohio, Apr 28, 24; married; c Patrick Brian. Educ: Mich State Univ; Wayne State Univ, LLB. Polit & Govt Pos: Chmn, Wayne Co Bd of Supvrs, Mich, formerly; deleg, Const Conv; Mayor, Wyandotte, Mich, 4 years, councilman, 6 years; Mich State Sen, 64- Bus & Prof Pos: Attorney-at-law. Mil Serv: Army; Purple Heart. Mem: Am Legion; VFW; Kiwanis; DAV; Eagles. Relig: Presbyterian. Mailing Add: 1822 Ford Ave Wyandotte MI 48192

MCCAULEY, MAURICE JOHN (R)
Minn State Rep
b Caledonia, Minn, June 7, 23; s John Joseph McCauley & Ella Scanlan M; m 1948 to Margaret Lee; c Janet, Debra, John, Colleen & Diane. Educ: Wis State Univ, LaCrosse, BS, 50; Univ Minn, Minneapolis, 47-48; Ariz State Univ, MS, 64. Polit & Govt Pos: Clerk, Houston Co Dist Court, Minn, 51-58; chmn, Winona Co Rep Party, 69-70; Minn State Rep, 71-, secy GOP policy comt, currently; mem sci & technol comt & chmn metrication subcomt, Nat Coun State Legis, currently; mem steering comt, First Cong Dist, Minn, currently. Mil Serv: Entered as Pvt, Marine Corps, 42, released as M/Sgt, 48, after serv in 2nd Marines, SPac, 43-44; Overseas Battle Ribbons. Publ: A thematic approach to physics, Sci Educ, 10/65; Try it on for size, Sci & Children, 10/69. Mem: Am & Minn Asn Physics Teachers; Winona Eagles; Winona Lions Club; Am Legion; VFW. Relig: Catholic. Mailing Add: 404 E Howard Winona MN 55987

MCCAVITT, LAWRENCE VINCENT (D)
b Brockton, Mass, Apr 5, 43; s Ernest James McCavitt & Mrs McCavitt (deceased); single. Educ: Stonehill Col, North Easton, Mass, AB in Polit Sci, 65; Pa State Univ, MA in Pub Admin, 66. Polit & Govt Pos: Planning asst, Boston Metrop Area Planning Coun, Mass, 66-70; research analyst, State Off of Planning, Commonwealth of Mass, 70-; deleg, Dem Nat Conv, 72; counr-at-lg, City of Brockton, 72- Relig: Roman Catholic. Mailing Add: 534 Ashland St Brockton MA 02402

MCCAW, CHARLOTTE LOUISE (R)
Chairwoman, Mercer Co Rep Cent Comt, Ill
b Rock Island, Ill, Dec 3, 02; d Frederick Robert Kuschmann & Mabel Louise McCarthy K; m 1924 to Cecil Richard McCaw; c Leonard Harry. Educ: Augustana Col (Ill), 1 year. Polit & Govt Pos: Rep precinct committeeman, Mercer Co, Ill, formerly; treas, Mercer Co Rep Cent Comt, formerly; chairwoman, currently; co-chmn, Citizens for Eisenhower-Nixon, Mercer Co, formerly. Bus & Prof Pos: Secy, McCaw Elec & Furniture, Inc, 24- Mem: Eastern Star; Women's Soc Christian Serv; Ill Fedn Rep Women; Mercer Co Rep Women's Club. Relig: United Methodist. Mailing Add: New Boston IL 61272

MCCLAIN, DAVID H (R)
Fla State Sen
b Macon, Ga, June 4, 33; s Joseph A McClain, Jr (deceased) & Laura Burkett M; m 1968 to Leslie McNevin; c Linda N. Educ: Duke Univ, BA, 57; George Washington Univ, MA, 61; Stetson Col Law, LLB, 61; Beta Theta Pi; Delta Theta Phi. Polit & Govt Pos: Legis liaison, Gov Off, Fla, 67; first vpres, Hillsborough Co Young Rep Club, 67-68, pres, 69-70; legal adv, Hillsborough Co Rep Exec Comt, 69-70; mem, Fla Law Rev Comn, 70-71; Fla State Sen, Dist 24, 70-; mem, Hillsborough Co Rep Club; vchmn, Bd Pub Rels & Conf Facilities, Tampa. Bus & Prof Pos: Law Off, McClain & Walkley, Tampa, Fla, 74- Mil Serv: Army, 1st Inf Div. Mem: Hillsborough Co Bar Asn; Tampa Jr CofC; Mason; Shrine; Interbay Sertoma Club. Honors & Awards: Tampa Jaycees Good Govt Award, 71; Outstanding Leadership in Traffic Safety, Independent Ins Agents Gtr Tampa; Green Cross Award, Gtr Tampa Citizens Safety Coun; Most Outstanding Freshman Rep Sen, 72; D B Mackay Award for dedication to Fla history, Tampa Hist Soc, 73. Relig: Protestant. Legal Res: 4611 Fig St Apt 201 Tampa FL 33609 Mailing Add: PO Box 1253 Tampa FL 33601

MCCLAIN, EDWARD FERRELL (D)
Wis State Rep
b Martinsburg, WVa, Aug 12, 35; s Russell Kenneth McClain & Faith Reynolds M; m 1964 to Mary Rosalind Moore; c Russell Edward Moore & Matthew Leyton. Educ: WVa Univ, AB, 61; Southern Ill Univ, MA, 63, PhD, 69. Polit & Govt Pos: Chmn, McCarthy Campaign, Marathon Co, Wis, 68; deleg, Dem Nat Conv, 68; chmn, Marathon Co, New Dem Coalition, Wis, 70; cand, State Sen, 29th Dist, 70; chmn, Marathon Co Dem Party, Wis, 71-; Wis State Rep, 75- Bus & Prof Pos: Ed, Preston Co News, Terra Alta, WVa, 58-59; instr philos, Hanover Col, 64-65; assoc prof philos, Univ Wis, Marathon Co Campus, 65- Mil Serv: Entered as Pvt, Army, 55, released as Cpl, 57, after serv in Hq, Pac. Mem: Am Asn Univ Prof; Am Philos Asn. Honors & Awards: Univ Wis Ctr Syst Teacher of the Year Award, 67. Mailing Add: 408 S Ninth Ave Wausau WI 54401

MCCLAIN, MICHAEL F (D)
Ill State Sen
Mailing Add: 4 N Branch Quincy IL 62301

MCCLAMROCK, MARGARET ELIZABETH (R)
Chmn, Grenada Co Rep Party, Miss
b Grenada, Miss, Jan 20, 30; d Francis Allen Kincaid & Mamie Riley K; m 1948 to Marcus Neil McClamrock; c Marcus Allen, Debra Frances, Margaret Gwen & Thomas Mike. Educ: Miss State Univ, 2 years. Polit & Govt Pos: Chmn, Grenada Co Rep Women, Phillips for Gov, Miss, 64 & 68; chmn, Grenada Co Rep Party, 67-; mem exec comt, Miss Rep Party, 74- Mem: Green Thumb Garden Club; Grenada Garden Club; Eastern Star; Grenada Cancer Soc. Relig: Presbyterian. Mailing Add: 29 Jones Rd Grenada MS 38901

MCCLANAN, GLENN B (D)
Va State Deleg
Mailing Add: 425 S Witchduck Rd Virginia Beach VA 23462

MCCLARY, TERENCE E (D)
Asst Secy & Comptroller, Dept Defense
b Lincoln, Nebr, Dec 1, 21; s Terence A McClary & Mildred A Wilson M; m to Florence H Harris; c Karyl Sue & Karyn Lou. Educ: Univ Nebr, Lincoln, 73-; mem, Cost Acct Standards Bd, 75- Bus & Prof Pos: Financial mgr, Gen Elec Co, Schenectady, NY, 49-64, mgr finance aircraft engine group, 64-69; vpres, controller & mem bd dirs, Sanders Assocs, Nashua, NH, 69-73. Mil Serv: Entered as Pvt, Army, 42, released as 1st Sgt, 46, after serv in 128th Inf Regiment, Pac, 44-46. Relig: Methodist. Mailing Add: 1225 Martha Custis Dr Alexandria VA 22302

MCCLASKEY, WALTER D (R)
Ohio State Rep
Mailing Add: 3434 Marion-Marysville Rd Marion OH 43302

MCCLATCHY, R A, JR (R)
Pa State Rep
Mailing Add: Capitol Bldg Harrisburg PA 17120

MCCLAUGHRY, JOHN (R)
Chmn, Caledonia Co Rep Comt, Vt
b Detroit, Mich, Sept 15, 37; s Richard Thornton McClaughry & Marian Williams M; m 1970 to Alice Hawkes Lamb; c three. Educ: Miami Univ, AB, 58; Columbia Univ, MS, 60; Univ Calif, Berkeley, MA, 63; Phi Beta Kappa. Polit & Govt Pos: Dir of research, Peterson Senate Campaign, Mich, 64; legis aide to Sen Winston Prouty, 65; dir of research, Percy Senate Campaign, Ill, 66; spec asst to Sen Charles Percy, 67; town moderator, Kirby, Vt, 67-; mem, Caledonia Co Rep Comt, Vt, 67-, chmn, currently; spec asst during campaign & transition

period to Richard M Nixon, 68; Vt State Rep, 69-73; mem, Nat Vol Serv Adv Coun, 73-75. Bus & Prof Pos: Pres, Inst Liberty & Community, 73- Mil Serv: Marine Corps Res, 66-, Maj. Publ: Expanded ownership, Sabre Found, 72; The troubled dream, Loyola Law J, winter 74; The Land Use Planning Act, Environ Affairs, winter 74. Legal Res: Kirby VT Mailing Add: PO Box 94 Lyndonville VT 05851

MCCLEAVE, MILDRED ATWOOD (R)
Mem, Rep State Cent Comt Colo
b Memphis, Tenn, Dec 19, 19; d Carl Rivers Poston (deceased) & Ellen Winston P; m to Ben Franklin McCleave, Jr; c Ben F, III, Robert (Bob) A, William (Bill) S & Bruce Poston. Educ: LeMoyne Col, BA, 41; Univ Denver, MA, 71; Delta Phi Delta; Scribblers Forum; Pan-Am Club; LeMoyne Players; Alpha Kappa Alpha; Tra-Co-Dram Drama Group. Polit & Govt Pos: Dist Capt, Rep Party, Denver, Colo, 60-; mem, Rep State Cent Comt Colo, 64-; mem, Denver Co Patronage Comt, 68-; alt deleg, Rep Nat Conv, 72. Bus & Prof Pos: Playground dir, Memphis, Tenn & Davenport, Iowa, 40-52; teacher, Memphis Pub Schs, 41-53; teacher, Denver Pub Schs, 58-; counr jr high sch, 71- Publ: The heritage and contributions of the Negro American, Denver Pub Sch Rev, 69. Mem: Denver Teachers' Club; Colo Personnel & Guid Asn; Colo Sch Counr Asn; NAACP; Eastern Star. Relig: Episcopal. Mailing Add: 2236 High St Denver CO 80205

MCCLELLAN, JOHN L (D)
US Sen, Ark
b Sheridan, Ark, Feb 25, 96; m 1937 to Norma Myers Cheatham. Polit & Govt Pos: Prosecuting attorney, Seventh Judicial Dist, Ark, 27-30; US Rep, Ark, 35-38; US Sen, Ark, 43-; deleg, Dem Nat Mid-Term Conf, 74. Bus & Prof Pos: Lawyer. Mil Serv: 1st Lt, ASSC, World War I. Publ: Crime without punishment, Duell, Sloan & Pierce, 62. Honors & Awards: George Washington Award, Freedoms Found, Valley Forge, Pa; Distinguished Pub Serv Award, Nat Tax Asn; Hatton W Summers Award, Southwestern Legal Found. Legal Res: Little Rock AR Mailing Add: 3241 New Senate Off Bldg Washington DC 20510

MCCLENDON, BURWELL BEEMAN, JR (R)
Mem, Miss State Rep Cent Comt
b Jackson, Miss, Dec 24, 30; s Burwell Beeman McClendon & Mae Allred M; m 1953 to Grace Jean Gillespie; c Marilyn Meek, Burwell Beeman, III & Barry Meek. Educ: Univ Miss, BA with distinction & LLB, 52; pres, Phi Delta Phi & Arnold Air Soc; Omicron Delta Kappa; Phi Eta Sigma; Pi Sigma Alpha; Pershing Rifles; Kappa Alpha Order. Polit & Govt Pos: Asst dist attorney, Hinds, Madison & Yazoo, Miss, 55-56; gen counsel, Miss Rep Party, 55-; chmn, Miss Young Rep Fedn, 57-61; mem exec comt, Nat Young Rep Fedn, 57-67, vchmn, 63-65, gen counsel, 65-67; chmn, Hinds Co Rep Exec Comt, 58-60; deleg, Rep Nat Conv, 60 & 64; chmn, Jackson Rep Exec Comt, 61-64; mem, Miss State Rep Cent Comt, 63-; pub mem, US State Dept Off Selection Bd, 72. Mil Serv: Entered as 2nd Lt, Air Force, 52, released as 1st Lt, 54; Capt, Air Force Res. Mem: Fed Commun Bar Asn; Kiwanis; Kappa Alpha Alumni Asn; CofC; Ole Miss Alumni Asn. Relig: Presbyterian. Legal Res: 4163 Dogwood Dr Jackson MS 39211 Mailing Add: 903 Deposit Guaranty Bank Bldg Jackson MS 39201

MCCLENDON, CAROL (D)
Dem Nat Committeewoman, Ohio
Mailing Add: 3627 E 108th St Cleveland OH 44105

MCCLERKIN, HAYES CANDOR (D)
b Texarkana, Ark, Dec 16, 31; s Hayes Candor McClerkin & Orlean Maloney M; m 1958 to Lillian Riggs; c Martha, Katherine & Lauren Hayes. Educ: Washington & Lee Univ, BS, 53; Univ Ark, LLB, 59; Blue Key; Delta Theta Phi; Beta Theta Pi. Polit & Govt Pos: Ark State Rep, Dist 38, 61-70, Speaker, Ark House Rep, 69-70; mem, Ark State Dem Comt, 71-74. Mil Serv: Entered as Seaman Recruit, Navy, 53, released as Lt, 56, after serv in USS Chilton APA-38, Atlantic Fleet, 53-56; discharged Lt, Naval Res, 67; Naval Occup Medal; Nat Defense Medal. Mem: Miller Co, Ark & Southwest Ark Bar Asns; Am Legion; VFW. Relig: Presbyterian. Legal Res: 7 Colonial Dr Texarkana AR 75501 Mailing Add: Suite 6 State Line Plaza Texarkana AR 75501

MCCLINTOCK, MARADA ANN (D)
Mem, Dem State Comt Mo
b Joplin, Mo, Sept 4, 50; d Albert August Henke & Edna Haddock H; m 1969 to Charles Michael McClintock. Educ: Crowder Col, Neosho, Mo, AA, 70; Mo Southern State Col, Joplin, BSEd, 72; Phi Theta Kappa. Polit & Govt Pos: Secy, Newton Co Dem Party, 72-; alt deleg, Dem Mid-Term Conf, 74; mem, Dem State Comt Mo, 74-; mem policy & planning & ethnic & minority comts, Mo State Dem Party, 75-76. Mem: Dem for Better Govt; Mo State Teachers Asn; East Newton Community Teachers Asn (secy, 73-); People for ERA. Mailing Add: 823 Hearrel Neosho MO 64850

MCCLORY, ROBERT (R)
US Rep, Ill
b Riverside, Ill, Jan 31, 08; s Frederick McClory & Catherine Reilly M; m to Audrey B Vasey (deceased); c Beatrice (Mrs Donald Etienne), Michael R & Oliver S; m 1969 to Doris Hibbard. Educ: L'Institut Sillig, Vevey, Switzerland, 25-26 & 28-29; Dartmouth Col, 26-27; Chicago-Kent Col Law, LLB, 32; Psi Upsilon; Phi Delta Phi. Polit & Govt Pos: Ill State Rep, 50-52; Ill State Sen, 52-62; US Rep, 13th Cong Dist, 63-; mem cong deleg, Inter-Parliamentary Conf, 64-, chmn, Educ, Sci & Cult Comt; participant, Ditchley Conf, London, 66; mem cong deleg, Stockholm Environ Conf, 72. Bus & Prof Pos: Lawyer, pvt practice, Chicago & Waukegan, 32-62. Mem: Chicago Law Club; Elks; Boy Scout Coun; Navy League; Lake Co Civic League. Relig: Christian Science. Legal Res: 340 Prospect Ave Lake Bluff IL 60044 Mailing Add: Rayburn House Off Bldg Washington DC 20515

MCCLOSKEY, JAY PATRICK (D)
Mem, Penobscot Co Dem Comt, Maine
b Bangor, Maine, Mar 20, 47; s Hugh Francis McCloskey, Jr & Mary Eleanor McCarthy M; single. Educ: Univ Maine, Orono, BA, 70; pres, Polit & Int Rels Club. Polit & Govt Pos: Mem, Gov Hon Comt on Maine Spec Olympics, 70; mem, Bangor Dem City Comt, 70-; mem, Penobscot Co Dem Comt, 70-; Maine State Rep, 71-72. Relig: Catholic. Mailing Add: 34 Second St Bangor ME 04401

MCCLOSKEY, PAUL NORTON, JR (R)
US Rep, Calif
b San Bernardino, Calif, Sept 29, 27; s Paul Norton McCloskey & Vera McNabb M; m 1949 to Caroline Wadsworth; c Nancy, Peter, John & Kathleen. Educ: Stanford Univ, BA, 50; Stanford Law Sch, LLD, 53; Phi Delta Phi; Phi Delta Theta. Polit & Govt Pos: Dep dist attorney, Alameda Co, Calif, 53-54; co-chmn, Young Lawyers for Nixon-Lodge, 60; Palo Alto chmn, Tom Coakley for Attorney Gen, Calif, 62; chmn, Spencer Williams for Attorney Gen, Calif, 66; speaker, George Christopher for Gov Campaign, 66; chmn, Critical Issues Conf, Calif Rep League, 67; US Rep, Calif, 67-; Presidential cand, 72. Bus & Prof Pos: Worked way through col & law sch holding various jobs such as laborer, hod carrier, garbage collector, athletic coach, semi-prof baseball player & law librn; mem law firm, Costello & Johnson, Palo Alto, Calif, 55-56; founding partner, McCloskey, Wilson, Mosher & Martin, Stanford, 56-67; lectr on legal ethics, Santa Clara & Stanford Law Schs, 64-67; spec counsel, Town of Woodside's Fight Against the Atomic Energy Comn Power Lines to the Stanford Linear Accelerator, 65-67. Mil Serv: Seaman 1/C, Navy, 45-47; 2nd Lt, Marine Corps, Korea, 50-52; Lt Col, Marine Corps Res, currently; Navy Cross; Silver Star; Purple Heart. Publ: United States Constitution: truth and untruth. Mem: Family Serv Asn; White House Conf on Civil Rights; Santa Clara Co Bar Asn (mem comt on legis & the jour); Alpine Little League; Am Arbit Asn. Honors & Awards: Named Young Man of the Year, Palo Alto Jr CofC, 61. Relig: Presbyterian. Legal Res: Portola Valley CA Mailing Add: 205 Cannon Bldg Washington DC 20515

MCCLOSKEY, ROBERT JAMES
Asst Secy State Cong Rels
b Philadelphia, Pa, Nov 25, 22; s Thomas McCloskey & Anna Wallace M; m 1961 to Anne Taylor Phelan; c Lisa Siobhan & Andre Taylor. Educ: Temple Univ, BS Jour, 53; George Washington Univ, 58-59. Polit & Govt Pos: Mem US Foreign Serv, 55-, assigned, Hong Kong, 55-57; publ officer, Dept State, 57-58, press officer, Off News, 58-60, dep dir, 63-64, dir, 64-66; assigned US Mission to UN, 60-62, spec asst, Bur Pub Affairs, Dept State, 62-63, dep asst secy state, 66-73, spec asst to Secy for Press Rels, Off Press Rels, 74-75; Asst Secy State Cong Rels, 75- Bus & Prof Pos: Engaged in hotel work, 45-50; newspaper reporter, 52-55. Mailing Add: Dept of State Washington DC 20520

MCCLUHAN, NEIL R (D)
b Sioux City, Iowa, May 14, 23; s John A McCluhan & Adah Kelly M; m 1945 to Angela C Camarda; c Mary, Leah, Barbara, John, Kelly, Richard & Joan. Educ: Univ Nebr, Lincoln, BSc in Bus Admin, 47; Creighton Univ, JD, 50; Sigma Alpha Epsilon; Delta Theta Phi. Polit & Govt Pos: Asst co attorney, Woodbury Co, Iowa, 59; city attorney, Sioux City, 60-66; chmn, Woodbury Co Dem Cent Comt, 66-68; committeeman, Iowa State Dem Cent Comt, Sixth Dist, 68-72; deleg, Dem Nat Conv, 72. Mil Serv: Entered as Aviation Cadet, Air Force, 43, released as 1st Lt, 45, after serv in 448th Bomb Group, ETO, 45; Air Medal; Distinguished Flying Cross. Mem: Sioux City Bar Asn; Gtr Sioux City Athletic Asn; KofC; Am Legion; VFW. Relig: Catholic. Legal Res: 810 35th St Sioux City IA 51104 Mailing Add: 503 Toy Nat Bank Bldg Sioux City IA 51101

MCCLUNG, DAVID CHARLES (D)
b Lansing, Mich, Sept 22, 26; s John William McClung (deceased) & Daisy Knight M; m 1946 to Mildred Kim Tai Fong; c Sharon Kim Nyuk. Educ: Univ Mich, BBA, MBA & LLB; Beta Gamma Sigma; Phi Kappa Phi; Alpha Kappa Psi. Polit & Govt Pos: Rep, Territory of Hawaii, 58-59, Hawaii State Rep, 59-62; deleg, Dem Nat Conv, 60, 64, 68 & 72, mem, Nat Platform Comt, 68 & 72; Hawaii State Sen, 67-74, majority leader, Hawaii State Senate, 67-68, pres, 68-74; chmn, Dem Party of Hawaii, formerly; deleg, Dem Nat Mid-Term Conf, 74. Bus & Prof Pos: Rep, Local Union, IBEW LU 1260, AFL-CIO, 56-58; exec secy, Cent Labor of Coun of Honolulu, AFL-CIO, 58-60; attorney-at-law, pvt practice, 60- Mil Serv: Entered as Seaman, Navy, 43, released as ARM 1/C, 46, after serv in Pac. Mem: Hawaii Bar Asn; Am Legion; Honolulu Press Club; Propeller Club; 1399th Engr Vet Club. Mailing Add: 3023 Pacific Heights Rd Honolulu HI 96813

MCCLURE, GARY LEE (R)
Chmn, Greene Co Rep Cent Comt, Ark
b Rector, Ark, Sept 30, 39; s Virgil C McClure & Ethel Lee M; m 1960 to Marilyn Kay Gordon; c Leianne Kaye, Lucinda Gaye & Gordon Michael. Educ: Murray State Univ, BS, 63. Polit & Govt Pos: Chmn, Greene Co Rep Cent Comt, Ark, 70-; alt deleg, Rep Nat Conv, 72; secy, Ark Rep State Cent Comt, 73- Mem: Kiwanis. Relig: Methodist. Legal Res: 701 Highland Paragould AR 72450 Mailing Add: PO Box 332 Paragould AR 72450

MCCLURE, HAROLD MILTON (R)
b Mendon, Ohio, Jan 13, 21; s Harold Milton McClure, Sr & Eva Marie C Stelzer M; m 1941 to Geraldine Adella Davis; c Mary Kathleen (Mrs James V Addy), Marie Kristine (Mrs Ronald L Christensen), Elizabeth Karin & Robert Kevin. Educ: Ohio State Univ, 39-40; Mich State Univ, 42; Univ Ark & Univ Mo, 42-45; Phi Delta Theta. Hon Degrees: LLD, Mich State Univ, 70. Polit & Govt Pos: Inaugural co-chmn, Mich Rep Party, 62, inaugural chmn, 64; co-chmn, Mich Rep State Finance Comt, 65-67, chmn, 65-66 & 69-70; finance chmn, Tenth Cong Dist Rep Party, 65-67; co-chmn, Romney for Pres Finance Comt, 68; alt deleg, Rep Nat Conv, 68; Rep Nat Committeeman, Mich, 68-72. Bus & Prof Pos: Owner & mgr, Alma Pipe & Supply, Mich, 38-39, Alma Drilling Co, 38-39, Allegan Pipe & Supply Co, 38-41 & McClure Drilling Co, 38-60; vpres, Mercer Oil Co, 48-51, pres, 51-62; pres & dir, McClure Oil Co, 50-; pres & dir, Old Dutch Refining Co, Muskegon, 52-54, Wis Petroleum Terminals Co, Milwaukee, Wis, 52-54, Mich Tankers, Inc, 52-54 & Rex Petroleum Corp, Alma, Mich, 54-55; pres & dir, McClure, Inc, Alma, 60-69; dir, Mich Nat Bank, Grand Rapids & Lansing, 64-; dir, Patrick Petroleum Corp, Jackson, 70- Mil Serv: Entered as Cadet, Air Force, 42, released as 2nd Lt, 45, after serv in Eastern Flying Training Command Hq, Res, 45-60. Mem: Am Petroleum Inst; Am Asn Oilwell Drilling Contractors; Interstate Oil Compact Comn; Independent Petroleum Asn Am; Mich Oil & Gas Asn. Honors & Awards: Off Emergency Planning Citation; Rep Nat Conv Deleg Mem. Relig: Methodist. Legal Res: 468 N Luce Ave Alma MI 48801 Mailing Add: PO Box 147 Alma MI 48801

MCCLURE, JAMES A (R)
US Sen, Idaho
b Payette, Idaho, Dec 27, 24; s W R McClure & Marie Freehafer M; m 1950 to Louise Miller; c Marilyn, David & Kenneth. Educ: Univ Idaho Col Law, LLB, 50; Phi Alpha Delta; Sigma Nu. Polit & Govt Pos: Prosecuting attorney, Payette Co, Idaho, 51-56; city attorney, Payette, 53-66; Idaho State Sen, Payette Co, 60-67; secy-treas, Little Willow Irrigation Dist, 62-66; mem, Idaho Const Rev Comn, 65-; US Rep, Idaho, 67-72; US Sen, 72-, mem budget comt, US Senate, 75- Mil Serv: Cadet, Navy, 42-45. Mem: Am Judicature Soc; Nat & Idaho Reclamation Asns; Am Legion; Mason. Relig: Methodist. Legal Res: 634 Hughes Dr Payette ID 83661 Mailing Add: US Senate Washington DC 20510

MCCLURE, JAMES J, JR (NON-PARTISAN)
Pres, Village of Oak Park
b Oak Park, Ill, Sept 23, 20; s James J McClure & Leslie Baker M; m 1949 to Carolyn Phelps;

c John Phelps, Julia Jean & Donald Stewart. Educ: Univ Chicago, BA, 42, Law Sch, JD, 49; ed-in-chief, Univ Chicago Law Rev, 49; Order of Coif; Delta Upsilon. Polit & Govt Pos: Comnr, Assembly of Mayors to Northeastern Ill Planning Comn, Chicago, 73-77; mem exec comt, Cook Co Coun Govts, 73-; pres, Village of Oak Park, 73-; chmn intergovt rels comt, Northeastern Ill Planning Comn, 74-; co-chmn, Bi-State Comn, Ind-Ill, 74- Bus & Prof Pos: Assoc, Hopkins, Sutter, Halls, DeWolfe & Owen, Chicago, 49-57; assoc, Gardner, Carton, Douglas, Roemer & Chilgren, 57-62; partner, Gardner, Carton, Douglas, Chilgren & Waud, 62- Mil Serv: Entered as Apprentice Seaman, Naval Res, 42, released as Lt, 46, after serv in Pac, USS SC 1025, comdr officer & USS Weber APD 75, exec officer, 43-46; Lt (Ret), Naval Res. Publ: Probate articles, Ill State Bar J. Mem: Am Col Probate Counsel; Christian Century Found (trustee & vchmn, 74-); Ill State Bar Asn (vchmn, Probate & Trust Law Coun, 74-); Chicago Bar Asn (mem probate exec & legis comt); United Christian Community Serv (asst secy). Honors & Awards: Silver Beaver & Distinguished Eagle Scout Award, Boy Scouts of Am, 64 & 70. Relig: Presbyterian; moderator, Presbytery of Chicago, 49. Mailing Add: 707 N Oak Park Ave Oak Park IL 60302

MCCLURE, JUNE ELINOR **(R)**
Chairwoman, Saguache Co Rep Party, Colo
b Center, Colo, Oct 23, 26; d Fred T Oliver & Maud Burnham O; m 1945 to John C McClure; c John F, Charles W, Rebecca S, Mark O & Mary C (Mrs Gilmore). Educ: Center High Sch, grad, 44. Polit & Govt Pos: Chairwoman, Saguache Co Rep Party, Colo, 74- Bus & Prof Pos: Pres, Am Legion Auxiliary 131, 48-49; pres, Rio Grande-Alamosa Co Legal Secretaries, 74-75. Mailing Add: 239 E Fifth Center CO 81125

MCCLURE, MARY ANNE **(R)**
SDak State Sen
b Milbank, SDak, Apr 21, 39; d Charles Cornelius Burges & Mary Lucille Whittom; m 1963 to Donald James McClure (Mike); c Kelly Joanne. Educ: Univ SDak, BA, 61; Univ Manchester, 61-62; Phi Beta Kappa; Alpha Lambda Delta; Guidon; Mortar Board; Alpha Phi. Polit & Govt Pos: Sch bd mem, Redfield Independent Sch Dist, 70-75; bd dirs, Assoc Sch Bds SDak, 72-74; SDak State Sen, 75- Bus & Prof Pos: Staff mem, US Senator Francis Case, Washington, 59-61; secy, SDak Legis, Pierre, SD, 63; exec secy, Frontier Airlines, Denver, Colo, 63-64; teacher, Pierre, SDak Pub Schs, 65-66, Redfield, SDak Pub Schs, 69-70. Mem: South Dakota Girls State (registrar, 72-). Honors & Awards: Outstanding Woman of Community, Redfield Jaycettes, 73. Relig: Congregational. Mailing Add: 910 E Second St Redfield SD 57469

MCCLUSKEY, DOROTHY SOEST **(D)**
Conn State Rep
b Middletown, Conn, June 28, 28; d Hugo Conrad Soest & Dorothy Hazen S; m to Donald Shepard McCluskey; c Peter Conrad, Martha Timmons & Christine Ann. Educ: Wheaton Col, BA, 49; Fulbright grant, Univ Oslo, 53-54; Yale Univ, MFS, 73. Polit & Govt Pos: Mem, North Branford Conserv Comn, 66-70, chmn, 67-70; dir, Conn Asn Conserv Comns, 69-71; mem, North Branford Planning & Zoning Comn, 70-75, secy, 72-74, chmn, 74; Conn State Rep, 75- Bus & Prof Pos: Proj mgr, Conn Inland Wetlands Proj, Ford Found Pilot Prog, Middletown, 73-74. Publ: Auth, Conservation Plan for North Branford, Conserv Comn, 70; co-auth, Implementation Aids for Inland Wetland Agencies, 73 & Evaluation of Inland Wetland & Water Course Functions, 74, Conn Inland Wetlands Proj. Mem: Nat Order Women Legislators; Nature Conservancy; League Women Voters; Friends of the Earth; North Branford Dem Women's Club. Honors & Awards: Pub Serv Award, League Women Voters, North Branford, 72. Relig: Episcopal. Mailing Add: 822 Forest Rd Northford CT 06472

MCCLUSKEY, MURRAY P **(D)**
Ala State Rep
Mailing Add: Box 599 Sylacauga AL 35150

MCCOLL, JOHN ANGUS **(R)**
Mem, Rep State Cent Comt, Calif
b San Diego, Calif, June 22, 28; s William Frazer McColl & Esther Ann DeVries M; m 1958 to Sharon Lupton; c Angus, William, Stuart & Theodore. Educ: Pomona Col, BA, 50; Stanford Univ, MBA, 53; Zeta Psi. Polit & Govt Pos: Mem, Rep State Cent Comt Calif, 64-; chmn bd trustees, Rep Assocs, San Diego, Calif, 69; mem, San Diego Co Rep Cent Comt, 69. Bus & Prof Pos: Vpres, Glore Forgan, William R Staats, 63-68; resident mgr, Blyth & Co, Inc, 68- Mil Serv: Entered as 2nd Lt, Army Res, 53, released as 1st Lt, 55, after serv in 2nd Engr Bn Combat, 2nd Div, 8th Army. Mem: San Diego YMCA. Relig: Episcopal. Legal Res: 5942 Henley Dr San Diego CA 92120 Mailing Add: 530 B St San Diego CA 92101

MCCOLLAR, MAURICE (MAC) **(DFL)**
Minn State Rep
Mailing Add: 3563 White Bear Ave St Paul MN 55110

MCCOLLISTER, BENJAMIN STEPHEN **(D)**
Nat Committeeman, Maine Young Dem
b Canton, Maine, July 13, 51; s Richard Ellsworth McCollister & Barbra Coffey Walker M; single. Educ: Ohio State Univ, 69; Univ Maine, Augusta, Ala, 72; Univ Maine, Farmington, 72-; student rep campus develop, Univ Maine, Augusta, 70-71, acad affairs, 71-72, student sen, 71, vpres senate, 71. Polit & Govt Pos: Pres, Canton Young Dem, 70-71; cent coordr, Maine Young Dem, 70-71, vpres, 70-71, pres, 71, nat committeeman, 72-; Young Dem rep, Oxford Co Comt, 70-72; pres, Univ Maine, Augusta Young Dem, 70-72; vchmn, Canton Dem Town Comt, 72-; alt deleg, Dem Nat Mid-Term Conf, 74. Mem: Maine Organic Farmers Asn. Relig: Protestant. Mailing Add: RD 1 Canton ME 04221

MCCOLLISTER, JOHN Y **(R)**
US Rep, Nebr
b Iowa City, Iowa, June 10, 21; s John M McCollister & Ruth Yetter M; m 1943 to Nanette Stokes; c John Stokes, Steven & Bruce. Educ: State Univ Iowa, BS in Com, 43; Phi Kappa Psi. Polit & Govt Pos: Mem, Douglas Co Rep Cent Comt, 58-62; chmn, Second Cong Dist Comt, 60-64; mem, Nebr State Rep Exec Comt, 60-64; deleg, Douglas Co Conv, 60, 62, 64, 66 & 68; chmn, Douglas Co Rep Finance Comt, 62-64; comnr, Douglas Co, 64 & 68; sr pres, Nebr Founder's Day, 68; deleg, Rep Nat Conv, 68; US Rep, Nebr, 71- Bus & Prof Pos: Sales rep, IBM Corp, Moline, Ill, 46-50, sales rep, Waterloo, Iowa, 50-52, spec rep meat packing, Chicago, Ill, 52-53; from sales mgr & vpres to pres, McCollister & Co, Omaha, 53-70; dir, Omaha Nat Bank, 66-71. Mil Serv: Entered as A/S, Navy, 42, released as Lt(jg), 46, after serv in USS Birmingham, Western Pac Theatre, 44-46. Mem: Kiwanis; Mason; Am Legion; Eagles; Omaha CofC. Honors & Awards: Silver Beaver Award, Boy Scouts. Relig: Presbyterian. Legal Res: Omaha NE Mailing Add: 217 Cannon House Off Bldg Washington DC 20515

MCCOLLOUGH, LUCILLE HANNA **(D)**
Mich State Rep
b Huron Co, Mich, Dec 30, 05; d William Hanna & Stella Stover H; m 1925 to Clarence Lindsay McCollough; c Clarence, Jr, Marilyn (Mrs Edwards) & Mich State Sen Patrick H. Educ: Western Mich Univ, grad, 23. Polit & Govt Pos: City councilman, Dearborn, Mich, 50-54; Mich State Rep, 31st Dist, 54-, chmn, Educ Comt, vchmn, Pub Health Comt, mem, Cols & Univs Comt, Retirement Comt & Youth Care Comt, Mich House Rep, currently. Bus & Prof Pos: Teacher, 23-24; pvt secy to personnel mgr, Graham Paige Motors, several years; secy stenographer, ins & real estate off. Mem: Women of the Moose; Ladies Auxiliary, VFW; League of Women Voters; Women's Polit Club Dearborn. Honors & Awards: Several awards for perfect attendance in Mich House Rep, 55-; Award for Distinguished Legis Leadership, Retail Gasoline Dealers of Mich, 71; Ruth Huston Whipple Award, Plymouth Bus & Prof Women's Club of Mich, 72; Award, Mich Asn for Children with Learning Disabilities, 72; Distinguished Serv Award, Mich Asn Sch Nurses, 73. Relig: Presbyterian. Mailing Add: 7517 Kentucky Ave Dearborn MI 48126

MCCOLLOUGH, PATRICK HANNA **(D)**
Mich State Sen
b Detroit, Mich, May 19, 42; s Clarence Lindsay McCollough & Lucille Hanna M; m 1975 to Sylvia Chappell. Educ: Mich State Univ, BA, 64; Univ Mich, MA, 67; Detroit Col Law, JD, 70; Blue Key; Lambda Chi Alpha; Delta Theta Phi. Polit & Govt Pos: Pres, Henry Ford Col & Mich State Univ Young Dem, 60-64; Dem precinct deleg, Dearborn, Mich, 64-; nat committeeman, Mich Young Dem, 65-67; staff mem, criminal div, Attorney Gen, Mich, summer 68; mem, Haber Polit Reform Comn, Mich Dem Party, 69-70; Mich State Sen, 71-, chmn municipalities & elec, vchmn com & mem judiciary comts, Mich State Senate, currently. Bus & Prof Pos: Teacher, Dearborn Schs, 64-71. Mem: Detroit & Mich Bar Asns; Community Task Force to Combat Drug Abuse; Detroit Inst Arts; Jaycees. Relig: Presbyterian. Mailing Add: 7425 Kentucky Dearborn MI 48126

MCCOLLUM, OTIS ROBERTS **(R)**
Mem, DC Rep Comt
b Reidsville, NC, 1930; m 1960 to Hilda Hutchins; c Courtney & Bradley. Educ: Univ NC, BS, 52; New York Univ, MBA, 62; Pi Kappa Phi. Polit & Govt Pos: Mem, DC Rep Comt, 73- Bus & Prof Pos: Vpres & trust officer, Nat Bank Washington, currently. Mil Serv: Army, 52-54. Mailing Add: 4825 Rodman St NW Washington DC 20016

MCCOLLUM, T HAYWARD **(D)**
Ga State Rep
Mailing Add: 701 Cordele Rd Albany GA 31705

MCCOLOUGH, CHARLES PETER **(D)**
Treas, Dem Nat Comt
b Halifax, NS, Aug 1, 22; s Reginald Walker McColough & Barbara Theresa Martin M; m 1953 to Mary Virginia White; c Peter, Andrew, Virginia, Ian & Robert. Educ: Osgoode Hall Law Sch, Toronto, 45-46; Dalhousie Law Sch, LLB, 47; Harvard Grad Sch Bus Admin, MBA, 49. Hon Degrees: LLD, Dalhousie Univ, 70. Polit & Govt Pos: Chmn, Finance Comt, Monroe Co Dem Party, NY, formerly; mem, Nat Adv Coun, Off Econ Opportunity, 66-67; mem, USO, 66-; treas, Dem Nat Comt, 73- Bus & Prof Pos: Vpres in charge sales, LeHigh Navig Coal Co, Philadelphia, Pa, 51-54; various positions, Xerox Corp, Rochester, NY, 54-60, vpres in charge sales, 60-63, exec vpres in charge opers, 63-66, pres, 66-71, chief exec officer, 68-, chmn & chief exec officer, Stamford, Conn, 71-, dir, Rank Xerox Ltd & Rank Orgn Ltd, London, Eng & Fuji Xerox Co Ltd, Tokyo, Japan, currently; dir, Coun for Financial Aid to Educ, Dalhousie Univ Found, Int Exec Serv Corps Rehabilitation Int, USA, First Nat City Bank, New York, First Nat City Corp, Overseas Develop Coun & Brunswick Sch, Greenwich; trustee, US Coun, Int CofC, Comt for Econ Develop, Rochester Inst Technol, St John Fisher Col & Manhattanville Col. Mil Serv: Naval Airman 2/C, Royal Navy, 44. Mem: Corp of Greenwich Hosp Asn; Bus Coun; Bus Roundtable; Coun on Foreign Rels; Harvard Club of New York. Honors & Awards: Pulse Man of the Year Award, 68. Relig: Roman Catholic. Legal Res: Broad Rd Greenwich CT 06830 Mailing Add: Xerox Corp Stamford CT 06904

MCCOMAS, ELIZABETH MAE VEITCH **(R)**
Mem, Rep State Cent Comt NMex
b Mesilla, NMex, June 17, 29; d Raymond J Veitch & Erminda J Fountain V; m 1952 to Dr Robert Emmett McComas; c Robert E, III, Timothy Stephen, Kathryn Elizabeth, Annemarie Minda, Mark Adrian, Rachael Erin & Johanna Magdalen. Educ: Hotel Dieu Sch Nursing, RN; St Louis Univ Sch Nursing, 2 years. Polit & Govt Pos: Rep precinct capt, Las Cruces, NMex, 61-64; pres, Rep Fedn Woman's Orgn, 64-67; co chairwoman, NMex Rep Party, 67-69, vchairwoman, 67-71; deleg & mem platform comt, Rep Nat Conv, 68; mem, Dona Ana Co Rep Exec Comt, currently; mem, Rep State Cent Comt NMex, currently; mem, Ballot Security for NMex & voter registr, currently. Mem: NMex Nurses Asn (prog chmn, 65, bd dirs, Dist 14, currently); Community Concert Asn (bd mem); Elks; Rep Federated Woman's Orgn; Am Red Cross. Honors & Awards: Local Rep Party awards for achievement. Relig: Catholic. Mailing Add: 1812 Apollo Dr Las Cruces NM 80081

MCCOMB, MARSHALL FRANCIS **(R)**
Assoc Justice, Supreme Court of Calif
b Denver, Colo, May 6, 94; s Harry McComb & Estelle Tredenick M; married. Educ: Stanford Univ, AB, 17; Yale Univ Sch Law, LLB cum laude, 19; Delta Chi. Hon Degrees: LLD, Loyola Univ, Calif & Univ San Fernando Valley Col Law. Polit & Govt Pos: Judge, Superior Court, Los Angeles, Calif, 27-37; Justice, Court of Appeal, Second Dist, Los Angeles, 37-56; Assoc Justice, Supreme Court Calif, 56- Mem: Soc Friendly Sons St Patrick Los Angeles; Elks (Past Exalted Ruler & Past Chief Justice Grand Forum); Calif Club; Los Angeles Country Club; Los Angeles Athletic Club. Legal Res: 215 S Occidental Blvd Los Angeles CA 90057 Mailing Add: Rm 4042 State Bldg San Francisco CA 94102

MCCONAUGHY, WALTER PATRICK
b Montevallo, Ala, Sept 11, 08; m to Dorothy Davis; c Patricia & Mary Drucilla. Educ: Birmingham-Southern Col, BA, 28; Duke Univ. Polit & Govt Pos: Career officer, US Dept of State Foreign Serv, 30-; first & second secy, Tampico, 30-33, Kobe, Osaka, Taiwan & Nagasaki, 33-41, Peiping, 41-42, La Paz, 42-44 & Rio de Janeiro, 44-47; Nat War Col, 47-48; consul, Shanghai, 48-50; consul gen, Hong Kong, 50-52; dir, Off of Chinese Affairs, 52-57; US Ambassador to Burma, 57-59; US Ambassador to Korea, 59-61; Asst Secy of State for Far Eastern Affairs, 61; US Ambassador to Pakistan, 62-66; US Ambassador to Repub of

China, 66-74. Bus & Prof Pos: High sch teacher, 28-30; instr, Ala Col, 29. Honors & Awards: State Dept Commendable Serv Award, 49. Legal Res: AL Mailing Add: c/o US Dept of State Washington DC 20520

MCCONKIE, JAMES WILSON, II (D)
b Salt Lake City, Utah, Jan 21, 46; s James W McConkie, Sr & Gwen Wirthlin M; m 1967 to Judith Evelyn Miller; c James Wilson, III & Bryant Joseph. Educ: Brigham Young Univ, BA, 70; Univ Utah, JD, 73; Phi Kappa Phi; Am Bar Asn; Blue Key (pres, BYU Chap). Polit & Govt Pos: Clerk, Attorney Gen, Utah, 72-73; admin asst to US Rep Gunn McKay, Utah, 73- Mem: Admin Asst Asn. Relig: Latter-day Saint. Legal Res: 199 W 3700 N Provo UT Mailing Add: 1427 Longworth Bldg Washington DC 20515

MCCONNAUGHEY, DOUGLAS STEVEN (D)
b Conway, Ark, Mar 3, 52; s George Donald McConnaughey & Melba Taylor M; single. Educ: Highline Col, Wash, AA, 73; Phi Theta Kappa. Polit & Govt Pos: Treas, Students for Jackson, 72; mem, King Co Dem Platform Comt, Wash, 72; deleg, Wash Dem State Conv, 72; deleg, Dem Nat Conv, 72; admin asst, Wash State Rep Frank Warnke, 73; chmn, Caucus for Dem Majority, Wash, 73- Bus & Prof Pos: Property appraiser, Pierce Co Assessor, Wash, 72. Mem: Hearst Soc for Broadcast (treas, 71-); Fed Way Dem Club (trustee, 72-); 30th Dem Dist Precinct Committeeman's Orgn; Retail Clerks Union. Honors & Awards: Voice of Democracy, VFW, 70. Relig: Southern Baptist. Mailing Add: 29806 Second Pl SW Federal Way WA 98002

MCCONNELL, A MITCHELL, JR
Acting Asst Attorney Gen, Off Legis Affairs, Dept Justice
Mailing Add: Dept of Justice Washington DC 20530

MCCONNELL, ANDREW E (D)
RI State Rep
Mailing Add: 101 Englewood Ave Pawtucket RI 02860

MCCONNELL, BARBARA WRIGHT (D)
Committeeperson, NJ State Dem Comt
b Nashville, Tenn, Oct 5, 36; d Carson Wright & Mildred Willeford; m to Terry J McConnell; c Abigail. Educ: Tenn Tech, BS, 57; Bus Club. Polit & Govt Pos: Admin secy, Congressman Joe L Evins, 58-65; mem & chmn, Hunterdon Co Bd Elec, 66-70; committeeperson, NJ State Dem Comt, 69-; mem, Dem State Policy Comt, 70-74; deleg, Dem Nat Mid-Term Conf, 74; mem, Nat Dem Charter Comn, 74-75; campaign mgr, Helen Meyner for Cong, 74- Bus & Prof Pos: Secy, NJ Div Tax Appeals, 74- Relig: Methodist. Mailing Add: RD 2 Flemington NJ 08822

MCCONNELL, DAVID MOFFATT (D)
b Chester, SC, June 12, 12; s Harvey E McConnell & Elizabeth Moffatt Simpson M; m 1952 to Ona Altman; c David M, Jr, Lynn Torbit & Joseph Moore. Educ: Davidson Col, BS summa cum laude; Harvard Univ Grad Sch Bus Admin, Rumrill Award Scholar, 33 & 34; Harvard Univ Law Sch; Georgetown Univ Law Sch & Grad Law Sch, JD, 39, LLM, 40; Phi Beta Kappa. Polit & Govt Pos: Secy & admin asst to US Sen James F Byrnes, 36-38; counsel to US Sen Comt on Govt Reorgn, 37-38; spec counsel to US Comnr Internal Revenue, 38-40; deleg, Dem Nat Conv, 48-72, mem exec comt, Platform Comt, 64-72, mem Platform Comt & Subcomt on Drafting the Platform, 68; comnr, NC Judicial Coun, 52-56; mem, NC Dem Exec Comt & chmn, NC Dem Comt on Credentials & Appeals, 52-60; chmn & secy, NC Bd of Elec, 58-64; organizer & vchmn, NC Businessmen's Comt, Lyndon B Johnson for President, 64; chmn, Mecklenburg Co Dem Exec Comt, NC, formerly; comnr, NC Comn to Revise the Revenue Structure; US Ambassador & Spec Adv, UN Econ & Social Coun, 68-69. Bus & Prof Pos: Attorney-at-law, Charlotte, NC, 46-; vpres & gen counsel, The Belk Dept Stores; gen counsel, The Leggett Dept Stores; chmn bd dir, Charlotte Div & mem gen bd dir, Southern Nat Bank; pres, Providence Realty Holding Co. Mil Serv: Entered as 1st Lt, Army, 40, released as Col, 46, after serv in Inf, China & Burma, Chief Legis Br, War Dept, Gen Staff G-1; Legion of Merit; Legion of Merit with Oak Leaf Cluster; Order of the Cloud & Banner, Nat Chinese; Am, European & Asiatic Pac Campaign Ribbons with Battle Stars. Publ: Doctrine of recoupment in taxation, Univ Va Law Rev. Mem: Mason; Shrine; Scottish Rite; Rotary; Am Legion. Relig: Presbyterian; mem bd dir, Billy Graham Evangelistic Asn. Legal Res: 920 Granville Rd Charlotte NC 28207 Mailing Add: Box 2727 Charlotte NC 28234

MCCONNELL, SAM A, JR (R)
Ariz State Rep
Mailing Add: 810 W Sheridan Williams AZ 86046

MCCONNELL, SAMUEL KERNS (R)
b Eddystone, Pa, Apr 6, 01; s Samuel K McConnell & Clara A Davis M; m 1925 to Helen C Marple; c Shirley. Educ: Univ Pa, BS in econ, 23; Theta Xi. Polit & Govt Pos: US Rep, Pa, 44-57; chmn, Montgomery Co Rep Party, Pa, 54-57. Bus & Prof Pos: Vpres, Woodcock, Moyer, Fricke & French, Inc, 61-63, pres, 63- Mem: United Cerebral Palsy Research & Educ Found (nat vpres); United Cerebral Palsy Asns, Inc; Franklin Lodge F&AM 135 (past master); Union League of Philadelphia; Univ Club, DC. Relig: Presbyterian. Mailing Add: Wynnewood Plaza Apt 507 Wynnewood PA 19096

MCCONWELL, KENNETH GEORGE (R)
Chmn, Hill Co Rep Cent Comt, Mont
b Havre, Mont, July 29, 42; s Carl A McConwell & Lillian Hobbs M; m 1962 to Joanne Marie Yeager; c John C, Cathrine M, Julie Ann & Marie L. Educ: Northern Mont Col, grad, 73. Polit & Govt Pos: Chmn, Hill Co Rep Cent Comt, Mont, 73- Bus & Prof Pos: In opers, Citizens Bank of Mont, 73- Mil Serv: Entered as E-1, Air Force, 62, released as E-4, 66. Mem: Elks; Optimists. Mailing Add: 1066 Lincoln Ave Havre MT 59501

MCCORKEL, FRANKLIN MYERS (R)
Lancaster Co Controller, Pa
b Dauphin Co, Pa, Aug 10, 20; s Daniel B McCorkel & Annie Myers M; m to Jean C Levens; c Joel D & Beth L. Educ: Syracuse Univ, 39-40; Franklin & Marshall Col, BS in Econ, 47. Polit & Govt Pos: Alt deleg, Rep Nat Conv, 68; Lancaster Co Controller, Pa, currently; treas, Lancaster Co Rep Comt, currently; vchmn, Pa State Rep Finance Comt, currently. Bus & Prof Pos: Dist mgr, New Holland Mfg Div, 47-50; co-founder, Aggregates Equipment, Inc, 50, vpres, 50-54, pres, 54- Mil Serv: Entered as Pvt, Army, 42, released as Capt, 46, after serv in Third Army, ETO, 44-46; Three Battle Stars. Mem: Am Legion; VFW; Lions (pres); Hamilton Club; Toastmasters. Relig: Presbyterian. Mailing Add: 44 Mayfield Dr Leola PA 17540

MCCORKEL, ZACK RESHESS (D)
b Marion Co, Ga, Mar 15, 01; s George Reshess McCorkle & Ada Hardridge M; m 1930 to Mary Cochran; c Betty (Mrs Allen) & Barbara (Mrs Hartley). Polit & Govt Pos: Chmn, Taylor Co Dem Comt, Ga, formerly; mem, Draft Bd, 45- Relig: Primitive Baptist. Mailing Add: Butler GA 31006

MCCORMACK, DAVID RICHARD (D)
VChmn, Fourth Cong Dist Dem Comt, Mich
b Macon, Ga, Apr 19, 45; s Richard McCormack & Margaret Piuarnik M; single. Educ: Yale Univ, BA, 67; Northwestern Univ, Evanston, MA, 69. Polit & Govt Pos: Residential col chmn, Yale Col Young Dem, 64-66; deleg, Mich Dem Conv, 68, 70 & 72; mem, Berrien Co Dem Comt, 70-, mem, Berrien Co Dem Exec Comt, 70-; nominee, US Rep, Fourth Dist, Mich, 70; chmn, Fourth Cong Dist Dem Comt, 71-73, vchmn, 73-; deleg, Dem Nat Conv, 72; ex-officio mem, Mich Dem State Cent Comt, 72-73; nominee, Mich State Rep, 44th Dist, 72. Bus & Prof Pos: Vista vol, Vols in Serv to Am, Crawfordville, Ga, 69-70; Vista recruiter, Volt Tech Corp, Chicago, Ill, 70; Outreach coordr, Planned Parenthood of Southwestern Mich, Benton Harbor, 71-72; exec dir, Am Cancer Soc, St Joseph, Mich, 73- Mem: Acad of Polit Sci; Ctr for Study of Dem Insts; Urban Am, Inc; Am Civil Liberties Union; Common Cause. Relig: Presbyterian. Mailing Add: 303 N Lincoln Ave Niles MI 49120

MCCORMACK, JOHN TIMOTHY (D)
Ohio State Sen
b Cleveland, Ohio, Aug 28, 44; s Earl Patrick McCormack (deceased) & June Whitcomb M; single. Educ: Miami Univ, BA; Cleveland Marshall Law Sch, JD. Polit & Govt Pos: City councilman, City of Euclid, Ohio, 70-72; Ohio State Rep, 73-74; Ohio State Sen, 75- Bus & Prof Pos: Self-employed attorney, 72- Relig: Roman Catholic. Mailing Add: 170 E 209 St Euclid OH 44123

MCCORMACK, JOHN W (D)
b South Boston, Mass; m to Harriet Joyce. Educ: Boston Pub Schs. Hon Degrees: LLD, Boston Univ, Holy Cross Col, Boston Col, Villanova Col, Tufts Col, Providence Col, Stonehill Col, Georgetown Univ, Cath Univ Am, Suffolk Univ & Staley Col. Polit & Govt Pos: Mem, Const Conv, 17-18; Mass State Rep, 20-22; Mass State Sen, 23-26, Dem Leader, Mass State Senate, 24-26; US Rep, Mass, 28-71, Dem Whip, US House of Rep, 47-48 & 53-54, Majority Leader, 49-52 & 55-61, speaker, 62-71. Mil Serv: World War I. Mem: Order of Malta; KofC. Honors & Awards: Peace Medal, Third Order of St Francis; Knight Comdr, Order of St Gregory the Great, with Star; Comdr, Legion of Honor, Repub of Philippines; Bellarmine Medal, 57; Cardinal Gibbons Medal, 63. Relig: Catholic. Mailing Add: 726 Columbia Rd Boston MA 02125

MCCORMACK, MIKE (D)
US Rep, Wash
b Basil, Ohio, Dec 14, 21; s Henry Arthur McCormack & Nancy Jane Jenkins M; m 1947 to Margaret Louise Higgins; c Mark Alan, Steven Arthur & Timothy Arnold. Educ: Univ Toledo, 39-43; Wash State Univ, BS, 48, MS in chem, 49; Alpha Chi Sigma; Sigma Chi. Polit & Govt Pos: Wash State Rep, 56-61; Wash State Sen, 16th Legis Dist, 61-70; US Rep, Wash, 71-; deleg, Dem Nat Conv, 72. Bus & Prof Pos: Instr chem, Univ Puget Sound, 49-50; chemist & engr, Gen Elec Co, 50-66; research scientist, Battelle Northwest, 66-70; nuclear energy consult, Wash State Asn Pub Utility Dists, 70. Mil Serv: Entered as Pvt, Army, 43, released as 1st Lt, 46, after serv in Airborne Inf, European-Am; World War II Victory & European & Am Theatre Medals. Publ: Washington state taxation and expenditure patterns, 64. Mem: Am Chem Soc; Am Nuclear Soc; Bonneville Power Admin Adv Coun; Wash Environ Coun; Grange. Legal Res: 1314 Hains Richland WA 99352 Mailing Add: 508 A St SE Washington DC 20003

MCCORMICK, C L (R)
Mem, Ill Rep State Cent Comt
b McCormick, Ill, Dec 1, 19; m to Erma Lee Turner; c Mike & Chris. Educ: Vienna Elem & High Sch, Ill. Polit & Govt Pos: Rep committeeman, Precinct One, Vienna, Ill, formerly; pres, Young Rep of Johnson Co; co clerk, Johnson Co, 50-58; Ill State Rep, until 74; chmn, Johnson Co Rep Party, formerly; mem, Ill Rep State Cent Comt, currently. Bus & Prof Pos: Formerly restaurant & taxi bus; real estate; farming. Mil Serv: Army, World War II. Mem: VFW; Am Legion. Relig: Baptist. Mailing Add: Box 547 Vienna IL 62995

MCCORMICK, CHARLES FRANCIS (D)
Committeeman, NY State Dem Comt
b Chateaugay, NY, Apr 5, 06; s John F McCormick & Mary McCallum M; m 1950 to Isabel McCollester; c Joan (Mrs George Tavernier), Ann, Teresa (Terry), Michael & Kathleen. Educ: Chateaugay Teachers Training Sch, 25; Clarkson Col Technol, 28-29. Polit & Govt Pos: Town supvr, Chateaugay, NY, 50-64; chmn, Franklin Co Dem Comt, 63-68; alt deleg, Dem Nat Conv, 68; committeeman, NY State Dem Comt, 68-; legislator, Franklin Co Dem Party, 70- Bus & Prof Pos: Teacher, 25-27; owner & operator, Dairy Farm. Mem: KofC (3 degree & 4 degree); Elks; Grange. Relig: Roman Catholic. Mailing Add: RFD 1 Chateaugay NY 12920

MCCORMICK, HAROLD L (R)
Colo State Sen
b Florence, Colo, May 16, 18; s B P McCormick & Anna Hoffman M; m 1941 to Jeanne R Rolfes; c Brian, Carole & Ellen. Educ: Univ Denver, BSC, 40; Omicron Delta Kappa; Beta Theta Pi. Polit & Govt Pos: Mem, Co Rep Cent Comt, 58; Colo State Rep, Fremont, Custer & Saguache Co, 60-72; Colo State Sen, El Paso, Fremont, Pueblo & Teller Counties, 72- Mil Serv: Entered as Pvt, Army Air Corps, 42, released as Capt, 46, after serv in Second Air Div, ETO, 43-45; Col, Res, 45-68; Presidential Unit Citation; ETO Ribbon; Six Battle Stars. Mem: Canon City CofC (pres, 59); Mason; Am Legion; VFW. Relig: Presbyterian. Mailing Add: 927 Greenwood Canon City CO 81212

MCCORMICK, HERALDINE (D)
Wash State Rep
Mailing Add: W 1829 Northridge Ct 4 Spokane WA 99208

MCCORMICK, HOPE (R)
VChmn, Rep Nat Comt
b New York, July 9, 19; d Alexander Taylor Baldwin & Loise Bisbee B; m 1940 to Brooks McCormick; c Martha (Mrs William O Hunt, Jr), Brooks, Jr, Mark & Abby. Educ: Ethel Walker Sch, Simsbury, Conn. Polit & Govt Pos: Ill State Rep, 65-67; deleg, Rep Nat Conv, 68 & 72; Rep Nat Committeewoman, Ill, 68-; vchmn, Rep Nat Comt, 72- Mem: Mus Sci &

Indust (bd trustees); Recording for Blind (bd gov); Chicago Symphony Orchestra (trustee); Art Inst Chicago (women's bd); Field Mus Natural Hist (women's bd). Relig: Episcopal. Legal Res: St James Farm Butterfield & Winfield Rds Warrenville IL 60555 Mailing Add: 1530 N State Pkwy Chicago IL 60610

MCCORMICK, JAMES CARLOS **(D)**
b Santa Barbara, Calif, Sept 7, 34; s James Phillip McCormick & Ruth Encinas M; m 1954 to Mercy Estrada; c Cynthia, Caprice, J Carlos & Camille. Educ: Univ Ariz, AB, 58; George Washington Univ, JD, 62; Delta Chi. Polit & Govt Pos: US Capitol police, US Senate, 58-60; staff aide, Kennedy for President, 60; exec coordr, Nat Viva Kennedy Clubs, 60-61; spec asst, Bur Inter-Am Affairs, US Dept State, 61-62; exec secy, Polit Asn Spanish Speaking Orgns, 61-63; asst chmn, Dem Nat Comt, 62-63; dep chmn, All Am Coun, 62-63; dir spec projs, Vista, Off Econ Opportunity, 65-66; alt deleg, Dem Nat Conv, 72. Bus & Prof Pos: Supreme pres, Alianza Hispano-Americana, 62-63; pres & gen mgr, Radio Sta KXEW, Tucson, 63-65; mgt consult, J C McCormick & Co, Phoenix, 66-75. Mem: GI Forum (nat vchmn, 60-). Relig: Roman Catholic. Legal Res: 6525 N 15th Ave Phoenix AZ 85015 Mailing Add: Suite 245-B 4350 E Camelback Rd Phoenix AZ 85018

MCCORMICK, KEITH C **(R)**
Ind State Sen
Polit & Govt Pos: Ind State Sen, 63-; Boone Co Rep Finance chmn; deleg, Rep State Conv. Bus & Prof Pos: Ins, real estate broker; chmn, Ind Real Estate Comn; vpres, Ind Real Estate Asn. Mil Serv: Air Force. Mem: Mason; Elks; Am Legion; Kiwanis; Lebanon CofC. Relig: Presbyterian. Mailing Add: 1018 N East St Lebanon IN 46052

MCCORMICK, THOMAS FRANCIS **(R)**
Pub Printer, US Govt Printing Off
b Gardner, Mass, Feb 20, 29; s Harold J McCormick & Florence R Mailloux M; m 1953 to Beverly G Acey; c Stephen, Harold, Laura & Ann. Educ: Holy Cross Col, Worcester, Mass, BS cum laude, 50. Polit & Govt Pos: Pub printer, US Govt Printing Off, Washington, DC, 73- Bus & Prof Pos: Financial mgt trainee, Gen Elec Co, Schenectady, NY, 53-56, mgr, Acct Oper, 56-58, traveling auditor, 58-60, mgr, Bus Analysis & Budgets/Corporate Staff, 60-65, mgr, Appropriations Analysis Oper, 65, financial analyst & admin asst to group vpres, Indust Group, New York, 65-67, gen mgr & treas, Maqua Co, Schenectady, 67-72, mgr, Power Generation Strategy Develop, New York, 72-73. Mil Serv: Entered as Ens, Navy, 50, released as Lt(jg), 53, after serv in TACRON-6, USS Siboney, VUE 112, Atlantic Fleet & NATO Command, 50-53. Relig: Roman Catholic. Legal Res: 22 Deacons Lane Wilton CT 06897 Mailing Add: 10020 Garrett Rd Vienna VA 22180

MCCORMICK, WILLIAM BLISS **(NON-PARTISAN)**
Mayor, Topeka, Kans
b Topeka, Kans, June 7, 27; s Joseph Bliss McCormick & Wilma Bergundthal M; m 1950 to Shirley Westfall; c Timili (Mrs James Gartner), Mary Jane, Lory Sue, Jamie Pat & Jennifer Bliss. Educ: Washburn Univ, BBA & LLB; Phi Alpha Delta. Polit & Govt Pos: Asst city attorney, Topeka, Kans, 59-69, mayor, 71- Legal Res: 500 Gage Ct Circle Topeka KS 66606 Mailing Add: Box 1052 Topeka KS 66603

MCCORMICK, WILLIAM E **(D)**
Committeeman, Ill Dem Cent Comt
b Ursa, Ill, May 17, 12; s John Thomas McCormick & Clora Luella Murrah M; m 1952 to Barbara Louise Cutforth; c Brent Alan, Karen Gail & Nancy Lynn. Educ: Western Univ, BS, 38, MS, 51; Univ Colo, summers, 52-55. Polit & Govt Pos: Dem precinct committeeman, Ill, 55-; committeeman, Ill Dem Representative Comt, 32nd Dist, 60-; city councilman, Crystal Lake, 61-73, city treas, 73- Bus & Prof Pos: Prin, grade sch, Ill, 34-38, high sch, 38-41; inspector, Powder & High Explosives, Iowa Ordnance, 41-43; sci teacher, 46-69; voc educ teacher, 69- Mil Serv: Entered as A/S, Navy, 43, released as 2/C ARTC, 45, after serv in Electronic Experimental Unit, Patuxent River, Md, 44-45. Mem: Ill Chem Teacher's Asn; Am Legion; Moose; Farm Bur; Mason. Relig: Protestant. Mailing Add: 168 Peterson Pkwy Crystal Lake IL 60014

MCCORQUODALE, JOSEPH CHARLES, JR **(D)**
Ala State Rep
b Salitpa, Ala, Dec 2, 20; s Joseph Charles McCorquodale & Winnie Lee Griffin M; m 1942 to Mary Elizabeth McCrary; c Joseph Charles III & Gaines Cowan. Educ: Marian Mil Inst, 1 year; Univ Ala, 2 years; Lambda Chi Alpha. Polit & Govt Pos: Mem bd of trustees, Jackson Schs, Ala, 54-58; Ala State Rep, 58-, vchmn, Ways & Means Comt, Ala House Rep, 68-, Speaker Pro Tem, 72-, chmn, Ala Legis Coun; trustee, Livingston Univ; chmn, Ala Forestry Comn; mem, State Ment Health Bd; chmn, Ala Toll Bridge Authority; mem, Gov Comt for Indust Develop. Bus & Prof Pos: Owner, McCorquodale Ins Agency; partner & pres, Overstreet & McCorquodale Forest Prod Inc; mem adv bd, First Fed Savings & Loan Asn. Mil Serv: Entered as Pvt, Army Signal Corps, 42, released as 1st Lt, 46, after serv in Air Corps 20th Bomb Group, Tinian Island, 43-46; Air Medal with 5 Oak Leaf Clusters. Mem: VFW; Am Legion; CofC; Optimist; Ala Alumni Asn. Honors & Awards: Gov Award for Outstanding Legislator in Conserv, 62; Capitol Press Awards, 67 & 71; Outstanding Mem of Legis Award, Ala Farm Bur, 68 & 72; Serv Award for Outstanding Work for Rural Ala; Jackson Man-of-the Year Award, 70; Hon Forester, Soc Am Foresters, 72. Relig: Methodist; Mem, Bd of Stewards, First Methodist of Jackson. Legal Res: Coffeeville Rd Jackson AL 36545 Mailing Add: PO Box 535 Jackson AL 36545

MCCOURT, JAMES P **(R)**
Ill State Rep
b Chicago, Ill, June 7, 24; s James J McCourt & Irene Hill M; m 1946 to Charlotte Beven; c J Patrick, Sean B, Brian J & Kevin D. Educ: Univ Notre Dame; Univ Okla, AB, 45; Harvard Grad Sch Bus; DePaul Univ, JD, 53. Polit & Govt Pos: Alderman, Evanston, Ill, 61-72; Ill State Rep, 73- Bus & Prof Pos: Instr, Univ Notre Dame, 46-48; attorney, Chicago & Evanston, Ill, 53, property mgt. Mil Serv: Lt(jg), Mem: Am, Chicago & Ill Bar Asns; Notre Dame Alumni Asn; KofC. Legal Res: 920 Madison St Evanston IL 60202 Mailing Add: 800 Custer Ave Evanston IL 60202

MCCOWN, DAVID HENRY **(D)**
Chmn, Lawrence Co Dem Exec Comt, Ohio
b Ironton, Ohio, Aug 31, 33; s Henry A McCown & Adrienne Tucker M; m 1955 to JoAnn Markins; c Kevin & Derek. Educ: Miami Univ, BS, 55; Univ Mich Law Sch, JD, 60. Polit & Govt Pos: City solicitor, Ironton, Ohio, 61-67; chmn, Lawrence Co Dem Exec Comt, 63- Bus & Prof Pos: Attorney, Liberty Federal S&L, 64-; attorney, Crowe, McCown & McCown, 66- Mil Serv: Entered as Ens, Navy, 55, released as Lt(jg), 57, after serv in Submarine Base, New London, Conn, 55-57. Mem: Am & Ohio Bar Asns; Am Trial Lawyers Asn; Jaycees; Elks. Relig: Presbyterian. Mailing Add: 1014 Pleasant St Ironton OH 45638

MCCOY, ALBERT DENIS **(NON-PARTISAN)**
Mayor, Aurora, Ill
b Aurora, Ill, June 25, 26; s Denis George McCoy & Katherine Longbein M; m 1954 to Mary Ann Malmborg; c Michael & Cara. Educ: Aurora Col; Univ Mont. Polit & Govt Pos: Mayor, Aurora, Ill, 65- Mil Serv: Entered Navy, 44, released as Signalman, 46, after serv in USS Monterey, Pac. Mem: US Conf Mayors; Ill Munic League (vpres); Ill Tollway Adv Bd. Mailing Add: 245 LeGrande Blvd Aurora IL 60506

MCCOY, BARRY MALCOLM **(D)**
Mem, NY State Dem Comt
b Trenton, NJ, Dec 14, 40; s Charles F McCoy & Leahmae Brown M; m 1970 to Tun-Hsu Tang. Educ: Calif Inst Technol, BS, 63; Harvard Univ, PhD, 67; Tau Beta Pi. Polit & Govt Pos: Mem, Suffolk Co Dem Comt, NY, 70-; alt deleg, Dem Nat Conv, 72; mem, NY State Dem Comt, Second Assembly Dist, 72- Bus & Prof Pos: Research assoc, State Univ NY Stony Brook, 67-69, asst prof, 69-74, assoc prof, 74- Publ: Co-auth, The two dimensional Ising model, Harvard Univ Press, 73. Honors & Awards: Alfred P Sloan Fel, 73-75. Relig: Methodist. Legal Res: 49 Thompson Way Path Setauket NY 11733 Mailing Add: Dept of Physics State Univ of NY Stony Brook NY 11790

MCCOY, CHARLEY ELVIS (CHARLEY) **(D)**
Miss State Sen
Mailing Add: Box 56 Wheeler MS 38880

MCCOY, DENNIS CHARLES **(D)**
Md State Deleg
b Baltimore, Md, May 26, 42; s Earl M McCoy & Helen M Coher M; m 1962 to Carolyn M Manieri; c Kimberly A & Dennis C, Jr. Educ: Univ Md, BS, 65; Univ Baltimore, LLB, 68; Loyola Col Md, MBA, 73; Sigma Alpha Epsilon. Polit & Govt Pos: Comnr, Md Criminal Injuries Compensation Bd, 69-75; treas, Criminal Justice Comn, 72-73; treas, Int Conf of Victims of Crime Bd, 73-75; Md State Deleg, 75- Bus & Prof Pos: Prod planner, Md Drydock Co, 63-65; teacher, Baltimore City Pub Schs, 65-66; agt, Md Dept Parole, 66-68; attorney, Sagner Stevan & Harris, 68-70; pvt law practice, 70- Mem: Jaycees; Toastmasters; Unity Dem Club, Inc (legal counsel); Md State Bar Asn; Am Trial Lawyers Asn. Relig: Catholic. Mailing Add: 2241 E Lake Ave Baltimore MD 21213

MCCOY, HOWARD WAYNE **(R)**
b Vicksburg, Miss, May 31, 23; s Howard Wayne McCoy & Gertrude Lassiter M; m 1955 to Marcie Kellan; c Howard Wayne, III. Educ: Univ Southern Calif, 46-47; Sigma Phi Epsilon. Polit & Govt Pos: Chmn, Warren Co Rep Party, Miss, 68-74; mem, State Exec Comt, Miss Rep Party, 68-74. Bus & Prof Pos: Claims supvr, Ins Co of NAm, Los Angeles, 63-67; securities & property mgr. Mil Serv: Entered as Pvt, Air Nat Guard, 43, released as M/Sgt, 61, after active serv with 146th Air Transport Wing, ETO, 44-45; Air Force Commendation Medal; ETO Medal with three Stars. Mem: Optimist Int. Relig: Episcopal. Mailing Add: 720 Ft Hill Dr Vicksburg MS 39180

MCCOY, LUCIAN MARION **(D)**
Chmn, Reagan Co Dem Party, Tex
b Eddy, Tex, Dec 19, 11; s James Marion McCoy & Minnie Harris M; wid; c James Miller. Educ: Bruceville-Eddy High Sch, Tex, 4 years. Polit & Govt Pos: Chmn, Reagan Co Dem Party, Tex, 70- Bus & Prof Pos: Rancher, self employed, 47- Mil Serv: Entered as Pvt, Army, 42, released as T-4, 46, after serv in 621st MPEG Co, Pac Theatre, 45-46; Am Campaign, Asiatic-Pac Campaign, World War II Victory & Japan Army of Occup Medals; Philippine Liberation Ribbon. Mem: Big Lake Masonic Lodge 1203, Chap 442 & Coun 360; Eastern Star; El Paso Consistory; Suez Temple; Am Legion 253. Relig: Baptist. Mailing Add: Box 821 Big Lake TX 76932

MCCOY, MARY ESTELLA **(D)**
Mem, Clark Co Dem Comt, Mo
b Wayland, Mo, Oct 27, 02; d Sampson Eagon & Virginia Mae Brammer E; m 1921 to Merryl Lynch McCoy; c Twila Mae (Mrs Otho Peters), Lucy Virginia (Mrs Robert Kullman), Theron Merryl & John Milan; three granddaughters. Educ: Wayland High Sch, two years; Campbell High Sch, two years. Polit & Govt Pos: Committeewoman, Madison Twp Dem Comt, 36-; mem, Clark Co Dem Comt, Mo, 38-, secy, 38-74. Publ: Correspondent, Clark Co Papers, 28-70. Mem: DAR. Honors & Awards: Celebrated 50th wedding anniversary, 71. Relig: Methodist. Mailing Add: RD 3 Kahoka MO 63445

MCCOY, R V, JR **(R)**
Chmn, Dickenson Co Rep Party, Va
b Va, Oct 25, 30; s Rufus V McCoy & Dema Lou Alexandria M; c James Rufus (Jamie). Educ: Lincoln Mem Univ, 47-51; Univ Va Exten Div, 54-55. Polit & Govt Pos: Chmn, Young Rep Club, Dickenson Co, Va, 54-58; chmn, Dickenson Co Rep Party, 58-63 & 66-; mem, Ninth Cong Dist Rep Comt, 66-; chmn, 40th Sen Dist Rep Party, 71-; mem, Va State Rep Cent Comt, 72-; app to Gov Godwin's Coal & Energy Comn, 75- Bus & Prof Pos: Agt, Nationwide Ins, 60-; mem bd dirs, Breaks Interstate Park Comn, Cumberland Plateau Planning Comn, Cumberland Plateau Criminal Comn, John Flannagan Water Authority & Temco Corp; mem bd dirs & past pres, Buchanan-Dickenson Rural Are Develop Corp. Mil Serv: Entered Army, 51, serv in Korea, 52-53; President Truman & President Rhee Citations; three Battle Stars. Mem: VFW; Goodfellows; Moose; United Commercial Travelers; Bus & Prof Asn. Honors & Awards: Richard A May Award for Va State's Top Co-City Rep Chmn, Va State Rep Conv, 72. Relig: Baptist. Mailing Add: Box 734 Clintwood VA 24228

MCCOY, WILLIAM, JR **(D)**
Ore State Rep
b Indianola, Miss, June 11, 21; s William McCoy & Lucy Lipscomb M; m 1951 to Gladys Sims; c Krista, William, Paul, Mary, Cecilia, Peter & Martha. Educ: Univ Portland, BA, 50. Polit & Govt Pos: Chmn, Multnomah Co Dem Cent Comt, Ore, 68-; alt deleg, Dem Nat Conv, 68 & 72; Ore State Rep, 15th Dist, 72- Mil Serv: Entered as Recruit, Navy, 42, released as Qm 3/C, 46, after serv in NPac Area. Relig: Catholic. Mailing Add: 6650 N Amherst St Portland OR 97203

MCCRACKEN, PAUL WINSTON **(R)**
b Richland, Iowa, Dec 29, 15; s Sumner McCracken & Mary Coffin M; m 1942 to Emily Ruth Siler; c Linda Jo & Paula Jeanne. Educ: William Penn Col, AB; Harvard Univ, MA & PhD

in Econ. Hon Degrees: LHD, William Penn Col; LLD, Albion Col. Polit & Govt Pos: Economist, US Dept of Commerce, 42-43; financial economist & dir research, Fed Reserve Bank of Minneapolis, Minn, 43-48; mem, Coun of Econ Adv, 56-59, chmn, 69-72; mem, President Kennedy's Task Force on the Domestic Econ Situation & the Balance of Payments, 61; mem, President's Comn on Budget Concepts, 67; delivered lect & held conf in Western Europe for US Dept State, Apr & May 68; adv, Secy US Treas, currently. Bus & Prof Pos: Eng teacher, Found Sch, Berea Col, 37-40; assoc prof, Sch of Bus Admin, Univ Mich, 48-50, prof, Grad Sch of Bus Admin, 50-65 & Edmund Ezra Day Univ Prof bus admin, 66-; lectr, Japan, summer 59, India, Dec 63 & the Netherlands, Jan 67; lectr, Seminar in Am Studies, Doshisha Univ & Univ Kyoto, summer 65. Publ: Public debt & economic stability, Yale Rev, 6/51; The role of the Council of Economic Advisers in government, Proc Conf on the Econ Outlook, Univ Mich, 59; Unemployment in an expanding economy—the long view, Mich Bus Rev, 7/64; plus others. Mem: Am Econ Asn; Am Finance Asn; Am Statist Asn; Cosmos Club, Washington, DC; Royal Econ Soc. Honors & Awards: Civic Award, Alpha Kappa Psi, Miami Univ, 57; Distinguished Faculty Award, Univ Mich, 59; Award of Merit, Alumni Asn, William Penn Col, 61. Relig: Presbyterian. Mailing Add: 2654 Hawthorn St Ann Arbor MI 48104

MCCRADY, BOB (D)
Chmn, Ellis Co Dem Exec Comt, Tex
b Waxahachie, Tex, Mar 8, 05; s William James McCrady & Willie Ann Hudson M; m 1930 to Lois Goodloe; c Yvonne (Mrs Alcorn) & Charles. Educ: Weatherford Col, AA, 26; Univ Colo, 27-28; Univ Wyo, 32; Univ Ark, BS, 35; Southern Methodist Univ, MA, 38; Psi Chi. Polit & Govt Pos: Supt, Ellis Co Pub Schs, Waxahachie, Tex, 38-48; chmn, Ellis Co Dem Exec Comt, 48- Bus & Prof Pos: Pres, Waxahachie CofC, 47-48; pres, Waxahachie Lions, 49-50; mem Bd Regents, NTex State Univ, 49-52. Publ: History of education in Ellis County, Libr Binding Co, Waco, 72. Relig: Presbyterian. Legal Res: Hwy 35E Waxahachie TX 75165 Mailing Add: PO Box 277 Waxahachie TX 75165

MCCRAE, WALLACE W (R)
Ore State Rep
Mailing Add: 1303 N W King Ave Pendleton OR 97801

MCCRARY, ROSCOE L (D)
Mo State Rep
Mailing Add: 40 Plaza Sq Apt 1004 St Louis MO 63103

MCCRARY, THOMAS (D)
Miss State Rep
Mailing Add: 216 McCrary Dr Columbus MS 39701

MCCRAW, DAN (D)
b Memphis, Tenn, Aug 3, 33; s James Otho McCraw & Madge Leon Gravette M; m 1954 to Joan Claire Brown; c Cassandra Lynn, Catherine Ann & Beverly Karen. Educ: Univ Ark, JD, 61; Pi Kappa Alpha; Delta Theta Phi. Polit & Govt Pos: Deleg, Seventh Ark Const Conv, 69 & 70; chmn, Garland Co Dem Cent Comt, 70-74. Bus & Prof Pos: Attorney, self employed, 61- Mem: Ark & Garland Co Bar Asns; Ark Trial Lawyers Asn; Am Judicature Soc; Oaklawn Lions Club. Relig: Episcopal. Legal Res: 1009 Second Hot Springs AR 71901 Mailing Add: 274 Hazel Hot Springs AR 71901

MCCRAY, BILLY QUINCY (D)
Kans State Sen
b Geary, Okla, Oct 29, 27; s John J McCray & Ivory B Jessie M; m 1951 to Wyvette M Williams; c Frankie Leen, Anthony B, Melodie C & Kent E. Educ: Langston Univ, 2 years; Colo State Univ, 1 year. Polit & Govt Pos: Comnr, Wichita Human Rels Comn, Kans, 61-64; mem, Mayors Adv Comt, Wichita, 64-65; Kans State Rep, 67-72; Kans State Sen, 73-; mem, Wichita Coun on Drug Abuse, currently; mem, Kans Drug Abuse Comn, currently; mem, 1202 Educ Comn, Kans Corrections Adv Bd, currently; mem, Kans Comn on Crime & Delinquency, currently. Bus & Prof Pos: Owner, McCray's Enterprises, 67-; indust photographer & writer, Boeing Airplane Co, currently. Mil Serv: Entered as Basic Airman, Air Force, 47, released as Airman 4/C, 51, after serv in 332nd Fighter Wing Training Command, Nellis Air Force Base, Las Vegas, Nev, 49-51. Publ: A tree by the hiway (poem), Bards & Poetry, 56. Mem: Langston Univ Alumni Club of Wichita, Kans; Mason. Relig: African Methodist Episcopal. Legal Res: 1532 N Ash St Wichita KS 67214 Mailing Add: 3800 S Oliver Wichita KS 67210

MCCRAY, JONATHAN FRANKLIN (R)
Chmn, Cleburne Co Rep Comt, Ark
b Bluefield, WVa, May 26, 04; s William Lee McCray & Rosabele Fisher M; m 1945 to Isabel Moore. Educ: Roanoke Col, 23-25; Mass Inst Technol, SB in EE, 25-29; Univ Md Law Sch, 36-38. Polit & Govt Pos: Committeeman, Ark Rep State Party, 68-71; chmn, Cleburne Co Rep Comt, Ark, 71- Bus & Prof Pos: Chesapeake & Potomac Tel Co in DC & Md, 29-67. Mem: Am Asn Advan Sci; Am Asn Retired Persons; Cleburne Co Hist Soc; Cleburne Co Elec Comn. Legal Res: Front St Heber Springs AR 72543 Mailing Add: Box 89 Heber Springs AR 72543

MCCREARY, RICHARD EDWARD, JR (R)
b Indianapolis, Ind, Jan 7, 17; s Richard E McCreary & Maude Clements M; m 1939 to Elizabeth Taggart; c Jack Taggart. Educ: Wabash Col, 35-36; Ind Univ, 37-38; Beta Theta Pi. Polit & Govt Pos: Chmn, Fayette Co Rep Party, Tex, formerly. Bus & Prof Pos: Rancher. Mil Serv: Baker 3/C, Navy, 43-45, with serv in Supply Depot, Pac, 45. Mem: Am & Tex Angus Asns. Relig: Methodist. Mailing Add: Rte 1 PO Box 290 Weimar TX 78962

MCCREEDY, HARRY DUANE (R)
b Washington, Iowa, Nov 21, 22; s Harry Duane McCreedy & Carrie Mae Evans M; m 1946 to Marilyn Tulare Morse; c Barbara Anne, Harry David, Vicki Lynn, Leslie Tulare & Thomas Morse. Educ: Iowa State Univ, DVM, 45; Alpha Gamma Rho. Polit & Govt Pos: Chmn, Davis Co Rep Cent Comt, Iowa, formerly. Mil Serv: Entered as Pvt, Army Specialized Training, 43, released as Pfc, 44. Mem: Am & Iowa Vet Med Asns; Mason; Rotary; Elks. Relig: Episcopal. Mailing Add: Rte 5 Bloomfield IA 52537

MCCROSKEY, JACK (D)
Colo State Rep
Mailing Add: 1219 E 11th Ave Denver CO 80218

MCCRUM, ROBERT D (R)
Kans State Rep
Mailing Add: 5606 W 69th Terr Prairie Village KS 66208

MCCUBBIN, CARROL J (R)
Mo State Rep
b Brumley, Mo, Sept 1, 20; m to Betty Gayle Gensert. Educ: Cent Mo State Col; Univ Mo, BSME. Polit & Govt Pos: Mo State Rep, 64-, asst minority floor leader, 76th Mo Gen Assembly. Bus & Prof Pos: Educator; teacher; city, co supt of schs; serv on many comt for furtherance of educ prog of schs; recreation bus. Mil Serv: Lt, Serv on Staff Comt 7th Fleet, World War II, 22 years serv, Naval Res. Mem: Brumley Masonic Lodge (past master). Honors & Awards: First Award for outstanding serv vocational educ in legis, Mo Vocational Educ Teachers. Relig: Baptist. Mailing Add: RFD 3 Eldon MO 65026

MCCUE, AGNES LOUISE (D)
VChairlady, Wethersfield Dem Town Comt, Conn
b Windsor Locks, Conn, Nov 9, 05; d Michael Joseph McCue & Mary Manhire M; single. Educ: Morse Bus Col; Hartford Secretarial Sch. Polit & Govt Pos: Secy, Wethersfield Dem Town Comt, Conn, 45-56, vchairlady, 56-; pres, Wethersfield Dem Women's Club, 49-51; secy, Hartford Co Fedn Women's Club, 63-; secy, Conn Ninth Sen Dist, 66; asst secy, Dem State Conv, 66. Relig: Roman Catholic. Mailing Add: 1 Center St Wethersfield CT 06109

MCCUE, JOHN B (R)
Pa State Rep
b Pittsburgh, Pa, June 22, 21; s Henry Michael McCue & Mary McCrossin M; m 1949 to Mary Helen Clapper; c Michael Brian & Patrick Alan. Educ: Pa State Col, BA, 42; Univ Pittsburgh, JD, 48; Pi Lambda Sigma; Scabbard & Blade; Phi Delta Phi; Theta Kappa Phi. Polit & Govt Pos: Asst dist attorney, Kittanning, Pa, 55; Pa State Rep, 63-64 & 71- Bus & Prof Pos: Attorney-at-law, Kittanning, Pa, 49- Mil Serv: Entered as Pvt, Army Air Force, 43, released as S/Sgt, 45, recalled as 1st Lt, 50-52, served in 8th Air Force, ETO, 44-45 & 28th Inf Div, European Command, 51-52; Col, Army Res; Air Medal with four Oak Leaf Clusters; Good Conduct Medal; Victory Medal; ETO Ribbon with four Battle Stars; Am Theatre Ribbon; Serv Ribbon; German Occup Medal; Res Medal; Pa Medals; Pa Commendation Ribbon. Mem: Nat Guard Asn; Elks; Eagles; Am Legion; VFW. Relig: Roman Catholic. Legal Res: RD 7 Kittanning PA 16201 Mailing Add: Capitol Bldg Harrisburg PA 17120

MCCUISTON, LLOYD CARLISLE, JR (D)
Ark State Rep
b Lucy, Tenn, Mar 26, 18; s Lloyd Carlisle McCuiston & Myrtle Ola Potts M; m 1947 to Olivia Lucretia Graham; c Diane Graham & Lloyd Carlisle, III. Educ: Univ Ark, BSCE, 41; Engr Soc; Kappa Sigma. Polit & Govt Pos: Circuit Court Clerk, 49-58; Justice of Peace, 59-60; Ark State Rep, 61-; mem, Ark Dem State Comt, currently. Bus & Prof Pos: Engr, US Corps of Engrs, 40-41; farmer, 46-; vpres, Russell Tractor Co, 63- Mil Serv: Entered as Midn, Navy, 42, released as Lt(sg), 46, after serv in Construction Bn, Pac Theatre, 44-45. Mem: Meadowbrook Country Club; Rotary; Am Legion; VFW; Farm Bur. Relig: Baptist. Mailing Add: 1004 Avalon West Memphis AR 72301

MCCUISTON, PAT M (D)
Ky State Sen
b Kirksey, Ky, Sept 8, 17; s Thomas Montie McCuiston & Flora Hamlin M; m 1940 to Clara Elizabeth Johnson; c Max Wayne, Jere Levy & John Dale. Educ: Murray State Univ, grad, 39. Polit & Govt Pos: Ky State Sen, Dist Three, 68- Bus & Prof Pos: Teacher, 39-45; exec, Hopkinsville CofC, Ky, 45-55; personnel dir, Thomas Indust, 45-48; banker, Trenton & Elkton, 48- Mem: Rotary Club; Woodmen of World. Relig: Baptist. Mailing Add: Planters Bank Trenton KY 42286

MCCULLEN, ALLIE RAY (R)
Exec Secy, Sampson Co Rep Exec Comt, NC
b Dunn, NC, Oct 12, 44; s Allie McCullen & Lalon Lee M; m 1971 to Shurley Louise Gill. Educ: NC State Univ, 63-65; Univ NC, AB, 69; Phi Eta Sigma. Polit & Govt Pos: Treas, Sampson Co Young Rep Club, NC, 60-61, vpres, 67-68; chmn, Jim Gardner for Gov Comt, Sampson Co, 68; auditor, Sampson Co, 68-; chmn, Sampson Co Rep Campaign Comt, 69-70; dir third dist, NC Young Rep Fedn, 69-70; chmn, Sampson Co Rep Exec Comt, 70-73, exec secy, 73- Bus & Prof Pos: Farmer, 60-; teacher, Wayne Co Bd Educ, 68- Mem: NC Asn Co Acct; Clinton Jr CofC; Kiwanis (vpres & pres); Am Farm Bur. Mailing Add: NC Rep Hq Suite 100 1417 Hillsborough St Raleigh NC 27605

MCCULLEN, JOSEPH THOMAS, JR (R)
Asst Secy of the Navy, Manpower & Reserve Affairs
b Philadelphia, Pa, Mar 15, 35; s Joseph Thomas McCullen & Sarah Ellen Berryman M; m 1958 to Eleanor Joan Houder; c Geoffrey, Jennifer & Justin. Educ: Villanova Univ, BA, 57; Johns Hopkins Univ, 60. Polit & Govt Pos: Exec dir, President's Comn Personnel Interchange, Washington, DC, 71-72; staff asst to the President, 72-73; Asst Secy of the Navy, Manpower & Reserve Affairs, 73- Bus & Prof Pos: Mgr col rels, Merck & Co, New York, 61-62, mgr planning & acquisitions anal, 62-64; sr vpres & partner, on leave, Spencer Stuart & Assocs, New York, 65- Mil Serv: Entered as A/S, Navy, 52, released as personnelman 3/C, 53; Naval Reserve, 53-56; entered as pvt, Army, 58, released as 1st Lt, 61, after serv in Chem Warfare Research, Edgewood Arsenal, Md, 59-61; Army Commendation Medal. Mem: Kenwood Country Club. Honors & Awards: Presidential Award for outstanding achievement as exec dir, President's Comn on Personnel Interchange, 72; Ohio State Univ Award for contrib to educ, 73; Admiral, Tex Navy, 75. Relig: Catholic. Mailing Add: 5512 Pollard Rd Washington DC 20016

MCCULLEY, J HENRY (D)
Ala State Rep
Mailing Add: PO Box 45 Wagerville AL 36585

MCCULLOCH, FRANK W (D)
b Evanston, Ill, Sept 30, 05; s Frank H McCulloch & Catharine G Waugh M; m 1937 to Edith F Leverton; c William H & Frank H, II. Educ: Williams Col, BA, 26; Harvard Univ Law Sch, LLB, 29; Phi Beta Kappa; Pi Delta Epsilon; Phi Gamma Delta. Hon Degrees: LLD, Chicago Theol Sem, Olivet Col & Williams Col. Polit & Govt Pos: Former mem, Regional War Labor Bd Panels, World War II; asst to US Sen Paul Douglas, 49-61; chmn, Nat Labor Rels Bd, Washington, DC, 61-70; mem & chmn, Civil Serv Comn Adv Comt on Hearing Exam, 62-69; mem Am deleg, Anglo-Am Conf on Admin Law, 69; roster of arbitrators, Fed Mediation & Conciliation Serv, 70-; mem, Va Comt Pub Employee Rights, 72-; mem, Ill State Employees

Labor Rels Coun, 73-; mem comt experts on appln conv & recommendations, Int Labor Orgn, 75- Bus & Prof Pos: Lawyer; indust rels secy, Coun Soc Action, Congregational-Christian Church, 35-46; dir labor educ div, Roosevelt Univ, Chicago, 46-49; vis prof, Sch Law, Univ NC, 71; mem pub rev bd, Int Union UAW, 71-; prof law, Sch Law, Univ Va, 71-, mem, Ctr Advan Stud, 71-74. Publ: Co-auth, The National Labor Relations Board (w Tim Bornstein), Praeger, 74. Mem: Chicago, Ill State, Am & Fed Bar Asns; Am Arbit Asn (mem nat panel, 44-). Relig: Congregational-Christian. Legal Res: 104 Falcon Dr Charlottesville VA 22901 Mailing Add: Sch of Law Univ of Va Charlottesville VA 22901

MCCULLOCH, ROBERT WINSLOW (D)
Mem, Gunnison Co Dem Exec Comt, Colo
b Kansas City, Mo, Mar 23, 10; s Albert Johnston McCulloch & Isabella Austin Winslow M; m 1933 to Margaret Elizabeth Young; c Robert Charles, Margaret Marie (Mrs Eastman) & Judith Anne (Mrs Hessel). Educ: Albion Col, AB, summa cum laude, 31; Univ Mich, MA, 32; PhD, 34; Delta Sigma Rho; Phi Kappa Phi; Phi Alpha Theta; Pi Gamma Mu; Pi Kappa Delta; Delta Tau Delta. Polit & Govt Pos: Mem, Gunnison Co Dem Finance Comt, Colo, 52-56; chmn, Gunnison Co Dem Campaign, 58-62; committeeman, Precinct 1, Gunnison Co, Colo, 58-63 & 70-; Colo State Sen, 62-65; mem, Colo Dem State Exec Comt, 64-66 & 73-75; chmn, Gunnison Co Dem Cent Comt, Colo, 64-69; mem, Gunnison Co Dem Exec Comt, 69-; deleg, Dem Nat Conv, 68. Bus & Prof Pos: Instr, Univ Tampa, 34-35; prof, Monmouth Col, 35-45; prof, Okla State Univ, 45-47; prof, Western State Col, 47-, dir grad studies, 49-64. Publ: Parliamentary Control: Question Hour in England's House of Commons, Univ Microfilms, Ann Arbor, Mich, 55; Inter-Institutional Cooperation: State Systems, Coun Grad Schs, 12/64; Intergovernmental Relations as Seen by Public Officials, Annals of Am Acad of Polit & Social Sci, 65. Mem: Am Asn of Univ Prof; Am Polit Sci Asn. Honors & Awards: Western Serv Award, Western Colo Coun of Boy Scouts, 57. Relig: Community Church. Legal Res: 500 N Taylor St Gunnison CO 81230 Mailing Add: PO Box 945 Gunnison CO 81230

MCCULLOCH, WILLIAM M (R)
b Holmes Co, Ohio; m 1925 to Mabel Harris; c Nancy & Ann (Mrs David Benson Carver); One granddaughter. Educ: Col Wooster; Ohio State Univ Col Law, LLB. Hon Degrees: LLD, Ohio Northern Univ. Polit & Govt Pos: Ohio State Rep, 5 terms, minority leader, Ohio House of Rep, 36-38, speaker, three terms; US Rep, Fourth Dist, Ohio, 47-72; mem, President's Comn on Causes & Prev of Violence; vchmn, Nat Rep Cong Campaign Comt; Cong Rep to Intergovt Comn on European Migration, mem, President's Comn on Civil Disorders & Comn on Govt Security, formerly. Bus & Prof Pos: Attorney-at-law. Mil Serv: World War II. Mem: Miami Co, Ohio State & Am Bar Asns; Rotary; Am Legion. Honors & Awards: Distinguished Alumni Award, Col Wooster, Ohio; named Rep of the Year, Harvard Univ Young Rep Club; Annual Watchdog of the Treas Award, Nat Asn Businessmen, Inc; Ohio State Univ Centennial Achievement Award, 70; Gov Award, Ohio, 71. Legal Res: Piqua OH Mailing Add: 4100 Cathedral Ave NW Washington DC 20016

MCCULLOUGH, BILLIE R (D)
b Cory, Ind, Sept 15, 25; s Emery McCullough & Edna Irene Price M; m 1950 to Margret Ruth Bettenbrock; c Lana Ruth (Mrs Blair) & Karla Kay. Educ: Kings Point, two years. Polit & Govt Pos: Mem twp adv bd, 54-56; clerk, Clay Circuit Court, 57-64; recorder, Clay Co, 65-71; precinct committeeman, 67, secy, Clay Co Dem Cent Comt, 68-69; chmn, Clay Co Dem Party, formerly. Mil Serv: Enlisted in Navy & traveled throughout world, 45-48. Mem: Brazil Exchange Club; Am Cancer Soc; Farm Bur; Ind Recorders Asn (pres, 70-); Ind Clerks Asn (pres, 61-). Relig: United Church of Christ. Mailing Add: Rte 1 Cory IN 47846

MCCULLOUGH, CALVIN R (D)
Del State Sen
b Wilmington, Del, 1902; s Robert McCullough & Amanda Davis M; m to Charlotte Brown; c Donall Lee, Robert W & Joyce Kay (Mrs Robert Peck). Educ: Boyd Bus Sch. Polit & Govt Pos: Del State Rep, 48-50; state supvr, Sch Bldgs & Grounds, 50-53; Del State Sen, 54-; deleg, Dem Nat Conv, 64, 68 & 72; comnr, Educ Comn of the States, Denver, Colo, 73- Bus & Prof Pos: Bldg contractor. Mem: Mason; Moose; Holloway Terr Improv Group (pres). Honors & Awards: Cert of Merit for outstanding contribution to educ as chmn of educ comt, Del State Educ Asn, 57. Relig: Baptist. Legal Res: 605 Central Ave Holloway Terr New Castle DE 19720 Mailing Add: Legislative Hall Dover DE 19901

MCCULLOUGH, ROBERT EARL (D)
b Lancaster, Mo, Apr 30, 26; s Earl McCullough & May Foglesong M; m 1954 to Mary Jane Dellinger; c Steven, Jane & Judy. Educ: Kirksville State Teachers Col, MA. Polit & Govt Pos: Chmn, Henry Co Dem Party, Iowa, formerly; mem, State Credentials Comn, 68- Mil Serv: Entered as A/S, Navy, 44, released as 1 SC 3/C, 47, after serv in Pac. Mem: Iowa State, Nat & Western Educ Asns; Masons; Am Legion. Relig: Lutheran. Mailing Add: Swedesburg IA 52652

MCCULLOUGH, ROLAND ALEXANDER (R)
Dir, Export-Import Bank of the US
b Spartanburg, SC, Nov 29, 17; s Ashton Alexander McCullough & Mary Belle Cannon M; m 1940 to Birdie Brown West; c Emily Alexandra (Mrs Robert Voorhees), Mary Cecilia (Mrs Joseph S Stall) & Margaret Ann. Educ: Spartanburg Jr Col, 35-37; Wofford Col, AB, 39, AM, 42. Hon Degrees: LLD, Wofford Col, 75. Polit & Govt Pos: Research & press secy, Gov James F Byrnes, SC, 51-54; admin asst, US Sen Strom Thurmond, SC, 55-57; mem, State Educ Finance Comn, 65-66; dir, Export-Import Bank of US, 69- Bus & Prof Pos: Sch teacher & adminr hosp investr & bus mgr, Spartanburg Co, SC, 39-44; managing ed, Spartanburg Herald & Sunday Herald-J, 44-50; vpres & sr vpres, SC Nat Bank, 57-69. Publ: Various by-line articles for Assoc Press, 43-50; Byrnes leads educational revolution, wire serv & numerous nat newspapers, 54; Political revolt in the South, US News & World Report, 5/56. Mem: Am Soc Newspaper Ed; Assoc Press Managing Ed Asn; Bank Mkt & Pub Rels Asn; Advert Club; Pub Rels Soc of Am. Relig: Baptist. Legal Res: Spartanburg SC Mailing Add: 7711 Bridle Path Lane McLean Hunt McLean VA 22101

MCCULLOUGH, WILLIAM TODD (D)
Miss State Rep
b Batesville, Miss, Oct 28, 03; married. Polit & Govt Pos: Miss State Rep, 48- Bus & Prof Pos: Cotton buyer; merchant; druggist. Mem: Farm Bur; CofC. Relig: Baptist; Bd of Deacons, Sunday Sch Teacher. Mailing Add: Box 82 Pope MS 38658

MCCUNE, JOHN ROBISON (R)
Okla State Sen
b Wilkinsburg, Pa, May 27, 26; s John Robison McCune & Mary Corson M; m 1953 to Nancy Raymond; c John R, Sarah W, Molly C, Laurie R & Carrie N. Educ: Princeton Univ, AB, 50; Univ Notre Dame, MA, 60. Polit & Govt Pos: Okla State Sen, Dist 47, 69-, minority whip, 71-73, asst minority floor leader, 75- Bus & Prof Pos: Sociologist, Mo Dept Corrections, 59-62; rehabilitation specialist, Okla Div Vocational Rehabilitation, 62-66; Owner, Triangle Petroleum Co, Inc, 66- Mil Serv: Entered as A/S, Naval Reserve, 44, released as Sonar Man 2/C, 46, after serv in USS Riddle DE-185, USS PC-1175, Pac; Two Battle Stars. Mem: Sertoma Int; CentrOK Tuberculosis & Respiratory Disease Asn; Okla Rehabilitation Asn; Okla Halfway House; Speck Homes, Inc. Relig: Presbyterian. Mailing Add: 3301 Quail Creek Rd Oklahoma City OK 73120

MCCUNE, WILLIAM (R)
Ariz State Sen
b Akron, Ohio, Nov 10, 44; s Paul Farrell McCune & Lenore Forest M; m 1971 to Diane Deborah (Debbie) Ponte; c Cara Lynn & Michael Eric. Educ: Phoenix Col, AA, 65; Ariz State Univ, BS in polit sci, 68; Gamma Rho. Polit & Govt Pos: Campaign coordr, Kans Rep State Cent Comt, 68-69; staff asst to Congressman Larry Winn, Jr, 69; mem, Northwest Phoenix Young Rep Club, Ariz, 69-; Ariz State Rep, Dist 20, 71-74; Ariz State Sen, 75- Bus & Prof Pos: Vpres, Behav Research Ctr, Phoenix, Ariz, 69-70; asst to pres, Ramada Inns Inc, 70-74; pres, Consumer Research Corp, Phoenix, currently. Mem: Foster Parents Orgn of Ariz; Fraternal Order of Police. Honors & Awards: Outstanding Young Man of Phoenix, Phoenix Jaycees; Outstanding Young Man of Ariz, Ariz Jaycees. Relig: Christian. Mailing Add: 4817 N 54th Dr Phoenix AZ 85031

MCCURLEY, ROBERT LEE, JR (D)
Secy, Ala Young Dem
b Gadsden, Ala, Sept 7, 41; s Robert Lee McCurley & Nell Sprayberry M; m 1969 to Martha Dawson; c Allison Leah. Educ: Univ Ala Col Eng, BSIE, 63, Law Sch, JD, 66; Pi Tau Chi; Lambda Chi Alpha. Polit & Govt Pos: Mem, Ala Dem Exec Comt, 69-70; pres, Etowah Co Young Dem, 70-72; Judge, Southside Recorders Court, 71-; mem, Etowah Co Dem Exec Comt, 71-; nat committeeman, Ala Young Dem, 72-74, secy, 74-; mem, Dem Nat Charter Comn, 73- Bus & Prof Pos: Dir, Ala Law Inst on leave from Rains, Rains, McCurley & Wilson, Attorneys, 67-75; instr, Gadsden State Jr Col, 67-75; mem staff, Ala Law Ctr; reporter, Ala Supreme Court; mem adv comt, Criminal Rules Procedure. Mil Serv: Entered as E-2, Army, 66, released as Capt (Ret), 72, after serv in Army Res, Civil Affairs Group. Mem: Am Bar Asn; Am Judicature Soc; Gadsden Jaycees; Kiwanis; Boy's Club. Honors & Awards: Outstanding Young Man of Ala, 71; Outstanding Young Man of Gadsden, 71; Key Man, Jaycees, 71. Relig: Baptist. Legal Res: Rte 10 Gadsden AL 35901 Mailing Add: Box 576 Gadsden AL 35902

MCCUSKEY, JOHN F (D)
WVa State Deleg
Mailing Add: State Capitol Charleston WV 25305

MCCUSKEY, LOWELL (R)
Chmn, Mo Rep State Comt
b Queen City, Mo, Aug 9, 30; s Joseph Thomas McCuskey & Annafae Figge M; m 1955 to Mariola Marie Pauley; c Richard, James, Tanya & Tamra. Educ: Univ Mo-Columbia, BSBA, 57, JD, 59; Alpha Kappa Psi; Phi Delta Phi. Polit & Govt Pos: Chmn, Jefferson City Rep Comt, 61-62; prosecuting attorney, Osage Co, Mo, 65-; treas, Mo State Rep Comt, 66-68, chmn, 74-; mem bd regents, Cent Mo State Univ, 74- Bus & Prof Pos: Dir educ, Mo Bar, 59-63; attorney-at-law, Linn, Mo, 63-; pres, Osage Co Abstr Co, 64- Mil Serv: Entered as Pvt, Army, 48, released as 1st Lt, 53, after serv in Far East Command, 52-53; Lt Col, Mo Nat Guard. Mem: Am Bar Asn; Bar Asn Metrop St Louis; Judge Advocates Asn; Lions; Nat Guard Asn of US. Relig: Methodist. Mailing Add: Drawer L Linn MO 65051

MCCUTCHEN, PLEASANT THEODORE (PAT) (D)
b Newnan, Ga, Apr 3, 02; s Pleasant Theodore McCutchen & Mai Close M; m 1930 to Irma Croker, wid 72; c P T, Jr & Samuel C. Educ: North Ga Col, 21-23; Atlanta Law Sch, LLB, 26; hon mem, Gridiron Soc; Pi Kappa Alpha. Polit & Govt Pos: Hearing officer, Wage Stabilization Admin; clerk, Ga State House of Rep, 43-46; deleg, Dem Nat Conv, 44 & 64; mem & secy, State Const Rev Comn, 44-45 & 62-63; exec secy to Gov, 46; secy-treas, State Bd of Workmen's Compensation, 47-48; vpres, Ninth Dist, Ga Munic Asn; attorney, Gilmer Co, Ga, 58-72; city attorney, East Ellijay, 60-; mem, State Budget Study Comt, 61-62; Ga State Rep, Gilmer Co, 61-62; mem, Ga State Dem Exec Comt, 63-66; mem & vchmn bd of trustees, State Employees Retirement Syst, 63-71; mem, Gilmer Co Dem Exec Comt, Ga, 70-72. Mem: State Bar of Ga (bd gov, 73-); NGa Area Planning & Develop Comn; Ellijay Lions; Gilmer Quarterback Club; Com Club, Atlanta. Relig: Methodist. Legal Res: Blue Ridge Rd Ellijay GA 30540 Mailing Add: PO Box 433 Ellijay GA 30540

MCCUTCHEON, ANDREW H, JR (D)
Mem, Henrico Co Dem Comt, Va
b Webster Springs, WVa, May 12, 27; s Andrew H McCutcheon & Elsie Hamrick M; m 1952 to Charlotte Andrews; c Sallie Baker. Educ: Univ Tenn, 44; Emory Univ & Ga Inst Technol, 45; Washington & Lee Univ, BA, 48; Sigma Delta Chi; Sigma Chi. Polit & Govt Pos: Admin asst to US Rep J Vaughan Gary, 60-64; admin asst to US Rep David E Satterfield, III, 65-67; specialist in cong affairs, Off Econ Opportunity, 67-68; Dem nominee for US Rep, Eighth Dist, Va, 68; chmn, Henrico Co Dem Comt, Va, 70-73, mem, 73- Bus & Prof Pos: Reporter, Richmond News Leader, Va, 49-60; dir pub affairs, Reynolds Metals Co, Richmond, currently. Mil Serv: Aviation Cadet, Navy, 45-46; Army Res. Mem: Southern Conf Sports Writers Asn (pres); Burro Club (secy); Pub Rels Soc Am. Relig: Episcopal. Mailing Add: 1003 Francisco Rd Richmond VA 23229

MCCUTCHEON, BILL (R)
Minn State Sen
Mailing Add: 2238 Edgebrook St Paul MN 55119

MCCUTCHEON, CHESTER M (R)
Mem Exec Comt, Cobb Co Rep Party, Ga
b Monroeville, Pa, Oct 30, 07; s William Erwin McCutcheon & Margaret Myers M; m 1944 to Hellen S Clawson; c Ronald R, Rev Brian L, Lynn Ellis (Mrs Earnest Mosley), Bruce A & Curtis W. Educ: High sch; various night schs & correspondence courses. Polit & Govt Pos: Treas, Cobb Co Rep Asn, Ga, 61-62, chmn, 62-64; chmn, Cobb Co Rep Exec Comt, 64-69; mem exec comt, Cobb Co Rep Party, 64-; co-chmn, Cobb Co Callaway for Gov Comt, 66. Bus & Prof Pos: Vpres, Fulton Fed Savings & Loan Asn, Atlanta, Ga, 48-; officer & dir, Southeastern Capital, Inc, Tuxedo Investment Co, Skyview Develop Co & Cherokee Enterprises, Investment Partnership. Publ: Various tech papers on savings & loan acct. Mem:

Nat Soc of Savings & Loan Controllers; Thesis Rev Bd; Am Savings & Loan Inst. Relig: Presbyterian. Mailing Add: 96 Whitlock Ave Marietta GA 30060

MCCUTCHIN, PAT WINSTON (R)
b Dallas, Tex, Jan 20, 42; s Robert M McCutchin & Verna Jones M; m 1961 to Nancy Padgett; c Matthew P. Educ: Univ Tex, Austin, BBA, 63; Alpha Delta Sigma; Alpha Epsilon Rho. Polit & Govt Pos: Chmn, Hockley Co Rep Party, Tex, formerly. Mem: Lions; Jaycees. Relig: Episcopal. Legal Res: 103 Redwood Levelland TX 79336 Mailing Add: Box 131 Levelland TX 79336

MCDADE, HELEN JACOBS (D)
Miss State Rep
Mailing Add: Box 112 DeKalb MS 39328

MCDADE, JOSEPH MICHAEL (R)
US Rep, Pa
b Scranton, Pa, Sept 29, 31; s John B McDade & Genevieve Hayes M; m 1962 to Mary Theresa O'Brien; c Joseph, Aileen, Deborah & Mark. Educ: Notre Dame Univ, BA, 53; Univ Pa Sch Law, LLB, 56; James Wilson Law Club. Hon Degrees: LLD, Univ Scranton, 69. Polit & Govt Pos: City solicitor, Scranton, Pa, 62; US Rep, Tenth Cong Dist, Pa, 63- Mem: Pa & Lackawanna Co Bar Asns; CofC; KofC; Elks. Honors & Awards: Nominated one of the ten most outstanding young men in the US, 64; Outstanding grad, Pa Sch Law; Captive Nations Scroll & Medal; Pres Medal, Maywood Col, 73. Relig: Roman Catholic. Legal Res: 1645 N Washington Ave Scranton PA 18509 Mailing Add: 4006 27th St N Arlington VA 22207

MCDANIEL, MARLIN K (R)
Ind State Sen
Educ: Purdue, BS; Ind Univ, LLB; George Washington Univ scholarship; Univ Oslo, Norway. Polit & Govt Pos: Chmn, Rep Nat Col, formerly; mem, Rep State Platform Comt, 64; chmn, Wayne Co Rep Party, Ind, 68-; Ind State Sen, currently. Bus & Prof Pos: Attorney; Spec agt, US Counterintelligence, formerly. Mil Serv: Officer, Ind Nat Guard. Mem: Co Bar Asn; Mason; Scottish Rite; Eagles; Elks. Relig: Presbyterian. Mailing Add: 34 S Seventh St Richmond IN 47374

MCDANIEL, RODGER EUGENE (D)
Wyo State Rep
b Leadville, Colo, Aug 14, 48; s Johnson Hall McDaniel & Betty Lou Swearingen M; m 1973 to Shari Rhodes; c John Rodger. Educ: Laramie Co Community Col, 69-70. Polit & Govt Pos: Chmn, committeeman & dist capt, Cheyenne Dem Precinct, 69-72; pres, Wyo Young Dem, 70-72; mem, Dem State Cent Comt, 70-; Wyo State Rep, 70- Bus & Prof Pos: Aide to Wyo Congressman Teno Roncalio; opers mgr, KCGO Radio, currently. Mil Serv: Officer cand, Army, 68-; Nat Guard Radio & TV Officer. Mem: GI Forum; Exchange Club; Jaycees; Young Men's Literary Club; Asn for Develop of Disabled. Mailing Add: 1944 Pershing Blvd Cheyenne WY 82001

MCDERMOTT, EDWARD ALOYSIOUS (D)
b Dubuque, Iowa, June 28, 20; s Edward L McDermott & Sarah Larkin M; m 1945 to Naola Spellman; c Maureen, Edward, Aloysious, Charles Joseph & Daniel John. Educ: Loras Col, BA, 39; Univ Iowa, JD, 42. Hon Degrees: JD, Xavier Univ, 62. Polit & Govt Pos: Deleg, Dem Nat Conv, 52, 60 & 64; mem, Iowa Dem Cent Comt, 56-60; co-chmn, Iowans for Kennedy, 60; dep dir, Off of Emergency Planning, 61-62, dir, 62-65; mem, Nat Security Coun; US Rep to Sr Comt & other comts, NATO, 62-65; chmn, President's Exec Stockpile Comt & mem, President's Comt Employ Handicapped, 62-65; chmn, Nat Civil Defense Adv Coun, 62-65; mem, President's Comt on Manpower, 63-65; chmn, Comt on Assumptions for Non-Mil Planning, 63-65; mem, Fed Reconstruction & Develop Comn of Alaska, 64-65; nat coordr, McGovern Campaign, 68; chmn, Nat Lawyers Comt for McGovern-Shriver, 72. Bus & Prof Pos: Mem legal dept, Travelers Ins Co, Omaha, Nebr, 42-43; mem legal dept, Montgomery Ward & Co, Chicago, 43-45; attorney, O'Connor, Thomas & O'Connor, 46-50; prof bus law & econ, Loras Col & Clarke Col, Dubuque, Iowa; partner, O'Connor, Thomas, McDermott & Wright, 51-61; partner, Hogan & Hartson, Washington, DC, 65-; vpres, Am Irish Found; bd regents, Univ Santa Clara; bd adv, Indust Col of Armed Forces; bd adv, Lynchburg Col; trustee, Colgate Univ, 71-; regent, Col Notre Dame, 72-; trustee, Loras Col, 75- Mem: DC Bar Asn; John Carroll Soc (pres, 73-); Am Judicature Soc; Int Asn Ins Counsels; Am Asn Ins Affils. Honors & Awards: Decorated Knight of Malta; Knight of Holy Sepulchre; Amvets Spec Silver Helmet Award, 63. Legal Res: 5400 Albermarle St NW Westmoreland Hills MD 20016 Mailing Add: 815 Connecticut Ave Washington DC 20006

MCDERMOTT, JAMES PATRICK (DFL)
Chairperson, 48th Senate Dist Dem-Farmer-Labor Comt, Minn
b Estherville, Iowa, Jan 18, 39; s Earl P McDermott & Marie M Moran M; m 1965 to Martha M Songer; c Phillip James. Educ: Univ Iowa, BA, 63; Col St Thomas, MAT, 65, MA, 69; Sophia Univ, summer 66; Univ Colo, Boulder, summer session, Amsterdam, 71. Polit & Govt Pos: Mem, Minn State Dem-Farmer-Labor Comt, Minn, 74- Bus & Prof Pos: Spec agt, Off Naval Intel, Dept Navy, Minneapolis & Chicago, 63-64; chairperson, Human Rights Comt, Local 710 Am Fedn Teachers, Minn, 65-67; chairperson, Human Rights Comt, Minn Fedn Teachers, 69-70, dir, Col Progs & Human Rels, 70-; teacher, Govt Guam, Agana, 65-67, Minn Pub Schs, Columbia Heights, 67-70. Mil Serv: Pvt, Army Nat Guard, 62. Mem: Local 1351 Roseville Fedn Teachers; St Paul Trades & Labor Assembly (deleg); Am & Minn Civil Liberties Union; Local 320 Educ Workers, Indust Workers of World. Mailing Add: 1279 Brighton Sq New Brighton MN 55112

MCDERMOTT, JIM (D)
Wash State Sen
Mailing Add: 1650 22nd Ave E Seattle WA 98105

MCDERMOTT, PATRICIA L (D)
Minority Floor Leader, Idaho House of Rep
b Washington, DC, Feb 19, 38; d Peter Alphonsus McDermott & Emily Louise Wolfe M; m 1971 to Richard H Bieber; stepchildren, Tamra Sue & Paul Richard Bieber. Educ: Creighton Univ, 55-56; Idaho State Univ, BA Polit Sci, 58; George Washington Univ, JD, 61; Georgetown Univ, LLM Labor Law, 63; Mortar Bd Pi Sigma Alpha; Pi Kappa Delta; Alpha Omicron Pi. Polit & Govt Pos: Pres, Bannock Co Young Dem, Idaho, 66-68; Idaho State Rep, Dist 34, 68-, minority floor leader, Idaho House of Rep, 75- Mem: Am & Sixth Dist Bar Asns; Am & Idaho Trial Lawyers Asns; Bus & Prof Women. Relig: Catholic. Mailing Add: PO Box 3 Pocatello ID 83201

MCDERMOTT, ROBERT HOGAN (R)
Finance Chmn, DC Rep Comt
b Minneapolis, Minn, May 22, 31; s James Francis McDermott & Corinne Hogan M; m 1957 to Mary Elizabeth Coudon; c Timothy Forbes & Martha Levering. Educ: Univ Minn, BA, 53; Georgetown Univ, 55-57; Sigma Alpha Epsilon. Polit & Govt Pos: Mem, DC Rep State Comt, 73-, finance chmn, 74-, mem, Exec Comt, 74- Bus & Prof Pos: Pres, McDermott Ins, Inc, Washington, DC, 59- Mil Serv: Seaman, Naval Res, 55-57. Mem: Univ Club Washington; Cong Country Club. Relig: Roman Catholic. Legal Res: 4323 Hawthorne St NW Washington DC 20016 Mailing Add: 888 17th St NW Washington DC 20006

MCDERMOTT, ROBERT JAMES (D)
Chmn, Hampton Dem Town Comt, Conn
b Hampton, Conn, Aug 6, 32; s Robert J J McDermott & Anna Fitzgerald M; single. Educ: Univ Conn, 50-54; Eastern Conn State Col, BS, 63; Univ Dramatic Club. Polit & Govt Pos: Mem, Hampton Dem Town Comt, Conn, 54-55, chmn, 70-; third selectman, Hampton, 54-55; justice of peace, Hampton, 62-; publicity chmn for Conn State Rep Cand, 66 & 68; Windham Co rep, Conn Educ Asn Polit Action Comt, currently. Bus & Prof Pos: Teacher Eng, Grove Sch, Madison, Conn, 57-62; teacher sci & music, Pomfret Community Sch, 63- Mil Serv: Entered as Pvt, Army, 55, released as Spec-4, 57, after serv in 365th Inf Regt, 1st Army Command, Ft Dix, NJ, 55-57; Good Conduct Medal; Citation from cmndg officer, Ft Dix, NJ. Mem: Nat Educ Asn; Conn Educ Asn (legis comn, 65-); Pomfret Teacher's Club; Little River Grange. Relig: Roman Catholic. Mailing Add: Old Rte 6 Hampton CT 06247

MCDEVITT, SHEILA MARIE (R)
Chairperson, Hillsborough Co Rep Exec Comt, Fla
b St Petersburg, Fla, Jan 15, 47; d Frank Davis McDevitt & Pauline Binns M; single. Educ: St Petersburg Jr Col, AA; Fla State Univ, BA. Polit & Govt Pos: Research asst to Legis Serv Bur, Tallahassee, Fla, 68-69; staff dir, Ga Const Rev Comn, Atlanta, 69-70; admin asst to Fla State Sen David McClain, 70-; cand for Fla State Rep, 74; chairperson, Hillsborough Co Rep Exec Comt, 74-; mem, Hillsborough Co Comn on Status of Women, 75. Mem: League of Women Voters; Youth for Understanding (bd dirs); San Carlo Opera Asn Fla (secy); Tampa Hist Soc; Tampa Preservation, Inc. Relig: Catholic. Legal Res: 405 Landmark Ct Apt 202 Tampa FL 33609 Mailing Add: PO Box 1253 Tampa FL 33601

MCDIARMID, DOROTHY SHOEMAKER (D)
Va State Deleg
b Waco, Tex, Oct 22, 07; d Daniel N Shoemaker & Frances Hartley S; m to Hugh McDiarmid; c Robert C & Mary S. Educ: Swarthmore Col, AB, 29; Delta Gamma. Polit & Govt Pos: Va State Deleg, 60-62, 64-70 & 72-; chmn, Fairfax Co Ment Health & Ment Retardation Serv Bd, 71- Bus & Prof Pos: Partner, McDiarmid Realty & Ins, 45-; vpres, Northern Va Properties, Inc, 60-; mem bd mgr, Swarthmore Col, 64- Publ: Richmond Report, Fairfax Pub Co, weekly column. Mem: Northern Va Ment Health Asn, Va Asn for Ment Health; Fairfax Hosp Asn; Bus & Prof Women's Club; League of Women Voters. Relig: Quaker. Legal Res: 9950 Meadowlark Rd Vienna VA 22180 Mailing Add: 390 Maple Ave E Vienna VA 22180

MCDONALD, ALBERT (D)
Ala State Sen
Mailing Add: 6800 Madison Pike Huntsville AL 35806

MCDONALD, B J (D)
Chairperson, Calhoun Co Dem Party, Mich
b Passaic, NJ, June 27, 33; s John Byron McDonald & Joan M; m 1963 to Nancy A Freeman; c Michael, Kelly & Stephen. Educ: Univ Notre Dame, 51-52; St Bonaventure Univ, 53; Western Mich Univ, 53, 56-57. Polit & Govt Pos: Chairperson, Calhoun Co Dem Party, Mich, 75-; chairperson, Third Dist Dem Party, 75-; admin asst to chmn judiciary comt, Mich House Rep, 75- Mil Serv: Army, 54-56, serv in Ger. Mem: Calhoun Co Substance Abuse Coun (chairperson, mem ment health bd); Am Fedn Grain Millers, AFL-CIO. Mailing Add: 121 Country Club Terr Battle Creek MI 49015

MCDONALD, DENNIS A (R)
Fla State Rep
b Brookfield, Ill, July 14, 38; s Dexter A McDonald & Eleanor Zymslowski M; m 1965 to Lois E Wilcox; c Douglas A & Daniel A. Educ: Jacksonville Univ. Polit & Govt Pos: Fla State Rep, 70- Mil Serv: Navy Air Force. Mem: Life Underwriters Asn; Pinellas Co Indust Coun (dir); St Petersburg Young Rep Club (pres, 70-71); Fla Fedn Young Rep (treas, 71). Honors & Awards: One of Top Ten Fla Young Rep, 70; Outstanding Freshman Rep Legislator, 70-72. Relig: Lutheran. Legal Res: 6829 16th Ave N St Petersburg FL 33710 Mailing Add: 300 31st St N Suite 638 St Petersburg FL 33713

MCDONALD, FELIX (D)
Tex State Rep
Mailing Add: 348 Austin Rd Edinburg TX 78539

MCDONALD, GEORGE FRANCIS, JR (D)
RI State Rep
b Providence, RI, Mar 28, 35; s George Francis McDonald, Sr (deceased) & Marguerite Murray M; m 1966 to Gloria Maria DiSandro. Educ: Providence Col, AB, 62; Suffolk Univ Law Sch, LLB, 67. Polit & Govt Pos: Press secy, Dem Gubernatorial Comt, RI, 64; RI State Rep, 69-; chmn, RI Bicentennial Comn. Bus & Prof Pos: Reporter, The Providence J, RI, 58-67; attorney-at-law, Breslin, Sweeney, Reilly & McDonald, Warwick, 72- Mil Serv: Entered as S/A, Navy, 53, released as CT 3/C, 56, after serv in Security Group, Bremenhaven, Germany, 54-56; Good Conduct Medal; German Occup Medal; Nat Defense Medal. Publ: Legalized gambling, Rhode Islander Mag, 67. Mem: RI Bar Asn (ed, annual); Am Bar Asn; Am Trial Lawyers Asn; Aurora Civic Asn. Honors & Awards: Award of Merit, New Eng Assoc Press Managing Ed Conf. Relig: Roman Catholic. Legal Res: 58 Frankfort St Cranston RI 02920 Mailing Add: 15 Spenstone Rd Cranston RI 02910

MCDONALD, JACK H (R)
b Detroit, Mich, June 28, 32; m 1953 to Joyce Isbell; c Michael & David. Educ: Wayne State Univ. Polit & Govt Pos: Supvr census in Wayne Co, Bur Census, Dept Com, 60; supvr, Redford Twp, 61-66; pres, Wayne Out-Co Supvrs Asn, 64; chmn, Wayne Co Bd Supvrs, 65; mem bd dirs, Mich Twps Asn & Supvrs Inter-Co Comt, formerly; US Rep, 19th Dist, Mich, 67-72; exec dir, Rep Cong Comt, 75- Bus & Prof Pos: Self-employed, contracting bus. Mem: Eagles; Moose; Optimist Club; hon mem Amvets. Honors & Awards: Distinguished Serv Award, Redford Twp Jaycees, 64; Outstanding Young Man of the Year, Detroit Jr Bd of Com, 65; Man of the Year, Tri-City Optimist, 66; Alpha Kappa Psi Civic Award, Univ

Detroit; Am Legion Citizenship Award. Relig: Presbyterian. Legal Res: 28100 Grand River Ave Farmington MI 48024 Mailing Add: 9514 Neuse Way Great Falls VA 22066

MCDONALD, JOHN CECIL (R)
Chmn, Rep State Cent Comt Iowa
b Lorimor, Iowa, Feb 19, 24; s Cecil F McDonald & Mary Elsie Fletcher M; m 1943 to Barbara Joan Berry; c Mary Elisabeth (Mrs Dell A Richard), Joan Frances & Jean Maurine. Educ: Simpson Col; Southern Ill Univ; Drake Univ Law Sch, LLB, 48, JD, 68; pres, Blackfriars; Alpha Psi Omega; Delta Theta Phi; Alpha Tau Omega. Polit & Govt Pos: Legal adv, Dallas Community Sch Dist, 53-69; legal adv, Dallas Co Bd of Educ; chmn Finance Comt, Dallas Co Rep Comt, 54-63, chmn, 63-68; co attorney, Dallas Co, 58-62, asst co attorney, 63-69; city attorney, Dallas Ctr, formerly; deleg, Rep Nat Conv, 64, deleg-at-lg, vchmn Iowa deleg & secy comt on call, 72; mem, Lincoln Club, 65-; mem, Rep State Cent Comt Iowa, 68-, chmn, 69-; mem, Gov Inaugural Comt, 69, 71, 73 & 75; chmn, Seventh Cong Dist Rep Comt, 68-69; mem, Rep Nat Comt, 69-, mem exec comt, 74-; hon mem, Gov Mil Staff, 71-73; chmn, Nat Rep State Chmn Adv Comt & Midwest Rep State Chmn Asn, 73- Bus & Prof Pos: Pvt law practice, Dallas Ctr, Iowa, 48-71; mem bd dirs, Dallas Ctr Promotions, Inc, 60-71; sr partner law firm, McDonald & Keller, 70- Mil Serv: Entered as Aviation Cadet, Air Force, 42; Col, Air Force Res, currently; Air Command & Staff Sch, 51; Nat War Col, 69; Am Campaign Medal; Asiatic-Pac Campaign Medal; World War II Victory Medal; Air Force Longevity Serv Award; Armed Air Forces Res Medal. Mem: US Supreme Court; US Court of Mil Appeals; US Air Force Acad (bd visitors, 75-); Dallas Center Rotary (pres); Farm Bur. Relig: Presbyterian. Legal Res: 1507 Vine St Dallas Center IA 50063 Mailing Add: 502 15th St Dallas Center IA 50063

MCDONALD, JOHN COOPER (D)
Mem, Ohio Dem Exec Comt
b Newark, Ohio, Nov 12, 36; s George Jennings McDonald & Isabelle Cooper M; m 1959 to Mary Jane Jagger; c Steven Jagger, Anne Cooper & Nancy Kendall. Educ: Denison Univ, AB with honors, 58; Ohio State Univ Col Law, JD, 61; Omicron Delta Kappa; Order of the Coif; Tau Kappa Alpha; Pi Sigma Alpha; Phi Delta Theta; Phi Delta Phi. Polit & Govt Pos: Mem, Licking Co Dem Exec Comt, Ohio, 61-, campaign chmn, 62; vpres & treas, Licking Co Men's Dem Club, 62-64; solicitor, Heath, Ohio, 62-65; dir, Licking Co Young Dem Club, 65-66; Ohio State Rep, 65-70, minority floor leader, Ohio House of Rep, 68-70; mem, Ohio Dem Exec Comt, 67-; deleg, Dem Nat Conv, 68; legis counsel to Gov, 71-72. Bus & Prof Pos: Partner, McDonald, Robinson, McDonald & Spahr, attorneys, 61-70; partner, Tingson, Hurd & Emens, Attorneys, 72- Publ: Judicial Protection of Minority Voting Rights, Ohio State Univ Law J, 61. Mem: Ohio State Bar Asn; Jaycees; Licking Co & Ohio State Hist Socs; League of Ohio Sportsmen. Honors & Awards: Winner, Am Col of Trial Lawyers Nat Moot Court Competition, 61; recipient, Newark Jaycees Distinguished Serv Award, 64, 66 & 67; John F Kennedy Pub Serv Award, 67; Named One of Ohio's Five Outstanding Young Men, Ohio Jaycees, 68; Recipient of Gov Award for Advan of Ohio, 68. Relig: Presbyterian. Mailing Add: 695 Snowdon Dr Newark OH 43055

MCDONALD, JOHN KENNETH (JACK) (R)
b Anaconda, Mont, Feb 17, 29; s Lennie McDonald & Margaret Murphy M; m 1965 to Marilyn McCafferty; c Deanna, Kenneth, Kelley, Laurel & stepchildren, Jeff & Wende. Educ: Mont State Univ, BA. Polit & Govt Pos: Mont State Rep, 65-66; Mont State Sen, 69-74; Rep cand for US Rep, Mont, 74. Bus & Prof Pos: Owner of cattle ranch, 16 years. Mem: Mont Stockgrowers Asn. Relig: Born Again Christian. Mailing Add: Belt MT 59412

MCDONALD, JOHN WESLEY (D)
Chmn, Berkeley Co Dem Exec Comt, WVa
b Greenspring, Va, May 8, 16; s John Edgar McDonald & Florence M; m 1937 to Dorothy DeHaven Barney; c Gary Wesley & John Richard. Educ: Bridgewater Col, 35-36. Polit & Govt Pos: Social worker, WVa Dept Pub Assistance, 37-43; acting postmaster, Martinsburg, WVa, 66-68; chmn, Berkeley Co Dem Exec Comt, 68-; assessor, Berkeley Co, 70- Bus & Prof Pos: Chmn, Berkeley Co Am Red Cross, 66-68. Mem: Moose; Berkeley Co Farm Bur. Relig: Methodist. Mailing Add: Rte 3 Box 106 Martinsburg WV 25401

MCDONALD, JOSEPH PAUL (R)
Chmn, Greer Co Rep Comt, Okla
b Mena, Ark, Jun 25, 14; s Charles Augustus McDonald & Mary Gray Moore M; m 1934 to Opal Irene Hamilton; c Maryanne (Mrs Ernest Leo Fite); one grandson. Educ: High sch; honor roll; student coun. Polit & Govt Pos: Mem, Okla Rep State Resolutions Comt, 62-64; chmn, Sixth Cong Dist Rep Comt, 62-67; chmn, Greer Co Rep Comt, 62-67 & currently; chmn, Okla Rep Cand Recruitment Comt, 63-64; mem, Okla Agr Prod Research Fund, 63-66; Okla mem, credentials comt & deleg, Rep Nat Conv, 64; mem, statement of principles comt, Okla Rep State Conv, 64. Bus & Prof Pos: Vpres, Honor Bilt Feed Mills, Inc, Mangum, Okla, 49- Mil Serv: Entered as Enlisted Res, Air Force, 41-44; student, Cent Instr Sch, Kelley Field, Tex, 41, then serv as flying instr, Air Force, 31 months. Mem: Am Radio Relay League (Okla asst dir); Masonic Grand Lodge of Okla (grand marshal, 65-66); Scottish Rite, Mason (32 degree); Am Legion; Farm Bur. Honors & Awards: Served on speaker's bur at state level; long-time master of ceremonies at Radio Conv & Old Settlers' Reunion & Fiddlin Contests; gen class amateur radio operator, W5CCV & mem Storm Warning Net, Okla, which originated tornado warnings serv now used throughout US & recognized by Fed Weather Bur. Relig: Methodist; Certified Lay-Speaker, Okla Conf of Methodist Church. Mailing Add: 425 W Monroe Mangum OK 73554

MCDONALD, LAUREN WYLIE, JR (BUBBA) (D)
Ga State Rep
b Commerce, Ga, Nov 24, 38; s Lauren Wylie McDonald, Sr & Kaythryn Nix M; m 1964 to Sunny Nivens; c Lauren Wylie, III. Educ: Univ Ga, BBA, 65; Sigma Chi. Polit & Govt Pos: Mem, Bd Comnrs, Jackson Co, Ga, 69 & 70; bd mgrs, Asn Co Comnrs Ga, 70-71; Ga State Rep, 71- Bus & Prof Pos: Pres, McDonald Hardware Co, Inc, 69- Mil Serv: Entered as Airman, Ga Air Nat Guard, 59, released as A/1, 65, after serv in Air Police & Band, Dobins Air Force Base, Ga. Mem: Commerce Jaycees; Commerce Fire Dept; Am Legion; Mason; Shrine. Honors & Awards: Jaycees Outstanding Young Man of the Year. Relig: Presbyterian. Mailing Add: Rte 3 Commerce GA 30529

MCDONALD, LAWRENCE PATTON (D)
US Rep, Ga
b Atlanta, Ga, Apr 1, 35; s Harold Paul McDonald & Callie Grace Patton; div; c Tryggvi Paul, Callie Grace & Mary Elizabeth. Educ: Davidson Col, pre-med, 51-53; Emory Univ Sch Med, MD, 57; Univ Mich, post-grad, 63-66; Phi Rho Sigma; Alpha Tau Omega. Hon Degrees: LHD, Daniel Payne Col, 71. Polit & Govt Pos: Chmn & vchmn, State Med Educ Bd, Atlanta, Ga, 69-74; US Rep, Ga, 75- Mil Serv: Entered as Lt, Navy, released as Lt Comdr, after serv as flight surgeon, COMICEDEFFOR; Air Force Commendation Medal. Polit & Govt Pos: Co-auth, Correlation of urinary output with serum & spinal fluid mannitol levels in normal & azotemic patients, In: J of Urology, William & Wilkins Co, 68; auth, Lobbies control the congress, In: Rev of the News, Vol 11, No 8, 2/76 & Gun control, In: Am Opinion, Vol XVIII, No 6, 5/75. Mem: John Birch Soc (nat coun); Nat Movement to Restore Decency (mem nat bd); Ga Right to Life Comt; Nat Rifle Asn; Nat Hist Soc. Relig: Independent Methodist. Legal Res: Cobb Co Marietta GA Mailing Add: 1641 Longworth House Off Bldg Washington DC 20515

MCDONALD, MARGARET ELLEN (R)
VChmn, Iowa State Rep Party
b Indianola, Iowa, Jan 10, 25; d Roscoe Simmons Hunget & Olive Sarchett H; m 1949 to James Lewis McDonald; c Bruce Cameron, Molly Sue & Amy Janette. Educ: Capital City Commercial Col, Des Moines, Iowa, grad, 43; Univ Iowa, 48-49. Polit & Govt Pos: Mem, Cherokee Co Rep Women, Iowa, 52-, vpres, 62-63; precinct committeewoman, Cherokee Co Rep Party, 63-64, vchmn, 65-70; vchmn, Sixth Cong Dist Rep Party, 70-73; vchmn, Iowa State Rep Party, 73- Mem: PEO; Iowa Children & Family Serv (co adv, 66-); Cherokee Symphony Guild. Relig: Presbyterian. Mailing Add: 607 W Bluff Cherokee IA 51012

MCDONALD, MARY JANE (D)
b Akron, Ohio, May 24, 37; d Paul Warren Jagger & Evelyn Conrad J; m 1959 to John Cooper McDonald; c Steven Jagger, Anne Cooper & Nancy Kendall. Educ: Denison Univ, BA, 59; Phi Beta Kappa; Mortar Bd; Kappa Delta Pi; Tau Kappa Alpha; Kappa Kappa Gamma. Polit & Govt Pos: Mem bd, Newark-Granville League of Women Voters, 61-64; first vpres, Licking Co Dem Women, 68-72; secy, Const Comt of Ohio Dem Party, 70-71; mem, Ohio State Dem Exec Comt, 71-75; chmn, Ohio Muskie for President Campaign, 72-73; mem, Judicial Selection Coun for Fifth Court of Appeals, 73-75; mem, Gov Judicial Selection Comt, 73-75; mem, Ohio Citizen's Task Force on Higher Educ, 73-75; mem campaign staff, Sen John Glenn, 74; mem policy bd, Ohio Citizens' Coun Health & Welfare, 75- Bus & Prof Pos: Teacher, Upper Arlington Jr High Sch, Columbus, Ohio, 59-60; trustee, Denison Univ, 71- Mem: Federated Dem Women of Ohio; 20th Century Club; Am Cancer Soc; Licking Co United Way (bd dirs, 74-); Arthritis Found. Honors & Awards: Outstanding Young Women of the Year, Licking Co, 68. Relig: Presbyterian. Mailing Add: 695 Snowdon Dr Newark OH 43055

MCDONALD, MILFORD EDGAR (D)
SC State Sen
b Honeapath, SC, Apr 17, 18; s Calvin C McDonald & Rosa Hinton M; m 1950 to Anne Harper Hall; c Rose Marie & Eddie. Educ: Erskine Col, AB, 43; Exten Course in Human Rels, Univ Buffalo, 49-50. Polit & Govt Pos: Secy bd trustees, Sch Dist 3, SC, 52-57; vchmn, Co Bd of Educ, 59-60; SC State Rep, 61-68; chmn, Co Dem Exec Comt, 62-66; SC State Sen, 68- Bus & Prof Pos: Cost acct, Riegel Mfg Co, 43; teacher & prin, Iva High Sch, 43-48; personnel off mgr, Jackson Mills. Mem: Co Hosp Asn; WOW (coun comdr); Lions; CofC; Am Red Cross. Relig: Baptist. Mailing Add: State House Columbia SC 29211

MCDONALD, ROBERT FAUCETTE (R)
Mem, Scott Co Rep Exec Comt, Miss
b Conehatta, Miss, Dec 23, 12; s Owen McDonald & Hattie Irene Woodward M; m 1938 to Annie Lucille May (deceased); m 1969 to Carrie Lee McCraney; c Willard, Elmer Dean, Rose Tjawan (Mrs Dennis Waite), Linda Faye (Mrs David Beard), Harold Owen, Mary Ann & Lucy Robert. Educ: Meridian Commercial Col, 2 years; Detroit Transmission Sch, Lansing, Mich, 1 month, 54. Polit & Govt Pos: Mem, Miss State Rep Exec Comt, 46-64; chmn, Scott Co Rep Party, Miss, 46-64; crew leader, Bur of the Census, 55-56 & 59-60; justice of the peace, 56-60; mem, Scott Co Rep Exec Comt, 64- Bus & Prof Pos: Parts mgr, Forest Auto Parts, Miss, 46-54; owner & operator, Cattle Ranch, Forest, Miss, 48-68; shop foreman, Ross Motor Co, Pelagatchie, 54-56; owner & operator, Country Corner Grocery, Forest, 56-61; mem staff maintenance dept, Sunbeam Corp, Forest, 61-64. Mil Serv: Entered Coast Guard, 43, released as A/S, 44. Mem: Mason; VFW; DAV; Farm Bur. Relig: Baptist. Mailing Add: Rte 1 Box 90 Newton MS 39345

MCDONALD, SID L (D)
Ala State Sen
b Springville, Ala, May 18, 38; s Leighton D McDonald & Marie Oliver M; m 1961 to Ann Burnham; c Foster Oliver, Kelly Marie & Wesley Leighton. Educ: Univ Ala, BS, 61; Phi Gamma Delta. Polit & Govt Pos: Ala State Rep, Seventh Dist, 66-74; Ala State Sen, 75- Bus & Prof Pos: Pres, Brindlee Mt Tel Co, Arab, Ala, 61- Relig: Methodist. Legal Res: 721 Sixth St NE Arab AL 35016 Mailing Add: Box 546 Arab AL 35016

MCDONALD, T H, SR (D)
Tex State Rep
Mailing Add: PO Box 155 Mesquite TX 75149

MCDONALD, TERRENCE JOHN (D)
b Dodgeville, Wis, July 29, 49; s Francis Leo McDonald & Agnes Reichling M; single. Educ: Wis State Univ, Platteville, 68-70; Univ Wis, Platteville, 71-72; Soc for the Perpetuation of Ronald. Polit & Govt Pos: Bd mem, Rural Family Develop Field Adv Bd, 69-70; vchmn, Univ Wis-Platteville Young Dem, 71-72; chmn, Lafayette Co Comt to Reelect US Rep Kastenmeier, Wis, 72; chmn, Lafayette Co Dem Party, 72-75. Bus & Prof Pos: Vista worker, Off of Econ Opportunity, Indiana, Pa, 70-71; counr, Neighborhood Youth Corps, Indiana Co, Pa, 72; supvr, Dick's Supermarket, Darlington, Wis, 72-73. Publ: Co-ed, Studies in bad housing in America, Rural Housing Alliance, Washington, DC, 70; co-auth, Caution: drinking this water may be hazardous to your health, Indiana Co Community Action Prog, Indiana, Pa, 71. Mem: Nat Vista Alliance; Indiana Co Housing Corp; Jaycees. Relig: Roman Catholic. Mailing Add: 304 North St Darlington WI 53530

MCDONOUGH, EDWARD FRANCIS (D)
Chmn, Rensselaer Co Dem Comt, NY
b Troy, NY, Dec 1, 32; s Edward F McDonough & Esther Minehan M; m 1961 to Marion Ruth McDonough; c Edward Gerard, Susan Ruth & Joanne. Educ: Siena Col (NY), BA, 59; pres, Troy Club; vpres, Vet Club; English Club. Polit & Govt Pos: City chmn, Troy Dem Comt, 62-64 & 66-68; chmn, Rensselaer Co Dem Comt, NY, 68-; admin asst to minority leader, NY State Assembly, 69-74, admin dir, 75; deleg, Dem Nat Mid-Term Conf, 74. Bus & Prof Pos: Salesman, Underwood Corp, 59-61; salesman, Aetna Life Ins Co, 61-63; asst mgr, Nat Life Ins Co, 63-64; owner, McDonough Ins Agency, 65- Mil Serv: Entered as Pvt, Army, 53, released as Pfc, 55. Mem: Hudson Valley Community Col (bd trustees, 71-); Troy Club;

Siena Alumni Asn; Elks; KofC. Relig: Roman Catholic. Legal Res: 1506 Sausse Ave Troy NY 12180 Mailing Add: PO Box 313 Troy NY 12181

MCDONOUGH, PETER J (R)
NJ State Sen
b Plainfield, NJ, Aug 24, 25; m to Elizabeth Driscoll; c Mary, Peter & Martha. Educ: St Lawrence Univ. Polit & Govt Pos: Mem, Union Co Welfare Bd & Bd Sch Estimate, NJ; mem, Finance, Pub Affairs, Admin & Rds & Bridges Comts; mem, Bd Chosen Freeholders, 60-63; NJ State Assemblyman, 63-74, chmn, Educ Comt & Comn to Study Child Labor Laws, NJ State Assembly, majority whip, 68-69, chmn, Comt Transportation, Pub Utilities & Motor Vehicles, 72-74; deleg, NJ Const Conv, 66; NJ State Sen, currently. Bus & Prof Pos: Vpres, Plainfield Lumber & Supply Co, until 70, pres, 70-; dir & vpres, J S Irving Co & Auto Fleet Leasing Co; dir, Morris Plains Lumber & Coal Co & Queen City Savings & Loan Asn; vpres, All State Cablevision. Mil Serv: Air Force, Japan & Pac Theater, World War II. Mem: NJ Lumber Dealers Asn; Kiwanis; VFW; Am Legion; Elks. Honors & Awards: Selected Young Man of Year, Jaycees, 58 & Man of Year, Plainfield Serv Clubs, 60; Nat Hemophelia Found Legislator of Year, 74. Relig: Roman Catholic. Mailing Add: 925 Oakwood Place Plainfield NJ 07060

MCDONOUGH, ROBERT PAUL (D)
b Parkersburg, WVa, Mar 13, 15; s Patrick J McDonough & Virginia Goff M; m 1941 to Martha Sinclair Smith; c Sara Katherine & Robert Sinclair. Educ: Univ Notre Dame, AB, 36. Polit & Govt Pos: Chmn, WVa Dem Exec Comt, 61-64; committeeman, Dem Nat Comt, 64-65; dir, WVa Dept Natural Resources, 65-66; Dem campaign chmn & alt deleg, Dem Nat Conv, 68, alt deleg, 72. Bus & Prof Pos: Consult, Matt Reese & Assoc, Washington, DC, 69-72; oil & gas develop bus, 72-; consult, currently. Mil Serv: Entered as Pvt, Infantry, 41, released as Capt, Corps Engrs, 45, after serv in 7th Army, ETO; Bronze Star. Legal Res: 809 1/2 Market St Parkersburg WV 26101 Mailing Add: 420 Argyle Dr Alexandria VA 22305

MCDONOUGH, WILLIAM J (D)
NH State Rep
Mailing Add: 287 Massabesic St Manchester NH 03103

MCDOUGALL, JACQUELYN HORAN (R)
b Wenatchee, Wash, Sept 24, 24; d John Rankin Horan & Helen Frampton Vandivort H; m 1947 to Robert Duncan McDougall; c Douglas John, Stuart Dean & Scott Horan. Educ: Wash State Univ, BA, 46; Sigma Phi Beta; Kappa Kappa Gamma. Polit & Govt Pos: Pres, Chelan Co Rep Women's Club, 54-56; chmn, Rep Neighbor to Neighbor Fund Drive, 58-59; state committeewoman, 60-70; from dist dir to first vpres, Wash State Fedn Rep Women, 59-69, pres, 69-71; app secy, Local Draft Bd 22, currently. deleg & secy Wash deleg, Rep Nat Conv, 60; secy, Wash Rep State Cent Comt, 62-64; app to Wash State Power & Energy Coun. Mem: Am Asn Univ Women (pres); Wenatchee YMCA (bd dirs); YMCA Youth & Govt Prog (dist chmn). Relig: Methodist. Mailing Add: 2 Horan Rd Wenatchee WA 98801

MCDOWELL, ALLEN JIM (R)
b Brunswick, Mo, Mar 12, 38; s Mildred Eastin M; m 1961 to Judith Feather. Educ: Univ Nebr, BS, 60; Kappa Sigma. Polit & Govt Pos: Newspaper ed, Live YR, Lancaster Co Young Rep, Nebr, 68-70, chmn, 70-71; hq chmn, Thone for Cong, 70-73; first dist dir, Nebr Fedn of Young Rep, 71-73; newspaper ed, Nebr Rep Party, 71-73, vchmn, 73-75; state chmn, Youth for the Reelection of the President, 72; chmn, Nebr Rep Party Exec Research Comt, 73. Bus & Prof Pos: Sales mgr, Laurence Homes Inc, 60-62; exec secy, Nebr Lumber Merchants Asn, 62-71; exec officer & secy-treas, Midwest Lumbermen's Inter-Ins Exchange, 67-; asst vpres, Alexander & Alexander, 72- Mil Serv: Entered as Pvt, Army Nat Guard, 56, released as SP-4, 59, after serv in 190 Tank Bn. Mem: Int Order of Hoo Hoo (pres, 67-68); Elks; Nebr Club; Country Club of Lincoln; Aircraft Owners & Pilot Asn. Honors & Awards: Aviation Comt Million Dollar Sales Club, Nat Asn of Home Builders, 61; Outstanding Man, Lancaster Co Young Rep, 71 & Nebr Fedn of Young Rep, 71. Mailing Add: 2924 S 26 Lincoln NE 68502

MCDOWELL, HENRY (D)
Ga State Sen
Mailing Add: 8303 Royal Oak Dr Savannah GA 31406

MCDOWELL, PETER LEE (R)
Mass State Rep
b Hyannis, Mass, June 5, 38; s Walter F McDowell & Anna Bendroth M; m 1961 to Patricia Kenney; c Laura, Mark, Patrick & Daniel. Educ: Gen Motors Inst, grad, 58; Mass Mil Acad, grad, 62. Polit & Govt Pos: Mem planning bd, Dennis, Mass, 65-70, town moderator, 72-; Mass State Rep, 75- Bus & Prof Pos: Dir, Cape Cod Coop Bank & Mass Moderators Asn, 73- Mil Serv: Entered as 2nd Lt, Mass Nat Guard, 63, released as 1st Lt, 68, after serv in Artillery. Mem: Cape Cod Bd Realtors; Rep Club Mass; Mass Asn of Realtors. Legal Res: 50 Dr Lord's Rd Dennis MA 02638 Mailing Add: 585 Main St Dennis MA 02638

MCDUFFIE, E M (PETE) (D)
Ga State Sen
b McRae, Ga, Apr 20, 38; s Muller McDuffie & Ruby Wilkes M; m 1960 to Margaret Thompson; c Greg. Educ: Brewton-Parker Jr Col, 56-58; Ga Southern Col, BS, 60; Mid Tenn State Univ, MEd, 67. Polit & Govt Pos: Ga State Sen, 19th Dist, 71- Bus & Prof Pos: Basketball coach & teacher, Milan High Sch, Ga, 60-63; basketball coach & teacher, Dodge Elem Sch, Eastman, 63-66, prin, 67- Mem: Ga & Dodge Co Asns Educators; Ga Dept Elem Sch Prin; Eastman Lions Club (vpres & bd dirs); Dodge Co CofC (pres). Relig: Methodist. Mailing Add: Rte 6 Eastman GA 31023

MCDUFFIE, JIM (D)
NC State Sen
Mailing Add: 1800 Eastway Dr Charlotte NC 28205

MCDUNN, HENRY J (D)
Chmn, Teton Co Dem Cent Comt, Mont
b Ft Benton, Mont, July 7, 26; s LeRoy Henry McDunn & Marie Qunell M; m 1951 to Eva Olson; c Charlotte (Mrs Goulet), Henry David, Richard, Ronald, John & Eva. Educ: High sch. Polit & Govt Pos: Secy, Dem Club, Teton Co, Mont, 61; secy, Teton Co Dem Cent Comt, 63, chmn, 64-70 & 71-, vchmn, 70-71. Bus & Prof Pos: Mgr, Stanford Coop Asn, 48, FUGTA Line Elevator, 51 & Dutton Coop Asn, 55- Mil Serv: Entered as A/S, Navy, 44, released as OM 2, 47, after serv in various Navy units, Pac Theatre, 45-47. Mem: KofC (recorder, 72-). Relig: Catholic. Mailing Add: Dutton MT 59433

MCEACHERN, BOB (DFL)
Minn State Rep
b St Paul, Minn, Mar 9, 27; s Albert McEachern & Grace Welker M; m 1949 to Dorothy Anderson; c Pat, Mary, Susie, Terry, Billy & Tommy. Educ: NDak State Univ, BS. Polit & Govt Pos: Minn State Rep, currently. Mil Serv: Navy, 4 years, World War II & Korea; Presidential Unit Citation. Relig: Catholic. Mailing Add: 601 N Walnut St Michael MN 55376

MCEACHERN, JOSEPH A (D)
NH State Rep
Mailing Add: 229 Sherburne Rd Portsmouth NH 03801

MCELHANEY, FRANK (D)
Ariz State Rep
Mailing Add: State Capitol Phoenix AZ 85007

MCELMURRAY, JEANNE FRANCES (D)
State Committeewoman, Dem Exec Comt, Fla
b Junction City, Kans, Mar 6, 21; d James Otto Delver & Elizabeth Stillie D; m 1944 to George Long McElmurray; c Guy James Burnett & Peter Delver. Educ: Junction City High Sch, Kans, grad, 39. Polit & Govt Pos: Precinct committeewoman, Sarasota Co Dem Exec Comt, Fla, 60-, chmn, 66-67; pres, Sarasota Dem Woman's Club, 64-65; vpres, Seventh Cong Dist Dem Woman's Club Fla, 65-66; pres, Cent Sarasota Dem Woman's Club, 65-67 & 69-; vchmn, Seventh Cong Dist Dem Exec Comt Fla, 66-; state committeewoman, Dem Exec Comt Fla, 66-; deleg, Dem Nat Conv, 68; vchmn, Sarasota-Manatee Airport Authority, 73- Mem: Siesta Key CofC; Sarasota Garden Club; Nat League of Am Pen Women; Sarasota Co Civic League; Sarasota Audubon Soc (pres). Honors & Awards: Community Leader of Am, 68; Only Hon Life Mem, Cent Sarasota Dem Women's Club; Beautification Comt, State CofC; Outstanding Dem Woman of Florida 1970, Dem Woman's Club of Fla. Relig: Protestant. Mailing Add: 1661 Sunrise Lane Sarasota FL 33581

MCELROY, LILLIAN MAE (R)
Iowa State Rep
b Maynard, Iowa, Apr 28, 17; d Harry LaVern Arthur & Carolyn Meyer A; m 1936 to Paul Edward McElroy, wid; c Sheryl Hunter, Sharon Hirz, Diane Obert & Paul Rodney. Educ: Upper Iowa Col, 34-36. Polit & Govt Pos: Iowa State Rep, 82nd Dist, 70-72, 97th Dist, 72- Mem: Fremon Co Farm Bur; PEO; Iowa Heart Asn; Iowa Fedn Rep Women; Community Club. Honors & Awards: Iowa State 4-H Alumni Award, Iowa Exten Serv, 58; Iowa Master Farm Homemaker, Wallaces Farmer, 59. Relig: Methodist. Legal Res: Rte 2 Percival IA 51648 Mailing Add: State House Des Moines IA 50319

MCELROY, NATALIE CHALONER (R)
Secy, NDak Rep State Comt
b East Hartford, Conn, Aug 15, 16; d Russell Smith Chaloner & Marion Davis C; m 1938 to John Edward McElroy, Jr; c John Edward, III, Peter Michael, James Chaloner & Katherine Marion. Educ: Lake Forest Col, 35-37; Univ Minn, Minneapolis, 37-38; Alpha Lambda Delta; Kappa Kappa Gamma. Polit & Govt Pos: Chmn, Dist 29 Rep Party, Jamestown, NDak, 72-; secy, NDak Rep State Comt, 74- Bus & Prof Pos: Secy, Marsh & McLennan, Minneapolis, Minn, 37-38; secy, Am Auto Ins Co, New York, 39-40; secy, McElroy Co, Jamestown, NDak, 70- Mem: PEO (state bd mem, 73-); Am Nat CowBelles; NDak CowBelles; SCent Achievement Ctr, Jamestown (bd mem, 71-). Honors & Awards: Robert A Taft Inst Govt Award, 74. Relig: Episcopal. Legal Res: Sydney ND Mailing Add: Box 810 Jamestown ND 58401

MCELROY, WILLIAM DAVID (D)
b Rogers, Tex, Jan 22, 17; s William D McElroy & Ora Shipley M; m 1940 to Nella Winch, div; m 1967 to Yerda Marlene Andregg; c Mary Elizabeth, Ann Reed, Thomas Shipley, William David, Jr & Eric Gene. Educ: Pasadena Jr Col, AA, 37; Stanford Univ, BA, 39; Reed Col, MA, 41; Princeton Univ, PhD, 43; Sigma Xi; Phi Beta Kappa. Polit & Govt Pos: Research assoc, Off Sci Research & Develop, 44-45; consult, Am Inst Biol Sci, Microbiol Adv Comt, Off Naval Res, 52-57; consult metabolic biol panel, Nat Sci Found, 55-58, div comt biol & med, 58-61, research facilities panel, 60-63, dir found, 69-72; consult sci adv comt, Dept Defense, 56-57; consult biochem stud panel, Nat Insts Health, 57-62; consult, Atomic Energy Comn, 58-63; consult bd sci counr, Nat Inst Arthritis & Metabolic Diseases, 59-63, mem coun, 64-68; mem, President's Sci Adv Comt, 62-66. Bus & Prof Pos: Instr biol, Johns Hopkins Univ, 46, asst prof, 46-48, assoc prof, 48-51, prof, 51-72, dir, McCollum-Pratt Inst, 49-69, chmn dept biol, 56-69; chancellor, Univ Calif, San Diego, 72- Publ: Co-ed, The chemical basis of heredity (w Bentley Glass), Johns Hopkins Press, 57; Cell physiology and biochemistry, Prentice-Hall, 61, 64 & 71; co-ed, Foundations of modern biology, ser (w C P Swanson), Prentice-Hall, 61-64. Mem: Am Chem Soc; Am Asn Advan Sci; Bot Soc Am; Soc Gen Psychologists; Am Soc Bact. Honors & Awards: Harvey Lectr, NY Acad Sci, 57; Barnett Cohen Award, Am Soc Bact, 58; Rumford Prize, Am Acad Arts & Sci, 64; Andrew White Medal, Loyola Col (Md), 71. Relig: Methodist. Legal Res: 9630 La Jolla Farms Rd La Jolla CA 92037 Mailing Add: Off of the Chancellor Univ of Calif San Diego La Jolla CA 92037

MCELWAIN, S MARION (D)
Founding Dir, State Speaker's Bur, Colo Dem Party
b Chicago, Ill, May 28, 32; d Herbert Wendall Holm & Mary Eleanor Stevenson H; m 1950 to William H McElwain; c Mary Kay (Mrs Gerald Malm), Martin William & Donna Marie. Educ: Univ Colo, Boulder, 59-63. Polit & Govt Pos: Committeewoman, Boulder Co Dem Party, Colo, 61-; treas, Boulder Co Dem Women's Club, 65-67, pres, 67-68, chmn nominating comt, 69; mem & area leader, Boulder Co Dem Exec Comt, 68-; founding dir, State Speaker's Bur, Colo Dem Party, 68-, cand for vchmn, 69; mem, Colo State Cent Comt, 68-; nominee, Boulder Co Treas, 70; co-chmn, Colo Legis Cand Comt, 70, chmn, 71; mem, Colo Dem State Finance Comt, 70-; admin asst to minority leader, Colo State Senate, 71-72; chmn, Dist 47 Dem Comt, currently; cand, House of Reps, Dist 52, 72; mem, 20th Judicial Nominating Comn, 72- Bus & Prof Pos: Self-employed acct; critic, Colo State Speech League, 66-; legis chmn, Boulder Bus & Prof Women, 73- Mem: Int Toastmistress Club; League of Women Voters; Colo Fedn Jane Jeffersons; Colo Coord Coun Women's Orgns; Nat Asn Parliamentarians. Relig: Catholic. Mailing Add: 4789 Briar Ridge Trail Boulder CO 80307

MCESSY, EARL F (R)
Wis State Rep
b Fond du Lac Co, Wis, Feb 12, 13. Educ: Marquette Univ, BS, 39. Polit & Govt Pos: Wis State Rep, 56-; undersheriff; traffic officer. Bus & Prof Pos: Factory laborer & purchasing agt,

formerly; real estate broker. Mil Serv: Navy, 42-46; SPac, 7 Battle Stars; 3 Spec Citations. Mem: Elks; Red Cross; PTA; Cent Educ Coun. Mailing Add: 361 Forest Ave Fond du Lac WI 54934

MCEVILLY, JAMES LAWRENCE (D)
Chmn, Grundy Co Dem Cent Comt, Ill
b Joliet, Ill, Apr 18, 26; s Lawrence McEvilly & Winifred Breen M; m 1949 to Anne Veronica Clennon; c Colleen, Patrick, Kathleen, Peggy, Kevin, Mary Lou, Brian & Kelly. Educ: Minooka High Sch, Ill, grad. Polit & Govt Pos: Precinct committeeman, Dem Party, Ill, 48-; chmn, Grundy Co Dem Cent Comt, 65- Bus & Prof Pos: Farmer, 25 years. Mem: KofC; Lions; Holy Name Soc of St Marys. Relig: Catholic. Mailing Add: RR 2 Minooka IL 60447

MCEVOY, JOHN THOMAS (D)
b Council Bluffs, Iowa, Apr 9, 37. Educ: Creighton Univ Law Sch, LLB, 61; Georgetown Univ Law Ctr, LLM, 64. Polit & Govt Pos: Asst to the Gen Counsel, Dept of the Army, 62-64; staff asst to spec asst to the Secy of Defense, 64-65; legis asst to US Sen Joseph D Tydings, Md, 66-68; staff dir, Comt on DC, US Senate, 68-70; admin asst to US Sen E S Muskie, Maine, 71-72; chief counsel, Budget Comt, US Senate, 74- Mil Serv: Entered as 1st Lt, Army, 61, released as Capt, 64, after serv in Judge Adv Gen Corps. Mailing Add: US Senate Washington DC 20510

MCEVOY, WILLIAM PETER (D)
Chmn, Boone Co Dem Party, Ky
b Forest Hills, Ohio, June 28, 15; s John McEvoy & Jennie Jameson M; m 1940 to Margaret L Kaelin; c Dennis Patrick. Educ: Centre Col, 35-39; Chase Col Law, JD, 42, 46-48; Beta Theta Pi. Polit & Govt Pos: Co attorney, Boone Co, Ky, 50-; past pres, Boone Co Dem Club; chmn, Boone Co Dem Party, currently; mem, Econ Develop Comn, Ky, currently; mem, Ky State Dem Cent Comt, currently. Bus & Prof Pos: Vpres, Northern Ky Indust Found, Covington, Ky, 58-; pres, Florence Deposit Bank, Florence, Ky, 59-; mem, Ky Develop Coun, Frankfort, 61-; mem bd dirs, Centre Col Alumni Asn, 70- Mil Serv: Entered as Pvt, Air Force, 42, released as 1st Sgt, 46, after serv in 7th Air Force, Pac Theatre, 45-46; Squadron Citation, Pac Theatre Opers; Good Conduct Medal; Victory Medal. Publ: Boone County Bar Association, Cincinnati Bar Asn, 72. Mem: Co Attorneys Asn Ky (pres); Florence Rotary Club; Am Legion; VFW; 40 et 8. Relig: Catholic. Mailing Add: 31 Lacresta Rd Florence KY 41042

MCEWEN, NEIL ALLAN (DFL)
Co Attorney, Pennington Co, Minn
b Hallock, Minn, Mar 19, 37; s Lorne Peter McEwen & Josephine Jensen M; m 1956 to Maxine; c Gregory & Gretchen. Educ: Univ NDak, BSBA, 62, Law Sch, JD; Beta Alpha Phi; ed, NDak Law Rev. Polit & Govt Pos: Chmn, Pennington Co Dem-Farmer-Labor Party, Minn, formerly; co attorney, Pennington Co, 70- Publ: Articles in NDak Law Rev. Mem: Elks; Eagles; Lions; Thief River CofC; Jaycees. Relig: Lutheran. Mailing Add: 226 S Maple Thief River Falls MN 56701

MCEWEN, ROBERT CAMERON (R)
US Rep, NY
b Ogdensburg, NY, Jan 5, 20; m to Anita Sharples; c Nancy & Mary. Educ: Univ Vt; Wharton Sch Finance, Univ Pa; Albany Law Sch. Polit & Govt Pos: NY State Sen, 54-64; US Rep, NY, 64- Mil Serv: Sgt, Air Force, World War II. Mem: Am Legion; VFW; Mason; Elks. Legal Res: RFD 2 Ogdensburg NY 13669 Mailing Add: House Off Bldg Washington DC 20515

MCEWEN, ROBERT DOUGLAS (R)
Ohio State Rep
b Hillsboro, Ohio, Jan 12, 50; s Dr D C McEwen & Ruth Robinson M; single. Educ: Univ Miami, BBA, 72; Ohio State Univ Col Law, 73-74; Sigma Chi; Omicron Delta Kappa. Polit & Govt Pos: Asst to US Rep William H Harsha, Ohio; Ohio State Rep, 77th Dist, 75- Mem: Rotary; Optimists Int; Jaycees; Farm Bur; Grange. Relig: Baptist. Legal Res: 124 Joy Ave Hillsboro OH 45133 Mailing Add: Ohio State Capitol Columbus OH 43215

MCFADDEN, DUANE P (MAC) (D)
Mont State Rep
Mailing Add: 1804 Fourth Ave N Great Falls MT 59401

MCFADDEN, ROBERT LAWRENCE (D)
SC State Rep
b Camden, SC, Aug 25, 29; s Lawrence Walker McFadden & Eunice Long M; m 1960 to Martha Anne Stewart; c Robert Lawrence, Jr & Sarah Anne. Educ: Duke Univ, BA, 51, LLB, 54; Delta Theta Phi. Polit & Govt Pos: SC State Rep, 61- Bus & Prof Pos: Lawyer, Gettys & McFadden, currently. Mil Serv: Army, 54-56. Mem: Elks; York Co Hist Soc; Kiwanis. Honors & Awards: 1960 Rock Hill DSA Award. Relig: Presbyterian; Deacon. Mailing Add: 949 Beverly Dr Rock Hill SC 29730

MCFADDEN, WILMOT CURNOW (D)
Committeewoman, Wyo State Dem Party
b Lead, SDak, Oct 30, 19; d William Curnow & Ingeborg Christianson C; m K Hamm, div; m 1965 to John McFadden; c Christina Hamm (Mrs Charles Bice). Educ: SDak State Col, Brookings; Univ Minn. Polit & Govt Pos: Committeewoman, Wyo State Dem Party, Sweetwater Co, 50-, vchairwoman, 63-64; pres, Sweetwater Co Dem Woman's Club, 52-54; deleg, Dem Nat Conv, 56 & 64; deleg, Wyo State Dem Conv, 68 & 70; mem Wyo adv bd, Fedn Comn on Civil Rights, 69- Publ: Compiler, Handbook for Wyoming library trustees. Mem: Fed Women's Clubs; Am Libr Asn; Am Legion Auxiliary; Does; Women's Dem Club. Honors & Awards: Nat Grolier Award, Nat Libr Week, 69. Relig: Congregational. Mailing Add: 28 Cedar Rock Springs WY 82901

MCFALL, DAVID MERRILL (D)
b Indianapolis, Ind, May 18, 31; s Rev Merrill B McFall & Mary Elizabeth Glossbrenner M; m 1951 to Patricia Louise Marlin; c Valerie Kay, David Marc, Robert Neil, Marlin Keith & Cristopher Merrill. Educ: Ind Univ, 48-51; Ind Col Mortuary Sci, Embalmer, 52. Polit & Govt Pos: Campaign mgr, Lee H Hamilton for Cong, 64, 66, 68, 70 & 72; admin asst to US Rep Hamilton, Ninth Dist, Ind, 65- Bus & Prof Pos: Embalmer & funeral dir, V L Poindexter & Day Funeral Homes, 52-54; salesman, Sun Life Assurance Co of Can, 54-55; claim agt, NY Cent RR, 55-61; field claim rep, State Farm Mutual Ins Co, 61-64; pres, McFall Claims Serv, 64-65. Mil Serv: Entered as Recruit E-1, Ind Nat Guard, 50, released as 1st Sgt, 56, after serv in Hq & Hq Battery, 38th Div Artil, Inf; Unit Commendation, 55. Publ: Aspects of crossing accident investigation, The Bull & The Chronicle, Asn Am RR & Nat Asn Rwy Trial Counsel, 2/61. Mem: Cong Secretaries Club; Rotary Int; Boy Scouts (mem exec bd, Hoosier Trails Coun); Sane Found of Ind, Inc (treas). Relig: United Methodist. Legal Res: 1011 Gaiser Dr Seymour IN 47274 Mailing Add: 2344 Rayburn House Off Bldg Washington DC 20515

MCFALL, JOHN J (D)
Majority Whip, US House Rep
b Buffalo, NY, Feb 20, 18; m to Evelyn Anklam M; c Joseph, Alicia & Sarah. Educ: Modesto Jr Col, 36; Univ Calif, AB, 38; LLB, 41. Polit & Govt Pos: Mayor, Manteca, Calif, 48-50; Calif State Assemblyman, 51-56; US Rep, Calif, 56-, Majority Whip, US House Rep, 72-; deleg, Dem Nat Mid-Term Conf, 74. Bus & Prof Pos: Lawyer, 46- Mil Serv: S/Sgt, Intel Corps, 42-46. Mem: Calif Bar Asn; Odd Fellows; Shrine; Mason; Scottish Rite. Legal Res: 316 W N St Manteca CA 95336 Mailing Add: 2346 Rayburn Bldg Washington DC 20515

MCFARLAND, DENNIS CLAUDE (D)
Minority Leader, SDak House of Rep
b Sioux Falls, SDak, Aug 29, 42; s Ernest Vincent McFarland & Evelyn Esther Hansen M; m 1965 to Janet Elaine Daniels. Educ: Univ Notre Dame, BBA, 64; Univ SDak, JD, 67; SDak State Univ, cert educator, 69. Polit & Govt Pos: SDak State Rep, 73-, chmn, Joint Senate-House Interim Rules Rev Comn, SDak Legis, 73-, Minority Leader, SDak House of Rep, 75- Bus & Prof Pos: Lawyer, 67-; teacher-debate coach, Baltic Independent Sch Dist, 67-71; dir forensics, Augustana Col (SDak), 72-73. Mem: Delta Theta Phi (chap pres, 64-); State Bar SDak; Minnehaha Co Legal Aid Asn (bd dirs, 70-); United Brotherhood Coun (vpres, 71-); Lutheran Social Serv Kinsman Youth Prog (vpres & bd dirs, 70-). Honors & Awards: Outstanding Young Men of Am, Univ SDak Alumni Asn, 73. Relig: Catholic. Legal Res: 1615 Dana Dr Sioux Falls SD 57105 Mailing Add: Suite 511 101 S Main Sioux Falls SD 57102

MCFARLAND, ERNEST WILLIAM (D)
b Earlsboro, Okla, Oct 9, 94; s William Thomas McFarland & Kesiah Smith M; m to Edna Eveland; c Jewell (Mrs Delbert Lewis). Educ: ECent State Teachers Col, Ada, Okla, 13-14; Univ Okla, AB, 17; Stanford Univ, JD, 21 & AM, 22. Hon Degrees: LLD, Univ Ariz, 50 & Ariz State Univ, 73. Polit & Govt Pos: Co Attorney, Pinal Co, Ariz, 24-30; Judge of Superior Court, Pinal Co, 35-41; US Sen, Ariz, 41-53, Majority Leader, US Senate, 51-53; Gov, Ariz, 55-59; chmn Ariz deleg, Dem Nat Conv, 64; Justice, Ariz Supreme Court, 65-71, Chief Justice, 69. Bus & Prof Pos: Pres, Ariz TV Co, Phoenix, 55- Mil Serv: Seaman, Navy, World War I; Lt Comdr, Naval Res, World War II. Mem: Am Legion; Mason; Shrine; Jester; KofP. Relig: Methodist. Legal Res: Florence AZ 85232 Mailing Add: 306 W Royal Palms Phoenix AZ 85021

MCFARLAND, GAIL EVELYN (D)
Committeewoman, East Hampton Dem Town Comt, NY
b Manhattan, NY, Apr 4, 42; d Allen Frankel & Florence Cohen F; m 1963 to Gary Ronald McFarland, wid, 71; c Milo & Kerry. Educ: Hofstra Univ, BA, 63; Southampton Col, Long Island Univ, 72-73. Polit & Govt Pos: Openhousing agt, Great Neck Comt for Human Rights, NY, 58-59; organizer for voter registr, Concerned Citizens of East Hampton, 70-71; organizer, South Fork Women's Liberation Coalition, 70-72; organizer & lobbyist, Comt for Legal Abortion, 71; deleg, Dem Nat Conv, 72; coordr, McGovern for President, East Hampton, 72; co-founder, first pres & deleg, South Fork New Dem Coalition, 72-73; committeewoman, East Hampton Dem Town Comt, 72-; deleg legis adv comt for Suffolk Co Dem Party, 73; asst to town leader, East Hampton Dem Party, 73-74; sr research assoc, NY State Assembly, currently; campaign mgr, Town Supvr Suffolk Co, 73-; ombudsman, East Hampton, 74; campaign mgr, First Assembly Dist, 74. Mem: Suffolk Co Women's Polit Caucus; East Hampton Town Dem Club. Mailing Add: 14 Blessing Rd Slingerlands NY 12159

MCFARLAND, GWEN NATION (D)
Committeewoman, Tenn State Dem Exec Comt
b Lawrenceburg, Tenn, July 4, 30; d James Luther Nation & Martha Owens N; m 1947 to George Henry McFarland; c Anthony Joel & Joni Elizabeth. Educ: George Peabody Col, BA, 52, MA, 63, PhD, 70; Kappa Delta Pi, Phi Delta Kappa. Polit & Govt Pos: Pres, Davidson Co Dem Women, 72, newsletter chmn, 73-; deleg, Dem Nat Conv, 72; secy, Nat Fedn Dem Women, 73-, newsletter chmn, 73-; newsletter chmn, Tenn Fedn Dem Women, 73-; committeewoman, Tenn State Dem Exec Comt, 74-; chairwoman, State Affirmative Action Comt, 75- Bus & Prof Pos: Teacher, Metrop Nashville Pub Schs, 52-65, elem prin, 65-70, dir career opportunities prog, 70-, coordr pre-serv teacher educ, 74- Publ: Utilization of Sensitivity Training as Inservice Education, Peabody Col, 70; Utilization of Paraprofessionals (course of study), privately published; Education-graduate level, Tenn Teachers, 63. Mem: United Teaching Profession (chmn Local Teachers Asn); Asn Supervision & Curriculum Develop; Asn Teacher Educators; Nashville Urban League (first vpres); Mayor's Adv Coun Youth Opportunity (second vchmn). Honors & Awards: Outstanding Serv Award, Metrop Nashville Educ Asn. Relig: Episcopal. Mailing Add: 828 Lemont Dr Nashville TN 37216

MCFARLAND, HELENE MORRIS (R)
Chmn, Castro Co Rep Party, Tex
b Castro Co, Tex, Mar 20, 19; d John Redwine Morris & Katie Mae White M; m 1938 to Gwen Ernest McFarland; c Sandra Gwen (Mrs Morgan), DeZane (Mrs Carter) & Kipa Wade. Educ: WTex State Univ, BS summa cum laude in Art Educ, 69, MA, 71; Tex Tech Univ, 74; Alpha Ki; Kappa Pi; Delta Zeta. Polit & Govt Pos: Precinct chmn, Castro Co Rep Party, Tex, 60-64, co vchmn, 64-68, chmn, 68- Bus & Prof Pos: Self-employed artist, farmer & homemaker, Windy Acres Farm, 38- Mem: Tex Fine Arts Asn; Amarillo Art Asn; Arney Community Club; WTex Watercolor Asn. Relig: Church of Christ. Mailing Add: Windy Acres Farm Rte 2 Happy TX 79042

MCFARLAND, JAMES THOMAS (R)
NY State Sen
b Buffalo, NY, Mar 13, 30; s Ralph J McFarland & Collette Roy M; m 1958 to Geraldine T Walsh; c Katherine, Susan, James T, Jr & Lynne. Educ: Canisius Col, BS, 51; Univ Buffalo Law Sch, LLB, 54, JD, 68; Gold Key Club. Polit & Govt Pos: Counsel, NY Assembly Health Comt, Joint Legis Comt on Housing & Urban Develop, 64; NY State Assemblyman, 66-72, chmn, Assembly Minority Subcomt on Medicaid Law of NY, NY State Assembly, chmn, Ways & Means Subcomt in Fields of Soc Serv & Health, & Joint Legis Comt on Commerce, Econ Develop, Tourism & Motor Boats, 69-71; chmn Assembly Rep Conf, 71-72; NY State Sen, 73-, chmn standing comt on corp, authorities & pub utilities & chmn subcomt on vet affairs, NY State Senate, currently. Bus & Prof Pos: Attorney, Buffalo, NY, 54- Mil Serv: Entered as Pvt, Army, 54, released as SP-3, 56, after serv in CIC, G-2, Fourth Army Hq, Fourth Army Area, Ft Sam Houston, Tex; Good Conduct & Sharpshooter Medals. Mem: Erie

Co & NY State Bar Asns; Erie Co Trial Lawyers Asn; Ken-Ton Rep Club; KofC. Honors & Awards: Portrait of the Year Award, Ken-Ton Young Rep Couples Club, 68; Citizen of the Year Award, Ken-Ton Jaycees, 69. Relig: Catholic. Mailing Add: 21 Grosvenor Rd Buffalo NY 14223

MCFARLAND, JOHN ALEXANDER, JR (D)
RI State Rep
b Westerly, RI, Mar 10, 42; s John Alexander McFarland & Marian Walton M; m 1965 to Peggy Guzeika; c Michelle. Educ: Univ RI, BS, 64; Univ NH, MS, 66; Alpha Zeta; Sigma Chi. Polit & Govt Pos: Chmn, N Kingstown Dem Town Comt, RI, 72-; RI State Rep, 73- Bus & Prof Pos: Teacher, N Kingstown, RI, 66-67; analytical chemist, Phillip Hunt Chem Corp, Lincoln, RI, 67- Mem: US Navy League. Relig: Protestant. Mailing Add: 55 Knollwood Circle North Kingstown RI 02852

MCFARLAND, LEONA MARIE (D)
Treas, CZ Regional Dem Party
b Boston, Mass, May 8, 28; d Alwin Karl Milch & Eleanor Anne McCarthy M; m 1958 to Edward A McFarland; c Renata Marie, Chantel Elizabeth, Brent Edward, Colin Patrick & Nicole Margaret. Educ: Bridgewater State Teachers' Col, BS Ed, 50, MEd, 52. Polit & Govt Pos: Vchmn, CZ Regional Dem Party, 68-70, treas, 72-; alt deleg, Dem Nat Conv, 72. Bus & Prof Pos: Elem & jr high teacher, Dennis, Mass, 51-54; elem & high sch teacher, Dept of the Air Force, Ger, 54-57 & 59-60, teacher & prin, Ger & France, 57-59; elem teacher, St Mary's Mission Parochial Sch, CZ, 67- Mem: Family Membership Spec Educ Asn CZ; Girl Scouts (asst leader, CZ Coun, 65-). Honors & Awards: Bronze Statuette, Girl Scouts, 71. Relig: Roman Catholic. Legal Res: 14820 NE Eighth Ct Miami FL 33161 Mailing Add: Box 936 Balboa CZ

MCFARLAND, MARY ANN (R)
b Detroit, Mich, June 5, 39; d Joseph Orlando Ciampichini & Anne Korpak C; m 1964 to Archie Alexander McFarland; c Linda & Gary. Educ: St Bernard's High Sch, Detroit, Mich, grad. Polit & Govt Pos: Admin asst, Los Angeles Co Rep Cent Comt, Calif, 67-68, mem from 65th Assembly Dist, 73-74; hq chmn, Rep Assembly Cand, 65th Dist, 68; alt, 65th Assembly Dist Rep Cent Comt, 68-70, mem, 70-74; mem, Calif Rep State Cent Comt, 69-72; campaign mgr, 31st Cong Dist Campaign, 70; chmn, 31st Cong Dist Rep Party, 73-74. Bus & Prof Pos: Pvt secy, H W Rickel & Co, Detroit, Mich, 55-60; free lance secy, 60-64; secretarial serv, self-employed, 71-74; salesman, Imperial Realty, Torrance, Calif; mem bd realtors, 74- Mem: Calif Rep Assembly; Inglewood Rep Women, Federated; PTA; Community Adv Coun (secy, 72-). Relig: Protestant. Mailing Add: 11121 Cedar Ave Inglewood CA 90304

MCFARLANE, WILLIAM D (D)
b Greenwood, Ark, July 17, 94; s Robert William McFarlane & Maggie Harris M; m 1923 to Alma Carl, wid, 38; m 1945 to Inez Bishop; c Mary, William D, Jr, Betty Ann, Barbara Frances & Robert Carl. Educ: Univ Ark, AB, 19; Chicago-Kent Col Law, LLB, 21, JD, 69; Tau Kappa Alpha; Delta Chi. Polit & Govt Pos: Tex State Rep, 23-27; Tex State Sen, 27-31; US Rep, Tex, 33-39; spec asst to Attorney Gen, 39-44; dir, Surplus Property Small War Plants Corp, 45-46; trial attorney, US Dept of Justice, 46-66. Bus & Prof Pos: Owner, Co Store, 14-18. Mil Serv: Entered as Pvt, Army, 18, released as 2nd Lt, 18, after serv in 87th Div, Camp Pike, Ark. Mem: Tex State & Young Co Bar Asns; Mason (32 degree); Shrine; Am Legion. Honors & Awards: Mem A Club, Univ Ark. Relig: Methodist. Mailing Add: 1410 Oak Hills Dr Graham TX 76046

MCFEE, SHIRLEY MILLER (R)
VChmn, Calhoun Co Rep Exec Comt, Mich
b Pontiac, Mich, Dec 2, 29; d Edwin Charles Miller & Flossie Murdick M; m 1952 to Robert Douglas McFee; c Bruce Charles, Russell Stuart & Carole Louise. Educ: Univ Mich, AB in Hist, 51; Western Mich Univ, MA in Polit Sci, 70; Phi Beta Kappa; Alpha Chi Omega. Polit & Govt Pos: Mem, Mich Third Cong Dist Rep Exec Comt, 64-70; mem, Calhoun Co Rep Exec Comt, formerly; alt deleg, Rep Nat Conv, 72; campaign staff, Mary Coleman for Supreme Court, 72; mem, State Off Compensation Comn, 72- Bus & Prof Pos: Teacher, Lakeview Sch Syst, Battle Creek, Mich, 53-56; instr, Albion Col, spring 69, Western Mich Univ, fall 69 & Kellogg Community Col, 70- Mem: Battle Creek Rep Women's Club; United Community Serv Bd Dirs; sustaining mem Jr League of Battle Creek. Relig: Congregational. Mailing Add: 611 Jennings Landing Battle Creek MI 49015

MCGAHN, JOSEPH L (D)
NJ State Sen
Mailing Add: State House Trenton NJ 08625

MCGAUVRAN, JOHN STANLEY (D)
NDak State Rep
b Langdon, NDak, Nov 8, 25; s Charles Randolph McGauvran & Maud Alice Symons M; m 1948 to Elaine Marvel Vollum; c Judith, Timothy, Mary Jo & Susan. Educ: Langdon Pub Schs, 12 years. Polit & Govt Pos: Precinct committeeman, NDak Dem Party; NDak State Rep, 71-; dir, NDak Sch Bd Asn for NE Dist, currently. Mem: KofP (past grand chancellor, NDak); Mason; Scottish Rite; NDak State Barley Show. Relig: Lutheran. Mailing Add: State Capitol Bismarck ND 58501

MCGAW, ROBERT WALTER (D)
Mayor, Rockford, Ill
b Rockford, Ill, Apr 9, 23; s James L McGaw & Loren M Lynch M; m 1946 to Peggy A Schindler; c Marlis Jean, Roberta Sue & Raymond William. Educ: Northern Ill Univ, BS, 50, MS, 66; Univ Ill; Wash Univ; Kappa Delta Pi. Polit & Govt Pos: Dem precinct committeeman, Ill, 50-; alderman, Rockford, Ill, 55-63; cand for Lt Gov, 60; co chmn, Dem Party, 62-64; deleg, Dem Nat Conv, 68 & 72; Dem cand for Mayor, Rockford, Ill, 72, Mayor, 73-; deleg, Dem Nat Mid-Term Conf, 74. Bus & Prof Pos: Teacher, High Sch, 50-68; prin, Rock Cut Teacher Training Sch, 68. Mil Serv: Entered as Pvt, Army, 42, released as Sgt, 46, after serv in 90mm Gun Bn; ETO, 44-46; Four Battle Ribbons. Mem: Ill Prin Asn; VFW; Mason (32 degree); Moose. Relig: Presbyterian. Mailing Add: 2016 E State St Rockford IL 61108

MCGEE, ARTHUR MARION (D)
Chmn, Cowlitz Co Dem Cent Comt, Wash
b Lake Stevens, Wash, May 23, 34; s William Walter McGee & Frances B Marquardt M; single. Educ: Pac Lutheran Univ, BA, 56; Lutheran Sch Theol, Chicago, MDiv, 61; Circle K Club. Polit & Govt Pos: Precinct committeeman, Lewis Co Dem Comt, Wash, 68-70; precinct committeeman, Cowlitz Co Dem Comt, 73-; chmn, Cowlitz Co Dem Cent Comt, 75- Bus & Prof Pos: Pastor, Troy Lutheran Church, Idaho, 61-65, Cent Lutheran Church, Morton, Wash, 65-69 & Gloria Dei Lutheran Church, Kelso, 69- Mem: Cowlitz Co & Kelso Ministerial Asns; Drug Abuse Prev Ctr (mem bd); Community Action Coun (mem bd). Relig: Lutheran. Mailing Add: 407 N Fifth Kelso WA 98626

MCGEE, CARL LOUIS (D)
Chmn, Caswell Co Dem Exec Comt, NC
b Lenoir, NC, Mar 31, 39; s Carl Dewey McGee & Thelma Beach M; m 1961 to Annette Law; c Brent & Shana. Educ: NC State Col, BS, 62; Western Carolina Univ, MA, 72; Farm House Fraternity. Polit & Govt Pos: Chmn, Caswell Co Dem Exec Comt, NC, 72- Bus & Prof Pos: Right of way agt, NC Hwy Comn, 64-69; prin, High Rock Sch & all schs in Caswell Co, NC, 69-70, Pelham Sch, 70-72 & Cobb Mem Sch, 72- Mem: Caswell Brotherhood Lodge 11, AF&AM (secy, 73-); Cobb Mem Ruritan Club (pres, 75); Boy Scout Troop 372 (asst scoutmaster). Relig: Presbyterian. Legal Res: Rte 1 Box 55 Ruffin NC 27326 Mailing Add: Rte 1 Box 546 Pelham NC 27311

MCGEE, GALE WILLIAM (D)
US Sen, Wyo
b Lincoln, Nebr, Mar 17, 15; s Garton W McGee & Frances McCoy M; m 1939 to Loraine Baker; c David Wyant, Robert Merrill, Mary Gale & Lori Ann. Educ: Nebr State Teachers' Col, BA, 36; Univ Colo, MA, 39; Univ Chicago, PhD, 47. Hon Degrees: LLD, Univ Wyo, Eastern Ky Univ, Am Univ, Seton Hall Univ & Allegheny Col. Polit & Govt Pos: US Sen, Wyo, 58-, mem, Senate Appropriations Comt, 59-, mem, Senate Foreign Rels Comt, 69-, chmn, Senate Post Off & Civil Serv Comt, 69-; deleg, Dem Nat Conv, 60, 64, 68 & 72. Bus & Prof Pos: Prof Am Hist, Crofton, Nebr High Sch, 36-37, Kearney, Nebr High Sch, 37-40, Nebr Wesleyan Univ, 40-43, Iowa State Univ, 43-44, Univ Notre Dame, 44-45, Univ Chicago, 45-46 & Univ Wyo, 46- Publ: The Responsibilities of World Power, Nat Press, Inc, 68. Mem: Am Asn Univ Prof; Am Hist Asn; Miss Valley Hist Asn; Am Asn for the UN; Coun on Foreign Rels. Relig: Presbyterian. Legal Res: Laramie WY Mailing Add: 7205 Marbury Rd Bethesda MD 20034

MCGEE, JAMES HOWELL (D)
Mayor, Dayton, Ohio
b Berryburg, WVa, Nov 8, 18; s Spanish McGee (mother deceased); m 1948 to Elizabeth McCracken; c Annette & Frances. Educ: Wilberforce Univ, BS, 41; Ohio State Univ Law Sch, LLB, 48; Alpha Phi Alpha. Polit & Govt Pos: City comnr, Dayton, Ohio, 67-70, mayor, 70- Bus & Prof Pos: Attorney-at-law, self-employed, 49- Mil Serv: Entered Army, 42, released 45, after serv in Africa, Sicily, Italy, France & Ger; Five Battle Stars. Mem: Ancient Square Lodge 40, F&AM; Prince Hall Affiliation Chap, RAM; Miami Consistory 26; Valley of Troy; NAACP. Relig: Protestant. Mailing Add: 1518 Benson Dr Dayton OH 45406

MCGEE, JOSEPH JAMES (R)
b New York, NY, Aug 7, 46; s James E McGee & Loretta McCormick M; single. Educ: Our Lady of Angels Sem, Albany, BA, 68; St John Univ (NY), 71; Am Univ. Polit & Govt Pos: Admin asst to US Rep Stewart B McKinney, Conn, currently. Legal Res: 56 Fairfield Beach Rd Fairfield CT 06430 Mailing Add: 2833 27th St NW Washington DC 20003

MCGEE, LEONARD ERWIN (D)
VChmn, Davis Co Dem Party, Utah
b Salt Lake City, Utah, June 3, 52; s Arden H McGee & Clara Brown M; single. Educ: Univ Utah, polit sci, 70-73; Pi Sigma Alpha; Skull & Bones. Polit & Govt Pos: Vpres, Univ Utah Young Dem, 70-72; state student coordr, Utah Citizens for McGovern, 71-72; alt deleg, Dem Nat Conv, 72; coordr, New Vote, 72; precinct chmn, Davis Co, Utah, 72-73, vchmn, Davis Co Dem Party, 73- Mailing Add: 297 E 1100 S Bountiful UT 84010

MCGEE, THOMAS W (D)
Mass State Rep
b Lynn, Mass; s Thomas McGee & Mary O'Shea M; m to Ann Sorrenti; c Four. Educ: Boston Univ, LLB, 53. Polit & Govt Pos: Mem, Ward Five City Coun, Mass; pres, City Coun, 58-61; deleg, Dem Nat Conv, 68; Mass State Rep, currently, majority leader, Mass House Rep, 69-; deleg, Dem Nat Mid-Term Conf, 74. Bus & Prof Pos: Ins; US Dept of Labor employee, formerly. Mil Serv: World War II, SPac. Mem: Am Legion; Amvets; DAV. Mailing Add: 9 Pine Rd Lynn MA 01904

MCGEE, WILLIAM SEARS (D)
Assoc Justice, Supreme Court of Tex
b Houston, Tex, Sept 29, 17; s James Butler McGee (deceased) & Alice Sears M; m 1941 to Mary Beth Peterson; c James Sears, Mary Gray (Mrs Neilson), Claire Sher, Alice, George Sears & Erwin Smith. Educ: Rice Univ, 35-37; Univ Tex, Austin, LLB, 40; Phi Delta Theta. Polit & Govt Pos: Co Judge, Harris Co, Tex, 48-54, Judge, 151st Dist Court, 54-55, Judge, 55th Dist Court, 58-68; Assoc Justice, Supreme Court, Tex, 69- Mil Serv: Entered as Ens, Naval Res, 43, released as Lt, 46, after serv in D E 363, Pac Theatre, 44-45. Mem: Am Judicature Soc; AF&AM; Scottish Rite; Sons of Hermann; SPJST Lodge. Relig: Episcopal. Mailing Add: 2300 Quarry Austin TX 78703

MCGHEE, GEORGE CREWS
b Waco, Tex, Mar 10, 12; s George Summers McGhee & Magnolia Spruce M; m 1938 to Cecilia Jeanne DeGolyer; c Marcia Spruce, George DeGolyer, Dorothy Hart, Michael Anthony, Cecilia Goodrich & Valerie Foster. Educ: Southern Methodist Univ, 28; Univ Okla, BS, 33; Oxford Univ, Rhodes scholar & DPhil, 37; Univ London, 37; Phi Beta Kappa; Sigma Xi. Hon Degrees: DCL, Southern Methodist Univ, 53; LLD, Tulane Univ, 57 & Univ Md, 65; DSc, Tampa Univ, 69. Polit & Govt Pos: Coord aid to Greece & Turkey, Dept of State, 47-49; asst secy of state, Near East, SAsian & African Affairs, 49-51, sr adv, NAtlantic Treaty Coun, Ottawa, 51, ambassador & chief, Am Mission for Aid to Turkey, 51-53, consult, Nat Security Coun & Comt Int Econ Growth, 58, mem, President's Comn to Study US Mil Asst Prog, 58-59, dir, Comt for Econ Develop, 57-, chmn, Policy Planning Coun & counsr, Dept of State, 61, Under Secy of State for Polit Affairs, 61-63, Ambassador to Fed Repub of Ger, 63-68, Ambassador-at-lg, 68-69; spec asst to the chmn, Urban Coalition, 69-70; chmn, Bus Coun for Int Understanding, 69-73; mem, Gov Comn for Econ Develop & Conserv, Va, 69- Bus & Prof Pos: Registered engr, Tex; oil geologist, 30-40; owner, McGhee Prod Co, 40-; dir, Mobil Oil Corp, currently dir, Procter & Gamble Co, currently; dir, Am Security & Trust Co, currently, chmn bd, Saturday Rev, currently. Mil Serv: Navy, 43-46; Lt Col, Air Force Res, 49-; Legion of Merit; Asiatic Ribbon with Three Battle Stars. Mem: Am Asn Petrol Geol; Soc Exp Geophys; Am Inst Mining, Metall & Petrol Engrs; Rotary; Century Asn. Honors & Awards: Hon fel, Queen's Col, Oxford Univ. Legal Res: Farmers' Delight Middleburg VA 22117 Mailing Add: 2808 N St NW Washington DC 20007

MCGILL, CHARLOTTE S (D)
Ky State Rep
Mailing Add: 3016 River Park Dr Louisville KY 40211

MCGILL, DUANE S (R)
Kans State Rep
b Grandview, Iowa, Apr 25, 22; s Jesse D McGill & Faith Stineman M; m 1954 to Wanda Crowe; c Pamela Jo & Scott Duane. Educ: Southwestern Col, BA, 51; Univ Kans, MA, 52. Polit & Govt Pos: Kans State Rep, 61-65 & 67-; mem, Comt on Interstate Coop, Kans, 63-64; deleg, Rep Nat Conv, 64. Bus & Prof Pos: Pres, Rapids Amusements, Inc, 59-61; mem bd dirs, Tom-Kat, Inc, 65- Mil Serv: Entered as Pvt, Army, 41, released as 1st Sgt, 45, after serv in Seventh Inf Div, Pac, 43-45; Am Defense Serv, Good Conduct & Asiatic Pac Campaign Medals; Philippines Liberation Ribbon with two Bronze Stars. Mem: Kans Restaurant Asn (bd of dirs, 59-); Kans Girl Scout Coun; Am Legion; VFW; Elks. Relig: Methodist. Mailing Add: Box 493 Winfield KS 67156

MCGILL, FRANK H (D)
SC State Rep
Mailing Add: 911 Highland Dr Kingstree SC 29556

MCGILL, LOVETTE EUNICE (D)
VChairwoman, Dade Co Dem Exec Comt, Fla
b Miami, Fla, Dec 16, 53; d James E Martin & Marion Walkine M; single. Educ: Miami-Dade Community Col, AA, 73; Univ Miami, currently; United Black Students of Miami-Dade Community Col. Polit & Govt Pos: Alt deleg, Dem Nat Conv, 72; vchairwoman, Dade Co Dem Exec Comt, Fla, currently; secy, Dade Co Black Caucus, currently. Relig: Catholic. Mailing Add: 4771 NW Sixth Ave Miami FL 33127

MCGILL, SAM P (D)
Ga State Sen
b Hartwell, Ga, Aug 30, 14; s Adolphus Cecil McGill & Lillian Norman M; m 1935 to Florence Clary; c Sam Clary & Kathryn (Mrs Jackson). Educ: South Ga State Col, grad. Polit & Govt Pos: Councilman, City of Washington, Ga, 44-54; Ga State Sen, 50th Dist, 59-60, 24th Dist, 65-, chmn agr comt, Ga State Senate, currently. Bus & Prof Pos: Partner, McGill Truck & Tractor Co, 39- & Wilkes Co Stock Yard, 50-; pres, Saluda Co Stock Yard, Inc, 57-; partner, Thomson Stock Yard, 63- Mem: Washington Lions Club; CofC (pres); Ga Farm Equip Asn; Ga Stock Yard Asn (pres); Ga Automobile Dealer's Asn (dir). Relig: Baptist. Legal Res: Tignall Rd Washington GA 30673 Mailing Add: PO Box 520 Washington GA 30673

MCGILLICUDDY, LILLIAN GRACE (R)
b Chicago, Ill, May 12, 93; d Gustave Flumey & Louise Peters F; m 1916 to Shelby M Boorhem; c Shelby (deceased) & William; m 1938 to Frank McGillicuddy (deceased). Educ: Chicago Teachers Col, 10-12. Polit & Govt Pos: Vchmn, Ark State Rep Comt, 40-64; deleg, Rep Nat Conv, 40, 44, 48, 52, 60, 64, 68 & 72; chmn, Hot Spring Co Comt, Ark, 42-48; chmn, Am Red Cross, Hot Springs, 42-48; pres, Malvern Rep Womens' Club, 46-48; pres, Pulaski Co Rep Womens' Club, Little Rock, 48-60; co-chmn, State Eisenhower Campaign, 52; Rep Nat Committeewoman, Ark, 64-72. Publ: Auth of column in Winthrop Rockefeller Campaigner, 63-64; contrib, Ark Outlook, 65- Mem: Nat Soc Arts & Letters; Nat League of Am Pen Women; Ark Fedn Rep Women; Ark Art Ctr; Fine Arts Club. Honors & Awards: Award for grad with highest scholastic average, Chicago Teachers Col; one of six leading Rep on Site Comt to select location of Rep Nat Conv, 68; Ark Young Rep held an Honor Night & initiated a Lillian McGillicuddy Scholarship Fund. Relig: Episcopal. Mailing Add: 463 Rivercliff Apts Little Rock AR 72202

MCGINLEY, DONALD F (D)
b Keystone, Nebr, June 30, 20; m 1947 to Evaleen Mueller; c One daughter. Educ: Univ Notre Dame, AB, 42; Georgetown Univ, LLB, 49. Polit & Govt Pos: Nebr State Sen, 55-58 & 63-64; US Rep, Nebr, 58-60; deleg, Dem Nat Conv, 64 & 68. Bus & Prof Pos: Lawyer; livestock farmer; reporter, copy ed, The Register, Denver, Colo, 45-46; mem bd, Mid-Plains Community Col, North Platte, Nebr, 66-; mem, Ogallala Libr Bd, 67- Mil Serv: Army Air Force, 42-45. Mem: Elks; Am Legion; VFW: KofC; Ogallala CofC. Relig: Catholic. Mailing Add: 401 E A Ogallala NE 69153

MCGINNESS, CHARLES LAWRENCE (D)
NH State Rep
b Dublin, NH, Mar 9, 1895; s James John McGinness & Margaret Mae Lahiff M; m 1924 to Anna Elizabeth Dunn. Educ: Bellows Falls, Vt, 3 years; Lebanon, NH, 5 years. Polit & Govt Pos: NH State Rep, 23 & Dist Seven, 71-; postmaster, 36-65. Mil Serv: Navy, 17-21. Mem: Am Legion; Patrons of Husbandry; World War I Barracks; KofC. Honors & Awards: Citation of dedicated & honorable serv, NH Chap Postmasters. Relig: Catholic. Mailing Add: 27 Prospect St Troy NH 03465

MCGINNIN, JAMES D (D)
Del State Rep
Mailing Add: 148 Cooper Rd Dover DE 19901

MCGINNIS, EDWARD FRANCIS (R)
b Chicago, Ill, Apr 10, 97; s Frank P McGinnis & Ellen Sutton M; m 1931 to Wilma Fay Hargrove. Educ: Chicago Col of Com. Polit & Govt Pos: Sgt at arms, US Senate, 47-48; chief sgt at arms, Rep Nat Conv, 60, 1st sgt at arms, 64, deleg, 68; mem, Rep State Comt, DC, formerly; chmn organizing comt, Vet for Nixon; nat co-chmn, Vet For Nixon-Agnew, 68; chmn vet comt, 1969 Inaugural; minority counsel, Comt Vet Affairs, US Senate, 71- Bus & Prof Pos: Invest banker, Chicago, Ill, 27-42; vpres & dir, Montgomery Fed Savings & Loan Asn; nat dir pub rels, Am Legion, 49-54; vpres, Seagram Distillers, 54-66. Mil Serv: Entered as Pvt, Army Air Corps, 17, released after serv as Aerial Machine Gunner, World War I, 19; re-entered as Lt, Naval Res, 42, serv in China-Burma-India, released as Comdr, OSS, 46; also serv as observer for Navy in Korea & Vietnam; Africa, China-Burma-India & Philippines Service Ribbons. Mem: Everett McKinley Dirksen Forum; Vets World War I; Am Legion; VFW; Amvets. Honors & Awards: Appointed to Am Battle Monuments Comt by Presidents Eisenhower, Johnson & Nixon. Relig: Roman Catholic. Mailing Add: 4201 Cathedral Ave Washington DC 20016

MCGINNIS, JAMES ALLAN (D)
Mem, NY State Dem Exec Comt
b Niagara Falls, Ont, Feb 17, 31; s James McGinnis & Florence C Allan M; m 1955 to Barbara Anne Noakes; c James Kevin, Maureen Eleanor, Kevin Sean, Barbara Anne, Brenda Eileen, Michael William, Patrick Allan & Mary Elizabeth. Educ: Bishop Duffy High Sch, grad; complete 4 year maintenance electricity course. Polit & Govt Pos: Dem committeeman, Niagara Co, NY, 62-75; chmn, North Tonawanda Dem City Comt, 66-70; mem, Niagara Co Alcoholic Beverage Control Bd, 66-70; mem, Niagara Co Dem Exec Comt, 66-75; deleg, Eighth Judicial Dist Dem Conv, 67; chmn, Niagara Co Dem Comt, 70-; mem, NY State Dem Exec Comt, 71-; mem, Nat Dem Comt, 75- Bus & Prof Pos: Maintenance supvr, duPont Co, 74- Mil Serv: Entered as A/S, Navy, 51, released as PO 3/C, 53. Mem: Am Legion. Relig: Roman Catholic. Mailing Add: 401 Evans St North Tonawanda NY 14120

MCGINNIS, PATRICK J (R)
Pa State Rep
Mailing Add: Capitol Bldg Harrisburg PA 17120

MCGLINCHEY, HERBERT J (D)
Treas, Philadelphia Co Dem Comt
b Philadelphia, Pa, Nov 7, 04. Educ: Pub & parochial schs, Philadelphia. Polit & Govt Pos: Supvr inspection, Eastern Dist, Pa Dept Labor & Indust, 35-37; alt deleg or deleg, Dem Nat Conv, 36-; US Rep, Pa, 45-47; mem, Tax Equalization Bd, 56-63; Pa State Sen, 64-72, chmn, Comt on Hwys, Pa State Senate, 71; treas, Philadelphia Co Dem Comt, 70- Bus & Prof Pos: Pres, Mfgs Sales & Equip Co; pres, Bd of Mercantile Appraisers of Philadelphia, 37-44. Legal Res: 596 E Geneva Ave Philadelphia PA 19120 Mailing Add: 4714 N Front St Philadelphia PA 19120

MCGLINN, FRANK C P (R)
Mem Adv Comt, Pa State Rep Finance Comt
b Philadelphia, Pa, Nov 19, 14; s Dr John A McGlinn & Emma F Potts M; m 1942 to Louise C Lea; c Marion (Mrs Myron E Lockwood, Jr), Alice Ashton, Louise Steuart (Mrs Donald Preston) & Ann Croasdale. Educ: Univ NC, AB, 37; Univ Pa, LLB, 40; LLD, Villanova Univ, 70; Phi Beta Kappa; Delta Kappa Epsilon; Sharswood Law Club. Polit & Govt Pos: Exec secy, Rep Finance Comt, Pa, 40-53, chmn, 63-65; alt deleg-at-lg, Rep Nat Conv, 40 & 52, deleg-at-lg, 64-72; chmn, Pa Fedn of Young Rep Clubs, 48-50; vpres, Nat Young Rep Fedn, 51-53; mem exec comt, Pa State Rep Comt, 48-50 & 63-71; vchmn, Rep Nat Finance Comt, 65-69, Pa chmn, 69-73, mem exec comt, 65-69 & 71-73; chmn exec comt, Pa State Rep Finance Comt, 65-68 & 71-74, mem adv comt, currently; mem, Comn Orgn Govt for Conduct Foreign Policy, currently; chmn, Reelect Sen Hugh Scott, Finance Comt, 70; Pa chmn finance comt Reelect the President, 72. Bus & Prof Pos: Marine counsel, Reliance Ins Co, 40-42; assoc, Pepper, Hamilton & Sheetz, Attorneys, 46-53; vpres & asst to pres, Al Paul Lefton Co, Inc, Advert, 53-57; exec vpres, Fidelity Bank, Philadelphia, Pa, 57-; trustee, Citizens Research Found, currently. Mil Serv: Entered as Ens, Naval Res, 42, released as Lt, 46, after serv in Mediterranean & Pac, 43-45; Purple Heart; Am & Asiatic Theaters & ETO Ribbons; Anzio, S France & Japan Campaign Ribbons. Mem: Union League; Philadelphia; Nat Conf of Christians & Jews (hon chmn); World Affairs Coun; Pub Rels Soc Am; KofM. Honors & Awards: Papal Knight, Equestrian Order St Gregory the Great. Relig: Roman Catholic. Legal Res: 729 Millbrook Lane Haverford PA 19041 Mailing Add: 135 S Broad St Philadelphia PA 19109

MCGLOTHLIN, DONALD A, SR (D)
Va State Deleg
b Honaker, Va, Feb 16, 26; s Jacob Stuart McGlothlin & Celia Ruth Jackson M; m 1947 to Mary Louise Williams; c Donald A, Jr, Mary Louise, Leah Anne, Sean Patrick & Kevin Timothy. Educ: Franklin & Marshall Col, BA, 54; Univ Pa, 46; Marshall Wythe Sch Law, Col of William & Mary, JD, 54; Phi Kappa Psi; Phi Alpha Delta. Polit & Govt Pos: Commonwealth attorney, Grundy, Va, 56-64; Va State Sen, 64-66; Va State Deleg, 68- Mil Serv: Navy, 43-46; CEng, Army, 48-50 & 51-52, Capt. Mem: Buchanan Co Bar Asn; Va State Bar; Mason (32 degree); Shrine; VFW; Am Legion. Relig: Methodist. Legal Res: 100 Granada St Grundy VA 24614 Mailing Add: PO Box 909 Grundy VA 24614

MCGLYNN, MARGARET L (D)
NH State Rep
Mailing Add: 64 Kinsley St Nashua NH 03060

MCGOUGH, KENT B (R)
Chmn, Ohio State Rep Cent & Exec Comt
b Harrod, Ohio, July 20, 17; s John M McGough & Mae Brown M; m 1940 to Wilda Mae Teter; c Sandra, Debra, Cynthia & John. Educ: Miami Univ, Oxford, Ohio, BA, 39; Sigma Nu. Polit & Govt Pos: Precinct committeeman, Allen Co Rep Party, Ohio, 50-; chmn, Rep Exec Comt, Allen Co, 52-; mem, State Rep Cent Comt, Fourth Cong Dist, 56-; alt deleg, Rep Nat Conv, 64 & 72, deleg, 68; treas, Ohio State Rep Cent & Exec Comt, 68-73, dir & legis div chmn, 72-73, chmn, 73- Bus & Prof Pos: Partner, McGough Ins Agency, Lima, Ohio, 46-; bd dirs, Relns Develop Corp, 71- Mil Serv: Entered as Pvt, Army, 45, released as M/Sgt, 46, after serv in Departmental Hq, Alaskan Theatre, 45-46. Mem: Am Inst for Property & Liability Underwriters, Inc; Mason; life mem Jr CofC; life mem Optimist Int; Capitol Hill Club, Washington, DC. Relig: United Methodist. Mailing Add: 1604 Shawnee Rd Lima OH 45805

MCGOVERN, FRANCIS LEO, III (R)
Chmn, Scituate Rep Town Comt, RI
b Providence, RI, Feb 20, 38; s Francis Leo McGovern, Jr & Margaret Mary Stewart M; m 1964 to Carole Louise Kettelle; c Kelly Ann & Jamie Lynn. Educ: Maine Maritime Acad, BS, 64; Young Rep Club. Polit & Govt Pos: Exec dir, Scituate Housing Authority, RI, 69-; chmn, Scituate Rep Town Comt, 74- Bus & Prof Pos: Engr-consult, Factory Mutual Eng Co, 66-72; engr-sales, Merchants & Bus Men's Mutual Ins Co, 72-74; safety & health officer, Univ RI, 74- Mem: Lions; Providence Eng Soc; Nat & RI Safety Coun; Nat Fire Protection Asn. Relig: Roman Catholic. Mailing Add: RD 2 Old Hartford Pike Scituate RI 02857

MCGOVERN, GEORGE (D)
US Sen, SDak
b Avon, SDak, July 19, 22; s Joseph C McGovern & Frances McLean M; m 1943 to Eleanor Faye Stegeberg; c Ann, Steven, Susan, Mary & Teresa. Educ: Dakota Wesleyan Univ, BA, 46; Northwestern Univ, MA, 49, PhD, 53. Polit & Govt Pos: Exec secy, SDak Dem Party, 53-55; US Rep, First Dist, SDak, 57-61; dir, Food for Peace Prog, 61-62; spec asst to President Kennedy; US Sen, SDak, 63-; Presidential cand, 68 & 72. Mil Serv: Entered as Air Cadet, Army Air Force, 43, released as 1st Lt, 45, after serv in ETO; Distinguished Flying Cross; Air Medal with Oak Leaf Clusters. Publ: A Time of War-A Time of Peace, 68 & An American Journey, 74, Random House; The Great Coalfield War (w L Guttridge), Houghton

Mifflin Co, 72; plus others. Mem: Kiwanis; Am Legion; VFW; Mason. Relig: Methodist. Legal Res: 103 E Third Mitchell SD 57301 Mailing Add: US Senate Washington DC 20510

MCGOVERN, TERRY P (D)
Conn State Rep
Mailing Add: 73 Birdsey St Bridgeport CT 06610

MCGOWAN, CHARLES M (D)
Mass State Rep
Mailing Add: State Capitol Boston MA 02133

MCGOWAN, EDGAR LEON (D)
b Conway, SC, June 1, 20; s Edgar Leon McGowan & Sarah Frances Mishoe M; m 1941 to Mildred Gene Parris; c Edgar Linden. Educ: Univ SC, BS, 47, MS, 50, LLB, 57; Beta Alpha Psi; Delta Sigma P. Polit & Govt Pos: City judge, Forest Acres, SC, 63-65, councilman, 65-71; secy, Richland Co Dem Party, 66-70; secy-treas, Dem Party of SC, 66-72; deleg, Dem Nat Conv, 68; comnr of labor, State of SC, 71- Bus & Prof Pos: Instr, Univ SC, 46-50, asst prof, 50-57, assoc prof, 58-71; pub acct, Columbia, SC, 47-50, CPA, 50-57; attorney-at-law, 57-71. Mil Serv: Entered as Pvt, Army, 41, released as Sgt, 45, after serv in 3104 Signal Unit, ETO, 44-45; Good Conduct Medal; European Theatre with Normandy, Northern France & Rhineland Battle Stars; Am Theatre of Opers Ribbons; World War II Victory Medal. Mem: Palmetto Club; Lions; F&AM; Consistory; Shrine. Relig: Methodist. Legal Res: 5067 Hillside Rd Columbia SC 29206 Mailing Add: PO Box 11329 Columbia SC 29211

MCGOWAN, MARION D (D)
SC State Rep
Mailing Add: Box 308 Warrenville SC 29851

MCGOWAN, MARY ELIZABETH (D)
b Akron, Ohio, May 25, 85; d James McGowan & Ellen Sweeney M; single. Educ: St Vincents Cath Sch; Bus Col, Akron. Polit & Govt Pos: Off court reporter, Summit Co Probate Court, Ohio, 40-60; Dem State Cent committeewoman, 14th Dist, Ohio, 38-; in charge Akron Off, Dept of Liquor Control; Dem Nat Committeewoman, Ohio, 52-56; Ohio State Rep, 14th Dist, 62-72; former asst secy, Liquor Control Comt & mem, Educ & Financial Insts Comts. Mem: Hon life mem Ohio Fed Dem Women; Akron Womens Dem Club; Fed Dem Women of Summit Co (campaign chmn); Adv Coun of Civic Unity; Cath Daughters of Am. Honors & Awards: Dem Woman of the Year, 65; Third award for work in the field of birth defects, Nat Found, 70; Award in gratitude for serv, Dem Party of Summit Co, 70. Relig: Catholic. Mailing Add: 1018 Copley Rd Akron OH 44320

MCGOWAN, SHERRY A (D)
Nat Committeewoman, Kans Young Dem
b Richmond, Va, May 11, 46; d Benjamin Stanley Smith & Imelda Catherine Dawson S; m 1965 to Jay Stevens McGowan. Educ: Univ Kans, 66-68; Washburn Univ, 70- Polit & Govt Pos: Exec secy, Kansans for Alternatives in 68, 67-68; secy & campaign mgr, Kansans for McCarthy, 68; McCarthy liaison for Kans deleg, Dem Nat Conv, 68, alt deleg, 72; campaign mgr, Swan for Cong, 68; campaign staff, Pendergast for President of Nat Young Dem, 69; founder & first chmn, New Dem Coalition of Kans, 69, secy, 70; publicity dir, Topeka New Dem Coalition, 69, chmn, 70; vchmn, Second Cong Dist Young Dem, 69, chmn, 70; speaker's dir, Kans Young Dem, 70 & 73, nat committeewoman, currently; precinct committeewoman, Shawnee Co Dem Cent Comt, 70 & 72-74; deleg, Second Dist Dem Conv, 72; deleg, Kans Dem State Conv, 72; Second Dist campaign mgr, McGovern-Shriver Presidential Campaign, 72; vpres, Women Aware, 72-73, coordr, 73-74; mem, Second Dist Dem Cent Comt, 73-; mem, Kans State Dem Comt, 75- Bus & Prof Pos: Waitress, Horseshoe Grill, Dighton, Kans, 63-65; nurses aide, Lane Co Hosp, 65; clerk, Egbert's Drugstore, 66; libr asst, Univ Kans, 66-68; secy, Capital Securities, Topeka, 69, licensed securities agent, 69-70; mgr, Swan Cards, 68-; secy staff develop, Topeka State Hosp, 70-72, secy, Psychol Dept, 72-73; secy, Spec Servs, 73-; owner & operator, Feminist Press, Topeka, currently. Publ: Ed, Proudly speaking, Topeka State Hosp, 70-72; & Behold the woman, Women Aware, 72 & 74-; auth, Poems, Inscape, 72; plus one other. Mem: Women's Int League for Peace & Freedom; Kansans Concerned about Vietnam; Topeka Peace Ctr (founding steering comt). Mailing Add: 1526 Harrison Topeka KS 66612

MCGOWAN, THOMAS F (R)
NY State Sen
Mailing Add: 117 Huntley Rd Buffalo NY 14215

MCGRAIL, STEPHEN JOHN (D)
Mass State Sen
b Melrose, Mass, Sept 23, 48; s Richard Joseph McGrail & Catherine Jackson M (deceased); single. Educ: Northeastern Univ, BS & BA, 71; Suffolk Law Sch, 72. Polit & Govt Pos: Selectman, Town of Wakefield, Mass, 71-73; Mass State Sen, Fourth Middlesex Dist, 73-; deleg, Dem Nat Mid-Term Conf, 74. Mem: Malden Vet of Irish Ancestry; Irish Am Asn, Inc; Moose; Eagles. Relig: Catholic. Mailing Add: 65 Hopkins St Wakefield MA 01880-

MCGRATH, CHARLES ROBERT (R)
b Oxnard, Calif, July 6, 37; s George Dominick McGrath & Mary Agnes Rover M; m 1961 to Beverlee Ellen Reed; c John Charles, Deborah June, Daniel Patrick & Bridget Nellie. Educ: Loyola Univ Los Angeles, BS, 59 & Sch Law, JD, 63; Alpha Delta Gamma. Polit & Govt Pos: Co-chmn, Ventura Co Comt to Reelect Gov Reagan, Calif, 70; pub mem, State Bd of Registr for Prof Engrs, 71-; Oxnard chmn, Comt to Reelect the President, 72; deleg, Rep Nat Conv, 72. Mil Serv: Entered as Pvt, Marine Corps Res, 59, released as Lance Cpl, 65, after serv in 4th Div, US, 59-65; E-3, Marine Corps Res; Marksmanship. Mem: Rancheros Adolfo; Rancheros Visitadores; Ventura Co 4-H Sponsors Club; Ventura Co Hist Soc; Ventura Co Econ Develop Asn. Mailing Add: PO Box 1232 Oxnard CA 93030

MCGRATH, DANIEL L (D)
b Ottawa, Ill, May 9, 38; s Burdette James McGrath & Anita Scherer M; m 1963 to Janet R Dobbs; c Patrick, Brendan & Molly. Educ: St Ambrose Col, BS, 63; Northern Ill Univ, MEd, 71. Polit & Govt Pos: Acct & asst to clerk, Second Dist Appellate Court, Ill, 64-68; educ specialist, Ill Educ Agency, 72-74; admin asst to US Rep Tim Lee Hall, Ill, 75- Bus & Prof Pos: Teacher, Ottawa, Ill, 69-71. Mil Serv: Entered as Spec Pvt, Army, 57, released as SP-5, 59, after serv in 9th Artil Div. Legal Res: 822 W Main St Ottawa IL 61350 Mailing Add: 5651 Ravenel Springfield VA 22151

MCGRATH, PHYLLIS ANN (R)
Acting Chmn, Young Rep Nat Fedn
b Benkelman, Nebr, Mar 15, 37; d Clyde Merle Ketler & Eva Marie Cooley; div; c John Robert & Jeffery Alan. Educ: Colo State Univ, 57-58; Univ Northern Colo, 58-59; bank mkt sch, Northwestern Univ, Evanston, grad, 70; Kappa Delta. Polit & Govt Pos: Co-chmn, Young Rep League, Colo, 67-69; local publicity chmn, Young Rep Nat Fedn, 69-71, secy, 71-73, co-chmn, 73-75, acting chmn, 75-; mem rule 29 comt, Rep Nat Comt, 73-75. Bus & Prof Pos: Legis chmn, Greeley Bd Realtors, 75- Mem: Greeley Bd Realtors; Colo & Nat Asn Real Estate Bds; Greeley United Fund. Relig: Methodist. Mailing Add: 1925 28th Ave Apt 22 Greeley CO 80631

MCGRATH, RICHARD J (D)
Mass State Rep
Mailing Add: State Capitol Boston MA 02133

MCGRATH, RICHARD M (D)
Mass State Rep
Mailing Add: State Capitol Boston MA 02133

MCGRATH, T ED (R)
Chmn, Mercer Co Rep Party, Pa
b Detroit, Mich, July 13, 19; s Archie A McGrath & Grace I Snyder M; m 1940 to Ruth Isabelle Romich; c Esther (Mrs Riccimoni) & Bonneva (Mrs Shontz). Educ: Thiel Col. Polit & Govt Pos: Committeeman, Mercer Co Rep Party, Pa, 48-75, asst chmn, 68-72, chmn, 72-; inspector II, Bldg & Safety, Pa Dept Labor, Mercer Co, 62-66, inspector I, 66-68. Mem: Grove City Rotary Club (pres, 75-); Mercer Co Sportsmen's Club; McKean Co Sportsmen's Club; Mercer Co Regional Planning Comn. Relig: Protestant. Mailing Add: RD 3 Werner Rd Greenville PA 16125

MCGRAW, ANDREW J (D)
Pa State Rep
b Sturgeon, Pa, Mar 9, 38; s Peter McGraw & Bridget Taggart M; m 1956 to Elaine J Matthews; c Andrew, Mark, Maureen, Michael & Melissa. Educ: Univ Pittsburgh, 62-66. Polit & Govt Pos: Pa State Rep, 67- Relig: Catholic. Mailing Add: Capitol Bldg Harrisburg PA 17120

MCGRAW, WARREN RANDOLPH (D)
WVa State Sen
b Mullens, WVa, May 10, 39; s Darrell V McGraw & Julia Zekany M; m 1961 to Peggy Ann Shufflebarger; c Warren Randolph, II, Helen Suzanne & Rebecca Lynn. Educ: Morris Harvey Col, AB in Polit Sci, Hist & Econ, 60; WVa Univ Grad Sch, 60; Wake Forest Univ, JD, 70; Pi Kappa Delta; Phi Alpha Delta. Polit & Govt Pos: Trial attorney, US Dept Justice, Washington, DC, 64-65; WVa State Deleg, Wyo Co, 68-72; deleg, Dem Nat Conv, 72; chmn, Wyo Co Dem Party, currently; WVa State Sen, 73-; deleg, Dem Nat Mid-Term Conf, 74. Mem: Wyo Co Bar Asn (pres); Am Bar Asn (mem, consumer affairs sub-comt); Am Judicature Soc; Am Soc Composers, Auth & Publ; Jaycees. Honors & Awards: First prize for Copyright Law. Relig: Methodist. Mailing Add: 101 Locust Pineville WV 24874

MCGREAVY, FRANCIS W (D)
RI State Rep
Mailing Add: 15 Bayview Ave Tiverton RI 02878

MCGREGOR, MARY MARTIN (D)
b Washington, DC, Oct 17, 43; d Oliver Houston Martin & Eileen Aldwell M; m 1965 to Robert Mar McGregor; c Michael Robert. Educ: Stanford Univ, BA, 65; Univ Mich, 66-68. Polit & Govt Pos: Deleg, Dem Nat Conv, 72; chmn vols, Colo Comt for McGovern, 72; precinct committeewoman, Denver Dem Party, Colo, 72- Mailing Add: 1465 S Elm St Denver CO 80222

MCGREGOR, NANCY ROHWER (R)
Mem Exec Bd, Wash State Fedn of Rep Women
b Spokane, Wash, Apr 9, 30; d Frederick H Rohwer & Annabelle Howard R; m 1954 to William McGregor; c DeEtte & Alyson. Educ: Univ Mex, 50-51; Vassar Col, BA, 52; Stanford Univ, 53-54. Polit & Govt Pos: Rep precinct committeewoman, Precinct 50, Whitman Co, Wash, 64-72; committeewoman, Wash Rep State Cent Comt, 64-68, vchmn, 68-71; mem exec bd, Whitman Co Rep Cent Comt, 64-72; mem exec bd, Whitman Co Rep Women's Clubs, 64-71; credentials chmn, Wash State Rep Conv, 66; deleg & mem, Platform Comt, Rep Nat Conv, 68; adv to exec bd, Wash State Fedn of Rep Women, 68, mem exec bd, 71-; secy, Nat State VChmn Asn, 69-71. Mem: Epton Soc for the Retarded; Champagne Charities, Spokane, Wash (secy & mem bd dirs); Eastern Wash Hist Soc; Wash State Wheat Growers Asn; St George's Sch, Spokane (bd trustees, 73-, exec bd, 74-). Relig: Episcopal. Legal Res: Hooper WA 99333 Mailing Add: 815 E 26th Spokane WA 99203

MCGREGOR, THOMAS EARL (D)
Vt State Rep
Mailing Add: RFD 3 Winooski VT 05405

MCGREW, FINLEY (R)
b Fairfield, Iowa, Mar 6, 08; s Harry L McGrew & Rose Culbertson M; m 1935 to Harriet G Leonard; c Jane (Mrs Robert Cram) & David F. Educ: Ohio Wesleyan Univ, AB, 31; Sigma Phi Epsilon. Polit & Govt Pos: Admin asst to US Rep John N Erlenborn, Ill, 65- Bus & Prof Pos: Assoc ed, Press Publ, Elmhurst, Ill, 46-61, ed, 61-62; ed, Glen Ellyn News & Wheaton Leader, Glen Ellyn, 62-65. Mil Serv: Specialist 1/C, Navy, 42-45. Mem: Nat Ed Asn; Ill Press Asn; AF&AM. Relig: Methodist. Legal Res: 194 Hawthorne Ave Ave Elmhurst IL 60126 Mailing Add: 4501 Arlington Blvd Apt 210 Arlington VA 22203

MCGREW, LESLIE FRANK (R)
Secy, Van Wert Co Rep Cent & Exec Comt, Ohio
b Cincinnati, Ohio, June 8, 99; s Charles Livingston & Mamie Steinmetz L; m 1922 to Dixie Mildred Fulton; c Elizabeth Jean (Mrs Otis Coon), Virginia Edythe (Mrs Forest Gribler) & Mildred Janet (Mrs William Pheanis). Educ: Woodward High Sch, Cincinnati, Ohio. Polit & Govt Pos: Councilman at large, Van Wert, Ohio, 48-49; Secy, Van Wert Co Rep Cent & Exec Comt, 64-; mem elec bd, Van Wert Co, 68- Bus & Prof Pos: Traffic mgr, Glenn L Martin Co, Cleveland, Ohio, 20-29; chief of stores & traffic mgr, Great Lakes Aircraft Co, 29-32; purchasing & sales mgr, Dunson Supply, Van Wert, Ohio, 32-39; coord material control & purchasing agent, Continental Can Co, 39-64. Mil Serv: Entered as Pvt, Marines, 18, released

as Cpl, 20, after serv in Third Regt, 44th Co, Dominican Repub, 18-20; Good Conduct Medal. Mem: Mason; Methodist Men's Club; DeMolay (adv); Am Legion; Eastern Star (Asst Grand Sentinel). Honors & Awards: Hon Lt Gov, State of Ohio, 71- Relig: Methodist; mem bd church properties & location, United Methodist Church, Defiance Dist, 66- Mailing Add: 628 N Market St Van Wert OH 45891

MCGREW, SAMUEL M (D)
Ill State Rep
Mailing Add: 2049 N Broad Galesburg IL 61401

MCGRIFF, JACK (D)
Chmn, Alachua Co Dem Exec Comt, Fla
b Live Oak, Fla, Nov 11, 20; s William Augustus McGriff & Bessie Colson M; m 1966 to Barbara Anne Bost; c Lee Colson, Martha Ann & Kathleen Ethel. Educ: Univ Fla, BAE, 47, MAE, 49; Columbia Univ, 50-51; Phi Kappa Phi; Kappa Delta Pi; Sigma Alpha Epsilon. Polit & Govt Pos: Chmn, Alachua Co Dem Exec Comt, 72-; regent, State Univ Syst Fla, 73-; bd mem, Local Govt Study Comn, 73- Bus & Prof Pos: Head coach & athletic dir, P K Yonge Lab Sch, Univ Fla, 46-48, asst prof phys educ, Univ, 49-53; owner & pres, Gator Sport Shop, Gainesville, 54-62; agent & owner, McGriff-Scarborough Ins Agency, 61-; pres, University City Bank, Gainesville, 72-74. Mil Serv: Entered as Aviation Cadet, Army Air Corps, 42, released as Capt, 46, after serv in US Training Command, 42-46. Mem: Life mem Million Dollar Round Table; life mem Nat Asn Life Underwriters; Fla Asn Life Underwriters; Gainesville Asn Life Underwriters; Alachua Co Taxpayers Asn. Honors & Awards: Dipl with honors, Univ Fla, 49; Outstanding Career Life Underwriter Award, Gainesville Asn Life Underwriters, 70. Relig: Baptist. Legal Res: 3431 NW 12th Ave Gainesville FL 32601 Mailing Add: PO Drawer M Gainesville FL 32601

MCGUFFEE, GEORGE ORVILLE (D)
Chmn, Catahoula Parish Dem Comt, La
b Aimwell, La, May 12, 08; s James Washington McGuffee & Minnie Bell Albritton M; m 1931 to Carrie Trisler; c George Leon. Educ: Lynn's Bus Col, Shreveport, La, 27. Relig & Govt Pos: Assessor, Catahoula Parish, La, 41-; chmn, Catahoula Parish Dem Comt, currently. Bus & Prof Pos: Mem exec bd, Southern Baptist Conv, Nashville, Tenn, 63-69; pres, La Baptist Exec Bd, Alexandria, 73-74. Mem: F&AM; Rotary; Int Asn Assessing Officers; La Assessor's Asn. Honors & Awards: Int Asn Assessing Officers 30 Year Serv Award; Outstanding Baptist Layman, La Baptist Brotherhood, 73, Outstanding Baptist Man, 74. Relig: Southern Baptist. Mailing Add: PO Box 237 Harrisonburg LA 71340

MCGUIRE, DON LOYE (D)
Chmn, Washington Co Dem Cent Comt, Ark
b Heber Springs, Ark, Aug 25, 34; s Loye Zem McGuire & Gladys Jones M; m 1964 to Billie Jo Weathers McGuire; c Melinda & Cheryl Garrison (step daughters) & Donell McGuire. Educ: La Polytech Inst, 53-55; Northeastern La Univ, 58-59; Sigma Kappa. Polit & Govt Pos: Vchmn, Washington Co Dem Cent Comt, Ark, 72-74, chmn, 74-; chmn, Washington Co Elec Comn, 74- Mil Serv: Entered as E-1, Army, 57, released as E-4, 58, after serv in XVII Airborne Corps, Ft Bragg, NC, 57-58. Mem: Fayetteville Lions Club. Relig: Presbyterian. Mailing Add: 940 Rush Dr Fayetteville AR 72701

MCGUIRE, E PERKINS (R)
b Boston, Mass, Oct 22, 04; s Clarence W McGuire & Evelyn Slattery M; m 1929 to Katherine Ward. Educ: Lowell Textile Inst, BTE & DSc. Polit & Govt Pos: Asst Secy of Defense, 57-61; mem, Washington, DC Rep Comt & vchmn finance comt, 62-68; chmn, DC Nixon Comt, 67-68; chmn, DC Deleg to Rep Nat Conv, 68; exec vchmn, Inauguration Comt, 69; chmn, Comn on Govt Procurement, 70-73. Bus & Prof Pos: Dir, Burlington Indusrs, Bunker Ramo Corp, Logetronics Corp & Southern Air Transport Co, currently. Mil Serv: Entered as Lt, Navy, 42, released as Comdr; Legion of Merit; Defense Pub Serv Medal. Relig: Catholic. Legal Res: 2420 Tracy Pl NW Washington DC 20008 Mailing Add: 800 17th St NW Washington DC 20006

MCGUIRK, HARRY J (D)
Md State Sen
b Baltimore, Md, Nov 7, 23; married. Educ: Univ Md; Cornell Univ. Polit & Govt Pos: Mem, Rent Adv Bd, Baltimore, Md, 51-, chmn, 52-53; mem, Zoning Comn, 58-; Md State Deleg, 60-67; Md State Sen, 67-; deleg, Dem Nat Conv, 68, alt deleg, 72; vchmn, Econ Affairs, Md State Senate, currently. Bus & Prof Pos: Mfr wood prod; real estate broker & consult. Mil Serv: Navy, 42-46. Mem: Elks (past Exalted Ruler, Baltimore Lodge 7); Walbrook Post 118, Am Legion (past Comdr); West Baltimore Bus Men's Asn. Honors & Awards: Man of the Year Award, 68. Legal Res: 310 Long Island Ave Baltimore MD 21229 Mailing Add: 908 Frederick Rd Baltimore MD 21228

MCGUIRK, JOHN F, SR (D)
Conn State Rep
Mailing Add: 6 Raymond Terr East Norwalk CT 06855

MCHAN, E V (R)
Idaho State Rep
Mailing Add: PO Box 126 Ketchum ID 83340

MCHARGUE, DANIEL STEPHEN, II (R)
Assoc Mem, Rep State Cent Comt Calif
b Torrance, Calif, Dec 2, 45; s Robert Morris McHargue & Margaret Henry M; m to Lynne Pound; c Kenneth Patrick & Daniel Frederick. Educ: US Naval Acad, 63-65; Occidental Col, AB, 67, MA, 69; Univ Southern Calif, 73-; Arnold Air Soc. Polit & Govt Pos: First chmn & charter mem, Los Angeles Co Campus Action Comt, 68-69; state vpres & Los Angeles area dir, Calif Col Rep, 68-69, exec dir, 69-70; admin asst to Calif State Assembly, 69-71; assoc mem, Rep State Cent Comt Calif, 69-; campaign mgr for Michael C Donaldson, 17th Cong Dist Rep Primary, 70; cand for elec to Los Angeles Community Col Bd Trustees, 71; mem, 41st Assembly Dist Rep Coord Comt, 71-72; deleg, Rep Nat Conv, 72; asst dir, Los Angeles Co Comt to Reelect President Nixon, 72. Bus & Prof Pos: Grad asst & teaching assoc, Occidental Col, 67-69, instr diplomacy & world affairs & acting chmn dept, 69-70; dir, Robert A Taft Inst Govt, instr polit sci & asst to pres, Pepperdine Univ, 71; head writer & research asst, KNBC-TV Pub Affairs Progs, 71; part-time instr, Occup Ctr, Los Angeles Valley & Pierce Cols, 71-72. Mil Serv: Midn, Navy, 63-65; serv at US Naval Acad; Air Force Res, 67-70; Distinguished Mil Cadet & Comdr, Air Force ROTC, Occidental Col. Mem: Am Asn Univ Prof; Calif Teachers Asn; Delta Phi Epsilon (nat vpres, 67-68 & 71-, nat secy collegiate affairs, 68-70); Phi Alpha Theta; Ephebian Soc Los Angeles. Honors & Awards: Col Rep of the Year, Calif Col Rep, 68-69. Relig: Baptist. Mailing Add: 5462 Ruthwood Calabasas CA 91302

MCHUGH, DOROTHY BARBREE (R)
Rep Nat Committeewoman, NY
b Oakland, Calif; d Joseph Barbree & Nellie Snowden B; m 1957 to Keith S McHugh; c Michael B & Harry. Educ: Univ Calif; Sigma Kappa. Polit & Govt Pos: Rep campaign mgr, New York, Mayoral Race, 61; Rep campaign mgr, NY Gubernatorial Race, 62 & 66; mem adv bd, New York Rep Women 63-; Rep Nat Committeewoman, NY, 63-; deleg, Rep Nat Conv, 68. Mem: Assistance League, Glendale, Calif; Women's Auxiliary Inst Phys Med & Rehab (dir, 59-); Asn Homemaker Serv. Mailing Add: 10 Gracie Sq New York NY 10028

MCHUGH, KATHLEEN ANN (D)
Nat Committeewoman, Young Dem of NMex
b Washington, DC, Aug 23, 53; d William James McHugh & Rosalina Salazar M; single. Educ: Univ NMex, 71- Polit & Govt Pos: Nat Committeewoman, Young Dem of NMex, 74- Mailing Add: Apt 134 2800 Lexington Pl NE Albuquerque NM 87112

MCHUGH, MATTHEW FRANCIS (D)
US Rep, NY
b Philadelphia, Pa, Dec 6, 38; s Peter F McHugh & Margaret Whalen M; m 1963 to Eileen Alanna Higgins; c Alanna, Kelli & Meg. Educ: Mt St Mary's Col (Md), BS, 60; Villanova Law Sch, JD, 63. Polit & Govt Pos: City prosecutor, Ithaca, NY, 68; dist attorney, Tompkins Co, NY, 69; mem, NY State Dem Comt, 72-74; US Rep, NY, 75- Mem: Am, NY & Tompkins Co Bar Asns; CofC (vpres, 73, pres, 74). Relig: Roman Catholic. Legal Res: 311 Richard Pl Ithaca NY 14850 Mailing Add: 1204 Longworth House Off Bldg Washington DC 20515

MCILVAIN, BILL D (R)
b Alma, Okla, Aug 28, 32; s Tommy O McIlvain & Birtie Chaudion M; m 1955 to Ila M Anderson; c Lavonda, Sandra, Larry & Mark. Educ: John Brown Univ, BSSE, 57; Univ Wyo, 58; State Teachers Col, Greeley, Colo, summers 58-60. Polit & Govt Pos: Wyo State Rep, 69-72; mem, Educ Comn of States, currently. Bus & Prof Pos: Mem staff, Summer Inst Ling, Peru; teacher, Int Sch of Kabul, 73- Mem: Gov Educ Comn; Cheyenne Classroom Teachers Asn; Cheyenne Educ Asn (pres, 69-); life mem Nat Educ Asn; Farm Bur. Honors & Awards: Teacher of the Year, Cheyenne. Relig: Baptist. Legal Res: 1109 Cactus Hill Rd Cheyenne WY 82001 Mailing Add: Kabul (ID) Dept of State Washington DC 20521

MCILVAINE, ROBINSON
b Downington, Pa, July 17, 13; m to Alice W Nicholson M; c Stevenson, Mia Carol, Ian & Katherine. Educ: Harvard Univ, BA, 35, grad work, 35-36. Polit & Govt Pos: Off of Asst Secy for Pub Affairs, 53; chmn, US Sect of Caribbean Comn, 53-56; Dep Asst Secy of State for Pub Affairs, 54-56; Dep Chief of Mission at Lisbon & Leopoldville; Ambassador to Dahoney; coordr, Nat Interdept Seminar, 64; head, Congo Working Group of State Dept, 64; spec asst, Off of Ambassador-at-lg Harriman, 65-66; co-dir, five W African Nations, State Dept, 66; US Ambassador to Guinea, 66-69; US Ambassador to Repub of Kenya, 69-73. Bus & Prof Pos: Dir African Opers, Wild Life Leadership Found, 73- Mil Serv: Comdr, Navy. Mailing Add: Wild Life Leadership Found Nairobi Kenya EAfrica

MCILVAINE, STEVENSON (D)
Mem, Fauquier Co Dem Comt, Va
b Washington, DC, Jan 11, 42; s Robinson McIlvaine & Jane Walker Stevenson M; single. Educ: Harvard Col, AB, 64; Harvard Lampoon, Phoenix SK. Polit & Govt Pos: Officer, US Foreign Serv, Dept State, Washington, DC & South Vietnam, 67-71; deleg, Va Dem Conv, 72; mem, Fauquier Co Dem Comt, 72-; treas & coordr, Va McGovern-Shriver Campaign Comt, Richmond, 72; dep press secy, Howell for Gov Campaign, 73; press secy & writer, Rufus Phillips for Cong, Fairfax Co, 74; admin asst, US Rep Robert B Duncan, Ore, 75- Bus & Prof Pos: First mate, Yacht Josefine, Deltaville, Va to Placentia, Brit Honduras, 71; free-lance writer & reporter, Weekly Newspapers in Va, 73. Mil Serv: Entered as 2nd Lt, Army, 64, released as 1st Lt, 66, after serv in WGer. Polit & Govt Pos: Series of local history articles, Fauquier Dem, 73-; Series of investigative reports on land-use issues, Loudoun Times-Mirror, fall 74. Relig: Episcopal. Legal Res: Eglinton Middleburg VA 22117 Mailing Add: c/o US Rep Robert Duncan 330 Cannon Off Bldg Washington DC 20515

MCILWAIN, WILLARD LEE (D)
Miss State Sen
Mailing Add: PO Box 558 Greenville MS 38701

MCINERNEY, KEVIN DENNIS (D)
b Chicago, Ill; s Patrick J McInerney & Shirley M McCann M; single. Educ: Chicago State Univ, BA in Social Sci, 73. Polit & Govt Pos: Deleg, Dem Nat Conv, 72. Mem: Independents for a New Chicago; Burlington Beach Improvement Asn (vpres, 73-). Relig: Roman Catholic. Mailing Add: Mail Route 31 Box 309B Valparaiso IN 46383

MCINERNEY, LINDA ANN (D)
Secy, Tyngsborough Dem Town Comt, Mass
b Lowell, Mass, Apr 19, 47; d Edward Anthony McInerney & Mary Robidouy M; single. Educ: Northern Essex Community Col, 67; Rivier Col, Nashua, NH, BA, 69; Suffolk Univ Law Sch, 70-72. Polit & Govt Pos: Secy, Tyngsborough Dem Town Comt, 68-; vchairwoman Mass deleg, Dem Nat Mid-Term Conf, 74. Bus & Prof Pos: Rural housing specialist, Community Teamwork, Inc, Lowell, Mass, currently. Relig: Roman Catholic. Mailing Add: Sherbrooke St Tyngsborough MA 01879

MCINNIS, DAVID FAIRLEY (D)
SC State Rep
b Timmonsville, SC, Aug 5, 34; s David F McInnis (deceased) & Louise DuBose M; m 1958 to Barbara Bruce; c Shawn, David F, Jr & Lee. Educ: Univ NC, AB, 57; Univ SC Law Sch, LLB & JD, 65; Phi Delta Phi; Kappa Alpha Order. Polit & Govt Pos: City judge, Sumter, SC, 66-70; SC State Rep, Dist 69, 75-, mem agr & natural resources & rules comts, SC House Rep, 75- Bus & Prof Pos: Attorney, David F McInnis, Sumter, SC, 65- Mil Serv: Entered as 2nd Lt, Air Force, 58, released as 1st Lt, 59, after serv in 9th Air Force; Capt, Air Force Res. Mem: Sumter Lions Club; Elks; SC Bar Asn; YMCA; Am Trial Lawyers Asn. Relig: Presbyterian. Legal Res: 702 Reynolds Rd Sumter SC 29150 Mailing Add: PO Box 1815 Sumter SC 29150

MCINNIS, WILLIAM DONALD (D)
Chmn, Union Co Dem Party, NC
b Udell Co, NC, Feb 21, 32; s George Franklin McInnis & Mable Triplet Lee M; m 1955 to Margaret Sechler; c William Douglas & David Lee. Educ: Univ Md, BS; Delta Sigma Phi. Polit & Govt Pos: Sch bd mem, Monroe City Schs, NC, 65-; pres, Union Co Young Dem, formerly; chmn, Union Co Dem Party, 73- Bus & Prof Pos: Mgr, M & J Financial Corp, Monroe, NC, 55-; pres, Old Georgetown, Inc, 69-; pres, Brookgreen Arms, Inc, 71-; owner, W D McInnis Construction Co, 75- Mil Serv: ROTC. Mem: Optimist; Moose; Shrine; Mason. Honors & Awards: Union Co Young Man of Year, Jaycees. Relig: Episcopal. Legal Res: 3010 Walkup Ave Rte 1 Monroe NC 28110 Mailing Add: PO Box 846 Monroe NC 28110

MCINTOSH, CARL DANIEL (R)
b Brownwood, Tex, May 17, 27; s Carl Daniel McIntosh & Blanche McKinley Eaton M; m 1948 to Janis Faye Hicks; c Carl Daniel, III, Donald Edward, Dewitt Hicks, Joel Eaton & Mary Lou. Educ: Tex Agr & Mech Univ, BS, 50. Polit & Govt Pos: Chmn, McLennan Co Rep Party, Tex, formerly. Bus & Prof Pos: Pres, Oasis Water Co, Waco & San Benito, Tex, 53-, Oasis Lawn Sprinkler Co, 63-, Waco Brick Mfg Co, Waco, 65- & Star Finance Corp, 67- Mil Serv: Entered as A/S, Naval Res, 45, released as Coxswain, 46, after serv in Naval Training Center, San Diego, Calif; Lt Col, Army Res, 493rd Engr Group, Dallas, Tex; Am Defense Medal; Army Res Medal; Army Occupation Medal; ETO Medal. Mem: Tex Soc of Prof Engrs; Rotary, Waco. Relig: Methodist. Mailing Add: 4824 Pecan Terrace Waco TX 76710

MCINTOSH, JAMES DAVID (D)
Chmn, W Carroll Parish Dem Exec Comt, La
b Rayville, La, Aug 21, 16; s John R McIntosh & Edna Brown; m 1948 to Kate White; c James D, Jr & Mary Kate. Educ: La State Univ, BA & JD, 33-39. Polit & Govt Pos: Asst dist attorney, Fifth Judicial Dist, La, 48-50; chmn, W Carroll Parish Dem Exec Comt, currently. Bus & Prof Pos: Partner, Law Firm McIntosh, Hester, Gilfoil & Fox, Oak Grove & Lake Providence, La, currently. Mil Serv: Entered as Pvt, released as 1st Lt, after serv in Counter Intel Corps, ETO, 42-46. Mem: Am Bar Asn; Am Trial Lawyers Asn; Lions; VFW; Am Legion. Relig: Methodist. Legal Res: McIntosh St Oak Grove LA 71263 Mailing Add: Box 207 Oak Grove LA 71263

MCINTOSH, WILLIAM M (D)
Committeeman, Wyo State Dem Comt
b Rawlins, Wyo, Oct 11, 18; s William P McIntosh & Bessie Morgan M; m 1942 to Virginia Beebe; c Ellen (Mrs Thomas E Murphree). Educ: Rawlins High Sch, 36. Polit & Govt Pos: Committeeman, Wyo State & Carbon Co Dem Comts, 70-; deleg, Dem Nat Conv, 72. Bus & Prof Pos: Rancher, Carbon Co, 36- Mem: Wyo Stockgrowers (exec comt, 70-); First Nat Bank (dir); Rawlins Rotary; Elks. Relig: Episcopal. Mailing Add: Lander Rte Rawlins WY 82301

MCINTYRE, BERNARD J (D)
Okla State Sen
Mailing Add: State Capitol Oklahoma City OK 73105

MCINTYRE, JACK W (R)
Ind State Rep
Mailing Add: PO Box 57 Lyons IN 47443

MC INTYRE, JAMES (D)
Pa State Rep
Mailing Add: Capitol Bldg Harrisburg PA 17120

MCINTYRE, ROBERT G (D)
Mo State Rep
Mailing Add: Cedar Hill MO 63016

MCINTYRE, THOMAS JAMES (D)
US Sen, NH
b Laconia, NH, Feb 20, 15; m 1941 to Myrtle Ann Clement; c Martha Grey. Educ: Dartmouth Col, 37; Boston Univ Law Sch, 40. Hon Degrees: LLD, Dartmouth Col, Univ NH, Nathaniel Hawthorne Col & Belknap Col. Polit & Govt Pos: Mayor, Laconia, NH, 49-51, city solicitor, 53; cand, US Rep, NH, 54; deleg, Dem Nat Conv, 56 & 68; chmn, Laconia Dem City Comt & Belknap Co Dem Comt; NH State Sen, 62-67; US Sen, NH, currently; deleg, Dem Nat Mid-Term Conf, 74. Bus & Prof Pos: Hon pres bd trustees, Taylor Home for Aged, 54-62. Mil Serv: Army, 42-46, serv in 376th Inf, 94th Div, Third Army; Maj (Ret); Combat Inf Badge; Bronze Star; Oak Leaf Cluster; Four Battle Stars. Mem: NH Bar Asn; Kiwanis; KofC; VFW; Am Legion. Legal Res: 45 Roundbay Rd Laconia NH 03246 Mailing Add: 2923 Garfield NW Washington DC 20008

MCIVER, EDGAR WILSON (R)
Committeeman, Ill Rep Cent Comt
b Roodhouse, Ill, June 30, 15; s Harold Anson McIver & Virginia Wilson M; m 1935 to Leona Ryan; c Harold A, John T & Mary Christine (Mrs Rust). Educ: Roodhouse High Sch, Ill, grad, 33. Polit & Govt Pos: Precinct committeeman, First Precinct, Roodhouse, Ill, 36-42; committeeman, Ill Rep Cent Comt, 15th Dist, 62-; dir, 20th Cong Dist Rep Adv Coun, Ill, 62-; mem, Nat Rep Cong Adv Comt, 62-; Green Co dir, US Rep Paul Findley's Vol for Findley, 62- Mem: AF&AM, Roodhouse, Ill; Kiwanis Int; United Transportation Union. Honors & Awards: Cong Cert of Recognition. Relig: Baptist. Mailing Add: 120 E Clay St Roodhouse IL 62082

MCKAMEY, LEO (D)
Mo State Rep
Mailing Add: 5260 Elmwood St Kansas City MO 64130

MCKAY, BRUCE ALAN (D)
b Portland, Ore, Dec 19, 14; s Paul McKay & Frieda Bleick M; div; c Bruce Alan, Jr. Educ: Univ Wash, 33-36; Theta Chi. Polit & Govt Pos: Deleg, Dem Nat Conv, 68 & 72; councilman, Renton, Wash, 69-70; chmn, 47th Legis Dist Dem Precinct Committeeman's Orgn, 68-72 & 11th Legis Dist Dem Precinct Committeeman's Orgn, 72- Bus & Prof Pos: Employee, Federal Works Agency, Navy Dept, 42-48; sales engr, Portland, Ore, 48-52; real estate salesman, Seattle, Wash, 52-53; field agt, Wash State Div Purchasing, 53-57; mem facil dept, Boeing Co, Renton, 57-70. Mem: Renton Dem Club (pres, 68 & 69), secy, 75-). Relig: Protestant. Mailing Add: 241 Factory Ave N Renton WA 98055

MCKAY, J CURTIS (R)
b Chicago, Ill, Oct 10, 26; s John L McKay & Theodora Bennett M; m 1965 to Ruth L Cary; c Thomas E, Joan E, Janet L, Kimberly C, Shane D & Holly. Educ: Grinnell Col, Grinnell, Iowa, BA, 51; Northwestern Law Sch, JD, 57; Sigma Delta Chi; Phi Delta Phi. Polit & Govt Pos: Wis State Assemblyman, 60-69, Majority Floor Leader, Wis State Assembly, 67-69; mem, Nat Legis Leaders Conf, 63-68; mem exec comt, Legis Conf, 65-67; Statutory chmn, Wis State Rep Party, 68-, mem exec comt, 68-, vchmn, 74-; chmn, Ozaukee Co Rep Party, 68-74. Bus & Prof Pos: Sr partner, McKay & Martin Attorneys at law, 69- Mem: Int Platform Asn; Am Judicature Soc; Airplane Owners & Pilots Asn; Nat Legis Leaders Conf; Rotary Int. Relig: Protestant. Legal Res: 534 N Washington Ave Cedarburg WI 53012 Mailing Add: W63-N650 Washington Ave Cedarburg WI 53012

MCKAY, JOHN PATTERSON (R)
Del State Rep
b Bowesmont, NDak, Oct 12, 15; s John Finlayson McKay & Jeanette Patterson M; m 1946 to Julia Ann Patterson; c John Jr, Richard & James. Educ: Univ NDak, BS Chem Eng, 38; Mass Inst Technol, MS Chem Eng Practice, 40; Sigma Tau; Phi Delta Theta. Polit & Govt Pos: Chmn, Dist 13 Rep Comt, Del, 70-74; Del State Rep, 74- Bus & Prof Pos: Tech & supvry positions with DuPont Chambers Works, Deepwater, NJ, 40-73, works engr, 73-75. Mem: Am Chem Soc; Am Inst Chem Engrs; Kennett Pike Asn; DuPont Lodge 29 AF&AM. Relig: Episcopal. Legal Res: West Farm Greenville DE 19807 Mailing Add: PO Box 3716 Greenville DE 19807

MCKAY, KOLN GUNN (D)
US Rep, Utah
b Ogden, Utah, Feb 23, 25; s James Gunn McKay & Elizabeth C Peterson M; m 1950 to Donna Beisinger; c Gunn Biesinger, Mavis, Marl Biesinger, Kolene, Carla, Ruston Biesinger, Chad Biesinger, Lon Biesinger (deceased), Ruth & Rachel. Educ: Weber State Col, grad; Utah State Univ, grad. Polit & Govt Pos: Utah State Rep & mem, Utah Legis Coun, 65-67; admin asst to Gov, Utah, 68-70; US Rep, Utah, 71-, mem, Appropriations Comt, US House Rep, 71- Mil Serv: Entered as A/S, Coast Guard, released as 3/C, PO, after serv in 12th Naval Dist. Mem: Am Legion; Meat Packers Union; Sons of Utah Pioneers. Relig: Latter-day Saint. Legal Res: 141 S 7600 E Huntsville UT 84317 Mailing Add: US House of Rep Washington DC 20515

MCKAY, MARTHA CLAMPITT (D)
Mem Charter Comn, Dem Nat Comt
b Winchester, Mass, May 16, 20; d Robert Hamilton Clampitt & Cornelia Morrison C; m 1941 to Herbert Stacy McKay; c Alexander Stacy, Brian McNeil & Anna Katherine. Educ: Univ NC, Chapel Hill, BA in Econ, 41; Alpha Delta Pi. Polit & Govt Pos: Precinct committeeman, Dem Party, NC, 50-60; secy, Precinct Dem Comt, 50-60; mem, Sixth Cong Dist Legis, Comt, 60-62; mem, NC Dem Exec Comt, 60-64; mem, Dem Nat Comt, 60-64, mem exec comt, 62-64, mem charter comn, 72-; consult, Off Inspection, Off Econ Opportunity, 65-; deleg, Dem Nat Conv, 72; chairperson policy coun, Nat Women's Polit Caucus, 72, mem, 72-; chairperson, NC Women's Polit Caucus, 72- Bus & Prof Pos: Mem, Comptrollers Staff, NC Shipbuilders, 42-45; self-employed, Acct & Food Serv Bus, 52-65; asst to exec dir, NC Fund, 66-67; dir spec proj, NC Manpower Develop Corp, 67-68; field exec, US R&D Corp, NY, 68-; pres, McKay & Assoc, 70- Mem: Nat Citizen's Comt Community Rels; Chapel Hill Country Club; NC Coun Human Rels (bd dirs); NC Consumers Coun (bd dirs). Relig: Presbyterian. Mailing Add: 406 Westwood Dr Chapel Hill NC 27514

MCKEE, CAROL B (R)
Young Rep Nat Committeewoman, Vt
b Montpelier, Vt, Oct 2, 42; d Bruno Bianchi & Mary B B; m to W Edson McKee. Educ: Montpelier High Sch, grad, 60. Polit & Govt Pos: Secy to Lt Gov, Vt, 65-66; secy to exec secy, Vt Rep State Comt, 65-66; dir, Washington Co Young Rep, 65-; mem, Montpelier Rep Comt, 65-; secy to Vt Speaker of the House, 66-68; exec secy, Vermonters for Rockefeller, 68; alt deleg, Rep Nat Conv, 68; justice of the peace, 68; mem, Bd of Civil Authority, 69-; secy to Secy of State, 69-72; mem, Washington Co Rep Comt, 69-; nat committeewoman, Vt Young Rep, 69-70; Young Rep Nat Committeewoman, Vt, 73- Bus & Prof Pos: Vt regional dir, Nat Ins Women's Asn, 63-64. Relig: Congregational. Mailing Add: Towne Hill Rd Montpelier VT 05602

MCKEE, MARVIN E (D)
Okla State Sen
Mailing Add: State Capitol Oklahoma City OK 73105

MCKEEVER, JUANITA M (D)
b Sioux Falls, SDak, Nov 1, 43; d Earl T McAtee & Edna Hansen M; m 1967 to Patrick James McKeever; c Patrick J, Jr, Cristin M, Devin T & Kyle M. Educ: Sioux Valley Hosp Sch Nursing, grad, 64. Polit & Govt Pos: Precinct committeewoman, 70-; deleg, Dem Nat Conv, 72. Bus & Prof Pos: Registered nurse, Mt Sinai Hosp, Miami Beach, Fla, 65-66, Sioux Valley Hosp, Sioux Falls, SDak, 66-67, St Joseph Hosp, Mitchell, SDak, 67 & Delaney Clinic, Mitchell, SDak, 68. Mem: Am Red Cross Nurse; SDak State Bd of Nursing; Beta Sigma Phi; Cath Daughters of Am; St Joseph Hosp Auxiliary. Honors & Awards: Outstanding Young Women of Am, 70. Relig: Catholic. Mailing Add: 106 W Prospect Pierre SD 57501

MCKEITHEN, JOHN JULIAN (D)
b Grayson, La, May 28, 18; s Jesse Jepheth McKeithen & Agnes Eglin M; m 1942 to Marjorie H Funderburk; c Jay, Fox, Rebecca, Melissa, Pamela & Jenneva. Polit & Govt Pos: La State Rep, 48-52; mem, La Pub Serv Comn, 54-62; Gov, La, 64-72; deleg, Dem Nat Conv, 68. Mil Serv: Army, Inf, 1st Lt. Mem: Am Legion; VFW; La Farm Bur; Delta Coun. Relig: Methodist. Mailing Add: Columbia LA 71418

MCKELVEY, ROBERT MORRIS (D)
Mem Exec Bd, SDak Dem Party
b Huron, SDak, Oct 11, 46; s William Hugh McKelvey & Francis Harter M; m 1966 to Rochelle Roberts; c George H. Educ: Augustana Col (SDak), 64-65; Black Hills State Col (SDak), BS Ed; Tau Kappa Epsilon, Kappa-Xi Chap Spearfish. Polit & Govt Pos: Chmn, Buffalo Co Dem Party, SDak, formerly; chmn, Region Seven Dem Party, 73-; mem exec bd, SDak Dem Party, 73- Bus & Prof Pos: Teacher, Hughitt Sch Hyde Co, SDak, 69-70; teacher, basketball & track coach, Gann Valley Elem Sch, 70- Mem: AF&AM. Relig: Protestant. Mailing Add: Box 105 Gann Valley SD 57341

MCKENNA, ARTHUR JAMES (D)
Mass State Rep
b Springfield, Mass, Nov 29, 14; s Jeremiah Francis McKenna & Elizabeth Mary Moriarty M; m 1938 to Rita Gladys Chapedelaine; c Arthur, Jr, Patricia, Ann Maria & John Paul. Educ: Cathedral High Sch. Polit & Govt Pos: City alderman, Springfield, Mass, 54-62; Mass State Rep, Fifth Hampden Dist, 63-; mem, Mass State Dem Comt, 64- Bus & Prof Pos: Mgr of Yankee Div, 51-55. Mil Serv: Seaman 1/C, Navy, 45. Mem: Am Legion; CIO Local 206; Am Bosch Inc. Relig: Roman Catholic. Mailing Add: 652 Chestnut St Springfield MA 01107

MCKENNA, DALE T (D)
Wis State Sen
Mailing Add: 336 E North St Jefferson WI 53549

MCKENNA, DENIS L (D)
Mass State Sen
Mailing Add: State Capitol Boston MA 02133

MCKENNA, ELLANORE LOUISE (D)
Chairperson, Third Cong Dist Dem Party, Colo
b Denver, Colo, June 23, 25; d Hammond Mathews & Edna Mitchell M; m 1949 to Robert Ludwig McKenna; c Marc Edward, Nancy Louise, Edna Elizabeth-Marie & Madeline Eileen (deceased). Educ: Colo Woman's Col, AA, 45; Univ Colo, BA, 48; Phi Theta Kappa; Beta Phi Gamma; Chi Omega. Polit & Govt Pos: Mem & vchmn, Colo State Bd for Voc Educ, 57-63; mem state exec comt, Golden Anniversary White House Conf on Children & Youth, 59-60; mem exec comt & past pres of bd, Southwest Colo Ment Health Ctr, Inc, 60-69; Dem precinct committeewoman, Precinct 5, La Plata Co, 62-69; mem of bd & vchmn, San Juan Basin Pub Health Unit, 63-72; vchmn, La Plata Co Dem Party, 69-71; La Plata Co Dem Exec Bd, 69-; alt deleg, Dem Nat Conv, 72; vchmn, Third Cong Dist Dem Party, Colo, 72-75; deleg, Dem Mid Term Conf, 74. Bus & Prof Pos: City ed, Durango News, 48-49. Mem: BR-PEO; Durango Reading Club; Durango League of Women Voters (former pres). Honors & Awards: State Am Asn Univ Women scholarship to attend Vassar Inst of Family & Community Living, Vassar Col, June-July, 55; Altrusa Club of Denver, Colo Activist Award, 73. Relig: Catholic. Mailing Add: PO Box 888 1623 Forest Ave Durango CO 81301

MCKENNA, MARLENE A (D)
b Providence, RI, May 3, 46; d Albert P Marcello & Katherine Gelfuso M; m 1973 to Keven Alexander McKenna; c Sean, Christopher & Damian. Educ: Skidmore Col, BA, 68; Ecole des Hautes Etudes Int, Paris, France, cert, 69; Univ RI, MA, 76; pres, Sr Class, 68, prin coordr for grad events. Polit & Govt Pos: Planner, Statewide Planning Prog, RI, 69-72; analyst for educ, State Budget Off of RI, 72-74; deleg, Dem Nat Mid-Term Conf, 74; mem policy & party orgn comt, Dem State Comt of RI, 75. Mem: Women's Polit Caucus; Common Cause of RI (lobbyist, 74-); RI Chap, Am Soc Pub Admin. Relig: Catholic. Mailing Add: 248 Mt Pleasant Ave Providence RI 02908

MCKENNA, ROBERT J (D)
RI State Sen
b Providence, RI, Feb 23, 31; s James C McKenna & Margaret V Gorman M; m 1956 to Mary Jean Kelly; c Robert, Margaret Ann, Mark, Raymond, Elizabeth, Paul & Patricia. Educ: Brown Univ, AB; Cath Univ Am, MA. Hon Degrees: DEd, Sem of Our Lady of Providence, 75. Polit & Govt Pos: Chmn, RI Comn State Govt Internships, 69-; secy, Comn on 200th Anniversary of RI Independence, 69-; secy, RI Bicentennial Found, 71-; mem, Brenton Point Comt, 71-; secy & mem exec comt, Ft Adams Found, 72-; mem, State Adv Bd of Libr Comnr, 73-; RI State Sen, Dist 50, 73-, vchmn, Spec Legis Comn to Study State Scholar Prog, 73-, mem, Spec Legis Study Comn on Post Baccalaureate Educ, 74-, chmn, Spec Legis Comn to Study Pub Health Impact on Abortions, 75-; RI Senate mem, Educ Comn to States, 73-; chmn, Am Irish Cult Exchange Comn, 74- Mil Serv: Entered as Pvt, Army, 53, released as SP-4, 56. Publ: Co-auth, The Supreme Court on abortion—a dissenting opinion, Cath Lawyer, winter 73. Mem: Christmas in Newport (mem bd dirs); RI Independence Commemorative at Newport, Inc (chmn bd); Seaport '76 Found, Ltd (vpres & dir); RI Hist Soc (mem finance comt); Newport Boys Club (mem bd dirs). Relig: Roman Catholic. Legal Res: 47 Everett St Newport RI 02840 Mailing Add: Salve Regina Col Ochre Point Ave Newport RI 02840

MCKENNA, WILLAFAY H (D)
Chairwoman, James City Co Dem Comt, Va
b Orange, NJ, Jan 26, 36; d Richard Lewis Hopkins & Elinor Lord H; m 1957 to Virgil V McKenna; c Quinn Hopkins & Elizabeth Conroy. Educ: Col of William & Mary, BS, 57; Univ SDak, 60; Col William & Mary, Marshall-Wythe Sch Law, 74; Kappa Alpha Theta. Polit & Govt Pos: Precinct chairwoman, LBJ Presidential Campaign Comt, 64; chairwoman, McCarthy for President Campaign, 68; co coordr, Humphrey Presidential Campaign, 68; deleg, Va Dem State Conv, 68, 70 & 72; coordr, Howell Gubernatorial Campaign, 69; dist chairwoman, Battle Gubernatorial Campaign, 69; Williamsburg-James City Co chairwoman, Rawlings Sen Campaign, 70; chairwoman, James City Co Dem Comt, 70-; chairwoman, 51st Dem House Dist Comt, 71-; deleg, Dem Nat Conv, 72; coordr, McGovern-Shriver, Spong & Downing Campaigns, 72-74; mem, Va Dem Platform Comt, 73; admin asst to Deleg George Grayson, Va House Deleg, 74. Bus & Prof Pos: Teacher spec educ, Devereux Found, Devon, Pa, 58-59; ed & alumni dir, Carleton Col, 59-60; social worker, NJ State Bd Child Welfare, New Brunswick, 60-62; research asst, Educ Testing Serv, Princeton, 62; research assoc, Col of William & Mary, 68- Mem: Danforth Found (assoc, 67-); Am Civil Liberties Union; Va Women's Polit Caucus; NAACP; League of Women Voters. Relig: Unitarian. Mailing Add: 117 Deer Spring Rd Williamsburg VA 23185

MCKENNEY, FRANK MEATH (D)
Committeeman, Ga State Dem Exec Comt
b Macon, Ga, Feb 1, 34; s Frank Miller McKenney & Isabel Meath M; single. Educ: Mercer Univ, AB, 56, Walter F George Sch of Law, Mercer Univ, LLB, 59. Polit & Govt Pos: Committeeman, Bibb Dem Exec Comt, 66-, chmn, 74-75; Ga State Dem Exec Comt, 71- Mil Serv: Entered as 2nd Lt, Army, 57, released as Capt, 67, after serv in Army Res. Publ: Personal Property and Sales, Mercer Law Rev, 60, 64, 66 & 69. Mem: Macon Legal Aid Soc (pres, 65, secy-treas, 71); Elks; Lions. Relig: Catholic. Mailing Add: Rte 13 Macon GA 30006

MCKENZIE, EARL EUGENE (R)
Mem, Scioto Co Rep Cent Comt, Ohio
b Lucasville, Ohio, Oct 9, 16; s Earl McKenzie & Margaret Fullerton M; m 1939 to Janice Joan Jones; c Betty Joan (Mrs David T Jenkins) & Ronald Eugene. Educ: Ohio Univ, BS in Educ, 38; Marshall Univ, MA in Sch Admin, 63; Kappa Delta Pi. Polit & Govt Pos: Secy, Scioto Co Rep Exec Comt, Ohio, 54-63, chmn, 63-72; mem, Scioto Co Rep Cent Comt, 54-; mem, bd of elec, Scioto Co Representative of Secy of State, 63- Bus & Prof Pos: Teacher & coach, Rush Twp Schs, McDermott, Ohio, 38-41; teacher, coach & athletic dir, Valley Local Schs, Lucasville, Ohio, 41-50, teacher, 50-62; dist mgr Fed Mutual Ins Co, 50-57; prin, Washington Local Schs, West Portsmouth, Ohio, 62-65, supt, 65- Mil Serv: Entered as Pvt, Army, 45, released as Sgt, 46, after serv in Hq, BTS, Ft Lewis, Wash, 45-46; Victory Medal. Mem: Ohio Sch Bd Asn; Nat Educ Asn; Am Asn of Sch Adminrs; Am Legion; Elks. Relig: Methodist. Legal Res: Broad St Lucasville OH 45648 Mailing Add: PO Box 686 Lucasville OH 45648

MCKENZIE, RICHARD WAYNE (D)
Miss State Rep
Mailing Add: Box 1403 Hattiesburg MS 39401

MCKENZIE, WILLIAM IRVING (D)
b Westhope, NDak, May 15, 04; s Thomas McKenzie & Catherine McNeill M; m 1942 to Dorthy Rinn; c Thomas C, James H & Kathleen A. Educ: Daybreak Sch, West Hope, NDak. Polit & Govt Pos: Precinct committeeman, 58-; vchmn, Douglas Co Dem Cent Comt, 60-62, treas, 62-64 & 66-70, chmn, 64-66 & 70-74; deleg, Wash Dem State Conv, 5 times. Mil Serv: Entered as CEM, Navy, 42, released as CEMPA, 45, after serv in 40th & 76th Construction Bn, Pac Theater; Pac & Asiatic Theater Ribbons; Presidential Unit Citation. Mem: Odd Fellows; IBEW; Mason; DeMolay (adv). Relig: Presbyterian. Legal Res: Rte 3 Box 3276 Wenatchee WA 98801 Mailing Add: PO Box 0146 East Wenatchee WA 98801

MCKERNAN, JOHN RETTIE, JR (R)
Maine State Rep
b Bangor, Maine, May 20, 48; s John Rettie McKernan (deceased) & Barbara Guild M; m 1970 to Judith Mary Files; c Peter Alexander. Educ: Dartmouth Col, BA, 70; Univ Maine Sch Law, Portland, 71-; Dragon Sr Soc; Heorot Fraternity. Polit & Govt Pos: Maine State Rep, 73- Mem: Student Bar Asn. Mailing Add: 256 Kenduskeag Ave Bangor ME 04401

MCKESSON, JOHN ALEXANDER, III (INDEPENDENT)
US Ambassador to Gabon
b New York, NY, Mar 29, 22; s John Alexander McKesson, II & Mildred Warner M; wid; c John Alexander, IV. Educ: Univ Paris, BesL, 39; Columbia Univ, AB, 41, MA, 42; Phi Beta Kappa. Hon Degrees: LLD, Eastern Mich Univ, 72. Polit & Govt Pos: Off dir, Dept State, Washington, DC, 61-70; counselor of embassy, Am Embassy, Dakar, Senegal, 64-67; US Ambassador to Gabon, 72- Mil Serv: Entered as Ens, Navy, 42, released as Lt, 46, after serv in Commun, Washington; Patrol Bombing Squadron, Europe, 42-46; Navy Unit Citation. Publ: The Schuman plan, Am Polit Sci Quart, 51. Mem: Am Foreign Serv Asn; Am Acad Polit Sci; Rotary; Metrop Club Washington, DC; Smithsonian. Honors & Awards: Comdr, Nat Order of Senegal, 67. Relig: Episcopal. Mailing Add: Dept of State (AF/C) Washington DC 20520

MCKEVITT, JAMES D (MIKE) (R)
Asst Attorney Gen, Off Legis Affairs, Dept Justice
b Spokane, Wash, Oct 26, 28; m to Doris Ellen Lester; c Kate & Julie. Educ: Univ Idaho, BA, polit sci, 51; Univ Denver Sch Law, LLB, 56. Polit & Govt Pos: Asst Attorney Gen, State Colo, 9 years; Dist Attorney, Denver, 67-68; US Rep, Colo, 71-73; deleg, Rep Nat Conv, 72; asst attorney gen, Off of Legis Affairs, Dept of Justice, 73- Bus & Prof Pos: Trial lawyer, 11 years. Mil Serv: Air Force, 2 years, serv as combat intel off, Korean Theatre Oper. Mem: Colo Dist Attorneys Asn (pres); Nat Dist Attorneys Asn (dir & vpres, chmn standing comt on fed legis). Honors & Awards: Distinguished Serv Award, Nat Dist Attorneys Asn, 69. Relig: Episcopal. Legal Res: Denver CO Mailing Add: US Dept Justice Washington DC 20530

MCKIBBEN, JADIE CLIFFORD (D)
b Polk Co, Ga, Dec 11, 99; s James William McKibben & Sara Winkles; m 1923 to Paschal Lovvorn; c Aline & Helen. Educ: High sch grad. Polit & Govt Pos: Chmn, Polk Co Dem Exec Comt, Ga, formerly. Bus & Prof Pos: Shoe repairman, 28-65. Mem: Mason. Relig: Baptist. Mailing Add: 133 Cobb St Cedartown GA 30125

MCKIBBIN, JOHN S (D)
Wash State Rep
Mailing Add: 11205 NE Tenth Ave Vancouver WA 98665

MCKILLEN, JEAN BARBARA (R)
Comnr, Calif Rep State Cent Comt
b Chicago, Ill; d James Arcus & Ethel Agate A; m 1932 to Bruce Abbott McKillen; c Zelma Ethelyn (Mrs Turner). Educ: Private tutoring, ballerina. Polit & Govt Pos: Held all pos up to supvr in filter stations, Bakersfield, Los Angeles & Oakland, 6th Army, Calif, 41-44; organizer & secy, Eden Area Rep Club, Calif Rep Assembly, 52-59; Parliamentarian, Chabot Rep Women's Federated Club, 66-68; comnr, Calif Rep State Cent Comt, 68-; deleg, State & Nat Rep Conv; coordr & hq mgr of numerous rep cand. Mem: Calif Federated Women's Clubs; Castro Valley CofC; Am Legion Auxiliary; Georgetown Divide Rep Women; Nat Grange (Patron of Husbandry). Honors & Awards: Castro Valley CofC Award for a civic proj; eleven Dist Awards, Calif Federated Women's Clubs. Relig: Protestant. Mailing Add: Box 291 Georgetown CA 95634

MCKIM, ADELE W (R)
VChmn, Bergen Co Rep Comt, NJ
b Little Falls, NJ, Sept 27, 14; d James C Marley & A Adele W Maass M; m 1937 to Thomas McKim; c Bonita Dorothy (Mrs Courtney John Dow) & Thomas Craigie; two grandchildren. Educ: Paterson Cent High Sch, 28-32; NY Sch Modeling, 34-35. Polit & Govt Pos: Chmn, Midland Park Rep Co Comt, NJ, 53-, munic chmn, 59-; secy & vpres, United Rep Club, Midland Park, 59-60; chmn dist 12, Bergen Co Rep Comt, 59, vchmn, 67-, regist chmn, 68-73; pres, Midland Park Rep Women Inc, 60-62, secy, 64-66; secy, Bergen Co Women's Rep Club, 63-67, mem bd trustees, 67-; mem, Bergen Co Rep Policy Comt, 67-; chmn, Women for Nixon, Bergen Co, 68; mem finance comt, NJ Fedn Rep Women, 69. Bus & Prof Pos: Treas, Midland Park Libr Bd of Trustee, 59- Mem: Ladies Auxiliary VFW (pres, 66-67); Am Legion Auxiliary; Daughters of Scotia (past chief daughter); Eastern Star; Midland Park Br Valley Hosp Auxiliary. Relig: Protestant. Mailing Add: 251 Park Ave Midland Park NJ 07432

MCKIM, GEORGE WILLIAM (R)
Mem Finance Comt, NMex Rep Party
b Clearwater, Nebr; s Lisbon Clarence (Posy) McKim & Elizabeth Anderson M; m 1936 to Della Harnish; c Barbara Jeanine. Educ: Wayne State Teachers Col, 21-25; Delta Sigma Rho; Tau Kappa Alpha. Polit & Govt Pos: Chmn, Bernalillo Co Rep Party, NMex, 55-58; Rep

cand, US Rep, NMex, 58; finance chmn, NMex Rep Party, 58-63 & 67-73, mem finance comt, currently. Mil Serv: Entered as A/S, Navy, 26, released as Radioman 3/C, 29, after serv aboard USS Omaha. Mem: Nat Asn Mutual Ins Agts (nat dir, 57-58, NMex vpres, 58-61, NMex dir, 67-); Mason; Elks; Toastmasters Int; Commun Chest (past mem bd dirs). Relig: Methodist; Treas, First United Methodist Church, 53- Mailing Add: 1406 Harvard NE Albuquerque NM 87106

MCKINLEY, IRA BLAKELY (R)
Chmn, House Dist 11 Rep Orgn, Alaska
b Detroit, Mich, Sept 28, 34; s Dr Lee L McKinley & Doris Blakely M; m 1961 to Pauline Joan Oeser; c Ira Blakely, Jr, Robert Paul, Susan Lee & Michael Dean. Educ: Univ Alaska, BEd, 58; Univ Mo, Kansas City Dent Sch, DDS, 66; Omicron Kappa Upsilon; Xi Psi Phi. Polit & Govt Pos: Rep precinct committeeman, Chugiak Area, Alaska, 58-60; deleg, Alaska, Rep State Conv, 60; state pres, Alaska Young Rep, 60-61; Rep precinct committeeman, Third Ward, Kansas City, Mo, 64; dist chmn, Kodiak Area Rep Party, Alaska, 67-70; chmn, House Dist 11 Rep Orgn, 67-; deleg, SCent Dist Rep Conv, 68; mayor, Kodiak, Alaska, 71- Bus & Prof Pos: Teacher, Chugiak, Alaska, 58-60, Anchorage, 60-61 & Kansas City, Kans, 61-62; dentist, Anchorage, Alaska, 66 & Kodiak, 66- Mil Serv: 2nd Lt, Army Chem Corps, 59; Army Nat Guard, 59-66, 1st Lt. Mem: Am Dent Asn; Mason; Shrine; CofC; Rotary. Relig: Church of God. Legal Res: 1110 Purtov Kodiak AK 99615 Mailing Add: Box 573 Kodiak AK 99615

MCKINNEY, DORIS MAY (R)
Mem, Calif Rep State Cent Comt
b Mill Valley, Calif, Nov 2, 22; d James Joseph O'Reilly & Alvena Von Fuchs; m 1941 to Byron Curtis McKinney; c James & Glenn. Educ: San Francisco City Col, AA. Polit & Govt Pos: Mem, Calif Rep Assembly, 64-66; mem, Nat City Civil Serv Comn, 65-, chmn, 70-; educ chmn, Southern Div, Calif Fedn Rep Women, 68-69; mem, Calif Rep State Cent Comt, 68-; corresponding secy, Chula Vista Rep Women's Club, 69-70, vpres, 70-; co-chmn orgn comt, San Diego Co Fedn Rep Women's Clubs, 70. Bus & Prof Pos: Dir music, Naval Air Sta Chapel, Kodiak, Alaska, 47-49, Naval Postgrad Sch Chapel, Monterey, Calif, 52-54 & Hickam Air Force Base, Honolulu, Hawaii, 59-60. Mem: San Diego Choral Club. Honors & Awards: Commun Serv Award, National City, Calif, 69. Relig: Evangelical Presbyterian. Mailing Add: 120 Valva Ave National City CA 92050

MCKINNEY, HELEN MATHEWS (R)
Mem, Idaho State Rep Cent Comt
b Idaho Falls, Idaho, Oct 30, 17; d Eugene W Mathews & Hilda Johnson M; m 1940 to Jack W McKinney; c John S. Educ: Univ Utah; Univ Idaho; Alpha Chi Omega. Polit & Govt Pos: Past secy & committeewoman, Idaho State Rep Cent Comt, mem, 50-; mem, Gov Status of Women's Comn, Idaho; Idaho State Rep, Dist 20-A, Lemhi, Anl & Custer Counties, 65-72, mem adv bd, Challis Nat Forest, Rep Caucus secy & vchmn, Appropriations Comt, Idaho House of Rep, formerly; mem, Lem Co Rep Women, 67- Bus & Prof Pos: Educator, jr high sch, 40-55. Mem: Bus & Prof Women's Club; Int Toast Mistress; Nat Educ Asn; N Idaho CofC (former vpres, pres, 73-74); Salmon Nat Forest (dir adv bd, 72-). Honors & Awards: Outstanding Citizen's Award, 65; Woman of the Year, 66. Relig: Episcopal. Mailing Add: 511 Second St N Salmon ID 83467

MCKINNEY, J E (D)
Ga State Rep
Mailing Add: 765 Shorter Terr NW Atlanta GA 30318

MCKINNEY, JAMES GROVER (R)
Mem, Rep State Cent Comt, Calif
b San Francisco, Calif, Oct 30, 45; s Byron Curtis McKinney & Doris O'Reilly M; m 1971 to Martia Ellen Trueblood; c Matthew Ethan. Educ: San Diego State Univ, BA, 68, MA; Pi Kappa Delta; Tau Kappa Epsilon. Polit & Govt Pos: Pres, Calif Col Young Rep, 67-68; chmn, Western Fedn Col Rep, 68-69; mem, San Diego Co Rep Cent Comt, Calif, 73-, chmn, 75; mem, Rep State Cent Comt, Calif, 74- Bus & Prof Pos: Prof, US Int Univ, 69-72; investment banker, Paine Webber, Jackson & Curtis, 72- Mem: Lions Int; Jaycees; Univ Club San Diego; Nat Forensic League. Honors & Awards: Outstanding Citizen Awards, Chula Vista Am Legion & National City VFW, 63; Bank of Am Award for Achievement in Foreign Langs, 63; First Place, Pac Southwest Collegiate Forensic Asn, 66. Relig: Presbyterian. Mailing Add: 625 E First St National City CA 92050

MCKINNEY, JAMES ROBIN (D)
Tenn State Rep
b Smith Co, Tenn, Mar 10, 31; s Theodore R McKinney & Pearl Bellar M; m 1955 to Dorothy Scudder; c J Robin & Bradley S. Educ: Tenn Technol Univ, 56; Nashville YMCA Night Law Sch, 64. Polit & Govt Pos: Tenn State Rep, 69-, Dem Whip, Tenn House Rep, 69-70, speaker, formerly; mem, Nat Conf State Legis Leaders, 69-70; exec mem, Southern Conf Legis, 71-; deleg, Dem Nat Conv, 72. Bus & Prof Pos: Pres, Madison Hillbilly Days, 67-68. Mil Serv: AM-2, Navy, 51-54; serv in Europe & SE Asia; Good Conduct Medal; Presidential Unit Citation; Korean Theatre Medal; Korean Presidential Citation; European & China Serv Medal; Marksmanship Medal. Mem: Lions; Madison Civic Club; Am Legion; VFW; F&AM. Honors & Awards: Distinguished Serv Award & Distinguished Young Man of the Year, Madison Jaycees, 66. Relig: Baptist. Legal Res: 110 Graycroft Madison TN 37115 Mailing Add: 608 Gallatin Rd N Madison TN 37115

MCKINNEY, JOSEPH EVANS (D)
b Elkton, Md, May 21, 13; s Joseph B McKinney & Bertha Payne M; m 1941 to Janet C Deibert; c Robert A & James C. Educ: Johns Hopkins, 35-37. Polit & Govt Pos: Eng aide, US Corps of Engrs, 37-44; pres, Cecil Co Young Dem, Md, 50-52; chmn, Cecil Co Dem Cent Comt, 58-66, mem, 70-74; co-chmn, East Shore Dem Comt, 58-66; deleg, Md Dem State Conv, 64; hon secy Md deleg & deleg, Dem Nat Conv, 64; vchmn, Md Dem State Cent Comt, 68-70; mem coun, Town of Elkton, 69- Bus & Prof Pos: Prod coord-sales, E I du Pont de Nemours & Co, Inc, 44- Mem: Assoc, Singerly Fire Co; Elkton Rotary Club; Cecil Co Hunter's Asn (secy); Ducks Unlimited; Kiwanis Club of Elkton. Relig: Methodist. Mailing Add: 405 Park Circle Elkton MD 21921

MCKINNEY, PAUL (D)
Pa State Sen
Mailing Add: 5741 Chestnut St Philadelphia PA 19139

MCKINNEY, PAUL CAYLOR (D)
Chmn, Montgomery Co Dem Party, Ind
b Otterbein, Ind, Aug 21, 30; s Theodore R McKinney, Sr & Sally B Caylor M; m 1966 to Irmingard E Kettemann; c Katherine Anne & Michael Andrew. Educ: Wabash Col, AB, 52; Fulbright scholar, Freiburg Univ, 55-56; Northwestern Univ, PhD, 58; Sigma Xi; Phi Lambda Upsilon; Sigma Pi Sigma; Delta Phi Alpha; Blue Key; Kappa Sigma; Alpha Chi Sigma. Polit & Govt Pos: Chmn, Montgomery Co Dem Party, Ind, 72- Bus & Prof Pos: Assoc prof chem, Wabash Col, 64- Mem: Am Asn Advan Sci; NY Acad Sci; Am Inst Chem. Mailing Add: 508 W Main St Crawfordsville IN 47933

MCKINNEY, ROBERT HURLEY (D)
b Indianapolis, Ind, Nov 7, 25; s E Kirk McKinney & Irene Hurley M; m 1951 to Arlene Allsopp; c Robert Carlton, Marni Frances, Kevin Kirk, Kent Allsopp & Lisa Carol. Educ: US Naval Acad, BS, 46; Ind Univ Law Sch, JD, 51; Phi Delta Phi. Polit & Govt Pos: Deleg, Ind State Dem Conv, 54, 56, 60, 64 & 68; chmn, Ind Dem Party, Kennedy for Pres Campaign, 60; deleg, Dem Nat Conv, 68 & 72; chmn, Ind Muskie for President Comt, 72. Bus & Prof Pos: Chmn, First Fed Savings of Indianapolis, 61-; pres, Jefferson Corp & Subsidiaries, 61-; partner, Bose, McKinney & Evans, Law Firm, 63- Mil Serv: Entered as Midn, Navy, 43, released as Lt Comdr, 53, after serv in Pac Theatre, 46-49 & 51-53, Lt Comdr, Naval Res; Pac Theatre Awards. Publ: Law Review articles. Mem: Am Bar Asn; Ind State Bar Asn (dir); Asn Life Ins Counsel; Boy Scouts (dir); Community Hosp (dir). Relig: Catholic. Legal Res: 7770 N Pennsylvania St Indianapolis IN 46240 Mailing Add: 1100 First Federal Bldg Indianapolis IN 46204

MCKINNEY, ROBERT M (D)
b Shattuck, Okla, Aug 28, 10; s Edwin S McKinney & Eva Moody M; m 1943 to Louise Trigg; m 1970 to Marie-Louise de Montmollin; c Robin. Educ: Univ Okla, AB, 32; Univ NMex, LLD, 64; Phi Beta Kappa; Phi Gamma Delta. Polit & Govt Pos: Chmn, NMex Econ Develop Comn & Water Resources Develop Bd, 49-51; Asst Secy of Interior, 51-52; chmn, Panel to Report to Cong on The Impact of the Peaceful Uses of Atomic Energy, 55-56; permanent US Rep to Int Atomic Energy Agency, Vienna, 57-58; dir, Rev of the Int Atomic Policies & Progs of the US, for Joint Comt on Atomic Energy, US Cong, 59-60; US Ambassador, Switz, 61-63; exec officer, Presidential Task Force on Int Investments, 63-64; US Rep to Int Centre for Settlement of Investment Disputes, Washington, DC, 67-; chmn, Presidential Comn on Travel, 68; deleg, Dem Nat Conv, 68. Bus & Prof Pos: Publ, The Santa Fe New Mexican; chmn, The New Mexican, Inc & Taos Publ Corp; dir, Copper Range Co, Surveyor Fund, Inc, Martin Marietta Corp & Trans World Airlines, Inc; pres, Robert Moody Found. Mil Serv: Entered as Lt(jg), Navy, 42, released as Lt, 45. Publ: On Increasing the Effectiveness of Western Science & Technology, 59; Review of the International Atomic Policies & Programs of the United States, for Joint Comt on Atomic Energy, US Cong, 59-60; The Red Challenge to Technological Renewal, 60. Mem: Foreign Policy Asn (dir); Am Soc of Newspaper Ed; Coun Foreign Rels; Am Newspaper Publ Asn; Am-Swiss Asn. Honors & Awards: Distinguished Serv Award, Univ Okla, 65. Relig: Christian Church. Legal Res: 202 E Marcy Santa Fe NM 87501 Mailing Add: PO Box 1705 Santa Fe NM 87501

MCKINNEY, STEWART BRETT (R)
US Rep, Conn
b Pittsburgh, Pa, Jan 30, 31; s James Polk McKinney & Clara Brett M; m 1954 to Lucie Bedford Cunningham; c Stewart Brett, Jr, Lucie Bedford, Jean Curry, Elizabeth Cunningham & John Polk. Educ: Princeton Univ, Class of 53; Yale Univ, AB, 58. Polit & Govt Pos: Conn State Rep, 67-70, minority leader, 69-70; US Rep, Fourth Dist, Conn, 70-; mem, Conn Transportation Authority, 71- Bus & Prof Pos: Past pres, CMF Tires Inc. Mil Serv: Entered as Pvt, Air Force, 51, released as Sgt, 55, after serv in US. Mem: Am Red Cross; Bridgeport Child Guid Clin (dir); Rehabilitation Ctr of Eastern Fairfield Co (dir); Rotary (vpres, Fairfield Club); Bridgeport CofC (dir). Relig: Episcopal; Mem of vestry, St Timothy's Church. Legal Res: 4480 Congress St Fairfield CT 06430 Mailing Add: PO Box 543 Fairfield CT 06430

MC KINNON, ALLAN R (D)
Mass State Sen
Mailing Add: 78 Cottage Lane Weymouth MA 02188

MCKINNON, CLINTON DOTSON (D)
b Dallas, Tex, Feb 5, 06; s John Clinton McKinnon & Tennie Hawkins M; m 1932 to Lucille Virginia McVey; c Clinton Dan, Michael D & Connie Lynn. Educ: Univ of Redlands, BA, 30; Univ of Geneva, Switz, post grad work, 30; Pi Chi; Sigma Delta Chi. Hon Degrees: DHL, Univ Redlands, 67. Polit & Govt Pos: US Rep, Calif, 49-52; vchmn, Calif Dem State Cent Comt, 52-54; deleg, Dem Nat Conv, 52 & 56; mem, Gov Bus Adv Coun; Disaster Gov of Calif; chmn, Indust Develop Comn, San Diego, 64-; chmn, San Diego Urban Coalition, 69-70. Bus & Prof Pos: Reporter, ed & adv mgr, various Southern Calif newspapers, 31-35; pres & gen mgr, Valley News Corp, 35-43; pres & publ, Valley Times, North Hollywood, 35-43; establisher, San Fernando Valley Times, 35, Los Angeles Aircraft Times, 40 & Long Beach Shipyard Times, 41; pres, publ & ed, San Diego Daily J, 44-48; pres, ed & publ, McKinnon Publ, San Diego, 45-48; owner, Radio Sta KSDJ, Columbia Affil, San Diego, 45-48; ed & publ, Los Angeles Daily News, 53-54; co-owner, Coronado J, 53-72; pres & publ, NShores Sentinel, 53-72; pres & gen mgr, Alvarado TV Co, Inc, KVOA-TV, Tucson, Ariz & KOAT-TV, Albuquerque, NMex, 55-63; pres, Sentinel Savings & Loan Asn, 63-68; owner, La Jolla Light J, 63-72; pres, San Diego Transit Corp, 67-72; secy, STex Telecasting Co, KIII-TV, Corpus Christi, Tex, currently. Mem: Rotary; Cuyamaca. Relig: Presbyterian. Legal Res: 1145 Pacific Beach Dr San Diego CA 92109 Mailing Add: PO Box 9417 San Diego CA 92109

MCKINNON, MICHAEL DEE (D)
Tex State Sen
b Los Angeles, Calif, June 12, 39; s Clinton D McKinnon & Lucille M; div; c Michael Dean & Mark Daniel. Educ: Univ Redlands, grad, 59; Harvard Grad Sch Bus, grad, TV Mgt, 68. Polit & Govt Pos: Tex State Sen, 20th Dist, 73- Bus & Prof Pos: Owner & oper mgr, KSON Radio Sta, San Diego, Calif; publ, La Jolla J, Calif; dir, KOAT-TV, Albuquerque, NMex; oper mgr, KIII-TV, Corpus Christi, Tex, exec vpres, pres, KIII-TV; pres, KXIX-TV, Corpus Christi. Mil Serv: Army. Mem: Tex Asn Broadcasters (pres, 71); Nat Asn Broadcasters; Broadcast Prom Asn; Asn Broadcast Execs of Tex; TV Bur Advert. Honors & Awards: Spec Citation for Serv to Mex-Am in Corpus Christi Area, Nat League of United Latin Am Citizens' Coun; Boss of the Year, Coastal Bend Chap, Nat Secy Asn, 70; Outstanding Young Man of the Year, Corpus Christi Jr CofC, 71; Citation for Personal Efforts During & After Hurricane Celia, President Nixon. Relig: Presbyterian. Legal Res: 5502 Ocean Dr Corpus Christi TX 78412 Mailing Add: PO Box 6669 Corpus Christi TX 78411

MCKINZIE, MYRTLE ANN (D)
b Houston, Tex, June 20, 44; d Livingston Jones & Lou Violet Thompson J; m 1962 to Lacy McKinzie, Jr; c Lacy, III & Larry Livingston. Educ: Tex Southern Univ, BA, magna cum laude, 73, Sch Law, 73-; Valedictorian, Phi Alpha Delta, Alpha Kappa Mu, Epsilon Psi. Polit

& Govt Pos: Deleg, Dem Nat Conv, 72; secy, 11th Sen Dist Dem Orgn, Tex, 72-73. Mem: Foster Place Area Civic Clubs (pres, 74-); Black Women for Polit Change (pres, 75-); Welfare Rights Orgn; Precinct 180 Club (chmn, 74-). Honors & Awards: Most Outstanding Woman, Precinct 180 Club, 73; Most Outstanding Women of 1974, Black Women for Polit Change, 75. Relig: African-Methodist-Episcopal; trustee, Walls Chapel AME Zion Church. Mailing Add: 3930 Porter Houston TX 77021

MCKISSACK, JIMMIE DON (D)
Ark State Rep
Mailing Add: PO Box 599 Star City AR 71667

MCKISSICK, HOWARD FRANK JR (R)
Mem, Nev Rep State Cent Comt
b Reno, Nev, May 5, 27; s Howard F McKissick, Sr & Frankie Porter M (deceased); m 1965 to Dorothy June Tutt; c Blair, twins Bruce & Pam, John, Patty & Molly. Educ: Univ Nev, BS, 50; Hastings Col Law, Univ Calif, JD, 53; Phi Kappa Phi; Order of the Coif; Sigma Nu; Phi Alpha Delta; Fleishmann Scholarship, 47-50, Wilson Scholarship, 53; Thurston Soc; student body pres, 52-53; Hastings Law Rev, 52-53. Polit & Govt Pos: Mem, Statute Revision Comn, Nev Supreme Court, 54-55; Nev State Assemblyman, 57-72, minority floor leader, Nev State Assembly, 59, Speaker of the Assembly, 69-71, chmn, Commerce Comt & mem, Judiciary & Labor Comts, 71-72; mem, Nev Rep State Cent Comt, currently. Bus & Prof Pos: Founder & instr, Nev Bar Rev Course, 55-60. Mil Serv: Navy, 45-46, Seaman 1/C, Serv in Amphibian Forces, SPac, 45-46; recalled 2nd Lt, Air Force, 50, serv Camp Stoneman, Calif. Publ: New laws of interest to Nevada lawyers, Nev State Bar J, spring 59, 61, 63, 67, 69 & 71; Demonstrative evidence in criminal cases, 69 & The new gun control law, 69, Am Trial Lawyers Asn; plus others. Mem: Am Bar Asn; Am Trial Lawyers Asn (state committeeman, 55 & 69-, Nev vchmn, legis sect, 69, student advocacy prog comt, 69, bd gov, 72-); Nat Soc State Legislators (secy, 70-71); Am Judicature Soc; Nat Asn State Legis Leaders (charter mem). Honors & Awards: Admitted to US Supreme Court, Court of Appeals & Dist Courts of Nev & Calif; registrant, John Appleman's Prof Trial Lawyers Seminar, Urbana, Ill, 69. Relig: Protestant. Mailing Add: 3075 Rustic Manor Circle Reno NV 89503

MCKITTRICK, DANIEL PATRICK (PAT) (D)
Mont State Rep
b Anaconda, Mont, Sept 24, 41; s Daniel Thomas McKittrick & Catherine Murphy M; m 1963 to Sharon Ann Graham; c Ann Marie, Tara Louise & Daniel Patrick. Educ: Carroll Col, BA, 63; Univ Mont, JD, 66; Delta Sigma Phi. Polit & Govt Pos: Law clerk, Mont Supreme Court, Helena, 66; pres, Mont Young Dem, 67-69; dep co attorney, Great Falls, 68; Mont State Rep, 71- Mem: Am & Mont Trial Lawyers Asns; Mont & Cascade Co Bar Asns; KofC. Honors & Awards: Outstanding Young Man Award; Outstanding Young Legislator, Eagleton Inst, Rutgers Univ, 71. Relig: Catholic. Mailing Add: 636 Carol Dr Great Falls MT 59405

MCKNEALLY, MARTIN B (R)
b Newburgh, NY, Dec 31, 15; s George F McKneally & Ellen Leahy M; single. Educ: Holy Cross Col, AB, 36; Fordham Univ Law Sch, LLB, 39. Polit & Govt Pos: Confidential secy, NY State Supreme Court Justice; pres bd educ, Newburgh, NY; mem, NY State Defense Coun, 60-68; coun, NY State Comn on World's Fair; spec coun to Lt Gov, NY State, 60-68; US Rep, NY, 69-70. Mil Serv: Army, 41, Maj, ETO & Pac Theatre; Decorated by France & Belgium. Mem: Am Legion (former state & nat comdr); hon Rotarian; March of Dimes (state pres, 5 years). Relig: Roman Catholic. Mailing Add: 329 First St Newburgh NY 12550

MCKNIGHT, CHARLES PEYTON (D)
Tex State Sen
b Alba, Tex, Dec 10, 24; s Charles Peyton McKnight (deceased) & Caudie Mae Jones M; m 1946 to Ann Cade; c Molly (Mrs Charles Hodges) & Jane (Mrs Bill Ratliff). Educ: ETex State Univ, 2 years; Tex A&M Univ, BA, 47; Univ Tex Law Sch, 1 year. Polit & Govt Pos: Tex State Rep, 49-51; mem, Sabine River Authority Bd, 51; US Marshal, Eastern Dist Tex, 53; mem bd of regents, Tex A&M Univ, 67-; mem, Tex State Dem Exec Comt, formerly; Tex State Sen, 73- Bus & Prof Pos: Independent oil operator, Tyler, Tex, currently; All Am Wildcatter, 73. Mil Serv: Entered Army Air Force, 43, released as 1st Lt, after serv in ETO; European Ribbon, Seven Battle Stars, Distinguished Flying Cross & Three Oak Leaf Clusters. Mem: ETex Hosp Found (mem bd); life mem ETex Peace Officers Asn; Willow Brook Country Club (bd dirs); Mason (32 degree); Shrine. Relig: Episcopal. Legal Res: PO Box 1031 Tyler TX 75701 Mailing Add: Capitol Bldg Austin TX 78711

MCKNIGHT, ROBERT ALLEN (R)
Research & Pub Rels Dir, Ohio Rep Hq
b Detroit, Mich, Apr 24, 43; s L Allen McKnight & Mildred Schwartz M; m 1966 to Jacqueline Sue Estes. Educ: Miami Univ, 61-62; Ohio State Univ, BA, 66, MA, 68; Kappa Tau Alpha; Sigma Delta Chi; Sigma Alpha Epsilon; Pub Rels Student Soc of Am; Young Rep; Pre-Law Club. Polit & Govt Pos: Pub Info Officer, Ohio Dept of Liquor Control, 67-69; chmn, Gov Rhodes Comt on Teenage Drinking, 66-69; pub rel counsel, City of Upper Arlington, Ohio, 68-70; publ & ed, Ohio Rep News, 69-; research & pub rels dir, Ohio Rep Hq, 69- Bus & Prof Pos: Staff writer, Defense Construction Supply Ctr, 65; advert copy-writer, 66; ed dir, Ctr for Voc & Tech Educ, 65-66; pub rels counsel, Columbus Air Conditioning, 69- Publ: Center with a future, Wonderful World of Ohio Mag, 3/67; The role of the public relations profession in the conception, production and implementation of institutional advertising, Ohio State Univ, 68. Mem: The Press Club of Central Ohio; Cap City Young Rep Club; City of Upper Arlington Fire Prev Control Bd. Honors & Awards: Hearst Found Award for Excellence in Newspaper Writing, 66, one of six student participants in Pub Rels Soc of Am Nat Conf, 66. Relig: Protestant. Legal Res: 2187 Arlington Ave Columbus OH 43221 Mailing Add: Suite 3300 50 W Broad St Columbus OH 43215

MCKNIGHT, ROBERT WAYNE (D)
Fla State Rep
b Port Chester, NY, May 11, 44; s Joel Roy McKnight & Gwendolyn Krumm; m 1970 to Susan Williams; c Michelle Elizabeth. Educ: Fla Southern Col, BS, 66; Fla State Univ, MBA, 67; Omicron Delta Kappa; Delta Sigma Pi; Beta Gamma Sigma; Pi Kappa Alpha. Polit & Govt Pos: Gov Comt for Employ of Handicapped, Miami, 72-74; Fla State Rep, 75- Bus & Prof Pos: Mkt rep, IBM, 67-72; dir mkt, Ire Financial Corp, 72-73; vpres, Werner, Wollack & Co, 73-74; partner, Segovia Investments Inc, 74- Mil Serv: Entered as 2nd Lt, Army, 68, released as 1st Lt, 70, after serv in Adj Gen Corps, Korea; Army Commendation Medal. Mem: Ment Health Asn (bd dirs); Young Dem (exec vpres); South Dade CofC; Tiger Bay Polit Club; Coral Gables CofC. Relig: Church of Christ. Mailing Add: 9703 S Dixie Hwy Suite 2B Miami FL 33156

MCKOWN, EDWARD G (R)
Chmn, Calhoun Co Rep Exec Comt, WVa
b Arnoldsburg, WVa, May 31, 15; s Isaac Delmar McKown & Emily Starcher M; m 1937 to Jewell Eleanore Wayne; c Marie, Mark, George, Clarence & Charles. Educ: Calhoun Co High Sch, Grantsville, WVa, 4 years. Polit & Govt Pos: Co rd supvr, State Rd Comn, WVa, 56-61; chmn, Calhoun Co Rep Exec Comt, 68- Bus & Prof Pos: Farmer & retail merchant, 45- Mem: Odd Fellows; Farm Bur; AFL-CIO. Relig: Protestant. Mailing Add: Box 65 Arnoldsburg WV 25234

MCLANE, SUSAN NEIDLINGER (R)
NH State Rep
b Boston, Mass, Sept 28, 29; d Lloyd Kellock Neidlinger & Marion Ruth Walker N; m 1948 to Malcolm McLane; c Susan B, Donald W, Deborah, Alan & Ann Lloyd; one grandchild. Educ: Mt Holyoke Col, 47-48. Polit & Govt Pos: NH State Rep, 69-, vchmn, Ways & Means Comt, NH House Rep, 71-72, chmn, Exec Departments & Admin Comt, currently. Relig: Protestant. Mailing Add: 5 Auburn St Concord NH 03301

MCLANE, WILLIAM JOHN (D)
Pa State Rep
b Scranton, Pa, Mar 5, 47; s John Thomas McLane & Miriam Gilroy M; single. Educ: Univ Scranton, BS in Polit Sci, 69, Grad Sch, 69-70; Col Young Dem Pa (first vpres); Polit Sci Club (pres); Univ Scranton Young Dem (pres). Polit & Govt Pos: Pa State Rep, 75- Bus & Prof Pos: Substitute teacher, Scranton Sch Dist, 70-71; Head Start dir, SLHDA, Scranton, 71-74. Mil Serv: Entered as 2nd Lt, Army Res, now Capt. Relig: Roman Catholic. Mailing Add: 2939 Birney Ave Scranton PA 18505

MCLAREN, RICHARD WELLINGTON (R)
b Chicago, Ill, Apr 21, 18; s Grover C McLaren & Nita Waggoner M; m 1941 to Edith Gillett; c Patricia M (Mrs MacDonald), Richard W, Jr, Sandra & James G. Educ: Yale Col, BA, 39; Yale Law Sch, LLB, 42; Phi Beta Kappa. Polit & Govt Pos: Asst Attorney Gen of the US, 69-72. Bus & Prof Pos: Assoc lawyer, Reavis & McGrath, New York, 46-49; partner, Chadwell, Keck, Kayser, Ruggles & McLaren, Chicago, Ill, 50-69. Mil Serv: Entered as Pvt, Air Force, 42, released as Capt, 46, after serv in Air Transport Command, US. Mem: Am, Fed, Ill & Chicago Bar Asns. Mailing Add: 855 Lamson Dr Winnetka IL 60093

MCLARTY, MACK (D)
Chmn, Ark Dem State Comt
Mailing Add: Plaza W Suite 900 Little Rock AR 72205

MCLAUGHLIN, J KEMP (D)
WVa State Deleg
Mailing Add: State Capitol Charleston WV 25305

MCLAUGHLIN, JOHN H (D)
NH State Sen
b Nashua, NH, Sept 21, 26; s John W McLaughlin (deceased) & Alice Martin M; m 1952 to Lilith Langley; c J Martin & Michael. Educ: Nashua Sr High Sch, grad, 44. Polit & Govt Pos: Mem, Nashua Bd Fire Comnr, 57-, chmn, 60-; NH State Sen, Dist 13, 72-, chmn pub health & state insts, NH State Senate, 73-, mem operating budget, capitol budget & legis comt for state prisons, 74- Bus & Prof Pos: Owner-pres, John W McLaughlin Co, 45- Mil Serv: Entered as Pvt, Air Force, 44, released as Cpl, 46, after serv in ETO. Mem: Motor Transport Asn NH (dir, 68-); Mayflower Warehousemen's Asn (dir, 57-59, secy-treas, 68-70, pres, 70-71); CofC (bd dirs, 71-); Rivier Col Adv Bd; St Joseph Hosp Bd Trustees. Honors & Awards: Man of Year Award, Nashua Jr CofC, 59; Warehouse of Year Award, Mayflower Warehousemen's Asn, 69; Commendation Cert, Am Legion, 70. Relig: Roman Catholic. Legal Res: 105 Connecticut Ave Nashua NH 03060 Mailing Add: 20 Progress Ave Nashua NH 03060

MCLAUGHLIN, LAWRENCE G (R)
NH State Rep
Mailing Add: 57 Marie Ave Nashua NH 03060

MCLAUGHLIN, MICHAEL EDWARD (D)
Asst Majority Leader, Mass House Rep
b Cambridge, Mass, Oct 27, 45; s John Joseph McLaughlin & Amelia Burlamachi M; m 1968 to Donna Christine Lorden; c Michael E, Jr & Matthew E. Educ: Burdett Col, Boston, 63-64; Lowell State Col, summer 65; Plymouth State Col, BE, 67; pres, Young Dem; Men's Athletic Asn; Student Coun. Polit & Govt Pos: Rep, Town Meeting, Billerica, Mass, 67-73, vchmn, Bd of Selectman, 69-72, chmn, Coun on Aging, 69-, mem, Sch Bldg Comt, 70-71, mem, Drug & Alcohol Abuse Comt, 70- & mem, Indust Comn, 70-; mem, Billerica Dem Town Comt, 70-; Mass State Rep, 71-, Asst Majority Leader, Mass House Rep, 73- Bus & Prof Pos: Varsity baseball coach & teacher, Billerica High Sch, Mass, 67-70. Mil Serv: Entered as E-1, Mass Nat Guard, 67, released as E-2, 71, after serv in Hq Troop. Mem: Mass Legis Asn; Mass Teacher's Asn; Elks; KofC; Mass Asn for Retarded Persons. Honors & Awards: Championship Baseball Coach's Award, Merrimack Valley Baseball League, 68 & 70; Outstanding Young Man of the Year, Jr CofC, 71; Distinguished Serv Award, DAV, 72; Outstanding Community Leader, Boy Scouts, 72. Relig: Roman Catholic. Mailing Add: 324 Treble Cove Rd Billerica MA 01862

MCLAUGHLIN, WILLIAM FRANCIS (R)
Chmn, Mich State Rep Cent Comt
b Syracuse, NY, Oct 10, 32; s Edward Joseph McLaughlin & Rosalind Couch M; m 1960 to Janet Ann Lemaster; c Michael, Patrick, Timothy & Sean. Educ: Lemoyne Col, 50-51, Univ Detroit, 51-56. Polit & Govt Pos: Rep cand for Mich State Legis, 62; mem, Macomb Co Bd of Canvassers, 63-64; chmn, Macomb Co Rep Comt, 63-65; mem, Mich State Fair Authority, 64; deleg, Rep Nat Conv, 64 & 72, alt deleg, 68; entertainment chmn, Mich Inaugural, 65; vchmn, Mich State Rep Cent Comt, 65-69, chmn, 69-; campaign coord, State Rep Campaign, 66 & 68; co-chmn, Govt Day-Mich Week, 69; mem, Rep Nat Comt, 69-; chmn, Northville Mich Week, 73. Bus & Prof Pos: Publicity & advert dir, Cinerama Music Hall, 56-65. Relig: Roman Catholic. Mailing Add: 592 Reed Northville MI 48167

MCLEAN, CLYDA EARLENE (R)
Secy, Young Rep Nat Fedn
b Yuba City, Calif, Feb 15, 40; d Clinton H Thomas & Eugenia Huxley T; m 1974 to Robert Dean Spence; c Martin & Stanley. Educ: Univ Alaska, acct, 62; Nat Tax Training Sch, cert of completion, 72. Polit & Govt Pos: Precinct committeewoman, Lane Co Rep Cent Comt,

Ore, 64-; co-chmn, Young Rep Fedn of Ore, 68-70; co-dir region IX, Young Rep Nat Fedn, 69-71, vchmn region IX, 71-73, secy, 73- Bus & Prof Pos: Asst, taxation dept, John D Shaw, Attorney-at-law, 62-65; owner-acct, Am Tax & Bookkeeping, 69- Mem: PTA; Ore Asn Tax Consult. Mailing Add: 240 Sterling Dr Eugene OR 97404

MCLEAN, JIM T (R)
Chmn, Davidson Co Rep Comt, Tenn
b Nashville, Tenn, Aug 16, 34; s George Gaines McLean & Grace Kindred M; m 1955 to Carole Leta Henry; c Jim T, Jr, Kerry S & Pamela K. Educ: Tenn Tech Univ, 54-55. Polit & Govt Pos: Chmn, Davidson Co Rep Comt, Tenn, 74- Bus & Prof Pos: Bd dirs, Home Builders Asn, Tenn, 73-75; bd dirs, Nashville Apt Asn, 75-76; vpres, Nashville Middle Tenn Home Builders, 75-76; bd dirs, Nat Asn Home Builders, 75-77. Mil Serv: Entered as Airman, Air Nat Guard, 53, released as Staff Sgt, 58, after serv in 118th Tactical Recognaissance Wing. Mem: Al Menah Shrine Temple; Nashville Mid-Tenn Home Builders Asn; Masonic Blue Lodge. Relig: Protestant. Mailing Add: 4032 Yoest Dr Nashville TN 37207

MCLEAN, RICHARD CAMERON (D)
b Denver, Colo, Nov 6, 31; s Leslie Robert McLean & Alberta Payne M; m 1955 to Carolyn Lee Lindseth; c Scott Cameron & Joan Carolyn. Educ: Stanford Univ, BA, 54; Univ Colo, LLB, 58; Phi Alpha Delta; Alpha Sigma Phi. Polit & Govt Pos: Law clerk, Tenth Circuit, US Court of Appeals, 58; Dem precinct committeeman, Colo, 60-65; mem, Dem Exec Comt, Boulder, Colo, 63-65; chmn, Boulder Co Dem Cent Comt, 65-66; chmn, Boulder Co Dem for McCarthy, 68; Councilman, Boulder City, 69-72, Mayor, 72-74. Bus & Prof Pos: Lawyer, Sheldon, Bayer, McLean & Glasman, 59- Mil Serv: Entered as 2nd Lt, Army, 55, released as 1st Lt, 57, after serv in Post QM, Ft Carson, Fifth Army, 56. Mem: Am & Colo Bar Asns; Law Club of Denver; Defense Research Inst; Int Asn Ins Counsel. Relig: Congregational. Mailing Add: 2345 Kohler Dr Boulder CO 80303

MCLELLAN, ROBERT (R)
b Kearney, Nebr, Mar 11, 23; both parents deceased; m 1946 to Helen Joyce Kidd; c Margaret, Jennifer, William & Katherine. Educ: San Jose State Col, BS, eng, 49; Santa Clara Grad Sch Bus, 52-53; Stanford Univ Grad Sch Bus, summer 59. Polit & Govt Pos: Dep asst secy for bus develop, Dept of Com, 69-70, asst secy domestic & int bus, 70-72. Bus & Prof Pos: From sales engr & sales mgr to gen mgr, FMC Int, 49-69, vpres, 60-69. Mil Serv: Aviation Cadet, Army, 44-46; Am Theatre Serv Medal; Good Conduct Medal; Victory Medal TAG TWX. Mem: President's Comn Personnel Interchange; Bd Foreign Serv; Foreign Direct Investment Appeals Bd; Econ Defense Adv Comt; Adv Comt Int Bus Prob. Relig: Protestant. Mailing Add: 526 Greenwood Ave Kenilworth IL 60043

MCLEMORE, CARL RAY (R)
Chmn, Lawrence Co Rep Party, Ala
b Moulton, Ala, Mar 1, 22; s Robert Emmett McLemore & Estie Sparks M; m 1952 to Jeffie Cowart; c Carla Susan, Stephen Ray & Lee Jeffrey. Educ: Samford Univ, BS, 54. Polit & Govt Pos: Chmn, Lawrence Co Rep Party, Ala, 67- Bus & Prof Pos: Pharmacist, York's Pharm, Birmingham, 52-53; pharmacist, Moulton Drug Co, 53-57; pharmacist & owner, The Drug Shop, 57- Mil Serv: Army. Mem: Nat Asn Retail Druggists; Mason; VFW; Boy Scouts; Am Legion. Mailing Add: 101 M St SE Moulton AL 35650

MCLENDON, JAMES ANDREW (D)
Ill State Rep
b Washington, Ga, May 7, 06; s Toombs McLendon & Fannie Willis M; m 1943 to Elnora Davis. Educ: Fisk Univ, AB; Northwestern Univ Sch of Law, JD; Alpha Phi Alpha; Frogs Club. Polit & Govt Pos: Master in Chancery, Chicago, Ill; Ill State Rep, currently. Mil Serv: Entered as Pvt, Army, 41, released as Maj, 46, after serv in Off of Judge Advocate Gen; Lt Col (Ret), Army Res; Army Commendation Medal. Mem: Chicago, Ill State, Am & Cook Co Bar Asns. Relig: Protestant. Legal Res: 1015 E Hyde Park Blvd Chicago IL 60615 Mailing Add: 100 N LaSalle St Chicago IL 60602

MCLENNAN, ROBERT M (R)
Calif State Assemblyman
b Shreveport, La, Dec 1, 15; s Walter P McLennan & Annie Horton M; m 1940 to Frances Powers; c Twyla (Mrs Thompson), Doug & Lee. Educ: Columbia Univ, BS; Loma Linda Univ, MD, 42. Polit & Govt Pos: Calif State Assemblyman, 73- Bus & Prof Pos: Physician, Southgate, Calif, 46-72. Mil Serv: Entered as 1st Lt, Army Air Corps, released as Capt, after serv in Pac Theatre, World War II. Mem: Am Acad Family Physicians; Los Angeles Co Med Asn; YMCA Century Club; Macpherson Soc. Honors & Awards: Outstanding Legislator, Calif Rep Assembly, 75, Los Angeles Co Fedn Rep Women, 75 & Orange Co Fedn Rep Women, 75. Relig: Seventh Day Adventist. Mailing Add: 8201 Fourth St Downey CA 90241

MCLEOD, DANIEL R (D)
Attorney Gen, SC
b Sumter, SC, Oct 6, 13; s Daniel Melvin McLeod & Bertie Estelle Guyton M; m 1962 to Virginia Barrett. Educ: Wofford Col; Univ of SC, LLB, 48. Polit & Govt Pos: Asst Attorney Gen, SC, 50-59, Attorney Gen, 59- Mil Serv: Navy, 40-45. Mem: SC, Richland Co & Am Bar Asns; SC Arch Coun. Relig: Methodist; Mem Off Bd, Washington St Methodist Church. Mailing Add: 4511 Landgrave Rd Columbia SC 29206

MCLEOD, DOROTHY THOMAS (R)
Cong Dist Chmn, Rep Party of Fla
b New Brunswick, NJ, Sept 29, 33; d Charles Williams Thomas & Betty Vallely T; m 1951 to Lorn Eugene McLeod; c Thomas Patrick & Laurie Susan. Educ: Palm Beach Jr Col, 62-63. Polit & Govt Pos: Precinct committeewoman, Palm Beach Co Rep Exec Comt, 62-70, dist committeewoman & chmn, formerly; vchmn, Young Rep of Palm Beach Co, 63-64; area chmn, Goldwater for President, 64 & Kirk for Gov, 66; chmn, Teens for Nixon, Palm Beach Co, 68; treas, Rep Club of the Palm Beaches, 68-69; area chmn, Palm Beach Co Rep Coord Comt, 68-70; campaign chmn, Bill James for Fla State Sen & Bill Cramer for US Sen, 70; alt deleg, Rep Nat Conv, 72; cong dist chmn, Rep Party of Fla, 72- Bus & Prof Pos: Lectr, Palm Beach Co, 67-69; dist mgr, 1970 Census, Palm Beach Co, 70. Mem: Rep Club & Young Rep Club of the Palm Beaches; Lantana Rep Club; Palm Beach Co Heart Asn (area chmn, 66-72). Honors & Awards: Girl of the Year, Beta Sigma Phi, Palm Beach Co, 64. Relig: Unity. Legal Res: 1011 Hansen St West Palm Beach FL 33405 Mailing Add: 3607A S Dixie Highway West Palm Beach FL 33405

MCLEOD, GEORGE CECIL, JR (D)
Miss State Sen
Mailing Add: Leakesville MS 39451

MCLEOD, PEDEN BROWN (D)
SC State Rep
b Walterboro, SC, Sept 3, 40; s Walton James McLeod, Jr & Rhoda Lane Brown M; m 1962 to Mary Waite Hamrick; c Mary Carlisle, Peden Brown, Jr, Rhoda Lane & John Reaves. Educ: Wofford Col, AB, 62; Univ SC Law Sch, JD, 67; Blue Key; Kappa Alpha Order. Polit & Govt Pos: Law clerk, US Dist Judge C E Simons, Jr, Charleston, SC, 67-69; city councilman, Walterboro, 70-72; secy, Colleton Co Dem Party, 70-72; SC State Rep, Colleton Co, 72-, mem ways & means comt, SC House of Rep, currently. Bus & Prof Pos: Attorney-at-law, Jeffries, McLeod, Unger & Fraser, Walterboro, 69-; dir, First Nat Bank in Orangeburg, Walterboro Br, 72. Mil Serv: Entered as 2nd Lt, Army, 62, released as 1st Lt, 64, after serv in 519th M I Bn, Third Army, 63-64. Mem: Colleton Co Bar Asn (secy, 69-); Moose; Elks; Lions; Am Legion (comdr, 71-72). Honors & Awards: Sr Order of Gnomes, Wofford Col, 62; Distinguished Serv Award, Walterboro Jaycees, 72. Relig: Methodist. Legal Res: 512 Hampton St Walterboro SC 29488 Mailing Add: Box 230 Walterboro SC 29488

MCLEOD, R C (R)
Mem, NDak State Rep Exec Comt
b Cando, NDak, June 13, 20; s D F McLeod & Emma O Reedy M; m 1943 to Mary Helen Bourdette; c Martha J (Mrs Eschweiler), Ronald B & Charles D. Educ: Univ NDak, BS, 41; Phi Delta Theta. Polit & Govt Pos: Secy, Dist Ten Rep Comt, NDak, 50-66, vchmn, 66-70, chmn, 70-74; mem, NDak State Rep Exec Comt, 70- Bus & Prof Pos: Secy-mgr, Towner Co Abstract Co, 46- & Farmers Mutual Ins Co, Cando, NDak, 63-; pres, NDak Asn Farm Mutual Ins Co, 65. Mil Serv: Entered as Pvt, Army, 43, released as NCO, 45, after serv in ETO, 44-45. Mem: Mason; Shrine; Am Legion; VFW; Elks. Relig: Methodist. Mailing Add: Cando ND 58324

MCLEOD, STEVEN BOYD (D)
Vt State Rep
b Barre, Vt, Aug 29, 50; s Harrison Lowell McLeod & Myrtle Boyd M; m 1972 to Kyle Ann Ingram. Educ: Boston Univ, BA, 72. Polit & Govt Pos: Vt State Rep, 73- Bus & Prof Pos: News-sports reporter, The Times-Argus, Barre, Vt, summer 68-72, 72-; promoter-gen mgr, Thunder Rd Int Speedbowl, 73- Publ: Five articles on Vermont's approach to environmental conservation, 5/15/72, Three articles on the devastating development of one of Vermont's most beutiful mountains, 7/19-21/72 & Series of articles on future development in Vermont, 1/73, The Times-Argus. Mem: Sigma Delta Chi; Common Cause; Friends of Spruce Mt. Honors & Awards: Dean's List, Boston Univ, 3 times. Mailing Add: 135 East St Barre VT 05641

MCLEOD, WILLIAM JAMES (D)
SC State Rep
b Timmonsville, SC, Mar 24, 19; s William Rogers McLeod & Ellen Byrd M; m 1948 to Sara A Carmichael; c William J, Jr & Martha A. Educ: Furman Univ, 36-39; Univ SC, LLB, 42; Omicron Delta Kappa; Kappa Alpha; Phi Delta Phi. Polit & Govt Pos: City recorder, Dillon, SC, 53-61; mem, co bd educ, Dillon Co, 61-63; mem & treas, Dunbar Mem Libr, Dillon, 63-; SC State Rep, Dillon Co, 66- Mil Serv: Entered as Pfc, Marine Corp, 42, released as Capt, 46, after serv in Pac Theatre, 43-46; SC Nat Guard, 49-, Col; Am Defense & Am Theater Medals; Asiatic Pac Theatre Ribbon with Two Battle Stars; Victory Medal; Army of Occup; Res Medal. Mem: Lions; Am Legion; VFW; CofC; Dillon Co Farm Bur. Relig: Methodist. Mailing Add: 600 E Jackson St Dillon SC 29536

MCLEOD, WILLIAM LASATER, JR
La State Rep
b Marks, Miss, Feb 27, 31; s William Lasater McLeod & Sara Macauley M; m 1962 to Lady Marilyn Cissie Qualls; c Sara Nelson, Martha Ellen & Ruth Elizabeth. Educ: Princeton Univ, BA magna cum laude, 53; La State Univ, JD, 58; Sigma Alpha Epsilon. Polit & Govt Pos: La State Rep, 34th Dist, 68- Mil Serv: Entered as Pvt, Army, 53, released as Cpl, 55, after serv in Field Artil. Mem: Salvation Army Adv Bd; Kiwanis; Southwest La Bar Asn (exec comt, 74-75); Calcasieu Area Coun Boy Scouts Exec Comt. Honors & Awards: Outstanding Young Man of Lake Charles, Lake Charles Jaycees, 64; Layman of the Year, Lake Charles Kiwanis, 71; Silver Beaver, Calcasieu Area Coun Boy Scouts, 75. Relig: Presbyterian; Elder, First Presby Church. Legal Res: 1614 22nd St Lake Charles LA 70601 Mailing Add: PO Box 3006 Lake Charles LA 70601

MCLEOD, WILLIAM MULLINS (D)
b Walterboro, SC, Aug 1, 42; s Walton James McLeod, Jr & Rhoda Lane Brown M; m 1965 to Maxine Walker Green; c Maxine Walker & William Mullins, Jr. Educ: Wofford Col, BA, 65; Univ SC Law Sch, JD, 68; Phi Delta Phi; Kappa Alpha Order. Polit & Govt Pos: Admin asst & dist adminr to US Rep Mendel J Davis, SC, 71- Bus & Prof Pos: Lawyer, Jefferies, McLeod, Unger & Fraser, 68- Mil Serv: Entered as 2nd Lt, Army Mil Intel, 68, released as 1st Lt, 70, after serv in 1st Field Force, Vietnam II Corps, 69-70; Capt, Army Res, Judge Adv Gen Corps, 70; Nat Defense Serv Ribbon; Vietnam Campaign Ribbon; Vietnam Serv Medal & Bronze Star. Mem: Am Judicature Soc; SC & Am Bar Asns; Am Legion; Shrine; Scottish Rite Mason (32 degree). Honors & Awards: SC All-State Football, 58; Fla All-City Football, City of Jacksonville, 60; Fla All-State Football, 60; Mark M Bradley Mem Award, Hall of Fame, Bolles Sch, 61. Relig: Methodist. Mailing Add: 311 Woodlawn St Walterboro SC 29488

MCLIN, CLARENCE JOSEF, JR (D)
Ohio State Rep
b East St Louis, Mo, May 31, 21; s Clarence Josef McLin, Sr & Rubie Thomas M; div; c Rhine Lana, Scherrie & Clarence Josef, III. Educ: Va Union Univ; Cincinnati Col of Embalming, grad. Polit & Govt Pos: Ohio State Rep, 36th Dist, currently; vchmn, Montgomery Co Dem Exec Comt; chmn, Dem Voters League; deleg, Dem Nat Conv, 68; chmn, Montgomery Co Voter's Registr Comt; first Negro appointee, House Rules Comt, Ohio State Dem Exec Comt; spec adv to Gov for minority group appointments, 70; co-chmn with John Glenn for Citizens for Gilligan for Gov; dir, Off of Minority Affairs, Ohio Dem Party, currently; deleg, Dem Nat Mid-Term Conf, 74. Bus & Prof Pos: Pres & mgr, McLin Funeral Home, Inc; bd mem, Goodwill Industs. Mil Serv: Entered as Pvt, Army, 42, released as Pfc, 44; Good Conduct Medal; ETO Medal. Publ: Guest columnist for the J Herald, series of 3 articles, 70. Mem: Elected Black Dem of Ohio (pres); Montgomery Co Funeral Dir Asn; Masonic Harmony Lodge, F&AM 77; VFW; Int Elks. Honors & Awards: One of the first elected Dem leaders; Outstanding Serv Award, US Marine Corps Recruiting Serv, 68. Relig: Baptist. Mailing Add: 1130 Germantown St Dayton OH 45408

MCLOONE, PHILIP JOSEPH (D)
Exec Treas, Miss Dem Party
b Brooklyn, NY, May 13, 21; s Philip McLoone & Mary Ferry M; single. Educ: Epiphany Col, 37-41; Cath Univ, Washington, DC; St Joseph Sem, Washington, DC, 41-47. Polit & Govt Pos: Deleg, Miss Loyalist Conv, 68; exec treas, Miss Dem Party, 68- Bus & Prof Pos: Asst pastor, New Orleans, La, Pass Christian, Miss, St Joseph, La, Beaumont, Tex, NALM & Washington, DC; pastor, St Joseph, Glenarden, Md, St Philip, New Orleans, La & Our Mother of Mercy, Pass Christian, Miss, currently. Mem: Pass Christian Progressive Civic League. Relig: Roman Catholic. Mailing Add: 3521 19th St Gulfport MS 39501

MCLOSKEY, ROBERT T (R)
b Monmouth, Ill, June 26, 07; s John A McLoskey & Lillian Shawler M; m 1929 to Elizabeth Dickson; c Robert D, Anne (Mrs Romine), Margaret Gail (Mrs McNitt) & Mary Alice (Mrs Toal). Educ: Monmouth Col, BS, 28; Theta Chi. Polit & Govt Pos: Mem bd, Co Tax Rev, Ill, 36-40; mem bd gov, Ill Young Rep, 40-44; field supvr, Ill Dept of Health, 41-48; alt deleg, Rep Nat Conv, 44 & 48; mem, Co Bd of Supvr, 48-50; co chmn, Rep Party, 50-60; Majority Whip, Ill Gen Assembly, 50-62; US Rep, Ill, 62-64. Bus & Prof Pos: Asst to pres, Bank, 29-32; funeral dir, Lugg & Holliday, 36-50; farm mgt, self-employed, 58-71; consult, Ill Coun for Branch Banking & Ill Tobacco Distributors, 65-71. Mem: Elks; Low Twelve Club; RAM; Farm Bur; CofC. Relig: Methodist. Mailing Add: RR 2 Lake Warren Monmouth IL 61462

MCLUCAS, JOHN L (R)
Secy of the Air Force
b Fayetteville, NC, Aug 22, 20; m 1946 to Patricia Newmaker Knapp; c Pamela (Mrs Jeffrey O Byers), Susan, John & Roderick. Educ: Davidson Col, BSc, 41; Tulane Univ, MSc in Physics, 43, Pa State Univ, PhD in Physics, 50. Polit & Govt Pos: Dep dir of defense research & eng, Tactical Warfare Progs, Dept of Defense, 62-64; Asst Secy Gen for Sci Affairs, NATO Hq, Paris, France, 64-66; Under Secy of the Air Force, 69-73, Secy of the Air Force, 73- Bus & Prof Pos: Co-founder or founder, several small businesses; vpres & tech dir, Haller, Raymond & Brown, Inc, State College, Pa, 50-57; pres, HRB-Singer, Inc, 58-62; pres & chief exec officer, Mitre Corp, Bedford, Mass & McLean, Va, 66-69. Mil Serv: Off, Navy, 43-46. Publ: Auth of numerous scientific articles. Mem: Fel Inst of Elec & Electronics Engrs; Chief Exec Forum; Nat Acad of Eng; Am Phys Soc; Am Inst of Aeronaut & Astronaut; Opers Research Soc of Am; Sigma Pi Sigma; Sigma Xi. Honors & Awards: Received Distinguished Pub Serv Award, Dept of Defense, 64 & Distinguished Pub Serv Award (First Bronze Palm), 73. Mailing Add: 6519 Dearborn Dr Falls Church VA 22044

MCMAHON, JAMES K (R)
Maine State Rep
Mailing Add: 41 Grove St Kennebunk ME 04043

MCMAHON, JAMES ROBERT, JR (D)
Chmn, Bourne Dem Town Comt, Mass
b Hartford, Conn, Oct 31, 29; s James R McMahon & Marion Edna Ryan M; m 1952 to Theresa Marie Prusko; c James Robert, III, William Joseph, Mary Theresa, John Thomas & Christine. Educ: Suffolk Univ, BS in bus admin; Suffolk Law Sch, JD, 70; Wig & Robe Soc. Polit & Govt Pos: Chmn, Dem Town Comt, Bourne, Mass, 56-64 & 68-; chmn, Barnstable Co Dem Comt, 57-58; Mass State Rep, Third Barnstable Dist, 65-66; mem, Finance Comt, Bourne, 65-66 & 72-, overseer pub welfare, 68, selectman & assessor, 68-70; deleg, Mass Dem State Conv, 70, mem speaker's staff, 72. Bus & Prof Pos: Attorney-at-law, Buzzards Bay, Mass, 71- Mem: Mass, Boston & Am Bar Asns; Mass Trial Lawyers Asn. Relig: Catholic. Mailing Add: 25 Canal View Rd Buzzards Bay MA 02532

MCMANIMON, FRANCIS J (D)
NJ State Assemblyman
Mailing Add: State House Trenton NJ 08625

MCMANUS, ANTHONY AIDAN (R)
NH State Rep
b Dover, NH, Mar 4, 39; s Patrick Henry McManus & Mary Cavanaugh M; m 1965 to Patricia Mary Dunigan; c Meghan, Brendan & Moira. Educ: Georgetown Univ, grad, 60; Boston Col Law Sch, grad, 63. Polit & Govt Pos: City attorney, Dover, NH, 67-73; mem adv comt, NH Rep State Comt, 73-74, mem steering comt, 75-; NH State Rep, 73-, vchmn judiciary comt, 73-; Strafford Co Rep chmn, 75- Bus & Prof Pos: Pub defender, Boston, 64-66; attorney, Dover, NH, 66- Mem: Am Bar Asn; NH Bar Asn (mem bd gov, 74-); Am Trial Lawyers Asn. Mailing Add: 52 Old Rochester Rd Dover NH 03820

MCMANUS, DONALD FRANCIS (D)
Exec Committeeman, Broome Co Dem Comt, NY
b Binghamton, NY, Dec 23, 17; s David F McManus & Agnes McCabe M; m 1958 to Ruth M Spalt; c Edward F, Kevin J & Maureen A. Educ: Georgetown Univ, BSS, 40; Union Univ, Albany Law Sch, LLB, 47. Polit & Govt Pos: Vchmn, Binghamton Housing Authority, NY, 50-52, counsel, 52-; chmn, Dem City Comt, Binghamton, 57; chmn, Broome Co Dem Comt, 57-63, exec committeeman, 57-; chmn, Sixth Judicial Dist Conv, 58-65; deleg, Dem State Conv, 58-66; deleg, Dem Nat Conv, 60, alt deleg, 64; judge, City Court, 64; counsel, Binghamton Urban Renewal Agency, 64-66; Dem cand for Justice, Supreme Court, Sixth Judicial Dist, 66. Mil Serv: Entered as Pvt, Army, 42, released as 1st Lt, 45; Asiatic-Pac Campaign Ribbon; Am Campaign Ribbon. Mem: Am, NY & Broome Co Bar Asns; Catholic Charities, Broome Co; KofC. Relig: Roman Catholic. Legal Res: 11 Edgebrooke Rd Binghamton NY 13903 Mailing Add: 29 Riverside Dr Binghamton NY 13901

MCMANUS, ELEANOR AGATHA (D)
Committeewoman, SDak Dem State Cent Comt
b Kimball, SDak, Dec 12, 94; d Simon Morgan & Catherine Coyle M; m to Leo McManus, wid; c Donna (Mrs William Tyrrell), Patricia (Mrs John Lehecka), William & Laverne (Mrs Harold Stone). Polit & Govt Pos: Vol worker for Sen George McGovern, SDak, mem staff, 68; worker for Robert Kennedy, Hubert Humphrey & Truman; campaign mgr, Kermit Sande, Attorney Gen, SDak; campaigned for Gov Kneip 2 times; membership chmn, Beadle Co Dem Women, 66-; committeewoman, Beadle Co Dem Comt, Hurin Precinct Two, 68-; committeewoman, SDak Dem State Cent Comt, 72-; alt deleg, Dem Nat Conv, 72. Bus & Prof Pos: Grade sch teacher, 7 years. Mem: Am Legion Auxiliary; St John's Hosp Auxiliary (membership chmn, 70-, pink lady chmn, 60-); St Martins Altar Soc; Cath Daughters. Honors & Awards: Lady Dem of SDak, SDak Fedn Dem Women, 72; Award for 1000 hours vol work, St John's Hosp, 72. Relig: Catholic. Legal Res: 578 Fourth St SW Huron SD 57350 Mailing Add: PO Box 359 Huron SD 57350

MCMANUS, JAMES HENRY (D)
Chmn, Tillman Co Dem Party, Okla
b Henrietta, Tex, Dec 4, 21; s John Henry McManus & Frances Ann Kelly M; m 1943 to Juanita E Calloway; c Carolyn Julane (Mrs Eddie Whitworth) & Joanna (Mrs Donnie Lawson). Educ: Chattanooga High Sch, grad. Polit & Govt Pos: Chmn, Tillman Co Dem Party, Okla, 67-; secy-treas, Okla, RR Maintenance Authority, 71- Bus & Prof Pos: Owner, Okla Farmers Union Agency, 57- Mil Serv: Entered as Pvt, Army, 42, released as T/Sgt, 46, after serv in 12th Armoured Div, ETO, 44-46; Good Conduct Medal; ETO Ribbon with Four Battle Stars. Mem: Mason (32 degree); Scottish Rite: (action comt); Kiwanis (past pres, Frederick); Am Legion Post 49 (finance officer); hon mem Tillman Co 4-H Club. Relig: Southern Baptist. Legal Res: 517 N 17th Frederick OK 73542 Mailing Add: Drawer F Frederick OK 73542

MCMANUS, JOHN BARTHOLOMEW, JR (D)
Chief Justice, NMex Supreme Court
b Wichita, Kans, June 13, 19; s John B McManus & Mary E Ressler M; m Mary Calnan; c Nancy, Jack, Terry Ann & Rick. Educ: Univ NMex, grad, 40; Georgetown Univ Law Sch, JD, 47; Delta Theta Phi; Sigma Chi. Polit & Govt Pos: Mem, NMex State Rep, 51-53; presiding judge, Second Judicial Dist Court, Albuquerque, 55-71; assoc justice, NMex Supreme Court, Santa Fe, 71-73, chief justice, 73- Mil Serv: Entered as Seaman 2/C, Navy, 41, released as Lt Comdr, 45, after serv in Naval Aviation, Pac Area. Mem: Am & NMex Bar Asns; Nat Conf of State Trial Judges (chmn, 67); NMex Judicial Conf (pres, 64-66); Elks; Am Legion. Honors & Awards: Outstanding Alumnus of Year, Georgetown Univ Law Ctr, 67. Relig: Catholic. Legal Res: 410 W San Mateo Dr Santa Fe NM 87501 Mailing Add: PO Box 848 Santa Fe NM 87501

MCMANUS, JOHN P (D)
Conn State Rep
Mailing Add: 16 Jesswig Dr Hamden CT 06514

MCMANUS, LEWIS NICHOLS (D)
WVa State Deleg
b Beckley, WVa, Sept 8, 29; s Joab L McManus & Mattie Ferguson M; single. Educ: Beckley Col; Morris Harvey Col, BA magna cum laude, 56. Polit & Govt Pos: WVa State Deleg, 64-, chmn, Finance Comt, WVa House of Deleg, 69-, Speaker, 71-; mem gov bd & exec comt, Southern Conf, Coun of State Govt, currently. Bus & Prof Pos: Gen ins bus. Mem: WVa Asn Realtors; WVa Hist Drama Asn (bd dirs, 67-); Elks; Moose; AF&AM. Relig: Presbyterian. Legal Res: 114 King St Beckley WV 25801 Mailing Add: PO Box 1818 Beckley WV 25801

MCMANUS, RICHARD JAMES (D)
b Brooklyn, NY, Apr 16, 45; s Richard Albert McManus & Janet Doris Cutler M; m 1967 to Mary Catherine Hinck. Educ: Yale Univ, BA, 67; Harvard Univ, JD, 72. Polit & Govt Pos: Munic leader, Monmouth Beach Dem Comt, NJ, 71-72; deleg, Dem Nat Conv, 72; exec bd mem, Monmouth Co Young Dem, 73-; deleg, Dem Nat Mid-Term Conf, 74. Bus & Prof Pos: Teacher, Mater Dei High Sch, New Monmouth, NJ, 68-69; news reporter, The Daily Register, Red Bank, NJ, 69-70; law secy, Appellate Div, Superior Court of NJ, 72- Mil Serv: Pfc, Army Res, 4 years. Mem: NJ State & Monmouth Co Bar Asns. Relig: Catholic. Mailing Add: 108 Hartsborne Rd Locust NJ 07760

MCMASTER, ARTHUR THOMAS (R)
Ill State Rep
b Oneida, Ill, June 21, 18; s A T McMaster & Hannah Eck M; m 1943 to Catherine O'Connor; c Tom, III, Mary (Mrs Stein), Peggy, James D & Martha. Educ: Knox Col; Phi Delta Theta. Polit & Govt Pos: Tax assessor, Copley Twp, Ill, 52-60, supvr, 60-70; chmn, Knox Co Bd Supvr, 66-70; chmn, Knox Co Bd Tax Rev, 66-70; Ill State Rep, 47th Dist, 71-, minority spokesman counties & townships legis comt, 73- Mem: Ill Asn Supvr & Co Comnr; Knox Co Fair Asn (dir, 69-); Knox Co Hist Sites Asn (dir, 70-); Mason (Past Master); Farm Bur. Relig: Presbyterian. Mailing Add: RR Oneida IL 61467

MCMASTER, FITZ-JOHN CREIGHTON (D)
Chmn, Fairfield Co Dem Party, SC
b Winnsboro, SC, June 13, 29; s Spencer Rice McMaster & Mary Frances Williford M; m 1955 to Anne Ashe Edmunds; c Sally Anne, William Spencer & Esther Ashe. Educ: Duke Univ, AB, 51; Omicron Delta Kappa; Kappa Alpha Order. Polit & Govt Pos: City comnr, Winnsboro, SC, 58-64; chmn, Fairfield Co Dem Party, 67- Bus & Prof Pos: Mgr, Winnsboro Petroleum Co, 53-69; trustee, Francis Marion Col & Col of Charleston; dir, Merchants & Planters Bank, 72- Mil Serv: Entered as 2nd Lt, Marines, 51, released as 1st Lt, 53, after serv in First Marine Div, Fleet Marine Forces, Pac, 52-53. Mem: Rotary; US Jaycees; CofC. Relig: Methodist. Mailing Add: 406 W High St Winnsboro SC 29180

MCMATH, GEORGE NOTTINGHAM (R)
Chmn, Rep Party Va
b Onley, Va, Aug 28, 32; m to Emma Allen Harlan; c Two daughters. Educ: Randolph-Macon Acad; Univ Va, BA; Am Univ, MA. Polit & Govt Pos: Va State Deleg, formerly; chmn, Rep Party Va, currently. Bus & Prof Pos: Pres, Eastern Shore News, Inc; pres, Va Press Asn, formerly; pres, Eastern Shore Indust Develop Corp; bd dirs, Farmers & Merchants Nat Bank. Mil Serv: Army, 54-56. Honors & Awards: Named Virginia's Most Outstanding Young Man, 65. Relig: Methodist. Mailing Add: Accomac VA 23301

MCMATH, SIDNEY S (D)
b Magnolia, Ark, June 14, 12; s Hal Pierce McMath & Nettie Sanders M; m to Anne Phillips; c Sandy, Phillip, Bruce & twins, Melissa & Patricia. Educ: Pub Schs of Hot Springs, Ark, 12 years; Univ Ark; Univ Ark Law Sch, 36; Blue Key; Sigma Alpha Epsilon. Polit & Govt Pos: Prosecuting attorney, 18th Judicial Dist of Ark; Gov of Ark, 48-51; nat chmn, Water Resources Conserv & Develop Comn; chmn, Interstate Oil Compact Comn; Ark State chmn, Humphrey-Muskie for President Campaign, 68; deleg, Dem Nat Conv, 68. Mil Serv: Marines, serv in Southwest Pac in World War II, 40-46, Maj Gen, Marine Corps Res, 46-71; Silver Star; Legion of Merit. Mem: Am Trial Lawyers Asn; fel, Int Acad of Trial Lawyers; VFW; Am Legion; Mason. Honors & Awards: One of 10 Outstanding Young Men of Am selected by Jr CofC, 49. Relig: Methodist. Legal Res: 711 W Third St Little Rock AR 72201 Mailing Add: 22 E Palisades Dr Little Rock AR 72207

MCMILLAN, BRUCE (R)
Wyo State Rep
Mailing Add: Riverview Rd Box 73 Riverton WY 82501

MCMILLAN, CLARA GOODING (D)
b Brunson, SC, Aug 17, 94; d William James Gooding & Mary Webb G; m 1916 to Thomas Sanders McMillan; wid; c Thomas S, Jr, James C, William Gooding, Edward Webb & Robert Hampton. Educ: Confederate Col; Flora McDonald Col. Polit & Govt Pos: US Rep, SC, 39-41; with Off Govt Reports, 42; info specialist, Off War Info, 42-45; legis asst, US Dept of State, 45-57. Bus & Prof Pos: Teacher, SC Pub Schs, 15-16. Relig: Presbyterian. Mailing Add: 2402 Hagood Ave Barnwell SC 29812

MCMILLAN, COLIN R (R)
NMex State Rep
Mailing Add: 714 Petroleum Bldg Roswell NM 88201

MCMILLAN, GEORGE (D)
Ala State Sen
Mailing Add: 1550 First Nat Southern Natural Bldg Birmingham AL 35203

MCMILLAN, GILBERT EDWARD (GIL) (R)
SC State Sen
Mailing Add: 402 Colleton Ave Aiken SC 29801

MCMILLAN, JOHN L (D)
b Mullins, SC, Apr 12, 02; s M L McMillan & Mary Alice Keith M; m 1936 to Margaret English. Educ: Univ NC; SC Univ Law Sch. Polit & Govt Pos: US Rep, SC, 39-73; US Rep Interparliamentary Union, London, 60 & Tokyo, 61; chmn, Dist Comt; vchmn, Agr Comt; Dean, SC Cong Deleg. Mem: Mason; 40 et 8; F Sexton Am Legion Post. Relig: Baptist. Legal Res: 410 Spruce St Florence SC 29501 Mailing Add: 4740 34th St N Arlington VA 22207

MCMILLAN, JOHN MURPHY, JR (D)
Ala State Rep
b Mobile, Ala, July 6, 41; s John Murphy McMillan, Sr & Madie Troutman M; m 1965 to Edith Kathryn Turner; c John Murphy, III & William Fleming. Educ: Southwestern at Memphis, BA in Econ, 63; Kappa Sigma. Polit & Govt Pos: Co comnr, Baldwin Co, Ala, 69-72; Ala State Rep, 74- Bus & Prof Pos: Dir, Southeastern Lumber Mfr Asn, 74- Mil Serv: S/Sgt, Ala Air Nat Guard, 187th TRG, 63-69. Mem: Bay Minette Kiwanis Club (pres, 70); Mason; Ala Dem Club; Ala Forestry Asn. Relig: Presbyterian. Mailing Add: PO Box 253 Stockton AL 36579

MCMILLAN, WANDA GOUGH (D)
Committeewoman, Western Dist Dem Exec Comt, Mont
b Helena, Mont, Jan 5, 34; d Page Albion Wilson & Fern Blanchard W; single; c Kim Marie, Joe, III & Page A. Educ: Helena Bus Col, 3 months; Univ Mont, 69. Polit & Govt Pos: Secy, Ravalli City Dem Women, Mont, 61-62, vpres, 63-64, pres, 65-66; secy & majority leader, Mont State Senate, 61-69; precinct committeewoman, Ravalli City Dem Party, 61-, dep registr, 63-, state committeewoman, 64-; vchmn, Ravalli City Dem Cent Comt, 62-64, elec judge, precinct six, 63-; secy, Mont State Dem Women, 63-65; crew leader, civil defense census, Ravalli & Granite; committeewoman, Western Dist Dem Exec Comt, 64- Bus & Prof Pos: Legal secy, Koch & McKenna, Mont, 65-67; Attorney Gerald Schultz, 67-69; vendor, liquor store, 69- Mem: Legal Secretaries; Mt Powell Econ Coun, Off Econ Opportunity (mem, 67-68, chmn, 69). Relig: Episcopal; Treas, St Paul's Episcopal Church. Legal Res: 401 N Second Hamilton MT 59840 Mailing Add: PO Box 414 Hamilton MT 59840

MCMILLAN, WILLIAM H (D)
NC State Rep
Mailing Add: 136 Rosemary Lane Statesville NC 28677

MCMILLEN, NANCY GAIL (D)
b LaPorte, Ind, July 17, 52; d Arthur D McMillen & Mildred Hagerty M; single. Educ: Lake Erie Col, 70- Polit & Govt Pos: Deleg, Dem Nat Conv, 72. Bus & Prof Pos: Caseworker, Lake Co Welfare Dept, Ohio, 72- Mailing Add: 44 Nelson St Painesville OH 44077

MCMILLIN, M JUNE (D)
VChmn, Douglas Co Dem Party, Kans
b Butler, Mo, Feb 7, 21; d L Lloyd Gaines & Ethel Coonrod G; m 1940 to Eugene S McMillin, wid; c Carol J (Mrs Hilton Nuffer) & Daniel A. Educ: Univ Kans, 1 year; Alpha Delta Pi. Polit & Govt Pos: Receptionist, Congressman Newell A George, Washington, DC, 58-60; pres, Douglas Co Dem Women's Club, Kans, 60-62; vchmn, Douglas Co Dem Party, 66-; precinct committeewoman, Lawrence Dem Party, Kans, 66-; secy, Third Dist Fedn Dem Women's Clubs, 66-; publicity chmn, Kans Fedn Dem Women's Clubs, 67-; deleg, Dem Nat Conv, 68; Dem vchmn, Third Dist, 68-70, secy, 72-; mem, Kans State Dem Exec Comt, 68-; mem, Nat Dem Comn on Deleg Selection & Party Structure, currently. Bus & Prof Pos: Advert & receptionist, Sta KLWN, Lawrence, 61-62; mgr & buyer, Kirsten's, 62-66; mgr & buyer, The Alley Shop, 66- Mem: Beta Sigma Phi; Am Legion Auxiliary; Dem Women's Clubs; Kans Dem Century Club; Lawrence CofC. Relig: Protestant. Mailing Add: Rte 4 Box 173 Lawrence KS 66044

MCMULLEN, MARY LOUISE (D)
b Santa Anna, Tex, Oct 23, 31; d Harry Brooks Baker, Sr & Louise Martha Mills B; m 1952 to James Abney McMullen, III; c Wade Hampton & Kay Louise. Educ: Univ Tex, Austin, 49-52; Delta Delta Delta. Polit & Govt Pos: Committeewoman, Tex State Dem Exec Comt, 67-72; chmn Voter Registrn Subcomt & vchmn Woman's Orgn Subcomt; alt deleg, Dem Nat Conv, 68 & 72. Mem: Ft Worth Lawyers Wives Club; Delta Delta Delta Alumnae Asn Ft Worth (pres); Woman's Club; Ft Worth Boys Choir Guild; All Saints Hosp Auxiliary. Relig: Episcopal. Mailing Add: 2432 Colonial Pkwy Ft Worth TX 76109

MCMULLEN, RALPH EDGAR, JR (R)
Nat Committeeman, Nev Young Rep Fedn
b Abilene, Tex, Aug 18, 44; s Ralph Edgar McMullen, Sr & Myra Laurette Donahoe Hobbs M; m 1971 to Vicky Jo Todd. Educ: San Jose City Col, 62-64; W Valley Col, Campbell, Calif, AA; San Jose State Col, BA; Merchandising Club; Student Body pres, San Jose City Col, 64. Polit & Govt Pos: Pres, San Jose City Col Young Rep, Calif, 62; pres, Campbell Young Rep, 65; dir, Calif Rep Assembly, 65; pres, W Valley Col Young Rep, 65; pres, Santa Clara Co Young Rep, 68; state chmn, US Servicemen for Max Rafferty for US Senate, 68; pres, Sparks Young Rep, Nev, 70; state chmn, Youth for Bill Raggio for US Senate, 70; mem, Washoe Co Rep Cent Comt, 70-73; state first vchmn, Nev Young Rep Fedn, 71, state chmn, 72, Nat Committeeman, 73- Bus & Prof Pos: Dept mgr, Sears Roebuck & Co, 69-71; gen mgr, First Chance Co, 71-72; dept mgr, Montgomery Wards, 73- Mil Serv: Entered as Pvt, Army Res, 66, released as S/Sgt, 72, after serv in Nev Air Nat Guard, Combat Support Group, 71-72; Top Secret Clearance, Army Security Agency. Publ: A strong national defense—America's key to freedom, Nat Guardsman, 6/71. Mem: Found for Supersonic & Environ Research (dir, 71-73); Am Security Coun (nat adv bd, 72-73); Am Nat Red Cross (first aid instr, 71-73); Nat Rifle Asn; Young Am for Freedom (chmn, Northern Nev, 73). Honors & Awards: Nat Membership Drive-Div C, Young Rep Nat Fedn, 73; Outstanding Young Man of the Year for 1972, Nev Young Rep Fedn, 73. Mailing Add: 210 Claremont Reno NV 89502

MCMURRAN, LEWIS ARCHER, JR (D)
Va State Deleg
b Newport News, Va, Apr 11, 14; m to Edith Margaret Lea; c Lewis Archer, III & Edith Lea. Educ: Washington & Lee Univ. Polit & Govt Pos: Va State Deleg, 48-, chmn Va adv legis coun, Va House Deleg, formerly, mem, currently; deleg, Dem Nat Conv, 48-68; mem, Dem Nat Platform Comt, 60-68; Comnr, Peninsula Port Authority of Va, formerly; chmn, Va Independence Bicentennial Comn; chmn, State Air Pollution Control Bd, formerly; pres, Young Dem Clubs of Va, formerly. Bus & Prof Pos: Secy-treas & dir, Citizens Rapid Transit Co, formerly; dir, Bank of Va-Peninsula; dir, Bank of Va Corp; dir, Peninsula Savings & Loan Asn. Mil Serv: Naval Res, World War II, Lt Comdr; Bronze Star (Combat V); Navy Commendation Medal. Mem: Peninsula CofC; Peninsula Indust Comn (chmn); Jamestown Found (chmn); Jamestown Corp (chmn, vchmn centennial coun 13 original states); War Mem Mus of Va (trustee). Honors & Awards: Hon officer, Order of the Brit Empire. Relig: Presbyterian. Legal Res: 1109 Riverside Dr Newport News VA 23606 Mailing Add: Rm 400 First & Merchants Bldg 2600 Washington Ave Newport News VA 23607

MCMURRAY, JOHN ODELL (R)
b Oakley, Idaho, May 20, 03; s John A McMurray & Louise Dahlquist M; m 1943 to Virginia Hume; c Michael Kay & John Patrick. Educ: Univ Idaho, BA, 27; Blue Key; Theta Nu Epsilon; Beta Theta Pi. Polit & Govt Pos: Mem, Idaho State Rep Finance Comt, 45-55; finance chmn, Ada Co Rep Party, 56-60; precinct committeeman, 56-61; chmn, Idaho State Rep Cent Comt, 61-69; deleg, Rep Nat Conv, 64, alt deleg, 68. Bus & Prof Pos: Vpres, McMurray Land & Livestock Co, 40-66; vpres & partner, Stein-McMurray Ins Agency, 43-66; mem, State Adv Comt, Small Bus Admin, 56-60; dir, Farmers & Merchants Bank, 69-; civilian aid to Secy of Army, 70-74. Mem: Elks; Arid Club; Hillcrest Country Club. Relig: Latter-day Saint. Mailing Add: 1207 Happy Dr Boise ID 83704

MCMURRAY, KAY
b Mar 18, 18; m to Roberta Jean Rankin; c Kathleen (Mrs Peter Wanger), Julia Lynn & Mollie R. Educ: Stanford Univ, AB, in Polit Sci, 40, Grad Sch Bus, MBA, 48. Polit & Govt Pos: Exec admin, Air Line Pilots Asn, Int, 53-71; consult, Govt Affairs, United Air Lines, 71-72; mem, Nat Mediation Bd, 72-, chmn, currently. Bus & Prof Pos: Co-pilot, United Air Lines, Inc, 40-42, capt, 42-49; asst to pres, Inland Empire Ins Co, 49-53; registered rep, Wegener & Daily, NY Stock Exchange, 49-53; legis rep, Western Hwy Inst, 49-53. Mailing Add: 4101 Cathedral Ave NW Washington DC 20016

MCMURTRIE, ALEXANDER B, JR (D)
Va State Deleg
Mailing Add: Suite 100 4615 W Broad St Richmond VA 23230

MCNAIR, ROBERT EVANDER (D)
Dem Nat Committeeman, SC
b Cades, SC, Dec 14, 23; s Daniel Evander McNair & Claudia Crawford M; m 1944 to Josephine Robinson; c Robert E, Jr, Robin Lee (Mrs Jon C Howell), Corinne Calhoun (Mrs James W Bolinds) & Claudia Crawford. Educ: Univ SC, AB, 47 & LLB, 48. Hon Degrees: Univ SC, Lander Col, Presby Col (SC), Furman Univ & Col Charleston. Polit & Govt Pos: SC State Rep, Allendale Co, 51-62; Lt Gov, SC, 62-65 & Gov, 65-71; chmn, Nat Conf Lt Gov, 65-66; chmn, Southern Regional Educ Bd, 67-68; deleg, Dem Nat Conv, 68 & 72; chmn, Educ Comn of the States, 68-69; chmn, Southern Gov Conf, 68-69 & chmn, Human Resources Comt, 69-70; chmn, Nat Dem Gov Conf, 68-69; states co-chmn, Coastal Plains Regional Comn, 67-68; states co-chmn, Appalachian Regional Comn, 70; vchmn, Dem Nat Comt, 69-70, Dem Nat Committeeman, SC, 70-, Dem Gov rep, Dem Nat Comt, 71-73, Dem Policy Coun, 72-; arrangements chmn, Dem Mid Term Conf, 74. Bus & Prof Pos: Attorney, McNair, Konduros, Corley, Singletary & Dibble, 71-; mem bd dirs, Investors Heritage Life Ins Co of the South, 71-; mem bd dirs, Airco, Inc, South Rwy Systs, R L Bryan Co, Ga-Pac Corps, Bankers Trust of SC & SC Found for Independent Cols; mem bd visitors, Presby Col (SC); mem bd trustees, Baptist Col at Charleston & Univ SC Bus Partnership Found; mem pres adv coun, Columbia Col. Mil Serv: Lt(jg), Naval Res, 42-46, 22 months with 7th Amphibious Forces, Pac Theatre. Mem: Lions; Am Legion; Kappa Sigma Kappa; Mason; Shrine. Relig: Baptist; Deacon & former Sunday Sch Teacher. Legal Res: 11 Sunturf Circle Spring Valley Columbia SC 29206 Mailing Add: Box J-1965 Jefferson Square Columbia SC 29201

MCNALLY, CECIL H (R)
Maine State Sen
Mailing Add: Box 448 Ellsworth ME 04605

MCNAMARA, EDWARD HOWARD (D)
Mayor, Livonia, Mich
b Detroit, Mich, Sept 21, 26; s Andrew Kurcina McNamara & Ellen Gertrude Bennett M; m 1948 to Lucille Yvonne Martin; c Colleen, Michael, Nancy, Kevin & Terence. Educ: Univ Detroit, PhB, 59. Polit & Govt Pos: Pres, Dearborn Twp Sch Bd, 54-59; councilman, Livonia, Mich, 62-, mayor, 70-; deleg, Southeast Mich Coun Govt, 71; chmn, Region III & mem finance & taxation comt, Mich Munic League, 71; mem, Wayne Co Bd Supvr; chmn, Wayne Co Legis Comt; Dem Precinct deleg; mem, Gov Spec Comt Land Use, 71-; mem environ comt, US Conf Mayors, 71-; chmn, Western Wayne Co Mayors Asn, 72- Bus & Prof Pos: With Mich Bell Tel Co, 48-70; mgr customer rels, 64-70; secy, Wil-O-Mac Corp, Livonia. Mil Serv: Entered as A/S, Navy, 44, released as Motor Machinist Mate, 46, after serv in Amphibious Attack Unit, Pac Theatre, 44-46. Mem: Southern Wayne Co CofC (vpres); Metrop Detroit Exec Coun; Rotary; KofC; Jr Achievement Adv Comt. Relig: Catholic. Mailing Add: 16501 Park Dr Livonia MI 48154

MCNAMARA, NELL GUY (D)
Educ: Morehead Col; Western State Col; Eastern State Col, AB, BS; Univ Ky. Polit & Govt Pos: Ky State Rep, 64-70; alt deleg, Dem Nat Conv, 72. Bus & Prof Pos: Teacher & Adminr; nurse's aid. Mem: Am Legion Auxiliary; Jr Red Cross; Womans Div Civil Defense; YWCA; Ky Hist Soc (mem exec comt). Mailing Add: Mt Sterling KY 40353

MCNAMARA, THOMAS R (D)
Va State Sen
Mailing Add: 1235 Virginia Nat Bank Bldg Norfolk VA 23510

MCNAMEE, NIKKI DIANE (D)
b Alexandria, Va, Apr 3, 46; d Gordon Orville Johnson & Inez Evelyn Arness J; m 1973 to Wallace W McNamee. Educ: Univ Md, 68-69. Polit & Govt Pos: Legis asst to US Rep James R Mann, SC, 75-. Mem: Capitol Hill Women's Polit Caucus; Nat Orgn Women. Mailing Add: 608 E St NE Washington DC 20002

MCNAMEE, RUTH B (R)
Mich State Rep
Mailing Add: 1271 Lakeside Birmingham MI 48009

MCNAUL, DAVID ANDREW (D)
Chmn, Clearfield Co Dem Comt, Pa
b Curwensville, Pa, Oct 8, 48; s Robert A McNaul & Eleanor Josephine McKeehan M; single. Educ: Pa State Univ, BS, 69. Polit & Govt Pos: Mem & vpres, Curwensville Borough Coun, Pa, 71-; mem, Community Action, Inc, Clearfield Co, 72-; chmn, Clearfield Co Dem Comt, Pa, 72-; pres, Curwensville Area Recreation Bd, 73-75; mem exec comt, Pa State Dem Comt, 75. Bus & Prof Pos: Teacher, Curwensville Area High Sch, 69- Mem: Pa State, Nat & Curwensville Area Educ Asns; KofC. Relig: Catholic. Mailing Add: 213 State St Curwensville PA 16833

MCNEELY, JAMES MICHAEL (D)
b Detroit, Mich, May 11, 30; s Edward McNeely & Mary L Sullivan M; m 1955 to Marialyce LaRock; c Mary Jo, Michael, Tim, Tom, Beth, Patti & Christopher. Educ: St Norbert Col, BA, 55; Wayne State Univ, MA, 60. Polit & Govt Pos: Dep chmn, Oakland Co Dem Comt, Mich, 62-65; dep chmn, Mich Dem State Cent Comt, 68-69, chmn, 69-73; chmn, 1968 Mich Register & Voter Comt, 68; dir, Nat Citizen's Conf State Legislatures, 73- Bus & Prof Pos: Pub rels, WBAY-TV, Green Bay, Wis, 53-55; teacher, Farmington Pub Schs, Farmington, Mich, 55-62. Mil Serv: Entered as Pvt, Army Inf, 51, released as S/Sgt, 53, after serv in 40th Inf Div, Korea, 52-53; Commendation Medal; Combat Inf Medal; Sygmund Rhee Unit Citation; Presidential Unit Citation. Mem: Mich Educ Asn (regional exec secy, 56-60); Oakland Co Comn on Econ Opportunity (exec dir, 65-68); Polit Sci Asn; Nat Educ Asn; NAACP. Relig: Catholic. Legal Res: 6346 Sporney Dr Brighton MI 48116 Mailing Add: 4722 Broadway Kansas City MO 64112

MCNEELY, JAMES W (D)
WVa State Deleg
Mailing Add: State Capitol Charleston WV 25305

MCNEELY, MATTHEW (D)
Mich State Rep
b Millen, Ga, May 11, 20; s Whaley McNeely & Nina Norton M; m to Beatrice; c Roy, Christopher, Clotelle, Camille & Cynthia. Educ: Highland Park Jr Col; Lansing Community Col, currently. Polit & Govt Pos: Pres, 18th & 20th Wards, Dem Club, Mich; vchmn, 16th Cong Dist Orgn, Detroit, 6 years; mem, Detroit Bd Educ Adv Comt Schs; Mich State Rep, 26th Dist, 64-; assoc speaker pro tempore, Mich House Rep, 69 & 71, speaker pro tempore, 73-, chmn comt ins & mem comts educ, pub utilities, tourist indust rels, legis coun & intergovt rels comt, currently; deleg, Dem Nat Conv, 72. Bus & Prof Pos: Consult, Mich State Bd Escheats; educ dir, Local 306, UAW, 4 years. Mem: Boy Scouts; NAACP; Mich Partners of Alliance (bd dirs); Nat Legis Black Clearing House (exec comt); Conf Ins Legis (secy, 74-). Relig: Baptist. Mailing Add: 3556 S Bassett St Detroit MI 48217

MCNEES, ALLEN (D)
Ala State Rep
Mailing Add: Rte 1 Vernon AL 35592

MCNEIL, JEAN MCINTYRE (R)
Mem, Calif Rep State Cent Comt
b West Kilbride, Ayrshire, Scotland, June 7, 11; d John McIntyre & Jean Cook M; m 1938 to John Edmund McNeil. Educ: Ardrossan Acad, 3 years; Gateside Hosp, Greenock, Scotland, Nurses training, RN. Polit & Govt Pos: Mem, Calif Rep State Cent Comt, 67-; mem, 12th Dist Cong Comt, currently. Bus & Prof Pos: Former staff nurse, Gateside Hosp, Greenock, Scotland, 18 months & former staff nurse, Mearnskirk Glasgow City Hosp; pvt duty nursing, 34-36; nurse & tutor, Mr George Dickinson's Home, Three Gables, York, Eng, 36-38; owner & operator, McNeil Nursing Home, Watsonville, 50-62. Mem: Rebekah; Watsonville Women's Club; Elks Ladies; Watsonville Community Hosp (mem serv league); Pajaro Valley Fedn of Rep Women (mem bd & parliamentarian, currently). Mailing Add: 21 St Francis Dr Watsonville CA 95076

MCNEIL, ROBERT D (D)
Mass State Rep
Mailing Add: State Capitol Boston MA 02133

MCNEILL, WELTON R (D)
b Ada, Okla, May 20, 17; s R H McNeill & Ethel Townsend M; m 1940 to Helen M Sallis; c Randy. Educ: High Sch, grad, 35. Polit & Govt Pos: Chmn, Okmulgee Co Dem Party, Okla, 64-72; alt deleg, Dem Nat Conv, 72. Mil Serv: Pvt, Army, 33-36, Nat Guard, 43-46, Sgt. Mem: United Glass & Ceramic Workers of NAm, AFL-CIO-CLC. Relig: Methodist. Mailing Add: 1016 W Tenth Okmulgee OK 74447

MCNEMAR, GEORGIA ARLONE (R)
b Portsmouth, Va, July 31, 33; d John Holland McNemar & Georgia Cartwright M; single. Educ: Norfolk Div, Col William & Mary; Va Polytech Inst, AA, 52; Wake Forest Col, BS, 54, Wake Forest Col Sch of Law, LLB, 56; Phi Alpha Delta; Pi Kappa Delta. Polit & Govt Pos: Magistrate, Charlotte Twp, Mecklenburg Co, NC, 58-60; ed, NCYR News, NC Young Rep Fedn, 59-60, gen counsel, 60-62; mem, Second Dist Rep Comt, 63-65; Second Dist rep, Young Rep Fedn, Va, 63-65; alt deleg, Rep Nat Conv, 64; hq coord, Rep Campaign Comt, Second Cong Dist, 64; librarian, Div Educ & Training Rep Nat Comt, 65-67; prog planning chmn, Nat Fedn of Rep Women, 68-69; mem staff, Criminal Div, US Dept Justice, 70- Bus & Prof Pos: Attorney-at-law, 56- Publ: Editing & Revision, GOP Leader's Manual, Ed Press, Hyattsville, Md, 66. Mem: NC State & Va State Bar Asns; Eastern Star; Northern Va Club; Int Toastmistress Club. Mailing Add: 216 Sixth St SE Washington DC 20003

MCNICHOL, BERNADETTE O (R)
NH State Rep
b Brooklyn, NY, July 20, 43; d Charles Kaiser & Margaret Oliver K; m 1965 to Robert Richard McNichol; c Bernadette Margaret & Mark Charles. Educ: New Eng Col, BS, 65; Newman Club (vpres). Polit & Govt Pos: Sch bd clerk, Bow, NH, currently; NH State Rep, 75- Bus & Prof Pos: Teacher, New York, NY, Bow, NH & North Sutton. Mem: Am Asn Univ Women (legis state chmn, 74-); Nat Order of Women Legislators. Relig: Catholic. Mailing Add: Allen Rd Bow NH 03301

MCNICHOLS, STEPHEN L R (D)
b Denver, Colo, Mar 17, 14; s William H McNichols & Cassie F Warner M; m 1942 to Marjory Roberta Hart; c Stephen L R, Robert M, William H, Mary Elizabeth & Marjory. Educ: Regis Col, PhB, 36; Cath Univ Am, LLB, 39. Polit & Govt Pos: Agt, Fed Bur Invest, 40; dep dist attorney, Denver, Colo, 41; from spec asst to Attorney Gen, US Dept Justice, 46-48; Colo State Sen, 49-54; Lt Gov, Colo, 54-56; Gov, Colo, 56-63; chmn, Nat Gov Conf, 59-60 & 60-61; Dem Nat Committeeman, Colo, until 72; nominee, US Sen, Colo, 68; deleg, Dem Nat Conv, 68. Bus & Prof Pos: Attorney, Denver, Colo, 48- Mil Serv: Lt Comdr, Navy, 41-46; Bronze Star. Mem: Am Bar Asn; Am Legion; VFW; Elks; KofC. Mailing Add: 400 Hilton Office Bldg Denver CO 80202

MCNULTY, MICHAEL ROBERT (D)
Mem, NY State Dem Comt
b Troy, NY, Sept 16, 47; s John Joseph McNulty, Jr & Madelon Frances Reinfurt M; m 1971 to Nancy Ann Lazzaro; c Michele Marie. Educ: Col of the Holy Cross, AB in Polit Sci, 69. Polit & Govt Pos: Staff mem comt on educ, NY Dem State Const Conv, 67; exec asst to Mayor, Green Island, NY, 69-70, supvr, Town of Green Island, 70-; deleg, Dem Nat Conv, 72; mem, NY State Dem Comt, 74- Bus & Prof Pos: Licensed rep, Berkshire Life Ins Co, Pittsfield, Mass, 70-; pres, Green Island Ins Agency, NY, 70-; registered rep, Berkshire Equity Sales, Inc, Pittsfield, Mass, 72-; licensed real estate rep, McNulty Real Estate, Green Island, NY, 73- Mem: Nat & NY State Asns of Ins Agents, Inc; Supvr & Co Legislator's Asn of the State of NY; Watervliet Rotary (vpres, 73, pres, 75); Sunnyside Ctr of Troy (dir, 71-). Relig: Roman Catholic. Mailing Add: 25 Swan St Green Island NY 12183

MCNUTT, D GAYLE (D)
b Comanche, Tex, Oct 4, 36; s Luther E McNutt (deceased) & Willie B Newby M; m 1958 to Esther R Edwards; c Linda, Gaye & Larry. Educ: Tex A&M Univ, BA, 59; Sigma Delta Chi. Polit & Govt Pos: Press secy, Lt Gov of Tex, 68-69; dir commun, Tex Dept Ment Health/Retardation, 69-70; admin asst to US Rep Bob Casey, Tex, 74- Bus & Prof Pos: Mil affairs ed, Abilene Reporter-News, Tex, 59-60; state ed, Capitol Bur Chief, Houston Post, Tex, 60-66; pub rels assoc, Tex Mid-Continent Oil & Gas Asn, 66-67; news ed, Dow Jones & Co, New York, 67-68; polit ed, Houston Chronicle, Tex, 70-74. Publ: Numerous articles dealing with polit affairs, publ by nat & regional newspapers & mag. Mem: Nat Press Club; Press Club of Houston; Burro Club; US House Rep Admin Asst Asn. Honors & Awards: Distinguished Reporting of Pub Affairs Award, Nat Polit Sci Asn, 63. Relig: Episcopal. Legal Res: 7318 Troulon Houston TX 77036 Mailing Add: 2256 Rayburn House Off Bldg Washington DC 20515

MCOMBER, W GORDON (D)
Mont State Sen
Mailing Add: Fairfield MT 59436

MCPARTLIN, ROBERT F (D)
Ill State Rep
b Chicago, Ill, Nov 2, 26; m to Geraldine Cronin; c Nine. Educ: St Ignatius High Sch; Campion High Sch, Prairie du Chien, Wis. Polit & Govt Pos: Ill State Rep, currently. Mil Serv: Marine Corps, 43-46. Mem: Amvets; KofC; Int Munic Signal Asn; IBEW. Mailing Add: 1104 N Lockwood Ave Chicago IL 60651

MCPEEK, BILLIE FAYE (D)
Mem, Orange Co Dem Cent Comt, Calif
b Morrilton, Ark, Feb 9, 31; d John Albert Spier & Hessie Hill S; m 1950 to Nathaniel Keith McPeek; c Michael Dwayne & Patrick Keith. Educ: Univ Calif, Irvine, 71-72; Golden West Col, Huntington Beach, AA, 72. Polit & Govt Pos: Vpres, Dem Women of Orange Co, Calif, 71-72, pres, 73-; del, Dem Nat Conv, 72; mem, Calif Dem State Comt, 72-74; mem, Orange Co Dem Cent Comt, 74- Bus & Prof Pos: Vpres, Credit Women's Breakfast Club NAm, 63-64, pres, 64. Mem: Epsilon Sigma Alpha, Int (educ dir, Alpha Theta, Bakersfield, Calif, 58, treas, Eta Lambda, Cortez, Colo, 59). Honors & Awards: Merit Award, Heart Asn, Cortez, 55; Cert of Merit, United Jewish War Vet, 70. Relig: Roman Catholic. Legal Res: 7140 Kelton Way Stanton CA 90680 Mailing Add: PO Box CI Westminster CA 92683

MCPHERSON, HARRY CUMMINGS, JR (D)
b Tyler, Tex, Aug 22, 29; s Harry Cummings McPherson & Nan Hight M; m 1952 to Clayton Read; c Courtenay & Peter. Educ: Univ of the South, BA, 49; Columbia Univ, 49-50; Univ of Tex Law Sch LLB, 56; Blue Key; Phi Alpha Delta; Sigma Alpha Epsilon. Hon Degrees: DCivil Laws, Univ of the South, 65. Polit & Govt Pos: Gen counsel, Senate Dem Policy Comt, 60-63; Dep Under Secy of the Army, Int Affairs, 63-64; Asst Secy of State, Educ & Cultural Affairs, 64-65; spec asst to the President, 65-66, spec counsel to the President, 66-69; vchmn bd trustees, John F Kennedy Ctr for Performing Arts, 69-; mem bd trustees, Woodrow Wilson Int Ctr for Scholars, 69-; mem bd dirs, coun on Foreign Rels; chmn, Domestic Affairs Task Force, Dem Adv Coun Elected Officials, Dem Nat Comt, currently. Bus & Prof Pos: Partner, Law Firm of Verner, Liipfert, Bernhard & McPherson, Washington, DC, 69- Mil Serv: Entered as Pvt, Air Force, 50, released as 2nd Lt, 53, after serv in Tactical Air Command, 52-53 & Hq, Europe, 53; Army Distinguished Civilian Serv Award, 64. Publ: Auth, A Political Education, Atlantic-Little, Brown, 72. Mem: Tex & DC Bar Asns; Coun on Foreign Rels. Honors & Awards: Arthur S Flemming Award, One of Ten Outstanding Young Men in Govt, 67. Relig: Episcopal. Mailing Add: 30 W Irving St Chevy Chase MD 20015

MCPHERSON, MICHAEL CLAUDE (D)
b St Louis, Mo, Nov 1, 31; s Earl C McPherson & Daisy L Bell M; div; c Tracy Ann. Educ: Stowe Jr Col, 49-52; Rutgers Univ, BS, 54; Alpha Phi Alpha. Polit & Govt Pos: Admin asst to US Rep William L Clay, Mo, 69- Bus & Prof Pos: Cartographer, Aeronaut Chart & Info Ctr, St Louis, Mo, 55-62; ins consult, Mutual of NY, 62-69. Relig: Catholic. Legal Res: 4642 Newberry Terr St Louis MO 63113 Mailing Add: 328 Cannon House Off Bldg Washington DC 20024

MCPHERSON, THOMAS ALLEN (D)
Fla State Rep
b Bement, Ill, Mar 26, 35; s A T McPherson & Doris Luttrell M; m to Sally Ann Webb; c Margaret Carol & Thomas Allen, Jr. Educ: Stetson Univ, BS, 58; Delta Sigma Phi. Polit & Govt Pos: Mayor, Cooper City, Fla, 63-65; Fla State Rep, 64-66 & 72- Bus & Prof Pos: Owner, Happy Cackle Egg Ranch, Cooper City, Fla, 58-; pres, High Rent Corp, currently; pres, Play Patch, Inc, 61- Mil Serv: Entered as 2nd Lt, Army, 58, released as 1st Lt, 59, after serv in Inf. Mem: Kiwanis; Farm Bur; Elks. Relig: Methodist. Mailing Add: 5273 SW 106th Ave Cooper City FL 33314

MCPHERSON, WILLIAM HAUHUTH (R)
Mem, Solano Co Rep Cent Comt, Calif
b Bremerton, Wash, May 16, 22; s James Gunn McPherson & Hertha Hauhuth M; m 1971 to Kim Denison; c Jon Lindsey, Jeanne Ann, Wendy Lou, Christina Marie & Nicette Keri. Educ: Shanghai Am Sch, China, grad, 40; Stanford Univ, AB in econ & hist, 48, JD, 51; Phi Alpha Delta. Polit & Govt Pos: Vpres, Calif Rep Assembly, 57-58; mem, Solano Co Rep Cent Comt, 52-, chmn, 54-56 & 64-66; mem, Calif State Rep Cent Comt, 54-66; chmn, Solano Co Nixon for President Comt, 72; mem, Gov Task Force Comt for Maritime Acad, 72. Bus & Prof Pos: Instr, Continuing Educ of Bar, Univ Calif; chmn, Solano Col Site Selection Comt, Calif, 66; pres, Vallejo Merchants & Property Owners Asn, 68-69; mem bd of gov, Calif Maritime Acad, 68, chmn, 69- Mil Serv: Entered as Pvt, Army, 43, released as Capt, after serv in ETO; Bronze Star with Oak Leaf Cluster; Combat Inf Badge; Commendation Medal. Mem: Am Bar Asn; Am Trial Lawyers Asn; Commonwealth Club of San Francisco; NBay United Crusade (dir, 56-64); Elks. Mailing Add: 7781 Silverado Trail Napa CA 94558

MCQUADE, HENRY F
Chief Justice, Idaho Supreme Court
b Pocatello, Idaho, Oct 11, 15; s Joseph McQuade & Mary Ellen Farnan M; m to Mary Elizabeth Downing; c Sharon (Mrs Leon Grisham), Dr Michael, Frances (Mrs Donald Horan), Robert, Joseph, Peter & William. Educ: Univ Idaho, BA, 40, LLB, 43. Polit & Govt Pos: Justice of the Peace, Latah Co, Idaho, 37-43; prosecuting attorney, Bannock Co, 47-51; judge, Fifth Judicial Dist, 51-56; justice, Idaho Supreme Court, 56-, chief justice, 71-72 & 75-; mem, Comn Nat Criminal Justice Standards & Goals, 71-73; app by President, Nat Hwy Traffic Safety Adv Comn, 72-75. Mil Serv: Entered Army, 43, released as Capt, 46, after serv in Intel Div, Sixth Army. Mem: Phi Alpha Delta; Am Red Cross (pres, Boise chap, 69-70). Mailing Add: Supreme Court Bldg 451 W State St Boise ID 83720

MCQUADE, J STANLEY (R)
Mem, Maine State Rep Comt
b Boston, Mass, Sept 28, 32; s John McQuade & Pearl G Flagg M; m 1955 to Rita E Pfeifer; c Glenn A. Educ: Indust Tech Sch, Boston, 50-51. Polit & Govt Pos: Mem, Saco Rep City Comt, 69-, publicity chmn, 70, chmn, 70-71; vchmn, York Co Rep Comt, 70-72; mem, Maine State Rep Comt, 71-, chmn, Exec Comt, formerly. Bus & Prof Pos: Mgr, Rockingham Elec Supply Co, Portland, 72- Mil Serv: Entered as Pvt, Army, 53, released as Sgt, 54, after serv in 40th Inf Div & KMAG, Korean Conflict, 53-54; Commendation Medal. Mem: AF&AM (Past Master). Relig: Protestant. Mailing Add: 451 Ferry Rd Saco ME 04072

MCQUADE, MARIAN HERNDON (R)
Sgt at Arms, Nat Fedn Rep Women
b Caperton, WVa, Jan 18, 17; d Charles Clarence Herndon & Lucille Dickerson H; m 1936 to Joseph Leo McQuade; c Shirley Buck (Mrs Davis), Patricia Evelyn, Dona Jo (Mrs Tobiasson), Kathleen Elizabeth, Joel Herndon, Charles Henry, Paul Daniel, William Robert, Thomas Allen, David Ray, Ruth Anne, Mary Virginia, George Richard, Margaret Lucille & Michael Patrick. Educ: Univ Tenn, Knoxville, 68-69. Polit & Govt Pos: Pres, Nicholas Co Rep Women, 60-64; dir, Third Dist Rep Women, WVa; sgt at arms, Nat Fedn Rep Women, 62-; second vpres, WVa Fedn Rep Women, 68-69; pres, Eisenhower Rep Women, Gauley Bridge, 69-; alt deleg, Rep Nat Conv, 72. Mem: Eastern Star; White Shrine of Jerusalem; United Daughters Confederacy; Charlton Heights Woman's Club; Fayette Co Comn on Aging. Honors & Awards: High Sch Honor Soc; WVa Mother of Year; Mrs Southern WVa; First Runner-up Mrs WVa Contest. Relig: Protestant. Mailing Add: Box 338 Gauley Bridge WV 25085

MCQUILLEN, MARY THERESA (D)
b Neah Bay, Wash, Mar 9, 32; d Walter Greene & Florence Tucker G; m 1955 to Ellis John McQuillen; c Teresa, Trudi, Wendy, Walter, Sean & Scott. Educ: Neah Bay High Sch, grad, 50. Polit & Govt Pos: Preinct committeeman, Jefferson Co Dem Party, 66-; state committeewoman, Jefferson Co Dem Cent Comt, 69-73, chmn, Jefferson Co Dem Cent Comt & Club, formerly. Mem: Rhododendron Toastmistress; Int Toastmistress (held off as secy, vpres & pres, 68-72 & secy, Coun Four, 70-71); Port Townsend Swim Club Parents; Asn of Concerned Townspeople. Honors & Awards: Cert for nomination Man of the Year Award, CofC, 70. Relig: Presbyterian; Held all offices from Circle Chairman to Presbyterial Pres, 66-73, Ruling elder on session; First Church 72- Mailing Add: 442 Cass St Port Townsend WA 98368

MCREYNOLDS, ELIZABETH SANFORD (R)
First VChmn, Shoshone Co Rep Cent Comt, Idaho
b Reno, Nev, Jan 15, 30; d John Sanford & Myrtle Helen Brooks S; m 1950 to Lauren Hall McReynolds, Jr; c Anne, Mary, James, Margaret & Graham. Educ: Univ Ore, BA, 50; Pi Lambda Theta. Polit & Govt Pos: Vchmn, Gooding Co Rep Cent Comt, Idaho, 58-60, precinct committeeman, 58-61, secy, 60-61; precinct committeeman, Shoshone Co Rep Cent Comt, 62-69, state committeewoman, 64-66, first vchmn, currently; pres, West Shoshone Rep Women, 63-65, exec dir, 65-69; chmn, First Dist, Idaho Fedn Rep Women, 64-66; vchmn, Idaho State Rep Cent Comt, 65-72; mem, Idaho Coun for Hosp Construction, 69; alt deleg, Rep Nat Conv, 72. Bus & Prof Pos: Teacher, Codornices Sch, Albany, Calif, 50-53; piano teacher, Kellogg, Idaho, 62-; kindergarten teacher, AAUW Kindergarten, 67; teacher, Sch Dist 391, 69- Mem: Calif & Nat Educ Asns; PEO. Mailing Add: 518 Second St Kellogg ID 83837

MCSPADDEN, CLEM ROGERS (D)
b Bushyhead, Okla, Nov 9, 25; s Herbert T McSpadden & Madalyn Palmer M; m 1962 to Donna Marie Casity; c Barton Casity. Educ: Univ Tex, BA; Redlands Univ; Okla State Univ, degree in animal husbandry. Polit & Govt Pos: Okla State Sen, 54-72, Asst Floor Leader, Okla State Senate, 61 & 63, Pres pro-tempore, 65-67, chmn, Appropriations & Budget Comt, 68-69; deleg, Dem Nat Conv, 68; US Rep, Okla, 72-75; deleg, Dem Nat Mid-Term Conf, 74. Bus & Prof Pos: Owner, Cattle Ranch, Northeastern Okla; nat TV sportscaster for world wide rodeos; rodeo announcer; vpres & dir, Cattlemen's Life Ins Co, Oklahoma City, 61-; contract dir, Rodeo Cowboy's Asn, 63-; real estate & property developer; gen mgr, Nat Finals Rodeo, Oklahoma City. Mil Serv: Navy V-12. Relig: Methodist. Mailing Add: RR 1 Chelsea OK 74016

MCSPEDON, THOMAS G (D)
Committeeman, Westchester Co Dem Comt, NY
b Yonkers, NY, Jan 29, 18; s Frank D McSpedon & Catherine Carroll M; m 1944 to Alice Gorman; c Thomas J. Educ: US Army Schs, Evening Adult Educ Classes. Polit & Govt Pos: Committeeman, Westchester Co Dem Comt, NY, 40-; mem, Bd Supvr, Westchester Co, 54-66, Dem minority leader, 60-61 & 64-65; Dem cand, NY State Assembly, 62; committeeman, NY State Dem Comt, 64-67; Dem cand, Mayor, Yonkers, 65; alt deleg, Dem Nat Conv, 64 & 68; chmn, Yonkers Dem City Comt, 67-70. Bus & Prof Pos: Various bldg & construction trades; supvr maintenance & dir, Munic Housing Authority, 60; secy, Job Develop Corp Yonkers, currently; chap mgr, Westchester-Fairfield Chap of Nat Elec Contractors Assoc, 70- Mil Serv: Entered as Pvt, Army, 43, released as T/Sgt, 46, after serv in Artil & Transportation Corps, Am & ETO, 43-45; Am Theatre Ribbon; European Theatre Ribbon; Good Conduct Medal. Mem: Am Legion; UN Asn; Elks; CofC; March of Dimes Heart Fund. Honors & Awards: Distinguished Serv Award Westchester Co; Citation Meritorious Serv, Am Legion. Relig: Roman Catholic. Mailing Add: 48 Emmett Pl Yonkers NY 10703

MCVEY, LAUDER TULLY (R)
b Vancouver, BC, June 7, 24; s James Lelin McVey & Belle Hukill Dilg M; m 1946 to Clara Elizabeth Chason; c Lauder Tully, Jr & Scott Douglas. Educ: Fla State Univ, 2 years; Univ of Fla, BIE, 53. Polit & Govt Pos: Chmn, Lowndes Co Rep Party, Ga, formerly. Bus & Prof Pos: Design engr, Food Machinery & Chem Corp, Lakeland, Fla, 53-55; indust engr & asst supt of power, Owens-Ill, Valdosta, Ga, 55- Mil Serv: Entered as Pvt, Army Air Force, 43, released as Cpl, 46, after serv in Detached Serv, 11th Air Force, Alaska, 43-46. Relig: Baptist. Mailing Add: 2314 N Toombs St Valdosta GA 31601

MCVEY, WALTER LEWIS, JR (R)
b Independence, Kans, Feb 19, 22; s Walter Lewis McVey & Nona Inge M; 2nd m 1964 to Velma Graham; c by 1st m Walter L, III & David Ayers. Educ: Univ Kans, AB, 47, LLB, 48, JD, 68; grad student, Ga State Univ, currently. Polit & Govt Pos: Kans State Rep, 49-52; Judge, Independence, Kans, 52-56; Kans State Sen, 57-61; US Rep, Third Dist, Kans, 61-63; exec dir, Fulton Co Rep Party, Ga, 64-65. Bus & Prof Pos: Attorney-at-law, Independence, Kans, 48-61; consult, Melpar, Inc, 63-64; staff counsel, Ga Munic Asn, Atlanta, Ga, 65-66; sr consult, McVey Consult Assocs, Atlanta, 66-; faculty mem polit sci, Ga State Univ & DeKalb Col, 68-, Mercer Univ, 71-73; attorney-at-law, Atlanta, Ga, currently. Mil Serv: Entered as Pvt, Army Air Force, 43, released as S/Sgt, 46. Publ: A federal-aids manual for municipalities, Ga Power Co, 66. Mem: Am, Ga State & Kans State Bar Asns; Am Legion; Elks. Honors & Awards: Nat speaker, McVey Speakers' Bur; photographer with contributions to various publ. Relig: Methodist. Legal Res: 712 E Paces Ferry Rd Atlanta GA 30305 Mailing Add: PO Box 18505 Atlanta GA 30326

MCVICKER, ROY HARRISON (D)
b Edgewater, Colo, Feb 20, 24; s Rev Roy H McVicker, Sr; m to Harriett Runge; c Bill, Theresa & Lisa. Educ: Denver Univ; Columbia Col, Columbia Law Sch. Polit & Govt Pos: Colo State Sen, 56-64; US Rep, Colo, 65-67; dir bi-nat develop, Agency for Int Develop, Dept of State, 67- Bus & Prof Pos: Lawyer, Wheat Ridge Colo, 53- Relig: Methodist. Mailing Add: 14405 Foothill Dr Golden CO 80401

MCVITTIE, WILLIAM JOHN (D)
Calif State Assemblyman
b Chicago, Ill, Oct 15, 38; s James McVittie & Kathleen Coonan M; m 1966 to M Cristina Arrosagaray. Educ: Univ Ill, BS, 60; Univ Southern Calif, JD, 64; Phi Eta Sigma; Phi Kappa Delta (vpres); Evans Scholars (pres); Com Club (pres); Pre-Law Club (pres); Varsity Debate Team; Activities Hon Soc. Polit & Govt Pos: City attorney, Chino, Calif, 70-74; chmn, San Bernardino Co Air Pollution Hearing Bd, 72-74; Calif State Assemblyman, 74- Bus & Prof Pos: Pub acct, Price Waterhouse & Co, Chicago, Ill, 59-60; spec agt, US Treas Dept, Los Angeles, Calif, 60-62; tax acct, Aerojet Gen Corp, Azusa, 62-64; tax attorney, Kaiser Aluminum Corp, Oakland, 64-65; pvt law practice, Chino, 65- Mil Serv: Air Force Res, 56-62. Legal Res: 1688 Redding Way Upland CA 91786 Mailing Add: Suite 5168 State Capitol Sacramento CA 95814

MCWHERTER, NED R (D)
Tenn State Rep
b Dresden, Tenn, Oct 15, 30; s Harmon R McWherter & Lucille Smith M; div; c Mickial R & Mary Lina Coppee (stepdaughter). Educ: Dresden High Sch, grad. Polit & Govt Pos: Tenn State Rep, 68-, speaker, Tenn House Rep, 73- Bus & Prof Pos: Self-employed. Mil Serv: Entered as Pvt, Army Nat Guard, 47, released as Maj, 69. Relig: Methodist. Mailing Add: Cedar St Dresden TN 38225

MCWHORTER, CLAYTON WARD (JIM) (R)
b Siloam Springs, Ark, Feb 24, 39; s Ward Tyler McWhorter & Gladys Clayton M; m 1966 to Michael Sharon Clark; c Clayton Ward, II. Educ: Univ Ark, BSBA, 61; Phi Delta Theta. Polit & Govt Pos: Committeeman, Third Dist Rep Orgn, Ark, 70; chmn, Benton Co Rep Comt, formerly; Rep State Committeeman, formerly; deleg, Rep Nat Conv, 72. Bus & Prof Pos: Sales mgr, Ozark Supply Co, 64-68, pres, 68- Mil Serv: Entered as 2nd Lt, Army, 62, released as 1st Lt, 64, after serv in 2nd Armored Div, Ft Hood, Tex, 62-64; Army Commendation Medal. Mem: Aircraft Owners & Pilots Asn; Bella Vista Country Club; Rogers CofC (agr comt). Relig: Protestant. Legal Res: 911 S 16th St Rogers AR 72756 Mailing Add: PO Box 429 Rogers AR 72756

MCWILLIAMS, CLETUS W (D)
Tenn State Rep
Mailing Add: 125 Third Ave N Franklin TN 37064

MCWILLIAMS, JOHN CECIL (D)
b New Diggings, Wis, Jan 4, 17; s Michael James McWilliams & Emma Jane Sullivan M; m 1942 to Mary Eileen Gille; c John Michael, Linda K, Daniel P, Timothy G, Vickie L & Julie Ann. Educ: New Diggings High Sch, grad, 34. Polit & Govt Pos: Chmn, New Diggings Town Dem Party, Wis, 55-67; mem, Bd La Fayette Co, 55-; various comts such as agr, fair bd, bonds & salaries, health, ment health, welfare & chmn bldg comt, Co Nursing Home, 62; pres, La Fayette Co Fair Bd; pres, Wis Asn Fairs, 67-68; chmn, La Fayette Co Dem Party, Wis,

formerly. Bus & Prof Pos: Mem, Civilian Conserv Corps, 34-35. Mem: FHA (committeeman); KofC (Past Grand Knight). Relig: Catholic. Mailing Add: Rte 1 Shullsburg WI 53586

MEACHAM, SHIRLEY (D)
Ark State Sen
Mailing Add: PO Box 566 Monroe AR 72108

MEAD, LARRY EDWARD (R)
Mo State Rep
b Avon, Ill, Mar 1, 38; s Ralph Donald Mead & Marie McFarland; m 1960 to Kathleen Phillips; c Stuart Blake & Angela Phillips. Educ: Western Ill Univ, BA in Agr, 61; Delta Sigma Phi. Polit & Govt Pos: Chmn, Mid-Mo Coun Govt, 70-; judge, Boone Co Court, 70-72; Mo State Rep, Dist 111, 72- Bus & Prof Pos: Ed, Sheepbreeder & Sheepman Mag, Columbia, Mo, 61- Publ: Several articles, Mo Municipal Review, 73 & 74. Mem: Rotary; CofC. Honors & Awards: Outstanding Local Jaycee President Award, 75; Alumni Achievement Award, Western Ill Univ, 75. Relig: Presbyterian; mem bd deacons. Legal Res: 1815 Highridge Dr Columbia MO 65201 Mailing Add: Rm 102B State Capitol Bldg Jefferson City MO 65101

MEADE, KENNETH ARNOLD (D)
Calif State Assemblyman
b Kentfield, Calif, Sept 27, 38; s Kenneth Jack Meade & Madeline Arnold M; m 1964 to Sharon Gilberd; c Kelly & Tyler. Educ: Univ Calif, Berkeley, AB, 61, Boalt Hall Sch Law, LLB, 64; Big C Soc; Chi Phi; Order Golden Bear. Polit & Govt Pos: Calif State Assemblyman, 12th Dist, 71- Bus & Prof Pos: Sr partner, Meade & Duane. Mem: Calif Trial Lawyers Asn; Calif State & Alameda Co Bar Asns; Boalt Hall Alumni Asn; Oakland Boys Club. Mailing Add: 3923 Grand Ave Oakland CA 94610

MEADER, GEORGE (R)
b Benton Harbor, Mich, Sept 13, 07; s Robert Eugene Meader & Jennie Editha Gibson M; m 1928 to Elizabeth Barbara Faeth; c Robert Eugene & Katherine Elizabeth (Mrs Vandelly). Educ: Ohio Wesleyan Univ, 23-25; Univ of Mich, AB, 27, Law Sch, JD, 31. Polit & Govt Pos: Charter bd mem, Mich Fedn Young Rep, 32; pres, Washtenaw Co Young Rep Club, Mich, 32; prosecuting attorney, Washtenaw Co, 41-43; counsel, Truman-Mead Spec Comt Invest Defense Prog, 43-45; chief counsel, Mead Spec Comt Invest Defense Prog, US Senate, 45-47; chief counsel, Fulbright Subcomt Invest Reconstruction Finance Corp, US Senate Banking & Currency Comt, 50; US Rep, Second Dist, Mich, 51-65; assoc counsel, Joint Comt on Orgn of Cong, 65-67, chief counsel, 67-68; counsel, Joint Comt Cong Opers, 71- Bus & Prof Pos: Counsel, Mich Merit Syst Asn, 39-41. Publ: Review of book entitled Congress, Its Contemporary Role, by Ernest Griffith, Mich Law Review, 6/56; Congressional investigations: importance of the fact-finding process, Univ of Chicago Law Review 51; Limitations on Congressional investigations, Mich Law Review, 4/49. Mem: Am & Dist of Columbia Bar Asns; Washington Kiwanis Club; charter mem, Former Members of Cong; Capitol Hill Club. Honors & Awards: Admitted to practice before US Supreme Court. Relig: Methodist. Legal Res: 3909 Walden Wood Ann Arbor MI 48105 Mailing Add: 3360 Tennyson St NW Washington DC 20015

MEADORS, ALBERT MURRIL (R)
Chmn, Wash Co Rep Cent Comt, Ind
b Salem, Ind, Mar 1, 01; s Elbert W Meadors & Lillie E Colglazier M; m 1928 to Ella Mae Frances Wilt. Educ: High Sch. Polit & Govt Pos: Deleg, Rep State Conv for many years; co relief chmn, co finance chmn, Wash Co Rep Cent Comt, Ind, 50-56, city chmn, 55-59, chmn, 58-; presidential elector, Ninth Dist Ind, 68; treas, Ind Ninth Dist Rep Cent Comt, 71- Bus & Prof Pos: Motor Truck & Bus Business & Wholesale Bus & Farm Produce, 21-50; farmer, 30-; milk procurement mgr, Kraft Foods Co, Chicago, 39-51; milk procurement, Salem Cheese & Milk Co, Salem, Ind, 51-; auto license br mgr. Mem: Red Men; KofP; Farm Bur; Lions (pres, Lion Tamer, 71-); State of Ind Coun, Sagamore of the Wabash. Relig: Christian Church NAm. Legal Res: 103 W Homer St Salem IN 47167 Mailing Add: PO Box 302 Salem IN 47167

MEADOWCROFT, WILLIAM HOWARTH (R)
Mem, Wash State Rep Finance Comt
b Seattle, Wash, Jan 30, 29; s Albert Henry Meadowcroft & Lillian Howarth M; m 1957 to Elizabeth Weyerhaeuser; c Laura Hunt, Elizabeth Mills, Anne Weyerhaeuser, Mark Howarth & David Walker. Educ: Univ Puget Sound; Harvard Bus Sch. Polit & Govt Pos: Co-finance chmn, Pierce Co Rep Finance Comt, 62-64; deleg, Rep Nat Conv, 64; precinct committeeman, Pierce Co Rep Cent Comt, 64-66; mem, Wash State Rep Finance Comt, currently. Bus & Prof Pos: Personnel asst, Weyerhaeuser Co, 49-52, mgr mkt planning, 54-60, new prod div, 60-65, asst to exec vpres, 65-68 & asst to pres, 68-; dir, Puget Sound Nat Bank, Tacoma, Wash, currently; trustee, Tacoma Art Mus. Mil Serv: Naval Air Reserve, 47-54. Mem: Elks; Tacoma Club; Univ Puget Sound (trustee); Wash Athletic Club; Tacoma Golf & Country Club. Relig: Episcopal. Mailing Add: 26 Country Club Dr SW Tacoma WA 98498

MEADOWS, HONEY LOU (D)
b Avery, Tex, Nov 24, 23; d William Elmer Brem & Lydia E Smith B; m 1942 to Noel N Douglas Meadows; c Huey P, Anita K (Mrs Puckett) & Andrea L (Mrs Barrientos). Educ: High Sch, Annona, Tex, 39-42. Polit & Govt Pos: Chmn & deleg, Precinct 72, 71-72; deleg, Dist Ten, Tarrant Co, Tex; deleg, Tex State Dem Conv; alt deleg, Dem Nat Conv, 72. Bus & Prof Pos: Court clerk, Town of Watauga, Tex, 69- Publ: DeKalb & Bowie Counties history & genealogy, 68. Honors & Awards: Distinguished Serv Awards, Tex State Hist Surv Comn, 66, 67 & 68. Relig: Baptist. Mailing Add: 6120 Maurie Circle Watauga TX 76248

MEAGHER, JOHN KIRBY (R)
b Syracuse, NY, Aug 29, 41; s Leo Meagher & Marion Kirby M; m 1964 to Laura Laree Youngblood; c Paul Joseph & Patrick John. Educ: Col William & Mary, AB, 63, Marshall-Wythe Sch Law, JD, 65; Famous Writers Sch, Westport, Conn, Cert of Recognition, 71; Kappa Sigma; Newman Club; Inter-Fraternity Coun. Polit & Govt Pos: Legis asst, US Rep Alexander Pirnie, NY, 65-70; spec asst & cong liaison, Off Secy, Dept Health, Educ & Welfare, Washington, DC, 70-71; dir cong rels, White House Spec Action Off for Drug Abuse Prev, 71-72; Asst Minority Counsel, US House Rep Comt on Ways & Means, 72-74; minority counsel, Ways & Means, 74- Publ: Why a department of human resources is needed now, Phi Delta Kappan, 9/71. Mem: US Supreme Court Bar; Bull Elephants Club; RAMS; Capitol Hill Club. Honors & Awards: Winner of Will Drafting Contest, Va Trust Co, Richmond, 65. Relig: Roman Catholic. Mailing Add: 6210 Foxcroft Rd Alexandria VA 22307

MEAKER, JOHN PALMER (R)
Vt State Rep
Mailing Add: Box 93 Waterbury VT 05676

MEANS, PAUL E (D)
Mass State Rep
Mailing Add: State Capitol Boston MA 20133

MEANS, STEPHEN ARDEN (D)
Mayor, Gadsden, Ala
b Gadsden, Ala, Jan 18, 46; s William Paschael Means & Elizabeth Cameron M; m to Connie Blanton. Educ: Auburn Univ, BA in Foreign Lang, 69; Univ Ala, Gadsden Ctr, 70-; Phi Kappa Tau; Circle K Int. Polit & Govt Pos: Mayor, Gadsden, Ala, 74- Mil Serv: Entered as Midn, Navy ROTC, 64, released 68, after serv in Auburn Univ Unit. Mem: League of Municipalities (exec & legis comt, 75-); Music Educators Nat Conf; Nat Asn Jazz Educators; Nat League of Cities; US Conf Mayors. Relig: Methodist. Legal Res: 605 S Fifth St Gadsden AL 35901 Mailing Add: c/o City Hall Gadsden AL 35901

MEANS, WILLIAM TOWNE (R)
Chmn, St Joseph Co Rep Cent Comt, Ind
b Chicago, Ill, Dec 13, 28; s Charles Edward Means & Ruth Towne M; m 1959 to Francianne Ivick; c Margaret Frances & Rachel Ruth. Educ: Univ Southern Calif, BA, 50; Univ Mich, LLB, 53; Delta Theta Phi. Polit & Govt Pos: City judge, Mishawaka, Ind, 64-72; chmn, St Joseph Co Rep Cent Comt, 72- Mem: Ind State, St Joseph Co & Am Bar Asns. Relig: Methodist. Legal Res: 828 W Mishawaka Ave Mishawaka IN 46544 Mailing Add: 402 Lincoln Way E Mishawaka IN 46544

MEARES, CARL WHITTEN (D)
b Fair Bluff, NC, Sept 10, 07; s Ellis Meares & Minnie Anderson M; m 1939 to Margaret Bracy; c Carolyn, Carl, Jr & Mary Lee. Educ: Mars Hill Col, 27-29; Univ NC, 29-31. Polit & Govt Pos: NC State Sen, 63-66; NC State Hwy Comnr, 66-69; alt deleg, Dem Nat Conv, 72. Bus & Prof Pos: Gen farm supply merchant; operator, tobacco warehouse; Ford automobile dealer; dir, First Union Nat Bank. Mem: Rotary; Shrine; Mars Hill Col (trustee). Relig: Baptist. Mailing Add: Box 187 Fair Bluff NC 28439

MEARS, ROGER CLIFTON, JR (D)
Chmn, Pulaski Co Dem Comt, Ark
b Monticello, Ark, May 21, 25; s Roger Clifton Mears & Linnie Langford M; div; m 1971 to Elsie Weaver; c Vicki Anne & Clifton Wayne Mears & Carl, Michael & Leslie Karen Williams. Educ: Univ Ark Fayetteville, BA, 48; Pi Kappa Alpha; Razorback Booster Club. Polit & Govt Pos: Chmn, Pulaski Co Elec Comn, Ark, 70-; chmn, Pulaski Co Dem Comt, 70-; mem, Ark State Dem Comt, 70-; deleg, Dem Nat Conv, 72. Bus & Prof Pos: Owner, laundry & cleaners, 54-62; agt, Union Life Ins Co, 62-65; secy-treas, Paramount Life Ins Co, 65-66; spec agt, Northwestern Mutual Life Ins Co, 66- Mil Serv: Entered as Pvt, Army, 48, released as noncommissioned officer, 49, after serv in 4th Div, US. Publ: Articles in several co publ. Mem: Million Dollar Round Table; Chartered Life Underwriters Asn (pres); Nat Asn Life Underwriters; Little Rock Life Underwriters Asn (pres); Mason. Relig: Baptist. Mailing Add: 5711 Country Club S Little Rock AR 72207

MEASER, GEORGE JOHN (R)
b Buffalo, NY, June 10, 25; s George J Measer, Sr (deceased) & Eugenie Snyder M (deceased); m 1948 to Joan Moesel; c George J, III, Karen G & Kimberly G. Educ: Rochester Inst Technol, grad, 48. Polit & Govt Pos: Deleg, Rep Nat Conv, 72; chmn, Newspapers to Reelect the President, 72. Bus & Prof Pos: Publ, Bee Publ, Inc, 48-; dir, Niagara Permanent Savings & Loan Asn; mem adv bd, Williamsville Off, Marine Midland-West; pres, Western NY Offset Press, Inc, 62- Mil Serv: Entered as Pvt, Army, 43, released as Pfc, 46, after serv in 88th Inf Div, Italy. Mem: NY Press Asn; Amherst CofC (pres, 72-73); Suburban Bd, Millard Fillmore Hosp (vpres, 72-73); Rotary; VFW; Am Legion. Relig: Roman Catholic. Mailing Add: 120 Oakgrove Dr Williamsville NY 14221

MEBUS, CHARLES FILLMORE (R)
Pa State Rep
b Abington, Pa, June 15, 28; s George Brinker Mebus & Estelle Claxton Negus M; m 1958 to Joy Campbell Robbins; c Lisa Jane Campbell. Educ: Pa State Univ, BS in Chem, 49 & BS in Sanit Eng, 51; Scabbard & Blade; Pershing Rifles; vpres, Sigma Alpha Epsilon, 50-51. Polit & Govt Pos: Mem, Young Rep Club of Cheltenham Twp, Pa, 56-60, mem bd dirs, 56-60, chmn, 60; mem, Montgomery Co Rep Comt, 60-74; mem bd dirs, Young Rep Fedn of Montgomery Co, 60-62, deleg, Pa Young Rep Conv, 60, 62 & 64; Pa State Rep, Third Legis Dist, 64-66, 154th Legis Dist, 66-, mem appropriations, urban affairs & local govt comts, Pa House Rep, currently, minority chmn local govt comt, 75-; mem, Pa State Planning Bd, 71-75; mem, Pa Local Govt Comn, 73- Bus & Prof Pos: Vpres, George B Mebus, Inc, 53-70, pres, 70- Mil Serv: Entered as 2nd Lt, Army Res, 49, released as Capt, 62, after serv in 354th Engrs. Construction Bn, Ger, 52-53; Ger Occup Medal; NATO Ribbon. Mem: Am Soc Civil Engrs; Consult Engrs Coun Pa; Nat Soc Prof Engrs; Am Water Works Asn; Am Soc Testing & Materials. Relig: Episcopal; lay reader, All Hallows Church, Wyncote, Pa. Legal Res: 214 Maple Ave Wyncote PA 19095 Mailing Add: Capitol Bldg Harrisburg PA 17120

MECHAM, LEONIDAS RALPH (R)
b Murray, Utah, Apr 23, 28; s Leonidas DeVon Mecham & Minnie Frame M; m 1950 to Barbara Folsom; c Mark L, Meredith, Richard O, Stephen F & Alison. Educ: Univ Utah, BS magna cum laude, 51; George Washington Univ, JD, 57; Harvard Univ, MPA, 64, fel pub admin, 65-66; Phi Kappa Phi; Phi Eta Sigma. Polit & Govt Pos: Legis asst to US Sen Wallace F Bennett, Utah, 52-58, admin asst & counsel, 58-65; asst to the pres for spec projs, Univ Utah, 65-67, vpres for econ & community develop, 67-69; spec asst to the Secy of Com for Regional Econ Coord, 69; exec secy, Fed Adv Coun on Regional Econ Develop, 69; fed co-chmn, Four Corners Regional Comn, 69-70; adv counsel, Pub Land Law Rev Comn, 69-70. Bus & Prof Pos: Vpres & gen counsel, Olympus Research Corp, Salt Lake City, Utah, 68-69; vpres, The Anaconda Co, 70- Mem: Am Soc Pub Admin; Am Polit Sci Asn; Utah & DC Bar Asns; Bus-Govt Rels Coun. Honors & Awards: Awarded one of the first four & the highest Cong Staff Fels by a bipartisan House-Senate Leadership Adv Comt for the Am Polit Sci Asn, 63. Relig: Latter-day Saint. Legal Res: Salt Lake City UT Mailing Add: 11337 Willowbrook Dr Potomac MD 20854

MECHEM, EDWIN LEARD (R)
b Alamogordo, NMex, July 2, 12; s Edwin Mechem & Eunice Leard M; m 1932 to Dorothy Ellen Heller; c Martha (Mrs M Vigil), John, Jesse (deceased) & Walter. Educ: NMex State

Univ, 30, 31 & 35; Univ Ark, LLB, 39. Polit & Govt Pos: With US Reclamation Bur, 32-35; agt, Fed Bur Invest, Tex, Ark & Calif, 42-45; Gov NMex, 51-54, 57-58 & 61-62; US Sen, NMex, 62-64; deleg, Rep Nat Conv, 68; US Dist Court Judge, 70- Bus & Prof Pos: Lawyer, 39-; partner, Darden, Mechem & Sage, Las Cruces, NMex, 65- Mem: Am Law Inst (mem comt on govt security). Relig: Methodist. Mailing Add: 316 W Parker Rd Las Cruces NM 88001

MEDAIRY, MARK CURTIS, JR (D)
Mem, Dem State Cent Comt, Md
b Baltimore, Md, Feb 2, 53; s Mark Curtis Medairy & Margaret Coakley M; single. Educ: Loyola Col, BS Bus Admin, 75. Polit & Govt Pos: Mem, Dem State Cent Comt, Md, 74- Bus & Prof Pos: Group sales rep, Sun Life Assurance Co of Canada, 75- Mem: Cent Dem Club; Rodgers Forge Community Asn. Relig: Roman Catholic. Mailing Add: 407 Murdock Rd Baltimore MD 21212

MEDDERS, MARION WARDNER (R)
Chmn, Autauga Co Rep Party, Ala
b Marion, Ala, Feb 5, 25; s Marion A Medders & Lola A M; m 1945 to Dorothy B; c Martha Lois, Davis Samuel & Mary Elizabeth. Educ: Cent Wesleyan Col, ThB, 45; Univ Ala; Troy State Col. Polit & Govt Pos: Mem, Ala State Rep Exec Comt, 66-71; chmn, Autauga Co Rep Party, Ala, 66- Bus & Prof Pos: Pastor, Prattville Wesleyan Church; pres, Acme Ins Agency, Prattville; Vet Admin compliance inspector. Mem: Civitan Int. Relig: Wesleyan. Legal Res: 893 Newton St Prattville AL 36067 Mailing Add: PO Box 422 Prattville AL 36067

MEDDERS, VERNON SHERWOOD (D)
Chmn, Bibb Co Dem Exec Comt, Ala
b Bibb Co, Ala, Mar 6, 19; s Minor Medders & M Lula Stewart M; m 1940 to Marguerite Cottingham; c Dan Sherwood & Roselyn (Mrs Pittman). Educ: Bibb Co High Sch, Ala, dipl, 39. Polit & Govt Pos: Chmn, Bibb Co Dem Exec Comt, Ala, 46- Bus & Prof Pos: Owner & operator, Cahaba Plumbing & Supply Co, Centreville, Ala, 46- Mil Serv: Entered as Electricians Mate, Navy, 44, released as EM 3, 46, after serv in Okinawa, 45-46; Warrant Off, Ala Nat Guard, currently; Good Conduct, Expert Rifleman & Okinawa War Time Serv Medals. Mem: Mason; Shrine; Lions Club; Elks (past Exalted Ruler several times). Relig: Southern Baptist. Mailing Add: 161 Riverside Dr Centreville AL 35042

MEDEARIS, ROBERT PARK (D)
Okla State Sen
b Tahlequah, Okla, Aug 17, 30; s Park Hinds Medearis & Carolyn Maratta M; m 1958 to Martha Elizabeth O'Neal; c Suzanne, Robert Park, Jr, John George & Frank Matthew. Educ: Tahlequah Cent High Sch, grad; Northeastern State Col, BA, 52; Tulsa Univ, grad sch, 2 years; Sigma Chi. Polit & Govt Pos: Secy-treas, Cherokee Co Dem Cent Comt, 62-68; Okla State Sen, 68- Bus & Prof Pos: Tulsa Fed Savings & Loan, Okla, 58-61; abstracter & fire casualty agt, Cherokee Capitol, Tahlequah, 61-; mem bd dirs, Liberty State Bank, 65- Mil Serv: Entered as Airman, Air Force, 52, released as Airman 1/C, 56, after serv in Security Serv, Far East Air Force, 54-56. Mem: Am Land Title Asn; CofC; Am Legion; Lions; VFW. Relig: Episcopal. Mailing Add: 1100 N Cedar Tahlequah OK 74464

MEDEIROS, JOHN J (R)
Hawaii State Rep
Mailing Add: House Sgt-at-arms State Capitol Honolulu HI 96813

MEDINA, REYNALDO S (D)
NMex State Rep
b Chama, NMex, Sept 11, 34; s J Florentino Medina (deceased) & Elvira Martinez M; m 1969 to Elvia Vidal Fuentes; c Joseph, IV, Diane, Gregg, Vickie, Kathleen, R Steven & Yolanda. Educ: NMex Highlands Univ, 55-56; Col Santa Fe, AA, 73; AZI; Newman Club. Polit & Govt Pos: NMex State Rep, Dist 41, 73- Mil Serv: Entered as Pvt, Air Force, 51, released as Sgt, 55, after serv in Seventh Fighter Bomber Wing, Korea-Far East Fifth Air Force, 52-55; Sgt, Air Force, 2 years, NY Air Defense Sector; Presidential Unit Citation; Korean, UN, Far East Air Force, China & Singman Rhee Citations; GC Ribbon; Far East Campaign. Mem: DAV; VFW; Jaycees; Job for Vet; KofC. Honors & Awards: All-Am Post Comdr, VFW, 65. Relig: Roman Catholic. Mailing Add: 59 Pinon Dr PO Box 676 Chama NM 87520

MEDLEN, WARREN RICHARD (R)
Chmn, Tenn Young Rep
b Woodbury, Tenn, Sept 6, 44; s Warren Howard Medlen & Margarete Ballentine M; m 1964 to Judy Carolyn Reeder; c Michael Adrian, Warren Edward & Nathaniel Brock. Educ: Cumberland Col; Univ Tenn, Knoxville. Polit & Govt Pos: Mem exec comt, DeKalb Co Rep Party, 68-; participant, Young Rep Leadership Training Sch & Region IV Training Sch, 70, Rep Cong Cand Sch, 70, Young Rep Nat Leadership Conf, 71-75, faculty mem, Tenn Young Rep Workshop, 72 & 74 & Rep Gov Conf, 74; Mid Tenn vchmn, Tenn Young Rep, 71-73, chmn, 73- Bus & Prof Pos: Partner, Southside Nursery, Smithville, Tenn, 65-74, owner, 74-; landscape supt, State Tenn, 71-73. Mem: Tenn & Mid Tenn Nurserymen's Asns; Southern Turfgrass Asn; DeKalb Co Welfare Adv Bd; DeKalb Co Young Rep Club (charter mem). Honors & Awards: Dist Chmn of the Year, Tenn Young Rep, 73. Relig: Methodist. Mailing Add: RR 1 Box 59 Smithville TN 37166

MEDLEY, DOLPHUS CLEVE (D)
SC State Rep
b Gaffney, SC, Aug 18, 23; s Dr Cleve Medley & Ila Bell Reynolds M; m 1947 to Dora Mae West; c Dolphus Carlton, Phillip West, Timothy Tyler, Joseph Shawn, Tonya Clevette & Leandra Alisa. Educ: Robinson Bus Col, 49-51. Polit & Govt Pos: SC State Rep, 71- Bus & Prof Pos: Mgr retail hardware, Mullinax Hardware, 49-61; credit dept, C&S Bank, Gaffney, SC, 61-69, field rep, WOW Life Ins Soc, 69- Mil Serv: Entered as A/S, Navy, 42, released as PO, 45, after serv in USS Murray, SPac, 43-45; 8 Awards; 13 Major Battle Stars. Mem: WOW; Mason; Civitans; Shrine. Relig: Baptist; past chmn bd deacons; Sunday sch teacher; dir training union. Mailing Add: RFD 5 Box 194 Gaffney SC 29340

MEDLOCK, THOMAS TRAVIS (D)
SC State Sen
b Joanna, SC, Aug 28, 34; s M K Medlock & Mayme DuBose M; single. Educ: Univ SC Law Sch, 56-59; Wofford Col, AB, 56; Phi Beta Kappa; Blue Key. Polit & Govt Pos: Asst Attorney Gen, SC, 61-62; SC State Rep, formerly; SC State Sen, 72- Bus & Prof Pos: Pvt law practice, Columbia, SC. Mem: United Cerebral Palsy of Midlands Carolina (pres). Mailing Add: State House Columbia SC 29211

MEEDS, LLOYD (D)
US Rep, Wash
b Dillon, Mont, Dec 11, 27; c Michael R, Marcia L & Michelle Jean. Educ: Everett Jr Col; Gonzaga University of Law, LLB, 58. Polit & Govt Pos: Elec Snohomish Co prosecuting attorney, Wash, 62; dep prosecuting attorney, Spokane & Snohomish Co; US Rep, Wash, 64-; deleg, Dem Nat Conv, 72. Bus & Prof Pos: Lawyer; admitted to Wash State Bar, 58; engaged in pvt practice of law in Everett, Wash, 2 years, in asn of Hunter, Meeds & French. Mil Serv: Navy, 46. Mem: Eagles; Wash State Bar Asn; Snohomish Co Bar Asn (vpres); Snohomish Co Young Dem (former pres); Phi Alpha Delta. Legal Res: Everett WA 98201 Mailing Add: US House of Rep Washington DC 20515

MEEK, ELSIE HELENA (D)
b Burke's Garden, Va, July 18, 27; d Leon Meek & Anna Laura McGinnis M; single. Educ: Marion Jr Col, grad, 47. Polit & Govt Pos: Receptionist, personal secy & caseworker, W Pat Jennings, 55-67; caseworker, Omar Burleson, 67-73; admin asst to US Rep George E Brown, Jr, Calif, 73- Mailing Add: 230 Ninth St NE Washington DC 20002

MEEKER, ANTHONY (TONY) (R)
Ore State Sen
b Amity, Ore, Mar 18, 39; s Phillip Edwin Meeker & Mable Iona Davis M; m 1962 to Carolyn Morton; c Tracy Michelle. Educ: Willamette Univ, BA, 61; Omicron Delta Kappa; Beta Theta Pi. Polit & Govt Pos: Ore State Rep, Fifth Dist, 69-72; Ore State Sen, 72- Bus & Prof Pos: Asst mgr, Burlingham Meeker Co, Amity, Ore, 66-69. Mil Serv: Entered as 2nd Lt, Air Force, 61, released as 1st Lt, 65, after serv in Strategic Air Command & Pac Air Force, US & Vietnam, 65; Two Oak Leaf Clusters; Air Force Commendation Medal. Mem: Am Legion; Lions; CofC; Ore Agr Bus Coun. Relig: Methodist. Mailing Add: 110 Rosedale Amity OR 97101

MEEKER, DAVID OLAN (R)
Asst Secy Community Planning & Develop, Dept Housing & Urban Develop
b Clifton Springs, NY, May 19, 24; s D Olan Meeker & Estelle Niemann M; m 1974 to Esther Stenzler; c Scott, Stone, Brett, Ann & Elizabeth. Educ: Yale Univ Dept Agr, BA, 50; Copenhagen Univ, Fulbright fel for advan study, 61, Grad Sch, cert archit, 62. Polit & Govt Pos: Dir, Model Cities Prog, Indianapolis, Ind, 68-69, dir, Dept Metrop Develop, 70-71, dep mayor, 72-73; Asst Secy Community Planning & Develop, Dept Housing & Urban Develop, 73- Bus & Prof Pos: Vpres, treas & dir, James Assocs, Inc, Architects & Engrs, 56-69. Mil Serv: Entered as Cpl, Army, 43, released as Lt Col(Ret), after serv in ETO, 43-45, Korea, 50-52. Mem: Fel Am Inst Architects; Am Inst Planners; Adv Coun on Hist Preservation; Domestic Coun (chmn, Fed Agency Bicentennial Task Force Subcomt & Long Range Econ Disaster Recovery Task Force). Honors & Awards: Man of Year in Construction, Ind Subcontractors Asn, 69; Good Govt Award, Indianapolis Jaycees, 71; Awards Prog, Prestressed Concrete Inst for Ind Univ Libr, 71; Award for Dedicated Serv & Prof Guid, Ind Limestone Inst of Am, 71. Relig: Presbyterian; Deacon, 69-73. Mailing Add: 210 I St SW Apt 713 Washington DC 20024

MEEKER, JAMES GEORGE (D)
b Jamestown, NDak, July 15, 37; s Donald Betts Meeker & Abigail W Klenk M; m 1960 to Jane F Sheridan; c Jeffrey Lynn, Julie Ann & John Donald. Educ: Jamestown Col, 55-57; Univ NDak, BA, 59; Pa State Univ, 65-66; Blue Key; Beta Theta Pi. Polit & Govt Pos: Admin asst to Sen Quentin N Burdick, NDak, 67-71; staff dir, Senate Judiciary Subcomt on Nat Penitentiaries, 71- Bus & Prof Pos: Dir of news & info, Univ NDak, 60-61; polit reporter, Fargo Forum, 61-65. Mem: US Senate Asn of Admin Asst. Honors & Awards: Fel, Wash Jour Ctr, 66-67. Relig: Presbyterian. Legal Res: 1442 14th St S Fargo ND 58102 Mailing Add: 8405 Buckhannon Dr Potomac MD 20854

MEEKER, LEONARD CARPENTER
b Montclair, NJ, Apr 4, 16; s Irving Avard Meeker & Elizabeth Louise Carpenter M; m 1947 to Christine Rhoda Halliday (deceased); m 1969 to Beverly Joan Meeker; c Richard Halliday, Charles Carpenter, Sarah Louise & Eliza Ann Hunt. Educ: Amherst Col, AB, 37; Harvard Univ, LLB, 40. Hon Degrees: LLD, Amherst Col, 67. Polit & Govt Pos: Off of Gen Counsel, Treas Dept, 40-41; Off of Solicitor Gen, Dept Justice, 41-42; with Off of Legal Adv, Dept State, 46-51, asst legal adv, 51-61, dep legal adv, 61-65, legal adv, 65-69; US Ambassador to Romania, 69-73. Bus & Prof Pos: Attorney, admitted to DC Bar, 40 & Calif Bar, 41. Mem: Am & Fed Bar Asns; Am Soc Int Law; St Nicholas Soc City of New York. Mailing Add: 3000 Chain Bridge Rd NW Washington DC 20016

MEEKS, JOHN NEAL (D)
Chmn, Stark Co Dem Party, Ohio
b Canton, Ohio, July 20, 31; s John H Meeks & Vergie Riel M; m 1958 to Joan D Bullard; c Sandra, John, David & Paul. Educ: Ohio Univ, BSC, 54; Blue Key; Theta Chi. Polit & Govt Pos: Dem precinct committeeman, Stark Co, Ohio, 60-; controller, Stark Co Engr Off, 62-66; mem, Stark Co Dem Exec Comt, 62-; Fed Aid coordr, Stark Co, 66-; vchmn, Stark Co Dem Party, formerly, chmn, 72-; founding mem, Citizens for Humphrey, 68; deleg-at-lg, Dem Nat Conv, 68; mem bd trustees, Multi-Co Juvenile Attention Ctr, 72-; mem exec comt, Ohio Dem Party, currently. Bus & Prof Pos: Gen agt, Mich Life Ins Co, 58-60; pres, McKinley Bus Col, Canton, Ohio, 60-62; pres, JM & Assocs, 66-; chmn, Urbanistics Inc. Mil Serv: Entered as 2nd Lt, Air Force, 54, released as 1st Lt, 57, after serv in 79th Fighter Bomber Squadron, 20th Fighter Bomber Wing, Royal Air Force Sta, Eng, Third Air Force, 55-57, Capt, Air Force Res. Mem: Elks; Ohio Univ Alumni (mem bd trustees); NAACP; Pro Football Hall of Fame Club; Fraternal Order Police Assocs. Honors & Awards: Awards from United Fund of Stark Co, YMCA & Salvation Army; Man of Year Award, Jefferson-Jackson Men's Club; Exec Order of Ohio Commodore. Relig: Presbyterian. Mailing Add: 3926 Harvard Ave NW Canton OH 44709

MEENAN, PATRICK HENRY (R)
Wyo State Rep
b Casper, Wyo, Sept 24, 27; s Hugh Martin Meenan & Margaret Kelly M; m 1950 to Shirley Louise Byron; c Maurya Ann, Kevin Patrick, Michael James & Patricia Kelly. Educ: Univ Notre Dame, BSC cum laude, 49. Polit & Govt Pos: Councilman, City of Casper, Wyo, 56-65, vmayor, 61, mayor, 62 & 65; US deleg, Int Union of Local Authorities, 61; Wyo State Rep, 69-, chmn joint Senate-House corp comt, 73- Bus & Prof Pos: CPA, Raab, Roush & Gaymon, 49-53, partner, 60-69; asst treas, Williston Oil & Gas Co, 53-55; partner, Meenan & Higgins, CPA, 55-60; pres, KATI & KAWY(FM), 64-; partner, Meenan, Miracle & Sherrill, CPA, 75- Mem: Am Inst CPA; Nat Asn Broadcasters; CBS Affil Asn; KofC; Notre Dame Alumni Asn (nat bd dirs, 72-). Honors & Awards: Jaycee Young Man of Year, 62; Distinguished Pub

Servant, 65; Jaycee Boss of Year, 66. Relig: Roman Catholic. Legal Res: 3070 E Fourth Casper WY 82601 Mailing Add: Box 481 Casper WY 82601

MEETZE, GEORGE ELIAS (D)
b Columbia, SC, June 24, 09; s Narvie Elias Meetze & Fannie Belle Leitzsey M; m 1936 to Margaret Allen; c George Allen & William Dagnall. Educ: Univ SC, AB cum laude, 30; NY Theol Sem, STB & STM; Lutheran Theol Southern Sem, 34; Sigma Phi Epsilon; Hermes Club. Hon Degrees: DD, Newberry Col, 56. Polit & Govt Pos: Chaplain, SC State Senate, 50- Bus & Prof Pos: Pastor, St Barnabas' Lutheran Church, Charleston, SC, 34-37, Grace Lutheran Church, Prosperity, 37-42 & Incarnation Lutheran Church, Columbia, 42-74. Publ: Prayers of the Chaplain, SC Senate-Bryan's Publ Co, Vols I-XXIII, 52-75. Mem: Lutheran Church Am (pres bd social missions, SC Synod); Am Cancer Soc (pres, SC Div & nat deleg); Rotary; Heptagon Club; Town & Gown Club. Honors & Awards: Serv to Mankind Award, Sertoma Clubs of Columbia, 71. Relig: Lutheran. Mailing Add: 1518 Wyndham Rd Columbia SC 29205

MEGA, CHRISTOPHER JOHN (R-CONSERVATIVE)
NY State Assemblyman
b US, Nov 15, 30; s Louis Thomas Mega & Palmina Parini M; m 1952 to Madelyn Barbara Friscia; c Christopher Louis, Jeffrey Joseph, Valerie Ann & Jacqueline Marie. Educ: St Francis Col, 48-50; Brooklyn Law Sch, LLB, 53; Phi Delta Phi. Polit & Govt Pos: NY State Assemblyman, 50th Dist, 74-, mem ins, banks, judiciary & elec law comts & select comt interstate coop, NY State Assembly, 75- Mil Serv: Entered as Pvt, Army, 53, released as Cpl, 55, after serv in Inf, Ft Dix. Mem: Bay Ridge Lawyers Asn Inc (pres, 75-); Dyker Heights Civic Asn; Mens Club Bay Ridge; NY State & Am Bar Asns. Honors & Awards: Civic Award, 50th Dist Rep Orgn, 74. Relig: Catholic. Mailing Add: 1022 80th St Brooklyn NY 11228

MEHLHAFF, DEAN O (R)
SDak State Rep
Mailing Add: Eureka SD 57437

MEHRENS, JOHN (SANDY) (D)
Mont State Sen
Mailing Add: 206 Evergreen Anaconda MT 59711

MEHRLE, KENNETH G (D)
b Cape Girardeau, Mo, Aug 19, 25; s Arthur J Mehrle & Anita Schwab M; m 1946 to Bettie L Fulbright; c Deborah Jeanne (Mrs David Headrick), Jane Ann & William Kent. Educ: Southeast Mo Univ; St Louis Col Pharm, BS in Pharm, 48; Kappa Psi. Polit & Govt Pos: Deleg, Girardeau Co Dem Conv, 72-; deleg, Mo Tenth Cong Dist Dem Party, 72; deleg, Mo Dem State Conv, 72; deleg, Dem Nat Conv, 72. Bus & Prof Pos: Pres, Mo State Bd Pharm, 63-65; mem bd dirs, Farmers & Merchants Bank, 70- Mil Serv: Army, 43-45, serv in 75th Div, ETO, 44-45, Purple Heart. Mem: Gamma Pi Chap, Kappa Psi; Nat Asn Retail Druggists (mem exec comt, 72-); CofC (vpres, 70-71); Navy League; Elks. Honors & Awards: Pres Award, Mo Pharm Asn, 64; King of Courtesy Award, Mo Pharm Travelers Asn, 66; Man of the Year Award, Sch Pharm, Univ Mo, 72. Relig: United Church of Christ. Mailing Add: 2460 Brookwood Dr Cape Girardeau MO 63701

MEIDINGER, ROLAND E (R)
b Fredonia, NDak, Apr 15, 13; s John J Meidinger & Amelia M; m 1962 to Shirley E Rolfs; c Andrea J. Educ: Univ of the Pac, BS, 36. Polit & Govt Pos: NDak State Sen, 53-65, mem, Legis Research Comn, NDak State Senate, 55-65; Rep Nat Committeeman, NDak, 63-68; mem, NDak Higher Educ Facilities Comn, 65-67; alt deleg, Rep Nat Conv, 68; deleg, NDak Const Conv, 70; elected deleg, Const Conv NDak & chmn, Comt Educ & Natural Resources, 70-72; civilian aide to Secy Army for NDak, Washington, DC & Presidio, Calif, 71- Bus & Prof Pos: Pres, State Bank of Streeter, 53-68; trustee, Jamestown Col, 56-; pres, R E Meidinger Co Inc, 61-; pres, Stutsman Co State Bank, 65- Mem: Mason; Shrine; Jester; Elks; Rotary. Honors & Awards: Jamestown Chamber Man of Year, 70. Relig: Methodist. Mailing Add: 733 Fifth St NE Jamestown ND 58401

MEIER, BEN (R)
Secy State, NDak
b Napoleon, NDak, Aug 1, 18; s Bernard Meier & Theresia Welzindeger M; m 1944 to Clara Kaczynski; c Lynn & Bernie. Educ: Dak Bus Col; Sch of Banking, Univ Wis. Polit & Govt Pos: Secy State, NDak, 54-; acting gov of NDak, 61; vchmn, Nat Conf States Bldg Codes & Standards, currently. Bus & Prof Pos: Farming, until 41; banking at Napoleon, Gackle & Hazleton, NDak, 8 years; real estate bus, Bismarck, 53-; pres, Mandan Security Bank, 59-70; dir, Dakota Bankers Trust, currently. Mem: Sons of Norway; NDak Heart Asn (chmn); Am Cancer Soc; NDak Bankers Asn; Nat Asn of Contracting Learning Agencies. Honors & Awards: NDak Nat Leadership Award of Excellence, Boys Scout Salute. Mailing Add: 105 Ave E Bismarck ND 58501

MEIER, BILL (D)
Tex State Sen
Mailing Add: 1004 W Euless Blvd Euless TX 76039

MEIER, CLAUDIA MARIE (DFL)
Minn State Rep
b Bismarck, NDak, Nov 6, 47; d Peter M Meier & Helen Kraft M; single. Educ: Col of St Scholastica, 65-66; Univ Minn, BS Nursing, 70. Polit & Govt Pos: Chairperson, Benton City Dem-Farmer-Labor Orgn, 74-75; Minn State Rep, Dist 18-A, 75- Bus & Prof Pos: Staff nurse, Northwestern Hosp, 70-71; mem, Stearns City Pub Health, St Cloud, Minn, 71-73; dir, Benton City Nursing Serv, Foley, 73-74; staff nurse, North Mem, Minneapolis, 74- Mem: Farmers Union; Minn Nurse's Asn; Minn Politically Involved Nurses; Rice Sportsman Club; Little Rock Lake Improv Asn. Relig: Catholic. Legal Res: RR 2 Rice MN 56367 Mailing Add: Rm 331 State Off Bldg St Paul MN 55155

MEIER, ERVIN A (R)
b Milwaukee, Wis, Sept 17, 97; s William Meier & Minnie Mahnke M; m 1928 to Olga Wolf; c Arlene M (Mrs Donald J Koch) & Çorene V (Mrs James O Klippel). Educ: Correspondence college courses. Polit & Govt Pos: Mayor, Wauwatosa, 64-74, & alderman. Bus & Prof Pos: Past immediate pres, League of Wis Munic. Mem: Milwaukee Typographical Union 23; Kiwanis; Mason; Shrine; KofP. Relig: Methodist; United Brethren Church. Legal Res: 2564 North 81st St Wauwatosa WI 53213 Mailing Add: 7725 West North Ave Wauwatosa WI 53213

MEIER, MARGARET KITCHEN (PEGGY) (D)
Committeewoman, Tenn Dem State Exec Comt
b Kingsclear, NB, Can, Dec 17, 31; d Delbert Elmo Kitchen & Ella Plume K; m 1956 to Homer Kay Meier; c Charles Edward, Stephen Frank & Susan Kay. Educ: Univ Tenn, Knoxville, BA, 75. Polit & Govt Pos: Chairperson, Oak Ridge Concerned Dem, 74-; committeewoman, Tenn Dem State Exec Comt, 74- Mem: Proj First Offender (bd dirs, Knoxville, 74-75); Vol Coordr for Anderson Co Juv Court; Roane Co Dem Women's Club (prog chairperson, 72-, legis chmn, 72-); Oak Ridge League Women Voters. Relig: Unitarian; bd dirs, Oak Ridge Unitarian Church, 72- Mailing Add: 113 Normandy Rd Oak Ridge TN 37830

MEIER, WILLIAM HENRY (D)
b Lincoln, Nebr, Dec 23, 04; s Otto William Meier & Mary G Bothwell M; m 1934 to Amelia Mabel Utter; c William E, Joel F & Sarah (Mrs Arnold Peterson). Educ: Univ Nebr, AB, 26, JD, 30; Paladian Lit Soc; Delta Theta Phi. Polit & Govt Pos: Spec agt, Fed Bur Invest, Denver, Colo & Birmingham, Ala, 30-31; Nebr State Rep, 32-34; attorney, Fed Land Bank, Omaha, 34-36; police magistrate, Minden, 38-40; chmn, Kearney Co Dem Cent Comt, 38-40 & 65-74; mem, Nebr State Dem Cent Comt, 40-42, chmn, 50-54 & mem, 54-58; govt appeal agt, Kearney Co Selective Serv, 40-42 & 48-49; asst US Dist Attorney, Omaha, 42-45; mem, Minden Sch Bd, 45-48 & pres, 46-48; mem, Kearney Co Selective Serv Bd, 45-47; Nebr Dem Pres Elector Designate, 48; chmn, Dem First Cong Dist Conv, 48-50; mem, Kearney Co Sch Reorgn Comt, 49-54; co attorney, Kearney Co, 59-67, dep co attorney, 67-74; city attorney, Minden, 70- Bus & Prof Pos: Mem, Matschullat, Meier & Matschullat, Attorneys, Lincoln, 30-33; attorney, Minden, 36-67; partner, Meier & Adkins, Attorneys, 67- Mem: AF&AM: Mason (32 degree); Shrine; Lions; Odd Fellows. Honors & Awards: Man of the Year, Minden CofC, 50; Cong Selective Serv Medal. Relig: Presbyterian. Legal Res: 305 N Tower Ave Minden NE 68959 Mailing Add: PO Box 267 Minden NE 68959

MEIERS, RUTH LENORE (D)
NDak State Rep
b Parshall, NDak, Nov 6, 25; d Axel Olson & Grace Williams O; m 1950 to Glenn E Meiers; c David E, Michael G, Monte C & Scott C. Educ: Univ NDak, BA, 46; Independent Students Asn; Women's Athletic Asn; Social Work Club; YWCA. Polit & Govt Pos: Bd mem, Upper Mo Dist Health Unit, 62-; vchmn, Dist Dem Nonpartisan League, 73-74; NDak State Rep, 75- Bus & Prof Pos: Caseworker, Mountrail Co Welfare Bd, 46-47, dir, 47-51, child welfare worker, 57-64. Mem: NDak Pub Health Asn; NDak Conf Social Welfare; Bus & Prof Women; Farmers Union. Relig: Lutheran. Mailing Add: Box 56 Ross ND 58776

MEINECKE, ROBERT LEE (R)
b Plainview, Tex, Dec 31, 30; s Robert Lee Meinecke & Nannie Wilson M; m 1951 to Patricia Mae Vaughn; c Jackye, Sheree & Mitzi. Educ: Tex Tech Col, BS in Agronomy, 53. Polit & Govt Pos: Chmn, Lamb Co Rep Party, Tex, formerly. Bus & Prof Pos: Farmer, currently. Mem: Tex Pecan Growers; Farm Bur. Relig: Methodist. Mailing Add: Rte 1 Olton TX 79064

MELAND, PETE H (D)
Alaska State Sen
b Postville, Iowa, Mar 21, 19; s Peter Meland & Mabel Meyer M; m 1940 to Lorraine Margaret Flaskerud; c David John. Educ: Postville High Sch, grad. Polit & Govt Pos: City councilman, Sitka, Alaska, 51-53; mem, Alaska Judicial Coun, 65-70; Alaska State Rep, formerly; Alaska State Sen, 72- Mem: Mason; Elks. Relig: Lutheran. Mailing Add: Box 53 Sitka AK 99835

MELCHER, JOHN (D)
US Rep, Mont
b Sioux City, Iowa, Sept 6, 24; m 1945 to Ruth Klein; c Terry, Joan, Mary, Robert & John. Educ: Univ Minn, 1 year; Iowa State Univ, DVM, 50; Phi Zeta. Polit & Govt Pos: City alderman, Forsyth, Mont, 53-55, mayor, 55-61; Mont State Rep, Rosebud Co, 61-62 & 69; Mont State Sen, 63-67; former mem, Mont Legis Coun; Dem Cand for US Rep, Mont, 66; US Rep, Mont, 69- Bus & Prof Pos: Partner, Yellowstone Valley Vet Clinic, Forsyth, Mont, 50-69; operator, cattle feedlot, 56-70. Mil Serv: Army, 43-45, with serv in 76th Inf Div, Third Army, ETO; Purple Heart; Combat Infantryman's Badge. Legal Res: Forsyth MT Mailing Add: Rm 1224 Longworth House Off Bldg Washington DC 20515

MELIA, JOHN F (D)
Mass State Rep
Mailing Add: State Capitol Boston MA 02133

MELICH, MITCHELL (R)
b Bingham Canyon, Utah, Feb 1, 12; s Joseph Melich & Mary Kalembar M; m 1935 to Doris Snyder; c Tanya (Mrs Noel L Silverman), Dr Michael E, Nancy (Mrs Timothy J Funk) & Robert A. Educ: Univ Utah, LLB, 34; Kappa Sigma. Polit & Govt Pos: City attorney, Moab, Utah, 34-55; co attorney, Grand Co, 40-42; Utah State Sen, 42-50, Minority Leader, Utah State Senate, 49-50; mem bd regents, Univ Utah, 59-64; Rep Nat Committeeman, Utah, 61-63; Rep cand for Gov of Utah, 64; consult on staff of Congressman Sherman P Lloyd, 67-68; former mem, Utah Legis Coun; former mem, Utah Colo River Water Bd; alt deleg, Rep Nat Conv, 68; solicitor, Dept of Interior, Washington, DC, 69-72. Bus & Prof Pos: Secy & dir, Utex Explor Co, Utah, 53-62; pres, Uranian Reduction Co, 54-62; consult to pres, Atlas Minerals, 62-67; mem bd dirs, Ideal Nat Ins, 62-69; mem bd, Salt Lake City First Security Bank, 62-69. Mem: Salt Lake City Coun Foreign Rels (chmn); Comt Designing Educ for Future; Utah Ballet Soc; Mason; Shriner. Honors & Awards: Distinguished Alumni Award, Univ Utah, 69; admitted to US Supreme Court, 71. Relig: Congregational. Mailing Add: 900 Donner Way Salt Lake City UT 84108

MELICH, TANYA MARIE (R)
b Moab, Utah, Apr 23, 36; d Mitchell Melich & Doris Marie Snyder; m 1962 to Noel Leo Silverman; c Karla Noelle & Evan Mitchell. Educ: Univ Colo, BA, cum laude, 58; Columbia Univ, MS, 61; Phi Beta Kappa; Pi Gamma Mu; Pi Sigma Alpha; Sigma Epsilon Sigma; Chi Omega. Polit & Govt Pos: Polit interne, Citizenship Clearing House, Ford Found, summer 56; asst to research dir, Lefkowitz for Mayor, 61; state campaign dep dir, Melich for Gov Utah, fall 64; dir research, Rep City Campaign, Lindsay for Mayor, fall 65; assoc to scheduling dir, Rockefeller for Gov, 66; dep dir, Nat Deleg Unit, Rockefeller for President, 68; research consult, Perrotta for Controller, fall 69; NY State research chmn, Goodell for Sen Campaign, 70; alt deleg, Rep Nat Conv, 72; dep dir, New York Campaign for the Comt to Reelect the President, fall 72. Bus & Prof Pos: Researcher-writer, Foreign Policy Asn, 62; nat elec research dir, Am Broacasting Co, 63-64; ed asst, John A Wells, 65-66; Gov Thomas E Dewey, 67-68; pub affairs writer, Allen-Van Slyck Group, 69-70; Philip Van Slyck, Inc, 71-72. Publ:

Co-ed, Peace: The Control of National Power, Beacon Press, 63; Thomas E Dewey on the Two-Party System, Doubleday, 66; auth, What is the energy crisis, Ripon Forum, 4/73, plus others. Mem: US Civil Rights Comn (NY State Adv Comn, 73-); Ripon Soc (nat chairperson, 74-); Manhattan Women's Polit Caucus (comt chmn, 72-); NY State Women's Polit Caucus (comt chmn, 71-72). Mailing Add: 115 E Ninth St 17A New York NY 10003

MELLADO, RAMON A (NEW PROGRESSIVE, PR)
Sen, PR Senate
b Carolina, PR, Oct 31, 04; s Antonio Mellado & Elena Parsons M; m to Rosario Gonzalez. Educ: Univ PR, BS, 27; Columbia Univ, MA, 40, EdD, 47; Phi Delta Kappa. Hon Degrees: LLD, Inter-Am Univ PR, 70. Polit & Govt Pos: Mem, Const Conv of PR, 51-52; secy of educ, Govt of PR, 69-72; Sen, PR Senate, 73- Bus & Prof Pos: Dean admin, Univ PR, 48-56, prof educ, Grad Sch, 57-68. Publ: Designing a Science Curriculum, Univ PR, 42; Culture & Education in Puerto Rico, PR Teachers Asn, 48; Puerto Rico y Occidente, Ed Cultura, Mejico, 63. Mem: PR Teachers Asn. Honors & Awards: Distinguished Serv Award, Red Cross; Beaver Scout, Boy Scouts; Distinguished Serv Award, Selective Serv. Relig: Catholic. Mailing Add: Cond Centrum Plaza Apt 4F Calle Mejico Hato Rey PR 00917

MELLAND, ROBERT BRUCE (R)
NDak State Sen
b Fargo, NDak, Aug 7, 29; s Russell O Melland & Gunvor Wichmann M; m 1949 to Helen Elaine Burau; c James Bruce & Deborah Jean. Educ: Jamestown Col, 47-48; Concordia Col, 48-49. Polit & Govt Pos: Deleg, NDak Rep State Conv, 51; mem adv comt, Stutsman Co Rep Party, 51-54, co patronage comt, 53-54, finance chmn, 64-66; NDak State Sen, Dist 29, 67-, Asst Majority Leader, NDak Senate, 69-71, vchmn appropriations comt, 73-, chmn legis coun & pres pro tem, 75- Mem: Elks; Mason; Shrine; Eagles; CofC. Relig: Lutheran. Legal Res: 225 Third Ave SE Jamestown ND 58401 Mailing Add: Box 112 Jamestown ND 58401

MELLEN, MELBA J (R)
Mem, Calif Rep State Cent Comt
b Bonham, Tex, Aug 5, 27; d Graham F Gurden & Ethel Russell G; m 1959 to Richard A Mellen; c Richard G, Mark S & Fredric A. Educ: Cent High Sch, Jackson, Miss, grad, 45; Millsaps Col, 45-47; Vikings, Millsaps Col. Polit & Govt Pos: Chmn, Bus Women's Comt, Rep Assocs, Los Angeles, Calif, 69-; mem, Calif Rep State Cent Comt, 69- Relig: Protestant. Mailing Add: 10724 Garfield Ave Culver City CA 90230

MELLINGER, SAUNDRA (D)
b Monongahela, Pa, June 23, 49; d Joseph H Barskite & Katherine Barle B; m 1967 to David L Mellinger; c Kimberlee, Michele & David. Educ: Monongahela High Sch, Pa, grad, 67. Polit & Govt Pos: Alt deleg, Dem Nat Conv, 72; vpres, Union Twp Dem Women's Club, 74- Mem: Dem Women's Club of Union Twp (soc chmn, 73); Young Dem Club of Wash Co (vchairwoman, 73). Relig: Catholic. Mailing Add: RD 2 Finleyville PA 15332

MELLO, DONALD RAY (D)
Nev State Assemblyman
b Owensboro, Ky, June 22, 34; s Jack Mello (deceased) & Gladys (Peggy) Jasper M; m 1956 to Barbara Jane Woodhall; c Donald Jack & David William. Educ: Univ Nev, 53-55; Lambda Chi Alpha. Polit & Govt Pos: Nev State Assemblyman, 63-, mem legis comn subcomt to study state hosp probs, 67-68, first alt, legis comn, 67-68, mem, 69-, chmn, 73-74, mem legis comn subcomt to study state uniform consumer credit code-consumer protection, 69-71, mem spec comt arts for Nev Legis Bldg, 69-, mem legis comn & interim finance comt, 71-, mem legis comn subcomt study Nev State Employees Retirement Bd, 71-72, mem spec comn to adv state controller, 73-, chmn ways & means comt, 73- Bus & Prof Pos: Brakeman, Southern Pac Co, 55-61, conductor, 61- Mil Serv: Inactive Naval Res. Mem: Elks; F&AM; Eagles; Sparks Dem Club; Brotherhood of Rwy Trainmen. Honors & Awards: Capt, Sparks High Sch Track Team, 53; Record Holder of 220 yd dash. Relig: Emmanuel Baptist. Mailing Add: 2590 Oppio St Sparks NV 89431

MELLO, PAMELA JEAN (D)
b Minneapolis, Minn, May 29, 53; d Dr Niels Rorholm & Jean Dagmar Clausen R; m 1974 to Paul M Mello. Educ: Univ NH, 71-72; Univ RI, grad, 75; Sailing Club. Polit & Govt Pos: Area coordr, Univ RI for McGovern Campaign, 72; deleg, Dem Nat Conv, 72. Mem: Young Dem RI. Relig: Protestant. Mailing Add: 322 Mitchell's Lane Middletown RI 02840

MELLOM, SHERWOOD ORLANDO (DFL)
Chmn, Kandiyohi Co Dem-Farmer-Labor Party, Minn
b Brandt, SDak, Feb 20, 24; s Peter Ole Mellom & Margaret Underland M; m 1948 to Charlotte Kathryn Blegen; c Kathryn Louise (Mrs Williams); Sherwood O, Jr, Cynthia Yvonne (Mrs Porter) & Kristen Ann. Educ: Luther Col, BA, 49. Polit & Govt Pos: Chmn, Kandiyohi Co Dem-Farmer-Labor Party, Minn, 74- Bus & Prof Pos: Teacher, Willmar Sr High Sch, Minn, 55- Mil Serv: Entered as Pvt, Marine Corps, 43, released as S/Sgt, 45, after serv in 4th Marine Div, SPac, 44-45; Army Res, 70, Capt(Ret); World War II Victory Medal; Asiatic-Pac Medal with 3 Bronze Stars; Presidential Unit Citation; Am Defense Medal; Res Medal; Navy Commendation. Mem: Am Fedn Teachers; Optimists; Am Legion; VFW; ROA. Relig: Lutheran. Mailing Add: 813 Irene Ave SE Willmar MN 56201

MELNICK, JOHN LATANE (D)
Va State Deleg
b Alexandria, Va, Apr 19, 35; s Norbert Melnick & Myrtle Waring M; m 1962 to Marjory Helter; c John Latane, II, Paul Helter & Marjory Kathleen. Educ: Roanoke Col, 53-55; Univ Va, BS in Com, 58, JD, 61; Alpha Kappa Psi; Delta Theta Phi; Sigma Chi. Polit & Govt Pos: Asst commonwealth attorney, Arlington, Va, 61-63; precinct chmn, Dem Comt, 64-67; pres, Young Dem Arlington, 65-66; chmn, Police Trial Bd, 68-72; Va State Deleg, 72- Bus & Prof Pos: Assoc, Kinney, Whitaker, Smith & Barham, 61-64; partner, Ball, McCarthy, Balle & Melnick, 64-67; partner, John L Melnick Attorney, 67-70; partner, Berryman, Melnick & Sanders, 70-; dir & off, United Savings & Loan Asn, 71- Mem: Am Judicature Soc; Kiwanis (dir & comt chmn, 61-); Mason; CofC; YMCA (dir, Arlington Co & vet mem, 63-). Relig: Methodist. Legal Res: 4710 N Dittmar Rd Arlington VA 22207 Mailing Add: 2400 Wilson Blvd Arlington VA 22201

MELNICK, ROWELL SHEP (D)
NH State Rep
b St Johnsbury, Vt, Apr 27, 51; s Charles Harrington Melnick & Barbara Rowell M; single. Educ: Harvard Col, BA, 73, Grad Sch, currently; Phi Beta Kappa. Polit & Govt Pos: NH State Rep, 75- Mailing Add: 16 Park Ave Littleton NH 03561

MELOY, FRANCIS EDWARD, JR
b Wash, Mar 28, 17; s Francis Edward Meloy & Anne Teresa Connor M. Educ: Am Univ, BA, 39; Yale Univ, MA, 42. Polit & Govt Pos: Mem, Diplomatic Serv, 46-, vconsul, Dhahran, Saudi Arabia, 46-49, assigned to Off of the Secy of State, 49-53, detailed to NATO Defense Col, Paris, France, 53, second secy & consul, Am Embassy, Saigon, Vietnam, 53, first secy & consul, 54, first secy & consul, Paris, France, 56-57, mem, US Mission to NATO, Paris, 57-58, detailed to Imperial Defense Col, London, Eng, 59-60, spec asst to Dep Under Secy of State for Polit Affairs, 60-62, dir, Off of Western European Affairs, 62-64, minister & dep chief of mission, Am Embassy, Rome, Italy, 64-69, US Ambassador to the Dominican Repub, 69-73, US Ambassador to Guatemala, 73- Mil Serv: Lt Comdr, Naval Res, 42-46. Mem: First Australia, New Zealand & US Coun Meeting, Honolulu, Hawaii (US deleg, 52); Tenth NATO Coun Meeting, Paris, France, (deleg, 52); Metropolitan Club; City Tavern Asn, Washington. Legal Res: 2909 P St NW Washington DC 20007 Mailing Add: Dept of State Washington DC 20521

MELOY, PETER MICHAEL (D)
Mont State Rep
b Helena, Mont, Oct 26, 42; s Judge Peter George Meloy & Harriett Cruttenden M; m 1967 to Claudia Montagne; c Maile & Colin. Educ: Univ Calif, Riverside, BA, 66; Univ Mont, Sch Law, 66-68, Grad Sch, MA, 69; Phi Sigma. Polit & Govt Pos: Dir legal servs, Mont Legis Coun, Helena, 71-74; mem steering comt, Montana McGovern for President Comt, 72; Mont State Rep, 75-, majority whip, Mont House Rep, 75- Bus & Prof Pos: Mem, Mont Bar, 71-; instr, Carroll Col, 74-; pvt law practice, Helena, Mont, 74- Mil Serv: Entered as Yn, Naval Res, 69, released as Yn2, 71, after serv in Staff Judge Adv, Commander-in-Chief Pac, 69-71; Joint Serv Commendation Medal. Mem: Northern Rockies Action Group (bd adv); Helena Symphony Soc (bd dirs); Attention Home Inc (bd dirs); Helena Farmers Market Inc (bd dirs); Mont Bar Asn. Honors & Awards: Freshman Legislator, Mont House of Rep. Mailing Add: 812 N Ewing Helena MT 59601

MELTON, EMORY L (R)
Mo State Sen
b McDowell, Mo, June 20, 23; s C R Melton & Pearly Wise M; m 1949 to Jean Sanders; c Stanley & Russell. Educ: Univ Mo, LLB, 45. Polit & Govt Pos: Prosecuting attorney, Barry Co, Mo, 47-51; treas, Barry Co Rep Cent Comt, Mo, formerly; Mo State Sen, 29th Dist, 73- Bus & Prof Pos: Pres, Melton Publ, Inc, 60- Mil Serv: Entered as Pvt, Army, 45, released as Sgt, 46, after serv in Criminal Invest Div, Pac Theater, 45-46. Mem: Mason; Lions. Relig: Baptist. Mailing Add: 201 W Ninth Cassville MO 65625

MELVIN, JARRETT GREEN (JERRY) (D)
Fla State Rep
b Bonifay, Fla, July 22, 29; s Carlton Alexander Melvin & Ruby Newton M; m 1968 to Patricia Ann Shelly Emminizer; c Shelly Ann, JayGee & Jarrett Green, II. Educ: Col Charleston, 2 years; Am Univ; Fla State Univ, Eglin AFB Exten; Pi Kappa Phi; Athletic Coun; Student Coun. Polit & Govt Pos: Pres, Okaloosa Co Young Dem, 56; nat committeeman, Fla Young Dem, 57; legis asst, US Rep Bob Sikes, 56-59; Fla State Rep, Seventh Dist, 68-; chmn, Okaloosa Co Dem Comt, Fla, currently. Bus & Prof Pos: Asst radio sta mgr, WCNH, Quincy, Fla, 50-54; writer, develop proj, Playground Daily News, Ft Walton Beach, Fla, 61-62; exec mgr Okaloosa Island Authority, 62-70, authority consult, 71; owner, J G Melvin Bus Serv, 63-; secy-treas, Prof Bldg, 66- Mil Serv: Nat Guard. Mem: Northwest Fla Press Club; Fla Pub Rels Coun; Kiwanis; CofC; Gulf Beach Resort Asn. Honors & Awards: Most Talented High Sch Sr, 47; Mr Col of Charleston, 48; Freshman CofC Scholarship, 55; Runner-up, Allen Morris Award, Outstanding Freshman Legis, 69. Relig: Methodist. Mailing Add: 840 Santa Rosa Ct OIB Ft Walton Beach FL 32548

MENAHAN, WILLIAM THOMAS (D)
Mont State Rep
b Anaconda, Mont, Aug 16, 35; s William T Menahan, Sr & Kathleen McNay M; m 1959 to Shirley Ann Jackson; c Patrick John, Kara Lynn & Michael Thomas. Educ: Carroll Col, degree, 63; Western Mont Col, 65-66. Polit & Govt Pos: Mont State Rep, Dist 19, 71- Mil Serv: Serv in Army Res. Mem: Am Fedn Teachers; KofC; Ancient Order of Hibernians; Elks; Anaconda Sportsmen. Relig: Catholic. Mailing Add: 1304 W Fifth St Anaconda MT 59711

MENAKER, EDWARD GOWARD (D)
Mem, Waynesboro Dem City Comt, Va
b Newark, NJ, Apr 10, 19; s George Menaker & Sara Goward M; m 1941 to Elizabeth Dresbold; c Richard Glen & Lawrence James. Educ: Columbia Col, AB, 38; Columbia Univ, MA, 39; Union Col, NY, 46-47. Polit & Govt Pos: Vchmn, Waynesboro Dem City Comt, Va, 65-66, chmn, 68-72, mem, 72-; mem bd trustees, Waynesboro Pub Libr, 66; deleg, Dem Nat Conv, 68; chmn, 15th Legis Dist Dem Comt, 70-72; mem, Waynesboro Recreation Comn, 72-, chmn, 73- Bus & Prof Pos: Teacher, Altaraz Sch, Monterey, Mass, 40-41; engr & various eng mgt pos, Gen Elec Co, Schenectady, NY & Waynesboro, Va, 46-; value control mgr, Compagnie Bull, Gen Elec, Paris, France, 67. Mil Serv: Entered as Pvt, Army, 42, released as Maj, 46, after serv in 308th Bombardment Group, 14th Air Force, China-Burma-India Theatre, 44-45, Maj (Ret), Air Force; Bronze Star Medal; Unit Citation; Theatre Ribbons with Six Battle Stars. Publ: Fundamentals of infrared hot box detection, IEEE Trans, 64. Mem: Nat Soc Prof Engrs; Inst Elec & Electronics Engrs; mem adv bd, Stonewall Jackson Area Coun, Boy Scouts. Honors & Awards: Silver Beaver Award, Boy Scouts. Relig: Jewish. Mailing Add: 1824 Westminster Rd Waynesboro VA 22980

MENDELSOHN, ROBERT H (D)
Supvr, San Francisco Co Bd of Supvr, Calif
b Iowa City, Iowa, Jan 11, 38; s Matthew Mendelsohn & Esther Jacobs M; m 1957 to Ingrid Levin; c Scott. Educ: Univ Calif, Berkeley, AB cum laude, 59; Coro Found, San Francisco, Cert, 61; Pi Sigma Alpha; Honor Student Soc; Interfraternity Scholastic Honor Soc. Polit & Govt Pos: Supvr community serv, San Francisco Redevelop Agency, Calif, 61-64; admin asst, State Sen J Eugene McAteer, 64-67; San Francisco vchmn, Kennedy for President Campaign, 68; state-wide chmn, Educators for Cranston, 68; deleg, Dem Nat Conv, 68; supvr, San Francisco Co & City Bd of Supvr, 68-; San Francisco co-chmn, Wilson Riles for State Supt Pub Instr, 69; co-chmn, Northern Calif Pub Off for McGovern, 72; mem, State Coastal Zone Conserv Comn, 73-; NCent Coast Regional Coastal Zone Conserv Comn, 73-; mem, Bay Area Sewage Servs Asn, 74 & Adv Comt Elec & Reapportionment, 75- Bus & Prof Pos: Asst prof polit sci, San Francisco State Col, 67-70; lectr, Nat Coun Jewish Women, 68-70; dir develop, Century Consult, Inc, 68-69; consult, Daniel Yankelovich, Inc, 68-69; lectr, Grad Sch Social Welfare, Univ Calif, Berkeley, 69; lectr, Polit Sci Dept, City Col of San Francisco, 70; proj adminr, Lawrence Halprin & Assocs, 70-72; independent consult, 73- Mil Serv: Entered as Pvt, Marine Corps Res, 56, released as Pfc, 62, after serv in Sixth Community

Co Fourth Marine Div. Publ: Voice of the People (w Florence Randall), Century Community, 69. Mem: Sickle Cell Anemia Research & Educ (mem bd dirs); Multi-Culture Inst (mem bd dirs); Proj ABLE (mem bd dirs); San Francisco Senior Ctr (mem bd dirs); B'nai B'rith Youth Orgn (mem bd dirs). Honors & Awards: One of Monthly Men Worth Watching, Gtr San Francisco CofC Mag, San Francisco Bus. Relig: Jewish. Legal Res: 2547 Lyon St San Francisco CA 94123 Mailing Add: 235 City Hall San Francisco CA 94102

MENDENHALL, ALICE MAE (R)
Chmn, Dickinson Co Rep Cent Comt, Iowa
b Lake Mills, Iowa, May 12, 15; d William Adolph Ottilie & Jennie Whyte O; m 1947 to Walter Leslie Mendenhall, Jr; c Walter Leslie; Educ: Coe Col, BA, 38; Univ Iowa, 41; Mu Phi Epsilon. Polit & Govt Pos: Vchmn, Dickinson Co Rep Cent Comt, Iowa, 63-73, chmn, 73- Bus & Prof Pos: Co-owner & mgr, Clements Beach Resort with husband, 47- Mil Serv: Entered as Ens, WAVES, 43, released as Lt(jg), 46. Relig: Presbyterian. Mailing Add: RR Box 9217 Spirit Lake IA 51360

MENDENHALL, EYVON (R)
Mem, Mo Rep State Comt
b Jaspar, Ark, June 8, 21; d Roscoe Conklin Stacey & Bessie Lee Allen M; wid; c Julia (Mrs Robert Feugate), Anita Jo & Stacey Taylor & Mary Ann Mendenhall. Educ: Southwest Mo State Univ, life teaching cert, 42; Alpha Sigma Tau. Polit & Govt Pos: Pres, Christian Co Rep Women's Club, Mo, 51-54 & Seventh Dist Rep Women's Club, 52-54; committeewoman, Jefferson Twp, St Louis Co, 59-; mem cand selection comt, St Louis Co Rep Cent Comt, 60-, vchmn, Co Comt, formerly; secy, Second Cong Dist, Mo, 64-65; vpres, Mo Asn Rep, 64-65, secy, 65-66; chmn, Mo-Ill Rep Seminar, 66-67; chmn twp redistricting comt, St Louis Co Coun, 71-72; deleg, Rep Nat Conv, 72; mem, Mo State Budget Comt, 72- & Mo Rep State Comt, 72- Bus & Prof Pos: Teacher, Sparta Sch Syst, Mo, 42-45; mgr drygoods store, Sparta, 44-69; mgt training prog, Transworld Airlines, Kansas City, Mo, 45; clerk of the court, Magistrate Third Dist Court, St Louis Co, 46- Mem: St Louis Co Magistrate Clerks Asn; Nat Asn Court Admin; White Shrine; Eastern Star (seven off, worthy matron, 52); Mo Libr Asn. Relig: Methodist. Mailing Add: 515 Lake Ave Webster Groves MO 63119

MENDENHALL, JOSEPH ABRAHAM
US Ambassador to Madagascar
b Calvert, Md, Jan 15, 20; s Joseph Edwin Mendenhall & Alice Brown M; m 1946 to Leone Reiber; c Penelope (Mrs Pestle), Priscilla & Anne. Educ: Univ Del, BA, 40; Harvard Univ Law Sch, 40-41; Univ Pa, 45-46; Phi Kappa Phi. Polit & Govt Pos: Vconsul, Istanbul, Turkey, 46-49; asst chief of Marshall Plan Mission, Reykjavik, Iceland, 49-51; econ & polit officer, Am Embassy, Bern, Switz, 52-55; int rels officer, Dept of State, Washington, DC, 55-59; polit counr, Am Embassy, Saigon, Vietnam, 59-62; dir of Far Eastern Regional Affairs, Dept of State, Washington, DC, 64-65; dir of US Agency for Int Develop Mission, Vientiane, Laos, 65-68, from dep to acting asst adminr for Vietnam, Agency for Int Develop, Washington, DC, 68-69; foreign serv inspector, Europe, Africa, MidE, 70-72; US Ambassador to Madagascar, 72- Mil Serv: Entered as Pvt, Army, 41, released as Capt, 46, after serv in numerous units & commands. Legal Res: Bayberry Farm East Haddam CT 06423 Mailing Add: La Fontanella Lucignano (Arezzo) 52046 Italy

MENDENHALL, SAMUEL BROOKS (D)
SC State Sen
b Rock Hill, SC, Jan 1, 36; s George Wallace Mendenhall & Margaret Love Good M; m 1962 to Carolyn King; c Robert Bratton & Mary Margaret. Educ: Univ SC, AB, LLB, 62; Phi Kappa Sigma; Omicron Delta Kappa; Kappa Sigma Kappa; Justice, Phi Alpha Delta; pres, Euphradian Lit Soc, 58-59; chmn, Univ Young Dem Club, 58. Polit & Govt Pos: Chmn, York City Hist Comt, SC; vchmn, Dem Party, Ebenezer Precinct, 62; SC State Rep, formerly; SC State Sen, 72- Bus & Prof Pos: Lawyer. Publ: Auth numerous articles on local hist & co-auth book, Plaxco-Robinson. Mem: Elks; Jaycees (secy); SAR (secy); SC Soc (dir); SC Hist Soc. Relig: Presbyterian. Mailing Add: Box 342 Rock Hill SC 29730

MENDEZ, JUSTO A (NEW PROGRESSIVE, PR)
Sen, PR Senate
b Lares, PR, Sept 8, 17; s Justo Mendez & Cristina Rodriguez M; m 1942 to Provi Oliver; c Provines (Mrs Humberto Torres), Justo & Lumen. Educ: Col Agr & Mech Arts, Mayaguez, PR, BS in Chem Eng, 42; Phi Sigma Alpha. Polit & Govt Pos: Chmn exec comt, Statehood Rep Party, PR, 66-67; first vpres, United Statehooders, 67-68; interim pres, New Progressive Party, 69; Sen & minority floor leader, PR Senate. Bus & Prof Pos: Chief chemist, Cent Los Canos, 42, gen supt, 46-58; exec vpres, Cent Fed Savings & Loan Asn, 58-64; pres, San Martin Mortgage & Investment Corp, 64-67. Mil Serv: Entered as Pvt, Army, 43, released as T/5, 46, after serv in Malaria Control Unit, Caribbean; Am Defense Medal; World War II Medal; Victory Medal; Good Conduct Medal. Polit & Govt Pos: Arecibo Harbor Feasibility Study, 51; Preliminary work with the filtration of effluences of rotary cane mud filters, annual meeting, Sugar Tech Asn, 54; Cooperative progress in Puerto Rico, 27th Session of the Am Inst Cooperativism, Purdue Univ, 55. Mem: PR Col Engrs, Architects & Surveyors; PR Chem Soc; Inter-Am Planning Soc; Prof Engrs; Lions Int. Relig: Catholic. Legal Res: C-71 Ebano St Golden Gate Develop Caparra PR 00920 Mailing Add: Condominio Torre de la Reina Ponce de Leon 450 Puerto de Tierra PR 00906

MENDEZ MOLL, JOSE (POPULAR DEMOCRAT, PR)
Sen, PR Senate
Mailing Add: State Capitol San Juan PR 00901

MENDOLIA, ARTHUR I (R)
Asst Secy Installations & Logistics, Dept Defense
Legal Res: DE Mailing Add: Dept of Defense Washington DC 20301

MENDOZA, ANGELES (NEW PROGRESSIVE, PR)
Sen, PR Senate
Mailing Add: State Capitol San Juan PR 00901

MENENDEZ-MONROIG, JOSE M (NEW PROGRESSIVE, PR)
Minority Leader, PR Senate
b San Juan, PR, June 22, 17; s Albert Seaman Menendez & Agustina Monroig M; m 1946 to Lyda M Cortada; c Jose Antonio & Michele Marie. Educ: Univ PR, BA, 39, LLB, 41; Phi Sigma Alpha; AFDA. Polit & Govt Pos: Assoc attorney, Pub Serv Comn, 46; adjudicator, Vet Admin, 47; Sen, PR Senate, 69-, minority leader, 73- Mil Serv: Entered as 2nd Lt, Army, 41, released as Capt, 46, after serv in 295th Inf, Caribbean Command, 41-45 & 296th Inf, Pac Theatre, 44-46; Caribbean & Pacific Theatre Medals. Mem: Am Bar Asn; Colegio de Abogados de PR; The Military Order of the World Wars. Relig: Catholic. Legal Res: 54 Krug St Santurce PR 00911 Mailing Add: PO Box 3183 San Juan PR 00904

MENES, PAULINE H (D)
Md State Deleg
b New York, NY, July 16, 24; d Arthur Benjamin Herskowitz & Hannah H; m 1946 to Melvin Menes; c Sandra Jill, Robin Joy & Bambi Lynn. Educ: Hunter Col, BA, 45; Norris '45-House Plan. Polit & Govt Pos: Secy, Prince Georges Co Independent Dem, Md, 62; chief clerk, Supvr Elecs, Md, 63; secy, Prince Georges Co Dem Steering Comt, 66; Md State Deleg, 67- Bus & Prof Pos: Economist, QmC, 45-47; geographer, Army Map Serv, 49-50; substitute teacher, Prince Georges Pub High Schs, Md, 65-66. Relig: Jewish. Mailing Add: 3517 Marlbrough Way College Park MD 20740

MENGDEN, WALTER HENRY, JR (R)
Tex State Sen
b Houston, Tex, Oct 25, 26; s Walter Henry Mengden, Sr & Eugenia Crawford M; m 1955 to June Shell; c Dorothea Eugenia, Walter Henry, III, Joseph Temple & John Shell. Educ: Univ Tex at Austin, BBA, LLB, DJ; Chi Phi. Polit & Govt Pos: Tex State Rep, 22nd Legis Dist, 71-73; Tex State Sen, 13th Sen Dist, 73- Bus & Prof Pos: Attorney-at-law & oil & gas consult, Houston, Tex. Mil Serv: Navy, 45-46; Army, 51-53. Relig: Catholic. Legal Res: 3730 Willowick Houston TX 77019 Mailing Add: PO Box 22837 Houston TX 77027

MENHORN, HARRY G, JR (D)
Pa State Rep
Mailing Add: Capitol Bldg Harrisburg PA 17120

MENKE, LESTER D (R)
Iowa State Rep
Mailing Add: RR Box 97 Calumet IA 51009

MENNENGA, JAY WARREN (D)
Iowa State Rep
b Belmond, Iowa, June 27, 43; s Alfred Mennenga & Marvieu Hansen M; m 1968 to Sonja Ann Boysen. Educ: Luther Col (Iowa), 61-63; Univ Northern Iowa, BS in Social Sci, 65, grad study polit sci, 71-; Sigma Tau Gamma. Polit & Govt Pos: Deleg, co, dist & Iowa State Dem Conv, 70; Iowa State Rep, 77th Dist, Clinton Co, 73- Mem: Nat, Iowa State & Clinton Educ Asns. Relig: Evangelical Free Church Am. Mailing Add: 1001 11th Ave N Clinton IA 52732

MENNING, MARION (MIKE) (DFL)
Minn State Rep
Mailing Add: Box 464 Edgerton MN 56128

MENOS, GUS G (D)
Wis State Rep
b Milwaukee, Wis, Dec 5, 20; s George Menos & Harriet Antonopolous M; m 1941 to Lillian M Pholie; c Jeffrey & Perry. Educ: Lincoln High Sch, grad, 38; Gemological Inst Am, grad, 56. Polit & Govt Pos: Wis State Rep, 11th Dist, 71-; mem, Interstate Coop Coun, 75- Bus & Prof Pos: Pres, Menos Jewelers & Carpetland, 56- Mil Serv: Army Air Force, Pfc, 46, serv in 419th Training Group. Mem: Local 248 AFL-CIO; Holy Name Soc; Lions; Elks. Relig: Catholic. Mailing Add: 1840 W Daisy Lane Glendale WI 53209

MENSCH, LYLE (D)
SDak State Rep
Mailing Add: Avon SD 57315

MENSCHEL, RONAY A (D)
b Washington, DC, May 5, 42; d Paul T Arlt & May Mooklar A; m 1974 to Richard L Menschel. Educ: Cornell Univ, BA, 64. Polit & Govt Pos: Admin asst to US Rep Edward I Koch, NY, 69- Mem: City Club of New York. Mailing Add: 19 E 80th St New York NY 10021

MENTA, GUIDO PAUL (D)
b New York, NY, June 29, 38; s Paul Menta & Mary Scalza M; m 1960 to Adrienne Tamburo; c Scott & Christopher. Educ: City Col New York, 59-61; Col New Rochelle, currently. Polit & Govt Pos: Deleg, Dem Nat Conv, 72. Bus & Prof Pos: Assoc dir polit action & legis, NY Dist Coun, 37, Am Fedn of State, Co & Munic Employees Union, AFL-CIO, 62- Mil Serv: Entered as Pvt, Army Nat Guard, 59, released as Cpl, 65, after serv in 42nd Inf Div. Mem: KofC; NY Dist Coun 37, Am Fedn State, Co & Munic Employees Union, AFL-CIO. Relig: Roman Catholic. Mailing Add: 1512 Library Ave New York NY 10465

MENTON, PAUL C (D)
VChmn, Mass State Dem Comt
b Cambridge, Mass, Apr 15, 25; s Patrick A Menton & Lucy A Comfort M; m 1950 to Mary T Regan; c Cbristopher, Robert, Jayne, Brian & Carol. Educ: Suffolk Univ Law Sch, LLB, 53. Polit & Govt Pos: Parole officer, Youth Serv Bd Comt, Mass, 51-53; mem, Watertown Sch Comt, 52-53; spec agt, Fed Bur Invest, 53-58; mem, Mass State Dem Comt, Fifth Dist, currently, vchmn, 68-; Mass State Rep, 59-72; asst counsel, Mass House Rep, 72- Bus & Prof Pos: Attorney-at-law, Watertown, Mass, 58- Mil Serv: Entered as Recruit, Marine Corps, 43, released as Cpl, 46, after serv in SPac Theater. Publ: Truth in lending. Mem: Mass Trial Lawyers Asn; Elks; KofC; Am Legion; Marine Corps League. Relig: Catholic. Mailing Add: 100 Robbins Watertown MA 02172

MENZA, ALEXANDER J (D)
NJ State Sen
b Newark, NJ, Mar 31, 32; s Alexander D Menza & Eleanor Cortese M; m 1955 to Carol Saunders; c Alexander D, Christopher, Philip & Jacqueline. Educ: Univ Wis, BS, 54; NY Univ Sch Law, JD, 58; Student Senate. Polit & Govt Pos: Attorney, Planning Bd, Hillside, NJ, 63-66 & Zoning Bd, 64-66; mem, Hillside Twp Comt, 67-71; mayor, 69; NJ State Assemblyman, 72-74; NJ State Sen, 75-, vchmn Senate judiciary comt, chmn joint legis subcomt ment health, chmn NJ drug comn, mem NJ ment health planning comt, mem insts, health & welfare comt, NJ State Sen, currently. Mil Serv: Entered as 2nd Lt, Army, 54, released as 1st Lt, 56, after serv in Mil Police, US; Commendation; Cert of Achievement. Publ: Intramural law review, New York Univ Law, 58. Mem: Am Bar Asn; Am Trial Lawyers Asn; NJ State Opera (bd dirs); Cerebral Palsy Ctr Union Co; Ment Health Asn Union Co. Honors & Awards: Distinguished Citizens Award, NJ Psychiat Asn, 75; Citizen of Year, NJ

Psychol Asn, 75. Relig: Presbyterian. Legal Res: 67 Georgian Ct Hillside NJ 07205 Mailing Add: 125 Broad St Elizabeth NJ 07201

MERCER, JOSEPH HENRY (R)
NMex State Rep
b Peoria, Ill, Feb 1, 37; s Maurice Dean Mercer & Dorothy Brickner M; m 1967 to JoAnn Swicegood; c Stephen, Jennifer & Matthew. Educ: Univ NMex, BA, 61; Harvard Univ, JD, 64; Tau Kappa Alpha; Phi Kappa Phi. Polit & Govt Pos: NMex State Rep, 75- Bus & Prof Pos: Chmn, Albuquerque Bar Asn Referral, NMex, 68-69; dir, NMex Legal Servs Corp, 73-75; vpres & dir, Prepaid Legal Serv Corp of NMex, 74-75. Mil Serv: Entered as Pvt, Army, 55, released as 1st Lt, 58, after serv in 267 Armored Field Artil Bn, Europe, 56-58; Good Conduct Medal. Mem: Am, NMex, Albuquerque Bar Asns; NMex Estate Planning Coun; Albuquerque Comt Foreign Rels (chmn). Honors & Awards: Distinguished Serv Award, NMex Bar Asn, 74. Relig: Protestant. Mailing Add: 3127 Carolina NE Albuquerque NM 87110

MERCER, WALLACE W (R)
Mont State Rep
b Roundup, Mont, Feb 13, 24; s Walter W Mercer & Fern E Hall M; m 1962 to Mary Joanne Crumbaker; c William W & James V. Educ: Univ Mont, Missoula, BS in Bus Admin, 49; Sigma Alpha Epsilon. Polit & Govt Pos: Mont State Rep, Dist Eight, 73- Bus & Prof Pos: Sales mgr, McKesson & Robbins, Billings, Mont, 56-63; mgr & owner, Empire Surg Supply, 64-68; co sales mgr, Rocky Mountain Surg Supply, Denver, Colo, 68-69; motel owner & mgr, Rimrock Lodge, Billings, 69- Mil Serv: Entered as Pvt, Army, 43, released as Sgt, 46, after serv in Inf, Pac, 45-46. Mem: Billings CofC (bd dirs, 71-); Rotary; Billings Hotel/Motel Asn; Al Bedoo Shrine; United Fund. Relig: Presbyterian. Mailing Add: 1914 Patricia Lane Billings MT 59103

MERCIER, RICHARD LOUIS (D)
Conn State Rep
b Norwich, Conn, Oct 13, 47; s Louis I Mercier & Doris A Monroe M; single. Educ: Marist Col & Sem, Framingham, Mass; Eastern Conn State Col. Polit & Govt Pos: Mem, Plainfield Dem Town Comt, Conn, 70-; assessor, Town of Plainfield, 72-; Conn State Rep, 72-; mem, Plainfield Charter Comn, 73- Bus & Prof Pos: Salesman, Quintal Real Estate, 73- Mem: KofC; Holy Name Soc; Lions. Relig: Catholic. Mailing Add: 7 Railroad Ave Plainfield CT 06374

MERCORELLA, ANTHONY J (D)
Councilman, New York, NY
b Mar 6, 27; s Sante Mercorella & Josephine Bozzuti M; m 1956 to Maria De Lucia; c Anne, Susan, Robert & Carole. Educ: Long Island Univ, AB, 49; NY Univ, 49; Fordham Univ Law Sch, LLB, 52. Polit & Govt Pos: Law asst, Civil Court, Bronx Co, New York, 55-65; NY State Assemblyman, 85th Dist, 66-72; councilman, New York, Seventh Cong Dist in the Bronx, 73- Bus & Prof Pos: Partner, Mercorella & Kase, New York, currently. Mil Serv: Entered in Navy, 45, released in 46, after serv in USS Helena, Pac & European Theatre; European & Pac Serv Awards. Mem: Sons of Italy; All-Am Coun, Nat Dem Comt; Nat Conf of Christians & Jews; Mary, Queen of Peace Coun, KofC; Insts of Appl Human Dynamics (dir, 71-). Relig: Roman Catholic. Legal Res: 1363 Astor Ave New York NY 10469 Mailing Add: 600 Madison Ave New York NY 10022

MERCURO, TOBIA GUSTAVE (R)
VChmn, Seventh Cong Dist, Va
b East Orange, NJ, Oct 30, 33; s Tobia Mercuro & Louise Pelosi M; m 1959 to Barbara Ann Beckwith; c Thomas Tobia, Virginia Louise & Rebecca Beckwith. Educ: Newark Col Eng, BS, Mech Eng, 55; Univ Wis, Milwaukee, 56-58; Xavier Univ, 59-60; Pi Tau Sigma. Polit & Govt Pos: Treas, Warren Co Rep Comt, Va, 66-68 & chmn, 68-70; chmn, 28th Legis Dist Rep Comt, Farquier, Rappahannock & Warren Co, 69-; vchmn & campaign chmn, Seventh Cong Dist, 70- Bus & Prof Pos: Supvr, mfg engr, Allis-Chalmers Mfg Co, Ohio, 55-61; asst plant mgr, Philip Carey Mfg Co, NJ, 61-63; vpres & gen mgr, Riverton Lime & Stone Co, Va, 63-71, pres, 71- Mem: Nat Limestone Inst (dir); Warren Co CofC (dir); Warren Co Indust Comn; Rotary; Izaac Walton League. Mailing Add: 325 Amherst Dr Front Royal VA 22630

MERIAM, HELEN (R)
Chmn, Lake Co Rep Party, Minn
b Sioux Falls, SDak, July 10, 20; d Roy Lester Ehlen & Louise Straghliati E; m 1949 to Arthur Adam Meriam; c David Anderson & Anthony A. Educ: Wash High Sch, 4 years; Univ Minn, Duluth, various courses. Polit & Govt Pos: Census taker, 60, census supvr, Lake Co, Minn, 70; chmn, Lake Co Rep Party, 69- Bus & Prof Pos: Ladies ready to wear mgt, Montgomery Ward & S & L Co, Sioux Falls, SDak; owner & mgr, Knife River Motel & Camper Park, 54-; mem bd dirs, Shore, Inc, 71- Publ: Newspaper articles. Mem: Lake Superior North Shore Asn (bd mem); Upper Respiratory Health Asn & Local Recreation Coun (mem bd); Citizens Adv Comt to Lake Co Sch Bd. Legal Res: North Shore Dr Knife River MN 55609 Mailing Add: PO Box 25 Knife River MN 55609

MERIDETH, H L, JR (SONNY) (D)
Miss State Rep
b Greenville, Miss, Dec 7, 30; married. Educ: Phi Alpha Delta. Polit & Govt Pos: Miss State Rep, 60-, chmn judiciary en banc, chmn judiciary A, mem ways & means comt & chmn income tax subcomt, mem ins comt & mem census & reapportionment comt, Miss House Rep, currently. Bus & Prof Pos: Attorney. Mem: Am Bar Asn; Exchange Club; Am Legion; VFW; CofC. Relig: Baptist. Mailing Add: Box 1498 Greenville MS 38701

MERLE, LYNN (D)
Mem, Cumberland Co Dem Exec Comt
b Vineland, NJ, Sept 10, 47; d Leslie Merle & Mary Martin M; single. Educ: Brandeis Univ, BA, 70; Univ Southern Calif, 72-73. Polit & Govt Pos: Mem, Vineland Vietnam Referendum Comt, NJ, 71; coordr, Cumberland Co Citizens for McGovern, 72; deleg & mem platform comt, Dem Nat Conv, 72; vol staff mem, US Sen Mike Gravel Campaign for Vice Presidency, 72; mem, Cumberland Co Dem Exec Comt, 73- Bus & Prof Pos: Libr asst, Mass Inst Technol/US Dept of Transportation, Cambridge, Mass, 69-71; libr asst, Univ Southern Calif Law Ctr, 73; librn/legal aid coordr, NJ State Prison, Leesburg, 74- Mem: Am Libr Asn; Exp in Int Living. Mailing Add: 529 Maurice River Blvd Vineland NJ 08360

MERLINO, JOSEPH PIEDMONT (D)
NJ State Sen
b Trenton, NJ, July 15, 22; s Pasquale Merlino (deceased) & Margarittia Fuccello M (deceased); m 1949 to Molly J McGoogan; c Claire Margaret, Mary Nell, Kate, James Richard & Joseph McGoogan. Educ: Col South Jersey, 40-42; Seton Hall Col, BSS, 48; Fordham Univ Law Sch, LLB & JD, 51; Int Rels Soc (pres, 46-47); Student Coun (pres, 47-48); Pre-Legal Soc (pres, 46-48); Glee Club (vpres, 47-48). Polit & Govt Pos: Attorney, Mercer Co Rent Control, NJ, 54-58; asst prosecutor, Mercer Co, 59-66; city attorney & dir, Dept Law, Trenton, 66-70; NJ State Assemblyman, Mercer Co, Dist 6-B, 68-72; NJ State Sen, Dist 6-B, 72-, vchmn ad hoc comt on energy & environ & Del-Raritan canal preservation study comn, NJ State Senate, 73- Bus & Prof Pos: Practicing attorney, Trenton, 52- Mil Serv: Pvt, Army, serv in 103rd Hosp Ship Co, ETO, 43-45. Mem: Am Bar Asn; Am Judicature Soc; Trenton Symphony Asn (dir); NJ Hist Comn; Int Narcotic Enforcement Officials Asn. Relig: Roman Catholic. Legal Res: 25 Whittier Ave Trenton NJ 08618 Mailing Add: 315 Market St Trenton NJ 08611

MERLO, JOHN (D)
Ill State Rep
b Chicago, Ill, Sept 12, 12; m to Meryle State; c Three. Educ: DePaul Univ; Phi Kappa Alpha. Polit & Govt Pos: Secy to Edward J Barrett, 44th Ward Committeeman, Ill, formerly; Ill State Rep, currently; alt deleg, Dem Nat Conv, 68; Dem committeeman, 44th ward. Bus & Prof Pos: Mem staff, Chicago Park Dist, 33- Mem: CofC; Holy Name Soc; Lake View Men's Club; Park West Community Asn; Lions. Honors & Awards: Outstanding Vol Award, March of Dimes, 62. Mailing Add: 3018 Sheridan Rd Chicago IL 60657

MERONEY, CLIFFORD CLINTON (D)
Chmn, Floyd Co Dem Exec Comt, Ga
b Floyd Co, Ga, Jan 29, 06; s Othir R Meroney & Mamie Harris M; m 1928 to Mary White; c Sara Kathryn (Mrs Toles, deceased). Educ: Edmonia Inst, Rome, Ga; Univ Ga, 39. Polit & Govt Pos: Mem, Floy Floyd Co Dem Exec Comt, Ga, 48-, secy-treas, 55-66, chmn, 66-; mem sub-comt on finance, Ga State Dem Exec Comt, 66-72; mem, Seventh Cong Dist Dem Exec Comt, 70-72. Bus & Prof Pos: Agency clerk, Cent of Ga Rwy Co, 25-30; cashier, W Point Pepperell, Lindale Plant, 30-70; owner, Creative Advertisers, Rome, Ga, 66- Mil Serv: S/Sgt, Ga State Guard. Mem: Mason; RAM; KT; AAONMS (ambassador, YAARAB Temple, 55-70); Shrine. Relig: Methodist. Mailing Add: 224 Flora Ave Rome GA 30161

MERRELL, HARVEY W (R)
Chmn, Grand Co Rep Party, Utah
b Murray, Utah, Mar 9, 28; s Charles W Merrell & Irene Webb M; m 1960 to Sheryl Christenses; c Melinda & Matthew. Educ: Univ Utah, BS in geol, 55, MS in geol, 58. Polit & Govt Pos: Chmn, Grand Co Rep Party, Utah, 72-; comnr, Grand Co, 75- Mil Serv: Entered as Pvt, Marine Corps, 46, released as Sgt, 51. Mem: Am Asn Petroleum Geologists; Am Inst Mining, Metallurgical & Petroleum Engrs; Soc Econ Geologists; Elks. Mailing Add: 546 Sundial Dr Moab UT 84532

MERRELL, NORMAN L (D)
Mo State Sen
Mailing Add: PO Box 117 Monticello MO 63457

MERRIAM, GENE (DFL)
Minn State Sen
b Minneapolis, Minn, Nov 1, 44; s George C Merriam & Frances Couillard M; m 1965 to Maureen Elizabeth Brown; c Jeffrey Vincent, Brian Patrick & Kathryn Jean. Educ: Univ Minn, BSBA, 67; Beta Alpha Psi. Polit & Govt Pos: Councilman-at-lg, Coon Rapids, Minn, 73-74; Minn State Sen, 75- Bus & Prof Pos: CPA, Minn, 70- Mil Serv: Entered as Pvt, Marine Corp Res, 62, released as Lance Cpl, 70, after serv in 26th Rifle Co, 62-70. Mem: Minn Soc CPA's; KofC; Asn for Retarded Citizens. Relig: Roman Catholic. Legal Res: 2924 116th Ave NW Coon Rapids MN 55433 Mailing Add: Rm 323 State Capitol St Paul MN 55155

MERRIAM, ROBERT EDWARD (R)
Chmn, Adv Comn Intergovt Rels
b Chicago, Ill, Oct 2, 18; s Charles Edward Merriam & Elizabeth Hilda Doyle M; m 1950 to Marguerite de Ternova; c Aimee Buch, Oliver & Monique. Educ: Univ Chicago, MA, 40; Psi Upsilon. Polit & Govt Pos: Alderman, Chicago, Ill, 47-55; asst dir, US Bur Budget, 55-58, dep dir, 58; dep asst to President, 58-61; co-chmn, Ill Comn Urban Area Govt, 69-74; chmn, Adv Comt Intergovt Rels, 69- Bus & Prof Pos: Pres, Spaceonics, Inc, Chicago, Ill, 61-64; pres, Univ Patents, Inc, 64-70; chmn, Planning Group, Urban Invest & Develop Co, 71-72, exec vpres, co, 72-; chmn bd, MGA Technol, Inc, 71- Mil Serv: Entered as Pvt, Army, 42, released as Capt, 46, after serv in 9th Army, ETO, 44-45; Bronze Star; Four Battle Stars. Publ: Auth, Dark December, Ziff-Davis, 47; co-auth, The American Government-Democracy in Action, Ginn, 54; co-auth, Going into Politics—A Guide for Citizens, Harper Bros, 57. Mem: Am Polit Sci Asn; Am Soc Pub Admin; Nat Acad Pub Admin. Mailing Add: 2340 N Lincoln Park W Chicago IL 60614

MERRICK, SAMUEL VAUGHAN (D)
b Cynwyd, Pa, Mar 24, 14; s Rodney K Merrick & Mary Gordon M; m 1947 to Eleanor Perry; c John Rodney, Melvin Gregory & Thaddeus. Educ: Univ Pa, BA, LLB; Phi Beta Kappa. Polit & Govt Pos: Spec asst gen counsel, Nat Labor Rel Bd, 50-55; staff mem, US Senate Labor Comt, 59-61; spec asst to the Secy of Labor for Legis Affairs, 61-68; spec counsel to Mayor, Boston, Mass, 68-71; dir cong rels, US Conf Mayors-Nat League of Cities, 71-72; consult on Govt Rels, 72- Relig: Catholic. Mailing Add: 401 N St SW Washington DC 20024

MERRILL, D BAILEY (R)
b Hymera, Ind, Nov 22, 12; s Harry D Merrill & Beatrice Bailey M; m 1939 to Josephine Drehrer. Educ: Ind State Univ, AB, 33; Ind Univ, JD, 37. Polit & Govt Pos: US Rep, Eighth Dist, Ind, 53-54. Bus & Prof Pos: Teacher, Hymera High Sch, Ind, 33-35; lawyer, Merrill, Schroeder, Johnson & Evans, 37-52 & 55- Mil Serv: Entered as Pvt, Army, 42, released as Capt, 46, after serv in 291st Field Artil Observation Bn, ETO. Mem: Rotary; Am Legion; VFW; Evansville Petrol Club; Nat Lawyers Club, Washington, DC. Relig: Baptist. Legal Res: 20 Adams Ave Evansville IN 47713 Mailing Add: 301 Union Fed Bldg Evansville IN 47708

MERRILL, FREDERICK THAYER JR (D)
b Washington, DC, Dec 17, 38; s Frederick Thayer Merrill & Edith Hall M; m 1965 to Jill Davidson; c Timothy Stokes & William Alexander. Educ: Cornell Univ, BA, 61; Delta Kappa Epsilon. Polit & Govt Pos: Legis coordr, Dem Study-Group, US House of Rep, 69-; deleg & mem credentials comt, Dem Nat Conv, 72. Bus & Prof Pos: Mem, Am Coun of Young Polit Leaders, Washington, DC, 68- Mil Serv: Entered as Pvt, Marine Corps Res, 63, released as Pfc, 66. Relig: Episcopal. Mailing Add: 2314 44th St NW Washington DC 20007

MERRILL, HUGH DAVIS (D)
Ala State Rep
b Anniston, Ala, Apr 2, 13; s Hugh Davis Merrill & Martha Chitwood M; m 1951 to Martha Holcombe; c Hugh, David, Paul & Nancy. Educ: Univ Ala, AB, 35, LLB, 37; Sigma Alpha Epsilon. Polit & Govt Pos: Deleg, Dem Nat Conv, 44, 52, 56 & 64; mem, Ala State Dem Comt, 51-58; Ala State Rep, 55- Mil Serv: Entered as Pvt, Army, 44, released as Lt, 46, after serv in Judge Adv Gen Dept. Mem: Mason; KofP; Kiwanis; Am Legion. Relig: Baptist. Legal Res: 2312 Ridgeview Rd Anniston AL 36201 Mailing Add: PO Box 1498 Anniston AL 36201

MERRILL, PELHAM JONES (D)
b Heflin, Ala, Dec 1, 07; s Walter Benjamin Merrill & Lilla Jones M; m 1936 to Gladys Morrison. Educ: Univ of Ala, AB, 26, LLB, 34. Polit & Govt Pos: Ala State Rep, 36-38 & 46-51, Speaker Pro Tem, Ala House Rep, 49-51; mem, Ala State Dem Exec Comt, 36-40; chmn, Cleburne Co Dem Exec Comt, 36-42; assoc justice, Supreme Court of Ala, 53-74. Mil Serv: Entered as 2nd Lt, Army Air Corps, 42, released as Maj, 46; Col (Ret), Air Force Res. Relig: Baptist. Mailing Add: 2008 Commodore St Montgomery AL 36106

MERRILL, PHILIP L (D)
Maine State Sen
b Portland, Maine, Nov 19, 45; s Earle L Merrill & Vena Mahar M; m 1967 to Linda Hilton; c Samantha M. Educ: Colby Col, BA, 68; Univ of Maine Law Sch, JD, 74. Polit & Govt Pos: Vchmn, Cumberland Co Dem Comt, Maine, 72-74; mem, Maine Dem State Comt, 74-; Maine State Sen, Dist Ten, 75- Bus & Prof Pos: Attorney-at-law, Portland, Maine, currently. Mil Serv: Entered as E-1, Army Nat Guard, 69, released as E-4, 75, after serv in Hq, 133rd Unit. Publ: Auth, 107th legislature & Maine's divorce laws, Church World, 75. Mem: Cumberland Co Bar Asn; Maine Asn of Retarded Citizens (dir, 74-); Portland Landmarks Asn; Maine Audubon Soc. Mailing Add: 140 William St Portland ME 04103

MERRILL, W ISRAEL (D)
Idaho State Rep
Mailing Add: 581 North Stout Blackfoot ID 83221

MERRIMAN, JOHN A (R)
Chmn, Polk Co Rep Party, Iowa
b Knoxville, Iowa, Aug 13, 42; s John W Merriman & Doris Henry M; single. Educ: Northwestern Univ, AB, 64; Columbia Univ, LLB, 67; Phi Alpha Delta; Evans Scholars. Polit & Govt Pos: Dep chmn, Young Rep Iowa, 70-72; campaign chmn for co & legis cand, 70 & 74; state pres, Rep Workshop, 71-72; campaign chmn for cong cand, 72; mem, Polk Co Rep Cent & Exec Comt, formerly; chmn, Polk Co Rep Party, 74- Bus & Prof Pos: Assoc, Gamble, Riepe, Mardin & Webster, 67-69; assoc coun, Equitable Life of Iowa, 67- Mil Serv: Lt Comdr, Naval Res, Judge Adv Gen Corps. Mem: Iowa Life Ins Asn (secy). Relig: Protestant. Mailing Add: 4290 NW 46th St Pl Des Moines IA 50323

MERRIS, CHARLES LARRY (R)
Nat Committeeman, SC Young Rep
b Pottsville, Pa, Apr 29, 44; s Bruce C Adams (stepfather) & Mary Christ A; m 1969 to Sandra Lee Miller. Educ: Fla Keys Jr Col, 66-67; Pa State Univ, 68. Polit & Govt Pos: Chmn, Greenville Co Young Rep, SC, 71-73; mem leadership comt, Greenville Co Rep Party, 72-73; precinct committeeman, 74-; chmn, SC Biennial State Conv, Greenville, 73; nat committeeman & mem exec comt, SC Young Rep, 74-; mem, Nat Young Rep Exec Comt, Washington, DC, 74- Bus & Prof Pos: Mem task force on legis action, Greenville Co CofC, 74-75. Mil Serv: Entered as E-1, Navy, 63, released as PO 3/C, 67, after serv in Air Traffic Control NAS Key West, Fla; Nat Defense Medal; Good Conduct Award. Mem: Mason (chaplain, Lodge 345). Relig: Lutheran. Mailing Add: Rte 3 Badger Dr Taylors SC 29687

MERRITT, GILBERT ROY (GIL) (R)
b Atchison, Kans, Feb 28, 41; s Thomas William Merritt, Sr & Virginia Skelley M; single. Educ: Baker Univ, BA, 63; Pi Kappa Delta; Alpha Psi Omega; Zeta Chi. Polit & Govt Pos: Chmn, Atchison Co Young Rep, Kans, 64-66; Rep precinct committeeman, Atchison, 65-66; vchmn, Kans Fedn Young Rep, 69; press secy, US Rep Larry Winn, Jr, Kans, 69-72; founding pres, House Rep Commun Asn, 69-70; exec dir, Nat Conf Econ in Govt, 72-73. Bus & Prof Pos: Pres, Hipsley & Co Int. Mem: Toastmasters Int; assoc mem, Rep Commun Asn; life mem, Capitol Hill Club. Honors & Awards: Toastmaster of the Year, Haworth, 67. Relig: Protestant. Legal Res: 1001 N 13th Atchison KS 66002 Mailing Add: 1001 Conn Ave NW Washington DC 20036

MERRITT, GILBERT STROUD, JR (D)
Treas, Tenn State Dem Exec Comt
b Nashville, Tenn, Jan 17, 36; s Gilbert Stroud Merritt & Angie Cantrell Merritt Donelson; wid; c Louise Clark, Gilbert Stroud, III & Rufus Elijah Fort. Educ: Yale Univ, grad, 57; Vanderbilt Law Sch, LLB, 60; Harvard Law Sch, LLM, 62. Polit & Govt Pos: City Attorney, Nashville Metrop Govt, 63-65; US Dist Attorney for Middle Tenn, Dept Justice, 65-69; treas, Tenn State Dem Exec Comt, currently. Mem: Nashville, Tenn & Am Bar Asns; Vanderbilt Law Alumni Coun (dir); Fisk Univ (mem bd dirs). Relig: Episcopal. Legal Res: 612 Fair St Franklin TN 37064 Mailing Add: 23rd Floor L & C Tower Nashville TN 37219

MERRITT, HUGH L (D)
VChmn, Surry Co Dem Exec Comt
b Mount Airy, NC, Apr 8, 08; s William E Merritt & Caroline Kochititzky M; m 1939 to Emma Rice; c Emma Jane, Julia Frances (Mrs Fuller), Nancy Elizabeth (Mrs Ball) & Hugh L, Jr. Educ: Univ NC, BS, 29; Alpha Kappa Phi; Pi Kappa Phi. Polit & Govt Pos: NC State Rep, 65-67; vchmn, Surry Co Dem Exec Comt, 68-; mem, NC Bd Water & Air Resources, 69- Bus & Prof Pos: Hosiery mfr & mem bd dir, Renfro Hosiery Mills Co, 65-68; mem bd trustees, Northern Hosp of Surry Co, 68-69; dir, Nat Asn Hosiery Mfrs, 68-69. Mem: Mason; KT; Shrine. Relig: Methodist. Mailing Add: Country Club Rd Mt Airy NC 27030

MERRITT, MILO (D)
Iowa State Sen
Mailing Add: 412 Ash Osage IA 50461

MERRITT, ROY DONALD (R)
Chmn, Sanders Co Rep Cent Comt, Mont
b Polson, Mont, Mar 13, 40; s Wallis Lowell Merritt & Marion Sederstrom M; m 1962 to Jean DeVoe; c Kendall Ray, Rachell Ann (deceased) & Kristin. Educ: Univ Mont, Econ Degree, 63; Delta Sigma Phi. Polit & Govt Pos: Chmn, Sanders Co Rep Cent Comt, Mont, 68-; mem, Local Co Govt Study Comn, 75- Bus & Prof Pos: Dir, Western Mont Stockgrowers Asn, 72- Mem: Mason (Master, 70, treas, 71-). Relig: Lutheran; vpres, Church Coun. Mailing Add: RR 2 Hot Springs MT 59845

MERRITT, TOM (R)
Ill State Sen
b Rossville, Ill, Oct 20, 11; m to Martha Sandusky; c Tom, Jr & Judy. Educ: DePauw Univ; Purdue Univ. Polit & Govt Pos: City treas, Ill, 37-41; mem bd supvrs, 47-64, Rep precinct committeeman, 50-; chmn, Vermilion Co Rep Cent Comt, 62-64; Ill State Sen, 53rd Dist, 65- Bus & Prof Pos: Owner, Tom Merritt & Co, gen ins, real estate & farm loan bus; dir & vchmn bd, Wellington State Bank. Mem: Hoopeston Rotary Club; Mason; Shrine; Moose; Farm Bur. Honors & Awards: Deleg, White House Conf on Children & Youth, 60. Relig: Methodist. Mailing Add: 858 E Lincoln St Hoopeston IL 60942

MERSHART, RONALD VALERE (D)
Chmn, Douglas Co Dem Party, Wis
b Chicago, Ill, Mar 24, 32; s Pascal Gerard Meerschaert & Margaret DeBender M; m 1965 to Eileen Frances DeGrand; c Marielle & Paul Valere. Educ: DePaul Univ, BA, 54, MA, 63; Univ Chicago, PhD, 69. Polit & Govt Pos: Statutory chmn, Douglas Co Dem Party, Wis, 70-, chmn, 72- Bus & Prof Pos: Assoc prof hist, Univ Wis-Superior, 69- Mem: Am Hist Asn; Acad Polit Sci; Soc for French Hist Studies; Am Civil Liberties Union; Am Legion. Relig: Roman Catholic. Mailing Add: 2421 Hughitt Ave Superior WI 54880

MERSHON, CREIGHTON E (D)
Mem, Jefferson Co Dem Exec Comt, Ky
b Louisville, Ky, Oct 13, 41; s E Olliver Mershon, Jr & Dorothy Hinkebein M; m to Kathryn T Marcil; c Creighton, Jr. Educ: Bellarmine Col, BA cum laude, 63; Univ Louisville Sch Law, JD, 68; Phi Alpha Delta. Polit & Govt Pos: Spec asst to mayor, Louisville, Ky, 69-73, alderman, 73-, pres, Bd of Aldermen, 73-74; mem, Louisville & Jefferson Co Dem Exec Comts, 72- Bus & Prof Pos: Vol, Peace Corps, Venezuela, 63-65; attorney, Greenebaum, Doll, Matthews & Boone, 68-69; attorney, pvt practice, Louisville, 69- Mem: Ky Arthritis Found (bd dirs); Louisville & Jefferson Co Crime Comn (bd dirs). Honors & Awards: Outstanding Young Man, Louisville Jr CofC, 73; Flur de Lis Award for Outstanding Serv to City of Louisville, 73. Relig: Catholic. Mailing Add: 2311 Raleigh Lane Louisville KY 40206

MERSHON, JOHN J (D)
NMex State Rep
b 1908. Educ: Okla Baptist Univ. Polit & Govt Pos: NMex State Rep, 59- Bus & Prof Pos: Farmer. Mem: Mason. Relig: Protestant. Mailing Add: PO Box 257 Cloudcroft NM 88317

MERTENS, CHARLES FRANKLIN (D)
NDak State Rep
b Devils Lake, NDak, Jan 3, 33; s Henry Mertens & Mary Vansteenvort M; m 1959 to Janet Marie Kuntz; c Richard Allen, Laura Ann, Kenneth Gerard, Jeanne Marie, Connie Jo & Craig Charles. Educ: St Mary's Acad High Sch, Devils Lake, NDak; Lake Region Jr Col, 50-51; Valley Jr Col, Van Nuys, Calif, AA, 52. Polit & Govt Pos: NDak State Rep Dist 15, 70-, mem appropriations comt, NDak House Rep, 71 & 73, mem legis res coun & chmn educ comt A & mem full budget rev comt, currently; chmn indust-bus & labor comt of legis coun & mem audit & fiscal rev comt, 75- Mem: NDak Milk Producers Asn; Nat Independent Dairies Asn (state dir); NDak Dairy Indust Asn; CofC; VFW. Relig: Catholic. Mailing Add: State Capitol Bismarck ND 58501

MERTZ, INEZ MADELINE (DFL)
b Sleepy Eye, Minn, Sept 4, 16; d Nicholas Mertz (deceased) & Ann G Seikora; single. Educ: Sleepy Eye Normal Training Dept, Minn, teaching cert, 34; Mankato State Col, BS, 65. Polit & Govt Pos: Vchairwoman, Brown Co Dem-Farmer-Labor Party, Minn, 60-61, secy, 62-72, chairwoman, 72-74; deleg to dist & state Dem-Farmer-Labor Conv, 62-70, co-chmn credentials comt at dist conv, 70; deleg, Dem Dist State & Co Conv, 72. Bus & Prof Pos: Rural teacher, Dist 44, Nicollet Co, 35-38, Dist 29, Brown Co, 38-41 & Dist 36, 41-53; teacher first grade, St Mary's Sch, Sleepy Eye, 53-73, teacher first grade & asst prin, 68-; remedial reading teacher during summer sch, Sleepy Eye Pub Sch, 68-70. Mem: Delta Kappa Gamma (treas, Alpha Iota chap); Reading Coun; Qui Vive Women's Club (treas); Dem-Farmer-Labor Women's Auxiliary; Qui Vive Federated Club (pres, 72-73). Honors & Awards: Received pins, cert & a plaque for 4-H serv & pin & cert for 25 years serv. Relig: Catholic. Mailing Add: 415 Second Ave NW Sleepy Eye MN 56085

MESHEL, HARRY (D)
Ohio State Sen
Mailing Add: 786 Fairgreen Ave Youngstown OH 44510

MESITE, PATSY J (D)
Conn State Rep
Mailing Add: PO Box 713 55 Edgewood Place Meriden CT 06450

MESKILL, THOMAS J (R)
b New Britain, Conn, Jan 30, 28; m to Mary T Grady; c Maureen, John, Peter, Eileen & Thomas. Educ: Trinity Col, BS, 50; Univ Conn Law Sch, 56; NY Univ Sch of Law; ed, Law Rev, Univ Conn. Polit & Govt Pos: Mayor, New Britain, Conn, 62-64; mem, Const Conv, Hartford, 65; US Rep, Conn, 66-70; Gov, Conn, 71-74; deleg, Rep Nat Conv, 72; judge, US Second Circuit Court Appeals, 75- Bus & Prof Pos: Attorney, corp counsel, 65-66. Mil Serv: 1st Lt, Air Force, 50-53. Mem: New Britain Jaycees; New Britain Found of Soc Agencies; KofC; Elks; Am Legion. Hon Degrees: Distinguished Serv Award, New Britain Jaycees, 64. Relig: Catholic. Mailing Add: 18 High Hill Rd Bloomfield CT 06002

MESSER, ERNEST BRYAN (D)
NC State Rep
b Waynesville, NC, Dec 21, 13; s Forrest W Messer & Effie Furr M; m 1936 to Jincy Owen Uryan C; m Mrs Clyde Poovey, Jr. Educ: Carson Newman Col, BA, 35. Polit & Govt Pos: Chmn, Haywood Co Dem Exec Comt, NC, 58-62; mem, Haywood Co Planning Bd; rep, Gen Assembly, 63; NC State Rep, currently. Bus & Prof Pos: Teacher & basketball coach, Haywood Co Sch, 35-39; supvr, Wood Procurement Dept, Champion Papers, Inc. Mil Serv: Lt, Navy, 42-45. Mem: Lions; Toastmasters; Am Legion; VFW; Haywood Co Ment Health Asn (bd dirs). Relig: Baptist; teacher, adult Sunday sch class. Mailing Add: 15 Forest View Circle Canton NC 28716

MESSER, MERLE AUBREY (R)
Chmn, Somerset Co Rep Comt, Maine
b Skowhegan, Maine, Aug 30, 44; s Ralph Waldo Messer & Clytie Batcher M; m 1967 to Donna Sargent; c Stephen & Aaron. Educ: Thomas Col, BSEd, 67. Polit & Govt Pos: Mem, Maine Second Cong Dist Comt, 73-; finance chmn, Anson Town Comt, 74-; chmn, Somerset Co Rep Comt, 74-; secy-treas, Maine Rep Co Chmn Asn, 74- Bus & Prof Pos: Owner & pres, Skowhegan Bus Sch, 68- Mil Serv: Entered as E-1, Navy, 67, released as E-4, 68, after serv in Staff Duty, San Diego, 67-68. Mem: Sch Admin Dist 74 (mem sch bd, 73-). Relig: Protestant. Mailing Add: Hilltop Rd Anson ME 04911

MESSINA, FRANCIS WILLIAM (R)
b New Haven, Conn, Aug 22, 13; s Pasquale Messina & Christina Mascola M; m 1940 to Marie Louise Donroe; c William Francis, Rita Marie (Mrs Dottori) & Lenora Ann (Mrs Bouchard). Educ: Hillhouse High Sch, New Haven, Conn, grad, 31. Polit & Govt Pos: First selectman, East Haven, Conn, 67-69, mayor, 69-; alt deleg, Rep Nat Conv, 72. Bus & Prof Pos: Pres, East Haven CofC, 62-65; dir, New Haven Real Estate Bd, Inc, 62-65; chmn, Conn Regional Coun Elected Off, 68-70; mem, Salvation Army Adv Bd, New Haven, 69-; dir, Comprehensive Health Planning, New Haven, 72- & Conn Conf of Mayors, 72- Mem: KofC; Am of Italian Descent; hon mem, New Eng Asn of Police Chiefs, Police Comnr Asn Conn & Conn State Asn Chiefs of Police. Honors & Awards: Outstanding Serv, East Haven CofC, 65, Cert of Participation, 69 & 72; Cert of Participation, Am Legion, 67; Leadership Award, East Shore Babe Ruth League, 67; Cert of Merit, Gtr New Haven Bd of Realtors, 69; Voice of Democracy Award, VFW, 70; Leadership Award, Realtors of Gtr New Haven, 70. Relig: Roman Catholic. Mailing Add: 22 Foote Rd East Haven CT 06512

METAYER, ELIZABETH NENER (D)
Mass State Rep
b Boston, Mass, Aug 21, 11; d John Willoughby Nener & Lucy Phillips N; m 1935, wid; m 1947 to Edward Achille Metayer; c Richard Edward & Gael Elizabeth (Mrs James Corbin, Jr). Educ: Harvard Univ, 2 years; Hickox Secretarial Sch, grad, 46. Polit & Govt Pos: Mem, Braintree Town Meeting, Mass, 55-; chmn, Braintree Tech Adv Comt on Transportation, 66-69; mem, Braintree Dem Town Comt, 67-; Mass State Rep, Norfolk Seventh Dist, 75- Bus & Prof Pos: Owner, Elizabeth N Metayer Secretarial Serv, Boston, 46-47. Publ: Cabbages and kings, weekly column, Braintree Observer Forum; columnist, various S Shore newspapers, 63- Mem: Braintree Point Woman's Club; Braintree Philergians; Braintree Hist Soc; Braintree League Women Voters; Mass State Fedn Women Clubs. Relig: Catholic. Mailing Add: 33 Arthur St Braintree MA 02184

METCALF, JACK HOLACE (R)
b Marysville, Wash, Nov 30, 27; s John Read Metcalf & Eunice Grannis M; m 1948 to Norma Jean Grant; c Marta Jean, Gayle Marie, Lea Lynn & Beverly Ann. Educ: Pac Lutheran Col, BA & BEduc, 51; Univ Wash, grad work, 65-66. Polit & Govt Pos: Wash State Rep, 60-64; pres, Wash Fedn Young Rep Clubs, 64; Wash State Sen, 21st Dist, 67-74; cand, US Sen, Wash, 68 & 74. Mil Serv: Pvt, Army, 46-47. Mem: Salvation Army (adv bd); Mukilteo Hist Soc; Lynnwood Kiwanis; Edmonds Rod & Gun Club; Snohomish Co Vols Am (bd dirs). Relig: Protestant. Mailing Add: 4469 S 3260 E Langley WA 98260

METCALF, LEE (D)
US Sen, Mont
b Stevensville, Mont, Jan 28, 11; m 1938 to Donna Hoover; c Jerry (foster son). Polit & Govt Pos: Assoc Justice, Mont Supreme Court, 46; US Rep, Mont, 53-54; US Sen, Mont, 60-; alt deleg, Dem Nat Conv, 72. Bus & Prof Pos: Lawyer. Legal Res: Helena MT Mailing Add: 427 Old Senate Office Bldg Washington DC 20510

METCALF, VERA MARIE (D)
Chairwoman, Trego Co Dem Comt, Kans
b Fort Scott, Kans, June 22, 45; d Clyde Eldon Ellington & Mildred Hultz E; m 1966 to Elmer Eugene Metcalf; c William Edward. Educ: Bronson High Sch, grad, 63; Nat Motel-Hotel Mgt, 70; Epsilon Sigma Alpha. Polit & Govt Pos: Chairwoman, Trego Co Dem Comt, 74- Bus & Prof Pos: Desk clerk & auditor, Holiday Inn, Hays, Kans, 70-74; real estate salesman, Marcotte Realty & Auction, 74- Mem: Kans Realtors Asn; Epsilon Sigma Alpha; WaKeeney Golf Club; Nat Womens Dem Orgn, (chmn, 74-75); Eastern Star. Relig: Methodist. Legal Res: 110 Easter Ave WaKeeney KS 67672 Mailing Add: 515 Russell Ave WaKeeney KS 67672

METCALFE, RALPH HAROLD (D)
US Rep, Ill
b Atlanta, Ga, May 30, 10; s Maj Clarence Metcalfe & Mayme Attaway M; m 1947 to Madalynne Fay Young; c Ralph H, Jr. Educ: Marquette Univ, PhB, 36; Univ Southern Calif, MA in Phys Educ, 39; Alpha Psi; Alpha Sigma Nu; pres of grad class. Polit & Govt Pos: Dr, Dept of Civil Rights, Comn on Human Rels, 45; Ill State Athletic Comnr, 49-52; committeeman, Third Ward Dem Comt, Chicago, Ill, 52-72, alderman, Chicago City Coun, Third Ward, 55-71, chmn, Comt Bldgs & Zoning, 65, pres pro tem, 69; alt deleg, Dem Nat Conv, 56 & 64, deleg, 68; Presidential Elector, 60; mem, Planning Comn, Chicago, 64; mem, Northeastern Ill Metrop Area Planning Comn, 69; US Rep, First Dist, Ill, 70-, mem, Interstate & Foreign Com Comt & Subcomt on Transportation & Com, Consumer Protection & Finance & Merchant Marine & Fisheries Comt, chmn, subcomts on Panama Canal & Oceanography, US House of Rep; mem, Dem Steering & Policy Comt; mem, Dem Study Group & mem, Exec Comt, formerly. Bus & Prof Pos: Track coach & instr polit sci, Xavier Univ, New Orleans, 36-42; mem bd dirs, Ill Fed Savings & Loan Asn, Chicago. Mil Serv: Entered as Pvt, Army, 42, released as 1st Lt, 45, after serv in Transportation Corps; Legion of Merit. Mem: Mahalia Jackson Scholar Found; Dr Martin Luther King, Jr Urban Progress Ctr comt on urban opportunity & co-chmn, subcomt on recreation & culture; NAACP; Amvets; Am Legion; Elks. Honors & Awards: Mem, US Olympic Teams, 32 & 34; first black Ill State Athletic Comnr; Mem Black Athletes Hall of Fame, US Track & Field Hall of Fame & Nat Track & Field Hall of Fame. Relig: Catholic. Legal Res: 4530 S Michigan Ave Chicago IL 60653 Mailing Add: 322 Cannon House Off Bldg Washington DC 20515

METELICA, JOHN (R)
Chmn, Leyden Rep Town Comt, Mass
b Leyden, Mass, Dec 2, 22; s Leonty Metelica (deceased) & Mary Verowka M (deceased); m 1948 to Margaret Louise Hallett; c Jacqueline Jeen, Nancy Jane & Michael John. Educ: Univ Mass, 2 years. Polit & Govt Pos: Local campaign coordr, Gov John Volpe, Mass, 68, Gov Francis Sargent, 70 & Rep Johnathon Healy, 70; chmn, Leyden Rep Town Comt, 71- Bus & Prof Pos: Sales mgr & owner, M & M Motors, 57-59; mgr & owner, Bridge of Flowers Cafe, 60-63; sales mgr, Henry M Kugler Autos, 64-69; machinist, Greenfield Tap & Die, 70- Mil Serv: Entered as Aviation Cadet, Air Force, 43, released as Sgt, 46, after serv in 5th Air Force, Southwest Pac, 45-46. Mem: Maple Valley Ski Area (ski ambassador); Elks; VFW. Relig: Russian Orthodox. Legal Res: Leyden MA Mailing Add: Leyden Rd Greenfield MA 01301

METRO, JAMES J (D)
Conn State Rep
Mailing Add: South Ellsworth Rd Sharon CT 06069

METTERT, ARLENE E (R)
Co-Chairwoman, Erie Co Rep Party, Ohio
b Athens Co, Ohio, Apr 16, 27; d Dow Dewey White & Florence Sedwick W; m 1947 to Paul Mettert; c Ronald P, Randall C, Kathy (Mrs Faetanini) & Jeffrey L. Educ: Margaretta High Sch, grad, 45. Polit & Govt Pos: Co-chairwoman, Erie Co Rep Party, Ohio, 74- Mem: Amvets Auxiliary. Legal Res: 1329 Stone St Sandusky OH 44870 Mailing Add: Bd of Elections Erie Co Court House Sandusky OH 44870

METZ, C BARNEY (D)
Chmn, St Clair Co Dem Party, Ill
b Dupo, Ill, May 24, 25; s Arthur Andrew Metz & Lillian Martin M; m 1946 to Alice Elizabeth Joshu; c Janice Cox, Knute, Jean Brown & Jacqueline. Educ: High sch. Polit & Govt Pos: Village bd of trustees, Dupo, Ill, 57-61; Sugarloaf Twp bd mgrs, St Clair Co, 59-65; mayor, Village of Dupo, 61-; chmn, St Clair Co Dem Party, Ill, 74-; St Clair co clerk, 74- Bus & Prof Pos: Chief clerk, St Clair Co Bd Assessors, 62-74. Mil Serv: Entered as Pvt, Army, 43, released as Cpl, 46, after serv in 689th Field Artillery, 3rd Army, ETO, 44-46; ETO Medal with Four Battle Stars; Good Conduct Medal; Unit Citations. Mem: Am Legion; life mem VFW; Belleville CofC. Mailing Add: 321 N Third Dupo IL 62239

METZ, REUBEN (R)
NDak State Rep
Mailing Add: State Capitol Bismarck ND 58501

METZ, SHARON KAY (D)
Wis State Rep
b Omro, Wis; d Henry Berthold Wiesner & Elfrieda Schmude W; m 1952 to Thomas O Metz; c Michael Lee, Mark Lane, Mitchell Lin & Matthew Laird. Educ: Univ Wis, Green Bay, 73- Polit & Govt Pos: Welfare comnr, Green Bay, Wis, 73-75; Wis State Rep, 75- Bus & Prof Pos: Admin asst, Action Prog, Univ Wis, Green Bay, 72-74. Mem: Womans Club Green Bay; Co-Care Neighborhood Orgn; United Way (bd dirs); Vol Comn Human Rights. Relig: Lutheran. Mailing Add: 816 Shawano Ave Green Bay WI 54303

METZEN, JAMES P (D)
Minn State Rep
Mailing Add: 401 Orchard Lane S St Paul MN 55075

METZENBAUM, HOWARD MORTON (D)
Mem, Ohio Dem State Exec Comt
b Cleveland, Ohio, June 4, 17; s Charles I Metzenbaum & Anna Klafter M; m 1946 to Shirley Turoff; c Barbara Jo, Susan Lynn, Shelley Hope & Amy Beth. Educ: Ohio State Univ, BA, 39, Law Sch, LLB, 41; Order of the Coif; Phi Eta Sigma; Tau Epsilon Rho. Polit & Govt Pos: Panel mem, War Labor Bd, 42-45; Ohio State Rep, 43-46; Ohio State Sen, 47-50, mem, Ohio Judiciary Coun, chmn, Judiciary Comt & vchmn, Rules Comt, Ohio State Senate, 49-50; mem, Ohio Bur Code Rev, 49-50; alt deleg, Dem Nat Conv, 64, deleg, 68; mem, Ohio Dem State Exec Comt, 66-; gold star mem, Ohio Dem Finance Comt, 69-; ex officio deleg, Dem Nat Mid-Term Conf, 74. Bus & Prof Pos: Chmn bd, Airport Parking Co Am, 58-66; trustee, Mt Sinai Hosp, Cleveland, Ohio, 61-, treas, 66-; dir, Capital Nat Bank, 62-68; chmn bd, ITT Consumer Serv Corp, 66-68; dir, Soc Nat Bank & Soc Corp, 68; chmn exec comt, ComCorp, 69- Mem: Am Bar Asn; Am Trial Lawyers Asn; Coun on Human Rels (mem bd); United Cerebral Palsy Asn (mem bd); Nat Coun on Hunger & Malnutrition (mem bd). Honors & Awards: Auth of Ohio Retail Installment Sales Act & numerous other legis enactments; Cath Interracial Justice Award; Towne Crier Award. Relig: Jewish. Legal Res: 18500 N Park Blvd Shaker Heights OH 44118 Mailing Add: 1770 Investment Plaza Cleveland OH 44114

METZGAR, EDITH CATHRINE (D)
VChairwoman, Holt Co Dem Cent Comt, Mo
b Fairfax, Mo, Dec 1, 18; d Robert Thomson & Lila Neta Curry T; m 1943 to Edgar Lee Metzgar; c Lila Lee, William Edward & Elizabeth Ann. Educ: Park Col, 1 year; Platt-Gard Bus Univ, St Joseph, Mo, secy course, 1 year. Polit & Govt Pos: Secy, Holt Co Dem Cent Comt, 62-64, vchairwoman, 68-; pres, Fed Women's Dem Club, Holt Co, 65-66, first vpres, 66-67, secy-treas, 68- Mem: Nat Farmers Orgn; Eastern Star. Relig: Presbyterian. Mailing Add: RR 1 Mound City MO 64470

METZGER, EDWARD (R)
NDak State Rep
b Willa, NDak, Apr 14, 27; s William Metzger & Elizabeth Miller M; m 1953 to Alyce Mae Ellison; c Edward J, Cynthia R, Marty Rae & Joy Marie. Educ: Hebron High Sch, grad, 45. Polit & Govt Pos: Co vchmn, NDak Dem Nonpartisan League; precinct committeeman, Dem Party, NDak, 63-66; NDak State Rep, 32nd Dist, 67- Mil Serv: Entered as Pvt, Army, 45, released as Sgt, 47, after serv in 907 Counter Intel Corps, ETO. Mem: Elks; Am Legion; VFW; Int Brotherhood Elec Workers; Bismarck Mfrs Trades & Labor Assembly. Relig: Lutheran. Mailing Add: 613 Remington Bismarck ND 58501

METZGER, RAY (D)
NDak State Rep
Mailing Add: State Capitol Bismarck ND 58501

METZNER, CARROLL E (R)
VChmn, Second Cong Dist Rep Party, Wis
b Milwaukee, Wis, Apr 24, 19; s Edwin F Metzner & Anna Mathilda Clara Henke M; m 1944 to Peggy Joan Hausse; c Bruce Carroll Stokes & Margot Andrea. Educ: Univ Wis Exten, 37-39; Northwestern Univ, BS, 41; Univ Wis Law Sch, LLB, 43. Polit & Govt Pos: Alderman, Madison, Wis, 51-56; Wis State Assemblyman, 54-58; secy, Citizens for Better Govt, 61-64; mem exec comt, Dane Co Rep Party, 61-65, chmn, 65-69; mem ins laws revision adv comn, Wis Legis Coun, 67-; alt deleg, Rep Nat Conv, 68 & 72; chmn, Second Cong Dist Rep Party, Wis, 69-73, vchmn, 73- Bus & Prof Pos: Attorney, Aberg, Bell, Blake & Metzner; dir & secy bd, Metropolitan Nat Bank, 73- Mem: Am Bar Asn; Fedn of Ins Counsel; Lions Int; Defense

Res Inst; Methodist Hosp. Relig: Congregational Christian. Legal Res: 733 Huron Hill Madison WI 53711 Mailing Add: United Bank Tower Madison WI 53701

MEYER, ARLIE H **(R)**
b St Charles, Mo, Aug 12, 05; s Edward Meyer & Sophie Griewing M; m 1933 to Flora Anna Haferkamp; c Donald Edward & Robert Allen. Educ: St Charles Pub Schs, 10 years. Polit & Govt Pos: City councilman, St Charles, Mo, 35-39; co assessor, St Charles Co, 53-65; Mo State Rep, 67-72; deleg, Rep Nat Conv, 72. Bus & Prof Pos: Real estate salesman; bd chmn, First State Bank of St Charles, Mo, 72- Mem: Mo Real Estate Asn; Elks (Exalted Ruler, Lodge 690); Moose; Am Red Cross; Mo State Assessors Asn. Relig: United Church of Christ. Mailing Add: 234 Thomas Ave St Charles MO 63301

MEYER, ARMIN HENRY
b Ft Wayne, Ind, Jan 19, 14; m 1949 to Alice James; c Kathleen Alice. Educ: Capital Univ, BA, 35, LLD; Ohio State Univ, MA, 41. Hon Degrees: LLD, Lincoln Col, 69, SDak Sch Mines & Technol, 72, Wartburg Col, 72 & Ohio State Univ, 72. Polit & Govt Pos: News ed, chief, Bur News, Off War Info, 44-45; pub affairs officer, Foreign Serv Auxiliary, Baghdad, 46-48; career officer, US Dept State Foreign Serv, 48-73, second secy, Baghdad, 48, first secy & consul, Beirut, 52-55, first secy, consul, Kabul, 55-57, dep dir, Off SAsian Affairs, 57-58, dep dir & dir, Off Near East Affairs, 58-60, dep asst secy state for Near East & SAsian Affairs, 61, US Ambassador to Lebanon, 62-65, US Ambassador to Iran, 65-69, US Ambassador to Japan, 69-72, spec asst to the Secy of State, 72- Bus & Prof Pos: Pub rels officer, 35-39; asst prof & dean of men, Capital Univ, 40-42; visiting prof, Am Univ, 74-75 & Georgetown Univ, 75- Honors & Awards: State Dept Meritorious & Superior Serv Awards, 58. Legal Res: Lincoln IL Mailing Add: 4610 Reno Rd NW Washington DC 20008

MEYER, CLARENCE ARDELL HENRY **(R)**
b Pender, Nebr, Sept 1, 10; s William C Meyer & Bertha Schultz M; m 1941 to Frances Boughn. Educ: Univ Nebr, AB, Univ Nebr Col Law, JD, 33; Sigma Alpha Epsilon; Phi Delta Phi. Polit & Govt Pos: Mem staff, US Dept Justice, 40-42 & Nebr Dept Labor, 46-49; asst attorney gen, Nebr, 49-52, Dep Attorney Gen, 52-60, Attorney Gen, Nebr, 60-75. Bus & Prof Pos: Lawyer, 33-40. Mil Serv: Entered as 2nd Lt, Air Force, 42, released as Maj, 46, after serv in Air Transport Command, China-Burma-India, 43-46; Bronze Star; Distinguished Unit Citation; Chinese Air Force Medal. Publ: State taxation in Nebraska, 1/55 & Analysis of business lotteries, 3/55, Nebr Law Rev; Arrest. search & seizure, Nebr State Bar J, 4/67. Mem: Am Law Inst; Am Legion; Nebr & Am Bar Asns. Honors & Awards: Lewis E Wyman Award, 65. Relig: Lutheran. Mailing Add: 3210 Van Dorn Lincoln NE 68502

MEYER, D WAYNE **(R)**
Chmn, Kingsbury Co Rep Party, SDak
b Erwin, SDak, May 1, 20; s Theodore H Meyer & Hazel Luders M; m 1942 to Audrey H Chester; c Joan (Mrs Jencks), Jerry W & Bruce D. Educ: SDak State Univ, 39-42. Polit & Govt Pos: Chmn, Kingsbury Co Rep Party, SDak, 71- Bus & Prof Pos: Vpres, Peoples State Bank, De Smet, SDak, 57- Mil Serv: Entered as Pvt, Air Force, 43, released as Pfc, after serv in Hq & Hq Squadron. Relig: Am Lutheran. Mailing Add: 304 Fourth Ave SW De Smet SD 57231

MEYER, J THEODORE **(R)**
Ill State Rep
b Chicago, Ill, Apr 13, 36; s Joseph Theodore Meyer & Mary E McHugh M; m 1961 to Mary Lou Bartholomew; c Jean Frances & J Theodore, III. Educ: John Carroll Univ, BS, 58; DePaul Univ Col Law, JD, 62. Polit & Govt Pos: Ill State Rep, 28th Dist, 66-72 & 74-, co-chmn joint House-Senate air pollution study comt, 67, chmn environ study comt, Ill House of Rep, 68, minority spokesman environ, energy & natural resources, 74-; chmn & founder, Midwest Legis Coun on Environ, Ten Midwestern States, US Environ Protection Agency, 71. Bus & Prof Pos: Self-employed attorney, 63- Mem: Am Bar Asn; Ill State Hist Soc; Oriental Inst, Univ Chicago; Nat Trust for Hist Preservation; Nat Wildlife Fedn. Honors & Awards: Ill Wildlife Fedn Appreciation Award, 72; Am Legion Expression of Appreciation, 72, Distinguished Lawyer Legislator, 72 & Comt on Courts & Justice Legislator Appreciation Award, 72; Environ Qual Award, Region V, US Environ Protection Agency, 74. Relig: Catholic. Mailing Add: 2355 W 111th St Chicago IL 60643

MEYER, JOHN **(D)**
Polit & Govt Pos: Mem, Dem Nat Comt, Ore, formerly. Mailing Add: PO Box 378 Canyonville OR 97417

MEYER, JOHN RICHARD (JACK) **(R)**
Chmn, Clay Co Rep Cent Comt, Ill
b Olney, Ill, Apr 5, 23; s Ralph G Meyer & Lena Bunnell M; m 1944 to Ruth Ann Schwager; c Carol, Paul & Janet. Educ: Wash Univ, LLB, 47, JD, 68. Polit & Govt Pos: Spec Asst Attorney Gen, Ill, 59-61 & 69-; chmn, Clay Co Rep Cent Comt, Ill, 68- Mil Serv: Entered as A/S, Naval Res, 43, released as Lt(jg), 45, after serv in LST Flotilla Staff, 36, Pac Theatre, 44-45. Mem: Ill State & Am Bar Asns; Ill & Am Trial Lawyer Asns; Kiwanis. Relig: Christian. Mailing Add: 717 N Main St PO Box 700 Flora IL 62839

MEYER, M BARRY **(D)**
b Charleston, WVa, Jan 4, 31; s Abe Meyer & Sophia Zimmerman M; m 1954 to Thelma Berch; c David, Deborah, Rebecca & Daniel. Educ: Univ Pa, BSE; Harvard Law Sch, LLB. Polit & Govt Pos: Chief counsel & chief clerk, Comt Pub Works, US Senate, 67- Mailing Add: 8508 Hunter Creek Trail Potomac MD 20854

MEYER, NORMAN J **(D)**
Mem, Orange Co Dem Cent Comt, Calif
b Wilkes-Barre, Pa, Aug 5, 30; s Nathan H Meyer & Helen Goldstein M; m 1953 to Shirley F Nast; c Lee Ann, Jack R, Neal J & Joanne. Educ: Syracuse Univ, 47-48; Pa State Univ, BS in physics, 51, MS in physics, 53; Univ Southern Calif, 52-53; Univ Calif, Los Angeles, PhD in physics, 59; Sigma Xi; Sigma Pi Sigma. Polit & Govt Pos: Mem, Orange Co Dem Cent Comt, Calif, 59-, vchmn, 60-62, chmn, 62-66; mem, Calif State Dem Party, 60-66, mem exec bd & steering comt, 62-66; deleg, Dem Nat Conv, 64; mem bd trustees, Fairview State Hosp, Costa Mesa, Calif, 64-68. Bus & Prof Pos: Sr engr, HRB-Singer, State College, Pa, 51-52; research scientist, Aeronutronic Div, Philco, Newport Beach, Calif, 59-61; staff physicist, Marshall Labs, Torrance, 61-62; dir, LTV Research Ctr, West Div, Anaheim, 62-70; vpres & mem bd dirs, Hearing Conserv Serv, Inc, Com, until 70; pres & prin scientist, OAS/Western Ocean & Atmospheric Sci, Inc, Santa Ana, 70-72; dir research, Wyle Labs, El Segundo, 73- Publ: Several tech articles, J of Chem Physics & J of Acoustical Soc of Am. Mem: Am Asn for Advan of Sci; Nat Acad Sci/Nat Research Coun, (Comt on Hearing, Bioacoustics & Biomech, 68-); Mason; Anti-Defamation League, Pac Southwest Region (regional adv bd), Orange Co Jewish Community Coun, (pres, 66-70). Relig: Jewish. Mailing Add: 2988 Ceylon Dr Costa Mesa CA 92626

MEYER, WALTER A **(D)**
NDak State Rep
Mailing Add: State Capitol Bismarck ND 58501

MEYER, WALTER L **(D)**
Mo State Rep
b St Louis, Mo, Feb 25, 23; s Lewis Meyer & Martha Hogan M; m 1943 to Audrey Merklin; c Lawrence, Daniel & Maureen. Educ: Mason Elem Sch & Southwest High Sch, St Louis, Mo. Polit & Govt Pos: Alderman, Bellefontaine Neighbors, Mo, 53-57, mayor, 57-63; St Ferdinand Twp Committeeman, 64-68; Mo State Dem Committeeman, formerly; Mo State Rep, 53rd Dist, St Louis Co, 62-, chmn comt rds & hwys, comt on educ, spec comt on airport develop & comn on ins, vchmn comt workmans compensation & comt interstate coop, Mo House Rep, currently; alt deleg, Dem Nat Conv, 72. Bus & Prof Pos: Secy-treas, steward, mem exec bd, Local 1102, IUE-AFL-CIO, currently, deleg, St Louis Labor Coun, currently. Mem: Northwest Kiwanis Club (pres); Christian Bros Col (exec bd); Hathaway Riverview Terrace Improv Asn; Red Cross for North St Louis Co (area chmn); Surrey Lane Athletic Asn. Relig: Catholic. Mailing Add: 9495 Yorktown Dr St Louis MO 63137

MEYER, WILLIAM BENEDICT **(D)**
Mem, Calif State Dem Cent Comt
b Santa Ana, Calif, Mar 13, 23; s J Meyer, Jr & Connie Chavez M; m to Barbara Wangsness; c Judy (Mrs Tom Leichtfuss), Susan McCrory, Roger P & Bruce M. Educ: Long Beach State Col, BA with honors, 52, MA, 53; Univ Calif, Los Angeles; Univ Southern Calif; Phi Theta Kappa. Polit & Govt Pos: Pres, Orange Dem Club, 64-65 & E Orange Co Dem Coun, 65-66; dir, 35th Cong Dist Calif Dem Coun, 66-67; chmn, Orange Co Dem Fedn, 67-69; mem, Orange Co Dem Cent Comt & chmn of Dem Clubs, 68-; mem, Calif Dem State Cent Comt, 68-; exec asst to Supvr Robert W Battin, First Dist, Orange Co, Calif, 72- Bus & Prof Pos: Counr, Orange Co Juv Hall, 45-54; pres, William B Meyer & Assoc, 45-; teacher, Fullerton Jr Col, 54-, on leave of absence, 72- Mil Serv: Pvt, Marine Corps, 44-45, with serv in 4th Bn, US; Good Serv Medal. Mem: Nat Educ Asn; Calif Asn of Teachers of English; Downtown Orange Businessmen & Property Owners Asn; Orange & Orange Co CofC; PTA. Relig: First Christian. Legal Res: 701 E Palmdale Ave Orange CA 92665 Mailing Add: PO Box 3525 Orange CA 92665

MEYERS, EMIL, JR **(R)**
Chmn, Napa Co Rep Cent Comt, Calif
b Wilmington, NC, July 27, 27; s Emil Meyers & Clyda Nolley M; m 1949 to Martha Isabelle Webb; c Christina (Mrs Conlee), Ronda Leigh & Emil Irvin. Educ: Napa Jr Col, AA, 48; Univ Calif, Berkeley, exten courses, 60. Polit & Govt Pos: Mem, Napa Co Rep Cent Comt, Calif, 70-73, chmn, 73-; mem, Rep State Cent Comt, Calif, 73- Bus & Prof Pos: Pres, Emil Meyers Construction, Inc, 59- Mil Serv: Entered as Seaman 2/C, Navy, 45, released as Seaman 1/C, 46, after serv in Air Wing; Am Theatre Medal; Good Conduct Medal. Mem: Elks; Solano-Napa Builders Exchange; Lions; PTA; Friends of Napa Co, RIA, Builders Exchange. Honors & Awards: Numerous awards, Lions Int, 61-; Citizen of the Month, CofC, 71; Builders Exchange Outstanding Contrib Award, 71. Relig: Protestant. Legal Res: 1830 Menlo Ave Napa CA 94558 Mailing Add: PO Box 236 Napa CA 94558

MEYERS, HANNES, JR **(R)**
Chmn, Ninth Cong Dist Rep Exec Comt, Mich
b Muskegon, Mich, Dec 11, 32; s Hannes Meyers, Sr & Ann Baker M; m 1958 to Marjorie Rodabaugh; c Hannes, IV, Steven Arthur & Mark Cameron. Educ: Calvin Col, BA, 55; Univ Mich Law Sch, JD, 58. Polit & Govt Pos: Treas, Ottawa Co Rep Party, Mich, 62-69; mem, Ninth Cong Dist Rep Exec Comt, 62-, chmn, 75-; mem, Ottawa Co Rep Exec Comt, 62-; mem, Rep State Cent Comt, 69-; chmn, State Officers Compensation Comn, 75- Bus & Prof Pos: City attorney, Hudsonville & Zeeland, Mich, 59- Mem: Ottawa Co Bar Asn (vpres, 74-); Mich Bar Asn; Calvin Col Alumni Asn; Delta Theta Phi; Am Judicature Soc. Relig: Christian Reformed. Mailing Add: 30 S Wall St Zeeland MI 49464

MEYERS, JAN **(R)**
Kans State Sen
Mailing Add: 8408 W 90th Overland Park KS 66212

MEYERSON, A FREDERICK **(D)**
NY State Sen
b Paterson, NJ, Feb 2, 18; s Max Meyerson & Rose Prince M; m 1947 to Shirley Kahan; c Gregory & Norma. Educ: St John's Univ, Col Arts & Sci, BA, 45, Law Sch, LLB, 43. Polit & Govt Pos: Admin asst to Congressman Eugene J Keogh; counsel, Joint Legis Comt Reapportionment; law secy, Justice Victor L Anfuso, Supreme Court, Kings Co, 63; law asst, Supreme Court, Kings Co, 67; law secy, Justice Abraham J Multer, Supreme Court, 68; NY State Sen, 15th Sen Dist, 69-; deleg, Dem Nat Mid-Term Conf, 74. Bus & Prof Pos: Mem Law Firm, Arab & Meyerson, 47- Mem: Temple Sinai (pres); 75th Precinct Youth Coun; East NY Community Activities (bd dirs); 38th Assembly Dist Regular Dem Orgn (exec mem); East NY Develop Corp (hon chmn). Relig: Hebrew. Legal Res: 14 Van Siclen Ct Brooklyn NY 11207 Mailing Add: 50 Court St Brooklyn NY 11201

MEYNER, HELEN STEVENSON **(D)**
US Rep, NJ
b New York, NY, March 5, 29; d William Edward Stevenson & Eleanor Bumstead Stevenson S; m 1957 to Robert Baumle Meyner. Educ: Colo Col, BA, 50. Hon Degrees: LLD, Colo Col, 73. Polit & Govt Pos: Comnr, NJ Rehabilitation, 61-; US Rep, NJ, 75- Bus & Prof Pos: Field worker, Am Red Cross, Korea, 50-52; guide, UN, New York, 52-53; travel adv, TWA Airlines, 53-56; spec asst, Adlai Stevenson Presidential Campaign, 56; columnist, Star-Ledger, Newark, NJ, 62-69. Mem: Rider Col (bd trustees, 71-); Newark Museum (bd trustees, 65-); Am Folk Art Museum (bd trustees, 72-). Relig: Presbyterian. Legal Res: 372 Lincoln Ave Phillipsburg NJ 08865 Mailing Add: 16 Olden Lane Princeton NJ 08540

MEYNER, ROBERT BAUMLE **(D)**
b Easton, Pa, July 3, 08; s Gustave Herman Meyner & Mary Sophia Baumle M; m 1957 to Helen Day Stevenson. Educ: Lafayette Col; Columbia Univ Law Sch. Polit & Govt Pos: NJ State Sen, Warren Co, 48-52; deleg, Dem Nat Conv, 48-68; Gov, NJ, 54-62. Bus & Prof Pos: Lawyer, 36-54; partner, law firm, Meyner, Landis & Verdon, 62-; adminr, Cigarette Advert Code, 64- Mil Serv: Entered as Lt(jg), Navy, 42, released as Comdr, Naval Res, 66. Mem:

Elks; Eagles; Odd Fellows; Moose; Am Legion. Legal Res: 372 Lincoln St Phillipsburg NJ 08865 Mailing Add: Suite 2500 Gateway I Newark NJ 07102

MEZVINSKY, EDWARD M (D)
US Rep, Iowa
b Ames, Iowa, Jan 17, 37. Educ: Univ Iowa, BA, 60; Univ Calif, MA & JD; Omicron Delta Kappa. Polit & Govt Pos: Legis asst to Congressman Neal Smith, Iowa, 65-67; Iowa State Rep, Johnson Co, 69-70; US Rep, Iowa, 72- Bus & Prof Pos: Lawyer, Iowa City. Honors & Awards: Presidential commendation for work to protect the public in areas of traffic & highway safety & meat inspection. Legal Res: Iowa City IA 52240 Mailing Add: US House of Rep Washington DC 20515

MICHAEL, JAMES HARRY, JR (D)
Va State Sen
b Charlottesville, Va, Oct 17, 18; s James Harry Michael, Sr & Reuben Shelton M; m 1946 to Barbara Elizabeth Puryear; c Jarrett Elizabeth & Victoria von der Au. Educ: Univ Va, BS, 40, Law Sch, LLB, 42; Omicron Delta Kappa; Raven Soc. Polit & Govt Pos: Va State Sen, 25th Dist, 68-; mem bd gov, Coun State Govt, 69-, mem exec comt, Southern Conf, 70- Bus & Prof Pos: Lectr, Univ Va Law Sch, 49-53; mem bd, Charlottesville Pub Schs, 51-62; exec dir, Univ Va Inst Pub Affairs, 52; mem bd gov, St Anne's Sch, Charlottesville, 52-; assoc judge, Juv & Domestic Rels Court, 54-67; spec master in patent cases, US Dist Court, Western Dist Va, 60- Mil Serv: Entered as Ens, Navy, 42, released as Lt Comdr, 46, after serv in various commands, Southwest Pac Theatre, 43-45; Comdr, Naval Res (Ret). Mem: Am Bar Asn; Nat Consumer Finance Asn; Am Trial Lawyers Asn; Am Judicature Soc; Elks. Relig: Episcopal. Legal Res: 900 Rugby Rd Charlottesville VA 22903 Mailing Add: PO Box 895 Charlottesville VA 22902

MICHAEL, PATRICIA M (R)
b Steubenville, Ohio, Dec 13, 26; d Frank P May & Mabel Cunningham M; m to Robert K Michael; c Terry, Randy & Pat. Educ: Univ Ill, BA; Soc Illustrators; Delta Gamma. Polit & Govt Pos: Vchmn, Colo State Rep Cent Comt, 67-71; deleg, Rep Nat Conv, 72; comnr, Colo Consumer Credit Comn, 72- Mailing Add: 7075 Roaring Fork Trail Gun Barrel Green Boulder CO 80302

MICHAELS, LEE STEPHEN (D)
b Auburn, NY, Dec 10, 40; s George M Michaels & Helen S Wetzler M; m 1965 to Sarah W Rumsey; c Rebecca Judith. Educ: Cornell Univ, AB, 62; Syracuse Univ Col Law, LLB magna cum laude, 67; Phi Kappa Phi; Order of Coif; Justinian Soc; Pi Lambda Phi. Polit & Govt Pos: Deleg, Dem Nat Conv, 72. Bus & Prof Pos: Attorney, Brown, Kelly, Turner, Hassett & Leach, Buffalo, NY, 67-69, Michaels, Cuddy & Bertrand, Auburn, 69-71 & Michaels & Michaels, 71- Mil Serv: Entered as Ens, Naval Res, 62, released as Lt(jg), 64, after serv in Pac Fleet, Destroyer Force, Pac Theatre, 62-64; Lt, Res, 6 years. Mem: Am & NY State Bar Asns; NY State & Am Trial Lawyers Asns; Booker T Washington Community Ctr (vpres, 72-). Relig: Jewish; Secy, B'nai Israel Congregation. Mailing Add: 27 E Genesee St Auburn NY 13021

MICHAELSON, JULIUS COOLEY (D)
Attorney Gen, RI
b Salem, Mass, Jan 26, 22; s Carl Michaelson & Celia Cooley M; m 1950 to Rita Castowitz; c Mark C & Jeffrey S. Educ: Boston Univ Law Sch, LLB, 47; Brown Univ, AM, 67. Polit & Govt Pos: Pub counsel, Utility Rate Cases, 57-58; deleg, State Const Conv, RI, 57-58; RI State Sen, 63-74, dep majority leader, RI State Senate, 69; deleg, Dem Nat Conv, 68; mem comt state-urban rels, Coun State Govts, 69; mem, RI Comn on Interstate Coop, 69; Attorney Gen, RI, 74- Bus & Prof Pos: Attorney, currently. Mil Serv: Entered as Pvt, Army, 43, released as 1st Lt, 46. Mem: RI Bar Asn (pres, 72-); Am Bar Asn; Nat Soc State Legislators (mem bd dirs, 66-); Am Arbit Asn. Relig: Jewish. Mailing Add: 78 Lorraine Ave Providence RI 02906

MICHALESKI, NANCY POPE (R)
b Augusta, Kans, Sept 13, 41; d Alfred Leroy Pope & Josephine Entwistle P; m 1965 to Stanley Joseph Michaleski, Jr. Educ: Univ Md, College Park, BS, 63; Alpha Gamma Delta. Polit & Govt Pos: Personnel officer, Cent Intel Agency, 63-67; research librn, Libr of Cong, 68-69; legis aide to US Rep Glenard P Lipscomb, 69-70; legis asst to US Rep John H Rousselot, Calif, 70- Bus & Prof Pos: Mem bd dirs, Bodanski's, Inc, 73- Mailing Add: 10121 Tenbrook Dr Silver Spring MD 20901

MICHALS, CHARLES (R)
b Cleveland, Ohio, Mar 3, 24; s Charles Michals (deceased) & Tessie Kyros M; m 1946 to Amelia Cocallas; c Mary Anne & Patricia Amelia. Educ: NY Univ, 43-44; Univ Calif Exten, cert in indust rels, 60. Polit & Govt Pos: Pres, Marin Co Young Rep, Calif, 62; chmn Goldwater Rally, Young Rep Nat Conv, San Francisco, 63; press aide, Rep Nat Conv, 64, alt deleg, 68; pres, Marin Co Rep Coun, 64; exec dir, Christopher for Gov Primary Campaign, Marin Co, 66; vchmn, Reagan for Gov Comt, Marin Co, 66; chmn, Marin Co Rep Cent Comt, 67-70 & 73-75; chmn, Bay Area Region Asn of Rep Co Cent Comt Chmn of Calif, 68-70; mem exec comt, Calif Rep State Cent Comt, 69-70; campaign consult, various campaigns, 70- Bus & Prof Pos: Legis analyst, govt rels dept, Standard Oil Co of Calif, 49-; participant, Conf for Bus Execs on Fed Govt Opers, Brookings Inst, summer 70. Mil Serv: Entered as Pvt, Army, 43, released as Sgt, 45, after serv in 104th Inf Div, ETO, 44-45; Bronze Star Medal; Three Battle Stars. Publ: Ed, Chevron Chemical News, 63-68; contrib, The Standard Oiler, 68- Mem: Commonwealth Club. Honors & Awards: Recipient of First Rep Man of Year Award, Marin Rep Coun, 69. Relig: Episcopal. Mailing Add: 71 Via Chaparro Greenbrae CA 94904

MICHAUX, HENRY M, JR (D)
NC State Rep
b Durham, NC, Sept 4, 30; s Henry M Michaux, Sr & Isadore Coates M; m 1966 to Joyce Millett; c Jocelyn Winston. Educ: NC Cent Univ, BS, 52, JD, 64; Rutgers Univ, New Brunswick, 54; Omega Psi Phi. Polit & Govt Pos: Asst Dist Attorney, Durham, NC, 69-72; NC State Rep, 72- Bus & Prof Pos: Exec vpres, Union Ins Realty Co, Durham, NC, 55-, Glenview Mem Park, 55- & Washington Terr Apt, Inc, Raleigh, 56-; real estate appraiser, Durham, 64-; practicing attorney, 66- Mil Serv: Entered as Pvt, Army, 52, released as Sgt, 54, after serv in 4005th Area Serv Unit, Ft Hood Army Hosp, Tex, 53-54; Nat Defense Serv Medal. Mem: Nat Asn Real Estate Brokers (asst gen counsel, 58-); Nat Bar Asn; Am Judicature Soc; Durham Comt Affairs of Black People; NAACP. Honors & Awards: Pub Affairs Award, Nat Asn Real Estate Brokers, 72; Serv Award, Local 77, Am Fedn State & Munic Employees, 72. Relig: Methodist. Legal Res: 1722 Alfred St Durham NC 27707 Mailing Add: PO Box 2152 Durham NC 27702

MICHEL, ROBERT HENRY (R)
US Rep, Ill
b Peoria, Ill, Mar 2, 23; s Charles John Michel & Anna Baer M; m 1948 to Corinne Ellen Woodruff; c Martin Scott, Bruce Woodruff, Laurie Lee & Robin Ward. Educ: Bradley Univ, BS in Bus Admin, 48; Sigma Nu; Pi Kappa Delta. Polit & Govt Pos: Admin asst to US Rep Harold Velde, 49-56; US Rep, 18th Cong Dist, Ill, 57-, chmn, Rep Campaign Comt, US House Rep, 73-74, minority whip, 74-; deleg, Rep Nat Conv, 64, 68 & 72, chmn subcomt on human concerns, Platform Comt, 72. Mil Serv: Entered as Pvt, Army, 42, discharged as disabled vet, 46, after serv as Combat Infantryman, Eng, France, Belgium & Ger; Bronze Star; Purple Heart & Four Battle Stars. Publ: REA encroachment—is the end in sight?, Pub Utility Surv, 5/65; Reorganization of the committees on government operations and minority control of investigations, In: We Propose: A Modern Congress, McGraw Hill, 66; Uncle Sam's feverish medical spending, Nation's Bus, 10/72; plus others. Mem: DAV; Am Legion; life mem, Mil Order of Purple Heart; life mem Amvets; hon mem Rotary Int. Honors & Awards: Distinguished Alumnus Award, Bradley Univ, 61. Relig: Apostolic Christian. Legal Res: 1029 N Glenwood Peoria IL 61606 Mailing Add: 2112 Rayburn House Off Bldg Washington DC 20515

MICHELS, JAMES ERNEST (R)
Chmn, Clay Co Rep Party, SDak
b Vermillion, SDak, Oct 23, 31; s Ernest T Michels & Gertrude Finnell M; m 1958 to Patricia Tarbell; c Mark, Matthew, Mary, Margaret & Marshall. Educ: Univ SDak, BA, 53; Phi Delta Theta. Polit & Govt Pos: Voter chmn, Pierre, SDak, 54, elec day chmn, 56, committeeman, SDak Rep Cent Comt, 57-60; chmn, Clay Co Rep Party, 66- Bus & Prof Pos: Stockbroker, Hanifen, Imhoff & Samford, Inc, Vermillion, SDak, 66- Relig: Catholic. Legal Res: 22 N Yale St Vermillion SD 57069 Mailing Add: Box 456 Vermillion SD 57069

MICHELSON, ROBERT (D)
Exec Bd Mem, Racine Co Dem Party, Wis
b St Louis, Mo, Dec 23, 44; s Isadore Michelson & Rose Goldman M; m 1974 to Carrie Ruth Wahlen. Educ: Univ North Wales, 65-66; Beloit Col, Porter Scholar, BA, 67; Duke Univ Law Sch, JD, 72; Beta Theta Pi. Polit & Govt Pos: Exec bd mem & trustee, Racine Co Dem Party, Wis, 73-; alt deleg, Dem Nat Mid-Term Conf, 74; munic court judge, Racine, Wis, 74-; bd mem, Southeast Wis Coun on Criminal Justice, 74- Bus & Prof Pos: Attorney-at-law, Goodman & Michelson, Racine, Wis, 73-; vpres, Resment, Inc, 75- Mil Serv: Entered as E-1, Army, 69, released as E-4, 70, after serv in 2nd Criminal Invest Div, Korea; Good Conduct Medal. Publ: Auth, A proposed role for rebuttable presumptions in antitrust restraint of trade litigation, Duke Law J, summer 72. Mem: Wis & Racine Co Bar Asns; Racine Jaycees. Honors & Awards: Samuel Mereno Taylor Hist Prize, Beloit Col, 67; Advocacy Award, Int Acad of Trial Lawyers, 72; Hervey Johnson Award, Duke Law J, 72. Relig: Jewish. Legal Res: 1629 S Wisconsin Racine WI 53403 Mailing Add: 440 Main St Racine WI 53403

MICHIE, THOMAS JOHNSON, JR (D)
Va State Deleg
b Pittsburgh, Pa, June 12, 31; s Thomas Johnson Michie & Cordelia Ruffin M; m 1955 to Molly Ingle; c Thomas Johnson, III, John Ingle, Edmund Ruffin & George Rust Bedinger. Educ: Trinity Col (Conn), AB, 53; Univ Va Law Sch, LLB, 56; St Anthony Hall; Delta Psi; Phi Alpha Delta. Polit & Govt Pos: Mem sch bd, Charlottesville, Va, 65-70; chmn planning bd, Charlottesville-Albemarle Voc-Tech Educ Ctr, 69-70; Va State Deleg, 70- Mil Serv: Entered as Ens, Navy, 56, released as Lt, 59, after serv in Serv Sch, Command Legal Off, San Diego, 57-59; Comdr, Naval Res. Mem: Am Bar Asn; Albemarle Hist Soc; Civic League of Charlottesville; Charlottesville Housing Found (dir). Honors & Awards: Man of the Year & Distinguished Serv Award, Jaycees, 63. Relig: Unitarian. Mailing Add: 2008 Greenbrier Dr Charlottesville VA 22901

MICHOT, LOUIS JOSEPH (D)
State Supt Pub Educ, La
b Lafayette, La, Nov 5, 22; s Louis Joseph Michot & Adele Domas M; m 1946 to Patricia Ann Smith; c Ann, Patrick, David, Timothy, Robert, Thomas, Michael & Yvonne. Educ: Univ Southwestern La, 39-41 & 45-46. Polit & Govt Pos: La State Rep, 60-64; mem bd educ, Second Pub Serv Dist, La, 68-72; State Supt Pub Educ, 72- Bus & Prof Pos: Exec vpres & gen mgr, Gtr Lafayette CofC, 53-57; asst to vpres, Air Transport Asn of Am, 57-59; dir franchise sales, Burger Chef Systs, Inc, 59-; pres, Louis J Michot & Assocs, Inc, 59- Mil Serv: Entered as Pvt, Marine Corps Res, 41, released as Sgt, 45, after serv in USS Enterprise, Southwest Pac Theatre, 43-45. Mailing Add: Dept of Pub Educ 626 N Fourth Baton Rouge LA 70802

MICKEL, CHARLES J (D)
SDak State Rep
b Winner, SDak, Dec 28, 38; s John P Mickel & Carrie Koellmann; div. Educ: Univ SDak, BA, 60, MA, 62, JD, 68; Phi Delta Phi; Tau Kappa Epsilon. Polit & Govt Pos: Dep state attorney, Pennington Co, SDak, 69-71, asst pub defender, 73-74; state crime comnr, State of SDak, 71-73; SDak State Rep, 75- Bus & Prof Pos: Partner law firm, Kandaras, Mickel & Moore, 73- Mil Serv: Entered as E-1, Army, 63, released as E-4, 65, after serv in Defense Intel Agency, Washington, DC, 63-65. Publ: Ed, SDak Law Rev, 67-68; Contempt without a cause, SDak Law Rev, 66-67. Mem: SDak & Pennington Co Bar Asns. Mailing Add: Box 1641 Rapid City SD 57701

MICKELSON, BOB J (D)
Chmn, Columbia Co Dem Cent Comt, Wash
b Wilson Creek, Wash, June 16, 21; s Eos Mickelson & Barbara Moore M; m 1946 to Donna M Cutts; c Helen Cristine & Stephanie Ann. Educ: Kinman Bus Univ; Idaho State Univ; Univ NMex. Polit & Govt Pos: Chmn, Columbia Co Dem Cent Comt, Wash, 64- Bus & Prof Pos: Former farm employ supvr & agr supvr; farm cost acct, Green Giant Co, currently, agr supt, 69- Mil Serv: Entered as Seaman, Navy, 42, released as SK 1/C, 53, after serv in Pac Area; Am Area & Asiatic-Pac Area Campaign Ribbons; Good Conduct & World War II Victory Medals. Mem: Am Legion; Wash State Big Game Coun; Columbia Co Sportsmen. Honors & Awards: Letterman in Football, Univ NMex, 45. Relig: Congregational. Mailing Add: 702 N First Dayton WA 99328

MICKELSON, FRANK LESLIE (D)
Mo State Rep
b Freeman, Mo, Jan 25, 11; s Frank C Mickelson & Elizabeth Crowl M; m 1939 to Alberta

Marie Rutt. Educ: Univ Mo-Columbia, BS, 33; Cent Mo State Col, 35. Polit & Govt Pos: Co treas & ex officio collector of revenue, Cass Co, Mo, 41-53; Mo State Rep, Dist 110, 53-57 & 63-72 & 75- Bus & Prof Pos: Teacher, 33-40 & 57-63; farmer; with Waddell & Reed Investment Co, Kansas City, Mo, 64- Mem: Farm Bur; Nat Farmer's Orgn; Mo Farmer's Asn; Lions; Mason. Relig: Baptist. Mailing Add: RD 1 Freeman MO 64746

MICKELSON, GEORGE SPEAKER **(R)**
SDak State Rep
b Mobridge, SDak, Jan 31, 41; s George Theodore Mickelson & Madge Ellen Turner M; m 1963 to Linda McCahren; c Mark, Amy & David. Educ: Univ SDak, BA, 63, JD, 65; Phi Delta Phi; Lambda Chi Alpha. Polit & Govt Pos: States attorney, Brookings Co, SDak, 71-74; SDak State Rep, 75- Bus & Prof Pos: Attorney, McCann, Martin & Mickelson, 68- Mil Serv: Entered as 2nd Lt, Army, 65, released as Capt, 67, after serv in Vietnam; Army Res, 67-; Army Commendation Medal with Oak Leaf Cluster; Vietnam Serv Medal. Mem: Shrine; Mason; Kiwanis; VFW; Am Legion. Relig: Methodist. Legal Res: 1911 Lincoln Lane Brookings SD 57006 Mailing Add: Drawer 248 Brookings SD 57006

MICKELSON, GRACE MAXINE **(D)**
SDak State Sen
b Rake, Iowa, May 22, 26; d Albert M Erdahl & Amanda Gunderson E; m 1947 to Dr John Chester Mickelson; c Judy (Mrs Brian Yeoman), John C, Jr, Barbara Jo & Becky Sue. Educ: Waldorf Col, Forest City, Iowa, AA, 45; Iowa State Univ, BA, 47; Univ Wyo, Eastern Mont Col & SDak Sch Mines 60's; Black Hills State Col, MSEd, 72; Alpha Delta Kappa. Polit & Govt Pos: Precinct committeewoman, 70-72; SDak State Sen, 72- Bus & Prof Pos: Teacher high sch math, Oxford, Iowa, 47-48, Casper, Wyo, 61 & Rapid City, SDak, 61- Mem: Nat Educ Asn; Bus & Prof Women (legis comt); Am Asn Univ Women; Int Toastmistress Clubs; Nat Asn Parliamentarians. Honors & Awards: Distinguished Alumni Award, Waldorf Col, 68; Outstanding Teacher in SDak, Black Hills State Col, 73. Relig: Lutheran. Mailing Add: 133 E St Charles St Rapid City SD 57701

MICKLE, JACK PEARSON **(D)**
Mayor, Columbus, Ga
b Auburn, Ala, Nov 14, 25; s John Flemuel Mickle & Fannie Cook M; m 1948 to Joyce Fields; c Jack Pearson, Jr, Cassandra Joy & Kelli Suzanne. Educ: Univ Ga Exten; Howard Col Exten; Am Inst Banking. Polit & Govt Pos: Congressional dist rep, Cong Jack Brinkley, 69-74; mayor, Columbus, Ga, 75- Bus & Prof Pos: Columbus Bank & Trust Co, 47-69; lab technician, Swift Spinning Mills; advert dept, Sears Roebuck & Co; Columbus Mfg Co. Mil Serv: Entered as Apprentice, Navy, 43, released as AOM 3/C, 46, after serv in Sq 5N, Naval Air Sta, Pensacola, Fla, 43-46. Mem: Optimist Club; US Safety Coun; Cong Club. Relig: Assembly of God. Legal Res: 2804 Roswell Lane Columbus GA 31906 Mailing Add: PO Box 1340 Columbus GA 31902

MICOLEAU, CHARLES JUDD **(D)**
b Englewood, NJ, Feb 8, 42; m 1967 to Judith Frary; c Tyler, Sandrine & Jennifer. Educ: Bowdoin Col, BA, 63; Sch Advan Int Studies, Washington, DC, MA, 65; Chi Psi. Polit & Govt Pos: Dir work training, Maine Health & Welfare Dept, 65-67; legis research dir, Maine Dem Party, 68-70; pres, Maine Young Dem, 68-70; exec asst to US Sen Edmund S Muskie, Maine, 70- Bus & Prof Pos: Exec secy, Casco Bay Island Develop Asn, 67; dir, Job Corps Recruitment, New Eng AFL-CIO Coun, 69. Publ: A proposal to reduce welfare costs, Maine Townsman, 12/66; The secret war: myths, morals & misconceptions, Cent Intel Agency, DC Heath & Co, 68. Legal Res: Augusta ME 04330 Mailing Add: 3179 Porter St NW Washington DC 20008

MIDDAUGH, JAMES MICHAEL **(R)**
Mem Exec Comt, Van Buren Co Rep Comt, Mich
b Paw Paw, Mich, Sept 4, 46; s Orson William Middaugh & Phyllis Jean M; single. Educ: Ferris State Col, 65-68; Western Mich Univ, BS in Sec Educ, 69; Student Sen, 66-67. Polit & Govt Pos: Vchmn, Van Buren Co Young Rep, Mich, 64-65; deleg, all Van Buren Co & Mich Rep State Conv, 65-73, chmn credentials comt, State Conv, 73; mem exec comt, Van Buren Co Rep Comt, 65-; exec dir, Mich Fedn Col Rep, 68; vchmn, Van Buren Co Rep Party, 68-70; mem, Fourth Dist Rep Comt, 70-73; admin asst, Mich State Sen Charles O Zollar, 70-; vchmn, Rep State Issues Comt, 74, chmn, 75- Bus & Prof Pos: Teacher, one semester. Mem: Mich Farm Bur; Western Mich Univ Alumni Asn; Ferris State Col Alumni Asn (pres, 75); bd mem, Ferris State Col Sch Gen Educ Alumni Asn. Honors & Awards: Outstanding Young Men Am, 72. Relig: Methodist. Legal Res: 603 W Michigan Ave Paw Paw MI 49079 Mailing Add: Box 240 State Senate Lansing MI 48902

MIDDENDORF, HENRY STUMP, JR **(CONSERVATIVE PARTY, NY)**
VChmn, NY Conservative Party
b Baltimore, Md, Feb 23, 23; s Henry Stump Middendorf & Sarah Kennedy Boone M; single. Educ: Harvard Univ, AB, 45, JD cum laude, 52; NY Univ, LLM, 57; ed, Harvard Law Rev, 51-52; Lincoln's Inn Soc Harvard Law Sch; treas, Harvard Lampoon; Hasty Pudding, Inst of 1770; Own Club Polit & Govt Pos: Mem, NY Co Rep Comt, 55-61; counsel, Nat Draft Goldwater Comt & Goldwater for President Comt, 62-64; mem, NY Conservative Party State Comt, 62-; chmn judicial selection comt, First Judicial Dist Conservative Party, 64-; chmn petitions comt, NY Co Conservative Party, 65-; chmn, NY Co Conservative Party Comt, 66-; mem, NY Conservative Party State Exec Comt, 66-; counsel, Nixon Finance Comt, 68; vchmn, NY Conservative Party, 70-, chmn law comt, 71- Bus & Prof Pos: Assoc, Milbank, Tweed, Hope & Hadley, 52-56 & Gilbert & Segall, 56-59; pvt practice of law, 59- Mil Serv: Entered as Pvt, Army, 44, released as 1st Lt, 46, after serv in Japanese Army of Occup. Publ: Ed, Law Today, 63- Mem: Am & NY State Bar Asns; Am Legion; Union Club; NY Genealogical & Biographical Soc. Relig: Episcopal. Legal Res: 236 E 36th St New York NY 10016 Mailing Add: 36 W 44th St New York NY 10036

MIDDENDORF, JOHN WILLIAM, II **(R)**
Secy of Navy
b Baltimore, Md, Sept 22, 24; s Harry Stump Middendorf & Sara Boone M; m 1953 to Isabelle J Paine; c Frances Paine, Martha Stone, Amy Ward, John William, IV & Ralph Henry. Educ: Holy Cross, BS, 45; Harvard Univ, AB, 47; NY Univ Grad Sch Bus Admin, MBA, 54. Polit & Govt Pos: Mem exec comt, Greenwich Rep Town Comt, Conn, 58-72; mem, Greenwich Representative Town Meeting, 60-72; treas, Rep Nat Comt, 64-69; mem, Conn State Rep Finance Comt, formerly; chmn, Greenwich Rep Town Finance Comt, formerly; mem, Rep Cong Boosters Club, 64-; deleg, Rep Nat Conv, 64 & 68; US Ambassador to the Netherlands, 69-74; Secy of Navy, 74- Bus & Prof Pos: Employee, Bank of Manhattan Co, 47-52; employee, Wood, Struthers & Co, 52-58, partner, 58-61; partner, Middendorf, Colgate & Co, 62- Mil Serv: Ens, Naval Res, 43-46; serv in Pac Theater. Publ: Investment Policies of Fire & Casualty Insurance Companies, 54. Mem: NY Hist Soc; Hoover Inst for War & Peace (bd dirs); US Olympic Comt for Field Hockey; US Naval Inst; Am Antiq Soc. Honors & Awards: Superior Honor Award, Dept of State; Brazil Grand Master of Order Naval Merit. Relig: Episcopal; former mem bd, Roundhill Community Church of Greenwich; hon mem, Church Coun, Eng & Am Episcopal Church, the Hague. Legal Res: 1453 Kirby Rd McLean VA 22101 Mailing Add: Dept of Defense Secy of Navy Washington DC 20350

MIDDLESWART, JAMES IRA **(D)**
Iowa State Rep
b Indianola, Iowa, Apr 8, 12; s David Allen Middleswart & Eva Morgan M; m 1936 to Geraldine Ann Denly; c Phyllis Ann (Mrs Robert Geyer), LaVerne David & Irene Marie (Mrs Roger Case). Educ: Simpson Col, 32. Hon Degrees: Bus Admin Degree, Simpson Col, 72. Polit & Govt Pos: Asst comnr, Soil Dist, Iowa; Iowa State Rep, 67-; chmn, Nat Resources Comt, 75- Mem: Nat Rehab Asn; Iowa State Hist Soc; Lions; Farm Bur; Isaac Walton League. Honors & Awards: Sweepstakes winner, Des Moines Register & Tribune Soil Conserv Contest, 65; WMT Sta Award, Outstanding Serv to Conserv as State Legis, 68. Relig: Methodist. Mailing Add: RR 2 Indianola IA 50125

MIDDLETON, CLYDE WILLIAM **(R)**
Ky State Sen
b Cleveland, Ohio, Jan 30, 28; s Edward George Middleton & Eleanor Mertz M; m 1954 to Mary Ann Janke; c Ann Eleanor, David Edward, Richard Carl & John Clyde. Educ: US Naval Acad, BS, 51; Xavier Univ, Ohio, MBA, 62; CLU, Am Col Life Underwriters, 70; Chase Col Law, Northern Ky State Col, JD, 74; Phi Kappa Psi. Polit & Govt Pos: Pres, Kenton Co Young Rep, Ky, 60-61; chmn, Kenton Co Rep Party, 61; Rep cand for Cong, Fourth Dist, 62 & 64; chmn, Fourth Dist Young Rep, 63; Ky State Sen, 24th Dist, 67- Bus & Prof Pos: Buyer, Procter & Gamble Co, Cincinnati, Ohio, 57-64; field underwriter, NY Life, Cincinnati Off, 64- Mil Serv: Entered as Seaman Recruit, Navy, 46, released as Lt(jg), 55, after serv in USS Menifee, Far East-Korean War, 51-53 & in USS Steinaker, East Coast-Mediter, 53-55, Comdr, Res, 55-74; World War II Victory, Japanese Occup, Nat Defense, China Serv; Korean War & UN Korean Medals. Mem: VFW; Covington Optimist Club. Honors & Awards: Hon Mention Award, Ky Pub Health Asn for work as chmn, Ky Comprehensive Health Planning Coun, 69. Relig: Lutheran. Legal Res: 30 Ft Mitchell Ave Covington KY 41011 Mailing Add: PO Box 546 Covington KY 41012

MIDDLETON, EARL MATTHEW **(D)**
SC State Rep
b Orangeburg Co, SC; s Samuel E Middleton & Ella Govan M; m 1946 to Bernice Bryant; c Anita (Mrs Alphonso Pearson), Kenneth Earl & Karen Denise. Educ: Claflin Col, AB, 42; Phi Beta Sigma. Polit & Govt Pos: SC State Rep, 75, chmn sub comt real estate, Labor Comt & Indust Comt, SC House of Rep, 75-; mem adv comt, US Civil Rights Comn, currently. Bus & Prof Pos: Real estate broker, Orangeburg, SC, 64-, ins agt, Casualty, 64- Mil Serv: Entered as Cadet, Air Force, 42, released as S/Sgt, 46, after serv in Port Bn; Good Conduct Medal. Mem: Nat Asns Real Estate Appraisers; Nat Asn Real Estate Bds; VFW Post 8166. Honors & Awards: Cert of Appreciation, Vol Serv to the Community, Salvation Army, 67; Cert of Appreciation, Five Years of Serv to Nation, President of the US, 73; Outstanding Achievement, Polit & Serv to Humanity, Omicron Chapter, Phi Beta Sigma, 75. Relig: Methodist. Legal Res: Whittaker Pkwy Orangeburg SC 29115 Mailing Add: PO Drawer 1305 Orangeburg SC 29115

MIDDLETON, EDWIN G **(R)**
Rep Nat Committeeman, Ky
b Louisville, Ky, June 11, 20; s Charles G Middleton & Anita Gheens M; m 1942 to Mary Jane Lampton; c Edwin Gheens, Anita G & Huntley L. Educ: Univ Va, BA, 41; Univ Louisville, LLB, 48. Polit & Govt Pos: Finance chmn, Citizens for Eisenhower, 52; chmn, Louisville & Jefferson Co Rep Exec Comt, 58-63; deleg, Rep Nat Conv, 64, chmn contest comt, 71-72; Rep Nat Committeeman, Ky, 65- Bus & Prof Pos: Partner, Middleton, Seelbach, Wolford, Willis & Cochran, 48; chmn, Louisville & Jefferson Co Children's Home, 56-60; trustee, Louisville Collegiate Sch, 56-, Louisville Country Day Sch, 57-64 & Univ Louisville, 64-, chmn trustees, 70-; dir & gen counsel, Am Life & Accident Ins Co; dir, Louisville Title Ins Co, 72- Mil Serv: Entered as Pvt, Marine Corps, 41, Ret as Maj, 46; Bronze Star; Purple Heart. Mem; Am, Ky & Louisville Bar Asns; Louisville Country Club (pres & dir). Legal Res: 6401 Transylvania Ave Harrods Creek KY 40027 Mailing Add: 501 S Second Louisville KY 40202

MIDDLETON, JOAN JOY **(R)**
b Dillsboro, Ind, Mar 6, 37; d Leroy Scott & Neva Philpot S; m 1955 to Joe C Middleton; c Susan, Faye & Ray. Educ: Dillsboro High Sch, Ind, grad, 55. Polit & Govt Pos: Precinct vcommitteeman, Dearborn Co, Ind, 64-; deleg, Ind Rep State Conv, 66; vchmn, Dearborn Co Young Rep, 66-70; nat committeewoman, Ind Young Rep Fedn, 70-72; mem & young Rep representative, Exec Comt Ind Rep Women's Fedn, 70-72; vchmn, Ninth Dist Young Rep, 71-73; mem youth comt, Ind Rep Platform Adv Comt, 72; prog chmn, Dearborn Co Rep Women's Fedn, 72-73; external awards co-chmn, Young Rep Nat Exec Comt, 73- Bus & Prof Pos: Admin reviewer, Sch Lunch Div, Ind Dept Pub Instr, 68-71 & 73-; field investr, Ind Dept Revenue, 72-73. Mem: Ind Sch Food Serv Asn; Ind PTA; New Horizon Rehabilitation Inc; Parent Teachers Orgn, Lawrenceburg; Lawrenceburg High Sch Band Boosters, Inc. Honors & Awards: Cert of Achievement, Dept of Pub Instr, 71; Serv Award, Ind Young Rep Fedn, 72. Relig: Lutheran. Mailing Add: Box 49 RR 2 Lawrenceburg IN 47025

MIDDLETON, MELVILLE PETER **(D)**
Iowa State Rep
b Cardiff, Wales, Apr 17, 46; s Ernest James Middleton & Millicent Hendrickson M; div; c Melville Peter, II & Meighan Rose. Educ: Rochester State Jr Col, AA, 66; Morningside Col, BS, 68; Univ Iowa, JD, 74; Alpha Phi Gamma. Polit & Govt Pos: Dir, Waterloo Comn on Human Rights, Iowa, 68-70; admin asst, Black Hawk Co Attorney's Off, 71; Iowa State Rep, 75- Bus & Prof Pos: Instr Black studies, Luther Col, 72; asst personnel & labor rels, Rath Packing Co, Waterloo, Iowa, 75- Mil Serv: Entered as A/S, Naval Res, 63, released as Seaman, 68, after serv in Surface Div. Mem: African Palace Youth Ctr (bd dirs); Rath Packing Co Mgt Club. Honors & Awards: Iowa State High Sch Wrestling Champion, 64; All Am, Nat Asn of Intercollegiate Athletics Wrestling Team, 67; Most Valuable Wrestler, NCent Conf, 67; Outstanding Young Man of Am, Jaycees, 70; Am Soc of Planning Officials Ford Found grant, 73-74. Relig: Baptist. Mailing Add: 211 Independence Ave Waterloo IA 50703

MIDGLEY, GRANT WINDER (D)
b Salt Lake City, Aug 2, 11; s John George Midgley & Anna Grant M; m 1942 to Marsha Ballif; c Marsha, John Ballif & Jane. Educ: Univ Utah, BS, 32; Phi Kappa Phi. Polit & Govt Pos: Utah State Rep, 41-44; Utah State Sen, 45-48; admin asst to US Sen Moss, Utah, 65-71; pub info specialist, Nat Park Serv, US Dept Interior, 71- Mailing Add: Nat Park Serv US Dept of Interior Washington DC 20240

MIEDEMA, ERNEST JOHN (R)
b Marion, NDak, Jan 5, 32; s Andrew Miedema & Ruth Rohrbeck M; m 1951 to Elinor Darlene Sortland; c Larry Ernest, Darryl Wayne & Gwen Lynette. Polit & Govt Pos: Rep precinct committeeman, 63rd Precinct, NDak, 64-; NDak State Rep, 24th Dist, 68-74; alt deleg, Rep Nat Conv, 72. Bus & Prof Pos: Owner, Auction City Sales Inc, NDak, 58- Mem: CofC (mem-off, Valley City Chap, 63-); Gtr NDak Asn; Rotary; Valley City Planning Comn (chmn). Relig: Free Lutheran; Mem coord bd, Asn Free Lutheran Congregations, 71- Mailing Add: 915 Second Ave NW Valley City ND 58072

MIEDUSIEWSKI, AMERICAN JOE (D)
Md State Deleg
b Baltimore, Md, Oct 17, 49; s Frank Joseph Miedusiewski & Frances Joan Jaskowiak M; single. Educ: Calvert Hall Col, grad, 67; Univ Baltimore, 70- Polit & Govt Pos: Md State Deleg, 74- Bus & Prof Pos: Br rep, Household Finance Corp, 69-71; spec agt, Am Nat Ins Co, 71-72; constable, Dist Court of Md, 72-74. Mil Serv: Entered as Airman Basic, Air Nat Guard, 69, released as Sgt, 75, after serv in 175th Tactical Fighter Group, Tactical Air Command. Mem: St Casimir's Holy Name Soc; St Patrick's Cath War Vet. Relig: Roman Catholic. Mailing Add: 625 S Luzerne Ave Baltimore MD 21224

MIELKE, JANET ALLEEN (D)
Mem-at-Lg, Dem Party Wis
b Edgerton, Wis, June 30, 37; d Theodore W Soergel (deceased) & Lena Ella Frank S; m 1959 to Eldred Melvin Mielke; c Gary Eldred, Gordon Allen, Doreen Lynn & Douglas Russell. Educ: Milton High Sch, grad; Salutatorian. Polit & Govt Pos: Mem, Rock Co Dem Women's Group, Wis, 65-73; treas, Rock Co Dem Party, 69, trustee, 70-71; secy, First Dist Statutory Comt, 70; mem, Wis State Dem Statutory Comt, 70-72; deleg, Wis State Dem Conv, 70, 71 & 72; Wis State Rep, 71-74; mem adv policy coun, Dem Nat Comt, 73; mem-at-lg, Dem Party Wis, 75- Mem: UAW Local 95 Auxiliary 8 (vpres); Milton East Mothers Club (vpres & prog chmn); Otter Creek Community Club. Relig: Lutheran; choir soloist, Mt Cavalry Lutheran Church. Mailing Add: Rte 1 Milton Junction WI 53564

MIERS, MORGAN L (D)
b Greensburg, Ind, Mar 22, 19; s Roy H Miers & Ruth Lundmark M; m 1946 to Nansi L Harries; c twins, David & Melodi. Educ: Purdue Univ, BSA, 41; Sigma Delta Chi; Sigma Nu. Polit & Govt Pos: Chmn, Decatur Co Dem Cent Comt, Ind, formerly; deleg, Dem Nat Conv, 64 & 68; treas, Ninth Dist Dem Cent Comt. Mil Serv: Entered as 2nd Lt, Army Artillery, 41, released as Capt, 46, after serv in 28th Inf Div, 108th Field Artillery & 229th Field Artillery, ETO; Bronze Medal; Purple Heart; ETO Ribbon. Mem: Mason; Scottish Rite; Elks; Am Legion; Farm Bur. Relig: Methodist. Mailing Add: RR 4 Greensburg IN 47240

MIGLAUTSCH, THOMAS JOHN (D)
b Milwaukee, Wis, Nov 1, 13; s Frank L Miglautsch & Clara Klann M; m to Dorothy Storer; c Karen (Mrs Soukup) & Thomas, Jr (deceased). Educ: Univ Mich, Ann Arbor, 35; Univ Wis, Milwaukee, 32-33 & 37-38; Teachers Lifetime Cert, Wis. Polit & Govt Pos: Chmn, Waukesha Co Dem Party, Wis, 54-56; chmn, Second Cong Dist Dem Party, 57-60; mem, Wis Dem Party State Admin Comt, 57-62; vchmn, Wis Gov Comn on Human Rites, 59-65; ed, chmn, Wis Democrat, 60; deleg, Dem Nat Conv, 60-72. Bus & Prof Pos: Pres, Advantage Ad, Inc, 47- Mailing Add: PO Box 8 Oconomowoc WI 53066

MIGLIACCIO, HELEN (D)
RI State Rep
b Red Bank, NJ, Nov 14, 42; d Robert Whitmarsh Drew & Thea Melchior D; m 1964 to John E Migliaccio; c Laura, Peter & John. Educ: Russell Sage Col, BA, 64. Polit & Govt Pos: RI State Rep, 74-; deleg & first vchmn RI Const Conv, 73; mem, Gov Permanent Adv Comn on Women, 75- Mem: Cranston Boys Club (bd); League of Women Voters; Edgewood Asn (bd); Pawtuxet Village Asn (bd); Volunteers in Cranston Schs (bd). Mailing Add: 126 Arnold Ave Cranston RI 02905

MIHALY, SERGE GEORGE (D)
Chmn, Trumbull Dem Town Comt, Conn
b Stratford, Conn, Oct 29, 33; s Joseph Mihaly & Gizella Steinhaus M; m 1959 to Elizabeth Chornock; c Serge George, Jr, Luke Bartholomew & Matthew Gedeon. Educ: NY Univ, BA, 54, Sch Law, LLB, 56. Polit & Govt Pos: Town rep, Trumbull Rep Town Meeting, Conn, 61, majority leader, 61-63, minority leader, 63-65; leader dist 2, Trumbull Dem Town Comt, 65-67, chmn, 67-; mem, Dem State Platform Comt, 70. Bus & Prof Pos: Adjuster, US Fidelity & Guaranty Co, 56 & 59; attorney, Mihaly & Mihaly, 59- Mil Serv: Entered as Pvt, Army, 57, released as Pfc, 59, after serv in 370th Armored Inf Bn, 11th Airborne Div. Mem: Southern Conn Claimsmen Asn; Trumbull Jr CofC; Trumbull Br YMCA; Trumbull Lions; Trumbull Hist Soc. Relig: Eastern Orthodox. Mailing Add: 111 Booth Hill Rd Trumbull CT 06611

MIHLBAUGH, ROBERT HOLLERAN (D)
Committeeman, Ohio State Dem Cent Comt
b Lima, Ohio, June 17, 32; s Edward P Mihlbaugh & Mary Holleran M; m 1960 to Barbara Synck; c Robert E H & Michael Patrick. Educ: Univ Notre Dame, BA with honors, 54, JD, 57. Polit & Govt Pos: Mem, Ohio State Adv Bd, Small Bus Admin, 65-68 & Nat Adv Bd, 66-68; committeeman, Ohio State Dem Cent Comt, 66-; deleg, Dem Nat Conv, 68; spec counsel to Attorney Gen, Ohio, 71-; committeeman, Ohio State Dem Exec Comt. Publ: Comprehensive Marketing Manual, Marathon Oil Co, 63; Sale-leaseback financing, Ohio Bar Asn, 3/63. Mem: Ohio State Bar Asn; Am Bar Asn; Elks. Relig: Catholic. Legal Res: 1471 W Market St Lima OH 45805 Mailing Add: Mihlbaugh Bldg Lima OH 45802

MIKESIC, DAVID PAUL (D)
Kans State Rep
b Kansas City, Kans, May 6, 44; s Anthony Michael Mikesic & Irene May Yarmek M; m 1970 to Janis Lee Heider; c Ashley Ann. Educ: Emporia Kans State Col, BA in Polit Sci & Hist, 66; Kans Univ, BSE Sec Educ, 67; Univ Ark, JD, 68-71; Phi Alpha Delta; Alpha Kappa Lambda. Polit & Govt Pos: Kans State Rep, 36th Dist, 73-, Dem Whip, 75- Bus & Prof Pos: Attorney; Asst Dist Attorney, 71- Mem: Am & Kans Bar Asns; Nat Dist Attorneys Asn; Slavic Am Civic Club; Blessed Sacrament Civic Club. Relig: Catholic. Mailing Add: 3116 W Barker Circle Kansas City KS 66104

MIKESIC, JOSEPH M (BABE) (D)
Kans State Rep
Mailing Add: 250 N 14th St Kansas City KS 66102

MIKSCH, EILEEN EVANS (R)
Chairwoman, Logan Co Rep Party, Ohio
b Crawford Co, Ohio, Nov 15, 26; d Arthur Thomas Evans, Sr & Edith Weeter E; m 1947 to Ronald James Miksch; c Thomas James & John Ronald. Educ: Miami Univ, 45-47. Polit & Govt Pos: Dir elec, Logan Co, Ohio, 60-; chmn, Logan Co Brown for Cong, 70 & Brown for Secy of State, 74; pres, Logan Co Rep Women, 71-74; secy credentials comt, Ohio State Rep Conv, 74; chairwoman, Logan Co Rep Party, 74- Bus & Prof Pos: Clerk, Lake Twp, Ohio, 74- Mem: Ohio Asn Elec Off; Co & State Asn Twp Trustees & Clerks; Ohio Asn of Garden Clubs. Relig: Presbyterian; treas, First United Presbyterian Church, Bellefontaine, 72- Mailing Add: 508 Woodland Dr Bellefontaine OH 43311

MIKULSKI, BARBARA ANN (D)
City Councilwoman, Baltimore, Md
b Baltimore, Md, July 20, 36; d William Mikulski & Christine Kutz M; single. Educ: Mt St Agnes Col, BA, 58; Univ Md, MSW, 65. Hon Degrees: LLD, Goucher Col, 73; DHL, Pratt Inst Planning & Archit, 74. Polit & Govt Pos: Polit worker, John F Kennedy for President, Md, 60; voter registr, Johnson for President, 64; First Dist coordr, Joseph D Tydings for Sen, Baltimore, 70; city councilwoman, Baltimore, 71-; spec adv to R Sargent Shriver, 72; chairwoman comn deleg selection & party structure, Dem Nat Comt, 73; mem, Gov Comn Struct & Governance Educ, currently; bd mem, Nat Urban Coalition, currently. Bus & Prof Pos: Teacher, Vista Training Ctr, Mt St Mary's Sem, Baltimore, Md, formerly; adminr dept social serv, Baltimore Health & Welfare Coun, formerly; adj prof sociol, Loyola Col (Md), 72-; auth & lectr, currently. Mem: League Women Voters; Women's Polit Caucus; Catalyst, Inc (bd mem). Honors & Awards: Nat Citizen of Year, Buffalo Am-Polit Eagle, NY, 73; Woman of Year, Bus & Prof Women's Club Asn, Baltimore, 73; Outstanding Alumnus, Univ Md Sch Social Work, 73 & Loyola Col (Md), 74; Nat Fel Award, Philadelphia Fel Comn, 74. Mailing Add: 309 Folcroft St Baltimore MD 21224

MIKVA, ABNER J (D)
US Rep, Ill
b Milwaukee, Wis, Jan 21, 26; s Henry Abraham Mikva & Ida Fishman M; m 1948 to Zorita Wise; c Mary Lane, Laurel Ida & Rachel Shaine. Educ: Univ Wis, 46-47; Washington Univ, 47-48; Univ Chicago Law Sch, JD, 51; Order of the Coif; Phi Beta Kappa; Phi Sigma Delta. Polit & Govt Pos: Law clerk to Justice Sherman Minton, US Supreme Court, 51-52; Ill State Rep, 56-66; US Rep, Ill, 69-72 & 75-, mem, Ways & Means Comt, US House of Rep, 75- Bus & Prof Pos: Partner, Devoe, Shadur, Mikva & Plotkin, Attorney's, 52-68; partner, D'Ancona, Pflaum, Wyatt & Riskind, 73- Mil Serv: Entered as Pvt, Air Force, 44, released as 2nd Lt, 45, after serv as navigator Air Force Training Command. Publ: Two perspectives on civil rights, 65 & The 91st Congress & the Constitution, 71, Univ Chicago Law Rev. Mem: Am Bar Asn; City Club of Chicago; Am Vets Comt; B'nai B'rith; Lions. Honors & Awards: Chosen Outstanding Freshmen Rep, Ill Newspapermen Covering Springfield, 56; Voted, One of Ten Oustanding Young Men of Chicago, Jr Asn Com & Indust, 61; Winner of Page One Award, Chicago Newspaper Guild, 65; Recipient for Five Straight Terms of the Best Legis Award, Independent Voters of Ill. Relig: Jewish. Mailing Add: 1015 Sheridan Rd Evanston IL 60202

MILANOVICH, FRED R (D)
Pa State Rep
Mailing Add: Capitol Bldg Harrisburg PA 17120

MILBANK, ROBBINS (R)
NH State Rep
Mailing Add: RFD Marlborough NH 03455

MILBURN, BERYL BUCKLEY (R)
b Los Angeles, Calif, Apr 2, 20; d Edmund Langford Buckley & Beryl Meeks B; m 1941 to Malcolm Long Milburn; c Beryl Langford, Malcolm Long, Jr & Michael Noyes. Educ: Univ Tex, BA, 41; Kappa Kappa Gamma. Polit & Govt Pos: Alt deleg, Rep Nat Conv, 56, deleg, 64-72; committeewoman, Rep State Exec Comt, Tex, 56-65, secy, 63-65; state dir, Woman Power for Tower Campaign, 66; pres, Tex Fedn Rep Women, 67-70; mem state adv comt, Women for Nixon, 68; vchmn, Tex State Rep Comt, 71-74. Mem: Jr League of Austin; Settlement Club; Pan-Am Round Table; Med Referral Serv; Tex Law Enforcement & Youth Found. Relig: Roman Catholic. Mailing Add: 2606 Pecos St Austin TX 78703

MILES, BERNARD (D)
Ga State Rep
Mailing Add: 2934 Peach Orchard Rd Augusta GA 30906

MILES, KATHERINE C KARWASINSKI (R)
State Chmn, Md Fedn Col Rep
b Washington, DC, Jan 12, 52; d Theo W Karwasinski & Mary Ellen Williams K; single. Educ: Col Notre Dame (Md), BA, 73. Polit & Govt Pos: Treas, Md Fedn Col Rep, 70-71, secy, 71-72, vchmn, 72, chmn, 72-; alt deleg, Rep Nat Conv, 72. Relig: Roman Catholic. Mailing Add: 1206 Palmer Rd Apt 9 Oxon Hill MD 20022

MILES, THOMAS JAMES (R)
Mem, Rep State Cent Comt Calif
b Dallas, Tex, Nov 6, s Thomas Miles & Hattie M Chandler M; wid; c Donnell O, Gregory T, Florence T, Lovette P, Thomas J, III & Antoinette. Educ: Golden Gate Col, grad, 52; Univ Calif Grad Sch, 1 year; Dale Carnegie Course, grad, 64; Lincoln Univ Sch, grad 71. Polit & Govt Pos: Vchmn, United Voters, Inc, 54; exec secy, Rep Group, Alameda Co, Calif, 66-69; chmn, Concerned Berkeley Citizens, 68; chmn, Alameda Co for Nixon-Agnew, 68; campaign mgr, Wysinger for Cong, 68; alt deleg, Rep Nat Conv, 68; chmn, 17th Rep Assembly Dist El Club Tejano, Rep Minority AdcAdv Comt & CalCalif Rep Assembly Urban Affairs Comt, 70; mem steering comt, Attorney Gen Evelle J Younger, 70; cand for 17th Assembly Dist, 70; pres, Emery-Oakland Rep Assembly, currently; Rep nominee for Calif State Sen, 11th Dist, 72; mem, Rep State Cent Comt Calif, 72-; mem, Alameda Co Rep Cent Comt, 72- Bus & Prof Pos: Pres, Thomas J Miles Realty & Finance Co, 60-, chmn, Monterey Savings Ctr, 67-; vpres, Urban Systs Develop, 71- Publ: Negro Buying Power, News Week, 64; Black

Business, Bay Viewer Mag, 67. Mem: Nat Notary Asn; US CofC; Boy Scouts; Kappa Phi; Nu Beta Epsilon. Honors & Awards: Award for outstanding coordr of workers in 17th Assembly Dist, Calif Co Cent Comt, 68; Outstanding Leadership Award, Phi Asn; seven awards for best sales approach, Dale Carnegie; Appreciation Award for sincere & devoted effort to Mex Am community, Bay Area Cong for Mex Am Affairs, 71. Relig: Methodist. Mailing Add: 3251 Grove St Oakland CA 94609

MILES, VICKI LYNN (D)
b Oklahoma City, Okla, Sept, 30, 53; d Charles Clifford Miles & Mary Lou Greenard M; single. Educ: Vassar Col, 71-; Univ Ghana at Legon, summer 73; Int Thespian Soc; Nat Fraternity of Student Musicians; Alpha Kappa Alpha. Polit & Govt Pos: Deleg, Dem Nat Conv, 72. Bus & Prof Pos: Tel news reporter, KWTV, Oklahoma City, currently. Honors & Awards: E K Gaylord Philanthropist Award, Okla Publ Co, 68; Gov, Okla Girls State, Okla Am Legion, 70; Pres Leadership Award, Pres of Okla Univ, 71. Relig: Protestant; secy youth dept, Progressive Nat Baptist Conv, 71-72. Legal Res: OK Mailing Add: Terrace Apt 16 Vassar Col Poughkeepsie NY 12601

MILES, WILLIAM JOSEPH (D)
b Paragould, Ark, Oct 4, 31; s Lovick P Miles & Pearl Fuqua M; m 1960 to Charlotte Elizabeth Loughery. Educ: Col of the Ozarks, BA summa cum laude, 53; Univ Ark, Fayetteville, MA, 55; Phi Alpha Theta; Alpha Chi. Polit & Govt Pos: Asst dir personnel prog mgt, Navy BuPers, Washington, DC, 65-67, asst dir systs design div, 67-74; admin asst to US Rep William Alexander, Ark, 74- Bus & Prof Pos: Spec events dir, Radio Sta KDRS, Paragould, Ark, 54-55. Mil Serv: Entered as Officer Cand, Navy, 56, released as Lt(jg), 59, after serv in Washington, DC; Comdr, Naval Res, 69. Publ: Auth, Navy personnel program management, Navy Mgt Rev, 65. Mem: Ark State Soc of Washington; House Rep Admin Assistants' Asn; Naval Reserve Asn; ROA. Honors & Awards: Outstanding Performance Eval Award, 4 times. Relig: Presbyterian. Legal Res: Arlington VA 22205 Mailing Add: 227 Cannon House Off Bldg Washington DC 20515

MILFORD, DALE (D)
US Rep, Tex
b Bug Tussle, Tex, Feb 18, 26; s Homer D Milford & Mary Mann M; m 1967 to Mary Michaelle Shattuck; c Stephen Craig & Shari. Educ: Baylor Univ, 53-57. Polit & Govt Pos: US Rep, 24th Dist, Tex, 73- Bus & Prof Pos: Weather observer, Civil Aeronaut Admin, Tex & NMex, 42-44; aircraft dealer & meteorologist, Waco, Tex, 57-59; consult meteorologist, Dallas, 59-64; consult aviation & meteorol, 64-73. Mil Serv: Entered as Pvt, Army, 44, released as Capt, 53, after serv in 185th Signal Bn, Aleutian Islands, Alaska & Europe, 44-50. Publ: Producer, Flight report (26 series of aviation documentaries TV film), 60 & Tornado (30-minute TV filmed documentary), 64, Syndicated. Mem: Prof mem Am Meteorol Soc; Aviation/Space Writers Asn; Confederate Air Force Flying Mus(adv coun, 63-); Quiet Birdmen. Honors & Awards: Am Meteorol Soc Seal of Approval for TV weather shows, 60. Relig: Lutheran. Legal Res: 211 W Main St Grand Prairie TX 75050 Mailing Add: PO Box 1450 Grand Prairie TX 75050

MILFORD, WILLIAM DOYLE (D)
Ga State Rep
b Toombs Co, Ga, Dec 15, 42; s Arthur Doyle Milford & Elizabeth Anderson M; m 1966 to Barbara Gail Ayers. Educ: Univ Ga, BBA, 66; Sigma Phi Epsilon. Polit & Govt Pos: Ga State Rep, 69- Bus & Prof Pos: Owner, supermkt & farmer, Hartwell, Ga, 68-69. Mil Serv: Entered as E-1, Army, 66, released as E-4, 68, after serv First Army Div. Mem: Jaycees; Am Legion. Relig: Baptist. Mailing Add: Rte 3 Hartwell GA 30643

MILLAR, RAYMOND IRVING (R)
Chmn, Voluntown Rep Comt, Conn
b Providence, RI, June 20, 30; s Raymond Irving Millar & Edna Muriel Meyer M; m 1964 to Judith Ellen Williams; c Deirdre Ellen & David Hanson. Educ: Univ RI, BS, 52; Phi Gamma Delta. Polit & Govt Pos: Assessor, Voluntown, Conn, 70-71; chmn, Voluntown Rep Comt, 70- Bus & Prof Pos: Exec vpres, Cent Adjust Serv, Inc, 69-; owner, Coastal Claims Serv, Groton, Conn, 72- Mil Serv: Entered as Pvt, Army, 53, released as Cpl, 55, after serv in 73rd AAA Bn (AW) (SP), Ger, 54-55. Mem: Nat Asn Independent Ins Adjusters; VFW; Elks; Voluntown Lions. Relig: Episcopal. Legal Res: N Shore Rd Voluntown CT 06384 Mailing Add: RFD 1 Voluntown CT 06384

MILLARD, ELIZABETH ST (R)
NH State Rep
Mailing Add: RFD 5 Penacook NH 03301

MILLEN, FLOYD H (R)
Speaker Pro Tem, Iowa House Rep
b Watertown, SDak, May 17, 19; s Homer E Millen & Pearle Wright M; m 1942 to Betty Coffin; c James Randall, Robert Gregg & David Craig. Educ: Iowa State Univ, 37-38; Nev Sch Mines, 39-41. Polit & Govt Pos: Iowa State Rep, Jefferson-Van Buren Co, 63-, Majority Floor Leader, Iowa House Rep, 67-68, Speaker Pro Tem, 69- Bus & Prof Pos: Pres, Valley Limestone & Gravel, Inc, 46- Mil Serv: Entered as Pvt, Army, 42, released as 2nd Lt, 46, after serv in 618th Light Engr Equip Co, Southwest Pac, Philippines, 45; Philippines Campaign. Mem: Am Mil Engr; CofC; Nat Limestone Inst; Am Roadbuilders Asn; Shrine. Relig: Methodist. Mailing Add: Box 68 Farmington IA 52626

MILLENSON, ROY HANDEN (R)
b Washington, DC, Oct 1, 21; s Joseph Millenson & Helen Handen M; m 1950 to Charlotte Katz; c Janet Ann, Michael Louis & Elliott Jacob. Educ: Wilson Teachers Col, Washington, DC, 39-40; Univ Pa, 44; George Washington Univ, AB, 47. Polit & Govt Pos: Legis & press asst, US Rep J K Javits, NY, 49-55; exec asst, US Sen J K Javits, NY, 57-59; mem, Eisenhower-Nixon Inaugural Comt, 53 & 57; mem, Rep State Comt, Washington, DC, 57-58; alt deleg, Atlantic Cong, London, Eng, 59; partic, White House Conf on Educ & on Health, 65; minority staff dir, Senate Comt on Labor & Pub Welfare, 65-74; partic, Int Cong Educ of Deaf, Stockholm, 70. Bus & Prof Pos: Washington nat rep, Am Jewish Comt, 59-65; staff dir, Educ Affairs, Asn Am Publs, 75- Mil Serv: World War II, 42-46; Army Air Corp; Air Force Res, Capt (Ret). Mem: Polit Sci Asn; Montgomery Co Mens Rep Club; Capitol Hill Club; Montgomery Col Bd Trustees (mem statutory nominating comt); Am Jewish Comt. Honors & Awards: John Fogarty Award, 68. Relig: Jewish. Mailing Add: 7013 Amy Lane Bethesda MD 20034

MILLER, ALEX (D)
b Juneau, Alaska, Oct 11, 22; s Charles Miller & Mary Pusich M; m 1948 to Doris Driscoll; c Alexis, Janice (Mrs Cook), Charles, Michael, Christine & Robert. Educ: Univ Wash, 2 years. Polit & Govt Pos: Dem Nat Committeeman, Alaska, until 73; deleg, Dem Nat Conv, 72. Mil Serv: Army, 42-46. Mailing Add: 969 Gold Beit Ave Juneau AK 99801

MILLER, ALVIN V (D)
Iowa State Rep
Mailing Add: RR 1 Box 167 Ventura IA 50482

MILLER, ANDREW PICKENS (D)
Attorney Gen, Va
b Fairfax, Va, Dec 21, 32; s Francis Pickens Miller & Helen Hill M; m 1954 to Dorothy Andrews Brown; c Julia, Pickens & Elise. Educ: Princeton Univ, AB, 54; Univ Va, LLB, 60; Phi Beta Kappa; Raven Soc; Omicron Delta Kappa; Order of the Coif; Dial Lodge; Phi Alpha Delta. Polit & Govt Pos: Pres, Young Dem Clubs of Va, 66-67; chmn, Washington Co Dem Comt, 67-69; deleg, Dem Nat Conv, 68; mem, Dem State Cent Comt, Va, 68-70; Attorney Gen, Va, 70-; chmn, Southern Conf of Attorneys Gen, 73-; chmn antitrust comt, Nat Asn Attorneys Gen, 71-, mem exec comt, 73-74. Bus & Prof Pos: Ed-in-chief, Va Law Rev, Charlottesville, Va, 59-60; assoc, Penn, Stuart & Stuart, Abingdon, Va, 60-63; partner, Penn, Stuart & Miller, 63-70. Mil Serv: Entered as 2nd Lt, Army, 55, released as 1st Lt, 57, after serv in 48th Field Artil Bn, 7th Div, Korea, 55-57. Publ: 200 Faces for the Future, Time Mag, 7/74. Mem: Va State Bar; Am Bar Asn (house of deleg, 71-); Am Judicature Soc (dir, 73-, mem exec comt, 74-); Am for Effective Law Enforcement, Inc (mem adv bd, 73-); Am Bar Found (fel, 74-). Honors & Awards: Jaycee Distinguished Serv Award, 63. Relig: Presbyterian; chmn bd deacons, Sinking Spring Presbyterian Church, 66-67. Legal Res: 13 Glenbrooke Circle W Richmond VA 23229 Mailing Add: Supreme Court Bldg Richmond VA 23219

MILLER, ANN FLOYD (R)
Co-Chairwoman, Harrison Co Rep Cent Comt, Ohio
b Freeport, Ohio, Nov 13, 36; d W Cecil Floyd & Thelma Mallernee F; m 1960 to Gene R Miller; c Susan Jean & Cynthia Ann. Educ: Kent State Univ, BA, 58; Theta Sigma Phi; Kappa Alpha Mu. Polit & Govt Pos: Pres, Lakeland Rep Women's Club, Ohio, 68-; co-chairwoman, Harrison Co Rep Cent Comt, 70-, treas, Harrison Co Rep Cent & Exec Comt, 72- Bus & Prof Pos: Soc ed, Fremont News-Messenger, Ohio, 58-60; court reporter, Manhattan Mercury, Kans, 60; teacher primary grades, Freeport, Ohio, 65- Mem: Eastern Star. Relig: Methodist. Legal Res: 110 High St Freeport OH 43973 Mailing Add: Box 75 Freeport OH 43973

MILLER, ANNETTA THELMA (D)
Mem Exec Comt, Oakland Co Dem Party, Mich
b Ft Wayne, Ind, Sept 8, 21; d Jacob Klein & Freda Sperling K; m 1945 to Sidney Miller; c Ronald, Frederick & Mark. Educ: Jewish Hosp Sch Nursing; Wayne State Univ. Polit & Govt Pos: Mem exec comt, Oakland Co Dem Party, Mich, 71-; deleg, Precinct & Mich Dem State Convs, 68-73; deleg, Dem Nat Conv, 72; Dem cand, 18th Cong Dist Primary, 70; mem, Mich State Bd Educ, 71-, treas, currently. Bus & Prof Pos: Adv comt, Mich Am Civil Liberties Union, 71-; adv bd, Mich Anti-Defamation League, 71-; nat vpres, Am for Dem Action, 72- Mil Serv: Entered as 2nd Lt, Army, 44, released, 45, after serv in 350 Sta Hosp, Nurse Corp, ETO. Publ: Teaching About Peace & War, Wayne State Univ, 74. Mem: Friends of WDET-FM (bd dirs, 75-); Ctr for Chap Chmns (adv bd). Honors & Awards: Award from Am for Dem Action, 74; Silver Scroll for the 25th Anniversary of the UN Declaration of Human Rights. Relig: Jewish. Legal Res: Huntington Woods MI 48070 Mailing Add: State Bd of Educ Lansing MI 48902

MILLER, ANTHONY P (D)
Conn State Sen
Mailing Add: 218 Charles St South Meriden CT 06450

MILLER, BERT F (D)
NDak State Rep
Mailing Add: State Capitol Bismarck ND 58501

MILLER, BRUCE A (D)
b Brooklyn, NY, Oct 11, 27; s Charles Miller & Lydia Barnett M; m 1961 to Edna Powell; c Powell, Ann & Elizabeth. Educ: Wayne State Univ, JD. Polit & Govt Pos: Chmn, Wayne Co Dem Comt, Mich, 71-74. Bus & Prof Pos: Partner, Miller, Klimist, Cohen, Martens & Sugarman. Mil Serv: Entered as Pvt, Army, 48, released as T/5, 50, after serv in Ft Knox, 2 years. Mailing Add: 2460 First National Bldg Detroit MI 48226

MILLER, C WENDELL (D)
Idaho State Rep
Mailing Add: 791 Skyline Dr Idaho Falls ID 83401

MILLER, CAROL CORINNE (R)
Chmn, Winnebago Co Rep Party, Iowa
b Peterson, Iowa, Nov 2, 20; d Hans William Christenson & Thora Beck C; m 1945 to Howard William Miller; c David, Curtis, Michael & Jeffery. Educ: Iowa State Col, BS, 45. Polit & Govt Pos: Chmn, Winnebago Co Rep Womens Club, 64-65; co-chmn, Winnebago Co Rep Party, Iowa, 65-74, chmn, 74- Bus & Prof Pos: Home economics teacher, Public Schs, Iowa, 43-47; home economist, Iowa State Univ Exten, 48-50; buyer, Miller Pharmacy Inc, 58- Mem: NIowa Home Economists; PTA; Alumni Asn Iowa State Univ; Iowa Womens Polit Caucus. Relig: Lutheran. Legal Res: 316 Sixth Ave NE Buffalo Center IA 50424 Mailing Add: Box K Buffalo Center IA 50424

MILLER, CHARLES P (D)
Iowa State Sen
b Harbor Beach, Mich, Apr 29, 18; s William H Miller & Anna V; m 1946 to Virginia Mae Ferrington; c Five sons & one daughter. Educ: Jr Col; Palmer Chiropractic Col. Polit & Govt Pos: Iowa State Rep, formerly; Iowa State Sen, Dist 42, 71- Bus & Prof Pos: Chiropractor, 52- Mil Serv: Navy, active duty, active res, 40-51. Mem: Chiropractic Soc Iowa; Toastmasters Int; Int Chiropractors Asn (first vpres, 70-); KofC; Eagles. Mailing Add: 801 High St Burlington IA 52601

MILLER, CHRIS (D)
Tex State Rep
b Boston, Mass, June 15, 26; d Charles Dana Chrisman (deceased) & Dorothy Noyce C; div;

c Louis Chrisman & Gerald Lee. Educ: Wheaton Col (Ill), 43-44; Mills Col (Calif), 44; Tex Christian Univ, 64-67. Polit & Govt Pos: Mem, Human Rels Comn, Ft Worth, Tex, 69-72; Tex State Rep, 73- Bus & Prof Pos: Advert mgr & pub rels aide, Ft Worth CofC, 67-68; neighborhood serv coordr & pub rels aide, Ft Worth-Tarrant Co Community Action Agency, 68-69; Chris Pub Rels, 69-72. Publ: Freelance feature writer, Ft Worth Star-Tel, 66- Mem: Women in Commun; Am Women in Radio & TV; founder Tex Women's Polit Caucus; League Women Voters (bd mem, 62-); Nat Orgn for Women (bd, 70-). Honors & Awards: Female Newsmaker 1972, Press Club of Ft Worth, 73; Eminent Individual, Am Women in Radio & TV, 74. Relig: Unitarian. Legal Res: Apt 24 2524 Ridgmar Ft Worth TX 76116 Mailing Add: PO Box 2910 House of Rep Austin TX 78767

MILLER, CLARENCE E (R)
US Rep, Ohio
b Lancaster, Ohio, Nov 1, 17; s Clarence E Miller, Sr & Delores LLoyd M; m 1936 to Helen Brown; c Ronald & Jacqueline (Mrs Thomas Williams). Hon Degrees: DPS, Rio Grande Col, Ohio. Polit & Govt Pos: Mem city coun, Lancaster, Ohio, 57-62 & 63, mayor, 64-65; US Rep, Tenth Dist, Ohio, 67-, mem appropriations comt, US House Rep, currently. Bus & Prof Pos: With Ohio Fuel Gas Co, 36; elec engr. Mem: Elks; YMCA; Ohio Valley Health Serv Found. Honors & Awards: Citation of Merit for Community Serv, Jr CofC. Relig: Methodist. Legal Res: 1430 E Main St Lancaster OH 43130 Mailing Add: 434 Cannon House Off Bldg Washington DC 20515

MILLER, CLINTON (R)
Va State Deleg
b Ferguson, NC, May 24, 39; s Sheridan Franklin Miller & Lizzie Funkhouser M; m 1964 to Linda Ann Emswiler; c Erin Paige & Sean Clinton. Educ: Columbia Univ, 59-60; Am Univ, BA in govt, 62; Washington & Lee Univ, LLB, 65; Phi Alpha Delta. Polit & Govt Pos: Commonwealth's attorney for Shenandoah Co, Va, Woodstock, 68-71; Va State Deleg, 72- Mem: Va Trial Lawyers Asn; Lions (third vpres, 73-); Odd Fellows; Va Heart Asn. Relig: Protestant. Mailing Add: PO Box 484 W Locust St Extended Woodstock VA 22664

MILLER, CLYDE L (D)
Secy of State, Utah
b Salt Lake City, Utah, Jan 1, 10; s Mark M Miller & Louella McArthur McMullin M; m 1954 to Reva Lee Carlson; c Roberta Lee, Clyde Alton, Carey Mae, Diane Marie, Linda Rae, Mark Miles, Daniel Duncan & Mathew Martin. Educ: Univ Utah, BS, 34. Polit & Govt Pos: Utah State Rep, 51-52; Utah State Sen, 59-64; Secy of State, Utah, 65- Mem: Nat Asn Secretaries of State (pres); South Salt Lake CofC; Int Footprinters Asn. Honors & Awards: Outstanding Alumnus of West High Sch. Relig: Latter-day Saint. Legal Res: 374 E Haven Ave Salt Lake City UT 84116 Mailing Add: Rm 203 State Capitol Bldg Salt Lake City UT 84114

MILLER, DARREL R (DFL)
Minn State Rep
married; c three. Polit & Govt Pos: Cand, Minn State Rep, 66; Co Bd Mem; Minn State Rep, 75- Bus & Prof Pos: Owns & operates 614 acre diary farm. Mem: New Haven Farmers Union; Dodge Co Fair Bd (dir). Honors & Awards: Olmsted Co Outstanding Young Farmer, 64. Relig: Methodist. Mailing Add: Pine Island MN 55963

MILLER, DAVID DOUGLAS (D)
Tenn State Rep
b Knoxville, Tenn, Apr 10, 43; s Dr Fred Dayton Miller & Ruth Heiskell M; m 1965 to Betty Lynn Roberts; c William Stephen & Martha Lee. Educ: Carson Newman Col; Debate Club. Polit & Govt Pos: Vchmn civil serv bd, City of Morristown, Tenn, 74-; Tenn State Rep, Tenth Dist, 75- Bus & Prof Pos: Farmer. Mil Serv: Entered as E-1, Army, 70, released as E-5, 72, after serv in 17th Cavalry 101st Air Borne Div, Vietnam, 71-72; Combat Infantryman's Badge; Bronze Star; Air Medal; Vietnam Campaign Ribbon with two Clusters. Mem: VFW; Am Legion; US Army Air Borne Asn; 101 Air Borne Asn; Farm Bur. Relig: Methodist. Mailing Add: 526 Lee Dr Morristown TN 37814

MILLER, DAVID LEE (D)
Kans State Rep
b Parsons, Kans; s Lewis Mervin Miller & Ruby Swenson M; single. Educ: Labette Community Jr Col, Kans, AA, 68; Kans State Col, Pittsburg, BSEd, 70 & MS, 73. Polit & Govt Pos: Vpres, Collegiate Young Dem, Parsons, Kans, 66-67, pres, 67-68, vpres, Pittsburg, 68-69; co-chmn, New Dem Coalition of Kans, 68-69; Kans State Rep, Sixth Dist, 73- Mil Serv: Entered as Pvt, Marine Corps, 71, released as Pvt, 71, after serv in Marine Corps Recruit Depot, 6 weeks, med discharge; Nat Defense Serv Medal. Mem: Elks; Am Legion; Laborer's Int Union. Relig: Methodist. Mailing Add: 2316 Belmont Parsons KS 67357

MILLER, DEAN E (D)
b Caldwell, Idaho, Sept 26, 22; s Dean W Miller & Mary Meek M; m 1945 to Josephine Ney; c Dean Joseph, Nicholas G, Thomas F, Mary M & Patrick J. Educ: Univ Idaho, LLB, 49; Phi Alpha Delta; Beta Theta Pi. Polit & Govt Pos: Co chmn, Dem Party, Idaho, 50-54; state committeeman, 54-56, regional coordr, 56-; chmn, Idaho McCarthy for President Campaign, 68; deleg, Dem Nat Conv, 68. Mil Serv: Entered as Pvt, Army, 42, released as 1st Lt, 45, after serv in 531 Field Artillery Bn, Cent & SPac, 43-45; Army Res (Ret); Asiatic-Pac Soc Ribbon; 3 Battle Stars; Philippine Liberation Medal. Mem: Am Bar Asn; Am Legion; Elks (pres, Idaho State Asn); Rotary Int; KofC. Relig: Roman Catholic. Mailing Add: 2201 Washington Caldwell ID 83605

MILLER, DOROTHY JENILEE (D)
First VPres, SCent Region, Nat Fedn Dem Women
b Dodge City, Kans, July 30, 24; d Cecil Ballard Middaugh & Ida Beatrice Cody M; m 1948 to Garnett Earl Miller; c Stephen Wayne & Mark William. Educ: Newton High Sch, Kans, 38-42; Rickay Career's Col, motel mgr, 71. Polit & Govt Pos: Dem precinct committeewoman, Fourth Ward, First Precinct, Newton, Kans, 54-; pres, Harvey Co Fedn Dem Club, 56-; prog chmn, Kans Fedn Women's Dem Clubs, 58-59; vpres, 63-66, pres, 66-71, treas, 75-, permanent mem exec bd; vchmn, Harvey Co Dem Cent Comt, 60-62; Dollar for Dem chmn, Kans Dem State Comt, 60, 62 & 63, Fourth Dist registr chmn, 62 & 64; deleg, Dem Nat Conv, 68; first vpres, SCent Region, Nat Fedn Dem Women, 73-, bylaws chmn, 75- Mem: Kans Day Women's Club; Native Sons & Daughters; VFW Auxiliary; Newton PTA Coun. Relig: Episcopal; past pres, Couple's Club & treas, Women's Orgn, St Matthews Episcopal Church, Newton, Kans. Mailing Add: 704 N Elm St Newton KS 67114

MILLER, EDGAR MERRELL (D)
b Lowville, NY, Nov 21, 24; s Stanley Brayton Miller & Charlotte Merrell M; m 1948 to Anne Terrell; c Lucinda Merrell, Christopher Terrell, Elizabeth Anne & Margaret Sanford. Educ: St Lawrence Univ, 42-43; Tufts Col Dent Sch, DMD, 47; Beta Theta Pi. Polit & Govt Pos: Alt deleg, Dem Nat Conv, 68, deleg 72; chmn, McCarthy for President, Lewis Co, NY, 68-69; chmn, McGovern for President, Lewis Co, 72. Bus & Prof Pos: Dentist, Lowville, NY, 47-; postgrad faculty, Univ Pa Sch Dent, 63-70 & Univ Detroit Sch Dent, 65-69. Mil Serv: Entered as Pvt, Army, 43, released as Pfc, 44; entered as Capt, Army, 51, released as Capt, 52, after serv in 23rd Inf, Korea, 51-52; Korean Combat Ribbon with 3 Battle Stars; Med Combat Badge; Bronze Star with Valour; Croix de Guerre. Publ: Co-auth, How to use personnel effectively, 7/65 & Dental auxiliaries: legal definition and modifications, 11/66, Dent Clin NAm; co-auth, Oral Lighting, J Am Dent Asn, 10/65. Mem: Am Dent Asn; Am Soc Prev Dent; Am Acad Dent Practice Admin; Acad Gen Dent; Fedn Dent Int. Honors & Awards: Exhibitor, Artists of Cent NY Show, Munson-Williams-Proctor Inst, 70. Relig: Universal Life Church; minister, 70- Legal Res: 7646 Collins St Lowville NY 13367 Mailing Add: Lewis Co Health Ctr Lowville NY 13367

MILLER, EDWARD BOONE (R)
b Milwaukee, Wis, Mar 26, 22; s Dr Edward A Miller & Myra Munsert M; m 1970 to Anne Harmon Chase Phillips; c Barbara (Mrs John W Link), Ellen, Elizabeth, Thomas; stepchildren: T Christopher & Sarah. Educ: Univ Wis, BA, 42, LLB, 47; Harvard Grad Sch Bus, 42-43; Order of the Coif; Phi Kappa Phi. Polit & Govt Pos: Indust mem, Regional Wage Stabilization Bd, 52; chmn, Nat Labor Rels Bd, 70-74. Bus & Prof Pos: Assoc attorney, Pope, Ballard, Kennedy, Shepard & Fowle, Chicago, 48-53, partner, 53-70. Mil Serv: Entered as Ens, Naval Res, 43, released as Lt, 46, after serv in Acorn 30, Pac, 45-46. Mem: Fed Bar Asn; Law Club Chicago; Lawyers Club DC; Cliff Dwellers Club. Relig: Congregational. Mailing Add: 5065 Macomb St NW Washington DC 20016

MILLER, ELIZABETH RUBY (R)
Iowa State Sen
b Marshalltown, Iowa, Aug 24, 05; d Stephen Shank & Lenora Burns S; m 1923 to John Bascom Miller; c John Bascom, Jr, Edward James, Mary Louise (Mrs Tom Speas) & Betty Arlene (Mrs Russell Weeden, Jr). Educ: Marshalltown High Sch, grad, 23. Polit & Govt Pos: Co pres, Iowa Fedn Rep Women, 65-66, state campaign chmn, 68-69; Iowa State Rep, 69-72; Iowa State Sen, Dist 20, 72- Bus & Prof Pos: Chmn, Home Nursing, Red Cross, 50-60; co rural chmn, Cancer Soc, 55-56. Mem: Gen Fedn Women's Clubs; Farm Bur; Iowa Hist Soc. Honors & Awards: Outstanding Civic Leader of Am, 67. Relig: Congregational. Mailing Add: RR 3 Marshalltown IA 50158

MILLER, ESTELLE LEE (R)
Chmn Educ Adv Comt, Nat Fedn Rep Women
b New York, NY, Nov 30, 29; d Dr Jacob Lieberman & Theresa Smith L; m to T E (Gene) Miller; c Lindajean Duff & Robert McCready. Educ: Brooklyn Col, BA, 49; Univ Wis, Law Sch, LLB, 54. Polit & Govt Pos: Mem trial staff, Antimonopoly Sect, Fed Trade Comn, 56-58; with gen counsel off, Fed Power Comn, 58 & Civil Aeronaut Bd, 58-61; founder, pres & life mem, Cobb Co Fedn Rep Women, Ga; participant in many Rep campaigns; mem, DC League Rep Women, 63-; state canvass chmn, Ga Rep Party, 64, exec dir finance, 67; bd dirs, Ga Fedn Rep Women, 64-67, pres, 65-67; Nat Fedn Rep Women participant, panel on develop int law, White House Conf Int Coop, 65; mem, Ga Rep State Exec Comt, 65-67; mem bd dirs, Nat Fedn Rep Women, 65-67 & 69-, chmn educ adv comt, 69-; participant, Rep Nat Comt Campaign Mgr Sch, 66; panelist, Rep Nat Comt Big City Workshop, Agnew for Gov, Md, 66; dir Women's Activities, Callaway for Gov, Ga, 66; mem task force const rev, Rep Nat Comt, consult, 69-; mem, Richard Nixon Assocs; assisting with President Nixon's Environ Merit Awards Prog in Ga, 72-; chmn, Lumpkin Area Bicentennial Comt, 75; chmn, Stewart Co Rep Party, 75- Bus & Prof Pos: Teacher, 49-51; lawyer. Honors & Awards: Awards for largest increase in membership & clubs while pres, Ga Fedn Rep Women, Nat Fedn Rep Women, 66, Citation for Dedicated Serv to Rep Ideals & Philos, 67. Relig: Episcopal. Mailing Add: Longview Farms RFD 1A Lumpkin GA 31815

MILLER, ETHEL ALLEN (R)
VChmn, Genesee Co Rep Comt, NY
b Rochester, NY, May 3, 04; d William V Allen & Blanche Bullock A; m 1925 to Francis James Miller, Sr; c Francis J, Jr, Joan E & Patricia (Mrs Webster A Chapman). Educ: Rochester Bus Sch, 2 years. Polit & Govt Pos: Pres & vpres, Genesee Co Women's Rep Club, NY, formerly; vpres & pres, Eighth Judicial Dist Women's Rep Club, formerly; vchmn, Genesee Co Rep Comt, 67- Mem: Eastern Star; Am Heart Asn; NY State Heart Asn (mem bd); Stafford Co Club. Relig: Presbyterian. Mailing Add: 53 Rochester St Bergen NY 14416

MILLER, FRANK (D)
Ky State Sen
Mailing Add: Rte 13 Box 216 Bowling Green KY 42101

MILLER, FRANK L (D)
Chmn, Beauregard Parish Dem Exec Comt, La
b Dry Creek, La, June 18, 10; s Samuel Nathan Miller & Emma Heard M; m 1931 to Versie Welborn; c Franklin D, Rose M (Mrs Manuel), William N, John R & Kathy M (Mrs Honea). Educ: La State Norm Col, BA, 31; Northwestern State Col La, MEd, 59; Sigma Tau Gamma; N-Club. Polit & Govt Pos: Chmn, Beauregard Parish Dem Exec Comt, La, 50-; chmn, 31st Legis Dist Dem Comt, 71-75. Bus & Prof Pos: Prin, Beauregard Parish Schs, La, 34-70. Mem: La Teachers' Asn; Nat Educ Asn; DeRidder Kiwanis; Mason; Beauregard Mem Hosp (bd dirs). Honors & Awards: Kiwanian of the Year, DeRidder Kiwanis Club, 67; Hon Chap Farmer, DeRidder High Sch Future Farmers Am, 68. Relig: Baptist; Deacon, Dry Creek Baptist Church. Mailing Add: PO Box 372 Dry Creek LA 70637

MILLER, GEORGE (D)
US Rep, Calif
b Richmond, Calif, May 17, 45; s George Miller, Jr (deceased) & Dorothy Rumsey M; m 1964 to Cynthia Caccavo Miller; c George, IV & Stephen. Educ: Diablo Valley Col, 66-67; San Francisco State Col, BA, Polit Sci, 68; Univ Calif at Davis Law Sch, JD, 72. Polit & Govt Pos: Chmn, Contra Costa Co Dem Cent Comt, 69-70; legis counsel, State Senate Majority Leader George Moscone, 69-73; Dem Presidential Elector, 72; US Rep, Calif, 75-, mem, Comt for a More Active, Effective Cong, US House Rep, 75-, mem, House Educ & Labor Comt, House Interior & Insular Affairs Comt, House Select Comt on Outer Continental Shelf & Cong Adv Bd of the Full Employment Action Coun, 75- Mem: Calif State Bar Asn; Davis Law Sch Alumni Asn; Martinez Dem Club; Common Cause. Legal Res: CA Mailing Add: 1532 Longworth House Off Bldg Washington DC 20515

642 / MILLER

MILLER, GEORGE M, JR (D)
NC State Rep
Mailing Add: 3862 Somerset Dr Durham NC 27707

MILLER, GEORGE PAUL (D)
b San Francisco, Calif, Jan 15, 91; s Joseph Miller & Margaret Anson M; m 1927 to Esther M Perkins; c Ann (Mrs Donald Muir). Educ: St Mary's Col, Calif, BS, 12. Polit & Govt Pos: Exec secy, Calif Div Fish & Game; Calif State Assemblyman, 52nd & 53rd sessions; adv to US Ambassador to UN on peaceful uses of outer space; US Rep, Calif, 44-72. Bus & Prof Pos: Civil engr. Mil Serv: Lt, Army, FA, 17; grad, 30th Class, Sch Fire, Ft Sill, Okla, 18. Mem: Nat Hist Publ Comn; Am Legion; Lions; Eagles; Elks. Mailing Add: 1424 Benton St Alameda CA 94501

MILLER, GEORGE WILLIAM (D)
NY State Assemblyman
b Rutherfordton, NC, Nov 19, 22; s George Louis Miller & Della Carpenter M; m 1947 to Alma Rose Adams; c Eric Loring. Educ: A&T Col, NC, BS, 43; Columbia Univ Sch Social Work, 48-50; Brooklyn Law Sch, LLB, 55; Omega Psi Phi. Polit & Govt Pos: Dep comnr, Dept of License, New York, 61-66; Dem dist leader, 72nd Ad, New York, currently; NY State Assemblyman, 71- Bus & Prof Pos: Attorney, Morris & Miller, 67-71; Legal Aide Soc. Mil Serv: Entered as Pvt, Army, 43, released as M/Sgt, 46, after serv in 243 Qm Bn, Southeast Asia & Okinawa, 45-46; Good Conduct Medal. Mem Harlem Lawyers Asn; 369th Vet Asn; NAACP (bd dirs); Elks; Omega Psi Phi. Relig: Episcopal. Mailing Add: 25 W 132nd St New York NY 10037

MILLER, HAINON A (D)
Miss State Rep
b Kosciusko, Miss, Oct 9, 30; s John Wesley Miller & Louise Johnston M; m 1956 to Lillian Henderson; c Nadalyn, Philip, Kendall, Melissa & Lyon. Educ: Miss Col, BA, 51; Tulane Univ, LLB, 54; Phi Delta Phi; Omicron Delta Kappa; pres, Student Body, 53-54. Polit & Govt Pos: Secy, Washington Co Dem Exec Comt, Miss, 55-60, mem, 55-67; Miss State Rep, 68- Bus & Prof Pos: Pres, Washington Co Bar Asn, 68-69. Mem: Am & Miss Bar Asns; Kiwanis; Boy Scouts (IR, 60-). Honors & Awards: Capt, Miss Col Track Team, 51, Tulane Univ, 53; Distinguished Serv Award, Jaycees, 57. Relig: Baptist. Legal Res: 1204 Waxhaw Dr Greenville MS 38701 Mailing Add: PO Box 1334 Greenville MS 38701

MILLER, HARLAN WALTER (D)
b Epperly, WVa, Sept 12, 20; s Clarence Preston Miller & Elsie Mae Trout M; m 1944 to Elaine Broyles Blake; c Joyce Elaine, Anita Roxie & Harlan Corbett. Educ: US Navy Turbo Elec Sch, Sound Motion Picture Tech Sch & Elec Sch. Polit & Govt Pos: Pres, Wetzel Co Young Dem, WVa, 58-61; secy exec comt, WVa State Young Dem, 59-61, mem, 61-64; chmn, Wetzel Co Dem Exec Comt, 64-72; mem, Grant Dist, Wetzel Co Dem Exec Comt, 68- Bus & Prof Pos: Electrician, Union Carbide Chem Co, 45- Mil Serv: Entered as A/S, Navy, 40, released as CPO, 45, after serv in SPac; SPac Theater, NAtlantic Theater & Asiatic Theater Ribbons. Mem: Mason (32 degree); Shrine; VFW; Am Legion; Pine Grove Sportsman Club. Relig: Methodist. Mailing Add: Hastings WV 26365

MILLER, HARRIET EVELYN (D)
b Council, Idaho, July 4, 19; d Colwell Miller & Vera Crome M; single. Educ: Whitman Col, BA, 41; Univ Pa, MA, 49; Univ Mont, grad study; Phi Beta Kappa; Psi Chi; Phi Kappa Phi; Alpha Chi Omega. Polit & Govt Pos: Secy, Missoula Co Young Rep, Mont, 52-53; nat committeewoman, Mont Young Rep, 54-56; supt pub instr, Mont, 57-68; cand, Dem nomination for Cong, First Dist, Mont, 68 & 72; mem, Dem Nat Platform Comt, 72- Bus & Prof Pos: Med technician, US Govt Civil Serv, Ft Lewis, Wash, 42-44; research chemist, Atlantic Refining Co, Philadelphia, Pa, 44-50; student personnel adminr, Univ Mont, 50-53, assoc dean of students, 54-56; free-lance writer, 53-54; pres, Harriet Miller Assocs, Mgt Consult, 69-; assoc dir, Nat Retired Teachers Asn & Am Asn Retired Persons, 74- Publ: Ed, Elephant Trumpetings, Mont Young Rep, 53-54; auth, Problems of financing quality education in Montana, Col Educ Rec, Univ Idaho, spring 65; Coyote Tales of the Montana Salish, 75. Mem: Gerontological Soc; World Future Soc; Am Mgt Asn; Nat Coun for Homemaker-Home Health Aide Servs, Inc (mem bd dirs); Northern Va Educ TV Asn (vpres). Relig: Methodist. Mailing Add: PO Box 1019 Helena MT 59601

MILLER, HERBERT J (D)
NY State Assemblyman
Mailing Add: 100-11 67th Rd Forest Hills NY 11375

MILLER, HILDRETH ESTHER (R)
Mem, Mich Rep State Cent Comt
b Udora, Ont, Can, Nov 3, 07; d James Edwin Peers & Zuleika Beare P; div; c James P, William Robert & Jon E. Educ: Uxbridge High Sch, grad, 26. Polit & Govt Pos: Comt mem, Eighth Cong Dist, 73-75; mem exec comt, Saginaw Co Rep Party, Mich, 75-, chmn, Sr Citizens Activities, 75-; mem, Mich Rep State Cent Comt, 75-; bd dirs & area coordr, Mich State Fedn Rep Women, 75- Bus & Prof Pos: Owner & operator, Employ Agency, 50-54; pvt duty nursing care, 55-59; acct, Melcraft Marine, 60-73. Mem: Saginaw Co Rep Women's Club (membership chmn, 75-); Eastern Star, Martha Washington Chap; Saginaw Area Christian Women's Club. Relig: Protestant. Mailing Add: 4440 Warren St Bridgeport MI 48722

MILLER, HYMAN M (R)
NY State Assemblyman
b Syracuse, NY; s Solomon J Miller & Fanny M; m to Anne; c Robert, Philip, Linda, Janis & Sharon. Educ: Western Md Col; Syracuse Univ. Polit & Govt Pos: Councilman, Dewitt, NY, 67-70; chmn, Dewitt Town Rep Comt, 70-; NY State Assemblyman, 119th Dist, 71- Mailing Add: 56 Lyndon Rd Fayetteville NY 13066

MILLER, JACK LEE (D)
b Lexington, Ky, Nov 29, 35; s I Jay Miller & Beatrice Frumberg M; single. Educ: Univ Ky, BA, 57, LLB, 62; Zeta Beta Tau; Hillel Found. Polit & Govt Pos: Asst Co Attorney, Fayette Co, Ky, 67-; chmn, Citizens for McGovern-Shriver, 72; deleg, Dem Nat Conv, 72. Mil Serv: Pfc, Army, 59; Capt, Res, 14 years. Mem: Ky Co Attorney's Asn; Phi Delta Phi; Kiwanis; Judge Adv Gen Sch Alumni Asn; ROA. Honors & Awards: Sixth Dist Outstanding Young Dem, Ky Young Dem, 70. Relig: Jewish. Mailing Add: 1920 Blairmore Rd Lexington KY 40502

MILLER, JERRY J (D)
Mayor, South Bend, Ind
b South Bend, Ind, Aug 31, 33; s Joseph Emmett Miller & Bernice H Gallagher M; m 1952 to Mary Lou Taylor; c Robert, Michael, Theresa & Beth. Educ: Purdue Univ Exten, Michigan City, 53; Ind Univ, South Bend, 54. Polit & Govt Pos: Vpres co comnrs, St Joseph Co, Ind, 69-70, pres, 71; chmn, Third Dist Dem Comt, 72-; mayor, South Bend, 72- Bus & Prof Pos: Ins agt, John Hancock Mutual Life, Michigan City, 54-58; ins agt, State Farm, South Bend, 58-71. Mem: Ind Asn Cities & Towns; US Conf Mayors; Nat League of Cities; KofC. Honors & Awards: Distinguished Serv Awards South Bend Jaycees, 68; Outstanding Dem of Ind, Ind Young Dem, 73. Relig: Catholic. Legal Res: 2610 S Twyckenham Dr South Bend IN 46614 Mailing Add: 1400 Co-City Bldg 227 W Jefferson South Bend IN 46601

MILLER, JOHN E (D)
Ark State Rep
b Melbourne, Ark, Mar 2, 29; s Green H Miller & Annie Gray M; m 1949 to Ruby Robertson; c David, Martha & Naomi. Educ: Ark State Col, BS, 49. Polit & Govt Pos: Co & circuit clerk, Melbourne, Ark, 52-56; Ark State Rep, 59- Bus & Prof Pos: Owner, John E Miller Ins Agency, 59- Mem: Farm Bur; Ark Co Clerk's Asn; Lions; Eastern Star; Mason (32 degree). Relig: Baptist. Mailing Add: PO Box 436 Melbourne AR 72556

MILLER, JOHN GUY (R)
b St Louis, Mo, Aug 20, 15; s Guy H Miller & Erma Moore M; m 1961 to Ann Jenson; c Vera. Educ: Univ Mo-Columbia, BS, 37. Polit & Govt Pos: Minority staff dir, US Senate Spec Comt on Aging, 61- Mil Serv: Marine Corps, 42-46. Legal Res: Hume MO 64752 Mailing Add: 5830 Oregon Ave NW Washington DC 20015

MILLER, JOHN (JACK) (D)
Fla State Rep
Mailing Add: 1351 Johnson St Hollywood FL 33020

MILLER, JOHN JOSE (D)
Calif State Assemblyman
b Savannah, Ga, July 28, 32; s Fred Miller, Sr & Minnie Emond M; m 1962 to Joyce Kolheim McNair; c Duncan McNair, Heather Joyce & Robin Hope. Educ: Talladega Col, AB, 54; Howard Univ Sch Law, JD, 57; Boalt Hall Law, Univ Calif, Berkeley, LLM Cand; Alpha Phi Alpha; Int House; class & student body pres & Avery Speech Award, Talladega Col, 54; WHC Brown fel, Howard Univ, 55-57; Walter Perry Johnson grad research fel law, Univ Calif, Berkeley, 58-59. Polit & Govt Pos: Mem, Berkeley Housing Adv & Appeals Bd, Calif, 62-65; mem, Bd Libr Trustees, Berkeley, 64-65; mem, Bd Educ, 64-66, pres, 65-66; Calif State Assemblyman, 13th Dist, 66-; deleg, Dem Nat Conv, 72. Bus & Prof Pos: Practicing attorney, San Francisco, Calif, currently. Publ: Assoc ed, Howard Law J, 67. Mem: Calif State Bar Asn; Am Acad Polit & Social Sci; Univ Calif Men's Faculty Club; Oakland grad Chap, Alpha Phi Alpha. Relig: Episcopal. Legal Res: Oakland CA Mailing Add: State Capitol Sacramento CA 95814

MILLER JOSEPH KERR (R)
Secy-Treas, Wyandot Co Rep Cent & Exec Comt, Ohio
b Upper Sandusky, Ohio, Dec 23, 08; s Harry Clay Miller & Eva Smith M; single. Educ: Upper Sandusky High Sch, Ohio. Polit & Govt Pos: Mem, Ohio State Rep Cent Comt, 40-69, secy-treas, 48-69; mem, City Coun, Upper Sandusky, 48-50; mem & secy-treas, Wyandot Co Rep Cent & Exec Comt, currently; mem, Bd Elec, currently. Bus & Prof Pos: Retired. Mem: Mason; AASR. Relig: Presbyterian. Mailing Add: 720 S Seventh St Upper Sandusky OH 43351

MILLER, JOSEPH S (D)
b Chilhowie, Va, Mar 2, 11; s Jason P Miller & Alice Crabtree M; m 1940 to Blanche Roberts; c Hilda Arlene (Mrs Frank M Wing, Jr). Polit & Govt Pos: Chmn, Washington Co Dem Comt, Va, formerly. Bus & Prof Pos: Plant engr, United Tel Syst, 41- Mem: RAM; KT; Shrine; Mason (32 degree); Independent Tel Pioneer Asn. Relig: Presbyterian. Mailing Add: 139 Terrace Dr Bristol VA 24201

MILLER, JUDITH LEE (D)
b Longview, Wash, Oct 14, 42; d W Wayne Doble & Virginia Wagner D; m 1961 to Alan William Miller; c Scott, Susan & Brian. Educ: Lower Columbia Col, 60-61; Ore State Univ, 70. Polit & Govt Pos: Vchmn, First Cong Dist Dem Comt, Ore, 68-70; vchmn, Polk Co Dem Party, 68-70, chmn, 70; mem exec comt, Ore Dem Party, 70-74; deleg, Dem Nat Conv, 72; mem, Monmouth City Coun, 75- Mailing Add: 453 Scott St Monmouth OR 97361

MILLER, JUSTINA MARIE (D)
Chmn, Greene Co Dem Exec Comt, Ohio
b Dayton, Ohio, Sept 26, 08; d Odgen Odell Wasson & Daisy E Hamilton W; m 1931 to Farrell Statia Miller; c Larry Farrell. Educ: Bliss Bus Col, Columbus, Ohio, grad, 28; action course in practical polit, 70. Polit & Govt Pos: Mem, Ohio Federated Dem Women, 25 years; mem, Greene Co Dem Cent Comt, 65-; mem, Greene Co Dem Exec Comt, 65-, secy, 66-68, vchmn, 69, chmn, 69-; committeewoman, Ohio State Dem Cent Comt, 66-; pres, Greene Co Dem Women's Club, 68-70; vchmn, Ohio State Dem Exec Comt, 69-; chmn, Greene Co Bd Educ, 70- Bus & Prof Pos: Owner, Justina's Women's Wear & Beauty Shop, Xenia, Ohio, 37-55; secy, Wright Patterson AFB, 56-63. Mem: Nat Fedn Bus & Prof Women's Clubs; Am Bus Women's Asn; Ohio Asn Elec Officers; Lambda Chi Omega; Eastern Star. Honors & Awards: Merit Award & Outstanding Performance Rating, Wright Patterson AFB. Relig: Methodist. Mailing Add: 152 W Market St Xenia OH 45385

MILLER, KAREN JENNINGS (D)
Del State Rep
Mailing Add: 836 Miller Dr Towne Point Dover DE 19901

MILLER, KEITH HARVEY (R)
b Seattle, Wash, Mar 1, 25; s Hopkins Keith Miller & Margaret Harvey M; m 1953 to Diana Mary Doyle. Educ: Univ Wash, BA, 52. Polit & Govt Pos: Alaska State Rep, 62-66; deleg, Rep Nat Conv, 64 & 72; Alaska, 66-69; Gov, Alaska, 69-71; Alaska State Sen, 73-75. Bus & Prof Pos: Pres, Olympia Holly Farm, Wash, 49-53; pres, United Collection Serv, Inc, Seattle, 54-57; homesteader, Talkeetna, Alaska, 59-62; pres, Alaska Local Develop Corp, 71- Mil Serv: Army Air Force, 43-45. Mem: Alaska Life Underwriters Asn; Moose; Lions; Explorers Club; Am Legion. Relig: Methodist. Mailing Add: PO Box 319 Palmer AK 99645

MILLER, KENNETH D (D)
Iowa State Rep
Mailing Add: RR 1 Independence IA 50644

MILLER, KENNETH J (D)
Chmn, Warren Co Dem Cent Comt, Ind
b Lafayette, Ind, Mar 29, 14; s James Miller & Emma Bates M; m 1935 to Dorothy Vinnetta Amick; c Ura Leslie, Karen Diane, Bertie Jane (Mrs Buchanan) & Kenneth J, II. Educ: Ind Cent Bus Col, Indianapolis, grad, 34. Polit & Govt Pos: Chmn, Warren Co Dem Cent Comt, Ind, 50-; mem, Warren Co Coun, 62-65 & 70-74; comnr, Warren Co, 65-69; alt deleg, Dem Nat Conv, 72. Mailing Add: RR 4 Attica IN 47981

MILLER, KEVIN GREY (R)
b Ferguson, NC, Sept 22, 30; s Sheridan F Miller & Lizzie F Funkhouser M; m 1959 to Frances Ann Thompson; c Stephanie Ann, Lora Gail & Kevin G, Jr. Educ: Madison Col, BA, 57, MS, 59; Pi Omega Pi. Polit & Govt Pos: Alt deleg, Rep Nat Conv, 72; chmn city comt, Harrisonburg, Va, 74- Bus & Prof Pos: High sch teacher, San Diego, Calif, 57-62; internal revenue agt, Charlottesville, Va, 64-69; asst prof bus admin, Madison Col, 69-; cert pub acct, Harrisonburg, Va, 71- Mil Serv: Entered as Pvt, Army, 48, released as Cpl, after serv in Far East Theatre, 49-51; Good Conduct Medal. Mem: Am Inst of Cert Pub Acct; Am Legion; Elks; Moose; Nat Exchange Club. Mailing Add: 417 Mountain View Dr Harrisonburg VA 22801

MILLER, LAURA ANNE (R)
Colo State Rep
b San Antonio, Tex, Oct 4, 19; d Kenneth Robert Wimer & Cecile Janin W; m 1942 to Robert William Miller; c Richard F & Patsy Ann (Mrs Marshall). Educ: Univ San Antonio, 36-38; Robert B Green Hosp, San Antonio, Tex, 39. Polit & Govt Pos: Rep committeewoman, Jefferson Co, Colo, 62-70; libr bd trustees, Jefferson Co, Colo Pub Libr, 67-; Colo State Rep, Dist 28, 71- Bus & Prof Pos: Med technologist, Austin State Hosp, Tex, 39-42. Relig: Episcopal. Mailing Add: 6100 W Bowles Ave Littleton CO 80123

MILLER, LINDA LEA MARGARET (D)
SDak State Rep
b Sioux Falls, SDak, Oct 27, 45; d Carl Thomas Crampton & Elenore Zehnpfennig C. Educ: Univ SDak, Vermillion, BS in Bus Educ, 67; Alpha Xi Delta. Polit & Govt Pos: SDak State Rep, Minnehaha Co, 73- Bus & Prof Pos: Teacher, Yankton Sr High Sch, SDak, 67-69 & Edison Jr High Sch, Sioux Falls, 69- Mem: Pi Omega Pi; SDak Educ Asn; Nat Bus Educ Asn (state membership dir, 67-); Nat Coun Teachers Social Studies; Am Asn Univ Women (pres, 70-). Relig: Roman Catholic. Mailing Add: 4100 W Mesa Pass Sioux Falls SD 57106

MILLER, LORNA MARIE (D)
b Valley City, NDak, Aug 27, 29; d John E Clancy & Frances Starke C; m 1958 to Anton J Miller; c Michelle, Renee & Shawn. Educ: Valley City State Teachers Col, NDak, 3 years. Polit & Govt Pos: Chmn, Barnes Co Young Dem, NDak, 45; chmn & nat committeewoman, NDak Young Dem, 51-56; secy-treas, Humphrey for President Comt, Eau Claire Co, Wis, 60; vchmn, Eau Claire Co Dem Party, 60; secy-treas, Chippewa Co Dem Party, 65, vchmn, 69; secy-treas, McCarthy for Pres Comt, Chippewa Co, 68; deleg, Dem Nat Conv, 68; exec dir, Friends of Don Peterson for Gov, 69-70; membership chmn, Eastern Dane Co Dem Party, Wis, 69-72; mem steering comt, Wis McGovern for President, 70-72; deleg, Dem Nat Conv, 72. Bus & Prof Pos: Teacher, Hazen, Ypsilanti, West Fargo, NDak, 49-51; fieldworker, NDak Farmer Union, 51-58; educ dept dir, Wis Farmers Union, 58-; exec dir, African-Latin Am Farm Coop Seminar, Nat Farmers Union & Agency Int Develop Contract, Kamp Kenwood, Chippewa Falls, Wis, summers 66 & 67; researcher, Ctr Appl Sociol, Univ Wis, 70-, asst dir, 70-72, asst to chancellor, Wis Univ Exten, 72- Mem: Comn Voc Opportunities for Rural Youth; Northern Great Lakes Resource Develop Comt; Nat Educ Asn; Farmers Union; Am Civil Liberties Union. Relig: Catholic. Mailing Add: 180 Columbus St Sun Prairie WI 53590

MILLER, MARC ERIC (D)
b New York , NY, Feb 8, 47; s Seymour Miller & Rosalyn Finkelstein M; m 1971 to Linda Bernstein. Educ: Princeton Univ, AB, 69; Harvard Univ Law Sch, JD, 72. Polit & Govt Pos: Personal aide, Basil A Paterson, Dem cand for Lt Gov, NY, 70; admin asst, US Rep Lester L Wolff, NY, 72- Mem: NY Bar. Relig: Jewish. Legal Res: 17 Wenwood Dr Brookville Glen Head NY 11545 Mailing Add: 2463 Rayburn House Off Bldg Washington DC 20515

MILLER, MARGARET (PEG) (R)
Mo State Rep
Mailing Add: 636 W Jackson Marshfield MO 65706

MILLER, MARIKO TERASAKI (D)
Mem Exec Comt, Dem Nat Comt
b Shanghai, China; d Hidenari Terasaki & Gwen Harold T; m 1953 to Mayne Williams Miller; c Robert Rush, Mayne Cole, Terence Haynes & Timothy Williams. Educ: ETenn State Univ, BA, 53. Polit & Govt Pos: Alt deleg, Dem Nat Conv, 72; mem steering comt, Nat Women's Polit Caucus, 72-; vchmn, Dem Party of Wyo, 73-; deleg, Dem Nat Mid Term Conf, 74; mem exec comt, Asn State Dem Chmn, 75-; mem, Dem Nat Comt, 75-, mem exec comt, 75- Mem: League of Women Voters; Am Civil Liberties Union; Common Cause; NAACP; Sierra Club. Relig: Unitarian. Mailing Add: 111 W 14th St Casper WY 82601

MILLER, MARJORIE M (D)
Wis State Rep
Mailing Add: 1937 Arlington Pl Madison WI 53705

MILLER, MARVIN EUGENE (R)
Pa State Rep
b Lime Rock, Pa, May 28, 27; s Roy Kling Miller & Emma Whitmyer M; c Marvin E, Jr & Lorrie L. Polit & Govt Pos: Dir, Lancaster Co Young Rep, Pa, 61-62; mem, Pa House Campaign Comt, 64 & 66; research aide & writer, Rep Floor Leader Staff, Pa House Rep, 66; Pa State Rep, 67-, minority chmn House comt labor rels, 71-72, vchmn, 73-, secy House comt law & justice, 73- Bus & Prof Pos: Sports ed & asst city ed, Intelligencer J, 46-58; ed, Lititz Record-Express, 58-60; reporter & asst ed, Lancaster New Era, 60-66; ed, Octorara Newspapers, 66- Mil Serv: Pvt, Marine Corps, 45, serv in Recruit Depot, Parris Island. Publ: Auth, The Republican Caucus, Am Polit Sci Asn, 71; The Church & the State, Moravian Church Am, 72. Mem: Lancaster Sportswriters & Broadcasters Asn. Honors & Awards: Winner, six statewide prizes in newspaper reporting, Pa Newspaper Publ Asn; Freedom in the Am Way Award, Sertoma, Lancaster, 72. Relig: Moravian Church. Legal Res: 2363 Oregon Pike Lancaster PA 17601 Mailing Add: 233 Frederick St Lancaster PA 17602

MILLER, MELVIN HOWARD (D)
NY State Assemblyman
b Brooklyn, NY, July 24, 39; s Henry Miller & Frieda Chaiet M; m 1961 to Elizabeth Mohr; c Susan & Lawrence. Educ: Brooklyn Col, BA, 61; NY Univ Sch Law, LLB, 64. Polit & Govt Pos: NY State Assemblyman, 44th Assembly Dist, 71- Bus & Prof Pos: Assoc, O'Dwyer & Bernstein, Esqs, NY, 64-67; Joseph Keller Esq, 67-69; Bluestone, Kleigman & Israel Esq, 69-71; partner, Sherman, Adolf & Miller Esq, 71- Mil Serv: Entered as Pvt, Army, 57, released as Pfc, 57, after serv in Mil Police. Mem: NY Co Bar Asn; Fidelity Lodge; KofP; Flatbush Comt for Youth; Midwood Community Coun. Relig: Jewish; bd trustees, Shaare Torah Congregation. Mailing Add: 301 Rugby Rd Brooklyn NY 11226

MILLER, MIDGE LEEPER (D)
Wis State Rep
b Morgantown, WVa, June 8, 22; d Lorimer Victor Cavins & Neva Adams C; m 1944 to H Dean Leeper, wid; m 1963 to Edward Ernst Miller; c Steven Lloyd, David Dean, Linda Jean & Kenneth Chandran Leeper & Mark Finley, Sterling Davey, Jeffrey Scoon, Nancy Jean & Randall Conrad Miller. Educ: Univ Mich, BS, 44; Yale Divinity Sch, audit, 54-57; Univ Wis, Madison, MA, 62. Polit & Govt Pos: Corresponding secy, Dane Co Dem Party, Wis, 1 year, vchmn, 66-67; dist rep, West Madison Dem Party, 3 years; deleg, Dem Nat Conv, 68, mem platform comt; mem, Wis State Steering Comt, McCarthy Campaign, 68; mem nat steering comt, New Dem Coalition, formerly, nat vchmn, 70-; Wis State Rep, Dane Co Third Dist, 71-72, Dist 77, 72-; mem nat policy coun, Nat Womens Polit Caucus, 71- Bus & Prof Pos: Prog dir, YWCA, Conn & Mich, 44-46; asst dean letters & sci, Univ Wis, 60-66, coordr univ relig activities, 66-68. Mem: YWCA. Relig: Methodist. Legal Res: 1937 Arlington Pl Madison WI 53705 Mailing Add: 48 North State Capitol Madison WI 53702

MILLER, MORTIMER MICHAEL (MIKE) (D)
Alaska State Rep
b Trinidad, Colo, July 17, 29; s L Hoy Miller & Juanita Risk M; m 1951 to Marilyn Bills; c Gail, Kevin & Shelley. Educ: Univ Wichita, BA, 51; Men of Webster. Polit & Govt Pos: Publicity dir, Alaska State Div Tourism, 60-70; assemblyman, City & Borough of Juneau, 66-70; Alaska State Rep, Dist Four, 70- Bus & Prof Pos: Free lance writer, Juneau, 70- Mil Serv: Army Res, 48-56. Publ: Off the Beaten Path in Alaska, 70, Soapy, 71 & Camping & Trailering in Alaska, 72, AlaskaBooks; plus articles in various mag & newspapers. Mem: Soc Mag Writers; Soc Am Travel Writers; Outdoor Writers Asn Am. Relig: Methodist. Mailing Add: Box 1494 Juneau AK 99801

MILLER, NATHAN H (R)
Va State Deleg
b Harrisonburg, Va, July 4, 43; s Garland Franklin Miller & Edith Huff M; single. Educ: Bridgewater Col, BA in Econ, 65; T C Williams Sch Law, Univ Richmond, LLB, 69; Phi Delta Phi. Polit & Govt Pos: Va State Deleg, City of Harrisonburg, Rockingham, Page & Shenandoah Co, 71-; Seventh Dist co-chmn, Comt to Reelect President, 72. Bus & Prof Pos: Vpres, Dominion Silo, 65; partner, Conrad, Litten, Sipe & Miller, 69; judge, Town Court of Timberville, Va, 71. Mem: Bridgewater Rotary; Bridgewater Col Alumni Asn; Harrisonburg Jaycees; Rockingham Male Chorus; Proj Concern (mem bd, 71-). Honors & Awards: Outstanding Young Man, Bridgewater Jaycees, 72. Relig: Church of the Brethren. Legal Res: Rte 2 Bridgewater VA 22812 Mailing Add: 218 E Market St Harrisonburg VA 22801

MILLER, NORMAN RODNEY (D)
b Winfield, Kans, May 20, 27; s Archibald R Miller & Jessie Geeslin M; m 1951 to Shirley Jean Shriver; c Andrew K, Jennifer Lou & Stanley J. Educ: Univ Kans, BS in Chem Eng, 50; Tau Beta Pi; Sigma Tau. Polit & Govt Pos: Dem precinct committeeman, Richland, Wash, 56-; chmn finance comt, Benton Co Dem Cent Comt, 65-66, chmn, 68-72; chmn, Dem Seeking a New World, Benton & Franklin Counties, 68; chmn, Tri-City Kennedy for President Comt, 68; chmn, Benton Co Dem Conv, 70; mem exec comt, Fourth Cong Dist Dem Coun, 71- Bus & Prof Pos: Engr & sr engr, Gen Elec, Richland, Wash, 50-62, supvr process analysis & eval, 62-66, corresponding secy, Gen Elec Technol Hazards Coun, 64-67, mgr process eval & control, 66-68; consult engr, Douglas United Nuclear, 68-71, mgr WPPSS proj sect, 71- Mil Serv: Entered as Seaman 1/C, Navy, 45, released as Seaman 1/C, 46, after serv in Naval Separations Ctr, 45-46. Mem: Am Nuclear Soc; Am Soc Metals; NAACP; YMCA. Mailing Add: 43 Ferry Rd Richland WA 99352

MILLER, OPAL (D)
Iowa State Rep
Mailing Add: RR 2 Rockwell City IA 50579

MILLER, PETER J (R)
Mem, Ill State Rep Comt
b June 16, 19; c five. Educ: Ill Mil Col, Abington; Northwestern Univ. Polit & Govt Pos: Park supvr, Chicago, Ill, 11 years; secy, Ill State Athletic Comn, 5 years; Ill State Sen, 2 terms; Ill State Rep, 56-72; mem, Ill State Rep Comt, currently; deleg, Rep Nat Conv, 68 & 72. Bus & Prof Pos: Paymaster, Sanit Dist, Chicago (formerly); phys educ teacher, parochial grammar schs (formerly); Olympic skating coach, 40 & 48. Mem: Cath Youth Orgn; Amateur Skating Unions of US. Legal Res: 1840 N Rutherford Ave Chicago IL 60635 Mailing Add: 5719 W Fullerton Chicago IL 60644

MILLER, PHYLLIS ANN (D)
Committeewoman, Dem Exec Comt, Fla
b Logan, WVa, July 16, 40; d Harold William Fleming & Dolly Beaver F; m 1960 to Wilton Royce Miller; c Billy & Melissa. Educ: Univ Fla, BAE, 62; Fla State Univ, grad work, 67-68; Delta Tau Kappa; Alpha Chi Omega. Polit & Govt Pos: Committeewoman, Dem Exec Comt, Fla, 70-; vchmn, Second Cong Dist, Dem Party Fla, 71-75, chmn, 75-, mem state budget & finance comt, 75-; deleg, Dem Nat Mid-Term Conf, 74. Bus & Prof Pos: Social worker, State Welfare Dept, 63-65; voc rehabilitation counr, Bur Blind Servs, 65-70. Mem: Fla Rehabilitation Asn; Leon Co Dem Woman's Club (3rd vpres, 75-). Relig: Methodist. Mailing Add: 1530 Crowder Rd Tallahassee FL 32303

MILLER, RALPH ROSS (D)
La State Rep
b Norco, La, Apr 27, 34; s Homer F Miller, Sr & Emma Cambre M; m 1959 to Anne M Blanchard; c Ross A, Gregory A, Maria C & Maureen J. Educ: La State Univ, BS, 56, JD & LLB, 58; Gamma Eta Gamma; Pi Tau Pi; Newman Club. Polit & Govt Pos: La State Rep,

Third Dist, 68-72, 56th Dist, 72- Bus & Prof Pos: Attorney-at-law, 59- Mil Serv: Entered as Pvt, Army, 61, released as S/Sgt, 62, after serv in 159th Evacuation Hosp, Ft Sill, Okla; Army Commendation Medal; La Cross. Mem: Am Bar Asn; 29th Judicial Dist Bar Asn; Nat Soc State Legislators; Norco CofC; Lions. Relig: Roman Catholic. Legal Res: 107 Apple St Norco LA 70079 Mailing Add: PO Box 190 Norco LA 70079

MILLER, RICHARD HAROLD (D)
Chmn, Mercer Co Dem Comt, Pa
b Beaver, Pa, May 22, 42; s Frank Harold Miller & Sarah I Kallenbaugh M; m 1969 to Gloria Mae Gill; c Mark. Educ: Lincoln High Sch, Ellwood City, Pa, grad, 60. Polit & Govt Pos: Chmn, Greenville City Dem Party, Pa, 68-70; mem, Greenville Planning Comn, 69-; mem steering comt, Pa State Dem Rules & Rev Comt, 70-72; chmn, Mercer Co Dem Comt, 70-; mem, Mercer Co Planning Comn, 72-; chmn, Solid Waste Mgt Comn, 73-74; mem, Mercer Co Indust Develop Authority, 72-; NW Pa coordr, Pa Dem State Comt, 73-; mem, Pa Dem State Platform Comt, 74. Mil Serv: Sgt, Army Res, until 72. Legal Res: 26 Chambers Ave Greenville PA 16125 Mailing Add: PO Box 56 Greenville PA 16125

MILLER, RICHARD L (D)
WVa State Deleg
Mailing Add: State Capitol Charleston WV 25305

MILLER, ROBERT BATES, JR (D)
Treas, Harrison Co Dem Exec Comt, WVa
b Clarksburg, WVa, Sept 23, 25; s Robert B Miller, Sr & Arline Kirby M; m to Anita Joyce Shreve; c Robert B, III, Annica, John G & Kirby. Educ: Washington-Irving High Sch, Clarksburg, grad, 43. Polit & Govt Pos: Mem, Harrison Co Dem Exec Comt, WVa, 64-, treas, 74-; ballot comnr, Harrison Co, 70-; deleg, Dem Charter Conf, Kansas City, Mo, 74; mem, First Cong Dist Dem Exec Comt, currently. Bus & Prof Pos: Chief of security, Benedum Airport, Clarksburg, currently. Mil Serv: Merchant Marine, serv in European & Mediter Theatres, 44 & 45. Mem: Clarksburg Little League (pres, 72-75); Moose. Relig: Methodist. Mailing Add: 123 Thompson St Clarksburg WV 26301

MILLER, ROBERT CHARLES (R)
b Keego Harbor, Mich, Dec 27, 27; s Clinton B Miller, Sr (deceased) & Marguerite Sievers M; m 1949 to Mary Lou Horsley; c Judith Ann, Todd Emerson & Robert C, Jr. Educ: Pontiac Sr High Sch, Mich, grad, 46. Polit & Govt Pos: Chief investr for Prosecuting Attorney, Oakland Co, Mich, 51-56; precinct deleg, Mich State Rep Conv, 52-58; vpres, Oakland Co Lincoln Rep Club, 54-56; pres, Pontiac Rep Club, 56; Rep nominee for Mich State Rep, 56; acting postmaster, Pontiac, Mich, 58-60; exec dir, Capitol Hill Asn & Club, DC, 62 & 63; exec secy, Eisenhower 73rd Birthday Dinner, 63; exec dir, D C Rep Comt, 63-65; state field dir, Rep Party of Wis, 65-71, dir polit div, 71; Rep committeeman, Precinct One, Ward Three, Madison, Wis, 67-72; mem exec comt, Dane Co Rep Party, Wis, 68-71; bus mgt specialist, US Small Bus Admin, 72-74; campaign dir, Kasten for Cong Comt, Ninth Dist Wis, 74; home secy, US Rep Robert W Kasten, 75- Bus & Prof Pos: Radio announcer, WCAR, Pontiac, Mich, 43-46, WTAC, Flint, 48-50; police officer, Pontiac Police Dept, 50-51; sales mgr, Cadillac-Oldsmobile Dealer, Pontiac, 56-62. Mil Serv: Entered as A/S, Navy Aviation, 46, released as Seaman 1/C, AMM, 48, after serv in Basic Training Squadron, Pensacola Air Base & Corey Field, Fla, 47-48; Am Theatre Ribbon & Victory Medal, World War II. Mem: Elks; East Side Bus Men's Asn. Relig: Methodist. Mailing Add: 333 Bishop's Way Brookfield WI 53005

MILLER, ROBERT HOWARD (R)
Mayor, Irvington, NJ
b Irvington, NJ, Sept 19, 18; s Joseph G Miller & Emily Goodwin M; m 1940 to Marion I Heidrich; c Robert H, Jr & Gary Richard. Educ: Drakes Bus Col, 37. Polit & Govt Pos: Mayor, Irvington, NJ, 74- Bus & Prof Pos: Dep Chief, Irvington Police Dept, retired. Mil Serv: Entered as Pvt, Army, 42, released as Sgt, 45, after serv in Air Corps. Mem: F&AM; Salaan Temple. Relig: Protestant. Legal Res: 899 Sanford Ave Irvington NJ 07111 Mailing Add: Town Hall Civic Sq Irvington NJ 07111

MILLER, ROBERT HUGH (R)
Kans State Rep
b Wellington, Kans, Aug 2, 44; s Ralph E Miller & Lizzie Clark M; single. Educ: Kans State Univ, BS, 67. Polit & Govt Pos: Mem exec bd, Kans Col Young Rep, 65-67; Rep precinct committeeman, Sumner Co, 66-; vpres, Kans Young Rep Fedn, 67-71, pres, 71-73; Kans State Rep, 80th Dist, 71-, chmn govt orgn comt, Kans House of Rep, currently; chmn, Sumner Co Rep Cent Comt; mem, Kans Rep State Comt. Bus & Prof Pos: Farmer, 59-; mem, Kans Pub TV Comn. Mil Serv: E-4, Air Nat Guard, 67-; Nat Defense Medal; Good Conduct Medal. Mem: White House Conf Children & Youth; Wellington Jaycees (pres); Farmers Coop Grain Asn; Am Legion. Relig: Presbyterian; mem bd trustees. Mailing Add: RR 2 Willington KS 67152

MILLER, ROBERT KEITH (D)
b Marshalltown, Iowa, July 10, 46; s Keith C Miller & Catherine E Patton M; m 1972 to Christine A Boos. Educ: Iowa State Univ, BS, 68, grad study, 69-70; Kappa Sigma. Polit & Govt Pos: Dist Rep, US Rep John C Culver, Iowa, 70-72; dir canvass, registr & elec day activities, Iowa Dem Party, 72; exec asst, US Sen Dick Clark, Iowa, 73- Relig: Methodist. Mailing Add: 248 Norman Dr NE Cedar Rapids IA 52402

MILLER, ROBERT LEE (R)
Chmn, Brule Co Rep Party, SDak
b Kimball, SDak, Feb 21, 37; s Arthur L Miller & Cecelia Schmitt M; single. Educ: St Mary's Col, BA; St Paul Sem, 1 year; Young Rep. Polit & Govt Pos: SDak State Sen, 71-74; chmn, Brule Co Rep Party, 75- Bus & Prof Pos: Farmer, Kimball, SDak, currently. Mil Serv: Entered as Airman Basic, Air Force, 61, released as Airman 1/C, 64, after serv in Acct & Finance, Hq 50TFWing, 59th Combat Support Group. Mem: Am Legion; KofC; Jaycees. Relig: Catholic. Legal Res: Cleveland Twp Kimball SD 57355 Mailing Add: RFD 2 Kimball SD 57355

MILLER, RONALD KNOX (R)
SDak State Rep
b Mitchell, SDak, Aug 10, 43; s Walter Carl Miller & Margaret Knox M; m 1965 to Patricia Leavitt; c Adria, Chandra & Aaron. Educ: Univ SDak, BA, 65, JD, 69; Phi Delta Phi; Alpha Tau Omega; Dakotans. Polit & Govt Pos: States attorney, Buffalo Co, SDak, 73-75; SDak State Rep, 18th Dist, 75- Mem: Am & SDak Bar Asns; Am & SDak Trial Lawyers Asns; Elks. Relig: Lutheran. Mailing Add: Kimball SD 57355

MILLER, ROY D (R)
Mem, Rep State Cent Comt Calif
b Okla, June 22, 33; s Frank R Miller & Nioma Bell M; m 1951 to Peggy Lewis; c Debra (Mrs Michael Bailey); Cynthia & Vicki. Educ: Yuba City Union High Sch, 4 years. Polit & Govt Pos: Chmn, Reagan for Gov Comt, Sutter Co, Calif, 66 & 70; assoc mem, Rep State Cent Comt, Calif, 69-71, mem, 71-, mem exec comt, 71-; vchmn, Sutter Co Rep Cent Comt, 70, chmn, 71-72. Mem: Yuba Sutter Painting & Decorating Contractors Am (pres, 60-); Northern Calif Bd Painting & Decorating Contractors Chaps; Valley Contractors Exchange (vpres, 71); Yuba City Rotary Club; Boy Scouts. Relig: Protestant. Mailing Add: 594 Darrough Dr Yuba City CA 95991

MILLER, ROY DAVID (R)
b Quincy, Mo, July 31, 95; s Lemon J Miller & Rosa Rich M; m 1919 to Nelle Mae Coyle; c Mary Frances (Mrs William L Brightwell), Marilyn Mae (Mrs Roy Young) & Dr Leroy J. Educ: Weaubleau Christian Col, 12-13; Springfield State Normal Sch, 15; Univ Mo, 16-17. Polit & Govt Pos: Mo State Rep, 27-28, chmn, Banks & Banking Comt, Mo House Rep, 27-28; bank exam, Mo, 27-33; presidential elector, 28; Mo State Sen, 43-47; chmn, Boone Co Rep Cent Comt, Mo, formerly. Bus & Prof Pos: Pub rels, 33-38, 41-42 & 48-53. Mil Serv: Entered as Seaman 3/C, Navy, 18, released as Ens, 22, after serv on Navy ships, 18-22. Mem: Am Legion; Pachyderm Club; Am Farm Bur; Am Angus Asn. Honors & Awards: Man of the Year, Mo Angus Asn, 55. Relig: Protestant. Mailing Add: 927 S Providence Columbia MO 65201

MILLER, SCOTT, JR (R)
b 1927. Educ: Univ Louisville Law Sch, LLB. Polit & Govt Pos: Mem, Young Rep Club; Ky State Sen, 58-75, chmn Rep caucus, 62; alt deleg, Rep Nat Conv, 72. Bus & Prof Pos: Attorney-at-law. Relig: Episcopal. Mailing Add: 26 Rio Vista Dr Louisville KY 40207

MILLER, STANLEY ALLEN (R)
Finance Chmn, Rep State Comt Pa
b Harrisburg, Pa, Aug 3, 28; s Sigmund Miller & Molly Abrams M; m 1949 to Shirley Tuck; c Marlene & Elliott. Educ: Wharton Sch of Com & Finance, 46-47; Univ Pa; Pi Tau Pi. Polit & Govt Pos: Spec asst to the Gov on Human Affairs & secy, Human Rels Comn, Pa, 67-69; secy, Dept of Pub Welfare, 70-71, chmn, Pa Securities Comn, 71; chmn, Health Ins Benefits Adv Coun of Health, Educ & Welfare, 71-; finance chmn, Rep State Comt, Pa, 75- Bus & Prof Pos: Pres & treas, Miller's Auto Supplies, Inc, 51-, Stanley Distributing Co, 51- Mem: Pa Asn for Retarded Citizens (bd dir, 71); Pa Asn for Ment Health (bd mem, 71-); Easter Seal Campaign (state chmn, 71-72); Holy Spirit Hosp (bd mgr, 74-); Goodwill Indust (bd dirs, 74-). Honors & Awards: Order of Merit, Boy Scouts Am, 66; Distinguished Serv Award, Am Histadrut Develop Found, 70; Award for Dedication & Improving Health Care for Children, Children's Hosp of Philadelphia, 70; Golden Sword Award, Am Cancer Soc, 70 & 72; Frontiersman Int Serv to Humanitiy Award, 73. Relig: Hebrew. Legal Res: 4713 Galen Rd Harrisburg PA 17110 Mailing Add: 200 S 18th St Harrisburg PA 17105

MILLER, STURGIS (D)
Ark State Rep
Mailing Add: Rte 7 Box 870 Pine Bluff AR 71601

MILLER, TED RAY (D)
Tenn State Rep
Mailing Add: 3313 Sunset Ave Knoxville TN 37914

MILLER, TERRY (R)
Alaska State Sen
b San Francisco, Calif, Nov 10, 42; s Conrad B Miller & Nellie W Wright M; m 1963 to Terry L Niemann; c Jennifer. Educ: Univ Alaska, BA, 65; Alpha Kappa Psi; Alpha Phi Omega. Polit & Govt Pos: North Pole City Coun, Alaska, 63-66; assemblyman, Fairbanks North Star Borough, 63-66, presiding off of assembly, 64-66; Alaska State Rep, 66-68; Alaska State Sen, 69-, mem, Finance Comt, Alaska State Sen, chmn judiciary comt, currently, majority leader, 71-73, pres, 73-75. Bus & Prof Pos: Businessman. Mailing Add: Box 80869 Fairbanks AK 99701

MILLER, THOMAS HENRY (R)
Ill State Rep
b Chicago, Ill, Jan 20, 36; s Andrew Peter Miller & Marguerite Hartman M; m 1957 to Eva Victoria Janik; c Linda Marie, Laura Lee, Lisa Victoria & Thomas Albert. Educ: Fox Bus Col, grad, 54. Polit & Govt Pos: Village trustee, South Holland, Ill, 65-72; deleg, Ill Const Conv, 70; Ill State Rep, Tenth Legis Dist, 73-; chmn, Little Calumet River Flood Control Coord Comn, 73- Bus & Prof Pos: Mgr off admin, Santa Fe Railway Co, 55- Mem: Kiwanis; Jaycees; Elks; KofC. Honors & Awards: Distinguished Serv Award as Community's Outstanding Young Man, Jaycees, 68. Relig: Roman Catholic. Legal Res: 15363 Ingleside Ave South Holland IL 60473 Mailing Add: 837 E 162nd St South Holland IL 60473

MILLER, THOMAS ROWLAND (D)
Treas, Jefferson Co Dem Comt, Ky
b Louisville, Ky, May 6, 06; s Thomas Richard Miller & Maud Isaacs M; m 1935 to Barbara Simmons. Educ: Univ Chicago, 23-25; Univ Louisville, 65-66. Polit & Govt Pos: Dem precinct capt, 60-68; Dem ward man, 64-68; cand for alderman, Louisville, Ky, 65; admin asst to comnr of hwys, 66-67; deleg, Dem Nat Conv, 68; treas, Jefferson Co Dem Comt, Ky, 68- Bus & Prof Pos: Restaurateur, Miller's Dairy Bar, Louisville, Ky, 39-45, Miller's Grill, 46-64 & Teeken's Bakery, 54-65; real estate salesman, McGill & McGill, 64-66; mgr, Alan Nash, Realtor, 68-69. Mil Serv: Entered as Pvt, Army, 43, released as Cpl, 46, after serv in 604th Ord Ammunition, Mediter Theatre, 44-46; Bronze Star. Mem: Louisville Bd Realtors; Cath Bus & Prof Men's Club; Esquire Club; NAACP; YMCA. Honors & Awards: Ky Col. Relig: Catholic. Mailing Add: 215 N 46th St Louisville KY 40212

MILLER, THOMAS V MIKE, JR (D)
Md State Sen
Mailing Add: 8808 Old Branch Ave Clinton MD 20735

MILLER, THOMAS WOODNUTT (R)
b Wilmington, Del, June 26, 86; s Charles Robert Miller & Abigail Morgan Woodnutt M; m 1913 to Katharine Tallman (deceased); c Thomas L & Mrs George P Bissell, Jr; m 1946 to Eleanor Taylor. Educ: Sheffield Sci Sch, Yale Univ, PhB, 08; Delta Phi; St Elmo Club, New Haven. Polit & Govt Pos: Secy State, Del, 13-15; US Rep, Del, 15-17; chmn, Del State Coun Defense, 17; alien property custodian, 21-25; mem, Am Battle Monuments Comn, 23-26;

founder, Nev State Park Syst, 35, chmn, Nev State Bank Comn, 35-37, 52-59 & 67-72; supvr, US Grazing Serv, Nev & Calif, 36-42; chmn, Nev State Coun Defense, 42-46; staff field rep, US Vet Employ Serv for Fourteen Western States, 46-57; mem, Nev Coun Civil Defense, 51-59; chmn, Park & Hort Comn, Reno, 63-66, mem, Recreation & Park Comn, 66-72. Bus & Prof Pos: Rolling mill foreman, Bethlehem Steel Co, South Bethlehem, Pa, 08-09; ranching & mining, Nev, many years. Mil Serv: Plattsburg Mil Training Camp, NY, 15; enlisted as Pvt, Inf, 17, released as Lt Col, 19, after serv in First Del Inf & 114th Inf, 29th Div, Ft McClelland, Ala, as Ord & Machine Gun Officer, 79th Div, AEF, 1 year, France, Meuse-Argonne Offensive, Lt Col, Res, 19-28, serv as Exec Officer, 315th Inf; cited in div orders by Commanding Gen 79th Div for gallantry in action under enemy fire & by Gen Persing for especially meritorious serv with the 79th Div, France; Purple Heart. Publ: Contrib, various conserv publ. Mem: Am Legion; F&AM; Shrine; Hist Soc Del & Nev; Navy League US. Relig: Episcopal; mem, Episcopal Found, Nev, 54-58, vestry, jr warden & sr warden & mem bishop's exec coun, 63-67, Trinity Church. Mailing Add: 1419 S Arlington Ave Reno NV 89502

MILLER, WALTER D (R)
SDak State Rep
Mailing Add: New Underwood SD 57761

MILLER, WARREN BAKER (D)
Chmn, Webster Co Dem Asn, Ky
b Bethany, Ill, Sept 27, 17; s Conda Cleveland Miller & Sallie Baker M; m 1954 to Nancy Rebecca Hockaday; c Nancy Jane, Robin Lyn & Warren Baker, Jr. Educ: Western Ky State Univ, 35-37; Univ Tenn, JD, 40; Debate Team. Polit & Govt Pos: Co attorney, Webster Co, Ky, 58-65; chmn, Webster Co Dem Asn, 68- Bus & Prof Pos: Field abstractor, Tenn Valley Authority, Murray, Ky, 41-44; enforcement attorney, Off Price Admin, Atlanta, Miami, 44-47; title examr, Tenn Valley Authority, Chattanooga, Tenn, 47-55; pvt law - practice Dixon, Ky, 55- Mem: Webster Co Bar Asn (secy-treas, 58-); Ky State Bar Asn; Univ Tenn Law Alumni; Lions. Honors & Awards: Robinson Medal, Western State Univ, 37. Relig: Cumberland Presbyterian. Legal Res: W Leiper St Dixon KY 42409 Mailing Add: Box 236 Dixon KY 42409

MILLER, WESLEY A (R)
Mo State Rep
Mailing Add: 801 E First Washington MO 63090

MILLER, WILLIAM ALBERT, JR (D)
Chmn, Fairfield Co Dem Cent Comt, Ohio
b Lancaster, Ohio, Apr 28, 23; s William A Miller & Ethel D Clark M; m 1943 to Helen T Rockey; c Cecilia Ann (Mrs John Carr), Penelope Susan (Mrs Robert Nihiser) & Doris L. Polit & Govt Pos: Mem city coun, Lancaster, Ohio, 56-68, pres, 63-64; mem, Fairfield Co Dem Exec Comt, 66-, chmn cent comt, 68-; chmn, Fairfield Co Bd Elec, 68-; deleg, Dem Nat Mid-Term Conf, 74. Bus & Prof Pos: Furnace room boy, Anchor Hocking Corp, Lancaster, Ohio, 41, moldmaker, 43-50, shift supvr, Mold Shop, 60-72, asst head dept, 72-; clerk, J A Mills Meats, 41-42. Mil Serv: Entered as A/S, US Coast Guard, 43, released as Seaman 2/C, 43, after serv out of US Port. Mem: Am Legion; Elks; DAV. Mailing Add: 617 E Main St Lancaster OH 43130

MILLER, WILLIAM MOSELEY (FISH BAIT) (D)
b Pascagoula, Miss, Sept 20, 09; s Albert Magnus Miller & Nettie Maddox M; m 1937 to Mable Breeland; c Sarah Patsy. Educ: Harrison-Stone-Jackson Jr Col, Miss; George Washington Univ Law Sch. Hon Degrees: LLD, Atlanta Law Sch. Polit & Govt Pos: Former messenger, House post off, asst sgt at arms & minority doorkeeper, US House Rep, doorkeeper, 48-; asst sgt at arms, Dem Nat Conv, 44, doorkeeper, 48, 52, 56, 64 & 68. Mem: Mason (33 degree); Scottish Rite; Shrine; Knight Comdr of Court of Hon, Grand Tiler. Honors & Awards: Ky Col; Ark Traveler; Hon Citizen, Tex; Adm, Gtr Navy, Nebr; Hon Citizen, Hattiesburg, Miss. Relig: Baptist. Legal Res: 2017 E Beach Dr Pascagoula MS 39567 Mailing Add: H-154 US Capitol Washington DC 20515

MILLER, ZELL BRYAN (D)
Lt Gov, Ga
b Young Harris, Ga, Feb 24, 32; s Stephen Grady Miller & Birdie Bryan M; m 1954 to Shirley Ann Carver; c Murphy Carver, Matthew Stephen. Educ: Young Harris Jr Col, 51; Univ Ga, AB, 57, MA, 58; 1 year's work toward PhD. Polit & Govt Pos: Mayor, Young Harris, Ga, 60; Ga State Sen, 40th Dist, 61-62, 50th Dist, 63-66; dir personnel, Ga Dept Corrections, 67-; exec secy, Gov Lester Maddox, Ga, 60-70; deleg, Dem Nat Conv, 72; Lt Gov, Ga, 75- Bus & Prof Pos: Prof. Mil Serv: Marine Corps, 53-56, Pvt-Sgt; Good Conduct Medal. Publ: The administration of E D Rivers as Governor of Georgia. Mem: Master Mason. Relig: Methodist; steward. Legal Res: 1012 Bailey Dr Norcross GA 30071 Mailing Add: State Capitol Atlanta GA 30334

MILLESON, RONALD KINSEY (D)
Chmn, Harrison Co Dem Cent & Exec Comt, Ohio
b Freeport, Ohio, Aug 11, 34; s Arthur H Milleson & Mary G Kinsey M; m 1956 to Carol Ann Carson; c Richard G, Mary Lynn, Greg Arthur & James Roland. Educ: Freeport Local High Sch, grad, 52. Polit & Govt Pos: Chmn, Harrison Co Cent & Exec Comt, Ohio, 62-; mayor, Freeport, 63-; vchmn, Ohio Chmn Orgn, 68-; deleg, Dem Nat Conv, 72. Bus & Prof Pos: Ins agt, 61-; vpres, Freeport Press, Inc, 63- Relig: Protestant. Mailing Add: 111 Philadelphia St Freeport OH 43973

MILLESON, WILLIAM THOMAS (D)
WVa State Deleg
b Springfield, WVa, Sept 16, 07; s Silas C Milleson & French Taylor M; m 1940 to Avery Heiskell Pancake; c Mary French (Mrs Barbe) & William Joseph. Educ: WVa Univ, BS Agr, 31; Theta Chi; Alpha Zeta. Polit & Govt Pos: WVa State Deleg, 37-42 & 75-; led People-to-People Goodwill Tours, Europe & Russia, 63, 66 & 70. Bus & Prof Pos: Livestock farmer; dir & vpres, First Nat Bank, Romney, WVa, 37-; dir, WVa State Farm Bur, 59-65; dir, Southern States Coop, Richmond, Va & Farmers Livestock Exchange, Winchester, Va, 63-; dir, Hampshire Develop Corp, Romney, WVa, 71- Mem: Lions; Clinton Lodge (Past Master); Ruritan; Aircraft Owners & Pilots Asn. Relig: Methodist. Mailing Add: Springfield WV 26763

MILLET, FRANK LINCOLN (R)
Chmn, Lancaster Rep Town Comt, Mass
b Brockton, Mass, Sept 14, 06; s Frank Holly Millet & Edith Emily Lincoln M; m to Grace Annie Peck; c Verrin Ralph Linwood, Thornton Ellsworth, Irville Lincoln, David Clark, Irene (Mrs Duval), Julia (Mrs Garvin), Elizabeth Jean (Mrs Kennedy) & Marilyn Joyce (Mrs Field). Educ: Atlantic Union Col, grad, 54; Worcester State Col, grad, 56, grad work, 60- Polit & Govt Pos: Dem nominee, Eighth Dist, Whitman, Abington & North Abington, Mass, 34 & 36; moderator, Lancaster Sewer Dist, 60-62 & 70-73; press secy, Southern New Eng Conf, 66; Rep nominee, 11th Worcester Dist, Lancaster, Clinton & Leominster, Ward Three, 70 & 72; secy bd health, Lancaster, 70-73, chmn, 73-; chmn, Lancaster Rep Town Comt, currently; secy & chmn planning bd, Whitman. Bus & Prof Pos: Pub sch teacher, North Brookfield, Mass, 56-57 & North Attleboro, 57-58; licensed practical nurse, Worcester State Hosp, 60-70, supvr nurses, 70-; social worker, Oxford, Mass, 61; reporter & spec writer, Clinton Daily Star, 68- Honors & Awards: Plaque, Sawyer St, South Lancaster, Mass. Relig: Seventh-day Adventist. Mailing Add: Old Common Rd Lancaster MA 01523

MILLETT, HAROLD (R)
SDak State Rep
b Sorum, SDak, Jan 7, 18; married; c Dean & Mark. Educ: Agr at State Col. Polit & Govt Pos: SDak State Rep, 62- Bus & Prof Pos: Rancher. Mem: Mason; VFW; Am Legion. Mailing Add: Reva SD 57651

MILLETTE, THEODORE JOSEPH (D)
Miss State Rep
b Greenville, Miss, Nov 11, 30; div. Educ: Univ Miss; Phi Delta Theta; M Club. Polit & Govt Pos: Miss State Rep, currently. Bus & Prof Pos: Real estate & ins; tug boat rentals. Mem: Elks; Moose; Am Legion; CofC; Rotary. Relig: Catholic. Legal Res: Tarbak Oaks Gautier MS 39553 Mailing Add: PO Box 1177 Pascagoula MS 39567

MILLHOUSE, CLIFFORD JOHN (R)
Treas, Mich Rep State Cent Comt
b Flint, Mich, Apr 25, 27; s Clifford Millhouse & Etta J Wolverton M; m 1949 to Helen Gene Graybill; c Marcia, Susan & David. Educ: Gen Motors Inst, BBA, 52; Sigma Alpha Epsilon. Polit & Govt Pos: Treas, Genesee Co Rep Comt, Mich, 67-69, chmn, 69-71, chmn, Seventh Cong Dist Rep Party, 71-73; treas, Mich Rep State Cent Comt, 71-. Bus & Prof Pos: Partner, Millhouse & Holaly, 60-; dir, Genesee Merchants Bank & Trust Co, 67- Mil Serv: Entered as Pvt, Air Force, 46, released as Cpl, 47, after serv in Air Univ, Maxwell Field, Ala. Mem: Am & Mich Asns; CPA; Flint Golf Club. Relig: Presbyterian. Legal Res: 1325 Beard Flint MI 48503 Mailing Add: 1800 Genesee Towers Flint MI 48502

MILLICAN, MANYON MEADOWS (R)
b Harriman, Tenn, Oct 16, 26; s Roscoe Claude Millican & Mary E M; m 1954 to Amelia Jean Wheeler; c Mark Steven, Janice Carlene & Barry Scott. Educ: Univ Chattanooga, 45-46, 48-49; Southern Col Pharm, Mercer Univ, BS, 52; pres, Kappa Psi, 52; Pi Kappa Alpha. Polit & Govt Pos: Precinct chmn, Jefferson Co Rep Party, Ala, 60, committeeman, 70; exec dir, Ala Rep State Comt, 62-67. Bus & Prof Pos: Pharmacist & med serv rep, CIBA Pharmaceutical Corp, 52-59 & Warner-Chilcott Labs, 59-62; mem staff, B D & F Assoc, polit fund raising firm; owner, Manyon Millican & Assoc, polit consult firm, currently. Mil Serv: Entered as A/S, Navy, 46, released as Seaman 1/C, 47, after serv in USS George K MacKenzie, Atlantic, 46-47. Mem: Am Pharmaceutical Asn. Relig: Baptist. Mailing Add: Frank WV 24937

MILLIGAN, THOMAS STUART (R)
Chmn, Ind Rep State Cent Comt
b Richmond, Ind, Oct 12, 34; s Scott Wallace Milligan & Elizabeth Taggart; m 1958 to Claire Ann Coble; c Michelle, Nancy & Stuart. Educ: Purdue Univ, BS, 56; Yale Univ, LLB, 59; Sigma Delta Chi; Iron Key; Beta Theta Pi. Polit & Govt Pos: Chmn, Wayne Co Rep Comt, Ind, 72-; chmn, Ind Rep State Cent Comt, 73-; mem exec comt, Rep Nat Comt, 75- Bus & Prof Pos: Attorney, Reller, Mendenhall, Kleinkuech & Milligan, Richmond, 59-75. Mem: Ind State Bar Asn; F&AM; Scottish Rite; Ind Farm Bur Fedn; Kiwanis Int. Honors & Awards: Young Man of the Year, Richmond Jaycees, Ind, 64; Distinguished Alumni, 4-H Clubs of Wayne Co, Ind, 74. Relig: Methodist. Legal Res: 532 Farlow Rd Richmond IN 47374 Mailing Add: 2 N Eighth St Richmond IN 47374

MILLIKEN, JAMES BUTLER (D)
Justice, Ky Court of Appeals
b Louisville, Ky, Aug 7, 00; s Herbert Bryan Milliken & Sarah Ann Neeld M; m 1938 to Janet Pugh; c Sara (Mrs James C Rogers) & Cindy. Educ: Centre Col, AB, 22; Yale Univ Sch Law, LLB, 26; Phi Kappa Tau. Polit & Govt Pos: City attorney, Southgate, 27-34; Ky State Rep, 34-35; mem, State Govt Reorgn Comt, 36; Workmen's Compensation Bd, 36-44 & Const Rev Comt, 47-51; justice, Ky Court of Appeals, 51- Bus & Prof Pos: Counsel for various co when in practice. Mil Serv: Army, 18. Mem: Am Bar Asn; Am Judicature Soc. Relig: Protestant. Mailing Add: 467 McDowell Rd Frankfort KY 40601

MILLIKEN, JOHN GORDON (D)
Chmn, Fifth Cong Dist Dem Cent Comt, Colo
b Denver, Colo, May 12, 27; s William Boyd Milliken & Margaret Marsh M; m 1953 to Marie Machell; c Karen Marie, Douglas Gordon, David Tait & Anne Alain. Educ: Yale Univ, BS in Indust Admin, 49, BE in Civil Eng, 50; George Washington Univ, 51-52; Univ Colo, MS in Mgt, 66, DBA, 69; Tau Beta Pi; Sigma Iota Epsilon; Beta Gamma Sigma; Sigma Xi. Polit & Govt Pos: Civil engr, US Dept Interior, Bur Reclamation, Denver, Colo & Washington, DC, 49-55; pres & dir, SE Englewood Water Dist, Colo, 63-; dir, South Englewood Sanit Dist, 65-; mem adv comt, Arapahoe Co Dem Cent Comt, 66-68, chmn, 69-71; Dem precinct committeeman, Arapahoe Co, 68-69; mem, Colo State Cent Comt, 69-; mem, Colo State Exec Comt, 71-; dir, South Suburban Metrop Recreation & Park Dist, 71-; chmn, Fifth Cong Dist Dem Cent Comt, Colo, 72- Bus & Prof Pos: Asst to plant mgr, Stanley Aviation Corp, Denver, Colo, 55-56; prin mgt engr adv progs & mgr orgn & procedures dept, Aerospace Div, Martin Marietta Corp, 56-64; mgt engr, Safeway Stores, Inc, 64-66; sr research economist & assoc prof, Denver Research Inst, Univ Denver, 66- Mil Serv: Entered as Pvt, Army, 45, released as Pfc, 46, after serv in Med Dept, Am Theatre, 45-46; World War II Victory Medal. Publ: Contract Research & Development Adjuncts of Federal Agencies (w J G Welles & others), 69 & Management methods from aerospace (w E Morrison), Harvard Bus Rev, 3-4/73; Federal Incentives for Innovation (w M Robbins & C Burke), Univ Denver Research Inst, 73; plus others. Mem: Acad Mgt; Yale Sci & Eng Asn; Nat Asn Bus Economists; Univ Denver Senate. Relig: Congregational. Mailing Add: 6502 S Ogden St Littleton CO 80121

MILLIKEN, ROGER (R)
b New York, NY, Oct 24, 15; s Gerrish Hill Milliken & Agnes Gayley M; m 1948 to Justine Van Rensselaer Hooper; c Justine Van Rensselaer, Nancy, Roger, Jr, David Gayley & Weston

Freeman. Educ: Yale Univ, AB, 37. Polit & Govt Pos: SC elector, Nat Elec, 56; deleg, Rep Nat Conv, 56, 60 & 72, deleg-at-lg, 64 & 68 & mem, Platform Comt, 56 & 60; state finance chmn, SC Rep Party, 59-63; mem, Rep Nat Finance Comt, 63-74. Bus & Prof Pos: Dir, Mercantile Stores Co, Inc, 39-, First Nat City Bank, NY, 47-, W R Grace & Co, 53- & Westinghouse Elec Corp, 62-; pres & dir, Deering Milliken, Inc, 47-; mem, Bus Coun; chmn, Greenville-Spartanburg Airport Comn; chmn bd trustees, Inst Textile Technol; mem bd trustees, Wofford Col. Relig: Episcopal. Legal Res: 627 Otis Blvd Spartanburg SC 29302 Mailing Add: PO Box 3167 Spartanburg SC 29302

MILLIKEN, WILLIAM GRAWN (R)
Gov, Mich
b Traverse City, Mich, Mar 26, 22; s James Thacker Milliken & Hildegarde Grawn M; m 1945 to Helen Wallbank; c William, Jr & Elaine. Educ: Yale Univ, BA, 46. Hon Degrees: LLD, Univ Mich, Eastern Mich Univ, Cent Mich Univ, Detroit Inst Technol & Western Mich Univ; LHD, Northern Mich Univ. Polit & Govt Pos: Chmn, Grand Traverse Co Rep Comt, 6 years; dir, Gtr Mich Found, comnr, Mich Waterways Comn, 47-55; mem, US State Dept Intercult Exchange Prog, WGer, 53; Mich State Sen, 60-64, Majority Floor Leader, Mich State Senate, 63-64; Lt Gov, Mich, 64-69, Gov, 69-; chmn, Rep Gov Conf, 71-72; tour of Soviet Union & Romania, US State Dept, 71; chmn, Midwestern Gov, 74. Bus & Prof Pos: Pres, J W Milliken, Inc, currently. Mil Serv: Entered as Pvt, Army Air Force, released as S/Sgt, after serv in 50 Combat Missions as Waist Gunner on a B-24; Purple Heart; Air Medal with 2 Oak Leaf Clusters; ETO Ribbon with 3 Battle Stars. Mem: Traverse City CofC. Relig: Congregational. Legal Res: Traverse City MI 49684 Mailing Add: State Capitol Bldg Lansing MI 48903

MILLIN, PAUL HASLET (R)
Chmn, Forest Co Rep Comt, Pa
b Warren, Pa, Feb 7, 44; s Hugh Wilson Millin & Alma Haslet M; m 1972 to Cynthia Faulkner; c David Jason, Christie Lynn & Jerome Frank. Educ: Maryville Col, BA, 66; Univ Tenn Col Law, JD, 69; Pi Gamma Mu; Phi Alpha Delta; Alpha Sigma. Polit & Govt Pos: Dist attorney, Forest Co, Pa, 71-; mem bd dirs, Warren-Forest Ment Health Serv, 72-; mem, Clarion-Forest-Venango-Warren Drug & Alcohol Planning & Implementation Coun, 73-; chmn, Forest Co Rep Comt, 73-; mem, Gov Justice Comn, Northwestern Pa, 74- Bus & Prof Pos: Mem law firm of Swanson, Bevevino & Millin, PC, Tionesta & Warren, Pa, 71- Mil Serv: Entered as Pvt, Army, 69, released as SP-4, 71, after serv in Judge Adv Sect, Ft Eustis, Va, 70-71; Unit Citation; Distinguished Serv Medal. Mem: Forest Co Bar Asn (pres, 73-); Lions; Elks; Mason; Shrine. Relig: Methodist. Legal Res: May St Tionesta PA 16353 Mailing Add: PO Box 477 Tionesta PA 16353

MILLIRON, JOHN PATRICK (D)
Pa State Rep
b Altoona, Pa, Sept 2, 47; s John Hiram Milliron & Zita Ann O'Friel; single. Educ: Duquesne Univ, 65-69. Polit & Govt Pos: Mem, Altoona Govt Study Comn, 73-; Pa State Rep, 74-, mem finance, transportation & urban affairs comts, Pa House Rep, 74, mem spec house comt on emergency health procedures, 75. Mem: Altoona Kiwanis Club; Altoona Jaycees; Blair Co Young Dem; Altoona KofC. Honors & Awards: Duquesne Univ Outstanding Sr Awards, 69. Relig: Roman Catholic. Legal Res: 2212 Second Ave Altoona PA 16602 Mailing Add: House of Rep PO Box 6 Main Capitol Bldg Harrisburg PA 17120

MILLS, BILLY GENE (D)
Councilman, Los Angeles City Coun, Calif
b Waco, Tex, Nov 19, 29; s Roosevelt Mills & Genevieve Donahue M; m 1953 to Rubye Maurine Jackson; c Karol M, Karen G, John S, William K & James E. Educ: Compton Col, AA, 49; Univ Calif, Los Angeles, BA, 51; Univ Calif, Los Angeles Law Sch, LLB, 54; Nu Beta Epsilon; Kappa Alpha Psi. Polit & Govt Pos: Dep probation officer, Los Angeles Co, 57-60; councilman, Eighth Dist, Los Angeles City Coun, Calif, 63-; chmn, Los Angeles Co Dem Cent Comt, 67-68; mem, Calif Coun Criminal Justice, 72- Bus & Prof Pos: Release engr, Douglas Aircraft Corp, 54-55; attorney-at-law, assoc with Herman English, 60-63. Mil Serv: Entered as Pvt, Army, 55, released as Specialist, 3/C, 57, after serv in Off Adj Gen, Far East Command. Mem: Am Bar Asn; Am Judicature Soc; F&AM (33 degree); Urban League; YMCA. Relig: Baptist; charter mem, Laymen's League, Trinity Baptist Church; mem bd trustees, Church of Relig Sci. Legal Res: 3621 Third Ave Los Angeles CA 90018 Mailing Add: Rm 237 City Hall 200 N Spring St Los Angeles CA 90012

MILLS, BRADFORD (R)
Pres & Chief Exec Officer, Overseas Pvt Investment Corp
b New York, NY, Dec 16, 26; s Dudley Holbrook Mills & Louise Morris M; m 1950 to Elizabeth Leisk; c Elizabeth Lee, Bradford Alan, Barbara Louise & Russ Dudley. Educ: Princeton Univ, BA, 48; Oxford Univ, 50-51; Cottage Club. Polit & Govt Pos: Asst to dir overseas territories div, Econ Coop Admin, Paris, France, 48-50; pres & chief exec officer, Overseas Pvt Investment Corp, Washington, DC, 71- Bus & Prof Pos: Former dir, Xtra, Boston, Mass, NAm Watch Co, New York, Scantlin Electronics, Inc, Los Angeles & Fed Petroleum, Inc, Oklahoma City, Okla; assoc & partner, F Eberstadt & Co, Inc, New York, 56-62; dir, Specialized Serv Inc, Atlanta, Ga & Princeton Packet, NJ, until 73; partner, NY Securities Co, 62-71. Mil Serv: Entered as Seaman, Navy, 44, released as Seaman 1/C, 46, after serv in Naval Off Training Prog & Fleet, LST 1011; Lt(jg), 52-55, Off Intel, Washington, DC. Mem: Coun Foreign Rels, NY; Mills Found, Princeton, NJ (pres); Links Club; Recess Club; Int Platform Asn. Relig: Presbyterian. Legal Res: Pretty Brook Rd RD 2 Princeton NJ 08540 Mailing Add: 1129 20th St NW Suite 702 Washington DC 20527

MILLS, ELLSWORTH LUTHER, II (R)
Committeeman, Ill Rep State Cent Comt
b Chicago, Ill, May 12, 26; s Ellsworth L Mills & Mary Roberts M; m 1949 to Betty Annette Masters; c Ellsworth L, III, Karen Clark, Martha Roberts & Juliana Knight. Educ: Missouri Valley Col, 44-45; Northwestern Univ, 46-47; Sigma Nu. Polit & Govt Pos: Precinct committeeman, Rep Party, Lake Co, Ill, 52-; chmn, Deerfield Twp Rep Party, 64-68; committeeman, Ill Rep State Cent Comt, 66-; mem, Lake Co Rep Cent Comt, 68- Bus & Prof Pos: Progressive student, Int Harvester, Memphis, 47-50; asst sales mgr, Bastian Blessing Co, Chicago, 50-66; sales rep, Joseph Dixon Crucible Co, Chicago, 66- Mil Serv: Entered as Aviation Cadet, Naval Air Corps, 44, released, 47, after serv in training units. Mem: Am Foundrymen's Soc; Liquified Petroleum Gas Asn; Am Legion; St Andrews Soc of Ill; Boy Scouts (leader, 61-). Relig: Episcopal. Mailing Add: 1870 Dale Ave Highland Park IL 60035

MILLS, GOVAN (D)
b Lake City, Kans, Oct 6, 07; s Govan Mills & Margaret Hittle M (Maggie); m 1930 to Margaret McKenzie; c Beulah Margaret (Mrs James C Harbaugh), Govan Clifton & Hannah Louise (Mrs Charles A Clarke). Educ: Kans State Univ, BS, 30; Sigma Phi Epsilon. Polit & Govt Pos: Secy-treas, Barber Co Dem Cent Comt, Kans, 36-38, chmn, formerly; twp treas, 38-44; precinct committeeman & mem, Dem Cent Comt, 52-60; alt deleg, Dem Nat Conv, 68. Bus & Prof Pos: Teacher, Haviland High Sch, Kans, 31-32, Lacrosse High Sch, 32-34 & Larned High Sch, 34-36; organizer & pres, SCent Tel Asn, Inc, 52-; owner, Mills Feed & Serv, 60-; pres & mgr, Mills Feed, Land & Cattle Corp, Lake City, currently. Mem: Barber Co Taxpayers Asn; Kans Fedn Taxpayers; Mason; Consistory; Shrine. Relig: Christian Church. Mailing Add: Mills Ranch Lake City KS 67071

MILLS, JACK D
Nebr State Sen
Mailing Add: Bing Springs NE 69122

MILLS, JAMES R (D)
Calif State Sen
b San Diego, Calif, June 6, 27; m 1959 to Joanna Rohrbough. Educ: San Diego State Col, BA, MA; Univ London. Polit & Govt Pos: Calif State Assemblyman, 60-66; Calif State Sen, 67-, Pres Pro-Tem, Calif State Senate, 71-; deleg, Dem Nat Conv, 68. Bus & Prof Pos: Teacher & writer; authority on hist of San Diego & Southern Calif. Mil Serv: Army, 50-53. Mem: Urban League; San Diego Hist Soc; CofC; Am Legion; NAACP. Mailing Add: 2656 Balboa Vista San Diego CA 92105

MILLS, KENNETH ADOLFO (D)
b San Francisco, Calif, Mar 20, 24; s Carley Mills & Beatrice Stahl M; m 1962 to Elizabeth Elstad; c Polly, Penny & John. Educ: Princeton Univ, AB, 48; Phi Beta Kappa; Dial Lodge. Polit & Govt Pos: Vchairperson, NY Comt Dem Voters, 67-69; deleg, Dem Nat Conv, 68 & 72; chairperson, New Dem Coalition, Manhattan, 69; mem, NY State Exec Comt, New Dem Coalition, 69-70, regional vchairperson, 71-72, admin vchairperson, 73-; leader, 66th Dem Assembly Dist, 69-; chairperson housing & zoning comt, Community Bd Eight, Manhattan, 73- Bus & Prof Pos: Dir creative servs, KATZ TV, New York, 48-; trustee, Princeton Broadcasting Corp. Mil Serv: Entered as A/S, Navy, 43, released as Seaman 3/C, 46; Good Conduct Medal. Mem: Broadcasters Prom Asn (pres). Mailing Add: 1349 Lexington Ave New York NY 10028

MILLS, KENNETH ARMOUR (D)
Maine State Rep
b Lynn, Mass, Sept 3, 99; s Frederick Ellsworth Mills & Edith Mavis Armour M; m to Irene Mae Hickey. Polit & Govt Pos: Vchmn, Eastport Dem Comt, Maine, 64-; committeemem, Washington Co Dem Party, 64-; Maine State Rep, 65-66 & 69-; mem, State Dem Platform Comt, 66-68; mem, Eastport City Coun, 68- Mil Serv: Pvt, Army, World War I, with serv in 40th Div, European Theatre. Mem: Am Legion; Border Hist Soc; Perry Improv Asn. Relig: Protestant. Mailing Add: 56 High St Eastport ME 04631

MILLS, KIRBY D (D)
La State Rep
Mailing Add: Rte 2 Box 190 Columbia LA 71418

MILLS, MAX MILO (R)
b Marshalltown, Iowa, Aug 26, 20; s Dr M M Mills & Reba Ferguson M; m 1945 to Carmel Bellini; c Sally (Mrs Bruce Loessin), Jeffrey & Carol. Educ: Univ Chicago, 40-42; Washington Univ, 46-47; Drake Univ, JD, 49; Order of the Coif; Delta Phi Delta. Polit & Govt Pos: Co attorney, Marshall Co, Iowa, 52-56; Iowa State Sen, 65-69; exec asst to Gov, 69-70; exec dir, Iowa Crime Comn, 69-70; regional dir, Region VII, Dept Health, Educ & Welfare, 70- Bus & Prof Pos: Attorney-at-law, Tye, Mills, Grimes & Peterson, 50-70; pres, McIntire Travel Co, 54-65 & Big Timber Cattle Co, 62-70; vpres, Tallyho Transport, 65-70; pres, Tallyho Oil Co, 66-69. Mil Serv: Entered as Pfc, Marine Corps, 42, released as Maj, 47, after serv in Pac Theatre, 43-45; Maj (Ret), Marine Corps Res; Two Purple Hearts; Commendation Medal; Bronze Star. Mem: Iowa State Bar Asn; Int Platform Asn; Lions; Am Legion; Masonic Bodies. Honors & Awards: Outstanding Young Man Award, 53; Eagle Scout. Relig: Episcopal. Mailing Add: 601 E 12th St Kansas City MO 64106

MILLS, MORRIS HADLEY (R)
Ind State Sen
b West Newton, Ind, Sept 25, 27; s Howard S Mills & Bernice Hadley M; m 1954 to Mary Ann Sellars; c Douglas, Frederic & Gordon. Educ: Earlham Col, AB, 50; Harvard Grad Sch Bus Admin, MBA, 52. Polit & Govt Pos: Ind State Rep, Marion Co, 69-73; Ind State Sen, 73- Bus & Prof Pos: Secy-treas, Maplehurst Farms, Indianapolis, Ind, 52-59, pres, 59-61; partner, Mills Bros Farms, 61-; dir, Maplehurst Farms, Inc, 71-; Marion Co Farm Bur Coop, 72- Mil Serv: Entered as Pvt, Army, 46, released as Tech 4/C, 47, after serv in Engrs, Japan, 46-47. Mem: Lions; Farm Bur; dir, Earlham Col Found. Relig: Friends. Mailing Add: 7148 W Thompson Rd Indianapolis IN 46241

MILLS, NEWT V (D)
b Calhoun, La, Sept 27, 99; s Henry E Mills & Minervia A Sanford M; m 1959 to Margaret Elizabeth Sunny. Educ: State Normal Col, La, 22; La Tech, 23-25; La State Univ, 29. Polit & Govt Pos: Mem, Presidential Electoral Col, 36; Col, staff of Gov R W Leche, La, 36-40; US Rep, Fifth Cong Dist, La, 37-43. Bus & Prof Pos: Real estate, farmer, timber, cattle, gas & oil; sch teacher & prin, 11 years. Honors & Awards: Honored recognition for participation in celebration of formation of Constitution, US Constitution Sesquicentennial Comn, 37. Relig: Assembly of God. Mailing Add: 715 Loop Rd Monroe LA 71201

MILLS, WILBUR D (D)
US Rep, Ark
b Kensett, Ark, May 24, 09; m 1934 to Clarine (Polly) Billingsley; c Martha Sue (Mrs David Jack Dixon) & Rebecca Ann (Mrs Richard Yates); 5 grandchildren. Educ: Hendrix Col; Harvard Law Sch. Polit & Govt Pos: Co & probate judge of White Co, Ark, 34-38; US Rep, Ark, currently, chmn, Comt on Ways & Means, US House of Rep, 58-74. Bus & Prof Pos: Lawyer. Mem: Mason (33 degree). Relig: Methodist. Legal Res: Kensett AR Mailing Add: 1136 Longworth Bldg Washington DC 20515

MILLS, WILLIAM DONALD (D)
NC State Sen
b Maysville, NC, Oct 8, 32; s Leo Bell Mills & Mildred Jones M; m 1952 to Donniere Morton;

c William Donald, Jr, Robert Duane & Kathy Darlene. Educ: ECarolina Univ, 50 & 53-54. Polit & Govt Pos: Onslow Co Comnr, NC, 59-64; NC State Rep, Fourth Dist, 65-68; NC State Sen, Sixth Dist, 71- Bus & Prof Pos: Appliance & furniture bus; trustee, Coastal Carolina Community Col, 65-; bd dirs, NC Merchants Asn, 67-; bd dirs, Jacksonville CofC, 68- Mil Serv: Army, 51-52, Cpl, E-4. Mem: Consistory; Moose; Eastern Star. Relig: Methodist; supt, Belgrade Methodist Church, 54-60, trustee, 62-; pres, Methodist Men's Club, 59-60. Legal Res: Rte 1 Box 107 Maysville NC 28555 Mailing Add: 818 New Bridge St Jacksonville NC 25840

MILLSPAUGH, GREGORY LOWELL (R)
Nat Committeeman, Nev Young Rep
b Pratt, Kans, Apr 21, 47; s Robert Lowell Millspaugh & Jean V I Cable M; single. Educ: Mass Inst Technol, BS in physics & BS in polit sci, 70; Univ Nev, Las Vegas, 74-75; Mass Inst Technol Lect Series Comt; Young Rep. Polit & Govt Pos: Treas, Clark Co Rep Cent Comt, Nev, 73; state chmn, Nev Young Rep, 73-75, nat committeeman, 75- Bus & Prof Pos: Nev licensed real estate broker-sales, 71-; systs analyst, Clark Co Dept Aviation, Las Vegas, 74- Mailing Add: 628 N 21st St Las Vegas NV 89101

MILMORE, THOMAS ALOYSIUS (D)
b Brooklyn, NY, Mar 21, 24; s Thomas Aloysius Milmore & Mary Smith M; m 1954 to Eleanor Bourne; c Susan, Thomas, Jr, Roland & Kevin. Educ: Columbia Univ, 1 year. Polit & Govt Pos: Comt mem, Weston Dem Town Party, Conn, 64, chmn, formerly. Bus & Prof Pos: Asst advert mgr, Philco, NY, 51-54; creative dir, Norm Advert, 54- Mil Serv: Entered as Pvt, Army, 42, released as Sgt, 45, after serv in 551st Field Artil Bn, ETO, 44-45. Relig: Catholic. Mailing Add: 155 Steephill Rd Weston CT 06880

MILNE, NORMAN F, JR (R)
NH State Rep
Mailing Add: 2159 Elm St Manchester NH 03104

MILSTEAD, GEORGE L (D)
b Ferriday, La, Dec 25, 22; s George L Milstead & Etta Mae Willis M; m 1949 to Clara Virginia Sutherland; c Barbara Ann. Educ: Am Univ, BS. Polit & Govt Pos: Admin asst to US Rep Jones, Ala, currently. Bus & Prof Pos: Supvr, Cent Intel Agency, 51-52; cong liaison rep, Civil Serv Comn, 56-63. Mil Serv: Air Force, 1st Lt, pilot, 416th Night Fighter Squadron, Europe; Maj, Air Force Res. Legal Res: 4205 Linden St Fairfax VA 22030 Mailing Add: 2426 Rayburn House Off Bldg Washington DC 20515

MILTICH, PAUL ANDREW (R)
b Virginia, Minn, Oct 30, 19; s Andrew D Miltich & Mary Pope M (deceased); m 1944 to Sylvia S Schumann; c Andrew Paul & Marianne April. Educ: Univ Minn, BS, 41 & postgrad work, 42; Delta Pi Lambda; Lambda Alpha Psi. Polit & Govt Pos: Dep comnr, Saginaw Co Pub Schs, Mich, 46; press secy to House Rep Leader, Gerald R Ford, 66-74; Spec Asst to President, 74-75; comnr, Postal Rate Comn, 75- Bus & Prof Pos: Teacher & drama dir, Breck Sch for Boys, St Paul, 41-42; teacher, Saginaw Pub Schs, Mich, 46; reporter & asst city ed, Booth Newspapers of Mich, 46-57; Washington Correspondent, 57-66. Mil Serv: Entered as Pvt, Army, 42, released as Cpl, 46, after serv in Transportation Corps, European Theater, 44-45; Good Conduct Medal; European Campaign Ribbon. Relig: Congregational; former mem bd of benevolences & social action bd. Mailing Add: 11104 Inwood Ave Silver Spring MD 20902

MILTON, JOHN (DFL)
Minn State Sen
Mailing Add: 4101 E County Line Rd White Bear Lake MN 55110

MIMS, LAMBERT CARTER
b Uriah, Ala, Apr 20, 30; s Jeff Carter Mims & Carrie Lambert M; m 1946 to Reecie Phillips; c Dale Phillips & Louis Daniel. Educ: Blacksher High Sch, Uriah, Ala, grad. Polit & Govt Pos: Pub works comnr, Mobile, Ala, 65-68, Mayor, 68- Bus & Prof Pos: Pres, Ala Chap, Am Pub Works Asn, 69-71, dir region IV, currently; mem, Human Resources Comt, Nat League Cities, Transportation Comt & Ala League Municipalities, currently. Publ: For Christ & Country, Fleming H Revell Co, 69. Mem: Kiwanis; CofC; F&AM; Scottish Rite (32 degree); Shrine. Honors & Awards: Outstanding Young Man, Mobile, Ala, 65. Relig: Baptist. Legal Res: 3005 Bryant Rd Mobile AL 36605 Mailing Add: 111 S Royal St Mobile AL 36601

MIMS, MASTON (D)
Ala State Sen
Mailing Add: Rte One Uriah AL 36480

MINEHART, THOMAS ZENO, II (D)
b Philadelphia, Pa, May 23, 07; s John R Minehart, MD & Katherine Violet Cosgrove M; m 1936 to Janet Mulvany; c Janet Elizabeth (Mrs Maupay), Thomas Z, III, Marylee, Charles R & John R. Educ: Temple Univ, AB, 29; Temple Univ Sch Law, LLB, 33; Blue Key; Theta Upsilon Omega. Polit & Govt Pos: Spec attorney, Commonwealth of Pa, 35; city councilman, Philadelphia, Pa, 36; chief area rent attorney, Off Price Admin, 43; auditor gen, Pa, 61-65, state treas, 65-69; chmn, Pa State Dem Comt, 66-70; deleg, Dem Nat Conv, 68. Bus & Prof Pos: Attorney-at-law. Mem: Philadelphia Bar Asn; Nat Asn State Auditors; Ft Washington Vol Fire Co; Gwynedd Valley Sportsmen's Club; Rainbow Fishing Club. Relig: United Church of Christ. Legal Res: 408 Bellaire Ave Ft Washington PA 19034 Mailing Add: 735 PSF Bldg 12 S 12th St Philadelphia PA 19107

MINER, DONALD (R)
Chmn, Concord Rep City Comt, NH
b Boston, Mass, Oct 25, 13; s Dr Walter Curtis Miner & Ethel Chase M; m 1936 to Ruth S Pratt; c Nancy (Mrs William Gruber), Sally (Mrs Peter Spinney) & Thomas Curtis. Educ: Springfield Col, 33-34; Boston Univ, 34-35. Polit & Govt Pos: Former mem, Hingham Town Adv Bd, Mass; mem, Concord Rep City Comt, NH, 55-71, chmn, 73-; supvr checklist, Ward 4, Concord, 66-; NH State Rep, 71-72; moderator, Ward 3, Concord, NH, 72-; mem steering comt, NH Rep State Comt, 73- Bus & Prof Pos: Sales rep, Herrick Co, South Boston, Mass, 38-57; NH sales rep, Brown-Wales Steel Co, Cambridge, Mass, 57-72; sales rep, Lyons Iron Works, Manchester, NH, 72- Mil Serv: Mass State Guard, World War II. Mem: Concord Rotary. Relig: Protestant. Mailing Add: 23 Auburn St Concord NH 03301

MINER, DOYLE C (R)
Idaho State Rep
b Teton City, Idaho, Dec 19, 28; s Merlon R Miner & Edith Hillman M; m 1948 to Doris Murri; c Diane (Mrs Neil Stoddard), Darla (Mrs Fred Martin), Denice, Daren & Danna. Educ: Idaho State Univ, BA; Phi Delta Chi. Polit & Govt Pos: City councilman, St Anthony, Idaho, 65-73; Idaho State Rep, 73- Mem: Lions; St Anthony CofC. Relig: Latter-day Saint. Mailing Add: Rte 1 Box 218A St Anthony ID 83445

MINER, MARJORIE M (R)
Chmn, Idaho Rep State Cent Comt
b Tulsa, Okla, June 22, 27; m 1949 to Gordon Miner; c James G & Casey H. Educ: Western NMex Univ, BS in Sec Educ, 48, grad study in elem educ, 51. Polit & Govt Pos: Pres, East Shoshone Rep Women's Club, Idaho, 68-70; chmn, Legis Dist Rep Party, 70-; vchmn, Idaho Rep State Cent Comt, 71-72, chmn, 72-; Rep Nat Committeewoman, Idaho, 72-, mem exec comt, formerly. Bus & Prof Pos: Teacher, Idaho, 48-52; substitute teacher & tutor, 63-68. Mem: PEO; Interagency Coun; Summer Sch Comt (treas); PTA; Eastern Star (past Worthy Matron). Relig: Episcopal; former adult leader, Episcopal Young Churchmen. Mailing Add: PO Box 538 Wallace ID 83873

MINER, RUTH (D)
Mem Exec Comt, Walworth Co Dem Party
b Galesburg, Ill, May 29, 20; d Albert Burns Miner & Anna Lee Dilworth M; single. Educ: Knox Col, Ill, 41; Univ Ill, Urbana, MA Polit Sci, 51; Univ Chicago Law Sch, JD, 53; Acad of Int Law, The Hague, Netherlands, summer 65; London Sch Econ, 65. Polit & Govt Pos: Mem exec comt, Walworth Co Dem Party, 71-; alt deleg, Dem Nat Conv, 72. Bus & Prof Pos: Prof, Univ Wis-Whitewater, 58- Mil Serv: Entered as A/S, WAVES, Naval Reserve, 42, released as SP(T) 1/C, 45, after serv in link trainer & celestial navigation training bases, Atlanta, Ga, Quonset Pt, RI & Pensacola, Fla. Mem: Ill Bar; Fed Bar; League of Women Voters; Am Civil Liberties Union. Relig: Protestant. Mailing Add: 327 Ann St Whitewater WI 53190

MINER, S NORTON (R)
b Salisbury, Conn, Mar 28, 11; s Samuel Corning Miner & Fanny Maria Peckham M; m 1937 to Isabel O Keller; c Linda (Mrs Malcolm MacLaren, Jr). Educ: Mass Inst Technol, BArch, 36; Phi Kappa Sigma. Polit & Govt Pos: Chmn, Salisbury Rep Town Comt, Conn, formerly. Mailing Add: Lime Rock Rd Lakeville CT 06039

MINETA, NORMAN YOSHIO (D)
US Rep, Calif
b San Jose, Calif, Nov 12, 31; m 1961 to May Hinoki; c David & Stuart. Educ: Univ Calif, Berkeley, BS, 53. Polit & Govt Pos: Comnr, San Jose Human Rels Comt, Calif, 62-64; comnr, San Jose Housing Authority, 66-67; councilman, San Jose City Coun, 67-71, vmayor, 68-71, mayor, 71-74; mem bd dirs, Nat League Cities; US Rep, Calif, 75- Bus & Prof Pos: Owner-Agt, Mineta Ins Agency. Mil Serv: Army, 53-56. Mem: Nat Conf Christians & Jews; Nat Urban Coalition; Japanese-Am Citizens League; Boy Scouts (bd dirs, Santa Clara Co Coun). Legal Res: 1564 Peregrino Way San Jose CA 95125 Mailing Add: US House Rep Washington DC 20515

MINGE, JERRY LEE (D)
b Rome, Ga, Sept 23, 34; s Willie Lee Minge & Mary Moore M; m 1958 to Carol Tilman Bland; c Mary Angela, Jennifer Bland & Anne Marguerite. Educ: Darlington Sch for Boys, 53; Univ Ga, BBA & LLB; Sigma Nu; Phi Delta Phi. Polit & Govt Pos: Ga State Rep, Floyd Co, Dist 13, 65-67; judge, Floyd City Court, 67-68; alt deleg, Dem Nat Conv, 72. Bus & Prof Pos: Partner, Hamilton, Anderson & Minge, Attorneys, 60- Mem: Am Bar Asn; Rome Jaycees; Young Dem; Elks; Mason. Relig: Baptist. Legal Res: 519 E Eleventh St Rome GA 30161 Mailing Add: 10 Saddle Mountain Rd Rome GA 30161

MINGLIN, HARRY J (R)
Chmn, Sac Co Rep Party, Iowa
b Lavinia, Iowa, Oct 2, 00; s William E Minglin & Dora King M; m 1924 to Muriel Ann Wheeler. Educ: Onarga High Sch, Ill, grad, 18. Polit & Govt Pos: Postmaster, Ulmer, Iowa, 39-45; finance chmn, Sac Co Rep Party, 58-61, chmn, 61-; alt deleg, Rep Nat Conv, 64, deleg, 72. Bus & Prof Pos: Owner & ed, Auburn Enterprise & Tri-Co Spec, 45- Mem: Lions; Farm Bur; York Rite; Scottish Rite Bodies; Commercial Clubs of Auburn, Lake View & Wall Lake. Relig: Methodist. Mailing Add: PO Box 1 Auburn IA 51433

MINISH, JOSEPH GEORGE (D)
US Rep, NJ
b Throop, Pa, Sept 1, 16; s George Minish & Angelina M; m to Theresa La Capra; c George, James & Joyce. Educ: Dunmore High Sch, Pa. Polit & Govt Pos: Mem, Newark Comt on Econ Develop, NJ; vchmn, Essex Co Welfare Fedn, 2 years, trustee, 6 years; US Rep, NJ, 63- Bus & Prof Pos: Exec secy, Essex-West Hudson Co CIO, 7 years; secy-treas, Essex-West Hudson Labor Coun AFL-CIO. Mil Serv: World War II. Mem: KofC; Ment Health Asn of Essex Co. Legal Res: West Orange NJ 07052 Mailing Add: Rm 2162 House Off Bldg Washington DC 20515

MINISTER, KINGSTON GLENN (R)
Colo State Sen
b Denver, Colo, June 20, 30; s Howard Minister & Amy Harris M; m 1959 to Cornelia Nell Quinlan. Educ: Univ Denver, BA, 54; Univ Northern Colo, Greeley, MA, 58; Phi Delta Kappa; Delta Sigma Phi. Polit & Govt Pos: Precinct committeeman, El Paso Co Rep Party, Colo, 64-68, chmn senate dist, 66-68; Colo State Sen, Dist 10, 69-, chmn finance comt, Colo State Senate, 71-72, chmn local govt comt, 73-74, chmn bus affairs & labor comt, currently. Bus & Prof Pos: Teacher, Jefferson Co Pub Schs, Colo, 54-59; prin, Limon Pub Schs, Colo, 59-60 & S A Wilsen Elem Sch, Widefield Sch Dist Three, Security, 60-; dir research & publ, Wickfield Sch Dist 3. Mil Serv: Entered as Pvt, Air Force, 50, released as Sgt, 51, after serv in 140th Med Div. Mem: Nat Educ Asn; Southern Colo Elem Prin; Colo Elem Prin; Colo Asn Sch Execs; Nat Sch Pub Rels Asn. Relig: Episcopal. Mailing Add: 331 Morningside Dr Security CO 80911

MINK, PATSY TAKEMOTO (D)
US Rep, Hawaii
b Maui, Hawaii, Dec 6, 27; d Mitama Takemoto; m 1951 to John Francis Mink; c Gwendolyn. Educ: Univ Hawaii, BA, 48; Chicago Law Sch, JD, 51; Delta Sigma Rho. Hon Degrees: LLD, Lindenwood Col, 65; LHD, Wilson Col, 65; Hon Degree, Duff's Inst; Chaminade Col, 75. Polit & Govt Pos: Charter pres, Young Dem Oahu, 54-56; attorney, Territorial Legis, 55 & 60; state pres, Young Dem, Hawaii, 56-58; Hawaii State Rep, 56-58; nat vpres, Nat Young Dem, 57-59; Hawaii State Sen, 58-59 & 62-64; US Rep, Hawaii, 65-, mem educ & labor comt, interior & insular affairs comt & budget comt, US House Rep, 65-, chmn subcomt mines &

mining, mem House-Senate ad hoc comt on poverty, 68, secy, Dem Caucus, 75-; secy, 89th Dem Cong Club, 65-; mem, Cong for Peace Thru Law, 65-, chmn US China Comt, 69-71, mem Foreign Policy-World Order Comt, currently; vpres, Dem Study Group, 67-71 & 75-, vchmn, Task Force on Educ, 71, mem, Cong Reform Task Force, 71; mem comn of rules rev, Dem Nat Conv, formerly, mem rules reform comn, 69-71; mem adv comt on state-urban rels, Coun State Govts, 68; Am Coun Young Polit Leaders, 69-71; nat adv bd, Nat Movement for the Student Vote, 71; vpres, Am Dem Action, 73-; deleg, Dem Nat Conv, 72; deleg, Dem Nat Mid Term Conf, 74. Bus & Prof Pos: Lectr, Univ Hawaii, 52-56 & 59-62; attorney-at-law, 53-65. Mem: Am Asn for UN; NAACP; Hawaii Asn to Help Retarded Children; YMCA. Honors & Awards: Community Speaker of the Year, Pac Speech Asn, 68; Alii Award, 4-H Clubs Hawaii, 69; Freedom Fund & Recognition Award, Honolulu NAACP, 71; Rehabilitation Serv Medallion, 71; Distinguished Humanitarian Award, St Louis YWCA, 72. Relig: Protestant. Legal Res: 94-1037 Maikai St Waipahu Oahu HI 96797 Mailing Add: 2338 Rayburn House Off Bldg Washington DC 20515

MINN, MOMI PEARL (D)
Dem Nat Committeewoman, Hawaii
b Honolulu, Hawaii, Jan 28, 20; d Hoon Ting & Healani Kuawela T; m 1942 to Philip P Minn; c Philip Nathan, Geraldine Healani, Michael Puiki & Phyliss Momi. Educ: Univ Hawaii. Polit & Govt Pos: Precinct secy, Dem Party, Hawaii; mem, Hawaii Co Dem Comt; Dem Nat Committeeman, Hawaii, 64-; Hawaii State Rep, 67-72; deleg, Dem Nat Conv, 72-; nat committeewoman, Dem Women's Fedn, 73- Mem: DAV Auxiliary; Women in Construction. Mailing Add: 3274 Lower Rd Honolulu HI 96822

MINNER, RUTH ANN (D)
Del State Rep
Mailing Add: RD 3 Box 694 Milford DE 19963

MINNICK, DANIEL JAMES, JR (D)
Md State Deleg
b Baltimore, Md, Oct 14, 25; s Daniel James Minnick, Sr & Dorothy Mary Mileski M; m 1958 to Eleanor Gail Moyer; c Deborah (Mrs Orby Knutson) & Cynthia Nadine; one grandchild. Educ: Dundalk Community Col; Athletic Club. Polit & Govt Pos: Md State Deleg, 67-, chmn protocol & co-chmn environ matters comt, Md House Deleg, 67- Bus & Prof Pos: Self-employed, Restaurant, 45- Mil Serv: Entered as Seaman, Navy, 43, released as Seaman 2/C, 46. Mem: Lions; VFW; Am Legion; Moose. Relig: Catholic. Mailing Add: 2421 Fairway Dundalk MD 21222

MINNIS, LEEOMIA WILLIAMS (D)
b Thomasville, Ga, May 30, 40; d Rev John B Williams & Julia Boyd W; div; c Tonya, Clement & Wilfred. Educ: Dade Jr Col, AA, 64; Univ Miami, BM, 66; Pi Kappa Lambda. Polit & Govt Pos: Campaigner, Hubert H Humphrey for President; deleg, Dem Nat Conv, 72. Mem: Dade Co Classroom Asn; Nat Educ Asn; Fla Vocal Teachers Asn; Am Choral Soc; Music Educators Nat Conf. Relig: Methodist; minister of music. Mailing Add: 2467 NW 99th St Miami FL 33147

MINOW, NEWTON NORMAN (D)
b Milwaukee, Wis, Jan 17, 26; s Jay A Minow & Doris Stein M; m to Josephine Baskin; c Nell, Mary & Martha. Educ: Northwestern Univ, BS, 49 & JD, 50; Order of the Coif; recipient, Wigmore Award. Hon Degrees: LLD, Brandeis Univ, 63, Univ Wis, 63; Northwestern Univ, 65; Columbia Col, 72. Polit & Govt Pos: Law clerk to Chief Justice of Supreme Court Fred M Vinson, 51-52; admin asst to Gov Adlai E Stevenson, Ill, 52-53; spec asst to Adlai E Stevenson in Presidential Campaigns, 52 & 56; gen counsel & secy, Nat Bus & Prof Comt for Kennedy-Johnson, 60; chmn, Fed Communication Comn, 61-63; alt deleg, Dem Nat Conv, 68, deleg, 72; chmn, 20th Century Fund Comn on Campaign Costs in the Electronic Era, 69-71. Bus & Prof Pos: Assoc, Mayer, Brown & Platt, 53-55; partner, Stevenson, Rifkind & Wirtz, 55-61; exec vpres, gen counsel & dir, Encycl Britannica, Inc, 63-65; trustee, Rand Corp, 65-75, chmn, 70-72; partner, Sidley & Austin & predecessor firm, 65-; dir, Stevenson Inst Int Affairs, 66-; dir, Fleming-Berger Fund, Inc, 68-; prof lectr, Medill Sch Jour, Northwestern Univ, 70-; bd gov, Pub Broadcasting Serv, 73-; dir, gen counsel, Aetna Life Ins Co, Ill, 73-; dir, gen counsel, Aetna Casualty & Surety Co, Ill, 73-; dir, Mayo Found, 73-; chmn bd overseers, Jewish Theological Sem, 74- Mil Serv: Entered as Pvt, Army, 44, released as Sgt, 46. Publ: Equal Time: the Private Broadcaster & The Public Interest, Atheneum Publ, 64; contrib, As We Knew Adlai, Harper & Row, 66; co-auth, Presidential Television, 73. Mem: Am Bar Asn; fel Am Bar Found; Univ Notre Dame (bd trustees); Chicago Educ TV (dir & hon chmn); Nat Acad TV Arts & Sci. Honors & Awards: Named One of Ten Outstanding Young Men in Chicago, Jr CofC & Indust, 60 & One of Ten Outstanding Young Men in US, 61; George Foster Peabody Award, 61. Relig: Jewish. Legal Res: 375 Palos Rd Glencoe IL 60022 Mailing Add: Rm 4800 One First Nat Plaza Chicago IL 60603

MINSHALL, WILLIAM E (R)
b East Cleveland, Ohio, Oct 24, 11; m to Frances Smith; c William Edwin, III, Werner Ellis & Peter Charles. Educ: Univ Va; Cleveland Law Sch, LLB. Polit & Govt Pos: Gen counsel to Maritime Admin, 53-54; US Rep, Ohio, 54-74; mem bd visitors to US Mil Acad, 61-62, US Naval Acad, 63-65 & 70-71 & US Air Force, 66-69; deleg, Rep Nat Conv, 68 & 72; mem bd regents, Smithsonian Inst, currently. Bus & Prof Pos: Attorney-at-law. Mil Serv: Enlisted 40 as Pvt, Army & serv in ETO, G-2 Sect, Hq III Corps, released 46, Lt Col. Legal Res: Lakewood OH 44107 Mailing Add: 2243 Rayburn House Off Bldg Washington DC 20515

MIOLA, MICHELE (D)
b Newark, NJ, Dec 30, 47; d Anthony Vincent Miola & Vera Ventre M; single. Educ: Bloomfield Col, 65-67; Upsala Col, BA in Psychol, 69; Rutgers Univ Grad Sch Social Work, New Brunswick, MSW, 71; treas, Phi Kappa Sigma. Polit & Govt Pos: Vol, McCarthy for President, 68; vol, Gibson Mayoral Race, Newark, NJ, 70; secy, City Wide Voters League, Newark, 70-; alt deleg, Dem Nat Conv, 72; mem, Essex Co Polit Caucus, 72- Bus & Prof Pos: Admin aide, United Community Corp, Newark, 65-67 & Timothy Still Prog, Upsala Col, 67-69; caseworker, Div Youth & Family Servs, Newark, 69-70; social worker, Bd Educ, Newark, 72-; social worker, Bessie Smith Health Ctr, Newark, currently. Mem: Nat Asn Social Workers; Acad Cert Social Workers; Am Civil Liberties Union; Nat Welfare Rights Orgn; Nat Orgn Women. Mailing Add: Apt 52-B 249 Belleville Ave Bloomfield NJ 07003

MIRABELLI, MICHAEL ANTHONY (D)
State Treas, Nev
b Union City, NJ, June 2, 22; s Carmen Mirabelli & Filomena Silvagni M; m 1974 to Carole McGilvrey; c Steve, Lynne, Royal, Jaime & Jeffrey. Educ: Univ Nev, Reno, BS, 51. Polit & Govt Pos: Co comnr, Washoe Co, Nev, 61-62; State Treas, Nev, 63- Mil Serv: Entered as Pvt, Army, 42, released as Sgt, 45, after serv in 8th Air Force, Medics, 43-45. Mem: Am Cancer Soc. Relig: Roman Catholic. Mailing Add: State Capitol Carson City NV 87901

MIRIKITANI, CARL KUNIO (R)
Second VChmn, Rep Party Hawaii
b Honolulu, Hawaii, Jan 16, 46; s Carl Mamoru Mirikitani & Hisa Yoshimura M; div; c Carl Kunio, II. Educ: Oberlin Col, AB, magna cum laude, 69; Univ Chicago Law Sch, JD, 72; Phi Beta Kappa; Order of the Coif. Polit & Govt Pos: Second vchmn, Rep Party Hawaii, 74-, rules chmn, 74- Bus & Prof Pos: Law clerk, O'Melveny & Myers, Los Angeles, Calif, 71; law clerk, hon Bernard H Levinson, Justice of the Supreme Court Hawaii, 72; assoc, Goodsill Anderson & Quinn, Honolulu, 72- Mem: Am & Hawaii Bar Asns. Legal Res: 225 Kaiulane Ave Apt 902 Honolulu HI 96815 Mailing Add: PO Box 3196 Honolulu HI 96801

MIRTO, PETER G (D)
NY State Assemblyman
Mailing Add: 180 Irving Ave Brooklyn NY 11237

MISCEVICH, GEORGE (D)
Pa State Rep
Mailing Add: Capitol Bldg Harrisburg PA 17120

MISHLER, EVERETT MONROE (D)
Assessor, Elkhart Co, Ind
b New Paris, Ind, Sept 29, 18; s Milton Mishler & Nina Moyer M; m 1939 to Kathryn Louise Stahly; c Kermit, Marlene, Jerry, Grace, Howard, Rex, Carolan & Dan. Polit & Govt Pos: Ind State Rep, Elkhart Co, 65-66; assessor, Elkhart Co, Ind, 71- Bus & Prof Pos: Pres, Elkhart Co Agr Soc, 71- Mem: Farm Bur; Nat Farmers Orgn; Elkhart Co Farm Bur Coop Asn. Relig: Church of the Brethren, mem gen bd, 69-70; dir, Elkhart Co Coun Churches, 69-71. Mailing Add: RR 1 New Paris IN 46553

MISKAVAGE, MARGARET BROWN (R)
Maine State Rep
b Presque Isle, Maine, Mar 21, 17; d Henry Chesley Brown & Caddie McEacheron B; m 1940 to Anthony Edward Miskavage; wid; c Toni (Mrs Paul Nelson) & John H. Educ: Cony High Sch, grad; Univ Maine, many adult educ courses in off mgt & supvry training. Polit & Govt Pos: Dep clerk of courts, Kennebec Co Courthouse, 59-61; off mgr, Attorney Gen Off, 65-73; admin asst clerk, Maine House Rep, 73-75; Maine State Rep, 75- Mem: Am Soc Pub Admin; Maine Women's Polit Caucus; Kennebec Co Women's Rep Club; Maine Hist Soc; Merrymeeting Bay Audubon Soc. Mailing Add: 6 Malta St Augusta ME 04330

MISKELLY, JOHN (D)
Okla State Sen
Mailing Add: State Capitol Oklahoma City OK 73105

MITCHELL, ALBERT KNELL (R)
b Clayton, NMex, June 25, 94; s Thomas Edward Mitchell & Linda Knell M; 2nd m 1957 to Natalie Galbraith; c Linda (Mrs Davis) & Albert Julian. Educ: Cornell Univ, 17; Gnome Club; Owl & Key. Polit & Govt Pos: NMex State Rep, 27-29; nominee, Gov, NMex, 37; US Sen, 41; mem & chmn, Rep Nat Conv Comts; committeeman, Rep Nat Comt, NMex, 42-65; vchmn, Rep Nat Comt, 62-65; mem, Nat Comn Food Mkt, 65-67. Bus & Prof Pos: Pres, T E Mitchell & Son, Albert, NMex, 34-; dir, Albuquerque Production Credit Corp, 38-, S E C Corp, El Paso, 39-, First Nat Bank, Raton, NMex, 40-, Ideal Basic Industries, Inc, 45-74 & Colo Interstate Corp, Colorado Springs, 55-75; chmn bd & dir, Nat Livestock Tax Comn, Denver, Colo, 57-70. Mil Serv: Pvt, Field Artil Officers Training, Camp Zachary Taylor, Louisville, Ky, 18. Mem: Am Nat Livestock Asn; Am Hereford Asn; Am Quarter Horse Asn; Mason (32 degree); Shrine. Relig: Episcopal. Mailing Add: Tequesquite Ranch Albert NM 87733

MITCHELL, BRUCE TYSON (R)
Mem, Rep State Cent Comt Calif
b San Francisco, Calif, Nov 6, 28; s John Robert Mitchell & Lorraine Tyson M; m 1951 to Adrienne Means Hiscox; c Mark Means. Educ: Stanford Univ, BA, 49, LLB, 51; El Cuadro Eating Club. Polit & Govt Pos: Chmn, Tri-City Young Rep, Calif, 57; mem, San Mateo Co Rep Cent Comt, 60-71, vchmn, 62-64, chmn, 64-71; mem, Rep State Cent Comt Calif, 64-; treas, Asn Rep Co Cent Comt Chmn of Calif, 67-71; alt deleg, Rep Nat Conv, 68. Bus & Prof Pos: Estate adminr, Crocker-Anglo Nat Bank, 55-57; sr counsel & asst secy, Utah Construction & Mining Co, 57- Mil Serv: Entered as Seaman, Navy, 52, released as Lt(jg), 55, after serv in Naval Forces Far East; Lt, Naval Res; Am Defense Medal; Korean & UN Campaign Ribbons. Mem: Am Bar Asn; Am Judicature Soc; Am Soc Corp Secretaries; Mason; Commonwealth Club of Calif. Relig: Congregational. Mailing Add: 165 Redwood Dr Hillsborough CA 94010

MITCHELL, BRYAN FRANKLIN (R)
Mem, Rep State Exec Comt WVa
b Petersburg, WVa, Aug 31, 27; s Bryan Mitchell & Esther Forman M; m 1965 to Grace Holden; c Tammy Ann & William Clifford. Educ: Washington & Jefferson Col; Pa State Col of Optometry; Honor Soc. Polit & Govt Pos: Mem, Grant Co Young Rep Club, WVa, 52; chmn, State Young Rep Club, 58; chmn, Grant Co Rep Comt, 60-; mem, Rep State Exec Comt WVa, 60- Bus & Prof Pos: Optometrist, 54- Mil Serv: Entered as Seaman, Navy, 65, released as Hosp Apprentice 1/C, 66. Mem: Am Optom Asn; Am Legion; Odd Fellows; Mason. Relig: Presbyterian. Legal Res: Judy St Petersburg WV 26747 Mailing Add: Box 38 Petersburg WV 26747

MITCHELL, CHARLENE (COMMUNIST PARTY)
Secy Comn on Black Liberation, Communist Party, US
b Cincinnati, Ohio, June 8, 30; d Charles Alexander & Naomi Taylor A; div; c Steven. Educ: Herzl Jr Col, AA, 50. Polit & Govt Pos: Mem, Ill State Bd, Labor Youth League, 49-55; admin secy, Southern Calif Communist Party, 57-60, chmn Negro comn, 63-67; mem nat comt, Communist Party, US, 57-; US Presidential cand, 68; secy, Comn on Black Liberation, 68-; exec secy, Nat Comt to Free Angela Davis, 70-72; exec secy, Nat Orgn Against Racist & Polit Repression, 73- Bus & Prof Pos: Head bookkeeper, importing firm, Southern Calif, 62-68; visiting lectr, African-Am Prog, Northwestern Univ, Evanston, Ill, 75. Mailing Add: 23 W 26th St New York NY 10010

MITCHELL, CHARLES B (D)
Miss State Rep
b Carthage, Miss, Dec 6, 25; s Clarence B Mitchell & Lessie Jolly M; m 1947 to Kathleen Yates; c Karen, Nancy & Jan. Educ: Millsaps Col, BA, 49; Lambda Chi Alpha. Polit & Govt Pos: Miss State Rep, Hinds Co, 68- Mil Serv: Entered as Pvt, Army, 44, released as Cpl, 46, after serv in 239th Gen Hosp, ETO, 44-46. Mem: Jackson Asn Life Underwriters; Miss Chartered Life Underwriters Asn; Kiwanis. Relig: Methodist; chmn bd stewards, Christ Methodist Church, 64-65. Legal Res: 5627 Concord Dr Jackson MS 39211 Mailing Add: PO Box 12301 Jackson MS 39211

MITCHELL, CLARENCE M, III (D)
Md State Sen
b St Paul, Minn, Dec 14, 39; married. Educ: Gonzaga High Sch, Washington, DC; Univ Md; Morgan State Col. Polit & Govt Pos: Mem, Young Dem Md; Md State Deleg, 63-67; Md State Sen, 67-; alt deleg, Dem Nat Conv, 68. Bus & Prof Pos: Pres, Real Estate Co. Mem: YMCA; NAACP; Kappa Alpha Psi; Baltimore Jr CofC. Relig: Methodist; mem off bd, Sharp St Methodist Church. Mailing Add: 1239 Druid Hill Ave Baltimore MD 21217

MITCHELL, CLEATIS GERALD (D)
Ore State Rep
b Nobell, Ark, Nov 20, 34; s Charles Leonard Mitchell & Alma Meyers M; m 1961 to Sandra Clary; c Elisabeth & Charles Taylor, Renee & Rodney Mitchell, Joy Salem & Becky Hunter. Educ: Southern Ore State Col, BS. Polit & Govt Pos: Ore State Rep, Dist 52, 75- Mil Serv: Entered as E-1, Army, 56, released as E-3, after serv in Mil Police, Sixth Army, 56-58. Legal Res: 243 Granite St Ashland OR 97520 Mailing Add: PO Box 131 Ashland OR 97520

MITCHELL, DALE W (D)
Utah State Rep
Mailing Add: 943 Serpentine Way Sandy UT 84070

MITCHELL, DONALD J (R)
US Rep, NY
b Ilion, NY, May 8, 23; m to Greta Levee; c Gretchen, Cynthia, Allen. Educ: Hobart Col; Columbia Univ, BS; Columbia Univ Teachers Col, MA. Polit & Govt Pos: Mem, Herkimer Town Coun, NY, 54-57; mayor, Herkimer, 57-60, mem zoning bd appeals, 63-64; NY State Assemblyman, 64-72, Majority Whip, NY State Assembly, 69-72; US Rep, NY, 73- Bus & Prof Pos: Optometrist, 50-; mem, NY State Bd Optom Examr. Mil Serv: Navy, World War II & Korea, 5 years. Mem: Naval rep three man mil adv comt, Optom Nat Orgn; Mohawk Valley Optom Soc; Boy Scouts; Kiwanis; Mason. Relig: First Methodist; mem off bd, Herkimer First Methodist Church. Mailing Add: Shells Bush Rd Herkimer NY 13350

MITCHELL, DOROTHY EVADEAN (R)
Mem Exec Bd, Vermilion Co Rep Cent Comt, Ill
b Oakwood, Ill, Aug 31, 19; d Wesley Thomas Richter & Mildred Eldridge R; m 1938 to George Harlan Mitchell; c Wesley Harlan; two grandchildren. Educ: Oakwood Twp High Sch, Muncie, Ill, 4 years. Polit & Govt Pos: Mem exec bd, Vermilion Co Permanent Rep Hq, 58-; police magistrate, Fairmount, Ill, 58-62, village clerk, 65-68; pres, Vermilion Co Rep Woman's Club, 60-; chairwoman, Vermilion Co Rep Party, Ill, formerly; mem exec bd, Vermilion Co Rep Cent Comt, 60-; precinct committeeman, 62-; bd mem, Ill Fedn Rep Women, 68-70. Bus & Prof Pos: Partner, Fairmount Sheet Metal, 58-; owner, Fairmount Hobby Shop, 71- Mem: Small Bus Admin (state adv coun); Am Legion Auxiliary; Danville Bus & Prof Women; Fairmount Federated Woman's Club. Relig: Methodist. Mailing Add: 200 N Main St Fairmount IL 61841

MITCHELL, ELIZABETH H (D)
Maine State Rep
Mailing Add: RFD 1 Augusta Vassalboro ME 04330

MITCHELL, GEORGE JOHN (D)
Dem Nat Committeeman, Maine
b Waterville, Maine, Aug 20, 33; s George J Mitchell & Mary Saad M; m 1959 to Sally Heath; c Andrea. Educ: Bowdoin Col, BA, 54; Georgetown Univ, LLB, 60; Sigma Nu. Polit & Govt Pos: Trial attorney, US Dept Justice, Washington, DC, 60-62; exec asst to US Sen Edmund S Muskie, 62-65; chmn, Maine Dem State Comt, 66-68; deleg, Dem Nat Conv, 68 & 72; Dem Nat Committeeman, Maine, 68-, mem exec comt, 74- Bus & Prof Pos: Attorney, Jensen & Baird, Portland, Maine, 65- Mil Serv: Entered as 2nd Lt, Army, 54, released as 1st Lt, 56, after serv in Army Counter Intel, Berlin, Ger, 55-56. Mem: Am Bar Asn. Relig: Roman Catholic. Mailing Add: 25 Channel Rd South Portland ME 04106

MITCHELL, GEORGE TRICE (R)
b Marshall, Ill, Jan 20, 14; s Roscoe Addison Mitchell & Alma Elizabeth Trice M; m 1941 to Mildred Aletha Miller; c Linda Sue (Mrs Keith L Miller) & Mary Kathryn (Mrs Michael V Drudge). Educ: Purdue Univ, BS in Mech Eng, 35, grad sch, 35-36; George Washington Univ, MD, 40; Smith-Reed-Russell Med Soc; Acacia; Alpha Kappa Kappa. Polit & Govt Pos: Mem state coun, Ill Med Polit Action Comt, 66-; alt deleg, Rep Nat Conv, 68, deleg, 72; mem multidiscipline accident invest team, Ill Dept Pub Safety, 69- Bus & Prof Pos: Gen practice med, Marshall, Ill, 46-; mem bd dir, First Nat Bank, 49-, vpres, 66-69, pres, 69- Mil Serv: Entered as 1st Lt, Army Med Corps, 41, released as Lt Col, 46, after serv in Army Air Force, Western Flying Training Command & Air Force Redistribution Command, 41-46. Mem: Am Med Asn; Ill State Med Soc; Am Acad Gen Practice; Mason (32 degree); Shrine. Honors & Awards: Distinguished Serv Award, Jaycees, 66. Relig: Methodist. Mailing Add: RR 2 Marshall IL 62441

MITCHELL, HUGH BURNTON (D)
b Great Falls, Mont, Mar 22, 07; s Harry Browne Mitchell & Mary Greening M; m 1937 to Kathryn Herkimer Smith; c Bruce C & Elizabeth S. Educ: Dartmouth Col, 25-29; Phi Kappa Psi. Polit & Govt Pos: US Sen, Wash, 45-46; US Rep, 1st Dist, Wash, 49-53. Bus & Prof Pos: Partner, Martin Van Lines, 53-60; chmn, Gaco Western, Inc, 56-; pres, Alaska Van & Storage Co, Inc, 56-; pres, Alaska Terminals, Inc & Alaska HHG Movers, Inc, 61-; pres, Mitchell Overseas Movers, 70- Mem: Comt Wash Tax Reform (chmn); CofC; Wash Athletic Club; Munic League Seattle: Former Mem Cong. Relig: Unitarian. Mailing Add: 3220 Magnolia Blvd W Seattle WA 98199

MITCHELL, J BERNARD (R)
Mo State Rep
Mailing Add: 547 Kings Dr Mt Vernon MO 65712

MITCHELL, JAMES L (R)
b Evanston, Ill, May 20, 37; s David B Mitchell & Sara McGinn M; m 1962 to Ann Elizabeth Stupple; c Caitlin & Andrew. Educ: Cornell Univ, BA, 59, Yale Univ Sch Law, LLB, 62; Order of the Coif. Polit & Govt Pos: Spec asst to the secy for policy develop, Dept Com, 72-73; gen counsel, Dept Housing & Urban Develop, 73-74, Under Secy, 74-75; assoc dir natural resources energy & sci, Off Mgt & Budget, 75- Bus & Prof Pos: Assoc, Mayer, Brown & Platt, Chicago, 66-69, partner, 69-72. Mil Serv: Entered as A/S, Navy, 62, released as Lt, 66, after serv in Judge Adv Gen Corps. Mem: Am, Ill & Chicago Bar Asns; Chicago Club; Capitol Hill Club. Legal Res: 744 Prospect Ave Winnetka IL 60093 Mailing Add: 4709 Dorset Ave Chevy Chase MD 20015

MITCHELL, KENRICK RUSSELL (R)
Chmn, Dixon Co Rep Cent Comt, Nebr
b Garden City, Kans, July 28, 04; s William Sherman Mitchell & Elizabeth Kenrick M; m 1928 to Faye Bacon; c Richard, William & Carol (Mrs Pearson). Educ: Wayne State Col, AB, 28; Univ Nebr, MA, 36. Polit & Govt Pos: Treas, Dixon Co Rep Cent Comt, Nebr, 58-60, secy, 60-74, chmn, 74- Bus & Prof Pos: Supt, Allen Consol Sch, Nebr, 36-68; retired. Mem: Mason (Past Master). Relig: Methodist. Mailing Add: Allen NE 68710

MITCHELL, MAXINE K (R)
Secy, Tuscarawas Co Rep Exec & Cent Comts, Ohio
b New Philadelphia, Ohio, Oct 4, 19; d Philip Getzman King & Etta Wilson K; m 1943 to Robert Wilson Mitchell; c Marilyn & Louise. Educ: Beckwith Bus Col, 1 year. Polit & Govt Pos: Secy, Ohio State Bur Motor Vehicles, 39; cashier, secy to chief auditor, Div Pub Assistance, Ohio State Dept Pub Welfare, 43; secy, US Dept Defense Transportation Corps of Engrs, 43; receptionist, Ohio State Hwy Dept, 47; mem, Tuscarawas Co Rep Bd Elections, 58-; secy, Tuscarawas Co Rep Exec & Cent Comts, 56-; mem, Nat & Ohio Fed Rep Women. Bus & Prof Pos: Secy to bldg engr, Kaiser Shipbuilding, Portland, Ore, 43-44; secy, Curtiss-Wright, 45. Mem: Beta Sigma Phi; Eastern Star; CofC; Union Hosp Auxiliary; Qui Vive Lit Club. Relig: Methodist. Mailing Add: 719 Oak St NW New Philadelphia OH 44663

MITCHELL, MIKE P (D)
Idaho State Sen
b Lewiston, Idaho, June 5, 25; s George F Mitchell & Loretta Geiseker M; m 1960 to Arlene R Harvey; c Christine, Cori & Molly. Educ: Univ Ore, BA in Jour; Phi Kappa Psi. Polit & Govt Pos: Idaho State Sen, currently. Mil Serv: Entered as A/S, Navy, 43, released as AMM 1/C, 45, after serv in Cent Pac & Japan, 44-45. Mem: CofC; Elks; Am Legion. Honors & Awards: Distinguished Serv Award, Jr CofC; Star Garnet Award, Idaho Hosp Asn. Relig: Catholic. Mailing Add: 316 Skyline Dr Lewiston ID 83501

MITCHELL, NICHOLAS WILFRED (D)
Mass Gov Councillor
b Fall River, Mass, Jan 15, 13; s John Mitchell & Malvina Lafleur M; m 1943 to Rita T Blake; c John B & Barbara A. Educ: Pvt tutoring & schooling for Registered Pharmacist, Mass, grad, 37. Polit & Govt Pos: Mem bd dir, Pub Welfare, Fall River, Mass, 53-56, city coun, 61-62 & 63-67, Dem committeeman, 65-, mayor, 68-71; gov councillor, First Dist, 64-68 & 69-; deleg, Dem Nat Conv, 68; exec dir, Fall River Indust Comn, currently; clerk, Bristol Co Juvenile Court. Bus & Prof Pos: Owner, Mitchell's Pharm, formerly. Mil Serv: Entered as Pvt, Army Air Force, 42, released as T/Sgt, 46, after serv in Eighth & Ninth Air Force, ETO, 43-46; Good Conduct Medal; ETO Ribbon; 2 Bronze Stars. Mem: Mass Pharmacist Asn; Fall River Druggist Asn; Southeast Mass Druggist Asn; Kiwanis; Ahepa. Relig: Catholic. Mailing Add: 105 Garden St Fall River MA 02720

MITCHELL, PARREN JAMES (D)
US Rep, Md
b Baltimore, Md, Apr 29, 22; s Clarence Maurice Mitchell & Elsie Davis M; single. Educ: Morgan State Col, AB, 50; Univ Md, College Park, MA, 52; Yale Univ, 57; Univ Conn, 60; Alpha Kappa Phi. Polit & Govt Pos: US Rep, Seventh Dist, Md, 71-; ex officio, Dem Nat Mid-Term Conf, 74. Bus & Prof Pos: Instr sociol, Morgan State Col, 53-54, prof, 68-70; probation officer, Supreme Bench of Baltimore City, 54-57, supvr domestic rels, 57-63; exec dir, Md Comn on Interracial Prob, 63-65; exec dir, Community Action Agency, 65-68. Mil Serv: Entered as Pvt, Army, 43, released as Capt, 46, after serv in Inf, Apennines; Purple Heart. Mem: Nat Asn Community Develop; Md Comt for Day Care. Relig: Episcopal. Legal Res: 951 Brooks Lane Baltimore MD 21217 Mailing Add: 414 House Off Bldg Washington DC 20515

MITCHELL, R CLAYTON, JR (D)
Md State Deleg
Mailing Add: Kentmore Park Kennedyville MD 21645

MITCHELL, RALPH WILSON (D)
Chmn, Shelby Co Dem Exec Comt, Ky
b Greensburg, Ky, Sept 30, 12; s William Wilson Mitchell & Harriet Hatcher M; m 1937 to Rena Holt Wadlington; c Ralph Seldon & Courtney W. Educ: Centre Col, AB, 33; Jefferson Sch Law, LLB, 39; Harvard Law Sch, 47; Beta Theta Pi. Polit & Govt Pos: Co judge, Shelby Co, Ky, 52-64; Ky State Rep, 58th Dist, 68-72; chmn, Shelby Co Dem Exec Comt, Ky, 72- Bus & Prof Pos: Clerical staff, Procter & Gamble, Cincinnati & Louisville, 33-41, salesman, Tenn & WVa, 41-42; contract rep, Curtis-Wright, Louisville, 42-43; attorney-at-law, Shelbyville, Ky, 47-; partner, Saunders, Mitchell & Mathis, 64-72, Mitchell & Mathis, 72- Mil Serv: Entered as Pvt, Marine Corps, 43, released as Sgt, 46, after serv in 12th Air Warning Squadron. Mem: Ky Bar Asn; Am Trial Lawyers Asn; Am Judicature Soc; Rotary. Relig: Presbyterian. Mailing Add: PO Box 367 Shelbyville KY 40065

MITCHELL, ROBERT E (R)
Treas, Los Angeles Co Rep Cent Comt, Calif
s Graham Mitchell & Helen Leonard M; m 1953 to Sarah S Christensen; c William, Susan, Cathleen & John. Educ: Univ Southern Calif, 48-53; Univ Southern Calif Law Sch, 53-56; Squires; Knights; Sigma Phi Epsilon; Blue Key; Skull & Dagger; pres, Asn Men Students. Polit & Govt Pos: Chmn, 66th Assembly Dist Rep Cent Comt & 19th Cong Dist Rep Cent, Calif, formerly; mem exec comt, Calif Rep State Cent Comt; alt deleg, Rep Nat Conv, 68; treas, Los Angeles Co Rep Cent Comt, 68-, chmn cand research & develop comt, mem budget & expenditures comt & exec comt, 68-; co-chmn ad hoc comt, Non-Partisan Citizen Comt, 69; chmn, State Benefits & Servs Adv Bd, Calif, currently, co-chmn, Task Force on Foster Care, currently. Bus & Prof Pos: Attorney, Iverson & Hogoboom, 56, Parker, Stanbury, Reese & McGee; attorney, self-employed, 63-72; partner, Mitchell & DiLoreto, 72- Mil Serv: Entered as Pvt, Army, 46, released as Cpl, 48, after serv in 24th Inf Div, Japanese Occup. Publ:

Children in waiting, 73; co-publ, Unplanned Parenthood. Mem: Norwalk CofC (bd dirs, 72-); Norwalk Kiwanis; Los Angeles United Way (exec bd mem & bd dirs, Los Angeles, bd dirs & chmn planning bd, Region III, Long Beach); Los Angeles Co Hist Soc; Los Angeles World Affairs' Coun. Relig: Protestant. Legal Res: 9415 Mesa Robles Whittier CA 90603 Mailing Add: 13917 San Antonio Dr Norwalk CA 90650

MITCHELL, ROBERT S (D)
Chmn, Tenth Cong Dist Dem Party, Mich
b Edenville, Mich, Mar 10, 22; s Estey William Mitchell & Mary Barron M; m 1953 to Carole Hunt. Educ: Flint Jr Col, Assoc in Eng, 47; Wayne State Univ, 47-48. Polit & Govt Pos: Chmn, Midland Co Dem Party, Mich, 54-59 & 63-68; chmn, Tenth Cong Dist Dem Party, 69- Mil Serv: Entered as Pvt, Air Force, 42, released as Cpl, 66, after serv in Continental US, 42-46. Relig: Methodist. Mailing Add: 2615 St Marys Dr Midland MI 48640

MITCHELL, THEO (D)
SC State Rep
Mailing Add: 522 Woodland Way Greenville SC 29607

MITCHELL, THOMAS (R)
b Ft Benton, Mont, Apr 27, 96; s Alexander Mitchell & Mary Ellen Coleman M; m 1919 to Bessie May Finck; c Warren T, T C & Donald R. Polit & Govt Pos: Rep precinct committeeman, Clark Co, Dubois, Idaho, 64-68; chmn, Clark Co Rep Cent Comt, formerly; mem sch bd, Jefferson Co West Side, 24-72; mem bd, Dubois City Coun, 60-74. Mil Serv: Entered as Fireman 3/C, Navy, 17, released as Engr, 2/C, 19. Mem: Lions; Am Legion; VFW. Relig: Christian. Mailing Add: PO Box 173 Dubois ID 83423

MITCHELL, WENDELL WILKIE (D)
Ala State Sen
b Montgomery, Ala, Sept 4, 40; s Furman Gastle Mitchell & Pearl Burnum M; m 1964 to Rosalind McBride; c Peter Maury & Wendelyn. Educ: Auburn Univ, BS, 62; Univ Ala, LLB, 65; Squires Sophomore Hon, pres, Pi Kappa Phi & Debate Team & Coun & ed, Tiger Cub, Auburn Univ; Phi Alpha Delta. Polit & Govt Pos: Admin asst to Congressman Tom Bevill, Ala, 67-68 & to US Sen James B Allen, 69-73; Crenshaw Co Solicitor, 72-74; Dem cand for Cong, Ala, 72; Ala State Sen, 74- Bus & Prof Pos: Partner, Law Firm of Hawkins, Rhea & Mitchell, Gadsden, Ala, 65-66; mem bd dir, Ala Christian Col, 69- Mem: US Senate Asn of Admin Asst; Ala Jaycees; Rotary; Ala Bankers Asn (counsel). Honors & Awards: Outstanding Jaycee Pub Speaker, Ala, 66. Relig: Church of Christ. Legal Res: W Sixth St Luverne AL 36049 Mailing Add: PO Box 225 Luverne AL 36049

MITCHEM, HINTON (D)
Ala State Rep
Mailing Add: PO Box 297 Albertville AL 35950

MITCHLER, ROBERT W (R)
Ill State Sen
b Aurora, Ill, June 4, 20; s John L Mitchler & Clara Rub M; m 1950 to Helen L Drew; c John Drew, Kurt David & Heidi Louise. Educ: Aurora Col, Ill, BS, 53. Polit & Govt Pos: Chmn, Kendall Co Young Rep Club, Ill; precinct committeeman, Kendall Co Rep Party, 63; Ill State Sen, 65- Bus & Prof Pos: Sales & pub rels, Northern Ill Gas Co, 58. Mil Serv: Chief Yeoman, Navy, Pac Theater, 41-46 & Japan & Korean Theaters, 50-52, mem, Mil Armistice Negotiations at Pan Mun Jom, Korea, on Staff of Adm C Turner Joy; 13 medals & decorations in World War II & Korean War, including Navy Commendation Ribbon & Combat V for combat serv in Korean War. Mem: Moose; Mason; Scottish Rite; Shrine; Am Legion. Relig: Methodist. Mailing Add: Hill Spring Oaks Oswego IL 60543

MITCHUM, TOMMY E (D)
Ark State Rep
b Batesville, Ark, July 17, 49; s John H Mitchum & Georgia P Burge M; m 1969 to Janet Sue Siler; c Brian Thomas. Educ: State Col Ark, currently. Polit & Govt Pos: Ark State Rep, 73- Bus & Prof Pos: With ins agencies, 69-75. Relig: Baptist. Legal Res: Star Rte M Batesville AR 72501 Mailing Add: PO Box 2082 Batesville AR 72501

MITTAN, RAY C (R)
Mich State Rep
Mailing Add: 530 Sherman Court Benton Harbor MI 49022

MITTELMAN, EUGENE (R)
b Brooklyn, NY, Nov 23, 35; s Irving Mittelman & Marion Hassin M; m 1958 to Jacqueline Gilbert; c Karen Sue & Deborah. Educ: Bard Col, AB, 57; Columbia Univ Sch Law, LLB, 61. Polit & Govt Pos: Minority counsel, Labor & Pub Welfare Comt, US Senate, 67- Bus & Prof Pos: Mem panel arbitrators, NJ Mediation Bd, 70- Mem: Am Bar Asn; Indust Rels Research Asn; Pub Serv Coun for Histadrut (vchmn, 69-). Legal Res: 3007 Doeg Indian Ct Alexandria VA 22309 Mailing Add: New Senate Off Bldg Washington DC 20510

MITTENBERG, DORA DALE (R)
b Dresden, Mo, Oct 29, 21; d Oscar Sitlington Siron & Ann Richter S; m 1947 to John Sievers Mittenberg. Educ: Cent Bus Col, Sedalia, Mo, 39-41. Polit & Govt Pos: Chairwoman, Randolph Co Rep Cent Comt, Mo, 70-73; treas, Rep Women of Randolph Co, 70-73; deleg, Rep Nat Conv, 72; collector of revenue, State of Mo, 73- Bus & Prof Pos: Secy, ins agency, Sedalia, Mo, 41-47; legal secy, Lamb & Semple, Moberly, 48-57; co-owner & mgr, Elec Motor & Pump Supply & Indust Elec Motor Serv, 57-67. Mem: Eastern Star; White Shrine of Jerusalem. Relig: Methodist; mem bd, Trinity United Methodist Church, currently. Mailing Add: 821 Monroe St Jefferson City MO 65101

MITTNESS, LEWIS T, JR (D)
Wis State Rep
b LaCrosse, Wis, July 29, 29. Educ: Wis State Col, BS, 54; Univ Wis, ME, 58. Polit & Govt Pos: Wis State Rep, 64-, chmn natural resources comt, Wis House Rep, currently. Bus & Prof Pos: Teacher & drive-in owner & mgr, formerly; real estate salesman, currently. Mil Serv: Army, 51-53. Mem: VFW; Am Legion. Mailing Add: 118 Sinclair Jamesville WI 53545

MITZMAN, NANCY CURTIN (D)
b Bellefonte, Pa, June 17, 38; d William Hurley Kerk & Nancy Curtin Kerk Eakin; m 1956 to Bud Mitzman; c Susan, Benjamin & Ged. Educ: Bellefonte Sr High Sch, grad, 56. Polit & Govt Pos: Campaign mgr, Suffolk Co Legis Thomas J Downey, 71, George McGovern for President, Suffolk Co, 72, Suffolk Co Legis Angela Christiansen, 73 & Cong Thomas J Downey, 74; committeewoman, Suffolk Co Dem Comt, 71-; deleg & whip, Nassau-Suffolk deleg, Dem Nat Conv, 72; mem, Suffolk Co Dem Exec Comt, 72-73; nat exec dir, New Dem Coalition, 73; representative, NY State Dem Women's Div, Region One, 75-; spec asst to US Rep Thomas J Downey, NY, 75-; vchairperson, NY State New Dem Coalition, 75- Mem: Suffolk Co Women's Polit Caucus (founder); NY State Women's Polit Caucus (co-chmn, Conv, 74, state rep, 74-75). Relig: Episcopal. Mailing Add: 3 Wren Dr Hauppauge NY 11787

MITZNER, JANICE L (D)
Committeewoman, Wash State Dem Comt
b Okanogan, Wash, May 3, 34; d Earl Burnett & Emma Dagnon B; m 1954 to Gaylord Harvey Mitzner; c Dianna, Sherry, Steven & Jeffery. Educ: Everett Bus Col, 53; Spokane Community Col, Wash, 72 & 73. Polit & Govt Pos: Pres, Southern Stevens Co Dem Women's Club, Wash, 60-72; deleg, Stevens Co Dem Conv, 60-72; Dem precinct committeewoman, Chewelah, Wash, 60-; coordr, Stevens Co for US Sen Warren G Magnusson, Wash, 64; coordr for US Rep Tom Foley, 64-68; mem platform comt, Wash State Fedn Dem Women, 66; committeewoman, Wash State Dem Comt, 68-; secy, Fifth Cong Dist, 68-72; deleg, Wash State Dem Conv, 68-72; co coordr, Women for Jackson, 70; deleg, Dem Nat Conv, 72; mem, Washington State Dem Resolutions Comt, 75- Bus & Prof Pos: Co-owner, Mitzner Machinery Co, Chewelah, Wash, 57-; realtor, Nine Pine Realty, 72- Mem: Nat Asn Real Estate Bd; Wash State Jaycee Auxiliary; Chewelah Chix's 4-H Club; Busy Bee 4-H Club. Honors & Awards: Nat 4-H Award, Mu Beta Beta, 55. Relig: Lutheran. Mailing Add: Rte 2 Box 105 Cozy Nook Rd Chewelah WA 99109

MIX, SHIRLEY V (R)
b Des Moines, Iowa, Nov 27, 34; d Lauren Smith & Evelyn Jordan S; m 1967 to Gale L Mix, II; c Sheri Lynn, Tracy Kay & Michelle Renee Van Buskirk. Educ: Boise Jr Col, 53-54; San Jose State Col, 54-55; Univ Idaho, currently; Delta Zeta. Polit & Govt Pos: Publ chmn, Ada Co Young Rep, 60's; nat committeewoman, Idaho Young Rep, 64-65; publ chmn, Latah Co Rep Cent Comt, 71-; pres, Latah Co Rep Women, 73-75. Bus & Prof Pos: Advert dir, Mercantile Stores, Inc, Boise, 62-65; staff writer & ed, Idaho Statesman Newspapers, Boise, 65-67; ed & pub rels dir, Hawaii Employers' Coun, Honolulu, 68-69; free lance writer, Lewiston Tribune & Idaho Statesman, 70-; partner, Western Home Ctr, Moscow, 73-; owner-mgr, Ad 1, Advert & Pub Rels, 74- Mem: Idaho Press Women; Nat Fedn Press Women; Toastmasters Int; Idaho Fedn Rep Women; Asn Hosp Pub Rels. Honors & Awards: Nat Fedn Press Women numerous state firsts from 65-; state first, Idaho Press Club, News Story, 66; nat second for feature writing, Nat Fedn Press Women, 74. Legal Res: 714 Indian Hills Dr Moscow ID 83843 Mailing Add: PO Box 8553 Moscow ID 83843

MIXSON, WAYNE (D)
Fla State Rep
Mailing Add: Caverns Park Rd Marianna FL 32446

MIYAKE, WILL EDWARD (R)
b Waimea, Hawaii, Dec 30, 45; s Noboru Miyake & Yone Kagawa M; m 1971 to Eleanor Fumi Nakaya; c Troy Kenji. Educ: Univ Hawaii, 66-69. Polit & Govt Pos: Deleg, Rep Nat Conv, 72; precinct pres, Kauai Co Rep Party, Hawaii, 72-; mem, Kauai Co Liquor Comn, 73- Bus & Prof Pos: Gen mgr, Waimea Garage Ltd, Kauai, Hawaii, 72- Mil Serv: Entered Army, 63, serv in Signal Corps & Vietnam, 63-66; Vietnam Serv Medal. Mem: West Kauai Bus & Prof Men's Asn (secy, 72-); West Kauai Jaycees (second vpres, 72-). Mailing Add: PO Box 433 Waimea HI 96796

MIZE, CHESTER L (R)
b Atchison, Kans, Dec 25, 17; m to Betty Muchnic; c David, Ann & Janet. Educ: Sch Bus Admin, Univ Kans, 35-39; Phi Delta Theta. Polit & Govt Pos: Mem, Atchison Pub Sch Syst Bd, Kans, formerly; mem bd trustees, Mt St Scholastica of Atchison; mem athletic bd, Univ NMex & farm, Atchison Co, Kans, formerly; US Rep, Kans, 65-70; chmn, US Tariff Comn, 71. Bus & Prof Pos: Treas, Blish, Mize & Silliman Hardware Do, 45-51; owner & operator cattle ranch, NMex & farm, Atchison Co, Kans, formerly; vpres, Valley Co, Inc, Gen Investment Co, 51-64. Mil Serv: Naval Res, 40; Navy, 41-45, SPac Theater; Lt Comdr, Naval Res. Mem: Am Legion; VFW; Kans Farm Bur; Elks; Kans CofC. Relig: Episcopal; vestryman, Trinity Episcopal Church. Legal Res: Atchison KS 66002 Mailing Add: 5416 Falmouth Rd Spring Hill Washington DC 20016

MIZE, DWIGHT WORKMAN (D)
Mem, Calif Dem State Cent Comt
b Tulsa, Okla, Apr 22, 29; s Dwight W Mize, Sr & Elnora Wyrick M; m 1950 to Joanne Lindamood; c Dwight Anthony, Michelle & Gregory Warren. Educ: St Peters High Sch, Joplin, Mo, dipl, 48. Polit & Govt Pos: Mem, Calif Dem State Cent Comt, 68-; mem, Small Bus Admin Adv Coun, 69-71; Dem nominee, 34th Senate Dist, 70; mem, Orange Co Dem Cent Comt, Calif, 71- Mem: Home Builder Asn Riverside & San Bernardino Counties; Nat Asn Home Builders. Relig: Catholic. Mailing Add: 2680 Garretson Ave Corona CA 91720

MIZE, MIKE (R)
Kans State Rep
Mailing Add: 712 N Springfield Anthony KS 67002

MIZELL, WILMER DAVID (VINEGAR BEND) (R)
Asst Secy Econ Develop, Dept Com
b Vinegar Bend, Ala, Aug 13, 31; s Walter David Mizell & Addie Turner M; m 1952 to Nancy Ruth McAlpine; c Wilmer David, Jr & James Daniel. Educ: Leakesville High Sch, Miss. Polit & Govt Pos: Chmn, Davidson Co Comn, NC, 66; US Rep, NC, 69-75; mem, Nat Adv Coun TAR; asst secy econ develop, Dept Com, 75- Bus & Prof Pos: Baseball pitcher, St Louis Cardinals, Pittsburgh Pirates & New York Mets, formerly; mem staff sales mgt & pub rels, Pepsi-Cola Co, NC, formerly. Mil Serv: Entered as Pvt, Army, 53, released 55, after serv in Hq Unit, Detachment 1, 3442 Area Serv Unit, Ft McPherson, Ga, 53-55. Mem: Am Legion. Honors & Awards: Athlete of the Year, Southern Baptist Sports Asn, 51; named to Nat League All-Star Baseball Team, 59; Distinguished Citizen's Award, George Washington Univ, 69; Watchdog of the Treas Awards, 91st, 92nd & 93rd Cong. Relig: Christian & Missionary Alliance; elder & lay speaker. Mailing Add: Dept of Commerce 14th & Constitution Ave NW Washington DC 20230

MIZUGUCHI, NORMAN (D)
Hawaii State Rep
Mailing Add: House Sgt-at-arms State Capitol Honolulu HI 96813

MOAKLEY, JOHN JOSEPH (D)
US Rep, Mass
b Boston, Mass, Apr 27, 27; s Joseph A Moakley & Mary Rita Scappini M; m 1957 to Evelyn Duffy. Educ: Univ Miami; Suffolk Univ Law Sch, LLB, 56. Polit & Govt Pos: Mass State Rep, 53-60, Dem Majority Whip, Mass House Rep, 57; Mass State Sen, 65-72; deleg, Dem Nat Conv, 68; mem, Boston City Coun, 71-72; US Rep, Ninth Dist, Mass, 73- Bus & Prof Pos: Attorney, 57-72. Mil Serv: Entered as Seaman 2/C, Navy, 43, released as Seaman 1/C, 46, after serv in Seabees, SPac; Philippine Liberation Medal. Mem: Mass Trial Lawyer's Asn; Am Legion; VFW; DAV; KofC. Relig: Catholic. Legal Res: MA Mailing Add: Rm 238 House Off Bldg Washington DC 20515

MOAN, RAYMOND CHARLES (D)
RI State Rep
b Providence, RI, Aug 23, 42; s Alfred R Moan & Marion Yeaw M; m 1965 to Annette L Peltier; c Jeffrey S. Educ: Bryant Col, 65. Polit & Govt Pos: Mem planning bd, Coventry, RI, 70-74, mem charter comn, 72; RI State Rep, 75- Bus & Prof Pos: Moan Bros Express, 66- Mil Serv: Entered as E-1, Navy, 60, released as PO E-5, 63, after serv in USS Forrestal. Mem: Elks; Lions; Teamsters Union. Relig: Catholic. Mailing Add: Town Farm Rd Coventry RI 02816

MOATS, HARRY E (R)
WVa State Deleg
Mailing Add: State Capitol Charleston WV 25305

MOATTS, MORRIS (R)
Chmn, Chilton Co Rep Exec Comt, Ala
b Clanton, Ala, Dec 21, 30; s Rudolph Moatts & Annie Bell Teel M; single. Educ: Athens Col, 56-57. Polit & Govt Pos: Circuit clerk, Chilton Co, Ala, 65-; chmn, Chilton Co Rep Exec Comt, 70-; mem, Ala State Rep Exec Comt, 71- Bus & Prof Pos: Mgr meat dept, A&P Tea Co, 49-58; owner, Pinedale Gardens Florist, 58- Mil Serv: Entered as Cpl, Army, 51, released as Sgt, 52, after serv in 933rd Field Artil, 31st Inf Div. Mem: Ala Asn Circuit Court Clerks & Registr; Ala Florist Asn; Chilton Co CofC; Am Legion. Honors & Awards: Young Man of Year, Jaycees, 59. Legal Res: Pinedale Rd Clanton AL 35405 Mailing Add: PO Box 741 Clanton AL 35405

MOBERLY, ISABEL CAROL (R)
Rep Nat Committeewoman, Mont
b Alliance, Alta, Sept 12, 09; d Carl J Quisberg & Elizabeth Hogan Q; m 1926 to Waldo Young Moberly. Polit & Govt Pos: Pres, Toole Co Rep Women's Club, Mont, 58-60; vpres, Mont Fedn Rep Women, formerly; vchmn, Mont Rep State Cent Comt, 64-; Rep Nat Committeewoman, Mont, 64-, mem exec comt, Rep Nat Comt, 64-68, vchmn, 72- Bus & Prof Pos: Vpres, W Y Moberly Inc, US Customhouse Broker, Sweetgrass, Mont, 55-68. Mem: Am Legion Auxiliary; Mont Girls State; Daughters of Nile; Eastern Star. Honors & Awards: Woman of the Year, Mont Fedn Bus & Prof Women's Clubs, 68. Relig: Methodist. Mailing Add: 485 Judy Ave Shelby MT 59474

MOBERLY, JANIE FERN (D)
Chmn, Curry Co Dem Cent Comt, NMex
b Melrose, NMex, Nov 8, 33; d Johnny Lloyd Elliott & Thelma Estell Gibbs E; m 1952 to Jacob Haskell Moberly; c Terry Lee, Tonya Jane, Kyle Haskell & Deirdre Estell. Educ: Eastern NMex Univ, AA, 55; Sigma Beta Chi. Polit & Govt Pos: Chmn precinct 34, Curry Co Dem Cent Comt, NMex, 63-71, chmn, 69-; co-chmn, Campaign for Congressman E S (Johnny) Walker, Curry Co, 64; deleg, NMex State Dem Conv, 66-70; mem, NMex Dem State Cent Comt, 69-71, dep registr, officer, Curry Co Bd Registr, 70- Bus & Prof Pos: Secy to agr instr, Eastern NMex Univ, 52-53; secy to mgr, Roosevelt Co Elec, Portales, 53-55; typist, Skelly Oil Co, Kansas City, Mo, 55-57, tank car recorder, 57-59. Mem: Curry Co Dem Women; Curry Co Young Dem; PEO; Beta Sigma Phi. Honors & Awards: Outstanding Girl of the Year, Xi Alpha Sigma chap, Beta Sigma Phi, 67; One of Am Outstanding Young Women, 67. Relig: Methodist; mem, Women Soc Christian Serv, Kingswood United Methodist Church. Mailing Add: 200 Murray Dr Clovis NM 88101

MOBERLY, STEPHEN C (R)
Ind State Rep
Mailing Add: 32 W Broadway Box 199 Shelbyville IN 46176

MOBLEY, CARLTON
Chief Justice, Ga Supreme Court
b Hillsboro, Ga, Dec 7, 06; s Jesse Aldine Mobley & Lillie Pearl Jackson M; m 1934 to Margaret Elrod; c Margaret Elrod. Educ: Mercer Univ, BA, LLB cum laude, 28; Sigma Pi; Delta Theta Phi. Polit & Govt Pos: US Rep, Ga, 32-34; secy, Exec Dept, 34-37; asst attorney gen, 41-42; presiding justice, Ga Supreme Court, 54-72, chief justice, 72- Bus & Prof Pos: Attorney-at-law, 37-41 & 46-54. Mil Serv: Lt Comdr, Naval Res, 43-46. Mem: Am, Ga & Macon Bar Asns; Kiwanis. Relig: Baptist. Mailing Add: 3163 Hakersham Rd NW Atlanta GA 30305

MOBLEY, ERNEST NELSON (R)
Calif State Assemblyman
b Shadyside, Ohio, Nov 1, 18; s B G Mobley & Ethel G Gatten M; m 1946 to Lillian Van Zant; c Jill. Educ: Ohio Univ, BS, 43; Tau Kappa Epsilon. Polit & Govt Pos: Co admin officer, Fresno Co, Calif, 56-62; city mgr, Santa Monica, 62-64; Calif State Assemblyman, 31st Dist, 67-; alt deleg, Rep Nat Conv, 72. Mil Serv: Entered as Pvt, Army, 43, released as Capt, 46, after serv in 6th Armored Div, 44th AIB, Europe, 44-46; Col, Calif Nat Guard, currently; Silver Star; Bronze Star with 2 Oak Leaf Clusters; Combat Inf Badge; 5 Battle Stars; Purple Heart. Mem: Farm Bur; Shrine; Scottish Rite; F&AM; Am Legion. Relig: Protestant. Legal Res: 907 N Oliver Sanger CA 93657 Mailing Add: 600 W Shaw Suite 210 Fresno CA 93704

MOBLEY, TOM (D)
Ky State Sen
Mailing Add: 302-2 Rockcliff Court Louisville KY 40218

MOCKLER, JAMES DAVID (R)
Wyo State Rep
b Lander, Wyo, Mar 9, 39; s Frank C Mockler & Esther Heyne M; m 1962 to Colleen Williams Mockler; c Richard W & Lana. Educ: Univ Wyo, BS, 61; Sigma Alpha Epsilon. Polit & Govt Pos: Wyo State Rep, Big Horn Co, 73-, chmn joint revenue comt, Joint House-Senate Revenue Comt, 75- Bus & Prof Pos: Co-owner, Mockler Ranch Co, Dubois, Wyo, 61-67; owner, Mockler Farms, Basin, 67-72, Mockler Land & Realty, Greybull, 71- Mem: Rotary Int; Elks; Boy Scouts Am (adv coun); Wyo Rep Party; Big Horn Co Search & Rescue. Relig: Catholic. Legal Res: 616 West A St Basin WY 82410 Mailing Add: PO Box 192 Greybull WY 82426

MOCULESKI, CHESTER FRANCIS (D)
b Chicago, Ill, June 9, 16; s Alexander Moculeski & Angeline Tabak M; m 1949 to Eleanor M Lewandowski; c Karen. Educ: Univ Chicago, BS, 39. Polit & Govt Pos: Dem precinct committeeman, Downers Grove Twp, DuPage Co, Ill, 60-; deleg, Dem Nat Conv, 68; vchmn, Downers Grove Twp Regular Dem Orgn, Ill, 70- Bus & Prof Pos: Chemist, Deavitt Labs, Chicago, 39-41; group leader, US Gypsum Research Lab, 41-43; tech rep, Rohm & Haas Co, Philadelphia, Pa, 43-49, Glyco Chem Co, Chicago, 49-57; sales mgr, Wallace Erickson Co, 57-59, Clintwood Chem Co, 59-62, vpres, 62-68, pres, 68- Mem: Am Chem Soc; Soc Cosmetic Chemists. Relig: Roman Catholic. Mailing Add: 325 W Ninth St Hinsdale IL 60521

MOE, DONALD M (DFL)
Minn State Rep
Mailing Add: 417 Grand Ave St Paul MN 55102

MOE, RICHARD (DFL)
b Duluth, Minn, Nov 27, 36; s Dr Russell James Moe (deceased) & Virginia Palmer M; m 1964 to Julia Neimeyer; c Eric Palmer, Andrew Neimeyer & Alexandra Julia. Educ: Williams Col, BA, 59; Univ Minn Sch Law, LLB, 66; Theta Delta Chi. Polit & Govt Pos: Admin asst to Mayor, Minneapolis, 61-62; admin asst to Lt Gov, 62-66; finance dir, Minn Dem-Farmer-Labor State Cent Comt, 67-69, chmn, 69-72; deleg, Dem Nat Conv, 72; admin asst to US Sen Walter F Mondale, Minn, 72- Mil Serv: Entered as Pvt, Minn Army Nat Guard, 60, released as SP-5, 66, after serv in artil. Mem: Minn Bar Asn; Asn Dem State Chmn (vpres); NAACP. Mailing Add: 443 Old Senate Off Bldg Washington DC 20510

MOE, ROGER DEANE (DFL)
Minn State Sen
b Crookston, Minn, June 2, 44; s Melvin Truman Moe & Matheldia Njus M; m 1964 to Nancy Lee Westgaard; c Dean Karl & Amy Lee. Educ: Mayville State Col, BS in Educ, 66; Moorhead State Col, summer 69; NDak State Univ, summer 70. Polit & Govt Pos: Ward deleg, Ada, Minn, 70; state deleg, Minn Dem-Farmer-Labor Party Conv, 70; Minn State Sen, 71- Bus & Prof Pos: Teacher, Ada High Sch, Minn, 66- Mem: Minn, Nat & Ada Educ Asns; Jaycees. Relig: Lutheran. Mailing Add: 706 E Third Ave Ada MN 56510

MOEHLMANN, NICHOLAS BRUCE (R)
Pa State Rep
b Reading, Pa, July 26, 38; s Ernst Otto Moehlmann & Helen Dietz M (deceased); m 1972 to Penelope Leighton Lowman; c David B. Educ: Yale Univ, BA, 60; Dickinson Sch Law, JD, 70. Polit & Govt Pos: Chmn, Lebanon Co Young Rep, Pa, 71-72; asst gen coun, Young Rep Pa, 72; Pa State Rep, 102nd Dist, 74- Bus & Prof Pos: Attorney-at-law, Lewis, Brubaker, Whitman & Christianson, Lebanon, Pa, 70- Mil Serv: Entered as E-1, Army, 61, released as E-5, 63, after serv in 513 Intel Corps Group, ETO. Mem: Am Legion; Lions Int; Pa Bar Asn; Richland Jaycees. Relig: Protestant. Legal Res: 1832 S Fifth Ave St Richland PA 17042 Mailing Add: 16 E Main St Richland PA 17087

MOELLER, JEANETTE (R)
VChmn, St Joseph Co Rep Party, Ind
b Milwaukee, Wis, Nov 6, 26; m 1949 to Lee Moeller; wid; c John & Wendy. Educ: Lawrence Univ, BS, 49; Ind Univ, MS, 74; Alpha Delta Pi; Delta Kappa Gamma. Polit & Govt Pos: Precinct committeewoman, Ind Rep Party; vchmn, St Joseph Co Rep Party, 72- Bus & Prof Pos: Teacher, J J O'Brien Sch, South Bend Sch Corp, 54-; mem, State Educ Comn, 73-, Teachers Credit Union Bd Dir, 74- & Bethany Lutheran Church Coun, 74- Mem: Civic Planning Asn; Am Asn Univ Women; Mayors Task Force on Educ; Nat Educ Asn; Int Sightseeing & Tours Asn. Relig: Lutheran. Mailing Add: 1164 E Victoria South Bend IN 46614

MOERSCHEL, W NEAL (R)
b Baltimore, Md, Dec 24, 30; s William George Moerschel & Emma Hevern M; m 1953 to Thelma Wright; c Susan, Leslie & Grant. Educ: Towson State Col, BS, 52; Johns Hopkins Univ, BS, 59; Delta Sigma Pi. Polit & Govt Pos: Councilman, Borough of Stratford, NJ, 62-63; nat committeeman, Del Fedn Young Rep, 67-68; Del State Rep, 31st Rep Dist, 68-73; admin asst, US Sen Roth, Del, 73- Bus & Prof Pos: Methods programmer, B&O RR, Baltimore, Md, 57-59; syst analyst, Honeywell Electronic Data Processing Div, Philadelphia, Pa, 59-65; mgr data processing, Speakman Co, Wilmington, Del, 65- Mil Serv: Entered as Seaman, Navy, 52, released as Lt(jg), 56, after serv in Patrol Squadron 24, Fleet Airborne Electronic Training Unit, Atlantic Fleet & Comdr Air Force, Atlantic Fleet. Mem: Nat Asn Accts. Relig: Lutheran. Mailing Add: 504 Old Orchard Circle Millersville MD 21108

MOFENSON, DAVID JOEL (D)
Mass State Rep
b Neptune, NJ, Feb 7, 43; s Jack Mofenson & Ruth Brown M; m 1972 to Caryn Goldberg. Educ: Tufts Univ, AB cum laude, 64; Boston Univ, JD, 67. Polit & Govt Pos: Mass State Rep, Newton, 71-; chmn, Newton Dem City Comt, Mass, 72- Relig: Jewish. Mailing Add: 6 Alban Rd Newton MA 02168

MOFFETT, ANTHONY (TOBY) (D)
US Rep, Conn
b Holyoke, Mass, Aug 18, 44; c Julia. Educ: Syracuse Univ, AB, 66; Boston Col, MA, 68. Polit & Govt Pos: Dir, Off Student & Youth, until 70; with Off US Comnr Educ, 69-70; staff asst to US Sen Walter Mondale, Minn, 70-71; dir, Conn Citizen Action Group, 71-74; US Rep, Conn, 75- Legal Res: RD 2 Unionville CT 06032 Mailing Add: US House Rep Washington DC 20515

MOFFETT, HUGH OLIVER (D)
Vt State Rep
b Cherryvale, Kans, Aug 17, 10; s Adam Moffett & Laura Wilkin M; m 1951 to Bette Little; c Molly (Mrs Frederick), Thomas & Mark. Educ: Univ Mo, BJ, 33. Hon Degrees: LLD, Monmouth Col, 59. Polit & Govt Pos: Vt State Rep, 75- Bus & Prof Pos: State ed, Des Moines Tribune, 33-44; war correspondent, Korea, Time Mag, 50-51; asst managing ed, Life Mag, 58-67. Publ: Moffett's travel in Soviet Union, 9/13/63 & Dr Schweitzer at 90, 67, Life Mag. Mem: Overseas Press Club. Mailing Add: 69 Park St Brandon VT 05733

MOFFITT, H LEE (D)
Fla State Rep
b Tampa, Fla, Nov 10, 41; s Benjamen Bascum Moffitt & Clara Stewart M; m 1971 to Karen Arlene Mathis. Educ: Univ SFla, BA, 64; Cumberland Law Sch, JD, 67; Phi Alpha Delta; Alpha Tau Omega. Polit & Govt Pos: Mem, Tampa Study Comn, Fla, 71-72; dir, Hillsborough Co Law Libr Bd, 73-74; Fla State Rep, 74- Bus & Prof Pos: Attorney, Straske & Moffitt, Tampa, 68- Mem: Hillsborough Co Bar Asn; Big Bros Tampa (dir, 72-); Fla Acad Trial Lawyers; Fla Bar Asn; Univ SFla Nat Alumni Asn (bd dirs, 75). Honors & Awards: Freedoms Found at Valley Forge Medal, 74. Relig: Methodist. Legal Res: 403 Barbara Lane Tampa FL 33609 Mailing Add: 1005 Exchange Nat Bank Bldg Tampa FL 33602

MOHN, LEO O (D)
Wis State Rep
Mailing Add: Woodville WI 54028

MOHR, HOWARD R (R)
Ill State Sen
Mailing Add: 1103 Troost Ave Forest Park IL 60130

MOILAN, WANDA DEVON (D)
b Huron, SDak, Apr 7, 34; d Frank J Jansen & Eva M Bootz J; m to Marvin W Moilan; c David, Eva & Jewel Beyer & Mark Moilan. Educ: High sch, Huron, SDak, grad, 53; Northwest Col Com, Huron, grad, 55. Polit & Govt Pos: Clerk, Off Beadle Co Treas, SDak, 55-59, dep co treas, 60-61; secy, Beadle Co Dem Cent Comt, 62-64 & 68-72, treas, 66-68, vchairwoman, formerly; dep registr deeds, Beadle Co, 65-71; admin asst, SDak State Fair, 71- Bus & Prof Pos: Head bookkeeper, Elks 444, Huron, 63-64. Mem: Beadle Co Dem Women; SDak State Employees Orgn; Am Cancer Soc (crusade chmn, standing comt, Beadle Unit, 70-); Am Legion Auxiliary; Am Lutheran Church Women. Honors & Awards: Ten Year Serv Award, Am Cancer Soc, Beadle Unit, 72. Relig: Lutheran. Mailing Add: 745 12th St SW Huron SD 57350

MOLER, JAMES M (D)
WVa State Deleg
Mailing Add: State Capitol Charleston WV 25305

MOLINA, MATILDA (D)
Mem, Dem Nat Comt, Hawaii
Mailing Add: Apt 205 430 N King St Honolulu HI 96817

MOLINARI, GUY VICTOR (R)
NY State Assemblyman
b New York, NY, Nov 23, 28; s S Robert Molinari & Elizabeth Majoros M; m 1956 to Marguerite Wing; c Susan. Educ: Wagner Col, BA, 49; New York Law Sch, LLB, 51; Phi Delta Phi; Kappa Sigma Alpha. Polit & Govt Pos: NY State Assemblyman, 60th Assembly Dist, 75- Bus & Prof Pos: Attorney, Staten Island, 53- Mil Serv: Entered as Pvt, Marine Corps, 52, released as Sgt, 53, after serv in 1st Marine Div, Korea, 52-53. Mem: Richmond Co Bar Asn; VFW; Sons of Italy (Giuseppe Lodge); Havol Mens Social Club. Relig: Catholic. Legal Res: 21 Merrick Ave Staten Island NY 10301 Mailing Add: 88 New Dorp Plaza Staten Island NY 10306

MOLINARO, CARMINE V, JR (D)
Comnr, Fayette Co, Pa
b Connellsville, Pa, Oct 26, 41; s Carmine V Molinaro, Sr & Anna K Matuschak M; single. Educ: St Vincent Col, BA magna cum laude, 63; Univ Pittsburgh Sch Law, JD, 66. Polit & Govt Pos: Mem, Fayette Co Planning Comn, Pa, 68-71; solicitor & treas, Fayette Co Dem Cent Comt, 68-72; chmn, Connellsville City Planning Comn, 70-; mem, Connellsville Area Regional Planning Comn, 70-; dir, Gtr Connellsville CofC, 70-; Fayette Co Comnr, 72- Bus & Prof Pos: Attorney-at-law, Molinaro, McCue & Wagner, Connellsville, Pa, 68- Mem: Pa Bar Asn; Delta Epsilon Sigma; Fayette Co Develop Coun; Am Fedn Musicians; KofC. Relig: Catholic. Mailing Add: Arch & Peach St Connellsville PA 15425

MOLINARO, GEORGE (D)
Wis State Rep
b Kenosha, Wis, Oct 1, 02. Educ: Bus Col. Polit & Govt Pos: Mem, Co Bd, Wis, 39-47; Wis State Rep, 46- Bus & Prof Pos: Automobile worker; bank pres. Mailing Add: 424 44th St Kenosha WI 53140

MOLINAROLI, LUCILE C (R)
Vt State Rep
Mailing Add: 46 Webster St Barre VT 05641

MOLL, OTTO RUDOLPH (R)
b Altamont, Ill, June 15, 99; s Rudolph Moll & Elizabeth Yagow M; m 1929 to Rachel E Hartmeister; c Judith (Mrs John Benwell) & David Eugene (deceased). Educ: McKendree Col, 1 year. Polit & Govt Pos: City treas, Altamont, Ill, 30-67; vchmn & chmn, Effingham Co Sch Survey Comt, 46-50; mem, Effingham Co Bd Sch Trustees, 50-; committeeman, Ill Rep State Cent Comt, 66-74. Bus & Prof Pos: Registered pharmacist, 23-; pharmacist & mgr drug store, 14-31. Mil Serv: Pvt, McKendree Students Army Training Corps Unit, 18. Mem: Am Legion; Lions Int; Int Lutheran Laymens League; Int Lutheran Hour. Relig: Lutheran. Mailing Add: Box 212 Altamont IL 62411

MOLLENKOPF, JANET ARLENE (R)
Mem, Columbiana Co Rep Cent Comt, Ohio
b Salem, Ohio, May 24, 31; d Walter O Cope & Velma Rudibaugh C; m 1951 to Paul Kenneth Mollenkopf; c Richard Lee & Sheryl Lynn. Educ: David Anderson High Sch, Lisbon, Ohio, grad, 49. Polit & Govt Pos: Secy, Columbiana Womens Rep Club, Ohio, 60-61; secy, Mid-Co Rep Club, 65-66; secy-treas, Columbiana Co Young Rep Club, 67-68; chmn, Columbiana Co Rep Party, 68-; asst clerk, Columbiana Co Bd Elec, 69-; mem, Columbiana Co Rep Exec Comt, 68-; Rep precinct committeewoman, Ctr Twp Northeast, 70-; mem, Columbiana Co Rep Cent Comt, 70- Bus & Prof Pos: Asst to secy, Columbiana Co Agr Soc, 63- Mem: Eastern Star; Mid-Co Rep Club; Columbiana Co Agr Soc. Relig: Methodist. Mailing Add: RD 5 39924 SR 517 Lisbon OH 44432

MOLLET, PEGGY EARLEEN (D)
b Fonda, Iowa, Mar 8, 30; d Earl Hucka & Leta Orwig H; m 1949 to Carl Norman Mollet; c Randall James, Douglas Carl, Kendell Lee, Marcia Jane, Cynthia Kay, Bradley David & Carleen Ann. Educ: Sch Cosmetology, Sioux City, Iowa, License. Polit & Govt Pos: Alt deleg, Dem Nat Conv, 72. Mem: Farmers Union; VFW Auxiliary; St Mary's Altar Soc. Mailing Add: RR 1 Burbank SD 57010

MOLLOHAN, ROBERT H (D)
US Rep, WVa
b Grantsville, WVa, Sept 18, 09; s Robert P Mollohan & Edith Witt M; m to Helen M Holt; c Robert H, Alan B & Kathryn M (Mrs Moats). Educ: Glenville Col; Shepherd Col. Polit & Govt Pos: Former chief miscellaneous tax div & cashier, US Internal Revenue Bur, WVa; dist mgr & state personnel dir, Works Projs Admin, formerly; state dir, 1940 Census; supt, WVa Indust Sch for Boys, formerly; US Marshal, Northern Dist, WVa, formerly; clerk, US Senate Comt on DC, formerly; US Rep, WVa, 53-56 & 69-; deleg, Dem Nat Conv, 72. Mem: Elks; Eagles; Moose. Relig: Baptist. Legal Res: Fairmont WV Mailing Add: 339 Cannon Off Bldg Washington DC 20515

MOLLOY, CLAUDE A (D)
Sen, VI Legis
Mailing Add: PO Box J Christiansted St Croix VI 00820

MOLLOY, JAMES HAGGIN (MIKE) (D)
Exec Dir, Fayette Co Dem Party, Ky
b Lexington, Ky, Aug 18, 33; s James Mulligan Molloy & Betty Haggin M; m 1957 to Forest Jean Sevy; c Forest Michael, James Huston & Patricia Anne. Educ: Transylvania Univ, BA, 57; Univ Louisville Sch Med, 58-61; Student Coun (vpres); Transylvania Day Chmn. Polit & Govt Pos: Exec dir, Fayette Co Dem Party, Ky, 70-; mem, Ky Dem State Cent Exec Comt, 70-; deleg, Dem Nat Mid-Term Conf, 74; state finance chmn, Wendell Ford for Senate Comt, 74-75. Bus & Prof Pos: Owner, Mt Brilliant Farm, 40-; pres, Lexington Welding Supply, 65- & 259 Corp, 66- Mil Serv: Entered as E-1, Army, 58, released as E-1, 59; Maj, Army Res, 58-; Honor grad, US Army Command & Gen Staff Sch, 72. Mem: Fraternal Order of Police; ROA; St Joseph Hosp (bd trustees); Lexington-Fayette Co Urban League (dir); Ky State Horse Park (adv comt). Honors & Awards: Banahan Award, Fayette Dem Exec Comt, 73. Legal Res: Mt Brilliant Farm Russell Cave Rd Lexington KY 40505 Mailing Add: PO Box 59 Lexington KY 40501

MOLLOY, VINCENT E (R)
Ill State Sen
Mailing Add: 733 S Cuyler Ave Oak Park IL 60304

MOLONEY, MICHAEL R (D)
Ky State Sen
Mailing Add: 605 Bank of Commerce Bldg Lexington KY 40507

MOLONY, JOSEPH P (D)
Mem-At-Lg, Dem Nat Comt
Mailing Add: 700 Pinetree Rd Pittsburgh PA 15243

MOLPUS, JAMES ERNEST (D)
Miss State Sen
b Philadelphia, Miss, Jan 24, 28; s Charles Miller Molpus & Mary Smith M; m 1951 to Clarkie Jean Stokes; c Wanda Kay, John, Fred & Robert. Educ: EMiss Jr Col, 2 years; Miss State Univ, MS; NC State Col, 1 year. Polit & Govt Pos: Miss State Sen, 68- Bus & Prof Pos: Owner, Molpus Entomological Serv, 55- Mil Serv: Entered as Pvt, Army, 46, released as Cpl, 48, reentered 51, released as M/Sgt, 52, after serv in 351st Inf Regt, Mediter Theatre, 46-48 & 932nd FA Bn, Continental Command, 51-53. Mem: Entomological Soc Am; Am Registry Cert Entomologists; Miss Agr Consults Asn; Rotary; Delta Coun. Honors & Awards: State Alumni of Year, 4-H Club. Relig: Baptist. Legal Res: 1402 May Clarksdale MS 38614 Mailing Add: Box 176 Clarksdale MS 38614

MONAGAN, JOHN STEPHEN (D)
b Waterbury, Conn, Dec 23, 11; s Charles A Monagan & Margaret Mulry M; m 1949 to Rosemary Anne Brady; c Charles A, Michael, Parthenia, Laura & Susan. Educ: Dartmouth Col, AB, 33; Harvard Law Sch, LLB, 37; Alpha Delta Phi; Sphinx. Polit & Govt Pos: Pres bd alderman, Waterbury, Conn, 40-42, mayor, 43-48; US Rep, Fifth Dist, Conn, 59-72; Cong deleg to European Conf NATO Parliamentarians, 60; mem coun Inter-Parliamentary Union, 65-69; deleg, Dem Nat Conv, 68. Bus & Prof Pos: Dir, Waterbury Savings Bank, 58- Mem: Fed Bar; US Supreme Court Bar; YMCA; Elks; Eagles. Relig: Roman Catholic. Mailing Add: 120 Hillside Ave Waterbury CT 06710

MONAGHAN, DIANA M (D)
b New York, NY, Sept 29, 37; d Edward N Myles & Margaret Craver M; div; c Patrick P, Jr & Matthew E. Educ: Woodrow Wilson High Sch, Washington, DC, grad, 56. Polit & Govt Pos: Precinct committeewoman, Hillsborough Co Exec Comt, Fla, 66-69 & Orange Co Exec Comt, 69-; exec vpres, Fla Young Dem, 69-71; spec asst to pres, Nat Young Dem Am, 70-71; state conv chairperson, Dem Women's Club Fla, 73, chairperson publicity comt, 73-74; deleg, Dem Nat Mid-Term Conf, 74. Bus & Prof Pos: Pres, PR Inc, currently; instr pub rels, Valencia Community Col, 75- Mem: Orlando Area Advert Fedn (bd dirs, 71-75); Fla Pub Rels Asn; Gtr Orlando Press Club; Dem Women's Clubs, Winter Park & Orlando. Honors & Awards: Outstanding Young Dem of Fla, Young Dem Fla, 69-70; Outstanding Achievement in Flame of Hope, Joseph P Kennedy, Jr Found, 70; Hon Texan, Gov Preston Smith, 70; Outstanding Serv, as bd of dirs, Orlando Area Advert Fedn, 72-73; Addy Award, First Place Complete Coordinated Campaign/Local, Orlando Area Advert Fedn, 74. Relig: Catholic. Mailing Add: 345 Merrie Oaks Rd Winter Park FL 32789

MONAGHAN, ROBERT LEE (R)
Chmn, Midland Co Rep Party, Tex
b Ft Worth, Tex, Sept 16, 23; s Johnnie Edgar Monaghan & Ruby Ferguson M; m 1964 to Virginia Phipps; c Cullen S, Patrick Kevin & Robert L, Jr. Educ: Univ Tex, Austin, BS in Petroleum Eng & JD; Alpha Tau Omega. Polit & Govt Pos: Pres, Midland Co Rep Men's Club, Tex, 69-70; chmn, Midland Co Rep Party, 70-; deleg, Rep Nat Conv, 72; mem, Tex Criminal Justice Coun, Midland Co, 72- Bus & Prof Pos: Landman, Standard Oil Co Tex, 51-53; gen mgr, Tex Crude Oil Co, 53-54; partner, C-M Oil Co, 54-56, pres, Cal-Mon Oil Co, 56- Mil Serv: Entered as Cadet, Air Force, 43, released as 2nd Lt, 45, after serv in 1st Air Force. Mem: Am Asn Petroleum Landmen; WTex Geol Soc; Soc Petroleum Engrs; Permian Basin Landman's Asn; Phi Delta Phi. Relig: Episcopal; past secy & mem vestry, Trinity Episcopal Church. Legal Res: 2007 Country Club Dr Midland TX 79701 Mailing Add: PO Box 2066 Midland TX 79701

MONAHAN, JOHN LEO (D)
b Newton, Mass, Mar 8, 33; s Francis Joseph Monahan & Mary F Quilty M; m 1963 to Annie Jean Franklin; c John Leo, Jr, Molly Lee, Kelly Jean & Joseph Franklin. Educ: Boston Col, BA, 59. Polit & Govt Pos: Secy to Majority Leader, US House Rep, 60-62, legis asst to Speaker John McCormack, 62-70, legis analyst, US House Rep, 71-72, legis asst, Majority Whip John J McFall, 73- Mil Serv: Entered as Pvt, Army, 55, released as Sgt, 57, after serv in 2nd Armored Div, Europe, 55-57. Relig: Roman Catholic. Mailing Add: 1 Infield Ct S Rockville MD 20854

MONAHAN, MAURICE BRICE (R)
Chmn, Millbury Rep Town Comt, Mass
b Montreal, Que, May 21, 26; s Maurice Brice Monahan & Muriel Ethel Taylor M; m 1948 to Dorothy Evelyn Gittus; c Brian Edward. Educ: Sir George Williams Univ, 2 years. Polit & Govt Pos: Mem, Millbury Rep Town Comt, Mass, 63-, chmn, 66-; mem & asst treas, Millbury Housing Authority, 67- Bus & Prof Pos: Sales & advert mgr, Hunter Douglas Ltd, Montreal, 53-; claim rep, Paul Revere Life Ins Co, Worcester, Mass, 57- Mil Serv: Pvt, Army Air Corps, 43-45, serv in USAAFTTC, US. Mem: AF&AM. Relig: Protestant. Mailing Add: 44 W Main St Millbury MA 01527

MONAT, RONALD S (D)
Chmn, Rock Co Dem Party Wis
b Janesville, Wis, Jan 19, 47; s Gordon C Monat & Helen A Hathorn; m 1969 to Margaret R Healy; c John G & Wendy A. Educ: Craig Sr High Sch, grad, 65; Black Hawk Vo-Tech, 71. Polit & Govt Pos: Chmn, Rock Co Dem Party Wis, 74- Bus & Prof Pos: Employed, Gen Motors Assembly Div, 65-; bargaining rep, UAW Local 95, 69-73, trustee, 73-75, 2nd vpres, 75- Mil Serv: Entered as Pvt, Army, 66, released as Sgt, 68, after serv in 9th Inf Div, Vietnam, 67-68; Nat Defense Serv Medal; Vietnam Serv Medal; Vietnam Campaign Medal; Combat Infantryman Badge; Expert M-14 & M-16; Army Commendation Medal for Meritorious Serv; Army Commendation Medal with V device & first oak leaf cluster for heroism. Mem: VFW, Kienow-Hilt Post No 1621; Janesville, Madison Area Community Action Prog Coun (bd mem, 74-); Janesville Paramedic Steering Comt. Honors & Awards: Proclamation, Janesville, Wis, 75. Mailing Add: 1263 E Milwaukee St Janesville WI 53545

MONCE, RAYMOND EUGENE (D)
Mem, Calif Dem State Cent Comt
b Indianapolis, Ind, Mar 8, 24; s Raymond Charles Monce & Mildred Olvey M; m 1955 to Doris Ruth Anderson; c Mark Douglas, Melissa Rae, Reginald Eugene & Gary Lee. Educ: Butler Univ, 46-48; Ind Univ, 48-50; Calif Western Univ, MSMS, 66; Western State Univ, JD, 75. Polit & Govt Pos: Mem, Wrightwood Sch Bd, Calif, 58; mem, San Diego Co Dem Cent Comt, 66-; mem, Calif Dem State Cent Comt, 68- Bus & Prof Pos: Aerospace eng & mgt, 48-69. Mil Serv: Entered as A/S, Navy, 43, released as Chief Electronic Technician, 46, after serv in USS Earl K Olsen, European & Asiatic-Pac Theatres, 43-46; Area Medals; Japanese Occup Ribbon. Mem: Nat Mgt Asn. Relig: Protestant. Mailing Add: 2035 Helix Spring Valley CA 92077

MONDALE, WALTER FREDERICK (DFL)
US Sen, Minn
b Ceylon, Minn, Jan 5, 28; s Reverend Theodore Sigvaard Mondale & Claribel Cowan M; m 1955 to Joan Adams; c Theodore Adams, Eleanor Jane & William Hall. Educ: Macalester Col, 46-49; Univ Minn, BA, 51, Law Sch, LLB, 56. Polit & Govt Pos: Spec Asst Attorney Gen, Minn, 2 years, Attorney Gen, 60-64; mem, President's Consumer Adv Coun, 62-64; mem credentials comt, Dem Nat Conv, 64, deleg, 68; US Sen, Minn, 64-, mem comt on labor & pub welfare, chmn subcomt children & youth, mem subcomts on health, educ, employ, manpower & poverty, handicapped, alcoholism & narcotics, arts & humanities, Nat Sci Found & RR retirement, mem comt on finance, chmn subcomt on state taxation of interstate com, mem subcomts health & int trade, spec comt on aging, chmn subcomt on retirement & the individual, mem subcomts on consumer interests for the elderly, employ & retirement incomes, health for the elderly & housing for the elderly, mem select comt on nutrition & human needs, US Senate, currently; ex officio, Dem Nat Mid-Term Conf, 74. Bus & Prof Pos: Attorney-at-law, Minneapolis, Minn, 56-60. Mil Serv: Entered as Pvt, Army, 51, released as Cpl, 53. Publ: Minnesota Corrupt Practices Act, Minn Law Rev, 55. Mem: Am Bar Asn; UN Asn of US; Sons of Norway; Eagles; Am Vets Comt, Am Legion. Honors & Awards: Averell Harriman Equal Housing Opportunity Award. Relig: Presbyterian. Mailing Add: 172 Fed Courts Bldg Minneapolis MN 55401

MONDANI, THOMAS P (D)
b Deep River, Conn, Aug 6, 34; s Frank Mondani & Ellen Campbell M; m 1960 to Henrietta Bloch; c Thomas, Jr & James. Educ: Univ Conn, BA, 56; Univ Hartford, MEd, 62. Polit & Govt Pos: Mem, Haddam Dem Town Comt, Conn, 64-74; Conn State Rep, 73rd Dist, 67-71; Conn State Sen, 71-73. Bus & Prof Pos: Salesman, Napier Co, 58-59; teacher, Moodus Schs, 59-63; dir of research, Conn Educ Asn, 63-71, exec secy, 71- Mil Serv: Entered as Pvt, Army, 56, released as Specialist 4, 58. Publ: The manual for teacher negotiators, Educators' Press, 66. Mem: Conn Educ Asn; Nat Educ Asn (life mem). Relig: Roman Catholic. Mailing Add: Timms Hill Rd Haddam CT 06438

MONDRAGON, ROBERT A (D)
Lt Gov, NMex
b La Loma, NMex, July 27, 40; s Severo Mondragon & Lucia Aragon M; m 1968 to Bell Urrea; c Julian Jaramillo, Geraldine Jaramillo & Robert Anthony. Educ: Albuquerque High Sch, grad, 58. Polit & Govt Pos: NMex State Rep, Bernalillo Co, 67-70; Lt Gov, NMex, 71-; deleg, Dem Nat Conv, 72. Mem: Albuquerque Goals Prog (exec comt); CofC; Lions; Am GI Forum; Fraternal Order of Police Assocs. Relig: Catholic. Mailing Add: Box 139-A Rte 1 Santa Fe NM 87501

MONDRES, MARVIN D (LUCKY) (R)
Cong Liaison Officer, Dept of Com
b New York, NY, June 16, 25; s Joseph R Mondres & Estelle Margolies M; m 1952 to Roberta Claire Leder; c Eric Myles & Gina Allyson. Educ: Cornell Univ, 42-44; Tau Epsilon Phi. Polit & Govt Pos: Vpres, Gtr Miami Young Rep Club, Fla, formerly; chmn, Fla Young Rep State Conv Comt, 52; organizer, Dade Co Fedn Young Rep Clubs, mem bd dirs in chg of all publicity & pub rels; Rep cand, Fla State Rep, 54; mem, Dade Co Rep Exec Comt; pres, West Broward Rep Club, formerly; mem, Broward Co Rep Exec Comt, 8 years, vchmn, 2 years; chief campaign coordr, J Herbert Burke Campaigns for Broward Co Bd Comnrs, 60 & 64 & US Rep, 66 & 68; vchmn, Broward Co Zoning Bd, Fla, 60-65; chief campaign coordr, J W Stevens Campaign, Broward Co Bd Comnrs, 62; mem, Broward Co Bd Adjust, 66; admin asst to US Rep J Herbert Burke, Fla, 67-69; cong liaison officer, Dept Com, 69-; Rep cand for US Cong, 13th Dist, Fla, 72. Bus & Prof Pos: Mfg rep, Miami, Fla, 46-48; life underwriter, Aetna Life Ins Co, 49-51; pres, Lucky's Furniture, Inc, Hollywood, Ft Lauderdale, Miami & West Palm Beach, Fla, 52-65. Mil Serv: Entered as A/S, Navy, 44, released as Seaman 1/C, 45. Mem: Hollywood Civitan Club; West Hollywood CofC; Cornell Univ Alumni Club; Fla State Soc in Washington (bd dirs). Relig: Jewish. Legal Res: Apt 1511 2750 N E 183rd St Miami FL 33160 Mailing Add: 9300 Arabian Ave Vienna VA 22180

MONETTE, CHARLES H (R)
Comnr, Socorro Co, NMex
b Belcourt, NDak, Mar 26, 37; s George J Monette & Frances Wynkoop M; m 1958 to Charlotte J Lackey; c Deborah, Denise, Daniel, David, Darren & Donald. Educ: Univ NMex, 58-62. Polit & Govt Pos: Vchmn, Socorro Co Rep Party, NMex, 64-67, chmn, 67-70; comnr, Socorro Co, 71- Bus & Prof Pos: Auto dealer, S-M Ford Co, Socorro, NMex, 62- Mil Serv: Entered as E-1, Air Force, 54, released as Airman 1/C, 58, after serv in various units, Korea, 55-56. Mem: NMex Auto Dealers Asn; Socorro KofC. Relig: Catholic. Legal Res: 407 Park SW Socorro NM 87801 Mailing Add: Box 1033 Socorro NM 87801

MONETTE, DELORES MARIE (D)
b Belcourt, NDak, July 25, 43; d Peter TurCotte & Elise Zaste Wilkie T; m 1963 to William Joseph Monette; c Michelle Renae & Montgomery Allen. Educ: Univ NDak, 69-70; NDak State Univ, Bottineau Br, AA, 72, Fargo, 72-; NAm Indian Asn; Young Dem; Student Senate Rep & bd mem, Student Affairs, 2 years; ed campus newspaper; pres, Indian Club. Polit & Govt Pos: Alt deleg, Dem Nat Conv, 72. Mem: Nat Indian Educ Asn. Relig: Catholic. Mailing Add: Box 359 Belcourt ND 58316

MONEY, ELDON A (D)
Utah State Rep
Mailing Add: RFD No 2 Box 11 Spanish Fork UT 84660

MONIER, ROBERT B (R)
NH State Sen
b Mar 5, 22; s Alexander G Monier & Abigail Mantle M; m 1965 to Claira Pirozzi; c Gregory B, David I, Stephen R & Kenneth P. Educ: Syracuse Univ, BA, 46, MA, 48, study, 54-56; Sigma Nu; Zeta Psi. Polit & Govt Pos: NH State Rep, 70-72; sr exec officer to Gov, NH, 72-74; NH State Sen, Dist 9, 75-, chmn exec dept & admin comt, NH State Senate, 75- Bus & Prof Pos: Prof & chmn geog & urban studies, St Anselm's Col, 64-; dir comprehensive planning, State of NH, 72-74. Mil Serv: Air Force, 48-58. Publ: Assoc auth & cartographic ed, Military Aspects of World Political Geography, Govt Printing Off, 59; Outline for Geographic Fundamentals (w Herbert J Vent), Peerless Press, 59; This is Our Nation (w Herbert J Vent), Websters Publ Co, 61. Mem: Am Inst Planners; Am Asn Geog (fel); VFW; Am Legion; Nat Coun Geog Educ. Relig: Catholic. Legal Res: 15 E Union St Goffstown NH 03045 Mailing Add: St Anselm's Col Manchester NH 03102

MONKS, JOHN (D)
Okla State Sen
Mailing Add: State Capitol Oklahoma City OK 73105

MONKS, NELL LUCILE (D)
Secy, Cooper Co Dem Party, Mo
b Pisgah, Mo, Oct 2, 02; d Oscar Harvey Born & Susan Wisdom B; m 1926 to Harry Ashley Monks; c Robert Ashley, William Oscar, Maude Lucile (Mrs Layne), Jerry Lee, Delia Sue (Mrs Berry), Tommie, Nancy Jane (Mrs Wright), Harry Ashley, Jr & Jimmy. Educ: Warrensburg Teachers Col; Sedalia Bus Col. Polit & Govt Pos: Secy, Cooper Co Dem Party, Mo, 68-; twp committeewoman, 5 years; worked in local elec for 24 years. Bus & Prof Pos: Teacher, Mt Pleasant Rural Sch, Cooper Co, Mo, 20-21; Davis, 22-23; Glendale, 23-26. Mem: Bunceton Exten Farm Club; Bunceton Garden Club; Tipton Garden Club. Relig: Baptist. Mailing Add: Tipton MO 65081

MONKS, ROBERT A G (R)
Mem, Cape Elizabeth Rep Town Comt, Maine
b Boston, Mass, Dec 4, 33; s G Gardner Monks & Katherine Knowles M; m 1954 to Millicent Sprague; c Melinda C & Robert C S. Educ: Harvard Col, BA, 54; Trinity Col, Cambridge Univ, 55; Harvard Law Sch, LLB, 58; Phi Beta Kappa. Polit & Govt Pos: Chmn, City of Cambridge Rep Comt, Mass, 66; finance chmn, Mass State Rep Comt, 67-68; deleg, Rep Nat Conv, 68; mem, Cape Elizabeth Rep Town Comt, Maine, 71- Bus & Prof Pos: Attorney, Goodwin, Procter & Hoar, Boston, 58-64, partner, 65; vpres, Gardner Assocs, Inc, 66-68; pres, C H Sprague & Son Co, now Sprague Securities, 68-71; partner, Ram & Co, 71- Legal Res: Richmond House Ram Island Farm Cape Elizabeth ME 04107 Mailing Add: 103 Exchange St Portland ME 04111

MONROE, DUFFIE GIBSON (R)
Chmn, Fort Bend Co Rep Party, Tex
b Houston, Tex, Jan 17, 31; s Perdon Duffie Monroe & Mary M; m 1953 to Charlene W Krizak; c Duffie W, Sharon Kay, Marshall B & Malcolm B. Educ: Univ Houston, 2 years. Polit & Govt Pos: Rep precinct committeeman, 60-64; vchmn, Ft Bend Co Rep Party, Tex, 64-66, chmn, 66- Bus & Prof Pos: Owner & vpres, Duffie Monroe & Sons Co; pres, Ameroil Corp & Petrol Chem Serv Inc. Mil Serv: Entered as Seaman, Navy, released as PO, after serv in Submarine Serv, 48-54; Good Conduct Medal; Korean Serv Ribbon. Mem: Tex Oil Jobbers Asn; Mason (32 degree); Shrine; VFW. Relig: Methodist. Mailing Add: PO Box 986 Rosenberg TX 77471

MONROE, W R JR (BILL) (D)
Iowa State Rep
Mailing Add: 911 North Sixth Burlington IA 52601

MONROE, WARREN LUDWIG (D)
Pres Pro Tem, Nev State Senate
b Rocklin, Calif, Apr 17, 06; s George Monroe & Alice Udbye M; m 1930 to Mary Kathleen Johnstone; c Lawrence K & James W. Educ: Univ Nev, AB; Nev Debate Soc. Polit & Govt Pos: Chmn, Humboldt Co Rep Comt, Nev, 32; chmn, Humboldt Co Bd Educ, 34-37; Nev State Rep, 41, 43 & 47; mem, Nev Fish & Game Comn, 47-54, chmn, 53; mem & past chmn & secy, Elko Co Dem Cent Comt; mem & past chmn, Nev Dem Cent Comt; Nev State Sen, Elko Co, 58-72, Nev State Sen, Northern Nev Dist, 72-, Majority Whip, Nev State Senate, 69-73, Pres Pro Tem, 75- Mil Serv: Entered as Pvt, Army, 43, released as Pfc, after serv in 106th Gen Hosp, ETO, 45. Mem: Nev State Press Asn; CofC; Rotary; Elks. Mailing Add: 100 Oak St Elko NV 89801

MONRONEY, A S MIKE (D)
b Oklahoma City, Okla, Mar 2, 02; m to Mary Ellen Mellon; c Michael. Educ: Univ Okla, BA, 24; Phi Beta Kappa; Phi Gamma Delta; Sigma Delta Chi. Hon Degrees: Colgate Univ, 48. Polit & Govt Pos: US Rep, Okla, 38-50; US Sen, Okla, 51-68; deleg, Dem Nat Conv, 68. Bus & Prof Pos: Reporter & polit writer, Okla News, 24-28; aviation & transportation consult, Washington, DC, 69-; mem bd dirs, Midland Mortgage Co, Calif. Honors & Awards: Collier's Award for Distinguished Cong Serv, 45; Wright Bros Mem Award, Nat Aeronaut Asn, 61; plus numerous others. Relig: Episcopal. Legal Res: 2760 32nd St NW Washington DC 20008 Mailing Add: 1701 K St NW Washington DC 20006

MONSEES, JANET LOUISE (R)
VChmn, Mo State Rep Comt
b Viola, Ark, Sept 30, 43; d Thomas Lee Hartin & Juanita Stone; m 1963 to Richard H Monsees; c Richard H, Jr, Scott Douglas & Robert Michael. Educ: Univ Mo-Columbia, 61-63. Polit & Govt Pos: Pres, Pettis Co Rep Women, 69-70; mem, Mo State Rep Comt, 72-, vchmn, 74- Bus & Prof Pos: Sales assoc, Monsees Realty Co, 64-; financial mgr, Monsees Develop Corp, 70-; financial mgr, A & R Industries, Inc, 74- Mem: PTA; Federated Music Club. Relig: Methodist; bd mem, United Methodist Church, Mailing Add: Rte 2 Hermosa Lake Sedalia MO 65301

MONSEES, RICHARD HENRY (R)
Chmn, Pettis Co Rep Comt, Mo
b Sedalia, Mo, Oct 11, 42; s Dick G Monsees & Ruby Bremer M; m 1963 to Janet Hartin; c Richard H, Jr, Scott Douglas & Robert Michael. Educ: Univ Mo-Columbia, BS Bus Admin, 64; Alpha Kappa Psi. Polit & Govt Pos: Mem, Pettis Co Rep Comt, 66-, chmn, 74-; pres & founder, Pettis Co GOP Club, 70-71; regional coordr, Fourth Cong Dist, Bond-For-Auditor Comt, 72 & Bond-For-Gov Comt, 74; mem, Governor's Club, 74- Bus & Prof Pos: Pres, Monsees Realty Co, 64-; exec-dir, Pettis Co United Fund, 64-65; vpres & secy, Monsees Develop Corp, 70-; pres, Maplewood Serv Co, 74-; pres, Brooking Park Geriatrics, Inc, 74- Mem: Nat Asn Home Builders (mem rural develop comt, 74-); Mo Asn Home Builders (chmn rural develop comt, 74-); Sedalia Bd Realtors; Spec Comt for Gifted Children; Sedalia Sch Dist 200; Nat Inst Real Estate Brokers. Relig: Methodist. Mailing Add: Rte 2 Heromsa Lake Sedalia MO 65301

MONSMA, STEPHEN VOS (D)
Mich State Rep
b Pella, Iowa, Sept 22, 36; s Martin Monsma & Marie Vos M; m 1964 to Mary Carlisle; c Martin Stephen & Kristin Joy. Educ: Calvin Col, AB, 58; Georgetown Univ, MA, 61; Mich State Univ, PhD, 65. Polit & Govt Pos: Mich State Rep, 75- Bus & Prof Pos: Asst prof, State Univ NY Col, Plattsburgh, 64-67; asst prof, Calvin Col, 67-69, assoc prof, 69-73 & prof, 73-74. Mil Serv: Army Res, 60-66. Publ: Auth, Am Politics, 1st ed, 69, 2nd ed, 73 & co-auth, The Dynamics of the American Political System, 72, Dryden Press; auth, The Unraveling of America, Inter-Varsity Press, 74. Mem: Mich Conf Polit Sci (pres, 74-75); Midwest Polit Sci Asn (exec coun mem, 72-75); Am Polit Sci Asn; Grand Rapids Urban League (vpres, 72-74). Relig: Christian Reformed. Legal Res: 829 N Kentview Dr NE Grand Rapids MI 49505 Mailing Add: State Capitol Lansing MI 48901

MONSON, ARCH, JR (R)
Mem, State Rep Cent Comt, Calif
b Thorntown, Ind, Nov 10, 13; s Arch Monson & Mabel Miller M; m 1959 to June Hammersmith; c Eminel, Arch, III, Dwight & Jay. Educ: Moral Twp Union High Sch, London, Ind, grad, 30. Polit & Govt Pos: Mem, United San Francisco Rep Finance Comt, Calif; tech consult to arrangements comt, Rep Nat Conv, 56, 64 & 68, deleg, 68; Northern Calif chmn, George Murphy for US Sen, 64, San Francisco co-chmn, 70; statewide coordr, Christopher for Gov Comt, 66; vchmn, State Finance Comt Reagan for Gov, 66; asst treas, Rep State Cent Comn, 67; co-chmn, Dobbs for Mayor Comt, San Francisco, 68; region II chmn, Nixon-Agnew Calif Campaign Comt, 68; presidential elector, Calif, 68; mem, State Rep Cent Comt Calif, 69- Bus & Prof Pos: Pres, Monson-Pac, Inc, 35; West Coast mgr, Autocall Div, Fed Sign & Signal Co, 45; owner-operator, St George Ranch, Geyserville, 59. Mem: Los Angeles Elec Club; Nat Elec Contractors Asn; San Francisco Rotary Club (vpres); Boy Scouts (nat exec bd); Bohemian Club. Honors & Awards: Silver Beaver, Silver Antelope & Silver Buffalo, Boy Scouts. Relig. Presbyterian. Legal Res: 2825 Broadway San Francisco CA 94115 Mailing Add: 360 Sixth St San Francisco CA 94103

MONSON, DAVID S (R)
State Auditor, Utah
b Salt Lake City, Utah, June 20, 45; s Smith Weston Monson & Dorothy Brammer M; m 1971 to Julianne Johnson; c David Johnson, Traci Lyn & Marianne. Educ: Univ Utah, BS in Acct, 70; CPA, 74; Delta Phi Kappa. Polit & Govt Pos: State auditor, Utah, 73- Bus & Prof Pos: Acct, Elmer Fox & Co, Salt Lake City, Utah, 70-72. Mil Serv: Entered as Airman Basic, Air Nat Guard, 67, released as Sgt, 73, after serv in 130 E I Squadron; Utah Air Nat Guard Achievement Award. Mem: Utah Asn CPA; Am Inst CPA; Western Coun State Govts (vpres); Nat Asn State Auditors, Comptrollers & Treas. Relig: Latter-day Saint. Legal Res: 1956 Michigan Ave Salt Lake City UT 84108 Mailing Add: Rm 221 State Capitol Salt Lake City UT 84114

MONSON, ROBERT JOSEPH (R)
VChmn, Dakota Co Rep Party, Minn
b Stillwater, Minn, June 10, 24; s Randolph Alvin Monson & Mathilda Lamere M; m 1946 to Lorraine Ann Pieruccioni; c Robert J, Jr & Michele L. Educ: St Paul Col Law, BSL, 50, LLB, 52, William Mitchell Col Law, JD, 69; Phi Beta Gamma. Polit & Govt Pos: Rep chmn, First Precinct, Mendota Heights, Minn, 61-67; chmn, Region Seven, Dakota Co Rep Party, 67-71; chmn, Dakota Co Nixon Comt, 68; vchmn, Dakota Co Rep Party, 71- Bus & Prof Pos: Attorney, pvt practice, 52- Mil Serv: Entered as Pvt, Air Force, 42, released as Sgt, 45, after serv in 398th Bomb Group, ETO, 44-45; Seven Battle Stars; ETO Ribbon; Good Conduct Ribbon. Mem: Am Bar Asn (mem, Standing Comt on Legis); Minn State Bar Asn (chmn, Legis Comt); Ramsey Co Bar Asn (mem, Ethics Comt, mem, Legis Comt); Am Arbit Soc (referee, 66-); KofC. Relig: Catholic. Mailing Add: 1018 Downing St St Paul MN 55118

MONTABON, DENNIS GENE (D)
Chmn, Lincoln Co Dem Party, Wis
b Tomahawk, Wis, Sept 30, 43; s Frank W Montabon & Laura Krubsack M; m 1967 to Julie Ann Bishop; c Frank Lloyd, Anthony Edward & Sara Nicole. Educ: Univ Wis-Madison, BS, 65; John Marshall Law Sch, JD, 72; Phi Alpha Delta. Polit & Govt Pos: Lincoln Co chmn, Earl for Attorney Gen Comt, 74; chmn, Lincoln Co Dem Party, Wis, 74-; mem, Northeast Criminal Justice Planning Coun & Wis Coun on Criminal Justice, 75- Bus & Prof Pos: Spec inspector, Bur of Alcohol, Tobacco & Firearms, US Treas Dept, 66-72; dist attorney, Lincoln Co, Wis, 73- Mem: Lincoln Co Bar Asn (secy-treas, 75-); Optimist (bd dirs, 75-); Nat & Wis Dist Attorney's Asns; State Bar Wis. Honors & Awards: Nat Off Task Force & High Qual Step Increase, Alcohol, Tobacco & Firearms, 69. Relig: Lutheran. Legal Res: 1105 E Third St Merrill WI 54452 Mailing Add: Courthouse 1110 E Main St Merrill WI 54452

MONTAGUE, DAVID NICHOLLS (R)
b New York, NY, Aug 23, 36; s Edgar Sclater Montague & Suzanne Garrett M; m 1958 to Carolyn Stewart Day; c Suzanne Stewart & David Nicholls, Jr. Educ: Univ Va, BA, 58; Law Sch, LLB, 61; Beta Theta Pi (vpres); T I L K A Soc; IMP Soc. Polit & Govt Pos: Chmn, Hampton City Rep Comt, Va, 68-70; first vchmn, Rep Party of Va, 68-72; mayor, Hampton, formerly. Bus & Prof Pos: Partner, Montague, Cumming & Watkins, Attorneys, 63-67; partner, Montague & Montague, Attorneys, 67- Mil Serv: Entered as 2nd Lt, Army, 61, released as 1st Lt, 62, after serv in Army Med Training Ctr, Brooke Army Med Ctr, Ft Sam Houston, Tex; Capt, Med Serv Corps, Army Res, 62-65. Mem: Hampton, Va State & Am Bar Asns; Va Trial Lawyers Asn; Va State Coun Higher Educ. Relig: Episcopal. Mailing Add: 29 Hampton Roads Ave Hampton VA 23361

MONTAGUE, JOANNE (D)
b Birmingham, Ala, Nov 10, 31; d Wayland Pharis Montague & Rachel Deanhardt M; single. Educ: Winthrop Col, AB, 54; Duke Univ, AM, 64. Polit & Govt Pos: Pres, Greenville Co Dem Women, SC, 72-74, mem exec comt, 74-; mem exec comt, Dem Women's Coun SC, 74-; alt deleg, Dem Nat Mid-Term Conf, 74. Bus & Prof Pos: Instr, Furman Univ, 68-71; ed trade mag, Southern Hosp/Munic South, 71-72; eval specialist, Piedmont Schs Proj, Greer, SC, 72- Mem: Nat, SC & Greenville Co Educ Asns; March of Dimes (mem bd, Greenville-Oconee-Pickens Chap, Mothers March chmn, 75 & 76). Relig: Baptist. Mailing Add: 202 Robinson St Greenville SC 29609

MONTAGUE, LEON ARTHUR (R)
Chmn, Shawassee Co Rep Party, Mich
b Owosso, Mich, Nov 28, 15; s Herbert W Montague & Achsah Maria Randt M; m 1949 to Elizabeth Roberts Chapelle. Educ: Cent Mich Univ, AB, 48; Northwestern Univ, DDS, 51; Univ Mich, Ann Arbor, MS, 56; Phi Kappa Phi; Omicron Kappa Upsilon. Polit & Govt Pos: Mem charter revision comn, Owosso, Mich, 63-64, mem city coun, 64-74, mayor, 70-74; chmn, Shawassee Co Rep Party, 74-; comnr, Shawassee Co, 75- Mil Serv: Entered as Yeoman 3/C, Navy, 42, released as Chief Yeoman, 46, after serv in Am & Pac Theatre. Mem: Am Asn Orthodontists; Am Dent Asn; Mich Soc Orthodontists; Rotary Int; Gideons Int (vpres local chap). Relig: Protestant. Mailing Add: 610 Fifth St Owosso MI 48867

MONTANO, ARMANDO (D)
NY State Assemblyman
b San Juan, PR, Oct 10, 28; s Armando Montano, Sr & Serafina Ramos M; m 1959 to Norma Silva; c Armando, Jr, Richard, Ronald & Marc. Educ: City Col New York, Bernard Baruch Br, 2 years. Polit & Govt Pos: Housing proj specialist, Housing & Develop Admin, New York, 66; founder, Robert F Kennedy Independent Dem Club, 66; NY State Assemblyman, 68- Bus & Prof Pos: Licensed ins & real estate broker, Montano Realty Co, Bronx, NY, 59- Mem: Inst Puerto Rican Urban Studies, Inc; CofC; Gtr NY Ins Brokers Asn; Puerto Rican Forum, Inc; Urban League of Gtr New York. Honors & Awards: Awarded Keys to Cities of Lackawanna, NY & San Juan, PR; John F Kennedy Libr for Minorities Award; Puerto Rican House Award. Relig: Catholic. Mailing Add: 634 Manida St Bronx NY 10474

MONTANO, GEORGE JOHN (R)
Chmn, New Haven Rep City Party, Conn
b New Haven, Conn, Sept 28, 27; s Charles P Montano & Lucia Macchiaroli M; m 1952 to Eleanor M DeCapua; c Ellyn & twins, John Charles & Stephen Michael. Educ: Holy Cross Col, BS in Econ, 50; Holy Cross Outing Club. Polit & Govt Pos: Chmn, New Haven Rep Adv Comt, Conn, 64-65; chmn, New Haven Rep City Party, 66-; deleg, Rep Nat Conv, 68; chmn, Conn Liquor Control Comn, 71- Bus & Prof Pos: Vpres, Maplewood Realty Corp, 50-; vpres, Montano Construction Co, 60-; pres, Nat Diversified Investors, 62-; vpres, Coop Credit Corp, 64-; owner, Am Credit Co, 71- Mem: New Haven Retail Credit Asn; Elks; Union League; Racebrook Country Club; St Aedan Holy Name Soc. Relig: Catholic. Mailing Add: 1169 Forest Rd New Haven CT 06515

MONTCHALIN, YVONNE (R)
Mem, Wash State Rep Cent Comt
b Siebert, Colo, Dec 9, 09; d Hubert Clyde Cornell & Byrde Stouffer C; m 1950 to Leon Paul Montchalin; c William Clyde & Karen (Mrs William A Allinger). Educ: Willamette Univ, JD, 30. Polit & Govt Pos: Title examr, Home Owners Loan Corp, 32-35; city attorney, Camas & Ridgefield, Wash, 45-50; dir, Skamania Co Sch Dist 2, 58-64; chmn, Skamania Co Civil Serv Comn, 59-65; mem, White House Conf Children & Youth, 60; mem, Wash State Rep Cent Comt, 64-, secy, 73-74; mem, Skamania Co Bd Educ, 60-66; mem, SW Wash Intermediate Sch Dist, 66-68. Bus & Prof Pos: Dir & corp secy, Wash State Bank, Washougal, 70. Publ: The Columbia River's thousand miles of river ramblings, Sea & Pac Motor Boat, 4-5/66, Northwest Passages, 69 & Trailerboats West, 70; Beacon rock in the gorge, Oregonian, 68. Mem: Wash State Bar Asn; Am Bar Asn; Am Judicature Soc; Int Platform Asn; Eastern Star. Relig: Methodist. Mailing Add: Rte 1 Box 1585 Washougal WA 98671

MONTGOMERY, A HAROLD (D)
La State Sen
b Humble, Tex, Apr 19, 11; s Allie H Montgomery & Martha Dean M; m 1945 to Azalee Wilson; c Hal. Educ: Univ Ark, BA & MA. Polit & Govt Pos: La State Sen, 60-68 & 72- Bus & Prof Pos: Sch teacher, 34-41; state supvr, Dept Educ, 41-45; state distributor of power equip, 45-; farmer & cattleman, 54-; dir, Peoples Bank & Trust, 58- & Lincoln Bank & Trust, 62- Mem: Mason (32 degree); Lions; Nat CofC; Soil Conserv Dist (state vpres). Honors & Awards: Nat Legislator of the Year Award. Relig: Methodist; state pres, La Methodist Laymen Asn. Mailing Add: Rte 1 Doyline LA 71023

MONTGOMERY, GEORGE F, SR (D)
Mich State Rep
b Ionia, Mich, Jan 13, 09; m to J Wortley; c George F, Jr & Alfred N. Educ: Univ Mich, AB, 29. Polit & Govt Pos: Mich State Rep, 45-46 & 59- Bus & Prof Pos: Teacher & research asst, Detroit Pub Schs, Mich. Mem: Detroit Fedn Teachers. Relig: Protestant. Mailing Add: 15792 Meyers Rd Detroit MI 48227

MONTGOMERY, GILLESPIE V (D)
US Rep, Miss
b Meridian, Miss. Polit & Govt Pos: Miss State Sen, 57-66; US Rep, Miss, 67-, mem, Vet Affairs Comt, US House of Rep, 69-, chmn, Select Comt on US Involvement in Southeast Asia, 71, mem, Armed Serv Comt, 71- Bus & Prof Pos: Life ins co officer & gen ins agent; pres, Cong Prayer Breakfast Group, 70. Mem: Mason; Moose; Scottish Rite; Shrine; Optimist Club. Relig: Episcopal. Legal Res: 3904 Country Club Blvd Meridian MS 39301 Mailing Add: 2367 Rayburn House Off Bldg Washington DC 20515

MONTGOMERY, HAROLD RONNIE (R)
b Rose Hill, Va, Dec 4, 38; s George Elmer Montgomery & Myrtle M; m 1968 to Sandra Kay Wilkinson. Educ: Va Polytech Inst & State Univ, BS, 61; Univ Tenn, JD, 67; Phi Alpha Delta; Lonesome Pine Southwest Va Student Asn; Ski Club. Polit & Govt Pos: Vchmn, Lee Co Rep Party, Va, 70-72; mem, Duffield Indust Authority, 71-, chmn, 72; alt deleg, Rep Nat Conv, 72; chmn, Lee Co Comt to Reelect the President, 72; mem, Lee Co Rep Exec Comt, 72-73; Commonwealths Attorney, Lee Co, 72-; mem, Law Enforcement Officers' Training Standards Comn, 72- Bus & Prof Pos: Attorney-at-law. Mil Serv: Entered as E-2, Navy, 61, released, 61, after serv in Officers' Candidate Sch, Newport, RI. Mem: Am & Va State Bar Asns; Va Commonwealths Attorney Asn; Va Trial Lawyers Asn; Am Judicature Soc. Honors & Awards: Distinguished Serv Award, Phi Alpha Delta, 67. Relig: Christian Church. Legal Res: Russell St Jonesville VA 24263 Mailing Add: PO Box 366 Jonesville VA 24263

MONTGOMERY, JOHN ALLEN (D)
Pres, Ala Young Dem
b Birmingham, Ala, Apr 3, 47; s John A Montgomery, Sr & Margaret Nash M; m 1968 to Jacqueline Jones; c Julia Louise & John Allen, III. Educ: Auburn Univ, BS, 69; Lambda Chi Alpha. Polit & Govt Pos: Spec asst in charge state off, US Sen John Sparkman, 71-; vchmn youth affairs, Ala Dem State Exec Comt, 74-; pres, Ala Young Dem, 74- Mem: Co United Appeal Dr (chmn); Civitan; Ala Lung Asn (bd mem). Honors & Awards: Selected as deleg to Soviet Union for polit seminar & study tour, Am Coun Young Polit Leaders, 74; nominated for Nat Outstanding Young Man of Year Award, 74. Relig: Methodist. Mailing Add: 1373 Willoughby Rd Birmingham AL 35216

MONTGOMERY, PAUL (D)
Committeeman, Wayne Co Dem Party, Mo
b Silva, Mo, Nov 4, 22; s Asa Lee Montgomery & Belvia Daggett M; m 1944 to Nell Parton. Educ: Elem sch, 8 years. Polit & Govt Pos: Committeeman, Wayne Co Dem Party, Mo, 70- Bus & Prof Pos: Farmer. Mem: AF&AM; Wayne Co Dem Club; Wayne Co Saddle Club, Inc. Relig: Protestant. Mailing Add: Star Rte Patterson MO 63956

MONTGOMERY, RAY HILLMAN (R)
Miss State Sen
Mailing Add: 139 S Liberty Canton MS 39046

MONTGOMERY, TERRY PATRICK (D)
Chmn, Sixth Cong Dist Dem Party, Minn
b McIntosh, SDak, Mar 21, 38; s Harry H Montgomery & Helen Payne M; m 1960 to Kathleen Clark. Educ: Univ Minn, Minneapolis, 56-57; St Cloud State Col, BS with honors, 62; Columbia Univ, MS with high honors, 63. Polit & Govt Pos: Mem, Minn State Dem Exec Comt, 68-70; cand for Cong, Sixth Dist, Minn, 70; mem, Minn Gov Crime Comn, 71-72; chmn, Sixth Cong Dist Dem Party, 71-; deleg, Dem Nat Conv, 72. Bus & Prof Pos: Reporter, Minneapolis Tribune, 63-64; instr Eng, St Cloud State Col, 64-66, asst to pres, 66-69, vpres, 69-; newsman, WCCO-TV, Minneapolis, 64-68; pres & owner, WKPM Radio, Princeton, Minn, 67- Mem: Nat Asn Broadcasters; Minn Broadcasters Asn; Sigma Delta Chi; KofC; St Cloud United Way (bd dirs). Honors & Awards: Distinguished Serv Award, St Cloud Jaycees, 68; One of Minn Ten Outstanding Young Men, Minn Jaycees, 69. Relig: Catholic. Mailing Add: RR 1 Sauk Rapids MN 56379

MONTILLA, CESAR ALBERTO, JR (R)
Chmn, PR Young Rep Fedn
b Santurce, PR, Sept 11, 42; s Cesar A Montilla & Margarita Emanuelli M; m 1967 to Mary Ann Byrne; c Lara Margarita & Maria Alejandra. Educ: Cornell Univ, 59-60; Univ PR, 60-61; Univ Fla, 61-65; Beta Theta Pi; Nu Sigma Beta. Polit & Govt Pos: Coun mem, Small Bus Adv Coun, 65-; chmn, PR Young Rep Fedn, 69- Bus & Prof Pos: Vpres, Blyth-Eastman Dillon & Co, Inc, 66-72; chmn bd, Securities Corp, PR, 72- Mil Serv: Entered as Pvt, Army, 62, released as Pfc, after serv in Mil Police, Regt 492, San Juan, PR, 63. Relig: Catholic. Mailing Add: 1825 Miosotis St Rio Piedras PR 00927

MONTOYA, GREGORY (D)
Tex State Rep
Mailing Add: General Delivery Elsa TX 78543

MONTOYA, HERBERT PATRICIO (D)
Mem, Alaska Dem State Cent Comt
b Bernalillo, NMex, Sept 7, 42; s Patricio Montoya & Edwina De La O M; m 1967 to Kay Sylvia Lamoreaux; c Pat, Kevin, Karen & Tim. Polit & Govt Pos: Precinct vchmn, NMex Dem Party, 64-66; precinct chmn, Alaska Dem Party, 66-; state coordr for pub disclosure law, 73-; mem, Dist Dem Comt, 69-71, chmn, 71-72; mem, Alaska Dem State Cent Comt, 73- Mem: PTA; City View Little League (bd, 68-73). Relig: Catholic. Mailing Add: 1560 Primrose Anchorage AK 99504

MONTOYA, JOSEPH M (D)
US Sen, NMex
b Sandoval Co, NMex, Sept 24, 15; m to Della Romero; c Joseph II, Patrick & Lynda. Educ: Regis Col, Denver, Colo; Georgetown Univ Law Sch, LLB, 38. Polit & Govt Pos: NMex State Rep, 36-40, Majority Floor Leader, NMex House of Rep, 38; NMex State Sen, 40-46 & 52-54, Majority Whip, NMex Senate, 40; Lt Gov, NMex, 46-48 & 54-56; US Rep, NMex, 57-64; deleg, Interparliamentary Conf, Warsaw, Poland, Orgn; nat co-chmn, Viva Kennedy Clubs, 60; deleg, Am-US Interparliamentary Conf, 61-65; US Sen, NMex, 64-, mem, Senate Comts on Appropriations & Pub Works Joint Comt Atomic Energy, Select Comt on Presidential Campaign Activities & former mem, Senate Comts on Agr & Forestry & Govt Opers; Off US Observer, Latin Am Parliamentary Conf, Lima, Peru, 65; deleg, Dem Nat Conv, 68; deleg, Dem Nat Mid-Term Conf, 74. Bus & Prof Pos: Attorney-at-law; actively engaged in various bus enterprises. Legal Res: Santa Fe NM 87501 Mailing Add: 5403 Surrey St Chevy Chase MD 20015

MONTOYA, RICARDO ANTHONY (D)
NMex State Rep
b Santa Fe, NMex, May 10, 37; s Dick Montoya & Fidelia Garcia M; single. Educ: NMex State Univ, 56-63; Sigma Alpha Epsilon. Polit & Govt Pos: NMex State Rep, Dist 45, 74-, mem bank & corp comt, labor comt, interim comt & water resources & conserv comt, NMex House Rep. Bus & Prof Pos: Pres, Montoya & Sons Elec Inc, 72-; pres & treas, Cordless Tela-Commun, Inc, 75-; owner, Montoya Bros Elec Co, 75- Mil Serv: Entered as S/A, Naval Res, 55, released as SN, 63. Mem: Elks; Jaycees. Relig: Catholic. Legal Res: 1329 Maes Rd Santa Fe NM 87501 Mailing Add: 321 Guadalupe Santa Fe NM 87501

MONTOYA, SAMUEL ZACHARY (D)
Justice, NMex Supreme Court
b Pena Blanca, NMex, Dec 2, 16; s Alfonso Montoya & Chonita Baca M; m 1943 to Carlota Quintana; c Mary Irene (Mrs Donald G Stevens) & Anita C. Educ: Univ NMex, AB, 36; Georgetown Univ Law Sch, LLB, 41; Pi Sigma Alpha; Gamma Eta Gamma. Polit & Govt Pos: Asst dist attorney, First Judicial Dist, Santa Fe, NMex, 47-49; mem city coun, Santa Fe, 50-54, city attorney, 55-59; treas, NMex Dem Party, 57-58; chmn bd dirs, NMex State Hosp, Las Vegas, 59-61; mem, NMex adv comt, Nat Comn on Civil Rights, 59-64; judge, First Judicial Dist, Santa Fe, 59-71; mem bd dirs, NMex Dept Pub Welfare, 64-65; justice, NMex Supreme Court, 71- Bus & Prof Pos: Pres, Santa Fe Co Bar Asn, 51-52; US deleg, Inter-Am Conf of Attorney Gens, 63; mem, Adv Coun Judges, Nat Coun on Crime & Delinquency, 68-71; vpres, Nat Coun Juv Court Judges, 69-71; pres, NMex Judicial Conf, 70-71. Mil Serv: Entered as Pvt, Army, 42, released as Maj, 45, after serv in Mil Railway Serv, NAm & European Theatres; Army Res, Ret; Five Battle Stars, Bronze Star Medal. Mem: VFW (Post 2951 Comdr, 49, State Judge Advocate, 52); Elks. Relig: Catholic. Mailing Add: 216 Sombrio Dr Santa Fe NM 87501

MONTOYA, THEODORE R (D)
NMex State Sen
b Bernalillo, NMex, Oct 24, 35; s Tomas O Montoya & Frances De La O M; m 1971 to Susan Lomax Ramsey; c Philip, Theodore R, Jr & Alicia Eileen. Educ: Georgetown Univ, BSS, 58; Law Sch, JD, 61; Delta Theta Phi. Polit & Govt Pos: NMex State Sen, 73- Mem: Am Trial Lawyers; Am & NMex Bar Asns. Relig: Roman Catholic. Legal Res: Box 331 Ranchos de Placitas Placitas NM 87043 Mailing Add: 420 Lomas Blvd NW Albuquerque NM 87101

MONTPLAISIR, J HENRY (R)
NH State Rep
Mailing Add: 285 Hawthorne St Manchester NH 03104

MOODY, DON A (D)
Nev State Assemblyman
Mailing Add: PO Box 1157 Hawthorne NV 89415

MOODY, JOHN OVERTON (D)
Chmn, Jay Co Dem Party, Ind
b Portland, Ind, July 7, 14; s George Draper Cleveland Moody & Mollie Evans M; m 1935 to Edna Ruth Platt; c Joy (Mrs Oral Dale Councilman). Educ: Portland High Sch, Ind, 4 years. Polit & Govt Pos: Chmn, Jay Co Dem Party, Ind, 69- Bus & Prof Pos: Owner, Moody's Barber Shop, Portland, Ind, 39-; leasee, Imes Barber Shop, 71- Mem: F&AM; Elks (twice pres, Past Exalted Rulers Club); Moose; Eastern Star; Portland Country Club (pres). Relig: United Church of Christ. Mailing Add: 634 E Water St Portland IN 47371

MOODY, WILLARD JAMES (D)
Va State Sen
b Franklin, Va, June 16, 24; m to Betty Glenn Covert. Educ: Norfolk Div, Col William & Mary; Univ Richmond, T C Williams Law Sch, LLB. Polit & Govt Pos: Va State Deleg, 56-68; alt deleg, Dem Nat Conv, 68; Va State Sen, 69- Mil Serv: World War II. Mem: Jr CofC; Am Bar Asn; Va Trial Lawyers Asn; Am Trial Lawyers Asn; CofC. Relig: Baptist. Mailing Add: PO Box 1138 Portsmouth VA 23705

MOON, CHARLES (D)
Wash State Rep
b Sheridan, Wyo, 1923; m to Ellen; c Three. Educ: Wash State Univ, BS, DVM. Polit & Govt Pos: Wash State Rep, currently. Bus & Prof Pos: Vet. Mil Serv: Army. Mailing Add: Rte 2 Box 427-A Snohomish WA 98290

MOON, MARJORIE RUTH (D)
Treas, State of Idaho
b Pocatello, Idaho, June 16, 26; d Clark Blakeley Moon & Ruth Gerhart M; single. Educ: Pac Univ, Ore, 44-46; Univ Wash, Seattle, AB, 48; Theta Sigma Phi; Phi Lambda Omicron. Polit & Govt Pos: Precinct committeeman, Idaho State Dem Cent Comt, 58, ed, Idaho Dem, 58-61; treas, State of Idaho, 63-; chmn, Idaho Comn on Women's Progs, 71-74; deleg, Dem Nat Conv, 72. Bus & Prof Pos: Reporter, Pocatello Tribune, Idaho, 44; reporter, Caldwell News-Tribune, 48-50; bur chief, Deseret News of Salt Lake City, Boise, 50-52; publ, Idaho Pioneer Statewide, 52-55; publ, owner & founder, Garden City Gazette, 54-68; partner, Modern Press Printing Plant, Boise, 58-60; partner, Sawtooth Lodge Guest Ranch, Grandjean, Idaho, 58-61. Mem: Idaho Press Women; Nat Fedn Press Women; Nat Asn Auditors, Comptrollers & Treas; Soroptimist (past pres, Boise Club). Relig: Congregational. Legal Res: 2227 Heights Dr Boise ID 83702 Mailing Add: PO Box 207 Boise ID 83701

MOONEY, ARTHUR AMOS (R)
Committeeman, Vt Rep State Comt
b Newport, Vt, Feb 5, 99; s Raymond James Mooney & Carrie Isabelle Magoon M; m 1943 to Lucille A Gardner; c Arthur Richard, Winston Charles, Robert Alan & Stephen James. Educ: Newport High Sch, Vt, 4 years. Polit & Govt Pos: Asst postmaster, Newport, Vt, 57; Justice of the Peace, Newport, Vt, 64-69; chmn, Newport Rep Town Comt, 67-69; Vt State Rep, Dist 17, 69-74; chmn, Orleans Co Rep Party, formerly; committeeman, Vt Rep State Comt, currently. Bus & Prof Pos: Trustee, Vt Baptist State Conv; pres, Vt-NH-Maine Postal Supvr, 59-60; vpres, Vt Credit Union League, 60-67. Mil Serv: Entered First Vt Vol Inf, Army, 17, released as Pfc, 19, after serv in 101 AMM TR 26th Div, AEF, 17-19; Reenlisted V6, Naval Res, 43, released as SP (M), 44. Mem: AF&AM; Am Legion; Vet World War I; Baptist Conv; Eastern Star. Honors & Awards: Recipient of Superior Achievement Award, US Post Off Dept. Relig: Baptist. Mailing Add: Bluff Rd Newport VT 05855

MOONEY, JAMES PIERCE (D)
b Fall River, Mass, May 28, 43; s James P Mooney (deceased) & Marie Antalek M; single. Educ: Univ RI, BA, 65; NY Univ Sch Law, JD, 70. Polit & Govt Pos: Cong liaison officer, US Equal Employ Opportunity Comn, 69-70, acting dir legis affairs, 70-71; spec asst to US Rep John Brademas, Ind, 71, admin asst, 71- Mem: Phi Alpha Theta; Pi Sigma Alpha. Legal Res: 514 Nanaquaket Rd Tiverton RI 02878 Mailing Add: Rm H-115 The Capitol Washington DC 20515

MOONEY, JOHN JOSEPH (D)
Mem, Canton Dem Town Comt, Mass
b Weymouth, Mass, Aug 14, 30; s John Joseph Mooney & Helen Doyle M; m 1952 to Winifred Theresa Fitzgerald; c John Daniel, Michael Gerard, Richard Francis, Paul William, Mark Fitzgerald, James Michael & Joan Marie. Educ: Northeastern Univ, 48-51; Boston Col Law Sch, 51-54; Loyola Univ Col Law, Chicago, JD, 55. Polit & Govt Pos: Mem, Personnel Bd, Town of Canton, Mass, 63-66, Zoning Bd Appeals, 66-68 & Canton Dem Town Comt, 68-; Mass State Rep, 69-72; mem, Spec Comn Judicial Reform, 71-72. Bus & Prof Pos: Attorney-at-law, Ill & Mass Bars, 55- Publ: Massachusetts adopts the doctrine of comparative negligence, New Eng Law Rev, fall 69. Mem: Mass & Norfolk Co Bar Asns; Nat Legislators Asn; Toastmasters (past pres); KofC. Relig: Catholic. Mailing Add: 281 York St Canton MA 02021

MOORE, ARCH A, JR (R)
Gov, WVa
b Moundsville, WVa, Apr 16, 23; s Arch A Moore & Genevieve Jones M; m 1949 to Shelley S Riley; c Arch A, III, Shelley Wellons & Lucy St Clair. Educ: Lafayette Col, 43; WVa Univ, AB, 48, Col Law, LLB, 51; pres, Beta Theta Pi, Coun of Fraternity Pres, Sr Men's Hon, Men's Ranking Hon & Law Sch Class, 51; Phi Delta Phi. Hon Degrees: PhD, Bethany Col, WVa Univ, WVa Inst Technol, Concord Col, Marshall Univ, Alderson-Broaddus Col & WVa Wesleyan Col. Polit & Govt Pos: WVa State Deleg, 52; US Rep, First Dist, WVa, 56-68, ranking mem, House Judiciary Comt, House Select Comt on Small Bus, House Subcomt on Immigration, House Spec Comt on Interstate Taxation & House Select Comt to Investigate Adam Clayton Powell; mem, Joint House-Senate Comt on Immigration & Nationality Policy & Select Comt on Western Hemispheric Immigration; deleg, Intergovt Comt on European Migration; mem, James Madison Mem Comt; deleg, Rep Nat Conv, 60 & 64, mem, Platform Comt & Platform Speaker, 64 & 68, deleg, 72; Gov, WVa, 69-; chmn, Nat Gov Conf, 71-72; mem, Rep Nat Comt, currently. Mil Serv: Entered as Pvt, Army, 43, released as Sgt, 45; Purple Heart; Combat Infantrymen's Badge; European Campaign Ribbon with Three Battle Stars. Mem: Am & WVa Bar Asns; 85th Cong Club (pres); Am Judicature Soc; WVa State Bar. Honors & Awards: Silver Beaver Award, Boy Scouts; Patriotic Serv Medal, Am Coalition of Patriotic Soc; Comdr & Grande Officiale, Order of the Merit, Italy; first WVa Gov to succeed himself to four year term. Relig: Methodist; Mem off bd, Simpson Methodist Church, Moundsville. Mailing Add: 507 Jefferson Ave Glen Dale WV 26038

MOORE, BIRDELL (D)
b Montford, Tex, June 29, 13; d Ed Chew & Georgia Davis C; div; c Josephine (Mrs Collins). Polit & Govt Pos: Community representor; representor for Assemblyman Leon Ralph; bd mem, Watts Found & Westminister Neighborhood Asn Inc; alt deleg, Dem Nat Conv, 72. Bus & Prof Pos: Chmn emergency treatment, Martin Luther King Hosp; chmn, Watts Found Vol Auxiliary; consult, Comt for State Crippled Children; professional writer. Publ: When You Go To the Doctor, US Dept Health, Educ & Welfare; Black mother's plea & Promise of strangers, In: From the Ashes, New Am Libr, 67; plus others. Mem: Child Care of 75; Urban Develop; Legal Aid Found Los Angeles; Nat Asn Black Women; Comprehensive Health Planning Coun. Honors & Awards: The Community's Artist Award, Cult Arts Prog; Dedicated Serv Award, Watts Found Vol Auxiliary; Resolution, Assemblyman Leon Ralph; Distinction Merit Award, Westminister Neighborhood Asn Inc. Relig: Baptist. Mailing Add: 9708 Beach St Los Angeles CA 90002

MOORE, C ROBERT
US Ambassador, Equatorial Guinea & Cameroon
b Galena, Ill, Aug 16, 15; m Joanna Daniels Moore; c Caroline, Cynthia & Letitia. Educ: Harvard Univ, BA, 35; NY Univ, MA, 40; Nat War Col, 55-56. Polit & Govt Pos: Mem staff, Off of Lend-Lease Admin, 43; with Foreign Econ Admin, Ankara, 43-46; career officer, US Dept of State Foreign Serv, 46-, mem staff, Am Embassy, Ankara, 46-48, officer-in-charge of Turkish Affairs, 49-52, first secy, Paris, 52-55, counr, Ankara, 56-59, counr & dep chief of mission, Phnom Penh, 59-62, counr & dep chief of mission, Damascus, 62-65, US Ambassador, Mali, 65-68, Dep Asst Secy for African Affairs, Dept of State, 68-72, US Ambassador, Equatorial Guinea & Cameroon, 72- Bus & Prof Pos: Investment reviewer, banking firm, 35-43. Legal Res: Seattle WA Mailing Add: Embassy Yaounde Dept of State Washington DC 20520

MOORE, CHARLES J (R)
RI State Rep
Mailing Add: 38 Avondale Rd Westerly RI 02891

MOORE, CHARLES RANDOLPH (D)
Ark State Rep
b Blytheville, Ark, Dec 31, 24; s Walter Ross Moore & Elizabeth Evans M; m 1955 to Sarah Laura Langston; c Ross Cleveland & Laura Elizabeth. Educ: Univ Miss, BA, 47; Pi Kappa Alpha. Polit & Govt Pos: Ark State Rep, 69- Mil Serv: Entered as Cadet, Air Force, 43, released as Cpl, 46, after serv in Air Sea Rescue, US, 45-46. Mem: Mississippi Co Farm Bur; Ark Jr CofC; Am Legion. Honors & Awards: Ky Colonel; Outstanding Young Man of Blytheville, Ark, 53. Relig: Methodist. Mailing Add: Rte 1 Box 179 Luxora AR 72358

MOORE, DANIEL KILLIAN (D)
Assoc Justice, NC Supreme Court
b Asheville, NC, Apr 2, 06; s Fred Moore & Lela Enloe M; m 1933 to Jeanelle Coutler; c Edith (Mrs Edgar B Hamilton, Jr) & Dan K, Jr. Educ: Univ NC, BS in Bus Admin, 27, Law Sch, Chapel Hill, grad, 28; Phi Beta Kappa; Pi Kappa Phi. Polit & Govt Pos: Former Dem precinct chmn; mem, Co & State Dem Exec Comts; mem, Cong Adv Comt; NC State Rep, 41-43; solicitor, 30th Judicial Dist, NC, 46-48; judge, Superior Court of NC, 48-58; counr & asst secy, Champion Papers Inc, 58-65; Gov, NC, 65-69; deleg, Dem Nat Convs; assoc justice, NC Supreme Court, 69- Bus & Prof Pos: Vchmn, NC Bd of Water Resources; former dir, Univ NC Alumni Asn, Univ NC Law Sch Found & NC RR; trustee, High Point Col, 66-; lawyer, Joyner, Moore & Howison, Raleigh, NC, 69. Mil Serv: Entered as Pvt, Army, 43, released as T-5, 45, after serv in ETO & Judge Adv Gen Off. Mem: Mason; Rotary; Civitan.

Relig: Methodist. Legal Res: 3621-E Anclote Arms Raleigh NC 27607 Mailing Add: Justice Bldg PO Box 1841 Raleigh NC 27602

MOORE, DON A (R)
Ill State Sen
b Chicago, Ill, Jan 1, 28; m to Verla; c Albert. Educ: Morgan Park Jr Col; John Marshall Law Sch, LLB, 50. Polit & Govt Pos: Rep committeeman, Bremen Twp, Ill, 56-; asst states attorney, 57-59; Ill State Rep, formerly; alt deleg, Rep Nat Conv, 68; Ill State Sen, 73- Bus & Prof Pos: Practicing attorney, 12 years. Mem: Am Judicature Soc; Lions; Boy Scouts; Moose; Mason; plus other civic, fraternal & charitable orgn. Mailing Add: 14636 S Long Ave Midlothian IL 60445

MOORE, DONALD ALFRED (D)
Vt State Rep
Mailing Add: RD 1 Cuttingsville VT 05738

MOORE, DOROTHA HUNTLEY (R)
Rep Nat Committeewoman, Ore
b Portland, Ore, Dec 29, 03; d John Clyde Huntley & Verna Lyman H; m 1925 to Collis Powell Moore; c David Huntley. Educ: Ore Col Educ; Univ Ore. Polit & Govt Pos: Mem exec comt, Ore State Rep Cent Comt, 46-56; chmn, Sherman Co Rep Comt, 52-56; Rep Nat Committeewoman, Ore, 56-, vchmn, Rep Nat Comt, 64-72; deleg, Rep Nat Conv, 72. Mem: Int hon Sigma Beta Phi; Eastern Star; DAR; Metrop Club; Rep Women's Fedn & Dalles Club. Relig: Presbyterian. Mailing Add: Box 225 Moro OR 97039

MOORE, DUDLEY SHIELDS (R)
b Sandusky, Ohio, May 24, 20; s Albert Henry Moore & Helen Shields M; m 1949 to Lynn Tanner; c Barbara Ann & James Dudley. Educ: Maryville Col, 42; Ind Univ Sch Dent, DDS, 44; Univ Calif & Northwestern Univ, post grad study; Delta Sigma Delta; col letter for swimming, 41-42. Polit & Govt Pos: Pres bd trustees, Santa Rosa Pub Libr, Calif, 56-72; chmn, Sonoma Co Rep Cent Comt, 62-69; mem, State Rep Cent Comt Calif, 62-69; from vchmn to chmn, First Cong Dist Rep Comt, 63-70; chmn, Dent Health Strike Force, State of Calif, 73-; chmn, Calif Dent Polit Action Comt. Bus & Prof Pos: Dentist & oral surgeon, currently; mem bd gov, Empire Col Law. Mil Serv: Entered as Pvt, Army, 43, released as Capt, 45, after serv in Dent Corps, 618th Med Co, 6th Army, 47; Lt Col, Air Force Res; Good Conduct Ribbon; Am Theater Ribbon; Victory Medal; Asiatic-Pac Theater Ribbon; Air Force Res Medal; Air Force Longevity Ribbon. Publ: Prof articles in J Fla Dent Asn, J Southern Calif Dent Asn & Sonoma Co Med Bull. Mem: Fel Int Asn Oral Surgeons; Calif Dent Asn (dir & mem exec comt, vpres & pres-elect, pres, 72-73); fel Am Col Dentists; fel Royal Soc Health, Eng; Pierre Fauchard Acad. Relig: Episcopal. Legal Res: 2160 Geary Dr Santa Rosa CA 95404 Mailing Add: 1173 Montgomery Dr Santa Rosa CA 95405

MOORE, EDDIE (R)
Wyo State Sen
Mailing Add: 630 Poplar Box 161 Douglas WY 82633

MOORE, ERNEST C (D)
WVa State Deleg
Mailing Add: State Capitol Charleston WV 25305

MOORE, FRED THURMAN (D)
SC State Rep
b Seneca, SC, June 30, 21; s Alger Earl Moore & Edith Betty Stancil M; m to Maude Elizabeth Williams; c Fredda (Mrs Billy Gilmer), Fred T, II & Betty Jo. Polit & Govt Pos: SC State Rep, 51-73 & 75-; agt, SC Law Enforcement Div; mem bd dirs, SC Rehabilitation Dept. Bus & Prof Pos: Publisher-ed, Honea Path Chronicle, 20 years; gen auctioneer & owner, Moore Auction Co; mem bd dirs, Grammer Guitar Co, Nashville, Tenn; agt, Moore Real Estate Co, Honea Path. Mil Serv: Enlisted, 42, Navy, released as PhM 1/C, 45, after serv in Pac & ETO; Purple Heart. Relig: Latter-day Saint. Mailing Add: Box 505 Honea Path SC 29654

MOORE, GEORGE MANSFIELD (R)
Comnr, US Tariff Comn
b LaGrange, Ky, Dec 9, 13; s George Mansfield Moore & Mary Elizabeth Johnston M; m 1946 to Mary Caroline McCullar; c George McCullar, James Alfred & Robert Mansfield. Educ: George Washington Univ, AB, 37, JD, 40; Kappa Sigma. Polit & Govt Pos: Chief counsel, Post Off & Civil Serv Comn, US House of Rep, 47-52; comnr, OS Civil Serv Comn, 53-57; exec asst to Postmaster Gen, Post Off Dept, 57-59, Dep Asst Postmaster Gen, 61, Asst Postmaster Gen, Bur of Transportation, 59-61; comnr, US Tariff Comn, 69- Bus & Prof Pos: Assoc, Galvin, Tracy, Goehegan, Levy & Milliken, Attorneys, Cincinnati, Ohio, 46, Fairbanks, Stafford & Fairbanks, Attorneys, DC, 52 & Ames, Hill & Ames, Attorneys, DC, 64-69. Mem: Am, DC & Ky State Bar Asns. Honors & Awards: Distinguished Serv Award, Post Off Dept, 60. Relig: Baptist. Legal Res: 1101 Highland Dr Silver Spring MD 20910 Mailing Add: US Tariff Comn Eighth & E Sts NW Washington DC 20436

MOORE, GERALD F (D)
Ariz State Rep
Mailing Add: 3321 W Vermont Phoenix AZ 85017

MOORE, HELEN HUNTER (D)
Committeewoman, Young Dem of Ala
b Mobile, Ala, Oct 17, 49; d Robert Hunter Moore & Ann Pennington M; div. Educ: Univ SAla, 70-72; Spring Hill Col, 74; Auburn Univ, currently. Polit & Govt Pos: Coordr, McGovern for President Campaign, Mobile, Ala, 72; pres, Mobile Co Young Dem, 73-74; alt deleg, Dem Nat Mid-Term Conf, 74; mem, Affirmative Action Comt, Ala, currently; committeewoman, Young Dem of Ala, 74- Honors & Awards: Deleg, US State Dept Seminar held in conjunction with Young Polit Leaders of Am, 75. Relig: Presbyterian. Mailing Add: 143 Cedar Crest Auburn AL 36830

MOORE, HERMAN AUBREY (D)
NC State Sen
b Greenwood, SC, Nov 8, 29; s Herman A Moore (deceased) & Emmie McConnell M; m 1950 to Bete Craig; c Leslie, Herman, III, Craig & Eric. Educ: Univ NC; Charlotte Col. Polit & Govt Pos: Pres, Mecklenburg Co Young Dem Club; secy, NC State Dem Exec Comt, 52-56; dinner chmn, Jefferson-Jackson Day Dinner, 55; NC State Sen, 64-, Pres Pro Tem, NC State Senate, 67-69; ex-officio, Dem Nat Mid-Term Conf, 74. Bus & Prof Pos: Dir & mem

exec comt, Am Credit Corp; state chmn, nat trustee & mem exec comt, Ducks Unlimited, Inc. Relig: Presbyterian. Mailing Add: Box 2665 Charlotte NC 28201

MOORE, J LEX (D)
Ark State Sen
Mailing Add: 315 S Spruce Harrison AR 72601

MOORE, J MAX (R)
Mem, Rep State Cent Comt, Calif
b Philadelphia, Pa, Sept 14, 19; s James Thaddeus Moore & Selma Gessler Steller M; m 1941 to Mary Cowles; c Ciss (Mrs Robert Harris, Jr), James Cowles & John B. Educ: Stanford Univ, AB, 41; Delta Kappa Epsilon. Polit & Govt Pos: Mem libr comn, City & Co of San Francisco, Calif, 56-59; pres, Bd of Permit Appeals, San Francisco, Calif, 59-63; acting mayor, City & Co of San Francisco, 63; mem, San Francisco Co Bd of Supvr, 63-64; chmn, San Francisco Co for Reagan, 66-69; chmn, San Francisco Co Rep Cent Comt, formerly; mem, Rep State Cent Comt Calif, currently; area chmn, Ed Reinecke for Gov, 74. Bus & Prof Pos: Pres, Moore Mfg, Inc, 53-73; pres, Moore Plastic Industs, Inc, 65-73; exec vpres, Moore Chem Corp, 60-73; vpres, Signature Transportation, Inc, 63-73. Mil Serv: Entered as A/S, Navy, 42, released as Lt(sg), 45, after serv in Supply Corps & Naval Air Training Command; Victory Medal; US Theatre Medal. Mem: Plastic Industs, Inc; Lowell Alumni Asn; Bohemian Club; Press Club; Rotary. Honors & Awards: Young Man of the Year, San Francisco, 55. Relig: Episcopal. Legal Res: 2470 Broadway San Francisco CA 94115 Mailing Add: Industrial Way & Moore Rd Brisbane CA 94005

MOORE, JACK KENNETH (R)
Mont State Rep
b Phenix City, Ala, Nov 9, 21; s Cecil Andrew Moore (deceased) & Mabel Pace M (deceased); m 1943 to Geraldine Hasquet; c Julienne A (Mrs Randolph Coley), Lance H, Craig C & Prentice J (Mrs William Kaste). Educ: Auburn Univ, 39-42; Univ Colo, 56-57; Univ Md, 60-61; Sigma Alpha Epsilon. Polit & Govt Pos: Mont State Rep, 75- Mil Serv: Entered as Cadet, Air Force, 42, released as Col, 71, after serv in ETO, 43-45, Caribbean Theatre, 46-49, Europe, 59-63, SE Asia, 66-67 & 69-70; Legion of Merit; Bronze Star; Meritorious Serv Medal; Air Force Commendation Medal with 2 Oak Leaf Clusters; World War II Victory Medal; Am Defense Serv Medal; Royal Thai Supreme Command Master Badge; Europe-EAfrica & Mid East Campaign Medals; Am Theater Campaign Medal; Vietnam Serv Medal. Mem: Air Force Asn (pres, Big Sky Chap); New Meadow Lark Country Club (pres); Cascade Co Bicentennial Comn (chmn); Kiwanis Int; Asn Am Rod & Gun Clubs Europe. Relig: Roman Catholic. Mailing Add: Apt 85 1200 32nd St S Great Falls MT 59405

MOORE, JAMES DOUGLAS (D)
Mont State Rep
b Helena, Mont, Nov 21, 44; s Orville Morris Moore, MD & Anna Dorthea Allen M; m 1970 to Margaret Chandler Sterling; c Sarah Allen & Meghan Chandler. Educ: Univ Colo, Boulder, BA, 68; Carroll Col, 66; Univ Mont, JD, 72; Phi Delta Theta. Polit & Govt Pos: Mont State Rep, Dist 18, 75- Bus & Prof Pos: Attorney, McGarvey, Moore & Lence, Kalispell, Mont, 72- Mil Serv: Entered as E-1, Army, 68, released as SP-5, 74, after serv in Army Res; Expert Marksman. Publ: Auth, Articles in Mont Law Rev. Mem: Am & Mont Trial Lawyers Asns; Mont Bar Asn; Northwest Mont Bar Asn (vpres). Relig: Episcopal. Mailing Add: 501 Sylvan Kalispell MT 59901

MOORE, JAMES EDWARD (D)
SC State Rep
b Laurens, SC, Mar 13, 36; s Roy Ernest Moore & Marie Elizabeth Hill M; m 1963 to Mary Alicia Deadwyler; c Erin Alicia & Travis Warren. Educ: Duke Univ, BA, 58, Law Sch, LLB, 61; Kappa Sigma; Phi Delta Phi. Polit & Govt Pos: Deleg, SC State Dem Conv, 64, 66 & 68; vpres, City Dem Club, Greenwood, 65, 66; SC State Rep, Greenwood Co, 69- Mil Serv: S/Sgt, Air Nat Guard, 58-64. Mem: Am Bar Asn; SC & Am Trial Lawyers Asns; A&FM; Moose, Relig: Baptist. Mailing Add: 212 Oak Ave Greenwood SC 29646

MOORE, JAMES P, JR (R)
Nat Exec Committeeman, SC Young Rep Fedn
b Greenville, SC, May 22, 41; s James P Moore & Rose Morgan M; m 1966 to Ellen Maultsby; c Ellen Rose & Elizabeth Ruth. Educ: St Andrew's Presby Col, BS, 65; Univ SC Law Sch, 69; Am Inst Banking, degree, 72; Phi Beta Lambda; Circle K; Phi Alpha Delta; Lancers. Polit & Govt Pos: Youth leader, Clemson Col Young Rep Club for Nixon, 60; chmn & founder, Scotland Co Rep Party & Goldwater for President, SC, 64; precinct organizer, John Lindsay for Mayor of New York, 65; chmn, Greenville Co Young Rep Club, 67-68; youth coordr, Greenville Co for Nixon, 68; treas, Greenville City Rep Party, 68-70; coordr & mem pub rels staff, Albert Watson Cand for Gov of SC, 70; Nat Exec Committeeman, SC Young Rep Fedn, 71-; youth coordr, SC Comt to Reelect the President, 72; campaign mgr, Wayne Whaltey Cand for US House of Rep, Fourth Dist, 72. Bus & Prof Pos: Owner, Moore Home Bldg Co, Greenville, SC, 65-69; asst trust officer, People's Nat Bank, 70-; pres, Fiberglass Industs, Inc, 72-73. Mil Serv: Entered as E-1, Army Signal Corps, 6O, released as E-5, 62, after serv in 111th Signal Corps, LB, Ft Gordon & Ft Benning, 60-62; Distinguished Serv Medal; Good Conduct Medal. Mem: Am & SC Banker's Asns; Am Inst of Banking; Nat Asn Real Estate Bd; SC Real Estate Bd. Relig: Presbyterian. Mailing Add: 311 Longview Terr Greenville SC 29605

MOORE, JAMES W (D)
Shelby Co Comnr, Tenn
b Paris, Tenn, Apr 24, 03; s James W Moore & Sally Gregson M; m 1940 to Kate Miles. Educ: Union Univ; Alpha Tau Omega. Polit & Govt Pos: Comnr, Memphis, Tenn, 60-66; comnr, Shelby Co, 66- Bus & Prof Pos: Prof baseball, 23-36, two world series, 30 & 31; taxi transportation, 36-52; bus transportation, 40-56; real estate, 56-60. Mem: Mason (32 degree); Shrine; four social clubs; Lions. Honors & Awards: Col on staff of Gov, Tenn & Gov, Ky. Relig: Presbyterian. Legal Res: 95 Hollyoke Lane Memphis TN 38101 Mailing Add: Court House Memphis TN 38103

MOORE, JERRY ALEXANDER JR (R)
Councilman, DC
b Minden, La, June 12, 18; s Jerry Alexander Moore, Sr & Mae Dee Abner M; m 1946 to Ettyce Herdon Hill; c Jerry, III & Juran D. Educ: Morehouse Col, BA, 40; Howard Univ, BD, 44, MA, 57; Phi Beta Sigma. Polit & Govt Pos: Mem, DC Rep Exec Comt, 67, chmn, formerly; alt deleg, Rep Nat Conv, 68; councilman, DC, 69-; mem, Transportation Planning Bd, Metrop Coun of Govts, currently. Bus & Prof Pos: Asst mgr, United Serv Orgn, New Orleans, La, 43; boy's work secy, YMCA, 44; personnel rels officer, Port of Embarkation, 44; asst to pastor, 19th St Baptist Church, DC, 45, pastor, 46- Publ: Look to This Day, privately publ, 49. Mem: NW Settlement House (bd dirs); Stoddard Baptist Home (bd dirs); Opportunities Industrializations Ctr (bd dirs); Washington Metrop Area Transit Authority (bd dirs). Relig: Baptist. Mailing Add: 1612 Buchanan St NW Washington DC 20011

MOORE, JOHN DENIS JOSEPH (R)
b New York, NY, Nov 10, 10; s John Denis Joseph Moore & Julia Frances Leader M; m 1936 to Mary Foote (deceased); c John Denis, Margaret Foote (deceased), Anne, MD (Mrs Arnold L Lisio), Julia (Mrs Allan Dean Converse, III), Mary Faith & Martha. Educ: Yale Univ, AB, 32, Law Sch, LLB, 35; Alpha Delta Phi; Phi Delta Phi. Hon Degrees: LLD, Suffolk Univ, 72. Polit & Govt Pos: Asst corp counsel, New York, 40-43; asst dist attorney, New York Co, 43-46; US Ambassador, Ireland, 69-75. Bus & Prof Pos: Lawyer, White & Case, 35-38; lawyer, Burlingame, Nourse & Pettit, 38-40; vpres, W R Grace & Co, New York, 46-69; dir, Grace Line, Inc, 53-69. Mil Serv: Pvt, NY Guard, 42-46, serv in 51st Regt. Mem: Am Bar Asn; US Inter-Am Coun; Ireland-US Coun; Coun for Latin Am; Yale Club, NY. Honors & Awards: Order of Sun, Peru; Knight of Malta, Vatican; Order of Merit, Ecuador; Order of Leopold II, Belgium; Gold Medal, Am-Irish Hist Soc, 66. Relig: Roman Catholic. Legal Res: NJ Mailing Add: Am Embassy Dublin Ireland

MOORE, JOHN J (D)
NY State Sen
b Wilkes-Barre, Pa, Sept 28, 21; s John J Moore & Margaret Boyle M; m 1973 to June P Dempsey; c Brian & Michael. Educ: Pace Univ, BBA, 55. Polit & Govt Pos: Mem community sch bd, Queens Dist 30, NY, 70-73; NY State Sen, Dist 14, 74- Bus & Prof Pos: Spec agt, Fed Bur Invest, 48-60; spec agt, NY State Comn Invest, 60-73. Mil Serv: Entered as Seaman 1/C, Navy, 42, released as Yeoman 2/C, 46, after serv in USS Haraden & USS Nields; 7 Combat Stars; Purple Heart. Mem: Soc Former Spec Agts of Fed Bur Invest; Am Legion; VFW; DAV; KofC. Relig: Catholic. Mailing Add: 22-48 80th St Jackson Heights NY 11370

MOORE, JOHN PAUL (D)
Miss State Sen
b Louisville, Miss, Aug 4, 30; s Clinton Moore & Berdie Elizabeth Clay M; m 1959 to Evelyn Jackson; c John Stuart, Bruce Alan, Ronald Scott & Teresa Ann. Educ: Miss State Univ, BBA, 57; Univ Miss, LLB, 59; Phi Alpha Delta. Polit & Govt Pos: Miss State Sen, Noxubee & Oktibbeha Co, 72- Mil Serv: Entered as Pvt, Air Force, 50, released as Sgt, 54, after serv in 5th Statist Serv, Eng, 52-54. Relig: Baptist. Legal Res: 205 Woodlawn Starkville MS 39759 Mailing Add: Box 924 Starkville MS 39759

MOORE, JOHN PORFILIO (R)
Attorney Gen, Colo
b Denver, Colo, Oct 14, 34; s Edward A Porfilio & Caroline Carbone P; m 1959 to G Joan West; c Edward Miles, Joseph Arthur & Jeanne Kathryn. Educ: Stanford Univ, 52-54; Univ Denver, BA, 56, LLB, 59; Phi Delta Phi; Alpha Sigma Phi. Polit & Govt Pos: Asst attorney gen, Colo, 62-68, dep attorney gen, 68-72, attorney gen, 72- Bus & Prof Pos: Pvt legal practice, Denver, Colo, 59-62. Mem: Nat, Am & Colo Bar Asns; Nat Asn of Attorneys Gen; Nat Organized Crime Prosecutors Asn (secy, 72-). Mailing Add: Attorney Generals Off State Capitol Denver CO 80203

MOORE, JONATHAN (R)
b New York, NY, Sept 10, 32; s Charles Frederick Moore, Jr & Adeline Reeves Nichols M; m 1957 to Katherine Weeks Andres; c Joan Brooke, Jennifer, Jocelyn Andres & Charles Frederick, IV. Educ: Dartmouth Col, AB cum laude, 54; Harvard Grad Sch Pub Admin, MPA, 57; Kennedy Inst of Polit, Harvard Univ, resident fel, 66-67 & fall 68. Polit & Govt Pos: Pub affairs asst, US Info Agency, Wash, Bombay & Monrovia, 57-59; legis asst to US Sen Leverett Saltonstall, Mass, 59-61; politico-mil affairs officer, Off of Int Security Affairs, Dept of Defense, 61-63, spec asst to Asst Secy of Defense, 63-64; spec asst to Asst Secy of State for Far Eastern Affairs, Dept of State, Dep Asst Secy of State for EAsian & Pac Affairs, 69-70; foreign affairs adv to Gov Romney in Nat Campaign, 67-68; foreign affairs adv to Gov Rockefeller in Nat Campaign, 68; counr, Dept Health, Educ & Welfare, 70-72; spec asst to Secy of Defense, 73- Relig: Protestant. Legal Res: Tonset Rd Orleans MA 02653 Mailing Add: 2407 Nordok Pl Alexandria VA 22306

MOORE, MARTHA CHRISTINE (R)
Rep Nat Committeewoman, Ohio
b Cambridge, Ohio, Nov 13, 18; d C Ellis Moore & Nannie B Hammond M; single. Educ: Wellesley Col, 36-37; Muskingum Col, BA, 40; Ohio State Univ, MA, 52; Columbia Univ, postgrad study, 59; hon mem Nat Collegiate Players. Polit & Govt Pos: Mem, State Rep Cent & Exec Comt Ohio, 50-, vchmn, 70-; mem, Guernsey Co Bd of Electors, 56-; alt deleg-at-lg, Rep Nat Conv, 60 & dist alt deleg, 64 & 72; mem, Guernsey Co Rep Exec Comt, 62-; precinct committeeman, Guernsey Co Rep Cent Comt, 64-; Rep Nat Committeewoman, Ohio, 72- Bus & Prof Pos: Teacher, Painesville, Ohio, 41-42; teacher, Cambridge, Ohio, 42-45; secy, Aluminum Co of Am, 45-47; assoc prof speech, Muskingum Col, 48- Mem: Speech Asn of Am; Speech Asn of Ohio; Am Asn Univ Women. Relig: United Presbyterian. Mailing Add: 501 Oakland Blvd Cambridge OH 43725

MOORE, OTIS H, JR (D)
Ala State Rep
Mailing Add: PO Box 44 Sterrett AL 35147

MOORE, PAUL M (D)
SC State Sen
Mailing Add: Spartanburg SC 29301

MOORE, PHYLLIS NORMAN (R)
Committeewoman, Rep State Exec Comt Fla
b Niles, Ohio, May 12, 23; d Earl Deadrick Norman & Julia Russell N; m 1954 to Sherwood Edgar Moore; c Michael Norman & Keith Erickson. Educ: St Elizabeth Sch Nursing, RN, 44; Univ Mo, AB, 50; Eng Honorary; Alpha Chi Omega. Polit & Govt Pos: Precinct committeewoman, Broward Co Rep Party, Fla, 62-70; committeewoman, Fla Rep State Exec Comt, 66-, vchmn, formerly; mayor, Lazy Lane, 68-; dist mgr, Bur of Census, 70. Mil Serv: Entered as 2nd Lt, Air Force, 45, released as 2nd Lt, 47, after serv in Nurse Corps. Mem: Am Nurses Asn; Am Red Cross; Am for Const Action; Am Conserv Union; Ft Lauderdale Rep Club. Relig: Episcopal. Mailing Add: 2200 Lazy Lane Ft Lauderdale FL 33305

MOORE, ROBERT D (D)
Chmn, Salt Lake Co Dem Comt, Utah

b Butte, Mont, Oct 24, 35; s William C Moore & Mary McGarvey M; m 1957 to Anne D McDonough; c Anne Katherine, Robert John & William Roger. Educ: Utah State Univ; Univ Utah, BSL, 56, Law Sch, JD; Phi Alpha Delta; Sigma Chi. Polit & Govt Pos: Attorney, Salt Lake Civil Serv, 60-61; dep attorney, Salt Lake Co, 61-63; voting dist deleg, Salt Lake Co, currently; mem, Utah State Cent Comt, currently; chmn, Salt Lake Co Dem Comt, 70-; deleg, Dem Nat Conv, 72. Mem: Utah Trial Lawyers Asn; Univ Club; Utah & Am Bar Asns; Bars of Circuit Court of Appeals, Fed & State Court. Relig: Catholic. Legal Res: 1529 Preston St Salt Lake City UT 84105 Mailing Add: Suite 400 Ten Broadway Bldg Ten W Third St S Salt Lake City UT 84101

MOORE, ROGER ALLAN (R)
b Framingham, Mass, Aug 8, 31; s Ralph Chester Moore & Mabelle Taft M; m 1955 to Barbara Lee Wildman; c Marshall Christian, Elizabeth Lee, Taft Hayden Davis & Allan Baron. Educ: Harvard Col, AB, 53, Harvard Law Sch, LLB, 56. Polit & Govt Pos: Col dir, Young Rep Nat Fedn, 51-53, vchmn, 53-57; mem, Bd of Foreign Scholar, US Dept of State, 54-58; exec dir, Mass Citizens for Eisenhower, 56; gen counsel, Mass Rep State Comt, 62-72; deleg, Rep Nat Conv, 64; counsel, Goldwater for President Comt, 64; parliamentarian, Mass Rep Conv, 64-72. Bus & Prof Pos: Legal asst to Attorney Gen of Mass, 53-56; attorney, Ropes & Gray, 56-66, partner, 67-; chmn bd, Nat Rev, Inc. Mem: Boston, Mass & Am Bar Asns. Relig: Episcopal. Legal Res: 26 W Cedar St Boston MA 02108 Mailing Add: 225 Franklin St Boston MA 02110

MOORE, ROWENA GENEVA (D)
Chairwoman, Douglas Co Dem Cent Comt, Nebr

b Meredian, Okla, Sept 10, 10; d Jethro James Moore & Anna Bell Jordan M; div; c Robert Eugene Rose & stepson, Thomas E Carodine. Educ: Bellevue Col, 1 year. Polit & Govt Pos: Chmn minorities comt, Nebr Dem State Cent Comt, 68-; alt deleg, Dem Nat Conv, 72; chairwoman, Douglas Co Dem Cent Comt, Nebr, currently; cand for Omaha City Coun, 73. Bus & Prof Pos: Partner & owner, Ann's Cafe, 44-60; pres, Moore & Rose Investment Enterprises, Inc, 70- Mem: UPAW AFL-CIO. Honors & Awards: Most Outstanding Orgn, United Community Serv, 72; Hon Mention, Nebr State Econ Develop Dept, 72. Relig: Methodist. Mailing Add: 2019 N 20th St Omaha NE 68102

MOORE, TOM (D)
Ariz State Sen

Mailing Add: 5809 S Liberty St Tucson AZ 85706

MOORE, TOM ROBERT (D)
Fla State Rep

b Clearwater, Fla, May 17, 40; s Edward Moore; m to Barbara Young; c Norman Thomas, Elizabeth Ann & Colin McRee. Educ: Univ Fla, BA/BS, 63, Col Law, JD, 66; Blue Key, vpres; Phi Kappa Tau. Polit & Govt Pos: Mem citizens adv comt, Tampa Bay Regional Planning Coun, Fla, 74-; mem, Pinellas Co Dem Exec Comt, 74-; Fla State Rep, 74- Bus & Prof Pos: Law prof, US Peace Corps, Liberia, Africa, 66-68; attorney, Moore, McDaniel & Tsonas, Clearwater, Fla, 74- Mem: Nat Audubon Soc (dir environ law div, Fla Audubon, 7-); Dem Clubs; Fla & Clearwater Bar Asns. Relig: United Church of Christ. Legal Res: 1567 Budleigh Clearwater FL 33516 Mailing Add: PO Box 4338 Clearwater FL 33518

MOORE, VINCENT E (R)
Kans State Sen

Mailing Add: 1316 Arrowhead Wichita KS 67203

MOORE, W D (BILL) JR (D)
Ark State Sen

Mailing Add: 1112 Green St El Dorado AR 71730

MOORE, W EDGAR (R)
Kans State Rep

single. Educ: Mid Am Nazarene Col, BS in Bus, 73. Polit & Govt Pos: Fed inspector, US Dept Agr, Kansas City, Kans, 41-72; Kans State Rep, 73- Bus & Prof Pos: Real estate broker, Agnes Gates Realty, Prairie Village, Kans, 73- Mem: Johnson Co Taxpayers Asn; Kiwanis Club (lt gov, 72-); Johnson Farm Bur; Grange; Toastmasters Club. Relig: United Presbyterian. Mailing Add: 127th St & Rogers Rd Olathe KS 66061

MOORE, W HENSON (R)
US Rep, La

b Lake Charles, La, Oct 4, 39; s Mr & Mrs W H Moore, Jr; m to Carolyn Ann Cherry; c William Henson, IV, Jennifer Lee & Cherry Ann. Educ: La State Univ, BA, 61, MA, 73; La State Univ Law Sch, JD, 65. Polit & Govt Pos: Mem, Rep State Cent Comt La, 71-75, chmn, State Research & Issues Comt, formerly; US Rep, Sixth Cong Dist, 75- Bus & Prof Pos: Mem, Dale, Owen, Richardson, Taylor & Matthews, 67-74, managing partner, 69-74. Mil Serv: Co Comdr, Army, 65-67. Mem: Am Legion; Rotary. Relig: Episcopal. Legal Res: Baton Rouge LA Mailing Add: 427 Cannon Off Bldg Washington DC 20515

MOORE, WALTER M (D)
Vt State Rep

b Proctor, Vt, Nov 20, 20; s Charles R Moore & Edna Manning M; m 1945 to Anita C Lefrancois; c Martha (Mrs Rideout), Suzanne (Mrs Martin), Mary Beth (Mrs Dawley), Margaret & James C. Educ: St Michael's Col, BA, 42, MA, 54. Polit & Govt Pos: Alderman, Rutland City, Vt, 72-; Vt State Rep, 75- Bus & Prof Pos: Eng teacher, Mt St Joseph Acad, 47- Mil Serv: Entered as Aviation Cadet, Army Air Force, 42, released as 1st Lt, 46, after serv in 90th Bomb Group, Southwest Pac Theater, 44-45; Air Force Res, Maj(Ret); Distinguished Flying Cross; Aid Medal. Mem: Vt Teachers Eng; KofC; Rutland Libr (trustee). Relig: Roman Catholic. Mailing Add: 12 Engrem Ave Rutland VT 05701

MOORE, WARREN C (D)
Ala State Rep

Mailing Add: Rte 3 Box 875 Huntsville AL 35806

MOORE, WILLIAM E, III (D)
b Barnsville, Ohio, Dec 15, 34; s Attorney William E Moore, Jr & Marjorie Taylor M; single. Educ: Ohio Northern Univ, BA, 56; Theta Alpha Phi; Sigma Pi. Polit & Govt Pos: Admin staff, State Treas, Ohio, 59-60; research asst to US Sen Ernest Gruening, Alaska, 67-69; admin staff, State Auditor, Ohio, 71-72; state coordr, Ohio Jackson for President, 72; deleg, Dem Nat Mid-Term Conf, 74. Bus & Prof Pos: Owner & publ, The Spirit of Democracy, 73- Mil Serv: Entered as E-1, Army, 57, released as E-3, after serv in Alaska Command, 57-58. Relig: Methodist. Mailing Add: 323 Eastern Ave Woodsfield OH 43793

MOORE, WILLIAM GRAHAM (R)
Mem, Conn State Rep Finance Comt

b New York, NY, Oct 21, 22; s Eugene M Moore & Margaret Graham M; m 1941 to Shirley Flower; c Megan, William G, Jr, Corwin F & Shirley. Educ: Yale Univ, BA; Delta Kappa Epsilon. Polit & Govt Pos: Mem, Greenwich Representative Town Meeting, Conn, 52-61; mem, Conn State Rep Finance Comt, 64-, vchmn, 65-66; Conn State Sen, 69-71; chmn, Conn State Bd Ment Health, 71-; chmn, Conn River Estuary Regional Planning Agency, 71- Bus & Prof Pos: Assoc ed, Column Mag, 47-49; reporter, Wall Street J, 49-53; assoc ed, Fortune Mag, 53-56; consult, Inquiry Eval, Inc, Indust Mkt Research, 56-61, pres, 61- Mil Serv: Entered as Pvt, Army, 42, released as T/Sgt, 45, after serv in Mil Intel Serv, 18th Airborne Corps, ETO, 44-45; Five Battle Stars. Publ: Poems, 1940-60, Poetry Asn Am, 61; articles & poems in Atlantic Monthly, New Yorker, Country J & others. Mem: Am Mkt Asn; NY Financial Writers Asn; CofC. Relig: Protestant. Mailing Add: Joshuatown Rd Lyme CT 06371

MOORE, WILLIAM J (R)
Pa State Sen

Mailing Add: 401 Beaver St Millertown PA 17062

MOORE, WILLIAM RUDY, JR (D)
Mem, Ark Dem State Comt

b Ft Smith, Ark, May 31, 43; s William Rudy Moore, Sr & Louise Burrow M; m 1968 to Judith Leigh Johnson; c Jason Tyler & Matthew William. Educ: Southern Methodist Univ, BA in Econ, 65; Am Univ, Cairo, 65-66; Univ Ark Sch Law, JD, 69; Cycen Fjodr; Phi Gamma Delta. Polit & Govt Pos: Ark State Rep, Washington Co, 71-75; mem, Ark Dem State Comt, 74- Bus & Prof Pos: Attorney-at-law, Wade, McAllister, Wade & Burke, 69- Mem: Rotary; CofC; Fine Arts Ctr (pres). Relig: Methodist. Legal Res: 1400 Cleveland St Fayetteville AR 72701 Mailing Add: PO Box 1000 Fayetteville AR 72701

MOORE, WILLIAM TYLER (D)
Tex State Sen

b Robertson Co, Tex, Apr 9, 18; s Ernest Boyd Moore & Ruby Closs M; m 1953 to Macille; c William Tyler, Jr. Educ: Tex A&M Univ, BBS, 40; Univ Tex, Austin, LLB, 49. Polit & Govt Pos: Tex State Rep, 47-49; Tex State Sen, 49-, pres pro tempore, Tex State Senate, 57. Bus & Prof Pos: Attorney-at-law, 48- Mil Serv: Entered as Pvt, Army, 43, released as S/Sgt, 46, after serv in 11th Air Force, Asiatic-Pac Theatre, 43-46. Mem: State Bar of Tex; VFW; Am Legion. Relig: Baptist. Legal Res: 1204 Sul Ross Bryan TX 77801 Mailing Add: PO Box 3967 Bryan TX 77801

MOOREHEAD, TOM V (R)
b Zanesville, Ohio, Apr 12, 98; s Thomas L Moorehead & Nellie Van Horn M; m to Louise Anderson; c Joan (Mrs Johnson), Janet (Mrs Freisinger), Tom V, Jr & Douglas A. Educ: Ohio Wesleyan Univ; George Washington Univ. Polit & Govt Pos: Councilman, Zanesville, Ohio, 34-38, mayor, 38-45; Ohio State Sen, 45-60, 63 & 67-68; US Rep, Ohio, 61-62. Bus & Prof Pos: Owner, Real Estate & Ins Agency. Mil Serv: Naval Air Force, 18. Relig: Presbyterian. Legal Res: 1515 Maple Ave Zanesville OH 43701 Mailing Add: 4 Main St Zanesville OH 43701

MOORES, HERVEY CUTHRELL (R)
Chmn, Killingworth Rep Town Comt, Conn

b Brooklyn, NY, July 28, 26; d Hugh Hamlin Cuthrell (deceased) & Faith Baldwin C; m 1961 to Chester Austin Moores, Jr; c Barbara (Mrs Limosani), Faith (Mrs Ploude), Laura (Mrs Davis), Elizabeth (Mrs Krulish), Philip & Marjorie. Educ: Roosevelt Hosp Sch Nursing, 43-46. Polit & Govt Pos: Deleg, 33rd Sen Dist, Rep Party, Conn, 74 & 35th Assembly Dist Rep Party, 75; chmn, Killingworth Rep Town Comt, 74-; adv, Coun on Foster Children, 75-; adv, Civil Preparedness, 75-; justice of the peace, Killingworth, 75- Mem: Emergency Med Technician Asn; Killingworth Grange (Fifth Degree). Relig: Congregational. Mailing Add: River Rd Rte 3 Killingworth CT 06417

MOORHEAD, ALEXANDER A, JR (INDEPENDENT CITIZENS MOVEMENT)
Sen, VI Legis

b Frederiksted, St Croix, VI, June 7, 45; s Alexander A Moorhead, Sr (deceased) & Ester Brow M; m 1974 to Maxine Benjamin. Educ: Moravian Col, BA, 66; Alpha Phi Omega. Polit & Govt Pos: Pres, Independent Dem, Frederiksted, 67-69; treas, 69-70; pres, Independent Citizens Movement Club, 70-71; chmn platform comt, Independent Citizens Movement Conv, 70; Sen, VI Legis, 71-, Minority Leader, 71-; vpres, Second Conv of VI, 71. Bus & Prof Pos: Acting mgr, Firm of Alexander Moorhead, 68- Mem: Jaycees. Honors & Awards: Senatorship & Distinguished Award, Jaycees. Relig: Moravian. Legal Res: 62 Smithfield Frederiksted St Croix VI 00840 Mailing Add: PO Box 187 Frederiksted St Croix VI 00840

MOORHEAD, CARLOS J (R)
US Rep, Calif

b 1922; m to Valery Joan Tyler. Educ: Univ Calif, Los Angeles; Univ Southern Calif, JD. Polit & Govt Pos: Pres, 43rd Dist Calif Rep Assembly, 59; mem, Rep State Cent Comt Calif, 67-; Calif State Assemblyman, formerly; US Rep, Calif, 73- Bus & Prof Pos: Lawyer, 24 years. Mem: State Bar of Calif; Glendale & Los Angeles Co Bar Asns; Asn of Former Calif Legislators; Judge Advocates Asn. Honors & Awards: Outstanding Legislator Award, Calif Rep Assembly, 67 & 69. Relig: Presbyterian. Legal Res: Apt C 1106 N Louise Glendale CA 91207 Mailing Add: 420 N Brand Blvd Rm 404 Glendale CA 91203

MOORHEAD, WILLIAM SINGER, (D)
US Rep, Pa

b Pittsburgh, Pa, Apr 8, 23; s William S Moorhead & Constance Barr M; m 1946 to Lucy Galpin; c William S, III, Lucy P Galpin, Stephen Galpin & James Barr. Educ: Yale Univ, BA, 44; Harvard Univ Law Sch, JD cum laude, 49. Polit & Govt Pos: Mem, Pittsburgh Art Comn; asst city solicitor, Pittsburgh, Pa, 54-57; secy, Allegheny Co Housing Authority, 56-58; US Rep, 14th Cong Dist, 59- Bus & Prof Pos: Partner, Moorhead & Knox, Attorneys, 49-70. Mil Serv: Entered as A/S, Naval Res, 43, released as Lt(jg), 46, after serv in Pac Theater; Am Campaign Ribbon; Philippine Campaign Ribbon with One Battle Star; Pac Campaign Ribbon with Five Battle Stars. Mem: Pittsburgh Child Guid Ctr (trustee); Tuberc League of Pittsburgh (trustee); Western Pa Conservancy (dir); Am Legion; Amvets. Relig: Episcopal.

Legal Res: 5226 Westminster Pl Pittsburgh PA 15232 Mailing Add: 2467 Rayburn House Off Bldg Washington DC 20515

MOOS, DONALD WILLIAM (R)
Dep Dir Region X, Environ Protection Agency
b Spokane, Wash, Mar 4, 23; s William F Moos & Clara Anna Koch M; m 1945 to Parmalee Jean Brouillard; c Merry Karlene & William H. Educ: City Col New York, 44; Wash State Univ, BS in Animal Sci, 47; Phi Kappa Phi; Alpha Zeta & Lambda Chi Alpha, Wash State Univ. Polit & Govt Pos: Precinct committeeman, Lincoln Co Cent Comt, Wash, 52-58; state pres, Wash Young Rep Fedn, 56-58; Wash State Rep, 58-65; temporary chmn, Wash State Rep Conv, 60, permanent chmn, 64; deleg, Rep Nat Conv, 64; former mem, Wash Water Pollution Comn, Wash Air Pollution Control Bd, Wash Water Resources Adv Coun, Gov Adv Coun on Nuclear Energy & Gov Adv Coun on Farm Labor; dir, Wash State Dept of Agr, 65-72; dep dir region X, Environ Protection Agency, 72- Bus & Prof Pos: Assoc ed, Western Livestock Reporter, Billings, Mont, 47-50; dir, Pac NW Grain & Grain Products, 56. Mil Serv: Entered as Pvt, Army, 42, released as S/Sgt, 45, after serv in 28th Div, 110th Inf, G Co, ETO, 42-45; ETO Ribbon, Three Major Campaigns; Purple Heart. Mem: Wash Asn Wheat Growers; Nat Asn State Depts of Agr (vpres, 71, pres, 72); Nat Meat & Poultry Inspection Adv Comt; Edwall Sch Bd; Pac Northwest Conf Methodist Church (bd educ). Honors & Awards: Outstanding Young Farmer Award, Spokane Jr CofC, 56; Hon Chap Farmer, Future Farmers of Am, 62; Medal for Outstanding Contributions to Am Agr, Fed Land Bank, 67. Relig: Methodist. Legal Res: Edwall WA 99008 Mailing Add: 2326 Vista Olympia WA 98501

MOOT, ROBERT C (D)
b Orange, NJ, June 1, 11; m to Helen Helms; c Karen, Robert, Jr & Gregory. Educ: NJ Schs. Polit & Govt Pos: Entered Fed Civil Serv, 46; comptroller, Bur of Supplies & Acct, Dept of the Navy, comptroller, Defense Supply Agency, Dept of Defense, 62-65, Dept Asst Secy of Defense for Logistics Serv, 65-66, Asst Secy of Defense, 68-72; dep adminr, Small Bus Admin, 66-67, chief officer, 67-68. Mil Serv: Army, World War II, released as Chief Warrant Officer. Honors & Awards: Recipient, Distinguished Civilian Serv Award with Bronze Palm & Meritorious Civilian Serv Award, Dept of Defense; Exceptional Civilian Serv Award & Meritorious Civilian Serv Award, Defense Supply Agency; Distinguished Civilian Serv Award, Small Bus Admin. Mailing Add: 4201 Woolls Pl Annandale VA 22003

MORAIN, FREDERICK GARVER (R)
Committeeman, Rep State Cent Comt Iowa
b Jefferson, Iowa, June 1, 41; s Frederick Elwyn Morain & Lois Irene Garver M; m 1965 to Clay Warwick Clement. Educ: Graceland Col, AA, 61; Univ Iowa, BA summa cum laude, 63; Yale Univ, MA, 65; PhD, 70; Phi Beta Kappa. Polit & Govt Pos: Chmn, Greene Co Rep Party, Iowa, 70-74; committeeman, Rep State Cent Comt, 75- Bus & Prof Pos: News ed & asst publ, Jefferson Bee & Herald Publ Co, Jefferson, Iowa, 67- Mem: Rotary; Greene Co Arts Coun. Honors & Awards: Eagle Scout, 57. Legal Res: 300 S Maple Jefferson IA 50129 Mailing Add: 214 N Wilson Jefferson IA 50129

MORALES, MARY FRANCES (D)
b Oneonta, NY, Oct 4, 5O; d Joseph William Morales & Thomasine Ross M; single. Educ: State Univ NY Col at Oneonta, 70-; secy, Art Club; Chantalles; publ chmn, Col Dem; Mask & Hammer. Polit & Govt Pos: Alt deleg, Dem Nat Conv, 72. Bus & Prof Pos: Summer recreation dir, City of Oneonta Recreation, NY, 68-71; publ chmn, Oneonta Art Ctr, 72-73. Mem: League of Women Voters; Community Art Ctr. Relig: Catholic. Mailing Add: 75 Main St Oneonta NY 13820

MORALES MELENDEZ, JOSE R (POPULAR DEMOCRAT, PR)
Rep, PR House Rep
Mailing Add: State Capitol San Juan PR 00901

MORALES RIVERA, GIL A (POPULAR DEMOCRAT, PR)
Rep, PR House Rep
Mailing Add: State Capitol San Juan PR 00901

MORALES RODRIGUEZ, TEOFILO (POPULAR DEMOCRAT, PR)
Rep, PR House Rep
Mailing Add: State Capitol San Juan PR 00901

MORAN, KIM (D)
Mem, Dem Nat Comt, Mich
Mailing Add: 28251 Emery Roseville MI 48066

MORAN, ROBERT DANIEL (R)
Chmn, US Occup Safety & Health Rev Comn
b Brewer, Maine, Oct 25, 29; s William H Moran (deceased) & Mary Ann Flynn M; m 1956 to Joan Ellen Leonard; c Kevin Leonard, Brian Cunningham, Mark McGuire, Sean Michael & Kathleen Kelly. Educ: Univ Maine, BA, 50; Boston Univ, LLB, 52; Georgetown Law Sch, grad study in law, 58; Am Int Col, grad study in bus admin, 63; Pi Kappa Delta, Order of Debate; Phi Delta Phi. Polit & Govt Pos: Legis counsel, Off of the Secy of Defense, Washington, DC, 55-56; pres, Springfield Young Rep Club, Mass, 57-58; treas, Mass Young Rep Asn, 61; deleg, Mass Rep State Conv, 62, deleg & mem rules comt, 66; pub adminr, Hampden Co, Mass, 62-67; mil aide to Lt Gov, Mass, 65-66; mem, Comtn to Study Financing of Polit Campaigns, 65-66; chmn, Springfield City Rep Comt, Mass, 65-69; chmn, Mass Bd of Conciliation & Arbit & Mass Minimum Wage Comn, 66-69; assoc comnr, Mass Dept of Labor & Industs, 66-69; alt deleg, Rep Nat Conv, 68; adminr wage & hour div, US Dept of Labor, 69-71; adminr of workplace standards, 71; chmn, US Occup Safety & Health Rev Comn, 71- Bus & Prof Pos: Attorney-at-law, 56-; labor arbitrator, 66- Mil Serv: Entered as Pvt, Army, 53, released as 1st Lt, 55, after serv in Off of Secy of Defense, Washington, DC, 54-55; Lt Col, Judge Adv Gen Corps, Army Res, 71- Publ: Massachusetts Municipal Collective Bargaining Manual (with others), Boston Col Bur of Pub Affairs, 68; State subsidized arbitration, Labor Law J, 10/68; Garnishment restrictions under federal law, Am Bar Asn J, 7/70. Mem: Indust Rels Res Asn; Boston Bar Asn (mem comt on arbit); Mass & Hampden Co Bar Asns; Bar of the Supreme Court of the US & the US Court of Mil Appeals. Honors & Awards: Radio Sta WACE Citation for Community Serv, 62. Relig: Roman Catholic. Legal Res: 258 Washington Blvd Springfield MA 01108 Mailing Add: US Occup Safety & Health Rev Comn 1825 K St NW Washington DC 20006

MORAN, ROBERT MARTIN (R)
NMex State Rep
b Tulsa, Okla, Nov 18, 28; s Edgar Francis Moran & Grace Marjorie Starr M; m 1959 to Brenda Anne Coogan; c Patricia Grace, Charles Edgar, Kathleen Ann, Andrew Joseph, Kevin Patrick, Ellen Marie & Timothy Mathew. Educ: Univ Notre Dame, BSME, 50. Polit & Govt Pos: NMex State Rep, Dist 62, 69- Bus & Prof Pos: Pres, Moran Co, 55-; dir, First Nat Bank, Hobbs, 69- Mem: Independent Petroleum Asn; NMex Oil & Gas Asn; Am Asn Oil Well Drilling Contractors; Hobbs United Fund; Rotary. Relig: Catholic. Legal Res: 1000 Walker Dr Hobbs NM 82240 Mailing Add: PO Box 1919 Hobbs NM 88240

MORANO, ALBERT PAUL (D)
b Paterson, NJ, Jan 18, 08; s Anthony Morano & Clementina Belmonte M; m 1933 to Millicent J Greco; c Anthony Albert & Clare Anita. Educ: Greenwich Pub Schs. Polit & Govt Pos: Exec secy to US Rep Albert E Austin, 39-41; exec secy to US Rep Clare Boothe Luce, 43-47; unemploy comnr, Fourth Cong Comn, 47-50; US Rep, Fourth Dist, Conn, 51-59; spec asst to US Sen Thomas J Dodd, 62-68; app by Gov Meskill to Bd of Parole, Conn, currently. Mem: Elks; KofC (4 degree); Soc of St Lawrence. Relig: Roman Catholic. Mailing Add: 7 Mallard Dr Greenwich CT 06830

MORANO, MICHAEL L (R)
Conn State Rep
Mailing Add: 44 Railroad Ave Greenwich CT 06830

MORANTE, JULIUS E (D)
Chmn, Farmington Dem Town Comt, Conn
b Plainville, Conn, June 10, 16; s Rollo Morante & Domenica D'Addario M; m 1941 to Anne Bucciacchio; c Charles A & Joanne M. Educ: Int Correspondence Schs, 41-43. Polit & Govt Pos: Mem, Farmington Dem Town Comt, Conn, 45-, chmn, 70-; councilman, Farmington, 58-61, vchmn, High Sch Bldg Comt, 61-62, mem, WDist Sch Bldg Comt, 62-63, Econ Develop Comn, 64-69 & Charter Revision Comn, 69-; mem, Gov Meskill's Housing Task Force, 71. Bus & Prof Pos: Order ed, Gen Elec Co, Plainville, Conn, 39-; owner, Jemco Co, 39-41, Ronne-Ann Gift Shop, New Britain, 45 & An-Mor Card Shop, Unionville, 70- Mem: KofC (Grand Knight & Knight of the Year); Farmington High Sch Booster Club (founder). Relig: Catholic. Mailing Add: 9 Cedar Lane Unionville CT 06085

MORASCO, SAMUEL A (D)
WVa State Deleg
b Grafton, WVa, Sept 24, 20; s John B Morasco & Theresa Tiano M; m 1951 to Rose Lee Jones; c David Lee. Educ: Penn Mutual Life Ins Sch, correspondence course; Aetna Life Ins Surety & Casualty Co; WVa Univ. Polit & Govt Pos: WVa State Deleg, 64-68 & 73- Bus & Prof Pos: Realtor; owner, Morasco's Agency, ins & real estate; pres, Grafton Area Develop Coun; dir, Sheltered Workshop. Mil Serv: 1st Sgt, Air Force, 42-46. Mem: Elks; Am Legion; KofC; Tygart Valley Develop Asn, Inc; Kiwanis. Honors & Awards: Outstanding Citizen Award, US Jaycees, 68. Relig: Catholic; pres, Parish Agency. Mailing Add: Brownlow Park Grafton WV 26354

MORDECAI, FRANK SELMER (R)
Chmn, Lamar Co Rep Party, Ala
b Fernbank, Ala, July 6, 88; s Marion Mordecai & Jane Atkins M; m 1906 to Arrie Ridgeway; c Marshall, Rudolph, Charlie Marion, Myrtle (Mrs Richards), Sarah Lee (Mrs Blair), Dot (Mrs May), Jo Fern (Mrs Jordon) & Faye (Mrs Stokes). Educ: Millport High Sch, grad, 06. Polit & Govt Pos: Chmn, Lamar Co Rep Party, Ala, 63- Mem: Odd Fellows. Relig: Baptist. Mailing Add: Lamar County Fund Bank Millport AL 35576

MOREAU, ART (D)
Wash State Rep
Mailing Add: 2101 Erie Bellingham WA 98225

MORELAND, C L (CLIFF) (D)
NMex State Rep
Mailing Add: Box 708 Tucumcari NM 88401

MORELAND, WILLIAM ALEXANDER (D)
WVa State Sen
b Morgantown, WVa, Apr 21, 16; s James R Moreland & Ethel Finnicum M; m 1940 to Ruth Russell Roberts; c Patricia Ann (Mrs A Wang). Educ: WVa Univ, AB, 38, Law Sch, LLB, 40; Kappa Alpha. Polit & Govt Pos: Mem, Suncrest City Coun, WVa, 46-47; mem, Morgantown City Coun, 48-50; WVa State Deleg, 51-58; WVa State Sen, 58-, Majority Leader, WVa State Senate, 60-68; mem, Co Dem Comt, 60- Mil Serv: Entered as 2nd Lt, Army, 41, released as Lt Col, 46, after serv in Am Inf Div, Far East Theater, 44; Lt Col, Army Res. Mem: Nat Conf State Legis Leaders; South Region Coun of State Govt; Rotary; Am Legion; VFW. Relig: Presbyterian. Mailing Add: 821-26 Monongahela Bldg Morgantown WV 26505

MORELLI, CARMEN (D)
Mem, Windsor Dem Town Comt, Conn
b Hartford, Conn, Oct 30, 22; s Joseph Morelli & Helen Carani M; m 1943 to Irene Edna Montminy; c Richard A, Mark D & Carl J. Educ: Boston Univ, BS in Bus Admin, 49, Sch Law, LLB, 52. Polit & Govt Pos: Asst prosecutor, Windsor, Conn, 57-58, town attorney, 61; mem, Windsor Dem Town Comt, 57-, treas, 60-64, chmn, 64-65; Conn State Rep, 59-60; mem, Charter Revision Comt, Windsor, 63-64, comnr, Windsor Town Plan & Zoning Comn, 65; rep, Capitol Region Planning Agency, 65-, chmn govt affairs comt & mem prog develop & rev, munic noise abatement & regional adv comts. Bus & Prof Pos: Attorney-at-law; arbitrator Am Arbit Asn, 64. Mil Serv: Entered as Seaman, Navy, 43, released as AMM 2/C, 45. Mem: Hartford Co, Conn State & Am Bar Asns; Conn Youth & Govt Comt; Elks. Relig: Catholic. Mailing Add: 41 Farmstead Lane Windsor CT 06095

MORENO, PAUL CRUZ (D)
Tex State Rep
b Alamogordo, NMex, Apr 28, 31; s Reyes Moreno & Avelina M; c Annette. Educ: Univ Tex, El Paso, BBA, Univ Tex, Austin, LLB; Delta Sigma Pi. Polit & Govt Pos: Tex State Rep, 66-72 & 75- Mil Serv: Entered as Pvt, Marine Corps, 48, released as S/Sgt, 52, after serv in 1st Marine Div, Korean War, 50-51; Korean Ribbon with 6 Stars; US Presidential Unit Citation with 2 Clusters; Korean Presidential Citation with 1 Cluster. Mem: Tex Bar Asn; Tex Trial Lawyers Asn; Elks; DAV; VFW. Honors & Awards: Outstanding Disabled Vet, 66.

Relig: Catholic. Legal Res: 2008 Atlanta St El Paso TX 79902 Mailing Add: House of Rep El Paso TX 79901

MORESHEAD, CHARLES E (R)
Polit & Govt Pos: Chmn, Maine Rep State Comt, until 73, gen counsel, 73- Mailing Add: 283 Water St Augusta ME 04330

MOREY, FRANCES HANS (D)
Nat Committeewoman, Young Dem of Tex
b Castroville, Tex, Sept 13, 42; d Gabriel R Hans & Fanny Bourquin H; div; c Gabriel Prowse & Travis Hood. Educ: Univ Tex, Austin, BS, 67. Polit & Govt Pos: Chairperson, Precinct 335, Travis Co, Tex, 72-; nat committeewoman, Young Dem of Tex, 74- Mailing Add: 901 W 24th Austin TX 78705

MORGAN, BARBARA (D)
Polit & Govt Pos: Mem, Dem Nat Comt, DC, formerly. Mailing Add: 3245 O St SE Washington DC 20020

MORGAN, CHARLIE O (D)
Okla State Rep
b Okemah, Okla, Oct 5, 31; m 1949 to Mattie L Burnett; c Dottie, Danny & Kenneth. Educ: Seminole Jr Col. Polit & Govt Pos: Mayor, Prague, Okla, 63-69; Okla State Rep, Dist 32, 73- Bus & Prof Pos: Pres, Morgan Well Servicing Co, Inc. Mem: Am Petrol Inst; Nat Oil Well Servicing Contractors Asn; Lions; Okla Independent Petrol Asn; CofC. Relig: Methodist. Legal Res: 1938 N Haynie Lane Prague OK 74864 Mailing Add: PO Box 666 Prague OK 74864

MORGAN, CLAUDE RUTLEDGE (D)
Chmn, Crenshaw Co Dem Party, Ala
b Luverne, Ala, May 19, 13; s Thomas Ira Morgan & Nellie Rutledge M; m 1936 to Sarah Davis; c Vivian (Mrs Preston Walker) & Claude Rutledge, Jr. Polit & Govt Pos: Chmn, Crenshaw Co Dem Party, Ala, 71- Bus & Prof Pos: Farmer; grocery merchant; asst rural letter carrier. Mem: Mason; Crenshaw Cattleman Asn; Crenshaw Hog Asn. Relig: Baptist. Mailing Add: Rte 1 Luverne AL 36049

MORGAN, CLYDE NATHANIEL (R)
b Belton, Tex, Nov 2, 23; s Xenophen William Morgan & Rhoda Ella Deck M; m 1951 to Birdie Joyce Palmer; c Clyde Nathaniel, Jr, Reinette Jean & Nancy Elaine. Educ: Abilene Christian Col, BS, 48; Univ Tex Med Br, MD, 53; Alpha Chi; Phi Omega Chi; Phi Rho Sigma. Polit & Govt Pos: Aircraft mechanic, Civil Serv, 41-43; precinct chmn, Taylor Co Rep Party, Tex, 64-65; alt deleg, Tex Rep State Conv, 64, deleg, 66, 68 & 72; chmn, Taylor Co Rep Exec Comt, 65-70; deleg, Rep Nat Conv, 68. Bus & Prof Pos: Physician & surgeon, 54-67; secy staff, Hendrick Mem Hosp, 56; dermatologist, pvt practice, 67- Mil Serv: Entered as Pvt, Army Air Force, 43, released as 1st Lt, 46, after serv in African & Mid East Theaters, 45-46 & spec assignment as personal pilot to King Ibn Saud, Saudi Arabia, 45; Am, ETO, African & Mid East Campaign Medals; Victory Medal. Publ: Patients like my drive-in office, Med Econ, 63; Time savers, Patient Care, 9/67; Automation, Firm Found, 4/69. Mem: Taylor-Jones Co Med Soc; Tex & Am Med Asns; Tex Acad Gen Practice; Am Acad Gen Practice. Honors & Awards: Med Econ Award, 63; Physician's Recognition Award, Am Med Asn, 69. Relig: Church of Christ. Legal Res: 1718 Cedarcrest Dr Abilene TX 79601 Mailing Add: 1166 Merchant St Abilene TX 79603

MORGAN, DALE EUGENE (D)
Chmn, Buchanan Co Dem Cent Comt, Mo
b Clarksdale, Mo, Jan 13, 30; s Eugene Arden Morgan & Fern Coffey M; m 1951 to Twyla Kathleen Critchfield; c Kathy Ann, Kayla Sue, Kenton Dale & Kerri Lynn. Educ: Faucett High Sch, Mo, 4 years. Polit & Govt Pos: Committeeman, Crawford Twp, 68-70; chmn, Buchanan Co Dem Cent Comt, Mo, 70-; chmn, Sixth Cong Dist Dem Party, 72-, mem, Sixth Cong Dist Club serv on Congressman Litton's Adv Coun, 73; deleg, Dem Nat Mid-Term Conf, 74. Bus & Prof Pos: Maintenance man, Carter-Waters Corp, Kansas City, Mo, 49-, plant mgr, 69- Mil Serv: Entered as Pvt, Air Force, 48, released as T/Sgt, 56, after serv in 126th Light Bombardment Wing, ETO during Korean Conflict, 51-52. Mem: Mason; Scottish Rite; Lions; Shriner's Moila Temple, St Joseph, Mo. Relig: Protestant. Mailing Add: Box 172 Faucett MO 64448

MORGAN, ELISE FOWLER (R)
Chmn, Laurel Co Rep Party, Ky
b McKee, Ky, Apr 18, 04; d John Fowler & Lou Hays F; m 1926 to Wathen Sandusky Morgan; c John W. Educ: Union Col (Ky), AB cum laude, 56; Eastern Ky Univ, MA, 58. Polit & Govt Pos: Chmn, Laurel Co Rep Party, Ky, 41-72 & 75- Bus & Prof Pos: Teacher, East Bernstadt Graded Sch, 29-51, prin, 51- Mem: Laurel Co Develop Asn. Honors & Awards: Outstanding Woman Rep, Laurel Co, 69. Relig: Reformed Church. Mailing Add: East Bernstadt KY 40729

MORGAN, FRED H (D)
Ky State Rep
b 1915; m 1936 to Zada L Brown; c Fred, Jr & Ron. Educ: Murray State Col. Polit & Govt Pos: Ky State Rep, 46-, spec session, Ky House of Rep, 49, Majority Leader, 56 & 68; city mgr, Paducah, 52 & 54-55. Bus & Prof Pos: Ins agt. Mem: Kiwanis; Moose. Honors & Awards: Kiwanian of Year, Paducah Club, 72. Relig: Presbyterian. Mailing Add: 2057 Broad St Paducah KY 42001

MORGAN, GEORGE HENRY (R)
Chmn, Bledsoe Co Rep Party, Tenn
b Benton, Tenn, Dec 14, 31; s Silas Marion Morgan & Mattie Bishop M; m 1952 to Willene J Frady; c James H, Gary J, Aundrea L & Charles M. Polit & Govt Pos: Chmn, Bledsoe Co Rep Party, 70-; mem welfare dept, Citizens Adv Comt, 71-; Col Aide de Camp to Gov Winfield Dunn, 71- Mil Serv: Entered as Pvt, US Army, 49, released as E-5, after serv in 82nd Airborne, US & ETO, 49-62; Parachutist Badge; Korean Defense; Good Conduct Medal. Mem: Mason; Am Legion; VFW. Relig: Protestant. Mailing Add: PO Box 74 Pikeville TN 37367

MORGAN, HERBERT DOYLE (D)
SC State Rep
b Six Mile, SC, Nov 28, 29; Herbert D Morgan, Sr & Christine Jones M; m 1956 to Kate Nimmons; c Jean N & Robert E. Educ: US Naval Acad, 47-48; Clemson Univ, BS, 50; Univ SC Law Sch, JD, 71; Phi Alpha Delta, Justice, 70. Polit & Govt Pos: Deleg, SC Dem State Conv, 58 & 62-74; alt deleg, Dem Nat Conv, 60, deleg, 64; committeeman, Oconee Co Dem Exec Comt, SC, 64-; SC State Rep, 67-68, 71-72 & 75-; deleg, Dem Mid Term Conf, 74; committeeman, SC Dem Exec Comt, 74- Bus & Prof Pos: Sales & mgt, Am Cyanamid Co, Wayne, NJ, 50-65; partner, Morgan, Sires & Brandt, Attorneys, Seneca, 71- Mil Serv: Officer, Army Res, 50-57. Mem: Am & SC Bar Asns; Rotary; AF&AM; Scottish Rite (32 degree). Honors & Awards: Young Man of the Year, Seneca, SC, 60. Relig: Presbyterian. Mailing Add: Box 215 Clemson Rd Seneca SC 29678

MORGAN, HERBERT F (D)
Fla State Rep
Mailing Add: 1148 Carissa Dr Tallahassee FL 32303

MORGAN, JACK H (D)
Chmn, Newton Co Bd of Comnr, Ga
b Newton Co, Ga, May 2, 19; s Joe Carter Morgan & Margaret Hays M; m 1945 to Barbara M Davis; c Barbara, Jack, Emily, Davis, John, William, Edna Sue & Can. Educ: Heart-Mixon High Sch, 36. Polit & Govt Pos: Ga State Rep, 63-64; chmn, Newton Co Bd of Comnr, 69- Bus & Prof Pos: Farmer; pulpwood dealer; grading contractor. Mil Serv: Navy Med Corps, World War II. Mem: Elks; Rotary. Relig: Methodist. Mailing Add: Rte 4 Covington GA 30209

MORGAN, JACK MAC GEE (R)
NMex State Sen
b Portales, NMex, Jan 15, 24; s George Albert Morgan & Mary Baker M; m 1947 to Peggy Cummings; c Marilyn, Rebecca, Claudia & Jack, Jr. Educ: Univ Tex, BBA, 48 & LLB, 50; Phi Delta Phi; Delta Sigma Pi. Polit & Govt Pos: NMex State Sen, 73-; mem, Southwest Regional Energy Coun. Mil Serv: Entered as A/S V-12, Navy, 42, released as Lt(jg), 46, after serv in USS Mitchell & USS Todd, SPac Theatre, 44-45; Asiatic Pac Area Serv Ribbon with 6 Stars; Philippine Liberation Ribbon with 1 Star. Mem: Am & NMex Bar Asns; Am Judicature Soc; Farmington Kiwanis; Southwestern Legal Found. Relig: Presbyterian. Legal Res: 4113 Skyline Dr Farmington NM 87401 Mailing Add: PO Box 2151 Farmington NM 87401

MORGAN, JOHN B (R)
NH State Rep
Mailing Add: Box 237 Peterborough NH 03458

MORGAN, JOHN HAYDEN (D)
Mo State Rep
b Wichita Falls, Tex, Nov 7, 33; s O E Morgan & Argie M; m 1953 to Jennie B George; c John H, Jr, Samuel D & Linda A. Educ: WTex State Univ, BBA, 55. Polit & Govt Pos: Mo State Rep, Dist 135, 71- Bus & Prof Pos: Farmer, Vernon Co, Mo, 65- Mil Serv: Entered as 2nd Lt, Army, 55, released as 1st Lt, 57, after serv in First Armored Div, Continental Army Command, 55-57. Mem: Elks; Mid-Continent Farmers Asn; Nat Asn Farmer Elected Committeemen. Relig: Presbyterian. Mailing Add: Rte 2 Nevada MO 64772

MORGAN, JOHN THACKERAY (R)
Vt State Rep
b Philadelphia, Pa, May 8, 11; s C Eldridge Morgan, III & Theresa Hamilton Fish M; m 1932 to Barbara Berry; c C Eldridge, IV, Deborah (Mrs Peter Van C Luquer) & Jeffrey Hall. Educ: Princeton Univ; Univ Va. Polit & Govt Pos: Vt State Rep, Dist 24, 71-74, Vt State Rep, Dist Windsor One, 75-; mem, Woodstock Bd Adjustment, 72- Bus & Prof Pos: Sr credit supvr, Nat City Bank, New York, 34-47; pres & treas, Tri-Com, Inc, 47-60; pres, John T Morgan Assoc, New York & Hartland Four Corners, Vt, 47-62; dir, Vt Beef Producers, 56-; dir, NE Angus Asn, 70-; pres, Vt Angus Asn, 70-; trustee, Univ Vt, 75- Mailing Add: South Woodstock VT 05071

MORGAN, KEN L (R)
NDak State Sen
b Fargo, NDak, 1915; m to Doris Ann Stevens. Educ: Leonard Pub Sch. Polit & Govt Pos: Numerous jobs during legis sessions, 35-; precinct committeeman, Barrie Twp & state cent committeeman, Richland City; mem senate, Richland City, 56; NDak State Sen, 67-, Pres Pro Tem, NDak State Senate, currently; vchmn agr comt, Midwest Coun State Govt, currently. Bus & Prof Pos: Farming. Mem: Mason; Shrine; Elks; Eagles; Farm Bur. Relig: Congregational. Mailing Add: Walcott ND 58077

MORGAN, MEL (D)
Mem, Dem Nat Comt, Idaho
Mailing Add: PO Box 951 Pocatello ID 83201

MORGAN, P J (R)
Mem, Douglas Co Bd Comnr, Nebr
b Omaha, Nebr, Apr 9, 40; s Paul B Morgan & Lucille Ellan M; m 1959 to Karen S Dillon; c Kimberly Sue & Paul Robert. Polit & Govt Pos: Nebr State Sen, Fourth Dist, 71-72; mem & comnr, Douglas Co Bd Comnr, Nebr, 75- Bus & Prof Pos: Real estate developer, Twin City Plaza, Inc, 61, vpres, 65-72, pres, 72-; owner, P J Morgan Co, 65- Mem: Omaha Home Builders Asn Bd; Cerebral Palsy Bd; Young Pres Orgn. Honors & Awards: One of Ten Most Outstanding Young Men of Omaha, 70. Relig: Episcopal. Mailing Add: 815 S 94th St Omaha NE 68114

MORGAN, PHILIP WILLIAM (R)
b Aberdeen, SDak, Nov 8, 21; s William Henry Morgan (deceased) & Julia Theresa Connelly M; single. Educ: St Thomas Col, 40-42; Univ Notre Dame, BSC, 47; Georgetown Univ Law Sch, JD, 51. Polit & Govt Pos: Asst US Attorney, Fairbanks, Alaska, 54-56; chief, Div of Alaskan Affairs, Dept of Interior, 56-59; chief counsel to minority rep, Invests Subcomt, Govt Opers Comt, US Senate, 59- Mil Serv: Entered as Pvt, Marine Corps, 43, released as 2nd Lt, 46, reentered as 1st Lt, 51, released as Capt, 52, after serv in III Amphibious Corps, Okinawa, Pac Theatre, 45-46 & Force Troops, Camp LeJeune, NC, 51-52; Col, Marine Corps Res, 68-; Pac Theatre Ribbon with One Battle Star. Mem: SDak & Am Bar Asns; Elks; Am Legion; VFW. Relig: Catholic. Legal Res: PO Box 133 Britton SD 57430 Mailing Add: 101 N Carolina Ave SE Washington DC 20003

MORGAN, ROBERT BURREN (D)
US Sen, NC
b Lillington, NC, Oct 5, 25; s James Harvey Morgan & Alice Butts M; m 1960 to Katie Owen;

c Margaret, Mary & foster son, Rupert. Educ: E Carolina Col, BS, 47; Wake Forest Univ, JD, 50; Phi Sigma Pi; Phi Alpha Delta. Polit & Govt Pos: Precinct worker, Dem Party, NC, 47-; clerk of Superior Court, Harnett Co, 50-54; NC State Sen, 55-57, 59-61 & 63-68, Pres Pro Tem, NC State Senate, 65-68; Attorney Gen, NC, formerly; US Sen, NC, currently. Bus & Prof Pos: Practicing attorney, 55-; chmn bd trustees, E Carolina Univ, 64-; sr partner, Morgan, Williams & Jones, Attorneys, 66-; dir, Home Savings & Loan Asn, Dunn NC & Justice Found of NC, Raleigh, 70- Publ: Youth & the law, Justice Found of NC, 72. Mil Serv: Entered as Seaman, Navy, 44, released as Lt, 53, after serv in Am Theater, 45-46 & Korean Theater, 52; Lt Comdr, Naval Res, 57-70; Lt Col, Air Force Res, 70-; Am Theater & World War II Ribbons; Korean War Ribbon with Battle Star; UN & Armed Force Res Medals; Navy Unit Citation. Mem: Am & NC Bar Asns; Am Trial Lawyers Asn; Rotary; Mason. Relig: Baptist. Legal Res: Morgan Dr Lillington NC 27546 Mailing Add: US Senate Washington DC 20510

MORGAN, THOMAS ELLSWORTH (D)
US Rep, Pa
b Ellsworth, Pa, Oct 13, 06; s William Morgan & Mary Lawson M; m 1937 to Winifred Strait; c Mary Ann (Mrs Gordon Youngwood). Educ: Waynesburg Col, BS, 30; Detroit Col of Med & Surg, BM, 33; Wayne Univ, MD, 34. Hon Degrees: LLD, Waynesburg Col, 65. Polit & Govt Pos: US Rep, Pa, 44-, chmn, House Comt on Int Rels, US House of Rep, currently; deleg, Dem Nat Conv, 68 & 72. Bus & Prof Pos: Physician, Fredericktown, Pa, 34- Mem: Numerous fraternal & civic orgns. Honors & Awards: Distinguished Serv Award, Wayne State Univ, 64. Relig: Methodist. Legal Res: Fredericktown PA 15333 Mailing Add: 2183 Rayburn House Off Bldg Washington DC 20515

MORGAN, THOMAS PHELPS (R)
Mem, Bernalillo Co Rep Cent Comt, NMex
b Roswell, NMex, Feb 15, 52; s Harold Maurice Morgan & Iverna Phelps M; m 1974 to Celeste Colberg. Educ: Ft Lewis Col, 70-72; Univ NMex, BA in Polit Sci & Hist, 74; secy, Col Rep. Polit & Govt Pos: Vchmn, Bernalillo Co Youth for Nixon, NMex, 68; mem, Albuquerque Youth Adv Comt to City Comt, 70; state chmn, Domenici for Gov, NMex, 70; dir state speakers bur, NMex Young Voters for the President, 72; deleg, NMex Rep State Conv, 72; deleg, Young Rep Nat Conv, 73 & 75; nat committeeman, NMex Young Rep Fedn, 73-74; Rep cand, NMex State Rep, Dist 22, 74; co-dir region XI, Young Rep Nat Fedn, 74-75; mem, NMex Rep State Cent Comt, 74-75; mem, Bernalillo Co Rep Cent Comt, NMex, 75- Bus & Prof Pos: Agent, Travelers Ins Corp. Mem: Orgn Am Historians; Western Hist Asn; Rocky Mt Ski Instr Asn. Relig: Presbyterian. Legal Res: 3956-2 Montgomery NE Albuquerque NM 87125 Mailing Add: PO Box 26263 Albuquerque NM 87125

MORGEN, GLADYS H (D)
Polit & Govt Pos: Mem, Dem Nat Comt, Wash, formerly. Mailing Add: W 2311 Walton Spokane WA 99205

MORGRAGE, BARRY C (D)
NH State Rep
Mailing Add: Mast Rd RFD 1 Goffstown NH 03045

MORI, S FLOYD (D)
Calif State Assemblyman
Mailing Add: State Capitol Sacramento CA 95814

MORIARTY, WILLIAM T (D)
Conn State Rep
Mailing Add: 29 Ransom Hall Rd Wolcott CT 06715

MORIN, BRUCE Q (D)
RI State Sen
Mailing Add: 9 Sweet Briar Lane West Warwick RI 02893

MORIN, LEATRICE (D)
Maine State Rep
Mailing Add: 27 Adelaide Rd Old Orchard Beach ME 04064

MORIN, VICKY LEE (D)
Pres, Mont Young Dem Clubs
b St Ignatius, Mont, June 5, 48; d Henry Marion Morin & Annabelle Lindsay M; single. Educ: Mont State Univ, BA in Govt, 70. Polit & Govt Pos: Vpres, Mont Univ Young Dem, 68; pres, Mont State Univ Young Dem, 68-69; treas, Mont Young Coun, 69; vchmn, Mont Young Dem Clubs, 69-70, pres, 70-; mem, Mont Dem Cent Comt, 70-71; deleg, Dem Nat Conv, 72. Mailing Add: Box 72 Ravalli MT 59864

MORIOKA, TED T (D)
Hawaii State Rep
b Honolulu, Hawaii, Nov 18, 21; s Kamekichi Morioka & Kikuno Sasagawa M; m 1945 to Alice U; c Daniel & Lyla. Educ: Univ Hawaii. Polit & Govt Pos: Mem eviction appeals bd, Hawaii Housing Authority, 59-61; mem traffic safety comn, City & Co of Honolulu, 59, civil serv comnr, 61-64; deleg, Dem Nat Conv, 64 & 68; Hawaii State Rep, Third Legis, 65- Bus & Prof Pos: Advert salesman, Hawaiian Tel Co, 47-53, commercial engr, 53-56, budget analyst, 57-63, asst to exec vpres, 63; asst to pres, 64-; dir & treas, All Hawaii Investment Corp Inc, 67-; dir, Waikiki Land Corp, 68- Mil Serv: Entered as Pvt, Army, 45, released as T-4, 47, after serv in Hawaii. Mem: Lions; Hawaii State CofC; YMCA; Honolulu Japanese CofC. Relig: Buddhist. Mailing Add: House of Rep State Captiol Honolulu HI 96813

MORIOKA, VINCE MATTHEWS (R)
b Honolulu, Hawaii, Oct 4, 54; s Edward Futaji Morioka & Sylvia Maile Moku M; single. Educ: St Louis High Sch, Honolulu, Hawaii, grad, 72. Polit & Govt Pos: Asst coordr, City & Co Off of Youth Activities, Honolulu, 70; asst exec dir, Young Voters for the President, Hawaii Comt to Reelect the President, 72; legis aide to Hawaii State Senate Minority Leader Wadsworth Yee, 73; staff asst to US Sen Hiram L Fong, Hawaii, 73-; second vchmn, Hawaii Rep Party, formerly. Bus & Prof Pos: Staff aide to exec dir, Pac & Asian Affairs Coun, Div of East-West Ctr, Univ Hawaii, 71; govt rels rep, Charley's Scenic Tours, Honolulu, 73. Relig: Roman Catholic. Mailing Add: 3516 Launa Pl Honolulu HI 96816

MORKEN, EDWIN DUANE, JR (R)
b Spokane, Wash, Oct 6, 31; s Edwin A Morken & Cletus E Gustufson M; m 1959 to Betty R Treu; c Nanette Susan. Educ: Pac Lutheran Univ, BA, 53; Wash State Univ, 53. Polit &

Govt Pos: Pres, Young Col Rep, Pac Lutheran Univ, 52-53; Rep precinct committeeman, Spokane, Wash, 61, Beaverton, Ore, 62; Rep precinct committeeman, Genesee, Idaho, 65-68; chmn, Latah Co Rep Party, 68-70; chmn, Fifth Legis Dist Rep Party, formerly. Bus & Prof Pos: Rancher. Mil Serv: Entered as Officer Cand, Navy, 53, released as Lt Comdr, 59, after serv in various commands, Pac & Continental; Lt Comdr, Naval Res, currently. Mem: Co Planning Comn; Co Adv Bd; Idaho Pea & Lentil Growers (pres); Idaho Wheat Growers; Civil Asn. Relig: Lutheran. Mailing Add: RFD 1 Genesee ID 83832

MORPHY, TED L (D)
Comnr-At-Lg, Lexington Co, SC
b Lexington, Ky, Nov 3, 33; s Lewis Harris Morphy & Jewel E Deal M; m 1958 to Barbara Ann Bowers. Educ: Columbia Bus Col, grad, 58. Polit & Govt Pos: SC State Rep, 65-66; comnr-at-lg, Lexington Co, 67- Bus & Prof Pos: Pres, Ted L Morphy Enterprises, Inc. Mil Serv: Army, 50-54; Paratroops, 82nd Airborne Div; retired for disability. Mem: West Columbia-Cayce CofC (bd dirs); Lexington CofC (bd dirs); Cayce-West Columbia Jaycees; Farm Bur; Civitans. Relig: Baptist. Mailing Add: Lexington SC 29072

MORRILL, WILLIAM A (R)
Asst Secy Planning & Eval, Dept Health, Educ & Welfare
Legal Res: VA Mailing Add: Dept Health Educ & Welfare Washington DC 20201

MORRIS, A BURR (D)
Chmn, Hartley Co Dem Exec Comt, Tex
b Ft Worth, Tex, Dec 14, 24; s Jake Newt Morris & Beulah Lee Burton M; m 1948 to Awand Irene McGarvin; c Cynthia (Mrs John J Leahy) & Arthur Ray. Educ: Tex Wesleyan Col, BA, 47; McCormick Theol Sem, MDiv, 50, 74-75. Polit & Govt Pos: Chmn, Hartley Co Dem Exec Comt, Tex, 73- Bus & Prof Pos: Pastor, First Presby Church, Memphis, Tex, 50-54, Canadian, 55-60, Dimmit, 62-65, McCamey, Tex, 66-69 & Dalhart, 69- Mil Serv: Entered as Pvt, Army Air Corps, 44, released as Pfc, 46; Chaplain, First Lt, Air Force Res, 52-53. Publ: Auth, Presbytery of Amarillo 1907-1959, Plains Presbytery, UPCUSA, 62. Mem: Dalhart Rotary; AF&AM. Relig: Presbyterian. Legal Res: 1307 Maple Dalhart TX 79022 Mailing Add: PO Box 188 Dalhart TX 79022

MORRIS, ARCHIE J (R)
Chmn, Macon Co Rep Party, Ga
b Montgomery Co, Ga, June 24, 30; s Archie J Morris & Esther Smith M; div; c Archie J, III, Carla, Shea & Melissa. Educ: Ga Teachers Col, BS, 51; Med Col Ga, MD, 57. Polit & Govt Pos: Mem, City Coun, Montezuma, Ga, 68-72; chmn, Macon Co Rep Party, 71-; alt deleg, Rep Nat Conv, 72; coroner, Macon Co, 73-; vchmn, Third Dist Rep Party, 73-; mem, Ga Rep State Cent Comt, 73- Bus & Prof Pos: Chief of surg, Riverside Hosp, Montezuma, Ga, 62-; mem bd dirs, Citizens Bank. Mil Serv: Entered as Pvt E-1, 51, released as Cpl, 53, after serv in 7th MASH Unit, 3rd Army, 51-53. Mem: Alpha Psi Omega; Theta Kappa Psi; Am Bd Surg; Am Col Surg; Am Med Asn. Relig: Baptist. Mailing Add: Walnut St Montezuma GA 31063

MORRIS, BARBARA ANN (R)
b Troy, NY, Nov 23, 43; d Robert Milton Morris & Sarah Beatrice Hancox M; single. Educ: High sch; pub admin intern, State of NY, 70. Polit & Govt Pos: Admin asst to admin dir, NY State Attorney Gen Off, 68-70; admin secy, US Rep Norman F Lent, Fourth Dist, NY, 71- Relig: Methodist. Legal Res: Apt 4 278 Pawling Ave Troy NY 12180 Mailing Add: 428 Cannon Bldg Washington DC 20515

MORRIS, BARBARA LEE PICKERAL (D)
Mem Exec Comt, Winchester Dem Town Comt, Va
b Winchester, Va, Oct 29, 43; d John Julian Pickeral, Sr & Dorothy Lee Wilkins M; div; c Laura Lee. Educ: Randolph-Macon Woman's Col, AB in Polit Sci, 66; Drew Univ, Jr Seminar at UN; Univ Va Grad Sch Educ, 67- Polit & Govt Pos: Page, Dem Nat Conv, 64; deleg, Va Young Dem Conv, 64-66 & 69-72; deleg, Biennial Young Dem Clubs of Am Conv, 65 & 73; pres, Randolph-Macon Woman's Col Young Dem, 65-66; mem exec comt, Col Fedn Young Dem Clubs of Va, 65-66; campaign worker, Young Virginians for Spong, 66; first vpres, Winchester-Frederick Co Young Dem, 67-68; coordr, Teen Dem Clubs of Va, 69-71; mem exec comt, Young Dem Clubs of Va, 69-, exec secy, 71-72, nat committeewoman, 72-74; deleg, Seventh Dist Dem Conv to nominate US House of Rep cand, 70; chmn Frederick Co, Duvall for US Senate, 70; area coordr, Rawlings for US Senate, 70; chmn, Educators for Williams, Seventh Dist US House of Rep race, 70; publicity chmn & mem exec comt, Winchester Dem Town Comt, 70-, secy, 74-; deleg, Va Nominating Conv for Lt Gov, 71; deleg, Va Legis & Sen Conv, 71; deleg, Va Dem State Conv, 72; chmn, Winchester Campaign for McGovern, 72; mem-at-lg, Va Dem State Cent Comt, 72-74. Bus & Prof Pos: Econ intern, Off Regional Econ, Bur Int Com, Dept Com, summer 65, econ asst, ITAD, summer, 66; hist teacher, John Mosby Acad, Front Royal, Va, 66-67; fifth grade teacher, Gore Elem Sch, 67-68; second grade teacher, Body Camp Elem Sch, Bedford, 68-69; third grade teacher, D G Cooley Elem Sch, Berryville, 69- Mem: Va Educ Asn (polit action comt, 72 & 74, bd dirs, 76-78); Clarke Co Educ Asn (secy, 70-71, chmn salary comt, 70-72, pres elect, 71-73, pres, 73-75, Dist N bd mem, 73-75, pres-elect Dist N, 74-76); Am Asn Univ Women (topic chmn, Winchester Br, 71-75); Blue Ridge Alumnae Chap, Randolph-Macon Woman's Col (pres, 72-76). Honors & Awards: Rusty Nail Award for Outstanding Mem, Clarke Co Educ Asn, 71; First Annual J Sargeant Reynolds Award for Outstanding Mem, Va Young Dem, 72. Relig: Methodist. Mailing Add: 316 W Leicester St Winchester VA 22601

MORRIS, BILL (D)
Ill State Sen
Mailing Add: 421 North Ave Waukegan IL 60085

MORRIS, BILL (R)
Kans State Rep
Mailing Add: 9822 Hardner Wichita KS 67212

MORRIS, BRAD (R)
Ore State Rep
Mailing Add: 516 Glairgeau Circle Medford OR 97501

MORRIS, BREWSTER HILLARD
b Bryn Mawr, Pa, Feb 7, 09; m to Ellen Downes. Educ: Haverford Col, BS, 30; Oxford Univ, BA, 32, BLit, 33. Polit & Govt Pos: Career officer, Dept of State Foreign Serv, 36-; vconsul, Montreal, 36-38, Vienna, 38, Dresden, 39, Berlin, 40-41 & Stockholm, 42-44; polit adv staff to US Mil Govt in Ger, 44-48; first secy, Moscow, 48-49, first secy, Frankfort, 49-51; mem

staff, Nat War Col, 51-52; mem staff, Off of German Affairs, 52-54; Foreign Serv Inspector, 54-57; counr, London, 57-60; minister-counr, Bonn, 60-63; US Ambassador, Chad, 63-67; asst chief of mission, Berlin, until 71. Bus & Prof Pos: Investment analyst, 34-36. Mailing Add: 430 Ridge Rd Tiburon CA 94920

MORRIS, BRUCE LEO (D)
Conn State Rep
b New Haven, Conn, Mar 28, 32; s Brass Morris & Leona Foreman M; m 1953 to Gwendolyn Davis; c Anthony E & Bruce V. Educ: New Haven Col, 56; Colonial Sch Tool Design, 59; Conn State Tech Inst, 61; Cent Conn State Col, 64. Polit & Govt Pos: Alderman, Dem Party, 62-68; mem, New Haven Dem Town Comt, 68-; Conn State Rep, currently. Bus & Prof Pos: Tool designer, M B Electronics, 59-65, Sargent & Co, 65-66 & self employed mfg engr, 66- Mil Serv: Entered as Pvt, Army, 53, released as Cpl, 55, after serv in Mil Police, West Point, NY; Nat Defense & Good Conduct Medals; Mem: Am Soc Tool Mfg Engrs; Int Elks. Relig: Catholic. Mailing Add: 280 Division St New Haven CT 06511

MORRIS, BURLENE (D)
Mem Exec Comt, Ga Dem Party
b Bartow Co, Ga, Jan 11, 35; d Theodore Jackson Hight & Smiley Lanham H; m 1956 to Harold Jefferson Morris. Educ: Shorter Col, 61-62; Chicago Sch Interior Design, dipl, 68. Polit & Govt Pos: Rec secy, Floyd Co Dem Asn, 74, 2nd vpres, 75-; bd dirs, Women's Dem League, 74-; mem exec comt, Ga Dem Party, 74-; mem, Ga Dem Party Charter Comn, 75- Bus & Prof Pos: Owner, Decorator Serv, Rome, Ga, 68-72. Mem: Rome-Floyd Co Humane Soc; Rome Area Heritage Found. Honors & Awards: Dem of the Year, Floyd Co Dem Asn, 74; Woman of the Year, Capotoline Chap, Am Bus Women's Asn, 70. Mailing Add: Bells Ferry Rd Rte 8 Rome GA 30161

MORRIS, CHRISTIAN PURTSCHER (R)
b Lima, Ohio, Nov 3, 30; s Christian P Morris (deceased) & Helen Stolzenbach M (deceased); m 1952 to Lillian Y Foehrenbach; c Debra Ann, Christian P, Jr, Mark Edward & David Remley. Educ: DePauw Univ, 48-50; Ohio State Univ, 54; Phi Sigma Alpha; Alpha Tau Omega. Polit & Govt Pos: Mayor, Lima, Ohio, formerly. Bus & Prof Pos: Owner & mgr, M&M Allsports, Inc, 54-60; owner & mgr, Morris Brothers Allsports, Inc, 60-65; mem bd dirs, North Main, Inc, until 65. Mil Serv: Entered as Seaman 2/C, Navy, 50, released as PO 1/C, 53; Korean War Ribbon; Mediter Theater of Oper Ribbon; Good Conduct Medal. Mem: Nat Sporting Goods Asn; Nat Congress of Parents & Teachers; Ohio Mayors Asn (bd dirs); Nat League of Cities; Ohio Munic League. Relig: Lutheran. Mailing Add: 429 S Jameson Ave Lima OH 45805

MORRIS, EARLE E, JR (D)
Lt Gov, SC
b Pickens, SC, July 14, 28; s Earle E Morris, Sr & Bernice Carey M; m 1972 to Carol Telford; c Lynda L, Carey M, Elizabeth M & Earle E, III. Educ: Clemson Univ, BS, 49; Blue Key; Phi Kappa Phi. Polit & Govt Pos: SC State Rep, 50-54; deleg, State & Co Dem Conv, 50-72; deleg, Dem Nat Conv, 52, 56 & 68; pres, Pickens Co Dem Party, 54, 65 & 66; SC State Sen, Pickens Co, 54-70, mem, Southern Regional Educ Bd Comn on Ment Illness, Atlanta, Ga, 58-; mem, Gov Adv Group on Ment Health Planning, 63-65; mem, Interagency Coun on Ment Retardation Planning, 64-; mem, Nat Adv Ment Health Coun, US Pub Health Serv, 65-; secy-treas, SC Dem Party, 65-66, chmn, 66-68; mem, Senate Interagency Coun on Aging, 66; Lt Gov, SC, 71- Bus & Prof Pos: Vpres & secy, Morris & Co, Inc, 50-; vpres & dir, Bankers Trust of SC, 56-; pres, Gen Ins Agency, 57-; secy, Carolina Investors, Inc, 63- Mil Serv: Maj, SC Army Nat Guard, 51- Mem: SC Ment Health Asn; SC Asn for Retarded Children; SC Voc Rehabilitation Asn (vpres); SC Crippled Children's Soc; Mason. Relig: Presbyterian; Elder & Clerk of the Session; trustee, Presby Church of SC. Legal Res: Rte 3 Pickens SC 29671 Mailing Add: Box 97 Pickens SC 29671

MORRIS, GLORIA GENEVIEVE (D)
Mem, Conn Dem State Cent Comt
b Willimantic, Conn, Aug 27, 23; d Charles Mazzola & Ana Castanza; m 1948 to Leo Ervin Morris, Sr; c Leo Ervin Morris, Jr. Educ: Univ Conn, BS, 45, Eastern Conn State Col, Teacher's Cert, 54; Delta Zeta, Gamma Beta Chap. Polit & Govt Pos: Chmn, Windham Dem Town Comt, Conn, 60-62; mem, Conn Dem State Cent Comt, 29th Dist, 60-, mem platform comt, 3 times; alderman, Second Ward, Willimantic, 61-63; comnr, Spec Revenue Comt, Conn, 71-; deleg, Dem Nat Conv, 72; deleg, Dem Nat Mid-Term Conf, 74. Bus & Prof Pos: Teacher, Mansfield, San Francisco & Windham, 45-60; asst instr, Eastern Conn State Col, 67-71. Mem: Conn State Employees Asn; Nat Asn State Racing Comnrs; US Trotting Asn; Windham Community Mem Hosp Asn; Eastern Conn Ment Health Asn. Relig: Roman Catholic. Mailing Add: 275 High St Willimantic CT 06226

MORRIS, HELENE M (R)
b Boston, Mass; wid. Educ: Lowell State Teachers Col; Boston Univ, grad study in bus admin. Polit & Govt Pos: Rep Nat Committeewoman, Fla, until 68; State Rep Committeewoman; state treas, Rep State Exec Comt; bd mem, Fla Fedn of Rep Women; mem, Women's Nat Rep Club, New York; vchmn Fla deleg, Rep Nat Conv, 64, alt deleg & mem host comt, 68, deleg, 72; Presidential Elector, Fla, 73. Bus & Prof Pos: Co-owner, M Bar M Ranch, Sarasota, Fla; pres & chmn bd, George L Mesker Steel Corp, Evansville, Ind & New Albany, Miss. Mil Serv: 2nd Lt to Maj, Women's Army Corps. Mem: Women's Auxiliary Mem Hosp; Sarasota Art Asn; Am Legion; Sarasota Co Bd of Zoning Appeals; Vis Nurse Asn. Honors & Awards: Champion of Independent Higher Educ, Pres of Independent Univs & Cols in Fla, 70. Mailing Add: Le Chateau 37 Sunset Dr Sarasota FL 33577

MORRIS, JAMES MCCULLUM (D)
SC State Sen
b New Zion, SC, Apr 24, 28; s Harrison McCullum Morris & Janie Marie Barker M; m 1946 to Dorothy Evelyn Coleman; m 1972 to Martha Pierce; c Sandra, Evelyn, Karen & Marian. Educ: Univ SC, LLB, 55; Wig & Robe; Phi Alpha Delta. Polit & Govt Pos: SC State Rep, Clarendon Co, 55-62; SC State Sen, Clarendon-Sumter Co, 62-66 & 68- Bus & Prof Pos: Lawyer & farmer, 55- Mil Serv: Pvt, Air Force, 46; reentered 50, released as S/Sgt, 51, after serv in Air Training Command & Troop Carrier. Mem: SC State Bar Asn; Ruritan; Mason; Am Legion. Relig: Methodist. Mailing Add: State House Columbia SC 29211

MORRIS, JAMES PAXTON (R)
b Tulsa, Okla, Aug 12, 35; s Carl Paxton Morris & Kathryn Cross M; m 1957 to Sara Ann Carpenter; c Janna Marie, Joseph Lee & James Paxton, Jr. Educ: Univ NMex, 53-57; Sigma Alpha Epsilon. Polit & Govt Pos: Secy-treas, Albuquerque City Campaign, NMex, 66; area coordr, Bernalillo Co Rep Party, 67, chmn, formerly; deleg, Rep Nat Conv, 68; campaign mgr & chmn, Pete Domenici for Gov, NMex, 70; co comnr, Bernalillo Co, 72-, chmn, Bernalillo Co Comn, currently. Bus & Prof Pos: Albuquerque chap, NMex Motor Carriers, 67-68, bd dirs & mem-at-lg, NMex Motor Carriers, 68-69; secy-treas, Commercial Warehouse Co, J P C & Sun City Transfer & Storage Co, Inc, currently. Mem: Delta Nu Alpha; Kiwanis; Mason; Shrine; Elks. Relig: Christian Science. Legal Res: 11401 Baldwin Ave NE Albuquerque NM 87112 Mailing Add: PO Box 853 Albuquerque NM 87103

MORRIS, JAY FLERON (R)
Pres, Md Fedn Young Rep
b Honolulu, Hawaii, Feb 21, 41; s I Sewell Morris & Joslin Fleron M; m 1959 to Angela Turner; c Jeffrey Fleron. Educ: Univ Md, BA, 63, grad sch, 63-65; Sch Advan Int Studies, Johns Hopkins Univ, 65-66; Tau Mu Epsilon (past pres); Phi Kappa Phi; Kappa Alpha Mu; Omicron Delta Kappa; Kappa Tau Alpha; Sigma Delta Chi (past pres & vpres); Student Pub Rels Asn (past pres & vpres); Pi Sigma Alpha. Polit & Govt Pos: Legis & research asst, US Sen James B Pearson, Kans, 67-71; pres, Prince George's Co Young Rep, 68-70; pres, Md Fedn Young Rep, 69-; chmn, Wash Coun Young Rep, 69-; senate chmn, Rep Capitol Hill Discussion Group; mem, Prince George's Co Rep 1970 Campaign Comt, 69-70; mem steering comt, Senate Legis Staff Club, 69-70; mem, Senate Staff Club & Bull Elephants, 69-70; exec vchmn, Prince George's Co Rep Cent Comt, 70-; chmn leadership training sch, Nat Fedn Young Rep, 71 & 72, auditor, Fedn, currently; admin aide, Co Exec W W Gullett, Prince George's Co Rep Exec Comt, Md, 71-; nat mgr for urban mass transit, Motorola, Commun & Electronics, Inc, Fed Prog Opers Div, Washington, DC. Mem: Adelphi Citizens Asn (bd gov); Prince George's Ment Health Asn (bd dirs); Prince George's Civic Asn (bd dirs); United Cerebral Palsy Asn Prince George's Co (bd dirs); Prince George's Citizens for Charter (chmn). Honors & Awards: Outstanding Man, Md Fedn Young Rep, 69 & 70; One of Outstanding Young Men in Am, Outstanding Am Found. Relig: Presbyterian. Mailing Add: 10816 Pleasant Acres Dr Adelphi MD 20783

MORRIS, JOHN EDWARD (D)
Del State Rep
Mailing Add: 5 East St Camden DE 19934

MORRIS, JULIUS D (D)
Conn State Rep
Mailing Add: 135 Marlin Rd New Britain CT 06053

MORRIS, KENNETH ELON (R)
Mem, NC State Rep Exec Comt
b New Bern, NC, Mar 26, 39; s Kenneth Elon Morris, Sr & Evelyn Smith M; m 1960 to Linda Rice; c Linda Katherine & Kenneth Elon, III. Educ: Univ NC, 2 years; Delta Kappa Epsilon. Polit & Govt Pos: Chmn, Craven Co Rep Exec Comt, NC, 69-72; mem, NC State Rep Exec Comt, 70- Bus & Prof Pos: Gen agent, Occidental Life of NC, 64-; pres, Carolina Growth, Inc, 67- Mem: Local & US CofC; New Bern Life Underwriters Asn; Nat Asn Health Underwriters. Honors & Awards: Nat Qual Award. Relig: Presbyterian. Legal Res: 4001 Country Club Rd New Bern NC 28560 Mailing Add: Drawer 550 New Bern NC 28560

MORRIS, LARRY WADE (D)
Ala State Rep
b Montgomery, Ala, Aug 16, 43; s Hoyt Morris; m to Beverly Jane Turner; c Mark, Clark, Benjamin & Kevin. Educ: Auburn Univ, BS, 65, Univ Ala Sch Law, JD, 68; Sigma Alpha Epsilon; pres, Law Sch. Polit & Govt Pos: City judge, Alexander City, Ala, 67-74; Ala State Rep, Dist 62, 75- Bus & Prof Pos: Partner, Radney & Morris, 67-73; pvt law practice, 73- Mil Serv: Entered as E-4, Nat Guard, 68, released as E-5, 74. Mem: CofC (pres); Kiwanis; Elks; Moose; Am Bar Asn. Relig: Methodist. Legal Res: 2010 Tracy Rd Alexander City AL 35010 Mailing Add: PO Box 811 Alexander City AL 35010

MORRIS, SAM CAMERON (D)
Chmn, Hoke Co Dem Exec Comt, NC
b Raeford, NC, Jan 16, 18; s Bruce Morris & Beulah Cameron M; m 1943 to Mary Alice Pernell; c Sarah Frances & John Arthur. Educ: Raeford High Sch. Polit & Govt Pos: Pres, Young Dem Club, 50-54; precinct chmn, Dem Party, NC, 54-58; chmn, Hoke Co Dem Exec Comt, 58-72 & 74- Mil Serv: Entered as Sgt, Army, 40, released as Capt, 46, after serv in Pac Theatre. Mem: Am Legion; Kiwanis. Relig: Presbyterian. Legal Res: 110 N Jackson St Raeford NC 28376 Mailing Add: PO Box 541 Raeford NC 28376

MORRIS, SAMUEL W (D)
Pa State Rep
Mailing Add: Capitol Bldg Harrisburg PA 17120

MORRIS, THOMAS GAYLE (D)
b Eastland Co, Tex, July 20, 19; s Robert Gayle Morris & Nancy Smith M; m 1947 to Corinne Stevens; c Thomas G, II & Elizabeth Jane. Educ: Univ NMex, BS in Civil Eng, 48; Sigma Chi. Polit & Govt Pos: Chmn, NMex Interstate Streams Comn; NMex State Rep, 53-58; US Rep, NMex, 58-68; mem, Nat Lewis & Clark Comn, 65; state treas, NMex Dem Party, 70. Bus & Prof Pos: Rancher & farmer; chmn bd, Am Bank of Com; dir & secy-treas, Benavidez Construction Co; chmn bd, Solo Eng; dir Bank Securities; consult to test dir, Atomic Energy Comn. Mil Serv: Navy, 37-44. Mem: Acad Polit Sci; Am Mgt Asn; Am Soc Pub Admin; Int Platform Asn; Am Nuclear Soc. Relig: Presbyterian. Mailing Add: 910 Warm Sands Dr SE Albuquerque NM 87123

MORRIS, THOMAS HANSLEY (D)
Chmn, Lenoir Co Dem Party, NC
b Halifax, NC, Apr 25, 36; s Ephriam Thomas Morris & Dorothy Hansley M; m 1964 to Ruby Hunter; c Thomas Hunter & Jessica Leigh. Educ: Wake Forest Univ, BA, 58, JD, 63; Phi Delta Phi; Sigma Chi. Polit & Govt Pos: Chmn, 25 Lenoir Co Bd Elecs, NC, 70-74; chmn, Lenoir Co Dem Party, 74- Mil Serv: Entered as Seaman, Navy, 59, released as PO 3/C, 61, after serv in USS Lorain Co, LST-1177. Mem: Am, NC & Lenoir Co Bar Asns; Rotary Int; Elks. Relig: Baptist. Legal Res: 3200 Hillman Rd Kingston NC 28501 Mailing Add: PO Box 396 Kinston NC 28501

MORRIS, WILLIAM HARRELL JR (R)
Mem Exec Comt, Tenn Rep Party
b Memphis, Tenn, Jan 5, 29; s William Harrell Morris & Rosaland Gooch M; m 1954 to Nancy Johnson; c George Robert & Mary Elizabeth. Educ: Univ Tenn, 2 years; Sigma Alpha Epsilon. Polit & Govt Pos: Co chmn for Goldwater, Tenn, 64; seventh dist chmn, Young Rep, 65 & 66; seventh dist campaign mgr for cong cand, 66; pres, Jackson-Madison Co Young Rep

Club, 66-67; chmn, Madison Co Elec Comn, 67, 68 & 71; chmn, Madison Co Rep Party, 67-70; deleg, Rep Nat Conv, 68; seventh dist chmn, Nixon-Agnew Campaign, 68; seventh dist chmn, Tenn Rep Party, 70-74; mem exec comt, 26th Sen Dist, 74-; exec asst to US Sen Bill Brock, currently; pres, Goals for Jackson, 74- Bus & Prof Pos: Pres, Gooch-Edenton Wholesale Hardware Co, Inc, 55- Mil Serv: Entered as Seaman, Navy, 51, released as PN-3, 53, after serv in Res. Mem: Jackson Rotary; Jackson Golf & Country Club (bd dirs); Youth Town of Tenn (vpres); Madison Co Cancer Soc (bd dirs); CofC (bd dirs). Honors & Awards: Tenn Young Rep of the Year, 67; City Maker Award, Jackson, Tenn, 68. Relig: Methodist. Mailing Add: 37 Carlisle Dr Jackson TN 38301

MORRISON, ANNE SAPP (R)
Chmn, Sixth Cong Dist Rep Party, NC
b Charlotte, NC, June 17, 30; d Charles Pinckney Sapp & Alene Stonestreet S; m 1951 to Daniel Baker Morrison; c Pamela Anne, Daniel Baker, Jr & Charles Sapp. Educ: Mary Washington Col, Univ Va, Fredericksburg, 48-49; Univ NC, Chapel Hill, grad of realtors inst, 72. Polit & Govt Pos: Pres, Greenville Co Rep Women's Club, SC, 62-64; mem exec bd, SC Fedn of Rep Women, 62-64; vchmn, SC Young Rep, 63-64, interim chmn, 64; precinct chmn, Rep Party, Greenville, 63-64; pub rels chmn, Buncombe Co Rep Women, NC, 65-66, vchmn, 66-67; vpres, Buncombe Co Young Rep, 66-67; pub rels chmn, 11th Cong Dist, Gardner for Gov, 68; pub rels chmn, NC Young Rep, 69-70, mem exec comt, 70-71; mem exec comt, Alamance Co Rep Party, 70-; pub rels chmn, Lowe for State Senate, 70; mem, NC State Rep Cent Comt, 70-; vchmn, Sixth Cong Dist Rep Party, 70-71; chmn, 71-; Alamance chmn, Ritchie for Cong. Mem: Nat Asn Realtors; Nat Inst Real Estate Brokers; Bd of Realtors, Burlington, NC; Burlington-Alamance CofC (vpres & bd dirs); Exec Club (bd dirs). Honors & Awards: Cert of Merit, SC Young Rep; Nominated for Outstanding Young Rep of NC. Relig: Church of Christ. Mailing Add: 916 W Davis St Burlington NC 27215

MORRISON, BETTY (D)
Ariz State Sen
Mailing Add: 4401 N 38th St Phoenix AZ 85018

MORRISON, DAVID EUGENE (R)
Asst Chmn, Nebr Rep State Cent Comt
b York, Nebr, May 6, 52; s Louis Eugene Morrison & Eleanor Ruth Curry M; single. Educ: Univ Nebr, Lincoln, 70-; Delta Sigma Rho, Tau Kappa Alpha; Phi Alpha Theta; Beta Theta Pi; second vpres, Builders, 73; chmn budget comt, Student Union Bd, 73-; Student Tribunal; co-chmn, Legis Liaison Comt, 71-72. Polit & Govt Pos: Pres, Kearney TAR, Nebr, 68-70; mem, Nebr Rep State Exec Comt, 72-; asst chmn, Nebr Rep State Cent Comt, 72-; alt deleg, Rep Nat Conv, 72. Mem: Nebr Coun of Youth (chmn, 71-72); Nebr Comt for Children & Youth. Honors & Awards: Deleg, Boys' Nation, Nebr Am Legion, 69; deleg, World Youth Cong, Lions, 69; Nebr State Youth Leadership Award, Nebr Elks, 70; Outstanding Achievement Award, Univ Nebr Innocents Soc, 72. Relig: United Methodist. Mailing Add: 1515 R St Lincoln NE 68508

MORRISON, DELESSEPS S, JR (D)
La State Rep
Mailing Add: 4418 Hamilton New Orleans LA 70118

MORRISON, DONALD RAY (R)
Mem Exec Bd, Chippewa Co Rep Party, Wis
b Santa Fe, NMex, Feb 27, 54; s Earl L Morrison & Hazel Hessinger M; single. Educ: Carleton Col, 72- Polit & Govt Pos: Chmn, Chippewa Co Young Rep, Wis, 69-72; deleg, Wis Rep State Conv & Tenth Cong Dist Rep Conv, 72; deleg, Rep Nat Conv, 72; student intern, US Rep Alvin O'Konski, 72; mem exec bd, Chippewa Co Rep Party, 72- Honors & Awards: Wingspread fel, Carleton Col, 73. Relig: Presbyterian. Legal Res: 507 W Willow St Chippewa Falls WI 54729 Mailing Add: Carleton Col Northfield MN 55057

MORRISON, EULA GRACE (D)
Chmn, Gladwin Co Dem Comt, Mich
b Ravenna, Ohio, Nov 5, 24; d Louis Harper & Belinda Dickenson H; m 1942 to Walter Morrison, Jr; c Harriette (Mrs Bongio Vanni). Educ: Bohecker Tech Sch, 40-41. Polit & Govt Pos: Chmn, Gladwin Co Dem Comt, Mich, 73; interim chmn, mem exec comt, Dem Women's Caucus, 73-; deleg, Dem Nat Conv, 72 & Dem Nat Mid-Term Conf, 74; Convenor, Dem Comt Unity Caucus, 75-; chairperson, Tenth Cong Dist Dem Comt, 75- Mem: VFW Auxiliary Post 7303 (treas, 71-). Relig: Methodist. Mailing Add: 696 Kathy Ct Beaverton MI 48612

MORRISON, FRANK B (D)
Pub Defender, Douglas Co, Nebr
b Golden, Colo, May 20, 05; m 1936 to Maxine Hepp; c Frank B, Jr, David J & Jean Marie. Educ: Kans State Col, BS, 27; Univ Nebr, JD, 31; Tau Kappa Epsilon; Phi Alpha Delta; Delta Sigma Rho; Pi Kappa Delta. Polit & Govt Pos: Co attorney, Red Willow & Frontier Co; Gov, Nebr, 60-67; pub defender, Douglas Co, Nebr, currently; deleg, Dem Nat Conv, 72. Bus & Prof Pos: Former farmer & teacher; lawyer; counsel for Frenchman-Cambridge Irrigation Dist, McCook Pub Power Dist & Twin Valleys Elec Mem Asn. Mem: Rotary Int (dist gov); Norris Mem Found (pres); McCook CofC (dir); Lutheran Med Ctr (trustee); Am Bar Asn. Legal Res: 13006 Shirley Omaha NE 68102 Mailing Add: County Court House Omaha NE 68102

MORRISON, JAMES HOBSON (D)
b Hammond, La, Dec 8, 08; s Benjamin M Morrison & Florence Hobson M; m 1940 to Marjorie Abbey; c James H, Jr, (Hobby) & Benjamin Abbey (Benjy). Educ: Tulane Univ, LLB, 35; Delta Tau Delta; Phi Delta Phi. Polit & Govt Pos: US Rep, La, 42-67. Bus & Prof Pos: Partner, Morrison & Higgins, currently. Mem: La State & Am Bar Asns; Eagles; Elks; City Club of Baton Rouge. Relig: Episcopal. Mailing Add: RR 3 Box 165 M Hammond LA 70401

MORRISON, JOHN J (D)
Conn State Rep
Mailing Add: 3 Eleanor Rd Enfield CT 06082

MORRISON, KATHRYN (D)
Wis State Sen
b Madison, Wis, May 22, 42; d Gould Morrison & Geraldine Andersen M; single. Educ: Univ Wis-Madison, BBA, 64, MBA, 65; Univ Minn, 69-70. Polit & Govt Pos: Mem, Platteville Sewer & Water, 73-; mem exec bd, Grant Co Dem Party, Wis, 73-; mem, Wis Coun on Criminal Justice, 75-; Wis State Sen, 17th Dist, 75- Mem: Am Econ Asn; Common Cause;

Womens Polit Caucus (state coordr, Nat Policy Coun, 73-74). Honors & Awards: CAROL Award, Platteville Jaycettes, 75. Legal Res: 885 Stonebridge Ave Platteville WI 53818 Mailing Add: 417 S Capitol Bldg Madison WI 53702

MORRISON, ROBERT LEE (D)
Chmn, Clark Co Dem Cent Comt, Nev
b Alpena, Mich, Feb 27, 24; s Dougal Lawrence Morrison & Jennie Manning M; m 1944 to Florence Rita Squire; c Robert Dougal, Anne Mary & Shannon Kathleen. Educ: Mich State Univ, BS, 48; Univ Mich, DrDentSurg, 51; Phi Kappa Phi; Omicron Kappa Upsilon; Delta Sigma Delta. Polit & Govt Pos: Precinct capt, Clark Co Dem Party, Nev, 64-65; chmn, Clark Co Dem Cent Comt, 68- Mil Serv: Entered as Air Cadet, Air Force, 42, released as 1st Lt, 45, after serv in WCoast Flying Training Command, Pilot. Mem: Am Dent Asn (vpres, 65-66, trustee, 67-); Elks; KofC. Relig: Catholic. Mailing Add: 1329 S Seventh Las Vegas NV 89104

MORRISON, SID (R)
Minority Orgn Leader, Wash House Rep
b Wash, 1933; s Charles Morrison; m to Marcella; c Four. Educ: Yakima Valley Col; Wash State Univ, 54. Polit & Govt Pos: Wash State Rep, 67-, chmn labor comt, Wash House Rep, 69-70, Asst Majority Floor Leader, 71-73, Minority Orgn Leader, 73- Bus & Prof Pos: Orchardist & nurseryman. Mem: Boy Scouts (leader); Grange; PTA; Mason. Relig: Methodist. Mailing Add: Rte 1 Box 220 AA Zillah WA 98953

MORRISON, THEODORE V, JR (D)
Va State Deleg
b Atlanta, Ga, June 15, 35; s Theodore V Morrison & Helen Sisson M; m 1956 to Audrey Powell; c Thomas Purnell & Charles Agustus. Educ: Emory Univ, BA, 57, LLB, 59; Alpha Tau Omega; Phi Delta Phi. Polit & Govt Pos: Va State Deleg, Newport News, 68-; mem, Va State Crime Comn, Interstate Coop Comn & Legis Rev & Audit Comn, currently. Bus & Prof Pos: Attorney-at-law, Saunders, Carlton, Morrison, Stephenson & Spratley, currently. Mil Serv: Entered as Pvt, Army Nat Guard, 59, released as Sgt, 65. Mem: Am Bar Asn; Am Trial Lawyers Asn; Am Judicature Soc; Nat Soc State Legislators (bd gov); Rotary. Honors & Awards: Distinguished Serv Award, Hampton Roads Jaycees, 68; Outstanding Young Man of 1968 Award, Va State Jaycees. Relig: Episcopal. Mailing Add: 2660 Washington Ave Newport News VA 23607

MORRISSETTE, GEORGE H (D)
NH State Rep
b Manchester, NH, Apr 5, 26; s Cleophas Morrissette & Marie Louise Bilopeau M; m 1944 to Lucienne; c Paul, Dennis, Linda & Paulette (Mrs Roy). Educ: NH Col, AS, 72; Univ NH, BS, 74; Franklin Pierce Law Ctr, 75- Polit & Govt Pos: NH State Sen, 72-73; NH State Rep, 75- Bus & Prof Pos: Pres, G M Plumbing Inc, 49-74, Reeds Ferry Supply Inc, 55- & G M Realty, 63- Mil Serv: Entered as Pvt, Army, 43, released as Sgt, 46, after serv in Army Air Force, Caribbean Theatre, 44-46; Air Force & Naval Res, 46-51. Mem: Sanitary Engr Asn; Joliette Club; Am Legion; Univ NH Alumni. Relig: Catholic. Mailing Add: 1630 Front St Manchester NH 03102

MORRISSEY, THOMAS LAWRENCE (D)
Chmn, Johnson Co Dem Cent Comt, Nebr
b Tecumseh, Nebr, Nov 23, 36; s Raymond B Morrissey & Florence Elizabeth Senneff M; m 1958 to Marie A Neukirch; c Timothy Paul, Elizabeth Ann & Theodore Raymond. Educ: Creighton Univ, MD, 60; Phi Alpha Delta. Polit & Govt Pos: Co attorney, Johnson Co, Nebr, 63-; chmn, Johnson Co Dem Cent Comt, 68-69 & 73- Bus & Prof Pos: Partner, Morrissey & Morrissey, Attorneys, Tecumseh, Nebr, 60-; chief counsel, Southeastern Nebr Crime Study Comn, 69. Mem: Nebr Co & Nat Dist Attorneys Asns; Tecumseh Country Club (pres); Kiwanis; CofC. Relig: Roman Catholic. Mailing Add: 962 N Fifth Tecumseh NE 68450

MORROW, FLOYD LEE (D)
City Councilman, San Diego, Calif
b Wichita Falls, Tex, Jan 20, 33; s William Frank Morrow & Lillian Shipp M; m 1954 to Marlene Patersen; c Darlene, Shawn & Lance. Educ: Univ Tex, BBA, 57, LLB, 59; Phi Alpha Delta. Polit & Govt Pos: Dep city attorney, San Diego, Calif, 63-65, city councilman, 65-; mem, San Diego Co Dem Cent Comt, 64-65. Bus & Prof Pos: Attorney, Ryan Aeronaut Co, 59-63; sr partner, Morrow & Young, 65- Mil Serv: Entered as Pvt, Marine Corps, 51, released as Sgt, 54, after serv in 1st Marine Div, Korea; Korean Campaign Ribbon with Three Battle Stars; Good Conduct, Nat Defense Serv & UN Serv Medals. Mem: San Diego Bar Asn; Calif & Tex State Bar Asns; San Diego Exchange Club; March of Dimes (co bd chmn). Relig: Lutheran. Mailing Add: 7132 Belden San Diego CA 92111

MORROW, JAMES ANTHONY (JIM) (D)
Miss State Rep
b Clovis, NMex, Sept 22, 23; single. Polit & Govt Pos: Miss State Rep, 52- Bus & Prof Pos: Farmer; lawyer; automobile dealer; merchant seaman. Mem: Am Legion; 40 et 8; Mason. Relig: Episcopal. Mailing Add: PO Box 73 Brandon MS 39042

MORROW, JOHN L (D)
NMex State Sen
Mailing Add: Box 111 Capulin NM 88414

MORROW, WILLIAM EARL, JR (R)
Rep Nat Committeeman, Nebr
b Alliance, Nebr, Aug 2, 30; s Wm E Morrow & Helen Young M; m 1953 to Dorothy McGinley; c Dorothy, Anne, Patricia, Catherine, William, Gertrude, John & Mary. Educ: Univ Nebr, BSC, 51, JD, 53; Phi Delta Phi; Sigma Chi. Polit & Govt Pos: Rep Nat Committeeman, Nebr, 75- Mil Serv: Entered as Ens, Navy, 53, released as Lt(jg), 56, after serv in Pac Fleet, 53-56. Relig: Catholic. Legal Res: 1703 S 108th St Omaha NE 68144 Mailing Add: 3535 Harney St Omaha NE 68131

MORSBERGER, LOUIS PHILLIP (D)
Md State Deleg
b Baltimore, Md, Aug 26, 29; s Emory Louis Morsberger; m 1954 to Jolene Truitt; c Lou Ann, Jeffrey Dallas & Mark Phillip. Educ: Catonsville Sr High, grad, 48; Baltimore Jr Col, 48. Polit & Govt Pos: Mem, Dem State Cent Comt, First Dist, Baltimore Co, Md, 66-74; deleg, Dem Nat Conv, 68; Md State Deleg, 75- Mil Serv: Entered as Pvt, Army, 51, released as Cpl, 53, after serv in Panama Canal Zone, 52-53; Good Conduct Medal. Mem: Boumi Temple; Elks; Ridgeway Dem Club; English Consul Dem Club; Consolidated Dem Club. Mailing Add: 612 Hilton Ave Baltimore MD 21228

MORSE, EVA MAE (R)
Vt State Rep
b South Fayston, Vt, Oct 28, 38; d Lawrence George Witham & Eloise Mae McCullough M; m 1956 to David Fred Morse, div; m 1974 to Allen George Sayers; c Sheila Kay, David Lindsay & Peter John. Educ: Montpelier High Sch, Vt, grad, 56, valedictorian. Polit & Govt Pos: Town clerk & treas, Calais, Vt, 63-, zoning adminr, 71-; Vt State Rep, 71-; dep sheriff, Washington Co Sheriff's Off, 72- Bus & Prof Pos: Trustee & bd dirs, Washington Elec Corp, 73- Relig: Methodist. Mailing Add: Calais VT 05648

MORSE, FRANK BRADFORD (R)
Undersecy Gen, UN
b Lowell, Mass, Aug 7, 21; s Frank Young Morse & Inez Turnbull Coffin M; m 1955 to Vera Francesca Cassilly; c Susanna Francesca & Anthony Bradford. Educ: Boston Univ, BS, 48, LLB, 49; Sigma Alpha Epsilon. Hon Degrees: DSc, Lowell Technol Inst; DPub Admin, Northeastern Univ. Polit & Govt Pos: City councilman, Lowell, Mass, 52-53; attorney, US Senate Comt on Armed Serv, 53-54; exec secy & chief asst to Sen Leverett Saltonstall, 55-58; dep adminr, Vet Admin, 58-60; US Rep, Mass, 61-72; alt deleg, Rep Nat Conv, 72; Undersecy Gen, UN, 72- Bus & Prof Pos: Law clerk, Chief Justice-Supreme Judicial Court of Mass, 49; attorney-at-law, Lowell, 49-53; faculty mem, Boston Univ, 49-53. Mil Serv: Entered as Pvt, Army, 42, released as 2nd Lt, 46. Mem: US-Mex Interparliamentary Group (US deleg); Interparliamentary Union (US deleg); Atlantic Coun (sponsor); 18-Nation Disarmament Conf, Geneva (adv); Coun of Europe (US rep). Legal Res: NY Mailing Add: 411 E 53rd St New York NY 10022

MORSE, GERALD IRA (R)
Vt State Sen
Mailing Add: Groton VT 05046

MORSE, ROBERT WARREN (D)
b Boston, Mass, May 25, 21; s Walter L Morse & Ethel E Prince M; m 1943 to Alice M Cooper; c Robert W, Jr, Pamela Dean & James Prince. Educ: Bowdoin Col, BS, 43; Brown Univ, ScM, 46, PhD, 49; Sigma Xi. Polit & Govt Pos: Asst Secy of Navy for Research & Develop, 64-66; chmn, Interagency Comt on Oceanography, Fed Coun for Sci & Technol, 64-66. Bus & Prof Pos: Asst prof physics, Brown Univ, 49-53, assoc prof, 53-58, prof, 58-64, head dept, 60-62, dean col, 62-64; chmn, Undersea Warfare Comt, Nat Acad Sci, 62-64; pres, Case Western Reserve Univ, 66-71; dir research, Woods Hole Oceanographic Inst, 71- Mil Serv: Entered as Ens, Navy, 43, released as Lt, 46. Publ: Over forty scientific papers in low temperature physics & acoustics. Mem: Am Acoustical Soc; fel Am Physical Soc; fel Am Acad Arts & Sci. Legal Res: Falmouth MA Mailing Add: Woods Hole Oceanographic Inst Woods Hole MA 02543

MORTIMER, G F (R)
SDak State Rep
Mailing Add: 1013 Kingsbury Belle Fourche SD 57717

MORTON, JOHN DUGGAN SR (R)
Treas, Coos Co, NH
b Berlin, NH, Mar 12, 37; s C Edward Morton & Marion Duggan M; m 1957 to Jacquelyn Mason; c John D, Jr & Karen Ann. Educ: Nichols Col, ABA, 57. Polit & Govt Pos: City councilman, Berlin, NH, 66-68; chmn, Coos Co Rep Party, 70-74; treas, Coos Co, 71- Bus & Prof Pos: Mgr trainee, Treadway Inns Inc, 58-59; mgr, Berlin-Gorham Fruit & Produce Co Inc, 59-60; ins underwriter, Retail Credit Co, 60-71; mgr, Montgomery Ward, 71- Mil Serv: Entered as Pvt, Army Res, 55, released as Pfc, 61. Mem: Kiwanis (past pres & current treas, Berlin Club, lt gov, New Eng Dist & treas, 71-74, New Eng Gov, 75-); Eagles; Athletic Booster Club Berlin; Boy Scouts (troop comt chmn); Berlin Sno-Riders. Relig: Protestant. Mailing Add: 130 Sweden St Berlin NH 03570

MORTON, MARGARET E (D)
Conn State Rep
Mailing Add: 25 Currier St Bridgeport CT 06607

MORTON, RICHARD G (R)
Maine State Rep
b Farmington, Maine, Aug 27, 18; s Lloyd B Morton & Gladys Matthieu M; m 1941 to Barbara Atwood; c Marilyn M (Mrs Daniel Hylan), Patricia Ann (Mrs Edward Larson) & Richard Matthieu. Educ: Univ Maine, BS in Mech Eng with highest distinction, 40; Sigma Alpha Epsilon; Tau Beta Pi; Phi Kappa Phi. Polit & Govt Pos: Mem sch bd, Farmington, Maine, 50-56, mem budget comt, 60-70; exec coun, State of Maine, 67-69; Maine State Rep, 73- Bus & Prof Pos: Pres, Morton Motor Co, Inc, Farmington, Maine, 56-; dir, Maine Automobile Dealers Asn, 62-70, pres, 68-69; dir, First Nat Bank, Farmington, 65-, chmn bd, 71- Mil Serv: Entered as 2nd Lt, Army, 42 released as Maj, 46, after serv in 377th AAA-AW Bn, European Theatre, 43-45; Bronze Star. Mem: Mason (Past Master, 51); Shrine; Am Legion. Honors & Awards: Time Mag Qual Dealer Award, 73. Relig: Congregational. Mailing Add: Box 224 Farmington ME 04938

MORTON, ROGERS CLARK BALLARD (R)
Secy of Commerce
b Louisville, Ky, Sept 19, 14; s David C Morton & Mary Ballard M; m 1939 to Anne Jones; c David & Anne (Mrs McCance). Educ: Yale Univ, AB, 37. Polit & Govt Pos: US Rep, Md, 62-71; deleg, Rep Nat Conv, 68 & 72; chmn, Rep Nat Comt, 69-71; Secy of the Interior, 71-75; Secy Commerce, 75- Bus & Prof Pos: Former farmer & businessman; experienced in bus mgt & pub rels; vpres, Ballard & Ballard, Louisville, Ky, 46-47, pres, 47-51, vpres, after co merged with Pillsbury Co, 51-52, dir & mem exec comt, 53-71; mem, Civilian Adv Bd, Air Training Command of Air Force, 56-63. Mil Serv: Entered as Pvt, Army, 41, released as Capt, 45, after serv in Field Artil. Mem: Soc of Cincinnati; Md Agr Soc Talbot Co (trustee); Wash Col, Chesterton, Md (bd gov & visitors); Chesapeake Bay Yacht Club. Relig: Episcopal. Legal Res: RD 1 Easton MD 21601 Mailing Add: Dept Commerce Washington DC 20230

MORTON, WARREN ALLEN (R)
Wyo State Rep
b Birmingham, Ala, Mar 22, 24; s Lindley C Morton & Ruth Goddard M; m 1946 to Katharine Hancock Allen; c Frederick Lee, Allen Salisbury, Robert Coleman & Warren Goddard. Educ: Yale Univ, chem eng, 45; Delta Psi. Polit & Govt Pos: Wyo State Rep, Natrona Co, 67-; Wyo Rep to Interstate Oil Compact Comn, 62-74. Bus & Prof Pos: Petrol engr, Morton & Sons, 46-52- mgr, MKM Oil Co, 52-; dir, Wyo Nat Bank, Casper, 70-; pres, Morton Bros Inc, 71- Mil Serv: Entered as A/S, Naval Res, 43, released as Ens, 46. Mem: Am Petrol Inst; Rocky Mountain Oil & Gas Asn; Wyo Asn Petrol Landmen; Am Asn Petrol Landmen; Independent Petrol Asn Am. Relig: Episcopal. Mailing Add: 241 E 12th St Casper WY 82601

MOSAKOWSKI, KENNETH ROBERT (INDEPENDENT-D)
Mem, Hampshire Co Dem Comt, Mass
b Somerville, Mass, Nov 25, 46; s Frank Mosakowski & Anne Ruth Milovitch M; single. Educ: Oxford Univ, 68; Smith Col, 69; Univ Mass, Amherst, BA, 69; Univ Theatre; Univ Reform Comt; Yahoo; Eng Dept Undergrad Coun. Polit & Govt Pos: Campaign mgr, Citizens for Gensheimer, South Deerfield, Mass, 70; campaign coordr, Western Mass Citizens for McGovern, 71-72; deleg, Dem Nat Conv, 72; campaign mgr, Citizens for Collins, Amherst, 72; mem precinct four, Amherst Town Meeting, 73-; mem, Amherst Comt on Pub Transportation, 73-75; mem, Amherst Dem Town Comt, Mass, currently; mem, Hampshire Co Dem Comt, Mass, currently; Dem cand for US Cong, 74. Bus & Prof Pos: Prog host & producer, Focus, Pub Affairs Series, Radio Sta WMUA, Univ Mass, Amherst, 68-, libr asst, 69-, instr, Proj Ten Polit Campaigns Seminar, 73- Mil Serv: Conscientious objector. Publ: The American way of truth, Spectrum Mag, spring 69; co-auth, Dorchester County, South Carolina: a struggle for human dignity, Comt on Poverty, Martin Luther King Coun, Univ Mass, Amherst, 2/70; Nixon budget cuts will hurt county students, farmers, Amherst Sunday Rec, 5/6/73. Mem: Friends Comt on Nat Legis (dist contact, 73-); Citizens for Participation in Polit Action (exec bd, 73-); Hampshire Co Garden Comt; Am Civil Liberties Union; Civil Liberties Union of Mass. Honors & Awards: Scholar, Nat Maritime Union, 65 & Univ Mass, 65. Relig: Humanist. Legal Res: 370 Northampton Rd Amherst MA 01002 Mailing Add: PO Box 197 Amherst MA 01002

MOSBACHER, EMIL, JR (BUS) (R)
b Mt Vernon, NY, Apr 1, 22; s Emil Mosbacher & Gertrude Schwartz M; m 1950 to Patricia Ryan; c Emil, III, Richard Bruce & John David. Educ: Dartmouth Col, BA, 43; Gamma Delta Chi. Hon Degrees: MA, Dartmouth Col, 63; LLD, Long Island Univ, 69. Polit & Govt Pos: Chief of Protocol, Dept of State, 69-72; chmn, NY State Racing & Wagering Bd, 73-74. Bus & Prof Pos: Trustee, Lenox Hill Hosp, 57-, chmn joint conf comt, 67-, mem exec comt, 67-; dir, Lily Tulip Cup Corp, 62-68; trustee, Dollar Savings Bank, 64-69 & 73-; mem exam comt, 67-69; dir, Police Athletic League, 67-69, Nat Life Ins Co, 68-69, Abercrombie & Fitch Co, 68-69 & United Merchants & Mfg Inc, 68-69 & 72-; real estate investor & independent oil & gas producer, NY, currently; dir, Chubb Corp, 72-; trustee, NY Yacht Club, 72-; mem, Chem Bank, Rockefeller Ctr Adv Bd, 72-; dir, Fed Ins Co, 72-; dir, Vigilant Ins Co, 72-; dir, Amax, 74-; dir, Hoover Inst on War, Revolution & Peace, 74-; chmn, Oper Sail, 76. Mil Serv: Navy, 43-46, Lt, with serv in Pac, VI & Washington, DC. Mem: Choate Club NY; Choate Assocs; Choate Father's Asn (vpres, 66, pres, 67-); Choate Sch (trustee, 68-); Dartmouth Col Clubs NY & Westchester (dir). Relig: Episcopal. Legal Res: Nipowin Island Mead Point Greenwich CT 06830 Mailing Add: 515 Madison Ave New York NY 10022

MOSCONE, GEORGE R (D)
Calif State Sen
b San Francisco, Calif, Nov 24, 30; s George Moscone & Lee Monge M; m to Eugenia Bondanza; c Jenifer, Rebecca, Christopher & Jonathon. Educ: Univ Pac, BA; Univ Calif Hastings Col Law, JD, 56. Polit & Govt Pos: Mem, San Francisco Co Dem Comt, Calif, 60-; mem, San Francisco Bd Supvrs, 63-66; Calif State Sen, 67- Bus & Prof Pos: Teacher law, Lincoln Univ, 60-64; attorney, Morgan & Moscone, San Francisco, 60-69 & Hansen, Bridgett, Marcus & Jenkins, 69- Mil Serv: Navy. Publ: Bang & superbangs (SST), Cry Calif, winter 68-69; Group legal services, Loyola Univ, Los Angeles Law Rev, 4/69; Fr Freedom of speech, Calif Libr Asn J, 69. Mem: Nat Soc State Legislators; Native Sons of Golden West. Honors & Awards: Sen of Year, Calif Trial Lawyers Asn; Award of Excellence, Calif Libr Asn. Relig: Roman Catholic. Legal Res: 90 Lansdale Ave San Francisco CA 94127 Mailing Add: 1 Kearny St San Francisco CA 94108

MOSELEY, DOUGLAS DEWAYNE (R)
Ky State Sen
b Bowling Green, Ky, Mar 24, 28; s J Lee Moseley & Eva Moore M; m 1954 to Betty Jean Wyant; c J Lewis, Rebekah Ellen & Leslie Anne. Educ: Western Ky Univ, 46-49; Ky Wesleyan Col, BA, 52; Emory Univ, BD, 58, ThM, 72. Polit & Govt Pos. Mem, Rep Nat Comt Speakers Bur, campaign speaker for Rep Party; alt deleg, Rep Nat Conv, 64; mem & vchmn, Ky State Personnel Bd, 68-70; dist mgr, Ky Dept Parks, 70-; mem, Ky State Parole & Probation Bd, 72-; Ky State Sen, 75- Bus & Prof Pos: Minister, Methodist Church, 46-; prof Bible, Lindsey Wilson Col, 60-64, vpres, 64-70; mem bd dirs & vchmn, Prof Serv, Inc, Louisville, Ky. Mem: Ky Jr Col Asn; Am Asn Univ Prof; Nat Asn Methodist Col Teachers; PTA; Rotary. Relig: Methodist. Mailing Add: Box 365 Columbia KY 42728

MOSELEY, MARTIN EDWARD (R)
Mem Exec Comt, Rutherford Co Rep Comt, Tenn
b Nashville, Tenn, Feb 19, 30; s William Edward Moseley & Margaret Pickens M; m 1953 to Jean Young; c Martin E, Jr & William D. Educ: George Peabody Col, BS, 53; Am Col Life Underwriters, CLU, 73; Phi Mu Alpha Sinfonia. Polit & Govt Pos: Comnr, Co Elec Comn, Tenn, 68-; chmn, Rutherford Co Rep Comt, formerly, mem exec comt, currently. Bus & Prof Pos: Teacher, Nashville City Schs, Tenn, 53-54; teacher, Williamson Co Schs, 54-55; asst plant mgr, Murfreesboro Pure Milk Co, Inc, 55-57, gen mgr, 66-68; gen mgr, Young-Moseley Inc, Murfreesboro, 57-66; agent, New Eng Mutual Life Ins Co, 68-; dir & secy bd, Citizens Cent Bank of Rutherford Co; trustee, Rutherford Hosp. Mil Serv: Entered Nat Guard, 30th Div, 8 years. Mem: Murfreesboro Asn Life Underwriters; Murfreesboro Rotary Club; Murfreesboro CofC; Stones River Country Club. Relig: United Methodist. Mailing Add: 1818 Riverview Dr Murfreesboro TN 37130

MOSER, JOHN RICHARD (R)
Chmn, Butler Co Rep Exec Comt, Ohio
b Hamilton, Ohio, Mar 5, 27; s John Jacob Moser & Magdalena Buchmann M; m 1952 to Shirley N Keats; c Linda Kay, Janet Lee & Donald K. Educ: Miami Univ, Ohio, BA, 50; Univ Cincinnati Col Law, LLB, 53; Acacia. Polit & Govt Pos: Asst prosecuting attorney, Butler Co, Ohio, 56-64; pres, Young Rep of Hamilton, 59; chmn, Butler Co Rep Exec Comt, 60-; deleg, Rep Nat Conv, 64. Mil Serv: Entered as Pvt, Army, 45, released as Sgt, 47, after serv in 4th Armored Cavalry, ETO. Publ: Miscellaneous law review articles while at Col Law, Univ Cincinnati. Mem: Butler Co, Ohio & Am Bar Asns; Am Trial Lawyers Asn; F&AM. Relig: Presbyterian; Elder. Mailing Add: 515 Northwood Terr Hamilton OH 45013

MOSER, LEROY ALVIN, (JR) (R)
Chmn, Grundy Co Rep Comt, Iowa
b Reinbeck, Iowa, Aug 20, 21; s Leroy Alvin Moser, Sr & Faye McInnes M; m 1941 to

Rosalyn Anna Robertson; c Gregg Alan, Geoffrey Linn, Gretchen (Mrs Swift) & Julie Ann. Educ: Iowa State Univ, 41-43; Delta Chi. Polit & Govt Pos: Clerk, Black Hawk Twp, Grundy Co, Iowa, 60; chmn, Grundy Co Rep Comt, 70- Bus & Prof Pos: Owner-publ, Reinbeck Courier, Iowa, 65; publ, Iowa Coiffeur News, 68. Mem: AF&AM; ElKahir Shrine; CofC; Lions; Iowa Press Asn. Relig: Protestant. Legal Res: 100 Ridge Reinbeck IA 50669 Mailing Add: 412 Main Reinbeck IA 50669

MOSER, RAYMOND (R)
Mem, Rep State Cent Comt Calif
b Sutton, Nebr, Jan 17, 31; s Theodore Moser (deceased) & Clara Hofmann M; m 1960 to Sandra Gillis; c Mark Raymond, Gail Adele & Dana Claire. Educ: Stockton Col, AA, 51; Univ Calif, Berkeley, BS, 53; Big C Soc; Kappa Sigma. Polit & Govt Pos: Pres, Elmwood-Claremont Rep Assembly, Calif, 61; vpres, Alameda Rep Assembly, 65; Rep nominee for Calif State Assembly, 14th Assembly Dist, 66 & 68; mem, Rep State Cent Comt Calif, 67-; ex-officio mem, Alameda Co Rep Cent Comt, 66-69; vchmn, Eastbay Rep Alliance, Alameda Co, Calif, 69; mem, Alameda Planning Bd, 70- Bus & Prof Pos: Salesman, Values, Inc Real Estate, 57-59; owner, Crest Investments, 60-67; owner, Ray Moser & Assoc, 67-69. Mil Serv: Entered as Off Cand, Navy, 53, released as Lt(jg), 56, after serv in USS Chemuno, Western Pac & WCoast; Lt Comdr, Naval Res, 62. Mem: Res Officers Asn; Rotary; Navy League; Alameda Co Steering Comt, Young Life. Relig: Protestant. Mailing Add: 913 Otis Dr Alameda CA 94501

MOSER, V JEAN (DFL)
Assoc Chairperson, Red Lake Co Dem-Farmer-Labor Party, Minn
b East Grand Forks, Minn, Dec 7, 38; d Leo James Cariveau & Violet Boushee C; m 1958 to William Henry Moser; c Susan Marie, Kimberly Jean, Karen Grace & William Joseph. Educ: Sacred Heart Sch, East Grand Forks, Minn, 12 years; Thief River Falls Jr Col, 72-73. Polit & Govt Pos: Mem, Minn State Dem-Farmer-Labor Cent Comt, 66-70; assoc chairperson, Red Lake Co Dem-Farmer-Labor Party, 66-; assoc chairperson, Senatorial Dist 1, Dem-Farmer-Labor Party, 72-74. Bus & Prof Pos: Teacher aide, St Joseph Grade Sch, fall 70. Relig: Catholic. Mailing Add: 212 Third St SW Red Lake Falls MN 56750

MOSES, ROBERT (R)
b New Haven, Conn, Dec 18, 88; s Emanuel Moses & Bella M; m 1915 to Mary Louise Sims; second m 1966 to Mary A Grady; c Barbara (Mrs Richard J Olds) & Jane (Mrs Frederic A Collins). Educ: Yale Univ, BA, 09; Oxford Univ, BA with honors in Jurisp, 11, MA, 13; Columbia Univ, PhD in Polit Sci, 14. Hon Degrees: Hon degrees from various cols & univs. Polit & Govt Pos: Munic investr, New York, 13; chief of staff, NY State Reconstruction Comn, 19-21; secy coalition comt, New York Munic Campaign, 21; secy, NY State Asn, 21-26; mem, State Fine Arts Comn, 24-27; pres, Long Island State Park Comn & chmn, State Coun of Parks, 24-63; chmn, Metrop Conf on Parks, 26-30; Secy of State, NY, 27-28; chief of staff, State Reorgn Comn, 27-28; chmn, NY Comt on Pub Improv, 27-28; Moreland Comnr to investigate State Banking Dept, 29; rep mem, Long Island Sanit Comn, 30; mem, NY Comn, Chicago Fair, 31; chmn, Emergency Pub Works Comn, 33; chmn, Jones Beach State Pkwy Authority & Bethpage Park Authority, 33-63; Rep cand for Gov, NY, 34; mem, Triborough Bridge Authority, 34, chmn, 36; sole mem, Henry Hudson Pkwy Authority & Marine Pkwy Authority, 34-38; New York Park Comnr, 34-60; deleg, Rep Nat Conv, 36; exec officer, New York World's Fair Comn, 36-40; deleg, NY State Const Conv, 38; chmn, Comt on Hwy, Pkwy & Grade Crossings, 38; sole mem, New York City Pkwy Authority, 38; chmn, State Comt on Postwar Employ, 42; mem, NY State Postwar Pub Works Comn, 42; mem, City Planning Comn, 42-60; chief exec officer, New York Tunnel Authority, 45-46; chmn, Consolidated Triborough Bridge & New York Tunnel Auth, 46-68; chmn, Mayor's Emergency Comt on Housing & Mayor's Comt for Permanent World Capitol, 46; coordr, New York Construction, 46-60; chmn, Mayor's Slum Clearance Comt, 48-60; mem, New York Traffic Comn, 49; adv, Nassau Co Transit Comn, 49; mem, Long Island RR Comn, 50; chmn, Power Authority of State of NY, 54-63; coordr of arterial projs, NY, 60-66; pres, NY World's Fair 1964-1965 Corp, 60-67; secy, Temporary State Comn on Protection & Preservation of the Atlantic Shorefront, 62; mem, Mitchel Field Adv Comt, 63-64; mem, New York Transportation Coun, 66-67; spec adv to Gov on Housing, 74-; mem, Temporary NY State Comn 200th Anniversary Am Revolution & 200th Anniversary of Creation of State of NY, 74- Bus & Prof Pos: Consult arterial plan, Pittsburgh Regional Planning Asn, 39; Centennial lectr, Duke Univ, 39; Godkin lectr, Harvard Univ, 39; Stafford Little lectr, Princeton Univ, 40; employed by State of Mich & Huron-Clinton Metrop Authority to rev hwy plans for Detroit region, 42; coordr, Surv of Congested War Prod Areas for Army & Navy Munitions Bd, 43; dir, Postwar Plan for Portland, Ore, 43; dir arterial plan, Baltimore, Md, 44; consult, Ill Superhwy Comn, 44; dir arterial plan, New Orleans, La, 46; consult on reconstruction of Postwar Ger, 47; consult on arterial syst, Caracas, Venezuela, 48; chief consult on pub works, Comn on Orgn of the Exec Br of US Govt, 48; consult, Arterial Syst, Hartford, Conn, 49; consult, Int Basic Econ Corp, 50; dir of report, Sao Paulo, Brazil, 50; report on expressway prog, New Britain, Conn, 51; dir of report, Canton, Ohio, 52; report on new city hall, Flint, Mich, 53; consult to chmn, Metrop Transportation Authority, 68-; trustee, Miner Inst, Chazy, NY, 71- Publ: Writer for mag & newspapers on govt, parks, pub works, housing & recreation; auth, LaGuardia; A Salute & a Memoir, 57 & A Tribute to Governor Smith, 62, Simon & Schuster; Public Works: A Dangerous Trade, 70. Mem: Manhattan Col (exec comt, 56-); Lincoln Ctr Performing Arts (dir, 60-69, dir emer, 69-); Phi Beta Kappa; Players & Lotos Clubs, New York; Southward Ho, Bayshore, NY. Honors & Awards: Nassau-Suffolk Hosp Coun Theodore Roosevelt Award & Nassau Co Recreation & Parks Soc Achievement Award, 68; Electoral Col Hall of Fame, 69-75; Pub Serv Award, Citizens Housing & Planning Coun, 69; Distinguished Serv Award, Coun Am Artist Socs, 72; plus many others. Mailing Add: 1 Gracie Terr New York NY 10028

MOSES, WILLIAM PRESTON (R)
Chmn, Contra Costa Co Rep Cent Comt, Calif
b San Francisco, Calif, Sept 29, 17; s Preston S Moses & Marie Calderella M; m 1944 to Margaret Walker; c Preston. Educ: Univ Calif, Hastings Col Law; San Francisco Law Sch. Polit & Govt Pos: Mem, Contra Costa Co Rep Cent Comt, Calif, 52-58 & 64-66, chmn, 66-; mem & pres, Contra Costa Co Sch Bd, 63-; mem exec comt, State Rep Cent Comt Calif, currently; mem, Calif State Water Comn, 67-; pres, Asn of Rep Co Cent Comt Chmn of Calif, 73- Bus & Prof Pos: Partner, Pelletreau, Gowen, Moses & Porlier, San Pablo, Calif, 60- Mil Serv: Entered as Cadet, Air Force, 41, released as 2nd Lt, 45, after serv in SPac. Mem: Contra Costa; Am & Calif Bar Asns; Am Legion (past comdr); Rotary. Relig: Protestant. Mailing Add: 5691 San Pablo Dam Rd El Sobrante CA 94806

MOSHER, CHARLES ADAMS (R)
US Rep, Ohio
b DeKalb Co, Ill, May 7, 06; m 1929 to Harriet Johnson; c Frederic A & Mary Jane. Educ: Oberlin Col, AB cum laude, 28. Polit & Govt Pos: Mem, Oberlin City Coun, Ohio, 45-51; Ohio State Sen, 51-61; vchmn, Ohio Sch Surv Comn, 54-55; Ohio Legis Serv Comn, 55-59; US Rep, Ohio, 61-; Oberlin Col Bd of Trustees, 64-70 & 73- Bus & Prof Pos: Employed on daily newspapers in Ill & Wis, 29-40; pres, Oberlin Printing Co, ed-publ of Oberlin News-Tribune, 40-62. Mem: Off of Technol Assessment (bd mem, 73-); Am Oceanic Orgn (chmn bd, 73-); US Merchant Marine Acad (bd vis, 67-75). Legal Res: Oberlin OH Mailing Add: 2368 Rayburn House Off Bldg Washington DC 20515

MOSHER, SOL (R)
Asst Secy for Legis Affairs, Dept of Housing & Urban Develop
b Chicago, Ill, Apr 14, 28; s Jacob Mosher & Blanch Becker M; m 1953 to Cora E Walker; c Janice May & Caryn Anne. Educ: Kansas City Jr Col, AB, 47; Univ Mo, Columbia, BJour, 49; Sigma Delta Chi; Sigma Alpha Mu. Polit & Govt Pos: Admin asst to Congressman Durward G Hall, Mo, 61-69; spec asst to Secy of Com for Cong Rels, US Dept of Com, 69-73; asst secy for legis affairs, Dept of Housing & Urban Develop, 73- Bus & Prof Pos: Sports ed, Mo Daily News Digest, Springfield, 54; news ed, Sta KICK, 54-56; news ed, KYTV, 56-58; civic affairs mgr, CofC, 58-60. Mil Serv: Entered as Pvt, Army, 50, released as 1st Lt, 53, after serv in 45th Div, Far East Command, 51-52. Mem: Bull Elephants; Mo Soc of Wash. Honors & Awards: Distinguished Serv Award, Springfield CofC. Legal Res: 2527 W Elm Springfield MO 65803 Mailing Add: 5010 Althea Dr Annandale VA 22003

MOSHIER, TERRY ALLEN (R)
Regional Dir Mgt & Budget, US Dept Interior
b Omaha, Nebr, July 18, 36; s Fredrick D Moshier & Vivian Rhodes M; m 1965 to Mary Helen Riddle; c Terry Allen, Jr & Douglas Rhodes. Educ: Carleton Col, BA, 58; Univ Nebr, MS, 61; Ga State Univ, MBA, 71; Sigma Xi. Polit & Govt Pos: Dir, Ga Young Rep, 63-67, nat committeeman, 67-68, chmn, 68-69; subcomt chmn, Fulton Co Rep Exec Comt, 64-65; mem awards comt, Nat Fedn Young Rep, 67-69; elector, Ga Rep Party, 68; alt deleg, Rep Nat Conv, 68; mem, Fifth Dist Rep Exec Comt, 68-; vchmn, Fulton Co Rep Party, 70-; regional dir mgr & budget, US Dept Interior, 72- Bus & Prof Pos: Tech rep, Union Carbide Corp, 60-64; pres, Moshier Shoe Co, 64-67; regional sales rep, PPG Indust, 67-71; mgr new bus develop, Mead Packaging, Atlanta, Ga, 71-72. Mem: Soc Paint Technol; Am Chem Soc; Nat Paint Varnish & Lacquer Asn. Relig: United Presbyterian. Mailing Add: 653 Starlight Dr Atlanta GA 30305

MOSK, EDNA MITCHELL (D)
b Winnipeg, Man, Can, Sept 16, 15; d M K Mitchell & Katharine Blond M; m 1936 to Justice Stanley Mosk; c Richard Mitchell. Educ: Univ Calif, Los Angeles, 3 years; Phi Sigma Sigma. Polit & Govt Pos: Mem, Calif Dem State Cent Comt, 60-62; mem exec comt, Econ Opportunity Coun, San Francisco, 67-69; deleg, Dem Nat Conv, 68; mem exec comt, Dem Finance Comt, Calif, 72- Bus & Prof Pos: Real estate broker. Mailing Add: 1200 California St San Francisco CA 94109

MOSK, STANLEY (D)
Assoc Justice, Calif Supreme Court
b San Antonio, Tex, Sept 4, 12; s Paul Mosk & Minna Perl M; m 1936 to Edna Mitchell; c Richard Mitchell. Educ: Univ Tex, 30; Univ Chicago, PhB, 33; The Hague Acad of Int Law, 70; Phi Sigma Delta. Hon Degrees: LLD, Univ of the Pac, 70 & Univ San Diego, 71. Polit & Govt Pos: Exec secy to Gov, Calif, 38-42; judge, Superior Court, 43-59; attorney gen, Calif, 59-64; assoc justice, Calif Supreme Court, 64- Bus & Prof Pos: Pres, Western Asn of Attorneys Gen, 63; chmn, San Francisco Film Festival, 67. Mil Serv: Pvt, World War II, serv in Coast Guard Temporary Res. Publ: Numerous articles in Am Bar J, UCLA, Stanford & Calif Law Rev & other legal periodicals. Mem: Am & Local Bar Asns; Am Judicature Soc; Am Legion; B'nai B'rith; Vista Del Mar Child-Care Serv. Legal Res: 1200 California St San Francisco CA 94109 Mailing Add: Supreme Court Bldg San Francisco CA 94102

MOSKOVITZ, MARK ELLIOTT (D)
b Waterbury, Conn, Dec 23, 52; s Norman Moskovitz & Bernice Jacobs M; single. Educ: Brooklyn Col, BA, 73. Polit & Govt Pos: Deleg, Dem Nat Conv, 72. Relig: Jewish. Mailing Add: 147 Beach 128th St Belle Harbor New York NY 11694

MOSKOW, MICHAEL HAROLD (R)
Asst Secy for Policy Develop & Research, US Dept Housing & Urban Develop
b Paterson, NJ, Jan 7, 38; s Jacob Moskow & Sylvia Edelstein M; m 1966 to Constance Bain; c Robert, Eliot & Lisa. Educ: LaFayette Col, AB, 59; Univ Pa, MA, 62, PhD, 65; Pi Lambda Phi. Polit & Govt Pos: Sr staff economist, Coun Econ Advs, 69-71; exec dir, Construction Indust Collective Bargaining, 70-72; Dep Under-Secy, US Dept Labor, 71-72, Asst Secy for Policy, Eval & Research, 72-73; Asst Secy for Policy Develop & Research, US Dept Housing & Urban Develop, 73- Bus & Prof Pos: Instr, Eastside High Sch, Paterson, NJ, 60-61; instr, Drexel Inst, 63-64, asst prof, 65-67; instr, LaFayette Col, 64-65; assoc prof, Temple Univ, 67-69. Mil Serv: Entered as 2nd Lt, Army, 59, released, 60. Publ: Auth, Teachers & Unions, Univ Pa Press, 66; Labor Relations in the Performing Arts: an Introductory Survey, Associated Coun for the Arts NY, 69; co-auth, Collective Bargaining in Public Employment, Random House, 70. Mem: Am Arbit Asn; Nat Panel of Arbitrators; Am Econ Asn; Indust Rels Res Asn. Honors & Awards: John H Allen Tax Essay Prize, Lafayette Col, 59, Class of 1936 Econ Prize, 59. Relig: Jewish. Legal Res: 32 Overlook Ave Paterson NJ 07504 Mailing Add: 451 Seventh St SW Washington DC 20410

MOSLEY, EDWARD REYNOLD (R)
Mem Exec Comt, State Rep Cent Comt Calif
b Chicago, Ill, Mar 30, 24; s Leroy Mosley & Mamie Watkins M; m 1965 to Marian June Kummerfeld; c Cary Jerome, Laura Dawn, Kia Marie, Edward Reynold, Jr, Christopher Reynold & Caroline Aileen. Educ: Univ Ill, Urbana, 42-44; Meharry Med Col, MD, 48; Alpha Phi Alpha. Polit & Govt Pos: Comnr, Fresno Co Parks & Recreation Comn, 57-67; mem, Mayor's Biracial Comt, 66-68; alt mem, Fresno Co Rep Cent Comt, 67-; chmn, Citizens Resource Comt, SCCCD, 69-70; mem, Minority Adv Comn, Gov Prog, 71-; mem exec comt, State Rep Cent Comt Calif, 71-; trustee, State Ctr, Community Col Dist, 7-- Bus & Prof Pos: Mem bd dirs, Wofford Oil Co, Kansas City, Kans, 63-; pres bd dirs, Westview Convalescent Hosp, Fresno, Calif, 67-; pres bd dirs, John Hale Med Ctr, 68-; regional med consult, Calif State Dept Rehabilitation, 70-; mem bd dirs, Fresno West Develop Co, 70- Mil Serv: Entered as 1st Lt, Army, 52, released as Capt, 54, after serv in Med Corps, Korean Theatre, 52-54. Publ: The efficacy of certain antacids on the treatment of peptic ulcer, J Nat Med Asn, 57. Mem: Am, Nat & Calif Med Asns; Am & Calif Soc Internal Med. Honors & Awards: Award of Meritorious Serv, Fresno Co, Calif. Relig: Methodist. Mailing Add: 3075 W Kearney Blvd Fresno CA 93706

MOSS, CHARLES HOLMES (D)
Chmn, Llano Co Dem Party, Tex

b Temple, Tex, Dec 11, 15; s Holmes Moss & Mae Ratliff M; m 1952 to Ruth Milliger; c Marla & Sally. Educ: Univ Tex, 2 years. Polit & Govt Pos: Chmn, Llano Co Dem Party, Tex, 64-Bus & Prof Pos: Rancher. Mil Serv: Entered as Pvt, Army, 41, released as M/Sgt, 45, after serv in Signal Corps in US. Mem: Mohair Prom Coun (dir); Llano Lions Club. Relig: Methodist; mem church bd. Mailing Add: Llano TX 78643

MOSS, FRANK EDWARD (D)
US Sen, Utah

b Salt Lake City, Utah, Sept 23, 11; s James Edward Moss & Maud Nixon M; m 1934 to Phyllis Hart; c Marilyn (Mrs Armstrong), Frank Edward, Jr, Brian Hart & Gordon James. Educ: Univ Utah, BA, 33; George Washington Univ, JD, 37; Order of the Coif; Phi Delta Phi; Phi Kappa Alpha. Hon Degrees: LLD, Univ Utah, 73. Polit & Govt Pos: City judge, Salt Lake City, Utah, 41-50; co attorney, Salt Lake Co, 51-58; US Sen, Utah, 59-, secy, Dem Conf, US Senate, 71-, chmn, Aeronaut & Space Sci Comt, 73-; deleg, Dem Nat Conv, 52-72. Mil Serv: Entered as 2nd Lt, Army Qm Corps, 42, released as Maj, 46, after serv in 8th Air Force, ETO; Col, Air Force Res. Publ: The Water Crisis, Praeger, 67. Mem: VFW; Am Legion; ROA. Relig: Latter-day Saint. Legal Res: Salt Lake City UT Mailing Add: 115 Russell Senate Off Bldg Washington DC 20510

MOSS, JAMES H (D)
SC State Rep
Mailing Add: Box 1107 Beaufort SC 29903

MOSS, JERROLD VICTOR (D)

b Farrell, Pa, Sept 10, 31; s Burton James Moss & Barbara Angstreich M; m 1960 to Marsha Graff; c Michael David & Meredith Susan. Educ: Pa State Univ, BA, 53; Univ Pa Law Sch, LLB, 57; Alpha Epsilon Pi. Polit & Govt Pos: Chmn, New Dem Coalition Eastern Montgomery Co, 69-71; committeeman, Cheltenham Twp Dem Party, Pa, 69-72; vchmn, New Dem Coalition, Pa, 70-71, chmn, 71-73; mem, Reform Comn, Dem State Party, Pa, 71-72; deleg, Dem Nat Conv, 72; mem bd dirs, Am Dem Action, 72-; chmn, Govt Study Comn of Cheltenham Twp, Pa, 74-75. Bus & Prof Pos: Attorney, 59- Mil Serv: Entered as Pvt, Army, 58, released as Sgt, 64, after serving six months at Ft Knox, Ky & six years, Mil Intel Res Unit, Philadelphia, Pa. Mem: Philadelphia Trial Lawyers Asn (bd dirs, 70-73, secy, 74); Am, Pa & Philadelphia Bar Asns; Asn Am Trial Lawyers. Relig: Jewish. Legal Res: 906 Rock Lane Elkins Park PA 19117 Mailing Add: 1201 Chestnut St Ninth Floor Philadelphia PA 19107

MOSS, JOHN EMERSON (D)
US Rep, Calif

b Hiawatha, Utah, Apr 13, 15; s John Emerson Moss & Della Mower M; m 1935 to Jean Kueny; c Jennifer (Mrs Michael Soderstrand) & Allison (Mrs Hillis Warren); grandchildren, Tabitha & Afton Warren. Educ: Sacramento Col. Polit & Govt Pos: Calif State Assemblyman, Ninth Dist, 48-52, asst Dem Floor Leader, Calif State Assembly, 49-52; US Rep, Calif, 52-, Dep Majority Whip, US House of Rep, 62-71, ranking majority mem, Subcom on Foreign Opers & Govt Info & chmn, Subcom on Com & Finance. Mil Serv: Navy, World War II. Legal Res: 2031 Eighth Ave Sacramento CA 95818 Mailing Add: Rm 2185 Rayburn House Off Bldg Washington DC 20515

MOSS, JOSEPH GIBSON (D)
Miss State Rep

b Jackson, Miss, Apr 26, 22; married. Educ: Sigma Delta Kappa. Polit & Govt Pos: Miss State Rep, 56- Bus & Prof Pos: Lawyer; farmer. Mem: Lions; Farm Bur; VFW. Relig: Methodist. Mailing Add: Drawer 49 Raymond MS 39154

MOSS, THOMAS WARREN, JR (D)
Va State Deleg

b Norfolk, Va, Oct 3, 28; s Thomas Warren Moss & Laura Burckard M; m to Jane Patricia Miller; c Elizabeth Ann, Susan Bruce & Thomas Warren, III. Educ: Va Polytech Inst, BS; Univ Richmond, LLB. Polit & Govt Pos: Exec vpres, Young Dem Club Va, formerly; pres, Young Dem Club Norfolk, formerly; mem steering comt, Dem Party Norfolk, 66-; Va State Deleg, currently; mem, Va Comn Children & Youth & Law Enforcement Off Training Standards Comn. Bus & Prof Pos: Attorney-at-law. Mil Serv: Korean War. Mem: Am Bar Asn; Va Trial Lawyers Asn; Mason; Scottish Rite; Shrine. Relig: Lutheran. Mailing Add: Suite 830 Maritime Tower Norfolk VA 23510

MOSS, TRUETT W (R)
Chmn, Seventh Cong Regional Dist, Ga

b Ranger, Ga, Mar 19, 30; s Grover Downey Moss & Clara Knight M; m 1957 to Yvonne Welch; c Kimberly, Jan, Amber & Truett W, II. Educ: Red Bud High Sch, Calhoun, Ga, grad, 47. Polit & Govt Pos: Chmn, Gordon Co Rep Party, Ga, 64-73; chmn, Seventh Cong Regional Dist, 73- Bus & Prof Pos: Mgr, Hatchery Div, Cotton Producers Asn, 53-61; agent, Prudential Ins Co, 61- Mil Serv: Entered as Pvt, Army, 51, released as Cpl, 53, after serv in Mil Police, ETO. Mem: Gordon Co & Ga Life Underwriters Asns; Elks; Moose; Mem Baptist Asn (clerk, 73-). Relig: Southern Baptist. Mailing Add: RD 1 Ranger GA 30734

MOSS, W F (D)

b Tenn, 1909; m to Golda Siler M; c Patsy Anne (Mrs Paul W Walker). Educ: Univ Chattanooga; Univ Tenn, BS; NC State Univ, MA. Polit & Govt Pos: Co agent, Rhea & Marshall Co, Tenn, 35; dist dairy specialist, Chattanooga Area, 47; asst comnr of agr, Tenn & comnr of agr, 53-70; asst to secy for Intergovt Affairs, US Dept Agr, currently. Bus & Prof Pos: Former teacher voc agr, Elkton & Jellico High Schs. Legal Res: TN Mailing Add: Off of the Secy US Dept of Agr Washington DC 20250

MOSTILER, JOHN L (D)
Ga State Rep

b Clifton, SC, Mar 9, 23; s William Callaway Mostiler & Carrie Lou Walker M; m 1946 to Nora Elizabeth Morgan; c Johnny Baxter & Donna Annette (Mrs Larry E Biles). Educ: NC State Univ, BS, 50; Delta Kappa Phi. Polit & Govt Pos: Ga State Rep, Dist 71, 75- Bus & Prof Pos: Textile mgt, Lynchburg, Va & Mass, 50-52; lumber salesman, Richmond, Va, 52-54; plywood warehouse mgt, Greensboro, NC, 54-58; plywood salesman, Southeast, 60-65; partner, Lumber Brokerage, Atlanta, Ga, 65-74; wholesale lumber broker, Griffin, 74- Mil Serv: Entered as Pvt, Air Force, 43, released as Cpl, 45, after serv in ETO. Relig: Baptist. Mailing Add: 1102 Skyline Dr Griffin GA 30223

MOTHERSHEAD, ANDREW O (D)
Md State Deleg

b Washington, DC, Oct 4, 26; s Andrew A Mothershead & Frances Boteler; m 1945 to Margaret Ann Mosako; c Diane (Mrs Downey). Educ: Hyattsville Sr High, 44. Polit & Govt Pos: Md State Deleg, First Legis Dist, Prince Georges Co, 67-70, 21st Legis Dist Prince Georges Co, 75- Mem: Kiwanis Int; Prince George's CofC; Univ Md Terrapin Club; Bd Trade. Mailing Add: 7112 Eversfield Dr Hyattsville MD 20782

MOTLOW, REAGOR (D)
Tenn State Sen

b Lynchburg, Tenn, Feb 15, 98; s Lem Motlow & Clara Reagor M; m 1928 to Jeanie Garth. Educ: Vanderbilt Univ, BA, 19; Alpha Tau Omega; Owl; Commodore. Polit & Govt Pos: Tenn State Rep, 41-62; Tenn State Sen, 16th Sen Dist, 65- Bus & Prof Pos: Farmer; vpres, Jack Daniel Distillery, Lynchburg, Tenn, 38-47, pres, 47-63, mem bd, 63-68; mem bd, Brown-Forman Distillers Corp, 63-68; dir & vpres, Farmers Bank, currently; mem bd trust, Vanderbilt Univ, currently. Mil Serv: 2nd Lt, Army, 18, serv in Inf, US. Mem: Am Soc Engrs; Elks; Rotary; Shrine; Am Legion. Relig: Protestant. Mailing Add: PO Box 202 Lynchburg TN 37352

MOTT, J THOMAS (DFL)
Secy, Dem-Farmer-Labor Party, Minn

b Rochelle, Ill, Nov 9, 49; s H L Mott & Janet Thomas M; single. Educ: Austin State Jr Col, Minn, AA, 70; Univ Minn, Minneapolis, BA, 72; William Mitchell Col Law, St Paul, 72-; Zeta Eta Chap, Phi Theta Kappa. Polit & Govt Pos: Co primary campaign coordr, Tom Olson for Cong & Earl Craig for Senate, Freeborn Co, Minn, 70; deleg, Freeborn Co Dem-Farmer-Labor Conv, 72, Second Cong Dist Dem-Farmer-Labor Conv, 72, alt deleg, 74, deleg, Minn Dem-Farmer-Labor Conv, 72, alt deleg, 74, deleg, Dem Nat Conv, 72; asst scheduling dir, McGovern for President, Minn Campaign, 72; mem, Dist & Minn State Dem-Farmer-Labor Cent Comts, 72-; chmn, Senate Dist 31 Dem-Farmer-Labor Party, 72-74, secy, 74- Mem: Law Sch Div, Am Bar Asn. Honors & Awards: Leadership Award, Austin State Jr Col, 70. Relig: Episcopal. Mailing Add: 305 Park Ave Albert Lea MN 56007

MOTT, ROGER ALAN (D)

b Moravia, NY, Aug 23, 50; s A Leonard Mott & Claire Jones M; single. Educ: Am Univ, BA in Polit Sci, 72. Polit & Govt Pos: Dist rep, US Rep Samuel Stratton, NY, 72-73, admin asst, 73- Mem: Admin Assistant's Asn. Legal Res: 18 Congress St Moravia NY 13118 Mailing Add: 100 S Van Dorn St Suite 301 Alexandria VA 22304

MOTT, SAMUEL D (D)
Chmn, New Shoreham Dem Town Comt, RI

b Block Island, RI, Dec 7, 09; s Alton H Mott & Clossie A Ball M; m 1955; c Susan Ellen, John R, James W, George D, Peter J, Alton H & S Douglas. Educ: Brown Univ, PhB, 32; Kappa Sigma. Polit & Govt Pos: Mem, Town Coun, Block Island, RI, 49-53, pres, 67 & 68, mem & chmn, Sch Comt, 49-53; RI State Rep, 61-62; chmn, New Shoreham Dem Town Comt, RI, 61- Bus & Prof Pos: Asst mgr wine steward & rm clerk, various Knott Hotels, New York, 33-43; asst mgr, Hotel Taft, 42-43, mgr, Hotel Blackstone & Hotel Albert, 43-46; asst mgr, Hotel Dixie, 45-46; owner & mgr, Narragawsett Inn, Block Island, RI, 46-; pres & mgr, Spring House Hotel, 52-; owner & mgr, The Oar Cafe & Lounge, 67-; owner & mgr, Dead Eye Dick's Cafe & Lounge, currently. Mem: Mason (32 degree); Block Island CofC (pres). Relig: Protestant. Mailing Add: Block Island RI 02807

MOTTL, RONALD M (D)
US Rep, Ohio

b Cleveland, Ohio, Feb 6, 34; s Milton Mottl & Anna Huml M; m 1969 to Debra Mary Budan; c Ron, Jr & Ronda. Educ: Univ Notre Dame, BS, 56, LLB, 57. Polit & Govt Pos: Asst dir law, Cleveland, Ohio, 58-60; councilman, Second Ward, Parma City Coun, 60-61, pres, 61-66; Ohio State Rep, Dist 51, 66-68; Ohio State Sen, Dist 24, 68-74; US Rep, 23rd Dist, Ohio, 75- Bus & Prof Pos: Attorney-at-Law, 57- Mil Serv: Pvt, Army, 57; Res, 5 years. Relig: Roman Catholic. Legal Res: 7713 Wake Robin Dr Parma OH 44130 Mailing Add: 5393 Pearl Rd Parma OH 44129

MOTTO, NICHOLAS M (D)
Conn State Rep
Mailing Add: 16 Griswold St Hartford CT 06114

MOULDS, ELIZABETH FRY (D)
Mem, Calif Dem State Cent Comt

b San Pedro, Calif, Nov 9, 41; d Donald Hume Fry, Jr & Pauline Fraser F; m 1964 to John Fryer Moulds, III; c Donald Bancroft & Gerald Bennett. Educ: Sacramento State Col, BA, 63; Univ Calif, Berkeley, MA, 64; Woodrow Wilson fel; Phi Kappa Phi; Young Dem. Polit & Govt Pos: Mem, Calif Dem State Cent Comt, 68- Bus & Prof Pos: Instr polit sci, Col of San Mateo, 64-66; asst prof polit sci, Calif State Univ, Sacramento, 66- Relig: Protestant. Mailing Add: 3013 Huntington Rd Sacramento CA 95825

MOUSER, COTYS MILNER (D)

b Antrim, La, Oct 3, 06; s Enoch Melvin Mouser & Hattie Jackson M; m 1933 to Vestal McKenzie Mathis; c Elizabeth (Mrs Frank C Fellows, Jr) & John Melvin. Educ: Univ Tex, Austin, BBA, 28; La State Univ, MA, 37; Univ Tex, Univ Denver & Ind Univ, Bloomington, summers 38-39 & 50; B Hall Asn. Polit & Govt Pos: Chief clerk, US Senate Comt Agr & Forestry, 51-53 & 54-74, asst chief clerk, 53-54; retired. Bus & Prof Pos: Auditor & head bus dept, Martin High Sch, Laredo, Tex, 29-40; instr bus admin, Sam Houston State Col, Huntsville, 40; auditor-bus mgr, assoc prof bus, Northwestern State Col, 40-51; teacher personal finance & bus math, part-time, Grad Sch US Dept Agr, 53- Publ: Syllabi for 1/2 Unit Courses in Retail Selling & Consumership, Tex State Bd Educ; compiler annual budgets, Northwestern State Col, 43-49 & Job Study Non Academic Personnel of State Colleges, La State Bd Educ, 50. Mem: Gulf Coast Sch Exec Asn (vpres); La State Teachers Asn Bus Educ Sect; La Col Conf Bus Adminr Sect (vpres); AF&AM; La Forestry Asn. Relig: Presbyterian; former chmn bd deacons, Natchitoches. Legal Res: Broadway & Main St Grayson LA 71435 Mailing Add: 7057 Western Ave NW Washington DC 20015

MOUTON, EDGAR G (D)
La State Sen

b Lafayette, La, Sept 22, 29; s Edgar G Mouton, Sr & Myrtle Grevemberg M; m 1952 to Patricia Dauphin; c Cheryl (Mrs James Lavin), Patti (Mrs Clay Judice), Katherine Ann & Mary Elizabeth. Educ: Tulane Univ, BA, 50; Tulane Univ Law Sch, LLB, 52. Polit & Govt Pos: La State Rep, Lafayette Parish, 64-66; La State Sen, Lafayette Parish, 66-, chmn, Senate,

Health, Educ & Welfare Comt, currently, mem, Senate Judicial Coun, currently; mem various Gov Comts, currently. Bus & Prof Pos: Attorney, Mouton, Roy, Carmouche, Hailey, Bivins & McNamara, 53- Mem: Muscular Dystrophy Asn Am (Nat vpres); Bar Asns; Kiwanis; Acadiana Alcoholic Coun (bd mem); Catholic Charities (bd mem). Mailing Add: 313 Dunreath St Lafayette LA 70501

MOWAT, JOHN S, JR (R)
Mich State Rep
Mailing Add: Rte 2 5022 Treat Rd Adrian MI 49221

MOWBRAY, JOHN CODE (D)
Assoc Justice, Nev Supreme Court
b Bradford, Ill, Sept 20, 18; s Thomas John Mowbray & Ellen Code M; m 1949 to Kathlyn Ann Hammes; c John Hammes, Romy Hammes, Jerry Hammes & Terry Hammes. Educ: Western Ill Univ, BA, 40; Notre Dame Law Sch, JD, 49. Polit & Govt Pos: Dep dist attorney, Clark Co, Nev, 49-53; US referee, State of Nev, 55-59; state dist judge, 59-67; assoc justice, Nev Supreme Court, 67- Mil Serv: Entered as Aviation Cadet, Army, 42, released as Maj, 46. Honors & Awards: Outstanding Alumni Award, Western Ill Univ, 71. Relig: Catholic. Legal Res: 1815 S 15th Las Vegas NV 89105 Mailing Add: Supreme Court Carson City NV 89701

MOWERY, MORRIS EVERETT (D)
WVa State Deleg
b Parkersburg, WVa, Jan 31, 42; s Morris Everett Mowery, Sr & Grace Newbanks M; m 1967 to Marlene Baron; c Grace Marie. Educ: WVa Univ, AB, 64, Col Law, JD, 68; Beta Theta Pi. Polit & Govt Pos: Asst prosecuting attorney, Wood Co, WVa, 73-74; WVa State Deleg, 75- Bus & Prof Pos: Resource develop specialist, WVa Univ Exten Serv, 68-70; staff attorney, NCent WVa Legal Aid Soc, 70-73; attorney, self-employed, Parkersburg, WVa, 73- Mem: WVa State Bar Asn; Wood Co Bar Asn (treas); Parkersburg YMCA (mem bd dirs). Relig: Presbyterian. Mailing Add: 1320 Market St Parkersburg WV 26101

MOWRER, GORDON BROWN (D)
Mayor, Bethlehem, Pa
b Bethlehem, Pa, Feb 9, 36; s Clifton E Mowrer & Margaret Brown M; m 1960 to Mary Thaeler; c George, Ruth & Margaret. Educ: Dickinson Col, BA, 59; Lehigh Univ, MA, 65; Kappa Sigma. Polit & Govt Pos: Councilman, Bethlehem, Pa, 72-74, mayor, 74- Bus & Prof Pos: Partner, Hampson-Mowrer Ins Agency, 59- Mil Serv: Entered as Seaman Recruit, Navy, 55, released as 3/C Personnel, after serv in Atlantic Fleet, USS Valley Forge as Educ Officer; Naval Res, 8 years. Mem: Nat & Pa League of Cities; Gov Justice Comn; US Conf Mayors; Rotary. Honors & Awards: Outstanding Young Man of Year, Bethlehem Jaycees, 68. Legal Res: 253 Bridle Path Rd Bethlehem PA 18017 Mailing Add: 10 E Church St Bethlehem PA 18018

MOWRY, JOHN L (R)
b Baxter, Iowa, Dec 15, 05; s William Mowry & Grace Lindsay Conn M; m 1941 to Irene Eudora Lounsberry; c Madelyn (Mrs Irvine). Educ: Ohio State Univ, 27-28; Univ Iowa, BA, 28, JD, 30; Sigma Chi; Phi Delta Phi; Iowa Law Rev. Polit & Govt Pos: Spec agent, Fed Bur Invest, 30-34; spec investr, Off of Thomas E Dewey, Spec Prosecutor, New York Co, NY, 34-36; Marshall Co attorney, Iowa, 38-41; dep comnr, NY State Liquor Authority, 45-47; mayor, Marshalltown, Iowa, 50-55; Iowa State Rep, 57-65 & 67-69; Iowa State Sen, 69-72; deleg, Rep Nat Conv, 72. Bus & Prof Pos: Pres, Evans Abstract Co & GMK, Inc. Mil Serv: Intel Div, Air Force, 41-45. Mem: Marshall Co & Iowa State Bar Asns; Former Agents of Fed Bur Invest; Marshall Co Hist Soc (trustee); Lions. Relig: Presbyterian. Legal Res: 503 W Main St Marshalltown IA 50158 Mailing Add: 25 N Center St Marshalltown IA 50158

MOWRY, SAMUEL ORIN (D)
Chmn, Williams Co Dem Party, Ohio
b Edgerton, Ohio, Apr 24, 23; s Samuel Orin Mowry, Sr & Ethel Marie Sucher M; m 1943 to Myra Blance Fritz; c Diane Lynette (Mrs Sailor) & Stanley Gene. Educ: Edgerton Local Sch, 12 years. Polit & Govt Pos: Precinct bd mem, St Joe Twp, Ohio, 48-58; co committeeman, Williams Co, 58-64; vchmn, Williams Co Dem Party, Ohio, 65-69, chmn, 69-; mem, Williams Co Elec Bd, 69- Mil Serv: Entered as Pvt, Army, 45, released as S/Sgt, 46, after serv in 6th Army Hq, Pac Theatre; Good Conduct Medal; Army of Occupation Medal in Japan; Asiatic Pac Theatre Ribbon; Philippine Liberation Ribbon; Victory Medal. Mem: Edgerton Lodge 357, F&AM; Knights of Constantine; Ohio Asn Elec Officials (first vchmn); Am Legion J D Smith Mem Post 10; Eagles. Relig: Methodist. Mailing Add: RR 1 Box 142 Edgerton OH 43517

MOYA, RICHARD A (D)
b Austin, Tex, Aug 14, 32; s Pete Moya & Bertha Ramos M; m 1953 to Gertrude Garza; c Lori & Danny. Educ: Durham's Bus Col, Austin, Tex, 51. Polit & Govt Pos: Deleg & sgt-at-arms, Tex Dem Conv, 72, deleg, 74; deleg, Dem Nat Conv, 72. Bus & Prof Pos: Chief investr, Legal Aid Serv, 70. Mil Serv: Entered as Cpl, Army, 53, released as Sgt 1/C, 55, after serv in Inf; Korean War Ribbon; UN Ribbon; Good Conduct Medal; Am Serv Ribbon. Mem: Pan Am Recreation Adv Bd; Capco (mem exec comt); Comprehensive Employ Training Act (exec comt); PTA. Relig: Catholic. Legal Res: 2211 Rebel Rd Austin TX 78704 Mailing Add: PO Box 1748 Austin TX 78767

MOYE, JAMES M (R)
b Laurel, Miss, Feb 9, 21; m 1944 to Mae Eleanor; c Marilyn & Jamie. Educ: Jones Co Jr Col; Southern Col of Optom, Memphis, Tenn. Polit & Govt Pos: Mem, Laurel Sch Bd, Miss, 61-66; chmn, Co Campaign for Gov, 63; mem, Miss Rep State Exec Comt, 64; alt deleg, Rep Nat Conv, 64, deleg, 68; vchmn, Miss State Rep Party, 66;chmn, Fifth Cong Dist Rep Party, 66-67; Rep Nat Committeeman, 68-72. Bus & Prof Pos: Optometrist; pres, Miss Optom Asn, 54-55; mem, State Bd of Examr in Optom, 56-61; mem, Am Optom Asn, 59-, chmn, Practice Mgt Comt, 63-65. Mem: Laurel CofC; Comt of 100; Local Red Cross (bd dirs). Honors & Awards: Distinguished Serv Award, Laurel Jaycees, 52. Relig: Presbyterian; Elder, Trinity Presby Church. Legal Res: 17 Glenwood Dr Laurel MS 39440 Mailing Add: 515 Fifth Ave Laurel MS 39440

MOYER, GLENN ROYDON (D)
Chmn, Lehigh Co Dem Comt, Pa
b Allentown, Pa, Aug 21, 29; s Carl E Moyer & Irene Sechrist M; m to Sandra Alexandra Logechnik; c four. Educ: Allentown High Sch. Polit & Govt Pos: Chmn, Lehigh Co Dem Comt, 66-; alt deleg, Dem Nat Conv, 68. Bus & Prof Pos: Owner, Glenn Moyer Ins & Real Estate Agency, currently. Mil Serv: Entered as Pvt, Army, 47, released as S/Sgt, 50. Relig: Unitarian. Mailing Add: 34 N 16th St Allentown PA 18102

MOYER, RUTH ELOISE (D)
b Ottumwa, Iowa, Feb 23, 17; d Andrew Julius Wind & Ada Mae Ward W; m 1947 to Donald Henry Moyer; c Linda Lou (Mrs Richard L Cox). Educ: Stephens Col, Assoc in Music. Polit & Govt Pos: Dep recorder, Wapello Co, Iowa, 53-74, co recorder, 74-; Dem precinct committeewoman, 56-; pres, Wapello Co Dem Women's Club, 60-62 & 64; mem, Gov Legis Comt, 64-; committeewoman, Fourth Cong Dist, Iowa, 64-74; secy, Iowa State Dem Comt, 64-74; mem comt for urban renewal, Mayor's Adv Coun, Ottumwa, 67-73; pres, Dem Women's Club, Wapello Co, 68-; coordr, Southeast Iowa, Dem Nat Telethon, summer 72; bd mem, Iowa State Dem Finance Comt, 72-74. Mem: Am Legion Auxiliary; VFW Ladies Auxiliary; Am Bus Women's Asn (rec secy, 74); Ottumwa Civic Music Asn (treas, 58-); West End Boosters Club. Relig: Presbyterian. Mailing Add: 308 E Elmdale Blvd Ottumwa IA 52501

MOYERS, JAMES ALLEN (R)
Chmn, Franklin Co Rep Party, Tex
b Knoxville, Tenn, Sept 2, 48; s Levi Jerry Moyers & Rosemary Garrett M; single. Educ: Baylor Univ, BBA, 71; ETex State Univ, MBA, 73; Beta Alpha Psi, Nat Acct Fraternity. Polit & Govt Pos: Chmn, Franklin Co Rep Party, Tex, 72- Bus & Prof Pos: Income tax consult, W N Chrisman, Pub Acct, Sulphur Springs, Tex, 73; instr acct, ETex State Univ, 74- Mem: Jaycees; Accts Soc ETex State Univ. Honors & Awards: Eagle Award, Boy Scouts Am, 65. Relig: Southern Baptist. Legal Res: PO Box 34 Winnsboro TX 75494 Mailing Add: PO Box 3035 ET Commerce TX 75428

MOYLAN, HAROLD THOMAS (D)
Nebr State Sen
b Bayard, Iowa, Mar 5, 03; s John Moylan & Margaret Ellen Ferris M; m 1929 to Margaret Ellen Emery; c James H, Joseph W, Mary Jean (Mrs Monte Taylor), Patrick F & Ann Marie (Mrs Mark Vanderloo). Educ: Creighton Univ, BA, 28. Polit & Govt Pos: Nebr State Sen, Dist 6, 65- Bus & Prof Pos: Real estate broker. Mem: Farm Bur; KofC; Eagles. Relig: Roman Catholic. Mailing Add: 3862 California St Omaha NE 68131

MOYLAN, KURT S (R)
Lt Gov, Guam
b Honolulu, Hawaii, Jan 14, 39; s Francis L Moylan & Yuk Lan Rose Ho M; m 1961 to Judith Ann Granchi; c Cassandra, Kaleo, Miki & Troy. Educ: Notre Dame Univ, BA in Econ, 61. Polit & Govt Pos: Sen, Guam Legis, 65-66, chmn comt on mil & vet affairs, mem pub works, econ develop, rules, munic affairs, pub health & welfare & judiciary comts; Secy, Guam, 69; Lt Gov, Guam, 71-; chmn, Gov Comn Delinquency, Crime & Law Enforcement, currently; chmn, Legis Rev Comt, currently. Bus & Prof Pos: Asst gen mgr, Moylan Motor Co, 63; gen mgr, F L Moylan Enterprises, 65; founder & pres, Moylan Col Fed Credit Union, 69; founder & owner, All-Am Ins Underwriters, 69; vpres & gen mgr, Pac Broadcasting Corp, currently; vpres, Air Pac Int Airlines, currently. Mem: Hawaiian Golf Club; SKAL Club; Nat Asn Secy State, Navy League; Guam Rifle & Pistol Club. Honors & Awards: One of four original incorporators of Rep Party of Guam; youngest Sen elected to Guam Legis. Relig: Roman Catholic. Legal Res: 23 Leticia Tumon Heights GU 96910 Mailing Add: Off of the Governor Agana GU 96910

MOYLE, JON (D)
Polit & Govt Pos: Chmn, Fla State Dem Party, formerly. Mailing Add: 707 N Flagler West Palm Beach FL 33401

MOYLE, MICHAEL J (R)
WVa State Deleg
Mailing Add: State Capitol Charleston WV 25305

MOYLE, SANDRA KAY (D)
Mem, Va State Dem Cent Comt
b Huntingdon, Pa, June 20, 49; d Ralph Cypher Moyle & Mary Abbott M; single. Educ: Va West Community Col, 2 years; Old Dom Univ, grad cum laude, 72. Polit & Govt Pos: Campaign aide, Fitzpatrick for Cong, 70; mem state exec comt & nat committeewoman, Young Dem Clubs Va, 7O-72; mem, Nat Young Dem, 70-72; mem, Va State Dem Cent Comt, 70- Bus & Prof Pos: Reporter, WARZ TV, Portsmouth, Va. Mailing Add: 1732 Yarmouth St Norfolk VA 23501

MOYNAHAN, THOMAS ALVIN (D)
b Indianapolis, Ind, Nov 16, 38; s Robert B Moynahan & Mary Louise Shiel Moynahan Frey; m 1964 to Jane Ellis Drury; c Kara Browning & Theodore Drury. Educ: Univ Notre Dame, BS, 60. Polit & Govt Pos: Deleg, Dem Nat Conv, 68; precinct committeeman, Marion Co Dem Cent Comt, Ind, 64-70, ward chmn, 68-; deleg, Dem Nat Mid-Term Conf, 74. Bus & Prof Pos: Pres, T A Moynahan Properties, Inc, 64- Mil Serv: Entered as Ens, Naval Res, 60, released as Lt, 64, after serv in USS San Pablo & USS Alcor; Lt, US Naval Res. Mem: Nat Asn Real Estate Bd; Young Pres Orgn; CofC; Inst of Real Estate Mgt; Nat Inst Real Estate Brokers. Relig: Roman Catholic. Legal Res: 4502 N Delaware St Indianapolis IN 46220 Mailing Add: 850 N Pennsylvania St Indianapolis IN 46204

MOYNIHAN, DANIEL PATRICK (D)
US Ambassador to UN
b Tulsa, Okla, Mar 16, 27; s John Henry Moynihan & Margaret A Phipps M; m 1955 to Elizabeth Therese Brennan; c Timothy Patrick, Maura Russell & John McCloskey. Educ: City Col New York, 43; Tufts Univ, BA cum laude, 48; Fletcher Sch Law & Diplomacy, MA, 49, PhD, 61. Hon Degrees: LLD, Fletcher Sch Law & Diplomacy. Polit & Govt Pos: Dir, PR Int Rescue Comt, 54; asst to secy, asst secy & acting secy to Gov, NY, 55-58; secy of pub affairs comt, NY State Dem Comt, 58-60; mem, NY State Tenure Comt, 59-60; dir, NY State Govt Research Proj, Syracuse Univ, 59-61; deleg, Dem Nat Conv, 60; spec asst to Secy of Labor, 61-62, exec asst, 62-63, Asst Secy of Labor for Urban Affairs, 69; counr to the President, 69-70; mem, President's Sci Adv Comt, 70-73; US Ambassador, India, 73-74; US Ambassador to UN, 75- Bus & Prof Pos: Dir, Mass Inst Technol-Harvard Univ Joint Ctr for Urban Studies, 66-69; prof educ & urban polit, Harvard Univ Grad Sch of Educ, 66-72 & 75- Mil Serv: Naval Res, 44-47. Publ: Co-auth, Beyond the Melting Pot (Anisfield Award, 63); Maximum Feasible Misunderstanding, Free Press, 69; auth of many articles. Mem: Am Acad Arts & Sci; Am Philos Soc; Cath Asn Int Peace. Honors & Awards: Recipient, Fulbright fel, London Sch Econ & Polit Sci, 50 & hon fel, 70; Arthur S Fleming Award, 56; Meritorious

Serv Award, Dept of Labor, 64. Relig: Catholic. Legal Res: 57 Francis Ave Cambridge MA 02138 Mailing Add: Off of US Ambassador to UN Dept of State Washington DC 20521

MOYNIHAN, KENNETH JAMES (D)
b Newport, RI, July 27, 44; s John Frances Moynihan & Claire Marie O'Connell M; m 1970 to Kathleen Marie Lucier. Educ: Holy Cross Col, AB, 66; Clark Univ, MA, 69, PhD, 73. Polit & Govt Pos: Mem steering comt, Worcester Area McCarthy for President Comt, Mass, 68; mem steering comt, Worcester Area Citizens for Participation Polit, 68-; vpres, Citizens' Plan E Asn, 70-; deleg, Dem Nat Conv, 72. Bus & Prof Pos: Asst prof hist, Assumption Col, 70- Mem: Am Hist Asn; Am Asn Univ Prof. Mailing Add: 83 Suomi St Paxton MA 01612

MOYNIHAN, TIMOTHY JOSEPH (D)
Conn State Rep
b East Hartford, Conn, July 28, 41; s Timothy J Moynihan & Irene Limburg M; m 1964 to Rosemary Lane; c Timothy, Susan & Patrick. Educ: St Michael's Col, BA, 63. Polit & Govt Pos: Mem, Dem Town Comt, East Hartford, Conn, 65-, dist chmn, 70-; mem, East Hartford Bd Educ, 66-69, chmn, 69-74; Conn State Rep, 75- Bus & Prof Pos: Asst vpres investment dept, J Watson Beach, 64- Mil Serv: Entered as Pvt E-1, Army Res, 63, released as S/Sgt E-6, 69, after serv in 76th Div. Honors & Awards: Jaycees Distinguished Serv Award, 71-72. Relig: Roman Catholic. Mailing Add: 190 Naubuc Ave East Hartford CT 06118

MRKONIC, EMIL (D)
Pa State Rep
Mailing Add: Capitol Bldg Harrisburg PA 17120

MRUK, WALTER J (D)
RI State Sen
Mailing Add: 61 Knotty Oak Rd Coventry RI 02816

MUCKLER, CARL HENRY (D)
Mo State Rep
b St Louis, Mo, May 13, 41; s William Christ Muckler & Jane Kiffmeyer; m 1967 to Ruth Mae Tumulty; c Matthew S & Melanie Jane. Educ: St Mary's Col (Minn), 63 & 70. Polit & Govt Pos: Mo State Rep, 56th Dist, 75- Bus & Prof Pos: Teacher, St Patrick High Sch, Chicago, Ill, 63-66, St Dominic High Sch, O'Fallon, Mo, 66-67 & Ritenour Sch Dist Overland, Mo, 69-74. Mil Serv: Entered as E-1, Army, 67, released as E-5 Adj Gen Corp, 67-69. Mem: Florissant Regular Dem Club; New Dem Coalition; St Louis Track Club. Relig: Catholic. Mailing Add: 1820 Arundel Dr Florissant MO 63033

MUDD, JOSEPH CHARLES (D)
Ill State Rep
b Peoria, Ill, May 1, 37; s William Charles Mudd & Lela W M; m 1954 to Judith Kay Nofsinger; c Joseph Richard, Timothy Mitchell & Elizabeth Anne. Polit & Govt Pos: Councilman, First Dist, Peoria, Ill, 69-75; Ill State Rep, 75- Bus & Prof Pos: Dept supvr, Keystone Steel & Wire Inc, Bartonville, Ill, 65-75. Mil Serv: Sgt, Air Force, 51-53, after serv in ETO, 52-53; Sgt, Air Force Res, 53-61; Good Conduct Medal; Marksmanship. Mem: Am Legion; South Side Businessmen's Club (vpres); Peoria Sportsman Club. Relig: Protestant. Legal Res: 1821 S Idaho Peoria IL 61605 Mailing Add: Rm 1131 House Rep Bldg Springfield IL 62706

MUDD, THERESE M (D)
Committeewoman, NY State Dem Party
b Denver, Colo, June 29, 31; d Marion Elliott Simmons & Helen Connell S; m 1955 to James F Mudd; c J Michael, Margaret M, Kevin J, Ellen M, T Andrew & Mary F. Educ: Immaculate Heart Col, BA, 53; Niagara Univ, MA, 74. Polit & Govt Pos: Secy, Calif State Young Dem, 53-54; committeewoman, Washington Co Dem Party, Okla, 59-60; committeewoman, Niagara Co Dem Party, NY, 66-; deleg, Dem Nat Conv, 72; committeewoman, 138th Dist, NY State Dem Party, 75- Bus & Prof Pos: Regional co-chmn, Christian Family Movement, Niagara Co, NY, 64-66; secy, Niaeara Co Migrant & Rural Ministry, 66-; secy bd dirs, Niagara Community Action Prog, 68-70, treas bd dirs, 70-71; coordr adult activities, United Cerebral Palsy Asn of Niagara Co, 73-; dir relig educ, St Peter's Church, Lewiston, NY, 74- Mem: Kappa Gamma Pi; Kappa Gamma Delta; Literacy Vol, Niagara Falls. Relig: Roman Catholic. Mailing Add: 610 Onondaga St Lewiston NY 14092

MUELLER, ALLAN GEORGE (D)
Mo State Rep
b St Louis, Mo, Dec 16, 42; s Aaron Barney Mueller & Theresa Marie Schlaffer M; m 1973 to Carol Coleman. Educ: St Mary's Univ (Tex), BBA, 65; Sigma Beta Chi. Polit & Govt Pos: Mo State Rep, Dist 62, 71- Bus & Prof Pos: Vpres, Land Systs, Inc. Mil Serv: Entered as Pvt, Marine Corps, 66, released as Capt, 68, after serv in 3rd Marine Div, SVietnam, 66-67; Presidential Unit Citation; Vietnamese Serv Medal; Nat Defense Medal; Vietnamese Campaign. Mem: 27th Ward Dem Club; Northside Independent Dem. Relig: Roman Catholic. Mailing Add: 1632 Veronica St Louis MO 63147

MUELLER, BARBARA SUE (D)
b East Lansing, Mich, Feb 8, 47; d William Harrison Coleman, II & Gertrude Esther Parker C; div; c Meredith Sue & Matthew Parker. Educ: Cleveland High Sch, grad with honors, 65. Polit & Govt Pos: Chmn, St Louis City Sch Tax Campaign, Md, 65; nat campaign staff, Robert F Kennedy Presidential Campaign Effort, 68; chmn, St Louis Coun Gun Control Petition Drive, 68; twp capt, George McGovern's Deleg Campaign, 72; dist chmn, George McGovern's Presidential Campaign Effort, 72; deleg, Mo Dem State Conv, 72; deleg, Dem Nat Conv, 72; cand for committeewoman, Gravois Twp, St Louis Co, 72; chairperson, City of Crestwood Youth Liaison Bd, 74; alt mem, President's Coun on Youth, 74; co-chairperson, City of Crestwood Recreation Bond Issue Bd, 74; St Louis Co Dem Telethon Coordr, 74; bd mem, Missourians for Honest Elec, 75. Mem: Nat & Mo Woman's Polit Caucus; Gravois Twp Dem Club (bd); Concord Twp Dem Club (bd); New Dem Coalition; PTA. Honors & Awards: Received Key to City of Crestwood, 74. Relig: Baptist. Mailing Add: 1035 Westglen Dr Crestwood MO 63126

MUELLER, C GEOFFREY (R)
Chmn, Rep Party of Calumet Co, Wis
b Appleton, Wis, Mar 10, 43; s Clarence A Mueller & Walburga L Thiel M; m 1973 to Angelika Franzciska Haas. Educ: St Norbert Col, BA, 65; Univ Wis-River Falls, 66; Univ Wis-Oshkosh, MA 73. Polit & Govt Pos: Chmn, St Norbert Col Young Rep, 62-64; precinct committeeman, Town of Harrison, Calumet Co, Wis, 66-68; village trustee, Village of Sherwood, Calumet Co, 68; secy, Calumet Co Hwy Safety Comn, 69; chmn, Rep Party of Calumet Co, 70- Bus & Prof Pos: Instr social studies, St Mary Cent High Sch, 67, dean of students, 68-72, chmn dept social studies, 70, admin asst, 73-; vpres, KMS, Inc, 70- Mem: Orgn Am Historians; Am & Wis State Hist Socs; Wis & Nat Coun of Social Studies. Relig: Roman Catholic. Mailing Add: 816 S Pierce Ave Appleton WI 54911

MUELLER, FREDERICK HENRY (R)
b Grand Rapids, Mich, Nov 11, 93; s John Frederick Mueller & Emma Matilda Oesterle M; m 1961 to Pauline Crane Kessler; c Frederick Eugene & Marcia Joan. Educ: Mich State Univ, BS, 14, LLD, 59; Tau Beta Pi. Polit & Govt Pos: Asst Secy of Com, 55-58, Undersecy of Com, 58-59, Secy of Com, 59-61. Bus & Prof Pos: Gen partner, Mueller Furniture Co, 14-55; pres & gen mgr, Grand Rapids Industs, Inc, 41-46; pres, Furniture Mutual Ins Co, 41-55; pres, Butterworth Hosp, 45-55; mem gov bd, Mich State Univ, 45-57; pres, United Hosp Fund, Inc, 48-55. Mem: Nat Asn Furniture Mfrs; Bus Coun; CofC; Mason (33 degree); Shrine. Mailing Add: Box 3436 Sarasota FL 33578

MUELLER, INEZ LEE (D)
Mem, Galveston Co Dem Exec Comt, Tex
b Live Oak Co, Tex, Nov 15, 16; d John Dobie & Alice Inez Coffman D; m to Hugo Albert Mueller; c Mitzi Inez (Mrs Vincent Maceo) & Tanya (Mrs A H Jaridly). Polit & Govt Pos: Mem steering comt, Galveston Co Dem Club, Tex, 60-66; presiding judge for co & state elec, 60-75; Galveston Co Dem chmn, Precinct 47, 60-; mem, Galveston Co Dem Exec Comt, 60-; mem, State Dem Exec Comt, Tex, 62-66; committeewoman, 17th Sen Dist Dem Exec Comt, 62-66; alt deleg, Dem Nat Conv, 68. Mem: OCAWIU; Galveston Co Civic Music Asn; Wild Country Civic Club; Order of Sons of Hermann. Relig: Methodist; Past primary Sunday sch supt, First Methodist Church of Texas City. Mailing Add: 816 13th Ave N Texas City TX 77590

MUELLER, JOHN FREDERICK (JACK) (R)
Chmn, Young Rep Nat Fedn
b Cheyenne, Wyo, Nov 10, 41; s Frederick John Mueller & Ellen Crago M; single. Educ: Univ Wyo, BA, 63, MEd, 70; Kappa Delta Pi; Omicron Delta Kappa; Iron Skull; Phi Epsilon Phi; Sigma Chi. Polit & Govt Pos: Chmn, Univ Young Rep, 60-63; educ sen, Student Body Senate, Univ Wyo, 61-62, pres pro tempore, 62-63; deleg, Young Rep Nat Conv, 61-71; deleg, Wyo Rep Conv, 62 & 66-74; region dir, Young Rep Nat Fedn, 63-65, nat vchmn, 65-67, regional co-dir, 69-71, chmn, 75-; chmn, Laramie Co Young Rep, 65-69; precinct committeeman, Laramie Co Rep Party, 66-68 & 70-; deleg, Rep Nat Conv, 68; Young Rep State Chmn, 69-72; nat committeeman, Young Rep League of Wyo, 71-; vchmn, Laramie Co Rep Cent Comt, Wyo, 72-74, chmn, 74- Bus & Prof Pos: Teacher, high sch, Tex, 63-64; teacher, high sch, Wyo, 64-65; dir civil defense educ, Wyo Dept Educ, 65-70, dir sch accreditation, 70-; consult driver educ, 67-70; mem state comt, NCent Asn of Secondary Schs & Cols for Wyo, 71- Publ: Emergency Operating Plans for Public Schools, Wyo Dept Educ, 69. Mem: Farm Bur; Wyo Hist Soc; Wyo & Laramie Co Hist Soc; Univ Wyo Alumni Asn. Honors & Awards: Sigma Chi Best Pledge, 59-60, Outstanding Senior, 63. Relig: Lutheran, Missouri Synod. Mailing Add: 3822 Capitol Cheyenne WY 82001

MUELLER, ROGER JOHN (R)
Chmn, Iowa Co Rep Party, Wis
b Milwaukee, Wis, Mar 4, 38; m 1965 to Mary F Hamilton; c Michael, Theresa & David. Educ: Univ Wis, BS Eng, 61; Marquette Univ, LLB, 65. Polit & Govt Pos: Chmn, Iowa Co Rep Party, Wis, 75- Bus & Prof Pos: Self-employed attorney, Hamilton & Mueller, Dodgeville, Wis, 66- Legal Res: RFD Dodgeville WI 53533 Mailing Add: PO Box 105 Dodgeville WI 53533

MUELLER, WALT (R)
Mo State Rep
Mailing Add: 17 E Glenwood Lane Kirkwood MO 63122

MUENSTER, THEODORE ROBERT (D)
b Beatrice, Nebr, Oct 15, 40; s Theodore R Muenster, Sr & Marcelene Goble M; m 1965 to Karen Nelsen; c Theodore, Mary & Thomas. Educ: Univ Nebr, BA in Hist & Polit Sci, 62, MA, 69; Pi Sigma Alpha. Polit & Govt Pos: Pres, Univ Nebr Young Dem, 61-62; regional dir, Young Dem Clubs of Am, 61-63; nat committeeman, Young Dem Clubs of Nebr, 62-64; spec asst to Gov, Minn, 63-64; alt deleg, Dem Nat Conv, 64; spec asst to US Rep Clair A Callan, 65-67; admin asst to Gov, SDak, 71- Bus & Prof Pos: Teaching asst, Univ Nebr, 63-64; placement specialist, Northern Natural Gas, 67; dir inst pub affairs, Univ SDak, 67-69, dir univ rels, 69-71. Mem: Am Soc Pub Adminr; Am Civil Liberties Union; Vermillion CofC. Relig: Unitarian. Legal Res: 2024 E Broadway Pierre SD 57501 Mailing Add: Off of the Governor Pierre SD 57501

MUGALIAN, RICHARD ARAM (D)
Ill State Rep
b Chicago, Ill, Apr 4, 22; s Levon Bedros Mugalian & Grace Bynderian; m 1946 to Lola Ouzounian; c Arthur, Ruth Anne & Stephen. Educ: Univ Ill, 44-45; Loyola Univ Med Sch, 45; Univ Chicago, BA; Univ Chicago Law Sch, JD. Polit & Govt Pos: Village Attorney, Palatine, Ill, 61-67; committeeman, Palatine Twp Dem Party, 70-75; Ill State Rep, Second Legis Dist, 73- Bus & Prof Pos: Partner law firm, Wooster & Mugalian, Chicago, Ill, 52- Mil Serv: Pvt Army, 43-46. Publ: Various articles, Ill Municipal League Mag. Mem: Chicago & Ill State Bar Asns; Chicago Coun Lawyers; Am Civil Liberties Union; Independent Voters Ill. Honors & Awards: Best Legislator of 1973, Independent Voters of Ill; Golden Award, Ill League of Conservation Voters, 73. Legal Res: 921 Sparrow Court Palatine IL 60067 Mailing Add: 105 W Adams Ct Chicago IL 60603

MULAR, JAMES THEODORE (D)
Mont State Rep
b Butte, Mont, Oct 23, 29; s Harry Mular & Lena Kwasnica M; m 1954 to Florence Ruth Johnson; c Mark James. Educ: Western Mont Col, 47-48; LaSalle Exten Univ, LLB, 65. Polit & Govt Pos: Secy-treas, Butte Labor Polit League, 56-58; chmn, Mont State Legis Comt, 68-; Mont State Rep, Dist 85, 75- Bus & Prof Pos: Claim clerk, Burlington Northern, 49-70; ticket agt, Amtrak, Butte, Mont, 70- Mil Serv: Entered as Pvt, Marine Corps, 45, released as Cpl, 46, after serv in 1st Amtrac Bn FMF Pac, Fleet Marine Force unattached Pac Theatre, 45-46 & Korean Theatre, 50-52; Good Conduct Medal; Sharpshooter. Mem: AF&AM; Am Legion; Elks; United Commercial Travelers; Brotherhood of Rwy Airlines Clerks. Legal Res: 3015 Busch St Butte MT 59701 Mailing Add: PO Box 3084 Butte MT 59701

MULARZ, RUTH LOUISE (D)
Mem Exec Comt, Pitkin Co Dem Party, Colo
b Chicago, Ill, Feb 1, 29; d Ernest W Larson & Sophia Markgraff L; m 1963 to Theodore L Mularz; c Anne Catherine & Mark Andrew. Educ: Carleton Col, BA in Econ. Polit & Govt Pos: Vchmn, Pitkin Co Dem Party, Colo, 69-70, mem exec comt, 70-; co-chmn & treas, Pitkin Co McGovern Campaign Comt, 72; Pitkin co coordr, Gary Hart for Senate. Bus & Prof Pos: Admin asst, Int Minerals & Chem Corp, Skokie, Ill, 53-59; exec secy for Herbert Bayer, Aspen, Colo, 59-63. Mem: League of Women Voters; Aspen Hist Soc (trustee); Aspen Valley Hosp Found (bd dirs). Relig: Lutheran. Mailing Add: White Horse Springs PO Box 166 Aspen CO 81611

MULCAHEY, RICHARD THOMAS (D)
Ill State Rep
b Rockford, Ill, Mar 22, 35; s Robert Thomas Mulcahey & Marcella Richardson M; m 1958 to Anna Mae Cox; c Richard Jr, Susan, Barbara, Martin, John & Megan. Educ: Univ Wis, BS, 62; Letterman's Club. Polit & Govt Pos: Ill State Rep, 75- Bus & Prof Pos: High sch teacher Am hist & govt, 62-75. Mil Serv: Entered as Pfc, Marine Corps, 54, after serv in 7th Marines 1st Div, Korea, 54-55; Presidential Unit Citation; Good Conduct Medal; Korean Campaign Ribbon. Mem: Elks; KofC; Lions; Galena Art Theatre; Ill Police Asn. Honors & Awards: Durand High Sch Yearbk Dedication, 69. Relig: Catholic. Legal Res: Rte 2 Durand IL 61024 Mailing Add: Box 107 Durand IL 61024

MULCAHY, EDWARD WILLIAM
Dep Asst Secy State African Affairs
b Malden, Mass, June 15, 21; s John Martin, Sr & Mary Alice Duffy M; m 1953 to Kathleen Lyon; c Anne Kathleen, John Lyon, Eileen Marie, Kevin Edward & Brian Martin. Educ: Tufts Univ, BA, 43; Fletcher Sch Law & Diplomacy, MA, 47; Zeta Psi. Polit & Govt Pos: Vconsul in charge, Am Consulate, Mombasa, Kenya, 47-49; vconsul, Munich, Ger, 49-50; Am consul, Asmara, Ethiopia, 50-52; chief, Near East, SAsian & African Br, Off Personnel, US Dept State, 52-54, officer in charge UN Trusteeship Affairs, Dept of State, 54-56, US mem, UN Visiting Mission to French & Brit Cameroons, 55-56; mem ed bd, Am Foreign Serv J, 53-56; first secy, Am Embassy, Athens, Greece, 56-59; Am consult, Salisbury, Fedn Rhodesia & Nyasaland, 59-62; officer in charge Rhodesian Zambian & Malawi Affairs, Dept of State, 62-64, dep dir, Off Eastern & Southern African Affairs, 64-66, dir, Off Eastern Affairs, 66, mem, Sr Seminar in Foreign Policy, 66-67; counr, Am Embassy, Tunis, Tunisia, 67-70; minister-counr, Am Embassy, Lagos, Nigeria, 70-72; Ambassador, Repub of Chad, 72-75; Dep Asst Secy State African Affairs, 75- Mil Serv: Entered as Pfc, Marine Corps, 43, released as 1st Lt, 46, after serv in B Co, 21st Marines, S & Cent Pac, 44-45; Capt, Res, 46-58; Silver Star; Purple Heart with Gold Star; Presidential Unit Citation; Navy Distinguished Unit Citation; Theater Medals. Publ: Auth several prof articles & numerous ed. Mem: Am Foreign Serv Asn; Third Marine Div Asn; founding & life mem Hellenic-Am Union, Athens; Friends of Fletcher Sch Law & Diplomacy (adv bd, 73). Relig: Roman Catholic. Legal Res: 712 W Encanto Blvd Phoenix AZ 85007 Mailing Add: Dept of State Washington DC 20520

MULICH, WM (BILL) (D)
Kans State Sen
Mailing Add: State Capitol Topeka KS 66612

MULITAUAOPELE, TAMOTU (NON-PARTISAN)
Sen, Am Samoa Legis
b Laulii, Am Samoa, Nov 10, 15; s Mulitauaopele Leana & Luaitupu L; m 1945 to Arieta Enesi; c Luela, Seine, Lago Lago, Faafetai, Paese, Tamotu & Enesi (Mrs T Pele). Educ: Marist Bros Jr High Sch, cert; Honolulu Police Acad, cert. Polit & Govt Pos: With judicial br, Govt Am Samoa, 38-39; copra export off, Off Attorney Gen, 39-41; chief of police, Govt Am Samoa, 41-57; Sen, Am Samoa Legis, 48- Bus & Prof Pos: Foreman, longshoreman. Relig: Congregational. Legal Res: Laulii Village Pago Pago American Samoa Mailing Add: PO Box 145 Pago Pago American Samoa

MULKERN, THOMAS J (D)
Maine State Rep
Mailing Add: 164 Falmouth St Portland ME 04102

MULLEN, MARTIN P (D)
Pa State Rep
b Philadelphia, Pa, July 29, 21; s John Mullen & Nellie McDermott M; m 1958 to Mary Barnett; c John J. Educ: Wharton Eve Sch, Univ Pa, cert of proficiency in bus admin; Brooklyn Law Sch; Temple Univ Sch Law, LLB. Polit & Govt Pos: Pa State Rep, 55- Bus & Prof Pos: Attorney. Mil Serv: Sgt, Air Force, 42-46, New Caledonia, Australia, Solomons, New Guinea & Philippines. Mem: Am Legion. Legal Res: 5332 Glenmore Ave Philadelphia PA 19143 Mailing Add: Capitol Bldg Harrisburg PA 17120

MULLEN, MARY PATRICIA (D)
b Anchorage, Alaska, Sept 5, 52; d Francis Edward Mullen & Margaret T Mack M; single. Educ: Kenai Peninsula Community Col, 71-72. Polit & Govt Pos: Alt deleg, Dem Nat Conv, 72. Bus & Prof Pos: Counr, Wildwood Boarding Home Complex, employed by Kenai Native Asn. Mem: Redoubt Toastmistresses Club (parliamentarian, 73); Alaska Conserv Soc; Kalifonsky Nordic Ski Club; Nat Women's Polit Caucus; Kenai Coun on Alcoholism. Honors & Awards: Youngest mem in hist of Alaska's deleg to Dem Nat Conv, 72. Relig: Catholic. Legal Res: Mullen Homestead Soldotna AK 99669 Mailing Add: Box 1210 Kenai AK 99611

MULLEN, MICHAEL M (D)
Pa State Rep
b Pittsburgh, Pa, Aug 21, 20; s Martin J Mullen & Elizabeth G O'Malley M; m 1941 to Katherine P McCarthy; c Michael M & Patrick M. Educ: Bus Training Col, dipl, 48. Polit & Govt Pos: Pa State Rep, 70-72 & 75- Mil Serv: Entered as Pvt, Army, 41, released as Sgt, 46, after serv in Inf & ACO, ETO, 43-46; Inf Badge; 3 Battle Stars. Mem: Elks; Moose; Munic Employees Union; CWV; Am Legion Post Five & Ralph McNulty Post. Relig: Catholic. Mailing Add: 4503 1/2 Corday Way Pittsburgh PA 15224

MULLER, ELLA ELIZABETH (R)
Mem, Rep State Cent Comt Calif
b Nashville, Ill, Feb 12, 94; d Samuel A Muller & Caroline Koenemann M; single. Educ: Southern Ill Univ, 1 year; Univ Calif, Los Angeles & Univ Southern Calif, summer semesters. Polit & Govt Pos: Precinct worker in city, co, state & nat campaigns; chmn, Campaign Hq, 54-; mem, Rep State Cent Comt Calif, 64-; mem, Los Angeles Co Rep Cent Comt, 48th Assembly Dist, 67-68. Bus & Prof Pos: Formerly teacher, Ill; mem staff, Criminal Div, Los Angeles Co Clerk's Off, 13 years. Mem: Eastern Star; Royal Neighbors of Am; Highland Park Rep Women, Federated. Honors & Awards: Presented a trophy for Dedicated Rep, Los Angeles Co, Rep Co Cent Comt, 71; Awarded a Resolution, Calif State Assembly, 71; Gold Membership Card & 50 Year Pin, Eastern Star, 72. Relig: Presbyterian. Mailing Add: 153 Roselawn Pl Los Angeles CA 90042

MULLET, MAURICE EUGENE (R)
Chmn, Holmes Co Rep Cent Comt, Ohio
b Millersburg, Ohio, Dec 17, 37; s Roy A Mullet & Alta Kandel M; m 1973 to Phyllis Shrock; c Kevin Eugene, Vonda Kathleen & Brett Everett. Educ: Goshen Col, BA, 59; Ohio State Univ Col Med, MD, 63. Polit & Govt Pos: Committeeman, Holmes Co Rep Cent Comt, Ohio, 72-, chmn, 74-; comnr, Holmes Co Gen Health Dist, 75- Bus & Prof Pos: Trustee, Joel Pomerene Mem Hosp, 66- Mem: Ohio State Med Asn (alt deleg, 72-); Ohio Acad Family Physicians; Am Acad Family Physicians; East Holmes Lions (zone chmn, 73-). Mailing Add: Buckeye Lane Box 260 Berlin OH 44610

MULLICAN, BRIAN LEE (R)
Mem, Mich Rep State Cent Comt
b Detroit, Mich, July 25, 43; s Mack Roger Mullican & Dorothy Hoppenrath M; m 1970 to Helen Elsa Gagern; c Adam Michael & Emily Marie. Educ: Detroit Inst Technol, 61-63; Lawrence Inst Technol, 65-66; Univ Mich, 73-; Circle K. Polit & Govt Pos: Mem, Mich Rep State Cent Comt, 75-; pres, Allen Park Rep Club, 75- Bus & Prof Pos: Auditor's asst, Security Bank & Trust Co, Allen Park, Mich, 68-72, mgr customer serv, 73. Mil Serv: Entered as Pvt E-1, Army, 66, released as SP-4, 68; Good Conduct Medal. Mem: Mich Asn Check Investrs (pres). Relig: Lutheran. Mailing Add: 15047 Philomene Allen Park MI 48101

MULLIGAN, CARY KAUFFMAN (D)
Chairperson, Josephine Co Dem Cent Comt, Ore
b Bethesda, Md, May 7, 44; d Draper L Kauffman, Rear Adm (Ret), US Navy & Margaret Cary Tuckerman K; m 1968 to Michael Anthony Mulligan; c Anne Kathryn. Educ: Wilson Col, 62-64; Univ Philippines, 68-69; George Washington Univ, BA, 73. Polit & Govt Pos: Asst to chief of staff, Md Const Conv, 67-68, asst archivist, 68; precinct committeewoman, Josephine Co Dem Cent Comt, Ore, 73-75, chairperson, 74- Bus & Prof Pos: Teacher, Am Sch, PR, 68-69; social worker, Multnomah Co Pub Welfare, Portland, Ore, 70-72; librn, Lake Forest Libr, Ill, 73 & Grants Pass Pub Libr, Ore, 74-75. Mem: Josephine Co Organic Gardening Club. Mailing Add: 1275 Summit Loop Rd Grants Pass OR 97526

MULLIGAN, JAMES H (D)
Mem, Wis Dem Party
b Everett, Wash, Oct 1, 31; s William P Mulligan & Ada Mongrain M; m 1959 to JoAnn Moskeland; c Nancy Ann, Michael James, Teresa Mary, Carol Joan & John Patrick. Educ: Univ Wash, BA, 57, MA, 60; Sigma Delta Chi. Polit & Govt Pos: Info dir, Upward Bound Off Econ Opportunity, Washington, DC, 68-69; mem, Wis Dem Party, 70-; deleg, Wis Dem Conv, 71 & 72; chmn, McGovern for President, Eighth Dist, Wis, 71-72, deleg, Dem Nat Conv, 72; campaign mgr, Cornell for Cong, Eighth Dist, Wis, 72; press asst, US Rep Brock Adams, Wash, 73- Bus & Prof Pos: Reporter, San Diego Union, Calif, 57-58; instr & pub rels dir, Casper Col, Casper, Wyo, 60-61; instr & pub rels dir, Western Wash State Col, 61-68; info dir, St Norbert Col, 69-72. Mil Serv: Entered as Pvt, Army, 51, released as Sgt, 53, after serv in 65th Regt, Korea, 52-53; Campaign Ribbons. Publ: No Longer a Wasteland, Off Econ Opportunity, 67; A World of Shadows, Rockefeller Found, 68; Talent search in the Mississippi Delta, Idea Mag & Am Educ, 69. Honors & Awards: Regional Honor Award, Am Col Pub Rels Asn, 65-66; Nat Honor Award, 67. Relig: Catholic. Legal Res: 1601 Patton St Green Bay WI 54301 Mailing Add: 8123 Lake Park Dr Alexandria VA 22039

MULLIGAN, JOHN J (D)
Vt State Rep
Mailing Add: Hydeville VT 05750

MULLIN, WILLIAM C (D)
Mass State Rep
Mailing Add: State Capitol Boston MA 02133

MULLINAX, EDWIN G (D)
Ga State Rep
Mailing Add: PO Drawer 1429 LaGrange GA 30240

MULTER, ABRAHAM J (D)
b Manhattan, NY, Dec 24, 00; s Max Multer (deceased) & Emma Rock M (deceased); m to Bertha L; c Robert K & Howard C. Educ: City Col New York, eve classes; Brooklyn Law Sch, LLB & LLM; pres, Marshall Soc; nat prector, Iota Theta. Hon Degrees: LLD, Yeshiva Univ. Polit & Govt Pos: Counsel to Dem leader, NY State Assembly & to many city, state & fed legis comts; spec counsel to mayor, New York; spec Asst Attorney Gen in elec matters, 10 years; former vchmn, Kings Co & NY State Dem Law Comts; former exec mem, pres, secy, chmn, Civil Serv Comt & organizer Civil Serv Sch, Kings Hwy Dem Club; former mem, NY State Dem Comt & Kings Co Dem Exec Comt; US Rep, NY, 47-67; Justice, Supreme Court of NY, 67- Bus & Prof Pos: Former mem, Rayfiel & Multer & Multer, Nova & Seymour. Mil Serv: Coast Guard Res, World War II. Mem: Fed, Inter-Am & Am Bar Asns; Am Soc Int Law; Asn of Supreme Court Justices. Relig: Jewish; hon pres, Temple Beth Emeth, hon pres, Brooklyn Jewish Community Coun & nat pres, Bnai Zion. Mailing Add: 1397 E 21st St Brooklyn NY 11210

MULVANEY, JAMES PATRICK (D)
Mo State Rep
Mailing Add: 5717 Beldon Dr Jennings MO 63136

MUNDT, GARY HAROLD (D)
b Hallam, Nebr, Aug 29, 43; s Harold John Mundt & Letty Stern M; single. Educ: Univ Nebr, BA, 67. Polit & Govt Pos: Deleg, Dem Nat Conv, 72; head, Register Youth 72, Denver, 72; asst to Denver coordr, McGovern Campaign, 72; mem staff, US Rep Pat Schroeder, Colo, 73- Mil Serv: Entered as 2nd Lt, Air Force, 67, released as Capt, 71, after serv in 22nd TRS, 432nd AMS, Tactical & Pac Air Commands, Udorn AFB, Thailand, 67-71; Capt, Res, 2 years. Mem: Vietnam Vet Against the War (regional coordr, 71-72); Young Dem (vpres, 72-73). Mailing Add: 1316 Dexter St Denver CO 80220

MUNFORD, DILLARD (R)
Mem, Rep Nat Finance Comt
b Cartersville, Ga, May 13, 18; s Robert Sims Munford & Katherine Aubrey M; m 1941 to Lillie Shepherd Davis; c Dillard, Jr, Page S, Mary Aubrey, Robert D & Henry A. Educ: Ga Inst Technol, BS in Mech Eng. Polit & Govt Pos: Past pres, Young Pres Orgn, Ga, 63; finance chmn, Howard Callaway for Gov, 64; mem, Ga State Rep Exec Comt & asst chmn, Exec Comt, 64-; first vchmn, Ga Rep Orgn, formerly; alt deleg, Rep Nat Conv, 68; mem, Rep Nat Finance Comt, currently; chmn, Ga State Rep Finance Comt to Reelect the President, 72. Bus & Prof Pos: Pres, Munford Co, 46-62; pres, Munford, Inc, 68-; chmn bd, Atlantic Co, 62-68; past div vpres, Nat Asn Mfrs; pres & chief exec officer, Jackson-Atlantic, Inc, 68-; chmn bd, Omni Group, currently. Mil Serv: Entered as 2nd Lt, Army, 42, released as Capt, 45, after serv in Aleutian Islands; Pac Campaign Ribbon. Relig: Methodist. Legal Res: 1065 W Paces Ferry Rd Atlanta GA 30327 Mailing Add: PO Box 7701 Sta C Atlanta GA 30309

MUNGER, MORGAN (R)
Idaho State Rep
Mailing Add: Ola ID 83657

MUNGER, WILLARD M (DFL)
Minn State Rep
b 1911. Educ: Univ Minn. Polit & Govt Pos: Minn State Rep, 55-65 & 67-; mem, Water Pollution Control Adv Comn; mem, Zoological Bd & Zoological Adv Comn; food sect chief, Off Price Stabilization; mem mkt inspection serv, dairy & food div, State Dept Agr & state grain inspection serv, Minn. Bus & Prof Pos: Pres, Willard Enterprises, Inc; former grocer. Mailing Add: 1121 70th Ave W Duluth MN 55807

MUNN, EARLE HAROLD (PROHIBITION)
Secy, Mich State Prohibition Comt
b Westlake, Ohio, Nov 29, 03; s Earle O Munn & Ella C Deming M; m 1926 to Luella Mae Asfahl; c E Harold, Jr & Lewis Edwin. Educ: Greenville Col, AB, 25; Univ Mich, AM, 28, grad courses, 38-39; Northwestern Univ, 37-38. Hon Degrees: DrEducAdmin, Hillsdale Col, 72. Polit & Govt Pos: Chmn, Mich State Prohibition Comt, 48-54, secy, 71-; mem, Nat Prohibition Comt, 52-, chmn, 56-71; Vice Presidential cand of Prohibition Party, 6O, Presidential cand, 64, 68 & 72; pres & treas, Nat Prohibition Found, 71- Bus & Prof Pos: Instr & dormitory supvr, Cent Acad & Col, 25-27; registr, acting dean & dir summer sch, Greenville Col, 28-37; teaching asst, Univ Mich, 38-39; assoc mgr, Munn Art Studio, 39-; assoc prof educ, Hillsdale Col, 39-72, emer prof, 72-, from asst dean to acad dean, 62-72; pres, WTVB Radio Sta, Coldwater, Mich, 54-68; mgr, WBSE Radio Sta, Hillsdale, 58-60; secy, WYNZ Radio Sta, Ypsilanti, 64-65. Relig: Free Methodist. Mailing Add: 3O6 N West St Hillsdale MI 49242

MUNOZ-MARIN, LUIS (POPULAR DEM, PR)
b San Juan, PR, Feb 18, 98; s Luis Munoz-Rivera & Amalia Marin; m to Ines Maria Mendoza; c Munita, Luis II, Vivian & Victoria. Educ: Georgetown Univ, 12-16. Polit & Govt Pos: Secy, Resident Comnr PR in Washington, DC, 16-18; PR Sen-at-lg, 32 & 65-72; founder & pres, Popular Dem Party, 38; pres, PR Sen, 41-48; gov, Territory of PR, 48-52; gov, Commonwealth of PR, 52-65; mem, Const Assembly PR, 51; formerly econ comnr for PR in US; mem gen secretariat, Pan-Am Conf, Havana. Bus & Prof Pos: Founder & ed, El Batey; ed & publ, La Democracia; ed, La Revista de Indies, 18-19. Publ: Borrones, 17; Madra Haraposa (in collab), 17; contrib, Am Mercury, Nation, New Repub & Foreign Affairs. Relig: Catholic. Mailing Add: Box 367 St Just PR 00750

MUNOZ-RIVERA, LUIS (D)
VPres, Dem Party of PR
b Cayey, PR, Apr 10, 16; s Jose Munoz & Clemencia Rivera M; m 1964 to Dulce Fernandez; c Luis & Marya. Educ: Univ PR, BBA, 51, LLB, 60; Syracuse Univ, MPA, 54. Polit & Govt Pos: Auditor, San Juan, PR, 47-54, dir of the budget, 54-59; mem cent bd, San Juan Popular Dem Comt, 50-; deleg, PR Const Conv, 51-52; PR State Sen, 61-68; treas, PR Dem State Comt, 62-; first vpres, San Juan Popular Dem Party, 65-69; deleg, Dem Nat Conv, 68; vpres, Dem Party of PR, 68- Mem: Am Bar Asn; Bar Asn of PR; PR Soc Pub Admin (vpres, 66-). Relig: Catholic. Legal Res: Apt 9W 61 King's Ct San Juan PR 00911 Mailing Add: Box 1892 Hato Rey PR 00919

MUNROE, DAVID A (R)
Committeeman, Idaho Rep Exec Comt
b Reno, Nev, Sept 25, 38; s Matilda Lalacona; m 1961 to Joyce R Spradling; c Mark David & Jason Spradling. Educ: Idaho State Univ, 59-64; Phi Sigma Kappa. Polit & Govt Pos: Precinct committeeman, Twin Falls Co, Idaho, 65-, mem exec bd, 65-; deleg, Idaho State Conv, currently; committeeman, Idaho Rep Exec Comt, currently; mem city council, Buhl, currently. Bus & Prof Pos: Gen mgr & owner, Dave Munroe Chevrolet Inc, Buhl, 73- Mem: Jaycees; Rotary; CofC; Methodist Youth Counselor. Honors & Awards: Distinguished Serv Award, Jaycees, 66; Citizen of the Week, Radio Sta KEEP, Twin Falls, 67. Relig: Methodist. Mailing Add: 904 11th N Buhl ID 83316

MUNSEY, EVERARD (D)
b Washington, DC, Sept 25, 33; s Virdell E Munsey & Mildred Wood M; m 1956 to Bernice Wilson; c Wanda Louise, Allan Coll, Andrew Everard & Carolyn Jane. Educ: Yale Univ, BA magna cum laude, 55; Harvard Univ, MPA, 67; Pi Sigma Alpha. Polit & Govt Pos: Legis asst to US Rep Henry Reuss, 63-68; vchmn, Arlington Co Dem Comt, Va, 65-66, chmn, 67-69; info coordr, United Dem for Humphrey, 68; deleg, Dem Nat Conv, 68; asst dir pub affairs for news & dir research, Dem Nat Comt, 68; mem, Arlington Co Bd, Va, 72-, vchmn, 72, chmn, 73-; vchmn, Northern Va Transportation Comn, 73-; mem, Nat Capital Region Transportation Planning Bd, 73-; chmn, Northern Va Transportation Comn, 74; dir, Washington Metrop Transit Authority, 75. Bus & Prof Pos: Reporter, Wash Post, 57-63; asst exec secy, Nat Planning Asn, 69-70, dep exec secy, 70-71, vpres, 71- Mil Serv: Entered as Pvt, Army, 55, released as Pfc, 57, after serv in 6966th Spec Detached Unit, 56-57. Mem: Am Polit Sci Asn; Am Acad Polit & Social Sci. Honors & Awards: Am Polit Sci Asn Distinguished Pub Affairs Reporting Award, 62 & Cong Staff Fel, 66-67. Relig: Congregational. Mailing Add: 3623 N 37th St Arlington VA 22207

MUNSON, DONALD FRANCIS (R)
Md State Deleg
b Hagerstown, Md, Dec 21, 37; s Donald Ray Munson & Mevis Rider M; m 1965 to Margaret Lucille Calandrelle; c Xanthy Marie. Educ: Johns Hopkins Univ, BA, 68. Polit & Govt Pos: Page, US House Rep, 53-55; Md State Deleg, 75- Bus & Prof Pos: Teacher, Frederick Co, Md, 69-75. Mil Serv: Army Res, 60-66. Mem: Rep Club Washington Co; Alsatia Club Inc; Exchange Club of Antietam; Washington Co Asn Retarded Children; Boy Scouts Dist Comt. Relig: Methodist. Legal Res: 117 W Magnolia Ave Hagerstown MD 21740 Mailing Add: 28 W Church St Hagerstown MD 21740

MUNSON, KAY M (R)
Colo State Rep
Mailing Add: 1419 Bellaire Dr Colorado Springs CO 80909

MUNSON, WILLIAM BEN, IV (D)
Tex State Rep
b Sherman, Tex, July 25, 42; s W B Munson & Martha de Golian M; m 1972 to Susan Ross Weber. Educ: Univ Notre Dame, BBA, 64; Univ Tex Sch Law, JD, 67; Phi Alpha Delta; Notre Dame Texas Club. Polit & Govt Pos: Admin asst, US Rep Ray Roberts, Fourth Dist, Tex; Tex State Rep, Dist 22, 72- Bus & Prof Pos: Attorney-at-law, Munson, Munson & Porter, 70- Mil Serv: Entered as 1st Lt, Army, 67, released as Capt, 69, after serv in Ord Corps, Continental Army Command; Capt, Res; Army Commendation Medal. Publ: Exclusive dealing under the Clayton Antitrust Act, Univ Tex Sch Law, 67. Mem: Am Bar Asn; Am Legion; Amvets; Rotary; Jaycees. Honors & Awards: Moot Court Competition Award, Univ Tex Sch Law, 67. Relig: Catholic. Mailing Add: 911 S Fairbanks Denison TX 75020

MUNTS, MARY LOUISE (D)
Wis State Rep
b Chicago, Ill, Aug 21, 24; d T Hunton Rogers & Elizabeth Vinsonhaler R; m 1947 to Raymond Munts; c Lisa (Mrs Redburn), Polly & Andrew. Educ: Swarthmore Univ, 41-44; Univ Chicago, MA, 45-47; Univ Wis, Law Sch, 71-75; Phi Beta Kappa. Polit & Govt Pos: Chmn, Assembly Environ Qual Comt; mem, Assembly Natural Resources Comt, Legis Coun Spec Comt on Lobbying Laws & Legis Coun Spec Comt on the Preserving Agr & Conserv Lands; chmn, Drafting Subcomt, 72-; Wis State Rep, 76th Assembly Dist, 72- Bus & Prof Pos: Research asst, US Dept Treasury, Paris, 47-48; instr, Sch Bus, Wilkes Col, Pa, 49-50; econ research assoc, Robert R Nathan Assocs, Bethesda, Md, 64-66; admis secy, Ctr for Develop, Univ Wis, 67-72. Publ: Co-auth, The Future of Small Business, Praeger, 67. Mem: Madison Asn for Retarded Children; Nat Conf State Legis (natural resources task force); Wis Women's Polit Caucus; Wis Dem Party Charter Comn (chmn); Portal Foster Ctr (exec bd). Honors & Awards: Madison Area Asn for Retarded Children Annual Recognition Award, 73, 74. Legal Res: 6102 Hammersley Rd Madison WI 53711 Mailing Add: 9 W Capitol Madison WI 53702

MURDOCK, NORMAN A (R)
Ohio State Rep
b Cincinnati, Ohio, Nov 6, 31; m to Patricia A Higgins; c Six. Educ: Xavier Univ, grad, 55; fel pub admin & grad intern, Univ Ala, summer 55; Col Law, Univ Cincinnati, JD, 68. Polit & Govt Pos: With Fed Bur Invest, 52-53; Dept Indust Rels, State of Ala, summer 55; clerk-treas, Delhi Twp, Ohio, 64-67; Ohio State Rep, 67-, mem taxation, govt opers & hwy comt, Ohio Gen Assembly, 67-68, vchmn ways & means comt, mem educ & reference comts, chmn House subcomt campus unrest, chmn health, educ & welfare comt, formerly, Asst Minority Leader, mem rules comt, educ comt, spec comt on finance & nat legis conf, 73-; mem, Select House-Senate Comt to Study Campus Unrest, 70 & comt to Study Govt Reorgn, 70; mem, Ohio Crime Comn, Gov Conf Aging & Educ Comn States; deleg-at-lg, White House Conf Aging, 72. Bus & Prof Pos: With Cincinnati Police Div, 53-55; dist scout exec, Boy Scouts, Dodge City, Kans, 56-59; pub acct, 59-; secy, managing off & mem bd, Oakmont Savings & Loan Co, Cheviot, Ohio, 63-65; practicing attorney, 68- Mil Serv: Capt, Army Res, 65. Mem: Am Bar Asn; Nat Asn Pub Acct; State Asn Twp Trustees & Clerks; Boy Scouts (troop committeeman); United Appeal. Honors & Awards: Outstanding Freshman, Ohio Gen Assembly, 68; Man of the Year in Polit, Price Hill Civic Club, Cincinnati, 69. Relig: Catholic; Mem, Archdiocesan Coun Cath Men; Holy Name Soc of Our Lady of Victory Church. Mailing Add: 628 Conina Dr Cincinnati OH 45238

MURFIN, WILLIAM FLOYD (R)
b Anderson, Ind, Aug 28, 25; s Floyd Frank Murfin & Della Fowler M; 2nd m 1962 to Jean Wilson; c Carole, Robyn, James, Charles & Harold. Educ: Ferris State Col, Big Rapids, Mich, BS, 50. Polit & Govt Pos: Chmn, Rep Activities Comt, Fla, 64-65; pres, Martin Co Young Rep Club, 65-66; chmn, Fla Rep State Exec Comt, 66-69; mem, Rep Nat Comt, 66-69; deleg, secy of host comt & chmn, Fla deleg, Rep Nat Conv, 68; assoc adminr, Small Bus Admin, Washington, DC, 69-70, dist dir, 7O-; state chmn & campaign mgr, Jack Eckerd for Gov, Fla, 70. Bus & Prof Pos: Mem, Fla Bd of Pharm. Mil Serv: Seaman, Navy, ETO, 43-46. Mem: Fla Bd of Pharm; Elks. Relig: Protestant. Legal Res: PO Box 723 Hobe Sound FL 33455 Mailing Add: 1001 Howard Ave Suite 1724 New Orleans LA 70113

MURPHY, ARTHUR G, SR (D)
Md State Deleg
Mailing Add: 4204 Ethland Ave Baltimore MD 21207

MURPHY, ARTHUR POWELL (D)
Idaho State Sen
b Sandpoint, Idaho, May 18, 98; s Thomas Edward Murphy & Mary Elizabeth Purdy M; m 1928 to Anietta Inola Rolfs; c Michael Arthur, Colleen Joyce (Mrs Cornell) & Terrance William. Educ: High Sch, Sandpoint, Idaho, 2 years. Polit & Govt Pos: Idaho State Rep, Shoshone Co, 37-41 & 43-51, Asst Majority Leader, Idaho House Rep, 41, Asst Minority Leader, 43, Minority Leader, 51; Idaho State Sen, 57-, Majority Leader, Idaho State Senate, 59, Minority Leader, 67, chmn Dem caucus, 69 & 73, mem legis coun, 67-73; deleg, Dem Nat Conv, 68. Mem: Mullan Coun; CofC (pres); United Crusade (dir); Cataldo Mission; Wallace Mus. Honors & Awards: Batting Awards & Diamond Lapel Button, Oakland Championship Coast League, 27. Relig: Presbyterian. Mailing Add: 127 Mill St Mullan ID 83846

MURPHY, BETTY SOUTHARD (R)
Chmn, Nat Labor Rels Bd
b East Orange, NJ, Mar 1, 28; d Floyd Theodore Southard & Thelma Casto; m 1965 to Dr Cornelius F Murphy; c Ann Southard & Cornelius F, Jr. Educ: Ohio State Univ, BA, 52; Alliance Francaise & Univ Sorbonne, Paris, 52-53; Am Univ Law Sch, JD, 58; Delta Delta Delta; Kappa Beta Pi. Hon Degrees: LLD, Eastern Mich Univ, 75. Polit & Govt Pos: Adminr, Wage & Hour Div, Dept of Labor, 74-75; chmn, Nat Labor Rels Bd, 75- Bus & Prof Pos: Reporter, United Press Int, 55-56; pub rels counr, Capitol Properties, Inc, 56-58; attorney, NLRB-Enforcement, 58-59; partner, Wilson, Woods & Villalon & Predecessors, 59-74; ed, Inter-Am Bar Asn Newslett, Am Univ Law Sch, 60-69, adj faculty, 72- Publ: Provisional Government of Vietnam Since 1945, 52; National labor relations act & comparative labor law,

IABA Conf, Bogota, 61 & Panama, 63. Mem: Int Ctr for Settlement of Investment Disputes (mem panel of conciliators); Ctr for Women in Med (nat adv coun); Am Univ (trustee); Mary Baldwin Col (chmn bd visitors, 73-). Honors & Awards: Dean's Scholar, Am Univ Law Sch, 56 & 57; Selected Rep for US at IV Cong Nacional de Abogados Colombianos, Colombian Bar Asn, Cucuta, Colombia, 63; Silver Medal as Outstanding Lawyer of 1967, Am Bar Asn, San Jose, Costa Rica. Legal Res: Annandale VA Mailing Add: 1717 Pennsylvania Ave NW Washington DC 20570

MURPHY, CHARLES J (D)
b Waterbury, Conn, Dec 27, 07; s Thomas F Murphy & Catherine Shortt M; m 1936 to Irene Lieber; c Philip. Educ: Col of the Holy Cross, AB, 31. Polit & Govt Pos: Asst to regional mgr, Home Owners Loan Corp, 34-44; mem bd educ, Middlebury, Conn, 65-69, mem, Indust & Develop Comn, 67-, mem, Retirement Comn, 70-; chmn, Middlebury Dem Town Comt, formerly. Bus & Prof Pos: Secy, First Fed Savings & Loan Asn, Waterbury, Conn, 44-73. Mem: Elks; KofC. Relig: Roman Catholic. Mailing Add: Whittemore Rd Middlebury CT 06762

MURPHY, CHARLES SPRINGS (D)
b Wallace, NC, Aug 20, 09; s William Murphy & Kate Westbrook M; m 1931 to Kate Chestney Graham M; c Courtenay, Westbrook & Elizabeth. Educ: Duke Univ, AB, 31, LLB, 34; Order of the Coif; Delta Sigma Phi; Pi Gamma Mu; Omicron Delta Kappa. Hon Degrees: LLD, Duke Univ, 67. Polit & Govt Pos: Pres, Nat Dem Club, formerly; mem, Off Legis Counsel, US Senate, 34-47; admin asst to President, US, 47-50; spec counsel to President, US, 50-53; counsel to Dem Nat Adv Coun, 57-60; Under Secy of Agr, 61-65; chmn, Civil Aeronaut Bd, 65-68; counr to President, US, 68-69. Bus & Prof Pos: Lawyer, Morison, Murphy, Clapp & Abrams, 53-61 & Morison, Murphy, Abrams & Haddock, 69-; mem bd trustees, Duke Univ, 70- Mem: Duke Sch Law (mem bd visitors); Am, DC, NC & Fed Bar Asns. Relig: Methodist. Mailing Add: Greenbriar Lane Annapolis MD 21401

MURPHY, CHARLOTTE ANN (R)
Chairwoman, Greene Co Rep Party, Ohio
b Dayton, Ohio, Apr 28, 26; d Christian H Wilkening & Hazel Koch W; m 1947 to Dr John E Murphy, Jr; c John Edward, III, Kevin Alan, Bradford James, Terrence Patrick & Constance Louise. Educ: Univ Cincinnati, 44-46. Polit & Govt Pos: Mem, Brown for Cong Comt, 66; chairwoman, Greene Co Rep Party, Ohio, 66-72; chairwoman, Greene Co Rep Exec Comt. Mem: Bellbrook-Sugarcreek PTA; Bellbrook Area Civic Coun; Bellbrook Mus Bd; Bellbrook Garden Club; Bellbrook Hist Comt. Relig: Lutheran. Mailing Add: 6730 Little Sugar Creek Rd Dayton OH 45440

MURPHY, DELBERT S (D)
Ky State Rep
Mailing Add: 1941 Lydia Dr Owensboro KY 42301

MURPHY, ELINORE JAMERSON (D)
Chmn, Monroe Co Dem Cent Comt, Ind
b Twin Falls, Idaho, July 21, 21; d James Mack Jamerson & Lucille Wilson J; m 1946 to Duncan Witten Murphy; c Duncan Mack. Educ: Colo Woman's Col, AA & AS, 41; Northwestern Univ, Evanston, BS, 43. Polit & Govt Pos: Clerk, Monroe Co Circuit Court, Ind, 70-; chmn, Monroe Co Dem Cent Comt, 72- Mailing Add: 705 Meadowbrook Bloomington IN 47401

MURPHY, FRANCIS (R)
NH State Rep
Mailing Add: 267 Webster St Manchester NH 03104

MURPHY, FRANK, JR (R)
Calif State Assemblyman
b Santa Cruz, Calif, Jan 19, 34; s John Francis Murphy & Marjorie Liebbrandt M; m 1962 to Christine A Allegrini; c Michel Louise, Katherine Anne, Erin Estelle & Lisa Marie. Educ: Univ Santa Clara, AB, 55, LLB, 57. Polit & Govt Pos: Consult, Joint Interim Comt on Equalization & Assessment Practices, Calif Legis, 57; Calif State Assemblyman, 28th Dist, 67-, chmn criminal procedure comt, Calif State Assembly, 69-70, Minority Whip, 71-73, Rep caucus chmn, 73- Bus & Prof Pos: Assoc, Murphy & Adams, 57-58 & 61-66; partner, Murphy & Murphy, 66-68, Murphy, Murphy & Black, 68-70, Murphy, Murphy, Black & Williams, 70-72, Murphy, Murphy, Black, Williams & Stevens, 72- Mil Serv: Entered as Lt(jg), Navy, 58, released as Lt, 61, after serv as Legal Off, Beeville, Tex, 58-59 & Long Beach, Calif, 59-61. Mem: Calif Bar Asn; Lions; Elks; KofC; Navy League. Relig: Catholic. Legal Res: 33 Eastridge Dr Santa Cruz CA 95060 Mailing Add: PO Box 634 Santa Cruz CA 95060

MURPHY, GEORGE A (R)
NY State Assemblyman
b Brooklyn, NY, Mar 16, 23; s Frank V Murphy & Catherine L Milroy M; m 1952 to Teresa M Short; c Michael, Timothy, Terrence, Mary, James, Maureen, Christopher, Marjorie & Paul. Educ: St Johns Univ Law Sch, LLB with honors, 49; Fordham Univ, BS cum laude, 51. Polit & Govt Pos: Councilman, Hempstead, NY, 63-71; NY State Sen, 71-72, NY State Assemblyman, 12th Dist, 73- Bus & Prof Pos: Attorney-at-law, Bellmore, NY, 49- Mil Serv: Entered as Pvt, Army, 43, released as 1st Lt, 46, after serv in China Serv Command, Europ & Am Theater, 43-46; Maj (Ret), Army Res; Theater Ribbons. Mem: Am Legion; Elks; Exchange; Nassau Co Bar Asn; KofC. Relig: Roman Catholic. Mailing Add: 3556 Tonopah St Seaford NY 11783

MURPHY, GEORGE LLOYD (R)
b New Haven, Conn, July 4, 02; s Mike Murphy; m 1926 to Julie Johnson M; c Dennis & Melissa (Mrs Robert W Ellis, III). Educ: Yale Univ. Polit & Govt Pos: Deleg to four Rep Nat Conv, in charge of progs, 56 & 60; chmn, Rep State Cent Comt, Calif, 53-54; US Sen, Calif, 64-71; chmn, Nat Rep Senate Comt, 67-69. Mem: AFL-CIO Affil Screen Actors Guild. Honors & Awards: Appeared in four Broadway shows & 45 motion pictures; recognized by Army, Navy, Marine Corps, Air Force & Coast Guard for activities in entertainment during World War II; received awards & honors from US Dept of State, Am Red Cross, Friendly Sons of St Patrick, Irish Am Soc, USO, Boy Scouts, Cancer Prev Soc & Univ Southern Calif; received first Nat Award given by Nat Conf Christians & Jews. Mailing Add: 807 N Rodeo Dr Beverly Hills CA 90210

MURPHY, IRA H (D)
Tenn State Rep
b Memphis, Tenn, Sept 8, 28; s George Murphy & Margaret Ross M; m to Rubye Bland.

Educ: Tenn State Univ, BS, 50; NY Univ, LLB, 55, LLM, 57; Kappa Delta Pi; Alpha Phi Alpha. Polit & Govt Pos: Tenn State Rep, Dist 6, 68- Bus & Prof Pos: Attorney at law, Memphis, Tenn. Mil Serv: Army. Mem: Mason; Shrine; Elks. Relig: Seventh Day Adventist. Legal Res: 411 S Orleans Memphis TN 38126 Mailing Add: 626 Vance Ave Memphis TN 38126

MURPHY, JACK M (R)
b Shoshone, Idaho, 1925; m 1946 to Cleora Nebeker; c Sheila, Maureen, Tim & Colleen. Educ: Idaho State Univ; Univ Utah, BS in Econ & Acct & LLB, 51. Polit & Govt Pos: Idaho State Sen, 53-66, Asst Minority Leader, Idaho State Senate, 59, Majority Leader, 61, Pres Pro Tem, 63-66; Lt Gov, Idaho, 67-75; chmn, Nixon for President, 68 & 72; deleg, Rep Nat Conv, 72. Bus & Prof Pos: Attorney; cattle rancher. Mem: Idaho State Bar; Legis Leaders Conf, White House; Coun of State Govt; Phi Alpha Delta; CofC (pres). Relig: Episcopal. Mailing Add: PO Box 666 Shoshone ID 83352

MURPHY, JACK REDMOND (R)
NDak State Rep
b Killdeer, NDak, May 17, 12; s Redmond Murphy & Elizabeth O'Neill M; m 1941 to Dorothy Mae Erickson; c Patty (Mrs Goodall), Mary (Mrs Moe), Joan (Mrs Braun), Leone (Mrs Dornheim), Hugh, Shirley (Mrs Meyer), Rose-Donna, Tom & Colleen. Educ: Col St Thomas, 1 year. Polit & Govt Pos: Mem, State Brand Bd, Bismarck, NDak, 55-, White House Conf, 60-, Sch Bd, Killdeer, 60-63 & Southwest Water Dist, 65; deleg, NDak State Rep Conv, 66, 68 & 70; NDak State Rep, 36th Dist, 71- Mem: NDak Stockmen's Asn; NDak Stockmen's Tax Comn; NDak Farm Bur (mem tax comt, 60-); Elks; KofC. Relig: Catholic. Mailing Add: Killdeer ND 58640

MURPHY, JAMES E (R)
b Laredo, Mo, Nov 6, 10; s John F Murphy & Ida Warren M; m to Sylvia J Brassett; c Mary Patricia. Educ: William Jewell Col, AB, 35; George Washington Univ, LLB, 39; Sigma Nu. Polit & Govt Pos: Mont mem, Columbia Interstate Compact Comn, 54-; mem, Pac Northwest River Basins Comn; Rep Nat Committeeman, Mont, 60-72; Mont State Rep, 67-72. Mil Serv: Entered as Pvt, Army, 42, released as 1st Lt, 46. Mem: Mont & Am Bar Asns; Mason; Shrine; Elks. Relig: Lutheran. Mailing Add: 604 Woodland Kalispell MT 59901

MURPHY, JAMES JEROME, JR (D)
Conn State Sen
b Norwich, Conn, Mar 1, 36; s James Jerome Murphy & Dorothy Smiley M; m 1958 to Barbara Elizabeth Olcott; c James Jerome, III, William Thomas, Kathryn Elin & Susan Deborah. Educ: Univ Conn, BA, 57, Sch Law, JD, 64; Lambda Chi Alpha. Polit & Govt Pos: Asst prosecutor, Tenth Circuit Court, NH, 66-68; vchmn town comt, Franklin Bd Educ, 68-71; Conn State Sen, 19th Sen Dist, 71- Bus & Prof Pos: Law partner, Gilman, Berberick & Murphy. Mil Serv: 2nd Lt, Army 58, serv in 6th Armored Cavalry. Mem: Am Bar Asn; Elks. Relig: Catholic. Legal Res: RFD 1 Pautipaug Lane North Franklin CT 06254 Mailing Add: 257 Main St Norwich CT 06360

MURPHY, JOHN (D)
Mont State Rep
Mailing Add: Box 40 Stanford MT 59479

MURPHY, JOHN E, JR (D)
Mass State Rep
b Richmond, Va, Apr 3, 43; s John E Murphy & Mariel Pierce M; m 1967 to Joan E Curran; c Maureen F & John E, III. Educ: Providence Col, AB, 65; Suffolk Univ Law Sch, LLB, 68. Polit & Govt Pos: Mass State Rep, 71- Bus & Prof Pos: Attorney-at-law, Murphy, Ryan & O'Keefe, 68- Mem: Mass Trial Lawyer Asn; Am Bar Asn; Elks; Ancient Order of Hibernians; KofC. Relig: Roman Catholic. Mailing Add: 21 Anne Dr Peabody MA 01960

MURPHY, JOHN F (R)
Chmn, Williamsburg Rep Town Comt, Va
b Roanoke, Va, Jan 18, 28; s Francis B Murphy & Wilma Paige Eversole M; m 1959 to Barbara Ann Collins; c Johanna Lee, R Cameron & Teresa Marie. Educ: Shenandoah Col & Conservatory of Music, Dayton, Va, 47-48; Concord Col, 48-49; Columbia Inst Radio Broadcasting, Philadelphia, 51-52. Polit & Govt Pos: Chmn, Williamsburg Rep Town Comt, Va, 70- Bus & Prof Pos: Chief engr, WBCI-WMBG Radio, Williamsburg, Va, 62-72; owner, John F Murphy Advert ency; consult engr; writer. Mil Serv: Entered as Pvt, Army, 54, released as Pfc, 56, after serv in Hq & Hq Co Alaskan Theatre, 55-56. Mem: Exchange Club of Gtr Williamsburg. Relig: Methodist. Mailing Add: 606 Richmond Rd Williamsburg VA 23185

MURPHY, JOHN FRANCIS (R)
b Orlando, Fla, Mar 1, 26; s John Francis Murphy & Myrtle O'Brien M; m 1970 to Mary Rutschman; c Kathleen Ann & Patricia Sue (Mrs Philip Beckhelm). Educ: Univ Calif, Los Angeles, NBC Radio Inst, cert, 47; Univ Ariz, 47-48; Alpha Epsilon Rho; Phi Kappa Psi. Polit & Govt Pos: Sr TV adv, US Info Agency, 69-72; dep dir commun, US Dept Interior, 72-73; admin asst to US Sen Barry Goldwater, Ariz, 73- Bus & Prof Pos: Exec producer, KPHO-TV, Phoenix, Ariz, 49-56; vpres news & pub affairs, KOOL Radio-TV, Phoenix, 56-69. Mil Serv: Entered as A/S, Navy, 44, released as ETM 3/C, 46, after serv in USS Ranger, Pac. Mem: Radio-TV News Dir Asn; Nat & Phoenix Press Clubs; Sigma Delta Chi; Cogswell Soc. Relig: Episcopal. Legal Res: 3839 E Whitton Phoenix AZ 85018 Mailing Add: 3001 Veazey Terr NW 1626 Washington DC 20008

MURPHY, JOHN FRANCIS (D)
Mem, Mass Dem State Comt
b Brockton, Mass, Oct 28, 38; s Ambrose Francis Murphy & Rose Etta Welch M; m 1959 to Caroline Elizabeth Corcoran; c John Francis, Jr, Julie Grace, James Ambrose & Jeanne Rose. Educ: Col of the Holy Cross, BS, 60; Boston Univ Law Sch, 2 years; founder, Holy Cross Young Dem. Polit & Govt Pos: Research asst to Secy of State Kevin White, Mass, 61, admin asst, 64, admin asst to Mayor Kevin White, Boston, 68-73; mem, Planning Bd, Brockton, Mass, 63, mem, Dem Ward Comt, 64, mem bd zoning appeals, 67; mem, Mass Dem State Comt, 64-; vchmn rules comt, Mass Dem State Conv, 66; pres, Mass Electoral Col, 68; chmn, Brockton Planning Bd, 72-76; dir occupancy, Boston Housing Authority, 73- Mem: KofC; Young Dem; Citizens Adv Comt for City of Brockton; Wimbeldon Beach Asn (pres); Lewis Bay Yacht Club. Relig: Catholic. Mailing Add: 144 Sunset Dr Brockton MA 02401

MURPHY, JOHN FRANCIS (D)
Vt State Rep
b Ludlow, Vt, Feb 22, 23; s Thomas James Murphy & Fern Agnes Batch M; m 1952 to Floribel Ann La Pine; c John Francis, Jr. Educ: High Sch. Polit & Govt Pos: Chmn, Rep Town Comt, Ludlow, Vt, 62-64, dist chmn, 64-66, co chmn, 64-68; Vt State Rep, 68- Relig: Catholic. Mailing Add: PO Box 125 Ludlow VT 05149

MURPHY, JOHN MICHAEL (D)
US Rep, NY
b Staten Island, NY, Aug 3, 26; s Frank Murphy & Florence M; m to Kathleen A Johnson; c Deirdre, John, Eve, Mark & Emily. Educ: Amherst Col; US Mil Acad, BSCE. Hon Degrees: LLD, Sung Kyun Kwan Univ, Korea. Polit & Govt Pos: Secy, Franklin Delano Roosevelt Comn; mem bd gov, Nat Dem Club; US Rep, 17th Dist, NY, 62-, mem interstate & foreign com comt, subcomt on Oceanography, chmn, Select Comt on Outer Continental Shelf, Merchant Marine & fisheries comt & chmn subcomt on Coast Guard, coast & geodetic surv & navig, 73-; deleg, Dem Nat Conv, 64, parliamentarian, 68; deleg, NY State Const Conv, 67. Bus & Prof Pos: Pres, Cleveland Gen Transport Co, Inc, 57-65; mem bd dirs, Empire State Hwy Transportation Asn, 60-67; bd trustees, Asn of Graduates & mem bd visitors, US Mil Acad. Mil Serv: Enlisted as Pvt, Army, 44, commissioned 2nd Lt, 45, served with 9th Inf Regt in Korea; discharged as Capt, 56; Purple Heart; Distinguished Serv Cross; Bronze Star with V & Oak Leaf Cluster; Commendation Ribbon with Oak Leaf Cluster; Combat Inf Badge; Parachute Badge; Korean Serv Medal with 6 Battle Stars & Chungmu Distinguished Serv Medal. Mem: Am Legion; VFW; KofC. Relig: Catholic. Legal Res: Staten Island NY Mailing Add: 2187 Rayburn House Off Bldg Washington DC 20515

MURPHY, JOHN R
Nebr State Sen
Mailing Add: 110 E 37th St South Sioux City NE 68776

MURPHY, JOSEPH E, JR (D)
Chairperson, Kitsap Co Dem Comt, Wash
b Benson, Minn, Jan 26, 40; s Joseph Earl Murphy, Sr & Lorraine Francais Wolffe M; m 1958 to Geraldine M Heber; c James, Theresa, Joseph & Robert. Educ: Flathead Co High Sch, grad, 58; numerous elec courses. Polit & Govt Pos: Precinct committeeperson, Precinct 48, Bremerton, Wash, 70-72 & Fairview, Kitsap Co, 72-74; precinct committeeperson, Kitsap Co Dem Comt, 74-, chairperson, 74- Bus & Prof Pos: Deleg, Cent Labor Coun Kitsap Co 71-72; deleg & mem exec bd, 72-74; mem, Wash State Retarded Children Asn, 73- Mil Serv: Entered as E-1, Army Nat Guard, 56, released as E-3, Hq Battery, Mont Nat Guard, 56-62. Mem: Mason; IBEW. Relig: Episcopal; vestryman. Mailing Add: PO Box 48 Tracyton WA 98393

MURPHY, JOSEPH EDWARD, JR (DFL)
b Minneapolis, Minn, Mar 13, 30; s Joseph E Murphy & Ann Hynes M; m 1958 to Diana Kuske; c Michael & John. Educ: Princeton Univ, AB, 52. Polit & Govt Pos: Chmn, 38th Legis Dist Dem-Farmer-Labor Party, Minn, formerly. Bus & Prof Pos: Asst vpres, Northwestern Nat Bank; dir, Midwest Radio TV, Inc. Mil Serv: Entered as Pvt, Army, released as 2nd Lt, 56, after serv in 1st Cavalry Div, Far East. Mailing Add: 2116 W Lake Isles Blvd Minneapolis MN 55405

MURPHY, LEWIS CURTIS (R)
Mayor, Tucson, Ariz
b New York, NY, Nov 2, 33; s Henry Waldo Murphy & Elizabeth Curtis M; m 1957 to Carol Carney; c Grey Curtis, Timothy Carney & Elizabeth Zane. Educ: Univ Ariz, BS in Bus Admin, 55, Col Law, LLB, 61; Sigma Chi. Polit & Govt Pos: City Attorney, Tucson, Ariz, 70-71, Mayor, 71-; chmn, Ariz Mayors & Munic Officers for the Reelect of President Nixon, 72; alt deleg, Rep Nat Conv, 72; mem, Gov Adv Comt on Intergovt Affairs, 72-; mem adv comt, US Conf Mayors, 73- Mil Serv: Entered as 2nd Lt, Air Force, 55, released as 1st Lt, 58, after serv in 6th Tow Target Squadron, Tokyo, Japan, 56-58. Mem: State Bar of Ariz; Pima Co Bar Asn; Phi Alpha Delta. Relig: Protestant. Legal Res: 3134 Via Palos Verdes Tucson AZ 85716 Mailing Add: PO Box 5547 Tucson AZ 85703

MURPHY, LORENA V (D)
b Providence, RI, Jan 31, 23; d Richard Percy Ward & Viola T McCallum W; m 1943 to Walter F Murphy; c Lynne & Richard. Educ: RI Col, BEd, 42; X-6 Club, French Club, Womens Athletic Club. Polit & Govt Pos: Secy, RI Womens Dem Club, 54-56; campaign vol worker for Elec of Julius Michelson for Attorney Gen, formerly; deleg, Dem Nat Mid-Term Conf, 74. Bus & Prof Pos: Critic teacher, North Providence Sch Dept, 55- Mem: Am Fedn Teachers (bd dirs); North Providence Womens Dem League; RI Womens Dem Club. Relig: Catholic. Mailing Add: 9 Raymond Ave North Providence RI 02911

MURPHY, MARY CATHERINE (DFL)
Chairperson, St Louis Co Dem-Farmer-Labor Party, Minn
b Duluth, Minn; single. Educ: Col St Scholastica, BA in Hist, 61; Univ Minn, summers 64, 68 & 69; Macalester Col, summer 70; State Univ NY; W R Coe fel in Am studies, summer 73. Polit & Govt Pos: Alt deleg, Dem Nat Conv, 64, deleg, 68; deleg, Minn Dem State Conv, 66-74; mem, Minn Dem-Farmer-Labor State Cent Comt, 65-, deleg, 68-; mem, Minn Dem-Farmer-Labor State Exec Comt, 69-, dir, 72-74; chairwoman, Eighth Cong Dist Dem-Farmer-Labor Party, 69-72; mem, Nat Dem Credentials Comt, 72; deleg, Dem Mid Term Conf, 74; chairperson, St Louis Co Dem-Farmer-Labor Party, Minn, 74- Bus & Prof Pos: Teacher, Duluth Cent High Sch, 64-; vpres, Duluth AFL-CIO Cent Labor Body, 72- Mem: Alpha Delta Kappa; Duluth Fedn of Teachers; Am Fedn Teachers; Am Asn for UN; Am Asn Univ Women. Relig: Roman Catholic. Mailing Add: 6794 Arrowhead Rd Duluth MN 55811

MURPHY, MATTHEW J, JR (D)
NY State Assemblyman
Mailing Add: 139 S Transit St Lockport NY 14094

MURPHY, MAURICE THOMAS (MOSS) (D)
Pub Rels Dir, Allegheny Co Dem Comt, Pa
b Pittsburgh, Pa, Sept 21, 35; s William A Murphy & Phyllis Siarkowski M; m 1959 to Carol Anton; c Maurice & Mary, William, James, Margaret, Gerard & Patrick Cauley. Educ: Duquesne Univ, BA, 58, studies for Dr, 71; Univ Pittsburgh, 63; Harvard Univ, 65; Phi Kappa Theta. Polit & Govt Pos: Pub rels dir, Allegheny Co Dem Comt, Pa, 72-; pub rels consult, Pa State Dem Comt, 75-; pub rels consult, Pa Liquor Control Bd, 75- Mem: Duquesne Univ Alumni (vpres, 72-); Pa Athletic Asn; Allegheny Club; Pittsburgh Press Club; Duquesne Golf Club. Mailing Add: 2771 Beechwood Blvd Pittsburgh PA 15217

MURPHY, MICHAEL DOLAN (D)
Tenn State Rep
b Nashville, Tenn, Sept 15, 43; s Percy Carnes Murphy & Margaret Catherine Dolan M (deceased); single. Educ: Vanderbilt Univ, BA in Polit Sci, 66, Law Sch, currently; Honors Prog. Polit & Govt Pos: Intergovt coordr, Off Local Govt, Tenn, 69; Tenn State Rep, 55th Dist, 70-; mem nat bd, Young Dem Am. Bus & Prof Pos: Admin asst, Off Civic Concern, Nashville, Tenn, currently; consult, State Off Local Govt. Mil Serv: Entered as 2nd Lt, Army, 67, released as 1st Lt, 68, after serv as Co Comdr, Vietnam, 68; 1st Lt, Army Res, 69. Mem: Am Soc Pub Admin; Nat Soc State Legislators; ROA; KofC; Urban League. Relig: Catholic. Legal Res: 219 Lauderdale Ave Nashville TN 37205 Mailing Add: G11 War Memorial Bldg Nashville TN 37219

MURPHY, MIKE (D)
Okla State Sen
Mailing Add: State Capitol Oklahoma City OK 73105

MURPHY, MILDRED ARLENE (R)
Chairwoman, Morrow Co Rep Party, Ohio
b Upper Sandusky, Ohio, Oct 2, 07; d John Squire Crawford & Nettie Furrow C; m 1932 to William Lowell Murphy, MD; c James & twins, Maeve & Michael. Educ: Ohio Wesleyan Univ, BA, 27, MA, 38; Delta Sigma Rho; Kappa Delta Pi; Pi Beta Phi; Clionian. Polit & Govt Pos: Neighbor-to-Neighbor chmn, Morrow Co Rep Party, Ohio, 64, chairwoman, 68-72 & 75-, precinct committeewoman, 68- Bus & Prof Pos: Speech teacher & debate coach, St Clairsville, Ohio, 27-28, 29-33; asst speech dept & freshmen women's debate coach, Ohio Wesleyan Univ, 28-29; Ohio State High Sch Debate Bd, Ohio State Univ, 32-33. Mem: Tuberc & Respiratory Disease Asn; DAR; Colonial Dames of Seventeenth Century; Eastern Star; Wedgwood Int Asn. Relig: Methodist. Mailing Add: 275 N Cherry St Mt Gilead OH 43338

MURPHY, MORGAN FRANCIS (D)
US Rep, Ill
b Chicago, Ill, Apr 16, 32; s Morgan Francis Murphy & Anne Burns M; m 1959 to Charlene Jurgensen; c Morgan, III, Michelle & Constance. Educ: Northwestern Univ, BS in Speech, 55; DePaul Univ Law Sch, JD, 63; Sigma Chi. Polit & Govt Pos: Comnr, Liquor License Bur, Chicago, formerly; US Rep, Ill, 71- Bus & Prof Pos: Attorney-at-law. Mil Serv: 1st Lt, Marine Corps. Mem: Am, Ill & Chicago Bar Asns. Relig: Roman Catholic. Legal Res: 10416 S Bell Chicago IL 60643 Mailing Add: US House of Rep Washington DC 20515

MURPHY, NAPOLEON BONAPART (D)
Ark State Rep
b Crossett, Ark, Sept 16, 21; s Charles Edward Murphy & Isadee McGound M; m to Maxine James; c James N, Ila Sue (Mrs Campbell) & Stephen E. Educ: Crossett High Sch, 40. Polit & Govt Pos: Ark State Rep, 59-, sr mem joint legis audit comt, Ark House Rep, 59-, speaker protem, 67-, mem house mgt comt, 69-, vchmn judicial comt, 71-, chmn house forestry comt, currently. Bus & Prof Pos: Dealer, Murphy Ford Co, Hamburg, Ark, 53- Mem: Prairie Lodge 465; Sahara Temple; Ark Consistory; Nat Legislator Asn. Relig: Baptist. Legal Res: South Main Hamburg AR 71646 Mailing Add: PO Box 556 Hamburg AR 71646

MURPHY, PATRICK M (D)
Nev State Assemblyman
Mailing Add: 100 N Arlington Ave Apt 9-K Reno NV 89501

MURPHY, PETER CONNACHER, JR (R)
Finance Chmn, Ore Rep State Cent Comt
b Portland, Ore, Sept 17, 36; s Peter C Murphy, Sr & Dorothy Zingleman M; m 1960 to Marcella Jubitz; c Peter C, III, Mark, Amanda, Anna & Marcella. Educ: Univ Notre Dame, BA, 58. Polit & Govt Pos: Deleg, Rep Nat Conv, 68; finance chmn, Ore Rep State Cent Comt, 68-; mem, Secy of Interior's Adv Bd on Nat Parks, Hist Sites & Landmarks, currently. Bus & Prof Pos: Gen mgr, Murphy Co, Portland, Ore, 61-; dir, Pac Logging Cong, 64-67 & 69-72; pres, Eugene Bombers Football Club, 65-68; pres, Continental Football League-Western Div, 66-67; dir, Condominiums Northwest, Salem, 69-72; chmn, Lane Co Cath Charities, 70. Mil Serv: Airman 2/C, Air Nat Guard, Ore, discharged, 64. Mem: Rotary; CofC; Eugene Country Club. Honors & Awards: Perfect Attendance Award, High Sch. Relig: Roman Catholic. Legal Res: 2820 City View St Eugene OR 97405 Mailing Add: 2820 City View St Eugene OR 97405

MURPHY, RICHARD E (D)
b Auburn, NY, Mar 26, 31; s Joseph A Murphy & Mary V Krupa M; m 1964 to Ann Reardon; c Clare, Kathleen & Mary. Educ: Cornell Univ, MA. Polit & Govt Pos: Nat polit dir, Serv Employees Int Union, AFL-CIO, 64- Relig: Roman Catholic. Legal Res: 414 W Braddock Rd Alexandria VA 22302 Mailing Add: 900 17th St NW Washington DC 20006

MURPHY, RICHARD JAMES (D)
Mem-at-Lg, Dem Policy Coun, Dem Nat Comt
b Baltimore, Md, Oct 15, 29; s James Fitzgerald Murphy & Thais Victoria Brady M; single. Educ: Univ NC, AB in Econ, 51, grad study, 52; Phi Beta Kappa; Phi Eta Sigma; nat pres, US Nat Student Asn, 52-53; Order of the Golden Fleece; Order of the Old Well; pres, NC State Student Legis. Polit & Govt Pos: Mem, US Nat Comn on UNESCO, 51-53; exec dir young Dem div, Dem Nat Comt, 56-61, mem comt on polit orgn, 58-60, mem-at-lg, Dem Policy Coun, 71-; exec secy, Young Dem Clubs of Am, 56-61; dir arrangements, Dem Platform Comt & assoc dir, Advan Platform Hearings, Dem Nat Conv, 60; nat coordr, Young Voters for Kennedy-Johnson, 60; alt mem, President's Comt on Employee Mgt Coop, 61; mem, Subcabinet Group on Civil Rights, 61-63; mem, Inaugural Comts, 61-65; asst postmaster gen, 61-69; nat chmn, Young Dem Nat Conv, 64 & 65; alt mem cabinet comt, Staff Retirement Systs, 65; conv mgr & dir conv activities, Dem Nat Conv, 72; asst to chmn, McGovern for President Campaign, 72; mem arrangements comt, Dem Mid Term Conf, 74; mem, Bi-Partisan Comn on Financing Nat Conv, 74. Bus & Prof Pos: Exec consult, Harbridge House, Washington, DC, 69-71; vpres, Warner Cable TV Corp, NY, 73- Mil Serv: Entered as Pvt, Army, 53, released as Pfc, 55, after serv in Army Ord Corps, Aberdeen Proving Grounds; Good Conduct & Nat Defense Medals. Publ: Assoc ed, Democratic Digest, 57-60; Crisis in public employee relations, Bur Nat Affairs, 11/70; Reflections on leaving public service, Pub Admin Rev, 11/69. Mem: Indust Rels Research Asn; Nat Civil Serv League. Honors & Awards: William A Jump Found Award for Meritorious Achievement in Pub Admin, 62; Benjamin Franklin Award, US Post Off Dept, 66; Award of Merit, US Treasury Dept, 68; John E Fogarty Pub Personnel Award, 69. Relig: Unitarian. Mailing Add: 9912 Harrogate Rd Bethesda MD 20034

MURPHY, RICHARD WILLIAM
US Ambassador to Syria
b Boston, Mass, July 29, 29; s John Deneen Murphy & Jane Diehl M; m 1955 to Anne Herrick Cook; c Katherine, Elizabeth & Richard. Educ: Philip Exeter Acad, 47; Harvard Col, BA, 51; Emmanuel Col, AB, 53. Polit & Govt Pos: Country dir, Arabian Peninsula Affairs, 70-71; Ambassador, Mauritania, 71-74 & Syria, 74- Mil Serv: Entered as Pvt, Army, 53, released as Pfc, 55. Honors & Awards: Superior Honor Award, Dept State, 69. Legal Res: 5610 Overlea Rd Sumner MD Mailing Add: Damascus Dept of State Washington DC 20520

MURPHY, ROBERT M (D)
Okla State Sen
Mailing Add: State Capitol Oklahoma City OK 73105

MURPHY, RODERICK PATRICK (R)
Chmn, Brimfield Rep Town Comt, Mass
b Cambridge, Mass, Mar 10, 39; s Thomas Edward Murphy & Helen Milan M; m 1962 to Jean Marie Michaud; c Jennifer Marie, Erin Maura, Deirdre Ann & Roderick Patrick, Jr. Educ: Boston State Col, 57-59. Polit & Govt Pos: Deleg, Mass Rep State Conv, 70 & 72; chmn, Brimfield Rep Town Comt, Mass, 70-; treas, Brimfield Citizen's Alliance, 72-; mem, Brimfield Housing Authority, 73-; dir, Worcester Co Rep Club, Mass; mem, Brimfield Hwys Comt, 75- Bus & Prof Pos: Sales mgr, COZ Chem Corp, Northbridge, 69-; proprietor, Windham Auto Supply, Putnam, Conn, 73- Mil Serv: Entered as Pvt, Army, 60, released as Pfc, 60, after serv in 1st Army Res Prog, 6 months; Res, 26th Yankee Div. Publ: Polit columnist for Palmer J Register, Mass, 72- Mem: St Joan of Arc Sch Comt, Southbridge; Soc Plastic Engrs; John Boyle O'Reilly Irish Am Club; Jaycees. Relig: Roman Catholic; Lector, St Christopher's Roman Cath Church, 70-, mem liturgy comt, 74- Mailing Add: Little Alum Pond Rd Brimfield MA 01010

MURPHY, ROGER P (R)
Wis State Sen
b Lancaster, Wis, Oct 17, 23; s Frank E Murphy (deceased) & Alice Petty M; m 1964 to Arlene Jane Laubenheimer; c Margaret Jane, Mark Patrick & Thomas Earl. Educ: Univ Wis, BS, 48, Law Sch, LLB, 51; Chi-Phi. Polit & Govt Pos: Pres, Wis Fedn Young Rep, 57-59; chmn, Region VIII, Nat Fedn Young Rep, 59-61; Waukesha Co Dist Attorney, 61-71; mem, State of Wis Crime Comn, 66-69; Wis State Sen, 33rd Dist, 71- Bus & Prof Pos: Pres, Wis Asn Dist Attorneys, 66-67. Mil Serv: Entered as Cadet, Army Air Corps, 42, released as 2nd Lt, 45, after serv in 306 Bomb Group, ETO, 44-45; Air Medal with Three Oak Leaf Clusters; ETO Medal & others. Mem: Am & Wis Bar Asns; Waukesha Co Rep Party; Am Acad Trial Lawyers; Waukesha Elks Lodge 400. Relig: Protestant. Mailing Add: 1012 Hawthorn Circle Waukesha WI 53186

MURPHY, RUPERT LEO
b Bromville, Ga, July 27, 09; s Luther H Murphy & Ardelia Woodruff M; m 1931 to Marion Kerlin; c Rupert L. Educ: Atlanta Law Sch, LLB, 38, LLM, 39; Delta Theta Phi; Delta Nu Alpha. Polit & Govt Pos: Pres & chmn, Gov S Traffic League, formerly; Comnr, Interstate Com Comn, 55- Bus & Prof Pos: Correspondent & rate clerk, Atlanta Freight Tariff Bur, Ga, 25-29; asst traffic mgr, Fulton Bag & Cotton Mills, Atlanta, 29-42; traffic mgr & attorney, Ga-Ala Textile Traffic Asn, Atlanta, 42-55. Mem: Am Bar Asn; Asn Interstate Com Comn Practitioners; Am Soc Traffic & Transportation; Nat Indust Traffic League; Mason. Relig: Presbyterian. Legal Res: Apt B-114 140O S Joyce St Arlington VA 22202 Mailing Add: Interstate Com Comn 12th St & Constitution Ave Washington DC 20423

MURPHY, TERRENCE DRAKE (R)
Nat Committeeman, Colo Young Rep
b Denver, Colo, Apr 26, 40; s Melven R Murphy & Kathleen Drake; m 1963 to Susan A McFarland; c Kissane, Kathleen & Megan. Educ: Colo State Univ, BS, 63. Polit & Govt Pos: Chmn, Douglas Co Young Rep Club, 68-70; state bd mem, Colo Young Rep, 70-, nat committeeman, 73-; committeeman Precinct Five, Douglas Co Rep Party, 70-75, co chmn, 75- Bus & Prof Pos: Dept head nondestructive testing, Gates Rubber Co, Denver, Colo, 67-74, shift supt trucking, 74- Mil Serv: Entered as 2nd Lt, Army, 63, released as 1st Lt, 65, after serv in 5th Inf Div, CONARC, 63-65; Capt, Army Res; currently; Silver Award, Excellence in Competition. Mem: Am Ord Asn; Am Soc Animal Sci; Boy Scouts; Am Soc Biol Sci. Mailing Add: PO Box 486 Castle Rock CO 80104

MURPHY, TERRY LAURENCE (D)
Mont State Sen
b Butte, Mont, Dec 5, 42; s Terence Joseph Murphy & Genevieve Watson M; single. Educ: Willow Creek High Sch, Mont, grad. Polit & Govt Pos: Mem, Whitehall Sch Bd, Mont, 66-72; Mont State Rep, 71-72; Mont State Sen, 75- Bus & Prof Pos: Dir, Mont Farmers Union, 68- Mem: Nat Farmers Union. Honors & Awards: Outstanding Conservationist, Jefferson Valley Conserv Dist, Mont, 73. Relig: Protestant. Mailing Add: Cardwell MT 59721

MURPHY, THOMAS BAILEY (D)
Speaker, Ga House of Rep
b Bremen, Ga, Mar 10, 24; s William Harvey Murphy & Leita Jones M; m 1946 to Agnes Bennett; c Michael L, Martha L, Marjorie Lynn & Mary June. Educ: NGa Col, 43; Univ Ga Law Sch, 49. Polit & Govt Pos: Chmn, Bremen Bd Educ, Ga; Ga State Rep, 61-, Admin Floor Leader, Ga House Rep, 67-71, Speaker Pro Tem, 71-74, Speaker, 74- Bus & Prof Pos: Attorney. Mil Serv: Navy, 43-46. Relig: Baptist. Mailing Add: PO Box 163 Bremen GA 30110

MURPHY, THOMAS J (R)
NY State Assemblyman
b Syracuse, NY, May 25, 30; s James A Murphy & Arlene Richman M; m 1954 to Mary Jane Dadey; c Thomas, William, James, Martin, Timothy, Vincent, Margaret & Martha. Educ: LeMoyne Col, 48-51; Syracuse Univ Col Law, LLD. Polit & Govt Pos: Supvr, Onondaga Co Bd Supvr, 65-67; legislator, Onondaga Co Legis, 68-70; NY State Assemblyman, 71- Bus & Prof Pos: Partner law firm, Deegan, Murphy & Dadey, Syracuse, NY, 60- Mem: NY State & Onondaga Co Bar Asns; Canal Museum, Onondaga Co (trustee); Kiwanis; LeMoyne Col Alumni Asn; Syracuse Univ Col Law Alumni Asn. Relig: Roman Catholic. Mailing Add: 314 Broadview Dr Syracuse NY 13215

MURPHY, WILLIAM MALCOLM, JR (D)
Del State Sen
b Americus, Ga, Dec 18, 27; s William Malcolm Murphy & Gussie Dell Harbuck M; single. Educ: George Washington Univ; Corcoran Sch Fine Arts; Ford Mkt Inst, New York, 62-68; Wesley Col, 68. Polit & Govt Pos: Vpres, Kent Co Young Dem, Del, 60-61, pres, 65-66, treas, 66-67; mem, Kent Co Dem Comt, 62-72; alt nat committeeman, Young Dem Am, 63-65, nat committeeman, 65-68; alt deleg, Dem Nat Conv, 64 & 68; mem, Dem State Comt, 66-; pres & founder, 31st Dist Dem Club, 68-69, bd dir, 69; dir, Kent Co Civil Defense, 69-71; Del State Sen, 18th Dist, 73- Bus & Prof Pos: Vpres & asst mgr, Murphy's Hardware, 64-; pres, Kennersley Marina & Yacht Club, 65-68. Mil Serv: Entered as Pvt, Army, 46, released as T/Sgt, 48, after serv in Am Theater. Mem: Prof Sales Mgrs; Kent Island Yacht Club; Kennersley Yacht Club; Moose; Del Arts Soc, Inc (treas & mem bd dirs). Relig: Presbyterian. Mailing Add: 1437 Nathaniel Mitchell Rd Dover DE 19901

MURPHY, WILLIAM R (INDEPENDENT)
Va State Deleg
Mailing Add: 9255 Lee Ave Manassas VA 22110

MURPHY, WILLIAM T (D)
b Chicago, Ill, Aug 7, 99; m to Rose McInerney; c William T, Jr, John P & Rosemary. Educ: Loyola Univ Law Sch, LLB, 26; Delta Theta Phi. Polit & Govt Pos: Alderman, Chicago City Coun, Ill, 35-59; Dem ward committeeman, 17th Ward, Chicago, 40-63; deleg, Dem Nat Conv, 44-56; US Rep, Ill, 59-71; mem, Can-US Interparliamentary Group, 60-68; mem NATO Interparliamentary Group, 16th Assembly, The Hague. Bus & Prof Pos: Prof engr; land surveyor; lawyer. Mil Serv: World War I. Honors & Awards: Commemorative Medal, Nat Assembly of SVietnam, 63; Tenth Commemorative Medal, Assembly of Captive Nations, 63; Commemorative Medal of the Knesset, Jerusalem, Israel, 66; rep of the Speaker of US House of Rep at dedication of new parliament bldg, Jerusalem, Israel, 66. Mailing Add: 4062 W 115th St Chicago IL 60653

MURRAH, WILLIAM NOLAN, JR (R)
Rep Nat Committeeman, Ga
b Columbus, Ga, Oct 27, 34; s William Nolan Murrah & Mary Huguley M; m 1955 to Barbara Ann Greene; c William Nolan & Lee Allan. Educ: Univ Ga, 3 years; Emory Univ Law Sch, AB & LLB; Harvard Law Sch, 1 year; SAE; Phi Delta Phi. Polit & Govt Pos: Chmn, Young Rep Club, Muscogee Co, Ga, 64-66; chmn, Muscogee Co Rep Comt, 66-68; chmn, Nixon-Agnew Comt, 68; deleg, Rep Nat Conv, 68; chmn, Third Cong Dist Rep Party, 68-71; co-chmn, Columbus Comt for Reelec of the President & chmn, Columbus Bus & Indust Comt, 72; Rep Nat Committeeman, Ga, 72- Bus & Prof Pos: Law asst, Supreme Court of Ga, 61; vpres, secy & gen counsel, Royal Crown Cola Co, 61- Mil Serv: Entered as 2nd Lt, Air Force, 58, released as Capt, 61, after serv in 3800 ABW, Maxwell AFB, Ala, 59-61. Mem: Am & Ga Bar Asns; Am Judicature Soc. Honors & Awards: Outstanding Young Man, Ga, 69. Relig: Baptist. Mailing Add: 1829 Park Dr Columbus GA 31906

MURRAY, CHARLES EDWARD (D)
Tenn State Rep
b Decherd, Tenn, Aug 16, 28; s Richard Oliver Murray & Patty Moffatt M; m 1969 to Sandra Gail Fields. Educ: Univ of the South, 46-49; Mid Tenn State Univ, BS, 51; YMCA Night Law Sch, JD, 65. Polit & Govt Pos: Asst dir, Tenn Aeronaut Comn, 65-67; Tenn State Rep, 15th Dist, 70-72, 49th Dist, 72- Bus & Prof Pos: Partner, Hickerson & Murray Law Firm, currently. Mil Serv: Navy, 51-53. Mem: Am Legion; Quiet Birdmen; Franklin Co CofC (dir, 71-). Relig: Protestant. Mailing Add: 101 Eighth Ave SW Winchester TN 37398

MURRAY, CLIFFORD GORDON, JR (D)
Chmn, Josephine Co Dem Cent Comt, Ore
b Los Angeles, Calif, Apr 21, 32; s Clifford Gordon Murray, Sr & Thelma Mae Kennison M; m 1963 to Pauline Meade Shier; c Melanie Ann, Michael Timothy & Diana Lynn. Educ: High sch, grad, 50; bus courses. Polit & Govt Pos: Vchmn, Dist 7 Sch Bd, 69-, chmn, 72-73; precinct committeeman, 70-; chmn, Josephine Co Libr Bd, 71-; treas, Josephine Co Dem Cent Comt, 71-72, chmn, 72-; mem, Josephine Co Bd Comnrs, 72. Bus & Prof Pos: Dir, Grants Pass & Josephine Co CofC; sports dir, KAGI Radio Grants Pass, Ore, 62-69, sales mgr, 64-69; sta mgr, KROW Radio, Dallas, Ore, 69; sports dir, KAJO Radio, Grants Pass, 69- Mil Serv: Entered as Seaman Recruit, Navy, 55, released as PO 2/C, 57, after serv in Cruiser Div 1, Pac Fleet, 56-57. Publ: Ed, Cruise Book, USS Bremerton, 57; Time out for sports, Grants Pass Bull, 67-68. Mem: Nat & Ore Sch Bd Asns; Ore Libr Asn; Elks; Josephine Co Babe Ruth League. Honors & Awards: Spoke Award, Grants Pass Jaycees, 64; Citizenship Award, Grants Pass Kiwanis, 68; Distinguished Serv Award, Grants Pass Jaycees, 69; Grants Pass Man of the Year, 72; Named State Judge, Voice of Democracy, VFW, 72. Relig: Grace Bible Church. Legal Res: 919 NE 11th St Grants Pass OR 97526 Mailing Add: PO Box 230 Grants Pass OR 97526

MURRAY, FRANK (D)
Secy of State, Mont
b Butte, Mont, Feb 28, 07; s Bernard Murray (deceased) & Harriet Tracey M (deceased); m 1935 to Geraldine Alice Jones. Educ: High sch & various home study courses. Polit & Govt Pos: Dep clerk & recorder, Silver Bow Co, Butte, Mont, 33-37; trustee, Sch Dist 1, Butte, 37-38; state store mgr, Mont Liquor Control Bd, 37-39; clerk, Mont Supreme Court, 42-57; deleg, Dem Nat Conv, 52, 64 & 68; Secy of State, Mont, 57- Mem: Nat Asn Secretaries of State; United Commercial Travelers of Am; Elks; Eagles. Legal Res: 825 Hauser Blvd Helena MT 59601 Mailing Add: State Capitol Helena MT 59601

MURRAY, FRANK JOHN (D)
b Bangor, Maine, Mar 12, 49; s Robert Emmett Murray & Laura Guite M; single. Educ: Univ Maine, Orono, BS, 72. Polit & Govt Pos: Deleg, Maine State Dem Conv, 70 & 72; coordr, Maine Young Dem, 70-, pres, 71-72; Maine State Rep, 71-74; deleg, Dem Nat Conv, 72. Mem: Nat Soc State Legislators; Bangor Jaycees. Honors & Awards: Youngest Mem of Maine Legis, 71-72. Relig: Roman Catholic. Mailing Add: 215 Maple St Bangor ME 04401

MURRAY, FRED E (R)
NH State Rep
Mailing Add: Box 178 Peterborough NH 03458

MURRAY, GEORGE E (R)
Mo State Sen
b St Louis, Mo, Aug 9, 23; s George E Murray & Marie C Straub M; m 1948 to Elizabeth Russell Cooper; c Elizabeth, George, III, Peggy & Mary Kathleen. Educ: Wash Univ, LLB & BS in BA, 48; Delta Theta Phi; Beta Theta Pi. Polit & Govt Pos: City Attorney, Fenton, Mo, 57-66; mem, Gov Comn Dent Care of Handicapped Children, 62-; Mo State Rep, 90th Dist, 67-74; Mo State Sen, 26th Dist, 75- Bus & Prof Pos: Pvt law practice, currently. Mil

Serv: Pvt, Army, 42-44. Mem: Elks; Am Legion. Relig: Catholic. Mailing Add: 3 Williamsburg Rd Creve Coeur MO 63141

MURRAY, HYDE H **(R)**
b Iola, Wis, Aug 2, 30; s Reid F Murray & Lyla G Hermanson M; m 1957 to Nancy Vander Hyde; c Reid James & Merri Carol. Educ: Univ Wis, BS in Agr, 52; Georgetown Univ Law Sch, LLB, 57; Alpha Zeta. Polit & Govt Pos: Attorney, Off Gen Counsel, Dept Agr, 57-58; counsel, Comt on Agr, US House Rep, 58-; mem platform staff, Rep Nat Conv, 64, 68 & 72. Mil Serv: Entered as 2nd Lt, Army, 52, released as 1st Lt, 54, after serv in Corps of Engrs; US Okinawa & Korea, 53-54; Capt (Ret), US Army Res; Korean Serv, Nat Defense & UN Medals. Mem: Fed Bar Asn; US Capitol Hist Soc; Cong Staff Club; Mason. Honors & Awards: Cong Secy of Year, Roll Call Newspaper, 67. Relig: Lutheran. Mailing Add: 432 Rosier Rd Oxon Hill MD 20022

MURRAY, JAMES B **(D)**
Va State Deleg
Mailing Add: Box 125 Earlysville VA 22936

MURRAY, JAMES W **(R)**
NH State Rep
Mailing Add: RFD 5 Wentworth Cove Rd Laconia NH 03246

MURRAY, JOHN HIRAM **(R)**
b Leavenworth, Kans, Jan 28, 14; s Roy Murray & Floy Burt M; m 1939 to Dorothy Lord; c Richard Lord & John Hiram, Jr. Educ: Univ Kans, LLB, 38, JD, 68; Delta Chi; Phi Alpha Delta. Polit & Govt Pos: Police judge, Leavenworth, Kans, 39-41, co attorney, 43-49; city attorney, Easton, 49; Kans State Rep, 49-57; deleg, Rep Nat Conv, 52; city attorney, Lansing, Kans, 57-71; Kans State Sen, 57-65; Comnr, Perry Dam, 64; city attorney, Basehor, Kans, 65; chmn, Leavenworth Co Rep Party, 66-74. Bus & Prof Pos: Law practice, 38-; attorney, Citizens' Mutual Bldg & Loan Asn, 49- Mil Serv: Entered as Ens, Navy, 44, released as Lt(jg), 46, after serv in Amphibious Forces, Pac Theater. Mem: Am Bar Asn; Am Judicature Soc; Lions; Mason (Past Grand Master, Kans, 61, mem, Kans Masonic Home Bd). Relig: Presbyterian; elder. Mailing Add: 1020 S Fourth St Leavenworth KS 66048

MURRAY, JOHN JOSEPH, JR **(R)**
Mayor, San Mateo, Calif
b San Francisco, Calif, July 18, 14; s John Joseph Murray, Sr & Margaret Rose Flaherty M; m 1940 to Hallie M Butler; c John Joseph, III, Jeanne Maureen & William. Educ: St Joseph's Col (Calif), AA magna cum laude, 34; Univ San Francisco, AB, 37; Univ Calif; Golden Gate Col, postgrad courses. Polit & Govt Pos: Mem staff, Dept of Social Welfare, Calif, 38-39; mem staff, San Francisco Pub Welfare Dept, 39-41; city councilman, San Mateo, 65, vmayor, 66-67 & 69-72, mayor, 67-68 & 72-, mem, San Mateo Coun of Mayors, chmn, 72-; mem exec comt, Regional Planning Comt, Bay Front Ad Hoc Subcomt, chmn, San Mateo Co Environ Qual Control Comt, deleg, Asn Bay Area Govt, 68; mem, San Mateo Co Rep Finance Comt, 69-70; mem, Rep State Cent Comt Calif, 69-70. Bus & Prof Pos: Columnist, San Francisco Cath Monitor & The Leader, 39-46; coordr, Bethlehem Steel Corp, San Francisco, 41-45; vpres, John J Murray Co, Inc, 46-54, pres, 54-68; vpres & exec dir, Peninsula Mfrs Asn, San Mateo, 68-71; sales exec, San Mateo Assocs, 72- Publ: Contrib, San Mateo Times, 61-, Burlingame Advan Star, 61-, Serra Int Mag, 61- & Western Cities Rev, 68- Mem: Painting & Decorating Contractors Asn; Univ San Francisco Alumni Asn; South San Mateo Home Owner's Asn; San Mateo Toyonaka Sister City Asn (bd dirs, 63-); Elks. Honors & Awards: Dist Gov Plaque & Int Off Plaque, Serra Int; Pres Award, St Mary's Col, Moraga, Calif; KofC Citizenship Plaque; Church of Jesus Christ of Latter-day Saints Brotherhood Award. Relig: Catholic. Mailing Add: 257 Del Mar Way San Mateo CA 94403

MURRAY, JOHN S **(R)**
Wash State Sen
Mailing Add: 8 W Roy St Seattle WA 98119

MURRAY, JOHN STEVENSON **(R)**
Iowa State Sen
b Ames, Iowa, Mar 22, 39; s William Gordon Murray & Mildred Furniss M; m 1973 to Robin Ruhe; c David Crighton. Educ: Cornell Univ, AB, 61; Columbia Univ, MA, 62; Univ Iowa, JD, 68; Phi Beta Kappa; Phi Kappa Phi; Order of the Coif; Sigma Phi Soc. Polit & Govt Pos: Exec asst to Gov Ray, Iowa, 70-72; Iowa State Sen, 21st Dist, 73- Bus & Prof Pos: Ed, Iowa Law Rev, 67-68; assoc attorney, Cleary, Gottlieb, Steen & Hamilton, New York, 68-70; attorney-at-law, Ames, Iowa, 72- Mil Serv: Entered as Pfc, Off Cand Sch, Marine Corps, 62, released as 1st Lt, 65. Publ: Adequate appellate review for indigents & Presidential Election Campaign Fund Act of 1966, Iowa Law Rev, 67. Mem: Iowa Bar Asn. Relig: Presbyterian. Mailing Add: 612 Stanton Ave Ames IA 50010

MURRAY, JOSEPH RENOLD **(D)**
SC State Rep
b Charleston, SC, June 17, 33; s Sam Murray & Jannie Jordan M; m 1965 to Carmen Simpson; c Anita Prestina, Michelle Nicole, Yvonne Renee & Joseph Renold, Jr. Educ: Univ Md, 61-63; Citadel, 68-69. Polit & Govt Pos: SC State Rep, 75- Mil Serv: Entered as Pvt, Air Force, 51, released as S/Sgt, 71, after serv in Med Servs, Europe & Continental US; Length of Serv Award with Four Oak Leaf Clusters; Good Conduct Medal with One Oak Leaf Cluster; Outstanding Unit Award with Two Oak Leaf Clusters. Mem: Am Legion, Herbert U Mack Post 241; United Retired Vet Am. Legal Res: 83 Hester St Charleston SC 29403 Mailing Add: PO Box 321 Charleston SC 29402

MURRAY, MARY DEPASQUALE **(D)**
VChmn, Milford Dem Town Comt, Mass
b Providence, RI, Feb 27, 91; d Antonio DePasquale & Maria Vitale D; wid of Judge William A Murray; c William A, Mary Norma (Mrs Thomas E Ervin) & Joseph E, MD. Educ: Framingham State Teachers Col, dipl, 11; Boston Univ & Harvard Col. Polit & Govt Pos: Trustee, Wrentham State Sch, Mass, 14 years; trustee, Belchertown State Sch, 1 term & Westboro State Hosp, 2 terms; deleg, Dem Nat Conv, 24-72. Bus & Prof Pos: Pub sch teacher, Milford, Mass, 11-14, eve sch teacher, 19-24; pub sch teacher, Hopedale, Mass, pvt sch teacher, 20-22. Mem: Cath Womans Club; Quinshipaug Womans Club; Ital Hist Soc of Boston; Am Legion Auxiliary; Ital Womans Club, Boston. Honors & Awards: Resolutions Award for 50 consecutive years as a State Committeewoman in Mass, Mass State Senate, 72. Relig: Catholic. Mailing Add: 19 Grant St Milford MA 01757

MURRAY, MICHAEL WEBSTER **(D)**
Mem Exec Comt, Ariz Dem Party
b Sioux Rapids, Iowa, July 9, 35; s Frank Murray & Myrna Webster M; m 1971 to Dorothy Banegas; c Michael J. Educ: St John's Univ (Minn), BS, 57; Univ Ariz, JD, 64; Phi Delta Phi. Polit & Govt Pos: Dem precinct committeeman, Pima Co, Ariz, 64-; pres, Young Dem of Gtr Tucson, 68; magistrate, City of Tucson, 68; deleg, Dem Nat Conv, 68; referee juv court, Pima Co Superior Court, 68-; mem exec comt, Ariz Dem Party, 68-; mem, Ariz Comn Party Struct & Deleg Selection, 69. Bus & Prof Pos: Attorney-at-law, Tucson, 64-; pres Southwestern Fiduciaries, Inc, Tucson, 69- Mil Serv: Entered as Pvt, Marine Corps, 56, released as 1st Lt, 60, after serv in 1st & 3rd Marine Div, 57-60; Res, 66-, Maj; Am Defense Ribbon. Mem: Am Trial Lawyers Asn (pres, Tucson chap); ROA (vpres); Young Dem of Ariz; Nucleus Club; Am Legion. Relig: Catholic. Legal Res: 321 E Glenn Tucson AZ 85708 Mailing Add: 705 Lawyers Title Bldg Tucson AZ 85701

MURRAY, RICHARD CHARLES **(D)**
b Greensburg, Pa, Dec 15, 49; s Clifton Coursen Murray & Betty Kuhn M; single. Educ: Indiana Univ Pa, BA cum laude, 72; Ohio State Univ, MA, 74; Pi Gamma Mu; Univ Senate. Polit & Govt Pos: Mem, Indiana Co Dem Exec Comt, Pa, 71-72; deleg, Dem Nat Conv, 72; legis intern, Ohio State Rep Barney Quilter, Majority Floor Leader, Ohio House of Rep, 72-73, legis asst, Speaker Pro Tem, currently. Honors & Awards: Leadership Trophy, Indiana Univ Pa Student Govt, 72; Contributing Effort, Red Cross for help in Pa flood relief, 72. Relig: Protestant. Mailing Add: 1214 Ashland Ave Columbus OH 43212

MURRAY, ROGER GOODMAN, JR **(D)**
Tenn State Rep
b Jackson, Tenn, Mar 3, 31; s Roger Goodman Murray & Agnes Mary Bradford M; stepmother, Ethel K; m to Judith Ligon; c Thomas David, Roger Goodman, III, Mona Melissa, Luanne & William Johnson. Educ: Union Univ, BA; Cumberland Sch Law, LLB; Alpha Tau Omega; Delta Theta Phi. Polit & Govt Pos: Asst city attorney, Jackson, Tenn, 63-67; Tenn State Rep, 73rd Dist, 73- Bus & Prof Pos: Attorney, Jackson, Tenn, 60-; pres & chmn bd, Murray Guard, Inc, 67- Mil Serv: Entered as Pvt, Army, serv in Signal Corps. Mem: Jackson Exchange Club; VFW; Moose Lodge; Am Legion. Relig: Methodist. Legal Res: 30 Royal Oaks Pl Jackson TN 38301 Mailing Add: 425 E Baltimore St Jackson TN 38301

MURRAY, THAD S **(INDEPENDENT)**
b Norfolk, Va, Oct 17, 19; s Charles B Murray & Blanche Thomas Spiers M; m 1949 to Nan Astin M; c Thad Neil & Stephen Kent. Educ: Randolph-Macon Col. Polit & Govt Pos: Admin asst, US Rep Porter Hardy, Jr, Va, 47-69; exec asst to US Sen Spong, Va, 69-73; admin asst, US Rep Robert W Daniel, Jr, Va, 73- Bus & Prof Pos: Off mgr, Norfolk Br, Giffels & Valet, Architects & Engrs, 42-44; dist mgr, Mass Mutual Life Ins Co, Norfolk, 44-45; publicity dir, Am Red Cross, Norfolk, 45-46; vpres, James & Murray, Inc, Real Estate & Ins, 45-47. Mem: Jaycees; Norfolk YMCA. Relig: Methodist. Mailing Add: 10513 Cedar Ave Fairfax VA 22030

MURRAY, THOMAS B **(D)**
Wis State Rep
Mailing Add: 1308 N 13th St Superior WI 54880

MURRELL, CECIL BOYD **(R)**
Mem, Rep State Cent Comt Calif
b Lebanon, Ky, Sept 11, 09; s Richard Murrell & Mary Carter M; m 1946 to Ursula Elizabeth Pruitt; c Mary Virginia (Mrs Williams). Educ: Univ Calif, Los Angeles, AB, 33; Hastings Col Law, 34-37. Polit & Govt Pos: Hearing examr, Los Angeles Police Dept, Calif, 57-; pres, Coun of Orgn Against Vice, Los Angeles, 60-; Rep nominee for Calif State Sen, 29th Sen Dist; mem adv comt, Dist Attorney of Los Angeles Co, Calif, 64-; mem, Rep Assocs, 65-68; mem exec comt, Los Angeles Co Rep Cent Comt, 66-68; mem, Rep State Cent Comt Calif, 66-; pres, Cosmopolitan Rep Voters Club, Inc, 68- Bus & Prof Pos: Sr partner, Murrell & Embry Real Estate Co, 46-; gen agt, Golden State Mutual Ins Co, Los Angeles, 57-60; publisher, Los Angeles Sun, 61-62. Mil Serv: Entered as Steward, Merchant Marine, 41, released as Lt(jg), 46, after serv in Far East Area. Publ: Series of articles in Los Angeles Times, Los Angeles Herald-Examr, neighborhood newspapers & some Negro publ, 60- Mem: Alumni Asn Univ Calif, Los Angeles; United Serv Orgn (bd dirs); NAACP. Honors & Awards: Cert of Appreciation, Boys' Clubs of Am, 66; Plaque of Appreciation for sponsoring Olympic Qualifying Trip of Los Angeles Group; other plaques for outstanding community serv. Relig: Presbyterian. Mailing Add: 2905 1/2 S Western Ave Los Angeles CA 90018

MURRY, JAMES WESLEY **(D)**
b Billings, Mont, Feb 6, 35; s Boyd Raymond Murry & Athleen Cowan M; m 1954 to Arlene Rowlan; c Patrick Lee, Cathy Ann, Timothy Kelly, Michael Sean & Kieran Thomas. Educ: Eastern Mont Col, 53-54 & 58-60. Polit & Govt Pos: Mem bd, Labor Appeals, Mont Dept Labor, 70-; deleg, Dem Nat Mid-Term Conf, 74. Bus & Prof Pos: Pres, Oil, Chem & Atomic Workers Int Union, Local 2-443, 65-66; dir polit educ, Mont State AFL-CIO, 66-68, exec secy, 68- Mem: US Savings Bond Drive Vol (Mont State Labor Chmn); Mont Comt for the Humanities; Rocky Mountain Labor Sch (mem bd controls, 68-); Nat AFL-CIO (adv comt to State & Local Cent Bodies, 70-); Am Trade Union Coun for Histadrut (co-chmn, 73-). Mailing Add: 3780 N Montana Ave Helena MT 59601

MURRY, OZELLA MAY **(D)**
VChmn, Phelps Co Dem Cent Comt, Mo
b High Gate, Mo, Mar 12, 00; d William S Murry & Belle McKinney M; div. Educ: St James High Sch, 4 years. Polit & Govt Pos: Committeewoman, Ward II, St James, Mo, 12 years; secy to State Rep Richard Smallwood, Dist 127, 66-; pres, Womens Dem Club, two terms; vchmn, Phelps Co Dem Cent Comt, 71- Mem: Eastern Star (Matron, 39). Relig: Baptist. Mailing Add: 602 S Jefferson St James MO 65559

MURTHA, JOHN PATRICK **(D)**
US Rep, Pa
b New Martinsville, WVa, June 17, 32; s John Patrick Murtha & Mary Edna Ray M; m 1955 to Joyce Bell; c Donna Sue, John Mark & Patrick Clark. Educ: Washington & Jefferson Col, 50-51; Univ Pittsburgh, BA, 61; Indiana Univ Pa, 62-65. Polit & Govt Pos: Dem nominee for US Rep, 68 & 74; Pa State Rep, 72nd Legis Dist, 69-74; US Rep, Pa, 75- Bus & Prof Pos: Mgr, Johnstown Minute Car Wash, 58-62, pres, 62-70; secy-treas & chmn bd, US Nat Car Wash, 66- Mil Serv: Entered as Pvt, Marine Corps, 52, released as 1st Lt, 55; Lt Col, Marine Corps Res, 68, served in SVietnam, 66-67; Am Spirit Honor Medal; Bronze Star; Two Purple Hearts; Vietnamese Cross of Gallantry; Presidential Unit Citation. Publ: Series of six articles,

Jungle Warfare, Res Marine, 61; Combat intelligence in Vietnam, Marine Corps Gazette, 1/68. Mem: Pa Wood Coun Boy Scouts (bd dirs); Community Nursing Serv (bd dirs); Mercy Hosp (bd dirs); Conemaugh Valley ROA. Mailing Add: 109 Colgate Ave Johnstown PA 15905

MUSCH, DONALD JOHN **(R)**
b Muskegon, Mich, Apr 17, 32; s Jacob E Musch & Ruth Bousema M; m 1958 to Salome Tanner; c Melissa Salome. Educ: Univ Colo, Boulder, BA, 58; Univ NC, Chapel Hill, LLB, 61; Univ London, cert African Law, 63; Phi Delta Phi; Int Rels Ceub; Ger Hon Club. Polit & Govt Pos: Mem, Loudoun Co Rep Comt, Va, 71-72; admin asst to US Sen William L Scott, Va, 73- Bus & Prof Pos: Foreign rep, Oceana Publ Inc, Dobbs Ferry, NY, 63-65; foreign rep, T H Miner & Assocs, Inc, Chicago, Ill, 65-68; Int Group, US CofC, Washington, DC, 68-72. Mil Serv: Entered as A/S, Navy, 51, released as CT2, 55, after serv in Naval Security Group, Washington, DC & London, Eng, 51-55. Publ: Kenya industrial court, EAfrican Law J, 67; ed, EAfrican Law J, Legal Publ Ltd, 66-68. Mem: Am & DC Bar Asns; Bar Asn of DC; Am Polit Sci Asn; Leesburg Rotary (dir, 73-). Relig: Episcopal. Mailing Add: PO Box 871 Middleburg VA 22117

MUSE, RAYMOND O'NEAL **(D)**
b Bryson City, NC, May 28, 28; s Harley Raymond Muse & Ida Chambers M; m 1946 to Doris Glenda Tallent; c Glenda Neil, Daniel, Rita Kim, Margaret Ann & Jeffery Scott. Educ: Swain Co Schs, 12 years; Swain Co High Sch, postgrad, bookkeeping & typing, 1 year. Polit & Govt Pos: Mem, Swain Co Sch Bd, 59-; chmn, Swain Co Dem Exec Comt, NC, formerly. Bus & Prof Pos: Mgr, Bennett's Drug Store, Bryson City, NC, 58- Mil Serv: Seaman 2-V6, Navy, 46. Mem: Jaycees; Maroon & White Club; Rotary; CofC (dir). Relig: Baptist. Mailing Add: Box 42 Bryson City NC 28713

MUSHIK, CORLISS DODGE **(D)**
NDak State Rep
b Hillsboro, NDak; d Kenneth M Dodge & Edith McDonald D; m 1950 to William Mushik; c Ross Dodge. Educ: Col of St Benedict, 41-42; Mary Col, 70. Polit & Govt Pos: Bd mem, Comn on Status of Women, 71; NDak State Rep, 71- Bus & Prof Pos: Bd mem & exec comt, NDak Am Revolution Bicentennial Comt, 71- Mem: League of Women Voters; Nat Women's Polit Caucus; PEO. Mailing Add: 608 Third St NW Mandan ND 58554

MUSKEY, NICHOLAS CHRIS **(R)**
Mem, Rep State Cent Comt Calif
b St Paul, Minn, Apr 21, 10; s Chris John Moschogianis & Kalliopi Yiannakoulis M; m 1941 to Claramay Franing. Educ: Univ Minn, 1 year; Univ Calif, Los Angeles, Exten Div, 1 year; City Col Los Angeles, Exten Div, 1 year; Univ Southern Calif, Exten Div, 1 year. Polit & Govt Pos: Rep precinct chmn, 42nd Assembly Dist, Calif, 52, registr chmn, 63-64; dir 21st Dist, Calif Rep Assembly, 60, dir 27th Dist, 61, pres 42nd Assembly Dist, 61-62, dir-at-lg, 66, vpres, 67, dir 28th Dist, 69, sgt at arms, 70-; mem, Rep State Cent Comt Calif, 63-, mem rules comt, 66-, sustaining mem; pres, Burbank Rep Assembly, 65; pres, All Rep Assembly, 66; vpres, Los Angeles Co Rep Assembly, 66-67; pres, Griffith Park Rep Assembly, 73-75. Bus & Prof Pos: Co-owner & mgr, Off Photos, Inc, Hollywood, Calif, 46-47; traffic mgr, Teleways Radio Prod, 48; asst mgr, Acousti-Glas, Inc, Burbank, 49-50; owner & operator, Magnolia Grill, North Hollywood, 50-51; asst mgr, Radio Sta KBLA, Burbank, 52-53; plant mgr, Rol-Fol Table Co, Inc, Van Nuys, 53-55; personnel dir, Hycor Div, Int Resistance Corp, Sylmar, 55-56; production mgr, Wizard Mfg Co, North Hollywood, 56; owner & operator, Blackwater Mining Co, Death Valley, 56-58; mgr, Bekins Film Ctr, Hollywood, 58-66; mgr, Producers Film Ctr, 66- Mil Serv: Entered as Pvt, Marine Corps, 40, retired as CWO-4, 66, after serv in 2nd Marine Div, SPac Theater, 40-46, Res, 46-66; 2 Presidential Citations; Res Medal; Pac Theater Medal; Am Theatre Ribbon. Mem: San Fernando Valley Youth Found Spotlighters; TV Film Asn (secy-treas); Southern Calif Motion Picture Coun (adv bd); 2nd Marine Div Asn (life mem); MCROA (life mem). Relig: Greek Orthodox. Mailing Add: 15751 Morrison St Encino CA 91436

MUSKIE, EDMUND SIXTUS **(D)**
US Sen, Maine
b Rumford, Maine, Mar 28, 14; s Stephen Muskie & Josephine Czarnecki M; m 1948 to Jane F Gray; c Stephen Oliver, Ellen (Mrs Ernest Allen), Melinda, Martha & Edmund S, Jr. Educ: Bates Col, BA, 36; Cornell Univ Law Sch, LLB, 39; Phi Beta Kappa; Delta Sigma Rho; Phi Alpha Theta. Hon Degrees: 26 from various cols & univs. Polit & Govt Pos: Maine State Rep, 46-51, Minority Leader, Maine House of Rep, 48-51; Maine dist dir, Price Stabilization, 51-52; Dem Nat Committeeman, 52-54; Gov, Maine, 55-59; US Sen, Maine, 59-, chmn intergovt rels subcomt of govt opers comt & subcomt on air & water pollution of pub works, US Senate, chmn budget comt, Asst Majority Whip, 66-, chmn Dem sen campaign comt, 67-69, chmn legis rev comt Dem policy comt, currently, chmn subcomt health of elderly, spec comt aging, currently; mem, Roosevelt Campobello Int Park Comn, currently; deleg, Dem Nat Conv, 68; Dem Vice Presidential Nominee, Bus & Prof Pos: Law practice, Waterville, Maine, 40-55. Mil Serv: Entered as Ens, Navy, 42, released as Lt(jg), 45, after serv as Eng Officer, European & Pac Theaters; 3 Battle Stars. Publ: Auth, Journeys, Doubleday & Co, 72. Mem: Maine & Mass Bar Asns; Commercial Law League; Lions; Amvets. Honors & Awards: First popularly elected Dem sen from Maine. Relig: Roman Catholic. Legal Res: Waterville ME 04901 Mailing Add: US Senate Washington DC 20510

MUSSER, VIRGIL LEE **(D)**
Pres, Young Dem Clubs of Am
b Marshallville, Ohio, Aug 3, 34; s Leland V Musser & Delpha Garman M; m 1955 to Dorothy Ann Hook; c Scott Alan & Julie Ann. Educ: Col of Wooster, BA, 56; Western Reserve Univ Sch Law, LLB, 59; Phi Alpha Delta; Pi Sigma Alpha. Polit & Govt Pos: Pres, Col Wooster Young Dem, 54-55; state coordr, Ohio Col Young Dem, 55; pres, Wayne Co Young Dem, 55, Young Dem of Cuyahoga Co, 56-57, Stark Co Young Dem, 64 & Ohio League of Young Dem Clubs, 64-66; pres, Young Dem Clubs of Am, 65-; city solicitor, Massillon, Ohio, 66-; cand, US House of Rep, 16th Dist, Ohio, 68, 70 & 72; deleg, Dem Nat Conv, 68. Mil Serv: Entered as Pvt, Army Res, 59, released as SP-4, 65. Mem: Ohio State Bar Asn; Col of Wooster Alumni Asn (nat pres, 69-); Am Asn Young Polit Leaders (pres); Jaycees; Urban League. Honors & Awards: First alt deleg, World Assembly of Youth Cong, Tokyo, 66. Relig: Methodist. Legal Res: 301 Sheri Dr NE Massillon OH 44646 Mailing Add: 510 Massillon Bldg Massillon OH 44646

MUSSEY, WILLIAM HOWARD **(R)**
Ohio State Sen
b Chicago, Ill, Aug 24, 13; s Charles F Mussey & Mabel Hill M; wid; m 1970 to Paula Mazel; c Elizabeth Jean & Ann Louise. Educ: Ohio State Univ, 31-35. Polit & Govt Pos: Ohio State Rep, 12th Dist, 67-72, Ohio State Sen, 72- Bus & Prof Pos: Gen mgr, Clermont Sun Publishing Co, Inc, 53-66; advert mgr, Clermont Courier, 67- Mil Serv: Ohio Nat Guard, 29-40; also entered as Pvt, Army, 42, released as Maj, 53, after serv in 37th & 33rd Inf Div, Korean Mil Advisor Group, SPac & Japan; President Commendation Medal, 2 awards; Philippine Campaign, Japan Occup, Am Theater & Korean Ribbons. Mem: Nat & Ohio Newspaper Asns; Cincinnati Advertisers Club; Am Legion; Batavia Businessmens Asn; F&AM. Relig: Presbyterian; chmn bd trustees, Batavia Presby Church. Mailing Add: 150 N Riverside Dr Batavia OH 45103

MUSTO, RAPHAEL **(D)**
Pa State Rep
Mailing Add: Capitol Bldg Harrisburg PA 17120

MUSTO, WILLIAM V **(D)**
NJ State Sen
b Union City, NJ, Mar 27, 17; m 1946 to Rhyta Palmerini; c Patrick & Patricia. Polit & Govt Pos: NJ State Assemblyman, 46-65, Minority Leader, NJ State Assembly, 53; mem bd comnr, Union City, NJ, 54-, Mayor, 62; NJ State Sen, 65- Bus & Prof Pos: Attorney-at-law. Mil Serv: Army, 4 years. Mem: Chmn many charity drives & affil with many civic, fraternal & church orgn. Relig: Catholic. Mailing Add: 321 23rd St Union City NJ 07087

MUTCH, DUANE **(R)**
NDak State Sen
b Grand Forks, NDak, May 13, 25; married; c Three. Educ: Pub schs. Polit & Govt Pos: NDak State Sen, 59-61 & currently. Bus & Prof Pos: Bulk oil distributor. Mil Serv: World War II. Mem: Am Legion; DAV. Mailing Add: State Capitol Bismarck ND 58501

MUTZ, JOHN M **(R)**
Ind State Sen
s John L Mutz & Helen Massie M; m 1958 to Carolyn Jane Hawthorne; c John Mark & Diana Caryl. Educ: Northwestern Univ, BS, 57 & MS, 58; Pi Alpha Mu; Beta Theta Pi. Polit & Govt Pos: Chmn, Allegheny Co Young Rep, Pa, 59-60; chmn, Lawrence Twp Young Rep, 64-65; Lawrence Twp chmn, Marion Co Rep Party, 66-67; Ind State Rep, 67-70; Rep cand for State Treas, Ind, 70; Ind State Sen, 72- Bus & Prof Pos: Vpres, Circle Leasing Corp, 62-; secy-treas, Louisville Food Systs, Inc, 64- Publ: Equipment leasing for financial institutions, Mid-Continent Bank, 65. Mem: Jr CofC. Mailing Add: 5940 E 79th St Indianapolis IN 46250

MYER, CALVIN HARLEY **(D)**
Treas, CZ Regional Dem Party
b Mansfield, Ohio, July 6, 32; s Calvin Charles Myer & Inez Louise Wright M; div. Educ: Ashland High Sch, Ohio, dipl, 49; US Air Force Inst & on base col exten courses in electronics. Polit & Govt Pos: Treas, CZ Regional Dem Party, 68- Bus & Prof Pos: Engr-in-chg, Caribbean Area Univac, Fed Syst Div, Sperry Rand Corp, 66- Mil Serv: Entered as Pvt, Air Force, 51, released as S/Sgt, 60, after serv in 1st Pilot Bomber Squadron, Fla, Caribbean, Ger & gen Western European area, 52-57; Ger Occup Medal; Good Conduct Medal with Cluster; Nat Defense Medal; UN Medal; Sharpshooter. Mem: Soc Philatelic Am; Am Philatelic Soc; Am Soc Repub Panama; VFW. Relig: Protestant. Mailing Add: PO Box 934 Albrook CZ

MYERS, ARCHIE **(D)**
Chmn, Green Co Dem Party, Wis
b Janesville, Wis, Nov 7, 20; s Archie S Myers & Helen Wilkinson M; m 1947 to Wanda Eileen Ableman; c Marilyn (Mrs Wm Smithyman), Carolyn & Deborah. Educ: Univ Tex, Austin, 38-40; Univ Wis-Madison, PhB, 42; Inst Int Affairs, Geneva, Switz, cert, 46; Sigma Phi Epsilon. Polit & Govt Pos: Chmn, Urban Renewal, Wis, 69-; chmn, Green Co Dem Party, 74- Bus & Prof Pos: Pres, Swiss Cheese Shops Inc, 74- Mil Serv: Entered as Pvt, Army, 43, released as T/Sgt, 46, after serv in 209th Signal Radar Maintenance Unit, ETO, 44-46; Good Conduct Medal; ETO Medal with three Battle Stars. Mem: Lions; Moose; Mason; Am Legion. Relig: Lutheran. Mailing Add: 1725 Lake Dr Monroe WI 53566

MYERS, BILL J **(D)**
Chmn, Bay Co Dem Exec Comt, Fla
b Panama City, Fla, Mar 29, 37; s Claude W Myers & Aline Ledbetter M; div; c Stephen W & Bettye J. Educ: Fla State Univ, BS, 59. Polit & Govt Pos: Chmn, Bay Co Dem Exec Comt, Fla, 75- Bus & Prof Pos: Acct, St Joe Paper Co, Jacksonville, Fla, 60-70; acct, Panama City, 70- Mil Serv: Entered as E-1, Nat Guard, 55, released as E-5, 64. Mem: Jaycees; Elks; CofC. Mailing Add: 5800 Lake Dr Panama City FL 32401

MYERS, CARROLL JEAN **(R)**
Chairwoman, Ashland Co Rep Orgn, Ohio
b Pittsburgh, Pa, Jan 11, 28; d Joseph Ralph Diehl & Dorothea Burns D; m 1955 to Phillip Alison Myers; c Gerald Lee Fife, Linda Louise (Mrs Paul E Thatcher, II), Holly Ann & Laurel Ann. Educ: Tiffin Univ, 45; Beta Sigma Phi. Polit & Govt Pos: Pres, Ashland Co Rep Womens Club, Ohio, 67-69; chmn, Ashland Co Neighbor to Neighbor Div, Ohio Rep Finance Comt, 68-73; chairwoman, Ashland Co Rep Orgn, 68-; off mgr to US Rep John M Ashbrook, Ashland, Ohio Off, 71-73; appointed as mem of Ashland Co Bd of Elect, 72-, chmn, 72 & 73; dist rep, 73- Bus & Prof Pos: Corp mem & off mgr, Myers Serv, Inc, 55- Mem: Ashland Co Rep Womens Club; Country Club of Ashland; Nat Secretaries Asn; Eastern Star. Relig: Protestant. Mailing Add: Rte 2 Box 49A Ashland OH 44805

MYERS, CLAY **(R)**
Secy of State, Ore
b Portland, Ore, May 27, 27; s Henry Clay Myers & Helen Mackey M; m 1955 to Elizabeth Lex Arndt; c Richard Clay, Carolyn Elizabeth & David Hobson. Educ: Univ Ore, BS, 49; Northwestern Col Law, 50-52; Lambda Chi Alpha, int pres; Sigma Nu Phi. Polit & Govt Pos: Asst Secy of State, Ore, 65-67, Secy of State, 68-; deleg, Rep Nat Conv, 68 & 72; chmn, Willamette Valley Environ Protection & Develop Planning Coun, 72-74; state chmn, Gov Comn on Youth, 69-74; mem exec comt, Nat Conf Lt Gov; chmn, Early Childhood Develop Task Force, 74- Bus & Prof Pos: Trust dept, First Nat Bank, 49-53; with Conn Gen Life, Ore, 53-62, state mgr, 60-62; vpres, Ins Co of Ore, 62-65. Mem: Portland City Club; Ecumenical Ministries of Ore (trustee); Boys & Girls Soc; Am Legion; Mason. Honors & Awards: DeMolay Legion of Honor. Relig: Episcopal; dep, nat conv Episcopal churches, 67, 69 & 71. Legal Res: 1610 Fir St S Salem OR 97302 Mailing Add: 121 State Capitol Salem OR 97310

676 / MYERS

MYERS, GARY A (R)
US Rep, Pa
b Toledo, Ohio, Aug 16, 37; s Arthur Hamilton Myers & Dorothea Isaly M; m 1963 to Elaine J Roppolo; c Michele Renee & Mark Christopher. Educ: Univ Cincinnati, Mech Eng, 60; Univ Pittsburgh, MBA, 64. Polit & Govt Pos: US Rep, Pa, 25 Dist, 75- Bus & Prof Pos: Coop student as a mech engr, Armco Steel Corp, 55-60, mech engr, 60-61, indust engr, 61-65; turn foreman, hot strip mill, 65-74. Mil Serv: Air Force Reserve, 61-68. Relig: Episcopal. Legal Res: 106 Shady Dr Butler PA 16001 Mailing Add: 1711 Longworth House Off Bldg Washington DC 20515

MYERS, HARDY (D)
Ore State Rep
Mailing Add: 132 NE Laurelhurst Place Portland OR 97232

MYERS, HAROLD ARTHUR (R)
Treas, Branch Co, Mich
b Ashley, Ind, July 25, 23; s Glen L Myers & Elta C Urey; m 1945 to Betty Jane Boyd. Educ: Purdue Univ, BS, 50. Polit & Govt Pos: Mem, Branch Co Planning Comn, Mich, 71-; chmn, Branch Co Rep Comt, 71-; treas, Branch Co, 73- Mil Serv: Entered as Pvt, Army Air Corps, 42, released as Col, Air Force, 69, after serv as bomber pilot, 9th Air Force, ETO; chief bomber br, Air Force Spec Weapons Ctr, Kirtland AFB, NMex, launch controller, Cape Kennedy, chief space support div, Hq Air Force Syst Command, Andrews AFB, Md; chief test div, Hq Air Force, Pentagon, DC; Legion of Merit, 11 Air Medals; 6 Air Force Commendation Medals; 4 Battle Stars, Europe; French Croix de Guerre with Palm. Mem: Air Force Asn; Coldwater Lake Asn (pres, 71-). Relig: Protestant. Mailing Add: 2053 Lake Dr RR 3 Coldwater MI 49036

MYERS, HIRAM KEITH, JR (D)
Chmn, Harmon Co Dem Party, Okla
b Utica, Mo, Sept 10, 31; s Hiram Keith Myers & Helena Mae Sherman M; m 1962 to Paula Deanne Bell; c Michelle Joyce, Hiram Keith, III, Lori Jean, Tamara Deanne & Dennis Bryan. Educ: Cent Mich Univ, BS, 56; Univ Tulsa, JD, 64; Alpha Psi Omega; Delta Pi Lambda; Tau Kappa Epsilon; Phi Alpha Delta. Polit & Govt Pos: Chmn, Harmon Co Dem Party, Okla, 67- Bus & Prof Pos: Mem bd dirs & past pres, Southwest Okla Legal Aid; mem bd regents, Altus Jr Col; mem bd dirs, Okla Tuberc & Respiratory Disease Asn, 71-, Okla Coun, Nat Coun on Crime & Delinquency, 72- Mil Serv: Navy, 48-52 & 56-57, Ens, serv in 6th Fleet; European Occup Medal; Meritorious Serv Medal. Publ: Article in Tulsa Bar J, 63. Mem: Am Trial Lawyers Asn; Okla Trial Lawyers Asn (bd dirs); Okla Bar Asn; Rotary. Relig: Baptist. Legal Res: 1223 N Sixth St Hollis OK 73550 Mailing Add: PO Box 186 Hollis OK 73550

MYERS, J W (D)
Wyo State Sen
b Evanston, Wyo, June 5, 07; m to Fern; c Four. Educ: Univ Wyo, BS. Polit & Govt Pos: Wyo State Rep, 4 years; Wyo State Sen, 55-71 & 72-, mem legis exec comt on reorgn state govt, 69- Bus & Prof Pos: Rancher. Mem: Mason; Wyo Farm Bur; Wyo Stockgrowers; Wyo Taxpayers; Wyo Develop Asn. Mailing Add: Rte 1 Box 97 Evanston WY 82930

MYERS, JAN (D)
Mem, Dem Nat Comt, Kans
b Coffeyville, Kans, Nov 14, 27; d Ernest E Royer & Frances Hodge R; m 1948 to Jack Allen Myers (deceased); c Marsha Jan, Monica Jane, Melisa Jo, Jack Allen, Jr & Frederick William. Educ: Cent Mo State Col, 47-48. Polit & Govt Pos: Co & dist officer, Johnson Co Young Dem, Kans, 54-62 & 63-66; precinct committeewoman, Johnson Co Dem Party, 56-62 & 65-; secy, Johnson Co Dem Women's Club, 57-59 vpres, 63-69, first vpres, 69-70; secy, Co Dem Comt, Midland, Mich, 62; vpres, Kans Fedn Women's Dem Clubs, 63-69, auditor, 69-; vchmn, Third Cong Dist Dem Party, Kans, 64-66; alt deleg, Dem Nat Conv, 64 & 68; Third Dist, Women Doer of 66; state chmn, Kans Women for Humphrey-Muskie, 68, Johnson Co chmn, 68; vchmn, Kans Dem State Comt, 75-; mem, Dem Nat Comt, Kans, 75- Mem: Kans Parent & Teachers Orgn; Boy Scouts; Camp Fire Girls; Girl Scouts. Relig: Presbyterian. Mailing Add: 3911 W 68th Terr Prairie Village KS 66208

MYERS, JIMMY LAIRD (R)
b Winston-Salem, NC, Mar 11, 53; s Tildren Ray Myers & Mattie Lois Laird M; single. Educ: Wake Forest Univ, BA, 75, deans list; Inter-Varsity Christian Fel; Intercollegiate Studies Inst; Young Am for Freedom. Polit & Govt Pos: Chmn, Davie Co Young Rep, 72-73; vpres, Wake Forest Univ Col Rep, 72-74, chmn, 74-75; secy, NC Fedn Col Rep, 73-74, vchmn, 74-75; mem, NC Young Rep, currently. Bus & Prof Pos: Sch bus driver, NC State Govt, 69-71; summer employee, R J Reynolds Tobacco Co, 71-74. Relig: United Methodist. Mailing Add: Rte 1 Box 213 Advance NC 27006

MYERS, JOHN T (R)
US Rep, Ind
b Covington, Ind, Feb 8, 27; s Warren E Myers & Myra Wisher M; m 1953 to Carol Carruthers; c Carol Ann & Lori Jan. Educ: Ind State Univ, BS, 51; Sigma Pi. Polit & Govt Pos: US Rep, Ind, 67- Mil Serv: Entered as Pvt, Army, 45, released as S/Sgt, 46, after serv in ETO; Maj, Army Res. Mem: ROA; VFW; Am Legion; Mason; Shrine. Relig: Episcopal. Legal Res: 921 Second St Covington IN 47932 Mailing Add: US House Off Bldg Washington DC 20515

MYERS, KENNETH MORTON (D)
Fla State Sen
b Miami, Fla, Mar 11, 33; s Stanley C Myers & Martha Scheinberg M. Educ: Univ NC, AB, 54; Univ Fla Law Sch, LLB, 57; Phi Beta Kappa; pres, Phi Alpha Delta; Pi Sigma Alpha; Tau Epsilon Phi; freshman swimming team; track & fencing teams; pres, Debate Coun; Student Coun; Student Hon Court; Order of Golden Fleece; exec ed, Univ Fla Law Rev; finalist champion, Law Sch Moot Court Competition. Polit & Govt Pos: Fla State Rep, 65-69; Fla State Sen, 69-, vchmn ways & means comt, chmn govt opers comt & mem rules & calendar comt, Fla State Senate. Mem: Am Bar Asn; Miami-Dade CofC. Honors & Awards: St Petersburg Times Capitol Press Poll, One of Ten Most Valuable Mem of House of Rep, 67; Miami Jr CofC Award, Outstanding Young Man of Miami, 67; Fla Jr CofC Award, One of Five Outstanding Young Men of Fla, 67; Allen Morris Award, Outstanding First Termer in Fla State Senate, 69; auth of significant legis completely revising Fla ment health laws, including estab of community ment health ctrs; auth, Fla Deceptive Trade Practices Act, Pollution Control Act & Community Ment Health Act. Relig: Jewish. Mailing Add: 1428 Brickell Ave Miami FL 33131

MYERS, MICHAEL (D)
Pa State Rep
Mailing Add: Capitol Bldg Harrisburg PA 17120

MYERS, ROBERT LEE, III (D)
Pa State Sen
b Camp Hill, Pa, May 15, 28; s Robert Lee Myers, Jr & Evelyn Mary Mentzer M; m 1958 to Helen Johnson; c Robert Lee, IV, Katharine Manley & William Frederick. Educ: Col of William & Mary, AB, 51; Dickinson Sch Law, LLB, 53; Theta Delta Chi; Corpus Juris Soc, Dickinson Sch Law. Polit & Govt Pos: Cand, Dist Attorney, Cumberland Co, Pa, 59; cong cand, 19th Cong Dist, Pa, 68; mem, Pa Dem State Comt, 72-; Pa State Sen, 74- Bus & Prof Pos: Secy & dir, Mt Allen Corp, Lemoyne, Pa. Mil Serv: Entered as Pvt, Army, 46, released as T-5, 47, after serv in 3rd Armored Cavalry, US, 46-47. Publ: Decedent's estates—conclusiveness of probate, Dickinson Law Rev, 52-53. Mem: Am Bar Asn; Am Trial Lawyers Asn; F&AM; Harrisburg Symphony Asn (trustee & vpres); Human Soc of Harrisburg (bd dirs). Relig: Presbyterian; deacon & secy bd trustees, Camp Hill Presby Church. Mailing Add: 2300 Market St Camp Hill PA 17011

MYERS, RODERICK DOUGLAS (R)
Chmn, Third Cong Dist Rep Cent Comt, Colo
b West Grove, Iowa, Oct 16, 32; s Raymond Carl Myers & LaVelle Lamb M; single; foster son, Charles T Conway. Educ: Univ Northern Colo, AB & teaching cert, 54, Colo State Bd Voc Educ, adult educ cert, 56; Colo State Univ & Adams State Col, adv study; Blue Key; Colvin Bus Soc; Distributive Educ Clubs Am; Int Rels Club; Pi Omega Pi; Sigma Phi Epsilon; Lambda Gamma Kappa; DeMolay Club; Canterbury Club. Polit & Govt Pos: Chmn, Colorado Springs High Sch Rep Club, 48-50; chmn, Colo State Col Young Rep League, 52-54; chmn, Pueblo Co Young Rep League, Colo, 58-62; cand for Colo State Rep, Pueblo Co, 58 & 60; committeeman & mem exec comt, Pueblo Co Rep Cent Comt, 58-65, chmn, formerly; chmn, Third Cong Dist Young Rep League, 60-62; bonus mem, Colo State Rep Cent Comt, 60-62; campaign mgr, State Supreme Court Justice, 62; pub rels dir, Third Dist Goldwater Campaign, 64; chmn, Third Cong Dist Rep Cent Comt, 71- Bus & Prof Pos: Coordr distributive educ, Pueblo Pub Schs, 54-; pres, Myers Enterprises, 57-62; owner, Myers Land & Cattle Co, 60-64; pres, Roderick Douglas Myers Found, 60-; vpres, King Bus Col Inc & Pueblo Employ Serv, 60-; owner, Trading Post Co, 62- Mil Serv: Entered as Pvt, Army, 55, released as 2nd Lt, 57, after serv in 554th & 89th Div, Antiaircraft; 1st Lt, Qm Corps, Army Res, 57-64. Mem: Nat Educ Asn; Nat Sales Exec Asn; Asn Sales Ralley Speakers; Pueblo CofC; YMCA. Relig: Episcopal. Mailing Add: The Mikado PO Box 158 Beulah CO 81023

MYLES, THOMAS EBERLY (D)
b Fayetteville, WVa, Oct 24, 22; s T A Myles & Rouena Eberly M; m 1943 to Virginia Lee Marshall; c Steven & Philip. Educ: WVa Inst Tech, AB, 46, Col Law, LLB, 49. Polit & Govt Pos: WVa State Deleg, 56-74, Majority Leader, WVa House Deleg, 57-60, 67-68, 71-72 & 73-; deleg, Dem Nat Conv, 72. Polit & Govt Pos: Attorney-at-law, Myles, Myles & Conrad, 48- Mil Serv: Entered as Pvt, Air Force, 42, released as S/Sgt, 45, after serv in 15th Air Force, ETO, 44-45; Purple Heart; Air Medal with 4 Oak Leaf Clusters; 5 Battle Stars. Mem: WVa Bar Asn; Am Legion; Mason; Shrine; Moose. Honors & Awards: Alumni of Year, WVa Inst Technol, 64. Relig: Presbyterian. Legal Res: 122 Goddard Ave Fayetteville WV 25840 Mailing Add: Drawer 60 Fayetteville WV 25840

N

NAADEN, LAWRENCE L (R)
NDak State Sen
Mailing Add: State Capitol Bismarck ND 58501

NABERS, LYNN (D)
Tex State Rep
b Brownwood, Tex, Mar 31, 40; s Joseph Dudley Nabers & Ima Lou Littlefield N; m 1959 to Mary Scott; c Joseph Scott & Timothy Lynn. Educ: NTex Univ, 58-59; Howard Payne Col, BS, 62; Baylor Univ, JD, 68; Phi Delta Phi; Lambda Chi. Polit & Govt Pos: Tex State Rep, 55th Legis Dist, 68- Bus & Prof Pos: Attorney-at-law, 68. Mem: Am Bar Asn; Brownwood CofC; Farm Bur; Sportsmans Club; Brownwood Jaycees. Relig: Baptist. Mailing Add: 4 Quail Creek Rd Brownwood TX 76801

NADASDY, LEONARD JOHN (R)
VChmn, Rep Party, Minn
b Brookings, SDak, Oct 6, 30; s Carl J Nadasdy & Claribel Hoehn N; div. Educ: Univ Minn, BA, 52; Sigma Phi Epsilon. Polit & Govt Pos: Chmn, Minn Col Reps, 51-52; chmn, Minn Young Rep League, 59-61; nat vchmn, Young Rep Fedn, 59-61, nat chmn, 61-63; vchmn, Rep Party Minn, 73- Bus & Prof Pos: Dir pub rels, NCent Wool Mkt Corp, 56-59; ed, Young Farmer, Gen Mills, Inc, 59-60, dir pub affairs, 65- Mil Serv: Entered as 2nd Lt, Army, 52, released as 1st Lt, 54, after serv as Pub Info Officer. Mem: Golden Valley Health Ctr & Hosp (mem bd gov, 72-); Minn Coun Delinquency & Crime (treas); Golden Valley CofC (exec comn, 72-); Am Numismatic Asn. Honors & Awards: Outstanding Man of Year, Minn Jaycees, 63; Distinguished Serv Award, Gtr Minn CofC, 68. Relig: Lutheran. Mailing Add: Loretto MN 55357

NADEAU, RICHARD JAMES (D)
Maine State Rep
b Sanford, Maine, Apr 17, 52; s J F Raymond Nadeau & Evelyn Richard N; single. Educ: Univ Maine, Orono, BA Sociol, 74; Sigma Phi Epsilon. Polit & Govt Pos: Maine State Rep, Dist 113, 75- Mem: KofC. Relig: Roman Catholic. Mailing Add: 5 June St Sanford ME 04073

NADER, ROBERT ALEXANDER (D)
Ohio State Rep
b Warren, Ohio, Mar 31, 28; s Nassif J Nader & Emily N; single. Educ: Ohio State Univ, 46; Adelbert Col, BA, 50; Western Reserve Univ Sch Law, LLB, 53. Polit & Govt Pos: City councilman & pres protem coun, Warren City, Ohio, 60-66; pres, Warren City Police & Fire Pension Bd, 60-66; Ohio State Rep, 98th Dist, 71-72, 55th Dist, 73-; Dem Exec & Precinct Comt. Bus & Prof Pos: Secy, Warren Equity Co, Warren City, Ohio, 56-; pres, Trumbull New

Theatre, 58; secy, PS, Inc, 64-; treas, Park-Porter Corp, 69-; trustee, Family Serv Asn, bd mem, Off Econ Opportunity, Trumbull Co, 70-72. Mil Serv: Entered Army, 46, released as Cpl, 48. Mem: Ohio Title Asn; Am Land Title Asn; Asn; Elks; KofC; Football Off Asn. Honors & Awards: 1945 All Ohio Football; 1947 All Fourth Army Football; Recipient of Outstanding Young Men of Am Award, 64; Community Action Award, Warren Area Bd Realtors, 67; Award, Am Arbit Asn, 65. Relig: Catholic. Mailing Add: 588 E Market St Warren OH 44481

NAFTALIN, ARTHUR (DFL)
b Fargo, NDak, June 28, 17; s Sandel Naftalin & Tillie Bresky N; m 1941 to Frances Marie Healy; c Mark, David & Gail. Educ: NDak Agr Col, 34-36; Univ Minn, BA, 39, MA, 42, PhD, 48. Hon Degrees: LLD, Univ NDak, 69. Polit & Govt Pos: Trustee, Nat Ctr Educ in Polit & Nat Inst Pub Affairs; secy to Hubert H Humphrey, Mayor, Minneapolis, Minn, 45-47; mem, Adv Comn Intergovt Rels; mem, Comn of Admin, Minneapolis, 54-60; bd dir, Citizens League of Gtr Minneapolis, 54-; consult, ICA, Mich State Univ Proj, Saigon, Vietnam, 57; mem Surgeon Gen adv comt urban health affairs, 62-; mayor, Minneapolis, 61-69. Bus & Prof Pos: Ed staff, Fargo Forum, 34-36; managing ed, Minn Daily, Univ Minn, 36-39, staff, 38-39; ed staff, Minneapolis Tribune, 39-41; instr, ASTP & teaching asst polit sci, 41-45; syndicated newspaper columnist, Minn Polit Roundup, Minn Newspapers, 45-54; assoc prof, Univ Minn, 47-54; consult pub affairs div, Ford Found, 60; prof pub affairs, Univ Minn, Minneapolis, 69-; chmn, Salzburg Seminar in Am Studies, 70; mem bd dirs, Augsburg Col, 73-; mem bd dirs, Farmers & Merchants Savings Bank, 73- Publ: Personality, Work, Community: An Introduction to Social Science (w others), 53. Mem: Nat Munic League; US Conf Mayors; Am Munic Asn; Am Soc Pub Admin; Nat League Cities. Honors & Awards: C C Ludwig Award for Outstanding Munic Serv, 69; Fel, Acad Contemporary Probs, Ohio State Univ, 75-; Cecil E Newman Humanitarian Award, Minneapolis Urban League, 75. Mailing Add: 66 Seymour Ave SE Minneapolis MN 55414

NAGELVOORT, BERNARD CHARLES (R)
b Detroit, Mich, Aug 7, 30; s Bernard August Nagelvoort & Caroline Lamport N; m 1957 to Mary Lucie Holmes; c Bernard Peter, Jonathan Holmes, Adam Winston & Charles Wendell. Educ: Mich State Univ, BS, 53; Univ Mich, MBA, 57; Alpha Zeta; Sigma Phi Epsilon. Polit & Govt Pos: Chmn, Newaygo Co Rep Comt, Mich, 60-62, secy, 63-64; admin asst to US Rep Vander Jagt, Mich, 66- Bus & Prof Pos: Mgt trainee, Gerber Prod Co, Fremont, Mich, 57-58, statist analyst, mkt research, 59-63, sr analyst, 63-66. Mil Serv: Entered as Pvt E-1, Army, 53, released as Cpl, 55 after serv in Finance Corps, Ger; Good Conduct Medal. Mem: Montgomery Environ Coalition. Honors & Awards: Young Man of Year Award, 62 & Outstanding Proj Chmn Award, 64, Jaycees. Relig: Congregational; trustee, Westmoreland Congregational Church, Md, currently. Legal Res: 5613 S Green St Fremont MI 49412 Mailing Add: 6200 Perthshire Ct Bethesda MD 20034

NAGLE, WILLIAM P, JR (D)
Mass State Rep
Mailing Add: State Capitol Boston MA 02133

NAHIL, SAM J (R)
NH State Rep
b Lawrence, Mass, Oct 3, 05; married; c One. Educ: Lawrence High Sch. Polit & Govt Pos: NH State Rep, 51-72 & 75-; Sullivan Co Comnr, 75- Bus & Prof Pos: Barber shop & real estate. Mem: Elks; CofC. Relig: Catholic. Mailing Add: 62 South St Claremont NH 03743

NAIFEH, JIMMY (D)
Tenn State Rep
Mailing Add: 620 Tipton Circle Covington TN 38019

NAITO, LISA (D)
Hawaii State Rep
b New York, NY, Dec 11, 34; d Louis Daniels & Bertha Ignatow D; m 1969 to Paul Katsumi Naito; c Lorelei Matsuko & Clay Joshua Naito & Vashti & Jonathon Gittler. Educ: Hunter Col, 52-54; Columbia Univ, 60; Univ Hawaii, 67. Polit & Govt Pos: Deleg, Dem Nat Conv, 72; precinct pres & state deleg, Hawaii Dem Party, 73-; comnr, Gov Comn on Status of Women, 74-; Hawaii State Rep, 74- Bus & Prof Pos: Citizens' Advocate, Self-Employed, Honolulu, Hawaii, 70- Publ: Citizen in a legislative maze, Honolulu Star Bull, 4/73; The prostitute as victim, 2/73 & Initiative and referendum, 2/74, Another Voice. Mem: Volunteer Info/Referral Serv (bd dirs); Kaimuki Bus & Prof Asn; Kapahulu Community Asn; Nat Womens' Polit Caucus. Relig: Buddhist. Legal Res: 3696 A Crater Rd Honolulu HI 96816 Mailing Add: House of Rep State Capitol Honolulu HI 96813

NAJARIAN, MARY (D)
Maine State Rep
Mailing Add: 173 Pleasant Ave Portland ME 04103

NAKASHIMA, NOBUO (D)
Chmn, White Pine Co Dem Comt, Nev
b Ely, Nev, July 3, 31; s Takichi Nakashima & Hide Ide N; m 1971 to Cheryl Katherine Johnson; c Michael Tak. Educ: White Pine Co High Sch, grad, 49. Polit & Govt Pos: Chmn Indian Housing, Dept Housing & Urban Develop, 64-70; precinct chmn, White Pine Co Dem Cent Comt, Nev, 70-72, vchmn, 70-72, chmn, 72-; mem, Nev Dem State Cent Comt, 72- Bus & Prof Pos: Vchmn, White Pine CofC, 60-61. Mil Serv: Entered as Pvt, Marine Corps, 52, released as Cpl, 54, after serv in 1st Marine Div, Korean Theatre, 52-53; Korean Theatre, UN & Nat Defense Medals; Ribbons. Mem: White Pine Jaycees. Honors & Awards: Distinguished Serv, White Pine Jaycees, 60. Relig: Catholic. Legal Res: 173 Fourth St Ely NV 89301 Mailing Add: PO Box 1042 Ely NV 89301

NAKATSUKA, LAWRENCE KAORU (R)
b Hanalei, Hawaii, Jan 27, 20; s Ichiro Nakatsuka & Yone Hashizume; m 1948 to Minnie Yamauchi; c Paul Takashi, Roy Hiroshi & Laura Naomi. Educ: Harvard Univ, Nieman fel, 51-52. Polit & Govt Pos: Press secy to Gov, Hawaii, 53-60; dep dir, State Dept Social Serv, 60-62; legis & exec asst to US Sen Hiram L Fong, Hawaii, 63-74; minority staff dir, Senate Post Off & Civil Serv Comt, 74- Bus & Prof Pos: Reporter, labor ed & asst city ed, Honolulu Star-Bull, 39-53; Hawaii correspondent, Christian Sci Monitor, Boston & Japanese Am Citizens League Newspaper, Pac Citizen, Los Angeles, 40-50. Mem: Nieman Fels; Am Soc Pub Admin; Am Pub Welfare Asn; Hawaii Pub Rels Asn; Honolulu Press Club. Honors & Awards: Guest of Japanese Govt for centennial observance of US-Japan Treaty of Amity & Com. Legal Res: 1335 Palolo Ave Honolulu HI 96816 Mailing Add: 2344 S Ode St Arlington VA 22202

NALDER, REBECCA A (D)
Utah State Rep
b Ogden, Utah, Sept 2, 31; d Dell H Adams & Sarah Kershaw A; m 1955 to Ned N Nalder; c Adam, Nathan & Eric. Educ: Utah State Univ, BS, 53; Chi Omega. Polit & Govt Pos: Mem, Layton City Planning & Zoning Comn, Utah, 69-71; Utah State Rep, 71-72 & 74- Bus & Prof Pos: Teacher elem educ, Davis Co Sch Bd, 53-70; teacher spec educ, ment retarded, 70. Relig: Latter-day Saint. Mailing Add: 144 Dixie St Layton UT 84041

NANCE, HANSLEE LEE (D)
b Aspermont, Tex, Nov 24, 27; s William Nance & Hellen Fields N; m 1953 to Lucy Margaret Palmer; c Helen (Mrs Raymond Hamilton), Carolyn Jean (Mrs Benny Jackson), Paula K, Hanslee, Jr, David Maurice, Dorothy Lucette, Bradshaw, Michaelle, Michael, Charlotte, Tonya & Sherill. Educ: Eastern NMex Univ, 56-58. Polit & Govt Pos: Coordr for McGovern, NMex, 72; deleg, Dem Nat Conv, 72; chmn environ bd, Clovis, 72-; mem, NMex Legis & Dem Coun, 73-; state chmn, NMex Black Assembly, 72- Bus & Prof Pos: Supvr of orderlies, Mem Hosp, Clovis, NMex, 45-; small janitor serv, 56-; massage & health club dir, Clovis YMCA, 66-; massage dir, Phys Ther Ctr, 64-71 & Days Rest Home, currently; vchmn, Licensed Practical Nursing Sch of Clovis, 72- Publ: Articles in Life & Sports Illustrated, 72 & Time, 73. Mem: Carver Br Libr (adv bd); NAACP. Honors & Awards: 25 Year Plaque, Mem Hosp, 69. Relig: Pentecostal. Mailing Add: 500 West St Clovis NM 88101

NANCE, KENNETH ROBERT (D)
Okla State Rep
b Mt Carmel, Ill, Oct 1, 41; s M J Nance & Leona Lee Pike N; m 1963 to Barbara Sue Hennessey; c Barry Wayne. Educ: Oklahoma City Univ, BA, 63, Sch Law, JD, 68; Univ Okla, 63-64; Kappa Alpha Order. Polit & Govt Pos: Research assoc, Okla Legis Coun, 64-67; dir, Okla Comn Fiscal Struct, 67; Asst Attorney Gen, Okla, 68; Okla State Rep, 68- Bus & Prof Pos: Attorney-at-law, 68- Mem: Am Bar Asn; Pi Sigma Alpha; Phi Delta Phi; Jaycees; CofC. Honors & Awards: Outstanding Young Man of Capitol, 68. Relig: Methodist. Mailing Add: 4806 S Western Oklahoma City OK 73109

NANGLE, JOHN FRANCIS (R)
Mem, St Louis Co Rep Cent Comt, Mo
b St Louis, Mo, June 8, 22; s Sylvester A Nangle & Thelma B N; m 1950 to Andrea Urseth; c John F, Jr. Educ: Univ Mo, BS in Pub Admin, 43; Wash Univ, JD & LLB, 48; Phi Delta Phi. Polit & Govt Pos: City attorney, Brentwood, Mo, 53-62; committeeman, Jefferson Twp Rep Party, 58-; mem, Rep State Comt, 58-72; mem, St Louis Co Rep Cent Comt, 58-, chmn, 60-61; pres, Mo Rep Vet League, 59-60; pres, Mo Asn Rep, 60-61; spec asst counr, St Louis Co, 62-; deleg, Rep Nat Conv, 68 & 72; Rep Nat Committeeman, Mo, 72-73; US Dist Judge, 73- Bus & Prof Pos: Lawyer, Clayton, Mo, 48- Mil Serv: Entered as Pvt, Army, 43, released as 1st Sgt, 46, after serv in 655th Engr Bn, ETO; Res, 46-63, Capt. Mem: Am Bar Asn; Mason (bd mem, Masonic Home of Mo, 71-); John Marshal Rep Club; Edgewood Children's Home (mem bd); Rotary. Honors & Awards: Mo Rep of Year Award, 70. Relig: Protestant. Mailing Add: 9 Southcote Rd Brentwood MO 63144

NAPOLITANO, FRANK ANTHONY (D)
Chmn, Mansfield Dem Town Comt, Conn
b Waterbury, Conn, June 6, 44; s Constantine Napolitano & Mary Finelli N; m 1967 to Jane Crommet; c Karrie & Kristi. Educ: Univ Conn, BA, 66, MA, 71; Phi Delta Kappa; Pi Sigma Alpha. Polit & Govt Pos: Chmn, Mansfield Dem Town Comt, Conn, 73- Bus & Prof Pos: Asst to dean student affairs, Univ Conn, 69-74; asst to vpres student affairs & serv, 74- Mil Serv: Entered as E-1, Army, 66, released as E-5, 69, after serv in 470th MI Group, Southern CZ, 67-68; Southern Command Cert Achievement. Mem: Nat Asn Student Personnel Adminr. Honors & Awards: Youngest town chmn in the state of Conn. Mailing Add: 32 Mansfield Apts Storrs CT 06268

NAPPER, HYACINTHE T (D)
b New York, NY, Feb 26, 28; d Charles Alexander Tatem & Georgiana Bergen T; m 1952 to Guy Napper; c Cynthia (Mrs Williams), Guy T, Jr & Geoffrey Alan. Educ: Fisk Univ, 45-47; Howard Univ, AB, 51; Alpha Kappa Alpha. Polit & Govt Pos: Admin asst to US Rep John Conyers, Mich, 65- Mem: NAACP; Urban League; Am Civil Liberties Union. Relig: Presbyterian. Legal Res: 3520 Pope St SE Washington DC 20020 Mailing Add: 2444 Rayburn House Off Bldg Washington DC 20515

NARAMORE, ALVIS (D)
Ala State Rep
Mailing Add: Fifth Ave & 19th St Jasper AL 35501

NARCISSE, LAWRENCE JOSEPH, III (D)
b Jeanerette, La, Oct 8, 41; s Lawrence Joseph Narcisse, Jr & Gertrude Millet N; m 1965 to Gaynell Madaline Sonnier; c Yvette Regina & Sheree Ann. Educ: Univ Southwestern La, BA, 64, MEd, 70. Polit & Govt Pos: Secy-treas, Jeanerette Planning Comn, La, 71-73; deleg, Dem Nat Conv, 72. Bus & Prof Pos: Teacher, Iberia Parish Sch Bd, La, 64- Mem: Nat Educ Asn; Jeanerette Area Alliance for Progress; CofC. Honors & Awards: Outstanding Male Educator, Grambling Alumni, 71. Relig: Catholic. Mailing Add: 515 Pellerin St Jeanerette LA 70544

NARDI, THEODORA P (D)
NH State Rep
Mailing Add: 776 Chestnut St Manchester NH 03104

NARDULLI, MICHAEL L (D)
Ill State Sen
Mailing Add: 2025 W Cortez St Chicago IL 60622

NARVID, ETHEL GALLAY (D)
Mem, Calif State Dem Cent Comt
b New York, NY; d James Gallay & Manya Helfant G; div; c Natalie & Michael. Polit & Govt Pos: Field secy to city councilman, Los Angeles, Calif, 56-60; mem exec comt, Calif Dem State Cent Comt, 60-64, finance dir, 70-72, mem, 70-; field rep to US Rep, 60-68; campaign mgr, Los Angeles City Councilman, Tom Bradley for Mayor, 72-73; chief regional coordr, 73- Bus & Prof Pos: Asst to pres, Coro Found, Los Angeles, Calif, currently; coordr, Calif Housing Coalition, currently. Mem: Jewish Fedn Coun of Los Angeles (mem community rels comt & urban affairs comn); Anti-Defamation League (mem regional bd & civil rights comt); Univ Judaism (pres adv comt). Relig: Jewish. Mailing Add: 2616 Hollyridge Dr Hollywood CA 90068

NASH, ADA RUTH (R)
b Plentywood, Mont, July 15, 25; d Joseph Henry Golterman & Mary Leo Lavengood G; m 1943 to Willard G Nash. Educ: High Sch, Plentywood, Mont. Polit & Govt Pos: Precinct committeewoman, Sheridan Co Rep Cent Comt, Mont, 58-, co vchmn, 63-66, chmn, formerly; vpres, Mont Fedn Rep Women, 59-65, pres, 65-67, state youth activities chmn, 67-69; pres, Co Rep Women's Club, 59-63; mem, Gov Comt Sch Found Prog, 61-63; vchmn, Mont State Rep Cent Comt, 69-71; state co-chmn, Comt to Reelect the President, 72. Bus & Prof Pos: Clerk, Sheridan Co Agr Stabilization & Conserv Serv, 43; secy, Sheridan Co Exten Serv, 43; bookkeeper, Nash Bros, Inc, 48-56. Mem: 4-H Club (leader, 51-); Cath Daughters; Redstone Homemakers; Sheridan Co Farm Bur; Redstone Parent Teachers Club. Relig: Catholic. Mailing Add: Box 136 Redstone MT 59257

NASH, DORRIS VALENTINE (D)
Chmn, Allen Co Dem Cent Comt, Kans
b Ada, Okla, Oct 9, 13; d David Edgar Barkley & Anna Lura Chipman B; div; c Richard Henry, III, Nancy Ann Sigg & Christina Kay (Walker). Educ: Shidler High Sch, Okla, grad, 31; Okla Sch Beauty Cult, Ponca City, grad, 34; Nat Honor Soc, 4 years. Polit & Govt Pos: Sponsor, Teen Age Dem, Shidler, Okla, 66-69; alt deleg, Fifth Dist & Kans State Dem Conv, 72; chmn, Allen Co Dem Cent Comt, Kans, 72-; committeewoman, Kans Dem State Comt, 73-, chmn resolutions comt, 74-; Allen Co chmn, Roy for Senate Campaign, 74. Bus & Prof Pos: Owner & operator, Dorris Nash Beauty Salon, Shidler, 63-70; dormitory mgr, Allen Co Community Jr Col, Iola, Kans, 69- Mem: Bus & Prof Women's Club (first vpres, 75-); Eastern Star (Worthy Matron, 69). Relig: United Methodist. Mailing Add: 1801 1/2 N Cottonwood Iola KS 66749

NASH, ERNEST W (R)
Mich State Rep
b Bay City, Mich, Sept 10, 30; s Ernest William Nash & Della Kaiser N; m 1949 to Marilyn Jane Balla; c Steven, Mark & Tracy. Educ: Mich State Univ, currently. Polit & Govt Pos: Mich State Rep, 75- Legal Res: 11480 Holt Rd Dimondale MI 48821 Mailing Add: State Capitol Bldg Lansing MI 48901

NASH, PETER GILLETTE (R)
b Newark, NY, Jan 4, 37; s Arthur E Nash & Marie Gillette N; m 1961 to Diane Engleson; c Kimberly T & Tamara M. Educ: Colgate Univ, AB, 59; NY Univ Sch Law, LLB, 62; Phi Beta Kappa; Pi Sigma Alpha (vpres); Order of the Coif; Lambda Chi Alpha; Phi Delta Phi (clerk). Hon Degrees: LLD, San Fernando Valley Law Sch, 71. Polit & Govt Pos: Confidential legal asst, NY Supreme Court, 62-63; bar exam grader, NY State Bd Law Examr, 63-64; assoc solicitor, US Dept Labor, 69-70, solicitor, 70-71; gen counsel, Nat Labor Rels Bd, Washington, DC, 71- Bus & Prof Pos: Assoc attorney, Wiser, Shaw, et al, 63-67, partner, 68-69. Mil Serv: 1st Lt, Air Force Res. Publ: Auth, Affirmative Action Under Executive Order 11246, 71; Recent Developments & a Look Ahead Under the National Labor Relations Act, 73; The Development of the Collyer Deferral Doctrine, 74; plus others. Mem: Am Bar Asn (labor law sect); Fed Bar Asn; Nat Panel Arbitrators, Am Arbit Asn; Admin Conf US; CofC (bd trustees). Relig: Protestant. Mailing Add: 12421 Over Ridge Rd Potomac MD 20854

NASH, PHILLEO (D)
b Wisconsin Rapids, Wis, Oct 25, 09; s Guy Nash & Florence Philleo N; m 1935 to Edith Rosenfels; c Maggie & Sally. Educ: Univ Wis, AB, 32; Univ Chicago, PhD, 37; Sr Honors, Wis; Sigma Xi; fel Am Anthrop Asn. Polit & Govt Pos: Admin asst to President US, 52-53; chmn, Dem Party of Wis, 55-57; Lt Gov, Wis, 59-61; asst to Asst Secy Interior, 61; comnr, Bur Indian Affairs, 61-66. Bus & Prof Pos: Lectr, Univ Toronto, 37-41; spec asst to Dir, Off War Info, 42-46; spec asst, White House Off, 46-52; pres, Biron Cranberry Co, 46-; consult anthropologist, 66-; research asst, Smithsonian Inst, Washington, DC, 68-70; adj prof, Am Univ, 71-73, prof, 73- Publ: Co-auth, Report to the Secretary of the Interior by Task Force on Indian Affairs, 61 & ed, Navajo Bordertown Dormitories, 65, US Dept Interior; auth, Briefing on Indian affairs, US House of Rep, 1/65; plus others. Mem: Am Asn Advan Sci (mem coun, 72-); Am Anthrop Asn (secy, Sect H, 74-); Anthrop Soc Washington; Soc Appl Anthrop; Wis Cranberry Growers Asn. Relig: Congregational. Mailing Add: 540 N St SW Washington DC 20024

NASH, ROBERT RHEA (R)
Chmn, Pickens Co Rep Party, SC
b Rockwood, Tenn, Aug 28, 38; s Thomas Burton Nash (deceased) & Dorothy Louise Rayburn N; m 1958 to Nancy Louise Earnhart; c Robert, Jr, Stephen Russell & Krista Lynn. Educ: Cent Wesleyan Col, AB, 61; NDEA fel, Clemson Univ, 63-66, MS, 64, PhD, 70; Sigma Xi; Gamma Sigma Delta. Polit & Govt Pos: Chmn, Cent Rep Precinct, SC, 66-70; chmn, Watson for Gov Comt, 70; deleg, SC State Conv, 72 & 74; chmn, Pickens Co Rep Party, 72- Bus & Prof Pos: Assoc prof sci, Cent Wesleyan Col, 66-75, prof, 75- Mil Serv: E-8 Army Res, 55-; SC Army Res & Columbia State Newspaper Component Achievement Award. Mem: Lions (pres-elect, 75-); Pickens Co Taxpayers Asn (dir, 75-). Relig: Wesleyan; treas, Cent First Wesleyan Church, 73- Legal Res: College St Exten Central SC 29630 Mailing Add: WRS PO Box 486 Central SC 29230

NASH, ROBIE LEE (D)
NC State Rep
b East Spencer, NC, Oct 5, 10; s Archie Lee Nash & Mary Lena Kennerly N; m 1936 to Ethel Peeler Arey; c John Lee, Samuel Arey & Lona (Mrs Jim Duggins). Educ: Boyden High Sch, 4 years. Polit & Govt Pos: City councilman, Salisbury, NC, 51-55; NC State Rep, 71-72 & 74- Bus & Prof Pos: Owner, Nash Body Co, 35-50, Nash Glass & Wheel Co, 50-60 & Nash Glass Co, 60-65. Mem: Lions; Mason. Relig: United Methodist. Mailing Add: 232 Richmond Rd Salisbury NC 28144

NASH, VICTORIA C (VICKI) (D)
Activities Coordr, Nev State Dem Cent Comt
b Buffalo, Kans, Apr 18, 15; d Garnet E Carpenter & Gladys Rozell Anderson C; m 1947 to William Michael Nash, Jr, wid; c William M, III, David J, Mary Jo, Thomas L, Anoinette Michele, Dorothy Renee & Paul Joseph; 10 grandchildren. Educ: Univ Toledo; Southwestern Univ; Hastings Col Law. Polit & Govt Pos: Hq mgr for Grant Sawyer for Gov, 58, precinct orgn, 62; precinct orgn chmn, Washoe Co, 58-60; publicity dir, Nev State Dem Cent Comt, 60-, secy, 64-66, activities coordr, currently; deleg, Western Dist Nev Women's Dem Clubs; exec dir, Nev Am Revolution Bicentennial Comn, Carson City, 72- Bus & Prof Pos: Church secy, Ohio, 32-39; law librn, Calif, 43-47; legis reporter & free lance polit columnist, 59-; owner & mgr, Vicki Nash Assocs, Inc, Advert Agency, 59-; legis reporter, Reno Newspapers, Inc & polit analyst, Reno Eve Gazette, 69-73. Mil Serv: Entered as Y 3/C, Coast Guard Res, 44, released as Y 2/C, 45. Mem: Nat Press Women; Soroptimists; Reno Press Club; Advert Club; Sigma Delta Chi. Relig: Catholic. Legal Res: 3250 Everett Dr Reno NV 89503 Mailing Add: PO Box 5477 Reno NV 89503

NASON, CHARLES P (R)
Vt State Rep
Mailing Add: Box 105 Chester VT 05143

NASSET, ROBERT M (R)
NDak State Sen
Mailing Add: State Capitol Bismarck ND 58501

NASSIKAS, JOHN NICHOLAS (R)
Chmn, Fed Power Comn
b Manchester, NH, Apr 29, 17; s Nicholas John Nassikas & Constantina Gagalis N (both deceased); m 1943 to Constantina Andreson; c Constance (Mrs John J Hohenadel, Jr), Mary (Mrs Robert C Hall), Elizabeth & John Nicholas, III. Educ: Dartmouth Col, AB, 38; Harvard Univ Grad Sch Bus Admin, MBA, 40, Law Sch, JD, 48; Kappa Kappa Kappa. Hon Degrees: LLD, Notre Dame Col (NH), 72. Polit & Govt Pos: Asst & dep attorney gen, State of NH, 50-53; chief counsel to Rep Minority, US Senate Commerce Comt, 68-69; chmn, Fed Power Comn, 69- Bus & Prof Pos: Mem, Water Resources Coun, 70-; mem, Admin Conf US, 70-; mem, Energy Resources Coun, 74-; mem adv comt, Am Enterprise Inst Nat Energy Proj, 74- Mil Serv: Entered as Ens, Naval Res, 42, released as Lt(sg), 46, after serv in Aviation Supply Off, Philadelphia, Pa. Publ: Auth, Coordination of electric power & environmental policy, Natural Resources Lawyer, 4/71; National energy & environmental policy, 6/71 & Countervailing pressures & the Fed Power Comn, 10/74, Pub Utilities Fortnightly. Mem: NH, Mass & Am Bar Asns; Jr Achievement of Metrop Washington (mem exec adv coun); Madeira Sch, Greenway, Va (mem bd dirs). Relig: Greek Orthodox. Legal Res: RD 4 Dunbarton NH 03104 Mailing Add: 4512 Potomac School Rd McLean VA 22102

NATALINO, MICHAEL VINCENT (D)
Conn State Rep
b New Haven, Conn, Jan 23, 20; s Arturo Natalino & Josephine Crisci N; m 1946 to Clementine Esposito; c Arthur, Gerald & Michael, Jr. Educ: New Haven Sch Systs, 12th grade. Polit & Govt Pos: Mem bd aldermen, 14th Ward, New Haven, Conn, 72-; Conn State Rep, 97th Dist, 75- Bus & Prof Pos: Pres & treas, Grand Fuel Oil Co, New Haven, Conn, 50- Mil Serv: Entered as Pfc, Army, 41, released as Cpl, 45, after serv in Armored Div, Pac Theatre, 43-45. Mem: Independent Conn Petrol Asn; Nat Fedn Independent Bus; St Jude Research Hosp (state dir). Honors & Awards: St Jude Research Hosp Award, 72; St Rose Holy Name Soc Award, 65; Dom Aitro Little League Award, 66. Relig: Catholic. Mailing Add: 135 Summit St New Haven CT 06513

NATCHER, WILLIAM H (D)
US Rep, Ky
b Bowling Green, Ky; m 1937 to Virginia Reardon; c Celeste (Mrs Jirles) & Louise (Mrs Murphy). Educ: Western Ky State Col, AB; Ohio State Univ, LLB. Polit & Govt Pos: Fed conciliation comnr, Western Dist Ky, 36-37; co attorney, Warren Co, Ky, 37, served three 4 year terms; pres, Young Dem Clubs Ky, 41-46; pres, Bowling Green Bar Asn, formerly; commonwealth attorney, Eighth Judicial Dist, 51-53; US Rep, Ky, 53-, mem comt appropriations, US House Rep. Bus & Prof Pos: Practicing attorney, Bowling Green, Ky, 34- Mil Serv: Navy, 42-45. Mem: Kiwanis Club; Odd Fellows; Am Legion Post 23; 40 et 8. Relig: Baptist. Legal Res: Bowling Green KY 42101 Mailing Add: 2333 Rayburn Bldg Washington DC 20016

NATHAN, HARDY LEWIS (R)
b New York, NY, May 14, 28; s Hardy A Nathan & Mary Civello N; m 1952 to Dorothy Ann Joyce; c Virginia J, Victoria A, Donald H & Christopher Y. Educ: Amherst Col, BA, 50; Kappa Theta. Polit & Govt Pos: Pres, Young Rep Club Northampton, Mass, 60; chmn, Northampton Rep City Comt, 64-66; exec asst to US Sen Edward Brooke, Mass, 68- Bus & Prof Pos: Salesman, Burlington Mills Corp, 50-53, agt-supvr, Phoenix Mutual Life Ins Co, Northampton, Mass, 54-68. Relig: Roman Catholic. Legal Res: 16 Massasoit St Northampton MA 01060 Mailing Add: 3202 White St Falls Church VA 22044

NATHAN, RICHARD PERLE (R)
b Schenectady, NY, Nov 24, 35; s Sidney Robert Nathan & Betty Green N; m 1957 to Mary McNamara; c Robert Joseph & Carol Hewit. Educ: Brown Univ, BA magna cum laude, 57; Harvard Univ, MPA, 59, PhD, 66; Phi Beta Kappa; Theta Delta Chi. Polit & Govt Pos: Legis asst to Sen Keating, NY, 59-62; dir domestic policy research, Gov Rockefeller, 63-64; assoc dir, Nat Adv Comt on Civil Disorders, Washington, DC, 67-68; chmn, President Nixon's Transition Task Forces on Pub Welfare & Intergovt Fiscal Rels, 68; asst dir, US Off Mgt & Budget, 69-71; Presidential app to Comn on Orgn of Govt of DC, 70-71; Dep Under Secy, Dept Health, Educ & Welfare, 71-72. Bus & Prof Pos: Research assoc, Brookings Inst, Washington, DC, 66-69, sr fel, 72-; prof lectr, Am Univ, 66-68. Publ: The policy setting: analysis of major post-Vietnam federal aid policy alternatives & The case for tax sharing—a political view, In: Revenue Sharing & Its Alternatives, Vol II, Joint Econ Comt, US Cong, 67; The potential impact of general aid for four selected states, In: Fiscal Issues in the Future of Federalism, Comt Econ Develop, 68; Jobs & Civil Rights, the Role of the Federal Government in Promoting Equal Opportunity in Employment & Training, US Comn Civil Rights, 69. Relig: Reform Jewish. Mailing Add: 7503 Cayuga Ave Bethesda MD 20034

NATHAN, THEODORA NATHALIA (TONIE) (LIBERTARIAN)
b New York, NY, Feb 9, 23; d Bennett Nathan & Salcha Ralska N; m 1942 to Charles Nathan; c Paul Steven, Lawrence Eugene & Gregory Charles. Educ: Univ Ore, BA in jour, 71, postgrad rhetoric, 72-73; Theta Sigma Phi; Guilder Soc. Polit & Govt Pos: Mem judicial comt, Nat Libertarian Party, 72-; cand for Vice President of the US, 72. Bus & Prof Pos: Owner, Valley Ins Agency, North Hollywood, Calif, 47-53; prof mgr, Chase Music Co, Sun Valley, 53-60; owner & interior decorator, Mr Charles Interiors, La Habra, 60-68; reporter & columnist, Valley News, Eugene, Ore, 71-72; producer, broadcaster doc & interviews, KVAL TV, Eugene, 71-72. Publ: The case of Mrs Quackenbush & urban renewal, Valley News, also half-hour doc KVAL, 8/71; Five part series, The 1990 plan-land use proposal, Valley News, 9-12/71; Libertarian views on Isms, Register-Guard, 3/75. Mem: Women in Commun, Inc; Rubicon Soc; Toastmistress; Metro Civic Club; Asn Libertarian Feminists. Honors & Awards: First Woman in Hist to Receive an Electoral Col Vote from Roger MacBride, Elector of Va, 72; Nominated for Phoenix Award, Soc for Individual Liberty, 73; Commendation Award, Anchorage Libertarians for Action, 73. Mailing Add: 2251 McMillan St Eugene OR 97405

NATION, BILL (D)
Mayor, Cheyenne, Wyo

b Lingle, Wyo, May 28, 25; s Wade Oliver Nation & Marie Voss N; div; c Michael, Martin, Nancy & Molly. Educ: Cheyenne Cent High Sch, grad, 43. Polit & Govt Pos: Mayor, Cheyenne, Wyo, 62-66, 73-; Wyo State Rep, Laramie Co, 63-64; mem, Wyo Recreation Comn, 67- Bus & Prof Pos: Real estate broker & photography bus. Mil Serv: Entered as Enlisted, Navy, 43, released as Gunner's Mate, after serv in Pac Theatre; Presidential Unit Citation. Mem: Salvation Army (adv bd); Wyo Asn Municipalities; Cheyenne Adv Coun on Naval Affairs; Lions Club; VFW (life mem Post 1881). Legal Res: 2221 Van Lennen Ave Cheyenne WY 82001 Mailing Add: PO Box 961 Cheyenne WY 82001

NATSIOS, ANDREW STEPHEN (R)
Mass State Rep

b Philadelphia, Pa, Sept 22, 49; s Basil Andrew Natsios & Eta Lappas N; single. Educ: Georgetown Univ, BA, 71. Polit & Govt Pos: Treas, Holliston Indust Develop Comn, Mass, 73-75; chmn, Holliston Rep Town Comt, 74-; Mass State Rep, 75-, mem comt taxation & comt urban affairs, Mass House Rep, 75- Bus & Prof Pos: Trust & estate asst, First Nat Bank Boston, 72-74. Mil Serv: 1st Lt, Army Res, 75. Mem: Jaycees; Holliston Militia Co. Relig: Congregational. Mailing Add: 392 Adams St Holliston MA 01746

NAUGHTON, EDWARD FRANKLIN (D)
Alaska State Rep

b Cordova, Alaska, June 14, 30; s Charles Colby Naughton & Emma Peterson N; m 1974 to Sharon Marie Cissna; c Thomas & Robin. Educ: Kodiak High Sch, Alaska, grad. Polit & Govt Pos: Assemblyman, Kodiak Island Burough, Alaska, 69-71; Alaska State Rep, 70- Mil Serv: Entered as Pvt, Army, released as Cpl, 53, after serv in Alaska, 51-53. Legal Res: Mill Bay Kodiak AK 99615 Mailing Add: Box 1097 Kodiak AK 99615

NAUJOCK, EVELYN KATSIS (R)
Mem, Rep State Cent Comt Calif

b Chicago, Ill, Dec 21, 20; d Sotirios Katsis & Panayiota Karageorge K; m 1942 to Claude Otto Naujock; c Frederick August & Claude Arthur. Educ: Austin High Sch, Chicago, Ill, grad, 39. Polit & Govt Pos: Mem, Rep State Cent Comt Calif, 67- Bus & Prof Pos: Secy-treas, Toolmasters, Inc, San Gabriel, Calif, 53- Mem: Eastern Star; East San Gabriel Valley Rep Women's Club; White Shrine of Jerusalem. Relig: Protestant. Mailing Add: 2832 E Lark Hill Dr West Covina CA 91791

NAULT, JULIA L (D)
VChmn, Maine Dem State Comt

b Machias, Maine, July 22, 34; d Julian W Davis & Edrie Whitney D; m 1957 to Marc A Nault; c Brian D & Michell C. Educ: Mary Washington Col, 52-54; Boston Univ, BA, 56. Polit & Govt Pos: Vchmn, Washington Co Dem Comt, Maine, 70-72, state committeewoman, 72-74; mem, State Bd Educ, 72-; vchmn, Maine Dem State Comt. Legal Res: Kennebec Rd Machias ME 04654 Mailing Add: PO Box 137 Machias ME 04654

NAVE, MARSHALL TONEY (R)
Tenn State Sen

b Elizabethton, Tenn, July 14, 29; s John L Nave & Gladys Arnold N; m 1962 to Nettie Lee Slemp; c Terri Sue. Educ: Steed Col Tech. Polit & Govt Pos: Vchmn, Carter Co Court, Tenn, 60-66; magistrate, Elizabethton, 60-66; Tenn State Sen, currently. Bus & Prof Pos: Dir, Carter Co Mem Hosp, chmn, East Tenn Hosp Asn, trustee, Carter Co Rescue Squadron. Mil Serv: Entered as Seaman, Navy, 43, released as PO 1/C, 46, after serv in SPac; Asiatic-Pac-European Theater Ribbons; Occup Medal; Am Campaign Ribbon; Presidential Citation. Mem: Nat Legis Comt; VFW; Elks; Moose; Am Legion (comdr). Honors & Awards: All Am VFW Comdr, 65. Relig: Methodist. Mailing Add: Box 591 Elizabethton TN 37643

NAVIN, JOSEPH M (D)
Mass State Rep
Mailing Add: State Capitol Boston MA 02133

NAVRATIL, ROBERT NORMAN (D)
Chmn, Blount Co Dem Party, Tenn

b New York, NY; s John Reginald Navratil & Ida Weissman N; m 1955 to Nancy Jane Naylor; c Rebecca Carol, Joseph Naylor & Angela Jane. Educ: Maryville Col, AB, cum laude, 54; Univ Chicago Law Sch, scholar, 54, JD, 57; Pi Kappa Delta; Alpha Sigma. Polit & Govt Pos: Chmn, Blount Co Dem Party, Tenn, 74- Mil Serv: Entered as Pvt, Air Force, 47, released as Cpl, 50, after serv in Europe & NAfrican Theatres, 48-49. Mem: Am & Blount Co Bar Asns; Tenn Bar Asn (deleg, 71-); Maryville-Alcoa Optimist Club; Blount Co CofC (pres, 73). Relig: Presbyterian. Legal Res: 2038 Eckles Dr Maryville TN 37801 Mailing Add: PO Box 647 Maryville TN 37801

NAWRATH, WILLIAM MICHAEL (D)
Vt State Rep

b Bennington, Vt, Apr 9, 47; s William Charles Nawrath, Jr & Elaine Griffith N; m 1973 to Rebecca Morse. Educ: Univ Vt, since 65. Polit & Govt Pos: Vt State Rep, Dist One, 75- Mil Serv: Entered as Pvt E-1, Army, 68, released as Sp-5, 71, after serv in Am Div, Vietnam, 70-71; Bronze Star with Oak Leaf Cluster; Good Conduct Medal. Mem: Nat Asn Concerned Vet. Relig: Episcopal. Mailing Add: River Rd Manchester Center VT 05255

NAYLON, RICHARD WILLIAM (D)

b Polo, Ill, May 26, 17; s Martin J Naylon & Teresa Meloy N; m 1940 to Edythe Mae Terrell; c James R, Carol Ann (Mrs King) & Joyce Elaine (Mrs Gray). Educ: Polo High Sch, dipl, 35. Polit & Govt Pos: Precinct committeeman, Ogle Co Dem Comt, Ill, 62-, vchmn, 66-68, chmn, formerly. Mem: Lions. Honors & Awards: Master Key Award, Lions Club. Relig: Catholic. Mailing Add: 201 W Webster St Polo IL 61064

NAYLOR, ROBERT WESLEY (R)
Mem Exec Comt, Rep State Cent Comt Calif

b Reno, Nev, Jan 21, 44; s Charles Irwin Naylor & Ruth Griswold N; m 1967 to Kathryn Lowry. Educ: Stanford Univ, AB, 66; Yale Univ Law Sch, JD, 69; El Toro Eating Club. Polit & Govt Pos: Staff asst, US Sen George Murphy, Calif, 65; pres, Stanford Area Young Rep, 65-66; state treas, Calif Young Rep Col Fedn, 65-66; assoc mem, Rep State Cent Comt, Calif, 66, mem, 73-; mem exec comt, 73-; exec asst to state co-chmn, Conn United Citizens for Nixon/Agnew, 68; pres, Yale Univ Law Sch Rep Club, 68-69; deleg & mem credentials comt, Rep Nat Conv, 72; chmn, San Mateo Co Young Voters for the President, Calif, 72; alt mem, San Mateo Co Rep Cent Comt, 72-; vchmn, Bay Area Rep Alliance, 74. Bus & Prof Pos: Attorney, Pillsbury, Madison & Sutro, San Francisco, 69-; dir opers, Orphans Airlift, San Francisco, 75. Mil Serv: Entered as 2nd Lt, Army, 69, released as 1st Lt, 71, after serv in Ft Sill, Okla, 69-70 & I Field Force Unit, Vietnam Theatre, 70-71; 1st Lt, Res; Bronze Star Medal; Oak Leaf Cluster; Vietnam Serv Medal. Publ: Ed, Stanford Daily, 64-65; auth, Why conservatives shun the campus, Los Angeles Times, 7/17/66. Mem: Phi Beta Kappa; Calif State, San Francisco & San Mateo Bar Asns; Commonwealth Club of Calif. Relig: Methodist. Mailing Add: 2308 Olympic Ave Menlo Park CA 94025

NAZARIO DE FERRER, SILA (NEW PROGRESSIVE, PR)
Sen, PR Senate
Mailing Add: State Capitol San Juan PR 00901

NEAL, EARL (D)
Mem, Dem Nat Comt, Ill
Mailing Add: 6032 S Michigan Chicago IL 60637

NEAL, HARVEY IVAN (R)
Chmn, Keya Paha Co Rep Party, Nebr

b North Platte, Nebr, Oct 3, 40; s John Ivan Neal & Onetta Harvey N; m 1963 to Janet Gray; c Jeffery Dean & Jacqueline Ann. Educ: Miltonvale Wesleyan Col, AA, 59; Univ Nebr, BS & JD; Phi Alpha Delta. Polit & Govt Pos: Chmn, Keya Paha Co Rep Party, Nebr, 66-; co attorney, Keya Paha Co, 67- Bus & Prof Pos: Partner, Weddel & Neal Attorneys, Springview, Nebr, 64-; First Nat Bank of Springview, 67-, owner, 100 Bar Ranch, 70-; dir, Keya Paha Feed & Supply, Inc, 72-; dir, Unorthodox Fiberglass Specialties, Inc, 72- Mem: Am, Nebr State & 15th Judicial Dist Bar Asns; Springview Serv Club. Relig: Methodist. Mailing Add: Box 127 Springview NE 68778

NEAL, JAMES HUSTON (D)
Miss State Rep
Mailing Add: 1952 Camellia Lane Jackson MS 39204

NEAL, JAMES THOMAS (R)

b Lebanon, Ind, Jan 5, 21; s Ralph B Neal & Josephine Honan N; m 1953 to Georgiana Davis; c Anne deHayden & Andrea Davis. Educ: Butler Univ, BS, 42; US Mil Acad, BS, 45; Sigma Chi. Polit & Govt Pos: Secy, Hamilton Co Rep Cent Comt, Ind, 50-57; secy, Ind Rep State Comt, 57-68, chmn, 72-73; deleg, Rep Nat Conv, 72; mem, Rep Nat Comt, 72-73. Bus & Prof Pos: Ed, Noblesville Daily Ledger, 50- Mil Serv: Entered as 2nd Lt, Army, 45, released as 1st Lt, 49, after serv in Constabulary Unit, European Theatre, 46-48. Mem: Hoosier State Press & Inland Press Asns; Am Legion; Community Serv Coun (vpres, 69-); Indianapolis Press Club. Honors & Awards: Ed of Year, Ball State Univ, 66; Rep Ed of Year, Ind Rep State Comt, 68. Relig: Catholic. Mailing Add: 7670 E 126th St Noblesville IN 46060

NEAL, JOE (D)
Nev State Sen
Mailing Add: 304 Lance Ave North Las Vegas NV 89030

NEAL, PATRICK K (D)
Fla State Rep

b Des Moines, Iowa, Mar 4, 49; s Paul Neal, Jr & Patricia Kelleher N; m 1974 to Mary-Lee Folks. Educ: Univ Pa, 67-71; Iowa State Univ, 71; Univ SFla, 72; Phi Kappa Sigma. Polit & Govt Pos: Secy, Manatee Co Dem Comt, 73, treas, 73-74; Fla State Rep, 74- Mil Serv: Entered as Pvt, Army Res, 69, released as 2nd Lt, 75, after serv in 231st Transportation Co, 72-75. Mem: Manatee Co CofC (dir, 74-75); Longboat Key CofC (dir, 74-); Local, State & Nat Bd Realtors; Nat Audubon Soc; League of Conservative Voters. Honors & Awards: Nat Merit scholar. Relig: Roman Catholic. Legal Res: 4105 16th Ave W Bradenton FL 33505 Mailing Add: Box 500 Longboat Key FL 33540

NEAL, SARAH LEE (D)
WVa State Deleg

b Whitaker, WVa, Feb 24, 24; d Joseph Ruffner Parcell & Frankie Kelley P; m 1941 to Clifton Perry Neal; c Cynthia (Mrs Robert Parker Vines), Clifton Perry, Jr & Carleton Patrick. Educ: Greenbrier Co Pub Schs, WVa; ins schs & exten courses. Polit & Govt Pos: Mem, WVa Dem State Exec Comt, 68-; dir area III, Gov Hwy Safety Comn; mem, Greenbrier Co Dem Women & WVa Fedn Women Voters; WVa State Deleg, 20th Dist, 72-, vchmn agr & natural resources comt, finance comt & comt on fed rels, WVa House of Deleg; mem adv comt, Southeastern Interstate Forest Fire Protection Compact, 73-; dir, Rainelle Libr Comn, 73- Bus & Prof Pos: Pres, Rainelle Woman's Club, 72-; legis dir, Rainelle. Bus & Prof Woman's Club, 73- Mem: Greenbrier Valley Hist Soc; Order of Rainbow for Girls (mother adv); Pocahontas Co Farm Bur; Probs of the Aged (interim comt). Relig: Methodist. Legal Res: 310 11th St Rainelle WV 25962 Mailing Add: House of Deleg Capitol Bldg 1800 Washington St Charleston WV 25305

NEAL, STEPHEN LYBROOK (D)
US Rep, NC

b Winston-Salem, NC, Nov 7, 34; s Charles H Neal & Mary Martha Lybrook N; m 1963 to Rachel Landis Miller; c Mary Piper & Stephen Lybrook. Educ: Univ Calif, Santa Barbara; Univ Hawaii, AB in Psychol. Polit & Govt Pos: US Rep, Fifth Dist, NC, 75- Bus & Prof Pos: Pres, Community Press, Inc & Suburban Newspapers, Inc, Winston-Salem, NC, 66-; pres, King Publishing Co, Inc, King, 66-; pres, Yadkn Printing Co, Inc, Jonesville, 69- Mem: NC Press Asn; Nat Newspaper Asn; Rotary; Sigma Delta Chi. Relig: Episcopal. Legal Res: 604 Archer Rd Winston-Salem NC 27106 Mailing Add: 7828 Southdown Dr Alexandria VA 22308

NEAL, VERNON (D)
Tenn State Sen

b Byrdstown, Tenn, Oct 10, 31; s Levi Piercen Neal & Mary Della Cope N; m 1958 to Mona Joyce Mahan; c Belinda Sue, Jeffrey Dale & Melissa Gail. Educ: Tenn Tech Univ, BS, 52; Univ Tenn, LLB & JD, 56; Phi Delta Phi. Polit & Govt Pos: City attorney, Algood, Tenn, 60-68; Tenn State Rep, Putnam Co, 62-66; Tenn State Sen, 13th Sen Dist, 66-, mem educ & judiciary comt, Tenn State Sen, 67-, vchmn spec legis improv comt, 72, chmn spec reapportionment comt, 73-; secy gen welfare & environ comt, 73-; chmn rules & calendar comt, 73-; mem, Gov Task Force for Vocational Rehabilitation, 68. Bus & Prof Pos: Attorney-at-law, Cookeville, Tenn, 57-; bd dirs, Voc Training Ctr, 67- & Baptist Student Union, Tenn Technol Univ, 72- Mem: Am Bar Asn; Mason; Optimist; Farm Bur. Relig: Baptist. Mailing Add: 1008 Oaklawn Dr Cookeville TN 38501

NEALE, BETTY IRENE (R)
Colo State Rep
b Hiawatha, Kans, May 20, 30; d Ira Arthur Overfield & Nellie Beaty O; div; c Dory Alan, Steven Michael & Scott Patrick. Educ: Hiawatha High Sch, grad, 48. Polit & Govt Pos: Rep committeewoman, Denver, Colo, 65-70, Rep dist capt, 70-; co-chmn, Denver Sch Bd Campaign, 69; alt deleg, Rep Nat Conv, 72; Colo State Rep, 75- Bus & Prof Pos: Printing clerk, Colo House of Rep, 69-71; fed grants asst, City Auditor's Off, Denver, 71- Mem: Eng Speaking Union; Denver Civic Ballet Guild; Denver Symphony Guild; Denver Lyric Opera Guild; Rep Roundtable. Relig: Presbyterian. Mailing Add: 759 S Hudson Denver CO 80222

NEALL, ROBERT RAYMOND (R)
Md State Deleg
b Baltimore, Md, June 26, 48; s William Wesley Neall & Doris McGinnis N; m 1970 to Margaret Lindsay Glendinning; c Robert R, Jr. Educ: US Mil Acad, 68-69; Anne Arundel Community Col, AA, 71; Univ Md, College Park, BA, 72; Univ Baltimore Sch Law, 73-; Delta Sigma Phi. Polit & Govt Pos: Legis asst to minority leader, Md State Senate, 73-74; Md State Deleg, 75- Bus & Prof Pos: Gen mgr, Davidsonville Supply Co, 68- Mil Serv: Entered as Seaman Recruit, Navy, 67, released as Cadet, US Mil Acad, 69, after serv in US Corps Cadets, 68-69; Nat Defense Serv Medal. Mem: All Hallows Parish; Anne Arundel Co Young Rep Club; South Anne Arundel Businessmens Asn; Annapolis Jaycees. Honors & Awards: Young Rep Man of the Year, Anne Arundel Co Young Rep Club, 73. Relig: Episcopal. Legal Res: Central Ave Davidsonville MD 21035 Mailing Add: PO Box 299 Davidsonville MD 21035

NEALSON, OTTO H (R)
Iowa State Rep
Mailing Add: 510 E Seventh West Liberty IA 52776

NEAS, RALPH GRAHAM, JR (R)
b Brookline, Mass, May 17, 46; s Ralph Graham Neas & Elsie Marie Barone N; single. Educ: Univ Notre Dame, AB, 68; Univ Chicago Law Sch, JD, 71. Polit & Govt Pos: Legis attorney for civil rights, Cong Research Serv, Libr of Cong, 71-73; legis asst to US Sen Edward W Brooke, Mass, 73-, chief legis asst, 74- Bus & Prof Pos: Law clerk, Kirkland & Ellis, Attorneys, Chicago, 69-71; lawyer, Am Bar Found, Chicago, summer 71. Mil Serv: Entered as 2nd Lt, Army, released as 1st Lt, 72, after serv in Adj Gen Corps, spring 72; 1st Lt, Army Res, 75. Mem: Am & Ill Bar Asns. Relig: Roman Catholic. Legal Res: 807 C St SE Washington DC 20003 Mailing Add: Off of Sen Edward W Brooke 421 Russell Senate Off Bldg Washington DC 20003

NEBLETT, HARRY EDWARD (D)
Miss State Rep
Mailing Add: Drawer 26 Jonestown MS 38639

NEBLETT, WILLIAM EDWIN (D)
Mem, Lunenburg Co Dem Comt, Va
b Lunenburg Co, Va, June 1, 96; s William Edwin Neblett & Rosa Hite N; m 1930 to Virginia Louise Akers; c Virginia Akers (Mrs Dan A Jones). Educ: William & Mary Col, 15-17; Washington & Lee Univ, LLB, 22; Kappa Sigma. Polit & Govt Pos: Commonwealth attorney, Va, 24-48; mem, Lunenburg Co Dem Comt, Va, 35-, chmn, 61-72; comnr accts, Lunenburg Co, 60. Mil Serv: Entered as Pvt, Army, 17, released as Cpl, 19, after serv in 318th Inf, 80th Div, Artois Sect, St Mihiel Meuse Argonne Forest, 18-19. Mem: Va Trial Lawyers Asn; AF&AM; RAM; Am Legion; Kiwanis. Relig: Episcopal. Mailing Add: Lunenburg VA 23952

NEDZI, LUCIEN NORBERT (D)
US Rep, Mich
b May 28, 25; m to Margaret Garvey; c Lucien A, Bridget K, Brendan T, Gretchen T & Eric. Educ: Univ Mich, AB in Econ, 48; Univ Detroit Law Sch, 49; Univ Mich Law Sch, JD, 51. Polit & Govt Pos: Wayne Co Pub Adminr, Mich, 55; deleg, Dem Nat Conv, 60 & 68; US Rep, Mich, 61-; US deleg, Interparliamentary Union. Bus & Prof Pos: Attorney-at-law. Mil Serv: World War II, 20 months overseas duty, Philippines & Japan; Korean War. Mem: Numerous community, fraternal & legal orgns. Relig: Catholic. Legal Res: Detroit MI Mailing Add: 2418 Rayburn House Off Bldg Washington DC 20515

NEEDHAM, DAISY EUDORA (R)
Mem, La State Rep Cent Comt
b St Helena Parish, La, Dec 26, 99; d Archie Carter Lambert & Sally Epperson L; m 1921 to Patrick Michael Needham; c Gerald. Educ: High Sch. Polit & Govt Pos: Mem, La State Rep Cent Comt, St Helena Parish, currently. Relig: Protestant. Legal Res: St Helena Parish Greensburg LA 70441 Mailing Add: RFD 1 Box 59 Kentwood LA 70444

NEEDHAM, THOMAS H (R)
b Providence, RI, June 30, 22; s Marcus J Needham (deceased) & Margaret A Brennan N (deceased); m 1947 to Ursula F McHale; c Clair Ann, Thomas W, Jane F & Mark W. Educ: Providence Col, PhB cum laude, 46; Boston Univ, JD, 48, LLM, 51; Theta Chap, Delta Epsilon Sigma; lit ed, 46 Yearbook, Providence Col; mem, Student Coun & sr class pres, Boston Univ. Polit & Govt Pos: Deleg, two const conv, 50's; vpres, Warwick Young Rep, RI, 54; asst city solicitor, Warwick, 54; mem trial coun, Dept Pub Works, 65-67; RI State Sen, Dist 13, 67-74, Dep Minority Leader, RI Senate, 71-74; alt deleg, Rep Nat Conv, 72. Bus & Prof Pos: Attorney, 48-; mem staff, Strauss, Factor, Chernick & Hillmann. Mil Serv: Entered as Pvt, Army, 42, released as Sgt, 46, after serv in 1282nd Combat Engrs, European & Pac Theatres, 43-46; Army Res, 50-, Lt Col, 68- Publ: Changes in Article XV of the US Code of Military Justice, RI Bar J. Mem: Legal Aid Soc (bd dirs, 60-); Nat Conf on Comnrs on Uniform State Laws (bd dirs, 63-); Am Bar Asn; Am Arbit Asn; US Court Mil Appeals. Relig: Roman Catholic. Mailing Add: 19 Berwick Lane Cranston RI 02905

NEEDHAM, WILLIAM FELIX, JR (R)
Finance Chmn, Llano Co Rep Party, Tex
b Wharton, Tex, Jan 9, 26; s William Felix Needham & Ollie Rae Elmore N; m 1951 to Virginia Ann McWhorter; c Nan, Margaret & William Kearby. Educ: Univ Tex, Austin, BA, 49; Univ Houston, BS in Pharm, 53; Kappa Kappa Psi; Canterbury Club. Polit & Govt Pos: Chmn, Llano Co Rep Party, Tex, 64-68, finance chmn, 68-; sch trustee, Llano Ind Sch Bd, 68-, pres, 71-72; vchmn, George Bush for US Sen, Tex, 70; chmn, John G Tower for US Sen, 72. Bus & Prof Pos: Pharmacist & partner, Corner Drug Store, Llano, Tex, 63-; consult, Llano Mem Hosp, Care Inn of Llano & Hill Country Manor, 70- Mil Serv: Entered as Seaman, Naval Res, 44, released as Pharmacist Mate 3/C, 46, after serv in Hosp Corps, Naval Hosp, Seattle, Wash. Mem: Tex Pharmaceutical Asn; Lions; Llano CofC; Boy Scouts; Highland Lakes Tourist Asn. Honors & Awards: Most Valuable Citizen of Llano, Llano CofC, 67. Relig: Episcopal. Mailing Add: Longhorn Lane Llano TX 78643

NEEDLE, HOWARD J (D)
Md State Deleg
Mailing Add: 507 Maryland Trust Bldg Baltimore MD 21202

NEELEY, W WALTER (D)
WVa State Sen
Mailing Add: State Capitol Charleston WV 25305

NEELY, CHARLES BATCHELLER, JR (R)
State Chmn, NC Fedn Young Rep
b Raleigh, NC, Dec 11, 43; s Charles Batcheller Neely & Nancy Maupin N; m 1972 to Laura Elizabeth Dalton. Educ: Univ NC, Chapel Hill, BA with honors, 65; Duke Univ Law Sch, JD, 70; Phi Alpha Delta. Polit & Govt Pos: State chmn, NC Fedn Young Rep, 72-; mem exec & cent comt, NC Rep Party & Wake Co Rep Exec Comt; asst gen counsel, Young Rep Nat Fedn, 73- Bus & Prof Pos: Partner, Maupin, Taylor & Ellis, Attorneys-at-Law, Raleigh, NC, 70- Mil Serv: Entered as Ens, Naval Res, 65, released as Lt(jg), 67, after serv in USS Regulus, Pac Fleet; Lt Comdr, Naval Res, 10 years; Nat Defense, Vietnam Campaign Ribbons. Mem: Am Bar Asn; ROA; Naval Reserve Asn (secy-treas, Wake Co Chap, 73-); CofC. Honors & Awards: Order of the Golden Fleece. Relig: Episcopal. Legal Res: 5420 Parkwood Dr Raleigh NC 27612 Mailing Add: PO Box 829 Raleigh NC 27602

NEELY, MARION ROBERT (R)
b Billings, Mont, Dec 7, 23; s Ralph Bilyeau Neely & Frances McCrary N; m 1952 to Marilyn Joan Long; c Robert H & Susan K. Educ: Univ Iowa, BSC & JD; Phi Delta Phi. Polit & Govt Pos: Asst attorney gen, Iowa Dept Justice, 59-61; asst bar examr, Iowa State Bar Examrs, 61-64; chmn, Johnson Co Rep Cent Comt, Iowa, formerly; police judge, Iowa City Police Court, 66-70. Bus & Prof Pos: Territory mgr, John Deere Plow Co, Moline, 51-56. Mil Serv: Entered as Pvt, Army, 43, released, 46, after serv in 94th Div, ETO. Mem: Am Bar Asn (Traffic Court Prog Comt, 69-); State Hist Soc Iowa (bd curators, 70-); Iowa Lincoln Club; Am Legion; Mason. Relig: Methodist; mem bd trustees, First United Methodist Church, 66- Legal Res: 1127 Wylde Green Rd Iowa City IA 52240 Mailing Add: 510 Iowa State Bank Bldg Iowa City IA 52240

NEELY, RICHARD (D)
Judge, WVa Supreme Court of Appeals
b Los Angeles, Calif, Aug 2, 41; s John Champ Neely & Elinore Forlani N; single. Educ: Dartmouth Col, AB, 64; Yale Law Sch, LLB, 67; Phi Delta Phi; hon mem, Phi Sigma Kappa. Polit & Govt Pos: Chmn, Marion Co Bd Pub Health, 71-72; WVa State Deleg, 71-72; Judge, WVa Supreme Court of Appeals, 73- Bus & Prof Pos: Lawyer, 69- Mil Serv: Entered as 1st Lt, Army, 67, released as Capt, 69, after serv in Civil Opers & Revolutionary Develop Support, Third Corps Tactical Zone, Repub of Vietnam; Bronze Star; Vietnam Honor Medal 1/C. Mem: WVa State Bar; WVa Bar Asn; Am Econ Asn; Moose; Am Legion. Relig: Episcopal. Legal Res: Pinelea Country Club Rd Fairmont WV 26554 Mailing Add: E-306 Capitol Bldg Supreme Court of Appeals Charleston WV 25305

NEFF, CLARENCE EVERETT (R)
Ill State Rep
b New Berlin, Ill, Aug 3, 09; s Jesse James Neff & Elizabeth Ferira N; m 1947 to Elaine Droste; c Janice Elaine & Charles Edward. Educ: Tristate Col, elec eng, 32, civil eng, 33; Phi Sigma. Polit & Govt Pos: Finance chmn, Henderson Co Rep Cent Comt, Ill, 50-56, chmn, 56-; mayor, Stronghurst, Ill, 50-63; Ill State Rep, 63- Bus & Prof Pos: Vpres, Monco Fertilizer Co, 59-64, pres, C E Neff Co, 41-, Bank of Stronghurst, 46- & Gladstone Grain Co, 60- Mem: Elks; Mason; Shrine; Warren Co YMCA (bd); Robert Morris Col (bd). Relig: Lutheran. Mailing Add: Stronghurst IL 61480

NEFF, EDWIN DEFREES (R)
Asst Pub Rels Dir, Rep Cong Comt
b Ft Collins, Colo, Jan 24, 12; s Charles Melvin Neff & Louis DeFrees N; m 1942 to Alice Fitzhugh; c Alice Louise & Carola Grayson. Educ: Dartmouth Col, AB, 35; Columbia Univ, MS, 36; Kappa Kappa Kappa. Polit & Govt Pos: Mem staff, Rep Cong Comt, 59-69, asst pub rels dir, 69- Bus & Prof Pos: Med & sci reporter, Washington Times-Herald, 37-41 & 45-52, chief ed writer, 52; press dir, US CofC, 52-59. Mil Serv: Entered as Ens, Naval Res, 42, released as Lt(sg), 45, after serv in Com 14, Commun, Pac Theatre, 43-45; Pac Theatre Ribbon. Mem: Nat Press Club; Capitol Hill Club. Relig: Protestant. Legal Res: MD Mailing Add: 5806 Ridgefield Rd Washington DC 20016

NEFF, FRANCINE IRVING (R)
Mem, Rep State Cent Comt NMex
b Albuquerque, NMex, Dec 6, 25; d Edward Hackett Irving & Georga Henderson I; m 1948 to Edward John Neff; c Sindle & Edward Vann. Educ: Cottey Jr Col for Women, 46; Univ NMex, BA, 48; Phi Theta Kappa; Mortar Bd; Phi Kappa Phi; Pi Lambda Theta; Sigma Alpha Iota; Alpha Delta Pi. Hon Degrees: DHL, Mt St Mary Col, 74. Polit & Govt Pos: Rep chmn, Precinct 294, Bernalillo Co, 66-70; NMex State Adv, TAR, 66-68; mem, NMex State State Young Rep Exec Bd, 66-68; NMex State chmn, Women for Nixon-Agnew, 68; deleg & mem permanent orgn, Rep Nat Conv, 68, deleg & mem rules comt, 72; mem, Rep State Cent Comt NMex, 68-74, mem exec & finance comts, 70-74; mem, Albuquerque Fedn Rep Women, 71-; mem, Bernalillo Co Exec Bd, 69; Rep Nat Committeewoman, NMex, 70-74, mem exec comt, 72-74; treas, Western States Rep Conf, 72-; Treas, US, 74-, nat dir US Savings Bond Div, 74- Mem: Exec Women in Govt; Rep Women's Fed Forum, Washington, DC; Rep Hispanic Assembly; Nat Fedn Bus & Prof Women's Clubs, Inc; Washington Heart Asn, Inc (Heart Sunday chmn, 75). Relig: Episcopal. Legal Res: 1509 Sagebrush Trail SE Albuquerque NM 87123 Mailing Add: Off of Treas of US 15th St & Pennsylvania Ave Washington DC 20220

NEFF, VERN C (R)
Chmn, Dist One Rep Party, NDak
b McClusky, NDak, Jan 17, 27; s Charles Neff & Martha Schindler N; m 1950 to Juanita I Jones; c Donna Lynn (Mrs Doug Hagen), Barbara (Mrs David Nash) & Charles. Educ: Univ NDak, BS in Commerce, 51, Sch Law, JD with honors, 52; Phi Alpha Delta; pres, Phi Alpha Theta; Blue Key; Univ NDak Sch Law Jr Bar; Order of the Coif; assoc ed, NDak Law Rev, 52; Alpha Tau Omega. Polit & Govt Pos: All off & various chairmanships, Dist One Rep Party, NDak, 53-, chmn, 74-; mem, NDak State Rep Cent Comt, 74- Bus & Prof Pos: Asst states attorney, Williams Co, NDak, 53-54; attorney/partner, Bjella & Jestrab Law Firm, Williston, 55-; city attorney, Grenora, 58- Mil Serv: Entered as Pvt, Army, 44, released as

S/Sgt, 46, after serv in 503rd Parachute Regt, 11th Airborne Div, Pac Theatre; Army Res, 46-52, 1st Lt. Mem: NDak State Hist Bd (vpres); Williston Chamber & Indust Develop Comt (past chamber pres); Williston Elks (Past Exalted Ruler, trustee, currently); Williston Shrine (past pres); NDak State Parks Adv Coun. Honors & Awards: Williston Distinguished Serv Award, 58; NDak Distinguished Serv Award, 58; Boss of Year Award, 72. Relig: Methodist. Legal Res: 417 E Eleventh St Williston ND 58801 Mailing Add: PO Box 1526 Williston ND 58801

NEFZGER, ANNA MARIE (D)
Chmn, McCone Co Dem Cent Comt, Mont
b Watkins, Mont, Apr 20, 26; d Daniel Schlenker & Olga Neuhardt S; m 1950 to Donald Deane Nefzger; c Daniel Charles, Deanna Rae & Darrell Allan. Educ: Castlemont High Sch, grad, 44; Helena Voc-Tech Ctr, Cert, 72. Polit & Govt Pos: Committeewoman, McCone Co Dem Cent Comt, Mont, 65-69, secy, 65-73, precinct committeewoman, 72-74, chmn, 73- Bus & Prof Pos: Treas, United Christian Church, 71. Mem: VFW Auxiliary (state pres, 70-71, legis chmn, 72-75); Past Dept Presidents' Club (pres, 74-75); McCone Women's Bowling Asn; Mont Farmer's Union. Relig: Congregational. Mailing Add: RR1 Box 53 Vida MT 59274

NEGLEY, HAROLD HOOVER (R)
Supt Pub Instr, Ind
b Indianapolis, Ind, Dec 13, 21; s Arthur O Negley & Alma Hoover N; m 1944 to Helen Davies; c Susan, Janet & Jeffrey. Educ: DePauw Univ, AB, 44; Butler Univ, MA, 47; Ind Univ, Bloomington, EdD, 62; Phi Kappa Phi; Phi Delta Kappa; Phi Gamma Delta. Polit & Govt Pos: Dir of curriculum, Dept Pub Instr, Ind, 67, Asst Supt, 68-70, Supt, 73- Bus & Prof Pos: Hist teacher, Arsenal Tech High Sch, 47-48 & Shortridge High Sch, 48-58 & 70; dir econ educ, Indianapolis Pub Schs, 59-60 & supvr inserv educ, 60-67; dir, Ball State Univ Prog Grissom AFB, 71-72. Mil Serv: Entered as Seaman, Navy, 43, released as Lt(jg), 46, after serv in 8th Amphibious Fleet, Mediter. Publ: Ed, Indiana Government, Elm, Inc, 68; co-auth, US History, J B Lippencott, 73; auth, The Humanities & the Social Studies, Nat Coun Social Studies, 69. Mem: Ind State Teachers' Asn; Adult Educ Asn; Nat Coun Social Studies; Ind Supt Asn; Mason. Relig: Methodist. Legal Res: 5802 San Clemente Indianapolis IN 46226 Mailing Add: Rm 227 Dept of Pub Instr State Capitol Bldg Indianapolis IN 46204

NEGRI, DAVID (D)
Mem, Calif Dem State Cent Comt
b Burbank, Calif, Jan 29, 27; s Morris Negri & Sarah Massoth N; m 1965 to Sharon Alleta; c Donald Howard, Debra Susan, Sharon Anne, Kari Alleta, Renea Sari & Brian David. Educ: Univ Calif, Los Angeles, AA, 51; Stanford Univ, BA, 52, LLB, 54; Phi Eta Sigma; Beta Gamma Sigma; mem, Moot Court Bd; co-chmn, Marion Rice Kirkwood Moot Court Competition. Polit & Govt Pos: Treas, San Fernando Valley Dem Club, Calif, 50; mem, Fernando Dem Club, 58; mem lawyer's comt, Rudd Brown for Cong, 58; 41st assembly dist coordr, Glenn Anderson for Lt Gov, 58; deleg, 21st Cong Coun, 58-60; deleg, 41st Assembly Dist Coun, 58-66; pres, San Fernando Dem Club, 59; discussion leader, Calif Dem Issues Conf, 59; chmn exec comt, Elec of Tom Carrell, 59-60; deleg, Dem Issues Conf & Endorsing Conv, 59-66; mem, Calif Dem State Cent Comt, 60, 62 & currently; mem, Los Angeles Co Dem Cent Comt, 60, 62, 64 & currently, secy, 60-62; trustee, 41st Assembly Dist Coun, 60-61; deleg, 22nd Cong Dist Coun, 60-66; mem, Adv Comt for Tom Carrell, 62 & 64; coordr, Gov Campaign for Northeast San Fernando Valley, 62; registr chmn, NE Valley Area, Los Angeles Co Comt, 63-64; vchmn, 22nd Cong Dem Coun, 64-65; deleg, Gov Conf Youth, 65; mem, Mex-Am Polit Asn; Calif State Assemblyman, 41st Dist, 66-68; Calif State Rep at Detroit Smog Hearings & Inspecting Rapid Transit Systs in Montreal & Toronto, Can, 68. Mil Serv: Entered as A/S, Maritime Serv, 44, released as Ens, 47, after serv as chief radio operator in High-Octane Tankers, SPac. Mem: San Fernando CofC; Elks; Am Bar Asn; Am Judicature Soc; San Fernando Lions. Relig: Jewish. Legal Res: 11806 Jellico Ave Granada Hills CA 91344 Mailing Add: 563 S Brand Blvd San Fernando CA 91340

NEIDEFFER, DAVID LEE (R)
Exec Dir, Md Rep Party
b Ann Arbor, Mich, Oct 1, 44; s Robert Lee Neideffer & Margaret O'Reardon N; m 1973 to Carole Morgan; c Lisa, Kimberly & Laura. Educ: Univ Louisville, BS in Com, 67; chmn, Deans Adv Comt, 66-67. Polit & Govt Pos: Regional dir, US Rep Gude, Md, 68; polit coordr, US Sen Mathias, Md, 68; pub rels chmn, Montgomery Co Cent Comt, 69; mem, 70 for 70 Comt, 70; regional dir, Kendall for Co Exec, 70; exec vpres, Young Rep, 70-71, pres, 71-72; exec dir, Md Comt to Reelect the President, 72; exec dir, Md Rep Party, 73- Bus & Prof Pos: Supvr new model introductions NAm, Gen Elec, Louisville, Ky, 63-67; sales mgr, Air Pollution Control Div, Am Air Filter, Kensington, Md, 67-72. Mem: Nat Asn Power Engrs. Honors & Awards: Outstanding Scholar & Serv, Univ Louisville, 66-67; Outstanding Precinct Chmn, Montgomery Co, 69-71; Outstanding Young Rep, Montgomery Co Young Rep, 70-72. Relig: Baptist. Legal Res: 8710 Liberty Lane Potomac MD 20854 Mailing Add: PO Box 108 Kensington MD 20795

NEIDER, C W (R)
Idaho State Rep
Mailing Add: West 210 Neider Ave Coeur d'Alene ID 83814

NEIDITZ, DAVID HENRY (D)
Conn State Sen
b Hartford, Conn, Nov 18, 30; s Moses Jacob Neiditz & Rachel Podnetsky N; m 1954 to Minerva Heller; c Jonathan Aaron & Robert Michael. Educ: Dartmouth Col, AB, 52; Harvard Univ Law Sch, JD, 55. Polit & Govt Pos: Conn State Rep, formerly; alt deleg, Dem Nat Conv, 72; Conn State Sen, currently. Bus & Prof Pos: Attorney, Hartford, 55- Mem: Comt Suggested State Legis, Coun, State Govt; Wadsworth Atheneum (trustee, 58-); YMCA (dir, Metrop Hartford, 71-); Hartford Pub Libr, Inst Living, St Francis Hosp (corporator, 71-). Honors & Awards: Outstanding State Legislator Award, Eagleton Inst Polit, Rutgers Univ, 70. Relig: Jewish. Mailing Add: 33 Fulton Pl West Hartford CT 06107

NEILL, JOHN ALEXANDER (D)
Miss State Rep
Mailing Add: Box 686 Laurel MS 39440

NEILL, KENNETH R (R)
Chmn, Mont State Rep Cent Comt
Mailing Add: 166 Riverview C Great Falls MT 59401

NEILS, BETTY JO (R)
Mem Exec Bd, Wash Fedn Rep Women
b Wenatchee, Wash, June 27, 19; d Joseph W Bouska & Florence Fry B; m 1943 to Edward Walter Neils; c Christopher B, David J & Eric W. Educ: Wash State Univ, BA, 40, BEd, 41; Nat Collegiate Radio Guild; Nat Collegiate Players; Pi Beta Phi. Polit & Govt Pos: Pres, Klickitat Co Women Rep Club, Wash, 52-53, secy, 53-54, pres, 58-60; prog chmn, Wash Fedn Rep Women, 54-55, treas, 67-71, mem exec bd, 72-; vchmn, Klickitat Co Rep Cent Comt, 60-67; vchmn, Wash State Rep Cent Comt, 71-72; deleg, Rep Nat Conv, 72, mem platform comt. Bus & Prof Pos: Asst dir audiovisual dept, Spokane Pub Schs, Wash, 41-42; dir sch of the air, Sta KOAC, Corvallis, Ore, 42-43 & currently; pres, KPFC Pub Progs; consumer mem, State Bd Nursing, currently. Publ: Now You Can Vote, 72. Mem: Preserv Gov Mansion Found (state bd mem); Tacoma Town Hall (bd mem). Relig: Lutheran; mem, Inter-Lutheran Comn Continuing Educ. Mailing Add: 12 Thornewood Lane SW Tacoma WA 98498

NEILS, HOWARD WILLIAM (R)
Chmn, Dist 32 Rep Party, NDak
b Bismarck, NDak, Nov 25, 29; s William Walter Neils & Katherine Kaelberer N; m 1956 to Dorothy Ann Anderson; c Jeffrey, Julie & Pamela. Educ: Bismarck Jr Col, AS, 49; Univ NDak, BS, 57; Sigma Tau. Polit & Govt Pos: Precinct committeman, Rep Party, NDak, 62-; chmn, Dist 32 Rep Party, 72- Bus & Prof Pos: Chem engr, Standard Oil Co, Ind, 57-64, process supt, 64-74. Mil Serv: Entered as Pvt, Air Force, 50, released as T/Sgt, 54, after serv in European Theatre. Mem: Am Legion; Am Inst Chem Engrs. Relig: Lutheran. Mailing Add: 2119 Assumption Dr Bismarck ND 58501

NEISEN, HOWARD J (DFL)
Minn State Rep
Mailing Add: 5150 Irondale Rd Moundsview MN 55112

NEISLER, ROBERT PRESTON (R)
Committeeman, SC State Rep Exec Comt
b Kings Mountain, NC, Aug 11, 36; s Joseph Andrew Neisler & Annie Lee Miller N; m 1959 to Nora Jane Deese; c Robert Preston, Jr, Matthew Ramseur & Christopher Edgar. Educ: Lenoir Rhyne Col, BS, 60; Sigma Phi Epsilon. Polit & Govt Pos: Deleg, SC State Rep Conv, 62; pres, Rep Party, Pageland Precinct, SC, 62-64; finance chmn, Chesterfield Co Rep Party, 64-66; state exec committeeman, SC State Rep Party, 64-66, adv, SC TAR, 66; deleg, Rep Nat Conv & SC rep to permanent orgn comt, 68; chmn, Fifth Cong Dist Rep Party, 68-70; mem, SC State Steering Comt, 69-70; orgn chmn, Ravenel for Gov; committeeman, SC State Rep Exec Comt, 71-; co chmn, Comt to Reelect the President, 72. Bus & Prof Pos: Pres, Chesterfield Yarn Mills, Pageland, SC, 59-; vpres, Lucky Strike Yarn Mills, Shelby, NC, 63- Mem: Jaycees; Chesterfield Co Soc Crippled Children & Adults; Chesterfield Co Asn Retarded Children (finance chmn, 68-). Relig: Associate Reformed Presbyterian. Legal Res: Rte 1 Pageland SC 29728 Mailing Add: Chesterfield Yarn Mills Pageland SC 29728

NEITZEL, ANGIE (D)
Polit & Govt Pos: Mem, Dem Nat Comt, Idaho, formerly. Mailing Add: 2741 Barton Rd Pocatello ID 83201

NEJEDLY, JOHN ALBERT (R)
Calif State Sen
b Oakland, Calif, Berkeley, BS, 35, Boalt Hall Sch Law, LLB, 41. Polit & Govt Pos: Dep dist attorney, Richmond, Calif, 46-58; city attorney, Walnut Creek, 46-58, gen counsel, Contra Costa Sanit Dist, 50-58; dist attorney, Contra Costa Co, Martinez, 58-69; Calif State Sen, Seventh Dist, 69- Bus & Prof Pos: Mem faculty, St Marys Col (Calif), 59-62 & eng exten, Univ Calif, 59-70. Mil Serv: Entered Air Force, 42, released as Warrant Off (jg), 46, after serv in Air Tech Intel, SPac Theatre. Mem: Am Legion; Sierra Club; Elks; Moose. Honors & Awards: One of Ten Outstanding Americans in Conserv, Am Motors Award, 65. Relig: Catholic. Legal Res: 400 Montecillo Dr Walnut Creek CA 94595 Mailing Add: 1393 Civic Dr Walnut Creek CA 94596

NELSEN, ANCHER (R)
b Renville Co, Minn, Oct 11, 04; s Nels Peter Nelsen & Elisabeth Anderson N; m 1929 to Ilo Irene Zimmerman, wid; c Richard, Bruce & Miriam (Mrs Sommerness). Educ: Brownton High Sch. Polit & Govt Pos: Minn State Sen, McLeod Co, 36-48; Lt Gov, Minn, 53; adminr, Rural Electrification Admin, 53-56; US Rep, Second Cong Dist, Minn, 59-74. Mem: AF&AM; Minn Farm Bur. Relig: Lutheran. Mailing Add: Rte 4 Hutchinson MN 55350

NELSON, BRUCE (R)
Minn State Rep
Mailing Add: R 1 Staples MN 56479

NELSON, C WILLIAM (BILL) (D)
Fla State Rep
Mailing Add: Rte 2 Box 162 Melbourne FL 32901

NELSON, CLARENCE A (R)
Treas, SC Rep Party
b Minn, Dec 17, 97; s Adolphus Nelson & Elsie Renberg N; m to Barbara Sawyer; c Mark. Polit & Govt Pos: Treas, SC Rep Party, 62-; alt deleg, Rep Nat Conv, 64-72; chmn, Saluda Co Rep Party, currently. Bus & Prof Pos: Trustee, Araxine Wilkins Found, 62-; vpres, Sawyer Corp, 66- Mil Serv: Entered as Pvt, Army, 17, released as Lt Col, 46, after serv in Engrs. Mailing Add: Box 235A Rte 3 Batesburg SC 29006

NELSON, DAVID ALDRICH (R)
b Watertown, NY, Aug 14, 32; s Carlton Low Nelson & Irene Aldrich N; m 1956 to Mary Ellen Dickson; c Frederick D, Claudia B & Caleb E. Educ: Hamilton Col, AB, 54; Cambridge Univ, 54-55; Harvard Law Sch, LLB, 58; Phi Beta Kappa; Emerson Lit Soc. Polit & Govt Pos: Gen counsel, Post Off Dept, 69-72, asst postmaster gen & gen counsel, US Postal Serv, 71- Bus & Prof Pos: Assoc, Squire, Sanders & Dempsey, Cleveland, Ohio, 58-67, partner, 67-69 & 72- Mil Serv: Off of the Gen Counsel, Dept Air Force, Washington, DC, 59-62; Maj, Air Force Res, 70. Mem: Cleveland, Am & Ohio State Bar Asns. Honors & Awards: Benjamin Franklin Award, 69. Relig: Congregational. Mailing Add: 2699 Wadsworth Rd Shaker Heights OH 44122

NELSON, DIXIE LEE (R)
b San Francisco, Calif, Mar 31, 31; d Irvin Heber Anderson & Dixie Doolittle A; m 1958 to Thomas Edward Nelson; c Eric Marshall, Katherine Lee, Elizabeth Ann & Patricia Marie. Educ: Univ Utah, BA, 60; Air Force ROTC Sponsor Corps. Polit & Govt Pos: Chmn, Benton Co Rep Affairs Coun, 65-66; vchmn, Wilson for State Rep Comt, 66; vchmn, Area Four, Benton Co Rep Party, 66-67, chmn, 67-68; chmn, Benton Co Rep Precinct Orgn, 67-68; vchmn, Montgomery for Secy of State Comt, 68; chmn, Benton Co Rep Cent Comt, 68-72; chmn precinct orgn, Rep State Cent Comt Ore, 70-, vchmn elec law reform, 70- Bus & Prof Pos: French teacher, Corvallis High Sch, Ore, 62-63; secy, Whitney Ball Ins, 64-65; Coop Mgrs Asn, 65-69. Relig: Episcopal. Mailing Add: 7015 NW Mountain View Dr Corvallis OR 97330

NELSON, DONALD T (R)
Ind State Rep
Mailing Add: 569 King Dr Indianapolis IN 46260

NELSON, EARL E (D)
Mich State Sen
Mailing Add: 519 McPherson Lansing MI 48915

NELSON, FRANK V (R)
Asst Attorney Gen, Utah
b Salt Lake City, Utah, Oct 22, 19; s N Fred Nelson & Florence Littlewood N; m 1947 to Jean Anderson; c Eric V, Jeff V, Kent A & Ron A. Educ: Univ Utah, BS, JD, 49. Polit & Govt Pos: Utah State Rep, 65-70; Asst Attorney Gen, Utah, currently. Mil Serv: Entered as Aviation Cadet, Navy, 42, released as Lt, 46, after serv in Navy Air Corps, Pac. Mem: Utah State Bar; Salt Lake Co Bar. Relig: Latter-day Saint. Mailing Add: 1866 Wasatch Dr Salt Lake City UT 84108

NELSON, GARY ALFRED (R)
Wash State Rep
b Spokane, Wash, Apr 11, 36; s Nels Alfred Nelson & Laura Marie Winberg N; m 1959 to JoAnne Laura Knutson; c Grant A, Geoffrey A & Gregory B; Educ: Wash State Univ, BS, 58; Univ Pa, 59; Univ Wis, MS, 63; Univ Wash, 64 & 65; Phi Kappa Tau; Tau Beta Pi; Sigma Tau; Phi Kappa Phi; Cougar Club. Polit & Govt Pos: Mem planning comn, Edmonds, Wash, 66-67, city councilman, 67-; Wash State Rep, 21st Dist, 73- Bus & Prof Pos: Mem bd dirs, Snohomist Co Emergency Dispatch Agency, 70-73; chmn, Snohomist Co Transit Bd, 71-73. Mil Serv: Entered as 2nd Lt, Air Force, 60, released as Capt, 62, after serv in 30th Air Div, Air Defense Command; Armed Forces Commun & Electronics Award. Publ: Becoming a professional engineer, Data Link Mag, 65. Mem: Inst Elec & Electronic Engrs; Registered Prof Engr of Wash; Jaycees (state dir, 64-); Edmonds Yacht Club. Honors & Awards: Outstanding Jaycee, Edmonds Jaycees, 66 & Distinguished Serv Award, 73. Relig: Lutheran. Mailing Add: 18423 High St Edmonds WA 98020

NELSON, GARY DEAN (D)
Regional Chmn, SDak State Dem Party
b Martin, SDak, July 15, 35; s Melvin T Nelson & Helen Westbrook N; m 1955 to Dorene A Williams; c Gwen Marie, Timothy Lane, Randall Dean, Mark Alan, Patricia Ann & Mary Ellen. Educ: High sch. Polit & Govt Pos: Regional chmn, SDak State Dem Party, 70-; mem, State Dem Party Exec Bd, 70-; deleg, Selection Comt for the Nat Conv, 71. Bus & Prof Pos: Farmer & rancher, currently; owner, Gary Nelson Ins Agency, 71-; state dir educ TV, SDak, 72. Mem: Nat Farmers Union. Mailing Add: Rural Box 4 Martin SD 57551

NELSON, GARY KENT (R)
b LaCrosse, Wis, July 12, 35; s Angus Nelson & Nora Nederloe N; m 1959 to Juanita Gay Moen; c Bradley, Byron, Douglas & Gregory. Educ: Ariz State Univ, BS, 57; Univ Ariz, LLB, 62; Phi Eta Sigma; Phi Kappa Phi; Delta Sigma Phi; Phi Delta Phi. Polit & Govt Pos: Law clerk to Justice Fred C Struckmeyer, Jr, Ariz Supreme Court, 62-63; Asst Attorney Gen, Ariz, 64-68, Attorney Gen, 68-74; mem, President's Consumer Adv Coun, Washington, DC, 71-; mem, Nat Adv Comn on Criminal Justice Standards & Goals, 71-73. Bus & Prof Pos: Assoc, Kramer Roche, Burch & Streich Law Firm, Phoenix, Ariz, 63-64. Mil Serv: Entered as 2nd Lt, Army, 57, released as 1st Lt, 59, after serv in Mil Intel Unit, 5th Army, 58-59; Capt, Res, 59-64. Mem: Am Bar Asn; Nat Asn Attorneys Gen; South Mountain Lions; Boy Scouts; Ariz State Justice Planning Agency (chmn). Relig: Lutheran. Mailing Add: 131 W Gary Way Phoenix AZ 85041

NELSON, GAYLORD ANTON (D)
US Sen, Wis
b Clear Lake, Wis, June 4, 16; s Dr Anton Nelson; m 1947 to Carrie Lee Dotson. Educ: San Jose State Col, 39; Univ Wis, law degree, 42. Polit & Govt Pos: Wis Legis, 48; Gov, Wis, 58-62; US Sen, Wis, 62-, chmn employ, poverty & migratory labor subcomt of labor & pub welfare comt, US Senate, chmn select comt on small bus, chmn pvt pension plans subcomt on senate finance comt & select comt on nutrition & human needs. Mil Serv: Army, 46 months, serv in Okinawa Campaign. Legal Res: Madison WI Mailing Add: Senate Off Bldg Washington DC 20510

NELSON, GORDON LEE (DFL)
b Minneapolis, Minn, May 1, 36; s Carl Barton Nelson & Muriel Johnson N; single. Educ: Univ Minn, Minneapolis, BA, 58, MA, 59; Luther Theol Sem, BD, 63; Univ Chicago, MA, 65, PhD, 72; Phi Beta Kappa. Polit & Govt Pos: Chmn, 34th Sen Dist Dem-Farmer-Labor Cent Comt, Minn, 70-72, chmn, 60th Sen Dist, 72-74; mem, Minn Dem-Farmer-Labor Cent Comt, 70-74; mem, Minneapolis Bd Estimate & Taxation, 73- Bus & Prof Pos: Instr, United Theol Sem, New Brighton, Minn, 66-67; asst prof sociol, Augsburg Col, 67- Publ: The Edge of the Ghetto, Seabury Press, 66. Mem: Midwest Sociol Soc; Am Sociol Asn; Soc for Sci Study Relig; Am Soc Christian Ethics; Am Asn Univ Prof. Relig: Lutheran. Mailing Add: 2550 39th Ave S Minneapolis MN 55406

NELSON, HAROLD C (R)
Mont State Sen
Mailing Add: 704 Third St SE Cut Bank MT 59427

NELSON, HELEN M (R)
Co Comnr, Grays Harbor Co, Wash
b Hoquiam, Wash; m 1933 to Lanpher Wyman Nelson. Educ: Inserv Mgt & Leadership Training Courses; Dale Carnegie Course, grad; Mid Mgt Training, Univ Southern Calif, 64. Polit & Govt Pos: Attended Fed Civil Defense Conf, Washington, DC, 51; mem, Mayor's Comt for New Libr, Aberdeen, Wash, formerly; civil defense secy, Grays Harbor Co Bd, formerly; mem, State Coun on Aging Comt, formerly; spearheaded reorganization, Grays Harbor Women's Rep Club, 57-58; precinct worker, State Grow Prog, 57-; committeewoman, Wash Rep State Comt, Grays Harbor Co, 60-64 & currently; hostess & observer, Rep Nat Comt Meeting, Seattle, Wash, 62; mem, Wash Rep State Cent & Exec Comts, 63-64; mem pub rels comt, Co Cent Comt & Women's Club; mem, Gov Comn Status of Women, 63-70; alt deleg, Rep Nat Conv, 64, observer & Nixon vol, 68 & 72; exec secy, Grays Harbor Co Rep Cent Comt, formerly, chmn, 74-; State Conf chmn, Washington, DC, 65; pres, Rep Women's Club, 65-66; Rep area co-chmn, Dist 2, Grays Harbor Co, 65-67; co comnr, Grays Harbor Co, currently; Rep precinct committeewoman, Aberdeen, 66-; deleg or alt deleg, All State Rep Conv; attended All Rep Women's Fedn State Conv, Conf & Dist & Workshop Meetings in Off Capacity; deleg, Rep Nat Comt, Women's Conf, Washington, DC, 69; dir, Cong Dist 3, Wash Fedn Rep Women, 70-74. Bus & Prof Pos: Vpres, Dean & Nelson Home Construction Co, formerly; dept head, Pac Northwest Bell, 42-62; co-owner & mgr, Nelde Manor Apt, Aberdeen, 60- Mem: United Way (bd dirs); Grays Harbor Soroptimist Club; Wash Fedn Bus & Prof Women's Clubs; Tel Pioneers of Am; VFW Auxiliary. Honors & Awards: Named State Woman of Achievement for Community Serv, Wash State Fedn Bus & Prof Women's Clubs, 61; Merit Cert, Am Red Cross & Nat Found Infantile Paralysis; Gold Key Award, Wash State Fedn Bus & Prof Women; First Heart Award, Grays Harbor Rep Party; Outstanding Woman of Achievement, League of Women Voters, 72. Relig: United Presbyterian; past pres, Womens Asn, United Presby Church, Aberdeen. Mailing Add: 600 N I St Aberdeen WA 98520

NELSON, HENRY ALBIN (R)
Mem, Hubbard Co Rep Exec Comt, Minn
b Oakes, NDak, Mar 23, 94; s John Nelson & Sophie Moberg N; m 1928 to Mabel Blanche Anderson. Educ: Gustavus Adolphus Col, 19-20; Univ NDak, JD, 24; Lambda Chi Alpha; Phi Alpha Delta. Polit & Govt Pos: Mem, Hubbard Co Rep Exec Comt, 63-; deleg, Minn Rep State Conv, 66-72; first asst chmn, Hubbard Co Rep Party, 69-, acting chmn, 70. Bus & Prof Pos: Law partner, Owens & Nelson, Williston, NDak, 24-36; with US Customs, 34th Dist, 36-60, Wages & Hours Comn, 52-60; retired. Mil Serv: Entered as Pvt, Army, 18, released as Pfc, 19, after serv in Co M, 140th Inf, 35th Div, France, 18-19; Purple Heart. Mem: NDak & Am Bar Asns; Mason; Am Legion. Relig: Protestant. Mailing Add: Rte 4 Box 121 Park Rapids MN 56470

NELSON, JAMES FREDERICK, JR (D)
Mem Exec Comt, Dem Party Ga
b Macon, Ga, Apr 12, 45; s James Frederick Nelson & Nina McQuaig N; m 1972 to Brenda Abernathy; c William Turner. Educ: Univ Ga, BBA, 67; Atlanta Law Sch, LLB, 70; Delta Theta Phi; Kappa Alpha Order. Polit & Govt Pos: Mem exec comt, Dem Party Ga, 74-; city court judge, Dublin, Ga, 74- Bus & Prof Pos: Partner, Nelson & Nelson, Attorneys, Dublin, Ga, 72- Mem: Dublin Rotary Club (treas, 73-75, bd dirs, 75-); Laurens Co Cancer Soc (bd dirs, 73-75); Toastmasters Int; Dublin Bar Asn (treas, 73, vpres, 74). Relig: Methodist; steward, First Methodist Church, 73-75. Legal Res: 1516 Woodrow Ave Dublin GA 31021 Mailing Add: 125 N Franklin St Dublin GA 31021

NELSON, JAMES LEE (R)
Chmn, Columbia Co Rep Cent Comt, Wash
b Bessmer, Mich, Sept 28, 35; s Roy M Nelson & Elizabeth Thenemann N; m 1956 to Diana Shirley Lemberg; c Jill, Kevin, James, Keith & Daniel. Educ: SDak State Univ, BS, 60. Polit & Govt Pos: Vchmn, Columbia Co Rep Cent Comt, Wash, 73-75, chmn, 75- Bus & Prof Pos: Mem bd dirs, Asn of Wash Bus, 71-; chmn, Wash Food Processors Coun, 73-74; mem bd dirs, Northwest Food Processors Asn, 74-, mem exec comt, 75- Mem: CofC (vpres, 74-75); Boosters Club; Dayton Days Inc. Mailing Add: 813 E Clay Dayton WA 99328

NELSON, JEANNE ROSS (R)
VChmn, Conn Rep State Cent Comt
b Melrose, Mass, May 25, 24; d Frank Artell Ross & Ida Fales; div; c Peter Ross, Jeffrey Scott & Debra. Educ: Univ Maine, Orono, AB, 45; Tri Delta. Polit & Govt Pos: Pres, Darien Women's Rep Asn, 67-70; vchmn, Darien Rep Town Comt, 72-74; vchmn, Conn Rep State Comt, 73- Mailing Add: 5 Oak Park Ave Darien CT 06820

NELSON, JOANI MICHAELLE (D)
b Ellendale, NDak, Apr 20, 56; d Donald Alfred Nelson (deceased) & Doris Guhin N; single. Educ: Northern State Col, 73-; managing ed col newspaper, Exponent, Col Dem, Newman Club & Nat Womens Polit Caucus; Quill & Scroll. Polit & Govt Pos: Cong Intern, US Sen James G Abourezk, 73; pres, Brown Co Young Dem, 73-74; first dist vpres, SDak Young Dem, 74-75; deleg, Dem Nat Mid-Term Conf, 74; legis intern, SDak Legis, 75. Bus & Prof Pos: Student secy speech dept, Admin Serv at Northern State Univ, 74; Mem: Nat Forensics League. Honors & Awards: KABY-TV Award for Speech; Aberdeen Am Legion Oratory Medal for taking First Place in Local Contest. Relig: Roman Catholic. Mailing Add: Apt 10 611 S Kline Aberdeen SD 57401

NELSON, JOE THOMAS (D)
b Munday, Tex, Oct 14, 23; s Clyde Nelson & Blanche N; m 1947 to Varina LeBeau; c Renee. Educ: NTex State Univ, BS in Biol, 48; Baylor Univ Col Med, grad, 51. Polit & Govt Pos: Deleg, Dem Nat Mid-Term Conf, 74. Bus & Prof Pos: Mem bd regents, NTex State Univ, 59-70; mem bd regents, Univ Tex Syst Bd, currently, chmn med affairs comt of bd, 71- Mem: Life mem Tex Med Asn (secy, Bd Trustees, past immediate chmn, Coun on Legis, mem exec bd & deleg to Am Med Asn, chmn of Tex deleg to Am Med Asn); Southern Med Asn (pres, 73-74 & dir, currently); Am Med Asn (mem bd trustees, 74-); Int Platform Asn; Newcomen Soc NAm. Honors & Awards: Citation for outstanding contrib to Am Community, Am Honorarium; Award for Leadership, WTex CofC, 66; Distinguished Serv Award, Southern Med Asn, 70; First Distinguished Alumnus Award, John Peter Smith Hosp; Outstanding Alumnus Award, Baylor Col Med, 73. Mailing Add: 201 S Waco St Weatherford TX 76086

NELSON, JOHN CLIFFORD (R)
Chmn, 63rd Rep Dist Cent Comt, Colo
b Walters, Okla, Dec 11, 21; s Edward Nelson (deceased) & Goldie Wills N; m 1944 to Eva Frances Schutte; c Jo Ann & Michael Jon. Educ: Cameron Jr Col, 6 months. Polit & Govt Pos: Rep committeeman, Precinct 14, Rio Grande Co, Colo, 64-66; deleg, Rep State Conv, 65; chmn, Rio Grande Co Rep Cent Comt, formerly; chmn, 63rd Rep Dist Cent Comt, Colo, 70-; secy, 33rd Sen Dist Cent Comt, Colo, 70- Bus & Prof Pos: Mgr-meat-cutter, Wholesale-Retail Meat Plant, 38-58; customer serv rep, Pub Serv Co, Colo, 58- Mil Serv: Entered as Pvt, Nat Guard, 39, released as Cpl, 40, after serv in Signal Sect-Battery D, 168th Field Artil. Mem: Elks; Monte Vista Lions Club (mem bd); Monte Vista Old Timers Boys

Baseball Asn (bd mem, treas); Monte Vista Country Club; San Luis Valley Chap, Nat Found (mem bd). Relig: Catholic. Mailing Add: Rte 2 Monte Vista CO 81144

NELSON, KNOX (D)
Ark State Sen
Mailing Add: 901 W 46th Pine Bluff AR 71601

NELSON, LEROY JAMES (D)
Mem, Mich Dem State Cent Comt
b Spalding, Mich, July 28, 22; s Hans Peter Nelson & Florence Mae Vincent N; m 1942 to Theadora Mae Fillion; c LeRoy William, Michael James, Sharman Ann, John Robert & Georgeanne Marie. Educ: Bay de Noc Community Col, credits; Mich Technol Univ, 1 year. Polit & Govt Pos: Treas, Powers Spalding Sch Bd, Mich, 49-53; br mgr, Secy of State, 56-66; Dem cand for Mich State Sen, 62 & 64; dir equalization dept, Menominee Co, Mich, 66-; deleg, Dem Nat Conv, 68; chmn, Menominee Co Dem Party, Mich, 68-72; mem exec comt, 11th Cong Dist Dem Party, 68-, chmn commun & educ, 69-; mem, Mich Dem State Cent Comt, 70-; Dem cand, Mich State Legis, 72. Mil Serv: Entered as Seaman 1/C, Navy, 42, released as SM 2/C, 45, after serv in 3rd & 5th Fleets, Asiatic-Pac Theatre & Philippine Liberation, 43-45. Mem: Int Asn Assessing Officers; Am Legion; KofC. Relig: Catholic. Mailing Add: Box 5 Powers MI 49874

NELSON, MARK DAVID (R)
b Milwaukee, Wis, Apr 23, 49; s David F Nelson & Elaine Muehl N; single. Educ: Dartmouth Col, BA, 71; Univ Wis Law Sch. Polit & Govt Pos: Youth for Nixon coordr, NH Primary, 68; Dartmouth legis intern, NH Legis, 69; voter serv chmn, New Eng Col Rep Fedn, 69-70; secy, NH Rep Col Caucus, 69-70; intern, US Rep Glenn R Davis, summer 70; deleg & mem comt of permanent orgn, Rep Nat Conv, 72; chmn, Second & Fourth Dist Young Wis Voters for the President, 72. Mem: Phi Beta Kappa; Order of the Coif. Relig: Lutheran. Mailing Add: Apt 211 920 E Mason St Milwaukee WI 53202

NELSON, MAURICE A (D)
Chmn, Cheyenne Co Dem Party, Nebr
b Cheyenne Co, Nebr, Mar 24, 10; s Edward M Nelson & Verda J Glassburn N; m 1931 to Enid L Edwards; c Nadine V (Mrs Cassata). Educ: Sidney High Sch, Nebr, grad, 28; Lincoln Airplane & Auto Sch, grad, 28. Polit & Govt Pos: Deleg, Cheyenne Co Dem Conv, 66-68; deleg, Nebr Dem State Conv, 70; chmn, Cheyenne Co Dem Party, 70- Bus & Prof Pos: Farmer, 30-70; retired. Mem: Cheyenne Co Rural Area Develop Comt; Elks. Relig: Protestant. Mailing Add: 2645 El Rancho Rd Sidney NE 69162

NELSON, RAYMOND (D)
Mem, RI Dem State Comt
b Providence, RI, Sept 2, 21; s Nels H Nelson & Lillie Swanson N; m 1943 to Shirley Alice Crane; c David C, Rebecca R & Marc A. Polit & Govt Pos: Admin asst to US Sen Claiborne Pell, RI, currently; mem, RI Dem State Comt, currently. Bus & Prof Pos: Reporter, Providence J, 46-60, bur chief, 50-60. Mil Serv: Entered as A/S, Navy, 42, released as PO 3/C, 45, after serv in ETO; Good Conduct Medal. Mem: Nat Press Club; US Sen Admin Asst & Personal Secy; US Sen Press Secy Club; Sen Staff Club. Relig: Lutheran. Mailing Add: 6118 Wilson Lane Bethesda MD 20034

NELSON, RICHARD THURLOW (R)
b Waupaca, Wis, Feb 23, 32; s Reuben Thorwaldt Nelson & Gertrude Elizabeth Mason N; m 1956 to Mary Lucile Delchamps; c Richard Thurlow, Jr, Robert Frederick & Wayne Stewart. Educ: Univ Wis, 50; Northwestern Prep Sch, Minneapolis, 51; US Naval Acad, BS, 55. Polit & Govt Pos: Vol campaign mgr, Edwards for Cong, Mobile, Ala, 68 & 70; prof campaign mgr, Blount for Senate Campaign, Montgomery, 71-72; prof campaign dir, Bafalis for Cong, Ft Myers, Fla, 72-73; admin asst, US Rep L A Bafalis, 73- Bus & Prof Pos: Mgt trainee, Delchamps, Inc, Mobile, Ala, 59-61, asst to vpres serv opers, 61-63, dir serv opers, 63-65, dir personnel, 65-67, vpres personel, 67-71. Mil Serv: Entered as Ens, Navy, 55, released as Lt(jg), 59, after serv in VF(AW)-4, VAW-12. Honors & Awards: Numerous state & local awards from Ala & Mobile Jaycees, 61-70. Relig: United Methodist. Legal Res: 4009 SE Tenth Ave Cape Coral FL 33904 Mailing Add: 9611 Jomar Dr Fairfax VA 22030

NELSON, ROBERT R (D)
WVa State Sen
b Boone Co, WVa, Oct 9, 35; s Joda Fulton Nelson & Opal W Hunter N; m 1960 to Mary Lucinda Abruzzino; c Phillip & Christine. Educ: Marshall Univ, AB in Polit Sci, 60, MA, 69; George Washington Univ. Polit & Govt Pos: WVa State Deleg, 64-72; WVa State Sen, 75-; admin asst to US Rep Ken Hechler, Fourth Dist, WVa, formerly. Mil Serv: Marine Corps, 53-57. Relig: Protestant. Legal Res: 1416 Washington Blvd Huntington WV 25701 Mailing Add: State Capitol Charleston WV 25305

NELSON, ROLF TIMOTHY (R)
Minn State Sen
b St Paul, Minn, Nov 23, 40; s Rev Dr Clifford Ansgar Nelson & E Bernice N; m 1970 to Phoebe Gail Hoiness; c Knute Timothy. Educ: Gustavus Adolphus Col, 59-60; Univ Singapore, Malaya, 60; Univ Minn, BA, 62, LLB, 65; Delta Theta Phi. Polit & Govt Pos: Precinct chmn, Robbinsdale Rep Party, Minn, 66; Minn State Rep, Dist 31-B, 66-72, Minn State Sen, Dist 43, currently. Bus & Prof Pos: Partner, Corrick, Miller, Meyer & Nelson, 66-69; Meyer & Nelson, 69-71 & Meyer, Nelson & Miller, 71- Mil Serv: Entered as Pvt, Army, 57, released as Sgt, 66; 66; Sgt Maj, Army Res. Mem: Am Bar Asn; Am Judicature Soc; North Hennepin Kiwanis; Minneapolis Urban League. Honors & Awards: One of Minn Ten Outstanding Young Men, Minn Jaycees, 70. Relig: Lutheran. Legal Res: 3820 Bassett Creek Dr Golden Valley MN 55422 Mailing Add: 3735 N Hwy 52 Robbinsdale MN 55422

NELSON, SHEILA DIANE (D)
Chmn, Pulaski Co Dem Comt, Va
b Pulaski, Va, May 23, 48; d Harvey Lewis Nelson & Helen Tilley N; single. Educ: Col William & Mary, 68; New River Community Col, Dublin, Va, 72-; Am Inst Banking, advan cert, 75. Polit & Govt Pos: Chmn, South Pulaski Precinct, Va, 71-73; secy-treas, Pulaski Co Dem Comt, 73-75, chmn, 75- Bus & Prof Pos: Numerous pos in credit, admin & auditing functions, Bank of Va-Pulaski, 68, control officer, 75- Mem: Va Fedn Bus & Prof Women's Clubs (state finance chmn); Am Inst Banking (pres, New River Valley Chap, 75-); Nat Asn Bank Women; Pulaski Co CofC (dir, Group V Young Bankers' Sect); Pulaski Co Dem Women's Orgn. Honors & Awards: First runner-up, Young Career Woman of Va, Va Fedn Bus & Prof Women's Clubs, 73; SAtlantic Regional Scholar Award, Nat Asn Bank Women,

75. Relig: Baptist. Legal Res: 410 Pulaski St Pulaski VA 24301 Mailing Add: PO Box 445 Pulaski VA 24301

NELSON, TALMAGE L (D)
b Ripley, Tenn, Nov 6, 89; m 1917 to Vicy Black; m 1958 to Sally Shoffner; m 1964 to Girlean Clifft; c Mrs Willie Lee Allen. Educ: Grade sch, tenth grade. Polit & Govt Pos: Chmn, Lauderdale Co Dem Exec Comt, Tenn, formerly. chmn & campaign mgr, John J Hooker, Jr for Gov, Tenn, 70. Bus & Prof Pos: Sch teacher, Home Co, Tenn, 31-16; owner & operator four dept stores, 20-63, retired. Mil Serv: Cpl, Army, AEF, 18. Mem: Col, Gov Staff, Tenn; Mason; Eastern Star; Am Legion; Am Farm Bur. Relig: Methodist. Mailing Add: 160 Lake Dr Ripley TN 38063

NEMELKA, DAVID ROBERT (D)
Utah State Rep
b Salt Lake City, Utah, Mar 30, 39; s Nephi Alma Nemelka & Ruth Hubold N; m 1962 to Ingrid Fritzen; c David Nephi, John Fritzen, Heidi, Joseph & Sonja. Educ: Univ Utah, BA, 65. Polit & Govt Pos: Utah State Rep, 73-; deleg, Dem Nat Mid-Term Conf, 74. Bus & Prof Pos: Asst dir, Ettie Lee Homes for Boys, Baldwin Park, Calif, 66-67; prog dir, Utah Boys Ranch, 68-69. Mil Serv: Entered as Pvt, Nat Guard, 62, released as 1st Lt. Relig: Latter-day Saint; high councilman, currently. Mailing Add: 54 S Seventh East Salt Lake City UT 84102

NEPSTAD, DOROTHY (R)
SDak State Rep
Mailing Add: 409 E Fifth Ave Mitchell SD 57301

NERGARD, CHARLES L (CHUCK) (R)
Fla State Rep
Mailing Add: 405 Abeto Lane Ft Pierce FL 33450

NERI, ROCCO (D)
NJ State Assemblyman
Mailing Add: State House Trenton NJ 08625

NERIN, WILLIAM F (D)
b Indianapolis, Ind, Jan 26, 26; s William Francis Nerin & Corine Rodier N; single. Educ: Glennon Col, BA, 47; Kenrick Theol Sem, St Louis, Mo, grad, 51; Columbia Univ Teachers Col, MA, 65. Polit & Govt Pos: Deleg, Dem Nat Conv, 72. Bus & Prof Pos: Marriage counr, Oklahoma City, 65-73; pastor, Community of John XXIII, 66-73; adminr, Discovery Child Develop Ctr, 67-73. Mil Serv: Capt, Air Force, 58-65, serv in Oklahoma City Air Defense Command, 59-65. Publ: Chap, In: Parish in Crisis, Soc of Divine Word, 67. Mem: Nat Coun Family Rels; Okla Health & Welfare Coun; Nat Asn of Laity; Family Growth Ctr, Inc. Honors & Awards: Vol of the Year Award, OEO-CAP Oklahoma City, 71. Relig: Catholic. Mailing Add: 205 NE 28th Oklahoma City OK 73105

NERMYR, ARNOLD (R)
NDak State Rep
Mailing Add: State Capitol Bismarck ND 58501

NERO, PAT (D)
RI State Sen
b Providence, RI, Sept 16, 19; m to Lee Geremia. Educ: Boston Univ, BM, 42, LLB, 44. Polit & Govt Pos: RI State Sen, 61-, mem Senate Dem steering comt, chmn comn to study minimum standards in music & arts; deleg, Const Conv, 58. Bus & Prof Pos: Prof violinist & conductor, mem, Providence Sch Dept & Recreation Dept, conductor, UF McCall Orchestra & Nickerson House Little Symphony, formerly; attorney-at-law. Mil Serv: Capt, Marine Corps, 3 years; RI Marine Corps Res, formerly. Mem: Am Bar Asn; Justinian Soc; Boston Univ Alumni Asn; Lions; KofC. Mailing Add: 1274 Narragansett Blvd Cranston RI 02905

NESMITH, OLE F (R)
Kans State Rep
Mailing Add: 2008 W 92nd Prairie Village KS 66206

NESSEN, RONALD HAROLD
Press Secy to the President
b Washington, DC, May 25, 34; s Frederick Edward Nessen & Ida Edith Kaufman N; m 1967 to Cindy Young Hi Song; c Caren Jayne & Edward Song. Educ: Am Univ, BA, 59. Hon Degrees: LLD, Heidelberg Col, 75. Polit & Govt Pos: Press secy to the President, 74- Bus & Prof Pos: Radio newscaster, WEPM, Martinsburg, WVa, 52-54 & WARL, Arlington, Va, 54-55; writer, Montgomery Co Sentinal, Rockville, Md, 55-56; ed, United Press Int, Washington, DC, 56-62; news correspondent, Nat Broadcasting Co, 62-74. Honors & Awards: George Foster Peabody Broadcasting Award, 64; George Polk Mem Award, Overseas Press Club, 67. Mailing Add: 5112 Baltimore Ave Bethesda MD 20016

NESSMITH, PAUL EDWARD, SR (D)
Ga State Rep
b Bulloch Co, Ga, Nov 24, 08; s Benjamin David Nessmith & Sally Moseley N; m 1936 to Eloise Smith; c Paul Edward, Jr & William Benjamin. Educ: Cave Spring Consol High Sch, 27. Polit & Govt Pos: Supvr, Ogeechee River Soil & Water Conserv Dist, 58-; Ga State Rep, 63-; mem, Ga Surface Mine Land Use Bd, 67-; mem, State Adv Comt for Voc Agr, 70- Bus & Prof Pos: Pres, Community Farm Bur, formerly; chmn, Southeastern Peanut Adv Comt, 61-; vpres & dir, Statesboro Fed Land Bank Asn, 61- Mem: Farm Bur; Nat Farmers Orgn; Bulloch Co CofC; KofP; Ton Per Acre Peanut Club. Honors & Awards: Ga Master Farmer, 61; Legis Conserv Award, Ga Sportsmen Fedn, 68; Outstanding Serv Award, Ga Farm Bur, 69. Relig: Baptist. Mailing Add: Rte 4 Statesboro GA 30458

NESTANDE, BRUCE (R)
Calif State Assemblyman
b Minneapolis, Minn, Jan 28, 38; m; c Barry & Brian. Educ: Univ Minn, BS; Loyola Univ, 69-70. Polit & Govt Pos: Rep nominee, 69th Assembly Dist, Calif, 68 & 70; mem, Orange Co Rep Cent Comt, 68-; mem, Rep State Cent Comt Calif, 68-, exec dir, 72-73; spec asst to Gov Ronald Reagan, 70-71 & 73-74; dir field opers, Calif Comt to Reelect the President, 72; Calif State Assemblyman, 75- Mil Serv: Entered as 2nd Lt, Marine Corps, 60, released as Capt, 64, after serv in Southeast Asia. Mem: Calif Adv Coun for Voc Educ; Am Legion; Cath Community Agencies of Orange Co (adv bd); Anaheim Union High Sch Dist Cert Personnel

Comt. Relig: Lutheran. Legal Res: Orange CA Mailing Add: State Capitol Sacramento CA 95814

NETHERCUTT, GEORGE R, JR (R)
b Spokane, Wash, Oct 7, 44; s George Rector Nethercutt & Nancy Sampson N; single. Educ: Wash State Univ, BA, 67; Gonzaga Univ Sch Law, JD, 71; Sigma Nu. Polit & Govt Pos: Law clerk, Judge William H Williams, Spokane Co Superior Court, Wash, 68-71; law clerk, Judge Raymond E Plummer, US Dist Court, Anchorage, Alaska, 71-72; staff attorney & legis asst, US Sen Ted Stevens, 73-74, admin asst, 74- Mem: Wash State Bar Asn; DC Bar Asn; Am Judicature Soc; Phi Alpha Delta; Spokane Club. Relig: Protestant. Legal Res: PO Box 1080 Anchorage AK 99510 Mailing Add: 411 Old Senate Off Bldg Washington DC 20510

NETHING, DAVID E (R)
NDak State Sen
Mailing Add: State Capitol Bismarck ND 58501

NETSCH, DAWN CLARK (D)
Ill State Sen
Mailing Add: 1700 N Hudson Chicago IL 60614

NETT, CARL ANTHONY (D)
Ky State Rep
b Louisville, Ky, Dec 2, 41; s Carl Raymond Nett & Agnita Bryan N; m 1972 to Barbara Ann Wimsatt. Educ: Bellarmine Col, BA, 63; Univ Louisville, 65-68; Oper Pride; exec vpres, Student Coun; NUB Tri-Col Coun. Polit & Govt Pos: Deleg, Dem State Conv, 68; precinct committeeman, Dem Party, 68-; Ky State Rep, 35th Dist, 70-, vchmn Jefferson Co legis deleg, Ky House Rep, 70-72, chmn interim joint subcomt cities of first & second classes, 70-72, mem legis study comn pub higher educ, 70-72, mem legis comts cities, bur orgns & prof hwys & traffic safety, 70-72, mem educ comt, 72-, vchmn appropriations & revenue comt, 72-; mem priorities comt, Louisville & Jefferson Co Health, Educ & Welfare Coun, 70-72. Bus & Prof Pos: Teacher, St Xavier High Sch, Louisville, Ky, 63-69; prin, Guardian Angels Elem Sch, Louisville, 70- Mem: Nat Asn Hist Soc; Am Heritage Soc. Honors & Awards: Scholar & Serv Award, PTA of Bellarmine Col; Community Award for Outstanding Contribution to Educ in Ky Gen Assembly, League of Cath PTA's, 72. Relig: Roman Catholic. Mailing Add: 1268 Lydia St Louisville KY 40217

NETTELS, GEORGE E, JR (R)
b Pittsburg, Kans, Oct 20, 27; m 1952 to Mary Joanne; c Christopher Bryan, Margaret Anne, Katherine Anne & Rebecca Jane. Educ: Univ Kans, BS in Civil Eng, 50; Tau Beta Pi; Omicron Delta Kappa. Polit & Govt Pos: Precinct committeeman, Kans Rep Party, 60-; mem, City Zoning Comt, 63-65; mem, Kans Comt Civil Rights, 65-; mem, Pittsburg Sch Bd, 65-; chmn, Kans State Rep Party, 66-68; deleg, Rep Nat Conv, 68. Bus & Prof Pos: Rock quarrying, John J Stark Contractors; pres, Midwest Minerals, Inc, 68-; chmn bd, McNally Pittsburg Mfg Corp, 70- Mem: Nat Limestone Inst, Washington, DC (chmn bd); Kans Limestone Asn; Kans State CofC (vpres). Relig: Presbyterian. Mailing Add: 509 W Quincy Pittsburg KS 66762

NETTLES, BERT (R)
Mem, Ala Rep State Exec Comt
b Monroeville, Ala, May 6, 36; s George Lee Nettles & Blanche Sheffield N; m 1967 to Elizabeth Duquet; c Jane Elizabeth, Mary Katherine & Susan Sheffield. Educ: Univ Ala, Tuscaloosa, BS, 58, LLB, 60; Omicron Delta Kappa; Tau Kappa Alpha; Beta Gamma Sigma; Alpha Tau Omega; Jasons. Polit & Govt Pos: Asst Attorney Gen, Ala, 60-61; chmn, Ala State Rep Conv, 68; Ala State Rep, 69-74, Minority Leader, Ala House Rep, 70-74; mem, Ala Rep State Exec Comt, 70-; pres, Ala Presidential Electors, 72. Bus & Prof Pos: Partner, Bryan, Nelson, Nettles & Cox, Lawyers, Mobile, Ala, currently. Mil Serv: Entered as 2nd Lt, Army, 60, released as Capt, 65, after serv in Army Res. Mem: Am Bar Asn; Right of Way Asn; Kiwanis. Honors & Awards: Algernon Sydney Sullivan Medallion, Univ Ala, 58. Relig: Episcopal. Legal Res: 136 Silverwood Mobile AL 36607 Mailing Add: PO Box 2232 Mobile AL 36601

NETZLEY, ROBERT E (R)
Ohio State Rep
b Laura, Ohio, Dec 7, 22; s Elmer Metzley & Mary Ingle N; m 1944 to Marjorie Lyons; c Kathleen, Carol Anne & Robert. Educ: Miami Univ, BS in Bus, 47; Phi Kappa Tau. Polit & Govt Pos: Pres, Miami Co Young Rep Club, Ohio, 52-54; chmn, Miami Co Rep Cent & Exec Comts, 58-; Ohio State Rep, Seventh Dist, 61- Bus & Prof Pos: Secy-treas & part owner, Netzley Oil Co, 47-; vpres, Romale Inc, 61- Mil Serv: Entered as A/S, Navy, 42, released as Ens, 46, after serv in Okinawa & Pac, 45; Purple Heart; Am & Pac Theaters. Mem: Am Legion; VFW; Miami Co Heart Coun; Grange; Laura Lions. Relig: United Church of Christ. Mailing Add: 2750 Pemberton Rd Laura OH 45337

NEU, ARLENE PETRICE (R)
Chairwoman, Hardin Co Rep Women, Ohio
b Kenton, Ohio, Jan 16, 09; d Oscar William Schwemer & Eliza Jane Whitmore S; m 1932 to Herman J Neu, wid. Educ: Ohio Northern Univ, 26-29; Findlay Col Music, 30. Polit & Govt Pos: Hardin Co chmn, Goldwater for President, 64; mem chmn, Hardin Co Women's Rep Club, Ohio, 64-65; chairwoman, Hardin Co Rep Women, 68-; mem, Fourth Cong Dist Rep Cent & Exec Comts, Ohio, 70-; trustee, Ohio Rep News, Inc, Columbus, Ohio, 70-; mem bd mgt, Ohio Fedn Rep Women's Orgn, 70-; mem, Ohio Rep State Conv, 70; Fourth Dist chmn, Guyer for Cong, 72. Bus & Prof Pos: Owner, NJ Neu Flag & Decorating Co, 34-; owner, Neu Apts, 37- Mem: Elks Ladies Club; Hardin Co Archaeol & Hist Soc; Hardin Co Farm Bur; Am Red Cross; Kenton Soroptimist Club Int. Honors & Awards: State membership award, Ohio Federated Women's Orgn, 64. Relig: United Church of Christ. Mailing Add: 334 N Main St Kenton OH 43326

NEU, ARTHUR ALAN (R)
Lt Gov, Iowa
b Carroll, Iowa, Feb 9, 33; s Arthur Nicholas Neu & Martha Margaret Frandsen N; m 1964 to Mary Naomi Bedwell; c Arthur Eric, Mary Martha & Poule Harold. Educ: Wentworth Mil Acad, 50-52; Northwestern Univ, BS in Bus Admin, 55; Northwestern Univ Sch Law, JD, 58; Georgetown Univ Sch Law, LLM in Taxation, 60; Acacia. Polit & Govt Pos: Iowa State Sen, 67-72; Lt Gov, Iowa, 73- Mil Serv: Entered as 1st Lt, Army, 58, released as Capt, 62, after serv in Judge Adv Gen Corps, Mil Dist, Wash. Mem: Iowa & Am Bar Asns; Rotary; Am Field Serv. Honors & Awards: Selected to attend Eagleton Inst Polit, Miami, Fla, 68. Relig: Presbyterian. Legal Res: 801 N Adams St Carroll IA 51401 Mailing Add: Box 276 Carroll IA 51401

NEUBERGER, KATHERINE (R)
Rep Nat Committeewoman, NJ
b New York, NY, Apr 30, 07; d Samuel Kridel & Elsie Wallach K; m 1929 to Harry H Neuberger; c Susan (Mrs Donald M Wilson), Joan (Mrs Henry M Woodhouse). Educ: Barnard Col, BA, 27; Columbia Univ, 32-33. Polit & Govt Pos: Mem bd, Monmouth Co Orgn Social Serv, 37-59; mem vpres & bd mgrs, NJ Reformatory for Women, 40-57; mem, NJ Law Enforcement Coun, 52-57, chmn, 54-57; deleg-at-lg, Rep Nat Conv, 60 & 64, alt deleg-at-lg, 68; Rep Nat Committeewoman, NJ, 61-, mem exec comt, Rep Nat Comt, 68-; mem, NJ Bd Higher Educ, 70- Bus & Prof Pos: Trustee, Montclair State Col, 67-70. Mem: Am Asn Univ Women; Cosmopolitan Club (New York); Family Serv Soc, Monmouth Co (mem bd, 59-); Nat Fedn Rep Women; NJ Fedn Rep Women. Relig: Episcopal. Mailing Add: 628 Middletown Lincroft Rd Lincroft NJ 07738

NEUBERGER, MAURINE BROWN (D)
b Cloverdale, Ore; m 1964 to Dr Philip Solomon. Educ: Ore Col Educ, Monmouth; Univ Ore; Univ Calif, Los Angeles. Polit & Govt Pos: Ore State Rep, 51-55; mem bd dirs, Am Asn for UN; mem, President's Comn on Status of Women; US Sen, Ore, 60-66. Bus & Prof Pos: Teacher in pub schs, Milton-Freewater, Newberg & Portland, Ore; writer & photographer. Relig: Unitarian. Mailing Add: 3000 NW Cornell Rd Portland OR 97210

NEUHAUS, RICHARD JOHN (D)
Mem Admin Comt, NY State New Dem Coalition
b Pembroke, Ont, May 14, 36; s Clemens Henry Neuhaus & Ella Prange N; single. Educ: Concordia Col, BA, 55; Concordia Theol Sem, BD, 60; Wash Univ, 57-60; Wayne State Univ, summer 58. Polit & Govt Pos: Chmn, Community Dist Planning Bd, Brooklyn, NY, 64-66, Williamsburg Community Progress Ctr, 65-66 & Brooklyn Dem Renewal, 67-68; deleg, Dem Nat Conv, 68 & 72; mem steering comt, Kings Co Dem Renewal, NY, 68-72; mem admin comt, NY State New Dem Coalition, 68-; Dem cand for Congressman, 14th Cong Dist, Brooklyn, NY, 70. Bus & Prof Pos: Pastor, St Paul's Lutheran Church, Massena, NY, 60-61; pastor, Church of St John Evangelist, Brooklyn, 61-; ed, Una Sancta, New York, 64-71; assoc ed, Worship Mag, Collegeville, Minn, 67-; chmn, NY Clergy Interrelig Coalition, 70-; assoc ed, Worldview, Jour Coun Relig & Int Affairs, NY, 72- Publ: Theology and the Kingdom of God, Westminster, 69; Movement & Revolution, Doubleday, 70; In defense of People, Macmillan, 71; plus others. Mem: Nat Comt for Sane Nuclear Policy (mem exec comt, NY Orgn, 67-); Lutheran Human Rels Asn; Clergy & Laymen Concerned about Vietnam (chmn, 64-); Nat Coun Churches; Nat Liturgical Conf. Honors & Awards: Cath Press Award, 68. Relig: Lutheran. Mailing Add: 195 Maujer St Brooklyn NY 11206

NEUMAN, JEROLD JOE (R)
Mem, Rep State Cent Comt, Calif
b Oelwein, Iowa, Mar 11, 31; s Emil William Neuman & Nancy Dudley N; m 1952 to Barbara Anne Huddleson; c Jerold Joe, Jr, Michael Aaron, Rachelle Anne, Renee Aline, Kenneth Eugene & Daniel Allen. Educ: Western Baptist Bible Col, BA, 57; Calif State Col, 59-60; San Jose State Col, 64; Univ Calif, Berkeley, 65; Chico State Col, 65, 66 & 69; Humboldt State Col, 66-67. Polit & Govt Pos: Mem, Trinity Co Rep Cent Comt, Calif, 66-, chmn, formerly; mem, Rep State Cent Comt Calif, 69- Bus & Prof Pos: Pastor, Community Church, Friant, Calif, 57-59; mgr paint stores, San Francisco, Oakland, San Jose & Hayward, Calif, 59-63; teacher, Ruth Sch, Calif, 63-64; teacher & prin, Hoaglin-Zenia Sch, 64-67; teacher & prin, Coffee Creek Sch, Trinity Center, Calif, 67-70; teacher, Foothill Elem Sch, Brown's Valley, 70- Mil Serv: Entered as SR, Navy, 58, released as CS 3, 52, after serv in China & Korean War. Mem: Calif & Trinity Co Teacher's Asns; Nat Educ Asn. Relig: Baptist. Mailing Add: Coffee Creek Sch Trinity Center CA 96091

NEUMANN, RAY A (R)
Treas, Ill Rep State Cent Comt
b Tazewell Co, Ill, Jan 11, 18; s Charles Adolph Neumann & Louisa Krause N; m 1942 to Thelma Eileen Connolly; c Celeste Rae, Charles Robert, Nancy Louise, Linda Sue, Ruth Ann, Ray Arthur, II & Diane Joy. Educ: Bradley Univ, BS, 38; MS, 56; Grad Sch Savings & Loans, Ind Univ, 51; Alpha Kappa Psi; Lambda Chi Alpha. Polit & Govt Pos: Pres, Peoria Co Young Rep, 54-56; councilman-at-lg, Peoria, 57-61; mem, Peoria Co Bd, 65-; mem, Ill Rep State Cent Comt, 18th Cong Dist, 70-, treas, 74- Bus & Prof Pos: Pub rels mgr, First Fed Savings & Loan Asn, 38-46, asst vpres, 46-51, vpres, 51-72, sr vpres, 72- Mil Serv: Maj, Army, 41-45, after serv in 82nd Airborne Inf, European Theatre; Six Battle Stars; French & Belgian Croix de Guerre; Queen Wilhelmina Medal; Two Presidential Citations. Publ: Auth, Large Association Management Policies, Trends & Ratios, US Savings & Loan League, 53. Mem: Kiwanis; Salvation Army Adv Bd; Am Mgt Asn; Bradley Alumni Asn; Bradley (trustee). Honors & Awards: Ill Distinguished Serv Award Winner, 49-50; Silver Beaver Award from Creve Coeur Coun, Boy Scouts of Am, 67; Golden Anniversary Award, Ill Dept Am Legion, 69; Peoria Advertising & Selling Club Award for Advertising Excellence, 72; Tri-Co Citizen of the Year, Kiwanis, 74. Relig: Lutheran. Mailing Add: 2917 W Wardcliffe Dr Peoria IL 61604

NEUMANN, ROBERT GERHARD (R)
US Ambassador to Morocco
b Vienna, Austria, Jan 2, 16; m to Marlen Eldredge; c Ronald E & Gregory W. Educ: Univ Rennes, Dipl Superieur, 36; Geneva Sch Int Studies, 37; Univ Vienna, 38; Amherst Col, MA, 40; Univ Minn, Shevlin fel, 40-41, PhD, 46; Haynes Found fel, 50-51; Social Sci Research Coun fel, 50-51; Fulbright fel, France, 54-55. Polit & Govt Pos: Adv, Secy to Defense, Int Security Affairs, Am deleg, NATO Ministerial Conf, Paris, 62; US Ambassador to Afghanistan, 66-73; US Ambassador to Morocco, 73- Bus & Prof Pos: Instr, State Teachers Col, Oshkosh, Wis, 41-43; lectr, Univ Wis, 46-47; prof, Univ Calif, Los Angeles, 57-69, dir, Inst Int & Foreign Studies, 59-65; ed writer, Los Angeles Times, 52-59; chmn, Int Rels Sect, Town Hall, 56-62; dir, Am Seminar in Polit Econ & Social Sci, Nice, France, 57. Mil Serv: Army, 42-46, Lt. Publ: European & Comparative Government, 68, 4th ed; The Government of the German Federal Republic, 66; plus articles. Honors & Awards: Hon Medal, Univ Brussels, 55; Legion of Honor, France, 57; Officers Cross, Order of Merit, Fed Repub of Germany, 63, Commander's Cross, 74; Order of the Star, Afghanistan, 73. Legal Res: 4312 Inglewood Blvd Los Angeles CA 90066 Mailing Add: US Embassy Rabat Morocco

NEVAS, ALAN HARRIS (R)
Conn State Rep
b Norwalk, Conn, Mar 27, 28; s Nathan Nevas & Eva Harris N; m 1959 to Janet Snyder; c Andrew B, Debra B & Nathaniel S. Educ: Syracuse Univ, AB, 48; NY Univ Sch Law, LLB, 51; Phi Epsilon Pi. Polit & Govt Pos: Pres, Westport Young Rep, Conn, 61-62; mem, Westport Co Bd Finance, 63-67, chmn, 67-70; mem, Westport Co Rep Town Comt, 64-72; Conn State Rep, 71-, Dep Majority Leader, Conn House Rep, 73- Mil Serv: Entered as Sgt, Army, 52, released as Sgt 1/C, 54, after serv in Judge Adv Gen Corps, Ft Dix, NJ, 52-54.

Mem: Conn Bar Asn; Jr Bar Asn Lower Fairfield Co; Westport Bar Asn (treas, 72-). Mailing Add: 4 Charcoal Lane Westport CT 06880

NEVILLS, WILLIE L (R)
Mem Bd Supvr, St Clair Co, Ill
b Scooba, Miss, May 28, 14; s Henry Nevills & Callie Nave N; div; c Dellar (Mrs Robert L Murphy) & Antoinette (Mrs James Davis). Polit & Govt Pos: Chmn, East St Louis Rep Party, Ill, currently; mem bd supvr, St Clair Co, currently; precinct committeeman, St Clair Co Rep Party, currently; spec investr, Attorney Gen Off, Mo. Mil Serv: T/5, Army, 41-45, with serv in 184 Qm, SPac Theatre; 5 serv medals. Mem: VFW. Relig: Protestant. Mailing Add: 1432 Market Ave East St Louis IL 62201

NEVINS, RICHARD (D)
Mem, Calif State Dem Cent Comt
b Los Angeles, Calif, Apr 21, 21; s Richard Nevins & Katharine Tilt N; m 1946 to Mary Lois Minton; c Richard, Jr, William McCay & Henry Minton. Educ: Yale Univ, AB, 42. Polit & Govt Pos: Southern chmn, Calif Fedn Young Dem, 54-56, pres, 56-58; mem, Los Angeles Co Dem Cent Comt, 54-58; mem, Calif State Dem Cent Comt, 54-; deleg, Dem Nat Conv, 56, 60, 64 & 72; mem, Calif State Bd Equalization, Fourth Dist, 59- Bus & Prof Pos: Ins solicitor, Marsh & McLennan, 46-58. Mil Serv: Entered as Pvt, Army, 43, released as Cpl, 46, after serv in Weather Serv, Air Force, US. Mem: Am Soc Pub Admin; Los Angeles Urban League; NAACP; Int Asn Assessing Officers; Nat Asn Tax Adminr. Honors & Awards: Earl Warren Award, Am Soc Pub Admin, 68, Adminr of Month, Nov, 72. Relig: Episcopal. Mailing Add: 561 Bradford St Pasadena CA 91105

NEW, JACK L (D)
State Treas, Ind
m to Corinne; c four. Educ: Ind Univ, 48. Polit & Govt Pos: Research dir, Ind Dem State Cent Comt, 48-51; dep dir & acting dir, Ind Off Price Stabilization, 51-53; mem, Hancock Co Coun, 59-60; exec secy to Gov Matthew E Welsh throughout Mr Welsh's term; State Treas, Ind, 65-66 & 71- Bus & Prof Pos: Operator, off furniture bus, 53- Relig: Methodist. Mailing Add: PO Box 73 Greenfield IN 46140

NEW, SHELLEY ROBINS (D)
b Philadelphia, Pa, Feb 4, 50; d Jerome Robins & Pearl Ruder R; m 1970 to Arnold Louis New. Educ: New Col of Hofstra Univ, BA, 70; Univ Pa, MGA, 72. Polit & Govt Pos: Alt deleg, Dem Nat Conv, 72; mem, McGovern-Shriver Steering Comt, Cumberland Co Dem Steering Comt, Pa, 72. Bus & Prof Pos: Admin asst, Found for Independent Cols Inc of Pa, 70-71; pub rels coordr, Harrisburg Hosp, 71-; pub rels, Hamilton Health Ctr, Harrisburg, 71- Mem: Pub Rels Soc of Hosp Asn of Pa; Am Hosp Asn; Am Soc Pub Rels Dirs; Womens Polit Caucus (pub rels co-chmn, Harrisburg, 73-); Harrisburg Women's Rights Movement. Relig: Jewish. Mailing Add: 7704 Doe Lane Philadelphia PA 19118

NEWBERG, ESTHER (D)
Exec Dir, NY State Dem Comt
b Middletown, Conn, Dec 25, 41; d Ivon Charles Newberg & Marion Fischer N; single. Educ: Wheaton Col, BA, 63, ed, Wheaton News. Polit & Govt Pos: Pres, Young Dem, Wheaton Col; chief clerk, Subcomt Exec Reorgn, US Sen Abraham Ribicoff, 65-68; staff asst to US Sen Robert F Kennedy, NY, 68; staff asst, Arthur Goldberg for Gov Campaign, 70-72; admin asst to US Rep Bella S Abzug, NY, 71-72; exec dir, NY State Dem Comt, 72-; deleg, Dem Nat Mid-Term Conf, 74. Bus & Prof Pos: Spec asst to vpres, Urban Inst, Washington, DC, 68-70. Relig: Jewish. Mailing Add: 800 Third Ave New York NY 10022

NEWBY, OLIN CARRIS (D)
Mem Rules Comt, Ga State Dem Party
b Twiggs Co, Ga, Aug 28, 39; s Olin P Newby & Sarah Lee Floyd N; m 1966 to Rosemary Flynt; c Olin C, Jr & Laura LaRose. Educ: Abraham Agr Col, AA, 59; Univ Ga, BS in Agr, 61, MEd, 68. Polit & Govt Pos: Wilkes Co chmn, Gov Campaign; mem, State Voc Educ Adv Bd, Ga; mem rules comt, Ga State Dem Party, 71- Mem: Am Voc Asn; Ga Educators Asn; Nat Voc Agr Teachers Asn; Wilkes Co Teacher Asn (pres, 68 & 71-); Int Asn Lions Clubs. Honors & Awards: Hon State Farmer Degree, Ga Future Farmer Asn; 100 Dist Gov Plaque, Int Asn Lions Clubs. Relig: Methodist. Legal Res: Lovelace Way Washington GA 30673 Mailing Add: PO Box 321 Washington GA 30673

NEWELL, DAVID R (D)
Chmn, Nebr Young Dem
b Oakland, Calif, Oct 14, 46; s Ivan Raymond Newell & Fern M Buchholz N; single. Educ: Univ Nebr, Omaha, BS in Educ, 71; Phi Alpha Theta. Polit & Govt Pos: Admin asst, Dir Dept Admin Serv, Nebr, 71-72; mem cent comt, Nebr Dem Party, 72, mem exec comt, 73-; nat committeeman, Nebr Young Dem, 72-73, chmn, 73- Bus & Prof Pos: Pres, Grad Student Asn, 72-73. Mil Serv: Entered as E-1, Army, 67, released as E-4, 69, after serv in 1st Brigade Reg Commun Group, RUN, 69; Army Commendation Medal; Good Conduct Medal; RUN. Mem: Nebr Civil Liberties Union; Nebraskans for Peace; Am Legion; Citizens for Environ Improv. Relig: Lutheran. Mailing Add: 24-35 Ellison Ave Omaha NE 68111

NEWELL, GRAHAM STILES (R)
Vt State Sen
b St Johnsbury, Vt, Nov 27, 15; s George Graham Newell & Maud Berry N; single. Educ: Univ Chicago, AB, 38, AM, 49. Polit & Govt Pos: Mem, Vt Comn Interstate Coop, 53-; Vt State Rep, 53-55 & 66-70; Vt State Sen, 55-65 & 71-; mem bd mgrs, Coun State Govts, 57-65; mem, Adv Comn on Intergovt Rels, 62-64. Bus & Prof Pos: Instr Latin, St Johnsbury Acad, Vt, 38-47; assoc prof, Lyndon State Col, 59-64, chmn dept social sci, 59-; prof, 64- Publ: Ed, 1966 Vermont Almanac & Government Guide, Vt Rep State Comt. Mem: Vt Hist Soc; Classical Asn New Eng; Am Hist Asn; Am Asn Univ Profs; Am Civil Liberties Union (dir Vt chap). Honors & Awards: Alumni Citation for Pub Serv, Univ Chicago, 61. Relig: Congregational. Mailing Add: 8 Park St St Johnsbury VT 05819

NEWHALL, DAVID, III (R)
b Philadelphia, Pa, Dec 6, 37; s David Newhall, Jr & Jane Martyn Dunn N; single. Educ: Princeton Univ, AB, 61; treas, Princeton Tower Club. Polit & Govt Pos: Admin asst to Richard S Schweiker, US Rep, Pa, 63-69; admin asst to US Sen Richard Schweiker, 69-; campaign asst to Gov William W Scranton, Rep Presidential Campaign, 64. Bus & Prof Pos: Reporter, Philadelphia Eve Bull, summers 55-57, full time, 58-59; mgr, Bell Tel Co Co, Pa, 61-63. Mem: Princeton Club Washington, DC; Princeton Tower Club (bd gov). Relig: Protestant. Legal Res: 411 Washington Lane Ft Washington PA 19301 Mailing Add: 521 Seventh St SE Washington DC 20003

NEWHARD, SCOTT DOUGLAS (D)
Iowa State Rep
b Anamosa, Iowa, Aug 23, 51; s Ivan Earl Newhard & Evelyn Jean Purcell N; single. Educ: Iowa Wesleyan Col, currently. Polit & Govt Pos: Iowa State Rep, 23rd Dist, 73- Mil Serv: SP-4, Nat Guard, 4 years. Mailing Add: 207 N High St Anamosa IA 52205

NEWHOUSE, GERALD FRANCIS (R)
Comnr, Alpena Co, Mich
b Alpena, Mich, Nov 27, 40; s Clarence J Newhouse & Frances C Raniszewski N; m 1968 to Kathryn Mae Beemer; c Kristyn Mae. Educ: Alpena Community Col, Assoc Polit Sci. Polit & Govt Pos: Treas, Alpena Co Rep Party, Mich, 66-68 & currently; comnr, Alpena Co, 68-; mem bd rev, Alpena Twp, 73- Bus & Prof Pos: Pres, KofC Credit Union, 67-73; pres, Local 237, AFL-CIO Barber Union, 69-70. Mem: Nat Barbers Asn; Nat Asn Cosmetologists & Barbers; Asn Comnrs; Jaycees; Alpena Exchange Club. Relig: Roman Catholic. Mailing Add: 109 Sunset Blvd Alpena MI 49707

NEWHOUSE, IRVING R (R)
Wash State Rep
b Mabton, Wash, Oct 16, 20; s John Newhouse & Tina Bos N; m 1945 to Ruth Gardner; c Joyce (Mrs Darrell Downing), James, Linda (Mrs Bruce Thomas), Laura, Daniel & Dorothy. Educ: Wash State Univ, BS, 43; Alpha Zeta; Mu Beta Beta; Alpha Gamma Rho. Polit & Govt Pos: Wash State Rep, Dist 15, 65-, Rep caucus chmn, Wash House Rep, 71-74; mem, Legis Coun, 67-73, chmn revenue & regulatory agencies, 71-73, Rep floor leader, 74- Bus & Prof Pos: Pres, Yakima Co Cattlemen, 55-57; pres, Wash Beef Coun, 58-59; pres, Yakima Co Farm Bur, 60-63; dir, Sunnyside Valley Irrigation Dist, 62-; dir, Valley Mem Hosp, 67- Mil Serv: Entered as A/S, Naval ROTC, 43, released as Lt(jg), 46, after serv in Landing Ship, Tanks, Pac, 43-45. Mem: Elks; Farm Bur; Wash Cattlemans Asn; Hop Growers of Am. Relig: Christian Reformed. Mailing Add: Rte 1 Box 130 Mabton WA 98935

NEWHOUSE, RICHARD H (D)
Ill State Sen
b Louisville, Ky, Jan 24, 24; s Richard H Newhouse & Annie Louise Singleton N; m to Katherine Vetterlein; c Suzanne, Richard & Holly. Educ: Boston Univ, BS, 50, MS, 52; Univ Chicago, JD, 60; Kappa Alpha Psi. Polit & Govt Pos: Ill State Sen, 24th Dist, 66-, mem appropriations, educ, judiciary & welfare comts, Ill State Senate; mem intergovt rels comn, Coun State Govt. Bus & Prof Pos: Practicing attorney, Chicago, Ill. Mil Serv: Entered as Pvt, Air Force, 43, released as S/Sgt, 45, after serv in 448th Signal Construction Unit, ETO, 43-45; 12 Battle Stars. Mem: Chicago Bar Asn; Black Legislators Asn; Coun on Diagnosis & Eval of Criminal Defendents; Adlai Stevenson Inst (fel); Ill State Hist Soc; Nat Urban Coalition. Honors & Awards: Best Legislator Award, Independent Voters of Ill; Best Legislator Award, Am Legion; Outstanding Pub Servant, Cook Co Bar Asn; Sen of Year, Baptist Ministers Conf Chicago. Relig: Protestant. Mailing Add: 5533 S Cornell Chicago IL 60634

NEWKIRK, ROSA H (D)
Committeewoman, Dem Party, Pa
b Richmond, Va, Dec 1, 28; d Charles Taylor Henderson & Emma Overton H; m 1948 to Kermit Liston Newkirk, Sr; c Kermit Liston, Jr, Charles Henderson & Bruce Howard. Educ: Community Col Philadelphia, 67. Polit & Govt Pos: Committeewoman, Dem Party, Pa, 60-; acct clerk, Orphan's Div Common Plea Court, 61-; mem bd gov, Dem Women's Club, 62-68; alt deleg, Dem Nat Conv, 68; treas, Concerned Women for Humphrey, 68; financial secy, Dem Women's Forum, 69. Bus & Prof Pos: Pres, Home & Sch Asn Kearny Sch, 62-64; pres, Northern Liberty Fed Credit Union, 66- Mem: Friend Neighborhood Guild (asst secy bd); St Paul Baptist Human Rel Comt (chmn housing); Penn Town Homes Improv Comt (pres); Philadelphia Comt to Aid Biafra Children (co-chmn). Honors & Awards: Citation from Human Rel Comn & Home & Sch Asn. Relig: Baptist. Mailing Add: Apt E 674 Franklin Pl Philadelphia PA 19123

NEWMAN, BOBBY GENE (D)
Ark State Rep
b El Dorado, Ark, Oct 1, 26; s Benton Albert Newman & Mary Roan N; m 1951 to Mary Elizabeth Raper; c Brad Kevin & Elizabeth Lacye. Educ: Ouachita Baptist Univ, BA, 50; Univ Tex, Austin, 50-51; Univ Ark, Fayetteville, MS, 51. Polit & Govt Pos: Justice of Peace, Smackover, Ark, 65-68; Ark State Rep, 69- Bus & Prof Pos: Mgr & vpres, Smackover Ins Agency, 60-70, pres, 70-; mem exec comt, Ark Asn Ins Agts, 66-67. Mil Serv: A/S, Navy, 44, released as F 1/C, 46, after serv in SPac, 45-46. Mem: Lions; Am Legion. Relig: Baptist. Mailing Add: Box 52 Smackover AR 71762

NEWMAN, CLARENCE BENTON (BUDDIE) (D)
Miss State Rep
b Valley Park, Miss, May 8, 21; married. Polit & Govt Pos: Miss State Sen, 48-52; Miss State Rep, 52-, mem & chmn House ways & means comt, mem legis recess study comt & House rules comt, Miss House Rep; mem, State Agr & Industrial Bd, State Comn Budget & Accounting; chmn, Southern Coun State Govt, formerly. Bus & Prof Pos: Farmer. Mem: Am Legion; 40 et 8; VFW; Delta Coun; Miss Mfg Asn. Relig: Baptist; mem bd deacons, Valley Park Baptist Church. Mailing Add: Box 200 Valley Park MS 39177

NEWMAN, CONSTANCE BERRY (R)
b Chicago, Ill, July 8, 35; d Joseph Alonzo Berry, MD & Ernestine Sigers B; m 1959 to Theodore Roosevelt Newman. Educ: Bates Col, AB, 56; Univ Minn Law Sch, BSL, 59. Hon Degrees: LLD, Bates Col, 72. Polit & Govt Pos: Personnel mgt officer, Dept Interior, 62-67; research analyst, Comn Polit Activity of Govt Personnel & Nat Adv Comn on Civil Disorders, 67; chief midwest sect, Migrant Div, Off Econ Opportunity, 67-69; spec asst to asst secy planning & eval, Dept Health, Educ & Welfare, 69-70, spec asst to secy, 70-71; dir, Vista, 71-73; comnr, Consumer Prod Safety Comn, 73- Honors & Awards: Bates Key, Bates Col, 56. Mailing Add: 7924 16th St NW Washington DC 20012

NEWMAN, CYNTHIA STAIR (R)
Rep Nat Committeewoman, Va
b Minneapolis, Minn, Mar 24, 22; d John Stewart Dalrymple & Bernice Barber D; m 1958 to Carson Boru Newman, wid; c Robert Hamill, Nancy Stair, Pamela Barbar Zimmerman, Tracy Stewart & Christopher Carson Newman. Educ: Smith Col, 39-42; Univ Va Law Sch, LLB, 44. Polit & Govt Pos: Vchmn, Va State Rep Party, 52-56 & 62-68, finance chmn, 59-62; Rep Nat Committeewoman, 56-58 & 68-; deleg, Rep Nat Conv, 56, 68 & 72; Secy of Commonwealth, Va, 70-74; app by President Nixon to Tourism Resources & Rev Comn, 71- Bus & Prof Pos: Attorney, UNRRA, 44-45; nat dir, Rep Open Forums, 46-48; asst to chmn, Rep Sen Comt, 48-50; pres, Waters Travel Serv, 63- Mem: Am & Va Bar Asns; Am Soc Travel

Agts; Soroptomists; Metrop Washington YWCA (bd dirs). Relig: Unitarian. Mailing Add: 3535 Half Moon Circle Falls Church VA 22044

NEWMAN, DAN L **(D)**
Mem Exec Bd Mont State Dem Party
b Butte, Mont, May 16, 37; s Dave Newman & Elve A Lundgren N; m 1957 to Dianna Mack; c Bradley, Lance & Dava Jean. Educ: Western Mont Col, BS; Humbolt State Col; Carroll Col. Polit & Govt Pos: Finance chmn, Mont State Dem Cent Comt, 64-; chmn, Lewis & Clark Co Dem Cent Comt, 66-72; mem exec bd, Mont State Dem Party, 67-, secy, formerly; asst, US Rep Arnold Olson, 68-72. Bus & Prof Pos: Teacher, 57-60; owner, Newman & Assocs, 60-68. Mem: Mont & Int Pilots Asns. Relig: Catholic. Legal Res: 1423 Stuart St Helena MT 59601 Mailing Add: 347 N Last Chance Gulch Helena MT 59601

NEWMAN, DANIEL F **(D)**
NJ State Assemblyman
Mailing Add: State House Trenton NJ 08625

NEWMAN, HAROLD TOLMAN **(D)**
Utah State Rep
b Bountiful, Utah, Feb 8, 16; s Otto Newman & Elvinia Tolman N; m 1936 to Joan Gilbert; c Harold Gilbert, Joan Carol (Mrs David Christensen); Jane Gayle (Mrs Robert Edwards) & Nancy Kathleen (Mrs Glen Ivie). Educ: Cyprus High Sch, grad; Utah Tech Col, 68-70. Polit & Govt Pos: Deleg, Co & Utah State Dem Convs, 20 years; Utah State Rep, 71- Mem: Boy Scouts. Honors & Awards: Silver Beaver Award, Boy Scouts. Relig: Latter-day Saint. Mailing Add: 4371 W 5255 South Kearns UT 84118

NEWSCHWANDER, CHARLES E **(R)**
Wash State Sen
b Tacoma, Wash, 1920; m to Emma N; c Four. Educ: Univ Puget Sound; Univ Ore Dent Sch. Polit & Govt Pos: Wash State Rep, formerly; Wash State Sen, currently. Bus & Prof Pos: Dentist. Mailing Add: 2140 Bridgeport Way Tacoma WA 98466

NEWSOM, DAVID D
US Ambassador to Indonesia
b Richmond, Calif, Jan 6, 18; m to Jean Craig; c John, Daniel, Nancy, Catherine & David. Educ: Univ Calif, Berkeley, BA, 38; Columbia Univ, MS, 40; Pulitzer traveling scholar, 40-41. Polit & Govt Pos: Third secy, Karachi, 47-50; career officer, US Dept of State Foreign Serv, 47-; second secy, Oslo, 50-51; second secy, Baghdad, 51-53; pub affairs officer, US Info Agency & consul, Baghdad, 53-55; officer in chg, Arabian Peninsula Affairs, 55-58; Nat War Col, 59-69; first secy, London, 60-62; dir, Off of NAfrica Affairs, 63-65; US Ambassador to Libya, 65-69; Asst Secy of State for African Affairs, 69-74; US Ambassador to Indonesia, 74- Bus & Prof Pos: Newspaper reporter, 38-41; newspaper publisher, 46-47. Mil Serv: Navy, Lt, 42-46. Honors & Awards: Commendable Serv Award, US Info Agency for Serv in Iraq, 55; Meritorious Serv Award, State Dept, 58; Career Serv Award, Nat Civil Serv League, 71; Rockefeller Pub Serv Award, 73. Legal Res: Berkeley CA Mailing Add: Dept of State Washington DC 20520

NEWSOM, GEORGE EDWARD **(R)**
b Berwick, Iowa, Aug 31, 19; s John B Newsom (deceased) & Alease S Hankie N (deceased); m 1937 to Mercedes M Zink. Educ: Des Moines Pub Schs, 24-36. Polit & Govt Pos: Precinct committeeman, Polk Co Rep Party, Iowa, 66-; deleg, Iowa Rep Conv, 68-74; mem, Polk Co Rep Cent Comt, 66-; campaign mgr, William H Huff for Iowa House Rep, 68; alt deleg, Rep Nat Conv, 68; zone leader, 21 precincts, Polk Co, 68 & 69; mem, Polk Co Rep Exec Comt, 69-; campaign chmn, Robert H Lounsberry, 74. Bus & Prof Pos: Gen contractor, 25 years. Mil Serv: Entered as Pvt, Army, 43, released as Sgt, 46, after serv in 690th Engr Base Equip Co, Pac Theatre, 44-46; Am Pac Theatre Ribbon; Victory Ribbon; Good Conduct Medal; Presidential Unit Citation. Mem: AF&AM; Mason (32 degree); Shrine; Elks; US Power Squadron. Honors & Awards: Rep Precinct Committeeman's Award, Polk Co Iowa, 66. Relig: Presbyterian. Mailing Add: 7202 Oak Brook Dr Urbandale IA 50322

NEWSOME, KENNETH WARREN **(D)**
b Raleigh, NC, June 18, 46; s Clarence S Newsome & Annie Lewis; m to Dixie Lee; c Brian C & Kimberly A. Educ: Ind Univ, Bloomington, BS, 69; Omega Psi Phi. Polit & Govt Pos: Deleg, Dem Nat Mid-Term Conf, 74. Mailing Add: Rte 2 Box 260D Ahoskie NC 27910

NEWTON, JOHN EDWARD
Judge, Nebr Supreme Court
b Ponca, Nebr, Apr 4, 04; s Oliver Isaac Newton & May Stough N; m 1940 to Bonnie Brownlee (deceased); c Merrily (Mrs Tunnicliff) & John Richard. Educ: Univ Nebr, LLB, 26; Phi Delta Phi. Polit & Govt Pos: Co attorney, Dixon Co, Nebr, 27-55; chmn, Dixon Co Rep Cent Comt, 38-54, mem, Rep State Cent Comt, 41-42; dist judge, Eight Judicial Dist, 57-67; judge, Nebr Supreme Court, 67- Bus & Prof Pos: Pres, Nebr Dist Judges Asn, 56. Mem: Am Bar Asn; Am Judicature Soc; AF&AM; Scottish Rite; Shrine. Relig: Lutheran. Legal Res: Ponca NE 68770 Mailing Add: 1301 J St Lincoln NE 68508

NEWTON, JON P **(D)**
Tex State Rep
Mailing Add: 301 E Huntington Beeville TX 78102

NEWTON, PHINEHAS STEWART, IV **(R)**
Chmn, Knox Co Rep Comt, Maine
b Boston, Mass, Feb 6, 26; s Phinehas Stewart Newton, III & Ethelyn Leone Olsen N; m 1948 to Frederica Kay Leach; c Edwina (Mrs Dana Taynton), Wendelin (Mrs Philip J Walsh), Phinehas Stewart, V & Frederic Leach. Educ: Bowdoin Col, BA, 48; Psi Upsilon. Polit & Govt Pos: Chmn, Rockport Rep Town Comt, Maine, 70-; chmn, Knox Co Rep Comt, 74- Mil Serv: Aviation Cadet during WW II, 44-45; entered as Ens, Navy, 50, released as Lt Comdr(Ret), 69, after serv in intel assignments, Japan, Taiwan, Cuba, San Diego & Washington, DC, 50-69; Naval Res Medal; Am Campaign & WW II Victory Medals; Nat Defense, Korean & UN Serv Medals. Mem: DAV (life mem); ROA (life mem). Relig: Protestant. Mailing Add: Pascals Ave Rockport ME 04856

NEWTON, POLLY **(D)**
b McKenzie, Tenn, June 19, 95; d Albert Newton & Lillie Warner N; single. Educ: Falls Bus Col, Nashville, 1 year; Bethel Col, 1 year. Polit & Govt Pos: Registr, Carroll Co, Tenn, 38-46; asst city clerk, McKenzie, 48-54; secy, Carroll Co Dem Exec Comt, formerly; chmn womens div, Carroll Co for Sen Albert Gore, 58; partic, Gov Ellington's Campaign, 66; bd mem, Carroll Co Dem Womens Club, 72- Bus & Prof Pos: Typing instr, Tolers Bus Col, Paris, Tenn, 53. Mem: Bus & Prof Womens Club; McKenzie Garden Club; McKenzie Friendship Club. Relig: Baptist. Mailing Add: 247 Main St McKenzie TN 38201

NEWTON, TOM V **(R)**
Chmn, Gonzales Co Rep Party, Tex
b Houston, Tex, Nov 4, 33; s Thomas V Newton & Maybell Williams N; m 1961 to Zilpha Cain; c Terry, Gary, Larry, Bobby & Sherry. Educ: Univ Houston, BBA, 56. Polit & Govt Pos: Chmn, Gonzales Co Rep Party, Tex, 72- Bus & Prof Pos: Tax acct, Continental Oil Co, Ponca City, Okla, 56-59; tax mgr, Crescent Corp, Tulsa, 59-60; tax acct, Peat Marwick Mitchell & Co, Houston, Tex, 60-63; owner, Tom Newton & Co CPA, Gonzales & Luling, 63- Mem: Am Inst CPA; Tex Soc CPA; Rotary; Elks. Relig: Baptist. Legal Res: Rte 1 Gonzales TX 78629 Mailing Add: Gonzales Bank Bldg Gonzales TX 78629

NEWTON, WILLMA HUMPHREYS **(R)**
Committeewoman, Ark Rep State Comt
b Jennings, La, Nov 2, 08; d William Fletcher Humphreys & Nellie Himler H; div; c William F Humphreys. Educ: Stephens Col, AA, 25; Univ Mo, 26; Univ Ark, Monticello, 54. Polit & Govt Pos: Committeewoman, Ark Rep State Comt & Calhoun Co Rep Comt, 69- Bus & Prof Pos: Abstractor, Lyon Abstr Co, Hampton, Ark & Ouachita Abstr Co, Camden, 48-65, Morton Abstr Co, Fordyce, 65-69, Guaranty Title Co, Hot Springs, 69-74 & Title Guaranty & Security Abstr Co, ElDorado, 74- Publ: Auth, One hundred twenty-five years of medicine and medical men Calhoun Co, Ark, 1850-1975 (in press) & My Dallas County (Ark) Notebook (in press), MP & Assocs, Hot Springs, Ark. Mem: Ark Genealogical Soc (dir, 62-, pres, 73, historian, 75); Ky & Hot Springs-Garland Co Hist Socs; Stephens Col Alumnae Asn (life mem). Honors & Awards: Pres Plaque for Distinguished Serv, Ark Genealogical Soc, 73. Relig: Christian Scientist. Mailing Add: 205 Newton Lane PO Box 41 Hampton AR 71744

NEYLAN, KATHLEEN MARY **(D)**
b Washington, DC, Sept 1, 44; d Charles Francis Newlan & Marguerite Kenneally N (both deceased); single. Educ: Univ Iowa, BA, JD, 67; Delta Gamma. Polit & Govt Pos: Deleg, Dem Nat Conv, 72, mem, Nat Dem Credentials Comt, 72; vpres, Clayton Co Young Dem, Iowa, 72-73; comnr, State Comn on the Status of Women, Iowa, 72-; mem, Nat Women's Polit Caucus; chmn structure & by laws comt, Iowa Womens Polit Caucus, 73- Publ: Articles for Nat Cath Sch Press Asn, 62 & Iowa Advocate, 67. Mem: Am Bar Asn; Young Lawyers Div of Iowa State Bar Asn (panels comt); Iowa Acad of Trial Lawyers; Iowa Community Theater Asn; Univ Iowa Alumni Asn. Relig: Roman Catholic. Legal Res: 210 1/2 S Main Elkader IA 52043 Mailing Add: 129 S Main Elkader IA 52043

NICELY, WILLIAM PERRY AMOS **(R)**
Mayor, Parkersburg, WVa
b Parkersburg, WVa, Oct 23, 22; s Perry Nicely & Anna Elizabeth Posey N; m 1947 to Marjorie Faith Meadows; c Cynthia Annette (Mrs Stephen N Honaker), Gregory Warren & William P A, Jr. Educ: Marietta Col, spec courses. Polit & Govt Pos: Bd dir, Union Mission; WVa State deleg, 54-58 & 64-70; dir, Wood Co Civil Defense, 59-65; dist supvr, Fourth Cong Dist Census, 60; deleg, Rep Nat Conv, 68, alt deleg, 72; mayor, Parkersburg, WVa, 70-73 & 74-; mem, Gov Comt on Crime, Delinquency & Correction. Bus & Prof Pos: Co-owner, Nicely Realty, Inc, 46-48; real estate developer, William P A Nicely, 48- Mil Serv: Entered as Pvt, Air Force, 43, released as Sgt, 45, after serv in 475 Bomber Squadron B-29's, Pac, Guam, Saipan & Iwo Jima, 44-45; Good Conduct Medal; Theater Ribbons & 3 Stars. Mem: Mason (32 degree); Shrine; Elks; Lions Int; Am Legion. Honors & Awards: 100% Dist Gov Award, 52; Outstanding Lions Serv Award Community Serv, 54, 56 & 60; United Fund Award, 66. Relig: Methodist. Mailing Add: 400 Camden Ave Parkersburg WV 26101

NICHOL, WILLIAM E
Nebr State Sen
Mailing Add: 722 Valleyview Dr Scottsbluff NE 69362

NICHOLAS, EUGENE JOSEPH **(R)**
NDak State Rep
b Rolette, NDak, June 14, 45; s Joseph Nicholas & Gladys Mincke N; m 1969 to Connie Mae Lee; c Joseph William & Jay Harold. Educ: NDak State Univ, degree in bus econ, 70; Tau Kappa Epsilon. Polit & Govt Pos: Deleg, NDak Const Conv, 70-72; NDak State Rep, 75- Bus & Prof Pos: Farmer, currently. Mem: Cando Lions (vpres, 74-); Towner Co Crop Improv Asn; NDak Farm Bur; Elks. Honors & Awards: Am Farmer Award, Future Farmers Am, 66; Outstanding Freshman Legislator, NDak House Rep, 75. Relig: Catholic. Mailing Add: 938 Fifth Ave Cando ND 58324

NICHOLAS, HARRY K **(R)**
b Dover, NJ, May 27, 23; m to Adelaide Amundsen; c three. Educ: Muhlenberg Col, BS, 44; Columbia Univ, MS, 51; Omicron Delta Kappa; Lambda Chi Alpha. Polit & Govt Pos: Apprentice training supvr, NJ Dept Educ, 46-50; info asst & Am House dir, US Info Agency, Ger, 54-57; info asst, US Rep Harold C Ostertag, NY, 57-64; admin asst, US Rep Barber B Conable, Jr, NY, 65- Bus & Prof Pos: Reporter, Newark News, NJ, 51-54. Mil Serv: Aviation Cadet, Navy, 44-45. Relig: Methodist. Legal Res: Annandale VA Mailing Add: 2228 Rayburn House Off Bldg Washington DC 20515

NICHOLS, DAVID A **(R)**
b Lincolnville, Maine, Aug 6, 17; s George E Nichols & Flora E Pillsbury N; single. Educ: Bates Col, AB magna cum laude, 42; Univ Mich, JD, 49; Delta Sigma Rho; Phi Beta Kappa. Polit & Govt Pos: Chmn, Maine Coun Young Rep, 50-54; pres, New Eng Coun Young Rep, 52-54; mem, Maine Exec Coun, 55-57; chmn, Maine State Rep Comt, 60-64; Rep Nat Committeeman, Maine, formerly. Bus & Prof Pos: Gen practice of law, Camden, Maine, 49- Mil Serv: Army Air Force, 42-45. Mem: Am Bar Found (fel); Am Bar Asn; Maine Trial Lawyers Asn; Rotary; Odd Fellows. Mailing Add: Box 76 Lincolnville ME 04849

NICHOLS, J HUGH **(D)**
Md State Deleg
b Sprott, Ala, Nov 27, 30; s Joseph Gordon Nichols & Roberta Stone N; m 1948 to Annie Sue Ratliff; c Duane Alryn, Sharon Kay, Gerald Hugh & Jonathan Gordon. Educ: Univ Md, Munich, Ger, 52-54; Univ Ala, AB, 57; Am Univ, MA, 67; Phi Beta Kappa; Pi Sigma Alpha; Phi Alpha Theta. Polit & Govt Pos: Deleg, Md State Dem Conv, 66; mem, Charter Bd, Howard Co, Md, 66-68, Planning Comn, 68-69 & Co Coun, 69-70; Md State Deleg, Howard Co, 70- Bus & Prof Pos: Analyst, US Govt, Ft Meade, Md, 57-59; sr methods specialist, RCA Corp, Washington, DC, 59-61; sr prog analyst, Int Elec Corp, Paramus, NJ, 61-63; sr scientist, Dunlap & Assoc, Washington, DC, 63-67; mgr plans & progs, Informatics, Inc, Rockville,

Md, 67-73; dir pub affairs, Ocean Data Systs, Inc, Rockville, 73- Mil Serv: Entered as Pvt, Army, 48, released as Sgt 1/C, 54, after serv in Army Security Agency, ETO & US, 48-54. Publ: County Home Rule in Maryland, Univ Microfilms, summer 67; General purpose file management, Pub Automation, 8/67; A close look at home rule, Am Co Mag, 2/70. Mem: Am Asn Advan Sci; Am Polit Sci Asn; Nat Munic League; Urban & Regional Info Sci Asn. Relig: Methodist. Mailing Add: 6117 Sebring Dr Columbia MD 21044

NICHOLS, MICHAEL COOPER (D)
Mem Exec Comt, Dem Party of Ga
b Birmingham, Ala, Feb 4, 52; s Fred William Nichols & Jeanette Cooper N; single. Educ: Brown Univ, BA with hons, 74; Emory Univ Law Sch, 74- Polit & Govt Pos: Mayor, Indian Springs Sch Community, Helena, Ala, 69-70; mem exec comt, Dem Party Ga, 37th Senate Dist, 74- Publ: Cities Are What Men Make Them, Birmingham, Alabama-1963, Univ Ala, 76. Mem: Am Civil Liberties Union; Midtown Atlanta Civic Asn. Honors & Awards: Harvard Book Award, Indian Springs Sch, 69 & Robert Kartus Award, 70. Relig: Jewish. Mailing Add: 903 Myrtle SE NE Atlanta GA 30309

NICHOLS, MILDRED THOMPSON (D)
Dem Nat Committeewoman, RI
b Hamilton, Va, Feb 23, 29; d Thomas Edward Thompson & Lillian Clark T; m 1950 to Charles Harold Nichols; c David, Keith & Brian. Educ: Hampton Inst, BS, 50, MA, 63; Delta Sigma Theta. Polit & Govt Pos: Dem Nat Committeewoman, RI, 72-; comnr, Dem Party Comn Party Structure & Deleg Selection, 73-74; comnr, RI Permanent Adv Comn Status Women, 73-; comnr, RI Port Authority & Econ Develop Corp, 74- Bus & Prof Pos: Instr Eng, Clark Col, 62-63; instr Eng, Berliner Wirtschaftschule, West Berlin, 63-65 & 68-69; assoc dir career counseling, Career Educ Proj, Providence, RI, 73-74, dir career counseling, 74- Mem: RI Women's Polit Caucus (policy coun, 72-); Opportunities Industrialization Ctr (bd mem, 73-); United Way (mem prog emphasis proj task force). Mailing Add: 56 Fosdyke St Providence RI 02906

NICHOLS, MILTON E (D)
Wyo State Rep
Mailing Add: 2698 Deming Blvd Cheyenne WY 82001

NICHOLS, ROBERT CECIL (D)
Tex State Rep
b Norphlet, Ark, July 15, 28; s John Henry Nichols & Nancy Phelps N; m 1948 to Lynda Hazel Slocum; c Joanne & Wayne. Educ: Kokomo High Sch, Miss. Polit & Govt Pos: Committeeman, Harris Co Dem Exec Comt, 59-67; Tex State Rep, 67-; alt deleg, Dem Nat Conv, 68. Bus & Prof Pos: Welder, Rheem Mfg, 48-; staff rep, USW, 69- Mem: USW, Local 2883. Relig: Baptist. Legal Res: 10907 Dunvegan Houston TX 77029 Mailing Add: PO Box 2910 Austin TX 78767

NICHOLS, WILLIAM FLYNT (D)
US Rep, Ala
b Amory, Miss, Oct 18, 18; s William Francis Nichols & Daisy Williams N; m 1943 to Carolyn Funderburk; c Memorie, Margaret Lynn & William Flynt. Educ: Auburn Univ, BS, 39, MS, 41; A Club; Blue Key; Scabbard & Blade; Gamma Sigma Delta; Omicron Delta Kappa. Polit & Govt Pos: Ala State Rep, 59-63; Ala State Sen, 63-66; US Rep, Ala, 67, mem house comt on agr, 67-69, app to house armed serv comt, 70, chmn Flag Day comt, House of Rep. Bus & Prof Pos: Agronomist & vpres, Sylacauga Fertilizer Co, 47-67; mem bd trustees, Auburn Univ, currently. Mil Serv: Entered as 2nd Lt, Army 42, released as Capt, 47, after serv in 45th Field Artil Bn, 8th Inf, Atlantic Theater, 42-47; Purple Heart; Bronze Star, 3 major battle stars & other awards. Mem: Mason; Shrine; Sylacauga Bd Educ; Am Legion; DAV. Honors & Awards: Progressive Farmer Man of Year Award; Most Outstanding Mem Ala Senate, Capitol Press Corps, 65. Relig: Methodist; past chmn bd, First Methodist Church. Legal Res: Capital Dr Sylacauga AL 35150 Mailing Add: 2417 Rayburn House Off Bldg Washington DC 20515

NICHOLSON, CARL JOSEPH (R)
Chmn, Nancock Co Rep Party, Ind
b Greenfield, Ind, Jan 16, 16; s Orval Leroy Nicholson & Effie Gilland N; m 1935 to Julian Elizabeth Dismore; c David, Joseph & Robert. Educ: Greenfield High Sch, 30-34. Polit & Govt Pos: Precinct committeeman, Hancock Co Rep Party, Ind, 37-66; trustee, Brandywine Twp, 54-58; inspector new rd construction, Ind State Hwy Dept, 54-58; dir, Ind Sch Lunch Div, Ind Dept Pub Instr, 67-69; mem exec comt, Ind Rep State Cent Comt, 68; educ consult, Ind State Supt Pub Instr, 69-7i; chmn, Hancock Co Rep party, currently; exec secy, Ind Real Estate Comn, 73- Bus & Prof Pos: Owner & operator farm, Greenfield, Ind, 35-58; ins agt, All Am Life & Casualty Co, Park Ridge, Ill, 58-66; mem bd, Ind Sch Food Serv Asn, 67- Mem: Mason; Moose; Hancock Co Farm Bur; Future Farmers Am (Ind state vchmn). Honors & Awards: Hoosier Farmer Award, 34; 25 Mem Pin Award, Masonic Lodge, 68. Relig: Methodist. Mailing Add: RR 4 Greenfield IN 46140

NICHOLSON, ELWYN J (D)
La State Sen
Mailing Add: 7300 Westbank Expressway Marrero LA 70072

NICHOLSON, JAMES RAY (R)
b Pensacola, Fla, Jan 17, 38; s James Titus Nicholson & Thelma Lee Miller N; m 1960 to Ethel Lucille Garner; c Sandra Kay, Lisa Ann & Jamie Lynn. Educ: Univ Fla, BME, 59, ME, 68. Polit & Govt Pos: Mem, Bd Social Welfare, Fla, 69-72; chmn, Escambia Co Rep Exec Comt, formerly. Bus & Prof Pos: Process engr, Monsanto Co, Pensacola, Fla, 59-64, sr engr, 64-67, group supvr, 68- Mem: Am Soc Mech Engrs; Moose; WOW; Fed Land Bank Asn. Relig: Baptist. Mailing Add: 6363 Appomattox Dr Pensacola FL 32503

NICHOLSON, RALPH WILLIAM (D)
b Chicago, Ill, Jan 30, 16; s Wheelock Steele Nicholson & Violet Israel N; m 1942 to Rosemary Elizabeth Kleutgen. Educ: Univ Chicago, AB, 36; Phi Kappa Psi. Polit & Govt Pos: Asst postmaster gen, Post Off Dept, 61-69; vpres finance & treas, Corp Pub Broadcasting, 69-72; Asst Postmaster Gen Policy Matters, US Postal Serv, 72-73, Sr Asst Postmaster Gen Finance Group, 73- Bus & Prof Pos: Ed, Gen Electric Co, 36-39; asst off of the pres, Univ Chicago, 39-41; various positions ending as mgr, New York off & dir, Fuller & Smith & Ross, 46-61. Mil Serv: Entered as Pvt, Marine Corps, 41, released as Capt, 46, after serv in Pac, 43-45; Letter of Commendation with Ribbon for Serv in Okinawa; Maj, Marine Corps Res, 46-57. Mailing Add: 15 Fourth St SE Washington DC 20003

NICHOLSON, W R (BILL) (D)
Ark State Rep
Mailing Add: 517 W Johnson Ave Osceola AR 72370

NICKEL, DIETER H (R)
Mem, Lincoln Co Exec Comt, Wis
b Minneapolis, Minn, July 27, 36; s Theodore Hoelty-Nickel & Irma VonHafen N; m 1961 to Pamela Wiedenheft; c Theodore Karl, Kathy Lyn & Timothy Kurt. Educ: Valparaiso Univ, BA, 58, LLB, 60; Pi Kappa Alpha; Phi Alpha Delta. Polit & Govt Pos: Dist attorney, Lincoln Co, Wis, 62-66; chmn, Rep Orgn Lincoln Co, 65-71; vpres, Merrill Area Schs Bd Educ, 67-71; mem, Lincoln Co Exec Comt, 71- Bus & Prof Pos: Pres, Church Mutual Ins Co, Merrill, Wis, currently. Mil Serv: Entered as Pvt, Marine Corps Res, 60, released as Cpl, 66, after serv in 95th Rifle Co, 61-66. Mem: Am Bar Asn; State Bar of Wis; Lincoln Co Bar Asn; Lions. Honors & Awards: Distinguished Serv Award, Jaycees, 70. Relig: Lutheran; pres, Trinity Lutheran Sch Bd, 71-75. Mailing Add: 1206 E Sixth St Merrill WI 54452

NICKELSON, ORABELL (D)
b SC, May 5, 28; d Artemus West & Lidie Reedy W; m to Joseph Nickelson, separated; c Darrell, Pearsall, Vanessa, Lula, Wesley, Kimberly, Tracy & Jamie. Educ: Bank St Col Educ, spec courses, summer 70. Polit & Govt Pos: Deleg, Dem Nat Conv, 72. Bus & Prof Pos: Social serv coordr, Day Care 100, Paterson, NJ, 70-71; asst supvr food serv, Paterson Bd Educ, 71- Mem: Passaic Co Legal Aide Soc (trustee); Paterson Welfare Rights Orgn (pres); Northside Forces of Paterson (pres); Area Coun I, Paterson (secy); Paterson Coalition (vpres). Honors & Awards: One of Mothers of the Year, Paterson, NJ, 72. Relig: Presbyterian. Mailing Add: 75 Jasper St Paterson NJ 07522

NICKERSON, EUGENE HOFFMAN (D)
b Orange, NJ, Aug 2, 18; s Hoffman Nickerson & Ruth Constance Comstock N; m 1943 to Marie-Louise Steiner; c Marie-Louise, Lawrie H, Stephanie W & Susan A. Educ: Harvard Univ, BA, 41; Columbia Univ Law Sch, LLB, 43; bd visitors, Columbia Law Sch. Hon Degrees: LLD, Hofstra Univ, 70. Polit & Govt Pos: Law secy to Judge Augustus N Hand, US Circuit Court of Appeals, 43-44; law secy to Chief Justice Harlan F Stone, US Supreme Court, 44-46; zone chmn, Roslyn Harbor, NH, 53-55; vchmn, Nassau Co Dem Comt, NY, 55-61; counsel, Gov Comt Pub Employee Security, 56-58; mem, Law Rev Comn, NY, 58-59; chmn transportation comt, Regional Coun, 62; officer, Roslyn Dem Club; co exec, Nassau Co, 61-70; chmn, Mitchel Field Planning Comt, 63; mem adv coun pub welfare, US Dept Health, Educ & Welfare, 64; mem pub off adv coun, Off Econ Opportunity, 66; deleg, Dem Nat Conv, 68 & 72. Bus & Prof Pos: Assoc law firm, Milbank, Tweed, Hope & Hadley, 46-51; mem law firm, Hale, Stimson, Russell & Nickerson, 52-61; partner, Nickerson, Kramer, Lowenstein, Nessen & Kamin, Attorneys at Law, 71- Publ: Ethics in government, New York, 64; Mobilize for democracy, 66; articles for law rev, legal & prof mag. Mem: Am & Nassau Co Bar Asns; Asn Bar of City of NY; Am Law Inst. Relig: Episcopal. Mailing Add: 495 Bryant Ave Roslyn Harbor NY 11576

NICKERSON, HERMAN, JR (R)
Adminr, Nat Credit Union Admin
b Boston, Mass, July 30, 13; s Herman Nickerson & Emma Eva Carver N; m 1939 to Phyllis Anne Winters; c John Herman & Dennis Anne (Mrs Frederick Higginbotham, III). Educ: Boston Univ, BSBA, 35. Polit & Govt Pos: Adminr, Nat Credit Union Admin, 70- Mil Serv: Entered as 2nd Lt, Marine Corps, 35, released as Lt Gen (Ret), 70, after serv in Korea, China, US Am Samoa, Far East Command, Pac & Vietnam; Army Distinguished Serv Cross; Distinguished Serv Medal with Gold Star; Silver Star; Legion of Merit with 2 stars; Bronze Star Medal; Air Medal; Presidential Unit Citation with 3 bronze stars; Navy Unit Citation; China Serv Medal with 1 star; Am Defense Serv Medal; Asiatic Pac Campaign Medal; Am Campaign Medal; World War II Victory Medal; Navy Occup Serv Medal; Nat Defense Serv Medal with 1 bronze star; Korean Serv Medal with 1 silver star; Repub Korea Presidential Unit Citation with 2 palms; Vietnam Serv Medal with 3 bronze stars; Repub Vietnam Presidential Unit Citation with 1 palm; Repub Vietnam Campaign Medal; plus many others. Mem: Boy Scouts (nat coun); Am Soc Mil Comptrollers; Nat Asn Uniformed Serv; Nat Rifle Asn; F&AM (Worshipful Master, Warren G Harding Lodge, Washington, DC, 73); plus many others. Honors & Awards: Boston Univ Alumni Pub Serv Award, 59; Ky Col. Relig: Protestant. Mailing Add: 2540 N Randolph St Arlington VA 22207

NICKINELLO, LOUIS R (D)
Mass State Rep
b East Boston, Mass, Sept 8, 40; s Anthony P Nickinello & Mary T Pedone N; m 1961 to Patricia Loynd; c Louis, Jeffrey, Gregory & Jodi Jin. Educ: Bentley Sch Acct & Finance, 59-62. Polit & Govt Pos: Mem, Natick Dem Town Comt, Mass, 66-; chmn bd pub works, Natick, 70-71; Mass State Rep, 71-, vchmn comt transportation, Mass House Rep, 72- Bus & Prof Pos: Asst treas, Nickinello Realty, 57-; treas, Bass River Sports World, West Yarmouth, Mass, 61-; clerk, Day Square Plumbing Co Inc, Natick, 62-70; asst treas, Nickinello Corp, Natick, 67-69 & Corral Motel, Yarmouth, 67- Mem: Kiwanis; Elks; Sons of Italy. Honors & Awards: Cert of Appreciation, Amvets, 73. Relig: Catholic. Mailing Add: 68 Pine St Natick MA 01760

NICOL, BETTY LOU (R)
Treas, Ohio Fedn Rep Women
b Columbus, Ohio, Dec 21, 22; d Joseph Chester Rogers & Lillian Marie Feigley R; m 1945 to Ralph Frank Edward Nicol; c Patricia Marie (Mrs Robert Lynch) & Roger Donald. Educ: Capital Univ, BS in Educ; Kappa Sigma Theta. Polit & Govt Pos: Pres, Union Co Fedn Rep Women, Ohio, 62-65; chairwoman, Union Co Rep Orgn, 66-; app to Mil Acad Rev Bd by US Rep Clarence Brown, 69-71; treas, Ohio Fedn Rep Women, 69-; committeewoman, Ohio State Rep Cent Comt, Seventh Dist, 74- Bus & Prof Pos: Teacher, Marysville High Sch, Ohio, 45-46. Mem: DAR (past nat officer, past state officer, past state chmn membership, Jr Am Citizens Comt & Motion Pictures Comt, past chap regent, chap bicentennial chmn, currently); Daughters Am Colonists (past state officer & chap regent, chap nat defense chmn, currently); Children of the Am Revolution; Eastern Star; Farm Bur Fedn. Honors & Awards: Endowment Pin, Children of Am Revolution, 68; Alumni Achievement Award, Capital Univ, 72. Relig: Methodist; officer, Women's Soc. Mailing Add: Rte 5 London Rd Marysville OH 43040

NICOLAS NOGUERAS, HIJO (NEW PROGRESSIVE, PR)
Sen, PR Senate
Mailing Add: State Capitol San Juan PR 00901

688 / NICOSIA

NICOSIA, D GREGORY (D)
b East Chicago, Ind, Dec 11, 47; s Dr John B Nicosia & Helen Migas N; m 1970 to Linda Rysiewicz; c Gina & Nicole. Educ: Parsons Col, BS, 69; Ind Univ, JD, 72; Alpha Chi Rho (ritual officer); parliamentarian, Student Body; Student Senate; Student Court Justice. Polit & Govt Pos: Staff asst, Lake Co Prosecutor's Off, Ind, 72; majority counsel, Comt on Rules, US House Rep, 73- Mem: Ind Bar Asn; Int City Mgrs Asn. Honors & Awards: Third Pl, Parsons Col Oratory Contest, 69. Relig: Roman Catholic. Legal Res: 3025 Harbor Dr Ft Lauderdale FL 33301 Mailing Add: 1843 W Windway McLean VA 22101

NIDECKER, JOHN EMANUEL (R)
b Philadelphia, Pa, Mar 30, 13; s Arnold Waldemar Nidecker & Anne Jane Williams N; m 1958 to Jeanne Kara Brodhead; c Arnold William & Stephen Andrew. Educ: Marine Corps Inst, 40; LaSalle Exten Univ, 54. Hon Degrees: BS, Cranston Univ, 74. Polit & Govt Pos: Spec asst to President, Washington, DC, 69- Bus & Prof Pos: Mem mkt staff, Sun Oil Co, 34-47; var mgt pos, Cities Serv Oil Co, 47-50; var mgt pos, Cities Serv Co, 50-60, bus develop mgr, 63-68; asst to pres, Int Bridge, Tunnel & Turnpike Asn, 60-61; mgr, Colonial Pipeline Co, 61-63. Mil Serv: Entered as Pvt, Marine Corps 36, released as Cpl, 40, after serv in 6th Bn. Publ: Ed, Compass, 56-60; ed, Angelus, 73-; auth, Poetry—Northern Virginia Bicentennial Book, 74. Mem: Mason; Shrine (32 degree); Int Asn Chiefs Police; Detective's Crime Clin. Honors & Awards: Outstanding Am Award, Friendship Vet Fire Engine Co; Civilian of Month Award. Relig: Episcopal; lay reader, 46 years. Mailing Add: 5 Atwell Ct Potomac MD 20854

NIEBLING, RICHARD F (D)
NH State Rep
Mailing Add: 27 Elliot St Exeter NH 03833

NIEFELD, JO ANN R (R)
b Barnesboro, Pa, June 19, 29; d Joseph Lewis Rogers (deceased) & Katharine Pierce R; m 1954 to Herbert Niefeld; c Debra Lea, Roger Elliot, April Lyn & Todd Andrew. Educ: Md State Teachers Col, 47-48; Strayer Sch Bus, 49. Polit & Govt Pos: Various pos, Md State & Montgomery Co Fedn of Rep Women, 52-; chmn, Montgomery Co Rep Cent Comt, Md, formerly; mem regional health adv comt, Region III, US Dept Health, Educ & Welfare, 70-; deleg, Rep Nat Conv, 72; staff mem & vol comt, Inaugural Comt, 72-73. Relig: Episcopal. Mailing Add: 11813 Timber Lane Rockville MD 20852

NIEHAUS, JOE (R)
Minn State Rep
Mailing Add: RR 3 Sauk Centre MN 56378

NIELSEN, CARL V (D)
Iowa State Rep
Mailing Add: 1507 Fourth St SW Altoona IA 50009

NIELSEN, HELGA RAGNHILD (DFL)
Chmn, McLeod Co Dem-Farmer-Labor Comt, Minn
b Hutchinson, Minn, Feb 25, 07; d Alfred Sorensen (deceased) & Sine Sorensen S (deceased); m to Nielsen Kusk Nielsen (deceased), wid; c Else (Mrs Paul Anderson) & Sine (Mrs Leif Duus). Educ: Minneapolis Bus Col, 24-25. Polit & Govt Pos: Secy/treas, McLeod Co Dem-Farmer-Labor Party, Minn, 48-68, chmn, currently; vchairwoman, Minn Dem-Farmer-Labor Party, 52-58, secy, 70-; dep registr at Hutchinson, 55-70; chairwoman, Second Cong Dist, Dem-Farmer-Labor Party, 58-69. Bus & Prof Pos: Off mgr, Burns Manor Munic Nursing Home, Hutchinson, 69-; mem, Gov Citizens Coun on Aging, 72- Mem: VFW Auxiliary Post 906 (life mem); Vale Rebekah Lodge; Eastern Star; Bus & Prof Women; Am Red Cross. Honors & Awards: Bus Woman of the Year, Hutchinson Bus & Prof Women's Club. Relig: Lutheran. Mailing Add: 635 Harmony Lane Hutchinson MN 55350

NIELSEN, J WERNER (R)
Chmn, Lyon Co Rep Party, Minn
b Tyler, Minn, Dec 25, 24; s Niels X Nielsen & Mary Jensen N; m 1948 to Donna Shirley Rowe; c Barry, Steven & Daniel. Educ: SDak State Univ, 1 year. Polit & Govt Pos: City alderman, Marshall, Minn, 64-69; precinct chmn, Marshall Rep Party, 65-67; first vchmn, Lyon Co Rep Party, Minn, 67-70, chmn, 70- Bus & Prof Pos: Construction supt, Rowe Construction Co, 50-61, secy-treas, Rowe-Nielsen, Inc, 61- Mil Serv: Entered as Seaman 1/C, Navy, 45, released as Yeoman 3/C, 46; Naval Res, 46-52. Mem: Southwest Builders Asn (vpres); Assoc Gen Contractors Minn; Am Legion; Rotary; Eagles. Relig: Protestant. Mailing Add: 907 W Main Marshall MN 56258

NIELSEN, KERMIT DUANE (DFL)
Secy, Carlton Co Dem-Farmer-Labor Party, Minn
b Cloquet, Minn, June 28, 41; s Lester H Nielsen & Charlotte Muermann N; m 1967 to Marilyn McGinn; c Chris. Educ: Univ Minn, Duluth, BS, 66. Polit & Govt Pos: Secy, Carlton Co Dem-Farmer-Labor Party, Minn, 69- Mil Serv: 1st Lt, Army Nat Guard, 71. Mailing Add: 734 Birch St Cloquet MN 55710

NIELSEN, LARRY DALE (R)
b Independence, Iowa, Oct 31, 46; s Dale William Nielsen & Verna Fulton N; m 1971 to Linda Sue Rehmke. Educ: Univ Iowa, BBA, 69. Polit & Govt Pos: Deleg, Rep Nat Conv, 72. Bus & Prof Pos: Sales br auditor, Deere & Co, 69; staff acct, McGladrey, Hansen, Dunn & Co, Cedar Rapids, Iowa, 71-72; CPA, Independence, 72- Mil Serv: Entered as 2nd Lt, Air Force, 69, released as 1st Lt, 71, after serv in Auditor Gen Unit, Patrick AFB, Fla, 70-71. Mem: Nat Asn Acct; Alpha Kappa Psi; Beta Alpha Psi. Relig: Methodist. Legal Res: Box 192 Van Horne IA 52346 Mailing Add: Box 188 207 Second Ave NE Independence IA 50644

NIELSEN, RAY (D)
Utah State Rep
Mailing Add: 628 N Milburn Rd Fairview UT 84629

NIELSON, GERALDINE R (R)
b Hunter, Utah; d Lon Rasmussen & Susan Lewis R; m to Dr Eldon D Nielson; c Dennis Lon, Karen Gae & Karla Sue. Educ: State Univ NY, Albany, 60-62; Univ NC, BS, 64 & MEd, 65; Sigma Alpha; Delta Pi Epsilon. Polit & Govt Pos: NC State Sen, 22nd Dist, 66-70; deleg-at-lg & mem platform comt, Rep Nat Conv, 68; corresponding secy, Nat Order of Women Legislators, 70-71, treas, 71-72, vpres, 72- Bus & Prof Pos: Off mgr, Freshmans Wholesale & Mfg Jewelry, Salt Lake City, Utah, 43-46; secy to the architect, Univ Ill, 47; teacher, Winston-Salem Bus Col, 66 & 68. Mem: League of Women Voters; YWCA (bd mem & treas, Evansville, Ind, 71-); Nat Educ Asn; Nat Bus Educ Asn. Honors & Awards: Hon Ky Col, Gov Louis B Nunn, 68. Relig: Unitarian. Mailing Add: 5808 Woodridge Dr Evansville IN 47712

NIEMEYER, ERNEST (R)
Ind State Sen
Mailing Add: PO Box 5 Lowell IN 46356

NIGH, GEORGE PATTERSON (D)
Lt Gov, Okla
b McAlester, Okla, June 9, 27; s Wilber R Nigh & Irene Crockett N; m 1963 to Donna Skinner Mashburn; c Mike Mashburn & Georgeann. Educ: Eastern Okla A&M Col, 46-48; East Cent State Col, BA, 50. Polit & Govt Pos: Okla State Rep, 51-59; Lt Gov, Okla, 59-63 & 67-; Gov, Okla, 63. Bus & Prof Pos: Teacher, McAlester High Sch, Okla, 51-58; grocery store, 54-62; pub rels, 63-66. Mil Serv: Entered as A/S, Navy, 46, released as Aviation Boatswain Mate 3/C, 47. Mem: Mason (32 degree); Shrine; Am Legion. Relig: Baptist. Legal Res: 8321 Picnic Lane Oklahoma City OK 73127 Mailing Add: State Capitol Bldg Oklahoma City OK 73105

NIGHSWANDER, ESTHER R (R)
NH State Rep
Mailing Add: RFD 4 Laconia NH 03245

NIKOLAY, FRANK LAWRENCE (D)
VChmn, Wis Dem Party
b Day, Wis, Sept 1, 22; s Jacob Nikolay & Anna Illig N; m 1957 to Mary Elizabeth Gisvold. Educ: Univ Wis, LLB, 48. Polit & Govt Pos: City attorney, Abbotsford, Wis, 48-; supvr, Clark Co, 49-51, supvr bd, 71-; dist counsel, Off Price Stabilization, Green Bay, 51; Asst US Attorney, 52, US Attorney, Western Dist, Wis, 52-54; Wis State Assemblyman, Clark Co, 59-65 & 68-71, Majority Floor Leader, Wis State Assembly, 65-66, asst Dem Floor Leader, 69-71; vchmn, Wis Dem Party, 63-; Dem cand, Lt Gov, Wis, 70; Deleg, Dem Nat Conv & chmn Wis McGovern deleg, 72. Mil Serv: Entered as Pvt, Wis Nat Guard, 40, released as 2/C PO, 46, after serv in 32nd Inf Div, Army, Navy Air Corps & Navy, SPac, 45-46; Judge Adv, Wis Army Nat Guard, 46-70; Col, Army Res, 70-; Asiatic Pac Theater Ribbon; Philippine Liberation, Japanese Occup & Pre-Pearl Harbor Medals. Mem: Am Bar Asn; Am Legion; VFW; KofC. Honors & Awards: Admitted to DC Bar, 72. Relig: Catholic. Legal Res: Abbotsford WI 54405 Mailing Add: Box 455 Colby WI 54421

NILES, ANITA GALE (D)
Kans State Rep
b Redding, Kans, Aug 3, 19; d David Arthur Thomas & Sadie Whittington T; m 1940 to Herbert Truman; c Sherril (Mrs Goering), Douglas, Jana (Mrs Springer), Clair & Rebecca. Educ: Emporia State Col, BS, 68, MS, 71. Polit & Govt Pos: Kans State Rep, 75- Bus & Prof Pos: Teacher, Osage City Schs, Osage City, Kans, 61- Mem: Farmers Union; Grange; Nat Farmers Orgn; Nat Educ Asn. Relig: Methodist. Mailing Add: Rte 2 Lebo KS 66856

NILES, IRVING RUSSELL (D)
Kans State Rep
b Olivet, Kans, Dec 12, 14; s Frank B Niles & Pearl Goodman N; m 1950 to Carrol Dean Ramsey; c Frank B, Nancy K & Norma D. Educ: Univ Kans, 32-34; Kans State Univ, BS in agr, 37. Polit & Govt Pos: Supvr, Osage Co Soil Conserv Dist, Kans, 51-; Kans State Rep, 55-57, 59-61 & 67-; mem, Osage Co Farm Home Admin Comt, 63-66. Bus & Prof Pos: Farmer; co-owner, Plodium Bowling Alley, currently. Mil Serv: Entered as A/S, Naval Res, 42, released as Lt, 46, after serv in Amphibious Div, SPac & Pac Theatres, 42-45; Pac Theatre Ribbon with 4 Battle Stars. Mem: Farm Bur; Grange; Am Legion. Relig: Methodist. Mailing Add: RR 2 Lyndon KS 66451

NILGES, AL J (D)
Mo State Rep
b Linn, Mo, Mar 14, 29; s Fred Nilges, Sr & Lena Voss N; m 1949 to Dorothy Ann Knoerr; c Lyle, Bruce, Beverly & Mark. Educ: Linn High Sch, Mo, grad, 47; ECent Jr Col, Union, Mo, summer 72. Polit & Govt Pos: Pres sch bd, Bourbon High Sch Syst, 64-67; pres, Crawford Co Dem Club, 66-69; Mo State Rep, Dist 126, 73- Bus & Prof Pos: Chmn, Bourbon Community Betterment Prog, 66-69. Mil Serv: Entered as Pvt, Air Force, 48, released as S/Sgt, after serv in 20th Bomb Group, Guam & Japan, 50-52. Mem: Am Legion; VFW; Bourbon Boosters Club. Relig: Catholic. Mailing Add: Box 97 Bourbon MO 65441

NIMMO, ROBERT P (R)
Calif State Assemblyman
Mailing Add: 1011 Pacific St San Luis Obispo CA 93401

NIMROD, JOHN J (R)
Ill State Sen
Mailing Add: 9216 Kildare Ave Skokie IL 60076

NIMS, STUART VICTOR (D)
NH State Rep
b Keene, NH; s Oscar B Nims & Charlotte Clerc N; m 1944 to Marjorie Ann Pierson; c Stuart Curtis, Martha Ann (Mrs Brynelsen), Debroah Joan & Laurie Louise. Educ: Univ Mass, 39-42; Augustana Col, BA in Econ, 50; Keene State Col, MEd, 65; Theta Chi. Polit & Govt Pos: NH State Rep, 75- Mil Serv: Entered as Pvt, Air Corps, 42, released as Maj, Air Force Res, 68, after serv in 541 Parachute Inf, 43-45 & 11th Airborne Div, Pac, 45-46; Maj(Ret), Air Force Res. Publ: Marketing of multiple line insurance, Annals Chartered Property & Casualty Underwriters, 4/63. Mem: AF&AM; Chartered Life Underwriters; Chartered Property & Casualty Underwriters. Relig: Unitarian. Mailing Add: 79 Maple Ave Keene NH 03431

NINBURG, DANIEL HARVEY (D)
Mem, Calif Dem State Cent Comt
b Newark, NJ, Apr 30, 28; s Samuel Hillel Ninburg & Beatrice Love Mecklin N; m 1966 to Margaret Mary Malley; c Michael Hillel & twins, Eliot Patrick & Rebecca Anne. Educ: Cornell Univ, AB, 49; Univ Zurich Sch Med, 54-55; Univ Buffalo Sch Med, MD, 59; Alpha Epsilon Delta; Alpha Omega Alpha; Sigma Alpha Mu; Nu Sigma Nu. Polit & Govt Pos: Mem, Campaign Cabinet, Richard T Hanna for Cong, 34th Dist, Calif, 64, 66 & 68; mem, Calif Dem State Cent Comt, 66-; co-chmn, Humphrey-Muskie Campaign, Orange Co, Calif, 68; cand for Calif Deleg to Dem Nat Conv, 68. Bus & Prof Pos: Chmn bd, Southland Ambulance Serv,

Inc, Buena Park, Calif, 62-; chief of staff, Anaheim Gen Hosp, 65-67; chmn bd, Studio Soest, Inc, Van Nuys, 66- Mem: Am Aerospace Med Asn; Am Acad Gen Practice; Anaheim CofC; Am Jewish Comt (chmn, Orange Co Chap, 66-). Relig: Hebrew. Legal Res: 1208 Rowan St Anaheim CA 92801 Mailing Add: 1781 W Romneya Dr Anaheim CA 92801

NINE, LOUIS (D)
NY State Assemblyman
b Puerto Rico, Dec 18, 22; s Jose Nine & Patvia Goyco N; m 1956 to Judy Bock; c Louis, Jr, Anna Christine & Joseph Louis. Educ: Fordham Univ, BS, 50; NY Univ Sch Law, 50-52. Polit & Govt Pos: Social worker, New York, 52-53; indust inspector, labor dept, State of NY, 55-70; NY State Assemblyman, 71- Bus & Prof Pos: Ins & real estate broker, 50- Mil Serv: Entered as Pvt, Army, 41, released as S/Sgt, 46, after serv in Inf. Mem: Hunt Point Community Corp (chmn); South Bronx Model Cities (chmn phys develop comt); NAACP. Honors & Awards: Award, J F Kennedy Libr for Minorities & R F Kennedy Found. Relig: Catholic. Mailing Add: 1424 Wilkins Ave Bronx NY 10459

NINOS, ANTHONY (D)
Committeeman, Fla State Dem Party
b Lockport, NY, Feb 7, 19; s Nickolas Ninos & Bessie Calafates N; m 1954 to Georgia G Georgas. Educ: Alfred Univ Exten, Lockport, 37-38; Alfred Univ, 38-41; Ceramic Eng Soc; Delta Sigma Phi. Polit & Govt Pos: Councilman, Cocoa, Fla, 59-63, mayor, 61-63; population comnr, Ninth Judicial Circuit, 64; comnr, Fla Dept Vet Affairs, 64-67; Fla State Rep, 66-67; chmn, Brevard Co Dem Exec Comt, 69-72; committeeman, Fla State Dem Party, 70- Bus & Prof Pos: Former pres & dir, Teletronics, Inc, Cocoa, Fla; former pres & dir, Boca Raton Enterprises; pres & dir, Laycock Brevard Co, Cocoa & Cocoa Enterprises, Inc, currently. Mil Serv: Entered as Pvt, Army, 42, released as Pfc, 45, after serv in 3rd Armored Div, ETO, 43-45; 4 Bronze Battle Stars; Distinguished Unit Badge; 2 Campaign Medals; Letter of Commendation. Mem: Fla Hotel & Motel Asn (dir); Cape Kennedy Restaurant Asn (dir); Elks; Am Legion (comdr); Kiwanis (pres). Legal Res: 112 Riverside Dr Cocoa FL 32922 Mailing Add: PO Box 1060 Cocoa FL 32922

NIQUETTE, JAMES RANDALL (D)
Vt State Rep
b Winooski, Vt, June 19, 48; s Russell F Niquette & Corine E Villemaire N; single. Educ: Mt Assumption Inst, 67; Norwich Univ, BA in Hist, 71. Polit & Govt Pos: Secy, Chittenden Co Transportation Authority, Vt, 73-74; Vt State Rep, 75- Bus & Prof Pos: Assoc realtor, Pomerleao Real Estate Co, 73- Relig: Catholic. Mailing Add: 41 E Allen St Winooski VT 05404

NIQUETTE, RUSSELL FRANK (D)
Vt State Sen
Mailing Add: 41 E Allen St Winooski VT 05404

NISHIMURA, DONALD S (D)
Hawaii State Sen
Mailing Add: Senate Sgt-at-Arms State Capitol Honolulu HI 96182

NISSEN, RALPH ALBERT (R)
Mem, Rep State Cent Comt Calif
b Livermore, Calif, July 2, 11; s Louis John Nissen & Florence Watkins N; m 1939 to Eleanor Marie Schneider; c Florence Jeanne (Mrs Peter Passof); Paula Louise (Mrs Harold Miller, Jr) & Louis John, III. Educ: Univ Calif, Davis, 35-36; Sacramento State Col, 61; Phi Alpha Iota. Polit & Govt Pos: Chmn, Williams Unified Sch Bd, Calif, 40-64; chmn, Colusa Co Rep Cent Comt, 56-60; mem, Rep State Cent Comt, Calif, 56-; Rep nominee, Fourth Dist, Calif State Sen, 63- mem, Gov Comn Foreign Trade, 66-; chmn, Calif Expos & Fair Exec Comt, 68- Bus & Prof Pos: Owner & mgr, Nissen Enterprises, farming, 37-69; dir, Bank of Agr, 67- Publ: Numerous articles on rice, Am Farm Bur. Mem: Rice Growers Asn Calif; Calif State Sen Agr Adv Bd; Irrigation Dist Asn; Calif Farm Bur Fedn; Odd Fellows. Honors & Awards: Calif 4-H Alumni Award, 59, Nat Finalist. Relig: Presbyterian. Legal Res: Husted Rd Williams CA 95987 Mailing Add: PO Box 216 Williams CA 95987

NISSLEY, ELEANORE STEFFENS (R)
Committeewoman, NJ Rep State Comt
b New York, NY; d Emil William Steffens & Gertrude Urchs S; m 1949 to Warren Walmer Nissley, Jr; c James Edward, Virginia Gale, Peter Bradford & Debra Lou. Educ: Skidmore Col; New York Univ, BS. Polit & Govt Pos: Committeewoman, Bergen Co Rep Comt, NJ, 53-; munic chmn, Ridgewood, NJ, 60-61; pres, Bergen Co Rep Women's Club, 62-68; officer, Bergen Co Rep Orgn, 62-; committeewoman, NJ Rep State Comt, Bergen Co, 64-, mem state exec bd; officer, NJ Fedn Rep Women, 65-67 & 68-70; deleg & mem platform comt, Rep Nat Conv, 68; campaign mgr, Bergen Co, 68; campaign coordr for Sen Case, Bergen Co, 73. Bus & Prof Pos: Sch teacher, Tucson, Ariz, formerly. Mem: Col Club Ridgewood; Bergen Co Boy Scout Coun (exec bd); Bergen Co Ment Health Bd (secy, 70-); Health & Welfare Coun Bergen Co (bd, 72-); Family Coun Bd, Ridgewood (vpres, 72-). Honors & Awards: Over the Top Award, Community Chest, 67. Relig: Presbyterian. Mailing Add: 145 Phelps Rd Ridgewood NJ 07450

NISWANDER, CALVIN ELROY (R)
Chmn, Lewis Co Rep Party, Idaho
b Winchester, Idaho, Apr 26, 25; s Virgil Elroy Niswander & Esther Lehman N; m 1947 to Kathleen Mae Smith; c Linda Louise, Carol Ann & Cheryl Marie. Educ: Univ Idaho, 2 years. Polit & Govt Pos: Pres, Clearwater Econ Develop Asn, 68-71; chmn, Lewis Co Rep Party, 68- Mil Serv: Entered as A/S, Navy, 44, released as AETM 1/C, 46, after serv on USS Ala, 45-46. Mem: Am Legion; Mason. Mailing Add: Craigmont ID 83523

NITZE, PAUL HENRY (D)
b Amherst, Mass, Jan 16, 07; s William A Nitze & Anina Hilken N; m 1932 to Phyllis Pratt; c Heidi, Peter, William, II & Anina. Educ: Harvard Univ, AB, 28; New Sch Social Res; Pratt Inst, Johns Hopkins Univ, LLD. Polit & Govt Pos: Finance dir, Off Coordr, Inter-Am Affairs, 41-42; chief metals & minerals br, Bd Econ Warfare, 42-43; dir foreign procurement & develop br, Foreign Econ Admin, 43-44; spec consult, War Dept; from dir to vchmn, US Strategic Bombing Surv, 44-46; dep dir, Off Int Trade Policy, 46-48; dep to asst secy for econ affairs, Dept State, 48-49, dir policy planning staff, 50-53; asst secy for int security affairs, Dept Defense, 61-63; Secy of Navy, 63-67; Dep Secy Defense, 67-69; mem, US deleg, Strategic Arms Limitation Talks, 69-74. Bus & Prof Pos: Chmn bd dirs, Aspen Skiing Corp, 46-; pres, Foreign Serv Educ Found, Washington, DC, 52-61; Dillon Read & Co, invest bankers, New York, 29-38, vpres, 39-41; pres, P H Nitze & Co, Inc, 38-39; bd overseers, Harvard Univ, 67-72; dir, Am Security & Trust Co, Washington, DC, 69-, Schroder's Ltd, London, Eng, 69- & Schroder's Inc, New York, 69-; trustee, Johns Hopkins Univ, 69-; trustee, Northwestern Mutual Life, Mortgage & Realty Investors, 71-; chmn adv coun, Johns Hopkins Sch Adv Int Studies, currently. Publ: US Foreign Policy, 45-55. Honors & Awards: Recipient, Medal for Merit. Legal Res: Bel Alton MD 20611 Mailing Add: 3120 Woodley Rd NW Washington DC 20008

NITZEL, CALLIE ANN (D)
b El Reno, Okla, Aug 27, 48; d Jean Leon Pazoureck & Betty Jo Chiles; m 1967 to Theodore Ray Nitzel; c Bradley Adam. Educ: El Reno Jr Col, 65-66; Okla State Univ, 66-68; Cent State Univ, 69-71; Young Dem; Lassos & Larriets. Polit & Govt Pos: El Reno Dem City co-chairwoman, 73-75; deleg, Dem Nat Mid-Term Conf, 74; vpres, Canadian Co Dem Women's Club, 75- Bus & Prof Pos: Legal secy, El Reno, Okla, 66-69; mem staff, Congressman Ed Edmondson, Oklahoma City, 72. Publ: Auth, Democrats hobnob with contenders, Yukon Rev, 12/74. Mem: Okla Fedn Dem Women; Okla State Univ Alumni Asn (pres, Canadian Co, 74-); El Reno Co Club; Farm Bur. Relig: Christian Church; bd dirs, First Christian Church, El Reno; deaconess. Mailing Add: 2607 Feddersen Dr El Reno OK 73036

NIX, CHARLES RAY (D)
Miss State Sen
Mailing Add: Westmoreland Heights Batesville MS 38606

NIX, EDMUND A (D)
Chmn, La Crosse Co Dem Party, Wis
b Eau Claire, Wis, May 24, 29; s Sebastian Nix & Kathryn Keirnan N; m 1968 to Mary Nagle; c Kim, Norbert, Mary Kay, Edmund, Jr & Michael. Educ: Univ Wis-Eau Claire, BS, 51; Univ Wis-Madison, LLB, 54, Grad Sch, 56; Phi Alpha Delta. Polit & Govt Pos: State chmn, Young Dem of Wis, 53-54; dist chmn, Ninth Cong Dist Dem Party, Wis, 58-59; dist attorney, Eau Claire Co, 58-64; cong nominee, Tenth Cong Dist Dem, 64; US attorney, Western Dist of Wis, 65-69; cong nominee, Third Cong Dist Dem, 72; chmn, La Crosse Co Dem Party, 72- Bus & Prof Pos: State chmn, Law Enforcement Comn of Wis Bar Asn, 69-70; state chmn, Joint Legis Task Force on Alcoholism, 72-; mem, Wis Health Policy Coun, 73- Mil Serv: Entered as Pvt, E-2, Army, 54, released as Pfc, 56, after serv in Guided Missile Prog. Publ: Legal implications of the new genetics, Viterbo Col, 5/73. Mem: Wis Bar Asn. Relig: Catholic. Mailing Add: 2525 Main St La Crosse WI 54601

NIX, KENNETH OWEN (R)
Ga State Rep
b Atlanta, Ga, Oct 4, 39; s Owen Nix & Helen Crawford N; m 1962 to Charlene Scroggs; c Kenneth Owen, Jr, William Keith, Kevin Crawford & Kimberley Charlene. Educ: Presby Col (SC), 57-59; Emory Univ, BA, 61, LLB, 64. Polit & Govt Pos: Judge, Smyrna, Ga, 70-71; Ga State Rep, Cobb Co Dist 20, Post 3, 73-, mem comts on motor vehicles, spec judiciary & univ systs, Gen Assembly Ga, 73- Bus & Prof Pos: Attorney, Ga Bar Asn, Smyrna, 65. Mem: Civitans; King Springs PTA, Smyrna (chmn, 71-); Oakdale Youth Football Asn (pres, 72-); Cobb Co Rep Party (conv chmn, 72). Honors & Awards: Outstanding Serv to Youth Award, South Cobb Civic & Athletic Asn, 70. Relig: Methodist; finance chmn, Bethany Methodist Church. Mailing Add: 3878 Manson Ave Smyrna GA 30080

NIX, ROBERT N C (D)
US Rep, Pa
b Orangeburg, SC, Sept 9, 05; s Nelson Cornelius Nix & Sylvia Benjamin N; m to Ethel Lanier; c Robert N C. Educ: Lincoln Univ, AB, 21; Univ Pa, LLB, 24; Omega Psi Phi. Polit & Govt Pos: Spec dep attorney gen, Escheats Div, Pa Dept of Revenue & spec asst dep attorney gen, Pa, 34-38; mem, Policy Comt, Dem Campaign Comt, Philadelphia, 53-, co-chmn, Inter-Rels Comt, 53-; deleg, Dem Nat Conv, 56, 60, 64 & 68; US Rep, Pa, Second Dist, 58- Bus & Prof Pos: Lawyer, 25- Mem: Philadelphia Bar Asn; NAACP; YMCA; Am Woodmen; Elks. Relig: Baptist. Legal Res: 2139 N 22nd St Philadelphia PA 19121 Mailing Add: 2201 Rayburn House Off Bldg Washington DC 20515

NIXON, CORWIN M (R)
Ohio State Rep
b Lebanon, Ohio, Mar 5, 16; s Morris Nixon & Blanche Stewart N; m to Eleanor Van Meter; c Karen (Mrs Donald Heaberlin, Jr) & Keith. Educ: Lebanon High Sch. Polit & Govt Pos: Co comnr, Warren Co, Ohio, 3 terms; Ohio State Rep, 63- Bus & Prof Pos: Pres, CofC; dir, Lebanon Citizens Nat Bank; dir, Cincinnati AAA Club. Mem: Mason; Elks; Kiwanis; Boy Scouts. Relig: Protestant. Mailing Add: PO Box 58 Lebanon OH 45036

NIXON, RICHARD (R)
b Yorba Linda, Calif, Jan 9, 13; s Francis A Nixon & Hannah Milhous N; m 1940 to Patricia Ryan; c Patricia (Mrs Edward Finch Cox) & Julie (Mrs Dwight David Eisenhower II). Educ: Whittier Col, AB, 34; Duke Univ Law Sch, LLB, 37; Order of Coif. Polit & Govt Pos: Attorney, Off Price Admin, Washington, DC, 42; US Rep, Calif, 47-50; US Sen, Calif, 50-53; Vice President, United States, 53-61; Rep Cand for President, United States, 60; Rep Nominee for Gov, Calif, 62; President, United States, 69-74, resigned 74. Bus & Prof Pos: Lawyer, Whittier, Calif, 37-42; counsel, Adams, Duque & Hazeltine, 61-63; mem, Mudge, Stern, Baldwin & Todd, 63-64; partner, Nixon, Mudge, Rose, Guthrie & Alexander, 64-67; partner, Nixon, Mudge, Rose, Guthrie, Alexander, & Mitchell, 67-68. Mil Serv: Naval Res, 42-46. Publ: Six Crises, 62. Mem: Whittier Col; Boys' Clubs of Am. Relig: Society of Friends. Mailing Add: San Clemente CA

NIXON, SAM A (R)
Chmn, Wilson Co Rep Party, Tex
b Galveston, Tex, June 28, 27; s Sam A Nixon (deceased) & Margaret Wooten N; m 1950 to Emilie Elizabeth Hughes; c Margaret Alice, Emilie Elizabeth, Janice Erin & Dorothy Hughes. Educ: Tex A&M Col, BS in Sci, 46; Univ Tex Med Br Galveston, MD, 50; Am Bd Family Practice, dipl, 70. Polit & Govt Pos: Chmn, Wilson Co Rep Party, Tex, currently. Bus & Prof Pos: Pvt practice med & surg, Nixon, Tex, 54-62, Floresville, Tex, 62-; builder & gen mgr, Floresville Nursing Home; owner & builder, Floresville Prof Bldg; chief of staff, Mem Hosp, Floresville, 68-72; staff, Holmes Mem Hosp, Gonzales; consult staff, Bexar Co Hosp Dist, San Antonio. Mil Serv: Entered Army Med Corps, 50, released, 54, after serv as 11th Field Artillery Bn Surgeon, Korea & Japan, 24th Div Artil Surgeon, Japan & Korea, Outpatient Clin, Brooke Army Hosp; Capt(Ret), Res, 62. Publ: Care of the geriatric patient, Caring; PKU & Rural Practice, GP Press; plus others. Mem: Am Acad Family Physicians (mem ad hoc comt on qual assurance of ambulatory care, 74-, vspeaker, Cong of Delegs, 74-); Tex Acad Family Physicians (deleg, 71-); Am Med Asn (coun on environ, occup & pub

health, 74-); Coun on Pub Rels & Pub Serv; Tex Med Asn (deleg, 62-). Mailing Add: 1608 Sixth St Floresville TX 78114

NIXON, SYDNEY THOMAS (R)
Vt State Rep
Mailing Add: 68 Oak Grove Brattleboro VT 05301

NIXON, WILLIE BERNARD SR (D)
b Rocky Point, NC, Mar 4, 23; s Elijah Nixon, Sr & Dora Carr N; m 1947 to Johnnie Mae Carr; c Willie Bernard, Jr & Vanesse Renee. Educ: Pender Co Training Sch, Rocky Point, NC, grad, 41. Polit & Govt Pos: City councilman, Burgaw, NC, 71-; deleg, Dem Nat Conv, 72; chmn, Pender Co Dem Exec Comt, formerly. Bus & Prof Pos: Mortician, Nixon's Mortuary, Burgaw, NC, 50-; merchant, Nixon's Food Bar & Grocery, 55- Mil Serv: Entered as Pvt, Army, 43, released as Sgt, 46, after serv in Transportation Unit, European Theatre, 43-46. Mem: NC A&T State Univ (trustee, 72-); Masons; Am Legion. Honors & Awards: Achievement Award for NC & SC, Sixth Dist of Omega Psi Phi, 72. Relig: Baptist. Legal Res: Corner of Smith & Satchwell St Burgaw NC 28425 Mailing Add: PO Box 454 Burgaw NC 28425

NOAH, DONALD WITHERELL (R)
Chmn, Mitchell Co Rep Cent Comt, Kans
b Beloit, Kans, Oct 3, 28; s Ralph Henry Noah & Grace Elizabeth Summers N; m 1953 to Maxine Noreen James; c Mark James & Michael Don. Educ: Univ Kans, AB, 50, LLB, 52; Phi Alpha Delta. Polit & Govt Pos: Secy-treas, Mitchell Co Rep Cent Comt, Kans, 58-64, chmn, 64-; city attorney, Beloit, Kans, 60-65. Mil Serv: Capt, Kans Nat Guard, 48-66. Mem: Am & Kans Bar Asns; Elks; Rotary. Relig: Methodist. Legal Res: 502 W Main Beloit KS 67420 Mailing Add: Box 298 Beloit KS 67420

NOAH, RAYMOND DOUGLAS (R)
b Hobbs, NMex, Oct 5, 32; s Raymond O Noah & Ruth Johnson N; m 1958 to Cynthia Garbrecht; c Raymond Douglas, Jr & Rebecca Lynn. Educ: Univ Tex, El Paso, BBA, 57; Southern Methodist Univ Sch Law, JD, 66; Phi Delta Phi; Phi Kappa Tau. Polit & Govt Pos: Mem, Dallas Co Rep Exec Comt, Tex, 68-72; mayor, Richardson, Tex, 68-73, mem, Richardson City Coun, 68-73; deleg, Tex Rep Conv, 68, 70 & 72; permanent chmn, Dallas Co 16th & Eighth Cong Dist Conv, 68, 70 & 72; dir, NCent Tex Coun Govt, 69-73, vpres, 70-71, pres, 71-72; deleg, Rep Nat Conv, 72; mem, Regional Develop Standards Comt, Regional Transportation Standards Comt & Regional Criminal Justice Standards Comt. Bus & Prof Pos: Attorney, Allen, Feigl & Noah, 67-; treas, Computer Info Mgt Co, 69-72; dir data processing, Southern Methodist Univ, 68-69. Mil Serv: Entered as Airman Basic, Air Force, 52, released as Airman 1/C, 56, after serv in US & Greenland. Mem: Am, Tex & Richardson Bar Asns; Richardson CofC (bd dirs); Dallas Co League Munic. Honors & Awards: Wall Street J Student Achievement Award for Excellence; Outstanding Bus Student, 57; Outstanding Toastmaster Award, 60; Outstanding Toastmaster Award Dallas Co, 67; Outstanding Polit Leader, 70, 71 & 72. Relig: Methodist; Trustee, Arapaho Methodist Church. Mailing Add: 2500 Overcreek Richardson TX 75080

NOBIS, ELIZABETH ANN (R)
Chmn, Clinton Co Rep Comt, Mich
b Longmont, Colo, Feb 13, 16; d Charles Frederick Johnson & Rosamay Hammond J; m 1966 to Paul W Nobis; c David F & Peter C Katt & stepchildren, Kenneth P, Larry M & Maralee J Nobis. Educ: Univ Colo, Boulder, BS, 39; Western Mich Univ, 53-54; Russell Sage Col, 62-63; Nat Honor Soc; Beta Sigma; Kappa Alpha Theta. Polit & Govt Pos: Vchmn, Clinton Co Rep Comt, Mich, 70-74, chmn, 75-; mem, Dist 10 Exec Rep Comt, 72-75, vchmn, 75- Bus & Prof Pos: Passenger serv rep, United Air Lines, Denver, Colo, 40-41; teacher, Brighton Pub Schs, Colo, 43-44, Vicksburg Pub Schs, Mich, 51-62 & 64-66, NColonie Pub Schs, Lathem, NY, 62-64 & St Johns Pub Schs, Mich, 66- Mem: Nat & Mich Educ Asns; Clinton Co Country Club; Farm Bur; Delta Kappa Gamma. Relig: Episcopal. Mailing Add: 5813 W Walker Rd Rte 2 St Johns MI 48879

NOBLE, BILL (D)
Ga State Rep
Mailing Add: 1523 Oakgrove Rd Decatur GA 30033

NOBLE, DAN D (R)
Colo State Sen
Mailing Add: Box 71 Norwood CO 81423

NOBLE, FREDA GOLDEN (D)
Chmn, Third Cong Dist Dem Comt, Ind
b Brook, Ind, Dec 27, 06; d Charles Lee Spitler & Lula Whiting S; m 1925 to John Edward Noble; c Richard Lee (deceased), Patricia (Mrs DeClercq), Norma (Mrs Kovach) & Kenneth George. Educ: Ind Univ Exten. Polit & Govt Pos: Clerk, Bd Pub Works & Safety, South Bend, Ind, 41-51; secy, Third Cong Dist Dem Comt, 53-66, vchmn, 66-70, chmn, 70-; vchmn, St Joseph Co Dem Party, 53-; city clerk, Sound Bend, 55-63; assoc dir, Dept Tourism, State of Ind, 64-67; mem bd registr, South Bend, 67-; deleg, Dem Nat Conv, 72. Mem: Bus & Prof Women's Club (state officer); South Bend Altrusa Club; Am Legion Auxiliary; 40 et 8; Gold Star Mothers. Honors & Awards: Dem of the Year, Young Dem, 61; Woman of the Year, Bus & Prof Women, 64. Relig: Roman Catholic. Mailing Add: 2820 Beechwood Lane South Bend IN 46615

NOBLE, IDA (D)
b Abilene, Tex, June 12, 26; d Birel Hickman & Panky Smith H; m 1944 to Wiley Noble, Jr; c Kathleen, Milo, Otis, Larry, Tommy, Norris, Doris, Johnny, Billy & Craig. Educ: Gen Educ Dipl. Polit & Govt Pos: Chairwoman, Maricopa Co Welfare Rights, Ariz, 68-; alt deleg, Dem Nat Conv, 72. Mem: Oper Leap (comnr, 71-). Honors & Awards: Cup Award, Citizens Comt for Better Health, 71. Relig: Baptist. Mailing Add: 4205 S 21st St Phoenix AZ 85040

NOBLE, JOHN H (R)
NH State Rep
Mailing Add: 4 Grant St Concord NH 03301

NOBLE, R ELAINE (D)
Mass State Rep
b New Kensington, Pa, Jan 22, 44; d Ronald Noble & Ruth N. Educ: Boston Univ, BFA, 66; Emerson Col, MS, 70; Harvard Univ, MEd, 74; Phi Delta Kappa. Polit & Govt Pos: Mass State Rep, 75-, mem educ comt, Mass State Legis, 75- Mailing Add: State Capitol Boston MA 02133

NOBLE, RAY EDWARD (D)
Chmn, Tipton Co Dem Comt, Ind
b Elwood, Ind, Nov 26, 36; s Arthur H Noble & Mildred E Teuscher N; m 1956 to Cynthia Ann Warner; c Tamera Gay & Mark Edward. Educ: Purdue Univ, BS, 58. Bus & Prof Pos: Precinct committeeman, Madison Twp, Tipton Co, Ind, 60-; chmn, Tipton Co Dem Comt, 74-, coun mem, 74- Bus & Prof Pos: Vpres, Ray Bros & Noble Canning Co, 58-67, pres, 67- Mem: Mason; Scottish Rite; Shrine (pres, Tipton Co Club, 75-); Kiwanis. Relig: Protestant. Mailing Add: PO Box 314 Hobbs IN 46047

NOBLIN, JIM (D)
Miss State Sen
b Jackson, Miss, Jan 24, 37; s Earl Noblin & Ivadell Warren N; m 1957 to Camelia Harvey; c David, Jeff & Dawn. Educ: Miss State Univ, BS, 58, MBA, 59; Phi Kappa Phi; Omicron Delta Kappa; Delta Sigma Pi. Polit & Govt Pos: Miss State Sen, 72- Bus & Prof Pos: Dir econ res, Miss Indust & Technol Res Comn, Jackson, 59-61; res dir, DeKalb Co CofC, Decatur, 61-62; chief economist, Michael Baker, Jr, Inc, Rochester, Pa, 62-66; pres, Magnadex, Inc, Jackson, Miss, 66- Mil Serv: Sgt 1/C, Army Res, 10 years. Publ: Ed, Encyclopedia of Mississippi manufacturers, 60, auth, Mississippi-Latin America Trade Opportunities, 61 & Expanding Mississippi's Economy, 61, Miss State Univ. Mem: Southern Indust Develop Coun; Soc Advan Mgt; Nat Asn Bus Econ; Nat Econ Club; Mgt & Tech Serv Adv Bd, Miss Res & Develop Ctr. Relig: Methodist. Mailing Add: 836 Briarfield Rd Jackson MS 39211

NOBLITT, HARDING COOLIDGE (D)
b Marion, NC, Oct 31, 20; s Walter Tate Noblitt & Nellie Mae Horton N; m 1943 to Louise Hope Lester; c Walter Thomas. Educ: Berea Col, BA, 42; Univ Chicago, AM, 47, PhD, 55; Phi Kappa Phi; Pi Gamma Mu; Tau Kappa Alpha; Pi Kappa Delta. Polit & Govt Pos: Deleg, Dem-Farmer-Labor State Conv, Minn, 58-64 & 68-70, alt deleg, 66 & 72, chmn platform comt, 68; youth coordr, 61-62; nominee for Cong, Seventh Dist, Dem-Farmer-Labor Party, 62; mem, Gov Citizens Coun on Aging, 63-68; co-chmn, Prof for Johnson-Humphrey, Minn, 64; deleg, Dem Nat Conv, 64; mem, Clay Co Dem Cent Comt, 66-72; chmn platform comt, Minn Dem Conv, 68, mem nominations comt, 70; mem, Seventh Cong Dist Exec Comt, Minn, 70-72; mem, Minn Higher Educ Coord Comn, 71-, secy, 74- Bus & Prof Pos: Asst prof, Concordia Col, Moorhead, Minn, 50-53, assoc prof, 53-56, prof, 56-, chmn dept polit sci, 64-; acting ed, Discourse: a review of the liberal arts, 59-60. Mil Serv: Entered as Pvt, Army, 43, released as T/Sgt, 46, after serv in 16th Armored Div, 79th Inf Div, 1st US Inf Div, ETO, 45-46; European-African-Mid Eastern Campaign Medal with Two Bronze Stars; Meritorious Serv Citation. Publ: Intentions of founding fathers in separating church & state, Discourse, 1/58; A case study in practical politics, In: Proc Minn Acad Sci, Vol 31, No 1. Mem: Am Polit Sci Asn; Acad of Polit Sci; Am Acad Polit & Social Sci; Am Legion; VFW. Relig: Presbyterian. Mailing Add: 2014 S Fourth St Moorhead MN 56560

NODDIN, HAROLD STAPLES (D)
b Bangor, Maine, Oct 22, 12; s George Heber Noddin & Harriet Staples N; m 1932 to Beatrice Gardiner; c George Harold. Educ: Bangor High Sch, grad, 32. Polit & Govt Pos: Alt deleg, Dem Nat Conv, 72. Bus & Prof Pos: Papermaker, Standard Packaging Corp, 42-68; secy-treas & asst to pres, Maine AFL-CIO, 68-73; dir, Bur of Labor, 73- Mem: Life mem United Paperworkers Int Union; Local 1826 AFSME; AF&AM (Past Master); York Rite. Relig: Methodist. Mailing Add: Rte 5 Leighton Rd Augusta ME 04330

NOE, JAMES ALBERT (D)
b West Point, Ky, Dec 21, 93; s John M Noe & Belle McRae N; m 1922 to Anna Gray Sweeney; c Gay, James Albert & Linda McRae. Educ: Country schs. Polit & Govt Pos: Former mem, Dem Nat Comt, La; La State Sen, 32-34 & 36-40; Lt Gov, La, 34-36, Gov, 36; deleg, Dem Nat Conv, 68, alt deleg, 72. Bus & Prof Pos: Owner-operator, plantations in Ouachita & Tensas Parishes; owner-operator, radio sta KNOE, KNOE FM & KNOE TV, Monroe, La & radio sta WNOE & FM, New Orleans, La; engaged in oil & natural gas bus in Ark, La & Tex. Mil Serv: Entered as Pvt, Army, released as Lt, after serv in 369th Inf, World War I. Relig: Presbyterian. Mailing Add: 529 Bienville St New Orleans LA 70130

NOEL, JAMES ELLSWORTH (R)
Chmn, Gove Co Rep Cent Comt, Kans
b Quinter, Kans, Aug 19, 28; s Floyd K Noel & Phyllis N Sharp N; m 1959 to Beverly Kay Shook; c Anna Thea, Floyd Garnett, Megan Michele & Nels Patric. Educ: Ft Hays Kans State Col, 46-47; Univ Kans, AB, 59, LLB, 60. Polit & Govt Pos: Co treas, Gove Co, Kans, 51-55 & 62-65, co attorney, 65-67; mayor, City of Grainfield, 61-62; precinct committeeman, Grainfield Twp, 66-68; chmn, Gove Co Rep Cent Comt, 68- Bus & Prof Pos: Gandy dancer, Union Pac RR, Grainfield, Kans, 47-51; bookkeeper & billing clerk, Grainfield Tel Co, Inc, 51, secy-treas, 60-; ins adjuster, Universal Adjustment & Inspection Co, Colby, 60-69. Mem: NW Kans Bar Asn; Kans Bar Asn; Mason; Lions; Theodore Gary Chap, Independent Tel Pioneer Asn. Relig: Methodist. Mailing Add: Grainfield KS 67737

NOEL, PHILIP WILLIAM (D)
Gov, RI
b Providence, RI, June 6, 31; s Seraphin Joseph Noel & Emma B Crudeli N; m 1956 to Joyce Anne Sandberg; c Linda Joyce, Joseph Walter, Lori Anne, Thomas Philip & JoAnne Marie. Educ: Brown Univ, AB in Econ, 54; Georgetown Univ, LLB, 57; Delta Tau Delta. Polit & Govt Pos: City councilman, Warwick, RI, 60-66, mayor, 67-72; deleg, Dem Nat Conv, 68; pres, RI League Cities & Towns, 70-72; Gov, RI, 73-; mem exec comt, Nat Gov Conf, 73-74; state co-chmn, New Eng Regional Comn, 74; vchmn, Dem Gov Conf, 74; mem US adv comn, Intergovt Rels, 75. Bus & Prof Pos: Attorney-at-law, 58-67. Mil Serv: Naval Res, 49-53. Mem: Am, RI & Kent Co Bar Asns; KofC; Elks. Honors & Awards: Distinguished Serv Award, RI & Warwick Jaycees; Providence J-Bull Man of Year Award, 73. Relig: Roman Catholic. Mailing Add: 21 Kirby Ave Warwick RI 02889

NOFZIGER, LYN (R)
Mem, Rep State Cent Comt Calif
b Bakersfield, Calif, June 8, 24; s Bennett R Nofziger & Rosalind Curran N; m 1947 to Bonnie Foster; c Susan & Glenda. Educ: Univ Calif, Los Angeles, 46; San Jose State Col, AB, 50. Polit & Govt Pos: Press secy to Ronald Reagan, 66; dir commun, Gov Ronald Reagan, Calif, 67-68, informal consult, currently; dep asst for cong rels, President Nixon, 69-71; dep chmn for commun, Rep Nat Comt, 71-72; Calif campaign mgr, President Nixon, 72; mgr, Reinecke for Gov Comt, 73; consult, Survival of Free Cong Comt, currently; mem, Rep State Cent Comt Calif, currently; mem, President's Comn on Personnel Interchange, 74- Bus & Prof Pos:

Reporter, ed & Wash correspondent, Copley Newspapers, 50-66; head, Lyn Nofziger Co, currently. Mem: Sigma Delta Chi; Nat Press Club. Mailing Add: Suite 833 Forum Bldg Sacramento CA 95814

NOGGLE, ABBY DEL (R)
Co-Chmn, Ind Young Rep
b Anderson, Ind, Dec 8, 44; d William Basil Porter & Kathryn Knight P; m 1966 to Jon Richard Noggle; c Andrea Dawn & Julie Renee. Educ: Anderson Col, BA in Music Educ, 68; Ball State Univ, MA in Music, 72; Camarada Social Club. Polit & Govt Pos: Asst dir, Madison Co Young Rep, Ind, 71-72, secy, 73-74, parliamentarian, currently; floor watcher, Rep State Conv, 72; conv site chmn, Ind Young Rep, 72-73, co-chmn, 74-; mem, Rep State Platform Comt, 74; precinct vcommitteeman, Stoney Creek & Madison Co, 74- Bus & Prof Pos: Choir dir, Victory Chapel Community Church, 75- Publ: Auth, IYRF brings back 1975 convention from Washington, DC, The Young Rep, 5-6/74; co-auth, Anderson to Host Constitutional Convention, The Young Rep, winter 75. Mem: US Auto Club (scorer, 68-); Anderson Jaycee Wives; Am Bible Soc (contribr). Honors & Awards: Bronze Hardcharger, 70 & Silver Hardcharger, 74, Nat Young Rep; Young Rep of the Year, Madison Co Young Rep, 72; Darling Award, 74 & Nominee for Jaycee Wife of the Year Award, Anderson Jaycee Wives, 74. Relig: Methodist. Mailing Add: 1216 Main St Lapel IN 46051

NOLAN, DAVID BRIAN (R)
b Washington, DC, Jan 1, 51; s Dr John Joseph Nolan & Mary Jane Donnelly N; single. Educ: Duke Univ, BA in Psychol, 73; Am Univ Sch Govt & Pub Affairs, MPA, 75; Southwestern Univ Sch Law, 74-; Worcester Col, Oxford Univ, 75; Tau Epsilon Phi; Delta Theta Phi. Polit & Govt Pos: Youth chmn, Les Phillips for Arlington Co Bd, Va, 68; organizer & marshall leader, Honor Am Day, Washington, DC, 70; Duke Club Chmn, Young Am for Freedom, 70-71; state bd mem, NC Young Am for Freedom, 70-73; pres, Duke Col Rep Club, 71-72; youth organizer, Jesse Helms for Senate, 72; alt deleg, Rep Nat Conv, 72; chmn, NC Fedn Col Rep, 72-73; state bd mem, NC Young Rep Fedn, 72-73; state bd mem, NC Rep Party Cent Comt, 72-73; exec dir, DC Col Rep Fedn, 74; organizer, Calif Young Rep Fedn, 75. Bus & Prof Pos: Cong intern for Hon Joel Broyhill (Tenth Va), summer 71; intern reporter & writer, Human Events, summer 72. Publ: A series of articles of Nixon versus McGovern, Duke Chronicle, 71-73. Mem: Alpha Phi Omega (treas, 71-73); Duke Interfraternity Coun (secy, 70-71); Mensa; Los Angeles Student Trial Lawyers Asn; Am Bar Asn (student div, regional chmn, pub contract law). Honors & Awards: Full tuition scholar to the Georgetown Inst on Comp Polit & Econ Systs, Charles Edison Youth Found, 71; Outstanding Col Rep of Year, Col Rep Fedn, 71; Dean's List, Duke Univ, 72 & 73. Relig: Roman Catholic. Legal Res: 2310 S Ft Scoll Dr Arlington VA 22202 Mailing Add: 330 S Berendo St Apt 114 Los Angeles CA 90020

NOLAN, HOWARD CHARLES, JR (D)
NY State Sen
b Albany, NY, Aug 24, 32; s Howard Charles Nolan & Helan A Burke N; m 1959 to Geraldine L Leonard; c Anne, Kathleen, Deborah, Robert, Donna, Lynn & Karen. Educ: Holy Cross Col, BS, 54; Union Univ, Albany Law Sch, JD, 57. Polit & Govt Pos: NY State Sen, 42nd Sen Dist, 75- Bus & Prof Pos: Mem bd dirs, Sisters of Mercy Bd Regents & Cath Youth Orgn, Albany Diocese, currently; mem bd trustees, St Gregory's Sch. Mil Serv: Entered as Pvt, Marine Corps, 57, released as Capt, 60, after serv in 2nd Marine Div, Camp Lejeune, NC, 58-60; Letter of Commendation. Mem: Serra Club of Albany; New York State Bar Asn; Albany Co Bar Asn (Grievance Comt); Marine Corps League; United Cerebral Palsy Asn. Honors & Awards: Outstanding Young Man of the Year Award & Award for Distinguished & Unselfish Serv, Jr CofC, 64; Award for Dedicated & Time Consuming Efforts, United Cerebral Palsy Asn, 69. Relig: Roman Catholic. Legal Res: 8 Birch Hill Rd Loudonville NY 12211 Mailing Add: 60 State St Albany NY 12207

NOLAN, MICHAEL THOMAS (D)
Chmn, San Luis Obispo Co Dem Cent Comt, Calif
b San Luis Obispo, Calif, Oct 5, 53; s Thomas Francis Nolan & Norma Clare Middleton N; single. Educ: Univ Notre Dame, 71-72; Calif Polytech State Univ, 72- Polit & Govt Pos: Coordr, San Luis Obispo Co Julian Camacho for Cong, Calif, 74; chmn, San Luis Obispo Co Dem Cent Comt, 75-; mem, Calif Dem Cent & Exec Comts, 75- Mem: El Moro Dem Club. Relig: Roman Catholic. Mailing Add: Rte 2 Box 784 San Luis Obispo CA 93401

NOLAN, MONICA (D)
Dem State Cent Committeewoman, Ohio
b Covington, Ky, Dec 28, 14; d James Lawrence Nolan & Mary Murphy N; single. Educ: Univ Cincinnati, AB, 35. Polit & Govt Pos: Adv comt, Cincinnati Pub Recreation Comn, Ohio; mem adv bd, Hamilton Co Welfare Dept; mem, Mayor's Comt on Youth, Cincinnati; mem steering comt, Hamilton Co Dem Party; deleg & mem rules comt, Dem Nat Conv, 56, deleg-at-lg, 64 & 68; Dem cand for US Rep, First Dist, Ohio, 62; Dem State Cent Committeewoman, Ohio, currently. Bus & Prof Pos: Registered rep of NY Stock Exchange, W E Hutton & Co, Cincinnati, Ohio. Mil Serv: Served with Am Red Cross in Greenland, India & Ger, World War II. Mem: Women's Nat Dem Club; Speakers Bur, NY Stock Exchange; Asn Alumnae of Sacred Heart; Women's Adv Comt, US Lawn Tennis Asn. Honors & Awards: Former Ohio State Tennis Champion; Mademoiselle Mag Award for Outstanding War Work, 43. Relig: Roman Catholic. Mailing Add: 3547 St Charles Pl Cincinnati OH 45208

NOLAN, RICHARD MICHAEL (D)
US Rep, Minn
b Brainerd, Minn, Dec 17, 43; s Henry Nolan & Mary Elwood N; m 1964 to Marjorie Langer N; c Michael, Leah, John & Katie. Educ: St John's Univ, 62; Univ Minn, BA Polit Sci, 66; Univ Md, 67. Polit & Govt Pos: Staff asst, Sen Walter Mondale, Minn, 66-68; Minn State Rep, 68-72; fed-state coordr for Minn House Rep, 73; US Rep, Minn, Sixth Dist, 75- Bus & Prof Pos: Admin asst to vpres, Fingerhut Corp, St Cloud, Minn, 73-74. Legal Res: Waite Park MN 56387 Mailing Add: 1107 Longworth Bldg Washington DC 20515

NOLAND, CHARLES PATRICK (D)
b Akron, Ohio, Aug 22, 52; s Charles Albert Noland & Viola St John N; single. Educ: Kent State Univ. Polit & Govt Pos: Alt deleg, Dem Nat Conv, 72. Mailing Add: 575 Center Rd Akron OH 44319

NOLAND, JAMES ALFRED, JR (R)
b Macks Creek, Mo, Feb 2, 27; s James Alfred Noland, Sr & Martha Allen N; m 1958 to Janice Mae Pueser; c Claire Ellen, Cynthia Janice & Cecilia Diane. Educ: Southwest Mo State Univ, BS in Educ, 63; Univ Mo, MA in Educ, 64. Polit & Govt Pos: Mo State Rep, 56-68; co tax collector, 58-; Mo State Sen, 68-74; Rep cand for US Rep, Md, 74. Bus & Prof Pos: Pub sch prin, 48-56; prof psychol, Cent Methodist Col, 65-66. Mil Serv: Entered as Pvt, Army, 45, released as Cpl, 47, after serv in 13th Air Force, Philippines, 46-47. Mem: AF&AM (Past Master, Sr Grand Deacon, currently); Linn Creek Odd Fellows (Past Noble Grand & Dist Dep Grand Master); Lake of the Ozarks Am Legion (Past Comdr); Eastern Star. Relig: Baptist. Mailing Add: Rte 1 Osage Beach MO 65065

NOLEN, JAMES RICHARD (D)
Mass State Rep
b Holyoke, Mass, Apr 17, 33; s James Robert Nolen & Katherine Dillon N; single. Educ: Harvard Col, AB; Columbia Univ, MS; Portia Law Sch, LLB, Valedictorian of Law Sch class. Polit & Govt Pos: Mass State Rep, 59-; alt deleg, Dem Nat Conv, 68. Bus & Prof Pos: Attorney-at-Law, 65- Mil Serv: Pvt, Army. Relig: Roman Catholic. Mailing Add: 25 Homecrest Ave Ware MA 01082

NOLIN, KARL (D)
Iowa State Sen
Mailing Add: Ralston IA 51459

NOLTING, FRED W (D)
Iowa State Sen
Mailing Add: 1716 Patton Ave Waterloo IA 50702

NOONAN, L W (D)
Ala State Sen
Mailing Add: 161 McGregor Ave Mobile AL 36608

NOONAN, NORMA CORIGLIANO (DFL)
Chairperson, Dist 39 Dem-Farmer-Labor Party, Minn
b Philadelphia, Pa, May 19, 37; d Domenic Corigliano & Amelia Stendardo C; m 1963 to Thomas S Noonan. Educ: Univ Pa, BA, 59; Ind Univ, Bloomington, MA, 62, PhD, 65; Phi Beta Kappa; Pi Sigma Alpha; Chi Omega. Polit & Govt Pos: Chairperson, Dist 39 Dem-Farmer-Labor Party, Minn, 74-; cand, Minn State Rep, Dist 39B, 74. Bus & Prof Pos: Asst prof polit sci, Western Ky Univ, 65-66; from asst prof to prof of polit sci, Augsburg Col, 66-, chairperson dept, 70- Publ: Auth, Study Guide: Soviet Politics & Government, Univ Minn, 74; co-ed, One January in Russia, Augsburg Col, 74. Mem: Minneapolis-St Paul Comt Foreign Rels; Am Asn Univ Prof (vpres, Minn Conf, 72-); Minn Polit Sci Asn (mem exec comt, 70-). Honors & Awards: Distinguished Teaching Award, Augsburg Col Sr Class, 72. Relig: Catholic. Mailing Add: 10224 Rich Rd Bloomington MN 55437

NORDBERG, NILS LOVERING (R)
Mass State Rep
b Woburn, Mass, Nov 6, 34; s Nils Lambert Nordberg & Eleanor Lovering N; m 1960 to Linda Chesley; c Ellen Lovering & Susan Currier. Educ: Cornell Univ, BS, 56; Alpha Tau Omega. Polit & Govt Pos: Rep precinct rep, Town Meeting, Reading, Mass, 63-69, mem, Rep Town Comt, 66-; Mass State Rep, 69- Mil Serv: Entered as 2nd Lt, Army, 56, Maj, Res, Army QmC, 56- Mem: Cornell Soc Hotelmen; Nat Restaurant Asn; AF&AM; Nat Fedn Independent Bus. Relig: Protestant. Mailing Add: 32 Pennsylvania Ave Reading MA 01867

NORED, ALVIN (R)
Chmn, Burnet Co Rep Party, Tex
b Ft Worth, Tex, Aug 12, 29; s Thomas Alvin Nored & Alberta Hampton N; m 1952 to Mildred Bloys; c Carolyn, Catherine & Jean. Educ: Tex Technol Col, BS, 51; St Mary's Univ Sch Law, JD, 68; Phi Delta Phi; Block & Bridle Club. Polit & Govt Pos: Deleg, Tex Rep State Conv, 64, 68 & 70; chmn, Burnet Co Rep Party, 70- Bus & Prof Pos: Attorney-at-law, 68- Mem: Tex Bar Asn; Rotary. Relig: Presbyterian. Mailing Add: 201 S Pierce Burnet TX 78611

NOREIKA, LOUISE A (D)
Finance Chmn, Fifth Dist Dem Cent Comt, Okla
b Burkburnett, Tex, July 10, 23; d Robert Edward Lee McMillian & Annie Cavin M; m 1944 to James G Noreika. Educ: Okla Oniv, 38-39; Okla City Univ, 41; Beverley Bus Col, Chicago, Ill, 46-47. Polit & Govt Pos: Precinct chmn, past 17 years & ward coordr for Village, Okla, currently; women's coordr, State Civil Defense Prog, 50-52; pub rels dir, Okla Semi-Centennial Comn, 56-58; secy, Okla State Legis, past 10 sessions; second vpres, State Fedn of Dem Women, 67-69; dep examr, State Exam & Inspector's Off, State Capitol, 67-69; alt deleg, Dem Nat Conv, 68; pres, Fifth Dist Federated Dem Women's Clubs, Okla, 69-72; finance chmn, Fifth Dist Dem Cent Comt, currently; employee, Off Community Affairs & Planning, State of Okla, currently. Bus & Prof Pos: Employed in radio & TV field on several occasions; free-lance pub rels & publicity for various orgn. Mil Serv: Entered as Pvt, Women's Air Corps, 42, released as Capt, 45, after serv in 3rd Air Force & 9th Air Force, ETO, 43-45; Five Battle Stars. Mem: Okla Pub Rels Asn; Northside Dem Women's Asn. Honors & Awards: Okla Woman of the Year, 57; Woman of the Year, Galatea Chap, Am Bus Women's Asn, 69. Relig: Catholic. Mailing Add: 2624 Abbey Rd Oklahoma City OK 73120

NORFOLK, NEVEDA BROOKS (VEDA) (R)
Mem, East Baton Rouge Parish Rep Exec Comt, La
b Baton Rouge, La, Dec 5, 29; d Laurance W Brooks & Neveda Stokes B; m 1951 to William Alvin Norfolk; c Veda Lynn, Claire Brooks, William Alvin, Jr & Nancy Ann. Educ: Sweet Briar Col, 46-47; La State Univ, BA, 50; Univ Miami, 51; Chi Omega. Polit & Govt Pos: Chmn, Baton Rouge, La, 68; pres, East Baton Rouge Parish Women's Rep Club, 69-71, mem, Rep Polit Action Coun, 69-71, vchmn, 71-; mem bd, La Fedn of Rep Women, 69-73; dist mgr, US Census Baton Rouge, 70; mem, East Baton Rouge Parish Issues Comt, 70-71; South regional chmn community serv & mem bd, Nat Fedn Rep Women, 70-71; mem, East Baton Rouge Parish Rep Exec Comt, 71-; horizons chmn, Exec Comt, Baton Rouge Bicentennial Comn, 72- Bus & Prof Pos: Secy to dean of women, Univ Miami, 51-52; stenographer, Humble Oil, Houston, Tex, 52-53. Mem: Baton Rouge Jr League (pres, vpres & treas); Baton Rouge Goals Cong; Found for Hist La (mem bd); YWCO (mem bd); Audubon Girls Scout Coun (mem bd). Relig: Episcopal; pres, Women of the Church, St James Episcopal Church, 72-74. Mailing Add: 3855 Churchill Ave Baton Rouge LA 70808

NORLAND, LOWELL E (D)
Iowa State Rep
Mailing Add: RR 1 Kensett IA 50448

NORMAN, DOVIE S (R)
VChmn, Simpson Co Rep Party, Miss
b Pinola, Miss, Jan 30, 15; d Robert Ernest Spencer & Ida Finch S; m 1936 to Thomas D Norman. Educ: High sch. Polit & Govt Pos: Vchmn, Simpson Co Rep Party, Miss, 64- Bus & Prof Pos: Merchant, 44. Relig: Baptist. Mailing Add: RR 2 Mendenhall MS 39114

NORMAN, LARRY ELLIS (R)
Mem, Vance Co Rep Exec Comt, NC
b Henderson, NC, May 1, 52; s James Ellis Norman & Chaney Fowlkes N; single. Educ: NC State Univ, 70- Polit & Govt Pos: Pres, Vance Co TAR, NC, 68-69; vpres, NC TAR, 68-69; chmn, Second Cong Dist Young Rep, 70-72; mem exec comt, NC Fedn Young Rep, 70-72; mem, Vance Co Rep Exec Comt, 7O-; alt deleg, Rep Nat Conv, 72; parliamentarian, Vance Co Young Rep, 73- Honors & Awards: Young Rep Man of the Year, NC Fedn of Young Rep, 72; youngest cand for Gen Assembly in NC hist, 72. Relig: Baptist. Mailing Add: 831 E Montgomery St Henderson NC 27536

NORMAN, SETH WALKER (D)
b Nashville, Tenn, Apr 6, 34; s Jack Norman & Carrie Sneed N; m 1958 to Mary Gennette Sain; c Thomas Jay, Frances Gennette & Jack. Educ: Vanderbilt Univ, 2 years; Nashville YMCA Night Law Sch, LLB; Sigma Chi. Polit & Govt Pos: Tenn State Rep, 83rd Gen Assembly, 62-64; pres, Davidson Co Young Dem, Tenn, 64-65; secy, Davidson Co Dem Primary Bd, 66-67; secy, Tenn State Dem Exec Comt, formerly; deleg, Dem Nat Conv & mem platform comt, 68. Mil Serv: Entered as Airman Basic, Air Force, 53, released as 1st Lt, 57, after serv in 581st Air Resupply Squadron, Far East Air Force & 3rd Air Transport Squadron, Mil Air Transport Serv, Capt, Res, 57-61; Nat Defense Serv Medal; Korean Conflict Medal; UN Medal. Mem: Tenn & Nashville Bar Asns; Davidson Co Trial Lawyers Asn; AAONMS; Royal Order of Jesters. Relig: Presbyterian. Legal Res: 4005 Newman Pl Nashville TN 37204 Mailing Add: 213 Third Ave N Nashville TN 37201

NORMAN, WILLIAM JAMES (BILL) (D)
Mont State Sen
b Minn, Apr 2, 22; m to Laura; c Daniel, Timothy & Margaret. Educ: MD & spec training in neurol. Polit & Govt Pos: Mont State Rep, formerly; Mont State Sen, currently. Bus & Prof Pos: Practicing physician. Mil Serv: Army Air Force, Pac Theatre, World War II. Mem: Mont Med Soc. Relig: Roman Catholic. Mailing Add: 440 Connell Missoula MT 59801

NORMAND, JAMES ARTHUR (D)
NH State Rep
b Manchester, NH, Dec 3, 53; s Lucien Joseph Normand & Lucille Beaudette N; single. Educ: Univ NH, 72-; Nat Inst Food Serv Indust scholar, N; Psi Epsilon; Young Dem; Sailing Club; Dean's List, 73, 74 & 75. Polit & Govt Pos: Mem, NH State Dem Comt, 74-; formerly, Hillsborough Co Dem Comt, NH, 74-; NH State Rep, 74- Bus & Prof Pos: Aide to coordr, Fed Funds, Manchester, NH, 74. Mem: Concerned Young Dem. Relig: Catholic. Mailing Add: 167 Morgan St Manchester NH 03102

NORPEL, RICHARD J, SR (D)
Iowa State Sen
Mailing Add: 1205 Mulberry St Bellevue IA 52031

NORQUIST, JOHN O (D)
Wis State Rep
Mailing Add: 2903 W National Milwaukee WI 53215

NORRELL, CATHERINE DORRIS (D)
b Camden, Ark; d William Frank Dorris & Lucinda Rose Whitehead D; m 1922 to W F Norrell, wid; c Julia J. Educ: Ouachita Baptist Col, 19-20; Univ Ark, 28. Polit & Govt Pos: US Rep, Ark, 61-63; dir, Dept State Reception Ctr, Honolulu; Dep Asst Secy State for Educ & Cult Affairs, Ark; mem, Women's Nat Dem Club; mem, Dem Wives Forum. Bus & Prof Pos: Dir, music dept, Ark A&M Col, 32-38; teacher pub schs, 20-24. Mem: Am Legion Auxiliary; Foreign Serv Asn; Nat Order Women Legis; Eastern Star (past Worthy Grand Matron); Former Mem Cong. Mailing Add: 3006 Pualei Circle Apt 203 Honolulu HI 96815

NORRIS, ALAN E (R)
Ohio State Rep
b Westerville, Ohio, Aug 15, 35; s James Russell Norris & Dorothy A Schrader N; m 1962 to Nancy Jeanne Myers; c Tom Edward Jackson & Tracy Elaine. Educ: Univ Paris, La Sorbonne, Cert, 56; Otterbein Col, BA, 57; NY Univ Sch Law, LLB, 60; Phi Alpha Theta; Theta Alpha Phi; Phi Sigma Iota; Phi Delta Phi; Pi Kappa Phi; Pi Kappa Delta; ed, Col Newspaper; 4 varsity letters, track. Polit & Govt Pos: Law clerk for Ohio Chief Justice Kingsley A Taft, 60-61; asst law dir, Westerville, Ohio, 62-67, chmn zoning bd, 62-67; committeeman, Franklin Co Rep Cent Comt, 62-; Ohio State Rep, 27th Dist, 67-, minority whip, 73-; chmn, Ohio Am Revolution Bicentennial Comn, 75- Bus & Prof Pos: Partner, Metz, Bailey & Norris, 62- Publ: Divorce reform, Ohio Style, 9/74; Legislative history of Ohio's new criminal code, Cleveland State Law Rev, winter 74; Divorce reform: Ohio's alternative to no-fault, State Govt, winter 75; plus others. Mem: Am Bar Asns; SAR; F&AM; Eastern Star; Kiwanis Int. Honors & Awards: Jaycee Distinguished Serv Award, 67. Relig: United Methodist. Mailing Add: Box 187 Westerville OH 43086

NORRIS, JAMES W (D)
Wyo State Sen
b Cheyenne, Wyo, Apr 15, 30; s William A Norris, Sr & Ethel Warlaumont N; single. Educ: Univ Wyo, BS, 53, LLB, 61; Kappa Sigma. Polit & Govt Pos: Wyo State Sen, 75- Bus & Prof Pos: Pres, The Timberline Corp, 56- & Wortham Machinery Co, 68-; assoc, Pattno & Norris, Attorneys, 61-63. Mil Serv: Entered as Pvt, Air Force, 51, released as 2nd Lt, 53, after serv in 1603rd Atld MATS, European Theatre, 52-53. Mem: Am & Wyo Bar Asns; Am Legion; KofC. Relig: Roman Catholic. Legal Res: 3408 Carey Ave Cheyenne WY 82001 Mailing Add: PO Box 349 Cheyenne WY 82001

NORRIS, JOHN M, II (R)
Maine State Rep
Mailing Add: 9 North Rd Brewer ME 04412

NORRIS, PALMER WHITTEN (PETE) (R)
Mem, Jefferson Co Rep Exec Comt, Ala
b Birmingham, Ala, Nov 29, 32; s Defour Witzar Norris & Callie Dee Shaw N; m 1962 to Ann Elizabeth Deaver; c Palmer Whitten, Jr & Melissa Ann. Educ: Univ Ala, BS, 57; Birmingham Sch Law, LLB, 62, JD, 68. Polit & Govt Pos: Rep precinct chmn, Jefferson Co Precinct 17, Ala, 63-; mem, Jefferson Co Rep Comt, 64-, legal counsel, 68-; Rep party poll watcher, 64 & 68; cand, Ala House of Rep, Pl 14 14th Dist, 66; coordr, Perry Hooper Campaign for US Sen, 68; deleg & permanent chmn, Jefferson Co Rep Conv, 68; recruitment chmn, Jefferson Co Rep Party, 68; deleg, Ala Rep Conv & mem resolutions comt, 68; alt deleg, Rep Nat Conv, 68; mem, Jefferson Co Rep Exec Comt, 68- Bus & Prof Pos: With Hayes Int Corp, 58; from clerk to asst auditor, First Nat Bank of Birmingham, 59-63; attorney-at-law, 63- Mil Serv: Entered as A/S, Navy, 51, released as YNT 3, 53, after serv in Transport Squadron 24, Fleet Aircraft Serv Squadron 76, PT Lyauty, French Morocco & London, Eng. Mem: Birmingham & Ala Bar Asns; Gardendale Libr & Accreditation Fund (founder). Relig: Conservative Baptist; mem bd deacons, First Conservative Baptist Church, training union dir, moderator bus meetings & substitute Sunday sch teacher. Legal Res: 1904 Norris Circle Fultondale AL 35068 Mailing Add: 2501 B N 30th Ave Birmingham AL 35207

NORRIS, RAYMOND (R)
b Waneta, Ky, Oct 28, 11; s Ben Norris & Maggie Lunsford N; m 1936 to Bessie Barnett; c Lewis Ray & Kenneth Leon. Educ: McKee High Sch, Ky, two years. Polit & Govt Pos: Mem sch bd, McKee, Ky, 42-; chmn, Jackson Co Rep Comt, formerly. Bus & Prof Pos: Bus driver, 30; salesman, 30-36; merchant, McKee, Ky, 37-69; real estate salesman. Mem: Mason. Honors & Awards: Twenty year pen, Ky Sch Bd Asn. Relig: Baptist. Mailing Add: Water St McKee KY 40447

NORRIS, RUSSELL EARL J (CONSERVATIVE, NY)
VChmn Southern Tier Region, Conservative Party, NY
b Johnson City, NY, Nov 23, 29; s Russell Earl Norris & Nora Bailey N; m 1952 to Winona Lillie Seislove; c Scott Royce, Anita Kay, Mark Andrew, John Russell & Lori Anne. Educ: Rochester Inst Technol, AAppl Sci, 50; Bucknell Univ, BS, 53. Polit & Govt Pos: Chmn, Conservative Party Club of Broome Co, NY, 62-64; vchmn Southern Tier Region, Conservative Party, NY, 63-; mem, Conservative Party State Exec Comt, 64- Bus & Prof Pos: Assoc tech writer, Int Bus Machines Corp, 67- Mil Serv: Entered as Pvt, Army, 53, released as Pfc, 55; after serv in Develop & Proof Servs Ord Corps, Aberdeen Proving Grounds; Good Conduct Medal. Mem: Am Ord Asn; Soc Tech Writers & Publ; Endicott Optimists' Club; Am Legion; Young Am for Freedom. Relig: Presbyterian. Mailing Add: 212 N Willis Ave Endwell NY 13760

NORRIS, WILLIAM ALBERT (D)
b Turtle Creek, Pa, Aug 30, 27, s George Norris & Florence Clive N; m to Merry Wiester; c Barbara, Donald, Kim & Alison. Educ: Princeton Univ, AB, 51; Stanford Univ, LLB, 54; Phi Beta Kappa; exec ed, Stanford Law Rev; Order of the Coif. Polit & Govt Pos: Mem, Calif State Dem Cent Comt, 59-66; campaign mgr, Rudd Brown Cong Campaign, 60; mem, Calif State Bd Educ, 61-67, vpres, 66-67, co-chmn, Southern Calif Campaign to Reelect Gov Brown, 62; deleg, Dem Nat Conv, 64, 68 & 72, mem rules comt, 68; chmn, Southern Calif Steering Comt, Campaign Against Proposition 14, 64; mem, Coord Coun Higher Educ, 64-66; treas, Thomas Braden for Lt Gov Campaign, 66; trustee, Calif State Cols, 67-71; vchmn, Kennedy Pres Campaign, Calif, 68; mem exec comt, Tom Bradley for Mayor Campaign, 69 & 73; co-chmn, Wilson Riles for State Supt of Pub Instr, 70; mem exec comt, Californians for McGovern, 71-72; pres bd comnrs, Los Angeles Police Dept, 73-74; Dem nominee, Attorney Gen, 74. Bus & Prof Pos: Spec asst attorney gen of Calif for Colorado River Litigation; assoc, Northcutt Ely, Washington, DC, 54-55; law clerk to Justice William O Douglas, US Supreme Court, 55-56; assoc, Tuttle & Taylor, 56-60, partner, 60-; spec counsel, President Kennedy's Comn Airlines Controversy, 61. Mil Serv: Navy, 45-47. Mem: Am, Calif State & Los Angeles Co Bar Asns; Town Hall, Los Angeles; Const Rights Found. Legal Res: 800 W First St Los Angeles CA 90012 Mailing Add: 609 S Grand Ave Los Angeles CA 90017

NORTH, FRANCES C (D)
Wash State Rep
Mailing Add: Box 441 North Bend WA 98045

NORTH, LOIS (R)
Wash State Sen
Mailing Add: 10126 Radford Ave NW Seattle WA 98177

NORTH, ROBERT (DFL)
Minn State Sen
Mailing Add: 1642 Blair Ave St Paul MN 55104

NORTH, SALLY ANNE (R)
Secy, 11th Dist Rep Comt, Mich
b Battle Creek, Mich, May 30, 34; d Sidney M Greensmith & Mildred E Brooks G; m 1953 to Walter H North; c Thomas Brian, David Allen & James Ryan. Educ: Battle Creek Cent High Sch, 4 years. Polit & Govt Pos: Mem, Calhoun Co Young Rep, Mich, 61-56; bd mem, Battle Creek Rep Women's Club, 64-; deleg, Mich Rep State Conv, 68-69; trustee, Moran Twp Bd Educ, 68-; chmn; Mackinac Co Rep Comt, 69-72; secy, 11th Dist Rep Comt, 69- Mem: Mackinac Straits Hosp Auxiliary. Honors & Awards: Outstanding Young Woman Award for Community Serv, Jaycee Auxiliary, 69. Relig: Protestant. Mailing Add: Boulevard Dr St Ignace MI 49781

NORTHACKER, PATRICIA JEANNE (R)
VChmn, Second Dist Rep Comt, Ind
b Lafayette, Ind, May 21, 24; d Carl E Bauer & Harriette Sharpe B; m 1945 to Fred John Northacker; c Michael Patrick, Julianne (Mrs Michael Meyerrose) & Nancy Lee. Educ: Purdue Univ, BS, 45, MS, 49; Alpha Lambda Delta, Delta Rho Kappa; Chi Omega Sorority. Polit & Govt Pos: Precinct vcommitteeman, Tippecanoe Co Rep Party, Ind, 51-56, 60-62; precinct committeeman, 56-59, co vchmn, 66-; dist vchmn, Second Dist Rep Comt; 74-; mem, Gov Task Force on Employ of Physically Handicapped, 75- Bus & Prof Pos: Secy to dir, Marian Darr, Clerical Personnel, Purdue Univ, 46-47; psychometrist, Purdue Admin Staff, 47-49; off mgr, Tippecanoe Co License Br 77, 69- Mem: Community Emergency Fund (adv bd, 74-); Vinton Home Demonstration Club (news chmn, 21 years); Alpha Chi Omega Mothers Club (pres, 75-); Ind Fedn Rep Women (state bd, 74-). Relig: United Methodist; Lafayette Trinity, Lay Deleg Annual Conf, 67- Mailing Add: 27 N 29th St Lafayette IN 47904

NORTHRUP, L DONALD (R)
Wyo State Sen
b Braymer, Mo, June 8, 06; m 1966 to Jane D Clark; c Two. Educ: Univ Iowa. Polit & Govt Pos: Mem adv coun, Big Horn Nat Forest; mem adv bd, Powell Research Sta; dir, Wyo Sch

Trustees Asn; pres, Big Horn Basin Sch Trustees Asn, formerly; mem, Powell Sch Bd, 15 years, clerk, 5 years, chmn educ comt; mem, Wyo Youth Coun; Wyo State Rep; Wyo State Sen, 67- Bus & Prof Pos: Farmer & feeder. Mem: Rotary Int; Masonic Lodge; Odd Fellows Lodge; Elks; Farm Bur. Relig: Methodist. Mailing Add: Star Rte Box 56 Powell WY 82435

NORTHUP, VYRON LESLIE (DFL)
Mem, Beltrami Co Cent Comt, Dem-Farmer-Labor Party, Minn
b Underwood, Minn, Sept 3, 10; s Archie A Northup & Myrtle O Johnson N; m 1936 to Helen Ruth Knox; c Lewis, Constance (Mrs Hallberg); Charles Vyron, Judith (Mrs Fowler), Richard, Diana (Mrs Morkassel), Dorothy (Mrs Persinger), Juanita, Ronald, Francis, Leanne & Darien. Educ: Eighth grade grad. Polit & Govt Pos: Mem commun comt, Agr Stabilization & Conserv Serv, 48-52 & 68-69; officer, Beltrami Co Dem-Farmer-Labor Party, 54-60, chmn, 69-72, mem, Cent Comt, 72-; assessor, Nebish Twp, Minn, 55-63, treas, 65-; chmn, Beltrami Co Farmers for Humphrey, 68; co chmn, Humphrey Vol, 70 & 72; co chmn, Farmers for McGovern, 72; mem, Minn State Dem-Farmer-Labor Cent Comt. Bus & Prof Pos: Carpenter, construct worker & farm hand, 25-36; with Civilian Conserv Corps, 33-34; farmer, 36-; truck driver, Knox Trucking, Bemidji, 38-46; part-time ins agent, Nat Farmers Union Ins Co, 56- Mem: Minn Farmers Union (Beltrami Co chmn, 53-72); Co Asn Twp Officers (bd dirs, 67-, co chmn, 68-72); Minn Asn Twp Officers (mem state comt, 70-); Rural Minn Concentrated Employ Prog (secy & mem bd, 67-); Moose. Relig: Lutheran; First treas, Pleasant Valley Lutheran Church, 58. Mailing Add: Puposky MN 56667

NORTON, FRANCIS CARLETON (R)
Chmn, Barnstable Rep Town Comt, Mass
b Hyde Park, Mass, Apr 5, 18; s John Francis Norton & Margaret Victoria Morris N; wid. Educ: Hobart Col, 1 year. Polit & Govt Pos: Chmn, Barnstable Rep Town Comt, Mass, 66-; mem, Rep Nat Comt, formerly. Bus & Prof Pos: Career life underwriter, New Eng Mutual Life Ins, 40-42; licensed Mass Real Estate Broker, currently. Mem: Hobart Col Club Boston; Century Club Hobart Col; Iedependent Mutual Agents of New Eng; Nat Asn Mutual Ins Agents; Barnstable Civic Asn. Relig: Episcopal; License Lay-Reader. Mailing Add: Rte 6-A PO Box 66 Cummaquid MA 02637

NORTON, FRED CARL (DFL)
Minn State Rep
b Minneapolis, Minn, Aug 19, 38; s Henry Wachs Norton & Lois Nash N; m 1952 to Martha C Holman; c Cynthia, Jeffrey Pierce & Katharine. Educ: Wesleyan Univ, BA, 50; Univ Minn, LLB, 55; Psi Upsilon. Polit & Govt Pos: Attorney, Dept Taxation, Minn, 55-56; spec asst attorney gen, 56-63, asst attorney gen, Minn, 63-66; mem, Minn State Dem-Farmer-Labor Cent Comt; Minn State Rep, Dist 46A, 67-, chmn appropriations comt, Minn House Rep, 73- Mem: Minn & Ramsey Co Bar Asns; Capitol Community Servs (bd dirs); Dale Selby Action Coun (bd dirs). Relig: Unitarian. Mailing Add: 701 Fairmount Ave St Paul MN 55105

NORTON, THOMAS C (D)
Mass State Rep
Mailing Add: State Capitol Boston MA 02133

NORTON, WILLIAM GEORGE (R)
Nat Committeeman, DC Young Rep Fedn
b Providence, RI, Apr 26, 51; s William Edgar Norton & Dorothy Lowe N; single. Educ: Georgetown Univ, BA, 73; Georgetown Univ Col Club. Polit & Govt Pos: Vchmn, RI TAR Fedn, 67-68; summer aide, US Agency Int Develop, 71-72; pres, Georgetown Univ Col Rep, 72-73; legis asst, US Sen Bill Brock, 73-; admin vpres, DC Young Rep Fedn, 74-75, nat committeeman, 75-; vpres, Arlington Co Young Rep, 75-; mem, Arlington Co Rep Comt, Va, 75- Mem: Georgetown Univ Metrop Washington Alumni Asn; Cardinal Soc Va. Honors & Awards: Chmn of the Year, DC Col Rep Fedn, 73. Mailing Add: 1301 N Kirkwood Rd Arlington VA 22201

NORVELL, DAVID L (D)
b Kansas City, Mo, Jan 31, 35; s Kenneth J Norvell & Mildred Lagers N; m 1957 to Marivee Trentman; c Teresa Jean, Connie, David, Jr, Felicia & John Leonard. Educ: Northeastern State Col, BS in Hist, 55; Okla Univ, LLB, 58; Delta Theta Phi; Phi Sigma Epsilon. Polit & Govt Pos: NMex State Rep, 63-71, Speaker, NMex House of Rep, 69-71; Attorney Gen, NMex, 71-74. Bus & Prof Pos: Partner, Blythe & Norvell Law Off, 59- Mem: Am Bus Club. Relig: Catholic. Legal Res: 2329 Calle Halcon Santa Fe NM 87501 Mailing Add: PO Box 2246 Santa Fe NM 87501

NORVELL, JOSEPH F (D)
Kans State Rep
Mailing Add: Box 991 Hays KS 67601

NOSZKA, STANLEY M (D)
Pa State Sen
Mailing Add: 5589 Bryant St Pittsburgh PA 15206

NOTT, RAY (D)
Wyo State Sen
Mailing Add: 560 College Dr Powell WY 82435

NOTTE, JOHN ANTHONY, JR (D)
b Providence, RI, May 3, 09; s John Anthony Notte & Eva Rondina N; m 1934 to Marie Joan Huerth; c John A, III & Joyce Ann. Educ: Providence Col, AB, 31; Boston Univ Sch Law, LLB, 35; Alpha Phi Delta. Hon Degrees: LLD, Univ RI. Polit & Govt Pos: Secy to US Sen Theodore Francis Green, RI, 48-56; pres, RI Young Dem, 49-50; Secy of State, RI, 57-58 Lt Gov, 59-60, Gov, 61-63. Bus & Prof Pos: Attorney & sr partner, Notte & Notte, 63- Mil Serv: Entered as Lt(jg), Navy, 43, released as Lt(sg), 46, after serv in African & Mediter Theaters, 43-45; ETO Ribbon with Two Bronze Stars; Mediter & Am Theater Ribbons. Mem: Am & RI Bar Asns; Elks, VFW; Am Legion. Relig: Roman Catholic. Mailing Add: 934 Industrial Bank Bldg Providence RI 02903

NOTTI, EMIL (D)
Polit & Govt Pos: Former chmn, Alaska State Dem Cent Comt. Mailing Add: 1905 W 47th St Anchorage AK 99502

NOVAK, BERNARD R (D)
Pa State Rep
Mailing Add: Capitol Bldg Harrisburg PA 17120

NOVAK, JAMES B, III (CONSERVATIVE, NY)
Mem, State Exec Comt, Conservative Party, NY
b Biste, Hungary, Sept 13, 13; s James B Novak & Mary Bidlen N; m 1935 to Catherine S Reese; c Catherine S, James B, IV, Warren C & Bruce P. Polit & Govt Pos: Chmn, Schoharie Co Conservative Party, NY, 63-, mem, State Exec Comt, currently. Mem: IUE, AFL-CIO, Local 301; NY State Civil Defense Commun; Schoharie Co Civil Defense Commun. Relig: Roman Catholic. Mailing Add: 5261 Ecker Hollow Rd Schoharie NY 12157

NOVAK, LARRY F (D)
b Valatie, NY, July 16, 22; s Martin M Novak & Mary Newrocky N; single. Educ: High sch grad. Polit & Govt Pos: Town chmn, Kinderhook, NY, 49-; chmn, Columbia Co Dem Party, formerly. Bus & Prof Pos: Owner, Novak Bowling Supplies, Albany, NY, 50-; pres, Valatie Savings & Loan, 67- Mil Serv: Entered as A/S, Navy, 42, released as B/M 1/C, 46; 12 Ribbons. Mem: VFW; Am Legion; St Clause Club; 12 Columbia Co Dem Clubs; Polish Community Club; Elks. Relig: Catholic. Mailing Add: Valatie NY 12184

NOVAK, LORRINE MARIE (D)
Mem, Defiance Co Dem Cent Comt, Ohio
b Chester, Pa, Feb 3, 48; d Walter J Novak & Josephine Melchiorre N; single. Educ: West Chester State Col, BS; Univ Pittsburgh Grad Sch Libr & Info Sci, ML; Phi Alpha Theta; Beta Phi Mu. Polit & Govt Pos: Deleg, Dem Nat Conv, 72; coordr, McGovern for President Campaign, Defiance Co, Ohio, 72; organizer, Spring-McGovern Campaign, 72; mem, Defiance Co Dem Cent Comt, 72- Bus & Prof Pos: Asst librn, Anthony Wayne Libr, Defiance Col, 70- Mem: Am & Ohio Libr Asns; Women's Equity Action League; Bus & Prof Women's Asn. Honors & Awards: August Alpers Award, Grad Sch Libr & Info Sci, Univ Pittsburgh, 70. Mailing Add: 712 N Clinton Defiance OH 43512

NOVAK, MICHAEL (D)
Mich State Rep
Mailing Add: 19658 Caldwell Detroit MI 48224

NOVAK, STEVEN G (DFL)
Minn State Rep
Mailing Add: 2110 14th St NW St Paul MN 55112

NOVICK, LEE ENGEL (D)
b Scranton, Pa, Jan 21, 32; d Louis Engel & Esther Blatt E; m 1961 to Jack Novick; c Mindy, David & Noah. Educ: Brooklyn Col, BA cum laude, 53; NY Univ, grad work, 53-54; Southern Conn State Col, grad work, 71- Polit & Govt Pos: Mem, Westchester Co Dem Comt, NY, 65-71; mem, NY State Dem Comt, 68-71; Dem cand, NY State Legis, 93rd Assembly Dist, 70; co-chairwoman, McGovern for President, Conn, 72; alt deleg, Dem Nat Conv, 72; deleg, Conn Dem State Conv, 72; chairwoman, Conn Women's Polit Caucus, 72- Bus & Prof Pos: Researcher in psychol, Payne Whitney Clin, NY Hosp, 53-54; mkt researcher, Inst for Motivational Research, Croton, 54-58; researcher, Dept Psychol, IBM, Yorktown Heights, 58-63; research assoc, Dept Socio-Med Research, Burke Found, White Plains, 66-70; lectr polit sci, Univ New Haven, currently. Publ: Co-auth, New Roles for Volunteers in Action Research Settings, Vol Admin, 69, In-Patient Social Relationships in a Rehabilitation Hospital: Implications for a Therapeutic Community, Nat Coun Health Serv Research, 69 & Community Influences on the Patient Care Process, US Pub Health Serv, 69. Mem: Women's Polit Caucus (nat policy coun, 72-); Nat Comt for Sane Nuclear Policy (nat bd, 72-). Relig: Jewish. Mailing Add: 62 Edgewood Way New Haven CT 06515

NOVINGER, GAIL HARVEY (R)
Mo State Rep
b Green Castle, Mo; s Isaac M Novinger & Fannie J Eitel N; m 1953 to Mary Francis Johnson; c James, Mark, Jane Ann & Carolyn. Educ: Northeast Mo State Univ, 47-49. Polit & Govt Pos: Mo State Rep, 75- Bus & Prof Pos: Chmn, Agribusiness Comn, Kirksville CofC, 67-73 & Adair Co Univ Exten, 68-72; committeeman, Boy Scouts, 68-74; vchmn bd supvrs, Adair Co Soil & Water Conserv Dist, 68-75; mem, Kirksville Bd Educ, 71-74. Mem: Lions; Moose; CofC; Chariton River Drainage Dist Bd; Adair Co Humane Soc (vpres). Relig: Presbyterian. Mailing Add: RR 2 Kirksville MO 63501

NOVOA-GONZALEZ, JOSE MIGUEL (POPULAR DEMOCRAT, PR)
Rep, PR House of Rep
b Penuelas, PR, Apr 17, 29; s Jose Novoa & Domitila Gonzalez N; m 1956 to Carmen Luz Loyola; c Jose Miguel, Carmen Ileana & Jose Edgardo. Educ: Univ PR, Rio Piedras, BBA; Cath Univ PR, JD. Polit & Govt Pos: Mem, Elec Local Bd, 65-72; mem, Cent Coun Popular Dem Party, 69-73, pres city local comt, 69-73; Rep, PR House Rep, Dist 23, 73- Bus & Prof Pos: Income tax inspector, Income Tax Bur, Ponce, 57-66; lawyer & notary pub, 66-73. Mil Serv: Entered as Pvt E-1, Army, 51, released as Pfc, 53, after serv in 296th Inf Unit, Losey Field, Juana Diaz, PR. Mem: Lawyer's Col PR; Penuelas Lions Club; Penuelas Baseball Club; PR Amateur Baseball Fedn. Honors & Awards: Best Zone Chmn, Dist 51-B, Lions Int, PR, 70; Year Exec, PR Amateur Baseball Fedn, 72. Relig: Catholic. Legal Res: 710 A Marin St Penuelas PR 00724 Mailing Add: PO Box 542 Penuelas PR 00724

NOVOTNY, ROBERT L (R)
Wyo State Sen
Mailing Add: Box 172 Kinnear WY 82516

NOWAK, HENRY JAMES (D-LIBERAL)
US Rep, NY
b Buffalo, NY, Feb 21, 35; s Joseph Jacob Nowak & Helen Batkiewicz; m 1965 to Rose Santa Lucia; c Diane & Henry Joseph. Educ: Canisius Col, BAA, 57; Univ Buffalo Law Sch, LLB, 61. Polit & Govt Pos: Attorney & counsel, State of NY, 62-64; asst dist attorney, Erie Co Dist Attorney Off, 64; confidential secy, Supreme Court Justice, Arthur J Cosgrove, 65; comptroller, Erie Co, NY, 66-70; US Rep, 37th Dist, NY, 75- Mil Serv: Entered as 2nd Lt, Army, 57, released as Capt, 62, after serv in Armor Br. Mem: NY State & Erie Co Bar Asn; Jr CofC; Prof Businessmen's Asn; Coun on Polish-Am Affairs. Honors & Awards: Canisius Col Athletic Hall of Fame, 67. Relig: Catholic. Legal Res: 31 Admiral Rd Buffalo NY 14216 Mailing Add: 1223 Longworth House Off Bldg Washington DC 20515

NOWLAN, JAMES DUNLAP (R)
b Kewanee, Ill, Sept 8, 41; s Robert J Nowlan & Barbara Dunlap N; single. Educ: Univ Ill, Urbana, BA with high honors in Polit Sci, 63, MA, 65, PhD in Polit Sci, 73; Skull & Crescent Soc; Sigma Nu. Polit & Govt Pos: Mem staff, Ill State Cent Comt, 63-64; Ill State Rep, 69-72; alt deleg, Rep Nat Conv, 72. Bus & Prof Pos: Ed, Stark Co News, 62-63; instr polit sci, Black Hawk E Col, Kewanee, Ill, 69-; asst prof polit sci, Western Ill Univ, 73-; lectr, Knox Col, 73- Mil Serv: Entered as 1st Lt, Army, 66, released as Capt, 68, after serv in Ft Gordon, Ga & 5th Army Hq, Ft Sheridan, Ill; Capt, Army Res, 68-; Army Commendation Medal. Mem: Sigma Delta Chi; Mason; Am Legion. Relig: Congregational. Mailing Add: 209 S Miller Toulon IL 61483

NOWLIN, JAMES ROBERTSON (R)
Tex State Rep
b San Antonio, Tex, Nov 21, 37; s William Forney Nowlin & Jeannette Robertson N; m 1973 to Kirsten Joan Wunderlich. Educ: Trinity Univ, BA & MA; Univ Tex Sch Law, JD. Polit & Govt Pos: Assoc legal counsel, labor & pub welfare comt, US Senate, 65-66; Tex State Rep, 67- Bus & Prof Pos: Attorney, San Antonio, 63-; instr Am hist, San Antonio Col, 64-65 & 71-73. Mil Serv: Entered as 2nd Lt, Army, 59, released as Capt, 68, after serv in Res, Ft Lee, Va, 59-60. Mem: Am Bar Asn; Am Judicature Soc; CofC; Research & Planning Coun. Honors & Awards: Outstanding Young Man of Year, Trinity Univ & San Antonio Jr CofC, 67. Relig: Presbyterian. Legal Res: 254 Tuxedo Ave San Antonio TX 78209 Mailing Add: 204 Edwards Bldg San Antonio TX 78217

NOWLIN, VAUGHAN BRIAN (D)
Chmn, Childress Co Dem Exec Comt, Tex
b Vernon, Tex, Jan 28, 43; s Chesnutt Vaughan Nowlin & Loura Ferne Brian N; single. Educ: Univ Tex, Austin, 61-63; Midwestern Univ, BA in Polit Sci, 68; Tau Kappa Epsilon. Polit & Govt Pos: Coordr, Purcell for Cong Comt, 68; deleg, Tex State Dem Conv, 68, 70 & 72; deleg, Dem Nat Conv, 72; chmn, Childress Co Dem Exec Comt, 72- Bus & Prof Pos: Owner, Vaughan B Nowlin Cotton Co, 69-, pres & chmn bd, Vaughan B Nowlin Co, Inc, 70-; pres & chmn bd, Childress Indust Investment Corp, 72- Mem: Am & Tex Cotton Asns; Tau Kappa Epsilon Alumni Asn; Rotary Int (dir, 72-); Elks. Relig: Methodist. Legal Res: 607 Third St NW Childress TX 79201 Mailing Add: PO Box 872 Childress TX 79201

NOWOTNY, GEORGE EDWARD, JR (R)
Chmn, Sebastian Co Rep Comt, Ark
b New Braunfels, Tex, Oct 18, 32; s George Edward Nowotny & Margaret Voight N; m 1954 to Lura Duff Elliston; c Edward Duff, George Edward, III & Addison Dance. Educ: Univ Tex, BS, 55; Phi Eta Sigma; Sigma Gamma Epsilon; Phi Beta Kappa; Delta Tau Delta. Polit & Govt Pos: Ark State Rep, 67-72, Minority Leader, Ark House of Rep, 67-72; committeeman, Nat Resources, Interstate Oil Compact Comn, 67-69; alt deleg, Rep Nat Conv, 68, deleg, 72; mem bd dirs, Southern Regional Bd, Nat Conf of Rep Legislators, 69-72; mem, Comprehensive Health Planning of Ark, 69-72; Ark state coordr for Reelec of the President, 72; chmn, Sebastian Co Rep Comt, 73-; consult, State Legis Leaders Found, Nat Conf State Legis Leaders, 73- Bus & Prof Pos: Geophysicist, affiliate of Standard Oil Co, Caracas, Venezuela, Havana, Cuba, Buenos Aires, Argentina, Okla, Utah & Mich, 56-61; consult geologist, Barton & Nowotny, Ft Smith, Ark, 61-63; owner, Nowotny & Co, real estate & personal investments, 63-; mem, Sparks Regional Med Ctr Adv Bd, 72- Mem: Am Asn Petroleum Geologists; Soc Explor Geophysicists; Asn Petroleum Landmen; Nat Exchange Club; Int Platform Asn. Relig: Episcopal; Past mem, Diocesan Exec Coun for Diocese of Ark, mem, Bishop's Standing Comt, 71- Mailing Add: 18 Berry Hill Ft Smith AR 72901

NOYE, FRED CHARLES (R)
Pa State Rep
b Harrisburg, Pa, May 13, 46; s Charles Arthur Noye & Marie Heckert N; m 1968, div. Educ: Harrisburg Area Community Col, AA, 66; Mansfield State Col, BS, 68; Shippensburg State Col, MEd, 70; Pi Gamma Mu; Kappa Delta Pi; Lambda Beta Phi. Polit & Govt Pos: Committeeman, Penn Twp, Pa, 70-; pres, Perry Co Young Rep, 70, chmn, 70-; Pa State Rep, 86th Dist, Perry-Juniata-Cumberland Co, 73- Bus & Prof Pos: Teacher, Cumberland Valley Sch Dist, 68-72. Mem: Harrisburg Consistory; Lions; Perry Co Hist Soc; Perry Co Farmers Asn; Juniata Jaycees. Honors & Awards: Scholar, Big 33, Inc, 66. Relig: Lutheran. Legal Res: RD 3 Duncannon PA 17020 Mailing Add: Captiol Bldg Harrisburg PA 17120

NUCKOLLS, HUGH PAUL (R)
Fla State Rep
b Hendersonville, NC, Oct 3, 41; s Hugh Allen Nuckolls & Minnie Calhoun N; m 1963 to Billie Jean Bowling; c Katherine Calhoun & Geoffrey Paul. Educ: Mars Hill Col, AB, 65; Cumberland Sch Law, Samford Univ, JD, 68; Phi Alpha Delta. Polit & Govt Pos: Western dist organizer, NC State Young Rep, 61-62; vchmn, NC Col Coun Young Rep, 62-63; charter pres, Lee Co Young Rep, Fla, 68-69, dir, 69-70; Asst Pub Defender, 71-72; Fla State Rep, Dist 91, 72- Bus & Prof Pos: Dir of student activities, Edison Community Col, Ft Myers, Fla, 68-71; attorney-at-law, Ft Myers, 71- Mem: Am Bar Asn; Jaycees; Kiwanis; Day-Care Adv Bd, Lee Co; Cancer Soc (dir, 69-). Honors & Awards: Admiralty Book Award, Am-Jurisp Publ Co, 66; Outstanding Young Educator, Edison Jr Col Student Govt, 71; Outstanding Young Men of Am, Mars Hill Col Alumni Asn, 73. Relig: Baptist. Legal Res: 1645 Newport Ct Ft Myers FL 33901 Mailing Add: Box 6631 Ft Myers FL 33902

NUCKOLLS, KENNETH RUSSELL (R)
Rep Nat Committeeman, Wash
b Westboro, Mo, Dec 12, 21; s Russell Kohler Nuckolls & Vesta Andrews N, m 1945 to Dorothy Ilene Kerr; c Ellen (Mrs Alan Rickis), Russell Kenneth & Sara Jo. Educ: Mont State Univ, 4 years; Alpha Gamma Rho. Polit & Govt Pos: Deleg, Wash State Rep Conv, 54-; Rep precinct committeeman, Bellingham, Wash, 57-, ward capt, 59-64; asst finance chmn, Whatcom Co Rep Party, 63-66, state committeeman, 65-66, chmn, 66-70 & 73-; pres, Wash Second Dist Rep Club, 64-66; mem, Gov Adv Comn, Wash, 64-; Rep Nat Committeeman, 71-; chmn, Western States Rep Conf, 71-73; deleg, Rep Nat Conv, 72. Bus & Prof Pos: Mem bd dirs, Mt Baker Recreation Co, 64-, pres, 67- Mil Serv: Entered as Cpl, Inf, 43, released as 1st Lt, 45, after serv in 35th Inf Div, ETO, 44-45. Mem: Kiwanis; United Good Neighbors; CofC; Elks; Bellingham Golf & Country Club. Honors & Awards: Outstanding Citizen Award, 67. Relig: Congregational. Mailing Add: PO Box 127 Bellingham WA 98225

NUCKOLS, PEGGY NOLTE (R)
Mem, Del State Rep Comt
b Milwaukee, Wis, June 26, 52; d Donald Carl Nolte & Greta June Hendrickson N; m. Educ: Univ Del, 70-73; Univ NC, Greensboro, BA, 75; Arts & Letters Soc; newspaper staff, Review. Polit & Govt Pos: Mem staff, Elec Hq, US Rep Pierre S duPont, IV, Del, 70; mem staff, Rep Nat Comt, summers 71 & 72; deleg & mem platform comt, Rep Nat Conv, 72; alt deleg, Del Rep State Conv, 72; mem, Del State Rep Comt, 73- Mem: Asn for the Awareness of Women Students; Del Young Rep. Relig: Episcopal. Mailing Add: 2403 Vanstory St Greensboro NC 27407

NUGENT, JAMES E (JIM) (D)
Tex State Rep
Mailing Add: 1223 Virginia Dr Kerrville TX 78028

NUGENT, JOHN JOSEPH, JR (D)
RI State Rep
Mailing Add: 25 Langham Rd Providence RI 02906

NUNES, FRANK L (R)
RI State Rep
Mailing Add: 127 W Main Rd Middletown RI 02840

NUNEZ, SAMUEL B, JR (D)
La State Sen
Mailing Add: 2501 Rosetta Dr Chalmette LA 70043

NUNN, LOUIE B (R)
b Mar 8, 24; m to Beula Cornelius Aspley; c two. Educ: Bowling Green Bus Univ; Univ Cincinnati; Univ Louisville, law degree. Hon Degrees: LLD, Univ Ky, Eastern Ky Univ, Murray State Univ, Lincoln Mem Univ & Pikeville Col. Polit & Govt Pos: Elected judge of Barren Co, Ky, 53; mgr, Eisenhower-Cooper-Morton Campaign, 56, Nixon Campaign, 60 & Cooper & Morton Campaigns, 60 & 62; deleg, Rep Nat Conv, 68 & 72; Gov, Ky, 67-71. Bus & Prof Pos: Sr partner & attorney, Stoll, Keenan & Park, Lexington, 72- Mil Serv: Army, World War II, 3 years. Mem: Mason (33 degree); Shrine; Am Legion (past Comdr, Barren Co Post); Glasgow PTA; Rotary; CofC. Honors & Awards: Named One of the Three Outstanding Young Men of Ky, 56. Relig: Christian Church; Chmn, Bd of Elders, First Christian Church of Glasgow. Mailing Add: 1867 Parkers Mill Rd Lexington KY 40504

NUNN, SAM (D)
US Sen, Ga
b Perry, Ga, Sept 8, 38; s Samuel Augustus Nunn & Elizabeth Canon N; m 1964 to Colleen O'Brien; c Mary Michelle & Samuel Brian. Educ: Emory Univ, AB, 60, Law Sch, LLB, 62; Bryan Honor Soc; Phi Delta Theta. Polit & Govt Pos: Ga State Rep, Houston Co, 68-72; US Sen, Ga, 72-; deleg, Dem Nat Mid-Term Conf, 74. Mil Serv: Seaman, Coast Guard, 59-68. Mem: Perry CofC; Mid Ga Planning Comn; Emory Univ Comt of 100. Honors & Awards: Five Outstanding Young Men in Ga, Jaycees, 71; Dist Attorneys Award as Outstanding Legislator, Ga Dist Attorneys Asn, 72. Relig: Methodist. Legal Res: Hawkinsville Rd Perry GA 31069 Mailing Add: 110 Russell Bldg Washington DC 20510

NUNN, WARNE (R)
b Spokane, Wash, Oct 14, 20; s Jack Crisp Nunn & Vera Blanche Anthony N; m 1943 to Delores Ruth Netz; c Kathryn (Mrs Bauck), Linda (Mrs Haines) & Robert. Educ: Willamette Univ, BA, 41; Phi Delta Theta. Polit & Govt Pos: Asst Pub Utilities Comnr, State of Ore, 52-56, dir, Dept Motor Vehicles, 56-57, Asst Secy of State, 57-59, exec asst to Gov, Ore, 59-66, admin asst to US Sen Mark O Hatfield, Ore, 67; exec reservist, Off Emergency Preparedness, 69-; exec dir, Ore Comt for Reelec of the President, 72; deleg, Rep Nat Conv, 72. Bus & Prof Pos: Asst vpres, Pac Power & Light Co, Portland, Ore, 67- Mil Serv: Entered as Pvt, Army, 42, released as Sgt, 45, after serv in Army Air Corps Training Command, 42-45. Mem: Pi Gamma Mu; Ore Tax Research (pres, 71-72); Portland Econ Develop Comt, Inc (pres, 72-); Portland Freight Traffic Asn (dir, 69-); Willamette Univ (vchmn bd trustees, 71-). Honors & Awards: Outstanding Alumni, Willamette Univ, 68. Relig: Lutheran. Mailing Add: 2405 Dellwood Dr Lake Oswego OR 97034

NUNNALLY, JAMES DAVID (D)
Miss State Rep
b Prentiss Co, Miss, Jan 15, 45; s J B Nunnally & Virginia Anderson N; m 1968 to Betty Jo Michael. Educ: Northeast Miss Jr Col, 67; Union Univ, 68; Univ Miss, BAE, 74. Polit & Govt Pos: Miss State Rep, Benton & Tappah Counties, 72- Bus & Prof Pos: Teacher, Henderson, Tenn, 68-69, Hornsby, 69-70 & Ashland, Miss, 70-72. Mem: CofC; Farm Bur. Relig: Church of Christ. Mailing Add: PO Box 53 Ripley MS 38663

NUNNERY, MELVIN ERNEST (ERNIE) (D)
SC State Rep
b York Co, SC, May 11, 51; s Jimmy Ernest Nunnery & Cora Emma Nunnery Simpson; single. Educ: Univ SC, BA, 72; Lambda Chi Alpha. Polit & Govt Pos: SC State Rep, 74-; mem govt & legis comt, SC Dem Party, 75- Mem: NChester Ment Retardation Day Care Ctr (mem adv comt). Honors & Awards: Youth of Year Award, SC Asn Retarded Citizens. Relig: Baptist. Mailing Add: Rte 1 Ft Lawn SC 29714

NUSSDORF, HARRY (D)
Mem, Queens Co Dem Comt, NY
b New York, NY, Dec 6, 47; s Oscar Nussdorf & Edith Posner N; m to Babette Albin. Educ: Univ Calif, Berkeley, 66; Queens Col, City Univ New York, BA, 71; Columbia Univ, MS, 73; Sigma Delta Chi; Mensa; pres, Queens Col Student Asn, 70-71. Polit & Govt Pos: Deleg, Dem Nat Conv, 72; mem, Queens Co Dem Comt, NY, 72-; mem, Legis Adv Comt, 27th Assembly Dist, Queens, 72- Honors & Awards: Reporting & Writing Award, Phoenix Press, 67; Distinguished Serv Medal, Queens Col, City Univ New York, 71. Relig: Jewish. Mailing Add: 142-01 59th Ave Flushing NY 11355

NUTE, HELEN ELIZABETH (D)
Mem, NH Dem State Comt
b North Conway, NH, Oct 25, 97; d Dexter Asbury Nute & Mary Virginia Eisele N; single. Educ: Radcliffe Col, AB, 19; Harvard Univ, EdM, 27; Univ St Andrews, summer 48; Univ Edinburgh, 48-49. Polit & Govt Pos: Supvr of Check List, Conway, NH, 68, mem munic budget comt, 68-75, trustee pub libr, 68-; chmn, Conway Dem Town Comt, 68-72; Dem cand for NH State Rep, 68-74; Dem cand for NH State Sen, 69; mem, NH Dem State Comt, 70-; alt deleg, Dem Nat Conv, 72; deleg, NH Const Conv, 74; chmn dist adv coun, NH State Libr Develop Prog, 74-75. Bus & Prof Pos: Teacher Eng, South Manchester High Sch, Conn, 23-26, Walnut Hill Sch, Natick, Mass, 26-28, Newton High Sch, 29-53, Emma Willard Sch, Troy, NY, 56-58 & Spaulding High Sch, Barre, Vt, 58-59; audio-visual consult & film librn, Am Bd Comnrs to Foreign Missions, 59-61; biweekly speaker, WBNC Radio, 74- Mil Serv:

Entered as Pvt, Army, 43, released as Cpl, 45, after serv in Woman's Army Corps, Transportation Corps, NY Port of Embarkation, Med Dept, Walter Reed Hosp & Camp Butner Gen Hosp, 45; Good Conduct Medal; World War II Victory Medal. Publ: Co-auth, The Teaching of English in the Secondary School, 27; auth, Inklings, articles in a weekly newspaper, North Conway Reporter, 52- Mem: Am Asn Univ Women (legis chmn, State of NH, 68-69, first vpres, Br, 68-70, legis chmn, 69-); Am Legion; Am Revolution Bicentennial Comn (chmn, Conway, 74-); Conway Hist Soc (pres, 73-); Soc for the Protection of NH Forests. Honors & Awards: Regional Women's Info Serv NH Award, 74. Relig: Congregational. Legal Res: Artists' Falls Rd North Conway NH 03860 Mailing Add: Hackmatack Hill North Conway NH 03860

NUTTER, GILBERT WARREN (R)
b Topeka, Kans, Mar 10, 23; s Coleman Evan Nutter & Rose Gilberg N; m 1946 to Jane Calvert Couch; c Coleman Alston, Jane Terry, Anne Elizabeth & William Warren. Educ: Univ Chicago, AB, 44, AM, 48, PhD, 49; Phi Beta Kappa. Polit & Govt Pos: Div chief, Cent Intel Agency, 52-53; Asst Secy of Defense for Int Security Affairs, 69-73. Bus & Prof Pos: Instr econ, Lawrence Col, 46-47; asst prof econ, Yale Univ, 49-56; mem research staff, Nat Bur Econ Research, 55-67; assoc prof econ, Univ Va, 57-58, prof, 58-67 & 73-, Paul Goodloe McIntire prof, 67-69, chmn dept econ, 62-66 & 67-69, assoc dir, Thomas Jefferson Ctr, 57-67, dir, 67-; adj scholar, Am Enterprise Inst, 73- Mil Serv: Entered as Pvt, Army, 43, released as S/Sgt, 46, after serv in 703rd CIC Detachment, ETO; Army Res, 1st Lt, 48-54; Bronze Star with Oak Leaf Cluster; Combat Infantryman's Badge; Three Battle Stars. Publ: Extent of Enterprise Monopoly in the United States, 51, Growth of Industrial Production in the Soviet Union, 62, & The Strange World of Ivan Ivanov, 68. Mem: Am & Southern Econ Asns; Am Asn Advan Soviet Studies; Mont Pelerin Soc. Honors & Awards: Gavel Award, Am Bar Asn, 68; Distinguished Pub Serv Medal, Dept of Defense, 72. Legal Res: Charlottesville VA 22902 Mailing Add: Am Enterprise Inst 1150 17th St NW Washington DC 20036

NUTTER, LLOYD BRODERICK (D)
Mem, Montgomery Co Dem Comt, Va
b Montgomery Co, Va, Dec 20, 07; s Samuel Edward Nutter & Valeria Robinson N, m 1958 to Nell Wills. Educ: Va Polytech Inst, BS, 30; Monogram Club. Polit & Govt Pos: Dist chmn, Blacksburg Mt Tabor Dist, 66-67; mem, Montgomery Co Dem Comt, 60-70 & 72-, chmn, 70-72; campaign mgr, Dem Ticket Gubernatorial, 69; chmn, 37th Sen Dist Dem Party, 71-74; Montgomery Co Pub Serv, currently; mem, New River Valley Dist Planning Comn, currently. Bus & Prof Pos: Teacher, Blackstone, Va, 30-38; farmer, Angus Beef Cattle Farm, 25 years; agency mgr, Va Farm Bur Ins Co, Richmond, Va, 57-68. Mil Serv: Capt, Army, 42-44, serv in Recruit Training Ctr. Mem: Montgomery Asn Life Underwriters; Hokie Club; Farm Bur; Lions Club. Honors & Awards: Hon mem, Future Farmers Am; Outstanding Leadership Award. Relig: Methodist. Mailing Add: PO Box 14 Blacksburg VA 24060

NYCKLEMOE, ARLEEN DELORIS (DFL)
b Fergus Falls, Minn, Apr 9, 30; d Elmer Fick & Emma Schleske F; m 1951 to Paul Hagen Nycklemoe; c Susan & Karen. Educ: Moorhead State Col, AE, 50. Polit & Govt Pos: Secy-treas, Fergus Falls Dem-Farmer-Labor Women's Orgn, Minn, 65-67, vpres, 69-; tri-chmn, Seventh Dist Women for Humphrey, 68; vchmn, Otter Tail Co Dem-Farmer-Labor Party, 68-74; deleg, Minn Dem-Farmer-Labor State Conv, 68-69; positions for local & co Dem-Farmer-Labor Convs; app, State Bd Community Cols, 74- Mem: Minn Dem-Farmer-Labor Women; Lake Region Hosp Auxiliary (second vpres, 70-71); Homemakers. Honors & Awards: VFW Recognition Award. Relig: Lutheran. Mailing Add: Rte 1 Minnehuta Dr Fergus Falls MN 56537

NYE, EDD (D)
NC State Sen
b Gulf, NC, Sept 12, 32; s Joseph Burke Nye & Vera Johnson N; m 1955 to Peggy McKee; c Shannon, Edward & Allison. Educ: Southeastern Community Col, AA, 70; NC State Univ, 70-72. Polit & Govt Pos: Comnr, Bladen Co, NC, 66-72; NC State Sen, 13th Dist, 74- Bus & Prof Pos: Agt, Nationwide Ins Co, 57- Mil Serv: Entered as Airman Basic, Air Force, 52, released as Airman 1/C, 56, after serv in Korea, 54-55. Mem: Mason; VFW; CofC. Relig: Baptist. Legal Res: Woodland Dr Elizabethtown NC 28337 Mailing Add: PO Box 8 Elizabethtown NC 28337

NYLAND, KENNETH EUGENE (D)
VChmn, Green Co Dem Comt, Wis
b Madison, Wis, Mar, 23, 33; s George Nyland (deceased) & Marie Terasa Nyland Wollin; m 1946 to Carol Marie Jelle; c Gregory A Wickersham & Amy Carol. Educ: Wis State Col, 55-56. Polit & Govt Pos: Chmn, Green Co Dem Comt, Wis, 69-71, vchmn, 71-; mem, Wis Dem Party, currently, mem, Second Dist Statutory Comt, 72; cand for Wis State Assemblyman, Green-Lafayette Dist, 70; munic justice, Village of New Glarus, 71-73. Bus & Prof Pos: Customer engr, Int Bus Mach Corp, Madison, Wis, 67- Mil Serv: Entered as Airman Recruit, Navy, 51, released as CPO, Naval Res, currently; Three Navy Good Conduct Medals; European Occup Medal; Nat Defense Medal. Mem: Wis Munic Justices Asn; Lions; Am Legion. Relig: American Lutheran. Legal Res: 1200 First St New Glarus WI 53574 Mailing Add: Box 188 New Glarus WI 53574

NYLEN, RAMONA FAITH (DFL)
Mem, Seventh Sen Dist Dem-Farmer-Labor Cent Comt, Minn
b Duluth, Minn, June 5, 37; d Casper Daniel Visina & Jean Salminen V; m 1963 to Dennis Lee Nylen; c Patrick Joseph. Educ: Cathedral High Sch, Duluth, Minn, 52-55. Polit & Govt Pos: Chmn, 59th Sen Dist Dem-Farmer-Labor Comt, Minn, 71-72; deleg, Duluth Coord Comt, 71-72; deleg, Duluth AFL-CIO Cent Body, dir, Comt on Polit Educ, 72-, secy, Eighth Dist, 72-; mem, Duluth City Charter Comn, 72-; mem bd dirs, Duluth Lighthouse for the Blind, 72-; mem, Seventh Sen Dist Dem-Farmer-Labor Cent Comt, 72- Bus & Prof Pos: Bookkeeper, Labor World, Inc, Duluth, Minn, 64- Mem: Nat PTA; Duluth Dem-Farmer-Labor Women's Club; Piedmont Heights Community Club; Retail Clerks Int Asn Local 1116; Blood Donors, Inc. Relig: Catholic. Mailing Add: 1719 Tyrol St Duluth MN 55811

NYSTROM, JOHN N (R)
Iowa State Sen
Mailing Add: PO Box 177 Boone IA 50036

O

OAKES, KERMIT W (R)
Kans State Rep
Mailing Add: 1502 Berkeley Rd Emporia KS 66801

OAKES, ROY SIDNEY (R)
VChmn, Hamblen Co Rep Party, Tenn
b Gresham, Ore, Sept 22, 28; s Henry Sidney Oakes & Gertrude Witt O; m 1952 to Elise Frazier; c Karen Jane & Timothy Frazier. Educ: Knoxville High Sch, 4 years. Polit & Govt Pos: Vchmn, Hamblen Co Rep Party, Tenn, 59-; mem, Morristown Sch Bd, 62-; magistrate, Hamblen Co Quarterly Court, 66-; alt deleg, Rep Nat Conv, 68. Bus & Prof Pos: Vpres-secy, Oakes Motor Co Inc, 50- Mil Serv: Entered as Pvt, Army, 47, released as T/Sgt, 51, after serv in Seventh Div, Pac Theatre, 47-49. Mem: F&AM; Kerbela Temple; Elks; Moose; Morristown Country Club. Relig: Presbyterian. Legal Res: 2007 Magnolia Ave Morristown TN 37814 Mailing Add: PO Box 8 Morristown TN 37814

OAKLEY, BRICE CASE (R)
Iowa State Rep
b Washington, Iowa, Feb 4, 37; s Robert Melvin Oakley & Helen Louise Case O; m 1957 to Bette Jeanne Michael; c Kristin, Kathlyn & Robert. Educ: Univ Iowa, BA, 58, LLB, 61; Phi Delta Phi; Delta Chi. Polit & Govt Pos: Chmn, Univ Iowa Young Rep, 60-61; chmn, State Col Young Rep of Iowa, 60-61; chmn, Polk Co Young Rep, 62-63; chmn, Second Dist Young Rep of Iowa, 63-64; dir, Clinton Community Sch Bd, 68-71; Iowa State Rep, 75- Bus & Prof Pos: Asst Attorney Gen, Iowa Dept Justice, 61-63; partner, Johnson, Oakley & Pfeffer, Attorneys, 63- Publ: Co-auth, Iowa Public Employment Act, 74 & Iowa Adoption Act, 75. Mem: Am Bar Asn; Rotary; Scottish Rite Bodies; Honors & Awards: Distinguished Serv Award, Clinton Jaycees, 66; Group Study Exchange Grant to Norway, Iowa Rotary, 69; Award of Merit, Clinton Community Sch Dist, 71. Relig: Methodist. Legal Res: 1 Heather Lane Clinton IA 52732 Mailing Add: Box 749 Clinton IA 52732

OAKS, STEVEN CLARK (D)
Chmn, Harris Co Dem Party, Tex
b Oakland, Calif, Mar 5, 38; s Robert Martin Oaks & Ruth Clark O; m 1961 to Susan Gresham; c Elizabeth & Mary. Educ: Col William & Mary, BA, 59; Univ Tex Law Sch, LLB, 62; Phi Alpha Delta; Eta Sigma Phi; Kappa Sigma. Polit & Govt Pos: Advan Man for Vice President Hubert Humphrey, Tex, 68; campaign mgr for Sen Lloyd Bentsen, 70 & Lt Gov Bill Hobby, 72; exec asst to Lt Gov, Tex, 73; chmn, Harris Co Dem Party, 74- Bus & Prof Pos: Partner, Butler, Binion, Rice, Cook & Knapp, Houston, Tex, 62- Mem: Am, Tex & Houston Bar Asns; Tex Bill of Rights Found (trustee); Am Judicature Soc. Relig: Episcopal. Legal Res: 1929 Sharp Pl Houston TX 77019 Mailing Add: 1100 Esperson Bldg Houston TX 77002

OATES, WILLIAM J, JR (D)
WVa State Sen
Mailing Add: 568 Sixth St Romney WV 26757

OATIS, KATHLEEN ANN (D)
Mem, Colo Dem State Cent Comt
b Denver, Colo, May 3, 51; d Robert N Ulmer & Eleanore H U; m 1971 to Mark Benton Oatis. Educ: Univ Colo, Boulder. Polit & Govt Pos: Deleg, Dem Nat Conv, 72; capt, Co Dem Party, Colo, 73-; mem, Colo Dem State Cent Comt, 73-; alt deleg, Dem Nat Mid-Term Conf, 74. Mem: Nat Orgn for Women; Nat Women's Polit Caucus; Community Workers of Am. Relig: Unitarian. Mailing Add: 6450 Pierce St Denver CO 80003

O'BANNON, FRANK LEWIS (D)
Ind State Sen
b Louisville, Ky, Jan 30, 30; s Robert Presley O'Bannon & Faith Dropsey O; m 1957 to Judith Mae Asmus; c Polly D, Jennifer Mae & Jonathan Lewis. Educ: Ind Univ, Bloomington, AB, 52, Sch Law, JD, 57; Phi Delta Phi; Phi Gamma Delta. Polit & Govt Pos: Dep prosecuting attorney, Third Judicial Dist, Ind, 58-70; town attorney, Corydon, Ind, 59-67; Ind State Sen, 70-, Minority Asst Floor Leader, Ind State Senate, 72- Mil Serv: Entered as 2nd Lt, Air Force, 52, released as 1st Lt, 54, after serv in Western Air Defense Command, 52-54. Mem: Am Bar Asn; Am Judicature Soc; Corydon CofC; Rotary; Mason. Honors & Awards: Distinguished Serv Award, Corydon Jaycees, 59. Relig: United Methodist. Mailing Add: Rte 6 Box 495 Corydon IN 47112

OBENSHAIN, RICHARD DUDLEY (R)
Co-Chmn, Rep Nat Comt
b Abingdon, Va, Oct 31, 35; s Samuel Shockley Obenshain & Josephine Mathews Dudley O; m 1961 to Helen Nottingham Wilkins; c Mark Dudley, Anne Scott & Kate Boyce. Educ: Bridgewater Col, BA, 56; NY Univ Sch Law, LLB, 59; Phi Delta Phi. Polit & Govt Pos: Chmn, Young Rep Fedn Va, 61-64; deleg, Rep Nat Conv, 64; Rep cand for Cong, Third Dist, Va, 64; Rep cand for Attorney Gen, Va, 69; chmn, Rep Party of Va, 72-74; mem, Rep Nat Comt, 72-74, co-chmn, 74- Bus & Prof Pos: Partner, Obenshain, Hinnant, Dolbeare & Beale, 70- Mil Serv: Marine Corps Res. Mem: Am & Va State Bar Asns; Am Judicature Soc; Va Commonwealth Univ (bd visitors, 70-); Masonic Lodge. Honors & Awards: One of Five Outstanding Young Men of Va, Jaycees, 70. Relig: Presbyterian. Legal Res: 5505 Toddsbury Rd Richmond VA 23226 Mailing Add: One North Fifth St Richmond VA 23219

OBER, ANN MORGAN (DFL)
Mem, Dem Nat Comt, Minn
b Duluth, Minn, Feb 3, 16; d George W Morgan & Cornelia Hollinshead M; m 1937 to Edgar B Ober, c Katharina (Mrs Richard Marx), Cornelia (Mrs Glenn Olsen) & Stephen Henry. Educ: Vassar Col, BA, 37. Polit & Govt Pos: Vchmn, Blue Earth Co Dem-Farmer-Labor Party, Minn, 54-56, chmn, 61-69; chmn, Second Dist Dem-Farmer-Labor Party, 69-73; deleg, Dem Nat Conv, 72; mem, Dem Nat Comt, Minn, 73- Mailing Add: 324 Woodlawn St Paul MN 55105

OBERMILLER, EDWARD (D)
Treas, Clinton Co Dem Cent Comt, Iowa
b Clinton, Iowa, Mar 6, 24; s Henry Obermiller & Alma Gladhill O; m 1945 to Claire Cramm; c John W & Susan. Educ: Clinton High Sch. Polit & Govt Pos: Treas, Clinton Co Dem Cent Comt, Iowa, 58-, ward committeeman, currently; deleg, Dem Nat Conv, 68; co coordr, John

C Culver Campaign, 69; mayor, Clinton, Iowa, formerly. Bus & Prof Pos: Millwright, Clinton Corn Processing Co, 48-65, safety coordr, 68-; bus rep, Local 6, Am Fedn Grain, 65-68. Mil Serv: Entered as A/S, Navy Air Force, 42, released as AMM 2/C, 45. Mem: Am Soc Safety Engrs; Clinton Indust Mgt Club; Clinton Engrs Club; Gateway Indust Mutual Aid; Int Mgt Coun (prog co-chmn). Relig: Lutheran. Legal Res: 530 Kenilworth Ct Clinton IA 52732 Mailing Add: PO Box 227 Clinton IA 52732

OBERQUELL, DIANE (D)
Mem, Dem Nat Comt, Wash
Mailing Add: 2814 Stark Lane Olympia WA 98506

OBERSTAR, JAMES L (D)
US Rep, Minn
b Chisholm, Minn, Sept 10, 34; m to Marilynn Jo Garlick; c Thomas Edward, Katherine Noelle & Anne Therese. Educ: Col St Thomas, Minn, BA summa cum laude, 56; Col Europe, Bruges, Belgium, MA, 57. Polit & Govt Pos: Admin asst to US Rep John A Blatnik, 65-74; adminr, House Pub Works Comt, 71-74; US Rep, Minn, 75- Legal Res: 317 Ninth St Chisholm MN 55719 Mailing Add: US House Rep Washington DC 20515

OBERWAGER, FRANCES ROBERTSON (R)
VChmn, Columbia Co Rep Comt, NY
b Salem, NY, Feb 22, 23; d James Wood Robertson & Julia Roche R; m to Edwin R Oberwager. Educ: Wash Acad, Salem, NY, grad; Albany Training Sch for Nurses, grad. Polit & Govt Pos: Vchmn, Columbia Co Rep Comt, NY, currently; ex-officio mem, Rep Clubs Columbia Co; pres, Women's Rep Club, Columbia Co; chmn, Rep Party Activities for Annual Columbia Co Fair; deleg, Annual Conv, Nat Fedn Women's Rep Clubs, Washington, DC; mem, Third Judicial Dist Rep Exec Comt; exec rep, Rep Women 28th Cong Dist Rep Women Women; former alt deleg, NY State Rep Comt State-Wide Gubernatorial Nominating Conv; coordr, Rep Mission 70 Campaign, Columbia Co, 70 & 71, coordr, Target 72 Proj, 72; hon chmn, Annual Fund Raising Picnic for Columbia Co Rep Comt, formerly; alt deleg, Rep Nat Conv, 72. Bus & Prof Pos: Mem staff & asst to supt, Child's Hosp, Albany, NY, 46-59, acting supt, 59-61. Mem: Eastern Star; Women's Club of Chatham; Kinderhook Garden Club, Inc; Columbia Golf & Country Club; Columbia Mem Hosp Auxiliary. Relig: Lutheran; Communicant, Christ Evangelical Lutheran Church. Mailing Add: Church St Ghent NY 12075

OBEY, DAVID R (D)
US Rep, Wis
b Okmulgee, Okla, Oct 3, 38; m 1962 to Joan Lepinski; c Craig David & Douglas David. Educ: Univ Wis, MA in Polit Sci, 60. Polit & Govt Pos: Mem, Admin Comt, Wis Dem Party; Wis State Assemblyman, 60-69; US Rep, Wis, 69-, past mem, House Comt on Pub Works, US House of Rep, 69, mem, Appropriations Comt, currently; mem, Dem Nat Steering & Policy Comt, currently. Bus & Prof Pos: Real estate broker. Mem: Optimists; KofC. Legal Res: 831 Dunbar St Wausau WI 54401 Mailing Add: 208 Cannon House Off Bldg Washington DC 20515

OBLINGER, JOSEPHINE KNEIDL (R)
VChairwoman, Sangamon Co Rep Party, Ill
b Chicago, Ill, Feb 14, 13; d Thomas William Harrington & Margaret Kneidl H; m 1940 to Walter L Oblinger; c Carl Douglas. Educ: Univ Ill, Urbana, BS, 33; Univ Detroit Law Sch, LLB, 43; Kappa Delta Pi; Sigma Delta Pi; Delta Delta Delta. Hon Degrees: LHD, Sioux Empire Col. Polit & Govt Pos: Asst supvr, Sangamon Co Bd Supvr, Ill, 55-62; chairwoman, Ill Women for Nixon, 60 & 68; co clerk, Sangamon Co, 62-70; twp clerk & assessor, Capital Twp, 62-70; asst dir, Ill Dept Registr & Educ, 70; exec dir, Gov Comt Vol Action, 70-; vchairwoman, Sangamon Co Rep Party, currently; alt deleg, Rep Nat Conv, 72; first vpres, Ill Fedn Rep Women, 72-74, pres, 74- Bus & Prof Pos: Teacher social sci, Lanphier High Sch, Springfield, Ill, 51-62; asst to the pres, Lincoln Land Community Col, 73- Publ: Recent decision ed, Univ Detroit Law Rev, 41-43; helped develop & write new tax redemption law, Ill, 70. Mem: Ill & Sangamon Co Bar Asns; Ill Fedn Teachers, AFL-CIO; Springfield & Sangamon Co Community Action, Inc; Sangamon Co Coun on Alcoholism & Drugs. Honors & Awards: John Hay fel, Williams Col, 60; Woman of the Year in Govt, Sangamon Co, 69. Relig: Methodist. Mailing Add: Box 82 RR 1 Sherman IL 62684

O'BLOCK, PATRICK MICHAEL (D)
Ill State Cent Committeeman, Fourth Dist
b Chicago, Ill, Sept 1, 19; s Mathew O'Block & Ellen Mullaney O; m 1941 to Helen P Burns; c Kenneth, Dennis, Patricia, Peggy, Kathy, Mickey & Nancy. Educ: Am Tech Soc Sch of Com. Polit & Govt Pos: Trustee, Hazel Crest, Ill, 60-62, mayor, 62-65; dir civil defense, Cook Co, Ill, 63-67 & 69-; committeeman, Thornton Twp Dem Party, 64-; secy, Ill Racing Bd, 67-69; deleg, Dem Nat Conv, 68, elected deleg, 72; dir, John F Kennedy Campaign for Thornton Twp, Ill; Ill State Cent Committeeman, Fourth Dist, 71- Bus & Prof Pos: Mgr, Superior Match Co, Chicago, 49-53; sales territory mgr, Diamond Nat Corp, 53-63. Publ: Lite up and live, Prog, Hwy Safety, Ill. Mem: Moose; Kiwanis; KofC. Honors & Awards: Recipient of Boy Scout Award, 64; Humanitarian South Suburban Mayors Award of Dedication; Gov of Ill Safety Award. Relig: Catholic. Mailing Add: 15126 Drexel Ave South Holland IL 60473

O'BRIEN, ANNA BELLE CLEMENT (D)
Tenn State Rep
Mailing Add: 36th Rep Dist Rte 1 Tansi Crossville TN 38555

O'BRIEN, BERNARD FRANCIS (D)
Pa State Rep
b Wilkes-Barre, Pa, Mar 5, 14; s Michael J O'Brien & Ellen Rogan O; m to Agnes McDonnell, wid; c Patricia (Mrs James Loughran), John, Eileen (Mrs James Halling), Bernard, Jr, Michael, Kevin, Joan, Daniel, Molly (Mrs Thomas Rutt) & Angle. Educ: Coughlin High Sch, Wilkes-Barre, Pa. Polit & Govt Pos: Pa State Rep, Wilkes-Barre Co, 62-70 & 73- Bus & Prof Pos: Stereotyper, Int Press. Mem: Allied Trades Coun; KofC; Eagles; Lions; Elks. Relig: Roman Catholic. Mailing Add: 28 Hillard St Wilkes-Barre PA 18702

O'BRIEN, DANIEL JOHN (D)
Dem Nat Committeeman, Vt
b Burlington, Vt, Dec 15, 33; s Leo O'Brien, Sr & Mary Mabel Hayes O; m to Sandra Corey; c Stephanie, Molly & Kerry K. Educ: Cathedral High Sch, Burlington, Vt. Polit & Govt Pos: Chmn, South Burlington Dem Town Comt, Vt, 57-62; mem, Comt on Town Govt, 58-69; Justice of the Peace, 60-; mem, Bd of Civil Authority, 60-; chmn, Chittenden Co Dem Comt, 62-64; chmn, Vt State Dem Comt, 64-68, chmn exec comt, 68-; mem, Vt State Bd of Health, 65-; Dem Nat Committeeman, Vt, 68-; mem bd gov, Med Ctr Hosp of Vt, 68-; mem, Small Bus Admin Adv Coun, Vt, 68-; deleg, Dem Nat Conv, 72. Bus & Prof Pos: Partner, O'Brien Bros Cattle Dealers, South Burlington, Vt, 57-; pres, Forest Park Realty Corp, 68-; vpres, Realty Sales Inc, 69- Mem: Vt Cattlemen's Asn; Farm Bur; North Farms; KofC; Eagles. Relig: Roman Catholic. Legal Res: 15O Old Farm Rd South Burlington VT 05401 Mailing Add: PO Box 2184 South Burlington VT 05401

O'BRIEN, DAVID FRANK (D)
b Litchfield, Ill, Nov 18, 36; s Maynard O'Brien & Estelle Gottrick O; m 1959 to Nancy Funkhouser; c James Frank, Rebecca Kathleen & Alice Margaret. Educ: Wabash Col, AB, 58; Univ Ill, Urbana, PhD, 62; Sigma Xi; Beta Theta Pi. Polit & Govt Pos: Mem, Rochester City Planning Comn, NY, 67-72; campaign coordr, 37th Cong Dist Citizens for Robert F Kennedy, 68; mem, Monroe Co Planning Coun, 68-69; vchmn, Dem Action Comt, 70-71, chmn, 71-72; alt deleg, Dem Nat Conv, 72; campaign coordr, Monroe Co Citizens for McGovern, 72; chmn, Monroe Co Dem Party City Issues Comt, 73. Bus & Prof Pos: Research chemist, Eastman Kodak Co, Rochester, NY, 62-64, sr research chemist, 64-67, research assoc, 67- Mem: Am Chem Soc; Soc Photographic Scientists & Engrs. Relig: Presbyterian. Mailing Add: 398 Beresford Rd Rochester NY 14610

O'BRIEN, DONALD EUGENE (D)
Dem Nat Committeeman, Iowa
b Marcus, Iowa, Sept 30, 23; s Michael John O'Brien & Myrtle Toomey O; m 1950 to Ruth Virginia Mahon; c Teresa, Brien, John & Schiuvaun. Educ: Creighton Univ, LLB, 48; Gamma Eta Gamma. Polit & Govt Pos: Co attorney, Sioux City, Iowa, 55-58, munic judge, 59-60; US Attorney, Northern Dist, Iowa, 61-67; campaign aide to Robert Kennedy, Iowa, Nebr & SDak, 68; conv coordr for Sen McGovern, 68; deleg, Dem Nat Conv, 68; Southern Calif coordr for Hubert Humphrey, 68; Tex & Southern Calif coordr for McGovern, 72; mem, Iowa Dem State Comt, 72-75; deleg, Dem Nat Mid-Term Conf, 74; Dem Nat Committeeman, Iowa, 75- Mil Serv: Entered as Pvt, Army Air Force, 42, released as 1st Lt, 45, after serv in 390th Bomb Group, ETO, 44-45; Distinguished Flying Cross; Five Air Medals; Presidential Citation. Mem: Iowa Bar Asn; KofC; Amvets; Am Legion. Relig: Catholic. Legal Res: 3140 Norman Dr Sioux City IA 51104 Mailing Add: 916 Grandview Blvd Sioux City IA 51101

O'BRIEN, DOROTHY GERTRUDE (D)
b DeKalb, Ill, Feb 8, 19; d James S O'Brien & Mary Carton O; single. Educ: St Joseph Hosp Sch Nursing, nursing dipl, 40; DePaul Univ, BS, 44, Law Sch, 54-56; Kappa Beta Pi. Polit & Govt Pos: Chairwoman, DeKalb Co Dem Cent Comt, Ill, 56-60; mem adv comt, Dem Nat Comt, 58-60; state chairwoman, Ill State Dem Cent Comt, 58-64; deleg & mem, Platform Comt, Dem Nat Conv, 60, 64 & 68; precinct committeewoman, Afton Twp Dem Party, 62-; Dem Nat Committeewoman, Ill, 64-72; mem defense adv comt on women in the serv, Defense Dept, 64-66; vchmn, Dem Midwest Conf, 65-67. Mil Serv: Entered as Asst Nurse Officer, US Pub Health Serv, 45, released as Sr Asst Nurse Officer, 52, after serv in Nutrition Div, 1 year & Venereal Disease Control Div, 6 years. Mem: St Joseph Hosp Alumnae Asn, Chicago; Women's Bd, St Joseph Hosp, Chicago; Am Legion Post 66; NAACP; Nat Farmers Union. Relig: Roman Catholic. Legal Res: Rte 2 DeKalb IL 60115 Mailing Add: 123 E Taylor St DeKalb IL 60115

O'BRIEN, GEORGE M (R)
US Rep, Ill
b Chicago, Ill, June 17, 17; s Matthew J O'Brien & Isabel Hyde O; m 1947 to Mary Lou Peyla; c Caryl Isabel (Mrs Timothy Bloch) & Mary Deborah (Mrs Richard L Pershey). Educ: Northwestern Univ, Evanton, AB, 39; Yale Law Sch, JD, 47; Phi Beta Kappa; Sigma Chi. Polit & Govt Pos: Mem, Will Co Bd Supvrs, Ill, 56-64; mem, Legis Adv Comt, Northeastern Ill Planning Comn, 71-72; Ill State Rep, 71-72; US Rep, 17th Dist, Ill, 73- Bus & Prof Pos: Partner, Gray, Thomas, Wallace & O'Brien, 54-66 & O'Brien, Garrison, Berard & Kusta, 66- Mil Serv: Entered as 2nd Lt, Air Force, 41, released as Lt Col, 45, after serv in 8th & 12th Air Force, ETO, 41-45; Bronze Star. Mem: Am, Ill, Chicago & Will Co Bar Asns; Trial Lawyers Asn of Ill. Relig: Catholic. Legal Res: Joliet IL Mailing Add: 422 Cannon House Off Bldg Washington DC 20515

O'BRIEN, J W, JR (D)
Va State Deleg
Mailing Add: 316 Constance Dr Chesapeake VA 23320

O'BRIEN, JAMES ANTHONY, JR (D)
Mass State Rep
b Fall River, Mass, June 22, 19; s James Anthony O'Brien & Mary V Connor O; m 1950 to Gertrude K Ready; c James A, III, Kathleen M & Timothy Patrick. Educ: Suffolk Univ, 46-47. Polit & Govt Pos: Mass State Rep, Sixth Bristol Dist, 61-, chmn comt on taxation, Mass House Rep, 68- Bus & Prof Pos: Sanit & health inspector, Fall River Health Dept, 47-61. Mil Serv: Entered as Pvt, Army, 42, released as Pfc, 46, after serv in 103rd Inf, European Theatre, 42-46; Good Conduct Medal; Purple Heart; 3 Battle Stars. Mem: Nat Legis Leaders; KofC; Elks; VFW; Am Legion. Relig: Roman Catholic. Legal Res: 37 Forest St Fall River MA 02721 Mailing Add: Rm 237 State House Boston MA 02133

O'BRIEN, JOHN FITZGERALD (D)
Committeeman, Ill Dem Representative Comt
b Springfield, Ill, May 6, 28; s Edward L O'Brien & Mary Murphy O; m 1961 to Sharon L Fassero; c Marjorie Ann, Polly Ann & Bridgett. Educ: Local sch. Polit & Govt Pos: Pres, Young Dem of Sangamon Co, 60-62; committeeman, Ill Dem Rep Comt, 62-; asst clerk, Ill House of Rep, 69-75; chief clerk, 75- Bus & Prof Pos: Owner, O'Brien Ins Agency, Springfield, Ill, 54- Mil Serv: Entered as Pvt, Army, 46, released as S/Sgt, 51, after serv in Second Inf Div, Korea, 50-51; Sgt Maj, Army Res, Ret; Combat Inf Badge. Mem: KofC; Elks; Sons of Erin (pres). Relig: Roman Catholic. Legal Res: 2427 Sussex Rd Springfield IL 62703 Mailing Add: PO Box 2376 Springfield IL 62705

O'BRIEN, JOHN F X (D)
Md State Deleg
b Baltimore, Md, Jan 26, 36; s John Mitchell O'Brien & Anne Zerhusen O; m 1966 to Mary Ellen Foppiano; c Kelly. Educ: Univ Baltimore, LLB, 64. Polit & Govt Pos: Md State Deleg, 67-; deleg, Dem Nat Conv, 72. Mil Serv: Entered as Pvt, Army, 56, released as Pfc, 58, after serv in 11th Armored Cavalry, Ger, 57-58. Relig: Roman Catholic. Mailing Add: 6410 Alta Ave Baltimore MD 21206

O'BRIEN, JOHN JOSEPH (D)
Vt State Sen
b New Bedford, Mass, Apr 29, 97; widower; c Two. Educ: New Bedford Schs. Polit & Govt Pos: Vt State Sen, 59-; mem, Lake Champlain Waterway Comn. Bus & Prof Pos: Sports promoter, formerly; retired. Mem: Elks (Past Exalted Ruler). Relig: Catholic. Mailing Add: 33 Hayden Pkwy South Burlington VT 05401

O'BRIEN, JOHN L (D)
Wash State Rep
b Seattle, Wash, 1911; m to Mary; c Six. Educ: Bus Col; Western Inst Prof Acct. Polit & Govt Pos: Wash State Rep, 41-, Majority Leader, Wash House Rep, 51 & 65, Minority Leader, 53, 63, 67 & 69, Speaker of the House, 55-62, chmn House minority exec comt, 71, Speaker Pro Tem, 73- Bus & Prof Pos: CPA. Mil Serv: Coast Guard; Temp Res. Mem: Eagles; KofC; Wash Athletic Club; Rainier CofC; Am Inst CPA. Mailing Add: 5041 Lake Washington Blvd S Seattle WA 98118

O'BRIEN, LAWRENCE FRANCIS (D)
b Springfield, Mass, July 7, 17; s Lawrence O'Brien, Sr & Myra Sweeney O; m 1944 to Elva Lena Brassard; c Lawrence Francis, III. Educ: Northeastern Univ, LLB, 42. Hon Degrees: PhD in Law, Western New Eng Col, 62, Villanova Univ, 66 & Loyola Univ, 67; PhD in Pub Admin, Northeastern Univ, 65; PhD in Humanities, St Anselm's Col, 66; PhD in Pub Affairs, Seton Hall Univ, 67; LHD, Am Int Col & Wheeling Col, 71; LLD, Xavier Univ, 71. Polit & Govt Pos: Dir orgn, Second Cong Dist Dem Campaigns, Mass, 46, 48 & 50; admin asst to US Rep Foster Furcolo, Mass, 48-50; dir orgn, J F Kennedy Senate Campaigns, Mass, 52 & 58; dir orgn, Kennedy-Johnson Campaign, 60; spec asst to President for Cong Rels, 61-65; dir orgn, Johnson-Humphrey Campaign, 64; Postmaster Gen, US Post Off Dept, 65-68; mem, Robert F Kennedy Presidential Campaign, 68; mem, Hubert H Humphrey Presidential Campaign, 68; chmn, Dem Nat Comt, 68-72. Bus & Prof Pos: Former mgr, family bus enterprises; bd pres & bus mgr, Western Mass Hotel Fund, 52-58; in pub rels, 58-60. Mil Serv: Army, 43-45. Publ: The O'Brien Manual, Dem Nat Comt, 60, revised 62, 64, 68 & 70. Mem: Elks; Am Legion. Mailing Add: 17 Kimball Cambridge MA 02140

O'BRIEN, LEO, JR (D)
b Burlington, Vt, Feb 5, 31; s Leo O'Brien, Sr & Mary Mabel Hayes O; m 1958 to Stella T Cotrupi; c Maureen, Leo, III, Kathleen, Bridget, Joanne & Patrick. Educ: St Michael's Col, 49-50; Univ Vt, BA in Polit Sci, 54-57. Polit & Govt Pos: Mem, South Burlington Dem Comn, Vt, 54-; mem, Chittenden Co Dem Comn, 56-; mem, South Burlington Planning Comn, 60-68; mem, Comn Admin Coord, Vt; Vt State Rep, 63-69, Minority Leader, Vt House of Rep, 66-68; trustee, Univ of Vt & State Agr Col, 65-71; assoc trustee, St Michael's Col, 67-; deleg, Dem Nat Conv, 68 & 72; mem, Interstate Coop Comn, 69-; Vt State Sen, Chittenden-Grand Isle Dist, 69-70; Dem cand for Gov of Vt, 70; spec asst to Gov, Vt, 73; Comnr Agr, State of Vt, 73-; deleg, Dem Nat Mid-Term Conf, 74. Bus & Prof Pos: Partner, O'Brien Brothers Cattle Sales, South Burlington, Vt, 57-; vpres, Forest Park Realty Corp, vpres, O'Brien Bros Agency, 69-; dir, Merchants Nat Bank, Burlington, 69- Mil Serv: Entered as Seaman Recruit, Navy, 50, released as PO 2/C, 54, after serv in Atlantic Fleet, 51-54; Nat Defense Serv Medal. Mem: Nat Asn State Dept Agr (2nd vpres); Burlington Veterans Club; Elks; Ethan Allen Club; Farm Bur. Honors & Awards: Distinguished Serv Award, Jr CofC, 64. Relig: Catholic. Legal Res: 200 Old Farm Rd South Burlington VT 05401 Mailing Add: PO Box 2184 South Burlington VT 05401

O'BRIEN, MARK D (D)
Ky State Rep
Mailing Add: 38 Meadowview Dr Louisville KY 40220

O'BRIEN, MARK PAUL (D)
Mem, Needham Dem Town Comt, Mass
b Boston, Mass, Jan 27, 51; s James Benedict O'Brien & Sarah Veronica Torpie O; single. Educ: Vesper George Sch Art, 70-72. Polit & Govt Pos: Mem, Needham Dem Town Comt, Mass, 70-; town meeting mem, Needham, 71-; coordr, Ninth Cong Dist. McGovern for President, 71-72; mem state steering comt, McGovern for President, 71-72; campaign mgr, Hubie Jones for Cong, Ninth Cong Dist, 72; alt deleg, Dem Nat Conv, 72; chmn, Needham Citizens for Participation in Polit Action, 72- Bus & Prof Pos: Mgr, Roche Bros Florist, 70-72; mgr, Temple Florist, 72- Relig: Quaker. Mailing Add: 49 Walnut St Needham MA 02192

O'BRIEN, MICHAEL J (D)
Mich State Sen
Mailing Add: 9396 Prest Detroit MI 48228

O'BRIEN, ROBERT (D)
Vt State Sen
Mailing Add: Tunbridge VT 05077

O'BRIEN, ROBERT S (D)
Treas, Wash
b Seattle, Wash, Sept 14, 18; s Edward Dennis O'Brien & Maude Ransom O; m 1941 to Kathryn Arvan. Polit & Govt Pos: Co treas, Grant Co, Wash, 51-65; Treas, Wash, 65-; chmn, Wash State Finance Comt, 65-; mem bd trustees, Wash State Teachers' Retirement Syst, 65-; mem, Wash State Data Processing Adv Bd, 67-; chmn, Wash State Law Enforcement Officers & Firefighters Retirement Bd, 69-; chmn, Wash State Pub Employees' Retirement Bd, 69-; chmn, Wash State Pub Deposit Protection Comn, 69- Mem: Elks (hon life mem); Olympia Yacht Club; Washington Athletic Club; Eagles; Moose. Honors & Awards: Award, Eagles; Leadership Award, Coun Co & City Employ & Fedn State Employ, AFL-CIO. Legal Res: 3213 Capitol Blvd Olympia WA 98501 Mailing Add: Legislative Bldg Olympia WA 98504

OBUCHOWSKI, MICHAEL JOHN (D)
Vt State Rep
Mailing Add: 24 South St Bellows Falls VT 05101

O'CALLAGHAN, DONAL N (MIKE) (D)
Gov, Nev
b La Crosse, Wis, Sept 10, 29; s Neil T O'Callaghan & Olive Berry O; m to Carolyn Randall; c Michael Neil, Brian Jack, Timothy Joe, Mary Colleen & Teresa Marie. Educ: Univ Idaho, BS & MEd, 56; Colo State Univ, grad work; Univ Nev, Las Vegas; Georgetown Univ & Claremont Grad Sch. Polit & Govt Pos: Chief probation officer & dir of court serv, Clark Co, Nev, 61-63; State Dir of Health & Welfare, 63-64; proj mgr dir, Job Corps Conserv Ctr, Washington, DC, 64-66; regional dir, Off of Emergency Planning, San Francisco, Calif, 67-69; Gov, Nev, 71-; Gov rep, Dem Nat Comt, 75- Bus & Prof Pos: High sch teacher govt & hist, 56-61; owner, Planning & Develop Corp, 1 year. Mil Serv: Marine Corps, Pac, 46-48; Marine Corps Res, 48-50; Air Force Intel, Alaska & Orient, 50-52; Army, Inf, Japan & Korea, 52-53; Purple Heart; Silver Star; Bronze Star V Device. Mem: Southern Nev Amateur Athletic Union; Lions Int (club pres & dept dist gov); KofC; VFW. Relig: Catholic. Legal Res: Governor's Mansion Carson City NV 89701 Mailing Add: State Capitol Carson City NV 89701

O'CALLAGHAN, PHYLLIS ANNE (D)
b Memphis, Tenn, Jan 10, 32; d Martin Francis O'Callaghan & Clarabealle Parham O; m 1967 to Charles Seaver Casazza. Educ: Memphis State Univ, BA, 53; St Louis Univ, fel, 53-57, MA, 55, PhD, 57; Gamma Pi Epsilon; Mortar Bd. Polit & Govt Pos: Legis asst to US Rep N N Craley, Jr, 65-67 & US Rep J Edward Roush, 67-69 & 71- Bus & Prof Pos: From asst prof to prof, St Mary's Col (Ind), 57-66; nat legis dir, Nat Fedn Bus & Prof Women's Clubs, Inc, 69-70; vis lectr, Georgetown Univ, 74-75. Publ: A selected bibliography on A Study of History by Arnold Toynbee, Hist Bull, 56; Clio Muses, Bull Hist Teachers Club Notre Dame Univ, 2-3/66; Spanning a Half-Century of Legislation, Nat Fedn Bus & Prof Women, Inc, 70. Honors & Awards: SPES UNICA Teaching Award, St Mary's Col (Ind), 66. Mailing Add: 5505 Uppingham St Chevy Chase MD 20015

OCASEK, OLIVER ROBERT (D)
Ohio State Sen
b Bedford, Ohio, Nov 2, 25; s Jack Barney Ocasek & Olive Drabek O; m 1955 to Virginia Mae Hejduk. Educ: Kent State Univ, BSc, 46, MA, 51; Western Reserve Univ, 51-56; Phi Delta Kappa; Asn Higher Educ; Nat Educ Asn; Sigma Nu. Polit & Govt Pos: Twp trustee, Sagamore Hills, Ohio, 49-60, precinct committeeman, 52-; Ohio State Sen, 58-, pres pro-tem, Ohio Senate, 75; pres, Young Dem Ohio, 62-64; vpres, Young Dem Am, 63-65; deleg, Dem Nat Conv, 72. Bus & Prof Pos: Teacher, Richfield High Sch, Ohio, 46-50 & Stow High Sch, 50-51; prin, Tallmadge High Sch, 51-60; instr, Kent State Univ, 60; from assoc prof to prof educ, Akron Univ, 61- Publ: School Finance, Ohio's Schs, 65. Honors & Awards: Distinguished legislator award from several orgns. Relig: Presbyterian. Mailing Add: 7665 Gannett Rd Northfield OH 44067

OCHOA, JOHN ROBERT (D)
b Pomona, Calif, June 25, 47; s Blas Ochoa & Bernardina Torres O; single. Educ: Calif State Univ, Fullerton, BA, 69, 69-; Delta Sigma Phi. Polit & Govt Pos: Vchmn, Community Life Comn, Pomona, Calif, 72-73; legis aide to US Rep Jim Lloyd, Calif, 75- Mil Serv: Entered as Pvt, Army, 69, released as Sgt E-5, 71, after serv in 2nd Armored Div; Army Commendation Medal. Relig: Protestant. Mailing Add: 2260 Virginia Ave Pomona CA 91766

OCKERMAN, FOSTER (D)
b Nelson Co, Ky, Sept 17, 20; s R F Ockerman & Anna Clara Sweazy O; m 1950 to Joyce Ann Harris; c Foster, Jr, Jefferson & Ann Ward. Educ: Univ Ky, BA & LLB. Polit & Govt Pos: City attorney, Lexington, Ky, 50-54; Ky State Rep, 54-59; comnr, Dept Motor Transportation, Commonwealth of Ky, 59-62; mgr, Successful Primary & Gen Elec Dem Gubernatorial Campaign, 63; chmn, Ky State Dem Cent Exec Comt, 64-66; chief legis asst to Gov, Ky, 66; mem, Transit Authority of Lexington, 73-74; vchmn, Lexington-Fayette Co Urban Airport Bd, 75. Bus & Prof Pos: Attorney-at-law, 46- Mil Serv: Entered as Seaman, Navy, 42, released as Lt, 46, after serv in Pac Theater. Mem: Am, Ky & Fayette Co Bar Asns. Honors & Awards: Gov Distinguished Award, Gov Edward T Breathitt, Ky, 66. Relig: Methodist. Legal Res: 211 S Hanover Ave Lexington KY 40502 Mailing Add: 259 W Short St Lexington KY 40507

OCKSRIDER, CHARLES BRIGHTBILL (R)
NMex State Rep
b Reading, Pa, Feb 8, 31; s Charles William Ocksrider & Dorothy Brightbill O; m 1953 to Bernece Cox; c Dean, Jonathan, Christopher & Rachel. Educ: Pa State Univ, BS, 52; Air War Col, grad, 71; Sigma Eta Alpha; Phi Kappa Tau. Polit & Govt Pos: Rep ward committeeman, Albuquerque, NMex, 65-67; mem exec comt, Peoples Comt for Better Govt, Albuquerque, 65-67; vchmn, Bernalillo Co Rep Party, 67-68; NMex State Rep, Dist, 30, 72- Bus & Prof Pos: Owner, Ocksrider Co, currently. Mil Serv: Entered as 2nd Lt, Air Force, 52, released as 1st Lt, 54, after serv in Alaska, 52; recalled as Maj, 68-69, Zone of Interior; Lt Col, Air Nat Guard, 55-, Dep Comdr, NMex, 55-; Air Force Commendation Medal. Mem: NMex Bd Realtors; Independent Ins Agents Asn NMex; Mason; Shrine; York Rite. Relig: Episcopal. Mailing Add: 1604 Cardenas Dr NE Albuquerque NM 87110

O'CONNELL, FRANK J (R)
Pa State Rep
Mailing Add: Capitol Bldg Harrisburg PA 17120

O'CONNELL, HELEN G (D)
Mont State Rep
Mailing Add: 703 Fourth Ave SW Great Falls MT 59404

O'CONNELL, JAMES J (D)
NH State Rep
Mailing Add: 81 Cottage St Portsmouth NH 03801

O'CONNELL, JOHN THOMAS (D)
b New York, NY, Dec 13, 43; s John Thomas O'Connell & Mary Tyson O; single. Educ: St Mary's Univ, AB, 65, Sch Theol, MTh, 69. Polit & Govt Pos: Alt deleg, Dem Nat Conv, 72. Bus & Prof Pos: Cath priest; assoc pastor, St Mary's Church, Far Rockaway, NY, 69-72; co-adminr, St Gertrude's Parish, 72-; dir, Rockaway Sr Citizen Ctr, currently. Mem: Rotary (bd dirs, 69-). Relig: Roman Catholic. Mailing Add: 230 Riverside Dr Apt 8G New York NY 10025

O'CONNELL, KENNETH JOHN (D)
Chief Justice, Ore Supreme Court
b Bayfield, Wis, Dec 8, 09; s Daniel W O'Connell & Kathryn B Smith O; m 1964 to Esther Foster; c Daniel & Thomas. Educ: Univ Wis-Madison, LLB, 33, SJD, 34; Omicron Delta Tau. Polit & Govt Pos: Employee, Wis Tax Comn, 34; chmn, Statute Rev Coun, Ore, 50-54; Assoc Justice, Ore Supreme Court, 58-70, Chief Justice, 70-; vchmn, Ore Const Rev Comn, 61-63; mem, Gov Judicial Reform Comn, 71-74. Bus & Prof Pos: Assisted in prep of restatement of Law of Property for Am Law Inst, 33-34; asst prof law, Univ Ore Law Sch, 35-40, assoc prof, 40-44, prof, 47-58; practice of law, O'Connell, Darling & Vonderheit, Eugene, Ore,

44-47; fel, Ctr for Advan Study in Behav Sci, 65-66; mem faculty, Appellate Judges Seminar, NY Univ Law Sch, 66 & 67. Publ: Personal Property Outlines (5), privately publ, 57; Oregon Laws on Surveying, State Agency; articles for Ore Law Rev, 36-67. Mem: Am & Ore State Bar Asns; Am Judicature Soc; Order of Coif. Honors & Awards: Law & Soc Award of Merit, Ore State Bar, 53; Distinguished Serv Award, Univ Ore, 67; Appointment to Order of Coif Second Triennial Awards Comt; Mem, Electoral Col of the Hall of Fame for Great Am, NY Univ, 70. Legal Res: 3393 Country Club Dr S Salem OR 97302 Mailing Add: Supreme Court Bldg Salem OR 97310

O'CONNOR, DENNIS (D)
Hawaii State Sen
Mailing Add: Senate Sgt-at-Arms State Capitol Honolulu HI 96813

O'CONNOR, GWENDOLYN MARIE (D)
Committeewoman, Maine State Dem Comt
b Bangor, Maine, Mar 21, 28; d Eric Godfred Jansson & Dorothy Kelleher J; m 1948 to Donald Timothy O'Connor; c Mary Edith, Ann Maureen, Christopher John, Dennis Charles, Kathleen Marie, Carol Jane, Kevin Joseph, Daisey Mae & Chee Von. Educ: John Bapst High Sch, Bangor, Maine, 4 years. Polit & Govt Pos: Committeewoman, Maine State Dem Comt, 68-; chmn, Dover-Foxcroft Town Dem Party, 70- Relig: Catholic. Mailing Add: 46 Court St Dover-Foxcroft ME 04426

O'CONNOR, J RAYMOND (R)
Treas, Winchester Rep Town Comt, Conn
b Winsted, Conn, Feb 18, 02; s John F O'Connor & Mary A Wheeler O; m 1932 to Jeannette Soucy; c John F & Robert E. Educ: Gilbert High Sch, 4 years. Polit & Govt Pos: Mem, Winsted Vol Fire Dept, 25-; mem bd finance, Winchester, Conn, 41-53; Conn State Rep, 51-53 & 55-57; chmn, Winchester Rep Town Comt, 66-70, treas, 70- Bus & Prof Pos: Asst engr, Conn Light & Power Co, 23-67, retired, 67. Mem: Elks; Union Engine Co One, Winsted Vol Fire Dept; Old Newgate Coon Club (secy). Relig: Roman Catholic. Mailing Add: 11 Cottage St Winsted CT 06098

O'CONNOR, JAMES A (D)
Conn State Rep
Mailing Add: PO Box 278 Danielson CT 06239

O'CONNOR, KAREN PAULA (R)
b Buffalo, NY, Feb 15, 52; d Robert Jeremiah O'Connor & Norma Wilton O; single. Educ: State Univ NY Col Buffalo, BA, 73; Polit Sci Forum. Polit & Govt Pos: Intern, Am Conservative Union, Washington, DC, 71; intern to US Rep Jack Kemp, NY, 72; off mgr, Comt to Reelect US Rep Kemp, 72; alt deleg, Rep Nat Conv, 72; dir vol, Comt to Reelect the President, Erie Co, 72; Erie Co coordr, Young Voters for the President, 72; coordr youth activities, Erie Co Rep Comt, 72; mem-at-lg, Erie Co Rep Exec Comt, 72; pres, 21st Century Young Rep Club, 72-; admin asst, Erie Co Legis, 73- Honors & Awards: Dean's List, State Univ NY Col Buffalo, 71-72. Relig: Roman Catholic. Mailing Add: 96 Burmon Dr Buffalo NY 14218

O'CONNOR, KATHLEEN T (D)
b Richland, Wash, Jan 13, 46; d John P Tordella & Mildred Rees T; m 1967 to J Kevin O'Connor; c Erin & Susan. Educ: Univ Del, BA, 68. Polit & Govt Pos: Deleg, Dem Nat Conv, 72; vchairperson, 26th Dem Rep Dist, Del, 72- Mem: Another Mother For Peace; New Dem Coalition. Relig: Roman Catholic. Mailing Add: 44 Bobby Dr Newark DE 19711

O'CONNOR, MICHAEL JOSEPH (D)
SDak State Sen
b Sioux Falls, SDak, Dec 15, 28; s Michael Joseph O'Connor (deceased) & Hazel Theresa Lundquist O; m 1950 to Barbara May Brown; c Deborah Ann, Michael Joseph, III, Theresa Louise & Mary Catherine. Educ: Univ SDak, 48-49; Augustana Col (SDak), BA, 51; Beta Theta Pi. Polit & Govt Pos: Precinct chmn, Co Dem Party, 69-70; pres, Dem Forum, 69-70; SDak State Rep, 71-72; SDak State Sen, 73-, chmn state affairs comt, SDak State Senate, vchmn judiciary comt & pres pro tem, currently. Bus & Prof Pos: Dir, Sioux Empire Fair, 64-; state chmn, Small Bus Admin Adv Bd, 67; pres, O'Connor Printers. Mil Serv: Entered as Pvt, Marine Corps, 46, released as Pfc, 48, after serv in SMS 33, 2nd Lt, Marine Corps Res, 48-51. Mem: CofC; SDak Commercial Printers Asn; SDak Jr CofC; Toastmasters; Sioux Falls Boys Club Bd. Honors & Awards: Distinguished Serv Award, 60; Outstanding Layman's Award, SDak Chiropractors Asn, 74. Relig: Baptist. Mailing Add: 1109 Lark Dr Brandon SD 57005

O'CONNOR, RODERICK HOWARD (D)
NH State Rep
b Brattleboro, Vt, Sept 27, 49; s Gerald Joseph O'Connor & Barbara Howard O; m 1967 to Melinda Jane Holden. Educ: Univ NH, BA, 71. Polit & Govt Pos: Youth deleg, NH Dem State Conv, 70, deleg, 72; coordr, Dover Muskie for President Comt, 72; coordr, Raiche for Gov, NH, 72; mem, NH Dem State Comt, 72-; secy, Strafford Co Dem Comt, 72-; NH State Rep, Strafford Co, Dist 15, 73- Bus & Prof Pos: Salesman, Bellamy Pontiac-Jeep, Inc, Dover, 73- Mem: Jaycees; Local 243, IUE; Am Civil Liberties Union; NH Social Welfare Coun; NAACP. Relig: Baptist. Mailing Add: 110 Henry Law Ave Dover NH 03820

O'CONNOR, SANDRA DAY (R)
b El Paso, Tex, Mar 26, 30; d Harry A Day & Ada Mae Wilkey D; m 1952 to John Jay O'Connor, III; c Scott, Brian & Jay. Educ: Stanford Univ, BA, 50, LLB, 52; Order of the Coif; bd ed, Stanford Law Rev. Polit & Govt Pos: Dep co attorney, San Mateo Co, Calif, 52-53; mem, Ariz State Personnel Comn, Maricopa Co Bd Adjust & Appeals, Gov Fannin's Comt Ment Health & Comt Marriage & Family Probs, formerly; Juvenile Court Referee, formerly; chmn vis bd, Maricopa Co Juv Detention Home, formerly; admin asst, Ariz State Hosp, 65; Asst Attorney Gen, Ariz, 65-69; Ariz State Sen, 69-75, Majority Leader, Ariz State Senate, 73-75; alt deleg, Rep Nat Conv, 72; mem, Ariz Adv Coun, Intergovt Rels, currently; judge, Superior Court, Maricopa Co, Ariz, 75-; mem, Nat Defense Adv Comn on Women in Serv. Bus & Prof Pos: Part-time employ, comt bar examr, State Bar Ariz; mem bd dirs, First Nat Bank of Ariz, 71-75. Mem: Maricopa Co Juv Court Study Comt; Stanford Club Phoenix (bd dirs); Heard Mus, Phoenix (vpres & mem bd trustees); State Bar Ariz (comt legal aid); State Bar Calif. Honors & Awards: Woman of Year Award, Phoenix Advert Club, 73. Relig: Episcopal. Mailing Add: 3651 E Denton Lane Paradise Valley AZ 85253

O'CONNOR, TIMOTHY J, JR (D)
Vt State Rep
Mailing Add: 13 Oak St Brattleboro VT 05301

O'CONNOR, TIMOTHY K (D)
NH State Rep
Mailing Add: 100 Rosedale Ave Manchester NH 03103

O'CONOR, ROBERT JR (R)
Committeeman, Tex State Rep Exec Comt
b Los Angeles, Calif, June 22, 34; s Robert O'Conor & Frances Robinson O; m 1961 to Ana Lourdes Navarrete; c Anne Frances, Robert Daniel & Elizabeth Christine. Educ: Univ Tex, Austin, BA, 56 & LLB, 57. Polit & Govt Pos: Chmn, Jack Cox for Gov Comt, Webb Co, Tex, 62; chmn, Webb Co Rep Party, 68-71; committeeman, Tex State Rep Exec Comt, 21st Sen Dist, 70-; deleg, Rep Nat Conv, 72. Mil Serv: Pvt, Army, 57; Capt, Res, 62-69. Mem: Am & Tex Bar Asns; Laredo Bar Asn; Tex Conf of Bar Pres (secy-treas, 70-); State Bar of Tex (dir, Family Law Sect, 70-). Relig: Catholic. Legal Res: 2702 Fremont Laredo TX 78040 Mailing Add: PO Box 298 Laredo TX 78040

ODA, HOWARD KAZUMI (R)
Hawaii State Rep
b Wahiawa, Hawaii, July 3, 31; s Joseph Tatsumi Oda & Hatsumi Ishi O; m 1954 to June Shizuko Eto; c Terri Jo & Robert Joe. Educ: Ohio State Univ, 54; La Crosse State Univ, BS, 58; Univ Hawaii, Prof Cert; Phi Kappa Epsilon; L Club. Polit & Govt Pos: Dist chmn, Wahiawa, Hawaii Rep Party, 65; Hawaii State Rep, 66-; deleg, State Const Conv, 68. Bus & Prof Pos: Teacher, Dept Educ, Hawaii, 58-66; supvr tax annuity, Grand Pac, Honolulu, 68. Mil Serv: Sgt, Army, 51-54, served in 343 Gen Hosp, Far East; UN Korean Unit Citation; Nat Defense Serv Medal. Mailing Add: House of Rep State Capitol Honolulu HI 96813

O'DANIEL, RICHARD TRUITT (D)
Chmn, Swisher Co Dem Party, Tex
b San Angelo, Tex, Oct 5, 08; s James Dial O'Daniel & Lillie Wilkins O; m 1929 to Zuleika Kendrick; c Donna (Mrs Harlan Vander Zee). Educ: High sch, Tulia, Tex. Polit & Govt Pos: Precinct chmn, Swisher Co Dem Party, Tex, 60-68, chmn, 68- Bus & Prof Pos: Rancher & farmer, Swisher Co, Tex, 29-; pres, Fed Land Bank, 48-; vpres, Tulia Develop Co, 60-; pres, Tulia Savings & Loan, 63-; dir, Hereford State Bank, 66-; vpres, Prairie Cattle Co, 69- Mem: Nat Farmers Union. Relig: Baptist. Mailing Add: 22 Circle Dr Tulia TX 79088

O'DAY, JOSEPH F (D)
Ind State Sen
Mailing Add: 311 Van Dusen Evansville IN 47711

ODEGAARD, GARY MARTIN (D)
Wash State Sen
b Bellingham, Wash, Feb 28, 40; s Harold Kristian Odegaard & Laurel Clark O; m 1963 to Kathleen Marit Fifield; c Gregory Martin & Jeffrey Arthur. Educ: Western Wash State Col, BA to 62; Univ Wash, currently, 63-67. Polit & Govt Pos: Wash State Sen, 20th Dist, 69-, mem ways & means & educ comt, Wash State Senate, 69-, mem parks & recreation comt, 73-, mem legis budget comt, 73- Bus & Prof Pos: Teacher, Centralia Community Col, 69- Mem: Int Reading Asn; Nat Educ Asn; Lewis Co Pomona Grange; Alpha Grange; Eagles. Honors & Awards: 500 Hour Award, Wash Educ Asn; Cert of Serv Award, Wash Asn Sheriffs & Police Chiefs, 72. Relig: Presbyterian. Mailing Add: 3415 Ives Rd Centralia WA 98531

ODELL, CHARLES (R)
b Salem, Mass, Jan 6, 28; s Harry Albert Odell & Edna Faulkner O; m 1956 to Dale Rolene Kelly Nichols; c David Lyle, Charles Dwight & Kelly Nichole. Educ: Western Wash State Col, BA, 52; chmn, Evergreen Student Conf, 51. Polit & Govt Pos: Treas, Wash State Young Rep, 57; pres, Kitsap Co Young Rep, 57; chmn, Kitsap Co Rep Cent Comt, 59-61 & 63-64; deleg, Rep Nat Conv, 64; admin asst to US Rep Thomas M Pelly, 65-71; cong liaison officer, Nat Oceanic & Atmospheric Admin, 71- Bus & Prof Pos: Teacher, South Kitsap Schs, 52 & 55-65. Mil Serv: Entered as A/S, Navy, 45, released as CS 3/C, 48. Mem: Am Legion; South Kitsap Active Club; South Kitsap Little League. Honors & Awards: South Kitsap Teacher of the Year, 63-64. Relig: Baptist. Legal Res: Kitsap County WA Mailing Add: 1112 Spotswood Dr Silver Spring MD 20904

ODELL, ROBERT P, JR (R)
Exec Dir, Nat Rep Finance Comt
b Nashua, NH, July 4, 43; m to Judith Fisher Odell; c Dawn Virginia & Robert P, III. Educ: Am Univ, BA, 66. Polit & Govt Pos: Exec dir, Nat Rep Finance Comt, 69- Mailing Add: 2811 Blaine Dr Chevy Chase MD 20015

ODEM, SUE EDNA (R)
Secy, Seventh Dist Rep Party, Tenn
b St Joseph, Tenn, July 3, 16; d William Luther Tidwell & Elizabeth Richardson T; m 1936 to Grady V Odem; c Kay (Mrs Rippy, Jr) & Susan. Educ: Florence Bus Col, Ala. Polit & Govt Pos: Co-chmn, Hardin Co Rep Party, 58-66 & 68-70; co-chmn, Pres Elec Campaign, 60; co-chmn, Sen Campaign, 62; alt deleg, Rep Nat Conv, 64; registr, Hardin Co Elec Comn, 65-66; Women's chmn for Nixon, Seventh Dist, Tenn Rep Party, 68; Women's chmn, Senate Campaign for Bill Brock, 70; secy, Seventh Dist Rep Party, 70-; publicity chmn, Hardin Co Fedn Rep Women's Club, currently. Bus & Prof Pos: News correspondent, Nashville Banner, Nashville, Tenn, 53-; news correspondent, Jackson Sun, Jackson, 58-; assoc ed, Savannah Courier Newspaper, 61-62. Publ: Several feature stories in various newspapers. Mem: Savannah Garden Club; Bridge Club; TVA Women's Club; Savannah Country Club. Relig: Methodist. Mailing Add: 2410 Park St Savannah TN 38372

ODGAARD, JOHN EDMUND (JACK) (R)
b Omaha, Nebr, Dec 4, 41; s Medrick C Odgaard & Hildegarde P Theewen O; m 1966 to Sandra Jean Johannes, c Eric Christopher, Jacqueline Terese, Nathan E & Marc Justin. Educ: Wayne State Col, 60-61; Univ Md, Heidelberg, WGer, 62-63; Univ Nebr, 65-66. Polit & Govt Pos: Admin asst to US Rep Dave Martin, Nebr, 69-74. Bus & Prof Pos: Reporter, Lincoln Eve J, Nebr, 65-66; polit features ed, Columbus Daily Tel, 66-69; dir & treas, Cong Employees Fed Credit Union, 71- Mil Serv: Entered 61, released, 64, after serv in 509th Airborne Inf, 8th Inf Div, Europe, 62-64; Army Commendation Medal; Good Conduct Medal; 8th Inf Div Noncommissioned Officer Acad Distinguished Grad; Parachutist Wings. Mem: Bull Elephants (mem steering comt, 73-); Sigma Delta Chi, Nat & Nebr; Nat & Nebr Press Photographers; Am Legion. Honors & Awards: Freedoms Found George Washington

Honor Medals, 62 & 64; Inland Daily Newspaper Asn First Pl Photo Series; Nebr Press Photographers Awards. Relig: Roman Catholic. Mailing Add: 1671 23rd Ave Columbus NE 68601

ODIERNA, ERNEST CARTER (D)
b New York, NY, Feb 22, 37; s Ernest Odierna & Gwendolyn Pollachek O; m 1961 to Camille Potenza; c Lisa Ann & Steven Jay. Educ: City Col New York, BS, 60; Baruch Col, MBA, 66. Polit & Govt Pos: Vchmn, Bronx Comt for Dem Voters, 70-74, chmn, 74-; state bd mem, NY Am for Dem Action, 71-; deleg, Dem Nat Conv, 72; admin vchmn, NY New Dem Coalition, 72-74. Bus & Prof Pos: Partner, Harvey J Krasner Assocs, Inc, Great Neck, NY, 66- Mem: Eng Rep Asn; Radio TV Square Club; City Col New York Alumni Asn. Relig: Ethical Culture. Mailing Add: 2430 Morgan Ave New York NY 10469

O'DOHERTY, KIERAN (CONSERVATIVE, NY)
State VChmn, Conservative Party, NY
b New York, NY, Aug 8, 26; s Edward O'Doherty & Mary Kirk O; married. Educ: City Col New York, AB, 50; Columbia Law Sch, LLB, 53; Phi Beta Kappa; Phi Alpha Delta. Polit & Govt Pos: Pres, City Col Young Rep Asn, NY, 49-50; exec mem, Queens Co Comt for Taft, 52; pres, Queens Co Young Rep Asn, 53-55; mem, Queens Co Rep Comt, 53-56; Conservative Party cand for US Sen, 62; Conservative Party cand for US Rep, 17th Cong Dist, 64; co-founder & first state chmn, Conservative Party, NY, 62, chmn, Nat Affairs Comt & mem, State Exec Comt, state vchmn, currently; mem, Adv Assembly, Am Conservative Union, 65-; Conservative Party Campaign Chmn, Wm F Buckley, Jr for Mayor, New York, 65; cand for Lt Gov, NY, 66; consult to US Secy Com, 71-72; comnr, US Foreign Claims Settlement Comn, 72-74; comnr, US Postal Rate Comn, 75- Bus & Prof Pos: Mgr, Stagshead Restaurant, Inc, 53-55; assoc, William G Mulligan, Esq, 55-57; assoc, Royall, Koegel & Rogers, 57-65; attorney-at-law, New York & Long Island, 65-71. Mil Serv: Entered as Pvt, Army, 44, released as Technician 5th Grade, 46, after serv in 4th Armored Div, ETO, 45-46. Publ: The Buckley campaign, Nat Rev Mag, 10/65. Mem: NY State Bar Asn; Cath War Vets; Comt for Monroe Doctrine; Comt on One Million Against Admission of Communist China to UN; Nat Adv Bd, Young Am for Freedom. Honors & Awards: Frequent panelist & debater, including many TV & radio appearances in New York. Relig: Roman Catholic. Legal Res: East Point Lane Hampton Bays NY 11946 Mailing Add: 360 First Ave New York NY 10010

ODOM, MARY HORNE (D)
NC State Sen
b Greenville, NC, Jan 29, 21; d John L Horne & Mamie Bagwell H; m 1943 to Leggette W Odom, Jr; c Leggette W, III, John H & J Phillip. Educ: ECarolina Teachers Col, AB; grad study, Univ NC, Chapel Hill & NC State Sen, 75- Bus & Prof Pos: Teacher, Scotland Co, NC, 22 years; co newspaper employee, The Laurinburg Exchange, 4 years; coordr of indust coop training, Scotland High Sch, Laurinburg, NC. Mem: Bus & Prof Women's Club; Nat Educ Asn; NC Asn of Educators; Lambda Chap, Delta Kappa Gamma; League of Women Voters. Honors & Awards: Named Tar Heel of the Week, News & Observer, 71; Named Woman of the Year, Lumberton BPW, 71. Relig: Presbyterian. Mailing Add: Box 7 Wagram NC 28396

O'DONNELL, ALLEN (D)
Chmn, Wayne Co Dem Comt, Nebr
b Brooklyn, NY, June 10, 31; s Lester O'Donnell & Isabel Creene O; m 1954 to Ann; c Kathleen Marie, Erin Maureen, Shannon Mary, Robin Andre & Kelly Marisa. Educ: Univ Southern Calif, MA, 68; Southern Ill Univ. Polit & Govt Pos: Chmn, Cape Girardeau Co New Dem Coalition, Mo, 70-71; vchmn, Mo New Dem Coalition, 71; chmn, Wayne Co Dem Comt, Nebr, 74-; chmn, First Cong Dist Dem Comt, 74-; mem exec comt, Nebr Dem Cent Comt, 74-; deleg, Dem Nat Mid-Term Conf, 74. Bus & Prof Pos: Instr polit sci, Southeast Mo State Univ, 68-71; assoc prof polit sci, Wayne State Col, Nebr, 71-, dir progs, Wayne Inst Pub Affairs, 75- Mil Serv: Entered as Pvt, Air Force, 48, released as Sr M/Sgt, after serv in Strategic Air Command, Europe, Far East & United Kingdom Theatres; Humane Action Medal. Mem: Nebr & Am Polit Sci Asns; Nebr Asn Ment Health (pres-elect, region IV); Lions Int. Honors & Awards: Gold Plaque for Serv, Cape Girardeau New Dem Coalition, 72; Student Senate Serv, Student Senate Wayne State Col, 73; Excellence in Teaching, Cardinal Blue, Wayne State Col, 74; Excellence in Teaching, Wayne State Found, Wayne State Col, 75. Relig: Roman Catholic. Mailing Add: 802 Lincoln Wayne NE 68787

O'DONNELL, DOROTHY S (D)
Mem, Dem Nat Comt, Mass
Mailing Add: 1 Archibald Circle Harwich MA 02671

O'DONNELL, HENRY JOSEPH, III (D)
Mass State Rep
b Lynn, Mass, Mar 13, 40; s Henry Joseph O'Donnell, Jr (deceased) & Dorothy V Dunn O; single. Educ: Salem State Col, BS, 62; Tufts Univ, MA, 63; Gen Elec fel, Boston Univ, 65; Harvard Univ, 66-67; State Univ NY Buffalo, EdM, 68-70; Kappa Delta Phi. Polit & Govt Pos: Mass State Rep, 70- Bus & Prof Pos: Teacher, Salem & Peabody Pub Sch Systs, Mass, 62-63; dir guid, Great Barrington, Mass, 63-65; state dir, Vt Neighborhood Youth Corps, 65-67; Pupil Personnel Serv, Vt State Dept Educ, 65-70; Nat Teachers Corps Prog, 66-68. Mem: Am Personnel & Guid Asn; Mass Legislators Asn; Common Cause; Asn Counr Educ & Supvr; Am Sch Counr Asn. Honors & Awards: Outstanding Young Men of Am, US CofC, 67; US Off Educ Research Asst grant; Nat Sci Found grant. Relig: Catholic. Mailing Add: 82 Washington Sq Salem MA 01970

O'DONNELL, JENNIFER MILDRED (R)
b Providence, RI, Mar 5, 49; d Joseph Henry O'Donnell, Jr & Yolande Cavedon O; single. Educ: Col Misericordia, BA, 71; Univ Conn, MA in Theatre Arts, 73; Glee Club; Lit Club; Educ Club. Polit & Govt Pos: Pres, TAR, North Smithfield, RI, 65-67; secy, State of RI TAR Fedn, 66-67; alt deleg, Rep Nat Conv, 72. Bus & Prof Pos: Receptionist-secy, George Cardono & Assocs Advert, Providence, RI, summer 69 & 70; instr music, speech & theatre, Mitchell Col, New London, Conn, 71- Mem: Nat Coun Teachers of Eng; Alumni Asn of Col Misericordia (dist chmn, 72 & 73); Univ Conn Alumni Asn; NSmithfield Rep Womens Club. Honors & Awards: Semifinalist, Budweiser Nat Folk Competition, 70. Relig: Catholic. Legal Res: 11 Getchell St North Smithfield RI 02895 Mailing Add: 717 Montauk Ave New London CT 06320

O'DONNELL, JOSEPH H, JR (R)
Mem Exec Comt, Rep State Cent Comt RI
b North Smithfield, RI, May 22, 25; s Joseph H O'Donnell, Sr & Anna McCarthy O; m to Yolande Cavedon; c Sharon, Diane, Jennifer, Ellen, Christopher & John. Educ: Providence Col; Maine Maritime Acad, grad. Polit & Govt Pos: Mem, North Smithfield Sch Comt, RI, 56-62; State Dir of Admin, 63-66; Lt Gov, RI, 66-68; mem exec comt, Rep State Cent Comt RI, 69-; former chmn, North Smithfield Rep Town Comt, mem, currently; mem, North Smithfield Town Budget Comt, 70-71. Bus & Prof Pos: Treas, Keough-Kirby Assocs, Inc, 63-; asst treas, Woonsocket Color & Chem Co; mem of corp, Hickory Color & Chem Co; dir, Woonsocket CofC, 71- Mil Serv: Merchant Marines. Mem: North Smithfield Asn Ins Agents (pres & dir, 70-72); RI Asn Ins Agents (comt on legis, 68-71); Nat Found Infantile Paralysis (chmn, Providence Chap); corp mem Woonsocket & Mercy Hosps; Mil Order of Officers of Foreign Wars. Relig: Catholic. Mailing Add: 11 Getchell St North Smithfield RI 02895

O'DONNELL, KATHLEEN (D)
Nat Committeewoman, Mass Young Dem
b Brockton, Mass, June 14, 49; d Charles Henry O'Donnell & Mary Haddad O; single. Educ: Univ Mass, Amherst, BA, 71; Am Univ, 71-72; Northeastern Univ, 72-73; Pi Sigma Alpha. Polit & Govt Pos: Vchmn, Hampshire Co New Voters Comt, Mass, 70-71; co-dir, Young Dem Register to Vote Comt, Mass Dem State Comt, 71; student coordr, Campaign US Sen Edward Kennedy, 70; secy, Col Young Dem Am, 71-72; nat committeewoman, Mass Young Dem, 72-; chairwoman, South Shore Woman's Polit Caucus, 72-; mem exec bd, Region I, Young Dem Am, 73-; Young Dem rep, Dem Action Comt, 73-; city coordr, Dukakis for Gov, Mass, currently; campaign mgr, Paul Harold for Quincy City Coun, currently; co-chairwoman, Quincy, Mayor's Comn on the Status Women, 74- Bus & Prof Pos: Teacher, Social Studies Dept, Quincy Pub Schs, Mass, 72- Mem: Nat Woman's Polit Caucus; Mass Woman's Polit Caucus (exec bd); Ward Two Civic Asn; Univ Mass Alumni Asn. Honors & Awards: Citation for serv & orgn work, Young Dem Am, 73. Relig: Catholic. Mailing Add: 26 Massachusetts Ave Quincy MA 02169

O'DONNELL, PATRICK EMMETT (R)
b New York, NY, Mar 17, 37; s Emmett O'Donnell & Lorraine Aintoinette O; m 1968 to Janet Eve Mottershead; c Patrick Justin & Hollace Tobin. Educ: Georgetown Univ, BA, 59; Am Univ Col Law, LLB, 62; Phi Alpha Delta. Polit & Govt Pos: Asst corp counsel, DC Govt, 63-69; legal asst to chmn, Fed Commun Comn, 69-71; staff asst to President, 71-73; Dep Asst Attorney Gen, US Dept Justice, 73; spec asst to President for Legis Affairs, 73- Mem: Am Bar Asn; DC Bar. Relig: Catholic. Legal Res: 4719 Butterworth Pl NW Washington DC 20016 Mailing Add: Spec Asst to President The White House Washington DC 20500

O'DONNELL, PETER, JR (R)
b Dallas, Tex, Apr 21, 24; s Peter O'Donnell & Annette Campbell O; m 1952 to Edith Jones; c Ann, Carol & Ruth. Educ: Univ of the South, BS, 47; Wharton Grad Div, Univ Pa, MBA; Phi Beta Kappa; Phi Delta Theta. Polit & Govt Pos: Mem, Task Force on Fed Fiscal & Monetary Policy, Rep Nat Comt, mem exec comt, Rep Nat Finance Comt, 64-70, Rep Nat Committeeman, Tex, 70-72; Rep chmn, Precinct 143, Dallas, 56-69; chmn, Dallas Co Rep Party, 59-70; chmn, Tex Rep Party, 62-70; chmn, Southern Asn Rep State Chmn, 65-70; deleg, Rep Nat Conv, 68. Mil Serv: Entered as Seaman, Naval Res, 43, released as Lt(jg), 46. Mem: Dallas Asn of Investment Analysts; Univ of the South (trustee); Univ Dallas & Grad Research Ctr (adv trustee); Southern Methodist Univ Found for Bus & Econ (trustee). Relig: Episcopal. Legal Res: 4300 St John's Dr Dallas TX 75205 Mailing Add: 4275 First Nat Bank Bldg Dallas TX 75202

O'DONNELL, ROBERT W (D)
Pa State Rep
Mailing Add: Capitol Bldg Harrisburg PA 17120

O'DONNELL, WILLIAM (D)
NMex State Rep
Mailing Add: 190 Townsend Terr Las Cruces NM 88001

O'DONNELL, WILLIAM JAMES, JR (D)
b Sandpoint, Idaho, June 2, 31; s William James O'Donnell, Sr & Edna M Keiser O; m 1952 to Lesley Marleen Mooney; c Alan D Kohal, Jacalyn Ann (Mrs Shaver) & Billie D (Mrs Alderman). Educ: Sandpoint High Sch, Idaho. Polit & Govt Pos: Precinct committeeman, Bonner Co Dem Cent Comt, Idaho, 68, chmn, 70-74. Mem: Int Woodworkers of Am Local 3-10; Elks. Relig: Methodist. Mailing Add: Box 36 Dover ID 83825

O'DONNELL, WILLIAM JOSEPH (D)
Assoc Judge, Md Court of Appeals
b Baltimore, Md, June 2, 16; s Joseph F O'Donnell & Mary K McCormick O (both deceased); m 1947 to Nancy Teresa Daniels; c Nancy (Mrs Burke), Kathleen (Mrs Weiss), Maureen, William D, Eileen & Dennis. Educ: Loyola Col(Md), AB cum laude, 37; Univ Md Sch Law, LLB with honors, Order of the Coif; Hist Acad; Bellarmine Debating Soc. Polit & Govt Pos: Law clerk to chief judge, Supreme Bench of Baltimore, Md, 37-41; gen counsel's off, Bd Econ Warfare, 41-42; asst states attorney, Md, 46-50; asst city solicitor, Baltimore, 50-51; state's attorney, Md, 62-64; assoc judge, Supreme Bench of Baltimore, 64-74; assoc judge, Md Court of Appeals, 74- Bus & Prof Pos: Enforcement attorney & spec asst to US Attorney, Off Price Stabilization, Baltimore, 51-52; attorney & counr at law, pvt practice, Baltimore, 52-62; instr criminal law, Univ Baltimore Law Sch, 58-74. Mil Serv: Entered as Ens, Naval Res, 42, released as Lt, 45, after serv in Naval Intel & Defense Counsel to Secy Navy Gen Court Martial, 44-45; Lt Comdr(Ret), Naval Res, 53; Atlantic Theatre & Victory Medals. Publ: Auth, Power of the state to impose medical treatment, Arch Environ Health & Md State Med J, 65-66; Criminal law & rules of criminal procedure in Maryland, Syllabus for Law Sch Use, 66; Search & seizure decisions as a result of Mapp v Ohio, Md Judicial Conf, 66. Mem: Loyola Col Alumni Asn; Barristers' Club of Baltimore; Friendly Sons of St Patrick; Am Legion; Am Bar Asn. Honors & Awards: Prize for Highest Standing in Corp Law, Univ Md Sch Law, 39; Award, Loyola Col Alumni Asn, 63; Rev Joseph M Kelly SJ Medal for Distinguished Serv as Alumnus, Loyola High Sch, 71. Relig: Roman Catholic. Legal Res: 219 Upnor Rd Baltimore MD 21212 Mailing Add: 620 Court House Baltimore MD 21202

O'DONNOHUE, DONNA STARR (D)
b Michigan City, Ind, Apr 25, 49; d David O'Donnohue, Jr & Dolores Kapica D; single. Educ: Univ London, 69; Mich State Univ, BA, 72; Univ Notre Dame, MA, 75. Polit & Govt Pos: Mem, Berrien Co Dem Exec Bd, 72-, chmn, 73; mem, Dem State Cent Comt, 73-; mem, Dem Women's Caucus, 73-; deleg, Dem Nat Mid-Term Conf, 74; co-chairperson Mich deleg, Women's Camp Conf, Washington, DC, 74; legis coordr to mayor, Benton Harbor, 73-74; Asst Secy of State, 74- Mem: Mich State Univ Alumni Club, Berrien Co (pres); Am Civil Liberties Union; NAACP; Am Asn Univ Women/NOW. Relig: Catholic. Legal Res: 13645 Red Arrow Hwy Harbert MI 49115 Mailing Add: Dept of State Lansing MI 48918

OEHMIG, DAN **(R)**
Tenn State Sen
Mailing Add: Tenth Sen Dist 909 Am Nat Bank Bldg Chattanooga TN 37402

OFFICER, ALBERT FITZPATRICK, JR (PAT) **(D)**
Chmn, Overton Co Dem Party, Tenn
b Livingston, Tenn, Mar 12, 34; s Albert Fitzpatrick Officer & Leliabel Dale O; m 1956 to Curtis Marie Dodson; c Albert Fitzpatrick, III, David Curtis, Michael Dale & Jane Ann. Educ: Tenn Technol Univ, BS, 56; Vanderbilt Univ, LLB, 61; Delta Theta Phi. Polit & Govt Pos: Asst dist attorney gen, Fifth Judicial Circuit, Tenn, 62-; Overton Co chmn for Lyndon B Johnson for President, 64; chmn, Overton Co Dem Party, 66-; chmn, Hubert H Humphrey for President Comt, Livingston, 68. Mil Serv: Entered as Pfc, Army, 56, released as Specialist 4, 58, after serv in Hq Detachment Med Training Ctr, Ft Sam Houston, Tex, 56-58. Mem: Am & Tenn Trial Lawyers Asns; Tenn Bar Asn; Nat Dist Attorney Asn; Am Judicature Soc. Relig: Disciples of Christ. Mailing Add: Officer Bldg SE Corner Pub Sq Livingston TN 38570

OFFICER, GEORGE B, JR **(R)**
Chmn, Third Dist Rep Party, NDak
b Ryder, NDak, Feb 5, 20; s G Blaine Officer & Petra Opheim O; m 1941 to Dorothy Burtness; c Michael & Rodney. Educ: High sch, grad, 37. Polit & Govt Pos: Chmn, Third Dist Rep Party, NDak, 74- Mem: Elks; NDak Farm Bur. Relig: Lutheran. Mailing Add: Box 267 Ryder ND 58779

OFFNER, PAUL **(D)**
Wis State Assemblyman
b Bennington, Vt, Aug 7, 42; s Richard Offner & Philippa Gerry O; single. Educ: Amherst Col, BA, 64; Princeton Univ, PhD, 70. Polit & Govt Pos: Legis asst to Sen Mondale, Washington, DC, 71; legis asst to Sen Nelson, 72; alt deleg, Dem Nat Mid-Term Conf, 74; Wis State Assemblyman, 75- Mem: Eagles; Farmers Union; Jaycees. Mailing Add: 1803 King St La Crosse WI 54601

OFFUTT, DAVID ALLEN **(R)**
b Independence, Mo, Jan 29, 40; s R S S Offutt & Iris Wood O; m 1963 to Laetitia A Warren; c Michael David. Educ: Univ Notre Dame, BA, 61; Boalt Hall Law Sch, Univ Calif, JD, 64. Polit & Govt Pos: Yuba Co chmn, Reagan for Gov, Calif, 66; chmn, Yuba Co Rep Cent Comt, formerly; gen chmn, Shumway for Cong, 68. Bus & Prof Pos: Chmn, Orgn & Exten Comt, Boy Scouts-Butte Area Coun, 67; assoc ed, Calif Trial Lawyers, 68-69. Mem: Calif & Am Trial Lawyers Asns; Yuba-Sutter & Am Bar Asns; Yuba-Sutter Tuberc Soc. Relig: Catholic. Mailing Add: PO Box 286 Marysville CA 95901

OGDAHL, HARMON T **(CONSERVATIVE)**
Minn State Sen
b Minneapolis, Minn, 1917; married; c Five. Educ: Univ Minn; Hamline Univ. Polit & Govt Pos: Alderman, Minneapolis, Minn, 13th Ward, 59-62; Minn State Sen, 62- Bus & Prof Pos: Vpres, First Fed Savings & Loan, currently. Mil Serv: Army, 42-46, Pac Theatre. Mailing Add: 5026 Morgan Ave S Minneapolis MN 55419

OGDEN, BARBARA LYNN **(R)**
Mem, WVa State Exec Comt
b Wallace, WVa, Oct 27, 38; d Lynn Ogden & Mildred Robinson O; single. Educ: Fairmont State Col, AB in Educ, 60; WVa Univ; Panhellenic; Young Rep; Wesleyan Found; Delta Zeta; Home Econ Club; FuSeFa Secretarial Club. Polit & Govt Pos: Vpres, Young Rep of WVa, 67-71, nat committeewoman, 71-74; mem bd dirs, Rep Youth Camp, 68-; mem, WVa State Exec Comt, 13th Sen Dist, 68-; mem, Gov Hwy Safety Comn, 69- Mem: Altrusa Club Clarksburg (corresponding secy). Relig: Protestant. Mailing Add: Apt 3 601 Collins Ave Clarksburg WV 26301

OGDEN, CARL **(D)**
Fla State Rep
b Jacksonville, Fla, Aug 27, 29; s Garrett Franklin Ogden & Catherine Cante O; m 1957 to Dorothy Christian Shook; c Bradley John & Gregory Carl. Educ: Jacksonville Univ, 2 years. Polit & Govt Pos: Fla State Rep, 68-, Majority Leader, Fla House Rep, formerly. Bus & Prof Pos: Pres, Carl Ogden Agency Inc, Jacksonville, Fla, 62- Mil Serv: Entered as Pvt, Air Force, 47, released as S/Sgt, 51, after serv in Alaskan Air Command, Korean Conflict. Mem: Mason; Optimist Int; Southville Businessmen's Club; Comt of 100; CofC. Honors & Awards: Outstanding Mem Award, Duval Deleg, 71; Outstanding Legislator Award, State Asn Opticians; Good Govt Award, Jacksonville Jaycees, 72. Relig: Presbyterian. Legal Res: 1107 Lido Rd Jacksonville FL 32216 Mailing Add: 4329 University Blvd S Jacksonville FL 32216

OGDEN, EDWIN BENNETT, JR **(R)**
Chmn, Adams Co Rep Party, Miss
b Chattanooga, Tenn, Aug 26, 04; s Edwin Bennett Ogden & Mary Curlett Broderick O; m 1936 to Nancy Hamilton Allen; c Nancy (Mrs Paul R Rogers), Mary (Mrs Martin Ratcliffe), Anne Louisa Wilkinson & Ellen Allen. Educ: Cathedral High Sch, Natchez, Miss. Polit & Govt Pos: Deleg, Rep Nat Conv, 68; mem, Adams Co Elec Comn, Miss, 69-72; chmn, Adams Co Rep Party, Miss, 69-70, finance chmn, 71-72, chmn, 72-; mem, La-Miss Regional Export Expansion Coun, Dept of Com, 69-; mem exec comt, Miss Rep Party, 72- Bus & Prof Pos: Civilian forage master, US Army Remount Depot, Camp Lee, Va, 19-20; partner, Ogden & Co, Havana, Cuba, 22-60, partner, Natchez, Miss, 60- Mil Serv: 2nd Lt, Army Res, 31-36. Mem: Am Club; Biltmore Forest Country Club; Boston Club; Miss Feed & Grain Asn; Natchez-Adams Co CofC. Relig: Catholic. Legal Res: 309 S Commerce St Natchez MS 39120 Mailing Add: PO Box 1106 Natchez MS 39120

OGDEN, HERBERT G **(R)**
Vt State Sen
Mailing Add: RFD 1 Windsor VT 05089

OGG, JACK CLYDE **(D)**
Tex State Sen
b Kansas City, Mo, Sept 7, 33; s William J Ogg & Mildred Owens O; m 1959 to Constance Sue Harner (Connie); c Kimbra Kathryn & Jon Christopher. Educ: Univ Houston, BS, 57; STex Col Law, LLB, 62; Phi Theta Kappa; Phi Kappa Alpha; Phi Alpha Delta; Inter-Fraternity Coun. Polit & Govt Pos: Tex State Rep, 67-72; Tex State Sen, Houston, 73- Bus & Prof Pos: Attorney-at-law, 62- Mem: Phi Alpha Delta Legal Fraternity Alumni Asn; Tex Bar Asn; Jr CofC; Univ Houston & STex Col Law Alumni Asn; Pi Kappa Alpha Alumni Asn. Honors & Awards: Outstanding Alumnus of Phi Alpha Delta Legal Fraternity, 68; Outstanding Alumnus of STex Col Law, 68; Outstanding Young Houstonian, 68; One of Five Outstanding Alumni of Pi Kappa Alpha Fraternity, One of Five Outstanding Young Texans, 69. Relig: Episcopal. Mailing Add: 761 Kuhlman Houston TX 77024

OGILVIE, OSCAR PHILLIPS **(D)**
Chmn, Red River Parish Dem Exec Comt, La
b Shreveport, La, Nov 5, 98; s Oscar Phillips Ogilvie & Anna Harper O; m 1922 to Sarah Elizabeth Brown; c Betty Jean (Mrs Fear, Jr). Polit & Govt Pos: Mem, Coushatta Town Coun, La, 28-32; mem, Red River Parish Dem Exec Comt, 32-, chmn, 36-; mayor, Coushatta, 40-46. Mem: Mason; Lions; Farm Bur. Relig: Methodist. Mailing Add: Box 383 Coushatta LA 71019

OGILVIE, RICHARD BUELL **(R)**
b Kansas City, Mo, Feb 22, 23; s Kenneth S Ogilvie & Edna Mae Buell O; m 1950 to Dorothy Louise Shriver; c Elizabeth. Educ: Yale Univ, BA, 47; Chicago Kent Col Law, LLB, 49; Beta Theta Pi; Phi Alpha Delta. Polit & Govt Pos: Chmn, Young Rep Orgn, Cook Co, Ill, 54; Asst US Attorney, Chicago, 54-55; spec asst to US Attorney Gen, 58-60; sheriff, Cook Co, Ill, 62-66; pres, Bd Comnrs, Cook Co, 66-69; deleg, Rep Nat Conv, 68; Gov, Ill, 69-73; deleg & chmn deleg, Rep Nat Conv, 72. Bus & Prof Pos: Partner law firm, Lord, Bissell & Brook, 50-58; Stevenson, Conaghan, Hackbert, Rooks & Pitts, 60-62; partner, Isham Lincoln & Beale, 73- Mil Serv: Entered as Pvt, Army, 42, released as Sgt, 45, after serv in 781st Tank Bn, ETO, 44-45; Purple Heart; ETO Ribbons. Mem: Am, Fed, Ill State & Chicago Bar Asns; Soc Trial Lawyers. Relig: Presbyterian. Mailing Add: 1500 Lake Shore Dr Chicago IL 60610

OGLE, ALICE NICHOLS **(R)**
Mem, Rep State Cent Comt Calif
b Azusa, Calif, Aug 6, 25; d Charles Leslie Nichols & Mary Murphy N; m 1948 to Robert Eugene Ogle; c Mary, Janet, John, Nancy, Vernon & Bobby. Educ: Occidental Col, BA, 48; Zeta Tau Zeta. Polit & Govt Pos: Chmn, 43rd Assembly Dist Rep Precinct Orgn, Calif, 66-71; vchmn steering comt, Los Angeles Co United Rep Precinct Orgn, 67-71; alt mem, Los Angeles Co Rep Cent Comt, 67-71, mem, 71-73, 75- mem, Rep State Cent Comt Calif, 67-, mem exec comt, 75-, state precinct co-chmn, 75-; regional co-chmn, Gov Reagan Reelec Comt, Los Angeles Co, 70; mem, Burbank City Charter Revision Study Comt, 70; mem, Inaugural Comt, Gov, Calif, 71; alt deleg, Rep Nat Conv, 72. Bus & Prof Pos: Teacher, Glendale Unified Sch Dist, 48; substitute teacher, Los Angeles City Schs, 70; secy & legal aide, LaFollette, Johnson, Horgan & Robinson, Los Angeles, 71- Mem: Nat Fedn Rep Women, Burbank; Los Angeles World Affairs Coun; La Providencia Guild of Children's Hosp; Town Hall of Calif. Honors & Awards: Calif Rep State Cent Comt Precinct Leadership Award, 68; Los Angeles Co Rep Cent Comt Nella Mae Howard Award for Outstanding Precinct Leadership, 71. Relig: Methodist. Mailing Add: 720 S Bel Aire Dr Burbank CA 91501

OGLE, ELLEN KNIGHT **(R)**
b Chicago, Ill, May 27, 03; d James Seaton Knight & Alma Matilda Fredrika Peterson K; m 1930 to Arthur Hook Ogle; c Jamie (Mrs Allen Osborne Shafer) & Carolyn (Mrs Norman Bluhm). Educ: Univ Wis, BA, 24; Art Inst Chicago, 25-27; Cleveland Art Inst, 44 & 45; Alpha Phi. Polit & Govt Pos: Rep precinct committeewoman, Broward Co, Fla, 63-70, dist leader of eight precincts, 70; finance chmn, Broward Co Rep Party, 65; mem, Fla Art Comn, 67-69; alt deleg, Rep Nat Conv, 68, deleg, 72; Women for Ruth Eckerd, Jack Eckerd Campaign, Broward Co, Fla, 70. Mem: Nat Bd Sponsors, Inst Am Strategy. Relig: Congregational. Mailing Add: 510 Lido Dr Ft Lauderdale FL 33301

OGLESBY, CATHERINE ELIZABETH **(R)**
b Liberal, Kans, Jan 27, 53; d Jamie White Oglesby & Delpha Elizabeth Folmer O; single. Educ: Univ Ga, grad, 75; Mortar Bd; Z-Club; Phi Mu; Univ Union; vpres, Panhellenic Coun; minister to alumni rels, Student Govt Asn. Polit & Govt Pos: Secy, Ga TAR, 67; secy, Univ Ga Young Rep, 71-72; alt deleg, Rep Nat Conv, 72. Mem: League Women Voters. Honors & Awards: Finalist in Miss Greek Week & Miss Homecoming, Univ Ga, 73. Relig: Presbyterian. Legal Res: 119 Parkway Dr Thomasville GA 31792 Mailing Add: PO Box 675 Thomasville GA 31792

OGONOWSKI, CASMER P **(D)**
Mich State Rep
Mailing Add: 16350 W Chicago Detroit MI 48228

O'GORMAN, FRANCIS EDMUND **(R)**
b New York, NY, July 18, 19; s John J O'Gorman & Elizabeth Sheehan O; m 1949 to Elizabeth McClelland; c Jean Mary, Kathleen, Christine; Francis E, Jr, Borbara Ann, Susan & Anne Elizabeth. Educ: Cath Univ Am, BA, 39; Fordham Univ Grad Sch English. Polit & Govt Pos: US Probation Officer, Mid Dist, Pa, 57-62; admin asst to US Rep Joseph McDade, Pa, 63- Bus & Prof Pos: Grammar sch teacher, St Bernard's Sch, New York, 39-40, high sch teacher, 40-41; high sch teacher, Barnard Sch for Boys, 46-49; instr Eng, Marywood Col, 49-57; instr Eng, Univ Scranton, 52-57. Mil Serv: Entered as Pvt, Army Air Force, 41, released as Capt, 46, after serv in 8th Air Force, Eng, 1st Air Div, ETO, 42-45; Lt Col, Air Force Res, inactive; Unit Citation; ETO Ribbon with Six Battle Stars; Am Theatre Ribbon; Victory Medal. Publ: Moon of the Devil (short story), 47; The Day of the Bomb, Sign Mag, 48; The Wheat, 53. Mem: Cath War Vet; Rotary; hon mem Lions Club, Carbondale, Pa; hon life mem TAR, Pa. Honors & Awards: Second Pl Award, Nat Short Story Contest for The Wheat, 53. Relig: Roman Catholic. Legal Res: 929 Grandview St Scranton PA 18509 Mailing Add: Off of Hon Joseph M McDade House of Rep Washington DC 20515

O'GRADY, EUGENE P **(D)**
Exec Dir, Ohio Dem State Exec Comt
b Cleveland, Ohio, July 18, 20; s Michael J O'Grady & Anne Sweeney O; m 1948 to Patricia Feller; c Michael P, Thomas J, Francis P, Mary Elizabeth, Mary Jude, Mary Anne, Richard K, Mary Catherine, Mary Rita, Mary Therese, Mary Christine & John E. Educ: John Carroll Univ, AB, 49; Cleveland Marshall Law Sch, 48-52. Polit & Govt Pos: Court bailiff & secy, Judge Donald F Lybarger, Common Pleas Bench & united appeal campaign mgr, Common Pleas Court, Cuyahoga Co, Ohio, 50-62; mem, Cuyahoga Co Dem Exec Comt, 17 years; chmn, Paul F Ward for Attorney Gen, 54; chmn, Suburban Elec Comt, 55; hq mgr, Bartunek for Mayor Campaign, 55; chmn, Young Dem for DiSalle for Gov, 58; past pres, Cuyahoga Co Young Dem; co-chmn, Young Dem for Kennedy; former state dir, US Savings Bonds Div & US Treas Dept; asst dir, Ohio State Dept Com, 62, dir, 62-63; vchmn, State Water Pollution Bd; gov rep, Interstate Oil Compact Comn & mem exec comt; mem, Ohio State Civil War Centennial Comn, 62-63; pub rels staff mem, Burr Commun Agency, Toledo-Cleveland, 63-; field dir, Elec of Int Pres of USW, I W Abel, 64-65; field dir, reelec campaigns of US Sen

Stephen M Young, Ohio, primary & gen elec, 64; field dir, defeat of Issue No 3-the 1964 lame duck session-apportionment plan adopted by the Rhodes Admin as part of his Four Issues Prog, 65; chmn, Ohio Dem Party, 68-72; exec dir, Ohio Dem State Exec Comt, currently. Bus & Prof Pos: Ins claims adjustor, Aetna Casualty & Surety Co, Ohio, 48-50. Mil Serv: Army Air Corps, 42-45, S/Sgt, with serv as Crew Chief, Athletic Dir, Tech Writer & Instr. Mem: John Carroll Alumni Asn; Hibernians; Holy Name Soc. Relig: Roman Catholic. Mailing Add: 1294 Bronwyn Ave Columbus OH 43204

O'HALLORAN, MARY (D)
Iowa State Rep
Mailing Add: 1939 College Cedar Falls IA 50613

O'HARA, JAMES GRANT (D)
US Rep, Mich
b Washington, DC, Nov 8, 25; s Raphael McNulty O'Hara & Neta Lloyd Hemphill O; m 1953 to Susan Puskas; c Ray, Thomas, Patrick, Brendan, Mary, Brigid & Neal. Educ: Univ Mich, AB, 54, LLB, 55. Polit & Govt Pos: US Rep, Mich, 59-; deleg, Dem Nat Conv, 60 & 68, chmn comt on rules & parliamentarian, 72; chmn, Dem Study Group, 67-68; chmn rules comn, Dem Nat Comt, 69-72; ex officio deleg, Dem Nat Mid-Term Conf, 74. Mil Serv: Army, 43, released as Sgt, 46, after serv in 11th Airborne Div, Pac Theater, 44-45. Mem: KofC; DAV; Am Legion; VFW; Amvets. Relig: Roman Catholic. Legal Res: 45306 Cass Ave Utica MI 48087 Mailing Add: 2241 Rayburn House Off Bldg Washington DC 20515

OHM, WILMA JEAN (D)
Pres, SDak Fedn Dem Women
b Lac qui Parle, Minn, July 4, 28; d J Earl Ruby & Myrtle Stone R; m 1947 to Albert A Ohm; c Albert Randall & Kevin Jay. Educ: High sch, Marietta, Minn. Polit & Govt Pos: Pres, SDak State Collectors Asn, 68-70, Beadle Co Women's Fedn, 68-69 & SDak Fedn Dem Women, 68-; mem exec bd, SDak Dem Party, 68-; mem, SDak State Fair Bd, 70-; pres, NCent Region, Nat Fedn Dem Women, 72-; regional chmn, SDak Dem Cent Comt, 74- Bus & Prof Pos: Tax collector, Beadle Co, SDak, 60-63; mgr, Huron Collection Agency, 63- Mem: Am Collectors Asn (dir, 70-); Huron Federated Bus & Prof Women (legis chmn, 70-72); Am Legion Auxiliary. Relig: Lutheran. Mailing Add: 679 First SW Huron SD 57350

OHMSTEDE, BRYCE ALTON (D)
b Guide Rock, Nebr, Jan 30, 24; s Gerhard Ohmstede & Louise Massinger O; m 1945 to Frances Woodside; c James Alton, Kenneth Paul & David Charles. Polit & Govt Pos: Alt deleg, Dem Nat Conv, 72; mem, Judicial Nominating Comn, Dist 10, Nebr, 73- Bus & Prof Pos: Farmer, Guide Rock, Nebr, 40- Mem: AF&AM; Scottish Rite, Hastings Consistory; Tehama Temple, Shrine; Webster Co Farmers Orgn. Relig: Unitarian. Mailing Add: Rte 1 Box 75 Guide Rock NE 68942

OHMSTEDE, FRANCES ELIZABETH (D)
Dem Nat Committeewoman, Nebr
b Formoso, Kans, Aug 15, 26; d Johnnie Charles Woodside & Wilma Evelyn Bottorf W; m 1945 to Bryce Alton Ohmstede; c James Alton, Kenneth Paul & David Charles. Polit & Govt Pos: Mem cent comt, Nebr State Dem Party, 66-72, mem exec comt, 70-72; Dem Nat Committeewoman, 72- Bus & Prof Pos: Teacher, Webster Co Rural Sch, Nebr, 43-45; farmer, Guide Rock, 45-75; bookkeeper, Guide Rock, 60-68. Publ: Auth, Historical jewels, Nebr Press Asn & Ak-Sar-Ben, 62. Mem: Eastern Star. Honors & Awards: Cent Dist Winner, Know Nebr Better, Nebr Press Asn & Ak-Sar-Ben. Relig: Unitarian. Mailing Add: Rte 1 Box 75 Guide Rock NE 68942

OHRENSTEIN, MANFRED (D)
NY State Sen
b Mannheim, Ger, Aug 5, 25; s Markus Ohrenstein & Fannie Hollander O; m 1957 to Marilyn Bacher; c Nancy Ellen & David Jonathan. Educ: Brooklyn Col, cum laude, 48; Harlan Fiske Stone scholar, Columbia Univ Law Sch, 51; Brooklyn Col Hon Soc. Polit & Govt Pos: Asst dist attorney, New York Co, NY, 54-58; NY State Sen, 61-, minority leader, currently. Bus & Prof Pos: Pvt law practice, 58-61; partner, Karpatkin, Ohrenstein & Karpatkin, 61-75; partner, Stein, Rosen & Ohrenstein, 75- Mem: New York Co Lawyers Asn; Am Civil Liberties Union; NY State Bd Am for Dem Action; NY Shakespeare Festival (mem bd). Relig: Jewish. Mailing Add: 215 W 90th St New York NY 11024

OKADA, HIDEO (D)
Committeeman, Hawaii State Dem Cent Comt
b Waipahu, Hawaii, June 15, 10; s Denjiro Okada & Matsu Imai O; m 1935 to Matsuko Hashinmoto; c Marlene Kikuko (Mrs Hirata), Glenn Kenji & Richard Masahiro. Educ: Mid-Pac Inst High Sch, Honolulu, Hawaii, grad, 32. Polit & Govt Pos: Deleg, Hawaii State Dem Conv, 48-68; vchmn, Oahu Co Dem Party, Hawaii, 64-66; chmn, Waipahu Dem Precinct Club, 66; campaign chmn for Mrs Patsy Young, State of Hawaii Const Conv, 68; committeeman, Hawaii State Dem Cent Comt, 69-; campaign chmn 20th dist for incumbent Gov John A Burns, 70; Dem precinct chmn, 20th Dist, Hawaii, 70- Bus & Prof Pos: Bus agent, ILWU, 50; mem adv coun, Leeward Oahu Community Col, 69. Mem: Waipahu Businessmen's Asn; Waipahu Young Farmers; Waiphau Orchid Soc; Waipahu Baseball Club (pres, 68, dir, 71-72); Waipahu Community Asn (vchmn, 71-72). Relig: Buddhist. Mailing Add: 94-111 Farrington Hwy Waipahu HI 96797

O'KEEFE, DANIEL EDWARD (D)
b Minneapolis, Minn, Dec 5, 52; s Edward O'Keefe (deceased) & Patricia Mitchell O; single. Educ: Vassar Col, 71- Polit & Govt Pos: Mem bd dirs, NY State Young Dem, 69-70; deleg, Nat Youth Caucus Conv, 71; committeeman, Dutchess Co Dem Comt, 71-74; ward chmn, Fifth Ward, Poughkeepsie Town Dem Comt, 71-72; dist researcher, Ralph Nader Study of Cong, 72; alt deleg, Dem Nat Conv, 72; deleg, Dem Nat Mid-Term Conf, 74; mem, Duchess Co Legis Dist IV, Poughkeepsie, 74- Relig: Catholic. Legal Res: 8 MacCracken Lane Poughkeepsie NY 12601 Mailing Add: Vassar Col Poughkeepsie NY 12601

O'KEEFE, JAMES L (D)
Pub Adminr, Cook Co, Ill
b Chicago, Ill, Jan 8, 10; s Raymond T O'Keefe & S Monahan O; m 1934 to Josephine Killian; c James L, Jr, William J & Dennis M. Educ: Northwestern Univ, BA, 31; Chicago-Kent Col of Law, JD, 36; Phi Delta Phi; Law Club; Phi Kappa Sigma. Polit & Govt Pos: Master in Chancery, Circuit Court, Ill, 45-65; deleg, Dem Nat Conv, 48-68, chmn host comt, 52 & 56; pub adminr, Cook Co, Ill, 61- Bus & Prof Pos: Sr partner, O'Keefe, O'Brien, Hanson & Ashenden, 37-; dir, Chessie System, Inc, Daniel Woodhead, Inc, Brinks, Inc & Nat Blvd Bank of Chicago, currently. Mem: Ill & Am Bar Asns; Chicago Club; Mid-Day Club; Metropolitan Club. Relig: Roman Catholic. Legal Res: 1420 N Sheridan Rd Wilmette IL 60091 Mailing Add: 5100 First Nat Plaza Chicago IL 60670

O'KEEFE, JEREMIAH JOSEPH, JR (D)
Miss State Rep
Mailing Add: Drawer O Biloxi MS 39530

O'KEEFE, MICHAEL HANLEY (D)
La State Sen
b New Orleans, La, Dec 1, 31; s Judge Arthur J O'Keefe, Jr & Eleanora Gordon O; m to Jean Ann Van Geffen; c Michael Hanley, Jr & Erin Elizabeth. Educ: Loyola Univ, BA, Sch Law, LLB; Blue Key. Polit & Govt Pos: Chmn, La Comn Interstate Coop; La State Sen, Fifth Dist, 57-, Pres Pro Tem, La State Senate, 72-, chmn coun govt reorgn & goals for La comt, state planning adv comn & gov comt on correctional treatment & rehabilitation, 70-; chmn, Comn Intergovt Rels, Goals for La & Regional Planning Forum; hon vchmn, La Comn on Status Women; mem, Joint Legis Comt Drug Abuse & Narcotics Rehabilitation Adv Coun; bd adv, La Coun Human Rels; found mem, Goals for New Orleans; deleg, Dem Nat Conv, 68. Bus & Prof Pos: Attorney & partner, O'Keefe, O'Keefe & Berrigan, New Orleans, La; mem faculty, Loyola Univ Eve Div, formerly. Mil Serv: Army, 2 years, serv as Asst Provost Marshal, Ft Hood. Mem: Am Bar Asn; Boy Scouts (cub scout master); Total Community Action, Inc (exec comt); Am Arbit Asn-Nat Panel Arbitrators; Coun State Govt. Honors & Awards: Outstanding Young Man of Year Award, Jr CofC, 64. Relig: Roman Catholic. Legal Res: 4 Gull St New Orleans LA 70124 Mailing Add: 813 American Bank Bldg New Orleans LA 70130

O'KEEFE, MICHAEL JOHN (D)
NH State Rep
b Portsmouth, NH, Mar 28, 47; s Jerome J O'Keefe & Mary Casa O; m 1968 to Ann Eileen Billbrough; c Mary Elizabeth, Jennie Kathleen & Michael John, Jr. Educ: Univ NH, BA cum laude, 72; MAT, 73. Polit & Govt Pos: Pres, Univ NH Young Dem, 69-70; chmn educ subcomt, NH Dem Platform Comt, 72; mem exec comt, NH Young Dem, 73-75; NH State Rep, 71-72 & 75- Bus & Prof Pos: Teacher, York High Sch, York, Maine, 72-; community prof, New Hampshire Col, Portsmouth, 74- Mil Serv: Entered as Airman, Air Force, 65, released as Sgt, 69, after serv in Security Serv, Korea & San Antonio, Tex, 66-69; Nat Defense Medal; Outstanding Unit Citation; Good Conduct Medal. Mem: Nat Educ Asn; Maine & York Teacher's Asn; NH Young Dem; Nat Coun for Social Studies. Relig: Roman Catholic. Legal Res: 100 Ledgewood Dr Portsmouth NH 03801 Mailing Add: Apt 9 100 Ledgewood Dr Portsmouth NH 03801

O'KEEFE, PETER J (D)
Pa State Rep
Mailing Add: Capitol Bldg Harrisburg PA 17120

O'KEEFFE, WHITNEY CARTER (R)
Mem, Ga Rep State Comt
b Brooklyn, NY, Jan 6, 35; s Edwin Hope O'Keeffe & Reba Carter O; m 1961 to Marion Eliza Gaines; c Whitney Carter, Jr & William Davis. Educ: Ga Inst Technol, BIE, 61; Wharton Grad Div, Univ Pa, MBA, 65; Chi Phi. Polit & Govt Pos: First vchmn, Fifth Dist Rep Party, Ga, 64-66; first vchmn, Ga Rep Party, 65-66; mem, Ga Rep State Comt, 64-; mem, Fulton Co Rep Comt, 64-; asst treas, Ga Finance Comt to Reelect the President, 72. Bus & Prof Pos: Asst treas, Trust Co of Ga, 62-69, group vpres, 69- Mil Serv: Entered as Pvt, Army, 57, released as SP-3/C, 58. Mem: Am Inst of Indust Engrs; Am Inst of Banking; US Jaycees; Atlanta Humane Soc (dir); Big Bros of Atlanta (bd trustees, 71-). Relig: Baptist. Mailing Add: 3916 Randall Farm Rd NW Atlanta GA 30339

O'KELLEY, ROBERT M (D)
Tex State Rep
Mailing Add: PO Box 10078 El Paso TX 79991

OKIYAMA, JESUS CARBULLIDO (D)
b Agat, Guam, Aug 2, 13; s Francisco K Okiyama & Ana C Carbullido O; m 1942 to Josefina M Leon Guerrero; c John Anthony & Frank Vincent. Educ: Guam High Sch. Polit & Govt Pos: Chmn, Com & Trade Comn Guam Cong, 46-50, chmn, Comt on Housing & Transportation, 50-52; chmn, Comt of Govt Opers, Guam Legis, 52-64, chmn, Far E Trade Mission, 56; Guam rep, SPac Econ Conf, 62; deleg, Hawaii Statehood Celebration; deleg, Dem Nat Conv, 64, 68 & 72; Dem Nat Committeeman, Guam, 64-72; Sen, Guam Legis, 66-72, spec asst to Minority Mem, 66; chmn foreign trade comt, Western State Conf. Bus & Prof Pos: Mgr wholesale div, Guam Commercial Corp, 46-52; pres & owner, Okie & Young Co, 56-62. Mem: Young Men League of Guam; Guam Eagle; Triple A Club of Yona. Relig: Roman Catholic. Mailing Add: Yona GU 96910

O'KONSKI, ALVIN E (R)
b Kewaunee, Wis; m to Veronica Hemming. Educ: Wis State Col, BEd; Univ Wis; Univ Iowa. Polit & Govt Pos: US Rep, Wis, 42-72, dean of Wis deleg; mem, Armed Serv Comt; pres, World Bill of Rights Asn, 45; former dir, Free World Forum & World League to Stop Communism; mem, Katyn Massaere Comt, 52. Bus & Prof Pos: Pres, WAEO-TV Inc, Rhinelander, Wis; former owner of WOSA & WLIN, radio sta at Wausaw & Merrill, Wis; former publ of newspaper, Hurley, Wis; taught at Itasca Jr Col in Minn, Ore State Col & Univ Detroit. Honors & Awards: Voted Most Distinguished Am for 45 by Foreign Lang Press for his work against communism; Awarded Polonia Restitutia, Highest Medal of Free Poland; ranked first among all Congressmen in Am Hist Test conducted by United Press; capt of debating team 3 years & pres of student body, 2 years, Wis State Col; capt, Univ Wis Big Ten Championship Debating Team. Mailing Add: Rhinelander WI 54501

OLDEN, DANA E (R)
NH State Rep
Mailing Add: RFD Old Carlemont Rd Charlestown NH 03603

OLDENDORF, YVETTE BOE (DFL)
b Bismarck, NDak; d Norman R Boe & Martha Gunville B; m to John P Oldendorf; c Brian Powell. Educ: Macalester Col, BA, 61; Univ Minn, Minneapolis, MA, 64. Polit & Govt Pos: Vchairwoman, Dakota Co Dem-Farmer-Labor Cent Comt, Minn, 68-69, chairwoman, 69-72; co rep, First Dist Dem-Farmer-Labor Cent Comt & Minn State Dem-Farmer-Labor Cent Comt, 68-; deleg, Dem Nat Conv, 72; co-chmn, First Cong Dist McGovern Campaign & mem, Minn State Exec Comt of McGovern Campaign, 72; co-founder & issues & prog coordr, Dem-Farmer-Labor Feminist Caucus, 73; metrop coordr, Minn Women's Polit Caucus, 73;

co-chairperson, Dem-Farmer-Labor Const Study Comn, 73; staff mem, Lt Gov Off, 73. Bus & Prof Pos: Instr social sci, Metrop State Jr Col, Minneapolis, 67; asst dir higher educ for low-income persons, Univ Minn, Minneapolis, 67-69; coordr common mkt progs, Minn State Col Syst, 69- Mem: Am Polit Sci Asn; West St Paul Dem-Farmer-Labor Club; Dem-Farmer-Labor Women's Caucus; Women Historians of the Midwest. Honors & Awards: Dewitt Wallace fel; Ordway scholar; Euland fel & Am Field Serv scholar. Mailing Add: 421 Ruby Dr West St Paul MN 55118

OLDHAM, DORTCH (R)
Chmn, Tenn Rep State Exec Comt
b Smith Co, Tenn, Aug 26, 19; s N E Oldham & Sally Gregory O; m 1948 to Lenore Huebner; c Dortch, Jr, Greg, Peter, Danny & Mark. Educ: Cumberland Col Tenn, 36-38; Univ Richmond, 39-41; Theta Chi. Hon Degrees: DH, Univ Richmond, 74. Polit & Govt Pos: State finance chmn for Sen Howard Baker, 71-72; chmn, Tenn Rep State Exec Comt, 74- Bus & Prof Pos: Pres, Southwestern Co, Nashville, Tenn, 60-72; co-founder & prin stockholder dir, Nasco, Inc, Springfield, 61-; dir, First Am Tenn Corp & First Am Nat Bank, Nashville, 69- Mil Serv: Entered as Cadet, Army Air Corps, 42, released as Capt, 46, after serv in Training Command, India & Okinawa. Mem: Nashville Rotary; Cumberland Col (trustee, 65-); Univ Richmond (trustee, 73-). Relig: Presbyterian. Mailing Add: 4390 Chickering Lane Nashville TN 37215

OLDS, GLENN A (R)
b Sherwood, Ore, Feb 28, 21; s Glenn Alvero Olds & Hazel Ross O; m 1944 to Eva B Spelts; c Linda (Mrs Ord Elliott) & Richard. Educ: Willamette Univ, AB magna cum laude, 42; Garrett Theol Sem, BD with highest distinction, 45; Northwestern Univ, Swift traveling fel, 44-45, MA with honors, 45; Yale Univ, Robinson fel, 45-46, PhD, 48; Omicron Delta Kappa; Tau Kappa Alpha; Blue Key; Omicron Delta Sigma. Hon Degrees: DD, Willamette Univ, 55; DH, Springfield Col, 65; Academico Honoris Causa, Mexican Acad Int Law, 67; Academician, China Acad, Taiwan, 67; LHD, Inter-Am Univ, PR, 68, Lake Land Col, Ill, 71 & Muhlenberg Col, 72; LLD, Univ Akron, 71; DLit, Univ Redlands, 74. Polit & Govt Pos: Mem, Am Seminar to Europe, 50; leader, Am Seminar to the Union of Soviet Social Repub, 57; consult to President Eisenhower, Stockholm Conf on Educ, 60 ,consult, Peace Corps, 51; consult, President's Coun on Juv Delinquency, 61-62; consult, President's Coun on Youth & Phys Fitness, 61-63; former consult, Disarmament & Arms Control Comn; consult, Govt of Liberia, 62; consult, Ministry of Educ, Nigeria, 62; spec asst to Sargent Shriver, War on Poverty, 64; mem exec comt, Alliance for Progress, Mass-Colombia, 64-65; chmn seminar educ & cult exchange, White House Conf on Int Educ, 65; convenor & host, NAm Conf on Univs Role in the Quest for Peace, Int Ctr, LI, 67, US Rep, Conf on Latin Am in the Last Quarter of the Twentieth Century, Mexico City, Mex, 68; US Rep, Conf on the Future of the UN, Dubrovnik, Yugoslavia, 68; spec asst for policy & manpower develop to President Richard M Nixon, 68-69; US Rep, Kyoto Conf on US-Japan Rels, 69; US Ambassador to the UN, Econ & Soc Coun, 69-71, chmn, Gov State Comt on UN, 73. Bus & Prof Pos: Student pastor, Methodist Churches, Harrisburg & Brooks, Ore, 39-40; dir youth, First Methodist Church, Salem, Ore, 40-42; dir youth, First Methodist Church, Oak Park, Ill, 43-45; dir, Wesley Found, Yale Univ, 45-47, asst instr philos, Univ, 46-47; asst prof, DePauw Univ, 47-48; assoc prof philos & ethics, Garrett Theol Sem & vis prof philos, Northwestern Univ, 48-51; chaplain & prof, Univ Denver, 51-54; dir, Cornell Univ United Relig Work, 54-58; pres, Springfield Col, 58-65; exec dean int studies & world affairs, State Univ NY Syst, 65-68; adv, Nat Asn of Int Rels Clubs, 67-68; consult, Universidad de Oriente, Venezuela, 68; pres, Kent State Univ, 71-; bd dirs, Coun Study of Mankind, 71-; pres bd dirs, Design Sci Inst, 72-; bd trustees, Interfaith Campus Ministry, 73-; chmn, Consortium Int Energy Research, 74-; Metropolitan Akron Jobs Coun, 74- Publ: Stress & Campus Response, 68; Fitness for the Whole Family, 64; Frontiers of Sch Law, 73; plus numerous articles & guest ed of Saturday Rev. Mem: Educ Futures Int (dir, 74-); Akron Art Inst (bd trustees, ex officio, 74-); Oceanic Soc (charter mem); Educ Opportunities for Minority Groups; Fourth Int Conf Unity Sciences (mem Am adv bd, 75-). Honors & Awards: Nat fel, Nat Coun on Relig in Higher Educ, 46; Outstanding Teacher Award, Univ Denver, 53 & 58; Outstanding Citizen Award, City of Springfield, Mass, 65. Relig: Methodist. Mailing Add: President's Home Kent State Univ Kent OH 44242

O'LEARY, CORNELIUS PETER (D)
Conn State Rep
b Hartford, Conn, Mar 27, 44; s Henry Edward O'Leary & Eleanor Frances Preli O; single. Educ: Williams Col, AB, 66; Trinity Col, 70- Polit & Govt Pos: Conn State Rep, 60th Dist, Windsor Locks-Enfield, 73-; mem, Windsor Locks Dem Town Comt. Bus & Prof Pos: Teacher, Windsor Locks High Sch, 70. Mem: Conn Educ Asn. Relig: Roman Catholic. Legal Res: 2 Fern St Windsor Locks CT 06096 Mailing Add: 60th District State Capitol Hartford CT 06115

O'LEARY, DONALD R (D)
Maine State Rep
Mailing Add: 157 S Main St Mexico ME 04257

O'LEARY, THOMAS FLEMING (D)
b North Grafton, Mass, Dec 15, 36; s Thomas F O'Leary & Agnes Fleming O; single. Educ: St John's Univ Sem, AB Philos, 59, MDiv, 63; Loyola Univ, Chicago, MRelEd, 73; Cath Univ, MChA, 74. Polit & Govt Pos: Consult to US Rep Harold D Donohue, 74-75; admin asst to US Rep Michael T Blouin, 75- Bus & Prof Pos: Roman Cath priest, Worcester Diocese, Mass, 63-73. Relig: Catholic. Mailing Add: 1114 D St SE Washington DC 20003

OLENICK, STEPHEN R (D)
Auditor, Mahoning Co, Ohio
b Youngstown, Ohio, Oct 18, 10; s Joseph Stephen Olenick & Veronica Yasechko O; m 1939 to Ann Slifka; c Bernice (Mrs Krispinsky), Carole (Mrs Morris) & Robert (deceased). Educ: South High Sch, Youngstown, Ohio, grad, 29. Polit & Govt Pos: City councilman, Youngstown, Ohio, 46-54; Ohio State Sen, 55-62; auditor, Mahoning Co, 62-; alt deleg, Dem Nat Conv, 64, deleg, 68; pres, Co Officers of Ohio, currently. Bus & Prof Pos: Supreme auditor, Slovak Cath Sokol, Passaic, NJ, 55-62, supreme treas, 62- Mem: United Appeal (chmn local govt div); Red Cross (dir); CofC; Baseball Town USA Oldtimers (vpres); Nat Amateur Baseball Fedn Champions (pitcher). Honors & Awards: Citation, Buckeye Sheriffs Asn; Citation, from Ohio Attorney Gen; CofC Award; Elected Mahoning Co Auditor with no opposition for the first time in 38 years. Relig: Roman Catholic; Councilman, St Matthias Church, 13 years. Mailing Add: 3022 Rush Blvd Youngstown OH 44502

OLESON, OTTO H (D)
NH State Rep
b Jefferson, NH, June 2, 15; s Otto W Oleson & Goldine Stellings O; m 1940 to Eilleen Garland; c Otto G, Eric J & Faith (Mrs Belanger). Educ: Berlin High Sch, NH, 4 years. Polit & Govt Pos: NH State Rep, 65-; deleg, Dem Nat Conv, 68. Mil Serv: Entered as CM 3/C, Navy, 43, released as CM 1/C, 45, after serv in Naval Construction Bn, Pac Theatre. Mem: Grange; Am Legion; F&AM. Relig: Protestant. Mailing Add: 10 Hamlin Ave Gorham NH 03581

OLHOFT, WAYNE LEE (D)
Minn State Sen
b Wheaton, Minn, Aug 1, 51; s John Karl Olhoft & Amanda Pochardt; single. Educ: Univ Minn, St Paul, 69-71; Minn Student Coop. Polit & Govt Pos: Minn State Sen, 73- Bus & Prof Pos: Game farm mgr, Herman, Minn, 71-72. Mil Serv: Entered as E-1, Army Nat Guard, 69, E-4, 3 years. Mem: Nat Farmers Orgn; Viking Sportsmen; Future Farmers of Am. Relig: Lutheran. Mailing Add: Herman MN 56248

OLIN, JACK D (R)
NDak State Rep
b Sims, NDak, Feb 12, 32; s Arthur L Olin & Delia Jacobson O; m 1956 to Velma Sailer; Scott K, Bruce W & Craig J. Educ: Bismarck Jr Col, 56-57. Polit & Govt Pos: NDak State Rep, Dist 37, 72- Mil Serv: Entered as Pvt, Army, 53, released as Cpl, 55, after serv in 801st Eng, Europe, 54-55. Mem: NDak Ready Mix & Concrete Prod Asn; Am Legion; Elks; Eagles; Lions. Relig: Lutheran. Legal Res: 1050 12th Ave W Dickinson ND 58601 Mailing Add: Box 726 Dickinson ND 58601

OLIPHANT, S PARKER (R)
Mem, DC Rep State Comt
b Washington, DC, Oct 26, 27; s A Chambers Oliphant & Ruth Larner O; m 1962 to Martha Carmichael; c Leonard Carmichael & Samuel Duncan. Educ: Princeton Univ, BS, 49; Dial Lodge. Polit & Govt Pos: Rep precinct worker, Washington, DC, 49-52, precinct chmn, 54-68; mem, DC Rep State Comt, 60- Bus & Prof Pos: Treas, William P Lipscomb Co, 49-71, pres, 71-; vpres, House Realty & Develop Co, 71- Mem: Columbia Hosp for Women; Spring Valley, Wesley Heights Citizens Asn; Wash Bldg Cong; Chevy Chase Club. Relig: Presbyterian. Mailing Add: 4977 Glenbrook Rd NW Washington DC 20016

OLIVEN, CONSTANCE F (D)
b New York, NY, Dec 4, 48, d Dr John F Oliven & Charlotte Bauchwitz O; single. Educ: Univ Wis-Madison, BA, 70. Polit & Govt Pos: Founding mem, Manhattan Women's Polit Caucus, NY, 71; mem, NY Co Dem Comt, 71-73; officer, Village Independent Dem Club, 71-; alt deleg, Dem Nat Conv, 72; deleg, First Dist Dem Judicial Conv, NY, 72; staff mem, McGovern for President Campaign, Mich, 72; research dir, Charles Pound for Co Exec, NY, 73- Bus & Prof Pos: Opers asst, WNET/Channel 13, New York, 71-72; broadcast opers supvr, WOR-TV, currently. Relig: Jewish. Legal Res: 49 W 12th St New York NY 10011 Mailing Add: 25 Lexington Dr Croton-on-Hudson NY 10520

OLIVER, COVEY THOMAS (D)
b Laredo, Tex, Apr 21, 13; s Pheneas Roan Oliver & Jane Covey Thomas O; m 1946 to Barbara Hauer; c Jane Covey, Lucy Boulware, Woodlief Hauer, Scotti Longan & Jefferson Thomas. Educ: Univ Tex, BA summa cum laude, 33 & LLB summa cum laude, 36; Columbia Univ, LLM, 53 & Jur Sci Dr, 54; Phi Beta Kappa; Phi Delta Phi. Polit & Govt Pos: Sr attorney, Bd of Econ Warfare, 42; chief econ controls sect, Am Embassy, Madrid, 42-44; head various divs, State Dept, 44-49; mem US deleg, Paris Peace Conf & other deleg, 46-49; Am mem, Inter-Am Juridical Comt, Orgn Am States, 63-; Ambassador Extraordinary & Minister Plenipotentiary to Colombia, 64-66; Asst Secy of State for Inter-Am Affairs, 67-69; US coordr, Alliance of Progress, 67-69; US exec dir, Int Bank for Reconstruction & Develop, Int Finance Corp, Int Develop Asn, 68-69; spec asst to Secy of Treas, 69- Bus & Prof Pos: Admitted to Tex Bar, 36; mem law faculty, Univ Tex, 36-41; prof law, Univ Calif, Berkeley, 49-56; prof law, Univ Pa, 56-69, Hubbell prof law, 69-; Fulbright scholar & lectr, Univ Sao Paulo, 63; mem bd of ed, Am J Int Law, 69- Publ: Co-auth, Restatement of the Foreign Relations Law of the US, 63 & The International Legal System with Documentary Supplement, 73; plus numerous articles. Mem: Am Soc Int Law (vpres, mem exec coun, 68-); Am Bar Asn; Int Law Asn; Foreign Serv Asn; Order of the Coif. Honors & Awards: Grand Cross, Order of Boyaca, Repub of Colombia, 66. Legal Res: 4210 Spruce St Philadelphia PA 19104 Mailing Add: 161 Law Bldg Univ of Pa Philadelphia PA 19174

OLIVER, FRANK LOUIS (D)
Pa State Rep
Mailing Add: Capitol Bldg Harrisburg PA 17120

OLIVER, ROBERT SPENCER (D)
b Newark, NJ, Nov 1, 37; s Robert Oliver & Mary Louise McClellan O; m 1958 to Florence Louise Marshall; c Jaquelin Ann, Martha Teel & Robert Spencer, Jr. Educ: Tex Christian Univ, BA, 60; George Washington Univ Sch Law, LLB, 67; Phi Kappa Sigma. Polit & Govt Pos: Pres, Tex Christian Univ Young Dem, 58-60; spec asst & press secy to US Sen Carl Hayden, Ariz, 62-67; chmn bd dirs, Young Dem Clubs Am, 64-65, vpres, 65-67, pres, 67-69; dir, Atlantic Asn Young Polit Leaders, 65-; admin asst to chmn, Dem Nat Comt, 67, dir youth affairs, 67-70, exec dir, Asn Dem State Chmn, 72-; chmn, Nat Young Citizens for Humphrey-Muskie, 68; exec dir, Am Coun Young Polit Leaders, 70- Mem: Am Polit Sci Asn. Relig: Episcopal. Mailing Add: 2617 Felter Lane Bowie MD 20715

OLIVIER, CHARLES J (R)
VChmn, Rockingham Co Rep Comt, NH
b New York, NY, Sept 27, 1914; s Charles C Olivier & Margaret Müller O; m 1938 to Helen Senko; c Denise, Richard A & Laurence C. Educ: Seamen's Inst Navigation Sch. Polit & Govt Pos: Selectman, Chester, NH, 56-65, mem sch bd, 65-68; chmn, Rockingham Co Rep Comt, 67-68, vchmn, 69-, mem exec comt, 73-; Rockingham Co chmn, Louis C Wyman for Cong, NH, 68 & 70; selectman, Town of Ellsworth, currently. Bus & Prof Pos: Sales mgr, NE Area, Wire Rope Mfg, 42- Mil Serv: Entered as Pvt, Army, 33, released as Pfc, 36, after serv in 27th & 18th Inf Div. Mem: Lions; NH & Maine Good Roads Asns; New Eng RR Club. Relig: Protestant. Legal Res: Ellsworth NH 03228 Mailing Add: Ellsworth Pond Rd West Campton NH 03228

OLKON, ELLIS (DFL)
Second VChmn, Fifth Cong Dist, Minn Dem-Farmer-Labor Party
b Minneapolis, Minn, Feb 11, 39; s Abe Olkon & Rose Fishbein O; m 1965 to Nancy

Katherine Hansen; c David Moses, Sara Esther & Deborah Miriam. Educ: Univ Minn, BA, 62; Tex Southern Univ, JD, 66. Polit & Govt Pos: Precinct chmn, 13th Precinct, Seventh Ward, Minneapolis Dem-Farmer-Labor Party, 70-75; deleg, Minn State Dem-Farmer-Labor Conv, 70 & 74; referee, Hennepin Co Conciliation Court, 71-72; mem bd dirs, Minn Am for Dem Action, 73-; second vchmn, Fifth Cong Dist, Minn Dem-Farmer-Labor Party, currently. Bus & Prof Pos: Hearing examr, State Dept Human Rights, Minn, 68-; law prof, Midwestern Sch Law, Hamline, 73-74. Publ: Pretrial release, Bench & Bar, 4/70. Mem: Hennepin Co Bar Asn (vchmn, Indust Rights & Responsibilities Comt); Minn State Bar Asn (mem Victimless Crime Comt); Am Bar Asn; Nat Asn Criminal Defense Lawyers. Relig: Jewish. Mailing Add: 3515 Zenith S Minneapolis MN 55416

OLKON, NANCY KATHERINE (DFL)
Dir, Fifth Cong Dist, Dem-Farmer-Labor Party, Minn
b Sioux Falls, SDak, Aug 26, 41; d James Conover Van Meter Hansen & Maybelle Katherine Anderson H; m 1965 to Ellis Olkon; c David Moses, Sara Esther & Deborah Miriam. Educ: Univ Minn, BA, 68; William Mitchell Col Law, JD, 70. Polit & Govt Pos: Precinct chmn, Minn Dem-Farmer-Labor Party, 70-, precinct deleg, 70-; deleg, Dem Nat Conv, 72; chairperson, House Dist 58B Dem-Farmer-Labor Party, 72-74; dir, Fifth Cong Dist, Dem-Farmer-Labor Party, 75- Bus & Prof Pos: Law partner, Olkon & Olkon, 68- Mem: Minn State Bar Asn (chairperson, Subcomt, 72-); Hennepin Co Bar Asn; Dem-Farmer-Labor Feminist Caucus (pres); Minn Women's Polit Caucus; Am for Dem Action (vpres & chairperson, Minn chap). Relig: Jewish. Mailing Add: 3515 Zenith Ave S Minneapolis MN 55416

OLKONEN, ELSIE SWAN (D)
Chmn, Island Co Dem Cent Comt, Wash
b Clinton, Wash, Oct 30, 17; d Evert Anders Swan & Anna Louise Nyman S; m 1942 to Albert Mathias Olkonen; c Gary, Selma Ann (Mrs Simon Delgado) & Evert. Educ: Langley High Sch, grad, 34. Polit & Govt Pos: Secy, Island Co Dem Cent Comt, Wash, 48-50, vchmn, 68-72, chmn, 72-; precinct committeeman, Deer Lake Precinct, 63-; vchmn, Tenth Legis Dist Orgn, 73- Bus & Prof Pos: Secy, Clinton Businessman's Asn, Wash, 69-71; assoc mem, Whidbey Island Realty Bd, 69-; sales assoc, Whidbey Realty, Inc, 70-; salesman rep, South Whidbey Broker's Asn, 73- Mem: Emblem Club; Am Legion Auxiliary; Am Lutheran Church Women; Clinton Progressive Asn; Wash State Dem Party. Relig: Lutheran. Legal Res: 4497 E Deer Lake Rd Clinton WA 98236 Mailing Add: PO Box 12 Clinton WA 98236

OLLWEILER, FRANCES B (D)
b New York, NY, Aug 24, 27; d Emil Berman & Cecelia Jack B; m 1948 to George J Ollweiler; c Kenneth D & Susan J. Educ: Davis & Elkins Col, 45-47; Phi Sigma Delta. Polit & Govt Pos: Secy, Kent Co Citizens for McGovern, Del, 72; alt deleg, Dem Nat Conv, 72. Bus & Prof Pos: Dir, Soroptimist Club, Dover, Del, 69-72. Mem: Century Club; Another Mother for Peace; 31st Dist Dem Club; Dover People for Peace (secy, 68-); PTA. Honors & Awards: Award of Merit, Dover YMCA, 69. Relig: Unitarian. Mailing Add: 1103 Westview Terr Dover DE 19901

OLMSTEAD, RALPH E (R)
Idaho State Rep
Mailing Add: Rte 2 Twin Falls ID 83301

OLSEN, ARNOLD (D)
b Butte, Mont, Dec 17, 16; s Albert Olsen (deceased) & Anna O; m to Margaret Williams; c Margaret Rae (Mrs David Childs), Anna Kristine & Karen Synneve. Educ: Mont Sch of Mines; Mont State Univ Law Sch, LLB; Phi Delta Phi. Polit & Govt Pos: Attorney Gen, Mont; US Rep, Mont, 60-70. Bus & Prof Pos: Lawyer. Mil Serv: Navy, World War II, 4 years overseas duty. Mem: Am Legion; VFW; Am Vet of World War II; Silver Bow Lodge 48 AF&AM; Scottish Rite. Mailing Add: Helena MT 59601

OLSEN, DENNIS M (R)
Chmn, Bonneville Co Rep Cent Comt, Idaho
b Blackfoot, Idaho, June 16, 30; s Melvin A Olsen & Doris Sparks O; m 1957 to Sheila Ann Sorensen; c Steven LaMar, Linda Le, Lori Ann, Timothy Morgan, Maria Kathleen, Nathan Miles, Mark Christian & Aaron Franklin. Educ: Idaho State Univ, 49-50; Brigham Young Univ, BS With Honors, 57; George Washington Univ, JD With Honors, 60; Order of the Coif; Phi Sigma Alpha; Phi Kappa Phi; Intercollegiate Knights. Polit & Govt Pos: Precinct committeeman, Bonneville Co Rep Comt, Idaho, 63-67; chmn, Bonneville Co Young Rep, 64-68; chmn, Dist 31 Rep Comt, 68-73; mem, Idaho Comn Fed Land Laws, 69-70; chmn, Region 7 Rep Comt, 73-; chmn, Bonneville Co Rep Cent Comt, 73-; mem, State Rep Exec Comt, 73- Bus & Prof Pos: Mem staff legal dept, J R Simplot Co, Boise, Idaho, 60-62; partner, Petersen, Moss, Olsen & Beard, Idaho Falls, 62- Mil Serv: Entered as Pvt, Air Force, 50, released as S/Sgt, 54, after serv in Air Training Command. Publ: Auth, Surface Reclamation Regulations on Federal & Indian Mineral Leases & Permits, 17th Annual Rocky Mountain Mineral Law Inst, 72. Mem: Lions; Idaho Trial Lawyers Asn; Seventh Judicial Dist & Idaho State Bar Asns. Honors & Awards: John Ben Snow Scholar, NY Univ Law Sch, 57, declined; George Washington Univ Law Sch Scholar, 57. Relig: Latter-day Saint. Mailing Add: 485 E St Idaho Falls ID 83401

OLSEN, VAN ROGER (R)
b Sanish, NDak, May 25, 33; s Oswald J Olsen & Nettie E Vanderhauf O; m 1958 to Myrna Louise Farroh; c Matthew G, Jennifer M & Susan E. Educ: Univ Mont, BA, 58; Phi Sigma Kappa. Polit & Govt Pos: Chmn, Cass Co Young Rep, NDak, 62-63; info dir, NDak Rep Party, 65; admin asst to US Rep Mark Andrews, NDak, 65- Bus & Prof Pos: Salesman, Yellow Pages, Northwestern Bell Tel Co, Minneapolis, Minn, 58-59; sales prom mgr, Farmhand Co, 59-60; acct exec, Flint Advert Agency, Fargo, NDak, 60-65. Mil Serv: Entered as E-1, Army, 54, released as E-4, 55, after serv in Vet Serv Corps, Hawaii, 14 months. Relig: Episcopal. Legal Res: 622 Crocus Dr Rockville MD 20850 Mailing Add: Off of Hon Mark Andrews House of Rep Washington DC 20515

OLSON, ALEC GEHARD (D)
Minn State Sen
b Mamre Twp, Kandiyohi Co, Minn, Sept 11, 30; s Axel Gehard Olson & Florence R Hoglund; m 1957 to Janice Ruth Albecht; c Alan G, Dennis A, Deron Jon & Eric W. Educ: High Sch, grad, 48; US Dept Agr Grad Sch, course in econ, 67. Polit & Govt Pos: Chmn, Kandiyohi Co Dem-Farmer-Labor Party, Minn, 54-57; Dem-Farmer-Labor chmn, Seventh Cong Dist, 58-62; US Rep, Minn, 62-66; asst to secy agr, US Dept Agr, 67; deleg, Dem Nat Conv, 68; Minn State Sen, 69- Bus & Prof Pos: Ins rep, Nat Farmers Union Serv Corp, 54-62; acct exec with investment firm, Kelly & Morey, 69- Mem: Nat Asn Security Dealers; Elks. Relig: Lutheran. Mailing Add: RR 1 Spicer MN 56228

OLSON, ALICE ADELE (R)
NDak State Rep
b Winnipeg, Man, May 24, 28; d Ames Carl Sangren & Olga Lutz S; m 1948 to Keith Cox Olson; c Linda Renee & Douglas Keith. Educ: Aaker's Bus Col, Grand Forks, NDak, grad, 46. Polit & Govt Pos: Vpres, Pembina Co Rep Women, NDak, 68-70, pres, 70-72; mem, NDak Rep Platform Comt, 72; NDak State Rep, 72- Bus & Prof Pos: Secy, Pembina Co Agt, NDak, 46-47 & Swift & Co, South St Paul, Minn, 47-48. Mem: Cavalier Study Club; Bathgate Homemakers Club (pres); Am Legion Auxiliary (vpres); Pembina Co Hosp Auxiliary; Pioneer Daughters & Hist Soc. Relig: Presbyterian; church organist & soloist. Mailing Add: State Capitol Bismarck ND 58501

OLSON, ALLEN INGVAR (R)
Attorney Gen, NDak
b Rolla, NDak, Nov 5, 38; s Elmer Olson & Olga Sundin O; m 1964 to Barbara Benner; c Kristin, Robin & Craig. Educ: Univ NDak, BSBA, 60, LLB, 63; Lambda Chi Alpha; Blue Key. Polit & Govt Pos: Asst dir NDak legis coun, NDak Legis Assembly, 67-69; Attorney Gen, NDak, 73- Bus & Prof Pos: Partner, Conmy, Rosenberg, Lucas & Olson Law Firm, Bismarck, NDak, 69-72. Mil Serv: Entered as 1st Lt, Army JAGC, 63, released as Capt, 67, after serv in Off Judge Adv Gen & US Army Europe, 64-67; Army Commendation Medal. Mem: Am Legion; Elks; Nat Asn Attorneys Gen; Am & NDak Bar Asn. Mailing Add: Star Rte 2 Bismarck ND 58501

OLSON, CLINTON L (R)
b Hitchcock, SDak, Mar 31, 16; s William Henry Olson & Allie Corinne Sparling O; m 1943 to Ethel Hoover Olson; c Merilee, Peter, David & Steven. Educ: Stanford Univ, BS, 39, MBA, 41; Nat War Col, 59-60; Theta Xi. Polit & Govt Pos: Foreign serv officer & sec secy, Am Embassy, Vienna, 48-52; Am consul, Martinique, French West Indies, 53-56; exec dir, Am Repub Affairs, Dept of State, 57-59; counr admin, Am Embassy, London, 60-62; counr econ affairs, Am Embassy, Vienna, 62-66; minister-counr, Am Embassy, Lagos, Nigeria, 66-70; sr inspector foreign serv, Dept of State, 70-72; US Ambassador, Sierra Leone, 72-74. Mil Serv: Entered as 2nd Lt, Army, 41, released as Lt Col, 46, serv in USSR, Iran & Iraq; Five Theatre Ribbons. Mem: Rolling Rock Club, Pa; Ross Mountain Club; Diplomatic & Consular Officers Retired; Foreign Serv Club. Mailing Add: Ross Mountain Club New Florence PA 15944

OLSON, DAGNY V (R)
Pub Relations Chmn, NDak State Rep Women
b Maddock, NDak, Aug 15, 14; d Bertheus Olson & Carolina Engen O; single. Educ: Minnewaukan High Sch, grad. Polit & Govt Pos: Reporter for NDak State, 11 sessions & one spec session; chmn fund raising events, Ramsey Co Rep Party, 7 years; pres, NDak Fedn of Rep Women, 67-71; deleg, Rep Nat Conv, 68 & 72; state chmn, NDak 1200 Rep Club, 71-; pub rels chmn, NDak State Rep Women, currently. Bus & Prof Pos: Off court reporter, Second Judicial Dist, NDak, 49- Mem: Bus & Prof Women's Clubs of NDak; Nat & NDak Shorthand Reporters Asns. Honors & Awards: Elected NDak Rep Woman of the Year, 69; honored by NDak Senate for 22 years serv as desk reporter, 73. Relig: Lutheran. Mailing Add: Box 618 Devils Lake ND 58301

OLSON, EMERALD L (R)
Chmn, Kearney Co Rep Party, Nebr
b Hildreth, Nebr, Mar 10, 07; s Orville A Olson & Emma Nyquist O; m 1931 to Clara H Johnson; c Richard E, Orville A & Muriel M (Mrs Lucky). Educ: Augustana Col (Ill), AB, 29; Univ Nebr-Lincoln, MA, 37. Polit & Govt Pos: Justice of the peace & clerk, Mirage Twp, Nebr, formerly; chmn, Kearney Co Rep Party, 74- Bus & Prof Pos: High sch teacher social sci, Sewal, Iowa, 29-31; teacher & athletic coach, Harlem, Mont, 31-32 & Axtell, Nebr, 34-37; farmer, 37-72; retired, 72. Mem: Lions; Nebr & Kearney Co Farm Bur; Boy Scouts. Relig: Lutheran. Mailing Add: Rte 2 Axtell NE 68924

OLSON, FLORENCE MAY (D)
VChmn, NDak Dem Non-Partisan League
b Enderlin, NDak, May 28, 20, d Oswald Hjalmer Sveum & Clara Olson S; m 1939 to Dale Conroy Olson; c Terry Dale & Kurt David. Educ: Enderlin Pub Sch, 12 years. Polit & Govt Pos: Dem precinct committeeman, Moore Twp, NDak, 58-; secy, Ransom Co Women's Dem Non-Partisan League, 60-62 & pres, 62-64; dist dir, Dem Non-Partisan League Women's Activities, 62-65; adv & organizer, Ransom Co Young Dem, 62-66; chmn, Ransom Co Dem Non-Partisan League Orgn, 62-68; chmn in charge of tent mgt & selling of novelties, Dem Non-Partisan League, Plowville, NDak, 64; vpres, NDak Women's Dem Non-Partisan League, 65-67, vchmn, 73-; state chmn, Nat Campaign Conf, Washington, DC & 4 for 66 Vol Prog, 66; campaign rep, state cand for labor, Earl Anderson, 66 & state cand for secy of state, Clara Wheelihan, 68; mem state campaign comt, 66 & 68; chmn Dist 27 & regional dir, Dem Non-Partisan League, 66-68; vchmn, NDak Dem Non-Partisan League, 66-; deleg, Dem Nat Conv, 68, served on, Rural Vol for Humphrey, 68; mem, Dem Nat Comt, formerly. Mem: Royal Neighbors of Am; Moore Hustler Homemakers; Am Legion Auxiliary; VFW Auxiliary. Relig: Lutheran. Mailing Add: Enderlin ND 58027

OLSON, GARY MILES (R)
b Portland, Ore, July 18, 31; s Reubin Alexander Olson & Greta Ehert O; single. Educ: Pac Univ, 55-59; treas, Assoc Students, 3 years; Intercollegiate Knights; Blue Key; Pi Delta Epsilon. Polit & Govt Pos: Committeeman, Cascade Precinct, Skamania Co, Wash, 65-; chmn, Skamania Co Civil Serv Comn, 66-; chmn, Skamania Co Rep Cent Comt, formerly; deleg, Rep Nat Conv, 72. Bus & Prof Pos: Salesman, NY Merchandise Co, Portland, Ore, 59- Mil Serv: Entered as Seaman Recruit, Navy, 50, released as YN 3, 54, after serv in Amphibious Force, USS LSM 161, Korean Conflict, 52-53; Good Conduct Medal; Nat Defense Serv Medal; UN Korean Serv, Two Stars; Korean Presidential Unit Citation. Relig: Protestant; Treas, North Bonneville Community Church, 10 years. Mailing Add: Box 97 R North Bonneville WA 98639

OLSON, HOWARD DEAN (DFL)
Minn State Sen
b Madelia, Minn, Aug 25, 37; s Edmund E Olson & Hannah R Noren O; m 1959 to Coleen Annette Skarphol; c Janae Jayne. Educ: Mankato State Col, 2 years. Polit & Govt Pos: Minn State Sen, 71- Bus & Prof Pos: Farmer. Mil Serv: Entered as Pvt, Nat Guard, 55, released as SP-5, 61, after serv in Battery A, 125th FA Bn, Viking Div. Relig: Lutheran. Mailing Add: RR 3 St James MN 56081

OLSON, JACK BENJAMIN (R)
VChmn, Rep Party of Wis
b Kilbourn, Wis, Aug 29, 20; s Grover Cleveland Olson & Jane Zimmerman O; m 1942 to Eleanor Jean Lang; c Sally Jane (Mrs Bracken), Jill Louise (Mrs Gaffney). Educ: Western Mich Univ, BS, 42; Kappa Sigma. Polit & Govt Pos: Chmn, Columbia Co Rep Club, 59-60; state chmn, Vice President Nixon Comt for the Presidency, 59-60; Lt Gov, Wis, 63-64 & 67-70, pres, Wis State Senate, 63-64 & 67-70; Rep cand for Gov, 70; mem, President's Air Quality Bd, 70-; mem, President's Environ Quality Comt, 71-; vchmn, Rep Party of Wis, 74- Bus & Prof Pos: Pres, State Tourist Coun, 52-57; co-owner, Olson Boat Corp, 60-; dir, Trade Mission to Europe, State of Wis, 64, exec chmn, World's Fair Comn, 64-65; chmn, March of Dimes Found, 65-69; co-owner, Olson Enterprises, Inc, 65- Mil Serv: Entered as Chief Specialist, Navy, 42, released as Lt(jg), 46, after serv as Comdr, PT Boat, NAtlantic, 44-45. Mem: Am Legion; VFW; DAV; Wis Dells Regional CofC; Wis State CofC (dir, 72-73). Honors & Awards: Distinguished Alumnus, Western Mich Univ, 66; Silver Anniversary Football Award, Sports Illustrated Mag, 66; Nat Theodore Roosevelt Conserv Award, Nat Conv Eagles Club of Am, 70. Relig: Presbyterian. Legal Res: 834 Meadow Lane Wisconsin Dells WI 53965 Mailing Add: Box 87 Wisconsin Dells WI 53965

OLSON, JOHN E (R)
Chmn, SDak Rep State Cent Comt
Mailing Add: PO Box 1099 Pierre SD 57501

OLSON, JOHN L
Minn State Sen
b Worthington, Minn, 1906; married; c Four. Educ: Nobles Co Pub Schs. Polit & Govt Pos: Minn State Sen, 58- Bus & Prof Pos: Livestock farmer; mem adv coun, Inst Agr, Univ Minn, 2 terms. Mem: Minn Swine Producers Asn; Minn Livestock Breeders Asn. Honors & Awards: Portrait in Minn Livestock Hall of Fame. Relig: Lutheran; Sunday sch supt, First Lutheran Church, Worthington, 29 years; secy churchmen, Lutheran Church Am. Mailing Add: 612 Lake St Worthington MN 56187

OLSON, KATHLEEN W (KAY) (R)
b Wood, SDak, Feb 22, 27; d James Harlan Danker & Theresa Cordes D; m 1951 to Eugene R Olson; c Warren E, Dale W & Barbara K. Educ: Univ SDak, BS, 50; Alpha Xi Delta. Polit & Govt Pos: Secy, Mellette Co Rep Party, SDak, 53-60, vchmn, formerly; deleg, Rep State Conv, 66; mem, Small Bus Admin Dist Coun, currently. Mem: Eastern Star; Am Legion Auxiliary; Gen Fedn of Women's Clubs. Relig: Methodist. Mailing Add: White River SD 57579

OLSON, LESLIE O (R)
Mem, Mo Rep State Cent Comt
b Bethune, Colo, Aug 13, 28; s Oscar A Olson & Iva May Rowbotham O; m 1958 to Anne Marie Granieri; c Leslie Anne, Michael Douglas & Lynda Marie. Educ: Univ Nebr, 53-54; Univ Colo, 55; Western State Col of Colo, BA, 57; Lambda Delta Lambda; Kappa Delta Mu; West State Col Vet Asn. Polit & Govt Pos: Cand, US Rep, Dist Four, Mo, 68; mem, Mo Rep State Cent Comt, 72- Bus & Prof Pos: Field engr, Defense Proj Div, Western Elec Co, Concord, Mass, Grand Forks, NDak & Montgomery, Ala, 57-61, planning engr, Mfg Div, Lee's Summit, Mo, 61-69; mem sch bd, R-7, Lee's Summit, Mo, currently. Mil Serv: Entered as Pvt, Marine Corps, 48, released as S/Sgt, 52, after serv in First Marine Air Wing, Korean Theatre, 50-51; Good Conduct Medal; Presidential Unit, Army Unit & Korean Presidential Unit Citations; Korean Serv & UN Serv Medals. Mem: Inst of Elec & Electronic Engrs; Kiwanis Int; Lee's Summit Club; VFW; Lee's Summit Rep Club. Honors & Awards: Registered prof engr, Mo. Relig: Protestant. Mailing Add: 820 Pleasant Dr Lee's Summit MO 64063

OLSON, LYNDON LOWELL, JR (D)
Tex State Rep
b Waco, Tex, Mar 7, 47; s Lyndon Lowell Olson, Sr & Frances McLaughlin O; m 1970 to Nancy Swenson. Educ: Baylor Univ, BA, 69, Baylor Law Sch. Polit & Govt Pos: Tex State Rep, 73-, chmn, Local Govt Comt, mem, Intergovt Affairs Comt, vchmn for appropriative matters, mem, Const Revision Comt, chmn subcomt on rules, Tex House Rep, 75- Bus & Prof Pos: Ranching; investments; attorney-at-law, Bryan, Wilson, Olson & Stem, currently. Mem: Lockwood Lodge Mason; Heart of Tex Coun Govts (mem transportation comt); Asn Locally Involved Vol Educ (chmn bd); Waco Asn for Retarded Citizens (legis chmn). Relig: Presbyterian, elder & col class teacher. Legal Res: 4142 Lake Shore Waco TX 76710 Mailing Add: 823 Washington Ave Waco TX 76702

OLSON, MAURICE ALAN (D)
SDak State Rep
b Pierpont, SDak, Apr 8, 26; s Olen Enger Olson & Alice Marie O; m 1950 to Mildred Aileen Erickson; c Debra Ann, Cynthia Ruth, Barbara Louise, Jerald Keith & Ronald Mark. Educ: Pierpont & Langford High Sch, grad; Augustana Col, SDak, 48-49; Kappa Theta Phi. Polit & Govt Pos: Precinct committeeman, Egeland Precinct, SDak, 60-64; pres, Day Co Dem Party, 66-70, SDak State Rep, 70-, chmn health & welfare comt, SDak House of Rep, 73-, mem exec bd, SDak Legis Research Coun, currently. Mil Serv: Entered as Pvt, Army, 50, released as Sgt, 52, after serv in 196th Regimental Combat Team, Alaska, 51-52; Good Conduct Medal. Mem: Nat Farmers Union; Nat Farmers Orgn. Relig: Lutheran. Mailing Add: RFD 2 Waubay SD 57273

OLSON, ROBERT CHARLES (R)
Mem, Winona Co Rep Comt, Minn
b Minneapolis, Minn, July 3, 34; s Charles Joseph Olson, Jr & Margaret Nelson O; m 1953 to Marjorie Marie Heutmaker; c Wendy Anne, Thomas Robert, Paul Joseph & Anne Marie. Educ: Univ Minn Exten Div, 56-62. Polit & Govt Pos: Mem, Winona Co Rep Comt, Minn, 63-, chmn, 65-67. Bus & Prof Pos: Mgr, NW Bell Tel Co, 62-67; instr, Am Inst Banking, 64-; gen mgr, Technigraph Corp, currently; pres & owner, Printing Design, Inc, Lake City, 71-; partner, The Imaginators, Lake City & Minneapolis, 72- Mil Serv: Entered as Recruit, Naval Air Res, 52, released as PO 3/C, 60, after serv in Air Support Squadron SF 612. Mem: Winona Rotary (dir, 65-); Winona CofC; Winona Jr Achievement; Winona Community Chest (pres & bd dirs); Kiwanis Int (vpres, 72-); Elks. Relig: Catholic. Mailing Add: Oakridge Lake City MN 55041

OLSON, RUSSELL A (R)
Wis State Rep
Mailing Add: 336th St Box 8 Bassett WI 53101

OLSON, STUART A (R)
Mont State Rep
b Lang, Sask, Nov 26, 08; s Christ Nils Olson & Clara Carlson O; m 1941 to D'Arline E Carrico; c Richard S & Ronald N. Educ: Univ Minn, MD, 35; Phi Beta Pi. Polit & Govt Pos: Med adv, Local Draft Bd, Dawson Co, Mont, 48-70; Mont State Rep, Dist 3, 71- Bus & Prof Pos: Asst chief surgeon, Northern Pac Beneficial Asn, 38-53, chief surgeon, 53-62; dist med examr, Northern Pac Rwy, 62-70 & Burlington Northern Rwy, 70- Mem: Am Med Asn; Am Col Surgeons; Mont State Bd Med Examr; Elem Sch Bd; Mason. Relig: Protestant. Mailing Add: Glendive Med Ctr Glendive MT 59330

OLSSON, ELEANOR (R)
b Elberta, Ala, May 19, 31; m 1956 to James Olsson; c Carol, James, Kurt & Lynn Marie. Polit & Govt Pos: Precinct deleg & chmn; vchmn, South Ottawa Co Women's Rep Club, Mich, 66-70, pres, 72-74; vchmn, Allegan Co Rep Exec Comt, 68-72 & 73-75, chmn, 72-73; mem credentials comt, Mich State Rep Conv, 71. Bus & Prof Pos: Statistician, gathering info & figures for scheduling, planning & projecting. Mem: PTA; W Mich PTA Conf; Philharmonic Club; Mich State Music Conv, Interlochen; DeGraaf Nature Ctr. Relig: Congregational; Choir mem, 18 years, chmn, Church Circle, 2 years. Mailing Add: 89 E 37th St Holland MI 49423

OLVER, JOHN WALTER (D)
Mass State Sen
b Honesdale, Pa, Sept 3, 36; s T Horace Olver & Helen Fulleborn O; m 1959 to Rose Alice Richardson; c Martha Jane. Educ: Rensselaer Polytech Inst, BS, 55; Mass Inst Technol, PhD, 61; Sigma Xi; Phi Lambda Upsilon. Polit & Govt Pos: Mass State Rep, Second Hampshire Dist, 69-72; Mass State Sen, Franklin-Hampshire Dist, 73- Bus & Prof Pos: Instr, Mass Inst Technol, 61-62; asst prof, Univ Mass, Amherst, 62-69. Publ: 14 articles in chem, anal research jour. Mem: Am Chem Soc; Electrochem Soc. Legal Res: 1333 West St Amherst MA 01002 Mailing Add: Box 855 Amherst MA 01002

O'MALEY, ROBERT L (R)
Ind State Rep
Mailing Add: 101 S Tenth St Richmond IN 47375

O'MALLEY, DAVID DONALD (D)
Wis State Rep
b Waunakee, Wis, Nov 12, 12; s Thomas P O'Malley & Martha Monks O; wid; c Thomas Patrick, Maureen & David, Jr. Educ: Univ Wis, 36-38. Polit & Govt Pos: Wis State Rep, 59-; treas, Dave Co Dem Statutory Comt, currently. Relig: Catholic. Mailing Add: 315 W Main St Waunakee WI 53597

O'MALLEY, JOHN F X (D)
b Brooklyn, NY, Apr 14, 49; s John O'Malley & Eileen Moogan O; m 1973 to Louise Anne Schrock. Educ: Fordham Univ, BS, 70; C W Post Col, Long Island Univ, MS, 73; pres, Fordham Univ Band. Polit & Govt Pos: Mem, Manhassett Dem Club, NY, 71; student coordr, Scientists & Engr for McGovern, 71; coordr, C W Post Students for McGovern, 71-72; deleg, Dem Nat Conv, 72; committeeman, Nassau Co Dem Party, NY, 73; mem, Lexington Dem Club, 73- Bus & Prof Pos: Research assoc, Dept Radiation Research, Nassau Co Med Ctr, 71-73; research asst, Rockefeller Univ, 73- Mem: Am Asn Advan Sci; Tissue Cult Asn; Mus Natural Hist, NY; Common Cause; Nassau Co Police Boy's Club. Relig: Roman Catholic. Mailing Add: 5 North Dr Plandome NY 11030

OMDAHL, LLOYD B (D)
b Conway, NDak, Jan 5, 31; s Lars Omdahl & Hannah Nelson O; m 1953 to Ruth Jones; c Scott, Becky & Nancy. Educ: Univ NDak, PhB, 53, MA, 62; Sigma Delta Chi; Blue Key. Polit & Govt Pos: Secy, NDak Nonpartisan League, 60-; mem, NDak Dem-Nonpartisan League Exec Comt, 60-68; admin asst to Gov Guy, 61-63, dir admin, 66-67; State Tax Comnr, 63-66; chmn, Grand Forks Home Rule Charter Comn, 69-74; deleg, Dem Nat Mid-Term Conf, 74. Bus & Prof Pos: Asst dir, State Safety Div, NDak, 54-55; dir, State Capitol News Serv, 55-56; planner, Civil Defense Survival Proj, 57-58; partner & mgr, Lloyds of Bismarck Advert Agency, 57-68; prof polit sci, Univ NDak, 67- Publ: Auth, Insurgents, Lakeland Color Press, 62; co-auth, North Dakota Government, Bur Govt Affairs, 73; auth, Unicameralism, Nat Civic Rev, 74. Mem: Am Soc Pub Admin. Honors & Awards: Outstanding Faculty Mem, Univ NDak, 71. Relig: Baptist. Mailing Add: 2624 Fourth Ave N Grand Forks ND 58201

O'MEARA, GEORGE F, JR (D)
State Committeeman, Mass Dem Party
b Lowell, Mass, June 29, 21; s George F O'Meara & Clara T Mahoney O; m 1956 to Estelle R Paguette; c George F, III, Mary K Peskovitz & Mark S. Educ: Lowell High Sch, 39. Polit & Govt Pos: State committeeman, Mass Dem Party, 64-; city coun, Lowell, Mass, 65-68; alt deleg, Dem Nat Conv, 68; fed-state liaison officer, Gtr Lowell Area Planning Comn, currently. Relig: Roman Catholic. Mailing Add: 521 Rogers St Lowell MA 01852

OMHOLT, ELMER V (R)
b Great Falls, Mont, Mar 29, 20; s Kristian Omholt & Ellen W Johnson O; m 1946 to Audrey Mae Haralson; c Kris Henry & Myrna Ellen. Educ: Northern Mont Col, 38-40. Polit & Govt Pos: Justice of the peace, Teton Co, Mont, 50; Mont State Rep, Teton Co, 51-55, chmn, Workmen's Compensation & Engrossing Comts, Mont House of Rep, vchmn, Mil Affairs Comt, mem Fish & Game Comt & Banking & Ins Comt; mayor, Dutton, Mont, 58; past mem, Teton Co Juv Court Bd; state ins comnr, investment comnr & fire marshal, 62-; State Auditor, Mont, formerly. Bus & Prof Pos: In auto implement bus, 45-50; with gen ins agency, 50-62. Mil Serv: Entered as Pvt, Army, 40, released as 1st Lt, 45, after serv in 34th Inf Div, European-African Theater; Purple Heart. Mem: Fedn of Ins Coun; Nat Asn Ins Comnrs; Am Red Cross (pres, Dutton Chap); Am Legion, 48 (dist comdr); DAV. Relig: Lutheran. Mailing Add: State Capitol Helena MT 59601

OMOHUNDRO, BAXTER HARRISON (R)
b Denver, Colo, Dec 27, 25; s Baxter Allen Omohundro & Mary Feree O; m 1944 to Shirley Arlese Spruill; c Sue Carol (Mrs Ronald Goble), Baxter Allen, Patricia (Mrs Thomas Williams) & Janet Lee. Educ: El Camino Col. Polit & Govt Pos: Dir pub info, Dept Health, Educ & Welfare, 69-71; commun dir, Rep State Cent Comt Calif, 73- Bus & Prof Pos: Reporter-photographer, Long Beach Independent Press-Tel, 48-57, regional bur chief, 57-61, city ed, 61-64; Wash correspondent, Ridder Newspapers, 64-69. Mil Serv: Entered as A/S, Navy, 43, released as Yeoman 2/C, 46, after serv in Landing Ship, Tank Flotilla 36 Staff, Asiatic-Pac Theatre, 45. Mem: Nat Press & Capitol Hill Clubs. Relig: Protestant. Mailing Add: Calif Rep State Cent Comt 926 J St Sacramento CA 95814

O'NEAL, ARTHUR DANIEL, JR (D)
Comnr, Interstate Com Comn
b Bremerton, Wash, May 15, 36; s Arthur Daniel O'Neal, Sr & Louise Nordahl O; m 1961 to Diane Gay Reedy; c Daniel Stewart, Reed Kazis, David Christopher & Beth Marie. Educ: Whitman Col, AB, 59; Univ Wash, JD, 65; Phi Delta Phi. Polit & Govt Pos: Staff counsel, Com Comt, US Senate, 66-67; legis counsel, US Sen Warren G Magnuson, Wash, 67-69; surface transportation counsel, Com Comt, US Senate, 69-71, transportation counsel, 71-73; comnr, Interstate Com Comn, 73- Mil Serv: Ens, Navy, 59, released as Lt(jg), 63, after serv in Destroyers, Pac & Vietnam. Publ: Co-auth, Study of the Penn Central & Other Railroads, Govt Printing Off, 72. Mem: Wash State Bar Asn. Relig: Protestant. Legal Res: 20156 Seventh NE Seattle WA 98155 Mailing Add: 1912 Torregrossa Ct McLean VA 22101

O'NEAL, B F, JR (R)
La State Rep
Mailing Add: 6449 Birnamwood Rd Shreveport LA 71106

O'NEAL, DUDLEY LEE, JR (D)
b Andalusia, Ala, Jan 13, 24; s Dudley L O'Neal (deceased) & Mary Louise Perrenot O; m 1951 to Mildred E Johns; c Dudley L, III, Lizabeth P & Francis W J. Educ: The Citadel, 41-43; Univ Ala, AB, 47, Univ Ala Law Sch, LLB, 50; Kappa Sigma; Phi Delta Phi. Polit & Govt Pos: Attorney, Dept Justice, 51; criminal investr, Fed Housing Admin, 53-54; trial attorney, Civil Serv Comn, 54-55; asst counsel subcomt housing, US Senate, 55-61, co-staff dir & chief counsel, 61-69 & staff dir & gen counsel, Banking & Currency Comt, 69- Bus & Prof Pos: Lawyer, Andalusia, Ala, 50-51. Mil Serv: Entered as Pvt, Army Corps Engrs, 43, released as Capt, 46, after serv in 6th Army Hq, Southwest Pac Theatre, 44-46, recalled as Capt, 51-52, serv in 866 Engr ANV Bn; Bronze Star with Oak Leaf Cluster; Legion of Merit; Army Commendation Medal with Two Oak Leaf Clusters. Mem: VFW; WOW. Relig: Episcopal; Trustee, Thomas Episcopal Church. Legal Res: Andalusia AL 36240 Mailing Add: 8611 Dixie Pl McLean VA 22101

O'NEAL, JOHN BARNWELL (D)
b Blackshear, Ga, Oct 22, 20; s John B O'Neal, Jr & Carol Anita Nelson O; m 1945 to Phyllis Johnson; c Patricia, Pamela, John, IV & Peggy. Educ: Univ Ga, BS; Med Col Ga, MD. Polit & Govt Pos: Mayor, Elberton, Ga, 54-56; mem, Gov Comn Efficiency & Econ in Govt, 62-66; deleg Dem Nat Conv, 64; mem, Ga State Dem Exec Comt, formerly. Bus & Prof Pos: Dir, First Nat Bank, Elberton, Ga; pres, Elberton Civic Ctr, 67- Mil Serv: Entered as 1st Lt, Army, 45, released as Capt, 48, after serv in Med Corps. Mem: Med Asn of Ga; Am Med Asn; Am Soc Abdominal Surgeons; Elberton CofC; Rotary Club Elberton. Relig: Methodist. Mailing Add: 33 Chestnut St Elberton GA 30635

O'NEAL, LINDA KAY (D)
Chmn, Trinity Co Dem Comt, Tex
b Angelina Co, Tex, July 16, 47; d Marvin Ellington Ivy & Kizzie Nolan I; m 1971 to Loy Mack O'Neal. Educ: Lamar Univ, 65-68. Polit & Govt Pos: Chmn, Trinity Co Dem Comt, Tex, 74- Mailing Add: Rte 1 Apple Springs TX 75926

O'NEAL, MASTON EMMETT, JR (D)
b Bainbridge, Ga, July 19, 07; s Maston Emmett O'Neal & Bessie Birch Matthews O; m 1934 to Mary Charlotte Tyson; c Susan Charlotte (Mrs Jerry M Bowden) & Maston Emmett, III. Educ: Marion Mil Inst, AA, 25; Davidson Col, AB, 27; Emory Univ Law Sch; Pi Kappa Alpha. Polit & Govt Pos: Solicitor gen, Albany Judicial Circuit, Ga, 40-64; US Rep, Second Dist, Ga, 65-70. Mil Serv: Entered as Seaman, Navy, 44, released as Lt, 46, after serv in Pac; Asiatic-Pac Campaign Medal with Battle Star; Navy Occupation Serv Medal with ASA Clasp; Am Campaign Medal; Victory Medal. Mem: Am & Ga Bar Asns; Solicitors Gen Asn of Ga (pres); Nat Asn of Co & Prosecuting Attorneys (dir); Scottish Rite. Relig: Presbyterian, Moderator, Presbytery of Southwest Ga. Mailing Add: 805 Alice St Bainbridge GA 31717

O'NEIL, CHARLES ROBERT (BOB) (R)
Wyo State Rep
b Big Piney, Wyo, Dec 2, 15; s Thomas Daniel O'Neil & Mary Ellen Searcy O; m 1956 to Helen Jenkins; c Thomas Daniel & Sandra Ellen. Educ: Colo & Utah Univ, 5 years; Sigma Nu. Polit & Govt Pos: Mayor, Big Piney, Wyo, 49-51; mem, Southwest Sch Bd, 49-57 & 70-, pres, 63-65; mem, Wyo Natural Resource Bd, 50-52; mem, Wyo Livestock & Sanitary Bd, 52-66; Wyo State Rep, 71- Mem: Elks; KofC; Wyo Stockgrowers; Wyo Hereford Asn. Honors & Awards: Outstanding Friend of 4-H, 68. Relig: Catholic. Mailing Add: Box 10 Big Piney WY 81313

O'NEIL, DORTHEA M (D)
NH State Rep
Mailing Add: 24 Roysan St Manchester NH 03103

O'NEIL, JAMES E (R)
Mem, NH Rep State Cent Comt
b New York, NY, Jan 22, 21; married; c Four. Educ: Univ NH. Polit & Govt Pos: Moderator, Sch Bd, NH; NH State Rep, 59-74; mem, NH Rep State Cent Comt, 68- Bus & Prof Pos: Sch consult. Mil Serv: Aviation Topographic Engrs, Pac. Relig: Protestant. Mailing Add: Box 151 Chesterfield NH 03443

O'NEIL, REGIS B, JR (R)
NY State Assemblyman
Mailing Add: 5 Woodcutters Lane Cold Spring Harbor NY 11724

O'NEIL, THOMAS VINCENT (D)
b Paterson, NJ, July 19, 47; s William T O'Neil & Josephine Venezia O; single. Educ: Rutgers Univ, BA, Law Sch, JD. Polit & Govt Pos: Counsel, NJ Dem Party, 73-; alt deleg, Dem Nat Mid-Term Conf, 74; chmn, Nat Gov Conf Task Force on Crime, 74-; legis counsel to Gov NJ, 74- Publ: Co-auth, Nixon—The end of justice, New Dem, 72. Legal Res: 786 Goffle Rd Hawthorne NJ 07506 Mailing Add: State House State St Trenton NJ 08608

O'NEILL, C WILLIAM (R)
Chief Justice, Ohio Supreme Court
b Marietta, Ohio, Feb 14, 16; s Charles Thompson O'Neill & Jessie Arnold O; m 1945 to Betty Estelle Hewson; c Charles William & Peggy. Educ: Marietta Col, AB, 38; Ohio State Univ Col Law, JD, 42; Phi Beta Kappa; Pi Kappa Delta; Delta Upsilon; Order of the Coif. Hon Degrees: LHD, Marietta Col, 53 & Bethany Col, 71; LLD, Defiance Col, 53, Ohio Univ, WVa Univ, Steubenville Col & Miami Univ, 57, Wilberforce Univ, Heidelberg Col & Bowling Green Univ, 58, Capital Univ, 71; DCL, Ohio Wesleyan Univ, 73. Polit & Govt Pos: Pres, Wash Co Young Rep Club, Ohio, 38; Ohio State Rep, 39-50, Speaker, Ohio House of Rep, 47-48, Minority Leader, 49-50; chmn, Ohio State Rep Conv, 58; Attorney Gen, Ohio, 51-56, Gov, 57-58; deleg, Rep Nat Conv, 52 & 56, vchmn, Ohio Deleg, 56; justice, Ohio Supreme Court, 60-70, Chief Justice, 70- Mil Serv: Entered as Pvt, Army, 43, released as S/Sgt, 46, after serv in 976th Engrs, ETO, 44-45; Normandy Campaign & Battle of the Bulge Ribbons. Mem: Am, Ohio State, Columbus & Wash Co Bar Asns. Honors & Awards: One of Ten Outstanding Young Men in the US, 51; Centennial Achievement Award, Ohio State Univ, 70; Ohio Bar Medal, Ohio State Bar Asn, 71. Relig: First Community Church. Mailing Add: 1560 London Dr Columbus OH 43221

O'NEILL, C WILLIAM, JR (R)
Ohio State Rep
Mailing Add: 935 Quay Ave Columbus OH 43212

O'NEILL, CATHY (D)
b New York, NY, July 12, 42; m to Brian O'Neill; c Colin & Conor. Educ: St Joseph's Col, BA, 64; Howard Univ, MSW. Polit & Govt Pos: Los Angeles field rep to US Sen John Tunney; Dem nominee, Calif State Senate, 72; mem steering comt & credentials chairperson, Calif Dem Party Exec Comt, 72-75; state educ comnr, Innovation & Planning, Calif, 73-; Dem cand for Calif Secy of State, 74; alt deleg, Dem Nat Mid-Term Conf, 74. Bus & Prof Pos: Teacher urban affairs, Univ Southern Calif, 72-74. Mem: Community Rels Conf of Southern Calif (legis chairperson); Nat Women's Polit Caucus; Women for Californians for Campaign Reform. Mailing Add: 412 Mt Holyoke Pacific Palisades CA 90272

O'NEILL, GARY THOMAS (R)
b Evergreen Park, Ill, Sept 28, 50; s Edmund B O'Neill & Adelaide C Tyler O; m 1973 to Ann Marie Byrnes. Educ: Univ Minn, Minneapolis, 68-69; Col St Thomas, 69-72. Polit & Govt Pos: Chmn, Minn TAR, 67-68; mem, Gov Comn on Voter Participation, 72; chmn, Minn Young Rep League, 72-74. Bus & Prof Pos: Pres, Sci Syst Corp, 72- Mem: Nat Fedn Independent Businessmen; Lions (first vpres, Chanhassen Club, 73-). Relig: Roman Catholic. Legal Res: 4439 Ellerdale Rd Minnetonka MN 55343 Mailing Add: PO Box 117 Chanhassen MN 55317

O'NEILL, JAMES E, JR (D)
Mich State Sen
Mailing Add: 1603 Spruce St Saginaw MI 48601

O'NEILL, JOSEPH THOMAS (R)
Minn State Sen
b St Paul, Minn, Nov 13, 31; s Joseph Thomas O'Neill & Marie Agnes O'Connell O; m 1954 to Marianne Kenefick; c Kathleen, Joseph, Maureen, Thomas, John, Michael, Kevin & Shelagh. Educ: Univ Notre Dame, BA, 53; Univ Minn Col Law, LLB; 56. Polit & Govt Pos: Minn State Rep, 67-71; Minn State Sen, 71- Bus & Prof Pos: Partner, O'Neill, Burke & O'Neill, currently. Mil Serv: Entered as Lt, Air Force, 56, released as Capt, 59, after serv in Judge Adv Br, Mil Air Transport Serv; Capt, Air Force Res. Mem: Fed Bar Asn; Am Judicature Soc; Jr Chamber Int Sen; St Paul Jr CofC. Relig: Roman Catholic. Mailing Add: 1381 Summit Ave St Paul MN 55105

O'NEILL, PAUL JOSEPH (R)
b Pleasantville, NJ, Feb 16, 13; s Paul J O'Neill, Sr & Kathryn Veronica Henderson O; m 1958 to Alyse Stern; c Paul, Jr & Paige; stepchildren, Pamela & Barton. Educ: Rider Col, BBA, 34; Naval War Col Staff Sch, 45; Skull & Sabres; first pres, Beta Zi Chap, Delta Sigma Pi; pres, Interfraternity Coun. Polit & Govt Pos: Pres, Action thru Voter Educ Club, 63-65; chmn, Dade Co Right to Vote Comt, Fla, 64; Rep nominee for US Cong, Third Dist Fla, 64; pres, Miami Shores Men's Rep Club, 64-65; Rep nominee, Fla State Legis, 65 & 66; chmn, Dade Co Rep Exec Comt, 66-69; mem, Fla State Comprehensive Health & Planning Comn, 68-69; app, Subversive Activities Control Bd, Washington, DC, 69- Bus & Prof Pos: Mgr, New Eng Br, Dorland Advert Agency, 38-41; secy-treas, Atlantic City Newspapers, NJ, 46-51; with Newberger & Co, NJ, 54-55; with A C Allen & Co, 56-57; assoc mgr, Hayden Stone, 60-66, mgr, Miami Br, 67-69. Mil Serv: Entered as Lt(jg), Navy, 42, released as Lt Comdr, 46, after serv in Naval Units, FAW 10, VP 11 & 101, SW Pac Theater & Philippines, 42-45; Comdr (Ret); mil ribbons & two battle stars. Mem: Am Legion; Acacia; Mason; Elks; Rep Clubs. Honors & Awards: Dir, Miss Am Beauty Pageant, Atlantic City, NJ, 47-55; letters in varsity track, football & swimming, Rider Col; Fla Outstanding Rep Co Chmn, 67. Relig: Presbyterian. Mailing Add: 811 Vermont Ave NW Washington DC 20445

O'NEILL, THOMAS P, JR (D)
Majority Leader, US House of Rep
b Dec 9, 12; s Thomas P O'Neill & Rose Ann Tolan O; m 1941 to Mildred Anne Miller; c Rosemary, Thomas III, Susan, Christopher & Michael. Educ: Boston Col, AB, 36. Hon Degrees: Boston Univ, Boston Col, Dunbarton Col & Suffolk Univ. Polit & Govt Pos: Mass State Rep, 37-52, Minority Leader, Mass State House of Rep, 47-48, Speaker of the House, 49-52; mem, Cambridge Sch Comt, 46-47; US Rep, Eighth Dist, Mass, 52-, mem, Rules Comt, US House of Rep, 54-72, Majority Whip, 71-72, Majority Leader, 72-; deleg, Dem Nat Conv, 68; mem, Dem Nat Comt; co-chmn, Dem Nat Cong Comt. Bus & Prof Pos: Ins bus. Legal Res: Cambridge MA Mailing Add: House Off Bldg Washington DC 20515

O'NEILL, THOMAS P, III (D)
Lt Gov, Mass
b Cambridge, Mass, Sept 20, 44; s Thomas P O'Neill, Jr & Mildred Miller O; m 1969 to Jacqueline Anne Demartino. Educ: Boston Col, BA, 68; Chorale. Polit & Govt Pos: Vchmn, Cambridge Dem City Comt, Mass, 68-72; chmn, Ward Ten Dem Comt, 68-72; mem, Ward 11 Dem Comt, 72-; Mass State Rep, Third Middlesex Dist, 73-, pres, Freshman Class of Mass State Rep, 73-74; Lt Gov, Mass, currently. Bus & Prof Pos: Stockbroker, Harris Upham & Co, Inc, 68- Mil Serv: Entered as Pvt, Army Res, 68, serv in 94th Army Res Command, Spec, currently. Mem: Mass Legislators Asn; Jr CofC (dir, 73-); Gtr Boston Asn of Retarded Citizens; Paraplegic Research Found, Inc (vpres, dir, 72-); KofC (4 degree); Amvets. Relig: Roman Catholic. Legal Res: 17 Harrison Ave Cambridge MA 02140 Mailing Add: State House Boston MA 02133

O'NEILL, WILLIAM A (D)
Chmn, Conn Dem State Cent Comt
Polit & Govt Pos: Conn State Rep, currently. Mailing Add: Meeks Point East Hampton CT 06424

706 / O'NEILL

O'NEILL, WILLIAM C (D)
RI State Sen
Mailing Add: 689 Boston Neck Rd Narrangansett RI 02882

ONWEILER, WILLIAM C (R)
Idaho State Rep
Mailing Add: 3710 Cabarton Lane Boise ID 83704

OPBROEK, FLORENCE M (D)
VChmn, Gregory Co Dem Comt, SDak
b Hartington, Nebr, Sept 9, 07; d Ferd Wiebelhaus & Anna Muellet W; wid; c Carole A (Mrs Meuting). Educ: Univ SDak, Springfield, summer 72. Polit & Govt Pos: Vchmn, Gregory Co Dem Comt, SDak, 70- Bus & Prof Pos: Co-owner of drugstore, Bonesteel, 30-65. Mem: Federated Women's Club (parliamentarian, 69-); Bonesteel Altar Soc. Relig: Catholic. Mailing Add: Bonesteel SD 57317

OPEDAHL, OLAF (D)
NDak State Rep
Mailing Add: State Capitol Bismarck ND 58501

OPFERKUCH, PAUL RAYMOND (R)
Treas, Delta Co Rep Comt, Mich
b Racine, Wis, June 10, 38; s John Thomas Opferkuch & Margaret Greis O; m 1970 to Rosa Maria Soto. Educ: Univ Wis-Milwaukee, BS, 60; Univ Wis-Madison, MS, 63; Phi Eta Sigma. Polit & Govt Pos: Mem, Delta Co Rep Comt, Mich, 69-71, chmn, 71-72, treas, 73-, mem exec comt, 73-; deleg, Mich Rep State Conv, 70, 71 & 72. Bus & Prof Pos: Claims adjuster, Social Security Admin, Chicago, Ill, 63-64; munic tax auditor, NJ Seibert CPA, Milwaukee, Wis, 64-67; secy-treas, Tax Researchers, Inc 67-69; asst prof polit sci, Bay de Noc Community Col, Escanaba, Mich, 69- Mem: Am & Midwest Polit Sci Asns; Mich Conf Polit Sci; Am Fedn Musicians; Kiwanis. Relig: Lutheran. Mailing Add: 1403 S 14th St Escanaba MI 49829

OPITZ, DAVID WILMER (R)
Wis State Rep
b Port Washington, Wis, Dec 15, 45; s Wilmer Charles Opitz & Ella Lonsdale O; single. Educ: Carroll Col(Wis), BS, 68; Beta Pi Epsilon. Polit & Govt Pos: Pub health biologist, Waukesha Co, Wis, 68-70; dir environ health, Ozaukee Co, 71-72; Wis State Rep, 73- Bus & Prof Pos: With Aqua-Tech, Inc, Port Washington, Wis, 71- Publ: The algae speciation of the outer reef of Port Maria Bay Jamaica, 3/68. Relig: Lutheran. Mailing Add: 2348 Shady Lane Saukville WI 53080

ORAMA MONROIG, JORGE (POPULAR DEMOCRAT, PR)
Rep, PR House of Rep
Mailing Add: State Capitol San Juan PR 00901

ORANGE, CHARLES (D)
NDak State Rep
Mailing Add: State Capitol Bismarck ND 58501

ORAZIO, ANGELO FRANK (D)
NY State Assemblyman
b Carolei, Cosenza, Italy, June 19, 26; s Domenic Orazio & Antonetta Pulicicchio O; m 1950 to Adeline Fata; c James Paul & Jeanne Marie. Educ: Rensselaer Polytech Inst, BEE, 47; Yale Univ, MEng, 48; Pi Mu Epsilon; Gamma Alpha. Polit & Govt Pos: Research assoc, Local Govt Select Comt, NY Assembly, 74; NY State Assemblyman, 15th Dist, 75- Bus & Prof Pos: Asst engr to sr engr, Sperry Gyroscope Co, Great Neck, NY, 48-62, eng sect supvr, 62-74, leave of absence, 75- Mil Serv: Entered as A/S, Navy, 44, released as Ens, 46, after serv in Naval Col Training Prog, US, 44-46; Lt(jg), Naval Res; Am Theatre & Victory Ribbons. Mem: Inst Elec & Electronics Engrs; Cellini Lodge, Sons of Italy (chaplain); Engr Asn; Air Force Asn (H H Arnold Chap); Nat Coun Cath Laity. Honors & Awards: Columbus Award, Fedn Ital-Am Polit Orgns, 71; Significant Achievement Award, H H Arnold Chap, Air Force Asn. Relig: Roman Catholic. Mailing Add: 18 Crescent Lane Albertson NY 11507

ORBECK, EDMUND N (D)
b West Union, Minn, Sept 16, 15; s Joseph S Orbeck & Mary E Gans O; m 1941 to Sherry C Hanson; c John E & Sharon L. Educ: Winona Teachers Col; Columbia Col. Polit & Govt Pos: City councilman, Fairbanks, Alaska, 57-59; Alaska State Rep, 55-57; Alaska State Sen, 60-61; Alaska State Rep, Dist 16, 64-72 & 75; State Comnr Labor, 75- Bus & Prof Pos: Bus mgr, Laborers Union, Fairbanks, Alaska, 50-75; mem, Community Col, Fairbanks, Alaska, 74-75. Mem: Toastmasters; Fairbanks Dem Club; Kiwanis; NAACP; Fairbanks Goldpanners (dir). Mailing Add: 1033 Lathrop St Fairbanks AK 99701

ORCUTT, GEIL (D)
Conn State Rep
Mailing Add: 44 Highland St New Haven CT 06511

ORCUTT, JOELLEN LINDH (D)
NH State Rep
b Wilmington, Del, July 22, 40; d John Lindh & Johanna McCarthy L; m 1961 to William Stanley Orcutt; c Kirsten & Marcia. Educ: Univ Del, BA, 62; Univ NH, MA, 73; Mortar Board. Polit & Govt Pos: NH State Rep, 73-74 & 75- Bus & Prof Pos: Jr high sch teacher, Manchester, Mich, 62-63; Eng teacher, High Sch, 63-64; Goffstown, NH, 64-67; Eng instr, Univ NH, Merrimack Valley Br, 70-72. Mailing Add: 7 Shirley Park Goffstown NH 03045

ORDMAN, ARNOLD (D)
Gen Counsel, Nat Labor Rels Bd
b Somersworth, NH, Feb 16, 12; s Maurice J Ordman & Anna Pierce O; m to Evelyn Ruth Sisson; c Edward Thorne & Alfred Bram. Educ: Boston Univ, AB, 33; Harvard Law Sch, LLB, 36; Phi Beta Kappa. Polit & Govt Pos: Mem, Nat Labor Rels Bd, 46-, chief counsel to chmn, 61-63, gen counsel, 63-; fed admin law judge, 72- Bus & Prof Pos: Pvt practice of law, Salem, Mass, 37-42. Mil Serv: Entered as Ens, Naval Res, 42, released as Lt(sg), 45, after serv in Pac; Certificate of Commendation; Atlantic, ETO, Pac, Iwo Jima & Okinawa Campaign Ribbons. Mem: Int Soc Labor Law & Social Action; Am Asn Advan Sci. Relig: Jewish. Mailing Add: 6313 Swords Way Bethesda MD 20034

ORE, ROBERT J (D)
Colo State Rep
Mailing Add: 33 Bramblewood St Pueblo CO 81005

O'REAR, OTERIA L (D)
b Tenn, Dec 18, 23; d Aulcie Ferguson & Annie Roundtree F; m 1944 to George W O'Rear, Jr; c Etoile L. Educ: Cent State Univ, BS, 65; Cent State Univ & Ohio State Univ, 66-69; Alpha Phi Gamma; Zeta Phi Beta. Polit & Govt Pos: Vchairperson, Ky Comn Women, 72-; alt deleg, Dem Nat Mid-Term Conf, 74; Washington precinct committeewoman, 74-; Cong Dist Rep to serv on comt to draft plan for deleg selection to 1976 Nat Conv, currently. Bus & Prof Pos: Teacher, Blytheville, Ark, 47-51; managing ed, Springfield Post, Ohio, 55-60; ed, Ohio Eagle, Dayton, 61-64; teacher, Cleveland, 65-70; secy-treas, O'Rear Enterprises Inc, Lexington, Ky, 70- Publ: Working With Disadvantaged Children, Cent State Univ, 67; Economics for Elementary School Children, Ohio Bd Educ, 68. Mem: Metro Environ Improv Comn (bd mem); Nat Woman's Polit Caucus (state policy coun); League Women Voters (treas); Nat Fedn Press Women; Bd Ky Press Women. Honors & Awards: Martha Holden Jennings Leader Award, 67; Affil Contractors Am Outstanding Community Serv Award, 74; Community Serv Award & Noteworthy American, Am Biog Inst Ed Bd, 74. Relig: Protestant. Mailing Add: 841 Charles Ave Lexington KY 40508

ORECHIO, CARL A (R)
NJ State Assemblyman
Mailing Add: State House Trenton NJ 08625

ORECHIO, CARMEN (D)
NJ State Sen
Mailing Add: State House Trenton NJ 08625

O'REILLY, THOMAS P (D)
Md State Sen
Mailing Add: 7107 Lois Lane Lanham MD 20801

ORESTIS, JOHN CHRISTOPHER (D)
Mem, Maine Dem State Comt
b Lewiston, Maine, Mar 8, 43; s Christos Orestis, II & Cecile Langelier O; m 1965 to M Kelsey; c Christos, III, Stephanos & Kelsey Anne. Educ: Georgetown Univ, AB, 65; Am Univ, JD, 68. Polit & Govt Pos: Staff aide to US Sen E S Muskie, 63-68; mem, Androscoggin Co Dem Comt, Maine, 68-73; mem, Lewiston City Dem Comt, 68-; city attorney, Lewiston, 70-72, mayor, 73-; Maine State Rep, 71-72; deleg, Dem Nat Conv, 72; bd dirs, Nat League Cities. Bus & Prof Pos: Attorney, Orestis & Garcia, Lewiston, Maine, 68-; vpres, Maine Municipal Asn. Mem: Am, Maine & Androscoggin Co Bar Asns; Am & Maine Trial Lawyers Asns. Relig: Roman Catholic. Mailing Add: 39 Wellman St Lewiston ME 04240

ORLANDI, O ROLAND (D)
Mass State Rep
Mailing Add: State Capitol Boston MA 02133

ORLANDO, QUENTIN R (D)
Pa State Sen
Mailing Add: 1024 W 22nd St Erie PA 16502

ORLANSKY, GRACE SUYDAM (D)
b New York, NY, Feb 14, 25; d Lawrence Chester Suydam & Louise English S; m 1952 to Jesse Orlansky; c Susan & Karen. Educ: Queens Col, BA, 45; NY Univ, MA, 52. Polit & Govt Pos: Deleg, Dem Nat Conv, 72 & Dem Nat Mid-Term Conf, 74; comnr, Md Fair Campaign Financing Comn, 75- Mailing Add: 7727 Rocton Ave Chevy Chase MD 20015

ORLEBEKE, CHARLES J (R)
b Grand Rapids, Mich, Oct 27, 34; s Joe Orlebeke & Wilhelmina Plekker O; m 1961 to Faith Holtrop; c Evagren, Alison & Britany. Educ: Calvin Col, BA, 57; grad study fel, Mich State Univ, 57-60, MA, 60, PhD, 65; Fulbright scholar, Univ Sydney, 60-61. Polit & Govt Pos: Research asst, Romney for Gov Comt, Mich, 62; admin asst to Gov Romney, 63-66, exec asst, 67-69; exec asst to Secy, Dept Housing & Urban Develop, Washington, DC, 69-70, Dep Under Secy, 70-72. Bus & Prof Pos: Dean, Col Urban Sci, Univ Ill, Chicago Circle, 73- Publ: The Calare By-Election, Australian Polit Studies Asn News, 2/61; Ambition and organization: The Liberal Party (N S W), Australian Polit, Cheshire, 66; Executive branch has new look, Mich Challenge, 2/67. Mem: Am Polit Sci Asn; Am Soc Pub Admin. Relig: Protestant. Mailing Add: Col of Urban Sci Univ of Ill at Chicago Circle Chicago IL 60680

ORLETT, EDWARD J (D)
Ohio State Rep
b Wheelersburg, Ohio, Oct 13, 33; s Joseph J Orlett & Mary E Miller O; single. Educ: Gen Motors Inst, BSME, 62; Univ Dayton, MBA, 69; Newman Clubs. Polit & Govt Pos: Mem, Trotwood City Coun, Ohio, 67-71; Ohio State Rep, 75- Bus & Prof Pos: Self-employed in real estate. Mil Serv: Entered as Pvt, Army, 54, released as Cpl, 56, after serv in 555th Engr Group, Ger, 54-56. Mem: VFW; Am Slovak Club; Dem Voters League; Montgomery-Greene Co Ment Health Asn. Honors & Awards: Cardinal Newman Award, John Henry Cardinal Newman Hon Soc, 62; Mem in Senate of Jr Chamber Int, 68; Liberty Bell Award for community serv, Dayton Bar Asn, 69. Mailing Add: 3 Cambridge Ave Dayton OH 45406

ORME, LILA MORTON (D)
Mem, Calif Dem State Cent Comt
b Chicago, Ill; d Evan John Morton & Delilah Munro M; div; c Lila Jeanne (Mrs Whitlow), Maynard E & Evan M. Educ: Univ Calif, Berkeley, BS & MS, 29; Beta Gamma Sigma; Gamma Epsilon Pi. Polit & Govt Pos: Mem, Calif Dem State Cent Comt, 44-; mem, Fresno Co Dem Cent Comt, 44-5O, exec secy, 48-50 & 58-60; mem campaign comts, Roosevelt-Truman & Downey, 44, Phillips, 46, Truman, 48, Sisk, 54 & 58 & Humphrey, 68; vchmn, Cong Dist Dem Cent Comt, 46-48; pres, Fresno Co Dem Women, 46-47 & 67-69, voter registrn chmn, 58-; alt deleg, Dem Nat Conv, 48; Fresno Co vchmn, Stevenson-Sparkman, 52; asst conv mgr, Calif Dem Coun, 58, 59 & 60; coordr, Registrn Drives, 58, 60 & 62; campaign coordr, Fresno Co Brown Campaign, 62; campaign coordr, Fresno Co Salinger Campaign, 64; managed hq, Trombetta, 67; managed hq, United Dem, 68 & 70; co women's chmn, Cranston Campaign, 68; co-chmn & mgr hq, Hardy for City Coun, 69; secy, Dem of Cent Calif, 69-; chmn, Fresno Co Dem Coun, 70-; mem, Valley Med Ctr Adv Comt, 71-; mgr, Muskie Hq, spring 72. Bus & Prof Pos: Copy writer, Honig-Cooper Advert, Seattle, Wash, 29-30; copy writer, J Walter Thompson, San Francisco, Calif, 32-35;

asst to advert mgr, United Prune Growers, 30-32; instr Eng, Fresno State Col, Calif, 55-56 & 60-61. Mem: Fresno Women's Civic Coun; Am Asn Univ Women; San Joaquin Valley Town Hall (bd dirs); PTA. Mailing Add: 1035 E Michigan Ave Fresno CA 93704

O'ROURKE, STEPHEN CHARLES **(D)**
RI State Rep
b New York, NY, Dec 26, 16; s Patrick O'Rourke & Bridget McCabe O; m 1941 to Jeanne Noel La Marche; c Stephen C, Jr & Denise Gibson. Educ: Manhattan Col, 33-35; US Naval Acad, BS, 39. Polit & Govt Pos: RI State Rep, 98th Dist, 73- Bus & Prof Pos: Prog mgr, Raytheon Co, Portsmouth RI, 59-64; motel owner-operator, Middletown, 64-72. Mil Serv: Midn, Navy, 35, released as Comdr, 59, after serv in Unrestricted Line Off, all Theatres; Purple Heart; Navy Unit Commendation; all Theatre Ribbons, from prior to World War II to end of Korean War. Mem: US Naval Inst; RI Eng Asn; Lions; Newport Preservation; KofC. Relig: Roman Catholic. Mailing Add: 48 Malbone Rd Newport RI 02840

OROZCO, JOSEPH WILLIAM **(R)**
Chmn, Los Angeles Co Rep Cent Comt, Calif
b Guadalajara, Mex, May 5, 21; s Joseph David Orozco & Mary Carmen O; m 1967 to Olga H Corrales; c David William, Margaret Cynthia, James Frances, Stephen William & Alexander Xavier. Educ: Los Angeles Trade Tech Col, grad, 40; Univ Puebla, MA in Econ. Polit & Govt Pos: Regional rep for Southern Calif, Gov Ronald Reagan, Calif, 67-68; mem bd trustees, Los Angeles Community Col Dist, 69-, pres, 69; asst secy, Los Angeles Co Rep Cent Comt, 71-72, first vchmn, 73-74, chmn, 75- Mil Serv: Chief Warrant Officer, Army, 42-45, serv in Mil Intel, ETO; (Ret). Mem: Am Soc Travel Agts; Am Legion; Am Col Trustees; ROA. Honors & Awards: Man of Year, Inter-Am Club, 67; Alumni of Year, Calif Jr Col Asn, 72; George Washington Honor Medal, Freedom Found, Valley Forge, 74. Relig: Catholic. Mailing Add: 1425 S Marengo Ave Alhambra CA 91803

ORR, A LORRAINE **(R)**
Mem, Nebr State Rep Cent Comt
b Nebr, 1921; d Owen Lee Maddox & Vivian Irene Headley M; m 1940 to James Wilson Orr; c Jeffrey Lee. Educ: San Francisco Bus Sch, 2 years. Polit & Govt Pos: Precinct committeewoman, Lincoln Co Rep Party, 2 years, vchmn, 4 years; pres, Lincoln Co Women's Rep Party, 4 years; mem, Nebr State Rep Cent Comt, 64-, vchmn, 64-67, chmn, 67-71, deleg, Rep Nat Conv, 72; state finance co-chmn, Nixon Comt, regional dir vol, Nixon Reelect Comt. Bus & Prof Pos: Bookkeeper, 42-58; worker, Opportunity Ctr Retarded Children; mem adv coun, Small Bus Admin. Mem: Ak-sar-ben; Nebr Bowling Asn; Lincoln Co Red Cross; North Platte Country Club; Elks. Relig: Presbyterian; Guild Pres. Mailing Add: 402 S Jefferson North Platte NE 69101

ORR, JOAN **(D)**
Iowa State Sen
Mailing Add: 10 Merrill Park Circle Grinnell IA 50112

ORR, KAY A **(R)**
Secy, Exec Comt, Nebr Rep Party
b Burlington, Iowa, Jan 2, 39; d Ralph Robert Stark & Sadie S; m 1957 to William Dayton Orr; c John William & Suzanne. Educ: Univ Iowa, 56-57. Polit & Govt Pos: Co-chmn, Lancaster Co Young Rep, Nebr, 66-67; Nat Committeewoman, Nebr Fedn of Young Rep, 67-68, vchmn, 69-70; vchmn, Lancaster Co Rep Party, 68-70, co-chmn, 72-; prog chmn, Exec Comt Nat Fedn Young Rep, 69-70; secy, Exec Comt, Nebr Rep Party, 70-; campaign coordr, Nebr Comt for Reelect of President, 72. Mem: Jr Women's Club (exec comt, 69-72); Lincoln Community Playhouse Guild; Lincoln Symphony Guild. Honors & Awards: Outstanding Young Rep Woman, Lancaster Co Young Rep, 69; Outstanding Young Rep Woman, Nebr Fedn of Young Rep, 69; Jr Vpres of Founders Day, Nebr Rep Founders Day Comt, 70; Golden Elephant Award, Nebr Rep Party, 72. Relig: Presbyterian. Mailing Add: 1610 Brent Blvd Lincoln NE 68520

ORR, ROBERT DUNKERSON **(R)**
Lt Gov, Ind
b Ann Arbor, Mich, Nov 17, 17; s Samuel Lowry Orr & Louise Dunkerson O; m 1944 to Joanne Wallace; c Robert D, Jr, Marjorie R & Susan (Mrs O Dunn). Educ: Yale Univ, BA, 40; Harvard Bus Sch, 42; Delta Kappa Epsilon; Scroll & Key. Hon Degrees: Hon degrees from Ind State Univ & Hanover Col. Polit & Govt Pos: Chmn, Ctr Twp Adv Bd, Ind, 50-54; treas, Vanderburgh Co Eisenhower Comt, 52; leader, Eval Team to Vietnam for Foreign Opers Div, 54; precinct committeeman, Rep Party, Ind, 54-62; alt deleg, Rep Nat Conv, 56; chmn, Ind Scranton Comt, 64; treas, Eighth Dist Rep Comt, 56-58; chmn, Vanderburgh Co Rep Cent Comt, 65-71; Ind State Sen, 68-72; Lt Gov, Ind, 73- Bus & Prof Pos: Exec vpres, Orr Iron Co, 46-60; vpres-dir, Hahn, Inc, 57-69; dir, Sign Crafters Inc, Evansville, 57-74, PAR Indust, 60-73, Dixson, Inc, Grand Junction, Colo, 62-, Erie Invest, Evansville, 65-73, & Indian Industs, 67-73; pres & dir, Indian Archery Corp, 62-65. Mil Serv: Entered as Pvt, Army, 42, released as Maj, 46, after serv in Qm Corps, Alaska, SW Pac, Philippines, Okinawa, Japan; Legion of Merit. Mem: Rotary; Evansville Country Club; Evansville Petroleum Club; Columbia Club; Hanover Col (trustee). Honors & Awards: Distinguished Serv Award, Jaycees, 53. Relig: Presbyterian. Legal Res: RR 8 Box 97 Evansville IN 47711 Mailing Add: Rm 333 State House Indianapolis IN 46204

ORR, ROY LEE **(D)**
Committeeman, Tex State Dem Party
b Dallas, Tex, Oct 2, 32; s Willis Walker Orr & Audra Hill O; m 1952 to Jessie Janice Gallagher; c Valorie Sue, Roxie Karen, Lei Ann & John Timothy. Polit & Govt Pos: Pres, De Soto Independent Sch Dist, Tex, 61-67; chmn, Charter Comn, City of De Soto, 68-69; committeeman, Tex State Dem Party, 23rd Senatorial Dist, 68-; chmn, Tex State Dem Exec Comt, 71-72; mayor, City of De Soto, 71-72; comnr, Dallas Co, 72- Mil Serv: Entered as Pvt, Air Force, 50, released as Sgt, 52, after serv in 443rd Troop Carrier Wing. Mem: Nat Asn Co Officials; Tex Co Judges & Comnr Asn; Am Bankers Asn; Tex Agents Asn; De Soto CofC. Honors & Awards: Outstanding Citizen Under Age 35, 63. Relig: Church of Christ. Legal Res: 320 Woodhaven Dr De Soto TX 75115 Mailing Add: Box 10 De Soto TX 75115

ORR, WILSON FRED, II **(D)**
b Atlanta, Ga, July 5, 41; s W Fred Orr, Sr & Cynthia Nance O; c Julie Theresa, Allison Margaret & Michael Fortson. Educ: Emory Univ, AB, 63, Law Sch, LLB, 65; Sigma Chi. Polit & Govt Pos: Mem, Ga State Dem Exec Comt, 71-74. Bus & Prof Pos: Partner, Orr & Federal, Attorney-at-Law, Decatur, Ga, 72- Mem: Phi Delta Phi; Am Bar Asn; Am Trial Lawyers Asn; Ga Conservancy, Inc; Am Judicature Soc. Relig: Protestant. Mailing Add: 1 West Court Sq Decatur GA 30030

ORRICK, WILLIAM HORSLEY, JR **(D)**
b San Francisco, Calif, Oct 10, 15; s William Horsley Orrick & Mary Downey O; m 1947 to Marion Naffziger; c Mary Louise, Marion & William H, III. Educ: Yale Univ, BA, 37; Univ Calif, LLB, 41. Polit & Govt Pos: Deleg, Dem Nat Conv, 56-68; Asst Attorney Gen, Civil Div, US Dept Justice, 61-62, Asst Attorney Gen, Antitrust Div, 63-65; dep undersecy state, US, 62-63; US Dist Judge, Calif Northern Dist, 74- Bus & Prof Pos: Assoc, Orrick, Herrington, Rowley & Sutcliffe, 41-50, partner, 50-60 & 65-75. Mil Serv: Entered Army, 42, released as Capt, 46, after serv in Mil Intelligence. Relig: Episcopal. Legal Res: 6 Presidio Terr San Francisco CA 94118 Mailing Add: 600 Montgomery St San Francisco CA 94111

ORRISON, CARROL PAYTON **(D)**
Wyo State Rep
b Sapulpa, Okla, May 19, 29; s Carl Orrison & Edythe Payton O; m 1950 to Barbara Colleen Kiehm; c Richard Carl & Debra Sue. Educ: Univ Wyo, 47; Allen Acad, Bryan, Tex, AS, 48; Univ Denver, 49. Polit & Govt Pos: Chmn, Wyo Aeronaut Comn, 71-; Wyo State Rep & mem appropriations comt, Wyo House Rep, 75- Bus & Prof Pos: Pres, Wyo Beer Wholesalers Asn, 73-75; dir, Rocky Mountain Beer Distributors Asn, 75- Mem: Kiwanis; CofC; Shrine; Mason; Elks. Mailing Add: 3634 Dover Rd Cheyenne WY 82001

ORSINI, JOSEPH LIONEL **(R)**
Alaska State Sen
b Staten Island, NY, May 18, 39; s Joseph Q Orsini & Gina Santiccioli O; m 1970 to Janice Victoria Nichols. Educ: Princeton Univ, BS, 60; Univ Alaska, Anchorage, MS, 64, MBA, 72; Sacramento State Col, BA, 70; Elm Club. Polit & Govt Pos: Alaska State Rep, formerly; Alaska State Sen, currently. Bus & Prof Pos: Jr engr, New York, 61; engr design & planning, Corps of Engrs, Anchorage & Sacramento, 64-69; asst prof eng mgt, Univ Alaska, Anchorage, 69-72; self-employed mgt consult, Anchorage, 73- Mil Serv: Entered as Pvt E-1, Army, 61, released as E-4, 64, after serv in Alaska, 61-64. Mem: Am Soc Eng Educ; Alaska Soc Prof Engrs; Data Processing Mgt Asn. Mailing Add: 2912 Alder Dr Anchorage AK 99504

ORTEN, BETTY **(D)**
Colo State Rep
b Washington, DC, Feb 3, 27; d Crawford McMann Kellogg & Mildred Tyler K; m 1951 to Russell Sage Orten; c Russell, Jerry, Frank & Bruce. Educ: Marin Jr Col, AA, 47; Univ Colo, BA, 49; Univ Denver, 51-52. Polit & Govt Pos: Mem, Dem Nat Comt, Colo, 72-74; Colo State Rep, 75- Mailing Add: 7978 Stuart Pl Westminster CO 80030

ORTH, ROBERT D **(R)**
Treas, Kans Rep State Comt
b Wichita, Kans, Dec 13, 35; s Wallace Edward Orth & Ethel McCoy O; m 1964 to Jeannie Karleen Johnson; c Fonda Michelle & Richard Edward. Educ: Wichita Univ, 53-59 & 62; Phi Delta. Polit & Govt Pos: Precinct committeeman, Sublette, Kans, 70; chmn, Sublette Rep Cent Comt, 70; justice of the peace, 70; treas, Kans Rep State Comt, 73- Bus & Prof Pos: Self-employed, 62; pres, Hasco, Inc, 72, Haskell Co Serv, Inc, 72 & Alfalfa, Inc, 72; bd dirs, McCoy Grain, 72; pres, Mid-Am Film Archive, Inc, 73; pres, Flicks, Inc, 73. Mil Serv: Entered as Recruit, Army, 59, released as Sgt, 62, after serv in 226th Signal Co, MSC Command, Korea, 60-62; Letter of Commendation. Mem: Am Legion; VFW (comdr, 69); life mem Sublette Jaycees; Kans Jaycees; Mason. Honors & Awards: Jaycee of the Year, Sublette Jaycees, 68, Distinguished Serv Award, 68; JCI Senator, Kans Jaycees, 70 & Jaycee of the Year, 71. Relig: Methodist. Mailing Add: 409 S Inman Sublette KS 67877

ORTIZ, DONALD JOSEPH **(D)**
Mem, NMex Dem State Cent Comt
b Santa Fe, NMex, Sept 19, 34; s Frank S Ortiz & Lucy Castillo O; m 1974 to Beverly Ann Garcia; c Rachel, Don, Carolyn, June & Donna. Educ: Univ NMex, BA, 59. Polit & Govt Pos: Nat committeeman, Young Dem NMex, 67; mem, NMex Dem State Cent Comt, 71-; deleg, Dem Nat Mid-Term Conf, 74. Bus & Prof Pos: Chmn bd, United Southwest Nat Bank, Santa Fe, NMex, 73- Mem: Elks; Toastmasters. Relig: Catholic. Legal Res: 526 Galisteo St Santa Fe NM 87501 Mailing Add: PO Box 1185 Santa Fe NM 87501

ORTIZ, RUDY A **(D)**
Dem Nat Committeeman, NMex
b Santa Fe, NMex, Nov 16, 32; s Tony J Ortiz & Luisita Perea O; m 1957 to Angeline Oyaca, div; c Marc R, Martin R, Marquita R & Marlisa R. Educ: Col Santa Fe, BA, 55; Univ NMex, grad study, 67- Polit & Govt Pos: Treas, Bernalillo Co Dem Party, NMex, 67-68, chmn, 69-; NMex state chmn, McCarthy for President Campaign, 68; deleg, Dem Nat Conv, 68; bd mem, New Dem Coalition, Nat Dem Party, 68-, Dem Nat Committeeman, NMex, 72-, mem exec comt, currently. Bus & Prof Pos: Ins examr, State of NMex, 55-67; dir, Repub Bank, Albuquerque, 72-; chmn dir, Employ Security Comn, NM, 75- Mil Serv: Entered Navy, 55, released as DK-3, 57, after serv in USS Nerus As-17. Mem: Nat Asn Life Co. Relig: Catholic. Legal Res: 1111 Cardenas Ave SE Albuquerque NM 87108 Mailing Add: PO Box 4O9 Albuquerque NM 87103

ORTIZ GORDILLS, HUMBERTO **(POPULAR DEMOCRAT, PR)**
Rep, PR House of Rep
Mailing Add: State Capitol San Juan PR 00901

ORTIZ-TORO, ARTURO **(R)**
b Ponce, PR, Nov 18, 96; s Carlos Ortiz de Landazuri y Rodas & Elisa del Toro Labarthe O; m 1918 to Zoraida Cordova Mattei; c Earline (Mrs Rogers), Lisette (Mrs Veve) & Arturo A. Educ: Univ Pa Law Sch, JD; pres, Phi Chi Delta. Polit & Govt Pos: Mem, Superior Bd of Health, PR, 26-40; First Asst Attorney Gen & Acting Attorney Gen, PR, 28-33; mem, San Juan Selective Serv Bd; Rep Statehood Party of PR; cand, Resident Comnr of PR; deleg, Rep Nat Conv, 52-68; PR State Sen, 60-68; chmn, PR Rep Party, 68-69, emer chmn, 69- Bus & Prof Pos: Pres, Furniture Finance Corp, 40; dir, El Faro Develop Corp; treas, Copa Construction Corp, currently. Mem: San Juan Chap, Am Legion; San Juan Chap, Univ Pa Club; Fed, Inter-Am & Am Bar Asns. Relig: Catholic. Mailing Add: Condominio Emajagua Apt 4A Nine Emajagua St Punta Las Marias Santurce PR 00913

ORZELL, JOHN J **(D)**
Vt State Rep
Mailing Add: RFD Box 184 West Rutland VT 05777

OSBORN, ELBURT FRANKLIN **(R)**
Dir, Bur of Mines
b Kishwaukee, Ill, Aug 13, 11; s William Franklin Osborn & Anna Sherman O; m 1939 to

Jean McLeod Thomson; c James Franklin & Ian Charles. Educ: DePauw Univ, BA, 32; Northwestern Univ, MS, 34; Calif Inst Technol, PhD, 37; Keramos; Phi Beta Kappa; Phi Kappa Phi; Phi Lambda Upsilon; Sigma Xi; Delta Tau Delta. DDSci, Alfred Univ, 65, Northwestern Univ, 72, Ohio State Univ, 72 & DePauw Univ, 72. Polit & Govt Pos: Dir, Bur of Mines, Dept of Interior, 70- Bus & Prof Pos: Teaching fel geol, Northwestern Univ, 32-34, instr, 37; teaching fel, Calif Inst Technol, 34-37; geologist, Val d'Or, Quebec, Can, 38; petrologist, Geophys Lab, Carnegie Inst, Washington, DC, 38-42; phys chemist, Div 1, Nat Defense Research Comt, Off Sci Research & Develop, 42-45; research chemist, Eastman Kodak Co, 45-46; prof geochem & chmn div earth sci, Col Mineral Industs, Pa State Univ, 46-52, assoc dean col, 52-53, dean, 53-59, vpres research, 59-70. Publ: Phase Equilibria Among Oxides in Steelmaking (w A Muan), Addison-Wesley, 65; Optimum composition of blast furnace slag as deduced from liquidus data for the quaternary system...(w R C DeVries, K G Gee & H M Kraner), J Metals, 1/54; Role of oxygen pressure in the crystallization & differentiation of basaltic magma, Am J Sci, 257: 609-647. Mem: Nat Acad Eng; fel Am Asn Advan Sci; fel Am Ceramic Soc; fel Am Geophys Union; fel Geol Soc Am. Honors & Awards: Regional Tech Meetings Award Medal, Am Iron & Steel Inst, 54; Nat Sci Found sr post doctoral fel, Cambridge Univ, 58; Mem Lectr, Am Ceramic Soc, 70; Roebling Medal, Mineralogical Soc Am, 72; John Jepson Award, Am Ceramic Soc, 73. Relig: Protestant. Legal Res: 300 E Irwin Ave State College PA 16801 Mailing Add: 3525 Hamlet Pl Chevy Chase MD 20015

OSBORN, GEORGE W (R)
VChmn, Greene Co Rep Comt, NY
b Windham, NY, July 24, 98; s George W Osborn & Clara Goslee O; m 1923 to Florence Dodge. Educ: Albany Bus Col. Polit & Govt Pos: Mem, Bd of Educ, Windham High Sch, NY, sch dir & town supvr, 16 years; vchmn, Greene Co Rep Comt, NY. Bus & Prof Pos: Owner, summer resort, Osborn House, Windham, NY, 15-46. Mem: Mason (Past Master, High Priest, Past Dist Deputy). Relig: Protestant. Mailing Add: Windham NY 12496

OSBORN, JONES (D)
Ariz State Sen
Mailing Add: State Capitol Phoenix AZ 85007

OSBORNE, EARL THOMAS (D)
Judge, Ky Court of Appeals
b Ballard Co, Ky, July 10, 20; s Willie Claude Osborne & Dovie Bradford O; m 1943 to Helen Cooper; c William P, Thomas Lee, Phyllis Jo & Debora Jane. Educ: Univ Ky, LLB, 50; Phi Alpha Delta. Polit & Govt Pos: Circuit judge, 42nd Judicial Dist, Ky, 57-67; judge, Ky Court Appeals, 67- Mil Serv: Entered as Pvt, Air Force, 40, released as 1st Lt, 45, after serv in 438 Troop Carrier Group, 90th T C Squadron, ETO, 43-45; Air Medal with Two Oak Leaf Clusters. Mem: Ky State & Am Bar Asns; Am Legion; VFW. Relig: Methodist. Mailing Add: Rte 1 Gilbertsville KY 42044

OSBORNE, EDWARD BERYL (D)
Chmn, Clermont Co Dem Cent & Exec Comts, Ohio
b Indian Hill, Ohio, July 30, 19; s Jesse Price Osborne & Jessie Jordan O; m 1941 to Rosemary White; c Karen. Educ: Wilmington Col, BS in Educ, 42; Univ Cincinnati Col Law, LLB, 48. Polit & Govt Pos: Secy, Clermont Co Dem Cent & Exec Comts, Ohio, 56-64, chmn, 64-; precinct committeeman, Dem Cent Comt, 56-; mem, Clermont Co Bd of Elec, 57-6O, chmn, 60- Mil Serv: Entered as Pvt, Army, 42, recalled, 51, released as 1st Lt, 52, after serv in 95th Div, 70th Div, 81st Div & 1st Cavalry, SPac & Korea, Japan, 42-46 & 51-52; Bronze Star; Second Award Combat Infantryman's Badge; Bronze Arrowhead; Pac Theater Ribbons with four Battle Stars; Japanese Army of Occup Medal; Korean Campaign Ribbon; Philippine Campaign Ribbon. Mem: Clermont Co & Ohio Bar Asns. Relig: Methodist. Mailing Add: 2262 Cedarville Rd Goshen OH 45122

OSBORNE, WILLIAM EDWARD (D)
Vt State Rep
Mailing Add: RD 2 Barre VT 05641

OSBOURN, D R (OZZIE) (D)
Mo State Rep
b Upton, Mo, Dec 14, 23; s Moses Henry Osbourn & Opal L Stottlemyre O; m 1950 to Lois M Meeker; c Doran M & Lori Lynn. Educ: Southwest Mo State Col, BS, 46; Univ Mo, Columbia, ME, 48; Phi Delta Kappa. Polit & Govt Pos: Mo State Rep, Dist 14, 67- Bus & Prof Pos: Athletic dir & basketball coach, Hannibal-LaGrange Col, 48-50 & Holy Rosary High Sch, 56-58. Mil Serv: Entered as Pvt, Army Air Force, 43, released as AC 44, after serv in 326CTD, Eastern Command, 43-44; Good Conduct Medal. Mem: Mo Jr Col Athletic Asn (vpres); Moose; Elks; Lions; Grange. Relig: Christian Church of NAm. Mailing Add: RR 3 Monroe City MO 63456

OSE, AL (D)
Alaska State Rep
Mailing Add: PO Box 832 Palmer AK 99645

OSGOOD, WILFRED BEEDE (R)
NH State Rep
b Haverhill, Mass, Aug 4, 11; s George Nowell Osgood & Mary Beede O; m 1946 to Donna M Tilton. Educ: Univ NH, 29-32; Mass Col Pharm, BS, 52; Phi Mu Delta. Polit & Govt Pos: Mem, NH State Bd Health, 58-61; mem, NH Comn Pharm & Practical Chem, 65-71; mem, Munic Budget Comt, Farmington, NH, 60-73; mem, Strafford Co Exec & Budget Comt, currently; NH State Rep, 75-, mem, Health & Welfare Comt, NH House Rep, 75- Bus & Prof Pos: Pres, Farmington Holding Corp, 60-65, NH Pharmaceutical Asn, 61-63, Farmington Indust Develop Corp, 67- & Farmington CofC, 73- Mailing Add: 15 Charles Farmington NH 03835

O'SHAUGHNESS, ROBERT E (D)
Ohio State Sen
Mailing Add: 405 E Town St Columbus OH 43215

OSHEIM, DONALD (R)
b Rosholt, SDak, Aug 20, 19; s Lawrence C Osheim & Anna Erdahl O; m 1942 to Reva Terry; c Elizabeth, David & Robert. Educ: Univ SDak, LLB, 48; Kappa Sigma; Delta Theta Phi. Polit & Govt Pos: City attorney, Watertown, SDak, 59-62; mem bd regents, Augustana Col, 68-; SDak State Rep & Speaker, SDak House of Rep, 71-72; deleg, Rep Nat Conv, 72. Bus & Prof Pos: Practicing attorney, Stover, Beardsley & Osheim, 52-56; practicing attorney, Beardsley, Osheim & Fox. Mil Serv: Pilot, Navy Air Corps, 41, released as Lt(sg), 45; Air Medal; Pac Theater Ribbon. Mem: Am & SDak Bar Asns; Elks (past Exalted Ruler); Lions. Relig: Lutheran. Mailing Add: 1381 Crestview Dr Watertown SD 57201

OSHEL, VAL (R)
b Harrisburg, Ill, Mar 5, 26; s James Clyde Oshel & Della McKinney O; m 1949 to Shirley Louise Walker; c Michael Val. Educ: Univ Ill, 47-48; Southern Ill Univ, 55-58. Polit & Govt Pos: City comnr, Harrisburg, Ill, 63-67; mayor, Harrisburg, 67-69; Rep cand, US Rep, Ill, 68 & 74; asst dir, Ill Dept Pub Works, 69-; dir, Ill Civil Defense Agency, 70- Mil Serv: Entered as A/S, Navy, 44, released as Signalman 3/C, 46, after serv in SPac Theatre, 45-46. Mem: Mason; Elks. Relig: Baptist. Mailing Add: 103 N Granger Harrisburg IL 62946

OSHIKI, KAZ (D)
b Hawthorne, Calif, Oct 25, 24. Educ: Drake Univ, BS; Univ Wis, MS. Polit & Govt Pos: Admin asst to US Rep Kastenmeier, Wis, currently. Mil Serv: S/Sgt, Army, World War II, with serv in South & West Pac. Mailing Add: 5600 Broad Br Rd Washington DC 20015

OSIECKI, CLARICE A (R)
Conn State Rep
Mailing Add: 9 Terra Glen Rd Danbury CT 06810

OSLER, DOROTHY K (R)
Conn State Rep
b Dayton, Ohio, Aug 19, 23; d Carl M Karstaedt & Pearl Tobias K; m 1946 to David K Osler; c Scott C & David D. Educ: Miami Univ, BS, 45; Phi Beta Kappa; Mortarboard; Les Politiques; Alpha Omicron Pi. Polit & Govt Pos: Town meet rep, Greenwich, Conn, 69-; Conn State Rep, 73- Mem: Am Asn Univ Women; League of Women Voters; Gtr Greenwich Rep Club; Eastern Greenwich Rep Women's Club. Relig: Christian Scientist. Mailing Add: 138 Lockwood Rd Riverside CT 06878

OSLUND, WALTER B (R)
Wyo State Rep
Mailing Add: 112 Highland Ave Newcastle WY 82701

OSTENDORF, ALVIN FRED (R)
Chmn, Washington Co Rep Party, Party, Ill
b Nashville, Ill, Dec 4, 25; s John Fred Ostendorf & Alvina Blumhorst O; m 1954 to Doris Laura Kersten; c Mary, John, Marsha & Marlene. Educ: LaSalle Exten Univ, LLB, 69. Polit & Govt Pos: Mem, Grad Sch Bd, Addieville, Ill, 57-66; precinct committeeman, Plum Hill Twp, 64-; chmn, Washington Co Rep Party, 68- Bus & Prof Pos: Farmer & trucker, 54- Mil Serv: Entered as Pvt, Nat Guard & Air Force, 48, released as Sgt, 57, after serv in 44th Div & 3310 T T Wing; Serv Ribbon. Mem: Farm Bur; Churchmen's Fel. Relig: United Church of Christ. Mailing Add: RR 2 Nashville IL 62263

OSTERBACK, ALVIN (D)
Alaska State Rep
Mailing Add: PO Box 71 Sand Point AK 99661

OSTERBACK, MARIE ERNA (D)
b Iktan, Alaska, July 30, 28; d Oscar Vanner & Alexandria Verskin V; m 1945 to Alvin Osterback; c David, Erna (Mrs Shearer), Svea (Mrs Myers) & Alvin Dwain. Polit & Govt Pos: Deleg, Dem Nat Conv, 72. Bus & Prof Pos: Owner-mgr, Sand Point Theatre, Alaska, 48-56, Marie's Variety Store, 58-62, Al & Marie's Coffee Shop, 59-68 & Shumigon Bakery, 69-72. Relig: Russian Orthodox. Mailing Add: Box 71 Sand Point AK 99661

OSTERBERGER, KENNETH E (D)
La State Sen
Mailing Add: 8874 Trinity Ave Baton Rouge LA 70806

OSTERLOH, HENRY JOE (D)
Ark State Rep
b Little Rock, Ark, Apr 23, 35; s Henry E Osterloh & Bernice Railey O; m 1959 to Shirley Ann Webster; c Schelle LeClair. Educ: Univ Ark, Little Rock, BS in Acct, 62; Ark Law Sch, LLB, 66; Kappa Sigma. Polit & Govt Pos: Mem, Pulaski Co Dem Comt, Ark, 70-72; Ark State Rep, 73- Bus & Prof Pos: Attorney-at-Law, Matthews, Purtle, Osterloh & Weber, Little Rock, Ark, 66- Mil Serv: Entered as Pvt, Army, 55, released as Cpl, 57, after serv in 510 Tank Bn, European Theatre, 56-57. Mem: Am Bar Asn; Ark Asn Criminal Defense Lawyers (treas); Optimist Club. Relig: Methodist. Legal Res: 4521 Greenway North Little Rock AR 72116 Mailing Add: 300 Spring St Little Rock AR 72201

OSTERTAG, HAROLD CHARLES (R)
b Attica, NY, June 22, 96; s Otto John Ostertag & Frances Julia Briem O; m 1919 to Grace Jean Bryson. Educ: Chamberlain Mil Inst. Polit & Govt Pos: NY State Assemblyman, 32-50; US Rep, 39th & 37th Cong Dist, NY, 50-64. Bus & Prof Pos: Asst vpres, Traffic Dept, New York Cent Syst. Mil Serv: Entered as Musician, Army, 17, released as Sgt, after serv in 55th Pioneer Inf, AEF. Mem: Elks; Am Legion; VFW; World War I Veterans; Farm Bur. Relig: Presbyterian. Legal Res: Westside Silver Lake Perry NY 14530 Mailing Add: 73 Palm Club Pompano Beach FL 33062

OSTHOFF, TOM (DFL)
Minn State Rep
Mailing Add: 766 W Maryland Ave St Paul MN 55117

OSTLING, RALPH A (R)
Mich State Rep
b Roscommon, Mich, July 3, 27; s John Enfred Ostling & Wilhemina Skagerberg O; m 1947 to Thela Catherine Dean; c Kurt Arthur. Educ: Cent Mich Univ, BS, 52; Mich State Univ, MS, 69. Polit & Govt Pos: Twp clerk, Gerrish Twp, Roscommon, Mich, 53-73; Mich State Rep, 103rd Dist, 73- Bus & Prof Pos: Sec educ teacher, Gerrish Higgins High Sch, Roscommon, Mich, 52-72. Mil Serv: Entered as A/S, Navy, 45, served in Pac Theatre, 45-47; Naval Res, 5 years. Relig: Lutheran. Mailing Add: RD 2 Box 475 Roscommon MI 48653

OSTLUND, JOHN C (R)
Wyo State Sen
b Gillette, Wyo, Sept 29, 27; s Axel W Ostlund & Mary S Roberts O; m 1952 to Mary V Ryan; c M M Peg, John C, Jr, Thomas A, Nancy E, Patrick J, Karin A, Jane E & James S.

Educ: US Naval Acad, BS, 49. Polit & Govt Pos: Chmn, Campbell Co Rep Comt, Wyo, 51-59; committeeman, Wyo Rep State Comt, 59-73; trustee, Univ Wyo, 69-73; Wyo State Sen, Campbell-Johnson Dist, 73- Bus & Prof Pos: Partner, Ostlund Investments, 60-; dir, Colo-Wyo Hotel & Motel Asn, 69-72; dir, Wyo Nat Corp, 69-; pres, Wyo Indust Develop Corp, 70-72; pres, Black Thunder Ranch Co, 72- Mil Serv: Entered as Midn, Navy, 45, released as Ens, 50, after serv in Mediter Fleet, 49. Mem: Rotary. Honors & Awards: Wyo Hon Mem, Alpha of Wyo Chap, Beta Gamma Sigma, Univ Wyo, 73. Relig: Catholic. Legal Res: 410 W Fifth St Gillette WY 82716 Mailing Add: 302 Douglas Hwy Gillette WY 82716

OSTROSKY, KATHRYN **(D)**
Alaska State Rep
Mailing Add: 423 E 12th Ave Anchorage AK 99501

O'SULLIVAN, WILLIAM HENRY **(R)**
Chmn, Smith Co Rep Party, Tex
b St James, NY, Apr 4, 23; s Patrick Henry O'Sullivan & Grace Finn O; m 1947 to Louise Marie Hoffmann; c Patrick Henry, John Dennis, Michael Francis, Christine Ann & William Henry. Educ: Syracuse Univ, BA, 50. Polit & Govt Pos: Precinct chmn, Tyler Rep Party, Tex, 67-73; chmn, Smith Co Rep Party, 73-; comnr, Tyler Airport Adv Comn, currently. Bus & Prof Pos: Sales mgr, Carrier Corp, Tyler, Tex, 57-59, qual control mgr, 59-60, sales mgr, 60-65, materials mgr, 65-69, prod mgr, 69- Mil Serv: Entered as Aviation Cadet, Navy, 43, released as Lt(jg), 46, after serv in Pac Theatre, 45-46. Mem: Am Inst Indust Engrs; Indust Mgt Club (adv bd); ETex Traffic Club; Tyler CofC (mem aviation comt). Relig: Roman Catholic. Mailing Add: 3209 Lynnwood Dr Tyler TX 75701

OSWALD, ROBERT HOLMES **(D)**
Chmn, Jackson Co Dem Exec Comt, Miss
b Birmingham, Ala, Jan 26, 28; s Charles Alfred Oswald, Jr & Jeannette Bibby O; m 1966 to Betty Jean Robinson; c Robert, Jr, Robyn & Rebecca. Educ: Millsaps Col, 46-47; Tulane Univ, 47-49; Jackson Law Sch, LLB, 51; Sigma Delta Kappa. Polit & Govt Pos: City prosecutor, Pascagoula, Miss, 53-56, city attorney, 56-60; chmn, Jackson Co Dem Exec Comt, 56-68 & 72-; secy, Young Dem of Miss, 57-59, pres, 61-63; chmn, Miss Dem Conf, 66. Bus & Prof Pos: Attorney-at-law, 52; co-ed, Gautier Independent, weekly newspaper, 71- Mil Serv: Entered as A/S, Navy, 45, released as Seaman 1/C, 46, after serv in USS Sargent Bay & USS Tripoli, Pac Theatre; Victory Medal; Asiatic-Pac Theatre Medal. Mem: Am, Miss & Jackson Co Bar Asns; Am Legion; Optimist Club, Pascagoula, Miss (pres, 69, lt-gov, Ala-Miss Dist, Int, 72-73). Relig: Baptist. Legal Res: Bayou Oaks Gautier MS 39553 Mailing Add: PO Box 189 Pascagoula MS 39567

OSWALD, ROBERT LEON **(R)**
Secy, Interstate Com Comn
b Glendale, Calif, Oct 31, 35; s Theodore Lewis Oswald (deceased) & Cora Ruth Youngberg O; m 1967 to Frances Dianne Biegelmeier, div; c Robert Scott. Educ: Univ Md, BA, 60; George Washington Univ Sch Law, JD, 64; First Honor Convocation; Delta Theta Phi. Polit & Govt Pos: Admin asst to Chief Hearing Examr, Interstate Com Comn, Washington, DC, 61-64, legal asst to Dir Bur Enforcement, 64-65, cong liaison officer, Interstate Com Comn, 69-, secy, 70-; spec asst for research & develop contracts to dir, Nat Career Inst, Nat Insts Health, 65-66; admin asst to US Rep William S Mailliard, Calif, 66-69; field rep, Ohio United Citizens for Nixon-Agnew, 68; staff asst, Rockefeller Cong Steering Comt, 68; assoc mem, Rep State Cent Comt Calif, 69- Mil Serv: Entered as Pvt, Air Force, 53, released as Sgt, 57, after serv in 1254th Air Transport Group, Wash; Group Conduct Medal; Nat Defense Medal. Mem: DAV. Honors & Awards: Outstanding Law Student Award, George Washington Univ Law Sch, 64; Outstanding Brother Award, Region Four, Four, Delta Theta Phi; Outstanding Serv Award, Student Bar Asn, George Washington Univ Sch Law; Achievement Cert, DC Bar Asn; Distinguished Scholar Cert, Univ Md. Relig: Protestant. Legal Res: 31709 Foxfield Dr Westlake Village CA 91361 Mailing Add: 1435 Fourth St SW Washington DC 20024

OTENASEK, MILDRED **(D)**
Dem Nat Committeewoman, Md
b Baltimore, Md, Feb 6, 14; d Frank Busick & Josephine Cook B; m 1937 to Dr Frank J Otenasek. Educ: Col of Notre Dame, Md, AB, 36; Johns Hopkins Univ, PhD, 39. Polit & Govt Pos: Vchmn, State Dem Cent Comt, Md, 48-56; pres, United Dem Women's Clubs of Md, 55-57; Dem Nat Committeewoman, Md, 56-, mem policy comt, Dem Nat Comt, 71, mem, Vice Presidential Comt, 73; deleg, Dem Nat Conv, 56-72, mem arrangements comt, 60, site comt, 64, allocation of deleg comt, 68 & credentiais comt, 64 & 68; chmn, Equal Employment Opportunities Comn, Baltimore, 60-62; co-chmn, Status of Women Comn, 64-66; mem, James Comn, 70; past mem, Port Authority Comt; past mem, Gov Reapportionment Comt. Bus & Prof Pos: Assoc prof econ, Trinity Col, 40-54; assoc prof econ & polit sci, Notre Dame Col, 54-72, prof econ & polit sci, 72- Mem: Cath Comn on Intellectual & Cult Affairs. Relig: Roman Catholic. Mailing Add: Highfield House 4000 N Charles St Baltimore MD 21218

OTIS, JAMES CORNISH, JR
Assoc Justice, Minn Supreme Court
b St Paul, Minn, Mar 23, 12; s James Cornish Otis & Winifred Brill O; m 1974 to Constance S Dillingham; c Emily R (Mrs Thach), James D & Todd H. Educ: Yale Univ, BA, 34; Univ Minn, LLB, 37; Phi Delta Phi; Zeta Psi. Polit & Govt Pos: Judge, Munic Court, St Paul, Minn, 48-54; judge, Second Dist Court, 54-61; assoc justice, Minn Supreme Court, 61- Bus & Prof Pos: Partner, Law Firm, Otis, Faricy & Burger, 37-48. Mem: Minn State & Am Bar Asns; Minn State Bar Found; Am Judicature Soc; Nat Coun Crime & Delinquency. Relig: Unitarian. Legal Res: 7 Crocus Hill St Paul MN 55102 Mailing Add: 230 State Capitol St Paul MN 55155

OTLOWSKI, GEORGE J **(D)**
NJ State Rep
Mailing Add: State House Trenton NJ 08625

O'TOOLE, DAN **(D)**
Mo State Rep
Mailing Add: 5082 Bristol Rock Rd Florissant MO 63033

O'TOOLE, WILLIAM R **(D)**
Mo State Rep
Mailing Add: 4712 Tamm St Louis MO 63109

OTSTOTT, JESSE LEE **(D)**
Chmn, Greeley Co Dem Cent Comt, Kans
b Athens, Ill, Jan 23, 11; s Jesse Hughie Otstott & Lola Mae Long O; m 1960 to Eva Marie Groff Warne; c Sammie Mauk, John, Robert, Delaine, Clark & Maynard Warne & Richard Eugene Otstott. Educ: Preston High Sch, Kans, 27-31. Polit & Govt Pos: Chmn, Greeley Co Dem Cent Comt, Kans, 50-; Greeley Co Centennial Chmn. Bus & Prof Pos: Sta agent, Mo Pac RR Co, 42- Mem: Transportation Commun Employees Union. Honors & Awards: 25 Year Pin, Mo Pac RR Co, 67. Relig: Catholic. Mailing Add: Box 248 Tribune KS 67879

OTT, ALEXANDER REGINALD **(D)**
Mem, Dem State Cent Comt, Mich
b Picayune, Miss, June 9, 31; s Fred Ott & Violette Armstrong O; m 1952 to Izolla Gaddies; c Alexander R, II, La Sharna M, Wendell W & Veronical Y. Educ: Alcorn Agr & Mech Col, Miss, 51-52; Dillard Univ, La, 54-55; Flint Col, Mich, 56-57. Polit & Govt Pos: Chmn, Genesee Co Dem Publicity Comt, Mich, 66-67; mem, Genesee Co Dem Exec Comt, 66-68; mem, Genesee Co Bldg Authority, Flint, 67-; mem, Dem State Cent Comt, Seventh Dist, 67-; deleg, Dem Nat Conv, 68. Bus & Prof Pos: Owner, Restaurant, Flint, Mich, 57-59; vpres, Local 659, UAW, Mich, 65-68; int rep, UAW, Flint, 68- Mil Serv: Entered as Basic Airman, Air Force, 52, released as Airman 1/C, 54, after serv in Mil Transportation, Far Eastern Air Command, 53; Good Conduct Medal. Mem: UAW; Genesee Co Bldg Authority Comt; Flint Urban League; NAACP; Flint Community Civic League. Relig: Protestant. Mailing Add: 753 Lyndon Ave Flint MI 48505

OTTE, CARL **(D)**
Wis State Assemblyman
b Sheboygan, Wis, June 24, 23; s John Otte & Magdalena Verconteren O; m 1949 to Ethel Dorothy Braatz; c Allen Carl, Jane Karen, Julie Beth & Lynn Carol. Educ: Central High Sch, Sheboygan, grad. Polit & Govt Pos: Mem co bd, Sheboygan, Wis, 62-68, parking comn, 65-68, adv comt community develop, 68-73, police & fire comn, 68-73; Wis State Assemblyman, currently. Mil Serv: Entered as Pvt, Army, 43, released as Pfc, 45, after serv in 478th Ord Evacuation Co, ETO, 44-45. Mem: Local 325 AMCBW; Local 95 Am Fedn Musicians; VFW; Am Legion. Relig: Lutheran. Legal Res: 1440 S 22nd St Sheboygan WI 53081 Mailing Add: 134 B South State Capitol Madison WI 53702

OTTE, PAUL JOSEPH **(R)**
WVa State Deleg
b Wheeling, WVa, Jan 9, 23; s Edward Henry Otte & Marie Morris O; m 1961 to Magdalen Ann Rickus. Educ: Army Provost Marshall Sch, 43-44; real estate course, cert, 74; WVa Northern Community Col, 75. Polit & Govt Pos: WVa State Deleg, 74-, mem health & welfare comt, polit sub-div, banking & ins comt, WVa Legis, 74- Bus & Prof Pos: Sales mgr & supvr, Steamway Carpet Cleaners & State Dry Cleaners, 40-; pub rels, State Sanitone & Otte Bros Cleaners, 75- & advert speciality, Wheeling, WVa & Martins Ferry, Ohio, 75- Mil Serv: Entered as Pvt, Air Force, 43, released as T-5, 45, after serv in 1296th MP Aviation, ETO, 44-45; ETO-Eisenhower Award; Good Conduct Medal; Cert of Achievement Award. Mem: Wheeling City Coun (co-chmn, Citizen's Adv Comt); KofC (4 degree); Serra Club of Wheeling (secy, 75-); Elks (mem entertainment comt, 75). Honors & Awards: Cert for 99% attendance at bus session, WVa Legis, 75. Mailing Add: 7 Oakmont Rd Wheeling WV 26003

OTTER, C L (BUTCH) **(R)**
Idaho State Rep
Mailing Add: 1105 N Ohio Caldwell ID 83605

OTTERBACHER, JOHN ROBERT **(D)**
Mich State Sen
b Grand Rapids, Mich, Nov 23, 42; s John Adalbert Otterbacher & Dena Dunn O; m 1966 to Christine Frances Nawrocki. Educ: Aquinas Col, Mich, BA, 66; St Louis Univ, MS, 68, PhD, 70. Polit & Govt Pos: Mem, Mich Dem State Party, 71-; chmn legis comt, Kent Co Dem Party, 71-, mem exec comt, 72-; Mich State Rep, 73-74, vchmn ment health comt & civil rights comt, mem urban affairs comt & youth care comt, Mich House Rep, 73-74; Mich State Sen, 75-, chmn health, social serv & retirement comt, Mich State Senate, 75-, chmn comt to investigate nursing homes, 75-, vchmn col & univs comts, 75-, vchmn agr & consumer affairs comt, 75-, vchmn vet affairs comt, 75- Bus & Prof Pos: Intern, John Cochrans Vet Hosp, St Louis, Mo, 2 years; asst prof & clin psychologist, Aquinas Col, Mich, 70-72. Publ: The development & evaluation of a state-trait measure of perceived guilt, J Clin & Consult Psychol. Mem: Kent Co Asn for Retarded Children (mem adv bd). Honors & Awards: Outstanding Young Man of Am, 72. Relig: Roman Catholic. Mailing Add: 412 Cedar NE Grand Rapids MI 49503

OTTERMAN, ROBERT JAMES **(D)**
Councilman, Akron, Ohio
b Akron, Ohio, July 29, 32; s John L Otterman & Marguerite Rauch O; m 1951 to Carolyn Marie Anzaldi; c John Robert & Robyn Marie. Educ: Akron Univ, BA in Social Studies, 58 & MA in Admin, 64; Lambda Chi Alpha. Polit & Govt Pos: Mem exec bd, Summit Co Young Dem, Ohio, 63-65 & 68-, second vpres, 65-66, first vpres, 66-67, pres, 67-68; precinct committeeman, Summit Co Dem Party, 65-, youth coordr, 67-, teen Dem adv, 68-; col adv, Akron Univ Dem Party, 67-; mem exec bd, Dem Cent Comt Summit Co, 67-; alt deleg, Dem Nat Conv, 68; chmn, Sixth War Dem Party, Akron, 70-; councilman, Sixth Ward, Akron, 70- Bus & Prof Pos: Rep, Akron Educ Asn, 64-65, legis chmn & mem bd dirs, 65-67; mem legis comt, Ohio Educ Asn, 65-66. Mil Serv: Entered as Pvt, Marine Corps, 50, released as Sgt, 54, after serv in 7th Marines, Korea, 52-53. Mem: Kent Area Pupil Personnel Coun; Hilltop Guid Coun; Akron Counr Asn; Ellet Citizens Asn; Summit Co Ment Health Asn. Honors & Awards: Spoke Award, Akron Jaycees, 65. Relig: Catholic; Pres, Cath Relig Prog, St Matthew Church. Mailing Add: 2125 Wedgewood Dr Akron OH 44312

OTTINA, JOHN RENALDO **(R)**
Asst Secy Admin & Mgt, Dept Health, Educ & Welfare
b Los Angeles, Calif, Nov 5, 31; s Louis Ottina & Mary Maga O; m 1952 to Martha Jean Furst; c John, James & David. Educ: Univ Calif, Los Angeles, BA, 53, MA, 55; Univ Southern Calif, PhD, 64. Polit & Govt Pos: Dep comnr educ, Dept Health, Educ & Welfare, 71-73, comnr educ, 73-74, asst secy admin & mgt, 74- Bus & Prof Pos: Teacher, Los Angeles City Sch, Calif, 54-58; engr, Lockheed Aircraft Corp, 56-58; vpres, Syst Develop Corp, 58-69; pres, World Wide Info, 69-71. Mem: Asn Comput Mach. Legal Res: CA Mailing Add: Dept of Health Educ & Welfare Washington DC 20201

OTTINGER, EDWARD E (R)
Mo State Rep
b St Louis, Mo, July 16, 34; s Alva Ottinger & Vera Hilbert O; m to Sue; c Edward E, Jr. Educ: Mo Univ, BS, 57. Polit & Govt Pos: Mo State Rep, 101st Dist, 68- Mil Serv: Entered as Seaman, Naval Air Res, 53, released as PO 3/C, 61. Mem: Real Estate Bd Metrop St Louis; Associated Ins Agts & Brokers; Nat Asn Independent Fee Appraisers; Real Estate Salesmen Asn of South St Louis; Toastmasters. Relig: Presbyterian. Mailing Add: 5912 Loughborough St Louis MO 63109

OTTINGER, RICHARD LAWRENCE (D)
US Rep, NY
b New York, NY, Jan 27, 29; s Lawrence Ottinger & Louise O; m to Betty Ann Schneider; c Ronald, Randall, Lawrence & Jenny Louise. Educ: Cornell Univ, BA, 50; Harvard Law Sch, LLB, 53; Georgetown Univ, grad study in int law, 60-61. Polit & Govt Pos: Contract mgr, Int Coop Admin, 60-61; second staff mem & dir prog, Latin Am, Western Coast, Peace Corps, 61-64; US Rep, NY, 25th Dist, 65-71, 75-; deleg, Dem Nat Conv, 68; Dem cand for US Senate, NY, 70. Bus & Prof Pos: Assoc, Cleary, Gottlieb, Friendly & Hamilton, corp & int law practice, 55-56; partner, Kridel & Ottinger, law firm, New York, 56-60; organizer, Grassroots Action, Inc, 71- Mil Serv: Entered Air Force, 53, released as Capt, 55. Mem: Inter-Am, Int & New York Bar Asns; UN Asn of US (nat bd dirs); Environ Defense Fund (bd dirs). Relig: Jewish; Temple Beth-El, Northern Westchester, NY. Legal Res: 235 Bear Ridge Rd Pleasantville NY 10570 Mailing Add: 2801 Tilden St NW Washington DC 20008

OTTLEY, ATHNIEL C (D)
Lt Gov, VI
b St Thomas, VI, Nov 8, 41; s Aubrey C Ottley & Iris Scatliffe O; div; c Angela, Alfreda, Alicia, Allan & Andre. Educ: RCA Inst of Technol, grad, 61; Ind Inst Technol, grad, 65; Phi Kappa Theta. Polit & Govt Pos: Sen, VI Legis, 70-73; Lt Gov, VI, 73- Bus & Prof Pos: Gen mgr, WSTA Radio, St Thomas, VI, 65-73. Mem: CofC; Rotary; Lions; Carnival Comt (chmn, 68-71). Relig: Catholic. Legal Res: North Star Village St Thomas VI 00801 Mailing Add: PO Box 450 St Thomas VI 00801

OTTLEY, EARLE B
Sen, VI Legis
Mailing Add: PO Box 4998 Charlotte Amalie St Thomas VI 00801

OTTO, GLENN E (D)
Ore State Rep
Mailing Add: 1225 E Columbia Troutdale OR 97060

OTTS, JAMES K (D)
NMex State Rep
b Oak Grove, La, Feb 7, 30; s Clarence M Otts & Jennie Tillery O; m 1948 to Mary Lou Thayer; c Vicki Lou & Kathy Dianne (Mrs Suttle). Educ: Southwestern Assemblies of God Col, 48; Univ Tenn, 48; NMex State Univ, Carlsbad, 63. Polit & Govt Pos: NMex State Rep, Dist 54, 75- Bus & Prof Pos: Owner & gen mgr, Southwest Air Conditioning, Carlsbad, NMex, 64-; pres layman coun, Southwestern Col, Waxahachie, Tex, 74- Mem: Contractors Asn; Kiwanis; CofC (comn chmn). Honors & Awards: Outstanding Layman, Southwestern Col, 72; Good Friend Award, Boy Scouts, 72; Outstanding Serv Award, Womens Missionary Coun, Dallas, Tex, 74. Relig: Assemblies of God. Legal Res: 1015 N Pate Carlsbad NM 88220 Mailing Add: Drawer 1300 Carlsbad NM 88220

OUDERKIRK, W STAN (R)
Ore State Sen
Mailing Add: 233 SE Penter Lane Newport OR 97365

OUTCHCUNIS, FLORENCE BACAS (D)
b Polichani, Epirus, Greece, Oct 14, 33; d Andrew Bacas & Theodora Pappacosta B; c Athena B & Theda A. Educ: Northeastern Univ, 67, Sch Law, 73-; Bridgewater State Col, 67-68; Massasoit Community Col, AS, 73. Polit & Govt Pos: Deleg, Dem Nat Conv, 72; Ward One Mem, Brockton Dem City Comt, Mass, 72-; mem, Consumers Adv Comn, Brockton, 73- Bus & Prof Pos: Legal Serv/Self-Help, Inc, 67-72; coordr, Welfare Dept, 74- Mem: CPPAX, Mass. Mailing Add: 72 Bassett Rd Brockton MA 02401

OUTLAND, GEORGE E (D)
b Santa Paula, Calif, Oct 8, 06; s Elmer Garfield Outland & Stella Martha Faulkner O; m 1938 to Ruth Merry, wid; c George Faulkner & John Warner; m 1971 to Martha Adams Avery. Educ: Whittier Col, AB, 28; Harvard Univ, AM, 29; Yale Univ, PhD, 37. Polit & Govt Pos: Mem, Calif State Dem Cent Comt, 42-52; US Rep, Calif, 43-46; deleg, Dem Nat Conv, 44 & 48; chmn, Calif State Dem Policy Comt, 46-48; mgr, Roosevelt for Gov Campaign, Primary Elec, 49-50. Bus & Prof Pos: Asst dir, Boys' Work, Hale House, Boston, 28-30; dir, Denison House, Boston, 29-33; dir, Boys' Work, Los Angeles Neighborhood House, 33-35; dir, Southern Calif Fed Transient Serv, 34-35; dir, New Haven Community Col, 35-36; instr, Yale Univ, 35-37; asst prof, Santa Barbara State Col, 37-43; prof, San Francisco State Col, 47-72; retired. Publ: Boy Transiency in America, Santa Barbara State Col Press, 39; Sociological Foundations of Education (w J Roucek), Crowell, 40; numerous articles in scholarly jours & two in Readers' Digest. Mem: Nat Comt for an Effective Cong; Consumers Union (bd dirs, 7 years); Pub Affairs Inst (bd dirs, 46-64). Honors & Awards: More than 20 appearances on nat broadcasts, including Town Meeting of the Air, Wake-up America & American Forum of the Air. Relig: Methodist Episcopal. Mailing Add: 2103 Ninth St Anacortes WA 98221

OUTLAW, NIGLE C (D)
b San Gabriel, Tex, May 9, 97; s Elmer Alpheus Outlaw & Zora Barclay O; m 1926 to Mildred Lorena Pate, wid; c Zora Anne (Mrs Evans) & Alma Louise (Mrs Boone). Educ: Baylor Univ, JD, 25; Senate & Barrister's Temple. Polit & Govt Pos: Spec co & dist judge on various occasions; co attorney, Crosby Co, Tex, 29-30; presidential elector, Tex Dem Party, 32 & 56; conciliation comnr, Fed Govt, 33-35; co surveyor, 39-40; co attorney, Garza Co, Tex, 41-42; appeal agent, Selective Serv, 42-62; chmn, Garza Co Dem Exec Comt, formerly; vchmn, Dem State Conv, 60. Mil Serv: Entered as Pvt, Army, 17, released as Sgt, 19, after serv in 3rd US Cavalry, France, 17-19; Victory Medal; French Campaign Ribbon. Mem: Garza Co, South Plains & Tex State Bar Asns; Am Legion; VFW. Relig: Methodist. Legal Res: Lubbock Rd Post TX 79356 Mailing Add: Box 206 Post TX 79356

OVERBY, HOWARD THOMAS (D)
Ga State Sen
b Buford, Ga, June 14, 15; s James Floyd Overby & Sallie Thomas O; m 1947 to Lalla Green Nimocks; c Currie Nimocks, Sally & Howard Thomas, Jr. Educ: Mercer Univ; Univ Ga, LLB, 37; Sigma Alpha Epsilon; Phi Alpha Delta. Polit & Govt Pos: Ga State Rep, 47-48, 51-52, 57-58 & 63-66; asst solicitor gen, Northeast Circuit, 49-50; Ga State Sen, 49-50, 55-56, 61-62 & 71-; Co Attorney, Hall Co, 57-58. Bus & Prof Pos: Attorney. Mil Serv: Army, World War II, 1st Lt. Mem: Mason; Shrine; Elks; Odd Fellows; Red Men. Relig: Baptist. Mailing Add: Box 636 Gainesville GA 30501

OVERHOUSE, MADGE VIRGINIA (D)
Northern Women's Div Chairperson, Calif Dem State Cent Comt
b The Dalles, Ore, July 29, 24; d Ralph Richard Jennings & Flossie Dixon J; m 1949 to Howard Guy Overhouse; c Richard Guy. Educ: San Jose State Univ, BA Hist 47; Kappa Delta Pi; Chi Omega. Polit & Govt Pos: Vol coordr, Santa Clara Co Dem Hq, 69-; co co-chmn women's div, Calif Dem State Cent Comt, 70-73, mem, 71-, mem rules comt, 73-75 & northern women's div chairperson, 75-; mem, Santa Clara Co Dem Cent Comt, 71-, vchmn, 73-74; co co-chmn, McGovern for President Comt, 72; Dem nominee, Calif State Assembly, 22nd Dist, 74; deleg, Dem Nat Mid-Term Conf, 74. Bus & Prof Pos: Librn, San Jose State Univ, 47-58 & San Jose City Col, 59- Mem: Commonwealth Club Calif; Century Club; Chi Omega, Iota Delta Chap (corp bd, 60-); Spartan Found. Mailing Add: 885 Pollard Rd Los Gatos CA 95030

OVERSTREET, RAYMOND D (R)
Ky State Rep
Mailing Add: PO Box 478 Liberty KY 42539

OWEN, BEN (D)
Miss State Rep
b Columbus, Miss, July 12, 21; s Frank Owen & Mary Askew O; m 1949 to Mary Jane Collins; div; c Lydia Watson, Frank Caleb, Marsha Ethridge, David Collins, Mary Jane & Judith Sharp. Educ: Univ Miss, BA, 42, LLB, 47; Phi Delta Theta. Polit & Govt Pos: Miss State Rep, 64- Mil Serv: Entered as Lt, Army, 42, released as Capt, 46, after serv in Pac Theater, 42-46. Mem: Am Bar Asn; Lowndes Co Farm Bur; Am Legion; VFW; Moose. Relig: Baptist. Legal Res: Rte 3 Box 136 Columbus MS 39701 Mailing Add: PO Box 1001 Columbus MS 39701

OWEN, DAVID (R)
Committeeman, Jefferson Co Rep Orgn, Ark
b Conway, Ark, July 26, 40; s W H Owen & Iris Searcy O; single. Educ: Ouachita Baptist Col, BA, 62. Polit & Govt Pos: Committeeman, Jefferson Co Rep Orgn, Ark, 72-, chmn, 73-74; treas, Jones for US Senate Campaign Comt, 74. Bus & Prof Pos: CPA, self-employed, 68- Mil Serv: Entered as Pvt, Army Nat Guard, 63, discharged, SP-5, 69. Mem: Ark Soc CPA's; Am Inst CPA's; Jaycees (govt affairs dir, treas, 70-71). Honors & Awards: Govt Affairs, Dir of the Year Award, Pine Bluff, Jaycees, 73-74. Relig: Baptist. Legal Res: 601 Idaho Pine Bluff AR 71601 Mailing Add: PO Box 8396 Pine Bluff AR 71601

OWEN, DAVID CARROLL (R)
b Hermitage, Ark, Aug 10, 38; s Robert Carroll Owen & Lois M Clanton O; m 1958 to Beverly Ann Lewis; c Debbie, Beth & Melissa. Educ: Ottawa Univ, BS in Bus Admin & Econ, 60; Ohio State Univ Grad Sch Mortgage Banking; Rutgers Univ, Grad Sch Banking. Polit & Govt Pos: Kans State Sen, 69-73; Lt Gov, Kans, 73-75. Bus & Prof Pos: Vpres, Overland Park State Bank, 62-70; exec vpres, Bob Owen & Co, 70-72; pres, First Nat Bank Shawnee Mission, 73-, chmn bd, currently; consult, US Info Agency; trustee, Ottawa Univ. Mil Serv: Army Res, 56-64. Mem: Nat Asn Real Estate Bds; Johnson Co Real Estate Bd; Kans Asn Realtors; Johnson Co Ment Health Asn; Kans Asn Retarded Children (dir). Honors & Awards: Nominated Little-All-Am Basketball Team, 60; Outstanding Young Legislator, Topeka Daily Capitol, 69; Outstanding Young Man, Overland Park Jaycees, 70; Outstanding Young Man of Am, Jaycees, 70; Youngest Elected State Official, 73. Relig: Baptist; Deacon, Leawood Baptist Church. Mailing Add: 7701 W 100th St Overland Park KS 66212

OWEN, ERNA LEE (D)
b Maysville, Mo, May 30, 13; d Guy Stanley Crabill & Opal Mae DeHart C; m 1937 to Clark Wade Owen; c Janice Lee (Mrs Eldon G Taylor). Educ: Maryville State Col, 1 year. Polit & Govt Pos: Social worker, Works Progress Admin, Maysville, Mo, 34-41, dist supvr, 36-41; committeewoman, DeKalb Co Dem Party, 34-55; off supvr, US Dept Agr War Bd, 42-44; committeewoman, Andrew Co Dem Comt, 55-74, secy, 56-74; secy & hostess, Sixth Cong Dist Dem Comt, 58-70; deleg & mem nominating comt, Mo State Conv; chmn, Sen Thomas Eagleton Campaign, Andrew Co, 68 & 74; observer, Dem Nat Mid Term Conf, 74. Bus & Prof Pos: Teacher, DeKalb Co Pub Schs, Mo, 32-34 & 50-52; tax consult, 41-69; exec secy, Savannah CofC, 66-; local registr vital rec, Andrew Co & Savannah, 66-; secy, Andrews Co Econ Opportunity Comn, 67-68; fee agent, Motor Vehicle Registr, Mo Dept Revenue, 66-, dep collector, Bur Photovision, 66- Mem: Bus & Prof Women's Club (legis comt, 69-72); Eastern Star (past matron, 55-56, installing officer, 59-62); Savannah CofC (legis & educ comts, 66-); Andrews Co Dem Club; Mo Dem Asn. Relig: Methodist. Mailing Add: Bolckow MO 64427

OWEN, GARY (D)
Mich State Rep
Mailing Add: 115 S Clubview Dr Ypsilanti MI 48197

OWEN, L DICK, JR (D)
Ala State Sen
b Bay Minette, Ala, Apr 10, 19; s L D Owen & Kate Lee O; m 1949 to Annie Ruth Heidelberg; c L D, III. Educ: Univ Ala, BS, 41; Pi Kappa Phi. Polit & Govt Pos: City councilman, Bay Minette, Ala, 60-63; judge probate, Baldwin Co, 63-64; Ala State Rep, 65-71; Ala State Sen, 71- Mil Serv: Entered as 2nd Lt, Army, 41, released as Capt, 46, after serv in 82nd A/B Div, NAfrica & ETO, 43-45; 2 Bronze Stars; Combat Inf Badge; ETO Theater Ribbon with 6 Campaign Stars; Lt Col (Ret), Army Res, 62. Mem: VFW; Am Legion; Mason; Shrine. Honors & Awards: Man of the Year, Bay Minette Jaycees. Relig: Baptist. Legal Res: 211 11th St Bay Minette AL 36507 Mailing Add: Box 45 Bay Minette AL 36507

OWEN, SANK EDWARD (R)
Chmn, Monroe Co Rep Party, Miss
b Aberdeen, Miss, Feb 12, 27; s Sank Owen (deceased) & Louise Howell O (deceased); single. Educ: Miss State Univ, BS, 47; George Peabody Col Teachers, MA, 55; vpres, YMCA, Miss State Univ; pres, Miss Club, George Peabody Col for Teachers. Polit & Govt Pos: Committeeman, Monroe Co Rep Party, Dist Two, Miss, 64-68; campaign mgr for Rubel Phillips, cand for Gov of Miss, Monroe Co, 67; chmn, Monroe Co Rep Party, Miss, 68-;

campaign mgr, Gil Carmichael for US Senate, 72; mem exec comt, Miss Rep Party, 74- Mil Serv: Entered as Recruit, Army, 50, released as S/Sgt, 52, after serv in 45th Inf Div, Korean Conflict, 51-52; Good Conduct Medal & Ribbons. Publ: Articles to Holly Springs, South Reporter, 1951-55; Why I chose Peabody, Peabody Reflector, 56. Mem: Miss, Amory & Monroe Co Educ Asns; Miss Folklore Soc; Marshall Co Educ Asn. Honors & Awards: Teacher of the Year, 60. Relig: Methodist. Legal Res: Rte 2 Box 18 Aberdeen MS 39730 Mailing Add: PO Box 182 Amory MS 38821

OWEN, WILLIAM SNEED (D)
Tenn State Rep

b Ocala, Fla; s Louis R Owen & Selma LaRue O; single. Educ: Univ Tenn, BS, 72. Polit & Govt Pos: Pres, Tenn Young Dem, 73-75; Tenn State Rep, 75- Bus & Prof Pos: Pres, Matrix Enterprises, currently. Mil Serv: Entered as Seaman, Navy, 69-70. Publ: Gerneric impact assessment of implementation of the MFBR, 73 & The Tellico Project, Oak Ridge Nat Lab, 74. Legal Res: 1160 Kenesaw Knoxville TN 37919 Mailing Add: Suite 209 War Mem Bldg Nashville TN 37219

OWENS, DOUGLAS WAYNE (D)
b Panguitch, Utah, May 2, 37; s Joseph Owens & Ruth Dodds O; m 1961 to Marlene Wessel; c Elizabeth, Doug, Sara, Stephen & Edward. Educ: Univ Utah, JD, 64. Polit & Govt Pos: Field rep, US Sen Frank E Moss, Utah, 65-68, admin asst, 71-72; Rocky Mt States coordr, Robert F Kennedy for President, 68; deleg, Dem Nat Conv, 68, mem, Platform Comt, 68; admin asst to US Senate Majority Whip Edward Kennedy, 69-70; US Rep, Dist Two, Utah, 73-74; Utah cand, US Senate, 74. Bus & Prof Pos: Lawyer, pvt practice, Salt Lake City, Utah, 65-68. Relig: Latter-day Saint. Mailing Add: 22 E First South Salt Lake City UT 84111

OWENS, EMMETT HENNINGTON (D)
Miss State Rep
Mailing Add: Box 10784 Jackson MS 39209

OWENS, HENRY, III (D)
Alderman, Louisville, Ky

b Belmont, Ky, Oct 25, 41; s Henry Owens, Jr & Johnella Terrell O; m to Janice Marie. Educ: Ky State Univ, BS, 67; Debate Club. Polit & Govt Pos: Alderman, City of Louisville, Ky, 71-; alt deleg, Dem Nat Conv, 72; mem bd, Mayors Comt Econ Develop, 72- Bus & Prof Pos: Mem bd, Enterprises Unlimited Inc, 69-; mem bd, Park Duvalle Neighborhood Serv Ctr, 73- Mil Serv: Entered as E-1, Army, 64, released as Pfc, after serv in Army Security Agency, Japan, 64-65. Mem: Nat Educ Asn; NAACP. Relig: Protestant. Legal Res: 3005 Virginia Louisville KY 40211 Mailing Add: 1201 S 36th St Louisville KY 40211

OWENS, HOWARD T, JR (D)
Conn State Sen

b Bridgeport, Conn, July 20, 34; s Howard T Owens & Clarisse Baillargeon O; m 1965 to Ann Ehrsam; c Caroline P, Howard T, III, Paul B & Martha. Educ: Holy Cross Col, BS, 56; Vanderbilt Univ Sch Law, LLB, 59. Polit & Govt Pos: Asst US Attorney, Dist of Conn, 63-65; tenants rep, State of Conn, 68-70; Conn State Sen, Dist 22, 75- Mil Serv: Entered as Pvt, Army, 57, released in 58; Army Res, 6 years. Mem: Am Bar Asn; Conn Bar Asn (pres, Jr Bar Asn, bd gov); Bridgeport Bar Asn. Relig: Roman Catholic. Mailing Add: 6 Pierce Ave Bridgeport CT 06604

OWENS, HUGH FRANKLIN (D)
b Muskogee, Okla, Oct 15, 09; s James Francis Owens & Elizabeth Turner O; m 1934 to Louise Simon; c Julie (Mrs William Charles Pickens). Educ: Univ Ill, AB, 31; Univ Okla, LLB, 34; Phi Delta Phi; Sigma Chi, Significant Sig Award. Polit & Govt Pos: Adminr, Okla Securities Comn, 59-64; comnr, Securities & Exchange Comn, Wash, 64-73, acting chmn, 4 months, 70 & 2 months, 73; chmn, Securities Investor Protection Corp, currently. Bus & Prof Pos: Assoc, Cummins, Hagenah & Flynn, Chicago, Ill, 34-36; assoc, Rainey, Flynn, Green & Anderson, Oklahoma City, Okla, 36-48; mem bd dirs, Salvation Army, Oklahoma City Community Fund, 38-41; partner, Hervey, May & Owens, Oklahoma City, 48-51; div attorney, Superior Oil Co, Midland, Tex, 51-53; gen counsel, Nat Assoc Petrol Co, Tulsa, 53; attorney-at-law, Oklahoma City, 53-59; mem part-time faculty, Oklahoma City Univ Law Sch, 57-64. Mil Serv: Naval Res, World War II. Mem: Bar, US Supreme Nat Asn RR & Utility Comnr; hon life mem Kans Bar Asn; Okla Bar Asn; Retired Officers Asn. Mailing Add: Securities Investor Protection Corp 900 17th St NW Capitol Washington DC 20006

OWENS, JAMES BENTLEY, JR (R)
Chmn, Jefferson Co Rep Party, Ala

b Birmingham, Ala, Aug 22, 27; s James Bentley Owens & Jesse Roys O; m 1952 to Kathleen Ross Fouchee; c James Bentley, III, Leslie Ross, Anne Roys & Harris Fouchee. Educ: Univ Ala, BS, 49, LLB, 52; Kappa Alpha. Polit & Govt Pos: Chmn, Jefferson Co Rep Party, Ala, 71- Bus & Prof Pos: Pres, Birmingham Asn Home Builders, 58-59; pres, Ala Asn Home Builders, 62-63. Mil Serv: Entered as A/S, Navy, 45, released as Seaman 1/C, 46, after serv in USS Merrimac, Pac, 45-46. Mem: Birmingham Asn Home Builders; Birmingham Bd Realtors; Birmingham Bar Asn; Lions. Relig: Baptist. Mailing Add: 3620 Westchester Circle Birmingham AL 35223

OWENS, JOSEPH E (D)
Md State Deleg
Mailing Add: Suburban Trust Bldg Rockville MD 20850

OWENS, MAJOR R (D)
NY State Sen

b Collierville, Tenn, June 28, 36; s Ezekiel Owens & Edna Davis O; m 1956 to Ethel Werfel; c Christopher, Geoffrey & Millard. Educ: Morehouse Col, BA; Atlanta Univ, MS. Polit & Govt Pos: Exec dir, Brownsville Community Coun, New York, 66-68; comnr, Community Develop Agency, New York, 68-72, dep adminr, 72-73; pres, Cent Brooklyn Mobilization, 73-; NY State Sen, 17th Dist, 75- Bus & Prof Pos: Assoc prof/dir, Columbia Univ, 73- Publ: Auth, Failures of libraries, Libr J, 5/70; Ways of implementing social policy to ensure maximum public participation & social justice for minorities, Comn XVI Int Conf Social Welfare, Hague, Netherlands, 8/72; Community media library program, New York Libr Asn Newsletter, 1/75. Mem: Black & Puerto Rican Legis Caucus; NY State Coun Black Elected Off; Cent Brooklyn Mobilization for Polit Action; Metrop Asn Voter Educ (founder); Alliance Inf & Referral Systs. Honors & Awards: Aware for Serv as a Sympathetic & Humane Adv of the Poor, 26th Dist Rep Orgn, 70; Proclamation of Major R Owens Day, Off of the Pres, Borough of Brooklyn, 71; Tribute Aware, Headstart Staff & Citywide Policy Coun, 71; Honoree Aware, Fedn Negro Civil Serv Orgn, Inc, 73; Awards in Black, Found for Researching Educ on Sickle Cell Disease, 73. Relig: Baptist. Mailing Add: 335 Wyona St Brooklyn NY 11207

OWENS, PEGGY JOYCE (D)
VChmn, Va State Dem Cent Comt

b St Paul, Va, Aug 7, 32; d Charles Henry Elmore & Myrtle Boyd E; m 1956 to Andrew Dow Owens; c Kellie Jane & Andrew Dow. Educ: Pulaski Hosp Sch Nursing, RN, 53; Med Col Va, 1 year. Polit & Govt Pos: Secy, Pulaski Young Dem, 58; secy, Pulaski Dem Women, 65-66, pres, 67-68; vchmn, Va State Dem Cent Comt, 68-, mem steering comt, 70-71; mem exec bd, Va Dem Women, 69; mem exec bd, Ninth Dist Dem Women, 69. Bus & Prof Pos: Registered nurse, Pulaski Hosp, 56. Mem: Beta Sigma Phi; Jr Women's Club; Women's Club; Music Club; Red Cross. Relig: Methodist. Mailing Add: 740 Prospect Ave Pulaski VA 24301

OWENS, RAY D (D)
Ga State Rep
Mailing Add: Rte 1 Appling GA 30802

OWENS, ROBERT I (D)
Mass State Rep
Mailing Add: State Capitol Boston MA 02133

OWENS, RONALD (D)
NJ State Assemblyman

b Newark, NJ, Feb 4, 30; s Leroy & Eleanor O; m to Louise Redding; c Randall Scott, Pamela Tracy. Educ: Rutgers Univ, BA, 53; Seton Hall Law Sch, 59. Polit & Govt Pos: Mem, Newark Bd Educ, NJ, 63-66; asst corp counsel, Newark, 66-70; NJ State Assemblyman, 66-, Asst Dem Leader, NJ Assembly, 71-, Speaker Pro Tem, 74-75. Bus & Prof Pos: Teacher, Newark Pub Sch Syst, NJ, 55-; law clerkship under Ferdinando J Biunno, Esq, Off US Rep Peter W Rodino, Jr, 59-; lawyer, Newark, currently. Mil Serv: Signal Corps, 53-55. Mem: Am Bar Asn; NAACP (exec bd, Newark Br). Honors & Awards: Legislator of Year, 70. Relig: Methodist. Mailing Add: 110 Hansbury Ave Newark NJ 07112

OWENS, RUTH JOHNSON (D)
Dem Nat Committeewoman, Ala

m to Wyatt Owens; c two. Polit & Govt Pos: Formerly active with Young Dem; personal secy, Gov Folsom, Ala, 55-58; Dem Nat Committeewoman, Ala, 60-, mem exec comt, Dem Nat Comt, 70-; deleg, Dem Nat Conv, 68 & 72. Mailing Add: 1208 Vista Lane Birmingham AL 35216

OWENS, STANLEY ALBERT (D)
Va State Deleg

b Canon, Ga, Feb 10, 07; m 1935 to Janet Rebecca Trusler; c Mary Oliver (Mrs Parkinson) & Stanley A, Jr. Educ: Emory Univ Law Sch, Atlanta; Univ Ga Law Sch, Athens, LLB, 31; Pi Kappa Alpha; Phi Alpha Delta. Polit & Govt Pos: Dir, Va State CofC, formerly; vpres, Commonwealth's Attorneys' Asn, 59; Commonwealth attorney, Prince William Co, 44-60; Va State Deleg, 60- Bus & Prof Pos: Lawyer; chmn bd, Tidewater Tel Co, Warsaw, Va, currently; chmn bd, First Colony Tel Co, Dulles Int Airport, currently; dir, pres & gen counsel, Piedmont Fed Savings & Loan Asn, Manassas; dir & chmn bd, First Va Bank-Manassas Nat. Mem: Kiwanis; Ruritan; Gtr Manassas CofC. Relig: Baptist. Mailing Add: PO Box 109 Manassas VA 22110

OWENS, THOMAS JEROME (D)
b Springfield, Ill, Oct 24, 20; s Harry Grant Owens & Nonie Bowe O; m 1948 to Lela Williams; c Terrance & Virginia L. Polit & Govt Pos: Chmn, Sangamon Co Dem Comt, Ill, formerly; supt bldgs & grounds, State of Ill, 70- Mil Serv: Entered as Pvt, Army, 42, released as M/Sgt, 46, after serv in 96th Inf Div, SPac. Mem: Ill Landscape Contractors Asn; Cent Ill Nurseryman's Asn; Ill Co Chmn Asn (vpres); Am Legion; VFW, 96th Inf Div Asn. Honors & Awards: Licensed Tree Expert. Relig: Catholic. Mailing Add: RR 2 Pleasant Plains IL 62677

OWENS, URIEL EDWARD (D)
b Ashdown, Ark, Mar 25, 37; s Chester Cole Owens & Frances Hughes O; m 1962 to Elaine Marie Browne; c Erica Elaine. Educ: Kansas City Jr Col, Mo, 63-64; Univ Kans, 68-71. Polit & Govt Pos: Alt deleg, Dem Nat Conv, 72. Mil Serv: Airman 3/C, Air Force, 55. Mem: Turner House, Inc (pres, 70-72); Kansas City Jaycees, Northeast Action Group; NAACP; Progress Inc. Honors & Awards: Leadership Award, Turner House, Inc, 72; Key to City of Kansas City, Kans, 74; Leadership Award, Nat Asn for the Advancement of Colored People, 74. Relig: Protestant. Mailing Add: 2454 N 37th St Kansas City KS 66104

OWENS, WALTER (D)
Ala State Rep
Mailing Add: 107 Court Sq W Centreville AL 35042

OWENS, WILLIAM (D)
Mass State Sen

b Demopolis, Ala, July 6, 37; s Jonathan Owens & Mary A Clemons O; m to Cora E Hilliard; c Laurel, Curtis, William & Adam. Educ: Boston Univ; Harvard Univ, MEd; Univ Mass, Amherst, Doctoral Cand. Polit & Govt Pos: Dir, Career Opportunities Prog, State Dept Educ, Mass; dir, Proj Jesi-Jobs & Educ for Self-Improv; Mass State Rep, formerly; mem, Mass Legis Black Caucus, currently; Mass State Sen, 75- Bus & Prof Pos: Owner-mgr, Sunrise 1-Hour Cleaners, Boston, Mass; educ dir, Urban League of Gtr Boston. Publ: Corporal punishment & physical abuse of children, Survival Mag, 69. Mem: Urban League of Gtr Boston (vpres); Boston Black United Front (bd mem); Nat Asn Sch Adminr; NAACP; Nat Educators Asn. Honors & Awards: Big Black Brother Alliance Award. Relig: Protestant. Mailing Add: 115 Hazelton St Boston MA 02126

OXENDINE, HENRY WARD (D)
NC State Rep
Mailing Add: PO Box 966 Pembroke NC 28372

OXFORD, CHARLES OLIVER (D)
Ga State Rep

b Americus, Ga, Mar 12, 41; s John Arnold Oxford & Marisue Oliver O; m 1966 to Lanier Harris Oxford. Educ: Univ Ga, BBA, 63; Univ Ga Sch Law, LLB, 65; Phi Delta Phi; Pi Kappa Alpha. Polit & Govt Pos: Ga State Rep, 70-, mem, Banks & Banking & Hwy Comts, Ga House Rep, secy, House Rep Appropriations Comt, currently; city attorney, Americus, 71-74. Bus

& Prof Pos: Law partner, Crisp & Oxford, Attorneys, 70-; dir, Sumter Co Bank, 74-; mem exec coun, Young Lawyers Sect Ga Bar Asn, 72. Mem: Kiwanis Club; Americus Jaycees; CofC; Americus-Sumter Co Cancer Asn (treas, 70-); Am Bar Asn. Honors & Awards: Distinguished Serv Award, Americus Jaycees, 75. Relig: Methodist. Mailing Add: 317 W College St Americus GA 31709

OXLEY, MICHAEL GARVER (R)
Ohio State Rep
b Findlay, Ohio, Feb 11, 44; c George Garver Oxley & Maxine Wolfe O; m 1971 to Patricia Pluguez; c Michael Chadd. Educ: Miami Univ, BA, 66; Ohio State Univ Col Law, JD, 69; Omicron Delta Kappa; Sigma Chi. Polit & Govt Pos: Intern, Off US Rep Jackson E Betts, Ohio, summer 65; admin asst, Lt Gov John W Brown, Ohio, 67-68; legal aide, Attorney Gen William B Saxbe, Ohio, 68-69; Ohio State Rep, 73- Mem: Am Bar Asn; Elks; Hancock Co & Henry Co Twp Trustees & Clerks. Honors & Awards: Balfour Province Award, Sigma Chi, 66; Outstanding Sr Man, Miami Univ, 66, Dept Govt Award, 66. Relig: Lutheran. Legal Res: 2800 S Main St Apt 108 Findlay OH 45840 Mailing Add: 301 E Main Cross St Findlay OH 45840

OZINGA, FRANK M (R)
Ill State Sen
b Chicago, Ill, Aug 30, 14; s Martin Ozinga & Wilma Hoving O; m 1938 to Grace Stob; c Wilma (Mrs Molenhouse), Martin F, Ronald, Janice (Mrs Hoffman) & Marcia. Educ: Cent YMCA Col, AA, 34; Chicago Kent Col Law, JD, 38. Polit & Govt Pos: Justice of the peace, Worth Twp, Ill, 37-41; Ill State Sen, Dist 8, 56-, chmn exec comt, Ill State Sen, 73- Bus & Prof Pos: Chmn bd & gen coun, First Nat Bank of Evergreen Park, Ill, 48- Mil Serv: Entered as Ens, Navy, 44, released as Lt(jg), 46, after serv in Judge Adv Gen Off, Pac, 46. Mem: Am Bar Asn; Am Judicature Soc; Nat Soc State Legislators; Lions; Am Legion. Relig: Christian Reform Church. Legal Res: 9626 S Homan Ave Evergreen Park IL 60642 Mailing Add: 3101 W 95th St Evergreen Park IL 60642

P

PAARLBERG, DON (R)
Dir of Agr Econ, US Dept of Agr
b Oak Glen, Ill, June 20, 11; s Henry P Paarlberg & Grace Int-Hout P; m 1940 to Eva Louisa Robertson; c Don, Jr & Robert Lynn. Educ: Purdue Univ, BS, 40; Cornell Univ, MS, 43, PhD, 46; Sigma Xi; Alpha Gamma Rho. Polit & Govt Pos: Asst to the Secy, US Dept of Agr, 53-57, asst secy, 57-58, dir of agr econ, 69-; spec asst to the President, 58-61, food for peace coordr, 60-61. Bus & Prof Pos: Prof, Purdue Univ, 46-53, Hillenbrand prof agr econ, 61-69. Publ: Food (w F A Pearson), Knopf, 44; American Farm Policy, Wiley, 64; Great Myths of Economics, New Am Libr, 68. Mem: Am Econ Asn; Am Agr Econ Asn; Am Farm Bur Fedn. Honors & Awards: Best Teacher Award, Purdue Univ, 61 & 68; Award for Distinguished Serv to Am Agr, Am Soc of Farm Mgrs, 66. Relig: Methodist. Legal Res: 1214 Hayes West Lafayette IN 47906 Mailing Add: 14 St & Independence Ave SW Washington DC 20250

PABST, RICHARD E (D)
Wis State Rep
Mailing Add: 5336 W Wells St Milwaukee WI 53208

PACARRO, RUDOLPH (D)
Councilman, City & Co of Honolulu, Hawaii
b Watertown, Honolulu, Hawaii, Oct 6, 27; s Frank Suan Pacarro & Juliana Adorna P; m 1950 to Mabel Jean Cortezan; c Rudolph, William, Catalino, Clarence Alexander & Randolph Scott. Educ: St Louis Co, Honolulu; Colo State Col Educ; Univ Hawaii. Polit & Govt Pos: Hawaii State Rep, 12th Dist, 63-71; councilman, City & Co of Honolulu, 71- Bus & Prof Pos: Asst mgr, Sky Room Restaurant, Int Airport, 59-61; realtor-salesman, Manoa Realty Co, 61-; pres, First Filipino Finance Corp, 63- Mem: Boy Scouts, (dist comnr Kam Dist); Kamehameha Lions; Maemae Sch PTA (pres); Filipino CofC. Relig: Congregational. Mailing Add: 1801 Wahine Pl Honolulu HI 96819

PACE, ANTHONY (R)
Committeeman, Suffolk Co Rep Comt, NY
b Bronx, NY, July 14, 27; s Frank Pace & Concetta Arrigo P; m 1951 to Filomena Cerone; c Mary Ann, Donna, Barbara & Frank. Educ: Fordham Univ, BS, 48; Brooklyn Law Sch, LLB, 51. Polit & Govt Pos: Committeeman, Suffolk Co Rep Comt, NY, 60-; pres, Ital-Am Rep Club, 61-66; asst town attorney, Islip Town, 63-66; town attorney, 67-68; pres, West Islip Rep Club, 66-68; asst co attorney, Suffolk Co, 68-72, sr asst co attorney, 72-; zone leader, Islip Rep Comt, 69-70, chmn, 70-; deleg, Rep Nat Conv, 72. Mil Serv: Entered as Pvt, Army, 45, released as Pfc, 46, after serv in First Army; Good Conduct Medal. Mem: Suffolk Co Bar Asn; Sequams Property Owners Asn. Mailing Add: 7 Sequams Lane N West Islip NY 11795

PACE, LORIN NELSON (R)
Utah State Rep
b Miami, Ariz, Aug 15, 25; s Levi Wilson Pace & Sentella Nelson P; m 1950 to Marilynn Haymore; c Grant Franklin, Lee Wendell, Stanley Lorin, Mark Leonard, Lorraine, Maurine, Lynn Haymore, Deanna, Bradley Wilson & Teresa. Educ: Brigham Young Univ, BA, 51; Univ Utah Col Law, LLB, 53, JD, 67. Polit & Govt Pos: Foreign serv officer, US Dept State, 55 & 56; Utah State Rep, Dist 17, 65-, Speaker, Utah House Rep, Dist 71, Minority Leader, 71; recruit chmn, Utah Rep State Exec Bd, currently. Bus & Prof Pos: Attorney-at-law, Richfield, Utah, 54 & 55, Salt Lake City, 60-; mission pres, Latter-day Saint Church, Argentina & Chile, 56-60. Mil Serv: Cadet, Air Force, World War II. Publ: Auth-publ, There ought to be a law. Mem: Utah Bar Asn. Honors & Awards: Silver Beaver Award, Boy Scouts. Relig: Latter-day Saint. Mailing Add: 2386 Olympus Dr Salt Lake City UT 84117

PACHECO, RICHARD (DICK) (D)
Ariz State Rep
Mailing Add: 232 Martinez St Nogales AZ 85621

PACHIOS, HAROLD CHRISTY (D)
b New Haven, Conn, July 12, 36; s Christy H Pachios & Lucy Cokkinias P; single. Educ: Princeton Univ, AB, 59; Georgetown Univ, JD, 65; Tiger Inn. Polit & Govt Pos: Cong liaison, Peace Corps, Washington, DC, 61-64; mem staff, Johnson-Humphrey Campaign, 64; mem, Off Econ Opportunity Task Force, 64-65; Assoc White House Press Secy, 65-67; dir scheduling & advan, Muskie for Vice President, 68; Calif coordr, Muskie for President, 72; deleg, Dem Nat Conv, 72. Bus & Prof Pos: Attorney & partner, Preti & Flaherty, Portland, Maine, 69- Mil Serv: Entered as Ens, Navy, 59, released as Lt(jg), 62, after serv in USS Randall, Atlantic Theatre. Mem: Am & Maine Bar Asns. Relig: Greek Orthodox. Mailing Add: Hunts Point Rd Cape Elizabeth ME 04107

PACK, DAVID M (D)
Attorney Gen & Reporter, Tenn
b Sevierville, Tenn, Nov 4, 21; m to Ruth Dixon; c Pamela Dixon & David, Jr. Educ: Univ of Tenn, AB & JD, 48. Polit & Govt Pos: Chancellor, 13th Chancery Div, 54-57; Asst Attorney Gen, Tenn, 57-63; Tenn State Comnr of Highways, 63-67; Tenn State Comnr of Ins & Banking, 67-69; Attorney Gen & Reporter, Tenn, 69- Bus & Prof Pos: Practiced law in Sevierville, Tenn, until 54. Mil Serv: Army, 42-46. Relig: Baptist. Mailing Add: Supreme Court Bldg Nashville TN 37219

PACKARD, DAVID (R)
b Pueblo, Colo, Sept 7, 12; s Sperry Sidney Packard & Ella Lorna Graber P; m 1938 to Lucile Salter; c David Woodley, Nancy Anne (Mrs Robin Burnett), Susan (Mrs Franklin M Orr) & Julie Elizabeth. Educ: Stanford Univ, BA, 34, EE, 39; Univ of Colo, 34; Alpha Delta Phi; Tau Beta Pi; Sigma Xi. Hon Degrees: ScD, Colo Col, 64; LLD, Univ of Calif, 66 & Cath Univ, 70; DLitt, Southern Colo State Col, 73; DEng, Univ Notre Dame, 74. Polit & Govt Pos: Dep Secy of Defense, 69-71. Bus & Prof Pos: Dir, Am Mgt Asn, 56-59, vpres-at-lg, 59-69; dir & mem exec comt, Stanford Research Inst, 58-69; mem adv bd, Hoover Inst on War, Peace & Revolution, 58-69; dir, Pac Gas & Elec Co, 59-69; dir, Calif State CofC, 62-69 & 71-; dir, Crocker-Citizens Nat Bank, 63-69; dir, Nat Merit Scholarship Corp, 63-69; dir, Gen Dynamics Corp, 64-69; dir, US Steel Corp, 64-69; chief exec officer, Hewlett-Packard Co, 64-69, chmn bd, 64-69 & 72-; mem bd dirs, Trans World Airlines 71-, Standard Oil of Calif, 71- & Caterpillar Tractor Co, 71- Mem: Nat Acad Eng; fel Inst of Elec & Electronics Eng; Trilateral Comn; Nat Coun US-China Trade; life mem Instrument Soc Am. Mailing Add: 1501 Page Mill Rd Palo Alto CA 94304

PACKARD, DAVID B (R)
NH State Rep
Mailing Add: RFD 1 Concord NH 03301

PACKWOOD, BOB (R)
US Sen, Ore
b Portland, Ore, Sept 11, 32; s Frederick William Packwood & Gladys Taft P; m 1964 to Georgie Ann Oberteuffer; c William Henderson & Shyla. Educ: Willamette Univ, AB, 54; NY Univ Sch Law, LLB, 57; Beta Theta Pi. Polit & Govt Pos: Chmn, Multnomah Co Rep Cent Comt, Ore, 60-62; Ore State Rep, 63-69; US Sen, Ore, 69-; deleg, Rep Nat Conv, 72. Mem: Ore Bar Asn. Honors & Awards: Arthur T Vanderbilt Pub Serv Award, NY Univ Sch Law, 69; Brotherhood Award, B'nai B'rith Anti-Defamation League, 71; Torch of Liberty Award, Anti-Defamation League, 71; Ore State Man of the Year Award, Nat Fedn Independent Bus, 71; Richard L Neuberger Award, Ore Environ Coun, 72. Relig: Unitarian. Legal Res: Portland OR Mailing Add: 1317 Dirksen Bldg Washington DC 20510

PADAVAN, FRANK (R)
NY State Sen
Mailing Add: 84-48 Radnor Rd Jamaica NY 11432

PADBERG, EILEEN E (R)
b Philadelphia, Apr 14, 44; d Caesar Badolato & Margaret Lawther B; div. Educ: Westminster High Sch, Calif grad, 62. Polit & Govt Pos: Secy, Anaheim Young Rep, Calif, 68-70; youth comt chmn, Orange Co Rep Cent Comt, 69-70; first vpres, Orange Co Young Rep, 69-71; chmn material procurement comt, Rep Assocs, Orange Co, 70-71; mem bd gov, 73-; mem, Rep State Cent Comt, 71-72; campaign coordr, Dannemeyer for Assembly, 72; alt deleg, Rep Nat Conv, 72; campaign coordr, Friends of Brad Gates for Sheriff, Orange Co, 74; advanceman, Flournoy for Gov, 74. Bus & Prof Pos: Exec secy, Robert Clay Pub Rels, 71; staff asst, Orange Co Employees Asn, 72, legis coordr, 72-; vpres, Rep Assocs. Honors & Awards: Orange Co Young Rep of the Year, 70; First Woman in Orange Co Rep Asn, 72. Relig: Catholic. Mailing Add: Apt 52 16661 McFadden Tustin CA 92680

PADDEN, JEFFREY D (D)
Mich State Rep
Mailing Add: 332 Riverside Dr Wyandotte MI 48192

PADGETT, C WARD (D)
Chief Mine Inspector, Okla
b Puxico, Mo, Dec 8, 10; s Charles Ward Padgett & Nell Smith P; m 1940 to Dorothy Nell Tate; c Vanetta Sue (Mrs James Welsh) & Charles Ward. Educ: Mining eng courses, Ind State Univ, Univ Ill & US Bur Mines exten classes; study of long wall mining, Eng. Polit & Govt Pos: Chief Mine Inspector, Okla, 63-; mem, Appeal Bd for Selective Serv, 4 years; chmn, Gov Coun Develop of Coal Indust in Okla; mem, Adv Comt Reclamation; Gov rep, Interstate Mining Compact, currently; mem solid fuels div, Off Energy Adv Coun & Gov rep on Midwest Gov Task Force on Energy & Environ, currently. Bus & Prof Pos: Mine Foreman, Little Betty Mining Corp, 35-38; mine foreman, Crescent Coal Co, 38-40, mine supt, 40-48; gen supt Ky operations, Bell & Zoller Coal Co, 48-53, gen supt all operations, 53-60; asst div supt of mining, Lone Star Steel Co, 60-63. Publ: Author of numerous papers on safety, production, long wall mining and other mining systems, publ in organizational proceedings. Mem: Nat Asn State Mine Inspection Agencies; Rotary; Shrine; Boy Scout Coun; Salvation Army (adv bd). Relig: Baptist. Legal Res: 528 E Seneca McAlester OK 74501 Mailing Add: 117 Capitol Bldg Oklahoma City OK 73105

PADGETT, DOROTHY B (D)
VChmn, Dem Women's Fedn
b Sandersville, Ga, Aug 26, 27; d Arthur A Bennett & Car Lou Lea Bruner B; m 1948 to W David Padgett; c Gail, Ted Ross, Nancy Elizabeth & Cameron Mitchell. Educ: Douglas Co High Sch, grad; Atlanta Div, Univ Syst Ga. Polit & Govt Pos: Women's coordr, Carter for Gov Campaign, 70; vchmn, Ga Dem Party, 70-74; mem, Dem Nat Comt, 72-74; vchmn women, Dem Women's Fedn, 73- Bus & Prof Pos: Cashier, Commercial Bank, Douglasville,

Ga, 44-46; bookkeeper, Fulton Fed Savings & Loan Asn, 46-49. Mem: Eastern Star; Douglas Co CofC; Garden Club Ga. Honors & Awards: Hon chap farmer, Future Farmers Am. Relig: Methodist. Mailing Add: 8550 Price Ave Douglasville GA 30134

PADILLA, HERNAN **(NEW PROGRESSIVE, PR)**
Alt Minority Floor Leader, PR House Rep
b Mayaguez, PR, May 5, 38; s Hernan Padilla & Luisa Ramirez P; m 1961 to Laura Cestero; c Herman F & Ingrid Y. Educ: Univ PR, BS, 59; Univ Md, MD, 63; Univ Hosp, Rio Piedras, PR Internal Med Specialty, 64-67; Rush Club, Univ Md Sch Med; Phi Sigma Alpha. Polit & Govt Pos: Mem, Young Rep, 64; deleg, Rep Nat Conv, 64; vpres, Polit Action Comt, PR Rep Party, 65; co-organizer, United Statehooders Asn, 67; vpres-at-lg, New Progressive Party Comt, PR, 68, rep-at-lg, 68-, chmn, 74-; Rep & majority floor leader, PR House Rep, 69-72, Rep-at-lg & alt minority floor leader, Floor Leader, 72- Bus & Prof Pos: Instr phys sci, Univ PR, 59, med, 67-69, asst attending in med, 69-, clin attending, 73- Mil Serv: Entered Army Nat Guard, 54, currently serv as Maj, MedC, Hq Detachment, PR Nat Guard. Publ: One year experience with closed kidney biopsies. Relig: Catholic. Mailing Add: GPO Box 70160 San Juan PR 00936

PAGE, HENRY H **(R)**
NH State Rep
Mailing Add: 24 Oak St Exeter NH 03833

PAGE, MATTHEW JOHN **(D)**
Chmn, Wash Co Dem Exec Comt, Miss
b Greenville, Miss, Nov 16, 29; s Johnny Page & Mollie Turnbull P; m 1960 to Vivian Miller Patton; c Letha Ann. Educ: Tougaloo Col, BS, 52; Meharry Med Col, MD, 56; Omega Psi Phi. Polit & Govt Pos: Mem, Miss Adv Comt, US Civil Rights Comn, 67-; deleg, Dem Nat Conv, 68, alt deleg, 72; vchmn, Wash Co Dem Orgn, Miss, 68-, chmn, Wash Co Dem Exec Comt, 68-; Dem Presidential Elector, Miss, 72. Bus & Prof Pos: Chmn bd dirs, Tri-State Products Corp & Renco Develop Corp, 72- Mil Serv: Entered as 1st Lt, Air Force, 57, released as Capt, 59, after serv in 40:81st Hosp Unit, Northeast Air Command, 57-59; Capt Air Force Res, 59-; Air Force Commendation Medal. Mem: Miss State Med Asn; Miss Coun on Human Rels (pres, 72-); Miss Comt for Humanities; Herbert Lee Commun Ctr; CofC. Honors & Awards: Rural Serv Award, Off Econ Opportunity, 68; Page-Moore Head Start Center dedicated in his honor, 72. Relig: Protestant. Legal Res: 239 N Florida St Greenville MS 38701 Mailing Add: 1659 E Union St Greenville MS 38701

PAGE, STANLEY HAYNES **(R)**
Conn State Sen
b New Haven, Conn, May 5, 42; s Harry Logan Page, Jr & Hazel Langdon P; m 1964 to Laura Dudley; c Claudia Haynes, Katharine Wilcox & Brian Langdon. Educ: Mitchell Col, AS, 62; New Haven Col, 62-63. Polit & Govt Pos: Mem, Guilford Rep Town Comt, Conn, currently, treas, 67-69, chmn, 69-73; justice of the peace, Guilford, 69-; admin asst, Gov Thomas Meskill, Conn, 71-73; Conn State Sen, 12th Dist, 73- Bus & Prof Pos: Vpres, Page Hardware & Appliance Co, Guilford, 63-71; mem, Guilford Adv Bd, Second New Haven Bank, 69-; mem, Community Adv Coun, Small Bus Admin, 70- Mem: Jaycees; Guilford Vol Fire Dept. Relig: Protestant. Mailing Add: 303 Murray Lane Guilford CT 06437

PAGEL, JOHN THEODORE **(R)**
b Wilkes Barre, Pa, Jan 13, 22; s John Theodore Pagel, Sr & Jessie Coons P; m 1945 to Mary Bradley Douglas; c John Theodore, Mary Lucile, Jessica Lynn & Jennifer Joyce. Polit & Govt Pos: First vchmn, Crawford Co Rep Comt, Ga, 60-64, chmn, 64-74. Bus & Prof Pos: Vpres, W F Bradley Lumber Co, 48-55; pres, Roberta Sand & Gravel Co, 60- Mil Serv: Entered as A/S, Navy, 41, released as Aviation Electrician 1/C, 46; Victory Medal; South Pac Theater Ribbon; Marshall Island Ribbon with Battle Star. Mem: Mason; Am Legion; Kiwanis Inst. Relig: Methodist. Mailing Add: Box 307 Roberta GA 31078

PAGLIARO, FRANK JOSEPH, JR **(R)**
Mem, San Francisco Co Rep Cent Comt, Calif
b New York, NY, Aug 10, 40; s Frank Joseph Pagliaro & Edith Bennett P; m 1969 to Bonnie Kay Dickason; c Jonathan Bennett & Jill Anna. Educ: Univ Vt, AB, 63; Hague Acad of Int Law, Netherlands, 65; Univ Va Law Sch, LLB, 66; Phi Alpha Delta; Pi Delta Epsilon; Sigma Nu. Polit & Govt Pos: Rep Assembly cand, San Francisco, Calif, 70; mem, Calif Rep State Cent Comt, 70-; mem, San Francisco Co Rep Cent Comt, 70-, gen counsel, 70-72; pres, San Francisco Young Rep, 70-72; mem bd dirs, Calif Rep Alliance, 71- & Calif Rep League, 71-; alt deleg, Rep Nat Conv, 72; Bay Area Dir, Young Voters for the President, 72. Bus & Prof Pos: Vpres & house counsel, Contel Construction Corp, San Francisco, Calif, 67-70; asst dist attorney, San Francisco, 71-73; attorney, Ropers, Majeski, Kohn, Bentley & Wagner, Redwood City, 73- Mil Serv: Entered as 2nd Lt, Army, 66, released as 1st Lt, 67, after serv in Mil Intel. Mem: Am, Calif & NY Bar Asns; Bar Asn of San Francisco; Columbus Civic Club. Mailing Add: 1337 Drake Ave Burlingame CA 94010

PAIEWONSKY, RALPH **(D)**
b St Thomas, VI, Nov 9, 07; s Isaac Paiewonsky & Rebecca P; married; c Two. Educ: NY Univ, BS in Chem, 30. Polit & Govt Pos: Mem, People's Party, VI, 36; organizer, Dem Club for participation in nat polit, 36; mem & chmn, Munic Comt, 36-46; chmn, Legis Assembly, VI, 36-46; chmn, St Thomas & St John Munic Coun, 36-46; mem of deleg to present needs of VI to Cong, 39; deleg, Dem Nat Conv, 40 & 44; Dem Nat Committeeman, VI, 40-60; mem, VI Senate Organic Act Adv Comt & Citizens' Adv Comt for Home Rule, 52-60; adv to Legis to Caribbean Comn, 58-60; chmn, Jackson-Jefferson Day Dinner, 58 & 60; mem, Spec Tax Comt for CofC & VI Legis to present VI tax legis case before Cong, 59-60; gen chmn, Gov Adv Comt on Tourism & Trade, 60; pres, VI Bd Trade, 60; hon mem, Inaugural Rule Comt, 60; Gov, VI, 61-69. Bus & Prof Pos: Mgr, St Thomas Apothecary Hall, 30; extensive research with sea water fermentation from which rum distillation process developed, 32; mgr, A H Riise Distilling Co, 33-49, pres, 49-; pres, Apollo Theater, Inc & Center Theater, Inc, 48-; pres, A H Riise, Inc, 49; mem bd dirs & pres W I Ins Co, 54-58; organizer, W I Bank & Trust Co, 54, mem bd dirs, chmn exec comt & vpres, 54-59; pres, W I Investment Corp, 54-58, mem bd dirs, 54-60. Mem: St Thomas Dem Club; Dem Capital Club (charter mem); F&AM (32 degree); Shrine; 750 Club. Relig: Hebrew. Mailing Add: Charlotte Amalie St Thomas VI 00801

PAINE, THOMAS OTTEN **(D)**
b Berkeley, Calif, Nov 9, 21; s George Thomas Paine & Ada Louise Otten P; m 1946 to Barbara Helen Taunton Pearse; c Marguerite Ada, George Thomas, Judith Janet & Frank Taunton. Educ: Brown Univ, AB, 42; Stanford Univ, MS, 47, PhD, 49; Sigma Xi; Delta Kappa Epsilon. Hon Degrees: DSc, Brown Univ, 69. Polit & Govt Pos: Chmn, Santa Barbara Scientist & Engrs for Johnson & Humphrey, 64; chmn spec task force, Dept of Housing & Urban Develop, 67; dep adminr, NASA, 68, acting adminr, 68-69, adminr, 69-70. Bus & Prof Pos: Research assoc, Stanford Univ, 47-49; research assoc, Gen Elec Research Lab, Schenectady, NY, 49-50, mgr, Gen Elec Meter & Instruments Lab, Lynn, Mass, 51-58, mgr eng applns, Gen Elec Research & Develop Ctr, Schenectady, NY, 58-63, mgr, Tempo, Gen Elec Ctr for Advan Studies, Santa Barbara, Calif, 63-68, vpres & group exec, Power Generation Group, Gen Elec Co, New York, 70-73, sr vpres, Gen Elec Technol Planning & Develop, 73- Mil Serv: Entered as Midn, Naval Res, 42, released as Lt, 46, after serv in Submarine Serv, Pac & Southwest Pac Areas, 42-46; Commendation Ribbon; Submarine Combat Award with Two Stars. Publ: Magnetic properties of fine particles, In: Magnetic Properties of Metals & Alloys, Am Soc for Metals, 59; Space and national security in the modern world, Air Force & Space Digest, 5/69. Mem: Am Astronaut Soc (fel); Cosmos Club; Explorers Club; Lotos Club; NAACP. Honors & Awards: Distinguished Serv Medal, NASA. Relig: Unitarian. Legal Res: Berkeley CA Mailing Add: General Electric Co Fairfield CT 06431

PAINES, GEORGE HERBERT **(R)**
Vt State Rep
Mailing Add: Box 345 Morrisville VT 05661

PAJCIC, STEVE **(D)**
Fla State Rep
Mailing Add: 3865 St Johns Ave Jacksonville FL 32205

PALAIA, LAWRENCE E **(D)**
Conn State Rep
Mailing Add: 536 Hollister St Stratford CT 06497

PALERM ALFONZO, JUAN A **(NEW PROGRESSIVE, PR)**
Sen, PR Senate
Mailing Add: State Capitol San Juan PR 00901

PALERM GUTIERREZ, JESUS E **(POPULAR DEMOCRAT, PR)**
Sen, PR Senate
Mailing Add: State Capitol San Juan PR 00901

PALLADINO, VINCENT OLIVER **(R)**
Mem, Watertown Rep Town Comt, Conn
b Waterbury, Conn, Apr 23, 29; s Vincent Aurelio Palladino & Aurora Oliver P; m 1952 to Marie Margaret Baumgartner; c Mark Oliver, Kim Marie, Eric Joseph & Kirk Vincent. Educ: Washington & Jefferson Col, BA, 51; Univ Conn, MA, 59; Lambda Chi Alpha. Polit & Govt Pos: Mem, Watertown Rep Town Comt, Conn, 63-, chmn, 64-66; charter mem, Young Rep Club of Watertown, 64-; chmn, Watertown Bd of Tax Rev, 68-71; vchmn, Watertown Police Comn, Conn, 72-; mem, Watertown Charter Rev Comn, 73. Bus & Prof Pos: Advert mgr, Town Times Newspaper, 61-62; ed & publ, Conn Jaycee J, 61-62; pres, Paldon Truck Serv, Inc, 61-; real estate broker, self-employed, 65-; ed & publ monthly newsletter, Rep Register, 64-66; teacher of Eng, Crosby High Sch, Waterbury, Conn, 66-; ed, Watertown Annual Town Report, 68 & 69. Mil Serv: Entered as Pvt, Army, 51, released as Cpl, 53, after serv in 71st Antiaircraft Artil Gun Bn, Ft Belvoir, Va. Publ: Town government change, Action, US Jr CofC, 62. Mem: Watertown CofC, (publicity dir, 63-64); Watertown Chap, Am Red Cross; Nat Rifle Asn; Miss Watertown Pageant Asn, Inc (chmn exec comt, 68-69); Libr Asn, Watertown-Oakville Libr (trustee, 73). Honors & Awards: Conn State Spark Plug Award, Conn Jaycees, 63; Outstanding Old Timer Award, 65; Jr Chamber Int Senate 3543, 63; Distinguished Serv Award, Watertown, Jaycees, 64; Distinguished Leadership Citation, presented by pres of Washington & Jefferson Col, 71. Relig: Roman Catholic. Mailing Add: 433 Woodbury Rd Watertown CT 06795

PALLERIA, FRANK ARTHUR **(D)**
Chmn, Edmunds Co Dem Cent Comt, SDak
b Haverhill, Mass, June 27, 48; s Antonio Joseph Palleria & Theresa Blair P; m 1972 to Christine Paulsen; c April Jean & Marianne. Educ: Huron Col, BM, 71; Western Conn State Univ, summer 73. Polit & Govt Pos: Chmn, Edmunds Co Dem Cent Comt, SDak, 73- Bus & Prof Pos: Dir music, Bowdle Pub Sch, SDak, 71-75; agt, Equitable Life of NY, Huron, 75- Mem: Nat & SDak Educ Asns; SDak Bandmasters Asn; Bowdle Educ Asn (pres). Honors & Awards: Life time pass to Huron Col Activities, 75. Relig: Methodist. Mailing Add: 148 14th SW Huron SD 57350

PALM, ED **(R)**
Chmn, Tarrant Co Rep Party, Tex
b Eastland, Tex, Mar 15, 34; s William Polk Palm & Frances Edmonds P; m 1957 to Rita Roberdeau; c Chris & Courtney. Educ: Univ Tex, BS, 57, MBA, 61; Kappa Sigma. Polit & Govt Pos: Precinct chmn, Dallas, 62-65; Ft Worth, 67-69; chmn, Tarrant Co Bush for Senate, Ft Worth, 70; chmn, Tarrant Co Rep Party, 70-, deleg, Rep Nat Conv, 72. Bus & Prof Pos: Cert pub accountant, Arthur Andersen & Co, Dallas, 61-65; vpres, Bldg Prod Wholesale, Inc, Ft Worth, 65-67; Ed Palm Co, Real Estate, currently. Mil Serv: Entered as 2nd Lt, Army, 57, released as 1st Lt, 59, after serv in 2nd & 4th Training Regt, Ft Leonard Wood, Mo, 57; Commendation Award with Pendant. Mem: Nat & Local Bd of Realtors; Century II Club; Ft Worth CofC; Rivercrest Country Club. Honors & Awards: Arthur Young & Co Scholarship, 60. Relig: Episcopal. Mailing Add: 6363 Lansdale Ft Worth TX 76116

PALM, NANCY DALE **(R)**
Chmn, Harris Co Rep Party, Tex
b Nashville, Tenn, Apr 14, 21; d Dillard Young Dale & Mary Bishop D; m 1942 to William Morrison Palm, MD. Educ: Vanderbilt Univ, BA, 42; secy & charter mem, Vanderbilt chap Mortar Board; Gamma Phi Beta; Athenians; Lotus Eaters; Int Rels Club. Polit & Govt Pos: Rep Precinct chmn, Dist 274, Harris Co, Tex, 64-68; vchmn, Harris Co Rep Party, 68, chmn, 68-; Presidential Elector, 68; deleg, Rep Nat Conv, 72. Bus & Prof Pos: Pub rels secy, Harris Co Med Soc, 51-57. Mem: Pro Am Houston Chap, Freedoms Found. Honors & Awards: Twenty-five years of med, civic, polit & soc serv work & extensive church work. Relig: Presbyterian. Legal Res: 612 E Friar Tuck Lane Houston TX 77024 Mailing Add: Suite 200 2626 Westheimer Houston TX 77006

PALMBERG, MAURICE EDWIN **(R)**
Mem, Nebr State Rep Cent Comt
b Aurora, Nebr, Feb 2, 32; s Edwin J Palmberg & Esther Swanson P; m 1954 to Barbara Ann Axelson; c Kurt Jeffrey & Karen Ann. Educ: N Park Col, AA, 52. Polit & Govt Pos: Chmn,

Hamilton Co Rep Cent Comt, Nebr, 64-74; mem, Nebr State Rep Cent Comt, 70- Bus & Prof Pos: Partner, Palmberg Auto Supply, Inc, 62. Mil Serv: Entered as Pvt, Army, 52, released as Cpl, 54, after serv in 5th Armored Div. Mem: Lions. Relig: Evangelical Covenant Church. Mailing Add: 1318 Tenth St Aurora NE 68818

PALMBY, CLARENCE DONALD (R)
b Eagle Bend, Minn, Feb 22, 16; s Ernest F Palmby & Addie Hartbeck P; m 1940 to Mildred Janet Davis; c Gail Alice (Mrs John Geidl), Philip David & Thomas Orin. Educ: Univ Minn, BS, 40. Polit & Govt Pos: Chmn, Garden City Rep Party, Minn, 53-55; chmn, Commodity Stabilization Serv State Comt, Dept of Agr, St Paul, 55-56, assoc dir, Grain Div, Commodity Stabilization Serv, Washington, DC, 56-57, dir, 57, dep adminr, serv, 57-58, assoc adminr, 58-61, pres, Commodity Credit Corp & Asst Secy of Agr for Int Affairs & Commodity Prog, 69-72; exec vpres, Feed Grains Coun, 61-69. Bus & Prof Pos: Farmer, 40-53; vpres, Continental Grain Co, New York, 72- Mem: Alpha Zeta; RAM; Farm Bur. Honors & Awards: Skelly Award for Superior Achievement in Agr, 55; Superior Serv Award, Dept of Agr, 60; Leader of Commerce Award, Ital Govt, 68. Relig: Methodist. Mailing Add: Continental Grain Co 2 Broadway New York NY 10004

PALMER, BEN E (D)
Ill State Sen
Mailing Add: 4250 N Marine Ave Chicago IL 60613

PALMER, BOB (D)
Mont State Rep
Mailing Add: 711 W Spruce Missoula MT 59801

PALMER, DWIGHT WENDELL (R)
Chmn, Telfair Co Rep Party, Ga
b Glenwood, Ga, Oct 17, 39; s James Aubrey Palmer & Juanita Windham P; m 1969 to Mary Vivion Young. Educ: S Ga Col, 57-59; Ga Southern Col, 59-60. Polit & Govt Pos: Chmn, Telfair Co Rep Party, Ga, 68- Bus & Prof Pos: Owner, Palmer Furniture Co, McRae, 64- Mil Serv: Entered as Pvt, Army, 61, released as SP-4, 64, after serv in 32nd Mil Police Detachment, Counter Intel, Europe, 61-64. Mem: Jaycees (Rebel Corps); CofC; Rotary; Telfair Co Libr Asn. Relig: Baptist. Mailing Add: PO Box 4 McRae GA 31055

PALMER, FRANCES BRANDT (R)
Chmn, Linn Co Rep Cent Comt, Iowa
b La Porte City, Iowa, Jan 2, 12; d Arnold Brandt, Sr & Ida May Jones B; m 1932 to Paul M Palmer; c Alice Florence (Mrs Russell D Werning). Educ: Kirkwood Jr Col, 69-70; Rep Polit Club. Polit & Govt Pos: Precinct committeewoman, Linn Co Rep Cent Comt, 58-, secy, 61-63, chmn, 74-; pres, Linn Co Rep Women's Eve Club, 61-63, treas, 74-; pres, Linn Co Rep Women's Morning Club, 63-65; pres, Second Dist Rep Women, 63-65; youth adv, Young Rep Linn Co, 64-; youth activities chmn, Iowa Fedn Rep Women, 67-69, conv & arrangements chmn, 69-71, finance co-chmn, 71-73. Mem: Women's Polit Caucus (steering comt, Linn Co, 75-); Cedar Valley Div, Iowa Heart Asn (bd mem, 73-76). Relig: Methodist. Mailing Add: Lincoln Heights Dr SE Cedar Rapids IA 52403

PALMER, GEORGE VINCENT (D)
b Schenectady, NY, Dec 5, 20; s Nicholas L Palmer & Evelyn Cruise; m 1972 to Elaine Ginet. Educ: Hobart Col, BA, 43; Cornell Univ, Army Specialized Training Prog, 43; Albany Law Sch, LLB, 49; Phi Beta Kappa; Justinian Soc; Law Rev Bd; ed, Hobart Col Student Newspaper. Polit & Govt Pos: Asst city attorney, Schenectady, NY, 50-51; town attorney, Rotterdam, 58-59 & 64-74; chmn, Schenectady Co Dem Comt, 61-74; mgr, Conv Campaigns for Rep Samuel S Stratton for Gov & US Senate nominations, 62 & 64; mem NY State Dem Exec Comt, 63-74; asst exec dir, NY State Bd Elec, 74- Mil Serv: Entered as Pvt, Air Force, 42, released as Sgt, 46, after serv in Western Flying Training Command. Mem: Schenectady Co Bar Asn; Am Legion Post 1005, Schenectady. Relig: Catholic. Legal Res: 2020 Lisa Lane Schenectady NY 12303 Mailing Add: 781 State St Schenectady NY 12307

PALMER, GLEN DANIEL (R)
b Yorkville, Ill, Mar 4, 93; s Daniel F Palmer & Harriett A Healy P; m 1936 to Grace Irene Lagerquist; c William A, Patricia (Mrs Kowal), Priscilla R & Glenda (Mrs Richter). Educ: Univ of Wis. Polit & Govt Pos: Supt, State Game Farm, Ill, 25-29; chmn, Kendall Co Rep Party, formerly; dep state treas, Ill, 51-53, dir of conserv, 53-61; asst to US Rep Charlotte T Reid, Ill, & in charge, 15th Dist Off, 63- Bus & Prof Pos: Dist & spec agent, Northwestern Mutual Life Ins of Milwaukee, Wis, 27- Mem: Lions; Izaak Walton League; Mason; Shrine & Consistory. Relig: Methodist. Mailing Add: Game Farm Rd Yorkville IL 60560

PALMER, GROVER ADDISON, JR (D)
b Lexington, NC, Aug 9, 25; s Grover Addison Palmer & Myrtle Younts P; m 1954 to Edna Vernelle Gilliam; c Kaye Vernelle. Educ: Lenoir Rhyne Col, AB, 47; Southern Col Optom, Memphis, OD, 49. Polit & Govt Pos: Mem bd aldermen, Town of Spencer, NC, 51-71; chmn, Rowan Co Dem Party, 71-74. Bus & Prof Pos: Optometrist, Salisbury, NC, 50- Mil Serv: Entered as A/S, Navy, 43, released as Ens, 46, after serv in USS Wheatear, 45-46; Lt Comdr (Ret), Navy, 25 years. Mem: Rotary (pres, 71-72); Salisbury-Rowan United Fund (dir, 73-); Salisbury-Rowan Merchants Asn (secy, 69-70, treas, 70-71); Salisbury-Rowan CofC; Rowan Co Fair Asn (secy-treas, 57-67). Honors & Awards: Distinguished Serv Award, Spencer Jaycees, 54. Relig: Lutheran. Legal Res: 420 Windsor Dr Salisbury NC 28144 Mailing Add: PO Box 4258 Salisbury NC 28144

PALMER, HAZEL (R)
b Climax Springs, Mo, Aug 11, 03; d John William Palmer & Nancy Jane Hutton P; single. Educ: Nat Univ Law Sch, George Washington Univ, JD, 32; past dean, Omicron Chap, Kappa Beta Pi; past pres, Cy Pres Club. Polit & Govt Pos: Asst prosecuting attorney, Pettis Co, Mo, 37-39, collector of revenue, 42-55; chmn, Pettis Co Rep Party, 42 & 64-67; past chmn, bus & prof women's comt, Nat Fedn Rep Women's Clubs; past mem bd, Mo Fedn Rep Women's Clubs; past pres, Pettis Co Rep Women's Clubs; past mem, Nat Security & Peace Subcomt, Rep Comt on Prog & Progress; cand for US Sen, Mo, 58; deleg & mem platform comt, Rep Nat Conv, 60, deleg-at-lg & mem credentials comt, 64; mem, State Rep Comt, 62-68; City & Co Rep Committeewoman; mem, Nat Adv Comt, Women for Nixon-Agnew, 68; mem, Citizens' Adv Coun on Status of Women, 69-; mem nat adv comt, Comt Reelec of President, 72; Magistrate Court Judge, 73- Bus & Prof Pos: Attorney-at-law, 32-73; partner, Palmer & Palmer, until 58. Mem: Women's Med Col Pa (nat bd); Eastern Star (Past Worthy Matron); Knife & Fork Club; Beta Sigma Phi (int hon mem). Honors & Awards: Hon Ky Col; Adm, Great Navy of Nebr, 58. Relig: Baptist; past chmn, Bd Trustees, First Baptist Church of Sedalia. Legal Res: 901 S Vermont Sedalia MO 65301 Mailing Add: Court House Sedalia MO 65301

PALMER, JOE H (D)
NC State Sen
Mailing Add: Rte 3 Clyde NC 28721

PALMER, JOHN ALBERT, JR (DFL)
Treas, Dakota Co Dem-Farmer-Labor Party, Minn
b Boulder, Colo, July 21, 33; s John Albert Palmer & Elizabeth Gambill P; m 1961 to Marjorie Indehar; c Nancy & Karen. Educ: Univ Colo, 51-54; Macalester Col, BA, 54-57; Univ Minn, Minneapolis, 57-58. Polit & Govt Pos: Precinct chmn, Burnsville Dem-Farmer-Labor Party, Minn, 63-71; treas, Burnsville Dem-Farmer-Labor Party State Conv, 70; treas, Dakota Co Dem-Farmer-Labor Party, 70- Bus & Prof Pos: Merchandising mgr, Minneapolis Star & Tribune Co, 65-71. Mem: 12-B Legis Dist Dem-Farmer-Labor Orgn. Relig: Methodist. Mailing Add: 1430 Valley Dr Burnsville MN 55378

PALMER, JOSEPH, II
b Detroit, Mich, June 16, 14; s Robert Woodbury Palmer & Helen Marie Bush P; m 1941 to Margaret McCamy Jones; c Joseph Woodbury, Heather Gordon & Thomas Jones. Educ: Harvard, SB, 37; Georgetown Sch of Foreign Serv, 37-38; Foreign Serv Sch, Dept of State, 41. Polit & Govt Pos: Foreign serv officer, Dept of State, 39-73, vconsul, Mexico City, 40-41 & Nairobi, Kenya, 41-45, asst chief, Div African Affairs, 45-49 & acting chief, 48, second secy & consul, London, 49-50, first secy & consul, 50-53, dep dir, Off European Regional Affairs, 53-56, dep asst secy state African affairs, 56-58, Am consul gen, Rhodesia & Nyasaland, 58-60, US Ambassador to Nigeria, 60-64, dir gen, Foreign Serv, 64-66, asst secy state African affairs, 66-69, US Ambassador to Libya, 69-72; retired. Mem: Am Foreign Serv Asn; Diplomatic & Consular Officers Retired; Sister Cities Int (bd dirs); Inst Int Policy (bd dirs). Honors & Awards: Distinguished Serv Award, US State Dept. Relig: Episcopal. Mailing Add: 5414 Kirkwood Dr Bethesda MD 20016

PALMER, LINWOOD E, JR (R)
Maine State Rep
Mailing Add: Nobleboro ME 04555

PALMER, R DON (D)
Mem, Tenn State Dem Exec Comt
b Calderwood, Tenn, Feb 8, 41; s Richard Daniel Palmer & Mildred Kirkland P; m 1963 to Virginia Anne Strange; c Pamela Kirkland & Rex Donald, Jr. Educ: Univ Tenn, Knoxville, BS, 63, JD, 65; Sigma Delta Chi, Phi Delta Phi, Kappa Sigma. Polit & Govt Pos: Mem, Tenn State Dem Exec Comt, 74- Mem: Am & Tenn Bar Asns; Asn of Trial Lawyers Am; Tenn Trial Lawyers Asn. Relig: Protestant. Legal Res: 1022 N Heritage Dr Maryville TN 37801 Mailing Add: 318 S Court St Maryville TN 37801

PALMER, RANDALL (R)
Kans State Rep
b Kansas City, Mo, Mar 11, 26; s A H Palmer & Retha Jones P; m 1946 to Shirley Lou Morris; c Paige (Mrs Detlefson) & Eric M. Educ: Cent Mo State Univ, 43-44; Univ Kans, BA, 48, Law Sch, JD, 49; Univ Mo-Kansas City, 50; Kans State Col Pittsburg, 51; Phi Alpha Delta. Polit & Govt Pos: Mem, Pittsburg Bd Educ, USD 250, Kans, 71-74, pres of bd, 73-74; Kans State Rep, Third Dist, 73- Bus & Prof Pos: Assoc, Keller & Wilbert, Pittsburg, Kans, 51-56, partner, Keller, Wilbert & Palmer, 56-64, & Keller, Wilbert, Palmer & Lassman, 64- Mil Serv: Entered as A/S, Navy, 43, released as Ens, 46, after serv in LCT Task Force 13, Pac, 45-46. Mem: Kans Bar Asn (mem exec coun, 73-); Kans Asn of Defense Counsel (secy-treas, 67-73, pres, 74-75); Nat Asn of Ins Attorneys (exec bd, 71-74); Am Legion Post 64; Crawford Co Hist Soc. Relig: Baptist. Mailing Add: 802 S Catalpa Pittsburg KS 66762

PALMER, ROMIE J (R)
Ill State Sen
Mailing Add: 2524 Burr Oak Ave Blue Island IL 60406

PALMER, VINCENT A (R)
Chmn, Wayne Co Rep Comt, NY
b Rochester, NY, Oct 6, 25; s Vincent A Palmer & Francis Ashley P; m 1962 to Eleanor C Filmer; c Scott Ashley & Craig Fillmore. Educ: Univ Rochester, 46-47; Rochester Inst of Technol, 46-47. Polit & Govt Pos: Chmn, Williamson Rep Comt, NY, 64-69; alt deleg, Rep Nat Conv, 68; chmn, Wayne Co Rep Comt, 68- Bus & Prof Pos: Secy, Cheetham & Ascherman, Inc, Williamson, NY, 63-; asst vpres, Egbert F Ashley Co, Rochester, 67- Mil Serv: Entered as Pvt, Army Air Force, 43, released as S/Sgt, 45, after serv in 466th Bomb Group, Eighth Air Force, ETO, 45; Air Medal, Four Oak Leaf Clusters. Mem: Upstate Chmn Asn (pres); Am Legion; Rochester Yacht Club; Pultneyville Civic Asn; Mason. Relig: Episcopal. Mailing Add: 215 E Lake Rd Pultneyville NY 14538

PALMER, WILLIAM DARRELL (D)
Iowa State Sen
b Iowa City, Iowa, Jan 13, 35; s George D Palmer & Florence I Middour P; m 1953 to Evelyn L Johnson; c William Nick, Tony Robert & Amanda Kaye. Educ: Life Underwriters Training Course, grad, 59; Col of Life Underwriters, currently. Polit & Govt Pos: Iowa State Rep, Polk Co, formerly; Iowa State Sen, Polk Co, 68- Bus & Prof Pos: Asst dist mgr, John Hancock Mutual Life Ins Co, 58; pres, Palmer & Assocs, Inc, Gen Ins Agency, currently. Mem: Mason; Life Underwriters Asn; Lions. Relig: Methodist. Mailing Add: 2948 Easton Blvd Des Moines IA 50317

PALMER, WILLIAM H (R)
b Oakdale, Nebr, Oct 1, 22; s Ernest W Palmer & Fannie G Guffey P; m 1950 to Elizabeth Jane Yoder; c Christine, Blaine, Myra & Katherine. Educ: Univ Nebr, BA, 48; Kappa Sigma. Polit & Govt Pos: Chief, Info Sect, Nebr Dept Rds & Irrigation, 50-53; state chmn, Nebr Young Rep, 57-58; mem, Nebr Rep Finance Comt, 58-59 & Nebr Rep State Cent Comt, 58-60; exec asst, US Rep Charles Thone, Nebr, 71- Bus & Prof Pos: Writer, Radio Sta KFAB, Omaha, 48-50; pub rels dir, Cudahy Packing Co, 54; pub rels acct exec, Bozell & Jacobs, Inc, 55-65, pub rels dir, Indianapolis, 65-68, pub rels accts mgr, Chicago, 69-71. Mil Serv: Entered as A/S Navy, 42, released as Lt(jg), after serv in USS Kershaw, Pac Theatre. Mem: Pub Rels Soc Am; Rep Commun Asn; Cong Staff Club; Bull Elephants; Capitol Hill Toastmasters (pres). Relig: Presbyterian. Legal Res: 2010 Stone St Falls City NE 68355 Mailing Add: 3445 Mildred Dr Falls Church VA 22042

PALMER, WILSON (D)
b 1917. Educ: Univ Ky. Polit & Govt Pos: Mem, Rural Elec Bd; mem, Hosp Bd; Ky State Sen, 62-75; alt deleg, Dem Nat Conv, 68; chmn, Harrison Co Dem Party, formerly. Bus & Prof Pos: Farmer. Mem: Farm Bur. Relig: Christian Church NAm. Mailing Add: Rte 3 Cynthiana KY 41031

PALMIERI, JAMES JOHN (D)
Conn State Rep
b Waterbury, Conn, Nov 30, 13; s Alphonse Palmieri & Marie Rosa Nervo P; m 1939 to Pauline Krowchenko; c Paula Marie, James, Jr & John. Educ: High Sch. Polit & Govt Pos: Conn State Rep, 62- Bus & Prof Pos: Sales rep, Metrop Life Ins, 41; proprietor, Palmieri Ins Agency, 55. Mil Serv: Entered as Pvt, Army, 42, released as S/Sgt, 45, after serv in 8th Inf, ETO; Bronze Star; Purple Heart; Presidential Citation; Combat Inf Badge. Mem: Elks; VFW; Ital Am Dem Club; KofC. Relig: Catholic. Legal Res: 65 Meriline Ave Waterbury CT 06702 Mailing Add: 51 W Maine St Waterbury CT 06702

PALMORE, JOHN STANLEY, JR (D)
Judge, Court of Appeals of Ky
b Ancon, CZ, Aug 6, 17; s John Stanley Palmore & Antoinette Gonzalez P; m 1938 to Eleanor Gertrude Anderson; c John W. Educ: Western Ky State Univ, 34-36; Univ Louisville, LLB, 39; Phi Alpha Delta. Polit & Govt Pos: Chief of legal br, Jeffersonville Qm Depot, Ind, 46-47; city prosecuting attorney, Henderson, Ky, 49-53, city attorney, 53-55; commonwealth's attorney, Fifth Judicial Dist, Ky, 55-59; judge, Court of Appeals of Ky, 59-, chief justice, 66 & 73. Bus & Prof Pos: Attorney-at-law, Henderson, Ky, 39-59. Mil Serv: Entered as A/S, Navy, 42, released as Lt, 46, after serv in Supply Corps, Pac Area, 45; recalled as Lt, Navy, 51, released 52, after serv in Bur Supplies & Accts, Washington, DC; Pac Theater Ribbon with One Star, Okinawa; Atlantic Theater & Victory Ribbons. Publ: After the verdict, Ky State Bar J, 1/62; Sentencing and correction—black sheep of the criminal law, Fed Probation, 12/62; Damages recoverable in a partial taking, Southwest Law J, 67. Mem: Moose; Elks; F&AM; Scottish Rite; AAONMS. Relig: Episcopal. Legal Res: 2018 Griffith Pl W Owensboro KY 42301 Mailing Add: Rm 224 State Capitol Frankfort KY 40601

PALMQUIST, DAWN ISABELLE (D)
VChmn, Plainville Dem Town Comt, Conn
b Lewisburg, Pa, Apr 30, 30; d Ford Bouton & Marjorie Davis B; m 1951 to Carl William Palmquist; c Carla, Kim, Holly & Gregory. Educ: Univ Scranton, 67; Univ Hartford, 69. Polit & Govt Pos: Census crew leader, Farmington, Berlin, Plainville, Bristol & Southington, Conn, 70-71; deleg, Conn Dem State Conv, 72; deleg, Dem Nat Conv, 72; chmn voter registr, Plainville Dem Town Comt, 72, Dem campaign coordr, 72, mem, 72-, vchmn, currently; deleg, Sixth Dist Dem Conv; co-chmn, Moffet for Cong Comt, Plainville; chmn, St Pierre for State Rep; co-chmn, Grasso for Gov. Bus & Prof Pos: Contract drafter, Aetna Life & Casualty Co, Hartford, 73- Mem: Plainville Human Rels Coun; Nat Woman's Polit Caucus; Box Proj (nat treas, 71-72). Relig: Lutheran. Mailing Add: 25 Beechwood Rd Plainville CT 06062

PALOMO, BENIGNO (R)
Sen, Guam Legis
Mailing Add: Guam Legis Box 373 Agana GU 96910

PALUMBO, BENJAMIN LEWIS (D)
b Boston, Mass, Mar 4, 37; s Guido Americo Palumbo & Stella Lombardo P; m 1961 to Magdalene Julia Palinczar; c Matthew Guy & Jason Michael. Educ: Rutgers Univ, New Brunswick, BA, 59, MA, 61; Kappa Sigma. Polit & Govt Pos: Admin asst, Gov Richard J Hughes, NJ, 63-65; dir res, NJ State Dem Comt, 65, dir pub affairs, 65-66; freeholder, Mercer Co Bd Freeholders, 66-67; exec asst, NJ Comnr Transportation, 67-70; admin asst, US Sen Harrison A Williams, Jr, NJ, 71-73; nat campaign dir, Bentsen in 76, 73- Bus & Prof Pos: Instr, Trenton Cent High Sch, NJ, 59-60; exec dir, Greater Princeton CofC, 61-63; asst dean, Woodrow Wilson Sch, Princeton Univ, 70-71. Mil Serv: Naval Res. Publ: Six months in London, Nat Acad Sci Hwy & Res Bd, 69. Mem: US Senate Asn Admin Assts & Exec Secys (treas, 71, vpres, 72, pres, 73); Nassau Club of Princeton, NJ; Am Club of London. Relig: Roman Catholic. Legal Res: 1204 S Oakcrest Rd Arlington VA 22202 Mailing Add: 505 C St NE Washington DC 20002

PALUMBO, MARIO JOSEPH (D)
WVa State Sen
b New York, NY, Apr 13, 33; s Jack Palumbo & Nancy Alfonso P; m 1969 to Louise Corey; c Christopher & Corey. Educ: Morris Harvey Col, BS, 54; Col Law, WVa Univ, LLB, 57; Order of the Coif; mem, Law Rev. Polit & Govt Pos: WVa State Sen, Eighth Dist, 69-, chmn judiciary comt, WVa State Senate, 73. Bus & Prof Pos: Partner, Law Firm of Woodroe, Kizer & Steed, Charleston, WVa, 58-69 & Campbell, Love, Woodroe & Kizer, 69- Mil Serv: Maj & Legal Officer, 130th Spec Opers Group, WVa Air Nat Guard Res. Mem: Am Bar Asn; WVa State Bar; Elks; Army & Navy Club; Tennis Club. Relig: Catholic. Mailing Add: 19 Bradford St Charleston WV 25301

PALUSKA, EVERETT CLIFFORD (R)
Chmn, Ellington Rep Town Comt, Conn
b Stafford Springs, Conn, June 19, 24; s William Paluska (deceased) & Nellie Meyer Paluska Pinney; m 1943 to Barbara Marie McLaughlin; c Everett Lloyd & Patricia Marie. Educ: Rockville Pub Schs, Conn, 8 years. Polit & Govt Pos: Prosecuting grand juror, Ellington Justice Court, Conn, 51-56, probation officer, 54-56; former treas & second vchmn, Conn Young Rep; chmn, Ellington Rep Town Comt, 52-72 & 75-; tax collector, Ellington, 57-; dep tax comnr, State of Conn, 71- Bus & Prof Pos: Indust salesman, Morton Salt Co, 55-71. Mem: AF&AM; Ital Soc Club; Ellington Grange; Ellington Cemetary Asn. Relig: Congregational. Legal Res: Snipsic Lake Rd Ellington CT 06029 Mailing Add: PO Box 261 Ellington CT 06029

PANCOAST, G SIEBER (R)
Pa State Rep
b Audubon, NJ, June 16, 14; s Garfield Pancoast & Frances M Rood; m to Muriel E Brandt; c Two. Educ: Ursinus Col, BS; Univ Pa, AM & PhD. Polit & Govt Pos: Vpres, Montgomery Co Boroughs Asn, Pa; mayor, Borough of Collegeville, 61-65; Pa State Rep, currently, chmn educ comt, Pa House Rep, 73-74; Pa Higher Educ Assistance Agency, 70-; mem, Gov Citizens Comn on Basic Educ. Bus & Prof Pos: Prof. Mil Serv: Naval Res, Ens & Lt(jg), 44-46. Mem: Several prof socs; Lions. Relig: United Church of Christ. Mailing Add: Capitol Bldg Harrisburg PA 17120

PANDICK, MARGARET L (D)
VChmn, Delaware Co Dem Comt, NY
b Delhi, NY; d Ernest A Leal & Margaret Simon L; m 1936 to Andrew Lawrence Pandick, wid 1963; c Linda A (Mrs Victor A Franzese) & Thomas O'Donnell. Educ: Delaware Acad, NY, grad, 29; Binghamton Beauty Sch, NY, 34. Polit & Govt Pos: Dep comnr, Delaware Co Bd of Elec, NY, 58-; secy & treas, Elec Comnr Asn, NY, 68-; vchmn, Delaware Co Dem Comt, 67- Bus & Prof Pos: Hair stylist, Jean King Studio, Bay Shore, Long Island, 35-36 & McLean's Dept Store, Binghamton, NY, 36-42. Mem: Bus & Prof Women; Village Improvement Soc, Delhi, NY. Relig: Presbyterian. Mailing Add: 15 Clinton St Delhi NY 13753

PANECALDO, LORETO ANTONIO, III (R)
Chmn, Butte Co Rep Cent Comt, Calif
b Yuba City, Calif, June 19, 48; s Loreto Antonio Panecaldo, Jr & Marjorie Isabelle Sarmento Thayer; single. Educ: Yuba Col, AA, 69; Calif Mkt Club; Young Rep. Polit & Govt Pos: Chmn, Butte Co Rep Cent Comt, Calif, 75-; mem, Rep State Cent Comt Calif & Calif Rep Assembly, currently. Mem: F&AM North Butte Lodge 230 (Past Master, 74); Commonwealth Club San Francisco; Butte Co Hist Soc (bd dirs); Bidwell Mansion Cooperating Asn; Life mem DeMolay, Sutter-Butte Chap. Honors & Awards: Outstanding Floral Design, Florists' Transworld Delivery Asn, 71; Outstanding Rep, South Butte Rep Women's Club, 75. Relig: Christian Scientist. Mailing Add: 1800 Hazel St Gridley CA 95948

PANEHAL, FRANCINE MARY (D)
Ohio State Rep
b Cleveland, Ohio, Oct 10, 25; d James Francis McAllister & Georgia Beyee M; m 1948 to Robert James Panehal; c Kathleen (Mrs Gallagher), Elise, Alexi, Robert, Jr & Gigi. Educ: Baldwin Wallace Col; Ursuline Col, BA, 48; Delta Phi Alpha, Newman Club, Writers Club. Polit & Govt Pos: Mem, Cleveland City Planning Comn, Ohio, 66-71 & Cleveland City Coun, Ward I, 71-73; Dem precinct committeeman, 71-; mem, Cuyahoga Co Dem Exec Comt, Ohio, 71-; Ohio State Rep, Dist 5, 75- Bus & Prof Pos: Head automotive order sales dept, Socony Vacuum Oil Co, Cleveland, 43-45; serv rep, Ohio Bell, 48-50. Mem: Ward I Dem Club; St Rose Parish Coun; Westside Irish Am Club. Honors & Awards: Outstanding German Student, Baldwin Wallace Col, 47. Relig: Catholic. Legal Res: 11502 Edgewater Dr Cleveland OH 44102 Mailing Add: Ohio House of Rep Columbus OH 43215

PANICHAS, GEORGE T (D)
RI State Rep
Mailing Add: 18 Mavis St Pawtucket RI 02860

PANKOPF, ARTHUR, JR
b Malden, Mass, Feb 1, 31; m; c three. Educ: Mass Maritime Acad, BS, 51; Georgetown Univ Sch Foreign Serv, BS magna cum laude, 56, Law Ctr, JD, 65. Polit & Govt Pos: Cargo preference specialist, US Maritime Admin, 61-62, subsidy opers examr, 62-65; minority counsel, Comt Merchant Marine & Fisheries, US House Rep, 65-69; minority counsel & staff dir, Comt on Com, US Senate, 69- Bus & Prof Pos: Third mate on SS Steel Director, Isthmian Steamship Co, Marine Opers, 51-53; third mate on SS Parismina, United Fruit Co, Marine Opers, 55; asst to dir transportation research, Georgetown Univ, 56-57; sales dept, Delta Air Lines, Inc, 57-58; mgt trainee & third & second mate on SS Alcoa Polaris, Alcoa Steamship Co, Marine Opers, 57-58; various positions with Trans Ocean Van Serv Div, Consol Freightways, Inc, 58-61. Mil Serv: Navy, 53-55, serv as navigator & opers officer, aboard USS Cavalier. Legal Res: 7819 Hampden Lane Bethesda MD 20014 Mailing Add: 5201 Dirksen Off Bldg Washington DC 20510

PANUZIO, NICHOLAS ARTHUR (R)
Mayor, Bridgeport, Conn
b Bridgeport, Conn, Oct 28, 35; s Nicholas Panuzio & Carmella Petrucelli P; m 1959 to June Bartram; c Susan Ann, Nicholas A, Jr & Thomas E. Educ: Univ Bridgeport, BS, indust rels & personnel mgt, 57. Polit & Govt Pos: Conn State Rep, 71-72; mayor, Bridgeport, Conn, 71-; mem adv bd, State Dept Community Affairs, 72-; exec bd mem, Conn Planning Comt on Criminal Admin, 72-; mem, President's Comn on Continuing Educ, 72-; comnr, Conn State Solid Waste Authority, 73; Rep cand for Gov, 75. Mem: Forum Club of the Ital Community Ctr; Jaycees; Hall Neighborhood House (bd dirs). Honors & Awards: Hon mem, Bridgeport Hosp Bd Dirs; Bridgeport's Outstanding Young Man, 66; Key Man Award & Pres Award, Conn Jaycees, 66 & 67; Jr Chamber Int Senator; One of 200 Future Leaders of Am, Time Mag, 75. Relig: Roman Catholic. Legal Res: 184 Ranch Dr Bridgeport CT 06606 Mailing Add: City Hall 45 Lyon Terr Bridgeport CT 06604

PAOLINO, THOMAS JOSEPH (R)
Assoc Justice, RI Supreme Court
b Providence, RI, Dec 4, 05; s Joseph Paolino & Elvira Cardarelli P; m 1932 to Florence Dolce; c Loreen Ann (Mrs Lepore), Thomas J, Jr, MD & Linda Vera (Mrs Raimondo). Educ: Brown Univ, AB, 28; Harvard Law Sch, LLB, 31; Phi Alpha Delta. Hon Degrees: LLD, Bryant Col, 64 & St Francis Col (Maine), 71. Polit & Govt Pos: Mem, Rep State Cent Comt, RI, 39-56; deleg, Rep Nat Conv, 40 & 44; mem, Wendell Willkie's Nat Adv Campaign Comt, 40; RI mem, Rep Nat Comt, 52-56; Rep candidate for cong, Second Cong Dist RI, 48; assoc justice, RI Supreme Court, 56- Bus & Prof Pos: Pvt law practice, 31-40; mem, Dooley, Dunn & Paolino, 40-56; chmn bd trustees, Roger Williams Col, 71-; mem corp, Miriam Hosp. Publ: A Digest of Rhode Island Zoning Cases, 60; Zoning-Its Growth and Development in Rhode Island, 63. Mem: Providence Athenaeum; Serra Club; KofC; St Laurence Coun; KofM. Honors & Awards: Outstanding Alumnus Award, Classical Varsity Club RI, 60; Knight of St Gregory, 67; Star of Solidarity, Repub Italy, 68. Relig: Roman Catholic. Legal Res: 35 Orchard Dr Cranston RI 02920 Mailing Add: Supreme Court of RI 250 Benefit St Providence RI 02903

PAPAN, LOUIS J (D)
Calif State Assemblyman
Mailing Add: 343-B Serramonte Plaza Daly City CA 94015

PAPANDREA, JOHN FRANCIS (D)
b San Giovanni Calabria, Italy, Aug 3, 34; s Joseph G Papandrea (deceased) & Rose M Mule P; m 1960 to Marianne Petrus; c Anne Marie, Mary Rose & John Francis, Jr. Educ: Fairfield Univ, BS, 56; Univ Conn Sch Law, LLB, 59; Acquinas Acad. Polit & Govt Pos: Mem, Charter Rev Comn, Meriden, Conn, 59-61; mem, Meriden City Coun, 62-66, minority leader, 62-64, majority leader, 64-66, chmn by-laws comt, 62-66, chmn zoning rev comt, 64-66; Conn State Rep, 78th Dist, 67-72, asst majority leader, Conn House of Rep, 69-70, dep majority leader, 71-72; mem, Gov Comns on Probate Rev & Youthful Wards of the State; mem, Gov Revenue

Task Force, 69; mem, New Eng Bd Higher Educ, 71-73; counsel, House Dem Caucus, Conn House Rep, 72-; mem, Conn Comn Arts, 73- Mil Serv: Pvt, Conn Nat Guard, 59-62. Mem: Conn Bar Asn (mem comn of rev of family law); Meriden Parents Without Partners, Meriden Ladin Am Soc (counsel); Unison Club; Mt Carmel Holy Name Soc; Meriden Latin Am Scholarship Comt. Relig: Roman Catholic. Mailing Add: 257 W Main St Meriden CT 06450

PAPE, CARL E (R)
b Clinton, Iowa, Mar 12, 10; s August C Pape & Anna D Jensen P; m 1932 to Helen A Nowak; c Robert C. Educ: Belvidere High Sch. Polit & Govt Pos: Hwy comnr, Belvidere Twp, Ill, 47-; dir, Twp Officials of Ill, 54-64 & 66-, first vpres, 64-65; precinct committeeman, Rep Party, 9 years; chmn, Boone Co Rep Party, formerly; deleg, Rep Nat Conv, 68. Mem: Lions Int (int counr, dist gov, 60-61). Relig: Protestant. Mailing Add: 1624 S State St Belvidere IL 61008

PAPEN, FRANK O'BRIEN (D)
NMex State Sen
b Las Vegas, NMex, Dec 2, 09; s John A Papen & Helen O'Brien P; m 1942 to Julia S Stevenson; c Frances Michele. Educ: De LaSalle Inst, Chicago, Ill. Polit & Govt Pos: NMex State Rep, 57-58; deleg, NMex Const Conv, 69; NMex State Sen, 69- Bus & Prof Pos: Pres, Loretto Develop Co, Shopping Ctr; pres, Frank O Papen & Co, Ins, 40-; dir, First Nat Bank Dona Ana Co, 54-, exec vpres, 57-60, pres, 60-; mem, NMex State Invest Coun, 63-67; mem, NMex Dept Develop Adv Coun, 67-68; mem, Govt Comt on Tech Excellence, Subcomt White Sands Space Shuttleport, 71; mem indust develop comt, Fedn Rocky Mountain States, 71- Mil Serv: Fourth Army liaison officer, ROTC Dona Ana Co, 68. Publ: Banking Progress Via Community Development, Burroughs Clearing House, 70. Mem: Las Cruces CofC; Kiwanis; Am Red Cross; Community Concert Asn; KofC (4 degree). Honors & Awards: Citizen of Year Award, NMex Asn Realtors, 68. Relig: Catholic. Legal Res: Rte 1 Box 2206 Las Cruces NM 88001 Mailing Add: First Nat Bank Dona Ana County 500 S Main St Las Cruces NM 88001

PAPY, CHARLES C, JR (D)
Fla State Rep
Mailing Add: 6400 SW 120th Ave Miami FL 33165

PAQUIN, KEITH DAVID (D)
Secy, Grant Co Dem-Farmer-Labor Party, Minn
b Round Prairie, Minn, Jan 10, 11; s Elias David Paquin & Eva Viola Shaw P; m 1932 to Ann Theresa Forster; c Dwayne F, Arlene (Mrs Whalen), Rosemary (Mrs Moreno), Dolores (Mrs Hartman), Lois (Mrs Segarra), Carol & David I. Educ: Univ Cincinnati, 33; Univ Minn, 60. Polit & Govt Pos: Deleg, Grant Co Dem-Farmer-Labor Party, 60, alt deleg, 70; secy, Grant Co Dem-Farmer-Labor Party, Minn, 70- Bus & Prof Pos: Dir, Herman Mkt, Minn, 60-69. Mil Serv: Entered as Pvt, Nat Guard, 27, released as S/Sgt, 33; awards for marksmanship. Publ: Auth of various articles in local papers. Mem: Minn Real Estate Asn; Columbia Mutual Fund Asn; Farmers Union; State of Minn Tax Asn; Am For Dem Action. Relig: Christian. Mailing Add: Herman MN 56248

PARADIS, AIME H (R)
NH State Rep
Mailing Add: Moose Club Park RFD 2 Goffstown NH 03045

PARADIS, HENRY LOUIS (D)
Chmn, Stafford Co Dem Party, NH
b Waterloo, Ont, Sept 5, 18; s George Paradis & Lydia Fountaine P; m 1940 to Mavis B Lance. Polit & Govt Pos: Chmn, Stafford Co Dem Party, NH, 74- Mailing Add: Box 335 Gonic NH 03867

PARCELL, LEW W (D)
Chmn, San Juan Co Dem Cent Comt, Colo
b Beverly, Ohio, Sept 17, 88; s William Parcell & Nellie Jane Deal P; m 1914 to Elva Jane Glanville; c Wallace G. Educ: Ohio Northern Univ. Polit & Govt Pos: Chmn, San Juan Co Dem Cent Comt, Colo, currently; mem, Colo Dem State Exec Comt, 69- Bus & Prof Pos: Owner, Silverton Elec Lighting Co, 16-66; owner, Circle Route Garage, 20-56. Mem: Elks; Rotary. Mailing Add: PO Box 67 Silverton CO 81433

PARDINI, A J (BUD) (R)
Wash State Rep
Mailing Add: E 1625 20th Ave Spokane WA 99203

PARDUE, ERWIN (R)
Mem, Rep State Cent Comt Calif
b Erwin, Tenn, July 22, 39; s Salomon Bradia Pardue & Berlyn Shell P; single. Educ: YMCA Jr Col, 2 years. Polit & Govt Pos: Mem, Rep State Cent Comt, Calif, 69-; mem, 20th Assembly Dist Rep Coun, 69-; mem, Calif Rep Assembly, 69-; mem, Calif Rep League, 69- Bus & Prof Pos: Pres, US Serv Bur, 70- Mil Serv: Seaman Recruit, Navy, 58; E-5, Naval Res, with serv in US Seventh Fleet, 62. Mem: Marine Exchange; Jr CofC; Optimist (vpres, El Camino chap); Club Sailors Union Pac. Relig: Baptist. Mailing Add: 510 Bush San Francisco CA 94108

PARDUN, PATRICIA JANE (R)
b Independence, Iowa, Oct 23, 24; d Allen Smith & Myra Mattice S; m 1943 to W Glen Pardun; c Paulette (Mrs Brossman), Anthony Allen & Pamela (Mrs Dunlap). Educ: Univ Dubuque, 1 year; Univ Iowa, 2 years. Polit & Govt Pos: Rep precinct committeewoman, Harrison Twp, Benton Co, Iowa, 53-68; vchmn, Benton Co Cent Comt, 54-58; pres, Rep Women's Club, 62-64; state prog chmn, Iowa Coun of Rep Women, 62-64; second dist vchmn, Iowa State Cent Comt Rep, 58-62, fourth dist vchmn, 64-68, state vchmn, 66-74; deleg, Rep Nat Conv, 68 & 72, mem, Nat Rules Comt, 72. Bus & Prof Pos: Secy, Buchanan Co Title & Loan, 41-43, Allen Smith, Attorney-at-law, 43-56 & Brandon Consol Sch, 56-58. Mem: Iowa Farm Bur; Navy Mothers; Am Legion Auxiliary; Federated Women's Club; Wapsipinicon Golf Club. Relig: Methodist. Mailing Add: RFD 1 Brandon IA 52210

PARELLA, GAETANO D (R)
RI State Rep
Mailing Add: 1255 Hope St Bristol RI 02809

PARENTEAU, CAROLYN BLANCHE (R)
Chmn, Northfield Rep Town Comt, Mass
b Gill, Mass, Jan 25, 21; d Frank A Zak & Mary Niedbala Z; m 1946 to Raymond J Parenteau. Educ: Nazareth Col, 40; Katherine Gibbs Secretarial Sch, 42. Polit & Govt Pos: Secy, Northfield Rep Town Comt, Mass, 53-65, vchmn, 66, chmn, 66-, mem-at-lg, Franklin Co Rep Club, 62-69; Northfield Rep coordr, Edward W Brooke for Attorney Gen Campaign Comt, 64 & for US Sen, 66; campaigner, Gov John A Volpe, 64 & 66, Lt Gov Elliot L Richardson, 64, Attorney Gen Elliot L Richardson, 66 & Lt Gov Francis Sargent, 66; campaigner, Mass State Rep Silvio O Conte, First Dist, 64 & 66, Mass State Sen Charles A Bisbee, Jr, Franklin-Hampshire Dist, 64, Mass State Sen John D Barrus, Franklin-Hampshire Dist, 66 & Mass State Rep Winston Healy, First Franklin Dist, 64 & 66; pres, Franklin Co Rep Women's Club, 65-67; campaign mgr, Attorney Raymond J Fontana for Gov Coun, Eighth Dist, 66-68; aide, Rep State Committeewoman, Franklin Co Dist, 68; chmn, Franklin Co Regist, Voter Drive, 68; mem nominating comt, Mass Fedn Rep Women, 69. Bus & Prof Pos: Owner & operator, Fairview Gardens Greenhouses, 51-69; secy/vchmn, Pioneer Valley Regional Sch Dist Comt, 61-69; mem, Rep Club of Mass, 67-69; secy & mem adv bd, Greenfield Community Col, 67-; mem, Greenfield Community Col Found, Inc, 69. Mem: Mass Flower Growers Asn; Mass Sch Comt Asn; Northfield Girl Scouts Little House (chmn & treas); Northfield Village Improve Soc (secy); Northfield Civic Coun. Honors & Awards: Appreciation Badge, Girl Scouts. Relig: Catholic. Mailing Add: 8 Main St Northfield MA 01360

PARHAM, BOBBY EUGENE (D)
Ga State Rep
Mailing Add: PO Box 606 Milledgeville GA 31061

PARIS, WILLIAM (BILL) (R)
Wash State Rep
Mailing Add: 620 Oregon Way Longview WA 98632

PARISH, RICHARD JUSTUS (DFL)
Minn State Rep
b Little Swan, Minn, Jan 4, 14; s John L Parish & Mary Ruth Sunburg P; m 1939 to Audrey Louise Hanson; c Carol (Mrs Compton), Mary (Mrs Gibson), Jane & Richard. Educ: Olivia High Sch, Minn; Hamline Univ, St Paul, BA; William Mitchell Col Law, JD; Kappa Phi Kappa. Polit & Govt Pos: Mem, secy-treas & pres, Sch Bd, Dist 281, Robbinsdale, 49-58; mem, Metrop Planning Comn, 57-58; Minn State Rep, 59-62 & 73-; Minn State Sen, 62-67 & 71-73. Bus & Prof Pos: Attorney-at-Law, 46- Mil Serv: Entered as Ens, Navy, 44, released as Lt(jg), 46, after serv in Armed Guard, Asiatic Pac; Am, Philippine & Asiatic Pac Campaign Ribbons. Mem: VFW; Am Legion; CofC; Minn Hist Soc; Shrine. Relig: Methodist. Legal Res: 2565 Vale Crest Rd Golden Valley MN 55422 Mailing Add: 3826 W Broadway Robbinsdale MN 55422

PARK, WILLIAM ANTHONY (D)
Attorney Gen, Idaho
b Blackfoot, Idaho, June 4, 34; s William Clair Park & Thelma Shear P; m 1961 to Elizabeth Jane Taylor; c Susan Elizabeth, William Adam & Patricia Anne. Educ: Boise Jr Col, Idaho, AA, 54; Univ Idaho, BA, 58, LLB, 63; Phi Alpha Delta; Kappa Sigma. Polit & Govt Pos: Pres, Ada Co Young Dem, Idaho, 65-66; chmn, 18th Dist Dem Orgn, 67-70; deleg, Dem Nat Conv, 68; Attorney Gen, Idaho, 71- Bus & Prof Pos: Self-employed attorney, 63-70. Mil Serv: Entered as Pvt, Army, 56, released as Pfc, 57, after serv in Qm Corps, Philadelphia Qm Depot. Mem: Idaho State & Boise Bar Asns; City Club of Boise; Crane Creek Country Club. Relig: Episcopal. Mailing Add: 315 Schmeizer Lane Boise ID 83706

PARKER, BARRY T (R)
NJ State Sen
b Mt Holly, NJ, Dec 12, 32. Educ: Bordentown Mil Inst, 50; Bucknell Univ, AB, 54; Rutgers Univ, LLB, 60. Polit & Govt Pos: NJ State Assemblyman, formerly; NJ State Sen, 75- Bus & Prof Pos: Attorney, Parker, McCay & Crisuolo, Mt Holly. Mem: NJ Compensation Asn; CofC (dir); Rotary; Elks; F&AM. Mailing Add: 115 High St Mt Holly NJ 08060

PARKER, CARL ALLEN (D)
Tex State Rep
b Port Arthur, Tex, Aug 6, 34; s Harvie A Parker & Juanita Christian P; m 1960 to Beverly Stiegler; c Valerie Lynn, Christian Ann & Carl Allen, Jr. Educ: Univ Tex, Austin, LLB & BA, 58; Phi Delta Phi. Polit & Govt Pos: Tex State Rep, 62-, Speaker Pro Tem, chmn calendar comt & mem appropriations comt, Tex House Rep, chmn penitentiaries, const amendments & judicial dist comts, formerly; Tex rep Nat Conf State & Legis Leaders, Washington, DC, El Paso, Tex & Salt Lake City, Utah. Bus & Prof Pos: Partner, Law Firm of Long, Parker & Glasscock. Mil Serv: Entered as Lt(jg), Naval Res, 58, Comdr, currently. Mem: Tex Trial Lawyers Asn; SJefferson Co Ment Health Soc; Lions; Jaycees; CofC. Honors & Awards: Outstanding Young Man in Port Arthur, Jaycees, 67. Relig: Baptist. Mailing Add: 3549 Sixth St Port Arthur TX 88640

PARKER, CLARE JOHN (D)
Vt State Rep
Mailing Add: 3 Hill Pl Springfield VT 05156

PARKER, DANIEL
Adminr, Agency Int Develop, Dept State
b Chicago, Ill, June 8, 25; s Kenneth Safford Parker & Mildred Gapen P; m 1945 to Sally Minor; c Geoffrey Safford, Steven Minor, Jennifer Parker Coleon & Sarah Clemens. Educ: Milton Col, BA, 47, DBA, 68, Harvard Univ, MBA, 49. Hon Degrees: LLD, Am Univ, 68. Polit & Govt Pos: Mem, Rep Nat Finance Comt, 61-73 & Wis Rep Finance Comt, 61-73; mem, Presidents Pub Adv Comt on Trade Policy, 68-69; adminr, Agency Int Develop, Dept State, 73-; President's Spec Coordr for Int Disaster Assistance, 75- Bus & Prof Pos: Dir research & prod develop, Parker Pen Co, 50, bd dirs, 50-73, secy, 51, exec vpres, 52-60, pres, 60-66, chmn bd, 66-73; dir, Merchants & Savings Bank, Janesville, Wis, 52-73; hon chmn bd trustees, Milton Col, 56-; dir, P W Minor & Son, Batavia, NY, 52-73, Omniflight, Inc, Janesville, 62-73 & Rexnord, Inc, Milwaukee, Wis, 64-73; trustee, Northwestern Mutual Life Ins Co, Milwaukee, 65-73 & Comt Econ Develop, Conf Bd, 65-; mem action comt for export promotion, Nat Export Expansion Coun, 66-68; dir, CPC Int, Englewood Cliffs, NJ, 66-73, Bank of Janesville, 61-73, S J Johnson & Son, Inc, Racine, Wis, 67-73 & Stewart-Warner Corp, Chicago, Ill, 69-73; adv coun, Midwest Vchmn Nat 4-H Clubs, 69-73; bd dirs exec comt, Overseas Develop Coun, 69-73; dir, M&S Bancorp, Janesville, Wis, 71-73, Oscar Mayer & Co, Madison, Wis, 71-73 & Overseas Pvt Investment Corp, 71-73, chmn, 73-, chmn

develop loan comt, 73- Mil Serv: Lt, Marine Corps, 42-46. Mem: Nat Asn Mfrs (chmn, 68, dir, hon vpres, 69-); Ft Lauderdale Yacht Club; Metrop Club; Capitol Hill Club; Janesville Country Club. Legal Res: 1000 E Milwaukee St Janesville WI 53545 Mailing Add: Agency for Int Develop Dept State Washington DC 20523

PARKER, DONAL IRWIN (D)
Chmn, Hempstead Co Dem Cent Comt, Ark
b Hope, Ark, July 17, 21; s Charles Conway Parker & Winnie Davis Woodall P; m 1959 to Mary Ellen Honeycutt; c Donna Marilyn & Paula Lee. Educ: Hope Pub Schs, grad, 39. Polit & Govt Pos: Mayor, Hope, Ark, 68-69; chmn, Hempstead Co Dem Cent Comt, 68-; secy, Hempstead Co Bd Elec Comnr, 68-; mem, Ark State Dem Comt, 74-76; mem rules comt, State Dem Conv, 74- Bus & Prof Pos: Dir advert, Star Publ Co, Hope, 54-73; pub rels dir, ACRC, Little Rock, 74-75; tax audit div, State of Ark, 75- Mil Serv: Entered as Pvt, Air Force, 42, released as Sgt, after serv in 359th Fighter Group, ETO, 43-45; Three Unit Battle Stars. Mem: Gov Adv Coun Voc-Tech Educ; VFW. Relig: Methodist. Legal Res: E 23rd St Hope AR 71801 Mailing Add: PO Box 11 Hope AR 71801

PARKER, DONALD CONANT (R)
Chmn, Bullock Co Rep Exec Comt, Ala
b Union Springs, Ala, July 27, 26; s Donald Wright Parker & Mabel Moore P; m 1947 to Alla Maye Springer; c Donald M, David C & Roger C. Educ: Auburn Univ, BS, 50; Phi Kappa Phi; Alpha Zeta; Xi Sigma Pi. Polit & Govt Pos: Secy, Bullock Co Rep Exec Comt, Ala, 62-64, chmn, 64-; vchmn, Bullock Co Bd of Educ, 62-68, chmn, 68-; mem, Rep State Exec Comt Ala, currently. Bus & Prof Pos: Partner, Springer Lumber Co, 51-, Builders Supply Co, 56- & Parker Bros, Union Springs, Ala, 63- Mil Serv: Entered as A/S, Navy, 44, released as RM 3/C, 46, after serv in Western Pac. Mem: Lions; Am Legion; Am Red Cross (chmn, Bullock Co chap). Relig: Presbyterian. Mailing Add: 209 W Hardaway Union Springs AL 36089

PARKER, GEORGE (R)
Chmn, Rep Party Wis
b Janesville, Wis, Nov 9, 29; s Russell Parker & Eleanor Jackson P; m 1951 to Nancy Bauhan; c George, Elizabeth, Martha & Patricia. Educ: Brown Univ, BA, 51; Univ Mich, MA, 52, Law Sch, 52; Psi Upsilon. Hon Degrees: LLD, Milton Col, 74. Polit & Govt Pos: Chmn, N Rock Co Rep Finance Comt, Wis, 58-70; chmn, Rock Co Rep Finance Comt, 70-71; chmn, First Cong Dist Rep Finance Comt, 71; chmn, Wis State Rep Finance Comt, 71-73; mem, Rep Nat Finance Comt, 71-73; alt deleg, Rep Nat Conv, 72; chmn, Rep Party Wis, currently; mem, Rep Nat Comt, 74- Bus & Prof Pos: Pres & chief exec officer, Parker Pen Co, 66- Mil Serv: Naval Res. Relig: Episcopal. Legal Res: 700 St Lawrence Ave Janesville WI 53545 Mailing Add: 219 E Court St Janesville WI 53545

PARKER, GERRY F, II (D)
NH State Rep
Mailing Add: 14 Webster St Nashua NH 03060

PARKER, H SHELDON, JR (R)
Pa State Rep
b Pittsburgh, Pa, Apr 14, 38; s H Sheldon Parker & Elizabeth Matthews P; m 1969 to Sara Ann Lawler; c Todd Sheldon & Scott Matthews. Educ: Williams Col, BA, 61; Univ Pittsburgh, MA, 65; Pi Sigma Alpha. Polit & Govt Pos: Committeeman, 45th Sen Dist Rep Party, Pa, 65-66; chmn, Mt Lebanon Twp Rep Party, 66; Pa State Rep, 67-, minority chmn comt on fed-state rels, Pa House Rep, 73; alt deleg, Rep Nat Conv, 68. Bus & Prof Pos: Investment broker, Parker/Hunter, Inc, Pittsburgh, currently. Mil Serv: Pvt, Nat Guard Res, 62-66. Publ: The State of Allegheny, 65. Mem: Pa Coun on the Arts; Pittsburgh Hist & Landmarks' Found. Relig: Presbyterian. Legal Res: 177 Sunridge Dr Pittsburgh PA 15234 Mailing Add: Capitol Bldg Harrisburg PA 17120

PARKER, JOHN F (R)
Mass State Sen
Mailing Add: State Capitol Boston MA 02133

PARKER, JOHN RAINEY, JR (R)
b Little Rock, Ark, Nov 12, 31; s John Rainey Parker & Ollie Leigh Marlette P; m 1960 to Jean Elizabeth Gale; c John Rainey, III & Sarah Elizabeth. Educ: Univ NC, AB in chem, 57, Law Sch; Pi Alpha Delta. Polit & Govt Pos: Cand, NC State Sen, 64; pres, Sampson Co Young Rep Club, 65-66; mem, Sampson Co Rep Exec Comt, formerly, chmn, 66-70; co attorney, Sampson Co, currently; mem, Comn on Uniform State Laws, currently. Bus & Prof Pos: Assoc, Butler & Butler, 57-63; attorney- at-law, 61-; bd dirs, NC Railroad. Mil Serv: Entered as Pvt, Army, 53, released as Sgt, 56, after serv in Korean Commun Zone & Japan; Good Conduct Ribbon. Mem: Am, NC & Sampson Co Bar Asns; NC State Bar; Clinton Jr CofC. Relig: Presbyterian. Legal Res: Rte 6 Box 196 Airport Rd Clinton NC 28328 Mailing Add: PO Box 27 Clinton NC 28328

PARKER, LEON DOUGLAS (R)
Chmn, Stanly Co Rep Exec Comt, NC
b Albermarle, NC, Oct 4, 20; s Raymond Swink Parker & Bessie Mae Arey P; m 1942 to Sue Louise Trott; c Sue Trott (Mrs McIntyre) & Ruth Arey. Educ: Wake Forest Col, 37-38. Polit & Govt Pos: Justice of the Peace, Stanly Co, NC, 62-68; vchmn, Stanly Co Rep Exec Comt, 64-68, chmn, 68-; magistrate, NC Dist Court, 68- Bus & Prof Pos: Newspaper prod, Stanly News & Press, Albemarle, NC, 17 years; owner-operator, Carolina Printing Co, 8 years. Mil Serv: Entered as Pvt, Army, 42, released as Cpl, 45, after serv in Mil Police, ETO, 43-45. Mem: Lions; DAV; VFW; Stanly Co Law Enforcement Officers Asn. Relig: Methodist. Legal Res: South Main St New London NC 28127 Mailing Add: Drawer 308 New London NC 28127

PARKER, LETHA MARY (R)
Mem, Kans Rep State Comt
b Clearwater, Kans, Dec 30, 05; d Joseph Harvey Kirk & Flora A Cummins K; m 1928 to Moses C Parker; c Dr Robert N, DVM, Dr Harold L, MD & Dorothy Anne (Mrs Ronald T McDonald). Educ: Emporia State Teachers Col & Friends Univ. Polit & Govt Pos: Rep committeewoman, Ninnescah Twp, Kans, 60; secy exec comt, Sedgwick Co Rep Cent Comt, 64-, mem adv comt, 70-72, area twp chmn, 70-72; mem, Co Campaign Comt for 72 Elec, 72; mem, Sedgwick Co Adv Bd, 69 & 70; alt deleg, Rep Nat Conv, 68; dir, Lincoln Rep Club, Fifth Dist; Rep ward chmn, Ninnescah Twp; mem, Kans Rep State Comt, Sedgwick Co Fifth Dist, 73- Bus & Prof Pos: Teacher, grade sch, 24-28 & 29-30 prin, Enterprise Sch, Wichita, Kans, 29-30; housewife, 41- Publ: Co-ed, Clearwater Hist Book, 61. Mem: Bus & Prof Womens Club; Local Womens Rep Club; Eastern Star (Worthy Matron, Ninnescah Chap & officer in Clearwater Chap, 63-). Honors & Awards: Mother of the Year, local chap, Bus & Prof Women's Club. Relig: Baptist. Mailing Add: RR Box 247 Clearwater KS 67026

PARKER, LEWIS W, JR (D)
Va State Deleg
Mailing Add: PO Box 366 South Hill VA 23970

PARKER, MAE FRANCES (D)
Committeewoman, Maine State Dem Comt
b New Gloucester, Maine, May 16, 05; d Harry Parker & Ethel Hunnewell P; single. Educ: Bliss Bus Col. Polit & Govt Pos: Secy, Durham Dem Town Comt, Maine, 48-54, chmn, 54-; secy, Androscoggin Co Dem Party, 54-70, vchairwoman, 72-; committeewoman, Maine State Dem Comt, 62- Bus & Prof Pos: Post stitcher, Shoe Shops, 36-70. Mem: Degree of Pocahontas No 33 (presiding off; Pocahontas, 70-74); New Gloucester Grange No 28 (past secy); Dem Women's Club of Androscoggin Co (vchairwoman, 72-74); Vol Fire Dept Auxiliary; Laspa Union (dir). Relig: Congregational. Legal Res: Durham ME Mailing Add: RD 1 Auburn ME 04210

PARKER, MANLEY CLARK (D)
Chmn, Lincoln Co Dem Party, NC
b Raleigh, NC, Aug 14, 42; s Dr Hermon M Parker & Virginia Clark P; m 1971 to Betty Curry. Educ: Univ NC, Chapel Hill, AB & JD; Phi Alpha Delta; Phi Eta Sigma; vpres & marshall, Class 68. Polit & Govt Pos: Pres, Lincoln Co Young Dem, NC, 71-72; chmn, Lincoln Co Dem Party, 72- Mem: Am & NC Bar Asns; Jaycees; Rotary; NC Trial Lawyers Asn. Relig: Unitarian. Legal Res: Rte 7 Box 157 Lincolnton NC 28092 Mailing Add: PO Box 754 Lincolnton NC 28092

PARKER, MARSHALL JOYNER (R)
Assoc Adminr, Procurement & Mgt Assistance, Small Bus Admin
b Seaboard, NC, Apr 25, 22; s Dr Carl P Parker & Bertha Joyner P; m 1943 to Martha Nimmons; c Anna, Susan & Alice. Educ: Univ NC, BS, 44; Sigma Nu. Polit & Govt Pos: City Councilman, Seneca, SC, 52-54; trustee, Oconee Co Bd Sch Trustees, 53-56; SC State Sen, 57-67; chmn, SC Tax Study Comt, 59-64; mem bd trustees, Columbia Col, SC, 63-69; Rep nominee, US Sen, SC, 66 & 68; deleg & chmn, SC deleg, Rep Nat Conv, 68; assoc adminr, Procurement & Mgt Assistance, Small Bus Admin, Washington, DC, 70-; mem, Nat Adv Coun on Exten & Continuing Educ, 72-; Rep cand, US House of Rep, SC, 74. Bus & Prof Pos: Businessman & owner, Oconee Dairies. Mil Serv: Marine Corps, 43-46. Mem: Sertoma; Am Legion; VFW. Relig: Methodist; Mem bd stewards & trustee, St Mark Methodist Church, Seneca, 47-56 & 68-70. Legal Res: Seneca SC 29678 Mailing Add: 220 M St SW Washington DC 20024

PARKER, MARTIN LEONARD (D)
Committeeman, Westchester Co Dem Comt, NY
b New York, NY, Apr 21, 21; s Harry Parker & Susan Jaffe P; m 1948 to Caroline Goldstein; c Andrew Charles, Frederick Lawrence & Suzanne Isabel. Educ: Duke Univ, AB, 42; Navy Supply Corps Sch, Harvard Univ Bus Sch, 42 & 44; Zeta Beta Tau; Hillel Found. Polit & Govt Pos: Committeeman, Westchester Co Dem Comt, NY, 60-; Dem-Liberal cand, NY State Assembly, 62; coordr, Westchester Co Campaign, Paul O'Dwyer for Senate, 68; deleg, Dem Nat Conv, 68 & 72; chmn, Briarcliff Manor Dem Comt, 68-; chmn, Concerned Dem of Westchester-Putnam, 68-; vchmn, NY State New Dem Coalition, 70-71; chmn, People for McGovern, Westchester Co, 72; deleg, Dem Nat Charter Conf, 74. Bus & Prof Pos: Mem bd trustees, NY Mil Acad, Cornwall-on-Hudson, NY, 63-71; acct exec mkt div, Reuben H Donnelley Corp, Mt Vernon, 47-70, sales mgr, 70- Mil Serv: Entered as Ens, Navy, 42, released as Lt, 46, after serv in Third Fleet, S Pac, 42-44; S Pac Theatre Medal; Am Theatre Medal; World War II Victory Medal; Citation from Task Group Comdr, Third Fleet Amphibious Forces. Mem: F&AM (Master, Loyalty Lodge 876, 57); Scottish Rite; Ancient Arabic Order of Nobles of the Mystic Shrine; Eastern Tennis Empires Asn; life mem US Law Tennis Asn. Relig: Jewish. Mailing Add: 39 Quinn Rd Briarcliff Manor NY 10510

PARKER, MARY EVELYN (D)
Treas, La
b Fullerton, La, Nov 8, 20; d Racia E Dickerson & Addie Graham D; m to W Bryant Parker (deceased); c Mary Bryant & Ann Graham. Educ: Northwestern State Col, BA, 41; La State Univ, Dipl Soc Welfare, 43. Polit & Govt Pos: Personnel adminstr, War Dept, 43-47; exec dir, La Dept Com & Indust, 48-52; Nat Dem Committeewoman, 48-52; chmn, La Bd Pub Welfare, 50-51; comnr pub welfare, La State Dept Pub Welfare, 56-63; comnr, Div Admin, La, 64-67; Treas, La, 68-; chmn, State Bond Comn, 68- Bus & Prof Pos: Social worker, La, 41-42; ed weekly newspaper, Oakdale, La, 47-48; life insurance salesman, Baton Rouge, La, 52-56. Mem: La Conf Social Welfare; White House Conf on Children & Youth; Women's Div, United Givers Fund Dr. Relig: Baptist. Mailing Add: State Capitol Baton Rouge LA 70809

PARKER, MIKE (D)
Wash State Rep
b Renton, Wash, May 23, 47; s E L Parker & Mary Cook P; m 1968 to Judith Mae Coon. Educ: Highline Community Col, grad, 67; Univ Puget Sound, grad, 70; Portland State Univ. Polit & Govt Pos: Wash State Rep, 73- Bus & Prof Pos: Coordr health & welfare progs, Riker Labs, 70- Mil Serv: Entered as Pvt, Nat Guard, 69, serv as 2nd Lt. Mem: Elks; Toastmasters; Jaycees; Kiwanis. Relig: Methodist. Mailing Add: 5434 S I Tacoma WA 98408

PARKER, NANCY BAUHAN (R)
Mem Exec Comt, Rep Party Wis
b Orange, NJ, Nov 30, 29; d Alexander Bauhan & Margaret Weedon B; m 1951 to George Safford Parker, II; c George Safford, III, Elizabeth Weedon, Martha Eleanor & Patricia Jeffris. Educ: Pembroke Col, Brown Univ, AB, 51; Univ Mich, 51-52. Polit & Govt Pos: Precinct survey worker, Janesville Rep Party, Wis, 60, voter registrn chmn, 62, campaign activities chmn, 64 & vchmn, 65-67; chmn, Mobilization of Rep Enterprise, Rock Co Rep Party, Wis, 66-69 & co-chmn, First Cong Dist Nixon for Pres Comt, 68; alt deleg, Rep Nat Conv, 68, deleg, 72; mem, Wis Develop Authority, 69-; vchmn, First Cong Dist Rep Party, 69-74; mem exec comt, Rep Party, Wis, 69-; mem, Rock Co Rep Party; sustaining mem, Nat Comt Rep Party. Mem: Janesville & Rock Co Fedn of Rep Women; Janesville Woman's Club; YMCA; Rock Co Hist Soc; Early Janesville Restoration Soc. Relig: Episcopal. Mailing Add: 700 St Lawrence Ave Janesville WI 53545

PARKER, RICHARD BORDEAUX
US Ambassador to Algeria
b Philippine Islands, July 3, 23; s Roscoe S Parker & Marguerite Blossom P; m 1944 to Jeanne

Jaccard; c Alison (Mrs Kenway), Jeffrey, Jill & Richard. Educ: Kans State Univ, BS, 47, MS, 48; Princeton Univ, 64-65; Delta Tau Delta. Polit & Govt Pos: US Foreign Serv, 49-, US Ambassador to Algeria, 75- Mil Serv: Entered as Pvt, Army, 43, released as 1st Lt, 47, after serv in 106th Div, ETO. Publ: Co-auth, Guide to Islamic Monuments of Cairo, AUC Press, 74. Mem: Mid East Study Asn; Royal Asian Soc; Am Foreign Serv Asn. Legal Res: c/o Robinson 55 Chumasero Dr San Francisco CA 94132 Mailing Add: Am Embassy Algiers Algeria

PARKER, ROBERT L (R)
Committeeman, Tex Rep State Exec Comt
b Roby, Tex, Dec 12, 23; s Tom H Parker & Thelma McCombs P; m 1943 to Dorothy G Stevenson; c Lynnda Diane, Robert Evans & Julie Anne. Educ: Tex A&M Univ, Agr, 40-46. Polit & Govt Pos: Finance chmn, Lamar Co Rep Party, 66-; alt deleg, Rep Nat Conv, 68, deleg, 72; deleg, Rep State Conv, 68, 70 & 72; committeeman, Tex Rep State Exec Comt, 69- Bus & Prof Pos: Instr agr, Rotan & Seymour Vocational Sch, Tex, 47-50; terracing contractor, 47-50; rancher & farmer, Paris, 50-54; exec vpres, Tex Sesame Growers Inc, 54-66; pres, Paris Milling Co, 66-, bd dirs, Liberty Nat Bank, Paris; bd mem, Paris Independent Sch Dist, 68-72. Mil Serv: Entered as Pvt, Army, 43, released as 1st Lt, 46, after serv in 380th Field Artil Bn, 102nd Inf Div, ETO, 44-45; Army Res: Bronze Star Medal; Europe-Africa-Mid East Campaign Medal with two Bronze Stars; Am Theatre Campaign Medal; World War II Victory Medal. Mem: Tex Seedsman Asn (first vpres); Southern Seedsman Asn; Tex Grain & Feed Asn; Nat Grain & Feed Dealers; Rotary. Relig: Methodist. Mailing Add: PO Box 690 Paris TX 75460

PARKER, ROBERT LEE (D)
Mem, Tex State Dem Exec Comt
b Houston, Tex, Apr 28, 29; s Charlie Duffield Parker & Ruth DeMoss P; m 1947 to Louise Ovalene Raby; c Robert Lee, Jr, Carol Ann (Mrs Medlin), Stephen Allen & Catherine Louise. Educ: Southwestern Col, 45-46. Polit & Govt Pos: Mem, Anderson Co Exec Comt, Tex, 74-; mem, Tex State Dem Exec Comt, Dist Three, 74-, mem nomination, affirmative action & credentials comts, 74- Bus & Prof Pos: Owner, Parker Elec Co, Palestine, Tex, 59- Mem: Palestine Rotary Club (pres, 75-); CofC; Int Fel of Flying Rotairians. Relig: Assembly of God. Legal Res: RR 3 Box 44P Palestine TX 75801 Mailing Add: PO Box 164 Palestine TX 75801

PARKER, WALTER E (D)
Tex State Rep
b Ft Worth, Tex, July 23, 17; s Lemuel Hicks Parker & Ethel Nancy Bradley P; m 1941 to Mildred Brock; c Walter E, Jr. Educ: NTex State Univ, BS, 40; Tex Christian Univ, MA, 47; Lambda Chi Alpha. Polit & Govt Pos: Chmn, Denton Park Bd, Tex, 58-63; mem, Denton Sch Bd, 67-68; Tex State Rep, Dist 25, Denton Co, 69-, mem appropriations comt, 69-, mem elec comt & vchmn environ affairs comt, 73- Bus & Prof Pos: Off, Nat Football League, currently; gen contractor. Mil Serv: Entered as Pvt, Air Force, 42, released as Capt, 46, after serv in 505th Heavy Bomb Group, SPac Theatre, 43-46; Capt, Air Force Res, Korea, 51-53. Mem: Southwest Football Off Asn; Mason; Shrine; Scottish Rite; Rotary. Relig: Methodist. Legal Res: 2911 Montecito Rd Denton TX 78201 Mailing Add: 725 First State Bank Bldg Denton TX 76201

PARKER, WILLIAM K (D)
Alaska State Rep
b Des Moines, Iowa, Sept 24, 44; s William R Parker & Veronica Kevane P; m 1970 to Peggy Mullen; c Mara. Educ: Immaculate Conception Sem, Conception, Mo, AB; St Joseph Sem, Yonkers, NY, 66-68. Polit & Govt Pos: Alaska State Rep, 73- Bus & Prof Pos: Sports ed, Anchorage Daily News, 69; counr, Kodiak Regional High Sch Dormitory, 70; educ specialist, Alaska State Econ Opportunity Off, 70-72; planner, Advocacy Planning Assocs, 72- Relig: Catholic. Mailing Add: 337 E Tenth Ave Anchorage AK 99501

PARKER, WILLIAM KING (R)
Chmn, Martin Co Rep Party, NC
b Windsor, NC, Mar 28, 93; s Henry King Parker & Lucy Barnard P; m 1962 to Ruth Willard Parker; c Elizabeth (Mrs Cone) & Burke Henry. Educ: Warrenton High Sch, NC, 2 years. Polit & Govt Pos: Dep collector, Fed Revenue Dept, 19-20; chmn, Martin Co Rep Party, NC, 69- Bus & Prof Pos: Salesman, Harrison Wholesale Co, Williamston, NC, 20-26; salesman, Standard Fertilizer Co, 26-32; farmer, 32-35; owner, Williamston Parts & Metal Co, 35- Mil Serv: Entered as Pvt, Army, 17, released as Cpl, 19, after serv in Co B, 120th Inf, 30th Div. Mem: Roanoke Country Club; Vet World War I; CofC. Honors & Awards: Distinguished Serv Award. Relig: Episcopal. Mailing Add: 401 E Franklin St Williamston NC 27892

PARKERSON, WILLIAM FRANCIS, JR (D)
Va State Sen
b Rocky Mount, NC, June 16, 20. Educ: Univ Richmond, BA, 41; Washington & Lee Univ, LLB, 47; Kappa Alpha; Phi Alpha Delta. Polit & Govt Pos: Commonwealth attorney, Henrico Co, Va, 57-61; Va State Deleg, 62-63; Va State Sen, 64- Bus & Prof Pos: Lawyer. Mil Serv: Col, Judge Adv Gen Corps, Army Res. Mem: Sons of the Revolution in State of Va. Relig: Episcopal. Mailing Add: Suite 904 700 Bldg Richmond VA 23219

PARKIN, JERRY DONALD (R)
b Anamosa, Iowa, Jan 5, 50; s Donald Francis Parkin & Alta Larson P; m 1974 to Randall Kay Gerdeman. Educ: Iowa State Univ, BS, 72; Drake Univ, grad work currently; Phi Gamma Delta; Tomahawk. Polit & Govt Pos: Research asst, US Sen Jack Miller, Iowa, 70; research asst, US Rep Fred Schwengel, Iowa, 71; youth coordr, Gov Robert Ray Comt, 71-72; staff asst, US Rep Fred Schwengel, 72; deleg, Rep Nat Conv, 72; community betterment specialist, Gov Off for Planning & Programming, 72-73, spec asst to dir, 74-; coordr, Gov Conf on Iowa in Year 2000, 74. Mem: Iowa Drug Abuse Adv Coun; Cardinal Key. Honors & Awards: Outstanding Alumnus, Alpha Iota Chap, Phi Gamma Delta, 73. Mailing Add: 2823 43rd St Des Moines IA 50310

PARKMAN, PERCY HOWARD (D)
Miss State Rep
Mailing Add: Box 224 Clinton MS 39056

PARKMAN, RALPH M (D)
Ga State Rep
Mailing Add: 584 N White St Carrollton GA 30117

PARKS, CATHERINE M (R)
Wyo State Rep
Mailing Add: Little Powder River Ranch Weston WY 82731

PARKS, JESSE L, JR (D)
Mem, Dem Nat Comt, Mass
b Cleveland, Ohio, May 1, 23; s Jesse L Parks, Sr & Annie D McCrary P; m 1948 to Lucille Goodson; c Donna, Jesse, Garry & Leslie. Educ: Oberlin Col, AB, 49; Univ Mich, Ann Arbor, AM, 50, PhD, 59. Polit & Govt Pos: Deleg, Dem Nat Conv, 72; mem, Dem Nat Comt, Mass, 72-; mem, Comt on Affirmative Action, currently. Bus & Prof Pos: From instr to asst prof health & phys educ, Dillard Univ, 50-55; teaching fel phys educ & research assoc, Univ Mich, Ann Arbor, 56-59; prof phys educ & dir athletics, SC State Col, 59-61; from assoc prof to prof, Springfield Col, 61- Mil Serv: Entered as Pvt, Army, 43, released as M/Sgt, 45, after serv in 176 Qm Bn Hq, ETO; Marksmanship Medal; Good Conduct Medal; 5 Battle Stars. Mem: Am Asn Health, Phys Educ & Recreation; Nat Col Phys Educ Asn for Men; Phi Epsilon Kappa; Am Asn Univ Prof. Honors & Awards: Danforth teacher grant, Univ Mich, Ann Arbor, 55-56; Distinguished Serv Award, Bethel African Methodist Episcopal Church, Springfield, Mass, 72; Hon Award, Northern Educ Serv, Springfield, 74. Relig: Methodist. Mailing Add: 123 Bronson Terr Springfield MA 01108

PARKS, RUTH ALLOTT (R)
Bd Dirs, Nat Fedn Rep Women
b Pueblo, Colo, Aug 3, 08; d Leonard John Allott & Bertha Louise Reese A; m to John Bert Parks; wid. Educ: Pueblo Jr Col, AA, 35; Univ Colo, 26 & 29. Polit & Govt Pos: Head, War Price & Rationing Bd, later Off Price Admin, 42-46; pres, Colo Fedn Rep Women, 53-54, bd dirs, 53-; bd dirs, Nat Fedn Rep Women, 53-, exec comt, 55-67, pres, 61-62; chmn, nominating comt, 67, bylaws, 68-; secy, Pueblo Co Rep Cent Comt, formerly, precinct committeewoman, 54-66, vchmn, Third Cong Dist, formerly; mem, Charter Conv, Pueblo, 54; Colo deleg-at-lg, Rep Nat Conv, 60; rep, White House Conf Children & Youth, 60, Int Coop, 65; mem, Comn to Study Structure, Functions & Finances of Colo, 62. Publ: Ed, The Republican clubwoman, Nat Fedn Rep Women, 61-62; auth, See how she runs (a guide for the woman candidate), Colo Comn on Status of Women, 72. Mem: St Mary-Corwin Hosp, Pueblo (lay adv bd, 65-); Altrusa Club Pueblo; Gen Fedn Women's Clubs; Colo Comn on Status of Women. Honors & Awards: One of twelve outstanding women in Colo, Denver Altrusa, 72; One of 32 Pueblo Women honored for Outstanding Leadership & Participation in Civic Affairs, Southern Colo State Col, 75. Relig: Episcopal; bd dirs, Episcopal Churchwomen, Diocese of Colo, 72. Mailing Add: 36 Villa Dr Pueblo CO 81001

PARNAGIAN, ARAM (R)
NH State Rep
b Lawrence, Mass, Apr 18, 05; s Ardash Parnagian & Mariam Ementian P; m 1934 to Siran Siranoosh Sarkisian; c Evelyn Miriam (Mrs Mamigonian) & Elaine Margaret (Mrs Hashem). Educ: Univ exten courses; Mass Radio Inst, 2 years; Lowell Inst, 2 years; Franklin Inst, 2 years. Polit & Govt Pos: Rep chmn, Ward Four, Dover, NH, 66-67; NH State Rep, Dist 19, 67-, vchmn transp comt, NH House Rep, currently; city chmn, Dover, Del, currently; chmn, New Co Court House & Admin Bldg, Stafford Co, NH, currently. Bus & Prof Pos: Real estate broker, NH; asst to mgr, Chelsea Radio, Chelsea, Mass, 24-28; mgr radio dept, Morgan Furniture, Boston, 28-30; pres, Am Radio Corp, NH, 34-35. Mem: Nat Soc State Legislators; US Power Squadrons (squadron comdr, dist legis officer); Mason; Scottish Rite; Shrine. Relig: Episcopal. Mailing Add: 6 Renaud Ave Dover NH 03820

PARNELL, DALE PAUL (INDEPENDENT)
b Monmouth, Ore, July 16, 28; s Archie S Parnell; mother deceased; m 1947 to Beverly Lush; c Sue, Paul, Teresa, Steve & Tim. Educ: Willamette Univ, BA, 51; Univ Ore MA, 56, DEd, 64; Phi Delta Kappa. Polit & Govt Pos: Precinct committeeman, Lane Co, Independent Party, Ore, 60-64; Supt Pub Instr, Ore, 68-74; chmn, Gov Sch Finance Task Force, Salem, 72-73; chmn, Nat Coun on Equality of Educ Opportunity, 73- Bus & Prof Pos: Teacher, Salem & Springfield, Ore, 50-54; vprin & prin, Springfield Sr High Sch, 54-60; supt, Lane Co Schs, Eugene, 60-64; pres, Lane Community Col, Eugene, 64-68; vis prof, Univ Ore, Eugene & Ore State Univ, Corvallis, summer 64-68; consult, Am Jr Col Asn on Develop Community Cols; bd trustee, Willamette Univ & Northwest Nazarene Col; chancellor, San Diego Community Col Dist, currently; consult ed, McGraw-Hill Publ Co; mem ed adv bd, Educ Digest. Publ: Auth, The Oregon way—career education, Am Voc J, 12/69; co-auth, Accountability; policies and procedures (four vols), Croft Educ Serv, Conn, 72; auth, Career education, US Off Educ, 73. Mem: Coun of Chief State Sch Off; Ore Community Col Asn; Ore Community Col Pres Coun; Am Asn Jr Cols; Nat Adv Coun Child Nutrition. Honors & Awards: Springfield Man of the Year Award, 66; State Golden Torch Award, Bus & Prof Women; Man of the Year Award, Ore Admin Mgt Soc, 66; hon mem, Future Farmers Am & Future Homemakers Am; Student Appreciation Award, Ore Community Col Student Asn, 72. Relig: Nazarene. Legal Res: 5167 Marlborough Ave San Diego CA 92116 Mailing Add: San Diego Community Col Dist 3375 Camino del Rio S San Diego CA 92108

PARNELL, DAVID RUSSELL (D)
NC State Rep
b Parkton, NC, Nov 16, 25; s John Quincy Parnell & Clelia Britt P; m 1948 to Barbara Anne Johnson; c David R, Jr, Anne J & Timothy S. Educ: Wake Forest Univ, BS, 49; Kappa Sigma. Polit & Govt Pos: Mem town bd, Parkton, NC, 59-63; mayor, 63-69; mem, Robeson Co Indust Develop Comn, 62-; mem, NC State Hwy Comn, 69-73; NC State Rep, 74- Bus & Prof Pos: Asst mgr, J Q Parnell, Inc, 50-56, exec vpres, 54-73, mgr, 56-, pres, 73-; owner & pres, Parnell Oil Co, 61-; bd dirs, First Union Nat Bank, 56- Mil Serv: Entered as Pvt, Army, 45, released as Cpl, 46. Mem: Parkton Ruritan Club. Relig: Baptist. Legal Res: Second St Parkton NC 28371 Mailing Add: PO Box 190 Parkton NC 28371

PARNELLE, ROSALIND CORRELL (R)
Exec Committeeman, SC Rep Party
b Lenoir, NC, Aug 6, 42; d John Horace Correll & Irene Boston C; m 1962 to Henry Manley Parnelle, Jr; c Cary Marie & Ellen Rebecca. Educ: Appalachian State Teachers Col, 60-61; Univ SC, 73-75. Polit & Govt Pos: Vchmn, Allendale Co Rep Party, SC, 70-74; mem, Allendale Co Social Serv Bd, 73-; exec committeeman, SC Rep Party, 74- Mem: Nat Found (co dir, 69-). Honors & Awards: Cert Appreciation, Dept Com, 70; Outstanding Serv Award, Nat Found, 73; Pres Honor Roll Award, Univ SC, 73-75. Mailing Add: PO Box 392 Allendale SC 29810

PAROLISE, JOSEPH L (D)
NH State Rep
Mailing Add: 15 Sandy Beach Rd Salem NH 03079

PARR, CHARLES H (CHARLIE) (D)
Alaska State Rep
Mailing Add: 6 1/2 Mile Chena Hot Springs Rd Fairbanks AK 99701

PARR, EDNAPEARL FLORES (R)
NH State Rep
b Brandon, Tex, Feb 15, 16; d Oscar Policarpio Flores & Nancy Maureen Landers F (deceased); m 1954 to Harry Parr; c Capt Neal Michael Parr. Educ: Sacramento City Col, AA; Strayer Jr Col, Washington, DC, 49-51. Polit & Govt Pos: Pres, Rep Federated Club of Hamptons, 59-61; recording secy, NH State Rep Comt, 63-64; field rep, NH State Rep Louis C Wyman, Sea Coast Div, NH, 63-68; chmn, Rockingham Co to Elect Richard Nixon, 68 & 72; NH State Rep, 73-, mem, Claims, Vet, Mil Affairs, & Ways & Means Comts, NH House of Rep, 72-; vchmn, Rockingham Rep Deleg, 75-; chmn, Rockingham Bicentennial Comt, 75- Bus & Prof Pos: Asst buyer, Weinstock-Lubin, Sacramento, Calif, 40-42; buyer, Erlebacher, Washington, DC, 49-51; merchandise mgr, Frank R Jelleff Inc, 51-54; broker, Real Estate of NH, 64-73. Mil Serv: Entered as WAVE, Navy, 42, released as HAC-1, 43, after serv in US. Publ: New Hampshire churches, DAR Mag, 2/67. Mem: Order of Women Legis; Nat Asn Parliamentarians; DAR (vpres gen, 72-75); Children of Am Revolution; Women's Federated Clubs of NH. Honors & Awards: Efficiency Award, Ground Observer Corps of US Air Force, 56; Achievement Award, State Civil Defense of NH, 57. Relig: Protestant. Mailing Add: 10 Emerald Ave Hampton NH 03842

PARRAN, JOHN THOMAS, JR (D)
VChmn, Charles Co Dem Cent Comt, Md
b Baltimore, Md, Feb 5, 26; s John Thomas Parran & Sarah Virginia Elliott P; m to Christel H. Educ: Charlotte Hall Acad; The Citadel; Univ of Md; BA, 50. Polit & Govt Pos: Pres, Young Dem of Charles Co, Md, formerly; Md State Deleg, 55-59; Md State Sen, 59-67; chmn, Tri Co Coun for Southern Md, 66-; vchmn, Charles Co Dem Cent Comt, Md, 70- Bus & Prof Pos: Real estate & ins broker, The Parran Agency, Indian Head, Md, currently; bd mem, Charles Co Community Col, 68-; mem adv bd, Md Nat Bank & Md State Savings & Loan Asn. Mil Serv: Army, 44-46. Mem: Charles Co CofC; Charles Co Jr CofC; Boy Scouts (regional dir); Indian Head Bus Asn; Lions. Relig: Episcopal. Mailing Add: Parran Lane Indian Head MD 20640

PARRATT, J EASTON (D)
Utah State Rep
Mailing Add: 4950 Wasatch St Murray UT 84107

PARRIS, BOB (D)
Okla State Sen
Mailing Add: State Capitol Oklahoma City OK 73105

PARRIS, STANFORD E (R)
b Champaign, Ill, Sept 9, 29; s Verne E Parris & Edna Long P; m 1951 to Jane McCullough; c Michael E, Ann M & Susan L. Educ: Univ Ill, BS, 50; George Washington Univ, JD, 58; Alpha Delta Phi. Polit & Govt Pos: Mem, Bd Supvrs, Fairfax Co, Va, 64-67; Va State Deleg, 69-72; US Rep, Eighth Dist, Va, 73-75; Rep cand, US House of Rep, Va, 74. Bus & Prof Pos: Pres, Woodbridge Chrysler-Plymouth Corp, 65-; vpres & mem, Bd Dirs, Paule of Va, Fairfax, 66-72; pres, Flying Circus Aerodrome, Inc, 70-; attorney & partner, Swayze, Parris, Tydings & Bryant, Fairfax, 72. Mil Serv: Entered as 2nd Lt, Air Force, 50, released as 1st Lt, 54, after serv in 31st Fighters Wing, Strategic Air Command, 51-54; Distinguished Flying Cross; Air Medal with Oak Leaf Clusters; Purple Heart; US & Korean Presidential Unit Citations. Mem: Fairfax Co YMCA (bd dirs); Rotary; Am Legion; CofC; Delta Theta Phi. Relig: Protestant. Legal Res: 7609 Manor House Dr Fairfax Station VA 22039 Mailing Add: 509 Cannon House Off Bldg Washington DC 20515

PARRISH, JIM (D)
Kans State Sen
b Great Bend, Kans, Aug 25, 46; s Maj Gen Clemont Crane Parrish & Ruth Elizebeth Cox P; m 1970 to Nancy Elaine Buchele. Educ: Pratt Community Jr Col, Kans, AA, 67; Kans State Univ, BS, 70; Washburn Univ Sch Law, Topeka, JD cum laude, 73; Phi Kappa Phi; Sigma Delta Chi; Blue Key; Phi Delta Theta. Polit & Govt Pos: Kans State Rep, 73-74; Kans State Sen, 75- Bus & Prof Pos: Sports ed & photographer, Pratt Daily Tribune, Kans, 66-67; news writer, photographer & relief ed, Manhattan Mercury Newspaper, Manhattan, Kans, 67-70. Mil Serv: Entered as 2nd Lt, Army Res, 70, 1st Lt, currently; Distinguished Mil Student, Kans State Univ. Mem: Sigma Delta Chi. Mailing Add: 909 Topeka Ave Topeka KS 66612

PARRISH, JOHN EDGAR, JR (JOHNNY) (D)
Ga State Rep
b Bulloch Co, Ga, June 30, 39; s John Edgar Parrish, Sr & Lula Shearouse P; m 1961 to Patricia Graham; c Bonnie, Patti Lu & John, III. Educ: Univ Ga, BBA, 62; GOP of Independent Men. Polit & Govt Pos: Ga State Rep, Dist 97, 75- Bus & Prof Pos: Ins adjustor, Crawford & Co, Waycross, Ga, 62-63; ins adjustor, Integon Corp, Winston-Salem, NC, 63-65, claims supvr, 66-67, agency secy, 67-68, mem, Pres Roundtable, 68-; pvt ins agency, Integon Corp, Columbus, Ga, 68- Publ: How to prevent cancelled appointments, Nat Ins Sales, 69. Mem: Columbus Life Underwriters Asn; St Anne Home & Sch Asn (pres); Kiwanis; Mason; Life Underwriters Polit Action Comt. Honors & Awards: New Man of Year, Integon Corp, 67-68 & 68-69, Life Award, 68-69 & 69-70, Nat Sales Achievement Award, 70-74; Outstanding Young Man of Year, Columbus Jaycees, 74. Relig: Methodist. Legal Res: 3327 Apache Dr Columbus GA 31904 Mailing Add: PO Box 6349 Columbus GA 31907

PARRISH, ROBERT AMBROSE (R)
Committeeman, Barton Co Rep Cent Comt, Kans
b Oklahoma City, Okla, Mar 3, 27; s George E Parrish & Leta Faye Dodson P; m 1949 to Mary Belle Pollock; c Cheryl C, Cynthia D & Robert A, Jr. Educ: Univ Kansas, Lawrence, BS, 50; Scabbard & Blade; Pershing Rifles; Sigma Nu; Alpha Kappa Psi. Polit & Govt Pos: Committeeman, Rep City Comt, Great Bend, 61; pres, Great Bend City Coun, 63; committeeman, Barton Co Rep Cent Comt, 66-, chmn, 68; chmn, Barton Co Rep Party, 68-72; mayor, Great Bend, 69- Bus & Prof Pos: Automobile dealer, Parrish Motor Co, Great Bend, Kans, 50- Mil Serv: Entered as Pvt, Army Air Force, 45, released as Cpl, 46, after serv in Air Training Command, US, Capt, Res, 46-54. Mem: Am Legion; Mason; Elks; Rotary. Relig: Protestant. Mailing Add: 1911 McKinney Dr Great Bend KS 67530

PARRISH, W F, JR (R)
Committeeman, Okla Rep Party
b Ada, Okla, Sep 8, 39; s William Fletcher Parrish & Helen Emeline Dawson P; m 1961 to Elizabeth Ann Tennis; c Laurie Ann & Cynthia Lynn. Educ: Univ Okla, 57-58; E Cent State Col, BA, 61; Univ Okla Col Law, LLB, 63; Phi Delta Phi. Polit & Govt Pos: Deleg, Rep Nat Conv, 68; committeeman, Okla Rep Party, 69- Bus & Prof Pos: Partner, Nicklas, Parrish & Saenz, Attorneys, 63- Publ: Numerous articles, Okla Law Rev, 61-64. Mem: Comanche Co & Okla Bar Asns; Am Judicature Soc. Honors & Awards: Commended by joint resolution of Okla Legis & by Okla Bar Asn for serv to Judiciary Comt in preparing & implementing statutes for judicial reform, 68. Relig: Presbyterian; Elder, Presby Church, Lawton, Okla. Legal Res: 1329 Cherry Lawton OK 73501 Mailing Add: 521 C Ave Lawton OK 73501

PARSHLEY, JAMES H (R)
NH State Rep
Mailing Add: Merrymeeting Lake New Durham NH 03855

PARSKY, GERALD LAWRENCE (R)
Asst Secy Trade, Energy & Financial Resources Policy Coord, US Dept Treas
b West Hartford, Conn, Oct 18, 42; s Isadore Parsky & Nettie Sanders P; m 1966 to Susan Haas; c Laura Haas & David Sanders. Educ: Princeton Univ, AB cum laude, 64; Univ Va, JD, 68; Princeton Univ Cottage Club. Polit & Govt Pos: Spec asst to under secy, US Treas Dept, 71-73, exec asst to dep secy, 73-74, asst secy trade, energy & financial resources policy coord, 74- Bus & Prof Pos: Eng master, Suffield Acad, Suffield, Conn, 64-65; assoc in law firm, Mudge, Rose, Guthrie & Alexander, New York, 68-71. Publ: The Environment of E M Forster, Princeton Univ, 64. Mem: NY & DC Bar Asns; Princeton Club NY; Univ Club DC. Honors & Awards: Citizenship Award & Athletic Award, Suffield Acad, 60 & Princeton Univ, 64; Exceptional Serv Award, US Treas Dept, 74; Ten Outstanding Young Men of Am, US Jaycees, 75. Mailing Add: 2911 45th St NW Washington DC 20016

PARSLEY, FRANCES ELAINE (R)
VChmn, Ky Rep Party
b Brownsville, Ky, Feb 28, 24; d Frederick Hilery Vincent & Mattie Meredilh V; m 1943 to Andrew Gus Parsley, Sr; c Nancy Sue & Andrew Gus, Jr. Educ: Western Ky Univ, 2 years. Polit & Govt Pos: Crew leader, Ky State Dept Com, 42-46; Rep precinct leader, Edmonson Co, 42-69; state chmn, Pyramaiding for, 62; co chmn, Friend for Morton, 62; state chmn, Nunn for Gov, 63; state chmn, Goldwater for Pres, 64; mem state bd, Ky Rep Clubs, 68; vchmn, Ky Rep Party, 68-; deleg, Rep Nat Conv, 72. Bus & Prof Pos: Elem Teacher, Edmonson Co, 42-46; recreation dir, Edmonson Co Recreation Dept, 72- Mem: Eastern Star; Brownsville Homemaker Club; Warren Co Rep Club; Univ High PTA. Honors & Awards: Church Attendance Awards; Citation for Record Attendance of Ky Rep State Cent Comt. Relig: Baptist. Mailing Add: PO Box 307 Brownsville KY 42210

PARSON, ELMER S, JR (R)
Secy, Wyo Rep State Comt
b Denver, Colo, Dec 26, 29; s Elmer S Parson & Ruth I Buchanan P; m 1953 to Mary Jean Reimer; c Dean R & Anne I. Educ: Univ of Colo, BA, 57. Polit & Govt Pos: Treas, Natrona Co Young Rep, Wyo, 61-62; ward capt, Natrona Co Rep Cent Comt, 62-67, chmn, 67-70; state committeeman, Wyo Rep Party, 66-67; secy, Wyo Rep State Comt, 68-; alt deleg, Rep Nat Conv, 72. Bus & Prof Pos: Explor geologist, Continental Oil Co, Casper, Wyo, 57-69; explor geologist, True Oil Co, 69, chief geologist, 73- Mil Serv: 2nd Lt, Army, 52-53, with serv in 459 Eng Bn, Korea. Mem: Am Asn Petroleum Geologists; Wyo Geol Asn; Rocky Mt Oil & Gas Asn; CofC; Wyo Oil Industs Comt. Relig: Methodist. Mailing Add: 3120 E Fifth Casper WY 82601

PARSONS, ALBERT ROY (R)
b Forrest, Ill, Nov 18, 00; s Albert Parsons & Flora Christoff P; m 1923 to Mabel Esther Mott; c Mary Carolyn (Mrs Chapman). Polit & Govt Pos: LaSalle Extension Univ, 2 year course salesmanship & Bus Mgt. Polit & Govt Pos: Mem sch bd, Monticello, Ill, 36-40; city clerk, Monticello, 37-69; Rep precinct committeeman, Piatt Co, 50-; secy, Piatt Co Rep Comt, formerly; twp supvr, Piatt Co Bd of Supvr, 67-, chmn, bd, 70- Bus & Prof Pos: Steam locomotive fireman, Chicago, Ill, 23-29; agent, Railway Express, Forrest & Monticello, 30-52; cashier, First State Bank, 53-67. Mem: AF&AM; Consistory; Mason; Farm Bur; Rotary. Relig: Methodist. Mailing Add: 504 E Lafayette St Monticello IL 61856

PARSONS, HAROLD PAUL (D)
Chmn, Harlan Co Dem Comt, Ky
b Barbourville, Ky, Oct 22, 37; s Curtis Sam Parsons & Estle Grant P; m 1956 to Barbara Ann Ballard; c Gregory & Bridgette. Educ: Union Col, AB, 58; Univ Ky, Lexington, 61-65. Polit & Govt Pos: Councilman, Evarts, Ky, 62-65; adv mgr, Harlan Co Referendum, 64-; alt deleg, Dem Nat Conv, 68; co-chmn, Harlan Co Dem Fund Raising Comt, 69; chmn, Harlan Co Dem Comt, 69- Bus & Prof Pos: Teacher, Harlan Co Bd of Educ, 58-; vpres, Mack's Super Mkts Inc, 63-; pres, Eastern Broadcasting, 66- Mem: Harlan Co CofC; F&AM; Evarts Lions Club (pres); Evarts Fish & Game Club. Relig: United Church of Christ. Mailing Add: Woodland Hills Harlan KY 40831

PARSONS, J GRAHAM
b New York, NY, Oct 28, 07; m to Margaret Boulton; c two daughters. Educ: Yale Univ, BA, 29; NY Univ Grad Sch Bus Admin; Phi Beta Kappa. Polit & Govt Pos: Career officer, US Dept of State Foreign Serv, 36-71, vconsul, Havana, Cuba, 36-38; vconsul, Mukden, 38-40, third secy, Ottawa, 40-42, asst chief, Div of Brit Commonwealth Affairs, 45, secy, US Sect, Permanent Joint Bd on Defense of Can & the US, 46-47, second secy, Rome, 47-48, first secy, New Delhi, 48-50, mem staff, Nat War Col, 50-51, dep dir & acting dir, Off of European Regional Affairs, 51-53, counsel, Tokyo, 53-56; US Ambassador, Laos, 56-58; Dep Asst Secy of State for Eastern Affairs, 58-59; Asst Secy of State for Far Eastern Affairs, 59-61; US Ambassador, Sweden, 61-67; sr foreign serv inspector, 67-69; State Dept Adv, Indust Col of the Armed Forces, 69-70; dep chmn, US Strategic Arms Limitations Negotiations Deleg, Vienna & Helsinki, 70-72, consult, State Dept, 71-74. Bus & Prof Pos: Security analyst, 31-32; pvt secy, US Ambassador, Japan, 32-36. Mailing Add: Box 621 Stockbridge MA 01262

PARSONS, JOHN WELSEY (R)
b Hartford, Iowa, June 27, 08; s Preston M Parsons & Frena M Laverty P; m 1942 to Ruth A Greenwalt; c Max, David & Pamela. Educ: Iowa State Univ, 2 years 6 months; Lambda Chi Alpha. Polit & Govt Pos: Finance chmn, Warren Co Rep Party, Iowa, 52-63, chmn, formerly; alt deleg, Rep Nat Conv, 64. Mem: Mason; Rotary. Honors & Awards: Simpson Col Distinguished Serv Award, 60. Relig: Methodist. Legal Res: 104 W Euclid Indianola IA 50125 Mailing Add: Box 292 Indianola IA 50125

PARSONS, RICHARD HUGO (D)
b McAlester, Okla, June 9, 36; s Alfred Richard Parsons & Veronica Hugo P; m 1958 to Catherine Ann Logan; Karen Ann, Anne Logan & Alfred Richard, II. Educ: Bradley Univ, BS, 58; Washington & Lee Univ, Sch Law, JD, 61; Phi Delta Phi; Sigma Phi Epsilon; Mu Eta Chi. Polit & Govt Pos: Campaign mgr, Blair for Recorder of Deed, 68 & 72; alt deleg, Dem Nat Conv, 72; comnr, Peoria Cable TV Comn, 72- Bus & Prof Pos: Asst secy, Chicago Title & Trust Co, 61-68; Attorney & organizing partner, Quinn, Parsons & Buckley, Peoria, 68-; pres & owner, Bankers Title Co, Ltd, 68-; dir, secy & counsel, Independence-Crown Assoc, Ltd, 69-; chmn bd dirs, Peacock Eng Co, Itasca, 72-; dir, Heights Bank, Peoria Heights, 73- Publ: Business editor, Washington & Lee Law Rev, 60-61. Mem: Ill State Bar Asn (merchantibility of title comt); Peoria Co Bar Asn (real estate law comt); Am Judicature Soc; Peoria Dem Chowder & Marching Soc (pres, 72 & 73); Mt Hawley Country Club, Peoria. Relig: Roman Catholic. Mailing Add: 7505 Hillrose Pl Peoria IL 61616

PARTEE, CECIL A (D)
Ill State Sen
b Blytheville, Ark; m to Paris A P; c Paris I & Cecile A. Educ: Tenn State Univ, BS cum laude bus admin; Northwestern Univ Law Sch, JD. Polit & Govt Pos: Pres, 20th Ward Reg Dem Orgn, committeeman, currently; asst state's attorney, Cook Co, Ill, 8 years; Ill State Sen, 66-, Minority Leader, Ill State Senate, currently; mem, Dem Nat Comt, 72-; deleg, Dem Nat Mid-Term Conf, 74. Mem: Cook Co, Chicago, Ill State & Am Nat Bar Asns; NAACP; Urban League. Relig: Congregational. Mailing Add: 100 N LaSalle St Chicago IL 60602

PARTRIDGE, BENJAMIN WARING, III (R)
b Greenwich, Conn, Nov 28, 44; s Capt Benjamin W Partridge, Jr & Cora Cheney P; single. Educ: Harvard Univ, 64; Yale Univ, BA, 67; Sr Hon Soc. Polit & Govt Pos: Admin asst, US Rep Richard W Mallary, Vt, 72-74; exec secy, Vt Rep Party, 72; chmn, Vt Fedn Young Rep, 72-73, nat committeeman, 73-; admin asst, US Rep Gary A Myers, Pa, 75- Bus & Prof Pos: Founder & chmn, Synstadt, Inc, Washington, DC, 71- Mil Serv: Entered as Ens, Navy, 67, released as Lt, 71, after serv in Danang, Vietnam, 69-70; Lt, Naval Res, currently; Navy Achievement Medal with Combat V, Vietnamese Cross Gallantry & several Campaign & Unit Awards. Publ: Auth weekly newspaper column, Vermonter in Washington, Brattleboro Reformer & Bennington Banner, 75- Mem: VFW; Am Legion; World Future Soc; Vt Hist Soc. Relig: Episcopal. Legal Res: West Townshend VT 05359 Mailing Add: 1711 Longworth Bldg Washington DC 20515

PARTRIDGE, SANBORN (R)
Vt State Sen
b Proctor, Vt, Apr 30, 15; single. Educ: Amherst Col, BA, 36; Harvard Bus Sch, 38; Yale Law Sch, LLB, 39; Yale Grad Schs, MS in Geol, 47; Sigma Xi; Phi Beta Kappa. Polit & Govt Pos: Town grand juror, 40-41; town agt, 42; mem, Rutland RR & Reapportionment Study Comt; Vt State Rep, 61-68; alt deleg, Rep Nat Conv, 68; Vt State Sen, 69- Bus & Prof Pos: Geologist; educator; former trustee, UVM; trustee, Proctor Free Libr. Mil Serv: Air Force, Pvt to 1st Lt, 42-46. Mem: Geological Soc Am; Appalachian Mountain Club; Sierra Club; Boy Scouts (pres, Green Mountain Coun); Am Bar Asn. Relig: Protestant. Mailing Add: 62 Ormsbee Ave Proctor VT 05765

PARYS, RONALD GEORGE (D)
Wis State Sen
b Milwaukee, Wis, Oct 7, 38; s Casimir George Parys & Gladys Bernice Olson P; m 1960 to Margarete Kauth; c Brian George, Cheryl Ann, Lynn Marie & Dawn Marie. Educ: Riverside High Sch, Milwaukee, 52-56; adv, Wis Acad Conf Student Govt. Polit & Govt Pos: Vchmn, 13th Ward Dem Party, Wis, 66-68; Wis State Assemblyman, 13th Dist, 65-69; Wis State Sen, Milwaukee Ninth Dist, 69- Bus & Prof Pos: Material control, Cornell Paper Prod, 56-57; buyer, Northwestern Food Prod Co, 57-59; foreman & purchasing supvr, Ben-Hur Mfg, 59-62; indust appraiser, Fidelity Appraisal Co, 62-65 & Am Appraisal Co, 65- Mil Serv: Entered as Pvt, Army Res, 55, released as S/Sgt E-6, 66, after serv in 84th Div. Mem: Polish Nat Alliance; 13th Ward Community Coun; Twin Arch Sportsman Club; Old Time Ball Player's Asn. Relig: Roman Catholic. Mailing Add: 1221 E Clarke St Milwaukee WI 53212

PASBACH, EARL FRANCIS (D)
RI State Rep
b Chicago, Ill, Nov 28, 29; s Earl F Pasbach & Mary White P; single. Educ: La Salle Acad, Providence, RI, 3 years; Providence Col, BS; Boston Col Law Sch, LLB; Albertus Magnus Club. Polit & Govt Pos: Legal asst, Off of Solicitor, US Dept Labor, 59-60; law clerk, Assoc Justice Thomas H Roberts, Supreme Court, RI, 61-62; attorney, Off Appeals, Nat Labor Rels Bd, Washington, DC, 62; RI State Rep, 87th Dist, 69- Mil Serv: Entered as Pvt, Army, 54, released as Cpl, 56, after serv in 3440th ASU, Ft Benning, Ga. Mem: Pawtucket Bar Asn; Lions. Relig: Roman Catholic. Mailing Add: 1000 Willett Ave East Providence RI 02915

PASCOE, D MONTE (D)
Chmn, Colo Dem Party
b Des Moines, Iowa, Jan 4, 35; s Donald Leslie Pascoe & Marjorie Powers P; m 1957 to Patricia Hill; c Sarah Lynn, Edward Llewellyn & William Arthur. Educ: Dartmouth Col, AB, 57; Stanford Univ Law Sch, LLB, 60; Psi Upsilon; Casque & Gauntlet. Polit & Govt Pos: State coordr, Humphrey for President, Colo, 68; Dem dist capt, Denver, Colo, 67-69 & 70-; chmn, Colo Dem Party, 73- Bus & Prof Pos: Partner, Ireland, Stapleton, Pryor & Holmes, 60- Mem: Law Club of Denver; Phi Delta Phi; Denver Club; Cactus Club; Colo Dartmouth & Stanford Asns. Relig: Presbyterian; Elder, Montview Blvd Presbyterian Church. Mailing Add: 744 Lafayette St Denver CO 80218

PASMA, JAMES JAY (D)
Committeeman, Mont Dem State Cent Comt
b Helena, Mont, Jan 16, 33; s Jay Peter Pasma & Elsie Pennington P; m 1955 to Virginia Mae Shaffer; c Zarren James, Victoria Star (Mrs Mitchell D Olson), Farol Marie & Zane Jay. Educ: GED, 53. Polit & Govt Pos: Chmn, Hill Co Dem Cent Comt, Mont, 65-72; secy, Mont State Senate, 67; finance chmn, Mont Dem State Cent Comt, 67-68, committeeman, 72-; deleg, Dem Nat Conv, 68; Dem cand, State Treas, 68; committeeman-at-lg, Mont State Dem Exec Comt, 68-70; state finance chmn, McGovern for President, 72; mem, State Dem Reform Comn, 73-; deleg, Dem Nat Mid-Term Conf, 74. Bus & Prof Pos: Pet shop owner, Havre, Mont, 68-70; prof artist, 70- Mil Serv: Entered as Pvt, Marine Corps, 52, released as Sgt, 55, after serv in Hq Co, Pearl Harbor, Hawaii, 53-55; 1st Sgt, Army Nat Guard, 55-68; Nat Defense Ribbon; Ten Year Armed Forces Reserve Medal; numerous State Nat Guard Medals. Mem: Hi-Line Art Asn; Miss Dem Scholar Pageant Comt (chmn). Relig: Episcopal. Legal Res: 5 Curve Dr Havre MT 59501 Mailing Add: PO Box 94 Havre MT 59501

PASSANNANTE, WILLIAM F (D)
NY State Assemblyman
b New York, NY, Feb 10, 20. Educ: NY Univ, grad, 40; Harvard Univ Law Sch, grad, 48. Polit & Govt Pos: Asst US Attorney for Southern Dist, NY, 48-53; legis counsel to pres, New York Coun, 54; NY State Assemblyman, 55-, chmn joint conf & chmn comts, NY Gen Assembly, currently. Bus & Prof Pos: Lawyer; dir, Charles Passannante Sons, Inc. Mil Serv: Army, 41-45. Mem: Fed Bar Asn; NY State Dist Attorneys Asn; Columbian Soc; KofC; Lions. Relig: Catholic. Mailing Add: 72 Barrow St New York NY 10014

PASSER, HAROLD CLARENCE (R)
b Lakefield, Minn, Nov 27, 21; s Clarence Walter Passer & Esther Nauman P; m 1966 to Astrid Louise Anderson Thurber; c David C, Jr & Christine L (Mrs Thomas Ervin). Educ: Harvard Univ, SB, 43, AM, 48; PhD, 50; Phi Beta Kappa. Polit & Govt Pos: Asst Secy of Com for Econ Affairs, US Dept of Com, 69-72. Bus & Prof Pos: Asst prof econ, Princeton Univ, 50-52; economist, Eastman Kodak Co, Rochester, NY, 52-69, asst treas, 73- Mil Serv: Entered as Ens, Navy, 43, released as Lt, 46, after serv in USS Young, DD580, Pac Theatre, 44-45, assigned to radar maintenance sch, Pac Fleet, Hawaii, 45-46. Publ: The electrical manufacturers, Harvard Univ, 53; Current international monetary problems, Bus Econ, winter 65-66; American economy in perspective, Orientacion Economica, 2/67. Mem: Fel Nat Asn Bus Economist; Am Econ Asn; Am Finance Asn; Conf Bus Economists. Relig: Presbyterian. Mailing Add: 133 Imperial Circle Rochester NY 14617

PASSMAN, OTTO ERNEST (D)
US Rep, La
b Washington Parish, near Franklinton, La, June 27, 00; married. Polit & Govt Pos: US Rep, La, 46- Bus & Prof Pos: Owner, Passman Investment Co, Monroe, La currently. Mil Serv: Officer, US Navy, World War II. Mem: Am Vet of World War II, Inc (past state comdr); Am Legion; Scottish Rite Mason (33 degree); Red Cross of Constantine of York Rite of Freemasonry; F&AM (past Grand Master, Grand Lodge of the State of La). Relig: Baptist. Legal Res: Monroe LA 71201 Mailing Add: House Off Bldg Annex Washington DC 20515

PASSMORE, CECIL, JR (D)
VChmn, Laurens Co Dem Party, Ga
b Dexter, Ga, Sept 8, 36; s Cecil Passmore, Sr & Effie Dunn P; m 1957 to Faye Collins; c Diana & Valena. Educ: Univ Ga Exten Syst, 1 year; Civil Serv Mgt Sch, grad, 64. Polit & Govt Pos: Vchmn, Laurens Co Dem Party, Ga, 70-; mem, Ga State Dem Exec Comt, 20th Sen Dist, 71-; State Comn on Compensation, 71- Bus & Prof Pos: Mgr civil serv, Robins Air Force Base, Ga, 55-67; partner, Knight-Passmore Ins Agency, Dexter, 68-; vpres, Knight State Bank, 68- Mil Serv: Entered as Pvt, Nat Guard, 54, released as M/Sgt, 65, after in Dublin Nat Guard. Publ: As I See It, weekly column, Laurens Co News, 68- Mem: Toastmasters (past gov dist 14, 68-70); Dexter Masonic Lodge 340 (past master, 59); PTA (pres, 68); Lions Club (pres, 66); Green Acres Golf Club (dir, 69-). Honors & Awards: Civil Serv Outstanding Performance Award, 66, Sustained Superior Serv Award & Mgr of Month Award, 67; Able Toastmaster Award, 68. Relig: Methodist; Mem admin bd & cert lay speaker. Mailing Add: Box 157 Dexter GA 31019

PASTER, HOWARD G (D)
b New York, NY, Dec 23, 44; s Alfred Paster & Hortense Zeltner P; m 1969 to Gail Kern. Educ: Alfred Univ, BA, 66; Columbia Univ, MS, 67; Pi Gamma Mu; Blue Key. Polit & Govt Pos: Admin asst to US Rep Lester L Wolff, NY, 67-71; spec asst to US Sen Birch Bayh, Ind, 71- Publ: The cyclamate story, Columbia Jour Rev, spring 70; Air & water, New Repub, 10/31/71; Intergovernmental regulations of Long Island Sound, On the Sound, fall 71. Mem: Sigma Delta Chi. Mailing Add: 313 E St SE Washington DC 20003

PASTOR, EDWARD LOPEZ (D)
Chmn, Dist 25 Dem Party, Ariz
b Claypool, Ariz, June 28, 43; s Enrique Perez Pastor & Margarita Lopez P; m 1965 to Verma Mendez; c Laura Ann. Educ: Ariz State Univ, BS in Chem, 65, Col Law, 71-; Newman Club; Arnold Air Soc; Young Dem; Irish Hall. Polit & Govt Pos: Chmn, UNIDOS con McGovern, 72; deleg, Dem Nat Conv, 72; deleg, Ariz Dem State Conv, 72; state committeeman, Ariz Dem Party, 72-; precinct committeeman, Maricopa Co Dem Party, Ariz, 72-; chmn, UNIDOS, 72-; chmn, Dist 25 Dem Party, 72- Bus & Prof Pos: Dep dir, Guadalupe, Ariz, 69-71; consult, Coun for Better & Equal Bus Opportunities, Washington, DC, 70; vpres, Maricopa Legal Aid Soc, Phoenix, Ariz, 71- Mem: Nat Resource Panel for the Spec Educ Prog, Univ Minn; Southwestern Coun on Educ & Leadership; Vesta Club; Student Bar Asn, Ariz State Univ (vpres, 72-73). Honors & Awards: Appreciation Award, City of Phoenix, 73. Relig: Catholic. Mailing Add: 3431 E Montecito Phoenix AZ 85018

PASTORE, JOHN O (D)
US Sen, RI
b Providence, RI Mar 17, 07; s Michelle Pastore & Erminia Asprinio P; m 1941 to Elena Elizabeth Caito; c Dr John O, Jr, Frances (Mrs Alfred Q Scheurer) & Louise Marie (Mrs Clifford M Harbourt). Educ: Northeastern Univ, LLB, 31. Hon Degrees: LLD, Providence Col, RI State Col & Brown Univ; EdD, RI Col of Educ; ScD, RI Col of Pharm & Bryant Col; Univ RI, Northeastern Univ, Salve Regina Col, New Bedford Inst Technol, Philadelphia Col of Textiles & Sci, Suffolk Univ & Villanova Univ. Polit & Govt Pos: RI State Rep, 35-37; asst attorney gen, RI, 37-38 & 40-44; lt gov, RI, 44-45, Gov, 45-50; US Sen, RI, 50-, vchmn, & past chmn, Joint Comt on Atomic Energy, US Senate; mem, US deleg Gen Assembly of UN, 55, cong adv to US Deleg with reference to establishing a new Int Atomic Energy Agency, 56; senate-designee, Geneva Conf on the Peaceful Uses of Atomic Energy, 55, 58 & 61; senate-designee, Intitial Conf on the Int Agency in Vienna, 57; keynote speaker, Dem Nat Conv, 64, deleg, 68 & 72. Legal Res: Cranston RI Mailing Add: 3215 New Senate Off Bldg Washington DC 20510

PASTORE, LOUIS H (D)
RI State Sen
Mailing Add: 8 Roanoke St Providence RI 02908

PASTRICK, ROBERT A (D)
Chmn, Lake Co Dem Cent Comt, Ind
b Gary, Ind, Nov 11, 27; s Andrew Pastrick (deceased) & Mary Oleska P; m 1954 to Ruth Ann Stolle; c Robert Scott, Michael Drew, David Joseph, Jennifer Ann, Mary Ruth, Susan Marie & Kevin Townsend. Educ: Univ Notre Dame, 45-47; Univ Denver, 49-50; St Joseph Col, 50-51. Polit & Govt Pos: Supvr, St Dept, City of East Chicago, 53-55, councilman, 55-64, br mgr, Bur Motor Vehicles, 60-64, city controller, 64-72, mayor, 73-; pres, Ind Young Dem, 54-61; dep treas, Lake Co, Ind, 55-60; chmn bd, Young Dem Am, 61-63; deleg, Dem Nat

Conv, 72; mem charter comt, Dem Nat Comt, currently; chmn, Lake Co Dem Cent Comt, 72- Bus & Prof Pos: Vpres, Oleska Funeral Home, East Chicago, 60-72. Mil Serv: Entered as Pvt, Army, 47, released as T/4, 49, after serv in Spec Serv. Mem: US Mayors' Conf; Ind Munic League; Elks; Moose; KofC; plus various civil & ethnic orgns. Mailing Add: 4525 Indianapolis Blvd East Chicago IN 46312

PASZTOR, LASZLO (R)
b Felso-Elemer, Yugoslavia, Sept 1, 21; s Karoly Pasztor & Maria Mayer P; m 1949 to Adel Bihari Nagy; c Laszlo, Jr. Educ: Peter Pazamny Univ, BS, 43, MS, 50; Univ Pittsburgh Grad Sch, MS in Chem, 63; Sigma Xi. Polit & Govt Pos: Hungarian co-chmn, Nationalities Div, Rep Nat Comt, 64, Hungarian adv, 68, dir heritage groups, 69-73, spec asst to chmn, 70-71, founder & chmn, Nat Rep Heritage Groups Coun, 71-74, hon chmn, 74-; Hungarian adv, Citizens for Goldwater, Western Pa, 64; mem adv bd, Rep Nat Comt, 71-73, ex officio mem exec comt, 72-74; co-chmn & dir, Heritage Groups for the Reelec of the President, 72. Bus & Prof Pos: Mgr, Prescription Pharm & Drugstore, Hungary, 43-44, diplomat, Hungarian Ministry Foreign Affairs, 44-45; pharmacist, 49-50 & 54-56; active leader, Hungarian Freedom Fighters & mem, Nat Revolutionary Coun, West Hungary, 56; research chemist, J & L Steel Corp, Pittsburgh, Pa, 57, sr research chemist, 60, research supvr, 63-69, consult, 73-74; mgr prod research, Dravo Corp, Pittsburgh, currently; mem adv bd, Talanta; ed, Magyar Szabadsagharcos & Hungarian Freedom Fighters, 67-69. Publ: More than 20 sci articles & several editorials in Hungarian language publ. Mem: Hungarian Freedom Fighters Fedn US (one of the founders, mem exec bd, 58-69, secy gen, 60-69, hon chmn, 63-); World Fedn Hungarian Freedom Fighters (secy gen, 64-69); Am Chem Soc; Soc Appl Spectroscopy; Am Soc Testing & Materials. Honors & Awards: Spec Merit Award, Am Iron & Steel Inst, 68; Man of Year, Hungarian-Am Asn, 72; Spec Merit Award, Wis Rep Heritage Groups Coun, 73; Spec Merit Award, Rep Heritage Groups Coun, 74; Award, Nat Rep Heritage Groups Coun. Mailing Add: 656 Greenlee Rd Pittsburgh PA 15227

PATCHETT, JOHN EARL (D)
Iowa State Rep
b Danville, Ill, Apr 12, 49; s Roy M Patchett & V Lorrea Weber P; m 1971 to Nancy Mona Kohrt. Educ: Eastern Iowa Community Col, Muscatine, 67-69; Univ Iowa, BA, 72. Polit & Govt Pos: State teen dem coordr, Young Dem Clubs of Iowa, 66-67, first dist committeeman, 67-69; state chairperson, Iowa Young Dem for Robert Kennedy, 68; campaign admin asst, William Gannon for Gov, 70; Iowa State Rep, 73- Mem: Univ Iowa Alumni Asn; Sierra Club; Civil Liberties Union; Common Cause; State Hist Soc Iowa. Relig: Protestant. Legal Res: Coralville Lake Terr North Liberty IA 52317 Mailing Add: Box 190 North Liberty IA 52317

PATE, JAMES L
Asst Secy Econ Affairs, Dept Com
Mailing Add: Asst Secy Econ Affairs Dept of Com Washington DC 20230

PATE, OSCAR PERRY (D)
Chmn, Sabine Co Dem Exec Comt, Tex
b Etoile, Tex, Dec 5, 95; s Wilber Franks Pate & Evaline Reynolds P; m 1920 to Vera J Bennett; c Mattie Pauline (Mrs N A Podhaiski), Oscar Glenn, Harold Valjean & Jane (Mrs Francis Rawson). Polit & Govt Pos: Supt of pub instr, Sabine Co, Tex, 19-23; chmn, Sabine Co Dem Exec Comt, 26-28 & currently; vet serv officer, Sabine Co, 58-66. Bus & Prof Pos: Independent contractor, 35-61. Mil Serv: Entered as Pvt, Army, 17, released as 1st Sgt, 19, after serv in Co A 360th Inf, 90th Div, Marne-St Mehiel-Muse-Argonne Offensive, 18; Purple Heart; Capt, Tex State Guard, 40-45. Mem: Tex Forestry Asn; Boy Scouts; Bronson Lodge 893 AF&AM; Dept of Tex Am Legion. Honors & Awards: Silver Beaver Award, Boy Scouts. Relig: Methodist. Mailing Add: PO Box 427 Hemphill TX 75948

PATEK, EUNICE JOAN (R)
VChmn, Livingston Co Rep Cent Comt, Mo
b Woonsocket, RI, Jan 15, 26; d Robert Gerald Dutton & Florence Hickman D (deceased); m 1947 to Byron Henry Patek; c Harry Robert & Keith Byron. Educ: Newport Hosp Sch Nursing, RN, 47; Beta Sigma Phi; Sorosis MFWC (pres). Polit & Govt Pos: Committeewoman, First Rep Ward, Chillicothe, Mo, 64-; vchmn, Livingston Co Rep Comt, 68- Mem: Hosp Auxiliary (life mem); Rep Womens Club. Relig: Episcopal. Mailing Add: 1816 Country Club Dr Chillicothe MO 64601

PATENAUDE, RICHARD A (D)
NH State Rep
Mailing Add: Box 517 150 Prospect St Berlin NH 03570

PATERO, JOSEPH D (D)
NH State Rep
Mailing Add: State House Trenton NJ 08625

PATERSON, BASIL ALEXANDER (D)
Dem Nat Committeeman, NY
b New York, NY, Apr 27, 26; s Leonard J Paterson & Evangeline Rondon P; m 1953 to Portia Hairston; c David A & Daniel A. Educ: St John's Col, BS, 48; St John's Univ Sch of Law, LLB, 51; Kappa Alpha Psi. Polit & Govt Pos: NY State Sen, 27th Dist, 65-70; deleg, Dem Nat Conv, 72; Dem Nat Committeeman, NY, 72-; vchmn, Dem Nat Comt, 72- Bus & Prof Pos: Attorney-at-law, Paterson, Michael, Dinkins & Jones, 68. Mil Serv: Pvt, Army, 43. Honors & Awards: Eagleton Inst of Polit Award, 67; Distinguished Serv Award, Guardians Asn NY Police Dept, 68; City Club of NY Award, 73; Black Expo Award, 73. Relig: Catholic. Mailing Add: 2186 Fifth Ave New York NY 10037

PATERSON, LLOYD H (R)
NY State Sen
Mailing Add: 1234 87th St Niagara Falls NY 14034

PATMAN, CARRIN MAURITZ (D)
Committeewoman, Tex State Dem Exec Comt
b Houston, Tex, Mar 1, 32; d Fred Mauritz & Carrin Foreman; m 1953 to William Neff Patman; c Carrin Foreman. Educ: Univ Tex, Austin, BA with honors, 54. Polit & Govt Pos: Dem precinct chmn, Precinct Five, Jackson Co, Ganado, 62-63; committeewoman, State Dem Exec Comt, 18th Sen Dist, 64-66 & 72-; Dem Nat Committeewoman, Tex, 69-72; mem, Gov Comn on Status of Women, 70-; deleg & mem permanent comt on rules, Dem Nat Conv, 72; mem, Nat Dem Party Comn on Deleg Selection, 72- Mem: Hon mem Delta Kappa Gamma; Jackson Co Hosp Auxiliary; Ganado Federated Women's Club; Austin Parents' League; Senate Ladies Club of Tex. Relig: Methodist; former exec bd mem, First Methodist Church of Ganado. Legal Res: PO Drawer A Ganado TX 77962 Mailing Add: 2702 Moonlight Bend Austin TX 78703

PATMAN, W N (BILL) (D)
Tex State Sen
Mailing Add: Drawer A Ganado TX 77962

PATMAN, WRIGHT (D)
US Rep, Tex
b Patman's Switch, Cass Co, Tex, Aug 6, 93; m 1919 to Merle Connor (deceased); m 1968 to Pauline Tucker; c Three. Educ: Cumberland Univ, LLB, 16. Polit & Govt Pos: Dist attorney, Fifth Judicial Dist, Tex, 5 years; Tex State Rep, 4 years; US Rep, Tex, 28-, chmn, Banking & Currency Comt, US House of Rep, formerly; vchmn, Joint House & Sen Defense Prod Comt, chmn, House & Sen Joint Econ Comt, currently; deleg, Dem Nat Mid-Term Conf, 74. Mil Serv: Army, 1st Lt, 17-19, machine gun officer. Mem: Elks; Mason; Eagles; Shrine; Am Legion. Relig: Baptist. Legal Res: Texarkana TX Mailing Add: 2328 Rayburn House Off Bldg Washington DC 20515

PATRICK, DAVID SCARBOROUGH
b Birmingham, Ala, Feb 13, 46; s Charles H Patrick & Mary Scarborough P; m 1967 to Sharon Spitzer. Educ: Samford Univ, BA in hist, 70, MA in hist, 71; George Washington Univ, MA in govt, 73; Pi Gamma Mu. Polit & Govt Pos: Admin asst to US Rep Bill Nichols, Ala, 72- Mem: Am Soc Pub Admin; US House Rep Admin Asst Asn. Honors & Awards: Colonial Dames Hist Essay Award, 71; Scottish Rite Fel, George Washington Univ, 71-72. Relig: Baptist. Legal Res: Rte 2 Box 1433 Pinson AL 35126 Mailing Add: 6630 Elk Park Ct Alexandria VA 22310

PATRICK, EDWIN EUGENE (R)
Chmn, Jennings Co Rep Party, Ind
b Jennings Co, Ind, Feb 8, 17; s Carl E Patrick & Hazel Jennings P; m 1938 to Maxine Dowell; c Larry. Educ: Vernon Sch, Vernon, Ind. Polit & Govt Pos: Chmn, Jennings Co Rep Party, Ind, 74- Bus & Prof Pos: Farmer, currently. Mailing Add: Rte 2 North Vernon IN 47265

PATRICK, JAMES FAIRCHILD
b Louisville, Ky, Feb 21, 09; s Samuel J Patrick & Virginia Fairchild P; m 1960 to Ruth Marie Hucaby. Educ: Univ Ky, 28; Pi Kappa Alpha. Polit & Govt Pos: Chmn, Wayne Co Rep Party, Ky, 62-64 & 68-74; admin asst to Hwy Comnr, 68- Bus & Prof Pos: Oil & gas operator, Ky, 39- Mem: Ky Oil & Gas Asn; Independent Petroleum Asn of Am; Mason; Shrine; Kiwanis. Relig: Baptist. Legal Res: 117 Michigan Ave Monticello KY 42633 Mailing Add: Box 381 Monticello KY 42633

PATRICK, LANGDON (D)
Ill State Sen
Mailing Add: 3014 W Jackson Blvd Chicago IL 60612

PATRICK, MARY LOUISE (R)
b St Paul, Minn, Feb 3, 29; d John H Stoffels & Anne M Conlin S; m 1953 to Richard A Patrick; c Mark S, Gregg A & Timothy K. Educ: Mech Arts High Sch, 4 years. Polit & Govt Pos: Ed, Okla Rep News, 66-72; secy, Okla Rep State Comt, 67-72; presidential elector, Okla, 72. Relig: Methodist. Mailing Add: 11605 Brandy Hall Lane Gaithersburg MD 20760

PATRIDGE, CORBET LEE (D)
Miss State Sen
b Ruleville, Miss, Sept 20, 23; married. Polit & Govt Pos: Field agt, Govt Bur; Miss State Rep, 56-60; Miss State Sen, currently. Bus & Prof Pos: Agriculturalist; teacher voc agr, formerly; pub rels rep, Nat Cotton Coun. Relig: Baptist. Mailing Add: PO Box 347 Schlater MS 38952

PATTEN, EDWARD JAMES (D)
US Rep, NJ
b Perth Amboy, NJ, Aug 22, 05 m 1936 to Anna Quigg; c Catharine M. Educ: Newark State Col; Rutgers Law Sch, LLB; Rutgers Univ, BS, Educ. Polit & Govt Pos: Pres bd, Salvation Army; mem, NJ Dem State Comt; chmn, Middlesex Co Dem Comt, 34-36; Mayor, Perth Amboy, 34-40; Co Clerk, Middlesex Co, 40-54; campaign mgr, Robert B Meyner, 53-57; Secy of State, NJ, 54-62; US Rep, NJ, 62-, mem, Appropriations Comt. Bus & Prof Pos: Lawyer, 27; teacher pub schs, 27-34. Mem: Eagles; Moose; Elks; Kiwanis; KofC. Honors & Awards: Recipient of Outstanding Citizenship Award from Am Heritage Found & B'nai B'riths Brotherhood Award. Legal Res: Perth Amboy NJ 08861 Mailing Add: US House of Rep Washington DC 20515

PATTEN, GROVER C (D)
Ga State Rep
Mailing Add: PO Box 312 Adel GA 31520

PATTEN, ROBERT L (D)
Ga State Rep
Mailing Add: Rte 1 Lakeland GA 31625

PATTERSON, E G (PAT) (R)
Wash State Rep
Mailing Add: NE 400 Campus Pullman WA 99163

PATTERSON, ED (D)
Ore State Rep
Mailing Add: 1608 Second St LaGrande OR 97850

PATTERSON, GRADY LESLIE, JR (D)
Treas, SC
b Abbeville Co, SC, Jan 13, 24; s Grady Leslie Patterson, Sr & Claudia McClain P; m 1951 to Marjorie Harrison Faucett; c Grady Leslie, III, Steven G, Marjorie Lynne, Laura Anne, Amy Susan & Mary Beth. Educ: Clemson Univ, 42-43; Univ Ala, 43; Univ SC, LLB, 50; Kappa Sigma. Polit & Govt Pos: Co serv officer, Abbeville Co, SC, 50; asst attorney gen, SC, 59-66, Treas, 67- Mil Serv: Entered as Pvt, Army Air Corps, 43, entered Res, as Lt, 46, after serv in 45th Fighter Squadron, Pac-Iwo Jima, 45; Air Force Res, serv during Korean War, 50-52; Berlin Call Up, 61-62; Col, SC Air Nat Guard, 47-, Opers Officer, 52-58; Air Medal with Two Oak Leaf Clusters; Presidential Unit Citation; Distinguished Unit Citation; Army

of Occup Medal; World War II Victory Medal; Am Campaign Medal; Nat Defense Serve Medal; Armed Forces Res Medal; Air Force Longevity Serv Award with Oak Leaf Cluster; Combat Readiness Medal; Small Arms Expert Marksmanship Ribbon, 20 year Res Medal; 20 year Active State Serv Medal; Berlin Crisis Medal. Mem: SC Bar Asn; Nat Asn of State Auditors, Comptrollers & Treas (vpres, 70-); Munic Finance Officers Asn; Am Legion; Mil Order of World Wars. Relig: Presbyterian. Legal Res: Tugaloo Ave Calhoun Falls SC 29628 Mailing Add: 3016 Petigru St Columbia SC 29204

PATTERSON, HELEN JO (D)
Chmn, Borden Co Dem Party, Tex
b Knapp, Tex, June 27, 30; d Robert Eugene Warren & Pearl Burney W; m 1965 to Royce Franklin Patterson; c Donna (Mrs Tommy Smith); Cynthia (Mrs Emmitt Hataway), Rhonda (Mrs Clay Copeland) & Tommy. Educ: High Sch, Fluvanna, Tex, grad, 47. Polit & Govt Pos: Chmn, Borden Co Dem Party, Tex, 74- Mem: 4-H Club (adult leader, 72-). Relig: Church of Christ. Mailing Add: Rte 1 Box 34 Fluvanna TX 79517

PATTERSON, J O, JR (D)
City Councilman, Memphis, Tenn
b Memphis, Tenn, May 28, 35; s Bishop J O Patterson, Sr & Deborah Mason P; m 1971 to Rose Elmer Kelly; div; c James O, III & Aaron L. Educ: Fisk Univ, AB, 58; De Paul Univ Law Sch, JD, 63; Blue Key; Alpha Phi Alpha; Phi Alpha Delta. Polit & Govt Pos: Tenn State Rep, 67-69; city councilman, Memphis, Tenn, 68-; Tenn State Sen, 69-74, Dem Whip, Tenn State Senate, 71-74. Bus & Prof Pos: Exec vpres, Tenn Funeral Syst, 64- Mem: Memphis & Shelby Co Bar Asns; NAACP; Am Trial Lawyers Asn; Goodwill Boys Club (bd dirs). Relig: Church of God in Christ. Mailing Add: Suite 216 227 S Main Memphis TN 38104

PATTERSON, JAMES F (R)
Comnr, Geauga Co, Ohio
b Cleveland, Ohio, Feb 16, 42; s Samuel A Patterson & Iona Lauser P; m 1963 to Nancy Wilson; c Susan Leigh, David Wilson & James William. Educ: Ohio State, BS, 64; Alpha Gamma Rho. Polit & Govt Pos: Mem, Geauga Co Libr Bd, Ohio, 67-68; mem, Geauga Co Bd Educ, 68; chmn, Geauga Co Rep Cent Comt, 68-70; comnr, Geauga Co, 69- Bus & Prof Pos: Farmer, Patterson Fruit Farm, 64- Mem: Ohio State Hort Soc; West Geauga Jr CofC; Ohio State Univ Alumni Asn; Ohio Farm Bur Fedn. Relig: Methodist. Mailing Add: 8765 Mulberry Rd Chesterland OH 44026

PATTERSON, JANE SMITH (D)
Chairperson, Guilford Co Dem Party, NC
b Wilmington, NC, Aug 27, 40; d Allie McCoy Smith & Emma Wright S; m 1961 to Henry Newton Patterson, Jr; c Henry N, V & Braxton Smith. Educ: Univ NC, Greensboro, 57-59; Univ NC, Chapel Hill, AB Polit Sci, 61. Polit & Govt Pos: First vpres, Guilford Co Young Dem Club, NC, 71-72; pres, Guilford Co Dem Women, 71-73; mem, Exec Comt, NC Dem Party, 71-; mem, Const & Bylaws Comt, NC Dem Women, 71-, chairperson, NC Dem Women's Conv, 71; policy counsel, NC Women's Polit Caucus, 71-, first vchairperson, 73-; mem, Nat Women's Adv Comt, McGovern/Shriver Campaign, 72; deleg, Dem Nat Conv, 72, secy, NC Deleg, 72; vchairperson, Guilford Co Dem Party, 72-75, chairperson, 75-; mem, Gov Adv Comt on Juvenile Detention, 72; mem, Gov Adv Comt on Youth Develop, 72-73; mem adv comn, US Civil Rights Comn, NC, 74- Bus & Prof Pos: Real estate broker & sales assoc, Zauber Realty Co, 72- Publ: Run, Jane, Run (How to be a delegate to a national convention), NC Women's Polit Caucus, 72. Mem: NC Asn of Realtor's, Inc; Greensboro Jr League; Nat Orgn Women; YWCA (bd dirs, 75-); Triad Sickle Cell Anemia Found (bd dirs). Honors & Awards: One of Ten Outstanding Young Dem, NC Young Dem Club, 72. Relig: Presbyterian. Mailing Add: 1004 Sunset Dr Greensboro NC 27408

PATTERSON, JERRY MUMFORD (D)
US Rep, Calif
b El Paso, Tex, Oct 25, 34; s Levin Mumford Patterson & Ella May Ferrier P; m 1955 to Mary Jane Crisman; c Patrick Alan & Jane Michelle. Educ: Calif State Univ, Long Beach, AB, 60; Univ Southern Calif, Los Angeles, 60-63; Univ Calif, Los Angeles Sch Law, JD, 66; Pi Gamma Mu; Phi Delta Phi; Sigma Chi; Sophos, Traditions Comt. Polit & Govt Pos: Mem, Santa Ana City Coun, Calif, 69-74; mem exec comt, Southern Calif Asn Govts, 69-74; vpres, Orange Co Div, Calif League of Cities, 72-73; chmn, Santa Ana Housing Authority, 72-74; chmn, Santa Ana Redevelop Agency, 73-74; chmn, Orange Co Sanitation Dists 1 & 7, 73-74; rep, Orange Co Intergovt Coord Coun, 73-74; mayor, Santa Ana, 73-74; chmn, Orange Co Manpower Area Planning Coun, 74; US Rep, Calif, 75- Bus & Prof Pos: Admin asst & personnel officer, City Garden Grove, Calif, 60-63; attorney, Santa Ana, 67- Mil Serv: Entered as Seaman Recruit, Coast Guard, 53, released as Hosp Corpsman 2/C, 57, after serv in 11th CG Dist, 53-57; Nat Defense Serv Award. Mem: Calif State Bar; Dem Club. Relig: Congregational. Legal Res: 2636 N Jessee Dr Santa Ana CA 92701 Mailing Add: 507 Cannon House Off Bldg Washington DC 20515

PATTERSON, JOHN GERALD (R)
Chmn, Brooke Co Rep Exec Comt, WVa
b Wheeling, WVa, Dec 15, 16; s John Fillmore Patterson & Marietta Poth P; m 1945 to Sara Julia Rosales Fortin; c Sandra (Mrs Meade) & Jo Anne (Mrs Ramming). Educ: Bethany Col, AB, 38; Univ Va, MA, 39; Univ Pittsburgh, 49-50; US Army Command & Gen Staff Col, 51-52; Pi Delta Epsilon; Kappa Alpha Order. Polit & Govt Pos: Mayor, Bethany, WVa, 63-67; chmn, Brooke Co Rep Exec Comt, 68- Bus & Prof Pos: Off mgt, Equitable Life Assurance Soc, NY, 39-41; prof polit sci, Bethany Col, 46-51 & 61-64; mgr, Easy Method Systs, Inc, 51-61; dir develop, Bethany Col, 64- Mil Serv: Entered as Pvt, Army, 41, released as Col, 46, after serv as Asst Chief of Staff Opers, Caribbean Defense Command; US Army Commendation; Am Defense Ribbon; Pac Theatre Ribbon; Am Theatre Ribbon. Mem: Am Polit Sci Asn; Am Hist Soc; Am Col Pub Rels Asn; Am Legion; Mason. Relig: Protestant. Mailing Add: 295 Lake Dr Bethany WV 26032

PATTERSON, JOHN MALCOLM (D)
b Goldville, Ala, Sept 27, 21; s Albert Love Patterson & Agnes Louise Benson P; m 1947 to Mary Jo McGowin; c Albert L, III & Barbara Louise. Educ: Univ Ala, LLB, 49, JD, 69; Phi Eta Sigma; Alpha Tau Omega; Phi Alpha Delta; Omicron Delta Kappa. Polit & Govt Pos: Attorney Gen, Ala, 55-59, Gov, 59-63. Bus & Prof Pos: Secy, Dewberry Drug Co, Inc, Birmingham, 60-; attorney, Patterson & Rinehart, Montgomery, 66-; assoc prof, Troy Univ, 73- Mil Serv: Entered as Pvt, Artil, 40, rêleased as Maj, 46; reentered serv as Maj, Artil, 51, released as Maj, 53, after serv in Africa, Italy & ETO; African, Italian, French & German Campaign Ribbons; Bronze Star Medal; Lt Col, Artil Res. Mem: Am Legion; VFW; WOW; Elks; Eagles. Relig: Methodist. Legal Res: 210 Felder Ave Montgomery AL 36104 Mailing Add: Suite 1100 Bell Bldg Montgomery AL 36104

PATTERSON, KAY (D)
SC State Rep
b Darlington, SC, Jan 11, 31; s James Hildred Patterson & Lelia Prince P; m 1955 to Jean James; c Eric & Pamela. Educ: Allen Univ, AB, 56; SC State Col, MEd, 71; Temple Univ. Polit & Govt Pos: Mem, Greenview Precinct Dem Exec Comt, SC, formerly; SC State Rep, Dist 73, currently, mem educ comt, SC House Rep, currently. Bus & Prof Pos: Teacher social studies & bus mgr, W A Perry Jr High Sch, Columbia, SC, 56-70; mem staff, SC Educ Asn, 70-; instr educ, Benedict Col, formerly. Mem: NEA; Omega Psi Phi; NAACP; CORE; Mason. Relig: Episcopal; secy-treas vestry, St Luke's Episcopal Church. Mailing Add: 6815 Gavilan Ave Columbia SC 29203

PATTERSON, LARRY SAMUEL (D)
Ark State Rep
b Bristol, Va, Aug 31, 42; s Herschel E Patterson & Dorcee Moore P; m 1966 to Jo Carol Cox; c Jan Kristen, Larry Samuel, Jr & Zane Blake. Educ: Southern State Col, Magnolia, Ark, BBA, 63; Vanderbilt Univ, JD, 66; Delta Theta Phi. Polit & Govt Pos: Juv court referee, Hempstead Co, Ark, 70-; Ark State Rep, Dist 20, 73- Bus & Prof Pos: Attorney-at-law, Hempstead Co, Ark, 66- Honors & Awards: Selected as One of Most Outstanding Young Men in Arkansas, Ark Jaycees, 70. Relig: Methodist. Legal Res: 1100 E Third St Hope AR 71801 Mailing Add: PO Box 276 Hope AR 71801

PATTERSON, PAT J (R)
Mem, Oklahoma Co Rep Exec Comt, Okla
b Oklahoma City, Okla, Mar 16, 20; s D Clarence Patterson & Alice Wattenbarger P; m 1943 to Ann Beard; c Nancy & James W. Educ: Univ Okla, 39-40; Oklahoma City Univ, LLB, 50; Sigma Alpha Epsilon. Polit & Govt Pos: Nominee, US Sen, Okla, 66; mem, Oklahoma Co Rep Exec Comt, 66-; deleg, Rep Nat Conv, 68; deleg to several state conv. Bus & Prof Pos: Acct-partner, Patterson Audit Co, Oklahoma City, 47-50; attorney-at-law, 50- Mil Serv: Flying Cadet, Army Air Force, 41, released as Lt Col, after serv in 5th Bomb Group, 13th Air Force, Southwest Pac Theatre, 44-45; Distinguished Flying Cross; Air Medal with 7 Clusters; Philippine Liberation Medal with Three Stars; Pac Theatre Medal with Nine Stars; Am Theater, Am Defense & World War II Victory Medals. Publ: Church School by Mail (3 vols), Episcopal Diocese of Okla, 60. Mem: Am Judicature Soc; various Bar Asns; Kiwanis; Am Legion. Relig: Episcopal. Legal Res: 1115 Huntington Oklahoma City OK 73116 Mailing Add: 6403 NW Grand Blvd Oklahoma City OK 73116

PATTERSON, RALPH (D)
Ark State Sen
Mailing Add: 2 Beresford Ct North Little Rock AR 72116

PATTERSON, RICHARD GEORGE (D)
Chmn, Wethersfield Dem Town Comt, Conn
b Manchester, NH, Oct 19, 29; s Raymond J Patterson & Albina Connolly P; m 1954 to Suzanne Laflamme; c Raymond, Louise & Daniel. Educ: Univ Conn, BA, 51, JD, 54. Polit & Govt Pos: Asst clerk, Hartford City & Police Court, 55-57; asst corp counsel, City of Hartford, Conn, 57-64; mem zoning bd of appeals, Wethersfield, 66-71; mem, Wethersfield Dem Town Comt, 70-, chmn, 72- Mem: Conn & Hartford Co Bar Asns; Elks; Sportmen's Club; Wethersfield Bus & Civic Asn; Univ Conn Club (pres, 70-71). Honors & Awards: Outstanding Alumnus Award, Hartford Chap, Univ Conn Alumni Asn, 72. Relig: Roman Catholic. Mailing Add: 137 Ox Yoke Dr Wethersfield CT 06109

PATTI, FRANK J (D)
La State Rep
Mailing Add: 113 Fort Jackson St Belle Chasse LA 70037

PATTISALL, RICHARD CHAPMAN (D)
Chmn, Roanoke Co Dem Comt, Va
b Norton, Va, Jan 29, 38; s Richard O'Dell Pattisall & Mary Coxe; m 1961 to Mary Jane Howard; c Richard Chapman Jr, Jennifer Howard & John James Benjamin. Educ: Univ NC, Chapel Hill, AB, 60, LLB, 62; Phi Gamma Delta. Polit & Govt Pos: Vpres, Halifax Co Young Dem Club, NC, 65; asst commonwealth attorney, Roanoke Co Va, 68; pres, Roanoke Co Young Dem Club, 68; substitute munic judge, Roanoke, 68; deleg, Dem Nat Conv, 68; vpres, Va Young Dem Club, 69; chmn, Roanoke Co Dem Comt, Va, 69-; Dem Cand, Va State Sen, 18th Dist, 70. Bus & Prof Pos: Attorney, Crew & House, Roanoke Rapids, 62-65; attorney & vpres, Roanoke Am Corp, Roanoke, Inc, 71-; pres, Va Airways Corp, 72- Mil Serv: Platoon Leaders Class Prog, Marine Corps, 59-60. Mem: Va & NC State Bar; Va State & Roanoke Bar Asns; Am Judicature Soc; Delta Theta Phi; Jaycees. Honors & Awards: Outstanding Leader, NC Dem Party, 65; named One of Outstanding Young Men of Am, 69. Relig: Presbyterian. Mailing Add: 4838 Buckhorn Rd SW Roanoke VA 24014

PATTISON, EDWARD W (D)
US Rep, NY
b Troy, NY, Apr 29, 32; s Edward H Pattison & Elisabeth Royce P; m 1951 to Eleanor Copley; c Mark, Lynn, Laura & Wendy. Educ: Cornell Univ, AB, 53; Cornell Univ Law Sch, LLB, 57. Polit & Govt Pos: Chmn, Sand Lake Dem Town Comt, 61-65; mem exec comt, Rensselaer Co Dem Comt, 62-64; treas, Rensselaer Co, 69-74; chmn, Rensselaer Co Citizens for Kennedy-Johnson, 60; cand, US Cong, 30th Cong Dist, 70; US Rep, 74- Bus & Prof Pos: Partner, Smith, Pattison, Sampson & Jones, Attorneys, 59-72, vpres, 72-74; vpres, Pattison, Herzog, Sampson & Nichols, PC, 74. Mil Serv: 1st Lt, Army, 54-56; after serv in adj gen off, El Paso, Tex. Publ: The Marketing of Property Acquired for Taxes, 72; How to Conduct a Tax Sale, 73. Mem: NY State & Rensselaer Co Bar Asns; Co Treas & Finance Officers Asn NY; Troy Club; Ft Orange Club. Legal Res: West Sand Lake NY 12196 Mailing Add: PO Box 474 West Sand Lake NY 12196

PATTISON, MARGE (D)
Mem, Dem Nat Comt, Wis
Mailing Add: 6407 Bridge Rd Apt 103 Madison WI 53713

PATTISON, ORVILLE HOYT (R)
NMex State Rep
m 1954 to Joy Bumgarner; c Rose Ellen, Roger, Melinda & Will. Educ: NMex State Univ, BS, Agr Eng with honors; Univ Dayton, 12 hours; Alpha Zeta; Sigma Tau; Tau Kappa Epsilon. Polit & Govt Pos: Rep party co chmn, NMex, formerly; mem, NMex Rep State Cent Comt, formerly; NMex State Rep, 62-, Minority Whip, NMex State House of Rep, 65-66, vchmn house agr comt, 69-, mem appropriations comt, currently. Bus & Prof Pos: Agr engr & farmer. Mil Serv: 1st Lt, Air Force, 52-54, served in Engr Air Research & Develop

Command, Wright-Patterson AFB, Ohio. Mem: Farm Bur; Clovis Stockyards Asn; NMex Wool Growers Asn; High Plains Prof Engrs; Water Inc (dir). Relig: Presbyterian; elder. Mailing Add: Box 58 Star Rte Clovis NM 88101

PATTON, AL (DFL)
Minn State Rep
Mailing Add: Box 8 Sartell MN 56377

PATTON, EDWIN GUY (D)
Chmn, Randolph Co Dem Comt, Mo
b Randolph Co, Mo, July 10, 04; s Lewis Edgar Patton & Emily Susan Snell P; m 1925 to Mary Margaret Wagoner; c Lewis Edwin & Mary Susan (Mrs Stansbekal). Educ: Moberly High Sch, Mo, grad, 23. Polit & Govt Pos: Chmn, Randolph Co Dem Comt, Mo, currently. Bus & Prof Pos: Retired. Mem: Mo Farmers Asn (bond sales supvr); Mason; Shrine. Honors & Awards: Legion of Honor DeMolay, 40; Knight York Cross of Honor, 50; Red Cross of Constantine, 75. Relig: Christian Church. Mailing Add: RR 3 Moberly MO 65270

PATTON, ELBERT EARL, JR (R)
Mem, Rep State Cent Comt, Ga
b Atlanta, Ga, June 27, 27; s Elbert Earl Patton & Ella Britt Hall P; m 1949 to Mary Louise Morris; c Thomas Earl, Richard Morris & Dorothy Louise. Educ: Ga Inst of Technol, BS, 49; Sigma Chi. Polit & Govt Pos: State campaign chmn, Young Rep Fedn & deleg, Young Rep Conv, 54-55; cand for Atlanta Aldermanic Bd, 65; mem, Atlanta, Fulton Co Local Govt Study Comn, 66; mem, Ga State Rep Comt & Ga Fifth Cong Dist Comt, 65; chmn, Fulton Co Rep Party, 66-68; Rep cand, US Sen, Ga, 68; mem, Rep State Cent Comt Ga, 68-; Ga State Sen, 69-73. Bus & Prof Pos: With Proctor & Gamble, 49-51 & Hungerford & Assocs, 54-57; dir of sales, Opelika Welding Machinery, Inc, 57-64; owner, Patton Assoc, 64- Mil Serv: Navy, 44-46; reentered serv as 2nd Lt, Air Force, 51, released as 1st Lt, 53, after serv in 62nd Troop Carrier Squadron, Japan-Korea Theater, 52-53; Air Medal with Three Battle Stars; Presidential Unit Citation with Two Oak Leaves; Korean Campaign & Southeast Asia Ribbons. Mem: Vchmn, Bd of Mgt, YMCA; Atlanta Quarterback Club; Capitol Hill Club; Cherokee Town & Country Club. Relig: Presbyterian. Legal Res: 669 Starlight Dr NE Atlanta GA 30342 Mailing Add: 38 Old Ivy Rd NE Atlanta GA 30342

PATTON, JOHN (R)
Minn State Sen
Mailing Add: 1007 S Moore Blue Earth MN 56013

PAUL, CONCETTA M (R)
Vt State Rep
b Troy, NY, June 29, 16; d Clarence C Milanese & Sadie Del Vecchio M; m 1944 to Joseph R Paul, wid; c Diane (Mrs Gerald Morrissey), Sandra M & Joseph R Paul. Educ: Allens Sch Com, grad, 32; Ideal Beauty Sch, grad, 33; Adult Eve Classes, grad, 36. Polit & Govt Pos: Second inspector, local elec, Vt, 59-; fund collecting, Rep Party, 71-; Vt State Rep, Dist 21, 73- Bus & Prof Pos: Mgr, Ideal Beauty Shop, Troy, NY, 35-44; vpres, Pauls Dry Cleaners, Rutland, Vt, 56. Relig: Catholic. Mailing Add: 225 N Church St Rutland VT 05701

PAUL, JOHN W (D)
Chmn, Dover-Foxcroft Co Dem Party, Maine
b Dover-Foxcroft, Maine, Oct 25, 25; s William L Paul & Anne M Parlia P; m 1946 to Donna Marie MsSorley; c Susan Anne & Elizabeth E. Educ: Milo High Sch, Maine, 4 years. Polit & Govt Pos: Mem, Milo Town Dem Comt, 50-66, chmn, 66-70; mem, Dover-Foxcroft Co Dem Comt, 66-, chmn, 70- Bus & Prof Pos: RR worker, Bangor & Aroostock RR, Derby, Maine, 25 years. Mil Serv: Entered as A/S, Navy Seabees, 43, released as Seaman 2/C, 46, after serv in Construction Bns, S Pac Theatre, 43-46; Bronze Star; Presidential Citation; Good Conduct Medal. Mem: Brotherhood Rwy Carmen; Brotherhood Firemen & Oilers. Relig: Methodist. Mailing Add: 36 First St Derby ME 04425

PAULEY, EDWIN WENDELL (D)
b Indianapolis, Ind, Jan 7, 03; s Elbert L Pauley & Ellen Van Petten P; m 1937 to Barbara Jean McHenry; c Edwin W, Jr, Stephen McHenry, Susan (Mrs French) & Robert Van Petten. Educ: Univ Calif, BS, 22, MS, 23. Hon Degrees: LLD, Univ Calif, 56. Polit & Govt Pos: Regent, Univ Calif, 39-, chmn bd regents, 56-58 & 60-62; petroleum coordr for European War on Petroleum Lend-Lease Supplies for Russia & the United Kingdom, 41; treas & secy, Dem Nat Comt, 41-43; indust & commercial adv, Tri-Part Potsdam Conf, 45; US Ambassador, Allied Comn on Reparations, 45-46 Spec Asst Secy of Army, 47; spec adv on reparations to Secy of State, 47-48; mem, Calif Dem State Cent Comt, formerly. Bus & Prof Pos: Founder & chmn bd, Pauley Petroleum Inc, Los Angeles, Calif; mem, bd trustees, Occidental Col; mem governing bd, Ga Mil Acad; dir, Western Airlines. Mem: Los Angeles World Affairs Coun (dir). Relig: Protestant. Legal Res: 9521 Sunset Blvd Beverly Hills CA 90210 Mailing Add: 10000 Santa Monica Blvd Los Angeles CA 90067

PAULEY, JACK L (D)
b Drybranch, WVa, Nov 30, 38; s Jess W Pauley & Belva Slack P; m 1969 to Nancy Stump; c Lisa Kay, Bradley James & Jack L, Jr. Educ: Morris Harvey Col, BA; Marshall Univ; Psi Sigma Psi; Tau Kappa Epsilon Int; Tau Kappa Epsilon. Polit & Govt Pos: Mem adv bd, 62-63; chmn, Membership Drive for Young Dem Club; pres, Morris Harvey Young Dem Club; WVa State Deleg, 64-66; clerk, Kanawha Co Court, 69-; deleg, Dem Nat Conv, 72. Bus & Prof Pos: Jr high sch teacher. Mem: Elks; Young Dem Club; Nat Educ Asn; WVEA; Am Fedn of Teachers. Relig: Baptist. Legal Res: 5305 Noyes Ave SE Charleston WV 25304 Mailing Add: PO Box 3226 Charleston WV 25332

PAULO, WALTER H (R)
b Mansfield, Ohio, 1902; s Andrew Paulo & Emma Isaly P; m 1928 to Dorothy M Catlin; c Gloria Jean (Mrs Jack J Meerman). Polit & Govt Pos: Ohio State Rep, Dist 83, 66-72, mem Agr & Conserv Comt, Com & Transportation Comt & Local Govt & Urban Affairs Comt, formerly; alt deleg, Rep Nat Conv, 72. Bus & Prof Pos: With Union Pac Rwy, Wyo & Mountain View Dairy, Calif, until 24; at various pos, Isaly Dairy Co, Youngstown, Ohio, 24-30, plant supt, 30-42, gen mgr, 42-46, exec vpres, gen mgr & secy, 46-61, pres, gen mgr & serv, 61-65; former dir, Mahoning Nat Bank; pub rels & outside sales for Pan Atlas Travel Serv. Mem: Heart Asn of Eastern Ohio (gifts chmn); Youngstown Area Develop Found (exec comt); Kiwanis Int; St Alban's Lodge, F&AM. Relig: Christian. Mailing Add: RR 2 Fairgrounds Blvd Canfield OH 44406

PAULSON, WILLIAM LEE
Assoc Justice, NDak Supreme Court
b Valley City, NDak, Sept 3, 13; s Alfred Parker Paulson & Inga Wold P; m 1938 to Jane Elizabeth Graves; c John Thomas & Mary Elizabeth. Educ: Valley City State Col, BA, 35; Univ NDak, LLB, 37, JD, 69; Beta Theta Pi; Phi Delta Phi. Polit & Govt Pos: States Attorney, Barnes Co NDak, 41-50; states attorney, Valley City, 59-66; Assoc Justice, NDak Supreme Court, 67- Bus & Prof Pos: Mem bd dirs, Am Nat Bank of Valley City, NDak, 38-; mem bd dirs, Valley City Civic & Com Asn, 60. Mem: Jaycees; Am Judicature Soc; NDak State Attorneys Asn; Elks; KofP; AF&AM. Relig: Episcopal; Chancellor of the Episcopal Church of NDak. Legal Res: 361 College St SW Valley City ND 58072 Mailing Add: 1009 E Highland Acres Rd Bismarck ND 58501

PAULUS, NORMA JEAN (R)
Ore State Rep
b Belgrade, Nebr, Mar 13, 33; d Paul Emil Petersen & Ella Marie Hellbusch P; m 1958 to William G Paulus; c Elizabeth & Fritz. Educ: Willamette Univ Sch Law, Law Degree, 62. Polit & Govt Pos: Mem, Salem Human Rels Comn, 67-70 & Marion-Polk Boundary Comn, 70-71; dir, Nat Soc State Legis, 71-72; Ore State Rep, 71- Bus & Prof Pos: Mem law firm, Paulus & Callaghan, Attorneys of Counsel, 75. Mem: Ore State Bar. Honors & Awards: First in Moot Court Competition, Willamette Law Sch, 62; Golden Torch Award, Bus & Prof Women Ore, 71; City Salem's Distinguished Serv Award, 71; Eagleton Inst Polit fel, 71. Relig: Protestant. Mailing Add: 3090 Pigeon Hollow Rd S Salem OR 97302

PAULY, HELEN (D)
b Galena, Mo, Mar 7, 05; d Jackson Grant Short & Permelia Long S; m 1922 to Fred W Pauly, wid; c Mary P & John Frederick. Educ: Ozark Wesleyan Acad; Wichita Bus Col. Polit & Govt Pos: Admin asst to US Rep O Clark Fisher, Tex, formerly. Mem: Eastern Star (past matron & past dist dep grandmatron); Church of Epiphany. Relig: Episcopal. Mailing Add: 5200 N Dixie West Palm Beach FL 33407

PAVICH, EMIL SAM (D)
Iowa State Rep
b Council Bluffs, Iowa, July 30, 31; s Guy Pavich & Josephine Pavelich P; single. Polit & Govt Pos: Pres, Pottawattamie Co Young Dem, 56; precinct committeeman, Pottawattamie Dem Comt, 58-; seventh dist committeeman, Iowa Young Dem, 59-60, vpres 60-62; treas, Pottawattamie Dem Cent Comt, Iowa, 64-66, chmn, formerly; mem, Govt Comt on Employ of the Physically Handicapped, 66-68; mem, Pottawattamie Co Welfare Bd, 72-, chmn, 73-; Iowa State Rep, currently. Mil Serv: Pvt, Army, 52-54. Mem: Local 50, Grain Millers Union; Iowa, Nebr & Pottawattamie Co Hist Socs; Am Polit Items Collectors; Council Bluffs Comt on Polit Educ. Relig: Catholic. Mailing Add: 1706 15th Ave Council Bluffs IA 51501

PAWLAK, PAUL, SR (D)
Conn State Rep
Mailing Add: 9 Grand St Seymour CT 06483

PAWLEY, WILLIAM DOUGLAS (R)
b Florence, SC, Sept 7, 96; s Edward Procher Pawley & Irene Wallace P; m 1919 to Annie Hahr Dobbs; div; m 1943 to Edna Earle Cadenhead; c William Douglas, Annie Hahr (Mrs Hobert Boomer McKay) & Irene Wallace (Mrs C Jackson Baldwin). Polit & Govt Pos: US Ambassador to Peru, 45-46; US Ambassador to Brazil, 46-48; deleg, Inter-Am Conf for Continental Peace & Security, Brazil, 47; spec asst to Secy of State, UN Gen Assembly, 48, deleg, Ninth Int Conf of Am States, Bogota, Columbia, 48; spec asst to Secy of Defense, Paris, & to Secy State, DC, 51; deleg, NATO Conf, Lisbon, 52; spec assignment, Dept of State, 54. Bus & Prof Pos: Pres, Co Nacional Cubana de Aviacion Curtiss, Havana, 28-32; pres, Intercontinent Corp, NY & China Nat Aviation Corp, Shanghai, 33, Hindustan Aircraft Corp, Bangalore, India, 40; pres & owner, Miami Transit Co & Miami Beach Rwy Co, 54-62; dir, Fla Nat Bank of Miami; pres, Talisman Sugar Corp, Fla, 64-72. Mem: Liberation of Cuban POW (sponsor's comt); Miami-Dade Community Col (trustee); Boy's Clubs Am (nat bd). Honors & Awards: Organized Flying Tigers, Am Vol Group, World War II, 40; US Medal for Merit; Air Medal, Peru; Grand Cross, Brazil; Grand Cross, Cuba. Legal Res: 2555 Lake Ave Sunset Island Miami Beach FL 33140 Mailing Add: 260 NE 17th Terr Miami FL 33132

PAXTON, JON BILLY (D)
Ky State Rep
Mailing Add: Country Club Subdiv Central City KY 42330

PAXTON, RALPH EUGENE (R)
Mem, Washington Parish Rep Comt, La
b Boone, Iowa, Dec 11, 01; s Charles Cook Paxton & Mary Catharine Teagarden P; m 1925 to Cleve Squires Welsh; c Ward Robert (deceased). Educ: Iowa State Univ, BS in Elec Eng, 24, EE, 29; Eta Kappa Nu; Kappa Sigma. Polit & Govt Pos: Mem, Rep State Cent Comt La, formerly; mem, Washington Parish Rep Comt, 73-; mem, Bogalusa Parks & Recreation Comt, currently. Mil Serv: Entered as Lt, Naval Res, 42, released as Lt Comdr, 45, after serv in Naval Mine Sweeping Trial Bd; Am Theater Ribbon; Chief of Naval Operations Letter of Commendation. Mem: Soc Am Military Engrs; Inst Elec & Electronics Engrs; Am Legion; Rotary. Relig: Protestant. Mailing Add: 1628 Piney Branch Rd Bogalusa LA 70427

PAYNE, ANNA LEE (R)
b Norton, Va, Feb 24, 32; d Willis Bozarth & Clara O'Neill B; m 1953 to Dr Roy A Payne; c Bruce David, Ginger Faye, Roy A, Jr & Jean Clare. Educ: Reed Col, BA, 53. Polit & Govt Pos: Precinct committeewoman, Clackamas Co Rep Cent Comt, Ore, 64-, precinct organizer, 66-69; vchmn, Ore Med Polit Action Comt, 68-69; mem, Budget Comt & Bd of Equalization, Clackamas Co, 68-; mem, Metrop Study Comn, 69-70; co-chmn, Ore Comt for Reelec of the President, 72; alt deleg, Rep Nat Conv, 72; coordr, Ore Inaugural Comt, 72-73. Bus & Prof Pos: Dir pub rels, Reed Col, 53-55; exec secy, Ore Acad of Gen Practice, 55-59. Mem: Clackamas Co Med Auxiliary (legis chmn, 65-68, pres, 68-69); Woman's Auxiliary to Ore Med Asn (ed, 61-63, legis chmn, 64-66, pres elect, 71-73, pres, 73-); Ore Zool Soc; PTA; North Clackamas CofC (educ comt, 71-). Relig: Protestant. Mailing Add: 2320 Ninth Ave Milwaukie OR 97222

PAYNE, FRANKLIN (D)
Mo State Sen
Mailing Add: 4128A Maffitt St Louis MO 63113

PAYNE, FREDERICK GEORGE (R)
b Lewiston, Maine, July 24, 04; s Frederick George Payne & Nellie Grant Smart P; m to Ella Hodgdon; c E Thomas & Putnam. Educ: Bentley Col of Acct & Finance, Boston, Mass; Kappa Pi Alpha. Polit & Govt Pos: Mayor, Augusta, Maine, 35-41; Comnr of Finance & Budget Dir, Maine, 40-42; Gov, 49-53; US Sen, Maine, 53-59. Bus & Prof Pos: Chief disbursement auditor, NE Div, Publix Theaters Corp, 25-29; gen mgr of theaters, Maine & NH Theater Co, 20-35; indust develop consult, Cent Maine Power Co, 37-40; bus & indust consult, self employed, 59- Mil Serv: Entered as Capt, Air Force, 42, released as Lt Col, 44; Air Force Commendation Medal. Publ: Author of legislation including Housing for Aged, Study of Effects of Atomic Fallout & Aid to Distressed Areas. Mem: Am Legion; Lions; numerous charitable orgns; Am Cancer Soc (chmn bd dirs, Maine Div, 71-). Honors & Awards: Bronze Medal, Am Cancer Soc. Relig: Protestant. Mailing Add: Main St Waldoboro ME 04572

PAYNE, GARY EDISON (D)
Okla State Rep
b Denison, Tex, Oct 31, 44; s Thomas Edison Payne & Jeanne Landram P; m 1966 to Suzanne Major Farris; c Robert Farris. Educ: Okla State Univ, BS, 65; Univ Okla Sch Law, JD, 69; Sigma Nu; Phi Alpha Delta; Young Dem; Student Union Activities Bd; Interfraternity Coun. Polit & Govt Pos: Committeeman, Okla State Univ Young Dem, 62-63; deleg, State Young Dem Conv; legis intern & asst bill drafter, Okla State Rep, 69-, Asst Majority Floor Leader, Okla House Rep, 69- Bus & Prof Pos: Attorney-at-law, Atoka, Okla, 69- Mil Serv: 1st Lt, Okla Nat Guard, 69- Mem: Am Bar Asn; Am Trial Lawyers Asn; Okla TB & Respiratory Disease Asn (co chmn, 72-); Jr CofC; Lions. Honors & Awards: Lew Wentz Scholar; Ford Found grant, 66-67; Citation of Merit, DAV. Relig: Baptist. Mailing Add: Box 250 Atoka OK 74525

PAYNE, JOHN FRANKLIN (D)
WVa State Deleg
b Brooksville, WVa, Aug 25, 25; s Joseph McCarthy Payne & Malinda Summerfield P; div; c Lana Kay, John Joseph & Franklin Andrew. Educ: Oklahoma City Univ, 46-47; Morris Harvey Col, 47-48. Polit & Govt Pos: App, Local Draft Bd 7, 67-73; WVa State Deleg, 75-, vchmn, State & Fed Affairs Comt, WVa Legis, 75- Bus & Prof Pos: Vchmn, Clendenin Bus Men Assoc, 64-; chmn, United Vets Asn, WVa, 71-74. Mil Serv: Entered as A/S, Navy, 43, released as PhM/2, 46, after serv in Marines 4th Div, Asiatic-Pac Theatre, 44-46; Pac Theatre Ribbon; Good Conduct; Presidential Unit Citation. Mem: Shrine; Mason; VFW (State Comdr); Am Legion; Moose. Honors & Awards: Outstanding Serv Award for Community Serv, VFW; Counsellor Cert of Appreciation, Dept Labor. Relig: Baptist. Legal Res: 143 Mary St Clendenin WV 25045 Mailing Add: 800 Morris St Charleston WV 25301

PAYNE, S TILFORD, JR (R)
Chmn, Louisville & Jefferson Co Rep Exec Comt, Ky
b Louisville, Ky, Sept 6, 14; s Tilford Payne & Ethel Longest P; m 1947 to Anne M Brown; c Anne Tilford & Edith Brown. Educ: Washington & Lee Univ, LLB, 37; Phi Delta Phi; Pi Kappa Alpha. Polit & Govt Pos: Chmn, Rep Policy Comt, 58-61; chmn, Louisville & Jefferson Co Rep Exec Comt, Ky, 63-70 & 74-; alt deleg, Rep Nat Conv, 68; mem, Ky State Rep Cent Comt, 68-71; vchmn, Third Cong Dist Rep Comt, Ky, 68-71; mem, Ky Comn Elec Finance, 70-73. Bus & Prof Pos: Treas, Louisville Bar Asn, 59, secy, 60. Mil Serv: Entered as Pvt, Marine Corps, 42, released as Comnr Warrant Officer, 46, after serv in 3rd Marine Air Wing, SPac; Pac Theater Ribbon. Mem: Am & Ky Bar Asns; Rotary; Salvation Army (adv bd, 65-); Planned Parenthood, Inc (treas, 72-). Relig: Presbyterian. Mailing Add: 2514 Poplar Crest Rd Louisville KY 40207

PAYTON, MICHAEL A (TONY) (R)
Regional Dir, Rep Nat Comt
b Spearville, Kans, Aug 31, 40; s Paul Winston Payton & Betty Wallingford Sowers P; div; c Michael Trent, Kirsti J & Peter Bradley. Educ: Kans State Teachers Col, 58-59; NMex State Univ. 59-60; Univ Ariz, part-time, 63-64; Orange Coast Col, part-time, 64-65. Polit & Govt Pos: Press dir & regional coordr, Fike for Gov Campaign, Nev, 70; campaign mgr, Towell for Cong Campaign, 72; admin asst, US Rep David Towell, Nev, 73-75; regional dir, Rep Nat Comt, currently. Bus & Prof Pos: Newspaper reporter, Ariz Daily Star, Tucson, 63-64; newspaper reporter, Orange Coast Daily Pilot, Costa Mesa, Calif, 64-65; publ-ed, The Record-Courier, Gardnerville, Nev, 65-70; publ-ed, Lovelock Review-Miner, Lovelock, Nev, 66-71. Mil Serv: Entered as Pvt, Army Nat Guard, 57, released as SP-4, 65, after serv in NMex Nat Guard, Clayton, NMex, 57-65. Mem: Sigma Delta Chi. Honors & Awards: Best News Series, Orange Co Press Asn, Calif, 65; 15 writing awards, Nev State Press Ans, 66-71; Best Column, Panhandle Press Asn, Tex, 72. Relig: Methodist. Mailing Add: PO Box 66 Gardnerville NV 89410

PAYTON, WILLIS OSBORNE (D)
Chmn, Valley Co Dem Party, Idaho
b Preston, Idaho, Dec 11, 11; s Chester Hall Payton & Louise Jacobson P; m 1933 to Opal Nevada Beard. Educ: West Jordan High Sch, grad. Polit & Govt Pos: Idaho State Rep, 51-53; Idaho State Committeeman, Valley Co, 51-55; deleg, Dem Nat Conv, 60, 64 & 68, chmn Idaho Deleg, 68; chmn, Valley Co Dem Party, Idaho, 66-; mem, Idaho Dem State Exec Comt, 66-; Idaho chmn, Humphrey-Muskie Campaign Comt, 68. Bus & Prof Pos: Pres, Payton Construction Co Inc, 57-66, chmn bd dirs, 66-; pres bd dirs, Centennial Corp Inc, 64- Mem: Idaho Lodge 1, AF&AM; Boise Consistory (32 degree); El Korah Temple, Shrine Club; Elks Lodge 310. Relig: Congregational. Mailing Add: W Lakeshore Dr McCall ID 83638

PEABODY, ENDICOTT (D)
b Lawrence, Mass, Feb 15, 20; s The Rt Rev Malcolm E Peabody & Mary Parkman P; m 1944 to Barbara Welch Gibbons; c Barbara, Endicott, Jr & Robert Lee. Educ: Harvard Col, AB, 42; Harvard Univ Law Sch, LLB, 48. Polit & Govt Pos: Gov Coun, Third Coun Dist, Mass, 55-56; cand for Attorney Gen, 56 & 58; cand for Gov, Mass, 60, 62 & 64, Gov, Mass, 63-64; deleg, Dem Nat Conv, 60, 64 & 68, first cand to run for Vice President in Dem Party, 72, finance chmn, Dem Nat Comt Comn on Selection of Vice President, 72; asst regional counsel, Off Price Stabilization; regional counsel & asst to dir, Small Defense Plant Admin, Boston, Mass; cand, US Sen, Mass, 66; asst dir Off of Emergency Preparedness, Exec Off of the President, 67-68; chmn sports comt, President's Comn on US-Mex Border Develop & Friendship, 67-69; deleg, Dem Nat Mid-Term Conf, 74. Bus & Prof Pos: Founder & partner, Peabody, Koufman & Brewer, 52-62; counsel, Roche & Leen, Boston, Mass, 65-66; founder & partner, Peabody, Rivlin & Lambert, Washington, DC, 69- Mil Serv: Entered as Ens, Navy, 42, released as Lt, 45, after serv in Submarine Serv, two war patrols in the Far East; Presidential Unit Citation; Silver Star; Commendation Ribbon. Mem: Harvard Varsity Club; Cambridge Tennis Club; Harvard Club of Wash; Harvard Law Sch Asn of DC; Wash Athletic Club. Honors & Awards: Knute Rockne Mem Trophy; Named Outstanding Football Player in New Eng, 41; Bulger-Lowe Trophy; Named One of the Seven Outstanding Young Men of Boston, 54; Elected to Nat Football Found Hall of Fame, 73. Relig: Episcopal. Legal Res: Cambridge MA Mailing Add: 1730 M St NW Washington DC 20036

PEABODY, MALCOLM E, JR (R)
Dep Asst Secy for Equal Opportunity, Dept of Housing & Urban Develop
b 1928; married; c Two. Educ: Harvard Col & Harvard Univ Grad Sch of Bus Admin, grad. Polit & Govt Pos: Exec secy, NY State Comn for Human Rights, formerly; chmn, Gov Adv Comt on Civil Rights, Mass, 63-64; chmn, Spec Legis Comn on Low Income Housing, Boston, 64-65; staff adv & mem Mayor's Comt on Minority Housing, Boston Redevelop Authority, 65-66; cand, US House of Rep, Third Mass Dist, 68; Dep Asst Secy for Equal Opportunity, Dept of Housing & Urban Develop, 69- Bus & Prof Pos: Merchandise mgr & controller, Butcher Polish Co, Malden, Mass; exec dir, Interfaith Housing Corp, Boston, 66-68. Mil Serv: Officer, Air Force, 52-53. Legal Res: MA Mailing Add: Dept of Housing & Urban Develop 451 Seventh St SW Washington DC 20410

PEACHES, DANIEL (R)
Ariz State Rep
b Kayenta, Ariz, Sept 2, 40; s (father deceased) & Adelaide P; m 1963 to Karen Russell; c Ives D & Arrow. Educ: Northern Ariz Univ, BS, 67; pres, Inter-Tribal Club, 67. Polit & Govt Pos: Mem, Ariz Comn Indian Affairs, 72-75; mem & vchmn, Nat Adv Coun Indian Educ, 73-; Ariz State Rep, 75- Mem: Nat Cong Am Indians; Black Mesa Rev Bd; Ariz Town Hall. Relig: Presbyterian. Legal Res: Box 762 Tuba City AZ 86045 Mailing Add: Box 784 Window Rock AZ 86515

PEACOCK, JOE N (D)
Ark State Rep
Mailing Add: Reynolds Dr McCrory AR 72101

PEADEN, R W (D)
Fla State Rep
Mailing Add: 7612 Pontiac Dr Pensacola FL 32506

PEAK, RAYMOND (D)
WVa State Deleg
Mailing Add: State Capitol Charleston WV 25305

PEAKES, JAMES L (D)
Maine State Rep
Mailing Add: Box 204 Dexter ME 04930

PEARCE, H NORWOOD (D)
Ga State Sen
Mailing Add: PO Box 2312 Columbus GA 31902

PEARCE, WILLIAM RINEHART (R)
Dep Spec Rep, Off of the Spec Rep for Trade Negotiations
b Coral Gables, Fla, Aug 12, 27; s Frank Pearce & Beatrice Rinehart P; m 1951 to Barbara Ann Smith; c Mary Ellen, Laurie Ann, William Owen & Elizabeth Jane. Educ: Univ Minn, BSL, 50, LLB, 52; Order of the Coif; Sigma Chi. Polit & Govt Pos: Mem, Hennepin Co Rep Selection Comt, Minn, 58; mem, Hennepin Co Rep Comt, 58-59, chmn, Hennepin Co Rep Poll Challenger Comt, 59; comnr, Housing & Redevelop Authority, Wayzata, 67-71; mem US deleg, Joint Study Group on Oilseeds, Fats & Oils, FAO-UNCTAD, London, 70; mem, President's Comn on Int Trade & Investment Policy, 70-71; dep spec rep, Off of Spec Rep for Trade Negotiations, 71- Bus & Prof Pos: Law dept, Cargill, Inc, Minneapolis, 52-57, asst vpres, 61-63, vpres, 63-71. Mil Serv: Entered as A/S, Naval Res, 45, released as Seaman 1/C, 46, after serv in V6; recalled as 2nd Lt, Air Force Res, 52-59. Mem: Coun Foreign Rels; Wayzata Country Club. Relig: Christian. Legal Res: MN Mailing Add: 7301 Masters Dr Potomac MD 20854

PEARCEY, RAY L (D)
b Oklahoma City, Okla; s Raymon Lewis Pearcey, Sr & Lamona Coley P; single. Educ: Univ Tulsa, 71-; Pres Club; pres, Student Asn, 73-, chmn, Acad Affairs Coun, 72-73. Polit & Govt Pos: Deleg, Dem Nat Conv, 72. Relig: Unitarian. Mailing Add: Apt 18H 2807 S Fifth Pl Tulsa OK 74104

PEARL, DOROTHY WAITE (R)
Chmn, Antrim Co Rep Party, Mich
b Kalamazoo, Mich, Feb 20, 96; d Benjamin Asa Waite & Nellie Fisher W; m 1919 to Norton Harris Pearl (deceased); c Ann (Mrs Bretz), Betty (Mrs Beeby), Jane (Mrs Martin) & Dorothy (Mrs Malasky). Educ: Western Mich Univ, 4 years; Wayne State Univ, grad work. Polit & Govt Pos: Dir women's prog, Mich State Civil Defense, 50-51; asst dir women's prog, Off Civil Defense, Washington, DC, 51-58; nat dir women's prog, Off Civil & Defense Mobilization, 58-64; chmn, Antrim Co Rep Party, Mich, 64-70 & 73-, mem exec comt, 70- Bus & Prof Pos: Teacher, Detroit Pub Schs, 18-40. Publ: Parliamentary points, 50. Mem: Am Legion Auxiliary, Gen Fedn Womens Clubs; DAR; Nat Asn Parliamentarians. Eastern Star. Relig: Episcopal. Mailing Add: PO Box 33 Eastport MI 49627

PEARMAN, VIRGIL L (D)
Ky State Rep
Mailing Add: 952 Woodland Dr Radcliff KY 40160

PEARRE, JEROME (R)
b Pontiac, Ill, May 25, 08; s Louis Victor Pearre & Mary Louise Kent P; m 1937 to Erma Williams; c James Alden & Victoria Louise (Mrs Bond). Educ: Dartmouth Col, AB, 30; Ill State Univ, BE, 31; Phi Beta Kappa; Phi Kappa Psi; Delta Omicron Gamma; Green Key. Polit & Govt Pos: Rep representative committeeman, 40th Ill Dist, 60-68. Bus & Prof Pos: Securities salesman, Morgan-Guaranty Bank, 30; hist instr, Pontiac High Sch, Ill, 32; city ed, Pontiac Daily Leader, 33-45, publisher, 45-; secy-treas, Pontiac Leader Publ Co, 45- Mem: Ill & Inland Daily Press Asns; Am Newspaper Publishers Asn; Pontiac Pub Libr Bd Trustees; Rotary; Elks. Relig: Protestant Episcopal. Mailing Add: 206 N Court St Pontiac IL 61764

PEARSON, CATHERINE A (D)
VChmn, Erie Co Dem Comt, Pa
b Washington, DC, Jan 20, 47; d George E Pearson & Marjorie Dean P; single. Educ: Calif State Univ, San Diego, AB with highest honors, 65; Georgetown Univ, PhD & JD cand; Pi

Sigma Alpha; Alpha Lambda Delta; Alpha Mu Gamma. Polit & Govt Pos: Committeewoman, Millcreek Twp Dem Comt, Erie Co, Pa, 70-; mem, Pa Dem State Comt, 72-74; mem, Comn on Status of Women, Pa, 72-; deleg-at-lg, Dem Nat Mid-Term Conf, 74; vchmn, Erie Co Dem Comt, Pa, 74- Bus & Prof Pos: Asst prof polit sci, Mercyhurst Col, 69-71; admin aide, Pa Legis Reapportionment Comn, 71; exec dir comt on educ, Pa House of Rep, 71-74; ed & publ, New Erie Dem, 71-; polit sci & publ consult, Pa & Washington, DC, 75- Publ: The functionalist approach to international law, J Int & Comp Studies, spring 68; The morality of the pursuit of power, Viewpoint, winter 68. Mem: Am Polit Sci Asn; Pa Right-to-Read Task Force. Honors & Awards: Nat Sci Found Grad Fel, 65. Relig: Catholic. Mailing Add: 1305 Greenfield Dr Erie PA 16509

PEARSON, ENID IRENE (R)
City Councilman, Palo Alto, Calif
b Venice, Calif, Aug 21, 24; d Arthur Williams & Gertrude Emelia Ortquist W; m 1951 to Paul Alfred Pearson; c Paul Arthur, Merit Lee, Barbara Emelia & Cecilia Irene. Educ: Mont State Univ, BA in chem, 47; Am Chem Soc. Polit & Govt Pos: Mem, Nat Redwood Scenic Rd & Trail Comt, 65-67; city councilman, Palo Alto, Calif, 65-, vice mayor, 73-74. Bus & Prof Pos: Chemist, Gen Elec Atomic Energy Plant, Hanford, Wash, 47-51; chemist, Stanford Res Inst, Calif, 51-52; secy-treas, Pearson Electronics, Inc, 58- Mem: Addison PTA (legis chmn, parliamentarian & treas, 57-65, coun rep & recording secy, 63); Palo Alto Residents' Asn (traffic chmn & co-founder, 59-61); Citizens for Regional Planning; Am Asn Univ Women (co-founder, Richland, Wash Bd, mem, Palo Alto br); Asn of Bay Area Govt (vchmn intergovt subcomt, Bay Resource Recovery Comt, 73). Honors & Awards: Co-sponsor Palo Alto Planning Ord, 60-62 & Reduction of Council Term from six to four years; sponsor, Palo Alto Park Dedication Charter Amendment. Relig: Protestant. Mailing Add: 1200 Bryant St Palo Alto CA 94301

PEARSON, J RICHMOND (D)
Ala State Sen
Mailing Add: 809 Bolin St SW Birmingham AL 35211

PEARSON, JAMES BLACKWOOD (R)
US Sen, Kans
b Nashville, Tenn, May 7, 20; m 1946 to Martha Mitchell; c Jim, Tom, Bill & Laura Alice. Educ: Duke Univ, 40-42; Univ Va Law Sch, grad, 50; admitted to the Bar, 50. Polit & Govt Pos: City attorney, Westwood, Fairway & Lenexa, Kans, 52-61; asst co attorney, 52-54; probate judge, Johnson Co, 54-56; Kans State Sen, 56-60; chmn, Kans State Rep Party for a short time; US Sen, Kans, 62- Bus & Prof Pos: Attorney-at-law. Mil Serv: Pilot, Navy, 43-46, based at Naval Air Sta, Olathe, Kans. Legal Res: Prairie Village KS 66208 Mailing Add: New Senate Off Bldg Washington DC 20510

PEARSON, JOHN LAFAYETTE (D)
Miss State Rep
Mailing Add: Box 565 Rosedale MS 38769

PEARSON, LLOYD EDWARD (R)
Mem, Bureau Co Rep Cent Comt, Ill
b Putnam Co, Ill, Feb 15, 10; s Edward William Pearson & Hannah Swanson P; m 1935 to Gwendolyn Marjorie Williams; c Judith Pearson (Mrs Lynn Andersen) & Jerome Lloyd. Educ: High Sch, grad, 27. Polit & Govt Pos: Rep precinct committeeman, Arispie Twp, Ill, 33-; mem, Bureau Co Rep Cent Comt, Ill, 33-; supvr, Arispie Twp, 57-; civil defense dir, Bureau Co, 62-64; mem, Bureau Co Exten Serv, 64-68, chmn, 3 years. Bus & Prof Pos: Farmer, 30- Mem: Perry Mem Hosp (adv bd, 40-); Tiskilwa Blue Lodge; Elks; Shrine; Consistory. Relig: Lutheran. Mailing Add: RFD 1 Tiskilwa IL 61368

PEARSON, LORENTZ CLARENCE (D)
Chmn, Madison Co Dem Cent Comt, Idaho
b American Fork, Utah, Jan 28, 24; s Clarence Norman Pearson & Johanna Peterson P; m 1952 to Ingvi Linnea Lindblad; c Suzanne (Mrs Lloyd Benson), Beth (Mrs Kem Cazier), Solveig, Ellen Lyn, Kjerstin & Laura. Educ: Utah State Univ, BS, 52; Univ Utah, MS, 52; Univ Minn, St Paul, PhD, 58; Phi Kappa Phi; Lambda Delta Sigma. Polit & Govt Pos: Adv, Ricks Col Young Dem, 60-; precinct committeeman, Fourth Precinct, Rexburg, Idaho, 70-72, 72-; chmn, Madison Co Dem Cent Comt, 74- Bus & Prof Pos: Teacher agr & biol, Ricks Col, 52- Mil Serv: Entered as Pvt, Army, 42, released as T-4, 46, after serv in Signal Corps, New Guinea & Philippines, 44-46; campaign ribbons. Publ: Primary productivity in a northern desert area, Oikos, Vol 15, 66; Principles of Agronomy, Reinhold van Nostrand, 67; Chap 11, In: Air Pollution & Lichens, Univ London Press, 74. Mem: Am Asn Advan Sci (fel, 63-); Botanical Soc Am; Ecol Soc Am; Idaho Acad Sci (pres, 73-74, ed, 75-); Rexburg Kiwanis Club. Honors & Awards: Nat Sci Found Res Fel, Uppsala Univ, 63-64. Relig: Latter-day Saint. Mailing Add: 366 S Third E Rexburg ID 83440

PEARSON, RONALD WALFRID (R)
b Pawtucket, RI, Apr 19, 46; s Per Walfrid Pearson (deceased) & Florence Forbes P; m 1968 to Patricia Ann Clark. Educ: Valparaiso Univ, BA, 68; Univ Notre Dame, MA, 70; Brown Univ, 70-72; Phi Sigma Epsilon. Polit & Govt Pos: Exec asst, US Rep John Ashbrook, 73- Bus & Prof Pos: Exec dir, WYCF, Inc, 72-73. Legal Res: VA Mailing Add: 1436 Longworth House Off Bldg Washington DC 20515

PEARSON, SHERRY CROSS (D)
b El Paso, Tex, July 28, 53; d Arthur Clifford Cross & Bernice Laird C; m 1973 to Robert Wayne Pearson. Educ: Durham Bus Col, 72. Polit & Govt Pos: Alt deleg, Dem Nat Conv, 72; mem, Tex Young Dem, 72- Bus & Prof Pos: Receptionist, Harris Co Adult Probation Dept, 73 & Thermotics Inc, Houston, Tex, 74; buyer, Petroleos Del Peru, Peruvian Oil Co Purchasing Div, 74- Relig: Methodist. Mailing Add: 15135 Memorial Houston TX 77024

PEASE, DONALD JAMES (D)
Ohio State Sen
b Toledo, Ohio, Sept 26, 31; Russell E Pease & Helen Mary Mullin P; m 1953 to Jeanne Camille Wendt; c Jennifer. Educ: Ohio Univ, BSJ & MA, 54; Univ Durham, Eng, 54-55; Phi Eta Sigma; Omicron Delta Kappa; Delta Tau Delta. Polit & Govt Pos: Chmn pub utilities comt, Oberlin, Ohio, 60-61; mem city coun, Oberlin, 62-64; Ohio State Sen, 65-66 & 75-; Ohio State Rep, 69-74; mem, Educ Comt of the States, Denver, 73- Bus & Prof Pos: Co-ed-publ, Oberlin News-Tribune, Ohio, 57-68, ed, 69- Mil Serv: Entered as 2nd Lt, Army, 55, released as 1st Lt, 57, after serv in QmC. Publ: Auth, The editor in politics, Grassroots Ed, 10/65; Teachers perform, Rockefeller Found Quart, 12/68; Higher education needs to lobby, Chronicle Higher Educ, 11/27/72; plus others. Mem: Int Conf Weekly Newspaper Ed; Sigma Delta Chi. Relig: Protestant. Mailing Add: 285 Oak St Oberlin OH 44074

PEASE, LUCILLE CURRIE (R)
Chmn, Ashfield Rep Town Comt, Mass
b Cornish, Maine, Mar 11, 25; d Eugene Kelvie Currie & Nora Pugsley C; m 1947 to Ralph Sanford Pease; c Norene. Educ: Fitchburg State Col, BSEd, 46. Polit & Govt Pos: Chmn, Ashfield Rep Town Comt, Mass, 65-; deleg, Mass Rep Conv, 66-70. Bus & Prof Pos: Teacher, Shrewsbury, Mass, 46, Newton, 46-48, Ashfield, 48-52 & Conway, 62- Mem: Am Legion Auxiliary; 40 et 8; Eastern Star; life mem Ashfield Hist Soc; Franklin Co Women's Rep Club. Relig: Protestant. Mailing Add: Main St Ashfield MA 01330

PEASE, ROGER DE VERE (R)
Committeeman, Rep State Cent Comt Iowa
b Littleton, Iowa, July 5, 30; s Lawrence A Pease & Grace Hayward P; m 1951 to Mary Ann Beatrice Herberg; c Lynell, Randy, Kevin & Lynor. Educ: High Sch, 4 years. Polit & Govt Pos: Chmn, Black Hawk Co Rep Party, Iowa, formerly; committeeman, Rep State Cent Comt Iowa, currently. Bus & Prof Pos: Cost anal clerk, John Deere Tractor Works, Waterloo, Iowa, 54- Mil Serv: Seaman Storekeeper, Naval Res, 52-53, with serv in USS Hickox, Korea. Mem: Mason (32 degree); AF&AM; Shrine; AAONMS; Eastern Star. Relig: Presbyterian. Mailing Add: 1299 St Andrews Ave Waterloo IA 50701

PEASE, VIOLET CALL (D)
State Committeewoman, York Co Dem Comt, Maine
b Levant, Maine, Feb 24, 27; d Elmer Call & Evelyn Leary C; m 1950 to Allen Gardner Pease; c Pamela Sue, Sanford Howard & Belinda Evelyn. Educ: Univ Maine, Farmington, BS, 49. Polit & Govt Pos: Vchmn, Buxton Dem Town Comt, 66; chmn, Hollis Dem Town Comt, 68-; state committeewoman, York Co Dem Comt, 68-; vchmn, Maine Dem State Comt, 68-73, chairperson, 73-74; mem, Nat Proj '70 Comn, Dem Nat Comt, 69, mem, Comt, 72-74, mem adv planning comt, currently; chmn, Maine Proj '70 Candidate Comt, 70; co-chmn, Maine Get-Out-the Vote Comt, 70, chmn, 72; deleg, Dem Nat Conv, 72. Bus & Prof Pos: Teacher home econ, Madison High Sch, Madison, Maine, 49-50; teacher home econ, Madison Twp High Sch, Groveport, Ohio, 52-53; mem advert staff, Ohio State J, Columbus, Ohio, 51-52; housewife, 54- Honors & Awards: Cert of Honor, Dem Nat Comt; membership drive winner, Maine Dem 500 Club, 69. Relig: Protestant. Legal Res: Hollis ME 04042 Mailing Add: 107 Grove St Augusta ME 04330

PEAVEY, JOHN THOMAS (R)
Idaho State Sen
b Twin Falls, Idaho, Sept 1, 33; s Arthur Jacob Peavey & Mary Thomas P; m 1957 to Luelle Lundgren; c David, Karen & Tom. Educ: Northwestern Univ, BS in Civil Eng; Phi Delta Theta. Polit & Govt Pos: Committeeman, Idaho Rep Party, 62-68; alt deleg, Rep Nat Conv, 68; chmn, Legis Dist 21 Rep Party, 68-69; Idaho State Sen, Dist 21, 69- Mil Serv: Entered as 2nd Lt, Marine Corps, 57, released as 1st Lt, 60, after serv US Naval Mission to Haiti, 59-60. Mem: Idaho Cattleman's Asn; Am Sheep Producers Coun (dir, 68-); Idaho Woolgrowers Asn; Elks. Relig: Methodist. Mailing Add: 904 Tenth St Rupert ID 83350

PEAVY, JAMES EDWIN (R)
Mem, Rep State Cent Comt Ga
b Cuthbert, Ga, Mar 22, 20; s John McKenzie Peavy & Addie Belle Peak P; m 1951 to Audrey Carolyn Beasley; c James E, Jr, & Julie Ann. Educ: Univ Ga, BBA, 47; Mercer Univ, AB cum laude, 48, Walter F George Sch Law, LLB cum laude, 49; Phi Alpha Delta; Kappa Sigma. Polit & Govt Pos: Asst secy, Rep Exec Comt, Ga, 64-66, mem, 64-68; mem, Rep State Cent Comt Ga, 64-; chmn, Ware Co Rep Comt, formerly; asst treas, Ga Rep Party, 66-68, parliamentarian, 68-69; vchmn, Eighth Dist Rep Comt, 68-72; mem, Ga Adv Comt, President's Cabinet Comt on Educ, 70-72. Mil Serv: Entered as Pvt, Air Force, 42, released as S/Sgt, 45, after serv in Hq USAFISPA & HQ SoPacBaCom, Asiatic Pac, 43-45; Asiatic-Pac Serv Medal with Bronze Star; Am Serv Medal; Victory Medal; Philippine Liberation Medal; Good Conduct Medal. Publ: Insurance sect in Mercer Law Rev, 56. Mem: Am Judicature Soc; Am Bar Asn; Waycross Bar Asn; Waycross Circuit Bar Asn (pres); Ga Exchange Clubs. Relig: Baptist. Mailing Add: 1504 Satilla Blvd Waycross GA 31501

PECK, BARBARA MAY (R)
Committeeman, Pinal Co Rep Comt, Ariz
b Jackson, Mich, May 11, 26; d Robert Frederick Rockwell & Mae Boger R; m 1952 to Vinton Meade Peck; c Ronald Craig, Pamela Mae & Patricia Meade. Educ: Jackson Bus Univ, 1 year. Polit & Govt Pos: Committeeman, Pinal Co Rep Comt, 62-, vchairwoman, 64-68, chmn, 68-72; vpres, Apache Junction Rep Women, 63, pres, 64, treas, 65, 68; dep registr, Pinal Co Recorder, 66-; alt deleg, Rep Nat Conv, 68 & 72; chmn of nominations, Ariz Fedn Rep Women, 68, membership chmn, 69, secy, 71-73, 1st vpres, 73-75, pres, 75- Bus & Prof Pos: Bookkeeper, Kennedy Hardware, Anchorage, Alaska, 51, 52; off mgr, Peck & Peck Construction, 59- Mem: CofC; Youth Boosters; Beta Sigma Phi; PTA; Apache Junction Soroptomist (first vpres). Honors & Awards: Named Woman of the Year by Beta Sigma Phi. Relig: Methodist. Legal Res: 1574 Boila St Apache Junction AZ 85220 Mailing Add: Rte 1 Box 1574 Apache Junction AZ 85220

PECK, GRACE OLIVIER (D)
Ore State Rep
Mailing Add: 2324 S E Ivon Portland OR 97202

PECK, RAYMOND STUART (D)
Mass State Rep
b New Bedford, Mass, Dec 10, 22; s Walter Peck & Gertrude E Costa P; m 1943 to Eleanor Louise Bouchie; c Robert Earl & Brenda Joyce. Educ: Dartmouth High Sch; Providence Bus & Trade; Kingston Trade. Polit & Govt Pos: Mem town meeting, Dartmouth, Mass, 51-66, mem, Recreation Comn, 59-62, mem, Bd Pub Welfare & selectman, 62-64; vet agt, 62-63; Mass State Rep, 64-; alt deleg, Dem Nat Conv, 68. Bus & Prof Pos: Owner, Smith Mills Sport Supply, 62-; owner, Dartmouth Golf Driving Range, currently. Mem: KofC, St Isidore; Farmer Coun; Rotary. Relig: Roman Catholic. Mailing Add: 25 Summit Ave North Dartmouth MA 02747

PECK, RUTH (R)
Ariz State Rep
Mailing Add: 510 East Medlock Dr Phoenix AZ 85012

PECK, WILLIAM R, III (D)
Secy-VChmn, Brown Co Dem Statutory Party, Wis
b Sigel, Wis, July 30, 31; s William R Peck, Jr & Alma M Lassa P; m 1956 to Sally Ann Neff; c William R, IV, David Brian & Steven Dwight. Educ: US Armed Forces Inst, Denver, Colo, 50-51, Naha AFB, Okinawa, 51-53 & San Jose State Col, 54; Western Adjustment & Inspection Co Sch, Chicago, Ill, 59; Liberty Sch of Claims Investigation, Libertyville, Ill, 60; Hon Order of Blue Goose Int. Polit & Govt Pos: Treas, Brown Co Dem Statutory Party, Wis, 61-63, secy-vchmn, 63-, vchmn, Third Assembly Dist, 63-; Eighth Dist Field Rep, John Kennedy for President Comt, 63; Eighth Dist field rep, Pat Lucey for Gov Comt, 66; treas, Eighth Cong Dist Wis for Johnson for President, 68; Brown Co Co-Chmn, Robert Kennedy for President Comt, 68; chmn, Muskie for President, Northeast Wis, 71-72; chmn, Cassie Danen Dinner, De Pere, 71; exec vchmn, De Pere Pat Lucey for Gov Dinners Comt, 71-72. Bus & Prof Pos: Charter mem, Nat Asn Legal Investrs; mem bd dirs, Nat Asn Fire Investrs, 68- Mil Serv: Entered as Airman Basic, Air Force, 50, released as S/Sgt, 54 after serv in Fighter Squadron, Naha AFB, Okinawa, Korean Conflict, 51-53, recalled as S/Sgt, Air Force, 54-59, Ground Observer Corps, Field Rep for Wis Civil Defense; Korean Ribbon; Good Conduct Medal; Overseas Far East. Mem: Brown Co Dep Sheriff Asn; Am Soc Notary Pub; Nat Asn of Missing Persons; Brown Co Adjusters Asn; Wis Consumer League (pres pro-tem, Green Bay chap). Relig: Catholic. Legal Res: 1646 Amy St Green Bay WI 54302 Mailing Add: 3731 Green Bay WI 54305

PEDEN, PRESTON E (D)
b Duke, Okla, June 28, 14; married; c Four. Educ: Univ Okla, AB, 36, LLB, 39. Polit & Govt Pos: Attorney for State Ins Fund, Okla, 39-42; US Rep, Okla, 46-47; counsel for Comt on Interior & Insular Affairs, US House of Rep, 49-53; regional counsel for Bur of Land Mgt, Dept of Interior, Alaska, 50; dir, Govt Affairs Div, Chicago Asn Com & Indust, 54- Bus & Prof Pos: Lawyer, 46- Mil Serv: Entered as Pvt, Army, 42, released as Capt, 46, after serv as Forward Observer, 87th Inf Div & Prosecutor & Judge in Mil Govt Courts of Upper Bavaria; Bronze Star. Mem: Okla & Ill State Bars. Mailing Add: 130 S Michigan Ave Chicago IL 60603

PEDERSEN, RICHARD F
US Ambassador, Hungary
b Ariz, Feb 21, 25; married; c Three. Educ: Univ Pac, BA, 46; Stanford Univ, MA, 47; Harvard Univ, PhD, 50. Hon Degrees: LLD, George Williams Col, 64, Univ of the Pac, 65. Polit & Govt Pos: With Dept of State, 50-, US Mission to UN, 53-69, adv on Econ & Soc Affairs, 53-56, adv on Polit & Security Affairs, 56-59, chief of Polit Sect, 59-64, counsr, US Mission, 64-66, sr adv to US Rep to UN, 66-67, dep US Rep in UN Security Coun, 67-69, counsr, US Dept of State, 69-73, US Ambassador, Hungary, 73- Bus & Prof Pos: Col instr in int rels, law & govt, 49-50. Mil Serv: Army, 43-45. Mem: Am Soc for Int Law; Am Foreign Serv Asn; Am Acad Polit & Soc Sci; YMCA (nat bd, 65-). Relig: Congregational. Legal Res: MD Mailing Add: Dept of State Washington DC 20521

PEDERSON, VERNON R (INDEPENDENT)
Assoc Justice, NDak Supreme Court
b Surrey, NDak, Sept 11, 19; s John Pederson & Tilda Torgerson P; m 1952 to Evelyn Kraby; c Kathy & Mary. Educ: Minot State Col, 37-40; Univ NDak, BSC, 46, LLB, 49, JD, 69; Phi Delta Phi; Tau Kappa Epsilon. Polit & Govt Pos: City justice, Minot, NDak, 49-51; spec agt-attorney, Off Price Stabilization, Fargo, 51-53; Spec Asst Attorney Gen, NDak, 53-74; Assoc Justice, NDak Supreme Court, 75- Bus & Prof Pos: Pres, Mo Slope Nursing Home, Bismarck, NDak, 70-71. Mil Serv: Entered as Pvt, Army, 41, released as S/Sgt, 45, after serv in 188th Field Artil, ETO, 43-45; 1st Lt(Ret), Judge Adv, Air Force Res, 56. Mem: NDak State & Am Bar Asns; Am Judicature Soc. Relig: Lutheran; pres, Good Shepherd Lutheran Church, Bismarck, 65-66. Mailing Add: 2029 Second St Bismarck ND 58501

PEDERSON, W DENNIS (DFL)
b Willmar, Minn, July 19, 38; s Oscar Pederson & Esther Ness Pederson (deceased); m 1962 to Sylvia Ruth Ostergaard; c Nathan John & Kristen Joy. Educ: Augsburg Col, BA, 60, Augsburg Theol Sem, BTh, 63; Univ Minn, Minneapolis, MHA, 66. Polit & Govt Pos: Chmn, Seventh Dist Young Dem-Farmer-Labor, 56-68; mem, Young People for Stevenson; chmn, Lutherans for Kennedy, Minneapolis, 59-60; chmn, Young Am for Kennedy-Johnson; chmn, Augsburg Col Students for Fraser, 62; finance chmn, Clay Co Dem-Farmer-Labor Party, 67-70; coordr, Clay-Wilkin Young Am Vol for Humphrey, 68; Dem-Farmer-Labor cand for Lt Gov, Minn, 70; Northwestern Minn advocate, Wendell R Anderson for Gov Vol Comt, 70-71; mem, Minn Dem-Farmer-Labor State Exec Comt, 71-72; staff asst, Off of Gov, Minn, 71-, legis coordr, currently. Bus & Prof Pos: Admin asst, Fairview Hosp, Minneapolis, Minn, 66-67; instr hosp admin, Univ Minn, Minneapolis, 66-67; asst prof hosp admin, Concordia Col (Moorhead, Minn), 67-70; exec dir, Northern Allied Health Inst, 69-70. Publ: A hospital system developed through a satellite system, US Surgeon Gen Report, 3/67; Emerging role of the chaplain in hospital patient care, 5/1/69 & Can more part-time nurses be recruited? 5/16/69, Hospitals. Mem: Minn Hosp Asn. Honors & Awards: Olaf Rogne mem Scholarship Award; Augsburg Gtr Alumni Grad Scholarship Award; Hosp Admin Class Award, 54; Outstanding Young Man of Moorhead, Minn, 70; Distinguished Serv Award, 70. Relig: Lutheran. Mailing Add: 4115 Burton Lane Minneapolis MN 55406

PEEBLES, ROBERT (R)
Secy, Scioto Co Rep Exec Comt, Ohio
b Portsmouth, Ohio, Feb 26, 08; s Samuel Coles Peebles & Helena Salmon P; div; c Pamela Lee. Educ: Ohio State Univ, BS, 31; Alpha Tau Omega. Polit & Govt Pos: Rep Precinct Committeeman, Scioto Co, Ohio, 46-; Sixth Dist Committeeman, Rep State Cent Comt, 50-54; area rep, programmed all housing for Atomic Installation in Portsmouth Area, Dept of Housing & Urban Develop, 52-54; secy, Scioto Co Rep Exec Comt, 69- Mil Serv: Entered as Lt, Army, 40, released as Maj, 46, after serv in 37th Div Field Artil, SE Pac, 42-45. Mem: Mason; Elks; Am Legion; VFW. Relig: Presbyterian. Legal Res: Rte 2 McDermott OH 45652 Mailing Add: Box 720 Portsmouth OH 45662

PEELER, JAMES ALFRED, JR (D)
Mem, Tenn Dem Exec Comt
b Covington, Tenn, Nov 8, 13; s James Alfred Peeler & Jennie Huffman P; m 1962 to Mildred Brown; c Meredith & James Alfred, III. Educ: Byars Hall High Sch, grad, 32. Polit & Govt Pos: Mem, Tenn Dem Exec Comt, 57-, chmn, formerly; deleg, Dem Nat Conv, 68 & 72. Bus & Prof Pos: Farmer & owner of cotton gin, Covington, Tenn, 32- Mil Serv: Entered as Pvt, Army, 42, released as 1st Lt, 46, after serv as Finance Officer, Far E Air Force, 43-46; Good Conduct Medal; Am Theatre Ribbon; Asiatic Pac Theatre Ribbon with two Bronze Serv Stars; World War II Victory Medal. Mem: Am Legion; VFW. Relig: Methodist. Mailing Add: 803 W Liberty St Covington TN 38019

PEEPLES, JACK TERRY (D)
Miss State Rep
b Greenwood, Miss, Jan 16, 44; s Jack Terry Peeples (deceased) & Mary Anne Holley P; m 1967 to Mary Dawn Boxx. Educ: Miss State Univ, BA, 66; Univ Miss, JD, 69. Polit & Govt Pos: Miss State Rep, 71- Mil Serv: Entered as 1st Lt, Army, 70, released as 1st Lt, 70, after serv in Air Defense Artil Sch, Ft Bliss, Tex; 1st Lt, Army Res, 70-; Nat Defense Medal; Rifleman's Expert Badge. Mem: Miss Bar Asn; Am Judicature Soc; Skuna Deer Club; CofC; Jaycees. Relig: Baptist. Mailing Add: PO Box 240 Coffeeville MS 38922

PEET, RICHARD CLAYTON (R)
b New York, NY, Aug 24, 28; s Charles F Peet & Florence Isaacs P; m 1956 to Barbara J McClure; c Victoria C, Alexandra C & Elizabeth E. Educ: Tulane Univ, BA, 50, JD & LLB, 53; Pi Kappa Alpha; Phi Delta Phi; Soc Droit Civil. Polit & Govt Pos: Attorney, Lands Div, Dept Justice, 55-56; asst to gen counsel, Dept Com, 57; prof staff, Senate Rep Policy Comt, 58; legis asst, US Sen Knowland, Calif, 58-59; assoc counsel, Antitrust Subcomt, House Judiciary Comt, 59-62; assoc minority counsel, House Pub Works Comt, 68- Bus & Prof Pos: Attorney, Washington, DC, 62-68; managing dir, Lincoln Research Ctr, 65-68; with RCP Assocs, 66-69. Mil Serv: Entered as Pvt, Army, 46, released as Sgt, 47, after serv in Korea. Publ: SAC's kissing cousins, 64 & Force de dissuasion, 65, Air Force & Space Digest; Goals for constructive opposition, Lincoln Research Ctr, 66. Mem: Int Inst Space Law; Int Astronaut Asn; Am Inst Aeronaut & Astronaut; Nat Space Club; Tulane Alumni Club of Washington (founder & pres, 60-). Honors & Awards: George Washington Medal, Freedom's Found of Valley Forge, 72. Relig: Christian. Legal Res: 4500 Vista del Monte Sherman Oaks Los Angeles CA 91403 Mailing Add: 824 Whann Ave McLean VA 22101

PEGUES, R LEIGH (D)
Ala State Rep
Mailing Add: 202 Early St Marion AL 36756

PEHLER, JAMES (JIM) (DFL)
Minn State Rep
Mailing Add: 734 14th Ave S St Cloud MN 56301

PEIRONNET, JAMES STEPHEN, JR (R)
NMex State Sen
b Oak Park, Ill, May 16, 36; s James Stephen Peironnet & Violette Haskin P; m 1958 to Charlotte Louise Ward; wid; c Cheryl Renee. Educ: Univ NMex, BA, 64; Delta Sigma Phi; Esquire Club. Polit & Govt Pos: NMex State Sen, Dist 15, 73-, mem educ & conserv comts, NMex State Senate, 73- Bus & Prof Pos: High sch teacher, Albuquerque Pub Schs, 65-70, team leader, 70- Mil Serv: Entered as Seaman Recruit, Navy, 54, released as PO, 59, after serv in USS Essex & USS Intrepid; PO 1/C, Naval Res, 15 years. Relig: Episcopal. Mailing Add: 4701 Comanche Rd NE Albuquerque NM 87110

PEIRSON, MARY WOOD (R)
Asst Secy, Del Rep State Comt
b Philadelphia, Pa, Apr 8, 22; d Edgar N Wood & Mary Hedderman W; m 1943 to David D Peirson; c Mary (Mrs Harris), Barbara (Mrs Mathers), David R, Kathleen, Patti Lynn & Donald James. Educ: Univ of Chattanooga, BS Chem, 42; Gamma Sigma Epsilon; Beta Beta Beta. Polit & Govt Pos: Alt committeewoman, St Georges Hundred, 58-69; asst secy, Del Rep State Comt, 62- Bus & Prof Pos: Chemist, Hercules Powder Co, Wilmington, Del, 42; chemist, Tenn Valley Authority, Chattanooga, Tenn, 43; teacher, St Paul's, Delaware City, Del, 66-69; real estate salesman, Peirwood Realty Co, currently. Mem: Am Asn of Univ Women; Bus & Prof Women; Farm Bur. Relig: Catholic. Mailing Add: RD 2 Box 43 Middletown DE 19709

PELIKAN, ROBERT L (D)
b Wis, Aug 11, 49; s Paul G Pelikan & Lois P; m 1970 to Ann Bartelmas; c Steven J & Cory. Educ: Waukesha High Sch, grad, 67. Polit & Govt Pos: Deleg, Dem Nat Mid-Term Conf, 74; membership secy, Waukesha Co Dem Party, 75- Bus & Prof Pos: Cost acct, Waukesha Foundry Co, 71- Relig: Methodist. Mailing Add: 1165 Whiterock Ave Apt 32 Waukesha WI 53186

PELL, CLAIBORNE (D)
US Sen, RI
b New York, NY, Nov 22, 18; s Hon Herbert Claiborne Pell & Matilda Bigelow P; m 1944 to Nuala O'Donnell; c Herbert III, Christopher, Dallas & Julia. Educ: Princeton Univ, AB cum laude, 40; Columbia Univ, AM. Polit & Govt Pos: Spec asst at San Francisco UN Conf; exec asst to RI Dem State Comn, 52 & 54; consult, Dem Nat Comt, 53-60; Dem Nat Registrn Chmn, 56; chief deleg tally clerk, Dem Nat Conv, 56, 60, 64 & 68, deleg, 68 & 72; with US Foreign Serv & State Dept, 7 years; US deleg to Intergovt Maritime Consultative Orgn in London, 59; vpres, Int Rescue Comt, until 60; mem, Nat Coun of Refugees; treas, Am Immigration Conf; US Sen, RI, 60-; deleg, Dem Nat Mid-Term Conf, 74. Bus & Prof Pos: Bus exec; investments. Mil Serv: Entered Coast Guard prior to World War II, released as Lt; Capt, Coast Guard Res, currently. Honors & Awards: Decorated by France, Italy, Portugal Liechtenstein & Knights of Malta. Legal Res: Newport RI Mailing Add: 325 Old Senate Off Bldg Washington DC 20510

PELLECCHIA, VINCENT OZZIE (D)
NJ State Assemblyman
Mailing Add: State House Trenton NJ 08625

PELLETT, WENDELL C (R)
Iowa State Rep
Mailing Add: 408 Maple Atlantic IA 50022

PELOQUIN, BRUCE SIMON (D)
Wis State Sen
b Chippewa Falls, Wis, Nov 3, 36; s Frank Simon Peloquin & Anna Marie Normand P; m 1967 to Stephanie Baker; c Tracy Claire & Dean Michael. Educ: Wis State Univ, BA in Bus & Psychol, 66; Univ Wis-Eau Claire, MSEd, 73; Beta Upsilon Sigma. Polit & Govt Pos: Co bd supvr, Chippewa Co, Wis, 64-66; Wis State Assemblyman, Chippewa Co, 65-70; mem exec comt, Chippewa Co Dem Party, 66; Wis State Sen, 71- Bus & Prof Pos: Supvr, US Rubber Co, Eau Claire, Wis, 58; clerical worker, Minn Mining & Mfg Co, 61. Mem: KofC. Honors & Awards: Various jour awards, Col & High Sch Publ. Relig: Catholic. Mailing Add: RR 5 Box 357 Chippewa Falls WI 54729

PELOQUIN, J CAMILLE (D)
RI State Rep
Mailing Add: 123 Albion Rd Manville RI 02838

PELOQUIN, J CAMILLE, SR (D)
RI State Rep
b Manville, RI, Jan 24, 28; s Theodore Peloquin (deceased) & Alma Dupuis P; m 1949 to Phyllis Cook; c J Camille, Jr, Linda Louise, Ronald N & Theodore A. Educ: RI Col. Polit & Govt Pos: Mem, Lincoln Dem Town Comt & Manville Dem Dist Comt, RI, 57; RI State Rep, 64- Bus & Prof Pos: Inspection & gage control; foreman, Anti-Submarine Warfare Div, Raytheon Co, 60- Mil Serv: Entered Army, 45, released as Sgt, 47, after serv in Inf as cook, Pac-Manila Theater. Mem: Manville Fireman's Asn & Fire Dept; Montcalm & Roosevelt Clubs; CofC. Relig: Catholic. Mailing Add: 1412 Old River Rd Manville RI 02838

PELOQUIN, RICHARD PAUL (D)
b Springfield, Vt, Mar 21, 44; s Wilfred Leonard Peloquin & Gertrude Paul P; m 1964 to Barbara DiBernardo; c Timothy Kierman & Rian Connor. Educ: Keene State Col, 63-64. Polit & Govt Pos: Deleg, NH Dem Conv, 72; deleg, Dem Nat Conv, 72; city councilman, Keene, NH, 72- Bus & Prof Pos: Field engr, IBM Corp, 67- Mem: Jaycees (secy, 70-71). Mailing Add: 308 Pearl St Keene NH 03431

PELOSI, RONALD (D)
Pres, San Francisco Bd of Supvr, Calif
b San Francisco, Calif, Nov 2, 34; s John Pelosi & Corinne Bianchi P; m 1956 to Barbara Newsom; c Brennan John, Matthew Francis & Laurence Kenelm. Educ: Stanford Univ, AB, 56; Georgetown Univ Grad Sch, 56-57. Polit & Govt Pos: Mem, San Francisco Co Dem Cent Comt, Calif, 60-64; mem, Calif State Dem Cent Comt, 62-64; mem, San Francisco Planning Comn, 64-67, pres, 66; deleg, Dem Nat Conv, 68; supvr, San Francisco Bd of Supvr, Calif, 68-, pres, 72- Bus & Prof Pos: Stockbroker, Brush Slocumb & Co, San Francisco, mem firm NY Stock Exchange, 57-61, J Barth & Co, San Francisco, mem firm, NY Stock Exchange, 57-61, J Barth & Co, 61-, Dean Witter & Co, San Francisco, 71-, Hambrecht & Quist, 73- Relig: Roman Catholic. Mailing Add: 18 Sixth Ave San Francisco CA 94118

PELOSI, THOMAS SANBAR (D)
Maine State Rep
b Portland, Maine, June 18, 44; s John M Pelosi & Mary Sanbar P; m to Ann Joyce; c Catherine Joyce & Sarah Ann. Educ: Univ Maine, Portland, BA, 68. Polit & Govt Pos: Maine State Rep, 75- Bus & Prof Pos: Owner real estate bus, Portland, Maine, 68- Relig: Catholic. Legal Res: 21 Massachusetts Ave Portland ME 04102 Mailing Add: State House Augusta ME 04330

PELTIER, HARVEY A, JR (D)
La State Sen
b Thibodaux, La, Jan 18, 23; s Harvey A Peltier & May Ayo P; m 1945 to Irma Geheeb; c Patricia E, Harvey A, III & Mary Ellen. Educ: Spring Hill Col, BS, 44. Polit & Govt Pos: La State Sen, 15th Sen Dist, 64- Bus & Prof Pos: Mem bd dirs, Bay Drilling Corp. Mil Serv: A/S, Navy, 43. Mem: Am Legion; Amvets; DAV; Nicholls Century Club; Nicholls Col Club. Honors & Awards: Named Outstanding Citizen by VFW; Grand Marshall, Thibodaux Fire Dept. Relig: Roman Catholic. Legal Res: 102 Cherokee St Thibodaux LA 70301 Mailing Add: PO Box 1097 Thibodaux LA 70301

PELTON, HORACE WILBUR (R)
Chmn, Wood Co Rep Exec Comt, Ohio
b Bloomdale, Ohio, Dec 16, 06; s Earl Theron Pelton & Lola Emerson P; m 1935 to Marjorie Burtsfield; c Rebecca (Mrs Clifton Babcock) & Thomas Earl. Educ: Bowling Green State Univ, BS, 29; Ohio State Univ, MD, 38; Sigma Alpha Epsilon. Polit & Govt Pos: Chmn, Wood Co Rep Exec Comt, Ohio, 74- Bus & Prof Pos: Teacher social studies & econ, Berea, Ohio, 29-43, Bowling Green, 45-47 & Findlay, 63-72; owner-operator farm, Wood Co, 43-; dir, Harcock-Wood Elec Coop, NBaltimore, Ohio, 56-64. Mem: Farm Bur (adv coun); Bloomdale Commercial Club. Relig: Christian; elder. Mailing Add: 6658 Eagleville Rd Bloomdale OH 44817

PELZER, MAX O (R)
b Griswold, Iowa, Nov 23, 31; s Irvin Pelzer & Dollie Sothman P; m 1955 to Bonnie Krueger; c Mark, Sheryl, Scott & Todd. Educ: Iowa State Univ. Polit & Govt Pos: Chmn, Emmet Co Rep Party, Iowa, formerly. Mil Serv: Entered as Seaman, Navy, 51, released as At-2, 55, after serv in Morocco. Mem: Kiwanis; VFW; Isaak Walton League; Farm Bur; Iowa Bar Asn. Relig: Methodist. Mailing Add: 408 N Eighth St Estherville IA 51334

PEMBERTON, MACK (R)
Ohio State Rep
Mailing Add: 2949 Crescent Dr Columbus OH 43204

PENA, ABE M (R)
b San Mateo, NMex, Nov 8, 26; s Pablo Pena & Pablita Marquez P; m 1955 to Viola Ruth Cisneros; c Ramona, Paula, Cecilia & Marco Jose. Educ: NMex State Univ, BS, 49; Fulbright scholar, Univ New South Wales, Australia, grad work, 54; Alpha Zeta; Agr Club; Block & Bridle; pres, Conquistadores. Polit & Govt Pos: Campaign mgr, Valencia Co Rep Party, NMex, 58; mem, State Agr Stabilization & Conserv Comt, 59-61; mem, Los Lunas Hosp & Training Sch, 60-61; mem state exec comt, NMex Rep Party, 60-62, vchmn, 71-72; mem, NMex Rep State Cent Comt, 61-71; bd mem & secy, NMex Livestock Bd, 67-71; dir, Peace Corps, Honduras, 72- Mil Serv: Entered as Pvt, Army, 50, released as Pvt, 52, after serv in Vet Serv. Mem: NMex Wool Growers Asn (vpres, 61-66, pres, 66-67); NMex Cattle Growers Asn (adv bd, 66-71); Valencia Co Farm & Livestock Bur (dir, 67-71); Grants-West Valencia CofC (dir, 62-64). Honors & Awards: Hon State Farmer, Future Farmers Am. Relig: Catholic. Legal Res: 700 Jefferson Grants NM 87020 Mailing Add: c/o Am Embassy Tequcigalpa Honduras

PENA, DENNIS S (D)
NMex State Rep
b Bosque, NMex, June 9, 35; s Justinian C Pena & Caroline Sais P; m 1957 to Patricia J Booth; c Mike, Mark, Caroline & Dave. Educ: Univ NMex Col Pharm, BS, 57; Kappa Psi; Alpha Phi Omega. Polit & Govt Pos: NMex State Rep, 75- Mil Serv: Entered as Recruit, Army, 59, released, 60, after serv in 2nd Gen Hosp, Landstuhl, Ger. Mem: NMex Pharmaceut Asn (pres, 74-; chmn nat legis comt, 75-); PTA; Am Automobile Asn (bd dirs); YMCA (bd dirs); NMex Heart Asn (bd dirs). Relig: Roman Catholic. Mailing Add: 5001 Sunningdale Ave Albuquerque NM 87110

PENA, MANUEL, JR (D)
Ariz State Sen
b Cashion, Ariz, Nov 17, 24; s Manuel Pena & Elvira Gomez P; m 1945 to Aurora Cruz; c Yolanda, Mary Ann, Henry, Estevan, Patricia, Geraldine & Manuel, III. Polit & Govt Pos: Comt mem, Ariz State Dem Party, 62-66, asst dir voter registr, 64; exec secy, State Athletic Comn, asst co chmn, Maricopa Co Dem Party & legis area chmn, Eighth Dist Dem Party, 64-66; Ariz State Rep, 67-73; Ariz State Sen, Dist 22, 73- Bus & Prof Pos: Pres, Pena Realty & Trust Co; owner, Pena Ins Agency, 51- Mil Serv: Entered as Pfc, 46, after serv in 31st Inf Regt, SPac Theatre. Mem: Am Legion; VFW. Relig: Catholic. Legal Res: 3728 W Willetta Phoenix AZ 85009 Mailing Add: PO Box 6482 Phoenix AZ 85005

PENA, R G (DANNY) (D)
Ariz State Rep
Mailing Add: 1847 North 39th Ave Phoenix AZ 85009

PENDERGAST, M ABBOTT (R)
Mem, Maine Rep State Comt
b Reading, Pa, Feb 20, 20; s Ralph E Pendergast & Ann Boone P; m 1950 to Margueritte Craig; c Margueritte Elizabeth, Craig Abbott & Margaret Anne. Educ: Penn State Exten Sch Metallurgy, 41-43; Univ Pa Exten, Wharton Sch Finance, 46-49. Polit & Govt Pos: Chmn, Kennebunkport Rep Town Comt, Maine, 52-56; committeeman, York Co Rep Comt, 56-60, chmn, 69-72; selectman, Town of Kennebunkport, 57-64, mem, Bd Selectmen, 73-, chmn, 75-; Maine State Rep, 64-68, secy, Pub Utilities Comt, Maine House Rep, 64-66; chmn, Transportation Comt, 66-68; mem, Maine Rep State Comt, currently. Bus & Prof Pos: Registered rep, Hayden Stone & Co, Portland, Maine, 59-62; registered rep, Bache & Co, Boston, 62-72; pres, Ocean Bluff Realty Co, Kennebunkport, 72- Mil Serv: Entered as Pvt, Army, 43, released as Pfc, 46, after serv in 11th Inf Bn, First Armored Div, Italy & 85th Mountain Inf Regt, 10th Div, ETO; ETO Ribbon with Four Battle Stars; Distinguished Unit Citation, Co B, 11th Inf, Plazzo, Italy; Good Conduct Ribbon; plus others. Mem: Webber Hosp Asn, Biddleford; Newcomen Soc NAm (Maine comt); AF&AM; St Amand Commandry; charter mem York Co Shrine Club & Kora Temple, Lewiston; US Coast Guard Auxiliary, Portsmouth, NH (past Flotilla Comdr). Relig: Congregational. Mailing Add: 450 Ocean Ave Kennebunkport ME 04046

PENDERGAST, PAUL EDWARD (D)
b Dalhart, Tex, Jan 15, 36; s J F Pendergast & Irene Harrington P; m 1966 to Sharon Ann Tork; c Amy. Educ: St Benedict's Col, AB, 58; Washburn Univ Law Sch, JD, 70; Phi Alpha Delta. Polit & Govt Pos: Asst to chmn, Dem Nat Comt, 61-64; staff asst, Off of Secy of Interior, 65; exec secy, Kans Dem State Comt, 65-69; exec asst to Gov, Kans, 67-68; admin asst to US Rep William R Roy, 71-75; admin asst to US Rep Martha Keys, currently. Mem: Kans & Am Bar Asns. Relig: Catholic. Legal Res: Topeka KS Mailing Add: 3418 Arrowhead Rd Topeka KS 66614

PENDERGRAFT, PHYLLIS M (R)
VChairwoman, Sixth Dist Rep Party, Va
b Henrico Co, Va, June 17, 37; m 1961 to Gradon O'Kelly Pendergraft, Jr; c Jimese Lynne. Educ: Clifton Force High Sch, Va, 4 years; Dunsmore Bus Col, Va, 52-53. Polit & Govt Pos: Pres, Waynesboro Rep Women, Va, 64-66; vchairwoman, Seventh Dist Rep Party, 66-72, Sixth Dist, 72-, chmn, Cands for Cong, 70, chmn, records comt, currently; temporary chmn, 19th Sen Conv, 67; deleg, State Rep Conv, 67, 68, 69; deleg, Nat Rep Conv, 68, served on platform comt, 68; mem, Robinson for Cong Adv Comt, & Garland for Sen Steering Comt, 70; arrangements chmn, Seventh Dist Rep Conv, 70; arrangements chmn, 15th Legis Dist, Va, 72- Bus & Prof Pos: Secy, Gen Elec Co, Waynesboro, Va, 59-67; receptionist, 67- Mem: Rep Women's Club; Waynesboro Friends of Libr; Waynesboro Choral Soc (secy); Int Platform Asn; Bus & Prof Women. Honors & Awards: Named to Gov Comm on Status of Women. Relig: Presbyterian. Mailing Add: 1308 Crofton Waynesboro VA 22980

PENDERGRASS, PAULA ARMBRUSTER (D)
Mem, Ark Dem State Comt
b Ft Smith, Ark, Aug 26, 36; d Paul Henry Armbruster & Alma Roberts A; m 1954 to John Frank Pendergrass; c John Paul. Educ: Ark Polytech Col, 54-56; Univ Ark, Fayetteville, 61; Assoc Women Students. Polit & Govt Pos: Mem, South Franklin Co Dem Women, Ark, 69-; dist circuit clerk, Franklin Co, 69-75, co libr trustee, 71-; mem, Ark Dem State Comt, 74-; chmn state libr trustees, Ark Libr Asn, 75- Publ: Co-ed, A Time of Change—A Centennial, Calvert-McBride, 74. Mem: Charleston CofC (bd dirs, 70-); Ark Farm Bur Fedn Auxiliary; Action Comt Rural Elec; Ark Sch Supvr Asn. Honors & Awards: Silver Medallion Award, Charleston CofC, 74. Relig: Methodist. Mailing Add: Rte 2 Box 113 Charleston AR 72933

PENDLETON, DON MILTON (R)
Chmn, Lincoln Co Rep Party, NC
b Lincoln Co, NC, Feb 12, 35; s Kermit Pendleton & Eula Beam P; m 1959 to Lessy Sain; c Don Milton, Jr & Kermit Clay. Educ: Wake Forest Law Sch, LLB, 58. Polit & Govt Pos: Chmn, Lincoln Co Rep Party, 65-; deleg, Rep Nat Conv, 72. Mem: Lincoln Co CofC. Relig: Baptist. Legal Res: 211 N Academy St Lincolnton NC 28092 Mailing Add: PO Box 159 Lincolnton NC 28092

PENDLETON, DONALD GREY (D)
Va State Deleg
b Lynchburg, Va, Jan 11, 32; m to Shirley Elizabeth Ewers. Educ: Phillips Bus Col; Lynchburg Col, BA, Polit Sci; Univ Va, LLB. Polit & Govt Pos: Asst trial judge, Amherst Co; pres, Young Dem Club, formerly; chmn, Dem Exec Comt; Va State Deleg, 66-; deleg, Dem Nat Mid-Term Conf, 74. Bus & Prof Pos: Attorney. Mil Serv: Korean War, 49-53. Mem: Am Trial Lawyers Asn; Ruritan; WOW; Mason; Odd Fellows. Legal Res: Vista Dr Amherst VA 24521 Mailing Add: PO Box 493 Amherst VA 24521

PENDLETON, EDMUND E (R)
Chmn, DC Rep State Comt
b St Louis, Mo, June 8, 22; s Edmund E Pendleton & Katharine Burum P; m to Josephine Culbertson; c 5 daughters. Educ: Wharton Sch Finance & Com Univ Pa, BS in Econ, 42; Georgetown Univ Law Sch, JD, 48; George Washington Univ Sch of Law, LLM, 50. Polit & Govt Pos: Pres, Young Rep Club of DC, 48-49 & 53-54; confidential asst to Asst Secy of Agr, US Dept of Agr, 55-57; counsel for minority, Senate Subcomt on Nat Policy Machinery,

60; mem, DC Rep State Comt & chmn, 69- Bus & Prof Pos: Attorney-at-law, Washington, DC, 48- Mil Serv: Army, 42-46. Mailing Add: 4727 Woodway Lane NW Washington DC 20016

PENELLO, JOHN ALLEN (D)
b Norfolk, Va, Aug 27, 09; s Francisco Penello & Maria Christina Toscana P; m 1939 to Doris Ridgely; c Anne (Mrs John Depenbrock), Doris (Mrs Curtis Ritter) & Cristine. Educ: Col William & Mary, BS, 34, LLB, 37; Omicron Delta Kappa; Alpha Phi Delta. Polit & Govt Pos: Chief exam, Nat Labor Rels Bd, Baltimore, Md & New York, 37-44, regional dir, St Louis, Mo & Minneapolis, Minn, 44-48, regional dir, Baltimore, Md, 48-72, assoc gen coun, Washington, DC, 58, bd mem, 72- Mem: Va Bar. Relig: Episcopal. Mailing Add: 55 Boone Trail Severna Park MD 21146

PENISTEN, GARY D
Asst Secy Navy Financial Mgt
Mailing Add: Dept of the Navy Pentagon Washington DC 20350

PENIX, BILL (D)
Secy, Craighead Co Dem Cent Comt, Ark
b Jonesboro, Ark, Oct 10, 22; s Roy Penix & Billie Broadway P; m 1945 to Marian Fox; c Susan Ellen (Mrs Mixon), Bill Jr, Charley & Jane Lee. Educ: Univ Ark, BA, 43, LLB, 49; Blue Key; Phi Alpha Delta; Sigma Chi. Polit & Govt Pos: Dep prosecuting attorney, Craighead Co, Ark, 49-55; secy, Craighead Co Dem Cent Comt, 58-; mem, Jonesboro Sch Bd, 67-; deleg, Dem Nat Conv, 68; state campaign mgr, Fulbright for Senate, 69; mem, State Dem Cent Comt, 69; mem, Ark State Dem Exec Comt, 70- Bus & Prof Pos: Lawyer, Penix & Penix, Jonesboro, Ark, 49- Mil Serv: Entered as Pvt, Army, 42, released as 1st Lt, 46, after serv in CHQ Signal Opers, Southwest-Pac, 44-46; Army Res, Maj (Ret); Asiatic-Pac Campaign Medal with three stars; Philippine Liberation Medal with two stars. Mem: Craighead Co, Ark & Am Bar Asns; Am Legion; Lions. Relig: Methodist. Legal Res: 1011 Neville Ave Jonesboro AR 72401 Mailing Add: PO Box 1306 Jonesboro AR 72401

PENIX, CHAUNCEY EDWARD (D)
b Big Spring, Tex, July 23, 03; s Stephen Austin Penix & Forra Argie Lindsey P; m 1925 to Mildred Tidwell. Educ: Univ Tex. Polit & Govt Pos: Co attorney, 27-30; asst dist attorney, Tex, 32-34; chmn, Young Co Dem Exec Comt, formerly. Bus & Prof Pos: Pres, Graham Fed Savings & Loan Asn, 52-66. Mil Serv: Entered as 2nd Lt, Army Air Force, 42, released as Lt Col, 45, after serv in ETO, 42-45; Bronze Star; French Croix De Guerre with Silver Star; Victory & Serv Medals. Mem: Tex Bat Asn; Am Legion; Mason; Eastern Star; Lions. Relig: Baptist. Mailing Add: Box 666 Graham TX 76046

PENNINGTON, GEORGE (RED) (D)
NMex State Rep
Mailing Add: Box 125 Bloomfield NM 87413

PENNINGTON, HARRY LUCAS (D)
b Wetumpka, Ala, Sept 3, 19, 19; s William Matthew Pennington & Bernadine Williams P; m 1964 to Mary Evelyn Higgins (deceased); c Harry Lucas, Jr & Mary Melanie; m 1972 to Marjory G Poundstone. Educ: Univ Ala, AB, 41, LLB, 50; Sigma Chi. Polit & Govt Pos: Circuit solicitor, Madison Co, Ala, 51-52; circuit judge, 23rd Judicial Circuit, 55-61; Ala State Rep, Madison Co, 63-71, chmn, Health Comt & mem, Ways & Means Comt, Ala House Rep; vchmn, Ala Space Sci Comn, 65-; pres pro tem bd of trustees, Florence State Univ, 68-71; exec secy, Gov Ala, 71- Bus & Prof Pos: Pres, Huntsville Lumber Co, Inc, 59-; chmn bd dirs, The Bank of Huntsville, 68- Mil Serv: Entered as 2nd Lt, Army, 41, released as Maj, 46, after serv in Coast Artil Corps, ETO, 45-46. Mem: Huntsville Lions; Am Legion (past comdr 2nd Dist Ala); VFW; Madison Co Ment Health Asn. Relig: Recipient of the Bonnie D Hand Award as the outstanding mem of the 1967 regular sessions, House of Rep, State of Ala, as selected by the vote of the members of the 1967 Capital Press Corps. Relig: Methodist. Mailing Add: 2811 N Fernway Dr Montgomery AL 36111

PENNINGTON, ROBERT MORRIS, JR (D)
b Woonsocket, SDak, May 4, 53; s Robert Morris Pennington & Ila Stagcberg P, single. Educ: Montgomery Jr Col, currently. Polit & Govt Pos: Mem, Montgomery Co Young Dem, Md, formerly; deleg, Dem Nat Conv, 72. Mem: Common Cause Inc; Ralph Nader Pub Citizen Inc. Relig: Unitarian. Mailing Add: 4810 Mercury Dr Rockville MD 20853

PENNINGTON, WILLIAM ALTON (INDEPENDENT)
Chmn, Va Independent Party
b Newport News, Va, Jan 13; 11; m to Margaret Allen. Educ: Col William & Mary, pre-med; Med Col of Va, MD, 37. Polit & Govt Pos: Dir & first pres, Va Wildlife Fedn; Va State Deleg, 60; chmn, George Wallace Campaign, Va, 68; chmn, Va Independent Party, 69- Bus & Prof Pos: Physician. Mil Serv: Entered Army, 42, released as Maj, Med Corps, 45; Bronze Star. Relig: Baptist. Mailing Add: Buckingham VA 23921

PENTA, ROBERT M (INDEPENDENT)
Mass State Rep
Mailing Add: State Capitol Boston MA 02133

PENTON, MARBY ROBERT (D)
Miss State Rep
b Gautier, Miss, Aug 23, 22; married. Polit & Govt Pos: Miss State Rep, currently. Bus & Prof Pos: Attorney-at-law; attorney, Ocean Springs Munic Separate Sch Dist. Mem: Commercial Law League; Jackson Co Legal Secy Asn (adv); Lions (exec comt, Ocean Springs Club); Cub Scouts; PTA. Relig: Protestant. Mailing Add: 206 Washington Ave Ocean Springs MS 39564

PENTONY, JOSEPH FRANCIS (D)
Tex State Rep
b Philadelphia, Pa, May 27, 38; s Frank Pentony & Eileen Coyne P; m 1968 to Carole Gentry; c Eileen & Joseph Francis. Educ: Univ Tex, Austin, PhD, 70. Polit & Govt Pos: Tex State Rep, 73- Bus & Prof Pos: Clin psychologist, Houston, Tex, 70-; psychologist & mem faculty, Univ St Thomas, 73-, head psychol dept, 73- Relig: Roman Catholic. Legal Res: 4834 Spellman Houston TX 77035 Mailing Add: PO Box 2910 Capitol Sta Austin TX 78767

PEPITONE, ANTHONY (R)
NH State Rep
Mailing Add: Box 267 Bethlehem NH 03574

PEPITONE, BYRON VINCENT (R)
Dir, Selective Serv
b New Brunswick, NJ, June 9, 18; s Joseph J Pepitone & Sarah F Byron P; m 1940 to Marolynn M Mills; c Byron Vincent, II & James Scott. Educ: Army Command & Gen Staff Col, grad, 44; Air Command & Staff Col, Air Univ, grad, 50; NATO Defense Col, grad, 55. Polit & Govt Pos: Officer, US Air Force, 42-70, including Air Univ, 46-50, Hq Air Force, 51-55, Supreme Hq Allied Forces Europe, 55-58, Off of Secy of Air Force, 67-70; dep dir, Selective Serv Syst, Washington, DC, 70-72, acting dir & dir, 72- Mil Serv: Entered as Pvt, Army Air Corps, 39, released as Col, 70 after serv in Air Force, ETO Eighth Air Force World War II & world wide, 42-70; Distinguished Serv Medal; Legion of Merit with two Oak Leaf Clusters; Army Commendation Medal with Oak Leaf Cluster; Air Force Commendation Medal. Mem: Am Legion; Retired Officers' Asn; Air Force Asn. Honors & Awards: Distinguished Serv Award, Selective Serv Syst, 72. Legal Res: 2111 Jeff Davis Hwy Arlington VA 22202 Mailing Add: 1742 F St Northwest Washington DC 20435

PEPPER, CLAUDE (D)
US Rep, Fla
b Dudleyville, Ala, Sept 8, 00; s J W Pepper & Lena C Talbot P; m 1936 to Mildred Irene Webster. Educ: Univ Ala, AB, 21; Harvard Law Sch, LLB, 24; Phi Beta Kappa; Kappa Alpha; Omicron Delta Kappa; Sigma Upsilon; Phi Alpha Delta; Blue Key. Hon Degrees: LLD, McMaster Univ, 41, Univ Toronto, 42, Univ Ala, 42 & Rollins Col, 44. Polit & Govt Pos: Mem, Fla State Dem Exec Comt, 28-29; Fla State Rep, Taylor Co, 29-30; mem, Fla State Bd, Pub Welfare, 31-32; mem, Bd Law Examr, 33-34; US Sen, Fla, 36-51, chmn, Senate Comt on Inter-Oceanic Canal & Subcomt on MidE, US Senate; US Senate deleg, Interparliamentary Union, The Hague, 38 & Dublin, 50; deleg & chmn Fla deleg Dem Nat Conv, 40 & 44, alt deleg, 48, 52, 56, 60, 64 & 68; US Rep, Third Cong Dist, Fla, 62-67, 11th Cong Dist, 67-72, 14th Cong Dist, 73-, mem Comt on Banking & Currency & Subcomt on Domestic Finance, Int Trade & Int Finance, US House Rep, 63-64, mem Rules Comt, 65-, chmn Select Comt to Investigate Crime & mem Comt on Internal Security, 69-; deleg, Dem Nat Mid-Term Conf, 74. Bus & Prof Pos: Teacher, pub schs, Dothan, Ala, 17-18; instr law, Univ Ark, 24-25; attorney-at-law, Perry, Fla, 25-30, Tallahassee, 30; Marfleet lectr, Univ Toronto, 42; officer & dir, Washington Fed Savings & Loan Asn, Miami Beach; attorney, Miami Beach, currently. Mil Serv: Pvt, Students Army Training Corps, Co A, Univ Ala, 18. Publ: Articles in law rev, mag & newspapers. Mem: 40 et 8; Mason; Shrine; Elks; Moose. Honors & Awards: Albert Lasker Pub Serv Award, 67; Eleanor Roosevelt-Israel Humanities Award, 68. Relig: Baptist. Legal Res: 2121 N Bayshore Dr Miami FL 33137 Mailing Add: Cannon House Off Bldg Rm 432 Washington DC 20515

PERAULT, FELIX R (D)
Mass State Rep
Mailing Add: State Capitol Boston MA 02133

PERCY, CHARLES HARTING (R)
US Sen, Ill
b Pensacola, Fla, Sept 27; 19; s Edward H Percy & Elizabeth Harting P; m 1943 to Jeanne Dickerson (deceased); c Sharon Lee, Valerie Jeanne (deceased) & Roger; m 1950 to Loraine Diane Guyer; c Gail & Mark. Educ: Univ Chicago, AB, 41; Phi Delta Phi; Alpha Delta Phi. Hon Degrees: LLD, Ill Col Col, 61, Roosevelt Univ, 61 & Lake Forest Col, 62; HHD, Willamette Univ, 62. Polit & Govt Pos: Spec ambassador & personal rep of the President to presidential inauguration ceremonies in Peru & Bolivia, 56; chmn, Rep Nat Finance Comt, 57-59; deleg & chmn platform comt, Rep Nat Conv, 60, deleg, 64, 68 & 72; US Sen Ill, 67-; mem, Nat Rep Sen Comt. Bus & Prof Pos: Sales trainee & apprentice, Bell & Howell, 38, mgr, War Coord Dept, 41-43, asst secy, 43-46, corp secy, 46-49, pres, 49-61, chief exec officer, 61, Harris Trust & Savings Bank, until 67. Mil Serv: Navy, Lt, 43-45. Mem: Chicago Asn Com; Photog Soc of Am; Chicago Club; Execs Club (dir); Commercial Commonwealth Club. Honors & Awards: One of Ten Outstanding Young Men, US Jr CofC, 49; World Trade Award, 55; Nat Sales Exec Mgt Award, 56; officer, French Legion of Honor, 61. Legal Res: Wilmette IL Mailing Add: 1200 New Senate Off Bldg Washington DC 20510

PEREZ, JOAQUIN ARRIOLA (D)
b Agana, Guam, Mar 14, 16; s Pedro Leon Guerrero Perez (deceased) & Ana Alvarez P (deceased); m 1939 to Macrene Aquiningoc; c Patricia (Mrs J P Castro), David Jose, Frank Anthony & Anne Julia. Educ: George Washington Univ spec prog pub admin, 64-65. Polit & Govt Pos: Acct clerk, Govt Guam, 35-46; chmn, Ways & Means Comt, Guam Legis, 48-50; Sen, Guam Legis, 50-61 & 68-72, vchmn, Rules Comt, 50-56, chmn, 56-61, chmn, Trade & Tourism Comt, 68-72; asst dir, Govt of Guam Pub Works, 61-67; chmn, Guam Dem Party, 71-72; chief judge, Island Court of Guam, currently. Bus & Prof Pos: Asst gen mgr, Guam Commercial Corp Inc, 46-49; pres & gen mgr, Island Serv-Co Inc, 49-53; pres & mgr, Perez Enterprise, Inc, 56- Mem: Young Men's League of Guam; Lions; PTA; Legis Leaders Conf Am (charter mem). Relig: Roman Catholic. Legal Res: Ipao-Tamuning GU 96910 Mailing Add: PO Box 373 Agana GU 96910

PEREZ, PEDRO DIAZ (PETE) (R)
Rep Nat Committeeman, Guam
b Agana, Guam, Aug 10, 11; s Feliz Flores Perez (deceased) & Josefa San Nicolas Diaz P (deceased); m to Antonia Camacho Untalan; c Frank Amado, Victor J, Peter Felix & Juanita Antonia (Mrs Pablo). Educ: Vellejo Jr Col, 51-53; Univ Denver, BSBA, 54; San Francisco State Col, 54-56. Polit & Govt Pos: Staff acct, US Navy Commands, 59-70; mem, Pub Health & Hosp Bd, Govt Guam, 66-68; chmn & mem, Civil Serv Comn, 68-70; mem, Guam Rep Cent Comt, 69-; exec asst, Gov Guam, 69-70; Sen, Guam Legis, 71-74; Rep Nat Committeeman, Guam, until 72 & 75- Bus & Prof Pos: Pub acct, licensed by Govt Guam, 68-71; opers mgr, Guam Savings & Loan Asn, 7O- Mil Serv: Entered as Seaman, 2/C, Navy, 41, released as Chief Yeoman, 46, after serv in Naval Sta, Guam & Lion Sic, Pac Theatre; prisoner of war, 41-44; Good Conduct Medal; Pac Theatre & US Defense Ribbons. Mem: Fed Govt Acct; VFW; Am Legion; NavMar Credit Union; Guam Club Am (first nat pres, 50). Relig: Catholic. Mailing Add: PO Box 3404 Agana GU 96910

PERINO, CARMEN (D)
Calif State Assemblyman
Mailing Add: 31 E Channel St Stockton CA 95202

PERINO, JOSEPH ORESTE (DFL)
b Alexandria, Minn, Oct 3, 54; s Joseph Oreste Perino & Margaret Filippone P; single. Educ: Univ Notre Dame, 72-; Nat Soc Prof Engrs. Polit & Govt Pos: Deleg, Douglas Co Dem-Farmer-Labor Conv, Minn, 72; deleg, Seventh Cong Dist Dem-Farmer-Labor Conv, 72; deleg, Minn Dem-Farmer-Labor State Conv, 72; alt deleg, Dem Nat Conv, 72. Bus & Prof

Pos: Secy & vpres, Perino Enterprises, Inc, 72- Mem: Boy Scouts. Honors & Awards: Eagle Scout, Boy Scouts, 70. Relig: Roman Catholic. Legal Res: 1205 Douglas St Alexandria MN 56308 Mailing Add: Howard Hall 318 Univ of Notre Dame Notre Dame IN 46556

PERK, RALPH JOSEPH (R)
Mayor, Cleveland, Ohio
b Cleveland, Ohio, Jan 19, 14; s Joseph C Perk & Mary Smrt P; m 1942 to Lucille Gagliardi; c Virginia (Mrs Bowers), Ralph J, Jr, twins, Kenneth & Thomas, Michael, Allen & Richard. Educ: Cleveland Col, Western Reserve Univ, eve courses; St John's Col (Ohio), eve courses. Hon Degrees: LLD, Ill Benedictine Col, 74. Polit & Govt Pos: Spec asst, Attorney Gen Off, 50-52; councilman, City of Cleveland, 53-62; auditor, Cuyahoga Co, Ohio, 62-71; mayor, Cleveland, 71- Mem: Citizens League of Cleveland; Gtr Cleveland Growth Bd; Nat Conf Christians & Jews; Urban League of Cleveland; US Conf Mayors (adv bd). Honors & Awards: Cath Man of Year, Diocese of Cleveland, 55; Outstanding Citizenship Award, VFW, 57; Freedom Award, Hungarian Freedom Fighters Fedn USA, 68; Fiorello LaGuardia Award, Eagles, 72. Relig: Roman Catholic. Legal Res: 3421 E 49th Cleveland OH Mailing Add: 601 Lakeside Ave Cleveland OH 44114

PERKINS, ARNOLD B (R)
NH State Rep
Mailing Add: Box Rd PO Box 125 Goffstown NH 03045

PERKINS, CARL D (D)
US Rep, Ky
b Hindman, Ky, Oct 15, 12; s J E Perkins & Dora Calhoun P; m to Verna Johnson; c Carl Christopher. Educ: Caney Jr Col; Lees Jr Col; Jefferson Sch of Law. Polit & Govt Pos: Commonwealth attorney from 31st Judicial Dist, Ky, 39; mem, Ky Gen Assembly, 40; Knott Co Attorney, 41-48; counsel, State Dept of Hwy, 48; US Rep, Ky, 48-, chmn, Educ & Labor Comt, US House of Reps, currently; ex-officio, Dem Nat Mid-Term Conf, 74. Bus & Prof Pos: Attorney-at-law. Mil Serv: World War II, ETO, participated in battle of N France, the Ardennes, The Rhineland & Cent Europe. Mem: Am Legion; Mason. Relig: Baptist. Legal Res: Knott Co KY Mailing Add: 2365 Rayburn House Off Bldg Washington DC 20515

PERKINS, CARROLL (D)
Iowa State Rep
Mailing Add: RR 3 Box 233 Jefferson IA 50129

PERKINS, MILDRED KELLEY (R)
b Littleton, NH, July 6, 08; d Fred Kelley & Carlotta Kimball K; m 1933 to Francis Eaton Perkins; c Harold Wilder & Francis Eaton, Jr. Educ: Plymouth State Col, BE, 30; Forensic Club; Pan Athenian. Polit & Govt Pos: Pres, Concord Women's Rep Club, NH, 51-52; asst treas, NH State Rep Comt, 52, asst chmn, 57 & 65-68; pres, NH Federated Rep Women's Clubs, 56-57; mem, Rev Comt, Nat Fedn Rep Women, 57, vchmn, Finance Comt, 58-59, prog chmn, 60, membership chmn, 61-64 & fourth vpres, 65-67; Rep Nat Committeewoman, NH, 68-72; mem, Youth & Govt Comt, 68- Bus & Prof Pos: Instr social sci, NH & NJ Pub Schs. Mem: Concord Bd Educ, NH; Eastern Star; Concord Women's Col Club; NH Lawyer's Wives Orgn (co-founder & dir); NH Hosp Auxiliary. Relig: Episcopal. Mailing Add: 5 Glendale Rd Concord NH 03301

PERKINS, PEGGY LYNN (D)
b Bunkie, La, Aug 25, 46; d David M Perkins & Gloria Brisolara P; single. Educ: La State Univ, Alexandria, 64-66; La State Univ, Baton Rouge, BS, 67, JD, 70; Alpha Delta Pi; Student Govt Asn. Polit & Govt Pos: Deleg, La Const Conv, 73-74; deleg, Dem Nat Mid-Term Conf, 74. Bus & Prof Pos: Attorney-at-law, Moreauville, La, 71- Mem: Am Bar Asn; Nat Bus & Prof Women's Club; Nat Platform Soc; La Civil Serv League; Avoyelles Parish Bicentennial Comt. Honors & Awards: Young Career Woman, La Fedn Bus & Prof Women's Club, 74-75; Alpha Delta Kappa Psi Chap First & Only Hon Membership, 74. Relig: Catholic. Mailing Add: Hwy 1 Moreauville LA 71355

PERKINS, RICHARD DALLAS (D)
Pres, Ohio Young Dem
b Steubenville, Ohio, Mar 13, 47; s Dallas Perkins & Marie Ward P; m 1973 to Elizabeth Dannenhaver; c Melissa. Educ: Steubenville Col, 65-67. Polit & Govt Pos: Pres, Jefferson Co Young Dem, 70-74; treas, Ohio Young Dem, 72-74, pres, 74-; councilman, City of Steubenville, 74- Bus & Prof Pos: Prod mgr, WSTV-TV, Steubenville, Ohio, 71-74 & acct exec, 74- Mem: Lions; IBEW. Mailing Add: 1904 McCauslen Manor Steubenville OH 43952

PERKINS, RUSSELL L (D)
NH State Rep
Mailing Add: 930 West Hollis St Nashua NH 03060

PERKINS, STEPHEN L (R)
Maine State Rep
Mailing Add: 805 Main St South Portland ME 04106

PERKINS, THOMAS RALPH (R)
Maine State Rep
b Patten, Maine, Feb 15, 31; s Henry G Perkins & Ruth Varney P; m 1953 to Mary Ann McVoty; c Kim Anne & Thomas R, Jr. Educ: Mass Col Pharm, BS in Pharm, 53; Kappa Psi. Polit & Govt Pos: Maine State Rep, Dist 43, currently, mem, Legal Affairs Comt & Liquor Control Comt, Maine House Rep, currently. Mem: Maine Pharmaceut Asn; Maine Pharmaceut Traveling Men's Asn; Mass Col Pharm (adv coun). Relig: Protestant. Mailing Add: Main St Blue Hill ME 04614

PERKINS, WILLIAM O, JR (D)
NJ State Assemblyman
Mailing Add: 314 Arlington Ave Jersey City NJ 07304

PERKINSON, MAURICE LEON (D)
Chmn, Oldham Co Dem Exec Comt, Ky
b Georgetown, Ky, Mar 18, 32; s O D Perkinson, mother (deceased); m 1955 to Barbara Jane Zuver; c Sharon & Sandra. Educ: Univ Ky, 50-52; Univ Miami, BBA, 58; Univ Louisville, JD, 63. Polit & Govt Pos: City attorney, LaGrange, Ky, 66-68; co attorney, Oldham Co, 72; chmn, Oldham Co Dem Exec Comt, 72- Mil Serv: SP-3, Army, 52-55, serv in 64th Tank Bn, Korea. Mem: Am, Ky & Oldham Co Bar Asns; Oldham Co Band Aids; Masons (Master, Fortitude Lodge 47, F&AM, 64-74). Mailing Add: 400 Kentucky Ave LaGrange KY 40031

PERKINSON, PATRICIA ROYAL (INDEPENDENT)
Secy of the Commonwealth, Va
b Middlesex Co, Va, July 18, 25; d Walter Albert Royal & Lucy Blakey R; m 1946 to Herbert R Perkinson, Jr; c Jean Tucker & H Russell, III. Educ: Va Commonwealth Univ, BS, 46, MS, 56. Polit & Govt Pos: Admin asst, Gov Mills E Godwin, Jr, Va, 66-70; admin asst to the Chancellor, Va Community Col Syst, 70-72; secy of the commonwealth, Va, 74- Bus & Prof Pos: Free lance pub rels, 46-66; newspaper columnist, Richmond Times-Dispatch, 48-66. Mem: Pub Rels Soc Am; Nat Asn Extradition Officials; Nat Asn Secy of State; Am Cancer Soc (Va div bd dirs); Va Lung Asn (bd dirs). Honors & Awards: Va Press Woman of the Year, Va Br Nat Fedn Press Women, 69. Relig: Presbyterian. Legal Res: 7702 Pinehill Dr Richmond VA 23228 Mailing Add: Ninth & Grace Sts Richmond VA 23219

PERLOFF, MIKE (D)
Ala State Sen
Mailing Add: 304-D Garden Lane Chickasaw AL 36611

PERPICH, ANTON JOHN (DFL)
Minn State Sen
b Carson Lake, Minn, Feb 10, 32; s Anton Perpich & Mary Vukelich P; m 1950 to Irene Kosiak; c Julie. Educ: Hibbing Jr Col, 51; Marquette Univ Sch Dentistry, 55. Polit & Govt Pos: Minn State Sen, Dist 6, 67- Bus & Prof Pos: Dentist, Am Dent Asn, 55- Mil Serv: Entered as 1st Lt, Air Force, 56, released as Capt, 58. Mem: Am Dent Asn. Legal Res: 4 Lakeside Dr S Eveleth MN 55734 Mailing Add: 108 N Third Ave Virginia MN 55792

PERPICH, GEORGE F (DFL)
Minn State Rep
Mailing Add: 814 NE Fifth Ave Chisholm MN 55719

PERPICH, RUDY GEORGE (DFL)
Lt Gov, Minn
b Carson Lake, Minn, June 27, 28; s Anton Perpich & Mary Vukelich P; m 1954 to Delores Helen Simich; c Rudy George, Jr & Mary Susan. Educ: Hibbing Jr Col, AA, 50; Marquette Univ, DDS, 54. Polit & Govt Pos: Mem, Hibbing Bd of Educ, Minn, 56-62; Minn State Sen, 62-70; Lt Gov, Minn, 70- Mil Serv: Army, 46-47. Mailing Add: 2123 Sixth Ave E Hibbing MN 55746

PERRI, FORTUNATO (R)
Pa State Rep
Mailing Add: Capitol Bldg Harrisburg PA 17120

PERRIN, CARL ELLIS (D)
Committeeman, Dem State Cent Comt Conn
b Ripton, Vt, May 24, 31; s Floyd E Perrin & Alice Hayes P; m 1951 to Dorothy Kerr; c Susan J (Mrs John Henry), Scott K, Carla E & Mark J. Educ: Hartford Pub High Sch. Polit & Govt Pos: Chmn, Cheshire Dem Town Comt, Conn, 60-67; committeeman, Dem State Cent Comt Conn, 13th Dist, 66-74, 34th Dist, 74-; selectman, Town of Cheshire, 69-71. Bus & Prof Pos: Mgr, Healthco/Keefe Dent, Hartford, Conn, 58- Mil Serv: Entered as Pvt, Air Force, 50, released as S/Sgt, 52, after serv in 103rd Fighter Squadron, Am Theater, 50-52. Relig: Congregational. Mailing Add: 227 Taylor Ave Cheshire CT 06410

PERRY, AUDREY EMILIE (R)
Chairwoman, Monroe Co Rep Comt, Mich
b Detroit, Mich, Sept 13, 28; d Louis T Hethke & Elizabeth A Wirgau H; m 1956 to Alvin E Perry; c James. Educ: Wayne State Univ, BS, 55, MS, 59; Univ Mich, 75; Phi Beta Kappa; Sigma Alpha Iota. Polit & Govt Pos: Dir State legis, Bus & Prof Women, 74-; organizer & exec coordr, State Women's Coalition, 75; chmn, Mich Rep Women's Caucus, 75; chairwoman, Monroe Co Rep Comt, 75- Bus & Prof Pos: Teacher & counr, Monroe Pub Schs, Mich, 66-74, asst prin, 74-; owner, Audara's Dress Shop, 70- Mem: Bus & Prof Women; Indust Rels Asn; Nat Orgn Legal Probs; Altrusa. Honors & Awards: Sword of Honor, Sigma Alpha Iota; Citizen of Year, Monroe Bus & Prof Women; Community Leader & Noteworthy Am Award, Bicentennial Ed. Mailing Add: 5469 Raven Pkwy Monroe MI 48161

PERRY, BOBBY GERALD (BG) (D)
Miss State Sen
b Memphis, Tenn, Sept 25, 31; single. Educ: Phi Alpha Delta; Phi Delta Epsilon; Phi Delta Kappa. Polit & Govt Pos: Miss State Sen, currently; mem, DeSoto Bd Realtors. Bus & Prof Pos: Real estate broker; attorney. Mem: Miss Farm Bur; N DeSoto Civil Club; Miss & Am Bar Asns. Relig: Lutheran. Mailing Add: PO Box 121 Horn Lake MS 38637

PERRY, DONALD CLEVELAND (R)
Mem Exec Comt, Union Co Rep Party, NC
b Monroe, NC, May 17, 40; s J J Perry & Ollie Chaney P; m 1962 to Edith Early; c Donica Nicole & Desha Christine. Educ: Wingate Jr Col, NC, AA, 60; Wake Forest Univ, BA, 62, Sch Law, JD, 64; Lambda Chi Alpha. Polit & Govt Pos: Mem exec comt, Union Co Rep Party, NC, 68-, legal counsel, 69-; Rep precinct chmn, Wingate Precinct, Union Co, 69-72; deleg, Rep Nat Conv, 72; Rep precinct chmn, Marshville Precinct, 72- Bus & Prof Pos: Attorney-at-law, Monroe, NC, 65- Mil Serv: Entered as 1st Lt, Air Force, 65, released as Capt, 68, after serv in Judge Adv Div, Air Training Command, 65-68; Capt Res, 68-72; Expert Marksman. Mem: Phi Alpha Delta; Phi Theta Kappa; Lions (pres, Wingate Club, 72-73); Union Co Combined Charities (pres, 72); Union Co CofC. Relig: Baptist. Mailing Add: Box 506 Rte 1 Wingate NC 28174

PERRY, ELDRIDGE WELLS (D)
b Buena Vista, Ga, Aug 31, 22; s Clarence Eldridge Perry & Mary Wells P; m 1943 to Doris Lillian Lane; c Mary Pauline. Educ: Abraham Baldwin Agr Col; Univ Ga. Polit & Govt Pos: Justice of the peace, 807th G M Dist, Ga, 52-; Ga State Rep, 57-58 & 63-66; Ga State Sen, 24th Dist, 59-60; chmn, Marion Co Dem Party, formerly. Bus & Prof Pos: Ins; grocery bus. Mem: Mason. Relig: Methodist. Mailing Add: Buena Vista GA 31803

PERRY, FELIX EDWIN (D)
Miss State Rep
Mailing Add: Box 345 Oxford MS 38655

PERRY, FLORENCE N (D)
b Zawiercie, Poland, Oct 6, 13; d Joseph Bookspna (deceased) & Anna Wainglick B (deceased); wid; c Joyce (Mrs Lupo), Donald William Grieshober & Samuel Arthur &

Kenneth Charles Perry. Educ: Acad High Sch, grad, 30. Polit & Govt Pos: Committeewoman, Sixth Ward 12th Dist, 62-74; treas, Dem Women's Coun Erie & Erie Co, 65-67, vpres, 67-69 & pres, 69-71; deleg, Dem Nat Mid-Term Conf, 74. Bus & Prof Pos: Bookkeeper, Post Jewelers, 41-50 & Village Hotel, 54-60; secy, Personnel Off, Erie, Pa, 62- Mem: Jewish War Vets Auxiliary; Downing Golf League; Ladies Major Bowling League (sgt-at-arms, 70-); City Hall Recreation (treas). Honors & Awards: Outstanding Dem Woman of the Year, 71; Honored by the Dem Women's Coun of Erie & Erie Co & by the Mayor; Plaque given by the Mayor & City Coun & other govt officials. Mailing Add: 2803 Melrose Ave Erie PA 16508

PERRY, FRANKLIN DELANO (R)
Exec Chmn, Warren Co Rep Party, Ohio
b Van Lear, Ky, Jan 21, 36; s William Jefferson Perry & Martha Jane Porter P; m 1963 to Lula June Smith; c Martha Lucille, Timothy Jon & Gregory Alan. Educ: Georgetown Col, Ky, BA, 61; Xavier Univ, MEd, 66, MA, 68; Vet Club; Young Rep; Varsity Football. Polit & Govt Pos: Campaign mgr, Powell for Cong, 70; chmn, Warren Co Rep Party, Ohio, 70-73, exec chmn, currently; dist rep, US Rep Walter E Powell, Ohio 24, 71-; deleg, Rep Nat Conv, 72. Bus & Prof Pos: Teacher & coach, Franklin City Sch Dist, Ohio, 62-66, elem prin, 71-; high sch, Col Corner Local Sch Dist, Ohio, 66; elem, South Lebanon, 67-69; elem & jr high, Mason Local Sch Dist, 70. Mil Serv: Entered as Basic Airman, Air Force, 54, released as A/1C, 58, after serv in 810th Supply Squadron, Biggs AFB, Tex, Strategic Air Command, 56-58; Outstanding Airman Award, Biggs AFB, 57; cert of achievement, Provisional Mil Assistance Adv Group, S Korea, 56; Good Conduct Medal, 56. Mem: Phi Delta Kappa; Int Men's Educ Fraternity; Ohio Educ Asn; Dept Elem Sch Prin; Warren Co Elem Prin Asn (pres-elect). Honors & Awards: Oustanding Achievement Award, Optimist Club, Franklin, Ohio, 64. Relig: Baptist. Mailing Add: 3623 McLean Rd Franklin OH 45005

PERRY, JESSE LAURENCE, JR (R)
VChmn, Tenn State Rep Finance Comt
b Nashville, Tenn, Oct 15, 19; s Jesse Laurence Perry & Mamie White P; m 1949 to Susan Taylor White (deceased); c Robert Laurence & Judith Foulds. Educ: Univ of the South, summa cum laude, 37; Vanderbilt Univ, BA, magna cum laude, 41; Harvard Univ, MBA, 43; Phi Beta Kappa; Omicron Delta Gamma; Pi Kappa Alpha. Polit & Govt Pos: Pres, Davidson Co Young Rep, Tenn, 41-48; nominee, Tenn State Rep, Sixth Dist, 48; chmn, Fifth Dist Rep Exec Comt, 50-54; campaign mgr, Mid Tenn, 56, 60 & 66; vchmn, Tenn Rep State Exec Comt, 56, vchmn, State Finance Comt & State Committeeman, currently; deleg, Rep Nat Conv, 60 & 68 & vchmn, Tenn Deleg, 60; mem spec comt urban develop, Rep Nat Exec Comt, 62. Bus & Prof Pos: Treas, J L Perry Co, Nashville, Tenn, 47-48, vpres, 49-54 & pres, 54- Mil Serv: Entered as Pvt, Army, 43, released as Capt, 46, after serv as Fiscal Dir, Finance Dept, Seventh Serv Command, 44-46. Mem: Am Acad Polit Sci; Nat Soc SAR; Am Legion; ROA; Elks. Honors & Awards: Hon col, Staff Gov Tenn. Relig: Episcopal. Mailing Add: 4434 E Brookfield Dr Nashville TN 37205

PERRY, JOHN B (D)
Mass State Rep
Mailing Add: State Capitol Boston MA 02133

PERRY, JOHN D (D)
NY State Sen
Mailing Add: 181 Lafayette Pkwy Rochester NY 14625

PERRY, MATTHEW (D)
Mem-at-Lg, Dem Nat Comt
Mailing Add: 924 Hampton St Columbia SC 29201

PERRY, NANCY MAYER (R)
b Seaford, Del, July 23, 44; d John Richard Miller & Alice Beebe M; m 1972 to Christopher Lawrence Perry; step-children, Kemberly Paige & Jeffrey Lawrence. Educ: Univ Del, 62-64, exten, 64-66. Polit & Govt Pos: Secy, Del State Fedn of Young Rep, 68-69; secy-polit aide, former Mayor Harry G Haskell, Jr, Wilmington, Del, 68-71; secy to chmn, Del Rep State Comt, 71-, acting secy, formerly. Relig: Episcopal. Mailing Add: 1408 Hamilton St Wilmington DE 19806

PERRY, PETER E (D)
Pa State Rep
b Philadelphia, Pa, June 22, 01; m 1926 to Rephaela Procopio; c Bernice G (Mrs Harry J Doyle), Richard P & Peter E, Jr. Polit & Govt Pos: Pa State Rep, 58- Bus & Prof Pos: Pres, Charles H Howell & Co, Inc; dir, E Germantown Bldg & Loan Asn. Mem: Nat Paint Salesmen's Club; W Oak Lane Lions; W Oak Lane Community Asn. Relig: Roman Catholic. Mailing Add: 1020 Lakeside Ave Philadelphia PA 19126

PERRY, ROBERT A (D)
Wash State Rep
b New York, 1921; wid; c Roberta Anne; Susan O & Lyn L. Educ: USMS Sch Eng. Polit & Govt Pos: Wash State Rep, currently, chmn legis ethics comt, Wash House Rep, currently. Mil Serv: Officer, Merchant Marine. Relig: Jewish. Mailing Add: 1154 N 92nd Seattle WA 98103

PERRY, T DUDLEY (D)
Ala State Sen
Mailing Add: PO Box 419 Tuskegee AL 36083

PERRY, WILLIAM H, III (R)
Mo State Rep
Mailing Add: 7 Colonial Dr Webb City MO 64870

PERRYMAN, AUDREY JOHNSTON (D)
b Pleasant Hill, Miss, Dec 8, 27; d Samuel Montgomery Johnston & Mattie Lauderdale; div; c Elizabeth P (Mrs Ausbon), Samuel Whitley & Frank Jason. Educ: Hernando Consol Sch, Miss, grad, 46. Polit & Govt Pos: Deleg, Dem Nat Mid-Term Conf, 74; secy, Dem Cong Dist 1, Miss, 75- Bus & Prof Pos: Operator, Southern Bell Tel & Tel Co, Hernando & Tupelo, Miss, 46-67; serv asst, South Cent Bell Tel Co, 67- Mem: Commun Workers of Am Int (secy, Local 10517, 67-); Tupelo Cent Labor Union, AFL-CIO (trustee, 73-). Relig: Presbyterian. Mailing Add: 703 W Jefferson Tupelo MS 38802

PERSKIE, STEVEN PHILIP (D)
NJ State Assemblyman
b Philadelphia, Pa, Jan 10, 45; s David M Perskie & Rosalie Glassman Perskie (both deceased); m 1968 to Barbara Fendrich. Educ: Yale Univ, BA, 66; Univ Pa Law Sch, JD, 69; NY Univ Law Sch, LLM in taxation, 70. Polit & Govt Pos: NJ State Assemblyman, 72-; chmn, Atlantic Co Dem Comt, currently. Bus & Prof Pos: Attorney, Cooper, Perskie, Neustadter & Katzman, Atlantic City, NJ, 69-; staff attorney, NJ Pub Defender, 70-71. Mem: Am Bar Asn; Stockton State Col Found (pres, 72-); Yale Alumni Comt; Margate Civic Asn; Jewish Community Ctr of Atlantic Co. Relig: Jewish. Legal Res: 9 E Gilmar Circle Margate NJ 08402 Mailing Add: 1125 Atlantic Ave Atlantic City NJ 08401

PERSON, CURTIS STANDIFER, JR (R)
Tenn State Sen
b Memphis, Tenn, Nov 27, 34; s Curtis S Person, Sr & Helen Hamilton P; m 1957 to Peggy Joyce Moore; c Kathleen, Curtis, III & Patrick. Educ: Memphis State Univ, BS, 56; Univ Miss, LLB, 59; Phi Alpha Theta; Phi Alpha Delta; Kappa Sigma; Memphis State Golf Team. Polit & Govt Pos: Spec dep sheriff, Shelby Co, Tenn, 60-; Tenn State Rep, 14th Dist, 67-69; Tenn State Sen, 69-, mem educ, judiciary & gen welfare comts, Tenn State Senate, secy Shelby Co legis deleg, 69, vchmn, 70-, secy Senate Rep caucus, 69-70. Bus & Prof Pos: Partner, Curtis Person Chevrolet Co, 53- Mem: Am Bar Asn; Memphis-Shelby Co Ment Health Asn (pres); Memphis State Univ Nat Alumni Asn (pres); Boy Scouts; Mason (32 degree). Honors & Awards: Tenn Outstanding Young Men of Year, Jaycees, 69; Memphis' Outstanding Young Man of Year, Jaycees, 69; Liberty Bell Freedom Award, Memphis-Shelby Co Bar Asn, 69. Relig: Presbyterian; jr deacon & Sunday sch teacher, Second Presby Church. Mailing Add: 208 Adams St Memphis TN 38103

PERSON, EARLE GEORGE, JR (D)
b Mt Vernon, Ill, Apr 28, 28; s Earle G Persons Sr (deceased) & Willie Claude Bryant P; m 1960 to Estelle M McCraty. Educ: Univ Ill, BS, 50; Creighton Univ Grad Sch, 53 & Sch Dent, DDS, 58; Omicron Kappa Upsilon; Alpha Sigma Nu; Alpha Phi Alpha. Polit & Govt Pos: Mem, Nebr Steering Comt McGovern for President, 71-72; chmn-founder, Right-on Comt of One Hundred for McGovern, 72; coordr, minorities, Nebraskans for McGovern, 72; chmn Nebr deleg, Nat Black Polit Conv, 72-, assemblyman, 72- Bus & Prof Pos: Mem bd dirs, KOWH AM-FM Radio, 70-73; deleg, Nebr Dent Asn, 70-73; chmn legis comt, Omaha Dent Soc, 71-73. Mil Serv: Entered as 2nd Lt, Army, 50, released 53, after serv in 5021 ASU, US, 50-53. Publ: Chap 13 In: Odyssey: journey through Black America, Putnam, 71; Decline becomes decay, The Chronicle, 68; Some have heart, AT & TJ, 69. Mem: Ill Soc Microbiol; Nebr Soc Clin Hypnosis (pres, 70-72); Am & Nebr Dent Asns; Comprehensive Health Asn of Omaha (pres, 73). Honors & Awards: Paynter Dent Med Award, Creighton Univ, 58, Donohoe Periodontal Award, 58; Owler's Serv Award, Masonic Lodge, 66; Award of Merit, Urban League of Nebr, 67; Meritorious Serv Award, Nebr Goodwill Indust, 71. Legal Res: 3212 Myrtle Ave Omaha NE 68131 Mailing Add: 3707 N 24th St Omaha NE 68110

PERSONS, OSCAR NEWTON (R)
Gen Counsel, Rep Party of Ga
b McCormick, SC, Jan 7, 39; s Abner Thaddeus Persons & Esther Dumas P; m 1966 to Barbara Burns; c Thaddeus William. Educ: Ga Inst Technol, BIE, 60; Emory Univ Law Sch, JD, 67; Beta Theta Pi. Polit & Govt Pos: Pres, Young Rep Club, Fulton Co, Ga, 66-67; chmn membership comt, Young Rep Nat Fedn, 67-69; asst gen counsel, Rep Party of Ga, 68-71, mem exec comt, 68-, gen counsel, 71- Bus & Prof Pos: Attorney-at-law, Alston, Miller & Gaines, Atlanta, Ga, 67- Mil Serv: Entered as Ens, Navy, 60, released as Lt(jg), 62, after serv in 7th Fleet Unit, Pac Theatre, 61-62. Mem: Am & Ga Bar Asns; Omicron Delta Kappa; Alpha Pi Mu; Pi Delta Epsilon. Relig: Presbyterian. Mailing Add: 1340 Peachtree Battle Ave Atlanta GA 30327

PERT, EDWIN HARRY (D)
b Bath, Maine, May 27, 33; s Perleston Lincoln Pert, Sr & Katherine M White P; single. Educ: Univ Maine, BA in Govt, 54; Sigma Phi Epsilon. Polit & Govt Pos: Publicity dir, Sagadahoc Co Dem Comt, 50, chmn, 54; publicity dir, Maine Dem State Comt, 51; pres, Young Dem Clubs of Maine, 52-53; exec secy, Maine Dem Party, 57-60; Maine State Rep, 99th Legis, 59-60; mem, Maine Civil War Centennial Comn, 59-60; secy, Maine State Senate, 65-68; Get Out the Vote coordr, Southern Sagadahoc Co, 70; chmn, Georgetown Dem Comt, 70-73; chmn bd selectmen, Town of Georgetown, 71-74; clerk, Maine House of Rep, currently. Bus & Prof Pos: News dir, Radio Sta WJTO, 61; state rep, Nat Found March of Dimes, 61-65; exec dir, Arthritis Found, 69-73. Mil Serv: Entered as 2nd Lt, Army, 55, released as 1st Lt, 57, after serv in 32nd Inf Regt, 7th Inf Div, Korea. Legal Res: Seguinland Rd Five Islands ME 04546 Mailing Add: PO Box 36 Bath ME 04530

PERTSCHUK, MICHAEL (D)
b London, Eng, Jan 12, 33; s David Pertschuk & Sarah Baumander P; m 1954 to Carleen Joyce Dooly; c Amy & Mark. Educ: Yale Univ, BA, 54, Sch Law, LLB, 59. Polit & Govt Pos: Legis asst, US Sen Maurine B Neuberger, Ore, 62-64; staff counsel, US Senate Com Comt, 64-68, chief counsel, 68-; consult, US Trade Missions to East Europe, 65-66; comnr, Nat Comn Prod Safety, 68-70. Bus & Prof Pos: Law clerk, Chief Judge Gus J Solomon, US Dist Court, Ore, 59-60; assoc, Hart, Rockwood, Davies, Biggs & Strayer, 60-62; chmn comt advert, packaging & promotion, Fed Bar Asn, 67-70 & mem comn automobile accident reparations, Am Bar Asn, 68-69; prof lectr, Am Univ, Washington Sch Law, 71-; adj prof, Georgetown Law Sch, 74- Mem: Univ Okla Law Ctr Comn; Nat Interagency Coun Smoking & Health. Relig: Ethical Humanist. Mailing Add: 3540 39th NW B644 Washington DC 20016

PESCE, MICHAEL L (D)
NY State Assemblyman
b Mola Di Bari, Italy, Mar 1, 43; s Francesco Pesce & Vincenza Micunco P; single. Educ: City Univ New York, BA, 64; New Sch Social Research, MA, 66; Univ Detroit Sch Law, JD, 69. Polit & Govt Pos: NY State Assemblyman, 73- Bus & Prof Pos: Social worker, New York Dept Social Serv, 66-68; attorney, Legal Aid Soc, 69-73. Publ: Notes on a blue collar reform movement, In: Pieces of a Dream, Ctr Migration Studies, 73. Mem: Delta Theta Phi; Common Cause; Van Westerhout Mola Club; La Casa Neighborhood Serv Ctr (bd dirs); South Brooklyn Health Ctr. Relig: Catholic. Mailing Add: 606 Henry St Brooklyn NY 11231

PESCI, FRANK BERNARD, SR (D)
Md State Deleg
b Raritan, NJ, Jan 6, 29; s Corrado Pesci & Rose L Perantoni P; m 1956 to Dorothy A Daly; c Cecilia C, Jane F, Barbara R, Marianna D, James C & Frank B, Jr. Educ: Seton Hall Univ, BS, 53; Cath Univ Am, MA, 56, PhD, 63. Polit & Govt Pos: Vchmn bd trustees, Prince

George's Community Col, Largo, Md, 69-71; Md State Deleg, 71- Bus & Prof Pos: Prof govt, Prince George's Community Col, 58-68, dean acad affairs, 62-66; assoc prof higher educ, Cath Univ Am, 68- Mem: Order Sons of Italy in Am. Honors & Awards: Outstanding Young Men of Am, 65. Relig: Catholic. Mailing Add: 8311 Fremont Pl New Carrollton MD 20784

PESEK, ROBERT JOSEPH (D)

Chmn, Lavaca Co Dem Party, Tex

b Sweet Home, Tex, Oct 14, 22; s Thomas James Pesek & Rosie Janak P; m 1950 to Amelia M Strauss; c Thomas Lee, Marianne, Judy Rose, Connie Sue & Joyce Marie. Educ: Tex Univ, BBA, 47; Harvard Univ; Tex Christian Univ; Delta Sigma Pi. Polit & Govt Pos: Pres, Lavaca Co Flood Bd, Tex, 64-66; chmn, Lavaca Co Dem Party, 73- Bus & Prof Pos: Dir, Monument Builders of Southwest, 65-66, pres, 69- Mil Serv: Entered as Seaman, Naval Res, 42, released as Lt(jg), 46, after serv in Amphibious Forces; Philippines & Okinawa Invasion Medals. Mem: KofC; Lions (pres, 69-); CofC (pres); Am Legion; VFW. Relig: Catholic; church bd, 68-70. Legal Res: 417 S Main St Hallettsville TX 77964 Mailing Add: PO Box 292 Hallettsville TX 77964

PESKIN, BERNARD M (D)

b Chicago, Ill, Sept 22, 22; m to Arlene P; c Barbara & Robert. Educ: Wilson Jr Col; Ill Inst of Tech; John Marshall Law Sch; Tau Epsilon Phi. Polit & Govt Pos: Ill State Rep, 4 terms, chmn, House Comt Banks & Savings & Loans, 74th Gen Assembly; Dem committeeman, Northfield Twp, 68-73; mem, Cook Co Dem Cent Comt, 68-73. Bus & Prof Pos: Self-employed. Mil Serv: Army Signal Corps in China Theatre of Operations. Mem: Am Chicago & Ill State Bar Asns; Decalogue Soc of Lawyers; B'nai B'rith. Honors & Awards: Best Legislator Award, Independent Voters of Ill, 72nd, 73rd & 74th Gen Assemblies; Distinguished Serv Award, Ill Welfare Coun, 65. Relig: North Shore Congregation Israel. Mailing Add: 7 Timber Lane Northbrook IL 60062

PESNER, LEON (D)

Committeeman, Rockland Co Dem Comt, NY

b Brooklyn, NY, May 7, 21; s Abraham Pesner & Mary Salkin P; m 1944 to Doris Elias; c Steven Marc, Alan Ira & Susan Minda. Educ: Spring Valley High Sch, NY, grad. Polit & Govt Pos: Committeeman, Rockland Co Dem Comt, NY, 58-, co chmn, 70-72; village chmn, Spring Valley Dem Comt, 60-65; receiver of taxes, Ramapo, 63; treas, Ramapo Dem Comt, 64-66. Bus & Prof Pos: Partner, Ramapo Mink Ranch, Monsey, NY, 43-58; self-employed, Leon Pesner Real Estate & Ins, Spring Valley, NY, 58- Mem: Rockland Hook & Ladder Fire Co (vpres); KofP; Rockland Co Fire Police Asn; Temple Beth El Men's Club; NY State Realtors. Relig: Hebrew. Mailing Add: 31 Singer Ave Spring Valley NY 10977

PETER, YERDA ELIZABETH (R)

VChmn Pub Rels, Nat Fedn Rep Women

b Buckfield, Maine, Dec 6, 11; d Fred Gray DaVee & Caroline Packard D; m 1952 to Charles Peter; c Adopted Nancy Gail & Carmine Enrico Leo. Educ: Woodstock High Sch, Bryant Pond, Maine, dipl, 28. Polit & Govt Pos: Mem, Portland Rep City Comt, 14 years, Cumberland Co Rep Comt, 12 years & First Cong Dist Rep Party, eight years; mem, Maine State Rep Comt, six years, secy, four years; deleg, Maine State Rep Conv, eight years; past vpres, Maine Fedn Rep Women, two years, pres, 69-73; past pres, Portland Club Rep Women, two years, past treas, two years, past prog chmn, two years, legis chmn, currently; mem, Windham Rep Womens Club; eight years; chmn women's activities, Nixon-Lodge Campaign, 60; chmn, Dimes for Nixon, Cumberland Co, 68; mem bd dirs, Nat Fedn Rep Women, deleg, nat women conf, vchmn pub rels, 73-; deleg & mem credentials comt, Rep Nat Conv, 68, deleg, 72. Mem: March of Dimes; Eastern Star; Madonna White Shrine; Rebekahs; Maine Victorian Soc. Honors & Awards: Maine Rep Woman of Year, 69; Woman of Year, Sta WLOB, Gtr Portland. Relig: Protestant. Mailing Add: 1501 Forest Ave Portland ME 04103

PETERNAL, NANCY FARRELL (D)

Wyo State Rep

b Lynn, Mass, Aug 26, 29; d John Bernard Farrell & Mary Tonry F; m 1953 to William W Peternal; c John Farrell & Kelly Ann. Educ: Emmanuel Col, AB, 50; Boston Univ; Univ Utah. Polit & Govt Pos: Vchmn, Lincoln Co Dem Cent Comt, 70-73, chmn, 73-; pres, Lincoln Co Dem Women's Club, 70-; mem, Wyo Comn on Status of Women, 71; Wyo State Rep, 71-73 & 75-; alt deleg, Dem Nat Conv, 72; committeewoman, Wyo State Dem Cent Comt, 72- Bus & Prof Pos: Teacher, pub schs, Kemmerer, Wyo, 50-53, 60- Mem: Nat & Wyo Educ Asns; Bus & Prof Women; League Women Voters; Canary Club. Honors & Awards: Distinguished Citizen Award, Kemmerer Boosters. Relig: Catholic. Mailing Add: 1001 Park Dr Kemmerer WY 83101

PETERS, ALICE BOYE (R)

Mem, Rep State Cent Comt Calif

b Sanger, Calif, Sept 11, 13; d Erik Albert Boye & Henrika Hansen; m 1933 to Arnold Davis Peters; c Robert D & Valerie (Mrs White). Educ: Univ Calif, Berkeley, 30-31. Polit & Govt Pos: Mem, Rep State Cent Comt Calif, 58-; secy, Alameda Co Rep Cent Comt, 62; secy, Fresno Co Rep Cent Comt, 69-71; chmn, Fresho Co Rep Coord Coun, 73- Mem: Beta Sigma Phi; Int Platform Asn. Relig: Episcopal. Mailing Add: 1425 N Farris Fresno CA 93728

PETERS, DELBERT DEAN (R)

Mem Exec Comt, Ada Co Rep Cent Comt, Idaho

b Erie, Ill, Sept 5, 21; s James H Peters (deceased) & Ethel M Echelbarger P; m 1942 to Faye Ann Miller; div; c William James, Jack D, Constance & Gene Raye. Educ: Grimms Sch Bus, Boise, Idaho, CPA, 53. Polit & Govt Pos: Precinct Committeeman, Ada Co, Idaho, 50-52 & 68-; staff asst, Nat Young Rep Conv, 62; comptroller, Idaho Rep State Cent Comt, 63-73, treas, 70-73; staff asst, Nat Rep Conv, 64; mem exec comt, Ada Co Rep Cent Comt, 68- Bus & Prof Pos: Cert pub acct, W Franklin Miller, CPA, Boise, Idaho, 60- Mil Serv: Entered as Pvt, Air Force, 42, released as T/Sgt, 45, after serv in 47th MR&R Squadron, ETO, 43-45. Mem: Boise Little Theatre Group; US Coast Guard Auxiliary. Relig: Baptist. Mailing Add: 627 Idaho Bldg Boise ID 83702

PETERS, HENRY H (D)

Hawaii State Rep

Mailing Add: House Sgt at Arms State Capitol Honolulu HI 96813

PETERS, J ELBERT (R)

VChmn, Ala Rep State Exec Comt

b Samson, Ala, Mar 2, 33; s Matthew M Peters & Willie Snow Hagan P; m 1956 to Melba Raines; c James Elbert, Jr & Carol Anita. Educ: Auburn Univ, BSEE, 58; grad study, Univ Ala, 62-64; Eta Kappa Nu; Tau Beta Pi; Lambda Chi Alpha. Polit & Govt Pos: Deleg, Ala Rep State Conv, 64, 68 & 70; Rep nominee for Tax Collector, Madison Co Ala, 66; ward chmn, Rep Party, Huntsville, Ala, 66-68; mem, Madison Co Rep Exec Comt, 66-, chmn, 70-74; alt deleg, Rep Nat Conv, 68; mem, Huntsville Bd of Appeals for Minimum Housing, 69-; Huntsville Sch Transportation Comt, 70; vchmn, Fifth Cong Dist Rep Comt, 70-74; mem, Ala Rep State Exec Comt, 70-, vchmn, 73-, mem platform comt, 70-74, mem bylaws comt, 71-74, chmn qualifications & elec comt, 74; chmn, State Rep Patronage Research Comt, 71-72; mem, Manpower Area Planning Comt, Huntsville, 70-72. Bus & Prof Pos: Instrumentation engr, Vitro Corp Am, 59-61; engr, Brown Eng Co, 61-65; engr Boeing Co, 65- Mil Serv: Entered as Pvt, Air Force, 50, released as S/Sgt, 54, after serv in Air Force Security Serv, 51-54. Mem: Inst Elec & Electronics Engrs; Am Ord Asn; Civitan Club; Air Force Asn; Am Legion. Relig: Church of Christ. Mailing Add: 1701 Jeannette Circle NW Huntsville AL 35805

PETERS, MARJORIE YOUNG (R)

NH State Rep

b Brooklyn, NY, Dec 6, 28; d Willard Voorhees Young & Matilda Miller Y; m 1952 to C Oswald Peters; c Clark Voorhees, Charles Young & Matilda. Educ: Lassell Jr Col, 48. Polit & Govt Pos: NH State Rep, 75-; mem, Bicentennial Comn, Bedford, 75- Mem: Bedford Hist Soc; Rep Womans Club, Amherst, NH. Relig: Presbyterian. Mailing Add: 3 Church Rd Bedford NH 03102

PETERS, MAXWELL (R)

Mem, Rep State Exec Comt, Ala

b Montgomery, Ala, Aug 14, 25; s William Marcus Peters, MD & Pearl Maxwell P; div; c William Marcus & Maxwell Lee. Educ: St John's Univ, Minn, 43-44; Univ Ala, BA, 49, LLB, 51. Polit & Govt Pos: Judge, Recorder's Court, Northport, Ala, 57-; exec dir, Northport Housing Authority, 60-62; vchmn, Tuscaloosa Co Rep Comt, 65-70; mem nominating comt, Rep State Conv, 66, 68 & 70; mem, Rep State Exec Comt Ala, 67-70 & 72-, mem steering comt, 74-; mem, State Rep Finance & Budget Comt, 67-69; deleg, Rep Nat Conv, 68 & 72; chmn, Seventh Dist Rep Comt, 74- Mil Serv: Entered as Pvt, Air Force, 43, released as S/Sgt, 46, after serv in Eighth Air Force, ETO, 45; Air Medal. Mem: Tuscaloosa Co, Ala & Am Bar Asns; Am Legion. Relig: Methodist. Legal Res: 302 Main Ave Northport AL 35476 Mailing Add: 312 First Nat Bank Bldg Tuscaloosa AL 35401

PETERS, PETER PIOTROWICZ (R)

Ill State Sen

Mailing Add: 5863 N Kolmar Ave Chicago IL 60630

PETERS, PHILIP L (R)

Chmn, Young Rep Fedn, Ore

b Portland, Ore, Oct 10, 40; s Charles L Peters & Rebecca G Gates P; m to Laurel A Ross; c Michael J, Ronald A & Stacey. Educ: Portland State Univ, BS Hist. Polit & Govt Pos: Co-chmn publ, Young Rep Fedn of Ore, 69-70, vchmn, 70-71, chmn, 71-; chmn, Multnomah Young Rep Club, 69-70; dir, Atiyeh for Gov campaign, 74. Bus & Prof Pos: US Peace Corps Vol, 62-64; pvt bus, 65-67 & 69-74; prof, Ore State Syst of Higher Educ, 67-69; life ins underwriter, Monarch Life Ins Co, 74- Legal Res: 305 SW 144 Beaverton OR 97005 Mailing Add: PO Box 3797 Portland OR 97208

PETERS, ROBERT G (D)

Ga State Rep

Mailing Add: PO Box 550 Ringgold GA 30736

PETERS, WILLIAM COOPER (D)

Mem, Colquitt Co Dem Exec Comt, Ga

b Moultrie, Ga, May 7, 22; s William Cleveland Peters & Elizabeth Cooper P; m 1950 to Ellen Brown; c John Clifton, Luellen, Floyd & Louise. Educ: Univ Ga, AB, 49, JD, 50; Kappa Sigma. Polit & Govt Pos: Justice of Peace, Ga, 53-71; mem, Colquitt Co Dem Exec Comt, 60-, chmn, formerly; co attorney, Colquitt Co, 67-70; mem, Ga State Dem Exec Comt, formerly; judge, Small Claims Court, 71-; recorder, City of Moultrie, 69- Bus & Prof Pos: Lawyer, 51- Mil Serv: Entered as Pvt, Army, 42, released as 1st Lt, 46, after serv in Air Transport Command, China-Burma-India, 44-46; Capt, Air Force Res; Air Medal with one Cluster. Mem: Kiwanis; Mason; Am Legion; Elk; VFW. Relig: Presbyterian. Legal Res: RR 6 Moultrie GA 31768 Mailing Add: PO Box 2 Moultrie GA 31768

PETERSEN, ARNOLD (SOCIALIST LABOR PARTY)

b Odense, Denmark, Apr 16, 85. Polit & Govt Pos: Nat secy, Socialist Labor Party, 14-69. Publ: Constitution of the United States, NY Labor News, Fifth Printing, 63, Theocracy or Democracy, 44 & Daniel De Leon, social architect, Vol I, 41, Vol II, 53. Mailing Add: 274 Highwood St Teaneck NJ 07666

PETERSEN, JANET JEAN (D)

b Omaha, Nebr, May 9, 18; d Herman Roy Kinsey & Verna Vesta Petty K; m to Arthur Peter Petersen; c Janet Jean (Mrs Nieto), Vee Ann Alyce (Mrs Wright), Arthur Victor & Harold Allan. Educ: St Catherine Sch Nursing, 68; Bellevue Col, BA, 71. Polit & Govt Pos: Pres, Sarpy Co Dem Cent Comt, formerly; alt deleg, Dem Nat Conv, 72; pres local unit, Nebr Fedn Dem Women, 72-; bd govs, Metrop Tech Community Col, 74- Bus & Prof Pos: Nurse, Dr Ben Ewing, Omaha, Nebr, 60-63 & Dr Jos McCaslin, 63-64; dept supvr, A Bergan Mercy Hosp, 64-65, RN coronary care, 68-71; nursing instr, Col St Mary (Nebr), 71-74. Mem: Nat League of Nursing; Am Asn Community & Jr Cols; Am Nurse Asn. Relig: Presbyterian. Mailing Add: 405 Bellevue Blvd North Bellevue NE 68005

PETERSEN, OPAL MAY (DFL)

VPres, First Dist Dem-Farmer-Labor Party, Minn

b St Paul, Minn, May 30, 24; d Emanuel Victor Nordlund & Martha May Rude N; c Nancy (Mrs James Linehan) & Daniel Paul & James Andrew Bartholomew. Educ: Minneapolis Bus Col, grad, 42; Univ Minn Exten, lifetime scholar. Polit & Govt Pos: Alt deleg or deleg, Co, Dist & State Dem-Farmer-Labor Convs, mem campaign comts for Cong Joseph E Karth, Sen Walter Mondale, Attorney Gen Spannaus & Gov Wendell Anderson; mem staff, Vice President Hubert H Humphrey, 68; Washington Co Coordr, H H Humphrey for Sen, 70, for President, 72; campaign mgr for Don Shaver & Dave Bieging for Minn State House of Rep, 70; mem, Minn State Dem-Farmer-Labor Cent Comt & State Exec Bd, currently; secy, Wash Co Dem-Farmer-Labor Party, currently; mem, Cent Comt & vpres, First Dist Dem Dem-Farmer-Labor Party, 72-; deleg, Dem Nat Conv, 72. Bus & Prof Pos: Off mgr, Brotherhood of Rwy Machinists, Dist 32, 57-60, Brotherhood of Maintenance of Way, 60-65 & Teamsters Local 974, 71-, off secy, Teamsters Local 471, 65-70. Mem: Off & Prof

Employees Union; Tops Club; Counter Weight Club; Camp Fire Girls; Club Scouts. Relig: Lutheran; Sunday Sch Teacher, 15 years. Mailing Add: 1109 S First Stillwater MN 55082

PETERSMEYER, VALLEA CORNELIA (R)
Mem, Warren Co Rep Party, Mo
b Hank Point, Mo, Feb 15, 11; d Allie Lee Monroe & Vina Iuka Trail M; m 1936 to Fredrick Detrich Petersmeyer; c Merly Fredrick. Educ: Cent Wesleyan Col, summers, 29-38; Northeast State Col, summer, 39. Polit & Govt Pos: Mem, Warren Co Rep Party, 60-, committeewoman, Elkhorn Twp, Ward Two, 60-; vpres, Warren Co Rep Comt, 62-66, chmn, 66-72. Mem: Rebekah; Band Booster's Club; Warrenton Study Club; Dorcas Soc; Parent-Teacher Orgn. Relig: Protestant. Mailing Add: 405 N 47th Warrenton MO 63383

PETERSON, ANDRIENNE TOSSO (D)
VChmn, Lake Co Dem Cent Comt, Colo
b Leadville, Colo, Oct 28, 24; d Andrew Tosso & Florence Maffei T; m to Leo V Peterson, wid; c Leandrea. Educ: Leadville High Sch, Colo, grad, 41. Polit & Govt Pos: Recording Secy, Lake Co Jane Jefferson Club, Colo, 58-60, vpres, 60-61, pres, 61-66; secy-treas, Lake Co Dem Cent Comt, Colo, 68-73, vchmn, 74-; secy, Fifth Judicial Dist, 68-70; secy, 35th Sen Dist, 68-70; secy, 61st Rep Dist, 74- Bus & Prof Pos: Deputy clerk, Lake Co Court, Leadville, 58-64; commodity clerk, Lake Co Welfare Dept, 62-65; eng secy, Bechtel Engrs, 65-67; med secy, Leadville Med Ctr, 67-70; chief acct, Lake Co, 70- Mem: Annunciation Church, Catholic Daughters Rosary & Altar Soc. Relig: Catholic. Legal Res: 135 E Third St Leadville CO 80461 Mailing Add: Box 558 Leadville CO 80461

PETERSON, BARBARA PRESTON (D)
Dem Nat Committeewoman, NDak
b Kenmare, NDa, July 19, 28; d Harry Earl Preston & Althea Hard P; m to Kermit Svein Peterson (deceased); c Stefan Kermit, Sarajane Althea, Seth Preston & Sabin Svein. Educ: Univ NDak, 3 years; Kappa Alpha Theta. Polit & Govt Pos: Pres, Minot Rep Women's Club, NDak, 66-68; deleg, Rep Nat Conv, 68; secy & vchairwoman, Fifth Dist Rep Party, 68; mem, Congressman Tom Kleppe Spec Comt, 68-69; Dem Nat Committeewoman, 72- Relig: Presbyterian. Mailing Add: New England ND 58647

PETERSON, BETTY ANN (D)
Mem, Colo Dem State Exec Comt
b Waco, Tex, July 12, 29; d James Herbert Guthrie & Verna Elsie Jones G; m 1952 to Wallace Bennett Peterson; c Wallace Bennett, Jr, Kenneth James, David Wayne, Kathryn Verna, Ronald Lee & Nancy Ann. Educ: Univ Tex, 48-49; Rosenberg Col, St Gallen, Switz, 49; European Command Finance Ctr, Friedborg, Ger, cert, 50. Polit & Govt Pos: Dist capt & committeewoman, Arapahoe Co Dem Party, Colo, 62-69, oper support chmn, 67-68; Arapahoe Co chmn, 35th Jefferson-Jackson Dinner, 67; mem, Colo State Credentials Comt, 68; Arapahoe Co Chmn, Ladies for Humphrey-Muskie, 68; chmn, Arapahoe Co Sen Dist 22, 68-; Arapahoe Co Campaign Chmn to Re-elect President Johnson, 68; mem, Colo Dem State Cent Comt, 68-69 & State Exec Bd, 69; chmn, Jefferson-Jackson 'Who Me' Luncheon, 69; mem, Colo Dem State Exec Comt, 69-; co & state deleg, Arapahoe Co Dem Party, 74. Bus & Prof Pos: Secy, War Crimes Trial, Dachau, Ger, 47; reservations clerk, Braniff Air Lines, Love Field, Dallas, Tex, 51; receptionist for Dr Cecil I Stell, Dallas, 52; model, The Parisian, Wichita Falls, 53. Publ: Feature ed, Petticoat Press, Sheppard AFB, Tex, 53-54. Mem: Easter Seal Soc; Englewood Jane Jefferson Club (officer); Lowry Retired Officer's Wives Club; East Arapahoe Coun Human Rels; Cherry Creek Woman's Club (parliamentarian, 70-). Honors & Awards: Centennial Dist Den Mother's Training Award, 65; Cert of Appreciation, Channel 6 Coun Educ TV, 68; Dem In 68 Award. Relig: Lutheran; Sunday sch dir, First Evangel Lutheran Church, Shreveport, La; Sunday sch teacher, Lutheran Church, Bossier City, La & Denver, Colo. Mailing Add: 2420 S Lima Denver CO 80232

PETERSON, C DONALD
Assoc Justice, Minn Supreme Court
b Minneapolis, Minn, Feb 2, 18; s Karl E Peterson (deceased) & Emma M Sellin P (deceased); m 1952 to Gretchen E Palen; c Barbara, Craig, Mark, Polly, Todd & Scott. Educ: Univ Minn, BA, with hon, 38; Univ Ill, JD, with hon, 41; Delta Sigma Rho. Polit & Govt Pos: Minn State Rep, 59-63; assoc justice, Minn Supreme Court, 67- Bus & Prof Pos: Sr partner, Howard, Peterson, LeFevere, Lefler & Hamilton, 55-66. Mil Serv: Air Force, 42-46, recalled as Maj, 50-51, serv as Judge Adv, Hq Far East Air Forces, Tokyo, 50-51; UN Medal; Bronze Star. Mem: Minn & Am Bar Asns; Am Law Inst; Minn Press Coun (chmn); Am Judicature Soc. Honors & Awards: State Original Oratory Champion, Col; Outstanding State Rep, Minn Legis, 60. Relig: Presbyterian. Mailing Add: 4809 Wilford Way Edina MN 55435

PETERSON, CARY (R)
Utah State Rep
Mailing Add: 406 E 500 N Nephi UT 84648

PETERSON, CHARLES R (D)
Okla State Sen
Mailing Add: State Capitol Oklahoma City OK 73105

PETERSON, CURTIS (D)
Fla State Sen
Mailing Add: 326 Senate Off Bldg Tallahassee FL 32304

PETERSON, DARREL LEE (R)
Minn State Rep
b Fairmont, Minn, Mar 8, 39; s Vernon Lynn Peterson & Helen Aagard P; m 1960 to Sharon Peryl Johnson; c Anne Kristen, Mary Kathryn & Elizabeth Catherine. Educ: Mankato State Col, 57-59; Univ Minn, BS, 61; Alpha Zeta. Polit & Govt Pos: Minn State Rep, 75-; mem task force on food supply & agr, Nat Conf State Legis, 75-; mem adv task force on small bus, Minn State Govt, 75- Bus & Prof Pos: Farmer, 61- Mem: East Chain Sportsman's Club (dir). Relig: United Methodist. Mailing Add: Rte 3 Fairmont MN 56031

PETERSON, DONALD OLIVER (D)
Dem Nat Committeeman, Wis
b Renville, Minn, Mar 9, 25; s Edgar Clarence Peterson & Jessie Henderson P; m 1946 to Roberta (Bobbie) Anne Taylor; c Gregory Alan, Terri Lynn, Stephanie Jo & Kirk Dale. Educ: Butler Univ, 43; Univ Minn, 46-47; Macalester Col, 48. Polit & Govt Pos: Various precinct & co Dem Party Off in Minn, SDak & Wis, 50-; chmn, Tenth Dist Dem Party, Wis, 67-68; del, Dem Nat Conv, 68; mem nat steering comt & past co-chmn, New Dem Coalition, currently; Dem Nat Committeeman, Wis, 71-; mem, Dem Charter Comn, 72-74; deleg, Dem Nat Mid-Term Conf, 74. Bus & Prof Pos: Vpres, Dadco Food Prod, Eau Claire, Wis, currently. Mil Serv: Entered as Pvt, Air Corps, 43, released as 1st Lt, 46, after serv in Fifth Air Force, SPac Theatre, 45-46; Air Medals. Relig: Unitarian. Mailing Add: 1406 State St PO Box 1107 Eau Claire WI 54701

PETERSON, ELLY M (R)
b New Berlin, Ill; m to Col William Peterson. Educ: William Woods Col; Northwestern Univ; Suburban Bus Col. Polit & Govt Pos: Aide to state chmn Lawrence Lindemer, Mich, 58-61; State Field Serv Mgr, 61; mem & former officer, Eaton Co & Charlotte Rep Comts; vchmn, Rep State Cent Comt, Mich, 61-65, chmn, 65-69; exec dir, Women's Div, Rep Nat Comt, 63, asst chmn, Rep Nat Comt, 64-70; Rep Nat Committeewoman, Mich, 68-70; Rep cand, US Sen, 64; addressed Rep Nat Conv, 64; deleg-at-lg, Rep Nat Conv, 68. Bus & Prof Pos: Hosp secy, Am Red Cross, 2 years overseas, former co pres & former dir, regional blood prog. Mem: Womens Campaign Fund; Deleg for Friendship Among Women (pres); Nat Ctr Vol Action. Relig: Congregational. Mailing Add: Rte 2 Charlotte MI 48813

PETERSON, ESTHER EGGERTSEN (D)
b Provo, Utah, Dec 9, 06; d Lars E Eggertsen & Annie Nielsen E; m 1932 to Oliver A Peterson; c Karen (Mrs Wieken), Eric Niels, Iver Echart & Lars Erling. Educ: Brigham Young Univ, AB, 27; Columbia Univ, MA, 30. Hon Degrees: Hon degrees from Smith, Bryant, Montclair, Simmons & Hood Cols, Carnegie Inst Technol, Northeastern Univ, Univ of Southern Utah, Western Col for Women, Univ Mich, Mich State Univ, Mercyhurst Col, Oxford Univ & Univ Utah. Polit & Govt Pos: Campaign worker, Dem Party, 42-46, 58-64 & 72; adv to US Del, Int Labor Orgn Conf, Geneva, Switz, 61 & 64; exec vchmn, President's Comt on Status of Women, 61-63; Asst Secy of Labor, 61-68, dir, Women's Bur, 61-64; spec asst to the President for consumer affairs & chmn, President's Comn on Consumer Interests, 64-68; mem bd, Nat Fair Campaign Practices Comt, currently. Bus & Prof Pos: Teacher indust dept, Boston YWCA; Winsor Sch & Br Agr Col, Cedar City, Utah, 27; asst dir educ, Amalgamated Clothing Workers of Am, 39-44, Wash legis rep, 45-48, legis rep, Indust Union Dept, AFL-CIO, 57-61; consumer adv, Giant Food Co, 70-; mem bd dirs, Nat Ctr for Resource Recovery. Mem: League of Women Voters; Am Asn Univ Women; Nat Consumers League; YWCA; Bus & Prof Women. Mailing Add: 7714 13th St NW Washington DC 20012

PETERSON, FRANK E (D)
NH State Rep
Mailing Add: 42 Hunking St Portsmouth NH 03801

PETERSON, GEOFFREY GISSLER (D)
b New York, NY, Feb 11, 46; s Roy Gerald Peterson (deceased) & Sigrid Marjorie Gissler P; m 1973 to Lynn Meredith Carey. Educ: Harvard Col, BA, 67; Georgetown Univ Law Ctr, JD, 71; Phi Alpha Delta. Polit & Govt Pos: Fed liaison, New Eng Regional Comn, 69; worked with Dem Polit Fund Raising for Phil Hoff & Sen Edward Kennedy, 70; chmn, Law Students for Dem Senate Victories in 70; legis asst, US Sen Abe Ribicoff, Conn, 71-74, admin asst, 75- Legal Res: 7 Scot-Alan Lane Westport CT 06880 Mailing Add: 507 Duke St Alexandria VA 22314

PETERSON, GEORGIA BODELL (R)
Utah State Rep
b Herriman, Utah; d Milton Bodell & Elizabeth Bodell Skanchy; m 1946 to Dr Ted T Peterson; c Craig Elwood & Elizabeth. Educ: Univ Utah. Polit & Govt Pos: Utah State Rep, 69-, mem educ, educ appropriations, polit subdiv & elections comts, Utah House Rep, formerly, chmn rules comt, formerly; vchmn bus & consumer western coun of state govts, currently, mem nat legis intergovt rels comt, 73-, mem comt health, educ & welfare, 73-, mem const rev comn, 71-, Asst Majority Whip, 73- Mem: Order of Women Legislators (deleg, 69-); Western Interstate Comn Higher Educ Conf; Utah Cong PTA; CofC; Rep Federated Clubs. Relig: Latter-day Saint. Mailing Add: 6417 Highland Dr Salt Lake City UT 84121

PETERSON, GUNNAR ARON JULIUS (R)
Chmn, Avon Rep Town Comt, Mass
b Svedala, Sweden, June 17, 00; s Hjalmar Sigfrid Peterson & Matilda Svenson P; m 1923 to Betty Carlson; c Earl Edmund & Elaine Marguerite (Mrs Sawler). Educ: High sch, Sweden, 15. Polit & Govt Pos: Chmn, Avon Bd Health, Mass, 44-65; chmn, Avon Rep Town Comt, 68- Bus & Prof Pos: Shipper, E C Hall Co, 24-62; foreman, Alfred G Peterson & Sons, Inc, 62- Mem: Scandinavian Fraternity of Am (former supreme officer); Vasa Order of Am; Southeastern Asn of Bd of Health (founder, first pres & hon exec bd mem, emer); YMCA; Mass Rep Comt. Relig: Lutheran. Mailing Add: 544 W Main St Avon MA 02322

PETERSON, HARRIETT MONROE (R)
Mem, State Rep Cent Comt Calif
b Hood River, Ore, May 14, 21; d George Henry Monroe & Carrie Candee M; m 1953 to Clarence W Peterson. Educ: Willamette Univ, BA, 43; Syracuse Univ, MA, 45. Polit & Govt Pos: Chaplain, Calif Fedn Rep Women, 55-60, recording secy, 61-63, pres cent div, 64-67, vpres from cent div, 68-69; Rep precinct worker, 12 years; mem, State Rep Cent Comt, Calif, 58-, mem exec comt, 67-70; pres, Tracy Rep Women, 62-63; alt deleg, Rep Nat Conv, 68. Bus & Prof Pos: Head resident of freshman dormitory, Univ of Redlands, 45-48; dean of women, Stockton Col, 48-51 & Col of the Pac, 48-53. Mem: PEO; Am Field Serv Comt; Tracy Women's Club; Hosp Auxiliary; Children's Home Soc (assoc mem). Honors & Awards: Jr Women's Club Citizen of the Year Award, Tracy, 61. Relig: Presbyterian. Mailing Add: 1457 Holly Dr Tracy CA 95376

PETERSON, HARRY L (D)
b Duluth, Minn, Feb 22, 40; s Harry Leonard Peterson & Pearl Rhode P; m 1963 to Sylvia Kay Brinkley; c Aaron. Educ: San Diego State Col, BA, 63; Univ Calif, Berkeley, MSW, 66; Harvard Med Sch-Mass Gen Hosp, Boston, cert, 69. Polit & Govt Pos: Deleg, Platform Comt, Wis State Dem Conv, 72; deleg, Dem Nat Conv, 72; chmn, Brown Co Citizens for McGovern-Shriver, Green Bay, 72; home asst, US Rep Robert J Cornell, Wis, 75- Bus & Prof Pos: Soc worker, Brown Co Guid Clin, Green Bay, Wis, 66-68; dir, Student Life Prog, Univ Wis-Green Bay, 69- Mil Serv: Entered as Pvt, Army Reserve, 60, released as Sgt, 66. Publ: Psychoanalysis and social work: the need for new ideas, New Perspectives, spring 67; A survey of community helpers, Hosp & Community Psychiat, 11/69. Mem: Nat Asn of Soc Workers; Acad of Cert Soc Workers; Am Asn Higher Educ; Am Civil Liberties Union (founder & vchmn, Northeastern Wis Chap, 68-71). Relig: Protestant. Mailing Add: 926 S Jackson St Green Bay WI 54301

PETERSON, HJALMAR REGINALD (R)
b Boston, Mass, Sept 26, 07; s Alfred G Peterson & Clara W Ostrom P; m to Ellen J Olson; c Joan (Mrs Allan MacEachern) & Janet (Mrs Paul Weatherbee). Educ: Bentley Col, grad; Boston Univ & Northeastern Univ, advan courses; past pres, Northeast Univ Small Bus Mgt Assocs. Polit & Govt Pos: Mem bd of gov, Commercial Club of Brockton, formerly; chmn, Cardinal Cushing Gen Hosp Fund Dr, formerly; chmn, Brockton City Rep Comt, Brockton City Rep Chmn, Mass, 45-49; mem, city coun, Brockton, 50-54, mayor, 56-57; deleg, Rep State Conv, 50-74; deleg, Rep Nat Conv, 56-72; chmn, Mass State Rep Finance Comt, formerly. Bus & Prof Pos: Pres, Alfred G Peterson & Sons, Inc & Mackedon Mfg Co, Inc; pres, Canvas Products Asn Int; dir, Mass Bank & Trust; past pres, New Eng Awning & Canvas Products Asn. Mem: Brockton CofC; Mason (32 degree); Paul Revere Lodge, Aleppo Temple Shrine; Elks; Vega Club. Relig: Baptist. Legal Res: 103 Braemoor Rd Brockton MA 02402 Mailing Add: 491 W Main St Avon MA 02322

PETERSON, IRENE M (D)
b Enid, Okla; d Frank Nathan Ludlum & Lillian Underkoffler L; div. Educ: Study of law, 27-35. Polit & Govt Pos: Vpres, Young Dem of Ill, 36-38; admin asst to US Rep Leonor K Sullivan, Mo, 67- Bus & Prof Pos: Secy, Sturtz & Ewan, Kewanee, Ill, 27-38; asst to trust officer, Security Trust Co, St Louis, Mo, 38-39; asst to chief counsel, pres & chmn bd, Mo Pac RR Co, 40-66; asst to publisher, St Louis Globe-Dem, 66. Mem: Bus & Prof Women's Club St Louis; Altrusa Club St Louis; Group Action Coun Gtr St Louis; Group Action Coun Women's Club. Honors & Awards: Outstanding Working Woman Award, Downtown St Louis, Inc, 64; Woman of Year Award, Bus & Prof Women's Club of St Louis, 72. Relig: Catholic. Legal Res: 4615 Lindell Blvd St Louis MO 63108 Mailing Add: Apt A-1009 1400 S Joyce St Arlington VA 22202

PETERSON, JACQUE P (D)
b Charleston, Ark, July 21, 31; d L A (Jack) Floyd & Verna Sharp F; m 1954 to Dr Sherman Peterson; c Brent, twins Kevin & Kimberly, & Scott. Educ: Ark Polytech Col, AA, 51; Henderson State Col, BSE, 53; Delta Kappa Pi; Heart & Key Home Econ Club. Polit & Govt Pos: Election clerk, Monticello, Ark, 69; asst coordr, Dale Bumpers Campaign, Drew Co, Ark, 70; mem, Inaugural Comt, Little Rock, Ark, 70 & 72; mem, Ark State Dem Cent Comt, formerly. Bus & Prof Pos: Instr home econ, Hughes High Sch, Ark, 53-54, Knobnoster High Sch, Mo, 55-56, Charleston High Sch, Ark, 58-59 & Siloam Springs High Sch, 63-68. Publ: College life today, Progressive Farmer Mag, 53. Mem: Delta Kappa Gamma; Ark Home Econ Asn; Ark Educ Asn; Am Voc Educ Asn; Ark Fedn Women's Clubs. Honors & Awards: Am Homemaker Degree & hon mem Ark Asn, Future Homemakers Am. Relig: Methodist. Mailing Add: 17 Nob Hill Cove Little Rock AR 72205

PETERSON, JAMES A (R)
NDak State Rep
Mailing Add: State Capitol Bismarck ND 58501

PETERSON, JAMES HARDIN (D)
b Batesburg, SC, Feb 11, 94. Educ: Univ of Fla, LLB, 14; Phi Alpha Delta; Fla Southern Col, Dr of Humanities, 47. Polit & Govt Pos: Spec counsel, W Coast Inland Navigation Dist, 51-; spec counsel, Territory of Guam, 51-52; chmn, comn of Appn of Fed Laws to Guam, 51; US Rep, Fla, 33-51; chmn, Dem Steering Comt, 33-51; Polk Co Solicitor, Fla, 23-31; Polk Co Prosecuting Attorney, 22-23; city attorney, Lakeland, Fla, 16 years. Bus & Prof Pos: Attorney. Mem: Lakeland Bar Asns; Am Judicature Soc; Kiwanis; Am Legion; Mason. Honors & Awards: Recipient of Awards, Nat Audubon Soc, 54; Fla Wildlife Conservation Award, 55; Certificate of Appreciation, Nat Conf of State Parks; Achievement Medal, Univ of Tampa; Distinguished Alumnus Award, Univ Fla, 63. Relig: Methodist. Mailing Add: 215 E Lime St Lakeland FL 33801

PETERSON, JOHN CHARLES (R)
b Topeka, Kans, Apr 15, 48; s Cecil Norvin Peterson & Helen Lyon P; single. Educ: Stanford Univ, AB, 70; Washburn Law Sch, 70-; Alpha Sigma Phi. Polit & Govt Pos: Kans State Rep, 55th Dist, 71-74; Rep cand for US Rep, Kans, 74. Bus & Prof Pos: Ins agt, Union Cent Life Ins Co, currently. Mem: Nat Asn Life Ins Underwriters. Honors & Awards: Gov, Kans Boys State; Kans State High Sch Debate & Oratory Champion; Third Pl, Nat Am Legion Oratory Champion; Serv to Educ Award, Eagleton Inst Polit, 72. Relig: Methodist. Mailing Add: 1600 High Topeka KS 66604

PETERSON, LEROY L (DFL)
b Cherokee, Iowa, Dec 27, 18; s Hans Peterson & Ruth Cashman P; m 1942 to Elizabeth J Waligura; c LeRoy L, Jr, Greg J, Karen A & Mary B. Educ: Barnum High Sch, Minn, 38. Polit & Govt Pos: Chmn, Ottertail Co Dem-Farmer-Labor Party, Minn, formerly. Bus & Prof Pos: Signalman, Burlington Northern RR, 41- Mil Serv: Entered as Pvt, Army, 42, released as Sgt, 45, after serv in 21st Chem Co, Africa, Sicily, Italy, France & Germany. Mem: Elks Lodge 1093; VFW; KofC 3118; Brotherhood of RR Signalmen 154. Relig: Catholic. Mailing Add: 905 Cleveland Ave N Fergus Falls MN 56573

PETERSON, LOIS GOODENOUGH (D)
b Springfield, SDak, Apr 13, 16; d Herbert Harold Goodenough & Florence Pearl G; m 1941 to Leroy Eric Peterson; c Karen (Mrs Donald Carpenter), Eric L & Kristin L. Educ: Southern State Teachers Col (SDak), Teacher's Cert, 34; Oberlin Col, AB, 37; Pi Kappa Delta; Delta Sigma Rho. Polit & Govt Pos: Mem, Swarthmore Dem Comt, 53-, chmn, 57-66; vchmn, Delaware Co Dem Comt, 64-70; deleg, Dem Nat Mid-Term Conf, 74; jury comnr, Delaware Co, Pa, currently. Bus & Prof Pos: Elem teacher, Newell, SDak, 34-35; elem teacher, Niles, Mich, 37-41; clerk-typist, Studebaker Aviation, South Bend, Ind, 41-42; reference asst, Swarthmore Col Libr, Pa, 60-65 & 68-; off mgr & secy, Delaware Co Dem Comt, Media, Pa, 65-68 & part-time, 68-73. Mem: Swarthmore League of Women Voters. Relig: Protestant. Mailing Add: 341 Vassar Ave Swarthmore PA 19081

PETERSON, LOWELL (D)
Wash State Sen
b Pateros, Wash, 1921; m to Ruth (deceased); c Lowell O, Cindee & Bart. Polit & Govt Pos: Councilman, Concrete, Wash, 57-60, Mayor, 60-63; Wash State Sen, currently. Bus & Prof Pos: Oil distributor. Mil Serv: Navy. Mem: Am Legion; Eagles; Elks. Mailing Add: Box 249 Concrete WA 98237

PETERSON, M BLAINE (D)
Utah State Rep
Mailing Add: 1018-26th St Ogden UT 84401

PETERSON, M F
Supt of Pub Instr, NDak
b Bowman Co, NDak; m 1938 to Gladys Swenson; c Gail, Carole & Pauline. Educ: Concordia Col, BA; Univ NDak, MSEd. Polit & Govt Pos: Past pres, Cent States Conf; mem exec comt, Midwest Work Conf on Rural Educ; Dep Supt of Pub Instr, NDak, 47, Supt of Pub Instr, 51-; former mem bd dirs, Coun of Chief State Sch Officers, pres, 67-68; exec dir & secy, State Bd of Pub Sch Educ. Bus & Prof Pos: High sch teacher, coach & supt, various schs, NDak. Publ: Ed, County Superintendents Handbook, 48 & 59, Compilation of School Laws of North Dakota, 55 & School Boards Manual, 66; plus others. Mem: Gtr North Dakota Asn; Mason; Kiwanis; NDak Educ Asn; NDak Asn of Sch Adminr. Relig: Lutheran. Mailing Add: State Capitol Bismarck ND 58501

PETERSON, MARION (D)
Mem, Dem Nat Comt, Utah
Mailing Add: 348 S Main St Salina UT 84654

PETERSON, MARTIN LYNN (D)
b Lewiston, Idaho, Apr 22, 43; s Conrad E Peterson & Charlotte Hoffman P; single. Educ: Columbia Basin Col, AS, 64; Univ Idaho, BA, 68; Sigma Delta Chi; state pres, Alpha Epsilon Rho, 66. Polit & Govt Pos: Mem staff, Congressman Compton I White Campaign, Idaho, 68; asst to US Sen Frank Church, 68-71; nat committeeman, Idaho Young Dem Clubs, 70-72; mem comt on party structure & deleg selection, Idaho Dem Party, 70-72; exec dir, Idaho Human Resource Develop Coun, Gov Off, 71-74; mem, Idaho Interagency Comt on Model Cities, 71-74; mem, Nat Coalition of Gov Manpower Policy Adv & Planners, 72-74; asst staff dir, Nat Gov Conf Adv Task Force on Human Resources, 72-73; mem, Human Resources Coun, Fedn of Rocky Mt States, 72-74; staff dir, Nat Gov Conf Adv Task Force on Human Resources, 73-74; coordr, Andrus for Gov Comt, 74; dir, Prog Develop & Opers, Asn of Idaho Cities, 75- Bus & Prof Pos: Mem staff, KUID-TV, Moscow, Idaho, 64-68. Mil Serv: Entered as Pvt, Army Nat Guard, 60, released as S/Sgt, 68, after serv in 148th Artil, Idaho Nat Guard. Mem: Elks; Idaho Dem Party; Boise Valley Fly Fishermen; Silver City Taxpayer's Asn; Common Cause. Honors & Awards: Idaho Citation Award, Int Asn of Personnel in Employ Security, 73. Relig: Methodist. Legal Res: 1429 E Euclid Boise ID 83702 Mailing Add: PO Box 173 Boise ID 83701

PETERSON, MERLE FRANCIS (D)
Chmn, Desha Co Dem Cent Comt, Ark
b Mt Carmel, Ill, Mar 6, 16; s Claude Roscoe Peterson & Edith Dixon P; m 1939 to Deloris Ellegood. Educ: Ark State Univ, Jonesboro, BS, 38. Polit & Govt Pos: Committeeman, Dem Party, Ark, 48-60; Ark State Sen, 61-66; deleg, Ark Const Conv, 69-; chmn, Desha Co Dem Cent Comt, Ark, 72-; chmn, Desha Co Elec Comt, 72- Bus & Prof Pos: Owner & mgr, Dumas Motor Co, 39- Mil Serv: Entered as Pvt, Air Force, 42, released as Capt, 45, after serv in 489th Squadron, 340th Bomb Group, Mediterranean, 43-45; NAfrican, Southern Italy, Sicily & Corsica Campaign Ribbons. Mem: Ark State Auto Dealers Asn; Dumas CofC; Lions; Am Legion; Farm Bur. Honors & Awards: Benjamin Franklin Quality Dealer Award, 69. Relig: Methodist. Legal Res: 117 Brasfield Dumas AR 71639 Mailing Add: PO Box 66 Dumas AR 71639

PETERSON, PETER G (R)
b Kearney, Nebr, June 5, 26; s George Peterson & Venet Paul P; m 1953 to Sally Hornbogen; c John, James, David, Holly & Michael. Educ: Mass Inst Technol, 44-45; Northwestern Univ, BS, summa cum laude, 47; Univ Chicago, MBA with honors, 51; Beta Gamma Sigma; Alpha Tau Omega. Polit & Govt Pos: Chmn planning comt, Ill Citizens for Eisenhower, 52; asst to the President for Int Econ Affairs, 71-72; Secy of Com, 72-73; ambassador & personal rep of the President, 73- Bus & Prof Pos: Exec vpres, Market Facts, Inc, Chicago, Ill, 47-53; vpres, gen mgr & asst to pres, McCann-Erickson, 53-58; exec vpres & dir, Bell & Howell, 58-61, pres, 61-63, pres & chief exec off, 63-68, chmn bd & chief exec off, 68-71; former dir, Am Express Co, First Nat Bank Chicago & Bell Tel Co; former trustee, Brookings Inst, Comt for Econ Develop & Nat Educ TV; bd trustees, Univ Chicago, currently. Publ: Contrib ed, Readings in market organization and price policies, 52. Mem: Econ, Chicago; Burning Tree Club; Chevy Chase Club. Honors & Awards: One of Ten Outstanding Young Men in US, US Jr CofC, 61. Mailing Add: Dept of Commerce Washington DC 20230

PETERSON, PHILIP F (R)
Maine State Rep
Mailing Add: Drawer M Caribou ME 04736

PETERSON, ROBERT EARL (R)
Deleg, Minn Rep State Exec Comt
b Glen, Minn, Feb 10, 27; s Brynolf C Peterson & Edith Barhite P; m 1953 to Doraine Lois Anderson; c Janet Lee, Robert Earl, Jr & Lisa Ann. Educ: Bethel Col, 47-49 Univ Minn, Minneapolis, BA, Econ, 51. Polit & Govt Pos: Campaign mgr, Anoka Co Rep Party, Minn, 62; third vchmn, Anoka Co Rep Comt, 63, chmn, 64-65, third dist chmn, 65-69; del, Rep Nat Conv, 68; deleg, Minn Rep State Exec Comt, 69- Bus & Prof Pos: Salesman, General Mills, 51-53; salesman, Standard Engineering, 53-54; supvr, Montgomery Ward, 55-56; materials mgr, Union Brass, 56-65; salesman-owner, Peterson Enterprises, 65- Mil Serv: Entered as Seaman 2/C, Navy, 45, released as Seaman 1/C, 46, after serv in Casu 33, Far East. Mem: Minn Soc for Indust Engrs; Twin City Purchasing Agents Asn; Nat Purchasing Agents Asn; Mfrs Agents Nat Asn; Carpenter's Union. Relig: Baptist. Mailing Add: 480 Rice Creek Blvd Minneapolis MN 55432

PETERSON, ROBERT W (R)
Auditor, NDak
b Williston, NDak, Jan 18, 29; s Carsten Peterson & Clara Solfest P; m 1950 to Beverly Henning; c Randy, Gary, Sonya & Mark. Educ: Concordia Col (Moorhead, Minn), BA, 51; Univ NDak, MS, 60. Polit & Govt Pos: Rep precinct comt, 63-67; NDak State Rep, Dist 1, 67-73; Auditor, NDak, 73- Bus & Prof Pos: Teacher high sch, NDak, 53-63; clin adminr, Western Dak Med Group, Williston, 63-73. Mil Serv: Entered as Pvt, Army, 51, released as Cpl, 53, after serv in Early Warning Radar, US, 51-53. Mem: Nat Asn State Auditors, Comptrollers & Treas; NDak Asn Clin Adminrs (pres, 70-71); Am Legion; Elks; Sons of Norway. Relig: Lutheran. Mailing Add: 621 Avenue C West Bismarck ND 58501

PETERSON, RUSSELL WILBUR (R)
b Portage, Wis, Oct 3, 16; s John Anton Peterson & Emma Marie Anthony P; m 1937 to Eva Lillian Turner; c Russell Glen, Peter Jon, Kristin Havill & Elin. Educ: Univ Wis, BS, 38, PhD, 42; Phi Beta Kappa; Sigma Xi; Phi Eta Sigma; Phi Lambda Upsilon. Polit & Govt Pos: Chmn, Finance Comt, Del State Rep Party, 65-68; Gov, Del, 69-73; chmn, Nat Adv Comn on

Criminal Justice Standards & Goals, 71-73; deleg, Rep Nat Conv, 72; chmn exec comt, Comn on Critical Choices for Am, 73, mem, 74-; chmn, President's Coun on Environ Qual. Bus & Prof Pos: Research mgr & supvr textile fibers dept, E I du Pont de Nemours & Co, Wilmington, Del, 46-51, tech supt, Seaford, Del & Kinston, NC, 51-52, asst plant mgr, Kinston, NC, 53-54, research dir, Wilmington, Del, 54, merchandising mgr, 54-55, research dir, 55-59, tech dir new prod, 59-62, dir research & develop div, develop dept, 63-69; chmn bd, Textile Res Inst. Publ: National environmental policy, In: Proc of First Symposium on RANN, 11/73; Nation's chief environmental adviser offers a long-range plan for energy, Smithsonian, 7/74; The quest for quality of life, BioScience, 3/75; plus others. Mem: Am Chem Soc; Am Asn Advan Sci; fel Am Inst Chemists; Mason; Grange. Honors & Awards: Commercial Develop Asn Annual Award, 71; Birdwatchers of Am Award, 71; Gold Medal Award, World Wildlife Fund, 71; Conservationist of Year, Nat Wildlife Fedn, 72; Parson's Award, Am Chem Soc, 74. Relig: Unitarian. Legal Res: 12 St Lawrence St Rehoboth Beach DE 19971 Mailing Add: Coun on Environ Qual 722 Jackson Pl Washington DC 20006

PETERSON, TALBOT (R)
b Neenah, Wis, Mar 22, 22; s Raymond A Peterson & Ruth Talbot P; m 1946 to Evelyn P DePuy; c Frances Strong & Michael Talbot. Educ: Lake Forest Col, 41-42; Northwestern Univ, Evanston, 42. Polit & Govt Pos: Chmn, Outagamie Co Young Rep, Wis, 50-51; chmn, Eighth Dist Young Rep, 52-53; chmn, Rep Party of Outagamie Co, 53-54; vchmn, Wis Rep State Statutory Comt, 62-63; chmn, Rep Party of Wis, 63-65; Rep Nat Committeeman, 63-65; deleg, Rep Nat Conv, 64 & 72; chmn, Eighth Dist Nixon for President Comt, 68; chmn, Area Eight Comt to Reelect the President, 72. Bus & Prof Pos: Asst to prod mgr, Valley Iron Works Co, Appleton, Wis, 46-52, sales rep, 52-55, secy, 55-57, secy & asst to the pres, 57-59, vpres, 59-64; dir mkt planning for paper indust, Allis Chalmers, Milwaukee, 65-68, gen mgr, Paper Mach Div, 68- Mil Serv: Entered as Pvt, Army, 42, released as 1st Lt, 46, after serv in 39th Inf, 9th Div, ETO, 44-46; Lt Col (Ret), Army Res, 17 years; Bronze Star Medal; Purple Heart; Distinguished Unit Citation; European Theater Ribbon; Combat Inf Badge. Mem: Reserve Officers Asn (Nat Jr Army VPres); Rotary; Am Legion; Tech Asn of Pulp & Paper Indust; Paper Indust Mgt Asn. Relig: Episcopal. Mailing Add: 1421 W Oakcrest Dr Appleton WI 54911

PETERSON, THOMAS J (D)
Maine State Rep
Mailing Add: Box 157 South Windham Windham ME 04082

PETERSON, VAL (R)
Co-Chmn, Wayne Co Rep Cent Comt, Nebr
b Oakland, Nebr, July 18, 03; s Henry C Peterson & Hermanda Swanberg P; m 1929 to Elizabeth Howells Pleak. Educ: Wayne State Col, AB, 27; Univ Nebr, AM, 31 & additional grad study, 31-33. Hon Degrees: LLD, Midland Col, Muhlenberg Col, Tex Lutheran Col, Fairleigh-Dickinson Univ & Stetson Univ. Polit & Govt Pos: Secy to Gov Dwight Griswold, Nebr, 41-42; mem, Mo Basin Inter-Agency Comt, 47-52; Gov, Nebr, 47-53; chmn, Mo River State Comt, 48-52; chmn, Nat Gov Conf, 52; admin asst to President Eisenhower, 53; sat in cabinet by presidential invitation & held cabinet status, participated in Nat Security Coun meetings & presided over several White House Gov & Mayor Conf, Eisenhower Admin; US rep, various NATO meetings; mem, Comn on Inter-Govt Rels, 53-55; Fed Civil Defense Adminr, 53-57; US Ambassador, Denmark, 57-61; deleg, Rep Nat Conv, 60-64, 68 & 72; chmn, Nebr State Centennial Comn, 61-62; regent, bd regents, Univ Nebr, 63-66, pres, 65; mem bd of trustees, People to People Inc, 67-, exec comt, 67-69, vchmn bd, 69-70; consult, Nat Comn on Causes & Prevention of Crime, 69; US Ambassador, Finland, 69-73; co-chmn, Wayne Co Rep Cent Comt, currently. Bus & Prof Pos: Instr, Nebr Pub Schs, 25-30; instr, Univ Nebr, 30-33; supt, Elgin Schs, 33-39; pub, Elgin Rev, 36-46; dir, J M McDonald Co, Hastings, Nebr, 56-66, vchmn bd, 61-66; vpres & adminr, J M McDonald Found, Inc, 61-65; dir, Investors Life Ins Co, Nebr, 61-69; pres, Wayne State Found, Wayne, 61-; chmn bd dirs, Life Investors Nebr, Omaha, 62-69; dir, First Nat Bank, Hastings, 63-69, hon dir, 70-; chmn bd, Investors Growth Indust, Inc, Omaha, 69, dir, 69-; dir, State Nat Bank & Trust Co, Wayne, 73-; dir-at-lg, Lower Elkhorn Natural Resources Dist; distinguished prof polit sci & polit affairs, Wayne State Col, currently. Mil Serv: Entered as Capt, Army Air Corps, 42, released as Lt Col, 46, after serv in Hq, China-Burma-India Theatre; Air Force Res, 46-63; Bronze Star Medal; Asiatic-Pac Theatre Serv Medal. Mem: Nat Press Club; Omaha Club; Lochland Country Club; York Rite; Scottish Rite. Honors & Awards: Am Red Cross Citation for Work in Disaster Relief; Decorated with Grand Cross of Dannebrog by King Frederick IX of Denmark; Int Serv Award, Kearney State Col, 69; Americanism Award for Outstanding Achievement & Patriotic Serv to our Nation, China-Burma-India Vet Asn, 73; Nebr Builders Award, Univ Nebr, Lincoln, 75. Relig: Lutheran. Mailing Add: 710 E Seventh St Wayne NE 68787

PETERSON, WALLACE CARROLL (D)
Mem, State Dem Cent Comt, Nebr
b Omaha, Nebr, Mar 28, 21; s Fred Nels Peterson & Grace Leila Brown P; m 1944 to Eunice Vivian Peterson; c Wallace C, Jr & Shelley Lorraine. Educ: Univ Nebr-Lincoln, BA, 47, MA, 48, PhD, 53. Polit & Govt Pos: Mem, State Dem Cent Comt, Nebr, 68-, ed, Nebr Dem, 74-; deleg, Dem Nat Mid-Term Conf, 74. Bus & Prof Pos: From instr to prof econ, Univ Nebr-Lincoln, 51-66, George Holmes prof, 66-, chmn dept, 65- Mil Serv: Entered as Pvt, Army, 42, released as Capt, 46, after serv in various theatres. Publ: Auth, The Welfare State in France, Univ Nebr, 60; Elements of Economics, 73 & Income, Employment and Economic Growth, 74, W W Norton. Mem: Am & Midwest Econ Asns; Am Asn Advan Sci; Am Asn Univ Prof; Asn Evolutionary Econ. Honors & Awards: Fulbright fel, France, 57-58, Greece, 64-65. Legal Res: 4549 South St Lincoln NE 68506 Mailing Add: Dept of Econ Univ Nebr-Lincoln Lincoln NE 68508

PETERSON, WALTER (R)
b Nashua, NH, Sept 19, 22; s Walter Rutherford Peterson & Helen Reed P; m 1949 to Dorothy Donovan; c Margaret & Andrew. Educ: Col William & Mary; Univ NH; Dartmouth Col, BA, 47; Beta Theta Pi. Polit & Govt Pos: Chmn, Hillsborough Co Rep Comt, NH, 52-64; mem, Budget Comt, Peterborough, 55-61; NH State Rep, 61-68, majority leader, NH House of Rep, 61-68, speaker, 65-68; Gov, NH, 69-73. Bus & Prof Pos: Realtor, The Petersons, Peterborough, 49-68; dir, Nat Asn Real Estate Bds, 58-62; pres, NH Realtors Asn, 60-61. Mil Serv: Naval overseas officer, 42-46. Mem: Lions; VFW; Am Legion; Elks; Grange. Relig: Episcopal. Legal Res: E Mountain Rd Peterborough NH 03458 Mailing Add: 42 Grove St Peterborough NH 03458

PETERSON, WARREN EDWARD (R)
Wash State Rep
b Nashville, Tenn, Feb 26, 40; s Alver Edward Nathaniel Peterson (deceased) & Mildred Larsen P; m 1975 to Barbara Elizabeth Schlag. Educ: Univ Pa Wharton Sch Econ, BS in Econ; Theta Xi. Polit & Govt Pos: Wash State Rep, 75- Bus & Prof Pos: Financial systs supvr, Boeing Co, 66- Mil Serv: Entered as Officer Cand, Navy, 62, released as Lt(jg), 66, after serv in USS Oriskany, Pac, 64-66; Lt, Naval Res; Vietnam Serv, Navy Unit Commendation. Mem: Young Rep of King Co; Seattle-King Co Am Revolution Bicentennial Comn. Relig: Presbyterian. Mailing Add: 1927 25th Ave E Seattle WA 98112

PETIT, MICHAEL DONALD (D)
b Hartford, Conn, Aug 3, 42; s Donald Raphael Petit & Jean Brunnell P; m 1972 to Caroline Roth. Educ: Fla State Univ, 62-66; George Washington Univ, 71; Sigma Delta Chi. Polit & Govt Pos: Press secy to US Rep Claude Pepper, Fla, 68-69; press secy, Select Comt on Crime, US House Rep, 69-71, info dir, 72-73; admin asst to US Rep William Gunter, Fla, 73-75; admin asst to US Rep William J Hughes, NJ, 75- Mil Serv: Army, 66-72. Publ: Co-auth & co-ed, Juvenile justice and corrections, 1/73 & auth & co-ed, Organized criminal influences in horse racing, 6/73, Select Comt Crime, US House Rep. Mem: Admin Asst Asn. Legal Res: 422 Rosaro Ave Coral Gables FL 33146 Mailing Add: 119 Eighth St SE Apt 202 Washington DC 20003

PETRAFESO, PETE (DFL)
Minn State Rep
Mailing Add: 3200 Virginia Ave S St Louis Park MN 55426

PETRAITIS, KAREL COLETTE (R)
Nat Committeewoman, Md Fedn Young Rep
b Chicago, Ill, Apr 4, 45; d Ferdinand John Petraitis & Dolores Karroll P; single. Educ: Univ Md, Mary Elizabeth Roby scholar, BA, 67, Grad Sch, 67-68, Law Sch, 68; George Washington Univ Law Ctr, JD, 71; Hasting Law Sch, 74; Phi Alpha Theta; Pi Sigma Alpha; John Marshall Pre-Law Hon; Univ Theatre; Young Rep; Govt & Polit Club; Freshman Orientation Bd. Polit & Govt Pos: Youth co-chmn, Agnew for Gov, Md, 66; youth coordr, Mathias for Senate, 68; hon sgt at arms, Rep Nat Conv, 68, Md Young Rep Conv coordr, 72; Prince Georges youth coordr, Beall for Senate, 70; adv, Prince Georges TAR, 70-74; law clerk, Prince Georges Co Off Law, 71-72, assoc co attorney, 72-; legal counsel, Region III Young Rep, 71-73; nat committeewoman, Md Fedn Young Rep, 71-; co-chmn young voters, Prince Georges Comt to Reelect the President, 72; dist chmn, Prince Georges Co Rep Party, 72-74; first sub-dist vpres, Prince Georges Young Rep, 72-74, legal counsel, 74-; secy, Co Coun Rep Clubs, 72-74; dir, Md Fedn TAR, 73-74. Bus & Prof Pos: Model, Hecht Co, Md, 59-62; pub rels dir & box off mgr, Summer Theatre, Univ Md, 65. Publ: Auth, Inside Marlboro—Communique, 71 & Trial by jury—Communique, 72, Prince Georges Co Rep Cent Comt; co-ed, Official Opinions of the Office of Law, Prince Georges Co Govt, 73 & 74. Mem: March of Dimes; Am Asn of Univ Women; University Park Rep Women's Club; Prince George's & Maryland Bar Asns. Honors & Awards: Best Actress, Washington Archdiocesean Play Festival, 60 & 61; Woman of the Year, Md Fedn of Young Rep, 70-71; Distinguished Vol Leadership, Nat Found of March of Dimes, 72; Nat Young Rep Woman of the Year, 73-75; One of Ten Outstanding Young Women Am, 74. Relig: Roman Catholic. Mailing Add: 7307 Radcliffe Dr College Park MD 20740

PETRARCA, JOSEPH A (D)
Pa State Rep
Mailing Add: Capitol Bldg Harrisburg PA 17120

PETREY, JOE BRADLEY (D)
b Montgomery, Ala, Sept 10, 52; s Walter Loyce Petrey & Susie Bradley P; m 1974 to JoAnne Smith; c Loyce Bradley. Educ: Univ Miss, 70; Univ Ala, 70-74; Pi Kappa Alpha. Polit & Govt Pos: Deleg, Nat Dem Conv, 72. Bus & Prof Pos: Officer & dir, W L Petrey Wholesale Co, Inc, 74- Relig: Methodist. Mailing Add: PO Box 48 Petrey AL 36062

PETRI, THOMAS E (R)
Wis State Sen
b Marinette, Wis; s Robert G Petri & Marian I Humleker P; single. Educ: Harvard Col, BA, 62, Harvard Univ Law Sch, LLB, 65. Polit & Govt Pos: Wis State Sen, 73- Bus & Prof Pos: Attorney, Petri Law Off, 72- Publ: Co-auth & ed, From Disaster to Distinction, Beacon Press, 65 & Election 64, Ripon Soc, 65; co-auth, Rights of mentally ill, Ripon Forum, 66. Mem: Am Bar Asn; Harvard Faculty Club; Harvard Club of NY; Madison Club. Mailing Add: Rte 3 Fond du Lac WI 54935

PETRIS, NICHOLAS C (D)
Calif State Sen
b Oakland, Calif, Feb, 23, 23; m 1951 to Anna Vlahos. Educ: Univ Calif, AB; Stanford Law Sch, LLB. Polit & Govt Pos: Vpres, Calif Dem Coun, San Francisco Bay Area, 56-58; Social Serv Bur; Bd Mgrs; mem, Redevelop Agency of Oakland, 57-58; Calif State Assemblyman, 58-66; Calif State Sen, 67- Bus & Prof Pos: Attorney-at-law. Mil Serv: Army, Antiaircraft Artil. Mem: Eagles; Mason; Am Hellenic Educ Progressive Asn; Mex Am Polit Asn; NAACP. Honors & Awards: Selected as Man of Year, Calif Kidney Found, 68; Legislator of Year Award, Calif Trial Lawyers Asn. Relig: Greek Orthodox. Legal Res: 6250 Fairlane Dr Oakland CA 94611 Mailing Add: State Capitol Sacramento CA 95814

PETRO, GEORGE (R)
Ga State Rep
Mailing Add: 3189 C Buford Hwy Atlanta GA 30329

PETRUCCI, ANTHONY MARK (D)
b Fayetteville, Ark, Nov 12, 41; s John Petrucci & Fay Henley P; single. Educ: Sacramento State Col, BA, 65, MA, 69. Polit & Govt Pos: Govt intern, Lt Gov Off, Calif, 64-65; admin asst, State Sen Fred Farr, 65-66; alt delg, Dem Nat Conv, 72. Bus & Prof Pos: Prof polit sci, Harrisburg Area Community Col, Pa, 69-; dir, City Internship Prog, Inc, 71-72. Mil Serv: Entered as Seaman, Navy, 59, released as PO 3/C, 62, after serv in USS Lexington, CVA-16, Aircraft Carrier, 7th Fleet, Far East, 60-62. Publ: Where have all the voters gone, Harrisburg Independent Press, 72. Mem: Foreign Policy Asn of Harrisburg (vpres, 71-73); Ctr for Dem Insts; Acad Polit & Soc Sci. Honors & Awards: Teacher of Year, Harrisburg Area Community Col Student Body, 71. Mailing Add: 216 Muench St Harrisburg PA 17102

PETRY, JOHN W (D)
b Laredo, Tex, Dec 25, 45; s Herbert Charles Petry, Jr & Josephine White P; m 1968 to Jill Lea Little; c Jana Lea & Jodi LaVerne. Educ: Trinity Univ (Tex), BS; St Mary's Univ (Tex), JD; Delta Pheta Phi. Polit & Govt Pos: Alt deleg, Dem Nat Conv, 72. Bus & Prof Pos: Partner, Petry, Moorhead & Petry Law Firm, 70- Mil Serv: Entered as 2nd Lt, Army, 67, released

as 1st Lt, 70, after serv in Air Defense; Capt, Army Res, currently. Mem: Border Dist, Tex & Dimmit Co Bar Asns; Lions (vpres, 72-73, dep gov, 74-75); assoc Bachelors Club of San Antonio. Relig: Episcopal. Mailing Add: Fourth & Houston Sts Carrizo Springs TX 78834

PETSKA, BEULAH M (D)
b Macon, Mo, Oct 16, 00; d Albert W Evans & Birdie Johnson E; m 1921 to Albert Petska; c Albert Michael. Educ: Brewer High Sch, dipl, 17; Chillicothe Bus Col, Mo, 18. Polit & Govt Pos: Committeewoman, Fourth Ward, Marceline City Dem Party, Mo, 56-; deleg, Mo State Dem Conv, 60-68; secy, Linn Co Dem Cent Comt, formerly. Bus & Prof Pos: Teacher, Rural Sch, Chareton Co Mo, 17-19; census enumerator, 50-60; sales clerk, 50- Mem: Am Red Cross (chmn, Linn Co home serv, 41-70); Marceline City Coun, Mo (citizens adv comt). Honors & Awards: Am Red Cross Grey Lady, Kans City Vet Hosp, 100 hours. Relig: Christian. Mailing Add: 313 E Lake St Marceline MO 64658

PETTAWAY, BRENDA CROMER (D)
Secy, Md Dem State Cent Comt
b Baltimore, Md, Nov 12, 45; d Ernest V Cromer & Margaret Marshall C; div; c Arlett H & Brian C. Educ: Morgan State Univ, BA in Socio-Psychol, 73; Loyola Col (Md), MS in Psychol-Counseling, 75. Polit & Govt Pos: Mem, Baltimore City Dem Cent Comt, 74-; secy, Md Dem State Cent Comt, 74- Bus & Prof Pos: Sr counr, Md State Drug Abuse Admin, 72-; sr counr, Harundale Youth Serv Bur, 72-74, asst dir & sr counr, 74-; probation counr, Md Juv Serv Admin, 74-75. Mem: Md Youth Serv Asn; Mid Atlantic States Conf of Correction; Youth Alternative Serv Asn; 5 & 5 Dem Club, Baltimore; Parents Comt-Boy Scouts Troop 282 (treas, 74-). Relig: Methodist. Mailing Add: 3013 Elgin Ave Baltimore MD 21215

PETTERSSON, CARL E (D)
Utah State Rep
Mailing Add: 3170 Dayton St Magna UT 84044

PETTIBON, GEORGE T (R)
b Rochester, Pa, Dec 13, 22; s Arthur W Pettibon & Hazel Sutherland P; m 1944 to Josephine P Phillips; c George T, II, Dean A, Lynn Dee & Timothy E. Educ: Washington & Jefferson Col, BS, 44; exten courses, Geneva Col, Pa State Univ & Univ Notre Dame; Beta Theta Pi. Polit & Govt Pos: Co comnr, Beaver Co, Pa, 68-; committeeman, Center Twp Rep, 68-; chmn, Beaver Co Rep Exec Comt, formerly; dir & chmn, Beaver Co Conserv Dist & Bd, 68-; mem, Southwest Pa Regional Planning Comn, 68-; chmn, Beaver Co Prison Bd, 68- Mil Serv: Lt (Ret), Navy; Asiatic, Pac Theatre, Philippine Liberation & Victory Medal. Mem: Pa Planning Asn (dir, 71); Nat Asn Counties (mem welfare comt); Rotary; Mason (32 degree). Relig: Protestant. Legal Res: 164 Stone Quarry Rd Beaver PA 15009 Mailing Add: 107-108 Beaver Trust Bldg Beaver PA 15009

PETTINE, RONALD JOSEPH (D)
Nat Committeeman, Pa Young Dem
b Norristown, Pa, May 6, 44; s Ernest James Pettine & Beatrice Talbot P; m 1965 to Elizabeth Newmiller; c Kristin & Gregory Sean. Educ: Villanova Univ, BS in polit sci, 65; vpres, Student Coun. Polit & Govt Pos: Pres, Montgomery Co Young Dem, 63-69; vpres, Pa Young Dem clubs, 64-66, nat committeeman, 70-; admin asst, Milton Shapp, Cand for Gov, Pa, 66; appointments secy, Gov Shapp, Pa, 70; dir, S Eastern Pa Citizens for Humphrey, 68; nat advanceman for Vice President Hubert Humphrey, 68; dep chmn, Pa Dem State Comt, 70-71; Dep Secy of State, Pa, 71-75; dir scheduling & advance, Udall for President, currently; mem, Comn on Vice Presidential Selection, Dem Nat Comt, 72. Bus & Prof Pos: Pres, Pettine Assocs, Polit Consult Firm, 67-68. Mil Serv: SP-4, Army Res; hon discharge, 72. Mem: Nat Asn Extradition Off; Am Dem Action; Pa Young Dem; Young Dem Am (regional dir, 73-); Young Dem Clubs Pa (pres, 72-). Honors & Awards: Outstanding Young Dem of Pa, 65. Relig: Roman Catholic. Legal Res: 1003 Maple St Conshohocken PA 19428 Mailing Add: 7740 Tiverton Dr Springfield VA 22150

PETTIS, SHIRLEY NEIL (R)
US Rep, Calif
b Mountain View, Calif, July 12, 24; d Dr Harold O McCumber & Dorothy O'Neil M; m Jerry L Pettis, wid; c Deborah Neil & Peter Dwight. Educ: Univ Calif; Andrews Univ; Pac Union Col. Polit & Govt Pos: US Rep, Calif, 75- Bus & Prof Pos: Self-employed, Magnetic Tape Duplicators & Audio Digest. Relig: Seventh-day Adventist. Legal Res: 24934 Tulip Ave Loma Linda CA 92354 Mailing Add: 1021 Longworth House Off Bldg Washington DC 20515

PETTY, JOHN R
b Chicago, Ill, Apr 16, 30; m 1957 to H Lee Mills; c Lawrence T, Robert D, George M & Victoria L. Educ: Brown Univ, 47-51. Polit & Govt Pos: Rapporteur, Coun on Foreign Rels, 53-61; mem, Export Subcomt, Defense Indust Adv Coun & Export Action Comt, Nat Export Expansion Coun, formerly; Dep Asst Secy for Int Affairs, Treas Dept, 66-68, Acting Asst Secy for Int Affairs, 68, Asst Secy for Int Affairs, 68-72. Bus & Prof Pos: Mem training prog, Chase Manhattan Bank, New York, 53-55, mem, Int Dept, Africa, Western European & Mid East Area, 55-61, asst treas, Western European Area, 58-61, asst vpres, Paris Br, 61-63, vpres & div exec Worldwide Projs Div, New York, 63-66; partner & dir, Lehman Brothers, 72-; dir, RCA Corp, Nat Broadcasting Corp, Hercules Inc, Nat US CofC, Foreign Bondholders Protective Coun & Econ Growth Ctr of Yale Univ. Mil Serv: Lt(jg), Destroyers, Pac Fleet, 51-53. Honors & Awards: Exceptional Serv Award, Treas Dept, 68; Received Arthur S Flemming Award as One of the Ten Outstanding Young Men in the Fed Serv in 68. Mailing Add: 37 W Lenox St Chevy Chase MD 20015

PETTY, JUDY CHANEY (R)
Nat Committeewoman, Ark Young Rep
b Little Rock, Ark, Sept 4, 43; d John T Chaney & Jostine Leming C; div; c Deborah Jo. Educ: Little Rock Univ, 61; Univ of Ark, 62. Polit & Govt Pos: Nat committeewoman, Ark Fedn Young Rep, 68-, chmn, 69-70; vchmn, Young Rep Nat Fedn, 71-, bd dirs, Am Coun Young Polit Leaders, formerly, co-chmn, currently. Mem: Ark Women's Polit Caucus (chmn Second Cong Dist, 72-). Honors & Awards: Ark Outstanding Young Rep, Ark Fedn Young Rep, 68, 69 & 70; mem, US Del, NATO Conf, Ger, 71. Relig: Baptist. Legal Res: 901 N McAdoo Little Rock AR 72207 Mailing Add: 1200 Tower Bldg Little Rock AR 72201

PEVETO, WAYNE (D)
Tex State Rep
Mailing Add: PO Box 189 Orange TX 77630

PEYSER, PETER A (R)
US Rep, NY
b Cedarhurst, NY, Sept 7, 21; s Percy A Peyser (deceased) & Rubye Hoeflick P; m 1949 to Marguerite Richards; c Penney, Carolyn, Peter, James & Tommy. Educ: Colgate Univ, BA, 43; Phi Kappa Psi. Polit & Govt Pos: Mayor, Irvington, NY, 63-70; US Rep, 25th Dist, NY, 71-72, 23rd Dist, 73-, mem, Subcomt Investigating Pension Reform, US House of Rep & Task Force on Drug Abuse, ranking minority mem, Subcomt on Family Farms & Rural Develop & House Educ & Labor Comt, mem, House Agr Comt, Subcomt on Manpower, Compensation & Health & Safety & Subcomt on Select Educ, US House Rep currently; mem bd dirs, Nat Comt for Student Vote, currently; mem, NY Cong Deleg, Steering Comt, currently; chmn, Cong Ad Hoc Comt against Heroin Maintenance, currently; chmn, Nat Adv Comt of the Odyssey House; mem bd trustees, Colgate Univ, currently. Bus & Prof Pos: Mgr, Peter Peyser Agency of Mutual of NY, 56-70. Mil Serv: Army Inf, 43-46; Capt, Army Res, 46; Combat Inf Badge; Belgian Fourragere; Presidential Unit Citation; Bronze Star Medal with three Battle Stars; Capt, NY Nat Guard, 46-58. Relig: Episcopal. Legal Res: Sunnyside Lane Irvington NY 10533 Mailing Add: 1133 Longworth House Off Bldg Washington DC 20515

PFAENDER, THOMAS PAINE (R)
b New Ulm, Minn, Jan 30, 98; s William Pfaender, Jr & Sophia Berndt P; single. Educ: Normal Col, Am Gymnastic Union, 25; Univ Minn, grad study; Phi Epsilon Kappa. Polit & Govt Pos: Exec secy, Brown Co Rep Hq, Minn, 64; chmn, Brown Co Rep Comt, formerly; Presidential Elector, 68. Bus & Prof Pos: Dir, dept of health & phys educ, New Ulm Pub Schs, Minn, 31-63; camp dir, St Louis Co 4-H Club Camp, 37-64. Mil Serv: Entered as Pvt, Inf, 16, released as Sgt, 17; Mex Border Serv & World War I Serv Ribbons. Mem: Am Legion; Mason; Fel Am Asn for Health, Phys Educ & Recreation; life mem Minn Asn Health, Phys Educ & Recreation; hon life mem St Louis Co 4-H Clubs. Honors & Awards: Decorated by Mexican Govt for fostering int cultural rels, 68. Relig: Unitarian. Mailing Add: 900 S Broadway New Ulm MN 56073

PFAFFENBERGER, GEORGE WILLIAM (R)
Chmn, Ninth Cong Dist Rep Party, Ind
b Indianapolis, Ind, Nov 10, 23; s George William Pfaffenberger & Gaynell Brietfield P; m 1943 to Edna Louise Mikels; c George William & Wallace Mikel. Educ: Sheilds High Sch, grad, 42. Polit & Govt Pos: Chmn, Jackson Co Rep Party, Ind, formerly; chmn, Ninth Cong Dist Rep Party, 70- Bus & Prof Pos: Treas, Empire Realty Corp, Seymour, Ind, 65; pres, Tote-A-Poke Fried Chicken, 69. Mem: Elks; Columbia Club; Exchange Club. Relig: United Methodist. Mailing Add: 1122 S Poplar Seymour IN 47274

PFAFFENBERGER, JANE ALICE (R)
Secy, Monroe Co Rep Cent Comt, Ind
b Indianapolis, Ind, Aug 29, 48; d Robert Thomas Taylor & Alice Hildebrandt T; m 1968 to George William Pfaffenberger, V; c Julie Anne & Katherine Marie. Educ: Ind Cent Col, 66-67; Purdue Univ, 67-69; Col Young Rep. Polit & Govt Pos: Secy, Monroe Co Rep Cent Comt, Ind, 74- Mem: Rep Women's Club; Exten Homemakers (secy). Relig: Methodist. Mailing Add: 3747 Oak Leaf Dr Bloomington IN 47401

PFALZGRAF, HAROLD ARCHER (R)
Chmn, Sumner Co Rep Comt, Kans
b McPherson, Kans, May 4, 33; s Charles Archer Pfalzgraf & Esther Brooks P; m 1953 to Carol Louise Ginavan; c Linda & Douglas. Educ: McPherson Col, BA, 59; Washburn Univ Sch Law, LLB, 62; Delta Theta Phi. Polit & Govt Pos: Asst Attorney Gen, Kans, 62-63; Probate & Juvenile Judge, Sumner Co, 63-66, Co Attorney, 67-; Rep Precinct Committeeman, 64-65; chmn, Sumner Co Rep Comt, 68-69 & 73-; pres, Fifth Cong Dist Lincoln Day Club, 69. Mil Serv: Entered as Pvt, Army, 53, released as Cpl, 55, after serv in 82nd Airborne-Paratroopers. Mem: Kans Bar Asn; Elks; Am Legion; CofC; Rotary. Relig: Methodist. Legal Res: 1115 N Jefferson Wellington KS 67152 Mailing Add: Court House Wellington KS 67152

PFEIFER, ELIZABETH J (R)
Rep Nat Committeewoman, Wis
b Madison, Wis, May 21, 31; m 1951 to Dr John Pfeifer; c John Steven, Jr, Mary Regina, Stanley Johnson & Catherine Isle. Educ: Univ Wis-Madison, 2 years. Polit & Govt Pos: Tel campaign chmn, Wis, 62; co-chmn, First John Byrnes Tribute, 63; mem credentials comt, Wis State Rep Conv, 64, hospitality chmn, 69; co-chmn, Goldwater Campaign & Goldwater Girl, 64; campaign coordr, Brown Co Rep Cand, 64; Brown Co Woman's Activity chmn for John Byrnes & Robert Warren, 64-66; mem, Human Rights Comn, 64-66; vchairwoman, Brown Co Rep Party, 64-68; mem, State Comt for Nixon, 68; Eighth Dist vchmn, Jack Olson for Lt Gov, 68; Eight Dist vchmn, Jack Olson for Gov, 70; treas, Brown Co Women's Fedn, 68-70; mem, Salute to John Byrnes 25th Anniversary Comt, 70; pres, Rep Women Brown Co, 70-71, bd mem, currently; deleg, Rep Nat Conv, 72; Rep Nat Committeewoman, Wis, 72-; mem state budget comt, Wis Fedn Rep Women, currently, treas, 70-; chmn elec workers, Third Precinct, Allouez, 69-72. Mem: DAR; PEO; Green Bay Serv League; Brown-Door-Kewaunee Dent Auxiliary (state legis chmn); Dent Wives (pres). Honors & Awards: Jaycettes Woman of the Year Award for Community Achievement, 61. Relig: Lutheran; Past Sunday Sch teacher, Grace Lutheran Church. Mailing Add: 3310 Michael Ct Green Bay WI 54301

PFEIFFER, ELLEN DORIS (D)
b Sapporo, Japan, July 17, 53; d Dr Cromwell Adams Riches & Victoria Kimbell R; single. Educ: Degrees in Polit Sci & Criminal Justice, Am Univ, 75. Polit & Govt Pos: Asst, US Senate Staff, Daniel K Inouye, 70-; deleg, New Voter Emergency Conf forming Nat Youth Caucus, 71; exec bd mem, Md Alliance for Dem Reform, 72-; deleg, Md New Dem Coalition Conv, 72; deleg, Youth Coalition '72 Nat Conv, 72; deleg, Am for Dem Action Nat Conv, 72; Md coordr, Nat Youth Caucus, 72; challenger, Md Deleg, Dem Nat Conv, 72, alt deleg, 72; mgr-organizer, McGovern Publicity Concerts, 72; boiler room coordr, Get Out the Vote Proj, McGovern Presidential Campaign, 72; campaign vol, Woodrow Allen for Md State Senate, 74. Mem: Nat Women's Polit Caucus; Md Young Dem (pres liaison); Nat Comt for Sane Nuclear Policy; Md Alliance for Dem Action (exec bd, 72-). Mailing Add: 7522 Arrowood Rd Bethesda MD 20034

PHEIFFER, WILLIAM TOWNSEND (R)
b Purcell, Okla, July 15, 98; s William Pheiffer & Susan Harrison P; m 1954 to Frances Uihlein. Educ: Univ Southern Calif; Univ of Okla; Chi Phi; Phi Alpha Delta; Delta Sigma Rho. Hon Degrees: Dr Honoris Causa, Univ Santo Domingo. Polit & Govt Pos: US Rep, 16th Dist, NY, 40-43; exec asst to chmn, Rep Nat Comt, 44-46; US Ambassador to the Dominican

Republic, 53-57; alt deleg, Rep Nat Conv, 68. Bus & Prof Pos: Mem, Bd of Dirs of various bus corp. Mil Serv: Capt, Army, 43-44, serv in Cavalry; Award of Merit. Mem: Mason; Am Legion (past past comdr); Metrop Club, New York; Lake Placid Club, Lake Placid, NY; Everglades Club, Palm Beach, Fla. Honors & Awards: Hon fel, Consular Law Soc. Relig: Unitarian. Mailing Add: 480 Park Ave New York NY 10022

PHELAN, ROBERT GERARD (D)
Mass State Rep
b Lynn, Mass, Mar 19, 33; s John Vincent Phelan & Helene A Crowley P; m 1959 to Shirley Ann Lipinski; c Robert G, Jr, Michael Thomas, John Timothy, Vincent Edmund, Nell Ann, Kathryn Marie, Peter Joseph & Elizabeth Ann. Educ: Col of the Holy Cross, BS, 54; Boston Col Law Sch, JD, 57. Polit & Govt Pos: Mass Land Court Title Exam, 57-; asst dist attorney, Eastern Dist Mass, 58-60; pub defender, Co of Essex, Commonwealth of Mass; Mass State Rep, Ninth Essex Dist, 73- Bus & Prof Pos: Practicing lawyer, Phelan & Phelan, Lynn, Mass, 57-; lectr criminal & const law, Northeastern Univ, 72-73. Mem: Lynn & Mass Bar Asns; Essex Co Bar Asn (exec comt, 66-67); Asn; Essex Co Dem Club; Ancient Order of Hibernians. Relig: Roman Catholic. Legal Res: 12 Kings Beach Rd Lynn MA 01902 Mailing Add: 33 Nahant St Lynn MA 01902

PHELPS, EDNA MAE (D)
Dem Nat Committeewoman, Okla
b Tulsa, Okla, June 12, 20; d William Harold Hough & Nedda Pearl Jerome H; m 1942 to Joe Elton Phelps; c Ronald Jerome & Joelton Mark. Educ: Okla State Univ, BA, 42; Okla Col Lib Arts, 60; Okla Univ, 65; Theta Sigma Phi; Kappa Delta Pi; Fourth Estate. Polit & Govt Pos: Publicity chmn, Seminole Co Dem, 63-65; pres, Seminole Co Dem Women's Club, 65-67; chmn of club pres comt, Okla Fedn Dem Women's Clubs, 65-67, immediate past pres; chmn, Precinct 1, Ward 4, Seminole Co, 65-69; deleg, Dem Nat Conv, 68 & 72, Okla rep, Credentials Comt, 68; chmn, Okla State Elec Bd, 70-; mem, Charter Comn, Dem Nat Comt, 73-, nat committeeman, 73-; deleg, Dem Nat Mid Term Conf, 74. Bus & Prof Pos: Ed, Okla Live Stock News; pub rels asst, Tulsa CofC. Mem: Seminole Pub Libr (bd trustees); Investment Club in Seminole Co; Seminole PTA; Mod Lit Club. Relig: Presbyterian; church women's auxiliary (past pres). Mailing Add: 916 Lee Ave Seminole OK 74868

PHELPS, GRACE LENORE (R)
VChairperson, DeKalb Co Rep Cent Comt, Ind
b DeKalb Co, Ind, Nov 16, 1900; d Alius Fry & Clara Ball F; m 1939 to Harvey Phelps. Educ: DeKalb Co Commmunity Schs. Polit & Govt Pos: Precinct vcommitteeman, City of Butler, DeKalb Co, 40-66, committeeman, 66-; secy, DeKalb Co Rep Cent Comt, 52-68, vice-chairperson, 68-; app co councilwoman, DeKalb Co, 69-70, elected, 71-74. Bus & Prof Pos: Off mgr, Ind & Mich Elec Co, 21-38; co treas dep, DeKalb Co, 39-42, co treas, 42-46; part-time, DeKalb Co Treas Off & Assessors Off, 46-52; off mgr, Marshall Clothing Mfg Co, Ind, 52-67. Mem: Butler Bus & Prof Womens' Club; Butler Am Legion Auxiliary; DeKalb Co Rep Women's Club. Honors & Awards: Named Woman of the Year by Butler Bus & Prof Womens' Club, 46, Fourth Dist Dir, 47-48; worked toward dedication of New Post Off Bldg in Butler, 58-61; Named Woman of the Year, Civic Orgns in Butler, 70. Relig: United Methodist. Mailing Add: 500 N Broadway Butler IN 46721

PHELPS, PAUL STEPHAN (D)
VPres, Ky Young Dem
b Louisville, Ky, July 25, 52; s Paul Phelps & Constance Blount P; single. Educ: Morehead State Univ, 71-73; Univ Louisville, BA, 75; Pi Sigma Alpha; Ky Student Govt Asn; Delta Tau Delta; Focal. Polit & Govt Pos: Dist chmn, Ky Young Dem, 72-73, vpres, 74-; chmn, Boyle Co Dem Party, 72-; deleg, Nat Young Dem, 73. Bus & Prof Pos: State comnr foreign deeds, Ky, 73-75; adminr, Danville Munic Court, 75- Mem: Jaycees; KofC; Ky Hist Soc; Am Fedn Musicians. Honors & Awards: Ky Admiral, 73; Dem Deserve Note, Ky Dem Party, 74; Outstanding Young Dem, Dem Women's Club, 75. Relig: Catholic. Mailing Add: 112 Wilderness Rd Danville KY 40422

PHELPS, THOMAS PRESTON (D)
Chmn, Adair Co Dem Party, Ky
b Burkesville, Ky, Dec 4, 24; s Claude Aaron Phelps & Willie Stephenson P; m 1946 to Virginia Finn; c Patty, Tommy & Kathy. Educ: Adair Co High Sch, Columbia, Ky, 40-44. Polit & Govt Pos: Chmn, Adair Co Dem Party, Ky, 73- Bus & Prof Pos: Mem, Dealer Coun, 66 & 68. Mil Serv: Entered as Pvt, Army, 43, released as Cpl, 46, after serv in SPac; Bronze Arrowhead; Five Battle Stars. Mem: Mason; VFW; Eastern Star (Worthy Grand Patron, 55); CofC (pres, 69). Relig: Methodist. Mailing Add: Miller Ave Columbia KY 42728

PHELPS, WILLIAM C (R)
Lt Gov, Mo
b Nevada, Mo, Apr 5, 34; s Dr & Mrs Dean H Phelps; m 1972 to Joanne Ronchetto Phelps. Educ: Univ Mo-Columbia, AB in econ & bus, 56, LLB, 59; Mystical Seven; Omicron Delta Kappa; Phi Eta Sigma; pres, Student Union Activities Bd; Beta Theta Pi; Phi Delta Phi. Polit & Govt Pos: Mo State Rep, 60-72, mem, Appropriations, Judiciary & Econ Comts & Rep Party Whip, Mo House Rep, formerly, mem, Joint Legis Comts Fiscal Affairs & Correctional Insts, formerly; state-wide campaign mgr for US Sen nominee Crosby Kemper, 62; Lt Gov, Mo, 73- Bus & Prof Pos: Teaching asst gen econ, Univ Mo-Columbia, formerly; assoc with law firm of Morrison, Hecker, Cozad, Morrison & Curtis, Kansas City, Mo, formerly. Mil Serv: Active duty, Army, 57; Capt, Army Res. Mem: Am & Kansas City Bar Asns; Lawyers Asn Kansas City; Mo Asn Rep, Kansas City Philharmonic Orchestra (trustee). Relig: Episcopal. Legal Res: 5016 Grand Kansas City MO 64112 Mailing Add: State Capitol Jefferson City MO 65101

PHILBROOK, BURNHAM JOHN (DFL)
Minn State Rep
b St Paul, Minn, Aug 28, 46; s Burnham LeRoy Philbrook & Margaret Bohen P; single. Educ: Univ Minn, BA, 69. Polit & Govt Pos: Minn State Rep, 75-; mem, President's Comt Employ Handicapped, currently. Bus & Prof Pos: Supvr, Univac, Div Sperry-Rand, 66-71; dir finance, United Shelter Corp, 72; dir finance & commun, Minn Pub Interest Research Group, 73-74. Mem: Roseville Citizen Action Group (steering comt); Minn Aesthetic Environ Task Force (chmn educ comt); Minn Bicentennial (mem horizon panel). Relig: Catholic. Legal Res: 2755 Rice St Roseville MN 55113 Mailing Add: 382 State Off Bldg St Paul MN 55155

PHILIP, JAMES PEYTON, JR (R)
Ill State Sen
b Elmhurst, Ill, May 26, 30; s James Peyton Philip, Sr & Elsa Gerhardt P; m 1964 to Judith Ann Haines; c Cynthia Kay & Jase. Educ: Kansas City Jr Col, 49-50; Kans State Col, 52-53. Polit & Govt Pos: Treas, Elmhurst Young Rep Club, Ill, 60; chmn, DuPage Co Young Rep Orgn, 61-63; admin asst to 14th Cong Dep Gov, Ill Young Rep Orgn, 61-63, admin asst to chmn bd, 63, Jr nat committeeman, 63-65, pres, 65-74; auditor, York Twp, 65-; Ill State Rep, 37th Dist, 66-72, Ill State Rep, 40th Dist, 72-74; chmn, DuPage Co Rep Cent Comt, 69-; Ill State Sen, 75- Bus & Prof Pos: Asst mgr, Edison Bros Stores, Inc, 49-53; sales rep, Pepperidge Farm, Inc, 53-54, sales prom supvr, 60, sales prom mgr, 60-62, dist sales mgr, 62- Mil Serv: Entered as Pvt, Marine Corps, 50, released as Cpl, 52. Mem: Suburban Bus Mgt Coun; Grocery Mgt & Sales Exec Club of Chicago; Am Legion; Elks; DuPage Shrine Club. Relig: Episcopal. Mailing Add: 488 E Crescent Elmhurst IL 60126

PHILLIPS, ALVAH H (D)
Chmn, Coventry Dem Town Comt, Conn
b Buffalo, NY, Aug 21, 28; s Alvah H Phillips & Queena P; m 1949 to Carol L Kelly; c A Gordon & Roger T. Educ: Allegheny Col, BS, 49; Univ Buffalo, MA, 52; Johns Hopkins Univ, PhD, 57; Phi Beta Kappa; Sigma Alpha Epsilon. Polit & Govt Pos: Chmn, Coventry Dem Town Comt, Conn, 70- Bus & Prof Pos: Research fel, Harvard Univ, 57-59; asst prof, Johns Hopkins Univ, 59-67; assoc prof, Univ Conn, 67- Mil Serv: Entered as Pvt, Army, 52, released as Cpl, 54, after serv in Chem Corps. Legal Res: Rte 44A Coventry CT 06238 Mailing Add: RFD 3 Box 535 Coventry CT 06238

PHILLIPS, ANDREW CRAIG (D)
Supt of Pub Instr, NC
b Greensboro, NC, Nov 1, 22; s Guy B Phillips; m 1943 to Mary Martha Cobb; c Martha Gatlin, Andrew Craig, Jr, Elizabeth Cobb & Eva Craig. Educ: Univ NC, Chapel Hill, MA, 46, EdD, 56. Polit & Govt Pos: Supt, Winston-Salem Schs, NC, 57-62; supt, Charlotte-Mecklenburg Schs, 62-67; State Supt Pub Instr, 69-; mem, Gov Comn to Study the NC Pub Sch Syst. Bus & Prof Pos: Admin vpres, Richardson Found, Greensboro, NC, 67-68. Mil Serv: Entered as Ens, Naval Res, released as Lt(jg), after serv in European & Pac Theatres, 43-46. Mem: Am Asn of Sch Adminr (mem exec comt); Nat Acad for Sch Execs (bd dir); Nat & NC Educ Asns; Divinity Sch Duke Univ (bd visitors). Honors & Awards: Winston-Salem Young Man of the Year, 57. Relig: Methodist. Legal Res: 2200 Barfield Court Raleigh NC 27609 Mailing Add: Rm 318 Educ Bldg Raleigh NC 27602

PHILLIPS, C EUGENE (R)
Chmn, Flathead Co Rep Cent Comt, Mont
b Peoria, Ill, July 12, 32; s Carl E Phillips & Bess Alexander P; m 1974 to Marlene Rae Spencer; c Stephen S, Audrey Ann, Cheryl E & Heidi I. Educ: Bradley Univ, 50-51; Colo State Univ, BS, 54; Univ Mont, LLB, 65; Tau Kappa Epsilon. Polit & Govt Pos: Mem, Mont State Const Conv Comn, 71-72; chmn, Flathead Co Rep Cent Comt, Mont, 71-; mem, Mont Rep State Exec Bd, 73- Mil Serv: Entered as Pvt, Army, 54, released as Cpl, 56, after serv in 11th Airborne Div. Mem: Am & Mont Bar Asns; Kalispell CofC (dir, 70-71 & 73-76, vpres, 71); Northwest Mont Bar Asn (pres, 70). Mailing Add: 159 Wedgewood Lane Kalispell MT 59901

PHILLIPS, CHANNING EMERY (D)
b Brooklyn, NY, Mar 23, 28; s Porter W Phillips, Sr & Dorothy A Fletcher P; m 1956 to Jane Nabors; c Channing Durward, Sheilah Nahketeh, Tracy Jane, Jill Celeste & John Emery. Educ: Va Union Univ, BA, 50; Colgate Rochester Divinity Sch, BD, 53; Drew Univ Grad Sch, 53-56; Alpha Kappa Mu; Alpha Phi Alpha. Hon Degrees: DD, Pac Sch Relig & Mary Holmes Col; LHD, Elmhurst Col. Polit & Govt Pos: Deleg, Dem Nat Conv, 68 & 72; chmn, DC Deleg & mem, Platform Comt, 68, mem, Rules Reform Comt, 69; Dem Nat Committeeman, DC, 68-72. Bus & Prof Pos: Exec pres, Housing Develop Corp, 67-74; vpres, Va Union Univ, 74- Mil Serv: Entered as Pvt, Air Force, 46, released as Sgt, 47 after serv in US, 46-47. Publ: The University and Revolution in the University and revolution, Am Univ. Mem: Am Civil Liberties Union (nat adv coun); Ctrs for Community Change (bd dirs). Honors & Awards: Pittsburgh Courier Top-Hat Award, 68; Man of the Year Award, Potomac Chap, Nat Asn Housing & Redevelop Off. Relig: United Church of Christ. Mailing Add: 3501 Moss Side Ave Richmond VA 23222

PHILLIPS, CHARLES EUGENE (R)
Chmn, Knox Co Rep Exec Comt, Ohio
b Mt Vernon, Ohio, Nov 25, 33; s Charles Cliffton Phillips & Anna Geneva Kirkpatrick P; m 1960 to Diana M James; c Douglas Michael, Charles Robert, Heidi Sue, James Eugene & Jason Lee. Educ: Cornell Univ, BS in Agr, 56; Alpha Gamma Rho. Polit & Govt Pos: Secy, Knox Co Rep Cent Comt, Ohio, 61-; chmn comnr, Knox Co Comn, 62-; secy, Knox Co Young Rep Club, 63; secy, Knox Co Rep Exec Comt, 65-70, chmn, 70-; mem, State Credentials Comt, Ohio State Rep Conv, 70; deleg, State Rep Conv, 71 & 72. Mem: Am Guernsey Cattle Club (dir, 73-, second vpres, 74-); Knox Co Farm Bur (vpres & trustee, 57-); Ohio Agr Serv (bd dirs, 74-); Ohio Guernsey Breeders Asn (pres, 72-); CofC. Honors & Awards: Cert of Merit, Mt Vernon Jaycees, 61-62; Outstanding Young Farmer, 65. Relig: Methodist; Bd Mem, Gay St Methodist Church, 60-65. Mailing Add: 11838 Banning Rd Rte 2 Mt Vernon OH 43050

PHILLIPS, CHARLES FRANKLIN, JR (R)
VChmn, Lexington Rep Comt, Va
b Geneva, NY, Nov 5, 34; s Charles F Phillips & Evelyn C Minard P; m 1957 to Marjorie Hancock; c Charles F, III, Susan H & Anne D. Educ: Univ NH, AB, 56; Harvard Univ, PhD in Econ, 60; Phi Beta Kappa; Pi Gamma Mu; Pi Sigma Alpha; Beta Gamma Sigma; Omicron Delta Epsilon; Beta Theta Pi; Sr Men's Honor Soc. Polit & Govt Pos: Mem, Buena Vista-Lexington-Rockbridge Rep Comt, Va, 59-64, chmn, 64-67; vchmn, Lexington Rep Comt, 67-; city coun, Lexington, Va, 67-71, mayor, 71-; app by President to Comn Rev Nat Policy on Gambling, 72- Bus & Prof Pos: Prof econ, Washington & Lee Univ, 59- Publ: Competition in the Synthetic Rubber Industry, Univ NC Press, 63; The Economics of Regulation, Richard D Irwin, Inc, 65, revised ed, 69; Registered Bank Holding Companies, Bd of Gov, Fed Reserve Syst, 67. Mem: Am & Southern Econ Asns; Am Mkt Asn; Omicron Delta Epsilon (vpres, 72-74, pres-elect, 74-); Lexington Kiwanis. Relig: Presbyterian. Mailing Add: 414 Morningside Dr Lexington VA 24450

PHILLIPS, CHARLES WILEY (D)
NC State Rep
b Randolph Co, NC, June 25, 97; s Jesse Lee Phillips & Fannie Waddell P; m 1924 to Lela Wade Phillips; c Wade, Carolyn, Charles, Jr & Barbara Ann. Educ: Univ NC, Chapel Hill, AB, 21; Columbia Univ, MA, 27. Hon Degrees: LLD, Univ NC, Greensboro, 67. Polit & Govt Pos: Pres, State Cong of PTA, NC, 43-45 & State Educ Asn, 45-46; NC State Rep, 65- Bus & Prof Pos: Prin, Greensboro Pub Schs, 12 years; dir pub rels, Woman's Col, Univ NC, 27 years; dir of exp in TV teaching in NC, 57-61; acting dir, Greensboro Div, Guilford Col,

65-66; retired. Mil Serv: Army, Cpl. Mem: NC Educ Asn; Rotary Int; Rotary Club of Greensboro. Relig: Methodist; Church sch teacher. Mailing Add: 210 S Tremont Dr Greensboro NC 27403

PHILLIPS, CHRISTOPHER HALLOWELL **(R)**
b Hague, Holland, Dec 6, 20; s William Phillips & Caroline Astor Drayton P; m 1943 to Mabel B Olsen; c Victoria P (Mrs Andrew Corbett Jr); Miriam O & David W. Educ: Harvard, BA, 43. Polit & Govt Pos: Mass State Sen, Second Essex Dist, 48-53; deleg, Rep Nat Conv, 52 & 60; Dep Asst Secy State, 53-57; US Civil Serv Comnr, 57; US Rep, Econ & Soc Coun, UN, 58-61, Dep US Rep, UN, 69-73; pres, Nat Coun for US-China Trade, 73- Bus & Prof Pos: Rep & second vpres, Chase Manhattan Bank, New York, 61-65; pres, US Coun Int CofC, 65-69. Mil Serv: Entered as Pvt, Army Air Corps, 42, released as Capt, 46, after serv in Supreme Comdr Allied Powers, Tokyo; Army Commendation Ribbon. Mem: Coun Foreign Rels; Am Acad Arts & Sci; Metrop Club, Washington, DC; River Club, New York; Tavern Club, Boston. Relig: Episcopal. Legal Res: 74 Eastern Ave Essex MA 01929 Mailing Add: 2801 New Mexico Ave NW Washington DC 20007

PHILLIPS, CLAIRE ADAMS **(R)**
b Detroit, Mich, Nov 3, 28; d William Albert Adams & Elizabeth Becker A; m 1952 to Robert Kay Phillips; c Elizabeth, Clark & Leigh Ann. Educ: Highland Park Jr Col, Mich, 46-48; Albion Col, BA; Univ Ariz, MEd. Polit & Govt Pos: Rep precinct committeewoman, Tucson, Ariz, 60-; secy, Pima Co Rep Cent Comt, 66-72; deleg, Rep Nat Conv, 72; secy, Ariz State Rep Cent Comt, formerly. Mem: Ariz Asn Teachers Math; Nat Coun Teachers Math; Pantano Rep Women (pres, 66-68); Eastern Star. Relig: Protestant. Mailing Add: 911 S Eli Dr Tucson AZ 85710

PHILLIPS, CLARENCE W **(D)**
Tenn State Rep
Mailing Add: 62nd Rep Dist Box 588 Shelbyville TN 37160

PHILLIPS, D J (JIM) **(D)**
Ariz State Rep
Mailing Add: 2400 South Kathleen Yuma AZ 85364

PHILLIPS, DAVID JULIUS **(D)**
b Lebanon, Pa, Oct 24, 24; s Lloyd W Phillips & Henrietta Hairhouse P; m 1950 to Lorraine F Burzynski; c Mary Margaret & John David. Educ: Woodrow Wilson High Sch, Long Beach, Calif, grad. Polit & Govt Pos: Staff aide, House Appropriations Comt, US House of Rep, 80th Cong; speech writer, Dem cand for US Rep, US Sen & Pres; founding mem, All-Ill Comt for Humphrey-Muskie; alt deleg, Dem Nat Conv, 72. Bus & Prof Pos: Staff reporter, Omaha World-Herald, Nebr, 48; ed & publisher, Washington Co Review Herald, 49-52; mem pub rels hq staff, Union Pac RR, 52-56; vpres, State Farm Ins Co, currently. Mil Serv: Entered as Pvt, Army Paratroops, 42, released as Sgt, 45, after serv in 101st Airborne Div, ETO, 44-45; Bronze Star; Army Commendation Medal; French Croix de Guerre; Belgian Croix de Guerre; Orange Lanyard, Holland; Presidential Unit Citations with Cluster; Combat Inf Badge; Parachutist's Badge. Mem: Pub Rel Soc of Am; Chicago, Nat & Overseas Press Club; Bloomington Country Club. Honors & Awards: Two Silver Anvil Trophies, Pub Rels Soc of Am; Pub Rels Award, Fedn for Railway Progress; Best Campaign Award, Chicago Publicity Club. Relig: Roman Catholic. Mailing Add: 104 S Ruth Rd Bloomington IL 61701

PHILLIPS, DAYTON EDWARD **(R)**
b Shell Creek, Tenn, Mar 29, 10; s Avery Phillips & Bertha Shell P; m 1960 to Jessie Lynnwood Hill; stepsons, Jeter E Wardrep, III & James C Wardrep; one grandchild. Educ: Milligan Col, Tenn; Univ Tenn Law Sch; Nat Univ Law Sch, JD. Polit & Govt Pos: Deleg, Rep Nat Conv, 3 times; co attorney, Carter Co, Tenn, 36-40; states attorney gen, Tenn, 40-46; US Rep, First Cong Dist, Tenn, 46-50; chancellor, First Judicial Div, Tenn, 52- Bus & Prof Pos: Pub sch teacher, 30-31; attorney-at-law, 34- Mil Serv: Enlisted Army, 42, released, 45, after serv in Counter Intel Corps, ETO; Five Battle Stars; ETO Ribbon; Good Conduct & Sharp Shooter Medals. Mem: Tenn Bar Asn; Shrine; Mason; Elks; VFW. Honors & Awards: Named Outstanding Hon Citizen of Year of Carter Co, 66. Relig: Baptist. Mailing Add: 1410 Burgie St Elizabethton TN 37643

PHILLIPS, ELIZABETH REED **(D)**
Committeeperson, Duval Co Dem Exec Comt, Fla
b New York, June 2, 47; d Glenn Reed & Aida Palermo R; m 1972 to Jerrold Keith Phillips. Educ: Univ Fla, BA, 69; Univ SFla, 70-71; Fla State Univ, 73-; Phi Kappa Phi. Polit & Govt Pos: Deleg, Dem Nat Conv, 72; comnr, Community Rels Comn, 72-; committeeperson, Duval Co Dem Exec Comt, Fla, 72- Bus & Prof Pos: High sch teacher, St Petersburg, Fla, 69-71; high sch teacher, Jacksonville, Fla, 71-72; counsr, NE Fla Comprehensive Drug Control, Inc, 72- Mem: Nat Orgn Women (bd mem, Jacksonville Chap, 71-); Fla Women's Polit Caucus; Jacksonville Women's Polit Caucus (legis chairperson, 72-); NAACP; League Women Voters. Relig: Roman Catholic. Mailing Add: 2877 Dickinson Rd Jacksonville FL 32216

PHILLIPS, GLEN EDWIN **(R)**
Chmn, Shelby Co Rep Exec Comt, Ohio
b Amanda, Ohio, Dec 22, 33; s Everett Meyers Phillips & Bernice Florence Drum P; m 1958 to Vanis Elaine Helman; c Cheryl & Brent. Educ: Manchester Col, BS, 61. Polit & Govt Pos: Rep precinct committeeman, Shelby Co, Ohio, 63-; mem, Shelby Co Bd Elec, 74-; chmn, Shelby Co Rep Exec Comt, 75- Bus & Prof Pos: Off mgr, Everyday Mfg Co Inc, 61- Mil Serv: Entered as E-1, Army Security Agency, 54, released as E-5, 57, after serv in Hq Co-ASA Europe, Frankfurt, Ger, 56-57. Relig: Church of the Brethren; treas, Trinity Church of the Brethren. Mailing Add: 510 Aurora Ave Sidney OH 45365

PHILLIPS, JACK W **(D)**
Ark State Rep
Mailing Add: PO Box 164 Ozark AR 72949

PHILLIPS, JIM **(D)**
Ariz State Rep
b Portsmouth, Ohio, June 1, 28; s Donald George Phillips (deceased) & Elizabeth Parsons P; m 1955 to Lettie Jean Palmer; c Donald James, Norman Eugene, Paul Edward & Elma Jean. Educ: Ariz Western Col, AA, 72. Polit & Govt Pos: Capt, Ariz Dept of Pub Safety, 52-75, retired, 75; Ariz State Rep, 75- Mil Serv: Entered as Pvt, Marine Corps, 45, released as Cpl, 47, after serv in 3rd Air Wing, Stateside; Good Conduct Medal. Mem: Southern Police Inst Alumni Asn; Elks; Moose; Yuma Hosp Gov Bd; Mason. Honors & Awards: Commendation Letter, Patrol Supt G O Hathway, 54; Award, Yuma Area Law Enforcement Asn, 74. Relig: Baptist. Mailing Add: 3285 E Hwy 80 Yuma AZ 85364

PHILLIPS, JIMMY **(D)**
b Angleton, Tex, May 17, 13; s Frank Phillips & Cora Cannan P; m 1938 to Esther Heyne; c Jimmy, Jr & Mike. Educ: Univ Tex, Law, 7 years. Polit & Govt Pos: Tex State Rep, 41-44; Tex State Sen, 47-61; deleg, Dem Nat Conv, 48-60, 64 & 68; mem, Tex Dem State Comt, formerly. Bus & Prof Pos: Lawyer, State of Tex Bar Asn, 41- Mil Serv: Entered as Pvt, Army, 43, released as Sgt, 45, after serv in Mil Intel. Mem: State Bar of Tex; Tex Ex-Students Asn; Brazoria Co Dem Club; Pres Club; CofC. Relig: Episcopal. Legal Res: Baileys Prairie Angleton TX 77515 Mailing Add: PO Box 1090 Angleton TX 77515

PHILLIPS, L L **(D)**
Ga State Rep
Mailing Add: Box 166 Soperton GA 30457

PHILLIPS, LEWIS MILTON **(D)**
b Macon Co, Ga, Apr 21, 21; s William Henry Phillips & Sue Oliver P; m 1944 to Constance Ann Fox; c Diane (Mrs Avret) & Patricia (Mrs Berry). Educ: Numerous mil schs; pre-flight col training; Univ Nebr, grad command pilot, 18 months. Polit & Govt Pos: Chmn, Scheley Co Dem Exec Comt, Ga, formerly. Bus & Prof Pos: Mgr, Ga Consol Construction Co, 50-52; owner & mgr, Phillips Lumber Co, 52-60. Mil Serv: Entered as Pvt, Air Force, 41, released as Capt, 45, after serv in Eighth Air Force, 385th Bomb Group, ETO, 44-45; Air Medal. Mem: Mason; Elks; Am Legion; Lions; Shrine. Relig: Baptist. Mailing Add: Box 321 Ellaville GA 31806

PHILLIPS, MARTHA HENDERSON **(R)**
b Washington, DC, Jan 27, 42; d Harry W Henderson & Eleanor H; m 1968 to Kevin P Phillips; c Elizabeth. Educ: Univ Md, BA, 65; Columbia Univ, MA, 71. Polit & Govt Pos: Legis secy, US Rep Melvin R Laird, 65-66; asst to chief spec projs, State Agency Coop Div, US Off Educ, 66-67; dir, House Rep Research Comt, US House Rep, 69-73, dir, House Rep Policy Comt, 74- Bus & Prof Pos: Develop officer, Teachers Col, Columbia Univ, 67-69. Mem: Am Educ Research Asn; Am Polit Sci Asn. Mailing Add: 5115 Moorland Lane Bethesda MD 20014

PHILLIPS, MICHAEL KEITH **(D)**
Ind State Rep
b Huntingburg, Ind, Sept 2, 43; s Lowell Truman Phillips & Ida Ruth Kelley P; m 1963 to Julie Mahon; c Mark, Jennifer, Stephanie & Jeffrey. Educ: DePauw Univ, BA in Polit Sci, 65; Ind Univ, Indianapolis Law Sch, JD, 69; Rector Scholar, Law J; Beta Theta Pi. Polit & Govt Pos: Vpres, Jefferson Jackson Club, DePauw Univ, 64-65; asst chmn, Ind State Dem Cent Comt, 65-69; asst div dir, Dem Nat Comt, 68; asst to vchmn, United Dem for Humphrey, 68; Ind State Rep, 71-73 & 75, majority leader, Ind House of Rep, formerly. Bus & Prof Pos: Attorney, 69- Publ: Quiet title action: proposal for reform, Ind Legal Forum, 69. Mem: Am Judicature Soc; Boonville Jr CofC; Kiwanis; Elks; F&AM. Honors & Awards: Outstanding Freshman State Rep, 71. Relig: Protestant. Legal Res: 608 Parkview Boonville IN 47601 Mailing Add: 1441 S First St Boonville IN 47601

PHILLIPS, NANCY LEE **(D)**
Third VPres, Okla Fedn of Dem Women
b Wewoka, Okla, Aug 4, 37; d Emory Lee Chaney & Hazel Williams C; m 1958 to Ted Morton Phillips; c Ted Steven & Stuart Chaney. Educ: Lindenwood Col, 1 year; Univ Okla, 2 years; Young Democrats. Polit & Govt Pos: Pres, Seminole Co Dem Women's Club, Okla, 64-65; pres, Fourth Dist, Okla Fedn of Dem Women's Clubs, 65-67, pres, Third Dist, 67-71, State chmn, Campaign 68 Comt, 68; Dist chmn, Operation Support Workshop, 67; State co-chmn nominating comt, Okla Dem Conv, 68; alt deleg, Dem Nat Conv, 68; chmn, Resolutions Comt, Okla Fedn Dem Women's Clubs State Conv, 68, chmn, Rules Comt, 69; third vpres, Okla Fedn of Dem Women, 71- Bus & Prof Pos: Flute instr, Seminole Jr Col, Okla, 72- Mem: CofC; Mod Lit Club (pres, 72-); Univ Okla Alumni Asn; Okla Press Asn; Cub Scouts (den mother, 69-). Relig: Presbyterian. Mailing Add: 1011 Hwy Nine W Seminole OK 74868

PHILLIPS, PARRIS JEROME **(D)**
Mem, Ga Dem State Exec Comt
b Atlanta, Ga, July 2, 48; s Paul Henry Lewis Phillips & Eloise Gail P; single. Educ: Morehouse Col, 72-; United Vets of Morehouse Col (pres). Polit & Govt Pos: Mem, Ga Dem State Exec Comt, 38th Dist, 74- Mil Serv: Entered as Pvt, Army, 68, released as SP 4/C, 70, after serv in 1st Inf Div, Asian Theatre, Vietnam Campaign, 68-69. Relig: African Methodist Episcopal. Mailing Add: 400 Fairburn Rd SW R150 Atlanta GA 30331

PHILLIPS, R T (TOM) **(R)**
Ga State Rep
Mailing Add: 1703 Pounds Rd Stone Mountain GA 30083

PHILLIPS, RALPH BOYD **(D)**
Committeeman, Baker Co Dem Comt, Ga
b Damascus, Ga, July 15, 03; s Benjamin Faulton Phillips & Rhodie Catherin Poole P; m 1932 to Verna Taylor; c Ralph Boyd, Jr. Polit & Govt Pos: Committeeman, Baker Co Dem Comt, Ga, 34-, secy-treas, 34-62; chmn, 62-72; justice of the peace, Ga, 36-69; mem, Gen Lewis B Hersey's Adv Bd, 27 years; cand for Ga state rep twice, for Ga state sen once, & for co comnr in 68. Bus & Prof Pos: Gen merchant, milling, farming & live stock raising since 18. Mem: Farm Bur. Relig: Church of God. Mailing Add: Rte 1 Damascus GA 31741

PHILLIPS, RICHARD I
b Artesia, NMex, Apr 2, 11; s Edward Frazier Phillips & Florence Idler P; m 1965 to Katherine Mayberry. Educ: Univ Nebr, 28-29; Univ Southern Calif, AB, 32, JD, 34; Phi Beta Kappa; Sigma Nu. Polit & Govt Pos: Second secy, Am Embassy, Montevideo, Uruguay, 46-48; second secy, Caracas, Venezuela, 48-51; polit adv to US Deleg to UN, Paris, France, 51-52; consul, Am Consulate, Nairobi, Kenya, 52-54; consul, Am Consulate, Guadalajara, Mex, 57-58; regional planning officer, Dept of State, 54-57, pub affairs adv, Bur of Inter-Am Affairs, Dept of State, 58-61, spec asst, Bur of Pub Affairs, 61-63, dir, off of news, 63-64, dep asst secy, 64-69, acting asst secy, 69-70; consul gen, Am Consulate, Monterrey, Mex, 70-71. Bus & Prof Pos: Attorney, Los Angeles, Calif, 34-35; auditor, Singer Sewing Machine Co, Argentina, 35-36; partner, Law firm of Marval, Rodriguez, Lareta & O'Farrell, Buenos Aires, 36-41; exec secy, Coord Comt for Uruguay, Montevideo, 41-45. Publ: Income tax laws of Argentina, Marval, Rodriguez, Lareta & O'Farrell, 39. Mem: State Bar of Calif; Am Club,

Buenos Aires, Argentina; Rotary Club; Am Asn, Montevideo, Uruguay; Int Club, Wash, DC. Honors & Awards: Distinguished Honor Award, Dept of State, 70. Relig: Protestant. Mailing Add: 3901 45th St NW Washington DC 20016

PHILLIPS, WATSON RANDOLPH (D)
Ga State Rep
b Shiloh, Ga, Mar 29, 40; s Thomas Watson Phillips & Ruth Chapman P; single. Educ: WGa Col, AB in Eng, 66. Polit & Govt Pos: City councilman, Shiloh, Ga, 64-66; Ga State Rep, Dist 38, 69-73, Dist 91, 75-; mem, Harris Co Dem Exec Comt, 72- Mem: CofC. Relig: Baptist. Mailing Add: Rte 1 Shiloh GA 31826

PHILLIPS, WILLARD L, JR (BILL) (R)
b Elkins, WVa, Apr 26, 41; s Willard Lewis Phillips & Norma Wiseman P; m 1965 to Marian Elaine Fusia; c Kristin E. Educ: Potomac State Col, AA, 61; WVa Wesleyan Col, BS, 64. Polit & Govt Pos: Dir, WVa Col Young Rep Clubs, 61-63; mem exec bd, Region III Col Young Rep, 61-63; mem col serv comt, Region III Young Rep Nat Fedn, 61-63, mem exec bd, 63-66; mem state exec comt, Young Rep WVa, 61-63, pres, 63-67; dir of orgn, Benedict for Cong Campaign, 62; dir of orgn, Benedict for US Senate, 64; dir of orgn, Randolph Co Rep Exec Comt, 62, secy-treas, 66; pres, Young Rep Club Randolph Co, 63; staff mem, State Rep Exec Comt, 64; city councilman, Elkins, WVa, 65; admin asst, US Rep Mizell, NC, 70-75; spec asst to the asst secy econ develop, Dept Com, 75- Bus & Prof Pos: Exec secy, WVa Pharmaceut Asn, 65-69, WVa Soc Prof Engrs, 67-69 & WVa Soc CPA, 68-69; spec asst to fed co-chmn, Appalachian Regional Comn, 69-70. Mem: Westwood Country Club; Cong Staff Club; Bull Elephants; Potomac State Col Alumni Asn (vpres); WVa Wesleyan Col Alumni Coun. Relig: United Methodist. Legal Res: Elkins WV Mailing Add: 14th & Constitution Ave NW Dept Com Rm 7804 Washington DC 20230

PHILLIPS, ZENO JOSEPH (D)
b West Columbia, Tex, Jan 31, 04; s Zeno J Phillips & Mary Narbon P; single. Educ: Sam Houston State Col, 21-24. Polit & Govt Pos: Admin asst to US Rep Omar Burleson, Tex, 41-72, secy, 72- Mil Serv: Entered as PO 1/C, Navy, 41, released as Chief PO, 45, after serv in 95th Naval Construction Bn, Pac Theatre. Mem: VFW; Am Legion; Cong Secy Club; Sons of the Repub of Tex. Relig: Presbyterian. Legal Res: Abilene TX Mailing Add: 2369 Rayburn Off Bldg Washington DC 20515

PHILLIPSON, HERBERT EMANUEL, JR (R)
Chmn, Cass Co Rep Party, Mich
b Dowagiac, Mich, Dec 25, 23; s Herbert E Phillipson & Florence Stern P; m 1952 to Dorothy Reasoner; c Jane Louise, Richard Herbert & Thomas David. Educ: Univ Mich, AB, 48, Law Sch, JD, 50. Polit & Govt Pos: City attorney, Dowagiac, Mich, 55-75; prosecuting attorney, Cass Co, 59-60; chmn, Cass Co Rep Party, 75- Mil Serv: Entered as Pvt, Air Force, 42, released as S/Sgt, 46, after serv in Pac Theatre, 43-46. Mem: Lions; Elks; Mich State Bar Asn (chmn civil procedure comt); Am Bar Asn. Legal Res: 502 Sunnyside Dr Dowagiac MI 49047 Mailing Add: 204 Commercial Dowagiac MI 49047

PHILPOTT, ALBERT LEE (D)
Va State Deleg
b Philpott, Va, July 29, 19; s John Elkania Philpott & Mary Gertrude Prillaman P; m 1941 to Katherine Apperson Spencer; c Judy (Mrs Marstiller) & Albert Lee, Jr. Educ: Richmond Col of Univ of Richmond, BA, 41; Univ Richmond Law Sch, JD, 47; Lambda Chi Alpha. Polit & Govt Pos: Commonwealth's Attorney, Henry Co, Va, 52-58; Va State Deleg, 58- Bus & Prof Pos: Attorney-at-law, 47- Mil Serv: Entered as Pvt, Army Air Force, 41, released as 1st Lt, 45, after serv in 2nd Air Force. Mem: Va State Bar; Elks; Moose; KofP; Am Legion (past Comdr, Bassett Post 11). Relig: Methodist. Mailing Add: Bassett VA 24055

PICKARD, ALBERT MARSHALL (R)
Chmn, Willacy Co Rep Party, Tex
b Pecan Gap, Tex, Aug 22, 22; s Lawrence E Pickard & Laura Ross P; m 1946 to Billie Conley; c Marsha Ann & Robert Marshall. Educ: Texas A&M Univ, DVM, 43. Polit & Govt Pos: Chmn, Willacy Co Rep Party, Tex, 63-; mem, US Indust Comt on Foot & Mouth Disease, 70- Bus & Prof Pos: Mem, Livestock comt, Rio Grande Valley Agr Adv Comt, 67-69. Mil Serv: Entered as Lt, Army, 43, released as Capt, 46, after serv in 124th Cavalry, China-Burma-India, 44-45. Publ: Brucellosis; Eradication vs Control, The Cattleman, 1/66. Mem: Rio Grande Valley Vet Med Asn (pres, 67-68); Tex Vet Med Asn; Farm Bur (vpres, Willacy Co Chap, 67-68, pres, Raymondville Chap, 68-69); Tex & Southwestern Cattle Raisers Asn; Rio Grande Valley Santa Gertrudis Breeders. Relig: Methodist. Legal Res: Two miles N Highway 77 Raymondville TX 78580 Mailing Add: PO Box 657 Raymondville TX 78580

PICKEL, THOMAS WESLEY, JR (R)
Chmn, Roane Co Rep Comt, Tenn
b Kingston, Tenn, Oct 13, 27; s Thomas Wesley Pickel, Sr & Mae Jackson P; m 1951 to Jane Coker Dunlap; c Laura (Mrs Dailey), Thomas Wesley, III & Margaret. Educ: Vanderbilt Univ, BE, 51; Univ Tenn, Knoxville, MA, 66; Univ Ill, Urbana-Champaign, PhD, 69; Tau Beta Pi; Sigma Xi. Polit & Govt Pos: Chmn, Roane Co Rep Comt, Tenn, 74-; mem, Roane Co Sch Bd, 75- Bus & Prof Pos: Sr supv engr, Humble Oil & Refining Co, 51-59; research engr, Union Carbide Corp Nuclear Div, 59-74 & dept mgr, 74- Mil Serv: Entered as Pvt, Air Force, 46, released as Sgt, 48. Mem: Nat Soc Prof Engrs; Am Inst Chem Engrs; Am Soc Mech Engrs; Rotary. Relig: Presbyterian. Mailing Add: PO Box 324 Kingston TN 37763

PICKERILL, MARY LOU (R)
Chmn, Otoe Co Rep Party, Nebr
b Kimball, Nebr, Oct 4, 31; d Raymond Wilson & Marion Noyes; m 1947 to Herbert M Pickerill; c Deborah (Mrs Gilbert), Mark, Julie, Kelly & Timothy. Educ: Syracuse High Sch, 47. Polit & Govt Pos: Chmn, Otoe Co Rep Party, 72, mem cent comt, 74-; mem, Nebr State Rep Cent Comt, 74- Mem: Eastern Star (assoc matron, 75). Relig: Methodist. Mailing Add: 1161 Thorne Syracuse NE 68446

PICKERING, CHARLES WILLIS (R)
Miss State Sen
b Hebron, Miss, May 29, 37; s Robert W Pickering & Lucille Anderson P; m 1959 to Margaret Ann Thomas; c Paige Elizabeth, Charles Willis (Chip), Allison Ann & Mary Christi. Educ: Jones Co Jr Col, 55-57; Univ Miss, BA with distinction, 59, LLB with distinction, 61; Phi Delta Phi; Omicron Delta Kappa; Tau Kappa Alpha (pres); Ole Miss Debate Club; Phi Kappa Phi; Pi Sigma Alpha; Claiborne Soc; Sigma Chi. Polit & Govt Pos: City prosecuting attorney, Laurel, Miss, 62; prosecuting attorney, Jones Co, 64-68; cand for state legis, 67; deleg, Rep Nat Conv, 68; mem, Am Fisheries Adv Comt, 70-71; Miss State Sen, 72- Bus & Prof Pos: Attorney-at-law, 61; assoc partner, Gartin & Hester, 61-62; partner, Gartin, Hester & Pickering, 62-71; partner, Pickering & McKenzie, currently. Mem: Kiwanis; Jaycees; Catfish Farmers of Am (pres); Am Red Cross (mem bd dirs, Jones Co Chap); Miss Farm Bur. Honors & Awards: Selected by Laurel Jaycees as Outstanding Young Man of the Year, 63 & Outstanding Civic Leaders of Am, 67; selected by Miss Jaycees as One of Three Outstanding Young Men of the Year, 63. Relig: Baptist; deacon, First Baptist Church, Laurel, teacher of adult Sunday sch class. Mailing Add: PO Box 713 Laurel MS 39440

PICKERING, GEORGE ROSCOE, JR (D)
Tenn State Rep
b Clarksville, Tenn, Aug 12, 12; s George Roscoe Pickering & Annie Geneva Nichols P; m 1934 to Dorothy Heflin; c Bobby Dean, William Howard & Linda Gail. Educ: Austin Peay State Univ, BS in Elem Educ, 33. Polit & Govt Pos: Tenn State Rep, 68- Bus & Prof Pos: Livestock specialist, Tenn Farm Corp, Clarksville, 40; farmer & livestock breeder, Pickering Farms, 60- Mem: Farm Bur; Tenn Livestock Asn. Relig: Church of Christ; deacon. Mailing Add: Rte 1 Adams TN 37010

PICKERING, THOMAS REEVE
US Ambassador, Jordan
b Orange, NJ, Nov 5, 31; s Hamilton R Pickering & Sarah P; m 1955 to Alice Stover; c Timothy Reeve & Margaret Stover. Educ: Bowdoin Col, AB, 53; Fletcher Sch Law & Diplomacy, Mass, MA, 54; Univ Melbourne, MA, 56; Phi Beta Kappa; Theta Delta Chi. Polit & Govt Pos: With Dept of State, 59-, intel research specialist, 60, foreign affairs officer, 61, detailed to Arms Control & Disarmament Agency, Geneva, with US Disarmament Conf Deleg, 61-64, Zanzibar prin officer, 65, Dar es Salaam dep chief of mission, 67, dep dir, Bur Politico Mil Affairs, 69, spec asst to Secy of State & exec secy, Dept of State, 73-74, US Ambassador, Jordan, 74- Mil Serv: Entered as Lt(jg), Navy, 56, released as Lt(jg), after serv in Fleet Intel Ctr, Atlantic, 57-59; Lt Comdr, Naval Res, 75. Mem: Coun on Foreign Rels; Int Inst Strategic Studies, London. Legal Res: Rutherford NJ Mailing Add: Amman Dept of State Washington DC 20520

PICKETT, DOVIE THEODOSIA (R)
Chmn, 13th Cong Dist Rep Comt, Mich
b Hinze, Miss, Nov 22, 21; d Joseph Thomas Carter & Lena Mary Lee C; m 1956 to Angelus Agustus Pickett, wid; foster child, Eddie Brown, Jr; one great granddaughter by marriage. Educ: Lewis Bus Col, 52; Int Data Processing Inst, grad, 56; Univ Mich Ctr for Adult Study, 69; Wayne Co Community Col, 72; Sigma Gamma Rho. Polit & Govt Pos: Precinct deleg, 13th Cong Dist Rep Comt, Mich, 54-, chmn, 69-; campaign chmn, Eisenhower-Nixon for President & Vice President, 13th Cong Dist Rep Hq Comt, 54; exec secy, 13th Cong Dist Rep Hq, 62-67; pres, 13th Dist Rep Womens Club, 63-67; secy, Womens Rep Fedn of Mich, 65-67; campaign coordr, 13th Cong Dist for President Nixon & US Sen Robert P Griffin, 72; mem, Electoral Col, Mich, 72; co-chmn, Mich Nat Black Comt for Reelec of President Nixon, 72; deleg, Rep Nat Conv, 72; mem, Mich Rep Nat Conv Rule 29 Comt, 76. Bus & Prof Pos: Clerical aide to Chief of Publ-Pub Rels, Mich Employ Security Comn, 67-68; mem, Clerical Staff, Gen Motors Corp, Detroit, 70- Mem: Nat Black Rep Coun (vpres); Equal Justice Coun (mem chmn); United Rep Mich (bd dirs); Capitol Hill Club; Int Platform Asn. Honors & Awards: Serv Award, Black Nat Vote Div, 72. Relig: Protestant. Mailing Add: 611 Chene St Detroit MI 48207

PICKETT, LAWRENCE EDWIN (R)
Chmn, Green Co Rep Party, Ky
b Greensburg, Ky, Nov 12, 17; s Henry Clayton Pickett & Bessie Rogers P; m 1939 to Ruby Christine Nienn; c Connie M (Mrs Driggers) & Lawrence E, Jr. Polit & Govt Pos: Jailer, Greensburg, Ky, 50-54, sheriff, 55; chmn, Green Co Rep Party, Ky, 58- Mem: CofC; Ky Fox Hunters Asn. Relig: Methodist. Mailing Add: 108 Riverview St Greensburg KY 42743

PICKETT, OWEN BRADFORD (D)
Va State Deleg
b Richmond, Va, Aug 31, 30; s Robert Lewis Pickett & Mary Judson Southworth P; m 1949 to Sybil Catherine Kelly; c Laura, Karen & Mary. Educ: Va Polytech Inst, BS; Univ Richmond, LLB. Polit & Govt Pos: Va State Deleg, 70-, mem revenue resources & econ comn & mem state govt mgt comn, Va House Deleg, 70- Mem: Moose; Am Inst CPA; Rotary; Ruritan; Phi Alpha Delta. Legal Res: 321 Apasus Trail Virginia Beach VA 23452 Mailing Add: Box 2127 Virginia Beach VA 23452

PICKETT, ROBERT MCQUILLIOUS (R)
b Daviess Co, Ind, Sept 25, 23; s Thomas Laiken Pickett & Belva Alyce White P; div; c Pricilla Jeanne. Educ: Washington High Sch, Ind, grad. Polit & Govt Pos: Rep precinct committeeman Daviess Co, Ind, 52-58; secy-treas, City Rep Comt, Washington, 53; chmn, Daviess Co Young Rep, 53-58; mem, Daviess Co Rep Finance Comt, 54; mgr License Br, Bur Motor Vehicles, 57-61; mem, Seventh Dist Rep Comt, 57-66, treas, 64-66; chmn, Daviess Co Rep Party, formerly; mem, Eighth Dist Rep Comt, 66-; treas, Win With Whitcomb Comt, 68; presidential elector, 68; mem exec comt, Rep State Comt, 68-; dir RR, Dept Pub Serv Comn, Ind, 69- Mem: Mason; Scottish Rite; Shrine; Elks; Moose. Relig: Protestant. Mailing Add: 12 Harned Ave Washington IN 47501

PICKETT, THOMAS AUGUSTUS (D)
b Travis, Tex, Aug 14, 06; s James D'Aubigne Pickett & Helen Augusta Mackey P; m 1938 to Alice Louise Watson; c Helen Louise, Alice Melinda. Educ: Palestine Bus Col; Univ of Tex. Polit & Govt Pos: US Rep, Tex, 45-51; dist attorney, Third Judicial Dist of Tex, 35-44; Co attorney, Anderson Co, Tex, 31-34. Bus & Prof Pos: Vpres, Asn Am RR, 61-67; vpres, Nat Coal Asn, 52-61; law practice in Palestine, Tex, formerly. Mailing Add: PO Box 1215 Leesburg FL 32748

PICKETT, WILLIAM A (D)
Mass State Rep
Mailing Add: State Capitol Boston MA 02133

PICKLE, J J (JAKE) (D)
US Rep, Tex
b Roscoe, Tex, Oct 11, 13; s J B Pickle & Mary P; married; c Peggy, Dick McCarroll & Graham McCarroll. Educ: Univ Tex, BA. Polit & Govt Pos: Area dir, Nat Youth Admin, 38-41; dir, Tex Dem State Exec Comt, 57-60; mem, Tex Employ Comn, 61-63; US Rep, Tex, 63-, mem Ways & Means Comt, US House Rep, 75- Bus & Prof Pos: Entered radio bus as one of the co-organizers of Radio Sta KVET, Austin, Tex; pub rels & advert bus. Mil Serv:

Navy, 3 years 6 months in Pac Theatre. Legal Res: Austin TX Mailing Add: 3900 Watson Pl Washington DC 20016

PICUCCI, ANGELO (D)
Mass State Rep
Mailing Add: State Capitol Boston MA 02133

PICZAK, JOHN P (D)
Chmn, Yates Co Dem Party, NY
b Rochester, NY, June 7, 40; s John Thomas Piczak & Bernice Zelazny P; m 1960 to Judy Casale; c Lisa, Steven & Matthew. Educ: State Univ NY Col Geneseo, BS in educ, 63; State Univ NY Albany Grad Sch Pub Affairs, PhD in polit sci, 70; Phi Sigma Epsilon. Polit & Govt Pos: Housing coordr, Monroe Co Human Rels Comn, NY, 66-67; intern, NY State Sen, 68-69; Upstate organizer, 34th Cong Dist Coalition for Muskie, 71-72; chmn, Yates Co Dem Party, 73-; research assoc, NY State Assembly, 75- Bus & Prof Pos: Assoc prof polit sci, Keuka Col, 71- Publ: County party chairmen of New York State: Their motivations, apprenticeships, & career aspirations, Int Rev Hist & Polit Sci, 5/74. Mem: Am & Northeastern Polit Sci Asns; Am Polit Item Collectors Asn; Ctr for Study of the Presidency. Mailing Add: Box 126 Keuka Park NY 14478

PIEKARSKI, STAN (D)
Mo State Rep
Mailing Add: 2547 A West Dodier St Louis MO 63107

PIEKOS, HENRY (R)
Chmn, Lee Rep Town Comt, Mass
b Cheshire, Mass, Feb 4, 26; s John Piekos & Karolina Bulsa P; m 1949 to Marcelline Labarge; c Claudia (Mrs Berry Scott), Larry H, Eleanor (Mrs Kent W Beam), Beverly J, Jennifer L & Daniel B. Educ: Berkshire Bus Col, grad, 48. Polit & Govt Pos: Selectman, Town of Cheshire, Mass, 58-61; chmn, Nixon Comt, Town of Lee, 68 & 72; mem, Berkshire Co Rep Asn, 68-73; selectman, Town of Lee, 69-71; campaign chmn, Town of Lee, Gov Francis Sargent, 70; chmn, Lee Rep Town Comt, 70-; mem, Selective Serv Local 44, 72. Bus & Prof Pos: Machinist, Gen Elec Co, Pittsfield, Mass, 51 & assembler of high voltage bushings, 69-; co-mgr, Marcy's Dress House, Lee, Mass, currently. Mil Serv: T-5, Army, 45-46, serv in 3rd Army, European, 45-46. Mem: IUE-CIO; Lions; Paper Town Pacers. Relig: Congregational. Mailing Add: 65 Housatonic St Lee MA 01138

PIEPLOW, E C (R)
Minority Leader, SDak State Senate
b Nov 9, 17; m 1939; c Mike. Educ: Kans State Univ, BS. Polit & Govt Pos: Past mem, Bd Educ & Park Bd, Aberdeen, SDak; SDak State Sen, 67-, Senate Minority Leader, currently; chmn, Local Govt Study Comn, currently; mem exec bd, Legis Res Coun, currently. Bus & Prof Pos: Formerly with Radio Sta KABR & KSDN; vpres, First Nat Bank of Aberdeen, currently. Mil Serv: Lt Comdr, Navy, World War II. Mem: Shrine; Elks; Am Legion; Lions; SDak Crippled Children (mem bd dirs). Relig: Presbyterian. Mailing Add: 1415 N Third Aberdeen SD 57401

PIER, CRAIG DONALD (D)
Chmn, Portage Co Dem Party, Wis
b Beloit, Wis, Jan 5, 43; s Donald Charles Pier & Margaret Ann Howell P; m 1966 to Romelle Lee Toppel; c Bryce Toppel & Brent Allen. Educ: Univ Wis, Madison, BS, 65. Polit & Govt Pos: Secy, Portage Co Dem Party, Wis, 68-70, vchmn, 70-73, mem-at-lg, 73-74, chmn, 74- Bus & Prof Pos: Teacher, Waunakee Sr High Sch, Wis, 66-67, Belmont Community Sch, 67-68 & Jacobs Jr High Sch, Stevens Point, 68- Mem: Stevens Point Area, Wis & Nat Educ Asns; Portage Co Preservation Asn (bd dirs, 69-). Mailing Add: 727 Second St Stevens Point WI 54481

PIERANNUNZI, CAMILLO A (D)
RI State Rep
Mailing Add: 757 Park Ave Woonsocket RI 02895

PIERAS, JAIME, JR (R)
Rep Nat Committeeman, PR
b San Juan, PR, May 19, 24; s Jaime Pieras & Ines Lopez-Cepero P; m 1953 to Elsie Castaner; c Awilda Ines & Jaime Roberto. Educ: Cath Univ Am, BA, 45; Georgetown Univ, LLB, 48; Phi Kappa; Nu Sigma Beta; Phi Delta Phi. Polit & Govt Pos: Gen counsel, Tourism Bur, PR, 53; mem, finance comt, San Juan Electoral Campaign, 60, chmn, 64; alt deleg, Rep Nat Conv, 64, deleg, 68 & 72; chmn finance comt, Statehood Rep Party, PR & mem, Polit Action Comt; Rep Nat Committeeman, PR, 68-; pres, Rep Nat Party of PR, 68- Bus & Prof Pos: Assoc, Luis E Dubon Law Off, 49-52 & Hartzell, Fernandez & Novas Law Off, 53-59; partner, Pieras & Torryella Law Off, 59- Mil Serv: Pvt, Army, 46-47; Victory Medal; Mediter Theater of Oper Ribbon; 2nd Lt, Army Res, 49-51. Mem: Am Bar Asn; Fed Bar Asn of PR; CofC; KofC; Rotary. Relig: Roman Catholic. Legal Res: One Washington Ave Condado San Juan PR 00907 Mailing Add: PO Box 507 Hato Rey PR 00919

PIERCE, CLARENCE ALBERT, JR (D)
Miss State Rep
b Thornton, Miss, Oct 1, 28; s Clarence Albert Pierce, Sr & Alice Vaiden Herring P; single. Educ: Univ Miss, 47-50; Beta Theta Pi. Polit & Govt Pos: Miss State Rep, 52-; chmn, Comt on Hwys & Hwy Finance, 70- Mem: Farm Bur; SAR; Omicron Delta Kappa; Mason. Relig: Episcopal. Mailing Add: Box 277 Vaiden MS 39176

PIERCE, DANIEL MARSHALL (D)
Minority Whip, Ill House Rep
b Chicago, Ill, Mar 31, 28; s Hyman A Pierce & Thelma Udwin P; m 1953 to Ellen M Field; c Andrew F, Anthony D & Theodore M. Educ: Harvard Col, AB, 49, Harvard Law Sch, LLB, 52; Lincoln's Inn Soc. Polit & Govt Pos: Vchmn, Lake Co Dem Cent Comt, Ill, 59-62; hearing officer, Ill Com Comn & Interstate Com Comn, 61-64; committeeman, Ill State Dem Cent Comt, 62-66 & 70-; mem, Ill Reapportionment Comn, 63; alt deleg, Dem Nat Conv, 64, deleg, 72; Ill State Rep, 65-, Minority Whip, Ill House of Rep, 71- Bus & Prof Pos: Partner law firm, Altheimer, Gray, Naiburg, Strasburger & Lawton, 66- Mil Serv: Entered as Pvt, Army, 52, released as Capt, Air Force, 54, after serv in Judge Adv Gen Dept, Flying Training Air Force. Mem: Am, Ill State & Chicago Bar Asns; Am Legion. Relig: Jewish. Mailing Add: 1923 Lake Ave Highland Park IL 60035

PIERCE, ELEANOR JEAN (R)
Chmn, Greene Co Rep Comt, Pa
b Waynesburg, Pa, June 28, 26; d S Earl Morris & Mae Cain M; m 1947 to Albert Norman Pierce, Jr; c Norman Lee, Mae Earlene (Mrs Glen Curfman) & Alberta Jean. Polit & Govt Pos: Chmn, Greene Co Rep Comt, Pa, 74- Relig: Baptist. Mailing Add: RD 5 Box 124B Waynesburg PA 15370

PIERCE, GRACE WAGNER (R)
Committeewoman, 31st Dist Rep Party, Del
b Coatesville, Pa, May 9, 26; d Jacob Heinly Wagner & Grace Quaintance Wallace W; m to Willard Lemar Pierce; c Linda Lee (Mrs Thomas Dolan), Barry Wallace Clark & Susan Butler. Educ: Goldey Col, 1 year; Wesley Jr Col, 1 year. Polit & Govt Pos: Rep committeewoman, 29th Dist, Kent Co, Del, 66-69; chmn of vol, Kent Co Rep Campaign, 68; deleg, Rep Nat Conv, 68; prog chmn, Del Fedn Rep Women, 68 & 69, pres, 70-; vchmn, Kent Co Rep Comt, 69-73; Kent Co chmn, Gov Peterson's Campaign Comt, 72; committeewoman, 31st Dist Rep Party, Del, 73- Bus & Prof Pos: Secy-treas, Pierce's Pharmacies Inc, Dover, Del, 58- Mem: Jr bd, Kent Gen Hosp; Palmer Home; Rehoboth Art League; Maple Dale Country Club; Wilmington Soc Fine Arts. Honors & Awards: Ribbons & awards for watercolors entered in art shows. Relig: Presbyterian. Mailing Add: 535 American Ave Dover DE 19901

PIERCE, JERRY T (R)
Okla State Sen
Mailing Add: State Capitol Oklahoma City OK 73105

PIERCE, RICHARD HERBERT (R)
Maine State Rep
b Waterville, Maine, Feb 3, 43; s Henry W Pierce & Beatrice Marshall P; single. Educ: Boston Univ, AB, 65; Univ Maine, MSEd, 73. Polit & Govt Pos: Maine State Rep, 75- Bus & Prof Pos: Dean students, Thomas Col, Waterville, Maine, 71-74. Mil Serv: Entered as E-1, Army Nat Guard, 68, released as Lt, 72. Mem: Am Legion; Elks; Gtr Waterville CofC (dir). Legal Res: 42 Roosevelt Ave Waterville ME 04901 Mailing Add: Box 120 State House Augusta ME 04333

PIERPONT, ROSS ZIMMERMAN (R)
Chmn, Third Legis Dist Rep Party, Md
b Woodlawn, Md, Sept 7, 17; s Edwin L Pierpont & Ethel Zimmerman P; m 1942 to Grace Schmidt; c Christine C. Educ: Univ Md Sch Pharm, BS, 37 & MD, 40; Kappa Psi. Polit & Govt Pos: Mem, Bd of Hosp Licensure, Md, 62-68; mem, Comprehensive Health Planning, 68-70; mem, Bd of Health Rev, 70-; deleg, Rep Nat Conv, 72; chmn, Third Legis Dist Rep Party, 72- Bus & Prof Pos: Chief of Surg, Harford Mem Hosp, Havre de Grace, Md, 46-56 & Md Gen Hosp, Baltimore, 60-; assoc, Dept Surg Anat, Univ Md, 46-, asst clin prof, Dept Surg, 62-; bd mem, Baltimore Ice Sports, 62-; bd mem, Md Old Line Ins Co, Annapolis, 68-; pres, Pierpont, Hebb & Finegan, Baltimore, 69- & Surgical Clinic, Havre de Grace, 69- Publ: Experience and the use of the Zimmerman type of hernioplasty: a new concept of the transversetis fascia, 10/59, Vagotomy and gastric drainage for peptic ulcer, 12/60 & Surgical management of duodenal ulcer, emphasis on vagotomy and gastric drainage, 4/67, The Am Surgeon. Mem: Am Med Asn; Southeastern Surg Conf; Am Col Surgeons; Univ Md Surg Soc; Kiwanis; Nat Rehabilitation Asn. Honors & Awards: Dipl, Am Bd of Surg, 47; fel, Am Col Surgeons, 57 & Southeastern Surg Cong, 57. Relig: Methodist. Mailing Add: 5602 Enderly Rd Baltimore MD 21212

PIERRE, WILFRED THOMAS (D)
b Lafayette, La, May 26, 46; s Mr Pierre (deceased) & Wilda Landor P; m to Carol Ann Guilbeaux. Educ: Univ Southwestern La, BA, 59; Alpha Phi Alpha. Polit & Govt Pos: Exec dir & coord voter educ proj, Black Alliance for Progress, Lafayette, La, 71-72; deleg, Dem Nat Conv, 72; mem bd dirs, Lafayette Coun on Human Rels; mem personnel adv comt, La State Dept Educ, coord interagency rels, 72-73, supvr vet educ training, 73, sr prog specialist, Bur Tech Assistance, 73- Bus & Prof Pos: Mem bd dirs, BLYM Corp. Mil Serv: Sgt, Marine Corps Res, 4 years, 6 months; Meritoriously promoted to Lance Cpl for outstanding performance in training. Mem: NAACP. Relig: Catholic. Mailing Add: 106 1/2 Lena St Lafayette LA 70501

PIERSOL, LAWRENCE L (D)
b Vermillion, SDak, Oct 21, 40; s Ralph N Piersol & Mildred Millette P; m 1962 to Catherine A Vogt; c William, Elizabeth & Leah. Educ: Univ Nebr, Lincoln, 58-59; Univ SDak, BA, 59-62, Law Sch, JD summa cum laude, 65; Omicron Delta Kappa; Phi Delta Theta. Polit & Govt Pos: Precinct committeeman, SDak, 70-; SDak State Rep, 71-74, Minority Whip, SDak State House Rep, 71-72, Majority Leader, 72-74; chmn, Citizens Comn on Exec Reorgn, 71-; mem, State Planning Coun, 71-; mem, State Judicial Coun, 71-; deleg, Dem Nat Conv, 72; mem, Nat Dem Party Presidential Selection Reform Comn, 73- Bus & Prof Pos: Assoc, Davenport, Evans, Hurwitz & Smith, Sioux Falls, SDak, 68-69, partner, 70- Mil Serv: Entered as 2nd Lt, Army, 62, released as Capt, 68, after serv in Judge Adv Gen Corps, 65-68; Army Commendation Medal. Publ: The abstention doctrine, SDak Law Rev, spring 64. Mem: SDak Trial Lawyers Asn; Am Bar Asn; State Judicial Coun; Rotary Club; KofC. Relig: Catholic. Mailing Add: 103 S Duluth Ave Sioux Falls SD 57105

PIERSON, JOHN JAY (R)
b Minneapolis, Minn, June 30, 17; s Roy Newton Pierson & Margaret Welles P; m 1960 to Jean Louise Stringer; c John J, Jr & Julia W. Educ: Univ Minn, Minneapolis, 35-38. Polit & Govt Pos: Chmn, Minn Rep Finance Comt, 71-74; deleg, Rep Nat Conv, 72. Bus & Prof Pos: Mem staff, Knoblauch & Pierson Eng Co, Minneapolis, Minn, 46-48, Russell Miller Milling Co, 48-61, Gold Eagle Wash, 61-63, Advance Floor Mach Co, Spring Park, 63-64 & Dain, Kalman & Quail, Inc, St Paul, 64- Mil Serv: Entered as Pvt, Army Air Corps, 41, released as T/Sgt, 45, after serv in 5th Air Force, 86th Fighter Bomber Group, ETO. Mem: Gow Sch (chmn bd trustees); Somerset Country Club (bd dirs); Minneapolis/St Paul Twin City Bond Club; Minn Club. Relig: Episcopal. Legal Res: 782 Hilltop Rd St Paul MN 55118 Mailing Add: 201 Am Nat Bank Bldg St Paul MN 55101

PIETRI, JOYCE ABBE (R)
Chairwoman, Houghton Co Rep Comt, Mich
b Neptune, NJ, Oct 18, 32; d Willis C Fitkin & Helen Shubert F; m 1954 to Raoul Pietri; c Joyce Abbe, Raoul, Jr & Willis A. Educ: Marjorie Webster Jr Col, AA, 53. Polit & Govt Pos: Chairwoman Nixon Hq, Houghton Co Rep Comt, Mich, 72, vchmn & chairwoman social events, 73-75, chairwoman, 75-; deleg, Mich State Conv, 73, chairwoman of deleg & deleg, 75; chairwoman, Gov Milliken Phone Ctr, Houghton Co, 74. Bus & Prof Pos: Teacher,

Meeting St Sch, Providence, RI, 69-71; teacher, Community Schs, Houghton, Mich, 72-75. Mem: United Fund (bd mem); Rep Women's Club. Relig: Episcopal; pres, Episcopal Church Women, Houghton, 73-75. Mailing Add: 1019 College Ave Houghton MI 49931

PIEVSKY, MAX (D)
Pa State Rep
Mailing Add: Capitol Bldg Harrisburg PA 17120

PIKE, OTIS GREY (D)
US Rep, NY
b Riverhead, NY, Aug 31, 21; s Otis G Pike & Belle Lupton P; m 1946 to Doris A Orth; c Lois, Douglas & Robert. Educ: Princeton Univ, AB magna cum laude in govt & polit, 46; Columbia Univ Sch Law, LLB, 48. Hon Degrees: LLD, Adelphi Univ, 64, Long Island Univ, 67. Polit & Govt Pos: Deleg, Dem Nat Conv, 52, 54 & 68; Justice of Peace, Riverhead, NY, 53-60, cand, 49; US Rep, NY, 61-, mem, House Armed Serv Comt, US House of Rep, 61-73, mem, Ways & Means Comt, 74- Bus & Prof Pos: With Griffing & Smith, 49-53; pvt practice, Riverhead, NY, 53- Mil Serv: Entered Navy Air Corps, 42, released as Capt, 46, after serv as Marine Corps Pilot, 14 months as dive bomber pilot in Solomon Island campaign & 8 months as night fighter pilot at Peleliu, Okinawa & Peking; Five Air Medals. Mem: Rotary; VFW; Am Legion; Suffolk Co Bar Asn; Riverhead Lodge F&AM. Honors & Awards: Annual Brotherhood Award, Odd Fellows Welfare Guild, 65; Medal of Merit, Jewish War Vet, Nassau-Suffolk Dist Coun, 65. Relig: Congregational; Past trustee, First Congregational Church of Riverhead. Legal Res: 132 Ostrander Ave Riverhead NY 11901 Mailing Add: 2428 Rayburn House Off Bldg Washington DC 20515

PIKE, THOMAS POTTER (R)
b Los Angeles, Calif, Aug 12, 09; s Percy Mortimer Pike & Elizabeth Potter P; m 1931 to Katherine Keho; c John Keho, Josephine (Mrs Barnes) & Mary Katherine (Mrs Coquillard). Educ: Stanford Univ, AB in Econ, 31; Alpha Delta Phi. Polit & Govt Pos: Chmn, Los Angeles Co Rep Finance Comt, Calif, 49-52; chmn, Calif Rep State Finance Comt, 52-53; Dep Asst Secy Defense, Supply & Logistics, 53-54, Asst Secy Defense, 54-56; spec asst to President Eisenhower, 56 & 58; spec asst to Secy Defense in charge of Mil Assistance Prog, 56-57; chmn, Calif Nixon for President, 60; vchmn, Los Angeles Co Nixon Finance Comt, 68; deleg, Rep Nat Conv, 68; vchmn, Calif Comt to Reelect Richard M Nixon, 72. Bus & Prof Pos: Mem staff, Repub Supply Co, Los Angeles, Calif, 31-38; pres & founder, Thomas P Pike Drilling Co, 38-53; chmn bd & chief exec officer, Pike Corp of Am, 58-65; vchmn bd, Fluor Corp, Ltd, currently. Mem: Calif Club; Bohemian Club; Univ Club; Valley Hunt Club. Relig: Roman Catholic. Mailing Add: 1475 Circle Dr San Marino CA 91108

PILCHER, JAMES BROWNIE (D)
Mem, Fulton Co Dem Exec Comt, Ga
b Shreveport, La, May 19, 29; s James Reese Pilcher & Mattie Brown P; m 1951 to Frances Maxine Pettit; c Lydia Dean, Martha Claire & Jay Bradley. Educ: La State Univ, BS, 52; John Marshall Univ, JD, 55; Emory Univ, 58; Kappa Phi Kappa; Nu Beta Epsilon. Polit & Govt Pos: Pres, Fulton Co Young Dem Club, Ga, 62-63; committeeman, Ga Dem State Exec Comt, 62-66; legal counsel to speaker of Ga House of Rep, 62-65; pres, Young Dem Clubs of Ga, 63-64; assoc city attorney, Atlanta, 65-70; mem, Fulton Co Dem Exec Comt, 66-, chmn, 69-72; mem, Fulton Co Dem Party. Bus & Prof Pos: Pres, Atlanta Health Coun, 66-; pres, Active Voters, 67-69. Mem: Atlanta Jaycees. Relig: Baptist. Legal Res: 434 Brentwood Dr NE Atlanta GA 30305 Mailing Add: Prof Bldg 1799 Lakewood Terr SE Atlanta GA 30315

PILLERS, GEORGE WYLIE, JR (R)
Chmn, Clinton Co Rep Cent Comt, Iowa
b Lincoln, Nebr, Aug 17, 14; s George Wylie Pillers & Caroline Gilster P; m 1940 to Esther Luella Brandt; c George Wylie, III & James Leigh. Educ: Col Bus Admin, BS, 35; Univ Nebr Col Law, JD, 37; Law Fraternity; Phalanx. Polit & Govt Pos: Purchasing & contracting officer, Ft Wayne Ord Depot, Mich, 41-43, fiscal officer, 43-44, chief stock control off, 44-45; renegotiation attorney, legal div, Off Chief Ord, Detroit, 45; chmn, Clinton Co Rep Cent Comt, Iowa, 62-; alt deleg, Rep Nat Conv, 72; mem, Clinton Airport Comn. Bus & Prof Pos: Sr partner, Pillers, Pillers & Pillers; vpres, Car Carrier Motor Sales. Mil Serv: Entered as 2nd Lt, Army, 40, released as Lt Col, 46, after serv in Qm Corps, Off Chief of Ord, Detroit, Mich; Cert of Commendation, Ord Dept; Army Inactive Res, 46-54. Mem: Am Bar Asn; Aircraft Owners & Pilots Asn; Nat Defense Transportation Asn; Am Legion; Rotary. Relig: Lutheran; Chmn bd dirs, Mo Synod, Iowa Dist East, 57-65. Legal Res: 1036 Fifth Ave N Clinton IA 52732 Mailing Add: Exec Plaza Bldg 1127 N Second St Clinton IA 52732

PILLOW, THEODORE EUGENE (D)
b Chicago, Ill, Aug 31, 51; s Frank Gordon & Ruby P Osby G; single. Educ: Parsons Col, 70-; Alpha Chi Rho. Polit & Govt Pos: Deleg, Dem Nat Conv, 72. Bus & Prof Pos: Student mgr, Saga Food Serv, Parsons Col, Fairfield, Iowa, 70- Honors & Awards: Deans List Parsons Col, 72. Relig: Catholic. Mailing Add: Apt 202 2727 S Indiana Chicago IL 60619

PILLSBURY, GEORGE STURGIS (R)
Minn State Sen
b Crystal Bay, Minn, July 17, 21; s John Sargent Pillsbury & Eleanor Lawler P; m 1947 to Sally Lucille Whitney; c Charles Alfred, George Sturgis, Jr, Sarah Kimball & Katharine Whitney. Educ: Yale Univ, BA, 42; Sigma Psi; Fence, Scroll & Key. Polit & Govt Pos: Minn State Sen, 33rd Dist, 71-73, 42nd Dist, 73-; chmn, Minn Rep Finance Comt, 73- Bus & Prof Pos: Vpres, Overseas Div, Pillsbury Co, Minneapolis, Minn, exec vpres, Co, group vpres, 46-69; dir & pres, Sargent Mgt Co, Minneapolis, 69- Mil Serv: Entered as Pfc, Marines, 43, released as 1st Lt, 46, after serv in Airborne Radio-Radar, Northern Philippines & Solomon Islands, 44-45; Presidential Unit Commendation. Mem: Woodhill Country Club (trustee); Minneapolis Club; Minneapolis Athletic Club; Minnetonka Yacht Club; Minn Club. Honors & Awards: Young Man of the Year, Minneapolis Jr CofC, 56; Distinguished Serv Award. Relig: Episcopal. Legal Res: 1320 Bracketts Point Rd Wayzata MN 55391 Mailing Add: 930 Dain Tower Minneapolis MN 55402

PILOT, LYNNE JOYCE (R)
b Cleveland, Ohio, May 10, 40; d Kenneth George Widlitz & Irene Darden W; m 1968 to Larry Robert Pilot; c Lawrence Robert, Jr & Tracy Lynne. Educ: John Carroll Univ, summer 57; Miami Univ, BS in Eng & Hist-Govt, 62, Educ Cert, Eng & Social Studies; George Washington Univ, Grad Studies in Polit Sci, 64; Nat Law Ctr, George Washington Univ, JD with honors, 69; Dean's List, high honors, 3 years, social chmn, Zeta Tau Alpha, 2 years, exec secy & mem exec coun, mem, House Coun, Assoc Women Students, Asn for Childhood Educ, Inter-Residence Coun & Sr Class Exec Bd, chmn, Sr Week Comt, queen, Newman Club, attend, Rose of Delta Sigma Pi & attend, Sesquicentennial Queen, Miami Univ; Student Bar; Kappa Beta Pi. Polit & Govt Pos: Admin & legis asst to US Rep Donald D Clancy, Ohio, 69- Bus & Prof Pos: Pvt law practice; legal bus agent, Diversified Food Enterprises. Mem: League of Women Voters; Va State & DC Bar Asns; Miami Univ Alumni Asn; Am Law Students Asn. Mailing Add: 1815 N Hartford St Arlington VA 22201

PINA, RONALD ANTHONY (D)
Mass State Rep
Mailing Add: State Capitol Boston MA 02133

PINANSKI, VIOLA R (R)
b Boston, Mass, June 24, 98; d Julius Rottenberg & Fannie Berg R; m 1920 to Abraham E Pinanski, wid; c Jean (Mrs Dietz), Joan (Mrs Morse), Jane & June (Mrs Schiff). Educ: Wellesley Col, BA & fel; Harvard Sch Educ; Shakespeare Soc; Wellesley Club. Hon Degrees: LHD, Suffolk Univ. Polit & Govt Pos: Mem adv comt, Brookline, Mass, 34-36, mem sch comt, 36-76; deleg, Rep Nat Comt, 51, 55, 59 & 62; US deleg, WHO, 57; deleg, Rep Nat Conv, 60; mem, Mass Civil Defense Comt & Harrington Willis Educ Comt. Bus & Prof Pos: Trustee, Peter Bent Brigham Hosp, New Eng Med Ctr, Beth Israel Hosp & Faulkner Hosp. Mem: Nat Inst Neurol Diseases (adv comt); hon life mem Am Hosp Asn; hon fel Am Col Hosp Adminr; WHO (dir, Nat Citizens Comt). Honors & Awards: Leadership Award, Nat Soc Christians & Jews. Relig: Jewish. Mailing Add: 1264 Beacon St Brookline MA 02146

PINCKNEY, KATHLEEN WELDON (KAY) (D)
b Griffin, Ga, June 18, 51; d Robert Howe Pinckney, OD & Kathleen Weldon P; single. Educ: Agnes Scott Col, BA, 73. Polit & Govt Pos: Chmn, Butts Co, Jimmy Carter for Gov, Ga, 70 & David Gambrell for US Senate, 72; alt deleg, Dem Nat Conv, 72; vpres, Agnes Scott Young Dem, Agnes Scott Col, 73. Mem: CHIMO of Agnes Scott; Dem Women of DeKalb Co, Ga; Ga Women's Polit Caucus. Honors & Awards: DAR Good Citizen, William McIntosh Chap, Jackson, Ga, 69; Citation of Merit, Muscular Dystrophy Asns of Am, Inc, 70. Relig: United Methodist. Mailing Add: 379 West Ave Box 3860 Jackson GA 30233

PINE, CHARLES WARREN (D)
Chmn, Ariz Dem Party
b Providence, RI, Feb 9, 15; s Charles Joseph Pine & Edna Kempf P; m 1970 to Selma Krantzow; c Charles Arthur & Elinor. Educ: Providence Eve Col, 34-37; Brown Univ, exten courses, 49-51. Polit & Govt Pos: Secy eighth ward comt, Providence Cent Comt, RI, 36-38, chmn speakers bur, 38; secy, Young Men's Dem League of RI, 38-41; deleg, Dem Nat Conv, 68; pub rels dir, Ariz Humphrey-Muskie Comt, 68; Dem precinct capt Maricopa Co, 68-; mem, Ariz Dem Leadership Conf, 69-; chmn, Dist 25, Maricopa Co Dem Comt, 70-72; mem, Ariz State Dem Exec Comt, 70-; chmn, Ariz Dem Party, 72-; mem, Dem Nat Comt, 72- Bus & Prof Pos: Newspaperman & free lance writer, New Eng newspapers, 34-42; managing ed, RI Herald News, 46, pres, Charles W Pine & Assoc, Providence, RI, 47-52; teacher, Providence YMCA Jr Col, 49-50; teacher, Johnson & Wales Bus Sch, 49-51; publicity dir, Valley Nat Bank of Ariz, 53-63; pres & owner, Charles W Pine & Assoc, Pub Rels & Advert, 63- Mil Serv: Entered as Pvt, Army Air Corps, 43, released, 44, after serv in Troop Carrier Command, 43-44. Publ: What should you expect of a public relations man?; Dispelling some myths about public relations; Moderation in politics, plus more than 40 others. Mem: Pub Rels Soc Am; CofC; Phoenix Art Mus; Am Legion; Nucleus Club of Maricopa Co. Honors & Awards: Cert Achievement, Indust Col of Armed Forces, 58; City Father Award, Phoenix City Coun, 60; Percy Award, Phoenix Pub Rels Soc, 61; Award for Extraordinary Community Serv, Maricopa Med Soc, 62; Advert Man of the Year Award, Phoenix Advert Club, 66. Relig: Congregational; moderator, Ariz Congregationalist Conf, 56-57; dir, Congregational Conf of Southern Calif & Southwest, 57-60. Legal Res: 1901 E Missouri Phoenix AZ 85014 Mailing Add: 5133 N Central Ave Phoenix AZ 85012

PINE, JAMES ALEXANDER (D)
b Princeton, WVa, Aug 12, 12; s Lewis Alexander Pine & Mary Bridges P; m 1944 to Charlotte Elissa Weikinger; c James Alexander, Frank Carlton, Mary Frederick & Nancy Lee. Educ: Univ WVa, BS, 38; Univ Md Law Sch, LLB, 44. Polit & Govt Pos: Counsel, Baltimore Co Bd of Co Comnrs, Md, 50-51; first co solicitor for Baltimore Co, 51-53; Md State Sen, Sen, 58-74, Majority Leader, Md State Senate, 62; deleg, Dem Nat Conv, 60-72; gen counsel, Pub Serv Comn Md, 74- Mem: Lions; Moose; Elks; Mason; Shrine. Honors & Awards: Legislator of the Year Award, Metrop Newspapers in Baltimore Area, 61. Relig: Baptist; former trustee, Calvary Baptist Church, Towson. Mailing Add: Thornhill Baldwin MD 21013

PINEO, FRED BENJAMIN, JR (D)
Mem, Washington Co Dem Comt, Maine
b Columbia Falls, Maine, July 19, 09; s Fred Benjamin Pineo & Lucy Higgins P; m 1931 to Shirley Grant; c Lucille (Mrs Charles Pittman), Bernice (Mrs Robert Gardner), Ellis L, Dale G & Loyce (Mrs Paul Worcester). Educ: Columbia Falls High Sch, Maine, 4 years. Polit & Govt Pos: Town chmn, Columbia Falls, Maine, 8 years & 68-; chmn, Washington Co Dem Comt, 62-66, treas, 66-72, mem, currently; mem, Maine Dem State Comt, 66-72; deleg, Dem Nat Conv, 68; chmn, Columbia Falls Dem Comt, currently. Mem: Subordinate, Pomona, State & Nat Granges; dep master, Maine State Grange. Relig: Methodist. Mailing Add: Columbia Falls ME 04623

PINES, LOIS G (D)
Mass State Rep
Mailing Add: State Capitol Boston MA 02133

PINKETT, FLAXIE MADISON (D)
b St Louis, Mo, Nov 30, 17; d John Randolph Pinkett & Flaxie Holcombe P; div. Educ: Howard Univ, BA, 36; Delta Sigma Theta. Polit & Govt Pos: Deleg, Dem Nat Conv, 68 & 72; mem, Mayor's Comt on Employ of Handicapped, 68; trustee, Bd of Higher Educ, DC, 68; mem, Dem Cent Comt, DC, formerly; Dem Nat Committeewoman, DC, 68-72; mem, Criminal Justice Coord Bd, 69; mem, Mayor's Comt on Crime & Delinquency, 69. Bus & Prof Pos: Mem, Pub Welfare Adv Coun, DC Dept Pub Welfare, 60-66; mem & chmn, Supt Adv Coun, DC Schs, 65-67; mem adv coun, Dept Voc Educ, DC, 67-68. Publ: Many shades of black, William Morrow & Co, 69; How to succeed in business by really trying. Mem: DC Health & Welfare Coun. Honors & Awards: Howard Univ Alumni Award, 64; Bus Woman of the Year Award, State Fedn Bus & Prof Women's Clubs, 68; Citizens Merit Award for pub serv, DC Bd Comnr; 9 awards for outstanding achievements in bus & community endeavors given by local bus & community orgn, 58-69. Relig: Episcopal. Legal Res: 4210 Argyle Terr NW Washington DC 20011 Mailing Add: 1507 Ninth St NW Washington DC 20001

PINKNEY, ARNOLD (D)
b Youngstown, Ohio, Jan 6, 31; s David E Pinkney & Catherine Davis P; m 1957 to Bettye Thompson; c Traci Lynne. Educ: South High Sch, Youngstown, grad, 48; Albion Col, BA, 52; Case Western Reserve Univ Law Sch, 54-55; pres, Independent Men's Club; treas, Athletic Club. Polit & Govt Pos: Pres, Cleveland Bd Educ, 67-, mem, 69; admin asst to Cong Staff of Hon Louis Stokes, 69; exec asst to Mayor Carl Stokes, Cleveland, 70-71; nat dep campaign mgr, Dem Nomination for President of Sen Hubert Humphrey, 72; mem, Nat Dem Party's Campaign Comt, 74; app mem, Cuyahoga Co Bd Elec, 74- Bus & Prof Pos: Partner, Pinkney-Perry Ins Agency, Cleveland, 61-65, pres, 65-73, chmn bd, 73-; mem bd trustees, Cent State Univ, 71-, pres bd, 72-; organizer & dir, First Nat Bank & Trust of Ohio-Cleveland, 73- Mil Serv: Entered as Pvt, Army, 52, released as Pfc, 54, after serv in Spec Serv, ETO, 53-55. Mem: Alpha Phi Alpha; life mem Life Underwriters Asn; life mem NAACP; Ohio Nat Sch Bd Asn (trustee); Nat Sch Bd Asn (mem Black Caucus). Honors & Awards: Million Dollar Round Table, Prudential Life Ins Co. Relig: Baptist. Legal Res: 16903 Eldamere Ave Cleveland OH 44128 Mailing Add: 2131 Fairhill Rd Cleveland OH 44106

PINKSTON, FRANK CHAPMAN (D)
Ga State Rep
b Ludowici, Ga, Feb 9, 23; s Alexander Gordon Pinkson, Sr & Kathleen Chapman P; m 1948 to Lucille Park Finney; c Frank Chapman, Jr & Calder Finney. Educ: Mercer Univ, Walter F George Sch Law, LLB, 47; Sigma Nu. Polit & Govt Pos: Ga State Rep, 81st Dist, 69- Mil Serv: Entered as Pvt, Army, 43, released as Cpl, 46, after serv in Finance Corps & Ordnance Corps, Eng, France, Belgium, Ger; Lt Col, Judge Adv Gen Corps, currently. Mem: Ga Bankers Asn (pres, Trust Div, 64-); Elks; Civitan Club; Nat Found; Boy Scouts. Relig: Baptist. Mailing Add: 3077 Stuart Dr Macon GA 31204

PINNEY, A SEARLE (R)
b New Milford, Conn, Sept 14, 20; s J Searle Pinney & Elsie Martha Lightfoot P; m 1953 to Evelyn Roberts. Educ: Tufts Univ, BA, 42; Harvard Univ Law Sch, LLB, 48. Polit & Govt Pos: Conn State Rep, 54-60; minority leader, Conn House of Rep, 59; chmn, Conn Rep State Cent Comt, 61-67; alt deleg, Rep Nat Conv, 68. Bus & Prof Pos: Attorney; town counsel, Brookfield, Conn; assoc, bd dirs, Fairfield Co Trust Co; corporator, Savings Bank of Danbury; trustee & treas, Wooster Sch. Mil Serv: Entered as Pvt, Air Force, 42, released as 2nd Lt, 45, after serv in ETO. Mem: Hon mem, Sheriff's Asn; Am, Conn & Danbury Bar Asns; Tufts Alumni Asn. Relig: Congregational. Legal Res: Brookfield CT 06804 Mailing Add: c/o Pinney Hull Payne & Van Lenten 26 West St Danbury CT 06810

PINNICK, SIRIA F (R)
b San Francisco, Calif, May 13, 26; d Joseph Pieri & Rita P; 1947 to Joseph Francis Pinnick; c Cristine, Patricia, Kathleen & Thomas. Educ: Commerce High Sch, grad, 43. Polit & Govt Pos: Deleg, Mich Rep State Cent Comt, 62-; vchmn, Newaygo Co Rep Party, Mich, formerly. Bus & Prof Pos: Reporter, Fremont Times Indicator-Weekly. Mem: Ramshorn Country Club (dir & secy); Gerber Hosp Auxiliary. Relig: All Saints Church. Mailing Add: 121 N Merchant Fremont MI 49412

PINSON, HARLEY FREDERICK (D)
b Oakland, Calif, July 8, 50; s Robert Franklin Pinson (deceased) & Borghilde Jorgensen P; m 1973 to Cynthia Ann West. Educ: Univ Calif, Santa Barbara, BA, 73; Univ of the Pacific Sch Law, currently. Polit & Govt Pos: Chmn, Laney Students for Jess Unruh, Oakland, Calif, 70; chmn, Univ Calif Santa Barbara Students for McGovern, 71-72; alt deleg, Dem Nat Conv, 72; mem, Santa Barbara Co Dem Cent Comt, 73-74; rep-at-lg, Isla Vista, Calif Community Coun, currently. Mem: F&AM; Sierra Club; Am Civil Liberties Union; Common Cause; Am for Dem Action. Mailing Add: 320-25th St Apt 4 Sacramento CA 95816

PINSON, JERRY D (D)
Committeeman, Ark Dem Party
b Harrison, Ark, Sept 7, 42; s Robert L Pinson & Cleta Keeter P; m 1964 to Jane Ellis; c Christopher Clifton. Educ: Univ Ark, BA, 64, Sch Law, JD, 67; Blue Key; Phi Eta Sigma; Sigma Alpha Epsilon. Polit & Govt Pos: Dep attorney gen, Ark, 67-70; campaign mgr, Joe Purcell for Gov, 70; committeeman, Ark Dem Party, 71- Bus & Prof Pos: Attorney-at-law, pvt practice, Harrison, Ark, 71- Mem: Am Bar Asn; Am Judicature Soc; Boone Co Bar Asn (vpres, 72-73); United Way of Boone Co, Ark, Inc, (pres, 74); Harrison Rotary (bd dirs, 75-). Relig: Methodist. Legal Res: 456 Skyline Dr Harrison AR 72601 Mailing Add: PO Box 1111 Harrison AR 72601

PINTAR, MICHAEL ANTHONY (DFL)
b Keewatin, Minn, May 13, 35; s Michael John Pintar & Ann Frances Podomanick P; m 1957 to Joelle Rae Gallant; c Charles Joseph, Michele Patrice & Michael Clement. Educ: Hibbing Jr Col, pre-law, 56; Bemidji State Col, BA in educ & hist, 58; Georgetown Univ, grad study; Tau Beta Gamma. Polit & Govt Pos: Mem, Minn Young Dem-Farmer-Labor Comt, 56-60; mem, Second Dist Exec Comt & State Cent Comt, Dem-Farmer-Labor Party & chmn, Sibley Co Dem-Farmer-Labor Party, 60-65; deleg, Dem Nat Conv, 64, alt deleg, 68; field rep, Minn Dem-Farmer-Labor Party, 65-71 & Eighth Dist Dem-Farmer-Labor Party, 69; mem, Humphrey-Muskie Comt, 68; state coord, Anderson For Gov, 70; spec asst to Gov Anderson, 71- Bus & Prof Pos: Instr Am hist & speech, Henderson Sch Syst, Minn, 60-64; educator social probs, Rush City High Sch, 64-65; gov rep, Upper Great Lakes Regional Comn, currently. Mil Serv: Entered as E-1, Army EGR, Recon, 58, released as E-4, 60. Mem: KofC; Elks. Relig: Catholic. Mailing Add: 110 Donovan Dr Grand Rapids MN 55744

PIPER, RODNEY E (D)
Ind State Sen
Mailing Add: PO Box 2816 Muncie IN 47304

PIPER, WILLIAM G (R)
Mem, Berks Co Rep Comt, Pa
b Philadelphia, Pa, Feb 16, 06; s Hugh B Piper & Rosina Goodman P; m to Ida C Greenawalt; c Susan C. Educ: Philadelphia pub schs. Polit & Govt Pos: Investr, Pa Liquor Control Bd, 34-43; mem, Spring Twp Sch Bd, 47; justice of the peace, 53-; pres, Pa State Claimmen's Asn, 54-55; Pa State Rep, 56 & 60-74; pres, Lincoln Park Civic League, 60; pres, Berks Co Magistrates Asn, 61; pres, Pa Magistrates Asn, 62; mem, Berks Co Rep Exec Comt, Berks Co Rep Comt & Berks Co Adv Coun, presently. Bus & Prof Pos: Mem, Pa State Hwy Patrol, 25-31; gen ins, 43- Mem: Fraternal Order of Police (Berks Co Lodge 71); CofC; Kiwanis Club of Reading; Mason. Relig: Community Church. Mailing Add: 202 Harvard Blvd Lincoln Park Reading PA 19609

PIPPIN, EARL CLAYTON (D)
Chmn, Montgomery Co Dem Exec Comt, Ala
b Troy, Ala; s L Devon Pippin & Lucy Howard P; m 1949 to Louise Dickinson; c Clayton, Lynn, Mark & Bill. Educ: Troy State Univ, 41-44; Huntingdon Col, BA, 53; Oxford Univ, MA, 56; Iota Lambda Sigma. Polit & Govt Pos: Mem, Nat Comn on Consumer Finance, currently; chmn, Montgomery Dem Exec Comt, Ala, 74- Relig: Unitarian. Legal Res: 1201 Magnolia Curve Montgomery AL 36106 Mailing Add: 605 Exec Bldg Montgomery AL 36104

PIRES, SHEILA ANN (D)
b Chicago, Ill, Apr 8, 49; d Edward Condon & Nancy Toomey C; m 1972 to Alexander John Pires, Jr. Educ: Boston Univ, BA, 71; Georgetown Univ, 72- Polit & Govt Pos: Legis asst to US Rep Lester L Wolff, NY, 71-74, admin asst, 74- Mem: US House Rep Admin Asst Asn. Mailing Add: 1516 44th St NW Washington DC 20007

PIRNIE, ALEXANDER (R)
b Pulaski, NY, Apr 16, 03; m to Mildred S; c Bruce R & Douglas J. Educ: Cornell Univ, AB; Cornell Law Sch, JD, admitted to the bar, 26; mem, Cornell Law Sch Coun. Polit & Govt Pos: US Rep, NY, 58-72, mem, Armed Serv Comt, US House Rep, formerly. Bus & Prof Pos: Formerly with Evans, Pirnie & Burdick, Law Firm, Utica. Mil Serv: Commissioned 2nd Lt, 24; vol for active duty, 42; released as Col after serv on staff assignments, ETO; Bronze Star & Legion of Merit. Mem: Judge Advocates Asn; Oneida Co Bar Asn; F&AM; Scottish Rite (32 degree); AAONMS (Past Potentate, Ziyara Temple). Mailing Add: 12 Slaytonbush Lane Utica NY 13501

PIRO, VINCENT JOSEPH (D)
Mass State Rep
b Somerville, Mass, May 15, 41; s Guy T Piro & Anna Lonardo P; m 1963 to Karen Lee Kelley; c Lisa Noelle, Vincent, Jr & Michael John. Educ: Salem State Col, BS in Educ, 64, MEd, 66; Beta Chi. Polit & Govt Pos: Mem, Dem Ward & City Comt, Mass, 63; local alderman, 65-, vpres, Bd Aldermen, 65, pres, 66; ex-officio mem, Sch Comt, 66; vchmn, Somerville Dem Comt, 68; Mass State Rep, 68-, Dem State Committeeman, Third Middlesex Dist, Mass House Rep, 72-, chmn, Comt Fed Financial Assistance & Asst Majority Leader, currently. Bus & Prof Pos: Elem sch teacher, Wakefield Syst, Mass, 64-69, asst prin, 66-69. Mem: Mass Teachers Asn; Mass Legislators Asn; Elks; Moose; Dante Club. Relig: Catholic. Mailing Add: 482 Medford St Somerville MA 02145

PIRTLE, MEL CARLTON (R)
Chmn, Henderson Co Rep Party, Tex
b Pittsburg, Tex, Nov 8, 40; s Guy Thomas Pirtle & Eileen Browning P; m 1961 to Janet Baskin; c Myra Jane, Melissa Jo & Mel Jason. Educ: Henderson Co Jr Col, Athens, Tex, AA, 61; ETex State Univ, BS, 64, ME, 68. Polit & Govt Pos: Chmn Precinct Four, Henderson Co, Tex, 69; chmn, Henderson Co Rep Party, Tex, 69-72 & 74- Bus & Prof Pos: Teacher sci & math, Caddo Mills High Sch, 64-65; teacher math, Mt Pleasant High Sch, 65-66; teacher math & sci, Athens High Sch, 66-69; teacher math, Malakoff High Sch, 69-70; supt schs, Murchison Pub Schs, 70- Mem: Tex State Teachers Asn; Kiwanis. Relig: Church of Christ. Mailing Add: Rte 3 Athens TX 75751

PISANI, JOSEPH R (R)
NY State Sen
b New Rochelle, NY, Aug 31, 29; s Louis M Pisani & Kathryn C Ferrara P; m 1953 to Joan L Marchiano; c Frank, Louis, Kathryn & Theresa. Educ: Iona Col, AB, 50; Fordham Univ, JD, 53; NY Univ Law Sch, 56; Fordham Law Rev Asn; Delta Theta Phi. Polit & Govt Pos: City prosecutor, New Rochelle, NY, 62-64, city councilman, 64-66; NY State Assemblyman, 66-72; NY State Sen, 72- Bus & Prof Pos: Partner, Gaynor, Freeman, Glick & Pisani, 58- Mil Serv: Entered as Seaman, Naval Res, 53, released as Lt(jg), 66, after serv in US, 53-56. Mem: NY State Bar Asn; CofC; KofC; Am Legion; Aviglianese Soc. Relig: Roman Catholic. Mailing Add: 18 Fairview Pl New Rochelle NY 10805

PISCOPO, PATSY J (R)
b Waterbury, Conn, July 14, 27; s John Piscopo & Filomena Minucci P; m 1955 to Frances B Laffey; c John E, Joyce R, Robert T, Nancy J & Linda P. Educ: Am Int Col, BA; Alpha Sigma Delta; Varsity Club. Polit & Govt Pos: Dir, Libr Bd, Thomaston, Conn, 58-60; chmn, Thomaston Rep Town Comt, 60-66; first selectman, Thomaston, 65-70; comnr, Dept Banking, State of Conn, currently; cand, US Rep, 74. Bus & Prof Pos: Teacher, Swift Jr High Sch, 52-65. Mil Serv: Entered as A/S, Navy, 45, released as Seaman 1/C, 46. Mem: Watertown Teacher's Asn; PTA; Am Legion; VFW; Am Int Col Alumni. Honors & Awards: Popularity Award, King of Winter Carnival, 50; Sportsmanship Award, 51; earned numerals in freshman year & letter in football, jr & sr years; capt rowing team, sr year, earned letter, 3 years. Relig: Catholic. Mailing Add: 38 Laurel Dr Thomaston CT 06787

PITCHER, GEORGE PAYTON (D)
Chmn, Craig Co Dem Party, Okla
b Miami, Okla, Jan 23, 19; s George B Pitcher & Margaret Payton P; m 1945 to Betty Jane Smith; c Stephanie (Mrs Carter F Sumner), Gregory P & Pamela Rae (Mrs Brad Schultz). Educ: Northeastern Okla Agr & Mech Col, 37-38; Univ Okla, LLB, BS & JD, 42; Phi Theta Kappa; Phi Delta Phi. Polit & Govt Pos: Co attorney, Craig Co, Okla, 47-51; Okla State Rep, 51-59; Okla State Sen, 59-61; chmn, Craig Co Dem Party, Okla, 69- Mil Serv: Entered as Pvt, Army Air Corps, 42, released as 1st Lt, 46, after serv in 42nd Bomb Group, 13th Air Force, Southwest Pac Theatre, 43-45; Air Medal with eight Clusters. Mem: Okla Bar Asn; Mason (32 degree); Shrine; Am Legion; VFW. Relig: Presbyterian. Mailing Add: 146 S Adair Vinita OK 74301

PITCOCK, LOUIS, JR (D)
Chmn, Young Co Dem Exec Comt, Tex
b Ft Worth, Tex, June 18, 24; s Louis Pitcock & Medora Shepherd P; m 1949 to Mary E McFarlane; c Ellen S (Mrs Charles F Morris), Louis, III & Thomas Carl. Educ: NTex State Univ, 41-42, grad sch, 73; Southwestern Univ, BA, 49; Phi Delta Theta. Polit & Govt Pos: Precinct 22 & 1 Dem chmn, 54-72; deleg, Dem State Conv, 54-; chmn, Dist Caucus Dem Party, 60-72; regent, Midwestern Univ, 68-74; chmn, Young Co Dem Exec Comt, 72- Bus & Prof Pos: Vpres & secy-treas, Pitcock Inc, Graham, 57- Mil Serv: Entered as Pvt, Air Force, 43, released as T/Sgt, 46, after serv in Command Hq, CBI Theatres, 43-46; Asia & China Theatre Campaign Ribbons. Mem: Rotary (secy); NTO&G Asn; West Tex Oil & Gas Asn; Graham CofC (vpres). Relig: Methodist; annual conf deleg, local, dist & conf offices. Mailing Add: PO Box 747A Graham TX 76046

742 / PITHOUD

PITHOUD, NAIDA (R)
Rep Nat Committeewoman, Wash
b Woodward, Iowa, June 14, 10; d Leon Edwin Mouser & Theda Rhoads M; wid; c Laurel Jean (Mrs Elden) & Ralph William McGinn, Jr. Educ: Jackson High Sch. Polit & Govt Pos: Precinct committeeman, 46-; vchmn, Clark Co Rep Party, Wash, 58-62, chmn, 62-74, state committeewoman, 74; Rep Nat Committeewoman, Wash, 74- Mailing Add: 2311 NE 119th St Vancouver WA 98665

PITSENBERGER, JULIA LOCKRIDGE (D)
WVa State Deleg
b May 2, 41; d Julian Field Lockridge & Jean Dever L; m 1962 to Thomas Morris Pitsenberger, DDS; c James Julian & Ashley Ann. Educ: WVa Univ, BS, 63, MA, 64; Delta Gamma. Polit & Govt Pos: WVa State Deleg, 74-, mem judiciary comt, banking & ins comt & redistricting comt, WVa Legis. Bus & Prof Pos: Dean of Women, Alderson-Broaddus Col, 66-70; asst dir counseling ctr, Davis & Elkins Col, 70-72; established elem guid prog, Randolph Co Schs, 72-73. Mem: Am Asn of Univ Women (state vpres); Jr Woman's Club of Elkins; Randolph Co Creative Art Coun; Randolph Co Health Info Bd; Nat Voc Guid Asn. Relig: Church of Christ. Mailing Add: 110 Westview Dr Elkins WV 26241

PITTENGER, JOHN CHAPMAN (D)
Mem, Lancaster Co Dem Exec Comt, Pa
b Philadelphia, Pa, May 23, 30; s Nicholas Otto Pittenger & Cornelia Chapman P; single. Educ: Harvard Col, BA, 51; Harvard Law Sch, LLB, 58. Polit & Govt Pos: Mem, Lancaster Co Dem Exec Comt, Pa, 60-; dist leader, Ninth Ward, Lancaster, 60-; Pa State Rep, 65-67 & 69-71, dir of research, Minority Caucus, Pa House Rep, 67-69; spec asst for legis, Off of Gov, Pa, 71- Bus & Prof Pos: Attorney-at-law, 58-65; adj instr govt, Franklin & Marshall Col, 60 & 63- Mil Serv: Entered as Pvt, E-1, Army, 52, released as 1st Lt, 55, after serv in Inf, Transportation Corps. Mem: Lancaster Co, Pa & Am Bar Asns. Relig: Society of Friends. Mailing Add: 307 N West End Ave Lancaster PA 17603

PITTMAN, RENA ARLENA (R)
b Guymon, Okla, Mar 19, 12; d John Wesley Jones & Rosa Huckleberry J; m 1934 to William Harold Pittman; c Carolyn Jean (Mrs Kirk), Pamela (Mrs Harris) & Larry. Educ: Tarleton State Col, 1 year. Polit & Govt Pos: Chmn, Comanche Co Rep Party, Tex, formerly. Mem: Par Country Club; Farm Bur. Relig: Baptist. Mailing Add: 204 E Pecan De Leon TX 76444

PITTMAN, WALTER JAMES, JR (D)
b Bailey, NC, Oct 7, 11; s Walter James Pittman & Leelah Shelton P; m 1951 to Mary Lucile Thomas; c Mary Lou & Walter James, III. Educ: Wake Forest Col, LLB, 34; Chi Tau; Gamma Eta Gamma. Polit & Govt Pos: Chmn, Wilson Co Bd of Elec, NC, 38-42; admin asst to US Rep L H Fountain, Second Dist, NC, 53- Relig: Methodist. Legal Res: 1614 W Nash St Wilson NC 27893 Mailing Add: 2188 Rayburn House Off Bldg Washington DC 20515

PITTS, JOSEPH R (R)
Pa State Rep
b Lexington, Ky, Oct 10, 39; s Joseph S Pitts & Pearl Jackson P; m 1961 to Virginia Pratt; c Karen R, Carol J & Daniel J. Educ: Asbury Col, AB, 61; West Chester State Col, MEd, 73. Polit & Govt Pos: Pa State Rep, 73- Bus & Prof Pos: Sci teacher, Great Valley High Sch, Pa, 69-73. Mil Serv: Entered as 2nd Lt, Air Force, 63, released as Capt, 69, after serv in 99th Bomber Wing, Strategic Air Command, 63-69; Air Medal with five Oak Leaf Clusters; Expert Marksman. Mem: Kennett Area Jaycees; Brandywine Valley Asn. Relig: Protestant. Legal Res: RD 1 Kennett Square PA 19348 Mailing Add: House of Rep Capitol Bldg Harrisburg PA 17120

PITTS, KNOX (D)
Chmn, Bedford Co Dem Exec Comt, Tenn
b Elkton, Tenn, Apr 28, 16; s Rufus Knox Pitts & Inez Puckette P; m 1938 to Mildred Steele; c Knox, III & John Steele. Educ: Oglethorpe Univ, AB, 35. Polit & Govt Pos: Admin asst to US Rep Joe L Evins, Tenn, 47; deleg, Dem Nat Conv, 56, 60, 64 & 68; chmn, Bedford Co Dem Exec Comt, Tenn, 55-; dep state campaign mgr for Lyndon Johnson, 64. Bus & Prof Pos: Owner, Knox Pitts Plumbing & Elec Supply Co, Shelbyville, Tenn, 47-; vpres, Roadsafe Emergency Vehicles Corp, currently. Mil Serv: Entered as Pvt, Army, 42, released as 1st Lt, 45, after serv in 147th Qm Depot Co, ETO, 43-45. Mem: Rotary; VFW, DAV; Nat Farm Orgn; Farm Bur. Mailing Add: 613 Kingree Rd Shelbyville TN 37160

PITTS, NOAH ODAS, JR (R)
Mem, NC State Rep Exec Comt
b Glen Alpine, NC, Apr 11, 21; s Noah Odas Pitts & Maude Simpson P; m to Sue Vance Pitts; c Elizabeth Hill, Barbara Gene, Noah Odas III & Grady Riggan. Educ: Duke Univ, 41-43; Kappa Alpha. Polit & Govt Pos: Chmn, Precinct Four, Burke Co, NY, 54-60; pres, Burke Co Young Rep, 58-59; chmn, Burke Co Rep Party, 60-; mem, NC State Rep Exec Comt, 60- Bus & Prof Pos: Vpres, Morganton Savings & Loan, 61-; vpres, Pitts Lumber, Inc, 61-; secy & treas, Burke Lumber, Inc, 61-; mem bd of trustees, Grace Hosp, 64-; mem, NC Nat Bank City Bd; vpres, Burke Construction Co, Inc, currently. Mil Serv: Entered as Ens, Navy, 43, released as Lt(jg), 45, after serv in Pac Theatre; ETO & Pac Theatre Ribbons. Mem: Carolina Builder's Asn (dir); Morganton CofC; Morganton Merchants Asn; Mimosa Hills Golf Club; Blowing Rock Country Club. Relig: Methodist. Legal Res: 308 Avery Ave Morganton NC 28655 Mailing Add: PO Box 338 Morganton NC 28655

PITTS, THOMAS LADD (D)
Chmn, Franklin Co Dem Party, Iowa
b Louisville, Ky, Feb 19, 26; s Thomas Ladd Pitts, Sr & Mable Irene Potts P; m 1951 to Susan Jane Roush; c Jennifer Jane. Educ: Auburn Univ, 48-50; Am Mgt Asn, courses; Cambridge Mgt Inst, courses; Squires; Student Coun; Agr Club; Ala Farmer. Polit & Govt Pos: Chmn, Franklin Co Dem Party, Iowa, 74- Bus & Prof Pos: Chmn legis comt, Ill Seed Dealers, Champaign. Mil Serv: Entered as Pvt, Army, 54, released as Pfc, 56. Mem: Rotary; Am Soc Agronomy; Am Seed Trade Asn; NCent Bd Realtors (dir). Relig: Methodist; lay speaker. Legal Res: 907 First Ave SE Hampton IA 50441 Mailing Add: Box 421 Hampton IA 50441

PIVONKA, CHARLES AUGUST (D)
b Timken, Kans, Aug 2, 04; s Frank Pivonka & Mary Bizek P; m 1929 to Ludmila Pechanec; c Maurice Charles & Barbara Jane (Mrs Robert Upson). Educ: Rush Co Sch Dist 19, 9 years. Polit & Govt Pos: Vchmn, Rush Co Dem Party, Kans, formerly. Bus & Prof Pos: Farmer & ins salesman; pres, Co Farmers Union; dir, Fed Land Bank Asn, Larned, Kans, currently. Mem: Lions; Farmers Union; Nat Farmers Orgn. Relig: Catholic. Mailing Add: Timken KS 67582

PIZZO, ANTHONY (D)
Ind State Rep
Mailing Add: Sare Rd Bloomington IN 47401

PLANT, AL O (D)
Del State Rep
Mailing Add: 523 Eastlawn Ave Wilmington DE 19802

PLANTE, KENNETH A (R)
Fla State Sen
Mailing Add: 2225 Via Tuscany Winter Park FL 32789

PLAS, JOSEPHINE PATRICIA (D)
Dem Nat Committeeman, Mass
b Ireland, Feb 29, 20; d Daniel McGrath & Hannah Sexton M; m 1946 to John W Plas; c Daniel Stuart. Educ: Victoria Univ, BA, 45. Polit & Govt Pos: Treas, Dem Club Marlboro, Mass, 69, vpres, 72-74, pres, 74-75; coordr, Drinan for Cong Comt, 70; deleg, Dem Nat Conv, 72; assembly coordr, Citizen for Polit Participation, 73-74; mem affirmative action comt, State Dem of Mass; mem, Dem Nat Comt, currently. Bus & Prof Pos: Notary pub, Mass, 73- Mem: League Women Voters; Common Cause; Friends of the Pub Libr; Hosp Auxiliary (legis chairperson); State Club Mass. Relig: Roman Catholic. Mailing Add: 83 Kingsview Rd Marlboro MA 01752

PLASTER, JAMES J (D)
Ala State Rep
Mailing Add: Rte 1 Box 193 Autaugaville AL 36003

PLATT, FAUN (R)
Chmn, Lenawee Co Rep Party, Mich
b Thawville, Ill, Jan 12, 02; m 1925 to Raymond F Platt; c Dr Thomas E & Richard. Educ: Ill Normal; Seina Heights Col; Mich State Univ. Polit & Govt Pos: Vchmn, Dist Rep Party, 2 years & reelected 2 years; vchmn, Lenawee Co Rep Party, Mich, 5 years, chmn, currently; former mem, Mich Rep State Cent Comt; alt deleg, Rep Nat Conv, 60, deleg, 72; del, Women's Fedn in Wash, 67; dist off secy, US Rep Hutchinson, Mich, 73- Bus & Prof Pos: Sch teacher, 15 years; juvenile co agent; probation officer for probate court. Mem: Grange; Eastern Star. Honors & Awards: Awarded Silver Plaque for Outstanding Work for the Rep Party, 68; Gold Engraved Medal for Outstanding Work in Rep Party as Co Chmn. Relig: Protestant. Mailing Add: 7616 Tipton Hwy Tipton MI 49287

PLATT, JOE-ANN ELIZABETH (R)
Nat Committeewoman, Young Rep of Iowa
b Moline, Ill, Sept 27, 33; d Joe W Sowder & Elizabeth G Fulton S; m 1952 to John B Platt, Jr; c Judith B, Jeb B, Jo-Ellyn E & Joe B. Educ: Awarded 4 year scholarship, Pa Col for Women, 51; Univ Md. Polit & Govt Pos: Vchmn, Scott Co Young Rep, Iowa, 60; campaign coord, J Kenneth Stringer Campaign for US Senate, 60; precinct committeewoman, Scott Co Rep Party, 60-; mem staff, Rep Nat Conv, 64; nat committeewoman, Young Rep of Iowa, 65-; state chmn, Young Iowans for Miller, US Sen Jack Miller Campaign, 66; coord, Scott Co Rep Campaign, 66-69; deleg-at-lg, Rep Nat Conv, 68; mem state adv comt, Richard Nixon for President, 68; state campaign coord, successful campaign of Lt Gov Roger W Jepsen, 68; chmn & nat secy, Iowa State Finance Comt, Young Rep Nat Fedn, formerly; mem, Iowa Comt to Reelect the President, 72; Scott Co chmn, Comt to Reelect US Sen Miller, 72; first dist cong campaign comt, James Leach for Congress, 74; Am Coun Young Polit Leaders. Bus & Prof Pos: Pres, JPD Co, Inc, The Home Place, 72-; secy, Platt & Assocs, Inc, currently. Mem: CofC (Womens Bur, Davenport Br); Davenport Human Rels Comn; Miss Valley Press Club (mem bd); Davenport Chap, Federated Women's Club of Iowa; trustee, Ava M Preacher Mem Trust. Honors & Awards: One of 15 deleg, US Dept of State to Europe, conf with young polit leaders from NATO countries, 70; Iowa Host Family for 3 day visit by 12 members of the KOMSOMOL from the USSR, on an official visit to the US as Future Polit Leaders. Relig: Episcopal. Mailing Add: 1122 W 51st St Davenport IA 52806

PLAWECKI, DAVID ANTHONY (D)
Mich State Sen
b Detroit, Mich, Nov 8, 47; s Edward J Plawecki & Lakadya C Popek P; m 1970 to Linda Rose Chantres. Educ: Gen Motors Inst Technol, BSME, 70. Polit & Govt Pos: Chmn, 15th Cong Dist Young Dem, 68-69; mem exec bd, Dearborn Heights Dem Club, 69-; 15th Cong Dist, 70-, 16th Cong Dist, 71-, 19th Cong Dist, 71-72 & 17th Cong Dist, 73-74; treas, 15th Cong Dist, 70; vchmn, Dearborn Heights Dem Club, 70-71; precinct deleg, Precinct 25, 70-; Mich State Sen, 71- Bus & Prof Pos: Engr coop student, Hydramatic Div, Gen Motors Corp, 65-69, jr engr, 70. Mem: Jaycees; Goodfellows; PLAV; KofC; Kingswood-Crestwood Civic Asn. Honors & Awards: Youngest elected sen in Mich hist. Relig: Catholic. Mailing Add: 1157 N Daly Dearborn Heights MI 48127

PLEASANT, RAY O (R)
Minn State Rep
Mailing Add: 9841 Xerxes Curve Bloomington MN 55431

PLESHAW, GERALDINE B (D)
Mem, Quincy City Dem Comt, Mass
b Boston, Mass; d James N Brown & Mary Burke B; m 1964 to Robert J Pleshaw; c Gregory J. Educ: Boston State Col, BSEd, 64; Northeastern Univ, MA Eng, 67. Polit & Govt Pos: Mem, Mass Dem State Comt, 68-72; mem, Boston Dem City Comt, 68-72; chairwoman, Boston Comn Status of Women, 69-; mem, Quincy City Dem Comt, 72-; staff asst to Mayor, Boston, 72- Bus & Prof Pos: Instr, Burdett Col, Mass, 65-68 & Boston State Col, 68-70; mem faculty, Kennedy Inst Polit, Harvard Sch Govt, 72- Mem: Mass Woman's Polit Caucus (chairwoman, 74-); Nat Woman's Polit Caucus (mem policy coun, Nat League Cities (regional rep, Women in Municipal Govt). Mailing Add: 128 Shore Ave Quincy MA 02169

PLEWA, CASMERE JOSEPH (R)
Mem, Macomb Co Rep Exec Comt, Mich
b Hamtramck, Mich, July 26, 26; s George Plewa & Mary Mazur P; m 1956 to Veronica Lucy Zwolak; c Robert, Michael & David. Educ: Univ Detroit, BME, 51; Tau Beta Pi; Pi Tau Sigma. Polit & Govt Pos: Mem, Warren Recreation Comn, Mich, 62-64; mem, Warren Libr Comn, 62-, chmn, 67-71 & 73-; precinct deleg, Rep Party, 62-; treas, Macomb Co Rep

Campaign Comt, 66; chmn, 12th Dist Rep Party, 67-69; deleg, Rep Nat Conv, 68; treas, Macomb Co Rep Exec Comt, 72-74, mem, 74-; mem, 18th Cong Dist Rep Comt, 73- Bus & Prof Pos: Sr mfg process engr, Fisher Body, GMC, 51-64; sr mfg process engr & cost analyst, Ford Motor Co, 64-70, sr mfg liaison engr, 70- Mil Serv: Entered as Pvt, Army, 44, released as T-5, 46, after serv in Gen Hq, Pac Theatre, 46; Presidential Citation; Overseas Serv Ribbons; Good Conduct Medal. Mem: Eng Soc Detroit; Bernadine Homeowners Asn. Honors & Awards: Bausch & Lomb Sci Award; Am Legion Sch Award. Relig: Roman Catholic. Mailing Add: 27761 Lorraine Warren MI 48093

PLEWA, JOHN ROBERT **(D)**
Wis State Rep
b Milwaukee, Wis; s Ervin Stanley Plewa & Helen Dombrowski P; single. Educ: Univ Wis-Whitewater, BEd, 68, cand for Master's degree, currently. Polit & Govt Pos: Vpres, 20th Assembly Dist Dem Party, Wis, 71-72; Wis State Rep, 20th Assembly Dist, 73- Bus & Prof Pos: Teacher, Milwaukee Area Tech Col, 68-73. Mem: Wis Fedn Teachers; Milwaukee Co Dem Party; Wilson Park Advan Asn. Relig: Catholic. Mailing Add: 1412 W Cudahy Ave Milwaukee WI 53221

PLOCK, RICHARD HENRY, JR **(R)**
Colo State Sen
b Burlington, Iowa, Feb 22, 36; s Richard Henry Plock & Helen Moulton Swisher P; m 1962 to Judith Marie Bishop; c William Henry & Christine Marie. Educ: Amherst Col, BA, 57; Univ Iowa Col Law, JD, 60; Phi Delta Phi; Psi Upsilon. Polit & Govt Pos: Asst city attorney, City & Co of Denver, 62-65; US Comnr, US Dist Court, Colo, 67-70; Colo State Sen, 70-, Asst Majority Leader, 73-75, Majority Leader, 75- Bus & Prof Pos: Assoc, Emil G Trott, Attorney-at-law, 60-61; assoc, Modesitt & Shaw, 62; partner, Shoemaker & Wham, 65-67; attorney, Richard H Plock, Jr, 67-69; partner, Clanahan, Tanner, Downing & Knowlton, 69- Mil Serv: Entered as 1st Lt, Air Force, 61, released as 1st Lt, 61, after serv in Judge Adv Gen Corps Res, Lackland AFB. Publ: Choice of law under federal tort claims act, Iowa Law Rev, 58. Mem: Am Bar Asn; Am Judicature Soc; Am Trial Lawyers Asn; Denver Law Club; Univ Club of Denver. Relig: Congregational. Legal Res: 1330 E Fourth Ave Denver CO 80218 Mailing Add: 1950 Western Fed Savings Bldg Denver CO 80202

PLOESER, WALTER CHRISTIAN **(R)**
b Jan 7, 07; s Christian D Ploeser & Maude E Parr P; m 1928 to Dorothy Annette Mohrig; c Ann (Mrs George E Berg) & Sally (Mrs William Chapel III). Educ: City Col Law & Finance, St Louis, Mo. Hon Degrees: LLD, Norwich Univ, 48; Dr Nat Univ Asuncion, Paraguay. Polit & Govt Pos: Mo State Rep, 31-32; founder & pres, Young Rep Fedn of Mo, 34-35; subcomt chmn, Rep Nat Prog Comt, 37-39; US Rep, Mo, 41-49; chmn, St Louis Co Rep Finance Comt, 52-56; US Ambassador to Paraguay, 57-59; Rep Nat Committeeman, Mo, 64-66; US Ambassador to Costa Rica, 70-72. Bus & Prof Pos: Chmn bd, Ploeser, Watts & Co, Ins, 33-; dir, Webster Groves Trust Co & Wehrenberg Theatres. Mem: Mason (33 degree); York Rite; Sovereign Grand Inspector Gen, Scottish Rite in Mo; Shriner (past potentate, Moolah Temple); Past Grand Master, Int DeMolay. Honors & Awards: Cert of Merit, US Navy, Freedom Found Award, 49; Grand Cross of Repub of Paraguay, 59. Relig: Christian Scientist. Legal Res: RR 1 Box 251 Manchester MO 63011 Mailing Add: 3633 Lindell Blvd St Louis MO 63108

PLOURDE, ROBERT E **(D)**
NH State Rep
Mailing Add: 15 Glass St Suncook NH 03275

PLOWMAN, FRANCIS WILDS **(R)**
Treas, Pa Rep State Comt
b Dover, Del, Oct 2, 02; s Garrett Hyuson Plowman & Beulah Wilds P; m 1940 to Elizabeth Crozer Birckhead; c Suzanne (Mrs Auten), Joan (Mrs Partridge) & Francis W, Jr. Educ: Washington & Lee Univ, BS, 24; Omicron Delta Kappa; Beta Gamma Sigma; Phi Epsilon Pi. Polit & Govt Pos: Finance chmn, Rep Party, Pa, 66-67; alt deleg, Rep Nat Conv, 68; treas, Pa Rep State Comt, 72- Bus & Prof Pos: Vpres & dir Scott Paper Co, Philadelphia. Mem: Union League. Relig: Episcopal. Mailing Add: Wildman Arms Swarthmore PA 19081

PLOWMAN, JOAN MARIE **(R)**
Committeewoman, Burlington Co Rep Comt, NJ
b Philadelphia, Pa, Mar 7, 51; d William Edward Plowman & Jeanette Calio P; single. Educ: Trenton State Col, 70. Polit & Govt Pos: Alt deleg, Rep Nat Conv, 72; chmn, Youth for Nixon, Burlington Co, NJ, 72; secy to William V Browne, admin asst to US Rep Edwin B Forsythe, NJ, 72-73; chmn, Burlington Co Youth for re-elec Gov Cahill, 73; campaign coordr, State Assembly cand, Ralph A Skowron, Dist 7, 73; committeewoman, Burlington Co Rep Comt, 72- Bus & Prof Pos: Secy to Twp Adminr of Riverside, NJ, 71-72; asst pension adminr, Am Fedn Musicians, Local 77, 74- Mem: Burlington Co Young Rep Club (vpres, 72-); Burlington Co Women's GOP; NJ Fedn of Rep Women. Relig: Roman Catholic. Mailing Add: 507 Cleveland Ave Riverside NJ 08075

PLUMADORE, HAYWARD HENRY **(R)**
Chmn, Franklin Co Rep Comt, NY
b Lyon Mt, NY, July 13, 13; s Herbert Plumadore & Ceceila Minney; m 1940 to May Furnia; c Jan H, Karen (Mrs Jurascheck) & Brett. Educ: St Lawrence Univ, BS, 40; Albany Law Sch, LLB, 43 & JD, 68; Xi Chap, Phi Sigma Kappa. Polit & Govt Pos: Supvr, Town of Harrietstown, NY, 50-55 & 58-61; chmn, Franklin Co Rep Comt, 52-62 & 67-; NY State Assemblyman, Franklin Co, 60-65; mem, NY Rep State Comt, 67- Bus & Prof Pos: Attorney-at-law, 43- Mil Serv: Pvt, NY Nat Guard, 35-38; entered as Ens, Navy, 43, released as Lt Comdr, 47, after serv in Amphibious Forces, European, NAfrican & Am Theatres; Lt Comdr, Inactive Naval Res, currently; Purple Heart; Am & NAfrican Theatre Ribbons; European Theatre Ribbon with Two Stars. Mem: Am Legion (Judge Advocate, Fourth Dist NY); VFW (Judge Advocate, St Lawrence Valley Coun); Elks; Moose; KofC (4 degree). Relig: Catholic. Legal Res: Lower Saranac Lake Saranac Lake NY 12983 Mailing Add: 52 Broadway Saranac Lake NY 12983

PLUMMER, JAMES WALTER
Under Secy, Air Force
b Idaho Springs, Colo, Jan 29, 20; s Edwin Leroy Plummer & Mary Frances Halliday P; m 1949 to Mary Anderson; c Robert B, John W, Janet C & Julia A. Educ: Univ Calif, Berkeley, BSEE, 42; Univ Md, MSEE, 53. Polit & Govt Pos: Head radio & commun, Electronics Test Div, Naval Air Test Ctr, Patuxent River, Md, 47-55; Under Secy, Air Force, 73- Bus & Prof Pos: Mem staff, Lockheed Missiles & Space Co, Sunnyvale, Calif, 55-62, dir mil progs, 62-65, vpres & asst gen mgr, 65-68, vpres & asst gen mgr research & develop, 68-69, vpres & gen mgr, 69-73. Mil Serv: Entered as Ens, Naval Res, 42, released as Lt Comdr, after serv in Pac Theatre, 46; Air Medal. Publ: Co-auth, UHF Propagation, John Wiley & Sons, 53. Mem: Am Inst Aeronaut & Astronaut (fel); Am Astronaut Soc (fel). Honors & Awards: Air Force Meritorious Serv Award; Silver Knight of Mgt Award, Lockheed Missiles & Space Co Mgt Asn, 67. Relig: Catholic. Legal Res: 2529 Lakevale Dr Vienna VA 22180 Mailing Add: Rm 4E-886 The Pentagon Washington DC 20330

PLUNKETT, CONNIE BERG **(D)**
Mem, Ga State Dem Exec Comt
b Woodward, Okla, July 1, 46; d Eric Wilhelm Berg II & Regena Black B; m 1967 to Thomas Sewell Plunkett. Educ: Wesleyan Col, Macon, Ga, GA, 68; cheerleader; Student Nat Educ Soc; Sweetheart Court, Sigma Nu, Mercer Univ; Alpha Beta Chi. Polit & Govt Pos: Campaign chmn for Gov Jimmy Carter, Carroll Co, Ga, 70; mem, Ga State Dem Exec Comt, 71-, vchmn, 73-74; mem, Carroll Co Dem Exec Comt, 72-; deleg & mem credentials comt, Dem Nat Conv, 72; mem, Nat Dem Charter Comn, 73-; mem, Dem Nat Comt, 73-74; deleg, Dem Nat Mid Term Conf, 74; mem, Ga State Dem Charter Comn; staff & advance work, Jimmy Carter Presidential Campaign, 75- Bus & Prof Pos: High sch teacher social studies, Bowdon, Ga, 68-69; asst advert mgr, Carroll Publ Co, Carrollton, 69-70. Mem: Nat Educ Asn; Carrollton Spade & Trowel Garden Club; Oak Mountain Pvt Acad (bd trustees, 73-); Lit-Mu Study Club. Relig: Episcopal. Mailing Add: W Club Dr Carrollton GA 30117

PLYLER, AARON WESLEY **(D)**
NC State Rep
b Union Co, NC, Oct 1, 26; s Isom F Plyler (deceased) & Ida Foard P; m 1948 to Dorothy Frances Moser; c Barbara (Mrs Faulk, Jr), Diane, Aaron W, Jr, Alan & Alton. Educ: Fla Mil Acad. Polit & Govt Pos: Chmn, Sutton Park Dem Precinct, Monroe, NC, formerly; NC State Rep, 33rd Dist, 74- Bus & Prof Pos: Pres & owner, Plyler Grading & Paving, Inc, 46-75; mem bd dirs, H R Johnson Construction Co, Inc, H R Johnson Realty Co, Inc & Am Bank & Trust Co, Monroe, NC, currently; pres, Hill Top Enterprises, Inc, currently; secy & treas, White Point, Inc, currently; vpres, Sturdibuilt, Inc, currently. Mem: Monroe-Union Co CofC (dir); Optimists; Rotary; Rolling Hills Country Club; Patrons Club Wingate Col. Honors & Awards: Man of Year, Monroe-Union Co CofC, 71. Relig: Presbyterian. Mailing Add: Rte 7 Box 62 Monroe NC 28110

PLYMAT, WILLIAM N **(R)**
Iowa State Sen
Mailing Add: 2908 Patricia Dr Urbandale IA 50322

POAGE, WILLIAM ROBERT (BOB) **(D)**
US Rep, Tex
b Waco, Tex, Dec 28, 99; s William A Poage & Helen Conger P; m 1938 to Frances Cotton. Educ: Univ Colo; Univ Tex; Baylor Univ, AB & LLB. Hon Degrees: LLD, Baylor Univ, 67. Polit & Govt Pos: Tex State Rep, 25-29; Tex State Sen, 31-37; US Rep, Tex, 36-, former chmn, Comt on Agr, US House of Rep; Am deleg to the Interparliamentary Union, 47- Bus & Prof Pos: Attorney-at-law, Waco, 24-36. Mem: Am Legion. Legal Res: 600 Edgewood Waco TX 76708 Mailing Add: Apt 1125 1200 N Nash Arlington VA 22209

POCHE, MARC B **(D)**
Exec Asst, Tenth Cong Dist Dem Party, Calif
b New Orleans, La, May 1, 34; s Marcel A Poche & Marie Belmar P; m 1956 to Therese Kremer; c Matthew, Anne & Michelle. Educ: Univ Santa Clara, BA summa cum laude, 56; Univ Calif, Berkeley, JD, 61; bd ed, Calif Law Rev; Alpha Sigma Nu. Polit & Govt Pos: Spec hearing officer, US Dept of Justice, 67-68; Dem nominee, Calif State Assembly, 25th Dist, 68; mem, Santa Clara Co Dem Cent Comt, 68-71; mem, Calif State Dem Cent Comt, 68-; exec asst, Ninth Cong Dist Dem Party, 69- Bus & Prof Pos: Attorney-at-law, San Jose, Calif, 62-; assoc prof law, Univ Santa Clara, 65-67, prof law, 69-; visiting prof law, Univ Calif, 73-74; asst to the gov & dir of prog & policy, State of Calif, currently. Mil Serv: Entered as 2nd Lt, Marine Corps, 56, released as 1st Lt, 58, after serv in 2nd Marine Air Wing, 56-58. Publ: Federal abstention doctrine, Calif Law Rev, 61; Uninsured motorist legislation in California, Hastings Law Rev, 62. Mem: Calif & Santa Clara Co Bar Asns; Am Asn Univ Counsel; Marine Corps Officers Asn; Sierra Club. Honors & Awards: Ryland Debate Prize. Relig: Catholic. Legal Res: 1650 University Ave San Jose CA 95126 Mailing Add: 999 W Taylor San Jose CA 95126

PODELL, BERTRAM L **(D)**
b Brooklyn, NY, Dec 27, 25; s Hyman Podell & Henrietta Menaker P; m 1953 to Bernice Posen; c Stephen, Ellen & Gary. Educ: St John's Univ, BA; Brooklyn Law Sch, LLB. Polit & Govt Pos: NY State Assemblyman, 54-68; US Rep, NY, 68-75; deleg, Dem Nat Mid-Term Conf, 74. Bus & Prof Pos: Attorney, Podell & Podell, Esquires, New York, currently. Mil Serv: Entered as Seaman, Navy, 44, released as HA 1/C, 46. Publ: Condemnation proceedings: protest of assessments, NY Law J, 12/67; Consolidation of local government as a greater means to economy and efficiency in New York State, 67; Joint Legislative Committee on Penal Institutions report, NY State Assembly, 68. Mem: Many civic & philanthropic orgn. Relig: Jewish. Mailing Add: 153 Rugby Rd Brooklyn NY 11226

PODESTA, ROBERT ANGELO **(R)**
b Chicago, Ill, Oct 7, 12; s Andrew D Podesta & Agnes Frazer P; m 1936 to Corrine Agnes Murnighan; Carol Ann (Mrs Brian Foley), Mary Ellen (Mrs Kevin Burke), Kathleen (Mrs John Mehigan) & Robert Anthony. Educ: Northwestern Univ, BS, 44. Hon Degrees: JD, St Mary's Col, Ind. Polit & Govt Pos: Rep cand, US Rep, Third Dist, Ill, 68; Asst Secy of Com for Econ Develop, Dept Com, 69-72. Bus & Prof Pos: Vpres, treas & dir, Julien Collins & Co, 45-49; managing partner, Cruttenden, Podesta & Miller, 49-63; sr vpres, mem exec comt & dir, Walston & Co Inc, 63-64; sr vpres, treas & dir, The Chicago Corp, 65-69. Mem: Nat Asn Securities Dealers; Asn Stock Exchange Firms; Investment Bankers Asn Am; gov, Midwest Stock Exchange; trustee, DePaul Univ. Relig: Catholic. Mailing Add: 9317 S Damen Ave Chicago IL 60620

POEPOE, ANDREW KELIIKUNIAUPUNI **(R)**
Hawaii State Rep
b Honolulu, Hawaii, May 2, 35; s Abraham Poaiki Poepoe & Dorothy Espinda P; m 1958 to Jaya L Ramulu; c Stephen & Alan. Educ: Yale Univ, BS, 57; Univ Hawaii, MBA, 71. Polit & Govt Pos: Vchmn, Eighth Dist Rep Party, Hawaii, 64-; Hawaii State Rep, 67-, Asst Minority Floor Leader & Minority Whip, Hawaii House of Rep, formerly, minority policy leader, 70-, minority leader, 74- Bus & Prof Pos: Indust engr, Castle & Cooke Terminals, 57-62 & Dole Co, 62- Mem: Soc Advan Mgt; Effective Citizens Orgn; Friends of the

East-West Ctr; Koolaupoko Hawaiian Civic Club; Jaycees. Relig: Congregational. Mailing Add: State Capitol Honolulu HI 96813

POERNER, JOHN H (D)
b D'Hanis, Tex, Nov 21, 32; s Henry Poerner & Mollie Zerr P; m 1953 to JoAnn Ney; c Margaret, Donna, Lucy, Cathy & Sarah Jo. Educ: St Mary's Univ, 1 year; various correspondence schs. Polit & Govt Pos: Tex State Rep, 69-74; deleg, Dem Nat Mid-Term Conf, 74. Mil Serv: Entered as Airman, Air Force, 51, released as S/Sgt, 55. Mem: Tex Surveyors Asn. Honors & Awards: Citizen of Year, Hondo, Tex, 61. Relig: Catholic. Mailing Add: Capital Sta Austin TX 78701

POFF, RICHARD H (R)
Justice, Supreme Court, Va
b Radford, Va, Oct 19, 23; m 1945 to Jo Ann Topper; c Rebecca Topper, Thomas Randolph & Richard H. Educ: Roanoke Col; Univ Va Law Sch, LLB; Sigma Nu Phi. Hon Degrees: LLD, Roanoke Col, 69. Polit & Govt Pos: US Rep, Va, 53-72; justice, Supreme Court, Va, currently. Mil Serv: B-24 bomber pilot; Distinguished Flying Cross. Mem: Lions; Mason (32 degree); Moose; Am Legion; VFW. Relig: Presbyterian. Mailing Add: 5001 Kingston Dr Annandale VA 22003

POGGIONE, P DANIEL (R)
Chmn, Washoe Co Rep Cent Comt, Nev
b Hollywood, Calif, June 2, 39; s Albert Poggione & Margaret Madden P; m 1962 to Joan Gale Buchanan; c Gina Marie, Peter Andrew & Leo Anthony. Educ: Univ Nev, Reno, BS, 64. Polit & Govt Pos: Nev State Assemblyman, 70-72, chmn labor-mgt comt, Nev State Assembly, 70-72; chmn, Washoe Co Rep Cent Comt, Nev, 74- Bus & Prof Pos: Owner, S&S Employ Serv, Reno, 69- & Poggione Enterprises, 72-; pres, Solar Control Co, 72- Mil Serv: Entered Air Nat Guard, 61, released as Pfc, 67. Mem: Builders Asn Northern Nev (bd dirs, 75-); Elks; Mens Golf Club; YMCA. Honors & Awards: Outstanding Legislator of 1971 Session, Nev Off-Rd Vehicle Asn. Relig: Catholic. Legal Res: 2370 Hunter Lake Dr Reno NV 89502 Mailing Add: 2095 Dickerson Rd Reno NV 89503

POHLENZ, DEAN (R)
b Blue Hill, Nebr, July 24, 20; s Chris P Pohlenz & Nettie Smith P; m 1942 to Mary Margaret Schmidt; c Paul Dean & Peggy J. Educ: Univ Nebr, 40; Indust Col of Armed Forces, 56-57; Sigma Delta Chi; Sigma Phi Epsilon. Polit & Govt Pos: Dep asst dir, Off Emergency Planning, Washington, 53-61; admin asst to US Sen Hruska, Nebr, until 72 & 75- Bus & Prof Pos: Reporter, Nebr State J, Lincoln, 37-53; lectr, Naval War Col & Indust Col Armed Forces. Mil Serv: Army, Pvt, 42-46, serv as correspondent with Stars & Stripes, ETO; Distinguished Serv Award; OCOM. Mem: Nebr State Soc. Relig: Methodist. Legal Res: Lincoln NE Mailing Add: 5303 Marlyn Dr Bethesda MD 20027

POINSATTE, STEPHEN T (D)
Ind State Rep
Mailing Add: 11322 Westwind Dr Ft Wayne IN 46825

POINTER, JAMES EDGAR, JR (D)
Chmn, Gloucester Co Dem Comt, Va
b Gloucester Co, Va, Sept 22, 22; s James Edgar Pointer & Lucy Lillie Minor P; m 1947 to Catherine Haseltine Jones; c James Edgar III & Steven David. Educ: Col William & Mary, BS, 43 & BCL, 47; Sigma Pi. Polit & Govt Pos: Acting commonwealth's attorney, Gloucester Co, Va, 53-54, commonwealth's attorney, 54-63; attorney, co sch bd, 54-74; secy-treas, Gloucester Co Dem Comt, 54-72, chmn, 72-; aide-de-camp to Gov of Va, 58-; comnr of accts, Gloucester, 62-; campaign mgr & area coord, Lyndon B Johnson Presidential Campaign, Va, 64; deleg, Dem Nat Conv, 64; Gloucester Co campaign mgr, William B Spong, Jr for US Senate, 66 & William C Battle for Gov of Va, 69. Bus & Prof Pos: Partner, Du Val & Pointer, 51-54; dir & asst secy, Bank of Gloucester, Va, 54-; dir, Francis N Sanders Nursing Home, Inc, 59-; partner, Pointer & Feild, Attorneys-at-law, Gloucester, 59-74. Mil Serv: Entered as Midn, Naval Res, 43, released as Lt(jg), 46, after serv in Pac Theatre, 44-45. Mem: Pres, CofC of Gloucester Co. Relig: Episcopal. Mailing Add: Gloucester VA 23061

POITEVINT, ALEC LOYD, II (R)
Chmn, Decatur Co Rep Party, Ga
b Bainbridge, Ga, Aug 28, 47; s Alec Loyd Poitevint & Joyce Lynn P; m 1971 to Doreen Stiles. Educ: Univ Ga, 65-70; Theta Chi. Polit & Govt Pos: Chmn, Decatur Co Rep Party, Ga, 75- Bus & Prof Pos: Vpres, Southeastern Minerals, Inc, Bainbridge, Ga, 73-74; exec vpres, Marshall Minerals, 73-75, pres, 75-; vpres, Bainbridge Container Corp, 73-; exec vpres, Southeastern Minerals Inc, 74- Mem: Nat Feed Ingredients Asn (vchmn membership); Ga Poultry Fedn (Poultry) Leaders Roundtable); Rotary; Boy Scouts Am; Comt of 100. Relig: Presbyterian. Legal Res: 2001 Twin Lakes Dr Bainbridge GA 31717 Mailing Add: PO Box 506 Bainbridge GA 31717

POKASKI, DANIEL FRANCIS (D)
Mass State Rep
b Boston, Mass, June 26, 49; s Joseph Martin Pokaski & Catherine Burns P; single. Educ: Boston State Col, BS, 71; Ski Club. Polit & Govt Pos: Mem, Mass Young Dem, currently, treas, 73-74; Mass State Rep, 17th Suffolk Dist & mem comt urban affairs, Mass House Rep, 75- Bus & Prof Pos: Educator, Boston Pub Schs, 72-75. Mil Serv: E-4 Yeoman, Naval Air Res, 71- Mem: Am Fedn Teachers; Am Legion; Holy Name Soc. Relig: Catholic. Legal Res: 40 Robinson St Dorchester MA 02122 Mailing Add: State House Boston MA 02133

POKORNY, GEORGE R (R)
Mem, Rep State Cent & Exec Comts, Ohio
b Cleveland, Ohio, Mar 29, 30; s Frank R Pokorny (deceased) & Helen Kusek P; m 1951 to Donna Marie Lotridge; c Judith Marie, Richard John & Michelle Marie. Educ: Bowling Green State Univ, AB, 47-50; Cleveland-Marshall Law Sch, JD, 58; Alpha Sigma Phi; Delta Theta Phi. Polit & Govt Pos: Committeeman, Cuyahoga Co, Parma 9E, Ohio, 65-; mem, Ohio State Rep Cent & Exec Comts, 21st Cong Dist, 66-68, 23rd Cong Dist, 70-; asst attorney gen, State of Ohio, 67. Bus & Prof Pos: Vpres, Alpha Sigma Phi Alumni Corp, 67-; mem adv finance comt, Parma Sch Bd, Ohio, 68-70; partner, Wochna Pokorny & Musiel, Attorneys-at-Law. Mem: Am Bar Asn; St Anthony Holy Name Soc; Parma Polish Am League; Parma Rep Club; Parma Ninth Ward Rep Club. Honors & Awards: Assistantship, Mt Holyoke Inst on UN, 50. Relig: Catholic; Mem, St Anthony Church Coun. Mailing Add: 2965 Alden Dr Parma OH 44134

POKORNY, PEGGY EDNA (D)
b Jamestown, NDak, Feb 8, 24; d Raymond Clark & Thelma Zimmerman C; m 1942 to Harold L Pokorny; c David, Antonia (Mrs Larry Pirkl), Richard, Janice (Mrs Gordon Tuel), Michael & Susan. Educ: St John's Acad, 41; Cent Dakota Bus Sch, 41. Polit & Govt Pos: Treas, Dist 29, NDak Dem Non-Partisan League, 68-70; vpres, NDak Dem Non-Partisan League Women's Orgn, 69-71, pres, 71-; endorsed cand for State Auditor, NDak Dem Non-Partisan League, 72; deleg, Dem Nat Conv, 72. Mem: United Transportation Union Auxiliary (legis rep, 70-); VFW Auxiliary; Am Legion Auxiliary; NDak Women's Polit Coalition; Nat Women's Polit Caucus. Relig: Catholic. Mailing Add: 401 Fourth Ave SE Jamestown ND 58401

POLAK, ANDREW JOSEPH (D)
NH State Rep
b Ludlow, Mass, Nov 22, 11; s Simon Polak & Theodora Pasek P; m to Stella Tomaski; c June (Mrs Ronald Morin) & Celia (Mrs John Bogaty). Educ: Fed Bur Invest Acad, Washington, DC, grad, 49. Polit & Govt Pos: NH State Rep, 75- Bus & Prof Pos: Chief of police, Hudson, NH, 45-72; retired. Mem: NH Chiefs Police; FBI Nat Acad; Hillsboro Co Law Enforcers; New Eng Chiefs Police. Honors & Awards: Fed Bur Invest Acad Award; Safety Awards, Automobile Asn Am, 65, 66, 67, 69, 71 & 72; Man of Year Award, 75. Mailing Add: 140 Melendy Rd Hudson NH 03051

POLAN, CHARLES M, JR (D)
WVa State Deleg
Mailing Add: State Capitol Charleston WV 25305

POLAND, KATHRYN ELEANOR (KAY) (D)
Alaska State Sen
b Portland, Ore, Oct 12, 19; d James Francis Kennedy & May V Jones K; div; c Patrick Kennedy, Kathleen Ann (Mrs Theodore Carlsen) & Shannon Elizabeth. Educ: Univ Wash, 37, 38 & 40; Moravian Col for Women, 38-39; Kappa Delta. Polit & Govt Pos: Chief clerk, Territorial Treas Off, Juneau, Alaska, 41-43; secy, US Wage & Hour Div, 44-45; jr acct, Dept of Taxation, 47-48; Alaska State Sen, 70- Bus & Prof Pos: Acct clerk, Juneau Cold Storage, 45-47; cannery acct, King Crab, Inc, Kodiak, 57-64; travel agent, Travel Ctr, 64-65; cannery acct, Kodiak Fisheries & Columbia Wards Fisheries, 66-70. Mem: Pioneers of Alaska; Kodiak CofC; League of Women Voters; Kodiak Area Native Asn. Relig: Roman Catholic. Legal Res: 1411 Kouskob Kodiak AK 99615 Mailing Add: PO Box 45 Kodiak AK 99615

POLANSKY, DANIEL J (R)
Treas, Kings Co Rep Comt, NY
b Brooklyn, NY, May 4, 06; s Harry Polansky & Minnie Cantor P; m 1931 to Eva Bresler; c Edwin Herbert & Sanford. Educ: St Lawrence Univ, LLB, 27; Kappa Phi Sigma. Polit & Govt Pos: Asst attorney gen, NY State Dept Law, 44-63, asst attorney gen in charge of labor bur, 63-; chmn bd dirs, 13th Assembly Dist Rep Club, 51-64, 42nd Assembly Dist Rep Club, 64-; alt deleg, Rep Nat Conv, 56 & 64; presidential elector, Rep Party, NY, 68; treas, Kings Co Rep Comt, 42nd Dist, currently; Rep cand, Dist Attorney of Kings Co, 73. Mem: Comt Labor & Indust Rels, Brooklyn Bar Asn; CofC; Canarsie Lodge, B'nai B'rith; Vanderveer Gardens Civic Asn. Honors & Awards: Cong Selective Serv Medal, 46; Vanderveer Garden Civic Asn Citation, 60; B'nai B'rith Citation, 63. Relig: Jewish. Mailing Add: 966 E 104th St Brooklyn NY 11236

POLISH, JOHN (D)
Nev State Assemblyman
Mailing Add: PO Box 1304 McGill NV 89318

POLITZER, S ROBERT (D)
Chmn, Marin Co Dem Cent Comt, Calif
b New York, NY, Sept 16, 29; s Sigmund Politzer & Emma Linzer P; m 1957 to Olive Webb; c Cassandra Deborah, Nicholas Charles (deceased), Adam Webb & Herissa Simone. Educ: Cooper Union Art Sch, New York, Archit, 52; Columbia Univ Sch Archit, 52-54. Polit & Govt Pos: Pres, Sausalito Dem Club, Calif, 63-64; chmn, Marin Co Coun of Dem Clubs, 64-65; First Cong Dist Dir, Calif Dem Coun, 65 67; vchmn, Marin Co Dem Cent Comt, 67-68, chmn, 68-; co-chmn, Sixth Cong Dist Dem Caucus, 68-; mem exec comt, Calif Dem State Cent Comt, 68-; dir, Marin Conserv League, 72- Bus & Prof Pos: Designer & job capt, John Carl Warnecks & Assocs, 61-63; project architect, Anshen & Allen, Architects, 63-68; prin, archit practice, 68-; guest lectr, Univ Ark Sch Archit, 72- Mem: Am Inst Architects; bd dirs, Marin Shakespeare Soc; trustee, Sausalito Found. Relig: Jewish. Mailing Add: 29 Glen Dr Sausalito CA 91965

POLK, WILLIAM BENJAMIN (R)
Ill State Rep
b Hamburg, Iowa, Jan 24, 30; s Warren McCain Polk & Carrie Belle Stubbs P; m 1958 to Mildred Ida Selander; c Morgan McCain & Nysha Alison. Educ: Univ Nebr, Lincoln, 51-53; St Louis Univ, 53-54; Phi Kappa Psi. Polit & Govt Pos: Dist rep, 19th Cong Dist, Ill, 66-73; vchmn, Rock Island Co Rep Cent Comt, 67-73; Ill State Rep, 73- Bus & Prof Pos: Chap mgr, Am Red Cross, 56-65. Mil Serv: Entered as Pvt, Marines, 48, released as Sgt, 52, after serv in Mil Police, Aleutian Islands, 50-52. Mem: Am Legion; Marine Corps League; Alcoholics & Narcotics Asn; Rock Island Co Welfare Coun; Moline Jaycees. Honors & Awards: Jaycee Int Sen, 67. Relig: Lutheran. Mailing Add: 4602 Eighth Ave Moline IL 61265

POLK, WILLIAM MERRILL (R)
Wash State Rep
b Cleburne, Tex, July 26, 35; s William Merrill Polk & Lucille Ray P; m 1958 to Karla Leopold; c Lucy Jennifer, Elizabeth Helena & Andrew James. Educ: Cornell Univ, BArchit, 58; Phi Kappa Sigma. Polit & Govt Pos: Precinct committeeman, Mercer Island Rep Party, Wash, 64-, area chmn, 65-66; cand chmn, 41st Dist Rep Party, Wash, 67-68, platform chmn, 70; pres, Downtown Young Rep Club, Seattle, Wash, 68-69, dir, 69-; Wash State Rep, 41st Legis Dist, 71- Bus & Prof Pos: Partner, Waldron & Pomeroy Architects, Seattle, Wash, 69-, secy corp, 70- Mil Serv: Entered as 2nd Lt, Army, 58, released as 1st Lt, 60, after serv in First Bn, 35th Artil, Ft Lewis, Wash, 59-60; Capt, Wash Army Nat Guard, 64- Mem: Am Inst Archit (corp mem, Seattle Chap); Seattle CofC; Seattle King Co Munic League; Col Club Seattle. Relig: Evangelical Covenant. Legal Res: 7220 92nd Ave SE Mercer Island WA 98040 Mailing Add: 422 Legislative Bldg Olympia WA 98504

POLLACK, MAURICE IRVINE (REECE) (R)
Dep Field Dir, Rep State Cent Comt Calif
b New York, NY, May 24, 40; s Harry Pollack & Birdie Stiller P; single. Educ: Univ Calif,

Los Angeles, BA, 71; Univ San Fernando Valley Col Law, 73-; Pi Gamma Mu; pres, UCLA Young Rep. Polit & Govt Pos: Area dir, Los Angeles Co Rep Comt, Calif, 72-73; regional vpres, Calif Young Rep, 72-75; dep field dir, Rep State Cent Comt Calif, 74- Mil Serv: Entered as Pvt, Marine Corps, 60, released as Cpl E-4, 64, after serv in 4th Rifle Co, Fleet Marine Force, Atlantic. Publ: Youth and the Republican Party, Truck Line, Los Angeles Co Rep Comt, 6/72; America the maligned, Points West, Westchester, Calif Rep, 10/74; The media and the GOP, The Challenge, Los Angeles Young Rep, 1/75. Mem: Los Angeles World Affairs Coun; Univ Calif Los Angeles Alumni Asn; US Marine Corps League; YMCA. Honors & Awards: Young Rep of Year, Los Angeles Co Young Rep, 72. Relig: Hebrew. Mailing Add: 8345 Dunbarton Ave Los Angeles CA 90045

POLLAN, CAROLYN JOAN **(R)**
Ark State Rep
b Houston, Tex, July 12, 37; d Rex Clark & Faith Basye C; m 1962 to George Angelo Pollan; c Cee Cee Lynn, Todd Angelo & Robert Edmond. Educ: New York Univ, 58; John Brown Univ, BS, Radio & TV, 59; Broadcasters Club; Engrs Club; ed, John Brown Univ Annual. Polit & Govt Pos: Five co chmn, Citizens for Nixon, 68; state chmn, Oper Lend-An-Ear for Ark Fedn Rep Women, 69; treas, Sebastian Co Rep Women's Fedn, 69-70, vpres, 70-71, pres, 71-; 13 co census coord, US Govt 1970 Census, Northwest Ark, 70; alt deleg, Rep Nat Conv, 72; mem by-laws & rules comt, Ark State Rep Conv, 72; co coord, Len Blaylock for Gov, 72; state chmn by-laws & revisions comt, Ark Fedn Rep Women, 72-; committeewoman, Ark State Rep Comt, Sebastian Co, 72-; secy, Third Dist Rep Comt, 72-; vchmn, Ark State Rep Party, 73-; Ark State Rep, 75- Bus & Prof Pos: Mem gen staff, KFPW Radio, 59-60; reservations staff, Cent Airlines, 60-62; co-owner & bookkeeper, Southwestern Boiler, Welding & Chem Co, 72-; owner, Ark Campaign Res, 72- Mem: PTA; Girl Scouts (leader); Friends of the Libr. Honors & Awards: Most Versatile Woman, John Brown Univ, 58 & 59. Relig: Southern Baptist. Mailing Add: 2201 S 40th Ft Smith AR 72901

POLLARD, ODELL **(R)**
Rep Nat Committeeman, Ark
b Union Hill, Ark, Apr 29, 27; s Joseph F Pollard & Beulah Scantlin P; m 1953 to Sammy Lane Lewis; c Laura Lane, Paula Lynn & Mark. Educ: Miss Col; Tulane Univ; Univ Ark, LLB. Polit & Govt Pos: Mem gen counsel, White Co Rep Comt, Ark, 2 years, 6 months, mem, 58-; mem, Ark State Rep Exec Comt, 60-; former mem & state chmn, Rep Nat Comt; deleg, Rep Nat Conv, 68; Rep Nat Committeeman, Ark, 73- Bus & Prof Pos: Attorney. Mem: Am, Ark & White Co Bar Asns. Relig: Methodist. Legal Res: 407 W Race Ave Searcy AR 72143 Mailing Add: PO Box 36 Searcy AR 72143

POLLARD, VIOLET MCDOUGALL **(D)**
b Glengarry Co, Ont, Can, July 17, 89; d Peter P McDougall & Ellen Robertson M; m 1933 to John Garland Pollard; wid. Educ: Regina Col, Sask & George Washington Univ Law Sch; Kappa Beta Pi. Polit & Govt Pos: Exec secy to four successive gov, Va, 19-33; alt deleg or deleg, Dem Nat Conv, 36-, mem platform comt; Dem nat committeewoman, Va, 40-68; chmn, Inter-Agency Comt on Recreation, 53-56. Bus & Prof Pos: Assoc dir, Va Mus Fine Arts, 40-56. Mem: Historic Richmond Found; life mem Asn for Preservation of Va Antiq; King & Queen Hist Soc; Va Mus Fine Arts; bd mem, Richmond Symphony Orchestra. Honors & Awards: Plaque, Va Recreation Asn, 54; Plaque, Bd Trustees, Va Mus Fine Arts, 56; Plaque for Patron of Arts, Federated Arts Coun of Richmond, 71. Relig: Presbyterian. Mailing Add: 1015 W Franklin St Richmond VA 23220

POLLOCK, ROBERT MICHAEL **(R)**
Chmn, Santa Cruz Co Rep Cent Comt, Calif
b Casselton, NDak, Feb 14, 26; s Michael Pollock & Geraldine Schipper P; m 1971 to Mildred Nordeen; c Janet, Pamela, Robert M, II & Lorna Gail Johnson. Educ: Dakota Bus Col, Fargo, NDak, grad, 46. Polit & Govt Pos: City councilman, Watsonville, Calif, 65-73; chmn, Santa Cruz Co Rep Cent Comt, 75- Bus & Prof Pos: Auditor, Standard Oil Co, 46-51; collection agency owner, Watsonville, Calif, 51-70; real estate broker, 71- Mil Serv: Entered as Fireman 2/C, Navy, 44, released as Machinist's Mate 3/C, 46, after serv in Pac Theatre. Mem: Rotary; Am Legion. Honors & Awards: Rotarian of the Year, 68. Legal Res: 604 Palm Ave Watsonville CA 95076 Mailing Add: PO Box 457 Watsonville CA 95076

POLONSKY, HELEN **(D)**
b New York, NY, Jan 11, 36; d Meyer Plancher & Mildred Sacs P; m 1957 to Jay B Polonsky; c Andrea Lee, Elizabeth Ann, Sara Michelle & Alexander Steven. Educ: Brooklyn Col, NY, BA, 57, grad work, 58-60; Gamma Sigma Sigma. Polit & Govt Pos: Deleg, Dem Nat Conv, 72; organizer, McGovern for President, 49th & 50th Assembly Dist, NY, 72. Bus & Prof Pos: Teacher of Eng, New York Schs, 57-62 & 73-75. Mem: B'nai B'rith Women (vpres, 75); PTA (corresponding secy, Pub Sch 102, 72-); Bridge Independent Dem (presiduim, 72-); Kings Co Dem Coalition (deleg-at-lg, 73); NY State New Dem Coalition (vchmn, 75). Honors & Awards: Fund Raising Award, B'nai B'rith Women, 72. Relig: Jewish. Mailing Add: 8008 Narrows Ave Brooklyn NY 11209

POMEROY, BENJAMIN SHERWOOD **(R)**
Mem, Legis Dist 62A Rep Comt, Minn
b St Paul, Minn, Apr 24, 11; s Benjamin A Pomeroy & Florence Anne Sherwood P; m 1938 to Margaret L Lyon; c Benjamin A, Sherwood R, Catherine Ann & Margaret Dawn. Educ: Iowa State Univ, DVM, 33; Cornell Univ, MS, 34; Univ Minn, PhD, 44; Phi Kappa Phi; Cardinal Key; Gamma Sigma Delta; Phi Zeta; Alpha Gamma Rho. Polit & Govt Pos: Chmn, Spec Comts to Nat Poultry Improv Plans, US Dept Agr, 48-72, mem, Adv Comt to Poultry Inspection, Consumer & Mkt Serv, 63; chmn, Adv Group to Vet Serv, Newcastle Disease, 71-; blockworker, 12th Precinct, Tenth Ward, Minn, 56-59, precinct officer, 59-60; chmn, 43rd South Legis Dist Rep Party, 60-61; chmn, Fourth Dist Rep Comt, 61-63 & 67-69; mem, Minn Rep State Exec Comt, 61-65 & 67-69; chmn, Ramsey Co Rep Comt, 61-65, mem, 65-71; deleg, Rep Nat Conv, 64; mem, Adv Comt on Vet Med, Food & Drug Admin, 65-67; mem, Minn Rep State Cent Comt, 65-71; mem, Legis Dist 62A Rep Comt, 72- Bus & Prof Pos: Instr, asst prof & assoc prof, Col Vet Med, Univ Minn, St Paul, 34-48, prof, 48-, head dept vet microbiol & pub health, 53-73, assoc dean col vet med, 70-74. Publ: Diseases of Parasites of Poultry (w Barger & Card), 58; contrib auth, Diseases of Poultry, Biester & Schwarte, 59 & 65 & Diseases of Poultry (ed, Hofstad), 72, Iowa State Univ. Mem: Sigma Xi (pres, Minn Chap, 73-74); Am Vet Med Asn; Soc Exp Biol & Med; Am Acad Microbiol; Am Col Vet Microbiol. Honors & Awards: Vet of Year, Minn, 70. Relig: Presbyterian. Mailing Add: 1443 Raymond Ave St Paul MN 55108

POMEROY, DUANE FRANKLIN **(R)**
Mem, Second Cong Dist Rep Comt, Kans
b Topeka, Kans, June 5, 52; s Sen Elwaine Franklin Pomeroy & Joanne C Bunge P; m 1973 to Deborah Kay Briggs. Educ: Kans State Teachers Col, 70-72; Washburn Univ, BA in Polit Sci, 75. Alpha Pi Omega. Polit & Govt Pos: Mem, Pomeroy for State Senate Comt, Kans, 68-; deleg, Kans Rep State Conv & Rep Dist Conv, 72 & 74; alt deleg, Rep Nat Conv, 72; mem, Second Cong Dist Rep Comt, 72-; precinct committeeman & ward captain, 73-; mem, Rep State Comt, 74-; supvr, Elec Bd, 74- Bus & Prof Pos: Clerk, Topeka Escrow Serv, Inc, 72-; teacher, Trinity Lutheran Church, 72-, church bd mem, 74-; apt mgr, 73-75; Lobbyist for Kansas Manufactured Housing & Recreational Vehicles Inst, 75- Honors & Awards: Letter in tennis, Kans State Teachers Col, 72 & Washburn Univ, 75; youngest deleg from Kans, Rep Nat Conv, 72. Relig: Lutheran. Legal Res: 1619 Jewell Topeka KS 66604 Mailing Add: 1412 W Fifth Topeka KS 66606

POMEROY, ELWAINE FRANKLIN **(R)**
Kans State Sen
b Topeka, Kans, June 4, 33; s Charles Franklin Pomeroy & Ada Frances Owen P; m 1950 to Joanne Carolyn Bunge; c Janella Ruth, Duane Franklin & Carl Fredrick. Educ: Washburn Univ of Topeka, AB, 55; Washburn Univ Sch Law, LLB, 57, JD, 69; Pi Gamma Mu; Pi Kappa Delta; Tau Delta Pi; Delta Theta Phi. Polit & Govt Pos: Rep precinct committeeman, Eighth Precinct, Eighth Ward, Kans, 61-; city attorney, Silver Lake, 64-74; Kans State Sen, 69- Bus & Prof Pos: Attorney-at-law, Topeka, Kans, 57-; dir & counsel, Topeka Teachers Credit Union, 57-; pres, Topeka Escrow Serv, Inc, 60-; sr partner, Pomeroy & Pomeroy, 64-; legal counsel, Kans Hwy Credit Union, 64- Publ: Contrib, Principles of Accounting, Pittman Publ Co, 57. Mem: Am Judicature Soc; Mason; Moose; Eagles. Relig: Lutheran. Legal Res: 1619 Jewell Topeka KS 66604 Mailing Add: 1415 Topeka Ave Topeka KS 66612

POMMERENING, GLEN EDWIN
Asst Attorney Gen for Admin, Dept of Justice
b Milwaukee, Wis, Sept 12, 27; s E C Pommerening & Emily Schinek R; m 1957 to Nancy Johnson; c William, David, Philip & Jean. Educ: Univ Wis, BS, 50, LLB, 53; Phi Eta Sigma; Sigma Chi. Polit & Govt Pos: Wis State Rep, 55-66; exec asst to Secy of Admin, State of Wis, 66-68, Dep Secy of Admin, 68-70; Dep Asst Attorney Gen for Admin, Dept of Justice, Washington, DC, 70-73, Acting Asst Attorney Gen for Admin, 73-74, Asst Attorney Gen for Admin, 74- Bus & Prof Pos: Pvt law practice, Milwaukee, Wis, 53-66. Legal Res: 8304 Weller Ave McLean VA 22101 Mailing Add: Dept of Justice Tenth & Constitution Ave Washington DC 20530

PONCY, CHARLES N **(D)**
Iowa State Rep
Mailing Add: 653 North Court Ottumwa IA 52501

PONDER, ZENO HERBERT **(D)**
Chmn, Madison Co Dem Comt, NC
b Madison Co, NC, Dec 20, 20; s Zadie Ponder & Emma Ramsey P; m 1942 to Nina Lou Rustin; c Z Herbert, Jr, Emagene (Mrs Marr), Wallace R & Ralph C. Educ: Mars Hill Col; NC State Univ, BS; Alpha Gamma Rho. Polit & Govt Pos: Chmn, Madison Co Bd Elec, 54-56 & Madison Co Bd Educ, 54-66; chmn, Madison Co Dem Exec Comt, NC, 58-60, 74-; deleg, Dem Nat Conv, 60 & 72; mem, Dem State Exec Comt, 74- Bus & Prof Pos: Pres, Zenina Farms, Inc, Marshall, NC, 60-, Ponderosa Homes, 62- & Zenina Lakes Inc, 63- Mem: Madison Co Farm Bur (bd dirs); NC Farm Bur (bd dirs & vpres); NC Farm Bur Mutual Ins Co (charter mem). Honors & Awards: Participated in Manhatten Proj & cited for contribution. Mailing Add: Rte 2 Marshall NC 28753

PONS, VICTOR MANUEL, JR **(POPULAR DEM, PR)**
Secy of State, PR
b Rio Piedras, PR, Apr 5, 35; s Victor M Pons & Carolina Nunez P; m 1960 to Carmen Luisa Rexach; c Carolina Sofia, Carmen Luisa, Victor Manuel & Juan Antonio. Educ: Swarthmore Col, 2 years; Univ PR, BA magna cum laude, 56, LLB magna cum laude, 59. Polit & Govt Pos: Mem, Coun on Higher Educ, PR, 66-71; chmn, Kennedy for President Comt, PR, 68; deleg, Dem Nat Conv, 68; mem cent coun, Popular Dem Party, PR, 68-69, pres electorate orgn unit, formerly, campaign mgr, 72; Secy of State, 73- Bus & Prof Pos: Assoc attorney, Fiddler, Gonzalez & Rodriguez, 59-62, partner, 63-72. Publ: Not guilty by reason of insanity (A commentary on Article 293 of the Code of Criminal Procedure), Revita Juridica, Univ PR, Vol XXVII; Apportionment of damages under the comparative negligence doctrine, Revista del Colegio de Abogados de PR, Vol XIX. Mem: PR, Am & Inter-Am Bar Asns. Relig: Roman Catholic. Legal Res: H-26 Villa Caparra Guaynabo PR 00619 Mailing Add: GPO Box P San Juan PR 00936

PONT, MARISARA **(D)**
Mem, Dem Nat Comt, PR
Mailing Add: 206 Ramirez-Baldrich San Juan PR 00918

PONTIUS, JOHN SAMUELS **(D)**
b Bethesda, Md, May 30, 45; s Harry Edgar Pontius & Kathryn Samuels P; m 1972 to Jane McAdams. Educ: Gettysburg Col, BA magna cum laude, 67; Univ Southern Calif, MPA, 70; Phi Beta Kappa; Pi Lambda Sigma; Phi Alpha Delta. Polit & Govt Pos: Admin asst, Los Angeles City Govt, Calif, 69-71; admin asst to US Rep, Charles W Wilson, Calif, 71- Mil Serv: E-4, Army Res. Publ: Is international relations part of political science, Gettysburg Rev, 6/67. Mem: Am Polit Sci Asn; Am Soc Pub Admin. Relig: Presbyterian. Mailing Add: 127 S Van Buren St Rockville MD 20850

POOL, RUSSELL FRANK **(R)**
b Rome, Ga, Aug 6, 38; s Russell P Pool & Myrtice Chapman P; m 1959 to Jane Spearman; c David John & Russell Scott. Educ: NGa Col, BS, 59. Polit & Govt Pos: Chmn, Jasper Co Rep Party, Ga, 70-74. Bus & Prof Pos: Owner, Pool Hardware, 68- Mil Serv: Entered as 2nd Lt, Army, 59, released as Maj (Ret), 68, after serv in Korea, Vietnam, Ger as Army Aviator, 59-68; Air Medal; Purple Heart; Commendation Medal; Bronze Star. Publ: Talking too much, Army Aviation, 64. Mem: ROA; Jasper Masonic Lodge; Monticello-Jasper Jaycees; Kiwanis (dir); Monticello-Jasper CofC. Relig: Methodist. Mailing Add: 445 College St Monticello GA 31064

POOLE, BAIN **(D)**
Ark State Rep
Mailing Add: 23 Plainview McGehee AR 71654

POOLE, VAN B **(R)**
Fla State Rep
b Jackson, Tenn, July 5, 35; s Martin Van Buren Poole & Louise Paul P; div; c Cynthia Lynn,

Kimberly Ann, Martin Devereaux & Katherine Kelly. Educ: Memphis State Univ, BS, 58; Humble Oil & Refining Co, mgt courses; Kappa Sigma. Polit & Govt Pos: Coordr, S Broward Campaign for Co Solicitor, James Geiger, 68; co-organizer & former dir, Gtr Hollywood Young Rep Club; mem, Ft Lauderdale Rep Club; Fla State Rep, 88th Dist, 70-72, Dist 84, 72-, chmn, Local Deleg Transportation Comt, mem, Elec, Ins, Finance & Taxation Comts & Campaign Spending Regulation Subcomt, Fla House Rep, formerly, liaison House & Senate, 70-72, deleg, Southern Legis Conv, 71, chmn, Broward Co Legis Deleg, mem, Appropriations, Educ & Environ Protection Comts, currently; mem cand selection comt & cong redistricting comt, Fla State Rep Party, 72. Bus & Prof Pos: With mkt dept, Humble Oil & Refining Co, 10 years; mgr life dept, Krieg, Kostas & Poole Ins, 68- Mil Serv: Cpl, Army Res. Mem: Nat Soc State Legislators; Hollywood Kiwanis Club; Gtr Hollywood CofC; KofC; Hollywood Comt 100. Honors & Awards: Outstanding New Jaycee, Memphis, 61, Tenn, 61; Hon Mention as Outstanding New Jaycees, US Jaycees, 61. Relig: Roman Catholic. Legal Res: 5801 SW 37th Ave Ft Lauderdale FL 33312 Mailing Add: 440 S Andrews Ave Ft Lauderdale FL 33301

POOR, RAYMOND JOHN (R)
Vt State Rep
Mailing Add: Box 144 Whitingham VT 05261

POOR, ROBERT LAWRENCE (R)
Chmn, Putnam Co Rep Comt, Ind
b Greencastle, Ind, Dec 5, 33; s John Lawrence Poor & Edna Hillis P; m 1955 to Barbara Ann Fuson; c Cynthia Lee & Lisa Ann. Educ: DePauw Univ, AB, 55; Lambda Chi Alpha. Polit & Govt Pos: Mem city coun, Greencastle, Ind, 63; chmn, Putnam Co Rep Comt, Ind, 65-; Ind Comnr, Wabash Valley Interstate Comn, 70-74; chmn, Ind Seventh Dist Rep Party, 72- Bus & Prof Pos: Vpres, Poor & Sons Inc, 58. Mil Serv: Entered as 2nd Lt, Air Force, 55, released as 1st Lt, 58, after serv in Continental Air Command, Bakalar AFB, 60; Capt, Air Force Res, 58- Mem: Nat Fertilizer Solutions Asn; Elks; Kiwanis; Am Legion; Ind Grain Dealers Asn. Relig: Christian. Mailing Add: 108 Northwood Blvd Greencastle IN 46135

POORBAUGH, JACK MORGAN (R)
Fla State Rep
b Cleveland, Ohio, Nov 3, 19; s John Milton Poorbaugh & Mianda Stewart P; m to Patty Sue; c John, Carl, Paul, Cathy & Jayne. Educ: Wash Univ, BS in Archit, 43. Polit & Govt Pos: Investr, US Sen, 47-53; pres, Boynton Beach-Ocean Ridge Rep Club, Fla, 66; Fla State Rep, currently. Bus & Prof Pos: Engr, Gill Construction Co, 53-55; owner, Archit Specialties, 55-60, gen contractor & owner, 66-72; gen sales mgr, Engineered Prod, 60-66. Mil Serv: Entered as Pvt, Marine Corps, 42, released as Sgt, 46. Mem: Mason. Relig: Protestant. Mailing Add: 10 River Edge Rd Jupiter FL 33458

POOVEY, JULIUS REID (R)
b Hickory, NC, Sept 24, 02; s Lloyd Willard Poovey & Nancy Thomas Reid P; m 1928 to Kathryn Violet Icard; c J Reid, Jr, James N, DDS, Maj William B & Nancy J (Mrs Walter N Yount). Educ: Weaver Col; Lenoir Rhyne Col, 19-22. Polit & Govt Pos: Magistrate, Hickory, NC, 50-62; former co secy, precinct chmn & precinct secy, Catawba Co Rep Comt; exec committeeman, NC Rep Exec Comt, formerly; NC State Rep, 66-68; NC State Sen, 68-70 & 72-74; mem, Catawba Co Bd Elec, 71-72; bd adv, NC Fedn Col Rep, 74- Mil Serv: Entered as Seaman 2/C, Coast Guard Res, 44, released as Seaman 1/C, 45, after serv in Chesapeake Bay, Md. Mem: Am Legion. Relig: Episcopal. Mailing Add: 61 20th Ave NW Hickory NC 28601

POPE, ALEXANDER H (D)
b New York, NY, June 4, 29; s Clifford H Pope & Sarah H Davis P; m 1950 to Harriet E Martin; c Stephen C, Virginia L & Daniel M. Educ: Univ Chicago, BA, 48, Law Sch, JD, 52; Phi Beta Kappa; Order of the Coif; pres, Univ Chicago Student Govt, 48-49; managing ed, Univ Chicago Law Rev, 51-52. Polit & Govt Pos: Mem nat bd, Vol for Stevenson, 52; vchmn, Los Angeles Co Dem Cent Comt, Calif, 58-59; legis secy, Calif Gov Off, 59-61; co-chmn, Los Angeles, Brown for Gov Comt, 62; Los Angeles finance chmn, Californians Against Proposition 14, 64; Los Angeles chmn, Calif Dem Coord Comt, 65, consult on SLos Angeles Riots, Calif Gov Off, 65-66; mem, Calif Hwy Comn, 66-70; assoc mem, Calif Dem State Cent Comt, 73-74; vpres, Los Angeles Bd Airport Comnrs, 73- Bus & Prof Pos: Partner, Fine & Pope, 57- Mil Serv: Entered as Pvt, Army, 52, released as Sgt, 54, after serv in 8th Army Hq, Korea, 53-54. Publ: Retroactivity of recognition of new foreign governments, 51 & Vertical forestalling under the anti-trust laws, Univ Chicago Law Rev, 52. Mem: Inglewood Dist Bar Asn (pres, 67); Am Civil Liberties Union; Am for Dem Action; Zero Population Growth. Relig: Unitarian. Legal Res: 7706 Boeing Ave Los Angeles CA 90045 Mailing Add: Suite 700 9800 S Sepulveda Blvd Los Angeles CA 90045

POPE, DONNA (R)
Ohio State Rep
b Cleveland, Ohio, Oct 15, 31; d John Emil Kolnik & Marie Theil K; m 1950 to Raymond L Pope; c Candace Rae & Cheryl Ann. Educ: South High Sch, grad, 49; Parma High Sch, spec adult courses, 62, 63 & 67. Polit & Govt Pos: Asst precinct committeeman, Parma, Ohio, 61-64, asst ward leader, 64-66, ward leader, 66-; precinct committeeman, Cuyahoga Co Rep Cent Comt, 64-; committeewoman, Rep State Cent & Exec Comt, Ohio, 66-72; mem, Cuyahoga Co Rep Exec Comt, 66-; bd mgr, Rep Women Ohio Fedn, 66- & Women's Rep Adv Bd, Cuyahoga Co, 68-; head, Cuyahoga Co Rep Booth Off Dept, Cuyahoga Co Bd of Elec, 68-72; Ohio State Rep, Dist 12, 72- Mem: Nat Soc State Legislators; Nat Orgn of Women Legislators; Int Platform Asn; Nat Travel Club; Nat Legis Conf Sci & Technol Comt. Relig: Catholic. Mailing Add: 3915 Longwood Ave Parma OH 44134

POPE, GEORGIA HELEN (R)
Mem, Rep State Cent Comt NMex
b Watonga, Okla, Jan 13, 32; d Arnold Julius Prickett & Fern Neal P; m 1952 to Leland Dean Pope; c Christy Lee & Julie Beth. Educ: Okla State Univ, 50-52. Polit & Govt Pos: Mem, Rep State Cent Comt NMex, 66-; chairwoman, Rep Party of McKinley Co, 66-68, chmn, 68. Bus & Prof Pos: Substitute teacher, Gallup-McKinley Co Schs, 57-61; ins agt, Nat Old Line Ins Co, 61-64, dist gen agt, 64-; owner-mgr, Jane's Fashions, 73- Mem: Soroptimist; Alpha Pi-Epsilon Sigma Alpha; Eastern Star (Past Matron); Shylock Investment Club; Past Matron's Club (past pres). Honors & Awards: Mem of the Wall of Fame of Nat Old Line Ins Co. Relig: Methodist; past pres of primary dept, past secy of the Sunday sch & teacher, Ninth Grade Sunday Sch Class, First United Methodist Church of Gallup. Mailing Add: 510 Julie Dr Gallup NM 87301

POPE, JACK (D)
Assoc Justice, Supreme Court of Tex
b Abilene, Tex, Apr 18, 13; s Dr Andrew J Pope & Ruth Taylor P; m 1938 to Allene Nichols; c Jackson & Allen. Educ: Abilene Christian Col, BA, 34; Univ Tex, LLB, 37. Polit & Govt Pos: Dist judge, 94th Dist Court, Tex, 46-50; assoc justice, Fourth Court of Civil Appeals, 50-65 & Supreme Court of Tex, 65- Bus & Prof Pos: Attorney-at-law, Corpus Christi, Tex, 37-46. Mil Serv: Seaman, Navy, 2 years. Publ: Numerous articles in law reviews & law journals. Mem: Am, San Antonio & Travis Co Bar Asns; Order of Coif; Phi Delta Phi. Honors & Awards: Silver Beaver Award, Boy Scouts; Rosewood Gavel Award, St Mary's Sch Law, 62. Relig: Church of Christ. Mailing Add: Supreme Court Bldg Capitol Station Box 12248 Austin TX 78711

POPE, JOANN (D)
VChairwoman, Mohave Co Dem Cent Comt, Ariz
b Kingman, Ariz, Nov 18, 45; d Virgil Harold Short & Betty Knowles S; m 1974 to Gary Ray Pope. Educ: Kingman High Sch, Ariz, grad, 62. Polit & Govt Pos: Chief dep recorder, Mohave Co, Ariz, 65-; pres, Kingman Dem Women's Club, 72-75; vchairwoman, Mohave Co Dem Cent Comt, 74-; secy, Ariz Fedn Dem Women's Club, 75. Mem: Mohave Co Daughters of Pioneers. Legal Res: 551 Simon Kingman AZ 86401 Mailing Add: PO Box 1288 Kingman AZ 86401

POPE, MARGARET GAFFIN (R)
b Philadelphia, Pa, Oct 15, 32; d Richard Birch Gaffin & Pauline Osborn G; m 1955 to Bruce Ben Pope; c Jessica Le Grand & Geoffrey Morton. Educ: Wheaton Col (Ill), BA, 56; Phi Mu. Polit & Govt Pos: Petition name gatherer to get Conservative Party on ballot, Bronxville, NY, 60; chmn, Nixon/Treen Hq, Thibodaux, La, 72; alt deleg, Rep Nat Conv, 72. Bus & Prof Pos: Personnel trainee, Campbell Soup Co, Chicago, 55-56; personnel mgr, Psychol Corp, New York, 57-60. Mem: Thibodaux Music Club (pres, 70-72); Amigas Club. Relig: Southern Baptist. Mailing Add: 201 Sycamore Dr Paducah KY 42001

POPHAM, BENJAMIN EUGENE (D)
b Cedartown, Ga, Feb 7, 17; s Benjamin Harrison Popham & Bessie Rutledge P; m 1941 to Frances Louciel Yoe; c Benjamin Eugene, Jr & Charles Ray. Educ: Southern Col Optometry, OD; Omega Epsilon Pi. Polit & Govt Pos: Mem, Ga State Dem Exec Comt, 71-74. Bus & Prof Pos: Employee, US Post Off, Cedartown, Ga, 38-47; pvt practice optometry, 51- Mil Serv: Enlisted, Army, 43-45, serv in 71st Inf Regiment, 44th Div, 7th Army, ETO, 44-45; Combat Inf Badge. Mem: Am Optometric Asn; Ga Optometric Asn; Kiwanis Int; Am Legion; CofC. Honors & Awards: Ga Optometrist of the Year Award, 59. Relig: Baptist. Legal Res: 1 Walton Way Rockmart GA 30153 Mailing Add: PO Box 505 Rockmart GA 30153

POPPEN, HENRY ALVIN (R)
SDak State Sen
b De Smet, SDak, Feb 12, 22; s Otto H Poppen & Sena Fransen P; m 1952 to Lorna Mildred Meyer; c Elizabeth Ann & Nanette Mildred. Educ: Huron Col, BA, 49. Polit & Govt Pos: Crew leader, 1959 Agr Census, Kingsbury-Miner Co, SDak, 59 & 60 Census, Kingsbury-Beadle Co, 60; chmn, Kingsbury Co Rep Party, 60-65; chmn & supvr, Spirit Lake Twp Bd, 64-; SDak State Sen, Dist 7, 67-, mem educ & agr comt, SDak State Senate, 67-70, chmn comt apportionment, elec, mil & vet affairs, 69-70. Bus & Prof Pos: Partner, Poppen Bros, De Smet, SDak, 54-69. Mem: Kingsbury Co Farm Bur; Mason; SDak Stockgrowers; Kingsbury Co Hist Soc (pres). Relig: Presbyterian. Mailing Add: RR 2 De Smet SD 57231

POPPER, DAVID HENRY
US Ambassador to Chile
b New York, NY, Oct 3, 12; s Morris Popper & Lilian Greenbaum P; m 1936 to Florence C Maisel; c Carol, Lewis, Katherine & Virginia. Educ: Harvard Univ, AB, 32 & AM, 34. Polit & Govt Pos: Specialist in int orgn affairs, Dept of State, 45, adv, US Deleg to UN Gen Assembly, 46-53 & prin exec officer, 49-50; asst chief div int orgn affairs, Dept of State, 48-49 & officer in charge, UN Gen Assembly Affairs, 49-51; dep dir, Off UN Polit & Security Affairs, 51-54 & dir, 54-55; dep US Rep for Int Orgn, Geneva, 56-59; dep US Rep, Conf on Discontinuance Nuclear Weapons Tests, Geneva, 59-61; sr adv disarmament affairs, US Mission to UN, 61-62; mem, US Deleg, NATO Ministerial Meetings, 62-65; dir, Off of Atlantic Polit & Mil Affairs, Dept State, 62-65; Dep Asst Secy State for Int Orgn Affairs, 65-69, Asst Secy of State for Int Orgn Affairs, 73-74; US Ambassador to Cyprus, 69-73; US Ambassador to Chile, 74- Bus & Prof Pos: Research assoc, Foreign Policy Asn, Inc, New York, 34-40 & assoc ed publ, 41-42. Mil Serv: Capt, CWC, Mil Intel Serv, AUS, 42-45. Publ: The puzzle of Palestine, 38; plus various articles in prof publs. Mem: Am Soc Int Law; Am Acad Polit & Soc Sci. Legal Res: Buffalo NY Mailing Add: Dept of State 2201 C St Washington DC 20520

POPPITI, MICHAEL (D)
Polit & Govt Pos: Former chmn, Del State Dem Cent Comt Mailing Add: 605 Market Towers Wilmington DE 19801

POQUETTE, RAY H (R)
Vt State Rep
Mailing Add: Alburg VT 05440

PORTER, ALBERT (D)
Chmn, Hood Co Dem Party, Tex
b Granbury, Tex, Oct 25, 94; s Luther Preston Porter & Amanda Massey P; m 1918 to Eula William (deceased); c William Norris, Doris Jean (Mrs Sweeney) & Garth Albert. Educ: Granbury High Sch, grad, 17. Polit & Govt Pos: Co clerk, Hood Co, Tex, 36-49 & 58-; chmn, Hood Co Dem Party, 58- Bus & Prof Pos: Owner, Grocery Store, Granbury, Tex, 23-34; supt, First Methodist Sunday Sch, 28-68; pres, Tri-Co Elec Coop, 42-; supvr, Hood-Parker Soil Conserv Dist, 51- Mem: WOW. Honors & Awards: Cert of Merit, Tex Bank & Trust Co, Dallas, Tex. Relig: Methodist. Mailing Add: PO Box 429 Granbury TX 76048

PORTER, ALBERT S (D)
b Nov 29, 04; s Albert S Porter, Sr & Lena May P; m to Genevieve S; c Lee A, Alan C & Carol S. Educ: Ohio State Univ, BCE, 28; Tau Beta Pi; Sigma Xi; Pi Mu Epsilon; Texnikoi; Sigma Phi Epsilon. Polit & Govt Pos: Deleg, Dem Nat Conv, 52, 64, 68 & 72; cand for mayor, Cleveland, Ohio, 53; chmn, Dem State Conv, 58 & 66; chmn, Cuyahoga Co Charter Comn, 59; Ohio Favorite Son Cand for President, 60 & 64; former chmn, Ohio Dem Exec Comt, at-lg-mem, currently; Dem Nat Committeeman, Ohio, 64-72; chmn, Cuyahoga Co Dem Cent Comt, 64-70. Bus & Prof Pos: Draftsman & asst engr, City Plan Comn & City Engrs Off, Columbus, Ohio, 25-29; engr & consult, Cleveland Hwy Research Bur, 29-32; asst to div engr,

POST / 747

Div 12, State Hwy Dept, Cleveland, 32-33; chief dep co engr, Cuyahoga Co, 33-41 & 46-47; Cuyahoga Co Engr, 47- Mil Serv: Civil Engr Corps, Navy, 41-46; Comdr, Naval Res. Mem: Am Soc Civil Engrs; F&AM; Lake Erie Consistory (32 degree); Am Legion; VFW. Honors & Awards: Engr of the Year, Cleveland Soc Prof Engrs & Cleveland Eng Soc, 64; KofC Civic Award for Commun Serv, 64. Relig: Episcopal. Legal Res: 31179 S Woodland Rd Cleveland OH 44115 Mailing Add: 1926 Standard Bldg Cleveland OH 44113

PORTER, CHARLES O (D)
b Klamath Falls, Ore, Apr 4, 19; s Frank Jason Porter & Ruth Peterson P; m 1943 to Priscilla Dean Galassi; c Donald Jason, Christopher Dean, Samuel Curry & Anne Julia. Educ: Harvard Col, BA, 44; Harvard Law Sch, LLB, 47. Polit & Govt Pos: Alt deleg-at-lg, Dem Nat Conv, 56, deleg-at-lg, 60, 64, 68 & 72; US Rep, Ore, 56-60; White House Consult, Food for Peace Prog, 61. Mil Serv: Entered as Pvt, Army, 41, released as 1st Lt, after serv in Hq, 9th Air Force; Maj, Air Force Res (Ret), 67; Four Battle Stars; Distinguished Unit Medal. Publ: Co-auth, The American Lawyer, Univ Chicago, 54; The Struggle for Democracy in Latin America, Macmillan, 61. Relig: United Church of Christ. Legal Res: 2680 Baker St Eugene OR 97403 Mailing Add: 200 Legal Ctr 858 Pearl St Eugene OR 97401

PORTER, CLOYD ALLEN (R)
Wis State Rep
b Huntley, Ill, May 22, 35; s Cecil William Porter & Myrtle Lucille Fisher P; m 1959 to Joan Ellen Hawkins; c Ellen Joan, Lee Ann, Jay Allen & Joli Sue. Educ: Univ Wis, 54. Polit & Govt Pos: Vpres bd dirs, Racine Co Planning Coun, Wis, 71-72; chmn, Town of Burlington, 71-75; mem, Racine Co Intergovt Coun, 71-75; mem, Racine Co Solid Waste Disposal Comt, 71-73; Wis State Rep, 43rd Dist, 72- Bus & Prof Pos: Partner, Cecil W Porter & Son Trucking, Burlington, 55-70; treas, Burlington Sand & Gravel Corp, 64-70; owner, Cloyd A Porter Trucking, 70-72; salesman, John Lynch Chevrolet-Pontiac, 71-72. Mem: Charter mem Burlington Jaycees; Wis Jaycees; Burlington Soap Box Derby Comt; Burlington Goodwill Industs; Little League Coach. Honors & Awards: Distinguished Serv Award, Burlington Jaycees, 69; Outstanding Local Pres Award, Wis Jaycees, 69, Outstanding State Vpres Award, 70 & One of Five Outstanding Young Men of Wis, 70; Outstanding Citizen Award, Burlington VFW, 72. Relig: Catholic. Mailing Add: Rte 3 Box 331 Burlington WI 53105

PORTER, DWIGHT J
b Shawnee, Okla, Apr 12, 16; m to Adele Ritchie; c Dwight A, James, Ellen, Barbara, Joan & Ritchie. Educ: Grinnell Col, BA, 38. Hon Degrees: LLD, Grinnell Col, 68. Polit & Govt Pos: Intern, Nat Inst of Pub Affairs, 38-39; with US Housing Authority, 39-41 & Dept of Agr, 41-42 & 45-48; asst personnel officer, Bd of Econ Warfare, 42; career officer, US Dept of State Foreign Serv, 48-, dep dir, Displaced Persons Comn, 48-49, chief mgt & budget div, US High Comnr for Ger, Frankfurt, 49-52, dep exec dir, Bonn, 52-54, first secy, London, 54-56, coordr, Hungarian Refugee Policies & Activities, 56-57, exec dir, Bur of Econ Affairs, 56-57, mem staff, Nat War Col, 57-58, spec asst to Under Secy for Polit Affairs, 58-59, counsel & dep chief of mission, Vienna, 59-63; Asst Secy State for Admin, 63-65; US Ambassador to Lebanon, 65-70; US Resident Rep, Int Atomic Energy Agency, Vienna, 70-75; dir inter-govt affairs, Westinghouse Elec Corp, Washington, DC, 75- Mil Serv: Capt, Marine Corps, 42-45. Legal Res: Omaha NE Mailing Add: 3327 Stuyvesant Pl NW Washington DC 20015

PORTER, E MELVIN (D)
Okla State Sen
b Okmulgee, Okla, May 22, 30; s Victor E Porter & Mary Cole P; m 1955 to Jewel Ewing; c E Melvin, II & Joel Anthony. Educ: Tenn State Univ, BS, 56; Vanderbilt Univ, LLB, 59; Sigma Rho Sigma; Kappa Alpha Psi. Polit & Govt Pos: Okla State Sen, 65- Mil Serv: Entered as Pvt, Army, 48, released as Cpl, 52, after serv in 93rd Engrs, Guam, 49-51. Mem: Am Bar Asn; Am Judicature Soc; NAACP; YMCA; CofC. Honors & Awards: Kappa of the Month. Relig: Baptist. Mailing Add: 2116 NE 23rd St Oklahoma City OK 73111

PORTER, FREDERICK ATHERTON (R)
b Bangor, Maine, Nov 22, 29; s Herbert E Porter (deceased) & Hazel Atherton P (deceased); m 1953 to Geraldine R Burgess; c Mark Andrew. Educ: Purdue Univ, 53-54; Univ Maine, Orono, BSEE, 57; Tau Kappa Epsilon; student chap, Inst Elec & Electronic Engrs. Polit & Govt Pos: Vpres, Souhegan Young Rep, 65-67; deleg, NH Rep State Conv, 68; mem adv bd, NH Voc-Tech Col, 68-; mem, Citizens Task Force, Concord, 69; NH State Sen, Dist 12, 69-74, Majority Leader, NY State Senate, 73-74; chmn, Amherst Rep Town Comt, 69-71; chmn comt on recreation & educ, NH Environ Coun, 70; alt deleg, Rep Nat Conv, 72. Bus & Prof Pos: Radio-TV engr, WFAU, Augusta, Maine, WTWO, Bangor & WBAA, Lafayette, Ind, 49-57; circulation agent, Bangor Daily News, Maine, 48-49; electronics engr, Page Commun Engrs, Washington, DC, 51-53 & Cent Intel Agency, 57-60; engr, prog mgr & mem corp tech staff, Sanders Assocs, Nashua, NH, 60- Mil Serv: Entered as Pvt, Army, 47, released as Pfc, 48, after serv in 9th Inf Div, US; Seaman, Naval Res, 48-53. Mem: Inst Elec & Electronic Engrs; NH Soc Registered Prof Engrs; Mason; CofC; Soc for Protection of NH Forests. Relig: Congregational. Mailing Add: Boston Post Rd Amherst NH 03031

PORTER, JOHN EDWARD (R)
Ill State Rep
b Evanston, Ill, June 1, 35; s Harry H Porter (deceased) & Florence B P; m to Kathryn Suzanne Cameron; c John Clark, David Britton & Ann Lindsay. Educ: Mass Inst Technol, 53-54; Northwestern Univ Sch Bus, BSBA, 57; Univ Mich Law Sch, JD with distinction, 61; Student Governing Bd; Alpha Tau Omega (pres); Norleggama Honor Coun; Interfraternity Coun (pres); Mich Law Rev (asst ed). Polit & Govt Pos: Gen Counsel, Cook Co Young Rep Orgn, 65; hq chmn, Evanston Citizen's for Ogilvie, 66; polit affairs vpres, Niles Twp Young Rep Orgn, 66; charter mem, Evanston Rep Workshops, 67; co-counsel, Evanston Rep Club, 67-70; pres, Evanston Young Rep Club, 68-69; precinct capt, Evanston Regular Rep Orgn, mem exec bd, 68- & co-chmn, Third Ward, 68-72; cand for Judge of Circuit Court of Cook Co, 70; Ill State Rep, First Dist, 72- Bus & Prof Pos: Attorney, Civil Div, Appellate Sect, US Dept of Justice, Washington, DC, 61-62 & self-employed, Evanston, Ill, 62-68; co-chmn lawyers sect, United Commun Serv of Evanston, 65 & chmn, 67; mem bd dirs, Legal Assistance Found of Cook Co, 67-72; temporary chmn, NCook Co Legal Adv Bd, 67 & bd mem, 67-72; bus & indust chmn, Evanston March of Dimes, 68 & 69; partner, Shanesy, Hobbs, Koch, Porter & Ball, 68-72; dir, Univ Club of Evanston, 69-71 & vpres, 71-72; sr partner, Porter & Hoffman, 72- Mil Serv: Army Res, 58-64, serv in Signal Corps, Ft Leonard Wood, Mo. Mem: Evanston CofC; Southeast Evanston Asn; East Evanston Community Conf; Evanston Hist Soc (trustee, 70-); Am Bar Asn. Relig: Presbyterian. Legal Res: 911 Sheridan Rd Evanston IL 60202 Mailing Add: 360 State Nat Bank Plaza Evanston IL 60201

PORTER, JOHN T (D)
Ala State Rep
Mailing Add: 1101 Montevallo Rd SW Birmingham AL 35211

PORTER, PAUL (D)
Mich State Rep
Mailing Add: 897 Central Rd Rte 1 Quincy MI 49082

PORTER, RALPH EVERETT (R)
b Maher, Colo, July 6, 02; s Everett H Porter & Cora J Flannary P; m 1925 to Marjorie O Peck; c Robert R, Jack E & Polly (Mrs Spann). Educ: Western State Col, AB, 27, AM, 55; Kappa Delta Mu; W Club. Polit & Govt Pos: Local councilman, 28; chmn, Colo State Rep Cent Comt, 52; Colo State Rep, Dist 58, 63-72. Bus & Prof Pos: Bus mgr, West State Col, 27-60; owner lumber co, 41-51; ranch & cattle owner & operator, 41-52. Mem: CofC (pres, Gunnison Chap, 33); Rotary (pres, Gunnison Club, 34); AF&AM (master, Gunnison Lodge, 34); Scottish Rite; Elks. Relig: Protestant. Mailing Add: Crested Butte Gunnison CO 81224

PORTER, ROBERT LAWRENCE (D)
Chmn, 20th Dist Dem Party, NDak
b Grandin, NDak, Apr 11, 26; s James F Porter & Lelah M Coleman P; m 1946 to Dolores M Tetzlaff; c Bonnie L & David R. Educ: Wahpeton Sci, 1 year. Polit & Govt Pos: Precinct committeeman, 20th Dist Dem Party, NDak, 54-, chmn, 65- Bus & Prof Pos: Dir, RRV Sugarbeet Coop, Hillsboro, NDak. Mil Serv: Entered as A/S, Navy, 44, released as WT 2/C, 46, after serv in USS Bootes Ak-99, Asiatic-Pac Theatre, 44-46. Mem: Elks; Eagles; Am Legion; VFW. Relig: Lutheran. Mailing Add: Grandin ND 58038

PORTER, VICTOR BUTLER (R)
Chmn, Adams Co Rep Cent Comt, Ind
b Decatur, Ind, Feb 3, 31; s Giles Porter & Velma Butler P; m 1950 to Kristine Striker; c John, Scott, Grant, Wayne, Jean & Ted. Educ: Purdue Univ. Polit & Govt Pos: Chmn, Adams Co Rep Cent Comt, 73- Bus & Prof Pos: Pres & chmn bd, Thunderbird Prod Corp, 74-; pres, Signa Corp, 70-73 & Duo Marine Corp, 58-70. Mem: Mason; Scottish Rite; Knights Templar; Shrine; Lions. Relig: Methodist. Legal Res: Rte 6 Decatur IN 46733 Mailing Add: PO Box 501 Decatur IN 46733

PORTER, WILLIAM JAMES
US Ambassador to Canada
b Stalybridge, Eng, Sept 1, 14; s William J Porter & Sarah Day P; m 1944 to Eleanore E Henry; c William James, Jr & Eleanor (Mrs Gentry Clark, III). Educ: Thibodeau Bus Col, 30-33. Polit & Govt Pos: With US Foreign Serv, 36-, served in Hungary, Iraq, Lebanon, Syria, Palestine, Cyprus, Morocco, Algeria & in several positions in Dept of State, 36-62; US Ambassador to Algeria, 62-65; Dep US Ambassador to Vietnam, 65-67; US Ambassador to Repub of Korea, 67-71; Chief US Negotiator, Paris Peace Talks, Paris, France, 71-73; Under Secy of State for Polit Affairs, 73-74; US Ambassador to Can, 74- Honors & Awards: Recipient Distinguished Honor Award, US State Dept, 66; President's Award for Distinguished Fed Civilian Serv, 67; Vietnam Serv Medal, 68. Legal Res: Westport Point MA 02791 Mailing Add: Dept of State Washington DC 20520

POSEY, JOHN PHILLIP (D)
b Dothan, Ala, Dec 4, 35; s James Herbert Posey & Marie Holloman P; m 1960 to Pauline Louise Stewart; c Heather Patrice & Laurel Marie. Educ: Univ Ga, BS, 58, MA, 59, PhD, 62; Phi Alpha Theta; Pi Sigma Alpha; Theta Chi. Polit & Govt Pos: Deleg, Loyal Dem of Miss Conv, 68; deleg, Dem Nat Conv, 68; mem exec comt, Humphrey-Muskie Campaign, Forrest Co, Miss, 68; chmn, Comt on New Ideas & Progs, Miss Dem Party, 68-69; mem, New Dem Coalition Ind, 69-; faculty moderator, Young Dem Club St Joseph's Col, 69-, coordr & faculty moderator, St Joseph's Col Students Hartke for Sen, 70-71. Bus & Prof Pos: Grad asst hist, Univ Ga, 58-61, student instr, 61-62; Nat Defense Educ Act instr, summer 66 & 67; asst prof, Va Polytech Inst, 62-66; asst prof, Appalachian State Univ, summer 63; assoc prof, Univ Southern Miss, 66-69; assoc prof hist, St Joseph's Col, Ind, 69-, dir, Non-Western Studies, 72- Publ: David Hunter Miller as an informal diplomat: the Fiume Question at the Paris Peace Conference, 4/67, Soviet propaganda, Europe, and the Russo-Polish War, 1920, 1/68 & From the Diary of A A Polovtsov: leadership in the Russo-Turkish War, 4/69, Southern Quart. Mem: Am Hist Asn; Am Asn for the Advan of Slavic Studies; Southern Conf on Slavic Studies; Ind Consortium for Int Progs (bd dirs); European Sect, Southern Hist Asn. Honors & Awards: Ford Found fel, Inst on Far Eastern Hist & Civilization, Fla State Univ, 65; US Off Educ grant for study in India, summer 72. Relig: Methodist. Mailing Add: 142 W Vine St Rensselaer IN 47978

POSNER, HERBERT A (D)
NY State Assemblyman
Mailing Add: 21-07 Elk Dr Far Rockaway NY 11691

POSNER, SEYMOUR (D)
NY State Assemblyman
b Bronx, NY, May 21, 25; s Nathan Posner & Fannie Gittleman P; m 1953 to Marilyn Deutsch; c Naomi Gila. Educ: City Col of New York, BS in Social Sci, 48; NY Univ, MA in Pub Admin; New Sch, Univ Paris. Polit & Govt Pos: Gen comt, NY Comt for Dem Voters; co-chmn, Vols for Stevenson in the Bronx, 52, Concourse-Jefferson Independent Dem, New York Dept of Welfare, NY & New York Housing Authority, State Rent Comn, formerly; NY State Assemblyman, 65- Bus & Prof Pos: Past dir, Bronx Div, Am Jewish Cong; moderator, Weekly Radio Discussion Series on Commun Probs, formerly; moderator, Urban League of Gtr New York, United Housing Found; pub rels dir, March on Washington, 63; conducts weekly pub serv prog, Ombudsman, Radio Sta WEVO, currently. Mil Serv: Inf World War II. Publ: Author of series of articles on housing probs, El Diaro De Nueva York. Mem: Jewish War Vets (Maccabean Post); Citizen's Union; NAACP; Nat Asn Intergroup Rels Officers; AFSCME; Am Jewish Cong. Relig: Jewish. Mailing Add: 1100 Grand Concourse Bronx NY 10456

POST, BONNIE (D)
Maine State Rep
Mailing Add: Box 458 Rockland Owls Head ME 04841

POST, RUSSELL LEE, JR (R)
Conn State Rep
b New York, NY, Jan 7, 37; s Russell Lee Post & Emily Davis Lord P; m 1960 to Linda Norton Ritchey; c Russell Lee, III, Lincoln Strong, Katherine Loring & Alison Ritchey. Educ:

Yale Univ, BA, 58, LLB, 61; Skull & Bones; Fence Club. Polit & Govt Pos: Mem & secy, Canton Zoning Comn, Conn, 67-72; mem, Canton Rep Town Comt, 67-; dep, Comn Personnel, State of Conn, 71-72; Conn State Rep, 73- Bus & Prof Pos: Partner, Shipman & Goodwin, Attorneys-at-Law, 61-71 & Post & Pratt, 73- Publ: Teacher labor relations in the 1970's, Educator's Negotiating Serv, 7/71; Long range implications of collective bargaining by teachers, Personnel News, Educ Serv Bur, 3/72; Report & recommendations of the Governor's Commission on Public Employment Relations, State of Conn, 1/73. Mem: Am, Conn & Hartford Co Bar Asns; Westledge Sch, Inc (chmn bd trustees); Mensa; Intertel. Relig: Episcopal; sr warden, Trinity Episcopal Church, 70-72. Mailing Add: Lawton Rd Canton CT 06019

POSTHUMUS, RICHARD EARL **(R)**
b Hastings, Mich, July 19, 50; s Earl Martin Posthumus & Lola Wieland P; m 1972 to Pamela Ann Bartz. Educ: Mich State Univ, BS with honors, 72; Alpha Gamma Rho, Tau Chap. Polit & Govt Pos: Legis asst to Mich State Rep John Engler, 100th Dist, 71; third vchmn, Mich Rep State Cent Comt, 71-74; campaign consult, Mich House Rep Republican Campaigns Comt, 72; deleg, Rep Nat Conv, 72, Kent Co Rep Conv, 72- & Mich Rep State Conv, 72-; exec vpres, Mich Beef Industry Comn, 74- Bus & Prof Pos: Pres, Mich Asn of Future Farmers of Am, 68-69; researcher, Exten Mkt, Mich State Univ, 71-72; exec vpres of growers, Farmers & Mfrs Beet Sugar Asn, Saginaw, Mich, 73-74. Publ: Ed, How to develop markets for US Agricultural and Food Exports, Coop Exten Serv, Mich State Univ, 73. Mem: Nat Future Farmers of Am Asn, Caledonia Chap. Honors & Awards: Most Outstanding Pub Affairs Mgr Grad, Agr & Econ Dept, Mich State Univ, 72. Relig: Church of the Brethren. Mailing Add: 4102 Segwun Lowell MI 49331

POSTON, BRYAN A **(D)**
La State Sen
Mailing Add: Hornbeck LA 71439

POSTON, ERNEST EUGENE **(D)**
Dem Nat Committeeman, NC
b Chesnee, SC, July 14, 18; s Summie Albert Poston & Minnie Conner P (both deceased); m 1939 to Dorothy Elizabeth Jenkins; c Robert Stephen, Gloria (Mrs Frank Helton, Jr) & Elizabeth (Mrs Robert C Lindemann). Educ: Gardner-Webb Col, AA, 43; Wake Forest Univ, BA, 44; Southern Baptist Theol Sem, MDiv, 47, ThM, 48, PhD, 50. Polit & Govt Pos: Dem Nat Committeeman, NC, 72- Bus & Prof Pos: Baptist minister, Wise & Rock Springs Churches, 43, Monterey, Swallowfield, Elk Lick & Dallasburg Churches, Ky, 44-50, Wallace Church, NC, 51-57 & First Baptist Church, Jonesboro, Ga, 58-59; head relig dept, Gardner-Webb Col, 59-61, pres, 61- Mem: NC Conf for Social Serv (vpres); Boy Scouts Am (mem exec comn, Piedmont Coun); Union Trust Co (mem bd dirs); Cleveland Savings & Loan Asn (mem bd dirs); Independent Col Fund of NC (treas). Honors & Awards: Alumnus of the Year Award, Gardner-Webb Col Alumni Asn, 67; Keynote Speaker for the Vance-Aycock Dinner, Asheville, NC, 72. Relig: Baptist, mem, First Baptist Church, Shelby, NC. Legal Res: Webb Knoll Riverbend Acres Shelby NC 28150 Mailing Add: Box 792 Boiling Springs NC 28017

POSTON, HOWARD HENRY, JR **(R)**
b Kingstree, SC, Oct 19, 29; s Howard H Poston, Sr & Henri Louise Johnson P; m 1951 to Mary Jo Stroud; c John Howard, Rebecca Louise, Mary Lella, Patricia Page. Educ: Duke Univ, AB, 51; Med Col of SC, MD, 55, Sigma Chi. Polit & Govt Pos: Med dir, Williamsburg Co Civil Defense, 60; chmn, Independent Voters of Williamsburg Co, 61-65; vchmn, Workman for Senate Comt, 62; chmn, Cand Evaluation Comt, Sixth Cong Dist, 62-65; mem, State Bd of Dirs, State Br, Am Polit Action Comt, 62-65; chmn, Williamsburg Co Goldwater for President Comt, 64; med adv, Local Selective Serv Bd, SC, 65-; chmn, Williamsburg Co Rep Party, 65-70 & 72-75; deleg, Rep Nat Conv, 68; chmn, Williamsburg Co Thurmond for Senate Comt, 72; chmn, Williamsburg Co Young for Cong Comt, 72. Bus & Prof Pos: Vpres, Seventh Med Dist, 59-60, pres, 69-70; alt deleg, SC Med Asn, 60-67, deleg, 68-; chief of staff, Williamsburg Co Mem Hosp, 69- Mil Serv: Entered as 1st Lt, Air Force, 56, released as Capt, 58, after serv in MedC, 6606th Air Force Hosp, Goose AFB, Labrador, 56-58. Mem: SC Acad of Family Practice; Williamsburg Co Med Soc; Am & Southern Med Asns; Am Acad of Family Practice; Moose. Relig: Methodist. Legal Res: 1505 Fulton Ave Kingstree SC 29556 Mailing Add: 1248 Longstreet Kingstree SC 29556

POSTON, JAMES RICHARD **(D)**
Chmn, Campbell Co Dem Exec Comt, Ky
b Covington, Ky, Feb 4, 25; s Cecil F Poston & Agnes Duvelius P; m 1953 to Shirley Frost; c Susan M, James R, Melinda M, Cindy M, Jay R, Diane M, Jennifer M, Jon R & Amy M. Educ: Denver Univ, AB, 47; Salmon P Chase Col Law, LLB, 51; Omicron Delta Kappa; Sigma Alpha Epsilon. Polit & Govt Pos: Alt deleg, Dem Nat Conv, 64 & 72; deleg, Ky Const Rev Assembly, 64-67; chmn, Dem Co Campaign, 65-68; chmn, Campbell Co Dem Exec Comt, 69-; judge, Campbell Co Juvenile Court, 74- Bus & Prof Pos: Counsel, Cinti Gas & Elec Co, 58-; bd regents, Northern Ky State Col, 74- Mem: Am, Ky & Campbell Co Bar Asns; Northern Ky CofC (bd dirs); Boy Scouts (bd dirs). Honors & Awards: Named Outstanding Young Man, Campbell Co, Ky, 61; Gov Award, Ky, 66. Relig: Catholic. Mailing Add: 131 Capri Dr Ft Thomas KY 41075

POSTON, RALPH R, SR **(D)**
Fla State Sen
Legal Res: 6282 SW 133rd St Miami FL 33156 Mailing Add: 3103 NW 20th St Miami FL 33142

POTESTA, RALPH J **(R)**
Ind State Sen
Mailing Add: 7332 Jackson Ave Hammond IN 46324

POTOCHNIK, STANLEY **(D)**
Chmn, Sheboygan Co Dem Party, Wis
b Sheboygan, Wis, Nov 15, 17; s John Potochnik & Mary Stajduhar P; m 1947 to Evelyn Gertrude Jacobs; c Kristi Ann & Timothy Mark. Educ: Univ Wis, BS in Mech Eng, 48; Ill Inst Technol, 50; Foreign Students Club. Polit & Govt Pos: Tech rep in radio, Off Strategic Serv, India & China, 44-45; vchmn, Sheboygan Co Dem Party, Wis, 60-62, treas, 63-64, chmn, 65-; exec bd mem, Sixth Cong Dist Dem Party, 65-66. Mem: Air Pollution Control Asn; Am Inst of Plant Engrs; Nat Rifle Asn; China-Burma-India Vet Asn; Boy Scouts. Relig: Methodist. Mailing Add: 2621 N Ninth St Sheboygan WI 53081

POTTER, CALVIN **(D)**
Wis State Rep
Mailing Add: 533 Lower Rd Kohler WI 53044

POTTER, CHARLENE MARIE **(D)**
Chmn, Neosho Co Dem Cent Comt, Kans
b Ft Scott, Kans, July 27, 45; d Charles S Grant, Jr & Darlene Marie Ball G; m 1967 to Delbert Loran Potter. Educ: Ft Scott Community Jr Col, 66-67. Polit & Govt Pos: Pres, Neosho Co Fedn Women's Dem Clubs, Kans, 72-; vchmn, Neosho Co Dem Cent Comt, 72-73, chmn, 74-; treas, Fifth Dist Fedn Women's Dem Clubs, 73-; auditor, Kans State Fedn Women's Dem Clubs, 73-; rec secy, SCent Region, Nat Fedn Women's Dem Clubs, 73- Bus & Prof Pos: Posting operator, Key Work Clothes, Ft Scott, Kans, 63-66; PBX operator, Mercy Hosp, Ft Scott, 66-67; secy, Western Ins Co, Ft Scott, 67-68; legal secy, William E Settle Attorney, also Co Attorney, Wilson Co, Fredonia, 68-70; secy & bookkeeper, Manley Steel Co, Inc, Chanute, 70-75. Mem: Neosho Co Dem Club; Nat Dem Club. Relig: United Methodist; chmn comt on social concerns, First United Methodist Church, Chanute, Kans. Mailing Add: 230 S Kansas Chanute KS 66720

POTTER, CHARLES EDWARD **(R)**
b Lapeer, Mich, Oct 30, 16; s Fred Potter & Sarah Elizabeth Converse P; m to Mary Elizabeth Bryant Wismer; c Henry Richards Wismer (deceased) & Wendy Wismer. Educ: Eastern Mich Univ, AB, 38. Hon Degrees: LLD, Eastern Mich Univ, 54, Hillside Col, Mich, 55. Polit & Govt Pos: Adminr, Bur Soc Aid, Cheboygan Co, Mich, 38-42; voc rehabilitation adv, Retraining & Reemployment Admin, Washington, DC, 46-47; US Rep, Mich, 47-52; US Sen, Mich, 52-59. Bus & Prof Pos: Real estate broker, securities broker & bus consult; vpres, Int Develop & Eng Corp; dir, Nat Capitol Life Ins Co; pres, Charles & Potter Co, 65-; sr partner, Potter & Kornmeier Int, currently. Mil Serv: Army, Maj, discharged 46; 28th Inf Div, wounded at Colmar, France, 45; decorated Silver Star; French Croix de Guerre with Silver Star; Purple Heart with two clusters. Publ: Days of shame, 65. Mem: Nat Rehab Asn (dir); Am Legion; DAV; Elks; Kiwanis. Honors & Awards: Goodwill Award, 57; Nat Rehabilitation Asn Pres Award, 54; VFW Award, 51; Hero of Month, DAV, 51; Named by US Jr CofC One of Ten Outstanding Young Men in Am, 51. Relig: Methodist. Legal Res: 5221 Kenewood Ave Chevy Chase MD 20015 Mailing Add: 1140 Connecticut Ave NW Washington DC 20036

POTTER, DAVID SAMUEL **(R)**
Under Secy Navy
b Seattle, Wash, Jan 16, 25; parents deceased; m 1945 to Juanita Mae Beck; c Diana (Mrs Paul Bankston); Janice, Tom & Bill. Educ: Yale Univ, BS Physics, 45; Univ Wash, PhD Physics, 51. Polit & Govt Pos: Asst Secy Navy Research & Develop, 73-74, Under Secy Navy, 74- Bus & Prof Pos: Jr physicist, Applied Res Lab, Univ Wash, 46-49, proj physicist, 50-53, sr physicist, 53-55, asst dir, 55-60; head sea opers dept, Defense Research Labs, Gen Motors Corp, 60-66, dir, 66-69, chief engr AC Electronics Div, 69-73, dir R&D, Detroit Diesel Allison Div, 73. Mil Serv: Entered as Seaman 3/C, Navy, 43, released as Ens, 46, after serv in Navy V-12 Prog, Yale Univ & USS Mount Katmai (AE-16). Publ: Publ over 30 prof publns, primarily in ocean sci & technol. Mem: Nat Acad Eng; Am Physical Soc; Acoustical Soc Am; Marine Technol Soc. Mailing Add: 1201 Ina Lane McLean VA 22101

POTTER, IRWIN LEE **(R)**
b Tower City, Pa, Oct 5, 09; s Harry Stewart Potter & Emma Wagner P; m 1928 to Dulcie H Horner; c Alan Lee. Educ: Southeastern Univ. Polit & Govt Pos: Chmn, Arlington Co Rep Comt, Va, 48-50 & Va Tenth Cong Rep Dist, 50-52; Rep cand, Va State Legis, 49; spec asst to Secy of Labor James P Mitchell, 54-55; asst to chmn, Rep Nat Comt, 55-66; chmn, Va Rep State Comt, 56-62; Rep Nat Committeeman, Va, 64-72; exec dir, Rep Cong Boosters Club; deleg, Rep Nat Comt, 68. Bus & Prof Pos: Partner, Potter & Wilt, 56-, Lee-Hi Indust Park, 63- & Maplewood Assocs; dir, Arlington Trust Co, Inc, 58- & Am Realty Trust, 66-; gen partner, Crystal Plaza Assocs, 66-; chmn bd, Frank R Jelleff, Inc, currently; pres, I Lee Potter Assocs, Inc, currently; mem bd, Wolf Trap Found for the Performing Arts, currently. Mem: Washington Golf & Country Club; Capitol Hill Club; AFL-CIO, Local 161, AFofM; Ctr Washington Cent Labor Coun, AFL-CIO. Relig: Baptist. Legal Res: 3120 N Wakefield St Arlington VA 22207 Mailing Add: 300 New Jersey Ave SE Washington DC 20003

POTTER, JOHN MELVIN **(R)**
b Wisconsin Rapids, Wis, Aug 16, 24; s Roy M Potter & Ruth C Crowns P; m 1951 to Kathleen Reeths; c Kevin, John & Greg. Educ: Univ Wis, LLB, 48; Phi Alpha Delta; Beta Theta Pi. Polit & Govt Pos: Deleg, Rep State Conv, Wis, 47-50 & 52-65; dist chmn, Young Rep, 48-50; dist attorney, Wood Co, 50-57; mem, Gov Comt on Cranberry Probs, Wis, 59; Wis State Sen, 61-65, chmn, Senate Rep Caucus, 63-64; deleg, Rep Nat Conv, 64, alt deleg, 72; chmn, Gov Conf on Water Probs, Wis, 65-66; chmn, State Bd Natural Resources, 69 & 70. Bus & Prof Pos: Partner, Graves, Casey & Potter, 48-52; pvt law practice, 52-61; partner, Brazeau, Brazeau, Potter & Cole, 61-66; partner, Potter, Wefel & Nettesheim, 67- Mil Serv: Entered as Pvt, Marine Corps, 43, released as 2nd Lt, 45, reentered 51, released as 1st Lt, 52. Mem: Wis Cranberry Growers; Elks; Kiwanis; Am Legion. Relig: Catholic. Mailing Add: 950 First Ave S Wisconsin Rapids WI 54494

POTTER, ORLANDO B **(D)**
b Ossining, NY, Jan 11, 28; s Frederick A Potter & Irene McWilliams P; m 1956 to Rose Ann Early; c Ann Brandreth & Matthew Early. Educ: Hamilton Col, BA, 50; Yale Univ, MA, 55; Am Univ, Washington, DC, 69; Pi Delta Epsilon; Delta Upsilon. Polit & Govt Pos: Legis asst to Sen Claiborne Pell, RI, 62-68; Dem-Liberal cand for US Rep, 68; admin consult to secy, US Senate, 69-75; staff dir, Fed Elec Comn, 75- Bus & Prof Pos: Reporter, Watertown Times, NY, 50; copy ed, Nippon Times, Tokyo, 52; ed writer & Washington correspondent, Providence J-Bull, RI, 55-62. Mil Serv: Army, 50-52, serv as Combat correspondent, Pac Stars & Stripes, Korea. Honors & Awards: Cong Staff Fel, Am Polit Sci Asn, 69. Relig: Protestant. Legal Res: Brandreth Park Long Lake NY 12847 Mailing Add: 4519 Klingle St NW Washington DC 20016

POTTER, PATRICIA RADCLIFF **(D)**
b Atlanta, Ga, Sept 17, 29; d Vincent Paul Radcliff & Mable Brock R; m 1957 to Robert Joseph Potter; c Robert Lee, Elizabeth Julian, Christina Bryan & Thomas Brock. Educ: WGa Col, AA, 49; Ga State Col for Women, BA, 51; Univ Nev, Reno, 69-71; honor bd, YWCA Cabinet, 50. Polit & Govt Pos: Staff mem, Sen Richard B Russell, 54-57; vol, Stevenson for President Washington Off, 56; pres, Ormsby Co Dem Women's Club, Nev, 64-66; chairperson, Northern Nev McGovern Reform Comn, 69; mem platform comt, Nev Dem State Conv, 70; vchairperson, Nev State Dem Cent Comt, 70-72, mem, 72-74; deleg & mem rules comt, Dem Nat Conv, 72; mem, Carson City Co Dem Cent Comt, 72-74; chairperson,

Carson City Co Park & Recreation Comn, 75-; mem, Nev Affirmative Action Comt, currently. Bus & Prof Pos: Teacher high sch, Lithonia, Ga, 51-53, jr high sch, Bladensburg, Md, 53-54, high sch, McLouth, Kans, 57-58, Mildred Bray Elem Sch, Carson City, Nev, 68-73 & Carson City Jr High Sch, 74- Mem: Carson City Co Teachers Asn; Nev State Teachers Asn; Nat Educ Asn; St Theresa's Parents Club; DAR. Relig: Presbyterian. Mailing Add: 1555 W King St Kings Canyon Rd Carson City NV 89701

POTTER, THOMAS EUGENE (R)
Chmn, Rep State Exec Comt, WVa
b Pittsburgh, Pa, June 20, 33; s Eugene William Potter (deceased) & Dorothy Studebaker P; m 1956 to Nancy Elizabeth Rapp; c Sharon Lynn, Barton Carl & Matthew Eugene. Educ: WVa Univ, AB, 55 & LLB, 57; Phi Alpha Delta; Sigma Phi Epsilon; Mountain; Sphinx; Fi Batar Cappar. Polit & Govt Pos: Pres, Young Rep Club, Kanawha Co, WVa, 63; chmn, Bd of Zoning Appeals, Charleston, 65-66; vchmn, Rep Revival in WVa, 65-66; city solicitor, Charleston, 67-68; mem, Munic Planning Comn, 67-68; WVa State Deleg, 67-74; chmn, Rep State Exec Comt, WVa, 68-; mem, Rep Nat Comt, 68-; deleg-at-lg, Rep Nat Conv, 72. Bus & Prof Pos: Lawyer & partner, Woodroe, Kizer & Steed, 60-68 & Jackson, Kelly, Holt & O'Farrell, 69- Mil Serv: Entered as 2nd Lt, Air Force, 57, released as 1st Lt, 60, after serv in Judge Adv Gen Off; Capt, Air Force Res, 68. Mem: Kanawha Co Legal Aid Soc; Kanawha Co, WVa & Am Bar Asns; Charleston Tennis Club. Honors & Awards: Named Young Man of the Year by Charleston Jr CofC. Relig: Presbyterian. Legal Res: 2 Bendcrest Charleston WV 25314 Mailing Add: 1601 Kanawha Valley Bank Bldg Charleston WV 25301

POTTER, WILLIAM SAMUEL (D)
b Clarksburg, WVa, Jan 10, 05; s Dorsey Read Potter & May Wheat P; m 1930 to Alice H Harvey; c Mary (Mrs Kitchel), Florence (Mrs Robb) & Renee (Mrs Sieglaff). Educ: Univ Va, LLB, 27; Phi Delta Phi; Order of the Coif; Phi Beta Kappa; Chi Phi. Polit & Govt Pos: Chmn, Seventh Ward, Wilmington, Del, 29; mem, Del Racing Comn, 39-45; Dem state chmn, Del, 42-45; deleg, Dem Nat Conv, 44, 52, 56, 60, 64, 68; Dem Nat Committeeman, Del, 55-72; mem, Bd of Visitors, Univ Va, currently. Bus & Prof Pos: Gen practice of law, Wilmington, Del, 27-; dir, Wilmington Trust Co, Shapdale, Inc, Hopeton Holding Co, Copeland-Andetot Found, Inc, Del Wild Lands, Inc, Del Park, Inc & Episcopal Church Sch Found, 48-; trustee, Winterthur Mus, 52- Publ: Co-auth, Delaware corporation annotated, 36. Mem: Soc of Colonial Wars; Del Racing Asn (dir); Wilmington Club; Wilmington Country Club; Farmington Country Club. Relig: Episcopal; chancellor, Episcopal Diocese of Del. Mailing Add: 5826 Kennett Pike Wilmington DE 19801

POTTINGER, J STANLEY (R)
Asst Attorney Gen Civil Rights Div, Dept of Justice
b Dayton, Ohio, Feb 13, 40; s John Paul Pottinger (deceased) & Eleanor Louise Zeller P; div; c Paul, Kathryn & Matthew. Educ: Harvard Col, BA, 62, Harvard Univ Law Sch, LLB, 65. Hon Degrees: LLB, Lincoln Univ, San Francisco, Calif, 75. Polit & Govt Pos: Campaign aide, Robert H Finch for Lt Gov of Calif, 66; gen counsel, San Francisco Co Rep Cent Comt, 67-68; assoc mem, Calif Rep State Cent Comt, 68; attorney, Region IX, Dept Health, Educ & Welfare, San Francisco, 69-70, dir, Off Civil Rights, Washington, DC, 70-73; asst attorney gen, Civil Rights Div, Dept of Justice, 73- Bus & Prof Pos: Assoc attorney, Broad, Khourie & Schultz, San Francisco, 65-69. Publ: Co-auth, Organization for local planning: the attitudes of directors, J Am Inst Planners, 1/67; auth, Book Rev of Manual of Federal Practice, Lavine & Horning, McGraw-Hill, 67, Calif Law Rev, 10/68; The drive toward equality, Change Mag, 10/72. Mem: Barristers Club, San Francisco; San Francisco & Calif State Bar Asns; Supreme Court Bar. Honors & Awards: Cert of Merit, Asn Mex-Am Educators, 72. Mailing Add: 7112 Laverock Lane Bethesda MD 20034

POTTORFF, WILLIAM THOMAS (D)
Chmn, Kit Carson Co Dem Party, Colo
b Dodge City, Kans, Nov 5, 14; parents deceased; m to Winnie C Cook; c Phyliss (Mrs Albrecht) & Sandra (Mrs Berry). Educ: Dodge City High Sch, Kans. Polit & Govt Pos: Chmn, Kit Carson Co Dem Party, Colo, currently. Bus & Prof Pos: Farmer, Stratton, Colo, currently. Mem: Rotary; Rocky Mountain Farmers Union; Colo Asn Wheat Growers. Relig: United Methodist. Mailing Add: 342 Iowa Stratton CO 80836

POTTS, DOROTHY ELLA (R)
Mem, Harris Co Exec Comt, Tex
b Muskogee, Okla, Mar 25, 21; d Abe Moore & Ella Thomas M; div; c James C, Willie L, Thomas B & Edward G. Educ: Houston Community Col, 71-73; Tex Southern Univ, 73-; Gamma Phi Delta; Orgn Rep Students. Polit & Govt Pos: Mem, Harris Co Rep Exec Comt, Tex, 68-; mem, Harris Co Pub Rels Comt, 68-; alt deleg, Rep Nat Conv, 72; mem health comt, Houston-Galveston Area Coun, 75- Mem: Life mem YWCA; Century Club; Houston CofC; UN Asn; NAACP. Honors & Awards: Awards, Nat Coun Negro Women, 72, Harris Co Rep Party, 73 & 74 & YMCA, 74. Relig: Baptist. Mailing Add: 6906 Cullen Blvd Houston TX 77021

POTTS, E D (D)
Ore State Sen
Mailing Add: 754 N E Madrone St Grants Pass OR 97526

POTTS, EDWARD ANDREW (R)
b Highland Park, Mich, Sept 20, 24; s Charles Heber Potts & Jessie Carmichael P; m 1946 to Lucille Jean Bell; c Lisa, Linda, Laura & Lyla Kathryn. Educ: Univ Mich, Ann Arbor, AB, 49; George Washington Univ, LLB, 52; Order of the Coif; Delta Theta Phi. Polit & Govt Pos: Staff vol, Nixon for President, Washington, DC, 60; Rep cand, US Rep, Fifth Dist, Md, 64; faculty adv, George Washington Univ Young Rep, 65; campaign mgr, Prince George's Co Spiro T Agnew Gubernatorial Campaign, 66; mem, Prince George Co Rep Cent Comt, 66-68; vchmn, 66-67, chmn, 67-68; chmn resolutions comt, Md Rep State Conv, 68; chmn, Nixon-Agnew, Third Legis Dist, Prince George Co, 68; chmn, Rep Founders Club Md, 68; mem, Scholars for Nixon Comt, Nixon Ballot Security Comt, Mathias for Senate Finance Comt, 68 & legis adv Comt Prince George Co Bd License Comnr, 68; spec campaign adv, Mathias for Senate, 68; consult, Off Secy & chmn, Rev Authority Civil Rights, Dept Health, Educ & Welfare, 68-; consult civil rights, US Comnr Educ, 71-; deleg, Rep Nat Conv, 72; mem, Nixon Ballot Security Comt, 74. Bus & Prof Pos: Prof law & assoc dean, Nat Law Ctr for Grad Studies, Proj & Research, George Washington Univ, 53- Mil Serv: Entered as A/S, Navy, 42, released as Aerographer's Mate, 46, after serv in USS Cabot, Fleet Air Wing 11, Naval Air Sta, NJ & SC; Capt, Naval Res, 46-; Atlantic Theatre Medal; World War II Victory Medal; Good Conduct Medal; twenty year commissioned serv with ten year hour glass device. Mem: Naval Res Off Asn; Am Legion; VFW; Prince Georges Co Rep Club; Free Masonry. Relig: Episcopal. Mailing Add: 7117 Westhaven Dr Camp Springs MD 20031

POTTS, LUCILLE BELL (R)
Prog Chmn, Nat Fedn Rep Women
b Greensburg, Pa, Mar 25, 24; d James Chester Bell & Elma Wagner B; m 1946 to Edward A Potts; c Lisa, Linda, Laurie & Lyla. Educ: Pa State Univ, 41-42; Gettysburg Col, 47; Univ Mich, AB, 49. Polit & Govt Pos: Pres, Prince Georges Co Fedn Rep Women, 65-67 & Prince Georges Co Bd Elec, 67-69; vchmn, Gov Study Comn Voc Rehabilitation, 67; prog chmn & mem bd dirs, Nat Fedn Rep Women, 69-; pres, Md Fedn Rep Women, 69-71; mem, Prince Georges Co Coun, 71-74; alt deleg, Rep Nat Conv, 72. Bus & Prof Pos: Acct, Navy Dept, Washington, DC, 49-51; substitute teacher, Prince Georges Co, Md, 62-64. Mil Serv: Entered as A/S, Navy, 44, released as SP-3, 46, after serv as Link Trainer instr, 44-46. Mem: Am Legion; Clinton Lady Lions; Nat Capital Coun Girl Scouts. Relig: Episcopal. Mailing Add: 7117 Westhaven Dr Camp Springs MD 20031

POUGH, W NEWTON (D)
VChmn, Orangeburg Co Dem Party, SC
b Orangeburg Co, SC, July 4, 21; s Willie Pough & Elizabeth Harrison P; m 1944 to Altamese Bell; c Carmen Rene. Educ: SC State Col, AB, 49, LLB, 52; Phi Beta Sigma. Polit & Govt Pos: Mem, Orangeburg Co Bar Libr Comn & Lower Savannah Region Comn; chmn bd, Orangeburg Area Ment Health; co committeeman, Orangeburg Co Dem Party, 68-72, vchmn, 72-; alt deleg, Dem Nat Conv, 72. Bus & Prof Pos: Gen coun, Hollydale Country Club & N Develop Corp, Inc, currently; assoc treas, Kahine Investment Club, Orangeburg, currently; secy-treas, Belleville Develop Corp, Orangeburg, currently; legal adv, AEAONMS & SC State Col, currently; chmn bd trustees, SC United Methodist Church Annual Conf, currently. Mil Serv: Entered as Pvt, Army Air Force, 42, released as S/Sgt, 46, after serv in 3rd Air Force, US, 42-46; Am Theatre Serv Ribbon; Good Conduct Medal; World War II Victory Medal. Mem: SC State Bar Asn; Am Trial Lawyers Asn; Mason (state grand trustee, 60-, 33 degree); Robert Shaw Consistory (comdr, 70); Shrine (past potentate). Honors & Awards: Sigma man of year, Phi Beta Sigma, 68 & 71; Outstanding achievement, Mason, 72, Shrine & Church, 73. Relig: Methodist. Legal Res: Rte 1 Belleville Rd Orangeburg SC 29115 Mailing Add: Box 1504 South Carolina State Col Orangeburg SC 29115

POULIN, RICHARD L (D)
NH State Rep
Mailing Add: Box 518 809 Kent St Berlin NH 03570

POULOS, WILLIAM FREDERIC (D)
Okla State Rep
b 1920. Educ: Univ Tex. Polit & Govt Pos: Okla State Rep, 65- Bus & Prof Pos: Securities dealer. Mem: Operation Rescue (chmn bd); Mason. Mailing Add: 505 N 70th East Ave Tulsa OK 74115

POULSEN, ANDREW W (R)
NH State Sen
b NJ, July 11, 15; s Niels Poulsen & Lilian Von Tell P; m 1938 to Greta Westin; c Philip W, Robert A, Linnea L, Margot A (Mrs Stephen Roy) & Peter N. Educ: Univ Maine, BS, 37; Xi Sigma Pi. Polit & Govt Pos: Selectman, Littleton, NH, 68-; NH State Sen, Dist 2, 71- Bus & Prof Pos: Dist supvr, US Forest Serv, 40-42; supt, Gillies Lumber Co, Waterboro, Maine, 42-45 & Champlin Lumber Co, Rochester, NH, 45-56; owner, Poulsen Lumber Co, Littleton, NH, 56-69; self-employed surveyor & forester, 69-; trustee, Franconia Col & dir, Littleton Savings Bank, currently. Mem: Elks. Relig: Congregational. Mailing Add: Littleton NH 03561

POUMELE, GALEA'I PENI (D)
Sen, Am Samoa Legis
b Fitiiuta, Manua'a, Dec 10, 24; s Poumele & Fofoa P; m 1946 to Gaoioi F Tufele; c Mrs Tai'ulagi T Asuega, Galea'i Peni, Jr, Taalolo P Galea'i, Pete P Galea'i, Seth P Galea'i, Clara P Galea'i, Tamara P Galea'i, Tasimaisaua P Galea'i & Pete P Galea'i, Jr. Educ: Admin Battery Coord AA Course, 55; LaSalle Exten Univ, home study, grad; Police Off Laws, 64-65; GMB Mil Sch, Great Lakes, Ill, 68. Polit & Govt Pos: Spec asst attorney gen, Govt Am Samoa, 67-68, parole & probation off, 67-68, spec investr, 67-68, dir civil defense, 68-70; Rep, Am Samoa Legis, 12th Dist, 71-72; Sen, Am Samoa Legis, First Dist, 72-, chmn govt oper comt, currently. Bus & Prof Pos: Contractor owner, Pala Construction Co, Am Samoa, 68-; personnel mgr, Star-Kist Samoa Inc, 71- Mil Serv: A/S, Navy, 43, released as Chief Gunners Mate, 67, after serv in Recruit Training Ctr, Amphibious Force Pac, Destroyer Force Pac, Fleet Training Command & Recruit Training Command, 55-67; World War II Victory Medal; Asiatic Pac Campaign; Good Conduct Medal; Rifle Expert Shooter; Pistol 45 Expert; Korean Campaign. Mem: Voc Sch; Comprehensive Health Planning Adv Coun, Govt Am Samoa; VFW; Safety Comt Rep; Fleet Reserve Asn. Mailing Add: Box 615 Nuu'uli American Samoa

POUNCEY, TAYLOR (INDEPENDENT)
Ill State Sen
Mailing Add: 1117 West 71st St Chicago IL 60621

POVLSEN, SHIRLEY (R)
Secy-Treas, Cassia Co Rep Cent Comt, Idaho
b Idaho Falls, Idaho, Feb 26, 27; d Rulon Ira Stoker & Louise Ellsworth S; m 1947 to Walter Charles Povlsen; c Catherine (Mrs Harwood); Robert, John, Eric & Lori. Educ: Woodbury Bus Col, 45-46. Polit & Govt Pos: Secy-treas, Cassia Co Rep Cent Comt, Idaho, 69-; treas, Fifth Region Rep Party, Idaho, 75- Bus & Prof Pos: Treas & tax collector, Cassia Co, Idaho, 69- Mem: Soroptimist Int (pres, 74-); Burley CofC (first vpres, 75-); Idaho Asn Co Treas (pres, 75-). Relig: Latter-day Saint. Legal Res: 85 Van Engelen Dr Burley ID 83318 Mailing Add: Box 983 Burley ID 83318

POWE, WILLIAM ALISON (R)
Mem, Forrest Co Rep Exec Comt, Miss
b Hattiesburg, Miss, Dec 19, 98; s William Alexander Powe & Pauline Lee P; m 1973 to Gladys T Evans; c Ellen Thomas & William A, Jr. Educ: Miss State Univ, BSci, 20; La State Univ, 21; Universidad Cent, Madrid, Spain, 26; Kappa Alpha; Lee Guard. Polit & Govt Pos: Elec comnr, Forrest Co, Miss, 68-72; mem, Forrest Co Rep Exec Comt, Miss, 68-, chmn, formerly. Bus & Prof Pos: Chemist, Guantanamo Sugar Co, Cuba, 21-24; supt of fabrication, Punta Alegre Sugar Co, 25-26; salesman, Oliver Continuous Filter Co, San Francisco, Calif, 26-34; owner, Powe Machinery Co, Havana, Cuba, 34-60; ed, Sugar J, 64-75. Mil Serv: Entered as Student, ROTC, 16, released as 2nd Lt, 21, after serv in Inf. Mem: Int & Am Soc of Sugar Cane Technologists; Miss Asn of Soil & Water Conserv Dist Comnr; Mason; Scottish Rite; Rotary. Honors & Awards: Silver Beaver Award, Boy Scouts. Relig: Episcopal. Mailing Add: 300 Sixth Ave Hattiesburg MS 39401

POWELL, ALVA LEE **(D)**
Kans State Rep
Mailing Add: 205 Brookside Dr Paola KS 66071

POWELL, AUSTIN CLIFFORD **(D)**
Mem, Frederick Co Dem Comt, Md
b Frederick, Md, Aug 11, 13; s James Kennedy Powell & Sadie Frances Meister P; m 1931 to Annabell Lee; c Edna Irene. Polit & Govt Pos: Vchmn, Md State Dem Cent Comt, 58-62, chmn, 62-66; chmn, Frederick Co Dem Comt, 68-72, mem, 72- Mem: Eagles; Moose; Jr Fire Co; Jeffersonian Dem Club. Relig: Episcopal. Mailing Add: 20 E Ninth St Frederick MD 21701

POWELL, C CLAYTON **(R)**
Mem, Ga State Rep Exec Comt
b Dothan, Ala, Apr 11, 27; s Mr Powell (deceased) & Evelyn Henderson P; m 1954 to Romae Turner; c C Clayton, Jr & Rometta E. Educ: Morehouse Col, AB; Ill Col Optom, BSc & OD; Beta Kappa Chi; Beta Sigma Kappa; Tomb & Key; Omega Psi Phi; Mu Sigma Psi. Polit & Govt Pos: Deleg, Ga State Rep Conv, 12 years; parliamentarian & mem, Ga State Rep Exec Comt, 65-; attended Presidential Inauguration, 69 & 73; deleg, Rep Nat Conv, 72; mem, Fulton Co Rep Exec Comt; chmn, Fifth Dist Rep Exec Comt; chmn Black vote div, Ga Comt to Reelect the President; spec asst to chmn, Rep Party, Ga. Bus & Prof Pos: Organizer & chmn, Metro-Atlanta OEP Study Group; chief of optom, Atlanta Southside Comprehensive Health Ctr. Publ: Glaucoma!!, Ga Optom Asn J, 9/52; The optometrist and comprehensive health centers, Am Optom Asn J, 6/71. Mem: Nat Eye Inst; Am Optom Asn (admin agencies comt, 71-73); Fifth Dist Optom Soc; Ga Optom Asn; Nat Optom Asn (pres). Honors & Awards: Outstanding Man of the Year, Clark Col, Morehouse Col, Morris Brown Col & Atlanta Grad Chap of Omega Psi Phi; Outstanding Achievement Award, Fulton Co Rep Club, Atlanta Postal Acad & Pine Acres Town & Country Club. Relig: Presbyterian. Legal Res: 403 Fielding Lane SW Atlanta GA 30311 Mailing Add: 565 Fair St SW Atlanta GA 30314

POWELL, CHARLES CARUTH **(D)**
Chmn, Coryell Co Dem Party, Tex
b Gatesville, Tex, Sept 22, 12; s William Lytle Powell, Sr & Eula Caruth P; m 1933 to Nancy Lou Routh; c Charles Caruth & William Elmo (deceased). Educ: John Tarleton State Col, 2 years. Polit & Govt Pos: Mayor, Gatesville, Tex, 56-59; chmn, Coryell Co Dem Party, 67- Bus & Prof Pos: Cotton ginner, Gatesville Gin Co, Tex, 33-69. Mem: Mason. Mailing Add: 1211 Bridge St Gatesville TX 76528

POWELL, CHARLES F **(D)**
SC State Rep
Mailing Add: Rte 4 Abbeville SC 29620

POWELL, CHARLES KENNETH **(R)**
b Greenwood, SC, Aug 11, 39; s Charles Willis Powell & Gladys Ouzts P; div. Educ: Clemson Univ, BS, 61; Univ SC, LLB, 64; Blue Key; pres, jr & sr class; mem, Student Senate; Speaker of House, SC Student Legis; chmn, Comt that Rewrote Law Sch Const. Polit & Govt Pos: Page, SC House of Rep, 61-64; speech writer & campaign aid for Floyd Spence, Rep cand for US Cong, Second Cong Dist, 62; worker, many Rep campaigns, Richland Co, SC, 62-70; cand, US House of Rep, Richland Co, 66; mem various comts for Sustaining Mem Dinners, 67-70; cand, SC State Sen, Richland Co, 68; chmn, Richland Co Rep Party, 70; chmn credentials comt, SC Rep Conv, 70; mem elec law study comt, SC Rep Party, 70, chmn, 71-75; mem, Draft Watson for Gov Comt, 70; mem, Gov Conf on Youth, 71; mem, Rep Nat Comt, 71-74. Bus & Prof Pos: Attorney, pvt practice, 64-69, Powell, Atria & Smith, formerly; sr partner, Powell & Smith, currently. Mem: SC Teenage Rep (first state adv); SC Bar Asn; Exchange Club; Mason (3 degree); Sons of Confederate Vet. Relig: Baptist; Sunday sch teacher, Shandon Baptist Church, ten years, past pres, Men's Brotherhood. Legal Res: 138 Cardiff Columbia SC 29209 Mailing Add: PO Box 5247 Columbia SC 29205

POWELL, CHARLES LEWIS **(D)**
b Ware Shoals, SC, June 18, 33; s Richard Powell & Cora Ferguson P; single. Educ: Lander Col, 55. Polit & Govt Pos: SC State Rep, until 72; alt deleg, Dem Nat Conv, 72. Bus & Prof Pos: Commercial agt, Seaboard Coast Line RR Co; farmer. Mil Serv: Army Res, 8 years. Mailing Add: RFD 4 Abbeville SC 29620

POWELL, EDWARD LEE **(R)**
Mem, NC Rep Exec Comt
b Mocksville, NC, Sept 21, 41; s Harrell Powell & Margaret Green P; m 1973 to Mary Elizabeth Bales. Educ: Univ NC, Chapel Hill, AB, 63; Wake Forest Univ Law Sch, JD, 67; Phi Delta Phi. Polit & Govt Pos: Mem, NC Rep Exec Comt, 72-; NC State Rep, 29th Dist, 72-74; NC Comnr Motor Vehicles, 75- Bus & Prof Pos: Attorney, Winston-Salem, NC, 69- Mil Serv: Entered as Pvt, Army, 67, released as SP-6, 69, after serv in Vietnam, Hq Long Binh Post, 68-69; Vietnam Campaign Medal; Vietnam Serv Medal; Nat Defense Serv Medal; Good Conduct Medal; Bronze Star Medal. Mem: NC State, NC, Forsyth Co & Forsyth Co Jr Bar Asns. Relig: Episcopal. Mailing Add: 415 S Main St Winston-Salem NC 27101

POWELL, FLOYD **(D)**
Maine State Rep
Mailing Add: Soldier Pond Wallagrass Place ME 04781

POWELL, HERBERT B **(INDEPENDENT)**
b Monmouth, Ore, July 13, 03; s Ira Clinton Powell & Lena Guenavier Butler P; m 1928 to Beryl King. Educ: Univ Ore, BS, 26; Command Gen Staff Sch, grad, 41; Nat War Col, 48-49; Phi Kappa Psi. Polit & Govt Pos: US Ambassador to New Zealand, 63-67. Mil Serv: Entered as Pvt, Ore Nat Guard, 19, released as Sgt, 26; entered as 2nd Lt, Army, 26, released as Gen, 61, after serv in Hawaii, 26-41, War Dept Gen Staff, 42, chief of staff, 75th Inf Div, European campaigns including Battle of the Bulge, 43-45, US Army Hq, Europe, 45-47, comdr, 17th Inf Regt advance on Yalu River, Korea, 50, dep G-1 manpower control & Army Gen Staff, 51-54; comdr, 25th Inf Div, 54-56, comdr US Army, Pac, 56; commandant, Army Inf Sch, Ft Benning & US Army Inf Ctr, 56-58; Dep Cmndg Gen, Res Forces, Continental Army Command, 58-60; Cmndg Gen, Third Army, 60; Cmndg Gen, Continental Army Command, 60-63; Comdr-in-Chief, Army Atlantic, Cuban Crisis, 60-63; Distinguished Serv Cross; Distinguished Serv Medal; Legion of Merit with Oak Leaf Cluster; Bronze Star with Two Oak Leaf Clusters; Air Medal; Commendation Medal; Purple Heart; Combat Inf Badge; Wings of Army Aviator; Czech War Cross; Ulch Distinguished Serv Medal; Presidential Citation, Repub Korea. Mem: Army & Navy Club; Am Foreign Serv Asn; Asn US Army; Nat Hist Soc. Relig: Episcopal. Legal Res: Little Cumberland Island GA 31520 Mailing Add: PO Box 3127 Jekyll Island GA 31520

POWELL, JERRY **(D)**
Ala State Sen
Mailing Add: PO Box 400 Eclectic AL 36024

POWELL, JOANNE **(D)**
Dem Nat Committeewoman, WVa
Mailing Add: PO Box 135 Romney WV 26757

POWELL, JOHN ALLEN **(D)**
Ore State Sen
b Lebanon, Ore, Dec 31, 47; s Melvin Kenneth Powell & Delta L Curtis P; m 1970 to Gladys Sue; c Mark A. Educ: Univ Ore, BS, 70. Polit & Govt Pos: Ore State Sen, 75- Bus & Prof Pos: Educator, Cent Linn High Sch, Ore, 70- Mailing Add: PO Box 92 Halsey OR 97348

POWELL, JOHN DUANE **(R)**
Committeeman, Mo State Rep Party
b Rolla, Mo, Dec 9, 25; s Frank Bowman Powell & Gertrude Carpenter P; m 1949 to Ruth Hawkins; c Jane, Anne & Frank Bowman. Educ: Univ Mo, Rolla, 43; Triangle. Polit & Govt Pos: Committeeman, Mo State Rep Party, 62-; treas, Phelps Co Rep Comt, 62-64 & 68-70; deleg, Rep Nat Conv, 64. Bus & Prof Pos: Secy-treas, Frank B Powell Lumber Co, currently; chmn, Adv Coun, Forestry Dept, Univ Mo, 64; chmn, Forestry Comt, Mo Conserv Fedn, 65-71; mem bd dirs, Mo State CofC, 67-71; pres, Mo Forest Prod Asn, 70-71. Mil Serv: Midn, Merchant Marine, 44-45; Pac Theater Ribbon. Mem: Rolla Lions (pres, 61); Rolla CofC (vpres, 54). Honors & Awards: Forest Conserv of the Year Award, Conserv Fedn Mo, Sears Found & Nat Wildlife Fedn, 68; Cert of Merit in Forestry, Univ Mo, 68; received Bronze Medallion & Centennial Cert, Univ Mo Sch of Agr, 70; Regional Tree Farmer of the Year, 74. Relig: Episcopal. Legal Res: 605 W 11th St Rolla MO 65401 Mailing Add: PO Box 576 Rolla MO 65401

POWELL, JOHN WILLIAM **(D)**
Miss State Sen
b Liberty, Miss, Mar 4, 28; s John Wesley Powell & Nan Bond P; m 1965 to Martha Ann Burris; c John Wesley. Educ: Southwest Miss Jr Col, Summit. Polit & Govt Pos: Miss State Sen, 60-; mem, Citizens Coun, presently. Bus & Prof Pos: Self-employed in cattle & timber. Mem: Mason; Shrine; Eastern Star; Miss Cattleman Asn; Farm Bur. Relig: Baptist. Mailing Add: Rte 2 Box 153 Liberty MS 39645

POWELL, KATHRYN (KATE) **(R)**
Finance Chmn, Mo State Rep Women's Fedn
b Calhoun, Mo, Sept 29, 07; d James Palistine Doss & Agnes Mae Mason D; m 1945 to Weston Powell, wid, 1963. Educ: Univ Mo, Midwest study seminar on US & Japan Rels, 66. Polit & Govt Pos: Davis Twp Committeewoman, Mo, currently; secy & membership chmn, Lafayette Co Federated Women's Rep Club, Mo, 60-62; secy, Fourth Dist Women's Federated Club, 60-64; state finance chmn, Mo State Rep Women's Fedn, currently, deleg, last three Nat Fedn Conv; vchmn, Lafayette Co Rep Cent Comt, 62-66 & 70-74; Mo Out State chmn, Wash Conf, 63; mem, Mo State Rep Comt, currently, mem, Budget Comt, 64-, vchmn, Mo State Rep Party, 64-66, chmn, 66; voted electoral col vote for Fourth Dist of Mo for Nixon-Agnew, 68; deleg, Mo State Rep Conv, 72; deleg, Rep Nat Conv, 72; bd mem, Three Co Show Me Regional Planning Comn, Coun on Aging, currently; app mem, Zoning Adjust Bd, Higginsville, currently; mem, Higginsville City Coun, 73-, chmn, Street Dept, mem, Admin Finance & Purchasing Bd, mem, Fire & Ambulance Bd & voting deleg, Show-Me Regional Planning Comn, currently. Bus & Prof Pos: Farm operator, Higginsville, Mo, formerly; columnist, Of Interest to Women, Lafayette Co Farm Bur Paper. Mem: Bus & Prof Women; Higginsville Park Bd; Rebekah Lodge 678 (Past Noble Grand); Farm Bur; Mo Farm Orgn. Honors & Awards: Livestock competition awards; invited to ride matched pair of parade horses in Cow Palace & Rose Bowl Parades; Gold Key Award, Nat Fedn of Rep Women; first woman in Mo & second in US to hold state chairmanship of Rep Party; first woman to be app to Zoning Adjust Bd of Higginsville. Relig: Christian Church. Mailing Add: 500 W 32nd St Higginsville MO 64037

POWELL, LEWIS F, JR
Assoc Justice, US Supreme Court
b Suffolk, Va, Sept 19, 07; m 1936 to Josephine Pierce Rucker; c Mrs Richard S Smith, Mrs Basil T Carmody, Mrs Christopher J Sumner & Lewis F, III. Educ: Washington & Lee Univ, BS magna cum laude, 29 & LLB, 31; Harvard Univ Law Sch, LLM, 32; Phi Beta Kappa. Polit & Govt Pos: Chmn spec comn which wrote mgr form of govt charter, Richmond, Va, 47-48; chmn, Richmond Pub Sch Bd, 52-61; mem, Va State Bd Educ, 61-69, pres, 68-69; mem, Nat Adv Comt on Legal Serv to the Poor, 65-66, mem, Nat Comn Law Enforcement & Admin of Justice, 65-67; mem, Va Const Rev Comn, 67-68; mem, Blue Ribbon Defense Panel to Study Dept of Defense, 69-70; assoc justice, US Supreme Court, 72- Bus & Prof Pos: Partner, Hunton, Williams, Gay, Powell & Gibson, Richmond, Va, 32-71; gen counsel, Colonial Williamsburg Found, mem bd trustees, 55-; mem bd trustees, Washington & Lee Univ, 64- Mil Serv: Entered as Lt, Army Air Force, 42, released as Col, 46, after serv in 319th Bombardment Group, 12th Air Force & Chief of Oper Intel, Strategic Air Forces, European & NAfrican Theatres; Legion of Merit; Bronze Star; Croix de Guerre with Palm. Mem: Am Bar Asn; Am Col Trial Lawyers; Am Bar Found. Honors & Awards: Hon Bencher, Lincoln's Inn, London. Legal Res: VA Mailing Add: US Supreme Court Washington DC 20543

POWELL, MARTHA BROWN **(R)**
Chmn, Isle of Wight Co Rep Party, Va
b Battery Park, Va, Sept 5, 26; d Robert Elmer Brown & Josie Lee Whitley B; m 1945 to James Melvin Powell, Sr; c Jacqueline Faye (Mrs Beacham), James Melvin, Jr (deceased) & Patricia Luellen; one grandchild. Educ: Smithfield High Sch, Va, grad, 44. Polit & Govt Pos: Organizer, Isle of Wight Co Rep Women's Club, 61, chmn, currently; alt deleg, Rep Nat Conv, 64, deleg & credentials chmn, 68; chmn, Isle of Wight Co Rep Party, 64-68 & 70-, secy, 68-70; former Fourth Dist rep, Va Fedn of Rep, second vpres, 72-74; eastern vchairwoman, Va Rep Party, 68-72. Bus & Prof Pos: Secy, R E Brown & Sons, 59-; off helper, Little's Supermkt, Smithfield, Va, 69-; agt, Div Motor Vehicles, Smithfield, Va, 73-74. Mem: Smithfield Recreation Asn; UDC. Relig: Pentecostal. Mailing Add: RFD 1 Box 75 A Carrollton VA 23314

POWELL, MARTIN E (R)
Vt State Rep
Mailing Add: Essex Center VT 05451

POWELL, MOZELLE JUANITA (D)
b Norfolk, Va, Dec 23, 43; d Wilson R Cole & Barbare Goodman C; m 1964 to Wendell Allen Powell; c Carl Arthur, Sharon Leigh & Allen Dee. Educ: Portsmouth Bus Col, 63-64. Polit & Govt Pos: Alt deleg, Dem Nat Conv, 72. Mem: UAW (committeeman, Local 1091, 67-70, chmn, 70-, pres, 71-); Ark State UAW (vchmn, Community Action Prog, 71-). Relig: Baptist. Legal Res: PO Box 263 Hope AR 71801 Mailing Add: Box 174 Rte 4 Hope AR 71801

POWELL, RICHARD EUGENE (R)
b Chicago, Ill, Sept 19, 47; s Raymond Henry Powell & Olivia Dotson P; m 1970 to Janet Louise Fuller. Educ: Ball State Univ, BS, 69; Alpha Phi Gamma; Sigma Delta Chi; Lambda Chi Alpha. Polit & Govt Pos: Press asst, US Rep David W Dennis, Ind, 70-72, admin asst, 73-75. Bus & Prof Pos: Staff reporter, The Muncie Star, Ind, 68-70. Relig: Protestant. Legal Res: Box 154 RR 7 Anderson IN 46011 Mailing Add: 3328 Gunston Rd Alexandria VA 22302

POWELL, ROBERT S (R)
Del State Rep
Mailing Add: 5455 Crestline Rd Wilmington DE 19808

POWELL, STANLEY M (R)
Mich State Rep
b Ionia, Mich, July 7, 98; married; c Patricia Ann, Ronald Herbert, Larry Burton, Rex Lynn. Educ: Mich State Univ, BS, 20; Pi Kappa Delta; Delta Sigma Rho. Polit & Govt Pos: Mich State Rep, 30-32 & 64-; mem, Mich State Fair Authority, 44-64; deleg, Const Conv, 61-62. Bus & Prof Pos: Farmer; served as legis counsel & dir pub affairs, Mich Farm Bur, 21-27 & 38-64; contrib ed, Mich Farmer Mag, 27-65. Mil Serv: World War I. Mem: Am Milking Shorthorn Soc; Farm Bur; Grange; Am Legion; Vets of World War I of the USA. Honors & Awards: Awarded citations & plaques by Mich State Univ, Mich Farm Bur, Mich State Grange, Mich Future Farmers of Am & Mich Asn of Teachers of Voc Agr. Relig: Baptist. Mailing Add: RFD 1 Box 238 Ionia MI 48846

POWELL, WALTER E (R)
b Hamilton, Ohio, Apr 25, 31; s Walter Powell (deceased) & Anna Parker P; m to Bobbi Powell; c Loren David & Stephen Walter. Educ: Heidelberg Col, BA in Hist, 53; Miami Univ (Ohio), MEd in Educ Admin, 61. Polit & Govt Pos: Clerk, City of Fairfield, Ohio, 56, mem, City Coun, 58; Ohio State Rep, Butler Co, 61-67; Ohio State Sen, Fourth Sen Dist, 67-70, vchmn, Finance Comt, Ohio State Senate; US Rep, Eighth Dist, Ohio, 71-75; chmn, Miami Valley Cong Coun, Ohio; treas, Ohio Cong Deleg. Bus & Prof Pos: Educator for 17 years as teacher, Fairfield Jr High Sch & prin, Fairfield W & Hopewell Elem Schs. Mem: Civitan Int (past Ohio gov); Fairfield CofC (charter mem); Butler Co Farm Bur. Honors & Awards: Man of Year, Fairfield, 59; Ky Col; One of Five Outstanding Freshmen Ohio Legis, 61; Doer's Award, Ohio Educ Asn, 65 & 67; Watchdog of the Treas Award, 72. Relig: Presbyterian; elder, Presby Church, Hamilton. Mailing Add: 6671 Wooden Shoe Dr Middletown OH 45042

POWELL, WESLEY (R)
b Portsmouth, NH, Oct 13, 15; s Samuel Wesley Powell & Mary Gosse P; m 1942 to Beverly Swain; c Samuel, Peter & Nancy. Educ: Univ NH; Southern Methodist Univ Col Law. Polit & Govt Pos: Asst to US Sen Styles Bridges; staff dir, US Sen, Comt on Appropriation & other comts, 40-43 & 46-49; Gov, NH, 59-63; chmn, US Gov Conf, 60-63; chmn, New Eng Gov Conf, 61-62. Bus & Prof Pos: Lawyer, publisher & businessman, 63- Mil Serv: Army Air Corps, Bomber Command, ETO. Mailing Add: Hampton Falls NH 03844

POWER, DOROTHY K (D)
Committeewoman, NJ Dem State Comt
b Elizabeth, NJ, July 14, 32; d Benjamin William Kanzler & Alice Bogda K; m 1954 to Edward J J Power; c Luisa (Mrs Brown), Maureen, Bonnie & Jenifer. Educ: Berkeley Secretarial Sch, East Orange, NJ, grad, 51. Polit & Govt Pos: Committeewoman, Middlesex Co Dem Orgn, NJ, 65-; vchmn, 70-74; legis secretarial aide, NJ State Assembly, Dist 17, 72-73; munic vchmn, Piscataway Dem Orgn, 68-70; committeewoman, NJ Dem State Comt, 74-; deleg, Dem Nat Mid-Term Conf, 74. Bus & Prof Pos: Mgt asst, Am Tel & Tel Co, 70- Publ: Ed, Treasury topics, monthly column, Am Tel & Tel Treas Dept, 75- Mem: Family Serv Asn Middlesex Co (bd dirs, 70-); Nat Secretaries Asn. Relig: Roman Catholic. Mailing Add: 304 Patton Ave Piscataway NJ 08854

POWER, MARY SUSAN (R)
VChairwoman, Craighead Co Rep Party, Ark
b Hazleton, Pa; d Dr Younger Lovelace Power & Cleo Boock P; single; c Catherine Laverne. Educ: Wells Col, BA, 57; Stanford Univ, MA, 59; Univ Ill, PhD, 61; attended Univ Exeter & Yale Univ Grad Sch. Polit & Govt Pos: Committeewoman, Snyder Co Rep Comt, Pa, 61-64; adv, Ark State Young Rep, 68-72; mem, Ark Rep Coun Arts & Sci, 70; deleg, Ark Rep State Conv, 70-72; vchairwoman, Craighead Co Rep Party, 71-; alt deleg, Rep Nat Conv, 72; secy, Rep Dist Comt, 72; coordr, Reelect the President, Craighead Co, 72; cong campaign cand comt & rep, Ark Fedn Rep Women, First Cong Dist; committeewoman, Ark Rep State Comt, 74- Bus & Prof Pos: Asst prof, Susquehanna Univ, 61-65; assoc prof, Univ Ark, 65-68 & Ark State Univ, 68-72. Publ: John Dickinson: freedom, protest, change, Susquehanna Studies, 71; John Dickinson: the Fabius Letters, Mod Age, 72. Mem: Am Asn Univ Prof; Am Polit Sci Asn; Phi Sigma Alpha. Relig: Lutheran. Mailing Add: 1922 Westwood Dr Jonesboro AR 72401

POWERS, ANNA BERTHA JOSEPHINE (D)
NDak State Rep
b Leonard, NDak, July 10, 12; d Julius Anderson & Inga Verding A; m 1930 to Edward Lancing Powers. Educ: Leonard High Sch, grad, 30; Leonard Adult Classes, 60. Polit & Govt Pos: Precinct committeeman, Dem Party, NDak, 50-; pres, NDak Dem Non-Partisan League Woman's Club, 60-; NDak State Rep, 61-66, 73-, vchmn social welfare comt, NDak House of Rep, 65; committeeman, NDak State Dem Cent Comt, 61-; mem, NDak Gov Comn on Status of Women, 63; deleg, Dem Nat Conv, 64; mem, Citizen's Adv Comt Hwy Beautification, 70-; NDak State Health Coun, 71-; pres, Provincial Women's Bd N, 71- Mem: Leonard Cemetery Asn (pres); Maple River Homemaker's Club; Region V Sr Citizen Coun (pres, 74-); Cass Co Sr Citizen Coun on Aging (pres, 73-). Relig: Moravian; elected to Provincial Women's Bd, Northern Prov, 66-, vpres, 69-; elder, local Moravian Church. Mailing Add: Leonard ND 58052

POWERS, ARTHUR B (D)
b New York, NY, June 28, 28; s Arthur Prosser Powers & Helen Boyd P; m Maryanne Thomas; c Arthur B, Jr, Juliann, Martha Grace, Christopher Stephen & Rebecca Elizabeth. Educ: Tufts Col; Tower Cross. Polit & Govt Pos: Chmn, Berlin Town Dem Party, Conn, 55-61; Conn State Rep, 59-61; first selectman, Berlin, Conn, 59-73, mayor, 73-; spec asst to US Sen Thomas J Dodd, Conn, 61-68; state chmn, Elec of Dem Legislators, 62; comnr, State Water Resources Comn, 63-72; campaign mgr for Rep Bernard Grabowski, 64 & for US Rep Ella T Grasso, Sixth Dist, Conn, 70; alt deleg, Dem Nat Conv, 64 & 72, deleg, 68; mem, Conn State Dem Cent Comt, 66-68. Bus & Prof Pos: Pres, Francis Maloney Ins Agency, Inc, 56; dir, Burritt Mutual Savings Bank, currently. Mem: New Britain YMCA (corporator); New Britain Gen Hosp (corporator). Relig: Protestant. Mailing Add: 857 Worthington Ridge Berlin CT 06037

POWERS, GEORGIA DAVIS (D)
Ky State Sen
b Springfield, Ky, Oct 29, 23; d Ben Montgomery & Frances Walker M; m 1973 to James L Powers; c William F Davis & Deborah P (Mrs Rattle) & Cheryl & Carlton Powers. Educ: Louisville Munic Col, 2 years. Polit & Govt Pos: Ky State Sen, 68- Bus & Prof Pos: Restaurant owner, 69-; owner coin laundry & cleaners, 70- Mem: YWCA; Louisville Urban League; NAACP. Honors & Awards: Kennedy-King Award, Young Dem Ky, 68; Alpha Kappa Alpha Award, 70; Zeta Phi Beta Award, 71. Relig: Protestant. Mailing Add: 733 Cecil Ave Louisville KY 40211

POWERS, JOHN E (D)
b South Boston, Mass, Nov 1, 10; m to Dorothy M Hutton; c John E, Jr & Dorothy (Mrs Richard Kelly); five grandchildren. Educ: Suffolk Univ Law Sch, JD, 69. Polit & Govt Pos: Mass State Rep, 39-46; Mass State Sen, 46-64; clerk, Mass Supreme Judicial Court, Suffolk Co, 64-; deleg, Dem Nat Conv, 68 & 72; Dem Nat Committeeman, Mass, 68-72; mem, Comn for Revision of Conv, Procedures & Rules for 1972 Dem Nat Conv, 69-72. Mem: Am, Mass & Boston Bar Asns. Relig: Catholic. Mailing Add: 158 M St South Boston MA 02127

POWERS, JOHN PIKE (D)
Tex State Rep
b Houston, Tex, May 1, 41; s John Pike Powers, Sr & Mary Groves P; m 1968 to Pamela Ann Honea. Educ: Lamar Univ, BA in Govt, 62; Southern Methodist Univ Law Sch, 62-63; Univ Tex Law Sch, JD, 65; Phi Delta Phi; Blue Key; Pi Kappa Alpha. Polit & Govt Pos: Tex State Rep, 72- Bus & Prof Pos: Attorney & partner, Strong, Pipkin, Nelson, Parker & Powers, Beaumont, Tex, 66- Mil Serv: Entered as Seaman Recruit, Coast Guard Res, 65, released as E-6, 71, after serv in Organized Res Training Unit, Port Security (operational), 65-71; Outstanding Reservist, 69. Mem: Am Bar Asn; Maritime Law Asn; Tex Asn Defense Counsel; Lions; State Jr Bar Tex (pres, 74-75). Honors & Awards: Outstanding Young Lawyer, Jefferson Co, 70; Outstanding Young Man, Beaumont Jaycees, 73; Boss of the Year, Beaumont Legal Secretaries Asn, 73; One of Five Outstanding Young Texans, Tex Jaycees, 73. Relig: Presbyterian. Legal Res: 2420 Harrison Beaumont TX 77702 Mailing Add: PO Box 1671 Beaumont TX 77704

POWERS, LAWRENCE F (D)
Vt State Rep
Mailing Add: North Bennington VT 05257

POWERS, WILLIAM MASTIN (D)
b McKenzie, Tenn, Sept 19, 13; s Mastin C Powers & Authea Greene P; m to Nevin M Bowles; c Paulette. Educ: Austin Peay State Univ; Mid Tenn State Univ, BS; Loyola Univ (La), DDS; Delta Sigma. Polit & Govt Pos: Field rep, Sixth Cong Dist for US Rep William R Anderson, Tenn, 65-73; chmn, Sixth Dist Dem Orgn, 66-68; chmn, Montgomery Co Dem, 72-75. Bus & Prof Pos: Pres, United Serv Orgn Operating Coun, 72-73, deleg, Nat Conv, 72-73. Mil Serv: Released as Capt in Army Dent Corps, 45; recalled as Capt, 54-56. Mem: Scottish Rite; Mason (32 degree, pres, Montgomery Co, 58); Shriner; Civitan Club; Am Legion; Farm Bur. Relig: Presbyterian; deacon, 71- Legal Res: 2134 Dogwood Lane Clarksville TN 37040 Mailing Add: 1722 Memorial Dr Clarksville TN 37040

POWERS, WILLIAM SHOTWELL (R)
b Elizabeth, NJ, June 7, 10; s James P Powers & May Statts P; m 1940 to Arlene Morrison Crane; c Jean P & Patricia C. Educ: Rutgers Univ, BS in Bus, 33, LLB, 36; Delta Upsilon. Polit & Govt Pos: Various pos, Rep Party, 33-; Colo State Sen, 55-56; Rep Nat Committeeman, Colo, 60-72. Bus & Prof Pos: Attorney & partner, Rothgerber Appel & Powers, 46- Mil Serv: Entered as Lt, Army, 40; released as Col, 46, after serv in Western Pac Area; Legion of Merit; Bronze Star; Pac Theater Ribbon; Col, Army Res. Mem: Am & Denver Colo Bar Asns; Am Legion; VFW. Relig: Presbyterian. Mailing Add: 745 S Steel St Denver CO 80209

POYNTER, BILL CHARLES (R)
Chmn, Miller Co Rep Comt, Ark
b Hillman, Ark, Sept 27, 35; s Sidney H Poynter & Nina Holman P; m 1956 to Martha Carolyn Scoggins; c Cynthia Ann, Janice Carolyn & Karen Elizabeth. Educ: Ark Polytech Col, BS in Sci & Math, 57; Nat Mil Honor Soc; Sci & Math Club. Polit & Govt Pos: Pres, Texarkana Young Rep, Ark, 62-63; deleg, Rep Nat Conv & Ark State Rep Conv, 64; chmn, Miller Co Rep Comt, Ark, 64-; mem, Ark Rep State Cent Comt, 64-66 & 70-; chmn, Miller Co Elec Comn, currently, exec secy, 70; mem, Texarkana Planning Comn, 70- Bus & Prof Pos: Geologist, Scoggins Independent Oil, 58-62; independent oil operator, 62-; trustee, Southern State Col, presently; mem, Interstate Oil Compact Comn, presently. Mil Serv: 2nd Lt, Army, 57-58; 1st Lt, 19th Corps, Army Res, 58-65. Mem: Shreveport Geol Soc; Kiwanis Int (bd dirs, Texarkana Club, vpres, 71-72); Am Red Cross (mem bd dir, Four State Chap). Relig: Baptist. Mailing Add: 11 Regency Texarkana AR 75501

PRAHINSKI, LEO FRANCIS XAVIER (D)
b Upper Darby, Pa, July 30, 41; s Arthur Leopold Prahinski & Dorothy Killian P; m 1965 to Margaret Elizabeth Stohr; c Kathleen Anne & Leo Dismas. Educ: Univ Md, College Park, BS, 66; Univ Md Law Sch, Baltimore, JD, 70; Delta Theta Phi; Newman Club. Polit & Govt Pos: Treas, Vol for Royal Hart Cong Campaign, 70-71; precinct chmn, Dem Party, College Park, Md, 71-; mem, College Park Citizen's Adv Bd, 71-; chmn, Prince George's Citizens for McGovern, 72; alt deleg, Dem Nat Conv, 72. Bus & Prof Pos: Contract adminr, Bendix Field Eng, 66-67; claims adjustor, State Farm Ins, 67-71; attorney-at-law, 71- Mem: Md & Prince

George's Bar Asns; College Park-Adelphi Jaycees (pres, 73-, state dir, 71-72); Eagles; Elks. Relig: Catholic. Mailing Add: 9525 49th Ave College Park MD 20740

PRAHL, NORMAN (DFL)
Minn State Rep
Mailing Add: Box 8 Keewatin MN 55753

PRANGER, ROBERT JOHN (INDEPENDENT)
b Waukesha, Wis, Nov 6, 31; s John William Pranger & Alpha Rasmussen P; m 1960 to Charlotte Gifford Evans; c Benjamin Charles, Melissa Claire & Christopher James. Educ: San Diego State Col, 49-52; Univ Calif, Berkeley, BA, 53, MA, 57, PhD, 61; Phi Beta Kappa. Polit & Govt Pos: Dep asst secy of defense for int security affairs, Dept of Defense, 69-71. Bus & Prof Pos: Instr polit sci, Univ Ill, Urbana, 60-61, asst prof, 61-65; asst prof, Univ Ky, 65-66, assoc prof, 66-68; lectr, Univ Calif, Berkeley, 66; assoc prof, Univ Wash, 69-71; resident scholar, Am Enterprise Inst, Washington, DC, 71-72, dir foreign & defense policy studies, 72- Mil Serv: Entered as Pvt, Army, 54, released as SP-3, 55, after serv in G-2, Caribbean, 54-55. Publ: Eclipse of Citizenship, Holt, 68; American Policy for Peace in the Middle East, 1969-1971, 71 & Defense Implications of International Indeterminacy, 72, Am Enterprise Inst; plus others. Mem: Am Polit Sci Asn. Honors & Awards: Woodrow Wilson fel, 59-60; Soc Sci Research Coun fel, 62-63; Meritorious Civilian Medal, Dept of Defense, 70, Meritorious Civilian Medal with Bronze Palm, 71. Relig: Protestant. Mailing Add: 4512 33rd St N Arlington VA 22207

PRATHER, ELLEN GENEVIEVE LOGAN (D)
Chmn, Linn Co Dem Cent Comt, Mo
b Hutchinson, Kans, July 29, 05; d Marcus Monroe Logan & Sarah Ellen Harris L; m 1922 to George Walter Prather; c Elizabeth Ann (Mrs Ellsberry), one grandchild. Educ: Browning High Sch. Polit & Govt Pos: Committeewoman, Linn Co Dem Party, Mo, 46-; deleg, Mo Dem State Convs, 46-; vchmn, Linn Co Dem Cent Comt, 66-74, chmn, 74-; past pres, Women's Dem Club. Bus & Prof Pos: Clerk, Post Off, 42; news reporter, Browning Leader Rec, Milan Standard & Daily News Bull. Mem: DAR; Am Legion Auxiliary; Browning Garden Club (secy); Rural Fire Asn; Woman Soc Christian Serv (pres). Relig: United Methodist; mem church bd & Sunday sch teacher, Browning United Methodist Church. Mailing Add: RR 3 Box 1 FF Browning MO 64630

PRATHER, JOSEPH W (D)
Ky State Sen
Mailing Add: 106 West Main St Vine Grove KY 40175

PRATT, JOHN ALDEN (R)
Chmn, Castine Town Rep Comt, Maine
b Woburn, Mass, May 22, 08; s Frank Leroy Pratt (deceased) & Lena Harrington P (deceased); m 1930 to Doris Madeline Wardwell; c John Wardwell. Educ: Colby Acad, New London, NH, grad, 26; Mass Inst Technol, 26-28; Sigma Chi. Polit & Govt Pos: Vchmn, Castine Town Rep Comt, 58-60, chmn, 60-; mem, Hancock Co Rep Comt, Maine, 60-, finance chmn, 60-71, chmn, 62-66; finance chmn, Second Dist, 67-69; State Finance Chmn Pro Tem, summer 69; chmn, Bd of Appeals of Zoning Ordinance, Town of Castine, Maine, 68. Bus & Prof Pos: Dist sales mgr, York-Shipley Mfg Co, York, Pa, 46-49 & Timken Silent Automatic Div, 49-57. Mil Serv: Warrant Officer, Naval Res, 43-46, serv in SPac & Atlantic Theaters; Campaign Ribbons; Inactive Res, 46-51. Mem: Hancock Lodge 4 AF&AM, Commandery, Shrine. Relig: Congregational. Mailing Add: Box 266 Green St Castine ME 04421

PRATT, RALPH DOMENICK (D)
Pa State Rep
b New Castle, Pa, July 7, 40; s Paul N Pratt & Ann M Morella P; m 1973 to Susan M Chaundy. Educ: Baldwin-Wallace Col, BS, 63; Univ Pittsburgh, MS, 71, Sch Law, JD, 70; Lambda Chi Alpha. Polit & Govt Pos: Health legal consult, Gov Off, Ill, 71-72; asst attorney gen, Dept Justice, Commonwealth of Pa, 72-74; Pa State Rep, 74- Bus & Prof Pos: Research chemist, Union Carbide Corp, Parma, Ohio, 63-65; chem process eng, Douglas Aircraft Corp, Santa Monica, Calif, 65-67; pvt law practice, Ellwood City, Pa, 72-74. Publ: Legal status of the physician's assistant, Physician's Assoc J, 4/72. Mem: Am & Pa Bar Asns; Moose; Kiwanis. Mailing Add: RD 1 Maidenblush Dr New Wilmington PA 16142

PRATT, ROBERT LEONARD (D)
b East Rockaway, NY, Jan 12, 47; s Leonard Charles Pratt & Florence Ranges P; single. Educ: Wesleyan Univ, BA with high honors, 69; Georgetown Univ Law Ctr, JD, 73; Harvard Univ, Kennedy Sch, MPA, 74. Polit & Govt Pos: From law clerk to chmn, Gen Servs Admin Bd of Contract Appeals, 73; legis asst, US Rep Robert F Drinan, 74- Bus & Prof Pos: Treas, co-founder & incorporator, What on Earth, Inc, 75- Mem: DC & Am Bar Asns. Legal Res: South Shelburne Rd Greenfield MA 01301 Mailing Add: 3002 Rodman St NW Washington DC 20008

PRAY, CHARLES P (D)
Maine State Sen
Mailing Add: 58 Forest Ave Millinocket ME 04462

PRAY, HARRY H (R)
NH State Rep
Mailing Add: 98 Sixth St Dover NH 03820

PREBENSEN, DENNIS MICHAEL (D)
Assoc Mem, Tewksbury Dem Town Comt, Mass
b Cambridge, Mass, Oct 14, 50; s Harold Leonard Prebensen, Sr & Catherine M Lawlor P; single. Educ: Lowell State Col, BA, 72. Polit & Govt Pos: Gov intern, Commonwealth of Mass, summer 71; alt deleg, Dem Nat Conv, 72; assoc mem, Tewksbury Dem Town Comt, 72- Mem: Am Acad Polit Sci; Am Hist Asn; Citizens for Participation in Polit Action. Mailing Add: 1224 Shawsheen St Tewksbury MA 01876

PRENDERGAST, JAMES FRANCIS (D)
Pa State Rep
b Easton, Pa, Feb 5, 17; s John L Prendergast & Elizabeth Hegarty P; m to Ann Naab; c Therese, Mary, Kathleen, John, Virginia, Timothy & James William. Educ: Lafayette Col, BA; George Washington Univ Law Sch, LLB; Sigma Nu. Polit & Govt Pos: Pa State Rep, 136th Legis Dist, 59-, Majority Caucus Secy, Pa State House of Rep, 65-66, Minority Caucus Chmn, 67-68, Majority Whip, 69-72, Dem Caucus Chmn, 73-74. Mil Serv: 1st Lt (Ret), Marine Corps Res; Purple Heart; Navy Cross in Pac. Mem: Am Legion; KofC; CWC; VFW; Pa Bar Asn. Legal Res: 340 Paxinosa Ave Easton PA 18042 Mailing Add: Capitol Bldg Harrisburg PA 17120

PRENDERGAST, RICHARD HALSEY (R)
b Oak Park, Ill, Oct 18, 45; s William Broderick Prendergast & Mary Comeford P; m 1973 to Paula J Peters. Educ: Villanova Univ, BA, 67; Univ Pa Wharton Grad Div, MBA, 69. Polit & Govt Pos: Admin asst, Anne Arundel Co Govt, Md, 69; campaign mgr, Holt for Cong Comt, 72; admin asst to US Rep Marjorie Holt, Md, 73- Bus & Prof Pos: Consult, Pop Coun, 70; mkt research asst, Md Nat Bank, 71. Mailing Add: Rte 1 Box 275A Dunkirk MD 20754

PRENTICE, CHARLES JAMES (R)
Okla State Rep
b Pittsburgh, Pa, Nov 9, 48; s Charles James Prentice, Sr & Harriet Falk P; single. Educ: Westminster Col (Pa), BA, 70; Alpha Psi Omega; Sigma Nu. Polit & Govt Pos: Deleg, Okla Rep State & Co Conv, 71-75; Okla State Rep, 72- Bus & Prof Pos: Commercial & indust real estate sales. Mem: Metrop Tulsa CofC; Eastbranch YMCA (mem bd dirs, 73-75); Southeast Jaycees. Relig: Episcopal. Legal Res: 2449 S 144th East Ave Tulsa OK 74134 Mailing Add: PO Box 45562 Tulsa OK 74145

PRENTICE, DIXON WRIGHT (D)
Justice, Ind State Supreme Court
b Sellersburg, Ind, June 3, 19; s Walter E Prentice & Maude Wilson P; m 1941 to Phyllis Catherine Ropa; c Penelope (Mrs Rauzi), Peter K & William W. Educ: Ind Univ Law Sch, LLB, 42; Phi Kappa Psi. Polit & Govt Pos: Justice, Ind State Supreme Court, 71- Bus & Prof Pos: Partner, Prentice & Prentice, Lawyers, Jeffersonville, Ind, 46-70. Mil Serv: Entered as Yeoman 3/C, Navy, 42, released as Lt, 46, after serv in Am, European-African & Asiatic Theatres; Intel, Naval Res, Lt Comdr (Ret). Mem: Am Judicature Soc; Ind State & Clark Co Bar Asns; Ind Judges Asn; Elks. Relig: Protestant. Legal Res: Blackison Mill Rd Jeffersonville IN 47130 Mailing Add: Rm 306 State House Indianapolis IN 46204

PRENTISS, WILLIAM CLARK (D)
Committeeman, Fla Dem State Comt
b Evanston, Ill, Apr 21, 32; s Clark Prentiss & Vera Palmer P; m 1957 to Sarah Frances Trawick; c William Clark, IV, Charles Trawick & Mary Elizabeth. Educ: Univ of South, George F Baker scholars, BA, 54; Univ Va, Woodrow Wilson Dept fel, 54, MA, 55; Univ Fla, Nat Defense Educ Act fel, 67, EdD, 69; Phi Beta Kappa; Phi Delta Kappa; Pi Gamma Mu; Alpha Psi Omega; Kappa Delta Pi; Alpha Tau Omega. Polit & Govt Pos: Mem, Orange Co Dem Exec Comt, Fla, 71-; chmn, McGovern Campaign, Cent Fla, 71-72; state bd dirs, Fla Concerned Dem, 73-; committeeman, Fla Dem State Comt, 74-; chmn rules comt, Fla Dem Party, 75- Bus & Prof Pos: Dean, Fla Mil Sch, 57-67; chmn social sci, Valencia Community Col, 69-75. Mil Serv: Entered as 2nd Lt, Air Force, 55, released as 1st Lt, after serv in 321st Bomber Wing, Strategic Air Command, 55-57. Publ: Co-auth, American Government: A Search for Freedom, Glencoe Press, 69. Mem: Orlando Community Correctional Ctr (adv bd); Youth Prog, Inc (bd dirs); Vol Serv Bur Orange Co (adv bd); Fla Asn Community Col. Mailing Add: 550 Arapaho Trail Maitland FL 32751

PRESCOTT, GEORGE A (R)
Mich State Sen
Mailing Add: 434 W Lake St Tawas City MI 48763

PRESLEY, ROBERT B (D)
Calif State Sen
b Tahlequah, Okla, Dec 4, 24; s Doyle O Presley & Ann Townsend P; m 1944 to Ahni Ratliff; c Marilyn (Mrs Raphael), Donna (Mrs Thurber) & Bobby. Educ: Riverside City Col, Calif, grad; Fed Bur Invest Nat Acad, Washington, DC; Univ Calif, Los Angeles & Univ Calif, Riverside, teaching credentials. Polit & Govt Pos: Undersheriff, Riverside, Calif, 62-74; Calif State Sen, 74- Mil Serv: Pfc, Army, 43-46, serv in 5th Army, Italy; Bronze Star. Mem: Riverside Co Law Enforcement Adminr Asn (pres); Fed Bur Invest Acad Assocs (pres, Calif chap); Riverside Co Peace Officers Asn; Air Force Asn; Riverside Family Serv Asn. Relig: Protestant. Mailing Add: 5508 Grassy Trail Dr Riverside CA 92504

PRESNAL, BILLY CHARLES (D)
Tex State Rep
b Bryan, Tex, Apr 26, 32; s Will Presnal & Margie Marquart P; m 1954 to Cecille D'Aun McCoy; c James Scott, Stephen Earl & DeAnna Kay. Educ: Tex A&M Univ, BS, 53, MS, 60. Polit & Govt Pos: Tex State Rep, 18th Dist, 69- Bus & Prof Pos: Instr, WTex State Univ, 53-54; civilian counr, Tex A&M Univ, 62-68. Mil Serv: Entered as 2nd Lt, Air Force, 54, released as 1st Lt, 56, after serv in Crew Training, Air Training Command. Mem: Farm Bur. Honors & Awards: First Runner-up, Outstanding Young Farmer of Tex, 66. Relig: Methodist. Mailing Add: PO Box 4142 Bryan TX 77801

PRESS, WILLIAM HANS (R)
Mem, DC Rep Cent Comt
b Washington, DC, July 29, 06; s Hans Jacob Press & Christine Miersen P; m 1932 to Mary Grand; c Christine (Mrs Heina). Educ: Univ Md, College Park, BS, 28; Phi Sigma Kappa. Polit & Govt Pos: Exec vpres, Metrop Washington Bd Trade, Washington, DC, 44-71; fuel oil coordr, 47-48; adv coun fed reports, Budget Bur, 48-57; chmn, Washington Metrop Area Jobs Coun, 67-; mem, DC Unemploy Compensation Bd, 70-; mem, DC Rep Cent Comt, 72-; chmn, Nat Capital Planning Comn, 73-74. Bus & Prof Pos: Ed, Jour, Am CofC Exec, 51-54; secy & dir, Belford Towers Mgt Co, Washington, DC, 69-, adv bd mem, Riggs Nat Bank, 71-; trustee, Med Serv DC, 71-, Consortium Univ DC, 71- & Nat Grad Univ, 73-; exec dir, Supreme Court Hist Soc, 75- Mil Serv: Entered as Capt, Army Engrs, 42, released as Lt Col, 45; Legion of Merit. Mem: DC hon life mem Am CofC Exec; Asn Oldest Inhabitants DC (pres, 72-73); Columbia Hist Soc (mgr, 69-); Mil Order World Wars DC Chap; hon life mem Metrop Washington Bd Trade. Honors & Awards: Washington Most Outstanding Citizen, Cosmopolitan Club, 71; Distinguished Citizen, DC City Coun, 71. Relig: Lutheran. Mailing Add: 1646 32 St NW Washington DC 20007

PRESSLER, LARRY (R)
US Rep, SDak
b Sioux Falls, SDak, Mar 29, 42; s Antone Pressler & Lorretta Claussen P; single. Educ: Univ SDak, BA, 64; Oxford Univ, Rhodes scholar, BS in Econ, 66; Harvard Univ, Kennedy Sch Govt, MA, 71; Harvard Law Sch, JD, 71; Phi Beta Kappa; Am Asn Rhodes Scholars. Polit & Govt Pos: Off legal adv to US Secy State, US Dept State, 71-74; aide, Sen Francis Case, formerly; US Rep, First Dist, SDak, 75- Mil Serv: Entered as 2nd Lt Army, 66, released as

1st Lt, 68, after serv in Hq USARV, Vietnam. Mem: VFW; Lions; Phi Beta Kappa Nat Asn; Am Legion; SDak Hist Soc. Honors & Awards: One of Four All-Am 4-H deleg to Agr Fair in Cairo, Egypt, 61, Nat 4-H Citizenship Award, 62; Report to the President 4-H Award, 62. Legal Res: SD Mailing Add: 1238 Longworth House Off Bldg Washington DC 20515

PRESTAGE, ETHEL MARIAN (R)
Mem, Rep State Cent Comt Calif
b Porterville, Calif, Nov 15, 99; d Clinton Ellsworth Martin & Nellie Alice Hall M; m 1920 to Edgar Lewis Prestage; c Lewis Ellsworth, Marcia Jeanette (Mrs Allen), Margaret Ellen (Mrs Winton) & Douglas Warren (deceased). Educ: Univ Calif. Polit & Govt Pos: Pres, Porterville Area Rep Women, Calif, 54-64, membership chmn, 65-; mailing chmn, Tulare Co Rep Party; mem, Rep State Cent Comt Calif, 54- Bus & Prof Pos: Bookkeeper, 17-20. Mem: Porterville State Hosp (adv bd); Porterville Women's Club (past pres, treas, 72-73); Porterville Garden Club (treas, 72-); Coun of Vol (ward brightening chmn, Porterville State Hosp, 69-); Tulare Co Crippled Children's Soc (bd mem). Honors & Awards: Named Porterville's Woman of the Year, 66. Relig: Methodist. Mailing Add: 219 S Westwood Porterville CA 93257

PRESTERA, G MICHELE (D)
WVa State Deleg
Mailing Add: State Capitol Charleston WV 25305

PRESTON, HOWELL F (R)
NH State Rep
Mailing Add: 117 Wakefield St Rochester NH 03867

PRESTON, ROBERT F (D)
NH State Sen
Mailing Add: 226 Winnacunnet Rd Hampton NH 03842

PRESTWOOD, COLON EDWARD (D)
b Lenoir, NC, Apr 23, 13; s James Sidney Prestwood & Cordelia Bush P; m 1934 to Nellie Pauline Ernest; c Billie Sue & William John Taylor, Jr. Educ: Oak Hill High Sch, 9 years. Polit & Govt Pos: Chmn, Caldwell Co Dem Exec Comt, NC, 66-74; mem, Indust Safety Adv Bd, State of NC Dept Labor, 69- Bus & Prof Pos: Foreman, Hibriten Furniture, 38-40; machine rm foreman, Bernhardt Furniture, 40-46, supt, 46-63, prod mgr, 63- Mem: Mason; York Rite; Shrine; Lions. Relig: Methodist. Mailing Add: 520 Mountain View Lenoir NC 28645

PRESTWOOD, RALPH (D)
NC State Rep
Mailing Add: 206 Friendly Park Lenoir NC 28645

PREWITT, TAYLOR ARCHIE (D)
b Selma, Ark, Oct 13, 86; s Zachary Taylor Prewitt & Cora Bell Lobbin P; m 1907 to Hughetta Duncan; c Cathryn (Mrs McDaniel), Taylor Archie Jr & Claudious Rowan. Educ: Hendrix Col. Polit & Govt Pos: Mem adv comt, Dept Health, Educ & Welfare, 62-66; chmn, Drew Co Dem Cent Comt, Ark, formerly, chmn elec comt, formerly. Bus & Prof Pos: Gen merchant; retired. Mem: State Schs for Deaf & Blind (bd mem for 24 years); Farm Bur; Local Mens Clubs. Relig: Methodist; mem, Church Gen Jurisdictional Bd. Mailing Add: Box 68 Tillar AR 71670

PREYER, LUNSFORD RICHARDSON (D)
US Rep, NC
b Greensboro, NC, Jan 11, 19; s William Yost Preyer & Mary Norris Richardson P; m 1946 to Emily Irving Harris; c L Richardson, Jr, Mary Norris, Britt Armfield, Jane Bethell & Emily Harris, II. Educ: Princeton Univ, AB, 41; Harvard Law Sch, LLB, 49. Hon Degrees: LLD, Elon Col & Univ NC, Greensboro, 72. Polit & Govt Pos: City Judge, Greensboro, NC, 53-54; State Superior Court Judge, NC, 61-63; US Dist Judge, NC, 63-64; US Rep, Sixth Dist, NC, 69- Bus & Prof Pos: Attorney, Preyer & Bynum, Greensboro, NC, 50-56; sr vpres & trust officer, NC Nat Bank, 64-68. Mil Serv: Entered as Lt(jg), Naval Res, 42, released as Lt, 46, after serv on destroyers, Atlantic & Pac Fleets, 42-46; Bronze Star. Mem: Am & NC Bar Asns; hon mem, Nat Boy Scout Coun. Honors & Awards: Greensboro Young Man of the Year Award, 54; Outstanding Civic Leader of the Year Award, Greensboro Inter-Club Coun, 68. Relig: Presbyterian; elder & teacher men's Bible class, First Presby Church. Legal Res: 603 Sunset Dr Greensboro NC 27408 Mailing Add: 403 Cannon House Off Bldg Washington DC 20515

PRIBYL, PATRICIA HEINZ (D)
b Owatonna, Minn, Aug 18, 47; d Marvin Heinz & Alice Byrnes H (deceased); m 1968 to James C Pribyl; c Sarah. Educ: Moorhead State Col, 65; Black Hills State Col, 69-70; Onandaga Community Col, 71-72. Polit & Govt Pos: Deleg, Dem Nat Mid-Term Conf, 74; secy to Lt Gov, SDak, 75- Mailing Add: 308 S Lincoln Pierre SD 57501

PRICE, ETHEL A (R)
Comnr, Luzerne Co, Pa
b Wilkes-Barre, Pa, Dec 5, 09; d Harry Aerenson (deceased) & Anna Bogart A (deceased); m 1937 to Oliver Jones Price, wid. Educ: Coughlin High Sch, Wilkes-Barre, Pa, grad, 27. Polit & Govt Pos: Secy, Wilkes-Barre City Coun, 32-37; app city councilman, Wilkes-Barre, 56, elected city councilman, 57-67; comnr, Luzerne Co, 68- Publ: Articles in Munic J, London, Eng, Pub Cleansing & Salvage, Edinburgh, Scotland, & Am City, New York. Mem: Luzerne Co Community Col (mem bd trustees); Jewish Home Scranton (mem bd dirs); Luzerne Co Asn Retarded Citizens (mem bd mem); Luzerne & Lackawanna Citizens' Coun for Clean Air (bd mem); Eastern Star (Past Matron). Relig: Jewish. Mailing Add: 27 W Hollenback Ave Wilkes-Barre PA 18702

PRICE, GEORGE (D)
Chmn, Guilford Dem Town Comt, Conn
b Paris, France, Jan 7, 39; married, c two. Educ: NY Univ, BAeroE, 58, MS, 66. Polit & Govt Pos: Mem, Econ Develop Comn, Guilford, Conn, 72-73; chmn, Guilford Dem Town Comt, 74- Bus & Prof Pos: Chief mkt planning, Sikorsky Aircraft, 71- Mil Serv: Entered as 2nd Lt, Air Force, 59, released as 1st Lt, 62; Capt, Air Force Res. Mem: Opers Research Soc Am; Am Helicopter Soc. Mailing Add: 79 Russet Dr Guilford CT 06437

PRICHARD / 753

PRICE, GEORGE A (R)
Md State Deleg
b Phoenix, Md, May 22, 26; married. Educ: Mercersburg Acad, Pa; Univ Md. Polit & Govt Pos: Md State Deleg, 63-; dir, Baltimore Co Conserv Dist & Tenth Dist Rep Club. Bus & Prof Pos: Farmer; chmn bd, Baltimore Co Petroleum Corp; mem, Md Nat Bank Adv Bd, currently. Mem: Baltimore Co Farm Bur; Md Angus Asn; Md Red Meat Coun (pres); Phi Kappa Sigma; Third Gunpowder Agr Club (treas). Mailing Add: Stockton Farm Phoenix MD 21131

PRICE, JAMES HOYT (D)
b Cedartown, Ga, Oct 27, 47; s Hoyt Hugh Price & Lucille Malone P; single. Educ: Norman Jr Col, Ga, 65-66; WGa Col, BS in Bus Admin, 70; Phi Beta Lambda; Bruins; WGa Pistol & Rifle Club. Polit & Govt Pos: Deleg, Dem Nat Conv, 72; co-chmn, Ga State Dem Charter, 31st Sen Dist, 74-; co-coordr Polk Co, Busbee for Gov, 74; chmn, Polk Co Youth for Busbee for Gov, 74. Bus & Prof Pos: Staff managerial analyst, Ga Dept of Transportation, 70-71; legis managerial analyst, Ga Gen Assembly, 71-72. Honors & Awards: Hon Ga Militia Comn, Gov Jimmy Carter, 71. Relig: Methodist. Mailing Add: 310 E Jule Peek Ave Cedartown GA 30125

PRICE, LINDA RICE (D)
b Norman, Okla, Sept 17, 48; d Elroy L Rice & Esther Wilson R; m 1970 to Michael Allen Price; c Justin R. Educ: Univ Okla, BA in Hist, 70, grad work, currently. Polit & Govt Pos: Coordr, McGovern Campaign, Kansas City, Kans, 72; deleg, Kans Dem State Conv & Fourth Dist Dem Conv, 72; campaign mgr, Barsotti for Cong, Fourth Dist, 72; alt deleg, Dem Nat Conv, 72. Bus & Prof Pos: Dir & founder, Univ Okla Crisis Ctr, 69-70; inhalation therapy technician, Bethany Med Ctr, Kansas City, 70-72; city planner, Seminole, Okla, 73-74 & Tecumseh, Okla, 74-75. Mem: Am Inst Planners. Relig: Presbyterian. Mailing Add: 1933 F Twisted Oak Dr Norman OK 73069

PRICE, MELVIN (D)
US Rep, Ill
b East St Louis, Ill, Jan 1, 05; s Lawrence Wood Price & Margaret Elizabeth Connolly P; m 1952 to Garaldine Freelin; c William. Polit & Govt Pos: Secy to US Rep Edwin Schaefer, 33-43; US Rep, Ill, 45-, chmn armed serv comt, US House Rep, 75- Bus & Prof Pos: Sports writer, East St Louis News-Rev, 25-27; correspondent, East St Louis, 27-33; correspondent, St Louis Globe Dem, 43-44. Mil Serv: Army, 43-44. Mem: Am Legion; KofC; Moose; Eagle; Elks. Relig: Catholic. Legal Res: 426 N Eighth St East St Louis IL 62201 Mailing Add: 2468 Rayburn House Off Bldg Washington DC 20515

PRICE, RICHARD A (DICK) (R)
Fla State Rep
Mailing Add: 400 Villa Grande Ave S St Petersburg FL 33707

PRICE, ROBERT DALE (R)
US Rep, Tex
b Reading, Kans, Sept 7, 27; s Ben F Price, Sr & Gladys A Watson P; m 1951 to Martha Ann White; c Robert Grant, Benjamin Carl & Janice Ann. Educ: Okla State Univ, BS in Agr, 51; Sigma Alpha Epsilon. Polit & Govt Pos: US Rep, Tex, 66-, mem, Comt on Agr Subcomts on Cotton, Livestock, & Grains, Dept Opers, Armed Serv Comt, Rep Policy Comt, Rep Comt on Comts & Subcomt on Research & Develop, US House Rep, currently; deleg, Rep Nat Conv, 68 & 72. Bus & Prof Pos: Rancher. Mil Serv: Entered as Airman, Air Force, 51, released as 1st Lt, 55, after serv in 51st Fighter Intercepters, Korea, 16th Squadron Jet Fighters, 53-54; 27 Combat Missions; Air Medal. Mem: Sigma Alpha Epsilon Alumni Asn; VFW; Am Legion; Kiwanis; Pampa CofC. Relig: Baptist. Legal Res: 2135 Charles Pampa TX 79065 Mailing Add: 1109 Villamay Blvd Alexandria VA 22308

PRICE, ROBERT EARLE (D)
Nev State Assemblyman
b DeLand, Fla, May 23, 36; s Robert E Price, Sr & Mary G Davis P; m 1970 to Brenda Joyce Denson; c William Randall, Sheri Elizabeth, Amber Lynn & Theresa Marie. Educ: Cheyenne Cent High Sch, Wyo, grad, 54. Polit & Govt Pos: Mem, Clark Co Dem Cent Comt, Nev, currently; Nev State Assemblyman, 74- Bus & Prof Pos: Bus mgr, IBEW Local Union, 357, 71-74. Mem: IBEW; North Las Vegas Rotary. Mailing Add: 1809 Renada Circle North Las Vegas NV 89030

PRICE, ROBERT LAVON (D)
Chmn, Elkhart Co Dem Party, Ind
b Milford, Ind, Nov 9, 24; s Charles Washington Price & Clara Mable Leatherman P; m to Isabelle Marie Culp; c Randall Louis, Michael Dale, Sharol Lynn (Mrs Dennis Robinson) & Cordell. Educ: Ind Univ Voc, 48-51. Polit & Govt Pos: Vprecinct committeeman, Clexe Twp, 56-69; chmn, Elkhart Co Dem Party, Ind, currently. Bus & Prof Pos: Local 464 chmn, Brotherhood of RR Clerks, Elkhart, Ind, 60-, vgen chmn, Lines West Syst Bd, Cleveland, Ohio, 67- Mil Serv: Entered as Pvt, Army, 43, released as S/Sgt, 45, after serv in Inf, Southwest Pac, 43-45; Bronze Star; Purple Heart; Combat Inf Badge. Publ: Ed, Dem Times, 72-75 & Pumpkin Vine, 75, privately publ; ed, Instructions for deputy registrars, Rooster Booster, 70. Mem: Lions; Am Legion; DAV; VFW. Relig: Protestant. Mailing Add: 28272 RR2 CR4W Elkhart IN 46514

PRICE, ROBERT ROSS (D)
Chmn, Jefferson Co Dem Exec Comt, Ohio
b Carrollton, Ohio, Nov 24, 26; s Robert Henry Price & Martha Jane Dunlap P; m 1967 to Judith Renee Kerr; c Karen Lee, Robert Kenneth, Linda Sue, Bruce Allan, Julia Adrianne & Heidi. Educ: Col of Steubenville, BS; Univ Pittsburgh, DDS; Psi Omega. Polit & Govt Pos: Precinct comt mem, Jefferson Co Dem Party, Ohio, 59-69; vchmn, Jefferson Co Dem Exec Comt, 67-68, chmn, 68-; mem, Ohio State Co Chmn Asn, 68-; alt deleg, Dem Nat Conv, 68; mem, Jefferson Co Bd Elec, 68-; mem exec comt, Ohio State Dem Party, 69- Mil Serv: Entered as Pfc, Army, 44, released as T-5, 46. Mem: Eagles; Elks; Mason; Moose; Shrine. Relig: Protestant. Mailing Add: 4349 Sunset Blvd Steubenville OH 43952

PRICHARD, W M (R)
b Dyersburg, Tenn, June 28, 13; s Jefferson R Prichard & Martha H White P; m 1939 to Mabel C Rambeau; c Philip M & Pamela N. Educ: Univ Tenn, grad, 35; Sigma Phi Epsilon; Biologia Society. Polit & Govt Pos: City councilman, Louisville, Ga, 53-57; chmn, Jefferson Co Rep Party, 64-74; mem regional adv comt, US Dept Agr, currently; chmn, Ga Soybean Commodity Comn, 71-73; mem, Ga Farm Bur Adv Comt Soybeans & Feed Grains, currently. Bus & Prof Pos: Played prof baseball, 35-37; proj mgr, Calloway Farms, Hamilton, Ga, 37-41; co agr agent, Ext Serv, 41-45; mgr & partner, Louisville Bonded Warehouse & Abbot &

Prichard, 45-59; owner & operator, Prichard Seed Farms, 59-; vpres & dir, Found Seeds, Inc, Athens, Ga; dir, First Nat Bank, Louisville Ga, currently. Mem: Farm Bur; Ga Crop Improv Asn (dir); Am Soybean Asn (dir); Kiwanis; CofC. Honors & Awards: Received first Distinguished Serv Award, Ga Chap, Am Soc Agronomy. Relig: Presbyterian. Legal Res: Avera Rd Louisville GA 30434 Mailing Add: PO Box 228 Louisville GA 30434

PRIDDY, DOTTIE (D)
Ky State Rep
Mailing Add: 3702 South Park Rd Louisville KY 40219

PRIEBE, BERL E (D)
Iowa State Sen
Mailing Add: RR 2 Box 145A Algona IA 50511

PRIESTLEY, WALLACE SCHUYLER (WALLY) (D)
Ore State Rep
b Portland, Ore, July 17, 31; s Wallace Soren Priestley & Florence Anne Winslow P; single. Educ: Univ Ore; Ore State Univ; Portland State Col; Sigma Chi. Polit & Govt Pos: Ore State Rep, currently. Mil Serv: Entered as E-1, Navy, 51, released as E-6, 54, Good Conduct Medal. Mailing Add: 2207 NE Ainsworth Portland OR 97211

PRIMEAU, LAWRENCE STEVEN (D)
Mem, Nebr State Dem Cent Comt
b Omaha, Nebr, May 25, 47; s Harry Miller Primeau, Jr & Mary Elizabeth King P; single. Educ: Creighton Univ, BA, 70; Univ Nebr Omaha, 71-72; Creighton Univ Grad Sch Bus Admin, 74- Polit & Govt Pos: Mem, Nebr State Dem Cent Comt, 72- & State Party Campaign Serv Comt, currently; asst chmn, Nebr Dem Party Const Rev Comt, 73-; alt deleg, Dem Nat Mid-Term Conf, 74. Bus & Prof Pos: Admin asst, Boys Town Sch Syst, 72- Mil Serv: Entered as 2nd Lt, Army, 70, released as 1st Lt, 71, after serv in Transportation Corp, Ft Eustis, Va, Baltimore Outport, Naha Port, Okinawa; 1st Lt, Army Res, currently. Mem: Common Cause (Second Cong Dist Nat Issues Coordr, 74-); Comt for New Polit Initiatives; Int City Mgrs Asn (jr mem, 73-); Boys Town Fed Credit Union (bd pres, currently); Boys Town Educ Asn. Relig: Roman Catholic. Legal Res: 7620 Pacific St Omaha NE 68114 Mailing Add: 709 N 33 St Omaha NE 68131

PRINCE, AUDREY P (D)
Secy, Anderson Co Dem Exec Comt, Tenn
b Loudon, Tenn, Aug 22, 24; d Samuel Jesse Parker & Lennie Christian P; m 1949 to Roland Prince; c Nancy L & Roland P. Polit & Govt Pos: Deleg, Tenn Limited Const Conv, 65; secy, Anderson Co Dem Exec Comt, 71-74; deleg, Dem Nat Conv, 72. Mem: League of Women Voters; Tenn Fedn Dem Women; Anderson Co Dem Women's Club (pres, 68, parliamentarian, 73). Relig: Presbyterian. Mailing Add: 178 California Ave Oak Ridge TN 37830

PRINCE, EUGENE AUGUSTUS (R)
b Thornton, Wash, July 31, 30; s Burdett H Prince & Lula Henning P; m 1960 to Sherri Knittle; c Stephan Randal & Suzanne M. Educ: Wash State Univ, BS, 52; Alpha Zeta; Alpha Gamma Rho. Polit & Govt Pos: Rep precinct committeeman, Whitman Co, Wash, 52-; bill clerk, Wash House of Rep, 59, asst chief clerk, 63-64, comt clerk, 65, sgt-at-arms, 67-; committeeman, Wash Rep Party, 62-64; chmn, Whitman Co Rep Party, 66-68 & 73-75; co-chmn platform comt, Rep State Conv, 68. Bus & Prof Pos: Farmer, 52- Mil Serv: Entered as 2nd Lt, Air Force, 54, released as 1st Lt, 56, after serv in Transportation, Air Research & Develop Command. Mem: Wash Asn of Wheat Growers; Mason; Grange; Farm Bur. Honors & Awards: Int Farm Youth Exchange Trip to Turkey Serv as Goodwill Ambassador, 52. Relig: Presbyterian. Mailing Add: Thornton WA 99176

PRINCE, JACK ALEXANDER (R)
Mem, Hall Co Rep Comt, Ga
b Spartanburg, SC, Sept 30, 28; s Alfred Bobo Prince & Mary Dunn P; m 1951 to Patricia Ann Jewell; c Deborah, Jesse & Rebecca. Educ: Brevard Jr Col; Univ NC, AB; Arnold Air Soc; Order of the Old Well; Student Assembly; Philantropic Literary Soc; Phi Kappa Phi. Polit & Govt Pos: Pres, Hall Co Young Rep Club, Ga, 60-64; chmn, Ninth Dist Goldwater for Pres Comt, 63-64; former mem, Ga State Rep Comt; alt deleg, Rep Nat Conv, 64; Rep cand, US Rep, Ninth Dist, Ga, 64; vchmn, Ninth Cong Dist Rep Comt, 64-66; mem, Hall Co Rep Comt, Ga, 64-, vchmn, 64-66. Bus & Prof Pos: Sales promotion mgr, J D Jewell, Inc, 54-57, gen sales mgr, 57-59 & vpres, 59-64; pres, Jack Prince, Inc, 65-; chmn bd, Precast Marble, Inc, Gainesville, Ga, 66- Mil Serv: Entered as Pvt, Army, 46, released as Capt, Air Force Res, 64, after serv in 188th Parachute Inf, 11th Airborne Div, Japanese Occup; Victory & Japanese Occup Medals; Parachutist Badge. Mem: Mensa; US Jaycees (past local pres, state vpres & nat dir); Jaycee Int Senate; Elks; Rotary; VFW. Relig: Episcopal; former sr warden & licensed lay reader. Mailing Add: 155 Piedmont Ave NW Gainesville GA 30501

PRINDIVILLE, RICHARD J (D)
NH State Rep
Mailing Add: 1152 Elm St Manchester NH 03103

PRINDLE, BARCLAY WARD (D)
Chmn, Sharon Dem Town Comt, Conn
b Sharon, Conn, May 31, 38; s Stuart E Prindle & Kathryn N O Ward P; m 1959 to Lynn Webster Hunter; c Jennifer Lynn & Tara Lynn. Educ: US Naval Schs, Newport, RI, cert, 58; Univ Md, overseas exten, cert, 60; Univ Conn, cert, 62. Polit & Govt Pos: Mem, Presidential Inaugural Honor Guard, Navy, 56; Dem cand, State Legis, 62; Justice of the Peace, Sharon, Conn, 64-; chmn, Sharon Dem Town Comt, 70-; chmn, Planning & Zoning Comn, 72- Bus & Prof Pos: Pres, Conn Grange Underwriters, 65-66. Mil Serv: Entered as Seaman Recruit E-1, Navy, 56, released as Disbursing Petty Off, E-4, 60, after serv in LST 1154, USS Tallahachie, Fleet Aircraft Squadron 107, Keflavic, Iceland, 58-59 & Little Creek Landing Opers, LST, 59-60. Mem: Int Asn Health Underwriters; Independent Mutual Agents Asn; Lions Int (pres, Sharon, Conn, 68-); Methodists Mens Club. Honors & Awards: Bronze 71 Award, Int Asn Health Underwriters, 72, Silver 72 Award, 73. Relig: Methodist. Mailing Add: Homefarm Sharon CT 06069

PRINGLE, AVIS WEAVER (R)
b Bassett, Va, June 5, 24; d Robert Edward Weaver & Avis Simmons Bassett W; m 1971 to James Moir Pringle; c Charles Stephen, Ralph J, Jr & Margaret Ann Helms. Educ: Salem Col (NC), AB, 46. Polit & Govt Pos: Deleg, Rep Nat Conv, 72; bd visitors, Radford Col, Va, 72- Bus & Prof Pos: Pres, Helms Veneer Corp, 66-68; vpres, Weaver Mirror Co, 67-71, pres, 71- Relig: Methodist. Mailing Add: Rte 1 Columbus Dr Bassett VA 24055

PRINGLE, EDWARD E
Chief Justice, Colo Supreme Court
b Chicago, Ill, Apr 12, 14; s Abraham J Pringle & Lena Oher P; m 1941 to Pauline Judd; c Bruce & Eric. Educ: Univ Colo, LLB, 36; Phi Alpha Delta; Phi Sigma Delta. Polit & Govt Pos: Dist judge, Denver, Colo, 57-61; chief justice, Colo Supreme Court, 61- Bus & Prof Pos: Practice of law, Denver, Colo, 36-57. Mil Serv: Pvt, Army Air Corps, 42. Publ: Co-auth, The expanding power of police to search and seize: effect of recent US Supreme Court decisions on criminal investigation, Univ Colo Law Rev, 68. Mem: Am Judicature Soc (chmn bd); Nat Ctr for State Courts (bd dirs); Nat Inst Justice (mem comn); Order of the Coif. Honors & Awards: Herbert Lincoln Harley Award, Am Judicature Soc, 73. Relig: Jewish. Mailing Add: State Capitol Denver CO 80203

PRINS, JOHN, JR (R)
Chmn, Pierce Co Rep Cent Comt, Wash
b Seattle, Wash, July 5, 21; s Dr John W Prins & Elizabeth Dunn P; m 1940 to Elizabeth Anderson; c John, III, Kathleen (Mrs Anderson) & Julie (Mrs Madsen). Educ: Univ Idaho, 40; Univ Calif, 41; Yakima Jr Col, 58; Univ Puget Sound, 59-60; Cent Wash State Col, 69. Polit & Govt Pos: Pres, Pierce Co Young Rep Club, 48; dir, Wash State Young Rep Fedn, 50; co chmn, Citizens for Eisenhower-Nixon, 54; treas, Pierce Co Rep Cent Comt, Wash, 68-72, chmn, 72- Bus & Prof Pos: Owner, John Prins & Co, Real Estate, 55- Mil Serv: Pvt, Army, 42-43. Mem: Elks Lodge 174; Tacoma CofC. Legal Res: 74 Orchard Rd Tacoma WA 98406 Mailing Add: 213 Security Bldg Tacoma WA 98402

PRIOLEAU, DIANE THYS (R)
Mem, Rep State Cent Comt Calif
b San Francisco, Calif, Apr 25, 34; d Edouard Thys & Beatrice Horst T; m 1957 to H Frost Prioleau; c Paul, Marc, Rene & Michelle. Educ: Wellesley Col, BA, 55; Phi Sigma. Polit & Govt Pos: Sector chmn, Sacramento Co Rep Precinct Orgn, Calif, 64; precinct chmn, Sacramento Co Citizens for Goldwater-Miller, 64; mem, Rep State Cent Comt Calif, 65-67, assoc mem, 67-69, mem, 69-; sector chmn, Alameda Co Rep Cent Comt, 68 & 70; precinct chmn & schedule coordr, Northern Calif Rafferty for US Senate, 68. Mem: Rep Assembly; Am Cancer Soc (dir, Alameda chap); Oakland Mus Asn; Calif Fed Rep Women; Alameda Cancer League (pres, 74-75). Relig: Episcopal. Mailing Add: 111 Woodland Way Piedmont CA 94611

PRIOLO, PAUL V (R)
Calif State Assemblyman
b San Francisco, Calif, July 14, 27; s Joseph Priolo & Pauline Pizzo P; div; c Jeffrey Paul & Jan Christine. Educ: Univ Calif, Berkeley, BA, 51; Phi Kappa Tau. Polit & Govt Pos: Calif State Assemblyman, 38th Dist, 67-, chmn, Comt on Elec & Const Amendments, Calif State Legis, 69-70, chmn, Comt on Planning & Land Use, 71-74, vchmn subcomt on coastal zone resources, 72- & mem joint comt on pub domain, resources & land use, local govt, energy & diminishing materials. Bus & Prof Pos: Merchandise trainee, The Emporium, San Francisco, Calif, 51-52; salesman, Gen Elec Co, 52; factory rep, Reynolds Metals Co, 52-55; partner, Stewart Photo & Sound Co, 55-67. Mil Serv: Entered as A/S, Naval Res, 45, released as Seaman 1/C, 46, after serv in Pac Theater; Pac Theater Ribbon; Victory Medal. Mem: Malibu Hist Soc; Nat Conf State Legis; life mem CofC & Jr CofC; Am Legion. Honors & Awards: Selected as Outstanding Young Man, Santa Monica, Calif, Jr CofC, 62; Distinguished Serv Award, Calif Asn Health, Phys Educ & Recreation, 73. Relig: Catholic. Legal Res: 21006 Pacific Coast Hwy Malibu CA 90265 Mailing Add: 4883 Topanga Canyon Blvd Suite 200 Woodland Hills CA 91364

PRIOR, EDWINA M (R)
VChmn, Nev State Rep Party
b Eureka, Calif, June 6, 10; d Edward A Melanson & Lillian Bond M; m 1935 to R M Prior; c Douglas E & Marie (Mrs Schou). Educ: Humboldt State Col, AB, 30. Polit & Govt Pos: Alt deleg, Rep Nat Conv, 72; vchmn, Nev State Rep Party, 72- Mem: Washoe Med Auxiliary; St Marys Med Auxiliary; Nev Art Gallery Rep Women; Humboldt Hist Soc. Mailing Add: 1555 Granite Dr Reno NV 89502

PRITCHARD, JOEL M (R)
US Rep, Wash
b Seattle, Wash, May 5, 25; m 1948 to Joan Sue Sutton; c Peggy, Frank, Anne & Jean. Educ: Marietta Col, 46-48. Polit & Govt Pos: Wash State Rep, 58-66; Wash State Sen, 66-70; US Rep, First Dist, Wash, 73- Bus & Prof Pos: Pres, Griffin Envelope Co, Seattle. Mil Serv: Army, 44-46. Legal Res: WA Mailing Add: 133 House Office Bldg Washington DC 20515

PRITZLAFF, JOHN CHARLES, JR (R)
Ariz State Sen
b Milwaukee, Wis, May 10, 25; s John Charles Pritzlaff & Elinor Gallun P; m 1951 to Mary Dell Olin; c Ann Olin, John C, Barbara Whitney & Richard Gallun. Educ: Princeton Univ. Polit & Govt Pos: Precinct committeeman & finance chmn, Rep Party, Milwaukee, Wis, 50-58; vchmn, Milwaukee Co Rep Exec Comt, 57-58; chmn, Maricopa Co Rep Finance Comt, Ariz, 60-63; Rep precinct committeeman, Phoenix, 60-72; Ariz State Rep, 63-69, Rep Whip, 65 & 66; field dir, Western Region, Rep Nat Comt, 64; mem, Rep Nat Finance Comt, 68 & 69; US Ambassador to Malta, 69-72; Ariz State Sen, 75- Bus & Prof Pos: Pres, Pritzlaff Hardware Co, Milwaukee, Wis, 56-58; vpres, Arrow Valve Co, Phoenix, Ariz, 59-60; exec vpres, Oxford Life Ins Co, Scottsdale, 60-62; chmn bd & treas, Repub Property, Inc, 60-69; dir, Phoenix Capital Corp, 62-; mem bd, Nashotah Episcopal Sem, Wis & Thunderbird Grad Sch Mgt, Phoenix, 68- Mil Serv: Entered as Pvt, Army, 43, released as T/Sgt, 45, after serv in PI Team, ETO; Good Conduct Medal; Presidential Citation; ETO Theatre Ribbons. Publ: Co-auth, Assistance to American business overseas, Dept of State & Com, 6/72. Mem: Nat Soc State Legis; San Pablo Home for Youth; Scottsdale Rotary; Scottsdale CofC; Phoenix Press Club. Relig: Episcopal. Legal Res: 4954 E Rockridge Rd Phoenix AZ 85018 Mailing Add: PO Box 202 Scottsdale AZ 85252

PRIVETT, ARNOLD REX (D)
b Maramec, Okla, May 28, 24; s Arnold Privett & Muriel P; m to Patricia Nichols; c Deborah Ann, Rex Nichols & Patricia Michelle. Educ: Okla State Univ, BA; Kappa Sigma. Polit & Govt Pos: Okla State Rep, Dist 35, 57-72, speaker, Okla House Rep, 67-72; deleg, Dem Nat Conv, 68; mem exec comt, Nat Conf State Legis Leaders, 69-72; mem, Okla Ambassadors Corps, 69; mem gov bd, Coun State Govt, 69-72; comnr, Okla Corp Comn, 73-75, chmn, 75- Mil Serv: Entered Army, 43, released, 46, after serv in Eng Corps, SPac, Okinawa & Saipan.

Mem: Pawnee Co Cattlemen's Asn; Pawnee Co CofC; Am Legion; Will Rogers Coun (coun mem); Bi-State Ment Health Found (bd dirs). Honors & Awards: Hon mem Pawnee Indian Tribe, given a headdress & name Bucks-Pa-Hut Pawnee-Nasharo, meaning Red Headed Pawnee Chief, 67. Relig: Methodist. Legal Res: Rte One Maramec OK 74045 Mailing Add: Okla Corp Comn Jim Thorpe Off Bldg Oklahoma City OK 73105

PROCTOR, HELEN JUNE (R)
Mem, Chatham Rep Town Comt, Mass
b Worcester, Mass, Oct 14, 17; d Ralph E Monigle (deceased) & Estelle Lind Monigle Boyd; m 1937 to Wesley Archer Proctor; c Cynthia (Mrs Edward C Kehoe, Jr), Louise (Mrs Richard L McKeon) & Wayne Archer. Educ: Commerce High Sch; Cape Cod Community Col, 71; cert real estate. Polit & Govt Pos: Hq secy, Leicester Rep Town Comt, Mass, 61 & 64, finance chmn, 64-68, social chmn, 64-68, chmn, 68-70; hq secy, John S Konrad for Mass State Rep, 62; town coordr, Stanley R Johnson & John C Miller for Mass State Rep, 64, town chmn, Edward W Brooke for US Sen, 66; Leicester campaign tel chmn, Richard M Nixon for President, 68; mem, Chatham Rep Town Comt, 72- Bus & Prof Pos: Bookkeeper, Independent Grocery Store, Worcester, Mass, 35-36; proprietor, The Treasure Chest Antiques, Chatham, 70-; realtor & proprietor, Treasure Chest Realty, Chatham, 72- Publ: Monthly articles for Mass State Fedn Women's Clubs as chmn community serv for Topic Mag, 65-67 & report of New Eng Conf, 68. Mem: Eastern Star, Spencerian Chap, (Past Matron); Rebekah (past noble grand Idun Rebekah Lodge); Chatham Woman's Club (pres, 74-); Leicester Woman's Club (organizer); Cape Cod Bd Realtors. Honors & Awards: Award of Merit, Mass Rep State Comt, 66. Relig: Protestant. Mailing Add: 409 Shore Rd Chatham MA 02633

PROCTOR, NANCY JEAN (D)
NH State Rep
b Keene, NH, Apr 24, 36; d Francis Leon Boufford & Marjorie B Hapward P; m 1956 to James Merton Proctor; c Jeffery Alan, Deanne Marie & Denise Ann. Educ: Jefferson High Sch, Keene, NH, grad, 75. Polit & Govt Pos: NH State Rep, Dist 14, 75-; treas, Cheshire Co Dem Comt, NH, 75- Bus & Prof Pos: Sales rep, Stone House Inc, 71-74. Mem: Consumers Utility Conf (secy). Relig: Baptist. Mailing Add: 187 North St Keene NH 03431

PROCTOR, RICHARD LEE (D)
Mem, Ark State Young Dem
b Wynne, Ark, Dec 7, 44; s Herbert Everett Proctor & Virginia Montgomery P; m 1971 to Irene Alice Nix. Educ: Ark State Univ, 62-64; Univ Ark, BS & JD, 68; Tau Kappa Epsilon; Student Bar Asn; Baptist Student Union; Circle K; Civic Club. Polit & Govt Pos: Mem, Ark State Dem Comt, 70-74, mem exec comt, 71-74; vpres, Cross Co Young Dem, 71-; mem, Ark State Young Dem, 71- Bus & Prof Pos: Partner, Proctor & Proctor Attorneys, 68- Mem: Cross Co, Ark & Am Bar Asns; Wynne Rotary Club. Relig: Baptist; deacon & pres, Baptist Men, Wynne Baptist Church. Legal Res: Crabb Lane Wynne AR 72396 Mailing Add: Box 468 Wynne AR 72396

PROFFER, MARVIN E (D)
Mo State Rep
b Cape Girardeau, Mo, Feb 3, 31; m 1954 to Marilyn Wilson; c Robert Kirk, Marian Louise & James Kent. Educ: Southeast Mo State Col, Cape Girardeau; Univ Mo, Columbia, BS in Educ & MEd. Polit & Govt Pos: Alderman, City Coun, Jackson, Mo; bd dirs, Cape Girardeau Co Dem Comt; hon col, Staff of the Late Gov James T Blair, Jr & Gov John M Dalton; Mo State Rep, Dist 156, 62-, chmn, Comt on Accts, Mo House of Rep, formerly, vchmn, Comt on Appropriations & mem, Roads & Hwys Comt. Bus & Prof Pos: Newspaper published & ed, ins agent & owner & operator of a printing & off supply bus, currently; theater mgr, formerly. Mil Serv: Army, 54-55. Mem: Rotary; Elks; Mason; AF&AM; Lions. Honors & Awards: Selected as Outstanding Young Man of Mo, 60; Nominee for One of Ten Outstanding Young Men of Am, 64. Relig: Presbyterian; elder, First Presby Church, Jackson Mo. Mailing Add: Rte 1 Jackson MO 63755

PROFFIT, HIGHT MOORE (D)
Wyo State Rep
b Goshen, NC, July 17, 11; s Robert Lee Proffit & Martha A McNeil P; m 1938 to Dorothy Ardelle Marsh; c Larry Mac, Donald Hight, Lola Emma (Mrs Baldwin) & Dorothy Deanne (Mrs Richins). Educ: Appalachian State Teachers Col, 1 year. Polit & Govt Pos: Mem, Uinta Co Comn, Wyo, 51-75; Wyo State Rep, 75- Bus & Prof Pos: Mem, Sulpher Creek Reservoir Bd, 54-; mem adult educ adv bd, Univ Wyo, 68-; mem, Land Use Adv Coun, 75- Mem: Boy Scouts (exec bd, Wyuta Dist, 65-); Wyo Farm Bur. Honors & Awards: Outstanding Co Official, Wyo Co Officers, 66; Outstanding Community Serv, Evanston CofC. Relig: Latter-day Saint. Mailing Add: Box 23 Rte 1 Evanston WY 82930

PROSSER, AUDREY BETTY (D)
Chmn, Bartholomew Co Dem Cent Comt, Ind
b Bloomington, Ind, Sept 7, 24; d Robert Lee Pardue & Katherine Kries P; m 1943 to Claude Milton Prosser; c Claudia, Stephen, Debra & Rebecca. Educ: High sch. Polit & Govt Pos: Precinct committeewoman, Bartholomew Co Dem Cent Comt, Ind, 68-, vchmn, 69-74, chmn, 74-; chmn, Columbus Dem City Comt, 71; deleg, Dem Nat Conv, 72. Relig: Methodist. Mailing Add: 1704 Central Ave Columbus IN 47201

PROSSER, DAVID THOMAS, JR (R)
b Chicago, Ill, Dec 24, 42; s David Thomas Prosser & Elizabeth Patterson P; single. Educ: DePauw Univ, BA, 65; Univ Wis-Madison, Law Sch, JD, 68; Sigma Delta Chi. Polit & Govt Pos: Pres, DePauw Univ Young Rep, 63-65; attorney-adv, Off of the Dep Attorney Gen, US Dept Justice, 69-72; deleg, Wis Rep Conv, 73 & 74; admin asst to US Rep Harold V Froehlich, 73-75; Bus & Prof Pos: Legal writing instr, Univ Wis-Madison, Law Sch, 67-68; lectr, Ind Univ, Indianapolis, Law Sch, 68-69; attorney, 75- Publ: Desecration of the American flag, Ind Legal Forum, fall 69. Mem: Am, Wis & Outagamie Co Bar Asns; Bar Asn of the Seventh Circuit. Relig: Presbyterian. Mailing Add: 821 E College Ave Appleton WI 54911

PROSSER, DEAN T, JR (R)
Wyo State Rep
Mailing Add: 1717 Alexander Ave Cheyenne WY 82001

PROTAN, JOHN (D)
Chmn, Boone Co Dem Party, WVa
b Holden, WVa, Dec 12, 21; s Mike Protan & Rose Telasky P; m to Doris Chingle; c Doris Mae, Connie Kay & John Michael. Polit & Govt Pos: Constable, Sylvester, WVa, 50-60, beer comnr, 60-64, sheriff, 64-; chmn, Boone Co Dem Party, WVa, 64- Mil Serv: Entered as A/S, Navy, released as PO 2/C, after serv in SPac. Mem: Elks; Moose; Am Legion; Mason. Mailing Add: Sylvester WV 25193

PROUDFIT, JOHN GRAHAM (R)
Asst Attorney Gen, NY
b Edinburgh, Scotland, July 13, 32; s Isabel Boyd P; single. Educ: Cornell Univ, BA, 54, Wharton Grad Sch, Univ Pa, MBA, 59; NY Univ Law Sch, LLB, 62. Polit & Govt Pos: Pres, Manhattan West Rep Club, NY, 67-69; Asst Attorney Gen, NY, 67-; alt deleg, Rep Nat Conv, 68; Rep cand, US Rep, NY, 68. Mil Serv: Entered as 2nd Lt, Air Force, 54, released as 1st Lt, 57, after serv in Korea & Air Defense Command; Res, Capt. Mem: Asn of the Bar of City of New York; Fed Bar Asn; Citizens Union; Sierra Club. Mailing Add: 215 W 90th St New York NY 10024

PROVOST, PAUL E (D)
NH State Sen
Mailing Add: 1790 Brown Ave Manchester NH 03103

PROXMIRE, WILLIAM (D)
US Sen, Wis
b Lake Forest, Ill, Nov 11, 15; s Dr Theodore Stanley Proxmire & Adele Flanigan P; m 1956 to Ellen Hodges; c Elsie Stillman, Theodore Stanley & Douglas Clark. Educ: Yale Univ, BA, 38; Harvard Bus Sch, MBA cum laude, 40, Sch Pub Admin, MPA, 48. Polit & Govt Pos: Wis State Assemblyman, 51-52; US Sen, Wis, 57-, chmn, House-Senate Joint Econ Comt, US Senate, 92nd Cong, chmn, Subcomt Priorities & Econ in Govt, mem, Subcomts Econ Progress, Fiscal Policy & Consumer Econ, chmn, Senate Banking, Housing & Urban Affairs Comt, mem, Senate Appropriations Comt, chmn, Subcomt Housing & Urban Develop-Independent Agencies, mem, Subcomts Labor-Health, Educ & Welfare & Related Agencies, Agr & Related Agencies, mem, Defense Subcomt Foreign Opers & mem, House Senate Joint Comt Defense Prod. Bus & Prof Pos: Polit & labor reporter, Capital Times, Madison, Wis, 49; reporter, Madison Union Labor News, Wis, 50; pres, Artcraft Press, Waterloo, Wis, 53-57. Mil Serv: Entered as Pvt, Army, 41, released as 1st Lt, 46, after serv in Counter-intel Corps. Publ: Report From Wasteland, America's Military Industrial Complex, Praeger, 70; Uncle Sam, Last of the Big Time Spenders, 72 & You Can Do It, 73, Simon & Schuster. Honors & Awards: Letter in football at Yale Univ; Yale boxing champion in 149-159 lb weight class. Relig: Episcopal. Legal Res: 4613 East Buckeye Rd Madison WI 53716 Mailing Add: 5241 New Senate Off Bldg Washington DC 20510

PRUITT, CHARLES W (D)
Tenn State Rep
Mailing Add: 1813 Hillside Ave Nashville TN 37203

PRUITT, DAVID CARL, III (R)
b Birmingham, Ala, Oct 15, 33; s David Carl Pruitt, Jr & Leo Reese P. Educ: Univ Ala, BS in Com, 55; Alpha Kappa Psi; Pi Kappa Alpha. Polit & Govt Pos: Admin asst to US Rep George Huddleston, Ala, 64-65 & to US Rep Jack Edwards, First Dist, Ala, 65- Bus & Prof Pos: Nat dir, Am Jr Miss Pageant, 60-64. Mil Serv: Entered as 2nd Lt, Army, 55, released as 1st Lt, 57, after serv in Qm Corps, Seventh Army, ETO; Outstanding Serv Cert. Mem: Mobile Jr CofC; Ala State Soc of Washington, DC; Univ Ala Alumni Asn. Relig: Methodist. Legal Res: 1250 Belle Chene Mobile AL 36609 Mailing Add: 2439 House Off Bldg Washington DC 20515

PRUITT, GLYNDON C (D)
Chmn, Gwinnett Co Dem Exec Comt, Ga
b Buford, Ga, Aug 25, 28; s Carl Clifford Pruitt & Pearl Peevy P; m to Deanna West; c Judy Lea, Carl Clifford, David & Glyndon Daniel. Educ: WGa Col; John Marshall Law Sch; Univ Ga, LLB, 50; Sigma Nu; Alpha Phi Omega. Polit & Govt Pos: Solicitor, City Court of Buford, Ga, 59-71; chmn, Gwinnett Co Dem Exec Comt, 70- Bus & Prof Pos: Attorney, Buford, Ga, 52- Mil Serv: T/Sgt, Army, serv in ETO. Mem: Am Bar Asn; Shrine; Mason; Lions; VFW. Relig: Methodist. Legal Res: 5459 N Richland Creek Rd Buford GA 30518 Mailing Add: PO Box 569 Buford GA 30518

PRUITT, IRA DRAYTON, JR (D)
b Pine Hill, Ala, Mar 4, 04; s Ira Drayton Pruitt & Mary Elizabeth Miller P; m 1935 to Elise Knox Cobb; c Ira Drayton, Jr. Educ: Univ Ala, LLB, 34; Phi Alpha Delta. Polit & Govt Pos: Mem town coun, Livingston, Ala, 36-51; circuit solicitor, 17th Judicial Circuit, 40-44; Ala State Rep, 44-74; deleg, Dem Nat Conv, 72. Bus & Prof Pos: Attorney-at-law, 34- Mem: Mason. Mailing Add: PO Drawer PP Livingston AL 35470

PRYOR, DAVID HAMPTON (D)
Gov, Ark
b Camden, Ark, Aug 29, 34; s William Edgar Pryor & Susan Newton P; m 1957 to Barbara Jean Lunsford; c David, Jr, Mark & Scott. Educ: Henderson State, Ark, 52-53; Ark Univ, BA, 57, Law Sch, LLB, 64; Blue Key; Sigma Alpha Epsilon; Phi Alpha Delta. Polit & Govt Pos: Ark State Rep, 61-66; US Rep, Ark, 67-72; deleg, Dem Nat Conv, 68; deleg, Dem Nat Mid-Term Conf, 74; Gov, Ark, 75- Bus & Prof Pos: Publ weekly newspaper, Ouachita Citizen, 57-60; law partner, Pryor & Barnes, 64-66; attorney, Little Rock, currently. Mem: Jr CofC; CofC. Honors & Awards: Selected One of Five Outstanding Young Men in Ark, Ark Jaycees, 67. Relig: Presbyterian. Mailing Add: State Capitol Little Rock AR 72201

PUCCINELLI, LEO JOHN (R)
b Fagnano, Lucca, Italy, Sept 8, 21; s Andrea Puccinelli & Gemma Lemucchi P; m 1949 to Gertrude Viola Ford; c Andrew James, Janet Lee, Gayle Ann & Carol Ann. Educ: Univ Nev, Reno, AB, 46; Univ San Francisco Sch Law, JD, 50; Sigma Alpha Epsilon. Polit & Govt Pos: Deleg, Nev Rep State Conv, 50-72; co-chmn, Nixon-Lodge Comt, Elko Co Nev, 60; vchmn, Elko Co Rep Party, 62-64; chmn adv bd, Nev Youth Training Ctr, 67-; mem, Gov Comt Juvenile Concerns, 68-71; mem, Pub Defender Selection Comn, 71-; alt deleg, Rep Nat Conv, 72; gov off rep, Inaugural of Nixon & Agnew, 73. Mil Serv: Entered as Pvt, Marine Corps Res, 42, released as S/Sgt, 45, after serv in Recruiting Serv. Mem: Elks (Exalted Ruler, 64-65); KofC; Am Legion (Comdr, 65-66); Rotary; Nev Jaycees (vpres, 56-57). Relig: Roman Catholic. Legal Res: 567 14th St Elko NV 89801 Mailing Add: PO Box 530 Elko NV 89801

PUCHALLA, ANDREW FRANCIS (D)
Chmn, Huntingdon Co Dem Comt, Pa
b Mt Union, Pa, Nov 15, 11; s Lawrence J Puchalla & Eva Suchanec P; m 1939 to Mary Jane Mickley; c Patricia Eva & Victoria Jane. Educ: High sch grad. Polit & Govt Pos: Chmn, Clark-Dillworth Campaign Comt, Pa, 62; chmn, Huntingdon Co Dem Comt, 64-; asst dir, Bur

Liquor Audits, Auditor-Gen Dept, Pa, 67-72, admin asst, 72- Bus & Prof Pos: Pres, Huntingdon Co Indust Develop Coun, Inc, Pa, 55-; mem bd, Mt Union Area Develop Corp, 58-, pres, 65- Publ: Industrial development in Huntingdon Co, Banker's Weekly, 5/28/58; coauth, article on indust develop, Indust Mkt Mag, 58; assisted in numerous develop articles, Tyrone Daily Herald, 60. Mem: Lions; KofC; Huntingdon Co Cancer Soc (exec bd); Mt Union CofC (pres). Honors & Awards: Assisted in formulating overall econ develop prog for Mifflin & Huntingdon Co, 62; took major part in fund raising for econ develop Huntingdon Co & Mt Union; represented Huntingdon Co at Indust Develop Show, NY Coliseum. Relig: Roman Catholic. Mailing Add: 125 S Division St Mt Union PA 17066

PUCINSKI, ROMAN C (D)

b May 13, 19; m to Aurelia Bordin; c two. Educ: Northwestern Univ; John Marshall Law Sch, Chicago. Polit & Govt Pos: Chief investr select comt of cong investigating mass murder by Communists of 15,000 Polish Army Officers in World War II; US Rep, 11th Cong Dist, Ill, 58-72, chmn, Standing Comt on Select Educ, US House Rep, 89th Cong, chmn, Standing Comt on Gen Educ, 90th & 91st Cong; alt deleg, Dem Nat Conv, 68; deleg, Dem Nat Mid-Term Conf, 74. Bus & Prof Pos: Staff reporter & writer for Chicago Sun-Times, 38-58. Mil Serv: Entered World War II as Pvt in 106th Cavalry, discharged as Capt; served with 20th Global (Superfort) Air Force; led his bomber group on first B-29 bombing raid over Tokyo, 44; subsequently flew 48 missions over Japan; awarded the Distinguished Flying Cross & Air Medal with Cluster. Relig: Roman Catholic. Mailing Add: 6301 N Louise Chicago IL 60646

PUFFER, KENNETH HART (R)

Mem, Kalkaska Co Rep Party, Mich

b South Boardman, Mich, Apr 14, 10; s George Wesley Puffer & Roma Thomas P; m 1935 to Lela Minear Baughman; c Phyllis A, Joan L (Mrs Kotcher) & Karen J. Educ: Western Mich Univ, BS, 35; Mich State Univ, MA, 49; Univ Mich, PhD, 59. Polit & Govt Pos: Chmn, Kalkaska Co Rep Party, Mich, 66-68, mem, 68-; deleg to various state conv of Kalkaska Co, currently. Bus & Prof Pos: Supt of schs, Flint Hoover, 53-56 & Stambaugh, 62-64; teacher, Flint, 57-62, 64-70; writer, 70- Publ: How Good Schools Are Run, Bond Wheelwright, 62; plus others. Mem: Mason; Int Platform Asn. Honors & Awards: Citation for assisting Upper Peninsula Creative Writers' Asn. Relig: Methodist. Legal Res: Rte 1 South Boardman MI 49680 Mailing Add: Pine Hills Farm South Boardman MI 49680

PUFFER, THOMAS RAY (R)

Mem, Rep State Cent Comt Calif

b Buffalo, NY, Mar 13, 31; s Ray H Puffer & Mildred I Pease P; m 1968 to Patricia Lamb; c Richard Scott & Lisa Karen. Educ: Hamilton Col, BA, 54; Univ Calif, San Diego, Cert of Indust Rels, 59; Theta Delta Chi. Polit & Govt Pos: Mem, San Diego Co Rep Cent Comt, Calif, 62-, treas, 69-72; mem, Rep State Cent Comt Calif, 66- Bus & Prof Pos: Managing dir, San Diego Employers Asn, Calif, 57- Mil Serv: Entered as 2nd Lt, Marine Corps, 54, released as Capt, 57, after serv in First Marine Div, Camp Pendleton, Calif, 54-57. Mem: San Diego Chap, Indust Research Asn; San Diego Active 20-30 Club; San Diego Co Welfare Bd; Youth Serv Bur Bd. Relig: Episcopal; vestry assoc, St Pauls Episcopal Church. Mailing Add: 7363 Florey St San Diego CA 92122

PUGEL, ROBERT JOSEPH (D)

Nat Committeeman, Colo Young Dem

b Pueblo, Colo, Aug 15, 41; s Joe E Pugel & Margaret E Jachetta P; m 1968 to Elke Marie Williamson. Educ: Pueblo Col, AA; Western State Col Colo, BA, & MA, magna cum laude; Univ London, int fel; Univ Denver; Kappa Delta Pi; Student Govt Club. Polit & Govt Pos: Nat committeeman, Colo Young Dem, 70-, mem exec coun; mem bd dirs, Denver Young Dem; precinct committeeman; chmn legis dist, Colo Dem Party; deleg, State Dem Conv; mem, Colo Dem Cent Comt; mem exec bd, Young Dem Clubs Am; research dir & chief speech writer, Dem campaigns, 70; mem, Am Coun Young Polit Leaders. Bus & Prof Pos: Teacher Eng, Pueblo South High Sch, Pueblo, Colo; instr, Southern Colo State Col & Univ Denver; prof Eng, Metrop State Col. Mem: Nat Educ Asn; Am Asn Higher Educ; Am Asn Univ Prof; Am Fedn Teachers; English Speaking Union (vpres, Denver Br, chmn & inter-US coordr younger mem group, chmn poetry reading group, deleg, Int Conf, Washington, DC & Bermuda). Relig: Catholic. Mailing Add: 7239 E Euclid Dr Englewood CO 80110

PUGH, J T (D)

NC State Rep

Mailing Add: 1413 Westmont Dr Asheboro NC 27203

PUGH, WARREN EDWARD (R)

Pres, Utah State Senate

b Salt Lake City, Utah, Dec 21, 09; s William E Pugh & Eva Murphy P; m 1933 to Leta Curtis; c Carol (Mrs Robert C Matheson), Lorin K & Donald E. Polit & Govt Pos: Mem, Utah State Rep, 59-60 & Utah Legis Coun, 67-68; chmn, Transportation & Pub Safety Standing Comn, 67-68 & 71-72; Utah State Sen, 67-, Majority Leader, Utah State Senate, 69-70, pres, 73-, chmn, Educ Subcomt, Joint Appropriations, 71-72, mem, Legis Coun Higher Educ Comt, 71-72 & Legis Coun Exec Comt, 73- Bus & Prof Pos: Owner-mgr, Cummins Diesel Sales Co; pres, Indust Develop & Sales Corp & Cummins Intermountain Idaho, Inc. Mem: Alta Club; Hidden Valley Country Club. Honors & Awards: Educ Serv Award, Granite Educ Asn, 73. Relig: Latter-day Saint. Mailing Add: 5124 Cottonwood Lane Salt Lake City UT 84117

PUGLIA, ANDREW ROBERT (D)

b Somerville, Mass, July 6, 48; s Andrew Puglia & Rose Tartaglia P; single. Educ: Univ Mass, BA, 70; Tufts Univ, MA, 73. Polit & Govt Pos: Sch committeeman, Somerville, Mass, 70-, chmn comt, 72-73, mem bd aldermen, 74-75, vpres bd, 75; deleg, Dem Nat Conv, 72; admin asst to Co Comnr S Lester Ralph, Middlesex Co, 73- Bus & Prof Pos: Staff mem, Somerville Recreation Comn, 66- Mem: Am Polit Sci Asn; Acad Polit & Soc Sci; Acad Polit Sci; Sons of Italy; Mass Citizens for Polit Action. Relig: Catholic. Mailing Add: 143 North St Somerville MA 02144

PULIDO, ALBERTO (D)

Dir Nationalities Div, Mich Dem State Cent Comt

b Laredo, Tex, June 7, 22; s Tomas Pulido & Ramona Zapata P; m 1952 to Domitila Serrato; c Teresa. Educ: Detroit Col Law, 49-50; Detroit Inst Technol, BA, 50; Univ Mich Exten Serv, 52, 59, 64 & 65; Wayne State Univ Law Sch, 56-57; Am Inst Banking; Gabriel Richard Inst, 66. Polit & Govt Pos: Pres, Latin Am Comt on Polit Action, Detroit, Mich, 58-59; right of way title analyst, Wayne Co Rd Comn, 58-63, appraisal reviewer, 63-67, negotiator, 67-; chmn Latin Am affairs, Nationalities Div, Mich Dem State Cent Comt, 64-, asst dir, 64-69, dir, 69-, mem policy adv comt, 65-66, mem exec bd, 16th Cong Dist, 66-, mem justice & equality comt, 68-; chmn & founder, Latin Am Dem Club of Mich, 64-; mem comt on apprenticeship info ctr, Mich Employment Security Comn, 64-; precinct deleg, Dem Co & State Conv, 64-; first vchmn citizens area adv comt, Total Action Against Poverty Area 2, Western Community Ctr, 65-66; mem mayor's policy adv comt, Total Action Against Poverty, 65-66; chmn property secy, Citizens Adv Comt, Western High Sch, Detroit Bd of Educ, 66-67; mem, Mayor's Comt on Neighborhood Conserv & Housing, 66-68; chmn & founder, Mich Huelga Comt, 66-; mem adv coun, Small Bus Admin, Mich, 67-68; alt deleg-at-lg, Dem Nat Conv, 68; state chmn & founder, Viva Humphrey Club, 68-; co-chmn, Jefferson-Jackson Dinner Ticket Comt, 16th Cong Dist, 69- Bus & Prof Pos: Painter & rough carpenter, Laredo, Tex, 41-43; gas welder, Briggs Mfg Co, Mack Plant, Detroit, Mich, 46-49; secy & law clerk to Charles C Benjamin, 46-49; abstractor & title examr, Burton Abstract & Title Co, 49-52; admin asst & chief mortgage closer, Indust Nat Bank of Detroit & later the Mfrs Nat Bank of Detroit, 52-56; real estate broker & ins agt, 57-58; gen mgr, Alamo Ins Agency, 58-; gen agt, Seguros Tepeyac, SA, 59-68; dir, Corktown Credit Union, 60-63, pres, 64-67. Mil Serv: Tank Comdr, Army, 43-46, with serv in Co C, 766th Tank Bn, Southwest Pac Theatre of Opers; Asiatic Pac Campaign Medal with One Bronze Star; Good Conduct Medal; Victory Ribbon with Four Overseas Serv Bars. Mem: Am Legion (comdr, Mex Am Post 505, 50-51 & various other positions); YMCA (chmn finance & property comt, Bd Mgt, Western Br, 65-); VFW; Am Fedn of State, Co & Munic Employees, AFL-CIO; Am Right-of-Way Asn. Honors & Awards: Thirteen Cert of Merit for the Most Outstanding Serv Officer, 15th Dist, Detroit Dist Asn, Am Legion; Two Departmental Meritorious Awards, Dept of Mich, Life Mem Award, Mexican Am Post 505; Three Silver Medals & Cert for being selected as Runner-Up for Mich Vet of the Year for 1963, 1965 & 1967; Cert Award in recognition of the outstanding meritorious serv in the field of constitution and by-law writing ability, Vernor-Junction Businessmen's Asn; Chamizal Medallion received from President Lyndon B Johnson in commemoration of the Chamizal Agreement between the US & the Repub of Mex. Relig: Catholic. Mailing Add: 3542 28th St Detroit MI 48210

PULLEN, KENT (R)

Wash State Sen

Mailing Add: 22844 172nd SE Kent WA 98031

PULLEY, WILLIAM W (R)

b Oxford, Ohio, Mar 7, 29; s Verlin L Pulley & Corola Wood P; m 1951 to Martha Lee Lesher; c William Lesher, Mary Lynn & Jeffrey Verlin. Educ: Dartmouth Col, AB, 50; Miami Univ, MBA, 56; Phi Beta Kappa; Beta Gamma Sigma; Phi Delta Theta. Polit & Govt Pos: Rep precinct committeeman, Ohio, 58; mem exec comt & area capt, Butler Co Rep Cent Comt, 60, chmn, formerly; deleg, Rep Nat Conv, 68. Bus & Prof Pos: Sales mgr, Capitol Varsity Co, 53, gen mgr, 66. Mil Serv: Res, Mil Intel, 51-57. Mem: Rotary. Relig: Methodist. Mailing Add: Capitol Varsity Cleaning Oxford OH 45056

PULLIA, SAL P (D)

Committeeman, Cook Co Dem Cent Comt, Ill

b Chicago, Ill, Aug 25, 47; s Frank Pullia & Lillian Falbo P; m 1972 to Karen Carpino. Educ: Northern Ill Univ, BS Finance. Polit & Govt Pos: Committeeman, Ill Proviso Twp, Cook Co Dem Cent Comt, currently; deleg, Dem Nat Mid-Term Conf, 74. Bus & Prof Pos: Ins broker & real estate broker; tax exten supvr, Cook Co Clerks Off, currently. Mem: Kiwanis; Tanagers Social & Athletic Club (secy); Fraternal Order Police; Italo-Am Lodge 9. Relig: Catholic. Legal Res: 1312 N 23rd Melrose Park IL 60160 Mailing Add: 1510 W Lake St Melrose Park IL 60160

PULLMAN, SAUL ARNOLD (D)

b Eastland, Tex, Nov 28, 40; s Henry Pullman & Tillie Engleberg P; single. Educ: Tex Christian Univ, BS in Com; Univ Tex, LLB; Phi Alpha Delta; Tex Christian Univ Ex-Lettermen's Asn. Polit & Govt Pos: Deleg, Dem Nat Conv, 72. Bus & Prof Pos: Attorney, State Bar of Tex. Mil Serv: Entered as Pvt E-1, Army, 65, released as Capt, 72, after serv in 1st Judge Advocate Gen Detachment. Mem: Tex Bar Asn; Rotary Int (past pres, 71-72); Farm Bur; Jaycees; CofC (dir). Mailing Add: 104 N Ammerman Eastland TX 76448

PURCE, THOMAS LESLIE (D)

Mem Exec Comt, Idaho State Dem Cent Comt

b Pocatello, Idaho, Nov 13, 46; s John William Purce; m 1969 to Carole. Educ: Idaho State Univ, BA, 69, MAEd, 70, EdD, 75; Kappa Alpha Psi. Polit & Govt Pos: Mem, Idaho State Housing Agency, Boise, Idaho, 73-76; mem exec comt, Idaho State Dem Cent Comt, 74-; vchmn, City Comn, Pocatello, 74- Bus & Prof Pos: Assoc, Idaho State Univ, 73-75, assoc counr educ & supvr, 73-75. Mem: Urban League Task Force; NAACP. Mailing Add: 1137 E Halliday Pocatello ID 83201

PURCELL, GRAHAM (D)

b Archer City, Tex, May 5, 19; s Graham B Purcell & Della Key P; m to Nancy Attebury; c nine. Educ: Tex A&M Col, BS Agr, 46; LLB, Baylor Univ Law Sch, 49. Polit & Govt Pos: Former Juvenile Court Judge of Wichita Co, Tex; former Judge, 89th Judicial Dist; US Rep, Tex, 62-72; mem, Nat Comn on Food Mkt, 64. Bus & Prof Pos: Practicing attorney, Big Spring & Wichita Falls, Tex, 49-55, Washington, DC, currently. Mil Serv: Army, 41, serv in Africa & Italy; Lt Col, Army Res, Armor, currently. Mem: Very active in work with juveniles, both as judge and civic worker; Boy Scouts of Am (dist chmn). Honors & Awards: Honored twice as Outstanding Citizen of Wichita Falls. Relig: Presbyterian; deacon, Fain Memorial Presbyterian Church of Wichita Falls. Legal Res: Wichita Falls TX Mailing Add: 9026 Old Mount Vernon Rd Alexandria VA 22309

PURCELL, JOE (D)

Lt Gov, Ark

Polit & Govt Pos: City attorney, Benton, Ark, 55-59; municipal judge, Benton & Saline Co, 59-66; Attorney Gen, Ark, 67-71; chmn, Ark State Dem Comt, 70-72; deleg, Dem Nat Conv, 72; mem, Dem Nat Comt, 72; Lt Gov, Ark, 75- Mailing Add: PO Box 25 Benton AR 72015

PURFEERST, CLARENCE M (D)

Minn State Sen

b Faribault, Minn, June 30, 28; s Mark P Purfeerst & Amelia Carpentier P; m 1949 to Rosemond Paquette; c Judith, Jane, Joe, James, Mary & Amy. Educ: High sch grad. Polit & Govt Pos: Minn State Sen, 73- Mailing Add: Rte 2 Faribault MN 55021

PURRINGTON, JOHN WARD (R)

Mem Exec Comt, Wake Co Rep Party, NC

b Raleigh, NC, June 1, 40; s Alfred Luther Purrington, Jr & Nella Grimes Ward P; m 1970 to Charlotte Camp Smith. Educ: Univ NC, Chapel Hill, AB, 62, JD, 67; Zeta Psi; Order of

Gimghoul. Polit & Govt Pos: Co-chmn, Wake Co Citizens for Nixon-Agnew, NC, 68; mem exec comt, Wake Co Rep Party, 70-, chmn, 71-72; mem, Fourth Dist Rep Exec Comt, 71-; mem exec comt, NC Rep Party, 72; NC State Rep, 73-74; chmn, Gov Adv Coun on Drug Abuse, 73-; cand US House of Rep, 74. Bus & Prof Pos: Research clerk, NC Supreme Court, 67-68; partner, Purrington & Purrington, Attorneys, 70- Mil Serv: Entered as Ens, Navy, 62, released as Lt (jg), 64. Mem: Wake Co Symphony Soc; Wake Co Ment Health Soc (bd dir); Raleigh CofC (bd dir); Kiwanis; United Health Serv (bd dir). Relig: Episcopal. Mailing Add: 2323 Churchill Rd Raleigh NC 27608

PURSELL, CARL D (R)
Mich State Sen
b Imlay City, Mich, Dec 19, 33; s Roy Pursell & Doris Perkins P; m 1956 to Peggy Jean Brown; c Philip, Mark & Kathy. Educ: Eastern Mich Univ, AB & MA; Tau Kappa Epsilon. Polit & Govt Pos: Comnr, Wayne Co, Mich, 69-70; Mich State Sen, 70- Bus & Prof Pos: Teacher, Livonia, Mich, 61-62; owner, Western Off Equip, Plymouth, 62-64; with Fehlig Real Estate, 64-69. Mil Serv: Entered as Lt, Army, 57, released as 1st Lt, after serv in Inf, 5th Army; Capt, Res, until 65. Honors & Awards: Outstanding Young Man of Year, Jaycees, 65; Outstanding Sen 70-71 by Leadership & Press. Legal Res: 46200 Territorial Rd Plymouth MI 48170 Mailing Add: Box 240 State Capitol Lansing MI 48902

PURTELL, WILLIAM ARTHUR (R)
b Hartford, Conn, May 6, 97; s Thomas M Purtell & Nora O'Connor P; m 1919 to Katherine E Cassidy; c William Arthur & Margaret Mary. Educ: Pub schs, Hartford; LLD, Trinity Col, Hillyer Col. Polit & Govt Pos: US Sen, Conn, 52, 53-58. Bus & Prof Pos: Pres, treas, gen mgr, Elec Soldering Iron Co, Deep River, Conn; vpres, treas, gen mgr, Sparmak Eng Corp, 38-52; pres, treas, gen mgr, dir, Holo-Krome Screw Corp, Hartford, 29-52; pres, treas, gen mgr, Billings & Spencer Co, Hartford, 37-44; dir, chmn exec comt, 44-47; also formerly dir, Colts Mfg Co, Hartford (Conn) Trust Co, Veeder-Root, Inc; also various pos other mfg concerns. Mil Serv: AEF, radio sect, Signal Corps, 18-19. Mem: Am Soc Metals; Am Supply & Machinery Mfrs Asn (dir); Am Legion. Honors & Awards: Recipient Citation Nat Conf Christians & Jews; Merit Award, Hardware Merchants & Mfrs Asn, 58. Relig: Roman Catholic. Legal Res: 514 Maple Ave Old Saybrook CT 06475 Mailing Add: PO Box 247 Deep River CT 06417

PURTLE, JOHN INGRAM (D)
Mem, Pulaski Co Dem Cent Comt, Ark
b Enola, Ark, Sept 7, 23; s John Wesley Purtle & Edna Ingram P; m 1951 to Marian Ruth White; c Jeffrey & Lisa Karen. Educ: Ark State Col, pre-law, 46-47; Univ Ark, JD, 50; Phi Alpha Zeta. Polit & Govt Pos: Ark State Rep, Faulkner Co, 51-53 & Pulaski Co, 69-70; mem, Pulaski Co Dem Cent Comt, Ark, 67-68 & 70-; mem exec comt, Ark Dem Party, 74- Mil Serv: Entered as Pvt, Army, 40, released as Lt, 45, after serv in 153rd Inf, Asiatic-Pac Theatre, 42-45, Lt Col, Res; Am Defense Medal; Good Conduct Medal; Am Theater Ribbon; Asiatic-Pac Ribbon; Aleutian Island Campaign Ribbon with Two Bronze Stars. Mem: Am Legion; VFW; Kiwanis; PTA; Ment Health Asn. Relig: Baptist; Deacon, Trustee. Mailing Add: 300 Spring Bldg Little Rock AR 72201

PURVES, PIERRE MAROT (R)
Dir of Statist Research, Nat Rep Cong Comt
b Philadelphia, Pa, Feb 22, 07; s Austin Montgomery Purves & Betsey Preston Coleman P; m 1939 to Mary Cornelia Gage; c Lloyd R, Nancy (Mrs Pollard) & Arthur G. Educ: Univ Pa, BA, 29, PhD, 36; Princeton Univ, MA, 30; St Anthony Hall. Polit & Govt Pos: Attache, Off of Polit Adv, SHAEF, Berlin, Ger, 45-46; polit officer, Off of Mil Govt for Bavaria, Munich, 46-49; polit adv, Off of Land Comnr for Bavaria, 49-51; research, Rep Nat Comt, 56; dir statist research, Nat Rep Cong Comt, 59- Bus & Prof Pos: Research asst, Oriental Inst, Univ Chicago, 36-44. Mil Serv: Pvt, Marine Corps Res, 44-45. Publ: Ed, Congressional vote statistics, 62, 64, 66, 68, 70 & 72 & Congressional district vote comparison, 64, 66 & 68, Nat Rep Cong Comt. Relig: Episcopal. Mailing Add: 4555 W St NW Washington DC 20007

PURVIS, PAUL FRANCIS (R)
b Rowan Co, Ky, May 12, 16; s Thomas L Purvis & Ollie H Carpenter P; m 1940 to Geneva Mildred Moore. Educ: Ashland Pub Schs, Ky, high sch dipl. Polit & Govt Pos: Chmn, Boyd Co Rep Exec Comt, Ky, 70-74. Bus & Prof Pos: Pres, Valley Auto Supply Co, Inc, currently, former exec vpres. Mil Serv: Entered as A/S, Navy, 43, released as Water Tender 1/C, 45, after serv in Amphibian Forces, ETO, Asiatic & Pac Theatres, 43-45; three Battle Stars. Mem: Ashland Rotary Club (dir); Am Legion; F&AM (master, Poage Lodge 325, 64). Honors & Awards: Ky Col. Relig: Protestant. Legal Res: 2605 Main St Ashland KY 41101 Mailing Add: 947 Winchester Ave Ashland KY 41101

PURVIS, PERRIN HAYS (D)
Miss State Sen
b Blue Springs, Miss, Feb 24, 18; m to Helen Foster. Educ: Univ Southern Miss, BS, 38; Sports Hall of Fame. Polit & Govt Pos: Miss State Sen, currently; mem, Miss Agr & Indust Bd, currently; mem exec comt, Miss Div Law Enforcement, currently; mem, Community Develop Found. Bus & Prof Pos: Gen ins agt; bd dir, First Citizens Nat Bank; vpres, WTWV Channel 9 TV; vpres, North Miss Realty Co. Mil Serv: World War II. Mem: Mason (32 degree); Shrine; WOW; Am Legion; 40 et 8. Relig: Methodist. Legal Res: 804 Oak-Grove Rd Tupelo MS 38801 Mailing Add: PO Box 791 Tupelo MS 38801

PURYEAR, BYRON NELSON (D)
Mem, Hampton Dem Exec Comt, Va
b Winston-Salem, NC, Sept 22, 13; s Royal Wendell Puryear & Beatrice Sharp P; m 1934 to Gladys Thornton Bizzell; c Alvin Nelson. Educ: Hampton Inst, trade dipl, 33. Polit & Govt Pos: Mem subcomt, Va Adv Legis Comt, Richmond, 67; mem, Hampton Dem Exec Comt, 67-68 & 69-; deleg, Va Dem State Conv, 68; alt deleg, Nat Dem Conv, 68; mem, Elec Laws Study Comn, 68-69; mem state comt, Howell for Gov, 69. Publ: Booklet on Democratic Candidates, Wilson & Andrews, 63; Hampton Institute; A Pictorial Review of its First Century, 1868-1968, Privately Publ, 67; Know Thy Neighbor. Mem: NAACP (exec bd mem); Am Civil Liberties Union; Nat Negro Bus League; Va Soc Prev Blindness (bd mem, 68-69); Penninsula Br Soc Prev Blindness (vchmn, 68-69). Honors & Awards: Nathan W Collier Meritorious Serv Award, Fla Mem Col, 65. Relig: Baptist. Mailing Add: 2705 Shell Rd Hampton VA 23361

PUTMAN, KATHLEEN HARVEY (R)
b Chicago, Ill, Aug 31, 13; d Frank William Harvey, Jr & Helen McJunkin H; m 1937 to Albert Michael Putman; c Rev Michael Dennis, Leigh Reding (Mrs Plagens), David Jeremy, Jonathan Christopher, Timothy Harvey & Mary Kathleen. Educ: St Mary's of Notre Dame; pres, Freshman Class. Polit & Govt Pos: Jefferson Co co-chmn, Citizens for Eisenhower, Ala, 52; mem, Jefferson Co Rep Exec Comt, 52-75; Ala co-chmn, Citizens for Eisenhower, 56 & Vol for Nixon, 60; campaign coordr, Ala Rep Cong Race, 60 & Jim Martin for Gov Race, 66; mem, Ala Rep State Exec Comt, 62-70; Justice of Peace, precinct 25, Jefferson Co, 64-68; campaign mgr, George Seibels, Jr for Mayor of Birmingham, 67 & for reelec, 71; spec asst to regional dir, Nixon Presidential Campaign, 68; Ala vchmn, Nixon Inaugural Ball, 69; dist mgr, Jefferson Co Decennial Census, 70; Regional dir, Census Employ Surv, 70. Mem: Children's Aid Soc; Cauldron Literary Club; Jr League of Birmingham; Highland Sewing Circle; Camellia Garden Club. Relig: Catholic. Mailing Add: 1200 Saulter Rd Birmingham AL 35209

PUTNEY, LACEY EDWARD (INDEPENDENT)
Va State Deleg
b Big Island, Va, June 27, 28; m to Elizabeth Harlow P. Educ: Washington & Lee Univ, BA & LLB. Polit & Govt Pos: Va State Deleg, 62-; mem, Va Income Tax Study Comn, 66-68; bd trustees, Va Baptist Hosp, Lynchburg. Bus & Prof Pos: Lawyer. Mil Serv: Air Force, 50-54. Mem: Am Legion; Bedford Rotary Club; Masons; Scottish Rite; Moose. Relig: Baptist. Mailing Add: Leggett Bldg Bedford VA 24533

PYFER, S CLARK (R)
Treas, Mont State Rep Cent Comt
b Townsend, Mont, Jan 17, 19; s Arthur A Pyfer & Lola A Dimock P; m 1946 to Mary Sasek; c Donald, Robert, Richard & William. Educ: Chillicothe Bus Col, Chillicothe, Mo, 38-39. Polit & Govt Pos: Precinct committeeman, East Helena, Mont, 50-; treas, Mont State Rep Cent Comt, 52-; mem, Bicentennial Comt, 74-; mem, Upper Midwest Coun, Ninth Fed Reserve Dist, 75- Bus & Prof Pos: Dir, Home Bldg & Loan Asn, 57-62, Union Bank & Trust Co, 62- & Mont Bd, Mountain Bell, 65-; chmn, Mont State Bd Exam Acct, 66-68; chmn, Livestock Export Ctr, 74- Mil Serv: Entered as Pvt, Army Air Force, 42, released as S/Sgt, 46, after serv in Med Detachment, US, 42-46. Mem: All Am Indian Hall of Fame (bd dirs, 72-); Kiwanis Int (int trustee); Mont Club; Algeria Shrine Temple; Am Legion. Honors & Awards: Hon Alumnus, Univ Mont; CPA of Year, 65. Relig: Presbyterian. Legal Res: 16 E Pacific East Helena MT 59635 Mailing Add: Box 752 East Helena MT 59635

PYLE, ERNEST GORDON (R)
NDak State Sen
b Harmony Twp, NDak, Apr 9, 24; s Kenneth Keith Pyle & Isabelle Roden P; m 1943 to Betty Lou Thompson; c Kenneth Lawrence, Richard Ernest, Gerald Gordon, Robert James & Marcia Lynn. Educ: West Fargo High Sch, grad, 42. Polit & Govt Pos: NDak State Sen, 22nd Dist, 67- Bus & Prof Pos: Farmer, Cass Co, NDak, 42- Mem: AF&AM (Casselton Lodge); Farm Bur; Casselton Community Club; Farmers Union. Honors & Awards: Outstanding Young Farmer, Jr CofC, 59. Relig: Lutheran. Legal Res: Sect 20 Harmony Twp ND Mailing Add: Box 570 Casselton ND 58012

PYLE, GLADYS (R)
b Huron, SDak, Oct 4, 90; d John Levis Pyle & Mamie I Shields P; single. Educ: Huron Col, AB, 11; Chicago Univ & Am Conservatory of Music, 11-12. Hon Degrees: LLD, Huron Col, 58. Polit & Govt Pos: SDak State Rep, 23-27; Secy of State, SDak, 27-31; secy, State Securities Comn, 31-33; alt deleg, Rep Nat Conv, 36, deleg, 40; US Sen, SDak, 38-39; mem & secy, SDak Bd of Charities & Corrections, 40-53. Bus & Prof Pos: Teacher, SDak High Schs, 12-20; life ins agent, Northwestern Mutual Life Ins Co, 49- Mem: Huron & SDak Life Underwriters Asn; Am Legion Auxiliary; Twentieth Century Study Club; PEO. Honors & Awards: First Lady of the Year, 52 & Order of the Rose, 70, Beta Sigma Phi; Named Hon Mem, Delta Kappa Gamma, 65; Selected Huron's Citizen of the Year, CofC, 65; Christian Citizenship Award, YWCA, 65. Relig: Presbyterian. Mailing Add: 376 Idaho SE Huron SD 57350

PYLE, HOWARD, III (R)
b Richmond, Va, Feb 1, 40; s Wilfrid Pyle & Anne Woolston Roller P; m 1965 to Caroline Oglesby Smith; c Elizabeth Roller & Howard IV. Educ: Princeton Univ, BA, 62; Univ Va Law Sch, JD, 67; Tiger Inn; Delta Theta Phi. Polit & Govt Pos: With Cent Intel Agency, 67-69; admin asst, US Rep Odin Langen, Minn, 69-70; admin asst, US Rep Hastings Keith, Mass, 71; Asst to Secy of Interior, Cong Liaison, 71-73. Bus & Prof Pos: Washington Rep, Standard Oil Ind, 73- Mil Serv: Entered as Ens, Navy, 62, released as Lt(jg), 64, after serv in USS English, DD-696, 62-63 & US Naval Air Sta, Corpus Christi, Tex, 63-64; Lt Comdr, Naval Res, 70-; Qualified Naval Parachutist. Mem: Va & DC Bar Asns; Aircraft Owners & Pilots Asn; Sons of Revolution in State Va; Country Club of Va. Honors & Awards: Licensed Fed Aviation Admin commercial pilot with single-engine, multi-engine & instrument ratings; Outstanding Young Men of Am, 72. Relig: Episcopal. Legal Res: Richmond VA Mailing Add: 4809 45th St NW Washington DC 20016

PYLE, ROBERT NOBLE (R)
b Wilmington, Del, Oct 23, 26; s Joseph Lybrand Pyle & La Verne Noble P; m 1950 to Edith Ayrault Rose; c Robert N, Jr, Mark C, Nicholas A & Sarah L. Educ: Dickinson Col, grad, 48; Univ Pa Wharton Grad Sch, 48; Phi Kappa Psi. Polit & Govt Pos: Researcher, US Sen John Williams, 53; admin asst to US Rep Herbert A Warburton, 53, US Rep Perkins Bass, 55-63 & US Rep Walter A Powell, 70; field man, Rep Nat Cong Comt, 58-74 & Rep Nat Comt, 74; consult, NY State Rep Comt, 61; treas, Md Charter Comt, 65; consult, US Rep Benjamin A Gilman, 72 & US Rep Margaret M Heckler, 74; adv to US Rep David F Emery, Maine, 75- Mil Serv: Entered as Pvt, Army, 45, released as Pfc, 46, after serv as reporter, Stars & Stripes, Europe; attended Nuremberg Trials, 46 & Paris Peace Conf, 46. Mem: Kenwood Country Club; Golden Triangle Golf Club. Honors & Awards: Subject of Wall St J article on How a Polit Field Man Operates?, 74. Relig: Presbyterian. Mailing Add: 3260 Arcadia Pl NW Washington DC 20015

PYLES, JOHN W (D)
Assessor, Monongalia Co, WVa
b Flemington, WVa, Jan 28, 33; s Melford J Pyles & Lucy L Scarcella P; m 1970 to Charlotte R Winebrenner. Educ: WVa Univ, BM & MA; Kappa Kappa Psi. Polit & Govt Pos: Former pres, Monongalia Co Young Dem Club; WVa State Legislator, 63-67; assessor, Monongalia Co, 69-; mem, Monongalia Co Dem Exec Comt, currently. Bus & Prof Pos: Pub sch teacher. Mem: Nat Educ Asn; WVa Assessor's Asn; Co United Fund (campaign chmn, 75). Relig: Baptist. Legal Res: 410 Wilbourn St Morgantown WV 26505 Mailing Add: Court House Morgantown WV 26505

PYLES, VERN (R)
Pa State Rep
Mailing Add: Capitol Bldg Harrisburg PA 17120

PYNE, LEE EDWARD (R)
Mem, Ashford Rep Town Comt, Conn
b Lynn, Mass, Oct 30, 08; s Okes Lee Pyne & Nellie Bishop P; m 1945 to Doris Laviolette Kearns. Educ: Boston Univ, BA & MA; Purdue Univ, prof cert; Phi Delta Kappa. Polit & Govt Pos: Justice of the Peace, Ashford, Conn, 58-62, mem, Bd Tax Rev, 60-, chmn, currently; mem, Ashford Rep Town Comt, 60-, chmn, 60-68; mem, Ashford Conserv Comn, 73- Mil Serv: Entered as Pvt, Army, 42, released as Sgt, 45, after serv in Med Corps, Am Theater. Mem: Conn Educ Asn; Nat Voc Guid Asn; Am Asn Sch Adminrs; AF&AM; Am Legion. Relig: Baptist. Mailing Add: RFD 1 Mansfield Center CT 06250

PYRROS, JAMES G (D)
b Detroit, Mich, Mar 10, 28; m 1965 to Betty Blougouras. Educ: Wayne State Univ, BA & LLB. Polit & Govt Pos: Aide to slum clearance dir, Detroit, Mich, 50-53; Asst Attorney Gen, Mich, 55-61; admin asst, US Rep Nedzi, Mich, currently. Mil Serv: Army, 53-55; Korean Serv & UN Serv Medals. Mailing Add: 4701 Willard Ave Chevy Chase MD 20015

Q

QUACKENBUSH, ROBERT L (R)
Wis State Rep
Mailing Add: 510 N Spring St Sparta WI 54656

QUAM, LESLIE JAMES (R)
b Toronto, SDak, Aug 23, 28; s Herman Quam & Jennie Haynes Q; m 1955 to Lois Maye Ramynke; c Lauren James. Educ: Toronto High Sch, 4 years. Polit & Govt Pos: Chmn, Deuel Co Young Rep SDak, 61-62; chmn, Deuel Co Rep Party, 62-67 & 73-75. Bus & Prof Pos: Farmer, Deuel Co, SDak, 47- Mil Serv: Entered as Pvt, Army, 52, released as Cpl, 53, after serv in 1st Div, Europe. Mem: Am Legion; Toronto Community Club. Relig: Lutheran. Mailing Add: Toronto SD 57268

QUARKER, DOROTHY ELAINE (D)
b Detroit, Mich, Feb 21, 22; d Anthony Henry Quarker, Sr (deceased) & Hortense Virginia Mann Q; single. Educ: Univ Detroit, BBA; Detroit Col Law & Washington Col Law, 56-59; Dean's Speech Key; Phi Gamma Nu. Polit & Govt Pos: Admin asst to US Rep Charles C Diggs, Jr, Mich, 55-, chief of staff for Washington-Detroit Cong Off, 72 & for House Rep DC Comt, 73; mem exec bd, 13th Cong Dist Dem Orgn, 68-; downtown forum co-chmn, Wayne Co Dem Comt, formerly. Bus & Prof Pos: Various positions as secy, secy to gen mgr & asst to off mgr, Great Lakes Mutual Life Ins Co, Detroit, Mich, 42-55, asst to the pres, 55; vis lectr black studies, Amherst Col, fall 72. Mem: Detroit Inst Com; Inner City Bus Improv Forum, Inc; NAACP. Relig: Protestant. Legal Res: Detroit WI Mailing Add: 1310 Longworth Bldg Washington DC 20515

QUARLES, CHARLES HARRISON (R)
Chmn, McCormick Co Rep Party, SC
b Abbeville, SC, July 17, 32; s Walter Yeldell Quarles & Mabel Reid Q; m 1953 to Hazel Reeves Gilliam; c Hazel LaMarr, Jan Kimberly (Mrs Goodwin), Charles Derrick & William Albert. Educ: Clemson Univ, grad, 55. Polit & Govt Pos: Chmn, McCormick Co Rep Party, SC, 74-; mem bd trustees, McCormick Co Sch Bd, currently. Bus & Prof Pos: Salesman, Cent Soya, 55-64; pres, Triple Q Farms, Inc, 64- Mem: Moose; Exchange Club; Farm Bur. Mailing Add: Triple Q Farms Rte 2 McCormick SC 29835

QUARLES, MARILYN (D)
Ala State Rep
Mailing Add: PO Box 214 Springville AL 35146

QUARLES, RAYMOND (RAY) (D)
Mo State Rep
Mailing Add: 4430 Dryden Ave St Louis MO 63115

QUATTROCCHI, ROCCO ANTHONY (D)
RI State Sen
b Providence, RI, Jan 13, 27; s John Quattrocchi & Vicenza Di Gennaro Q; m 1951 to Dolores R De Rosa; c John Joseph, Cynthia Ann & Joseph Anthony. Educ: Univ RI, BS, 51; Phi Kappa Theta. Polit & Govt Pos: RI State Rep, Seventh Dist, 69-70; RI State Sen, Fourth Dist, 71-, Dep Majority Leader, RI State Senate, 73- Mil Serv: Entered as Pvt, Army, 45, released as Sgt, 46, after serv in Signal Corps, Iceland, 45-46. Relig: Catholic. Mailing Add: 15 Messina St Providence RI 02908

QUEENSEN, KEITH ALAN (DFL)
Mem, 39th Dist Dem-Farmer-Labor Exec Comt, Minn
b St Louis, Mo, May 14, 55; s Kenneth Robert Queensen & Doris Gillmeth Q; single. Educ: Univ Minn, Minneapolis, 73- Polit & Govt Pos: Mem, 39th Dist Dem-Farmer-Labor Exec Comt, Minn, 73-; corresponding secy, Third Dist Dem-Farmer-Labor Exec Comt, 73-; deleg, Dem Nat Mid-Term Conf, 74; mem, Minn Dem-Farmer-Labor Const Comn, 75- Bus & Prof Pos: Part-time employee, Art Gallery, Univ Minn, 74- Honors & Awards: Martin Luther King Scholar, Univ Minn, 73-77, William A Schaper Mem Scholar, 74-75. Mailing Add: 4456 W 76th St Edina MN 55435

QUIE, ALBERT HAROLD (R)
US Rep, Minn
b Dennison, Minn, Sept 18, 23; m 1948 to Gretchen Hansen; c Fredric, Jennifer, Daniel, Joel & Benjamin. Educ: St Olaf Col, BA in Polit Sci, 50. Hon Degrees: LLD, Buena Vista Col, 71; Gettysburg Col, 72; Capital Univ, 74 & Gallaudet Col, 74; DPS, Greenville Col, 73; Degree, St Olaf Col, 73. Polit & Govt Pos: Former dir, Soil Conserv Dist, Md; former mem, Sch Bd; Minn State Sen, 54-58; US Rep, Minn, 58-, ranking Rep mem, House Educ & Labor Comt, US House Rep, currently; deleg, Rep Nat Conv, 68. Bus & Prof Pos: Farmer. Mil Serv: Pilot, Navy, World War II. Honors & Awards: Citation for Legis Statsmanship, Learning Disabilities Asn, 69; Annual Award, Nat Coun Local Admin, 71; Annual Award, Am Voc Asn, 72; Nat Milk Producers Fedn Award, 74; Nat Coun Independent Cols & Univs Award, 75. Legal Res: Dennison MN 55018 Mailing Add: 2182 Rayburn House Off Bldg Washington DC 20515

QUIGLEY, JAMES MICHAEL (D)
b Mt Carmel, Pa, Mar 30, 18; s James Quigley & Helen C Laughlin Q; m 1941 to Genevieve C Morgan; c Ann, Joan, Claire, James, Jr, Mary & Elizabeth. Educ: Villanova Univ, AB, 39; Dickinson Law Sch, LLB, 42. Polit & Govt Pos: US Rep, Pa, 54-56 & 58-60; asst secy, US Dept Health, Educ & Welfare, 61-65; chmn, Fed Water Pollution Control Admin, 65-68. Bus & Prof Pos: Vpres, US Plywood Champion Papers Inc, 68- Mil Serv: Lt, Naval Res, 43-46. Mem: Pa & Dauphine Bar Asns. Mailing Add: 605 E 14th St New York NY 10009

QUIGLEY, JOHN PATRICK (D)
NH State Rep
b Nashua, NH, Dec 5, 31; s James David Quigley & Elsie Pelkey Q; m 1957 to Jeanne H Morin; c Linda M, John P, Jr, Colleen A, Kellie J & Kathryn N. Educ: Nashua High Sch, NH, grad, 49. Polit & Govt Pos: NH State Rep, 75- Bus & Prof Pos: Owner, Quigley's Serv Sta, 54- Mil Serv: Entered as Pvt E-2, Army, 51, released as Sgt, 54, after serv in 11th Eng Combat Bn, Korea, 51-53; Korea Serv Medal with 4 Bronze Stars; UN Serv Medal; Nat Defense Serv Medal. Mem: Am Legion; VFW. Relig: Catholic. Mailing Add: McCrady Dr Hudson NH 03051

QUILLEN, FORD C (D)
Va State Deleg
b Gate City, Va, Sept 21, 38; s Cecil D Quillen & Louise Carter Q; m 1960 to Barbara Gail Burdette; c Madre, Carter & Lenoir. Educ: Univ Tenn, BS, LLB, 66; Phi Gamma Delta. Polit & Govt Pos: Va State Deleg, 70-, mem, Age of Majority Study Comn, Va House of Deleg, 71-72, mem, Legis Process Study Comn, 72- Mil Serv: Entered as 2nd Lt, 61, released as 1st Lt, 63, after serv in 3rd Inf Div. Mailing Add: Box 186 Gate City VA 24251

QUILLEN, GEORGE ROBERT (R)
Co Treas, Kent Co, Del
b Ocean View, Del, Oct 28, 28; s Robert Henry Quillen & Cora Derrickson Q (deceased); single. Educ: Beacom Bus Col, cert, 50. Polit & Govt Pos: Del State Rep, 29th Dist, 67-69, 33rd Dist 69-72, chmn, Natural Resources Comt & mem, Hwy & Pub Safety Comt, Del House Rep, 68-70; co receiver of taxes & co treas, Kent Co, Del, 72- Mil Serv: Sgt, Army, 50-52, serv in 1st Med Bn, 1st Inf Div, Ger, 51-52. Mem: Am Legion; Kent Co Archaeol Soc. Relig: Episcopal. Legal Res: 40 Commerce St Harrington DE 19952 Mailing Add: PO Box 247 Harrington DE 19952

QUILLEN, JAMES HENRY (R)
US Rep, Tenn
b Wayland, Va, Jan 11, 16; s John A Quillen (deceased) & Hannah Chapman Q; m 1952 to Cecile Cox. Hon Degrees: LLD, Steed Col, 63. Polit & Govt Pos: Tenn State Rep, 55-63, Rep Floor Leader, Tenn House Rep, 59; deleg-at-lg, Rep Nat Conv, 56, deleg, 64, 68 & 72; US Rep, First Dist, Tenn, 63-, ranking minority mem House rules comt, US House Rep, currently, mem stand official conduct comt, mem Rep leadership. Bus & Prof Pos: Pres, Kingsport Develop Co, Inc, Gen Contractors, Inc, Ins Inc, Model City Investment Corp & Real Estate-Loans, Inc, 52-63; dir, Kingsport Nat Bank, 59-; chmn bd, Wofford Bros, Johnson City, Tenn, 62-63 & Johnson City Ins Agency, Inc, currently. Mil Serv: Entered as Ens, Navy, 43, released as Lt, 46, after serv in Pac, 45-46; Atlantic & Pac Theater Ribbons. Mem: Lions; CofC; Am Legion; VFW. Relig: Methodist. Legal Res: 1501 Fairidge Pl Kingsport TN 37664 Mailing Add: 102 Cannon House Off Bldg Washington DC 20515

QUILTER, BARNEY (D)
Ohio State Rep
Mailing Add: 641 Woodville Rd Toledo OH 43605

QUINE, JOHN DAY (R)
Mayor, Meriden, Conn
b Bangor, Maine, Feb 10, 34; s James Patrick Quine & Marion Day Q; m 1957 to Sandra Whalen; c Catherine, Laura & Lisa. Educ: Holy Cross Col, BA, 56; Univ New Haven, Cert in Bus Admin, 68. Polit & Govt Pos: Chmn, Code Enforcement Appeal Bd, Meriden, 65-72; chmn, Quinnipiac River Study Comt, 70-72; chmn, Rep Town Comt, 73; comnr, Tri-State Regional Planning Comt, 74-75; mayor, Meriden, 74- Bus & Prof Pos: Sales mgt, Xerox Corp, 62-72; pres, Nutmeg Copy Ctr, 72- Mil Serv: Entered as 2nd Lt, Air Force, 56, released as 1st Lt, 59, after serv in 310th Bomb Wing, Strategic Air Command, 56-59. Mem: Rotary; Appalachian Mountain Club. Relig: Roman Catholic. Mailing Add: 21 Harvard Ave Meriden CT 06450

QUINLAN, CLARENCE (R)
Colo State Rep
Mailing Add: 27 Sixth Ave Antonito CO 81120

QUINLAN, JOHN M (R)
b Natick, Mass, July 11, 35; s Arthur William Quinlan & Margaret Everett Q; single. Educ: Harvard Col, AB, 57. Polit & Govt Pos: Mem, Dover Rep Town Comt, 56-69; spec asst, US Sen Leverett Saltonstall, Mass, 60-62; mem, Nat Asn of State Legislators, 65-74, Mass Legislators Asn, 65-74 & Norwood Rep Town Comt, 69; exec dir, Mass Coun for Const Reform, 63-64; Mass State Sen, Second Dist, Norfolk, 65-74; pres, Norfolk Co Rep Club, 66-; chmn, Comt for Const Conv, 67-; known nat, United Citizens for Nixon-Agnew, 68; deleg, Rep Nat Conv, 72. Bus & Prof Pos: Govt & hist teacher, Franklin Pub Schs, Mass, 57-60. Mil Serv: A/2C, Air Force Res, 57-63. Mem: Mass Adv Coun Educ; Nat Comt Pub Schs; Mass Audubon Soc; Nat Found March of Dimes (spec gifts chmn, Mass Bay Chap); Am Fedn Musicians. Honors & Awards: One of Mass Ten Outstanding Young Men, Gtr Boston Jr CofC, 66; One of 36 Outstanding Legislators, Eagleton Inst of Polit; Seminar on Improv of State Legis. Relig: Roman Catholic. Legal Res: 401 Engamore Lane Norwood MA 02062 Mailing Add: 11 Crestwood Circle Norwood MA 02062

QUINLAN, WILLIAM LOUIS (D)
Ky State Sen
b Louisville, Ky, Dec 25, 30; s Raymond A Quinlan & Marie Veith Q; m 1949 to Geneva Ann Gordon; c William L, Jr, David R, Robin M & Cindra A. Educ: Univ Louisville, BSC, 59. Polit & Govt Pos: Precinct capt, Grassroots Dem Club, Ky, 69-, pres, 70-71; Ky State

Sen, Seventh Dist, 72- Bus & Prof Pos: Sr indust engr, Ford Motor Co, Louisville Assembly Plant, 57- Mil Serv: Entered as Pvt, Army, 52, released as Cpl, 53, after serv in 5th RCT Unit, Korea, 52-53; UN Serv Ribbon; Korean Serv Ribbon. Mem: Am Legion; VFW; Pleasure Valley Lions. Relig: Catholic. Mailing Add: 8214 Seaforth Dr Louisville KY 40258

QUINN, A THOMAS (D)
b Los Angeles, Calif, Mar 14, 44; s Joseph Martin Quinn & Grace Cooper Q; m 1964 to Daniela Marie Buia; s Douglas Tyrone & Laurel Jean. Educ: Calif State Col, Los Angeles, 62; Northwestern Univ, BS, 65. Polit & Govt Pos: Chmn, Los Angeles Qual Educ Comt, Calif, 69-70; campaign mgr, Edmund G Brown, Jr for Secy of State, Calif, Los Angeles & San Francisco, 70; Dep Secy of State, Calif, formerly. Bus & Prof Pos: Pres, Radio News West, Los Angeles, 67-70; vpres, City News Serv, 68-70. Mem: Radio & TV News Asn Southern Calif; Gtr Los Angeles Press Club; Gtr Los Angeles Jr CofC; Nat Asn Broadcast Employees & Technicians. Mailing Add: Apt 4001 107 S Broadway Los Angeles CA 90012

QUINN, CHARLES LEWIS (R)
State Chmn, Ind Young Rep Fedn
b Garrett, Ind, Dec 23, 43; s Franklin Charles Quinn & Goldie Ellen Lewis Q; single. Educ: Manchester Col, AB, 64; Ind Univ Sch Law, JD, 67; Phi Delta Phi; Manchester Christian Asn; Methodist Student Movement; Men's Residence Coun; Kappa Tau Iota; Student Bar Asn. Polit & Govt Pos: Elect bd sheriff, Garrett, Ind, 62; pres, Manchester Col Rep Club, 62-64; precinct committeeman, Garrett, 62-66; pres, Manchester Student Orgn for Goldwater, 64; mem, Ind Univ Rep Club, 64-67; legal counsel, Ind Young Rep Fedn, 70, nat committeeman, 71-73, state chmn, 73-; mem, Youth for Adair for Cong Comt, 70; dir, DeKalb Co Young Rep, 70-73; mem, DeKalb Co Rep Cent Comt, 70-73; asst chmn, Garrett Rep City Comt, 71; mem credentials comt & deleg, Young Rep Nat Conv, 71; mem, Young Rep Nat Fedn, 71-, mem const rev comt, 72; chmn, Northern Ind Young Voters for the President, 72; coord, Young Voters for the President, Rep Nat Conv, 72; co coord, Bloom for Cong Comt, 72; mem platform comt & deleg, Ind Rep State Conv, 72, deleg, 74; mem statewide voter registr comt, Ind Rep State Cent Comt, 72, mem opposition research comt, 73; mem Am deleg, Am Coun of Young Polit Leaders Conf, 73; co coordr, Helmke for Cong Comt, 74; mem, Gov Statutory Adv Comt Child Ment Health; mem, Gov Youth Adv Coun. Bus & Prof Pos: Mem legal dept, Midwest United Life Ins Co, Ft Wayne, Ind, 67-68; law clerk, Judge Dale J Myers, Allen Superior Court, 68-69; gen partner, Smith & Quinn, Auburn, 69- Mem: Int Acad Criminol; Int Platform Asn; Nat Consumer Finance Asn; DeKalb Co Hist Soc; Auburn CofC (mem bd dirs, 72-). Honors & Awards: Bronze Medallion for Meritorious Serv, Northeast Ind Chap of Am Heart Asn, 72 & Silver Medallion for Meritorious Serv, 73; Best Proj in fund raising of Young Rep Leadership Conf, Young Rep Nat Fedn, 73 & Best Proj in Spec Non-Polit Projs of Young Rep Leadership Conf, 73; Pres Award, Auburn CofC, 74. Relig: Methodist. Legal Res: 115 Clark St Garrett IN 46738 Mailing Add: 12th & Jackson Sts Auburn IN 46706

QUINN, DORIS MARILYN (D)
Mo State Rep
b Independence, Mo, July 15, 23; d Earnest Hays Allison & Ethel Marie Ferman A; m 1948 to Jack Elliott Quinn; c Curtis Lee & William Craig. Educ: Univ Mo, BJour; Theta Sigma Phi. Polit & Govt Pos: Committeewoman, Independence Twp Dem Party, 73-74; Mo State Rep, 40th Dist, 75- Bus & Prof Pos: Indust ed, Various Co, 51-; employee, Remington Arms Co, Lake City AAP, currently. Mem: Women's Polit Caucus; Nat Fedn Press Women; Int Asn Bus Communicators; Women in Commun, Inc. Honors & Awards: Matrix Honoree, Women in Commun, Inc, 74. Relig: Methodist. Mailing Add: 3302 N Osage Independence MO 64050

QUINN, DWIGHT WILSON (D)
NC State Rep
b York, SC, Sept 12, 17; s William Lytle Quinn & Lucy Wilson Q; m 1936 to Marion Elizabeth Isenhour; c Mrs Lester U Dodge. Educ: Night & correspondence schs. Polit & Govt Pos: Pres, Cabarrus Co Young Dem Club, NC, 48, served on various state comts; precinct registr, 48-50; NC Med Care Comn; NC State Rep, 51-; mem, Gov Comn Reorgn State Govt, 59-60, chmn, 61-62; mem, Gov Comt Juvenile Delinquency, Los Angeles, Calif, 60; deleg, Dem Nat Conv, 60 & 68; mem exec comt, NC Citizens Comt Better Schs, Inc. Bus & Prof Pos: Supvry capacity, Cannon Mills Co. Mil Serv: Army, 44-45. Mem: Rotary; AF&AM; Scottish Rite; Shrine; Oasis Temple. Honors & Awards: Kannapolis Man of the Year, Jaycees, 48; Amvets Nat Distinguished Serv Award for Outstanding Community Serv, 53. Relig: Lutheran; mem church coun, secy congregation, gen supt, Sunday Sch; pres, Brotherhood, Sunday sch teacher & mem archit & planning comt, Kimball Mem Lutheran Church. Legal Res: 213 S Main St Kannapolis NC 28081 Mailing Add: PO Box 314 Kannapolis NC 28081

QUINN, JAMES E (D)
RI State Rep
Mailing Add: 755 Dexter St Central Falls RI 02863

QUINN, JOHN ROBERT (D)
Conn State Rep
b Bridgeport, Conn, Nov 29, 48; s Thomas V Quinn & Mary D Cacioppo Q; m 1969 to Barbara Jean Ventrice; c Kimberly Ann, Colleen Marie & Kelly Ann. Educ: Sacred Heart Univ, BA, 70; Univ Bridgeport, MS in Psychol, except for thesis; Sigma Psi Delta; Freshman Class Pres; Student Govt. Polit & Govt Pos: Pres, Fairfield Young Dem, Conn, 71-72; rep, Fairfield Dem Town Meeting, 71-73; chmn, Fourth Cong Dist Young Dem, 72-73; leader, Fairfield Dem Town Comt, Fifth Dist, 72-; Conn State Rep, 132nd Dist, 75- Bus & Prof Pos: Counr, Dept of Children Youth Serv, Bridgeport, Conn, 71-73; head diagnostic counr, Dept of Corrections, North Ave Jail, Bridgeport, 73; exec dir, Fairfield Drug Adv Bd Inc, 73- Mem: Fairfield Day Center; Barnum Festival Soc; KofC; Conn Youth Serv Asn; Conn Child Welfare Asn. Relig: Roman Catholic. Mailing Add: 245 Sunnyridge Ave Fairfield CT 06430

QUINN, KATHERINE T (D)
Mem, Dem Nat Comt, Conn
Mailing Add: 525 Main St Hartford CT 06103

QUINN, PHILIP ANDREW (D)
b Worcester, Mass, Feb 21, 10; s James Henry Quinn & Dorothy Mulrone Q; single. Polit & Govt Pos: Mass State Rep, 49-64; Mass State Sen, 65-72; alt deleg, Dem Nat Conv, 68 & 72. Bus & Prof Pos: Proprietor, Hotel Massasoit, Spencer, Mass, 35-; owner, John J Brown Ins Agency, 58- Mil Serv: Entered as Pvt, Air Force, 42, released as S/Sgt, 45, after serv in 302nd Air Serv Group, India & Burma, 45; India-Burma Ribbon with three Battle Stars. Mem: KofC; Am Legion; VFW. Relig: Roman Catholic. Mailing Add: 101 Main St Spencer MA 01562

QUINN, ROBERT E (D)
Va State Deleg
Mailing Add: 113 Marvin Dr Hampton VA 23666

QUINN, ROBERT H (D)
b Boston, Mass, Jan 30, 28; m to Claudina Mainini Pyne; c Andrea, Michael, Elaina & Stephanie. Educ: Boston Col, AB, 52; Harvard Law Sch, LLB, 55. Polit & Govt Pos: Mass State Rep, 57-69, speaker, Mass House Rep, 67-69; Attorney Gen, Mass, 69-75. Bus & Prof Pos: Attorney-at-law. Mem: Nat Asn Attorneys Gen. KofC; Boston Col Alumni Asn; Boston Col Varsity Club; Harvard Law Sch Asn of Mass. Legal Res: 32 Auckland St Boston MA 02125 Mailing Add: Peabody Brown Rowley & Storey One Boston Pl Boston MA 02108

QUINN, RODNEY S (D)
Maine State Rep
Mailing Add: 15 Green St Gorham ME 04038

QUINN, VICTOR H (R)
Mem, Maury Co Rep Exec Comt, Tenn
b Lula, Ga, Oct 29, 25; s Herbert Quinn & Minnie Q; m 1948 to Jean Westmoreland; c Victor H, Jr, Suzanne & Michael. Polit & Govt Pos: Mem, Maury Co Rep Exec Comt, Tenn, 48-, secy, 48-60, chmn, 64-74; mgr, Maury Co Nixon Campaign, 60; magistrate, Maury Co Court, 60-66; finance chmn, Sixth Cong Dist Rep Party; jury comnr, Middle Tenn Dist Fed Court, 64-66. Bus & Prof Pos: Employee, Commerce Union Bank, 54-64, asst cashier, 64-65, asst vpres, 65-66. Mil Serv: Entered as A/S, Navy, 43, released as Aviation Radioman 2/C, 47, after serv in Patrol Bomber Squadron 108, Pac, 44-47. Mem: Jaycees; Am Legion; Rotary; Maury Co Ment Health Asn; Maury Co Cancer Soc. Honors & Awards: Selected Maury Co Outstanding Young Man of Year, 61. Relig: Church of Christ. Mailing Add: RR 6 Columbia TN 38401

QUINN, WALTER A, JR (D)
RI State Rep
Mailing Add: 19 Elmhurst Ave Providence RI 02908

QUIRK, JOHN A (D)
b Hastings, Nebr, June 11, 51; s John Pierce Quirk & Helen Anderson Q; single. Educ: Harvard Col, AB magna cum laude, 73. Polit & Govt Pos: Alt deleg, Nebr Dem State Conv, 72, deleg, 74; deleg, Dem Nat Conv, 72. Mem: Common Cause. Relig: Lutheran. Mailing Add: 408 Forest Blvd Hastings NE 68901

QUIRK, ROBERT JOSEPH (D)
Mayor, Cuyahoga Falls, Ohio
b Kearny, NJ, Sept 25, 31; s William A Quirk & Helen C Toomey Q; m 1957 to Dorothy Ann McCartan; c Cynthia Ann, Mary Ann, Marjorie Ann & James Edward. Educ: Potomac State Col, AA, 56; Univ Pittsburgh, BA, 58. Polit & Govt Pos: Sixth ward councilman, Cuyahoga Falls, Ohio, 67-71, mayor, 74- Mil Serv: Entered as Pvt, Army, serv in 3rd Div, Korea; Combat Inf Badge; Korean Campaign Medal with Five Battle Stars. Mailing Add: 317 Van Buren Ave Cuyahoga Falls OH 44221

R

RAASCH, MARY ELIZABETH (R)
b Aroya, Colo, Feb 7, 09; d William Henry Rowe Ching & Annie Jardine C; m 1931 to Earl Raasch; c Robert W, Marjorie M (Mrs Poppen) & Richard E. Educ: SDak State Univ 1 year; Watertown Bus Univ, 6 months. Polit & Govt Pos: Vchmn, Hamlin Co Rep Party, SDak, 61-74. Bus & Prof Pos: Bookkeeper, auto co, Watertown, SDak, 29-31. Mem: Eastern Star; Fidelus Study Club; Rep Federated Club. Relig: Presbyterian. Mailing Add: Rural Route Castlewood SD 57223

RABBITT, RICHARD J (D)
Mo State Rep
b St Louis, Mo, Oct 30, 35; m 1962 to Teresa Marie Molloy; c Michael Patrick, Richard J, Jr, Daniel Timothy, Maureen Molloy, Sheila Marie & Terese Lenore. Educ: St Louis Univ Grad Sch, BS in Polit Sci & LLB. Polit & Govt Pos: Mo State Rep, 60-, speaker, Mo House of Rep, 73- Bus & Prof Pos: Attorney-at-law. Mem: KofC (First Grand Knight, Past Grand Knight & trustee, Coun 5181). Honors & Awards: City of Hope Humanitarian Award, 75. Relig: Catholic. Mailing Add: 4340 Forest Park St Louis MO 63108

RABEDEAUX, W R (R)
Iowa State Sen
Mailing Add: 514 E Wate St Wilton IA 52778

RABINOWITZ, JAY ANDREW (D)
Chief Justice, Alaska Supreme Court
b Philadelphia, Pa, Feb 27, 27; s Milton Rabinowitz & Rose R; m 1957 to Ann Marie Nesbit; c Judith, Mara, Sara & Max. Educ: Syracuse Univ, BA, 49; Harvard Law Sch, LLB, 52. Polit & Govt Pos: Asst US attorney, Territory of Alaska, 58-59; dep attorney gen, Alaska, 59-60, superior court judge, 60-65; assoc justice, Alaska Supreme Court, chief justice, 73- Mil Serv: Entered as Pvt, Army Air Corps, 45, released as Pfc, 46, after serv in US. Relig: Jewish. Legal Res: Yankovitch Rd Fairbanks AK 99701 Mailing Add: State Capitol Juneau AK 99801

RACE, HOWARD EVERETT (R)
Mem, Milwaukee Co Rep Coun, Wis
b Rome, NY, May 9, 18; s Homer D Race & Estelle Maude Herman R; m 1944 to Mary Theresa Thiery. Educ: Milwaukee Sch Eng, BSEEP; Sigma Pi Rho. Polit & Govt Pos: Chmn, 15th Ward Rep Party, Milwaukee, 15th Dist, 61-62; mem, State Cent Comt, 62 & 64; alt deleg, Rep Nat Conv, 64; Gov campaign coordr, Fourth Cong Dist, 64; deleg & membership chmn, Milwaukee Co Rep Coun, 64, mem, 66-; deleg & mem exec comt,

Ninth Dist Rep Party & chmn, 18th Ward, 66- Bus & Prof Pos: Sr Prof Engr, Allen Bradley, 52- Mil Serv: Entered as A/S, Navy, 42, released as AMM 2/C, 45. Mem: Plastics Engrs Soc; Inst Elec & Electronics Engrs; Am Legion. Mailing Add: 8605 W Glendale Ave Milwaukee WI 53225

RADACK, JEROME D (D)
SDak State Rep
b Yankton, SDak, July 13, 42; s Darrell Radack & Darlene Ramsdell R; m 1960 to Diane M Christopherson; c Cheri, John, Jennifer & Robert. Educ: Univ SDak, Vermillion, BA, 67, MA, 69; Univ Nebr, Lincoln, grad work; Phi Alpha Theta; Phi Eta Sigma; Phi Beta Kappa. Polit & Govt Pos: SDak State Rep, 73- Bus & Prof Pos: Asst prof, Yankton Col, SDak, 70-71; owner pvt bus, 71- Mil Serv: Entered as Pvt, E-1, Army, 60, released as Sp-5, 63, after serv in Army Res Control Group 14 Army Corps, 60-63; Good Conduct Medal. Mem: Sertoma Club; UFO; Mason (32 degree). Mailing Add: 706 Locust Yankton SD 57078

RADANT, KENNETH RAYMOND (R)
b Owosso, Mich, Jan 1, 36; s Raymond Radant & Josephine Kovacic R; m 1957 to Marjorie Ellen White; c Karen, Steven & Joellyn. Educ: Alma Col, 3 years; Mich State Univ, BA, 58; Tau Kappa Epsilon. Polit & Govt Pos: Chmn, Barry Co Rep Party, Mich, 65-74; alt deleg, Rep Nat Conv, 68; vchmn, Barry Co Bd Comnr, Mich, 68- Bus & Prof Pos: Pres & gen mgr, WBCH AM-FM, Hastings, Mich, 62- Mem: Rotary; Elks. Honors & Awards: Outstanding Serv Award, Jr CofC. Relig: Episcopal. Mailing Add: 646 W Walnut St Hastings MI 49058

RADCLIFFE, CHARLES W (R)
b Oolitic, Ind, Nov 20, 25; s George Charles Radcliffe & Grace Sears R; m 1966 to Shirley Caron; c Suzanne Caron. Educ: Bates Col, AB, 50; Univ NH, 51-52; Georgetown Univ Sch Law, LLB, 59; Delta Sigma Rho. Polit & Govt Pos: Asst to chmn, Sen Commerce Comt, 53; legis asst to US Sen Upton, NH, 54; asst dir, White House Conf on Educ, 55-56; legis specialist, US Off Educ, 56-62; minority counsel, House Educ & Labor Comt, US House Rep, 63- Bus & Prof Pos: Lawyer, Ruben, Karr, Barrett & Radcliffe, 62-63. Mil Serv: Seabees, serv in Naval Construction Bn, Pac Theatre, 45-46. Relig: Anglican. Legal Res: Annapolis MD Mailing Add: 2174 Rayburn House Off Bldg Washington DC 20515

RADER, BOBBY JEWETT (R)
Chmn, Rep State Cent Comt Calif
b Tecumseh, Okla, Feb 23, 26; s M C Rader & Alice Harbor R; m 1945 to Clarice Jean Brundege; c Robin Jean & Susan Myrl. Educ: Okla Univ, 1 year. Polit & Govt Pos: Mem, Calif Rep State Cent Comt, 65-74, chmn, 74- Bus & Prof Pos: Mgr Visalia yard, United Lumber Yards, Calif, 50-60; owner, Mother Lode Lumber Co, Mariposa, currently. Mil Serv: Merchant Marine. Mem: Elks; F&AM; Lions. Relig: Church of Christ. Mailing Add: PO Box 96 Hwy 140 Mariposa CA 95338

RADER, JOAN SPERRY (R)
Mem, Conn Rep State Cent Comt
b Brooklyn, NY, July 11, 34; d Edward Goodman Sperry & Mary Elizabeth Garvin S; m 1958 to William Donald Rader; c Elizabeth, Judith & Jennifer. Educ: Vassar Col, BA, 56. Polit & Govt Pos: Mem, Conn Rep State Finance Comt, 69-71; mem, Conn Rep State Cent Comt, 72- Bus & Prof Pos: Asst to exec dir, Far East-Am Coun of Com & Indust, New York, 57-68. Honors & Awards: Hal Hammond Award, Greenwich Young Rep, 70. Mailing Add: 2 Walsh Lane Greenwich CT 06830

RADER, JOHN L (D)
Alaska State Sen
b Howard, Kans, Feb 11, 27; s Mr & Mrs Ralph R Rader; m 1951 to Carolyn Weigand; c Tim, Matthew & Janet. Educ: Univ Ore; Stanford Univ; Univ Kans, BS in Bus Admin, 48 & LLB, 51. Polit & Govt Pos: City attorney, Anchorage, Alaska, 54-55; State Attorney Gen, Alaska, 59-60; Alaska State Rep, 61-68, Floor Leader, Alaska House of Rep, 63-64; mem bd, Gtr Anchorage Health Dist; Alaska State Sen, 68- Bus & Prof Pos: Mem, Indust Rels Dept, Lago Oil & Transport, Netherlands, WI, 48; employee, FE Co, 49; partner, McCutcheon, Nesbett & Rader, 51-54 & Hartlieb, Groh & Rader, 55-58 & 61-62; part-time instr real estate law, Anchorage Community Col, 57; attorney-at-law. Mil Serv: Naval Res, 45-46. Mem: Alaska Bar. Honors & Awards. Received Young Man of Year Award, Anchorage Jr CofC, 60. Mailing Add: Box 2068 Anchorage AK 99501

RADER, STEVEN PALMER (R)
Chmn, NC Fedn Col Rep
b Charlotte, NC, Dec 30, 52; s Alvin Marion Rader, Jr & Shirley Palmer R; single. Educ: Duke Univ, Nat Merit scholar, 71-75, BA, 75; Tau Epsilon Phi. Polit & Govt Pos: Pres, Duke Univ Col Rep, 72-74; sgt-at-arms, NC Fedn Col Rep, 72-73, vchmn, 73-74, chmn, 74-; mem exec bd, NC Conservative Soc, 73-75; mem exec comt, Mecklenburg Co Rep Party, 73-, chmn precinct 38, 74-; mem, Rep State Exec & Cent Comts, NC, 74-; mem, Col Rep Nat Comt, 74-; mem, NC Young Rep Exec Comt, 74-75. Mem: Blue Ridge Numismatic Asn; Carolina World Coin Asn; Duke Univ Interfraternity Coun; De Tocqueville Soc. Honors & Awards: Eagle Scout, Boy Scouts, 69; Col Rep of the Year, NC Fedn Col Rep, 75; Leon Schneider Mem Scholar, 75. Relig: Lutheran. Legal Res: 4438 Univ Dr Charlotte NC 28209 Mailing Add: PO Box 9307 Duke Sta Durham NC 27706

RADEWAGEN, FRED (R)
b Louisville, Ky, Mar 20, 44; s Hobart Fred Radewagen & Mildred Carlsen R; m 1971 to Amata Catherine Coleman; c Erika Catherine. Educ: Northwestern Univ, Evanston, BA, 66; Georgetown Univ, MSFS, 68; Delta Tau Delta, pres, Nat Capital Alumni Chap, 71-75. Polit & Govt Pos: Research asst, Rep Nat Comt, 67-68; off mgr, United Citizens for Nixon/Agnew, 68; off mgr, Inaugural Comt, 68-69; Washington liaison officer, High Comnr of Trust Territory of Pac Islands, 69-71; staff coordr, Territorial Affairs, Dept of Interior, 71- Mem: DC Young Rep; Northwestern Univ Alumni Asn; Everett McKinley Dirksen Rep Forum; Ill State Soc of Washington, DC; Capitol Hill Club. Relig: United Presbyterian. Legal Res: 1245 Taft Ave Berkeley IL 60163 Mailing Add: 103 E Luray Ave Alexandria VA 22301

RADNEY, TOM (D)
Mem, Ala State Dem Comt
b Wadley, Ala, June 18, 32; s James Monroe Radney & Beatrice Simpson R; m 1962 to Madolyn Boyd Anderson; c Margaret Ellen, Sara Frances, Hollis Lee & Thomas Anderson. Educ: Auburn Univ, BS & MS, 52; Univ Ala, LLB, 55; Phi Kappa Tau; Phi Alpha Delta. Polit & Govt Pos: Deleg, Dem Nat Conv, 60 & 68; judge, Alexander City, Ala, 62-68; Ala State Sen, 66-70; mem, Ala State Dem Comt, 70-; mem, Ala Bd Bar Comnr, 70- Mil Serv: Entered as Pvt, Army, 55, released as Capt, 59, after serv in Judge Adv Gen Corps. Mem: Am Legion; Kiwanis; Elks; Mason; Shrine. Relig: Methodist. Legal Res: 234 Ridgeway Dr Alexander City AL 35010 Mailing Add: Box 443 Alexander City AL 35010

RADO, STUART ALAN (D)
b Atlanta, Ga, Nov 17, 45; s Jerome Rado & Jeanne Gusman R; single. Educ: Univ Ga, BBA, 71; secy, Zeta Beta Tau. Polit & Govt Pos: Alt deleg & vol coord transportation comt, Dem Nat Conv, 72. Bus & Prof Pos: Proj coord, Third Century, USA, 72; exec dir, Nat Network of Youth Advisory Boards Project. Publ: Youth Advisory Boards: Organize, Advise, Implement; free lance writer. Mem: Gtr Miami Jaycees (mem vpres, 74-75); Young Dem Club Dade Co (bd dirs, 72-); Tiger Bay Club; Univ Ga Alumni Soc (pres Miami chap, 74-75); Orange Bowl Staging Comt. Relig: Jewish. Legal Res: 1500 W 23rd St Sunset Isle 3 Miami Beach FL 33140 Mailing Add: PO Box 402036 Ocean View Br Miami Beach FL 33140

RADOSEVICH, R WAYNE (D)
NMex State Sen
b Gallup, NMex, June 17, 45; s Joseph J Radosevich & Doris E Leahy R; m to Mary Ann Salas; c John Joseph & Michael Dwayne. Educ: Gallup High Sch, grad, 62. Polit & Govt Pos: Pres, McKinley Co Young Dem, 68-70, mem adv comt, 70-72; mem, NMex Dem Cent Comt, 69-72; mem, McKinley Co Exec & Adv Comts, 70-72; mem, NMex Dem Compilation Comt, 70-72; pres, NMex Young Dem, 70-72; chmn, UNDay, 2 years; mem, Attorney Gen Staff, NMex, 71-72; NMex State Sen, Dist Four, 72-; hon mem, McKinley Co Coun Govts, 72- Bus & Prof Pos: Gen mgr, J B Tanner Shopping Ctr, 64-69; partner, B J Livestock & Pinon Co, 66-69; owner, Wayne's Shell Serv, 69- & Wayne's East Chevron, 71- Mem: Coatians; Odd Fellows. Honors & Awards: Outstanding Orgn Award for NMex, 3 years; Outstanding Young Dem, 4 years. Relig: Catholic. Mailing Add: 624 McKee Dr Gallup NM 87301

RADWAY, LAURENCE INGRAM (D)
Chmn, NH Dem State Comt
b Staten Island, NY, Feb 2, 19; s Frederick & Dorothy R; m 1949 to Patricia Ann Headland; c Robert Russell, Carol Sinclair, Michael Porter & Deborah Brooke. Educ: Harvard, BS, 40, PhD, 50; Phi Beta Kappa. Polit & Govt Pos: Civilian aide to Secy of Army; chmn, platform comt, NH Dem Party, 58-60; chmn, Grafton Co Dem Comt, 58-62; mem, NH Dem State Comt, 58-62, chmn, 75-; prof nat security affairs, US Nat War Col, 62-63; deleg, Dem Nat Conv, 64, alt deleg, 72; NH State Rep, 68-72, asst Dem leader, NH House Rep, 70-72. Mil Serv: Entered as Cpl, Army, 43, released as Capt, 46, after serv in Transportation Corps, ETO & US, 43-46. Publ: Soldiers and Scholars, Princeton Univ Press, 57; Military Behavior in International Organization, Free Press of Glencoe, 62; Foreign Policy and National Defense, Scott, Foresman & Co, 69. Mem: Am Polit Sci Asn; Coun on Foreign Rels; Am Legion. Relig: Protestant. Mailing Add: 22 Occom Ridge Hanover NH 03755

RADZWILLAS, ALDONA (D)
Conn State Rep
Mailing Add: 325 Northfield Dr Bridgeport CT 06606

RAE, MATTHEW SANDERSON, JR (R)
Mem, Calif State Rep Cent Comt
b Pittsburgh, Pa, Sept 12, 22; s Matthew Sanderson Rae & Olive Waite R; m 1953 to Janet Hettman; c Mary-Anna S, Margaret S & Janet S. Educ: Duke Univ, AB, 46, LLB, 47; Stanford Univ, 51; Phi Beta Kappa; Omicron Delta Kappa; Phi Eta Sigma; Tau Psi Omega; Sigma Nu; Phi Alpha Delta. Polit & Govt Pos: Pres, South Bay Young Rep, 56; parliamentarian, Los Angeles Co Young Rep, Calif, 56; pres, 46th Assembly Dist Rep Assembly, 57; asst treas, Calif Rep Assembly, 57-58; vpres, Los Angeles Co Rep Assembly, 59-64; vchmn, 17th Cong Dist Rep Party, 60-62; mem, Los Angeles Co Rep Cent Comt, 60-64; vchmn, 28th Cong Dist Rep Party, 62-64; chmn, 46th Assembly Dist Rep Party, 62-64; pres, Calif Rep League, 66-67; mem, Calif State Rep Cent Comt, 66-, mem exec comt, 66-67. Bus & Prof Pos: Asst to dean, Duke Univ Sch Law, 47-48; assoc Off of Karl F Steinmann, Baltimore, Md, 48-49; nat field rep, Phi Alpha Delta Law Fraternity, 49-51; research attorney, Calif Supreme Court, 51-52; assoc, Darling, Hall, Rae & Gute, 53-55, partner, 55- Mil Serv: Entered as Aviation Cadet, Army Air Corps, 43, released as 2nd Lt, 45, after serv in Training Command, US, 43-45. Mem: Am Bar Asn; State Bar Calif (chmn, Probate & Trust Law Comt, 74-75); Phi Alpha Delta (supreme justice, 72-74); Am Legion (comdr, Allied Post, 69-70); Town Hall Calif (pres, 75). Relig: United Presbyterian. Legal Res: 600 John St Manhattan Beach CA 90266 Mailing Add: Rm 400 523 W Sixth St Los Angeles CA 90014

RAFFL, KENNETH ALBERT (R)
Mem, Ill Rep State Cent Comt
b Redbud, Ill, Nov 17, 13; s Oswald Raffl & Adeline Bromleve R; m 1938 to Luella Schuette; c John David. Polit & Govt Pos: Rep precinct committeeman, Ill, 60; chmn, Randolph Co Rep Party, 64-74; mem, Ill Rep State Cent Comt, currently. Bus & Prof Pos: Salesman, Liggett-Meyers, 35-38 & Weeke Wholesale Co, 39- Mem: Boy Scouts (instnl rep). Relig: Catholic. Mailing Add: 269 Summit St Redbud IL 62278

RAFTERY, FRANK (D)
Mem-at-Lg, Dem Nat Comt
Mailing Add: 1750 New York Ave NW Washington DC 20006

RAGGE, EVERETT KENNETH (D)
Committeeman, Ark State Dem Party
b Uniontown, Ark, Oct 6, 34; s Claud Roosevelt Ragge & Hazel Morrison R; m 1956 to Katherine Tyler; c Phyllis M, Sanford K & Susan J L. Educ: Poteau Community Col, Poteau, Okla, AA, 2 years. Polit & Govt Pos: Committeeman, Ark Young Dem Exec Comt, 64-68 & Ark State Dem Party, 68- Bus & Prof Pos: Dir civil defense, Crawford Co, Ark, 62-66; pres, Crawford Co Bd of Realtors, 66 & Van Buren CofC, 67. Mil Serv: Entered as Pvt, Army, 53, released as E-6, 59, after serv in White House Staff Exec Detachment, 57-59; Presidential Citation; White House Serv Commendation. Mem: Ark Real Estate Asn; Nat Asn Real Estate Bd; F&AM; Scottish Rite; Shrine. Relig: Protestant. Legal Res: 4 Vista Hills Circle Van Buren AR 72956 Mailing Add: PO Drawer A Van Buren AR 72956

RAGGIO, WILLIAM J (R)
Nev State Sen
Mailing Add: PO Box 3137 Reno NV 89505

RAGSDALE, ALBERT GEORGE (D)
Chmn, Phillips Co Dem Cent Comt, Ark
b West Helena, Ark, May 23, 13; s George William Ragsdale & Agnes Snyder R; m 1931 to Gladys Jane Kendal; c Norma Sue (Mrs Surman). Educ: Woodruff High Sch, West Helena,

Ark, 10 years. Polit & Govt Pos: Chmn, Phillips Co Dem Cent Comt, Ark, 65-; secy, Phillips Co Elec Comnr, 65- Bus & Prof Pos: Owner, Albert Ragsdale Serv Sta, 40-; consignee, Cities Serv Oil Co, 40- Mem: Shrine. Relig: Methodist. Mailing Add: 317 Elm Helena AR 72342

RAGSDALE, EDWIN H (R)
Va State Deleg
Mailing Add: Rte 14 Fort Brady Rd Richmond VA 23231

RAGSDALE, MIKE (R)
Ore State Rep
Mailing Add: 6520 S W Murray Blvd Beaverton OR 97005

RAGSDALE, PAUL BURDETT (D)
Tex State Rep
b Mt Haven, Tex, Jan 14, 45; s Emmittee R, father deceased; single. Educ: Univ Tex, Austin, BA in Sociol, 66. Polit & Govt Pos: Tex State Rep, Dallas Co, Dist 33N, 72- Bus & Prof Pos: Social scientist, Tracor, Inc, Austin, 66-68; chief planning & eval, Crossroads Community Ctr, Dallas, 68-72. Mem: Black United Fund (bd dirs); Progressive Voters League; Black Legis Caucus; Tex Blac Polit Caucus. Honors & Awards: Outstanding Orchestra Mem, Univ Tex, Austin, 62. Relig: Methodist. Mailing Add: 5710 E Thornton Freeway Dallas TX 75232

RAHALL, NICK JOE, II (D)
b Beckley, WVa, May 20, 49; s Nick Joe Rahall & Mary Alice Rahall R; m 1972 to Helen Oliver McDaniel. Educ: Duke Univ, AB, 71; George Washington Univ, 71-72. Polit & Govt Pos: Treas, NC Col Fedn Young Dem, 68-69; vpres, Duke Univ Young Dem, 69-70, pres, 70-71; asst press liaison, US Senate, 71-72; deleg, Dem Nat Conv, 72; aide, US Senate Majority Whip, Robert C Byrd, WVa, 72; asst, US Senate Majority Secy, 72-74; deleg, Dem Nat Mid-Term Conf, 74. Bus & Prof Pos: Mail carrier, US Senate Post Off, summer 69, laborer, US Senate Serv Dept, summer 70; bid dirs, Rahall Commun Corp; pres, Mountaineer Tour & Travel, Inc. Mem: Beckley Jaycees; Beckley Young Dem Club; Common Cause; Beckley Rotary; Mason. Honors & Awards: Outstanding NC Young Dem, NC Young Dem Club, 71; Outstanding Young Man Award, Beckley Jaycees, 73-74. Relig: Presbyterian. Mailing Add: 504 Carriage Dr Beckley WV 25801

RAICHE, ROBERT EDWARD (D)
Mem, NH Dem State Comt
b Manchester, NH, Feb 18, 37; s Edward Raiche & Lucienne Harris R; m 1958 to Mary Elizabeth Duval; c Robert Edward, Jr, Denise Anne, Maureen Elizabeth, Donna Marie & Kathleen Joyce. Educ: Nathaniel Hawthorne Col, BA, 67. Polit & Govt Pos: Mem, NH Dem State Comt, currently; NH State Rep, 65-72, minority leader, NH House Rep, 69-72; alt deleg, Dem Nat Conv, 68, deleg, 72; chmn, Hillsborough Co Dem Party, 69-70. Bus & Prof Pos: Instr & adminr, Nathaniel Hawthorne Col, 68- Mil Serv: Entered Marine Corps, 55, released as Sgt, 61. Mem: KofC. Relig: Roman Catholic. Mailing Add: 957 Somerville St Manchester NH 03103

RAILE, J L (R)
Chmn, Dist 30 Rep Party, NDak
b Stutsman Co, NDak, July 28, 12; s Jacob Raile & Christina Martell M; m 1934 to Lydia Wanner; c Edwin, Lawrence, Frances, Charlene, James, Vernon & Sherwin. Polit & Govt Pos: Chmn, McIntosh Co Livestock Asn, 46-58; chmn, Non-Partisan League, 48-54; chmn, Tri-Co Fair Asn, 50-68; NDak State Rep, 71-73; chmn, Dist 30 Rep Party, NDak, 71-; dir, Wishek Hosp Asn, 73- Bus & Prof Pos: Pres, Raile Equip Inc, 60- Relig: Lutheran. Mailing Add: Wishek ND 58495

RAILSBACK, TOM (R)
US Rep, Ill
b Moline, Ill, Jan 22, 32; m to Patricia Sloan; c Kathryn, Julia, Margaret Ann & Lisa. Educ: Grinnell Col, BA in Eng, 54; Northwestern Univ Law Sch, JD, 57; sr class pres, Grinnell Col; pres, Phi Delta Phi, Northwestern Univ; Phi Gamma Delta. Hon Degrees: LLD, Monmouth Col. Polit & Govt Pos: Ill State Rep, 63-66; US Rep, 19th Dist, Ill, 66-; deleg, Rep Nat Conv, 72. Bus & Prof Pos: Attorney, assoc with father, Fred H Railsback, Ill, 57-63; assoc, Graham, Califf, Harper, Benson & Railsback, Attorneys, 63-69. Mil Serv: Army, 57-59, serv in Legal Assistance Off, Ft Riley, Kans. Mem: Ill State Bar Asn; Jr CofC; Elks; Blackhawk Chap, Am Red Cross (bd dirs); Grinnell Col Alumni Bd Dirs (pres). Honors & Awards: Distinguished Serv Award, Jaycees, 64; Moline's Outstanding Young Man of Year, 64; Alumni Award for Distinguished Serv, Grinnell Col, 73; Flandrau Award, Nat Coun on Crime & Delinquency, 74. Relig: Congregational. Legal Res: 2800 12th St Moline IL 61265 Mailing Add: 2431 Rayburn House Off Bldg Washington DC 20515

RAINBOLT, JOHN VERNON (MIKE) (D)
b Abbott, Tex, June 23, 14; s John Bellfield Rainbolt & Venda Gray R; m 1938 to Mary Alice Power; c John V, II, Elizabeth (Mrs Marshall) & Charles. Educ: Univ Okla. Polit & Govt Pos: Chmn, Washita Co Dem Party, Okla, 39, 43, 52 & 56; deleg, Dem Nat Conv, 64, 68 & 72; chmn, Fourth Dist Dem Cent Comt, Okla, 66-73; majority counsel agr comt, US House of Rep, 74- Mil Serv: Merchant Seaman, Navy, 43-45. Mem: Am Asn Petroleum Landmen; Okla City Landmen's Asn; CofC; Okla Good Roads Asn; Okla & Am Title Asns. Relig: Presbyterian. Mailing Add: Box 248 Cordell OK 73632

RAINEY, DONALD GLENN (D)
b Mayfield, Ky, Aug 14, 31; s Frank Paul Rainey & Maudie R; m 1953 to Geraldine Edwards; c Denis Glenn, Julie Lynn & Jill Marie. Educ: Union Univ, BA, 53; Ga Inst Technol, MS, 54; Univ Pittsburgh, 54-55; Sigma Alpha Epsilon. Polit & Govt Pos: Chmn, Gov Campaign, Tenn, 67, Gov field rep & mem, Gov Staff, 68-; deleg, Tenn State Dem Conv, 68; deleg, Dem Nat Conv, 68; mem, Tenn Conserv Comn, 68-; Madison Co chmn, US Sen Campaign, 70; mem, Tenn Higher Educ Comn, 70- Bus & Prof Pos: Engr, Westinghouse Elec Corp, 57-60; instr, Union Univ, 60-62, mem bd trustees & exec comt, 70-; pres, Rainey Furniture Co, Inc, 62-; mem bd dirs, Nat Bank Com & Tenn Retail Furniture Assocs, 70-; mem exec comt, Southern Baptist Found, 72- Mil Serv: Entered as Pvt, Army, 55, released as Specialist, 57, after serv in 3rd Inf, Ft Benning, Ga. Publ: Purchasing News, 59. Mem: Purchasing Agents Asn; Retail Merchants Coun (chmn); Retail Furniture Dealers Asn Tenn; Jackson CofC; Jackson Retail Furniture Dealers Asn. Honors & Awards: Community Award, Jackson State Community Col, 62; Cited by Jackson CofC, 62-65; Spec Citation, Union Univ, 63; Jackson's Young Man of Year, 65; Human Rels Award, Lane Col, 68. Relig: Baptist; Deacon, W Jackson Baptist Church. Mailing Add: 841 Skyline Dr Jackson TN 38301

RAINEY, HOWARD (D)
Ga State Rep
b Crisp Co, Ga, Aug 21, 27; s Dallas Rainey & Essie Lewis R; m 1949 to Mildred Edge; c Marsha Lynn & Howard Mark. Educ: Ga Southwestern Col, 47. Polit & Govt Pos: Ga State Rep, 61- Bus & Prof Pos: Income tax acct; real estate agent; retail furniture operator. Mil Serv: Ga Nat Guard. Mem: Farm Bur; WOW; Lions; Jr CofC. Relig: Baptist. Mailing Add: 201 Eighth St S Cordele GA 31015

RAINS, ALBERT M (D)
Dem Nat Committeeman, Ala
b De Kalb Co, Ala, Mar 11, 02, s Elbert Rains & Louella Campbell R; m 1939 to Allison Blair. Educ: Jacksonville State Col; Univ Ala. Hon Degrees: DLL, Jacksonville State Univ, 72. Polit & Govt Pos: Dist attorney, Etowah Co, Ala, 32-36; Ala State Rep, 42-44; US Rep, Ala, 45-65; Dem nat committeeman, Ala, currently; deleg, Dem Nat Comt, 72. Bus & Prof Pos: Attorney, Rains & Rains; chmn bd, First Ala Bank Gadsden; mem bd dirs, First Ala Bancshares, Inc. Publ: With Heritage So Rich, Random House, 66. Mem: Am & Ala Bar Asns; Lions; Mason; Newcomen Soc. Relig: Baptist. Legal Res: 221 Alpine View Gadsden AL 35901 Mailing Add: Suite 204 First Alabama Bank Bldg Gadsden AL 35901

RAINS, DON (D)
Tex State Rep
Mailing Add: 503 Indiana San Marcos TX 78666

RAINS, HOBDY G (D)
Secy, Ala Dem State Exec Comt
b DeKalb Co, Ala, Mar 29, 12; s Will G Rains & Ola Hamrick R; m 1945 to Constance N Goldman. Educ: Howard Col; Univ Ala, AB & LLB; Pi Kappa Alpha. Polit & Govt Pos: Prison supt, Ala, 39-42 & parole officer, 42-44; secy, Ala Dem State Exec Comt, currently. Bus & Prof Pos: Lawyer, 45- Mil Serv: Nat Guard, 3 years, served in Qm Band. Mem: Am Bar Asn; Etowah Co Bar Asn; Odd Fellows; Mason; Shrine. Relig: Baptist. Mailing Add: 112 Gwindale Rd Gadsden AL 35902

RAINS, OMER L (D)
Calif State Sen
b Kansas City, Mo, Sept 25, 41; s Roy M Rains & Janice Cochran R; div; c Kelly & Mark. Educ: Univ Calif, Berkeley, BA, 63; Boalt Hall Sch Law, JD, 66; Phi Alpha Delta. Polit & Govt Pos: Calif State Sen, 74-, chmn comt elec & reapportionment, subcomt, polit reform, vchmn joint legis comt rev elec code, Calif mem, judiciary comt, bus & professions comt & comt ins & financial insts, Calif State Senate, 74-, chmn, joint legis comt legal equality & joint comt pub domain, 75- Mem: Am & Calif Bar Asns; Calif Trial Lawyers Asn; Sierra Club; Ventura CofC. Honors & Awards: Distinguished Serv Award, presented to Ventura's outstanding citizen, 71; commendations from Univ Calif Alumni Asn, Cities of Ventura & Camarillo, Co of Ventura & Ventura Port Dist. Relig: Protestant. Legal Res: 4059 Ocean Dr Oxnard CA 93030 Mailing Add: 5082 State Capitol Sacramento CA 95814

RAINWATER, WALLACE EUGENE (GENE) (D)
Ark State Sen
b Fort Smith, Ark, Nov 4, 24; s Wallace B Rainwater & Nona B Plunkett R; single. Educ: Col of The Ozarks, 42-43; Ark A&M Col, 43-44; Northwestern Univ, 44. Polit & Govt Pos: Ark State Rep, 12th Dist, 67-70; Ark State Sen, 71- Bus & Prof Pos: Pres, Rainwater Trucking Co Inc, Fort Smith, currently. Mil Serv: Entered as A/S, Navy, 42, released as Ens, 46, after serv in Standard Landing Craft Unit 62, recalled to active duty, 50, released as Lt, 52, duty in Korea & Japan; Comdr, Naval Res. Mem: Nat Soc State Legislators; ROA; Exchange Club; Am Legion; Mason. Relig: Methodist. Mailing Add: Box 98 Greenwood AR 72936

RAISCH, WM (BILL) (R)
Mo State Rep
Mailing Add: 9904 Vasel Affton MO 63123

RAIT, GEORGE (D)
NDak State Sen
b Noonan, NDak, Dec 5, 07; s Robert Rait & Williamina Morrison R; m 1947 to Olga Hanson. Educ: Long Creek Sch, 8 years. Polit & Govt Pos: Community committeeman, Agr Adjust Agency, NDak, 37-44; bd mem, Farmer Home Admin, 42-46; first chmn, Soil Conserv Dist, 46-50; NDak State Sen, 65-, mem, Legis Coun, NDak State Senate, 67-, mem, Finance & Tax Comn, 67-, mem, Coun of State Govt on Social Welfare, 69-, mem, Legis Coun & chmn, Subcomt on Polit Subdiv, 71- Bus & Prof Pos: Mem, Divide Co Fair Asn, 47-57; mem bd, Burke Divide Elec Coop, 52-, pres, 64-71; bd mem, Upper Mo Gen & Transmission Coop, 64-, pres bd, 70-; mem, Midwest Elec Consumers Asn, 64-71. Mem: Farmers Union. Honors & Awards: Soil Conservation Awards; State Rural Elec Dir of the Year Award, 70. Relig: Protestant. Mailing Add: Noonan ND 58765

RAKESTRAW, PRISCILLA B (R)
Rep Nat Committeewoman, Del
Mailing Add: 2 Woodshaw Dr Newark DE 19711

RAKESTRAW, W VINCENT (R)
b Dayton, Ohio, July 6, 40; s David W Rakestraw & Lou Ann Hobbs R; m 1963 to Penny Lynn Blackford. Educ: Ohio Univ, BSJ; Capital Univ, Franklin Law Sch, JS; Sigma Delta Chi; Sigma Chi. Polit & Govt Pos: Asst Attorney Gen, Ohio, 68-69; legis dir, Sen William B Saxbe, 69-74; Asst Attorney Gen, Legis Affairs, Dept Justice, 74-75; Counsel to Ambassador India, Dept State, 75- Mem: Am, Fla, DC & Ohio Bar Asns. Legal Res: 16 Highland Rd Dar-Lin Estates Martins Ferry OH 43935 Mailing Add: New Delhi Dept of State Washington DC 20520

RALPH, LEON DOUGLAS (D)
Mem, Dem Nat Comt, Calif
b Richmond, Va, Aug 20, 32; s Arthur Ralph & Leanna Woodard R; m 1972 to Pamela L Joynes; c Martha B, Ruth L & Leon A. Educ: Univ Colo; Valley Col, AA, 61. Polit & Govt Pos: Chmn, Los Angeles Co Youth for Kennedy Orgn, Calif, 60; chmn, 62nd Assembly Dist, Los Angeles Co Dem Comt, 62-66; dir health orgn, Dem Party, Calif, 63-64; coord for President Johnson's Campaign, 64; admin asst to Speaker, Calif House Rep, 64-66 & consult to Speaker; Calif State Assemblyman, 66-, chmn, Assembly Subcomt on Urban Probs, 68-; Cent Los Angeles campaign mgr for US Sen Robert F Kennedy, 68; deleg, Dem Nat Conv, 68 & 72; mem, Dem Nat Comt, 72- Bus & Prof Pos: Logistics analysts, NAm Aviation, 59-62. Mil Serv: Entered as Pvt, Air Force, 50, released as S/Sgt, 54, after serv in Provost Marshalls

Off, Air Defense Command Hq; Good Conduct & Nat Defense Medals. Publ: Auth, California Freeway-Housing Law for Poor People, 68. Mem: Mason; Boy Scouts; NAACP (life mem). Relig: Methodist; Trustee, Grant AME Church. Legal Res: 10615 State St South Gate CA 90280 Mailing Add: 1922 E 103rd St Los Angeles CA 90002

RALPH, S LESTER (D)
Mayor, Somerville, Mass
b Lynn, Mass, July 9, 31; s Albert Ralph & Grace Dawe R; m 1964 to Joyce Palmer; c Sarah, Thomas & Jennifer. Educ: Boston Univ, BA, 54, MA, 59, Sch Law, LLB, 63; Episcopal Theol Sch, MTS, 56. Hon Degrees: DD, Episcopal Theol Sch, 73. Polit & Govt Pos: Mayor, Somerville, Mass, 70-; comnr, Middlesex Co, 72- Bus & Prof Pos: Asst rector, Christ Episcopal Church, Waltham, Mass, 59-60 & Grace Episcopal Church, Medford, 60-62; teacher, Chapel Hill Sch, Waltham, 60-63; instr, New Eng Sch Law, 64-67; lawyer, Waltham, 64-69; rector, Christ Episcopal Church, Somerville, 64-; instr, Northeastern Univ, 67-69. Publ: Auth, Methods of Practice in Massachusetts, suppl, 2nd ed, 66 & 68. Mem: Am & Mass Bar Asns. Honors & Awards: Distinguished Pub Serv Award, Gen Alumni Asn, Boston Univ, 71, Collegium of Distinguished Alumni, 74. Relig: Episcopal. Legal Res: 73 Wheatland St Somerville MA 02145 Mailing Add: 93 Highland Ave Somerville MA 02143

RALSTON, DAVID EDMUND (R)
Mem, Ga Rep State Cent Comt
b Ellijay, Ga, Mar 14, 54; s David Willard Ralston & Ernestine Pettit R; single. Educ: Young Harris Col, 72-73; NGa Col, 73-; Phi Theta Kappa. Polit & Govt Pos: Dir, Ninth Dist, Ga Young Rep, 71-; alt deleg, Rep Nat Conv, 72; staff aide, John Savage for Lt Gov Campaign, 74; mem, Ga Rep State Cent Comt, currently. Mem: Ga Conservancy. Honors & Awards: Ga Del to 1972 US Senate Youth Prog, William Randolph Hearst Found, 72. Relig: Baptist. Mailing Add: Big Creek Rd Ellijay GA 30540

RALSTON, RAYMOND EDWARD (D)
Chmn, Warren Co Dem Party, Pa
b Sheffield, Pa, Feb 21, 19; s Lynn Russell Ralston & Angeline Corbran R; m 1940 to Verna Janette Wenstran; c Kenneth, Dr Terrance, Mavis (Mrs Spencer) & Brenda (Mrs Short). Educ: Sheffield High Sch, grad, 36. Polit & Govt Pos: Committeeman, Dem Party Sheffield, Pa, 62-; chmn, Warren Co Dem Party, 68-; investr, Pub Assistance Audits, 70- Bus & Prof Pos: Packer, Penn Bottle Co, 37-44; owner & operator of a dairy farm, 48-66; tool dresser to drilling contractors, 66-68; grinder, Stack Pole Carbon Co, 68-70. Mil Serv: Entered as A/S, Navy, 44, released as Seaman 1/C, 46, after serv in SPac, 46-47; Pac Theater Ribbon. Mem: Moose; Am Fedn State, Co & Munic Employees; United Commercial Travelers; Sheffield Forest Indust Hist Mus; Pa Dept Forest & Waters (forest fire warden). Relig: Methodist. Mailing Add: Box 4 Star Rte Sheffield PA 16347

RAMBEAU, IONE (D)
Polit & Govt Pos: Former mem, Dem Nat Comt, Idaho Mailing Add: 227 Prospect Lewiston ID 83501

RAMBERG, CHARLES HENRY (D)
Mem, Hinds Co Dem Exec Comt, Miss
b Washington, DC, Dec 4, 43; s Vernon Charles Ramberg & Norma Boie R; m 1972 to Mary Leah Frank. Educ: Davidson Col, AB, 65; Georgetown Univ Law Ctr, JD, 71; Phi Eta Sigma; Sigma Nu. Polit & Govt Pos: Admin asst, Hon Charles Evers, Fayette, Miss, 69-70; scheduler, Evers for Gov Campaign, 71; alt deleg, Dem Nat Conv, 72; mem, Hinds Co Dem Exec Comt, 72-; secy, Fourth Cong Dist Caucus, 72- Bus & Prof Pos: Staff attorney, Community Legal Serv, Jackson, Miss, 71- Mil Serv: Entered as 2nd Lt, Army, 65, released as 1st Lt, 67, after serv in 101st Airborne Div, 65-67; Res Capt, Army, 1 year; parachutist. Mem: Am Va & Miss State Bar Asns; NAACP; Am Civil Liberties Union (pres, Jackson Area Chap). Mailing Add: Box 22571 Jackson MS 39205

RAMBO, CARROLL ANN (D)
Secy-Treas, Fourth Dist Dem Cent Comt, Okla
b Hillsboro, Ill, Feb 24, 44; d Albert Robert Imle & Virginia Brinton I; m 1969 to G Dan Rambo. Educ: Univ Ill, Champaign-Urbana, BA, 71; Shi-Ai; Torch; Shorter Bd; Alpha Chi Omega. Polit & Govt Pos: Mem, Gov Comn Status Women, Okla, 72; secy-treas, Fourth Dist Dem Cent Comt, Norman, 73-; deleg, Dem Nat Mid-Term Conf, 74. Relig: Lutheran. Mailing Add: 511 Chautauqua Ave Norman OK 73069

RAMBO, G DAN (D)
b Marietta, Okla, Apr 23, 28; s Joseph Daniel Rambo & Mae Belle Raum R; m 1969 to Carroll Ann Imle. Educ: Univ Okla, BBA in Bus, 51, MS in Geol, 55 & JD, 65; Phi Eta Sigma; Delta Sigma Pi; Sigma Gamma Epsilon; Sigma Xi; Sigma Alpha Epsilon; Delta Theta Phi; Scabbard & Blade. Polit & Govt Pos: Chmn, Cleveland Co Dem Party, Okla, 65-69; co chmn, Fred Harris Campaign Orgn; state coordr in states of Wash & Ore & asst coordr for Southern Calif, deleg search oper & campaign orgn, Humphrey-Muskie Campaign; mem, Dem Nat Comt, 68; deleg, Dem Nat Conv, 68, alt deleg, 72; state campaign coord, David Hall for Gov, Okla, 69-70; chief legal aide, Off of Gov David Hall, formerly. Mil Serv: Entered as Pvt, Marine Corps, 46, released as Pfc, 47, after serv in Signal Bn, First Marine Div; Army Res, 49-53, 2nd Lt. Mem: Am Asn Petroleum Geologists; Am Bar Asn; Lions; CofC; Cleveland Co Community Action Found, Inc (chmn, 67-72). Relig: Presbyterian. Mailing Add: 511 Chautauqua Ave Norman OK 73069

RAMIREZ, E ALICE (D)
Mem, Calif Dem State Cent Comt
b Los Angeles, Calif, Apr 29, 28; d Vicente M Contreras & MaRefugio Vasquez C; m 1953 to Concepcion Ramirez; c Steven, Marie Concepcion, Alice, Anthony, Sylvia & Debbie. Educ: Instituto Tecnico Industrial de Agua Caliente, Mexico, 4 years; Metrop Bus Col, Los Angeles, Calif, 49. Polit & Govt Pos: Treas, Echo Park Dem Club, Calif, 64, pres, 65-67 & 69; mem, Calif Dem State Cent Comt, 66-; chmn, 29th Cong Dist Coun, 68; field rep to Assemblyman David A Roberti, 70-; asst secy, Los Angeles Co Dem Comt, 69-, third vchmn, 73- Mem: Dem Women's Forum; Latin Alliance Club; life mem PTA; Mexican-Am Polit Asn; Polit Action League of Mex Am. Relig: Catholic. Mailing Add: 2207 Lyric Ave Los Angeles CA 90027

RAMMELL, ARTHUR LEON (ART) (D)
Chmn, Teton Co Dem Party, Idaho
b Tetonia, Idaho, June 17, 01; s George Fredrick Rammell & Josephene Nielsen R; m 1925 to Pearl Daniels; c Glenda (Mrs Robert Green) & George Daniels; eight grandchildren. Polit & Govt Pos: Chmn, Teton Co Dem Party, Idaho, currently. Bus & Prof Pos: Life time farmer & rancher. Relig: Latter-day Saint. Mailing Add: 402 N Main Tetonia ID 83452

RAMOS COMAS, JORGE A (POPULAR DEMOCRAT, PR)
Rep, PR House of Rep
Mailing Add: State Capitol San Juan PR 00901

RAMOS VAELLO, RAMON (NEW PROGRESSIVE, PR)
Rep, PR House of Rep
Mailing Add: State Capitol San Juan PR 00901

RAMOS YORDAN, LUIS ERNESTO (POPULAR DEM, PR)
Popular Dem Speaker, PR House Rep
b Ponce, PR, Feb 2, 15; s Federico Ramos Antonini & Felicita Yordan R; m 1943 to Lenabelle Smith; c Harry Luis & Lysa Lee. Educ: Lincoln Univ, BS, 41; Faculty of Med, Nat Univ Med, MD, 47; Grad Sch Pub Health, Columbia Univ, MPH, 54. Polit & Govt Pos: Consult indust med & occup health, Dept of Labor, PR, 55-56 & Dept Health, 58-59; consult indust med & safety, PR House Rep, 67-68; Rep, PR House Rep, 69-, Popular Dem Party Floor Leader, 69-73, Popular Dem Speaker, 73-; mem bd dirs, Popular Dem Party, PR, 69- Bus & Prof Pos: Prof pub health, Col Pharm, Univ PR, 48-50 & Inst Labor Rels, 59-68; med dir, Arroyo City Hosp, 49-51 & Arecibo Dist Hosp, 51-53; pres hosp, Dr Ramos-Yordan Inc, 57-; pres, Lenabelle & Burhans Lab, Inc, 57-70 & Ramos & Smith Realty, Inc, 64- Mil Serv: Entered as Capt, Army, 56, released as Maj, 58, after serv in MedC, Chief Prev Med-Med Intel, Far East Command. Publ: Pathogenesis of Sprue, Mex, 47; Industrial hygiene & occupational disease in Puerto Rico, Indust Med & Surv, 2/58. Mem: Med Asn PR; Am Indust Med Asn. Honors & Awards: Sport Hall of Fame, PR Academia Internationalis-Lex et Srientia, 72; Hall of Fame Hispanic Int Research Inst, 73. Relig: Catholic. Legal Res: 40 SO & De Diego Ave La Riviera Rio Piedras PR 00921 Mailing Add: Ave De Diego Esquina 40S Urbanizaction La Riviera Rio Piedras PR 00924

RAMPTON, CALVIN LEWELLYN (D)
Gov, Utah
b Bountiful, Utah, Nov 6, 13; s Lewellyn S Rampton & Janet Campbell R; m 1941 to Lucybeth Cardon; c Margaret, Janet, Anthony & Vincent. Educ: Univ of Utah, JD, 40; George Washington Univ; Bar & Gavel Law Soc. Hon Degrees: LLD, Univ Utah, 70. Polit & Govt Pos: Admin asst to US Rep J W Robinson, 36-38; co attorney, Davis Co, Utah, 39-41; Gov, Utah, 65-; deleg, Dem Nat Conv, 68 & 72; chmn, Nat Gov Conf, 74-75; pres, Coun State Govts, 74-75. Bus & Prof Pos: Attorney-at-law, 40. Mil Serv: Nat Guard, 32-37; entered as 2nd Lt, Army, 37, released as Maj, 45, after serv in ETO & US Army Claims Comn; Res Col, Army Field Judiciary Serv; Bronze Star; Army Commendation Ribbon with Rhineland & WGer Battle Stars. Mem: Int Acad of Trial Lawyers; The New Coalition (chmn, 74-75); Brigham Young Univ Master Pub Admin Asn. Honors & Awards: Environ Planning Guide Distinguished Serv Award; Outstanding Pub Admnr of the Year, Inst Govt Serv, 71; Presidential Citation, 73; Citation from US Dept Justice Bur Narcotics & Dangerous Drugs; Brotherhood Award, Utah Chap Nat Conf Christians & Jews, 73. Relig: Latter-day Saint. Legal Res: 1270 Fairfax Rd Salt Lake City UT 84103 Mailing Add: Governor's Office State Capitol Salt Lake City UT 84114

RAMSAY, JOHN ERWIN (D)
Chmn, Rowan Co Dem Party, NC
b Salisbury, NC, Sept 23, 15; s John Ernest Ramsay & Elizabeth Craige R; m 1945 to Jean Anne Ferrier; c Anne Ferrier (Mrs Frank L Saunders, Jr), John Erwin, II, Kerr Craige & George Bard Ferrier. Educ: Univ NC, Chapel Hill, BA, 38; Yale Univ Sch Archit, BFA & MA, 41; Di Senate, pres; Sigma Nu. Polit & Govt Pos: Chmn, Rowan Co Dem Party, NC, 75- Mil Serv: Entered as Pfc, Army, 42, released as Lt, Naval Res, 46, after serv in Pac Interp Squadron 1, SPac & Washington, DC, 43-46. Mem: Nat Coun Archit Regist Bd; fel Am Inst Archit; NC Symphony; Rotary. Honors & Awards: Awards of Merit for Farm Colony Bldg, 55, Residence of Mr & Mrs John Erwin Ramsay, 55 & Am Sq, Furniture Display, Martinsville, Va, 60, NC Chap, Am Inst Archit; Cert of Recognition for Milford Hills Methodist Church, Bishop's Comt, 63. Relig: Presbyterian. Legal Res: 119 Pine Tree Rd Salisbury NC 28144 Mailing Add: PO Box 1285 Salisbury NC 28144

RAMSEY, CLAUDE (R)
Tenn State Rep
Mailing Add: Ramsey Forgey Rd Rte 1 Harrison TN 37341

RAMSEY, HARVEY KENNETH (R)
Chmn, Knox Co Rep Cent Comt, Ind
b Vincennes, Ind, Jan 21, 18; s John A Ramsey & Nora Mayall R; m 1940 to Alma B Newton; c Paula A, Patrick H & Christopher A. Educ: Ind Univ; Phi Alpha Delta. Polit & Govt Pos: Prosecuting attorney, Knox Co, Ind, 51-59; town attorney, Bruceville, 56-66; city attorney, Vincennes, 64-66; chmn, Knox Co Rep Cent Comt, 64- Mil Serv: Entered as Pvt, Air Force, 41, released as Sgt, 45; Air Medal; Asiatic-Pac Theater & Am Theater Ribbons. Mem: KofC (3 degree & 4 degree); Am Legion; VFW; 40 et 8; Elks. Relig: Catholic. Legal Res: 1203 Busseron Vincennes IN 47591 Mailing Add: 118 N Seventh Vincennes IN 47591

RAMSEY, J W (BILL) (D)
Ark State Rep
Mailing Add: 406 E Graham St Prairie Grove AR 72753

RAMSEY, PETER E (R)
NH State Rep
Mailing Add: 31 Dunbar St Keene NH 03431

RAMSEY, RICHARD RALPH (R)
Iowa State Sen
b Osceola, Iowa, Nov 23, 40; s Joseph Dean Ramsey & Ardis Ruth Bowlsby R; m 1968 to Natalie Judy Green; c Adam Todd. Educ: Univ Northern Iowa, BA, 64; Univ Iowa, Col Law, JD, 66; Sigma Tau Gamma; Phi Delta Phi. Polit & Govt Pos: Prosecuting attorney, Clarke Co, Iowa, 68-73; chmn, Clarke Co Rep Cent Comt, formerly; Iowa State Sen, 47th Sen Dist, 73- Bus & Prof Pos: Attorney-at-law, Osceola, Iowa, 66- Mil Serv: Entered as Pvt, Army, 66, released as SP-5, 68, after serv in 35th Eng Group, Vietnam, 67-68; Army Commendation Medal; Good Conduct Medal. Mem: Osceola Lions; Osceola Jaycees (pres & secy); Am Legion (serv officer); Clarke Co Tuberc Asn (chmn mem gifts); Farm Bur. Relig: Protestant. Mailing Add: 707 S Fillmore St Osceola IA 50213

RANDALL, ANTHONY T (R)
NH State Rep
Mailing Add: Adams Ave Seabrook NH 03874

RANDALL, BILL (D)
Ark State Rep
Mailing Add: 116 Rose Hot Springs AR 71901

RANDALL, DONALD MILLARD (D)
Mo State Rep
b St Joseph, Mo, Dec 1, 26; s Don C Randall & Thelma Lester R; m 1945 to Evelyn Norris; c Donald O, Thomas & Eddie D. Educ: Benton High Sch, 4 years; Mo Western Col, short courses. Polit & Govt Pos: Dem committeeman, 11th Ward, 63-70; chmn, Dem Co Comt, 64-70; Mo State Rep, Eighth Dist, 71- Bus & Prof Pos: Steamheat serviceman, St Joseph Light & Power Co, 53- Mil Serv: Entered as Pvt, 45, released as Pfc, 46, after serv in Mil Police, ETO & Atlantic-Pac Theatre, 45-46; M/Sgt, Air Force Res, 49-; several medals. Mem: Mason; Am Legion; Eagles; IBEW; CofC; Mo Nat Guard Asn. Relig: Protestant. Mailing Add: 4011 Pickett Rd St Joseph MO 64503

RANDALL, KENNETH ALLAN (R)
NH State Rep
b Franklin, New Hampshire, Dec 14, 32; s Earle Francis Randall & Helen Thompson R; m 1961 to Elaine Coddington; c Katherine Anne. Educ: Plymouth State Col, BE, 54; Univ NH, 72-75. Polit & Govt Pos: Comnr, Gunstock Recreation Area, 61-68; treas, Tilton, NH, 62-, mem budget comt, Tilton, 72-; sch dist moderator, Winnisquam Regional Sch Dist, 74-; NH State Rep, Belknap Co Dist Three, 75- Bus & Prof Pos: Teacher bus educ, Tilton-Northfield High Sch, 58-65; instr electronic data processing, NH Tech Inst, 65- Mil Serv: Entered as Airman Basic, Air Force, 54, released as Airman 1/C, 57, after serv in Air Training Command. Mem: F&AM Doric Lodge. Relig: Congregational. Mailing Add: Calef Hill Rd Tilton NH 03276

RANDALL, ROBERT WHITE (D)
Wash State Rep
b Chicago, Ill, Nov 18, 21; s Harry L Randall & Pauline White R; m 1946 to Lorna Lee Cooper; c Robert W, Jr, Bruce L & Jane Lee. Educ: Univ Wash, BS, 43; Ill Col Optom, OD, 49; Phi Gamma Delta. Polit & Govt Pos: Wash State Rep, Dist 23, 69-, chmn revenue & taxation comt, Wash House Rep, 73- Bus & Prof Pos: Optometrist, 59-; mem, Bremerton Sch Bd, Wash, 65-72, chmn, 70-71. Mil Serv: Entered as Cadet, Army Air Force, 43, released as 1st Lt, 45, after serv in 82nd Fighter Group, ETO, 44-45; Capt, Air Force Res, currently; ETO Medal; Air Medal with 5 Oak Leaf Clusters; Distinguished Flying Cross. Mailing Add: 3040 Marine Dr Bremerton WA 98310

RANDALL, WILLIAM CLARENCE (D)
Ga State Rep
b Macon, Ga, Oct 14, 43; s William Phillip Randall & Elizabeth Hudson R; m 1962 to Lauretta Lois Fults; c Dawn Michelle, Lance Jeffrey, Allison Germaine & Nikki Tere. Educ: Morgan State Col, BA, 65; Emory Univ Sch Law, JD, 69. Polit & Govt Pos: Deleg, Dem Nat Conv, 72; Ga State Rep, 75- Mem: Gamma Eta Gamma; Am Bar Asn; NAACP; Prince Hall Mason; Elks. Relig: Protestant. Mailing Add: 349-A Grant Ave Macon GA 31201

RANDALL, WILLIAM J (D)
US Rep, Mo
b Independence, Mo, July 16, 09; m to Margaret L; c Mary (Mrs Garland Wilson, III). Educ: Jr Col, Kansas City, Mo; Univ of Mo; Kansas City Sch of Law; Univ of Kansas City. Polit & Govt Pos: Judge, Jackson Co Court, Mo, 46-59; US Rep, Mo, 59- Mil Serv: World War II, serv in Amphibious Unit, SW Pac & Philippines. Legal Res: 201 S Pleasant Independence MO 64050 Mailing Add: US House of Rep Washington DC 20515

RANDLE, RODGER A (D)
Okla State Sen
Mailing Add: State Capitol Oklahoma City OK 73105

RANDOLPH, EDWARD G, JR (D)
La State Rep
Mailing Add: 1801 Bush Ave Alexandria LA 71301

RANDOLPH, JENNINGS (D)
US Sen, WVa
b Salem, WVa, Mar 8, 02; s Ernest Randolph & Idell Bingman R; m 1933 to Mary Katherine Babb; c Jennings, Jr & Frank Babb. Educ: Salem Col, grad, 24; Tau Kappa Alpha. Hon Degrees: Hon degrees from various cols & univs. Polit & Govt Pos: Mem, President's Comt on Employ of the Handicapped; deleg, Dem Nat Conv, 48, 52, 56, 64 & 68; US Rep, WVa, 33-47; US Sen, WVa, 58-, chmn, Comt Pub Works, mem, Comt Labor & Pub Welfare, Comt PO & Civil Serv, Comt Vet Affairs, Spec Comt Aging & Dem Sen Campaign Comt, US Senate, currently; mem US deleg, Interparliamentary Union, Rome, 62; US deleg, NATO Parliamentarian's Conf, Paris, 62; Tenth Mex-US Interparliamentary Conf, US, 70 & Mex-US Interparliamentary Conf, Guanajuato, 73. Bus & Prof Pos: Ed, Green & White, 22-23 & The Message, Salem, WVa, 22-25; mem ed staff, Clarksburg Daily Telegram, WVa, 24-25; assoc ed, WVa Rev, 25-26; hon trustee, prof of pub speaking & journalism & dir athletics, Davis & Elkins Col, 26-32; trustee, Salem Col; asst to pres & dir pub rels, Capital Airlines, 47-58; former co-owner & assoc ed, Randolph Enterprise-Rev, Elkins; former faculty mem, Leadership Training Inst; former instr effective speaking, Southeastern Univ & dean, Col Bus & Financial Admin. Publ: Co-auth, Mr Chairman, Ladies & Gentlemen, Judd & Detweiler, Inc, 39; auth, Going to Make a Speech?, Capital Airlines, 48, contrib, nat mags. Mem: Youth Gov Conf (nat sponsoring comt, 62-); Moose; Nat Aeronaut Asn; Nat Blinded Vet Asn (adv comt); Nat Asn Physically Handicapped. Honors & Awards: Vocational Rehabilitation Award, 70; City of Hope Med Award, 71; Cabell Co Asn Ment Retarded Children, 71; Leadership Award, President's Comn Employ Handicapped, 72; Migel Medal, Am Found for the Blind, 72; plus many other awards from nat prof orgns. Relig: Seventh Day Baptist. Legal Res: 206-8 Davis Ave Elkins WV 26241 Mailing Add: 4608 Reservoir Rd NW Washington DC 20007

RANDOLPH, LLOYAL (D)
Md State Deleg
Mailing Add: 3400 Woodbrook Ave Baltimore MD 21216

RANDOLPH, PAUL J (R)
Ill State Rep
b Logan Co, Ill, Sept 5, 05; married. Educ: Millikin Univ; Univ Ill. Polit & Govt Pos: Ill State Rep, 13th Dist, 54- Bus & Prof Pos: In mkt, Atlantic Richfield Co. Mem: Mason (32 degree); Scottish Rite; Shrine; Moose; Kiwanis. Relig: Presbyterian; trustee & elder, Fourth Presby Church, Chicago. Mailing Add: 850 N DeWitt Pl Chicago IL 60611

RANDOLPH, SANNA POORMAN (D)
b Baton Rouge, La, Apr 27, 42; d Glenn William Poorman & Louise Gueno P; m 1967 to Edward (Ned) Gordon Randolph, Jr; c Sanna Aimee & Edward Gordon, III. Educ: Smith Col, Jr year abroad at Univ Geneva & Inst for Advan Int Studies, BA, 64; Columbia Univ, summer 64; Syracuse Univ, Peace Corps Training, 64; Tulane Univ, Russian lang courses, 67. Polit & Govt Pos: Deleg, Dem Nat Conv, 72; mem exec comt, La Comt for Humanities, 72-; bd mem, Dem Alliance, 72-; mem, La Bicentennial Comn, 73-; mem, Alexandria City Charter Comn, 73. Bus & Prof Pos: Teacher, Peace Corps in EAfrica, 64-66 & Head Start, New Orleans, 67; coordr, Cenla Community Action Agency, Alexandria, 69. Mem: Inter-Racial Coalition (secy, 70); Prison Reform Steering Comt (publicity chmn, 72-73); Smith Col Alumnae Club; Rapides Parish Sch Vol Prog (lang enrichment chmn & publicity chmn, 72-); Poor Man's Supper, Alexandria (co-chmn, 73-). Mailing Add: 2517 Avenue B Alexandria LA 71301

RANDOLPH, SUZANNE FURNEAUX (D)
VChmn Budget & Finance, Tex State Dem Party
b St Louis, Mo, Mar 22, 39; d John Lakeman Furneaux & Sue Mae Hammett F; m 1962 to George Randolph; c John Frederick, Cameron & Amy Lynn. Educ: Univ Tex, Austin, 57-59; Gamma Phi Beta. Polit & Govt Pos: Vchmn budget & finance, Tex State Dem Party, 74-; committeewoman, Tex State Dem Exec Comt, Sen Dist 13, 74- Bus & Prof Pos: Pub rels-fund raiser, Oper Peace of Mind, Nat Runaway Hotline, also co-auth of hotline idea for Tex Gov Dolph Briscoe, 73- Mem: Bayou City Dem Women (treas, 75-76); Fiestas Patrias (adv bd, 75); Women of Rotary; Mus of Fine Arts. Relig: Episcopal. Mailing Add: 7803 Meadowglen Houston TX 77042

RANER, GUY HAVARD, JR (D)
Mem, Los Angeles Co Dem Cent Comt, Calif
b Vicksburg, Miss, Nov 7, 19; s Guy Havard Raner, Sr & Caroline Lorraine Campbell R; m 1941 to Jane Anne Law; c James G, Daniel L & Janice A. Educ: Univ Miss, 37-40; Univ Mo, Columbia, BJ, 42; Univ Calif, Los Angeles, Sec Teaching Credentials, 46; Univ Southern Calif, MA in Polit Sci, 56; San Fernando Valley State Col, Sec Admin Credentials, 65; Tau Kappa Alpha. Polit & Govt Pos: Cand, Calif State Assembly, 64th Dist, 68; mem, Calif Dem State Cent Comt, 68-70; mem, Los Angeles Co Dem Cent Comt, 68- Bus & Prof Pos: Govt & hist teacher & chmn social studies dept, Canoga Park High Sch, Los Angeles City Unified Sch Dist, 46-72, curriculum adv, Mgt Info Div, Systems & Prog Br, Los Angeles City Schs, 72-74. Mil Serv: Entered as Yeoman 3/C, Naval Res, 42, released as Lt, 55, after serv in Patrol Squadron 94, Fleet Air Wing 16, Harvard Commun Sch, USS Bougainville, USS Shangri-La & Sch of Naval Justice, Newport, RI, World War II, 42-45, Brazil, Pac; Korean War, 51-52; Atlantic & Pac Area Ribbons; Reserve Medal. Publ: Co-ed, Land Of The Free and Its Critics, Calif Teachers Asn, 67; Polling the teachers, Calif Social Sci Rev, 10/64; How Free is the Free Secondary School?, J of Sec Educ, 3/65. Mem: Nat Educ Asn; UN Asn; NAACP; Am For Dem Action; Calif Dem Coun. Honors & Awards: Recipient of JFK Award for Meritorious Serv in the Field of Human Rels. Mailing Add: 22331 Devonshire St Chatsworth CA 91311

RANEY, JOHN NATHAN (R)
Chmn, Brazos Co Rep Party, Tex
b Huntsville, Tex, Apr 4, 47; s James Nathan Raney & Maurine Key R; m 1974 to Elizabeth Hodges. Educ: Tex A&M Univ, BBA in Mkt, 69; Alpha Phi Omega. Polit & Govt Pos: Chmn, Brazos Co Rep Party, Tex, 71- Bus & Prof Pos: Owner-mgr, Tex Aggie Bookstore, College Station, 69- Mil Serv: Entered as Pvt, Tex Army Nat Guard, 69, released as 1st Lt, after serv in Co C, 1st Bn (Abn), 143rd Inf, 69-75. Mem: AF&AM (Worshipful Master, Brazos Union Masonic Lodge 129, 74-75); Scottish Rite (32 degree, Houston Consistory); AAONMS (Arabia Temple, Houston). Relig: Methodist. Mailing Add: 3410 Sandra Dr Bryan TX 77801

RANGEL, CHARLES B (D)
US Rep, NY
b New York, NY, June 11, 30; s Ralph Rangel & Blanche Wharton R; m 1964 to Alma Carter; c Steven & Alicia. Educ: NY Univ, BS, 57; St John's Law Sch, LLB, 60 & JD, 68; Phi Alpha Delta; Alpha Phi Alpha. Polit & Govt Pos: Asst US Attorney, NY Dept Justice, 61; counsel to Assembly Speaker, NY Assembly; counsel, New York Housing Authority & President Johnson's Draft Rev Comt; NY State Assemblyman, 72nd Assembly Dist, Harlem, 66-70; US Rep, NY, 70-, mem, Ways & Means Comt, US House Rep, 74-; deleg, Dem Nat Mid-Term Conf, 74. Mil Serv: Entered as Recruit, Army, 48, released as Sgt, 52, after serv in Second Inf Div, Korea, 50-51; Purple Heart; Bronze Star; four Battle Stars; Presidential Citations. Mem: NY State Bar Asn; 369th Vet Asn; NAACP; Nat Asn State Legislators. Honors & Awards: Father of the Year. Relig: Catholic. Mailing Add: 74 W 132nd St New York NY 10037

RANKIN, DORIS BROOKS (D)
Mem, Dem Nat Comt, Ohio
b Cincinnati, Ohio, Oct 20, 29; d Roscoe Southgate Brooks, Sr & Zola Banks B; m to William Theodore Rankin I; wid; c William T, II, Prince A & Robin L. Educ: Walnut Hills High Sch, Cincinnati, Ohio, 46; Xavier Univ, 63-65; Univ Cincinnati, 69. Polit & Govt Pos: Pres, Harriet Tubman Black Women's Dem Club, 71-73; parliamentarian, Ohio Black Women's Leadership Caucus, formerly, pres, currently; mem, Hamilton Co Women's Dem Club, 71-, League of Women's Voters, 71-, Federated Dem Women of Ohio, 72-, Independent Voters of Ohio, 72-; Ohio Black Polit Assembly, 72-; Dem Nat Comt, Ohio, 72-, vchairperson commun & projections for Black Caucus; mem state planning coun, Nat Mus Afro-Am Hist & Cult, currently. Bus & Prof Pos: Pres, Rankin, Sells, Turner & Assocs, Inc, 72- Publ: Why A Black Women's Political Organization, 71. Mem: Women's City Club; Am Soc Planning Off. Honors & Awards: Golden Mike Award, Radio Station WCIN, 71. Relig: Protestant. Mailing Add: Apt 3 566 Torrence Lane Cincinnati OH 45208

RANKIN, HARRY LONGINO, JR (R)
b Columbia, Miss, Nov 4, 26; s Harry Longino Rankin & Tommye Bridewell R; m 1950 to Olive Elizabeth Clower; c Marianne, Thomas Stephen Clower, Elizabeth Carolyn & Christopher Harry Lee. Educ: Univ Ala, Tuscaloosa, BS in Banking, 48; La State Univ Sch of Banking of the South, 59; Harvard Univ Sch of Bus, sr bank officers seminar, 60; Army

Finance Sch, 50; Air Command & Staff Sch, Maxwell AFB, Ala, Squadron Officers course, 51; Officers Training Sch, Shepard AFB, Tex, 64; Nat War Col, Washington, DC, defense strategy seminar, 65; Pi Tau Chi (nat pres, 70-); Sigma Chi; Alpha Chi Omega. Polit & Govt Pos: Col, Miss Militia, 48; mem, Nat States Rights Party, 48-49; chmn, Marion Co Rep Exec Comt, formerly. Bus & Prof Pos: Teller, Citizens Bank, Columbia, Miss, 48-50, cashier, 56-57, vpres, 52-62 & 69-; exec vpres, 62-69; pres, The Rankin Co, 69- Mil Serv: Cadet Pvt, USCC, USMA, 45; re-entered as 2nd Lt, Air Force, 50, released as Capt, 55, after serv in Japan; Maj, Miss Air Nat Guard, 63-70; Lt Col, Air Force Res, 70-; World War II Victory, Nat Defense Serv, Korean Serv, Air Force Longevity, Air Force Res, & UN Serv Medals. Mem: Am Legion; VFW; Shrine; Mason; Rotary. Honors & Awards: UDC Award; Cross of Mil Serv, World War II & Korea. Relig: Episcopal; licensed lay-reader, 67- Legal Res: 1927 Orchard Dr Columbia MS 39429 Mailing Add: PO Box 391 Columbia MS 39429

RANKIN, JAMES W (D)
Ohio State Rep
Mailing Add: 3461 Evanston Ave Cincinnati OH 45207

RANKIN, OTWELL C (D)
VChmn, Kenton Co Dem Exec Comt, Ky
b Harrison Co, Ky, June 23, 16; s Grover C Rankin & Alice Mae Townsend R; m 1940 to Katherine Prather; c Richard, Thomas & Harry. Educ: Eastern State Col, Ky, BS, 38; Xavier Univ, Ohio; Univ Cincinnati; Phi Kappa Tau. Polit & Govt Pos: Vchmn, Kenton Co Dem Exec Comt, Ky, 59-; mem bd of dirs, Fed Home Loan Bank, Cincinnati, 63-; alt deleg, Dem Nat Conv, 68. Bus & Prof Pos: Vchmn bd of dirs, YMCA, 64- Mem: CofC. Relig: Methodist. Mailing Add: 114 Graves Ave Erlanger KY 41018

RANNEY, ZILPAH FAY (R)
Chmn, Pittsfield Rep Town Comt, Vt
b Pittsfield, Vt, May 1, 90; d Harris Guernsey Ranney & Caroline Gibbs R; single. Educ: Univ Vt, BA, 16; Boston Univ Col Lib Arts, MA, 38; Delta Delta Delta. Polit & Govt Pos: Mem, Women's Rep Club, Vt, currently; chmn, Women's Rep Club, Pittsfield, currently; past state secy, Order Women Legislators; trustee, Pub Moneys, currently; former secy & treas, Pittsfield Rep Town Comt, chmn, currently; Vt State Rep, 61-65; mem, Vt Rep State Comt & Rutland Co Rep Comt, currently; Pittsfield Planning Comn, formerly; mem, Bicentennial Comt, Pittsfield, 75. Bus & Prof Pos: Secy-treas, Mt Wilcox Water Asn, Inc, formerly; retired high sch teacher; trustee, Pub Libr, Pittsfield, formerly. Mem: Nat Soc New Eng Women; Ladies Union; DAR (Vt State Historian, State Off & Chap Regents Club); Nat Fedn Rep Women; Am Asn Univ Women. Honors & Awards: Trustee Emeritus, Roger Clark Mem Libr, Pittsfield, Vt. Relig: Methodist. Mailing Add: Park Circle Dr Pittsfield VT 05762

RANSDELL, WILLIAM GARLAND, JR (D)
Chmn, Wake Co Dem Exec Comt, NC
b Fuquay-Varina, NC, Mar 11, 30; s William Garland Ransdell, Sr & Elva Clifton R; m 1958 to Sara Anne Shea; c William Garland, III. Educ: Univ NC, Chapel Hill, BS, 52; Univ NC Law Sch, Chapel Hill, JD with honors, 58; Phi Alpha Delta. Polit & Govt Pos: Asst dist solicitor, NC, 59-62, dist solicitor, 63-72; mem, Gov Comt on Law & Order, 70-73; chmn, Wake Co Dem Exec Comt, NC, 74- Bus & Prof Pos: Partner law practice, Ransdell & Ransdell, 58-62, 73- Mil Serv: Entered as Pvt, Army, 52, released as Sgt, 54, after serv in 101st Airborne Div, Am Theater, 52-54. Publ: Execution-Supplemental proceedings on creditor's bill in NC, 57 & Administrative law-judicial review in state & federal courts—determination of validity of rules & regulations before their application in specific cases, 58, NC Law Rev. Mem: Wake Co, NC & Am Bar Asns; NC State Bar; North Ridge Country Club (pres). Legal Res: 604 Marlowe Rd Raleigh NC 27609 Mailing Add: PO Drawer 1430 Raleigh NC 27602

RANSFORD, PAUL ALLAN (R)
Chmn, Tuscola Co Rep Party, Mich
b Highland Park, Mich, July 8, 35; s Maurice C Ransford & Margaret Robins R; m 1966 to Ann Luther; c Charles, John & Kathryn. Educ: Wayne State Univ, grad, 56. Polit & Govt Pos: Chmn, Tuscola Co Rep Party, Mich, 75- Bus & Prof Pos: Owner, Tuscola Co Abstract Co, Mich, 71- Mem: Am & Mich Land Title Asns, Caro CofC (dir). Relig: Protestant. Mailing Add: 231 Golfview Caro MI 48723

RANSOHOFF, BABETTE STRAUSS (R)
b New York, NY, Mar 25, 04; d Martin Strauss & Annie Jackson S; m 1926 to Arthur Lee Ransohoff; c Martin, Jackson & Barbara (Mrs Howard Burnett). Educ: Vassar Col, BA, 25. Polit & Govt Pos: Mem, Charter Rev Comn, Stamford, Conn, 44-48, mem, Stamford Housing Authority, 44-50, clerk & mem bd rep, 49-54; trustee, Ferguson Libr, 65-; mem, State Rep Platform Comt, 50; chmn, Fairfield Co Eisenhower-Nixon Campaign, 56; vchmn & mem exec comt, Rep Nat Comt, 59-65, mem platform comt, 60; campaign chmn, Lowell P Weicker, Jr for US Rep, Conn, 68; mem, State Libr Bd, 73- Publ: What's The US to You? A Quiz, League of Women Voters of US, 48; Is politics your job?, The Methodist Woman, 50; Where does Christian citizenship start?, Methodist Church, 50. Mem: Nat Soc for Prevention of Blindness; Stamford Mus (trustee). Mailing Add: Wyndover Lane N Stamford CT 06902

RANSON, JOHN S (JACK) (R)
Chmn, Kans Rep State Comt
b Wichita, Kans, Aug 16, 29; m 1951 to Dolores; c Cynthia, Patricia, John & Melissa. Educ: Univ Kans, BSBA, 51. Polit & Govt Pos: State finance chmn, Rick Harman Gubernatorial Primary Campaign, 68, campaign chmn, 70; treas, Kans Rep State Comt, 68-69, chmn, 72-; Sedgwick Co chmn, Jim Pearson Sen Campaign, 72; mem, Rep Nat Comt, currently. Bus & Prof Pos: Pres, Ranson & Co, Inc, Investment Bankers, 53- Mil Serv: Supply Corps Off, Navy, 51-53. Mem: Wichita Crime Comn (bd dirs). Relig: Episcopal. Mailing Add: 328 S Terrace Dr Wichita KS 67218

RANSON, SAMUEL LEE (R)
Chmn, Buckingham Co Rep Party, Va
b Dillwyn, Va, Feb 21, 23; s Radford Bennett Ranson, Sr & Norah Estelle Fitzgerald R; single. Educ: Dillwyn High Sch, Va, grad, 40. Polit & Govt Pos: Chmn, Buckingham Co Rep Party, Va, 64- Bus & Prof Pos: Merchant, Ranson Bros, Dillwyn, Va, 46- Mil Serv: Entered as Pvt, Army, 42, released as Cpl, 46, after serv in Signal Corps, US, 42-46; Sharp Shooter, Good Conduct & Am Victory Medals. Mem: Lions; Am Legion; RAM (past High Priest); Shrine; Mason (past Master, Illustrious Master & Annointed High Priest, 3 times). Relig: Baptist. Mailing Add: PO Box 72 Dillwyn VA 23936

RAO, ANTHONY L, JR (D)
RI State Rep
Mailing Add: 35 Messer St Providence RI 02909

RAPAICH, MARGUERITE CECILLE (R)
b Waterbury, Conn, Feb 1, 23; d Clinton A Fitch & Anne Marie Cote F; m 1949 to Dan Rapaich; c Mark, Diane Marie, Amy Linda, Ellen Elaine & Lisa Anne. Polit & Govt Pos: Secy, Dickinson Co Rep Comt, Mich, 65-67 & 69-71, vchmn, 67-69 & 71-74. Bus & Prof Pos: Stenographer, Burkart-Schier Chem Co, Chattanooga, Tenn, 41-44, secy, 47-49 secy, law off, 45-47 & Royal Bond, Inc, St Louis, Mo, 49-51. Relig: Roman Catholic. Mailing Add: Star Rte 2 Box 330 Iron Mountain MI 49801

RAPOPORT, LORIE JEAN (DFL)
Secy, 30th Legis Dist Dem-Farmer-Labor Party, Minn
b Spirit Lake, Iowa, July 24, 35; d Mervyn Benjamin Fronk & Viola Ruth Williams F; m 1954 to Lawrence Gordon Rapoport; c Sara Elizabeth, Michelle Ann, Mia Lynn & Judith Lee. Educ: State Univ Iowa, one year. Polit & Govt Pos: Third vchairwoman, Third Dist Dem-Farmer-Labor Party, Minn, 70-; secy, 30th Legis Dist Dem-Farmer-Labor Party, Minneapolis, 70- Relig: Hebrew. Mailing Add: 2407 Flag Ave S St Louis Park MN 55426

RAPOPORT, NATALIE (D)
Conn State Rep
b Waterbury, Conn, Apr 22, 27; d Benedict M Rabinowitz & Polly Kraft R; m 1946 to Samuel Rapoport; c Cheryl (Mrs Arnold Kramer) & Jeffrey. Educ: Univ Conn, 44-46. Polit & Govt Pos: Deleg, Conn Dem State Conv, 68, 70 & 72 & Dem Nat Conv, 72; Conn State Rep, Waterbury, 73- Bus & Prof Pos: Teacher, Conn, 64-72. Mem: Nat Women's League (pres, Conn Br); Am Cancer Soc (state bd dirs); Hadassah (chmn, Am Affairs); Jewish War Vet Ladies Auxiliary (David L Fannick Post 91). Honors & Awards: Spec Events Award, Am Cancer Soc, 66, 68 & 70. Relig: Jewish. Mailing Add: 273 Columbia Blvd Waterbury CT 06710

RAPOSA, MANUEL, JR (D)
Mass State Rep
Mailing Add: State Capitol Boston MA 02133

RAPP, STEPHEN JOHN (D)
b Waterloo, Iowa, Jan 26, 49; s Spurgeon John Rapp, Jr & Beverly Leckington R; single. Educ: Harvard Col, AB cum laude, 70; Columbia Univ Law Sch, 71-72; Drake Univ Law Sch, JD with honors, 73; Hasty Pudding-Inst of 1770; Order of the Coif. Polit & Govt Pos: Research asst, Off of US Sen Birch Bayh, Ind, 70; community prog asst, US Dept Housing & Urban Develop, Chicago, 71; Iowa State Rep, 73-74; cand, US Rep, Iowa, 74. Bus & Prof Pos: Attorney, Lindeman & Yagla, Waterloo, Iowa, 74- Mem: Am & Iowa State Bar Asns; Am Civil Liberties Union. Honors & Awards: Nat championship, Voice of Democracy Competition, VFW, 67; Golden Eagle Award, Am Acad Achievement, 67. Relig: Methodist. Mailing Add: 309 Allen St Waterloo IA 50701

RAPPAPORT, SAMUEL (D)
Pa State Rep
b Philadelphia, Pa, Aug 25, 32; s Joseph Rappaport & Goldie Evans R; m 1975 to Rivka Schnurmann. Educ: Temple Univ, AB, 54; Columbia Univ, LLB, 57; Univ Pa Grad Sch, 60-61. Polit & Govt Pos: Deleg & co-chmn, Comt on Home Rule of Local Govt, Pa Const Conv, 67-68; spec adv, Pa Local Govt Comn, 68-70; alt deleg, Dem Nat Conv, 68; Pa State Rep, 71-, chmn comt on ethics, Pa House of Rep, currently; mem, Pa Bi-Centennial Comn, 74- Bus & Prof Pos: Lawyer, Rappaport & Furman, Esqs, 60-; assoc consult, Div Housing & Community Renewal, State of NY, 63-64. Mil Serv: Entered as recruit, Army, 57, released as Sp-4, 59, after serv in Third Med Bn, ETO, 58-59. Mem: Pa, Philadelphia & Am Bar Asns; Am Acad Polit & Social Sci; B'nai B'rith. Relig: Jewish. Mailing Add: Capitol Bldg Harrisburg PA 17120

RAPPEPORT, MICHAEL ARNOLD (D)
b Brooklyn, NY, Oct 24, 37; s Moses Rappeport & Lili Sirota R; m 1959 to Joyce Albin; c Joshua & Beth. Educ: Rensselaer Polytech Inst, BS in Physics, 57; Yale Univ, MEE, 58; NY Univ, PhD in Statist, 68; Alpha Epsilon Pi. Polit & Govt Pos: Deleg, Dem Nat Conv, 72; treas, Middlesex Co McGovern for President, 72; mem finance comt, NJ McGovern for President, 72. Bus & Prof Pos: Mem tech staff, Bell Tel Labs, Holmdel, NJ, 59-66, supvr, 66-67; dir statist serv, Opinion Research Corp, Princeton, 68-72, vpres, 72-; contrib ed, Washington Monthly Mag, Washington, DC, 72- Publ: The kids will be more than just younger, 9/70 & The cities turn a corner, 3/72, Washington Monthly; co-auth, Liberals are infiltrating the House, Washington Post, Outlook Sect, 3/71. Mem: Am Polit Sci Asn; Am Asn for Pub Opinion Research; Am Civil Liberties Union (bd dirs, NJ, 71-). Relig: Jewish. Mailing Add: 68 High St Metuchen NJ 08840

RAPPLEYEA, CLARENCE D (R)
NY State Assemblyman
Mailing Add: 11 Ridgeland Rd Norwich NY 13815

RARICK, JOHN RICHARD (D)
b Waterford, Ind, Jan 29, 24; m to Marguerite Gertrude Pierce; c John Richard, Jr, Carolyn Cheri & Laurie Lee. Educ: Ball State Teachers Col, 42 & 44-45, La State Univ, 43-44; Tulane Univ Law Sch, JD, 49. Polit & Govt Pos: Dist judge, 20th Judicial Dist, La, 61-66; US Rep, La, 67-75. Bus & Prof Pos: Attorney. Mil Serv: Army, World War II, three years; Two Battle Stars for Rhineland & Ardennes campaigns; Bronze Star; Purple Heart; prisoner of war, Germany, four months. Mem: Mason (32 degree, KCCH & Knight Templar); Am Legion; Shrine; Eastern Star; Moose. Honors & Awards: Liberty Award, Cong of Freedom; Distinguished Serv Award, Am for Const Action; Toured Rhodesia & met with Prime Minister Ian Smith, 67; addressed Freedom Day Rally, Asian People's Anti-Communist League, Taiwan, 68; German Volksunion, Nurnberg, 72, Mainz, 73; George Washington Honorary Medal, Freedom Valley Forge. Relig: Baptist. Mailing Add: Drawer E St Francisville LA 70775

RASMUSSEN, A L (SLIM) (D)
Wash State Sen
b Everett, Wash, 1909; m to Eleanor; c four. Educ: Tacoma Pub Schs. Polit & Govt Pos: Wash State Rep, 8 terms; Wash State Sen, formerly & 75-; mayor, Tacoma, formerly. Bus & Prof Pos: Railroad machinist, Northern Pac RR. Mailing Add: 5414 A St Tacoma WA 98408

RASMUSSEN, A T (TOM) (R)
Mont State Rep
Mailing Add: 1300 North Montana Helena MT 59601

RASMUSSEN, DENNIS F (D)
Md State Deleg
Mailing Add: 8009 Yellowstone Rd Kingsville MD 21087

RASMUSSEN, DENNIS L
Nebr State Sen
Mailing Add: RR Scotia NE 68875

RAST, ELSIE SUTHERLAND (D)
VChmn, Lexington Co Dem Party, SC
b Columbia, SC, Nov 11, 31; d Cecil Conway Sutherland & T Lesta Powell S; m 1954 to James Fort Rast; c James Carlisle & William Fort. Educ: Wesleyan Col (Ga), AB, 53; Ariz State Univ, MA, 59; Univ SC, MM, 71. Polit & Govt Pos: Off mgr state hq, John West Campaign for Lt Gov, 66, organizer vol, Gubernatorial Campaign, 70; vchmn, Lexington Co Dem Party, SC, 71-; deleg, Lexington Co, SC State & Dem Nat Conv, 72; cand SC House of Rep, 72; mem, SC Dem Party Reorganization Comt, 73; mem, Lexington Co Coun, 73-, vchmn, 75-; mem, Lexington Co Bicentennial Comt, 74- Bus & Prof Pos: Teacher math & social studies, Columbia, SC, 52-54 & Kyrene Sch, Tempe, Ariz, 58-60; teacher math & govt, Lexington Dist I, SC, 67- Mem: Lexington Co Educ Asn (pres, 74-75); Am Legion; VFW; Lexington Co Hist Soc (pres, 71-73); League of Women Voters. Relig: Methodist. Mailing Add: Pelion SC 29123

RATHBUN, FRANK HUGO (D)
b Philadelphia, Pa, Oct 3, 24; s Frank Hugo Rathbun & Florence McLean R; m 1970 to Hazel Josephine Matcham; c Charity Theresa, Frank Hugo, III, Rebecca Rae & Charles Frederick. Educ: Wayne State Univ, BA, 51. Polit & Govt Pos: Admin asst to US Rep William D Ford, 15th Dist, Mich, 65- Bus & Prof Pos: Newspaper reporter, Mellus Newspapers, Lincoln Park, Mich, 51-64. Mil Serv: Entered as Pvt, Marine Corps, 42, released as S/Sgt, 46, after serv in Second Marine Div, SPac, 42-44; Guadalcanal, Tarawa, Saipan & Tinian Campaign Ribbons; Presidential Unit Citation. Mem: Mason; Shrine; Eagles; Lincoln Park Jaycees; Lincoln Park Hist Soc. Legal Res: Taylor MI 48180 Mailing Add: 11308 Popes Head Rd Fairfax VA 22030

RATHE, BARBARA A (D)
b New Orleans, La, Sept 24, 24; d Gustave Henry Rathe & Euxenia Baccich R; single. Educ: Sacred Heart Convent, Loyola Univ South, New Orleans, La. Polit & Govt Pos: Exec secy to US Rep Hale Boggs, La, 49-72; admin asst to US Rep Lindy Boggs, 73- Relig: Roman Catholic. Legal Res: 3915 St Charles Ave Apt 202 New Orleans LA 70115 Mailing Add: 1656 32nd St NW Washington DC 20007

RATHLESBERGER, JAMES HOWARD (INDEPENDENT)
b Pittsburgh, Pa, May 2, 48; s Howard E Rathlesberger & Jean Heiden R; single. Educ: Univ Calif, Berkeley, BA, 71. Polit & Govt Pos: Research dir, League of Conserv Voters, Washington, DC, 71-72; legis asst to US Rep Henry S Reuss, 73-75; staff dir, Environ Study Conf, US House Rep, 75- Publ: Ed, Nixon and the Environment, Village Voice Books, 72. Honors & Awards: Hon Citizen of Paola, Kans, Mayor of Paola, 68. Relig: Episcopal. Mailing Add: Apt 1 105 Sixth St NE Washington DC 20002

RATLIFF, GERALD R (D)
Chmn, Tom Green Co Dem Party, Tex
b San Angelo, Tex, Dec 25, 38; s Ray Ratliff & Evelyn Summy R; m 1960 to Beverly McCollum; c Merritt & Jefferson. Educ: NTex State Univ, BS, 60; Univ Houston, JD, 67; Phi Delta Phi. Polit & Govt Pos: Chmn, Tom Green Co Dem Party, Tex, 72- Bus & Prof Pos: Attorney, Hardeman, Kever, Ratliff & Fohn, 73. Mil Serv: Lt, Marine Corps, 61; Capt, Res. Mem: Tom Green Co & Tex State Bar Asns; Tex Trial Lawyers Asn. Relig: Presbyterian. Legal Res: 635 S Jefferson San Angelo TX 76901 Mailing Add: PO Drawer 1588 San Angelo TX 76901

RATLIFF, JAMES B (R)
Ariz State Rep
Mailing Add: 11030 Arron Circle Sun City AZ 85351

RATTLEY, JESSIE MENIFIELD (D)
Mem, Dem Nat Comt, Va
b Birmingham, Ala, May 4, 29; d Alonzo Bedell Menifield & Altona Cochran M; m 1952 to Robert Louis Rattley; c Florence E & Robin A. Educ: Hampton Inst, BS in bus admin & secretarial sci, 51; Alpha Kappa Alpha. Polit & Govt Pos: Councilwoman, Newport News, Va, 70-; first vchmn, Va State Dem Party, 72-; mem, Dem Nat Comt, Va, currently, mem credentials comt & by-laws comt, currently; first vchmn, Newport News City Dem Exec Comt, currently; pres, Peninsula Coord Comt, currently; second vchmn, Nat Black Caucus of Local Elected Officials, Houston, Tex, 74; deleg, Dem Nat Mid-Term Conf, 74; chmn, Southeast Community Neighborhood Study Comt, Newport News Planning Comn, currently; app by Gov to serve on Criminal Justice & Crime Prev Task Force for Volunteerism & Spec Task Force to Study Va Jails, 74; app to assist Dept Educ & Ment Health & Ment Retardation, 75. Bus & Prof Pos: Estab, Bus Dept, Huntington High Sch, 51; founded, Peninsula Bus Col, 52, owner, operator & prof, 52- Mem: Dem State Chmn Asn (treas, 75-); Nat Asn Negro Bus & Prof Women's Clubs (hon mem); NAACP (life membership); Va Black Elected Off Orgn (mem exec comt); Nat League of Cities (vchmn effective govt policy comt, 74-). Honors & Awards: Plaque for Outstanding & Dedicated Serv, Zeta Lambda Chap, Alpha Phi Alpha; Resolution of Appreciation, Newport News Planning Comn, 75; Plaque in Recognition of Serv Rendered During Black Hist Week at Ft Monroe, 75; Plaque for Outstanding Community Serv, Pandora Lodge 2 & White Rose Beauty Temple 89, Int Elks, 74; Plaque for Distinguished Serv to Alpha Kappa Alpha from Epsilon Omega Chap, 74. Relig: Presbyterian. Mailing Add: 529 Ivy Ave Newport News VA 23607

RATTLIFF, HERMAN W (R)
Ky State Rep
b Summersville, Ky, Apr 2, 26; s James William Rattliff & Estill Dobson R; m 1951 to Jewell Merritt; c David Brian & Kristi Lynn. Educ: Campbellsville Col, 2 years; Woodward Sch Photog, 1 year. Polit & Govt Pos: Pres, Taylor Co Young Rep, Ky, 53-54; vpres, Ky Young Rep, 54, dist chmn, 55-56, nat committeeman, 64-65; precinct chmn, Taylor Co Rep Party, 57-69; Ky State Rep, 29th Dist, 68-72, 51st Dist, 72- Bus & Prof Pos: Partner photog studio, Campbellsville, 49-; farmer & Charolais breeder, currently. Mil Serv: Entered as Pvt, Army, 45, released as S/Sgt, 47, after serv in 557th Signal Bn, SPac Theater, 45-46; Good Conduct Medal; SPac Theater Ribbon. Mem: Ky Prof Photographers Asn; Prof Photographers Asn Am; Am Legion; Farm Bur; Jaycees. Honors & Awards: Outstanding Serv Awards, Taylor Co Jaycees, 65, 67 & 68; Outstanding Young Rep Ky, 66. Relig: Methodist. Mailing Add: Rte 3 Campbellsville KY 42718

RAU, DUANE (R)
NDak State Rep
Mailing Add: State Capitol Bismarck ND 58501

RAUB, BRIAN DAVID (R)
b Grove City, Pa, Aug 5, 53; s Paul Lester Raub, D O & Miriam Smith R; m 1972 to Annalyse Callahan. Educ: Yale Univ, BA in Polit Sci, 75; Harvard Bus Sch, 75- Polit & Govt Pos: Alt deleg, Rep Nat Conv, 72; campaign chmn, Witt for Sheriff Comt, 75. Bus & Prof Pos: Advert sales mgr, Yale Banner Publ, Inc, 72, bus mgr, 73-74, gen mgr, 74-75; bus mgr, New J, 72, publ, 74-75. Mem: Yale Polit Union; Yale Rep Club (campaign coordr, 71-). Relig: Methodist. Legal Res: Rte 5 Mercer Rd Greenville PA 16125 Mailing Add: PO Box 509 Greenville PA 16125

RAUB, FRIEDA WRIGHT (R)
VPres, Montgomery Co Rep Cent Comt, Md
b New Brunswick, Can; parents deceased; m 1936 to Archie Maxwell Raub; c Richard Albert & David Wright. Educ: Upsala Col, East Orange, NJ, BS. Polit & Govt Pos: Committeewoman, Essex Co, NJ, 54-60; precinct chmn, Montgomery Co, Md, 62-, regional chmn, 71-, vpres, Montgomery Co Rep Cent Comt, 75-; mem, Bd License Comnr, Montgomery Co, 72- Bus & Prof Pos: Substitute sch teacher, Montgomery Co, Md, 60- Mem: Suburban Hosp Auxiliary (pres, 70-72); Rock Creek Women's Rep Club (polit educ chmn); Women's Comt for Nat Symphony; Montgomery Co Thrift Shop (pres, 74-); Salvation Army Auxiliary. Relig: Methodist. Mailing Add: 5614 Jordan Rd Bethesda MD 20016

RAUCH, MARSHALL ARTHUR (D)
NC State Sen
b New York, NY, Feb 2, 23; s Nathan A Rauch & Tillie Wohl R; m 1946 to Jeanne Girard; c Ingrid, Marc, Peter, Stephanie & John. Educ: Duke Univ, 44; Zeta Beta Tau; pres, Varsity Basketball. Polit & Govt Pos: Mayor pro tem, Gastonia, NC, 52-54 & 61-63, city councilman, 52-54 & 61-65; NC State Sen, 29th Dist, 67- Bus & Prof Pos: Chmn bd, dir & treas, Pyramid Mills Co, Inc, Pyramid Dye Corp, Homeside Yarn, Inc, Nile Star, Inc & Gastonia Dyeing Corp; dir & treas, E P Press, Inc & The Rauch Found, Inc; dir, Darby Chem Co, Southern Invest Corp, Sedgefield Realty Co, Majestic Ins Financing Corp & Advan Invest Fund; mgr, Narco Molding Co. Mil Serv: Entered as Pvt, Army, 43, released as Pfc, 45, after serv in ETO; Combat Infantry Medal; European Theater & Occupation Ribbons. Mem: NC Comt on Population & Family (chmn, 68-); B'nai B'rith (Frank Goldberg Lodge); Nat Coun Am Jewish Joint Distribution Comt; Mason; Shrine. Honors & Awards: Nat Recreation Citation, Nat Recreation Asn, 65; Named Man of the Year, Gaston Co Omega Psi Phi, 66, NC Health Dept, 68 & Gastonia Red Shield Boys Club, 70; Nat Recreation Citation, Nat Recreation Asn, 65; Nat Coun Christians & Jews Brotherhood Award, 69. Relig: Jewish. Mailing Add: 1121 Scotch Dr Gastonia NC 28052

RAUH, JO ANN (R)
VChmn, Woods Co Rep Party, Okla
b Alva, Okla, July 17, 33; d Russell Clarkson Kasparek & Helen Nevora Snyder K; m 1965 to John Harry Rauh; c Billy D, Charley M, Glenda J, Sharry L & Larry B Wimmer. Educ: Hardtner High Sch, Hardtner, Kans, grad, 51. Polit & Govt Pos: Precinct chmn, Woods Co Rep Party, Okla, 66-73, vchmn, 70- Relig: Lutheran. Mailing Add: 727 Maple Alva OK 73717

RAUH, JOSEPH L, JR (D)
b Cincinnati, Ohio, Jan 3, 11; s Joseph L Rauh & Sara Weiler R; m 1935 to Olie Westheimer; c B Michael & Carl S; three grandchildren. Educ: Harvard Col, BS, 32, Law Sch, LLB, 35; Phi Beta Kappa. Polit & Govt Pos: Counsel to various govt agencies, 35-36 & 39-42; law secy to Supreme Court Justices Cardozo & Frankfurter, 36-39; gen dep housing expediter, Vet Emergency Housing Prog, 46-47; deleg, Dem Nat Conv, 48, 52, 60 & 64, counsel to Miss Freedom Dem Party, 64, credentials coordr for Sen McCarthy, 68, counsel for Sen McGovern on Calif challenge, 72; vchmn, DC Dem Cent Comt, 52-64, chmn, 64-67; nat chmn, Am for Dem Action, 55-57, vchmn, currently. Mil Serv: Entered as 1st Lt, Army, 42, released as Lt Col, 45, after serv as Exec Officer, G-5, Hq, Southwest Pac Area; Legion of Merit; Philippine Distinguished Serv Star. Publ: Various articles on civil rights & civil liberties. Mem: UAW (Wash counsel); Leadership Conf on Civil Rights (gen counsel); NAACP (nat bd). Honors & Awards: Hon fel, Univ Pa Law Sch, 70; Florina Lasker Civil Liberties Award, 65; Isaiah Award, Am Jewish Comt, 72. Relig: Jewish. Legal Res: 3625 Appleton St NW Washington DC 20008 Mailing Add: 1001 Connecticut Ave NW Washington DC 20036

RAUSCH, EUGENE E (D)
Chmn, Union Co Dem Exec Comt, Ohio
b Marysville, Ohio, Aug 25, 10; s John M Rausch & Caroline Rausch R; m 1935 to Mary Jo Main; c Lynn (Mrs Beasley). Educ: Marysville High Sch, Ohio, 4 years. Polit & Govt Pos: Chmn, Union Co Dem Exec Comt, Ohio, 30-; mem, Young Dem State Exec Comt, 32-36; chmn, Union Co Bd of Elec, 36- Bus & Prof Pos: Asst mgr & mgr, City Loan Co, Marysville, Ohio, 35-61; pres, Fuller Monument Works Inc, 60- Mil Serv: Entered as Pvt, Army, 43, released as Sgt, 46, after serv in MIS, ETO, 44-46. Mem: Elks; Moose; Am Legion; VFW; 40 et 8. Relig: Lutheran. Mailing Add: 230 Grand Ave Marysville OH 43040

RAUSCH, RICHARD L (D)
b Perry, Iowa, Nov 11, 35; s Leland Rausch & Ruth Aylwood R; single. Polit & Govt Pos: Mem staff, Congressman Neal Smith, Washington, DC, 60-62; exec dir youth div, Dem Nat Comt, 62-64; dep chmn Vista recruitment, Off Econ Opportunity, 66-70; exec dir, Set the Date Now, 71-72; dep chmn cong rels, McGovern for President Comt, 72; deleg, Dem Nat Mid-Term Conf, 74; mem staff, Dem Caucus, US House Rep, 75- Mil Serv: Army, 58-60, Pfc. Publ: Toward Democratic Victories, Dem Nat Comt, 63. Mem: Am Dem Action; Washington, DC Task Force on Neighborhood Adv Couns. Relig: Roman Catholic. Mailing Add: 220 Second St SE Washington DC 20003

RAUSCHENBERGER, JOHN KENNETH (R)
b Elgin, Ill, June 30, 22; s Carl L Rauschenberger & Laura Eaton R; m 1947 to Shirley Mae Westerbeck; c Laurel Ann, John K, Jr, Thomas E, Carol Jean, Steven J & Keith W. Educ:

Ellis Bus Col, 42. Polit & Govt Pos: Precinct committeeman, Rep Party, Ill, 62-; mem, Kane Co Bd of Supvrs, 63-; chmn, Kane Co Rep Cent Comt, 66-74; alt deleg, Rep Nat Conv, 72. Bus & Prof Pos: Pres, Rauschenberger Furniture Co. Mil Serv: Entered as Pvt, Army, 43, released as Sgt, 45, after serv in 92nd Chem Mortar Bn, ETO; ETO Ribbon with five Battle Stars. Mem: Kiwanis; Fox River Valley Coun Boy Scouts; Elks. Relig: Episcopal. Mailing Add: 637 Prospect St Elgin IL 60120

RAVNHOLT, EILER CHRISTIAN (D)
b Milltown, Wis, Feb 21, 23; s Ansgar B Ravnholt & Kristine Petersen R; m 1947 to Edna Joyce Collis; c Eliszabeth, Ann, Margarete, Jane & Christopher. Educ: Niagara Univ, 43-44; Univ of Minn, BS, 48; Univ of Southampton, Eng, 49-50. Polit & Govt Pos: Chmn, Blue Earth Co Dem-Farmer-Labor Party, Minn & first vchmn, Second Cong Dist Dem-Farmer-Labor Party, 60-62; deleg, Dem Nat Conv, 60, alt deleg, 64; asst librn, US Senate, 62-65; asst to the Vice President, 65-69; admin asst, US Sen Daniel K Inouye, Hawaii, 69- Bus & Prof Pos: Teacher, Mankato Pub Schs, Minn, 52-62. Mil Serv: 104th Inf Div, ETO, 44-46. Publ: Teachers in politics, Minn Educ J, 3/59; Nomination and election of the President & Vice President of the United States, GPO, 64. Mem: Nat & Minn Educ Asns. Relig: Unitarian. Mailing Add: 3566 Raymoor Rd Kensington MD 20795

RAWLINGS, GEORGE CHANCELLOR, JR (D)
Dem Nat Committeeman, Va
b Fredericksburg, Va, Nov 7, 21; m 1954 to Rosalie Dabney Saunders R. Educ: Randolph-Macon Col, BA; Univ Va, LLB; Kappa Alpha Order. Polit & Govt Pos: Va State Deleg, 64-70; Dem nominee, US Sen, Va, 70; Dem Nat Committeeman, 72- Bus & Prof Pos: Lawyer. Mem: 39th Judicial Circuit; Va Asn Ment Health (Frank C Pratt Chap), Elks; Moose; KofP. Relig: Baptist. Mailing Add: 405 Amelia St Fredericksburg VA 23401

RAWLINGS, MAURICE EDWARD (D)
Justice, Iowa Supreme Court
b Onawa, Iowa, Aug 17, 06; s Ed Eugene Rawlings & Effie Miller R; m 1928 to Helen C Fowler; c Richard Ray (deceased), Maurice F, William J, Janet (Mrs Pulscher), Mary (Mrs Gaukel) & Robert C. Educ: Univ Iowa, 25-27; SDak Univ Col Law, JD, 30; Phi Gamma Delta. Polit & Govt Pos: Co attorney, Woodbury Co, Iowa, 35-43; Off Price Admin dir, Iowa-SDak-Nebr, 43-47; corp counsel, Sioux City, Iowa, 48-51; mem, Sioux City Sch Bd, 55-58; judge, Fourth Judicial Dist, 58-65; justice, Iowa Supreme Court, 65- Bus & Prof Pos: Adv coun, Sgt Floyd Area Boy Scouts, 60-; adv bd, Boys & Girls Home, 62-68; bd dirs, Goodwill Industs, Sioux City, Iowa, 64- Mil Serv: Army Res, 37-42, Capt, serv in Judge Adv Gen Dept, Seventh Serv Command. Publ: Constitutional balance between fair trials and free press, Drake Law Rev, 12/67; Castellation of the citadel, SDak Law Rev, spring 71. Mem: Am & Woodbury Co Bar Asns; Iowa Bar Asn (uniform jury instr comt, 63-68); Am Legion (Comdr, 49-50). Honors & Awards: Distinguished Serv Award, Woodbury Co Bar Asn, 68; Judge of the Year Award, Lawyers Chataqua, 70. Relig: Episcopal. Legal Res: 3433 Court St Sioux City IA 51104 Mailing Add: 608 Court House Sioux City IA 51101

RAWLINGS, ROB ROY (D)
RI State Sen
b Westerly, RI, Feb 20, 20; m to Barbara T. Educ: Univ RI; Duke Univ. Polit & Govt Pos: Mem, RI State Dem Comt, 62; mem, Richmond Tax Study Comt, 62-63; RI State Sen, 64-66, 71-72 & 75- Bus & Prof Pos: Self-employed, Meadow Brook Golf Course. Mem: Hope Valley Grange (past Master); CofC; Hope Valley Vol Fire Asn; Richmond PTA (vpres); Chariho-Exeter Credit Union (mem bd dirs & vpres). Mailing Add: Wyoming RI 02898

RAWLINGS, WILLIAM VINCENT (D)
Va State Sen
b Capron, Va, Aug 17, 13; s Edgar Eley Rawlings & Irma Vincent R; m 1942 to Novella Howard Pope; c Elizabeth C, Arthur P & Novella Vincent. Educ: Va Mil Inst, BS, 35; Univ Va, LLB, 38; Phi Alpha Delta; Phi Kappa Sigma. Polit & Govt Pos: Mayor, Capron, Va, 48-50; mem, Southampton Co Sch Bd, 5-56, chmn, 56-62; mem, Southampton Co Dem Comt, 52-; mem exec comt, Farmers for Kennedy-Johnson, 60; mem, Pres Nat Agr Adv Comt, 61-65; chmn, Gov Opportunities in Agr Study; Va State Sen, 62-, chmn Dem steering comt, Va State Senate, 74-; chmn, Rural Virginians for Johnson-Humphrey, 64; state campaign mgr, William C Battle, Cand for Gov, J Sargeant, Cand for Lt Gov & Andrew P Miller, Cand for Attorney Gen, Va; dist campaign mgr for Rep Watkins M Abbitt, 70. Bus & Prof Pos: Attorney-at-law, 37-41; exec secy & gen counsel, Asn Va Peanut & Hog Growers, 50-69. Mil Serv: Entered as 1st Lt, Army, 41, released as Lt Col, 46, after serv in ETO, 44-46; Col, Army Res, 47; Legion of Merit; Bronze Star; Croix de Guerre; three Campaign Stars. Mem: Farm Bur; Ruritan; Grange; Am Legion; Farmers Union. Honors & Awards: Man of the Year in Serv to Va Agr, Awarded by Progressive Farmer Mag, 66; Va Poultry Fedn Serv to Agr Award, 69. Relig: Methodist. Mailing Add: PO Box 126 Capron VA 23829

RAWSON, ROGER F (D)
Utah State Rep
Mailing Add: 5151 W 4000 S Hooper UT 84315

RAY, BILL (D)
Alaska State Sen
b Anaconda, Mont, Apr 6, 22; s Eli Ray & Marchette Victoria Isabella Sabella R (deceased); m 1946 to Jeanette Pauline Haas; c Terry Haas & Bill Carter. Educ: Wallace High Sch, Idaho, 38. Polit & Govt Pos: Mem, Fish & Game Adv Bd, Alaska, 55-59; chmn, Alcoholic Beverage Control Bd, 59-64, dir, 63-64; Alaska State Rep, Fourth Dist, 65-70; Alaska State Sen, 71-, mem finance & state affairs comts, Alaska State Senate, 71- Bus & Prof Pos: Owner, Bill Ray's Liquor Stores (3), 48-66. Mil Serv: Entered as A/S, Navy, 42, released as Chief Radioman, 46, after serv in NPac & SPac Command Admin; Am Theater, Asiatic-Pac & Good Conduct Ribbons; Victory Medal. Mem: Am Legion; Elks; Rotary; Alaska Pioneers; Alaska Native Brotherhood. Honors & Awards: Nat Edgar Award, 63; recognized sport fishing expert (Salmon). Relig: Episcopal. Mailing Add: 165 Behrends Ave Juneau AK 99801

RAY, DIXY LEE
b Tacoma, Wash, Sept 3, 14; d Alvis Marion Ray & Frances Adams R. Educ: Mills Col, BA, 37, MA, 38, LLD, 67; Stanford Univ, PhD & Van Sicklen fel, 45. Hon Degrees: Hon degrees from St Martins Col, 72; Hood Col, 73 & Seattle Univ, 73. Polit & Govt Pos: Mem, Presidential Task Force Oceanog, 69; mem, Atomic Energy Comn, 72-74, chmn, 73-74; Asst Secy State Oceans & Int Environ & Sci Affairs, 74-75. Bus & Prof Pos: Teacher pub schs, Oakland, Calif, 38-42; John Switzer fel, Stanford Univ, 42-43; assoc prof zool, Univ Wash, 45-72; mem exec comt, Friday Harbor Labs, 45-60; spec consult biol oceanog, Nat Sci Found, 60-62; dir, Pac Sci Ctr, Seattle, 63-72; chief scientist & vis prof, Stanford Res Vessel TE VEGA, Int Indian Ocean Expedition, 64. Publ: Marine Boring & Fouling Organisms, 59; plus others. Mem: Danish Royal Soc Natural Hist. Honors & Awards: William Clapp Award, Nat Asn Corrosion Engrs, 59; Seattle Maritime Award, 66; Frances K Hutchinson Medal, Garden Club Am, 73. Legal Res: WA Mailing Add: Rte 1 Box 135A Stephens City VA 22655

RAY, GEORGE E (D)
Ga State Rep
Mailing Add: 1073 S Indian Creek Dr Stone Mountain GA 30083

RAY, HECTOR (D)
NC State Rep
Mailing Add: 306 Dunbar Dr Fayetteville NC 28303

RAY, JOE F (D)
Ark State Sen
b Havana, Ark, Sept 21, 11; s Joseph Ray & Cathrine Scott R; m 1969 to Maxine Mildred Jones. Educ: Col of Ozarks, 33-36. Polit & Govt Pos: Chmn, Ark Poultry & Livestock Comn, 56-67; mem adv bd, US Dept Agr, 57-61; dir, Ark Agr Stabilization & Conserv Serv, 62-63; chmn, Yell Co Dem Cent Comt, Ark, formerly; Ark State Sen, 73- Bus & Prof Pos: Pres, Joe Ray Inc, Danville, Ark, 40-66. Mem: Mason; Lions; Ruritan; Ark Poultry Fedn; Farm Bur. Relig: Protestant. Mailing Add: Rte 1 Box 96 Havana AR 72842

RAY, ROBERT D (R)
Gov, Iowa
b Des Moines, Iowa, Sept 26, 28; s Clark A Ray & Mildred Dolph R; m 1951 to Billie Lee Hornberger; c Randi Sue, Lu Ann & Vicki Jo. Educ: Drake Univ, BA in Bus Admin, 52, JD, 54; Order of the Coif; Alpha Zeta. Hon Degrees: Hon doctorate from various cols & univs. Polit & Govt Pos: Chmn, Rep State Cent Comt, Iowa, 63-67; chmn, Midwest Asn Rep State Chmn, 65-; chmn, Nat Rep State Chmn Asn, 67-72; Gov, Iowa, 68-; chmn, mem exec comt, mem comt rural & urban develop & mem comt natural resources & environ mgt, Nat Gov Conf; mem, Adv Comn Intergovt Rels; vpres exec comt, Coun State Govt; mem, President's Nat Reading Coun; deleg, Rep Nat Conv, 72; chmn, Midwest Gov Conf, 72; chmn policy coun, Rep Gov Asn, 75-; Bus & Prof Pos: Attorney-at-law, Lawyer, Lawyer & Ray, Des Moines, Iowa, 54-69. Mil Serv: Army, 46-48. Mem: Am Trial Lawyers Asn; Delta Theta Phi; Geol Bd Iowa (chmn); Iowa Exec Coun (chmn); Make Today Count (hon bd mem). Honors & Awards: Nat Distinguished Serv Award, Future Farmers Am, 70; Distinguished Alumnus Award, Drake Univ. Relig: Christian Church; former elder & deacon, Sunday sch teacher, currently. Legal Res: 917 California Dr Des Moines IA 50312 Mailing Add: State Capitol Des Moines IA 50319

RAYBELL, GLENNA J (D)
b Poulsbo, Wash, June 29, 32; d Glen E Raybell & Ruby E Nupp R; single. Educ: Univ Puget Sound, 50-52; Mary Col, BS, 61; Univ Ill, MSocWork, 71. Polit & Govt Pos: Mem, NDak Comn Status Women, 72-73; mem exec comt, NDak Dem-NPL Party, Burleigh Co, 72-74, mem state platform comt, 74; pres & founder, NDak Women's Coalition, 73-74; mem, NDak State Parole Bd, 73-74; deleg, Dem Nat Mid-Term Conf, 74; bd mem & founder, NDak Coord Coun Equal Rights Amendment, 74- Bus & Prof Pos: Psychologist, Chicago Bd Health, Ment Health Div, 68-72; dir, Psychotherapy & Family Counseling Serv, Bismarck, NDak, 72-74; supvr & caseworker, Cath Family Serv, Bismarck, NDak & Bad Axe, Mich, 74-75; outreach social worker, Vet Admin Ctr, Sioux Falls, SDak, 75- Publ: Columnist, Nat Farmer's Orgn Info, NDak, 74-75. Mem: Nat Coalition of Am Nuns (bd mem); Feminists for Life, Int; Nat Women's Polit Caucus; Nat Asn of Social Workers; Nat Coun for Social Studies. Relig: Catholic. Legal Res: Rte 2 Box 119 Bismarck ND 58501 Mailing Add: 705 N Elmwood Ave 205 Sioux Falls SD 57104

RAYBURN, B B (SIXTY) (D)
La State Sen
Mailing Add: 606 Ave B Bogalusa LA 70427

RAYMAR, ROBERT SOL (D)
b Somerville, NJ, Sept 20, 47; s Sidney Raymar & Renee Bibasse R; single. Educ: Rutgers Univ, 65-67; Princeton Univ, AB, 69; Yale Law Sch, JD, 72; Phi Beta Kappa; Zeta Beta Tau. Polit & Govt Pos: Youth coordr, US Rep James Howard, NJ, 68; field coordr, George McGovern Presidential Campaign, 72; deleg-at-lg & mem credentials comt, Dem Nat Conv, 72; issues-field aide, Brendan Byrne Gubernatorial Campaign, 73; asst counsel, Gov Brendan Byrne, NJ, 74-75; Dep Attorney Gen, NJ, 75. Bus & Prof Pos: Legis asst, Gov Richard J Hughes, NJ, 68-69; law clerk, US Dist Court Judge Leonard I Garth, 72-73. Mil Serv: Army ROTC. Publ: Prison mail censorship and the first amendment, Yale Law J, 11/71; Judicial Review of Credentials Contests: The 1972 Dem Nat Conv, George Washington Law Rev, 11/73. Honors & Awards: Outstanding Freshman, Rutgers Univ Class of 1969, 66. Relig: Jewish. Mailing Add: 33 Codington Pl Somerville NJ 08876

RAYMOND, ARTHUR (R)
NDak State Rep
b Winner, SDak; s Enoch Wheeler Raymond & Mary Frazier R; m 1950 to Rose Marie Schone; c Arthur, Jr, Eric, Mary, Mark & Rebekah Rae. Educ: Dakota Wesleyan Univ, BA, 51. Polit & Govt Pos: NDak State Rep, 71- Bus & Prof Pos: City ed, Mitchell Daily Repub, SDak, 53-61; managing ed, Williston Herald, NDak, 61-65; Sunday ed, Grand Forks Herald, NDak, 65-71. Mil Serv: Entered as Pvt, Army, 42, released as 1st Lt, 46, after serv in 35th Inf Div, ETO. Relig: Episcopal. Mailing Add: 2111 University Ave Grand Forks ND 58201

RAYMOND, ARTHUR CHARLES (D)
Maine State Rep
b Lewiston, Maine, Apr 25, 33; s Marcel Levasseur (stepfather) & Antoinette Sirois L; single. Educ: St Dominic High Sch, grad, 52. Polit & Govt Pos: Mem planning bd, Lewiston, Maine, 69-70, mem health & welfare bd, 70-75; Maine State Rep, Dist 6, 75- Bus & Prof Pos: Wholesale & retail buyer, Bauer Howe Co, Lewiston, Maine, 57- Mil Serv: Entered as Pvt, Army, 53, released as SP-2, 56, after serv in 7th Corp Artil, Ger; ETO & NATO Ribbons; Letter of Recommendation from Gen Hamelette. Mem: Am Snowshoe Union; Int Snowshoe Union (lt gov, 74-75); Pastime Club; Am Legion; Maine Marching Ambassador's (bd dirs). Relig: Roman Catholic. Mailing Add: 66 Summer St Lewiston ME 04240

RAYMOND, JOSEPH ROBERT (D)
b Brooklyn, NY, Oct 12, 39; s Joseph Raymond & Frances Ciauri R; m 1967 to Emily Elizabeth Levering Royer. Educ: Georgetown Univ, AB, 61, LLB, 64. Polit & Govt Pos: Pres, Md Young Dem, 67-68; deleg, Dem Nat Conv, 68 & 72; Md State Deleg, 71-74; chmn, Md

New Dem Coalition, 71-72; chmn, Md McGovern for President Primary Campaign, 72. Bus & Prof Pos: Asst State Attorney, Baltimore City, Md, 66-68 & Asst City Solicitor, 70-71; Asst Attorney Gen, State of Md, 68-70. Mil Serv: Entered as 2nd Lt, Army, 64, released as Capt, 66, after serv in Artil Br. Mem: Md State & Am Bar Asns; Am Coun of Young Polit Leaders (bd mem, 70-); Citizens Comn on Md Govt; Md Asn for Ment Health. Relig: Roman Catholic. Legal Res: 1417 Park Ave Baltimore MD 21217 Mailing Add: 9 W Hamilton St Baltimore MD 21202

RAYMOND, MORRIS DEAN (D)
Mem, Dodge Co Dem Party, Nebr
b Columbus, Nebr, Aug 26, 27; s Theodore Hastings Raymond & Lillian Ruth Kluver R; m 1955 to Elizabeth Josephine Leenerts; c twins Roberta & Rebecca, Raymond, Randall, Eric, Jeanna & Lisa. Educ: Kramer High Sch, Columbus, Nebr, dipl, 45; La Salle Exten Univ, 1 year. Polit & Govt Pos: Ward chmn, Fremont City Dem Party, Nebr, 67-68; chmn, Dodge Co Dem Party, 70-72, vchmn, 72-74, mem, 74- Bus & Prof Pos: Owner, Raymond Serv Co, 63-67; notary pub, 70-; income tax serv, 71- Mem: Dodge Co Dem. Honors & Awards: Outstanding Dem for Dodge Co, 70-72. Relig: Catholic. Mailing Add: 1214 N Pebble St Fremont NE 68025

RAYNARD, SHIRLEY M (D)
Committeewoman, Mass Dem State Comt
b Lynn, Mass, Aug 30, 42; d Lyle Austin Paul & Blanche Louise Tisdell P; m 1961 to Edward L Raynard; c Robert Allen & William Douglas. Educ: Am Univ, 60-62; Boston Univ, BA, 64. Polit & Govt Pos: Comitteewoman, Mass Dem State Comt, 73-; chairperson, Middleton Dem Town Comt, 73-; comnr, Middleton Charter Comn, 73-74; deleg, Dem Nat Mid-Term Conf, 74. Bus & Prof Pos: Social worker, Beverly, Mass, 64-67; consult, Educ Develop Ctr, 71-74; librn, Flint Pub Libr, 74- Mem: Nat Asn Social Workers (fed legis alert coordr); Coun on Aging (secy); Mass Libr Asn (legis coordr); Middleton Community Servs (bd dirs); Mass Bay United Fund. Relig: Protestant. Mailing Add: 53 Boston St Middleton MA 01949

RAYSON, LELAND HOMER (D)
Ill State Rep
b Oak Park, Ill, Aug 23, 21; s Ennes Charles Rayson & Beatrice Margaret Rowland R; m 1944 to Barbara Ellen Chandler; c Ann Louise, John, William, Anthony, Leland, James & Thomas. Educ: Coe Col, 40-41; Univ Rochester, AB, 46; Northwestern Law Sch, JD, 49; Dean's List Scholarship; Alpha Delta Phi; Phi Alpha Delta. Polit & Govt Pos: Sch bd mem, Tinley Park, Ill, 50-54, police magistrate, 51-53, police comnr, 54-55; twp assessor, Bremen Twp, 53-61; pres, Bremen Twp Regular Dem Orgn, 54-; alt deleg, Dem Nat Conv, 60; Justice of the Peace, Bremen Twp, 61-65; comnr, Ill Comn on Law Income Housing, 65-67; Ill State Rep, 65-; comnr, Ill Family Law Study Comn, 67-; dir, Am for Dem Action, 68- Bus & Prof Pos: Attorney, Rayson, Williams, Pisani & Rayson, Tinley Park, Ill, 49-; dir, Palos-Worth Reporter, Worth, 60-; community prof, Gov State Univ, 75- Mil Serv: Entered as Seaman, Navy, 43, released as Lt (jg), 46, after serv in Pac Theatre, 44-45; Lt Comdr, Naval Res, 68; Battle Star Ribbons for Pac Theatre, Leyte Invasion & Lingayen Gulf Invasion; Am, Pac & Philippines Theatre Ribbons. Publ: Face the facts as they are, IVI Bellringer, 5/65; Abortion law reform in Illinois, Student Law J, 12/68; Rights & liabilities of family members, Ill Inst for Continuing Legal Educ, Ill State Bar Asn, 3/69. Mem: Nat Soc State Legislators; Chicago Coun on Foreign Rels; Lions; CofC; World Serv & Finance Comn of the United Methodist Church. Honors & Awards: Best Freshman Citation, 66 & Best Legislator Awards, Independent Voters of Ill, 66, 68, 70, 72 & 74. Relig: Protestant. Legal Res: 6500 W 166th St Tinley Park IL 60477 Mailing Add: 16740 S Oak Park Ave Tinley Park IL 60477

REA, PAULINE HELEN (R)
VChmn, Fremont Co Rep Cent Comt, Iowa
b Sidney, Iowa, Mar 14, 12; d Clinton J Sanderson & Martha Jane Barrett S; m 1932 to Verbyl L Schnepp, div; m 1974 to M Gerald Rea; c Danny Lee (deceased); stepson Clifford. Educ: Riverton High Sch, grad, 30; Teachers Col, 3 summers, Teacher's Cert, Cedar Falls. Polit & Govt Pos: Rep precinct committeewoman, Prairie Twp, Fremont Co, Iowa, 41-; pres, Fremont Co Rep Women, 64-66; vchmn, Fremont Co Rep Cent Comt, 64-; membership chmn, Iowa Fedn of Rep Women, Seventh Dist, 65-66, pres, 67-69, state membership chmn, 70-71, 1st vpres, 72-73, state pres, 74-; deleg, Rep Nat Conv, 68 & 72; mem nominating comt, Nat Fedn Rep Women, 74. Bus & Prof Pos: Sch teacher, Fremont Co Schs, Iowa, 30-32, substitute teaching, 33-58; secy, bookkeeper & agent, Schnepp Ins Agency, Sidney, Iowa, 50-; secy & bookkeeper, Schnepp Motor Co, 58-61; employee, Co Treas Off, Sidney, Iowa, 72- Mem: Local, civic & community clubs & orgns. Relig: Protestant; Held off in church & women's orgn, taught Sunday Sch & directed progs, Farragut Congregational Church. Legal Res: RFD Prairie Twp Fremont Co Sidney IA 51652 Mailing Add: Rte 1 Sidney IA 51652

READ, MAURICE W (R)
NH State Rep
b Derry, NH, Dec 26, 03; s John Louis Read & Edith Willey R; m 1926 to Dorothy Holbrook; c Charles L & Priscilla (Mrs Perry). Educ: Columbia Univ, 3 years; Cent Col Com, 1 year. Polit & Govt Pos: NH State Rep, 69-; chmn, Gov Comt for Affairs of the Elderly. Bus & Prof Pos: Self employed. Mem: Mason; Kiwanis; Am Asn Retired Persons (asst to state dir). Honors & Awards: Cert Master Watchmaker, Horological Inst of Am & Am Watchmakers Inst. Relig: Protestant. Mailing Add: 16 Chester Rd Derry NH 03038

READ, WILLIAM BROOKS (D)
Mem, Dem State Cent Comt, La
b Baton Rouge, La, Aug 4, 26; s Frank Clifford Read, Sr & Margaret Huck R; m 1949 to Maureen Hushar; c Jennifer, Heather & Wendy. Educ: La State Univ, 41-42 & 48-49; Northwestern Univ, 42-43. Polit & Govt Pos: Mem, Gov Adv Comt on State Penitentiary, 64; mem, Dem State Cent Comt, La, 67-; deleg, Dem Nat Conv, 68; mem, Family Court Adv Comt, East Baton Rouge Parish, 69-; press secy to Gov, La, 69-70; La Dem Presidential Elector, 72; deleg, Dem Conf on Party Orgn & Policy, 74. Bus & Prof Pos: Gen mgr, WNAT Radio, Natchez, Miss, 51; prod mgr, Liberty Broadcasting Syst, Dallas, Tex, 51-52; owner-mgr & free-lance writer, Voi-Serv, Dallas, Tex & Baton Rouge, La, 53-54; news dir, WBRZ-TV, Baton Rouge, La, 55-64; pres, Brooks Read & Assocs, Inc, 64- Mil Serv: Entered as Pvt, La Nat Guard, 48, released as 1st Lt, 55, after serv in Mil Intel, Army Res. Mem: Sigma Delta Chi; Press Club of Baton Rouge; Capitol Correspondents Asn of La; Baton Rouge CofC (govt affairs comt); Pub Affairs Res Coun. Relig: Episcopal. Legal Res: 1525 Cloverdale Ave Baton Rouge LA 70808 Mailing Add: PO Box 2345 Baton Rouge LA 70821

READING, JOHN HARDEN (R)
Mayor, Oakland, Calif
b Glendale, Ariz, Nov 26, 17; s Cecil Virgil Reading & Lillian May Ingram R; m 1941 to Hazel Mary Swortfiguer; c Joanna Lee (Mrs Negley) & Ronald James. Educ: Univ Calif, BS, 40. Polit & Govt Pos: Mayor, Oakland, Calif, 66- Mil Serv: Entered as Flying Cadet, Air Force, 40, released as Col, 46, after serv in Second Air Command. Relig: Protestant. Mailing Add: 4735 Sequoyah Rd Oakland CA 94605

READINGER, DAVID M (R)
Iowa State Rep
Mailing Add: 4300-67th St Urbandale IA 50322

REAGAN, RONALD WILSON (R)
b Tampico, Ill, Feb 6, 11; s John Edward Reagan & Nelle Wilson R; m 1952 to Nancy Davis; c Maureen Elizabeth, Michael Edward, Patricia Ann & Ronald Prescott. Educ: Eureka Col, BA, 32; Tau Kappa Epsilon. Hon Degrees: MA, Eureka Col, 57. Polit & Govt Pos: Mem, Rep State Cent Comt Calif, 64-66; Gov, Calif, 66-75; deleg, Rep Nat Conv, 68 & 72; chmn, Rep Gov Asn, 68-73. Bus & Prof Pos: Sports announcer, Radio WHO, Des Moines, 32-37; motion picture actor, Warner Bros, Univ, 37-54; player & prod supvr, Gen Elec Theatre, 54-62; host & part-time performer, TV series, Death Valley Days, 62-66. Mil Serv: Entered as 2nd Lt, US Cavalry Res, released as Capt, 46, after serv in 18th Army Air Force Base Unit, Ft Mason, 42-46. Publ: Where's the Rest of Me, Duell-Sloane & Pierce, 65. Mem: Am Fedn Radio & TV Artists; Screen Actors Guild; Who's Who in Am Polit (adv comt, 69, 71 & 73); Lions; Friars. Honors & Awards: Great Am of the Decade Award, Va Young Am for Freedom, 60 & 70; Man of the Year Free Enterprise Award, San Fernando Valley Bus & Prof Asn, 64; Am Legion Award, 65; Horatio Alger Award, 69; George Washington Honor Medal Award, Freedoms Found Valley Forge, 71. Relig: Christian Church. Mailing Add: Pacific Palisades CA 90272

REARDON, ALBERT JOSEPH (D)
NH State Rep
b Nashua, NH, Mar 3, 05; s Timothy Reardon & Josephen Diggins R; m 1923 to Alice Gamache. Educ: High Sch, Nashua. Polit & Govt Pos: NH State Rep, 75- Mem: KofC; Am Legion. Mailing Add: 20 Ferson St Nashua NH 03060

REARDON, HAROLD E (R)
Finance Chmn, Humboldt Co Rep Party, Calif
b Cresco, Iowa, Oct 20, 08; s Charles John Reardon & Mary Hogan R; m 1937 to Ethel Rait; c Robert Charles & Harold E, Jr. Educ: NDak State Univ, BS, 34. Polit & Govt Pos: Finance chmn, Humboldt Co Rep Party, Calif, 55- Bus & Prof Pos: Secy & treas, Bridgeville Lumber Co, 50-; owner, HE Reardon Realtor Co, 49- Mil Serv: Entered as Lt(jg), Navy, 41, released as Lt Comdr, 45, after serv in Pac Theater, 42-44; Capt, Res, 44-58; Commendation from Secy of Navy. Mem: Am Soc Mil Engrs; Mason (32 degree); Shrine; Nat Farm Bur; Lions. Relig: Protestant. Mailing Add: 5169 Leonard Dr Eureka CA 95501

REARDON, JOHN F (R)
Idaho State Rep
Mailing Add: 3100 North Five Mile Boise ID 83702

REARDON, TERRENCE JAMES (D)
Mem, Contra Costa Co Dem Cent Comt, Calif
b Oakland, Calif, July 6, 50; s John Reardon & Marian Walsh R; single. Educ: Calif State Univ, Fresno, BA Social Sci, 73; Sigma Alpha Epsilon. Polit & Govt Pos: Deleg, Dem Nat Mid-Term Conf, 74; mem, Contra Costa Co Dem Cent Comt, Calif, 75- Bus & Prof Pos: Staff asst, Congressman George Miller, 75- Mem: Contra Costa Co Fedn Dem Clubs (pres, 75-); Sunrise Optimist Club Concord (community serv chmn). Relig: Roman Catholic. Mailing Add: 343 Glacier Dr Martinez CA 94553

REARDON, WILLIAM J (D)
Kans State Rep
b Kansas City, Kans, June 24, 41; s Joseph F Reardon & Helen Cahill R; m 1963 to Kathleen T Page; c Ann, Coki & Kerry. Educ: Donnelly Jr Col, AA, 61; Rockhurst Col, BA, 63; Univ Mo-Kansas City, MA, 70. Polit & Govt Pos: Alt deleg, Kans State Dem Conv, 72; Kans State Rep, Dist 37, 75- Bus & Prof Pos: Teacher social studies, Miege High Sch, 63- Relig: Catholic. Mailing Add: 2206 Everett Kansas City KS 66102

REAVES, BETTY ANNE (D)
Committeewoman, NJ Dem State Comt
b Hazard, Ky, Oct 8, 23; d James Hogg Cornette & Margaret Fitzpatrick C; m 1946 to William Curtiss Reaves. Educ: Hazard High Sch, grad, 42. Polit & Govt Pos: Mem, Ocean Co Dem Comt, 63-; mem, Ocean Co Bd of Elec, 72-74; committeewoman, NJ Dem State Comt, 69- Bus & Prof Pos: Treas, City Hazard, Ky, 43-44; secy, Beau Brummel Ties Inc, 46-58 & Toms River Chem Corp, 58-74; production scheduler, Ciba-Geigy Facil, Toms River, 75- Mem: Eastern Star; DAR; Am Audubon Soc; Am Cancer Soc (bd mgr). Relig: Presbyterian. Mailing Add: 1170 Marlane Rd Toms River NJ 08753

REAVES, GINEVERA N (D)
Chairperson, First Cong Dist Dem Party, Miss
b Greenwood, Miss, Jan 21, 25; d Symiel Tyler Nero & Mary Smith N; m 1948 to Henry Eugene Reaves, Sr; c Naomi Normene (deceased) & Henry Eugene, Jr. Educ: Rust Col, BA, 51; Univ Chicago, MA, 54. Polit & Govt Pos: Chairperson, First Cong Dist Dem Party, Miss, 72-; alt deleg, Dem Nat Mid-Term Conf, 74; mem, Miss State Affirmative Action Comt, 75. Bus & Prof Pos: Teacher, Miss Pub Schs, 42-64; asst prof, Rust Col, 64- Mem: Phi Delta Kappa; Delta Sigma Theta; Benton Co NAACP (pres); Am Asn Univ Women (local legis chairperson); Miss Teachers Asn. Honors & Awards: Runner-up Teacher of the Year, Rust Col, 66; Sargent Shriver Award for alleviating poverty in rural Am, 66; Miss Finer Womanhood Award, Zeta Phi Beta, 68; Teacher of the Year, Rust Col-Zeta Phi Beta, 72; Ginevera Reaves Day, Benton Co NAACP, 75. Mailing Add: Rte 2 Box 126 Holly Springs MS 38635

REAVES, HENRY L (D)
Ga State Rep
b Kissimmee, Fla, Aug 7, 19; s Coy Reaves & Blanche Nance R; m 1948 to Frances Barker; c Henry L, Jr & Joan A. Educ: Osceola High Sch, 37. Polit & Govt Pos: Ga State Rep, 63- Bus & Prof Pos: Farmer; cattleman; asst mgr, Agr Bus Servs, Southern Rwy. Mil Serv: 1st Lt, Army Air Force, World War II, ETO. Mem: Elks; Quitman Rotary Club; Brooks Co Livestock Asn; Brooks Co Farm Bur (secy-treas). Relig: Baptist. Mailing Add: RFD 2 Quitman GA 31643

REAVLEY, THOMAS MORROW (D)
Assoc Justice, Supreme Court, Tex
b Quitman, Tex, June 21, 21; s Thomas Mark Reavley & Matty Morrow R; m 1943 to Florence Montgomery Wilson; c Thomas Wilson, Marian, Paul Stuart & Margaret. Educ: Stephen F Austin Col, 37-39; Univ Tex Law Sch, BA, 42; Harvard Law Sch, LLB, 48. Polit & Govt Pos: Co attorney, Nacogdoches Co, Tex, 51; Secy of State, Tex, 55-57; dist judge, 167th Judicial Dist, Tex, 64-68; assoc justice, Supreme Court, Tex, 68- Mil Serv: Entered as Ens, Navy, 43, released as Lt, 45, after serv in USS Cogswell & USS Ticonderoga. Relig: Methodist. Legal Res: 1312 Meriden Lane Austin TX 78703 Mailing Add: Supreme Court of Tex Austin TX 78711

REBERGER, J PHILIP (R)
b Caldwell, Idaho, Apr 3, 42; s George Arthur Reberger & Dorothy Beall R; m 1964 to Nancy Jean Yount; c John Philip, Jr & Diane Elizabeth. Educ: Univ Idaho, BS in Bus, 64; Intercollegiate Knights; Sigma Nu. Polit & Govt Pos: Dep dir campaign div, Rep Nat Comt, 70-71, exec asst to dep chmn & polit div dir, 71-73; consult & dep dir, Mills Godwin for Gov of Va Campaign, 73; admin asst to US Sen Harry F Byrd, Jr, Ind, 73- Mil Serv: Entered as Ens, Navy, 64, released as Lt, 70, after serv as staff pilot to Comdr in Chief Pac, 66-70; two Air Medals, Vietnam Serv, five Awards. Mem: DeMolay. Relig: Presbyterian. Mailing Add: 8230 The Midway Annandale VA 22003

RECHTIN, EBERHARDT (R)
Asst Secy For Telecommun, Dept of Defense
b Orange, NJ, Jan 16, 26; s Eberhardt Carl Rechtin & Ida Pfarrer R; m 1951 to Dorothy Diane Denebrink; c Andrea Compton, Nina, Julia Anne, Erica & Mark Eberhardt. Educ: Calif Inst Technol, BS in Eng, 46, PhD, 50; Tau Beta Pi; Sigma Xi. Polit & Govt Pos: Dir, Adv Research Projs Agency, Dept of Defense, 67-70, prin dep dir, Defense Research & Eng, 70-73, asst secy for telecommun, 73- Bus & Prof Pos: From research engr to asst dir for tracking & data acquisition, Jet Propulsion Lab, Calif Inst of Technol, 49-67. Mil Serv: Entered as A/S, Naval Res, 43, released as Lt, 58, after serv in Continental US, 43-46; Theater Ribbon. Publ: Articles on space communication, Astronaut, 62-67. Mem: Fel Am Inst Aeronaut & Astronaut; fel Inst Elec & Electronics Engrs; Nat Acad of Eng; Int Astronaut Fedn (academician). Honors & Awards: NASA Medal for Exceptional Sci Achievement. Relig: Protestant. Legal Res: 6904 Old Gate Lane Rockville MD 20852 Mailing Add: Dept of Defense Pentagon Washington DC 20301

RECKDAHL, JOAN MARIE (DFL)
Chairwoman, Meeker Co Dem-Farmer-Labor Party, Minn
b Hutchinson, Minn, Aug 27, 36; d Henry Frederick Schramm & Bertha Duesterhoeft S; m 1958 to Jerome Nels Reckdahl; c Beth Laurel, Keith Jerome, Kathryn Joan, Benjamin Bryant, & Andrea Joy. Educ: Concordia Col (St Paul), AA, 56; Univ Minn, Minneapolis, BS, 59. Polit & Govt Pos: Chairwoman, Meeker Co Dem-Farmer-Labor Party, Minn, 70-; mem, Sixth Dist Dem-Farmer-Labor Party Exec Comt, 72-, chmn subdist three, 72-; assoc chairperson, Minn Sen Dist 22, Dem-Farmer-Labor Party, 72-; mem, Minn Dem-Farmer-Labor State Cent Comt, 72- Bus & Prof Pos: Teacher, Immanuel Lutheran Sch, Minneapolis, Minn, 59-61; teacher Eng, Grove City High Sch, 61-64, 70-71. Mem: Am Asn Univ Women; Grove City Women's Club; Minn & Nat Educ Asns; Crow River Regional Libr Bd (trustee, 75-). Relig: Lutheran. Mailing Add: 318 S Third St Grove City MN 56243

RECKMAN, ROBERT FREDERICK (R)
Comnr, Hamilton Co, Ohio
b Cincinnati, Ohio, Apr 7, 22; s William A Reckman & Florence Apel R; m 1945 to Mary Carleen Stone; c Robert C, Richard F & Mark S. Educ: DePauw Univ, AB, 43; Univ Cincinnati, LLB, 48; Phi Beta Kappa; Phi Eta Sigma; Sigma Delta Chi; Blue Key; Beta Theta Pi. Polit & Govt Pos: Ohio State Rep, 52-68, acting speaker, Ohio House Rep, 65-66; comnr, Hamilton Co, 71- Bus & Prof Pos: Dir, The Columbia Savings & Loan Co, 47-, pres, 68-; partner, Wood, Lamping, Slutz & Reckman, 61-; dir, Globe Off Equip & Supplies Co, 64- Mil Serv: Entered as Pfc, Marine Corps, 43, released as Lt(jg), Naval Air Corps, 46. Mem: Cincinnati Club; Cincinnatus Asn. Relig: Presbyterian. Legal Res: 330 Warren Ave Cincinnati OH 45220 Mailing Add: 900 Tri-State Bldg Cincinnati OH 45202

RECORD, LOUIS D, JR (R)
NH State Rep
Mailing Add: 9 Reservoir St Nashua NH 03060

RECTOR, WILLIAM GORDON (BILL) (D)
Wyo State Sen
b Des Moines, Iowa, July 22, 22; s Jesse Rector & Viola O'Conner R; m 1950 to Norma Louise Watkins; c William Gordon, Jr & Christine Louise. Educ: Kearney State Col, BS, 43. Polit & Govt Pos: Wyo State Rep, 59-65; Wyo State Sen, 67- Bus & Prof Pos: Owner of restaurant & drive in; dir, First Cheyenne State Bank, 71- Mil Serv: Marine Corps, 6 years. Mem: Elks; Am Legion; VFW; Exec Club; Optimists Club. Relig: Catholic. Mailing Add: 301 W Fifth Ave Cheyenne WY 82001

RECTOR, WILLIAM LEE (R)
Committeeman, Rep Party of Tex
b Shawnee, Okla, Nov 30, 19; s William Lee Rector & Mary Elizabeth Reese R; m 1943 to N Jane Fielder; c Nancy Jane & Lee Anne. Educ: Okla State Univ, BS, 40; Okla Univ, MD, 43; Am Bd Internal Med, dipl; Blue Key; Phi Beta Pi. Polit & Govt Pos: Committeeman, Rep Party Tex, 64-, chmn, Task Force on Human Rights & Responsibilities, 66-; deleg, Rep Nat Conv, 68 & 72; permanent chmn, Tex Rep State Conv, 70; mem, Regional Health Adv Comt, Dept Health, Educ & Welfare, 70; mem, Nat Census Adv Comt on Privacy & Confidentiality, Dept Com, 72- Bus & Prof Pos: Practicing physician, Med & Surg Clin, Wichita Falls, Tex, 50- Mil Serv: Entered as 1st Lt, Army, 43, released as Capt, 45. Mem: Am Col Physicians. Honors & Awards: Altrusa Distinguished Civic Serv Award, 63. Relig: Protestant. Legal Res: Apt A101 4021 Taft Wichita Falls TX 76308 Mailing Add: 1518 Tenth St Wichita Falls TX 76301

REDDEN, JAMES ANTHONY (D)
State Treas, Ore
b Springfield, Mass, Mar 13, 29; s James Anthony Redden & Alma Cheek R; m 1950 to Joan Ida Johnson; c James Anthony, Jr & William Francis. Educ: Boston Univ, 49-51; Boston Col Law Sch, LLB, 54. Polit & Govt Pos: Chmn, Jackson Co Dem Comt, Ore, 57-59; Ore State Rep, 19th Dist, 63-69, minority leader, Ore House of Rep, 67; deleg, Dem Nat Conv, 68; mem, State of Ore Pub Employee Rels Bd, currently; State Treas, Ore, 73- Mil Serv: Entered as Pvt, Army, 46, released as Pfc, 48, after serv in 118th Sta Hosp, Japan; Japan Occup Medal. Mem: Ore Bar; Mass & Jackson Co Bar Asns; Am Judicature Soc. Relig: Catholic. Legal Res: 546 Welcome Way Salem OR 97302 Mailing Add: Office of State Treasurer State Capitol Salem OR 97310

REDDICK, DONNA LYNN (R)
b Pomona, Calif, Mar 5, 45; d Lyndall Leon Palmer & Christine Tucker P; div. Educ: Kilgore Col, Tex. Polit & Govt Pos: Co chmn, San Bernardino Co Young Rep, Calif, 67-68; mem, Calif Rep State Cent Comt, 67-73; asst secy, Calif Young Rep, 68-69; consult, Calif State Senate Rep Caucus, 69-71; Young Rep Nat Committeewoman, 70-71; co-chmn, Young Rep Nat Fedn, 71-73; admin asst, State Sen H L Richardson, Calif, 71-73; ex officio mem, Rep Nat Comt, 71-73; pub rels consult, state & local campaigns, Tex, 72; deleg, US Youth Coun, 72-; mem, Tex Young Rep, currently. Bus & Prof Pos: Legal secy, San Bernardino, Calif, 63-66; legis secy, Calif State Sen, 67-70. Relig: Lutheran Missouri Synod. Legal Res: 312 Ruthlynn Longview TX 75601 Mailing Add: PO Box 1086 Longview TX 75601

REDDING, ROBERT S (D)
Md State Deleg
Mailing Add: PO Box L Bowie MD 20715

REDENBO, MILDRED IRENE (R)
VChmn, Logan Co Rep Party, Nebr
b Royal, Nebr, Mar 8, 17; d Clarence D Curtis & Mary Calista Voorhies C; m 1944 to William Alanzo Redenbo, wid 1966; c Kathleen Jean (Mrs Cross) & Mary Lu (Mrs Coventon). Educ: Wayne State Col, AA, 37, BA, magna cum laude, 41; Kearney State Col, MS, 69, postgrad, 69-72; Kappa Mu Epsilon; Sadalis Latini. Polit & Govt Pos: Vchmn, Logan Co Rep Party, Nebr, 64- Bus & Prof Pos: Teacher, Dixon, Nebr, 37-39, Stapleton, 39-41, Sioux City, Iowa, 41-44, San Diego, Calif, 44-45 & Stapleton, Nebr, 47-49; bookkeeper & buyer, Redenbo's Shopping Ctr, 47-66; guid counr, Stapleton Sch Dist R-1, 67- Publ: Auth, Freedom-not license, Freedom's Found, 70. Mem: Nebr State & Nat Educ Asns; Logan Co Teachers Asn; Am Legion Auxiliary; Sand Hills Area Regional Progress Club. Honors & Awards: Attended Presidential Inauguration, 68; Schoolmen Medal, Freedom's Found, 71. Relig: Presbyterian. Mailing Add: Box 177 Stapleton NE 69163

REDFORD, MACK ANDY (R)
b Wendell, Idaho, July 16, 37; s John Edgar Redford & Viola Palmer R; m 1966 to Nancy Jean Tefft; c Holly Jean. Educ: Univ Idaho, BS in Agr Econ, 61, JD, 67; Alpha Tau Omega. Polit & Govt Pos: Police Judge, City of Moscow, Idaho, 65-67; Asst Attorney Gen, Idaho, 67-68, Chief Criminal Dep Attorney Gen, 68-70; chmn & comnr, Idaho Comn for Pardons & Paroles, 68-70; mem Idaho Police Off Standards & Training Comn, 69-71; state campaign chmn, Robert M Robson for Attorney Gen, 70; Dep Pub Defender, state campaign chmn, Robert M Robson for Attorney Gen, 70-; consult on criminal rules, Idaho Supreme Court, 71-; alt deleg, Rep Nat Conv, 72. Bus & Prof Pos: Territory salesman, Firestone Tire & Rubber Co, Salt Lake City, Utah, 61-64; partner, Webb, Tway, Redford & Johnson, 70- Mil Serv: Entered as Pvt, E-1, Army, 59, released as Pvt, E-3, 61, after serv in 11th Corps Hq, St Louis, Mo; Soldier of the Month, 11th Corps. Mem: Am Judicature Soc; Chi Alpha Delta; Elks; Idaho Lincoln Day Banquet Comt; Univ Idaho Alumni (mem exec bd, 71-). Mailing Add: 5007 Greenbrier Dr Boise ID 83705

REDLIN, ROLLAND (D)
NDak State Sen
b Lambert, Mont, Feb 29, 20; m to Christine Nesje; c Ilene, Jeannette, Lisa, Daniel & Steven. Educ: Univ Wash; NDak State Col, Minot, exten courses. Polit & Govt Pos: Nominee, NDak State Rep, 52; NDak State Sen, 58-64 & 73-; US Rep, NDak, 64-66; Dem cand for US Rep, NDak, 66 & 68. Bus & Prof Pos: Bank vpres & agr rep; farming. Relig: Lutheran; pres, Christ Lutheran Church, Minot, 73- Mailing Add: Box 1090 Minot ND 58701

REDMAN, CHARLES LEE, JR (D)
b Jackson, Ga, Apr 26, 14; s Charles Lee Redman & Mary Strickland R; m 1940 to Jean Butrick; c Janet Lee, Mary Christine & Charles Lee III. Educ: Univ Ga, LLB, 36; Command & Gen Staff Col; Army War Col; Univ Pittsburgh; Sigma Delta Kappa. Polit & Govt Pos: Various pos with Army, including, Commander, European Exchange System; Exec Officer, Off Asst Secy of Army & Dep Chief of Staff, Army Materiel Command; admin asst to US Rep John J Flynt, Jr, Ga, 66- Mil Serv: Entered as Lt, Army, 40, released as Col, 66; Legion of Merit with Three Oak Leaf Clusters; Bronze Star Medal; Air Medal; Eight Battle Stars & others. Publ: Various articles on mgt of tech data & configuration mgt. Mem: Dept of Defense Comt on Tech Data & Configuration Mgt. Mailing Add: 10014 Morningside Court Fairfax VA 22030

REDMAN, JAMES L (D)
Fla State Rep
b Plant City, Fla, Jan 19, 32; s J W Redman & Madaline Miller R; m 1957 to Ruby Jean Barker; c Susan, Pam & Jeanne. Educ: Univ Fla, BSBA, 53, LLB, 58; Phi Kappa Phi; Kappa Alpha. Polit & Govt Pos: Assoc City Judge, Plant City, Fla, 60-65; Dem precinct committeeman, 62-66; Fla State Rep, 66- Mil Serv: Entered as 2nd Lt, Air Force, 54, released as 1st Lt, 56, after serv with Auditor Gen, Tactical Air Command, European Theater. Mem: Fla Bar Asn; Am Judicature Soc; Lions; Fla Cattlemen's Asn; Fla Citrus Mutual. Relig: Baptist. Legal Res: Keene Rd Plant City FL 33566 Mailing Add: PO Drawer TT Plant City FL 33566

REDMAN, RICHARD ELSON (R)
Co-Chmn, Rep State Finance Comt Iowa
b Elko, Nev, Sept 5, 38; s Corwin Elson Redman & Mary Polich R; m 1969 to Jeanette McKellar Remsburg; c Jacklyn Lou & Stephanie Anne. Educ: State Univ Iowa, BA, 60. Polit & Govt Pos: Exec secy, Young Rep Iowa, 60-63; orgn dir, Rep State Cent Comt, Iowa, 63-65, finance secy, 65-66, exec secy, 66-69; pres, Redman Resources, Rep Fund Raisers, 69-; co-chmn, Rep State Finance Comt Iowa, 75- Mem: Des Moines Club. Relig: Presbyterian. Mailing Add: Edgeland Farm Carlisle IA 50047

REDMAN, ROBERT CLAYTON (R)
Chmn, Tenth Dist Rep Party, Mich
b Almā, Mich, Feb 10, 37; s T Clayton Redman & Nora E Morse R; m 1959 to Carolyn Taylor; c Thomas Clayton & Robert LeClair. Educ: Ferris State Col, grad, 59; Mich State Univ Grad Sch, 2 years. Polit & Govt Pos: Chmn, Missaukee Co Rep Comt, Mich, 70-72; chmn, Tenth Dist Rep Party, Mich, 72- Bus & Prof Pos: Vpres & dir, T C Redman, Inc, Lake City, Mich, 59-; teacher, Alma High Sch, 61-63; part owner & chmn bd, Redman Agency, Inc, Lake City, 64-; pres, Lake City CofC, 65-; pres, Lake City Indust Develop Comt, 66-;

mem, Ferris Col Alumni Bd, 68- Mem: Rotary; Ferris Col Alumni Asn (pres, 72-). Relig: Methodist. Legal Res: 241 Nora Dr Lake City MI 49651 Mailing Add: 130 S Main St Lake City MI 49651

REDMOND, CLARICE T (D)
Mem, Maine State Dem Comt
b Madison, Maine, Sept 11, 11; d Joseph A Gallant & Sylvia L G; wid; c John F & Sylvia M. Educ: Madison High Sch, Maine. Polit & Govt Pos: Mem, Maine State Dem Comt, 70- Mem: Daughters of Isabella. Relig: Catholic. Mailing Add: 13 Rowell St Madison ME 04950

REDMOND, JAMES M (D)
Iowa State Sen
Mailing Add: 617 19th St SE Cedar Rapids IA 52403

REDMOND, MARCIA LOUISE (R)
Chairwoman, Paulding Co Rep Comt, Ohio
b Buffalo, NY, Apr 24, 37; d George Leslie Rhodes & Grace Hutchison R; wid; c William Puehn, Laura, Jennifer, Patrick & Brenda. Educ: Amherst High Sch, grad, 55. Polit & Govt Pos: Chairwoman, Paulding Co Rep Comt, Ohio, 74- Bus & Prof Pos: Serv rep, NY Tel Co, Buffalo, 56-59; mgr, D&P Motor Sales, Defiance, 73-74; decorator, Sherwin-Williams Co, 74- Mem: Eagles, Aeria 2405. Relig: Lutheran. Mailing Add: RD 149 RR 5 Defiance OH 43512

REDMOND, WILLIAM A (D)
Ill State Rep
b Chicago, Ill, Nov 25, 08; m to Rita Riordan; c Mary, William Patrick & Colleen. Educ: Marquette Univ; Northwestern Univ, JD. Polit & Govt Pos: Village attorney; sch bd attorney; Ill State Rep, currently; chmn, Du Page Co Dem Party, 73- Bus & Prof Pos: Pvt law practice, Chicago, 34-42. Mil Serv: Naval Res, released, 46, as Lt Comdr. Mem: Am Legion; Lions; KofC. Mailing Add: 250 Tioga Bensenville IL 60106

REDNOUR, JOHN (D)
Mem, Dem Nat Comt, Ill
Mailing Add: 933 S Lake Dr Duquoin IL 62832

REED, ALAN BARRY (D)
Mem, Bernalillo Co Dem Cent Comt, NMex
b Leavenworth, Kans, June 28, 40; s Warren Lillard Reed & Violet Seichepine R; m 1962 to Shari Laine Waetzig; c Selena Eden. Educ: Univ Kans, BA, 62, MA, 64; Univ Tex, PhD, 71; Univ Calif, Los Angeles, MLS, 73; Pi Sigma Alpha. Polit & Govt Pos: Alt deleg, Dem Nat Conv, Nebr, 68; deleg, Travis Co Dem Party, Tex, 72; mem, Bernalillo Co Dem Cent Comt, NMex, 73-; alt deleg, Dem Nat Mid-Term Conf, 74. Bus & Prof Pos: Analyst in Am foreign policy, Libr Cong, Washington, DC, 63-64; asst prof polit sci, Univ Nebr, 67-68; pres, Mosaic Corp, 68-72; asst prof librarianship & polit sci, Univ NMex, 73- Publ: Auth, Legislative politics (film), Filmhouse, Austin, Tex, 69; co-auth, A Quasi-Cabinet for New Mexico, State NMex, 75; auth, The Bibliotheque Royale de Belgique as a national library, J Libr Hist, 1/75. Mem: Albuquerque Comt Foreign Rels; NMex Coun Crime & Delinquency (chmn comt detention & insts, 74-); NMex Dem Coun (state bd mem); Albuquerque Press Club; Gtr Albuquerque Libr Asn. Mailing Add: 2723 McEarl SE Albuquerque NM 87106

REED, ANCIL MASON (R)
Committeeman, Ark Rep State Comt
b Blytheville, Ark, Mar 1, 29; s Lawrence Neill Reed & Ruth Weidemeyer R; div; c Ralph David, Amanda Ruth & William Mitchell. Educ: Hendrix Col, AB, 51; Univ Ark, Fayetteville, LLB, 58, JD, 70; Alpha Psi Omega; Int Rels Club. Polit & Govt Pos: Doorkeeper, US House Rep, Washington, DC, 51-52; lab technician, Ark Hwy Dept, Little Rock, 54; Asst Attorney Gen, Ark, 58-61; committeeman, Ark Rep State Comt, 74- Bus & Prof Pos: Assoc attorney, Talley & Owens, Little Rock, 58; attorney, Thompson, Thompson & Reed, Little Rock, 61-63; title examr, escrow officer, Pac Gas & Elec Co, San Francisco, 63-74; attorney, Reed & Reed, Heber Springs, Ark, 74- Mil Serv: Entered as A/S, Navy, 46, released as Seaman 1/C, 48, after serv in Naval Radio Sta, Haiku-Heeia, Hawaii; Victory Medal. Publ: Auth, One Man's Opinion (column), Hendrix Col Profile, 50. Mem: Cleburne Co Bar Asn; Am Legion; Cleburne Co Hist Soc; Toastmasters Int. Honors & Awards: Cert of Award as Instr, US Naval Res, 51; Cert of Appreciation, Kiwanis Club, Little Rock, 61. Relig: Methodist. Legal Res: Rte 4 Box 300 Heber Springs AR 72543 Mailing Add: 305 W Searcy St Heber Springs AR 72543

REED, AUDRA KNOX (D)
b Orient, Iowa, Dec 23, 05; s William Henry Reed & Emma Ann Witham R; m 1928 to Lela Ann Whitaker; c Lloyd Knox, Rex Whitaker & Audrey Ann Freihofner (Mrs Anton). Educ: Greggs Bus Col, Twin Falls, 24-26. Polit & Govt Pos: Precinct committeeman, Maroa Dist, Twin Falls Co, Idaho, 44-; state committeeman, Twin Falls Co, 70-; deleg, Idaho State Conv, six times; alt deleg, Dem Nat Conv, 72; committeeman, Idaho State Dem Party, formerly. Mem: Odd Fellows (Filer, Idaho Noble Grand, 45); Mason (Filer); RAM; El Korah Temple, Shrine, Boise; Oasis Shrine Club, Buhl. Relig: First Christian. Mailing Add: Rte 1 Filer ID 83328

REED, BETTY LOU (R)
Ill State Rep
b Flint, Mich, Mar 23, 27; d Clifford J Ledrow & Mary Johnson L; m 1947 to Richard C Reed; c Nancy & Sally. Educ: Flint Cent High Sch, 44. Polit & Govt Pos: Mem exec comt, West Deerfield Twp Young Rep, 59-60; pres, West Deerfield Twp Rep Women, 62-64; chmn, Lake Co Rep Party, 64-70; precinct committeeman, West Deerfield Twp 5, 64-; exec dir, Ill Women for Nixon-Agnew, 68; asst supvr, West Deerfield Twp, 69-; committeewoman, Ill Rep State Cent Comt, 70-; Ill State Rep, 75- Mem: Comt of Deerfield, Inc; Infant Welfare Soc of Chicago, Deerfield Wing. Relig: Episcopal. Mailing Add: 927 Holly Court Deerfield IL 60015

REED, CLARKE THOMAS (R)
Chmn, Miss Rep Party
b Aug 4, 28; s Lyman Harlan Reed & Kathryn Reynolds R; m 1957 to Julia Brooks; c Julia Evans, Clark T, Jr & Reynolds Crews. Educ: Univ Mo, BS in Econ, 50; Phi Gamma Delta. Polit & Govt Pos: Chmn, Washington Co Rep Party, Miss, 62-65; finance chmn, Miss Rep Party, 65, chmn, 66-; mem, Rep Nat Comt, 66-, mem, Exec Comt, 73-; deleg & chmn, Miss Deleg, Rep Nat Conv, 68 & 72; chmn, Southern Asn Rep State Chmn, 69- Bus & Prof Pos: Pres, Reed-Joseph Co, 52- Mil Serv: Entered as 2nd Lt, Air Force, 53, released as 1st Lt, 55; Commendation Ribbon. Mem: Young Presidents Orgn. Relig: Presbyterian. Legal Res: Bayou Rd Greenville MS 38701 Mailing Add: Box 894 Greenville MS 38701

REED, GEORGE JOSEPH (R)
b Haigler, Nebr, May 31, 14; s Edwin W Reed & Cleo Randall R; m 1938 to Lois Goetze; c George Calvert. Educ: Pasadena Col, AB, 38, Univ Southern Calif, grad work, 48. Hon Degrees: Three LLD degrees. Polit & Govt Pos: Dep probation officer, Los Angeles Co, Calif, 38-46; field dir, Calif Youth Authority, 46-49; dep dir, Minn Youth Conserv Comn, 49-53; chmn, Youth Correction Div, US Bd of Parole, 53-57, mem, US Bd of Parole, 57-, chmn, 57-64, 69-72, vchmn, 72-; dir, Nev Dept of Parole & Probation, 65-67 & Lane Co Juvenile Dept, Eugene, Ore, 68-69. Bus & Prof Pos: Prof of criminology, Col of the Sequoias, 67-68. Mil Serv: Navy, 41-44. Publ: Crime Prevention and Community Organization, State of Minn, 50; Parole better protects society, Vital Speeches of the Day, 11/58; Treating the youthful offender, Southwest Legal Found, 59. Mem: Fel Am Acad of Criminology; Am Correctional Asn; Nat Parole Coun; Nat Coun on Crime & Delinquency; Prof Coun on Probation & Parole (exec bd). Honors & Awards: Award, Outstanding Pres Alumni Asn, Pasadena Col; Spec Award of Recognition, Am Legion; Membership in Spec Awards for Serv to Humanities, Nat Exchange Clubs of Am. Relig: Protestant. Legal Res: 1925 Coventry Way Eugene OR 97405 Mailing Add: 4201 Cathedral Ave NW Washington DC 20016

REED, GLENN EDWARD (R)
Chmn, Skagit Co Rep Cent Comt, Wash
b Seattle, Wash, Apr 3, 44; s Glenn Walker Reed & Geraldine Lyon R; m 1963 to Anita Constance Mihos; c Tina Marie & Trisha Elizabeth. Educ: Loyola Univ Sch Law, JD; Univ Nev, Las Vegas, BS in Bus Admin; Phi Kappa Phi; Alpha Kappa Psi, past pres, Eta Lambda Chap. Polit & Govt Pos: Chmn, Skagit Co Rep Cent Comt, Wash, 75- Bus & Prof Pos: Asst attorney gen, Wash, 73-74; sole practitioner, 74- Mil Serv: Entered as E-1, Air Force, 62, released as E-4, 64, after serv in Tactical Air Command. Mem: Boy Scouts (mem exec bd, Mt Baker Area Coun, 74-); Am Legion; Elks; Kiwanis. Honors & Awards: Distinguished Serv Award, Alpha Kappa Psi, 69; Am Jurisp Award, Bancroft-Whitney, 73. Legal Res: 115 S Fifth St Mt Vernon WA 98273 Mailing Add: 709-711 S First St Mt Vernon WA 98273

REED, GORDON WIES (R)
Mem, Nat Rep Finance Comt
b Chicago, Ill, Nov 20, 99; s Frank Reed & Mary Wies R; m 1967 to Genevieve Funston; c Tom & step daughter Susan Logan. Educ: Univ Ill, Urbana, BS, 22. Polit & Govt Pos: Chmn, Rep Citizens Comt, Conn, 62-65 & Rep Finance Comt, 64-65; deleg, Rep Nat Conv, 68; mem, Nat Rep Finance Comt, 69- Bus & Prof Pos: Chmn, Tex Gulf Prod Co, 41-64; chmn finance comt, Am Metal Climax, 64- Mil Serv: Pvt Army, 18; asst dir aluminum & magnesium div, War Prod Bd, 41-44; spec asst to chief of staff, US Air Force, 50-54; Civilian Air Medal, 55. Publ: Reed Report on Military Air Transport Service, US Air Force, 58. Relig: Methodist. Mailing Add: 100 Clapboard Ridge Rd Greenwich CT 06830

REED, JOHN HATHAWAY (R)
b Ft Fairfield, Maine, Jan 5, 21; s Walter Manley Reed, Sr & Eva Seeley R; m 1944 to Cora Davison; c Cheryl Diane & Ruth Ann. Educ: Univ Maine, BS, 42; Phi Eta Kappa. Hon Degrees: LLD, Ricker Col & Univ Maine. Polit & Govt Pos: Maine State Rep, 55-57; Maine State Sen, 57-59, pres, Maine State Senate, 59; Gov, Maine, 60-67; mem, Nat Transportation Safety Bd, Washington, DC, 67-69, chmn, 69- Bus & Prof Pos: Dir, Reed Farms, Inc, Ft Fairfield, Maine, 42- Mil Serv: Entered as Storekeeper 3/C, Naval Res, 42, released as Lt(jg), 45, after serv in Cub 17, Okinawa, Pac, 45. Mem: Rotary; VFW; Am Legion; Shrine; Mason. Relig: Congregational. Legal Res: Ft Fairfield ME 04742 Mailing Add: 410 O St SW Washington DC 20024

REED, MAXINE GRESHAM (R)
Committeewoman, Ark State Rep Comt
b Fordyce, Ark, Sept 9, 05; d John William Gresham & Annie Louise Russell G; div; c Mary Aline (Mrs Bland) & John Robert. Educ: Fordyce High Sch, grad. Polit & Govt Pos: Dep circuit clerk, Drew Co, Ark, 6 years; acct mgr, Dallas Co Hosp, Fordyce, 6 years; mgr, Food Coupon Off, 5 years. Relig: Episcopal. Mailing Add: 611 W Second St Fordyce AR 71742

REED, MICHAEL ALLEN (D)
Chairperson, Page Co Dem Cent Comt, Iowa
b Clarinda, Iowa, June 29, 47; s Allen Elmer Reed & Susan Marilyn Shields R; m 1965 to Linda Marie Riddle; c Todd Allen, Michael Allen, Jr & Robert Allen. Educ: Iowa Western Community Col, Clarinda, 65-66. Polit & Govt Pos: Chairperson, Page Co Dem Cent Comt, Iowa, 72- Bus & Prof Pos: Turret lathe operator, Lisle Corp, Clarinda, Iowa, 66-; emergency med technician-ambulance, Clarinda Vol Fire Dept, 72- Mem: IAMAW (recording secy, Local 1300, 69-71, pres, 72-); Southwest Iowa Labor Coun AFL-CIO (vpres, 72-); Iowa State Coun of Machinists AFL-CIO (vpres, 75-); Clarinda Vol Fire Dept (treas, 73-); Iowa Heart Asn (instr basic life support). Relig: Protestant. Mailing Add: 615 N 16th St Clarinda IA 51632

REED, MICHAEL LEE (D)
b Durant, Okla, Sept 9, 37; s I N Reed & Daisy L Derrick R; m 1968 to Stephanie Williams. Educ: Wash Univ, AB, 61; Univ Okla, LLB, 62; Phi Delta Phi; Sigma Nu. Polit & Govt Pos: Mem staff, Gov Okla, 60-62, counsel to Gov, 62; asst to US Sen J Howard Edmondson, Okla, 63-64; legis asst to US Rep Carl Albert, Okla, 64- Mem: Fed & Okla Bar Asns. Relig: Methodist. Legal Res: Durant OK 74701 Mailing Add: 913 Enderby Dr Alexandria VA 22302

REED, NATHANIEL PRYOR (R)
Asst Secy Interior for Fish, Wildlife & Parks
b New York, NY, July 22, 33; s Joseph Verner Reed & Permelia Pryor R; m 1965 to Alita Davis Weaver; c Nathaniel Pryor, Jr, Alita Pryor & Adrian William. Educ: Trinity Col (Conn), BA, 55; St Anthony Hall; Delta Psi. Hon Degrees: DPS, Univ Fla, 72. Polit & Govt Pos: Co-chmn, Fla Bd Antiq, 62-63; spec asst to Gov for the Environ, Fla State Govt, 67-71; mem, Fla Bd of Pollution Control Comn, 68; chmn, Fla Dept Air & Water Pollution Control, 69-71; Asst Secy Interior for Fish, Wildlife & Parks, 71- Bus & Prof Pos: Vpres, Hobe Sound Co, Fla, 60-71. Mil Serv: Entered as 2nd Lt, Air Force, 55, released as Capt, 59, after serv in Intel ETO, NAfrica & MidE, 55-59. Mem: Jupiter Island Club; The Links; Seminole; The Angler's Club; Chevy Chase Club. Honors & Awards: Awards, Garden Club of Am & Fla Wildlife Fedn, 70, Trop Audubon Soc, 71; Outdoorsman of the Year, Fla Outdoor Writers Asn, 71-72; Alumni Award, Trinity Col (Conn), 72. Legal Res: Jupiter Island Club PO Box 375 Hobe Sound FL 33455 Mailing Add: 2900 Woodland Dr NW Washington DC 20008

REED, NORMAN EARL (R)
Vt State Rep
Mailing Add: Chandler Rd Box 61 White River Junction VT 05001

REED, ROBERT GORDON, JR (R)
b Kenton, Ohio, Sept 21, 36; s Robert Gordon Reed & Eva Mae Campbell R; single. Educ: Ohio State Univ, BA, 58, LLB, 60; Phi Delta Phi. Polit & Govt Pos: Chmn, Hardin Co Rep Cent Comt, Ohio, 68-74. Bus & Prof Pos: Partner, Hanna & Reed, Kenton, Ohio, 64- Mil Serv: Entered as 1st Lt, Army, 61, released as Capt, 64, after serv at Judge Adv Gen Sch, Charlottesville, Va, 61-64; Army Commendation Medal. Mem: Hardin Co & Logan Co Bar Asns; Grange; Elks; Kiwanis. Relig: United Presbyterian. Mailing Add: RR 1 Belle Center OH 43310

REED, SAM GLEN (R)
Nat Committeeman, United Tex Young Rep Fedn
b Ft Worth, Tex, Jan 7, 46; s Sam Strong Reed & Cora Lawrence R; single. Educ: Panola Col, AA, 66; Stephen F Austin State Univ, BBA, 69; Alpha Kappa Psi. Polit & Govt Pos: State chmn, Tex Young Rep Fedn, 73-74, young adult coun chmn, United Tex Rep Youth, 74-75, nat committeeman, United Tex Young Rep Fedn, 75-; chmn, Bastrop Co Rep Party, 74- Bus & Prof Pos: Teacher, Wortham Independent Sch Dist, Tex, 69-71; teacher, Bastrop Independent Sch Dist, 71-74. Mem: Kiwanis; Bastrop Co Young Adult Rep Club (pres, 74-); Explorer Scout Post 187 (adult leader); PTA. Honors & Awards: Outstanding Young Adult Rep in Tex, United Tex Rep Youth, 75. Relig: Episcopal. Mailing Add: PO Box 632 Bastrop TX 78602

REED, SAM SUMNER (R)
Asst Secy State, Wash
b Portland, Ore, Jan 10, 41; s Donald Blackhall Reed & Geraldine J Sumner R; m 1963 to Margery Ann Nichols; c Kristen Louise & David Sumner. Educ: Wash State Univ, BA, 63, Coulter Found Scholar & Kappa Sigma Scholar, MA in Polit Sci, 68; Phi Alpha Theta; Pi Sigma Alpha; Kappa Sigma. Polit & Govt Pos: Admin asst, Secy State A Ludlow Kramer, Wash, 66; exec dir, Gov Urban Affairs Coun, 67-69; Asst Secy State, 69-; state dir, Campaign to Reelect Secy State A Ludlow Kramer, 72. Bus & Prof Pos: Teacher hist & lit, Olympia Sch Dist, Wash, 63-64; dean of men's staff, Wash State Univ, 65-67. Publ: Auth, Urban Washington: Apathy or Action?, Wash State Printer, 68; Factional Power Struggles in Washington State Republican Party, Wash State Univ, 68; The unliberated American male, Human Affairs Coun News, 72. Mem: Common Cause; Olympia Racquet Club; Ballet Northwest; Ore Shakespearean Asn. Legal Res: 2512 Angela St SE Lacey WA 98503 Mailing Add: Asst Secy State Legis Bldg Olympia WA 98504

REED, SAMUEL LEE (R)
Ind State Rep
b Selma, Ind, July 29, 34; s Merritt Camillus Reed & Ivy Jane Williams R; m 1955 to Joan Carol Guinn; c Scott Lindsay, Craig Samuel, Steven Andrew & Jennifer Gwynne. Educ: Ind Univ, Bloomington, BS, 56, JD, 59; Phi Gamma Delta. Polit & Govt Pos: Dep prosecuting attorney, Del Co, Ind, 60-63, drainage bd attorney, 68-72; twp attorney, Union Twp, 63-67; town attorney, Albany, 66-72 & Selma, 68-71; mem & pres, Muncie Community Sch Bd, 68-72; Ind State Rep, 72-, mem budget comt, Ind House of Rep, 74-, ranking minority mem ways & means comt, 75- Bus & Prof Pos: Pres, Eastern Ind Community TV, Inc, 71-; community adv coun, Ind Univ Med Sch, 73- Mem: Muncie-Delaware Co CofC (bd dirs, 74-); Blue Key; Muncie Exchange Club (pres, 65-); YWCA (bd trustees, 69-); Boy Scouts (exec bd, 69-). Honors & Awards: Big Ten Medal, Ind Univ, 56; Distinguished Serv Award, Muncie Jaycees, 68. Relig: Presbyterian. Legal Res: 76 Warwick Rd Muncie IN 47304 Mailing Add: 320 S High St Muncie IN 47305

REED, STEPHEN RUSSELL (D)
Pa State Rep
b Chambersburg, Pa, Aug 9, 49; s Galen Berkeley Reed, Sr (deceased) & Jane Louise Leach R; single. Educ: Dickinson Col, Carlisle, Pa, 67-68; Harrisburg Area Community Col, Pa, 70-72; Kappa Kappa; Alpha Epsilon Tau; Harrisburg Area Community Col Student Govt Pres. Polit & Govt Pos: Founder & past pres, Dauphin Co Teenage Dem, Pa, 65-69; founder & past pres, Pa Teenage Dem, 67-69; chmn, Pa Youth for Humphrey, Muskie & Clark, 68; pres, Dauphin Co Young Dem, 69-; US Cong campaign dir, Pa 17th Dist, 70; co-founder & past chmn, Pa Community Col Student Govt Asn, 70-71; nat committeeman, Col Young Dem of Pa, 70-72; mem exec comt, Dauphin Co Dem Comt, 70-; chmn, Dauphin Co Dem Platform Comt, 71; chmn, Pa Asn of Col & Univ Student Govts, 71-72; chmn, Mayor's Youth Adv Task Force, City of Harrisburg, 71-73; chmn, Adult Educ Adv Coun, Harrisburg Sch Dist, 71-; chmn, Col Young Dem of Am Nat Conv, 71 & 73; Dauphin Co Bd of Assistance, Pa Dept of Pub Welfare, 72-74; chmn, Dem Party, Harrisburg, 72-74; Nat Committeeman, Young Dem of Am, 72-74; US Regional Secy, Region II, 73-74; registr, Pa Health Dept, 72-74; Pa State Rep, 75- Bus & Prof Pos: Consumer adv, Pa Ins Comnr, 71-75; chmn, Cent Pa Health Security Action Coun, 72-75; chmn, Orgn & Planning Comt to Tri-County Manpower Planning Coun, 72-74; mem, Labor Mkt Adv Coun, 73-75. Publ: The mechanics of politics: organization, administration & community service, Cent Pa Conf of Young Dem, 71, reprinted, 72; Community college alumni: a new force in the educational system, Pa Community Col Alumni Asn, 73; ed, The Pennsylvanian, Pa Young Dem Newspaper, 71, 72 & 73. Mem: Jednota (Cath Slovak Union); Elks; Dauphin Co NAACP; Gtr Harrisburg Area YMCA (bd dirs, 74-). Honors & Awards: Outstanding Young Dem of Pa, Pa Young Dem, 71; Distinguished Leadership Award, Harrisburg Area Community Col Student Govt, 71; Outstanding Young Man of Am, 72 & 74; Distinguished Serv Award, Harrisburg Jaycees, 73; Presidents Leadership Award, US Jaycees, 73. Relig: Roman Catholic. Mailing Add: Capitol Bldg Harrisburg PA 17120

REED, SUE MABEL (R)
Historian, Nat Fedn Rep Women
b Alexander, Iowa, Feb 19, 10; d Lupke Schulte & Mabel Bell S; m 1941 to William Jap Reed; c Dianne (Mrs Bozarth). Educ: Des Moines Univ, 27-28; Univ Commerce, Des Moines, secy, 1 year; Delta Gamma Chi. Polit & Govt Pos: Supvr & adminr, qm & war ord, War Dept, Des Moines, Iowa, 35-45; chief jour clerk, Iowa House Rep, 55-73; state pres, Iowa Fedn Rep Women, 63-64; deleg, Rep Nat Conv, 64; membership chmn, Nat Fedn Rep Women, 68-70, historian, 72-; pub rep, State Iowa Med Assistance Adv Coun, 69-72; Polk Co coordr & state vol chmn, Comt for Reelec of the President, 72. Mem: Eastern Star; YWCA; Des Moines Women's Club; Drake Alumni Asn. Relig: Protestant. Mailing Add: 1314 48th St Des Moines IA 50311

REED, THOMAS (D)
Ala State Rep
Mailing Add: Drawer EE Tuskegee Institute AL 36088

REED, THOMAS BRUCE (R)
Exec Dir, Mo Fedn Young Rep
b St Louis, Mo, July 27, 45; s James A Reed & Mary Millar R; single. Educ: Cent Mo State Col, BA, 68; secy of state, Mo Intercollegiate State Legis, 65-66. Polit & Govt Pos: Pres, Cent Mo State Col Young Rep, 65-66; asst to chmn, Mo Rep State Comt, 69-; exec dir, Mo Fedn Young Rep, 70-, pres, Capitol Region Young Rep, 71-72, treas, 72-; mem, Friends of Richard Nixon, 72- Mil Serv: Entered as Pvt, Army, 67, released as SP-4, 69, after serv in K-75th Rangers, Vietnam, 68-69; Combat Infantryman's Badge; Bronze Star; Air Medal; Army Commendation Medal; Vietnam Serv Medal; Vietnam Campaign Medal; Good Conduct Medal. Mem: Am Legion. Relig: Presbyterian. Legal Res: Rte 2 Box 12 Pacific MO 63069 Mailing Add: PO Box 73 Jefferson City MO 65101

REEL, WILLIAM A, JR (D)
SC State Rep
Mailing Add: 205 Lynch Edgefield SC 29854

REES, G STANFORD (R)
Utah State Sen
Mailing Add: Gunnison UT 84634

REES, GROVER JOSEPH, III (R)
Mem Exec Comt, Young Rep Nat Fedn
b New Orleans, La, Oct 11, 51; s Grover Joseph Rees, Jr & Patricia Byrne R; m 1972 to Helene Marie Maiorano; c Grover J, IV. Educ: Yale Univ, BA, 75; Yale Calliopean Soc. Polit & Govt Pos: Justice of the Peace, New Haven, Conn, 73-75; chmn, 23rd Ward Rep Comt, 73-75; mem exec comt, Young Rep Nat Fedn, 74-; chmn, Conservative Campaign Comt, 75-; dir, Comt for Responsible Youth Polit, 73- Bus & Prof Pos: Asst ed, Battle Line, Am Conservative Union, 71; press asst, US Rep David Treen, 73; exec dir, Conn State Taxpayers Asn, 73-75; assoc, Grover Rees Jr & Assocs, Lafayette, La, 75- Mem: KofC; Young Am for Freedom. Honors & Awards: First Prize, Gardner-White Sr Prize Debate, Yale Polit Union, 72. Relig: Roman Catholic. Mailing Add: 2301 Pine St Lafayette LA 70501

REES, HELEN (D)
Dem Nat Committeewoman, Mass
Mailing Add: 119 Colchester St Brookline MA 02146

REES, THOMAS L (D)
Chmn, Mitchell Co Dem Party, Tex
b San Angelo, Tex, Dec 14, 39; s Horace B Rees & Margaret Holland R; m 1962 to Margaret Diane; c Thomas L, Jr, Melanie Diane & Reagan Carter. Educ: Rice Univ, BS & BA, 62; Baylor Univ, LLB, 65; Phi Delta Phi. Polit & Govt Pos: Chmn, Mitchell Co Dem Party, Tex, 67-; deleg to Rules & Regulation 24th Cong Dist, 68-; vpres, Colo Independent Sch Dist, Colorado City, Tex, 68-69; pres, 69- Bus & Prof Pos: Partner, Thompson & Rees, 65-69. Mem: State Bar of Tex; Mitchell Co & Am Bar Asn; Scottish Rite. Honors & Awards: Distinguished Young Man of Mitchell Co Tex. Relig: Methodist. Legal Res: 644 Chestnut Colorado City TX 79512 Mailing Add: Box 1007 Colorado City TX 79512

REES, THOMAS M (D)
US Rep, Calif
b Los Angeles, Calif, Mar 26, 25; s Caradoc Rees & Mildred Melgaard R; m 1960 to Leanne G Boccardo; c Evan B & James C. Educ: Occidental Col, BA, 50; Univ Calif, Berkeley, Boalt Hall, 50-51. Polit & Govt Pos: Mem, State Dem Cent Comt, Calif, 54-56; Calif State Assemblyman, 55-62; deleg, Dem Nat Conv, 56, 60, 64 & 68; Calif State Sen, 62-65; mem, Calif Comn of the Californias, 63-66 & Calif Arts Comn, 63-66; US Rep, 23rd Cong Dist, Calif, 65- Bus & Prof Pos: Pres, Compania Del Pacifico, 52-; mem bd, Conoisseur Wine Imports, Inc, 65-68; attorney, Calif. Mil Serv: Served as combat infantry man, World War II in 89th Inf Div, Third Army, ETO; Combat Inf Badge; ETO Medal with two Battle Stars; Am Theater Ribbon; Bronze Star Medal. Mem: Los Angeles Mus of Art Assoc; Los Angeles World Affairs Coun; Los Angeles Opera Asn; Am Legion. Relig: Episcopal. Legal Res: 1673 Waynecrest Dr Beverly Hills CA 90210 Mailing Add: 1112 Longworth House Off Bldg Washington DC 20515

REESE, BOB L (R)
Committeeman, Rep State Cent Comt La
b Arcadia, La, Apr 29, 29; s Lester Lynn Reese & Martha Beard R; m 1954 to Gwen Thomas. Educ: La Tech Univ, 2 years. Polit & Govt Pos: Committeeman, Rep State Cent Comt La, 68-; chmn, Natchitoches Parish Rep Exec Comt, 69-; mem polit action coun bd, La Rep Party, 69- Bus & Prof Pos: Owner, Residential Designers & Builders, 56- Mil Serv: Entered as Pvt, Air Force, 48, released as S/Sgt, 53, after serv in Far East Air Material Command, 49-52. Mem: Nat Homebuilders Asn (chmn, Natchitoches); Lions. Relig: Baptist. Mailing Add: PO Box 2667 Natchitoches LA 71457

REESE, D LEON (D)
Utah State Rep
Mailing Add: 2889 South 8560 W Magna UT 84044

REESE, DELIGHT HARMON (R)
NH State Rep
b Springfield, Mass, Sept 18, 38; d Charles Warren Harmon & Dorothy Mossman H; m 1961 to Donald Reese; c Charles Christopher & Jeffrey Donald. Educ: Bates Col, BA, 61. Polit & Govt Pos: Mem sch bd, Hampstead, NH, 71-74 & chmn, 74-75; NH State Rep, Dist 6, 74- Bus & Prof Pos: Legal secy, Providence, RI, 56-57; co-founder, co-dir & teacher, Gingerbread House Kindergarten, Hampstead, NH, 66-71. Mem: Salem Ment Health Clin (bd dirs, 75-); Orgn of Women Legislators. Relig: Protestant. Legal Res: Main St Hampstead NH 03841 Mailing Add: Box 145 Hampstead NH 03841

REESE, ELOIS HAMILL (R)
VChmn, Hockley Co Rep Party, Tex
b Clarksville, Tex, Aug 8, 17; d Thomas Jefferson Messick & Sarah Ann Edwards M; m to L Peyton Reese; c Richard Peyton, Jane, Sue Beth & Robert Arther. Educ: Tex Tech, 2 years. Polit & Govt Pos: Vchmn, Hockley Co Rep Party, Tex, 60-; sponsor, Hockley Co TAR, 70-; dist dir, Tex Fedn Rep Women, 70- Mem: Eastern Star; Rep Womens Club; Home

Demonstration Club; Tex Farm Bur; Levelland Country Club. Relig: Baptist. Legal Res: 310 12th St Levelland TX 79336 Mailing Add: Box 242 Levelland TX 79336

REESE, MATTHEW ANDERSON (D)
b Huntington, WVa, Aug 9, 27; s Matthew Anderson Reese, Sr & Gladys Lee Willis R; m 1950 to Martha Lee Sedinger; c April Lee, Holly Dean & Timothy Anderson. Educ: Marshall Univ, BA, 50; George Washington Univ, 55; Omicron Delta Kappa. Polit & Govt Pos: Staff asst to Congressman M G Burnside, WVa, 55-57; exec secy, Young Dem Clubs WVa, 59-60; exec dir, WVirginians for Kennedy, 60; spec asst to adminr, Small Bus Admin, 61; dir opers, Dem Nat Comt, 61-65, mem, Dem Charter Comn, 73-74; dep dir, WVa Dept Natural Resources, 65-66. Bus & Prof Pos: Head, Matt Reese & Assocs, Polit Consult, 66-; sr partner, Reese, Whelan, Nace & Murphine, 73- Mil Serv: Entered as Pvt, Army, 46, released as Sgt, 47, after serv in Air Corps, US; reentered as 2nd Lt, 51, released as 1st Lt, 53, after serv in TranspC, Korea, 52-53; various awards. Mem: Am Asn Polit Consult (pres). Honors & Awards: Outstanding Citizenship Award, Am Heritage Found, 66. Relig: Presbyterian. Legal Res: 1040 Bellview Pl McLean VA 22101 Mailing Add: 1625 Massachusetts Ave NW Washington DC 20036

REESE, PAUL FRANCIS (D)
b Parkersburg, WVa, June 14, 40; s William Warren Reese & Ethel Francis R; m 1958 to Nita Ruth Freed; c Michael Paul & John Edward & Angela Roberta. Educ: Glenville State Col, AB, 72. Polit & Govt Pos: Committeeman, Wood Co Dem Exec Comt, WVa, 66-74, chmn, 70-72; mem, Wood Co Bd Educ, 74- Bus & Prof Pos: Co-owner & vpres, Rafferty Appliance, Inc; co-owner, Home Discount Ctr; co-owner, Russel's Trailer Park; owner, Reese Ins Agency. Mem: Nat Life Underwriters Asn; Boy Scouts; AF&AM. Relig: Baptist. Legal Res: Rte 2 Box 71A Waverly WV 26184 Mailing Add: PO Box 1974 Parkersburg WV 26101

REEVES, ALBERT L (R)
b Steelville, Mo, May 31, 06; s Albert L Reeves & Martha Ferguson R; m 1935 to Eleanor Louise Glasner; c Elaine Louise (Mrs Padovani), Martha Emilie & Nancy Lee. Educ: William Jewell Col, BA, 27; Univ Mo, LLB, 31; Kappa Sigma; Phi Delta Phi; Pi Kappa Delta; Delta Sigma Rho. Polit & Govt Pos: Treas, Jackson Co Rep Comt, Mo, 34-36; US Rep, Mo, 47-48. Bus & Prof Pos: Partner, Michaels, Blackmar, Newkirk, Eager & Swanson, Kansas City, Mo, 31-46; partner, Cummings, Sellers, Reeves & Connor & predecessor firms, Washington, DC, 49-58; sr vpres, dir & secy, Utah Int, Inc, Calif, 58-75; dir & secy, Marcona Corp & subsidiaries, 61-74, sr vpres, 75-; dir, Bay Area Educ TV, 70-; dir, French Bank Calif; chmn, SAFE, Int, 71-74, dir, currently. Mil Serv: Entered as Capt, Army, 42, released as Lt Col, 46, after serv in Mo River Div, Corps of Engrs; China-Burma-India Theater of Opers; Motor Transport Command, 468th Qm Group & 1905th Aviation Bn; China-Burma-India & Z I Ribbons. Mem: Am Soc of Int Law; Acad of Polit Sci; DeMolay (Legion of Honor); World Affairs Coun of Northern Calif (trustee); World Trade Club of San Francisco (pres, 65-68). Relig: Episcopal. Legal Res: 2225 Forest View Ave Hillsborough CA 94010 Mailing Add: Marcona Corp One Maritime Plaza San Francisco CA 94111

REEVES, BRUCE MANNING (D)
Maine State Sen
b RI, Dec 10, 35; s Charles M Reeves & Minna C Connors R; m 1959 to Polly Rice Reeves; c Phoebe & Charles. Educ: Harvard Univ, AB, 57; Boston Univ Sch Bus Admin, 59-61. Polit & Govt Pos: Maine State Sen, Dist 20, 75-, chmn, Joint Select Comt on Jobs, Maine Legis, 75- Bus & Prof Pos: Founding mem, Maine Organic Farmers Asn, 70-72. Mem: Audubon Soc Maine. Mailing Add: Beech Hill Rd East Pittston ME 04345

REEVES, HELEN GRAYSON (R)
VChairwoman, Columbia Co Rep Party, Ark
d Thomas Samuel Grayson & Mary Elizabeth Hayes G; m 1927 to Thomas Hal Reeves, wid; c Katheryn (Mrs J L Jean) & Ann (Mrs Eddy); three grandchildren. Educ: Henderson State Col, BA, 25. Polit & Govt Pos: Chmn fund raising, Eisenhower Campaign, Columbia Co, Ark, 52; pres, Columbia Co Rep Women, 67-68, chmn, 68-; chmn fund raising, Nixon Campaign, Columbia Co, 68; alt deleg, Rep Nat Conv, 68; vol worker, Rep Cands, Ark, 70-; treas, Ark Fedn of Rep Women, 71-72; vchairwoman, Columbia Co Rep Party, currently. Bus & Prof Pos: Vpres, Farmers Bank & Trust Co Magnolia, Magnolia, Ark; pres, Reeves Land & Timber Develop; chmn, City Planning Comn, 62-66; owner, Red Bird Lumber Co. Mem: PTA (pres, 36-38); Band Parents (pres, 45); Quota Club (pres, 50-51 & 73-, lt gov, 54); Sorosis Club (pres, 35-36). Relig: Church of Christ. Mailing Add: 1105 Lawton Circle Magnolia AR 71753

REEVES, J H (RIP) (R)
Kans State Rep
Mailing Add: 1464 Perry Wichita KS 67203

REEVES, R B (BREEZY) (D)
Miss State Sen
b Pike Co, Miss, Aug 1, 28; married. Polit & Govt Pos: Miss State Sen, currently. Bus & Prof Pos: Lawyer. Mem: Sigma Nu; CofC; KofP; Lions; Am Legion. Relig: Baptist. Mailing Add: 820 Northwest St McComb MS 39648

REFIOR, EVERETT LEE (D)
Mem Exec Comt, Walworth Co Dem Party, Wis
b Donnellson, Iowa, Jan 23, 19; s Fred C Refior & Daisy E Gardner R; m 1943 to Marie Emma Culp; c Gene Allan, Wendell Frederick, Paul Douglas & Donna Marie. Educ: Iowa Wesleyan Col, BA, summa cum laude, 42; Univ Chicago, MA, 55; Univ Iowa, PhD, 62; Iota Phi; Pi Kappa Delta; Alpha Psi Omega; Order of Artus; Independent Men's Club (pres); Wesley Club (vpres); Ed, Tiger 1 year 6 months. Polit & Govt Pos: City chmn, UN Day Comt, Whitewater, Wis, 60, mem, 62-; deleg, Wis Dem Conv, 64, 66, 68, deleg & mem resolutions comt, 69-; precinct committeeman, Third Ward, Whitewater, 66-; chmn, Walworth Co Dem Party, 69-72, mem exec comt, 73-; mem, Gov Comn on UN, 71- Bus & Prof Pos: Instr econ & bus, Iowa Wesleyan Col, 47-50; teaching asst social sci, 50-51; res asst, Bur Labor & Mgt, Univ Iowa, 51-52, instr mgt & social sci, 54-55; assoc prof econ, Simpson Col, 52-54; asst prof econ, Wis State Univ-Whitewater, 55-62, assoc prof, 62-64, prof, 64-, chmn dept econ, 66- Mil Serv: Entered as Pvt, Army, 43, released as Pfc, 46, after serv in 163rd Gen Hosp, Europe, 44-46. Publ: Estimating the labor supply in a rural community (w K E Larsen), Bur Labor & Mgt, Univ Iowa, 54; Flexibility in manpower utilization, Univ Iowa, 62; Income-leisure choices of college faculty members, Midwest Econ Asn, 63. Mem: Indust Rels Res Asn (adv bd, Wis Chap); Asn Wis State Univ Faculties; World Federalists USA (Founder, Whitewater Chap, pres, 60-68, vpres midwest region, 61-63 & 67-69, pres midwest region, 69-71, nat exec coun, 68-, US voting deleg, World Cong, Ottawa, 70, Brussels, 72); Walworth Co UN Asn (prog chmn, 65-69); Am Civil Liberties Union. Relig: United Methodist; lay speaker; mem, Wis Conf Bd Christian Soc Concerns, 62-69, 71- Mailing Add: 205 N Fremont St Whitewater WI 53190

REGAN, CAROL BOYD (D)
VChmn, Charleston Co Dem Party, SC
b Miami Beach, Fla, Dec 24, 41; d Ralph Benjamin Boyd & Rae Russell B; m 1962 to William Bennett Regan; c Kelly Kathleen. Educ: Col Charleston, BS, 63; Alpha Kappa Gamma; Senior Select; Chi Omega; pres, Athletic Asn; Newman Club; Yearbook Staff. Polit & Govt Pos: Mem, City of Charleston Human Rels Comn, 71-; Charleston Co Social Serv Bd, 71-; deleg, Dem Nat Conv, 72; vchmn, Charleston Co Dem Party, 72-74. Mem: Charleston Co Dem Women's Club (prog comt chmn, 73-75); Ward 3 Dem Club (vpres, 72); League of Women Voters (vpres & bd mem, 71-72); YWCA Gtr Charleston (bd mem, 75-). Relig: Roman Catholic. Mailing Add: 47 Hasell St Charleston SC 29401

REGAN, PAT (D)
Mont State Sen
Mailing Add: 204 Mountain View Billings MT 59101

REGAN, RAYMOND RICHARD (R)
Chmn, Dona Ana Co Rep Party, NMex
b Buffalo, NY, May 26, 39; s R R Regan & Helen Susan Keysa R; m 1963 to Joan Martha Knoth; c Brian Keith & Kristina Erin. Educ: US Mil Acad, West Point, BS, 61; Univ NMex Sch Law, JD, 68, pres, Student Bar Asn, 67-68. Polit & Govt Pos: Co campaign coordr for US Sen Pete V Domenici, NMex, 71-72; chmn, Dona Ana Co Rep Party, 74- Bus & Prof Pos: Pres, Ray R Regan, Ltd, Las Cruces, NMex, 74- Mil Serv: Entered as 2nd Lt, Army, 61, released as Capt, 65, after serv in 17th Bn, 35th Artil, ETO, 62-65; Airborne & Ranger Medals. Publ: Buy-sell agreements for legalus smarticus, Law Off Econ & Mgt, 3/72; A single-entry timekeeping system, Practical Lawyer, 4/73 & Law Off Mgt Manual, 8/74; Mini-management memos, NMex State Bar Bull, 74-75. Mem: NMex & Colo Bar Asns; Am Bar Asn (nat chmn, Timekeeping Sect); West Point Alumni; Rotary Club Las Cruces. Honors & Awards: Award of Merit, State Bar NMex, 72; US Law Week Award, 67-68. Legal Res: 1820 Apollo Dr Las Cruces NM 88001 Mailing Add: PO Drawer 518 Las Cruces NM 88001

REGAN, WALTER JOSEPH (D)
Vt State Rep
Mailing Add: 60 Ferris St St Albans VT 05478

REGNER, DAVID JOSEPH (R)
Ill State Sen
b Chicago, Ill, Mar 19, 31; s Joseph H Regner & Catherine Schram R; m 1957 to Joan Catherine Scanlan; c David Michael. Educ: DePaul Univ Eve Sch, BS, 59. Polit & Govt Pos: Rep block capt, 38th Ward, Chicago, Ill, 55-56; campaign chmn, Elk Grove Twp Percy for Gov Campaign, 63; pres, Young Rep, Elk Grove Twp, 64; vpres, Elk Grove Twp Rep Orgn, 64, dep committeeman, 65; auditor, Elk Grove Twp, 65-66; secy platform comt, Ill State Rep Conv, 66, mem, 68 & 70; Ill State Rep, Third Dist, 67-73; Ill State Sen, 73-, secy, Rep Senate Caucus, Econ & Fiscal Comn, Ill State Senate, currently, vchmn, currently, State Property Ins Study Comn, currently; chmn, Legis Info Systs Comt. Bus & Prof Pos: Self-employed ins sales, currently; pres, Regner Enterprises Inc; pres, Lynbird Air Charter, Inc. Mem: Cook Co Auditors Asn (nominating comt & vpres); Chicago Jaycees; Mt Prospect Jaycees; Ill Jaycees; CofC. Honors & Awards: Outstanding Local Pres & Active Jaycee, Ill Jaycees, 63, Outstanding State VPres, 64; Spark Plug Awards, Mt Prospect Jaycees, 64 & Chicago Jaycees, 65; Cert of Merit, Ill Jaycees, 65. Relig: Roman Catholic. Mailing Add: 910 S See Gwun Ave Mt Prospect IL 60056

REGNIER, RICHARD OLIN (R)
Chmn, Fifth Dist Rep Party, Ind
b Huntington, Ind, Sept 3, 29; s Coleman Franklin Regnier & Ruth Plumley R; m 1954 to Margaret Ann Peters; c Risa Ann, Mark Randall & David Brian. Educ: Wabash Col, AB, 51; Ind Univ, LLB, 54; Phi Kappa Psi. Polit & Govt Pos: Co Attorney, Tipton Co, Ind, 57-61, prosecuting attorney, 62-66; finance chmn cent comt, Tipton Co Rep Party, 60-64, chmn, 66-74; chmn, Fifth Dist Rep Party, 70- Mil Serv: Entered as Pvt, Army, 54, released as Spec 3/C, 56. Mem: Tipton Co & Ind State Bar Asns; Rotary (pres, Tipton Club, 59-60); F&AM; CofC (pres, 60-61, dir, 61, 62, 65 & 66). Relig: Methodist. Mailing Add: 322 Columbia Ave Tipton IN 46072

REGULA, RALPH S (R)
US Rep, Ohio
b 1924. Educ: Mt Union Col, BA; William McKinley Sch of Law, LLB. Polit & Govt Pos: Mem, Ohio State Bd Educ, 60-64; Ohio State Rep, 65-66; Ohio State Sen, 67-72; mem, President's Comn on Financial Structure & Regulation, 70-72; deleg, Rep Nat Conv, 72; US Rep, 16th Dist, Ohio, 73- Legal Res: 8787 Erie SW Navarre OH 44662 Mailing Add: 1729 Longworth Bldg Washington DC 20515

REHDER, MERLYN ALBERT (R)
Chmn, Sioux Co Rep Cent Comt, Iowa
b Hawarden, Iowa, Aug 22, 31; s Albert Marcus Rehder & Frieda Lange R; m 1969 to Phyllis Joan Dean; c Teresa Deann. Educ: SDak State Univ, BS with honor, 60, grad sch, 60-63; Blue Key; Alpha Zeta. Polit & Govt Pos: Representative div agr, Bd Control, SDak State Univ & finance chmn, 59-60; prog chmn, SDak State Univ Young Rep, 61-63; deleg, Nat Leadership Training Sch Young Rep, Washington, DC, 62 & 64; deleg, Nat Young Rep Conv, 63 & 67; asst chmn, SDak Fedn Young Rep, 63; counr, Nat TAR Camp, Lake Herman, SDak, 63 & 64; prog chmn, Sioux Co Young Rep, 64-67; counr, Iowa TAR Camp Boone, 66; chmn, Sioux Co Rep Cent Comt, 68- Bus & Prof Pos: Investment coun, Life Investors Inc, Cedar Rapids, Iowa, 65-; bus mgr & treas, Sioux Empire Col, Hawarden, 66- Mil Serv: Entered as Pvt, Army, 53, released as Cpl, 55, after serv in Co C 47th Eng Comouflage Bn, Fort Riley, Kans, & 5th Army, Chicago, Ill, 53-55; Good Conduct Medal. Mem: Nat Asn Life Underwriters; Hawarden Kiwanis Club; Sioux Co Farm Bur; Hawarden CofC; Am Legion. Honors & Awards: Fortunaires, Life Investors Inc, 69, 71 & 72; Nat Sales Achievement Award, 72. Relig: Lutheran. Legal Res: 1020 Ave N Hawarden IA 51023 Mailing Add: Box 112 Hawarden IA 51023

REHNQUIST, WILLIAM HUBBS
Assoc Justice, Supreme Court of US
b Milwaukee, Wis, Oct 1, 24; s William Benjamin Rehnquist & Margery Peck R; m 1953 to Natalie Cornell; c James, Janet & Nancy. Educ: Kenyon Col, 43; Stanford Univ, BA & MA, 48, LLB, 52; Harvard Univ, MA, 49; Phi Beta Kappa; Order of the Coif; Phi Delta Phi. Polit

& Govt Pos: Mem, Nat Conf Comnrs on Uniform State Laws, Ariz, 63-69; asst attorney gen, Off of Legal Counsel, US Dept of Justice, 69-71; assoc justice, Supreme Court of US, 72- Bus & Prof Pos: Law clerk, Robert H Jackson, US Supreme Court, Washington, DC, 52-53; attorney, Evans, Kitchel & Jenckes, Phoenix, Ariz, 53-55; partner, Ragan & Rehnquist, 56-57, Cunningham, Carson & Messenger, 57-60 & Powers & Rehnquist, 60-69. Mil Serv: Entered as Pvt, Army Air Corps, 43, released as Sgt, 46, after serv in Weather Serv, Africa-Middle East Theater. Publ: Supreme Court law clerks, US News & World Report, 12/57; The bar admission cases, J Am Bar Asn, 3/58; Subdivision trusts and the Bankruptcy Act, Ariz Law Rev, winter 61. Mem: Maricopa Co, Am & Fed Bar Asns; State Bar of Ariz; Nat Conf Lawyers & Realtors. Relig: Lutheran. Legal Res: VA Mailing Add: Supreme Ct of the US Washington DC 20543

REICHARD, LOIS L (R)
Chairwoman, Lorain Co Rep Cent Comt, Ohio
b Detroit, Mich, Jan 3, 31; d George H Berg & Audrey A Ehlke; m 1950 to Robert Hyland; c Lynne Carol (Mrs Hreha), Gail Louise, Steven Hyland & R James. Educ: Bowling Green State Univ, 47-49; Kent State Univ, 64-65; Chi Omega. Polit & Govt Pos: Pres, Elyria Rep Woman's Club, 72-73; chairwoman, Lorain Co Rep Cent Comt, Ohio, 73- Bus & Prof Pos: Vpres, Lorain Co Legal Secys, 69-71. Mem: Orgn Eastern Stars; Elyria Ice Hockey Boosters Club. Relig: Lutheran. Mailing Add: 1094 N Pasadena Ave Elyria OH 44035

REID, CHARLOTTE T (R)
b Kankakee, Ill, wid; c Frank R III; Edward Thompson; Patricia (Mrs Lindner) & Susan. Educ: Ill Col Jacksonville, Ill. Hon Degrees: LLD, Ill Col, 71 & John Marshall Law Sch, 71. Polit & Govt Pos: US Rep, 15th Dist, Ill, 63-71; comnr, Fed Commun Comn, 71- Bus & Prof Pos: Under the name of Annette King, served as NBC Staff Vocalist; vocalist for 3 years, Don McNeill's Radio Prog. Legal Res: 183 S Fourth St Aurora IL 60505 Mailing Add: 1200 N Nash Arlington VA 22209

REID, DAVID EDWARD, JR (D)
b Asheville, NC, July 30, 32; s David Edward Reid & Susan Elias R; m 1958 to Beverley Jacqueline Rippard; c Rebekah Beverley, Jacqueline Susan & David Edward, III. Educ: Univ NC, AB, 56, Law Sch, LLB, 59; Phi Alpha Delta. Polit & Govt Pos: Research asst to Chief Justice, NC Supreme Court, 59-60; state pres, NC Young Dem Clubs, 62; chmn, State Dem Jefferson-Jackson Day Dinner, 63; city attorney, Greenville, NC, 65-; NC State Rep, 68-70; deleg, Dem Nat Conv, 72. Mem: AF&AM; Moose; Kiwanis; CofC; Merchants Asn. Relig: Episcopal. Legal Res: 1600 E Fifth St Greenville NC 27834 Mailing Add: PO Box 375 Greenville NC 27834

REID, HAROLD W (D)
Idaho State Rep
Mailing Add: Rte 2 Box 34 Craigmont ID 83523

REID, HARRY M (D)
b Searchlight, Nev, Dec 2, 39; s Harry Reid & Inez Jaynes R; m 1959 to Landra Gould; c Lana, Rory & Leif. Educ: Col South Utah, AS, 59; Utah State Univ, BS, 61; George Washington Univ, LLB & JD; Phi Kappa Phi; Pi Sigma Alpha; Phi Alpha Theta. Polit & Govt Pos: City attorney, Henderson, Nev, 63-65; Nev State Assemblyman, Dist Four, 69-71, mem judiciary & elec comts, Nev State Assembly, 69-71; Lt Gov, Nev, 71-74. Mem: Nat Inst Munic Law Off; Legal Aid Soc; Am Cancer Soc; Nev State Athletic Comn (judge, 65-); Nat Conf Lt Gov (exec comt). Relig: Latter-day Saint. Mailing Add: 4601 Gretel Circle Las Vegas NV 89102

REID, LUKE HARMON (R)
Chmn, Atoka Co Rep Comt, Okla
b Norman, Okla, Oct 11, 03; s Harmon Reid & Marry Keelton R; m 1944 to Effie. Educ: High sch. Polit & Govt Pos: Deleg, Rep Nat Conv, 24, 40, 52 & 60; chmn, Atoka Co Rep Comt, Okla, currently. Mem: Odd Fellows. Relig: Baptist. Mailing Add: Box 303 Caney OK 74533

REID, MARTHA LOUISE (R)
VChmn, Rep Party Alaska
b Bellingham, Wash, Dec 6, 23; d Edgar S Hungerford & Caroline Gallup H; m 1945 to Glenn W Reid; c Jean (Mrs David Ellis), Glenn W, Jr & Celia H. Polit & Govt Pos: Vchmn, Alaska Rep Party, currently; deleg, Rep Nat Conv, 72. Relig: Presbyterian. Mailing Add: PO Box 521 Petersburg AK 99833

REID, OGDEN ROGERS (D)
b New York, NY, June 24, 25; s Ogden Mills Reid & Helen Rogers R; m 1949 to Mary Louise Stewart; c Stewart, Elisabeth, Michael, Ogden, William & David W. Educ: Yale Univ, AB, 49; Brandeis Univ, fel; Bar-Ilan Univ, Israel, fel; Phi Gamma Delta; Sigma Delta Chi. Hon Degrees: LLD, Adelphi Col, 60 & Jewish Theol Sem, 61; Dr Hebrew Letters, Dropsie Col, 61. Polit & Govt Pos: US Ambassador Israel, 59-61; chmn, NY Comn for Human Rights, 61-62; chmn, NY Int Off Visitors Off, 62; US Rep, 24th Dist, NY, 62-75. Bus & Prof Pos: Pres, NY Herald Tribune Societe Anonyme, 53-58; pres & ed, NY Herald Tribune, Inc, 55-59; dir, Panama Canal Co, 56-59; trustee, Hampton Inst; mem comt grad sch, Yale Univ Coun, 68- Mil Serv: Entered as Pvt, Army, 43, released as 1st Lt, 46, after serv in 11th Airborne Div; Capt, Army Res; Chevalier of the Legion of Honor. Mem: 369th Vets Asn; Atlantic Coun of US (dir); Coun Foreign Rels; Nat Inst Soc Sci (vpres, Westchester Dist); 11th Airborne Div Asn (1st pres). Honors & Awards: Southern Cross of Brazil, 56. Relig: Presbyterian; elder, Rye Presby Church. Mailing Add: Ophir Hill Purchase NY 10577

REIDA, LARRY (R)
b Grinnell, Iowa, Sept 18, 35; s T W Reida & Bernice Lyman R. Educ: Iowa State Col, 53-54; State Univ Iowa, BSc, 58, JD, 60. Polit & Govt Pos: Treas, Lancaster Co Young Rep, 66; legis asst, US Rep Robert Denney, 66-68; minority counsel, Select Comt on Crime, US House Rep, 69-70; assoc gen counsel for legis, Interstate Com Comn, 71-74; assoc minority counsel, House Comt on Pub Works & Transportation, 75- Bus & Prof Pos: Gen practice of law, Nebr, 60-66. Legal Res: Arlington VA 22204 Mailing Add: 2165 Rayburn House Off Bldg Washington DC 20515

REIDER, ROBERT W (D)
b Oak Harbor, Ohio, May 5, 16; s Otto E Reider & Laura Williamsen R; m 1945 to Annette Wendt; c Robert W, Jr. Educ: Ohio Univ, BS in journalism, 39; Omicron Delta Kappa; Blue Key; J-Club; Sigma Delta Chi; Sigma Pi. Polit & Govt Pos: Ohio State Rep, 48-54; nominee for Secy of State, Ohio, 54; mem, Ohio State Dem Cent Comt, 58-72, chmn, 68-72; mem, Ohio State Dem Exec Comt, 58-72; mem, Pub Utilities Comn, 59-60; deleg, Dem Nat Conv, 60, 64 & 68, deleg-at-lg & mem, Credentials Comt, 64; Ohio Lake Lands Adminr, 72-75. Bus & Prof Pos: Publisher & treas, Exponent Pub Co, 45-50; pres & founder, Ohio Radio, Inc, 61- & Cablevision Corp of Ohio, 72- Mil Serv: Entered as Pvt, Army, 42, released as T/Sgt, 45, after serv as Spec Agent, Counter Intel Corps, 970th Detachment, ETO, 1st Lt, Inactive Army Res; French Croix de Guerre with Silver Star, 44; Am Campaign Serv Medal; Europe-Africa-Mid East Campaign Medal with three Bronze Stars. Mem: Sigma Delta Chi; Elks; Eagles; Moose; CofC. Relig: Lutheran. Legal Res: 2184 N Carriage Lane Port Clinton OH 43452 Mailing Add: PO Drawer A Port Clinton OH 43452

REIDY, FRANK J (D)
NH State Rep
Mailing Add: 36 Fenton St Manchester NH 03102

REIFF, ARTHUR FREDERICK (D)
Mem, Ohio State Dem Cent Comt
b Hamilton, Ohio, Nov 21, 36; s Arthur Sylvester Reiff & Georgia Tuggle R; m 1972 to Carol Lee Stegner. Educ: Otterbein Col, 55; Univ Cincinnati, 62; Zeta Phi. Polit & Govt Pos: Fairfield Twp Trustee, Butler Co, Ohio, 62-70; mem, Ohio State Dem Cent Comt, 24th Dist, 65-67 & 70-; comnr, Butler Co, 71- Bus & Prof Pos: Real estate broker & developer, Hamilton, Ohio. Mil Serv: Entered as Airman, Air Force, 55, released as Airman 2/C, 59; Good Conduct Medal. Mem: Hamilton-Fairfield Bd Realtors; Fairfield Sportsmans Club; Asns Twp Trustees & Clerks (local & state); Nat Rifleman Asn. Relig: Baptist. Mailing Add: 5945 Allison Ave Hamilton OH 45011

REILLY, ANNABELLE WILSON (D)
b Washington, Pa, June 5, 26; d Stanley Corbett Wilson & Helen Johnston W; m to James Joseph Reilly, Jr, wid; c William Lawrence, Paula Ann (Mrs Michael W Markley) & David John. Educ: Carnegie Inst Technol, night sch, 38-42. Polit & Govt Pos: Washington Co chairperson, Gov George C Wallace for President Comt, 66-72; Western Pa State chairperson, Wallace for President, 72-; mem, Gov Wallace Staff, 72-; deleg, Dem Nat Mid-Term Conf, 74. Bus & Prof Pos: Selector-packer & tester, Hazel Atlas 1, Glass Bottle Blowers Union, 41-45; outfitter & welder trainee, USW, Am Bridge, Aliquippa, Pa, 45; asst occup therapist, Mayview State Hosp, 57-58 & 67-68. Mem: Pa Asn Notaries; Concerned Taxpayers League of Washington Co (founder & chairwoman); CofC of US; Sch Surv Group (assoc mem); Western Pa Artists. Honors & Awards: Hon Lt Col, Ala Militia. Relig: Presbyterian. Legal Res: 270 Shirls Ave Washington PA 15301 Mailing Add: PO Box 168 Washington PA 15301

REILLY, CHARLES T (D)
Chmn, RI State Dem Cent Comt
Mailing Add: 10 Mosher Dr Barrington RI 02806

REILLY, EDWARD FRANCIS, JR (R)
Kans State Sen
b Leavenworth, Kans, Mar 24, 37; s Edward Francis Reilly & Marian Sullivan R; single. Educ: Univ Kans, BA, 61; Sigma Alpha Epsilon. Polit & Govt Pos: Kans State Rep, 63-64; Kans State Sen, 64-; deleg, Rep Nat Conv, 68. Bus & Prof Pos: Vpres, Ed Reilly & Sons, Insurers-Realtors, 61-; vpres, First State Bank of Lansing, 66-68; pres, Continental Developers, 66- Mem: Elks (past Exalted Ruler); Eagles; KofC; Kiwanis; People to People. Honors & Awards: Henry Leavenworth Award, Asn US Army, 60; Outstanding Young Man of Am, US Jaycee Publ, 65; Distinguished Serv Award, Jaycees, 69. Relig: Catholic. Mailing Add: 1412 S Broadway Leavenworth KS 66048

REILLY, JANE BERNADETTE (R)
Mem, Rep State Cent Comt Calif
b San Francisco, Calif, June 26, 29; d Bernard Reilly & Jane Walsh R; single. Educ: Univ San Francisco, theol, 63-64; Golden Gate Col, acct, 65; San Francisco City Col, hotel restaurant, 70-73; Alliance Francais, 72-73. Polit & Govt Pos: Assoc mem, Rep State Cent Comt Calif, 67-68, mem, 69-; mem, Comt to Elect Rep State Assembly, 69. Bus & Prof Pos: Prof model, 52-55; IBM Keypunch operator, Pac Fruit Express, 52-55, tab operator, 55-64, revising clerk, 64-66, gen clerk, 66-69, comput programmer, 69; acct clerk, C&H Sugar, 69- Mem: Calif Pac Club (bd dirs); Railway Clerks Union. Relig: Catholic. Mailing Add: 343 20th Ave San Francisco CA 94121

REILLY, JOSEPH MATTHEW (R)
NY State Assemblyman
b Glen Cove, NY, July 21, 27; s T Joseph Reilly & Catherine McCormach R; m 1959 to Margaret Mary Power; c Joseph M, Jr, John P, Margaret C & Paul C. Educ: Rider Col, BSEd, 52; Hofstra Univ, MSEd, 53. Polit & Govt Pos: Comnr acct, Glen Cove, NY, 56-61 & mayor-supvr, 62-65; NY State Assemblyman, 66-, chmn, Standing Comt on Labor, NY State Assembly, currently. Bus & Prof Pos: Teacher, North Shore Sch Dist, 53-61; stock broker, Paine, Webber, Jackson & Curtis, 66-69; banker, Franklin Nat Bank, 70- Mil Serv: Entered as A/S, Navy, 45, released as Seaman 1/C, 46. Mem: Nat Asn Security Dealers; Am Legion; KofC; Ancient Order of Hibernians; Glen Cove Rep Club. Honors & Awards: Hon Order of Gen Pulaski. Relig: Roman Catholic. Mailing Add: 7 Hickory Lane Glen Cove NY 11542

REILLY, KEVIN P (D)
La State Rep
Mailing Add: 763 Mouton Ave Baton Rouge LA 70806

REIMERS, ROBERT F (R)
NDak State Rep
b Carrington, NDak, June 15, 23; m 1945 to Carol Margaret Fortney; c two. Educ: NDak State Univ of Agr & Applied Sci. Polit & Govt Pos: NDak State Rep, 61-, chmn, Appropriations Comt, NDak House of Rep, 71-73, chmn, State Budget Bd, 69-73. Bus & Prof Pos: Farming, grain elevator & seed bus in NDak; bus & farming interests in Tex. Mem: Elks; Mason; Shrine; Jamestown Shrine Club (pres); also farm orgns. Honors & Awards: Outstanding Young Farmer Award, 57; Fed Land Bank Leadership in Community Serv Award, 67. Relig: Congregational. Mailing Add: RR 3 Box M-40 Carrington ND 58421

REINHARDT, JOHN EDWARD (INDEPENDENT)
Asst Secy State Pub Affairs
b Glade Spring, Va, Mar 8, 20; s Edward Vinton Reinhardt & Alice Miller R; m 1947 to Carolyn Daves; c Sharman R (Mrs Lancefield), Alice N (Mrs Jeffers) & Carolyn C. Educ: Knoxville Col, AB, 39; Univ Chicago, 39-40; Univ Wis, MS, 47, PhD, 50; Alpha Phi Alpha. Polit & Govt Pos: Cult officer, Am Embassy, Manila, Philippines, 56-58; dir, Am Cult Ctr,

Kyoto, Japan, 58-63; cult attache, Am Embassy, Tehran, Iran, 63-66; dep asst dir for Far E, US Info Agency, Washington, DC, 66-68, asst dir for Africa, 68-70, asst dir for Far E, 70-71; US Ambassador to Nigeria, 71-75; asst secy state for pub affairs, Dept State, 75- Bus & Prof Pos: Instr Eng, Knoxville Col, 40-41 & State Teachers Col (Fayetteville, NC), 41-42; prof Eng, Va State Col, 50-55. Mil Serv: Entered as Pvt, Army, 42, released as Lt after serv in 93rd Div, Pac, 45-46. Mem: Mod Lang Asn Am; Am Foreign Serv Asn (vpres, 66-). Honors & Awards: Career Serv Award, Nat Civil Serv League, 71; Edward R Murrow Award, Fletcher Sch, Tufts Univ, 73. Relig: Methodist. Legal Res: 6801 Laverock Ct Bethesda MD 20034 Mailing Add: Dept of State Washington DC 20520

REINHARDT, STEPHEN (D)

b New York, NY, Mar 27, 31; m to Mary Treman; c Mark, Justin & Dana. Educ: Pomona Col, BA cum laude, 51; Yale Law Sch, LLB, 54; Order of the Coif. Polit & Govt Pos: Chmn resolutions comt, Calif Dem Coun, 61, chmn elec reform comt, 62-63; mem, Calif Adv Comn Civil Rights, 63-74, vchmn, 65-74; exec comt mem, Dem State Cent Comt, 64-66, legal counsel, 66-68; deleg, Dem Nat Conv, 68, deleg & mem rules comt, 72; Dem Nat Committeeman, Calif, 68-72, mem exec comt, 69-72; pres, Los Angeles Bd Recreation & Parks Comnrs, 74; mem, Coliseum Comn, Los Angeles, 74- Bus & Prof Pos: Assoc, O'Melveny & Myers, Los Angeles, 57-59; assoc, Bodle & Fogel, 59-66; partner, Bodle, Fogel, Julber & Reinhardt, 66- Mil Serv: Entered as 2nd Lt, Air Force, released as 1st Lt, after serv in Gen Counsel Off. Mem: Am Bar Asn (mem labor coun, 74-); Calif State Bar; US Supreme Court; Bar of DC. Legal Res: 9544 Lime Orchard Rd Los Angeles CA Mailing Add: 5900 Wilshire Blvd Los Angeles CA 90010

REINTSEMA, ROBERT ARNOLD (R)

Dep Under Secy Cong Affairs, Dept Com

b Brooklyn, NY, Sept 13, 37; s Herman Arnold Reintsema & Margaret Beck R; m 1960 to Carmen A; c Laura, Carl & Robin. Educ: Alfred Univ, BFA, 59; George Washington Univ, MBA, 75; Blue Key; Kappa Psi Upsilon. Polit & Govt Pos: Chmn, Fairfield Co Young Rep, 64 & 65; campaign mgr, Miller for Congress Comt, Lancaster, Ohio, 66; admin asst, US Rep Clarence Miller, Ohio, 67-74; dep under secy for cong affairs, US Dept Com, 74- Bus & Prof Pos: Indust designer, Anchor Hocking Glass Corp, Lancaster, Ohio, 62-66. Mil Serv: Entered as 2nd Lt, Army, 60, released as 1st Lt, 62, after serv in 2nd EASC, Ft Lewis, Wash, 60-62; Capt Army Res. Mem: Am Ceramic Soc. Relig: Methodist. Legal Res: 1340 Shumaker Ave Lancaster OH 43130 Mailing Add: Rm 5835 14th & Constitution Ave US Dept Com Washington DC 20230

REISCH, HAROLD FRANKLIN (R)

Mo State Rep

b Springfield, Ill, Aug 5, 20; s Elmer J Reisch & Belle Hergett R; m 1944 to Bessie Louise Thatcher; c Sally Louise (Mrs Ralph Warmack) & Susan Kay (Mrs Richard Berkley). Educ: Ill Wesleyan Univ, BS, 42; United Theol Sem, MDiv, 48. Polit & Govt Pos: Mo State Rep, 110th Dist, 69- Bus & Prof Pos: Exec bd, Mo Coun of Churches; pres, Nat Marketron Inc; pastor, Church of Distinction; pres, Downtown Merchants Inc, 67-68. Mil Serv: Entered as Chaplain, Army, 44, released as Capt, 46, after serv in 1149th Combat Engr Co, ETO, 44-46; Cert Meritorious Serv. Mem: CofC; Farm Bur. Honors & Awards: Globe Dem Award for Meritorious Pub Serv; Legis Conservationist Award, Mo Conserv Fedn. Relig: Christian. Mailing Add: 1013 Falcon Dr Columbia MO 65201

REISING, GREGORY S (D)

Ind State Rep

Mailing Add: 650 South Lake St Gary IN 46403

REISSING, THEODORE CHARLES, SR (R)

Mem, 17th Cong Dist Rep Exec Comt, Mich

b Hopkins, Mich, Nov 5, 03; s Charles George Reissing & Mary Ellinger R; m 1933 to Helen Martha Lauffer; c Theodore Charles, Jr, Sue Ann (Mrs William Mohney) & Michael George. Educ: Univ Mich, BA in sci, 24; Sigma Pi. Polit & Govt Pos: Mem, 17th Cong Dist Rep Exec Comt, Mich, 59-; mem, Mich Rep State Cent Comt, 61-74, chmn, 65-68; deleg & mem rules comt, Rep Nat Conv, 64. Mem: Assoc mem Inst of Elec & Electronics Engrs; Univ Mich Alumni (vpres, Nat Bd Govs); Wayne Co Human Rels Comt; Mason; Washtenaw Country Club. Relig: Presbyterian. Mailing Add: 17225 Patton Detroit MI 48219

REITEN, CHESTER (R)

NDak State Sen

Mailing Add: State Capitol Bismarck ND 58501

REMMERT, PETE (R)

Mem Exec Bd, Nat Young Rep Orgn

b Woodford Co, Ill, Sept 11, 34; s Edwin Remmert & Berdina Hartman R; m 1961 to Patricia Ann Martino; c Lynne & Denise. Educ: El Paso High Sch, grad, 52. Polit & Govt Pos: Pres, Woodford Co Young Rep, Ill, 67-71; auditor, Ill Young Rep Orgn, 69-71, dep down state vchmn, 70-71, exec dir, 71-; mem, Gov Adv Coun, 69-73; supvr, Property Control Sect, Dept Gen Serv, 70-73; precinct committeeman, Woodford Co Rep Cent Comt, 70-, chmn, 72-; mem exec bd, Nat Young Rep Orgn, 73-; supvr property control, Comptroller's Off, State of Ill, 73- Bus & Prof Pos: Owner, R&W Outdoor Advert Co, 63- Mil Serv: Entered as E-1, Army, 57, released as SP-4, 59, after serv in 80th Missile Bn, S European Task Force, Italy, 57-59; Good Conduct Medal; S European Task Force Award. Mem: Am Judicature Soc; Farm Bur; VFW; Am Trap Shooters Asn; Rep Co Chmn of Ill Asn. Honors & Awards: Indian Award, Ill Young Rep Orgn, 69; Outstanding Young Rep in Ill. Relig: Lutheran. Mailing Add: RR 1 Secor IL 61771

RENCHER, RONALD LYNN (D)

Speaker, Utah House Rep

b Hawthorne, Calif, July 6, 41; s Joseph Lynn Rencher & Aften Flake R; m 1964 to Eileen Bunnell; c Rachel, Jefferson, Jennie & Lynette. Educ: Univ Colo, 59-60, Law Sch, 65-66; Brigham Young Univ, BA, 65; Univ Utah Law Sch, JD, 68. Polit & Govt Pos: Utah State Rep, 45th Dist, 71-, Minority Whip, Utah House Rep, 73-74, mem, Utah Legis Coun, 73-74, mem, Legis Mgt Comt, 75, Speaker, 75- Bus & Prof Pos: Attorney-at-law, Kunz, Kunz & Rencher, Ogden, Utah, 68- Mem: Utah State Bar; Am Trial Lawyers Asn; Weber Co Bar Asn. Relig: Latter-day Saint. Legal Res: 1269 Binford Ogden UT 84401 Mailing Add: Suite 7 Bank of Utah Plaza Ogden UT 84401

RENDLEN, ALBERT L (R)

Polit & Govt Pos: Former chmn, Mo State Rep Cent Comt Mailing Add: Rendlen Bldg Hannibal MO 63401

RENDLEN, CHARLES EARNEST, JR (R)

Chmn, Marion Co Dem Comt, Mo

b Hannibal, Mo, Aug 9, 19; s Charles Earnest Rendlen & Norma Lewis R; m 1948 to Shirley Ann Raible; c Charles Earnest, III, Branham, Jeffry Raible & Cynthia M. Educ: William Jewell Col, BA, 41; Univ Mich, JD, 48; Phi Delta Phi; Phi Gamma Nu; Sigma Nu. Polit & Govt Pos: Asst, Rep Nat Conv, 48; chmn, Rep Cent Comt, Mo, 50-60; chmn, Ninth Cong Dist Rep Party, 52-56; spec asst to Attorney Gen of Mo, 68-74; mem, Mo State Rep Comt, 74-; chmn, Marion Co Dem Comt, currently. Bus & Prof Pos: Managing partner, Rendlen, Rendlen & Ahrens, 54-; pres, Hannibal Found, 67-, Master Machinist, 68- & Canon Land Co, 72- Mil Serv: Entered as Pvt, Army, 41, released as Capt, 45, after serv in 7th VII Corps, ETO, 44-45; Ret, Res; Bronze Star with Oak Leaf Cluster; Bronze Arrowhead (D-Day Landing). Publ: Auth, Use of Counter Battery Artillery, US Army, 45; articles in Mo Bar J, 62, 66 & 67, article in Mo Asn Trial Attorneys, 63. Mem: Mo Bar Asn; Hannibal Community Chest. Honors & Awards: Citation of Serv, Mo Bar Asn, 66; Pace Setter Award, City of Hannibal, 68; Legion of Merit, awarded by Gov Bond of Mo, 72. Mailing Add: 508 Country Club Hannibal MO 63401

RENDON, RALPH ALBERT (R)

Mem, Rep State Cent Comt Calif

b Los Angeles, Calif, Mar 15, 37; s Ralph Alex Rendon & Concha Duarte R; m 1973 to Tinina Ann Vaughn. Educ: Univ Southern Calif, BA, 59; Delta Sigma Phi; Trojan Knights; Trojan Squires. Polit & Govt Pos: Bd dirs, Coun Latin Am Rep Orgns, 67-; mem, Los Angeles Dist Attorney's Adv Coun, Calif, 67-; mem, Rep State Cent Comt Calif, 67-; mem, Rep Assocs San Diego Co, 72-; app to State Attorney Gen Citizens Adv Coun, 72-; app by San Diego Co Bd Supvr to Human Resources Agency Adv Bd, 73-; app to Calif State Hosp Bd, 74- Bus & Prof Pos: Self-employed pub rels counr, Beverly Hills, Calif, until 62; acct exec, Bates Assocs, Whittier, 62-64; asst pub rels dir, McFadden, Strauss, Eddy & Irwin, Palm Springs, 64; acct exec, John R MacFaden, Los Angeles, 64-70; vpres & secy, Bruce Farley Corp, San Diego, 70-, vpres & secy, SeaCoast Financial Corp, secy, SeaCoast Escrow Corp, Bruce Farley Develop Corp & Bruce Farley Mkt Corp, 72- Mil Serv: Entered as Airman Basic, Calif Air Nat Guard, 60, released as Sgt, 66. Mem: Trojan Club; Town Hall of Calif; Jr CofC; San Diego Civil Light Opera Asn; Rep Assocs San Diego Co (bd dirs). Honors & Awards: Recipient of Calif State Assembly & Los Angeles City Coun Resolutions, 68. Relig: Catholic. Mailing Add: 386 Rosecrans St San Diego CA 92106

RENFROW, EDWARD (D)

NC State Sen

b Johnston Co, NC, Sept 17, 40; s Donnie Tildon Renfrow & Ila Mae Lewis R; m 1960 to Rebecca Stephenson; c Candace & Paige. Educ: Hardbargers Bus Col, bus admin & acct, 60; Phi Theta Pi. Polit & Govt Pos: Treas, NC Dem Exec Comt, 73-74; NC State Sen, 75- Mil Serv: Entered as Pvt, Army Nat Guard, 63, released as SP-4, 67, after serv in 30th Inf Div. Mem: NC Soc Accts (pres, 72-73); Smithfield-Selma CofC (pres-elect, 73-74); Nat Soc Pub Accts (speaker, 72-); Johnston Baptist Asn (treas, 73-); NC State Baptist Conv (gen bd exec comt, 70-74). Honors & Awards: Distinguished Serv Award, Smithfield Jaycees, 73; The Old North State Award, 72. Relig: Baptist. Legal Res: 131 Castle Dr Smithfield NC 27577 Mailing Add: PO Box 731 Smithfield NC 27577

RENGO, RAYMOND ARDEN (R)

Chmn, Manistee Co Rep Comt, Mich

b Manistee, Mich, Apr 4, 28; s Emil Jacob Rengo & Sadie J O Johnson R; div; c Becky, Amy, Lisa & Sarah. Educ: Mich State Univ, BA, 50; Delta Chi. Polit & Govt Pos: Chmn, Manistee Co Rep Comt, Mich, 74- Bus & Prof Pos: Trustee, Manistee Intermediate Sch Dist, Mich, 68-; pres, Kaleva Norman Sch Bd, 10 years; trustee & finance chmn, Westshore Hosp, Manistee, 73-; mem fuel oil comt, Nat Oil Jobbers Coun, 74-; vpres, Mich Petrol Asn, 75- Mil Serv: Entered as 2nd Lt, Army, 53, released as 1st Lt, 55. Mem: Shrine; Elks. Relig: Lutheran. Mailing Add: 9200 Aura St Kaleva MI 49645

RENICK, RICHARD RANDOLPH (D)

Fla State Sen

b Bronx, NY, Oct 14, 30; s Ralph Apperson Renick & Rosalie Marie Dwyer R; m 1968 to Valerie E Phillips; c Deborah Kathleen & Karen Valerie. Educ: Univ Miami, 2 years. Polit & Govt Pos: Fla State Rep, 66-72; Fla State Sen, 75- Bus & Prof Pos: TV film dir, WTVJ, Miami, Fla, 50-59; with Renick Prod, 60-69. Mil Serv: Entered as 2/C Seaman, Navy, 47, released as Radio Seaman, 50, after serv in USS Conserver, Pac. Mem: Int Photographers Local 666; Am Legion; Kiwanis; Elks; KofC. Relig: Catholic. Legal Res: 13440 SW 80th Ave Miami FL 33156 Mailing Add: 1828 Ponce de Leon Blvd Coral Gables FL 33134

RENNEKE, EARL WALLACE (R)

Minn State Sen

b St Peter, Minn, Mar 10, 28; s John Gottfried Renneke & Olga Strand R; m 1951 to Marjorie Elizabeth Eckberg; c Rochelle, Lynnette & Kristin. Educ: Univ Minn, Minneapolis, 1 year. Polit & Govt Pos: Vchmn, Sibley Co Rep Party, Minn, 66-67, chmn, 68-69; Minn State Sen, Dist 15, 69-72, Dist 23, 72- Mem: Minn Farm Bur Fedn. Relig: Lutheran. Mailing Add: Rte 2 Le Sueur MN 56058

RENNINGER, JOHN S (R)

Pa State Rep

b Philadelphia, Pa, Oct 10, 24; s Francis Xavier Renninger & Mary Robinson R; m to Katharine Steele; c Ann, Molly, Sally & Patrick. Educ: Drexel Inst Technol; Univ Ore; Univ Pa, BA & LLB; assoc ed, Law Rev. Polit & Govt Pos: Past pres, Bucks Co Estate Planning Coun, Pa; Pa State Rep, 64-, mem, Consumer Protection & Urban Affairs Comts, Pa State House of Rep, currently. Bus & Prof Pos: Attorney. Mil Serv: Army Air Force, 42-46, Sgt; Ens, Naval Res; Asiatic Pac Theater Serv Medal with Bronze Star. Mem: Bucks Co, Philadelphia & Pa Bar Asns; Am Legion. Relig: Former warden, vestryman, & chmn, Bldg Fund & Diocesan Rep, St Luke's Church, Newtown. Mailing Add: Capitol Bldg Harrisburg PA 17120

RENO, DONALD F (D)

Chmn, Harney Co Dem Comt, Ore

b Okmulgee, Okla, Oct 3, 34; s William E Reno & Mabel B Carpenter R; m to Ruth M Oswold; c Don, Jr, Donetta, Barbara & Louise. Educ: Idaho State Univ, BA, 61; Brigham Young Univ, MA, 67. Polit & Govt Pos: Chmn, Harney Co Dem Party, 73- Bus & Prof Pos: Prin, Pocatello Sch Dist 25, Idaho, 61-73; asst supt, Harney Co Dist 1, Burns, Ore, 73- Mil Serv: Entered as Pvt, Army, 52, released as Sgt, 54. Mem: Lions; Adminr Asn. Relig: Latter-day Saint. Mailing Add: Box 717 Hines OR 97720

RENO, OTTIE WAYNE (D)
Chmn, Pike Co Dem Exec Comt, Ohio

b Pike Co, Ohio, Apr 7, 29; s Eli Enos Reno & Arbannah Jones R; m 1947 to Janet Gay McCann; c Ottie Wayne, II, Jennifer Lynn & Lorna Victoria. Educ: Franklin Univ, AA in bus admin, 49; Col Law, LLB, 53; Capital Univ, JD, 66. Polit & Govt Pos: Asst prosecuting attorney, Pike Co, Ohio, 53-54, recorder, 56-73; secy, Pike Co Dem Cent Comt, 56-70; mem, Scioto Valley local bd of educ, Pike Co, 62-66; Ohio Dem State Cent Committeeman, Sixth Cong Dist, 69-70; chmn, Pike Co Dem Exec Comt, 70-; deleg, Dem Nat Conv, 72; judge, Probate & Juvenile Divisions, Common Pleas Court, Pike Co, 73- Bus & Prof Pos: Cook, Mills Restaurants, Columbus, Ohio, 50-53; attorney-at-law, Pike Co Bar Asn, 53- Mil Serv: Entered as Recruit, Ohio Nat Guard, 48, released as Pvt, 51, after serv in Serv Co, 166th Regt Combat Team, Inf. Publ: The Story of Horseshoes, Vantage Press, Inc, 63; Pitching Championship Horseshoes, A S Barnes & Co, 71; Horseshoe pitching, a perfect farm hobby, Successful Farming Mag, 8/65. Mem: Pike Co Bar Asn; YMCA; Farm Bur; Nat Farmers Orgn. Relig: Protestant. Mailing Add: Rte 5 Box 305 Lucasville OH 45648

RENSTROM, DARRELL GEORGE (D)
Utah State Sen

b Ogden, Utah, June 5, 31; s Arnold P Renstrom & Ruby Salt R; m 1970 to Jane Elizabeth Chugg; c Chantile, Wendy, Timothy Simmons, Natasha & Zachary. Educ: Univ Utah, BS, 55; George Washington Univ, JD, 58; Phi Delta Phi. Polit & Govt Pos: Publicity dir, Univ Utah Young Dem, 54-55; clerk, US House of Rep, 55-66; prosecuting attorney, Weber Co, Utah, 59-63, chief prosecuting attorney, 63-66, fed aid coordr, 66; pres, Weber Co Young Dem, 61-63; chmn, Utah Dem State Conv, 62; nat committeeman, Utah State Young Dem, 62-64; chmn const & bylaw comt, Nat Conv Young Dem of Am, 63, chmn credentials comt, 65 & 69; deleg, Dem Nat Conv, 64; chmn, Northwestern Conf Young Dem of Am, 63-65; chmn, Weber Co Dem Party, 65-67; chmn nat membership comt, Young Dem of Am, 67-69; attorney & legis consult, Nat Educ Asn, 67-; Utah State Sen, 73- Bus & Prof Pos: Teacher, Arlington Co Pub Schs, 56-58; secy-treas, Weber Co Bar Asn, 60. Mil Serv: Entered as Pvt, Marine Corps, 52, released as Sgt, 54, after serv in Third Marine Inf Div, Japan, 53-54; UN, Korean Theater of War & Overseas Ribbons. Mem: Utah State, DC & Am Bar Asns; Nat Educ Asn; Kiwanis Serv Club. Honors & Awards: Outstanding Young Dem of Utah, 63; Outstanding Young Dem of Am, 65. Relig: Latter-day Saint; Master M-Man Award. Mailing Add: 1990 N Mountain Rd North Ogden UT 84404

RENSTROM, SARAH BROWN (D)
b Mishawaka, Ind, Jan 9, 43; d Corder Travis Brown & Vera Caruthers B; div. Educ: Macalester Col, BA, 65; Mich State Univ, 67-68; Western Mich Univ, 70-71. Polit & Govt Pos: Mem exec comt, Kalamazoo Dem Party, 70-; chairperson, Kalamazoo Co Dem Party, 71-72; deleg from Third Cong Dist to Mich Dem State Cent Comt, 71-; deleg & vchairperson, Mich McGovern deleg, Dem Nat Conv, 72; mem, Mich Steering Comt for McGovern for President, 72; comnr, Kalamazoo Co, 13th Dist, 72-74. Bus & Prof Pos: Teacher of French, Mason High Sch, Mich, 65-69; secy, Kalamazoo Implementation Comn, 72-73; relocation coordr, Sr Serv, Inc, Kalamazoo, 73-74; SCent Mich Comn on Aging, 74- Mem: League of Women Voters; Am Civil Liberties Union; Nat Orgn of Women. Mailing Add: 513 Davis Kalamazoo MI 49007

RENTSCHLER, WILLIAM HENRY (R)
b Hamilton, Ohio, May 11, 25; s Peter Earl Rentschler & Barbara Schlosser P; m to Martha G Snowdon; c Sarah Y, Peter F, Mary A, Phoebe M & Hope Snowdon. Educ: Princeton Univ, BA in Hist, 49. Polit & Govt Pos: Pres, Ill Young Rep, 57-59; mem, Rep Comt on Prog & Progress, 59; campaign chmn, Nat Young Rep Fedn, 59-60; cand, US Sen, Ill, 60; Ill chmn, Win with Nixon-Lodge Campaign, 60 & Registr & Get-Out-Vote Dr, 62; deleg, Rep Nat Conv, 64 & 72; chmn selection comt, Rep Blue Ribbon Legis Cand, Ill, 64; chmn polit strategy comt, Percy for US Sen Campaign, 66; mem exec comt, United Rep Fund of Ill, 63-69; Ill chmn, Nixon/Agnew Campaign, 68; spec adv, President Nixon's Nat Prog for Vol Action, 69; Rep cand for US Sen, Ill, 70; co-founder & chmn, Citizens for a Stronger Rep Party, 70. Bus & Prof Pos: Reporter & asst to exec ed, Minneapolis Star & Tribune, 49-52; second vpres, Northern Trust Co, 53-56; pres, Stevens Candy Kitchens, Inc, 57-66; pres, Martha Washington Kitchens, Inc, Ill, 66-68; entrepreneur-investor, 70-73; independent bus & financial consult, 74- Mil Serv: Entered as A/S, Navy, 43, released as PO 3/C, 46, after serv in US. Publ: Weekly syndicated column, Viewpoint from Mid-America, 80 newspapers; various articles for periodicals; plus two books. Mem: Colonial Club of Princeton; Econ & Exec Clubs of Chicago; Tavern Club; Onwentsia Club. Honors & Awards: Buddy Hackett Youth Award, 68; Man of the Year, Cook Co Young Rep, 71; trustee, Goodwill Indust; dir, Better Boys Found. Mailing Add: 361 Cherokee Rd Lake Forest IL 60045

RENWICK, WILLIAM F (D)
Pa State Rep

b St Marys, Pa, Dec 30, 15; Lawson Renwick & Julia Bucheit R; m to Aurelia O'Donnell; c Kathleen, Jack & Joe. Educ: St Marys Cent Cath High Sch, 34. Polit & Govt Pos: Mem, St Marys Borough Coun, 45-49; Pa State Rep, 54- Mil Serv: Marine Corps, World War II. Mailing Add: Capitol Bldg Harrisburg PA 17120

REPICCI, FRANCIS C (D)
Chmn, Genesee Co Dem Comt, NY

b Batavia, NY, Aug 9, 44; s John Repicci, Jr & Clara DiPiazza R; single. Educ: St Bonaventure Univ, BA, 66, study, 67; Bryant Stratton Bus Inst, real estate & real estate appraisal cert, 71. Polit & Govt Pos: Secy-treas, Genesee Co Dem Comt, NY, 67-69, chmn, 69-; cand for deleg, Dem Nat Conv, 68; spec asst to State Chmn for Upstate NY, 68-71; aid, adv & state organizer for Theodore Sorenson for US Senate race, 69-70; Upstate NY Coordr, John V Lindsay Presidential Campaign, 72; comnr, Genesee Co Bd Elec, 74- Bus & Prof Pos: Proprietor, Bel-Air Motel, Batavia, NY, 67-; social studies teacher, Elba Cent Sch, 67-68; proprietor, Tekee's Motel & Concord Inn Restaurant, 68- Mem: Nat Educ Asn; Lions Int; Upstate NY Dem Co Chmn Asn (chmn, 72-). Relig: Catholic. Mailing Add: 110 Naramore Dr Batavia NY 14020

REPKO, ANDREW (R)
Polit & Govt Pos: Conn State Rep, 55-66; Conn State Sen, 67-68; chmn, Willington Rep Town Comt, formerly. Mailing Add: West Willington CT 06279

REPLOGLE, JAMES WALTER, JR (R)
Chmn, Wayne Co Rep Party, Ga

b Darke Co, Ohio, Feb 27, 21; s James Walter Replogle & Gaye Marie Dunn R; m 1944 to Helen Whiteman; c Janis, John & James. Educ: Univ Fla, BME, 52; Benton Eng Soc. Polit & Govt Pos: Chmn, Wayne Co Rep Party, Ga, 73- Bus & Prof Pos: Develop engr, Carbide & Carbon, Oak Ridge, Tenn, 52-55; sr proj engr, Panellit Serv Corp & Panalarm, Skokie, Ill, 60-61; shift supt, ITT Rayonier, Jesup, Ga, 61-71, asst utilities supt, 71-74 & tech asst to mgr, 74- Mil Serv: Entered as Pvt, Army, 45, released as S/Sgt, 47, after serv in 160th TC Harbor Craft Co, Caribbean Defense Command; Presidential Unit Citation; Good Conduct Medal. Mem: Tech Asn Pulp & Paper Indust (mem steam & power comt); Instrument Soc Am (secy, Jacksonville Sect); VFW; Mason; Shrine. Relig: Methodist. Mailing Add: 676 S Elm Jesup GA 31545

REPLOGLE, LUTHER IRVIN (R)
b Tyrone, Pa, Mar 2, 02; s Charles Brumbaugh Replogle & Anna Mock R; m 1970 to Lorene Whitham Ingalls. Educ: US Naval Acad, 2 years. Polit & Govt Pos: Mem Foreign Serv Selection Bd, Washington, DC, 65; US Ambassador to Iceland, 69-72. Bus & Prof Pos: Founder & pres, Replogle Globes, Chicago, 30-69. Mil Serv: Midn, Navy, 20-22. Mem: Metrop Club, Washington, DC; Chicago Club; Chicago Yacht Club; Belvedere Club, Charlevoix. Relig: Presbyterian. Mailing Add: 1040 Lake Shore Dr Chicago IL 60611

REPPA, JEROME J (R)
Ind State Rep

Mailing Add: 7017 Indianapolis Blvd Hammond IN 46324

RESCIA, GEORGE FRANK (R)
Chmn, Ludlow Rep Town Comt, Mass

b Springfield, Mass, Feb 18, 30; s Frank Rescia & Lydia Lora R; m 1951 to Elizabeth Grace Nedeau; c Daniel George, Lynda May, Cynda May & Elizabeth Lora. Educ: Springfield Tech High, 45-47. Polit & Govt Pos: Chmn, Ludlow Elem Sch Surv, Mass, 62-65; dist coordr, Edward W Brooke for Attorney Gen, 64 & 66 & US Sen, 68; chmn, Ludlow Elem Sch Bldg Comt, 64-; mem, Ludlow Finance Comt, 67-, vchmn, 69-70; chmn, Ludlow Rep Town Comt, 68- Bus & Prof Pos: Dept mgr & salesman, Sears Roebuck & Co, 53-63; agt, Prudential Ins, 64-67; mgr & owner, Frank Realty, 66-; investr, Dept Labor & Indust, 67- Mem: KofC; Mass State Employees Asn; Ludlow Jaycees; Boys Club Alumni; Chicopee Country Club. Relig: Catholic. Mailing Add: Marion Circle Ludlow MA 01056

RESTON, TOM (D)
Secy, Dem Party, Va

b New York, NY, July 4, 46; s James Barrett Reston & Sarah Fulton R; single. Educ: Harvard Univ, AB, 68; Univ Va Sch Law, JD, 74. Polit & Govt Pos: Secy, Dem Party Va, 72- Bus & Prof Pos: Attorney, Hogan & Hartson, 74- Mem: Va State Bar; DC Bar; Am Bar Asn. Relig: Episcopal. Legal Res: 825 Dolley Madison Blvd McLean VA 22101 Mailing Add: 815 Connecticut Ave NW Washington DC 20006

REUSS, FREDERICK M, JR (R)
Mem, Queens Co Rep Comt, NY

b Richmond Hill, NY, Dec 4, 32; s Frederick M Reuss & Elizabeth R Sullivan R; m 1968 to Tria Gaffikin. Educ: Fordham Col, BS; Univ Pa Law Sch, JD. Polit & Govt Pos: Nat chmn, Col Comt for Taft, 52; chmn col div, NY State Young Rep, 52-53; admin asst to Comnr of Corrections, New York, 57-58; chmn, Parents & Taxpayers, 63-; asst to Chmn of Ways & Means Comt, 70-72; Rep cand, NY State Assemblyman, 29th Assembly Dist, 65; pres, Midland Rep Club, Queens Village, 65-68; chmn, Citizens Crime Comn, Queens Co, 65-; cand, Deleg to Const Conv, NY, 66; alt deleg, Rep State Conv, 66; chmn, Citizens Comt for Nixon-Agnew, Sixth Cong Dist, NY, 68; deleg, Rep Nat Conv, 68; arbitrator, Civil Court of the City of New York, 72- Bus & Prof Pos: Pvt practice of law, New York, 57-63, Hollis, NY, 63-70, Bellerose, 70- Mem: Am Judicature Soc; KofC; Order of Lafayette; Floral Park-Bellerose Rep Club; Young Am for Freedom. Honors & Awards: Numerous awards by civic & other orgns for work in fields of Educ & Community Crime Control. Relig: Roman Catholic. Mailing Add: 248-50 Jericho Turnpike Bellerose NY 11426

REUSS, HENRY S (D)
US Rep, Wis

b Milwaukee, Wis, Feb 22, 12; m 1942 to Margaret Magrath; c Christopher, Michael, Jacqueline & Anne. Educ: Cornell Univ, BA; Harvard Law Sch, LLB; vpres, Chi Psi Alumni Asn; past pres, Cornell Alumni Asn of Wis; bd of alumni visitors, Harvard Law Sch, 57-60; bd of visitors, Cornell Univ. Polit & Govt Pos: Asst corp counsel, Milwaukee Co, Wis, 39-40; asst gen counsel, Off Price Admin, Washington, DC, 41-42; dep gen counsel, Marshall Plan, Paris, France, 49; spec prosecutor, Milwaukee Co Grand Jury, Wis, 50; personal counsel to Secy of State Fred Zimmerman in Reapportionment Case, Wis Supreme Court, 53; mem, Milwaukee Sch Bd, 53-55; US Rep, Wis, 54-, chmn, House Comt on Banking, Currency & Housing, currently; del, Dem Nat Conv, 68. Bus & Prof Pos: Lawyer; lectr; writer; former pres, White Elm Nursery Co, Hartland, Wis; former dir, Marshall & Ilsley Bank, Milwaukee & Niagara Share Corp, Buffalo, NY. Mil Serv: 2nd Lt, Army, 43-45, served in 63rd & 75th Inf Div; chief, Price Control Br, Off of Mil Govt for Germany, 45; Awarded Bronze Star Medal for action at crossing of Rhine & Bronze Stars for Normandy, Northern France & Cent Germany. Publ: The Critical Decade, 64; Revenue Sharing, 70. Mem: Jr Bar Asn (vchmn); Milwaukee Co Bar Asn (chmn constit & citizenship comt); Foreign Policy Asn (vchmn); Children's Serv Soc (dir); Milwaukee City Club. Legal Res: Milwaukee WI 53200 Mailing Add: 2186 Rayburn House Off Bldg Washington DC 20515

REVELES, ROBERT APODACA (D)
b Miami, Ariz, Nov 25, 32; m 1959 to Carlotta Norris; c Robert Gregory, Rachel Antonia, Rebecca Maria, Sara Christina & Ruth Elizabeth. Educ: Univ Md, Overseas Prog, 53-54; Georgetown Univ Sch Foreign Serv, BSFS, 62. Polit & Govt Pos: Secy to US Rep Stewart L Udall, Ariz, 56 & 58-61; secy to US Rep Morris K Udall, Ariz, 61-63 & spec asst, 66-68; legis asst to US Rep George F Senner, Jr, Ariz, 63-64; admin asst to US Rep Paul J Krebs, NJ, 64-66; exec secy to US Rep Frank Thompson, Jr, NJ, 69- Mil Serv: Entered as Pvt, Air Force, 52, released as Airman 1/C, 55, after serv in Hq, Allied Air Forces Southern Europe, NATO. Mem: VFW; Am GI Forum; Nat Orgn for Mexican-Am Serv. Relig: Catholic. Legal Res: Miami AZ Mailing Add: 7621 Kingsbury Rd Alexandria VA 22310

REVELLE, J GUY, SR (D)
NC State Rep

Mailing Add: Conway NC 27820

REVELLE, RANDY (D)
City Councilman, Seattle, Wash

b Seattle, Wash, Apr 26, 41; s Judge George Henry Revelle, Jr & Evelyn Alice Hall; m 1967 to Ann Carol Werelius; c Lisa Ann. Educ: Princeton Univ, BA, 63; Woodrow Wilson Sch Pub & Int Affairs, hon grad, 63; Univ Nancy, 63-64, Rotary Found Fel for Int Understanding;

Harvard Law Sch, JD, 67; Princeton Quadrangle Club. Polit & Govt Pos: Dem precinct committeeman, King Co Dem Party, Wash, 70-; city councilman, Seattle, 74-; mem, Metro Coun, 74- Bus & Prof Pos: Asst ed, Off Asst Secy Defense, Syst Anal, 67-69, ed, 69-70; assoc attorney, Perkins, Coie, Stone, Olsen & Williams, 70-73. Mil Serv: Entered as 1st Lt, Army, 67, released as Capt, 69, after serv in Off Asst Secy Defense, Syst Anal, 67-69; Distinguished Mil Grad (ROTC); Secy of Defense Medal. Mem: Am, Wash State & Seattle-King Co Bar Asns; Seattle-King Co Munic League; CHECC on Seattle City Govt; Allied Arts of Seattle. Relig: Episcopal. Legal Res: 2809 39th Ave W Seattle WA 98199 Mailing Add: 1112 Seattle Munic Bldg Seattle WA 98104

REVENS, JOHN COSGROVE, JR (D)
RI State Sen
b Providence, RI, Jan 29, 47; s John C Revens & Rita M Williams R; m to Susan L Shaw. Educ: RI Jr Col, AA, 66; Providence Col, BA, 69; Suffolk Univ Law Sch; Dillon Club; St Thomas More Club (secy); Political Union (pres, Dem Caucus). Polit & Govt Pos: Page, RI House of Rep, 65-66, asst head page, 67, head page, 68; RI State Rep, 69-74; vchmn, New Eng Bd Higher Educ, 70-; vol coordr, Elec Campaign Gov Philip W Noel, 72; Warwick coordr, Elec Campaign Attorney Gen Julius Michaelson, 74; RI State Sen, 75-, mem judiciary & labor comts & chmn permanent med educ comn, RI State Senate. Mem: KofC; Warwick Police Athletic League; Greenwood Improvement Asn; Sienna Club St Catherine's Church; Indust Nat Bank Scholar Comt. Honors & Awards: Bishop Hendricken High Sch Letterman's Club Alumni Man of the Year, 69. Relig: Roman Catholic. Mailing Add: 360 Chapmans Ave Warwick RI 02886

REVERCOMB, CHAPMAN (R)
b Covington, Va, July 20, 95; s George A Revercomb & Elizabeth Chapman R; m 1926 to Sara Venable Hughes; c William George, Anne R (Mrs Graney) & James. Educ: Washington & Lee Univ, 14-16; Univ Va, LLB, 19; Omicron Delta Kappa; Phi Delta Phi; Delta Sigma Rho; Raven Soc; Phi Kappa Sigma. Polit & Govt Pos: Mem, WVa State Rep Comt, 33-34; pres, Young Rep League, 35-36; chmn, WVa State Rep Judicial Conv, 36; US Sen, WVa, 43-49 & 56-59; del, Rep Nat Conv, 68 & 72. Mil Serv: Entered as Pvt, Army, 17, released as Cpl, 18, after serv in Battery A, 35th Regt, CAC, USA. Mem: WVa State Bar Asn; Am Legion; Elks; Rotary; hon mem Amvets. Relig: Presbyterian. Legal Res: 917 Edgewood Dr Charleston WV 25302 Mailing Add: 821 Kanawha Valley Bldg Charleston WV 25301

REX, FRANCES LILLIAN (R)
VChmn, Summit Co Rep Comt, Ohio
b Akron, Ohio, Aug 17, 11; d Grover Cleveland Wellspring & Ethel Martin W; m 1930 to Leroy Harry Rex; c Linda Sue (Mrs Donald Joseph Blaz). Educ: Akron Pub Schs. Polit & Govt Pos: Off mgr, Summit Co Rep Hq, 49-; pres, Ohio Coun Rep Women, Summit Co, 56-58; vpres, Ohio Fedn Rep Womens Orgns, 62-64; pres, Franklin Twp Rep Orgn; committeewoman, Ohio State Rep Comt, 62-64; precinct committeewoman, Summit Co Rep Comt, 62-; mem, Summit Co Rep Exec Comt, 62-; vchmn, Summit Co Rep Cent Comt, 62-; deleg, & secy deleg, Rep Nat Conv, 72. Relig: Methodist. Legal Res: 706 W Nimisila Rd Akron OH 44308 Mailing Add: 1004 First Nat Tower Akron OH 44308

REX, PEARL TEENIE (R)
VChmn, Rich Co Rep Party, Utah
b Lonetree, Wyo, Aug 19, 17; d Evan Molbourn Bullock & Teenie S Malin B; m 1935 to Robert R Rex; c Ronald D, Norman Dale, Nina (Mrs John L Christensen), Capt Robert Alan (MIA, Vietnam), Douglas, Steven, Darlene (Mrs Dave Wightman), Bettie (Mrs Jim Armstrong), Curtis, Charmaine & Julie. Educ: South Rich High Sch, dipl, 34; Brigham Young Univ, leadership sessions. Polit & Govt Pos: Vchmn, Rich Co Rep Party, Utah, 68-; voting deleg, Utah Rep Conv, 68-; chmn & charter mem, Rich Co Rep Women, 71- Bus & Prof Pos: Newspaper reporter, Uintah Co Herald, 47-68; newspaper reporter, Salt Lake Tribune & Deseret News, 63-68; news reporter, Radio Sta KEVA-Evanston, Wyo, 65-66; ins agt, Co Mutual Life & Utah Farm Bur Ins Co, 61-75. Mem: Utah Farm Bur (chmn & info chmn, Rich Co, 61-); Rich Co March of Dimes (chap chmn, 50-); Utah State; Cowbelle Princess Pageant; Utah State Dairy Wives (pres, 74-75, chmn state dairy princess pageant, 75); Rich Co RC&D Indust Comt (chmn, 74-75). Honors & Awards: Utah Farm Bur Membership Award, 67, 70 & 74; Nat Found March of Dimes Chap & Regional Award for Outstanding Achievement, 71. Relig: Latter-day Saint; Woodruff Stake Mutual Improv Asn & Ward Drama dir, 53-70; Ward Sunday Sch Teacher, 63-75. Legal Res: Park Lane Randolph UT 84064 Mailing Add: Box 252 Randolph UT 84064

REXACH BENITEZ, ROBERTO (POPULAR DEMOCRAT, PR)
Rep, PR House of Rep
Mailing Add: State Capitol San Juan PR 00901

REYES, BEN T (D)
Tex State Rep
Mailing Add: 1006 Zoe Houston TX 77020

REYNOLDS, BENJAMIN J (R)
Committeeman, Chester Co Rep Party, Pa
b West Grove, Pa, Jan 29, 27; s S Evan Reynolds & Carsye Bower R; m to Eleanor Marshall; c three. Educ: Kennett Consol Sch. Polit & Govt Pos: Pres, Southern Chester Co Young Rep, Pa, formerly; chmn, Mason Dixon Task Force, Pa-Md-Del Water Proposal; dir, Chester Co Develop Coun, Pa; New Garden Twp supvr, 60-65; committeeman, Chester Co Rep Party, 62-; Pa State Rep, 64-72. Bus & Prof Pos: Dairy farmer & retailer. Mem: Chester Co Hist Soc; Chester Co Fireman's Asn; assoc Fraternal Order of Police; CofC. Mailing Add: RD 1 Avondale PA 19311

REYNOLDS, CATHERINE COX (D)
Mayor, West Hartford, Conn
b Hartford, Conn, Feb 27, 28; d Berkeley Cox & Margaret Stuart C; m 1957 to Philip R Reynolds; c Mary, Frances & Philip, Jr. Educ: Sweet Briar Col, AB, 49; Univ Hartford, MPA, 70. Polit & Govt Pos: Mem charter revision comn, West Hartford, Conn, 64-65, mem town planning & zoning comn, 67-70, mem town coun, 71-, mayor, 73-; dir, Conn Conf Mayors & Munic, 74-; mem exec comt, Capitol Region Coun Govts, 74- Mem: Health Planning Coun; Gtr Hartford Process (bd mem); Capitol Higher Educ Serv (bd mem). Relig: Episcopal. Mailing Add: 43 Montclair Dr West Hartford CT 06107

REYNOLDS, DOROTHY L (D)
Idaho State Rep
Mailing Add: 1920 Howard Caldwell ID 83605

REYNOLDS, EDWARD HARRIS (D)
Asst Attorney Gen, Ala
b Notasulga, Ala, Oct 7, 18; s Edward Harris Reynolds & Vivian Wise R; m 1948 to Sarah Elizabeth Avant; c Edward Harris, Jr & Jeanne. Educ: Ala Polytech Inst, BS, 40; Univ Ala, LLB, 43; Phi Gamma Delta. Polit & Govt Pos: Ala State Sen until 66; Asst Attorney Gen, Ala, 66-, chief, State Lands Div, 67- Mil Serv: World War II; served in Pac Area, Philippine Islands, Japan & Hawaii; was in War Crimes Div, Tokyo, 1 year. Mem: Mason. Relig: Methodist. Mailing Add: Notasulga AL 36866

REYNOLDS, HOBSON RICHMOND (R)
b Winton, NC; s Refus Reynolds & Julia Belle R; m 1926 to Evelyn Crawford. Educ: Waters Normal Inst & NC Bus Col. Hon Degrees: LLD, Bethune-Cookman Col, 48, Allen Univ, 63. Polit & Govt Pos: Pa State Rep, 34 & 38; selected by President Franklin D Roosevelt as an observer at formation of UN Orgn; referee in workmen's compensation, Pa Labor Comn, 50-55; Consul of Liberia; deleg & seconded nomination of Dwight D Eisenhower, Rep Nat Conv, 52, deleg, 56 & 72; alt deleg-at-lg, 68; app by President Eisenhower as asst to Comnr Fed Housing; mem, Pa Constitutional Conv, 68. Mem: F&AM (past Grand Master, Prince Hall Affil of Pa); Nat Urban League (bd mem); Bethune-Cookman Col, Fla (trustee); Cheyney State Col, Pa (chmn bd trustees); Elks (Grand Dir, Dept Civil Liberties, 39-60; Grand Exalted Ruler, 60). Honors & Awards: Distinguished & outstanding pub serv, selected by Afro-American newspaper, placed on its honor roll, 49-50. Relig: Baptist; chmn trustee bd, Wayland Temple Baptist Church, Pa. Mailing Add: 1522 N 16th St Philadelphia PA 19121

REYNOLDS, JAMES JOSEPH (D)
b Brooklyn, NJ, Jan 8, 07; s James J Reynolds & Katherine Mahoney R; m 1965 to Helen May. Educ: Columbia Univ, AB, 28. Polit & Govt Pos: Under Secy of Labor, formerly. Bus & Prof Pos: Pres, Am Inst Merchant Shipping, currently. Mailing Add: 1625 K St NW Washington DC 20006

REYNOLDS, JOHN W (D)
b Green Bay, Wis, Apr 4, 21; s John W Reynolds & Madge Flatley R; m 1942 to Patricia Ann Brody, wid; m 1971 to Jane Conway; c Kate M, Molly, Jimmy & Joe. Educ: Univ Wis, BS, 46, LLB, 49. Polit & Govt Pos: Attorney Gen, Wis, 59-63; del, Dem Nat Conv, 60 & 64, vchmn, 64; Gov, Wis, 63-65; US Dist Judge, Eastern Dist, Wis, 65- Bus & Prof Pos: Attorney-at-law, Green Bay, Wis, 49- Mem: Am, Wis & Brown Co Bar Asns. Mailing Add: 4654 N Woodburn Milwaukee WI 53211

REYNOLDS, MARIAN KAYE (D)
Kans State Rep
b Dodge City, Kans, Feb 16, 50; d Mark LeVern Schartz & Betty Henning S; m 1973 to Jay Don Reynolds; c Kansas Mark Henry. Educ: Dodge City Community Jr Col, 68; Parks Bus Col, grad, 69. Polit & Govt Pos: Kans State Rep, Dist 115, 75- Bus & Prof Pos: Loan clerk, Midland Mortgage Co, Denver, Colo, 69-70; legal secy, Frigon Law Off, Cimarron, Kans, 70-71 & Akin & Stanford Law Off, Dallas, Tex, 71-73; exec secy, Cimarron Ins Co, Cimarron, Kans, 73-75. Relig: Catholic. Legal Res: Box 707 Cimarron KS 67835 Mailing Add: House of Rep Topeka KS 66612

REYNOLDS, RANDALL O (D)
Va State Deleg
Mailing Add: Box 304 Chatham VA 24531

REYNOLDS, RICHARD FLOYD (R)
Tex State Rep
b Franklin Co, Ohio, Sept 23, 27; m 1953 to Lois Joanne Loiry; c Brad, Guy, Jack, Eric & Ann. Educ: Ohio State Univ, BSBA; Bliss Col; Southern Methodist Univ. Polit & Govt Pos: City councilman, Richardson, Tex, 63-66, mayor pro-tem, 69-70; dir, NCent Tex Coun Govt, currently, mem, Planning Comn, currently; Tex State Rep, Dist 33-P, 72- Bus & Prof Pos: Secy & financial vpres, Ben Griffin Enterprises, Inc, Dallas, currently; mgt consult, Richardson, currently; pres, Macatee Capital Corp, Dallas; financial vpres, Col Inns of Am, Inc. Mil Serv: Entered Army, 2nd Lt (ONG). Relig: Methodist. Legal Res: 427 Fall Creek Richardson TX 75080 Mailing Add: 2186 Promenade Ctr Richardson TX 75080

REYNOLDS, ROBERT CHARLES (R)
Mass State Rep
b Rochester, NH, Nov 6, 34; s Everett Leon Reynolds & Anne Eckles R; m 1952 to Carol Everlena Norris; c Robert C, Jr, Raymond Scott, Ralph Alan & Richard Leon. Educ: Boston Univ; Suffolk Law Sch. Polit & Govt Pos: Town moderator, Northborough, Mass; Mass State Rep, Worcester's 23rd Dist, 69- Bus & Prof Pos: Practicing attorney, R R Reynolds, Northborough, Mass, currently; pres, Renco Ins, 62- & Renco Realty, Westboro, 65-; partner law off, Gallagher & Reynolds, currently. Mil Serv: Airman 1/C, Air Force, 52-56. Mem: Mass Bar Asn; Am Trial Lawyers Asn; Lions; Am Legion; Aleppo Temple Lodge. Relig: Protestant. Legal Res: 20 Solomon Pond Rd Northborough MA 01532 Mailing Add: 5 W Main St Northborough MA 01532

REYNOLDS, ROBERT JACKSON (D)
Chmn, Montgomery Co Dem Exec Comt, Ky
b Joplin, Mo, May 5, 10; s Roy Randolph Reynolds & Roberta Katherine Taulbee R; m 1931 to Anne Kenney Prewitt; c Elizabeth (Mrs Carr) & Robert Jackson, Jr. Educ: Univ Mo, 2 years; Sigma Nu. Polit & Govt Pos: Mem, Ky Tuberc Sanatoria Comn, 48-50; Ky State Sen, 50-58; Dem precinct committeeman, Montgomery Co, Ky, 56-; chmn, Montgomery Co Dem Exec Comt, 60- Bus & Prof Pos: Owner, R J Reynolds, Gen Contractor, 45-; pres, Hwy Concrete Pipe, Inc, 49-, Hwy Drainage Pipe, Inc, 54- & Mt Sterling Broadcasting Corp, 56-; vpres, Capitol Broadcasting Corp, 62- & Del-Marysville Broadcasting Corp, 64- Mem: Assoc mem, Am Soc Civil Engrs; life mem, Ky Sheriff's Asn; hon mem, Ky Hwy Employees Ten-To-Forty Club; assoc mem, Islamorada Fishing Guides Asn, Fla. Relig: Christian Church. Legal Res: Rte 2 Mt Sterling KY 40353 Mailing Add: PO Box 373 Mt Sterling KY 40353

REYNOLDS, ROBERT LEONARD, JR (D)
Mem Bd, Dane Co Dem Party, Wis
b Madison, Wis, June 11, 30; s Robert Leonard Reynolds & Sarah Chickering R; m 1952 to Marjorie Jill Bump; c Anne T, Robert L, III & Daniel C. Educ: Univ Wis, Madison, BA, 53, LLB, 60. Polit & Govt Pos: Alderman, Madison, Wis, 64-68; del, Dem Nat Conv, 68; mem bd, Dane Co Dem Party, 68-, chmn, 71-72. Bus & Prof Pos: Trust officer, Security State Bank, Madison, 62-68; practicing attorney, Madison, 68- Mil Serv: Entered as Lt, Army, 53,

released as 1st Lt, 55; Army Res, 55-60, Capt. Mem: Wis & Dane Co Bar Asns. Relig: Episcopal. Mailing Add: 2327 Eton Ridge Madison WI 53705

REYNOLDS, RUSSELL JOSEPH (D)
Conn State Rep
b New Haven, Conn, Mar 19, 41; s John Russell Reynolds & Helen Adams R; m 1972 to Joan Marie Czapleski; c Matthew David. Educ: St Bonaventure Univ, BA cum laude, 62; Southern Conn State Col, MS in Urban Studies, 72; Fairfield Univ, continued studies. Polit & Govt Pos: Conn State Rep, Dist 116, 75- Bus & Prof Pos: Research analyst asst to Fed Coordr, West Haven, 71-72; proj dir, Proj Naugatuck Valley, Health Transportation, Dept Health, Educ & Welfare, 72-74; self-employed transportation consult, Conn & NY, 75- Mem: West Haven Jaycees; West Haven Auxiliary Police (secy); Dem Town Comt. Relig: Christian. Mailing Add: 893 First Ave West Haven CT 06516

REYNOLDS, S SEELEY, JR (D)
Vt State Sen
Mailing Add: RD Salisbury VT 05769

REYNOLDS, STEVE (D)
Ga State Sen
b Jackson Co, Ga, June 6, 20; s Waldo Bryant Reynolds (deceased) & Lalyer Evans Crowe R; m 1939 to Rebecca Harper; c David W. Educ: Southern Bus Col, 1 year; La Salle Exten Univ, 3 years. Polit & Govt Pos: Ga State Sen, Dist 48, currently. Bus & Prof Pos: Former pres & gen mgr, Cent Containers Co, Inc; pres & gen mgr, Reynolds Oil Co, currently. Mil Serv: Entered as Pvt, Army, 44, released as T-5, 46, after serv in Army Inf, US. Mem: Am Legion; Kiwanis; PTA; Farm Bur. Relig: Presbyterian; elder. Legal Res: 297 Craig Dr Lawrenceville GA 30245 Mailing Add: PO Box 303 Lawrenceville GA 30245

REYNOLDS, W J (BILL), JR (D)
Ky State Rep
b 1920. Educ: Univ Ky; Morehead State Col. Polit & Govt Pos: Ky State Rep, 64-; alt deleg, Dem Nat Conv, 68, deleg, 72. Bus & Prof Pos: Right-of-way supvr, United Fuel Gas Co. Mil Serv: Army Air Force. Mem: Am Legion; VFW; Mason; PTA; Big Sandy Develop Corp. Relig: Christian. Mailing Add: PO Box 56 Allen KY 41601

REZ, DONALD GARY (D)
b San Antonio, Tex, July 7, 53; s Lt Col Orville Clinton Rez & Francis Jaquelan Boyd R; single. Educ: Washington Workshop Found, Washington, DC, 71; Tarleton State Col, 72-; pres, Soc Sci Club, 72- Polit & Govt Pos: Page, US House of Rep, 71; state exec committeeman, Tex Young Dem, 71-72; deleg, Dem Nat Conv, 72; co youth coordr, Briscoe for Gov Comt, 72; dist youth coordr, Sanders for Senate Comt, 72; pres, Tarleton State Col Young Dem, 72- Bus & Prof Pos: Attend, Weem's Enco Serv Sta, 69-71. Publ: Page-eye view of Congress, Stephenville Daily Empire-Tribune, 7/71. Mem: Student Adv Comn, Washington Workshops Found; US Lawn Tennis Asn T Award, Tarleton State Col, 72. Mailing Add: 1880 Kingland Stephenville TX 76401

RHETT, HASKELL E S (D)
b Evanston, Ill, Aug 29, 36; s Haskell Smith Rhett & Eunice Emery R; m 1961 to Roberta Teel Oliver, div; c Kathryn Emery & Cecily Coffin. Educ: Hamilton Col, BA, 58; Cornell Univ, univ scholar, 64, Nat Defense fel, 66, MA, 67, PhD, 68; Univ London, 66-67; Pi Delta Epsilon; Sigma Phi. Polit & Govt Pos: Co-chmn, Bucks Co Pa, Citizens for McGovern, 72; alt deleg, Dem Nat Conv, 72. Bus & Prof Pos: Asst dir admissions, Hamilton Col, 61-62, asst to pres, 62-64; res asst, Cornell Univ, 64-66; res assoc, Univ London, 66-67; dir prog develop, Educ Testing Serv, 67-73; assoc dir, Nat Longitudinal Study, US Off Educ, 72-73; Asst Chancellor Higher Educ, NJ, 73- Mil Serv: Entered as Seaman Apprentice, Navy, 58 & released as Lt, 61 after serv in Heavy Attack Squadron 5, US Sixth Fleet; Bombardier & Navigator Awards. Publ: The Massachusetts State College System—a Guide to Admissions and Financial aid Information, Col Entrance Exam Bd, 72; The University Grants Committee and the New British Universities, Hist Educ Soc, 72; The National Longitudinal Study of the High Sch Class of 1972, Am Educ Res Asn, 73. Mem: Soc Res in Higher Educ, Ltd, London; Am Asn Higher Educ. Relig: Episcopal. Mailing Add: ETTL Farm Rosedale Rd Princeton NJ 08540

RHINEHART, SHELBY AARON (D)
Tenn State Rep
b Monterey, Tenn, May 5, 27; s Shelby A Rhinehart & Laura Underwood R; m 1952 to Margret Wrenn; c Shelby Porter & James Barney. Educ: Tenn Tech Univ; Stamford Univ; Rho Chi. Polit & Govt Pos: Mem, Bd of Educ, Spencer, Tenn, 56-; chmn, Van Buren Co Dem Exec Comt, 58-; Tenn State Rep, 59-63 & 71-; mayor, Spencer, 63- Bus & Prof Pos: Owner, Spencer Drug Co, 56- Mil Serv: Entered as Pvt, Army, 44, released as Sgt, 51, after serv in Army Ord, Pac, 46 & 51; South West Pac & Good Conduct Medals; World War II & Korean Victory Medals; Korean Serv Medal. Mem: Mason; Am Legion; Civitan; Am & Tenn State Pharmaceutical Asns. Relig: Baptist. Mailing Add: Spencer Drug Co Spencer TN 38385

RHINELANDER, JOHN BASSETT (R)
Gen Counsel, Dept Health, Educ & Welfare
b Boston, Mass, June 18, 33; s Frederic W Rhinelander & Constance Templeton R; m 1962 to Jeanne Elizabeth Cattell; c John Richard, Margaret Templeton, Katherine Pierson & Thomas Bassett. Educ: Yale Univ, BA, 51; Inst d'Etudes Polit, Paris, 55-56; Univ Va Law Sch, LLB, 61. Polit & Govt Pos: Spec civilian asst to Secy, Dept Navy, Washington, DC, 66-68; chief counsel & acting dep dir, Off Foreign Direct Investment, Dept Com, 68-69; dep legal adv, Dept State, 69-71; legal adv, US Strategic Arms Limitation Talks, 71-72; gen counsel, Dept Health, Educ & Welfare, 73- Bus & Prof Pos: Ed-in-chief, Va Law Rev, 60-61; law clerk, Justice John M Harlan, US Supreme Court, Washington, DC, 61-62; attorney, Davis, Polk & Wardwell, New York, 62-66; partner, Liebman, Williams, Bennett, Baird & Minow, Washington, DC, 72; partner, Sidley & Austin, 72-73. Mil Serv: Entered as Pvt, Army, 56, released as SP-3, 58, after serv in 44th Missile Bn. Publ: Co-ed & auth chap, SALT: The Moscow Agreements & Beyond, Free Press, 74. Mem: NY, DC & US Supreme Court Bar; Arms Control Asn; Coun Foreign Rels. Mailing Add: 6115 Ramshorn Pl McLean VA 22101

RHOAD, W D (D)
SC State Rep
Mailing Add: Box 508 Bamberg SC 29003

RHOADES, ANNA ROSA (R)
VChmn, Ocean Co Rep Exec Comt, NJ
b Basel, Switz, Oct 9, 13; d Jacob Hirschbiegel & Mary Steiner H; div; c Linda (Mrs Grissett) & Judith. Educ: Lakewood High Sch, NJ, 4 years. Polit & Govt Pos: Head clerk, Ocean Co Court House, Toms River, NJ, 40-; admin asst & secy, Lakewood Rep Munic Comt, 58-73; mem exec bd, NJ VChmn Asn, 65-69, vchmn, Cent Region, 70-71; vchmn, Ocean Co Rep Exec Comt, 65- Mem: Ocean Co Sheltered Workshop (bd dirs, vpres, 72-); Toms River Bus & Prof Women's Club (recording secy, 72- & corresponding secy, 73-74); Ocean Co Employees Fed Credit Union (bd dirs); Lakewood Rep Club; Ocean Co Hist Soc (trustee, 62-73, vpres, 72-). Honors & Awards: 20 Year Pin, Ocean Co March of Dimes; Chmn Dist Plaque. Relig: Lutheran. Mailing Add: 5 S Oakland St Lakewood NJ 08701

RHODE, LEO (R)
Alaska State Sen
Mailing Add: Rm 608 Baranoff Hotel Juneau AK 99801

RHODES, ALFRED HENRY, JR (D)
VChmn, Third Cong Dist Dem Party, Miss
b Midnight, Miss, Mar 16, 41; s Alfred Henry Rhodes & Willie Mae Hall R; m 1963 to Lottie Mary William; c William Wyatt & Romula P. Educ: Utica Jr Col, Miss, AA, 59-61; Tougaloo Col, BA, 64; Jackson State Col, MS, 70; Omega Psi Phi. Polit & Govt Pos: Vchmn, Third Cong Dist Dem Party, Miss, currently; secy, State Exec Comt, Miss Freedom Dem Party, currently; mem, State Exec Comt, Young Dem Clubs of Miss, currently; deleg, Dem Nat Conv, 68; chmn, Hinds Co Dem Exec Comt, 69-72. Bus & Prof Pos: Dir, Miss Prof, Nat Fedn of Settlements & Neighborhood Centers, currently; commun organizer, Child Develop Group, 65-66; teacher, Hinds Co Pub Schs, 65-66; consult, Miss Med & Surg Asn, 67; consult, Michael Schwerner Mem Fund, 68-69; consult, Nat Coun Negro Women, 69; Ford Found Leadership Develop fel, 70-71. Mem: Jackson Urban League (mem bd); Bethlehem Ctr & Commun Serv Asn (chmn bd). Relig: Baptist. Mailing Add: 1557 Reddix St Jackson MS 39209

RHODES, DONALD H (D)
Va State Deleg
b Norfolk, Va, Mar 17, 33; s Early Clemons Rhodes & Ivy Mae Harris R; m 1959 to Anna Margaret Young; c Donald, Jr & Chester. Educ: Univ Va, Charlottesville, BS, 55, JD, 61; Phi Kappa Psi; Delta Theta Phi. Polit & Govt Pos: Mem, City Coun, Virginia Beach, Va, 70-, mayor, 70-72; Va State Deleg, 75- Bus & Prof Pos: Asst city attorney, Norfolk, Va, 61-62; pvt law practice, Virginia Beach, 62-68, partner, Owen, Guy, Rhodes & Betz, 68- Mem: Thalia Civic League; Princess Anne Ruritan Club; Va Soc Crippled Children & Adults (vpres, currently); March of Dimes (treas, Tidewater Va Chap, currently); AF&AM. Relig: Protestant. Legal Res: 621 Heron Point Circle Virginia Beach VA 23452 Mailing Add: PO Box 62204 Virginia Beach VA 23462

RHODES, FRED BURNETT (R)
Dep Adminstr Vet Affairs, Vet Admin
b Washington, DC, Dec 17, 13; s Fred B Rhodes & Florence Shuffle R; m 1956 to Winona Henderson. Educ: Colgate Univ, AB, 36; Univ Md, LLB, 41; Sigma Nu. Polit & Govt Pos: Exec dir, Joint Comt on Atomic Energy, 47-49; chief counsel, Comt on Armed Serv, US Senate, 53-55, gen counsel, Vet Admin, 60-61; minority counsel, Comt on Appropriations, US Senate, 62-64, secy & staff dir, Policy Comt, 64-69; dep adminstr vet affairs, Vet Admin, 69- Bus & Prof Pos: Pvt law practice, 55-60. Mil Serv: Entered as Pvt, Army, 41, released as Maj, 47, after serv in Manhattan Eng Dist; recalled, Army, 51-53; Commendation Ribbon & other awards for Atomic Bomb Proj; Col, Army Res, 64. Mem: Am Bar Asn; Nat Lawyers Club; Potomac Appalachian Trail Club; Army Navy Country Club; Capitol Hill Club. Relig: Southern Baptist. Legal Res: 3101 N Peary St Arlington VA 22207 Mailing Add: Vet Admin Bldg Suite 1001 801 Vermont Ave NW Washington DC 20420

RHODES, GEORGE MILTON (D)
b Reading, Pa, Feb 24, 98; m 1921 to Margie Seiverling. Educ: Reading Pub Schs. Polit & Govt Pos: Mem rationing bd, War Manpower Comt; US Rep, Pa, 48-68. Bus & Prof Pos: Printer; bus mgr; labor ed & labor rep; pres, Reading & Berks Co Cent Labor Union, AFL, 22 years; bd mem, Reading Housing Authority. Mil Serv: Vet of World War I. Mem: Coun of Soc Agencies; Commun Gen Hosp; YMCA. Mailing Add: 505 Brighton Ave Reading PA 19606

RHODES, JAMES ALLEN (R)
Gov, Ohio
b Coalton, Ohio, Sept 13, 09; s James Llewellyn Rhodes & Susan Howe R; m 1941 to Helen Rawlins; c Susan (Mrs Richard Moore); Saundra (Mrs John Jacob) & Sharon; 3 grandchildren. Educ: Ohio State Univ. Hon Degrees: Hon degrees from numerous cols & univs. Polit & Govt Pos: Auditor, Columbus, Ohio, 39-42, mayor, 42-53; State Auditor, Ohio, 53-63, Gov, 63-70 & 75-; deleg, Rep Nat Conv, 72. Bus & Prof Pos: Founder develop firm, James A Rhodes & Assocs, currently. Publ: Johnny Shiloh, Bobbs-Merrill Co, 58; The Trial of Mary Todd Lincoln, 59; The Court-Martial of Commodore Perry, 60. Mem: Amateur Athletic Union; US Olympic Comt; Pan-Am Games. Honors & Awards: Recipient of the Silver Keystone Award by Boys Clubs of Am & the Helms Found Award. Relig: Presbyterian. Mailing Add: 2375 Tremont Rd Columbus OH 43221

RHODES, JERI A (D)
b Benton Co, Mo, Sept 23, 17; d Franklin Dewitt Allen & Laura Alexander A; m to E L Rhodes, MD; c Charlu. Educ: Central Mo State Univ, BS, 41. Polit & Govt Pos: Vchmn, Benton Co Dem Comt, Mo, formerly. Mailing Add: Warsaw MO 65355

RHODES, JOHN J (R)
US Rep, Ariz
b Council Grove, Kans, Sept 18, 16; s J J Rhodes & Gladys Thomas R; m 1942 to Mary Elizabeth (Betty) Harvey; c John J, III, Thomas H, Elizabeth Campbell & James Scott. Educ: Kans State Col, BS, 38; Harvard Law Sch, LLB, 41; Blue Key; Beta Theta Pi. Polit & Govt Pos: Vchmn, Ariz Bd of Pub Welfare, 51-52; US Rep, First Dist, Ariz, 52-, minority leader, US House Rep, 74-; deleg, Rep Nat Conv, 72; mem exec comt, Rep Nat Comt, 74- Bus & Prof Pos: Vpres, Farm & Home Life Ins Co, Phoenix, 51- Mil Serv: Entered as 1st Lt, Army Air Force, 41, released as Lt Col, 46, after serv in Air Force Training Command; Col (Ret), Judge Adv Gen Corps, Army Res. Mem: Scottish Rite (33 degree); SAR; Elks; Am Legion (past sr vcomdr); CofC. Relig: Methodist. Legal Res: 1114 N Cherry St Mesa AZ 85201 Mailing Add: H-230 The Capitol Washington DC 20515

RHODES, JOSEPH, JR (D)
Pa State Rep
Mailing Add: Capitol Bldg Harrisburg PA 17120

RHODES, NINA (D)
Mem, Calif Dem State Cent Comt
b Brooklyn, NY, Jan 8, 34; d Jack Fried & Clare Forman F; div; c Ross Benett, Laura Raven & Camila. Educ: Hollywood High Sch, Calif, grad. Polit & Govt Pos: Chmn fund raising, Young Prof for Kennedy, Calif, 68, committeewoman, Gala Finance Comt for Kennedy under Warschaws, 68; deleg, Dem Nat Conv, 68; mem bd dirs, Dem Womens Forum, Calif, 68-, mem adv bd, 71-; mem, Calif Dem State Cent Comt, currently. Bus & Prof Pos: Actress, NBC & Screen Gems, currently. Mem: Screen Actors Guild; Am Fedn TV & Radio Artists. Relig: Jewish. Mailing Add: 4342 Nogales Dr Tarzana CA 91356

RHODES, SAMUEL THOMAS (R)
NC State Rep
b Wilmington, NC, Oct 12, 44; s Samuel Thomas Rhodes & Dorothy Williamson R; single. Educ: Univ NC, Chapel Hill, BA, 66; Auburn Univ, MS, 69; NC State Univ, work toward PhD. Polit & Govt Pos: NC State Rep, 73- Bus & Prof Pos: Instr, Cape Fear Tech Inst, 69- Publ: Published two papers relating to ecology in scientific journals. Mem: Ecol Soc Am; Int Oceanog Found; Am Mus Nat Hist; Am Inst Biol Sci; Eastern Star. Relig: Baptist. Mailing Add: PO Box 3251 Wilmington NC 28401

RHODES, THOMAS WALLACE (D)
Chmn Troup Co Dem Exec Comt, Ga
b La Grange, Ga, Sept 7, 28; s Thomas Lawson Rhodes & Leila Belle Griggs R; m 1960 to Edna Earle Mallory. Educ: La Grange High Sch, 42-46; Perry Bus Sch, 46. Polit & Govt Pos: Mem, Sixth Cong Dist Dem Comt, Ga, 66-70; mem, State Bd Family & Children Serv, 67-69; mem, Children & Youth, 69-; mem, Troup Co Dem Exec Comt, 66-67, chmn, 67-; mem, Ga State Dem Exec Comt, 67- Bus & Prof Pos: Rhodes, Inc, La Grange, Ga, 54- Mem: Moose. Relig: Methodist. Legal Res: 502 S Lewis St La Grange GA 30240 Mailing Add: Box 605 La Grange GA 30240

RHODES, WILLIAM CHARLES (D)
Miss State Sen
Mailing Add: PO Box 805 Pascagoula MS 39567

RHODES, WILLIAM EMERSON (D)
b Syracuse, NY, Dec 6, 39; s Frank George Rhodes & Elenita Elizabeth Ryan R; m 1963 to Jo Ann Frances Meyer; c Brian Patrick & Kevin Michael. Educ: Syracuse Univ, BS, 61; New York Inst Finance, 68. Polit & Govt Pos: Twp trustee, Delhi Twp, Hamilton Co, Ohio, 69-; mem, Dist 13 Crime Coun, Cincinnati, 70-72; mem, Ohio Local Govt Serv Comn, 72-74; deleg, Dem Nat Mid-Term Conf, 74; mem, Hamilton Cable TV Study Comt, 74-; mem, Gtr Cincinnati Fed Exec Bd, 74- Bus & Prof Pos: Prog dir, air personality, Radio Sta WSAI, Cincinnati, 61-66; air personality, Radio Sta CKLW, Detroit, 66-67; broadcast acct exec, Radio Sta WSAI, Cincinnati, 67-68; registered rep, W E Hutton & Co, 68-71; registered rep, Harrison & Co, 71- Mem: Cincinnati Stock & Bond Club; Delhi Twp & Hamilton Co Dem Party; Western Hills Civil Planning Coun (mem exec, policy & steering comts); Ohio Asn Twp Trustees & Clerks; Am Fedn Radio & TV Artists. Honors & Awards: Cincinnati's Most Popular Disc Jockey, Billboard Mag, 65. Relig: Roman Catholic. Mailing Add: 421 Sunaire Terr Cincinnati OH 45238

RIBAK, ABRAHAM D (D)
Tex State Rep
Mailing Add: 2722 Gainesborough San Antonio TX 78230

RIBICOFF, ABRAHAM A (D)
US Sen, Conn
b New Britain, Conn, Apr 9, 10; m to Lois Mathes; c Peter & Jane. Educ: NY Univ; Univ Chicago Law Sch, LLB, 33. Hon Degrees: Hon degrees from 20 cols & univs. Polit & Govt Pos: Conn State Rep, 38-42; munic judge, Hartford, 41-43 & 45-47; US Rep, Conn, 48-52; Gov, Conn, 54-61; Secy of Health, Educ & Welfare, 61-62; US Sen, Conn, 62-; deleg, Dem Nat Conv, 72; deleg, Dem Nat Mid-Term Conf, 74. Bus & Prof Pos: Lawyer, Hartford, Conn. Legal Res: Hartford CT Mailing Add: 321 Old Senate Off Bldg Washington DC 20510

RICE, CARL VENTON (D)
b Lovilla, Iowa, Mar 27, 98; s Walter S Rice & Ida Isabelle Chamberlain R, wid; c Ruth Isabelle (Mrs Jefferson Mitchell), Carlene Virginia (Mrs George Lind), Mary Elizabeth (Mrs Samuel Wells) & Grace Lucille (Mrs John A Muder, Jr). Educ: Kans Univ, LLB & LD, 18; Delta Theta Phi. Polit & Govt Pos: Chmn, Labette Co Dem Party, Kans, 22-34; chmn, Dem Cong Dist, 26-28; chmn platform comt, State Dem Conv, 28, 30, 32 & 38; mem, Kans State Hwy Comn, 31-33; deleg, Dem Nat Conv, 32, 40, 44, 48, 52 & 60, mem platform comt, 32 & 60, mem credentials comt, 56, alt deleg, 36, 64 & 68; counsel, Reconstruction Finance Corp, Kans, 33-49 & State Bank Dept, 37-39; Dem Nat Committeeman for Kans, 44-52; dir, Kans Emergency Resources Mgt Plan, 67-; mem, Urban Renewal Comn, Kansas City, 67- Mil Serv: Entered as Pvt, Army, 18, released as Sgt Maj, 19 after serv in Field Artil. Mem: Am Bar Asn; Am Legion; CofC; Kans City Club; Univ Club. Relig: Protestant. Mailing Add: 2108 Washington Blvd Kansas City KS 66102

RICE, CHARLES E (CONSERVATIVE)
b New York; m 1956 to Mary E Mannix; c John Laurence, Mary Frances, Anne Patricia, Joseph Patrick, Charles Peter, Jeanne Elizabeth, Teresa Helen, Kathleen Bernadette & Ellen Mary. Educ: Col Holy Cross, AB, 53; Boston Col Law Sch, LLB, 56; NY Univ, LLM, 59 & JSD, 62. Polit & Govt Pos: State vchmn, Conservative Party, NY, 62-69; chmn, United Conservatives of Ind, Inc, 72- Bus & Prof Pos: Lectr hist & polit sci, C W Post Col, 59-62; lectr & vis asst prof, NY Univ Sch of Law, 59-62; prof law, Fordham Univ Sch of Law, 60-69; prof law, Univ Notre Dame Sch of Law, 69- Mil Serv: Entered as 2nd Lt, Marine Corps, 56, released as 1st Lt, 58, after serv at Air Sta, Quantico, Va, 57-58; Maj, Marine Corps Res, currently. Publ: Freedom of Association, NY Univ, 62; The Vanishing Right to Live, 69; Authority & Rebellion: The Case for Orthodoxy in the Catholic Church, Doubleday, 71; plus others. Mem: Am & NY State Bar Asns. Relig: Roman Catholic. Mailing Add: 12622 Dragoon Trail Mishawaka IN 46544

RICE, DECKIE M (D)
Chmn, Idaho Dem Party
b Nashville, Tenn, May 20, 24; d Hallie Decker Martin & Carrie B Freeman M; m 1947 to Ralph Estes Rice, Jr; c Patricia (Mrs John Todd Nelson) & Karen Estes. Educ: Ward Belmot Jr Col, grad, 44; Univ Tenn, Knoxville, BA, 46; Idaho State Univ, 68-69; Alpha Omicron Pi. Polit & Govt Pos: Precinct committeeman, Idaho Falls, Idaho, 62-; chmn, Idaho Dist 30 Dem Party, 68-; deleg, Dem Nat Mid-Term Conf, 74; mem, Dem Charter Comn, 74; chmn, Idaho Dem Party, 75- Bus & Prof Pos: Chemist, Oak Ridge Nat Lab, 46-48 & Argonne Nat Lab, 48-51; teacher, Idaho Dist 91, 70- Mem: League of Women Voters; Am Asn Univ Women; Girl Scouts; Am Fedn Teachers. Mailing Add: 119 S Lloyd Circle Idaho Falls ID 83401

RICE, EDMUND BURKE
b Cambridge, Mass, Feb 19, 49; s Edmund Townsend Rice & Catherine Burke R; single. Educ: Colgate Univ, BA, 70; Pi Sigma Alpha. Polit & Govt Pos: Projs asst to US Rep Margaret Heckler, Mass, 71-72, legis asst, 72-73, spec asst, 73-75, admin asst, 75- Mil Serv: SP-5, Army Res. Legal Res: 24 Belair Rd Wellesley MA 02181 Mailing Add: 330 Fifth St SE Washington DC 20003

RICE, EDWARD WILLIAM (R)
Idaho State Rep
b Great Falls, Mont, July 24, 11; s Robert W Rice & Laura S Martin R; m 1940 to Patricia Murray Arnold; c Barbara B (Mrs Wescott) & Catherine M (Mrs Green). Educ: Univ Kans, BS, 35, Sch Law, LLB, 38, JD, 68; Sigma Chi; Phi Delta Phi. Polit & Govt Pos: Mem, Boise Civil Serv Comn, Idaho, 53-61; City Coun, Boise, 61-65, pres, 65; Idaho State Rep, Dist 15, 69-, chmn judiciary & rules comt, Idaho House of Rep. Bus & Prof Pos: Pres, Doctors Bus Bur, Boise, Idaho, 50-; med mgt consult, 50- Mil Serv: Entered as Lt (jg), Naval Res, 43, released as CDR, 46, after serv as CO, USS Fairbault, Am & Pac Theatres, World War II, 43-46. Publ: Author of various articles in Physicians Mgt; ed consult, currently. Mem: Med-Dent Hosp Bur Am; Am Legion; Mason; Shrine; Boise CofC. Relig: Protestant. Mailing Add: 1214 Johnson Boise ID 83705

RICE, JAMES I (DFL)
Minn State Rep
Mailing Add: 2220 Vincent Ave N Minneapolis MN 55411

RICE, JOHN S (D)
b Adams Co, Pa, Jan 28, 99; m to Luene Rogers; c Ellen F. Educ: Gettysburg Col, BS, 21. Hon Degrees: LLD, Temple Univ. Polit & Govt Pos: Pa State Sen, 32-40, majority floor leader, Pa State Senate, 37, pres pro tempore, 38; first chmn, Pa Salvage Dr, 41; Dem nominee for Gov, Pa, 46; secy, Dept Property & Supplies, 56-57; Secy, Commonwealth of Pa, 58-61; US Ambassador to Netherlands, 61-64; chmn, Pa State Dem Cent Comt, 59-61 & 65-66; deleg, Dem Nat Conv, 68. Bus & Prof Pos: Former dir, Gettysburg Nat Bank; pres, Rice, Trew & Rice Co, Biglerville, Pa, 29-55; trustee, Gettysburg Col, 39-, chmn bd trustees, 55-61; trustee, Gettysburg Lutheran Theol Sem, 41-55; pres, State Container Co, 47-55. Mil Serv: Entered as Pvt, Army, World War I, re-entered Army Air Force, 42, released as Col, 45; Col (Ret), Army Res; Legion of Merit. Mem: Am Legion; VFW; Mason; Elks. Relig: Lutheran. Mailing Add: Apt 216B 1750 S Ocean Lane Ft Lauderdale FL 33316

RICE, LYLE K (R)
Vt State Rep
Mailing Add: 15 Harvard St Rutland VT 05701

RICE, THOMAS J, SR (R)
La State Rep
Mailing Add: 420 Aurora Ave Metairie LA 70005

RICE, VIRGIL THOMAS (R)
b La Harpe, Ill, June 29, 20; s Vilas E Rice & Jane N Robertson R; m 1969 to Phyllis Ann Carpenter; c Lesley Jean, Sharon Leilani & Clayton Taylor. Educ: Univ Ill, BA, 41; Univ Ill Col Law, JD, 48; Phi Sigma Kappa; Phi Delta Phi. Polit & Govt Pos: Vpres, 37th Precinct, Fourth Rep Dist, Hawaii, 53-55; deleg, Hawaii State Rep Conv, 53-75; chmn, 17th Rep Dist Comt, Hawaii, 55-60; mem, Honolulu Co Rep Comt, 56-60, chmn, 69; mem, Hawaii Homes Comn, 60; mem, chmn & secy, State Transportation Adv Comn, 60-64; vchmn various precincts in Hawaii, 60-69; chmn, Rep Party of Hawaii, 69-71, mem exec comt, 69-73; mem, Rep Nat Comt, 69-71; deleg, Rep Nat Conv, 72, mem platform comt; mem, State of Hawaii Reapportionment Comn, 73; mem, State Adv Comt Spec Educ, 75- Bus & Prof Pos: Assoc law off of James P Blaisdell, 48-50, assoc & partner, Blaisdell & Moore Attorneys, 53-61, partner, Moore, Torkildson & Rice, 61-64, Quinn & Moore, 64, Rice & Lee, 64-71, Rice, Lee & Wong, 72- Mil Serv: Entered as Leading Aircraftsman, Royal Can Air Force, 41, transferred to US Army Air Corps, 43, released as Capt, 45, after serv in 415th Squadron, Royal Can Air Force, 43-44 & Air Transport Command, 44-45, ETO; Capt, US Air Force, 50, released as Maj, 53, after serv in Pac Div, MATS, Hawaii; Lt Col (Ret), Air Force Res, 69; Distinguished Flying Cross; Air Medal with three Oak Leaf Clusters; Nat Serv Defense Medal; Can Vol Serv Medal with Maple Leaf Clasp; Res Medal. Mem: Life mem, Child & Family Serv; charter mem, Hawaii Planned Parenthood; Health & Community Serv Coun of Hawaii (mem bd, 72-, pres, 74-); Am Judicature Soc; Am Bar Asn (chmn family law comt, 74-). Relig: Protestant. Legal Res: Apt 707 2877 Kalakaua Ave Honolulu HI 96815 Mailing Add: Suite 410 735 Bishop St Honolulu HI 96813

RICE, WALTER LYMAN (R)
s Carl J Rice & Milda Orfield R; m 1960 to Inger Vestergaard; c Lisa Milda & John Eric. Educ: Univ Minn, BA; Harvard Law Sch, LLB; Phi Beta Kappa; Sigma Delta Chi; Chi Phi. Polit & Govt Pos: Spec asst to US Attorney Gen; US Ambassador to Australia, 69-73. Bus & Prof Pos: Prosecuting attorney, US Dist Court, NY; gen counsel, Reynolds Metals Co, 41, vpres & dir, 42, pres, Reynolds Mining Corp, 43; pres, Caribbean Steamship Co, Reynolds Haitian Mines, Guianan Mines & Lydford Enterprises, Inc, 44-68; chmn policy comt, US CofC, 65-66, dir, 60-69, vpres, 67-69. Publ: Drafted Fed Anti-Racketeering Act for Cong, 34. Mem: Country Club of Va; Harvard Club; Cong Country Club. Mailing Add: 1000 Old Lock Lane Lock Island Richmond VA 23226

RICH, JOE LYNN (D)
b Wellington, Tex, May 12, 24; s Otto Brian Rich & Allie Green R; m 1945 to Linda Margaret McGee; c Mark William, Lynn Brian, Alison & Jody. Educ: North Tex State Univ, 40-42; Univ Tex, Austin, BS in Archit, 51. Polit & Govt Pos: Dem precinct chmn, Dallas Co, Tex, 56-66; city councilman, Irving, 57-59; chmn, Dallas Co Dem Party, formerly; deleg, Dem Nat Conv, 68. Bus & Prof Pos: Partner, Wright-Rich & Assoc, Architects, 54- Mil Serv: Entered as Aviation Cadet, Navy, 42, released as Lt Comdr, 54, after serv in 211, 201 & 48 Patrol Squadron, S Am & Korea, 42-54. Mem: Am Inst of Architects; Construction Specifications

Inst (pres, Dallas Chap, 63). Relig: Presbyterian. Legal Res: 1500 Colony Dr Irving TX 75060 Mailing Add: 2727 Cedar Springs Dallas TX 75201

RICH, KERRY (D)
Ala State Rep
Mailing Add: Rte 12 Gadsden AL 35901

RICH, WAYNE SCHERMERHORN (R)
NH State Rep
b Bridgewater, Maine, Mar 30, 12; s Nathan Harold Rich & Myrtle Schermerhorn R; m 1937 to Caroline Toole; c Harold T, Margaret (Mrs Rapp), Virginia (Mrs Augustini), Barbara (Mrs Merriman), Judith C & Christine. Educ: Univ Maine, Orono, BS in Agr Chem, 34, grad work, 34-35; Cornell Univ, 49; Univ NH, 65-67; Alpha Zeta; Phi Kappa Phi; Alpha Gamma Rho. Polit & Govt Pos: NH State Rep, Ward Five, Dist 18, 73-, mem, State Inst Comt, NH House Rep, currently, chmn, State Hosp Subcomt, currently; Merrimack Co Deleg Exec Comt, 75-; Merrimack Co Exten Serv Coun, 75- Bus & Prof Pos: Asst exten ed, Maine Coop Exten Serv, Orono, 34-35, co 4-H agent, Lewiston, 35-46 & NH Coop Exten Serv, Concord, 46-69; adv bd, Salvation Army, Concord Area, 73- Publ: Ed, Nonagon, Bull of NH Numismatic Asn, 63- Mem: NH Numismatic Asn (corresponding secy & ed, 63-); NH Collectors Club (corresponding secy, 60-); Merrimack Co 4-H Found (dir, 72-); hon mem Merrimack Co 4-H Adv Coun. Honors & Awards: Distinguished Serv, Nat 4-H Club Agents Asn, 55; Spec Award for Outstanding Serv, New Eng Numismatic Asn, 71. Relig: Protestant. Legal Res: 11 South St Concord NH 03301 Mailing Add: Box 391 Concord NH 03301

RICHARD, BARRY SCOTT (D)
Fla State Rep
b Miami Beach, Fla, Mar 28, 42; s Melvin J Richard & Janet Shecter R; m 1967 to Margaret Sokal; c Todd. Educ: Univ Miami, AB, 64, JD, 67; Phi Delta Phi; Omicron Delta Kappa. Polit & Govt Pos: Asst attorney gen, Fla, 71-72, dep attorney gen, 72-74; Fla State Rep, 74- Bus & Prof Pos: Attorney, currently. Mil Serv: Entered as Lt(jg), Navy, 68, released as Lt, 70, after serv in Judge Adv Gen Corps, Naval Hosp, Oakland, Calif; Spec Commendation. Relig: Jewish. Legal Res: 4714 SW 67th Ave Miami FL 33155 Mailing Add: PO Box 557395 Miami FL 33155

RICHARD, GRAHAM ARTHUR (D)
Ind State Sen
b Cleveland, Ohio, Jan 1, 47; s Arthur C Richard & Anne Stillings R; m 1970 to Beverly Anne Quandt; c Heather Anne. Educ: Princeton Univ, BA, 69. Polit & Govt Pos: Ind State Sen, 75- Bus & Prof Pos: Teacher, Bishop Dwenger High Sch, 69-70; legis asst, Ind House Rep, 71; admin asst, Ind State Supt Pub Instr, 71-72; independent educ consult, 72- Legal Res: 3319 S Harrison St Ft Wayne IN 46807 Mailing Add: 927 S Harrison St Ft Wayne IN 46802

RICHARDS, FRANK F (R)
NH State Rep
Mailing Add: Great Bay Dr Greenland NH 03840

RICHARDS, GEORGE LAMONT (R)
Utah State Rep
b Salt Lake City, Utah, Jan 17, 18; s LeGrand Richards & Ina Ashton R; m 1941 to Edna Fae Firmage; c G LaMont, Jr, Charlotte R (Mrs Harrison), John Lawrence & Shauna Fae. Educ: Univ Colo, Boulder, 43; Northwestern Univ, Midn Sch, 44; Univ Utah, BS, 46; Pi Kappa Alpha. Polit & Govt Pos: Utah State Rep, 74- Mil Serv: Entered as Yeoman 3/C, Navy, 42, released as Lt, after serv in Amphibious Training Command, Pac, 44-46; Lt, Naval Res. Publ: Auth, LeGrand Richards Speaks, Deseret News Press, 71. Mem: Salt Lake Country Club; Alta Club; Balboa Bay Club; Indian Wells Country Club. Relig: Latter-day Saint. Mailing Add: 2315 E 13th South St Salt Lake City UT 84108

RICHARDS, HAROLD LELAND (D)
b Port Hope, Mich, Mar 7, 08; s Lewis James Richards & Emma Anderson R; m 1930 to Blanche I McNair; c Robert R, Donald B, Mary Lou (Mrs Lively) & Marjorie Ann (Mrs Nilsen). Educ: Port Hope High Sch, 23-27. Polit & Govt Pos: Former cand for Co Register of Deeds, 77th Dist Mich State Rep & Huron Co Clerk, Mich; mem exec bd, Econ Opportunity Agency; mem, Huron Co Planning Comn; membership chmn, Huron Co Dem Party, 53-64, chmn, formerly; councilman & city comnr, Harbor Beach, 64-66; deleg, Mich Dem State Conv, 65, 67, 68 & 70; mem exec comt, Sheltered Workshop & Finance Comt, Huron Co Comt on Polit Educ; Thumb Area, AFL-CIO Coun, chmn, currently; cand, Mich State Rep, 77th Dist, 70-72; committeeman, Eighth Dist Dem Steering Comt, 71- Bus & Prof Pos: Crew Leader, Hercules, Inc, formerly, retired, 73. Mem: UAW (vpres & chmn ins comt & community serv comt, Local 812, 71-73); Harbor Beach Community Fed Credit Union, (vpres, 71-72, pres, 73-); Huron AFL-CIO Coun, (secy, 66-); hon life mem Huron Co Hist Soc (vpres, 71-72, pres, 73-). Honors & Awards: Huron Co Dem Party Award, 68. Relig: Reorganized Latter-day Saint; Presiding minister, Harbor Beach Reorganized Church of Jesus Christ of Latter-day Saints; chmn brochure comt, church sch dir, Eastern Mich Dist, 72-73. Mailing Add: 233 S Third St Harbor Beach MI 48441

RICHARDS, PAMELA JANE
b Joliet, Ill, Apr 6, 48; d Robert John Richards & Betty Todd R; single. Educ: Northern Ill Univ, 66-71; Sigma Kappa. Polit & Govt Pos: Admin asst to US Rep William H Harsha, Ohio, Sixth Dist, 71- Mailing Add: 2024 Peach Orchard Dr Falls Church VA 22043

RICHARDS, PAUL THOMAS (D)
Mont State Rep
b Helena, Mont, July 27, 54; s Jerrold Reeves Richards & Belle Calkins R; m 1974 to JoAnne Jordan. Educ: Univ Mont, 72-73; Evergreen State Col, 73-74. Polit & Govt Pos: Mont State Rep, Dist 32, 75- Bus & Prof Pos: Page, Mont State Senate, 69; janitor, 70-71; musician, 71-72; appliance delivery, Cummins Elec, 72-73; research assoc, Thurston Regional Planning Coun, Olympia, Wash, 74; auto body repairman, 74- Publ: Co-auth, White Is, Grove Press, 70; plus many news arts in Mont periodicals. Mem: Common Cause; Am Civil Liberties Union; Mont Wilderness Asn; Northern Plains Resource Coun. Honors & Awards: Honors Scholars, Univ Mont, 72-74; Youngest Appointee, Mont Adv Coun Children & Youth; Youngest Appointee, State Supt Drug Educ Consortium; Youngest Legislator in US. Mailing Add: 1002 Wilder Helena MT 59601

RICHARDS, RICHARD (R)
b Ogden, Utah, May 14, 32; s Blaine Boyden Richards & Violet G Williams R; m 1954 to Annette Bott; c Julie, Richard Albert, Jan & Amy. Educ: Univ Utah, JD. Polit & Govt Pos: Chmn, Utah Young Rep, 60-61; admin asst to US Rep Laurance J Burton, Utah, 63-64; former chmn, Utah Rep State Cent Comt; mem, Rep Nat Comt, dep chmn, 71-73; deleg, Rep Nat Conv, 68 & 72. Mil Serv: Entered as Pvt, Army, 52, released as 2nd Lt, 55. Mem: Am Bar Asn. Honors & Awards: Utah Jaycee Award, 68; Outstanding Young Man of Utah, 68. Relig: Latter-day Saint. Mailing Add: 4753 Madison Ave Ogden UT 84403

RICHARDS, WILLIAM LOUIS (R)
Mem, Rep State Cent Comt Nev
b Houston, Tex, Dec 21, 22; s John Donald Richards & Katherine Phillips R; m 1969 to Margie Ann Grosskopf; c Lynn Anne (Mrs Davis), Laura Catherine (Mrs Crum) & William L, Jr. Educ: Col of the Sacred Heart, Victoriaville PQ, 39; Kings Col, Oxford Univ, 40-41; Southern Methodist Univ Sch Law, LLB, 50; Phi Alpha Delta; Phi Eta Sigma; Psi Chi; Kappa Sigma. Polit & Govt Pos: Deleg, Rep Nat Conv, 48, 56 & 64, alt deleg, 72; mem, Rep State Cent Comt Nev, currently, state conv chmn, 74; mem, Nev Comn Crime, Delinquency & Corrections, currently; Bus & Prof Pos: Pvt law practice, Dallas/Houston, Tex, 49-66; judiciary, 68- Mil Serv: Pilot Off, Royal Air Force, 41-43; Flying Off, US Army Air Corps, 44-46, serv in Fifth Air Force Far East; Capt, Air Force, 51-53, serv in 18th Air Force, Korean Conflict; Brit Distinguished Serv Order, Distinguished Flying Cross, Air Force Cross, Maltese Cross; Am Soldiers Medal, Three Distinguished Flying Crosses; five Air Medals. Mem: State Bar of Tex; Am Bar Asn; Mil Order World Wars. Relig: Anglican. Mailing Add: Nevada Supreme Court Bldg Carson City NV 89701

RICHARDS, WILLIAM SIDNEY (R)
Mem, Marin Co Rep Cent Comt, Calif
b San Jose, Calif, Nov 22, 10; s Charles M Richards, MD & Alice Rodgers R; m 1947 to Emily White; c William S, III, James E, John R & Cynthia A. Educ: Stanford Univ, AB, 31, MBA, 38; Kappa Alpha. Polit & Govt Pos: Mem, Marin Co Rep Cent Comt, Calif, 67-; mem, Calif Rep State Cent Comt, 69-74. Mil Serv: Army, 31-61, Col (Ret), after serv in ETO, 45, Far East Command, 52-55, & US, 31-44, 46-52 & 55-61; Bronze Star Medal; Army Commendation Medal with Oak Leaf Cluster. Mem: Asn of the US Army. Relig: Protestant. Mailing Add: 118 Linden Lane San Rafael CA 94901

RICHARDSON, BOBBY HAROLD (D)
Ky State Rep
b Barren Co, Ky, Nov 25, 44; s Robert E Richardson & Nina Tucker R; m 1970 to Elaine Alexander. Educ: Western Ky Univ, BA, 65; Univ Ky, JD, 68; Delta Theta Phi. Polit & Govt Pos: Master Comnr, Barren Co, Ky, 68-72; Ky State Rep, 72- Bus & Prof Pos: Dir, First Fed Savings & Loan Asn, Glasgow, Ky, 69- Mem: Ky Bar Asn; Glasgow Lions; Barren Co Farm Bur. Relig: Baptist. Legal Res: Rte 7 Glasgow KY 42141 Mailing Add: 117 E Washington St Glasgow KY 42141

RICHARDSON, DAVID P, JR (D)
Pa State Rep
Mailing Add: Capitol Bldg Harrisburg PA 17120

RICHARDSON, DON WENDELL (D)
Miss State Rep
Mailing Add: Box 9332 Jackson MS 39206

RICHARDSON, ELEANOR L (D)
Ga State Rep
Mailing Add: 755 Park Lane Decatur GA 30033

RICHARDSON, ELLIOT LEE (R)
US Ambassador to Great Britain
b Boston, Mass, July 20, 20; s Edward P Richardson (deceased) & Clara Shattuck R (deceased); m 1952 to Anne Francis Hazard; c Henry Shattuck, Anne Hazard & Michael Elliot. Educ: Harvard Col, AB, cum laude, 41; Harvard Law Sch, LLB, cum laude, 47. Polit & Govt Pos: Asst to Sen Leverett Saltonstall, Mass, 53-54; asst to Gov Christian A Herter, 55-56; asst secy for legis, US Dept Health, Educ & Welfare, 57-59, acting secy, 58; US Attorney for Mass, 59-61; spec asst to the Attorney Gen, US, 61; Lt Gov, Mass, 65-67; Attorney Gen, Mass, 67-69; Under Secy of State, 69-70; Secy of Health, Educ & Welfare, 70-73; Secy of Defense, 73; Attorney Gen of US, 73; US Ambassador to Great Britain, 75- Bus & Prof Pos: Assoc, Ropes, Gray, Best, Coolidge & Rugg, Law Firm, 49-53 & 54-56; lectr law, Harvard Law Sch, 52; partner, Ropes & Gray, 61-62 & 63-64. Mil Serv: Entered as Pvt, Army, 42, released as 1st Lt, 45, after serv in Fourth Inf Div, ETO; Bronze Star Medal; Purple Heart with Oak Leaf Cluster; Combat Med Badge; ETO Medal with Five Battle Stars. Publ: Poisoned politics, Atlantic Monthly, 61; Judicial intervention in the civil rights movement, Boston Univ Law Rev, 66; Responsibility and responsiveness: the HEW potential for the seventies, 72; plus others. Mem: Fed, Mass & Am Bar Asns; Harvard Col (mem bd overseers, 68-70); Am Acad Arts & Sci. Relig: Unitarian. Legal Res: Brookline MA Mailing Add: Dept of State Washington DC 20521

RICHARDSON, EUGENE ALLISON (R)
Comnr, Linn Co, Ore
b Turpin, Okla, May 9, 24; s C Lester Richardson & Evelyn Tina Solano R; m 1954 to Elizabeth Ann Workman; c Cindy Ann, Lori Carol & Cheri Lynn. Educ: Herbert Hoover High Sch, Glendale, Calif. Polit & Govt Pos: Mem, Rep Party Precinct Comt, Ore, 62-64; comnr, Linn Co, 69- Mil Serv: Entered as MM 3/C, Navy, 42, released as MM 2/C, 46, after serv in 98th Construction Bn, S Pac; reenlisted CD 2/C, 50-51, Korea. Mem: Elks; Mason; Am Legion, (past comdr, Post 10, Albany, Ore); Beaver Boys State Chmn for Albany; DeMolay (Dad Adv). Relig: Presbyterian. Mailing Add: 1615 S Sherman Albany OR 97321

RICHARDSON, EVELYN D (D)
Mem, Dem Nat Comt, Pa
Mailing Add: 6908 Kedron St Pittsburgh PA 15204

RICHARDSON, H L (BILL) (R)
Calif State Sen
b Terre Haute, Ind, 1927; m to Barbara Budrow; c Laurie, Carrie & Doug. Educ: Olympic Col; Cornish Conserv, Seattle, Advert Degree. Polit & Govt Pos: Mem, Calif Rep Assembly, United Rep Calif & Rep State Cent Comt; Calif State Sen, 67-; Minority Whip, Calif State Senate, currently, vchmn elec & reapportionment comt, mem agr & water resources, educ, revenue & taxation comts & select comt on penal insts, currently; mem, Rep State Cent Comt Calif, currently. Bus & Prof Pos: Graphic arts & advert bus, formerly. Mil Serv: Naval Air Force, 46. Publ: Slightly to the Right. Mem: Nat Riflemen's Asn (bd dirs); Safari Club. Honors

& Awards: Outstanding Legislator Award, Calif Dist Attorneys Asn, Calif Correctional Officers Asn & Calif Southern Coun of Conservation Clubs, 68, 70 & 72; George Washington Award, Freedom Found Valley Forge. Mailing Add: 735 W Duarte Rd Arcadia CA 91006

RICHARDSON, HENRY BOYD (R)
NH State Rep
b Johnstown, SC, Apr 6, 17; s Thomas Richardson (deceased) & Elvira Jones R; m 1950 to Katherine Albright; c Gale Renney, Portia Lee & Eric Boyd. Educ: Baldwin-Wallace Conservatory of Music, Berea, Ohio, 36-37; Wilberforce Univ, BS, 43; Warton Am Tech Sch, 46; Alpha Phi Alpha; pres, Scroller Club, Kappa Alpha Psi; Spectators Club of Arts. Polit & Govt Pos: NH State Rep, 75-, mem, Educ Claims Comt & Vet & Mil Affairs Comts, NH House Rep, 75- Mil Serv: Entered as Pvt, Army, 42, released as Maj, 73, after serv in Ord Corp, ETO, Far East Command & Vietnam Command, 44-70; Legion of Merit; Meritorious Serv; Bronze Star; Air Medal; Army Commendation Medals; Korean Expeditionary Medal; Presidential Unit Citation; Korean Presidential Unit Citation; Good Conduct Medal with Seven Claspknots; plus 13 other serv medals covering three wars. Mem: F&AM (Asst Dept Grand Master, Paris, France, 66-); Lions Int (health officer, Greenville, NH, 74-); Nashua Voc-Tech Col (mem craft comt, 74-); NH Adv Coun for Voc-Tech Educ; Am Judicature Soc. Honors & Awards: First Black ever elected to the NH Gen Court. Relig: Protestant. Mailing Add: PO Box 154 Greenville NH 03048

RICHARDSON, JAMES M (R)
Chmn, Cumberland Co Rep Comt, Maine
b New York, NY, Oct 4, 40; s Donald S Richardson & Evelyn Lafferty R; single. Educ: Franklin & Marshall Col, BA, 63; Colgate Univ, 73-74. Polit & Govt Pos: Finance chmn, Cumberland Co Rep Comt, Maine, 70-73; field dir, Monks for US Sen Comt, 71-72; exec dir, Maine finance comt to Re-elect the President, 72; mem, Maine State Rep Comt, 72-74; chmn, Cumberland Co Rep Comt, 74- Bus & Prof Pos: Teacher & adminr, North Yarmouth Acad, Maine, 64-67; pres, J M R Corp, Cumberland, 67-71; registered rep, Hornblower & Weeks Hemphill, Noyes, 72- Mem: Rep Co Chmn Asn; Muscular Dystrophy Asn (bd dir, 74-). Mailing Add: 15 Mill Ridge Rd Cumberland Center ME 04021

RICHARDSON, JOHN, JR (R)
Asst Secy for Educ & Cultural Affairs, Dept of State
b Boston, Mass, Feb 4, 21; s John Richardson & Hope Hemenway R; m to Thelma Ingram; c Eva (Mrs Karoly Selek Teleki), Teren, Hope H, Bonnie Catherine & Hetty L. Educ: Harvard Col, BA cum laude, 43, Harvard Law Sch, LLB, 49. Polit & Govt Pos: Asst Secy for Educ & Cultural Affairs, Dept of State, 69-, Acting Asst Secy for Pub Affairs, 71- Bus & Prof Pos: Attorney-at-law, Sullivan & Cromwell, 49-55; assoc & partner, Paine, Webber, Jackson & Curtis, 57-61; pres, Free Europe, Inc, New York, 61-68. Mil Serv: Entered as Lt, Army, 43, released as Capt, after serv in 17th Airborne Div, Parachute Artil, ETO, 43-46; Bronze Star. Publ: Chap, In: Peace and War in the Modern Age, Doubleday & Co, 65. Mem: New York Bar Asn; Coun on For Rels; Int Rescue Comt (bd, 57-61 & 68-69); For Policy Asn (bd, 58-68); NAACP. Legal Res: McLean VA Mailing Add: Rm 6218 Dept of State Washington DC 20520

RICHARDSON, MABEL LOWE (R)
NH State Rep
b Randolph, NH; d Thaddeus Sobiesky Lowe & Frances Hinds Jenkins L; m to Herbert Randall Richardson; c Dr Edwin H & Dwight B. Educ: Univ NH, summer credits; Keene State Col, summer credits. Polit & Govt Pos: NH State Rep, 47-48 & 68-, during interim served in every app position within NH Gen Court; chairwoman, NH Rep State Comt, formerly; mem, Legis Coun, currently; mem exec comt, Coos Co, currently; sponsor, Search & Rescue Bill for protection of persons lost in White Mountains of NH; mem, Coos Co Finance Comt, currently; serving on Land Appraisal for State of NH, currently. Bus & Prof Pos: Pub rels consult, 36-69. Mem: Jefferson Ctr Higher Learning (trustee); Grange; Am Legion Auxiliary; Rebekah; 4-H Club. Relig: Protestant. Mailing Add: Randolph NH 03593

RICHARDSON, RAY (R)
Ind State Rep
Mailing Add: 103 Walnut St Greenfield IN 46140

RICHARDSON, TRUMAN (D)
b Ardmore, Okla, Feb 10, 27; s J W Richardson & Pauline Hendricks; single. Educ: Univ Okla, BA, MA; George Washington Univ; Phi Beta Kappa; Phi Eta Sigma; Sigma Delta Chi. Polit & Govt Pos: Admin asst to US Rep Tom Steed, Okla, 54- Bus & Prof Pos: Former city ed, Shawnee News-Star; instr hist & jour, Okla Baptist Univ, 53-54; spec lectr hist, 63. Relig: Methodist. Legal Res: 502 N Aydelotte Shawnee OK 74801 Mailing Add: 2037 N Kensington Arlington VA 22205

RICHARDSON, WILLIAM ALLEN, JR (D)
Tenn State Rep
b Culleoka, Tenn, Mar 20, 32; s William Allen Richardson, Sr & Alvy Holt R; m 1953 to Peggy Belle Ashburn; c Allen, Joy, Brett, Stanley, Rene, Carlton, Amy & Logan. Educ: Tenn Technol Univ, BS, 54; Harding Grad Sch Relig, MA, 62. Polit & Govt Pos: Tenn State Rep, 64th Dist, 74- Bus & Prof Pos: Civil engr, Tenn Valley Authority, Maps & Surv Div, 54-55; missionary, Church of Christ Mission, Korea, 58-71; surveyor, Southern Land & Assocs, 72- Mil Serv: Entered as 2nd Lt, Army, 55, released as 1st Lt, 58, after serv in 51st Signal Bn, 8th Army, 57-58. Mem: Am Col Surveyors of Tenn; Farm Bur; Civitan Club; JOUAM. Relig: Church of Christ. Mailing Add: Rte 2 Culleoka TN 38451

RICHER, STEPHEN BRUCE (D)
b Newark, NJ, Aug 18, 46; s Seymour Albert Richer & Rosalind Greenberg R. Educ: Princeton Univ, AB, 68; secy & trustee, Circle K; ed-in-chief, Princeton Yearbook. Polit & Govt Pos: Chmn, Morris Co Young Citizens for Johnson, NJ, 64; pres, Princeton Univ Young Dem, 66-67; nat chmn, Students for Robert F Kennedy, 67-68; coun cand, Randolph Twp, NJ, 68, councilman, currently; registr chmn, Morris Co Dem Orgn, 69; cand, NJ State Assemblyman, Dist 10-A, 69; chmn, NJ Young People for Williams, 70; pres, NJ Young Dem, 70-72; mem, NJ State Dem Policy Coun, 70-71; pres, Randolph Twp Dem Club, 71; mem nat comt, Young Dem Clubs of Am, 70-72; chmn, Randolph Twp Dem Comt, 71-72; chmn, Morris Co Mayor's Ball, 72; chmn, Randolph Twp Redistricting Comt, 72-73; chmn, Morris Co Dem Comt, NJ, 72-75; dep dir, NJ Am Revolution Bicentennial Comn, currently. Bus & Prof Pos: Teacher, Newark Pub Schs, NJ, 68-69; acct mgr, NJ Bell Tel Co, 69-70; field rep, Tailored Tours of Trenton, 70-74. Mem: Dover Kiwanis Club (vpres, 71-73 & pres, 73-74); Jaycees; Urban League; Boy Scouts; Princeton Club of NY. Honors & Awards: Amvets Nat Scholarship; Degree of Distinction, Nat Forensic League; German Lang Award; Eagle Scout; Elks Leadership Award. Relig: Jewish. Mailing Add: 7 Farview Ave Randolph NJ 07801

RICHERT, CAROL CLOUSER (D)
b Cleveland, Ohio, Aug 28, 40; d John Burton Clouser & Mary Kerekes C; m 1965 to Kent David Richert; c Kristen Tsehai, Colene Lishan, David Andreas & Karen Justine. Educ: Mt Union Col, BA, 62; Univ Iowa, 67. Polit & Govt Pos: Chairperson, Bonneville Co Dem Women Club, Idaho, 70-71; precinct committeeperson, Bonneville Co Dem Cent Comt, 70-72, chairperson, formerly. Mailing Add: 715 Terrace Dr Idaho Falls ID 83401

RICHEY, THOMAS BRUCE (R)
Ariz State Rep
b San Benito, Tex, Oct 31, 19; s McMurry Richey & Ruby Smith R; m 1945 to Barbara Jane Samuelson; c Leslie Jane & Philip McMurry. Educ: Tex A&M Univ, BS, 41; Cavalry Sch, 42; Army Aviation Sch, 55; Signal Officer Advan Course, 58; US Army Command & Gen Staff Col, 60; US Air War Col, 65; George Washington Univ, MSIA, 65. Polit & Govt Pos: Ariz State Rep, Dist Nine, 73- Bus & Prof Pos: Mgr, Western Wool & Mohair Co, San Angelo, Tex, 45-48; area mgr, Kaman Sci Corp, Sierra Vista, Ariz, 69-70; asst mgr develop, Lockheed Electronics Co, Tucson, 70-72. Mil Serv: Entered as 2nd Lt, Army, 41, retired as Col, 68, after serv in 12th Cavalry Regt, 1st Cavalry Div, US, Australia, New Guinea, Philippines & Japan, 41-45, US, Korea & Japan, 48-61, Joint Chiefs of Staff & Co Off, 11th Signal Group, 62-68; two Legion of Merits; three Bronze Star Medals; two Air Medals; Joint Serv Commendation Medal; Combat Inf Badge; Sr Army Aviator; Joint Chiefs of Staff Badge. Publ: Auth of many articles in sch publ & acad papers. Mem: Sierra Vista CofC; Indust Develop Corp (bd dirs, 69-); Ariz Tuberc & Respiratory Disease Asn; Rotary Int; Ariz Bicentennial Comn. Relig: Methodist. Legal Res: Santa Cruz Co AZ Mailing Add: PO Box 1941 Sierra Vista AZ 85635

RICHMOND, FREDERICK W (D)
US Rep, NY
b Mattapan, Mass, Nov 15, 23; c William. Educ: Harvard Univ, 42-43; Boston Univ, BA, 45. Polit & Govt Pos: Pres, Gtr New York Urban League, 59-64; New York City Taxi & Limousine Comnr, 70-72; New York City Human Rights Comnr, 64-70; councilman, City Council, New York, 73-75, mem coun finance, state legis, indust rels & charter & govt opers comts, 73-74; US Rep, NY, 75- Bus & Prof Pos: Chmn, Nat Urban League Equal Opportunity Conf, 55; chmn bd, Carnegie Hall Corp, 60-; chmn bd, Walco Nat Corp, 60-; budget dir, NY State Coun Arts, 65-74; founder, Brooklyn Businessmen's Comt for Employ Ex-Offenders, 72- Mil Serv: Navy, 43-45, Radioman 3/C, Pac Theatre. Legal Res: 43 Pierrepont St Brooklyn NY 11201 Mailing Add: US House Rep Washington DC 20515

RICHMOND, LINDELL BRUCE (D)
Ill State Rep
b Williamson Co, Ill, Oct 17, 20; s John Moore Richmond & Dottie Martin R; m 1941 to LaCleeta Maude Patterson; c Randall B, Michael P & Susan K (Mrs David Stover). Educ: Fed Art Sch, Minneapolis, 37-38; Southern Ill Univ, Carbondale, 39-40. Polit & Govt Pos: Alderman, Murphysboro City Govt, 57-70, mayor, 70-75; Ill State Rep, Dist 58, 75- Bus & Prof Pos: Co-owner, Artcraft Sign Serv, 46- Mil Serv: A/S, Naval Res, 43-45. Mem: Hon life mem Elks; Eagles; Moose; AFL-CIO. Honors & Awards: State pres, Ill Elks Asn, 63; Man of Year, Murphysboro CofC, 72. Relig: Presbyterian. Mailing Add: 404 S 20th St Murphysboro IL 62966

RICHMOND, RONALD R (RON) (R)
Fla State Rep
Mailing Add: 1205 Park Dr New Port Richey FL 33552

RICHTER, ANNE THORBECK (DFL)
Assoc Chairperson, Senate Dist Ten Dem-Farmer-Labor Party, Minn
b Churches' Ferry, NDak, June 15, 11; d George Thorbeck & Synneva Erie T; m 1940 to Paul Richter; c Mary Ann, Paulette, Philip & Paul. Educ: Univ Minn, St Paul, BSEd, 37; Gamma Omicron Beta. Polit & Govt Pos: Secy, Wadena Co Dem Party, Minn, 50-55, chairwoman, 55-65 & 70-71; deleg, Dem State Conv, 52-; vchairwoman, Seventh Dist Dem-Farmer-Labor Party, 64-68, assoc chairperson, 71-74; deleg, Dem Nat Conv, 68 & 72; vol state chmn, Gov Wendell Anderson Campaign, 74; assoc chairperson, Senate Dist Ten Dem-Farmer-Labor Party, currently; mem, Community Corrections Bd Wadena & Todd Co, 74- Bus & Prof Pos: Teacher home econ, Barnesville, Minn, 37-38; home supvr, Farm Security Admin, Fergus Falls, Minn, 38-39; state 4-H staff, Univ Minn Exten Serv, 39-40; dist home mgt supvr, Farm Security Admin, Brainerd, 40-42; spec teacher, Wadena High Sch, 66-69. Mem: Wadena Housing & Redevelop Authority (secy); Am Red Cross (vol consult, 70); Fergus Falls Community Col (adv bd, 71-). Honors & Awards: Girl Scout Thanks Badge, 52; Univ Minn Alumni Serv Award, 63; Outstanding 4-H Alumni Award, Minn, 65; Community Serv Award, Wadena CofC, 72. Relig: Catholic. Mailing Add: 415 Seventh St SW Wadena MN 56482

RICKELS, JUDON (R)
Chmn, Dickens Co Rep Party, Tex
b Spur, Tex, Aug 12, 31; s Mardist Adrian Rickels & Marguerite Aston R; m 1953 to Patsy Parks; c Brent Parks & Julie. Educ: Baylor Univ, BBA, 52, MA in econ, 53. Polit & Govt Pos: Chmn, Dickens Co Rep Party, Tex, 70-; councilman, Spur, 70- Bus & Prof Pos: Owner, Rickels Motor Co, Spur, Tex, currently. Mem: Mason. Relig: Methodist. Legal Res: 1023 W Third St Spur TX 79370 Mailing Add: PO Box 666 Spur TX 79370

RICKENBACH, JOEL (R)
SDak State Rep
Mailing Add: Oelrichs SD 57763

RICKENBACKER, WILLIAM FROST (INDEPENDENT)
b Beverly Hills, Calif, Mar 16, 28; s Capt Eddie Rickenbacker & Adelaide Frost R; m 1955 to Alexandra Harriman Leys, div, 73; c James Edward & Thomas; m 1973 to Carroll Lee Douglass. Educ: Harvard Univ, AB cum laude, 49. Polit & Govt Pos: Mem State Exec Comt, Conservative Party, NY, 62-73. Bus & Prof Pos: Research analyst, Smith, Barney & Co, 55-58; invest adv, 58-61; sr ed, Nat Rev, 61-69; mem ed adv bd, Mod Age & Relig & Soc & ed, Rickenbacker Report, currently; pres, Rickenbacker Report Corp & Rickenbacker Enterprises, Inc, 69-; publ, Financial Book Digest, 71- Mil Serv: Entered as Aviation Cadet, Air Force, 51, released as 1st Lt, 55, after serv in various air transport units including continental US, Europe & Korea, 52-53; Air Medal with clusters; UN Theater Ribbon; Korean Ribbon. Publ: Wooden Nickels, 66 & Death of the Dollar, 68, Arlington; ed, The

Twelve Year Sentence, 73; plus others. Mem: Philadelphia Soc; Spec Interests (exec secy); Stephen Decatur Soc; Am-African Affairs Asn. Honors & Awards: First place, Nat Steinway Piano Competition, 35; Westchester Jr Champion golf, 48-49; co-medalist, New Eng Intercollegiate Golf Championship, 49. Relig: Congregational. Mailing Add: Box 1000 Briarcliff Manor NY 10501

RICKENBAKER, DUDLEY GENE (R)
Mem Exec Comt, SC Rep Party
b St Matthews, SC, Feb 6, 41; s Charlie Dudley Rickenbaker & Margaret Crider R; m 1963 to Mary Kaye Thomas; c Vonda Kaye & Christie Kaye. Educ: Univ SC, BS, 63, Law Sch, JD, 66; Phi Alpha Delta. Polit & Govt Pos: Asst US attorney, Dist SC, Dept Justice, 70-71; exec asst for legal affairs, Gov Off, SC, 75-; mem exec comt, SC Rep Party, 75- Bus & Prof Pos: Partner, Rogers, Riggs & Rickenbaker, Attorneys-at-law, Sumter, SC, 72-75. Mil Serv: Entered as 1st Lt, Air Force, released as Capt, 70, after serv in 363rd Combat Serv Group, Tactical Air Command; Capt, Air Force Res, 71-; Air Force Commendation Medal; Outstanding Young Judge Adv, 9th Air Force. Mem: Am & SC Bar Asns; Mason, Izlar Lodge 177; Am Legion; Sumter Co Unit Am Cancer Soc (bd dirs). Relig: Baptist. Mailing Add: 514 Mattison Ave Sumter SC 29150

RICKERT, FLORENCE EVELYN (D)
Chairperson, Grundy Co Dem Party, Iowa
b Luverne, Minn, Aug 13, 14; d Herman August Rickert & Emma Ella Karlsen D; single. Educ: High sch, Worthington, Minn, grad, 31. Polit & Govt Pos: Precinct woman, Reinbeck, Blackhawk Twp, Iowa, 62-; vchmn, Grundy Co Dem Party, 68-72, chairperson, 72-; advocator welfare answering serv, 74-75. Bus & Prof Pos: Bookkeeper, Reinbeck Motor Co, Iowa, 60-64, Culligan Softwater Serv, 60-71 & Del Williams Ford-Mercury, Inc, 71-72. Mem: Bus & Prof Women's Club; Eastern Star (treas); Am Legion Auxiliary; White Shrine of Jerusalem; Grundy Co Farm Bur (twp chmn). Relig: United Church of Christ; Sunday Sch Teacher, currently. Mailing Add: 208 Clark St Reinbeck IA 50669

RICKERT, ROBERT TAYLOR (DFL)
Chmn, Jackson Co Dem-Farmer-Labor Party, Minn
b Rupert, Idaho, Feb 13, 16; s Fred Rickert & Florence E Taylor R; m 1941 to Hilda M Ackermann; c Judith Ann, Leslie Robert & Marvin LeRoy. Educ: Lakefield High Sch, 2 years. Polit & Govt Pos: Chmn, Jackson Co Dem-Farmer-Labor Party, Minn, 67-, chmn, Jackson Co Housing & Develop. Bus & Prof Pos: Farmer, 40- Mem: Farmers Exchange; Double H Local; Post Local; Jackson Co Lakes & Rivers Asn (pub rels dir, 72-); Minn Farmers Union (secy, 72-); Lutheran Laymens League (dist chmn). Relig: Lutheran. Mailing Add: RFD 3 Okabena MN 56161

RICKETTS, LIESE L (D)
b Ger, Mar 17, 20; d John Borchardt & Anna Braeger B; m 1948 to William C Ricketts; c Liese Palao & William C, Jr. Educ: Lutheran High Sch, Milwaukee, 38; Univ Chicago, PhB, 43. Polit & Govt Pos: Deleg, Dem Nat Conv, 72; cand for twp supvr, Crete Twp, 73. Mem: UN of Ill (bd dirs); Welfare Coun of Chicago (adv bd); League of Women Voters (bd dirs); Eastern Will Co Dem (secy). Relig: Catholic. Mailing Add: Nacke Rd Crete IL 60417

RICKMAN, HERBERT PAUL (D)
Exec VChmn, New York City Dem Comt
b New York, NY, July 31, 31; s Louis Rickman & Ida Greenfield R; single. Educ: NY Univ, BA, 51, LLB, 54. Polit & Govt Pos: Spec asst to US Attorney, Southern Dist NY, 61-62; exec asst to state chmn, NY State Dem Comt, 63-66; exec dir, NY Citizens for McCarthy, 68; deleg, Dem Nat Conv, 68; dep campaign mgr for US Rep James H Scheuer for Mayor, 69; exec vchmn, New York City Dem Comt, 70- Bus & Prof Pos: Attorney, McLaughlin, Stickles, McKean & Hayden, 56-60; exec dir, Am for Permanent Peace in Mid East, 67- Mil Serv: Entered as Pvt, Army, 53, released as Pfc, 55. Publ: Contrib, Chicago, 1968, 10/68. Mem: Nat Dem Club; Bronx-Nat Conf Christians & Jews (dir). Relig: Hebrew. Mailing Add: 1060 Park Ave New York NY 10028

RIDDAGH, ROBERT W (R)
Majority Whip, Del House Rep
b 1914; m 1945 to Anne Mary Lupo; c Robert L. Polit & Govt Pos: Mayor, Smyrna, Del, formerly; Del State Rep, 66-, chmn, Judiciary Comt, Del House Rep, 66-, mem, Joint Const Rev Comt, Comsumer Affairs Comt & Agr Comt, 66-, Majority Whip, 70- Bus & Prof Pos: Welding supvr, Philadelphia Navy Yard; mgr, Am Stores Co; owner, Towne Cleaners. Mem: AF&AM (past Master, Harmony Lodge 13); Smyrna-Clayton Bus Develop Asn (treas). Relig: Methodist. Mailing Add: 24 Lake Dr Smyrna DE 19977

RIDDER, RUTHE B (D)
Wash State Sen
b Pullman, Wash, June 13, 29; d Fred H Burmaster & Esther L Johnson B; m 1950 to Robert Carl Ridder; c Janet R (Mrs Blume), Robert (Andy), Susan, David & William. Educ: Univ Wash, B Sci, 50; Phrateres Int. Polit & Govt Pos: Wash State Sen, 73-, chmn, Senate Labor Comt, 75- Mem: Rainier Beach Women's Club (co-pres, 74-); South Shore PTA (co-pres, 74-); Rainier CofC. Relig: Lutheran. Mailing Add: 5809 S Roxbury Seattle WA 98118

RIDDICK, FRANK H (D)
Ala State Rep
Mailing Add: 2920 Hillsboro Rd SW Huntsville AL 35805

RIDDLEBERGER, JAMES W
b Washington, DC, Sept 21, 04; m to Amelie Otken; c Three. Educ: Randolph-Macon Col, AB, 24; Georgetown Univ, MA, 26. Hon Degrees: LLD, Randolph-Macon Col. Polit & Govt Pos: Research asst, Libr Cong, 24-27; US Tariff Comn, 27-29; career officer, US Dept State Foreign Serv, 29-68, second secy, Geneva, 30-36 & Berlin, 36-41, first secy, London, 42-43, chief div cent European affairs, 44-47, counr, Berlin, 47-49; dir, Off Polit Affairs, Frankfort, 49-50, ECA, Paris, 50-52 & Bur Ger Affairs, Dept of State, 52-53, US Ambassador to Yugoslavia, 53-58 & Greece, 58-59, dir, Int Coop Admin, 59-61, spec asst to Secy of State, 61, chmn, Develop Assistance Comt to Orgn for Econ Coop & Develop, 61-62, US Ambassador to Austria, 62-68; chmn, Population Crisis Comt, 69- Bus & Prof Pos: Asst prof int rels, Georgetown Univ, 26-29. Mem: Diplomatic & Consular Officers Retired. Mailing Add: 440 N Main St Woodstock VA 22664

RIDEOUT, HARRY FREEMAN (D)
Maine State Rep
b Presque Isle, Maine, Mar 3, 42; s Harry R Rideout & Winnifred Plissey R; m 1966 to Sharon Ilene Sponberg; c Hollie Jane & Shari Jo. Educ: Washburn High Sch, dipl, 60. Polit & Govt Pos: Maine State Rep, 75- Bus & Prof Pos: Owner, Harry's Grocery, Rideout's Market & Rideout's Apts, Presque Isle; co-owner, Roy's Army & Navy, Presque Isle; owner, Coffee Shop, Washburn. Mil Serv: Entered as Pvt, Army, 60, released as E-4, 62, after serv in Engr Corps. Mem: Washburn Masonic Lodge 193; Anan Temple, Shrine; Aroostook Shrine Club; Presque Isle Fish & Game. Relig: Protestant. Legal Res: State Rd Mapleton ME 04757 Mailing Add: RFD 2 Presque Isle ME 04769

RIDER, HARRY DURBIN (D)
Mem Exec Comt, Pa State Dem Comt
b Baltimore, Md, Dec 15, 05; s Harry Durbin Rider & Amedia Whelan R; m 1928 to Catherine Antoinette Hulitt; c Kathleen May, Dixie Gale (deceased), James Turner, Harry Durbin, Bonnie Lea, Marilyn Effie & Carletta Sylvia. Educ: Harford Seminary. Polit & Govt Pos: Secy, Pocono Mountain Dem Club, 61-63, treas, 64-66; mem exec comt, Monroe Co Dem Party, 63-66; deleg, Dem Nat Conv, 64; committeeman, Pa State Dem Comt, 66-, mem exec comt, 70- Bus & Prof Pos: Owner & mgr, Rider Decorating Co, 35-65; dir, Burnley Workshop, 64-66; dir, Camp Moll for Retarded, 66- Mem: Monroe Co Asn for Retarded Children (dir); Pa Asn for Retarded Children (state bd dirs); Patriotic Order Sons of Am; Boy Scouts (comnr). Relig: Methodist. Legal Res: Paradise Cresco PA 18320 Mailing Add: Box 114 Cresco PA 18326

RIDER, JOSEPH ALFRED (R)
Mem, Calif Rep State Cent Finance Comt
b Chicago, Ill, Jan 30, 21; s Dr Dean L Loller Rider & Dr Jeannette L Leszczynski R; m 1943 to Graclynn L Rice; c Charles & Dean. Educ: Univ Chicago, SB, 42, fel, 50-51, PhD in Pharmacology, 51, Sch Med, MD, 44; Am Bd Internal Med, dipl; Am Bd Gastroenterol, dipl; Sigma Xi. Polit & Govt Pos: Mem pesticides & alt study sect, Food & Drug Admin, 67-70; mem, Calif Rep State Cent Finance Comt, currently; mem adv bd, Calif Bur Repair Serv, pres adv bd, 73- Bus & Prof Pos: Intern, Presby Hosp, Chicago, Ill, 44-45; resident med, Univ Tex, Galveston, 47-49; resident, Univ Chicago, 49-50, instr med, 51-52; asst prof med, Univ Calif Sch Med, San Francisco & asst chief gastrointestinal clin, 53-59, asst clin prof med, 59-66; dir gastrointestinal research lab, Franklin Hosp Found, 63-; mem staff, St Mary's Hosp, San Francisco. Mil Serv: Capt, Army MedC, 45-47, with serv as Chief of Med, 172nd Sta Hosp; Am Theatre Medal; World War II Victory Medal; Army of Occup Medal. Publ: Disturbances in Gastrointestinal Motility, C C Thomas, 59; Gastric & duodenal ulcers, Encyclop Britannica, 61; The digestive system, In: Better Homes & Gardens Family Medical Guide, Meredith Press, 64; plus others. Mem: Am Col Physicians (fel); Am Gastroenterological Asn (fel); Myasthenia Gravis Found; Am Asn Advan Sci; Am Fedn Clin Research. Honors & Awards: Cert of Merit, Am Med Asn Sci Exhib, 70; Billings Bronze Medal, 61, First Prize, 61 & 62 & Hull Gold Medal Award, 67. Relig: Methodist. Legal Res: 10 Charles-Dean Rd Mill Valley CA 94941 Mailing Add: Suite 900 350 Parnassus Ave San Francisco CA 94117

RIDER, ROBERT EARL, SR (D)
Chmn, Marshall Co Dem Cent Comt, Iowa
b Toledo, Iowa, Dec 25, 21; s Clifford Earl Rider & Myrtle Justus R; m 1946 to Dorothy Mae Wickersham; c Robert Earl, Jr, Patricia Eileen (Mrs Freiburg), Ronald Leroy & Nancy Lee (Mrs Albers). Educ: Garwin High Sch, Iowa, 39. Polit & Govt Pos: Iowa State Rep, 65-69; committeeman, Washington Twp, Iowa, 66-71; finance chmn, Marshall Co Dem Cent Comt, 71-72, chmn, 72- Mem: Franklin Mint Collectors Soc; Moose; Farm Bur. Honors & Awards: Master Lamb Producer, Sheep Growers, 60. Relig: Congregational. Mailing Add: Rte 3 Marshalltown IA 50158

RIDGEWAY, WILLIAM GILBERT (R)
Committeeman, Ill Rep State Cent Comt
b Coulterville, Ill, Mar 6, 27; s William Clayton Ridgeway & Margaret Elizabeth Penrod R; m 1950 to Elizabeth Ann Greer; c Carol Ann. Educ: Southern Ill Univ, BA, 49; Univ Ill Col Law, LLB & JD, 68; Phi Alpha Delta. Polit & Govt Pos: State's attorney, Jackson Co, Ill, 56-64, pub defender, 67-68, spec asst attorney gen, 69-; committeeman, Ill Rep State Cent Comt, 66- Mil Serv: Entered as Pvt, Army, 45, released as Pfc, 46, after serv in Finance, Fifth Army, Ft Sheridan, Ill. Mem: Am Bar Asn; CofC (dir); Lions; Mason; Shrine. Relig: Methodist. Legal Res: 712 N Sixth St Murphysboro IL 62966 Mailing Add: 18 1/2 S Tenth St Murphysboro IL 62966

RIDINGS, C LESLIE, JR (R)
Del State Rep
b Wilmington, Del, Oct 11, 26; s Clayton L Ridings & Frances Besten R; m 1952 to Marie T Berl; c Clayton L, III, Elizabeth M & Barbara Anne. Educ: Univ Del, BS, 51; Univ Pa; Am Col Life Underwriters, CLU, 67; Kappa Alpha Order. Polit & Govt Pos: Committeeman, Elec Dist, Del, 64-71, chmn, 71-74; Del State Rep, 74- Bus & Prof Pos: Mgr, Home Life Ins Co, Channing Co & Travelers, 60-69; pres, Brandywine Pension Consult, Heather Agency Inc & Brandywine Enterprises Ltd, 69- Mil Serv: Entered as Seaman, Navy, 44, released as Lt(jg), 59, after serv in regular & res, Pac Theatre, 44-46; Am Theatre, Pac-Philippines-Japan Occup Medals. Mem: Am Soc Chartered Life Underwriters; Am Soc Pension Actuaries; Nat Asn Life Underwriters; Nat Asn Security Dealers; Estate Planning Coun Del. Relig: Episcopal. Mailing Add: 3201 Kammerer Dr Delwynn Wilmington DE 19803

RIECHMANN, HOWARD CHRIST (R)
Mem, Ill Rep State Cent Comt.
b Valmeyer, Ill, July 21, 22; s George Riechmann & Louise Kruse R; m 1944 to Melba Ida Ritzel; c Jane Marie & John Howard. Polit & Govt Pos: Chmn, Monroe Co Rep Cent Comt, Ill, formerly; mem, Ill Rep State Cent Comt, currently. Bus & Prof Pos: Pres, Monroe Serv Co, 61-64; dir, First Nat Bank, Columbia, Ill, 66- Mem: Monroe Co Farm Bur; Monroe Co Tuberc Asn; KofC; Ill Polled Hereford Asn; Monroe Co Fair Asn (vpres). Relig: Catholic. Mailing Add: RFD 1 Valmeyer IL 62295

RIECKER, MARGARET ANN (RANNY) (R)
Rep Nat Committeewoman, Mich
b Ann Arbor, Mich, Nov 9, 33; d Dr Harry A Towsley & Margaret Dow T; m 1955 to John E Riecker; c John Towsley & Margaret Elizabeth. Educ: Carleton Col, BA, 54; Mt Holyoke Col, 54-55. Polit & Govt Pos: Vchmn, Midland Co Rep Comt, Mich, 62-66, chmn exec comt, 70-; vchmn, Tenth Cong Dist Rep Party, 64-68, spec asst to State Chmn for Women's Activities, 66-68; deleg, Rep Nat Conv, 68 & 72; first vchmn, Mich State Rep Cent Comt, 69-; vchmn, Mich State Rep Finance Comt, 70-73; Rep Nat Committeewoman, Mich, 70-, mem exec comt, Rep Nat Comt, 70- Mem: Bd Town & Campus & Women's Bd, Northwood Inst. Relig: Protestant. Mailing Add: 3211 Valley Dr Midland MI 48640

RIEDY, JOHN R (D)
SDak State Sen
Mailing Add: Thunder Hawk SD 57655

RIEGER, WILLIAM W (D)
Pa State Rep
Mailing Add: Capitol Bldg Harrisburg PA 17120

RIEGLE, DONALD W, JR (D)
US Rep, Mich
b Flint, Mich, Feb 4, 38; s Donald W Riegle; m 1972 to Meredith Ann White. Educ: Univ Mich, BA, 60; Mich State Univ, MBA, 61; Harvard Univ Bus Sch, doctoral cand. Hon Degrees: LLD, St Benedict's Col & Defiance Col, 70. Polit & Govt Pos: US Rep, Mich, 66-, mem int rels comt, US House of Rep, currently. Bus & Prof Pos: Faculty mem, Mich State, Boston & Harvard Univs, formerly; financial specialist, IBM Corp, 61-64. Publ: O Congress, Doubleday & Co, 72. Honors & Awards: Named One of Ten Outstanding Young Men of Nation in 1967, US Jr CofC; One of Two Best Congressmen of Year, Nation Mag, 67. Legal Res: Flint MI 48502 Mailing Add: 438 Cannon House Off Bldg Washington DC 20515

RIEHLE, THEODORE MARTIN, JR (R)
b New York, NY, Dec 20, 24; s Theodore Martin Riehle & Mary Dunlap R; m 1958 to Hope Maynard; c Theodore M, III, Dunlap Bowditch & Parker Maynard. Educ: Choate Sch, Conn, 38-41; Cornell Univ, 41-42; NY Maritime Acad, 42-44; Kappa Sigma. Polit & Govt Pos: Vt State Rep, 66-69; chmn, Chittenden Town Rep Comt, formerly; finance chmn, Davis for Gov, 70; mem, Vt State Rep Comt, formerly. Bus & Prof Pos: Exec vpres & dir, Master Rule Mfg Co, 47-57. Mil Serv: Entered as Ens, Navy, 44, released as Lt(jg), 46, after serv in Atlantic & Pac; Comdr, Naval Res; Three letters of commendation from Chief of Naval Opers. Relig: Protestant. Legal Res: 495 Spear St South Burlington VT 05401 Mailing Add: Box 2165 South Burlington VT 05401

RIEKE, MARY W (R)
Ore State Rep
Mailing Add: 5519 SW Menefee Dr Portland OR 97201

RIESS, EILEEN KATHLEEN (D)
Chairperson, Sanilac Co Dem Party, Mich
b Detroit, Mich, Sept 27, 16; d Francis William Shea & Grace Albertene Selee S; m 1937 to William Joseph Riess; c William Joseph, Jr. Educ: East Detroit High Sch, grad, 35. Polit & Govt Pos: Vchairperson, Sanilac Co Dem Party, Mich, 70-74, chairperson, 75- Mailing Add: 3820 W Downington Rd Snover MI 48472

RIETZ, KEN (R)
b Oshkosh, Wis, May 3, 41; s Howard K Rietz & Catherine Abbey R; single. Educ: George Washington Univ, 60-64; pres, Phi Sigma Kappa. Polit & Govt Pos: Publicity dir, Wis Young Rep, 65; mem, Sixth Dist Exec Comt, Wis Rep Orgn, 66; campaign dir for US Rep William Steiger, 66 & 68, legis asst, 66-68; assoc, Treleaven Assocs, 68-; asst community dir & info dir, Rep Nat Comt, 69; campaign dir for Bill Brock, US Senate race, 70; dir, Young Voters for the President, 71-72; group dir, 73 Inaugural Comt, 72-73; dir New Majority campaign for 74, Rep Nat Comt, 73- Bus & Prof Pos: Vpres, Allison, Treleaven & Reitz, 71; vpres & mem bd, Holder-Kennedy, Inc, Nashville, Tenn, 71. Mil Serv: Midn, US Naval Acad. Relig: Methodist. Legal Res: Westover MD Mailing Add: 310 First St SE Washington DC 20003

RIFFE, VERNAL G, JR (D)
Speaker Pro Tem, Ohio House of Rep
b New Boston, Ohio, June 26, 25; s Vernal G Riffe, Sr & Jewell Adkins R; m 1948 to Thelma Cooper; c Cathy (Mrs Skiver); Verna Kay, Mary Beth & Vernal G, III. Educ: Ohio Univ, Portsmouth; Miami Univ, Ins Agency Mgt Sch. Polit & Govt Pos: Ohio State Rep, 22nd Dist, 59-, Speaker Pro Tem, Ohio House of Rep, 73-, mem, Legis Serv Comn & vchmn, Legis Off Bldg Comn, currently. Bus & Prof Pos: Pres, Sherman, Riffe & Bennett Ins Agency, Inc; vpres & bd mem, Merchants' & Mfrs' Mutual Ins Co; bd mem, Mark Man Investment Co. Mil Serv: Entered as Pvt, Air Force, 43, released as S/Sgt, 45, after serv in 15th Air Force, Italy, Mediterranean Theater, 44-45; Good Conduct Medal; Am Campaign Medal; European-African-Mid Eastern Campaign Medal with 9 Bronze Stars; World War II Victory Medal. Mem: Mason (32 degree); Shrine; Scottish Rite; Am Legion; Bus & Prof Mens Asn. Relig: Protestant. Legal Res: 422 Center St New Boston OH 45662 Mailing Add: Ohio House of Rep State House Columbus OH 43215

RIFKIN, JULIE KAYE (R)
Mem, Nat Fed Rep Women
b Conn; m; c Laurence A. Polit & Govt Pos: Mem, Cent Calif Educ TV Corp, 52-, pres, North-Cent Area; mem, Sacramento Appeals Rev Bd; mem comt, Study Unification of City & Co Health Dept; mem exec comt, Betterment of Parking Conditions & Traffic Comt, Sacramento; mem, Sacramento Regional Arts Coun, Calif; campaign chmn, Ivy Baker Priest for State Treas, 66 & 70; mem, Behavioral Sci Bd, 69-; mem, Rep State Cent Comt Calif, currently; mem, Nat Fedn Rep Women, currently; chmn, Calif State Bd Behav Sci Examr, currently. Bus & Prof Pos: Participant, Workshops, Stanford Univ; mem, CofC Study Conf for Indust Col of Armed Forces Nat Resources; participant progs & workshops for Youth Welfare, Crime & Juv Justice, Social Welfare & Ment Health; deleg, Western Cong UNESCO, mem bd dirs, 1 year. Mem: Women's Coun; Am Col Nursing Home Adminrs (fel); Soroptimist; Sacramento Soc Crippled Children (bd dirs); Am River Hosp Auxiliary. Honors & Awards: Meritorious Serv Award, Nat Red Cross & Women of the Year Award Distinguished Community Serv, 66; judge, Miss Sacramento Contest; Guide Dogs for the Blind, Inc Serv Award. Mailing Add: 1206 43rd St Sacramento CA 95819

RIFORD, LLOYD S, JR (R)
NY State Assemblyman
Mailing Add: West Genessee St Rd Auburn NY 13020

RIGAU, MARCO ANTONIO, JR (POPULAR DEMOCRAT, PR)
Dir, Commonwealth PR Dem Comt
b Boston, Mass, Aug 16, 46; s Marco A Rigau & Alice Jimenez R; m to Maria Moran; c Maria Teresa. Educ: Univ PR, BA magna cum laude, 65, LLB magna cum laude, 69; Harvard Univ, LLM, 70; Inst Polit Studies, Costa Rica, dipl, 65; Lincoln's Inn Soc; Phi Sigma Alpha. Polit & Govt Pos: Pres, Popular Dem Party-Univ Students Asn, PR, 64-65; asst, Sen Robert F Kennedy's Off, NY, 66; mem, Robert F Kennedy for President Comt, PR, 68; chmn, McGovern for Pres Comt, 72; deleg, Dem Nat Conv, 72; dir, Commonwealth PR Dem Comt, 72-, mem ruling cong, 75- Bus & Prof Pos: Res assoc, Grad Sch Pub Admin, Uni prof social sci, 66-69, res assoc, Inst Urban Law, Sch Law, 66-69; prof law, Interam Sch, 70-73; law practice, 74- Publ: Co-auth, Teach-ins, teach-outs & education: th dissent, San Juan Rev, 4/66; auth, El derecho a la ciudadania y la ciudadania 7 la ciudadania Americana de los Puertorriquenos-Afroyim v Rusk, 68 & El Estado Libre Asociado de Puerto Rico vs Rosso, 69, Rev Jur Univ PR. Mem: Interam Soc Planning; Bar Asn Commonwealth PR (const law comt); Am Bar Asn; Ateneo Puertoriqueno. Legal Res: Blvd del Valle 274 San Juan PR 00901 Mailing Add: PO Box 1678 San Juan PR 00903

RIGEL, WILLIAM EDWARD (R)
Ariz State Rep
b Sherwood, Ohio, May 23, 15; s Adam F Rigel & Cecelia Konzen R; m 1956 to Esther Bunk. Educ: Ohio State Univ, BS in Educ, 38; Columbia Univ, MA in Pub Law & Govt, 52. Polit & Govt Pos: Ariz State Rep, Dist 28, 75-, vchmn banking & ins comt, mem ways & means, govt opers & co & munic comts, currently. Bus & Prof Pos: Eng specialist, Northrop Corp, Calif, 65-66. Mil Serv: Entered as 2nd Lt, Army, 39, released as Col, 64, after serv in Europe, NATO, Alaska; Legion of Merit; Bronze Star; Combat Inf Badge; European Campaign Medal. Mem: ROA; Scottsdale CofC. Relig: Catholic. Mailing Add: 7680 E Coolidge St Scottsdale AZ 85251

RIGGS, ELEANOR COX (R)
b Terre Haute, Ind, Jan 28, 34; d Wilson Naylor Cox, Jr & Dorothy Valentine C; m 1955 to Wendell A Riggs, MD; c Steven J, David Cox & Andrew Cromwell. Educ: Ind Univ, AB, 55; Phi Beta Kappa; Alpha Lambda Delta; Pi Lambda Theta; Kappa Kappa Gamma. Polit & Govt Pos: Treas & vpres, Rep Women's Club of Tippecanoe Co, 67-71, pres, 71-; Rep precinct committeeman, 70-71; alt deleg, Rep Nat Conv, 72. Bus & Prof Pos: Housewife. Mem: League of Women Voters; Tippecanoe Co Med Auxiliary; Home Hosp Auxiliary; St Elizabeth's Hosp Auxiliary; Lafayette Country Club. Relig: American Baptist. Legal Res: 3503 S Ninth St Rd Lafayette IN 47905 Mailing Add: 3503 S 100 E Lafayette IN 47905

RIGGS, JOHN ARTHUR (D)
VChmn, Washoe Co Dem Party, Nev
b Los Angeles, Calif, Nov 29, 46; s Robert Clarence Riggs & Marguerite E Konsella R; single. Educ: Univ Md, Ansbach, Ger, 67-68; Univ Nev, Reno, BS, 72, grad study, 72-; SDX; Circle-K. Polit & Govt Pos: Pres, Washoe Co Young Dem, Nev, 70-72; vpres, Young Dem Nev, 72-73, pres, 73, nat committeeman, 73-; dir Region VII, Young Dem Am, 74-; vchmn, Washoe Co Dem Party, 74-; historian, Nev Dem Cent Comt, 74- Bus & Prof Pos: Credit investr, Reno Check Cashing Serv, Nev, 70-72; acad instr, Nev State Prison, Carson City, 72-; consult criminal justice, US Jaycees, Tulsa, Okla, 74- Mil Serv: Entered as E-1, Army, 66, released as E-5, 69, after serv in 4th Bn, 23rd Inf, 25th Inf Div, Republic of Vietnam, 68-69; Bronze Star; Purple Heart with Oakleaf Cluster; Army Commendation Medal; Combat Inf Badge; Good Conduct Medal; Vietnam Serv with Four Stars; South Vietnam Serv with Scroll; Am Defense Serv Medal; Combat Drivers Badge; Expert Rifle Badge. Publ: Ed & publ of newspaper, Sagebrush II, 72-74. Mem: Phi Delta Kappa; Jaycees (pres, Sparks; criminal justice chmn, Nevada); life mem DAV; KofC; Am Correctional Asn. Honors & Awards: Freedoms Found Honor Cert, Valley Forge, Pa, 66; Outstanding Serv Award, Washoe Co Young Dem, 73; Outstanding Young Educator, Nev Jaycees, 74-75; Distinguished Serv Award, Sparks Jaycees, 75; Outstanding Young Nevadan, Nev Jaycees, 75. Relig: Catholic. Mailing Add: 610 Mill Reno NV 89502

RIGGS, MELVIN DAVID (D)
Okla State Rep
b Sand Springs, Okla, Nov 29, 37; s James Ray Riggs & Thelma Beatrice Fisher R; m 1959 to Dora Arleen Hoppes; c Lisa Rene, Michael Eric, Jennifer Lee, Andrea Lynn & Aaron David. Educ: Phillips Univ, BA; Univ Okla, MA; Univ Tulsa, JD. Polit & Govt Pos: Okla State Rep, 71-, chmn, Pub Safety & Penal Affairs, Okla House Rep, 73-, mem, Const Rev & Regulatory Serv, Criminal Jurisp, Rules & Revenue & Taxation, currently. Bus & Prof Pos: Ed, Tulsa Law J, 67. Publ: Mental illness and criminal responsibility. Mem: Okla & Am Bar Asns; Nat Coun on Crime & Delinquency; Youth Serv Tulsa, Inc; Okla Health & Welfare Asn. Honors & Awards: Outstanding Athlete Award, Phillips Univ, 58; Order of the Curule Chair, Univ Tulsa Law Sch, 68; Outstanding Legislator, Okla Observer, 73 & 74. Legal Res: 6722 W Admiral Tulsa OK 74127 Mailing Add: 1640 S Boston Tulsa OK 74119

RIGGS, WARREN ELWOOD (R)
Chmn, Camden Co Rep Party, NC
b Old Trap, NC, May 5, 27; s Charlie Sawyer Riggs & Ella Hubbard R; m 1948 to Jessie Mae Wright; c Gale Raynette, Warren Curtis & Michael Cary. Educ: Shiloh High Sch, 11 years. Polit & Govt Pos: Treas & secy, Camden Co Rep Party, NC, 66-68, chmn, 68- Bus & Prof Pos: Asst mgr, Freezer Locker Co, 48-56; farmer & merchant, self-employed, 56- Mil Serv: Entered as A/S, Navy, 45, released as Seaman 1/C, 46, after serv in USS Saidor CVE 117 & USS Amphion AR 13, Pac Theatre & Atlantic Theatre. Mem: Mason; NC Farm Bur; Nat Farmers Orgn. Relig: Methodist. Mailing Add: Box 160 Shiloh NC 27974

RIGNEY, HARLAN (R)
Ill State Sen
Mailing Add: RR No 1 Red Oak IL 61066

RIHERD, HUBERT MILTON (D)
Chmn, Osceola Co Dem Exec Comt, Fla
b Centralia, Ill, Mar 7, 21; s John Milton Riherd & Lalla Brown R; m 1953 to Carmen Cyr; c Charlotte (Mrs Alan Baker) & John P. Educ: Southern Ill Univ, Carbondale, BS, 47; Univ Calif, Los Angeles, 51-52; Western Mich Univ, MA, 68. Polit & Govt Pos: Chmn, Osceola Co Dem Exec Comt, Fla, 74- Mil Serv: Entered as Pvt, Army Air Force, 43, retired as Maj, 65, after serv in Weather Serv, Mil Air Transport Serv, 47-65; World War II Victory Medal; Am, Asiatic-Pac Campaign Medals; Air Force Commendation Medal; Air Force Outstanding Unit Award; Nat Defense Serv Medal. Mem: Retired Officers Asn; Elks (trustee, 71-); Nat Educ Asn; Fla Teaching Profession; Osceola Co Educ Asn (treas, 72-). Relig: Baptist. Mailing Add: 816 Canterbury Lane Kissimmee FL 32741

RIJKEN, MAX CH (D)
Ore State Rep
b Tjipatat, Java, Indonesia, Mar 24, 20; s Eduard Rijken & Louise Elizabeth van Haasen R; m 1946 to Leginah bin Kario; c Samsudin, Hedy Louise & Randy Paul. Educ: Dutch High Sch, 5 years. Polit & Govt Pos: Chmn, Lincoln Co Dem Cent Comt, Ore, 70-72; Ore State Rep, 75- Bus & Prof Pos: Rubberplanter, Cultuur Maatschappij, Bagdjanegara, Indonesia, 39-41; employee, Ruys' Handels Vereinging Import-Export, Batavia, Java, 48-50; employee,

Dasaad Musin Concern Djakarta, 50-52, sales, Nilai Inti Sari Penjimpan, 52-54; inspector, Onderlinge s'Gravenhage, IJmuiden, Holland, 54-57 & NEZIFO, 57-59; in charge sales orgn, NUT Hospitalization Ins Co, 59-62. Mil Serv: Entered as Pvt, Dutch Army, 37, released as Sgt 1/C, 38, after serv in Mt Artillery, 1st Div; reenlisted 41-48; prisoner of war, 42-45. Mem: AF&AM; Ore State Grange. Relig: Presbyterian; ruling elder, First Presby Church, Newport. Legal Res: 1250 NW Lake St Newport OR 97365 Mailing Add: PO Box 576 Newport OR 97365

RILES, WILSON CAMANZA (D)
Supt Pub Instr, Calif
b Alexandria, La, June 27, 17; s Wilson Roy Riles & Susie Anna Jefferson R; m 1941 to Mary Louise Phillips; c Michael Leigh, Narvia (Mrs Ronald Bostick), Wilson C, Jr & Phillip Gregory. Educ: Northern Ariz Univ, BA, 40, MA, 47. Hon Degrees: LLD, Pepperdine Col, 65. Polit & Govt Pos: Mem, President Johnson's Task Force on Urban Educ Opportunities; chmn, President Nixon's Task Force on Urban Education, 69; mem, Nat Adv Comt on Teacher Corps; mem adv comt, Calif Legis Joint Comt Higher Educ; mem ad hoc comt financial statist for urban educ, US Off Educ; Supt Pub Instr, Calif, 71-; mem, Nat Coun Educ Research, 73. Bus & Prof Pos: Adminr & teacher, Ariz Pub Schs, 40-54; exec secy, Pac Coast Region, Fel for Reconciliation, 54-58; bur chief intergroup rels, dir compensatory educ & assoc supt pub instr, Calif Dept Educ, 58-65, dep supt pub instr for prog & legis, 65-71. Mil Serv: Entered as Pvt, Army Air Corps, 43, released as Sgt, 46, after serv in 2143 AAFBU, Tuskegee, Ala, 43-46. Publ: Articles in Calif Educ, Educ Leadership, Calif Teachers Asn J, plus others. Mem: Phi Delta Kappa; NEA; Calif Cong Parents & Teachers. Relig: Methodist. Legal Res: 4246 Warren Ave Sacramento CA 95822 Mailing Add: 721 Capitol Mall Sacramento CA 95814

RILEY, BOB COWLEY (D)
Gov, Ark
b Little Rock, Ark, Sept 18, 24; s Columbus Allen Riley & Winnie Mae Craig R; m 1956 to Claudia Zimmerman; c Megen. Educ: Univ Ark, BA, 50, MA, 51, EdD, 57; Univ Calif, Jr Col Credential, 56; Nat Defense Educ Act Inst, Univ Nebr, 68; Phi Eta Sigma; Phi Alpha Theta; Phi Delta Kappa; Blue Key; Psi Chi; Alpha Phi Omega; Sigma Chi. Polit & Govt Pos: Ark State Rep, 48-50, parliamentarian, Ark House Rep, 69-; founder & first pres, Univ Ark Young Dem Club; mem, Arkadelphia City Coun, 60-64; fire comnr, Arkadelphia, Mayor, 65-66; consult, Mitchellville Community Develop Proj, 68; deleg, Dem Nat Conv, 68; solicitor fire & casualty ins, Ark Ins Dept; Lt Gov, Ark, 70-74, Gov, 74- Bus & Prof Pos: Broker, Freeling Ins Agency, Little Rock; instr, Little Rock Univ, 51-55; prof hist & polit sci, Ouachita Baptist Univ, chmn div social sci & dept polit sci, 60- Mil Serv: Entered as Pvt, Marines, 41, released as Cpl, 45, after serv in 2nd & 3rd Div, 2nd & 9th Regt, Pac Theater, 42-45. Publ: They Never Came Back, Purdue Univ, 59; The Party That Almost Was, monograph, 60 & The Reorganization of the Arkansas State Legislature, monograph, 69, Pioneer. Mem: Am Polit Sci Asn; Am Asn Univ Prof; Nat Coun Social Studies; Am Inst Parliamentarians (cert, 73); DAV. Honors & Awards: Blinded Vet Asn Nat Achievement Award, 63; Distinguished Serv Award, Ark Munic League; Fifth Person in Nation to Receive Ambassador Award, Am Coun of Blind. Relig: Baptist. Legal Res: 1076 N Phelps Circle Arkadelphia AR 71923 Mailing Add: Dept of Polit Sci Ouachita Baptist Univ Arkadelphia AR 71923

RILEY, CATHERINE I (D)
Md State Deleg
b Baltimore, Md, Mar 21, 47; d Francis Worth Riley & Catherine Cain R; single. Educ: Towson State Col, BA, 69; Towson State Col Alumni Asn. Polit & Govt Pos: Md State Deleg, 75-, mem environ matters comt, Md House Deleg, 75-, mem joint subcomt preservation agr land, 75- Bus & Prof Pos: Bacteriologist, Baltimore City Hosps, Md, 69-72; legis aide, Md House Deleg, 73, legis asst, 74; consult, Div Alcoholism Control, 73. Publ: Co-auth, A backbench view of the legislature, Baltimore Morning Sunpapers, 1/25/75. Mem: Orgn Women Legislators (secy, 75-); Young Dem Md (vpres, 75); United Fund Cent Md (bd dirs, 75-); Harford Co Dem Club. Honors & Awards: United Fund Community Serv Award, 73 & 74; Bel Air Jaycees Pub Serv Award, 74; Nat Orgn Women Serv Award, 74. Legal Res: 747 Roland Ave Bel Air MD 21014 Mailing Add: 20 Office St Bel Air MD 21014

RILEY, DORIS J (D)
NH State Rep
Mailing Add: 1475 Hooksett Rd Hooksett NH 03106

RILEY, EDWARD PATTERSON (D)
b Barnwell, SC, Oct 27, 00; s Richard Wilson Riley & Meta Dowling R; m 1927 to Martha Dixon; c Edward Patterson, Jr & Richard Wilson. Educ: Furman Univ, LLB. Polit & Govt Pos: Chmn, Co Dem Party, SC, 54-56; exec committeeman, SC Dem Party, 58-60, chmn, 60-64; attorney, Greenville Co, 58-59; deleg, Dem Nat Conv, 60. Mil Serv: Entered as Lt, Navy, 42, released as Lt Comdr, 45, after serv in Pac Theater; Asiatic Theater, Philippine Liberation, Victory & Am Theater Medals. Mem: SC Bar Asn; Am Judicature Soc; Kiwanis; Am Legion (comdr, Post 3, 54); Mason; Elks. Honors & Awards: Ky Col. Relig: Methodist. Legal Res: 218 Henrietta St Greenville SC 29601 Mailing Add: PO Box 10084 Greenville SC 29603

RILEY, JAMES N (D)
Mo State Rep
Mailing Add: 7363 Goff Ave Richmond Heights MO 63117

RILEY, JOHN R (D)
Ga State Sen
Mailing Add: PO Box 9641 Savannah GA 31402

RILEY, LAKE (R)
b Benton, Ky, May 20, 17; s Lex G Riley & Oma Johnston R; m 1935 to Leeoda Fooks; c William M, Alevate (Mrs Warren), Galon & James H. Educ: Freed-Hardeman Col. Polit & Govt Pos: Mem, Marshall Co Bd Educ, 64-; chmn, Marshall Co Rep Exec Comt, Ky, formerly. Bus & Prof Pos: Dir, Ky Coop Coun, 62-66; pres, Marshall Co Soil Improvement Asn, 62-: pres, Valley Co Ky Coop, 62- Mem: Marshall Co Farm Bur; United Asn Plumbing & Pipe Fitting Local 184. Relig: Church of Christ; minister. Mailing Add: Rte 6 Benton KY 42025

RILEY, RICHARD WILSON (D)
SC State Sen
b Greenville, SC, Jan 2, 33; s Edward Patterson Riley & Martha Elizabeth Dixon R; m 1957 to Ann Osteen Yarborough; c Richard W, Jr, Anne Y, Hubert D & Theodore D. Educ: Furman Univ, AB, 54; Univ SC Law Sch, Student page, SC State Senate & state vpres, Young Dem, 58-59; SC State Rep, 63-66; SC State Sen, Greenville Co, 66- Bus & Prof Pos: Vpres, Young Lawyers Club, Greenville, 61. Mil Serv: Entered as Ens, Navy, 54, released as Lt(jg), 56, after serv in Mine Force. Mem: Simpsonville & Mauldin Rotary Club; Jaycees; pres, Furman Univ Alumni Asn, 68-69. Relig: Methodist. Legal Res: 200 Sunset Dr Greenville SC 29605 Mailing Add: State House Columbia SC 29211

RILEY, TIMOTHY CROCKER (R)
Mem, Rep State Cent Comt, Calif
b Wilmington, Del, Oct 10, 46; s William Hale Riley & Mary Turner Brown R; m 1974 to Cindy Ann Smith; c Shannon. Educ: Loyola Univ Los Angeles, BA, 68; Calif State Univ, Fresno, MA, 75; Delta Sigma Phi. Polit & Govt Pos: Chmn, Loyolans for Ronald Reagan, 66; pres, Loyola Univ Young Rep, 67-68; co chmn, Youth for Sen Murphy, 70; state chmn, Citizens Opposing Marijuana Initiative, 72; nominee, Calif State Assembly, 74; area dir, Los Angeles Rep Exec Comt, 72, mem exec comt, 75-; mem, Rep State Cent Comt Calif, 75- Bus & Prof Pos: Govt teacher, Fowler High Sch, 69-71; exec dir, Prof Educators Group, 73- Mem: Am Polit Sci Asn; Los Angeles Co Museum Art; Am Fedn Arts; Am Conservative Union. Relig: Episcopal. Legal Res: 5000 Centinela Ave Los Angeles CA 90066 Mailing Add: 253 N Canon Dr Beverly Hills CA 90210

RILEY, TOM JOSEPH (R)
b Cedar Rapids, Iowa, Jan 9, 29; s Joseph W Riley & Edna Kyle R; m 1952 to Nancy Evans; c Pamela Jo, Peter Craig, Lisa Ann, Martha Sue, Sara Lynne & Heather Lee. Educ: State Univ Iowa, BA, 50, Col Law, JD, 52; Alpha Tau Omega; Delta Theta Phi. Polit & Govt Pos: Iowa State Rep, Linn Co, 61-65; chmn, Gov Adv Comt on Aging, 64-65; Iowa State Sen, 23rd Sen Dist, 65-68 & 71-74; Rep cand for US Rep, Second Cong Dist, Iowa, 68 & 74; mem, Iowa State Comn on Aging; deleg, White House Conf on Aging, 71. Bus & Prof Pos: Practicing attorney, Simmons, Perrine, Albright & Ellwood, 54- Mil Serv: 1st Lt, Air Force, 52-54, serv in Judge Adv Gen Dept, Air Training Command. Publ: Response to Crisis, Basset Publ Co, 68. Mem: Am Bar Asn; fel Iowa Acad Trial Lawyers; World Peace Through Law Ctr; Mason; Am Legion. Honors & Awards: Outstanding Freshman Legislator, Des Moines Press & Radio Club, 61. Relig: Presbyterian. Legal Res: 3610 Clark Rd Cedar Rapids IA 52403 Mailing Add: 1215 Merchants Nat Bank Bldg Cedar Rapids IA 52401

RINALDO, MATTHEW JOHN (R)
US Rep, NJ
b Elizabeth, NJ, Sept 1, 31; s Matthew J Rinaldo, Sr & Ann Papaccio R; single. Educ: Rutgers Univ, BSc, 53; Seton Hall Univ, MBA, 59; NY Univ, 64-69; Acct Club; Finance Club; Mgt Club. Polit & Govt Pos: Chmn, Young Rep, Union, NJ, 61-63; pres, Bd of Adjust, 62-63; freeholder, Union Co, 63-64; NJ State Sen, Dist Nine, 68-72; US Rep, 12th Cong Dist, NJ, 73-, mem interstate & foreign com comt, US House Rep, currently, mem Merchant Marine & fisheries comt, currently. Bus & Prof Pos: Instr, Rutgers Univ, 63-72. Publ: The businessmen's responsibility in politics, The Enterprise, spring 68. Mem: Am Soc Pub Admin; Nat Munic League; NJ Heart Asn (bd trustees); Union Co Heart Asn (bd dir); Boys' Club of Union (bd dirs). Honors & Awards: Outstanding Young Man of the Year, Union CofC, 65; Knight of Year, Union KofC, 68; Man of Year, Union chap of Unico Nat, 70 & Plainfield chap, 72; Man of Year, Union B'nai B'rith, 73. Relig: Roman Catholic. Mailing Add: 142 Headley Terr Union NJ 07083

RINAS, B JOSEPH (D)
Iowa State Rep
Mailing Add: 1100 English Blvd Marion IA 52302

RINEHART, D ELDRED (R)
b Smithsburg, Md, Nov 13, 03; s John J Rinehart & Carrie Needy R; m 1923 to Mary Edith Davis; c John H, Mary Susan (Mrs Harold L Elgin); seven grandchildren. Educ: Pub Schs, Washington Co, Md. Polit & Govt Pos: Chmn, Washington Co Rep Cent Comt, Md, 42-52; mem, Md State Apple Comn, 46-48; mem comt on agr, Rep Nat Comt, 48; deleg, Rep Nat Conv, 48 & 56, alt deleg, 52 & 64, deleg & chmn of deleg, 60, deleg mem arrangements comt & chmn subcomt on transportation, 68; mem, Md Racing Comn, 51, chmn, 52-59 & 67-69; chmn, Md Rep State Cent Comt, 52-62; mem, Rep Nat Comt, 52-62; Rep Nat Committeeman, Md, 64-69; chmn, Md Farm Phase-Out Comt, 67-68; mem, Renegotiation Bd, 69- Bus & Prof Pos: Farmer, Glen Afton Farms, currently; orchardist, pres & treas, Rinehart Orchards, Inc, currently; dir, Citizens Nat Bank & Trust Co, Waynesboro, Pa, currently. Mem: Md State Hort Soc (pres); Waynesboro Hosp, Pa (mem bd mgr); Md Coop Guernsey Breeders Asn; Interstate Milk Producers Asn; Mason (32 degree). Legal Res: Glen Afton Farms RFD 2 Smithsburg MD 21783 Mailing Add: 2000 M St NW Washington DC 20446

RING, CAROLYN LOUISE (R)
Chairwoman, Minn Rep State Cent Comt
b Minneapolis, Minn, Aug 12, 26; d Milford O McLean & Bessy Martin M; m 1947 to Ward D Ring; c Linda, Peggy, Diane & Ward, Jr. Educ: Univ Minn, 3 years; Pi Beta Phi. Polit & Govt Pos: Chairwoman, Rep Party, Richfield, Minn, 60-62; secy, Third Dist Rep Party, 63-65, chairwoman, 65-67; chairwoman, Hennepin Co Rep Party, 67-; deleg, Rep Nat Conv, 68; vchairwoman, Minn Rep State Cent Comt, 70-73, chairwoman, 73- Relig: Presbyterian. Mailing Add: 6304 Russell Ave S Richfield MN 55423

RING, CHARLES WARREN (R)
Mem, Maine Rep State Comt
b Fall River, Mass, Apr 2, 36; s Charles Warren Ring (deceased) & Constance Varney R (deceased); m 1960 to Margaret Rowlands Thomas; c Elizabeth B, Constance V, Mary T & John P. Educ: Hamilton Col, AB, 59; Inst Educ Develop, Harvard Bus Sch, 70; Alpha Psi Omega; Theta Delta Chi. Polit & Govt Pos: Mem, Brunswick Rep Town Comt, 59-, chmn, 67-69; mem, Brunswick Bd Selectmen, 63-67, chmn, 67; mem, Brunswick Bd Assessors, 63-67; mem, Cumberland Co Rep Comt, 64-; mem, Maine State Rep Comt, 68- Bus & Prof Pos: Develop officer, Bowdoin Col, 61-67, exec secy, 67-71, vpres, 71- Mil Serv: Entered as Seaman, Navy, 60, released as Seaman, 61, after serv in Brunswick Naval Air Sta. Mem: Boy Scouts (bd dirs); Brunswick Village Improv Asn (bd dirs); Rotary (bd dirs); Kennebec Squadron of US Power Squadron; Navy League. Relig: Protestant. Mailing Add: Adams Rd Brunswick ME 04011

RING, ELEANOR REYNOLDS (R)
b Tunkhannock, Pa, Aug 19, 05; d Ziba Wells Reynolds & Belle Stewart R; m to Stanhope Cotton Ring, wid; c Stewart A & Mrs Robert Taylor Scott Keith, Jr. Educ: Univ Calif. Polit

& Govt Pos: Pres, Coronado Rep Women Fedn, Calif, 58-59; vchmn, Bob Wilson Campaign, 60; alt deleg, Rep Nat Conv, 60, 64 & 68; pres, San Diego Co Fedn, 61-62; mem, Coronado City Coun, 63-66; vchmn, San Diego Co Rep Cent Comt, 65-66, campaign chmn, 73; Rep Nat Committeewoman, Calif, 68-72; deleg, Rep Nat Conv, 72. Relig: Episcopal. Mailing Add: 801 Tolita Ave Coronado CA 92118

RINGSAK, ELTON W (R)
NDak State Sen
b Grafton, NDak, Nov 18, 15; married; c five. Educ: Univ NDak. Polit & Govt Pos: NDak State Sen, 57- Bus & Prof Pos: Attorney-at-law. Mem: Am Legion; DAV; Mason; Shrine; Eagles. Mailing Add: State Capitol Bismarck ND 58501

RINI, DOMINIC WILLIAM (D)
Mem Exec Bd, Will Co Dem Party, Ill
b New Orleans, La, Sept 7, 06; s Louis Rini & Rose Vazzano R; m 1927 to Ann Sineni; c Sarah (Mrs Terry Aversa) & Louis V. Educ: Various classes & courses in bus admin & mgt; E I DuPont, US Rubber & UniRoyal Supvry develop training. Polit & Govt Pos: Committeeman, Will Co Dem Party, Ill, 49-, mem exec bd, 59-; construction supvr, State Ill, 60-65; committeeman, 42nd Dist Dem Party, 62-; New Lenox Twp Dem chmn, currently; precinct committeeman, 42nd Rep Dist Chmn, 70-; mem educ prog for precinct comt, Will Co, currently. Bus & Prof Pos: Stock clerk, Int Harvester, 24-25; shipping foreman, Bankers Thrift Corp, 25-30; mgr, Goldblatts, 32-34; gen foreman, Stone & Webester, 40-41; road supvr, US Rubber Co, 44-46; sales supvr, Electrolux Co, 46-51. Mem: Dem Orgn Club. Honors & Awards: Man of Year, UniRoyal Supvr, 69. Relig: Catholic. Mailing Add: 2425 Erskine Rd Joliet IL 60432

RIPP, WILLIAM ROBERT (R)
SDak State Sen
b Dimock, SDak, Dec 30, 24; s Henry Peter Ripp & Bertha Kabeiseman R; single. Educ: Parkston High Sch, SDak, 42. Polit & Govt Pos: Chmn & secy, Co Exten Bd, 58-68; coun mem, State Exten Adv Coun, 64-67; chmn Cross Plains twp, SDak, 68-, precinct committeeman, 70-, SDak State Sen, 70- Bus & Prof Pos: Pres, sch bd, 60-69; mem bd, Sioux Valley Milk Producers, Mitchell, SDak, 65-69; Eastern SDak Milk Producers, Sioux Falls, 67-70; mem, Land O'Lakes, Inc. Mem: KofC; Poland China Record Asn; SDak Dairy Herd Improv Asn; Holstein Friesian Asn Am. Relig: Catholic. Mailing Add: Dimock SD 57331

RIPPER, JACK DORLAND (D)
Ore State Sen
b Bingen, Wash, May 29, 20; s Percy Gilbert Ripper & Oris Loughary R; m 1942 to Nellie Christine Andersen; c John Gilbert, Susan Kay (Mrs Gary Combs) & Richard William. Educ: Univ Ore, 39-42; Portland State Col, BS, 64; Delta Upsilon. Polit & Govt Pos: Mem, North Bend Planning Comn, Ore, 59-60, chmn, 61; mem, gov comn on youth, 69; Ore State Rep, Dist 16, Coos Co, 69-73; adv comt, Ore Dunes Nat Recreation Area, 72-; Ore State Sen, 73-, vchmn, State & Fed Affairs Comt, Ore State Senate, 73-, co-chmn, Joint Comt, Prof Responsibility, 73-, mem, Land Use & Environ & Appropriation & Ways & Means Comt, 73-; mem, Law Enforcement Coun, 73. Bus & Prof Pos: Owner & operator of restaurants, North Bend, Ore, 43-60; educator hist dept, North Bend Sch Dist, 64-69. Mem: Ore Educ Asn; Nat Educ Asn; Elks; Lions; Western Rivers Girl Scout Coun (bd mem). Relig: Episcopal. Legal Res: Saunders Lake North Bend OR 97459 Mailing Add: Box 489 North Bend OR 97459

RIPPEY, CATHERINE NORRIS (D)
b New Bedford, Mass, Dec 14, 25; d Walter Vincent Moriarty & Marion Rigby M; m 1960 to John Newton Rippey; c Christopher & Jonathan V Hall & Patrick M Rippey. Educ: RI State Col, BS, 47; Alpha Delta Pi. Polit & Govt Pos: Deleg, Dem Nat Conv, 72. Bus & Prof Pos: Transitional first grade teacher, Charlestown Sch, RI, 66- Mem: Am Civil Liberties Union RI Affiliate (vchmn, 73-); New Dem Coalition; Womens Polit Caucus South Co (speakers bur, 75). Relig: Unitarian. Mailing Add: 25 Hillcrest Rd Wakefield RI 02879

RISCH, JAMES E (R)
Idaho State Sen
b Milwaukee, Wis, May 3, 43; s Elroy A Risch & Helen B Levi R; m 1968 to Vicki L Choborda; c James E, II & Jason S. Educ: Univ Idaho, BS, 65, JD, 68; Xi Sigma Pi; Phi Delta Theta. Polit & Govt Pos: Prosecuting attorney, Ada Co, Idaho, 70-74; Idaho State Sen, Dist 18, 74- Bus & Prof Pos: Attorney-at-law, 68-; instr, Boise State Univ, 68- Relig: Catholic. Mailing Add: Rte 3 Boise ID 83705

RISENHOOVER, TED M (D)
US Rep, Okla
b Stigler, Okla, Nov 3, 34; m to Carol Coshow; c Dorothy & Billy. Educ: Univ Ala, 60-61; Northeastern State Col, BS, 65. Polit & Govt Pos: Okla Crime Comnr; US Rep, Okla, 75- Bus & Prof Pos: Newspaper publ; pres, Web Offset Printers, Inc, Tahlequah, Okla. Mem: Okla Press Asn; Nat Newspaper Asn; Lions; Kiwanis; Phi Delta Epsilon. Legal Res: PO Box 496 Tahlequah OK 74464 Mailing Add: US House Rep Washington DC 20515

RISH, WILLIAM J (BILLY JOE) (D)
Fla State Rep
Mailing Add: 1017 Marvin Ave Port St Joe FL 32456

RISHER, WILLIAM RHETT (R)
b Ehrhardt, SC, July 22, 27; s James F Risher & Emma Jane Varn R; m 1971 to Joyce Benton Griffin; c Barbara Kay, Jane Wilkie & William Rhett, Jr. Educ: The Citadel, BS; Univ NC; Sigma Pi Sigma. Polit & Govt Pos: Chmn, Bamberg Co Rep Party, SC, formerly; alt deleg, Rep Nat Conv, formerly. Bus & Prof Pos: Headmaster, Carlisle Mil Sch, 56- Mil Serv: Army Res. Mem: Mason (Past Master); Shrine; SC Jaycees (pres); US Jaycees (vpres). Relig: Methodist. Legal Res: S Carlisle St Bamberg SC 29003 Mailing Add: Carlisle Military Sch Bamberg SC 29003

RISPOLI, MARCELLO (D)
Del State Rep
b Italy, Mar 27, 14; s Thomas Rispoli & Camille Parisi R; m 1935 to Anna Mary Grandell; c Thomas, Andrew, Mary Ellen (Mrs Wilkinson) & Andrew. Polit & Govt Pos: Del State Rep, 72- Mailing Add: 1412 W Seventh St Wilmington DE 19805

RISSER, ANDREW WARNER (D)
b Madison, Wis, Jan 14, 29; s Fred E Risser & Elizabeth Warner R; m 1957 to Judith Louise Mayer; c Martha Kay, Laura Lee & Kathleen Ann. Educ: Eastern Wash Col, BA, 50; Wis State Univ, Madison, LLB, 58. Polit & Govt Pos: Mem exec bd, Eau Claire Co Dem Party, Wis, 59-65; deleg, State Dem Conv, 59-65; alt deleg, Dem Nat Conv, 60 & 64; Dem precinct committeeman, Fall Creek, Eau Claire Co, 60-; cand, Wis State Assembly, 62; mem, Dem Nat Comt, Wis, 62-72. Mem: Am & Wis Co Bar Asns; Fall Creek Parents Club. Relig: Protestant. Mailing Add: 8215 Chestnut St Wauwatosa WI 53213

RISSER, FRED A (D)
Pres Pro Tem, Wis State Senate
b Madison, Wis, May 5, 27; married; c Three. Educ: Univ Wis, BA; Univ Ore, LLB, 52. Polit & Govt Pos: Wis State Assemblyman, 56-62; deleg, Dem Nat Conv, 60 & 64, Presidential Elector & chmn, State Electoral Col, 64; Wis State Sen, 62-, asst minority leader, Wis State Senate, 65-67, minority leader, 67-75, pres pro tem, 75-, chmn senate orgn comt & joint orgn comt, chmn interstate coop comn, chmn bldg comn subcomt on admin affairs, chmn spec comt on criminal penalties, vchmn bldg comn & vchmn bond bd. Bus & Prof Pos: Attorney-at-law. Mil Serv: World War II. Mem: Ore, Wis & Dane Co Bar Asns. Mailing Add: 140 W Wilson St Madison WI 53703

RITCHIE, JOHN, JR (R)
b Seattle, Wash, June 25, 32; s John Ritchie, III & Sarah Wallace R; m 1970 to Virginia Hutcheson; c Thomas Ritchie. Educ: Univ Va, Charlottesville, BA, 54; Harvard Law Sch, LLB, 60; Omega Delta Kappa; St Elmo Club. Polit & Govt Pos: Exec dir, Richmond Forward, 67-69; campaign coordr, Gubernatorial Campaign of Linwood Holton, 69-70; exec asst to Gov, Commonwealth of Va, 70- Bus & Prof Pos: Law practice, Hunton, Williams, Gay, Powell & Gibson, 60-67. Mil Serv: Entered as Ens, Navy, 54, released as Lt, 62, after serv in USS Dyess & USS Loeser, NAtlantic, Mediter & Caribbean Theaters, 54-57 & 61-62. Mem: Am Bar Asn; Big Bros of Richmond; Kiwanis; Westwood Racquet Club. Relig: Episcopal. Legal Res: 106 N Plum St Richmond VA 23220 Mailing Add: Governor's Off State Capitol Richmond VA 23219

RITTER, GEORGE JOSEPH (D)
Conn State Rep
b New York, NY, Mar 26, 20; s Charles Joseph Ritter & Gertrude Sternberg R; m 1946 to Patricia Kingsley Sleezer; c Martha Kingsley, Scott Robinson, Thomas Drummond, Penn Joseph & John Lathrop. Educ: Rutgers Col of Rutgers Univ, AB, 41; Yale Univ Law Sch, LLB, 46, Sterling Fel, 46-47. Polit & Govt Pos: Corp counsel, Hartford, Conn, 56-58, dep mayor & mem city coun, 59-69; mem, Hartford Charter Rev Comn, 53, 57 & 65; vchmn, Gtr Hartford Mass Transit Dist, 63, chmn, 63-; mem exec comt, Community Renewal Team, 64-; Conn State Rep, 69- Bus & Prof Pos: Exec dir of Conn Coun 16, Am Fedn of State, Co & Munic Employees, AFL-CIO, 48-50; chmn, Comt on Admin Law & Practices, Conn State Bar Asn, 57; sr partner, Ritter & Berman, Attorneys, currently. Mil Serv: Entered as Pvt, Army, 43, released as S/Sgt, 45, after serv in Eighth Army Hq, Far East; 3 Battle Stars; Northern Solomons, Cebu in the Philippines & Leyte in the Philippines; Presidential Unit Citation. Mem: Civitan Club; VFW; Am Vet Comt. Relig: Quaker. Legal Res: 248 N Whitney St Hartford CT 06103 Mailing Add: 266 Pearl St Hartford CT 06103

RITTER, JAMES PIERCE (D)
Pa State Rep
b Allentown, Pa, Oct 30, 30; s Pierce Albert Clairius Ritter & Rose Deutsch R; m 1951 to Faye Eilleen Morrissey; c Karen Anne, Steven Pierce & David James. Educ: Allentown High Sch, grad, 48; Int Correspondence Sch, 50. Polit & Govt Pos: Alderman, Allentown, Pa, 62-; Pa State Rep, 65- Bus & Prof Pos: Draftsman, Pa Power & Light Co, 54-58; design draftsman, Lehigh Struct Steel Co, 58-63; designer & checker, F W Armitage Co, Inc, 63-64. Mil Serv: Entered as Pvt, Army, 51, released as Sgt 1/C, 54, after serv in Army Security Agency, US. Mem: Pa Magistrates Asn; Lehigh Valley Minor Judiciary Asns; Patriot Order, Sons of Am; Police Athletic League (bd dirs); various fraternal orgns & Dem clubs. Honors & Awards: Rose grower, numerous ribbons. Relig: Lutheran. Mailing Add: Capitol Bldg Harrisburg PA 17120

RITTER, MABEL LOUISE (R)
b Houston, Ark, Nov 9, 29; d Hubert Alderson Hill & Ruth Freeman H; m 1950 to Loren Eugene Ritter; c Mickey Jean (Mrs Danny Hill), Kathryn Louise, Ruth Leann, David Frank, John Alan, Jayne Alice, Loren Edward & Rita Gayle. Educ: Bigelow Sch, 4 years. Polit & Govt Pos: Secy, Perry Co Rep Party, Ark, 66-68, chmn, formerly. Mem: St Boniface Altar Soc; Union Exten Homemakers Club; Perry Co Exten Homemakers Club. Relig: Catholic. Mailing Add: Rte 1 Box 22 Bigelow AR 72016

RITTER, THOMAS DRUMMOND (D)
Mem, Hartford Dem Town Comt, Conn
b New Haven, Conn, Nov 24, 52; s George Joseph Ritter & Patricia Kingsley Sleezer R; single. Educ: Amherst Col, formerly; Univ Conn Law Sch, currently; Theta Delta Chi. Polit & Govt Pos: Deleg, Conn Dem State Conv, 72; deleg, Conn State Senate Conv, 72; alt deleg, Dem Nat Conv, 72; exec asst to chmn, Hartford Dem Town Comt, 74, mem, 75- Mem: West End Civic Asn (exec bd, 74-). Relig: Quaker. Mailing Add: 891 West Blvd Hartford CT 06105

RITVO, LUCILLE B (D)
b July 11, 20; d Asher Bernstein, MD & Pauline Copel B; m 1941 to Samuel Ritvo, MD; c Jonathan Isaac, David Zvi & Rachel Zeporah. Educ: Sullin's Jr Col, Bristol, Va, 35-36; Mt Holyoke Col, AB, 40; Yale Univ, MA, 63, PhD, 72. Polit & Govt Pos: Mem, Woodbridge Pub Health Nurses Comt, Conn, 57-60; treas, Third Cong Dist, Eugene McCarthy Campaign, 67-68; deleg, Third Cong Dist Dem Conv, 68 & 72; alt deleg, 14th Sen Dist Conv to elect state Cent Committeeman & Committeewomen, 68; alt deleg, Conn Dem State Conv to Elect Nat Deleg, 68 & 72, deleg, 74; secy, Caucus of Conn Dem, 68-74; coordr, Third Cong Dist, Joe Duffey for Sen Campaign, 69-70; acting registr of voters, Dem Party, Conn, 69-70, registr, 70-; coordr, Third Cong Dist, McGovern for President Campaign, 71-72; alt deleg, Dem Nat Conv, 72; deleg, Dem Nat Mid-Term Conf, 74; mem steering comt, Conn Women's Polit Caucus, 74- Bus & Prof Pos: Field secy, New Eng Am Friends Serv Comt, 40-41; educ & recreation dir, Coop Consumers of New Haven, 41-42; recreation dir, Univ Wis Sch Worker, summers 42 & 43; ed asst, Univ Minn Press, Minneapolis, 42-43; acct exec asst, Speir & Sussman Book Advertisers, New York, 43-44; recreation dir, Hudson Shore Labor Sch, NY, summers 44 & 45; club dir, 92nd YM-YWCA, New York, 45-48; dir placement & career counseling, Albertus Magnus Col, New Haven, 69-73; lectr psychol, 72-73; lectr hist sci & med, Yale Univ, 74. Publ: Co-auth, Ernst Kris, Uomo Universales, Psychoanal Pioneers, 67; Evolution & development in psychoanalysis, Evolution & Develop Behavior, 71; auth, Carl Claus as Freud's professor of the new Darwinian biology, J Int Psychoanal Asn, 72. Mem: Group Appl Psychoanal; Oral Hist Asn; Int Soc Hist Behavioral Sci; Registr of Voters Asn

Conn; League Women Voters. Relig: Conservative Judaism. Mailing Add: 1221 Race Brook Rd Woodbridge CT 06525

RIVERA, JERRY MANALISAY (R)
Sen, Guam Legis
b Agana, Guam, Feb 2, 46; s Jesus Santos Rivera & Socorro Castro Manalisay R; m 1972 to Katherine Rose Salvatierra Baker; c Douglas Jason Baker. Educ: Univ Colo, Boulder, 64-66; Acadia; Alpha Phi Omega. Polit & Govt Pos: State chmn, Vet Day, Guam, 71 & 72; mem, Civil Serv Comn, 71-72; Sen, Guam Legis, 73- Bus & Prof Pos: Proprietor, Golden Enterprises, 72- Mil Serv: Entered as Pvt E-1, Army, 66, released as Capt, 70, after serv in 9th Inf Div, Vietnam & Royal Thai Army Vol Force Spec Liaison Sect, 2nd Field Force, Vietnam, 69-70; Res, Capt; Bronze Star with First Oak Leaf Cluster; Campaign Ribbons; Vietnam Serv Medal. Mem: Jaycees; VFW; Navy League; Air Force Asn (bd mem, 72-); Propeller Club of the US. Relig: Roman Catholic. Legal Res: 3 Marianas Terr Yigo GU Mailing Add: PO Box 8486 Tamuning GU 96911

RIVERA ORTIZ, GILBERTO (POPULAR DEMOCRAT, PR)
Sen, PR Legis
b Humacao, PR, Apr 20, 32; s Gervasio Rivera & Perfecta Ortiz R; m 1956 to Melania Rivera; c Erving, Wanda & Wilma G. Educ: Univ PR, BA, 58; Northwestern Univ, MA, 61, doctoral studies, 62. Polit & Govt Pos: Sen, PR Legis, 71- Bus & Prof Pos: Assoc prof, Univ PR, 60-70. Mil Serv: Entered as Pvt, Army, 53, released as Cpl, after serv in Co 2, 2nd Bn, 33rd Inf Regt, CZ, 53-55. Mem: Educ Comn of the States; PR Teacher Asn. Honors & Awards: Hon Cert, Pittsburgh Univ; PR Civil Defense Award. Relig: Catholic. Mailing Add: Villa Universitaria Second St K-14 Humacao PR 00661

RIVERS, JOHN STAINSBY (R)
b Detroit, Mich; s John Francis Rivers & Lillian Stainsby R; m 1951 to Joycelyn Ann Pellegrini; c Diane & Caroline. Educ: Univ Houston, 51-52; Univ Tenn, 54-55; Univ Md, 56-59; Univ Ala, 60-63; Univ Omaha, BGE, 64; Am Univ, 70-71. Polit & Govt Pos: Admin asst to US Rep David C Treen, La, 73- Mil Serv: Entered as Pvt, Air Force, 48, released as Lt Col, 71, after serv at Pentagon, 69-71; Distinguished Flying Cross with one Oak Leaf Cluster; Meritorious Serv Medal; Bronze Star; Air Medal with twelve Oak Leaf Clusters; Combat Readiness Medal; Presidential Unit Citation; Air Force Outstanding Unit Award with three Oak Leaf Clusters; Good Conduct Medal; Am Defense Serv with one Bronze Serv Star; Korean Serv Medal; Air Force Longevity Serv Award; Small Arms Expert Marksmanship; Armed Forces Expeditionary Medal; Vietnam Serv Medal with two Bronze Serv Stars; UN Serv Medal; Vietnam Air Serv Medal; Vietnam Gallantry Cross with Palm; Repub of Vietnam Commendation Medal. Relig: Catholic. Legal Res: 6205 Boutall St Metairie LA 70003 Mailing Add: 9440 Shouse Dr Vienna VA 22180

RIVERS, NATHANIEL J (NAT) (D)
Mo State Rep
Mailing Add: 5475 Cabanne St Louis MO 63112

RIVERS, RALPH JULIAN (D)
b Seattle, Wash, May 23, 03; s Julian Guy Rivers & Louisa Lavoy R; m 1928 to Lina Carol Caldwell; m 1955 to Martha Marie Quehl; c Julian Ralph & Joyce Carol (Mrs Mansfield). Educ: Univ Wash, LLB, 29; Sigma Chi; Phi Alpha Delta. Hon Degrees: LLD, Univ Alaska, 74. Polit & Govt Pos: US Dist Attorney, Fourth Judicial Div Dist of Alaska, 33-44; Attorney Gen, Alaska, 45-49; chmn, Employ Security Comn Alaska, 50-52; mayor, Fairbanks, 52-54; Sen, Alaska Territory, 55; second vpres, Alaska Const Conv, 55-56; US Rep elect under Alaska-Tenn Plan, 57-58; US Rep, Alaska, 59-67; deleg, Dem Nat Conv, 68. Bus & Prof Pos: Attorney-at-law, Fairbanks, Alaska, 31-33 & 49-57 & 67-70; retired. Mem: Alaska Bar Asn; Elks; Pioneers of Alaska; SAR; Soc Mayflower Descendants. Mailing Add: 2027 Grandview Ave Chehalis WA 98532

RIVINIUS, ALBERT L (R)
NDak State Rep
Mailing Add: State Capitol Bismarck ND 58501

RIZZO, FRANCIS LAZZARO (D)
Mayor, Philadelphia, Pa
b Philadelphia, Pa, Oct 23, 20; s Raffaele Rizzo & Theresa Ermino R; m 1942 to Carmella Silvestri; c Francis Silvestri, Jr & Joanna Ellen. Polit & Govt Pos: Mayor, Philadelphia, Pa, 72- Bus & Prof Pos: Patrolman, City of Philadelphia, 43-51, sgt, 51-54, capt, 54-59, inspector, 59-64, dep police comnr, 64-67, police comnr, 67-71. Mem: Southeastern Pa Police Chiefs Asn; Fraternal Order of Police; Del Valley Regional Planning Comn (chmn, 72-); Lions; Sons of Italy. Honors & Awards: Lowest Crime Rate Among Ten Largest Cities in Nation for Past Five Years, Crime Comn Philadelphia, 69; J Edgar Hoover Award, Nat VFW, 69; Dir Honor Award, US Secret Serv, Treas Dept, 69; many civic, local, regional & prof awards. Relig: Roman Catholic. Legal Res: 8224 Provident St Philadelphia PA 19150 Mailing Add: Rm 215 City Hall Philadelphia PA 19107

RIZZOLO, VICTOR A (R)
NJ State Assemblyman
Mailing Add: State House Trenton NJ 08625

ROACH, CRISS WARREN (D)
b Bolckow, Mo, June 17, 23; s Walter P Roach & Abbie Criss R; m 1944 to Doris Audrey Alkire; c Phyllis E (Mrs Hendricks), Priscilla A (Mrs Stuart), Charles Randall & Gerald Wayne. Educ: High Sch, Maryville, Mo, 4 years. Polit & Govt Pos: Chmn, Andrew Co Dem Comt, Mo, formerly; sales tax auditor, Mo Dept Revenue, 58-63; colonel, Gov Hearnes' Staff, 64; dairy inspector, Mo Dept Agr, 64-; chmn, Sixth Dist Dem Party, 66. Bus & Prof Pos: Farmer, Andrew Co, 41- Mil Serv: Entered as Pvt, Army, 43, released as Sgt, 46, after serv in 755th Field Artil, Ninth Div, ETO, 44-45; Presidential Unit Citation; Purple Heart. Mem: Am Legion; VFW; Mason. Relig: Protestant. Mailing Add: RR 1 Bolckow MO 64427

ROACH, WILLIAM D (D)
Ind State Rep
b West Terre Haute, Ind, Oct 21, 31; s James Roach & Francis Cash R; m 1951 to Setsuko Uesugi; c Deborah Ann, Kathleen Ann, William D, Jr, Patricia Ann & Susan Ann. Educ: Ind State Univ, Terre Haute, BS, 60, MA, 62; Ind Univ, Bloomington, 2 years. Polit & Govt Pos: Ind State Rep, 75-, ranking majority mem pub policy & vet affairs, Ind State Legis, 75- Bus & Prof Pos: Instr polit sci, Ind State Univ, 65-70; gen contractor & owner, Roach & Co Construction, Terre Haute, 70- Mil Serv: Entered as Pvt E-1, Army, 50, released as Cpl, 52, after serv in 2nd Inf Div, Korea & Japan. Mem: VFW; F&AM; Local 133 Carpenters Union; Young Dem; Kerman Grotto. Relig: Presbyterian. Mailing Add: Rte 1 Box 449 West Terre Haute IN 47885

ROACH, WILLIAM NEALE (D)
Dir Pub Rels, Dem Nat Cong Comt
b Chevy Chase, Md, Dec 29, 12; married; c Four. Polit & Govt Pos: Organizer of campaign & registr comts in many states & fund raising progs in major cities for Dem Party; serv in admin, exec & Cong liaison positions with Dem Nat Comt; mgr, Dem Nat Conv, 44, 48, 52 & 56; exec dir, Dem Sen Campaign Comt, 56; dir, Dem Cong Dinners, Washington, DC, 60, 64 & 66-69; asst chmn, Presidential Inaugural, 61; exec dir, Presidential Inaugural Comt, 65; dir pub rels, Dem Nat Cong Comt, 65- Bus & Prof Pos: Consult, Neale Roach Assocs, 57- Mailing Add: 3201 Winnett Rd Chevy Chase MD 20015

ROARK, WILSON EUGENE (R)
b Plainview, Tex, Oct 28, 26; s Cloyd E Roark & Lucy Lagow R; m 1950 to Wanda Lu Hill; c Jonathan Gene & Cynthia Lu. Educ: La State Univ Sch Med, MD, 49. Polit & Govt Pos: Chmn, McCurtain Co Rep Party, Okla, formerly. Mil Serv: Entered as 1st Lt, Air Force, 50, released as Capt, 53, after serv in 307th Bomb Wing, Strategic Air Command; Maj, Air Force Res, 61. Mem: Lions; Okla Med Soc; Am Med Asn. Relig: Baptist. Mailing Add: 410 S Park Dr Broken Bow OK 72748

ROBACH, ROGER J (D)
NY State Assemblyman
Mailing Add: 171 Hewitt St Rochester NY 14612

ROBARDS, MARY PATRICIA (D)
Committeewoman, Tex State Dem Exec Comt
b Laredo, Tex, June 26, 44; d Henrey Eugene Robards & Esther Small R; single. Educ: St Mary's Univ (Tex), BA in Int Rels, 66, JD, 74; Pi Gamma Mu. Polit & Govt Pos: Committeewoman, Tex State Dem Exec Comt, 74- Bus & Prof Pos: Bus agt, Local 171 AMCBW, 74-75; attorney-at-law, 75-; secy, Labor Coun for Latin Am Advan, San Antonio, Tex, currently. Mem: Tex Bar Asn; Coalition of Labor Union Women; Bexar Co Dem Women; AMCBW, AFL-CIO. Mailing Add: 2609 W Woodlawn San Antonio TX 78228

ROBB, ROBERT CLIFTON, JR (R)
b Harrisburg, Pa, Aug 13, 45; s Robert Clifton Robb & Pauline Mickle R; single. Educ: Univ Ky, BA, 68, Eta Sigma Phi. Polit & Govt Pos: Advanceman campaign staff, US Sen Richard S Schweiker, Pa, 68; confidential asst to asst adminr, Gen Serv Admin, 69; asst to Gov Raymond J Broderick, Pa, 70; admin asst to US Rep Albert W Johnson, Pa, 71-73 & 75-; polit consult to Andrew L Lewis, Jr, 73-75. Mem: Univ Ky Alumni Asn. Relig: Lutheran. Mailing Add: 107 November Dr Camp Hill PA 17011

ROBBENNOLT, GENE (D)
SDak State Rep
b Gettysburg, SDak, Mar 8, 36; s Maxwell Robbennolt & Mary McDonnell R; m 1955 to Donna Bown; C Mark, Michelle & Stephan. Polit & Govt Pos: Dem Co Chmn, 60-72; SDak State Rep, Dist 19, 73- Bus & Prof Pos: Owner-operator, farming, Potter Co, SDak, 58- Mil Serv: Entered as Pvt, Army, 54, released as Cpl, 56, after serv in 176th AAA Missile Bn, Media, Pa. Mem: Farmers Union; Nat Farmers Orgn. Relig: Catholic. Mailing Add: Gettysburg SD 57442

ROBBIE, JOSEPH, JR (D)
Mem Finance Coun, Dem Nat Comt, Fla
b Sisseton, SDak, July 7, 16; s Joseph Robbie, Sr & Jennie Ready R; m 1942 to Elizabeth Ann Lyle; c Diane Elizabeth, David Lyle, Janet Lee, Joseph Michael, Kathleen Mary (deceased), Lynn Margaret, Deborah Ann, Timothy John, Brian Peter, Daniel Thomas & Kevin Patrick. Educ: Northern State Teachers Col, 35-38; Univ SDak, AB, 43, LLB, 46; Degree Spec Distinction in Oratory & Debate, Pi Kappa Delta; Nat Discussion Debate Champion, Tau Kappa Alpha; Sigma Tau Delta. Hon Degrees: LLD, Biscayne Col, 70. Polit & Govt Pos: Dep State Attorney, Davison Co, SDak, 47-49; cand for Gov, SDak, 48; chmn, SDak State Dem Cent Comt, 48-50; SDak State Rep & Minority Leader, SDak House Rep, 49-51; regional counsel, Acting Regional Enforcement Dir, 51-52; regional dir, Off Price Stabilization, 52-53; chmn, Minn Adv Comt to Dem Nat Comt, 54-58; cand for US Cong, Minn, 56 & 58; exec secy, Legal Counsel Comn Munic Annexation & Consol Minn Legis, 57-59; charter mem & secy-treas, Twin Cities Metrop Planning Comn, Minn, 57-67; chmn, Minn Munic Comn, 59-65; campaign chmn, Humphrey for President, Charleston, WVa, 60; spec counsel, Comt for Hearings to Create Dept Urban Affairs, US Senate, 61; fund raising rep, Humphrey for Vice President, 64; chmn, Dade Co Dem Exec Comt, Fla, 72-74; mem, Fla Dem Exec Comt, 72-74; mem finance coun, Dem Nat Comt, currently. Bus & Prof Pos: Attorney-at-law, 46-; instr econ, Dakota Wesleyan Univ, 46-51; debate coach & speech instr, Col St Catherine, 53-54; exec secy & dir, Minn Candy & Tobacco Distributors Asn, 59-; pres & managing gen partner, Miami Dolphins, Ltd, 65-; bd trustees, Jackson Mem Hosp, 73- Mil Serv: Entered as Seaman, Naval Res, 41, released as Lt(jg), 45, after serv with 7th Amphibious Force, Pac Fleet, SW Pac, 45; Bronze Star & Leyte, Brunei Bay & Tarakan Invasion Ribbons; Intel Officer, Naval Res, until 65. Publ: Report of Committee on Municipal Annexation & Consolidation, 59 & Report of Commission on Municipal Laws, 63, Minn Legis Research Comt; Ethics in government, Va Law Rev, 61. Mem: Am Bar Asn; Am Judicature Soc; Nat Munic League; Am Trial Lawyers Asn; Am Friends of Hebrew Univ (fel). Honors & Awards: Good Samaritan Award, Variety Club Gtr Miami, 70; Nat Football League Owner of Year, Minutemen of Minneapolis & St Paul, 71; Prof Football Exec of Year, LI Athletic Club, 72; Meritorious Pub Serv Citation, Dept Navy, 73-74; Silver Medallion, Nat Conf Christians & Jews, Fla Region, 73. Relig: Catholic. Legal Res: 1301 NE 100th St Miami Shores FL 33138 Mailing Add: 330 Biscayne Blvd Miami FL 33132

ROBBINS, HERSHEL M (D)
Mont State Rep
Mailing Add: 915 First St E Roundup MT 59072

ROBBINS, WILLIAM RAYMOND (R)
b Spickard, Mo, May 30, 16; s Albert Raymond Robbins & Agnes Nigh R; m 1950 to Marilyn Henderson; c Meredith Nadine & Marsha Gail. Educ: Trenton Jr Col, AA; Univ Mo, BS in Agr; Alpha Gamma Rho; OEBH. Polit & Govt Pos: Chmn, Grundy Co Rep Cent Comt, Mo, formerly; mem, Mo Rep State Comt, 66-68. Bus & Prof Pos: Mem pub rels staff, Fed Land Bank of St Louis, 39-42; mkt news reporter, US Dept Agr, 42; dir & vpres, Farmers Mutual Windstorm Ins Co, 46-59; secy-mgr & treas, Farmers Mutual Ins Co of Grundy Co, 59- Mil

Serv: Entered as Pvt, Marine Corps, 42, released as Capt, 51, after serv in Marine Air Wing, Pac Theater, 43-46, Res, Capt (Ret). Mem: Mason; KT; Shrine; Am Legion; CofC. Relig: Disciples of Christ. Mailing Add: 515 DeBolt Trenton MO 64683

ROBERGE, A ROLAND (R)
b North Battleford, Sask, May 13, 33; s Albert J Roberge & Marie Anna Trottier R; m 1957 to M Sheila Skeffington; c Carolyn & John. Educ: St Anselm's Col, BS, 57; Columbia Univ Grad Sch Bus, MS, 59. Polit & Govt Pos: Manchester chmn, NH Comt for Reelec of President, 71-73; treas, NH Rep State Comt, formerly. Bus & Prof Pos: Asst vpres, Harris Upham & Co, Manchester, 69- Mem: Am Cancer Soc, NH Div; NH Easter Seal Soc (chmn, Manchester); Kiwanis; Joliet Club. Honors & Awards: Editorial praising orgn leadership for Reelec of President Nixon, Manchester Union Leader, 72. Relig: Catholic. Mailing Add: 101 Magnolia Rd Manchester NH 03104

ROBERSON, JAMES H (D)
Tenn State Sen
Mailing Add: 711 Graycroft Madison TN 37115

ROBERT, ERNEST (R)
Chmn, Granby Rep Town Comt, Mass
b Granby, Mass, Oct 11, 05; s Ernest Robert & Angliana Perneault R; m 1932 to Viola Theroux; c Wilfred F & Jeannette R (Mrs Molin). Educ: Granby Schs, 14-18. Polit & Govt Pos: Chmn, Granby Rep Town Comt, Mass, 49-; supt-treas, Granby, 50-58. Mem: New Eng Milk Producers Asn; Cath Men Club (vchmn). Relig: Catholic. Mailing Add: 164 South Granby MA 01033

ROBERTI, DAVID A (D)
Calif State Sen
b Los Angeles, Calif, May 4, 39; s Emil Roberti & Elvira Ligrano R; m 1968 to June Joyce. Educ: Loyola Univ, Los Angeles, BA, 61; Univ Southern Calif Law Sch, JD, 64; Univ Southern Calif Law Rev. Polit & Govt Pos: Mem, Calif Dem Coun; chmn, Los Angeles Co Young Dem, 65; dep attorney gen, Calif, 65-66; Calif State Assemblyman, 48th Dist, 67-71, chmn, Comt Labor Rels, Calif State Assembly, 71; Calif State Sen, 71-, chmn majority caucus, Calif State Senate, 74- Relig: Roman Catholic. Legal Res: 2634 Hollyridge Dr Los Angeles CA 90068 Mailing Add: State Capitol Sacramento CA 95814

ROBERTO, MARCUS AURELIUS (D)
Ohio State Rep
b New Milford, Ohio, Nov 26, 30; s Americo Dominic Roberto & Anna Laurito R; m 1957 to Marjorie Jean Hope; c Cathleen (Mrs Richard Rufener), John, Elizabeth & Marcus. Educ: Kent State Univ, BS, 57, MA, 60; Akron Sch Law, JD, 72; Nat Educ Honor Soc. Polit & Govt Pos: Ohio State Rep, 71- Bus & Prof Pos: Teacher & attorney, Ravenna, Ohio, 57- Mil Serv: Entered as Pvt, Air Force, 50, released as S/Sgt, 54, after serv in Eastern Air Defense Command. Mem: Rotary Int; Am Legion; Grange. Honors & Awards: Martha Holden Jennings award, 67-68. Relig: Protestant. Mailing Add: 3377 Summit Rd Ravenna OH 44266

ROBERTS, ANTHONY ALONGI (R)
Mem, Los Angeles Co Rep Cent Comt, Calif
b Rochester, NY, July 17, 24; s Alfonso Alongi & Angela Farruggia A; m 1955 to Arlyn Kuhn; c Dorian Lee & Stephen. Educ: La Salle Exten Law Sch. Polit & Govt Pos: Unit chmn, United Rep of Calif, 68-72; mem, Calif State Rep Cent Comt, 68-72; mem, Los Angeles Co Rep Cent Comt, 72-; mem, Gtr Whittier Calif Rep Assembly, 69. Bus & Prof Pos: Exec secy & partner, Am Land, Del Mar Village & Am Cal Corps, 62-65; vpres & gen mgr, Niagara Invest Co, Inc, 65- Mil Serv: Entered as A/S, Naval Res, 43, released as HA 1/C, 45, after serv in Pac Theatre, 44-45. Mem: Town Hall of Calif; Rotary Int; Whittier CofC; Calif State CofC; KofC. Relig: Catholic. Legal Res: 13206 Philadelphia St Whittier CA 90602 Mailing Add: Box 548 Whittier CA 90608

ROBERTS, B K (D)
Justice, Fla Supreme Court
b Sopchoppy, Fla, Feb 5, 07; m 1937 to Mary Newman; c Mary Jane & Thomas. Educ: Univ Fla, JD, 28; Phi Alpha Delta; Alpha Kappa Psi; Blue Key; Gold Key; Delta Chi; vpres, Sr Class. Hon Degrees: LLD, Univ Miami, 54. Polit & Govt Pos: Justice, Fla Supreme Court, 49-, chief justice, 53-54, 61-63 & 71-72; chmn, Fla Judicial Coun, 62-; mem, Fla Const Rev Comt & chmn, Subcomt on Human Rights, 66; chmn, Judicial Admin Comn, 71-72. Bus & Prof Pos: Attorney, Tallahassee, 28-49; vpres, Tallahassee Bank & Trust Co, 48-49. Mil Serv: Coast Guard; asst legal officer, 6th Naval Dist, staff mem, Dist Coast Guard Off, US Shipping Comnr, Port of Jacksonville. Mem: Am Bar Asn; Am Law Inst; Am Judicature Soc; Nat Conf Chief Justices; Int Bar Asn. Honors & Awards: Distinguished Citizen Award, Stetson Law Col, 62. Relig: Presbyterian. Legal Res: Meridian Pl Tallahassee FL 32303 Mailing Add: Supreme Court Bldg Tallahassee FL 32304

ROBERTS, BETTY R (D)
Ore State Sen
b Arkansas City, Kans, Feb 5, 23; d David Murray Cantrell & Pearl Higgins C; m 1968 to Keith D Skelton; c Dian (Mrs Odell), John Rice, Jo & Randall Rice. Educ: Portland State Col, BS; Univ Ore, MS; Northwestern Sch Law, Lewis & Clark Col, LLB. Polit & Govt Pos: Sch bd mem, Lynch Sch Dist, Portland, Ore, 60-66; Ore State Rep, Dist 6, 65-68; deleg, Dem Nat Conv, 68 & 72; Ore State Sen, 69- Bus & Prof Pos: Dean of girls, Reynolds High Sch, Troutdale, Ore, 58-60; teacher, Centennial High Sch, Gresham, 60-62; teacher, David Douglas High Sch, Portland, 62-66; teacher, Mt Hood Community Col, Gresham, 67-; attorney-at-law, currently. Mem: Ore & Nat Educ Asns; Am & Ore Bar Asns; League of Women Voters. Legal Res: 319 SE Gilham Portland OR 97215 Mailing Add: Boise Cascade Bldg SW Fourth St at Market St Portland OR 97201

ROBERTS, BILL (D)
Ala State Sen
b Mobile, Ala, Jan 6, 41; s William Leslie Roberts & Josie Lee Stevens R; single. Educ: Auburn Univ, 4 years; Univ SAla, 4 years, Phi Delta Theta. Polit & Govt Pos: Ala State Rep, formerly; Ala State Sen, currently. Bus & Prof Pos: Adminr, Cogburn Nursing Home of Mobile, Ala, 65-70. Mil Serv: Airman 1/C, Air Force Res, 65. Relig: Baptist. Mailing Add: Rte 1 Box 278 Theodore AL 36582

ROBERTS, CLINT, JR (R)
SDak State Sen
Mailing Add: Presho SD 57568

ROBERTS, DAVID EARL (D)
Ark State Rep
b Jacksonville, Ark, Dec 14, 23; s Dave A Roberts & Rubie Rogers R; m 1949 to Marion Knowles; c Debra (Mrs Rogers) & Patricia Lynn. Educ: Univ Wichita. Polit & Govt Pos: Ark State Rep, 73-; chmn, North Little Rock Planning Comn. Mil Serv: Entered as Pvt, Air Force, 42, released as Col, after serv in various units, 72. Mem: Rotary; Mason, Shrine; North Hills Country Club; Home Builders Asn. Relig: Methodist. Mailing Add: 3419 N Hills Blvd North Little Rock AR 72116

ROBERTS, DONALD DUANE (R)
Chmn, Lincoln Parish Rep Orgn, La
b Jamestown, NDak, Feb 18, 29; s Calvin Boyd Roberts & Irma Roberts R; m 1952 to Ann Marie Valenti; c Marie Therese, Marie Christine, Marie Kathleen, Susan Marie, Robert Joseph & Maribeth. Educ: Jamestown Col, BS, 50; Loyola Univ, Ill, MS, 57, Am Chem Soc fel, PhD, 62. Polit & Govt Pos: Chmn, Lincoln Parish Rep Orgn, 66-; mem, Rep State Cent Comt La, 66- Bus & Prof Pos: Research chemist, Sherwin Williams, Chicago, 52-54; group leader, Borg Warner Corp, DesPlaines, 54-58; research chemist, Am Oil Co, Whiting, Ind, 58-60; prof, La Tech Univ, 63- Mil Serv: Entered as Cadet, Navy, 48, released 49, after serv in Naval Flight Sch, Pensacola, Fla, 48-49. Publ: Auth, 25 sci papers, J Organic Chem. Mem: Sigma Xi; Am Chem Soc; La Independent Sch Asn (pres, 72-). Honors & Awards: Research grants from Research Corp Am & Am Chem Soc Petroleum Research Fund. Relig: Roman Catholic. Mailing Add: 2101 Cypress Springs Ave Ruston LA 71270

ROBERTS, DONUS DAN (D)
b Chamberlain, SDak, July 19, 37; s Daniel Paul Roberts & Ester Foreman R; m 1962 to Lovila Zoellner; c Robyn Renae. Educ: Univ SDak, Springfield, BS, 59; Univ Nebr, Lincoln, 60; Northwestern Univ, Evanston, MA, 64; Stanford Univ, 67; Macalester Col, 70; Colo State Univ, 71; Sigma Delta Nu. Polit & Govt Pos: Financial & campaign coordr, Codington Co Dem Party, SDak, 70-71, chmn, formerly. Bus & Prof Pos: Field personnel, Rogers Indust, Chicago, Ill, 59-60; teacher & dir forensics & chmn lang arts dept, Watertown Pub Schs, SDak, 60-; asst prof, Mich State Univ, 69. Publ: Extemp: a new emphasis, J Speech Asn SDak, 65; co-auth, Ethics in research & speaking, Issues Mag, 2/72. Mem: SDak Speech Adv Comt; Speech-Commun Asn SDak; Nat Forensic League Dist Comt (chmn, 62-); Speech Commun Asn Am (legis assembly); Am Forensic Asn. Honors & Awards: Community Leader, CofC, US, 68; Outstanding Educator, Jr CofC, 69; Coe Scholar, Coe Humanities Found, 70; Outstanding Alumnus, Univ SDak, Springfield, 73. Relig: Lutheran. Mailing Add: 1281 Second St NW Watertown SD 57201

ROBERTS, EDWARD CALHOUN (D)
Secy, Richland Co Dem Party, SC
b Columbia, SC, Oct 17, 37; s John Cornelius Roberts & Cecilia Allen R; m 1967 to Margaret Coons; c Kathryn Alexandria. Educ: Univ SC, AB, 59, JD, 62; Georgetown Univ Law Ctr, LLM, 63; Blue Key; Sigma Alpha Epsilon. Polit & Govt Pos: US Comnr, Spartanburg, SC, 66-67; nat committeeman, SC Young Dem, 69-71 & 73-; secy, Richland Co Dem Party, 70-; acting secy, SC Dem Party, 73. Bus & Prof Pos: Attorney-at-law, Spartanburg, SC, 64-67; asst counsel, SC Elec & Gas Co, 67. Mil Serv: Entered as Pvt, Marine Corps Res, 63, released as S/Sgt, 69, after serv in Amma Co, Columbia, SC. Publ: Co-auth, Freedom From Federal Establishment: The Formation & History of the First Amendment Religion Clauses (w C J Antieau & A T Downey, III), Bruce Publ Co; Criteria for award of foreign air route to American Air Carrier, SC Law Rev, 15: 867 & 16: 263. Mem: Am Bar Asn (antitrust, corp, banking & bus & pub utility sect); SC Bar Asn (chmn comt rev SC corp law); KofC; Jaycees. Relig: Roman Catholic. Legal Res: 8 Woodhill Circle Columbia SC 29209 Mailing Add: Box 764 Columbia SC 29202

ROBERTS, FRANK LIVEZEY (D)
Ore State Sen
b Boise, Idaho, Dec 28, 15; s Walter Scott Roberts & Mary Elizabeth Livezey R; div; c Mary Linda & Leslie. Educ: Pac Univ, Forest Grove, Ore, BA, 38; Univ Wis, PhM, 43; Stanford Univ, PhD, 54. Polit & Govt Pos: Chmn, Multnomah Co Dem Cent Comt, 60-63; mem, Portland Metrop Study Comn, 64-; mem, Mt Hood Community Col Bd, 65-; permanent chmn, Ore Dem State Conv, 66; Ore State Rep, Sixth Dist, 67-72; deleg, Dem Nat Conv, 68; Ore State Sen, 75- Bus & Prof Pos: Prof speech, Portland State Univ, 46-, dean undergrad studies & assoc dean faculty, 63-66. Mil Serv: Entered as Aviation Cadet, Army, 43, released as 1st Lt, 46, after serv in Army Airways Commun Serv, ETO, 46. Publ: Basic Parliamentary Procedure, Rigdon, 66. Mem: Portland City Club. Mailing Add: 223 NW 103rd Ave Portland OR 97220

ROBERTS, GEORGE B (R)
Majority Leader, NH House of Rep
b Andover, Mass, June 13, 39; s George B Roberts; m 1967 to Margaret Edmunds. Educ: Univ NY, BS & MPA; Sigma Alpha Epsilon. Polit & Govt Pos: Mem adv coun, Nat Conf State Legis Leaders; mem, Nat Soc State Legislators & Nat Legis Conf; deleg, NH State Rep Conv, 66, 68, 70-72; NH State Rep, 67-69 & 71-, majority leader, NH State House of Rep, 71-, chmn, Rules Comt, Belknap Co Deleg, Labor Study Comt, Subcomt Data Processing & Off Space Study Comt, 71-, mem, State Interstate Coop Comt, Exec Depts & Admin Comt, Legis Coun Subcomt & Appropriations Comt, 71-; deleg, Rep Nat Conv, 72. Mil Serv: Entered as Seaman, US Coast Guard, 57, released as Qm II, 59, after serv in NAtlantic; Qm II, US Coast Guard Res, 63. Publ: Application of Data Processing for Municipalities, 67; Comparisons of Organizational Behavior in Government & Business Structures, 68. Mem: Am Heritage Soc; Acad Polit Sci; Soc Protection of NH Forests; Lakes Region Ment Health Clin (bd dirs). Honors & Awards: Outstanding legislator of the Year, NH, Eagleton Inst Polit, 73. Relig: Protestant. Legal Res: Meeting House Rd Gilmanton Iron Works NH 03837 Mailing Add: State House Concord NH 03301

ROBERTS, HARRY (R)
Secy, Wyo Rep State Cent Comt
b New York, NY, Dec 10, 17; s Albert S Roberts & Nathalie Harrison R; m 1942 to Louise Littleton; c Marion (Mrs Rankin), Sheila (Mrs Anderson), Susan (Mrs Hubbell), Joan (Mrs Fitch) & Virginia. Educ: Yale Univ, BA, 39; Univ Md, 46; Zeta Psi. Polit & Govt Pos: Chmn, Gov Comt Educ, 63-65; mem, State Bd Educ, 63-70; Supt Pub Instr, Wyo, 66-70; cand for cong, 70; Wyo Transportation mem, Fed Rocky Mountain States, 71-; secy, Wyo Conserv & Land Use Comn, 73-; secy, Wyo Rep State Cent Comt, 73- Bus & Prof Pos: Mgr & vpres, D Cross Cattle Co, 51-66; admin asst to Hatrue Jr, True Oil Co, 70- Mil Serv: Entered as A/S, Navy, 41, released as Lt, 45, after serv in submarine SS 241, Pac, 43-45; various ribbons; Submarine Combat Medal. Mem: Rocky Mountain Oil & Gas Asn; Rotary; Am Legion; Farm Bur; Mason. Relig: Episcopal. Mailing Add: 233 E 12th St Casper WY 82601

ROBERTS, HOLLIS E (D)
Okla State Sen
Mailing Add: State Capitol Oklahoma City OK 73105

ROBERTS, JAMES HAZELTON (R)
Mem, Rep State Exec Comt WVa
b Parkersburg, WVa, Aug 26, 25; s Leslie Van Dyke Roberts & Dorothy Folts R; m 1952 to Patricia Higgins; c Sara Dorothy, Charlotte Ann & Christine Lee. Educ: Ohio State Univ, BS; Univ Mich, MS; Kappa Alpha; Phi Epsilon Kappa; Lettermans Club. Polit & Govt Pos: Chmn, Co Rep Exec Comt, WVa, 57; deleg, Rep Nat Conv, 60 & 68; mem, Rep State Exec Comt WVa, 64- Mil Serv: Entered as Seaman, Navy, 43, released as Athletic Specialist, 46; Good Conduct, Victory & Asian-Pac Ribbons. Mem: Am Legion; Lions; Moose; VFW; Farm Bur. Relig: Methodist. Mailing Add: Elizabeth WV 26143

ROBERTS, JAMES WILLIAM (R)
Chmn, Asotin Co Rep Cent Comt, Wash
b Colfax, Wash, Mar 15, 28; s James Richard Roberts & Evelyn Johnston R; m 1948 to Frances Louise Spooner; c Kenneth Lee, Christopher Allen & Vickie Jo. Educ: Clarkston High Sch, grad, 48; Lewis Clark Normal Sch, 63. Polit & Govt Pos: Assessor, Asotin Co, 71-; chmn, Asotin Co Rep Cent Comt, Wash, 71- Bus & Prof Pos: Bldg contractor, Clarkston, Wash, 60- Mil Serv: Entered as Pvt, Marine Corps, 44, released as Sgt, 50, after serv in Asiatic Theatre, 44-46. Mem: Mason; Shrine; Am Legion; Grange. Relig: Church of God. Mailing Add: 2545 Reservoir Rd Clarkston WA 99403

ROBERTS, JOE R (D)
Mont State Sen
Mailing Add: c/o Don's Men's Store Libby MT 59923

ROBERTS, JOHN B (R)
Maine State Sen
Mailing Add: 6 Washington St Sanford ME 04073

ROBERTS, KENNETH ALLISON (D)
b Piedmont, Ala, Nov 1, 12; s John Franklin Roberts & Josephine Burton R; m 1953 to Margaret Hamilton McMillan; c Margaret Hamilton & Allison McMillan. Educ: Samford Col, 29; Univ Ala, LLB, 35; Alpha Tau Omega; Phi Alpha Delta; Blue Key. Polit & Govt Pos: Mem, State Bd Vet Affairs; Ala State Sen, 42; US Rep, Ala, 51-65; mem, Nat Hwy Safety Adv Comt, 67- Bus & Prof Pos: Attorney-at-law, Anniston, Ala, 35, 45-50 & Talladega, 37-42; pres, Piedmont Develop Co. Mil Serv: Entered as Ens, Navy, 42, released as Lt, 46, after serv in USS Micka, Atlantic & Pac Theaters, 44-46; Lt Comdr, Naval Res (Ret); Atlantic & Pac Theater Ribbons. Mem: Ala & DC Bar Asns; Am Legion; Mason; Lions. Legal Res: 429 Belleville Ave Brewton AL 36426 Mailing Add: 7106 Plantation Lane Rockville MD 20852

ROBERTS, LILLIAN (D)
b Chicago, Ill; d Henry Davis & Lillian Henry D; div. Educ: Univ Ill, 44-45. Polit & Govt Pos: Deleg, Dem Nat Conv, 72. Bus & Prof Pos: Nurse's aide, Univ Chicago-Lying In Hosp, 45-51, operating room technician, 51-58; organizer, dist coun 19 & 34, Am Fedn State & Munic Employees, 58-65, div dir, local 420, Am Fedn State, Co & Munic Employees, NY, 65-67, assoc dir dist coun 37, 67- Mem: Ctr for Mediation & Conflict Resolution (bd dirs); Cornell Univ Sch Indust & Labor Rels (coun); Women's Prison Asn & Home (bd, 71-); Comprehensive Health Planning Agency of New York; Health Ins Plan of Gtr New York (bd). Honors & Awards: Serv Award, Am Fedn State, Co & Munic Employees, 65; A Phillip Randolph Award for Person who has done most for Negro-Labor Alliance, 68 & 69; New Leadership Award, Am Dem Action, 70; Women of Year Award, NAACP, New York Br, 71; Sixth Annual Award, Michael Schwerner Mem Comt, 72. Relig: Protestant. Mailing Add: 626 Riverside Dr New York NY 10031

ROBERTS, MARY LINDA (WENDY) (D)
Ore State Sen
b Ill, Dec 19, 44; d Dr Frank L Roberts & Mary L Charleson R; single. Educ: Portland State Univ, summer 63; Chinese-Japanese Lang Inst, Univ Colo, summer 64; Univ Ore, BA, 65; Univ Wis-Madison, MA, 71; Chi Delta Phi. Polit & Govt Pos: Ore State Rep, 73-75; Ore State Sen, 75- Bus & Prof Pos: Caseworker III, Multnomah Co Juvenile Court, 71-72; real estate, 73- Mem: Am Fedn State Co & Munic Employees, Local 88. Relig: Unitarian. Legal Res: 835 NE 118th Portland OR 97220 Mailing Add: Ore State Senate Salem OR 93710

ROBERTS, RAY (D)
US Rep, Tex
b Collin Co, Tex, Mar 28, 13; s Roy C Roberts (deceased) & Margaret Emma R; m to Elizabeth Bush; c Mrs Tom Murray, III. Educ: Tex A&M Univ; NTex State Univ; Tex Univ. Polit & Govt Pos: Mem staff, US Rep Sam Rayburn, Tex, formerly; Tex State Sen, 55-62; US Rep, Tex, 62- Mil Serv: Navy; Capt (Ret), Naval Res. Legal Res: McKinney TX 75069 Mailing Add: Rayburn House Off Bldg Washington DC 20515

ROBERTS, RICHARD W (R)
Dir, Nat Bur Standards
b Buffalo, NY, Jan 12, 35; s William B Roberts & Eugena Cook Pratt R; m 1956 to Carol J Elmer; c Beth C & William C. Educ: Univ Rochester, BS, 56; Brown Univ, PhD, 59; Phi Beta Kappa; Sigma Xi; Theta Chi. Polit & Govt Pos: Dir, Nat Bur Standards, 73- Bus & Prof Pos: Res scientist, Chem Res Div, Gen Elec Co, 60-65, mgr, Center's Struct & Reactions Br, 65-68 & Center's Phys Chem Lab, 68, res & develop mgr mat sci & eng, 68-73. Publ: Co-auth, Ultrahigh Vacuum & Its Applications (w T A Vanderslice), Prentice-Hall, 63 & 64; co-ed, Annual review of materials science, Annual Rev Inc, currently. Mem: Am Chem Soc; Am Phys Soc; Am Nuclear Soc; AAAS; Am Inst Chem. Relig: Protestant. Mailing Add: 9310 Hollyoak Dr Bethesda MD 20034

ROBERTS, SANDRA LEVINSON (D)
b Santa Rosa, Calif, Dec 20, 46; d Herman Levinson & Doris Thorson L; m 1969 to Alan Arthur Roberts. Educ: Univ Calif, Berkeley, 64-66; Univ Calif, Santa Barbara, BA in Eng, 68, Standard Elem Credential, 69; Univ Colo, Boulder, Sch Pub Admin, 73- Polit & Govt Pos: Alt deleg, Dem Nat Conv, 72; off mgr, Boulder Co Dem Hq, Colo, 72; polit educ chmn, Dem Women of Boulder Co, 72-73, vpres, 73- Bus & Prof Pos: Elem teacher, Marymount Jr Sch, Santa Barbara, Calif, 69-70; librn, Boulder Pub Libr, Colo, 71-72. Mem: Colo Dem Women's Caucus. Mailing Add: 1999 Bluebell Ave Boulder CO 80302

ROBERTS, SHARRON DALE (D)
Mem, Ga State Dem Exec Comt
b Gainesville, Ga, Mar 24, 50; d Joe White & Beatrice Vickers W; m 1973 to Johnny Franklin Roberts. Educ: Gainesville Jr Col, AA, 70; NGa Col, BA in hist, 71; Sigma Delta Upsilon. Polit & Govt Pos: Mem, Ga State Dem Exec Comt, 74- Relig: Assembly of God. Mailing Add: Rte 12 Box 733 Gainesville GA 30501

ROBERTS, TERRY LEE (R)
Nat Committeeman, Ga Fedn Young Rep
b Tampa, Fla, Oct 12, 45; s F Claude Roberts & Eva Mitchell R; div; c Chad Justin. Educ: Embry-Riddle Aeronaut Univ, BS, 71; Sigma Chi. Polit & Govt Pos: Chmn, Embry-Riddle Young Rep, 70-71; 1st vchmn, Fla Col Young Rep, 71-72; vchmn polit affairs, Clayton Co Young Rep Club, 72-74; sixth dist dir, Ga Fedn Young Rep, 73-74, chmn, 74-75, nat committeeman, 75-; campaign mgr, Harold Dye for Gov, 74. Bus & Prof Pos: Salesman, Jean Rick Realty, Jonesboro, Ga, 71-73, training dir, 73-74, sales mgr, 74- Mil Serv: HM3, Naval Res, 65-71. Mem: Clayton Co Bd Realtors; Ga & Nat Asn Realtors. Legal Res: 685 Roundtree Rd J-74 Riverdale GA 30274 Mailing Add: 148 S Main St Jonesboro GA 30236

ROBERTS, TOMMY ED (D)
Ala State Rep
Mailing Add: Rte 4 Box 293-E Decatur AL 35601

ROBERTS, VIRGIL DEAN (D)
Wis State Rep
b Mindoro, Wis, Apr 13, 22; s Earl Edwin Roberts & Eva Radcliffe R; m 1945 to Alice Marie Evenson; c Ann (Mrs Don Campbell), Joan (Mrs Jake Schaller), Gordon & Janet. Educ: Winona State Col, 59-60. Polit & Govt Pos: Clerk, Mindoro Sch Bd of Educ, 50-58; Wis State Rep, 71- Bus & Prof Pos: Train dispatcher, Milwaukee RR, Wis, 43- Mem: Toastmasters Int; Lions; Am Train Dispatchers Asn. Relig: Lutheran. Mailing Add: 308 Park Lane Holmen WI 54636

ROBERTS, VIRGIL H (R)
b Augusta, Ill, June 29, 16; s Herman Roberts & Iva Harris R; m 1938 to Mildred Kathryn Ayers; c Mary Ruth (Mrs John Phillips), Shirley Jean (Mrs Kay Lord), Bettie Kathryn (Mrs Kieth White), Ronald Glenn & Paul Herman. Educ: Augusta High Sch, 4 years. Polit & Govt Pos: Secy, Augusta Bd Educ, Ill, 46-51, pres, 61-64; supvr, Birmingham Twp, 50-; precinct committeeman, Birmingham Twp Rep Party, 50-; chmn, Schuyler Co Rep Party, formerly. Bus & Prof Pos: Lifetime farmer. Mem: Mason; Consistory; Shrine; Farm Bur. Relig: Methodist. Mailing Add: Rte 1 Augusta IL 62311

ROBERTS, WILBER ESTES (D)
Mem, Dent Co Dem Party, Mo
b Salem, Mo, Oct 7, 09; s Thomas Mattison Roberts & Alberta Hayes R; m 1930 to Bonnie Jewel Black; c Ronald Dean & Lavonne Silva. Educ: New Home Sch, 8 years. Polit & Govt Pos: Mem, Dem Comt, 58-63; chmn, Dent Co Dem Party, Mo, 58-70, mem, 70- Bus & Prof Pos: Contractor. Mem: Odd Fellows. Relig: Southern Baptist. Mailing Add: Rte 3 Salem MO 65560

ROBERTS, WILLIAM (R)
Idaho State Rep
Mailing Add: Rte 4 Box 300 Buhl ID 83316

ROBERTS, WILLIAM LEE (D)
Ky State Rep
Mailing Add: PO Box 694 Pikeville KY 41501

ROBERTSON, CAROL (R)
VChmn, Ellis Co Rep Party, Okla
b Gage, Okla, Dec 25, 13; d Lewis Hampton Long & Louis E Geier L; m 1934 to Roma C Robertson. Educ: High Sch, Shattuck, Okla & exten classes in Bible, bookkeeping, art & psychol, 35-36 & 51-61. Polit & Govt Pos: Precinct chmn, Ellis Co Rep Party, Okla, 59-60, vchmn, 61-62, 63-66 & 75-, chmn, 66-67, 67-68; deleg, Rep state & dist conv, 61-; mem, Rep State Comt, 61-, mem rules & order comt, 62, resolutions comt, 64 & resolutions comt in the dist, 68; mem, State Rep Party Auditing Comt, 67-68; alt deleg-at-lg, Rep Nat Conv, 68; mem, Gov Comt Children & Youth; State Committeewoman, Okla Rep Party, 69-74; co coordr, Bartlett for Gov & Thompson for Lt Gov, 70 & Dewey F Bartlett for US Senate & Nixon for President, 72; mem, Okla State Legis Campaign Comt, 70-; coordr, Henry Bellmon for US Senate Campaign & James Inhofe for Gov, 74. Bus & Prof Pos: Merchant, music store, 46- Mem: Bus & Prof Women; Westerner Art Club; Missionary Orgn; Shattuck CofC; Ellis Co Sportsman Club. Relig: Christian; adult Bible teacher. Legal Res: 811 S Locust Shattuck OK 73858 Mailing Add: PO Box 111 Shattuck OK 73858

ROBERTSON, DONALD B (D)
Md State Deleg
b Washington, DC, Oct 6, 31; s Nathan Wood Robertson & Elizabeth R; m 1959 to Marion Ostrom; c Stephen, Anne, Thomas & John. Educ: Oberlin Col, BA, 53; Columbia Law Sch, LLB, 58; Phi Delta Phi. Polit & Govt Pos: Mem & vchmn, Citizens Comt of Chevy Chase, Sect III, 68-71; Md State Deleg, 71-, chmn, Montgomery Co Deleg, 71- Bus & Prof Pos: Attorney-at-law, Washington, DC & Md, 61- Mil Serv: Entered as Ens, Navy, 53, released as Lt(jg), 55, after serv in USS Hickox (DD673), Atlantic Fleet. Publ: Co-auth, Recent developments in natural gas regulation by the FPC, 16th Oil & Gas Inst I, 65; contrib auth, Natural gas, Report Sec Mineral Law, Am Bar Asn, 66. Legal Res: 7003 Delaware St Chevy Chase MD 20015 Mailing Add: Rm 222 House Off Bldg Annapolis MD 21404

ROBERTSON, EDWARD D (D)
Ala State Rep
b Northport, Ala, Oct 16, 30; s J D Robertson & Myra Marie Parsons R; m 1950 to Sarah Imogene Moore; c Donna Marie. Educ: Gorgas High Sch, 12 years. Polit & Govt Pos: City councilman, Northport, Ala, 64-67; Ala State Rep, 67- Bus & Prof Pos: Vpres, Local 351, United Rubber Workers, 65-67. Mem: United Rubber Workers. Relig: Baptist. Mailing Add: Box 331 Northport AL 35476

ROBERTSON, GEORGE LOUIS (R)
Chmn, Minnehaha Co Rep Party, SDak
b Sioux Falls, SDak, Dec 7, 47; s Howard Jerome Robertson & Louise Fangmeier R; m 1968 to Nancy Anne Westre; c Clayton. Educ: Yankton Col, 65-68. Polit & Govt Pos: Chmn,

Minnehaha Co Rep Party, SDak, 75-; mem, SDak Rep Party Exec Comt, 75- Bus & Prof Pos: Exec dir, Gtr Sioux Falls Safety Coun, 69-73; safety engr, Maryland Casualty Co, El Paso, Tex, 73-74; dir personnel & safety, Jack Rabbit Lines, Sioux Falls, SDak, 74- Mem: Gtr Sioux Falls Safety Coun (mem bd dirs, 74-); Sioux Falls Morning Optimists; Sioux Empire Drug Educ Comt; SDak Gov Adv Coun on Occup Safety & Health. Legal Res: 1205 Pam Rd Sioux Falls SD 57105 Mailing Add: 301 N Dakota Ave Sioux Falls SD 57102

ROBERTSON, JAMES TAYLOR, JR (D)
Chmn, Westmoreland Co Dem Comt, Va
b Richmond, Va, Feb 26, 23; s James Taylor Robertson & Dorothy Sage R; m 1947 to Paula D Gabler; c Sarah (Mrs deG Pretlow); James Taylor, III, Samuel Creed & Archer Sage. Educ: Hampden-Sydney Col, BS, 43; Univ Va, LLB, 49; Theta Chi. Polit & Govt Pos: Chmn, Westmoreland Co Dem Comt, Va, 75-; chmn, Dem Senate Dist Comt, 75- & Dem House of Deleg Dist Comt, 75- Bus & Prof Pos: Partner, Hutt & Robertson, Attorneys-at-law, 51- Mil Serv: Entered as A/S, Naval Res, 43, released as Lt(jg), 46, after serv in Pac Fleet, 44-46; several theatre campaign and/or occup ribbons with stars. Mem: Va State Bar; Northern Neck & 15th Judicial Circuit Bar Asns. Relig: Protestant. Mailing Add: Montross VA 22520

ROBERTSON, JOHN ANDERSON (R)
VChmn, Rep State Exec Comt, Ala
b Cleveland, Ohio, Sept 9, 31; s William Monroe Robertson & Pauline Slusher R; m 1954 to Faye Samford; c John Anderson, Jr & Polly Connor; m 1972 to Patricia Ramaage Bryan; c Patricia & Lee Bryan. Educ: Auburn Univ, BS, 53; Sigma Alpha Epsilon. Polit & Govt Pos: Chmn, Indust Develop Bd & mem, Aviation Bd, Fairhope, Ala, 65-, mem, City Coun, 68-72; chmn, Baldwin Co Rep Exec Comt, Ala, 66-70; mem, Rep State Exec Comt Ala, 66-, vchmn, 70-; vchmn, Second Cong Dist Rep Party, 66- Bus & Prof Pos: Brokerage consult, 60-62; dist mgr, Conn Gen Life Ins Co, 62-63; partner, Huffman-Robertson Ins Agency, 64-; pres, Barons Motel & Rest Inc, currently. Mil Serv: Entered as Airman Basic, Air Force, 53, released as Airman, 2/C, 55. Mem: Eastern Shore CofC; Eastern Shore Jr CofC. Relig: Methodist. Mailing Add: PO Drawer D Fairhope AL 36532

ROBERTSON, JOHN OTHO, JR (R)
b Poplarville, Miss, Jan 8, 21; s John Otho Robertson & Carrie Stewart R; m 1961 to Mary Prudence Marchman; c George Bruce, Wendell Marion, John Douglas & Mary Patricia. Educ: Pearl River Jr Col, Poplarville, Miss, 38-40; Univ Mich, Ann Arbor, 40-42; Univ Ga, BSA, 58. Polit & Govt Pos: Chmn, Oglethorpe Co Rep Party, Ga, formerly. Mil Serv: Entered as Pvt, Army, 42, released as Lt Col, 62, after serv in 17th Airborne & 1st Armored Div, European Theatre & Far East, 42-62; Silver Star. Publ: Ed, Georgia Stockman, Ga Livestock Asn, 63-72. Mem: Ga Livestock Asn (exec vpres, 62-); Flaga Sheep Producers Asn (secy, 63-). Relig: Protestant. Mailing Add: Maxeys GA 30671

ROBERTSON, ROGER (D)
Kans State Rep
Mailing Add: 228 E Sixth Hutchinson KS 67501

ROBERTSON, RUTH ELIZABETH (R)
VChmn, 18th Cong Dist Rep Party, Mich
b Kansas City, Mo, Apr 10, 17; d Walter Ervin Maloy & Mary Baird M; m 1941 to Paul Corwin Robertson; c Paul C, Jr, Mary Jane (Mrs Bower); Martha Ruth; Julia Evelyn, David Wilson & John Baird. Educ: Kansas City Jr Col, 35-36; Univ Mich, AB, 39. Polit & Govt Pos: Neighbor-to-neighbor worker, Rep Party, Mich, 60-69; precinct deleg, Mich Rep Party, 63-65 & 68-; chmn, Oakland Co High Sch Prog, Mich, 64-65; pres, Beverly-Franklin Rep Women, 65; pres, Oakland Co Coun Rep Women's Clubs, 66-67; deleg, state & nat fedn conv, 67; mem exec comt, Oakland Co Rep Comt, 67-68; deleg, Rep Nat Conv & Mich deleg, Nat Platform Comt, 68; comnr, Mich State Civil Serv Comn, 68-; vchmn, 18th Cong Dist Rep Party, Mich, 69- Mem: Am Asn Univ Women; Univ Mich Alumnae Club; League of Women Voters. Relig: Presbyterian. Mailing Add: 25665 River Dr Franklin MI 48025

ROBERTSON, STOKES VERNON (INDEPENDENT)
Assoc Justice, Supreme Court, Miss
b Hattiesburg, Miss, Nov 9, 12; s Stokes Vernon Robertson & Sudie Mason Burt R; m 1945 to Una Lurline Caldwell; c Stokes V, III, David G & Helen C. Educ: Millsaps Col, 29-32; Univ Miss, BA, 33 & LLB, 35; Sigma Upsilon; Pi Kappa Delta; Omicron Delta Kappa; Phi Delta Phi; Kappa Alpha. Polit & Govt Pos: Chancery Judge, Fifth Chancery Court Dist, Miss, 55-66; Assoc Justice, Supreme Court, Miss, 66- Mil Serv: Entered as Capt, Army, 40, released as Lt Col, 45, after serv in 31st Inf Div & Mobile Qm Bn, US & SW Pac Theatres; Col (Ret) Army Res, Judge Adv Gen Corps, 60; Presidential Unit Citation; SW Pac Theatre Medal with 3 Battle Stars. Mem: Hinds Co & Miss State Bar Asns; Kiwanis; Am Legion. Relig: Presbyterian. Legal Res: 2246 N Cheryl Dr Jackson MS 39211 Mailing Add: PO Box 117 Jackson MS 39205

ROBEY, FRANK C, JR (D)
Md State Deleg
Mailing Add: 3830 Monterey Rd Baltimore MD 21218

ROBILLARD, MARC (D)
NH State Rep
Mailing Add: 23 Hough St Dover NH 03820

ROBILLARD, ROY (D)
La State Rep
Mailing Add: Morganza LA 70759

ROBINSON, ALBERT LEE (R)
Ky State Rep
b Clay Co, Ky, Dec 19, 38; s Roscoe Robinson & Vernia Lee Johnson R; m 1962 to C Lucille Morgan; c Maria Francine & Stephen Albert. Polit & Govt Pos: State treas, Ky Young Rep, 70-71; Ky State Rep, 72- Bus & Prof Pos: Co-owner & sales mgr, Robinson Sausage Co, 58-73. Honors & Awards: Most Colorful Legislator, Ky Press Orgn, 72. Relig: Church of God. Mailing Add: Pittsburg KY 40755

ROBINSON, ANTHONY MARK (D)
Nat Committeeman, RI Young Dem
b Providence, RI, Jan 16, 49; s Vincent John Robinson & Mary Ellen R; single. Educ: Univ RI, BA, 72; Am Univ, MPA, 73, MBA, 75; Sigma Chi. Polit & Govt Pos: Pres, RI Young Dem, 71-73; nat committeeman, 73-; deleg, Dem Nat Conv, 72; dir, Youth for Sen Pell, 72; staff mem, McGovern for President, NH Primary, 72. Mem: Am Soc Pub Admin; RI Common Cause (mem steering comt). Relig: Catholic. Legal Res: 79 Whittier Rd Pawtucket RI 02861 Mailing Add: c/o US Sen Pell Senate Off Bldg Washington DC 20510

ROBINSON, BILL (D)
Okla State Sen
Mailing Add: State Capitol Oklahoma City OK 73105

ROBINSON, CARLOS R (R)
Mem, NMex State Rep Exec Comt
b Clovis, NMex, Mar 20, 30; s Carlos R Robinson & Iva B Hymen R; m 1969 to Carol Lynn Nieburger; c Gary Lee, Gregory Stephen, Frances Ann, Patrick Ashton & Michael David. Educ: St Michael's Col, NMex, 54; Univ NMex, BA in Bus Admin, 57; Sigma Chi. Polit & Govt Pos: Secy, Gov, NMex Port Entry Adv Comt, 67-; alt deleg, Rep Nat Conv, 68, deleg, 72; chmn, Grant Co Rep Party, NMex, 68-69; mem, Rep State Cent Comt NMex, 71-; regional vchmn, NMex Rep Party, 73-; mem, NMex State Rep Exec Comt, 73-; vchmn, Sandoval Co Rep Party, formerly, chmn, currently. Mil Serv: Entered as Pvt, Army, 51, released as 1st Lt, 53, after serv in 7th Inf Div, Artil, Korea, 52-53; Bronze Star Medal; Commendation Medal with Oak Leaf Cluster; Korean Serv Medal with 2 Battle Stars; UN Serv Medal; Nat Defense Serv Medal. Mem: Jaycees; Elks. Relig: Methodist. Legal Res: Jemez Dam Rd Bernalillo NM 87004 Mailing Add: PO Box 118 Bernalillo NM 87004

ROBINSON, CHARLES EDWARDS (D)
b Ashville, Ala, July 10, 39; s John Roland Robinson & Jane Dozier R; m 1961 to Mary Anne Lowery; c Charles Edwards, Jr & Thomas Dozier. Educ: Univ Ala, BA, 62; Cumberland Sch Law, Howard Col, JD, 65; Phi Alpha Delta; Kappa Alpha Order. Polit & Govt Pos: Chmn, St Clair Co Dem Party, Ala, formerly; Dist Attorney, 30th Judicial Circuit of Ala, 71- Bus & Prof Pos: Partner, Embry & Robinson, Attorneys-at-law, 65-71. Mem: Ala & Nat Dist Attorney's Asn; Mason; Pell City Jaycees; St Clair Co Cattlemens Asn. Honors & Awards: Outstanding Law Enforcement Off, Ala Jaycees, 71. Relig: Methodist. Mailing Add: Rte 3 Box 529 Pell City AL 35125

ROBINSON, CHARLES K (R)
VChmn, Park Co Rep Party, Colo
b Uhrichsville, Ohio, Sept 15, 07; both parents deceased; m 1931 to Marge Welsh; c Charles K, Jr & John Welsh. Educ: Denison Univ, BA in Govt, 30; Sigma Alpha Epsilon. Polit & Govt Pos: Vchmn, Park Co Rep Party, Colo, currently. Mem: Lions Int. Mailing Add: Willo Wisp Rte 1 Pine CO 80470

ROBINSON, CHARLES R (D)
Tenn State Rep
Mailing Add: 1317 Riverwood Dr Nashville TN 37216

ROBINSON, CHARLES W (D)
Under Secy Econ Affairs, Dept State
Mailing Add: Dept State 2201 C St Washington DC 20520

ROBINSON, CLARENCE B (D)
Tenn State Rep
Mailing Add: 1909 E Fifth St Chattanooga TN 37404

ROBINSON, CLOYD ERWIN (D)
Iowa State Sen
b Norway, Iowa, Apr 25, 38; s Earl Roy Robinson & Florence Gerard R; m 1956 to Shirlene Rose Rimrodt; c Rustin, Shawn & Shelly. Educ: Univ Mo, 68; Univ Wis, 70. Polit & Govt Pos: Iowa State Sen, 22nd Dist, 71-72, 14th Dist, 72- Bus & Prof Pos: Prod leadman, Quaker Oats Co, Cedar Rapids, Iowa, 61-73; vpres, Hawkeye Labor Coun, 70. Mil Serv: Naval Res, 55-63. Mem: Linn Co Retarded Childrens Asn; Nat Founders Club; United Cereal Workers. Honors & Awards: Founders Club Award, Iowa Credit Union League for organizing Quaker Oats Credit Union, 65. Relig: Methodist. Mailing Add: 404 Cherry Hill Rd SW Cedar Rapids IA 52405

ROBINSON, CLYDE RAYFORD (D)
Chmn, Miller Co Dem Comt, Mo
b Linn Creek, Mo, Mar 29, 10; s Bertie Clyde Robinson & Lena Davis R; m 1932 to Pebble Wilma Hill. Educ: Bagnell High Sch, 4 years. Polit & Govt Pos: Chmn, Miller Co Dem Comt, Mo, currently. Bus & Prof Pos: Bldg contractor, retired. Mil Serv: Entered as Pvt, Army, 43, released as T-5 after serv in Corps Engrs, Asiatic-Pac Theater, 44-45; Good Conduct Medal; Asiatic Pac Medal. Mem: Mason (hon mem of all temples in Mo); Shrine. Relig: Baptist. Mailing Add: Box 408 Lake Ozark MO 65049

ROBINSON, DAVE M (R)
Chmn, Dist Eight Rep Party, NDak
b Bismarck, NDak, Aug 1, 18; s George Marshall Robinson & Helen Clark R; m 1942 to Sheila Alice Crowley; c Janet, Matthew & Stephen. Educ: NDak State Univ, BS in Agr. Polit & Govt Pos: NDak State Sen, Eighth Dist, 63-72; chmn, Dist Eight Rep Party, NDak, 75- Mem: NDak Stockmen's Asn; Co Agr Improv Asn; Garrison Sportsmen's Club; Mason; Elks. Honors & Awards: Soil Conserv Award, Swift Tripper. Relig: Protestant. Mailing Add: Coalharbor Stock Farm Coleharbor ND 58531

ROBINSON, DONALD LOUIS (D)
b Ottawa, Ill, Dec 8, 36; s Arthur Robinson & Louise Freebury R; m 1962 to Sara Katharine Moore; c Marshall Jackson & Margaret Moore. Educ: Northwestern Univ, BA in Hist, 58, MA, 59; Am Univ, PhD, 63; Alpha Phi Omega; Phi Mu Alpha; Phi Alpha Theta; Pi Gamma Mu; Alpha Tau Omega; Pi Sigma Alpha; Am Univ Hon Soc. Polit & Govt Pos: Co-chmn, Speakers Bur, Young Citizens for Johnson-Humphrey Campaign, 64; admin asst to US Rep Henry S Reuss, 63-74; co-chmn, Bi-Partisan Intern Proj, US House of Rep, 69-71, US Cong, 72-; exec asst to chmn, Comt Banking, Currency & Housing, US House Rep, currently. Bus & Prof Pos: Assoc prof polit sci, George Washington Univ, currently; adj assoc prof polit sci, Boston Univ, currently. Mil Serv: Entered as Ens, Navy, 59, released as Lt(jg), 62, after serv as Chief, Naval Opers. Mem: Am Polit Sci Asn; Am Civil Liberties Union; Am for Dem Action. Relig: Episcopal. Mailing Add: 1817 Kenyon St NW Washington DC 20010

ROBINSON, ERROL WAYNE (R)
Rep Chmn, 27th Legis Dist, Wash
b Downey, Idaho, Nov 23, 23; s Thomas Arnold Robinson & Nettie L Johnson R; m to Carla

Ruth Harris; c E Wayne, Jr, Carla Rose, Rhea Ann & Helen Ruth. Educ: US Naval Acad, Annapolis, BS, 45; Univ Wash, MS in Eng, 58. Polit & Govt Pos: Chmn, Madison Co Rep Exec Comt Ala, 65-66; cand, Third Dist, Ala State Senate; mem, Ala Rep State Exec Comt, formerly; Rep chmn, 27th Legis Dist, Wash, 70- Bus & Prof Pos: Eng supvr, Boeing Co, 55-70; dist mgr, Field Enterprises Educ Corp, 70- Mil Serv: Entered as Midn, Navy, released as Lt, World War II & Korean Conflict; Air Medal with Gold Star; Presidential Unit Citation; Korean Serv, Asian Occup, Am Theater, Pac & Victory Medals. Mem: Lions. Relig: Latter-day Saint. Mailing Add: 2401 David Ct Pl E Tacoma WA 98424

ROBINSON, GROVER C, III (D)
Fla State Rep
Mailing Add: 781 Connell Dr Pensacola FL 32503

ROBINSON, HENRIETTA (D)
Mem, Mich State Dem Cent Comt
b St Petersburg, Fla, Nov 1919; d James Neal & Irene Smith N; div; c Valerie Cynthia (Mrs Louis Muse), Alexander Givens & Charlotte Robinson. Educ: Gibbs Trade & Bus Sch, Practice Nurse, 52; Mumford Bus Sch, Real Estate Law, 58; Wayne Co Community Col, 72; Univ Mich. Polit & Govt Pos: Tenth Precinct Citizen Rep; mem, Women Pub Affairs Comt; charter mem, Coun Precinct Deleg, Dem Precinct 17 Deleg, Dist 22, 60-; mem, Mich Black Caucus, 68; alt deleg, Dem Nat Conv, 68; mem, Mich State Dem Cent Comt, 70-; vpres, Detroit House of Correction Comn, 71-; pres, Dexter-Grand River Livernois Asn, formerly; pres, Otsego Block Club, formerly; deleg, Tenth precinct of Detroit Police Dept, City Wide Coun & chmn, City Wide Youth Coun, 73-74. Bus & Prof Pos: Supvr of Dainty Maid Products, Detroit Area, 51-53; real estate saleswoman, 69- Mem: Nat Coun Negro Women; Escalator's Club; Am Bridge Asn. Honors & Awards: Awarded Trophy for Most Beautiful Block in a 50 Block Radius, Bond Bilt Construction Co. Relig: Baptist. Mailing Add: 9320 Otsego Detroit MI 48204

ROBINSON, JAMES KENNETH (R)
US Rep, Va
b Frederick Co, Va, May 14, 16; m to Kathryn M R. Educ: Va Polytech Inst, 37, BS in Hort. Polit & Govt Pos: Va State Sen, 66-71; US Rep, Seventh Dist, Va, 71- Bus & Prof Pos: Fruit grower, packer, farmer & businessman; mem bd visitors, US Air Force Acad, currently. Mil Serv: Inf, 4 years, Maj. Mem: Rotary; Izaak Walton League; Am Legion; Va Farm Bur Fedn; Boy Scouts (adv). Honors & Awards: Meritorious Serv Award for Serv to Va Agr, Va Polytech Inst, 63; Man of Year in Serv to Va Agr, Progressive Farmer Mag, 64. Relig: Quaker. Legal Res: PO Box 407 Winchester VA 22601 Mailing Add: US House of Rep Washington DC 20515

ROBINSON, JANE W (R)
Fla State Rep
Mailing Add: 715 Carambola Dr Merritt Island FL 32922

ROBINSON, JOHN ALEXANDER, III (D)
Pres, Young Dem Ala
b Jasper, Ala, Apr 23, 42; s John Alexander Robinson, Jr & Reba Sherer R; m 1969 to Nancy Louise Carver; c John Alexander, IV. Educ: Univ Ala, BS, 67. Polit & Govt Pos: Campaign mgr, Dunn for City Coun, 68 & McLain for Sen, 70; coordr, Wall for City Coun, 70; finance chmn, Saucier for City Coun, 72; pres, Young Dem Am, 73. Bus & Prof Pos: Asst to pres, Am Southern Publ Co, 66-67; mkt rep, IBM Corp, 67-73. Mil Serv: Entered as Airman Basic, Air Force, 60, released as Airman 1/C, 63, after serv in 609th Radar Squadron, Air Defense Command, 61-63. Mem: Lamar Soc; Civic Club Coun of Huntsville & Madison Co; Jaycees; Family Coun Asn; Vol Action Ctr of Huntsville/Madison Co. Honors & Awards: Distinguished Serv Award, Jaycees, 72, One of Four Outstanding Young Men of Ala, 72; Outstanding Young Men of Am, 72. Relig: Methodist. Mailing Add: 12008 Camelot Dr SE Huntsville AL 35803

ROBINSON, L W (HAP) (R)
Chmn, Davis Co Rep Cent Comt, Utah
b Farmington, Utah, Nov 19, 01; s William Oliver Robinson & Lucy Clark R; m to Jannetta Knowlton; c Stephen Lamond, Richard Knowlton, Jo Ann (Mrs Robert Ellis Freed), J Clark & David A. Educ: Utah State Univ, BS, 25. Polit & Govt Pos: Chmn, Dist 58 Rep Party, Utah, 66-68; chmn, Dist 7 Vote Turnout, 70-71; chmn, Davis Co Rep Cent Comt, 71- Bus & Prof Pos: Dir, Cache Valley Breeding Asn, Utah, 50-60, vpres, 60-68; dir, Federated Milk Producers, 52-58; vpres, Utah Dairy Coun, 54-58. Mem: Utah Soc Farm & Ranch Mgrs & Appraisers. Relig: Latter-day Saint. Mailing Add: 242 Spencer Circle Farmington UT 84059

ROBINSON, PALMA LUTHER (R)
Tenn State Rep
b Erwin, Tenn, June 2, 21; s Thomas Edward Robinson & Nora Roland R; m 1942 to Ruth Marie May; c Robert David & Pamela May. Educ: ETenn State Univ, 1 year. Polit & Govt Pos: Chmn, Fourth Dist Rep Party, Tenn, 64-68; Tenn State Rep, First Dist, 70- Bus & Prof Pos: Dairy farmer, 47- Mil Serv: Entered as Air Cadet-Pvt, Air Force, 42, released as Capt, 47, after serv in 301st Troop Carrier Squadron, ETO, 44-45; Lt Col, Air Force Res, 68-; Air Medal with Oak Leaf Cluster; Theatre Serv Medal; European-African-Middle Eastern Serv Medal; World War II Victory Medal. Mem: Dairymen Inc (vpres); Elks; VFW; Moose; Farm Bur. Honors & Awards: Progressive Farmers Master Farmer Award Fed Land Banks Commemorative Medal for contrib to agr; Tenn Outstanding Young Farmer, 55; Progressive Farmer's Man of the Year in Serv to Agr in Tenn, 72. Relig: Presbyterian. Mailing Add: Rte 1 Jonesboro TN 37659

ROBINSON, PAUL RANDALL (R)
Chmn, Cedar Co Rep Party, Nebr
b Sioux City, Iowa, July 10, 37; s Philip Hunter Robinson & Lucile Randall R; m 1963 to Marcia Deanne Nepstad; c Kristen & Paul, Jr. Educ: Univ Wyo, BA, 59; George Washington Univ, JD, 64; Sigma Chi. Polit & Govt Pos: Legis asst to Congressman Ralph F Beerman, 61-64; dep clerk to Nebr Legis, 65; mem, Nebr Rep State Cent Comt, 65-; chmn, Cedar Co Rep Party, currently. Bus & Prof Pos: Attorney in pvt practice, Hartington, Nebr, 65- Mil Serv: Entered as 2nd Lt, Army, 59, released as 1st Lt, 61, after serv in Air Defense Command, Boston, 60-61. Mem: Am Bar Asn; Mason. Relig: Congregational. Mailing Add: 218 N Broadway Hartington NE 68739

ROBINSON, RALPH DUANE (R)
Chmn, Cleveland Co Rep Party, NC
b Celo, NC, Sept 28, 32; s James Edward Robinson & Blanche Beatrice Buchanan R; m 1954 to Mary Frances Tysinger; c Kimball Duane, Jeffrey Neil & Christopher Edward. Educ: Appalachian State Univ, BS in Math, 55; NC State Univ, BSChE, 58. Polit & Govt Pos: Chmn, Cleveland Co Rep Party, NC, 69- Bus & Prof Pos: Supt, PPG Indust, Shelby, NC, 59-63; gen mgr, Shelby Plastics Corp, 63-66; gen mgr & vpres, Printing & Packaging, Inc, 66-68; gen mgr, Craftspun Yarns, Div BVD, Kings Mt, 68-70; gen mgr & vpres, Ferguson Gear Co, Gastonia, 70-; pres, FRK Industs, Inc, Shelby, currently. Mem: Am Inst Chem Engrs; Soc Plastic Engrs; Am Chem Soc; Jaycees. Relig: Methodist. Mailing Add: Box 1785 Shelby NC 28150

ROBINSON, RICHARD (D)
Calif State Assemblyman
Mailing Add: 822 N Broadway Santa Ana CA 92701

ROBINSON, ROBERT E (D)
Nev State Assemblyman
Mailing Add: 3000 W Charleston Blvd Suite 5 Las Vegas NV 89103

ROBINSON, SAM PERRY, JR (R)
Chmn, Hunt Co Rep Party, Tex
b Brockport, NY, Mar 5, 43; s Sam Perry Robinson & Lollie Lavender Lathem R; single. Educ: ETex State Univ, BS, 70, MS, 72; Lambda Chi Alpha; Pre-Law Club; Finance Club; Ins Club; Young Rep. Polit & Govt Pos: Regional dir col coun, Tex Young Rep, 66-67, dist committeeman, 67-68, chmn state voter registr, 70; pres, ETex Young Rep, 67-69; staff aide, United Citizens for Reagan, Miami, 68; exec comt, Tex Students for Reagan, 68; Bronze, Silver & Gold Hardcharger, Young Rep Nat Fedn, 68, chmn absentee voters prog; deleg, Young Rep Nat Fedn Nat Conv, 69; deleg, Tex State Rep Conv, 70; chmn, Hunt Co Rep Party, 70-; campaign chmn, United Citizens for Perry, 70; admin aide, State Rep Will Lee & Sid Bowers, Tex House of Rep, 71; field rep, Bob Daniels for Cong, 72. Bus & Prof Pos: Educator. Mem: Psi Chi; Rio Grande Valley Counr Asn; Kiwanis; Int Platform Asn. Relig: Episcopal. Mailing Add: 2719 Kipling E Houston TX 77006

ROBINSON, SARA KATHARINE MOORE (D)
b Chicago, Ill, June 23, 38; d Herbert Jackson Moore & Margaret Emma Roberts M; m 1962 to Donald Louis Robinson; c Marshall Jackson & Margaret Moore. Educ: Beloit Col, BA, 59; Columbus Sch Law, Cath Univ Am, JD, 65; rush chmn, Kappa Alpha Theta; Young Dem; Kappa Beta Pi; assoc ed & ed-in-chief, Legal Issue. Polit & Govt Pos: Campaign secy, Wis Humphrey for President Comt, 59; exec secy to US Rep Henry S Reuss, 59-65, legal asst, 65-72, counsel, 73- Publ: Legislative reapportionment: in court & congress, Kappa Beta Pi Quart, 12/64. Mem: Kappa Beta Pi (dean); Am Civil Liberties Union; Powerhouse, Inc (bd dirs); Wash Half-Way Home for Women (chmn bd dirs). Relig: Episcopal; mem bd dirs, St Stephen's Enterprises, Inc; former jr warden, Church of St Stephen & The Incarnation. Mailing Add: 1817 Kenyon St NW Washington DC 20010

ROBINSON, SHIRLEY A (D)
Mem, Dem Nat Comt, Mich
b Detroit, Mich, June 11, 42; d Walter Thomas Robinson & Alma Hughey R; single. Educ: Elsa Cooper's Sch Court Reporting, grad, 64; Wayne State Univ, BA, 74. Polit & Govt Pos: Secy to US Rep John Conyers, Jr, Mich, 65; secy, US Embassy, New Delhi, India, 65-66; exec secy, Off of Vice President Hubert H Humphrey, 67-68; staff aide, US Rep, James H Scheuer, NY, 68-70; field rep, Mich Dem State Cent Comt, 70-72; deleg, Dem Nat Conv, 72; mem, Dem Nat Comt, 72- Bus & Prof Pos: Prog specialist, Housing Develop Corp, Detroit, Mich, 72-73. Mem: NAACP (chairperson, Urban Affairs Comt, 73-). Relig: Methodist. Mailing Add: 1017 Trevor Pl Detroit MI 48207

ROBINSON, STEPHEN C (R)
Exec Secy, Rep State Cent Comt Iowa
b Des Moines, Iowa, Sept 7, 35; s Stephen Robinson & Ada Curtis R; m 1957 to Margaret Davis; c Stephen Davis & John W. Educ: Graceland Jr Col, AA, 55; Univ Iowa, BA, 58; Drake Univ, LLB, 62. Polit & Govt Pos: Exec dir, Polk Co Rep Party, Des Moines, Iowa, 65-67; asst attorney gen, State of Iowa, 67; secy, Exec Coun of Iowa, 67-69; exec secy, Rep State Cent Comt, 69-73; Asst Attorney Gen, Iowa, 73- Mem: Iowa & Am Bar Asns. Relig: Reorganized Latter-day Saint. Legal Res: 1135 46th St Des Moines IA 50311 Mailing Add: Dept of Justice Capitol Complex Des Moines IA 50319

ROBINSON, W LEE (D)
Ga State Sen
Mailing Add: 864 Winchester Circle Macon GA 31204

ROBINSON, WILLIAM DWIGHT (D)
Vt State Rep
b St Stephen, NB, Can, May 4, 43; s William F Robinson & Olive Libby R; m 1966 to Judith Ann Burden; c William Allen & Andrew Peter. Educ: Northeastern Univ, BA, 66; Cornell Univ Law Sch, JD, 69; Phi Kappa Phi; Phi Sigma Alpha; Phi Alpha Theta. Polit & Govt Pos: Mem, Colchester Bd Educ, Vt, 72-75; Vt State Rep, Dist 1-2, 74- Bus & Prof Pos: Attorney-at-law, Colchester, Vt, 71- Mem: Am, Vt, Chittenden Co & Wis Bar Asns; Colchester Boys' League. Honors & Awards: Vchancellor, Cornell Moot Court Bd, 68-69. Legal Res: 30 Village Dr Colchester VT 05446 Mailing Add: PO Box 113 Colchester VT 05446

ROBINSON, WILLIAM G (R)
Mass State Rep
Mailing Add: Mass House Rep State Capitol Boston MA 02122

ROBINSON, WILLIAM PETERS, SR (D)
Va State Deleg
b Norfolk, Va, Mar 15, 11; s William Charles Robinson & Avis Peters R; c William P, Jr. Educ: Howard Univ, BS, 32, MA, 35; NY Univ, PhD, 50; Omega Psi Phi; Phi Alpha Theta; Sigma Rho Sigma. Polit & Govt Pos: Admin asst, Dept Agr, Washington, DC, & analyst, Prog Surveys Div, formerly; consult, Off Econ Opportunity for Va, Washington Off; coordr seminar, Solving Urban Probs Through Community Develop, State Planning Dept, Richmond, Va; dir, Conf of Newly Elec Black Local Off of Va, Ctr For Govt Studies, Washington, DC; dir, Educ Prof Develop Act, Civics Inst, US Dept Health, Educ & Welfare, 67-68 & 68-69; Va State Deleg, 70-, mem, Comts Educ, Health, Welfare, Insts & Rd, Va House Deleg, 72- Bus & Prof Pos: Instr dept polit sci, Howard Univ; asst to pres, Morris Brown Col, Ga; chmn dept polit sci, Tex South Univ; Cent State Col, Ohio; dir div liberal arts, Alcorn Col, Miss; pres faculty senate, Norfolk State Col, Va, 70, dir, Lyman B Brooks

Debate Team, chmn dept polit sci & dir div of soc sci, currently. Publ: First Fair Housing Legislation enacted by Va Gen Assembly; Legislative progress of minority groups in United States & Nature of political prejudice, J Soc Sci Teacher; plus one other. Mem: Am Polit Sci Asn; Asn Soc Sci Teachers; Nat Coun for Soc Studies; Asn for Study of Negro Life & History; Elks. Honors & Awards: Gold Key Awards for Most Outstanding Contrib to Opera & for Partic & Extra Curricular Scholarship; Man of the Year, Omega Psi Phi; teaching fel, dept polit, Univ NC, Chapel Hill. Relig: Episcopal. Mailing Add: 958 Anna St Norfolk VA 23502

ROBINSON, WINTHROP LINCOLN (R)
Chmn, Taunton Rep City Comt, Mass
b Taunton, Mass, Sept 11, 05; s Chester Winthrop Robinson (deceased) & Alice Maud Lincoln R (deceased); m 1960 to Amy Mildred Cousins. Educ: High Sch, grad, 24; Int Accts Soc, Alexander Hamilton Inst, Chicago, Ill. Polit & Govt Pos: Taunton Area coordr for former US Rep Lawrence E Curtis for US Sen, Mass, 63, committeeman & treas, Taunton Ward 5; finance chmn, Taunton Area, Mass State Rep Comt, 63-66; mem, Bristol Co Rep Club, 65-, dir, 71-; chmn, Taunton Rep City Comt, currently; mem, Taunton Coun Aging, currently; Taunton area coordr for the reelection of President Nixon, 72. Bus & Prof Pos: Bldg contractor, Taunton, Mass, 35-66; notary pub, currently; corporator, Morton Hosp & Bristol Co Savings Bank, currently. Mem: Ment Health Bargain Bazaar Thrift Shop (dir); Jolly Sr Citizens Club (vpres); Taunton Redevelop Authority (secy); Taunton Area Ment Health Clin (dir); Mass Rep City Chmn Asn. Relig: Baptist. Mailing Add: 5 Jefferson Ave Taunton MA 02780

ROBRECHT, RAYMOND R (R)
Va State Deleg
Mailing Add: 9 S College Ave Salem VA 24153

ROBSION, JOHN MARSHALL, JR (R)
b Barbourville, Ky, Aug 28, 04; s John Marshall Robsion & Lida Stansberry R; m 1949 to Laura Selinda Edwards. Educ: Union Col Acad, Barbourville, 19; George Washington Univ, JD, 26; Georgetown Univ; Nat War Col, 54. Hon Degrees: LLD, Union Col, 69. Polit & Govt Pos: Cong Secy, 20-26; Speaker of Little Cong, 26; chief of law div, US Bur Pensions, 29-32, mem, Bd Vet Appeals, 32-35; gen counsel, Rep Party, Ky, 38-42; exec secy, Young Rep Nat Fedn, 40-42; spec circuit court judge, 46-52; US Rep, Ky, 53-59; deleg, Interparliamentary Union Conf, Helsinki, 55, Bangkok, 56 & London, 57; deleg, Rep Nat Conv, 56 & 60; cand, Gov, Ky, 59; chmn, Rep Adv Comt, SFla, 66-68. Bus & Prof Pos: Attorney-at-law, Barbourville, 26-29, Louisville, 35-42, 46-52 & 59-; trustee, Ky Jockey Club, 60-65. Mil Serv: Army, 42-46; mem staff Gen Mark Clark, Italy & Austria. Mem: Union Col (trustee); Gtr Decisions Comt, Ky; Amvets; Am Legion; DAV. Relig: Christian Church. Mailing Add: 2500 E Las Olas Blvd Ft Lauderdale FL 33301

ROBSON, ROBERT MORGAN (R)
Region Chmn, Idaho Rep Exec Comt
b Kellogg, Idaho, Nov 28, 21; s Ira A Robson & Margaret Mary Morgan R; m 1944 to Catherine Penelope Agee; c Catherine Lynn (Mrs Spurway), James Allen, Margaret Leslie & Robert Agee. Educ: Univ Idaho, LLB; Pi Delta Phi. Polit & Govt Pos: Prosecuting attorney, Idaho Co, Idaho, 51-53, Trust Territory of the Pac Islands, 55-57; city attorney, Kellogg, Idaho, 58-62; attorney general, Idaho, 69-71; region chmn, Idaho Rep Exec Comt, currently. Bus & Prof Pos: Attorney-at-law, 49- Mil Serv: Entered as Seaman 2/C, Navy, released as Lt(jg), after serv in Naval Air Training Command, VC-27 Jeep Carrier Squadron, 42-45. Mem: Fed & Idaho Bar Asns; AF&AM; Am Judicature Soc. Relig: Episcopal. Legal Res: 333 S Straughan Boise ID 83701 Mailing Add: Box 1346 Boise ID 83701

ROCCO, SAL (D)
Mich State Rep
Mailing Add: 33560 Somerset Dr Sterling Heights MI 48077

ROCH, DONALD EDMOND (R)
Mem Exec Comt, RI Rep State Cent Comt
b West Warwick, RI, Sept 12, 31; s Joseph Gaspard Roch & Georgianna Boudreau R; m 1953 to Mary Bernice Lombardi; c Julie, Paula & Janine. Educ: Univ RI Exten, 67-68. Polit & Govt Pos: Mem, RI Rep State Cent Comt, 67-, mem exec comt, 68-, admin asst, 70, mem nominating comt, 71; chmn, West Warwick Rep Town Comt, 69-71; RI State Sen, West Warwick, 71-74. Bus & Prof Pos: Radio announcer, French, West Warwick, RI, 56-58; salesman, Metrop Life Ins, 58- Mil Serv: Navy, 50-51. Mem: Am Legion; Ins Workers Int Union; Lions; Sons of Italy; Club Frontenac. Honors & Awards: Selected Outstanding Legislator, Rutgers Univ Eagleton Inst Polit, 73. Relig: Catholic. Mailing Add: 10 Brayton St West Warwick RI 02893

ROCHELEAU, RICHARD (D)
NDak State Rep
Mailing Add: State Capitol Bismarck ND 58501

ROCHELLE, ROBERT THOMAS (D)
Chmn, Wilson Co Dem Exec Comt, Tenn
b Nashville, Tenn, Nov 25, 45; s James Marcellus Rochelle & Katherine Purnell-Rochelle Oakley; m 1973 to Janice Gail Johnson. Educ: Cumberland Col, 64-65; Mid Tenn State Univ, BS, 66; Univ Tenn, Knoxville, JD, 69. Polit & Govt Pos: Pres, Wilson Co Young Dem, Tenn, 72-75; vchmn, Wilson Co Dem Exec Comt, 74-75, chmn, 75-; attorney, Wilson Co, 74-76. Mil Serv: Entered as E-1, Army, 69, released as E-5, 71, after serv in 1st Single Brigade, Vietnam, 70-71; Bronze Star. Mem: Am & Ten Bar Asns; Lebanon-Wilson Co CofC; West Wilson Co CofC; Univ Tenn Alumni Asn. Legal Res: 730 W Main St Lebanon TN 37087 Mailing Add: 212 E Main St Lebanon TN 37087

ROCHESTER, MATTILYN TALFORD (D)
Mem-at-lg, Dem Nat Comt
b Chester Co, SC, May 14, 41; d Lonnie Talford & Maggie Macon T; m 1963 to Reverend Enoch Benjamin Rochester; c Enoch Benjamin, II & Mattilyn Corelia. Educ: Mt Holyoke Col, 61; Univ Wis, Madison, summer 62; Johns Hopkins Univ, 63; Bennett Col, Greensboro, NC, BS, 62; Glassboro State Col, MA, 66; Sigma Rho Sigma; Omicron Eta Chi; Alpha Kappa Alpha, Theta Pi Omega Chap. Polit & Govt Pos: Co committeewoman, 34th Dist, Willingboro Dem Munic Comt; mem, Burlington Co Dem Comt; mem, Burlington Co Dem Women's Club; mem, Willingboro Dem Club; mem, NJ New Dem Coalition; mem state exec comt, McGovern for President; deleg & mem rules comt, Dem Nat Conv, 72; mem-at-lg, Dem Nat Comt, 72- Bus & Prof Pos: Math teacher, John T Williams Jr High Sch, Charlotte, NC & Adult Educ, Burlington; instr, Multi-Dist Inst for Polit Educ for High Sch Students; math & social sci teacher, Samuel Smith Sch Burlington. Mem: Nat Educ Asn; Nat Coun Teachers of Math; NAACP (vpres, Burlington Co Br); Bennett Col Alumnae (pres, SJersey A Area); League of Women Voters. Honors & Awards: Outstanding Serv to the Community, Alpha Kappa Alpha Sorority, Inc, Theta Omega Chap. Relig: African Methodist Episcopal Zion. Mailing Add: 32 Trebing Lane Willingboro NJ 08046

ROCK, D ALAN (R)
NH State Sen
Mailing Add: 25 Woodland Dr Nashua NH 03060

ROCK, PHILIP JOSEPH (D)
Ill State Sen
b Chicago, Ill, May 4, 37; s Joseph J Rock & Kathryn Crimmins R; m 1964 to Sheila Graber; c Kathleen, Meghan, Colleen & John Joseph. Educ: Loyola Univ Sch Law, JD, 64. Polit & Govt Pos: Committeeman, Ill State Dem Cent Comt, 70-; Ill State Sen, 71-, asst minority leader, Ill State Senate, 73- Bus & Prof Pos: Attorney at law. Mem: Chicago, Ill & Am Bar Asns. Relig: Roman Catholic. Mailing Add: 5840 Midway Park Chicago IL 60644

ROCKEFELLER, JOHN DAVISON, IV (D)
b New York, NY, June 18, 37; s John Davison Rockefeller, III & Blanchette Hooker R; m 1967 to Sharon Percy. Educ: Harvard Univ, AB, 61. Polit & Govt Pos: Philippine opers officer, Peace Corps, Washington, DC, 62-63; Indonesian opers officer, State Dept, 63-64; mem staff community develop, Off Econ Opportunity, Charleston, WVa, 64-66; WVa State Deleg, 66-68; Secy of State, WVa, 69-72; alt deleg, Dem Nat Conv, 72. Bus & Prof Pos: Pres, WVa Wesleyan Col, 73- Publ: The Japanese student, New York Times Mag, 6/60 & Life, 6/60. Relig: Presbyterian. Legal Res: 1515 Barberry Lane Charleston WV 25314 Mailing Add: WVa Wesleyan Col Buckhannon WV 26201

ROCKEFELLER, NELSON ALDRICH (R)
Vice President, US
b Bar Harbor, Maine, July 8, 08; s John D Rockefeller, Jr & Abby Aldrich R; m 1930 to Mary Todhunter Clark, div, 3/62; m 1963 to Margaretta Fitler Murphy; c Rodman C, Ann (Mrs R Coste), Steven C, Mary (Mrs Thomas Morgan), Michael C (deceased), Nelson, Jr & Mark F. Educ: Dartmouth Col, AB in Econ, 30; Phi Beta Kappa. Polit & Govt Pos: Coordr Inter-Am Affairs, 40-44; Asst Secy of State for Am Repub Affairs, 44-45; chmn, Int Develop Adv Bd, 50-51; chmn, President's Adv Comt on Govt Orgn, 53-58; chmn, Spec Comt on Reorgn Defense Dept, 53; Under Secy, Dept Health, Educ & Welfare, 53-54; Spec Asst to the President for Foreign Affairs, 54-55; chmn two studies, NY State Const, 56-59; Gov, NY, 59-73; Presidential cand, 60, 64 & 68; mem, Adv Comn Intergovt Rels, 65-69; personal rep of the President to Latin Am, 69; founder & chmn, Comn on Critical Choices for Americans, 73-75; Vice President, US, 74-; vchmn, Domestic Coun, Exec Off of the President, 75- Relig: Baptist. Legal Res: Pocantico Hills Tarrytown NY 10591 Mailing Add: Exec Off White House 1600 Pennsylvania Ave Washington DC 20500

ROCKWELL, ELIZABETH ADAMS (R)
Ariz State Rep
Mailing Add: 308 E Palm Lane Phoenix AZ 85004

RODBY, LEO BERNARD, JR (D)
Dem Nat Committeeman, Hawaii
b Wahiawa, Hawaii, Jan 12, 26; s Leo R Rodby & Carita Fisher R; m 1954 to Kuulei E Directo; c Leilani, Timothy, Leo, III, Walter & Peter. Educ: Va Jr Col, 2 years. Polit & Govt Pos: Various precinct & dist off, Dem Party, Hawaii, 54-65; mem, Hawaii Dem State Cent Comt, 65-66, treas, 66-68; treas, Dem State Campaign Comt, 66; alt deleg, Dem Nat Conv, 68 & 72; Dem Nat Committeeman, Hawaii, 68-; deleg, Dem Nat Mid-Term Conf, 74. Bus & Prof Pos: Pres & gen mgr, Wahiawa Distributors Ltd, Wahiawa, Hawaii, 48-; pres, Wahiawa Community Asn, 54; treas, Trinity Lutheran Church & Sch, 54-; pres, Wahiawa Hosp Asn, 64-68. Mil Serv: Entered as A/S, Navy, 43, released as Qm 2/C, 46, after serv in Landing Craft, Pac, 44-46. Mem: Bishop Museum Asn; Honolulu Acad Arts; Hawaii Canoe Racing Asn; Lions. Honors & Awards: Named Jr CofC Young Man of Year, 54. Legal Res: 1828 Eames St Wahiawa HI 96786 Mailing Add: PO Box 70 Wahiawa HI 96786

RODDA, ALBERT S (D)
Calif State Sen
b Sacramento, Calif; m to Clarice Horgan; c Mary Elizabeth, Steven Holliway & Margaret Anne. Educ: Stanford Univ, PhD in hist. Polit & Govt Pos: Mem, Sacramento Co Dem Cent Comt, Calif, 52-58; Calif State Sen, 58- Bus & Prof Pos: Instr econ & hist, Sacramento City Col. Mil Serv: Naval Res, World War II. Mailing Add: 4048 Capitol Bldg Sacramento CA 95814

RODDEY, FRANK LANEY (D)
SC State Sen
b Lancaster, SC, Feb 3, 27; s Elliott B Roddey & Beulah Mae Laney R; m 1947 to Ophelia Melbrae Taylor; c Glendora (Mrs Roy Small, III), Sunni Leigh (Mrs W Glen Parker) & Jan T. Educ: Davidson Col, 44; Univ SC, 47-48; Sigma Chi. Polit & Govt Pos: Mem, Lancaster City Coun, SC, 52-59; SC State Sen, Dist Six, 63-, chmn, Commerce & Mfg Comt, SC State Sen, 69- Bus & Prof Pos: Owner, Frank L Roddey Ins. Mem: Mason, Jackson Lodge 53; Shriner Hejaz Temple; CofC(bd of dir); United Fund (bd of dir); Jaycees. Honors & Awards: Young Man of the Year, 56. Mailing Add: State House Columbia SC 29211

RODDY, JOSEPH P (D)
Mem, State Dem Comt, Mo
b St Louis, Mo, Nov 4, 19; s Joseph J Roddy & Ann Flood R; m 1954 to Lucille L Baumann; c Mary C, Joseph D, Daniel M & Mark S. Educ: St Louis Univ, 37-38. Polit & Govt Pos: Alderman, 17th Ward, St Louis, Mo, 53-68; committeeman, 17th Ward Dem Comt, St Louis, 68-; treas, Dem City Campaign Comt, 69-; mem, State Dem Comt, 70-; deleg, Dem Nat Mid-Term Conf, 74. Bus & Prof Pos: Owner, Joseph P Roddy Ins Co, 58- Mem: Chouteau Lions (vpres); Optimists West (vpres); Manchester-Chouteau Businessmen (bd dirs); Mid-Town Neighborhood Improv Asn (vpres). Relig: Catholic. Mailing Add: 4529 Gibson St Louis MO 63110

RODERICK, GERALD JOHN (D)
Mo State Rep
b Upton, Mo, Dec 22, 24; s Leonard Wheeler Roderick & Gracie Baker R; div; c Sherri, Darrell, Kerry & Lisa. Educ: Univ Mo-Columbia, BA, 50, MEd, 52; Phi Sigma Gamma; Phi Delta Kappa. Polit & Govt Pos: Bd dirs, Dem Unlimited, 70; mem, Mo State Dem Party,

currently; Mo State Rep, 19th Dist, 73- Bus & Prof Pos: Chmn dept gen practice, Kansas City Col Osteopathic Med, 68, chmn intern comt, 69-, chief of staff, 70-71. Mil Serv: Entered as Seaman 2/C, Navy, 43, released as Pharmacist 3/C, 46, after serv in Seventh Amphibian, Pac Theatre, 44-45; Am & Asiatic Medals. Mem: Am Col Gen Practitioners; Mo Asn Osteopathic Physicians & Surgeons (deleg, 60-); VFW (med adv, Post 5606, 59-); Am Legion (med adv, Post 61, 59-); 40 et 8 (grand med, 66-); Claycomo Lions. Relig: Baptist. Mailing Add: 56 Northeast 69 Hwy Kansas City MO 64119

RODEY, PATRICK MICHAEL (D)
Alaska State Sen
b San Francisco, Calif, Jan 22, 43; s James Rodey & Leora Phillips R; div. Educ: Univ Alaska, BEd, 66; Chico State Univ, 66-67; Univ Ariz, JD, 73; Phi Alpha Delta. Polit & Govt Pos: Alaska State Sen, 75- Bus & Prof Pos: Attorney, currently. Relig: Episcopal. Mailing Add: 3940 Spenard Rd Anchorage AK 99503

RODGER, RONALD ALAN (D)
b Blue Island, Ill, Oct 3, 44; s Alexander S Rodger & Anne F Milmine R; single. Educ: Northern Ill Univ, BSEd, 68, MA, 70, PhD, currently; John Marshall Law Sch, 68-; Upper Classmen's Award, 66; Chicago Coun on Foreign Rels. Polit & Govt Pos: Legis aide to State Rep Leland H Rayson, Ill, 68-; speaker for US Sen George McGovern, SDak, 72; cand, US Rep, Ill, 74. Bus & Prof Pos: Teacher, Sch Dist 65, Evanston, Ill, 68-69; teacher, Sch Dist 218, Oak Lawn, 70- Publ: Paris peace talks, Northerner, 70; The Democratic National Convention 1972, Worth-Palos Reporter, 71. Mem: Nat Hist Asn; Lit Guild; Ill & Nat Educ Asns. Honors & Awards: George M Pullman Found scholar, 66. Relig: Protestant. Mailing Add: 16719 Lakewood Tinley Park IL 60477

RODGERS, DAVID H (R)
Mayor, Spokane, Wash
b New Albany, Ind, Aug 10, 23; s Clarence Earl Rodgers & Gladys Hardy R; m 1965 to Naomi Fowle; c Nancy (Mrs Varnador) & Maureen Fowle & John T, Rebecca J, Brian A & Janet P Rodgers. Educ: Purdue Univ, BS, 47; Sigma Alpha Epsilon. Polit & Govt Pos: Precinct committeeman, Rep Party, Wash, 52-54; Rep Dist Leader, Spokane, Wash, 52-54; pres, Spokane Co Rep Club, 54-56; chmn, Spokane Co Rep Party, 56-58; mem, Wash State Rep Exec Bd, 56-60; Rep State Committeeman, Wash, 58-60; Mayor, Spokane, 67- Bus & Prof Pos: Mgr group & pension dept, Aetna Life Ins Co, Spokane, 49- Mil Serv: Navy, 45, Ens, serv in Underwater Demolition Team. Mem: Boy Scouts (bd, Inland Empire Coun); Mason; Kiwanis; YMCA. Relig: Presbyterian. Legal Res: 4511 S Madelia Spokane WA 99203 Mailing Add: 654 City Hall Spokane WA 99201

RODGERS, HENRY L (D)
Presiding Justice, Supreme Court, Miss
b Philadelphia, Miss, Apr 6, 03; s Henry Herman Rodgers & Ettie Lee Brantley R; m 1929 to Leola Edwards. Educ: Miss Col, 20-22; Cumberland Univ, BA, 22; Univ Miss, LLB, 27. Polit & Govt Pos: City attorney, Louisville, Miss, 45-46; dist attorney, Fifth Judicial Dist, 46-51, circuit judge, 51-61; Justice, Supreme Court, Miss, 61- Mil Serv: Miss Nat Guard, 29-35, Hq Co, 155th Inf, 31st Div, Army, 43-44, 2nd Lt, 240 AAA East Coast Defense, Newport, RI. Publ: Search & seizure, 12/56 & Process, 8/59, Miss Law J. Mem: Miss Bar Asn; Sons of Confederate Vets; Am Legion; 40 et 8; Shrine. Relig: Methodist. Legal Res: 431 N Spring Louisville MS 39339 Mailing Add: State Capitol Jackson MS 39205

RODGERS, KENNETH DAVID (R)
b Canton, Ohio, Jan 26, 41; s John Rodgers & Mabel Clark R; m 1961 to Elizabeth Margaret Jenkins; c Kenneth David, Jr & Lloyd Kevin. Educ: Kent State Univ, 60-61. Polit & Govt Pos: Vchmn, Dougherty Co Young Rep, Ga, 68-70; chmn, Dougherty Co Rep Party, formerly; alt deleg, Rep Nat Conv, 72. Bus & Prof Pos: Vpres opers, Davis Bros of Albany Inc, 63-73. Mem: Ga Restaurant Asn; Albany Boys Club; CofC. Honors & Awards: Restaurateur of Year, Ga Restaurant Asn, 72; Food Serv Award, Fla State Univ, 72. Relig: Catholic. Legal Res: 2603 Northgate Rd Albany GA 31705 Mailing Add: 813 Highland Ave Albany GA 31701

RODGERS, LOUISE V (D)
Mem, Ala State Dem Exec Comt
b New Market, Ala, May 4, 20; d William Roe Vandiver & Lillie Henshaw V; m 1938 to Walton White Rodgers; c William Stanley, Kenneth White & Augustus Donnell. Educ: New Market High Sch, grad, 38; Alverson-Draughon Bus Col. Polit & Govt Pos: Co off mgr, DeGraffenried for Gov, Ala, 62 & co mgr, 62-66; off mgr, Glenn Hearn for Mayor, 64; co off mgr, Gilchrist for Gov & Madison Co Dem Cand Comt, 66; vchmn women's div, Madison Co Dem Party, 67, chmn, formerly; alt deleg, Dem Nat Conv, 68; mem, Ala State Dem Exec Comt, 70- Bus & Prof Pos: Bookkeeper & co-owner, Maple Ridge Hatchery, 45-62; free lance pub rels dir, 62- Mem: Press Club; Int Concert Mgrs Asn; Arts Coun, Inc; Phi Sigma Alpha; Civic Club Coun. Honors & Awards: Outstanding Serv Awards from Salvation Army, United Givers Fund, Fantasy Playhouse, Civil Club Coun, Bus & Prof Women's Club, Cancer Soc, March of Dimes & Heart Asn; Good Neighbor Award. Relig: Presbyterian. Mailing Add: 208 White St NE Huntsville AL 35801

RODGERS, SARAH JANE (D)
VPres, Okla Fedn Dem Women
b Stillwater, Okla, Aug 10, 27; d James Edward Berry & Edwina Morrison B; m 1949 to James William Rodgers, Jr; c James William, III, Robert Berry, Becky & Beverly. Educ: Sullins Col, 44-45; Okla State Univ, BA, 48; Kappa Alpha Theta. Polit & Govt Pos: Dist vpres, Okla Fedn Dem Women, 69-71, dist pres, 71-75, state vpres, 75-; precinct chmn, Hughes Co Dem Party, Okla, 69-73; alt deleg, Dem Nat Conv, 72; mem exec comt, Okla State Dem Cent Comt, currently. Mem: Holdenville City Libr Bd; Okla Comn Educ; Hosp Auxiliary (treas, currently). Honors & Awards: Outstanding Dem Woman of Okla, Okla Fedn Dem Women's Clubs, 71. Relig: Episcopal. Mailing Add: 121 N Lowe Holdenville OK 74848

RODHAM, A DAVID (R)
Mass State Rep
b Medford, Mass, Nov 26, 38; s Arthur Rodham & Edith Kingman R; m 1960 to Kathryn Gail Doherty; c Rebecca, Kathryn & David. Educ: Huntington Prep, 58; Univ Mass, 59-60. Polit & Govt Pos: Parks & cemetary, Lynnfield, Mass, 65-69, selectman, 69-75, chmn bd, 71-72 & 74-75; Mass State Rep, 75- Mem: Lynnfield AF&AM Lodge; Shrine; Rotary Int; Mass Selectmans Asn. Relig: Episcopal. Mailing Add: 665 Lowell St Lynnfield MA 01940

RODINO, PETER WALLACE, JR (D)
US Rep, NJ
b Newark, NJ, June 7, 09; m to Marianna Stango; c Margaret Ann (Mrs Charles Stanziale, Jr) & Peter, III; one grandchild. Educ: Univ Newark, JD, 37. Polit & Govt Pos: Nat chmn, Columbus Found, Inc, formerly; spearheaded drive against Communism in Apr 1948, elec in Italy; US deleg, Intergovt Comt Europ Migration, 62-, chmn, 71-72; deleg, NAtlantic Assembly, NATO, chmn sci & tech comt & working group on control of narcotics, currently; US Rep, 10th Dist, NJ, 48-, dean, NJ Cong Deleg, US House Rep, currently, Asst Majority Whip, mem steering comt & chmn immigration & nationality subcomt, formerly, chmn comt on judiciary, 73- Bus & Prof Pos: Attorney-at-law. Mil Serv: One of First enlisted men to be commissioned overseas; First Armored Div & Mil Mission Italy Army; discharged 46 as Capt; Bronze Star & other decorations. Honors & Awards: Order of Merit, Ital Repub, Star of Solidarity, Cavaliere de Gran Croce of Order Al Merito della Repubblica; knighted by former King Umberto of Italy; Knight of the Order Crown of Italy; Knight of St Maurizio Lazzaro; Ital Cross of Merit; plus many others. Legal Res: 205 Grafton Ave Newark NJ 07104 Mailing Add: 2462 Rayburn House Off Bldg Washington DC 20515

RODRIGUES, THOMAS J (D)
RI State Rep
Mailing Add: 742 Jepson Lane Middletown RI 02840

RODRIGUEZ, DAVID (R)
Mem, Rep State Cent Comt Calif
b Holtville, Calif, Feb 27, 35; s Bishan Sidhu & Simona Rodriguez; m 1956 to Seferina Magallanez; c Monica Lynn, David Keith & Michael George. Educ: Am River Col, 62. Polit & Govt Pos: Span Speaking Rep Conf, 68-; mem, Rep State Cent Com Calif, 71- Bus & Prof Pos: With Aerojet-Gen Corp, Sacramento, Calif, 58- Mil Serv: Sgt 1/C, Calif Nat Guard, 54-66. Mem: Overall Econ Develop Prog, Placer Co; Mex-Am Scholarship Asn Placer Co; KofC Coun 4540 (grand knight); Placer Co Ment Retardation Asn (bd mem); Ahepa. Relig: Catholic. Mailing Add: 511 Vine Way Roseville CA 95678

RODRIGUEZ, JEANNE E (R)
Secy, State Rep Party, Fla
b Thompsonville, Conn; d Joseph Frank D'Agostino & Antoinette Avignone D; wid; c Mark A & John J. Educ: Boston Univ, eve. Polit & Govt Pos: Orange Co Rep Women's Club Orange Co, Fla, 47; chmn, Youth for Eisenhower, Fla, 51; deleg, Rep Nat Conv, 52 & 72; coordr, Nixon for President, 68; women's chmn, Nat Alliance of Businessmen, 70; mem, Nat Adv Comt to Reelect the President, 72; mem adv comt, Small Bus Admin, Fla, 75-; secy, State Rep Party, 75- Mem: Winter Park (bd dir); Orlando CofC (bd dirs); Drug Abuse Coun, Orange Co; Newman Student Community Ctr Coterie (pres); Morning Star (vpres). Relig: Catholic. Mailing Add: 409 Melanie Way Maitland FL 32751

RODRIGUEZ TORRES, JULIO I (POPULAR DEMOCRAT, PR)
Sen, PR Senate
Mailing Add: State Capitol San Juan PR 00901

RODROCK, JACK L (D)
Kans State Rep
b Garden City, Kans, Dec 24, 49; s Whitford (Rod) Rodrock & Vera Turner; m 1973 to Jeanne Speer. Educ: Garden City Community Jr Col, 73- Polit & Govt Pos: Kans State Rep, 75- Mil Serv: Entered as E-1, Army, released as Acting E-5, after serv in 82nd Mil Police, 82nd Airborne Div, Ft Bragg, NC, 70-72. Mem: VFW; Leoti Jaycees; Kans Livestock Asn; Kans Farm Bur. Mailing Add: Box 159 Leoti KS 67361

ROE, DAVID K (DFL)
Mem-At-Lg, Dem Nat Comt
Mailing Add: 179 Peninsula Rd Minneapolis MN 55441

ROE, ELBERT OLIVER (D)
Ind State Rep
b Mishawaka, Ind, Mar 22, 14; s Glenn Earl Roe & Florence Williamson R; m 1934 to Marjorie Calbeek; c Janet (Mrs Loren Brumbaugh), Stephen & Mary Jayne (Mrs Robert Huff). Educ: Ligonier High Sch, grad, 32. Polit & Govt Pos: Trustee, Perry Twp, Noble Co, Ind, 59-67; supvr, Soil & Water Conserv, Noble Co, 57-; state pres, Ind Soil & Water Conserv Dists, 68-69; mem, Noble Co Community Develop Comt, 71-; Ind State Rep, 75- Bus & Prof Pos: Self-employed livestock & grain farmer. Mem: Farm Bur; Nat Farmers Union; Nat Farmers Orgn; Farm, Labor, Small Bus; Taxpayers, Inc. Relig: Methodist. Mailing Add: Rte 3 Ligonier IN 46767

ROE, JERRY D (R)
Exec Dir, Mich Rep State Cent Comt
b Conrad, Mont, May 18, 36; s Howard O Roe & Ialene B Freel R; m 1965 to Shirley Carol Hands; c Jason & Samantha. Educ: Northern Mont Col, 1 year; Col Great Falls, BA, 58; mem student coun. Polit & Govt Pos: Chmn, Col Great Falls Rep Club, 56-57, Mont Fedn Col Rep Clubs, 57-58 & Cascade Co Young Rep, 57-58; exec dir, Minn Young Rep League, 59-61; exec dir, Nat Fedn Young Rep, 61-63; dir orgn, Mich Rep Party, 63-69; precinct deleg, 13th Precinct, Ward 4, Lansing, 65-71, 13th Precinct, Ward 4, Rep Club, 65-70; Rep dist rep for US Congressman Garry Brown, 67-69; exec dir, Mich Rep State Cent Comt, 69-; mem adv bd, Young Rep Nat Fedn, 71; app, Mich Hist Comn, 72, pres, 75; chmn, Mich Rep Bicentennial Comt. Bus & Prof Pos: Mem bd, Cleary Col, 73-75. Mil Serv: Mont & Minn Army Nat Guards; Mont Air Nat' Guard. Mem: Mich Hist Soc (bd dirs); Am Polit Items Collectors Asn (pres, currently); Am Polit Sci Asn; US Cong Secy Club; Mason. Relig: Methodist. Mailing Add: 4 Locust Lane Lansing MI 48910

ROE, JOHN B (R)
Ill State Sen
Mailing Add: RFD 1 Rochelle IL 61068

ROE, ROBERT A (D)
US Rep, NJ
b Wayne, NJ, Feb 28, 24. Educ: Ore State & Wash State Univs. Polit & Govt Pos: Committeeman, Wayne Twp, NJ, 55-56; mayor, Wayne, 56-61; freeholder, Passaic Co, 59-63, dir bd chosen freeholders, 62-63; NJ State Cabinet, comnr, Conserv & Econ Develop, State NJ, 63-69; US Rep, Eighth Dist, NJ, 69-, mem pub works & transportation comt, US House of Rep, chmn econ develop subcomt, water resources subcomt & surface transportation subcomt, mem comt sci & technol, mem domestic & int sci planning & anal

subcomt, mem space, sci & applns subcomt & aviation & transportation, research & develop, currently; Mil Serv: World War II, serv in Reconnaissance Force, ETO; Bronze Star. Mem: 89th Div Soc World War II (nat vpres); Elks; Optimist; Am Legion; Boy Scouts (nat coun). Honors & Awards: Hon Fel Award, Am Acad Med Adminr, 71; Inst Appl Psychother Cert of Appreciation, 72; Nat Small Bus Asn Citation Award, 72; Nat Humanitarian Award, Joint Handicapped Coun, Nat Soc Handicapped, 72; Cited by President's Comt on Employ of Handicapped, 72. Legal Res: Wayne NJ Mailing Add: US House Rep Washington DC 20515

ROE, TEDDY W (D)
b Imperial, Nebr, Mar 21, 34; s Wallace H Roe & Coryelle Miller R; m 1967 to Marcie Rivin; c Timothy. Educ: Eastern Mont Col, 51-53; Mex City Col, summer 58; Univ Mont, BA in Jour, 59; Univ Buenos Aires, 60; Georgetown Univ, MA in Russian Area Studies, 65; Johns Hopkins Sch Advan Int Studies, 68-; Kappa Tau Alpha; Phi Kappa Phi. Polit & Govt Pos: Am Polit Sci Asn Cong Fel, Off US Rep Armistead Selden, Ala, 62 & Off US Sen Mike Mansfield, Mont, 62; prof staff man, Dem Policy Comt, US Senate, 62-65; asst to majority leader, 62-70, prof staff mem, Off Secy for Majority, 65-69, asst secy for majority, 70-71; legis aide, US Rep John Melcher, Mont, 72-73; exec secy, US Sen Lee Metcalf, Mont, 73- Bus & Prof Pos: Reporter & photographer, Great Falls Leader Mont, summer 59; ed writer, Des Moines Register, Iowa, 59-60. Mil Serv: Entered as Pvt, Army, 55, released as Cpl, 57, after serv in 7th Inf Regt, 3rd Div. Honors & Awards: Recipient of Inter-Am Press Asn Fel Award for 1 year spent in Argentina, 60; Am Polit Sci Asn Cong Fel Award, 61-62; Am Polit Sci Asn Cong Staff Fel Award, 68 for study & travel in Latin Am & the Soviet Union. Relig: Protestant. Legal Res: MT Mailing Add: 140 N Early St Alexandria VA 22304

ROEBUCK, ELMO D
Sen, VI Legis
Mailing Add: PO Box 477 Charlotte Amalie St Thomas VI 00801

ROEDER, JOHN (R)
Ariz State Sen
Mailing Add: 6265 E Catalina Dr Scottsdale AZ 85251

ROEHRIG, STANLEY HERBERT (D)
Hawaii State Rep
b Honolulu, Hawaii, Mar 11, 39; s Kenneth William Roehrig & Ethel Seivers R; m 1965 to Janice Hodapp; c Ginger Allison & Jill Ilima. Educ: Brown Univ, AB in Physics, 61; Univ Wash Law Sch, JD, 65; Phi Gamma Delta. Polit & Govt Pos: Dep Attorney Gen, State of Hawaii, 65-66; Dep Co Attorney, Co of Hawaii, 66-67; fund raising chmn, Co Dem Party, Hawaii, 66, co-chmn, rallies, 66, chmn, resolutions comt, 68; Pub Defender, Hawaii Co, 67-68; Hawaii State Rep, 70- Mem: Civitan Club; Hilo Jaycees; Farm Bur; Big Island Comt of Alcoholism; Comt on Aging. Honors & Awards: One of Three Outstanding Young Men, Hawaii State Jaycees, 69; one of five nat recipients, Freedom Guard Award for Excellence in Pub Serv, 71. Relig: Christian. Legal Res: 25 Akepa St Hilo HI 96720 Mailing Add: House of Rep State Capitol Honolulu HI 96813

ROETHLER, KENNETH J (D)
Chmn, Kossuth Co Dem Cent Comt, Iowa
b Bode, Iowa, Oct 17, 22; s Phillp Roethler & Veronica Faber R; m 1945 to Dolores May Kollasch; c ten. Educ: Eighth grade. Polit & Govt Pos: Chmn, Kossuth Co Dem Cent Comt, Iowa, 72- Bus & Prof Pos: Farming. Mil Serv: Entered as Pvt, Army, 43, released as Cpl, 45, after serv in Europe. Mem: VFW. Mailing Add: RR 1 Box 142 Algona IA 50511

ROFF, HADLEY REA (D)
b Fresno, Calif, Dec 16, 31; s Fay Freeman Roff & Gertrude Olive Rea R; wid; c James Michael, Timothy Charles & Kelly Killoran. Educ: Stanford Univ, BA, 54; Sigma Delta Chi; Delta Upsilon. Polit & Govt Pos: Campaign mgr, Calif State Controller Alan Cranston, 66; confidential secy, Mayor Joseph Alioto, San Francisco, 67-70; press secy, US Sen John V Tunney, Calif, 70-72, admin asst, 72-; dep press secy, Muskie for President, 72. Bus & Prof Pos: Reporter, San Francisco News/News-Call Bull/Examr, 55-66. Honors & Awards: McQuade Award, Cath Newsman Asn, San Francisco, 62. Mailing Add: 5925 Autumn Dr McLean VA 22101

ROGERS, BARBARA RADCLIFFE (R)
Mem, NH Rep State Comt
b Bedford, Ind, Apr 23, 39; d George Charles Radcliffe & Liddie Bacom R; m 1967 to Stillman D Rogers; c Juliette. Educ: Boston Univ, AB, 61. Polit & Govt Pos: Vchmn, Mass Young Rep, 60-61; mem, Washington, DC staff, US Rep James C Cleveland, NH, 63, dist rep, 69-73; legis asst, US Rep Edward J Gurney, Fla, 65-67; polit speech writer, Libr Cong, Washington, DC, 68; asst chmn, Keene Rep City Comt, NH, 70; pres, Cheshire Rep Women's Club, 71; co coordr, Comt for Reelection of the President, 72; chmn, Cheshire Co Rep Comt, 72-73, mem, currently; asst chmn, NH State Rep Comt, 73-74, mem, currently; deleg, NH Const Conv, 74, vchmn jour comt; mem, Keene Planning Bd, 74-; mem, Keene Community Develop Comn; state chmn, Wyman for Senate Campaign, 74- Bus & Prof Pos: Free lance writer & lectr. Mem: Old Homestead Garden Club; Cheshire Co Hist Soc. Relig: Episcopal. Mailing Add: 10 Old Walpole Rd Keene NH 03431

ROGERS, BENJAMIN D, JR (R)
Chmn, Norfolk Rep Town Comt, Mass
b Norwood, Mass, Dec 13, 19; s Benjamin D Rogers & Alice Wyman R; m 1947 to Elizabeth Conklin Fenn; c Margaret F (Mrs England), Kimball W, Benjamin D, III & Joanna W. Educ: Dartmouth Col, 38-40; Theta Delta Chi. Polit & Govt Pos: Mem, Norfolk Rep Town Comt, 52-, secy, 64-68, chmn, 68-70 & 73-; mem, Zoning Bd Appeals, 63-70. Bus & Prof Pos: Vpres & treas, Heritage Publ Co, Inc, currently. Mil Serv: Entered as Pvt, Army, 42, released as 1st Lt, 46, after serv in Mil Intel, ETO, 3rd Army, 43-45. Mailing Add: 2 Holbrook St Norfolk MA 02056

ROGERS, BETH (R)
Rep Nat Committeewoman, Kans
m 1946 to Richard D Rogers; c Letitia Ann, Cappi & Kurt. Educ: Kans State Univ, BS in Music Educ, 43. Polit & Govt Pos: Mem, Riley Co Rep Women, Kans; mem prog comt, Kans Fedn Rep Women; Rep precinct committeewoman; mem, Comt to Reelect a Rep Gov; Rep Nat Committeewoman, Kans, 71; deleg, Rep Nat Conv, 72. Mem: Manhattan Music Club; PEO; Kappa Kappa Gamma (alumni pres). Relig: Presbyterian; church organist. Mailing Add: 919 Fairway Dr Manhattan KS 66502

ROGERS, BOBBY WAYNE (D)
NC State Rep
b Henderson, NC, June 19, 34; s Hartwell B Rogers & Rena Gentry R; m to Nancy Bell; c Samuel J, Rena E, Michael F & Matthew H W. Educ: NC State Col, BSCE; George Washington Univ, LLB. Polit & Govt Pos: Solicitor, Vance Co Recorders Court, NC, 64-68; asst solicitor, Vance Co Superior Court, 64-68; chmn, Vance Co Dem Exec Comt, 66-68; NC State Rep, 16th Dist, 71-73, 13th Dist, 73- Bus & Prof Pos: Naval architect, Bushps, Washington, DC, 59-63; attorney-at-law, 63- Mil Serv: Entered as Recruit, Navy, 52, released as AT-3, 55. Mailing Add: PO Box 696 Henderson NC 27536

ROGERS, BYRON GILES (D)
b Hunt Co, Tex, Aug 1, 00; s Peter Rogers & Minnie M Gentry R; m; c Mrs Hollis Martin & Byron, Jr. Educ: Univ Okla, 19-22; Univ Colo, Univ Denver, 23-25, LLB; Phi Alpha Delta. Polit & Govt Pos: City attorney, Las Animas & co attorney, Bent Co, Colo; Colo State Rep, 31-35, Speaker, Colo Gen Assembly, 33; with Dept Agr & Nat Recovery Admin, Washington, DC, 33-34; Asst US Attorney, Dist Colo, 34-36; app Attorney Gen, Colo, 35, elected, 36-38; state chmn, Dem State Cent Comt, Colo, 41-42; pub mem, War Labor Bd, 42-45; co chmn, Denver Dem Cent Comt, 45-50; US Rep, Colo, 50-70. Bus & Prof Pos: Law practice, Las Animas, Colo, 25-33. Mil Serv: Army, 18. Mem: Am Bar Asn; Lions Int; Mystic Shrine; Elks; Am Legion. Relig: Baptist. Mailing Add: 666 Gaylord Denver CO 80206

ROGERS, CHLOE (D)
Co Recorder, Mineral Co, Colo
b Sanford, Colo, Aug 23, 18; d George Ernest Wright & Fannie Jane Morgan W; wid; c Lonnie Milton & Dannie Edward. Educ: Sanford High Sch, Colo. Polit & Govt Pos: Clerk & recorder, Mineral Co, Colo, 58-; vchairwoman, Mineral Co Dem Party, 60- Honors & Awards: Colo Dept Revenue Serv Award. Relig: Latter-day Saint. Mailing Add: Creede CO 81130

ROGERS, FREDERICK MARSHALL (FRED) (D)
Miss State Rep
Mailing Add: 1823 Thirty-fourth St Meridian MS 39301

ROGERS, GEORGE (D)
Mass State Rep
b New Bedford, Mass, Aug 2, 35; s M F Rogers & Rose Soares R; single. Educ: Providence Col, AB, 58; Bridgewater State Col, 59-60; Boston State Col, 65; New Bedford Club of Providence Col. Polit & Govt Pos: Mass State Rep, 65-70; Mayor, New Bedford, 70-71; deleg, Dem Nat Conv, 72; Mass State Sen, 75- Bus & Prof Pos: Teacher, Fairhaven High Sch, Mass, 58-61; pub rels dir, Atlantic Ten Pin Lanes, Fairhaven, 59-61 & Holiday Lanes, South Dartmouth, 61-64; teacher-coach, New Bedford Voc High Sch, 61-64. Mem: Nat Educ Asn; Mass Teachers Asn; Mass Coaches Asn; Nat Soc State Legislators; Am Voc Asn. Honors & Awards: Dean's List, Providence Col. Relig: Roman Catholic. Mailing Add: 23 Robeson St New Bedford MA 02740

ROGERS, GEORGE LESTER (R)
Exec Committeeman, Dillon Co Rep Party, SC
b Dillon, SC, Apr 28, 22; s Lacey B Rogers & Nettie Harrelson R; m 1945 to Mary White Clardy; c George Darryl & Samuel Norman. Educ: Univ NC, 2 years; Chi Phi. Polit & Govt Pos: Treas, Dillon Co Rep Party, 64-70, chmn, formerly, exec committeeman, currently. Bus & Prof Pos: Spec rep, NY Life Ins Co, 55-; secy-treas, G & R Enterprises, Inc, 70-; owner, Rogers Realty Co, 70- Mem: Top Club; Lions; Mason; Shrine. Relig: Methodist. Legal Res: 1512 E Washington St Dillon SC 29536 Mailing Add: PO Box 967 Dillon SC 29536

ROGERS, GEORGE WINTERS, JR (D)
Miss State Rep
b Vicksburg, Miss; s George W Rogers & Marion Todd R; m 1953 to Muriel Oulpe; c Paul, John, Peter & Elizabeth. Educ: Yale Univ, BA, 49; Oxford Univ, MA, 51; Univ Miss, LLB, 54; Phi Delta Phi; Omicron Delta Kappa; Tau Kappa Epsilon; Phi Kappa Phi; Sigma Alpha Epsilon. Polit & Govt Pos: Miss State Rep, 52-64 & 69-, chmn, Comt on Educ, Miss House of Rep, 72-; mem, Miss Cent Data Processing Authority, 70-, chmn, 72-; mem, Southern Regional Educ Bd, 73- Bus & Prof Pos: Partner, Teller, Biedenharn & Rogers, Law Firm, 54-; dir, Vicksburg Small Bus Investment Co, 60- Mil Serv: Entered as Pvt, Army, 45, released as Sgt, 47, after serv in Counter Intel Corps, Japan, 46-47. Publ: Co-auth, Yesterday's Constitution Today, Univ Miss, 60. Mem: Am Judicature Soc; Rotary; Y's Mens Club; Am Legion; Elks. Relig: Presbyterian. Legal Res: Rte 6 Box 279 Vicksburg MS 39180 Mailing Add: PO Box 22 Vicksburg MS 39180

ROGERS, GLENN K (DOC) (D)
Wyo State Sen
b Girard, Kans, July 26, 00; s Benjamin Adelbert Rogers & Bell Britton R; m 1924 to Mary Ethola Read; c Mary Lee (Mrs Donald I Meyer). Educ: Baker Univ, AB, 24; Univ Wyo, MA, 37; Kans Univ & Southern Methodist Univ, grad study; Kappa Delta Pi; Sigma Phi Epsilon; B Club; Radio Club; letters in baseball, basketball & track. Polit & Govt Pos: Wyo State Sen, Laramie Co, 67- Bus & Prof Pos: Coach & high sch prin, Kanorado, Kans, 24-26; coach & sci teacher, Wheatland, 27-38; high sch sci teacher, Cheyenne, Wyo, 38-66 & coach, 38-44; broker, Prudential Ins Co of Am, 43-; owner, lapidary shop, Doc's Rock's, Cheyenne. Publ: Book reviewer on physics & geol, Wyo Libr Roundup. Relig: Protestant. Mailing Add: 312 E Pershing Blvd Cheyenne WY 82001

ROGERS, J ROBERT (D)
WVa State Sen
Mailing Add: State Capitol Charleston WV 25305

ROGERS, J STANLEY (D)
Tenn State Rep
b Kilpatrick, Ala, Mar 2, 39; s Walker A Rogers & Annie May Gilbreath R; m 1961 to Patricia Ann Cooper; c J Stanley, Jr & Amy Lee. Educ: Mid Tenn State Univ, BS, 61; Vanderbilt Univ Law Sch, JD, 64; Phi Kappa Delta; Delta Theta Phi. Polit & Govt Pos: City attorney, Manchester, Tenn, 68-; mem, Coffee Co Dem Exec Comt, 68-, chmn, 68-70; Tenn State Rep, 71-, Dem Whip, Tenn House Rep, 71, Majority Leader, 73- Bus & Prof Pos: Attorney, Rogers & Parsons, 64- Mem: Tenn Munic Attorneys Asn; Tenn Trial Lawyers Asn; CofC; Rotary; Jaycees. Honors & Awards: Robert A (Fats) Everett Mem Award State Tenn, 71; Outstanding Young Man of the Year, Manchester, Jaycees, 70. Relig: Presbyterian. Mailing Add: 100 North Spring Street Manchester TN 37355

ROGERS, JOHN (D)
Secy of State, Okla
b Clinton, Okla, Aug 15, 28; s John Marvin Rogers & Annette Ann Jaworsky R; m to Jeannie Thompson; c John Marvin, III & Mary Annette. Educ: Oklahoma City Univ & Univ Okla. Polit & Govt Pos: State Sen-at-lg, Okla, 64; Secy of State, Okla, 67-; mem, State Bd Equalization; comnr, Land Off; ex officio mem, State Bldg Bonds Comn, Okla Funding Bond Comn, Employee's Retirement Bd, State Emergency Fund Bd & State Salary Admin Bd. Bus & Prof Pos: Partner, Rogers & Rogers, Accts, 50; exec vpres & dir, Stemen Labs, Trade-Mart Dept Stores; sr partner, Jefferson Interests, Okla Drainboard & other corps, 64. Mil Serv: Entered as Pvt, Marine Corps, 46, released as Cpl, 48, after serv in 1st Div, Japan; Reentered as Pvt, Army, 53, released as Sgt 1/C, 55, after serv in 45th Inf Div, Korean Conflict. Mem: Nat Asn Secy of States; Pilots Int Asn; Platform Speakers Asn; Oklahoma City Speaker's Forum; Am Legion. Relig: Disciples of Christ. Mailing Add: 211 State Capitol Bldg Oklahoma City OK 73105

ROGERS, JOHN D (D)
NMex State Sen
Mailing Add: 329 Rover Los Alamos NM 87544

ROGERS, JOHN I, III (D)
SC State Rep
Mailing Add: Box 47 Bennettsville SC 29512

ROGERS, JOHN MARVIN (D)
State Examr & Inspector, Okla
b Bessie, Okla, Apr 24, 00; s John Lafayette Rogers & Martha Ellen Hatchett R; m 1922 to Annette Ann Jaworsky; c Roberta Mae (Mrs Henry R Krueger) & John Marvin. Educ: Hills Bus Col, Oklahoma City, 1 year; Univ Okla, 2 years; Oklahoma City Univ, 2 years. Polit & Govt Pos: State Examr & Inspector, Okla, 59- Mem: Okla Soc CPA; Am Inst CPA. Relig: Christian. Legal Res: 3408 NW 60th St Oklahoma City OK 73112 Mailing Add: PO Box 53311 Oklahoma City OK 73105

ROGERS, JOHN RICHARD (D)
b Ashburn, Ga, June 30, 24; s Edwin A Rogers & Ella Mae Evans R; m 1953 to Reginald Ann Cox; c Sylvia, Dawn & Starr. Educ: Univ Ga, JD, 49; Phi Eta Sigma; Blue Key; Phi Alpha Delta; Sigma Chi. Polit & Govt Pos: Chmn, Turner Co Dem Exec Comt, Ga, until 66; mem, Ga State Dem Exec Comt, formerly. Bus & Prof Pos: Vpres, First Fed Savings & Loan Asn, Turner Co, 62-; pres, Monroe Mall Corp, 65- Mil Serv: Entered as 2nd Lt, Army, 44, released as 1st Lt, 46, after serv in Marine Supply Depot, Manila, Philippine Islands. Mem: Am Bar Asn; Am Judicature Soc; Am Trial Lawyers Asn; Mason; Shrine. Relig: Methodist. Legal Res: E Madison Ave Ashburn GA 31714 Mailing Add: PO Box 304 Ashburn GA 31714

ROGERS, JOSEPH OSCAR, JR (R)
Exec Committeeman, SC Rep State Cent Comt
b Mullins, SC, Oct 8, 21; s Joseph O Rogers & Lila McDonald R; m 1949 to Kathleen Brown; c Pamela, Joseph O, III & Timothy Julian. Educ: The Citadel, 3 years; Univ SC, LLB. Polit & Govt Pos: SC State Rep, 55-66; Rep cand for Gov, SC, 66; deleg, Rep Nat Conv, 68; US Attorney for Dist of SC, 69-; exec committeeman, SC Rep State Cent Comt, 74- Bus & Prof Pos: Attorney-at-law, 50- Mil Serv: Entered as Pvt, Army Engrs, 43, released as Sgt, 46, after serv in African & European Theaters. Mem: Mason; Civitan; Am Legion; Farm Bur. Relig: Methodist; lay leader, Manning Methodist Church. Mailing Add: PO Box 487 Manning SC 29102

ROGERS, LLOYD EMMETT (D)
b Lexington, Ky, Aug 31, 09; s Charles V Rogers & Ardena Tune R; m 1929 to Frances Phelps; c Emmett Vinson & Charles William Carter. Educ: Univ Ky, BA, 33; George Washington Univ Law Sch, LLB, 38; Georgetown Univ Law Sch, LLM, 40. Polit & Govt Pos: Comnr finance, Cynthiana, Ky, 46-51; Ky State Rep, 56th Dist, 54-56; city attorney, Cynthiana, 66-67; alt deleg, Dem Nat Mid-Term Conf, 74; comnr juv cases, Harrison Co Court, 75- Mem: F&AM; Cynthiana Lions; Am Acad Polit & Social Sci; Ky Bar Asn (mem house deleg, 66-); Harrison Co Hist Soc (pres). Relig: Presbyterian. Legal Res: 107 Charlotte Dr Cynthiana KY 41031 Mailing Add: PO Box 342 Cynthiana KY 41031

ROGERS, MYRTLE BEATRICE (R)
NH State Rep
b Haverhill, Mass, Mar 24, 25; d Rufus Cecil Fanjoy & Rose Chabot F; m 1952 to Roland Irving Rogers; c Richard F Newhall & Rebecca J & foster children, Mark A Swasey & Mary A Rogers. Educ: Haverhill High Sch, Mass, grad, 43. Polit & Govt Pos: Secy-treas, Newton Conserv Comt, NH, 67-; deleg, Rockingham Co Rep Comt, 73-; NH State Rep, 73-; deleg, NH Rep Const Conv, 74-; deleg, NH Rep State Comt, 75- Mem: NH Hist Soc (founder & chmn); NH Bicentennial Comt (chmn); 4-H Leader. Relig: Christian Church; mem budget & activities comt, First Christian Church, Newton. Legal Res: Gale Village Rd Newton NH 03858 Mailing Add: RD 2 Box 435 Newton NH 03858

ROGERS, NORMAN G (D)
Iowa State Sen
Mailing Add: RR 2 Adel IA 50003

ROGERS, PAUL GRANT (D)
US Rep, Fla
b Ocilla, Ga, June 4, 21; s Dwight L Rogers & Florence Roberts R; m to Rebecca Bell; c Rebecca Laing. Educ: Univ Fla, AB, 42; George Washington Univ, 46; Univ Fla Law Sch, LLB, 48; pres, Fla Blue Key; nat debate champion, Tau Kappa Alpha. Hon Degrees: LLD, Fla Atlantic Univ, Univ Md & George Washington Univ; DSc, Univ Miami, LHD, Nova Univ & New York Med Col. Polit & Govt Pos: US Rep, Sixth Dist, Fla, 55-66, Ninth Dist, 66-72, Dist 11, 73-, mem interstate & foreign com & merchant marine & fisheries comts & chmn subcomt health & environ, US House Rep; deleg, Dem Nat Conv, 68. Mil Serv: Entered Army, 42, released as Maj, 46, after serv in Field Artil ETO; Bronze Star Medal; 2 Battle Stars. Legal Res: West Palm Beach FL 33401 Mailing Add: 2407 Rayburn House Off Bldg Washington DC 20515

ROGERS, RICHARD ADAMS (R)
Mass State Rep
b Northampton, Mass, July 8, 30; s Myron Mathew Rogers & Marjorie Olive Adams; m 1951 to Joan Irene Falvey; c Myron Edward, Kathleen Sue, Mark Bradford, Leisa Joan, Richard Adams, Jr & Jodi Elizebeth. Educ: Am Int Col, 52-53; Holy Cross, 54-56; Northeastern Univ, 56-61. Polit & Govt Pos: Mem, Zoning Bd Appeals, Westboro, Mass, 72-74; Mass State Rep, 18th Worcester Dist, 75- Bus & Prof Pos: Pres-treas, F&H Transportation Co, Worcester, 54- Mil Serv: Entered as Pvt, Air Force, 48, released as Sgt, 52, after serv in 3605 Hq, EADF & TC, 48-52. Mem: Lions Int (P/P Westoro-P/ZC Dist 33A); Worcester Traffic Asn; AF&AM. Relig: Protestant. Legal Res: 98 South St Westborough MA 01581 Mailing Add: Drawer C Westborough MA 01581

ROGERS, RICHARD D (R)
Kans State Sen
Mailing Add: 919 Fairway Dr Manhattan KS 66502

ROGERS, RUSSELL (D)
Mem Exec Comt, Ark Dem State Comt
b El Dorado, Ark, Oct 8, 44; s Frank Haltom Rogers & Lucy Russell R; m to Anne Elizabeth Heinold; c Matthew Timothy & Alexander Russell. Educ: Hendrix Col, 62-63; Univ Ark, Fayetteville, JD, 68; Pi Kappa Alpha. Polit & Govt Pos: City attorney, Des Arc, Ark, 70-71; mem exec comt, Ark Dem State Comt, 74-; chmn bd control, Ark State Hosps, 74- Publ: Co-auth, Arkansas Local Court Judges' Manual, Ark Judicial Dept, 71. Mem: Rotary; Ark Bar Asn; Ark Co Bar Asn (pres, 74-); Ark Jaycees. Legal Res: 1804 Fairway Stuttgart AR 72160 Mailing Add: PO Box 365 Stuttgart AR 72160

ROGERS, STANLEY (D)
Mem, Calif State Dem Cent Comt
b Los Angeles, Calif, Feb 28, 34; s Murray Harold Rogers & Rose Mednick R; m 1959 to Jane Hope Fegen; c Susan Louise, John Stuart, Kenneth Andrew & Steven Michael. Educ: Princeton Univ, 56; Univ Calif, Los Angeles Sch Law, LLB, 59; ELM Club. Polit & Govt Pos: Pres, West Side Dem Club, West Los Angeles, 62-63; chmn, 59th Assembly Dist Coun, Calif, 64; mem, Los Angeles Co Dem Cent Comt, 67-, chmn 59th Dist deleg, 68-74; vchmn, 26th Cong Dist Coun, 68; deleg, Dem Nat Conv, 68; mem, Calif State Dem Cent Comt, 69 & 75- Bus & Prof Pos: Law clerk to Fed Dist Court Judge, Los Angeles, 59-60; assoc, Little, Curry & Hagen, Los Angeles, 60-63; partner, Rogers & Harris, Los Angeles, 63-; arbitrator, Am Arbit Asn, 67- Mem: Los Angeles Co, Calif State & Beverly Hills Bar Asns; Am Judicature Asn; PTA (adv coun, Warner Ave Elem Sch & Emerson Jr High Sch). Relig: Jewish. Mailing Add: 661 Warner Ave Los Angeles CA 90024

ROGERS, STILLMAN D (R)
Mem, NH Rep State Comt
b Nashua, NH, Mar 6, 39; s Norman B Rogers & Claire Noel R; m 1967 to Barbara Radcliffe; c Juliette. Educ: Harvard Col, AB, 61; Am Univ, Washington Col Law, JD, 68; Phi Alpha Delta. Polit & Govt Pos: Chmn, Strafford Co Cong Campaign, NH, 62; mem bd dirs, NH Legal Assistance, 69-72; co chmn, US Rep James C Cleveland, NH, 70; mem, Cheshire Co Rep Comt, 71-, chmn, 71-72; mem, NH Rep State Comt, 71-; moderator, Ward Four, Keene, 72-74; mem, NH Rep State Finance Comt, 73-75; mem bd visitors, US Air Force Acad, 74-; deleg, NH Rep Conv, 74. Bus & Prof Pos: Attorney, Faulkner, Plaut, Hanna & Zimmerman, 68- Mil Serv: Entered as 2nd Lt, Army, 62, released as 1st Lt, 65, after serv as Commanding Officer, 57th APU, Southern European Task Force, 62-65. Mem: Am Bar Asn; Harvard Club of Boston; Cheshire Co Hist Soc (vpres, 73-); Harvard Club of NH (pres, 74-); Lions. Relig: Roman Catholic. Mailing Add: 10 Old Walpole Rd Keene NH 03431

ROGERS, THELMA THARP (R)
Rep Nat Committeewoman, NC
b Elkin, NC; d Noah W Tharp & Alice Council T; m 1924 to Louis Godger Rogers; c Catherine (Mrs Buchanan) & Louis G, Jr. Educ: Winthrop Col. Polit & Govt Pos: Vchmn, Mecklenburg Co Rep Exec Comt, NC, 46-53; organizer, Mecklenburg Co Rep Womens Club, 53; bd mem, Mecklenburg Co Social Planning Comt, 56-60; deleg & mem platform comt, Rep Nat Conv, 56, 60 & 64, mem arrangements comt, 64, 68 & 72, deleg & mem rules comt, 72; mem, NC Rep State Cent Comt, 56-; bd mem, NC Fedn Rep Women; Rep Nat Committeewoman, NC, 56-, mem site selection comt, 59-60 & 75, comt on conv reform, 66, exec comt, 72-; mem, Nat Adv Comt, White House Conf on Aging, 58-59 & Gov Coord Comt on Aging, 59-60; mem, Comt on Oper Dixie, 58-62; mem, Gov Comt on Status of Women, 64. Publ: Mental health program in Mecklenburg County, In: History of Mecklenburg County, 60. Mem: Myers Park PTA; Mecklenburg Co Ment Health Asn; NC Ment Health Asn (bd mem); Charlotte City Club; Erosophian Book Club. Relig: Methodist; mem off bd, Myers Park Methodist Church, 62-65. Mailing Add: Rte 3 Box 251 A Charlotte NC 28210

ROGERS, THOMAS CHARLES (R)
b San Francisco, Calif, Dec 26, 24; m; c Cecile, Christine, Thomas, Harry & Helen. Educ: Univ Southern Calif, 42 & 43; Loyola Univ Los Angeles, BBA, 49. Polit & Govt Pos: Finance chmn, John Schmitz for Sen, 64-65, campaign chmn, primary, 66; finance chmn, Orange Co Rep Cent Comt, Calif, 66-69, chmn, 69-72; dir, 32nd Agr Dist Fair, 69-; vpres, Rep Co Chmn Asn, 71-; planning chmn, Calif Rep State Comt, 72- Bus & Prof Pos: Dir, Una Voce, New York, 66-; dir, Cath welfare, Cath Youth Orgn, Cath Coord Agency, 65- Mil Serv: Entered as Pvt, Army, 43, released as T/Sgt, 46, after serv in 544th Boat & Shore Regt, SPac, Philippines & Japanese Theatres, 44-46; 2nd Lt, Army Res, 46-54. Publ: Papal principles of social reconstruction applied to civil rights legislation, Ensign, 63. Mem: Credit Mgrs Asn; Calif Cattlemens Asn; Am Angus Asn. Honors & Awards: Annual Wanderer Forum Award, 69. Relig: Roman Catholic. Mailing Add: 29361 Spotted Bull Way San Juan Capistrano CA 92675

ROGERS, TOM (R)
Okla State Sen
Mailing Add: State Capitol Oklahoma City OK 73105

ROGERS, WALTER E (D)
b Texarkana, Ark, July 19, 08; s Peter Gordon Rogers & Emma Gertrude Caperton R; m 1936 to Catherine R Daly; c John E, Thomas Kelly, Walter Ed, Jr, Robert Joseph, Susan Daly (Mrs James C Healey, Jr) & Mary Catherine. Educ: Austin Col; Univ Tex. Polit & Govt Pos: City attorney, Pampa, Tex, 38-39; dist attorney, 31st Judicial Dist, Tex, 41-45; US Rep, 18th Dist, until 67. Mil Serv: Entered as Maj, Army Res, 51, released as Lt Col, after serv in Judge Adv Gen Corps. Mailing Add: 6219 Kennedy Dr Chevy Chase MD 20015

ROGERS, WILL (D)
b Bessie, Okla, Dec 12, 98; s John L Rogers & Martha Ellen Hatchett R; m 1945 to Ruby Thomas; c Nell (Mrs Sonnenfeld) & Kenneth Duggin. Educ: Cent State Univ, BS, 26, AB, 29; Univ Okla, MS, 30; Pi Kappa Alpha. Polit & Govt Pos: US Rep, Okla, 33-43; asst adminr solid fuels, Dept Interior, 43-45; asst to Secy Agr, US Dept Agr, 46-47, Admin Judge, 47-70.

Bus & Prof Pos: Teacher, Okla Pub Schs, 17-24; supt schs, Rush Springs, Okla, 26-27, Chattanooga, 27-28 & Moore, 28-33. Mem: Okla Bar Asn; Fed Trial Exam Conf; Okla Educ Asn; Mason; Shrine. Relig: Baptist. Mailing Add: 2611 N Nelson Arlington VA 22207

ROGERS, WILLIAM DILL
Asst Secy State Inter-Am Affairs & Coordr Alliance for Progress

b Wilmington, Del, May 12, 27; s Louis Frederick Rogers & Margaret Dill R; m 1951 to Suzanne Rochford; c William Dill & Daniel Rochford. Educ: Princeton Univ, AB with honors, 48; Yale Univ, LLB, 51. Polit & Govt Pos: Law clerk, Judge Clark, 51-52; law clerk, Supreme Court Justice Reed, 52-53; spec dep attorney gen, Hawaii, 60-62; spec counsel to US Coordr Alliance for Progress, 62-63; dep US Coordr Alliance for Progress, dep adminr, Agency Int Develop, 63-65; alt US rep, Int-Am Econ & Social Coun, 64-65; Asst Secy State Inter-Am Affairs & Coordr Alliance for Progress, 74- Bus & Prof Pos: From assoc to partner, Arnold, Fortas & Porter, Washington, 53-62; partner, Arnold & Porter, 65-; pres, Ctr Inter-Am Rels, New York, 65-70. Publ: The Twilight Struggle, 67. Mem: Am Soc Int Law; Coun Foreign Rels. Honors & Awards: Distinguished Honor Award, Agency Int Develop, 65; Fel Hudson Inst. Legal Res: 2 Jefferson Run Rd Great Falls VA 22066 Mailing Add: 1229 19th St NW Washington DC 20036

ROGERS, WILLIAM JOSEPH (D)
Wis State Rep

b Kaukauna, Wis, Dec 9, 30; s Claude Joseph Rogers & Lucille Reichel D R; m 1956 to Kay Ludke; c Michael, Steven, Patrick, Laureen, Kevin, Amy, Scott, Corey & twins, Heather & Holly. Educ: St Norbert Col, BS in Hist & Spanish, 58; Mex City Col, 1 year. Polit & Govt Pos: Councilman, Kaukauna City Coun, Wis, 60-; Wis State Rep, 62- Bus & Prof Pos: Teacher, Menasha, Wis, 58-62. Mil Serv: Pvt, Army, 52-54, serv in Mil Police, Europe & Korean Conflict. Mem: VFW; KofC; Am Legion. Relig: Catholic. Mailing Add: 1800 Peters Rd Kaukauna WI 54130

ROGERS, WILLIAM PIERCE (R)

b Norfolk, NY, June 23, 13; s Harrison A Rogers & Myra Beswick R; m 1936 to Adele Langston; c Dale Rogers (Mrs Marshall), Anthony Wood, Jeffrey Langston & Douglas Langston. Educ: Colgate Univ, AB, 34; Cornell Law Sch, LLB, 37; Sigma Chi; Delta Theta Phi; Order of the Coif; assoc ed, Cornell Law Quart. Polit & Govt Pos: Asst Dist Attorney, New York Co, 38-42 & 46-47; chief counsel, Senate War Investigating Comt, 47-48; chief counsel, Senate Invests Subcomt, Exec Expenditures Comt, 48-50; Dep Attorney Gen, US, 53-57, Attorney Gen, 57-61; mem US deleg, Twentieth Gen Assembly of UN, 65; Secy of State, 69-73. Bus & Prof Pos: Mem, Dwight, Royall, Harris, Koegel & Caskey, New York & Washington, DC, 50-53; firm, Royall, Koegel, Rogers & Wells, 61-69; ltd partner, Dreyfus & Co, 63-; sr partner, Rogers & Wells, 73-; dir, Merrill Lynch & Co, Inc & Gannett Co, Inc; mem int adv bd, Sperry Rand Corp; mem NAm adv bd, Volvo of Am Corp. Mil Serv: Entered as Lt(jg), Naval Res, 42, released as Lt Comdr, 46, after serv in Air Group 10, Pac. Mem: Metrop Club; Chevy Chase Club; Sky Club; Bar Asn of City of New York; Burning Tree Club. Honors & Awards: Presidential Medal of Freedom. Relig: Presbyterian. Mailing Add: 7007 Glenbrook Rd Bethesda MD 20014

ROGERS, WILLIAM RICHARD, JR (BILL) (R)
Ore State Rep

b Ben Wheeler, Tex, Dec 8, 29; s William Richard Rogers & Elva Rollins R; m 1951 to Mary Ellin Johnson; c William Richard, Kerrie (Mrs Parrish) & Colleen. Educ: Univ Omaha, BGE, 64. Polit & Govt Pos: Ore State Rep, Dist 44, 75- Mil Serv: Entered as Pvt, US Air Force, 58, released as Maj (Ret), 69. Mem: Mason; Horticultural Soc; Nut Growers Soc. Relig: Southern Baptist. Mailing Add: PO Box 109 Vida OR 97488

ROGERSON, ROY HAROLD (R)
WVa State Sen

b Wheeling, WVa, Jan 16, 29; s J Russell Rogerson & Lilly Fisher R; m 1951 to LaVerne Yoho; c Christine A, Marsha J, Lavon E & Susan L. Educ: Washington & Jefferson Univ, 46-47; WVa Univ, BSChE, 51; Sigma Gamma Epsilon. Polit & Govt Pos: WVa State Deleg, formerly, minority chmn, House Finance Comt; WVa State Sen, 73- Bus & Prof Pos: Chem engr, Corps of Engrs, US Army, 51-55 & chem div, PPG Indust, Inc, 55- Mem: Northern WVa Sect, Am Inst Chem Engrs; Am Inst Chem Engrs; 4-H (local club orgn leader); Marshall Co 4-H Leaders Orgn; Marshall Co Exten Serv Comt (chmn). Relig: Presbyterian. Mailing Add: RD 1 Moundsville WV 26041

ROGG, HERBERT A (D)
Kans State Rep

Mailing Add: 312 E Sixth Russell KS 67665

ROGOVIN, MITCHELL (D)

b New York, NY, Dec 3, 30; s Max Shea Rogovin & Sayde Epstein R; m 1954 to Sheila Anne Ender; c Lisa Shea, Wendy Meryl & John Andrew. Educ: Syracuse Univ, AB, 52; Univ Va Law Sch, LLB, 54; Georgetown Univ Law Ctr, LLM, 60; Phi Delta Phi. Polit & Govt Pos: Asst to Comnr, Internal Revenue Serv, 61-65; Chief Counsel, 65-66; Asst Attorney Gen, Dept Justice, 66-69. Bus & Prof Pos: Partner, Arnold & Porter, Washington, DC, currently. Mil Serv: Entered as Pvt, Marine Corps, 54, released as 1st Lt, 58; Capt, Marine Corps Res. Publ: The Charitable Enigma: Commercialism, Univ Southern Calif Tax Inst, 64; The four R's: rulings, regulations, reliance & retroactivity, Taxes Mag, 12/65; Revenue procedure 64-19, Practical Lawyer, 2/66. Mem: Fed Bar Asn; Am Bar Asn; Common Cause (gen counsel); Int Fiscal Asn (vpres, US Br); Nat Legal Aid & Defenders Asn (dir). Relig: Hebrew. Mailing Add: 4500 Klingle St NW Washington DC 20036

ROHLFING, FREDERICK W (R)
Hawaii State Sen

b Honolulu, Hawaii, Nov 2, 28; s R R Rohlfing & Kathryn Coe R; m 1952 to Joan Halford; c Frederick W, III, Karl A & Eric Bradford. Educ: Yale Univ, BA, 50; George Washington Univ Law Sch, JD, 55; Phi Delta Phi; Beta Theta Pi. Polit & Govt Pos: Chmn, Oahu Young Rep, Hawaii, 57-58; dist chmn, 17th Rep Dist Comt, 58-59; Hawaii State Rep, 59-66, chmn, House Rep Campaign Comt, 62; minority floor leader, Hawaii House of Rep, 62-65, minority leader, 65-66; Hawaii State Sen, 66-; asst minority leader, Hawaii State Senate, 66-68; minority policy leader, 69-; deleg, Rep Nat Conv, 68 & 72; Rep cand for First Cong Dist; mem intergovernmental rels comt, Nat Legis Conf. Bus & Prof Pos: Assoc attorney, Moore, Torkildson & Rice, 55-61; attorney-at-law, 61-63 & 70-; partner, Rohlfing, Nakamura & Low, 63-68; Hughes, Steiner & Rohlfing, 68-70; pvt practice, 70- Mil Serv: Entered as Seaman Recruit, Navy, 51, released as Lt(jg), 54; Capt, Naval Res, currently. Publ: Should the political parties be reformed, & if so, how?, Ripon Forum, summer 70. Mem: Downtown Exchange; Naval Reserve Asn; Navy League; Waialae Golf Club; 200 Club. Honors & Awards: Norman S Hall Football Award, Yale, 50; William B Stephenson Award, Outstanding Hawaii Naval Reservist, 68-69. Relig: Protestant. Mailing Add: c/o Senate Sgt at Arms State Capitol Honolulu HI 96817

ROHLFING, GLENICE FITCH (R)

b De Soto, Mo, July 8, 05; d Glenn Scott Fitch & Ethel Pigueron F; m 1932 to Dr William A Rohlfing; c Ann (Mrs Greene). Educ: Southeast Mo Teachers Col, 23; Cent Wesleyan Col, 26-29; Northwestern Univ, Evanston, 29. Polit & Govt Pos: Committeewoman, St Francois Twp, Flat River, Mo, 62-72; deleg, Rep Dist Conv & Mo Rep State Conv, 64, 68 & 72; deleg, Rep Nat Conv, 72. Mem: DAR; PEO; Mineral Area Hosp Auxiliary; Federated Garden Club; Monday Book Club (pres, 40-). Relig: Protestant. Mailing Add: 807 W Main Flat River MO 63601

ROHLSEN, HENRY E (R)
Rep Nat Committeeman, VI

b St Johns, VI, Oct 6, 16; m to Joyce E. Educ: Air Force Tech & Flying Sch. Polit & Govt Pos: Sen, VI Legis, formerly; admin, St Croix, VI, formerly; deleg, Rep Nat Conv, 72; Rep Nat Committeeman, VI, 72-; pres, St Croix Br Progressive Rep Party. Bus & Prof Pos: Owner auto dealership & heavy equip rental bus. Relig: Lutheran. Mailing Add: Box 85 Christiansted St Croix VI 00820

ROHRER, GRACE JEMISON (R)
VChmn, NC State Rep Party

b Chicago, Ill, June 14, 24; d Howard Allan Jemison, Sr & Carolina Bishop J; wid; c David Allan, Donald Elmore & Robert Bruce. Educ: Western Md Col, BA, 46; Salem Col, Teaching Cert; Wake Forest Univ, MA, 69; Trumpeters; Phi Alpha Mu; Argonauts; Mortar Board. Polit & Govt Pos: Elec clerk, Mt Tabor, Winston-Salem, NC, 60-62, precinct chmn, 60-64; mem, Forsyth Co Rep Exec Comt, 60-70; precinct secy, Ardmore Sch, Winston-Salem, 68-70, precinct chmn, 70-; mem exec comt, NC Fedn Rep Women, 70-; mem state exec comt, state cent comt & vchmn, NC State Rep Party, 70-; deleg, Rep Nat Conv, 72; mem policy coun, NC Women's Polit Caucus, 72-; cand, Secy State, 73; Secy Cult Resources, State of NC, 73- Bus & Prof Pos: Rep, Forsyth Co Kindergarten Asn, Asn for Childhood Educ Int, 66-; mem adv coun, Small Bus Admin, 70-72. Mem: Am Mus Asn; NC State Kindergarten Asn; NC CofC; Nature Sci Guild; Soroptimist. Honors & Awards: Award for Outstanding serv to Choral Arts in Forsyth Co presented by the Singers' Guild, 66. Relig: Episcopal. Mailing Add: 2404 H Still Forest Pl Raleigh NC 27607

ROHRER, JANET EDNA (D)

b Aberdeen, SDak, Aug 2, 10; d William Mason & Edith Tassell M; m 1934 to Eugene Charles Rohrer; c Roger Leigh & Audrey Frances (Mrs Henderson). Educ: Faith High Sch, SDak, grad, 33. Polit & Govt Pos: Vchmn, Ziebach Co Dem Comt, SDak, formerly. Bus & Prof Pos: Clerk, Faith Livestock Commun Co, 68-; rancher's wife, currently. Relig: Methodist. Mailing Add: PO Box 205 Faith SD 57626

ROJAS, PAUL G (D)
Mo State Rep

Mailing Add: 2008 Jefferson Kansas City MO 64108

ROLAPP, R RICHARDS (R)

b Los Angeles, Calif, Dec 31, 40; s Ralph Thatcher Rolapp & Barbara Richards R; m 1963 to Marilyn Johnson; c Todd Johnson, Juliane & Brian Johnson. Educ: Brigham Young Univ, BS, 64; Harvard Law Sch, JD, 67. Polit & Govt Pos: Chmn, Vol for Ernest L Wilkinson for US Sen, Utah, 64; spec counsel, Nixon Campaign, Washington, DC, 68; assoc gen counsel, Presidential Inaugural Comt, 69; spec asst to Dep Attorney Gen, Dept Justice, 69-71, chief anal & eval sect, Internal Security Div, 71; dir, Attorney Gen Employ Prog for Honor Law Grad, 70-71; exec secy, Spec Presidential Task Force on Narcotics, Marihuana & Dangerous Drugs, 70. Bus & Prof Pos: Law clerk, Iverson & Hogoboom, Los Angeles, Calif, 66; assoc, Wilkinson, Cragun & Barker, Washington, DC, 67-69; attorney, Smathers & Merrigan, Washington, DC, 71-73. Publ: The private college & student discipline, Am Bar Asn J, 2/70. Mem: Thoroughbred Club Am; Am, Fed & DC Bar Asns; Md Horse Breeders Asn. Honors & Awards: Student Body Pres, Brigham Young Univ, 63-64; Jr CofC Award as One of Am Outstanding Young Men, 70. Relig: Latter-day Saint. Legal Res: CA Mailing Add: 15325 Quail Run Dr Darnestown MD 20760

ROLDE, NEIL RICHARD (D)
Maine State Rep

b Boston, Mass, July 25, 31; s L Robert Rolde & Lillian Lewis R; m 1960 to Carlotta Florsheim; c Claudia Cathrene, Nicolette Adrienne, Andrea Jacqueline & Danielle Louise. Educ: Yale Univ, BA; Columbia Univ Sch Jour, MS; Elizabethan Soc; Manuscript Soc. Polit & Govt Pos: Consult to Maine Fed-State Coordr, Augusta, 67-68; mem, Gov Task Force on Oceanography, 67-68; mem, Maine Comn on Arts & Humanities, 67-; co-chmn, Town of York Conserv Comt, 67-70; deleg, Dem Nat Conv, 68; Dem Cand, State Senate, Dist 1, 68; Maine trustee, New Eng Aquarium, Boston, 68-; chmn, York Dem Town Comt, Maine, 68-; spec asst to Gov Kenneth M Curtis, 68-, press secy, currently; mem, Gov Task Force on Human Rights, 68-; Dem Cand, State Rep, Maine; mem platform comt, Maine Dem State Conv, 70 & 72, campaign coordr, Reelection Campaign for Gov Kenneth M Curtis, 70, campaign coordr, Violette for Cong Comt, 72; Maine State Rep, 73-, Majority Leader, Maine House Rep, 75- Bus & Prof Pos: Scriptwriter, Louis De Rochemont Assocs, New York, 56-; exec, R&S Construction Co, Boston, Mass, 58-60; free lance writer, currently. Mem: Theatre by the Sea Portsmouth, NH; York Fish & Game Asn; Seacoast Coun Race & Relig, Portsmouth, NH (mem steering comt); York Co Community Action Bd (bd dirs); Maine Audubon Soc (trustee, 73-). Honors & Awards: Dean's prize, Yale Univ. Legal Res: Sewall's Hill York ME 03909 Mailing Add: Box 304 York ME 03909

ROLISON, JAY P, JR (R)
NY State Sen

Mailing Add: 150 Kingwood Park Poughkeepsie NY 12603

ROLLINS, JOHN ERROLL (D)
Mo State Rep

b Monett, Mo, Oct 28, 40; s John B Rollins & Doris A Turner R; m 1964 to Linda L Schell; c John S, Michael L & Leigh K. Educ: Univ Mo-Rolla, 58-60; Lincoln Univ, 62-64; Kappa Alpha Order. Polit & Govt Pos: Mo State Rep, 47th Dist, 75- Bus & Prof Pos: Br mgr, Interstate Securities Co, 68-75. Mil Serv: Entered as Pvt, Marines, 60, released as Cpl. Mailing Add: Rte 10 Columbia MO 65201

ROLLINS, JOHN HERBERT (R)
Maine State Rep
b Dixfield, Maine, Nov 29, 10; s Warren W Rollins & Mary Ridley R; m 1929 to Theda Lois Packard; c Warren F & Lauren D. Educ: Stephens High Sch, grad. Polit & Govt Pos: Maine State Rep, 71- Bus & Prof Pos: With Oxford Paper Co, Rumford, Maine, 48- Relig: Baptist. Legal Res: Dixfield ME 04224 Mailing Add: East Dixfield ME 04227

ROLLINS, KENNETH B (INDEPENDENT)
Va State Deleg
Mailing Add: Box 803 Leesburg VA 22075

ROLLINS, WALTER (D)
WVa State Deleg
Mailing Add: State Capitol Charleston WV 25305

ROLVAAG, KARL FRITJOF (DFL)
b Northfield, Minn, July 18, 13; s Ole Edvart Rolvaag & Jennie Berdahl R; m 1943 to Florence Boedeker; c Paul & Kristin. Educ: St Olaf Col, BA, 41; Univ Minn Grad Sch, 46; Univ Oslo, Am-Scandinavian Found Fel, 47-48. Hon Degrees: LLD, St Mary's Col, 64. Polit & Govt Pos: Cand for Cong, 46, 48 & 52; state chmn, Dem-Farmer-Labor Party, 50-54; deleg, Dem Nat Conv, 52, 60 & 64; Lt Gov, Minn, 55-63, Gov, 63-67; exec dir, Midwest Humphrey for President Comt, 59-60; Ambassador to Iceland, 67-69. Bus & Prof Pos: Vpres, Group Health Mutual Ins Co, 56-59; vpres, Interfinancial Corp, Minneapolis, Minn, 69-; dir, Franklin Nat Bank, Minneapolis, 69- Mil Serv: Entered as Pvt, Army, 41, released as Capt, 47, after serv in 4th Armored Div, 3rd Army, ETO, France; Silver Star; Purple Heart; Presidential Unit Citation; Croix de Guerre. Publ: History of the Democrat-Farmer-Labor Party, Minn Heritage, 58. Mem: Norweg-Am Hist Soc; Minn Hist Soc; VFW; DAV; Am Legion. Honors & Awards: Distinguished Alumnus Award, St Olaf Col, 59. Relig: Lutheran. Mailing Add: 311 Manitou St Northfield MN 55057

ROMAN CARDONA, JOSE R (POPULAR DEMOCRAT, PR)
Rep, PR House Rep
Mailing Add: State Capitol San Juan PR 00901

ROMANELLI, JAMES A (D)
Pa State Rep
Mailing Add: Capitol Bldg Harrisburg PA 17120

ROMANO, JOHN A (R)
RI State Rep
b New York, NY, Aug 20, 23; s Michael Romano & Concetta DeRienzis R; m 1955 to Teresa M Palermo; c Teresa Phyllis & John Michael. Educ: La Salle Acad, Providence, RI, 41; Univ RI, BA in Econ, 72; Theta Delta Chi. Polit & Govt Pos: RI State Rep, Dist 44, 73- Bus & Prof Pos: Retired naval officer. Mil Serv: Capt, Navy, 42-70, serv in Naval Aviation, executing officer, Naval Air Sta, Quonset Point, RI, 42-70; Letter of Commendation; China Serv Medal; World War II Victory Medal; Korean Serv Medal. Mem: Navy League; Preservation Soc; Am Legion. Relig: Catholic. Legal Res: 41 Division St East Greenwich RI 02818 Mailing Add: PO Box 281 East Greenwich RI 02818

ROMANO, SAM (D)
Ill State Sen
b Chicago, Ill; c two; six grandchildren. Educ: Chicago pub schs; eve classes at Lewis Inst & YMCA. Polit & Govt Pos: Ill State Rep, 5 terms; Ill State Sen, 66- Bus & Prof Pos: Practicing tax acct; sr partner, Rapid Bus Serv, a bookkeeping serv & ins firm. Mem: Civic & church activities. Mailing Add: 2347 S Oakley Ave Chicago IL 62552

ROME, LEWIS B (R)
Conn State Sen
b Hartford, Conn, Sept 12, 33; s Albert H Rome & Celia M R; m 1954 to Ann Nicolle; c Thomas, Richard, Deborah & David. Educ: Univ Conn, Storrs, BA, 54, Hartford, LLD, 57. Polit & Govt Pos: Councilman, Bloomfield, Conn, 62-70, mayor, 66-70; chmn, Region Coun Elected Officials, Hartford, 68-70; Conn State Sen, 71-, majority leader, Conn State Senate, 73-, minority leader, 75-; alt deleg, Rep Nat Conv, 72. Bus & Prof Pos: Attorney, Rome & Case, 57- Mem: Am, Hartford Co & Conn Bar Asns. Honors & Awards: Outstanding Sen, Eagleton Inst of Polit, 72. Mailing Add: 443 Simsbury Rd Bloomfield CT 06002

ROMER, HAROLD WILLIAM (D)
Chmn, Mercer Co Dem Exec Comt, Ohio
b St Henry, Ohio, Sept 21, 94; s Joseph John Romer & Anna Hartings R; m 1922 to Anna Josephine Haas; c Donald Edward & Joan (Mrs Clarence Scott Braun). Educ: St Henry Pub Sch, Ohio, grad, 11. Polit & Govt Pos: City councilman, Coldwater, Ohio, 37-41; chmn, Mercer Co Dem Party, 51-56 & 59-69; chmn, Mercer Co Dem Exec Comt, 51-; Ohio State Rep, Mercer Co, 59-66; deleg, Dem Nat Conv, 68. Bus & Prof Pos: Mgr, Romer's Store, St Henry, Ohio, 15-23; clerk in training, S H Kress Co, Nashville, Tenn, 23-24; mgr & co-owner, Romer Dry Goods Co, Coldwater, Ohio, 24-29; owner, Romer's Store, 29-55 & 66-69, mgr, 56-65. Mem: Elks; KofC. Honors & Awards: Honored as the outstanding polit leader in Mercer Co, 66; steered formation of a hospital dist for seven twps of Mercer Co & passage of bond issue for hospital expansion. Relig: Catholic. Legal Res: 803 W Main St Coldwater OH 45828 Mailing Add: PO Box 83 Coldwater OH 45828

ROMERO, LOUIS J (D)
NMex State Rep
Mailing Add: 505 W Mesa Gallup NM 87301

ROMERO, MOISES (R)
Secy, Mora Co Rep Cent Comt, NMex
b Cleveland, NMex, Mar 27, 00; s David Romero & Cicilia Bernal R; m 1927 to Fidela Cahcon (deceased); m 1939 to Sofia Padilla (deceased); m 1950 to Carmelita Montoya; c Antonia (Mrs Fred Apdoca), Barney, Precilla (Mrs Jose F Garcia), Henry (deceased), Floraido, Jose, Videlita, Leonor, Luciano (deceased), Maria, Bertha (deceased) & stepchildren, Maximinio, Maria (Mrs Val Gonzales) & Aurora (Mrs Processo Chavez). Educ: Adult educ under Works Prog Admin. Polit & Govt Pos: Dep co clerk, NMex, 42-46; clerk, Bur Revenue, 51-62; chmn, Mora Co Rep Party, 57-58; counr, Social Security, 69-70; secy, Mora Co Rep Cent Comt, NMex, 71-; colonel aide-de-camp, Staff of NMex State Gov, currently. Bus & Prof Pos: Pub sch teacher, 20-34; farmer, Cleveland, NMex, 62- Relig: Catholic. Mailing Add: PO Box 63 Cleveland NM 87715

ROMINE, CHARLES EVERETT, JR (R)
VChmn, WVa State Rep Exec Comt
b Spencer, WVa, Jan 16, 36; s Charles Everett Romine, Sr & Shirley Reed R; m 1957 to Phyllis Cremeans; c Charles E, III, David C, Bradley R & Anne E. Educ: Marshall Univ, 4 years; Sigma Phi Epsilon. Polit & Govt Pos: WVa State Deleg, 69-74; vchmn, WVa State Rep Exec Comt, 71- Bus & Prof Pos: Local agt, State Farm Ins Co, 58- Mem: Huntington Life Underwriters Asn; Cabell-Huntington Mental Health Asn; Huntington Jaycees; Kyova Goodwill Industs, Inc; Marshall Univ Alumni Asn (bd dirs). Honors & Awards: Outstanding Young Man of 1968, Huntington, WVa. Relig: United Methodist. Legal Res: 5257 Pearidge Rd Huntington WV 25705 Mailing Add: PO Box 2225 Huntington WV 25723

ROMINES, ARCHIE N, SR (D)
Ky State Rep
Mailing Add: 13312 Tennis Blvd Valley Station KY 40272

ROMINGER, JAMES CORRIDON (R)
Chmn, Stephens Co Rep Party, Tex
b Cisco, Tex, Apr 27, 20; s C V Rominger & Myrtle Robinson R; m 1959 to Muriel Jean Henderson; c James Whitney, Kurt Gideon, Jett Daniel & Stuart Robinson. Educ: Tex A&M, BA, 41. Polit & Govt Pos: Precinct chmn & chmn, Stephens Co Rep Party, Tex, currently; pres, Sch Bd, 63- Bus & Prof Pos: Acct, Chem Process Co, 47-56, B J Serv, Borg Warner, 56-59 & Sheets & Walton Drilling Co, 59-65; vpres, Citizens Nat Bank, Tex, 65- Mil Serv: Entered as 2nd Lt, Army, 41, released as Maj, 46, after serv in 1st Armored Div, Africa & Italy, 42-45; Col, Army Res, 66; Bronze Star; Purple Heart; African & Ital Campaign Ribbons. Mem: Lions; Am Legion; Elks. Relig: Roman Catholic. Mailing Add: 600 S Mistletoe Breckenridge TX 76024

ROMNEY, GEORGE WILCKEN (R)
b Chihuahua, Mex, July 8, 07; s Gaskell Romney & Anna Amelia Pratt R; m 1931 to Lenore LaFount; c Lynn (Mrs Loren Keenan), Jane (Mrs Bruce Robinson), Scott & Mitt. Educ: Univ Utah; George Washington Univ. Hon Degrees: More than a dozen hon doctorates. Polit & Govt Pos: US deleg, Int Labor Conf, 46-; deleg & vpres, State Const Conv, Mich, 61-62; Gov, Mich, 63-69; deleg, Rep Nat Conv, 68; Secy, Housing & Urban Develop, 69-72. Bus & Prof Pos: Rep, Aluminum Co Am, 30-39; mgr, Automobile Mfrs Asn, 39-48; asst to pres & vpres, Nash-Kelvinator Corp, 48-54; bd chmn & pres, Am Motors Corp, 54-62. Mem: Automobile Mfrs Asn; Automotive Coun for War Prod; Citizens for Mich. Relig: Latter-day Saint. Mailing Add: Valley Rd Bloomfield Hills MI 48013

ROMNEY, JEAN A
Sen, VI Legis
Mailing Add: PO Box 604 Christiansted St Croix VI 00820

ROMNEY, MILES (D)
Mont State Sen
b Hamilton, Mont, Dec 6, 00; s Miles Romney & Elizabeth Rosetta Robbins R; m 1925 to Ruth Gray. Educ: US Mil Acad, 18-19; George Washington Univ, 19 & 20-21; Univ Mont, BA, 22; Kappa Sigma; Delta Sigma Chi. Polit & Govt Pos: Deleg, Mont State Dem Conv, 22-; committeeman, State Dem Cent Comt, Ravalli Co, 40-; deleg, Dem Nat Conv, 56 & 60; Mont State Rep Dist 25, 67-71; deleg, Mont State Const Conv, 72; secy, Mont State Dem Exec Comt, formerly; Mont State Sen, 75- Bus & Prof Pos: Worked on various newspapers; comt clerk, Pub Lands Comt & clerk, Off Document Room, US House Rep, formerly; dir, Motor Vehicle Dept, Mont RR Comn, 36-37; ed & publ, Western News, Hamilton, Mont, 37- Mem: Mont State Press Asn; AF&AM; Eagles; Elks; Ravalli Co Fish & Wildlife Asn. Legal Res: 425 S Third St Hamilton MT 59840 Mailing Add: PO Box 633 Hamilton MT 59840

ROMNEY, VERNON (R)
Attorney Gen, Utah
b Colonia Juarez, Mex, July 3, 96; s Miles Park Romney & Catherine Jane Cottam; m 1923 to Lois Bradford (deceased); c Vernon B, Ralph Bradford, Rowena (Mrs Boyd Busath), Yvonne (Mrs Grant Dixon) & John B; m 1964 to Helen Hackett Brown; stepchildren, Marilyn (Mrs Benair Hansen), Jacqueline (Mrs Darwin Anderson) & Thomas Vernon Brown. Educ: George Washington Univ, JD, 22; Phi Delta Phi; pres, Utah Legal Club of George Washington Univ, 20-22. Polit & Govt Pos: Mem, Utah Rep State Exec Comt, 36-62; chmn, Salt Lake Co Rep Comt, 42-44; deleg, Rep Nat Conv, 44, 48 (seconded nomination of Sen Robert A Taft for President), 52, 60 & 64; Rep Nat Committeeman & Rep State Chmn, Utah, 44-50 & 58-62; chmn, Rep State Chmn Orgn Midwest & Rocky Mountain States, 49-50; mem cent campaign comt, Sen Robert Taft for President, campaign mgr for Northwestern US; chmn, Comn Utah State Indian Affairs, 59; mem civic comt, Salt Lake City, 66-, Attorney Gen, Utah, 73- Bus & Prof Pos: Secy, Romney Lunt Land & Livestock Co, 14-24; Western mgr, Nat Wool Warehouse & Storage Co, 18-20; Western rep, Am Sheepbreeder, 18-20; attorney, Romney & Nelson, Salt Lake City, 22-; trustee, Robert A Taft Mem Found, 54-; vpres, State Savings & Loan Asn, secy, Utah Comt for Int Contact, 64-72; mem, Nat Lawyers' Comt John Marshall Mem Bldg Fund, Freedoms Found at Valley Forge, 65- Mem: Am Bar Asn; George Washington Univ Alumni Asn; George Washington Law Asn; US Savings & Loan League; CofC. Honors & Awards: Alumni Serv Award, George Washington Univ Gen Alumni Asn, 65. Relig: Latter-day Saint. Mailing Add: 404 Kearns Bldg Salt Lake City UT 84101

RONAN, JAMES A (D)
b Chicago, Ill, July 2, 04; s James Ronan & Katherine McDonald R; m 1929 to Margaret Mary Maloney; c Margaret (Mrs Stephen K Healy), James, John & Martin. Educ: Univ Notre Dame, AB, 26; Loyola Univ, JD, 31. Polit & Govt Pos: Ill Indust Comn, 49-53; deleg, Dem Nat Conv, 52-72; chmn, Ill State Dem Party, 52-60; Dem Nat Committeeman, Ill, 60-72; dir, Ill State Finance, 61-69. Bus & Prof Pos: Pres, James Ronan Co, 26-; attorney-at-law, 32- Mem: Ill Workmans Compensation Bar Asn; South Shore Country Club; KofC; Cath Lawyers Guild. Relig: Catholic. Mailing Add: 834 W Fulton Chicago IL 60607

RONAYNE, MAURICE E, JR (D)
Mass State Rep
Mailing Add: State Capitol Boston MA 02133

RONCALIO, TENO (D)
US Rep, Wyo
b Rock Springs, Wyo, Mar 23, 16; s Frank Roncalio & Ernestina Mussi R; m 1962 to Cecelia Waters Domenico; c Teno Frank & John Waters; stepchildren, Carol, David, Joan & Louis.

Educ: Univ Wyo, LLB, 47. Polit & Govt Pos: Mem staff, US Sen O'Mahoney, 41; asst clerk, US Senate Libr, 41; dep prosecuting attorney, Cheyenne, Wyo, 50-56; chmn, Wyo State Dem Cent Comt, 57-61; vchmn Wyo deleg, Dem Nat Conv, 60, deleg, 64-72; mem, Interstate Comn, Potomac River Basin, 61-63; chmn, US Sect, Int Joint Comn, Washington, DC, 61-63; US Rep, Wyo, 65-66 & 70-, mem interior & insular affairs comt, US House Rep, 65-67 & 71-, mem pub works comt, 71-, mem joint comt on atomic energy, 73-; Dem Nat Committeeman, Wyo, 69; mem bd dirs, John F Kennedy Ctr for Performing Arts, 71- Bus & Prof Pos: Ed, Wyo Labor J, 49; law practice, Cheyenne, 49-; chmn bd, Cheyenne Nat Bank, 60-68. Mil Serv: Army, Capt, World War II. Mem: Am & Wyo Bar Asns; Lawyer-Pilots Asn (area pres). Legal Res: 3024 Capitol Ave Cheyenne WY 82001 Mailing Add: 1529 Longworth Bldg Washington DC 20515

RONCALLO, ANGELO D (R)
b Port Chester, NY, May 28, 27; s Anthony Roncallo & Connie Prochilo R; m 1952 to Priscille Pouliot; c Marc, Paul, John, Jean & James. Educ: Manhattan Col, BA, 50; Georgetown Univ, JD, 53; Delta Theta Phi. Polit & Govt Pos: Dep co attorney, Nassau Co, NY, 58-60, comptroller, 67-72; counsel, Joint Legis Comt, 61-63; councilman, Oyster Bay, 65-67; alt deleg, Rep Nat Conv, 68, deleg, 72; chmn, Oyster Bay Rep Comt, NY, 68-; US Rep, NY, 73-74. Bus & Prof Pos: Sr partner, Roncallo, Leff, Weber & Shapiro, 73- Mil Serv: Entered as Pvt, Army, 44, released as Pfc, 46, after serv in 130th Sta Hosp. Mem: NY State Bar Asn; Cath Lawyers Guild; KofC; VFW; Elks (Exalted Ruler); Am Arbit Asn. Honors & Awards: Annual Alumni Achievement Award, Georgetown Alumni Club of Metrop Washington, DC, 73. Mailing Add: 226 Toronto Ave Massapequa NY 11758

RONIGER, PASCAL ALLEN (R)
Kans State Rep
b Hymer, Kans, Nov 10, 14; s Charles Roniger & Anna H Allen R; m 1941 to Martha Sharer; c Ann (Mrs William A Hussong) & John Charles. Educ: Kans Univ, AB, 39, grad work in bact, 39-41; Phi Chi. Polit & Govt Pos: Rep precinct committeeman, Diamond Twp, Chase Co, Kans, 58 & 59, 69-; Kans State Rep, 61st Dist, 69-71, 71st Dist, 72-74, 70th Dist, 74- Bus & Prof Pos: Serologist, NMex State Bd of Health, 41-42; Riley Co sanitarian & milk inspector, Kans State Bd of Health, 42-51; farmer & stockman, Chase Co, 51- Mil Serv: Entered as Ens, Navy, 44, released as Lt(jg), 46, after serv in Pac Fleet; Lt, Naval Res, 46-51. Mem: Am Legion; Farm Mgt Asn; Chase Co Soil Conserv; Flint Hills Rural & Elec Co-op (dir, 64-); State Asn Kans Watersheds (dir, 74-). Honors & Awards: Banker's Award for Soil Conserv Work. Relig: First Christian. Mailing Add: RR 1 Burdick KS 66838

ROOD, EDWIN CYRIL (CY) (R)
Chmn, Gem Co Rep Cent Comt, Idaho
b Emmett, Idaho, Nov 17, 40; s Sherman M Rood & Edna M Funk R; m 1963 to Ruth Ann Frennd; c Christine E & Martin A. Educ: Univ Idaho, BA in Polit Sci, 68, JD, 70; Young Rep. Polit & Govt Pos: Prosecuting attorney, Gem Co, Idaho, 73-; chmn, Gem Co Rep Cent Comt, 74- Bus & Prof Pos: Law clerk, Aitken, Schauble & Shoemaker, Pullman, Wash, 68-70; law clerk, US Dist Court, Boise, Idaho, 70-72; attorney-at-law, Emmett, Idaho, 72- Mil Serv: Entered as Seaman Recruit, Navy, 61, released as FT 2, 65, after serv in USS Galveston CLG-3 & USS Columbus CG-12, Pac Fleet, 61-65. Mem: Idaho & Am Bar Asns; Third Dist Bar Asn (secy-treas, currently); Nat Dist Attorneys Asn. Legal Res: East Locust Emmett ID 83617 Mailing Add: PO Box 216 Emmett ID 83617

ROOD, PAUL WILLIAM (R)
Mem, Rep State Cent Comt Calif
b Seattle, Wash, Nov 28, 53; s Dr Donald Bryan Rood & Beatrice Clarke R; single. Educ: Claremont Men's Col, 72-; James Madison Soc; Young Rep; Intercollegiate Studies Inst. Polit & Govt Pos: Chmn, NCalif Youth for Nixon, 67-68; mem, Rep State Cent Comt Calif, 70-; mem youth adv comn, Dept Transportation, 71-; alt deleg, Rep Nat Conv, 72. Relig: Orthodox Presbyterian. Legal Res: 1038 Pinenut Ct Sunnyvale CA 94087 Mailing Add: Story House Claremont Men's Col Claremont CA 91711

ROODKOWSKY, ALICE MAY (R)
Secy, Mass Rep State Comt
b New York, NY, Oct 10, 21; d Otto Juenger & Mary M Queenan J; m 1947 to Nikita D Roodkowsky; c Tatiana, Mary & Alexandra. Educ: Hunter Col; Packard Commercial Sch. Polit & Govt Pos: Deleg, Mass Rep State Conv, 66, 70 & 72, temporary secy, 72; deleg, Worcester Conf, 67; campaign coordr, Mass State Sen William I Randall, 66; mem, Natick Rep Town Comt, 66-, secy, 66-68; mem & secy, Mass Rep State Comt, 68- Bus & Prof Pos: Admin asst to Coordr Student Serv, Wellesley Col, currently. Relig: Roman Catholic. Mailing Add: 10 University Dr Natick MA 01760

ROOK, DORIS MAE (R)
b Washington, DC, June 22, 21; d Charles Willard Rook & Ruth Kelly R; single. Educ: George Washington Univ, AA, 48; Strayers Bus Col, 1 year. Polit & Govt Pos: Secy, Dept Army, 41-45; exec secy, US Rep Carl T Curtis, Nebr, 45-55, US Sen Carl T Curtis, 55-63, admin asst, 63- Mem: Eastern Star. Relig: Episcopal. Mailing Add: 103 Granville Dr Silver Spring MD 20901

ROOKS, JAMES ORVILLE (R)
Mem, Rep State Cent Comt Ga
b Jackson, Ga, Mar 22, 22; s James Howard Rooks & Fannie Willard R; m 1945 to Peggy Marilyn Sanders; c Denise (Mrs Ricks), Anita & Melanie. Educ: Md Inst Fine Arts, Baltimore, 3 years. Polit & Govt Pos: Vchmn, Henry Co Rep Comt, Ga, 66-68, chmn, 68-72; mem, Ga Sixth Dist Rep Comt, 67-; mem, Rep State Cent Comt Ga, 68- Bus & Prof Pos: Printer, Jackson Progress-Argus, Jackson, Ga, 46-49; engraver, Baltimore Type Corp, Md, 49-58; printer-pressman, Advertiser Printing Co, McDonough, Ga, 58-69. Mil Serv: Entered as Pvt, Air Force, 42, released as T/5, 45, after serv in Airborne Engrs, Fifth Air Force, Pac Theatre, 43-45; Good Conduct Medal; Asiatic-Pac Ribbon with 3 Bronze Stars; Presidential Unit Citation; Among first 500 flown into Japan to make preparations for surrender & occup, 8/45. Publ: Republican viewpoint, weekly column, Weekly Advertiser. Mem: Kiwanis. Relig: Baptist. Mailing Add: 105 Carmichael St McDonough GA 30253

ROONEY, FRED B (D)
US Rep, Pa
b Bethlehem, Pa, Nov 6, 25; s Fred B Rooney & Veronica K McGreevy R; m 1963 to Evelyn Davis Lisle; c Timothy Craig, Martha Lisle & Gregory Hart. Educ: Univ Ga, AB in Bus Admin, 50. Hon Degrees: LLD, Moravian Col, 72. Polit & Govt Pos: Pres & reorganizer, Young Dem Club of Northampton Co, Pa, 56; Pa State Sen, 58-63, mem, Bethlehem Housing Authority, 58-59; Pa State Rep, 15th Dist, 63-66; US Rep, Pa, currently. Mil Serv: 515th Paratroop Inf Regt, 13th Airborne Div, ETO. Publ: Power as part of the Tocks Island Reservoir, 5/65 & Europe says: It (the big blackout) couldn't happen here, 5/65, Pub Utilities Fortnightly. Mem: Am Legion; Amvets; VFW; CWV; KofC (Past Grand Knight). Relig: Catholic. Legal Res: 27 E Church St Bethlehem PA 18018 Mailing Add: 3150 Highland Pl NW Washington DC 20008

ROONEY, JAMES F (D)
Wis State Rep
b Racine, Wis, Sept 29, 35; s C J Rooney & Mabel Beherend R; m 1960 to Nancy Lee Schulz; c Erin Marie, James Connell, John Connell & Richard Connell. Polit & Govt Pos: Mem, Racine Co Bd Supvr, Wis, 66-; chmn, Racine Harbor Comn, 68-73; Wis State Rep, 73- Bus & Prof Pos: Bus mgr, Nielsen & Maden Eng, 56- Mil Serv: Entered as Pvt, Army, 54, released as Pfc, 56. Mem: Am Cong Surv & Mapping; Racine Yacht Club. Relig: Catholic. Legal Res: 1500 Michigan Blvd Racine WI 53402 Mailing Add: Room 312 W State Capitol Madison WI 53702

ROONEY, JOHN J (D)
b Brooklyn, NY, Nov 29, 03; m to Catherine Kramm Curran; c John James, Jr, Edward Patrick, Arthur Patrick & William Edward Curran & Mary Ann (Mrs Michael G Farrell). Educ: St Francis Col; Fordham Univ Sch Law, 25. Hon Degrees: LLD, St Francis Col, Brooklyn. Polit & Govt Pos: Asst dist attorney, Kings Co, NY, 40-44; US Rep, NY, 43-74; off observer, First Bikini Atom Test; off observer, Japanese Peace Conf, 51; deleg, Dem Nat Mid-Term Conf, 74. Bus & Prof Pos: Attorney-at-law. Mem: Ecclesiastic Order of St Gregory the Great (Knight Comdr with Star); Elks (Past Exalted Ruler); Ancient Order of Hibernians in Am; St Patrick Soc of Brooklyn; VFW. Honors & Awards: Royal Order of the Phoenix, Govt of Kingdom of Greece; Grande Ufficiale, Order of Merit, Repub of Italy; recipient of Polonia Restituta, highest award of the Free Polish Govt in Exile, London; hon fel, Hebrew Univ of Jerusalem. Mailing Add: 217 Congress Brooklyn NY 11201

ROONEY, JOHN JOSEPH (D)
b Chadron, Nebr, Nov 30, 15; s William Peter Rooney & Armena Broghamer R; m 1937 to Velma Kruse; c Armena (Mrs Taylor), Velma Ruth (Mrs Yeargain), Margaret, Kathryn (Mrs Cooper), Jean (Mrs Robinson) & John. Educ: Univ Minn; Univ Colo, AB & LLB. Polit & Govt Pos: Spec agt, Fed Bur Invest, 41-58; precinct committeeman, Dem Party, Wyo, 58-; mem staff, US Sen J J Hickey, 61-63; Wyo State Rep, 65-70; mem, Statute Revision Comn, 65-70; chmn, Wyo Dem State Cent Comt, 65-70; deleg, Dem Nat Conv, 68 & 72; city attorney, Cheyenne, 68-70; Dem nominee, Gov, 70; attorney, Laramie Co Sch Bd, 74- Relig: Catholic. Mailing Add: 420 W 28th St Cheyenne WY 82001

ROONEY, RICHARD V (D)
Treas, Swift Co Dem Party, Minn
b Appleton, Minn, Aug 20, 22; s George P Rooney & Muriel McLaughlin R; m 1944 to Ione M; c Patrick R, Mary Ann, E Colleen & Gerri Kay. Educ: Col St Thomas, BA, 49. Polit & Govt Pos: Treas, Swift Co Dem Party, Minn, 66- Bus & Prof Pos: Owner, Rooney Ford Sales, Benson, Minn. Mil Serv: Entered as Pvt, Army, 41, released as Cpl, 45, after serv in 34th Inf Div, European-African & Italy Theatres, 42-44. Relig: Catholic. Mailing Add: 314 Sanford Rd Benson MN 56215

ROORDA, WALTER JOHN (R)
Ind State Rep
b De Motte, Ind, Sept 20, 30; s Albert Frank Roorda & Gertrude Walstra R; m 1949 to Alberta Klemp; c Kathleen Sue, Karen Louise, Marvin Allen, Milton Ryan, Mark Walter, Mitchell Albert & Krista Marie. Educ: De Motte Pub Schs, grad. Polit & Govt Pos: Mem, Jasper Co Young Rep, Ind, 58; precinct committeeman, Keener Twp E, Jasper Co, 62-; pres, Northern Jasper Co Young Rep, 64-65; secy, Jasper Co Rep Cent Comt, 64-66, treas, 66-68; Ind State Rep, Jasper, Porter & Pulaski Counties, 68- Bus & Prof Pos: Owner, Al's Upholstery Shop, 60, The Roorda Furniture Co, 65. Mem: Nat Fedn of Independent Bus; Nat Retail Furniture Asn; De Motte CofC. Relig: Christian Reformed Church. Mailing Add: 408 15th St SE De Motte IN 46310

ROOS, LAWRENCE K (R)
b St Louis, Mo, Feb 1, 18; s Sol Roos & Selma Kalter R; m 1955 to Mary Watson; c Pamela, Mary Ellen, Jennifer & Lawrence K, Jr. Educ: Yale Univ, BA, 40. Hon Degrees: LLD, Univ Mo, St Louis, 75. Polit & Govt Pos: Mo State Rep, 46-50; supvr, St Louis Co, Mo, 62-74; Rep nominee for Gov, Mo, 68; app by President Nixon to Adv Comn on Intergovt Rels; mem, President's Comn on Jobs for Viet Nam Vets, 71; chmn, Mo Comt for Reelec of the President, 72; deleg, Rep Nat Conv, 72; Rep Nat Committeeman, 73-74. Bus & Prof Pos: Pres, Mound City Trust Co, St Louis, Mo, 50-62; chmn bd, First Security Bank of Kirkwood, 50-62; exec vpres & dir, First Nat Bank, St Louis, currently. Mil Serv: Entered as Pvt, Army, 41, released as Maj, 45, after serv in ETO, 42-45; 5 Battle Stars; Bronze Star Medal. Mem: Nat Asn Counties (bd dirs); Woodrow Wilson Int Ctr for Scholars (adv comt); Beta Gamma Sigma; Alpha Kappa Psi (hon mem). Honors & Awards: Mo Rep of Year Award, 72; Anti-defamation League Torch of Liberty Award, 74; St Louis Globe-Dem Man of Year, 75. Relig: Jewish. Mailing Add: 943 Tirrill Farms Rd St Louis MO 63124

ROOSA, BENJAMIN P, JR (R)
NY State Assemblyman
b Beacon, NY, Nov 22, 31; s Benjamin P Roosa & Marion Fleming R; m 1958 to Elizabeth Haeberlin; c Elizabeth Anne, Nancy Marion, Benjamin P, III & Robert August. Educ: Columbia Col, AB; Albany Law Sch, JD; Phi Gamma Delta. Polit & Govt Pos: Attorney, Town of East Fishkill, NY, 57-64; legislator, Dutchess Co Bd Rep, 72; NY State Assemblyman, 73- Mem: Salvation Army Adv Bd (pres); Fishkill Rural Cemetary (trustee); Highland Hosp (trustee); Kiwanis; CofC. Relig: Protestant. Legal Res: Hickman Dr Hopewell Junction NY 12533 Mailing Add: 398 Main St Beacon NY 12508

ROOT, HARMER F (R)
Mem, LaCrosse Co Rep Exec Comt, Wis
b Walla Walla, Wash, Nov 4, 14; s Herbert D Root & Hope Harmer R; m 1939 to Elsie D Boudreau; c Kathleen D (Mrs Weibel), Dennis M & Mary Ellen. Educ: St Thomas Col, BA, 37; Univ Minn Grad Sch, 38 & 39. Polit & Govt Pos: Chmn, LaCrosse Co Rep Party, Wis, 67-72; mem, LaCrosse Co Rep Exec Comt, Wis, 72- Bus & Prof Pos: Pub sch teacher, 37-; supvr parochial schs, 46-48; assoc prof, Wis State Univ Syst, 48-52; investment exec, NY Stock Exchange-Am Stock Exchange & all prin exchanges, 59- Mem: Kiwanis; LaCrosse Country Club. Relig: Catholic. Legal Res: 520 South 11 LaCrosse WI 54601 Mailing Add: Box 937 LaCrosse WI 54601

ROOT, HELEN (D)
Mem, Dem Nat Comt, Mich
Mailing Add: 1729 N Broadway Hastings MI 49058

ROOT, MARV (R)
Dir, Rep State Cent Comt Ore
b Caldwell, Idaho, Aug 13, 42; s Lloyd Joseph Root & Rosabelle Huston R; m 1970 to Jennifer Corinne Smith. Educ: Seattle Pac Col, BA in Sociol, 64; Western Evangel Sem, 64-67; Sigma Alpha Kappa. Polit & Govt Pos: Chmn, Western Fedn Col Rep, 65-67; deleg, Rep Nat Conv, 68 & 72, secy, Ore deleg, 68; nominee, US Rep, Second Dist, Ore, 68; dir, Rep State Cent Comt Ore, 72- Bus & Prof Pos: Free lance pub rels consult, 64-; dir on-the-job manpower develop & training prog, Ore Automotive Wholesalers Asn, 67-68; radio commentator, Marv Root Legis Report, 69; dir mkt, MECO Motel Equip Co, 69-70; pres, Hospitality & Instnl Sales Corp, 70- Mem: Jaycees; Ore Wheat Growers League; Ore Farm Bur Fedn; YMCA; Kiwanis (dir, 72-). Honors & Awards: Named One of Outstanding Young Men in Am, 67; Pres & Valedictorian, Madras High Sch, Ore. Relig: Free Methodist. Legal Res: 36 Craven Rd Bend OR 97701 Mailing Add: PO Box 628 Bend OR 97701

ROSA, PAUL JAMES, JR (R)
Chmn, Ridgefield Rep Town Comt, Conn
b Stamford, Conn, Aug 11, 27; s Paul James Rosa & Anna Annunziato R; m 1957 to Kathryn Venus. Educ: Univ Conn, BS in Mech Eng, 49; Kappa Sigma. Polit & Govt Pos: Vpres, New Canaan Young Rep Club, Conn, 50-52; mem, Ridgefield Zoning Comn, 61-65; mem, Ridgefield Rep Town Comt, 64-, chmn, 66-; vchmn, Ridgefield Planning & Zoning Comn, 65-66; chmn, 24th Sen Dist Conv, 66; vchmn, Rep Fifth Cong Dist Orgn, 67-68 & 72-74; deleg, Rep State Conv, 68-74, mem comt resolutions, 70; deleg, Fifth Cong Dist Conv, 74; mem, Ridgefield Parks & Recreation Comn, 74- Bus & Prof Pos: Mgr inventory mgt, Perkin-Elmer Corp, 73- Mil Serv: Entered as Seaman, Navy, 45, released as Seaman 1/C, 46. Mem: Am Prod & Inventory Control Soc; Soc Mfg Engrs; KofC; Ital Am Mutual Aid Soc; Univ Conn Club. Relig: Roman Catholic. Mailing Add: 75 Olmstead Lane Ridgefield CT 06877

ROSCHE, RICHARD JOSEPH (D)
Committeeman, Erie Co Dem Party, NY
b Buffalo, NY, Nov 25, 45; s Raymond Rosche & Dorothy R; m 1969 to Margaret Raynor. Educ: Canisius Col, BA, 68; State Univ NY, JD, 71; Am Hist Honor Soc; Pi Gamma. Polit & Govt Pos: Alt deleg, Dem Nat Conv, 72; committeeman, Erie Co Dem Party, NY, 72- Bus & Prof Pos: Assoc attorney, Ralabate, Nicosia & Nicosia, Buffalo, 72- Mil Serv: Entered as 2nd Lt, Army Res, 68, 1st Lt, currently. Publ: They shoot students, State Univ NY at Buffalo, 3/72. Mem: Am, NY & Erie Co Bar Asns. Legal Res: 716 Brisbane Blvd Buffalo NY 14203 Mailing Add: 204 Auburn Buffalo NY 14213

ROSE, ALEX (LIBERAL, NY)
VChmn, NY Liberal Party
b Warsaw, Poland, Oct 15, 98; s Hyman Royz & Faiga Halpern R; m 1920 to Elsie Shapiro; c Mrs Carmy Schwartz & Herbert. Polit & Govt Pos: Vchmn, NY Liberal Party, currently; assisted in organizing Am Labor Party, 36, state secy & dir, 36-44; Presidential elector for Franklin D Roosevelt, 40, Harry S Truman, 48, Lyndon B Johnson, 64 & Hubert H Humphrey, 68; Liberal-Dem deleg-at-lg, NY State Const Conv, 66; dir, Welfare Island Planning & Develop Corp, 68-, mem bd dir, New York Pub Develop Corp, 68- Bus & Prof Pos: Vpres, United Hatters, Cap & Millinery Workers Int Union, 25, pres, 50-; headed appeals comt, AFL-CIO Conv which expelled IBT, 57. Mil Serv: Brit Army, 18-20. Mailing Add: 245 Fifth Ave New York NY 10016

ROSE, CHARLES, III (D)
US Rep, NC
b Fayetteville, NC, Aug 10, 39; m 1962 to Sara Louise Richardson; c Charles G, IV. Educ: Davidson Col, AB, 61; Univ NC Law Sch, LLB, 64. Polit & Govt Pos: Chief dist court prosecutor, 12th Judicial Dist, NC, 67-70; US Rep, Seventh Dist, NC, 73- Bus & Prof Pos: Lawyer. Legal Res: NC Mailing Add: Rm 1724 House Off Bldg Washington DC 20515

ROSE, IVAN W (D)
Ark State Rep
b Flippin, Ark, Nov 26, 25; s W E Rose & Louisa Lee R; m 1944 to Betty Ruth Wood; c Judy R & Gary Lynn. Educ: St Louis Col Pharm. Polit & Govt Pos: Ark State Rep, 65- Mem: Ark Pharmaceut Asn; Lions; Am Pharmaceut Asn; Nat Asn Retail Druggists. Relig: First Christian. Mailing Add: 124 W Walnut Rogers AR 72756

ROSE, JOE (R)
Chmn, Eddy Co Rep Cent Comt, NMex
b Carlsbad, NMex, June 24, 31; s Jess Rose & Johnnie Nichols R; m 1954 to Anne Howard; c Allen, Gregory & Melanie. Educ: Abilene Christian Col, 50-51; Eastern NMex Univ, BA, 57; Vet Club; Geography Club; Bus Assocs. Polit & Govt Pos: Alderman, Carlsbad City Coun, NMex, 62-66; campaign mgr, Eddy Co Rep Party, 62; mem, Eddy Co Rep Cent Comt, 62-, chmn, 67- Bus & Prof Pos: Pres, NMex Sand & Gravel Asn, 60-64; mem bd, Nat Ready Mix Concrete Asn, 66-68. Mil Serv: Entered as Pvt, Army, 51, released as 1st Lt, 54, after serv in Eighth Army Ord, Far East Command, Korea, 51-54; Commendation Medal; UN, Korean & Good Conduct Medals. Mem: Rotary; VFW; Boy Scouts (dist chmn); CofC (bd dirs, Carlsbad Chap, 68-). Relig: Church of Christ; deacon. Mailing Add: PO Box 220 Carlsbad NM 88220

ROSE, JONATHAN CHAPMAN (R)
Dir Off of Policy & Planning, Dept of Justice
b Cleveland, Ohio, June 8, 41; s H Chapman Rose & Katherine Cast R; single. Educ: Yale Univ, AB, 63; Harvard Univ Law Sch, LLB cum laude, 67; Zeta Psi; Lincoln's Inn. Polit & Govt Pos: Law clerk to Justice Ammi Cutter, Supreme Judicial Court, Mass, 67-68; staff asst, White House, 69-71, spec asst to the President, 71-72, gen counsel, Coun on Int Econ Policy, 72-74; assoc dep attorney gen, Dept of Justice, 74, dir off of policy & planning, 74- Mil Serv: Entered as 2nd Lt, Army, 69, released as 1st Lt, 74. Mem: Mass, DC & Am Bar Asns; US Court of Appeals; US Dist Court for DC. Relig: Episcopal. Legal Res: 12407 Fairhill Rd Cleveland OH 44120 Mailing Add: 501 Slaters Lane Alexandria VA 22314

ROSE, KATHLEEN BLOUNT (R)
VChmn, Henry Magisterial Dist, Hanover Co Rep Comt, Va
b Pine Beach, Va, Aug 26, 08; d John Gardner Blount & Marye Alice Grubbs B; wid; c Bettye Jean (Mrs Marvin A Moore) & Jeanette (Mrs William Lloyd Pierce). Educ: Smithdeal-Massey Bus Col; Richmond Prof Inst, real estate appraisal, med asst & med secy; courses sponsored by Univ Richmond; completed advert & surv interviewing course, Universal Schs, Dallas, Tex; courses in income tax, Federated Tax Serv. Polit & Govt Pos: Freight classifier, Transportation Dept, Qm Depot, 42-45; exec secy, Rep Party, Va, 64-69, liaison, 64-69, in charge reservations & ticket sales, numerous fund-raising dinners & projects, 65-, campaign materials coordr, 66-68; chmn voter registr & ways & means comt, Hanover Co Rep Comt, 68-70; hon sgt at arms, Rep Nat Conv, 68; deleg & conv coordr, Va State Conv, 68, deleg, 70-75; chmn, Henry Magisterial Dist, Hanover Co Rep Comt, Va, 73-74, vchmn, 74- Bus & Prof Pos: Notary pub, 48-; real estate broker, 52-; co-owner, Auto Machine Shop, 54-56; dealer, Paragon Homes, Inc, NY, 58-60; advert counr, Geiger Bros, Lewiston, Maine, 58-70; arranged scenic & hist bus tours & accommodations; prof interviewer including surveys, currently. Mem: Real Estate Women Va, Inc; Parliamentary Law Club Richmond; Daughters of Am; Am Cancer Soc; Eastern Star. Relig: Baptist; Sunday sch teacher; deaconess, chmn bd deaconesses; choir leader. Mailing Add: 2532 New London Rd Mechanicsville VA 23111

ROSE, ROBERT EDGAR (D)
Lt Gov, Nev
b Orange, NJ, Oct 7, 39; s Edgar Oscar Rose & Loretta Kane R; m 1963 to Elizabeth Peterson. Educ: Juniata Col, Simpson Mem Scholar, 57-61, BA with honors in Hist, 61; NY Univ Sch Law, Root-Tilden Scholar, 61-64, LLB, 64; Root-Tilden. Polit & Govt Pos: Vpres, Sierra Dem Club, 65-66; pres, Young Dem Nev, 67-68, western regional dir, 68-; deleg, Dem Nat Conv, 68; state chmn, Nev Dem Party, 68-70; dist attorney, Washoe Co, 71-; Lt Gov, Nev, currently. Bus & Prof Pos: Law clerk, Nev Supreme Court, 65; partner, law firm, Goldwater, Taber, Hill & Rose, 65- Mem: Nev State Bar Asn; YMCA; Washoe Co Cancer Soc (bd dir); Nev State Cancer Soc; Inter-Tribal Coun Nev (bd dirs). Relig: Episcopal. Legal Res: 1907 S Arlington Ave Reno NV 89502 Mailing Add: State Capitol Carson City NV 89701

ROSE, STUART PAUL (D)
Mem Exec Comt, Fla Dem Party
b Miami, Fla, May 20, 46; s Frank A Rose & Miriam Safer R; m 1972 to Avis Small. Educ: Univ Miami, BBA, 69. Polit & Govt Pos: Pres, Univ Miami Young Dem, 68-69; vpres, Dade Co Young Dem, Fla, 68-69; field dir, Fla Primary, George McGovern for President, 71-72; admin asst to Attorney Gen Robert Shevin, Fla, 71-72; campaign mgr, US Rep William Lehman, Fla, 72; Dem elector, State Fla Presidential Elec, 72; bd mem, Fla Conf Concerned Dem, 72-; mem exec comt, Fla Dem Party, 72-; pres, Young Dem Clubs Fla, 72- Bus & Prof Pos: Asst, Robert S Hurwitz & Assocs, 69-71; self-employed, Stuart P Rose & Assocs, 73- Mem: Gtr Miami Jaycees. Honors & Awards: Outstanding Serv Award, Univ Miami Student Govt, 69, Young Dem Fla, 71 & 72. Relig: Jewish. Legal Res: 604 NW 179th St Miami FL 33169 Mailing Add: Suite C 352 NE 167th St North Miami Beach FL 33162

ROSE, THOMAS CHAPIN (R)
Ill State Rep
b White Hall, Ill, Dec 8, 32; s George Lyndell Rose & Florence Chapin R; m 1954 to Harriet McLaughlin. Educ: Univ Ill, AB, 54; Univ Mich, JD, 59; Phi Eta Sigma; Sachem; Ma Wan Da; Sigma Chi. Polit & Govt Pos: City Attorney, Jacksonville, Ill, 61-64; trustee, Oaklawn Tuberc Sanatorium, 62-66; asst states attorney, Morgan Co, 64-66; Ill State Rep, currently, mem, Budgetary Comn & vchmn, Appropriations Comt, Ill House of Rep; chmn, Rules Comt of the Nat Legis Conf. Bus & Prof Pos: Instr, Ill Col, 65. Mil Serv: Entered as 2nd Lt, Army, 54, released as 1st Lt, 56, after serv in Security Agency. Mem: Morgan Co Bar Asn; Jacksonville Area Asn for Retarded Children (bd dirs); Jacksonville Symphony Soc; Visiting Nurses Asn; Kiwanis. Relig: Presbyterian. Mailing Add: 6 Westwood Place Jacksonville IL 62650

ROSE, WALDO BENNETT (R)
Ohio State Rep
Mailing Add: 330 S Charles St Lima OH 45805

ROSEDALE, PETER KLAUS (D)
RI State Rep
b Germany, July 14, 31; s Otto Julius Rosedale & Martha R; m 1969 to Beverly Ann Costantino. Educ: Col Gen Educ, Boston Univ, AA, 51, sch law, LLB, 54. Polit & Govt Pos: City councilman, Providence, RI, 59-62; judge, Providence Munic Court, 62-67; mem, Providence Dem Dist Comt, 62-69; RI State Rep, 69- Mil Serv: Entered as Pvt, Army, 54, released as Specialist, 56, after serv in Qm Corp. Mem: B'nai B'rith; instnl rep, Boy Scouts, Troop Ten. Relig: Jewish; bd dir, Temple Beth-Israel. Legal Res: 127 Gallatin St Providence RI 02907 Mailing Add: 424 Hospital Trust Bldg Providence RI 02903

ROSEDALE, RALPH EIDON (R)
b Whittier, Calif, Apr 6, 33; s Selmer M Rosedale & Margaret Carline White R; m to Pauline Erma Uuskallio; c David, Barbara & Margaret. Educ: Fullerton Jr Col, AA, 52. Polit & Govt Pos: Chmn, Tulare Co Rep Cent Comt, Calif, 56-74; officer, Rep State Cent Comt Calif, 71; pres, Asn Rep Co Cent Comt Chmn, Calif, 71-; deleg Rep Nat Conv, 72. Bus & Prof Pos: Farmer. Mem: Farm Bur. Relig: Society of Friends. Mailing Add: 10181 Ave 416 Dinuba CA 93618

ROSEFF, RICHARD (D)
b Dover, NJ, May 19, 54; s Albert S Roseff & Ruth Reibel R; single. Educ: Amherst Col, 72-; Phi Gamma. Polit & Govt Pos: Alt deleg, Dem Nat Conv, 72; dep, voter registr drive, Morris Co Bd Elec, NJ, 72 & 73. Relig: Jewish. Legal Res: 35 Elliot Rd Parsippany NJ 07054 Mailing Add: Box 399 Station 2 Amherst MA 01002

ROSELL, ANTOINETTE FRASER (R)
Mont State Sen
b Princeton, Ill, Sept 18, 26; d Robert Berkely & Rosebel Walter Fraser; m 1957 to Earl Leonard Rosell, Jr; c Rene Fraser. Educ: Mont State Univ, BA, Psychol, 48; Univ Oslo, dipl, 51; Columbia Univ, MA, Student Personnel Admin, 52. Polit & Govt Pos: Secy, Mont Young Rep, 54-56, nat committeewoman, 57-59; secy, Yellowstone Co Young Rep, 57-58; by-laws chmn, Mont Fedn Rep Women; Mont State Rep, 57-58, 61-62 & 63-64, vchmn, educ comt, Mont House Rep; Mont State Sen, 67-, vchmn, Comn Exec Reorgn, Mont State Senate, 69-70, Legis Comt Sch Laws, 69-70, Legis Coun, 71-72, subcomt schs & cols, 71-, Comt Univ Duplication, 71-72, asst minority floor leader, 75-; mem, State Supt Coun for Disadvantaged, 71-73; mem intergovt rel comt, Nat Legis Conf, 71-, comt on training, 73-, exec comt, 73-; mem exec bd, Nat Conf State Legis, 75- Bus & Prof Pos: Dean of girls, Missoula Co High Sch, 50-51; dir student activities, Eastern Mont Col Educ, Billings, 54-56; girl counr, Youth Guid Coun, 58-59 & 61-67; partner, ET Ranch, 59-; guid counr, Lincoln Jr High Sch, 67-;

dir, R B Fraser, Inc; Fraser Land & Livestock Co; dean of girls, Billings Sr High Sch. Mem: Nat Order Women Legislators; League Women Voters; Am Legion Auxiliary; Am Asn Univ Women; Mont Personnel & Guid Asn. Honors & Awards: One of Three Women of the Year, Mont Fedn Bus & Prof Women, 57, Woman of the Year, 67. Relig: Presbyterian. Legal Res: 4200 Rimrock Rd Billings MT 59102 Mailing Add: Box 45 Capitol Bldg Helena MT 59601

ROSELLINI, ALBERT D (D)
b Tacoma, Wash, Jan 21, 10; s John Rosellini & Annunziata Pagni R; m 1937 to Ethel K McNeil; c John M, Janey (Mrs Campbell), Sue, Lynn & Albert D, Jr. Educ: Univ Wash; Phi Alpha Delta; Tau Kappa Epsilon. Polit & Govt Pos: Dep prosecutor, King Co, Wash, 35-41; Wash State Sen, 39-57; Spec Asst Attorney Gen, Wash, 41-46; Gov, Wash, 57-65; deleg, Dem Nat Conv, 68. Bus & Prof Pos: Lawyer, 33- Mem: Kiwanis; Moose; Eagles; Elks; KofC. Relig: Catholic. Legal Res: 6320 NE 57th Seattle WA 98105 Mailing Add: 3737 Seattle First Bank Bldg Seattle WA 98154

ROSELLINI, EVELYN ELIZABETH (D)
b Sapulpa, Okla, Feb 7, 17; d Victor Edwards & Ethel Gambill E; m 1939 to Dean Rosellini; c Philip Edward & Deanne Marie. Educ: High Sch. Polit & Govt Pos: Adminr, Dem Polit Campaigns, Hugh J Rosellini for State Supreme Court Judge & Albert D Rosellini for Gov, Wash, 56-64; secy, Wash State Dem Comt, 61-72; deleg, Dem Nat Conv, 64-72; campaign coordr, Warren G Magnuson for Sen Campaign, 68 & 74. Bus & Prof Pos: Secy legal dept, State Liquor Control Bd, 35-39. Relig: Catholic. Mailing Add: 5404 NE Windermere Rd Seattle WA 98105

ROSEMOND, JOHN HENRY (D)
City Councilman, Columbus, Ohio
b Jacksonville, Fla, Oct 17, 17; s John H Rosemond, Sr (deceased) & Ida Belle Taylor R (deceased); m 1943 to Rosalie Edge; c John Henry, Jr, Janith Sheryl & Ronald Eliott. Educ: Fla A&M Univ, BS, 41; Howard Univ, MD, 51; Omega Psi Phi. Polit & Govt Pos: Cand, Franklin Co Coroner, Ohio, 64; alt deleg, Dem Nat Conv, 68; city councilman, Columbus, Ohio, 69-, cand for mayor, 75. Bus & Prof Pos: Civilian physician, US Army Hosp, Ft Belvoir, Va, 52-53; pvt practice med, Columbus, Ohio, 53-; staff mem, Mt Carmel, Grant, St Anthony, Ohio State Univ & Childrens Hosps, Columbus, Ohio. Mil Serv: Entered as Pvt, Army Air Corps, 43, released as 1st Lt, 46, after serv in 477th Composite Group, Navigator-Bombardier, US, 45-46. Mem: Am & Nat Med Asns; Am Acad Gen Practice; Flying Physicians Asn; Sigma Phi Phi. Honors & Awards: Named Nat Omega Man of Year, 70; Columbus UN Day Award of Honor, 68; Voted Gen Practitioner of Year, Nat Med Asn, 70; Gen Practitioner of Year, Ohio Acad Family Physicians, 74. Relig: Presbyterian; ruling elder, Bethany Presby Church. Mailing Add: 3300 E Livingston Ave Columbus OH 43227

ROSEN, ALEX (D)
b Brooklyn, NY, Feb 20, 31; s Simon Rosen & Sadie Schechter R; m 1952 to Bernice Federman; c Ricki, Peter & David. Educ: Univ Calif, Berkeley, AB, 51; Univ Calif Med Sch, San Francisco, MD, 55; Phi Beta Kappa; Sigma Xi; Alpha Omega Alpha. Polit & Govt Pos: Chmn, McGovern Orgn, Metuchen, NJ; alt deleg, Dem Nat Conv, 72. Bus & Prof Pos: Surgeon, Sayreville Med Group, 62-73; chief surg, South Amboy Mem Hosp, 69-73. Mil Serv: Entered as Asst Surgeon, USPHS, 55, released as Sr Asst Surgeon, 60. Mem: Med Soc NJ; Am Col Surgeons (fel); Am Civil Liberties Union, NJ. Relig: Hebrew. Mailing Add: 251 E Chestnut Ave Metuchen NJ 08840

ROSEN, JEROME ALLAN (D)
Chmn, Columbia Dem Town Comt, Conn
b Willimantic, Conn, June 20, 36; s Louis Rosen & Eva Rottner R; m 1961 to Harriet Weitzman; c Rochelle K & Jonathan A. Educ: Yale Univ, BA, 58; Harvard Univ Law Sch, JD, 61. Polit & Govt Pos: Asst prosecutor, Circuit Court, Conn, 64-67; town counsel, Windham, 69-; chmn, Columbia Dem Town Comt, 71- Bus & Prof Pos: Attorney & partner, Lane & Rosen PC, Willimantic, 67- Mem: Am Bar Asn; Conn Trial Lawyers Asn; Rotary; Eastern Conn State Col Found (secy, 73-). Honors & Awards: President's Award, Willimantic YMCA, 73. Relig: Jewish. Mailing Add: Pine St Columbia CT 06237

ROSEN, LESTER L (R)
b Wichita, Kans, Nov 21, 24; s Herman Rosen & Dena Wishnuff R; m 1948 to Barbara Bernice Shustorman; c Cynthia Kay, Sandra Ellen & Edward Howard. Educ: Univ Wichita, AB, 46-49; Pi Alpha Pi. Polit & Govt Pos: Admin asst to US Rep Garner Shriver, Kans, currently. Mil Serv: Army, T/5, 44-45. Mem: Wichita Advert Club (vpres & pres); Wichita Pub Rels Soc; Am Col Pub Rels Soc; Wichita-Sedgwick Co Ment Health Asn. Relig: Jewish. Legal Res: 5705 Rockhill Rd Wichita KS 67208 Mailing Add: 7 Fulham Ct Silver Spring MD 20902

ROSENAU, FRED W (D)
Kans State Rep
b Shawnee, Kans, May 7, 22; s John W Rosenau & Louise Stangle R; m 1952 to Betty M Hines; c Mark O, Ken F & Rita L. Polit & Govt Pos: Mem bd educ, Turner Unified Dist 202, 65-; Kans State Rep, Dist 35, Wyandotte Co, 66- Bus & Prof Pos: Excavating contractor, Kansas City, Kans, 28 years. Mil Serv: Army Anti-Aircraft Training Bn, 42. Mem: Kans State Sch Bd Asn; Lions; Mid-Co Dem Club, Wyandotte Co. Mailing Add: 3050 S 65th Kansas City KS 66106

ROSENBAUM, PAUL A (R)
Mich State Rep
Mailing Add: 312 Crary St Apt 3N Marshall MI 49068

ROSENBAUM, POLLY (D)
Ariz State Rep
m 1939 to William George Rosenbaum, wid. Educ: Univ Colo, BA; Univ Southern Calif, MEd. Polit & Govt Pos: Ariz State Rep, currently. Bus & Prof Pos: Teacher, formerly; stenographer; gen girl Fri in copper & asbestos industs, law, real estate appraisal, savings & loan; co clerk & recorder's offices; dent receptionist. Mem: Globe Bus & Prof Women's Club; Zonta Int; Gila CO Tuberc Control Bd; Winkleman Chap, Eastern Star (Past matron). Mailing Add: Box 609 Globe AZ 85501

ROSENBAUM, RICHARD MERRILL (R)
Chmn, NY Rep State Comt
b Oswego, NY, Apr 8, 31; s Jack M Rosenbaum & Shirley Gover R; m 1958 to Judith Kanthor; c Amy Michel, Jill Margret, Matthew Adam & Julie Fay. Educ: Hobart Col, BA, 52; Cornell Law Sch, LLB, 55, JD, 70; Phi Phi Delta. Educ: Town justice, Penfield, NY, 61-62; exec committeeman, Penfield Rep Party, 62-; legislator & asst majority leader, Monroe Co Legis, 67-68; deleg, Rep Nat Conv, 68; chmn, Monroe Co Rep Party, 68-70; Justice, Supreme Court, NY, 70-; chmn, NY Rep State Comt, 73-; mem, Rep Nat Comt, 73-; chmn, Northeast Rep State Chmn Asn, currently; chmn, Rep Nat Task Force, currently. Publ: They Said It Couldn't Be Done, Great Lakes Press, 70. Mem: Am Bar Asn; Am Arbit Asn; Am Trial Lawyers Asn; NY State Supreme Court Justice Asn; Phi Delta Phi. Honors & Awards: Named Man of Year, City of Rochester Puerto Rican Soc, 69. Relig: Jewish. Legal Res: 21 E Bayberry Rd Glenmont NY 12077 Mailing Add: NY Rep State Comt 315 State St Albany NY 12210

ROSENBAUM, STEVEN RAY (D)
b Mangum, Okla; s Finis Leo Rosenbaum & Lucille Lewis R; single. Educ: Okla State Univ, 70-71; Southwestern State Col, 71-72; Univ Tex, El Paso, 72-73. Polit & Govt Pos: Vpres, Southwestern State Col Young Dem, 71-72; deleg, Dem Dist Conv, Lawton, Okla, 72 & Okla State Dem Conv, 72; alt deleg, Dem Nat Conv, 72; Young Dem adv to US Sen Edmondson, Okla, 72; state treas, Okla Young Dem, 72-73; youth dir, Greer Co Dem Party, 72-73; campaign aide to Okla State Rep Victor Wickersham, 60th Dist. Mem: Okla Water Inc. Honors & Awards: Outstanding Young Dem, Okla Fedn Young Dem, 73; House Joint Resolution Commendation. Relig: Church of Christ. Mailing Add: 1912 N Oklahoma Dr Mangum OK 73554

ROSENBERG, ALEX JACOB (D)
Leader, 67th Assembly Dist Dem Party, NY
b New York, NY, May 25, 19; s Israel Rosenberg & Lena Zar R; m 1941 to Dorothy Hardy; c Lawrence & Andrew. Educ: Albright Col, 36-38; Philadelphia Textile Col, 38-40; Sigma Phi Tau. Polit & Govt Pos: Leader, 67th Assembly Dist Dem Party, NY, 65-, state committeeman, currently; deleg, Comt Dem Voters, 65-68; deleg, New Dem Coalition, 68-; deleg, Dem Nat Conv, 68 & 72; deleg, Comt Dem Alternatives, 68-69. Bus & Prof Pos: Pres, Anserphone, 59-65; partner, Northeast Mgt & Develop Co, 66-69; vpres, Starfax Corp, 69-70; pres, Transworld Art Corp, 70- Mil Serv: Entered as Cadet, Air Force, 42, released as Lt, 45, after serv in Fourth Photo Reconnaissance Squadron Hq, 43-45. Mem: Metrop Coun; Am Jewish Cong; Community Planning Bd; West Side CofC (vpres); Givat Haviva, Hadera, Israel (trustee). Legal Res: 277 West End Ave New York NY 10023 Mailing Add: 600 Fifth Ave New York NY 10020

ROSENBERG, MARLENE (D)
b Brooklyn, NY, Apr 20, 46; d Joseph Rosenberg & Irene Turkin R; single. Educ: Brooklyn Col, BA, 67; Rutgers Univ, MLS, 68. Polit & Govt Pos: Deleg, Dem Nat Mid-Term Conf, 74. Bus & Prof Pos: Sr librarian, Brooklyn Pub Libr, 68- Mem: Brooklyn Libr Guild (pres, Local 1482, Am Fedn State, Co & Munic Employees, AFL-CIO, 72-); Nat Asn Female Execs. Relig: Hebrew. Mailing Add: 222 Lenox Rd Brooklyn NY 11226

ROSENBERG, MARVIN (D)
b New York, NY, Aug 22, 06; s David Rosenberg & Annie Schwartz R; m to Helene Feller; c Ellen (Mrs Tovatt), David & Linda. Polit & Govt Pos: Chmn, Nat Exec Comt, Am for Dem Action, 57-58, nat vchmn, 59-; chmn, Eastern Div, Humphrey for President Comt, 60; nat treas, Humphrey for Vice President Comt, 64; deleg, Dem Nat Conv, 64 & 68; chmn finance comt, Citizens Comt, O'Connor for Gov, NY, 66; mem nat adv comt, Econ Develop Admin, 66-69; chmn, NY State Humphrey-Muskie Campaign Comt, 68; chmn finance comt, Dem for Lindsay, 69; exec chmn finance comt, Samuels for Gov, 70 & 74; treas, NY Humphrey for President Comt, 72; coordr, Task Forces/Finance Comt, Abraham Beame for Mayor, 73. Bus & Prof Pos: Pres, Cameo Curtains Inc, 38- Mem: City Athletic Club. Relig: Jewish. Legal Res: 2 West 67th St New York NY 10023 Mailing Add: 261 Fifth Ave New York NY 10016

ROSENBERGER, FRANCIS COLEMAN (D)
b Manassas, Va, Mar 22, 15; s George L Rosenberger & Olive Robertson R; m 1966 to Astra Brennan. Educ: Univ Va, 32-36 & 37-40; George Washington Univ, JD, 42. Polit & Govt Pos: Attorney, US Senate Comt on Small Bus, 42; Subcomt of US Senate Comt Mil Affairs, 42-46; attorney mem, Bd Rev, Off Price Admin, 46; attorney, Subcomt US House Rep Comt Expenditures in Exec Depts, 47-48; US Senate Comt on Judiciary, 49-50; legis asst to US Sen Harley M Kilgore, WVa, 51-55; prof staff, US Senate Comt on Judiciary, 55-; adv, US deleg, Geneva, 55 & 56, Vienna, 73. Bus & Prof Pos: Book reviewer, Richmond Times-Dispatch, 38-40, Washington Post, 40-43, NY Herald Tribune Book Rev, 45-62 & Washington Star, 67-71; mem ed bd, Fed Bar J, 57-63. Publ: Ed, Virginia Reader: A Treasury of Writings from the First Voyages to the Present, E P Dutton & Co, 48 & Octagon Books, 72; Jefferson Reader: A Treasury of Writings About Thomas Jefferson, E P Dutton & Co, 53; plus others. Mem: Fed Bar Asn; Cosmos Club, Washington, DC. Honors & Awards: Cong fel, Am Polit Sci Asn, 63; Cert Commendation for Scholarly Editing, Am Asn State & Local Hist, 71; co-organizer, Annual Confs on Washington, DC Hist Studies; ed bd, Washington Studies, George Washington Univ; ed seven vol of rec, Columbia Hist Soc, distrib by Univ Press Va. Relig: Presbyterian. Mailing Add: 6809 Melrose Dr McLean VA 22101

ROSENBLATT, JOSEPH B (D)
Mem, New York Co Dem Comt, NY
b New York, NY, Aug 28, 22; s Samson Rosenblatt & Jeannette Wacht R; m 1955 to Sheila Burger; c Jill Marion, Sarah Jane & Samuel Wacht. Educ: Syracuse Univ, 40-43. Polit & Govt Pos: Pres, NY Young Dem Club, 55-56; chmn, Borough Pres Planning Bd, 60-63; alt deleg, Dem Nat Conv, 64; deleg, NY State Dem Comt, 66; mem exec comt, East Side Dem Club, New York, vpres, currently; mem, New York Co Dem Comt, currently. Bus & Prof Pos: Pres, real estate comt, Young Men's Bd Trade, 54; pres, Joseph B Rosenblatt Assocs, 10 years; mem housing comt, Real Estate Bd New York, 62-; pres, Property Maintenance Co, 63- Mil Serv: Entered as Pvt, Army, 43, released as T/5, 45, after serv in 5th Amphibious Force, Asiatic Theater; Bronze Battle Star; Navy Commendation Letter. Mem: Henry Kaufmann Campgrounds (bd dirs); United Jewish Appeal (leadership coun); Citizens Union; Coun on Parks. Relig: Jewish. Mailing Add: 993 Park Ave New York NY 10028

ROSENFELD, MITCHELL ALLAN (R)
b Philadelphia, Pa, Nov 24, 28; s Solomon C Rosenfeld & Betty Shenkman R; m 1956 to E Louise James; c Erik J, Beth A & Steven J. Educ: Temple Univ, BS, 50; Armed Forces Info Sch, Ft Slocum, NY, 52; Beta Gamma Sigma; Pi Gamma Mu; Phi Alpha Theta; Sigma Delta Chi; ed & managing ed, Temple Univ News. Polit & Govt Pos: Pub info dir, Montgomery Co, Pa, 63-66; pub rels dir, Montgomery Co Rep Comt, 63-69; admin asst to US Rep Lawrence Coughlin, Pa, 69- Bus & Prof Pos: Gen mgr, Inter-Co Publ Co, Conshohocken, Pa; reporter & rewriteman, Delaware Co Daily Times, Philadelphia Daily News & Philadelphia Eve & Sunday Bull; pub rels dir, World Mutual Health & Accident Ins Co, King of Prussia, 66-68. Mil Serv: Entered as Pvt, Army, 51, released as Pfc, 52, after serv in 47th Inf Div,

Stateside. Mem: Nat Press Club; Fed Ed Asn. Relig: Jewish. Legal Res: PA Mailing Add: 7111 Thrasher Rd McLean VA 22101

ROSENHEIM, ROBERT CHATWELL **(R)**
b Williamson, WVa, June 15, 09; s William Spiller Rosenheim & Frances Harris R; m 1932 to Frances Elizabeth Dillman; c Jane Taylor. Educ: Marshall Col, AB, 30; Harvard Bus Sch, 43; Sigma Alpha Epsilon. Polit & Govt Pos: Chmn, Citizens for Eisenhower, Bonhomme Twp, St Louis Co, Mo, 52; precinct committeeman, Denver, Colo, 57-59; mem, Colo Rep State Cent Comt, 59-63; bonus mem, Denver Co Rep Cent Comt, 59-66; comnr, Denver Urban Renewal Comn, 61-70, chmn, 69-70; deleg, Rep Nat Conv, 64; region VIII adminr, Dept Housing & Urban Develop, 70- Mil Serv: Entered as Pvt, Army Air Force, 43, released as Capt, 46. Mem: Rocky Mountain Beverage Asn; Kiwanis; Columbine Country Club; Lincoln Club. Relig: Episcopal. Mailing Add: 3203 S Milwaukee Denver CO 80210

ROSENSHINE, DONALD LOUIS **(D)**
Md State Deleg
b Weirton, WVa, June 29, 43; s Morton Harry Rosenshine & Frances Cooper R; m 1967 to Nancy Rosenfield; c Jessica Elise. Educ: Washington & Jefferson Col, BA, 65; Univ Baltimore Sch Law, LLB, 69; George Washington Univ, 70-71; Pi Lambda Phi. Polit & Govt Pos: Mem, Annapolis Dem City Cent Comt, Md, 73-74; Md State Deleg, 75- Bus & Prof Pos: Transportation planner, Rural Community Bus Lines, 70-72; dir community leadership info serv, Md Dept Employ & Social Serv, 72-74; consult, Community Enterprise Develop Asn, Annapolis, 75- Mem: Annapolis Waterfront Asn; Common Cause; Chesapeake Environ Protection Asn; Chesapeake Bay Found; Rural Community Bus Lines (bd mem). Legal Res: 761-D Fairview Ave Annapolis MD 21403 Mailing Add: Rm 212-B House of Deleg Off Bldg Annapolis MD 21404

ROSENSTREICH, JUDY PATTON **(R)**
Vt State Rep
Mailing Add: Maple St Waterbury Center VT 05677

ROSENTHAL, BEATRICE HOLT **(D)**
Dem Nat Committeewoman, Conn
b Brooklyn, NY, June 7, 00; d Hamilton Holt (deceased) & Alexina Smith H (deceased); m 1950 to Joseph S Rosenthal; c William Holt, Joseph H & Grace (Mrs W R Hayes). Educ: Columbia Teachers Col, 17-18. Polit & Govt Pos: Pres, Conn Federated Dem Women's Clubs, formerly; chmn, Waterford Dem Town Comt, formerly; mem, Nat Adv Comt on Polit Orgn; deleg local & state Dem Convs, 48-; deleg, Dem Nat Conv, 48-, mem site & credentials comt, 68; committeewoman, 20th Dist, Conn Dem State Cent Comt & State Party Rules Comt, formerly; Justice of the Peace, Waterford, Conn, formerly; Dem Nat Committeewoman, 60-; co-chmn, Conn Dem Speakers Bur, 68; mem, Conn Comt for Rev Party Rules, currently; mem, Waterford Indust & Develop Comn, currently; mem, Conn Hist Comn & Conn Personnel Appeals Bd, formerly; mem, Dem Charter Comn, 74. Mem: Norwich State Hosp (pres bd trustees); Mystic Oral Sch for Deaf (pres bd trustees, 60-); Roseland Park & Eugene O'Neill Theater for Performing Arts; Antiquarian & Landmarks Soc (pres, 65-); State Bd Humane Soc. Honors & Awards: Woman of the Year, Niantic News, Conn, 62. Mailing Add: Rope Ferry Rd Waterford CT 06385

ROSENTHAL, BENJAMIN STANLEY **(D-LIBERAL)**
US Rep, NY
b New York, NY, June 8, 23; s Joseph Rosenthal & Ceil Fischer R; m 1950 to Lila Moskowitz; c Debra & Edward. Educ: Long Island Univ & City Col New York; Brooklyn Law Sch, LLB, 49; New York Univ, LLM, 52. Polit & Govt Pos: US Rep, NY, 62-, mem nat comn food mkt, 66, foreign affairs comt, govt oper comt, spec inquiry on invasion of privacy, chmn spec inquiry on consumer representation in fed govt, mem steering comt, Men of Cong for peace through law, US House Rep, currently, chmn subcomt on Europe, foreign affairs comt, 71- Bus & Prof Pos: Practicing attorney, 49-70. Mil Serv: Entered as Pvt, Army, 43, released as T/5, 46, after serv in Iceland. Mem: Queens Co, NY State & Am Bar Asns. Relig: Jewish. Legal Res: 88-12 Elmhurst Ave Elmhurst NY 11373 Mailing Add: House Off Bldg Washington DC 20515

ROSENTHAL, HERSCHEL **(D)**
Calif State Assemblyman
b St Louis, Mo, Mar 13, 18; s Saul Hyman Rosenthal & Minnie Berkowitz R; m 1946 to Patricia P Staman; c Joel & Suzanne. Educ: Univ Calif, Los Angeles Col Eng, 36-39. Polit & Govt Pos: Comt mem, Los Angeles City Dollars for Dem, Calif, 58; chmn, Los Angeles Co Dollars for Dem, 60; mem, Los Angeles Co Dem Cent Comt, 60-70; deleg, Dem Nat Conv, 72; comnr, Los Angeles Community Redevelop Agency, 73-74; Calif State Assemblyman, 45th Dist, 75- Bus & Prof Pos: Vpres, Ad Type Serv Co, Inc, Los Angeles, Calif, 46- Mil Serv: Entered as Seaman, Navy, 44, released as Aerographers Mate 3/C, 46, after serv in Asiatic Pac, 44-46. Mem: Int Typographical Local 174; Trade Compositors & Typographers Group; Westside Jewish Community Ctr; Am Civil Liberties Union; Comt Liberal Representation. Relig: Jewish. Legal Res: 1427 N Poinsettia Pl 209 Los Angeles CA 90046 Mailing Add: Rm 5160 State Capitol Sacramento CA 95814

ROSENTHAL, JACK H **(D)**
Chmn, Newtown Town Dem Comt, Conn
b New York, NY, Aug 6, 19; s Irving A Rosenthal & Anne Shafter R; m 1942 to Annabelle Pokress; c Herbert C. Educ: Roosevelt High Sch, Yonkers, NY. Polit & Govt Pos: Selectman, Newtown, Conn, 55-59, mem bd finance, 63-; chmn, Newtown Town Dem Comt, 67- Bus & Prof Pos: Salesman, Metrop Life Ins, Mutual of Omaha & Nationwide Ins Co, 46-; sales mgr, Nationwide Ins Co, 63. Mil Serv: Entered as Pvt, Army, 41, released as S/Sgt, 45, after serv in 69th Sta Hosp, NAfrica, 42-43. Legal Res: 70 Main St Newtown CT 06470 Mailing Add: Box 305 Newtown CT 06470

ROSENTHAL, TAMAR NAOMI **(D)**
b Tulsa, Okla, July 6, 54; d Norbert Leon Rosenthal & Geraldine Hellman R; single. Educ: Univ Okla, 72-73; mem, Pres Adv Comt Minority Affairs, 72-73; student congresswoman, 73-; Emory Univ, AB, 75. Polit & Govt Pos: Alt deleg, Dem Nat Conv, 72. Mem: Sierra Club; Friends of the Earth. Honors & Awards: Lit Award for Eyrie, High Sch Anthology, 71; Stipe Award, Emory Univ. Relig: Jewish. Mailing Add: 3633 E 48th St Tulsa OK 74135

ROSENZWEIG, HARRY **(R)**
Chmn, Ariz Rep State Comt
b Phoenix, Ariz, July 8, 07; s Isaac Rosenzweig & Rosa Gross R; m 1958 to Sandy Pollack; c Diane (Mrs Jack Hardy), Harry, Jr & Burke. Educ: Univ Ariz & Univ Mich, 26 & 27. Polit & Govt Pos: City councilman, Phoenix, Ariz, 50-53; finance chmn, Maricopa Co Rep Comt, 52; finance chmn, Ariz Rep State Comt, 60-62, chmn, 65-; mem, Rep Nat Comt, 65-; deleg, Rep Nat Conv, 72. Bus & Prof Pos: Partner, Rosenzweig's Jewelers, 28- Mem: Mason (32 degree); Thunderbirds; Sun Angel Found; Better Bus Bur; Retail Jewelers of Am. Relig: Jewish; trustee, Temple Beth Israel. Legal Res: 512 W Flynn Lane Phoenix AZ 85013 Mailing Add: 35 N First Ave Phoenix AZ 85003

ROSEWELL, EDWARD JOSEPH **(D)**
Treas, Cook Co, Ill
b Chicago, Ill, Dec 8, 28; s Andrew Rosewell & Edna M Maquire R; single. Educ: DePaul Univ, PhB, 61, Law Sch; John Marshall Law Sch. Polit & Govt Pos: Chmn, Cook Co Young Dem, 63-64; nat registr chmn, Johnson-Humphrey Presidential Campaign, Young Dem Clubs Am, first vpres, formerly; mem platform comt, Ill Dem Party, 64-72; alt deleg, Dem Nat Conv, 64-72, coordr, Chicago Host Comt, 68; mem, Inaugural Comt for President Johnson & Vice President Humphrey, 65; pres, Ill Young Dem, 66-69; exec dir, Ill State Toll Hwy Comn, formerly; comnr, Chicago Park Dist, formerly; treas, Cook Co, Ill, currently. Bus & Prof Pos: Vpres, Continental Ill Nat Bank, 69-74. Mil Serv: Army, 2 years, released as Sgt, attended personnel & finance sch. Mem: Am Inst Banking; Order of St Philip; Garfield Park Improv Asn; WSide Area Planning Bd (asst dir); Our Lady of Sorrows Holy Name Soc. Mailing Add: Apt 2512 300 N State St Chicago IL 60610

ROSKIE, GEORGE F **(R)**
Mont State Sen
Mailing Add: 3440 Sixth Ave S Great Falls MT 59405

ROSOW, JEROME MORRIS **(INDEPENDENT)**
b Chicago, Ill, Dec 2, 19; s Morris Rosow & Mary Cornick R; m 1941 to Rosalyn Levin; c Michael & Joel. Educ: Wright Jr Col, AAB, 40; Univ Chicago, BA cum laude, 42. Polit & Govt Pos: Position classification analyst, Dept Army, Washington, DC, 42-43; dir compensation, orgn & methods, War Assets Admin, 46-48; orgn examr & asst mgr, Wage & Salary Div, Off Secy Army, 48-51; dir policy & salary, stabilization bd, Econ Stabilization Agency, 52-53; Asst Secy of Labor for Policy, Eval & Research, Dept Labor, 69-71; US deleg, Ministers Econ Conf, Orgn Econ Coop & Develop, Paris, 70, chmn, Tech Experts Meeting on Multinationals, 72; chmn, Int Seminar Advances in Work Orgn, 73; chmn, President's Adv Comt on Fed Pay, currently; consult, Comptroller Gen, US, currently; mem, Nat Comn on Productivity & Quality of Work, 74-; deleg, Int Seminar Worker Participation, 75. Bus & Prof Pos: Mem staff, Creole Petroleum Corp, Standard Oil, Caracas, Venezuela, 53-55, various exec pos, employee rels dept, Standard Oil, NJ, 55-; mem bus adv research comt, Bur Labor Statist, 58-65; mem & chmn coun compensation, Nat Indust Conf Bd, 59-66; assoc, Columbia Univ Seminar on Labor, 61-; dir, Voc Adv Serv, New York, 61-69, chmn finance comt, 62-65; consult, US Bur Budget & US Civil Serv Comn, 64; mem bd trustees, Nat Comt Employ Youth, 65-, trustee, Young Audiences, 74-; mgr employee rels dept, ESSO Europe, Inc, London, Eng, 66-69; planning mgr pub affairs, Exxon Corp, New York, 71-; adv comt, Econ Develop, 71-; mem, Bus Adv Comt Nat Planning Asn, 72-; Mil Serv: Entered as Pvt, Army, 43, released as Chief Warrant Officer, 46, after serv in Qm Corps. Publ: Ed, American Men in Government, Pub Affairs Press, 49; numerous articles relating to industrial relations & compensation matters in prof jour including Harvard Bus Rev & Nat Indust Conf Bd Record. Mem: Indust Rels Research Asn (exec bd); Am Mgt Asn; Univ Club, New York; Fed City Club, Washington, DC. Relig: Jewish. Mailing Add: 117 Fox Meadow Rd Scarsdale NY 10583

ROSS, BEN BARRON **(D)**
Ga State Rep
Mailing Add: PO Box 245 Lincolnton GA 30817

ROSS, CHARLES DOUGLAS **(R)**
Mem, Montgomery Co Rep Exec Comt, Ohio
b Shelby, Ohio, July 1, 34; s Loren C Ross & Mary Agnes R; m 1957 to Lois Huston; c Robert Douglas & Anne Elizabeth. Educ: Purdue Univ, BSME, 57; Am Univ, LLB, 61; Gimlet Club; Lambda Chi Alpha. Polit & Govt Pos: Staff, Young Rep Pres, Dayton, Ohio, 64; campaign chmn & mgr, Whaler for Cong Comt, 66; state orgn dir, Saxbe for Senate Comt, 68; chmn, Montgomery Co Rep Party, 70-73, mem exec comt, currently; mem, Montgomery Co Bd Elections, 71-; deleg, Rep Nat Conv, 72; campaign dir, Ohio Comt to Reelect the President, 72. Bus & Prof Pos: Attorney, Marechal, Biebel, French & Bugg, 61-69, Young & Alexander, 70-73 & Ross & D'Amico, Dayton, 74- Mil Serv: Entered as 2nd Lt, Army, 57, released as 1st Lt, 58, after serv in Off Basic, Ft Sill, Okla, Capt, Judge Adv Gen Corps, Army Res, retired, 69. Mem: Am, Ohio & Dayton Bar Asns. Relig: Presbyterian. Mailing Add: 188 Lookout Dayton OH 45419

ROSS, CHARLES ROBERT **(R)**
b Middlebury, Vt, Feb 24, 20; s Jacob Johnson Ross & Hannah Elizabeth Holmes R; m 1948 to Charlotte Sells Hoyt; c Jacqueline Hoyt, Peter Holmes & Charles Robert, Jr. Educ: Univ Mich, AB, 41, MBA & LLB, 48. Polit & Govt Pos: Mem, Burlington Bd Alderman, Vt, 57-59; chmn, Vt Pub Serv Comn, 59-61; comnr, Fed Power Comn, 61-68; comnr, Int Joint Comn, 62-; consult, New Eng Regional Comn, 68-70; consult, US Dept Justice, 69-70. Bus & Prof Pos: Instr, Ore State Col, 48-49; adj prof, Univ Vt, 69-74. Mem: Am & Vt Bar Asns. Mailing Add: Box F Hinesburg VT 05461

ROSS, CLAUDE G
b Chicago, Ill, Oct 26, 17; m to Antigone Peterson; c Two. Educ: Univ Southern Calif, BA, 39; Phi Beta Kappa; Phi Kappa Phi; Delta Phi Epsilon. Polit & Govt Pos: Career officer, US Dept of State Foreign Serv, 40-, Mexico City, 40-41, Quito, Guayaquil, 41-45, Athens, 45-49, Noumea, 49-51, Washington, DC, 51-54 & Beirut, 54-56, Nat War Col, 56-57, counr, Cairo, 57-60 & Conakry, 60-62, dep dir, Off of African & Malagasy Union Affairs, 62-63, US Ambassador to Cent African Repub, 63-67, Haiti, 67-69 & Tanzania, 69-72; Dep Asst Secy of State for African Affairs, 72-74, sr foreign serv inspector, 74, consult to Dept State, 75- Bus & Prof Pos: With Los Angeles Daily News, 34-35. Legal Res: 3257 Worthington St NW Washington DC 20015 Mailing Add: Dept of State Washington DC 20520

ROSS, DAVID GRAY **(D)**
Md State Deleg
b Quanah, Tex, Aug 9, 35; s Lee Roy Ross & Ethel Cass R; m 1966 to Jane Noel Lewis. Educ: George Washington Univ, 53-55; Am Univ, BS, 60, Washington Col Law, JD, 64; Omicron Delta Kappa; Delta Theta Phi; Alpha Tau Omega; Alpha Phi Omega. Polit & Govt Pos: Asst corp counsel, DC Govt, 65-67; assoc co attorney, Prince George's Co, Md, 67-68; master of juvenile causes, Prince George's Co Circuit Court, 68-70; chmn bd trustees, Prince George's

Community Col, 69-70; Md State Deleg, 70- Bus & Prof Pos: Partner, Ross, Luchte, Murray, Redding & Devlan, Attorneys, Bowie, Md, 64- Mil Serv: Entered as Pvt, Army, 55, released as Sgt, 58, after serv in 260th AAA Group; Maj, Army Nat Guard, currently; Nat Defense Medal; Armed Forces Res Meritorious Serv Medal. Publ: The foreign student program at American University, The Lodestar, Vol II, No 2; Mobilization 1961, 64; The real (estate) cost of delinquency, Realtor, Vol XXXVIII, No 9. Mem: Am, DC, Md & Prince George's Co Bar Asns. Honors & Awards: Young Man of the Year, City of Bowie, Md, 68; Young Man of Southern Prince George's Co, 69; One of Five Outstanding Young Men of Md, 70. Relig: United Methodist. Legal Res: 12406 Whitehall Dr Bowie MD 20715 Mailing Add: PO Box Z Bowie MD 20715

ROSS, DONALD ROE (R)
b Orleans, Nebr, June 8, 22; s Roe M Ross & Leila Reed R; m 1943 to Janice Cook; c Susan Jane (Mrs Randall Moody), Sharon Kay (Mrs Kenneth Stephan), Rebecca Lynn, Joan Christine (Mrs Tom C Wilson) & Donald Dean. Educ: Univ Nebr, LLB, 48; Delta Theta Phi. Polit & Govt Pos: Mayor, Lexington, Nebr, 52-53; US Dist Attorney, Nebr, 53-56; chmn, Douglas Co Rep Party, 57-58; gen counsel, Nebr Rep Party, 57-58; Rep Nat Committeeman, Nebr, 58-70, mem exec comt, Rep Nat Comt, 64-70, vchmn, 65-70; US Circuit Judge, Eighth Judicial Circuit, 71- Bus & Prof Pos: Partner, law firm, Cook & Ross, Lexington, Nebr, 48-53 & Swarr, May Royce, Smith, Andersen & Ross, 56-71. Mil Serv: Entered as Cadet, Air Force, 42, released as Maj, 46, after serv in 306th Bomb Group, 8th Air Force, Eng, 43-45; Distinguished Flying Cross with Oak Leaf Cluster; Air Medal with 5 Clusters. Mem: Am, Nebr & Omaha Bar Asns; Am Legion; Mason. Relig: Congregational. Legal Res: 9921 Broadmoor Dr Omaha NE 68114 Mailing Add: US Courthouse 215 N 17th St Omaha NE 68101

ROSS, EDNA GENEVIEVE (R)
Registr Chmn, Ariz State Rep Exec Comt
b Wheeling, WVa, Mar 2, 16; d Eugene Edwin Reed & Stella May McConnaughy R; m 1934 to Andrew Wilson Ross; c Kenneth Reed, Ellen Penelope (Mrs Lewis Kruse) & Carolyn Jennifer (Mrs William R Donges). Educ: Univ Ariz, 2 years. Polit & Govt Pos: Rep precinct committeeman, Pima Co, Ariz, 49-; ward committeeman, Tucson, 60-73; secy exec comt, Pima Co Rep Comt, 63-73, vchmn, 66-73; mem, Ariz Rep State Comt, 63-; secy, Tucson Trunk 'N Tusk Club, 67-72; deleg & secy credential's comt, Rep Nat Conv, 68; mem, Bi-Partisan Elec Reform Comt, Pima Co, 69; registr chmn, Ariz State Rep Exec Comt, 71-; spec events chmn, Comt to Elect Gene Savoie to Cong, Dist 2, Ariz, 72; publicity chmn, Pima Co Rep Women, 72-73; campaign chmn, Legis Cand Dan Eckstrom, Dist 10, 72; mem, Comt to Reelect the President, 72; mem, Basic Concepts Comn, Ariz Dept Educ, 72-73; adv comt, Re-elect Barry Goldwater, 74; registr chmn, Pima Co, 75. Bus & Prof Pos: Bus mgr, Tucson Ariz Boys Chorus, 49-51; dist mgr, Cong Dist 2, Bur Census, Dept Com, 70; adv counsel, Robert A Taft Inst Govt, 72- Mem: Suburban Women's Club; Tucson Women's Symphony; Ariz Prof Engrs Auxiliary; Mrs Wrights Pueblo Juniors; Univ Ariz Faculty Wives. Honors & Awards: Art Wales Citizenship Award, Pima Co Rep Orgn, 70; Serv Award, Dist 10, Pima Co Rep Comt, 72. Mailing Add: 3117 E 29th St Tucson AZ 85713

ROSS, HOPE SNIDER (D)
b Vonore, Tenn, May 23, 10; d Henry Tipton Snider & Iris Ellis S; m 1931 to George T Ross, MD; c Julia (Mrs Douglas Grossman), Mary Ruth (Mrs Tom Huntington) & Gerald Henry. Educ: Tenn Wesleyan Univ, 26-27; Maryville Col, AB, 31; Univ Okla Sch Med, MD, 35; Crippled Children's Hosp, Oklahoma City, internship, 35-56; North Hudson Hosp, Weehawken, NJ, resident in med & anesthesia; Commonwealth fel, Harvard Univ, 43. Polit & Govt Pos: Deleg, White House Conf on Educ, 55; Hon Col, Gov Staff, 62; alt deleg & alt asst secy Okla deleg, Dem Nat Conv, 64, physician, Okla deleg, 72; mem finance adv comt, Okla Dem Cent Comt, 65; med consult comt on physicians participation, Medicare Adv Comt, 65 & Social Security Admin, currently; presidential elector, 68; mem, President's Comt on Employ of Handicapped, 68-69; mem, Defense Adv Coun on Women in Serv, 68-; mem, White House Conf on Employ of Handicapped, 73; mem bldg comt, Okla Dem Party, currently. Bus & Prof Pos: Sch physician, Phillips Univ, 38-42; area consult, Okla Voc Rehabilitation, 64-; mem liaison comt, Okla Acad Gen Practice & Univ Okla Sch Med, 65; mem, Garfield Co Health Bd, 66-; mem, Gov Comt on Children & Youth, 69; mem planning comt, Okla Regional Med Progs, bd dirs, St Mary's Hosp Sch Nursing & Gov Adv Comt for Statewide Planning for Voc Rehabilitation Serv & bd mem, Okla Rehabilitation Asn, currently. Publ: Problems of deep anesthesia, Southern Med J, 6/41. Mem: Acad Polit Sci; Am Med Asn; Am Acad Gen Practice; Am Acad Family Physicians (fel); Am Med Women's Asn. Honors & Awards: Nominated for President Johnson's Nat Talent Bank by Dem Cent Comt, Okla, 65; Int Hon Mem, Beta Sigma Phi. Relig: Methodist; mem off bd, First Methodist Church of Enid. Legal Res: 28 Woodlands Enid OK 73701 Mailing Add: 1101 E Broadway Enid OK 73701

ROSS, JIM BUCK (D)
Comnr Agr & Com, Miss
b Pelahatchie, Miss, Aug 14, 17; s E N Ross & Emma Jones R; m 1941 to Margaret Spann; c James Hall & Mary Gwendolyn. Educ: Miss State Univ, 4 years; Jackson Sch Law. Polit & Govt Pos: Mayor, Pelahatchie, Miss, 55-59; Miss State Sen, 64-68; Comnr Agr & Com, Miss, 68- Bus & Prof Pos: Farm equip dealer & cotton grower, Rankin Co, Miss, 45-57. Mil Serv: Entered as Pvt, Army, 44, released as 1st Lt, 46, after serv in SPac, 44-46. Mem: Nat Asn State Dept Agr; Southern Asn State Dept Agr; Gamma Sigma Delta; Miss Econ Coun. Relig: Methodist. Legal Res: Pelahatchie MS 39145 Mailing Add: State Capitol Jackson MS 39205

ROSS, JOHN CURLEE, JR (D)
Miss State Rep
Mailing Add: Box 191 Corinth MS 38834

ROSS, RICHARD C (R)
NY State Assemblyman
b New York, NY, May 5, 27; s Louis H Rosoff & Mollie Silverman R; m 1952 to Joan A Flug; c Marcia, William & Andrew. Educ: NY Univ, BA, 49, Sch Law, JD, 50, Grad Sch Law, LLM, 53. Polit & Govt Pos: Counsel, NY State Legis, 54-63; supvr, Westchester Co Bd Supvr, NY, 64-65; councilman, City Coun Mt Vernon, 66-72; NY State Assemblyman, 73- Bus & Prof Pos: Attorney-at-law, Mt Vernon, NY, 50- Mil Serv: Entered as A/S, Navy, 45, released as Pharmacist's Mate 3/C, after serv in First Spec Marine Brigade, Caribbean, 46. Publ: Subrogation under the Federal Tort Claims Act, NY Univ Law Rev, 49. Mem: NY Tennis Club (pres, 72); Boy Scouts (neighborhood comnr); Lions; F&AM; Am Legion. Relig: Jewish; Trustee, Men's Club, Free Synagogue of Westchester. Mailing Add: 24 Palmer Ave Mt Vernon NY 10552

ROSS, ROY R (D)
Ky State Sen
b Flat Gap, Ky, May 14, 15; s Marion S Ross & Della Wheeler R; m 1942 to Agnes Daniel; c Ruth Ann (Mrs Don Brickley), Peggy Alice (Mrs Wayne Castle), Donald R & Jackie A. Educ: Morehead State Univ, 38-39; Western State Univ, 39-41. Polit & Govt Pos: Court clerk, Johnson Co, Ky, 66-70; Ky State Sen, 25th Dist, Boyd, Lawrence & Johnson Co, 72- Bus & Prof Pos: Teacher, Johnson Co Sch Syst, Ky, 41-52; farm placement rep & interviewer, Exam Employ Serv, 52-60; mgr & owner, R & D Aluminum Co, 62-65; grade foreman, Peter Kewitt Construction Co, two years; land agt, Ridgeway Fuel Corp, 73- Mem: Paintsville Kiwanis; Farm Bur; Eastern Ky Teachers Asn; Granddaddy Hunt & Game Club; F&AM. Honors & Awards: Ky Col, Gov Edward Breathitt. Relig: Protestant. Mailing Add: 407 N Madison Louisa KY 41230

ROSS, SAMUEL A (D)
Pa State Rep
b Sumter, SC, Jan 24, 14; s Rev Augusta Ross & Sarah Ann Phelps R; m 1941 to Mildred Ransome; c Cordell (Mrs Samuel) & Marvin A. Educ: Bordentown Manual Training Indust Sch, cert, 27; NC Mutual Ins Training Sch, cert, 41; Ins Soc Philadelphia, cert, 62. Polit & Govt Pos: Committeeman & treas, Third Ward Dem Exec Comt, 58-75; Pa State Rep, 191st Dist, 75- Bus & Prof Pos: Salesman, Progressive Life Ins Co, NJ, 36-37, reporter & columnist, NY Amsterdam News, 37-39; agt, NC Mutual Life, 39-42 & Bankers Life & Casualty, Chicago, Ill, 43-52; pres, Ross Famous Fashions, Philadelphia, Pa, 43-52; dir, 20th Century Modeling & Charm Sch, Philadelphia, 46-52; pres, Ross Ins Agency, 65- Relig: Protestant. Mailing Add: 6140 Carpenter St Philadelphia PA 19143

ROSS, YAN MICHAEL (R)
b New York, NY, Dec 2, 42; s Dr Herman J Ross & Pauline C R; m 1968 to Kathleen Browne; c Matthew Kennett & Elizabeth Feiga. Educ: Princeton Univ, AB, 64; Yale Law Sch, JD, 67; Woodrow Wilson Sch Pub & Int Affairs; Barristers' Union; Phi Alpha Delta; Princeton Stock Anal & Investment Club (founder & pres); Am Whig-Cliosophic Soc. Polit & Govt Pos: Minority counsel, Comt on Banking & Currency, US House Rep, 70-75; alt US exec dir, Inter-Am Develop Bank, 75- Mil Serv: Entered as Officer Trainee, Air Force, 67, released as 1st Lt, 70, after serv in Strategic Air Command & Hq Command, 68-70. Mem: US Supreme Court & DC Bars; Inter-Am, Am & Fed Bar Asns; Capitol Hill Club. Mailing Add: 6008 Cobalt Rd Bethesda MD 20016

ROSSETTI, FRANK G (D)
Polit & Govt Pos: NY State Assemblyman, 43-44 & 54-72; exec mem, Kanawha Club, Regular Dem Orgn of 72nd Assembly Dist; deleg, Dem Nat Conv, 68; chmn, NY Co Dem Party, formerly; alt deleg, Dem Mid-Term Conf, 74. Bus & Prof Pos: Vpres, Oper Plasterers & Cement Masons Int Asn. Mem: Holy Name Soc; KofC; Elks; Soc of Tammany or Columbian Order. Mailing Add: 342 Madison Ave New York NY 10017

ROSSIDES, EUGENE TELEMACHUS (R)
b Brooklyn, NY, Oct 23, 27; s Telemachus Rossides & Anna Maravel R; m 1961 to Aphrodite Macotsin; c Gale Daphne, Michael Telemachus, Alexander Demetrius & Eleni Ariadne. Educ: Columbia Col, BA; Columbia Law Sch, LLB; Sigma Chi; Phi Delta Phi. Polit & Govt Pos: Criminal law investr, New York Co Dist Attorney's Off, NY, 52; asst attorney gen, NY, 56-58; special asst to Under Secy of Treas, 58-61, Asst Secy of Treas, 69-73. Bus & Prof Pos: Attorney-at-law, Rogers & Wells, New York, 54-56 & 61-69, partner, 66-69 & 73- Mil Serv: 2nd Lt, Air Force, 52-53, with Air Materiel Command, Wright-Patterson AFB; Capt, Air Force Res, 53- Publ: Helping a client cope with foreign unfair competition, Bus Lawyer, 4/73. Mem: Acad Polit Sci; Am & Fed Bar Asns; Am Polit Sci Asn; NY State Dist Attorneys Asn. Honors & Awards: Received Rolker Prize, Columbia Col; Columbia Univ Medal for Excellence, 72; Young Lawyer's Award, Columbia Law Sch Alumni Asn, 72. Relig: Greek Orthodox; mem Archdiocesan Coun, Greek Orthodox Church of N & S Am. Mailing Add: 3666 Upton St NW Washington DC 20008

ROSSITER, MICHAEL ANTHONY (D)
b Yankton, SDak, Aug 25, 35; s Lawrence Rossiter & Florence Lase R; m 1962 to Theodora Horn; c Cecilia Marie, Lawrence Dominic, Peter Anthony & Rachel Mary. Educ: Creighton Univ, BS in BA, 59; Delta Sigma Phi. Polit & Govt Pos: Chmn, Yankton Co Dem Party, SDak, 64-66 & 68-70; vol, McGovern Campaign, 71-72; committeeman, SDak Dem State Cent Comt, 72-74. Bus & Prof Pos: Acct-exec, Rossiter Ins, 59-62, Fuller Brush Co, 62 & Orchard & Wilhelmco, 62-63; owner, Rossiter Ins, 62-65; pres, Rossiter Agency, Inc, 65- Mil Serv: Entered as E-1, Army, 56, released as E-4, 57, after serv in 267th Field Artil, 5th Corps, Ger. Mem: KofC; Yankton CofC. Relig: Catholic. Legal Res: 300 E Fifth Yankton SD 57078 Mailing Add: Box 570 Yankton SD 57078

ROSTENKOWSKI, DAN (D)
US Rep, Ill
m to LaVerne Pirkins; c Four. Educ: Loyola Univ, Polit & Govt Pos: Ill State Rep, 68th Gen Assembly; Ill State Sen, 33rd Sen Dist, 69th & 70th Gen Assemblies; US Rep, Ill, 58-, chmn, ways & means comt, mem, Subcomt on Trade & Chmn, Health Subcomt, currently; US House Rep, chmn Dem caucus, 67-70; deleg, Dem Nat Conv, 60, 64, 68 & 72. Mil Serv: Inf, Korea, 2 years. Mem: VFW. Legal Res: Chicago IL Mailing Add: US House of Rep Washington DC 20515

ROSTKER, SKIPPER (D)
Southern Secy, Calif Dem State Cent Comt
b Kenosha, Wis, Mar 24, 19; s Morris Rostker & Anna Raitchick R; m 1944 to Patricia Murphey; c Terry Murphey, Steven L, Margaret A & Vivion Jo. Educ: Northwestern Univ; Univ Ariz; Pomona Col. Polit & Govt Pos: Dem precinct worker, 25 years; officer, Hastings Ranch Dem Club, FRD Dem Club, Los Angeles Co Cent Comt & local cong dist orgn; mem, Dem State Cent Comt, 10 years, Los Angeles Co Grand Jury, 66; southern secy, Calif Dem State Cent Comt, currently. Mem: UN Asn (bd mem, Pasadena Area); NAACP; Farm Workers; Small Bus Adv Bd; Pasadena Community Hosp. Honors & Awards: Award from Urban League for being one of three plaintiffs who filed law suit against Pasadena Sch Bd in 67 thru 70 to force integration; resulted in landmark decision requiring integrated schs. Mailing Add: 3426 Barhite St Pasadena CA 91107

ROSTOW, WALT WHITMAN (D)
b New York, NY, Oct 7, 16; s Victor Aaron Rostow & Lillian Helman R; m 1947 to Elspeth Vaughan Davies; c Peter Vaughan & Ann Larner. Educ: Yale Univ, BA, 36, PhD, 40; Balliol Col, Rhodes Scholar, 36-38. Polit & Govt Pos: Asst chief, Ger-Austrian Econ Div, Dept of State, 45-46; asst to exec secy, Econ Comn for Europe, 47-49; dep spec asst to President for

nat security affairs, 61; counr & chmn policy planning coun, Dept of State, 61-66; US Rep (Ambassador), Inter-Am Comt, Alliance for Progress, 64-66; spec asst to the President, 66-69. Bus & Prof Pos: Instr econ, Columbia Univ, 40-41; Harmsworth prof Am hist, Oxford Univ, 46-47; Pitt prof Am hist, Cambridge Univ, 49-50; prof econ hist, Mass Inst Technol, 50-60; staff mem, Ctr Int Studies, 51-60; prof hist & econ, Univ Tex, Austin, 69- Mil Serv: Maj, Off Strategic Serv, Army, 42-45; Legion of Merit; Hon Order Brit Empire. Publ: The Stages of Economic Growth, 60 & 71; The Diffusion of Power, Macmillan, 72; How It All Began, 75; plus others. Mem: Cosmos Club, Washington, DC; Elizabethan Club, New Haven. Honors & Awards: Presidential Medal of Freedom with distinction, 69. Mailing Add: 1 Wildwind Point Austin TX 78746

ROTELLI, DELBERT LEROY (R)
Mem, Rep State Cent Comt Calif
b Sonora, Calif, Sept 8, 34; s Anelo Rotelli & Treana Pretto R; m 1958 to Kathleen Rohrman; c Larry & Vickie. Educ: Col San Mateo, AA, 55; Idaho State Col, BA, 57; Tau Kappa Epsilon; I Club. Polit & Govt Pos: Councilman, Sonora, Calif, 64-68; mem, Rep State Cent Comt Calif, 68-69 & 71-; supvr, Tuolumne Co, currently. Mem: Sonora Area Bus Asn (pres); Sonora Elks Club (Exalted Ruler); KofC; Ital Cath Fedn (pres); Sonora Vol Fireman. Relig: Catholic. Legal Res: 250 E Pasadena Ave Sonora CA 95370 Mailing Add: PO Box 297 Sonora CA 95370

ROTENBERG, JON FRED (D)
b Boston, Mass, Oct 21, 47; s Harold Rotenberg & Fay Amgott R; single. Educ: Ohio Univ, BSE, 69. Polit & Govt Pos: Legis aide to US Rep Thomas P O'Neill, Jr, 70; Mass State Rep, 71-74; Dem cand for US Rep, Mass, 74. Mailing Add: 476 Heath St Brookline MA 02167

ROTH, GERALD IRWIN (D)
Mem Exec Comt, Lehigh Co Dem Party, Pa
b Allentown, Pa, July 2, 31; s Eugene Jerome Roth & Juliet Weiss R; m 1953 to Selma Barbara Grossman; c Judd Kevin, Kyle Richard, Adam Morris, Douglas Craig & Melissa B. Educ: Univ Calif, Los Angeles, BA, 52; Northwestern Univ, JD, 56; Phi Alpha Delta; Order of the Coif; Phi Epsilon Pi. Polit & Govt Pos: Deleg, Dem Nat Conv, Pa, 68 & 72; mem exec comt, Lehigh Co Dem Party, 71-; deleg, Dem Nat Mid-Term Conf, 74; comnr, Lehigh Co Charter Study Comn, 74- Bus & Prof Pos: Spec asst, State Attorney Gen Off, Calif, summer 55; attorney-at-law, Calif & Pa, 56-; prof law, Univ Calif, Los Angeles, 56-57; instr law, Northwestern Univ, 57-59. Publ: Freedom from arbitrary removal in the classified civil service—real or illusory & Changes in board interpretation, Sect 8(b) 4(A) Taft-Hartley, Northwestern Univ Law Rev, 55. Mem: Calif & Pa State Bar Asns. Relig: Jewish. Mailing Add: 1048 N 27th St Allentown PA 18104

ROTH, IRVING LEROY (D)
Wyo State Rep
b Warren, Ore, July 28, 26; s Severin Roth & Olga Matson R; m 1950 to Vera Louise Adams; c Larry Lee & Shelley Louise. Educ: Scappose High Sch. Polit & Govt Pos: Precinct committeeman, Sweetwater Co, Wyo, 54-; vchmn, Sweetwater Co Dem Party; vchmn, Sweetwater Co Recreation Bd, currently; vchmn, Castle Rock Hosp Dist, currently; Wyo State Rep, 73- Bus & Prof Pos: Pres, Adams Sales, Inc, Green River, Wyo, 60-74, chmn, 74- Mil Serv: Navy Construction Bn, 43-46. Mem: Elks; Masonic Blue Lodge; Korein Temple Shrine. Honors & Awards: Boy Scouts Am Century Club, 73. Relig: Union Congregational Church. Legal Res: 412 Tollgate Ave Rio Vista Green River WY Mailing Add: Box 432 Green River WY 82935

ROTH, TOBIAS A (R)
Wis State Rep
b Oct 10, 38; s Kasper Roth & Julia Roehrich R; m 1964 to Barbara Fischer; c Toby, Jr & Vickie. Educ: Marquette Univ, BA, 61. Polit & Govt Pos: Wis State Rep, 42nd Dist, 73- Mil Serv: Entered as Pvt, Army, 63, released as 1st Lt, 69, after serv in 44th Gen Hosp. Relig: Roman Catholic. Legal Res: 417 E Longview Dr Appleton WI 54911 Mailing Add: 1525 W Wisconsin Ave Appleton WI 54911

ROTH, WILLIAM VICTOR, JR (R)
US Sen, Del
b Great Falls, Mont, July 22, 21; s William V Roth, Sr & Clara Nelson R; m 1965 to Jane K Richards; c William V, III & Katharine Kellond. Educ: Univ Ore, BA, 44; Harvard Bus Sch, IA, 43, MBA, 47; Harvard Law Sch, LLB, 49. Polit & Govt Pos: Pres, State Fedn Young Rep of Del, 56-58; pres, New Castle Co Young Rep, Del, 59-60; chmn, Rep State Comt & mem, Rep Nat Comt, 61-64; chmn, Del Comn on Modernization of State Laws, 61-67; US Rep, Del, 67-70; US Sen, Del, 71- Bus & Prof Pos: Sr counsel, Hercules Inc, Wilmington, Del, 50-66. Mil Serv: Entered as Pvt, Army, 43, released as Capt, 46, after serv in Mil Intel, Psychol Warfare Br & Info Chief, Japanese Radio in Hq, Supreme Command Allied Powers. Am Theater Serv Medal; Asiatic Pac Serv Medal with 3 Bronze Stars; Bronze Star Medal; Distinguished Unit Citation; World War II Victory Medal; Army of Occup. Mem: Del State Bar; State Bar of Calif; Am Legion; VFW; Harvard Club of New York. Relig: Episcopal. Legal Res: Old Kennett Rd Wilmington DE 19807 Mailing Add: 4327 Dirksen Senate Off Bldg Washington DC 20510

ROTHMAN, KENNETH J (D)
Mo State Rep
b St Louis, Mo, Oct 11, 35; m 1965 to Geraldine Jaffe; c David Haron. Educ: Washington Univ, St Louis, AB, LLB; Sigma Alpha Mu; Phi Delta Phi; Eta Sigma Phi classical lang hon fraternity. Polit & Govt Pos: Asst prosecuting attorney, 59-61; pres, Hadley Twp Dem Club, 60-62; Mo State Rep, 62- Bus & Prof Pos: Attorney, pvt practice of law, 59- Mil Serv: Mo Air Nat Guard, 53-62; active duty, Berlin Crisis, 61-62. Mem: Mason. Relig: Jewish. Mailing Add: 90 Aberdeen Place Clayton MO 63105

ROTHROCK, THOMAS JEFFERSON (D)
Va State Deleg
b Monticello, Ind, Dec 20, 32; s John Allen Rothrock & Eva Friend R; m 1959 to Jeanette C Carroll; c Jefferson & Bradley. Educ: Univ Md, College Park, BS, 55; George Washington Univ Sch Law, JD, 61; Phi Eta Sigma; Scabbard & Blade; Delta Sigma Phi. Polit & Govt Pos: Mem, Arlington Co Dem Comt, 62-66; mem, Fairfax Co Planning Comn, 67-71; vchmn, Fairfax Co Dem Comt, 69-71; Va State Deleg, 71- Bus & Prof Pos: Pres, NVa Jr Bar Asn, 66-67; mem, Fairfax City CofC, 68-; pres, Fairfax Legal Aid Soc, 70-71. Mil Serv: Entered as 2nd Lt, Air Force, 55, released as 1st Lt, 57, after serv in Off Spec Invest. Relig: Protestant. Legal Res: 10820 Windermere Rd Fairfax Station VA 22039 Mailing Add: PO Box 325 Fairfax VA 22030

ROTHWELL, ROBERT LEE (D)
VChmn, Grant Co Dem Cent Comt, Nebr
b Hyannis, Nebr, June 15, 19; s George W Rothwell & Gladys N Crouch R; m 1943 to Ann T Yockey; c Robert G, John H, Rick T, George A & Lynne Ann. Educ: Univ Nebr, BSc in Agr, 40; Kappa Sigma; Block & Bridle Club. Polit & Govt Pos: Co comnr, Nebr, 49-57; mem, Exten Bd, 47-69; vchmn, Grant Co Dem Cent Comt, 50-; pres, Sandhills Fire Protection Dist, 58-73; secy, Grant Co Weed Dist, 66. Mil Serv: Entered as Pvt, Army Air Corps, 42, released as 1st Lt, 45. Mem: Nebr Stock Growers Asn; Sandhills CofC (pres, 68); Mason; Scottish Rite; Shrine. Mailing Add: Hyannis NE 69350

ROTTMANN, FRED EDWARD (R)
b Saginaw, Mich, Feb 17, 99; s Fred Rottmann & Lilly Ellen Wallin R; m 1970 to Henrietta S Schmohe Owlett Gordon; c Sgt Earl D. Educ: Bldg Foreman & Drafting Course, Chicago, 22 & 23. Polit & Govt Pos: Councilman from First Ward, City of Ithaca, NY, 40-43, supvr, 44-48; Rep precinct committeeman, Precinct 23, Pasco Co, Fla, 58-; bldg inspector, City of Port Richey, 60-63, city clerk, 62-65, mem, City Coun, 66-67, pres, 67; chmn, Pasco Co Rep Exec Comt, formerly. Bus & Prof Pos: Carpenter & builder, Mich & NY State, 14-32; roofing & remodeling, NY State, 32-56. Mem: F&AM; W Pasco Co Rep Club; Pioneer Fla Mus Asn, Inc. Honors & Awards: Resolution 15 for outstanding work as city clerk, Port Richey, Fla, 65, Resolution Four, Water Comnr & Pres, City Coun, 68. Relig: Lutheran. Mailing Add: 101 Boulevard Port Richey FL 33568

ROUDEBUSH, RICHARD L (R)
Adminr, Vet Admin
b Noblesville, Ind, Jan 18, 18; s Roy L Roudebush & Mae R; m to Marjorie Elliott; c Karen & Roy. Educ: Butler Univ, BS in Bus Admin, 41; Sigma Chi. Polit & Govt Pos: US Rep, Ind, 60-70; chmn, Vet Div, Rep Nat Comt; mem, Ind Rep Speakers Bur; cand, US Sen, 70; Asst Dep Adminr for Cong Rels, Vet Admin, 73-74, Adminr, 74- Bus & Prof Pos: Partner, Roudebush Comn Co, Indianapolis, Ind, formerly. Mil Serv: Army, 41-44; serv in Mid East, NAfrica & Italy; five Battle Stars. Mem: VFW (nat comdr, 57-58, Nat Chief of Staff, 54, State Comdr, 53-54, Dept Serv Officer, 8 years, State Legis Chmn, 3 years, State Poppy Chmn, 5 years); Am Legion; Amvets; Mason; Shrine. Honors & Awards: Cited by Fed Bur Invest Dir J Edgar Hoover & numerous groups, including Am for Const Action & Civic Affairs Asn. Relig: Refuge Christian Church. Legal Res: RR 3 Box 23-A Noblesville IN 46060 Mailing Add: Vet Admin Washington DC 20420

ROUNICK, JACK A (R)
b Philadelphia, Pa, June 5, 35; s Philip Rounick & Nettie Brownstein R; m 1970 to Noreen Anne Garrigan; c Ellen Lynn, Eric Scott & Amy Joy. Educ: Univ Mich, BBA, 56, Univ Pa, JD, 59; McKean Law Club. Polit & Govt Pos: Committeeman, Plymouth Twp Rep Party, Pa, 61-63; chmn, Norristown Young Rep, 62; mem & chmn, Plymouth Twp Indust Develop, 63-65; spec asst attorney gen, Pa, 63-71; finance chmn, Pa Young Rep, 64-66, treas, 66-68, chmn, 68-70; mem, Pa Rep Finance Comt, 64-70; mem, Pa Rep Exec Comt, 68-70; mem exec comt, Young Rep Nat Fedn, 69-71. Bus & Prof Pos: Attorney & partner, Israelit & Rounick, Ardmore, Pa, 60-67, Moss, Rounick & Hurowitz, Norristown, 68-73 & Pechner, Sacks, Dorfman, Rosen & Richardson, 73- Mem: Am, Pa & Montgomery Co Bar Asns; Practicing Law Inst; Exodus Lodge, B'nai B'rith. Relig: Jewish. Legal Res: 435 Militia Hill Rd Fort Washington PA 19034 Mailing Add: 68-70 E Penn St Norristown PA 19401

ROUNTREE, HERBERT HORTON (D)
NC State Rep
b Farmville, NC, May 5, 21; s Charles Stanley Rountree & Madeline V Horton R; m 1946 to Helen Elizabeth Lotz; c Kathryn, Dorene, Charles S, III & Mary Helen. Educ: Univ NC, AB, 43; Univ NC Law Sch, LLB, 50; Delta Theta Phi. Polit & Govt Pos: Solicitor, Pitt Co Recorder's Court, NC, 51-53; comnr, Farmville, 55-57; mem loan comt, State Employers Credit Union, 58-62; asst attorney gen, State of NC, 59-62; mem, Gov Indust Financing Study Group & NC Judicial Coun, 61-62; NC State Rep, Pitt Co, 67-; mem, Salvation Army Adv Bd & mem, NC Courts Comn, 69- Mil Serv: Entered as Aviation Cadet, Navy, 43, released as Lt(jg), 46, after serv in Pac, 45-46; Am & Pac Theater Ribbons. Mem: Am Judicature Soc; Kiwanis; Farmville Masonic Lodge 517, New Bern Consistory 3, AASR, Sudan Temple, AAONMNS of New Bern, NC; Farmville Am Legion Post 151; Greenville Lodge 885, Moose; Greenville Lodge 1645 Elks; Burnette-Rouse Post 9081, VFW. Honors & Awards: Outstanding Citizens Award, City of Greenville, NC, 71. Relig: Episcopal. Legal Res: 112 E Third St Greenville NC 27934 Mailing Add: 1209 Drexel Lane Greenville NC 27834

ROUNTREE, WILLIAM CLIFFORD
b Columbia, SC, Sept 24, 41; s William Clifford Rountree & Lila Odell Cowley R; m 1966 to Bonnie Beth Salisbury; c Scott William. Educ: Fla Southern Col, BA, 63; Vanderbilt Univ Sch Law, JD, 66; Omicron Delta Kappa; Phi Delta Phi; Pi Kappa Alpha (pres); Supreme Court Justice, Student Govt, Fla Southern Col, 62; Head coach, Vanderbilt Univ Soccer Team, 63-66. Polit & Govt Pos: Legis asst, Congressman John Dellenback, Ore, 69-71; minority counsel, Comt on Merchant Marine & Fisheries, US House Rep, 71-73; asst gen counsel for legis, US Dept Com, 73-75; asst dir, Fed Govt Affairs, Standard Oil Co (Ohio), 75- Bus & Prof Pos: Attorney, Law Firm of Reed, Smith, Shaw & McLay, Washington, DC, 68-69. Mil Serv: Entered as 2nd Lt, Army, 66, released as Capt, after serv in US Army Intel, US Army Intel Command, Baltimore, Md, 66-68; Capt, Army Res; Army Commendation Medal; numerous Letters of Commendation for exemplary performance of varied intelligence duties. Mem: Fla Southern Col Alumni Asn (vpres); Capitol Hill Chap, US Jaycees (chmn bd). Honors & Awards: Outstanding Graduating Sr, Pi Kappa Alpha, 63; Three Year Letterman, Varsity Soccer, Fla Southern Col, 59-63. Relig: Protestant. Mailing Add: 11622 Foxclove Rd Reston VA 22091

ROUNTREE, WILLIAM M
b Swainsboro, Ga, Mar 28, 17; m to Suzanne McDowall; c Susan. Educ: Columbus Univ, LLB, 41. Polit & Govt Pos: Acct-auditor, US Treas Dept, 35-41; budget officer, Off Lend-Lease Admin, 41-42; asst to dir, Am Econ Opers, Mid East, 42-45; career officer, Dept of State Foreign Serv, 46-, econ adv, Bur Near East, SAsian & African Affairs, 46-47, spec asst to Am Ambassador, Greece, 47-49, dir & dep dir, Off Greek, Turkish & Iranian Affairs, 49-52, counr, Ankara, 52-53, minister counr, Tehran, 53-55, dep asst secy for Near East, SAsian & African Affairs, 55-56, asst secy, 56-58, asst secy for Near Eastern & SAsian Affairs, 58-59; US Ambassador to Pakistan, 59-62, Sudan, 62-65, SAfrica, 65-70 & Brazil, 70-74. Honors & Awards: Superior Serv Award, 52; Nat Civil Serv League Career Serv Award, 57. Legal Res: FL Mailing Add: Dept of State Washington DC 20505

ROURKE, RAYMOND F (D)
Mass State Rep
Mailing Add: State Capitol Boston MA 02133

ROURKE, RUSSELL ARTHUR (R)
b New York, NY, Dec 30, 31; s Francis Xavier Rourke & Ethel Johnson R; m 1961 to Judith Anne Muller; c Patricia Anne, Elizabeth & Mary Frances. Educ: Univ Md, BA, 53; Georgetown Univ Law Sch, LLB, 59; Delta Theta Phi; Pi Sigma Alpha; Sigma Chi. Polit & Govt Pos: Admin asst to US Rep John R Pillion, 61-64 & US Rep Henry P Smith, III, 65-74; dep to presidential counsellor, John O Marsh, Jr, 74- Bus & Prof Pos: Law clerk, Keogh, Carey & Costello, 59-60. Mil Serv: Entered as Officer Cand, Marine Corps, 53, released as 1st Lt, 56, after serv in 1st Marine Aircraft Wing, Korea, 55; Lt Col, Marine Corps Res, 55-; Nat Defense Serv Medal. Mem: DC Bar Asn; Navy League; Univ Md Alumni Asn; ROA; Am Legion. Relig: Roman Catholic. Legal Res: Lewiston NY Mailing Add: The White House Washington DC 20500

ROUSAKIS, JOHN PAUL (D)
Mayor, Savannah, Ga
b Savannah, Ga, Jan 14, 29; s Paul V Rousakis & Antigone Alexopoulos R; m 1953 to Irene Fotopoulos; c Rhonda, Paul, Thea & Tina. Educ: Univ Ga, BBA, 52. Polit & Govt Pos: Comnr, Chatham Co, Ga, 65-70; Mayor, Savannah, Ga, 70-; mem bd dirs, Nat League Cities; co-chmn, Environ Quality Comt, US Conf Mayors, mem legis action comt, currently; vchmn, Coastal Area Planning & Develop Comn; mem, Mayors Adv Comt Nat Coun for Urban Econ Develop. Bus & Prof Pos: Self-employed ins broker, 53- Mil Serv: Entered as Pvt, Army, 53, released as Sgt, 56, after serv in Counter Intel Corps, Second Army. Mem: Sertoma; Ga Municipal Asn (first vpres); Ga Motion Picture & TV Adv Comt; Am Revolution Bicentennial (regional co-chmn); Shrine. Honors & Awards: Selected Outstanding Young Man of Savannah, 62; selected One of Five Outstanding Young Men in Ga, 62. Relig: Greek Orthodox. Legal Res: 1905 Colonial Dr Savannah GA 31406 Mailing Add: PO Box 1027 Savannah GA 31402

ROUSE, FRANKLIN ARTHUR (R)
b Lenoir Co, NC, June 3, 38; s Samuel Earl Rouse & Mary Linville R; wid; c Elizabeth Eaton (Betsy). Educ: Valdosta State Col, 56-57; NC State Univ, BSCE, 61; Sigma Phi Epsilon. Polit & Govt Pos: Pres, NC State Col Young Rep, 60-61; mem exec comt, Lenoir Co Rep Party, 70-71; mem exec comt, NC Rep Party, 70-71; chmn, Lenoir Co Young Rep Club, 70-71; orgn chmn, NC Fedn Young Rep, 70-71, exec secy, 71; chmn, NC Rep Party, 71-73. Bus & Prof Pos: Estimator-engr, Dickerson, Inc, Monroe, NC, 61-63; pres, SMS, Inc, Kinston, NC, 63-, Williams Concrete Prod Corp, 68- & Farvendco, Inc, 71- Mil Serv: Entered as Pvt, Marines, 59, released as Pfc, 65, after serv in active duty, 6 months, inactive Res, 5 years. Mem: Jaycees; Elks; Kinston Country Club. Honors & Awards: NC Grassroots Award, NC Fedn Young Rep, 70, Young Rep Man of Year, 71, Sr Party Award, 72. Relig: Baptist. Mailing Add: 2103 Stanton Rd Kinston NC 28501

ROUSE, FREDERICK OAKES (R)
Chmn, Great Lakes Basin Comn
b Bay City, Mich, Apr 10, 26; s Frederick Oliver Rouse & Margaret Oakes R; m 1951 to Barbara Ellen Henry; s Stephen, Mary & John. Educ: Port Huron Jr Col, AA, 48; Univ Mich, 48-49; Olivet Col, BA in Econ, 51; Scabbard & Blade; pres, Phi Alpha Pi, 50. Polit & Govt Pos: Precinct worker & deleg, Co Conv, 58-67; chmn, City of St Clair Rep Party, 60-63; mem, St Clair Co Bd of Supvrs, Mich, 61-70; deleg, Rep State Conv, 61-67, chmn, 65; chmn, St Clair Co Rep Comt, Mich, 63-69; deleg, Rep Nat Conv, 68; chmn, St Clair Co Bd of Comnrs, 69-70; app chmn, Great Lakes Basin Comn by President Nixon, 69- Bus & Prof Pos: Gen sales mgr, Marysville Printing Co, 56-58; sales rep, Esterling Tri-Craft Press, Inc, 58-61; vpres sales & mem bd dirs, Gilson Press, 61-64; exec vpres, gen mgr & mem bd dirs, Indust Printing Corp, 64-67; vpres, Acorn Press, 67-69. Mil Serv: Entered as Pvt, Army Air Force, 44, released as Cpl, 46, after serv in 9th Air Force, ETO, 44-46; Good Conduct Medal; ETO & Am Theatre Ribbons; Victory Medal; Army of Occup Medal. Mem: Adcraft Club of Detroit; Graphic Arts Asn of Mich; Rotary; Elks; Am Legion. Relig: Episcopal. Mailing Add: 729 N Riverside Ave St Clair MI 48079

ROUSE, STEWART A (D)
Vt State Rep
Mailing Add: PO Box 907 White River Junction VT 05001

ROUSEK, ROBERT RONALD (R)
Dir Commun, Rep Nat Comt
b Burwell, Nebr, Oct 15, 24; s Charles Henry Rousek & Emma Gross R; m 1951 to Jean Marie McDonald; c Kathleen Anne. Educ: Univ Omaha, BSc in Gen Educ. Polit & Govt Pos: Treas & vpres, Lake View Terr Rep Club, Calif, 66-68; alt mem, Los Angeles Co Rep Cent Comt, 67-69; mem, Rep State Cent Comt Calif, 69-73; Asst State Treas, Calif, 69-73; pres, Sierra Rep Orgn, 72-73; exec asst to co-chmn, Rep Nat Comt, 73-, dir commun, 73- Bus & Prof Pos: News exec, Int News Serv, 50-58; regional membership exec, The Assoc Press, 58-62; vpres, Kennett Pub Rels Assocs, Los Angeles, 62-65; pub rels acct dir, MacManus, John & Adams, Inc, Los Angeles, 65-69. Mil Serv: Entered as Seaman, Maritime Serv, 42, released as Ens, 45, after serv in Atlantic & Indian Oceans, 42-45. Relig: Roman Catholic. Mailing Add: 11201 Vale Rd Oakton VA 22124

ROUSH, GLENN ARTHUR (D)
Chmn, Glacier Co Dem Cent Comt, Mont
b Helena, Mont, Jan 25, 34; s Robert A Roush & Agnes Morgan R; m 1958 to Ardith Campbell; c Kay Leann, Ryan Robert, Neal John & Glenda Agnes. Educ: Cut Bank High Sch, grad, 52. Polit & Govt Pos: Secy-treas, Glacier Co Dem Cent Comt, Mont, 65-69, chmn, 69- Bus & Prof Pos: Gas well operator, prod & transmission, Mont Power Co, 55- Mil Serv: Entered as Pvt, Army, 53, released as Cpl, 55, after serv in Inf, US, 53-55; Good Conduct Medal. Mem: OCAWIU (pres, Dist 2, Coun, 72-73); Elks; Cut Bank Optimist Club; Cut Bank Quarterback Club. Relig: Lutheran. Legal Res: 121 Eighth Ave SE Cut Bank MT 59427 Mailing Add: Box 195 Cut Bank MT 59427

ROUSH, J EDWARD (D)
US Rep, Ind
b Barnsdall, Okla, Sept 12, 20; s Herman A Roush & Eva B Fisher R; m 1943 to Pauline Borton; c David, Joel, Melody & Robin. Educ: Huntington Col, AB, 42; Ind Univ Sch Law, LLB, 49; Phi Delta Phi. Polit & Govt Pos: Ind State Rep, 49-50; prosecuting attorney, Huntington Co, 54-58; US Rep, Fifth Dist, Ind, 59-68, US Rep, Fourth Dist, 70-; deleg, Dem Nat Conv, 68 & 72. Bus & Prof Pos: Mem bd trustees, Huntington Col, 49- Mil Serv: Entered as Pvt, Army, 42, released as Capt, 46, after serv in combat in Europe with 99th Inf Div; recalled to active duty, 50, released, 52; Maj, Army Res; Combat Inf Badge; Bronze Star Medal; Two Battle Stars; Am Theater, European Theater, Victory & Army of Occupation Ribbons. Mem: Am, Ind & Huntington Co Bar Asns; Am Legion; VFW. Relig: United Brethren in Christ. Mailing Add: 2340 College Ave Huntington IN 46750

ROUSSE, JEANNE LAURA (D)
Secy & Treas, Williamstown Dem Town Comt, Vt
b Williamstown, Vt, Feb 7, 16; d Hormidas J Rousse & Laura Longchamp R; single. Educ: Holy Ghost Convent, 30. Polit & Govt Pos: State committeeman, Vt Dem Party, 25 years; secy to Secy of State, Vt, 65 & Dep Secy of State, 65-69; secy & treas, Williamstown Dem Town Comt, 68-; secy, State Legis Coun, Vt, 69; asst, Coord Title IV Prog, Free Pub Libr, 69-; payroll supvr, Vt Treas Off, 69-; mem, Williamstown Planning Comn, 71-; mem, Cent Vt Planning Comn, 73-; mem, Pub Records Bd, State of Vt, 73-; mem, Orange Co Dem Comt, currently. Bus & Prof Pos: Clerk, Cert Div, Rock of Ages Corp, 42-65; local news reporter, Times-Argus, Barre, Vt, 12 years. Mem: Altrusa; Canadian Club; Red Cross vol, Cent Vt Hosp, Berlin. Honors & Awards: Good Neighbor Award, 55; Women Doers Award, Wash-Orange Co Dem Women's Club, 67; Bishop Fund Appeal Cert for active participation in diocesan prog for charities & develop, 68. Relig: Catholic. Legal Res: Cogswell Williamstown VT 05654 Mailing Add: Graniteville VT 05654

ROUSSEAU, LAURENT L (D)
RI State Sen
b Fall River, Mass, Mar 18, 44; s Roland A Rousseau & Lucienne Laliberte R; m 1967 to Jane D Chase; c Kathleen A, Jennifer C & Michael G. Educ: Providence Col, AB, 66; Notre Dame Law Sch, JD, 69; Delta Epsilon Sigma. Polit & Govt Pos: Mem & pres, Portsmouth Town Coun, RI, 70-74; RI State Sen, 74- Bus & Prof Pos: Attorney-at-law, Moore, Virgadamo, Boyle & Lynch, 69- Mem: KofC (Grand Knight, 74-); Rotary (treas, 75-); Am, RI & Newport Co Bar Asns. Relig: Roman Catholic. Mailing Add: 112 Watson Dr Portsmouth RI 20871

ROUSSEAU, OMER A (D)
NH State Rep
Mailing Add: 58 Sullivan St Claremont NH 03743

ROUSSELOT, JOHN HARBIN (R)
US Rep, Calif
b Los Angeles, Calif, Nov 1, 27; s Harbin Michon Rousselot & Mary Gibson R; c Craig Nobel, Robin Lee & Wendy Gibson. Educ: Principia Col, BA in Polit Sci & Bus Admin, 49. Polit & Govt Pos: Mem, Los Angeles Co Rep Cent Comt, Calif & vchmn, 55-58; deleg, Rep Nat Conv & pres, Calif Young Rep, 56; mem exec comt, State Rep Cent Comt Calif, 56-57 & 60-61; US Rep, 25th Dist, Calif, 61-63, US Rep, 24th Dist, Calif, 70-, mem, Comt on Banking & Currency, US House of Rep, 70-, mem, Post Off & Civil Serv Comts, currently. Bus & Prof Pos: Owner & pub rels consult, John H Rousselot & Assocs, 54-58; nat dir pub info, Fed Housing Admin, 58-60; nat dir pub rels, John Birch Soc, 63-66; publ, Am Opinion Mag, 64-; mgr consult, 67- Mem: Nat Press Club; Capitol Hill Soc; Pub Rels Soc of Am. Relig: Church of Christ, Scientist. Legal Res: 735 W Duarte Rd Suite 403 Arcadia CA 91006 Mailing Add: 1706 Longworth House Off Bldg Washington DC 20515

ROUTHIER, DONALD ROLAND (D)
b Somersworth, NH, Apr 25, 52; s Roland Routhier & Verta Ferland R; single. Educ: Univ NH, currently; Phi Kappa Theta; univ sen, mem senate judiciary comt. Polit & Govt Pos: Dem ward representative, Somersworth, NH, 71-; youth coordr, Somersworth Dem Party, 71-; co-chmn, McGovern for President, Somersworth, NH Primary & Gen Elec, 72; alt deleg, Dem Nat Conv, 72; mem, El Regional Planning Comn, 72. Relig: Roman Catholic. Mailing Add: 303 Main St Somersworth NH 03878

ROUTON, BONNIE ANTHONY (R)
Finance Chairwoman, Hempstead Co Rep Comt, Ark
b Murfreesboro, Ark, Jan 15, 30; d Graydon William Anthony & Nina Nelms A; m 1949 to William Ralph Routon; c William Ralph, Stephen Anthony, Jane Marie & John Graydon Nelms. Educ: Monticello Col, 47-49; Henderson State Teachers Col, 49-51. Polit & Govt Pos: Charter mem, Hempstead Co Rep Women, Ark, 53; comt chmn, Hempstead Rep Women, 60-69; finance chmn, Hempstead Co Rep Comt, 66 & 69, campaign mgr, 66-68, finance chairwomen, 68-; alt deleg, Rep Nat Conv, 68; sponsor, TAR, 69. Bus & Prof Pos: Reporter, Hope J, 49; asst to coordr, Hope Pub Schs, 50-51. Mem: Ark Arts Ctr; Hempstead Co Rep Women; Hope Country Club; Great Decisions; PTA. Relig: Methodist. Mailing Add: 601 E 14th Hope AR 71801

ROUYER, ALWYN R (D)
Mem, Idaho State Dem Cent Comt
b New Orleans, La, Nov 3, 41; s Alwyn R Rouyer & Claire Puyaer R; m 1965 to Catherine Rice; c Cathlene & Anne. Educ: Univ Southwestern La, BA, 63; Georgetown Univ, MA, 66; Tulane Univ, PhD, 71; Delta Sigma Phi. Polit & Govt Pos: Deleg, Dem Mid-Term Conf, 74; mem, Idaho State Dem Cent Comt, 75- Bus & Prof Pos: Prof, Univ Idaho, 70- Publ: Co-auth, Social, Economy & Voting Characteristics of Idaho Precincts, Univ Idaho Research Found, 73; auth, Political recruitment and political change in Kenya, J Developing Areas, 75. Mem: Am & Idaho Polit Sci Asns; Am Fedn Teachers. Legal Res: 415 N Hayes Moscow ID 83843 Mailing Add: Dept of Polit Sci Univ Idaho Moscow ID 83843

ROVE, KARL CHRISTIAN (R)
Chmn, Col Rep Nat Comt
b Denver, Colo, Dec 25, 50; s Louis Claude Rove & Reba Wood R; single. Educ: Univ Utah, 69-71; George Mason Univ, 73-75; Pi Kappa Alpha-Alpha Tau Chap. Polit & Govt Pos: Exec dir, Col Rep Nat Comt, Washington, DC, 71-73, chmn, 73-; mem exec comt, Rep Nat Comt, 73-, spec asst to chmn, 74-75, spec asst to co-chmn, 75-; spec asst, Dir Polit Research Div, 75; legis asst to US Rep Richard Mallary, Vt, 73-74; mem, Rule 29 Comt, Rep Reform Comn, 73-75. Mem: Royal Trampoline Soc. Relig: Lutheran. Legal Res: 112 N Patrick St Alexandria VA 22314 Mailing Add: 310 First St SE Washington DC 20003

ROVNER, ROBERT ALLEN (R)
b Philadelphia, Pa, Sept 28, 43; s Edward H Rovner; m 1965 to Susan Cohen; c Steven & Daniel. Educ: Temple Univ, BS, 65, Law Sch, JD, 68; pres, Student Body, 64-65, pres, Law Sch Student Body, 67-68; Tau Epsilon Rho; Alpha Phi Omega. Polit & Govt Pos: Asst Dist Attorney, Philadelphia, Pa, 68-70; Pa State Sen, Sixth Dist, 70-74, chmn, Statewide Comt that successfully repealed sales tax on text books; statewide chmn, Young Voters to Reelect

the President Comt, Pa, 72; deleg, Rep Nat Conv, 72. Bus & Prof Pos: Attorney-at-law; lectr, Temple Univ & Nat Inst for Admin of Justice. Mem: Mason; KofP; Masonic Law Enforcement Lodge; Lt Charles Freedman Post 706; Philadelphia Jaycees. Honors & Awards: Golden Slipper Young Achiever Award, 72; Winged Foot Award & Man of the Year, Eastern Pa Podiatry Asn, 72; First Hon Mem, Our Lady of Consolation Holy Name Soc; Oxford Circle Realty Serv Award & Hon Lifetime Mem, 72; Man of the Year, B'nai B'rith Law Enforcement Lodge, 73. Legal Res: 9675 Sandanne Rd Philadelphia PA 19115 Mailing Add: One Bustleton Pike Feasterville PA 19047

ROWAN, CARL THOMAS (INDEPENDENT)
b Ravenscroft, Tenn, Aug 11, 25; s Thomas David Rowan & Johnnie Bradford R; m 1950 to Vivien Louise Murphy; c Barbara, Carl Thomas & Geoffrey. Educ: Tenn State Univ, 42-43; Washburn Univ, 43-44; Oberlin Col, AB, 47; Univ Minn, MA, 48. Hon Degrees: LittD, Simpson Col, 57, Hamline Univ, 58, Oberlin Col, 62, Col Wooster, 68 & Drexel Inst Technol, 69; LHD, Washburn Univ, 64, Talladega Col, 65, St Olaf Col & Knoxville Col, 66; LLD, Howard Univ, Alfred Univ & Temple Univ, 64, Atlanta Univ, 65, Allegheny Col, 66, Colby Col, 69 & Univ Notre Dame, 73; DPA, Morgan State Col, 64; Elijah P Lovejoy fel, Colby Col, 68. Polit & Govt Pos: Dep Asst Secy of State for Pub Affairs, Dept of State, 61-63; US Ambassador, Finland, 63-64; dir, US Info Agency, 64-65. Bus & Prof Pos: Copywriter, Minneapolis Tribune, 48-50, staff writer, 50-61; columnist, Chicago Daily News, Publ Newspaper Syndicate, 65- Publ: South of Freedom, 52; The Pitiful & the Proud, 56; Go South to Sorrow, 57. Honors & Awards: Contrib to Am Democracy Award, Roosevelt Univ, 64; Distinguished Serv Award, Capital Press Club, 64; Nat Brotherhood Award, Nat Conf Christians & Jews, 64; Am Southern Regional Press Inst Award, 65; Liberty Bell Award, Howard Univ, 65. Mailing Add: 3116 Fessenden St NW Washington DC 20008

ROWAN, JOHN PATRICK (D)
Mem, Queens Co Dem Exec Comt, NY
b New York, NY, Sept 18, 45; s Patrick J Rowan & Dorothy W McLaughlin R; single. Educ: Queens Col, BA, 71; Hunter Col, MS, 73; Pi Sigma Alpha; Polit Sci Club; Vietnam Vet Against the War. Polit & Govt Pos: Mem, Queens Co Dem Exec Comt, NY, 72-; deleg, Queens Co Judicial Conv, 72-74; NY state dir, Vets for McGovern, 72; community bd coordr to Borough Pres Robert Abrams, Bronx, 73; community liaison to Congressman Benjamin S Rosenthal, 73-; deleg, Dem Nat Mid-Term Conf, 74. Bus & Prof Pos: Long line technician, Am Tel & Tel, 64-69; urban corp worker, Addiction Serv Agency, 70. Mil Serv: Entered as Airman, Air Force, 65, released as Sgt, 67, after serv in Security Serv, US, Japan & Vietnam, 67; Nat Serv Medal; Vietnam Serv Medal. Publ: Co-auth, The Vietnam veteran blues, NY Times, 3/74. Mem: Am for Dem Action (nat bd); Am Legion; Cath War Vet; Community Planning Bd; Woodside-Elmhurst Dem Club. Relig: Roman Catholic. Mailing Add: 42-65 80th St Elmhurst NY 11373

ROWE, AUBY, JR (D)
Ark State Rep
b Magnolia, Ark, June 2, 19; s Auby Rowe & Ruth Linton R; m 1943 to Billye Gibson; c Auby, III, Tim & Barbara. Educ: Southern State Col, 39-40. Polit & Govt Pos: Mem Magnolia City Coun, Ark, 50-51; Ark State Rep, 71- Bus & Prof Pos: Explor mgr, McAlester Fuel Co, 22 years; self employed, oil oper, lease broker & real estate broker, currently. Mil Serv: Entered as Pvt, Army, 40, released as Capt, 48, after serv in Alaska & Europe, 41-42, 44-45; Purple Heart; Bronze Star. Mem: Am Asn Petrol Landmen; Independent Producers Asn Am; Mason; Am Legion. Relig: Baptist. Legal Res: 1608 S Lakewood Magnolia AR 71753 Mailing Add: PO Box 786 Magnolia AR 71753

ROWE, HARRIS (R)
Chmn, Morgan Co Rep Cent Comt
b Jacksonville, Ill, 1923; m to Alice Mary R; c Sally, Mary & Millicent. Educ: Ill Col; Northwestern Univ Law Sch. Polit & Govt Pos: Alderman, Jacksonville, Ill, 8 years; former Ill State Rep; chmn, Morgan Co Rep Cent Comt & mem, Ill Rep State Cent Comt, currently. Bus & Prof Pos: Attorney & ins exec. Mem: Morgan Co Polio Found (chmn); Kiwanis; Mason; Elks; Am Legion. Relig: Presbyterian. Mailing Add: 1152 W State Jacksonville IL 62650

ROWE, HORTENSE C MILLIGAN (R)
VChmn, Rep Party, VI
b Frederiksted, St Croix, VI, Oct 21, 38; d Hugh Milligan & Marie Sackey M; div; c Marc Alyn. Educ: Inter-Am Univ, PR, BA, 62; Caribbean Orgn. Polit & Govt Pos: Acct, VI Corp, VI Dept Interior, 62-64; vchmn, Rep Party, VI, 68-; mem, VI Comn on Status of Women, 69-71; mem, VI Small Bus Develop Agency, 70-74; VI comnr, Conserv & Cult Affairs, 72-75. Bus & Prof Pos: Acct & off mgr, Harvlan, Inc, 64-68; acct, Andreas Esberg & Co, 68-; acct, Alan Bronstein & Co, 69, resident mgr, 69-; chmn & mem bd dirs, St Croix Community Econ Develop Corp Inc, 72-; vchmn & mem bd dirs, Tri-Island Econ Develop Coun, Inc, 72- Mem: Bus & Prof Women's Club; Fedn Bus & Prof Women's Clubs (vpres, 69-71); VI Businessmen's Asn (bd dirs, treas, 72-); Friends of Denmark Soc; St Croix Community Theatre. Relig: Roman Catholic. Mailing Add: PO Box 194 Frederiksted St Croix VI 00840

ROWE, MARIE RICH (R)
VChmn, Mecklenburg Co Rep Party, NC
b Rock Hill, SC, May 19, 08; d William Thomas Rich & Ennis Culler R; m 1928 to Oliver Reagan Rowe; c O Reagan, Jr, Lynda (Mrs Rankin) & Ralph Burnett (deceased). Educ: Univ NC, Greensboro, 25-28; Univ NC, Chapel Hill, BS in Pub Admin, 34; Adelphian Soc. Polit & Govt Pos: Cand, NC State Rep, 58; pres, Mecklenburg Co Rep Women's Club, 58-60; precinct committeewoman, Mecklenburg Co Rep Party, 58-68, vchmn for spec events, 68 & 69, vchmn, Party, 72-, finance chmn, currently; mem, Eisenhower's Comt of 44 on Prog & Progress, 59; dist rep, NC Fedn of Rep Women, 60-64, area vpres, 64-68, pres-elect, 68, pres, 69-; alt deleg-at-lg, Rep Nat Conv, 68; mem, Mayor's Comt City Develop of a Govt Ctr, 68; mem, NC Rep State Cent Comt, 68-69; NC state chmn, Nixon's Cult & Fine Arts Comt, 68-69; state chmn, Hostess-Tel Comt, Reelect Nixon Comt, 72; deleg, Rep Nat Conv, 72; mem steering comt, Rep Gov Elect, 72. Mem: NC Award Comn (chmn, 74-); Teen-Age Summer Employ (Mecklenburg Co chmn); Am Asn Univ Women; Salvation Army Auxiliary (pres, 75-); life mem Charity League, Inc. Honors & Awards: Sr Rep Party Award, NC Young Rep, 75. Relig: Methodist; Bd trustees, Myers Park United Methodist Church. Mailing Add: 2823 Providence Rd Charlotte NC 28211

ROWELL, EDWARD LEONIDAS (R)
Exec Committeeman, SC Rep Party
b Tampa, Fla, July 31, 28; s Elijah Hendrix Rowell & Sallie Bass R; m 1954 to Etta Mae Charpia; c Sallie Elizabeth, Hendrix Leonidas, Marcus Pinckney & Melinda Lucille, stepchildren, Lloyd Dean Clayton, Wanda Marie (Mrs Veno) & Deborah Jean (Mrs McNeil). Educ: Baptist Col at Charleston, 71- Polit & Govt Pos: Exec committeeman, SC Rep Party, Dorchester Co, 72- Bus & Prof Pos: Tool engr, Artex Corp, Summerville, SC, 56; plant engr, Bird & Son, Charleston, 57; chief engr & opers mgr, Craver Industs, 57-60; owner & gen mgr, Pyramid Enterprises, Summerville, 60- Mil Serv: Entered as Seaman Recruit, Navy, 50, released as Machinist Mate 1/C, 54, after serv in USS Harry F Bauer DM 26, Atlantic Mine Force, 51-54; Good Conduct Medal. Mem: Am Inst Indust Engrs (pres, SC Low Country Chap 151, 70-71); Soc Mfg Engrs; AF&AM (worshipful master, 66-67). Relig: Protestant. Mailing Add: Rte 1 Box 365 Summerville SC 29483

ROWELL, JAMES VICTOR (R)
Exec Committeewoman, SC Rep State Comt
b Trio, SC, Sept 18, 39; s Ervin Robert Rowell & Hallie Boykin R; m 1963 to Pearl Casselman; c Linda Karen. Educ: Univ SC, 3 years. Polit & Govt Pos: SC State Rep, 69-72; exec committeeman, SC Rep State Comt, 74- Bus & Prof Pos: Mgr, Rowell Bros, Trio, 62-66, owner, 66- Mem: Mason; Jr CofC. Relig: Methodist. Legal Res: Trio SC 29595 Mailing Add: PO Box 208 Trio SC 29595

ROWELL, RUTH ELIZABETH (R)
NH State Rep
b Everett, Mass, June 12, 27; d Fielding Taylor & Agnes Anderson T; m 1947 to Edward Richard Rowell; c Julie Anne, Jane Elizabeth, Thomas Richard, Timothy Earle, Stephen Taylor & Peter Edward & Patricia & Fred Riley. Educ: Univ NH, 44-46; Theta Upsilon. Polit & Govt Pos: NH State Rep, 73- Bus & Prof Pos: Bookkeeper, Barrington Sch Dist, NH, 61-71 & Leon C Calef Inc, Barrington, 64-72. Mem: Order Women Legislators; Pioneer Girls. Relig: Evangelical Free Church. Mailing Add: PO Box 13 Barrington NH 03825

ROWEN, ELIZABETH GORE (R)
Mem, State Rep Cent Comt Calif
b Marks, Miss, Jan 30, 20; d Weaver Ellis Gore & Bessie Griffin G; m 1942 to James Alan Rowen; c Diane (Mrs Stephen R Adams) & Patricia (Mrs R P Ritter, Jr). Educ: Hinds Jr Col, Raymond, Miss, 2 years. Polit & Govt Pos: First Cong Dist dir, Calif Rep Assembly, 65 & 66, dir-at-lg, 69; assoc mem, State Rep Cent Comt Calif, 67, mem, 68-69 & 73-; precinct chmn, Marin Co Rep Cent Comt, 67-68, vchmn comt, 70-73, alt mem, 73-; comnr, Calif Hosp Comn, 72-; Marin bd mem, Bay Area Social Planning Coun, 73; bd mem, Marin Rep Coun, 73. Mem: Marin Coalition (exec comt mem, 74); San Francisco Home Health Serv (bd mem, 75); Eastern Star; Napa State Hosp, Adv Bd for the Ment Disordered (chmn, Canteen Bd, 70-); Marin Federated Rep Women. Honors & Awards: Cert of Appreciation, Girl Scouts, 61; Grand Cross of Colors, Order of Rainbow for Girls, 63; Selected as Woman of Year, Marin Charter Chap, Am Bus Women's Asn, 65. Relig: Protestant. Mailing Add: 360 Johnstone Dr San Rafael CA 94903

ROWLAND, JOHN PATRICK (R)
b El Monte, Calif, July 12, 37; s Thomas A Rowland & Erma M Cole R; m 1961 to Virginia Annette Patton; c Thomas A, Carrie A & Colleen V. Educ: Univ Southern Calif, BS, 59, MBA, 60; Beta Gamma Sigma; Tau Kappa Epsilon; Pi Sigma Epsilon. Polit & Govt Pos: Admin asst to US Rep Charles E Wiggins, Calif, 69- Bus & Prof Pos: Reporter, El Monte Herald, Calif, 58-60, advert prom mgr, 60-61; mgr, El Monte-South El Monte CofC, 61-67; dir cong action, US CofC, Washington, DC, 67-69. Mil Serv: M/Sgt, PIO, Calif Nat Guard, 55-63. Mem: Cong Secy Club; KofC; Boys Club San Gabriel Valley. Honors & Awards: Tom May Mkt Award; Am Mkt Award; Young Man of the Year Award, El Monte, 63. Relig: Catholic. Legal Res: 1005 Greendale West Covina CA 91791 Mailing Add: 2315 Jackson Pkwy Vienna VA 22180

ROWLAND, MICHAEL YOUNG (D)
Tenn State Rep
b Knoxville, Tenn, Sept 6, 42; s Elmo Rowland & Ernest Lou Young; m 1968 to Elizabeth Ann Noblett. Educ: E Tenn State Univ, BA, 64; Univ Tenn Col Law, Knoxville, JD, 70; Pi Gamma Mu. Polit & Govt Pos: Dem nominee & cand for state rep, Dist 18, Tenn, 72; deleg, Dem Nat Conv, 72; Tenn State Rep, 75- Bus & Prof Pos: Attorney-at-law assoc, Haynes, Gilreath & Cary, Knoxville, 71-72; attorney-at-law, Gilreath, Carpenter, Rowland & O'Conner, Knoxville, 73- Mil Serv: Entered as 2nd Lt, Army, 64, released as Capt, 68, after serv in 1st Inf Div, SVietnam & 8th Inf Div, Ger, 64-68; Capt, Inactive Res, 7 years; Army Commendation Medal; Combat Infantryman Badge; Ranger Tab; Airborne Wings; Bronze Star with Two Oak Leaf Clusters. Mem: Knoxville Barrister's Club; Knoxville, Tenn & Am Bar Asns; Am & Tenn Trial Lawyers Asns. Relig: Protestant. Mailing Add: 707 Gay St SW Knoxville TN 37902

ROWLEY, BERT WALLACE (D)
La State Rep
Mailing Add: 2512 Rosetta Dr Chalmette LA 70043

ROWLEY, EVELYN FISH (R)
Chmn, Morris Rep Town Comt, Conn
b Southington, Conn, Mar 15, 27; d J Hamilton Fish & Hazel Shepard F; m 1956 to James William Rowley; c James E, (Jed), Eileen Harriet & Corinne Elizabeth. Educ: Univ Conn, BS, 49; Block & Bridle Club. Polit & Govt Pos: Vchmn, Morris Rep Town Comt, Conn, 64-66, chmn, 66-; deleg or alt deleg, Cong, Sen or Assembly Dist Conv, 65, 66, 67 & 68; deleg, Conn Rep State Conv, 66, 67, 68, 69 & 70; mem, Litchfield Co Rep Orgn, currently; Justice of Peace, 65-71; secy, Morris Youth Adv Coun, 71-; mem, Bd Tax Rev, 72- Mem: Litchfield Co Tax Off; Morris Youth Adv Coun (chmn, 72-); charter mem Morris Thrift Shop Comt; Morris Friendly Serv; Morris Serv Unit, Salvation Army (secy). Relig: Episcopal. Mailing Add: Straits Turnpike Lane Morris CT 06763

ROY, WILLIAM ROBERT (D)
b Bloomington, Ill, Feb 23, 26; s Elmer Javan Roy & Edna Blanche Foley R; m 1947 to Jane Twining Osterhoudt; c Robin Jo, Randall Jay, Richelle Jane, William Robert, Jr, Renee Jan & Rise Javan. Educ: Ill Wesleyan Univ, BS, 46; Northwestern Univ Med Sch, BMed, 48, MD, 49; Washburn Univ Sch Law, JD with honors, 70; Am Bd Obstet & Gynec, dipl; Sigma Chi. Polit & Govt Pos: Deleg, White House Conf Children & Youth, 60; US Rep, Kans, 71-74; Dem cand, US Senate, Kans, 74; ex officio deleg, Dem Nat Mid-Term Conf, 74. Bus & Prof Pos: Intern, Evanston Hosp Asn, 49-50; resident obstet & gynec, City of Detroit Receiving Hosp & Wayne State Univ, 50-53; pres, Stormont Vail Hosp Med Staff, 65-66; mem clin fac, Kans Univ Med Sch. Mil Serv: Entered as Lt, Air Force, 53, released as Capt, 55, after serv in US, 53-55. Publ: Article in Washburn Univ Sch Law, spring 70; The Proposed Health Maintenance Organization Act of 1972, 72. Mem: Shawnee Co Med Soc; Kans Obstet Soc;

Kans Med Soc (mem house of deleg, 5 times, chmn reference comts & vspeaker of house, chmn comn on educ); Kansas City Gynecologic Soc; fel Am Col Obstet & Gynec. Honors & Awards: One of estimated 210 people in US & only person in Cong to ever serve with both Med & Law degrees. Relig: Methodist; Chmn social concerns work area, First United Methodist Church, Topeka; mem expenditures comt, Kans Conf Fund for Reconciliation of United Methodist Church. Mailing Add: 909 Topeka Blvd Topeka KS 66612

ROYALL, KENNETH CLAIBORNE, JR (D)
NC State Sen
b Warsaw, NC, Sept 2, 18; s Kenneth Claiborne Royall & Margaret Pierce Best R; m 1945 to Julia Bryan Zollicoffer; c Kenneth C, III, Jere Zollicoffer & Julia Bryan. Educ: Univ NC, AB, 40; Univ Va Law Sch, 40-41; Wake Forest Col Law Sch, 41-42; Delta Kappa Epsilon. Polit & Govt Pos: Mem, Durham Co Sch Bd, 57-66, chmn, 59-66; NC State Rep, 67-72, chmn, subcomt health, NC House Rep, 69, chmn, Appropriations Comt, NC House Rep, 71-72; mem, NC Legis Bldg Gov Comn, 67-72; NC State Sen, 73- Bus & Prof Pos: Owner retail furniture store. Mil Serv: Entered as Pvt, Marine Corps, 42, released as Maj, 45, after serv in 2nd Bn, 3rd Marine Corps, SPac; Bronze Star with Combat V. Mem: Southern Retail Furniture Asn; NC Merchants Asn (dir); Rotary; Elks; Durham CofC (dir, 62-73, vpres, 72-). Relig: Episcopal; Jr Warden, 59, Sr Warden, 64; Mem vestry, 3 terms. Legal Res: 64 Beverly Dr Durham NC 27707 Mailing Add: PO Box 8766 FH Sta Durham NC 27707

ROYBAL, BEN (D)
NMex State Rep
Mailing Add: 301 Second SW Albuquerque NM 87101

ROYBAL, EDWARD R (D)
US Rep, Calif
b Albuquerque, NMex, Feb 10, 16; m 1940 to Lucille Beserra; c Lucille, Lillian & Edward R, Jr. Educ: Univ Calif, Los Angeles; Southwestern Univ. Hon Degrees: LLD, Pac States Univ. Polit & Govt Pos: Mem, Los Angeles City Coun, Calif, 49-62, pres pro tempore, 61-62; US Rep, Calif, 62- Bus & Prof Pos: With Civilian Conserv Corps until 35; dir health educ, Los Angeles Co Tuberc & Health Asn, 42-49; social worker & pub health educator, Calif Tuberc Asn; pres, Eastland Savings & Loan Asn. Mil Serv: Army, 44-45. Mem: KofC; Am Legion. Relig: Catholic. Legal Res: Los Angeles CA Mailing Add: US House of Rep 2404 Rayburn Bldg Washington DC 20515

ROYCE, FREDERICK HENRY (R)
Chmn, Clallam Co Rep Cent Comt, Wash
b Sheboygan, Wis, May 17, 34; s Frank F Royce & Caroline Pungarcher R; m 1955 to Carol Morgan; c Fred, Jr, Arthur & Susan. Educ: Univ Wis-Madison, BS, 56; Alpha Phi Omega. Polit & Govt Pos: Precinct committeeman, Clallam Co Rep Cent Comt, Wash, 66-74, orgn chmn, 68-70, state committeeman, 72-73, chmn, 75- Bus & Prof Pos: Process engr, ITT Rayonier Inc, 56-63, asst tech supt, 65-71 & tech supt, 71-; develop engr, Wis Alumni Research Found, 63-65. Mem: Am Inst Chem Engrs; Tech Asn Pulp & Paper Indust; Citizens Adv Group for Schs (vpres, 70); Port Angeles Symphony Bd Dirs (pres, 72-74). Relig: Episcopal. Mailing Add: 326 W Columbus Ave Port Angeles WA 98362

ROYSE, ALVIN LEE (R)
NDak State Rep
b Bismarck, NDak, Jan 29, 50; s Homer L Royse & Gladys Hepper R; single. Educ: Bismarck Jr Col, AAA, 70; Univ NDak, BSBA in Acct & Bus Law, summa cum laude, 72, MS in Acct & Bus Law, 73; Beta Alpha Psi (vpres); Phi Theta Pi; Sigma Alpha Epsilon (pres); Blue Key; Circle K. Polit & Govt Pos: State chmn, NDak Col Rep, 70-71; mem, NDak Rep Exec Comt, 70-71; mem, Dept of Youth Affairs, NDak Rep Party, 71; deleg, Young Rep Nat Conv, 71 & 73; deleg, NDak Rep State Conv, 72; youth coordr, Larsen for Gov, 72; NDak State Rep, Dist 34, 72-; nat committeeman, Young Rep, 73. Bus & Prof Pos: Instr econ, Bismarck Jr Col, NDak, 73-; acct, Royse Produce, Inc, Mandan, 73- Mem: Am Asn Acct; Elks; NDak Jaycees. Honors & Awards: Wall St Journal Award, Univ NDak, 72; Grad Sr of Year in Bus, Delta Sigma Phi, 72; Outstanding Freshman Rep, Grand Forks Herald, 73. Relig: Protestant. Legal Res: Box 9 Rte 1 Mandan ND 58554 Mailing Add: 715 N 40th Apt 308J Grand Forks ND 58201

RUANE, J MICHAEL (D)
Mass State Rep
Mailing Add: State Capitol Boston MA 02133

RUANE, PAUL G (R)
Chmn, Northumberland Co Rep Party, Pa
b Carbondale, Pa, July 31, 33; s Joseph Ruane & Mary Burke R; m 1963 to Anita Ellen Barni; c Paul Patrick & Susan. Educ: EStroudsburg State Col, BS in Educ, 55; Bucknell Univ, MS in Educ, 59. Polit & Govt Pos: Pa State Rep, until 74; chmn, Northumberland Co Rep Party, Pa, 75- Mil Serv: Entered as Pvt, Army, 55, released as Cpl, after serv in Nike Guided Missile Ban, Milwaukee, Wis, 57; Sgt, Army Res, 59; Good Conduct Medal. Mem: Pa State & Nat Educ Asns; Elks; CWV; KofC. Relig: Roman Catholic. Mailing Add: 415 Banyan St Shamokin PA 17872

RUANE, ROBERT M (D)
NJ State Assemblyman
Mailing Add: State House Trenton NJ 08625

RUBEL, RANDY LEE (D)
Chairperson, Jackson Co Dem Cent Comt, Iowa
b Bellevue, Iowa, Feb 23, 51; s Leo Charles Rubel & Darlene Michels R; single. Educ: Loras Col, BA, 73; Delta Epsilon Sigma. Polit & Govt Pos: Precinct chmn, Jackson Twp, 72-74; chairperson, Jackson Co Dem Cent Comt, 74- Mem: Bellevue KofC (Grand Knight, 74-); Bellevue Jaycees; Bellevue Ambulance Vol. Honors & Awards: Maxima Cum Laude Grad & Regents scholar, Loras Col; State of Iowa scholar. Relig: Roman Catholic. Mailing Add: 111 1/2 N Second Bellevue IA 52031

RUBEN, IDA GASS (D)
Md State Deleg
b Washington, DC, Jan 7, 29; d Sol Gass & Sonia E Darman G; m 1948 to L Leonard Ruben; c Garry, Michael, Scott & Stephen. Educ: Univ WFla, Univ Pittsburgh, Temple Univ & Western Md Col, seminars & workshops in human rels, group dynamics, leadership training, orgn develop & consult, sensitivity training, prob-solving & decision-making, behav modifications & psychol of personality. Polit & Govt Pos: Precinct coordr, Tydings for Senate, active in Johnson for President & mem, Inaugural Ball Comt for Johnson-Humphrey, 64; mem, Sickles for Gov Comt, advan for Attorney Gen & Comptroller Cand in Montgomery Co, 66; co-chairperson, Montgomery Co for Washington Metrop VPresident Humphrey Birthday party, off asst, Humphrey for President Montgomery Co, Humphrey for President Comt Statewide fund-raiser, citizens for Humphrey Comt, Housewives for Humphrey Comt, chairperson, Humphrey Fashions & Lunch & active in Schweinhaut for Cong, 68; active in Tydings for Senate, Boggs for Cong & Dem for the 70's, 70; chairperson, 3B Caucus Fund Raiser McGovern for President, 72; chairperson, Annual Montgomery Co Dem Ball, mem, Eastern Montgomery-Kensington-Wheaton Dem Club, Western Suburban Dem Club, Women's Suburban Dem Club, Women's Polit Caucus of Md & Women's Polit Caucus of Montgomery Co, 73; Md State Deleg, Dist 20, 75- Bus & Prof Pos: Admin & legal secy, Dept of Justice, 47-51. Mem: B'nai B'rith Women (mem, int bd, currently, conduct & moderate leadership training & community serv workshops, 60-); DC Legal Aid Soc; Anti-Defamation League Regional Bd; Jewish Mem Hosp Asn (exec bd mem); Serv Guild of Washington. Relig: Jewish. Mailing Add: 11 Schindler Ct Silver Spring MD 20903

RUBEN, ROBERT CHARLES (D)
b Minneapolis, Minn, Feb 16, 23; s Albert G Ruben & Ruth Bachman R; m 1946 to Margit Marquis; c Katherine & Peter Charles. Educ: Univ Ore, 1 year; Santa Monica Jr Col, ABA, 42; Ariz State Teachers Col, 1 year. Polit & Govt Pos: Admin asst to US Rep James C Corman, 69- Mil Serv: Entered as A/S, Navy, 41, released as Lt(jg), 46, after serv in Naval Res, Pac Theatre, 45-46. Mem: Nat Asn Broadcast Engrs & Technicians. Mailing Add: 4137 Woodbine St Chevy Chase MD 20015

RUBENFELD, ABBY ROSE (D)
b Oneonta, NY, Oct 10, 53; d Milton Rubenfeld & Judy Rosen R; single. Educ: Princeton Univ, 75; pres, class of 75, 71-72. Polit & Govt Pos: Alt deleg, Dem Nat Conv, 72. Bus & Prof Pos: Coordr, Nat Women's Rowing Asn Nat Championship Regatta, 75. Mem: Friends of Princeton Women's Rowing (founder & pres, 73-); Mercer Co Women's Polit Caucus (coordr, 72). Honors & Awards: Outstanding Mem, Keyettes, 71. Relig: Jewish. Mailing Add: 2168 Sparrow Ct Sarasota FL 33579

RUBENS, KENT (D)
Ark State Rep
Mailing Add: 388 Three Forks Rd Apt 3 West Memphis AR 72301

RUBIN, HYMAN (D)
SC State Sen
b Charleston, SC, Jan 21, 13; s Joseph Rubin & Bessie Peskin R; m 1940 to Rose Rudnick; c Jane & Hyman, Jr. Educ: Univ NC, 2 years; Univ SC, AB, 35; Phi Beta Kappa; Tau Epsilon Phi. Polit & Govt Pos: City councilman, Columbia, SC, 52-66 & mayor pro tempore, 56-66; SC State Sen, 66-; chmn, Richland Co Legis Deleg, currently; mem, Gtr Columbia Human Rels Coun, currently. Bus & Prof Pos: Partner, J Rubin & Son Co, wholesale textiles & apparel, 35- Mem: Nat Asn Textile & Apparel Wholesalers; Columbia Civitan Club; Elks; Shrine; Mason. Relig: Jewish. Legal Res: 2428 Wheat St Columbia SC 29205 Mailing Add: State House Columbia SC 29211

RUBINO, THEODORE SALVATORE A (R)
Chmn, Chester Co Rep Comt, Pa
b Malvern, Pa, Nov 27, 11; s Joseph Rubino & Raphaela Modano R; single. Educ: Pa State Univ. Polit & Govt Pos: Clerk, Bd Elec, Malvern, Pa, 41; pres, Malvern Coun, 52; sheriff, Chester Co, 63; chmn, Chester Co Rep Comt, 64-; Chester Co comnr, 4 years, chmn bd comnrs, currently; mem, State Rep Exec Comt, currently. Bus & Prof Pos: Supvr stone prod, Warner Co, Pa; owner-operator, Knickerbocker Sanit Landfill, 52-; bd dirs, Cent-Penn Nat Bank & First Am Modern Enterprises; mem, Del River Basin Comn & exec comt, Cath Charities of Chester Co; sustaining mem, Boy Scouts; chmn, Indust & Commercial orgn for Chester Co Heart Asn, Southeastern Pa; dir, Chester Co Fund; Sierra Club. Mem: Malvern Civic Asn; Lions; Malvern Fire Co; Paoli Massacre; Chester Co Group of Layman's Week-End Retreat League (assoc capt). Honors & Awards: Humanitarian Award, Chester Co Heart Asn & Chester Co Multiple Sclerosis Soc, 71; Italian Merit Award, Italian Social Club of West Chester, 73; Good Samaritan Award, Safety Coun. Relig: Roman Catholic. Legal Res: Old Lincoln Hwy Malvern PA Mailing Add: 21 S Church St West Chester PA 19380

RUBY, DONALD W (R)
b Detroit, Mich, Apr 25, 30; s Harold E Ruby & Kathryn Bolin R (deceased); m 1951 to Valonda M Viso; c Kathryn M, Donald D & Teresa L. Educ: Ind State Univ, Terre Haute, BA. Polit & Govt Pos: Legis asst to US Rep Richard L Roudebush, Ind, 66-69, admin asst, 69-70; admin asst to US Rep Elwood H Hillis, Ind, 70- Bus & Prof Pos: City ed, Daily Clintonian, Clinton, Ind, 52-54; reporter, Indianapolis Star, 54-62; legis asst, Indianapolis CofC, 62-66. Mil Serv: Entered as Pvt, Army, 50, released as Cpl, 52, after serv in 20th Inf Div, European Theatre. Relig: Roman Catholic. Legal Res: 442 S Fifth St Clinton IN 47842 Mailing Add: 1475 Danville Rd Woodbridge VA 22191

RUBY, ELLIS SCOTT (R)
Chmn, Garden Co Rep Party, Nebr
b Broadwater, Nebr, June 15, 21; s Clarke Ellis Ruby & Audra Scott R; m 1951 to Irple Gibson; c Barbara Ann, Susanna Jo & James Ellis. Educ: Univ Nebr, BS, 47, MSc, 48; Tex A&M Col, PhD, 51. Polit & Govt Pos: Chmn, Garden Co Rep Party, Nebr, 68- Bus & Prof Pos: Asst prof, Univ Ark, 51-53; mgr, Rushcreek Land & Livestock Co Arabian Horse Div, 53- Mem: Sigma Xi. Relig: Presbyterian. Mailing Add: Lisco NE 69148

RUBY, JOHN ALLEN (D)
Dep Treas, Ind
b Indianapolis, Ind, Oct 21, 35; s Harold Allen Ruby & Helen Siler R; m 1966 to Merna Mosel; c Ellen Suzanne & John Allen, II. Educ: Purdue Univ, BS, 57; Ind Univ, MBA, 59; Pi Kappa Phi. Polit & Govt Pos: Asst exec secy, Pub Employees Retirement Fund of Ind, 61-63, exec secy, 67-69; mgt analyst, Dept Admin, 63-65; pres, Tenth Dist Young Dem, 63-65; Ind State Rep, 65-66; patronage asst, Ind Dem State Cent Comt, 65-66; pres, Ind Young Dem, 65-67; Dep Treas, Ind, 71- Bus & Prof Pos: Acct, Gen Motors Corp, 57; asst to pres, Rushville Nat Bank, 59-61; sr acct mgr, Trust Dept, Ind Nat Bank, 69-71. Mem: Indianapolis Soc Financial Analysts; Nat Asn State Retirement Adminr; Nat Asn State Social Security Adminr. Relig: Christian Church. Legal Res: 510 N Main Carthage IN 46115 Mailing Add: Rm 242 State House Indianapolis IN 46204

RUCHO, JOHN (D)
Mass State Rep
Mailing Add: State Capitol Boston MA 02133

RUCKDESCHEL, JOHN DOUGLAS, JR (D)
b Newburgh, NY, July 26, 49; s John Douglas Ruckdeschel, Sr & Naomi Marie Krom R; single. Educ: Orange Co Community Col, AA, 69; Hofstra Univ, 69-70; St Luke's Hosp, Clin Lab Asst, Am Soc Clin Pathologist, 72. Polit & Govt Pos: Committeeman, Newburgh City Dem Comt, 71-72, mem exec comt, 72-; youth coordr, Citizens for Congressman Dow, 72; deleg, Dem Nat Conv, 72; co-coordr, City of Newburgh McGovern for President, 72; co-coordr, Speakers Bur, Orange Co Citizens for McGovern, 72. Mem: Orange Co Coalition for Peace & Justice (Newburgh co-coordr, 73-). Relig: Methodist. Mailing Add: 36 Hudson View Terr Newburgh NY 12550

RUCKELSHAUS, WILLIAM DOYLE (R)
b Indianapolis, Ind, July 24, 32; s John K Ruckelshaus & Marion Doyle R; m 1962 to Jill Elizabeth Strickland; c Catherine, Mary, Jennifer, William & Robin. Educ: Princeton Univ, AB cum laude, 57; Harvard Law Sch, LLB, 60; Cottage Club, Princeton Univ. Polit & Govt Pos: Dep Attorney Gen, Ind, 60-63; chief counsel, Attorney Gen Off, Ind, 63-65; minority attorney, Ind State Sen, 67-69; Ind State Rep, 67-69, majority leader, Ind House of Rep, 67-69; Rep nominee, US Sen, Ind, 68; asst attorney gen, Civil Div, Dept of Justice, 69-70; adminr, Environ Protection Agency, 70-73; acting dir, Fed Bur Invest, 73; Dep Attorney Gen, 73-74. Bus & Prof Pos: Attorney-at-law, Ruckelshaus, Bobbit & O'Connor, 60-68. Mil Serv: Entered as Pvt, Army, 53, released as Sgt, 55, after serv in US. Publ: Reapportionment—a continuing problem, Res Gestae, 63. Mem: Indianapolis, Ind & Am Bar Asns; Am Polit Sci Asn; Indianapolis Coun of Foreign Rels. Honors & Awards: Named Outstanding Rep Legislator in Ind House of Rep by the Working Press, 67; Ind Broadcasters Asn Award for Outstanding First Year Legislator in the House, 67; named Man of the Year, Indianapolis Jaycees. Relig: Roman Catholic. Legal Res: 4320 N Meridian Indianapolis IN 46208 Mailing Add: 11124 Luxmanor Rd Rockville MD 20852

RUCKER, CALVIN (D)
Tex State Rep
Mailing Add: Rte 1 Box 762 Cedar Hill TX 75104

RUCKER, NANNIE GEORGE (D)
Mem, State Dem Exec Comt Tenn
b Murfreesboro, Tenn; d D George Flowers & Mamie Ransom F; m James Isaac Rucker; c Theresa Ann (Mrs Miller Harris). Educ: Tenn State Univ, BS, 50, MS, 58; Fisk Univ, 52; Tuskegee Inst, 54; Alpha Kappa Mu; Delta Kappa Gamma; Sigma Gamma Rho. Polit & Govt Pos: Mem, State Dem Exec Comt, Tenn, 70-; rec secy, Tenn State Fedn Dem Women, 70-; mem, Women's Round Table, 70-; mem, Women's Caucus, 71-; deleg & secy, Tenn Deleg, Dem Nat Conv, 72; vpres, Rutherford Co Dem Women's Fedn, currently. Mem: Mid Tenn Teachers Asn; Int Reading Asn (pres, 72); Am Asn Univ Women; Rutherford Co Teachers Asn; Mid Tenn Coun Int Reading Asn (secy). Honors & Awards: Testified for Fed Aid to Educ, Washington, DC, Southern Asn, 47 & 49; Nannie G Rucker Day, Mr Frank Ely & Mrs Brown, Doylestown, Pa, 49. Relig: Baptist. Mailing Add: 619 Johnson St Murfreesboro TN 37130

RUD, RICHARD WAYNE (DFL)
Chmn, Olmsted Co Dem-Farmer-Labor Party, Minn
b Kasota, Minn, Feb 21, 32; s Melvin O Rud & Marietta K Bartels R; m 1951 to Phyllis Ann Hoffmeister; c Steven Wayne, Kevin Scott, Norma Jean (Mrs Bruce R Anderson) & Jay Brian. Educ: Austin Voc-Tech Sch, 58-59. Polit & Govt Pos: Chmn, Olmsted Co Dem-Farmer-Labor Party, Minn, 74-; mem, Dem-Farmer-Labor State Cent Comt, 74- Bus & Prof Pos: Mem staff, PBX Dept, Northwestern Bell Tel Co, 52- Mil Serv: Entered as Pvt, Army, 50, released as Sgt, 52, after serv in Am Theatre; M/Sgt, Army Res, 58. Mem: United Way Olmsted Co (bd dirs, 70-); Commun Workers Am (pres, Local 7203, 68-); Boy Scouts. Honors & Awards: Silver Beaver, Boy Scouts, 73; Helping Hand Award, United Way, 72; George Meany Award, 74. Relig: Presbyterian. Mailing Add: 1711 25th St SE Rochester MN 55901

RUDDY, MARGARET EVA (D)
b Utica, NY, Dec 24, 51; d Jeremiah E Ruddy & Elizabeth Joseph R; single. Educ: Utica Col, BA magna cum laude, 73; Dean's High Honor List, 69- Polit & Govt Pos: Tri-co coordr of youth, Ottinger for Sen Campaign, NY, 70; publicity dir, Bryant for Co Exec Campaign, 71; coordr of vol, Lindsay for President, Fla Primaries, 72; field coordr, McGovern for President, 72; deleg, Dem Nat Conv, 72; coordr of vol & advance person, Castle for Cong Campaign, 31st Cong Dist, 72; mem, Oneida Co Dem Adv Comt, 72- Bus & Prof Pos: Asst instr, Campaign Mgt Course, Utica Col, 72-73. Mem: Utica Col (asst coach, Debate Club, 70-, mem, Social-Cult Comt, Faculty Affairs Comt, Speaker Bur & councilwoman, Col Coun, 72-). Honors & Awards: Second Pl, Oneida Co Lions Club Annual Speaking Contest, 70; cand for Nat Symp on the Presidency, 73. Relig: Roman Catholic. Mailing Add: 1108 Taylor Ave Utica NY 13501

RUDDY, PHILIP CULKIN (D)
b Aurora, Ill, Sept 9, 41; s Clarence John Ruddy & Dorothy Culkin R; m 1965 to Colleen Murray; c Philip Culkin, Jr & Erin Colleen. Educ: Univ Notre Dame, AB, 63 & JD, 66. Polit & Govt Pos: City Attorney, Aurora, Ill, 69-72, corp counsel, 72-; deleg, Dem Nat Conv, 72. Bus & Prof Pos: Law clerk for Chief Justice, Ill Supreme Court, 66-68; assoc, Ruddy, Myler, Bartsch Law Firm, 66- Mem: Ill & Kane Co Bar Asns; Moose. Honors & Awards: Distinguished Serv Award, Aurora Jaycees, 70; Outstanding Young Man Award, Ill Jaycees, 70. Relig: Roman Catholic. Legal Res: 241 Le Grande Blvd Aurora IL 60506 Mailing Add: 111 W Downer Pl Aurora IL 60504

RUDDY, ROBERT EDWARD (R)
Dep Under Secy for Field Opers, Dept of Housing & Urban Develop
b Aberdeen, SDak, June 8, 36; s Edward Vincent Ruddy & Bernice Elliott R; m 1970 to Shelby Jean Anderson; c Robin Elizabeth & Mark Edward. Educ: Northern State Col, 57-59; Univ SDak, Vermillion, BA, 61; George Washington Univ Law Sch, JD, 64; Omicron Delta Kappa; Pi Sigma Alpha; Pi Kappa Delta; Sigma Alpha Epsilon. Polit & Govt Pos: Asst Attorney Gen, SDak, 64-65; legis asst to US Sen Karl E Mundt, 65-71; spec asst to the Secy, Dept Com, 71-73; dep under secy for field opers, Dept Housing & Urban Develop, 73- Mil Serv: Entered as Pvt, Army, 55, released as Sgt, 57, after serv in 40th AAA Brigade, Japan, 56-57. Mem: SDak Bar Asn; VFW; KofC; Capitol Hill Club. Relig: Catholic. Legal Res: 112 S Arch St Aberdeen SD 57401 Mailing Add: 9106 Drumaldry Dr Bethesda MD 20034

RUDE, ARTHUR HERMAN (R)
Fla State Rep
b Chicago, Ill, July 27, 26; s Arthur William Rude & Mildred Chott R; m 1952 to Catherine Boyd Erskine; c Sharyn Elizabeth, Leisa Beth & John Arthur. Educ: Univ Ill, BS in archit, 50. Polit & Govt Pos: Precinct committeeman, Rep Exec Comn, Broward Co, Fla, 62-; mem, Ft Lauderdale Bd of Rules & Appeals, 64-; Fla State Rep, 67-70 & 72-; mem, Urban Transportation Adv Coun, US Dept Transportation, 73- Bus & Prof Pos: Architect, 57- Mil Serv: Entered as A/S, Navy, 44, released as Qm 2/C, 46, after serv in USS LCI (L) 871, Asiatic-Pac Theater, 44-46; also serv in USS Boxer CV-21 in Korean Conflict, 51-53; Comdr, Construction Bn, Civil Eng Corps, Naval Res; Letter of Commendation; Presidential Unit Citation & Korean Presidential Unit Citation; Good Conduct, Am Defense, Victory & Japanese Occupation Medals; Asiatic-Pac & Korean Theater Campaign Medals; Korean, China & UN Serv Medals; Philippine Liberation Medal. Mem: Navy League, Navy Acad Found; ROA; Am Legion; VFW; Amvets. Honors & Awards: Archit Design Award; Exemplary Serv in Behalf of Ment Health. Relig: Grace Brethren Church. Mailing Add: 630 NE 14th Ave Ft Lauderdale FL 33304

RUDERMAN, JEROLD ROBERT (R)
Regional Co-Dir, Nat Young Rep
b Watertown, NY, Mar 28, 43; s Joseph Ruderman & Sylvia Sapp R; m 1965 to Terry Schwartz; c Jill Ellen. Educ: Cornell Univ, BA, 64, Law Sch, JD, 67; Phi Delta Phi; Tau Epsilon Phi. Polit & Govt Pos: Pres, West Bronx Young Rep Club, 68-70; gen counsel, New York Dept of Real Estate, 69-71; chmn, NY Young Voters for the President, 72; pres, NY Young Rep Club, 72-73; regional co-dir, Second Dist, Nat Young Rep, 72- Bus & Prof Pos: Partner, Rood, Schwartz & Cohen, Attorneys, 71- Mem: Am & NY Bar Asns; Asn of Bar of New York. Honors & Awards: Outstanding Judicial Dist Leader, NY State Young Rep, 72. Mailing Add: 18 Ridgedale Rd Scarsdale NY 10583

RUDERMAN, RUTH (D)
Mem, Dem Nat Comt, Ind
b Noble Co, Ind; d Don Brown & Ina B; m 1936 to Morris Ruderman, wid. Educ: Purdue Univ. Polit & Govt Pos: Vchmn, Allen Co Dem Cent Comt, Ind, 4 terms; deleg, Dem State Conv, 12 times; Dist Dem Party, 2 terms; mem, Ind Dem State Cent Comt, currently; mem, Dem Nat Comt, currently; exec bd dirs, Allen Co Dem Club; Dep Registr Allen Co, currently. Bus & Prof Pos: Employee, Hillman China Co, 7 years; operator, resident agt & secy-treas, A & M Ruderman Farms, Inc; employ specialist, City of Ft Wayne, currently. Mem: State Dem Womens Club Fedn; Allen Co Dem Luncheon Club; Eagles; Eastern Star; Allen Co Dem Club (exec bd dirs, currently). Honors & Awards: Nat Sigma Beta Girl of the Year Award, Chi Eta Chap, Sigma Beta. Relig: Jewish. Mailing Add: Box 56 Huntertown IN 46748

RUDICEL, CHANDLER CLIFTON (D)
Chmn, Reno Co Dem Party, Kans
b Rush Center, Kans, Nov 15, 05; s Thomas Clifton Rudicel & Laura McClintock R; m 1958 to Velma Jewel Hanselman. Educ: High Sch, La Crosse, Kans, 20-24; GED & 2CX, 51. Polit & Govt Pos: Exec secy, Reno Co Dem Cent Comt, Kans, 66-68; precinct committeeman, SReno Twp, Hutchinson, 66-; Presidential Elector, 68; chmn, Reno Co Dem Party, 68-72 & 74-; chmn, Reno Co Comt McGovern for President, 70. Mil Serv: Entered as Pvt, Army, 26, released as Lt Col, 60, after serv in Army & Air Force, Australia, New Guinea, Korea, China, Japan, Okinawa & France, 41-60. Mem: Lions Int; ROA; Retired Officers Asn. Mailing Add: 15 Glass Manor Lane Hutchinson KS 67505

RUDMAN, WARREN BRUCE (R)
Attorney Gen, NH
b Boston, Mass, May 18, 30; s Edward G Rudman & Theresa Levonson R; m 1952 to Shirley Heckert; c Laura, Alan & Debra. Educ: Valley Forge Mil Acad, 45-48; Syracuse Univ, BS, 52; Boston Col Law Sch, JD, 60. Polit & Govt Pos: Fiscal agent for Gov Walter Peterson 1968 Campaign; spec counsel to Gov Walter Peterson, NH, 69-70; Attorney Gen, NH, 70-; pres, Nat Asn Attorneys Gen, 75. Bus & Prof Pos: Founder & chmn bd of trustees, Daniel Webster Jr Col & New Eng Aeronaut Inst, 65-; mem, Stein, Rudman & Gormley, Nashua, NH, 60-70. Mil Serv: Entered as 2nd Lt, Army Inf, 52, released as Capt, 54, after serv in 2nd Div, Korea, 52-53; Bronze Star; Combat Infantryman's Badge; Korean Campaign, Three Battle Stars; Presidential Unit Citation; Korean Presidential Unit Citation. Publ: Co-auth, New Hampshire's business profits tax, NH Bar J, Vol 12, No 3. Mem: Am Legion. Legal Res: Indian Rock Rd Nashua NH 03060 Mailing Add: 208 State House Annex Concord NH 03301

RUDNICK, IRENE K (D)
SC State Rep
Mailing Add: Box 544 Aiken SC 29801

RUDOLPH, CHARLES R (D)
Corp Comnr, NMex
b Las Vegas, NMex, Oct 4, 41; s Charles B Rudolph & Lucy Trujillo R; m 1965 to Lorraine Lucero; c Michelle Charlaine & Charles Eric. Educ: Highland Univ, BA, 65; Howard Law Sch; Kappa Theta; Forensic Club. Polit & Govt Pos: Policeman, US Capitol, Washington, DC, 65-69; fed investr, Equal Employ Opportunity Comn, Albuquerque, NMex, 69-70; exec dir, Human Rights Comn, Santa Fe, 71-74; Corp Comnr, 75- Mem: Albuquerque Optimist Club; Eagles; Elks; Fraternal Order Police; Santa Fe Jaycees. Relig: Catholic. Mailing Add: 143 Rio Seco Santa Fe NM 87501

RUDY, C GUY (D)
Chmn, Centre Co Dem Comt, Pa
b Centre Hall, Pa, Nov 21, 36; s Clarence R Rudy & Esther R Stoner R; m 1956 to Ruth Alice Corman; c Douglas Guy, Donita Ruth & Dianna Faith. Educ: Lock Haven State Col, 54-56; Pa State Univ, University Park, 70- Polit & Govt Pos: Representative, Cent Pa Dem Coun, 72-; mem, Pa State Adv Bd, Col Young Dem, 72-; mem, Rural Develop Coun of Cent Pa, 72-; chmn, Centre Co Dem Comt, Pa, 72- Bus & Prof Pos: Pres, Rud-Cor Enterprises, 66- Mem: Pa Mobile Housing Asn (dir, 68-); Centre Co Mobile Housing Asn (dir, 68-); Centre Co Agr Exten Serv (dir, 71-); Scottish Rite. Relig: Methodist. Mailing Add: RD 1 Centre Hall PA 16828

RUDY, RUTH CORMAN (D)
Regional Dir, Pa Fedn Dem Women
b Millheim, Pa, Jan 3, 38; d Orvis E Corman & Mabel Stover R; m 1956 to C Guy Rudy; c Douglas G, Donita R & Dianna F. Educ: Pa State Univ, University Park, 69-73; Carnegie Inst, grad, X-ray Technol. Polit & Govt Pos: Area vchmn, Centre Co Dem Comt, 72-74;

regional dir, Pa Fedn Dem Women, 73-; deleg, Dem Nat Mid-Term Conf, 74. Bus & Prof Pos: Admin asst, Pa Dept Agr, Harrisburg, 74; bus mgr, Rud-Cor Enterprises, Centre Hall, Pa, 74- Mem: Centre Area Health Coun (bd dir, 74-); Centre Co Exten Adv Coun (bd dir, 73-); Penns Valley Health & Welfare Asn (bd dir, 70-); Eastern Star (marshall, Centre Chap 207, 74-). Relig: Methodist. Mailing Add: RD 1 Centre Hall PA 16828

RUED, ROYDEN DALE (R)
NDak State Rep
b Palermo, NDak, Jan 22, 26; s John J Rued & Bendicte Sathre R; m 1948 to LaVerne H Mattfeld; c Douglas & Susan. Educ: NDak State Univ, 45-47; Minot State Col, BS, 50; Tau Kappa Epsilon. Polit & Govt Pos: NDak State Rep, 72- Bus & Prof Pos: Owner, Rued Ins Agency, 53- Mil Serv: Entered as V-5, Naval Air Corps, 44, released as V12A, 44. Mem: Am Legion; DAV (life mem); Nat Asn Independent Ins Agents; Civil Air Patrol; Minot Country Club. Relig: Lutheran. Legal Res: 47 Country Club Acres Minot ND 58701 Mailing Add: Box 1666 Minot ND 58701

RUEFF, MARGARET LILLIAN (R)
Chairwoman, Butler Co Rep Party, Ky
b Jefferson Co, Ky, Oct 20, 22; d Robert E Lee Fight & Anna Jean Oliver F; m to William E Rueff, Jr; c Gerald Lee, R Michael, Kenneth C, Rebecca Ann, Theresa H & Margaret Elaine. Educ: Spencerian Commercial Col, Louisville, Ky, Acct, 40; Univ San Antonio, 45-46. Polit & Govt Pos: City treas, Lynview, Ky, 53-54; secy, First Magisterial Dist Rep Club, 60-61; co campaign chairwoman, Nixon for President, 68; pres, Butler Co Women's Rep Club, 69-72; chairwoman, Butler Co Rep Party, 72-; chmn sr citizens comt, Ky Fedn Rep Women, 74-75. Bus & Prof Pos: Mgr & secy-treas, Ky Mirror & Plate Glass Co, Louisville, 46-60; law clerk & off mgr, Rueff & Moore, Attorneys, Morgantown, 67- Publ: Co-ed, Monitor Herald (monthly newspaper), 62-64. Mem: Ky Bar Auxiliary. Relig: Protestant. Legal Res: Green Acres Lane Morgantown KY 42261 Mailing Add: PO Box 476 Morgantown KY 42261

RUEHLMANN, EUGENE P (R)
City Councilman, Cincinnati, Ohio
b Cincinnati, Ohio, Feb 23, 25; s John F Ruehlmann & Hattie Mehrckens R; m 1947 to Virginia M Juergens; c Virginia, Peter, Margaret, Andrea, Gregory, James, Mark & Richard. Educ: Univ Cincinnati, BA with honors in Polit Sci, 48; Harvard Law Sch, LLB, 50; Phi Beta Kappa; Omicron Delta Kappa; Beta Theta Pi. Hon Degrees: LLD, St Xavier Univ, 71. Polit & Govt Pos: City Councilman, Cincinnati, Ohio, 59-, chmn, Capital Improv Comt & Finance Comt & vchmn, Urban Develop & Pub Utilities Comt, Cincinnati City Coun, 61-; VMayor, Cincinnati, 63-67, Mayor, 68-71; chmn, Ohio Mayors for Nixon Campaign, 68; chmn, Reelect the President Campaign, Hamilton Co, Ohio, 72. Bus & Prof Pos: Partner, Law Firm of Strauss, Troy & Ruehlmann, 52- Mil Serv: Marine Corps, 43. Publ: State taxation of radio & TV, Univ Cincinnati Law Rev, 1/51. Mem: Am, Ohio & Cincinnati Bar Asns; Western Hills Country Club; Cincinnatus Asn. Honors & Awards: McKibbon Medal Award Winner, Univ Cincinnati, 47; Cincinnati's Outstanding Young Man of the Year, 60; Distinguished Am Award for serv in connection with the new stadium in Cincinnati, Nat Football Found & Hall of Fame. Relig: Presbyterian. Legal Res: 4966 Cleves Warsaw Pike Cincinnati OH 45238 Mailing Add: 1800 First Nat Bank Bldg Cincinnati OH 45202

RUEL, ALFRED J (D)
NH State Rep
Mailing Add: 6 Harding Ave Gonic NH 03867

RUFFIN, JAMES EDWARD (D)
b Tipton Co, Tenn, July 24, 93; s John Brahan Ruffin & Mary Culbreath R; m 1933 to Grace Gresham. Educ: Drury Col, AB, 16; Cumberland Univ, LLB, 20; Lambda Chi Alpha; All-Mo Valley Tackle, football & recordholder, Mo Inter-collegiate discus throw, 15. Polit & Govt Pos: US Rep, Mo, 33-35; spec asst attorney gen of US, 35-53. Mil Serv: 1st Lt, Army, 17-19, serv as Comdr, Co M, 53rd Pioneer Inf, France, also serv as Capt, Judge Adv Gen Dept, Army Res, 24-26. Mem: Mo Bar Asn; Mil Order of World Wars; Mo State Hist Soc; 40 et 8; Am Legion. Relig: Methodist. Mailing Add: 82O S McCann Ave Springfield MO 65804

RUFFIN, WILLIAM T (D)
Miss State Rep
Mailing Add: Box 217 Bay Springs MS 39422

RUGGIERO, PHILIP S (D)
Pa State Rep
b Washington Twp, Pa, Mar 4, 28; s Stephen Ruggiero & Angeline Natalizio R; single. Educ: Temple Univ, Col Liberal Arts, 50, Sch Law, LLB, 53. Polit & Govt Pos: Hearing examr, Bur Traffic Safety, Pa, 55-61; chmn, Northampton Co Area Three Dem Party, 60-; asst dist attorney, Northampton Co, 64-; Pa State Rep, 137th Dist, currently. Mem: Northampton Co & Pa Bar Asns. Relig: Catholic. Legal Res: 920 North Main St Bangor PA 18013 Mailing Add: Capitol Bldg Harrisburg PA 17120

RUIZ, ISRAEL JR (D)
NY State Sen
Mailing Add: 952 Anderson Ave Bronx NY 10452

RUMERY, MYRON G A (D)
Nebr State Sen
b Julesburg, Colo, July 29, 05; s Henry Leslie Rumery & Medora Blanche Runyan R; m 1934 to Mattie Ella Washburn; c Margene (Mrs Robert Phares) & Myron Leslie. Educ: Grand Island Col, 25-28; Univ Nebr, BS, 32, grad study, 41-42; Colo State Univ, 56-57; Gamma Sigma Delta. Polit & Govt Pos: Nebr State Sen, 75- Bus & Prof Pos: Teacher high sch, 28-31 & 32-43; staff mem, North Platte Sta Animal Sci Research & Admin, Univ Nebr, 43-73. Publ: Co-auth, Feeding Brown Swiss & Holstein steers for beef, 56 & Irrigated bromegrass, intermediate and tall wheatgrass pastures for dairy cows, 64, Nebr Bull; auth, Feeding pelleted corn fodder and corn silage to dairy cows, J Dairy Sci, 69. Mem: Rotary; Odd Fellows (grand master, jurisdiction Nebr); Am Soc Animal Sci; Nebr Acad Sci; Nebr Asn Baptist Churches (pres). Honors & Awards: Churchmen's Award, Cent Baptist Seminary, Kansas City, Kans. Relig: Baptist. Mailing Add: 1905 Cedarberry Rd North Platte NE 69101

RUMFORD, WILLIAM BYRON, SR (D)
b Courtland, Ariz, Feb 2, 08; s Chauncey Goodrich Rumford & Margaret Lee Johnson R; m 1932 to Elsie Rebecca Carrington; c William B & Elsie Rebecca, II. Educ: Univ Calif Col Pharm, Berkeley, PhG, 31, Univ Calif, Berkeley, AB in Polit Sci, 48, MA in Pub Admin, 59; Alpha Phi Alpha; Sigma Pi Phi. Polit & Govt Pos: Calif State Assemblyman, 48-66, chmn, Pub Health Comn, Calif State Assembly, 15 years; asst to dir, Regional Opers, Fed-State Coop, Fed Trade Comn, 72- Bus & Prof Pos: Owner, Rumford's Pharm, Berkeley, Calif. Publ: Housing & Health, Calif Health, 60. Mem: Mason; Shrine; Commonwealth Club of Calif; Berkeley Commons Club; John F Kennedy Univ, Martinez, Calif (trustee). Honors & Awards: Pharm Col Alumni of the Year, 65; Named one of Univ Calif Most Distinguished Grads, Calif Monthly Mag, 3/68; Distinguished Achievement & Notable Serv Award, Univ Calif, Berkeley, 70; mem, Berkeley Fellows. Relig: Methodist. Legal Res: 1998 Ward St Berkeley CA 94703 Mailing Add: 3003 Van Ness St NW Washington DC 20008

RUMLER, JAMES RICHARD (D)
b Madison Co, Ind, Apr 5, 30; s Walter Kenneth Rumler, Sr & Dorothy Reed R; m 1954 to Norma Lee Huffman; c Michele Ann & Michael Alan. Educ: Pendleton High Sch, grad, 48. Polit & Govt Pos: Precinct committeeman, Carmel Twp, Hamilton Co, Ind, 60-; chmn, Clay Twp, Hamilton Co, 68-71; chmn, Hamilton Co Dem Party, 71-74. Bus & Prof Pos: Eng supvr, J M Rotz Engr Co Inc, Indianapolis, 61- Mil Serv: Entered as Pvt, Army, 48, released as Pfc, 50, after serv in 813 Engr Aviation Bn, Alaska, 49-50; Pfc, Army, 50, Korea, 1 year; M/Sgt, Res, 53-59; Korean & UN Medals. Mem: Am Legion (comdr, dist vcomdr); VFW; 40 et 8 (chef de gar, 64-70). Relig: Protestant. Mailing Add: 1335 W Main St Carmel IN 46032

RUMMAGE, FREDERICK CHARLES (D)
Md State Deleg
b Hunlock Creek, Pa, Mar 27, 31; s Walter Eugene Rummage & Hilda Croop R; m 1953 to Loretta Cecilia Formulak; c Kama Croop & Frederick, Jr. Educ: Bloomsburg State Col, BS; Univ Miami, JD; Kappa Delta Pi; Phi Sigma Pi; Delta Theta Phi. Polit & Govt Pos: Md State Deleg, 67- Bus & Prof Pos: Exec dir, Nat Found, Washington, DC, 59-62; house counsel, Nat Asn of Elec Co, 62-65; exec secy & counsel, Educators' Asn, Prince George, Md, 65- Mil Serv: Entered as Pvt, Army, 56, released as Lt, 58, after serv in Army Intel, Metrop Dist, Washington, DC, 56-58. Mem: Fla & Washington, DC Bars; Dem Clubs; Rotary. Relig: Protestant. Legal Res: 6300 George Washington Dr Camp Springs MD 20031 Mailing Add: 8008 Old Marlboro Pike Forestville MD 20028

RUMSFELD, DONALD (R)
Asst to the President
b Chicago, Ill, July 9, 32; s George Rumsfeld & Jeannette Husted R; m 1954 to Joyce Pierson; c Valerie Jean, Marcy Kay & Donald Nicholas, Educ: Princeton Univ, AB, 54. Polit & Govt Pos: Admin asst to US Rep David Dennison, Ohio, 58; staff asst to US Rep Robert Griffin, Mich, 59; US Rep, Ill, 63-69; dir, Off of Econ Opportunity, 69-70; asst to the President, 69-70, counr to the President, 70-73; dir, Cost of Living Coun, US Econ Stabilization Prog, 71-73; US Ambassador to NATO, 73-74; asst to President Ford, 74- Bus & Prof Pos: Registered representative, A G Becker & Co, Inc, 60-62. Mil Serv: Entered as Ens, Navy, 54, released as Lt(jg), 57, after serv as Naval Aviator; Comdr, Naval Res, currently. Honors & Awards: All Navy Wrestling Champion, 56. Relig: Protestant. Legal Res: 1373 Ashland Lane Wilmette IL 60091 Mailing Add: White House Off 1600 Pennsylvania Ave Washington DC 20500

RUNDLE, EARL CLIFFORD (R)
NDak State Rep
b Dickinson, NDak, May 9, 06; s Philip Henry Rundle & Rachel Thompson R; m 1933 to Elinor Aird; c Rachel (Mrs Hoovestol), Don Philip & Lynne (Mrs Carlson). Educ: Univ Mont, 24-26; Dickinson State Col & NDak State Univ, 28-29; Sigma Delta Chi. Polit & Govt Pos: Supvr, Dovre Twp, NDak, 28-37; mem sch bd, Dovre Consol Dist, 33-37; committeeman, AAA Co, 34-36; mem, Co Selective Serv Bd, 6 years & Co Rationing Bd, 2 years; city auditor, Marmarth, 40-45; city auditor & pres sch bd, New England, NDak, 49-59; deleg, many NDak State Conv; precinct committeeman & co secy, Rep Party; NDak State Rep, 39th Dist, 65-; elected deleg, State Const Conv, 72; mem, NDak Heritage Comn, 73- Bus & Prof Pos: Teacher, country schs, 27-29; owner & operator, Rundle Ranch, New Eng, 27-; ed & publ Slope Messenger, Marmarth, 37-59; pres, Register Publ Co, Chamberlain, SDak, 58-60. Mil Serv: Pvt, Army, 44-45. Mem: Mason; Shrine; Royal Order of Jesters; Lions; Am Legion. Relig: Congregational. Mailing Add: Rundle Ranch New England ND 58647

RUNKLE, JERRY CHLOYD (R)
b Pisgah, Iowa, Sept 27, 15; s Jerry Franklin Runkle & Chloie Scherer R; m 1938 to Wilma Irene Michael; c Jane Catherine & Jerry Michael. Educ: Univ Northern Iowa, BS, 38; Univ Iowa, MA, 42; Univ Calif, Berkeley, 48-50; summers, Northwestern Univ, 45, Univ Minn, 58, Univ Va, 64 & Univ Calif, Los Angeles, 67. Polit & Govt Pos: Chmn, Decatur Co Rep Cent Comt, Iowa, 68-74. Bus & Prof Pos: Teacher, Clarence Pub Sch, Iowa, 38-42; teacher, DeWitt Pub Sch, Iowa, 42-43; prof econ, Graceland Col, 42- Mem: Am Econ Asn; Midwest Econ Asn; Am Asn Univ Prof. Relig: Reorganized Latter-day Saint, Evangelist. Mailing Add: 202 N Silver St Lamoni IA 50140

RUNNELS, HAROLD LOWELL (D)
US Rep, NMex
b Dallas, Tex, Mar 17, 24; s Elbert Dewey Runnels & Stella McCutcheon R; m 1944 to Dorothy Francis Gilland; c Michael Lowell, Phillip Harold, Dewey Mathew & Eydie Francis. Educ: Cameron State Agr Col, Lawton, Okla, 43. Polit & Govt Pos: Clerk, Fed Bur Invest, 42; NMex State Sen, 60-70; US Rep, Second Dist, NMex, 71- Bus & Prof Pos: Mgr, Magnolia Amusement Co, 45-51; partner, Southland Supply Co, 52; owner & mgr, RunCo Acidizing & Fracturing & Runnels Mud Co. Mil Serv: Pvt, Air Force Res, 42. Mem: Am Petroleum Inst; Permiam Basin Petroleum Asn; CofC; Mason (32 degree); Shrine. Relig: Baptist. Legal Res: 218 S Seventh Lovington NM 88260 Mailing Add: 1535 Longworth House Off Bldg Washington DC 20515

RUNNELS, JOSEPH L (PETE) (D)
Chmn, Orange Co Dem Comt, Tex
b Alice, Tex, July 3, 43; s Joe Mixon Runnels & Inez Harter R; m 1965 to Carol Jean Wilcox; c Joseph Lance & Jason Edward. Educ: Sam Houston State Univ, BBA, 65; Kappa Alpha. Polit & Govt Pos: Deleg, Dem Nat Conv, 72; chmn, Orange Co Dem Comt, Tex, 72-; admin asst to co judge, 73-; mem adv bd, Const Revision Comn, 73- Mem: Lions; Jaycees; Optimist. Relig: Baptist. Mailing Add: 3609 Edgemont Orange TX 77630

RUNYAN, S H (HAL) (R)
Ariz State Sen
Mailing Add: PO Box 1072 260 Bird Lane Litchfield Park AZ 85340

806 / RUPP

RUPP, DANIEL GABRIEL **(D)**
b Hays, Kans, Mar 11, 36; s Gabriel Frederick Rupp & Josephine Anna Wolf R; m 1967 to Sandra Sue Gerber; c Jo Ellen. Educ: St Benedict's Col (Kans), BA, 58; Ft Hays Kans State Col, MS, 59; Univ Kans, 62-65. Polit & Govt Pos: Mem, Coun on Econ Anal, State of Kans, 67-69; alt deleg, Dem Nat Conv, 72; mem nat comt, Campaign for Human Develop, 73-; mayor, Hays, Kans, 75- Bus & Prof Pos: Mem faculty senate exec comt, Ft Hays Kans State Col, 71-73. Mem: Nat Geog Soc; Nat Asn Intercol Athletics (eligibility comt, Dist Ten, 72-); Kiwanis (Lt Gov, Div VIII, Kans Dist, 72-73); US Cath Bishops Adv Coun (layman rep, Div IX, 72-, vchairperson, 75); Salina Diocesan Pastoral Coun (pres, 72-). Relig: Roman Catholic. Mailing Add: 206 W 34th Hays KS 67601

RUPPE, PHILIP E **(R)**
US Rep, Mich
b Laurium, Mich, Sept 29, 26; m 1957 to Loret Miller; c five. Educ: Cent Mich Univ; Univ Mich; Yale Univ, 48. Polit & Govt Pos: Mich Indust Ambassador, 2 years; US Rep, Mich, 67- Bus & Prof Pos: Pres & gen mgr, Bosch Brewing Co, 55-65; dir, Commercial Nat Bank of L'Anse, 62- Mil Serv: Ens, Naval Res, 48; Navy, 52, Japan & Korea. Mem: Am Legion; VFW; Houghton Rotary Club. Legal Res: Woodland Rd Houghton MI 49931 Mailing Add: 203 Cannon House Off Bldg Washington DC 20515

RUPRECHT, MARY MARGARET **(DFL)**
Chmn, 60th Sen Dist Dem-Farmer-Labor Party, Minn
b O'Neill, Nebr, Oct 20, 34; d Charles Ellsworth Wyant & Mary Cuddy W; m 1955 to Gregory Earl Ruprecht; c Mary Debra & Sharie Marie. Educ: Col St Benedict (Minn), 54-56; Am Inst Banking, basic cert, 69, gen cert, 70, standard cert, 71; Int Rels Comt; Thespian Club; Modern Dance Club. Polit & Govt Pos: Secy, Aitkin Co Dem-Farmer-Labor Precinct Caucus, Minn, 60; deleg, Aitkin Co Conv, 60-62; pres, Women's Liberal Orgn, Aitkin Co, 60-65; secy, 60th Legis Dist Dem-Farmer-Labor Orgn, 66; alt deleg, Eighth Dist & Minn State Dem-Farmer-Labor Conv, 66 & 70, deleg, 68; mem, Duluth Dem-Farmer-Labor Club, 66-; mem, Women for Humphrey Comt, 68; chmn, 60th Sen Dist Dem-Farmer-Labor Party, 68-, chmn screening comt, 70-; vchmn, Duluth Dem-Farmer-Labor Coord Comt, 68-; secy, Eighth Cong Dist Dem-Farmer-Labor Party, 68-, finance dir, 72-; treas, Rep Sam Solon's Campaign, 70 & 72; secy, St Louis Co Dem-Farmer-Labor Party, 70-71, treas, 71-73; assoc chairwoman, Seventh Sen Dist Dem-Farmer-Labor Party, 72-, mem screening comt, 72-73. Bus & Prof Pos: Receptionist & cashier, Rural Elec Coop, Aitkin, Minn, 54-55; secy, Wyant Law Off, 57-64; dist clerk, US Soil Conserv Dist, 58-65; publ, The Shopper, 60-63; secy commercial loan, Northern City Nat Bank, Duluth, 65-71; off mgr, Fryberger, Buchanan, Smith, Sanford & Frederick, 71- Publ: How to Construct Word Processing Procedures Manual, Mod Off Procedure, 5/72; Word processing in a law office, Law Off Econ & Mgt, 6/73. Mem: Minn-Arrow Nat Asn Secy; Am Inst Banking (secy, 66-67, asst women's chmn & publicity chmn, 67-68, women's chmn, 68-69, dist 10 mem nat women's comt, 69-70, chmn nat women's comt, 70-71); Int Word Processing Asn (chmn exec comt, 72-); Int Platform Asn; Bus & Prof Women's Asn, Duluth. Honors & Awards: Fourth Pl Trophy, Regional Am Inst Banking Speech Contest, 69. Relig: Catholic. Mailing Add: 140 W Myrtle St Duluth MN 55811

RURAK, JAMES P **(D)**
Mass State Rep
Mailing Add: State Capitol Boston MA 02133

RUSH, CARLETON K **(R)**
Mem, Mich Rep State Cent Comt
b Stanton, Mich, Nov 20, 24; s Oratio R Rush & Clara Baldwin Sackett R; m 1947 to Dorothy M DeMeritt; c Douglas Kenneth, Vicki Marie & Philip Thomas. Educ: Mich State Univ, BS, 47; Tau Beta Pi; Sigma Alpha Epsilon. Polit & Govt Pos: Precinct deleg, Huron Twp, Mich, 64-; deleg, Mich State Rep Conv, 64-; trustee, Huron Bd Educ, 65-; mem, Mich Rep State Cent Comt, 69-, vchmn, Ways & Means Comt, 69-71, chmn, 71-; mem, Rep 15th Cong Dist Exec Comt, 69-71; chmn, 15th Dist Lincoln Day Banquet Comt, 70-72; Mich state deleg, Regional Rep Conf, Indianapolis, 71 & Nat Leadership Conf, Washington, DC, 72; deleg, Rep Nat Conv, 72; chmn, Mich Transportation to Conv & Inauguration, 72-73. Bus & Prof Pos: Asst engr, Creole Petroleum Corp, Maracaibo, Venezuela, 47; jr engr, Off Engr & Asst City Engr, City of Midland, Mich, 48-52; city mgr, Vassar, Mich, 52-54; partner & gen mgr, E & B Enterprise, Romulus, Mich, 54-63, pres, E & B Mfg Co, Inc, Romulus, 63- Mil Serv: Entered as Pvt, Army, 44, released as Cpl, 46, after serv in Airborne Div, Am Theatre, 44-46; Sharp Shooter; Good Conduct. Mem: Mich Soc Prof Engrs; Lions. Relig: Methodist. Mailing Add: 29620 King Rd Romulus MI 48174

RUSH, CAROLYN SUE **(R)**
VChairwoman, Ark Rep State Comt
b Russellville, Ark, Oct 9, 33; d Modie Daniel Morgan & Ora May Morgan M; m 1953 to Marshall Neil Rush; c Stephanie Ann, Kathryn Sue, Allison Lee & Marshall Morgan. Educ: Tex Univ for Women, 2 years; Singing Stars. Polit & Govt Pos: Mem, Young Rep Club of Jefferson Co & Jefferson Co Rep Women's Club; second vchairwoman, Jefferson Co Rep Cent Comt, 51-65; nat committeewoman, Young Rep Ark, 62-63; secy, Fourth Cong Dist, 63; pres, Jefferson Co Rep Women's Orgn, 63-64; vchairwoman, Ark Rep State Comt, 64-; deleg, Rep Nat Conv, 68 & 72. Mem: PTA (bd mem, Lakeside Sch Chap); Time Club; League of Women Voters; Jaycee Auxiliary (secy); South Regional VChairwoman Asn (chmn, 70). Relig: Baptist. Mailing Add: 209 W Harding Pine Bluff AR 71601

RUSH, DEWEY DAVENT **(D)**
Ga State Rep
b Glennville, Ga, May 16, 16; s Lewie Leroy Rush & Amy Procell R; m 1938 to Una Mae Weathers; c Derrel D, Quinton S, Aris Dianne (Mrs Wilson), Lynn Gail & David Roy. Educ: Glennville High Sch. Polit & Govt Pos: Ga State Rep, 75th Dist, Tattnall & Long Cos, 65- Mem: Masons; Lions; Farm Bur. Relig: Missionary Baptist. Mailing Add: RR 4 Box 262 Glennville GA 30427

RUSH, DORIS MITCHELL **(R)**
Chairwoman, Metcalfe Co Rep Party, Ky
b Edmonton, Ky, Apr 30, 34; d Guy Mitchell & Adele Gassaway M; m 1954 to Robert Gentry Rush, Jr; c Patty Lynn. Educ: Edmonton High Sch, grad, 52; Spencerian Bus Sch, 53. Polit & Govt Pos: Chairwoman, Metcalfe Co Rep Party, Ky, 59-; pres, Metcalfe Co Rep Women's Club, 70- Bus & Prof Pos: Secy-bookkeeper, Ashland Oil & Ref Co, Edmonton, Ky, 52-60, B & C Chevrolet Co, 2 years & Bell's Sales & Serv, 2 years; dent asst, Dr J M Hays, 66- Mem: Metcalfe Co Rep Women's Club; Edmonton Woman's Club. Honors & Awards: Dwight D Eisenhower Award. Relig: Methodist. Mailing Add: Edmonton KY 42129

RUSH, HENRI FRANCIS, JR **(R)**
b St Louis, Mo, Aug 9, 37; s Charles Henri Rush & Vivian Evans R; m 1959 to Jeanne Jacobson; c Cynthia Evans & Michelle Lynds. Educ: Univ Minn, BA, 59, Law Sch, 59-60; Georgetown Law Ctr, LLB, 63; pres, Phoenix Soc; Minn Men's Res Asn; Univ Rep Club; Georgetown Univ Law J. Polit & Govt Pos: Chmn, Pine Co Rep Party, 57-59; mem, Minn Rep State Cent Comt, 57-59; mgt analyst, Admin Div, US Dept of Justice, 62-63; dir, Speakers Bur, John V Lindsay, New York, 65; staff, Off Gen Counsel, Interstate Com Comn, 66-68; chmn, 34th & Tenth Precincts, DC, 68-71; mem, DC Rep Cent Comt, 69-72; minority staff counsel, Senate Comt Com, 70-72; dep adminr, Fed Railroad Admin, US Dept of Transportation, 72- Bus & Prof Pos: Assoc, Donovan, Leisure, Newton & Irvine, New York, 63-66; assoc, Swidler & Belnap, Washington, DC, 68-70. Mem: Bars of the US Supreme Court, Second Circuit Court of Appeals, Dist Court for the Southern Dist of NY, DC & State of NY. Relig: Presbyterian. Mailing Add: 3110 44th St NW Washington DC 20016

RUSH, KENNETH
US Ambassador, France
b Walla Walla, Wash, Jan 17, 10; s David Campbell Rush & Emma Kate Kidwell R; m 1937 to Jane Gilbert Smith; c George Gilbert (deceased), David (deceased), Malcolm, Cynthia Shepherd (Mrs Thomas J Monahan), John Randall & Kenneth. Educ: Univ Tenn, AB, 30; Yale Univ, JD, 32; Phi Beta Kappa. Hon Degrees: LLD, Tusculum Col, 61. Polit & Govt Pos: Mem, President Johnson's Comt on Foreign Trade Policy, 68-69; mem, Secy of Com Comt on Foreign Direct Investment, 69; US Ambassador, Ger, 69-72; Dep Secy of Defense, Pentagon, Washington, DC, 72-73; Dep Secy of State, Dept of State, 73-74; Secy State ad interim, 73; counr to President for Econ Policy, 74; mem, Nat Security Coun, formerly; chmn Coun on Int Econ Policy, formerly; mem, President's Comt on East-West Trade Policy, President's Food Comt, Coun on Wage & Price Stability, Comt on Energy & Joint Presidential-Cong Steering Comt for the Conf on Inflation, currently; US Ambassador, France, 74- Bus & Prof Pos: Assoc, Chadbourne, Parke, Whiteside & Wolfe, New York, 32-36; asst prof, Duke Univ Law Sch, 36-37, mem law dept, Union Carbide Corp, 36 & 37-54, vpres, 49-61, exec vpres, 61-66, chmn gen operating comt, 65-69, pres & mem exec comt, 66-69, dir, 58-69; dir, Bankers Trust Co, 66-69; dir, Amstar Corp, 62-69; chmn bd, Mfg Chemists Asn, 66-67, dir, 65-67. Mem: Am Bar Asn; Coun on Foreign Rels; Univ Tenn (develop coun, 63-); The Univ Club, NY. Honors & Awards: Grand Cross of the Order of Merit, Fed Repub of Ger, 72; Distinguished Pub Serv Medal, Dept of Defense, 73. Relig: Episcopal; former Vestryman & Sr Warden. Legal Res: North Manursing Island Rye NY 10580 Mailing Add: Am Embassy APO New York NY 09777

RUSH, PAULA SHAYE **(D)**
Mem, Ky Dem State Cent Exec Comt
b Knoxville, Tenn, Nov 19, 48; d Louis Valenti & Dorothy Seals V; single. Educ: Morehead State Univ, Ky, acad scholar, 66-68; Alpha Gamma Epsilon. Polit & Govt Pos: Fourth Dist youth chmn, Ford for Gov Primary Campaign, Ky, 71, state youth dir, Gen Elec, 71; rec secy, Ky Young Dem, 71-72, nat committeewoman, 72-73; mem, Ky Dem State Cent Exec Comt, 71-; Fourth Dist youth chmn, Huddleston for Senate, 72; youth lobbyist, Dem Nat Conv, 72; exec bd mem, Dem Women's Club of Ky, 72-73. Bus & Prof Pos: Admin asst state & local govt rels, Procter & Gamble, Cincinnati, Ohio, 68- Mem: Kenton Co Young Dem; Ky Comn on Women. Honors & Awards: Ky Col, State of Ky, 72; Citizen of the Day, Avco Broadcasting, 73. Relig: Baptist. Mailing Add: Apt 1 525 W Chelsea Circle Ft Mitchell KY 41017

RUSH, SAMUEL LEE **(R)**
b Alexandria, La, Apr 27, 92; s William Slade Rush & Betty Harwell R; m 1912 to Fannie Winfree; c Stanley, Florine (Mrs Blount), Juanita (Mrs Reynolds), R L & Vanelda (Mrs Elliott). Polit & Govt Pos: Mem, Electoral Col, 52; committeeman, La Rep State Cent Comt, 52-70; chmn, Allen Parish Rep Cent Comt, La, 70-74. Bus & Prof Pos: Sawmill supt, Hillyer Deutsch Edwards, Inc, 27-57. Relig: Methodist. Mailing Add: 403 A Maple St Oakdale LA 71463

RUSH, WILLIAM **(D)**
Md State Deleg
b Belfast, Northern Ireland, Nov 3, 19; married. Educ: Pub schs, Belfast & Baltimore Co. Polit & Govt Pos: Md State Deleg, 63- Mil Serv: Army. Mem: Mason; Am Legion; VFW; Parkville Golf Club; Sportsman Club. Mailing Add: 3307 E Putty Hill Ave Baltimore MD 21234

RUSHTON, ROBERT ARCHIE **(D)**
Mem, Ga State Dem Exec Comt
b Dublin, Ga, July 6, 43; s Archie Sime Rushton & Bettye Jane Johnson R; single. Educ: Univ Ga, BBA, 65; Demothenians; Phi Kappa; Rho Epsilon. Polit & Govt Pos: Pres, Univ Ga Young Dem, 64; mem, Ga State Dem Exec Comt, 71- Bus & Prof Pos: Vpres, R & R Builders, Inc, 62-; pres, Rushton Assocs Realty, Inc, 69- Mem: Int Coun Shopping Ctrs; Nat, Ga & Marietta Asns Real Estate Bds; Nat Inst Real Estate Brokers. Relig: Methodist. Legal Res: 217 Holt Rd Marietta GA 30060 Mailing Add: PO Box 838 Marietta GA 30060

RUSK, DEAN
b Cherokee Co, Ga, Feb 9, 09; s Robert Hugh Rusk & Frances Elizabeth Clotfelter R; m 1937 to Virginia Foisie; c David Patrick, Richard Geary & Margaret Elizabeth. Educ: Davidson Col, BA, 31; St John's Col, Oxford Univ, Rhodes scholar, 33, MA, 34; Phi Beta Kappa; Kappa Alpha. Polit & Govt Pos: Spec asst to Secy of War, Patterson, 46-47; dir, Off UN Affairs, Dept of State, 47-49, Asst Secy of State, 49, Dep Under Secy of State, 49-50, Asst Secy of State for Far Eastern Affairs, 50-51, Secy of State, 61-68. Bus & Prof Pos: Asst prof govt, Mills Col, 34-38, dean of faculty, 38-40; pres, Rockefeller Found, New York, 52-61; prof law, Univ Ga Law Sch, 70- Mil Serv: Entered as Capt, Army, 40, released as Col, 46, after serv in Inf & Gen Staff; Legion of Merit with Oak Leaf Cluster; Hon Col, Army Res. Relig: Presbyterian. Mailing Add: 1 Lafayette Sq 620 Hill St Athens GA 30601

RUSS, JOSEPH, IV **(R)**
Finance Chmn, Humboldt Co Rep Cent Comt, Calif
b Eureka, Calif, July 25, 36; s Joseph Russ & Annette Tamboury R; m 1963 to Karen Lane; c Renee & J Lane. Educ: Univ Calif, Berkeley, BS, 59. Polit & Govt Pos: Mem, Rep State Cent Comt Calif, 64-68; vchmn, First Cong Dist Rep Comt, 64-; chmn, Humboldt Co Rep Cent Comt, 66-68, finance chmn, 68-; deleg, Rep Nat Conv, 68, alt deleg, 72. Bus & Prof Pos: Dir, Bank of Coleta, 64-; vchmn, Humboldt Co Planning Comt, 66-69. Mil Serv: Entered as Pvt, Marine Corps Air Res, 59, released as Cpl, 64, after serv in HMR 769; Honor Man of Platoon. Mem: Calif Asn Future Farmers of Am; Humboldt Co Cattlemen's Asn; Humboldt Co Farm Bur; Native Sons of Golden West; Commonwealth Club of Calif. Honors & Awards: Am Farmer Award. Relig: Catholic. Mailing Add: Bunker Hill Ranch Ferndale CA 95536

RUSSEK, TRULA WELLS (R)
b Brenham, Tex, Feb 27, 21; d Robert Rush Wells & Trula Harbert W; m 1944 to I Warren Russek; c Myra. Educ: Sullins Col (Va), 38-39; Univ Tex, Austin, BBA, 42. Polit & Govt Pos: Pres, La Fedn Rep Women, 65-67, mem bd, 65-; mem bd, Nat Fedn Rep Women, 65-70; mem, La Platform Comt, 66 & 74; chmn, Rep Precinct Three, Ward Ten, Lafayette, 67-71; chmn, S La Women for Nixon, 68; chmn, La Hostess-Bus Tel Prog to Reelect the President, 72; deleg & mem credentials comt, Rep Nat Conv, 68 & 72; vchmn, Lafayette Parish Polit Action Comt, 72-74, chmn, 74- Mem: Lafayette Parish Heart Coun (treas, 63-); Galvez Chap, DAR; Southwest La Geophys Auxiliary; Lafayette Geol Auxiliary; Chez Amis (pres, 73). Honors & Awards: Rep Woman of the Year, La Fedn of Rep Women, 69 & Runner-up to Rep Woman of the Year, Nat Fedn of Rep Women, 69. Relig: Episcopal. Mailing Add: 110 Hampton Rd Lafayette LA 70501

RUSSELL, CHARLES HINTON (R)
b Lovelock, Nev, Dec 27, 03; s Robert James Russell & Ellen Daisy Ernst R; m 1939 to Marjorie Ann Guild; c Clark George, Virginia Ellen, Craig Robert, Charles David & James Todd. Educ: Univ Nev, AB, 26. Polit & Govt Pos: Nev State Assemblyman, 35-40; Nev State Sen, 41-46, pres pro tem, Nev State Senate, 43; US Rep, Nev, 47-49; mem, Comn on Foreign Econ Coop, 49-50; Gov, Nev, 50-58; dir, US Opers Mission, Asuncion, Paraguay, 59-63. Bus & Prof Pos: Teacher, 26-27; mine off, Ruth, Nev, 28-29; ed, The Ely Rec, 29-46; dir develop & asst to pres, Univ Nev, Reno, 63-69. Mem: Mason; Shrine. Relig: Episcopal. Mailing Add: 302 N Minnesota St Carson City NV 89701

RUSSELL, DAVID OWEN (R)
Committeeman, Ark Rep State Comt
b North Little Rock, Ark, July 18, 52; s Oscar Garland Russell, Jr & Reba Lynn Faulk R; single. Educ: Univ Ark, Fayetteville, BA, 74; Omicron Delta Kappa; Acacia; Order of Omega & Cardinal XX. Polit & Govt Pos: Committeeman, Ark Rep State Comt, 72-; reelec press secy to Cong John P Hammerschmidt, 74. Bus & Prof Pos: Reporter & photographer, Forrest City Times-Herald, Ark, summers 72 & 73; reporter-photographer, Springdale News, 74; sports ed & chief photographer, Malvern Daily Rec, 74- Relig: Assemblies of God. Mailing Add: Apt 9 615 Garland St Malvern AR 72104

RUSSELL, DONALD STUART (D)
b Lafayette Springs, Miss, Feb 22, 06; s Jesse L Russell & Lula R; m 1929 to Virginia Utsey; c Donald Stuart, Mildred Pendleton, Walker Scott & John Richardson. Educ: Univ SC, AB, 25, LLB, 28; Univ Mich, grad work in law, 29; Phi Beta Kappa. Hon Degrees: LLD, Wofford Col, Lander Col, The Citadel, Univ SC, Clemson Univ & C W Post Col, LI Univ. Polit & Govt Pos: Mem, Price Adjust Bd, War Dept, Washington, DC, 42; asst to Dir of Econ Stabilization, 42; asst to Dir of War Mobilization, 43; dep dir, Off War Mobilization & Reconversion, 45; Asst Secy of State for Admin, 45-47; mem, SC Pub Sch Curricula Comt; mem, Hoover Comn on Govt Reorgn; mem, Wriston Comn on Reorgn Foreign Serv, 54; Gov, SC, 63-65; US Sen, SC, 65-66; US Dist Judge, SC, 67-71; US Circuit Judge, 71- Bus & Prof Pos: Lawyer; pres, Univ SC, 52-57. Mil Serv: Army, Maj, 44, SHAEF. Mem: Converse Col (chmn bd trustees); Emory Univ (chmn bd trustees); Spartanburg Jr Col (chmn bd trustees); Mason; Rotary. Relig: Methodist. Legal Res: 716 Otis Blvd Spartanburg SC 29302 Mailing Add: Fed Bldg Spartanburg SC 29301

RUSSELL, DORIS MAE (R)
Chmn, Hancock Co Rep Comt, Maine
b Washington, DC, Sept 13, 26; d Earl Middleton Mackintosh & Dorothy Zellers M; m 1947 to Robert Foster Russell, MD; c Penny (Mrs Ronald L Terry), Ronald Bruce, Michael Laurance, Heather Lynne, Robin Lance & Kelly Andrews. Educ: Briarcliff Col, AB, 47; Univ Maine, 68. Polit & Govt Pos: Mem, Gov Comt on Children & Youth, Maine, 60-66; vchmn, Hancock Co Rep Comt, 72-75, chmn, 75-; mem, Castine Bd of Appeals, 72- Bus & Prof Pos: Mem, Castine Sch Comt, 7 years, chmn, 3 years; proprietor, Used Bookstore, 66-; chmn, Sch Union 93, 69-70. Mem: Castine Community Hosp (bd mem, 50-72); Northeast Chap Maine Maritime Acad (treas, 72-75); Witherle Mem Libr (trustee), 74-); Girl Scouts (leader, 57-60, 71-73, coordr & treas, 73-). Honors & Awards: Boy Scouts Award, 59. Relig: Episcopal. Legal Res: Battle Ave Castine ME 04421 Mailing Add: Box 63 Castine ME 04421

RUSSELL, F DANIEL (D)
RI State Sen
b Providence, RI, Feb 18, 20; s Thomas Russell & Ellen E Grady R; m 1946 to Edith Holden; c David Holden, F Daniel, Jr, Pamela Ann, Ardith Jane, Heidi Christina, Meredy Paula, Erica Elizabeth, Andrew Jeremy & Roanne Jessica. Educ: Providence Col, BS in Biol, 43; Jefferson Med Col, 45-46; Tufts Univ Sch Dent, DMD, 50; Phi Alpha Sigma. Polit & Govt Pos: Sch Comt, Town of Smithfield, 56-64, conserv comt chmn, 67-74, planning bd chmn, 69-75; RI State Sen, 75- Mem: Lions; Dem Town Comt. Relig: Catholic. Mailing Add: Burlingame Rd RFD 4 Esmond RI 02917

RUSSELL, FRED J (R)
b Edmonton, Alta, June 9, 16; s Fred H Russell (deceased) & Agnes Maye Clements R (deceased); div; c Terry Lee (Mrs Benjamin F Hayes) & Fred B. Educ: Univ Calif, Los Angeles, Exten Div, 37-41. Polit & Govt Pos: Dep dir, Off of Emergency Preparedness, Exec Off of the President, 69-70; Under Secy of Interior, 70-71; US Ambassador to Denmark, 71-72. Bus & Prof Pos: Asst to asst gen mgr, Douglas Aircraft Co, Santa Monica, Calif, 36-42; asst works mgr, Timm Aircraft Corp, Van Nuys, 42-45; pres & gen mgr, Weiser Co, South Gate, 45-68; pres, various construction co, 48-; pres, Russell Properties Co, Los Angeles, 64-69; exec, mfg & subdiv, commercial & indust develop, pub utility. Mil Serv: Entered as Pvt, Marine Corps Res, 35-39 with serv in 13th Bn. Mem: Los Angeles Country Club; Calif Club; Burning Tree Club, Bethesda, Md. Mailing Add: PO Box 54228 Los Angeles CA 90054

RUSSELL, HENRY PHILLIP, JR (D)
Ga State Sen
b Milledgeville, Ga, July 14, 16; s Henry Phillip Russell, Sr & Lelia Harris R; m 1937 to Myrtis Wynnette Dekle; c Henry Phillip, III & Sally Wynnette. Educ: Thomasville High Sch, 34. Polit & Govt Pos: Thomas Co Comnr, Roads & Revenue, Ga, 57-65; Ga State Rep, 63-72; Ga State Sen, 75- Bus & Prof Pos: Owner, Russell Dairy Farm. Mil Serv: Entered as Seaman 2/C, Navy, 44, released as Radarman 2/C, 46, after serv in Amphibious Corps, Pac Theatre, 44-46; Asiatic-Pac Ribbon with two stars. Mem: Moose; Elks; VFW; Am Legion; Farm Bur. Relig: Presbyterian. Mailing Add: Rte 1 Boston GA 31626

RUSSELL, JAMES (JAY) (D)
Mo State Rep
b St Louis, Mo, Nov 4, 28; m 1955 to Delphie Mann; c Jeanne & Jim. Educ: Univ Mo, Columbia. Polit & Govt Pos: Mo State Rep, 62-; deleg, Dem Nat Mid-Term Conf, 74. Bus & Prof Pos: Restaurant owner. Mil Serv: Marine Corps. Mem: KofC. Relig: Catholic. Mailing Add: 700 Bellarmine Lane Florissant MO 63031

RUSSELL, JAMES L (JIM) (D)
Mo State Rep
b Savannah, Mo, Sept 13, 38; s John Bedford Russell & Beatrice Hoshor R; m 1963 to Kathryn Carter; c Kim, Jamie & Matthew. Educ: Univ Mo-Columbia, BS, 61, MS, 67. Polit & Govt Pos: Mo State Rep, 75- Mem: AF&AM. Relig: Protestant. Mailing Add: Rte 3 Savannah MO 64485

RUSSELL, JEAN ALBACH (R)
VChmn, Routt Co Rep Party, Colo
b Omaha, Nebr, Mar 8, 34; d John Solon Albach & Beatrice Leighton A; m 1958 to Richard W Russell; c Clayton, Elizabeth & David. Educ: State Univ Iowa, MA, 56; Kappa Kappa Gamma. Polit & Govt Pos: Vchmn, Routt Co Rep Party, Colo, 69- Mem: Jr League of Des Moines, Iowa. Relig: Episcopal. Mailing Add: Box W Steamboat Springs CO 80477

RUSSELL, JOHN DAVIDSON (D)
Ga State Rep
b Decatur, Ga, May 13, 46; s Alex Brevard Russell & Sarah Eaton R; single. Educ: Univ Ga, AB, 68; Chi Phi. Polit & Govt Pos: Ga State Rep, 73- Bus & Prof Pos: Asst adminr, Russell Nursing Home, 70- Mil Serv: Entered as Officers Cand, Marine Corps, 66, released as 1st Lt, 71, after serv in Fleet Marine Force, Pac, 70; Navy Commendation Medal. Mem: Am Legion. Relig: Presbyterian. Mailing Add: Rte 2 Box 588 Winder GA 30680

RUSSELL, JOHN THOMAS (R)
Republican Floor Leader, Mo House of Rep
b Lebanon, Mo, Sept 22, 31; s Aubrey F Russell & Velma F Johnson R; m 1951 to Margaret Ann Carr; c John Douglas, Georgia Jeanette & Sarah Melissa. Educ: Drury Col, Springfield, Mo, 3 years. Polit & Govt Pos: Mo State Rep, Laclede Co, 62-66, 125th Dist, 67-, minority whip, Mo House of Rep, 67-71, Republican floor leader, 71-; deleg, Rep Nat Conv, 72. Bus & Prof Pos: Dir & officer, Laclede Metal Prod Co & Detroit Tool & Eng Co, Lebanon, 57- & Gen Aluminum Supply Co, Kansas City, 59-; So-Mo Transportation Co, Lebanon, 60; partner, Faith Leasing Co, Lebanon, 69- Mil Serv: Entered Air Force, 51, released as Airman 1/C, 54. Mem: Kiwanis; Am Legion; Mason (32 degree); Scottish Rite; Lebanon CofC. Relig: Southern Baptist. Legal Res: W City Rte 66 Lebanon MO 65536 Mailing Add: Box 93 Lebanon MO 65536

RUSSELL, LLOYD A (R)
Committeeman, Cattaraugus Co Rep Comt, NY
b East Otto, NY, July 4, 21; s Lester W Russell & Ada Dreier R; m 1943 to Margaret Bailey; c Cheryl Jean (Mrs Pauly). Educ: Agr Tech, Alfred, NY, 38-39. Polit & Govt Pos: Justice of Peace, East Otto, NY, 59-64; town committeeman, East Otto, 62; committeeman, Cattaraugus Co Rep Comt, NY, 62-; mem, Cattaraugus Co Civil Serv Comn, 64-, chmn, 66-; NY State Assemblyman, 66-72. Mil Serv: Entered as Pvt, Air Corps, 42, released as Flight Officer, Glider Pilot, 45, after serv in First Provisional Glider Group, Asiatic Theatre, 44. Mem: Am Legion; Farm Bur; Dairymen's League; Grange; Cattaraugus Co Magistrates' Asn. Relig: Methodist. Mailing Add: East Otto NY 14729

RUSSELL, MADELEINE H (D)
Mem, Dem Nat Comt, Calif
Mailing Add: 3778 Washington St San Francisco CA 94118

RUSSELL, NEWTON R (R)
Calif State Sen
b Los Angeles, Calif, June 25, 27; s John Russell & Amy Requa R; m 1953 to Diane Henderson; c Steve, Sherry & Julie. Educ: Univ Southern Calif, BS in bus admin; Univ Calif, Los Angeles & Georgetown Univ, postgrad study; Squires; Delta Tau Delta; Alpha Kappa Psi. Polit & Govt Pos: Former precinct chmn; Calif State Assemblyman, 62nd Dist, Los Angeles Co, 64-74; Calif State Sen, Dist 21, 74-, vchmn pub employ & retirement, ins & financial insts comts, Calif State Senate, currently, mem pub utilities, transit & energy comts; mem, Educ Innovation & Planning Comn, Comn for Econ Develop & Am Revolution Bicentennial Comn. Bus & Prof Pos: Spec agt, Northwestern Mutual Life Ins Co, 54- Mil Serv: Entered as A/S, Navy, World War II, released as Seaman 1/C, Mem: Rotary; Am Legion Post 250; CofC; Boy Scouts (mem-at-lg); Masters Men. Relig: Presbyterian. Legal Res: Tujunga CA 91042 Mailing Add: Rm 26 815 S Central Glendale CA 91204

RUSSELL, NORMA C (D)
SC State Rep
Mailing Add: 92 Nob Hill Rd Columbia SC 29210

RUSSELL, PATRICIA T (D)
NH State Rep
Mailing Add: 74 Beech St Keene NH 03431

RUSSELL, RUTH (D)
b Gallatin, Tenn, Feb 28, 08; d Frank Bernard Seay & Nancy Jackson S; m 1927 to Oscar Alexander Russell. Educ: Gallatin Pvt Inst, 25-27. Polit & Govt Pos: Court reporter, Sumner, Trousdale, Wilson & Macon Co, Tenn, 28-58; dep clerk, Chancery Court, Sumner Co, Tenn, 46-59; mem, Tenn Dem Exec Comt, 46-59, chmn, 56-59; Dem Nat Committeewoman, Tenn, 57-72; deleg, Dem Nat Conv, 68. Bus & Prof Pos: Dir, First Mortgage Co. Mem: A R C (registrn chmn, Sumner Co); Tenn Clerks Asn; Eastern Star (past matron); Gallatin Bus & Prof Women's Club (past pres & chmn, career adv). Honors & Awards: Named Bus Woman of the Year, 56. Legal Res: Gallatin TN 37066 Mailing Add: Court House Gallatin TN 37066

RUSSELL, THEODORE HENRY (D)
Chmn, Kennebec Co Dem Comt, Maine
b Waterville, Maine, Nov 6, 25; s Clyde E Russell & Doris Garland R; m 1948 to Ethelyn Bradstreet; c Bonnie Ellen, Franklin Arthur, Andrew Nelson, Mark Theodore, Lucinda Ethel, Steven Clyde, Barbara Lynne, Beth Ann & Doreen Doris. Educ: Colby Col, AB, 47; Bates Col, Navy V-12 Prog, 3 semesters; Univ Notre Dame, Naval Midn Sch, 1 semester; Delta Upsilon. Polit & Govt Pos: State committeeman, Maine Dem State Comt, 62-66; chmn, Kennebec Co Dem Comt, 67-; deleg, Dem Nat Conv, 68 & 72. Bus & Prof Pos: Local rep, Eastern States Farmers Exchange, Winslow, Maine, 53-58; agent, State Farm Ins Co, Waterville, 59-61, agency mgr, Augusta, 61- Mil Serv: Entered as A/S, Navy, 44, released

as Lt, 53, after serv in USS N K Perry, ComDes Pac, 45-46 & 6th Fleet, 51-53; World War II Victory, Am Theater & Asiatic-Pac Theater Medals. Mem: Kennebec Valley Life Underwriters Asn; Maine Dairymen's Asn; Maine Breeding Coop; Winslow Grange (past master); VFW (past comdr, Ernest A Rutter Post). Honors & Awards: Recipient of awards for ins & farm work. Relig: United Church of Christ. Legal Res: RFD 5 Augusta ME 04330 Mailing Add: 114 State St Augusta ME 04330

RUSSELL, WALTER BROWN, JR (D)
Ga State Rep
b Greensboro, NC, July 24, 29; s Walter Brown Russell & Dorothea Bealer R; m 1954 to Nancy Hinton; c Walter B, III, Emily, Betty Hinton, Stuart Brevard & Anne Minetree. Educ: Duke Univ, 45-46; US Mil Acad, West Point, BS, 51; Sigma Alpha Epsilon. Polit & Govt Pos: Ga State Rep, Dist 53, 70- Bus & Prof Pos: Attorney, Russell & Nardone, Decatur, Ga, 71- Mil Serv: Entered as 2nd Lt, Army, 51, released as Lt Col, 66, after serv in 82nd Airborne Div, 7th Inf Div, Korea, 1st Air Cavalry, Vietnam, 51-66; Silver Star; Legion of Merit; Distinguished Flying Corss; Bronze Star; Air Medal; Army Commendation Medal; Korea & Vietnam Campaign Ribbons; Combat Inf Badge; Master Parachutist Badge; Sr Army Aviator Wings; Ranger Tab. Mem: Am Legion; Rotary; Burns Club of Atlanta. Relig: Episcopal. Mailing Add: 921 Nottingham Dr Avondale Estates GA 30002

RUSSO, FREDERICK N DELLO (D)
Mass State Rep
Mailing Add: State Capitol Boston MA 02133

RUSSO, JOHN FRANCIS (D)
NJ State Sen
b Asbury Park, NJ, July 11, 33; s John Russo & Philomena Appicelli R; m 1957 to Mary Ann Carrigan; c Kathleen, Carol & John, Jr. Educ: Univ Notre Dame, BA cum laude, 55; Columbia Univ Law Sch, LLB, 58. Polit & Govt Pos: Ocean Co Prosecutor, NJ, 60-70; chmn, Ocean Co Dem Comt, formerly; NJ State Sen, 75- Bus & Prof Pos: Partner, Russo & Courtney, currently. Mem: NJ & Ocean Co Bar Asns; Am & NJ State Trial Lawyers Asns; Am Judicature Soc. Relig: Catholic. Legal Res: 488 Madison Ave Toms River NJ 08753 Mailing Add: 616 Washington St Toms River NJ 08753

RUSSO, MARIUS THOMAS (D)
Chmn, East Lansdowne Town Dem Comt, Pa
b New York, Jan 1, 22; s Rocco Russo & Carmella Romano R; m 1946 to Irene D Durant; c Irene S, Beth Ann & Thomas R. Educ: US Army Sig Corps Radio Sch, 42. Polit & Govt Pos: Coun mem, East Lansdowne Borough, Pa, 54-, pres of coun, 62-; chmn, East Lansdowne Town Dem Comt, 60-; deleg, Dem Nat Conv, 64. Bus & Prof Pos: Vpres, E B Krausen Inc, 61- Mil Serv: Entered as Pvt, Army, 42, released as T-5, 45, after serv in 1373rd Sig Unit, ETO; ETO, Rhineland & Cent Europe Serv Medals; World War II Medal; Am Serv Medal; Europe-Africa-Mid East Serv Medal; Good Conduct Medal. Mem: Am Legion (chaplain, George Washington Post). Honors & Awards: Awarded membership to Chapel of Four Chaplains Honor Roll. Relig: Catholic. Mailing Add: 111 Beverly Ave E Lansdowne PA 19050

RUSSO, MARTIN A (D)
US Rep, Ill
b Chicago, Ill, Jan 23, 44; m to Karen Jorgensen; c Tony. Educ: DePaul Univ, BA, 65, Col Law, JD, 67; Delta Theta Phi; Blue Key; Alpha Phi Delta. Polit & Govt Pos: Law clerk, Hon John V McCormack, Ill Appellate Court, 67-68; asst states attorney, Cook Co, 71-73; US Rep, Ill, 75-, vchmn freshman task force on tax reform, US House Rep, 75-, mem judiciary & small bus comts, 75- Bus & Prof Pos: Attorney. Mem: Tinley Park Jr CofC; Sons of Italy; Am & Ill Bar Asns; Joint Civil Comt Ital-Am (life mem). Honors & Awards: One of Roseland's Ten Outstanding Young Men, Chicago Jr Asn Com & Indust, Gateway Br, 68. Relig: Roman Catholic. Legal Res: 1127 W 127th Pl Calumet Park IL 60643 Mailing Add: US House Rep Washington DC 20515

RUSSO, PAUL ANTHONY (R)
Exec Asst, Rep Nat Finance Comt
b Newport, RI, Dec 8, 42; s Gabriel D Russo & Mary C Wogan R; m 1963 to Mary Jane Sisson; c Deborah Ann, Michael Paul & James Anthony. Educ: Rogers High Sch, Newport, RI, dipl, 60; Int Bus Mach Educ Ctr, Boston, Mass, 65; NAm Inst Syst & Procedures, Newport Beach, Calif, 69-71. Polit & Govt Pos: Mem, Jamestown Rep Town Comt, RI, 65-70, chmn, 68-70; mem, RI State Rep Cent Comt, 66-67; mem, Jamestown Town Coun, 67-69; secy, 47th Representative Dist Rep Comt, RI, formerly; exec asst, Rep Nat Finance Comt, 75- Bus & Prof Pos: Sr programmer-analyst, Stanwick Corp, Newport, RI, 65-67; sr syst analyst, Bostitch, Inc, East Greenwich, 67-68; mgr tech opers, Appl Comput Sci, Providence, 68-70; mgr syst & data processing, Campanella Corp, Warwick, 70- Mil Serv: Entered as Pvt E-1, Marine Corps, 60, released as Cpl E-4, 64, after serv in 1st Marine Aircraft Wing, DaNang, S Vietnam, 61-62; Good Conduct Medal; Am Defense Award. Mem: Asn Syst Mgt; Data Processing Mgr Asn; Jamestown Hist Soc; Jamestown Rotary Club. Relig: Roman Catholic. Mailing Add: 300 New Jersey Ave SE Washington DC 20003

RUSSO, WILLIAM ANDREW (R)
Exec Dir, NC Rep Party
b Ottawa, Kans, Oct 24, 49; s Frank Russo & Dorothy Jo Witt R; m to Jennifer Page Smith. Educ: Univ NC, Chapel Hill, AB, 71; Cath Univ Law Sch, 73-74; Lambda Chi Alpha. Polit & Govt Pos: State dir, Youth for Nixon-Agnew, NMex, 68; mem, Rep Nat Finance Comt, 70; young voters dir, Nat Rep Cong Comt, 71, southern states campaign dir, 72; pres & legis asst to US Rep James T Broyhill, NC, 73-; exec dir, NC Rep Party, 74- Relig: Episcopal. Mailing Add: 4705-A Edwards Mill Rd Raleigh NC 27612

RUSSUM, JULIUS FRANKLIN (D)
Chmn, DeSoto Co Dem Comt, Miss
b Flora, Miss, Feb 18, 95; s Wilson Frank Russum & Cornelia Hospon R; m 1922 to Beatrice Brunson; c Lawrence Brunson & Betty (Mrs Manning). Educ: Miss State Univ, BS, 21; George Peabody Col, MA, 28; Phi Delta Kappa. Polit & Govt Pos: Chmn, DeSoto Co Dem Comt, Miss, 48- Bus & Prof Pos: Supt, Hernando Schs, Miss, 36-45; supt educ, DeSoto Co, Miss, 48-56. Mil Serv: Entered as Pvt, Army, 18, released as Wagoner, 19, after serv in 304th Am Tr, 79th Div, Argonne Forest, France. Mem: Miss & Nat Educ Asns; Miss & Nat Dept of Supt; Mason. Relig: Baptist; Deacon, Hernando Baptist Church. Mailing Add: 138 East St Hernando MS 38632

RUST, GARY W (R)
Mo State Rep
Mailing Add: 700 North Pacific Cape Girardeau MO 63701

RUSTAD, ELMER LEWIS (R)
b Wakonda, SDak, Aug 11, 08; s John Rustad & Hannah Forsethlien R; m 1932 to Berniece Elizabeth Hillery; c Patricia (Mrs W J Herrmann) & Robert L. Educ: Sioux Falls Col, BA cum laude, 29; Univ Minn, MA, 37. Polit & Govt Pos: State dir, US Savings Bonds Div, SDak, 41-52, dir sales, Washington, DC, 52-66, asst nat dir, 66-69, nat dir, 69-72. Bus & Prof Pos: Supt schs, Egan, SDak, 29-34; jr high sch prin, Aberdeen, 34-41. Mil Serv: Entered as Lt(jg), Navy, 43, released as Lt Comdr, 46, after serv in Navy Air Training, Pac Theatre. Mem: Lions; Civic Clubs; Am Legion. Honors & Awards: Meritorious Serv Award, US Treas Dept; nominee, Civil Servant of the Year, 70. Relig: Baptist. Mailing Add: 2019 Lorraine Ave McLean VA 22101

RUSTAD, GERALD (D)
Chmn Dist One, NDak Dem Non-Partisan League
b Williston, NDak, Feb 28, 44; s Herman Rustad & Marion Brisson R; m 1968 to Dawn Lea Duncalf; c Jennifer Karn & Joshua Buchanan. Educ: Univ NDak, BA, 66, Sch Law, JD, 66; Theta Chi. Polit & Govt Pos: Committeeman, Precinct 73, Williston, NDak, 70-; chmn Dist One, NDak Dem Non-Partisan League, 70-; state finance comt mem, NDak Dem Non-Partisan League Party, 73- Bus & Prof Pos: Asst States Attorney, Williams Co, NDak, 69-; partner, Anseth & Rustad, Law Firm, Williston, 71- Publ: Assoc ed, NDak Law Rev, 68. Mem: Am & NDak Bar Asns; Nat Dist Attorneys Asn; Am Trial Lawyers Asn; Elks. Relig: Protestant. Legal Res: 501 E 11th St Williston ND 58801 Mailing Add: Box 476 Williston ND 58801

RUTH, EARL BAKER (R)
Gov, Am Samoa
b Spencer, NC, Feb 7, 16; s Earl Monroe Ruth & Marion Beatrice Ruth Butler; m 1938 to Jane Wiley; c Billie Jane (Mrs Frank Foil), Earl Wiley, Marian Ann (Mrs Joe Reber) & Jacqueline Dell (Mrs Clay Burleson). Educ: Univ NC, AB, 38, MA, 42 & PhD, 55. Polit & Govt Pos: City councilman, Salisbury, NC; US Rep, Eighth Dist, NC, 69-74; Gov, Am Samoa, 75- Bus & Prof Pos: Teacher & coach, Chapel Hill High Sch, Chapel Hill, NC, 38-39; teacher & coach, Piedmont Jr High Sch, Charlotte, NC, 39-40; shipping dept, McCrary Mills, Asheboro, NC, 40; asst supt, NC State Parks, 41; grad asst, Dept Phys Educ, Univ NC, 41-42; dir recreation, Kings Mountain, NC, 45; asst football coach, baseball coach, basketball coach, athletic dir, chmn dept phys educ & dean students, Catawba Col, 46-68. Mil Serv: Entered as Ens, Navy, 42, released as Lt, 45, after serv in USS St George. Mem: Nat Sportscasters & Sportswriters Awards Prog (mem of original comt & past pres); Am Legion; VFW; Civitan; Elks. Relig: Presbyterian. Legal Res: Box 4293 Salisbury NC 28144 Mailing Add: Govt House Pago Pago American Samoa

RUTH, IRLEY GALE (R)
Mem, Schuyler Co Rep Party, Mo
b Downing, Mo, May 19, 32; s John Raymond Ruth & Millie Wheeler R; single. Educ: Downing High Sch, Mo, 4 years; Devey Tech Sch, Chicago, Ill, 2 years. Polit & Govt Pos: Mayor, Downing, Mo, 56-58 & 68-; mem, Schuyler Co Rep Party, 62-, chmn, 68-74. Bus & Prof Pos: Mem bd dirs, C & E Mfg Corp, Memphis, Mo, 64-66; dir, Ruth Enterprise, Downing, Mo, presently. Mil Serv: Entered as Pvt, Army, 52, released as Sgt, 55, after serv in 8th Army, Korean Theatre, 53-54. Mem: Odd Fellows; VFW. Relig: Protestant. Mailing Add: Box 39 Downing MO 63536

RUTHERFORD, CLARA BERYL (R)
Chmn, Tulare Co Rep Cent Comt, Calif
b Porterville, Calif, Mar 2, 12; d Harry Abbey Wilcox & Jessie Jefford W; m 1933 to Kenneth Carr Rutherford; c Jane (Mrs Barry V Smith), Anne (Mrs John F Johnson) & Alan. Educ: Porterville Jr Col, AA, 31. Polit & Govt Pos: Asst clerk, Selective Serv Bd, Porterville, Calif, 41-42; secy, Calif Rep Assembly, Porterville Area, 65-66, vpres, 67, pres, 68, dir-at-lg, 72-; mem, Tulare Co Rep Cent Comt, 67-, secy, 70-72, chmn, 73-; mem, Rep State Cent Comt Calif, 67-; mem, Tulare Co Citizens' Welfare Adv Comt, 71-, secy, 72- Bus & Prof Pos: Bookkeeper & comptometer operator, Pig 'n' Whistle Corp, Los Angeles, Calif, 31-37; bookkeeper, Claubes Prescription Pharm, Porterville, 48-60. Mem: Farm Bur; Am & Tulare Co Cowbelles; Calif Cowbelles (chmn consumer educ, chmn nominating comt, 73-); Calif Cattlemen's Asn. Relig: Congregational. Mailing Add: 33195 Success Valley Dr Porterville CA 93257

RUTHERFORD, THOMAS TRUXTUN (D)
NMex State Sen
b Columbus, Ohio, Mar 3, 47; s James William Rutherford & Elizabeth Whiting Colby R; m 1965 to Linda Sue Rogers; c Jeremy Todd. Educ: Univ NMex, BBA, 70. Polit & Govt Pos: Ward committeeperson, Bernalillo Co Dem Party, NMex, 71-; nominee, Dem Party Cand for NMex State Sen, 72; founding officer, NMex Youth Caucus, 72-; mem, NMex Attorney Gen Environ Adv Comt, 72- & Bernalillo Co Dem Cent Comt, 72-; NMex State Sen, 73- Bus & Prof Pos: Prog coordr, KOB Radio, Albuquerque, 68-71, sta mgr, KOB-FM, 71-72; vpres, World Hot Air Balloon Championships, Inc, 72- Mem: Albuquerque Press Club; Nat Asn Broadcasters; Balloon Fedn of Am; Albuquerque Aerostat Ascension Asn. Honors & Awards: Numerous awards for commercial & promotional excellence, Albuquerque Advert Club, 70-72; youngest State Sen ever elected in NMex. Relig: Episcopal. Mailing Add: 729 Loma Vista NE Albuquerque NM 87106

RUTKOWSKI, JAMES ANTHONY (D)
Wis State Rep
b Milwaukee, Wis, Apr 6, 42; s Anton Bernard Rutkowski & Grace Jankowski R; single. Educ: Marquette Univ, BS, 64, Law Sch, JD, 66; Delta Theta Phi. Polit & Govt Pos: Trustee, Village of Hales Corners, Milwaukee Co, Wis, 70; Wis State Rep, Dist 23, 71- Bus & Prof Pos: Practicing attorney, Mount & Keck, Milwaukee, Wis, 66; Brendel & Hughes, Wauwatosa, 66-67; pvt practice, Milwaukee, 68- Mil Serv: Entered as Pvt E-1, Army Res, 67, released as Pvt E-2, 68, after serv in Active Duty Training, Sch Army Security Agency, Ft Devens, Mass; Spec-4, Army Res, 71. Mem: Milwaukee Jr Bar Asn; Jaycees; KofC. Relig: Roman Catholic. Legal Res: 10223 Kay Pkwy Hales Corners WI 53130 Mailing Add: 108-N State Capitol Madison WI 53702

RUTLEDGE, DAVID KEITH (R)
Chmn, Independence Co Rep Comt, Ark
b Batesville, Ark, Dec 25, 42; s Leslie Rutledge & Ona Pearson R; m 1970 to Nancy Carol

Leonard; c Joel Alan. Educ: Univ Ark, Fayetteville, BA & JD; Phi Alpha Delta. Polit & Govt Pos: Chmn, First Cong Dist Rep Party, Ark, 72 & Independence Co Rep Comt, 72-; exec committeeman, Ark State Rep Party, 73- Mil Serv: Entered as Pvt, Army, 60, released as SP-5, 63, after serv in V Corps, ETO, 60-63. Mem: Ark Bar Asn; Independence Co Bar Asn (pres, 71-72); Batesville Area CofC; Batesville Jaycees (pres, 72-73); Farm Bur. Honors & Awards: Fel Inst Polit in Ark. Legal Res: Gen Delivery Huff AR 72545 Mailing Add: PO Box 2738 186 Broad St Batesville AR 72501

RUTOWSKI, JOHN A (D)
Md State Deleg
Mailing Add: 314 Washburn Ave Baltimore MD 21225

RUWE, L NICHOLAS (R)
Asst Chief of Protocol, Dept of State
b Detroit, Mich, Sept 22, 33; s Lester Frederick Ruwe & Ruth Maude Devoy R; single. Educ: Brown Univ, BA, 55; Univ Mich Grad Sch Bus Admin, 56; Psi Upsilon. Polit & Govt Pos: Mem presidential campaign staff & nat adv staff, Nixon-Lodge, Washington, DC, 60; dir scheduling & itinerary, John G Tower for Sen Campaign, Tex, 61; co-campaign dir for John W Goode, Jr, 20th Cong Dist, Tex, 61; mem, Gubernatorial Campaign Staff of Richard Nixon, Los Angeles, Calif, 62; campaign mgr, Mayoralty Race, Houston, Tex, 63; scheduling & itinerary, Charles Percy Gubernatorial Campaign, Ill, 64; dir scheduling & itinerary for Richard Nixon Presidential Campaign, 64; mem, Advance Staff of Richard Nixon, New York, 66 & Campaign Staff of Richard Nixon, Ill, 68; asst chief of protocol, Dept of State, 69-; asst to Herbert G Klein, Dir of Commun, 70- Relig: Roman Catholic. Legal Res: 217 Touraine Rd Grosse Pointe MI 48236 Mailing Add: Dept of State Washington DC 20520

RYALS, JOHN L (D)
Fla State Rep
Mailing Add: 221 North Kings Ave Brandon FL 33511

RYAN, AILEEN BARLOW (D)
Councilman, New York City Coun
b Bronx, NY; m to E Gerard Ryan, wid; c Gerald, Alanna & Francis X. Educ: Hunter Col; NY Law Sch. Polit & Govt Pos: Vpres, Siwanoy Dem Clubs; unit mgr, New York Census Bur; mem, NY State Dem Women; NY State Assemblywoman, 58-66; councilman-at-lg, New York City Coun, 66-; deleg, Dem Nat Conv, 72. Bus & Prof Pos: Teacher & supvr educ, Mus of City of New York; bd adv, Bronx Commun Col. Mem: Bronx Red Cross (bd dirs); Nat Multiple Sclerosis Asn (bd dirs); Bus & Prof Women's Club; League of Women Voters. Mailing Add: 2051 St Raymonds Ave Bronx NY 10462

RYAN, ANDREW W, JR (R)
NY State Assemblyman
b Plattsburgh, NY, June 13, 31; s Andrew W Ryan, Sr & Lillian MacDougal R; m 1974 to Ellen Moe; c Maura Ann & Andrew W, III. Educ: Georgetown Univ, BSSS, Albany Law Sch, LLB. Polit & Govt Pos: Confidential Supreme Court Clerk, NY, 59-63; NY State Assemblyman, 111th Assembly Dist, 69-; secy, Clinton Co Rep Comt. Bus & Prof Pos: Attorney-at-law, pvt practice, 60-62; assoc with John P Judge, 62-65; assoc with Fitzpatrick, Bennett & Tromblley, 65-70; pvt practice, 70-71; Ryan & Lahtinen Law Firm, 71-73; pvt practice, 73- Mil Serv: Entered as 2nd Lt, Army Artil, 55, released as 1st Lt, 56, after serv in 760th Bn Artil, Ger. Mem: Clinton Co Bar Asn; NY State Trial Lawyers Ask; Elks; Rod & Gun Club; KofC; Kiwanis. Relig: Catholic. Legal Res: Apt 40G Adirondack Lane Plattsburgh NY 12901 Mailing Add: 51 Clinton St Plattsburgh NY 12901

RYAN, CHARLES J, JR (D)
Committeeman, Prince George's Co Dem Party, Md
b Southbridge, Mass, Sept 15, 36; s Charles J Ryan & Doris Olney R; m 1958 to Michele King; c Charles J, III & Kimberly Michele. Educ: Georgetown Univ, BS, 58; Univ Md, MA, 74; Polit Sci Asn; Delta Phi Epsilon; Gamma Rho Sigma. Polit & Govt Pos: Admin dir, Lawyers' Comt for Civil Rights, Washington, DC, 66-69; dir polit research, Muskie Elec Comt, 70-72; committeeman, Prince George's Co Dem Party, Md, 70-; exec asst to Gov Marvin Mandel, Md, 73- Bus & Prof Pos: Prof, Prince George's Community Col, 74-75. Mil Serv: Entered as 2nd Lt, Army, 58, released as 1st Lt, 60, after serv in 116th Counter-Intel Corps Unit, Washington, DC. Publ: Auth, Political History of the American Trade Union Movement, 66. Mem: Bowie Dem Club; 14th Dist Dem Club; Dem Forum; Coalition for Dem Majority; Coalition for Support of Handicapped Children. Relig: Roman Catholic. Mailing Add: 3007 Bendix Lane Bowie MD 20715

RYAN, GEORGE HOMER (R)
Ill State Rep
b Maquoketa, Iowa, Feb 24, 34; s Thomas Jefferson Ryan, Sr & Jeanette Bowman R; m 1956 to Lura Lynn Lowe; c Nancy, Lynda, Julie, Jo Anne, Jeanette & George Homer, Jr. Educ: Ferris State Col, Big Rapids, Mich, BS in pharm, 61. Polit & Govt Pos: Asst supvr, Kankakee Co Bd, Ill, 66-73, chmn, 72-73; Ill State Rep, 43rd Dist, 73-, mem revenue comt, Ill legis invest comt, minority spokesman appropriations comt & mem space needs comn, Ill House of Rep. Bus & Prof Pos: Vpres, Ryan Pharmacies, Kankakee, Ill, 52- Mil Serv: Entered as Pvt, Army, 54, released as Sp-1, 56, after serv in Korea, 55-56. Relig: Methodist. Mailing Add: 912 S Greenwood Ave Kankakee IL 60901

RYAN, HEWSON ANTHONY
b New Haven, Conn, June 16, 22; s James Patrick Ryan & Clara Hewson Sprightley R; m 1949 to Helene Elizabeth Lecko; c Anthony H & Anne S. Educ: Yale Univ, BA, 47, MA, 48; Univ Madrid, PhD, 51. Polit & Govt Pos: Foreign serv assignment to Colombia, 51-54, Bolivia, 54-56 & Chile, 56-61, appt career minister, 69, US Ambassador, Honduras, 69-73; asst dir, US Info Agency, 61-64, assoc dir, 65-66, dep dir, 66-69; diplomat in residence, Fletcher Sch Law & Diplomacy, Tufts Univ, 73-75; dep asst secy of state for Inter-Am Affairs, 75- Mil Serv: Entered as Pvt, Army, 42, released as T/Sgt, 46, after serv in 271st Inf Regt, ETO, 44-46; Combat Inf Badge; Bronze Star Medal. Publ: Various articles in scholarly jour on Spanish lit & bibliography, 53-60. Mem: Latin Am Studies Asn; Am Acad Polit & Social Sci; Foreign Serv Asn; Overseas Press Club, New York; DACOR, Washington. Honors & Awards: Distinguished Serv Award, US Info Agency, 64; Presidential Citation, 65; Order of Morazan, Honduras, 73. Mailing Add: 6109 Robinwood Rd Bethesda MD 20034

RYAN, HOWARD CHRIS (R)
Justice, Ill Supreme Court
b Tonica, Ill, June 17, 16; s John F Ryan & Sarah Egger R; m 1943 to Helen Cizek; c John F, Elizabeth & Howard C, Jr. Educ: LaSalle-Peru Oglesby Jr Col, AA, 36; Univ Ill, BA, 40, JD, 42; Phi Alpha Delta. Polit & Govt Pos: Asst States Attorney, LaSalle Co, Ill, 52-54, Co Judge, 54-57; Circuit Judge, 13th Judicial Circuit, Ill, 57-68, Chief Judge, 64-68; Appellate Court Justice, Third Judicial Dist, 68-70; Supreme Court Justice, State of Ill, 70- Bus & Prof Pos: Attorney-at-law, Decatur, Ill, 46-47; attorney-at-law, Peru, 47-57. Mil Serv: Entered as Pvt, Army Air Force, 42, released as 1st Lt, 45, after serv in Air Transport Command, 42-45. Mem: Am Judicature Soc; Am, Ill & LaSalle Co Bar Asns; Ill Judges Asn; Mason (33 degree). Relig: Methodist. Mailing Add: Box 53 Tonica IL 61370

RYAN, JOHN C (R)
Mo State Sen
married; c two daughters; two grandchildren. Polit & Govt Pos: Chmn, Pettis Co Rep Comt, Mo; mem bd regents, Cent Mo State Col; Mo State Sen, 67- Bus & Prof Pos: Mem bd dirs, Mo State Bank; vpres, Bryant Motor Co; farmer, Pettis Co & bus in Sedalia. Mem: Mason; Shrine; Kiwanis; Elks; Black Angus Asn. Relig: Methodist; chmn bd trustees, Wesley Methodist Church. Mailing Add: Walnut Hills Rte 3 Sedalia MO 65301

RYAN, LEO JOSEPH (D)
US Rep, Calif
b Lincoln, Nebr, May 5, 25; s Leo Joseph Ryan & Autumn Mead R; c Christopher, Shannon, Patricia, Kevin & Erin. Educ: Creighton Univ, BS, 49, MS, 51. Polit & Govt Pos: City Councilman, South San Francisco, 56-62, Mayor, 62; Calif State Assemblyman, 63-72, mem, Assembly Rules, Ways & Means Com & Pub Utilities & Educ Comts & Joint Comt on Textbooks & Curriculum; adv, Compensatory Educ Comn, Calif, 66; deleg, Dem Nat Conv, 64 & 68; US Rep, Calif, 73-, mem, Govt Opers Comt & Foreign Affairs Comt, US House of Rep, 73- Bus & Prof Pos: Exec vpres, Pension Investment Corp, 66. Mil Serv: Entered as A/S, Navy, 43, released as Seaman 1/C, 46, after serv in Submarine Force, Pac Fleet, 44-45. Publ: Understanding California Government & Politics, 66 & USA/From Where We Stand, 70, Fearon Publ. Mem: Nat Am Revolution Bicentennial Comn; Elks; Moose; Commonwealth Club. Legal Res: South San Francisco CA Mailing Add: 119 Cannon Bldg Washington DC 20515

RYAN, MARGARET MARY (D)
Secy, Lake Co Dem Exec & Cent Comts, Ohio
b Painesville, Ohio, Jan 15, 25; d Francis Patrick Ryan & Irene Dowling R; single. Educ: Ursuline Col (Ohio), AB, 46. Polit & Govt Pos: Mem, Lake Co Dem Cent Comt, Ohio, 60-; mem, Lake Co Dem Exec Comt, 62-; trustee, Morley Libr Bd, Lake Co, 65-71; secy, Lake Co Dem Exec & Cent Comts, 68-; trustee, Eastern Lake Co Dem Club, 69-; trustee, Lake Co Dem Women's Club, 69-; trustee, Lakeland Community Col, 72-; mem, Lake Co Bd Elec, 74- Bus & Prof Pos: Teacher, St Mary Sch, Painesville, Ohio, 46-; secy, St Mary Church, Painesville, 46- Mem: Nat Cath Educ Asn; Ursuline Col Alumnae Asn, Federated Dem Women Ohio; Lake Co Dem Women's Club; West Lake Co Dem Club. Relig: Roman Catholic. Mailing Add: 311 Rockwood Dr Painesville OH 44077

RYAN, MATTHEW J (R)
Rep Whip, Pa House of Rep
b Philadelphia, Pa, Apr 27, 32; s Thomas F Ryan & Kathleen Mullin R; m 1956 to Mary Jane Mullray; c five. Educ: Villanova Univ, BS, JD. Polit & Govt Pos: Pa State Rep, 63-, chmn, Rep Policy Comt, Pa House of Rep, 71-72, Majority Whip, 73-74, Rep Whip, 75- Bus & Prof Pos: Attorney. Mil Serv: 1st Lt, Marines, 54-56; Marine Corps Res, 52-60. Mailing Add: House PO Box 2 Main Capitol Bldg Harrisburg PA 17120

RYAN, PAUL J (R)
NH State Rep
Mailing Add: Box 166 Danbury NH 03230

RYAN, ROBERT JOSEPH
Asst Secy Gen, UN
b Hatfield, Mass, July 11, 14; m to Mary Frances O'Leary; c Robert James & Thomas. Educ: Univ Mass, 32-34; Columbus Univ, LLB, 40. Polit & Govt Pos: Career officer, US Dept of State Foreign Serv, 37-, clerk, 37-42, asst chief, Div of Dept Personnel, 42-50, asst chief, Div of Foreign Serv Personnel, 50-53, chief, Personnel Opers Div, 53-55, exec dir, Bur of Near East, SAsian & African Affairs, 55-58, Nat War Col, 58-59, counr, Paris, 59-64, US Ambassador, Niger, 64-68, Dep Asst Secy State, 68-69, Dir Mgt Serv, UN, 69-72, Asst Secy Gen, 72- Mem: DC Bar Asn; Am Foreign Serv Asn; Am Mgt Asn. Honors & Awards: Superior Serv Award, 54, Dept of State; Commendable Serv Award, 50. Mailing Add: 340 E 64th St New York NY 10021

RYAN, THOMAS (LIBERAL)
Married; c eight. Polit & Govt Pos: Cand, Minn State Sen, 66; former Minn State Rep; former Spec Asst US Dist Attorney; Spec Asst Attorney Gen, State of Minn; alt deleg, Dem Nat Conv, 72. Bus & Prof Pos: Attorney. Mil Serv: Navy. Mailing Add: Seventh Ave NE Sandstone MN 55072

RYAN, THOMAS F (TOM) (D)
Mo State Rep
Mailing Add: 10513 E 42nd St Apt A Kansas City MO 64133

RYAN, THOMAS P, JR (D)
Mayor, Rochester, NY
b Rochester, NY, Dec 4, 29; s Thomas Patrick Ryan, Sr & Delia Mulkeen R; m to Charlotte Carpenter; c Mary. Educ: Aquinas Inst, Rochester; St Bonaventure Univ, 52; Syracuse Univ Sch Law, 57. Polit & Govt Pos: Mem, Monroe Co Bd Supvr, NY, 62-67; city councilman, Rochester, 68-, mayor, 74- Bus & Prof Pos: Partner, Kennedy & Ryan, Rochester, NY, 57- Mil Serv: Entered as Pvt, Marine Corps, 46, released as Cpl, 48. Mem: NY State Bar Asn (judicial comt). Relig: Catholic. Mailing Add: 439 Rocket St Rochester NY 14609

RYAN, TIMOTHY THOMAS (D)
Mo State Rep
b Oklahoma City, Okla, Sept 18, 38; s William Patrick Ryan & Mary Elizabeth McGury R; m 1966 to Mary Ann Ferry; c Timothy Thomas, Jr & Michael David. Educ: Univ Mo, 56-61. Polit & Govt Pos: Mo State Rep, 71- Bus & Prof Pos: Owner, Ryan Brokerage Co, 67- Mil Serv: Entered as Pvt, Marines, 62, released as Cpl, 66, after serv in Fourth Div, 62-66. Relig: Catholic. Mailing Add: 10513 E 42nd St Apt A Kansas City MO 64133

RYAN, WILLIAM A (D)
Mich State Rep
b Morgantown, WVa, May 2, 19. Educ: High sch grad. Polit & Govt Pos: Mich State Rep, 58-; deleg, Dem Nat Conv, 68. Bus & Prof Pos: Ed, The Wage Earner, formerly; pres, financial secy, Local 104, UAW, formerly. Mil Serv: Marines. Mem: Cath Interracial Coun; Nat Cath Soc Action Conf. Relig: Roman Catholic. Mailing Add: 1582 Defer Place Detroit MI 48214

RYAN, WILLIAM MURRAY (R)
NMex State Rep
b Central, NMex, July 22, 22; s James Stanton Ryan & Lyda Murray R; m 1945 to Marian E Buchella; c William Murray, Jr, Kathleen Mary, Robin Patricia & twins, Kerry Frank & Kevin Frank. Educ: NMex State Teachers Col, 40-42; US Mil Acad, BS, 45. Polit & Govt Pos: Mem & chmn, Silver City Sch Bd Educ, NMex, 59-65; NMex State Rep, Grant Co, 69-; chmn, Rep State Cent Comt NMex, formerly. Mil Serv: Entered as Cadet, US Mil Acad, 42, released as 1st Lt, 49. Mem: Am Inst Mining Engrs; KofC; VFW; Am Legion. Relig: Catholic. Legal Res: 1709 W Sixth St Silver City NM 88061 Mailing Add: Box 110 Silver City NM 88061

RYBACKI, RAY J (D)
Mem, Cook Co Dem Cent Comt, Ill
b Chicago, Ill, May 19, 31; s Anton Rybacki & Lottie Wisowaty R; m 1953 to Jacqueline Mary Murphy; c Charlotte, Pamela, Jacqueline & Patricia. Educ: Wilson Jr Col, Chicago, Ill, 50-51; Bradley Univ, 52-53; Roosevelt Univ, BS, 53. Polit & Govt Pos: Pres, Palos Twp Young Dem, Ill, 61-63; vchmn, Cook Co Young Dem, 61-63; vpres, Palos Twp Dem Orgn, 62-65; Dem cand for Cong, Fourth Cong Dist, 64-66; Dem Committeeman, Palos Twp, 65-; alt deleg, Dem Nat Conv, 68; mem, Cook Co Dem Cent Comt, currently. Bus & Prof Pos: Indust salesman, Fullerton Metals, Chicago, Ill, 56-57, Kasle Steel Corp, 57-60, Craname, Inc, 60-63 & US Steel Supply, Div of US Steel, 63-65; arbitrator, Ill Indust Comn, 65- Mil Serv: Entered as Pvt, Army, 53, released as Pfc, 55, after serv in 1st Specially Organized Electronic Warfare Counter-Measures Unit, Ft Bliss, Tex, 54-55. Mem: KofC. Relig: Catholic. Mailing Add: 11917 Timber Lane Dr Palos Park IL 60464

RYBURN, BENNIE, JR (D)
Ark State Rep
b Rison, Ark, July 26, 34; s Bennie Ryburn, Sr & Virginia Morrison R; m 1961 to Judith McKenney; c Bennie, III, Angelia Dawn & Ray Morrison. Educ: Univ Ark & Ark A&M Col, 52-57. Polit & Govt Pos: Ark State Rep, currently. Bus & Prof Pos: Owner & gen mgr, Ryburn Motor Co, 58-; pres, Ryburn Ins Inc, 61-; pres, First State Savings & Loan, 66-; mem bd dirs, Commercial Bank & Trust Co, 69- Relig: Baptist. Legal Res: 1 Westood Lane Monticello AR 71655 Mailing Add: Box 390 Monticello AR 71655

RYDER, KENNETH, JR (D)
Pres, Young Dem Del
b Bryn Mawr, Pa, July 25, 40; s Kenneth Ryder, Sr & Helen McNally Nielson R; m 1962 to Betty Jean Carey; c John Kenneth & Michele Jean. Educ: Univ Del, 2 years. Polit & Govt Pos: Exec secy, Young Dem Del, 69, pres, 70-; vpres, State Young Dem, 69-70; vpres, Kent Co Young Dem, 70; vpres, 32nd Dist Dem Club, 70; mem, Dem Renewal Comn & Revolutionary War Bicentennial Comt, 70-; committeeman, 32nd Dist Dem Party, Del, 71- Bus & Prof Pos: Asst results engr, Dover, Del, 61-64; skilled technician, Gen Foods, Dover, 64- Mil Serv: Entered as E-1, Navy, 58, released as E-5, P-1, 61, after serv in Atlantic Fleet, 59-61; Letter of Commendation. Mem: Felton High Sch Alumni Asn; Felton Commun Fire Co. Relig: Methsdistx Relig: Methodist. Mailing Add: RD 3 Box 382 Felton DE 19943

RYLANCE, DAN FREDERICK (D)
NDak State Rep
b Fargo, NDak, June 10, 42; s Donald Rylance & Laura Mae Gumb R; m 1964 to Billie Jo Elliott; c Keli Erin & David Elliott. Educ: Am Univ, cert arch admin, 67; St Johns Univ, BA, 64; Univ NDak, MA, 64; Univ Mo-Columbia, 69-70. Polit & Govt Pos: Dem-Non-Partisan League Cand, Secy of State, 72; Dem precinct committeeman, 72-; NDak State Rep, 18th Dist, 74- Bus & Prof Pos: Research asst, Univ NDak, 66-67, archivist, 67-69, curator & asst prof hist, 71. Publ: Gerald P Nye, NDak Quart, 69; William Langer and the themes of North Dakota history, SDak Hist, 72; co-auth, Years of Despair, North Dakota in the Depression, Oxcart Press, 74. Mem: Am Asn Univ Prof; Orgn of Am Historians; Western Hist Asn. Mailing Add: 924 Sunset Dr Grand Forks ND 58201

RYMER, THOMAS ARRINGTON (D)
Md State Deleg
b Asheville, NC, Feb 10, 25; s Furman Houston Rymer & Amy Collins R; separated; c Gary, Thomas & Ronnie. Educ: Cornell Univ, BCE, 48; George Washington Univ, JD, 56; Sigma Chi. Polit & Govt Pos: Attorney, Calvert Co, Md, 66-70; Md State Deleg, 70- Bus & Prof Pos: Construction engr, Secy of Defense, 46-65; attorney-at-law, 65- Mil Serv: Entered as Ens, Navy, 43, released as Lt(jg), after serv in Seabees, Pac, 43-46; Theatre Ribbons, Expert Rifle & Pistol. Mem: Am Legion; Elks; Bd of Trade. Relig: Methodist. Mailing Add: Box 283 Prince Frederick MD 20678

RYS, C GUS (R)
NJ State Assemblyman
Mailing Add: State House Trenton NJ 08625

RYSKIND, MARY HOUSE (R)
Secy, Los Angeles Co Rep Cent Comt, Calif
b Oklahoma City, Okla, May 28, 04; d Julius Temple House & Flora Smith H; m 1929 to Morrie Ryskind; c Ruth (Mrs Ohman) & Allan H. Educ: Univ Chicago, PhB, 23; Columbia Teachers Col, post-grad work, 27; Phi Upsilon. Polit & Govt Pos: Mem, Rep State Cent Comt Calif, 52-56 & 66-74; mem, Los Angeles Co Rep Cent Comt, 43rd Assembly Dist, Calif, 67-, vchmn, 69-70, secy, 70-, mem, Exec Comt, 70- Mem: Beverly Hills Br, West Los Angeles Chap, Am Nat Red Cross. Honors & Awards: Outstanding Serv to Los Angeles Co Rep Cent Comt. Mailing Add: 605 N Hillcrest Rd Beverly Hills CA 90201

S

SAAR, T D, JR (TED) (D)
Kans State Sen
Mailing Add: 903 Kings Hwy Pittsburg KS 66762

SAARI, LEONARD W (D)
b Superior, Ariz, May 25, 22; s Leonard Saari (deceased) & Aina Koskiniemi S; m 1951 to Ruth Desiree Simon; c Neilton Jared. Educ: Univ Wash, BA, 51; Sigma Delta Chi. Polit & Govt Pos: Legis asst to US Rep Brock Adams, Wash, 65-67; econ develop specialist, Econ Develop Admin, 67-69; admin asst to US Rep Lloyd Meeds, Wash, 69- Bus & Prof Pos: Reporter, Tacoma News Tribune, 53-69; ed, Lodge 751, Int Asn Machinists, 59-64. Mil Serv: Entered as Pvt, Army, 46, released as T-5, 48, after serv in Develop Det, Signal Corps. Mem: IAMAW; Nat Press Club; Capitol Dem Club. Honors & Awards: Distinguished Serv Award, Tacoma-Pierce Co Asn for Ment Health; Assoc Press Photog Award. Relig: Unitarian. Legal Res: Lynnwood WA Mailing Add: 412 Underhill Pl Alexandria VA 22305

SAARI, RUTH DESIREE (D)
b Berlin, Ger, July 29, 29; d Manfred Simon (deceased) & Margot Goldsmith S; m 1951 to Leonard W Saari; c Neilton Jared. Educ: Univ Wash, BA, 51; Theta Sigma Phi. Polit & Govt Pos: Mem, Pierce Co Adv Coun to Wash State Bd Against Discrimination, 54-56; Dem precinct committeeman, 31st Dist, Wash, 60-64, secy, 62-64; deleg, Wash State Dem Conv, 62-68; Dem precinct committeeman, 35th Dist, Wash, 66-69; voter registr, King Co, 67-69; founding mem, Nat Citizens for Humphrey, 68; mem, Wash State Dem Comn on Party Struct & Deleg Selection, 69; deleg, Dem Nat Conv & hon secy of Wash Deleg, 68, mem, Rules Comt, 72; pub info specialist, Jackson for President, Washington, DC, 71-72. Bus & Prof Pos: Copy writer, KBKW Radio, Aberdeen, Wash, 51-52; reporter, Upper Valley Rev, Naches, 52; copy writer, KTNT-TV & Radio, Tacoma, 53-54; pub info specialist, Pierce Co Civil Defense, 54-56; pub info specialist, Heart Asn, Washington, DC, 65-66. Mem: Univ Wash Alumni Asn; Theta Sigma Phi Prof Chap; PTA. Honors & Awards: Several awards for poetry. Legal Res: Lynnwood WA Mailing Add: 412 Underhill Pl Alexandria VA 22305

SABATINI, FREDERICK ANTHONY (R)
Co Attorney, Cass Co, Ind
b Chicago, Ill, Oct 16, 37; s Fausto J Sabatini & Josephine Marocco S (deceased); single. Educ: Ind Univ, AB, 60, JD, 64; Phi Delta Phi; Blue Key; Sigma Nu. Polit & Govt Pos: Mem staff, US Rep Charles A Halleck, 62-65; chmn, Cass Co Young Rep, Ind, 65-66; deleg, Ind State Rep Conv, 66, 68 & 70; chmn, Cass Co Rep Party, 66-74; Co Attorney, Cass Co, 69-; exec comdr, Ind State Chmn of Nat Rep of Italian Descent; mem, Ind Legis Local Govt Study Comn. Bus & Prof Pos: Attorney, Hanna, Small, Sabatini & Becker, 65- Mil Serv: Pvt, Army, 60; Army Res. Mem: Am, Ind & Cass Co Bar Asns; Elks; Logansport Jr Achievement (bd of dirs). Honors & Awards: Logansport Outstanding Young Man, 67-68. Relig: Catholic. Legal Res: 1129 Erie Ave Logansport IN 46947 Mailing Add: 208 Fourth St Logansport IN 46947

SABBOW, FRITZ T (D)
NH State Rep
Mailing Add: 30 Lincoln St Laconia NH 03246

SABEL, JOSEPH H (D)
Chmn, Levy Co Dem Party, Fla
b Pittsburgh, Pa, Mar 13, 13; s Joseph Sabel & Katherine Kamins S; m 1974 to Adelaide Jones; c Shirley (Mrs Robert Iman) & Jo Ann (Mrs John Bitzer). Educ: Hazelwood High Sch, Pittsburgh, 27-28; Harvard Bus Admin spec prog, 56-57; Harvard-Yale Club. Polit & Govt Pos: Dep secy of labor & indust, State of Pa, 57-58; mem, Mayor's Comn on Human Rels, Pittsburgh, 59-63; vchmn, Levy Co Planning Comn, Fla, 72-; chmn, Levy Co Dem Party, 74-; mayor, Yankeetown, 75- Bus & Prof Pos: Mem bd dirs, Blue Cross of Western Pa, 60-73; pres local 590, Amalgamated Food Employees Union, Pittsburgh, 62-73; vpres, Pa State Fedn of Labor, 70-73. Publ: Ed, Labor Paper, The 590 News, 62-73. Mem: Amalgamated Food Employees Union; Mason (32 degree); Shrine; Am Asn Retired Persons (exec bd mem, Inglis-Yankeetown, 73-). Honors & Awards: Man of Year Award, Pittsburgh Jr CofC, 64; Community Chest Award, 68; Serv Award, AMCBW. Relig: Methodist. Legal Res: Star Rte 1 Box 22 Yankeetown FL 32698 Mailing Add: Box 280 Town Hall Yankeetown FL 32698

SABENS, MARSHALL T (R)
b Burlington, Vt, May 1, 26; s Harold T Sabens & Freda Bliss S; m 1954 to Joan Coffman; c Elizabeth & George. Educ: Univ Vt, BA, 51; Sigma Alpha Epsilon. Polit & Govt Pos: Treas, Vt Rep State Comt, 66-74. Mil Serv: Army, 45-47. Mem: Rotary; March of Dimes (treas, Vt State Chap). Relig: Episcopal. Mailing Add: 4 Highland Ave Montpelier VT 05601

SABLAN, RUDOLPHO G (D)
Lt Gov, Guam
Mailing Add: Congress Bldg Agana GU 96910

SABO, MARTIN OLAV (DFL)
Speaker, Minn State House of Rep
b Crosby, NDak, Feb 28, 38; m 1963 to Sylvia Ann Lee; c Karin Margaret & Julie Ann. Educ: Augsburg Col, BA, cum laude, 59. Polit & Govt Pos: Minn State Rep, 61-, Minority Leader, Minn House Rep, 69 & 71, Speaker, 73 & 75; vpres, Nat Cong State Legis, currently, mem intergovt rels comt; partic, Eagleton Inst for Young Legislators, 72. Bus & Prof Pos: Salesman, Aetna Life Ins Co, 61-; mem bd regents, Augsburg Col, currently. Honors & Awards: Man of Year, Minneapolis Jaycees, 73-74; One of Ten Outstanding Young Men of Year, Minn Jaycees; One of 200 Rising Young Leaders in Am, Time Mag. Relig: Lutheran; treas, Trinity Lutheran Church. Mailing Add: Minn House of Rep State Capitol St Paul MN 55155

SABONJIAN, ROBERT V (R)
Mayor, Waukegan, Ill
b Waukegan, Ill, Jan 4, 16; s Lazurus Sabonjian & Zaruhey Mooradian S; m 1947 to Lorene Terrill; c Dana Jo & Robert Glen. Educ: High Sch. Polit & Govt Pos: Alderman, Second Ward, Waukegan, Ill, 51-52 & 55-57, mayor, 57-; acting postmaster, US Post Off, Waukegan, 52-54. Bus & Prof Pos: Owner, Dutch Mill Dry Cleaners, 48-57; dir, Bank of Waukegan, 63-66. Mil Serv: Entered as A/S, Coast Guard, released as Boatswain Mate 2/C, 45, after serv in SPac; Asiatic Pac Medal; Good Conduct Medal; Pearl Harbor Medal; Am Theater Medal; Victory Medal. Mem: Eagles; Moose; DAV; Am Legion; VFW. Relig: Disciples of

Christ. Legal Res: 410 Flossmoor Waukegan IL 60085 Mailing Add: City Hall 106 N Utica St Waukegan IL 60085

SABOTA, FRANCIS ROBERT (D)
Mem, Wallingford Dem City Comt, Conn
b Wallingford, Conn, Jan 23, 19; s John Bartholomew Sabota & Katherine Sczerba S; single. Educ: Yale Univ, BS in Indust Eng, 48; Univ Conn, LLB, 58; Tau Beta Pi. Polit & Govt Pos: Mem, Planning & Zoning Comn, 53-65, chmn, 58-60; mem, Wallingford Dem City Comt, Conn, 55-; prosecutor, Munic Court, 59-60; mem, Bd of Finance, 61; Conn State Rep, 63-66; Judge of Probate, 67- Bus & Prof Pos: Attorney-at-law, 58- Mil Serv: Entered as 2nd Lt, Army, 41, released as Capt, 46, after serv in Pac Theater. Mem: Elks; Am Legion; KofC. Relig: Catholic. Mailing Add: 12 Lake St Wallingford CT 06492

SACHS, ALICE (D)
Leader, 66th Assembly Dist Dem Party, Manhattan, NY
b Kansas City, Mo; d Charles Sachs & Flora Weil; single. Educ: Wellesley Col, BA; Sorbonne, Cert d'Etudes Francaises; Durant scholar; Phi Beta Kappa. Polit & Govt Pos: Founder, Lexington Dem Club, NY, 49, mem exec comt, 50-; leader, 66th Assembly Dist Dem Party, Manhattan, 53-; cand, NY State Assembly, 56, 58 & 60; mem gen comt, NY Comt Dem Voters, 59-; mem adv coun, NY Young Dem Club, 59-65; cand, NY State Senate, 62; chmn, Dem Human Rels Comt, NY Co, 62-63; mem, State Dem Platform Comt, 64. Bus & Prof Pos: Ed, Crown Publ, Inc, 39- Mem: Commun Planning Bd Eight; Women's City Club; League of Women Voters; Citizens Union; Am for Dem Action. Mailing Add: 140 E 63rd St New York NY 10021

SACHS, ARTHUR S (D)
Chmn, Orange Dem Town Comt, Conn
b New Haven, Conn, Feb 26, 27; s Louis Sachs & Jessie Slater S; m 1950 to Marilyn Markle; c Nancy, David, Karen, Peter, Jimmy & Laurie. Educ: Yale Col, AB, 49, Law Sch, LLB, 52. Polit & Govt Pos: Chmn, Conn Personnel Appeals Bd, 59-70; mem, Orange Bd Educ, 60-73; mem, Conn Aeronaut Comn, 67-71; chmn, Orange Dem Town Comt, 68- Bus & Prof Pos: Partner, Sachs, Sachs, Giaimo & Sachs, 52- Mil Serv: Entered as Seaman 1/C, Navy, 45, released as R T M 3/C, 46, after serv in USS Eyms 80, Atlantic, 46. Publ: Co-auth, Vertical integration in the oil industry, Yale Law J, 52. Mem: Am, New Haven & Conn Bar Asns. Relig: Jewish. Mailing Add: 1014 Grassy Hill Rd Orange CT 06477

SACKETT, EVERETT BAXTER (R)
NH State Rep
b Buffalo, NY, Dec 1, 01; s Edward Everett Sackett & Ella Grove S; m 1925 to Martha E Rowley. Educ: Hamline Univ, BA, 23; Univ Minn, Minneapolis, MA, 25; Columbia Univ, PhD, 30. Hon Degrees: LLD, Univ NH, 67. Polit & Govt Pos: Town moderator, Lee, NH, 52-, mem bd adjustment, 64-; chmn sch bd, Oyster River Cooperative, NH, 53-61, sch moderator, 63-74; deleg, NH Const Conv, 56, 64 & 74; NH State Rep, 75- Bus & Prof Pos: Asst dir jr div, League Red Cross Soc, Paris, France, 28-30; dir research, Panama Canal Zone Schs, 30-35; instr, Grad Sch Educ, Harvard Univ, 38; prof educ & dean students, Univ NH, 46-59, chmn dept educ, 59-62, dean, Col Liberal Arts, 62-67. Publ: Co-auth, Our Schools, Harper Bros, 39; auth, New Hampshire's University, NH Publ Co, 75; auth, A Plan for Postsecondary Education in NH, Postsec Educ Comn, 73. Mem: Am Asn Univ Prof; Nat Educ Asn. Legal Res: Rte 155 Lee NH Mailing Add: RFD 2 Box 111 Dover NH 03820

SACKETT, JOHN C (R)
Alaska State Sen
b Huslia, Alaska, June 3, 44; s James Sackett & Lucy Vent S; single. Educ: Ohio Univ; Univ Alaska, BA in Acct, 72; Alpha Kappa Psi. Polit & Govt Pos: Pres, Tanana Chiefs Conf, 66-69; participant, Eagleton Inst Legis Reform, Rutgers Univ, formerly; Alaska State Rep, 66-70; Alaska State Sen, currently, mem comts finance, rules, labor & mgt, Alaska State Senate, currently; chmn bd, Alaska Fedn of Natives, 73-74; mem adv comt on Alaska Power Surv, currently; mem, Northwest Adv Comt & Pac Northwest Regional Adv Comt, Nat Park Serv, currently; mem nat adv bd coun, Bur of Land Mgt, currently; mem nat adv environ health sci coun, Nat Insts Health, 74- Bus & Prof Pos: Chmn bd, The Tundra Times, 73-74, mem adv bd, currently; pres & chmn bd, Doyon, Ltd, currently; mem bd dirs, Alaska Int Industs, currently; mem bd trustees, Alaska Methodist Univ, currently; mem student orientation serv adv bd, Univ Alaska, currently; mem bd dirs, Visual Arts Ctr, currently; chmn bd, Int Tech, Ltd, 75- Mailing Add: Box 65 Galena AK 99741

SACKETT, WALTER W, JR (D)
Fla State Rep
b Bridgeport, Conn, Nov 20, 05; s Walter Wallace Sackett, Sr & Hermine Archambault S; m 1972 to Sophie Georgeff Strickland; c Monica Ann, Walter Wallace, III, John A (adopted, deceased) & Charles A Dunn, MD. Educ: Harvard Univ, 22-23; Univ Miami, AB, 32; Univ Ala, 32-34; Rush Med Col, MD, 38; Phi Chi; Sigma Xi; Iron Arrow. Polit & Govt Pos: Fla State Rep, 66- Bus & Prof Pos: Instr anat, Univ Ala, 34-36, instr obstetrics, student health phys, 39-40; prof anat, Col Mortuary Sci, St Louis, 36-37; intern, Berwyn Hosp, Ill, 37-38 & St Lukes Hosp, St Louis, 38-39; resident, Charity Hosp, Natchez, Miss, 40-41; gen practice med, 41-; mem, Med Res Found, Univ Miami, 50-53; pioneer oral polio vaccine in newborns, 60-61; bd dirs, Physicians & Surgeons Underwriters Corp Adv Comt Poliomyelitis, Surgeon Gen US, 60-61; consult diabetes & arthritis, US Pub Health Serv, 61-62; mem staff, Doctors' Hosp, Jackson Mem Hosp, Variety Children's Hosp, Baptist Hosp & Coral Gables Hosp; secy, Dade Co Hosp, 62- Publ: Bringing up babies, 62; contrib to popular mags & prof jours plus TV & radio lects. Mem: Fla Acad Gen Practice; Pan Am Med Asn (chmn, NAm, 62-); Moose. Honors & Awards: Outstanding Alumni Award, Univ Miami, 57. Relig: Roman Catholic. Legal Res: 333 University Dr Coral Gables FL 33134 Mailing Add: 2500 Coral Way Miami FL 33145

SACKETT, WAYNE B (R)
Mich State Rep
b Gobles, Mich, July 16, 07; s Fred Sackett & Bessie M Olmstead S; m 1933 to Zelma Irene Roberts; c Nancy (Mrs Kaiser), Diane (Mrs Bumpus) & Ruthann (Mrs Solomon). Educ: Wolf Point High Sch, Mont, Dipl. Polit & Govt Pos: Pres & founder, Portage Rep Orgn, 64-67; Mich State Rep, 69- Bus & Prof Pos: Decorating contractor, 20 years. Mem: Westwood Vol Fire Dept, 25 years; F&AM; Kiwanis (pres); Mason; Grange. Relig: Presbyterian. Mailing Add: 515 Larkspur Portage MI 49081

SACKS, ALEXANDER (R)
b New York, NY, Nov 11, 09; s Barnett Sacks & Eva Molloy S; m 1941 to Vera Peskin; c Nina Flora Ramos. Educ: City Col of New York, 27-29; Brooklyn Law Sch, LLB, 32; New Sch Social Res, 39-40; NY Univ Grad Sch Pub Admin, 41-42. Polit & Govt Pos: Spec attorney, Dept Justice, Washington & NY, 42-47; financial consult, Supreme Hq, London, on assignment by Attorney Gen of US, 45; attorney & sr economist, Off of Mil Govt, Berlin & Frankfurt, 47-49; cand for US Rep, 23rd Cong Dist, NY, 68; cand for judge, Civil Court, 69 & 72; mem exec comt, Bronx Rep Co Comt, 69-73, counsel to chmn, 71-73; confidential counsel, NY State Court of Claims, 71-75. Bus & Prof Pos: Attorney, consult economist & pub affairs specialist in pvt practice, 50-71 & 75- Publ: Numerous articles & monographs on both domestic & foreign industrial, financial & political problems. Mem: Fed Bar Asn; Nat Econ Club; Am Conservative Union; B'nai B'rith. Relig: Jewish. Legal Res: 201 E Mosholu Pkwy Bronx NY 10467 Mailing Add: 888 Seventh Ave New York NY 10019

SACKS, STANLEY ELLIOTT (D)
b Norfolk, Va, May 27, 22; s Herman Abraham Sacks & Sallie F Feldman S; m 1953 to Carole Freedman; c Andrew Michael & Betty Ann. Educ: Washington & Lee Univ, AB, 46, Law Sch, LLB, 48; Phi Beta Kappa; Order of the Coif; Zeta Beta Tau. Polit & Govt Pos: Mem, Dem City Comt, precinct committeeman, Precinct 23; mem, Norfolk City Dem Steering Comt, Kennedy Campaign, 60; mem, speaker's comt, Dem Campaign Comt for Presidential Elec, 64; deleg, Va State Dem Conv, 64; alt deleg, Dem Nat Conv, 64, deleg, 68 & 72; Va State Deleg, 65-74. Bus & Prof Pos: Chmn, Bank of the Commonwealth, Norfolk, Va, currently. Mil Serv: Entered as Pvt, Air Force, released as Sgt, after serv in Pac Theater. Publ: Preservation of the civil jury, Washington & Lee Law Rev, Uninsured motorist law, Trials & Tort Trends & Effective use of pleadings in opening statement, Personal Injury Annual, 64. Mem: Bar Found Comt, Va State Bar; chmn, Continuing Legal Educ Comt, Norfolk-Portsmouth Bar Asn; fel, Int Acad Trial Lawyers; Va Trial Lawyers Asn. Relig: Jewish. Legal Res: 6058 Newport Crescent Norfolk VA 23505 Mailing Add: 405 First & Merchants Bank Bldg Norfolk VA 23510

SADDLEMIRE, CARL LEWIS (R)
Chmn, Tioga Co Rep Comt, NY
b Owego, NY, Sept 7, 14; s Dalton F Saddlemire & May Signor S; m 1937 to Lucille Bogart; c Ann, Ruth & Richard D. Educ: Univ Mich, AB, 35; Cornell Univ, MA, 36; Pi Delta Phi. Polit & Govt Pos: Clerk, Bd Supvrs, Tioga Co, NY, 47-57, treas, 58-; chmn, Tioga Co Rep Comt, 64- Publ: Chmn ed comt, Manual for Clerks of Bd of Supvrs, publ in conjunction with Cornell Univ. Mem: Elks (past exalted ruler, Owego Lodge 1039); Tioga Co Hist Soc (dir); Paget-Price Home for Retired Presby Ministers (dir); Tioga Co Soil & Water Conserv Dist (treas & mgr); Dist Forest Practice Bd. Relig: Presbyterian. Mailing Add: Treasurer's Off Owego NY 13827

SADLER, RICHARD SHERMAN (D)
Wyo State Sen
b Hawarden, Iowa, Sept 10, 28; s Edward Anthony Sadler & Elsie June Sherman S; m 1952 to Mary Aliene Dusterhoft; c Edward Allen, Richard Paul & Connie Louise. Educ: St Mary's High Sch, Clinton, Iowa. Polit & Govt Pos: Financial secy, Clinton Co Young Dem, Iowa, 52-53; Dem precinct committeeman, Natrona Co, Wyo, 66-; deleg, Dem Nat Conv, 68; chmn, Natrona Co Dem Party, Wyo, 68, mem exec bd, 69-; deleg, Wyo State Dem Conv, 68, 70 & 72; Wyo State Rep, 70-74; Wyo State Sen, 75- Bus & Prof Pos: Round house foreman, Chicago & North Western Trans Co, 54- Mil Serv: Seaman, Navy, 46-49, US Navy, Pac Fleet; World War Victory Medal; Good Conduct Medal. Mem: IBEW; KofC; Elks Lodge 1353. Relig: Catholic. Mailing Add: 4000 Arroyo Casper WY 82601

SADOWSKY, EDWARD L (D)
City Councilman, New York
b Brooklyn, NY, Feb 6, 29; s David Sadowsky & Bina Greenberg S; m 1953 to Jean T Fishkin; c Richard, Nina & Jonathan. Educ: NY Univ, AB, 50; Columbia Univ, LLB, 53. Polit & Govt Pos: City Councilman, New York, 62-; alt deleg, Dem Nat Conv, 68, deleg, 72. Bus & Prof Pos: Partner, Tenzer, Greenblatt, Fallon & Kaplan, Attorneys, New York, currently. Mil Serv: Entered as Pvt, Army, 53, released as SP-4, 55. Relig: Jewish. Mailing Add: 13-15 160th St Beechhurst New York NY 11357

SAEGER, RICHARD THOMAS (D)
Mem Exec Comt, Dem Party Ga
b Allentown, Pa, Mar 19, 42; s Warren Thomas Saeger & Mildred Steifel S; m 1965 to Marie A Augello; c Mary Elizabeth, Katherine Eileen & Richard Thomas, Jr. Educ: Moravian Col, BA, 69; Miami Univ, MA, 70, PhD, 73. Polit & Govt Pos: Mem exec comt, Dem Party Ga, 74- Bus & Prof Pos: Plant mgr, Lehigh Frocks, Inc, Nazareth, Pa, 65-69; teaching fel, Miami Univ, 71-72; asst prof polit sci, Valdosta State Col, 72- Mil Serv: Entered as Pvt, Army, 61, released as Pfc, after serv in 517 Ord Co, 7th Army, ETO, 62-64. Publ: Co-auth, Marx & the religious: the gnostic perspective, Philos Today, 6/73. Mem: Am, Southern & Ga Polit Sci Asns; Am Asn Univ Prof (exec comt, 74-75). Honors & Awards: Grad asst, Miami Univ, 69, NDEA fel, 70-72. Relig: Unitarian. Mailing Add: 1304 Iola Dr Valdosta GA 31601

SAGARDIA SANCHEZ, ANTONIO (POPULAR DEMOCRAT, PR)
Rep, PR House Rep
b San Sebastian, PR, Sept 13, 13; s Antonio Sagardia Torrens & Damasa Sanchez S; m 1932 to Emma Perez Cancio; c Emma (Mrs Mercedes), Antonio, Jose M & Reinaldo. Educ: High Sch, grad, 32; Grad of Com, 36. Polit & Govt Pos: Mem, Munic Assembly, San Sebastian, PR, 60-64; Rep, PR House Rep, 64- Mem: San Sebastian High Sch Teachers & Fathers Asn; Cancer Soc San Sebastian; Am Red Cross, San Sebastian; Rotary. Relig: Catholic. Legal Res: Condominio de la Riena 5D Ave Ponce de Leon 450 Puerta de Tierra PR 00906 Mailing Add: Calle Munoz Rivera 26 Altos San Sebastian PR 00755

SAGGESE, ALFRED E, JR (D)
Mass State Rep
b Winthrop, Mass, Nov 21, 46; s Alfred E Saggese & Louise F Cuddi S; m 1974 to Donna Marie Corso; c Joanna. Educ: Univ Mass, Amherst, grad, 68; Suffolk Univ Law Sch, grad, 71; Sigma Phi Epsilon. Polit & Govt Pos: Mass State Rep, 75- Honors & Awards: Moot Court Award, Suffolk Univ Law Sch. Relig: Catholic. Mailing Add: 32 Underhill St Winthrop MA 02150

SAGGIOTES, JAMES A (R)
NH State Sen
Mailing Add: 23 Summit Rd Newport NH 03773

SAIA, DAVID JOSEPH (JOE) (D)
Comnr, Crawford Co, Kans
b Chicopee, Kans, May 2, 04; s Phillip Saia & Elizabeth Piraro S; m 1957 to Olga Emma Leon;

c Philip J & Betty Jo (Mrs Sol Hammons). Educ: Frontenac Pub Sch, 8 years. Polit & Govt Pos: Comnr, Crawford Co, Kans, 38-; deleg, Dem Nat Conv, 72. Bus & Prof Pos: Saia Appliance & Furniture, Frontenac, Kans, 40-; Saia Explosives Co, Inc, 62- Mem: Eagles; Elks; Lions; Frontenac Civic Club. Relig: Catholic. Mailing Add: 611 S Harris Frontenac KS 66762

SAIKI, PATRICIA (R)
Hawaii State Sen
b Hilo, Hawaii, May 28, 30; d Kazuo Fukuda & Shizue Inoue F; m 1954 to Stanley Mitsuo Saiki; c Stanley M, Jr, Sandra S, Margaret C, Stuart K & Laura H. Educ: Univ Hawaii, BS. Polit & Govt Pos: State secy, Rep Party of Hawaii, 64-66 & state vchmn, 66-68; research asst, State Senate Rep, 66-68; deleg, Hawaii Const Conv, 68; alt deleg, Rep Nat Conv, 68; Hawaii State Rep, 17th Dist, 68-70, Ninth Dist, 70-74, asst rep floor leader, Hawaii House Rep, 70-74; Hawaii State Sen, 75- Bus & Prof Pos: Teacher, Punahou Sch; Kaimuku Intermediate & Kalani High, 12 years; dir, Amfac Inc; dir, Hawaiian Airlines. Mem: President's Adv Coun on Status of Women; Hawaii Pac Col (dir); Boy Scouts (bd Aloha Coun); Western Ment Health Coun; Hawaii Special Olympics for Retarded Children (chmn). Honors & Awards: Most promising Legislator, Eagleton Inst, Rutgers Univ, 70. Relig: Episcopal. Mailing Add: Senate Sgt at Arms State Capitol Honolulu HI 96813

ST ANGELO, GORDON (D)
b Huntingburg, Ind, July 20, 27; s George St Angelo & Lillian N S; m 1952 to Beatrice Larsen; c Paul, Kurt & John. Educ: NCent Col, BA in Polit Sci, 50. Polit & Govt Pos: Precinct Committeeman, Dubois Co, Ind, 53-56; chmn, Dubois Co Dem Party, 56-64; chmn, Eighth Dist Dem Party, 60-65; pres, Eighth Dist Young Dem, 2 years; state campaign chmn, Branigin for Gov, 64; chmn, Ind State Dem Cent Comt, 65-74; mem field staff for Congressman Winfield Denton, Favorite Son Primary, 68; mem, Branigin for Pres Campaign & nat vchmn, Humphrey for Pres, 68; deleg, Dem Nat Conv, 68 & 72. Bus & Prof Pos: Pres & gen mgr, St Angelo's Inc, Huntingburg, Ind, 52-64; chmn bd, ITAN, Inc, currently. Mil Serv: Entered as Seaman, Navy, 45, released as Yeoman 3/C, 46, after serv in Am Theater; Victory Medal; Am Theater Ribbon. Mem: Elks; Jaycees; Am Legion; Kiwanis; Huntingburg Country Club. Relig: Presbyterian; Elder, Second Presby Church, Indianapolis. Mailing Add: 311 W Washington Indianapolis IN 46204

ST GEORGE, KATHARINE (R)
b England; m to George Baker St George; c one. Polit & Govt Pos: Dir & mem bd gov, Women's Nat Rep Club; chmn, Orange Co Rep Comt, NY; former pres , Bd Educ, Tuxedo, NY & mem town bd, 15 years; deleg & parliamentarian, 64 & 68; US Rep, 27th Dist, NY, 47-65, Asst Rep Party Whip, US House Rep, formerly; dir, Women's Nat Rep Club; adv comt, Rep Bus Women's Club, New York. Bus & Prof Pos: Dir, Tuxedo Hosp, formerly. Mem: DAR; Rockland Co Bus & Prof Women's Club; Comt of One Million Against the Admis of Communist China to UN (cong endorser). Relig: Episcopal. Mailing Add: Pepperidge Rd Tuxedo Park NY 10987

ST GERMAIN, FERNAND JOSEPH (D)
US Rep, RI
b Blackstone, Mass, Jan 9, 28; m to Rachel O'Neill; c two. Educ: Providence Col, BPhilos, 48; Boston Univ Law Sch, LLB, 55. Hon Degrees: LLD, Providence Col, 65; DCL, Our Lady of Providence Sem, 68. Polit & Govt Pos: RI State Rep, 52-60; deleg, RI Const Conv, 55; pres, Woonsocket Young Dem; mem nationalities div, Dem Nat Comt; US Rep, RI, 60-; deleg, Dem Nat Conv, 64, 68 & 72. Bus & Prof Pos: Lawyer. Mil Serv: Army, 49-52. Mem: RI & Woonsocket Bar Asns; Am Legion. Legal Res: Woonsocket RI Mailing Add: 2136 Rayburn House Off Bldg Washington DC 20515

ST JOHN, FINIS (D)
Ala State Sen
Mailing Add: PO Drawer K Cullman AL 35055

ST LAWRENCE, JOSEPH THOMAS (D)
Treas, Rockland Co, NY
b Sayville, NY, Aug 9, 13; s John St Lawrence & Winifred McTernan S; m 1941 to Marguerite Clinton Downey; c Joseph, Timothy, Christopher & George. Educ: Cortland State Teachers Col, BS; NY Univ, MA; Col of William & Mary, Univ Ariz & Harvard Univ, grad work. Polit & Govt Pos: Councilman, Ramapo Town, NY, 61-64; NY State Assemblyman, 64-68; deleg, NY State Const Conv, 67; Rockland Co Legislator, Charter Legis, 69; Rockland Co Treas, 70- Bus & Prof Pos: Fulbright prof, US State Dept, 53-54; dir phys educ, Suffern High Sch, 45-64. Mil Serv: Entered as CPO, Navy, 42, released as Lt(jg), 45, after serv in 3rd Fleet, Pac Theatre; Presidential Citation; Seven Campaign Medals & Six Battle Stars. Mem: Ramapo Dem Club; KofC; Holy Name Soc; Parents Club of Sacred Heart Sch; Am Legion. Honors & Awards: Established six collegiate track & field rec. Relig: Roman Catholic. Mailing Add: 5 Campbell Ave Suffern NY 10901

ST ONGE, DOUG (DFL)
Minn State Rep
Mailing Add: RR 4 Box 387 Bemidji MN 56601

ST PIERRE, DONALD R (D)
Conn State Rep
Mailing Add: 6 River Edge Court Plainville CT 06062

SAKIMA, AKIRA (D)
Hawaii State Rep
Mailing Add: House Sgt-at-Arms State Capitol Honolulu HI 96813

SALANSKY, JAMES MICHAEL (D)
Chmn, Flathead Co Dem Cent Comt, Mont
b Great Falls, Mont, Feb 4, 27; s John A Salansky & Helen Check S; m 1956 to Joan Pagano; c Susan, Diane, Mark & Marie. Educ: Cath Univ of Am, BA, 53; Georgetown Univ Law Sch, JD, 56; Sigma Beta Kappa. Polit & Govt Pos: Co attorney, Flathead Co, Mont, 63-66; chmn, Flathead Co Dem Cent Comt, Mont, 72- Mil Serv: Entered as Pvt, Army, 45, released as T/5, 47, after serv in Hq, US. Mem: Am & Mont Bar Asns; KofC; Elks; CofC. Relig: Roman Catholic. Mailing Add: 121 Birch Rd Kalispell MT 59901

SALAS, G RICARDO (R)
Sen, Guam Legis
b Agana, Guam, Nov 14, 23; s Jose Salas & Clotilde San Nicolas Santos; m 1951 to Rosa Teresita Leon Guerrero Perez; c Richard Conrad Perez (adopted), Ronald Perez & Kathleen Angelica P. Educ: San Francisco City Col, 46-47; Doane Col, BA, 49; Univ Chicago Col Law & Hastings Col Law, 57-58; Delta Kappa Pi. Polit & Govt Pos: Asst budget off, Govt of Guam, Agana, 52; Internal Revenue Agt, acct, & Dep Comnr of Revenue & Taxation, 52-57; dep comnr of ins, Dept Adminr of Securities & Comn Licenses & Registr, 61-63; Sen, Guam Legis, 64-66 & 73-, chmn Rules Comt, 64-66, Comt Finance & Taxation, 64-66 & 73-; second vpres, Rep Party of Guam, 68-; Rep Nat Committeeman, Guam, until 69; mem, Rep Nat Comt, 73-74, deleg, Rep Nat Conv, 72. Bus & Prof Pos: Chief clerk & asst oper officer, Bank of Am, Guam Br, Agana, 50; acct & officer mgr, Standard-Vacuum Oil Co, 51-52; purchasing agt, Pac Construction Co, Inc, Los Angeles Off, Calif, 60; asst mgr opers officer & acct, Bank of Hawaii, Guam Br, 63-66; owner, gen mgr, real estate broker, property mgr & appraiser, Salas Agency Corp Guam, 66- Mil Serv: Prisoner of War, Guam, 41-44. Mem: Lions; Young Men's League of Guam; Am Red Cross. Relig: Catholic. Mailing Add: PO Box 373 Agana GU 96910

SALAZAR, NICK L (D)
NMex State Rep
Mailing Add: Box 773 San Juan Pueblo NM 87566

SALCHERT, JOHN JOSEPH (DFL)
b Minneapolis, Minn, Aug 9, 36; s Hubert Salchert (deceased) & Helen Mary Ley S (deceased); m 1957 to Dolores Elsie DeMars; c Michael, Mark, Annamarie, Julie & Stephen. Educ: Col St Thomas, 54-57; Univ Minn, BS, 57, MD, 61; Phi Beta Pi. Polit & Govt Pos: VChmn, Hennepin Co Dem-Farmer-Labor Party, Minn, 62-64; Dem-Farmer-Labor chmn, Third Ward, Minneapolis, 62-64; mem, Minn State Comn Against Discrimination, 63-66; mem, Hennepin Co Park Bd, 65-66; Minn State Rep, Dist 54A, 66-74; mem, Minn State Dem-Farmer-Labor Cent Comt, 67-; mem bd dirs, Hennepin Co Daytime Activity Care Ctr, currently; deleg, Dem Nat Conv, 68 & 72. Mil Serv: 1st Lt, Army Nat Guard, 62, Maj, 204th Med Bn, 62- Mem: Am Acad Gen Practice (comt med educ, 67, alt deleg, 69); Am Med Asn; Am Asn Col Physicians; Minn Med Asn (comt med educ, 67); Moose. Relig: Roman Catholic. Mailing Add: 2120 Memorial Pkwy Minneapolis MN 55412

SALE, FOREST (AGGIE) (D)
Ky State Rep
Mailing Add: 520 Beaumont Ave Harrodsburg KY 40330

SALEEBY, EDWARD ELI (D)
SC State Sen
b Hartsville, SC, Sept 8, 27; s Eli A Saleeby & Creola Stokes S; m 1951 to Willie Meta Calcutt; c Edward Eli, Jr, Mary Kay & Holly Ann. Educ: Univ SC, LLB, 49, JD, 70; Phi Kappa Alpha (pres); Omicron Delta Kappa. Polit & Govt Pos: SC State Rep, 51-58; SC State Sen, 73- Bus & Prof Pos: Bd of trustees, Univ SC, Columbia, SC, 61-72, Coker Col & Byerly Hosp, currently. Mem: Kiwanis; Scottish Rite Mason; Darlington Co Red Fez Club. Legal Res: West Home Ave Hartsville SC 29550 Mailing Add: Box 519 Hartsville SC 29550

SALEM, JOSEPH JOHN (D)
Tex State Rep
b Corpus Christi, Tex, Dec 29, 20; both parents deceased; m 1943 to Christine Louise Aboud; c Christine, Joe, Jr & Sam II. Educ: Air Force cadet training, grad. Polit & Govt Pos: Sustaining mem, Nat Dem Comt; mem, Nueces Co Dem Orgn; State Rep, Tex, 69- Bus & Prof Pos: Businessman, developer & investor, Corpus Christi, Tex. Mil Serv: Entered as Pvt, Air Force, 41, released as 1st Lt & acting Capt, 45; serv as fighter pilot, asst squadron comdr & supvr instrument training. Mem: Optimists; Lebasyr Club; Am Legion (past comdr); Nueces Co Vets Asn (founder); KofC. Honors & Awards: Little League Ball Park named in his hon; recipient of Gov award for dedicated service to the handicapped; Optimists awards; Corpus Christi Police Officers Asn Award of Appreciation for Contribution to Better Law Enforcement; winner Outstanding Retailer of the Year award, nationwide jewelers category, Brand Names Foundation. Relig: Catholic. Mailing Add: PO Box 6642 Corpus Christi TX 78411

SALERNO, MARY J (D)
VChairlady, Lackawanna Co Dem Comt, Pa
b Old Forge, Pa, Nov 11, 23; d Peter J Connors & Nora Lally C; m 1949 to Edward L Salerno; c Nora (Mrs Michael Katz), Mary Kay & Edward G. Educ: Lackawanna Jr Col, Bus Degree. Polit & Govt Pos: Mem, Lackawanna Co Dem Exec Comt, Pa, 65-; vchairlady, Lackawanna Co Dem Comt, 69- Bus & Prof Pos: Clerk, US Govt, Washington, DC, 42-47; salesman & mgr, Stanly Home Prod, Westfield, Mass, 47-71; clerk, Magistrate Talerico, Old Forge, Pa, 71- Mem: Magistrate Secretarial Asn; Am Cancer Soc; Am Legion Auxiliary; PTA; Lackawanna Co Ladies Dem Club (exec comt). Relig: Catholic. Mailing Add: 716 Beech St Old Forge PA 18518

SALFI, DOMINICK J (R)
b Philadelphia, Pa, Aug 29, 37; s Domenic Salfi & Madeline Lombardi S; m to Doris Margaret Gay; c Dea Gay, Dominick Joseph, Dawn Ann & Don Christopher. Educ: Univ Fla, BA, 58, Law Sch, JD, 61; Delta Upsilon; Delta Theta Phi. Polit & Govt Pos: Legal asst, Orange-Seminole deleg, Fla Legis, 67; state attorney, 18th Judicial Circuit, Fla, 67-69, circuit court judge, 70-; chmn, Seminole Co Rep Exec Comt, 69-70; legal adv, Fla State Rep Exec Comt, 69-; Seminole Co committeeman, Fla State Rep Comt, 70- Bus & Prof Pos: Law partner, Hornsby, Johnson, Yurko & Salfi, 61-65; law partner, Fishback, Davis, Domenick, Troutman & Salfi, 66-70. Mem: Am, Orange Co & Seminole Co Bar Asns; NY & Fla Trial Lawyers Asns. Relig: Catholic. Mailing Add: Box 19 Rte 1 Longwood FL 32750

SALIBA, ALFRED J (R)
Chmn, Houston Co Rep Exec Comt, Ala
b Dothan, Ala, Feb 22, 30; s Joseph E Saliba & Marcia Accawie S; m 1955 to Henrietta Carpenter; c Annamarie, Alfred, Jr & James Mark. Educ: Univ Ala, BS in Civil Eng; pres, Eng Sch; pres, Sigma Phi Epsilon; Omicron Delta Kappa; Jasons; Chi Epsilon; Alpha Phi Omega; Pershing Rifles; Cotillion Club. Polit & Govt Pos: Orgn dir, Houston Co Rep Exec Comt, Ala, 62-65, chmn, 65-; mem, Rep State Exec Comt Ala, 66- Bus & Prof Pos: Owner & mgr, Alfred Saliba Homes Inc, 55- Mil Serv: Entered as 2nd Lt, Air Force, 53, released as 1st Lt, 65, after serv in 1503rd Air Installations Squadron, Japan; Korean Serv Medal; UN Serv Medal; Nat Defense Serv Medal; Capt, Air Force Res, currently. Mem: Dothan Home Builders Asn; Dothan Jr CofC; United Fund; Dothan Rotary Club. Relig: Presbyterian; Elder. Legal Res: 3201 Ridgewood Dothan AL 36301 Mailing Add: PO Box 1076 Dothan AL 36301

SALICHS, JOSE E (NEW PROGRESSIVE, PR)
Rep, PR House Rep
Mailing Add: State Capitol San Juan PR 00901

SALINGER, PIERRE EMIL GEORGE (D)
b San Francisco, Calif, June 14, 25; s Herbert Salinger (deceased) & Jehanne Bietry S; m 1965 to Nicole Helene Gillmann; c Marc, Suzanne, Stephen & Gregory. Educ: Univ San Francisco, BS in Hist, 47. Polit & Govt Pos: Investr, Senate Select Comt on Improper Activities in the Labor & Mgt Field, 57-59; press secy to US Sen Kennedy, Mass, 59-60; press secy to the President, 61-64; US Sen, Calif, 64-65; former mem, Calif Dem State Cent Comt; deleg, Dem Nat Conv, 68. Bus & Prof Pos: Reporter & night city ed, San Francisco Chronicle, 46-55; guest lectr jour, Mills Col, 50-55; contrib ed, Colliers Mag, 55-56; col & univ lectr, 60-69; vpres, Nat Gen Corp, 65; vpres int affairs, Continental Airlines & vpres & dir, Continental Air Serv Inc, 65-68; chmn bd, Gramco Int & Gramco Sales Corp, 68-69, dep chmn, Gramco Ltd, London, 70-; sr vpres, Amprop Inc, 69-70. Mil Serv: Entered as A/S, Navy, 43, released as Lt(jg), 46, after serv in Pac Area; Navy & Marine Corps Medal. Publ: With Kennedy, 66 & A Tribute to Robert F Kennedy, 68, Doubleday; ed, A Tribute to John F Kennedy, Encycl Brittanica, 64. Mem: Nat Press Club; Robert F Kennedy Mem Found (trustee). Mailing Add: 1438 N Kings Rd Los Angeles CA 90069

SALISBURY, GEORGE R (D)
Wyo State Rep
Mailing Add: Savery WY 82332

SALISBURY, WALLACE DANIEL (R)
Chmn, Plainfield Rep Town Comt, Conn
b Canterbury, Conn, June 6, 22; s Wallace J Salisbury & Fanny Boglich S; m 1945 to Elaine Marion Ducat; c Linda May (Mrs Long), Robert A, Wallace D, Lloyd T, Rodney H & Paul G. Educ: Plainfield High Sch, grad, 41; Life Underwriter Training Coun, grad, 67. Polit & Govt Pos: Mem, Plainfield Rep Town Comt, Conn, 62-69, chmn, 69-72 & 75-; coordr sportsmen against Dedario, NEastern Conn Campaign, 70. Bus & Prof Pos: Foreman, Townshend Furniture Co, Vt, 46-48; chief set up man, Am Screw Co, Willimantic, Conn, 48-62; agt, Metrop Life Ins Co, 62- Mil Serv: Entered as A/S, Navy, 42, released as PO 1/C, 46, after serv in USS Anthony & USS Mugford, Asiatic Pac Theatre, Solomon Islands, 43-45; Good Conduct Medal; Three Bronze Stars; Am Defense Medal. Mem: Nat Asn Life Underwriters; Eastern Conn Life Underwriters Asn; Conn Asn Life Underwriters; Mason; Nat Rifle Asn. Relig: Baptist. Mailing Add: RFD Spaulding Rd Plainfield CT 06374

SALKIND, MORTON (D)
NJ State Assemblyman
Mailing Add: State House Trenton NJ 08625

SALLADE, GEORGE WAHR (D)
Chmn, Second Dist Dem Comt, Mich
b Ann Arbor, Mich, Nov 16, 22; s James A Sallade & Nathalie Wahr S; m 1945 to Charlotte Haas; c Natalie Ann, Elizabeth Lee, James Edward & Barbara Jean. Educ: Univ Mich, AB, 43; Phi Alpha Delta; Sigma Delta Chi; Sigma Phi. Hon Degrees: LLD, Univ Mich, 61. Polit & Govt Pos: Councilman, Ann Arbor, Mich, 50-52, pres, Coun, 53-55; Mich State Rep, 55-60; chmn, Washtenaw Co Dem Comt, 65-69; Dem cand for Mich State Sen, 66 & 70; Dem cand for Mich State Rep, 68; mem, Second Cong Dist Dem Comt, 69-71, chmn, 71-; Dem cand, Prosecuting Attorney, Washtenaw Co, 72. Mem: Washtenaw Co, Mich & Am Bar Asns; Am Trial Lawyers Asn; Mason; Moose; Rotary. Honors & Awards: Outstanding Young Man Award, 54. Relig: Episcopal. Mailing Add: 2307 Hill St Ann Arbor MI 48104

SALMAN, DAVID M (D)
NMex State Rep
Mailing Add: Box 1307 Las Vegas NM 87701

SALMON, NANCY PILSON (D)
b Los Angeles, Calif, Oct 8, 26; d Raymond Huston Pilson & Emily Earl P; div; c Victoria Anne. Educ: Univ Calif, Los Angeles. Polit & Govt Pos: Deleg, Ind Dem State Conv, 68, 70 & 72; deleg, Dem Nat Conv, 72; mem credentials comt, Dem Nat Comt, 72; co-chmn, Seventh Dist Dem for McGovern President Comt, 72; mem, McGovern Women's Adv Coun, 72; secy deleg selection & affirmative action comt, Ind Dem Party, 74; deleg, Dem Nat Mid-Term Conf, 74. Bus & Prof Pos: Admin asst, Int Prog in Taxation, Harvard Law Sch, 58; secy, City of Bloomington, 73-74, housing code officer, 74- Mem: Bloomington Civil Liberties Union (bd mem, 69-); Ind Civil Liberties Union (state bd mem, 73-); Planned Parenthood Asn of Monroe Co (bd mem, 68-73). Mailing Add: 2345 Browncliff Rd Bloomington IN 47401

SALMON, THOMAS P (D)
Gov, Vt
b Cleveland, Ohio, Aug 19, 32; m to Madeleine G Savaria; c four. Educ: Boston Col, AB, 54, Law Sch, LLB, 57; NY Univ Law Sch, LLM (Taxation), 58. Polit & Govt Pos: Justice of the Peace, Rockingham, Vt, 59, mem, Town Coun, 59-72, mem, Temporary Adv Comn on Sch Dist Reorgn; Munic Judge, Bellows Falls, 63-65; deleg, Dem Nat Conv, 64, 68 & 72; Vt State Rep, 65-73; chmn, Windham Co Dem Party, 67-; Gov, Vt, 73- Bus & Prof Pos: Attorney-at-law; pres, Bellows Falls Area Develop Corp; dir, Vt Nat Bank. Mem: Am, Vt & Windham Co Bar Asns; Rotary; Elks. Relig: Catholic. Mailing Add: 24 Atkinson St Bellows Falls VT 05101

SALOOM, EUGENE GEORGE (R)
Pa State Rep
b Mount Pleasant, Pa, Sept 22, 34; s George Saloom & Isabell Karfelt S; m 1958 to Nancy Lou Newill. Educ: Elon Col, 55-57; Pittsburgh Inst Mortuary Sci, Grad, 55; Alpha Pi Delta. Polit & Govt Pos: Pa State Rep, 67- Bus & Prof Pos: Owner, Eugene G Saloom Funeral Home, Mt Pleasant, Pa, 60- Mil Serv: Entered as Pvt, Army, 58, released as SP-4, 60, after serv as Qm; Good Conduct Award. Mem: Nat Funeral Dirs Asn; Elks; Odd Fellows; Moose; Grange. Relig: Protestant. Mailing Add: Capitol Bldg Harrisburg PA 17120

SALOPEK, FRANK (D)
NMex State Rep
b El Paso, Tex, Feb 26, 32; s David Salopek & Mary Tomason S; m 1961 to Oleta Dean Wall; c Frank Paul, Kary Samuel & Gregory Vide. Educ: NMex State Univ, BS agr, 54. Polit & Govt Pos: NMex State Rep, Dist I, 71- Bus & Prof Pos: Farmer. Mil Serv: Entered as Lt, Air Force, 55, released as Capt, 57, after serv in 815 Troop Carriers Squadron, Far Eastern.

Mem: Mesilla Coop Gin (bd dirs). Relig: Catholic. Mailing Add: Rte 2 Box 735 Las Cruces NM 88001

SALTMARSH, SHERMAN W, JR (R)
Mass State Rep
Mailing Add: State Capitol Boston MA 02133

SALTONSTALL, JOHN LEE, JR (D)
b Beverly, Mass, Apr 20, 16; s John Lee Saltonstall & Gladys Rice S; m 1943 to Margaret Louise Bonnell; c Stephen Lee, Sarah Bonnell (Mrs D'Antonio) & Thomas Lee. Educ: Harvard Univ, AB, 38; Yale Law Sch, LLB, 41. Polit & Govt Pos: Attorney, Dept War, Washington, DC, 41-43; prin mediation officer, Nat War Labor Bd, Washington, DC, New York & Chicago, 43-45; mem, Mass Dem State Comt, 52; dep gen counsel, Dept of the Army, Washington, DC, 52-53; deleg-at-lg, Dem Nat Conv, 60 & 72; chmn, Mass Transportation Comn, Mass, 63-64; vchmn, Boston Home Rule Comn, 68-71; mem coun, Boston City Coun, 68-72. Bus & Prof Pos: Assoc, Hill & Barlow, Esqs, Boston, 45-49, partner, 49-68, of counsel, 68-73, partner, 73-; pres & dir, Boston Harbor Assocs, Inc, 74- Publ: Auth, article, In: Mass Law Quart; co-auth, article, In: Boston Bar J. Mem: Am & Boston Bar Asns; Mass Bar Asn (comt future planning, 75-); Asn Bar of City of New York; Am Law Inst. Relig: Unitarian. Legal Res: 85 E India Row Boston MA 02110 Mailing Add: 225 Franklin St Boston MA 02110

SALTONSTALL, LEVERETT (R)
b Newton, Mass, Sept 1, 92; s Richard Middlecott Saltonstall & Eleanor Brooks S; m 1916 to Alice Wesselhoeft; c Leverett, Jr (deceased), Rosalie (deceased), Emily (Mrs Byrd), Peter Brooks (deceased), William Lawrence & Susan. Educ: Harvard Univ, BA, 14, LLB, 17; hon mem Phi Beta Kappa; Hasty Pudding; Porcellian Club; Delta Kappa Epsilon; Sigma Kappa. Polit & Govt Pos: Alderman, Newton, Mass, 20-22; Asst Dist Attorney, Middlesex Co, 21-22; Mass State Rep, 23-37, Speaker, Mass State House of Rep, 8 years; Gov, Mass, 38-44; US Sen, Mass, 44-67; deleg, Rep Nat Conv, 68 & 72. Bus & Prof Pos: Former dir, Nat Shawmut Bank of Boston & Boston Safe Deposit & Trust Co, Mass; lawyer, Gaston, Snow, Saltonstall & Hunt, Boston, 19-28; vchmn, MBUF, 67-; trustee of IVEST, formerly. Mil Serv: 1st Lt, Army, 17-19, serv in Field Artil. Mem: Mason (32 degree); Elks; Am Legion; Ancient & Hon Artil Co; hon mem Rotary. Honors & Awards: Capt, Harvard Second Crew, which won the Grand Challenge Cup at Henley, 14; mem, Harvard Hockey Team. Relig: Protestant. Mailing Add: Smith St Dover MA 02030

SALTONSTALL, WILLIAM LAWRENCE (R)
Mass State Sen
b Newton, Mass, May 14, 27; s Sen Leverett Saltonstall & Alice Wesselhoeft S; m 1953 to Jane Chandler; c William L, Jr & Abigail. Educ: Harvard Col, AB, 50; Harvard Bus Sch, MBA, 52. Polit & Govt Pos: Campaign worker, Saltonstall for Sen, 54 & 60 & Whittier for Gov, 56; mem staff, Sen L Saltonstall, 59-60, admin asst, 61-66; Mass State Sen, 66- Bus & Prof Pos: Security Analyst, New Eng Mutual Life Ins Co, Boston, Mass, 52-58. Mil Serv: Entered as A/S, Navy, 45, released as Qm 3/C, 46. Relig: Protestant. Mailing Add: 388 Summer St Manchester MA 01944

SALTSMAN, GEORGE J (D)
Chmn, Fifth Dist Dem Non-Partisan League Party, NDak
b Maxbass, NDak, Dec 22, 23; s George E Saltsman, Sr & Alice Hirengen S; m 1948 to Mary Prisizney; c George E, III, William E & Craig E. Educ: Williston High Sch. Polit & Govt Pos: State legis chmn, Brotherhood Locomotive Engrs, 59-64; chmn, Fifth Dist Dem Non-Partisan League Party, NDak, 74- Bus & Prof Pos: Locomotive engr, Burlington Northern RR, 42-; owner, Jet Cafe, Ruthville, 62-63; co-owner, Fourth Ave Realty, 65-66 & Trader Realty, 67; partner & secy-treas, Owner Direct Real Estate Co, 68-70. Mil Serv: Entered as Pvt, Marine Corps Res, 43, released as Pfc, 45, after serv in Co-5th Fleet, Pac Theatre; six Battle Stars. Mem: Brotherhood Locomotive Engrs; Elks; Mason; Am Legion; VFW. Honors & Awards: Gov Meritorious Award for polit in Dem Non-Partisan League Party, 64. Relig: Episcopal. Mailing Add: 926 Third St SE Minot ND 58701

SALVATORE, FRANK A (R)
Pa State Rep
Mailing Add: Capitol Bldg Harrisburg PA 17120

SALVATORE, MICHAEL JOSEPH (D)
b Jeannette, Pa, Oct 30, 33; s Joseph X Salvatore & Pauline Mastracchio S; single. Educ: Jeannette Pub Schs, grad, 51; Greensburg Bus Sch, 51-52; Univ Pittsburgh, continuing educ classes, 55 & various night sch classes, 73. Polit & Govt Pos: City councilman, Jeannette, Pa, 72-; deleg, Dem Nat Mid-Term Conf, 74. Bus & Prof Pos: Production scheduler, Robertshaw Controls, New Stanton, Pa, 52-75; purchaser-dispatcher, West End Builders, Jeannette, 75-Mil Serv: Entered as Pvt, Army, 56, released as E-4, 58, after serv in Hq & Hq Battery, Ft Bliss, Tex, 57-58; Good Conduct Medal. Mem: KofC (3 & 4 degree); Jeannette Rotary Club (dir & sgt-at-arms); Jeannette Am Legion. Relig: Roman Catholic. Mailing Add: 1115 Thompson St Jeannette PA 15644

SALZMAN, HERBERT
Exec VPres, Overseas Pvt Investment Corp
b New York, NY, May 2, 16; s William Salzman & Minnie Reich S; m 1947 to Rita Fredricks; c Anthony David & Jeffrey Jonathan. Educ: Yale Univ, BA, 38; Navy Supply Corps Sch, Harvard Univ, 42; Columbia Univ Grad Sch Bus, 56. Polit & Govt Pos: Asst adminr, Off Develop Finance & Off Pvt Resources, Agency for Int Develop, 66-70, mgr transition to Overseas Pvt Investment Corp, 70-71, exec vpres, Corp, 71- Bus & Prof Pos: Vpres, Standard Bag Corp, 38-59, pres, 59-66. Mil Serv: Entered as Ens, Navy, 41, released as Lt Comdr, 46. Publ: How to Reduce & Manage Political Risks in Developing Countries, Prentice-Hall. Mem: Adlai Stevenson Inst Int Affairs, Chicago (bd); Kennedy Ctr Prod Inc, Washington, DC (bd); Int Club, Washington, DC; Fed City Club; Cedar Point Yacht Club. Relig: Jewish. Mailing Add: 2700 Virginia Ave NW Washington DC 20037

SALZWEDEL, PEARL R (DFL)
b Chicago, Ill, Feb 28, 27; d Eric Ernquist & Ragnhild Holmquist E; m 1947 to Ray Salzwedel; c Carolyn, Ray Eric, John, Laurie, Thomas & Dennis. Educ: High sch, Chicago, Ill, 3 years. Polit & Govt Pos: Chairwoman, Jackson Co Dem-Farmer-Labor Party, Minn, 69-74. Mem: Am Legion Auxiliary; VFW Auxiliary. Relig: Protestant. Mailing Add: RR 1 Lakefield MN 56150

SAMBERSON, C GENE (D)
NMex State Rep
Mailing Add: Box 1298 Lovington NM 88260

SAMPOL, WILLIAM, JR (R)
Mem, Kings Co Rep Comt, NY
b New York, NY, Apr 8, 41; s William Sampol, Sr & Esther Soto S; m 1966 to Rosella Pepe. Educ: Univ Havana, BA, 62. Polit & Govt Pos: Kings Co campaign chmn, US Sen James Buckley, 70; mem, Kings Co Rep Comt, 70-; pres, 42nd Assembly Dist Rep Orgn, 70-; judicial deleg, Kings Co, 71 & 72; first vpres, Kings Co Young Rep, 71-; hon deleg, Rep Nat Conv, 72; coordr, Kings Co Comt to Reelect the President, 72; exec asst, Kings Co Comt, 72-; dir security, Kings Co, NY Rep Party, 72- Bus & Prof Pos: Pres, Nat Polygraph Assoc, 68-, Nat Silent Majority, Inc, 69 & Highlawn Mgt, 70- Mem: Douglas MacArthur Rep Club (bd mem, 70-); Marine Park Civic Asn; Mill Basin Civic Asn; Ryder Civic Asn (pres, 66-). Honors & Awards: Man of the Year Award, Cath War Vet, 70; Spec Citation, VFW, 70 & Jewish War Vet, 70. Relig: Catholic. Mailing Add: 1810 E 49th St Brooklyn NY 11234

SAMPSON, ARTHUR F (R)
b Fall River, Mass, Oct 8, 26; s Arthur F Sampson, Sr & Dora S (both deceased); m 1947 to Blanche Bouffard; c Arthur F III, Philip R, Jason & Matthew. Educ: Univ RI, BS (magna cum laude), 51; George Washington Univ, 71-73. Polit & Govt Pos: Secy admin & budget secy, Commonwealth of Pa, 62-69; comnr, Fed Supply Serv & Pub Bldg Serv, Gen Serv Admin, 69-72, acting adminr, 72-73, adminr, 73-75. Bus & Prof Pos: Various mgt pos, Gen Elec, 51-62. Mil Serv: Entered as Pvt, Army Air Corps, 44, released as Cpl, 47, after serv in Italy one year with Occup Forces. Publ: GSA advocates new financing techniques for public buildings, Archit Rec, 9/71; GSA's systems approach to life safety in structure, Fire J, 9/72; Government as a market . . . , Systs Bldg News, 8/73; plus one other. Mem: Nat Capital Planning Comn; Adv Coun on Hist Preservation; Bldg Research Adv Bd; Joint Financial Mgt Improv Prog (chmn). Honors & Awards: Man of Year, Am Pub Works Asn; Man of Year, Soc Fire Protection Engrs; hon mem, Am Inst Architects; hon mem, Fed Govt Acct Asn. Relig: Catholic. Legal Res: 19 Oak Ave Camp Hill PA 17011 Mailing Add: 1315 Fourth St SW Washington DC 20024

SAMPSON, CURTIS ALLEN (R)
Dir, Renville Co Rep Party, Minn
b Hector, Minn, July 6, 33; s Selmer B Sampson & Sophie Sjogren S; m 1954 to Marian Arlys Walter; c Paul Curtis, Randall David, Russell Steven & Susan Joy. Educ: Univ Minn, BBA with Distinction, 55; pres, Beta Alpha Psi, 54-55; All Univ Cong. Polit & Govt Pos: Co chmn, John Zwach Campaign, 67 & 72; chmn, Renville Co Rep Party, Minn, 67-69, dir, 71-; mem site comt, Rep State Conv, 68; conv chmn, Sixth Cong Dist Rep Conv, 69; chmn, Schafer for Rep, 70; committeeman, Small Bus Admin Adv Comt, 71-72, ACE Vol, Small Bus Admin Active Corp of Execs, 72- Bus & Prof Pos: Various mgt & financial pos, NAm Commun Corp & Predecessor Co, 55-68, exec vpres & treas, 68-70; secy & dir, Hector Indust Corp, Hector, Minn, 58-; pres & treas, Commun Systs, Inc, 70-; dir, Midwest Bean Co, Hector, 72-, Oakdale Country Club, Buffalo Lake, 72-, H G Fischer Co, Franklin Park & Afton House Corp, Excelsior, 73- Mem: US Tel Asn; Independent Tel Pioneer Asn; AF&AM (past master, Hector Lodge); Civic & Com Asn; Kiwanis. Relig: Lutheran. Mailing Add: 50 Parkview Lane Hector MN 55342

SAMS, H WILLIAM, JR (R)
Ga State Rep
b Atlanta, Ga, Nov 4, 39; s Herbert William Sams & Mary Francis Brooke S; m 1961 to Patricia Hale; c Herbert William, III & Haley Brooke. Educ: Emory Univ, BA, 61; Univ Ga Sch Law, JD, 63; Phi Alpha Delta; Beta Theta Pi. Polit & Govt Pos: Chmn, Richmond Co Rep Party, Ga, 70-71; mem, Ga Rep State Exec Comt, 71-72; chmn, Tenth Cong Dist Rep Party, 72-73; alt deleg, Rep Nat Conv, 72; Ga State Rep, 73- Bus & Prof Pos: Attorney, Lester & Lester, 64-67, Harrison, Jolles & Sams, 67-70 & Sams & Dunstan, 70- Mem: Am & Augusta Bar Asns; State Bar of Ga; Kiwanis Club of Augusta. Honors & Awards: Outstanding Young Man of Year, Richmond Co Jaycees, 73; One of Five Outstanding Young Men in Ga, Ga Jaycees, 74. Relig: Methodist. Mailing Add: 17 Rockbrook Rd Augusta GA 30904

SAMUEL, HOWARD DAVID (D)
b New York, NY, Nov 16, 24; s Ralph E Samuel & Florence Weingarten S; m 1948 to Ruth H Zamkin; c Robert Harry, Donald Franklin & William Howard. Educ: Dartmouth Col, BA, 48; Phi Beta Kappa. Polit & Govt Pos: Chmn, White Plains City Dem Comt, NY, 60-64; alt deleg, Dem Nat Conv, 64; vchmn, Westchester Co Dem Comt, 59-70, registr chmn, 64, campaign chmn, 65; mem, NY State Dem Adv Comn, 69-; mem, Nat Manpower Adv Comt, 69-; mem, Comn Population Growth & Am Future, 70-72; exec dir, Nat Labor Comt for McGovern-Shriver, 72; mem, Nat Dem Charter Comn, 73-; deleg, Dem Nat Mid-Term Conf, 74. Bus & Prof Pos: Vpres, Amalgamated Clothing Workers Am, AFL-CIO, 49-64 & 66-; vpres, New Sch Social Res, 65. Mil Serv: Entered as Pvt, Army, 43, released as Sgt, 46. Publ: Co-auth, Congress at Work, 52 & Government in America, 57, Holt; ed, Toward a Better America, Macmillan, 68. Mem: NY Urban Coalition; Carnegie Corp (trustee, 71-); Common Cause (gov bd, 71-). Mailing Add: 7 Sherman Ave White Plains NY 10605

SAMUEL, NOBLE B (INDEPENDENT CITIZENS MOVEMENT)
Sen, VI Legis
b Cruz Bay, St John, VI, Mar 26, 26; s Henry Samuel & Amelia Janet Bastian S; m 1952 to Elaine Hazell; c Bernice & Gilbert. Educ: Charlotte Amalie, grad. Polit & Govt Pos: Sen, VI Legis, 73- Mil Serv: Entered as Pvt, Army, 52, released as Cpl, 54, after serv in 223rd Inf Regt, 40th Div, Korea, Far E Command, 52-53; Bronze Medal; Good Conduct Medal. Mem: Explorers Club; Lions Club; Boy Scouts. Relig: Lutheran. Mailing Add: Cruz Bay St John VI 00830

SAMUEL, RICHARD IRVING (D)
Mem, Dem Nat Comt, NJ
b Brooklyn, NY, Feb 21, 40; s Alexander Samuel & Mollie Fleischer S; m 1961 to Ellen Ruth Sherman; c Miriam Sharon & Joanne Marcia. Educ: Rensselaer Polytechnic Inst, BEE, 61; Boston Col Law Sch, LLB, 65; George Washington Univ Law Sch; Alpha Epsilon Pi. Polit & Govt Pos: Alt deleg, Dem Nat Conv, 68, deleg & mem, Rules Comt, 72; chmn, Vol for McCarthy, 12th Cong Dist, NJ, 68; NJ Temporary Rep, Nat Steering Comt of New Dem Coalition, 69; mem, Dem Nat Comt, NJ, 72-, co-chmn bylaws comt, Dem Nat Comt, 75; deleg & NJ rep on rules & amendments comt, Dem Nat Mid-Term Conf, 74. Bus & Prof Pos: Elec engr, Raytheon Co, Lexington, Mass, 61-63; elec engr, Harvard Univ, 63-65; mem patent staff, Western Elec Co, Washington, DC, 66; mem patent staff, Bell Tel Lab, Murray Hill, NJ, 66-; patent attorney, Lerner, David, Littenberg & Samuel, Westfield, NJ, 70- Mem: NJ Patent Law Asn. Relig: Jewish. Legal Res: 526 Lenox Ave Westfield NJ 07090 Mailing Add: 195 Elm St Westfield NJ 07090

SAMUELS, HOWARD JOSEPH (D)
b Rochester, NY, Dec 3, 19; s Harry L Samuels; m 1942 to Barbara J Christie; div; m 1973 to Antoinette Chautemps; c William Christie, Susan Carey, Catherine Christie, Victoria, Howard Christie, II, Barbara Christie, Jacqueline, Janine & Camille. Educ: Mass Inst Technol, BS in Bus Eng Admin, 41. Polit & Govt Pos: Chmn admin comt, NY State Dem Adv Coun, 63-66; chmn, Citizen's Comt for an Effective Const, 65-66; Dem nominee for Lt Gov, NY, 66; leader, Campaign to Convene NY State Const Conv, 67; Under-Secy of Com, Washington, DC, 67-68; deleg, Dem Nat Conv, 68 & 72; nat adminr, Small Bus Admin, Washington, DC, 68-69; mem, Mayor's Narcotics Coun, New York, currently. Bus & Prof Pos: Vis lectr, New Sch for Social Research, spring 69, fall 73 & 75; vpres, Mobil Chem Corp & gen mgr plastics div, Macedon & New York, NY; founder, Kordite Corp, Macedon, NY; pres & chmn bd, Off-Track Betting Corp, 70-74. Mil Serv: Entered as 2nd Lt, Army, 41, released as Lt Col, 45, after serv on staff of Gen George S Patton, 3rd Army, Europe; cited as an outstanding officer on the staff of Gen George S Patton. Publ: An Insufficient House, 65; numerous articles & essays in periodicals & mag on finance, Black econ develop & educ. Mem: Pub Educ Asn; Am Histadrut Cult Exchange Inst; Am-Israel Pub Affairs Comt (exec comt); Ad Hoc Comt of New Yorkers Against Anti-Ballistic Missiles (sponsor); Am Jewish Comt (bd gov, currently). Honors & Awards: Fel, Brandeis Univ. Relig: Jewish. Legal Res: 7 W 81st St New York NY 10024 Mailing Add: 355 Lexington Ave New York NY 10017

SAMUELS, MICHAEL ANTHONY (R)
US Ambassador to Sierra Leone
b Youngstown, Ohio, Apr 4, 39; s Lou Emmanuel Samuels & Myrrel Friedman S; m 1969 to Susan Hassman; c Joel Hassman. Educ: Yale Univ, BA, 61; Columbia Univ Teachers Col, MA, 62, PhD, 69; Univ London, 62. Polit & Govt Pos: Legis mgt officer, Dept of State, 70-73, exec asst to Dep Secy State, 73-74; staff asst to the President, White House, 74; US Ambassador to Sierra Leone, 75- Bus & Prof Pos: Sec sch teacher, Northern Nigeria, 62-64; sr staff mem, Ctr Strategic & Int Studies, Georgetown Univ, 68-70. Publ: Ed, The Nigeria-Biafra Conflict, Ctr Strategic & Int Studies, Georgetown Univ, 67; auth, Education in Angola, 1878-1914, Teachers Col, Columbia Univ, 68; co-auth, Portuguese Africa: A Handbook, Praeger, New York & Pall Mall, London, 69. Mem: African Studies Asn; Int Studies Asn. Legal Res: 2713 Woodley Pl Washington DC 20008 Mailing Add: Freetown Dept of State Washington DC 20520

SAMUELSON, DON W (R)
b Woodhull, Ill, July 27, 13; s Fred W Samuelson & Nellie Johnson S; m 1936 to Ruby A Mayo; c Steve & Donna. Educ: Knox Col. Polit & Govt Pos: Idaho State Sen, 60-66; Gov, Idaho, 67-71; deleg, Rep Nat Conv, 68; regional rep for US Dept Transportation, NW Fed Regional Coun, 71- Mil Serv: Entered as Seaman 1/C, 46, after serv in Am Theater. Mem: Am Legion; Elks; Kiwanis; Nat Rifleman's Asn; Pend Oreille Gem Club & several other sportsmen's orgn. Relig: Methodist. Legal Res: N Boyer Sandpoint ID 83864 Mailing Add: Apt 601 507 W Mercer Seattle WA 98119

SAMUELSON, DONALD B (DFL)
Minn State Rep
b Brainerd, Minn, Aug 23, 32; s Walter H Samuelson & Ellen Gallagher S; m 1952 to Nancy O'Brien; c Stephen, Laura, Paula & Christine. Educ: Washington High Sch, Brainerd, Minn. Polit & Govt Pos: Chmn, Sixth Dist Comt on Polit Educ, Minn, 60-66; mem, State Cent Comt, Dem-Farmer-Labor Party, 64-66; chmn, Crow Wing Co Dem-Farmer-Labor Party, formerly; Minn State Rep, 68- Bus & Prof Pos: Construct foreman, Bor-Son Construct Co. Mem: Elks; Eagles; Moose; Bricklayers Union (secy); Minn AFL-CIO (vpres); Housing & Redevelop Authority; Brainerd Trades & Labor (pres). Relig: Catholic. Mailing Add: 1018 Portland Ave Brainerd MN 56401

SAMUELSON, LILLIAN THOMPSON (D)
b Boydton, Va, July 13, 26; d Ralph Washington Thompson & Hallie Wootton T; m 1947 to Dale Silas Samuelson; c Ralph Dale & Ann Elizabeth. Educ: Va Polytech Inst, 45-47; Ill Inst Technol, BS, 49. Polit & Govt Pos: Committeewoman, Johnson Co Dem Party, Kans, 60-62; alt deleg-at-lg, Dem Nat Conv, 72. Bus & Prof Pos: Test engr, Sears Roebuck & Co Test Labs, Chicago, Ill, 48-50; supvr research test kitchen, Hotpoint, Inc, Chicago, 50-52; homemaker & prof vol, Long Island, NY, Bucks Co, Pa, Dallas, Tex, Princeton, NJ, Johnson Co, Kans & Schenectady, NY, 52-71; mgr & owner, Am Indian Treasures, Guilderland, NY, 71- Publ: Ernest Smith, Seneca artist, Am Indian Crafts & Cult, 5/73. Mem: Am Home Econ Asn; Nat Cong Am Indians; Asn Am Indian Affairs; Am Indianist Soc. Mailing Add: 19-19 Inwood Terr Schenectady NY 12303

SANASARIAN, HAROUT O (D)
Wis State Rep
b Baghdad, Iraq, Mar 29, 29; s Onnig Sanasarian & Julia Ibrahim S; m 1964 to Joy Anne Draak; c Julie & John. Educ: Univ Wis, Milwaukee, BA in Polit Sci, 61. Polit & Govt Pos: Chmn, Armenians for Proxmire, Wis, 64; chmn, Third Ward Dem Unit, 66; prog chmn, Fourth Ward Dem Unit, 68; Wis State Rep, 26th Dist, 69-, mem, Health & Soc Serv Comt, Wis House Rep, 71-, chmn, Commerce & Consumer Affairs Comt, 71-, mem, Munic Comt, Printing Comt & Spec Comt to Investigate Utility Price Discrimination, 73-; deleg, Five Wis State Dem Conv, chmn platform on consumer protection, 70; mem platform comt, Milwaukee Co & Wis Dem Parties, various years; mem, Gov Task Force on Consumer Protection, 71; deleg & mem platform comt, Dem Nat Conv, 72; mem, State Energy Conserv Adv Coun, currently; mem spec energy task force, Nat Conf State Legis, currently; mem regulatory adv comt, Fed Energy Admin, currently. Bus & Prof Pos: Coordr, export work, Allis Chalmers Mfg Co, 61-65; teacher high sch civics, Milwaukee Pub Schs, 67-68. Publ: State utility regulation, Milwaukee J, 72; Can the Public Service Commission serve the public interest, Capitol Times, 72; In Wisconsin—a consumers bill of rights, State Govt, summer 72; plus others. Mem: Am Acad Polit & Soc Sci; Milwaukee Teachers Union; Milwaukee Art Ctr; Int Inst Milwaukee & Holiday Folk Fair (mem bd dirs). Honors & Awards: Consumers Friend in the Legis, Gtr Milwaukee Consumers League. Relig: Armenian Apostolic. Legal Res: 1246 N Cass St Milwaukee WI 53202 Mailing Add: Room 146 N State Capitol Madison WI 53702

SANBORN, BLAKE PAUL (R)
Mayor, Whittier, Calif
b Pomona, Calif, Oct 7, 24; s Carl H Sanborn & Sallie Dossett S; m 1949 to Mae Louise Moore; c Jennifer & Shelley. Educ: Pomona Col, BA, 49; Kappa Delta. Polit & Govt Pos: Town chmn, Ramsay for Cong, 62; pres, Whittier Young Rep, 63; deleg, Los Angeles Co

Young Rep, 63; victory squad chmn, 66th Assembly Dist Goldwater Campaign, 64; town chmn, Wiggins for Cong, 66 & 68; city councilman, Whittier, Calif, 68-73, mayor pro tem, 70, mayor, 73-; mem bd dirs, Whittier Rep Club, 69; chmn, Lincoln Club & Nixon Homecoming, 69; city of Whittier deleg, President Nixon's Inauguration, 69. Bus & Prof Pos: Dist mgr, Farmers Ins Group, 56-69; pres, Capital Leasing Corp, 69- & Blake P Sanborn Ins Agency, currently. Mil Serv: Entered as Seaman, Navy, 42, released as Lt Naval Aviator, 53, after serv in VB-14 World War II, Fasron Seven, Korean Action, recalled, 42-47 & 52-53; Naval Res, 53-56; Designated Naval Aviator. Mem: President's Coun; Whittier Exchange Club (pres); CofC (pres). Relig: Lutheran. Mailing Add: 8607 LaTremolina Lane Whittier CA 90605

SANBORN, LEONARD FOGG (R)
NH State Rep
b East Hartland, Conn, Oct 20, 03; s Rev Edward Stevens Sanborn & Dr Martha Pike S; m 1926 to Dorothy Rae; c Dorothy Elizabeth (Mrs Blank), John Leonard, Judith Sargent (Mrs Levis), Philip Moseley, Edwin Charles & Donald Pike. Educ: Worcester Polytech Inst, BS, 25; Sigma Phi Epsilon. Polit & Govt Pos: Moderator, Town of Kingston & Kingston Sch Dist, NH; NH State Rep, Dist Nine, 73- Bus & Prof Pos: Construction engr, Bahama Islands, Vt, Fla & NY, 25-31; & Mass, NH & Maine, 44-50; newspaper mgr, Bahama Islands, 35-40; construction engr, Fay, Spofford & Thorndike, Inc, Boston, 50-70; assoc, Hamilton Eng Assocs, Inc, Nashua, NH, 71. Mem: Fel, Am Soc of Civil Engrs; Mason. Relig: United Church of Christ. Legal Res: Depot Rd Kingston NH 03848 Mailing Add: PO Box 83 Kingston NH 03848

SANBORN, WILLIAM E (R)
NH State Sen
Mailing Add: Deerfield NH 03037

SANCHEZ, ADRIAN CRUZ (D)
Sen, Guam Legis
b Agana, Guam, Sept 26, 19; s Simon A Sanchez & Antonia Santos Cruz S; m 1974 to Joung Choon Park; c Doris M, Diana J T, Josephine R T & Adrian Frank. Educ: San Diego State Univ, 45-47; Univ Md, 58; Univ Guam, AA & BA, 73; United Vet Asn. Polit & Govt Pos: Asst dir pub health & welfare, Govt of Guam, 64-68, dir dept corrections, 68-70, dep dir dept pub works, 70-71; Sen, Guam Legis, 71- Bus & Prof Pos: Chmn bd dirs, Marianas Realty, 71-74; pres, Sanchez Realty Inc, 70-, Sanchez Enterprises Inc, 71-, Irek Guam Inc, Guam & Philippines, 71- & Socio Construction Co Inc, 72- Mil Serv: Entered as A/S, Navy, 38, released as Master CPO, 64, after serv in various task forces, 5th & 7th Fleets, Pac; Good Conduct Medal; Asiatic Pac & European Theatre Medals; Philippines Liberation Medal. Mem: VFW; Press Club; Lions. Honors & Awards: Distinguished Serv Award, Am Cancer Soc & Nat Tuberc & Respiratory Disease Asn. Relig: Catholic. Legal Res: Tamuning GU Mailing Add: PO Box 1161 Agana GU 96910

SANCHEZ, COSME FILIBERTO, JR (D)
Chmn, Costilla Co Dem Party, Colo
b Chama, Colo, Mar 13, 45; s Cosme Sanchez, Sr & Mary T Trujillo S; m 1969 to Rose Ann Mondragon; c Ann Rose & Cosme F, III. Educ: High sch. Polit & Govt Pos: Chmn, Costilla Co Dem Party, Colo, 69-; co treas, Costilla Co, 71- Mil Serv: Entered as E-1, Army, 65, released as E-4, 67, after serv in Vietnam, 66-67; Good Conduct Medal; Vietnam Serv Medal. Mem: Am Legion; VFW; KofC; Head Start (chmn, Conyor Costilla Policy Coun). Legal Res: 602 Costilla San Luis CO 81152 Mailing Add: PO Box 406 San Luis CO 81152

SANCHEZ, PHILLIP VICTOR (R)
US Ambassador to Honduras
b Pinedale, Calif, July 28, 29; s Jesus Visgues Sanchez & Josefina Tafoya S; m 1951 to Juanita Martinez; c Mark, Cynthia, Rand, Phillip & Marina. Educ: Fresno State Col, BA, 53, MA, 72; Sigma Delta Pi; Phi Mu Alpha; Sigma Chi; Sigma Tau. Polit & Govt Pos: Admin asst, US Property & Disbursing Off, State of Calif, 50-54, personnel officer, 54-56; admin analyst, Fresno Co, 56-57, sr admin analyst, 57-62, admin officer, 62-71; asst dir opers, Off Econ Opportunity, Washington, DC, 71-, nat dir, 71-73; US Ambassador to Honduras, 73- Bus & Prof Pos: Ed, The Pinedale Local, 57-58. Mil Serv: Entered as Recruit, Calif Army Nat Guard, 47, Lt Col, Army Res, currently; State of Calif Commendation with Oak Leaf Cluster, Medal of Merit; 20 Years Serv Medal; Armed Forces Res Medal; Calif Drill Honor Award for 20 Years Perfect Attendance. Publ: A Master Plan for Alcoholic Rehabilitation, 53; The Effects of the Last Ten Years of the Supreme Court on Contemporary Public Administration, 68; An Approach to Public Administration for the Twentieth Century Metropolitan Community, 69. Mem: US Jaycees; Commonwealth Club Calif; Western Govt Res Asn; Am Soc Pub Admin; Am Acad Polit Sci. Honors & Awards: Man of the Year, Fresno Commun Serv Orgn, 59; Fresno Outstanding Young Man, Jaycees, 63; Calif Five Outstanding Young Men, Calif Jaycees, 64; Medal of Merit, State of Calif, 66; Significant Sig Award, Sigma Chi Int, 73. Relig: Roman Catholic. Legal Res: 1015 E Alluvial Fresno CA 93726 Mailing Add: c/o Am Embassy APO New York NY 09887

SANCHEZ, RAYMOND G (D)
NM State Rep
Mailing Add: Box 1966 Albuquerque NM 87103

SANCHEZ-VILELLA, ROBERTO
b Mayaguez, PR, Feb 19, 13; s Luis Sanchez-Frasqueri & Angela Vilella-Velez; m 1936 to Conchita Dapena-Quiñones; c Evelyn (Mrs Salomon Monserrate) & Vilma (Mrs Salvador Marquez); m 1967 to Jeannette Ramos-Buonomo; c Robert Jose & Olga Elizabeth. Educ: Ohio State Univ, BCE, 34; Tau Beta Pi; Theta Xi. Polit & Govt Pos: Sub-Comnr of the Interior, PR, 41-42; dir, Transportation Authority, 42-45; adminr, Capital of PR, 45-46; spec asst to Pres, PR Sen, 46-47; exec secy, Govt of PR, 49-51; Secy of Pub Works, 51-59; Secy of State, PR, 52-64; Gov, PR, 64-68; pres, People's Party, PR, 68-73. Bus & Prof Pos: Resident engr, Caribe Hilton Hotel, 47-48. Publ: Funcion y Accion de la Rama Ejecutiva; Elite, Pobreza y Poder Politico. Mem: PR Col Engrs; Am Soc Pub Admin. Honors & Awards: Am Soc Pub Admin Annual Award, 63. Relig: Catholic. Mailing Add: Box 4109 San Juan PR 00905

SAND, ERVIN HERMAN (DFL)
Chmn, 16th Senate Dist, Dem-Farmer-Labor Comt, Minn
b St Martin Twp, Minn, Feb 16, 26; s Leo M Sand & Katherine Thull S; m 1948 to Elizabeth C Kraemer; c James, Joyce, Judy & Eldred Dingmann & Dennis, Dale, Leo, Thomas & Brian, Mary Kay (deceased), Diane (deceased) & Mary Lou (deceased). Polit & Govt Pos: Mem sch bd, New Munich, Minn, 49-52; city coun, Albany, 58-67, city assessor, 68-69; vchmn, Stearns Co Conv, 68-74; deleg, Minn State Conv, 68, 70, 72 & 74; chmn, 16th Senate Dist, Dem-Farmer-Labor Comt, 74- Bus & Prof Pos: Farmer, New Munich, Minn, 48-54; artificial inseminator, Albany, 53-70; seed & real estate sales broker, 70- Mem: KofC; Lions; CofC; Farmers Union; Farm Bur. Relig: Catholic. Mailing Add: Seventh St & Second Ave Albany MN 56307

SAND, PAUL M
Assoc Justice, NDak Supreme Court
b Balta, NDak, Oct 21, 14; s Paul A Sand & Clara Vetsch S; m 1952 to Gloria Gray; c Sheila (Mrs Rodney Kuhn). Educ: Univ NDak Law Sch, LLB, 41; JD, 69. Polit & Govt Pos: Asst attorney gen, NDak, 49-63, first asst Attorney Gen, 63-75; assoc justice, NDak Supreme Court, 75- Mil Serv: Entered as Pvt, Army, 41, released as Lt Col, 46, after serv in XXIII Corps, US Berlin Dist & War Crimes Comn in ETO; Army Res (Ret). Mem: Am Bar Asn; Am Judicature Soc; NDak State Bar; Lions. Relig: Catholic. Mailing Add: 1022 Eighth St Bismarck ND 58501

SANDA, KRISTA LINNEA (R)
VChairwoman, Minn State Rep Party
b Detroit Lakes, Minn, Dec 26, 37; d Karrol Ingvald Gandrud & Luella Elizabeth Meyer G; m 1956 to Donald James Sanda; c John Howard, Karin Marie, Steven Emil, Timothy James, Paul George & David Christopher Gandrud. Educ: St Cloud State Col, 55-57, Alpha Psi Omega scholar, 55; Minerva Soc. Polit & Govt Pos: Chairwoman, Todd Co Rep Comt, Minn, 66-68; mem, Rep Legis Campaign Comt, 66-68; mem, Minn State Rep Cent Comt, 66-; chairwoman, Seventh Cong Dist Nixon for President, Minn, 68; mem, Minn Rep State Exec Comt, 68-; chairwoman, Seventh Cong Dist, Minn, 68-73; chairwoman, Head for Gov, 70; deleg & chmn permanent orgn comt, Rep Nat Conv, 72; mem, Jon Haaven for Cong Comt, Minn, 72; vchairwoman, Minn State Rep Party, 73-; chmn, Minn Rule 29 Comt, 74-75; chmn, State Off Comt, 74-; get-out-the-vote chmn, Tom Hagedorn for Cong, 74 & Bruce Nelsen for House Rep, 74. Bus & Prof Pos: Substitute teacher, Staples Pub Schs, Minn, 58-62; welcome neighbor hostess, Staples CofC, 62-65; soc ed, World Weekly Newspaper, Staples, 68; exec secy, Benson Optical Lab, Staples, 68-73, customer rels expediter, 73- Publ: Ed, The college chronicle, St Cloud State Col, 56; auth, Crashing with dignity—an afternoon with H H H, 6/70 & From terror to triumph—an account of the 1972 G O P National Convention, 8/72, World Newspaper, Staples. Mem: Todd Co Cancer Soc (unit pres, 70-); United Fund Bd (residential chmn, Staples, 71-72); Nat Women's Polit Caucus, Minn; Staples Faculty Wives Club. Relig: Am Lutheran. Mailing Add: 603 N Ninth St Staples MN 56479

SANDACK, A WALLY (D)
b Chicago, Ill, June 26, 13; s Jack M Sandack & Ethel Grossman S; m 1940 to Helen Frank; c Nancy (Mrs Borgenicht), Roger D, Richard P, Arthur F & Susan. Educ: Univ Utah, JD. Polit & Govt Pos: Chmn, Salt Lake Co Dem Comt, Utah, 54-57; deleg, Dem Nat Conv, 56, 60 & 68; mem, Utah State Legis Coun, 65-66; chmn, Utah State Dem Comt, 67-68; regent, Univ Utah, 69. Bus & Prof Pos: Attorney, Sandack & Sandack, 37- Mil Serv: Entered as A/S, Navy, 42, released as Lt, 45, after serv in Pac Theatre. Relig: Jewish. Mailing Add: 26 N Wolcott St Salt Lake City UT 84103

SANDE, KERMIT ANDREW (D)
b Huron, SDak, Feb 23, 43; s Andrew Hanson Sande & Helen Busch; single. Educ: Augustana Col, BA, 65; George Washington Univ, summer 65; Univ SDak, JD, 68; Kappa Theta Phi. Polit & Govt Pos: Mem staff, Sen George McGovern, Washington, DC, summer 65; cand for Comnr of Sch & Pub Lands, 68; deleg, Dem Nat Conv, 68 & 72; legis counsel, SDak Dem Party, 68 & exec secy, 69-70; Beadle Co States Attorney, 71-72; Attorney Gen, SDak, 73-75. Bus & Prof Pos: Practicing attorney, 68-71. Mil Serv: Naval Res. Publ: Loyalty oaths, the US Supreme Court & South Dakota's loyalty oath requirement, spring 67 & South Dakota's bad check statutes, winter, 68, SDak Law Rev. Mem: Am & SDak Bar Asns; Phi Delta Phi; life mem SDak Law Rev Asn; Nat Dist Attorneys Asn. Honors & Awards: Nat Honor Soc; SDak Boys State; SDak & US Jaycees Freedom Guard Awards, 72. Relig: Lutheran. Legal Res: 1631 Illinois Ave SW Huron SD 57350 Mailing Add: Box 51 Pierre SD 57501

SANDEL, JERRY WAYNE (D)
NMex State Rep
b Woodson, Tex, May 25, 42; s Wayne Sandel & Sally Martin S; m 1964 to Nancy Potts; c Michelle (Mlle). Educ: Tex Technol Col, BA, 65; Univ Tex Sch of Prod Rig Oper, 1 year; Soc for Advan of Mgt; Circle K. Polit & Govt Pos: Alt deleg, Dem Nat Conv, 68; pres, Young Dem, Farmington, NMex, 68-; NMex State Rep, 71- Bus & Prof Pos: Pres, Totah Rental & Equipment Co Inc, Aztec, NMex & vpres, Aztec Well Servicing Co, currently. Mem: Am Petroleum Inst; NMex Lawman Asn; Mason; Elks. Honors & Awards: Participant, Presidents Council Youth Orgn; participant in Project Gasbuggy, first nuclear detonation for industrial application. Relig: Christian Church NAm. Mailing Add: 107 W 32nd St Farmington NM 87401

SANDERS, CARL EDWARD (D)
b Augusta, Ga, May 15, 25; s Carl T Sanders & Roberta Jones S; m 1947 to Betty Bird Foy; c Betty Foy & Carl E, Jr. Educ: Univ Ga, LLB, 47; Chi Phi; Phi Delta Phi. Polit & Govt Pos: Ga State Rep, 54-56; Ga State Sen, 18th Dist, 56-62, Floor Leader, Ga State Senate, 59, Pres Pro Tem, 60-62; mem, US Intergovt Comn of Fed-State Rels, 63-65; Gov, Ga, 63-67; chmn rules comt, Dem Nat Conv, 64; mem exec comt, Nat Gov Conf, 64-65; chmn, Appalachian Gov Conf, 64-65; vchmn, Southern Gov Conf, 65-66, counsel, 66-; chmn, Southern Region Educ Bd, 65; mem, Nat Comn on Urban Affairs, 67; mem adv coun, Off Econ Opportunity, 67; mem, Nat Citizens Comt for Pub TV; mem bd dirs, Pub Broadcasting Corp, 68-70. Bus & Prof Pos: Attorney-at-law; mem firm, Hammond, Kennedy & Sanders, Augusta, 48-52; sr mem, Sanders, Thurmond, Hester & Jolles, Augusta, 52-62; sr mem, Sanders, Hester, Holley, Ashmore & Boozer, formerly; partner, Law Firm of Troutman, Sanders, Lockerman & Ashmore, Atlanta, currently; mem bd dirs & exec comt, Fuqua Industs, Inc; mem adv comt, Cent of Ga RR; mem bd dirs, exec comt & finance comt, First Ga Bank; bd dirs, First RR & Banking Co. Mil Serv: Entered Air Force, released as 1st Lt, after serv as first pilot of a B-17 heavy bomber. Mem: Am & Ga Bar Asns; Lawyers Club of Am; Ga Conservancy; Am Legion. Honors & Awards: Selected Young Man of the Year, Augusta Jaycees, 55; honored by Ga Jaycees as One of Five Outstanding Young Georgians, 59; Golden Key Award, Nat Educ Asn, 65; Athletic Hall of Fame, 68; Pres, Univ Ga Alumni Soc, 69-70. Legal Res: 3488 Tuxedo Rd NW Atlanta GA 30305 Mailing Add: 1500 Candler Bldg Atlanta GA 30303

SANDERS, DONALD GILBERT (R)
b St Louis, Mo, Apr 26, 30; s Howard W Sanders & Ann M Schmitz S; m 1952 to Dolores L Henderson; c Deborah Ann, Michael Steven & Matthew Henderson. Educ: Univ Mo, 47-49, LLB, 54; Wash Univ, 50-51; Alpha Gamma Rho; Phi Alpha Delta. Polit & Govt Pos:

City Attorney, Columbia, Mo, 56-58; Asst Prosecuting Attorney, Boone Co, Mo, 59; spec agent, Fed Bur of Invest, Birmingham, Ala & Miami, Fla, 59-64, supvry spec agent, Washington, DC, 64-69; chief counsel, US House of Rep Comt on Internal Security, 69-73; dep minority counsel, US Senate Select Comt Presidential Campaign Activities, 73-74; sr prog analyst, US Atomic Energy Comn, 74-75; dep asst secy legis affairs, US Dept Defense, 75- Bus & Prof Pos: Pvt practice of law, Columbia, Mo, 56-59. Mil Serv: Entered as 2nd Lt, Marine Corps, 54, released as 1st Lt, 56, after serv in Legal Off, Camp Pendleton, Calif, 55-56. Mem: Am & Mo Bar Asns; US Supreme Court Bar; Soc Former Spec Agents Fed Bur of Invest; Am Legion. Relig: Methodist. Legal Res: 6423 Rotunda Ct Springfield VA 22150 Mailing Add: Pentagon Washington DC 20301

SANDERS, E C (SANDY) (D)
Okla State Rep
b Cordell, Okla, July 24, 20; s Edward Clinton Sanders & Carmen Lima Montgomery S; m 1942 to Ruth Charlotte Baumgart; c Edward Clinton & Charlotte (Mrs William Strain). Educ: Southwestern State Teachers Col, 37 & 38. Polit & Govt Pos: Okla State Rep, 70- Mem: Oklahoma City CofC; Oklahoma City Exchange Club. Relig: Am Lutheran. Mailing Add: 3128 NW 35 Oklahoma City OK 73112

SANDERS, FRANK (D)
b Tarboro, NC, July 30, 19; m to Mary Ellen Gilbert; c Douglas & Frank, Jr. Educ: Armstrong Jr Col, Savannah, Ga, grad; George Washington Univ Law Sch, grad; Univ Md, MA in Govt & Polit. Polit & Govt Pos: Mem staff, Comt on Appropriations, US House of Rep, 19 years, staff asst, Subcomt on Mil Construction & Subcomt on Defense Dept; Asst Secy of the Navy for Installations & Logistics, 69-71, Asst Secy for Financial Mgt, 71-72, Under Secy of the Navy, 72-73. Bus & Prof Pos: Pres, Logistics Mgt Inst, 73-74; vpres, Signal Corp, 74- Mil Serv: Entered as Pvt, Army, 41, released as Capt, 45, after serv in Intel & Surv Sect of Div Artil Staffs of the 85th & 34th Inf Div; Lt Col, Army Off Res Corps; Bronze Star; European Theater Ribbon with Three Battle Stars. Mem: Gospel Mission, DC; Wash Bible Col (trustee); assoc Inst for Strategic Studies, London; Psi Sigma Alpha. Relig: Presbyterian; Elder, Fourth Presby Church. Mailing Add: 12413 Over Ridge Rd Potomac MD 20854

SANDERS, HAROLD BAREFOOT, JR,
b Dallas, Tex, Feb 5, 25; s Harold Barefoot Sanders & May Elizabeth Forester S; m 1952 to Jan Scurlock; c Janet Lea, Martha Kay, Mary Frances, Harold Barefoot, III. Educ: Univ Tex, BA, 49, LLB, 50; Phi Delta Phi; Phi Delta Theta. Polit & Govt Pos: Tex State Rep, 52-58; Dem nominee, US Rep, Tex, 58; US Attorney, Northern Dist, Tex, 61-65; Asst Dep US Attorney Gen, 65-66, Asst Attorney Gen, US, 66-67; legis counsel to President Lyndon B Johnson, 67-69; Dem nominee, US Sen, Tex, 72. Bus & Prof Pos: Assoc, Storey, Sanders, Sherrill & Armstrong, Dallas, 50-52; partner, Sanders & Sanders, 51-61; partner, Clark, West, Keller, Sanders & Ginsberg, Dallas, Tex, 69- Mil Serv: Lt(jg), Naval Res, World War II. Mem: Am & Dallas Bar Asns; Fed Bar Asn; State Bar Tex; Tex Ex-Students Asn. Honors & Awards: Distinguished Serv Award, Dallas Fed Bar Asn, 64. Relig: Methodist. Legal Res: 7326 Malabar Lane Dallas TX 75230 Mailing Add: 2424 First Nat Bank Bldg Dallas TX 75202

SANDERS, JAMES WILLIS (R)
Mem, Ill Rep State Cent Comt
b Marion, Ill, Sept 20, 23; s Lawrence A Sanders & Minnie Harris S; m 1947 to Myrla Leach; c Jane, Larry, John, Gail & Ann. Educ: Univ Ill, BS, 48; John Marshall Law Sch, 51. Polit & Govt Pos: Chmn, Williamson Co Rep Party, Ill, formerly; mem, Ill Rep State Cent Comt, currently; Spec Asst Attorney Gen, Ill, 69-; deleg, Rep Nat Conv, 72. Mil Serv: Entered as Pvt, Army, 42, released as T/Sgt, 47, after serv in 310th Inf, 78th Div, ETO, 44; Purple Heart. Mem: Williamson Co Bar Asn; Rotary; Ill Jr Col Bd (bd mem, 71-); Ill Asn of Sch Bds (bd, 68-); Cent Midwestern Regional Educ Lab, Inc (bd, 70-). Relig: Methodist. Mailing Add: 208 N Market St Marion IL 62959

SANDERS, JOE WILLIAM (D)
Chief Justice, Supreme Court of La
b Pleasant Hill, La, May 31, 15; s Oliver Lud Sanders & Ozie Allen S; m 1940 to Marie Sistrunk. Educ: La State Univ, BA, 35; LLB, 38; Phi Kappa Phi; Omicron Delta Kappa; Gamma Eta Gamma; Pi Sigma Alpha; Pi Gamma Mu; Theta Xi. Polit & Govt Pos: La State Rep, 40-44; deleg, Dem Conv, 52; chmn, East Baton Rouge Parish Juv Comn, 51-54; judge family court, East Baton Rouge Parish, 54-60; mem adv coun judges, Nat Coun Crime & Delinquency, 55-; assoc justice, Supreme Court of La, 60-73, chief justice, 73- Bus & Prof Pos: Attorney-at-law, Many, La, 38-42; attorney-at-law, Baton Rouge, 46-54; chmn, Blue Ridge Training Inst of Southern Juv Court Judges, 57. Mil Serv: Capt, Army, 42-46. Mem: Am & La Bar Asns; Am Judicature Soc; Nat Coun Juv Court Judges; Coun La State Law Inst; Am Law Inst. Legal Res: 209 Lovers Lane Dr Baton Rouge LA 70806 Mailing Add: 301 Loyola Ave New Orleans LA 70112

SANDERS, ROBERT DONALD (R)
VChmn, Howard Co Rep Comt, Mo
b Glasgow, Mo, May 14, 31; s Edward Charles Sanders & Luella Hilderbrand S; single. Educ: Glasgow High Sch, 50. Polit & Govt Pos: Vchmn, Howard Co Rep Comt, Mo, 74- Relig: Protestant. Legal Res: 630 Saline St Glasgow MO 65254 Mailing Add: PO Box 93 Glasgow MO 65254

SANDERS, ROBERT R (R)
State Printer, Kans
b Mulvane, Kans, Jan 4, 03; s William Bernard Sanders & Marietta Clerk S; m 1922 to Letha Gwendolyn King; c Dona Jeanne (Mrs Ralph H Woertendyke) & Robert Dana. Educ: Plainville & Manhattan High Schs, Kans. Polit & Govt Pos: State Printer, Kans, 65- Bus & Prof Pos: Owner, Globe-Sun Printing Co, Salina, Kans, 44-65. Mem: Kiwanis; Mason (32 degree); Shrine; Elks; Int Typographic Union. Relig: Methodist. Legal Res: 944 Highland Salina KS 67401 Mailing Add: 201 W Tenth Topeka KS 66612

SANDERS, SHERRY E (D)
Chairperson, Marshall Co Dem Cent Comt, Iowa
b Custer, SDak, Dec 24, 39; d Clifford Benjamin Kelley & Alyce Harmes K; m 1960 to Arthur L Sanders; c Lynda Lee, Kristen Kay & Terry Jay. Educ: Black Hills State Col, 58-59. Polit & Govt Pos: Precinct committeeperson, Marshall Co Dem Cent Comt, 72; dist liaison person, Third Cong Dist, Iowa, 72-74; coordr, Marshall Co McGovern Campaign, Iowa, 71-72; deleg, Dem Nat Conv, 72; secy, Marshall Co Dem Cent Comt, Iowa, 73-75, chairperson, 75- Bus & Prof Pos: Realtor assoc, Fiscus Real Estate, Marshalltown, Iowa, currently. Mem: Nat & Iowa Asns Realtors; Dem Women's Club; Toastmistress Club; Blue & Gold Club. Relig: Methodist. Mailing Add: 27 S First St Marshalltown IA 50158

SANDERS, SYLVIA (D)
Treas, 11th Dist Dem Orgn, Mich
b Detroit, Mich, Jan 15, 31; d John Nicoara & Draga Bugarin N; div; c Brandon Michael. Educ: Univ Mich, Ann Arbor, AB, 52; Detroit Col Law, LLB, 58. Polit & Govt Pos: Co coordr, McGovern for President, Mich, 72; deleg, Mich Dem State Cent Comt, 73; deleg, Dem Mid-Term Conf, 74; treas, 11th Dist Dem Orgn, 74- Bus & Prof Pos: Secy-treas, Otsego Co Abstr Co, 63-71, pres, 71- Mem: State Bar Mich; Mich Land Title Asn (chmn const & by-laws comt, 72-); Am Land Title Asn. Legal Res: 880 North Dr Rte 4 Gaylord MI 49735 Mailing Add: 120 E Main St Gaylord MI 49735

SANDERS, W T, JR (BILL) (R)
SC State Rep
Mailing Add: 3620 Deerfield Dr Columbia SC 29204

SANDERS, WILFRED LEROY, JR (D)
Coordr, First Cong Dist Dem Comt, NH
b Marlboro, Mass, Nov 20, 35; s Wilfred L Sanders, Sr & Rose A Harpin S; m 1959 to Mary Jo; c Elizabeth Rose, Jonathan Lee & Steven Mark. Educ: Univ NH, BA, 59; Boston Col Sch Law, LLB, 62; Sigma Alpha Epsilon (pres); Newman Club (vpres); Class Pres, Univ NH. Polit & Govt Pos: Secy, NH Const Conv, 65; chmn, Rockingham Co Dem Comt, 65-68; chmn, NH State Dem Conv, 66, 68 & 70; deleg, Dem Nat Conv, 68; coordr, First Cong Dist Dem Comt, 68- Bus & Prof Pos: Lectr, Univ NH, 69- Mil Serv: Entered as Pvt, NH Nat Guard, 58-66. Mem: Am Trial Lawyers Asn; Am, NH & Rockingham Co Bar Asns; Jaycees. Relig: Roman Catholic. Mailing Add: 21 Exeter Rd Hampton NH 03842

SANDERSON, JAMES ELMER (R)
Exec Secy, Vt Rep State Comt
b East Burke, Vt, May 9, 44; s Kenneth Edward Sanderson, Sr & Marjorie Burrington S; single. Educ: Univ Vt, 62-63; Lyndon State Col, 64-67. Polit & Govt Pos: Moderator, Burke Town Meeting, Vt, 66-; chmn, Burke Rep Town Comt, 67-; mem, Caledonia Co Rep Comt, 67-; Dep Secy of State, Vt, 69-; vpres, Vt Young Rep, 70; exec secy, Vt Rep State Comt, 73- Mem: Iroquois Dist, Long Trail Coun Boy Scouts (advan chmn); Burke Mt Club; Green Mt Club; Vt Philatelic Soc. Legal Res: East Burke VT 05832 Mailing Add: RD 2 Montpelier VT 05602

SANDGRUND, HYLA ZONA (D)
b Rochester, NY, July 12, 25; d Irving Van Dilla & Fannie Cohen; m 1957 to Morris Sandgrund; c David Michael & Robert Max. Educ: Benjamin Franklin High Sch, 43. Polit & Govt Pos: Mgr hq, Campaign for a Dem Alternative, Rochester, 68; McCarthy for President, 68; exec comt, Coalition for Independent Candidacy, 68; secy, New Dem Coalition, 68-69; deleg, Dem Nat Conv, 72; coordr, Another Woman for McGovern, 72. Bus & Prof Pos: Traffic mgr, WARC, Rochester, 47-49; secy, Rochester Asn for UN, 52-55; Sutherland, Linowitz, Williams, Attorneys, 55-56; Rabbi Philip S Bernstein, Temple Brith Kodesh, 56-58. Mem: Rochester Area Women for Peace (coordr, 71-); Metro-Act of Rochester; Am Civil Liberties Union; Nat Woman's Polit Caucus; Nat Orgn Women. Mailing Add: 92 Shepard St Rochester NY 14620

SANDIFER, CECIL T (D)
SC State Rep
Mailing Add: Box 97 Westminster SC 29693

SANDISON, GORDON (D)
Wash State Sen
b Washington, Feb 20, 20; s Arthur T Sandison & Martha Davison S; m 1943 to Muriel Lane; c Gordon T, Colin Douglas, Bruce Malcolm, Derek Ian & Trevor Russell. Educ: Univ Idaho; Seattle Univ, BS, 41; Alpha Tau Omega. Hon Degrees: LLD, St Martin's Col, 71. Polit & Govt Pos: Wash State Rep, 5 terms, 47-58; mem Western Interstate Comn for Higher Educ, 59-, exec bd mem, 63-68, chmn, 67-68; chmn, Wash State Legis Coun on Higher Educ, 65-69; mem, Educ Comn of the States, 65-, Wash comnr, 67-; Wash State Sen, 59-, chmn, Interim Comt Higher Educ, Wash State Senate, mem, Steering Comt, 73- Bus & Prof Pos: Owner, Gordon Sandison Ins, 49-; dir, Port Angeles Savings & Loan, 68-; real estate bus; dir, Land Title Ins Co. Mil Serv: Entered as Pvt, US Marine Corps, 41, released as Capt, 45, after serv in Third Marine Div, SPac, 42-45. Mem: Elks; Eagles; VFW; Grange; Am Legion. Honors & Awards: Distinguished Serv Award, Pac Lutheran Univ, 71. Relig: Protestant. Legal Res: 2501 S Cherry St Port Angeles WA 98362 Mailing Add: PO Box 2025 Port Angeles WA 98362

SANDLIN, HUGH C (D)
NC State Rep
Mailing Add: Rte 3 Box 333 Jacksonville NC 28540

SANDMAN, CHARLES W, JR (R)
b Philadelphia, Pa, Oct 23, 21; s Charles W Sandman & Rose Frasch S; m 1948 to Marion Louise Cooney; c Carol, William, Marion, Robert, Charles & Richard. Educ: Temple Univ, 40-42; Rutgers Law Sch, 45-48; Theta Kappa Phi. Polit & Govt Pos: Deleg, Rep Nat Conv, 56-68; NJ State Sen, 56-66, Majority Leader, Senate, 62 & 63, pres, 64 & 65; US Rep, NJ, 67-74; chmn, Cape May Co Rep Party, NJ, 71-74; cand, US House Rep, NJ, 74. Bus & Prof Pos: Solicitor, West Cape May, NJ, 50-66, Lower Twp, 51-61, First Nat Bank of Stone Harbor, 57- & Cape May, 57 & 64- Mil Serv: Entered as Aviation Cadet, Air Force, 42, released as Flight Officer, 45, after serv in 483rd Bomb Group, 840th Bomb Squadron, 15th Air Force, ETO, 44; ETO Ribbon; Air Medal with Two Gold Crosses. Mem: Rotary Int; Am, NJ & Cape May Co Bar Asns; VFW. Relig: Catholic. Mailing Add: Erma Park Rd Cape May NJ 08204

SANDNESS, CLAIRE A (R)
NDak State Sen
Mailing Add: State Capitol Bismarck ND 58501

SANDOVAL, ALICIA CATHERINE (D)
b Glendale, Calif, May 2, 43; d Crescent D Sandoval & Lucy Sauceda S; single. Educ: Immaculate Heart Col, 61-64; Univ Calif, Los Angeles, BA, 66; Univ Southern Calif, MS, 70; Theta Iota Pi. Polit & Govt Pos: Orgn chmn, Dem Southern Calif; San Fernando Valley chmn, Comt to Elect Pierre Salinger to US Senate, 64; San Fernando Valley chmn, Comt to Reelect Gov Pat Brown, 66; secy, Educators Comt to Elect Humphrey, Southern Calif, 68; mem, Calif Dem State Cent Comt, 68-74; app to mayor's adv comt on Greek Theater by Hon Tom Bradley, 75. Bus & Prof Pos: Teacher Eng, Roosevelt High Sch, Los Angeles, 67-69,

asst girls vprin, currently; supvr Eng instr, San Fernando Valley State Col, Educ Opportunities Prog, summer session, 69; assoc producer, Mex-Am Heritage Series, NBC, 70-71; dir field serv, United Teachers Los Angeles, 70- Mem: Asn Mex-Am Educators; Educ Issues Coord Comt; Latin-Am Civic Asn; Mex-Am Polit Asn; Van Nuys Dem Club (rec secy). Honors & Awards: Hon panelist with Vice President Humphrey on Press Conference (TV Show), summer 68; Mayor's Cert for Outstanding Community Involvement, Hon Tom Bradley, 74. Relig: Catholic. Mailing Add: 5209 N Babcock Ave North Hollywood CA 91607

SANDOVAL, HILARY JOSEPH, JR (R)
b El Paso, Tex, Jan 29, 30; s Hilary Joseph Sandoval, Sr & Theodora Aguirre S; m 1951 to Dolores B Morales; c Mary Dolores, Irene Roberta, Hilary Joseph, III, George Edward & Anthony F. Educ: Univ Ariz, BA; Univ Mex; Tex Technol Col. Polit & Govt Pos: Chmn, El Paso Co Rep Exec Comt, Tex, 62; asst chmn, Tex Rep Party, 66; adminr, Small Bus Admin, 69-70. Bus & Prof Pos: Pres, Sandoval News Serv, Inc, 53- Mil Serv: Entered as Pvt, Army, 51, released as Capt, 53; Capt, Army Res, currently. Mem: El Paso Club, Sales & Mkt Execs Int; Mid-Am Periodicals Distributors Asn; Bur of Independent Publ & Distributors; League of United Latin Am Citizens Coun 8; El Paso Rotary Club. Honors & Awards: Sales Exec of the Year Award, El Paso Club, Sales & Mkt Execs Int, chosen Most Valuable Mem of the Lulac Dist 4, 66-67; Tex State Man of the Year, Air Force Asn, 68. Relig: Catholic. Mailing Add: 9917 Fenway El Paso TX 79925

SANDOVAL, PAUL (D)
Colo State Sen
Mailing Add: 3647 Vallejo Denver CO 80223

SANDS, EDWARD PAUL (D)
b Lincoln, Nebr, Apr 27, 50; s Stanley Hugh Sands & Nancy Ann Platt S; single. Educ: Duke Univ, AB, 74; Univ Nebr Col Law, 74-; chmn, Duke Univ Young Dem Club, 69-70; deleg, Col Young Dem Clubs Am Conv, 69 & 70. Polit & Govt Pos: High sch students coordr, Nebr McCarthy for President Campaign, 68; campaign worker, Durham, NC Humphrey-Muskie Campaign, 68; deleg, NC State Young Dem Conv, 70; campaign worker, Gore for Senate Campaign, Memphis, Tenn, 70; nat field staff, McGovern for President Campaign, 71-72, Washington, DC & six states; deleg, Lancaster Co & Nebr State Dem Conv, 72; alt deleg, Dem Nat Conv, 72. Mem: Nebr Young Dem Club; Am Civil Liberties Union. Relig: Jewish. Mailing Add: 2601 Woodscrest Ave Lincoln NE 68502

SANDS, ERNEST MONROE (R)
NDak State Sen
b Pincher Creek, Alta, Can, Apr 30, 22; s Monroe Edwin Sands & Anna Barr S; m 1944 to Ione Yeager; c Nancy (Mrs Terry Krumwiede) & William Ernest. Educ: Univ NDak, BS in Bus Admin, 43; Phi Delta Theta. Polit & Govt Pos: City comnr, Velva, NDak, 60-62, mayor, 62-70; pres, NDak League of Cities, 66; NDak State Sen, 67- Bus & Prof Pos: Owner, Sands Funeral Home, 47- & Sands Dept Store, currently. Mil Serv: Entered as Pvt, Army Air Force, 43, released as 1st Lt, 45, after serv in 8th Air Force, European Theatre, 44-45. Mem: Am Legion; VFW; Mason; Elks; CofC. Relig: Methodist. Mailing Add: One Main St Velva ND 58790

SANDS, NANCY PLATT (D)
b St Louis, Mo, Oct 12, 24; d Edward Grover Platt & Helen Sommers Waldheim P; m 1947 to Stanley Hugh Sands; c Edward Paul, Alan Platt, David Stuart, Stephen Scott & Pamela Ann. Educ: Conn Col, BA, 46; Cum Laude Soc. Polit & Govt Pos: Alt deleg, Nebr Dem State Conv, Lincoln, 72; deleg, Lancaster Co Conv, Lincoln, 72; deleg, Dem Nat Conv, 72. Mem: Dem Women's Club; Family Serv Asn; Lincoln Gen Hosp Auxiliary; Lincoln Symphony Guild; Sheridan PTA. Mailing Add: 2601 Woodscrest Ave Lincoln NE 68502

SANDSTROM, ELSA (R)
Nat Americanism Chmn, Nat Fedn Rep Women
b Chicago, Ill; married. Polit & Govt Pos: Women's chmn, Nixon-for-Gov Comt, Santa Clara Co, Calif, 62, women's chmn, Goldwater for President Comt, 64; deleg, Rep Nat Conv, 64 & 72; Rep Elector, Tenth Cong Dist, 64; mem exec comt, Rep State Cent Comt Calif, currently; pres, Los Altos Rep Women, Calif Fedn Rep Women, 60, vpres, Northern Div, 62-63, Americanism chmn, State Fedn, 66-68, vpres, 68-69, pres, 71-72; mem, Reagan for Gov Campaign Comt, 70; mem bd dirs, Nat Fedn Rep Women, 71-, nat Americanism chmn, currently; mem adv bd & Calif chmn of vol & state women's chmn, President's Campaign Comt, 72; Presidential Elector & secy, Electoral Col, 72; mem, Calif Am Revolution Bi-Centennial Comn, 72-; Rep Nat Committeewoman, 74-; plus numerous off & chairmanships in vol polit. Mailing Add: Hi Valley Ranch Stonyford CA 95979

SANDUSKY, JOHN THOMAS, JR (D)
Ala State Rep
b Mobile, Ala, Mar 28, 34; s John Thomas Sandusky, Sr & Beatrice Brooks S; m 1968 to Bonnie Hawkins; c Julie Lynn, Jamie Elaine, Gayle J Miller, Jr & Damon Alfred Miller. Educ: Auburn Univ, 51-56; Theta Chi. Polit & Govt Pos: Ala State Rep, 75- Mem: Mobile Area CofC; Auburn Alumni Asn. Honors & Awards: Outstanding Towne Men of Ala, 64. Relig: Baptist. Legal Res: 2113 Knollwood Dr Mobile AL 36609 Mailing Add: PO Box 9132 Mobile AL 36609

SAN FELIPPO, RONALD S (D)
b Milwaukee, Wis, Aug 8, 46; s Michael J San Felippo & Anne Levy S; m 1975 to Andrea Spheeris. Educ: Univ Wis-Milwaukee, 65-67; Marquette Univ, 67-68. Polit & Govt Pos: Wis nat committeeman, Young Dem, 67-69; mem campaign staff, Milwaukee Mayor Maier, 67; mem, Milwaukee UN Comn, 67; vchmn statutory comt, Milwaukee Dem Statutory Party, 68-; trustee, Milwaukee Libr Bd, 68-72; nat vpres, Young Dem Clubs Am, 69-71; exec dir, US Sen William Proxmire Campaign Staff, 70; treas, Wis Libr Trustees, 70-71; dir, Milwaukee Sch Bd, 71-, pres, 72-75; adminr, Emergency Govt, Wis, currently. Bus & Prof Pos: Supvr, Northwestern Mutual Life Ins Co, 68-73; vpres, Wis No Fault Ins Co, Inc, 73-75; trustee, Milwaukee Teachers' Retirement & Annuity Bd, 73-75. Mem: Wis Acad Arts, Letters & Sci; Old Time Ball Players Asn; Milwaukee Ment Health Asn. Relig: Catholic. Mailing Add: 7820 W Grantosa Dr Milwaukee WI 53218

SANFORD, BERNARD H (R)
b Oshkosh, Wis, Sept 29, 01; m 1924 to Sarah Rostagno; c Helen June & Donna Marie. Polit & Govt Pos: Mem, Bd of Canvassers & chmn, Dickinson Co Rep Party, Mich, formerly. Bus & Prof Pos: Dist mgr; ins counr; speaker at high schs. Mem: Mason; Eastern Star & others. Legal Res: Hamilton Lakes Vulcan MI 49892 Mailing Add: Box 26 Norway MI 49870

SANFORD, CALVIN G (R)
Va State Deleg
Mailing Add: Box 91 Hague VA 22469

SANFORD, I S (D)
Miss State Sen
b Jones Co, Miss, June 28, 10; married. Polit & Govt Pos: Mem, Pub Serv Comn; chancery clerk; Miss State Rep, 40-44; Miss State Sen, currently. Bus & Prof Pos: Farmer. Mem: VFW; Mason; Shrine; Am Legion. Relig: Baptist. Mailing Add: PO Box 55 Collins MS 39428

SANFORD, MARIE (R)
Chairwoman, 23rd Dist Rep Party, Ill
b North English, Iowa, May 19, 16; d Jake Smith & Ida Miller S; m 1936 to Dan H Sanford; c Jeffrey Alan. Polit & Govt Pos: Chmn, Crawford Co Rep Comt, 67-74; mem ethnic res comt, Ill Rep State Cent Comt, 71-; bd dirs, Ill State Fedn Rep Women, 71-; chairwoman, 23rd Dist Rep Party, currently. Bus & Prof Pos: Pres, D&M Rentals, Inc, 57- Mem: Bus & Prof Women's Club (treas); Crawford Co Rep Women's Club; Robinson CofC; Camp Fire Girls; Robinson Sr Women's Club. Honors & Awards: Hall of Fame, Dale Carnegie Alumni Asn. Relig: Jewish. Mailing Add: 607 Woodland Dr Robinson IL 62454

SANFORD, TERRY (D)
b Laurinburg, NC, Aug 20, 17; s Cecil L Sanford & Elizabeth Martin S; m 1942 to Margaret Rose Knight; c Elizabeth Knight & James Terry. Educ: Univ NC, AB, 39, Law Sch, JD, 46. Polit & Govt Pos: Pres, NC Young Dem Clubs, 49-50; NC State Sen, 53, deleg, Dem Nat Conv, 56-68; Gov, NC, 61-65; nat chmn, Citizens for Humphrey-Muskie, 68; chmn, Dem Charter Comn, 72-, chmn exec comt, 74; deleg, Dem Nat Mid-Term Conf, 74. Bus & Prof Pos: Lawyer, Sanford, Cannon, Adams & McCullough, 65- & dir, A Study of Am States, Duke Univ, 65-67; pres, Urban Am, Inc, 68-69; pres, Duke Univ, 69- Mil Serv: Entered as Pvt, Army, 42, released as 1st Lt, 45, after serv in 517th Parachute Combat Team, ETO, 43-45; Bronze Star; Purple Heart. Publ: But What About the People?, Harper & Row, 66; Storm Over the States, McGraw-Hill, 67. Mem: Am Bar Asn; Am Judicature Soc; Am Acad Polit & Social Sci. Relig: Methodist. Mailing Add: PO Box 1366 Durham NC 27702

SANGER, RICHARD CALVIN (R)
b New York, NY, Aug 12, 30; s Edmund P Sanger & Clara Wilde S; m 1954 to Eleanor Matejcek; c Robert Calvin. Educ: Trinity Col, BA, 52; Univ Conn Sch Law, LLB, 61; Delta Kappa Epsilon. Polit & Govt Pos: Chmn, Canton Rep Town Comt, Conn, 67-74. Mil Serv: Entered as 2nd Lt, Air Force, 52, released as Capt, 58, after serv in 28th SRW, Strategic Air Command, 53-58; Res, 58-69, Maj; Commendation Ribbon. Mem: Am, Conn & Hartford Co Bar Asns; Lions Int. Relig: Congregational. Mailing Add: Mohawk Dr Canton CT 06019

SANGMEISTER, GEORGE EDWARD (D)
Ill State Rep
b Frankfort, Ill, Feb 16, 31; s George Conrad Sangmeister & Rose Johnson S; m 1951 to Doris Marie Hinspeter; c George Kurt & Kimberly Ann. Educ: Joliet Jr Col, 49-51; Elmhurst Col, BA, 57; John Marshall Law Sch, Chicago, LLB, 60, JJD, 70; Delta Theta Phi. Polit & Govt Pos: Justice of the Peace, Will Co, Ill, 61-63, Magistrate of the Circuit Court, 63-64, State's Attorney, 64-68; bd trustees, Sch Dist 210, 70-73; Ill State Rep, Dist 42, Will Co, 73- Mil Serv: Entered as Pvt, Army, 51, released as Sgt, 53, after serv in Inf, US, 51-53. Mem: Frankfort CofC; Frankfort Lions; Family Counseling Agency; Am Legion; Salvation Army. Honors & Awards: Attorney of the Year, Will Co Legal Secretaries, 67. Relig: Protestant. Mailing Add: S Wolf Rd Mokena IL 60448

SANSTEAD, WAYNE GODFREY (D)
Lt Gov, NDak
b Hot Springs, Ark, Apr 16, 35; s Godfrey A Sanstead & Clara Buen S; m 1957 to Mary Jane Bober; c Timothy Wayne & Jonathan Paul. Educ: St Olaf Col, BA in Speech & Polit Sci, 57; Northwestern Univ, MA in Pub Address & Group Commun, 66; Univ NDak, EdD, 74. Polit & Govt Pos: NDak State Rep, Fifth Legis Dist, 64-70; NDak State Sen, 70-72; const conv deleg, 70-; Lt Gov, NDak, 72- Bus & Prof Pos: Dir debate, Luverne High Sch, Minn, 59-60; dir forensics, Minot Sr High Sch, 60-69. Mil Serv: Entered as Pvt, Army Res, 57, released as Pfc, 59, after serv in Intel Ctr, Baltimore, Md. Mem: Speech Asn of Am; NDak Speech Asn (pres); Phi Delta Kappa; Am Forensic Asn; Am Civil Liberties Union. Honors & Awards: Degree of Distinction, Pi Kappa Delta Minn Beta Chap, 57; Degree of Distinction, Nat Forensic League, 62; Outstanding Young Speech Teacher Award, Cent States Speech Asn, 63; Minot & NDak Jaycees Outstanding Young Educator Awards, 67; Distinguished Serv Award, Outstanding Young Man, Minot Jaycees, 70. Relig: Lutheran; Chmn, Western NDak Res & Social Action Comt, Am Lutheran Church. Mailing Add: 823 Ninth Ave NE Minot ND 58701

SANTANGELO, FRANCIS J, SR (D)
Md State Deleg
Mailing Add: 7509 Chesapeake St Landover MD 20785

SANTARELLI, DONALD EUGENE (R)
b Hershey, Pa, July 22, 37; s Ambrose Santarelli & Ercolina Altobelli S; m 1966 to Anne Constance Dunlap; c Louisa Rush. Educ: Mt St Mary's Col, 55-59; Va Law Sch, LLB, 62; Univ Va Grad Sch, 62-64; Eli Banana; Delta Kappa Epsilon; Pi Delta Epsilon. Polit & Govt Pos: Asst, Corp Coun, DC, 65-66, Asst US Attorney, 66-67; minority counsel, Comt on Judiciary, US House of Rep, 67-69; spec counsel, Subcomt on Const Rights, Comt on Judiciary, US Senate, 69; Assoc Dep Attorney Gen, Dept of Justice, 69-73, adminr, Law Enforcement Assistance Admin, 73-74; mem, Task Force on Legal Rights & Justice, White House Conf on Youth, 70-71. Bus & Prof Pos: Law clerk, US Dist Judge Thomas J Michie, Fourth Circuit Court, 64-65. Mem: Va State & Am Bar Asns; Judicial Conf of DC; Univ Va (bd visitors, 70-). Relig: Roman Catholic. Mailing Add: 224 N Royal St Alexandria VA 22314

SANTIAGO-CAPETILLO, WILFRIDO (POPULAR DEMOCRAT, PR)
Rep, PR House Rep
b Utuado, PR, Oct 19, 39; s Miguel Santiago & Julia Capetillo S; m 1966 to Daisy Marcano. Educ: Univ PR, Rio Piedras, BA, 62; Inter-Am Univ PR, Hato Rey, real estate, 65. Polit & Govt Pos: Pres, Youth Coun, San Juan, PR, 59-65; mem island party coun, Popular Dem Party, 61-; spec asst to exec dir, Housing & Urban Renewal Corp, 62-65; exec secy, Pub Work Comt, Senate PR, 65-66; treas, Popular Dem Party, Seventh Precinct, 65-69; asst dir, Commun Action Dept, San Juan, 66-69; dir alumnae off, Univ PR, Mayaguez, 69-71; vpres, San Juan Popular Dem Party Cent City Comt, 69-; precinct pres, Popular Dem Party, 39th Precinct, 69-; Rep, PR House Rep, 73- Publ: Fundamentals of the Commonwealth Puerto

Rico, J Interam Dem Sch, 65. Mem: Lions Club (vpres, 68-). Honors & Awards: Distinguished Serv Award, Et-Olympus Club, 61; civic work award, Lions Club, 70. Relig: Catholic. Mailing Add: 2107 Sirce St Apolo Rio Piedras PR 00927

SANTIAGO GARCIA, PRESBY **(POPULAR DEMOCRAT, PR)**
Rep, PR House Rep
Mailing Add: State Capitol San Juan PR 00901

SANTIESTEBAN, HUMBERTO TATI **(D)**
Tex State Sen
b El Paso, Tex, Nov 3, 34; s Ricardo Santiesteban, Jr & Carmen Leyva S; m 1956 to Ruby Sue McMillen; c Valori Lynn, Stephanie Diane & Ricardo Tati. Educ: NMex Mil Inst, BA with honors, 56; Univ Tex Sch Law, Austin, LLB, 62; Spanish Honor Soc; Letterman's Club; pres & chmn bd gov, Student Bar Asn; Praetor; Dean's List. Polit & Govt Pos: Mem, El Paso Zoning Bd of Adjust, Tex, 63-65; Tex State Rep, Dist 67-1, 67-72; vchmn, Fed-State Rels; chmn, Mex Am Legis Deleg; Tex State Sen, 73- Bus & Prof Pos: Partner, Law Firm, Paxson & Santiesteban, 62- Mil Serv: Entered as 2nd Lt, Army, 56, released as 1st Lt, 59, after serv in Airborne Inf & Mil Police, 56-59; Jungle Warfare & Ranger Airborne Badge. Mem: Am & Tex State Bar Asns; Am & Tex Trial Lawyers Asns; CofC; Am Arbit Asn (nat panel of arbitrators); League of United Latin Am Citizens. Honors & Awards: Distinguished Mil Student; Cadet Col; Univ Tex Law Sch Dean's List; recognition for work on State Legis Criminal Jurisp Comt, Tex Bar Asn. Relig: Roman Catholic. Legal Res: 601 La Cruz El Paso TX 79902 Mailing Add: Suite 14K El Paso Nat Bank Bldg El Paso TX 79901

SANTINI, JAMES DAVID **(D)**
US Rep, Nev
b Reno, Nev, Aug 13, 37; m to Ann Marie Crane; c David, Lisa, Kerrie, Lori & Mark. Educ: Univ Nev, BS, 59; Hastings Col Law, JD, 62. Polit & Govt Pos: Dep dist attorney, Clark Co, Nev, 68-69; from dep pub defender to pub defender, 68-70; justice of the peace, 70-72; dist court judge, Clark Co, 72-74; US Rep, Nev, 75- Bus & Prof Pos: Attorney-at-law; instr, Univ Las Vegas, 67-71; lectr, Nat Legal Aid & Defender Asn, 68; lectr, Practicing Law Inst, 68-70; lectr, Am Acad Judicial Educ, 71-74; lectr, Nat Col State Judiciary, 73; owner & lectr, Nev Bar Rev, 70-74; bd mem & chmn, Southern Nev Mus, 68-74. Mil Serv: Army, 63-66. Mem: Nev Judges Asn (pres, 71). Honors & Awards: Order of Merit of Ital Rep, Ital Consultate, San Francisco, Calif, 72; One of the three outstanding pub defenders in the nation, Nat Legal Aid & Defender Asn, 68. Legal Res: 1500 E Charleston Las Vegas NV 89104 Mailing Add: US House Rep Washington DC 20515

SANTONI, GEORGE JOSEPH **(D)**
Md State Deleg
b Baltimore, Md, Mar 4, 39; s George Howard Santoni & Mary Matarazzo S; m 1969 to Concetta Francis Comi; c Darlene & Donna. Educ: Patterson Park High Sch, grad, 57. Polit & Govt Pos: Md State Deleg, 46th Dist, 75-; chmn, Harbour Tunnel Truck Study Comn, 75- Bus & Prof Pos: Gen mgr, Real Estate Serv Inc, 65-67; pres, United Construction Co Inc, 67-69; chief operating officer, Comi Vending Serv Inc, 69-74; financial consult, Inervest Capitol Corp, 74-75. Mem: Old Glory Dem Club; Sons of Italy; Freedom to Choose Dem Club; Polish Home Club. Honors & Awards: Ital of Year, Belair Rd Lodge, Sons of Italy, 74; Gov Citation, Gov of Md, 74, Dedicated to Serv Award, 75; Pres Award, Pres of City Coun, 74. Mailing Add: 3921 Lyndale Ave Baltimore MD 21213

SANTOS, ALFRED **(R)**
Chmn, Cumberland Rep Town Comt, RI
b Buenos Aires, Argentina, July 19, 40; s Armenio Santos & Isaura Delgado S; m 1963 to Lydia Pestana; c Steven. Educ: Bryant Col, BSBA, 62; Kappa Tau. Polit & Govt Pos: Chmn, Cumberland Rep Town Comt, RI, 75-; deleg, RI State Rep Cent Comt, 75- Bus & Prof Pos: Salesman, Aetna Ins Co, 74- Mil Serv: Entered as Pvt, Army, 63, released as Lt, 69, after serv in 1043rd Ord Co, RI Nat Guard. Mem: Jaycees; Mason; Cumberland Beagle Club. Honors & Awards: Key Man of Year, Cumberland-Lincoln Jaycees. Relig: Catholic. Mailing Add: 104 New York Ave Cumberland RI 02864

SANTOS, FRANK **(D)**
Sen, Guam Legis
Mailing Add: Guam Legislature Box 373 Agana GU 96910

SANTOS, VELMA MCWAYNE **(R)**
Hawaii State Rep
b Kula, Maui, Hawaii, Dec 8, 30; d William Lilinoe McWayne & Helen Hoohoku M; m 1955 to Louis Santos; c Alexa-Helene, Ilona-May, Leslie-Ann & Mark McWayne. Educ: Univ Mich, Ann Arbor, 48-50; Univ Hawaii, BA, 52. Polit & Govt Pos: Chmn & mem, Comt on Status of Women, Maui, Hawaii & Civil Serv Comt, Maui Co, 72-74; Hawaii State Rep, Dist 6, 74- Bus & Prof Pos: Teacher, Keokea Sch, Kula, Maui, Hawaii, 52-54, Kahului Sch, Kahului, 54-55 & Wailuku Elem, 55-74. Mem: Maui & Hawaii State Teachers Asns; Hawaii Fedn Bus & Prof Women's Clubs (pres, 73-74); Delta Kappa Gamma Hon Soc; Maui Asn to Help Retarded Children. Honors & Awards: Career Woman of the Year, Nat Fedn of BPW Clubs, Inc, 70; Outstanding Elem Teacher of Am, Outstanding Elem Teachers of Am, Bd Adv, 74. Relig: Catholic. Mailing Add: 253 Awapuhi Pl Wailuku HI 96793

SANTUCCI, JOHN J **(D)**
NY State Sen
Mailing Add: 111-29 116th St South Ozone Park NY 11420

SANXTER, JOAN M **(R)**
VChmn, Steuben Co Rep Comt, Ind
b Fremont, Ind, Oct 19, 22; d Lewis C Schaeffer & Maizie Mountz S; wid; c Kathleen (Mrs Millican), Charles L & Thomas W Nedele. Educ: High Sch, grad. Polit & Govt Pos: Chmn, Steuben Co Rep Comt, Ind, 62-; secy, Fourth Dist Rep Cent Comt, 72- Bus & Prof Pos: Clerk, City Court, Angola, Ind, 63-68; mgr license br 4, Angola, 69. Mem: Angola Bus & Prof Womens Club; Am Legion Auxiliary; Rep Women's Club. Relig: Christian Science. Mailing Add: 811 Stevens St Angola IN 46703

SAPERSTEIN, ESTHER **(D)**
Ill State Sen
b Chicago, Ill; wid; c Sidney & Natalie. Educ: Northwestern Univ. Polit & Govt Pos: Mem, Mayor's Juvenile Welfare Comt & Comt on Human Rels, Chicago, Ill; Ill State Rep, 57-66; Ill chmn, Comn Ment Health & Ment Retardation, 65-; Ill State Sen, 66-, chmn, Educ Comt, Ill State Senate; Ill chmn, Comn Status of Women; alderman, 49th Ward, Chicago, 75- Mem: Women's Auxiliary, Bernard Horwarch Ctr (bd); Zionist Orgn (exec comt); one of the founders of City of Hope; League of Women Voters; Pub Affairs of Metrop YWCA. Honors & Awards: Mrs Ment Health of Ill, 65; First Dem woman to be elected Ill State Sen in 149 years; Woman of the Year in Pub Serv, 71; Freedom Award, Roosevelt Univ, 73. Relig: Jewish; North Shore B'nai B'rith. Mailing Add: 1316 W Arthur Chicago IL 60626

SAPINSLEY, LILA MANFIELD **(R)**
Minority Leader, RI State Senate
b Chicago, Ill, Sept 9, 22; d Jacob Manfield & Doris Silverman M; m 1942 to John M Sapinsley; c Jill S (Mrs James Mooney), Carol S (Mrs Alan Rubenstein); Joan & Patricia. Educ: Wellesley Col, BA, 44. Hon Degrees: DPS, Univ RI, 71; DPed, RI Col, 73. Polit & Govt Pos: Chmn, Bd Trustees State Cols, RI, 67-70; RI State Sen, 75-, Minority Leader, RI State Senate, 75- Mem: Butler Hosp (vpres bd, 71-); Miriam Hosp (bd). Honors & Awards: Distinguished Alumnus Award, Wellesley Col, 74; JFK Award, RI Col, 75. Relig: Jewish. Legal Res: 25 Cooke St Providence RI 02906 Mailing Add: Rm 314 State House Providence RI 02903

SARAPO, DONATO FRANK **(R)**
Treas, Lenawee Co Rep Party, Mich
b New York, NY, July 2, 25; s Donato Frank Sarapo, Sr & Teresa Miglionico S; m 1947 to Lois Marie Miller; c Terry Lee (Mrs Merle Humphrey), Nora Lynn, Guy Donato & David Wayne. Educ: Columbia Col, BA, 49; NY State Med Col, MD, 52. Polit & Govt Pos: Rep precinct leader, Eighth Precinct, Adrian, Mich, 58-61; deleg, Mich State Rep Conv, 59-68; chmn, Adrian City Rep Party, 61-62; chmn, Adrian Twp, Lenawee Co Rep Party, 63-69; mem exec comt, Lenawee Co Rep Party, 64-, treas, 67-; mem platform comt, Second Cong Dist Rep Party, 66, mem exec comt, 68-69; alt deleg, Rep Nat Conv, 68. Mil Serv: Entered as Pvt, Army, 43, released as Pfc, 46, after serv in Army Specialized Training Prog, 346th Inf Div, ETO & Pac Theater of Opers, 43-46; Good Conduct Medal; Combat Infantry Badge. Mem: Am, Mich State & Lenawee Co Med Asns; Mich Asn of Professions; Am Col Physicians. Relig: Catholic. Legal Res: 4314 Evergreen Dr Adrian MI 49221 Mailing Add: Mill St Professional Bldg Adrian MI 49221

SARASIN, RONALD A **(R)**
US Rep, Conn
b Fall River, Mass, Dec 31, 34; s Joseph A Sarasin & Mary D Pereira S; m 1958 to Marjorie Ann Grazio; c Michael A. Educ: Univ Conn, BS in Bus Admin, 60; Univ Conn Sch Law, JD, 63. Polit & Govt Pos: Corp counsel, Beacon Falls, Conn, 63-72; Conn State Rep, 95th Assembly Dist, 69-72, asst minority leader, Conn House of Rep, 71-72, US Rep, Conn, 73-, mem house comt educ & labor, select comt aging, mem Rep task force on energy & environ, mem policy comt & cong comt, ranking mem agr labor subcomt, US House Rep, currently. Bus & Prof Pos: Asst prof law, New Haven Univ, 64-67. Mil Serv: Navy, 52-56. Mem: Am, Conn & New Haven Co Bar Asns; Valley Bar Asn (pres, 71-72); Am Arbit Asn. Honors & Awards: Distinguished Serv Award, Lions Club of Beacon Falls, 69. Relig: Roman Catholic. Legal Res: 155 Munson Rd Beacon Falls CT 06403 Mailing Add: 229 Cannon House Off Bldg Washington DC 20515

SARBANES, PAUL SPYROS **(D)**
US Rep, Md
b Salisbury, Md, Feb 3, 33; s Spyros P Sarbanes & Matina Tsigounis; m 1960 to Christine Dunbar; c John Peter, Michael & Janet. Educ: Princeton Univ, AB, 54; Oxford Univ, Rhodes scholar & BA with First Class Honours, 57; Harvard Law Sch, LLB Cum Laude, 60; Phi Beta Kappa. Polit & Govt Pos: Asst to chmn, Coun Econ Adv, Washington, DC, 62-63; exec dir, City Charter Revision Comn, Baltimore, Md, 63-64; exec dir, Md Citizens for Johnson-Humphrey, 64; Md State Deleg, 66-70; state coordr, Kennedy for President Comt, 68; US Rep, Third Dist, Md, 71- Bus & Prof Pos: Assoc, Baltimore Law Firm of Venable, Baetjer & Howard, 65-70. Mem: Am, Md & Baltimore City Bar Asns. Relig: Greek Orthodox. Legal Res: 320 Suffolk Rd Baltimore MD 21218 Mailing Add: 317 Cannon House Off Bldg Washington DC 20515

SARCONE, CHRISTINE MARY **(D)**
b Des Moines, Iowa, Feb 25, 54; d James Vincent Sarcone & Jessie Presnall S; single. Educ: Barry Col, Fla, currently. Polit & Govt Pos: Deleg, Dem Nat Conv, 72. Mem: Nat Honor Soc, Nat Bus Honor Soc. Relig: Catholic. Mailing Add: 1310 SW Broad Des Moines IA 50315

SARGENT, FRANCIS W **(R)**
b Hamilton, Mass, July 29, 15; s Francis W Sargent (deceased) & Margery Lee S; m 1938 to Jessie Fay; c Fay (Mrs James McLane), Jessie (Mrs Brian Flynn) & F Williams, Jr. Educ: Mass Inst Technol, Spec Degree in Archit, 39. Hon Degrees: LLD, Univ Mass, 71; DPA, Suffolk Univ, 71; DSc, Lowell Technol Inst, 71. Polit & Govt Pos: Dir, Mass Div Marine Fisheries, 47-56; chmn, Atlantic States Marine Fisheries Comn, 56-59; comnr, Mass Dept Natural Resources, 56-59; exec dir, US Outdoor Recreation Resources Rev Comn, Washington, DC, 59-62; comnr, Mass Dept Pub Works, 63-66; Lt Gov, Mass, 66-69, Gov, 69-74. Bus & Prof Pos: Architect, Coolidge, Shepley, Bulfinch & Abbott, 39-41; architect, Sargent & Sweeney, 41-42; founder-owner, Goose Hummock Shop, Inc, Orleans, Mass, 46- Mil Serv: Entered as 2nd Lt, Army, 42, released as Inf Capt, 46, after serv in 10th Mt Div, ETO; Bronze Star; Purple Heart with Oak Leaf Cluster; European Theatre Medal with Battle Stars, Brazilian Govt Medahlia di Guerra-Skier. Mem: Corp, Boston Mus Sci; New Eng Aquarium, Boston (trustee); Trustees of Reservations (trustee); Harvard Univ Vis Comt; Old Sturbridge Village (overseer). Honors & Awards: Annual Awards, Trustees of Reservations, 59, New Eng Outdoor Writers, 63 & Nat Wildlife Asn, 70; Award, Boston Col Symp on Conserv & Recreation; Annual Award for a Beautiful Am, Holiday Mag, 70. Relig: Protestant. Mailing Add: Farm St Dover MA 02030

SARK, GUY O **(R)**
Chmn, Pickaway Co Rep Exec Comt, Ohio
b Ashville, Ohio, Oct 21, 02; s John H Sark & Anna Markwood S; m 1923 to Leona Wright; c Ruth Ann (Mrs Swisher), Eleanor (Mrs Foreman) & Virginia Lee (Mrs Bowers). Polit & Govt Pos: Chmn, Pickaway Co Rep Exec Comt, Ohio, 68- Bus & Prof Pos: Asst cashier, City Nat Bank & Trust Co, Columbus, Ohio, 20-67. Mem: Mason; RAM (past Grand Marshal). Honors & Awards: Knight of the York Cross of Honour; Grand Encampment K T Cross of Honor. Relig: Protestant. Mailing Add: 215 E Main St Ashville OH 43103

SASLOW, MICHAEL GEORGE **(D)**
Publicity Dir, Benton Co Dem Cent Comt, Ore
b Rochester, NY, Apr 8, 37; s George Saslow & Julia Ipcar S; m 1959 to Carol Ann Griffiths.

Educ: Harvard Col, AB, 60; Univ Calif, Berkeley, PhD, 66; US Pub Health Serv fel. Polit & Govt Pos: Vol work, Dem Party, St Louis, Mo, Cambridge, Mass & Albany, Calif, 48-65; Dem committeeman, Precincts, 46-63; Dem committeeman, Seattle, Wash, 65-69; vchmn, 46th Legis Dist, 66; cand, Wash State Senate, 46th Legis Dist, 66; dist chmn, 46th Legis Dist, 67-68; consult, Seattle-King Co Econ Opportunity Bd, 67-68; educ dir, Young Dem of Wash State, 67-68; first cong dist coordr, McCarthy for President, 68; chmn, First Cong Dist Dem Caucus, 68; mem grievance comt, Wash State Dem Conv, 68; deleg, Dem Nat Conv, 68; deleg, King Co Dem Exec Bd, Wash, 69; publicity dir, Benton Co Dem Cent Comt, Corvallis, Ore, 69-; chmn, Nursing Task Force, State of Ore Comprehensive Health Planning Authority, 72- Bus & Prof Pos: Lectr & res asst prof psychol, Univ Wash, 65-67; asst dir, Wash-Alaska Regional Med Prog, Seattle, 68-69; asst prof teaching res div, Ore State Syst of Higher Educ, Monmouth, 69-, assoc prof & dir health manpower proj, 71- Publ: Washington Democratic Council Precinct Committeeman's Campaign Handbook (w Carol A Saslow), Mimeographed, 68; plus others. Mem: Western Psychol Asn; Asn Am Historians; Acoust Soc Am; Seattle Urban League; North Cascades Conserv Coun. Honors & Awards: Presidential Youth Opportunity Award, 68. Mailing Add: Rte 1 Box 414 Philomath OR 97370

SASSER, JAMES G (D)
Ala State Rep
Mailing Add: 1208 Skipperville Rd Ozark AL 36360

SASSER, JAMES RALPH (D)
Chmn, Tenn State Dem Exec Comt
b Memphis, Tenn, Sept 30, 36; s Joseph Ralph Sasser & Mary Nell Gray S; m 1962 to Mary Ballantine Gorman; c James Gray & Elizabeth Ballantine. Educ: Univ Tenn, 54-55; Vanderbilt Univ, BA, 58; Vanderbilt Univ Sch Law, JD, 61; Phi Delta Phi; Kappa Sigma. Polit & Govt Pos: Chmn, Tenn State Dem Exec Comt, 73-; southern vchmn, Asn Dem State Chmn, 75- Bus & Prof Pos: Attorney, Goodpasture, Carpenter, Woods & Sasser, 61- Mil Serv: Lance Cpl, Marine Corps Res, 58-65. Mem: Am Bar Asn; Nat Conf Christians & Jews (bd mem, Nashville Chap); UN Asn (past pres); Nashville Comt on Foreign Rels; Am Judicature Soc. Relig: Protestant. Mailing Add: 6027 Hillsboro Rd Nashville TN 37215

SATTER, ROBERT (D)
Gen Counsel, Dem Majority, Conn State Legis
b Chicago, Ill, Aug 19, 19; s Henry Satter & Patty Salvin S; m 1946 to Ruth Lyttle; c Richard, Mimi, Susan & Jane. Educ: Rutgers Univ, AB, 41; Columbia Univ Law Sch, LLB, 47; Phi Beta Kappa. Polit & Govt Pos: Mem, Newington Develop Comn, Conn, 58-72, chmn, 67; mem, Newington Charter Comn, 59, 61 & 68; Conn State Rep, 59-65; mem, Bd of Finance, Newington, 61-66; mem, Conn Adv Comt to US Comn of Civil Rights, 65-; gen counsel, Dem Majority, Conn State Legis, 67-72 & 75-, gen counsel, Dem Minority, 73-75. Bus & Prof Pos: Mem bd of ed, Conn Bar J, 62-; mem bd dirs, numerous corps; lectr polit sci & admin law, Grad Sch Polit Sci, Univ Conn, 69- Mil Serv: Entered as Midn, Naval Res, 42, released as Lt(sg), 46, after serv in Pac, 42-46; Lt, Naval Res; Pac Theater Campaign Ribbon & Seven Battle Stars. Publ: How to pass your law, Progressive Mag, 59; Lawyer as lobbyist, 60 & False arrest: compensation & deterrence, 12/69, Conn Bar J. Mem: Conn Bar Asn; Hartford Commun Coun; Family Serv Soc (bd dirs, 66-); Columbia Law Sch Asn (vpres); Westledge Sch, Simsbury Conn (chmn bd trustees). Honors & Awards: Doubles tennis champion, Newington, 59-69 & singles tennis champion, 2 times. Legal Res: 75 Brookside Rd Newington CT 06111 Mailing Add: 60 Washington St Hartford CT 06106

SATTERFIELD, DAVID E, III (D)
US Rep, Va
b Richmond, Va, Dec 2, 20; s David E Satterfield, Jr & Blanche Kidd S; m 1943 to Anne Elizabeth Powell; c David E, IV & John B. Educ: Univ Richmond, 39-42; Univ Va, LLB, 47; Phi Gamma Delta; Phi Alpha Delta. Polit & Govt Pos: Asst US Attorney, 50-53; city councilman, Richmond, Va, 54-56; Va State Deleg, 60-64; US Rep, Va, 64- Mil Serv: Entered as Seaman 2/C, V-5, Navy, 42, released as Lt, 45, after serv as Fighter Pilot; Capt, Naval Res, 46-; Air Medal with Three Gold Stars; Purple Heart. Mem: Richmond & Va Bar Asns; Kiwanis; Univ Richmond (bd trustees); Naval Aviation Museum (trustee). Relig: Episcopal. Legal Res: 511 St Christopher's Rd Richmond VA 23226 Mailing Add: House of Rep Washington DC 20515

SATTERTHWAITE, CAMERON B (D)
b Salem, Ohio, July 26, 20; s William David Satterthwaite & Mabel Cameron S; m 1950 to Helen Elizabeth Foster; c Mark Cameron, Tod Foster, Tracy Lynn, Keith Alan & Craig Evan. Educ: Col Wooster, BA; Ohio State Univ, 2 years; Univ Pittsburgh, PhD; Sigma Xi; Sigma Pi Sigma. Polit & Govt Pos: Sch dir, Monroeville, Pa, 59-61; Dem nominee, US House of Rep, 22nd Dist, Ill, 66; deleg, Dem Nat Conv, 68 & 72; chmn, Independent Dem Coalition, 69. Publ: 15 articles in sci jour. Mem: Am Phys Soc; AAAS; Fedn Am Scientists (dir, 64-65, vchmn, 67, chmn, 68); Urban League; Am Civil Liberties Union. Relig: Society of Friends. Mailing Add: 101 E Florida Ave Urbana IL 61801

SATTERTHWAITE, HELEN FOSTER (D)
Ill State Rep
b Blawnox, Pa, July 8, 28; d Samuel James Foster & Lillian Schreiber F; m 1950 to Cameron B Satterthwaite; c Mark Cameron, Tod Foster, Tracy Lynn (Mrs Roger Phillips), Keith Alan & Craig Evan. Educ: Duquesne Univ, BS, 49. Polit & Govt Pos: Ill State Rep, 52nd Legis Dist, 75-, vchmn Dem study group, Ill House Rep, 75 & 76. Bus & Prof Pos: Chemist, E I du Pont de Nemours & Co, Inc, Wilmington, Del, 51-53; natural sci lab asst, Univ Ill, Urbana, 67-74. Mem: United Way of Champaign Co (bd mem, 71-); League of Women Voters; YWCA; Nat Orgn for Women. Relig: Religious Soc of Friends. Legal Res: 101 E Florida Ave Urbana IL 61801 Mailing Add: 505A E University Ave Champaign IL 61820

SATTES, FREDERICK LYLE (D)
WVa State Deleg
b Charleston, WVa, Nov 14, 43; s Frederick Lyle Sattes, Sr & Katharine Backus S; single. Educ: Purdue Univ, BSME, 66; WVa Univ, JD, 71. Polit & Govt Pos: WVa State Deleg, Kanawha Co, 74- Mil Serv: Entered as 2nd Lt, Army, 66, released as Capt, 68, after serv in Vietnam, 67-68. Mem: Am Soc Mech Engrs; Phi Alpha Delta; Am & WVa Bar Asns. Relig: Presbyterian. Legal Res: 2000 Kanawha Ave SE Charleston WV 25304 Mailing Add: 12 Capitol St Charleston WV 25301

SATTLER, KEITH PAUL (D)
Chmn, Walla Walla Co Dem Party, Wash
b Cottonwood, Idaho, Jan 24, 44; s Joseph Sebastian Sattler & Rose Harmon S; m 1965 to Myra Ann Ellis; c Krisann & Troy. Educ: Wash State Univ, BS, 72; Beta Alpha Psi; Acct Club; Vietnam Veterans. Polit & Govt Pos: Finance chmn, Walla Walla Co Dem Party, WA, 73-74, chmn, 74- Mil Serv: Entered as A/S, Navy, 61, released as Personnelman 3/C, 64, after serv in USS Midway CVA, Pac, 62-64; Vietnam Serv Medal. Mem: Walla Walla Area CofC (bd dirs, 73-); Blue Mountain Action Coun (bd dirs, 73-); Walla Walla Jaycees (vpres & bd dirs, 72-); Beta Alpha Psi; Elks. Honors & Awards: Grad with distinction, Wash State Univ; Outstanding Local Jaycee & Distinguished Serv Award, Walla Walla Jaycees; Outstanding Regional Jaycee, Wash State Jaycees. Relig: Catholic. Mailing Add: 319 Locust Walla Walla WA 99362

SATZ, ARNOLD (R)
b Minneapolis, Minn, Dec 30, 20; s Samuel Satz & Bertha Shulman S; m 1945 to Marjorie Fisher; c Karen Rita & David Lawrence. Educ: Univ Minn, BMetall Eng, 43; Tau Beta Pi; Sigma Alpha Sigma. Polit & Govt Pos: Bd mem, New Castle Area Sch Bd, Pa, 64-68; chmn, Lawrence Co Rep Comt, 65-72; alt deleg, Rep Nat Conv, 72. Bus & Prof Pos: Pres, New Castle Foundry Co, 47-; vpres, Gallagher Bros, Inc, 58-; bd mem, Peoples Bank of Western Pa, 64-; vpres, Am Clay Machinery, Inc, 68- Mem: Am Foundrymen's Asn; Jameson Mem Hosp (bd); Lawrence Co US Savings Bond Prog (chmn). Relig: Jewish. Mailing Add: 311 Sumner Ave New Castle PA 16105

SAUER, CHARLES ANDREW (D)
Vt State Rep
b Mineola, NY, Oct 19, 30; s Charles Francis Sauer & Dorothy Walsh S; m 1965 to Mary Jane; c Janet Violia, Charles Andrew, John Joseph, Susan Marie, Donald James & Stephen Michael. Polit & Govt Pos: Second asst fire chief, Bennington Rural Fire Dept, Vt, 71-73, first asst fire chief, 73-; Vt State Rep, 73- Bus & Prof Pos: Roofing foreman, Monument Roofing & Sheet Metal Co, 59- Mil Serv: Entered as Pvt E-1, Army, 51, released as Pfc, 53, after serv in Army Security Agency, Ft Devens, Mass, 51-53. Mem: KofC. Relig: Roman Catholic. Mailing Add: RD 2 Bennington VT 05201

SAUER, WALTER CHARLES
First VPres & VChmn, Export-Import Bank of US
b Jersey City, NJ, Mar 5, 05. Educ: Princeton Univ, AB, 28; Yale Univ, LLB, 31. Polit & Govt Pos: First vpres & vchmn, Export-Import Bank of the US, currently. Bus & Prof Pos: Attorney-at-law. Legal Res: Univ Club 1135 16th NW Washington DC 20036 Mailing Add: Export-Import Bank of the US Lafayette Bldg 811 Vermont Ave NW Washington DC 20571

SAUNDERS, CHARLES BASKERVILLE, JR (R)
b Boston, Mass, Dec 26, 28; s Charles B Saunders & Lucy Carmichael S; m 1950 to Margaret Shafer; c Charles B, III, George C, Margaret K, Lucy C & John R. Educ: Princeton Univ, AB, 50; Univ Cottage Club. Polit & Govt Pos: Legis asst to US Sen H Alexander Smith, NJ, 57-58; spec asst to Asst Secy for Legis Elliot L Richardson, Dept Health, Educ & Welfare, 58-59, admin asst to Secy Arthur S Flemming, 59-60, Dep Asst Secy for Legis, 69-71, Dep Asst Secy for Educ, 73-74; mem, Montgomery Co Bd of Educ, Md, 66-70; mem bd trustees, Montgomery Jr Col, 69-70; dep comnr external rels, US Off Educ, 71-73. Bus & Prof Pos: Newspaper reporter, Ogdensburg J, NY & Hartford Times, Conn, 50-53; asst dir pub rels, Trinity Col, 53-55; asst dir pub info, Princeton Univ, 53-57; asst to the pres, Brookings Inst, Washington, DC, 61-69; dir govt rels, Am Coun Educ, 75- Publ: The Brookings Institution; A Fifty-Year History, Brookings Inst, 66; Upgrading the American Police, Brookings, 70. Relig: Presbyterian. Mailing Add: 7622 Winterberry Pl Bethesda MD 20034

SAUNDERS, EMILY C (D)
Maine State Rep
Mailing Add: Paradise Rd Bethel ME 04217

SAUNDERS, ROBERT B, JR (D)
b Hardin, Mont, Oct 11, 29; s Robert B Saunders & Mattie Bundy S; m 1955 to Patricia Anne Nelson; c Robert Douglas & Lisa Anne. Educ: Mont State Univ, BS, 52; SEA Social Fraternity. Polit & Govt Pos: Chmn, Big Horn Co Cent Comt, Mont, 67-69; chmn, Mont State Dem Cent Comt, 69-72. Bus & Prof Pos: Owner & operator, Retail Lumber Bus, 15 years. Mil Serv: Entered as 2nd Lt, Air Force, 52, released as 1st Lt, 55, after serv in 8th Air Force. Mailing Add: 410 Silver Lane Billings MT 59102

SAUNDERS, ROBERT L, JR (BOB) (D)
Fla State Sen
b Quitman, Ga, Jan 22, 29; s Robert L Saunders, Sr & Lois Patrick S; m 1951 to Millicent Johns; c Sandra Lynn & Robert L, III. Educ: Univ Fla, AA, 51. Polit & Govt Pos: Fla State Sen, Fifth Dist, 68- Bus & Prof Pos: Pres, Fla Petroleum Marketers Asn. Mem: CofC (dir, Gainesville area); dir, Alachua Co United Fund; Rotary. Honors & Awards: Runner-up for the Outstanding First Termer in the Fla State Senate. Relig: Episcopal. Legal Res: 1705 NW 26th Way Gainesville FL 32601 Mailing Add: 1831 NW 13th St Gainesville FL 32601

SAVAGE, CHARLES R (D)
Wash State Rep
b La Farge, Wis, 1906; m to Helen S; c two. Educ: High sch; some spec training. Polit & Govt Pos: US Rep, Wash, 1 term; Wash State Rep, currently. Bus & Prof Pos: Logger. Mailing Add: 2011 King St Shelton WA 98584

SAVAGE, JOHN PATRICK (R)
b New Haven, Conn, Aug 14, 43; s John Francis Savage & Dorothy Ryan S; single. Educ: Marquette Univ, BS, 65, JD, 67; Alpha Sigma Nu; Delta Theta Phi. Polit & Govt Pos: Cong dist chmn, Wis Fedn Young Rep, 64-67, nat committeeman, 67-69; orientation comt chmn, Young Rep Nat Fedn, 67-69, asst gen counsel, 69-73; Rep committeeman, Village of Fox Point, Wis, 68-72; young Rep representative to Wis State Rep Exec Comt, 69-71; vchmn, NShore Rep Club, 71-73; Milwaukee Co Rep Speakers' Bur Chmn, 72-; treas, Sensenbrenner Campaign Comt, 70-; mem media liaison comt, Milwaukee Soc. Bus & Prof Pos: Dir, Property Taxpayers' Union; dir & legal counsel, Family Found Inc, currently. Mil Serv: Capt, Army Res, 67- Mem: Milwaukee & Wis Bar Asns; Milwaukee Jr Bar Asn; Milwaukee Jaycees (legal counsel, 71-); Eagles. Honors & Awards: Ky Col. Relig: Roman Catholic. Mailing Add: 2531-B W Clybourn St Milwaukee WI 53233

SAVAGE, JOHN S (R)
Nebr State Sen
b Denver, Colo, June 25, 05; s Gilbert L Savage & Eunice Cummings S; m 1930 to Marie Schofield; c John Schofield & Patricia Ann (Mrs Robert J Russell). Educ: Univ Nebr, 2 years; Sigma Alpha Epsilon. Polit & Govt Pos: Nebr State Sen, 71-, mem exec comt, Nebr State Legis, 73- Bus & Prof Pos: Reporter-photographer, Omaha Bee-News, 28-32; Omaha

World-Herald, 32-70. Mem: Omaha Press Club (past pres, exec vpres & dir, 70-); Nebr Press Photographers (First President's Award, 68); Nat Press Photographers Asn (life mem & past regional dir); Mason (past Master); Scottish Rite (33 degree). Honors & Awards: Outstanding Contrib to Journ Award, Univ Nebr, Omaha, 57; Prof Achievement Award, Creighton Univ Sch Journ, 70; Nat Pres Photographers Asn, Presidents Medal, 64; Award of Merit for Excellence in News Photography, Univ Nebr Lincoln, 72. Relig: Methodist. Mailing Add: 7321 Miami St Omaha NE 68134

SAVAGE, WALLACE HAMILTON **(D)**
b Houston, Tex, Nov 21, 12; s Homer H Savage & Mary Wallace S; m 1940 to Dorothy Harris; c Virginia Wallace & Dorothy Harris. Educ: Univ Va, BS, 33; Harvard Univ, JD, 36; Univ Colo, fel, 36-37. Polit & Govt Pos: Mayor-pro-tem, Dallas, Tex, 47-49, mayor, 49-51; chmn, Dallas Co Dem Party & State Dem Party, 52-54; Dallas Co chmn & nat vchmn, Citizen's Comn, Hoover Report, 52-54; mem, Dir Citizen's Comt Reorgn Exec Br Govt, 54-59. Bus & Prof Pos: Partner, Lane, Savage, Counts, & Winn & dir, Lakewood Bank & Trust Co, currently. Mil Serv: Comdr, Naval Res, 41-45. Mem: Tex, Am & Dallas Bar Asns; Dallas Country Club; Idlewood Club. Relig: Episcopal; Parish chancellor & church vestryman. Legal Res: 5703 Swiss Ave Dallas TX 75214 Mailing Add: PO Box 9706 Dallas TX 75214

SAVELKOUL, HENRY JEROME **(R)**
Minn State Rep
b Lansford, NDak, July 1, 40; s Harry N Savelkoul & Mary Davis S; m 1964 to Margaret Ann Sykes; c Patricia Ann & Donald Wayne. Educ: St Thomas Col, lib arts, 4 years; Univ Minn Law Sch, JD, 65; Alpha Kappa Psi; Delta Theta Phi. Polit & Govt Pos: Secy, Freeborn Co Rep Party, Minn, formerly; Minn State Rep, currently. Bus & Prof Pos: Counsel, Christian, Slen, Savelkoul, Johnson & Broberg, Albert Lea, Minn, 65- Mem: Am & Minn Bar Asns. Honors & Awards: Bush Found Fel Award. Relig: Roman Catholic. Mailing Add: 1100 Cedar Albert Lea MN 56007

SAVELL, CYNTHIA TOBY **(D)**
Mem Exec Comt, NJ Young Dem
b Brooklyn, NY, Nov 25, 42; d Lawrence Savell & Shirley Ashendorf S; div. Educ: Fairleigh Dickinson Univ, 60-63; Hackensack Hosp Sch Nursing, NJ, RN, 72; Felician Col, Lodi, NJ, 73- Polit & Govt Pos: Secy, Bergen Co Young Dem, NJ, 70-71, pres, 71-72, chmn exec comt, 72-73; cong vpres, NJ Young Dem, 70-71, nat committeewoman, 72-74, mem exec comt, 73-; scheduling coordr, Bergen Co Senate Nominees, 71; advancewoman, Hubert H Humphrey for President, 71-72, asst to dir polit opers, 72. Bus & Prof Pos: Nurse, Saddle Brook Hosp, NJ, 70- Mem: Am Nurses Asn. Honors & Awards: Young Woman Dem of the Year, NJ Young Dem, 73. Relig: Jewish. Mailing Add: 265 Beech St Hackensack NJ 07601

SAVICKAS, FRANK DAVID **(D)**
Ill State Sen
b Chicago, Ill, May 14, 35; s Frank L Savickas & Estelle Ivaskevich S; m 1954 to Adrienne C Shenoha; c Michael David, Linda Diane & Sharon Eileen. Educ: Wildon Jr Col, 2 years. Polit & Govt Pos: Ill State Rep, 27th Dist, 66-72; Ill State Sen, 73- Mem: KofC (4 degree); Lithuanian CofC; Chicago Journeyman Plumbers Local Union 130; Moose; Riano Soc Club. Relig: Catholic. Mailing Add: 6940 S Artesian Ave Chicago IL 60629

SAVILLA, ROLAND **(D)**
WVa State Sen
Mailing Add: State Capitol Charleston WV 25305

SAWICKI, JOHN GERALD **(R)**
Mem, Rep State Cent Comt Calif
b Denver, Colo, Jan 10, 43; s Walter J Sawicki, Jr & Mary K Christensen S. Educ: Big Bend Commun Col, Moses Lake, Wash, AA, 65; Gonzaga Univ, 64-65; Eastern Wash State Col, BA, 66; McGeorge Sch Law. Polit & Govt Pos: Campaign mgr, Douglas A McKee, 61st Assembly Dist, 68, Dr William Vickery-Carbell-McKee, Culver City Sch Bd, 68, John T LaFollette, 28th Cong Dist, 69 & James L Flournoy, Secy of State, 69; mem, 61st Calif Assembly Dist Cent Comt, 68-69; vpres, Los Angeles Co Young Rep, 69-; mem, State Rep Cent Comt Calif, 69-; alt, Los Angeles Co Rep Cent Comt, 69; asst dir, Calif Off Econ Opportunity, 70-72; western states field dir, Spec Ballots Div, Comt for the Reelec of the President, 72; spec consult legal serv, Exec Off of the President, 72-73; vpres consumer affairs, The Larwin Group, 73- Mil Serv: Entered as Airman 3/C, Air Force, 61, released as Airman 1/C, 64, after serv in 568th Strategic Missile Squadron, Strategic Air Command, 61-64; Good Conduct Medal; Outstanding Airman of the Year Award. Mem: Los Angeles World Affairs Coun; Los Angeles Co World Trade Asn. Relig: Catholic. Mailing Add: 1740 Roosevelt San Diego CA 92109

SAWYER, CHARLES **(D)**
b Cincinnati, Ohio, Feb 10, 87; s Edward Milton Sawyer & Caroline Butler S; m to Margaret Johnston (deceased); m 1942 to Elizabeth L de Veyrac; c Anne Sawyer Greene (Mrs John Bradley), Charles (deceased), Jean Johnston (Mrs John J Weaver), John & Edward. Educ: Oberlin Col, AB, 08; Univ Cincinnati, LLB, 11. Hon Degrees: LLD, Univ Cincinnati, 50; plus numerous others. Polit & Govt Pos: Mem, Cincinnati City Coun, Ohio, 11-15; Lt Gov, Ohio, 33-35; mem, Dem Nat Comt, Ohio, 36-44; Dem cand for Gov, Ohio, 38; Ambassador to Belgium, Minister to Luxembourg, 44-46; Secy of Com, 48-53; mem, Comn on Money & Credit, 59-60. Bus & Prof Pos: Sr partner law firm, Taft, Stettinius & Hollister, Cincinnati; dir numerous corps; chmn, Cincinnati Commun Chest, 54; chmn, Cincinnati United Appeal, 55-60; Citizens Develop Comt, Cincinnati; hon trustee, Oberlin Col. Mil Serv: Entered Army, 17, released as Maj, 19, after serv in Inf, AEF, 18-19. Mem: Am, Fed & Ohio Bar Asns; Mason; Cincinnati Queen City Club. Relig: Episcopal. Legal Res: 95 E Fountain Ave Glendale OH 45246 Mailing Add: 2513 Central Trust Tower Cincinnati OH 45202

SAWYER, ED **(D)**
Ariz State Sen
Mailing Add: 1205 Fifth Ave Safford AZ 85546

SAWYER, EUGENE, JR **(D)**
b Greensboro, Ala, Sept 3, 34; s Eugene Sawyer, Sr & Bernice Mauldin S; m 1955 to Celeste Cavalier Banks; c Shedrick Eugene, Sheryl Celeste & Roderick Terrence. Educ: Ala State Col, BS, 56; Alpha Phi Alpha. Polit & Govt Pos: Area chmn, Young Dem Cook Co, Ill, 61-62; chmn regist, Young Dem Ill, 64-65; committeeman, Sixth Ward Dem Orgn, 68-74, alderman, 71 & 75; deleg, Dem Nat Conv, 72. Mem: Miss State Teachers Asn; Woodlawn Boys Club (bd dirs); Wisdom Lodge 102; Pkwy Community Ctr (bd dirs); Plumbers Union; Hull House Asn (bd trustees); NAACP. Relig: Methodist. Legal Res: 7406 S Wabash Ave Chicago IL 60619 Mailing Add: 511 E 75th St Chicago IL 60619

SAWYER, F GRANT **(D)**
Dem Nat Committeeman, Nev
b Twin Falls, Idaho, Dec 14, 18; s Harry W Sawyer & Bula Cameron S; m 1946 to Bette Norene Hoge; c Gaile Louise. Educ: Linfield Col, 38-39; Univ Nev, BA, 41; George Washington Univ Law Sch, 41-42; Georgetown Univ Law Sch, DJS, 48; pres, Alpha Tau Omega. Hon Degrees: LLD, Univ Nev & Linfield Col. Polit & Govt Pos: Chmn, Elko Co Dem Comt, formerly; presiding officer, Dem State Conv, Nev, formerly; dist attorney, Elko Co, Nev, 50-58; chmn, Nev Dem Comt, 55; deleg, Dem Nat Conv, 56-72; mem, Nat Dem Platform Comt, 58-60, 64, 68 & 72; mem bd regents, Univ Nev, 57; Gov, Nev, 59-67; chmn, Nat Gov Conf & pres, Coun State Govt, 64-65; chmn, Western Gov Conf, 65-66; Spec US Ambassador to Paraguay, 68; Dem Nat Committeeman, Nev, 68- Bus & Prof Pos: Mem bd of trustees, John F Kennedy Libr. Mil Serv: Entered as Pvt, Army, 42, released as 1st Lt, 46, after serv in Pac Theater. Mem: Nat Dist Attorneys Asn (dir); Nev Dist Attorneys Asn (pres); Elko Co Bar Asn (pres); Am Bar Asn; Am Judicature Soc. Honors & Awards: Outstanding Young Dem of Nev, 55; Elko Young Man of Year, 52. Relig: Baptist. Legal Res: 6985 Mira Vista Las Vegas NV 89120 Mailing Add: 302 E Carson Las Vegas NV 89101

SAWYER, FERN **(D)**
Chmn, Lincoln Co Dem Party, NMex
b Buchannen, NMex, May 17, 17; d Uyless Devoe Sawyer & Dessie Lewis S; div. Educ: Tex Tech Col, 2 years; Univ NMex, 1 year; Alpha Delta Pi. Polit & Govt Pos: Chairwoman, Lincoln Co Dem Party, NMex, 62-66, chmn, 66-70 & 73-; alt deleg, Dem Nat Conv, 68. Bus & Prof Pos: Prof rodeo performer, 20 years; Hereford cattle rancher. Mem: Rodeo Cowboys Asn. Honors & Awards: Won World's Championship for riding cutting horses & Girl's All Around World Championship of 47. Relig: Episcopal. Mailing Add: Nogal NM 83341

SAWYER, FORREST LAMAR **(R)**
Chmn, Cherokee Co Rep Party, Ga
b Robbinsville, NC, Apr 20, 32; s Charlie DeWitt Sawyer & Viola Brock S; m 1949 to Frankie Dunn; c Forrest Lamar, Jr. Educ: Mercer Univ, 53-54; John Marshall Law Sch, 54-56. Polit & Govt Pos: Deleg, Ga State Rep Conv, 70; treas, Cherokee Co Rep Party, Ga, 72-73 & 74-75, chmn, 75- Bus & Prof Pos: Construction eng, State of Ga, 49-54; stock & bond broker, Atlanta, 56-66; construction eng, 66- Mil Serv: Entered as Pvt, Ga Nat Guard, 50, 1st Sgt, currently, serv in Co A, 1st Bn, 121 Inf; Res Forces Medal; State Active Serv Medal; State Serv Medal; Good Conduct Medal. Mem: Mason; Shrine; Moose; Nat Hist Soc; Smithsonian Asn. Relig: Protestant. Mailing Add: 171 Cartersville Rd City 3 Canton GA 30114

SAWYER, LEONARD ALSON **(D)**
Speaker, Wash House of Rep
b Puyallup, Wash, May 18, 25; s Alson L Sawyer & Velma MacDonald S; m 1950 to Beverly M Farrell; c Carla, Colleen, Cynthia, L Clark & Craig. Educ: Univ Puget Sound, BA, 48; Univ Wash, law degree, 51; Kappa Sigma. Polit & Govt Pos: Dep prosecuting attorney, Prosecutor's Off, Wash, 52-55; Wash State Rep, 55-, majority whip, Wash State House of Rep & chmn, Joint Interim Comt on Hwys, Wash Legis, 65-66, minority leader, formerly, speaker, 73-; mem, Seattle World's Fair Comn, 58-62; mem exec bd, Western Conf State Gov, 65-66; mem, President's Motor Vehicle Safety Adv Coun, 67-68. Mil Serv: Entered as A/S, Navy, 43, released as Ens, 46, after serv as Port Dir, Post Off, Pac & China, 45-46; Pac & China Campaign Ribbons. Mem: Coun of State Govts; Eagles; Elks; VFW; Am Legion. Relig: Presbyterian. Legal Res: Rte 3 Box 1990 Sumner WA 98390 Mailing Add: 2723 E Main Puyallup WA 98371

SAWYER, MRS U D (DESSIE) **(D)**
Dem Nat Committeewoman, NMex
b Tex; wid; c Fern & Merle (Mrs Jeff Good). Polit & Govt Pos: Precinct chmn, Dem Party, NMex; mem & former chmn, Lea Co Dem Cent Comt; chairwoman, NMex Dem Party, formerly; Dem Nat Committeewoman, NMex, 48-; deleg, Dem Nat Conv, 68. Mem: March of Dimes (chmn, 27 years); March of Dimes for NMex (hon chmn); Jr Col Found (chmn restoration comt, Old Lincoln Co, 18 years). Mailing Add: Box 1000 Tatum NM 88267

SAXBE, CHARLES ROCKWELL (ROCKY) **(R)**
Ohio State Rep
Mailing Add: 176 S Main St Mechanicsburg OH 43044

SAXBE, WILLIAM B **(R)**
US Ambassador to India
b Mechanicsburg, Ohio, June 24, 16; s Bart Saxbe & Faye Carey S; m 1940 to Ardath Kleinhans; c Juli (Mrs C S Lopeman), Bart & Rocky. Educ: Ohio State Univ, AB & LLB; Chi Phi; Phi Delta Phi. Polit & Govt Pos: Ohio State Rep, 47-54, Majority Leader, Ohio State House of Rep, 51-52 & Speaker of the House, 53-54; Attorney Gen, Ohio, 57-58 & 63-68; chmn, Ohio Crime Comn, 67-68; US Sen, Ohio, 69-74; deleg, Rep Nat Conv, 72; Attorney Gen US, 74-75; US Ambassador to India, 75- Mil Serv: Entered as Pvt, Ohio Nat Guard, 37, released as Col, 66, after serv in Inf, Air Force; active duty, World War II & Korean Conflict. Mem: Am Judicature Soc; Am Legion; Amvets; Ohio Grange; local, state & nat Bar Asns & other fraternal, serv & civic groups. Relig: Episcopal. Mailing Add: Rte 2 Mechanicsburg OH 43044

SAXON, JAMES J **(D)**
b Toledo, Ohio, Apr 13, 14; s Samuel Joseph Saxon & Catherine Ann Mulhanney S; m 1944 to Dorothy Stewart Bell; c James J, Jr, Stephen, Dorea, Kevin, Catherine & Lucy. Educ: St John's Col, AB; Georgetown Univ Law Sch, LLB; Cath Univ Am, post-grad work in econ & finance. Polit & Govt Pos: Treas attache, Treas Dept, 41-42, Philippines, economist & spec asst to dir div monetary res, Off of Int Finance, 42-45, asst to Secy of Treas, 45-50, spec asst gen counsel, 50-52, comptroller of currency, 61-66. Bus & Prof Pos: Counsel, Am Bankers Asn, 52-56; attorney, First Nat Bank of Chicago, 56-61; dir, Amax Financial Corp, San Francisco, Am Life Ins Co & Am Fletcher Corp, Indianapolis, currently; practicing attorney, Washington, DC, currently; dir, Sterling Nat Bank & Standard Prudential Corp, New York, Nat Homes Corp, Lafayette & Univ Computing Corp, Dallas, Tex. Mem: Ill Bar; Cong Country Club, Bethesda, Md. Relig: Catholic. Mailing Add: 6024 Western Ave Chevy Chase MD 20015

SAXVIK, ROBERT WILLIAM **(D)**
Idaho State Sen
b Spring Grove, Minn, Jan 13, 30; s Gilbert Morton Saxvik & Amanda Johnson S; m 1958

to Marilyn Anne DeMers; c Robin Margaret & Eric Bradley. Educ: Western Wash State Col, BA in Educ, 58. Polit & Govt Pos: Idaho State Sen, Legis Dist 26, 71- Bus & Prof Pos: Vpres & control mgr, KBAR Radio, Burley, Idaho. Mil Serv: Entered as Airman 3/C, Air Force, 51, released as S/Sgt, 55, after serv in Strategic Air Command, Korean War, 52; Air Medal with Oak Leaf Cluster. Mem: Nat Asn Broadcasters; Idaho State Broadcasters Asn; Idaho Golf Asn; Cassia Mem Hosp (bd mem, 72-); Rotary. Relig: Lutheran. Mailing Add: 1319 W 16th Burley ID 83318

SAYER, JAMES A (R)
NH State Rep
Mailing Add: Cluffs Crossing Rd Box 3 Salem NH 03079

SAYLER, HENRY B, JR (R)
Fla State Sen
b Savannah, Ga, Jan 16, 21; s Henry B Sayler & Jessie Dixon S; m 1947 to Wyline Chapman; c Lee, Alan, Robin & Van. Educ: US Mil Acad, BS, 43. Polit & Govt Pos: Fla State Sen, 20th Dist, currently. Bus & Prof Pos: Dir, Bank of Seminole, 60-; secy-treas, Fliteair, Inc, 72-; pres, Security Planning of Fla, Inc, 62-; dir, Founders Life Assurance Co, 63- Mil Serv: Entered as 2nd Lt, Air Force, 43, released as Lt Col, 55, after serv in 8th Air Force, Eng as fighter pilot, final assignment, AIr Force Missile Test Ctr; Distinguished Flying Cross; Air Medal with 6 Clusters; Am Theater Ribbon; European Theater Ribbon; Am Defense & Victory Medals. Mem: Nat Asn Life Underwriters; Kiwanis. Honors & Awards: Fla Badminton Champion, Doubles. Relig: Methodist. Mailing Add: 220 Rafael Blvd St Petersburg FL 33704

SAYLOR, JOHN THOMAS (D)
Mem, Pa Dem State Comt
b Bellefonte, Pa, Nov 24, 31; s Philip P Saylor & Kathryn M Hoy S; single. Educ: Northwest Mo State Col, 51; Univ Scranton, 55; Pa State Univ, BA, 58, MEd, 59. Polit & Govt Pos: Dem committeeman, Bellefonte Borough, Pa, 61-62 & 70-75; treas, Centre Co Dem Comt, 62-68, secy, 68-70 & 72-75, mem exec comt, 62-; treas, Young Dem Club of Centre Co, 64-70; inspector of elec, Bellefonte Borough N Ward, 65-75; secy, 34th Pa Dist Dem Const Deleg Nominating Conv, 67; alt deleg, Dem Nat Conv, 68; mem, Pa Dem State Comt, 72-, mem, Pa Dem State Exec Comt, 74-; alt deleg, Dem Nat Mid-Term Conf, 74. Bus & Prof Pos: Rehabilitation counr, Pa Bur Voc Rehabilitation, Pittsburgh, 59-60; teacher, Bellefonte Sch Dist, 60; tech writer, HRB-Singer, Inc, State College, Pa, 61- Mil Serv: Entered as Pvt, Air Force, 51, released as S/Sgt, 55, after serv in Strategic Air Command, Strategic Air Command Hq, Omaha, Nebr, 51-54; Nat Defense Serv Medal. Mem: Logan Vol Fire Co, Bellefonte, Pa; Centre Co Vol Firemen's Asn; Cent Dist Vol Firemen's Asn of Pa; Toastmasters Int; Am Legion. Relig: Catholic. Mailing Add: 238 N Penn St Bellefonte PA 16823

SAYLOR, STANLEY RAYMOND (R)
Chmn, Snyder Co Rep Comt, Pa
b Beavertown, Pa, Dec 17, 16; s William H Saylor & Ida Doebler S; m 1947 to Beatrice Elizabeth Lepley. Educ: High sch. Polit & Govt Pos: Pres, Beavertown Borough Coun, Pa, 47-61; mem, Pa State Rep Comt, 58-60; chmn, Snyder Co Rep Comt, 60- Bus & Prof Pos: Pres, Beavertown Develop Co. Mil Serv: Entered as Pvt, Army, 42, released as S/Sgt, 45, after serv in ETO, 44; European Theater Ribbon with Four Battle Stars; Bronze Star. Mem: F&AM (past Master); Harrisburg Consistory; Zembo Temple; VFW; Am Legion. Relig: Lutheran. Mailing Add: Beaver Springs PA 17812

SAYRE, CLYDE O (R)
Conn State Rep
b Mineola, NY, June 26, 40; s George Milton Sayre & Caroline Melton S; m 1960 to Karen E Singelton; c Shayne, Michael, Judy & Elizabeth. Educ: State Univ NY Canton, AAS, 59; Zeta Alpha Phi. Polit & Govt Pos: Conn State Rep, 72-, ranking mem, Govt Admin & Policy Comt, Conn Gen Assembly, 74-, mem, Gov Econ Adv Task Force, 75-; vchmn, Watertown Bicentennial Comn, currently. Bus & Prof Pos: Vpres, Bozzuto-Sayre Ins Inc, 73- Mem: Watertown Jaycees. Honors & Awards: Watertowns Outstanding Young Man, DSA, 73. Relig: Congregational. Mailing Add: 647 Park Rd Watertown CT 06795

SAYRE, ROBERT MARION
b Hillsboro, Ore, Aug 18, 24; s William Octavius Sayre & Mary Brozka S; m 1951 to Elora Amanda Moyhihan; c Marian Amanda, Robert Marion & Daniel Humphrey. Educ: Willamette Univ, BA summa cum laude, 49; George Washsngton Univ, JD, 56; Stanford Univ, MA, 60. Hon Degrees: LLD, Willamette Univ, 65. Polit & Govt Pos: Career officer, Dept of State Foreign Serv, 49-, econ adv on Latin Am, 50-52, mil adv, 52-57, officer in charge, Inter-Am Security Affairs, 57, chief polit sect, Embassy, Lima, Peru, 57-59, financial adv, Embassy, Havana, Cuba, 60, exec secy, Task Force on Latin Am, State Dept, 61, officer in charge, Mexican Affairs, 61-63, dir, 64, dep dir, Off of Caribbean & Mexican Affairs, 63-64, sr staff mem, White House, 64-65, dep asst secy, Bur of Inter-Am Affairs, 65-68, US Ambassador to Uruguay, 68-69, US Ambassador to Panama, 69-74. Mil Serv: Capt, Army, World War II; Col, Army Res. Mem: DC Bar; Blue Key; Phi Delta Theta; Phi Eta Sigma; Tau Kappa Alpha. Relig: Methodist. Mailing Add: 3714 Bent Branch Rd Falls Church VA 22041

SCACCIA, ANGELO M (D)
Mass State Rep
Mailing Add: State Capitol Boston MA 02133

SCAGLIA, PHILLIP P (D)
Mo State Rep
b Pueblo, Colo, Oct 6, 18; m 1964 to Patricia Lee Lyons; c Phillip Patrick. Educ: Univ Mo, Kansas City. Polit & Govt Pos: Mo State Rep, 64-; chmn & one of the organizers of Dem Citizens Asn Jackson Co, Inc. Bus & Prof Pos: Merchant, 39-57; prin underwriter, United Funds Inc, Kansas City; real estate & ins broker, Waddell & Reed, Inc. Mem: KofC; Elks; St Vincent DePaul Soc; Rockhurst Hon Dirs Asn. Relig: Catholic. Mailing Add: 4640 Forest Kansas City MO 64110

SCALES, JOHN NEIL (D)
b Trafford, Pa, Dec 3, 32; s A C Scales & Gladys Neil S; m 1956 to Joan Shirley Mathes; c Laura Elizabeth, Lisa Anne, Gretchen Suzanne & John Neil, Jr. Educ: Yale Univ, AB, 54; Harvard Law Sch, LLB, 58. Polit & Govt Pos: Vchmn, Westmoreland Co Redevelop Authority, 62-69; asst dist attorney, Westmoreland Co, Pa, 66-69, dist attorney, 70-72; deleg, Pa Const Conv, 67-68; chmn, Pa Dem State Comt, 70-72; Pa State Sen, 73-74. Bus & Prof Pos: Partner, Scales & Shaw, 58- Mem: Am, Pa & Westmoreland Co Bar Asns; president's adv coun, Seton Hill Col; Jeanette Dist Mem Hosp (bd dirs); Westmoreland Girl Scout Coun (bd dirs). Relig: Presbyterian. Mailing Add: 236 Maple Dr Maplewood Terr Greensburg PA 15601

SCALI, JOHN (D)
Polit & Govt Pos: Former UN Ambassador Legal Res: DC Mailing Add: 799 United Nations Plaza New York NY 10017

SCALIA, ROBERT CHARLES (R)
Asst Regional Adminr, Dept of Housing & Urban Develop
b Dansville, NY, Aug 28, 34; s Charles Scalia & Anna Walker S; m 1955 to Bonnie Elaine Anderson; c Michael & Russell Mark. Educ: Monterey Peninsula Col, AA, 60; Calif State Col at Fresno, BA, 63; Univ Calif, Santa Barbara, 67-68; Artus Hon Econ Soc. Polit & Govt Pos: Labor Policy Asn trainee, Redevelop Agency, Fresno, Calif, 62-63, relocation finance officer, Seaside, 63-64, exec dir, Crescent City, 64-65, exec dir, Santa Maria, 65-69; gen dep, Dept of Housing & Urban Develop, 69-71, asst regional adminr commun develop, Region Ten, 71-; adv to President's personal rep, Hurricane Agnes Flood Disaster, 72-73. Bus & Prof Pos: Br mgr, Sequoia Mortgage, San Jose, Calif, 64; asst regional adminr, Region X, Dept of Housing & Urban Develop, Renewal & Housing Mgt Off, 70- Mil Serv: Entered as Pvt, Army, 55, released as SP-3, 57, after serv in Adj Gen Corps, Calif & Alaska. Mem: Nat Asn of Housing & Redevelop Officers; Santa Maria Retarded Children's Coun (steering comt); World Affairs Coun. Mailing Add: 1105 147th Pl NE Bellevue WA 98004

SCAMMAN, WALTER DOUGLAS, JR (R)
NH State Rep
b Concord, NH, Nov 26, 41; s Walter Douglas Scamman & Frances Gile S; m 1963 to Stella Emanuel; c Kimberly Diane & twins, Karl Michael & Kirk Quentin & Bruce Douglas. Educ: Univ NH, BA in Polit Sci, 64; Phi Mu Delta. Polit & Govt Pos: Auditor, Stratham Sch Dist, NH, 64-65; town auditor, Stratham, 65-67; chmn, Stratham Rep Party, 65-69; mem, sch bd, Stratham, 67-73; NH State Rep, 69-; alt deleg, Rep Nat Conv, 72. Bus & Prof Pos: Owner & operator, Dairy Farm, Stratham, 64- Mem: Univ NH Alumni Asn; Rotary. Honors & Awards: Outstanding Young Farmer in NH, 69. Relig: Congregational. Mailing Add: River Rd Stratham NH 03885

SCAMMON, RICHARD MONTGOMERY
Dir Elec Res Ctr, Govt Affairs Inst
b Minneapolis, Minn, July 17, 15; s Richard Everingham Scammon & Julia Simms S; m 1952 to Mary Stark Allen; c Anne Valerie. Educ: Univ Minn, AB, 35; Univ Mich, MA, 38; London Sch Econ, cert, 36. Polit & Govt Pos: Dep mil gov, US Off Mil Govt, Kreis Mergentheim, Württemberg, Ger, 45, polit officer, Land Baden-Württemberg, 45-46, chief polit activities br, Civil Admin Div, Ger, 46-48; chief div res for Western Europe, Dept of State, 48-55; dir elec res ctr, Govt Affairs Inst, 55-; chmn, US Deleg to Observe Elec in USSR, 58; dir, Bur Census, Dept Com, 61-65; chmn, President's Comn on Registrn & Voting Participation, 63; chmn, Select Comn on Western Hemisphere Immigration, 66-68; mem, US Deleg to UN Gen Assembly, 73. Bus & Prof Pos: Asst in polit sci, Univ Mich, 37-38; res secy, Radio Off, Univ Chicago & assoc producer, Univ Chicago-NBC Round Table, 39-41. Mil Serv: Army, 41-46, released as Capt. Publ: Ed, America Votes, Vols 1-10; co-auth, This USA, Doubleday, 65; The Real Majority, Coward-McCann, 70; plus others & contrib to jour. Mem: Am Polit Sci Asn; Am Acad Polit & Social Sci; Acad Polit Sci; Can Polit Sci Asn; Who's Who in Am Polit (mem adv comt, 67-). Legal Res: 5508 Greystone St Chevy Chase MD 20015 Mailing Add: 1619 Massachusetts Ave NW Washington DC 20036

SCANLAN, CHARLES FRANCIS (R)
Chmn, Wilson Co Rep Orgn, Kans
b St Louis, Mo, Aug 15, 29; s Frank D Scanlan & Opal Holmes S; m 1953 to Billie Loflin; c Shawn Duggan & Kevin Patrick. Educ: Univ Kans, AB in Polit Sci, 53; Southern Methodist Univ Sch Law, 56. Polit & Govt Pos: Precinct committeeman, Fredonia, Kans, 66-; chmn, Kans Citizens for Reagan, 68; mem, Kans Nixon-Agnew Comt, 68; chmn, Wilson Co Rep Orgn, 68-; exec secy, Kans Rep Party, 69, exec dir, 71-72; legis counsel, Kans State Dent Asn, currently; admin asst, US Sen James Pearson, 70. Bus & Prof Pos: Asst exec dir, Tex United Fund, 56-57; exec dir, Tyler Tex United Fund, 58-61; exec dir, Lubbock United Fund & Commun Coun, 62-63; owner & publ, Fredonia Daily Herald, Kans, 63- Mil Serv: Entered as 2nd Lt, Air Force, 54, released as 1st Lt, 55, after serv in 1804 AACS Wing, Alaska Air Command; various serv awards. Publ: Organizational and fund raising manuals; Inside Kansas, syndicated weekly polit column, 52 Kans daily & weekly newspapers, 72- Mem: United Commun Funds & Coun Am; Fredonia CofC; Fredonia Planning Comn; Southeast Kans Hwy Asn (pres, 68-); Kans State CofC (comt, 68-). Relig: Catholic. Mailing Add: 1005 Madison Fredonia KS 66736

SCANLAN, ROBERT JOSEPH (R)
b Miles City, Mont, Jan 30, 20; s Joseph Dominic Scanlan & Sarah M McDougal S; c R Joseph, Salli P (Mrs Bennett) & Allan M. Educ: Custer Co Jr Col, 40-41. Polit & Govt Pos: Publicity chmn, Custer Co Rep Party, Mont, 60-65, finance chmn, 63-64; deleg, Mont Rep Conv, 64; deleg, Rep Nat Conv, 64; aide to US Rep John J Rhodes, First Cong Dist, Ariz, 66- Bus & Prof Pos: Publ, Miles City Star, Miles City, Mont, 51-65; gen mgr, Star Printing Co, Inc, 51-65, pres, 61-65. Mil Serv: Entered as PO 3/C, Navy, 41, released as PO 1/C, 45, after serv in Pac Theater; Admiral's Commendation Medal; Pac Theater Campaign Ribbon; Good Conduct Medal. Publ: Weekly personal column, Scanning the News with Scanlan, Miles City Daily Star, Mont, 60-65. Mem: Rotary; Am Legion; DAV; Elks; Nat Cowboy Hall of Fame. Relig: Catholic. Mailing Add: 6040 Fed Bldg 230 N First Ave Phoenix AZ 85025

SCANLAN, SUSAN FRANCES (D)
Committeewoman, Maine Dem Party
b Portland, Maine, July 7, 48; d John J Scanlan & Patricia Fox S; single. Educ: Univ Maine, BA. Polit & Govt Pos: Staff asst to US Rep Peter Kyros, Maine, 69-71; committeewoman, Maine Dem Party, 70-; staff asst to US Sen Edmund Muskie, Maine, 71- Relig: Catholic. Mailing Add: 388 Woodford St Portland ME 04103

SCANLON, JOSEPH (D)
Mem, RI Dem Exec Comt
b Fall River, Mass, Mar 30, 30; s John T Scanlon & Eva Armstrong S; m 1952 to Jeannine Pelletier; c Deborah Geralyn, Stephen Joseph & Susan Elizabeth. Educ: BMC Durfee High Sch, 48. Polit & Govt Pos: Mem, RI Dem Exec Comt, 73- Mil Serv: Entered as Pvt, Army, 53, released as Cpl, after serv in Mil Police, Pac Theatre. Relig: Catholic. Legal Res: 29 Fir Ave Tiverton RI 02878 Mailing Add: 200 Fogarty Fed Bldg Providence RI 02903

SCANNELL, WILLIAM FRANCIS (R)
b Chicago, Ill, Nov 23, 23; s Albert Terence Scannell & Florence O'Connor S; m to Louise Bouchard; c Frances & Terence. Educ: Kenyon Col, 45; Univ Va Law Sch, LLB, 49; Sigma Phi Epsilon. Hon Degrees: LLD, Univ Va Law Sch, 72. Polit & Govt Pos: Committeeman, Ill Rep State Cent Comt, 62, secy, 69-74; engr, Agreements Div & admin asst, Right-of-Way Div, Cook Co Hwy Dept, Ill, 68-, gen counsel, Med Ctr Comn & spec asst to Attorney Gen, State of Ill, 69- Bus & Prof Pos: Lawyer, Gen Practice, Va, 48 & Ill, 49-; pres, Archer Iron Works, Inc, Chicago, Ill, 50-67. Mil Serv: Entered as Pvt, Army, 43, released as Lt(jg), after serv in Engrs Corps, ETO; Lt(jg) (Ret), Naval Res. Mem: Am, Va & Ill Bar Asns; Am Legion; Calumet City CofC. Mailing Add: 290 S Yates Ave Calumet City IL 60409

SCARBOROUGH, DAN IRVING (D)
Fla State Sen
b Hortense, Ga, Feb 6, 33; s Robert H Scarborough & Vivian Strickland S; m 1952 to Virginia Louise Zipperer; c John Robert, Vicki Elizabeth, Lynn & Karen. Educ: Univ Fla, 52-53. Polit & Govt Pos: Fla State Rep, 66-68; Fla State Sen, Tenth Dist, 68- Bus & Prof Pos: Owner-pres, Answer Phone of Jacksonville, St Augustine, currently. Mil Serv: Sgt, Marine Corps Res, 52-59. Mem: Masons; Scottish Rite; Shrine; Fla-Ga High Sch Football Off Asn; St Johns Flying Club. Honors & Awards: Allen Morris Award, Outstanding First Term Senator. Relig: Methodist. Legal Res: 4538 Ortega Farms Circle Jacksonville FL 32210 Mailing Add: 404 W Monroe St Jacksonville FL 32202

SCARBOROUGH, FRANKLIN A (R)
Chmn, Bleckley Co Rep Party, Ga
b Cochran, Ga, Feb 14, 09; s John W Scarborough & Carrie Harold S; m 1937 to Muriel McIntyre; c Paul O, Nancy M (Mrs Burson), Timothy F & J S. Educ: Bleckley Co Schs. Polit & Govt Pos: Chmn, Bleckley Co Rep Party, Ga, 68-72 & 75-; mem, Ga Rep State Cent Comt, 69; dir, Small Bus Admin, Ga, Region, 70. Bus & Prof Pos: Maintenance off, Bell Aircraft, 41-45, White Trucks Div, 45-53 & J M Huber Corp, 53-69; retired farmer & cattleman, Scarborough Farms, 69- Mem: Ga Farm Bur. Relig: Baptist. Mailing Add: Rte 2 Cochran GA 31014

SCARBOROUGH, HOMER M, JR (D)
b Macon, Ga, July 20, 41; s Homer M Scarborough, Sr & Mrs Vivian Keeling Tew; single. Educ: Univ Ga, JD, 66. Polit & Govt Pos: Ga State Rep, 69-72; mem, Bibb Co Dem Exec Comt, 71-74. Bus & Prof Pos: Attorney-at-law, Macon, Ga, 66- Mem: Ga Bar Asn; Moose; Phi Alpha Delta; Elks. Relig: Methodist. Mailing Add: 206 Am Fed Bldg Macon GA 31201

SCARCELLI, VINCENT F (D)
b Philadelphia, Pa, June 16, 14; s Frank Scarcelli & Rose Dodara S; m to Nancy Sue Russo; c Vincent, Jr, Philomena, Patricia. Educ: Secretarial Sch of Philadelphia; Mastbaum Voc Sch. Polit & Govt Pos: Pa State Rep, 54-67; mem, 48th Ward Dem Exec Comt; deleg, Dem Nat Mid-Term Conf, 74. Bus & Prof Pos: Owner, mgr, confectionery bus; operated a butter & egg rte; supervised receiving & shipping depts, Edward Tailoring Co, 14 years. Mem: Int Brotherhood of Teamsters (shop steward, local 830); Bartenders & Hotel Workers Union; Ambler; Order of Brotherly Love; VFW (hon mem, Post 3094). Relig: Catholic. Mailing Add: 2103 S Lambert St Philadelphia PA 19145

SCARDINO, ANTHONY, JR (D)
NJ State Sen
Mailing Add: State House Trenton NJ 08625

SCARLETT, FLOYD M (D)
Chmn, Harper Co Dem Party, Kans
b Okla, Aug 30, 06; s Mack A Scarlett & Nettie B Freeman S; m to Dorothy Farrell; c Sandra J (Mrs Beem). Educ: Cent Col (Okla), 29. Polit & Govt Pos: Chmn, Harper Co Dem Party, Kans, currently. Bus & Prof Pos: Owner, Scarlett's Int Harvester Dealership, Harper, Kans; owner, Scarlett's Case Dealership, Harper. Mem: Mason (past Master, 32 degree); Harper CofC (pres); Harper Co Fair (chmn). Mailing Add: Box 275 Harper KS 67058

SCELSI, JOSEPH S (D)
Mass State Rep
Mailing Add: State Capitol Boston MA 02133

SCHAAF, DAVID D (DFL)
Minn State Sen
Mailing Add: 6550 East River Rd Apt 215 Fridley MN 55432

SCHAAP, GEORGE ALDARUS (R)
b Sacramento, Calif, Aug 11, 19; s George Aldarus Schaap, Sr & Maybelle Nirod Niestrath S; m 1942 to Phoebe Ann Lewis; c Pamela Ann (Mrs MacKean) & Craig Aldarus. Educ: Santa Rosa Jr Col, AA, 40; Univ Calif, Los Angeles, 41-42; Calif Col Med, MD, 46; Univ Vienna, 56-57. Polit & Govt Pos: Rep campaign dir, Fifth Sen Dist, Calif, 61; chmn, Colusa Co Rep Cent Comt, formerly; area chmn, NCent Co Rep Party, 69. Bus & Prof Pos: Sr resident in med, Los Angeles Co Hosp, 47-48; pvt practice of med, Colusa Co, Calif, 48-; resident in surgery, Gen Hosp, Linz, Austria, 57-58; pres, Valley West Convalescent Hosp, Williams, Calif, 65- Mem: Am & Calif Med Asns; Tri Co Med Soc; Mason; Farm Bur. Honors & Awards: County Fair Share Quota 100%, 64-68. Relig: Protestant. Mailing Add: 426 Webster Colusa CA 95932

SCHABARUM, PETER F (R)
Chmn Bd of Supvr, Co of Los Angeles, Calif
b Los Angeles, Calif, 1929; m 1957 to Gerry Ann Curtice; c Laura, Frank & Tom. Educ: Univ Calif, Berkeley, BS in Bus Admin. Polit & Govt Pos: Foreman, Los Angeles Co Grand Jury, 65; Calif State Assemblyman, 67-72; mem, Rep State Cent Comt Calif, currently; supvr, First Dist & chmn bd supvr, Co of Los Angeles, 72- Bus & Prof Pos: Pres & owner of real estate investment co. Honors & Awards: Mem, San Francisco 49'ers Pro-Football Team, formerly; former All-Coast Football Player. Mailing Add: 500 W Temple St Los Angeles CA 90012

SCHACHTER, MARVIN (D)
Mem, Calif Dem State Cent Comt
b New York, NY, May 17, 24; s Max Schachter & Fanny Javits S; m 1956 to Esther Adler; c Pamela & Amanda. Educ: Univ Chicago, Cert in Russian Studies, 43; Univ Minn, Cert in German Studies, 44; Brooklyn Col, BA; Univ Colo, MA, 50; Cambridge Univ, Econ Res, 51-52; Phi Gamma Mu. Polit & Govt Pos: State issues chmn, Calif Dem Coun, 58-59, state legis chmn, 67-68; mem, Kennedy Campaign Comt, 60; chmn, 42nd Assembly Dist Dem Party, 60-61; mem, McCarthy Campaign Comt, 68; mem, Cranston Campaign Comt, 68; mem, Bradley Campaign Comt, 69; mem, Calif Dem State Cent Comt, 69-; chmn comt law & justice, Los Angeles Bicentennial Comn. Bus & Prof Pos: Buyer, May Co, 55-62; merchandise mgr, Shoe Corp of Am, 62-63; vpres, R B Mfg Co, 63-64; vpres, Vol Merchandise, Inc, 64-74, pres, 74- Mil Serv: Entered as Pvt, Army, 43, as Pfc, 46, after serv in Mil Intel. Mem: Am Econ Asn; Am Civil Liberties Union (vchmn nat bd dirs, 75-); Am Civil Liberties Union of S Calif (pres & bd dirs); Los Angeles Town Hall. Relig: Jewish. Mailing Add: 300 California Terr Pasadena CA 91105

SCHAEFER, FRANCES DARRAH (R)
Mem, Orleans Parish Rep Exec Comt, La
b New Orleans, La, Dec 28, 38; d Louis James Darrah & Patti Trim D; m 1960 to E Gordon Schaefer, Jr; c E Gordon, III, Frederick Darrah & Anne Worsley. Educ: Duke Univ, 56-59; Tulane Univ, BA, 60; Alpha Phi. Polit & Govt Pos: Secy, La Young Rep Fedn, 63-67; New Orleans Women's Rep Club, 63-69; hq chmn, Metrop Dist, La Rep Party, 66-68; vchmn, Orleans Parish Polit Action Coun, 67-68; vchmn, Orleans Parish Rep Exec Comt, 67-70, mem, 67-; alt deleg, Rep Nat Conv, 68 & 72. Bus & Prof Pos: Dist field supvr, US Census Bur, 70; commun organizer, Irish Channel Action Found, 70-72; employ counr, Snelling & Snelling of Metairie, 72-73. Mem: League of Women Voters; New Orleans Philharmonic Symphony Soc (jr comt); New Orleans CofC Auxiliary. Relig: Presbyterian. Mailing Add: 5818 Chestnut St New Orleans LA 70115

SCHAEFER, RICHARD MAX, JR (D)
b Greenacres, Wash, Nov 8, 16; s Richard Max Schaefer & Edith Kuchenbuch S; m 1942 to Mildred Bostick; c Richard Max, III & Janice K. Educ: Wash State Univ, BA in Econ, 41; Montezuma Club of Stimson Hall; Assoc Chemists. Polit & Govt Pos: Precinct committeeman, Lewiston Orchards 9, Idaho, 60-; vchmn, Nez Perce Co Dem Cent Comt, 69-70; deleg, Idaho State Dem Conv, 72 & 74; alt deleg, Dem Nat Conv, 72. Bus & Prof Pos: Instr preflight physics & aeronaut, Wash State Univ, 42-45; teacher math, S Kitsap High Sch, Port Orchard, Wash, 45; bus agent, Carpenter's Union, 47; owner & operator, R M Schaefer Lumber Co, Lewiston, Idaho, 49- Mil Serv: Entered as Pvt, 45, released as T/5, 46, after serv in Army Med Corps, US, 45-46; Sharp Shooter; Victory Medal. Mem: Idaho State Grange; Nat Farmers Union; Am for Dem Action; Am Vet Comn; Am Civil Liberties Union. Relig: Protestant. Mailing Add: 1331 Ripon Lewiston ID 83501

SCHAEFER, WILLIAM DONALD (D)
Mayor, Baltimore, Md
b Baltimore, Md, Nov 2, 21; s William Henry Schaefer & Tululu Skipper S; single. Educ: Univ Baltimore, LLB, 42, LLM, 52. Polit & Govt Pos: City councilman, Baltimore City Coun, 55-67, pres, 67-71; mayor, Baltimore, Md, 71- Bus & Prof Pos: Attorney, Pvt Practice, 45- Mil Serv: Entered Army, 42, released as Maj, 45, after serv in Med Unit, ETO, 42-45; Col, Army Res. Mem: Many current mem in prof orgn, clubs & civic orgn. Honors & Awards: Citation for Promotion of the Fine Arts, Artists Equity Asn, 63; First Annual Civic Statesmanship Award, Citizens Planning & Housing Asn, 65; Citation for Distinguished Contrib to Retarded Children, Baltimore Asn of Retarded Children, 69; Man of the Year, Baltimore Asn of Retarded Children, 71; Alumni of the Year, Univ Baltimore Law Sch, 72; plus many others. Relig: Episcopal. Legal Res: 620 Edgewood St Baltimore MD 21229 Mailing Add: 230 City Hall Baltimore MD 21202

SCHAFER, ALAN HELLER (D)
b Baltimore, Md, Jan 12, 14; s Samuel I Schafer & Wilhelmina Heller S; m to Helen Swinson (deceased); c William H, Richard H & Frederic R. Educ: Univ SC, AB in Jour, 34; Sigma Delta Chi; Pi Lambda Phi; Clariosophic Soc. Polit & Govt Pos: Chmn, Dillon Co Dem Party, SC & Exec Comt, formerly; deleg, Dem Nat Conv, 68. Bus & Prof Pos: Chmn & pres, Schafer Distributing Co, Inc, 35-, Palmetto Properties, Inc & Modern Music Co, 46-69, South of the Border Co, 50- & Ace-Hi Advert Corp, 60- Mil Serv: Entered as Pvt, Army, 43, released as Pfc, 45, after serv in 4th Serv Command, Atlanta, Ga, 43-45. Mem: Am Legion; VFW; Mason; Shrine (bd gov & Shrine Bowl, Greenville Crippled Children's Hosp). Relig: Jewish. Mailing Add: Hwy 57 Dillon SC 29536

SCHAFFER, ARCHIBALD RICHARD, III (D)
b Ft Smith, Ark, Jan 7, 48; s A R Schaffer & Margaret Flanagan S; m 1968 to Rebecca Faith Evans; c Mary Faith & Archibald R, IV. Educ: Ark State Univ, 65-67; Univ Ark, BA, 69, Med Sch, 69-70, Law Sch, 71-73. Polit & Govt Pos: Admin asst to Gov, Dale Bumpers, Ark, 71-75, admin asst to US Sen Bumpers, 75- Legal Res: Charleston AR 72833 Mailing Add: 5809 Ogden Rd Bethesda MD 20016

SCHAFFER, GLORIA WILINSKI (D)
Secy of State, Conn
b New London, Conn, Oct 3, 30; d Arthur Wilinski & Charlotte Reiner W; m 1949 to Eugene Schaffer; c Susan & Stephen. Educ: Sarah Lawrence Col. Polit & Govt Pos: Conn State Sen, 59-71; Secy of State, Conn, 71-; deleg, Dem Nat Conv, 72. Mem: New Haven Commun Coun (bd dirs); Urban League; Conn Hosp Planning Comn; Order of Women Legislators; White House Conf Educ (rep, Conf & mem, Nat Educ Comn). Honors & Awards: Nat Merit Award, Coun Crime & Delinquency; Award, Nat Cystic Fibrosis Soc, Conn Asn Hearing Impaired Children & Conn Asn Voc Insts; Jewish War Vet Citation; Nat Human Rels Award, Nat Conf Christians & Jews; Dist Serv Award, New London Co Bar Asn, 74. Legal Res: Tumblebrook Rd Woodbridge CT 06525 Mailing Add: State Capitol Hartford CT 06115

SCHAFFER, JACK RAYMOND (R)
Ill State Sen
b Chicago, Ill, Dec 10, 42; s Raymond Paul Schaffer & Frances Barter S; m 1969 to Linda L Bellerud. Educ: Northern Ill Univ, BS. Polit & Govt Pos: Founding mem & membership chmn, Northern Ill Univ Young Rep, 60, pres, 61-62; chmn, Youth for Nixon, Northern Ill Univ, 60 & Youth for Dirksen, 62; resolutions chmn, Ill Young Rep Col Fedn, 61, pres, 63-64; mem, McHenry Co Young Rep, 61-, pres, 65-66; participant, Proj Eagle Eye, Chicago, 62; deleg, Nat Young Rep Conv, 63 & 69; committeeman, Algonquin Twp 17, 64-; nat dir, Region Five Col Young Rep, 64; vchmn, Ill Youth for Goldwater, 64; fieldman, 23rd Dist Young Rep Nat Fedn, 64; dist gov, 12th Cong Dist, Ill Young Rep Orgn, 65, membership chmn, 69, state chmn, 69-; mem exec comt, McHenry Co Rep Cent Comt, 65, mem, 68-, mem, Patronage Comt, 68-; chmn, Rep Comt for McHenry Co Fair, 68; downstate chmn, One Million Young People for Nixon, 68; auditor, McHenry Co, 68-; mem, Ill Tollway Adv Bd & Gov Adv Bd, 69-; chmn, McHenry Co Awards Dinner, 70; campaign coordr, Kucharski for State Treas, 70; participant, Nat Young Rep Training Sch, 70; chmn, Algonquin Twp Rep Cent Comt, 70-; Ill State Sen, 73- Mil Serv: Entered as Pvt, Army, 65, released as Sgt, 67, after serv in B/3/70, Germany. Mem: Ill Asn Co Auditors (secy-treas, 69-); Spring Beach Improv Asn

(trustee); Am Legion; Jaycees; Farm Bur. Honors & Awards: Outstanding Col Young Rep Award, 64. Mailing Add: 56 N Williams St Crystal Lake IL 60014

SCHAFFER, LARRY D (R)
b Emmet, Nebr, Oct 12, 28; s Dewey Cramer Schaffer & Elizabeth Gribble S; m 1948 to Lois Cole; c Elizabeth & Dewey, II. Educ: Univ Nebr, 46-47; Sigma Nu. Polit & Govt Pos: Chmn, Holt Co Rep Party, Nebr, formerly. Mem: Boy Scouts (dist chmn, Sandhills Dist); Mason; Shrine; Am Quarter Horse Asn; Nebr Stockgrowers. Relig: Presbyterian. Mailing Add: 412 N Second O'Neill NE 68763

SCHALLER, BARRY RAYMOND (R)
b Hartford, Conn, Nov 23, 38; s Raymond T Schaller & Mildred McCollum S; m 1962 to Deborah Douglas; c Katherine Deborah, Jane Elizabeth & Peter Douglas. Educ: Yale Col, BA, 60, Law Sch, LLB, 63; Phi Delta Phi. Polit & Govt Pos: State youth chmn, Conn Alsop for Gov Comt, 62; coordr, Stelio Salmona for Cong, 66; chmn, Branford Rep Town Comt, 67-70; counsel to Minority Leader, Conn House of Rep, 69-; mem, Conn Rep State Cent Comt, 70-74; mem, Conn Bd of Pardons, 71-; mem, Conn Planning Comt on Criminal Admin, 72- Bus & Prof Pos: Partner, Bronson & Rice, Attorneys, New Haven, 63- Mem: Conn & Am Bar Asns; US Dist & US Supreme Courts; US Court of Appeals, Second Circuit. Relig: Episcopal; Vestryman, Trinity Church, Branford, Conn, 72- Mailing Add: 114 Flax Mill Rd Branford CT 06405

SCHANZLE, ELLEN JOSEPHINE (D)
b Evansville, Ind, Jan 20, 50; d George Herman Schanzle & Marion Winter S; single. Educ: Eastern Ill Univ, BS, 72, MA cand psychol, currently; Psi Chi; student sen, 68-71, senate secy, 71-73, pres, 73- Polit & Govt Pos: Deleg, Dem Nat Conv, 72. Mem: Am Civil Liberties Union (vchmn, 72-73); Asn of Ill Student Govt. Mailing Add: Apt 212 2400 Nantucket Charleston IL 61920

SCHAUFELE, WILLIAM EVERETT, JR
b Lakewood, Ohio, Dec 7, 23; s William Elias Schaufele & Lillian Bergen S; m 1950 to Heather Moon; c Steven William & Peter Henry. Educ: Yale Univ, BA, 48; Columbia Univ, MIA, 50. Polit & Govt Pos: Career officer, Foreign Serv, US State Dept, 50-, resident officer, Pfaffenhefen an der Ilm, Ger, 50-52, resident officer, Augsburg, 52, vconsul, Duesseldorf, 52-53, vconsul, Munich, 53-56, mem staff, State Dept, 56-59, consul, Casablanca, 59-63, consul, Bukavu, 63-64, officer in charge, Congolese Affairs, 64-65, dep dir, Cent African Affairs, 65-67, dir, Cent WAfrican Affairs, 67-69, US Ambassador to Upper Volta, 69-71, sr adv to US Permanent Rep to UN, 71-73, US Dep Rep on UN Security Coun, 73-75, Inspector Gen of Foreign Serv, 75- Mil Serv: Army, 43-46, ETO. Legal Res: 32150 Lake Rd Avon Lake OH 44012 Mailing Add: Dept of State Washington DC 20520

SCHEAFFER, JOHN E (R)
Pa State Rep
b Pottstown, Pa, Aug 28, 16; s Grover C Scheaffer & Bertha Bewley S; m 1947 to Lillian A Serwatka; c two. Educ: New Cumberland High Sch; Harrisburg Acad & Univ Ala. Polit & Govt Pos: Pa State Rep, 70-; mem, Cumberland Co Rep Finance & Exec Comts, Pa. Bus & Prof Pos: Sales exec, currently. Mil Serv: Mem, 504th Parachute Inf, 82nd Airborne Div, Army, 40-45; Silver Star; Bronze Star; Purple Heart. Mem: West Shore CofC; West Shore Kiwanis; Harrisburg Area CofC; Cumberland Co Indust Authority (chmn, 69-); West Shore Country Club. Honors & Awards: Sword of Hope, Cancer Soc. Legal Res: 5 Amherst Dr Camp Hill PA 17011 Mailing Add: Capitol Bldg Harrisburg PA 17120

SCHECHTER, MAURICE (D)
Mo State Sen
b St Louis, Mo, June 27, 07; m 1931 to Bess Ragin Schechter; c Stanley I, Judith Kay (Mrs Siegel); four grandchildren. Educ: Wash Univ; City Col Law & Finance, LLB. Polit & Govt Pos: Charter mem & first pres, Creve Coeur Twp Dem Club, St Louis Co; Mo State Rep, 34-48; Mo State Sen, 60- Bus & Prof Pos: Practicing attorney, 28- Mem: Scottish Rite; Mason; Shrine; B'nai B'rith; Lawyers Asn St Louis. Relig: Jewish. Mailing Add: 41 Country Fair Lane Creve Coeur MO 63141

SCHECTER, SHELDON DALE (D)
Co-Chmn, Ohio New Dem Coalition
b Cleveland, Ohio, Dec 1, 26; s Morris Schecter & Betty Romanoff S; m 1963 to Renee Louise Fried; c Mark Byron, David Michael & Cynthia Elise. Educ: Western Reserve Univ, BA, 50, LLB, 53; Pi Sigma Alpha; Omicron Sigma Alpha; Tau Epsilon Rho. Polit & Govt Pos: Vchmn, Cleveland Am for Dem Action, Ohio, 67-68; Ohio & Cleveland Co-Chmn, McCarthy for President Comt, 68; alt deleg, Dem Nat Conv, 68, deleg for McGovern & asst floor leader, Ohio McGovern Deleg, 72; co-chmn, Ohio New Dem Coalition, currently; mem, Inaugural Comt for Gov John J Gilligan, 71; Cuyahoga Co co-chmn, McGovern for President Comt Primary Campaign & Ohio State polit dir, Gen Elec, 72. Mil Serv: Pvt, Army, 45-46, with serv in Mil Police, Italy; Good Conduct Medal; Mediter Theatre Medal. Mem: Ohio, Cleveland & Cuyahoga Bar Asns; Citizen League; City Club. Relig: Jewish. Mailing Add: 3605 Ingleside Rd Shaker Heights OH 44122

SCHEDLER, SPENCER JAIME (R)
b Manila, Philippine Islands, Oct 23, 33; s Edmund W Schedler; m 1969 to Judy Hamilton. Educ: Univ Tulsa, BS in Petroleum Eng, 55; Harvard Bus Sch, MBA, 62; Phi Kappa Gamma; Sword & Key. Polit & Govt Pos: Asst Secy of the Air Force for Financial Mgt, 69-73. Bus & Prof Pos: Petroleum engr, Humble Oil & Refining Co, Tulsa, 58-60; cost analyst & asst to chmn of the bd, Houston Oil Field Material Co, Tex, 62; financial analyst, Sinclair Oil Corp, Tulsa, Okla, 63, asst dir budgets, New York, 65, mgr budgets & financial analysis, 66, mgr budgets & analysis, 67; exec vpres, Hycel Inc, Houston, Tex, 73; gen mgr & asst to exec vpres finance & admin, Continental Can Co, Inc, New York, currently. Mil Serv: Entered as 2nd Lt, Air Force, 55, released as 1st Lt, 58, after serv in 41st Fighter-Interceptor Squadron, Guam, 57-58; Capt, Air Force Res. Mem: Union League Club New York. Honors & Awards: Exceptional Civilian Serv Award, Air Force. Mailing Add: SAFFM Rm 4E 978 Pentagon Washington DC 20330

SCHEELHAASE, LYLE (D)
Iowa State Rep
Mailing Add: RR 2 Moville IA 51039

SCHEIDEL, THEODORE C, JR (D)
Chmn, Burlington Town Dem Comt, Conn
b Burlington, Conn, July 8, 44; s Theodore Charles Scheidel, Sr & Catherine Teresa Flood S; single. Educ: Univ Hartford, 2 years. Polit & Govt Pos: Comnr, Burlington Town Planning & Zoning, Conn, 68; chmn, Burlington Town Dem Comt, 70- Bus & Prof Pos: Mem staff, Conn Bank & Trust Co, 67- Mil Serv: Entered as Pvt E-1, Army, 65, released as Sgt E-5, 67, after serv in 3rd Brigade, 4th Inf Div, Vietnam, II FFV, 66-67; Good Conduct Medal with Bronze Star. Mem: Burlington Vol Fire Dept (secy); Burlington Men's Club; Green-Erickson Post 122 Am Legion (adj & finance officer); Farmington Valley Stamp Club. Relig: Roman Catholic. Mailing Add: RD 1 Covey Rd Unionville CT 06085

SCHEIDT, VIRGIL D (R)
Chmn, Bartholomew Co Rep Cent Comt, Ind
b Columbus, Ind, Sept 23, 28; s Harry Scheidt & Mildred Armuth S; m 1949 to Bettie L Todd; c Don Randall, Deborah Diane, Warren Ray & Christie Cheryl. Polit & Govt Pos: Treas, Bartholomew Co, Ind, 62-70; chmn, Bartholomew Co Rep Cent Comt, 65-; state chmn co off, 65 & 66; nat dir co off, 65 & 66; chmn, Ninth Dist Rep Cent Comt, 66-70; deleg, Rep Nat Conv, 68. Honors & Awards: Jr CofC Good Govt Award, 62; First runner-up, Outstanding Co Treas, US, 65. Relig: Lutheran. Legal Res: RR 2 Columbus IN 47201 Mailing Add: Rep Hq 422 1/2 Fifth St Columbus OH 47201

SCHEIERMAN, MABEL M (R)
VChmn, Fifth Cong Dist Rep Party, Colo
b Stratton, Colo, Feb 27, 19; d Joseph W Garner & Sarah S Hampton G; m 1952 to Kenneth Scheierman. Educ: Blair's Bus Col, Colorado Springs, 36-37; Anderson Col, 44-45. Polit & Govt Pos: Vchmn, Kit Carson Co Rep Party, Colo, 60-71, chmn, 71-74; secy, Third Cong Dist Rep Party, formerly; vchmn, Fifth Cong Dist Rep Party, 72-, vchmn, Sen Dist 35, 72-, co-chmn, Rep Dist, 64 & 72- Bus & Prof Pos: Mem, Stratton Sch Accountability Comt, currently. Mem: Keep Colo Beautiful (bd); M S A Club (treas, formerly, vpres, 72-74); Am Nat Cowbelles; Chapel of Hope (co chmn); Colo Fedn Women's Clubs (ed chmn, 72-74). Relig: Church of God; Secy prog comt, Colo Conf of the Church of God; state secy, Woman's Missionary Soc. Mailing Add: Rte 1 Stratton CO 80836

SCHEPERS, MARLYN GLENN (D)
Chairperson, Muscatine Co Dem Cent Comt, Iowa
b Lost Nation, Iowa, Jan 7, 33; s Glenn Schepers & Ruth Hohn; m 1968 to Mary Ann Hogan; c Rae Lynn, Erich Tyson & Malia Ann. Educ: Iowa State Univ, BS, 55; Univ Liberia, 59; Univ Ill, Champaign, 63; Muscatine Community Col, 64; Univ Iowa, MS, 69; Phi Eta Sigma. Polit & Govt Pos: Treas, Muscatine Co Dem Cent Comt, Iowa, 68-71, chairperson, 71-; bd mem, Muscatine Library, 74. Bus & Prof Pos: Design engr, Stanley Eng Co, Muscatine, Iowa, 55-57, 60-73; hydrologist, Stanley Eng Co Africa, Liberia, 58-60; sr struct engr, Stanley Consults, Inc, Muscatine, Iowa, 74- Mil Serv: Entered as Pvt, Army, 55, released as SP-3, 57, after serv in 12th Engr Bn, Eighth Div, Seventh Army, Germany, 56-57; Good Conduct Medal; Commendation for Voluntary Librarian from Eighth Div Commander. Mem: Am Soc Civil Engrs; Int Conf Large Elec Systs; Am Civil Liberties Union (treas & bd mem, Hawkeye Area Chap, 74); AF&AM Harbor Lodge, Lost Nation. Relig: Presbyterian. Mailing Add: 413 W Third St Muscatine IA 52761

SCHERER, GORDON HARRY (R)
b Cincinnati, Ohio, Dec 26, 06; s John E Scherer & Minnie Kuehnle S; m 1933 to Virginia Mottern; c Gordon Mottern & Suzanne (Mrs Louiso). Educ: Univ Cincinnati, Salmon P Chase Col of Law, LLB, 29; Order of Curia; Phi Alpha Delta. Hon Degrees: LLD, Institutum Divi Thomae, 62. Polit & Govt Pos: Pres, Young Rep Club of Hamilton Co, Ohio, 33-34; asst prosecuting attorney, Hamilton Co, 33-40, dir of safety, 43-44; mem, Cincinnati City Coun, 45-49; vpres, Hamilton Co Rep Club, 38-42; chmn, Robert A Taft Citizens Comt for US Senate, 50; US Rep, Ohio, 53-62; chmn, Hamilton Co Rep Party, 62-68; mem, Ohio Rep State Cent & Exec Comts, 62-70; mem, Hamilton Co Bd of Elec, Ohio, 67; mem, Task Force on Crime & Delinquency, Rep Nat Comt, 68; deleg, Rep Nat Conv, 64 & 68, mem platform comt, & Nixon floor mgr for Ohio deleg, 68; mem, Ohio Supreme Court Comn on Grievances & Discipline, 70-; US Rep to UN, 72-73; US deleg to UN, 74- Bus & Prof Pos: Mem, bd of dirs, Universal Guaranty Life Ins Co of Ohio, 63- Publ: Key targets of the Communists, Am Legion Mag, 8/62; Are Americans aware? Vital Speeches, 8/58; I was a target, Readers Digest, 7/54. Mem: US Comn to UNESCO; DeMolay Legion of Honor; Mason (33 degree); Cincinnati Southern Railway (trustee); Am for Const Action (bd of trustees). Honors & Awards: Recipient, Patriotic Serv Awards from Am Coalition of Patriotic Soc, Am Legion & DAR. Relig: Protestant. Mailing Add: Carew Tower Cincinnati OH 45202

SCHERER, GORDON M (R)
b Cincinnati, Ohio, Aug 1, 38; s Gordon Harry Scherer & Virginia Mottern S; m 1961 to Judith Marjorie Myers; c Gordon W & Steven M. Educ: Univ Cincinnati, BA in polit sci, 61; Salmon P Chase Col Law, JD, 66; Phi Alpha Delta; Sigma Alpha Epsilon. Polit & Govt Pos: Ohio State Rep, formerly; alt deleg, Rep Nat Conv, 72. Bus & Prof Pos: Mem, Govt Affairs Br, Cincinnati Real Estate Bd, Ohio, 62-66; assoc, P G Graves Inc, Indust Realtors, 62-66; attorney-at-law, Scherer & Scherer, currently. Mem: Mason (32 degree); Scottish Rite; Shrine. Relig: Presbyterian. Mailing Add: 2857 Springwood Court Cincinnati OH 45211

SCHERESKY, LAURENCE THEODORE (R)
b Max, NDak, Feb 5, 29; s Joseph J Scheresky & Dorothy Dassenko S; m 1953 to Lenore Irene Hines; c Katherine, Kari Lynn, Kimberly Ann & Barry Jay. Educ: Minot State Col, 2 years; NDak State Univ, 1 year. Polit & Govt Pos: Agr Stabilization & Conserv Serv Committeeman, Ward Co NDak, 59-61, chmn, 61-62; chmn, Fourth Dist Rep Party, formerly; pres, United Pub Sch Bd Seven, 69- Mem: NDak Farm Bur; Am Farm Bur Fedn; NDak Durum Growers Asn; NDak Stockmen's Asn; Ward Co Red Cross (dir, 72-). Honors & Awards: Named Outstanding Young Farmer, Ward Co, NDak, 60 & 65; Runnerup for Outstanding Young Farmer, NDak, 65. Relig: Seventh Day Adventist. Mailing Add: Des Lacs ND 58733

SCHERLE, WILLIAM J (R)
b Little Falls, NY, Mar 14, 23; m 1947 to Jane Goldapp; c William David & John Robert. Educ: Southern Methodist Univ, BS Admin. Polit & Govt Pos: Chmn, Mills Co Rep Cent Comt, 3 terms; Iowa State Rep, 60-66, mem, Legis Research Comt, Iowa House Rep, Fifth Dist, 66; US Rep, Iowa, formerly; mem, Nat Rivers & Harbors Cong; asst dep adminr, Agr Stabilization & Conserv Serv, Dept of Agr, 75- Bus & Prof Pos: Grain & livestock farmer; asst div mgr George D Barnard Co, Dallas, Tex. Mil Serv: Vet of World War II; Naval Res. Mem: Nat Livestock Feeders Asn; Am Nat Cattlemen's Asn; Farm Bur; Elks; Am Legion. Honors & Awards: Silver Medallion on Space & Rocketry, German-Am Cong; Hon Hungarian Freedom Fighter; Nat Legislators Award, SAR; Bulgarian Nat Liberty Award; State Man of the Year Award, Nat Fedn Independent Bus, 72. Relig: Catholic. Legal Res:

RFD Henderson IA 51541 Mailing Add: Agr Stabilization & Conserv Serv Dept of Agr Washington DC 20250

SCHERMERHORN, RICHARD E (R)
NY State Sen
Mailing Add: 12 Idlewild Park Dr Cornwall-on-Hudson NY 12520

SCHEUER, JAMES H (D)
US Rep, NY
b New York, NY, Feb 6, 20; m to Emily; c four. Educ: Swarthmore Col, AB; Columbia Law Sch, LLB; Harvard Grad Sch of Bus Admin, degree in indust admin. Polit & Govt Pos: Developer of residential community in eight cities under the Fed Urban Renewal prog; deleg to four UN Conf on housing & urban probs & human rights; economist, US Foreign Econ Admin, 45-46; mem of legal staff, Off of Price Stabilization, 51-52; US Rep, NY, 64-72, 75-; deleg, Dem Nat Conv, 68, 72; Cong adv to US deleg, UN Conf for Adoption of Protocol on Psychotropic Substances, Vienna, 71. Bus & Prof Pos: Writer & lectr. Mil Serv: Flight instr, Army, 43-45. Publ: To Walk the Streets Safely, Doubleday, 69. Mem: Bar Asn of New York City; Nat Panel of Arbitrators, Am Arbit Asn; Citizens' Housing & Planning Coun of New York (pres); Nat Housing Conf (bd mem); Bronx Boys Club (dir). Legal Res: Bronx NY Mailing Add: 3238 R St NW Washington DC 20007

SCHIAPPA, GERARD FRANCIS (R)
b Scranton, Pa, Dec 11, 38; s Frank Peter Schiappa & Isabel K McDonald S; m 1964 to Jane Leishear Thompson. Educ: Univ Md, 4 years. Polit & Govt Pos: Staff asst to US Rep Joe Skubitz, Kans, 62-64; staff investr for minority, House Comt on Publ Works, 64-66; spec asst to US Sen Louis C Wyman, NH, 67-69, admin asst, 69- Mil Serv: Entered as Pvt, Army, 57, released as Cpl, 59. Mem: Cong Secretaries Club; Bull Elephants Club; Fed Ed Asn. Relig: Lutheran. Legal Res: 10616 Seneca Ridge Dr Gaithersburg MD Mailing Add: 1409 Dirksen Senate Off Bldg Washington DC 20510

SCHIEFFELIN, JOSEPH B (R)
Colo State Sen
b New York, NY, Jan 18, 27; married; c Three. Polit & Govt Pos: Colo State Rep, one term; precinct committeeman, 6 yrs; Colo State Sen, 67-, majority leader, Colo State Senate, 73- Bus & Prof Pos: Ins agt. Honors & Awards: Man of the Year, local press of Lakewood & Wheatridge, Colo. Mailing Add: 11674 Applewood Knolls Dr Lakewood CO 80215

SCHIEFFER, JOHN THOMAS (D)
Tex State Rep
b Ft Worth, Tex, Oct 4, 47; s John E Schieffer & Gladys Payne S; single. Educ: Univ Tex, Austin, BA, 70, MA, 72; Phi Delta Theta. Polit & Govt Pos: Tex State Rep, 73- Relig: Presbyterian. Legal Res: 4500 Williams Rd Ft Worth TX 76116 Mailing Add: 1105 Ridglea State Bank Bldg Ft Worth TX 76116

SCHIEL, DONALD CARL (D)
VChmn, Redwood Co Dem Party, Minn
b Brainerd, Minn, Sept 21, 38; s Carl Peter Schiel (deceased) & Helen Parrish S; m 1964 to Rita Gail Loken; c Bradley Donald & Robert Alan. Educ: Washington High Sch, Brainerd, Minn, grad, 56. Polit & Govt Pos: Secy, Becker Co Dem Party, Minn, 66; chmn, Redwood Co Dem Party, 70-74, vchmn, currently; mem, Minn State Dem Cent Comt, 70-; mem exec comt, Sixth Dist Dem Comt, 72-; chmn, Sixth Dist Cong Club, 72-; adv, Richard Nolan. Bus & Prof Pos: Secy & bus rep, Brainerd Bldg Trades, 62-63; owner & gen mgr, Redwood Broadcasting, Inc, 66- Mil Serv: Entered as Pvt, Army Nat Guard, 56, released as Pfc, 63, after serv in Inactive Res. Mem: Nat Asn Broadcasters (trustee & mem bd dirs of TV & radio polit action comt); Minn Broadcasters Asn (vpres & chmn legis comt, 72-); Lions (pres, 72); Redwood Falls CofC. Honors & Awards: Cert of Appreciation, Minn Asn Retarded Children; Boss of Year, Redwood Falls Jaycees. Relig: Methodist. Legal Res: 303 Smith Dr Redwood Falls MN 56283 Mailing Add: 303 Smith Dr Redwood Falls MN 56283

SCHIFTER, RICHARD (D)
b Vienna, Austria, July 31, 23; s Paul Schifter & Balbina Blass S; m 1948 to Lilo Krueger; c Judith (Mrs Alter), Deborah E, Richard P, Barbara F & Karen E. Educ: City Col NY, BS Soc Sci, summa cum laude, 43; Yale Law Sch, LLB, 51; Phi Beta Kappa. Polit & Govt Pos: Mem, Md State Bd Educ, 59-, vpres, 67-; mem bd visitors, Md Sch Deaf, 60-; chmn, Montgomery Co Dem Cent Comt, 66-70; vchmn, Md Dem State Cent Comt, 67-70; deleg, Dem Nat Conv, 68; mem bd dirs, Coalition for a Dem Majority, 72- Bus & Prof Pos: Assoc, Fried, Frank, Harris, Shriver & Kampelman, 51-57, partner, 57- Mil Serv: Entered as Pvt, Army, 43, released as T/Sgt, 46, after serv in T-Force, 12th Army Group, ETO, 44-45. Mem: Am Bar Asn. Relig: Jewish. Mailing Add: 6907 Crail Dr Bethesda MD 20034

SCHILFFARTH, RICHARD ALLEN (R)
Chmn, Ninth Dist Rep Party, Wis
b Milwaukee, Wis, Apr 24, 31; s Herman T Schilffarth & Elizabeth Rausch S; m 1953 to Marlene Thiele; c Christine Lynn & Richard Allen. Educ: Univ Wis, BBA, 53; Delta Tau Delta. Polit & Govt Pos: Deleg, Wis State Rep Conv, 61-72; deleg, Rep Nat Conv, 68; chmn, Wis State Get-Out-The-Vote, 68 & 72; chmn, Ninth Dist Rep Party, Wis, 73- Bus & Prof Pos: Mgr, E F Hutton & Co, Milwaukee, currently. Mil Serv: Entered as 2nd Lt, Army, 53, released as 1st Lt, 55 after serv in 4th Armored Div. Mem: Dominican Col (vpres, dir); Friends of Art-Milwaukee (mem bd); Delta Tau Delta Alumni Club of Milwaukee. Relig: Lutheran. Mailing Add: 15025 Cascade Dr Elm Grove WI 53122

SCHILLER, JAMES JOSEPH (D)
Mem, Ohio State Dem Exec Comt
b Cleveland, Ohio, July 1, 33; s Jacob Peter Schiller & Helen Elizabeth Tosh S; m 1964 to Sara Brooke Wilson; c Charles Alexander, Brooke VanGeem & Kristan Wilson. Educ: Case Western Reserve Univ, BS, 55; Univ Mich, JD, 61; Theta Tau; Phi Delta Phi; Pi Delta Epsilon; Beta Theta Pi. Polit & Govt Pos: Co-chmn, John J Gilligan Gubernatorial Campaign, Cuyahoga Co, Ohio, 70; mem, Ohio State & Cuyahoga Co Dem Exec Comts, currently; dep registr motor vehicles, Cuyahoga Co, 71-75; cand for deleg to Dem Nat Conv on Muskie Slate, 72; campaign dir, US Sen Howard M Metzenbaum, 74. Bus & Prof Pos: Partner, Zellmer & Gruber, Lawyers; secy & counsel, Community Telecasters of Cleveland, Inc, 63- Mil Serv: Entered as Ens, Navy, 55, released as Lt(jg), 58, after serv in Patrol Squadron 16 & Fleet Air Wing 11, Jacksonville, Fla, Iceland & Northern Europe, 55-58; Lt Comdr, Naval Res, 55-; Armed Serv Medal. Mem: Am & Ohio Bar Asns; Cleveland Bar Asn (mem legis comt, 68-); City Club. Relig: Episcopal. Legal Res: 3311 Maynard Ave Shaker Heights OH 44122 Mailing Add: 1010 Leader Bldg Cleveland OH 44114

SCHIMEK, DIANNA RUTH (D)
Committeewoman, Nebr Dem State Cent Comt
b Holdrege, Nebr, Mar 21, 40; d Ralph William Rebman & Elizabeth Julia Wilmot R; m 1963 to Herbert Henry Schimek; c Samuel Wolfgang & Saul William. Educ: Colo Woman's Col, AA, 60; Univ Nebr, Lincoln, 60-61; Nebr State Col, BA in Ed, magna cum laude, 63, grad work, 63-; Pi Gamma Mu. Polit & Govt Pos: Committeewoman, Nebr Dem State Cent Comt, 69-70, 72-; lobbyist & state telethon coordr, 74-75; vchairwoman, Adams Co Dem Party, 69-70; pres, Lancaster Co Dem Woman's Club, 74-; vpres, Nebr Fedn Dem Women, 74-; area rep, Nebr Dem State Exec Comt, 74; deleg, Dem Nat Mid-Term Conf, 74. Bus & Prof Pos: Teacher, Limon Pub Schs, Limon, Colo, 63-64; substitute teacher, Hastings Pub Schs, Hastings, Nebr, 64-65, 68-70, teacher, 65-68; substitute teacher, Lincoln Pub Schs, Lincoln, Nebr, 73- Mem: PEO; League Women Voters; Women's Polit Caucus; Order of Eastern Star. Honors & Awards: Outstanding Sr Award, Pi Gamma Mu, Nat Social Sci, 63. Relig: Unitarian. Mailing Add: 2321 Camelot Ct Lincoln NE 68512

SCHIMMEL, ALLAN D (R)
b Sioux Center, Iowa, June 18, 40; s A Arie Schimmel & Magdalena Scheffer S; single. Educ: Northwestern Col, BA, 62; Univ Iowa, MA, 66. Polit & Govt Pos: Legis asst, US Rep Fred Schwengel, Iowa, 63-64, admin asst, 67-73; admin asst to US Rep Howard W Robison, NY, 73-75. Mem: Am Polit Sci Asn; bd trustees, Northwestern Col. Relig: Protestant. Mailing Add: 413 W Hayes Davenport IA 52803

SCHINAGLE, ALLAN CHARLES (R)
Chmn, Geauga Co Rep Party, Ohio
b Cleveland, Ohio, June 7, 30; s Elmer William Schinagle & Mildred Handler S; m 1956 to Cynthia Robinson; c Cheryl Lynn, Allan Charles, Holly Anne & Penny Sue. Educ: Miami Univ, BS in BAdmin, 53; Sigma Alpha Epsilon; Delta Sigma Pi. Polit & Govt Pos: Precinct committeeman, Geauga Co Rep Party, Ohio, 69-, chmn, 71-; chmn, Geauga Co Rep Cent Comt, 70-74; chmn, Geauga Co Rep Exec Comt, 71- Bus & Prof Pos: Rep, Aetna Life, Cleveland, Ohio, 53-54 & Louisville, Ky, 54-65, mgr, Cleveland, 65-71, sr acct supvr, 71-74, sr acct exec, 74- Mil Serv: Entered as A/S, Navy, 48, released as Seaman 1/C, 49, after serv in USS William T Powell, 48-49. Mem: Rotary; YMCA (bd of mgrs); Ohio Asn Life Underwriters; Cleveland Growth Asn. Relig: Presbyterian. Mailing Add: Hillbrook Estate Lane East Hunting Valley OH 44072

SCHINDLER, ORVILLE (R)
NDak State Rep
Mailing Add: State Capitol Bismarck ND 58501

SCHIPPER, DORIS ANN (D)
VChmn, Ripley Co Dem Cent Comt, Ind
b Batesville, Ind, Apr 15, 43; d William Albert Gutzwiller & Elizabeth M Miller G; m 1975 to Gerald L Schipper. Educ: Xavier Univ (Ohio), night classes; Ind Univ Exten, night classes. Polit & Govt Pos: Secy-treas, Ripley Co Young Dem, Ind, 60-64; Dem precinct vcommitteeman, Batesville, 64-65, precinct committeeman, 65-; vpres, Ninth Dist Young Dem, 66-69, pres, 69-71; deleg, Ind State Dem Conv, 66, 68, 70 & 72; deleg, Dem Nat Conv, 72; pres, Ripley Co Women's Dem Club, 68-69; nat committeewoman, Ind State Young Dem, 69-73; mem, Ind Dem Platform Comt, 70 & 74, deleg, Young Polit Leaders Nat Foreign Policy Conf, State Dept, 70; mem campaign staff, Mary Aikens for Auditor of State, 70; Ripley Co coordr, Matt Welsh for Gov, 72; vchmn, Ripley Co Dem Cent Comt, 74- Bus & Prof Pos: Vpres, W A Gutzwiller Co, Inc, Batesville, Ind, 65-71; secy, Bruns-Gutzwiller, Inc, 72- Mem: Assoc Gen Contractors of Ind (legis comt, 70); Batesville CofC; Phi Beta Psi. Relig: Roman Catholic. Mailing Add: 106 S Second St Batesville IN 47006

SCHIRGER, WILLIAM EDWARD (D)
b Somerville, NJ, July 13, 35; s Joseph Charles Schirger & Veronica Jakubick S; m 1962 to Carolyn Ann Collins; c Suzanne, Kathleen & John. Educ: St Peter's Col, NJ, BS in Govt, 58; Univ Notre Dame, JD, 63. Polit & Govt Pos: Campaign coordr for Adlai Stevenson III, 66; asst attorney gen, State Ill, 66-69; chmn, Winnebago Co Dem Party, 68-74; assoc judge, Winnebago Co, 69. Bus & Prof Pos: Chmn bd, Northwest Publ Co, 67- Mil Serv: Entered as 2nd Lt, Army, 58, released as Capt, 65, after serv in Inf; Capt, Army Standby Res. Publ: Guide to Estate Planning, 63; Economic Rebirth of Germany, Pavaun, 57. Mem: Winnebago Co & Ill State Bar Asns; Am Trial Lawyers Asn; Comt Ill Govt (bd dirs); Elks. Relig: Catholic. Legal Res: 2504 Harlem Blvd Rockford IL 61103 Mailing Add: 704 N Church St Rockford IL 61101

SCHISLER, CAROLYN KAY (D)
Chairwoman, Fulton Co Dem Comt, Ill
b Galesburg, Ill, Mar 6, 34; d Charles Cochran & Carrie C; m 1957 to Gale Schisler; c Kimberley Joy, Pamela Jill & Kurt Jeffrey. Educ: Univ Ill, Urbana, 52-54; Delta Zeta. Polit & Govt Pos: Chairwoman, Fulton Co Dem Comt, Ill, 68-; deleg & co-chairperson Ill deleg, Dem Nat Mid-Term Conf, 74; committeewoman, 19th Dist State Cent Comt, Ill, 74- Bus & Prof Pos: Field inspection supvr, Secy of State, Springfield, 72- Mem: London Mills Woman's Club; London Mills Community Asn; Women of the Moose; Fulton Co League of Dem Women. Relig: United Methodist. Mailing Add: Box 114 London Mills IL 61544

SCHISLER, D GALE (D)
Ill State Rep
b Knox Co, Ill, Mar 2, 33; s D Claire Schisler & Doris Jacobs S; m 1957 to Carolyn K Cochran; c Kimberley Joy, Pamela Jill & Kurt Jeffrey. Educ: Western Ill Univ, BS in Educ, 59; NE Mo State Teachers Col, MA in sch admin, 62; West Ill Univ Alumni Asn. Polit & Govt Pos: US Rep, 19th Dist, Ill, 65-66; Ill State Rep, 69- Bus & Prof Pos: Teacher & coach, Elem & Jr High Schs, London Mills, Ill, 59-60, prin, 60-64. Mil Serv: Entered as A/B, Air Force, 52, released as Airman 1/C, 55; Good Conduct Medal. Mem: Spoon River Valley Teachers Asn; Mason, Shrine, Mohammed Temple; Am Legion; Amvets (life mem); Fulton Co Farm Bur. Honors & Awards: Mem European Serv Volleyball Championship Team; France All Star Football Team. Relig: Methodist. Mailing Add: Box 114 London Mills IL 61544

SCHLEF, EARL L (D)
Mo State Rep
Mailing Add: 1672 Maldon Lane Dellwood MO 63301

SCHLEICHER, BEN T (R)
b Rockford, Ill, Oct 10, 16; m 1936 to Evelyn Waltz; c Ben K & Sally Jo (Mrs Ross). Educ: Rockford Cent High Sch, dipl, 34. Polit & Govt Pos: Supv for Gov Woodward, Rockford,

Ill, 37-57; alderman, Seventh Ward, Rockford, Ill, 48-57, mayor, formerly. Relig: Lutheran. Mailing Add: City Hall 425 E State Rockford IL 61604

SCHLEIN, BETTY GOLDMAN (D)
VChairwoman, NY State Dem Cent Comt
b Brooklyn, NY, Apr 1, 31; d Paul Goldman & Estelle Oremland G; m 1953 to Richard Schlein; c Carol, Alan & Michael. Educ: Cornell Univ, BA, 52; Columbia Univ, MA, 53; Alpha Epsilon Phi. Polit & Govt Pos: Committeewoman, Nassau Co Dem Party, 13th Assembly Dist, 55th Elec Dist, NY, 70-; deleg, Dem Nat Conv, 72; committeewoman, NY State Dem Cent Comt, 13th Assembly Dist, 72-, vchairwoman, 74- Mem: Nat Orgn for Women (polit action coordr, Long Island Chap, 70-, pres, 73-); Am for Dem Action (bd dirs, 71-); Am Civil Liberties Union (bd dirs, Nassau Chap, 71-). Relig: Jewish. Mailing Add: 2261 Helene Ave Merrick NY 11566

SCHLENKER, GERALD (D)
Mem, Calif Dem State Cent Comt
b Buffalo, NY, Dec 6, 36; s Elmer C Schlenker & Marie Lexner S; m 1957 to Elizabeth Bye; c Sandra. Educ: NY Univ Col, Buffalo, BS, 62; San Diego State Col, MA, 68; Kappa Delta Pi; Phi Alpha Theta. Polit & Govt Pos: Nominee for Calif State Assemblyman, 76th Assembly Dist, 68; mem, San Diego Co Dem Cent Comt, Calif, 68-; mem, Calif Dem State Cent Comt, 68-; pres, Downtown Dem of San Diego, Calif, 69-; chmn, Educators for Sen James R Mills, 40th Sen Dist, 70. Bus & Prof Pos: Teacher, Sweet Home Cent Schs, Calif, 62-63, Sweet Water United High Sch Dist, 63-70; bd dirs, Combined Health Agencies, San Diego, 69-; asst prin, San Dieguito United High Sch Dist, 70- Mil Serv: Entered as Airman Basic, Air Force, 54, released as Airman 2/C, 58, after serv in 30th Air Transport Squadron, Mil Air Transport Serv; Good Conduct Medal; Air Crew Members Badge. Publ: The internment of the Japanese, Star News, 5/68. Mem: Am Fedn of Teachers; bd dirs, Multiple Sclerosis Soc, San Diego, 69-; Econ Educ Coun; Calif Asn Sec Sch Adminr; South Bay Hist Soc. Honors & Awards: One of San Diego's Ten Outstanding Young Men, 68. Relig: United Church of Christ. Mailing Add: 6564 Jackson Dr San Diego CA 92119

SCHLESINGER, JAMES RODNEY (R)
Secy of Defense
b New York, NY, Feb 15, 29; s Julius Schlesinger & Rhea Rogen S; m 1954 to Rachel Mellinger; c Cora K, Charles L, Ann R, William F, Emily, Thomas S, Clara & James R. Educ: Harvard Univ, AB in Econ summa cum laude, 50, Frederick Sheldon Prize fel, 50-51, AM in Econ, 52, PhD in Econ, 56; Phi Beta Kappa. Polit & Govt Pos: Acad consult, Naval War Col, 57, consult bd gov, Fed Reserve Bd, 62-63; consult, Bur of the Budget, 65-69, asst dir, 69-70, acting dep dir, 69-70; asst dir, Off of Mgt & Budget, 70-71; chmn, Atomic Energy Comn, 71-73; dir, Cent Intel Agency, 73; Secy of Defense, 73- Bus & Prof Pos: Asst prof econ, Univ Va, 55-58, assoc prof, 58-63; sr staff mem, Rand Corp, Santa Monica, Calif, 63-67, dir strategic studies, 67-69. Publ: The Political Economy of National Security, Frederick A Praeer, 60; Organizational Structures & Planning, Nat Bur of Econ Research, 67, reprint from Issues in Defense Economics distributed by Columbia Univ Press; Systems analysis & the political process, J Law & Econ, 10/68. Relig: Lutheran. Mailing Add: 3601 26th St N Arlington VA 22207

SCHLICKMAN, EUGENE F (R)
Ill State Rep
b Dubuque, Iowa, Dec 17, 29; s Leander L Schlickman & Helen Juergens S; m 1951 to Margaret J Muraski; c J Andrew, Stephen E, Mary Elizabeth & Monica Ann. Educ: Loras Col, Dubuque, Iowa, BA, 51; Georgetown Univ Law Ctr, LLB, 56. Polit & Govt Pos: Statistician, Dept Labor, 52-53; trustee, Arlington Heights, Ill, 59-64; Ill State Rep, 65-, chmn, Elem & Sec Nonpublic Schs & Zoning Laws Study Comns & Legis Adv Comt to Northeastern Ill Planning Comn, Ill House Rep; Wheeling Twp Rep Committeeman, 66-69. Bus & Prof Pos: Asst to exec vpres, Corn Indust Research Found, 53-56; research dir, Nat Foundry Asn, 56-60; labor rels specialist, Ekco Prod Co, 60-64; partner, Burfeind & Schlickman, 64- Publ: Labor relations in foundry industries, Labor Law J, 7/57; Suburban Cook County politics, New City, 11/65. Mem: Am, Ill & Northwest Suburban Bar Asns; KofC; CofC. Honors & Awards: John Howard Asn Award, 67; Outstanding Legislator Award, Rutgers Univ, 66; Jaycee Man of the Year, Arlington Heights, Ill, 60. Relig: Roman Catholic. Legal Res: 1219 E Clarendon Arlington Heights IL 60004 Mailing Add: 116 W Eastman Arlington Heights IL 60004

SCHLIENTZ, KENNETH M (R)
NMex State Sen
Mailing Add: Box 1005 Tucumcari NM 88401

SCHLITZ, LESTER E (D)
Va State Deleg
Mailing Add: PO Box 1137 Portsmouth VA 23705

SCHLOR, GEORGE F (D)
Del State Sen
Mailing Add: 114 N Franklin St Wilmington DE 19805

SCHLOSSER, JAMES DOUGLAS (R)
b Jamestown, NDak, Aug 13, 37; s Reynold Martin Schlosser & Marie Huilk S; m 1962 to Sharon Jean Martin; c Leslie Anne, Lynne Marie, Laurie Kay & Mark Allen. Educ: Marquette Univ, Milwaukee, Wis, 55-56; St John's Univ, Minn, BA in polit sci, 59; Univ NDak Sch Law, JD, 62; Law Rev Staff; Phi Alpha Delta. Polit & Govt Pos: Chmn, Univ NDak Young Rep, 59-61; Rep campaign dir, Stutsman Co, 60; mem exec comt, Midwest Col Fedn Young Rep, 60-62; mem exec comt, NDak Young Rep, 60-68, chmn, 61-63 & vchmn, 62-64; asst state attorney, Stutsman Co, 62-63; exec secy, NDak Rep Party, 63-65; ed, NDak Young Rep Spokesman, 65-67; asst attorney gen, NDak, 65-73; campaign dir, Rep Tom Kleppe, Second Dist NDak 66 & 68; chmn, NDak Rep Conv, 72. Publ: Assoc ed, The campus conscience magazine, 61; Eminent domain & land condemnation in North Dakota, NDak Law Rev, 1/62. Mem: YMCA (bd dirs, 68-, pres, 73-74); Mary Col, Bismarck, NDak, (trustee, 69-); Elks; Eagles; KofC. Honors & Awards: Gov, Boys State, 54; King, Univ NDak Law Sch, 62; Outstanding Sr Award, 62; Little All-Am Football, 54; Prin research asst, Agr Law Inst, 61-62; Chosen Outstanding Young Man, Bismarck, NDak & NDak, 69. Relig: Catholic. Legal Res: 1017 Cottage Dr Bismarck ND 58501 Mailing Add: Box 1762 Bismarck ND 58501

SCHLOSSTEIN, FREDERIC W, JR (D)
Mass State Sen
Mailing Add: State Capitol Boston MA 02133

SCHLOTFELDT, RICHARD DANIEL (D)
b Vancouver, Wash, Dec 20, 42; s Fredrick Joseph Schlotfeldt & Rose Monahan S; single. Educ: Univ Colo, Boulder, summers 65 & 66; Univ Portland, BA, 65; Cath Univ Am, 66-67; Univ Md, College Park, MS, 73. Polit & Govt Pos: Alt deleg, Dem Nat Conv, 72. Bus & Prof Pos: Assoc sci programmer, Sperry Univac, 67-68, sci programmer, 68-71, sr syst design engr, 72- Mem: Asn Comput Mach; Inst Elec & Electronics Eng; Common Cause; Prince Georges Co Young Dem. Relig: Roman Catholic. Mailing Add: Apt 805 6200 Westchester Park Dr College Park MD 20740

SCHLUETER, IRENE SELMA (R)
Chmn, Marathon Co Rep Party, Wis
b Rib Falls, Wis, Apr 9, 12; d August Schlueter & Anna Schulz S; single. Educ: Marathon Co Normal Sch, Wis, grad, 29. Polit & Govt Pos: Pres, Marathon Co Rep Women, Wis, 65-70; Rep precinct committeeman, Wausau, 66-68 & 72; vchmn, Marathon Co Rep Party, 69-70, chmn, 70- Bus & Prof Pos: Elem sch teacher, Berlin, Wis, 29-31; ins clerk, Employers Ins Co of Wausau, 31-36, off supvr, Milwaukee, 36-39 & New York, 39-41, syst analyst, Wausau, 41-59, comput prog analyst, 59-61, mgr comput prog, 61-64, research analyst-mkt, 64-70 & educ programmer, 70- Mem: Altrusa Club of Wausau, Inc; Mayor's Comn on Status of Women; Wausau Area Taxpayer's League (pres 74-); Wausau Hosp Vols (pres, 75-); Marathon Co Hist Soc (secy, 72-). Relig: Lutheran. Mailing Add: 3203 11th St Wausau WI 54401

SCHLUTER, NANCY HURD (R)
Committeewoman, NJ State Rep Comt
b Buffalo, NY, Jan 1, 29; d Laurance Lankler Hurd & Nancy Albright H; m 1950 to William Everett Schluter; c William E, Jr, Nancy C, Sally Ruth, Peter Laurance, Stephen Albright & Philip H. Educ: Smith Col, 3 years; Univ Buffalo, 1 year. Polit & Govt Pos: Pres & co-founder, Hopewell Valley Young Rep, 58-59; treas & vpres, Mercer Co Young Rep, 58-61; pres & founder, Mercer Co Women's Rep Fedn, 61-65; committeewoman, Mercer Co Rep Comt, 65-; vpres, NJ Fedn Rep Women, 65-74, chmn, A Day for the President, 72; committeewoman, NJ State Rep Comt, 65-; munic chmn, Pennington Rep Party, 66-; women's chmn, NJ Presidential Campaign, 68; mem, NJ State Health Planning Coun, 71-; mem, NJ Rep State Platform Comt, 71; co chmn, Re-elect the President Comt; vchmn, Mercer Co Charter Study Comn, 73-74. Honors & Awards: State Award for Efforts on Behalf of Soviet Jewry, Jewish War Vet, 72. Relig: Presbyterian. Mailing Add: 205 S Main St Pennington NJ 08534

SCHMA, DONALD WILLIAM (R)
Chmn, Monterey Co Rep Cent Comt, Calif
b Evanston, Ill, July 16, 32; s John William Schma & Suzanne Kremer S; m 1956 to Marjorie Bray Cohen; c Douglas, Kathryn, Jennifer, Peter, Elizabeth & Sarah. Educ: Purdue Univ, Lib Arts, 53; Northwestern Univ, DDS, 57; Univ Calif, San Francisco, postgrad work, 58; Phi Gamma Delta; Delta Sigma Delta. Polit & Govt Pos: Mem, Rep State Cent Comt Calif, 68-; mem, Monterey Co Rep Cent Comt, 68-69 & chmn, 69-; mem, Calif Co Chmn Asn; chmn, 34th Assembly Rep Comt; area coordr, Ronald Reagan for Gov Campaign, 70. Bus & Prof Pos: Dentist, self-employed, 57-; trustee, Northwood Inst, Midland, Mich, 72-, pres, currently. Mil Serv: Entered as Ens, Navy, 56, released as Lt, 60, after serv in Fleet Activities, Sasebo, Japan. Mem: Calif & Am Dent Asns; Monterey Inst Foreign Studies, (trustee, 69-); Int Platform Asn; Commonwealth Club, Calif; Anti-Poverty Coord Coun (exec bd). Relig: Roman Catholic. Legal Res: Ronda Rd Pebble Beach CA 93953 Mailing Add: 400 Pacific Monterey CA 93940

SCHMAEDECKE, WILLIAM L (R)
Ky State Rep
Mailing Add: PO Box 546 Covington KY 41011

SCHMALZL, KURT CHARLES (R)
Secy, Logan Co Rep Cent Comt, Ill
b Lincoln, Ill, Mar 21, 06; s Johann C Schmalzl & Anna Louise Ziegler S; m 1928 to Lois Naoma McKinney. Educ: High Sch, class 25. Polit & Govt Pos: Justice of the Peace, East Lincoln Twp, Ill, 46-50; town auditor, East Lincoln, 60-; vchmn, Logan Co Rep Cent Comt, 48-52, secy, 52- Mem: Nat Asn Independent Ins Agents; Nat Asn Mutual Ins Agents. Relig: Evangelical Lutheran Church Mo Synod. Mailing Add: 503 N Sherman St Lincoln IL 62656

SCHMIDHAUSER, JOHN RICHARD (D)
b Bronx, NY, Jan 3, 22; married; c Steven, Paul, Thomas, John Christopher, Martha, Sarah & Susan. Educ: Univ Del, BA, 49; Univ Va, MA, 52, PhD, 54; Phi Beta Phi; Phi Beta Kappa. Polit & Govt Pos: Precinct committeeman & chmn, Johnson Co Dem Party, Iowa; US Rep, Iowa, 64-66; mem, Nat Comt on Tax Justice, formerly. Bus & Prof Pos: Prof polit sci, Univ Iowa, 54-73; prof polit sci & chmn dept, Univ Southern Calif, 73-; assoc ed, Pub Law & Judicial Behavior, Western Polit Quart, 73- Mil Serv: Enlisted man in US Navy including duty on the aircraft carrier USS Bon Homme Richard, Philippine campaign, the Battle of Okinawa, & final assault on Japan under Adm Halsey, Aug 1941 to Dec 1945. Publ: Constitutional Law in the Political Process, Rand McNally, 63; Congress & the Supreme Court (w Larry L Berg), Free Press, Macmillan, 71; co-auth, Political Corruption in America (w Larry L Berg & Harlan Hahn), Gen Learning Publ Co, 75; plus others. Mem: Am Asn of Univ Profs; Am Polit Sci Asn. Honors & Awards: Univ Va Sesquicentennial Award for Pub Serv, 1969. Relig: Unitarian Church. Mailing Add: 136 W 64th Place Inglewood CA 90302

SCHMIDT, ADOLPH WILLIAM (R)
b McKeesport, Pa, Sept 13, 04; s Adolph Schmidt & Louise S; m 1936 to Helen S Mellon; c Helen S M (Mrs William F Claire) & Thomas M. Educ: Princeton Univ, AB, 26; Harvard Univ, MBA, 29; Univ Dijon, Univ Berlin & Univ Paris, Cert, 26-27. Hon Degrees: LLD, Univ Pittsburgh, 54, Univ NB, 73; LHD, Chatham Col, 65. Polit & Govt Pos: Chmn, Pa State Planning Bd, 55-67; US deleg to Atlantic Cong, London, 59 & to Atlantic Conv of NATO Nations, Paris, 62; adv, US deleg to Econ Comn for Europe, Geneva, 67; dir, Population Crisis Comt, Washington, DC, 67-69 & Environ Fund, 73-; US Ambassador to Can, 69-74. Bus & Prof Pos: Officer, Mellon Nat Bank & affiliated orgns, Pittsburgh, Pa, 29-42; trustee, Old Dominion Found, 41-69; vpres & gov, T Mellon & Sons, Pittsburgh, Pa, 46-69; pres & trustee, A W Mellon Educ & Charitable Trust, 50-65; chmn bd of visitors & gov, St John's Col (Md), 56 & 62; mem grad coun, Princeton Univ, 56-59; trustee, Carnegie Inst, currently.

Mil Serv: Entered as Capt, Army, 42, released as Lt Col, 46, after serv in Inf, Off Strategic Serv, African & European Theatres & Allied Control Comn, Berlin; Bronze Star; two Battle Stars. Mem: Atlantic Inst, Paris; Southwestern Pa Regional Planning Comn (chmn); Pittsburgh Regional Planning Asn (dir); Urban Redevelop Authority (vchmn); Atlantic Coun of the US, Washington, DC. Honors & Awards: David Glick Award, World Affairs Coun, 64; Benjamin Rush Award, Allegheny Co Med Soc. Relig: Presbyterian. Mailing Add: RD 4 Ligonier PA 15658

SCHMIDT, ALEXANDER MACKAY
Comnr, Food & Drug Admin
b Jamestown, NDak, Jan 26, 30; s Theodore G Schmidt & Marion W MacKay S; m 1952 to Patricia Ann White; c Susan Jane & Sarah Ann. Educ: Northwestern Univ, BS, 51; Univ Utah Col Med, MD, 55, Affiliated Hosps, intern med, 55-56, resident, 58-60, Col Med, research fel cardiol, Dept Internal Med, 60-62; Alpha Omega Alpha. Polit & Govt Pos: Chief continuing educ & training br, Div Regional Med Progs, Nat Insts Health, 67-68; mem, Utah State Gov Comt on Eradication of Tuberc & Air Pollution; mem med educ comt, Health Educ Comn, Ill State Bd Higher Educ, 68-; mem, Health Facil & Resources Task Force, Comprehensive Health Care Planning, 69-; mem rev comt, Ill Regional Med Progs; co-chmn rev comt, Div Regional Med Progs, Health Serv & Ment Health Admin, 70-; co-chmn, State Ill Interagency Task Force on Health Manpower, 71-; mem, Nat Task Forces in Areas of Adult Educ, Continuing Educ, Med Sch Affairs; comnr, Food & Drug Admin, 73- Bus & Prof Pos: Instr med, Univ Utah Col Med, 62-64, dir cardiovascular lab, 62-68, lectr physiol, 64-66, instr, 66-68, dir planning, Cardiovascular Research & Training Ctr, 66-67 & asst dean, Col Med, 67-68; exec assoc dean & assoc prof med, Univ Ill Col Med, 69-70 & prof med & dean, Abraham Lincoln Sch Med, 70-73. Mil Serv: Army, 56-58. Publ: Hemodynamic effects of exercise in patients with aortic stneosis (w F L Anderson, T J Tsagaris, G Tikoff, J L Thorne & H Kuida), Am J Med, 46: 872; auth, The university and social needs of the 70's, Ill Med J, Vol 137, No 2 & Medical education without schools, In: The Changing Medical Curriculum, Josiah Macy, Jr Found, 72; plus others. Mem: Am Fedn Clin Res; Am & Utah Thoracic Soc; Am Med Asn; Utah Co Med Soc. Honors & Awards: John & Mary R Markle Scholar in Acad Med; Best Teacher Award, Class of 1968. Legal Res: 5307 Wapakoneta Rd Bethesda MD 22016 Mailing Add: Rm 14-81 5600 Fishers Lane Rockville MD 20852

SCHMIDT, ARTHUR LOUIS (R)
Ky State Rep
b Cold Spring, Ky, May 1, 27; s Joseph Edwin Schmidt & Elizabeth Bertsch S; m 1951 to Marian Seibert; c Karen Ann & Marianne. Educ: Univ Ky, 57-58. Polit & Govt Pos: Treas, Campbell Co Young Rep Party, 57; co chmn, Campbell Co Young Rep, 58 & 59; state chmn, Young Rep Clubs of Ky, 59 & 60; mem, Ky State Rep Cent Comt, 60-; city coun, Cold Spring, 62 & 63; Ky State Rep, 64, 65 & 68-; deleg, Rep Nat Conv, 64, 68 & 72; mem, Tax Appeal Bd, Cold Spring, 66. Bus & Prof Pos: Plant dept, Cincinnati Bell Tel Co, 46-55, commun consult, 55-58, eng tech, 58-62 & mkt develop supvr, 62; mem bd dir, Lakeside Place Home for the Aged, 62 & 63; mem bd dir, Bank of Alexandria, 67-; mem bd dir, Northern Ky CofC, currently. Mil Serv: Entered as A/S, Navy, 45, released as Seaman 1/C, 46, after serv in Asiatic Pac Area, 45-46; Victory Medal; Am Area Campaign Medal; Asiatic Pac Area Campaign Medal; Japan Occup Medal. Mem: KofC; Holy Name Soc; YMCA; Lakeside Place Asn; United Appeal (chmn). Relig: Catholic. Mailing Add: 134 Winters Lane Cold Spring KY 41076

SCHMIDT, EARL WILLIAM (R)
Wis State Rep
b Birnamwood, Wis, Mar 11, 36; s Frederick William Schmidt & Erma Laura Kufahl S; m 1974 to Judy Diane Eckardt; c Jill. Educ: Univ Wis-Madison, BS, 62, MS, 64. Polit & Govt Pos: Wis State Rep, 75- Bus & Prof Pos: Dist attorney, Shawano & Menominee Co. Mem: Am, Wis State & Shawano Co Bar Asns. Relig: Lutheran. Mailing Add: Rte 3 Box 1-C Shawano WI 54166

SCHMIDT, FREDERICK D (D)
NY State Assemblyman
b Queens, NY, June 30, 32; m to Julia Casassa; c four. Educ: Holy Trinity High Sch; St John's Col. Polit & Govt Pos: NY State Assemblyman, 64-72, 75- Bus & Prof Pos: Trial attorney, firm of Terhune, Gibbons, & Muluehill. Mil Serv: 1st Lt, Marine Corps. Mem: NY State Bar Asn; Fordham Law Alumni; St Thomas Holy Name Soc; Moose; Am Legion; Steben Soc; hon mem, Richhaven Little League; chmn, Interfaith Christmas Procession. Mailing Add: 85-14 86th St Woodhaven NY 11421

SCHMIDT, RONALD GARRARD (R)
b Turlock, Calif, Apr 22, 36; s Reinhold Schmidt & Gertrude Kerley S; div. Educ: San Jose State Col, BA, Pub Rels, 59; Blue Shield; Alpha Tau Omega. Polit & Govt Pos: Admin asst, Gov Tom McCall, Ore, 67-74; mem, President's Adv Comt on Arts, 70-; chmn, Ore Traffic Safety Comn, formerly; mem, Adv Comt to John F Kennedy Ctr for Performing Arts, Washington, DC, currently; founding dir, Portland Ctr for Visual Arts; mem, Gov Comt on Interstate Coop, currently. Bus & Prof Pos: Vpres pub rels, William Dawkins & Assocs, Portland & Medford, Ore, 59-60; pub rels counr, Pub Rels Counr, San Francisco, Calif, 60-61; pub rels dir, Lloyd Ctr, Portland, Ore, 61-67. Mem: Pub Rels Soc Am; Ore Newspaper Publ Asn; Univ Club of Portland; City Club of Portland; Portland Art Asn. Honors & Awards: Award of Excellence, Pub Rels Soc of Am, 61. Relig: Episcopal. Mailing Add: 688 Rural Ave S Salem OR 97302

SCHMIT, LORAN (R)
Nebr State Sen
b Butler Co, Nebr, Aug 13, 29; m 1950 to Irene JoAnn Squire; c Marcia, Steven, Mary, Julie, John, Michele, Susan, Jeanie, Lori & Mike. Educ: Univ Nebr, BS, 50. Polit & Govt Pos: Chmn, Butler Co Rep Party, Nebr, formerly; Nebr State Sen, Dist 23, 69- Bus & Prof Pos: Pres, Mid-Am Helicopter Serv, Inc, currently; Owner, Farm, Butler Co, Nebr, currently. Relig: Catholic. Legal Res: Box 121 Bellwood NE 68624 Mailing Add: State Capitol Lincoln NE 68509

SCHMIT, NICHOLAS MATTHEW (NICK) (D)
Chmn, 26th Dist Dem Non-Partisan League Exec Comt, NDak
b Wyndmere, NDak, s Nicholas Schmit Sr & Rose Woodle S; m 1942 to Eleanore Klosterman; c Kairouan (Mrs Moffett), Mary, Nicholas M, III, Anthony & Patricia. Educ: Wyndmere Public Schools. Polit & Govt Pos: NDak State Sen, 53-55; city councilman, Wyndmere, NDak, 54-56; mem adv comt, NDak Dem Non-Partisan League Legis Group, 66-; mem exec comt, NDak Dem Non-Partisan League Century Club, 67-; alt deleg, Dem Nat Conv, 68; campaign comt mem, US Senate Comt, 68; mem, NDak Dem Non-Partisan League Exec Comt, 68-; chmn, 26th Dist Dem Non-Partisan League Exec Comt, currently; deleg, NDak State Const Conv, 70. Bus & Prof Pos: Pres, Schmit Inc, Wyndmere, NDak, 61- Mil Serv: QmC, Army, 42-45; Marksmanship Medal. Mem: NDak Bldg Mover's Asn; Elks; Am Legion; KofC; Wyndmere Commercial Club. Relig: Roman Catholic. Mailing Add: Wyndmere ND 58081

SCHMITT, C L (D)
Pa State Rep
b Pittsburgh, Pa, May 8, 12; s Ludwig Schmitt & Hattie Primbs S; m 1935 to Sally Lou Byers; c Patty Lou (Mrs Martini), James P, Susan J & David L. Educ: Univ Pittsburgh. Polit & Govt Pos: Mem city coun, New Kensington, Pa, 50-54; Pa State Rep, 64- Bus & Prof Pos: Owner, C L Schmitt Real Estate & Ins, 44- Mem: Soc Real Estate Appraisers (SRA Degree); New Kensington Bd Realtors (past pres); Lions Int (Int counr, 44-); KofC; Moose; Holy Name Soc. Relig: Catholic. Mailing Add: 1015 Edgewood Rd New Kensington PA 15068

SCHMITT, EARL JOSEPH (D)
La State Rep
Mailing Add: 606 Opelousas Ave New Orleans LA 70114

SCHMITT, JOHN WILLIAM (D)
Mem-At-Large, Dem Nat Comt
b Milwaukee, Wis, Feb 3, 20; s Joseph Charles Schmitt & Margaret Nowak S; m to Anna Stockman; c James John, Jane Catherine, Jeffrey Robert & John Joseph. Educ: Univ Wis Exten, 39-40. Polit & Govt Pos: Alt deleg, Dem Nat Conv, 68; Mem-at-large, Dem Nat Comt, 72- Bus & Prof Pos: Corresponding & recording secy, Brewery Workers AFL-CIO, 52-60; exec vpres, Wis State AFL-CIO, 60-66, pres, 66- Mil Serv: Entered as Pvt, Army, 42, released as Sgt, 45, after serv in Hq Fifth Army, Africa-Italy Theatre, 43-45; Good Conduct medal; Two Battle Stars; Am Theatre Ribbon; Europe-Africa-Middle East Theatre Ribbon; Four Overseas Serv Bars; One Serv Stripe, Victory Medal. Mem: Milwaukee Co Planning Comn; Wis Adv Comt Unemploy Compensation & Workmen's Compensation; Wis Equal Employ Opportunity Asn; Nat Conf Christians & Jews; Cath Interracial Coun. Relig: Catholic. Legal Res: 6155 W Goodrich Ln Milwaukee WI 53223 Mailing Add: 6333 W Bluemound Rd Milwaukee WI 53213

SCHMITZ, JOE W (D)
Chmn, Carroll Co Dem Comt, Iowa
b Carroll, Iowa, July 23, 32; s Henry Schmitz & Sophia S; m 1951 to Esther Niehus; c Diane, Debra, Doan, Dan, Dorene, Donna, Denise & Darlene. Polit & Govt Pos: Twp clerk, Carroll Co, Iowa, 8 years; chmn, Carroll Co Dem Comt, currently. Bus & Prof Pos: Farmer, currently. Mem: KofC; Elks. Relig: Catholic. Mailing Add: RR 1 Carroll IA 51401

SCHMITZ, JOHN G (R)
b Milwaukee, Wis, Aug 12, 30; s Jacob J Schmitz & Wilhelmina Frueh S; m 1954 to Mary E Suehr; c John P, Joseph E, Jerome T, Mary Kay, Theresa Ann, Elizabeth L & Philip J. Educ: Marquette Univ, BS, 52; Long Beach State Col, MA, 60; Claremont Grad Sch, 61-66; Phi Alpha Theta. Polit & Govt Pos: Mem, bd dirs, Orange Co Conserv Coord Coun, formerly; faculty adv, Santa Ana Col Young Rep, formerly; chmn, Orange Co Coord Rep Assembly, twice; mem, Calif Rep Assembly, United Rep of Calif & Calif Young Rep; Calif State Sen, Orange Co, 64-66, 34th Sen Dist, 66-70; chmn local govt comt, Calif State Sen, formerly; presidential cand for Am Independent Party, 72. Bus & Prof Pos: Instr philos, hist & polit sci, Santa Ana Col, 60- Mil Serv: Entered as Officers Cand, Marine Corps, 52, released as Cpl, 60, after serv in VMF 114, VMO 2 & others, Cherry Point, NC, Okinawa, Japan & El Toro, Calif, 54-60; Lt Col, Marine Corps Res, currently. Mem: Am Legion; Mil Order of World Wars; KofC; Order of the Alhambra; John Birch Soc. Honors & Awards: Statesman of the Year Award, We The People, Phoenix, Ariz; Man of the Year Award, Cong of Freedom, 72; Outstanding Citizen Award, Am Citizens of German Descent, 72. Relig: Roman Catholic. Legal Res: 10 Mission Bay Dr Corona Del Mar CA 92625 Mailing Add: Dept of Political Science Santa Ana College Santa Ana CA 92706

SCHMITZ, ROBERT JOSEPH (DFL)
Minn State Sen
b Jordan, Minn, Apr 23, 21; s Jacob Schmitz & Mary Lambrecht S; m 1947 to Grace Savage; c Susan, Murray, Kristine, Robin & Karen. Educ: Jordan High Sch, grad. Polit & Govt Pos: Chmn, Scott Co Dem-Farmer-Labor Party, Minn, 63-66; supvr, Scott Soil & Water Conserv Dist, 66-74; chmn, 2nd Dist Dem-Farmer-Labor Party, Minn, 72-74; Minn State Sen, Dist 36, Scott & Carver Co, 74- Bus & Prof Pos: Chmn, Scott Co Farmers Union, 60-64; dir, Northwestern State Bank of Jordan, 66-; pres, New Prague Mutual Fire Ins Co, 68-74; owner, Schmitz Farm Equip, 69-; pres, Jordan Commercial Club, 73-74. Relig: Catholic. Mailing Add: RR 1 Jordan MN 55352

SCHMULTS, EDWARD C (R)
Under Secy of the Treas
b Paterson, NJ, Feb 6, 31; s Edward M Schmults & Mildred Moore S; m 1960 to Diane Beers; c Alison C, Edward M & Robert C. Educ: Yale Univ, BS, 53; Harvard Law Sch, LLB cum laude, 58. Polit & Govt Pos: Gen counsel, US Treas, 73-74, Under Secy of the Treas, 74- Bus & Prof Pos: Assoc, White & Case, Attorneys, New York, 58-65, partner, 65-73. Mil Serv: Entered as 2nd Lt, Marines, 53, released as 1st Lt, 55, after serv in 3rd Marine Div; Capt, Marine Res. Publ: Various articles in legal publ on corp & securities law subjects. Mem: Various prof orgns. Honors & Awards: Treasury's Alexander Hamilton Award. Relig: Episcopal. Mailing Add: 7301 Brennon Lane Chevy Chase MD 20015

SCHNAITTER, SPENCER J (D)
Ind State Rep
Mailing Add: 449 Bellaire Dr Madison IN 47251

SCHNATMEIER, OMAR LOUIS (R)
Mo State Rep
b St Charles, Mo, July 21, 08; s August F Schnatmeier & Mary Teckemeier S; m 1936 to May L Bohrer; c Karen (Mrs Ted Smith). Educ: Northeast Mo State Univ; Washington Univ. Polit & Govt Pos: Sheriff, St Charles Co, Mo, 41-45; Mo State Rep, Dist 52, 51-53 & 72-; US marshal, Eastern Dist Mo, 53-61; police judge, St Charles, Mo, 63-72. Bus & Prof Pos: Ed & publ, St Charles Publ Co, Mo, 45-49; personnel adminr, McDonnell-Douglas Corp, St Louis, 61-74. Mem: Masons; charter & life mem St Charles Hist Soc. Relig: United Church of Christ. Mailing Add: 1901 Elm St St Charles MO 63301

SCHNEEBELI, HERMAN THEODORE (R)
US Rep, Pa
b Lancaster, Pa, July 7, 07; s Alfred Schneebeli & Barbara Schneider S; m 1939 to Mary Louise Meyer; c Marta & Susan. Educ: Dartmouth Col, AB, 30; Amos Tuck Sch, Dartmouth Grad Sch, MCS in Bus Admin, 31; Theta Delta Chi. Polit & Govt Pos: Mem, Williamsport Sch Bd, Pa, formerly; US Rep, Pa, 60- Bus & Prof Pos: Comn distributor, Gulf Oil Corp, 39-; Buick automobile dealer, Muncy Motor Co, 48-65; dir, Fidelity Nat Bank of Williamsport, 58-72. Mil Serv: Entered as Lt, Army, 42, released as Capt, 46, after serv in Ord Dept as Exec & Commanding Officer, three different high explosive plants, US. Mem: Williamsport Hosp (bd mgrs); Williamsport Indust Comt; Am Legion; Elks; Kiwanis. Honors & Awards: Recipient Meritorious Community Serv Award presented by Grit. Relig: Episcopal; Vestryman. Legal Res: 870 Hollywood Circle Williamsport PA 17701 Mailing Add: 1336 Longworth House Office Bldg Washington DC 20515

SCHNEIDER, ALLAN IVAN (R)
b Scotland, Nov 15, 29; s Ivan Earp Schneider & Jean Simpson S; m 1963 to Margaret Varner; c David, Sandra, Bruce & Laura. Educ: Baylor Univ, LLB, 58; Phi Delta Phi. Polit & Govt Pos: Co Chmn, Rep Party Tex, formerly. Bus & Prof Pos: Attorney-at-law, 58-66. Mil Serv: Entered as Pvt, Air Force, 47, released as T/Sgt. Mem: Tex State Bar Asn; Rotary; CofC. Relig: Methodist. Legal Res: 489 Schneider Giddings TX 78942 Mailing Add: Box 87 Giddings TX 78942

SCHNEIDER, CURT THOMAS (D)
Attorney Gen, Kans
b Coffeyville, Kans, Oct 12, 44; s John William Schneider & Ellen Fern Haddock S; m 1972 to Barbara Marie Gonzales. Educ: Coffeyville Jr Col, grad; Pittsburg State Col, grad; Univ Kans Law Sch, grad. Polit & Govt Pos: Attorney Gen, Kans, 75- Bus & Prof Pos: Chief of Litigation, Hwy Comn, Topeka, Kans, 69-72 & Attorney Gen Off, 72-75. Mem: Kans Drug Abuse Comn; Gov Comt on Criminal Admin; Nat Wildlife Fedn; Kans Univ Law Soc; Kans Univ Alumni Asn. Mailing Add: 1829 Pembroke Lane Topeka KS 66604

SCHNEIDER, J GLENN (D)
Ill State Sen
Mailing Add: 21 St Columbia St Naperville IL 60540

SCHNEIDER, JOHN DURBIN (D)
Mo State Sen
b St Louis, Mo, Mar 1, 37; s F John Schneider & Kathleen Durbin S; m 1961 to Mary Jo Steppan; c Anne Marie, John Steppan & Robert Durbin. Educ: St Louis Univ, BS & JD, 60; Phi Delta Phi. Polit & Govt Pos: Mo State Rep, Dist 26, 69-70; Mo State Sen, Dist 14, 70- Bus & Prof Pos: Attorney, Transit Casualty Co, 60-65, chief trial attorney, 65-70. Mil Serv: Entered as Pvt, Army, 61, released as Pfc, after serv in Res. Mem: St Louis Bar Asn. Relig: Catholic. Mailing Add: 2259 Ainsworth St Louis MO 63136

SCHNEIDER, MARLIN DALE (D)
Wis State Rep
b La Crosse, Wis, Nov 16, 42; s Donald M Schneider & Elva M Peterson S; m 1973 to Georgia Jean Johansen. Educ: Univ Wis-La Crosse, BS, 65; Univ Wis-Stevens Point, 68-; Sigma Tau Gamma. Polit & Govt Pos: Wis State Rep, 71- Bus & Prof Pos: Teacher, Lomira High Sch, Wis, 65-66; teacher, Lincoln High Sch, Wisconsin Rapids, 66-71. Mem: Nat Conf State Legis (mem intergovt rels comt); AF&AM (Local 610). Relig: Lutheran. Legal Res: 921 Washington St Wisconsin Rapids WI 54494 Mailing Add: 131A South State Capitol Madison WI 53702

SCHNEIDER, MORRIS H (D)
Mem, Nassau Co Dem Comt, NY
b New York, NY, Aug 15, 10; s Philip Schneider & Bessie Haas S; m 1937 to Estelle I Simon; c Alan & Betsy. Educ: St John's Univ, BS, 32, Sch Law, JD, 35; past pres, Sigma Lambda Tau. Polit & Govt Pos: Pres, Rockville Centre Dem Club, NY, 55-57; committeeman, Rockville Centre Zone, Dem Party, 55-; mem, Affiliated Young Dem, NY, 55-; trustee & mem, Citizens Party, Rockville Centre, 60-; mem, Nassau Co Comt for Aged, 64, Nassau Co Off Econ Opportunity & Nassau Co Youth Bds, 65-, Nassau Co Crime Coun, 67-, Nassau Co Health & Welfare Coun & Nassau Co Supreme Court Libr Bd; chmn & mem, Nassau Co Traffic Safety Coun; mem, Nassau-Suffolk Comprehensive Health Planning Coun; co attorney, Nassau Co, 65-71; mem, Nassau Co Dem Comt & leader, Rockville Centre Dem Orgn, currently; dir, Nassau Co Planning Comn, 71-72; corp counsel, Long Beach, NY, 74- Bus & Prof Pos: Exec secy & counsel, Metrop Contractors Asn, 41-62 & Nat Refrigeration & Air Conditioning Contractors Asn, 48-50. Mem: Herzl Lodge KofP (past chancellor); Mason; Nat Asn Co Civil Attorneys (dir, 67-); Nat Inst Munic Law Officers; NY State Co Attorneys Asn. Relig: Hebrew. Mailing Add: 386 Raymond St Rockville Centre NY 11570

SCHNEIRSOHN, ERIC ELI (D)
Mem, Calif Dem State & Cent Comt
b Montreal, Que, Nov 5, 26; s Soloman Schneirsohn & Frima Freedman S; m 1955 to Estey Evelyn Olsen; c Daniel, Frima, Karen, Michael, Julie & Victoria. Educ: Univ Southern Calif, 54; Calif State Univ, Los Angeles, BA, 55. Polit & Govt Pos: Dir, Coord Coun, 20th Cong Dist, Calif, 72-73; pres, Glendale Dem Club Forum, 72-74; deleg, Dem Nat Mid-Term Conf, 74; mem, Calif State & Cent Comts, currently. Bus & Prof Pos: Owner, London Book Co & Xanadu Interiors, 56-75; sr appraiser, Am Soc 69- Mil Serv: Pvt, Army, 44-45. Publ: Ed, Private Diaries & Letters of Captain Hall, London Book, 74; auth, Appraisal of manuscripts from Presidential papers to Hollywood movie & TV scripts, Am Soc Appraisers, 75. Mem: Rotary; Brand Cult Arts Asn; Am Acad Polit & Social Sci; Protect Our Mountains. Honors & Awards: Brom Medal, Sister City Comt, 72; Judge, Glendale Beautiful Comt, 73. Mailing Add: 2510 Gardner Pl Glendale CA 91206

SCHNELL, GARY LYNN (R)
Treas, NDak Young Rep
b Greeley, Colo, May 13, 51; s Raymond C Schnell & Geneva Grasl S; m 1972 to Jane M Noble. Educ: NDak State Univ, 69-72; Alpha Gamma Rho. Polit & Govt Pos: Pres, NDak State Univ Col Rep, 70-71; precinct committeeman, Dist 21, Precinct 12, 71-72; nat committeeman, NDak Young Rep, 71-73, treas, 73-; alt deleg, Rep Nat Conv, 72. Bus & Prof Pos: Campaign asst, Win with Wilhite Comt, 72; auctioneer, Schnell Livestock Auction Mkt, 72- Mem: Livestock Merchandising Inst (bd gov, 71-); Elks; NDak Stockmen's Asn. Honors & Awards: Jr world champion auctioneer, Nat Livestock Auction Mkts Asn, 70. Relig: Catholic. Mailing Add: Box 1209 Dickinson ND 58601

SCHNELLER, RICHARD FRANCIS (D)
Conn State Sen
b New York, NY, Mar 21, 22; s Julius Schneller & Helen Efros S; m 1946 to Nancy Suisman; c Deborah Pepper, Juliet Van Eenwyk & Marie. Educ: Yale Univ, BS, 43. Polit & Govt Pos: Mem & chmn, Regional Dist Four Bd of Educ, 53-63; mem bd trustees, Univ Conn, 57-65; mem, Essex, Conn Bd of Finance, 64-70; mem, Conn Dem State Platform Comt, 72-74; chmn, Essex Dem Town Comt, Conn, 71-; Conn State Sen, 20th Dist, 75- Bus & Prof Pos: Pres, Verplex Co, Essex, 46-72; pres, Marich Realty Corp, 72- Mil Serv: Entered as Midn, Navy, 43, Lt(jg), 46, after serv in Amphibious Forces, SPac, 44-45; Unit Citation. Mem: World Bus Coun; Chief Exec Forum. Legal Res: Crosstrees Hill Rd Essex CT 06426 Mailing Add: Box 205 West Ave Essex CT 06426

SCHOEBERLEIN, ALLAN L (AL) (R)
Ill State Rep
b Aurora, Ill. Educ: Bus Col. Polit & Govt Pos: Chmn & mem Kane Co Bd Supvr, Ill, 4 years; alderman, First Ward; mayor pro tem, 18 years; vpres, Ill Munic League, 16 years; Rep precinct committeeman, 32 years; chmn precinct orgn, 4 years; Ill State Rep, 62- Bus & Prof Pos: Salesman, All-Steel Equip Inc. Mem: Moose (fel degree); YMCA; Elks; Aurora Sportsmen's Club; active mem in numerous other civic & social orgns. Mailing Add: 1543 Downer Place Aurora IL 60506

SCHOECK, JEAN (D)
Secy, Wyo Dem State Cent Comt
b Rosiclare, Ill, Oct 14, 23; d Charles Leonard Schoeck & Viola Wilson S; single. Polit & Govt Pos: Secy to Mayors Ben Nelson & Ed Warren, 48-52; alt deleg, Dem Nat Conv, 52 & 56, deleg & mem, Comt on Selection of Chmn for Nat Conv, 60; secy to Sen Joseph C O'Mahoney, 54; secy to co attorney Walter B Phelan, 54-57; secy, Wyo Dem State Cent Comt, 57-61 & 62-; mem, Gov Adv Comt on Civil Defense, 59-60; secy to Theodore C Sorensen, Spec counsel to President John F Kennedy, 60-61; secy, Gov Herschler's Inaugural Comt, 75. Bus & Prof Pos: Secy to Teno Roncalio, state chmn, attorney & banker, 57-60; owner, Jeanne's Secretariat, Cheyenne, Wyo, 62- Publ: I've got 35,000 bosses, The Denver Post, 50; East meets West, Tavern Talk, 53; Out where the West begins, Seydell Quart, Belgium, 51. Mem: Eastern Star, Oak Leaf Chap; Beta Sigma Phi Epsilon Chap; Cheyenne Kennel Club (vpres, 68-); VFW Auxiliary. Honors & Awards: Named Community Leader of Am, 68. Relig: Protestant. Mailing Add: 3315 Cribbon Ave Cheyenne WY 82001

SCHOEL, RICHARD GEORGE (R)
Finance Chmn, Union Co Rep Party, NJ
b Chicago, Ill, Nov 4, 20; s Richard George Schoel & Marguerite Mendenhall S; m 1944 to Helen Shirley Cathcart; c Marguerite Lynn (Mrs Conn) & Kenneth Richard. Educ: Univ Mich, BSE, 43; Scabbard & Blade; Delta Tau Delta; Alpha Phi Omega. Polit & Govt Pos: Mem, Bd of Educ, Hicksville, NY, 53-55; mem, Union Co Rep Comt, NJ, 61-64, mem exec comt, 62-64; chmn, Goldwater Campaign, Westfield, 64; chmn, Union Co Rep Citizens Comt, 65-66; chmn, Union Co Rep Party, 68-73, finance chmn, 73- Bus & Prof Pos: Asst sales mgr, Solventol Chem Prod, Detroit, Mich, 46-48; asst to gen mgr, John Robert Powers Prod, New York, NY, 48-49; asst sales mgr, Clairol, Inc, 49-50; brand mgr, Lever Bros Co, 50-55; prod group dir, Johnson & Johnson, New Brunswick, NJ, 55-69, dir mkt info, 69- Mil Serv: Entered as Sgt, Army, 43, released as Capt, 46, after serv in 13th Ord Bomb Disposal Squad, Mediterranean Theatre of Opers, 45-46; Soldiers Medal. Mem: NJ Epilepsy Found (bd trustees, 73-); F&AM. Relig: Orthodox Presbyterian. Mailing Add: 642 Summit Ave Westfield NJ 07090

SCHOENBERGER, CHARLOTTE SALLY (R)
VChmn, State Sen Dist 23, Colo
b Lehighton, Pa, Dec 21, 17; d Hubert Hager & Margaret Laury H; m 1940 to Morton W Schoenberger; c Susan (Mrs Bruce MacQueen). Educ: Mt Sinai Hosp Nurses Training Sch, RN, 40. Polit & Govt Pos: Blockworker, Tioga Co Rep Party, NY, 59-63, committeewoman, 62-66; financial secy, Boulder Co Rep Party, Colo, 67-68; secy, Boulder Co Rep Cent Comt, 68-72, dist capt, 73-74, bonus mem, 74-75; co-chmn, Comt to Reelect the President, Boulder Co, 72; co-chmn, Comt to Elect Vanderhoof for Gov, 74; vchmn, State Sen Dist 23, Colo, 75- Bus & Prof Pos: Gen duty nurse, Mt Sinai Hosp, Philadelphia, Pa, 40; vis nurse, Community Nurse Asn, Lehighton, 40-47; med secy, Gnaden Huetten Hosp, Lehighton, 47-52; off nurse, Dr Irving Dolsky, Linden, NJ, 52-59. Mem: Eastern Star; Boulder Women's Club; Boulder Women's Rep Club; Morning Forum Rep Women, Boulder. Relig: Protestant. Mailing Add: 7660 Ferris Way Boulder CO 80303

SCHOENBERGER, MARALYN MORTON (D)
State Committeewoman, Maine Dem Party
b Pittsburgh, Pa, Oct 1, 29; d Stanley Francis Morton & Eleanor Birdetta Hill M; m 1952 to Dr Walter Smith Schoenberger; c Karen. Educ: Peabody High Sch, Pittsburgh, 43-47; Gimbel Bros Scholarship, Bellefield Sch, Pittsburgh, Pa, 47-48, retailing post grad cert; Univ Maine Col Arts & Sci, 67-68. Polit & Govt Pos: Dem cand Maine House Rep, 65 & 68; mem, Bd Voter Registr, Orono, 66-68; justice of the peace, Penobscot Co, 67-; mem finance comt, 500 Club, Dem Party Maine, 68 & 69; state committeewoman, Maine Dem Party, Penobscot Co, 68-; lobbyist, Maine Chiropractic Asn, 69; deleg, White House Conf on Children & Youth, 70; chmn health subcomt, Gov Comn on Children & Youth, Maine, 70-; vchmn, Orono Dem Party, 70-; mem & legis liaison, Orono Conserv Comn, 70-; mem finance comt, Maine Dem State Comt, 70-; mem, Health Coun of Maine, 71-; alt deleg, Dem Nat Mid-Term Conf, 74. Bus & Prof Pos: Bookkeeper, Mellon Nat Bank & Trust Co, 48-50; receptionist & secy, Harbison Walker Refractories, 50-53; libr asst, Fletcher Sch Law & Diplomacy, 53-54, proctor, 54-56; secy & admin asst, registr office, Univ Maine, 61-64. Mem: Counr, Am Legion Dirigo Boys State, 68-; citizens adv comt, Am Studies Prog, Orono High Sch, 70-; League of Women Voters US; Thursday Wives Club; YWCA. Relig: Presbyterian. Mailing Add: 25 College Heights Orono ME 04473

SCHOENECK, CHARLES A (R)
Mem, NY Rep State Comt
b Syracuse, NY, Feb 3, 12; s Charles A Schoeneck & Louise E Kappesser S; m 1946 to Elizabeth Ellen Brandt; c Charles A, III & Elisabeth N. Educ: Syracuse Univ, AB, 33; Harvard Univ Law Sch, LLB, 36; Sigma Alpha Epsilon. Polit & Govt Pos: Mem, NY Rep State Comt, 52-, chmn, 67-69; NY State Assemblyman, 55-60, Majority Leader, NY State Assembly, 59-60; mem, Rep Nat Comt, 67-69; deleg & chmn NY deleg, Rep Nat Conv, 68. Bus & Prof Pos: Attorney-at-law, Bond, Schoeneck & King, 36- Mil Serv: Entered as Pvt, Army, 42, released as Capt, 45, after serv in 37th Inf Div, Asian Pac, 43-45; Combat Inf Badge; Bronze Star Medal. Mem: Onondaga Co, NY State & Am Bar Asns; Am Legion. Relig: Episcopal. Mailing Add: 110 Juneway Rd Syracuse NY 13215

SCHOFIELD, JACK LUND (D)
Nev State Sen
b Douglas, Ariz, Apr 25, 23; s Thomas Theron Schofield & Della Larson S; m 1941 to Alene Earl; c Camille Alene (Mrs Farmer), Pamela (Mrs Bananto), Jacqueline (Mrs Taylor), Jill (Mrs Toddre), Jack Lund, Jr & Christopher Earl. Educ: Univ Utah, BS; Univ Nev, Reno, ME. Polit & Govt Pos: Secy, Paradise Valley Improv Asn, 54-55, pres, 55-56; bd mem, Paradise Valley Town Bd, 55-65; Nev State Assemblyman, 70-74; Nev State Sen, 75- Bus & Prof Pos: Pres, Apt Owner's Asn, 64-65. Mil Serv: Entered as Pvt, Army Air Corps, 43, released as 1st Lt, 46, after serv in 22nd Bomb Squadron, 341st Bomb Group, 14th Air Force, Flying Tigers, 45-46; recalled as 1st Lt, Air Force, 51-53, 4th Tow Target Squadron, Tactical & Continental Air Command, 51-53; honorably discharged, 1st Lt, 59; Asiatic Pac Theatre Campaign Medal with 2 Oak Leaf Clusters; Presidential Unit Citation; World War II Victory Medal. Mem: Sertoma; Hump Pilot's Asn; Am Soc of Pub Adminr; Am Legion; VFW. Honors & Awards: Parade Marshall, Helldorado, Las Vegas, 72, North Las Vegas Christmas Parade, 72, Tournament of Roses, Pasadena, 73 & Henderson Indust Days, Nev, 73. Relig: Latter-day Saint. Mailing Add: 1308 S 8th St Las Vegas NV 89104

SCHOFIELD, JAMES W (D)
Nev State Assemblyman
Mailing Add: 1740 Howard Ave Las Vegas NV 89104

SCHORGL, JAMES JOSEPH (JOE) (D)
Mo State Rep
b Kansas City, Mo, Sept 13, 22; s James Joseph Schorgl (deceased) & Catherine Burns S (deceased); m 1948 to Helen Marie Rice; c Patricia, Denise & Elizabeth. Educ: NE High Sch, Kansas City, Mo, grad, 39. Polit & Govt Pos: Mo State Rep, Ninth Dist, 69- Bus & Prof Pos: Switchman, Mo Pac RR, Kansas City, Mo, 46-69; partner, J & L Elec, 54-69. Mil Serv: Entered as Pvt, Army, 42, released as Pfc, 45, after serv in Third Inf Div, ETO, 42-46. Mem: Dem Good Govt Asn; KofC; Am Legion; Northeast Community Coun; East Side Community Coun. Relig: Catholic. Mailing Add: 637 Brighton Kansas City MO 64124

SCHORR, ROBERT JEFFREY (R)
Nat Committeeman, Mich Young Rep Nat Fedn
b Detroit, Mich, Oct 30, 41; s Robert William Schorr & Margretta Jones S; single. Educ: Wayne State Univ, 66; Sigma Delta Chi Jour Fraternity; Tau Kappa Epsilon. Polit & Govt Pos: Newsletter & publicity chmn, Oakland Co Young Rep, 71-73; precinct deleg, 18th Mich Cong Dist, 72-; mem, Mich State Rep Comt, 74-; nat committeeman, Mich Young Rep Nat Fedn, 74-; app mem, Mich Rep Bicentennial Comt, 75- Bus & Prof Pos: Teacher Am hist, Cabrini High Sch, 66-68; pub rels, Detroit Race Course, 65-68; free lance pub rels & prom work, 69-73; rep, Investors Diversified Serv, Sales, 69-73; pub rels staff, Campbell-Ewald Advert Co, 74- Mem: Sigma Delta Chi; Prof Journalistic Soc; Detroit Hist Soc (publicity chmn); Mich Bicentennial Rep Comt. Honors & Awards: Teke-of-year Award, Col Award, 64. Relig: Christian Scientist. Mailing Add: 2424 Coolidge Troy MI 48084

SCHOSBERG, PAUL ALAN (D)
b New York, NY, Apr 6, 37; s Eugene Louis Schosberg & Thelma Siegel S; m 1958 to Jane Mindlin; c Jill Ernestine & Richard Eugene. Educ: Middlebury Col, BA, 59; Columbia Law Sch, 59-61. Polit & Govt Pos: Admin asst to US Rep, Richard L Ottinger, NY, 65-71; campaign coordr, Ottinger for Cong, 64 & campaign dir, 66 & 68; admin asst, US Rep, Herman Badillo, NY, 71- Bus & Prof Pos: Bur mgr, Westchester Co Publ, 63-64, night city ed, 62-63 & reporter, 61-62. Publ: Auth, See How They Run, Chilton, 64 & The Picture Life of Herman Badillo, Franklin Watts, 72. Legal Res: 25 Iverness Rd Scarsdale NY 10583 Mailing Add: 12225 Thoroughbred Rd Herndon VA 22070

SCHOUWEILER, EILEEN CAFFREY (R)
Secy, Washoe Co Rep Cent Comt, Nev
b Reno, Nev, Dec 1, 31; d Willis Wilson Caffrey & Dorothy Snyder C; m 1954 to Robert Leroy Schouweiler; c John Willis & Paul Robert. Educ: Briarcliff Col, 49-51; Stanford Univ, BA, 53. Polit & Govt Pos: Pres, Rep Women's Club, Reno, Nev, 59-61; vchmn, Washoe Co Rep Cent Comt, 71-74, secy, 74-; mem, Nev State Rep Cent Comt, 71- & Nev State Rep Exec Comt, 74-; deleg, Rep Nat Conv, 72. Mem: St Mary's Hosp Guild (publicity chmn, 74-75); Washoe Med Ctr Women's League; Trinity Episcopal Church Women. Honors & Awards: Dauphine Award, St Mary's Hosp Guild, 67. Relig: Episcopal. Mailing Add: 123 Greenridge Dr Reno NV 89502

SCHRADE, JACK (R)
Calif State Sen
b Williamsport, Pa, May 25, 02. Educ: Pa & NY Schs. Polit & Govt Pos: Calif State Assembly, 54; Calif State Sen, 62-, chmn, Rules Comt & Pres Pro Tem, Calif State Senate, 70-; deleg, Rep Nat Conv, 72. Bus & Prof Pos: Retired rancher & businessman; dir, Southland Savings & Loan Asn. Mem: Rotary; Eagles; Elks; Moose; El Cajon Valley Club. Mailing Add: 1904 Hotel Circle San Diego CA 92108

SCHRADER, BEVERLY SUE (R)
b Rockford, Ill, Oct 8, 44; d Clarence J Thompson & Dorothy Wahl T; m 1972 to Donald Lee Schrader; c Marvin Wesley. Educ: Valparaiso Univ, BS in Elem Educ, 66; Univ Iowa, cert in orthoptics, 67. Polit & Govt Pos: Secy, Young Rep League of Wyo, 69-72; Rep precinct committeewoman, Laramie Co, Wyo, 70-72; treas, Laramie Co Young Rep, 70-72; deleg, Nat Rep Conv, 72; state committeewoman from Laramie Co, Wyo State Young Rep, 72-73. Bus & Prof Pos: Orthoptist, Cheyenne Eye Clin, 67- Mem: Mariners; DePaul Hosp Guild; Zonta; Am Asn Univ Women; Women's Civic League. Relig: Presbyterian. Mailing Add: 2815 Deming Blvd Cheyenne WY 82001

SCHRADER, LEO W (D)
Mo State Rep
b Joplin, Mo, Oct 25, 38; s Leo Ray Schrader & Helen Marguerite Woodford S; m 1960 to Cean G Carter; c Kara Lee & Marady Lynn. Educ: Southwest Mo State Col, 56-57; Univ Ark, BSBA, 60; Univ Mo Sch Law, LLB, 63. Polit & Govt Pos: Asst prosecuting attorney, Jasper Co, Mo, 65-66; Mo State Rep, 69- Mil Serv: Army, 64-65, 1st Lt, serv in 69 Signal Bn. Mem: Optimist. Relig: Protestant. Mailing Add: 815 N Byers Joplin MO 64801

SCHRADER, ROBERT GALT (R)
Supt Pub Instr, Wyo
b Canon City, Colo, July 1, 28; s Galt Schrader & Mildred Knox S; m 1951 to Virginia Ann Evans; c Robert Melvin, Andrew Galt & Amy Ann. Educ: Park Col, BA, 51; Univ Wyo, MEd, 58, EdD, 65. Polit & Govt Pos: Supt pub instr, Wyo, 71-; mem steering comt, Educ Comt of the States; coun chief, State Sch Officers; mem, Higher Educ Coun, Community Col Comn, State Land Bd, Farm Loan Bd, Charities & Reform Bd, State Liquor Comn & State Bd Deposits. Bus & Prof Pos: Teacher, Thermopolis High Sch, Wyo, 54-58; prin, Kemmerer High Sch, 58-60; supt, Shoshoni Schs, 61-63 & Cody Schs, 63-70; trustee, Univ Wyo, currently. Mil Serv: Entered as Pvt, Marine Corps, 46, released 47, reentered 51, released as Sgt, 53. Mem: Nat Educ Asn; Phi Delta Kappa; AF&AM; Scottish Rite; Rotary. Relig: Presbyterian. Legal Res: 500 Killarney Dr Cheyenne WY 82001 Mailing Add: State Off Bldg W Cheyenne WY 82002

SCHRADER, RONALD FREDERICK (D)
b Brainerd, Minn, Dec 8, 38; s Fred John Schrader & Eleanore Rose Flansberg S; m 1961 to Judith Delores Fitch; c John Frederick, Connie Rose & Michael Thomas. Educ: Brainerd Jr Col, 2 years; Bemidji State Col, BS, 62; Claremont Grad Sch; Colo Col; Ore Col of Educ. Polit & Govt Pos: Vchmn, Wadena Co Dem-Farmer-Labor Party, 67-68; campaign chmn, Bergland Campaign Comt, 70; admin asst, US Rep Bob Bergland, Minn, 71- Bus & Prof Pos: Modern probs instr, Wadena Pub Schs, Minn, 63-70. Mil Serv: Entered as Pvt, Minn Nat Guard, 56, released as Sgt E-5, 63. Publ: Isn't it time, Minn Fedn of Teachers Newspaper, 69. Mem: Minn & Am Fedn Teachers. Relig: Catholic. Legal Res: 512 Irving Wadena MN 56482 Mailing Add: 1008 Longworth House Off Bldg Washington DC 20515

SCHRAEDER, FRED JOSEPH (D)
Ill State Sen
b Iroquois Twp, Ill, Dec 26, 23; s Fred A Schraeder & Iva Marie Roth S; m 1946 to Helen Ruth Wilson; c Ivan L, Fred M & Kevin H. Educ: High sch, spec courses at higher level. Polit & Govt Pos: Vchmn, Peoria Co Dem Cent Comt, Ill, 57-63, chmn, formerly; Ill State Rep, formerly; arbitrator, Indust Comn, Ill, 61-64; Ill State Sen, 75- Bus & Prof Pos: Chmn, Peoria-Tazewell Indust Union Coun, AFL-CIO, 54-57, vchmn & chmn, Peoria-Tazewell Labor Coun, 57-61; bus rep & pres, Int Union of United Brewery Workers of Am, Local 77, 54-61; restaurant owner, 65- Mil Serv: Pvt, Army, serv in Amphibious Engrs, Asian Theater; Asian & Pac Theater Ribbons. Relig: Roman Catholic; past chmn, Christian Family Movement, Peoria Diocese. Mailing Add: 205 E Arcadia Ave Peoria IL 61603

SCHRAEDER, VERNON VIRGIL (D)
Comnr, Hodgeman Co, Kans
b Burdett, Kans, Dec 24, 17; s Frank Schraeder & Clara Pivonka S; m 1947 to Mildred Rice; c James J & Jo Lana. Educ: Ft Hays, Kans State Col, AB, 40; Phi Sigma Epsilon. Polit & Govt Pos: Co comnr, Hodgeman Co, Kans, 57-; pres, Co Comnrs Asn, 62; mem gov comn on criminal admin, 69. Bus & Prof Pos: Rancher, 47- Mil Serv: Entered as Aviation Cadet, Army Air Force, 40, released as Capt, 45, after serv in Eighth Air Force, ETO, 43-44; Unit Citation; Air Medal with Three Oak Leaf Clusters; Distinguished Flying Cross. Mem: Am Legion; Lions. Relig: Methodist. Mailing Add: Jetmore KS 67854

SCHRAG, LLOYD (R)
b Marion, SDak, Jan 10, 15; m 1939 to Lorraine Miller; c Lois Kay & Larry James. Educ: High Sch. Polit & Govt Pos: Co comnr, 52-56; Turner Co Crop Improv Asn; SDak State Sen, 58-72; deleg, Rep Nat Conv, 72. Bus & Prof Pos: Farming. Relig: Mennonite. Mailing Add: Marion SD 57043

SCHREIBER, ANN F (D)
b Maywood, Ill; d Emil A Schrieber & Pauline Winkler S; single. Educ: Proviso High Sch, Maywood, Ill, 4 years. Polit & Govt Pos: Admin asst to US Rep Edgar A Jones, 49-54; admin asst to US Rep John F Baldwin, 54-66; exec secy to US Rep Jerome R Waldie, Calif, formerly. Bus & Prof Pos: Secy to dir, Eng Dept, Fred S James Co, Inc, Chicago, Ill, 37-40; passenger dept rep, Santa Fe RR, 40-44; secy to assoc dir, Nat Physicians Comt, 44-49. Mem: Cong Staff Club; Calif State Soc. Relig: Protestant. Mailing Add: 700 New Hampshire Ave NW Washington DC 20037

SCHREIBER, BILL (R)
Minn State Rep
Mailing Add: 10001 Zane Ave N Brooklyn Park MN 55443

SCHREIBER, JOHN PAUL (R)
b Windthorst, Tex, Sept 13, 13; s T A Schreiber & Clara Hoff S; m 1938 to Gertrude Mary Zotz; c Jo-Ann (Mrs Gilbert Murillo), Ronald J, David A, Raymond J, John P, Jr, Margaret (Mrs James Baumhadt) & Janie H. Polit & Govt Pos: Mem sch bd, Windthorst Pub Schs, Tex, 56-58; chmn, Archer Co Rep Party, formerly. Mem: KofC; Farm Bur. Relig: Catholic. Mailing Add: Rte 1 Box 34 Windthorst TX 76389

SCHREIBER, MARTIN JAMES (D)
Lt Gov, Wis
b Milwaukee, Wis, Apr 8, 39; s Martin Eugene Schreiber & Emeline Kurz S; m 1961 to Elaine Ruth Thaney; c Katherine, Martin, Kristine & Matthew. Educ: Valparaiso Univ; Marquette Univ, LLB; Univ Wis-Milwaukee, grad student in urban affairs. Polit & Govt Pos: Wis State Sen, 63-70, chmn Dem caucus, Wis State Senate, formerly; cand for Lt Gov, Wis, 66; mem pub policy comt, Wis Asn for Ment Health, 67-68; Lt Gov, Wis, 71-; mem exec comt, Nat Conf Lt Gov; Wis Nursing Home Ombudsman; chmn, Wis Coun for Consumer Affairs & Wis Ins Laws Revision Comt; mem, Interstate Coop Comn; chmn, Wis Am Revolution Bicentennial Comn; mem bd dirs, Community Training & Develop Corp; mem bd trustees, Gtr Wis Found, currently. Bus & Prof Pos: Attorney-at-law. Mem: Am Coun to Improve our Neighborhoods; Wis Acad Sci, Arts & Letters; AFL-CIO Locals 9 & 113; Midtown Neighborhood Improv Asn; Coop West Side. Relig: Lutheran. Mailing Add: State Capitol Rm 22E Madison WI 53711

SCHREIER, HAROLD (D)
SDak State Sen
Mailing Add: Rte 3 Flandreau SD 57028

SCHREINER, L D, JR (R)
Committeeman, Rep State Comt Okla
b Weatherford, Okla, June 30, 32; s L D Schreiner Sr & Josephine Sugden S; m 1952 to Ginger D Gravlee; c Larry Allen & Angela Renee. Educ: Southwestern State Col, BS, 58. Polit & Govt Pos: Chmn, Custer Co Rep Party, Okla, 69-71; committeeman, Rep State Comt Okla, 71-; cand, Okla State Rep, Dist 57, 72. Bus & Prof Pos: Farmer-rancher, Schreiner Charolais Farm, 56-; real estate broker & ins agent, Schreiner Ins Agency, 58- Mil Serv: Entered as Airman Recruit, Navy, 51, released as AD-3, 55, after serv in several units, Korea &

Southeast Asia, 54. Mem: Am Legion; VFW. Relig: Methodist. Legal Res: 700 Santa Fe Dr Clinton OK 73601 Mailing Add: PO Box 355 Clinton OK 73601

SCHRETTE, ROLAND DONALD (R)
Mem, Rep State Cent Comt Calif
b Renton, Wash, Apr 25, 29; s Almond Donald Schrette & Ruby Beaudry S; m 1954 to Hildegard Grete Duser; c Kristi Lynn & Thomas Henry. Educ: Napa Col, AA, 51. Polit & Govt Pos: Mem finance comt, Napa Co Rep Cent Comt, Calif, 67-, chmn cand comt, 68-69; mem, Rep State Cent Comt, Calif, 69- Bus & Prof Pos: Sales mgr & secy-treas, Henry Duser Co Inc, Napa, Calif, 53-66; owner, Paine's Cocktail Lounge, 66-71; mem staff, NY Life Ins Co, 71-, mem, Top Club, 72. Mil Serv: Entered as Pvt E-1, Army, 51, released as Cpl, 53, after serv in 508th Airborne, Ft Benning, Ga, 3rd Army, 52-53. Mem: Nat Asn Life Underwriters; Active 20-30 Club Int; Elks. Honors & Awards: Dist Gov, Northern Calif; Active 20-30 Clubs Outstanding Governor Award, 64-65. Relig: Catholic. Mailing Add: 2109 Trower Ave Napa CA 94558

SCHRICKER, KENNETH M (R)
Wis State Rep
Mailing Add: RR 2 Spooner WI 54801

SCHROEDER, ALFRED GUSTAV (R)
Justice, Kans Supreme Court
b Newton, Kans, June 5, 16; s Gustav D Schroeder & Grete Janzen S; m 1942 to Katheryn Marie Diel; c John Scott, Hedy Marie & Marilyn Sue. Educ: Bethel Col, 2 years; Kans State Col, BS in Agr with high honors, 37; Harvard Law Sch, LLB, 40; Phi Kappa Phi; Alpha Zeta; Farm House. Polit & Govt Pos: Probate & co judge, Harvey Co, Kans, 47-53; dist judge, Ninth Judicial Dist, Harvey & McPherson Co, 53-57; justice, Kans Supreme Court, 57- Bus & Prof Pos: Law practice, Newton, Kans, 40-42. Mil Serv: Entered as Pvt, Air Force, 42, released as 1st Lt, 46, after serv in Hq Off, Lake Charles Army Air Force Base, 42-46; Res, 46-50, Capt; Good Conduct Medal. Publ: Opinions written in Kans Off Supreme Court Reports from 1/57 to present. Mem: Am & Kans Bar Asns; Phi Alpha Delta. Honors & Awards: Winner State Coop Mkt Exam, 4-H, 35. Relig: Protestant. Mailing Add: 825 Buchanan Topeka KS 66606

SCHROEDER, CLARENCE HENRY (R)
b San Antonio, Tex, June 1, 18; s Frederick Nathaniel Schroeder & Theresa Manka S; single. Educ: Tex Col of Arts & Indust, 1 year; Univ of Tex, 3 years. Polit & Govt Pos: Chmn, Duval Co Rep Party, Tex, formerly. Bus & Prof Pos: Comn agent, Mobil Oil Corp, 45- Mil Serv: Entered as Pvt, Army, 40, released as T/3, 45, after serv in Div Surg Off, 2nd Inf Div, ETO. Mem: Rotary; KofC; VFW; Curcillos; Univ Tex Alumni Asn. Relig: Catholic. Legal Res: Box 246 San Diego TX 78384 Mailing Add: Gravis St San Diego TX 78384

SCHROEDER, FREDERICK CARL (R)
Wis State Rep
b West Bend, Wis, Jan 19, 10; s Herbert Schroeder & Minnie Gumm S; m 1931 to Molly Weddig; c William Carl. Educ: High Sch, West Bend. Polit & Govt Pos: Wis State Rep, 64-, mem, Comt on Commerce & Consumer Affairs & Comt on Agr, Wis House of Rep, currently. Bus & Prof Pos: Farmer & dairy operator. Mem: Wash Co Holstein Asn (bd dirs); Nat Coun of Churches; Wash Co Dairy Herd Improv Asn (bd dirs); Lions; Moose. Honors & Awards: Progressive Breeder Award of the Holstein-Friesian Asn of Am; 4-H Alumni Award, Wis, 67. Relig: United Church of Christ. Legal Res: 2472 Hwy 143 West Bend WI 53095 Mailing Add: Rm 335-E N Wisconsin State Capitol Madison WI 53702

SCHROEDER, LAVERNE W (R)
Iowa State Rep
b 1933; married. Polit & Govt Pos: Hardin Twp Bd of Trustees, Iowa, 64-66; Iowa State Rep, 67-71 & 73-; Iowa State Sen, 71-73. Bus & Prof Pos: Farmer. Mil Serv: Army, Korean War, 53-55. Mem: Farm Bur; Am Legion Post 725 (2nd vcomdr). Mailing Add: Route 1 McClelland IA 51548

SCHROEDER, LEAH WEBB (D)
b Ft Worth, Tex, Aug 19, 44; d Farris Baxter Webb & Margaret Lee Baden W; m 1967 to Richard E Schroeder. Educ: La State Univ, Baton Rouge, BA, 65; Univ Chicago, MA, 68; Phi Kappa Phi; Mu Sigma Rho; Alpha Lambda Delta; Delta Phi Alpha; Pi Sigma Alpha; La State Univ Union; Baptist Student Union. Polit & Govt Pos: Legis asst, US Rep Bill Nichols, Ala, 69-70; admin asst, Gillis Long Gubernatorial Campaign, La, 70-71; admin asst, US Rep Gillis W Long, La, 73- Bus & Prof Pos: Exec asst to pres, Steele & Utz, Washington, DC, 72. Mem: La State Univ Alumni Asn (pres, 74-); Am Polit Sci Asn. Honors & Awards: Woodrow Wilson Found fel, 65-66; fel, Ctr for Comp Study of Polit Develop, Univ Chicago, 66-67, univ fel, 66-68. Relig: Baptist. Legal Res: 5712 Mildred St Alexandria LA 71301 Mailing Add: 1125 Independence Ave SE Washington DC 20003

SCHROEDER, LLOYD G F (D)
Chmn, Allamakee Co Dem Party, Iowa
b Postville, Iowa, Feb 8, 10; s John A Schroeder & Amanda Oldag S; div; c Ken, Keith, Wayne & Marion (Mrs George Frederich). Polit & Govt Pos: Chmn, Allamakee Co Dem Party, Iowa, 72- Bus & Prof Pos: Ins agt, 40- Mem: Brotherly Love Masonic Lodge (Past Master, 57); Eastern Star (Worthy Patron, 57); Commercial Club. Relig: Lutheran. Mailing Add: 123 S Lawler Postville IA 52162

SCHROEDER, LUELLA RUTH (D)
Secy, Butler Co Dem Exec Comt, Ohio
b Newport, Ky, May 27, 22; d August Bartley Thomas & Evelyn Brown T; m 1946 to William Ben Schroeder. Educ: Berea Col, AB, 44; Univ Cincinnati Grad Sch, 45-46. Polit & Govt Pos: Off mgr, Butler Co Citizens for Gilligan Sen Campaign, Ohio, 68; asst & exec secy, Butler Co Dem Party Chmn Richard N Koehler, 69-71; deleg, Dem Nat Conv on Policies & Procedures, 74; secy, Butler Co Dem Exec Comt, 75- Bus & Prof Pos: Asst to ed, Screen Process Mag, Cincinnati, 53-56; off mgr & bookkeeper, Butler-Warren-Clinton Co AFL-CIO Labor Coun, Hamilton, 72-, rec secy, 72- Mem: Off & Prof Employees Int Union; League of Women Voters of Hamilton-Fairfield Area (nominating Comt chairperson, 73-75); Nat Orgn for Women; YWCA. Honors & Awards: You've Come a Long Way Baby, Butler Co Chap, Nat Orgn for Women, 74. Relig: United Methodist. Mailing Add: 790 Walter Ave Fairfield OH 45014

SCHROEDER, MARTHA K (D)
Chmn, Hot Springs Co Dem Cent Comt, Wyo
b Donnybrook, NDak, May 7, 03; d Edward M King (deceased) & Anna Martha Powers K (deceased); m 1927 to Lawrence John Schroeder (deceased); c Shirley Ann (Mrs Crawford). Educ: Minot State Teachers Col, teachers cert elem educ, 23; Riverton Col Exten, psychol course. Polit & Govt Pos: Committeewoman, Hot Springs Co Dem Cent Comt, Wyo, 60-66, chmn, 66-; deleg, Dem Nat Conv, 72; mem, Wyo Comn Status Women, 75- Bus & Prof Pos: Teacher, NDak & Mont, 22-27; Bookkeeper, Maytag Co & J C Penney Co, 27-35; bookkeeper & clerk, Holiday Inn, currently. Mem: St Frances Altar Soc (parliamentarian, 66-69); Beta Sigma Phi (dir, Alpha Zeta chap, 66-); Big Horn Basin Women in Community Serv, (proj dir, 64); Thermopolis Toastmistress Club (pres, 62-67 & 70-71, treas, 73-74); Thermopolis Women's Club (pres, 75-). Honors & Awards: Outstanding Toastmistress for Thermopolis Club, 68-69. Relig: Catholic. Mailing Add: 1136 Amoretti Thermopolis WY 82443

SCHROEDER, PATRICIA (D)
US Rep, Colo
b Portland, Ore, July 30, 40; d Lee Combs Scott & Bernice Lemoin S; m to James White Schroeder; c Scott & Jamie. Educ: Univ Minn, Minneapolis, BA, magna cum laude, 61; Harvard Law Sch, JD, 64; Sigma Epsilon Sigma; Phi Beta Kappa; Chi Omega; Mortar Bd. Polit & Govt Pos: Precinct committeewoman, Denver Dem Party, 68-70; US Rep, First Dist, Colo, 73- Bus & Prof Pos: Field attorney, Nat Labor Rels Bd, Colo, Wyo & Utah, 64-66; lectr & law instr, Community Col Denver, 69-70, Univ Denver, Denver Ctr, 69 & Regis Col (Colo), 70-72; hearing officer, Colo Dept of Personnel, 71-72; legal counsel, Planned Parenthood of Colo. Mem: Am Bar Asn; League of Women Voters; Nat Orgn of Women; Nat Women's Polit Caucus. Relig: United Church of Christ. Legal Res: 1440 High St Denver CO 80210 Mailing Add: 1131 Longworth House Off Bldg Washington DC 20515

SCHROEDER, RHEA (R)
Committeewoman, Idaho Rep State Cent Comt
b Sugar City, Idaho, June 1, 28; d Fremont Fullmer & Golda Richman F; m 1955 to Neil S Schroeder; c Scott, Randy, Garin & Karin. Educ: Ricks Col, BS, 52; Lambda Delta Sigma; Valkyries. Polit & Govt Pos: Committeewoman, Idaho Rep State Cent Comt, 68-; exec secy, Idaho Young Rep, 70-72. Bus & Prof Pos: Legal secy, Rexburg, Idaho, 47- Mem: Madison Co Heart Asn (chmn, 70-); Idaho Heart Asn (dir, 74-). Relig: Latter-day Saint. Legal Res: Rte 1 Box 8 Rexburg ID 83440 Mailing Add: 30 S Second West Rexburg ID 83440

SCHROEDER, WILLIAM L (D)
Chmn, Comal Co Dem Party, Tex
b Littlefield, Tex, Aug 14, 40; s L Lloyd Schroeder & E Ruth Wells S; m 1962 to Audrey Jean George; c Christopher Scott & Eric Christian. Educ: NTex State Univ, BA; Univ Kans Law Sch, JD; Phi Alpha Delta; Kappa Sigma. Polit & Govt Pos: Chmn, Comal Co Dem Party, Tex, 73-; asst dist attorney, Comal-Caldwell Co, 73-; mem, Alamo Area Coun Govts Criminal Justice Coun, 74- Bus & Prof Pos: Vpres & exec bd, Community Coun of SCent Tex, 75- Mem: Tex Bar Asn; Tex Trial Lawyers Asn; Tex Dist & Co Attorney's Asn; New Braunfels Jaycees. Relig: Roman Catholic. Mailing Add: 753 Encino Dr New Braunfels TX 78130

SCHROEHER, KATHY JEAN (D)
b Rockville Centre, NY, July 16, 49; d William Louis Schroeher & Caroline Limbach S; single. Educ: Univ Va Mary Washington Col, BA, 71; Cath Univ Am Columbus Sch Law, currently; Pi Gamma Mu; Mortar Board. Polit & Govt Pos: Legis aide to US Rep John G Dow, 71-72; legis asst to US Rep William Lehamn, 73-74; legis asst to US Rep Dave Evans, Ind, 75- Legal Res: 23 Greenridge Ave Garden City NY 11530 Mailing Add: 636 G St SE Washington DC 20003

SCHROM, EDWARD JOSEPH (DFL)
Minn State Sen
b Albany, Minn, Mar 17, 11; s John H Schrom & Julia Grausam S; m 1936 to Dorothy Eva Beumel; c Kenneth (deceased), Donald & Eileen (Mrs William Nathe). Polit & Govt Pos: Deleg-at-lg, Dem Nat Conv, 68; Minn State Sen, Dist 26, 70-72, Dist 16, 72- Mem: KofC; Albany Sportsman's Club; Albany Golf Club; Farmers Union; Township Treasurer. Relig: Catholic. Mailing Add: Rte 2 Albany MN 56307

SCHRON, NANCY JANE (R)
b Jersey City, NJ; d Herold Godsall Schron & Catherine Kirkpatrick S; single. Educ: Kean State Col, BSEd; Sigma Kappa Phi. Polit & Govt Pos: Secy, EOrange Co Policy Comt, NJ, 62-73, first ward chmn, 72-73; councilwoman, EOrange, 70-, chmn, Pub Affairs Comt, 70-73, chmn, Legis Comt, 70-73, chmn, Sanitation Comt, 2 years, EOrange City Coun; pres & mem exec bd, First Ward Rep Club, 71-73; alt deleg, Rep Nat Conv, 72. Bus & Prof Pos: Kindergarten teacher, EOrange Sch Syst, currently. Mem: PTA (mem exec bd, Franklin Sch, vpres, secy & rep to three state conv); EOrange Kindergarten Asn (vpres, secy); NJ Fedn Rep Women; Federated Rep Clubs of Essex Co; Easter Seal Soc. Honors & Awards: East Orange Woman of Year, 74. Relig: Episcopal. Mailing Add: 48 Fulton St East Orange NJ 07017

SCHROTE, JOHN E (R)
b Findlay, Ohio, May 6, 36; s Millard L Schrote & Alberta Ellis S; m 1957 to Rachel Daly; c James D & Gretchen L. Educ: Ohio State Univ, BS, 58; Univ Cincinnati, 58-59; Miami Univ, 59-60; Xavier Univ, MBA, 64; Tower Club; Saddle & Sirloin Club; Intramurals. Polit & Govt Pos: Page, Ohio House Rep, spec session, 57; mem, Warren Co Goldwater for President Comt, 64; secy, Warren Co Young Rep, 65; regional dir, Lukens for Cong Comt, 66; mem, Warren Co Rep Cent Comt, 65-68; Warren Co chmn, Herbert for State Treas Comt, 66; deleg, Ohio Young Rep State Conv, 66, 67 & 68; alt deleg, Rep State Conv, 66; mem, Franklin City Recreation Bd, 66; admin asst, US Rep, D E (Buz) Lukens, 67-71; advan man & hotel chmn, Citizens for Reagan Comt, Rep Nat Conv, 68; asst to exec dir, Inaugural Ball Comt, 69; mem, Cloud for Gov Finance Comt, 70; consult govt mgt, pub & govt affairs, 71; nat field rep, Comt to Reelect the President, 72; spec asst to assoc dir, Off Econ Opportunity, 71-72, prin asst to acct dir, 72-73; spec asst to Secy US Dept Agr, 73- Bus & Prof Pos: Buyer & expediter, McGraw Construction Co, Middletown, Ohio, 58-59; buyer, Armco Steel Corp, 59-66. Mem: Bull Elephants Club; Congressional Secy Club; Warren Co Youth Coun (trustee); Poky Griffith Dist Comt Boy Scouts. Relig: Episcopal. Legal Res: 601 Dorset Dr Middletown OH 45042 Mailing Add: 2301 Cheshire Lane Alexandria VA 22307

SCHUBERT, CARROLL WAYNE (D)
b Corpus Christi, Tex, Oct 21, 47; s Adolph Carl Schubert & Alma Capeheart S; single. Educ: Tex A&M Univ, BS in agr econ, 69; Univ Tex Sch Law, Austin, JD, 73; Alpha Zeta; Phi Alpha Delta. Polit & Govt Pos: Pres, Brazos Co Young Dem, Tex, 67-68; mem exec comt, Young

Dem Clubs of Tex, 67-, treas, 69-71; pres, Tex A&M Young Dem, 68-69; deleg, Tex State Dem Conv, 70; staff, Tex State Dem Party, 70-71; legis aide, Tex State Sen Wayne Connally, 71-72; treas, Young Dem Clubs of Am, 71-73. Mil Serv: Entered as 2nd Lt, Army, 73, released as 2nd Lt, 73, after serv in Transportation Off Basic Course; 1st Lt, Army Res, 4 years. Mem: Am Bar Asn; State Bar Tex. Relig: Lutheran. Mailing Add: Rte 2 Box 51 Robstown TX 78380

SCHUBERT, RICHARD FRANCIS
Undersecy of Labor
b Trenton, NJ, Nov 2, 36; s Yaro Schubert & Frances Mary Hustak S; m 1957 to Sarah Jane Lockington; c Robyn Denise & David Mark. Educ: Eastern Nazarene Col, BA, 58; Yale Law Sch, LLB, 61. Polit & Govt Pos: Exec asst to Undersecy of Labor, Dept of Labor, 70, exec asst to Secy of Labor, 70-71, solicitor of labor, 71-73, Undersecy of Labor, 73- Bus & Prof Pos: Arbit attorney, Dept Labor Rels, Bethlehem Steel Co, 61-66; asst mgr labor rels, 66-70, asst to vpres indust rels, 73-; bd trustees, Eastern Nazarene Col. Mem: Pa & Northampton Co Bar Asns; Am Iron & Steel Inst; Am Arbit Asn; Philadelphia Delta; East Nazarene Alumni Asn. Relig: Church of Nazarene. Legal Res: 1435 Hardy St McLean VA 22101 Mailing Add: Dept of Labor Dept Labor Bldg 14th St & Constitution Ave Washington DC 20210

SCHUCHHARDT, LUETTA JUNE (D)
Chairwoman, Ziebach Co Dem Party, SDak
b Raton, NMex, Nov 15, 44; d Garland Leon Arnold & Etta Gibson A; m 1972 to Donald Ervin Schuchhardt; c Robin Lee. Educ: Phillips Univ, BS, 67; First Mile; Tenth Muse. Polit & Govt Pos: Chairwoman, Ziebach Co Dem Party, SDak, 74- Bus & Prof Pos: Recreation worker, Am Red Cross, San Antonio, Tex & Okinawa, 67-69, recreation supvr, Korea, Japan & Ft Carson, Colo, 69-72. Mem: Beta Sigma Phi (pres, 75-76); Merifu Exten (vchairwoman, 74-75); Beef Promoters. Relig: United Church of Christ. Legal Res: RR Dupree SD 57623 Mailing Add: Box 264 Dupree SD 57623

SCHUCK, ERNEST F (D)
NJ State Assemblyman
b Bridgeboro, NJ, Mar 1, 19; m to Elizabeth McNichols; c Maryanne, Bernadettee & Ernest, Jr. Educ: Rutgers Univ Col, Camden, NJ. Polit & Govt Pos: Councilman, Borough of Barrington, 66-67, mayor, 67-74; NJ State Assemblyman, 75-, mem insts, health & welfare comt, munic govt comt & sub-comt on health state, NJ State Assembly, 74-75. Bus & Prof Pos: Supvr, Bell Tel Co, 20 years. Mil Serv: Released from Army, 52, after serv in Artillery Unit. Mem: Barrington Businessmen's Asn; Barrington Lions Club; NJ State Bicentennial Comn; Camden Co Mayor's Asn; NJ Conf Mayors (dir). Honors & Awards: Hon mem Jaycees. Mailing Add: 34 Enders Dr Barrington NJ 08007

SCHUCK, JAROLD RAYMOND (R)
b Marinette, Wis, July 16, 36; s Raymond William Schuck & Kathryn Scherer S; m 1959 to Susan Jennifer Rouse; c Christopher Raymond, Gregory Karl, Stephen Elliot & Daniel Jason. Educ: Univ Wis, BS, 60. Polit & Govt Pos: Dir, Radio & TV, Wis Rep Party, 60-62; pub rels dir, 65-71; admin asst to Lt Gov Jack B Olson, 64-65; staff mem, Gov Warren P Knowles, 65; admin asst, US Rep John W Byrnes, Wis, 71-72; admin asst, US Rep Charles E Chamberlain, Mich, 72-75. Bus & Prof Pos: Pub rels dir, GEX Milwaukee Corp, 62-64. Mil Serv: Entered as Pvt, Army, 54, released as Specialist 3/C, 56, after serv as Teletype Operator, Army Commun Ctr, Germany; Expert Carbine; Good Conduct Medal; Nat Defense Serv & Army Occup Medals. Relig: Roman Catholic. Mailing Add: 1532 Winding Waye Lane Wheaton MD 20902

SCHUCKER, ALBERT EDWIN (R)
Councilman, Reading, Pa
b Reading, Pa, Sept 1, 22; s Edwin A Schucker & Lizzie R Knoll S; m 1949 to Lillian A; c Suzanne M & Nancy A. Educ: Chicago Tech, Specialized Construction, 41; Wharton Sch, Univ Pa. Polit & Govt Pos: Councilman & dir streets & pub improvs, Reading, Pa, 63- Bus & Prof Pos: Gen mgr, Edwin A Schucker Construction Co, 54-; owner, Schucker Construction Co, 59- Mil Serv: Entered as Pvt, Army, 42, released as Cpl, 43, after serv in 305th Ord Regt. Mem: Mason; Shrine; Am Pub Works Asn; bldg construction orgns; many civic groups. Relig: Protestant. Legal Res: 1510 Greenview Ave Reading PA 19601 Mailing Add: Luzerne & Warren Sts Reading PA 19601

SCHUELEIN, WILLIAM M (D)
Okla State Sen
b Akron, Ohio, Aug 7, 27; s William F Schuelein & Gladys E Morton S; m 1949 to Frances J Hill; c Shelly J (Mrs Brooks) & James W. Educ: Northeastern Okla Agr & Mech Sr Col, 48-49. Polit & Govt Pos: Sheriff, Ottawa Co, Miami, Okla, 63-73; Okla State Sen, 73- Bus & Prof Pos: Service Sta, 49-63; Real Estate, 74- Mil Serv: Entered as Pvt, Army, 46, released as Tech Sgt, 48, after serv in 24th Inf Div, Japan. Mem: VFW; Am Legion; Booster Clubs. Honors & Awards: All Around Athlete, Sr Year High Sch; Am Legion Award in Law Enforcement. Relig: Presbyterian. Mailing Add: 806 Jefferson Blvd Miami OK 74354

SCHUETT, WARREN (D)
NDak State Rep
Mailing Add: State Capitol Bismarck ND 58501

SCHULER, JOHN HAMILTON (R)
Mem, Rep State Exec Comt, Ala
b Birmingham, Ala, Oct 15, 26; s Robert Eustace Schuler & Doris Moughon S; m 1954 to Elizabeth Ann Locke Mattison; c George A Mattison, IV, Elizabeth Locke, John Hamilton, Jr & Robert Eustace, II. Educ: Auburn Univ, BS Indust Mgt, 52; Sigma Alpha Epsilon. Polit & Govt Pos: Del, Rep Nat Conv, 64 & 68; state finance chmn, Rep Party, Ala, 64-66; mem, Rep State Exec Comt, 64-; campaign mgr, Nixon-Agnew Comt, 67-68; mem, Rep Nat Finance Comt, 64-; finance chmn, Ala Comt to Reelect the President, 72. Bus & Prof Pos: Chmn bd, Anderson Elec Corp, 69-73; pres, Leaf Ind Inc; pres, Schuler Investment Co, Inc, Birmingham, 72- Mil Serv: Entered as Seaman, Coast Guard, 44, released as Seaman 1/C, 46, after serv in Pac Theatre, 44-46. Mem: Auburn Alumni Eng Coun; Assoc Indust of Ala; Birmingham Area CofC. Relig: Episcopal. Legal Res: 2964 Cherokee Rd Birmingham AL 35223 Mailing Add: PO Box 23 Trussville AL 35173

SCHULER, LOUIS EUGENE (R)
b Griswold, Iowa, Feb 9, 22; s George A Schuler & Iona Kreamer S; m 1948 to Mildred Hines; c George Richard, Louis Eugene, Jr, Herbert Theodore, Mark Luther & Helen Elisabeth. Educ: Grinnell Col, BA, 43; Drake Univ, summer 43; State Univ Iowa, JD, 49; Friars, pres,

Gamma Eta Gamma, Univ Iowa, 49. Polit & Govt Pos: City attorney, Clear Lake, Iowa, 56-, city attorney, Ventura, 60- & Thornton, 68-; chmn, Cerro Gordo Co Rep Cent Comt, 68-74. Bus & Prof Pos: Partner, Boyle, Schuler & Oltrogge, 49- Mil Serv: Entered as Pvt, Air Force, 43, released as S/Sgt, 46, after serv in 20th Air Force, Asiatic Theatre, 45-46; Good Conduct Medal & Asiatic Theatre Medal. Publ: Articles in Iowa Law Rev, 49. Mem: Am Judicature Soc; Am Trial Lawyers Asn; 12th Judicial Dist Bar Asn; Cerro Gordo Co Bar Asn; VFW. Honors & Awards: Boss of the Year, Clear Lake, Iowa, 67. Relig: Lutheran. Mailing Add: 408 N Shore Dr Clear Lake IA 50428

SCHULLER, KERRY ANNE (D)
b Tillamook, Ore, Aug 21, 44; d Max Thane Honey & Jean Tinnerstet H; m 1968 to Charles Richard Schuller. Educ: Ore Col Educ, BS, 66. Polit & Govt Pos: Co-chmn, Coun Dem Women, Knoxville, Tenn, 71-; campaign dir, McGovern for President, Knox Co, Tenn, 72; alt deleg, Nat Dem Conv, 72; deleg, Co, Dist & State Conv, Dem Party, Tenn, 72. Bus & Prof Pos: Teacher, Eugene Pub Schs, 66-68; owner, African Imports, 70-71. Mem: League of Women Voters; Dem Womens Roundtable. Relig: Protestant. Mailing Add: 1529 Whitower Rd Knoxville TN 37919

SCHULTHEIS, BRUCE E (R)
b Tacoma, Wash, Apr 19, 41; s Bernard Earl Schultheis & Myrtle Lund S; m 1971 to Mary Elizabeth Carlisle; c Robert Bruce. Educ: Cent Wash State Col, BA, 63; Willamette Univ, JD, 66. Polit & Govt Pos: Dep prosecuting attorney, Yakima Co, Wash, 66-68; legis asst to US Rep H W Pollock, Alaska, 68-69; admin asst, 69-70; staff attorney to US Sen Ted Stevens, Alaska, 70-71; chief legis div, off asst secy policy & int affairs, Dept Transportation, 71-74; spec asst to Secy, Dept Interior, 74- Bus & Prof Pos: Vpres, Western Growth Ind Inc, 68- Mil Serv: Capt Army Res, Judge Adv Gen Corps. Mem: Wash & Am Bar Asns. Mailing Add: Box 2276 Anchorage AK 99501

SCHULTZ, CLARENCE G (R)
NDak State Sen
Mailing Add: State Capitol Bismarck ND 58501

SCHULTZ, JAY (R)
NDak State Sen
Mailing Add: State Capitol Bismarck ND 58501

SCHULTZ, MARILYN FRANCES (D)
Ind State Rep
b Alexandria, La, Jan 7, 44; d Frank William Schultz & Catherine Smith S; m 1972 to Alfred I Towell. Educ: Univ Tex, BA, 64, MA, 68. Polit & Govt Pos: Ind State Rep, 51st Dist, 73-; deleg, Dem Nat Mid-Term Conf, 74. Mailing Add: 814 N Washington Bloomington IN 47401

SCHULTZ, MARILYN L (MRS FRANK) (D)
b Augusta, Ga, Jan 7, 36; d Col Kenneth Smith & Mildred Pangburn S; m 1955 to Frank Lewis Schultz; c Karen Ann & Stephen Lewis. Educ: Univ Tex, 53-55; Univ Mex; Pan-Am Univ, currently; Gamma Phi Beta. Polit & Govt Pos: Deleg, Dem Nat Mid-Term Conf, 74. Bus & Prof Pos: Pres, Gallery Editions, Ltd. Mem: McAllen Jr Serv League; PEO; Pan-Am Round Table; Music Festival Bd. Relig: Methodist. Mailing Add: 600 Sunset Dr McAllen TX 78501

SCHULTZ, WALDEMAR HERBERT (D)
Treas, Fourth Dist Dem Orgn, Wis
b Milwaukee, Wis, Dec 3, 21; s Walter J Schultz & Emma L Sievert S; single. Educ: St Olaf Col; Univ Wis. Polit & Govt Pos: Membership chmn, West Allis-West Milwaukee Unit Dem Party, 46-71, treas, 49, 55-69 & 73-, vchmn, 69-70, chmn, 70-72; mem, state & co platform comts & Dem Const Comt, 48; Dem committeeman, Fourth Ward, 50-64, Second Ward, 64-72, mem, Second Aldermanic Dist, 72-; chmn, Eighth Sen Dist Dem Party, 50 & 65; secy, Milwaukee Co Dem Statutory Comt, Wis, 52-; treas, Milwaukee Co Dem Party, 60-63; alt deleg, Dem Nat Conv, 64; asst to chmn, Dem State Conv; state legis chmn, Wis Conf of Br, NAACP, 68-73, second vpres, 73-; treas, Fourth Dist Dem Orgn, 69-; mem cent comt, Wis Dem Statutory Comt, 70-; mem, Wis Dem State Cent Comt, 72- Mil Serv: A/S, Navy, 43-44. Publ: Why I am a Democrat—The Creed of your US Senator, Congressman & Assemblyman, Artcraft Press; A Democratic Profile—Waldemar Schultz—Christian, Milwaukee Sentinel Press. Mem: West Allis NAACP (treas, 69-); Milwaukee Conf of the Am Lutheran Churchmen (second vpres, 69-); Century Club. Relig: Lutheran. Mailing Add: 1968 S 72nd St West Allis WI 53219

SCHULZE, RICHARD T (R)
US Rep, Pa
b Philadelphia, Pa, Aug 7, 29; s John L Schulze, Jr & Grace Taylor S; m 1955 to Anne (Nancy) Lockwood; c Karen Lockwood, Richard Taylor, Jr, Michael Scott & Linda Anne. Educ: Univ Houston; Villanova Univ; Temple Univ. Polit & Govt Pos: Mem, Chester Co Rep Comt, 60-67, pres, Upper Main Line Young Rep Club, 62-63; first vpres, Chester Co Fedn Young Rep Clubs, 63-64; pres, 64-65; mem, Chester Co Rep Exec Comt, 64-67; chmn nominating comt, Pa State Young Rep Biennial Conv, 66; chmn, Tredyffrin Twp Rep Comt, 66-67; chmn, Richard Nixon Day, 68; registr, Wills & clerk of Orphans' Court, Chester Co, Pa, 68-70; Pa State Rep, 157th Dist, 70-74; US Rep, Pa, 75- Bus & Prof Pos: Partner, Home Appliance Ctr, Paoli, Pa, 50- Mil Serv: Entered as Pvt, Army, 51, released as Cpl, 53. Mem: Archaeol Inst Am; Thomson Lodge 340, F&AM; Chester Co Coun, Boy Scouts Am; Great Valley Asn; Circus Saints & Sinners Club Am. Honors & Awards: Jaycee of the Year, Upper Main Line Jaycees, 59; Dist Merit Award & Scoutmasters Key Award, Great Valley Dist, Boy Scouts Am. Relig: Presbyterian. Mailing Add: Swedesford Rd Box 512 RD 1 Malvern PA 19355

SCHUMACHER, ANITA M A (R)
Exec Mem, SDak Rep Women's Fedn
b Douglas Co, SDak, Sept 7, 14; d William C Wenzel & Johanna Mattheis W; m 1934 to Herbert J Schumacher; c Darleen Anne (Mrs James Kautz) & Harold H. Educ: Grad of Dale Carnegie; Epsilon Sigma Alpha. Polit & Govt Pos: Precinct woman, Rep Party, Hutchinson Co, SDak, 48-; committeewoman, SDak Rep State Cent Comt, 58-65, vchmn, formerly; chmn, Hutchinson Co Rep Finance Comt, 58-65; organizer & chmn, Parkston Rep Women's Fedn, 59-65; deleg & hon chmn, SDak del, Rep Nat Conv, 60; area chmn, Rep Campaign, 60; mem, Gov Gubbrud Steering Comt, 60; mem, SDak State Fair Bd, 61-71, vpres, 63-64; mem, State Rep Adv Comt, 65-; exec mem, SDak Rep Women's Fedn, 65- Bus & Prof Pos: Acct, Parkston Automobile Agency, 48-; pres, Bus Mgt Coun, Omaha Zone, 62-63. Honors & Awards: Cert of Award for Outstanding Achievement in Acct; Award, Dale Carnegie Best

Prepared Speech; Citizen of the Week, Sioux Falls Argus Leader Newspaper. Relig: Am Lutheran. Mailing Add: 707 N Monroe Pierre SD 57501

SCHUMACHER, WAYNE (DFL)
Minn State Rep
Mailing Add: RR 1 Glenwood MN 56334

SCHUMAKER, WM (BILL) (R)
Wash State Rep
Mailing Add: 208 W Fifth Colville WA 99114

SCHUMANN, MERRITT J (R)
Committeeman, Rep Party of Tex
b New Braunfels, Tex, June 16, 28; s Herbert O Schumann & Meta Krause S (deceased); m 1950 to Iris Timmermann; c Sharon Lynn, Sandra Kay, Susan Jeannine, Sara Christine & Sheila Anne. Educ: Univ Tex, BBA, 50. Polit & Govt Pos: Mem & treas, bd of trustees, New Braunfels Independent Sch Dist, 56-59; chmn, Comal Co Rep Party, Tex, 62-66 & 68-75; mem, Elected Charter Comn, New Braunfels, 66; chmn, Good Govt League of New Braunfels, 66 & 67; mem, Rep Task Force on Educ, 67; committeeman, Rep Party of Tex, 68-, state chmn for 50 targeted counties, 70. Bus & Prof Pos: Pres, New Braunfels Indust Found, 67- Mil Serv: Entered as Ens, Navy, 50, released as Lt, 53, after serv in Sea Duty, USS Pritchett DD561, Korean Theatre; UN & Korean Medals; Admirals Commendation, Outstanding Supply Dept on DesLant Atlantic Fleet. Mem: San Antonio Chap, Chartered Life Underwriters (vpres, currently); San Antonio Chap, Col of Life Underwriters; Longhorn Club; Comal Co Steering Comt (chmn); YMCA. Honors & Awards: Named Outstanding Jaycee of the Year, 59-60; Besserung Award, 66. Relig: United Church of Christ; pres, United Church of Christ, New Braunfels. Mailing Add: 1079 Fredricksburg New Braunfels TX 78130

SCHUMER, CHARLES E (D)
NY State Assemblyman
b Brooklyn, NY, Nov, 50; s Abraham Schumer & Selma Rosen S; single. Educ: Harvard Col, BA, 71; Harvard Univ Law Sch, JD, 74; Phi Beta Kappa; Signet Soc. Polit & Govt Pos: Mem, Nat Comt for Effective Cong, currently, asst dir, 72; mem staff, US Sen Claiborne Pell, RI, 73; chief aide to NY State Assemblyman Steven Solarz, 73-74; NY State Assemblyman, 75- Bus & Prof Pos: Assoc, Paul, Weiss, Rifkind, Wharton & Garrison, 74; study group leader, John F Kennedy Inst Polit, 75. Mem: B'nai B'rith; Jewish War Vet; 61st Precinct Community Coun; Harvard Col Fund. Honors & Awards: David Mason Little scholar, Harvard Univ; Root-Tilden scholar, NY Univ. Relig: Jewish. Mailing Add: 1755 E 13th St Brooklyn NY 11229

SCHUNEMAN, CALVIN W (R)
Ill State Sen
Mailing Add: 409 Dale Ave Prophetstown IL 61277

SCHURTER, MARION EVELINE (R)
VChmn, Fifth Cong Dist Rep Party, Kans
b Redford, NY, Sept 23, 16; d Edgar John Haley & Esther Ada Hanlon H; m 1942 to Roy William Schurter. Educ: Midwest Inst, 65-66; Kans State Teachers Col, summers 66 & 67; Univ Kans, correspondence sch, 68. Polit & Govt Pos: Precinct committeewoman, Rep Party of Kans, 58-72; vchmn, Greenwood Co Rep Cent Comt, 58-64, chmn, 64-72; vchmn, Fifth Cong Dist Rep Party, Kans, 62-; state committeewoman, Farmers Home Admin, 70; dist mgr, Bur of Census, 70. Mem: Kans Fedn Rep Women. Relig: Catholic. Mailing Add: RD 3 Eureka KS 67045

SCHUSTER, JOHN CONRAD (D)
Chmn, Skagit Co Dem Comt, Wash
b Spokane, Wash, Jan 8, 45; s Frank Osborn Schuster & Iris Conrad S; m 1966 to Virginia Jane Allison; c Carolyn & Franklin. Educ: Gonzaga Univ, 63-65; Eastern Wash State Col, BA, 67; Western Wash State Col, MEd, 71. Polit & Govt Pos: Chmn, Skagit Co Dem Comt, Wash, 75- Bus & Prof Pos: Salesman, Wash Water Power Co, 63-67; warehouseman, Nabisco, 67-68; teacher social studies & drama, Burlington-Edison Sch Dist, 68-71; pres, Burlington-Edison Educ Asn, 70-71; vprin, Burlington-Edison High Sch, 71- Mem: Asn Wash Sch Prins (state legis comt); Eastern Wash State Col Alumni Asn (pres, 75-); KofC (Dep Grand Knight, 74-75). Relig: Roman Catholic. Mailing Add: 3340 E Division Mt Vernon WA 98273

SCHUSTER, NANCY P (D)
b Atlanta, Ga, Feb 15, 31; d Joseph James Pence & Elizabeth Adams P; m 1955 to Edgar Howard Schuster; c Nina & William. Educ: Hahnemann Hosp, Philadelphia, RN, 51; Univ Pa, BA, 56. Polit & Govt Pos: Coordr, Shapp for Gov, Cheltenham Twp, Pa, 54 & McCarthy for President, 56; co-coordr, Reece for Senate, Montgomery Co, 58; committeewoman, Cheltenham Twp Dem Party, 60-; vchmn, McGovern for President, Montgomery Co, 72; deleg, Dem Nat Conv, 72. Mem: Am for Dem Action (vchmn, Southeastern Pa Chap, 69-); New Dem Coalition. Mailing Add: 7301 Granite Rd Melrose Park PA 19126

SCHUSTER, RODERIC E (D)
NDak State Sen
b Minot, NDak, May 10, 41; m 1970 to Kay Kallas; c Matthew. Educ: NDak State Univ, BS, 68; Univ NDak, JD, 72. Polit & Govt Pos: NDak State Sen, Dist 21, 74- Bus & Prof Pos: Partner, Schuster, Ramlo & McGuire, Attorneys, Fargo, 72- Mil Serv: Entered as E-1, Army, released as E-4, after serv in Vietnam, 65-66. Mem: Am & NDak Bar Asns; VFW; Am Legion; KofC. Mailing Add: 1428 S 15th Fargo ND 58102

SCHUTTER, BETTY RUGEN (R)
b Evanston, Ill, Apr 10, 19; d Fred A Rugen & Kathrine Haupt R; m 1942 to John Maurice Schutter, MD; c John Maurice, Jr, Margaret (Mrs Gene Kiekhaefer), James Fredrick, Stephen Richard & Anne Elizabeth. Educ: State Univ Iowa, BA, 41. Polit & Govt Pos: Deleg, Rep Nat Conv, 72; pres, Iowa Fedn Rep Women, 71-74. Bus & Prof Pos: Teacher & speech therapist, SDak Sch for Deaf, 41-42; speech therapist in pvt practice, 45- Mem: Nat Fedn Rep Women (adv bd, 72-73); League of Women Voters; Meals on Wheels, Inc; Community Concert Asn (bd mem); Am Asn Univ Women (bk sale chmn; bk discussion chmn). Honors & Awards: Merit Mother of Iowa, Am Asn Univ Women, 71; Iowa Mother of the Year, 73. Relig: Methodist; librarian, United Methodist Church, 71- Mailing Add: 218 Fair St Algona IA 50511

SCHUTZ, VICTOR (DFL)
Minn State Rep
Mailing Add: Goodhue MN 55027

SCHWAB, C B (R)
Chmn, Jefferson Co Rep Comt, Nebr
b Morrowville, Kans, Jan 22, 22; s John Benjamin Schwab & Jessie Mallery S; m 1940 to Mildred I Stewart; c Ronald L & Lana A (Mrs Criner). Educ: Kans State Univ, DVM, 44; Block & Bridle; Jr Am Vet Med Asn. Polit & Govt Pos: Precinct chmn, Second Ward, Fairbury, Nebr, 48-58, 63-64 & 70-; mem, City Coun, Fairbury, Nebr, 50-52, mem, Sch Bd, 52-55, Mayor, 69-; chmn, Jefferson Co Rep Comt, 64- Bus & Prof Pos: Veterinarian. Mil Serv: Entered as Pvt, Army, 45, released as Cpl, 46, after serv in 970 Counter Intel Corps, ETO; ETO Serv Medal. Mem: Mason; Elks; VFW; CofC; Am Vet Med Asn. Honors & Awards: Silver Beaver Scout Leaders Award; Veterinarian of the Year, Nebr, 69. Relig: Presbyterian. Mailing Add: 1210 B Fairbury NE 68352

SCHWAB, ELEANOR ANNE (D)
b Philadelphia, Pa, Mar 1, 31; d Walter Benjamin Schwab & Anna McHale S; single. Educ: Temple Univ, AB, 55; NY Univ, MA, 56. Polit & Govt Pos: Vchmn, Brookings Co Dem Cent Comt, SDak, 67-68; chmn, Brookings Co McCarthy for President Comt, 68; mem, J Abourezk for Senate Comt, 72; deleg, SDak Dem Nomination Conv, 72; deleg & mem credentials comt, Dem Nat Conv, 72; precinct committeewoman, Second Ward Dem Party, 72- Bus & Prof Pos: Instr polit sci, Hofstra Col, 57 & NY Univ Sch Com, 57-59; research asst, Int City Mgrs Asn, Chicago, 59-61; instr govt & pub affairs, Southern Ill Univ, Edwardsville, 61-66; asst prof polit sci, SDak State Univ, 66-75, assoc prof, 75- Publ: Co-auth, Study guide for management training program, 60, auth, City policies & programs for the aging population, 60 & Training programs for state & local management personnel, 61, Int City Mgrs Asn. Mem: Am Polit Sci Asn, Women's Polit Caucus; Mid West Polit Sci Asn; Am Soc Pub Admin; Mid West Pub Admin Soc; Pi Gamma Mu. Honors & Awards: Grad asst, dept govt, NY Univ, 56-57, Penfield Fel, Grad Sch Arts, 57-58; Ford Fel, Ford Found, 71. Mailing Add: 618 Heritage Dr Brookings SD 57006

SCHWABE, MAX (R)
Mem, Boone Co Rep Comt, Mo
b Columbia, Mo, Dec 6, 05; s Dr George W Schwabe & Lulu M Stotts S; m 1930 to Georgia May Ashlock; c June & Maxine Lusk. Educ: Univ Mo. Polit & Govt Pos: US Rep, Mo, 43-49; state dir, Farmers Home Admin, US Dept Agr, 53-61; mem, Boone Co Rep Comt, Mo, currently; deleg & mem, Platform Comt, Rep Nat Conv, 72. Bus & Prof Pos: Underwriting supvr, MFA Mutual Ins Co, Columbia; retired. Relig: Christian Church. Mailing Add: 2105 S Country Club Dr Columbia MO 65201

SCHWALLER, WILLIAM ANTON (R)
Chmn, Miller Co Rep Cent Comt, Mo
b Eugene, Mo, Apr 27, 17; s William Herman Schwaller & Jennie Sanning S; m 1939 to Alvina Marie Jurgensmeyer; c Mary (Mrs Raymond), Carol (Mrs Sexton), Thomas, Robert & Jennie (Mrs Cronkite). Polit & Govt Pos: Mem, Mo Rep State Comt, 70-72; chmn, Miller Co Rep Cent Comt, Mo, 70- Bus & Prof Pos: Pres, St Elizabeth Ins Co, Miller Co, Mo, 35-; farmer. Mem: Osage River Flood Control Asn; KofC, Marys Home; Marys Home Cemetery Asn; Mo Farmers Asn. Relig: Roman Catholic. Mailing Add: RR 1 Eugene MO 65032

SCHWANER, ANNIE MAE (R)
NH State Rep
b Carnesville, Ga, Apr 24, 12; d Charles Holman Ginn & Mary Elizabeth Terrell G; m to Nelson Marshall Schwaner (deceased); c Audrey M (Mrs David L Barker), Susan A (Mrs Anthony D Iannuccillo), Marsha M (Mrs Walter E Karbowsky), Gordon W & N Marshall. Educ: Ga, SC & Va Schs. Polit & Govt Pos: NH State Rep, 63-; past pres, Plaistow Rep Women's Club; mem, Rep Town Club; mem, State Security Task Force & Price Stabilization Bd; mem, Const Conv, 64; mem State Selective Serv Syst, 70-; mem exec bd, Rockingham Co Legis Deleg, 73-75. Bus & Prof Pos: Va newspaper reporter & columnist, formerly; columnist, Wonder City Wanderings, The Progress Index, Petersburg Va. Mem: Seacoast Regional Develop Asn, New Market, NH (vpres, 72-74); State Order Women Legislators (pres, 73-74); Plaistow Civic Orgn (founder & pres); Am Judicature Soc; mem for various orgns & fund drives. Honors & Awards: Cert of Merit, Am Mother's Comt, 60; Bronze Medallion, NH Heart Asn. Relig: Catholic; mem, Diocesan Sch Bd, 63-70 & adv bd, Holy Angels Parish. Legal Res: Elm St Plaistow NY 03865 Mailing Add: Box 236 Plaistow NH 03865

SCHWARTZ, AARON ROBERT (D)
Tex State Sen
b Galveston, Tex, July 17, 26; s Joseph Schwartz & Clara Bulbe S; m 1951 to Marilyn Ruth Cohn; c Robert A, Richard A, John R & Thomas L. Educ: Tex A&M, pre-law, 44 & 46-47; Univ Tex, LLB, 51. Polit & Govt Pos: Asst attorney, Galveston Co, Tex, 51-54; Tex State Rep, 54-58; Tex State Sen, 17th Dist, 60-, pres pro tem, Tex State Senate, 66; chmn, Tex Coun on Marine-Related Affairs; chmn, Coastal States Orgn. Mil Serv: Seaman 1/C, Naval Res, 44-46, serv in Pac, 45-46; 2nd Lt, Air Force Res, 48-53. Relig: Jewish. Mailing Add: 10 S Shore Dr Galveston TX 77550

SCHWARTZ, B D (D)
NC State Rep
Mailing Add: 205 Forest Hill Dr Wilmington NC 28401

SCHWARTZ, EDNA BARBARA (D)
Chmn, Weston Dem Town Comt, Mass
b Boston, Mass, May 19, 09; d Abram Smith & Louise Halter S; m 1941 to Edward Lester Schwartz; c Andrea (Mrs Saiet). Educ: Emerson Col, BLit, 34; Portia Law Sch, LLB, 39. Polit & Govt Pos: Deleg, Mass State Dem Conv, 32; mem, Brookline Dem Town Comt, 32-38; mem exec comt, Newton Dem City Comt, 60-65; pres, Dem Women on Wheels, 62-64; state chmn, Operation Support, 62-68; mem adv coun, Mass State Small Bus Admin, 64-66; mem, Weston Dem Town Comt, 66-70, treas, 70-72, vchmn, formerly, chmn, currently; deleg, Dem Nat Conv, 68. Publ: Personality Improvement, Barnes & Noble, 40; The Best I Know, Waverly, 41. Mem: Nat Coun Jewish Women (pres Gtr Boston Sect, vpres, New Eng Regional Div); Brandeis Women's Auxiliary; Jewish Children & Family Serv (women's comt); Women's Div, Gtr Boston Chap, Mass Heart Asn, Inc (pres, 72-); Prospect Valley Br, Mass Cancer Soc (chmn spec events, 74-). Mailing Add: 17 Ledgewood Rd Weston MA 02193

SCHWARTZ, GEORGE X (D)
Mem, Dem Nat Comt, Pa
b New York, NY, Jan 28, 15; s Max Schwartz & Ida Ochroch S; m 1937 to Jerre Davidov; c William G, Marjorie (Mrs Richard Dilsheimer) & Susan. Educ: Temple Univ, BS, 36, Law Sch, LLB, 40; Pyramid; Alpha Epsilon Pi. Polit & Govt Pos: Legal consult, Redevelop Authority, Philadelphia, Pa, 52-60; Pa State Rep, 53-60; city councilman, Philadelphia, 60-, majority floor leader & chmn, finance comt, City Coun, 62-71, pres, 72-; committeeman, 34th Ward Dem Exec Comt, Philadelphia Dem City Exec Comt, 62-; deleg, Dem Nat Conv, 64, 68 & 72; mem, Dem Nat Comt, 72-; mem, Pa Dem State Comt, 72-; deleg, Dem Nat Mid-Term Conf, 74. Bus & Prof Pos: Partner, Blank, Rome, Klaus & Comisky, Attorneys, 62-71; dir, Philadelphia Conv & Tourist Bur; Food Distribution Ctr; Philadelphia Housing Develop Corp; Philadelphia Indust Develop Corp; Univ City Sci Ctr Corp; Fairmount Park Comn; Free Libr Philadelphia; Old Philadelphia Develop Corp; Philadelphia Port Corp; Philadelphia Authority Indust Develop; WHYY-TV Educ Radio & TV. Mem: Victory Lodge, Independent Order of B'rith Sholom; Justice Lodge, B'nai B'rith; Overbrook Park Wolfe Baron Lodge, B'rith Sholom; Green Valley Country Club; Locust Club Philadelphia. Relig: Jewish; mem bd & past pres, Beth David Reform Congregation; mem exec comt & past pres, Reform Synagogues Gtr Philadelphia, past pres, Synagogue Coun Philadelphia. Mailing Add: 1421 Walnut St Philadelphia PA 19102

SCHWARTZ, JOSEPH WILLIAM (D)
Conn State Sen
b Bridgeport, Conn, Dec 22, 50; s James Peter Schwartz & Natalie Postol S; single. Educ: Union Col, BA, 72. Polit & Govt Pos: Justice of the Peace, Easton, Conn, 73-75; secy, Easton Dem Town Comt, 74; Conn State Sen, 75-, chmn, elections comt, Conn Gen Assembly, 75-, vchmn regulated activities comt, 75- Bus & Prof Pos: Mgr, James P Schwartz Real Estate Agency, 73- Mem: Gtr Bridgeport Bd Realtors (assoc mem); Fairfield Bd Realtors (assoc mem & mem prof standards comt). Relig: Jewish. Mailing Add: 78 Blanchard Rd Easton CT 06612

SCHWARTZ, RAMON, JR (D)
SC State Rep
b Sumter, SC, May 25, 25; S Raymon Schwartz & Madge Grossman S; m 1950 to Rosa Weinberg; c Barbara, Ramon, III, Milton & Bill. Educ: Univ SC, AB & LLB; Omicron Delta Kappa; Kappa Sigma Kappa. Polit & Govt Pos: Judge, Munic Court, Sumter, SC, 53-57 & 60-64; chmn, Sumter Co Libr Bd, 61-68; chmn, Sumter Housing Authority, 65-68; SC State Rep, 69- Mil Serv: Entered as Pvt, Army, 43, released as Pfc, 46, after serv in ETO. Mem: Sumter CofC; Sumter Rotary Club; Am Legion; VFW; Elks. Honors & Awards: Outstanding Young Man of Year Award, Sumter, SC, 57. Relig: Episcopal. Legal Res: 214 Haynsworth St Sumter SC 29150 Mailing Add: Law Range Sumter SC 29150

SCHWARTZ, ROBERT A D (D)
Chmn Northern Div, Calif Dem State Cent Comt
b Chicago, Ill; s Charles P Schwartz & Lavinia D Schulman S; c Robert D, Stevon S, Paul D, Donald C & David R. Educ: Univ Chicago, 40-42; Mass Inst Technol, BS, 44; Golden Gate Univ, MBA, 68, Law Sch, JD, 74. Polit & Govt Pos: Chmn, Alameda Co Brown for Gov Campaign, Calif, 73-74; chmn gen voc adv comt, Peralta Community Col Dist, 73-; chmn northern div, Calif Dem State Cent Comt, 75- Bus & Prof Pos: Pres & chmn bd, United Plastics Corp, Oakland, Calif, 54-; vpres, Schwartz & Lindheim Inc, 59-; pres, Western States Equip Co Inc, 62- Mil Serv: Entered as Ens, Navy, 44, released as Lt, 46, after serv in Advan Base, Combat Commun Training Ctr, Pac Theatre. Publ: Ed, Plastics education—now?, Soc Plastics Engrs, 70; co-ed, Skills used by attorneys, Golden Gate Law Rev, 73. Mem: Soc Plastics Engrs; Illuminating Eng Soc; Piedmont Boy Scouts Coun; Alameda Co Bar Asn. Honors & Awards: First Pl Lighting Award, Golden Gate Illuminating Eng Soc, 58; Second Pl Lighting Award, West Coast Illuminating Eng Soc, 58; Life Mem, Calif PTA, 70. Mailing Add: 81 Kimberlin Heights Dr Oakland CA 94619

SCHWARTZKOPF, SAMUEL (D)
Mayor, Lincoln, Nebr
b Lincoln, Nebr, Jan 12, 16; s William Schwartzkopf & Katherine S; m 1941 to Dorothy J Anderson; c Louis A, Christine Cay & Suzanne. Educ: Univ Nebr, Lincoln, BA, 40. Polit & Govt Pos: Mayor, Lincoln, Nebr, 67- Mil Serv: Entered as Pvt, Air Force, 42, released as Capt, 46, after serv in 46 in 3rd Force. Mem: Mason; Am Legion; Sertoma; US Conf Mayors; Nat League Cities. Relig: Protestant. Legal Res: 930 Eldon Dr Lincoln NE 68510 Mailing Add: City-County Bldg Lincoln NE 68508

SCHWARZ, JOHN JOSEPH HENRY (R)
Mem, Mich Rep State Cent Comt
b Chicago, Ill, Nov 15, 37; s Frank W Schwarz & Helen Brennan S; m 1971 to Anne Louise Ennis; c Brennan Louise. Educ: Univ Mich, AB, 59; Wayne State Univ, MD, 64; Nu Sigma Nu; Sigma Chi. Polit & Govt Pos: Mem, Calhoun Co Rep Exec Comt, Mich, 74-; mem, Mich Rep State Cent Comt, 75- Bus & Prof Pos: Faculty, Harvard Med Sch, 72-74; physician, 74- Mil Serv: Entered as Lt, Navy, 65, released, 67, after serv in Med Corps Vietnam & asst naval attache, US Embassy, Indonesia, 65-67; Lt Comdr, Naval Reserve, 70; Joint Services Commendation Medal. Mem: Soc Med Consultants to the Armed Forces; Am Acad Ophthalmology & Otolaryngology; Am Med Asn. Relig: Roman Catholic. Legal Res: 251 Central St Battle Creek MI 49017 Mailing Add: 612 Michigan Nat Bank Battle Creek MI 49014

SCHWEDER, J MICHAEL (D)
Pa State Rep
Mailing Add: Capitol Bldg Harrisburg PA 17120

SCHWEIGERT, THOMAS F (R)
b Detroit, Mich, Sept 29, 17; s Thomas H Schweigert & Marie Martinek S; m 1943 to Margaret Chapman; c Frank Thomas, Ralph Fred & Charles James. Educ: Mich State Univ, BS in forestry, 39; Xi Sigma Pi; Phi Delta Theta. Hon Degrees: LLD, Northern Mich Univ, 72. Polit & Govt Pos: Forester, US Forest Serv, 39-43 & 46-48; supvr, Emmet Co, Mich, 55-61; Mich State Sen, 37th Dist, 61-71, former minority leader & pres pro tempore, Mich State Senate; Acting Lt Gov, Mich, 69-71; fed co-chmn, Upper Great Lakes Regional Comn, 71-73; US comnr, Delaware River Basin Comn, 73- Bus & Prof Pos: Consulting forester & land surveyor, self-employed, 48-71. Mil Serv: Entered as Pvt, Army, 43, released as 1st Lt, 46, after serv in Inf & 17th Major Port, US & ETO, 45-46; US Theater, ETO, Occupation & Victory Ribbons. Mem: Soc Am Foresters; Mich Forestry & Park Asn; Kiwanis; Mason; KT. Honors & Awards: Distinguished Serv to Agr Award, Mich State Univ; Distinguished Citizen Award, Lake Superior State Col. Relig: Christian Science. Legal Res: L'Arbre Croche PO Box 637 Petoskey MI 49770 Mailing Add: 700 New Hampshire NW Washington DC 20037

SCHWEIKER, RICHARD SCHULTZ (R)
US Sen, Pa
b Norristown, Pa, June 1, 26; s Malcolm Alderfer Schweiker & Blanche Schultz S (deceased); m 1955 to Claire Joan Coleman; c Malcolm C, Lani L, Kyle C, Richard S, Jr & Lara Kristi. Educ: Pa State Univ, BA, 50; Phi Beta Kappa. Hon Degrees: Numerous degrees from various cols & univs. Polit & Govt Pos: Alt deleg, Rep Nat Conv, 52 & 56, deleg, 72; mem, Pa Rep State Exec Comt; US Rep, 13th Dist, Pa, 61-69, mem, House Armed Serv & Govt Opers Comts; US Sen, Pa, 69-, mem labor & pub welfare comt, ranking mem health subcomt, mem appropriations comt, mem select comt nutrition & human needs, US Senate, mem, Technol Assessment Bd, mem select comt to study intelligence activities. Mil Serv: Enlisted in Navy, World War II, served aboard aircraft carrier. Mem: Navy League; VFW; Rotary; Amvets; Anthracosilicosis League Pa. Honors & Awards: Bringer of Light Award, Jewish Nat Fund, 71; Samuel H Daroff Humanitarian Award, Antidefamation League, B'nai B'rith, 71; Nat Asn Ment Health Award, 74; Israel Prime Ministers Medal, 74; Opportunities Industrialization Ctr Key Award, 74; plus others. Relig: Schwenkfelder Church. Legal Res: Worcester PA Mailing Add: Senate Off Bldg Washington DC 20510

SCHWEINHAUT, MARGARET COLLINS (D)
Md State Sen
b Georgetown, Md, Dec 1, 04; d Lewis F Collins & Mary Ann Fitzpatrick C; m to Judge Henry A Schweinhaut; wid; c Joan (Mrs Michael Delehanty) & Mary Ann (Mrs William Thebus). Educ: George Washington Univ, 2 years; Nat Univ Law Sch, 1 year. Hon Degrees: LLD, St Joseph Col, 71. Polit & Govt Pos: Dem precinct chmn, Montgomery Co, Md, 50-56; Md State Deleg, 55-61; app, Md State Sen, 61, elec, 66-, chmn, Exec Nominations Comt, currently. Bus & Prof Pos: Chmn, Md Comn on Aging, 59-; mem, Health, Educ & Welfare Adv Comt on Aging, 65- Mem: League of Women Voters; Bus & Prof Woman of Wheaton. Honors & Awards: Citation, Nat Coun Sr Citizens; Citation of Merit, Wheaton Sr Citizens. Relig: Catholic. Mailing Add: 3601 Saul Rd Kensington MD 20795

SCHWEITZER, MELVIN L (D)
Counsel, NY State Dem Comt
b New York, NY, Oct 27, 44; s Irving Schweitzer & Betty Schreter S; m 1972 1972 to Maxine Roth. Educ: New York Univ, BA with honors in Govt, 66; Fordham Univ, JD, 69; Pi Sigma Alpha; Perstare et Praestare. Polit & Govt Pos: Committeeman, NY State Dem Comt, 68-70, counsel to adv coun task force on campaign financing, 73, counsel & chmn law comt, 75-; mem transition panel, New York Comptroller's Off, 73-74; mem spec adv comt, NY State Bd Elec, 75- Bus & Prof Pos: Attorney, Rogers & Wells, New York, 69- Relig: Jewish. Mailing Add: 55 E Ninth St New York NY 10003

SCHWEND, RENATO TIMOTHY (R)
b Bronx, NY, July 31, 23; s Henry A Schwend & Lillian F Marchetti S; m 1948 to Marjorie E Raymond; c Keith Renato, Jeffrey Stephen, David Michael, Elaine Susan, Robert Timothy & Roberta Marjorie. Educ: Nichols Col, ABA, 48. Polit & Govt Pos: Tax collector, Thompson, Conn, 63-; chmn, Thompson Rep Town Comt, formerly. Bus & Prof Pos: Supt, Am Optical Co, 58- Mil Serv: Entered as Pvt, Army, 43, released as Sgt, 46, after serv in 20th A F, China-Burma-India, Okinawa, 44-46; China-Burma-India Ribbons. Mem: VFW; Am Legion; Civil Defense (coordr); Little League (pres); Eastern Conn Police Asn (charter mem). Relig: Catholic. Mailing Add: Blain Rd North Grosvenordale CT 06255

SCHWENGEL, FRED (R)
b Franklin Co, Iowa, May 28, 07; s Gerhardt Schwengel & Margaret Stover S; m 1931 to Clara Ethel Cassity; c Frank & Dorothy (Mrs Cosby). Educ: Northeast Mo State Teachers Col, BS, 30; State Univ Iowa, grad work, 35-36; Lincoln Mem Univ, Sullivan Award. Hon Degrees: LHD, Lincoln Col; LLD, Pearsons Col, 59. Polit & Govt Pos: Chmn, A'dair Co Young Rep, Mo, 35-36 & Scott Co Young Rep, 38-39; Rep Cong committeeman, Scott Co, Iowa, 38-55; dist chmn, Iowa Young Rep, 39-40; Iowa State Rep, Scott Co, 44-54; US Rep, First Cong Dist, Iowa, 54-64 & 66-73. Bus & Prof Pos: Gen agent, Am Mutual Life Ins Co, 38-55. Mil Serv: Entered as Pvt, Nat Guard, 33, released as Sgt, 37. Mem: US Capitol Hist Soc (pres); Rep Heritage Found (pres); Lincoln Group, Washington, DC, 56-; Phi Sigma Epsilon (life coun). Relig: Baptist. Legal Res: 3311 W Locust St Davenport IA 52804 Mailing Add: 200 Maryland Ave NE Washington DC 20515

SCHWENGELS, FORREST VICTOR (R)
Iowa State Sen
b Sheffield, Iowa, Aug 27, 15; s Gerhardt Schwengels & Grace Stover S; m 1943 to Betty Pickett; c Forrest Victor, II, Paul F & Suzanne K. Educ: Ind Univ, MA, 63; Phi Kappa Phi; Phi Sigma Epsilon. Polit & Govt Pos: Iowa State Sen, 73- Bus & Prof Pos: Dir of develop, Parsons Col, 72- Mil Serv: Entered as Cadet, Air Force, 42, released as Lt Col, 63, after serv in 305th Bombardment Air Wing, Strategic Air Command, 42-63; Am Theatre Occup Medal, Germany; Airlift Medal, Nat Defense Medal; Air Force Commendation Medal, Humane Action; Secy of Defense Medal; Order of Phoenix, Rank of Commander, Govt of Greece. Mem: Elks; Shrine; Mason; Am Legion; VFW. Relig: Presbyterian. Mailing Add: RR 2 Box 247 Fairfield IA 52556

SCHWENK, EDWIN MILLER (R)
Chmn, Suffolk Co Rep Comt, NY
b Southampton, NY, Dec 5, 23; s Edwin Schwenk & Rosalind Miller S; m 1947 to Diana K Barnes; c Diana B, Jr, Edwin Christopher & Kathryn. Educ: Colgate Univ, BA, 47; Phi Kappa Psi. Polit & Govt Pos: Chmn, Suffolk Co Rep Comt, 67-; mem, Suffolk Co Rep Club, 67-, chmn bd gov, 68-; deleg, Rep Nat Conv, 68 & 72; mem exec comt, NY Rep State Comt, 68-; trustee, Power Authority State NY, 72-74; chmn, NY State Sports Authority, 74- Bus & Prof Pos: Vpres, E Schwenk's Dairy, Inc, 46-; pres, Katrinka Dairy Stores, 61-; dir, Tinker Nat Bank, 63-67, vpres, 65-67; bd trustees, Molloy Cath Col Women, 71-, Dowling Col, 72- & Kaufman Fund, Inc, 72- Mil Serv: Entered as A/S, Navy, 43, released as Lt, 46, after serv in Atlantic Fleet, 43-45. Mem: Stalwarts Club; Elks; Mason; Rotary; VFW. Relig: Methodist. Legal Res: Hampton Park Southampton NY 11968 Mailing Add: Edge of the Woods Rd Southampton NY 11968

SCHWETHELM, A C (D)
Chmn, Kendall Co Dem Comt, Tex
b Comfort, Tex, Aug 6, 31; s Chester A Schwethelm & Julia Seidensticker S; m 1951 to Marilyn Fortner; c Julia May, Otto Chester, Marilyn Sue & Jean Marie. Educ: Draughon's Bus Col, bus degree, 48; San Antonio Col, night sch, 57- Polit & Govt Pos: Precinct chmn,

Dem Party, Tex, 52-60; chmn, Kendall Co Dem Comt, Tex, 60- Mem: Comfort CofC (pres, 56, chmn indust comt, 62-); Lions; Hermann Sons Lodge; Soc Real Estate Appraisers (SRA designation, 71-); Am Inst Real Estate Appraisers (RM designation, 72-). Honors & Awards: Named Man of the Year, Comfort CofC, 58. Relig: Baptist. Legal Res: US 87 E Comfort TX 78013 Mailing Add: Box 248 Comfort TX 78013

SCHWOPE, MARY KAY (D)
Wyo State Rep
b Rock Springs, Wyo, July 21, 17; d Charles Alfred Viox, Sr & Mary Frances Moriarty V; m 1940 to Eldridge Lawson Schwope; c Michael Lawson, Fachon J (Mrs Murphy), Patricia K (Mrs Murphy) & Madalaine M (Mrs Connolly). Educ: Green River High Sch, Wyo, grad, 35; Nat Security Seminars, Cheyenne, 61 & 66; Fed Civil Defense Sch, Alameda, Calif, 62. Polit & Govt Pos: Dem precinct committeewoman, Laramie Co, 57-67; secy, Laramie Co Fair Bd, 66-; vchmn, Laramie Co Cent Comt, 71-73, dist capt, 73-75; Wyo State Rep, 75- Mem: Am Legion Auxiliary; Int Toastmistress; Dem Women's Club; Union Pac Old Timer's; Exec Club. Honors & Awards: Woman of the Year, Am Legion Auxiliary Unit Six, 72; Woman of the Year, Cheyenne Toastmistress Club. Relig: Catholic. Mailing Add: 900 Foyer Ave Cheyenne WY 82001

SCHYE, ELMER (R)
Mont State Rep
Mailing Add: Box 504 White Sulphur Springs MT 59645

SCIBELLI, ANTHONY M (D)
Mass State Rep
Mailing Add: 200 Maple St Springfield MA 01105

SCIRICA, ANTHONY J (R)
Pa State Rep
Mailing Add: Capitol Bldg Harrisburg PA 17120

SCOFIELD, CHARLES (R)
NDak State Rep
Mailing Add: State Capitol Bismarck ND 58501

SCOGIN, EDWARD C (D)
La State Rep
Mailing Add: Rte 1 Box 603 Slidell LA 70458

SCOPER, VINCENT GRADIE, JR (R)
Miss State Rep
Mailing Add: Box 2366 Laurel MS 39440

SCORESBY, CLIFFORD NORMAN (R)
Idaho State Rep
b Queensland, Australia, Feb 26, 01; s William Scoresby & Jessie Ann Higgs S; m 1924 to Johanna L Horman; c Fern (Mrs Lynn Benson), Clifford William, Leah (Mrs Harry Thacker), Charles, Mary Lou (Mrs Doyle Rilndsbaker), Marilyn (Mrs Niel Sargent), Fred, Harold & John F. Educ: Idaho Falls High Sch, 2 years. Polit & Govt Pos: Mem, Iona Village Bd, Idaho, 30-46; sch trustee, Independent Sch Dist Five, 34-48; dir, Progressive Irrigation Dist, 44-69; mem selective serv bd number ten, Bonneville Co, 53-69; Idaho State Rep, 67- Mem: Farm Bur. Relig: Latter-day Saint. Mailing Add: Box 102 Iona ID 83427

SCOTT, ANNA WALL (D)
Committeeman, Ill Dem State Cent Comt
b Fulton, Ky; d Thomas Porter & J Roggie Patton P; m to John Scott; c Harvey Wall. Educ: Univ Ill, Urbana, BS in Sociol, MEd in Social Sci & MSW. Polit & Govt Pos: Mem, Human Rels Comn, Urbana, Ill, 70-74; deleg, Dem Mid-Term Conf, 74; mem, Fair Housing Bd, Urbana, Ill, 74-; committeeman, Ill Dem State Cent Comt, 21st Cong Dist, 74-; mem credentials comt, Dem Nat Comt, currently; vchmn, Ill Dem Party, currently. Bus & Prof Pos: Pub aid case worker, Champaign, Ill, 65-68; psychiat social worker, Danville & Champaign, 68-; instr, Parkland Community Col, Champaign, 69- Mil Serv: Entered as Pvt, Women's Army Corps, 44, released as Cpl, 47, after serv in 5th Serv Command, 44-47; Good Conduct Medal in Am Theatre of Opers. Mem: NAACP (chmn educ, Champaign Co Chap, 70-); Am Sociol Soc; Nat Asn Social Workers; Caucus of Black Sociologists; League of Women Voters. Honors & Awards: Outstanding Honors, Victory Temple 530, Daughters of Elks, 68. Mailing Add: 309 W Michigan Ave Urbana IL 61801

SCOTT, BARBARA GARRETT (D)
Secy, Warren Co Dem Party, Tenn
b Overton Co, Tenn, Sept 23, 29; d Oren R Garrett & Beatrice Gunnels G; m 1948 to Melvin E Scott; c Melanie Ann & James Nathan. Educ: Tenn Technol Univ, BA, 65; Purdue Univ, Lafayette, MA, 69; Univ Tenn, Knoxville, PhD, cand in Eng, 71-; Sigma Tau Delta; Phi Kappa Phi; Howard Scholarship Award, 65. Polit & Govt Pos: Mem, Vol Women's Roundtable, 70-; secy, Warren Co Dem Party, 71-; deleg, Dem Nat Conv, 72; pres, Warren Co Dem Women's Club, 72- Bus & Prof Pos: Operator & supvr, Gen Tel Co, McMinnville, Tenn, 48-57; clerical worker, Standard Newspapers, 57-58; bookkeeper, Maxwell & Co Acct, 61-68; instr Eng, Tenn Technol Univ, 65-68; teaching asst, Purdue Univ, Lafayette, 68-69; instr, Motlow State Community Col, 69-71; teaching asst, Univ Tenn, Knoxville, 71- Mem: Tenn Educ Asn; Mod Lang Asn; Delta Kappa Gamma; Am Asn Univ Women. Honors & Awards: Delta Kappa Gamma Spec Scholarship, 72. Relig: United Methodist. Mailing Add: Rte 1 Rock Island TN 38581

SCOTT, BEATRICE NORMADINE (R)
b Gentry, Ark, July 25, 30; d Glenn Oliver Beckwith & Velma Lee Hardy B; m 1959 to Buford Scott; c Harold Leon, Glenn Arthur, Buford Lee, Rebecca Lynne & James Kent (deceased). Polit & Govt Pos: Past chmn for many Rep cand; pres, Stanton Co Women Rep Club, 60 & 62; co-dir, First Dist & Fifth Dist, Kans Fedn Rep Women, 62, dir, First Dist, 62-66; first alt deleg, Rep Nat Conv, 64; exec mem bd, Rep Assocs of Southwest Kans; precinct committeewoman; co-chmn for gubernatorial cand Rick Harman, First Dist; secy-treas, Stanton Co Taxpayers Fedn; Rep State Subdist, Finance Chmn; regional chmn, Nat Rep Comt-Action Now, 70-; dist coordr, Rep Nat Comt Mission 70's, 70- Bus & Prof Pos: Asst buyer, corset dept, Crosby Bros, Topeka, Kans, 58-59. Mem: Cosmos Club (pres); Hellou Leborium Club (secy-treas); Methodist Women Soc; Kans Flying Farmers; Sweet Adalines, Inc. Honors & Awards: Name included on the Rep Mem at Gettysburg, Pa. Relig: Baptist. Sunday Sch instr. Mailing Add: 5600 W 18th Terr Topeka KS 66604

SCOTT, BOBBY KENNETH (R)
Chmn, Pulaski Co Rep Comt, Ark
b Gravette, Ark, Oct 6, 33; s Kenneth Scott & Jeffa Beck S; m 1954 to Annice Embrey; c Beverly Ann, Debbie Lynn & Sheryl Kay. Educ: Univ Ark Sch Law, LLB, 58. Polit & Govt Pos: State committeeman, Benton Co Rep Comt, Ark, 58-60; city attorney, Rogers, Ark, 60-62; legal aide to Gov, Ark, 67-69; Comnr of Revenues, State of Ark, 69-70; chmn, Pulaski Co Rep Comt, Little Rock, Ark, 72- Mil Serv: Entered as Pvt, Army Nat Guard, 50, released as Cpl, 52, after serv in Z Battery 936th Field Artillery Bn, I Corp, Korea, 51-52; Routine Korean War Awards. Mem: Ark & Pulaski Co Bar Asns. Relig: 6th & Izard Church of Christ. Legal Res: 7304 Woodside Lane Little Rock AR 72205 Mailing Add: 420 Tower Bldg Little Rock AR 72201

SCOTT, BOYD FRANKLIN (R)
NMex State Rep
b Bon Ami, La, Dec 28, 11; s Boyd Jefferson Scott & Alice Lyons S; m 1934 to Josephine Cotter; c Marcialea (Mrs Matlock) & Dennis Jefferson. Educ: Baylor Univ, 29; Sul Ross State Col, 30-32; Alpha Psi Omega. Polit & Govt Pos: Mayor, Farmington, NMex, 68-74; NMex State Rep, 75- Bus & Prof Pos: Resident mgr, Frontier Theatres, Inc, Roswell, NMex, 48-54, dist mgr, Pecos, Tex, 54-57, vpres & asst gen mgr, Dallas, 57-62; secy-treas & gen mgr, Allen Theatres, Inc, Farmington, NMex, 63- Mem: NMex Theatre Asn; Mason; Elks; Community Concert Asn (dir, 75-). Honors & Awards: Citizen of the Year, Farmington CofC, 74. Relig: Presbyterian. Mailing Add: 1404 Camina Contenta Farmington NM 87401

SCOTT, DAVID (D)
Ga State Rep
Mailing Add: 190 Wendell Dr SE Atlanta GA 30315

SCOTT, DONALD B (D)
Wyo State Rep
Mailing Add: 3001 Monte Vista Torrington WY 82240

SCOTT, EDWARD SMITH (R)
Mem, Rep State Cent Comt Colo
b Denver, Colo, Aug 4, 28; s Jesse Carl Smith & Iola Verne Steveson S; m 1948 to Dorothy Edna Schmid; c Christopher, Bradford, Wendy, Rebecca, Cynthia & Jonathan. Educ: Univ Denver & Univ Wash, 45. Polit & Govt Pos: Councilman, Englewood, Colo, 55-57, mayor, 57-60; comnr, Arapahoe Co, 61-65; Colo State Sen, 65-69; Chmn for Nixon, Arapahoe Co, Colo, 68; secy, Arapahoe Co Rep Party, 69-70; chmn for Congressman Brotzman, Jefferson Co, 70, pres, Brotz-Men, 72; mem Rep State Cent Comt, Colo, 72- Bus & Prof Pos: Staff announcer, KLZ Radio, Denver, 47-49; staff performer, CBS-WBBM, 49-53; free lance performer, Chicago, Ill, 53; free lance Radio-TV performer, Denver, Colo, 53-61; pres, KLAK Radio, 61- Mem: Lakewood CofC, Colo (pres, 70-71); Denver CofC; Advert Club of Denver, Colo Broadcasters Asn; Denver Press Club. Honors & Awards: Selected as Colo Young Man of the Year, 59. Relig: Lutheran, Missouri Synod. Mailing Add: 3400 S Reed Lakewood CO 80227

SCOTT, EUGENE W, JR (D)
Chmn, Natchitoches Parish Dem Exec Comt, La
b Natchitoches, La, July 29, 38; s Eugene Whitcomb Scott, Sr & Lela Orr S; m 1958 to Shirley Ann Ackel; c Sadie, Eugene W, III & Craig. Educ: Northwestern State Col, BS, 60; Pi Kappa Phi. Polit & Govt Pos: Mem, Northwest Fish & Game Comn, 72-; chmn, Natchitoches Parish Dem Exec Comt, La, 75- Bus & Prof Pos: Gen mgr, secy-treas, Scott-Gatragan Agency, Ltd, Ins, 70-; owner, Scott Agency, Real Estate, 62- Mil Serv: Entered as 2nd Lt, Army, 60, released as 1st Lt, 62, after serv in 78th Artillery, 2nd Armored Div, 60-62; Cert of Achievement. Mem: La Asn Ins Agts; Nat Asn Ins Agts; Am Legion. Mailing Add: 130 Jefferson St Natchitoches LA 71457

SCOTT, GEORGE WILLIAM (R)
Wash State Sen
b Seattle, Wash, July 9, 37; s Arthur Pousette Scott & Eleanor Irene Bleasdale S; m 1965 to Carol Susan Rogel. Educ: Whitworth Col, BA, 59; Univ Wash, MA, 66, PhD, 70; Phi Alpha Theta. Polit & Govt Pos: Precinct Committeeman, 32nd Dist, 66-68; Wash State Rep, 46th Dist, 68-70; Wash State Sen, 46th Dist, 70- Bus & Prof Pos: Mem, faculty, Seattle Community Col, 69- Mil Serv: Entered as 2nd Lt, Marines, 59, released as Capt, 66, after serv in Third Marine Div, Okinawa from 59-62; Marines Res, 62-67. Mem: Seattle Munic League; Lions; Rotary; Am Legion; Mason. Mailing Add: 2530 NE 105th Place Seattle WA 98125

SCOTT, HAROLD JOSEPH (D)
Mich State Rep
b Flint, Mich, Oct 5, 38; s Harold Leroy Scott & Irene Archambault S; m 1960 to Jacqueline Isabelle Dombrosky; c Harold Anthony, John Charles, Ann Marie & Michael Andrew. Educ: Univ Mich, BA, 60; Wayne State Univ, MA, 64. Polit & Govt Pos: Mich State Rep, 80th Dist, 73- Bus & Prof Pos: Teacher, Wyandotte Schs, Mich, 61-67, Indian River Jr Col, Ft Pierce, Fla, 67-68, Grand Blanc Schs, Mich, 68-69 & Mt Morris Schs, 69-72. Mem: KofC. Relig: Roman Catholic. Legal Res: 3526 Blue Lake Dr Flint MI 48506 Mailing Add: Mich House of Rep Capital Bldg Lansing MI 48933

SCOTT, HUGH (R)
Minority Leader, US Senate
b Fredericksburg, Va, Nov 11, 00; s Hugh Scott & Jane Lee Lewis S; m 1924 to Marian Huntington Chase; c Marian (Mrs Concannon) & eight grandchildren. Educ: Univ Pa, 18; Randolph-Macon Col, AB, 19; Univ Va, LLB, 22; Balliol Col, Oxford, Michaelmas term, vis fel, 67; Phi Beta Kappa; Tau Kappa Alpha; Phi Alpha Delta; Alpha Chi Rho (nat pres, 42-46). Hon Degrees: Numerous degrees from various cols & univs. Polit & Govt Pos: Asst dist attorney, Philadelphia, Pa, 26-41; US Rep, Pa, 41-58, nat chmn, Rep Party, 48-49; mem, Bd Visitors, Naval Acad, 48, & Univ Va, 71; chmn, Bd Visitors, Merchant Marine Acad, 59, Coast Guard Acad, 63; chmn, Eisenhower Hq Comt, mem personal staff & chmn regional orgn, Eisenhower Campaign, 52; gen counsel, Rep Nat Comt, 55-60, ex officio mem, 74-; US Sen, Pa, 58-, mem, Comts on Foreign Rels, Judiciary, Rules & Admin Comts & Rep Policy, US Senate, currently, US deleg, Int Orgn meetings in Uruguay, India, Switz, Australia, Can, Germany, France & Gt Brit, vpres, Rep Sen Campaign Comt, Asst Floor Leader, 69, Minority Leader, 69-, mem, Joint Comt on Printing, Rep Coordr Comt & Joint House-Senate Rep Leadership Comt, currently; mem Bd of Regents, Smithsonian Inst, currently; Nat Visitor Facilities Adv Comn, Interparliamentary Union; vpres, US deleg, currently; deleg, Rep Nat Conv, 68 & 72, vchmn, Platform Comt, 68; co-chmn truth squad, Rep Presidential Campaign, 68. Bus & Prof Pos: Counsel to firm of Obermayer, Rebmann, Maxwell & Hippel,

Philadelphia. Mil Serv: Entered as Lt, Naval Res, 42, released, 46, after serv with NAtlantic Patrol, Occup of Iceland, Pac Theater & Occup of Japan with Third Amphibious Force, also served temporary duty aboard carrier Valley Forge & at Naktong in Korean War, 50; Capt (Ret), Naval Res; Navy Commendation Ribbon; Philippine Liberation Medal; Atlantic Convoy M Medal. Publ: The Golden Age of Chinese Art: The Lively T'ang Dynasty, Charles E Tuttle Co, 66; How to Run for Public Office & Win, The Nat Press, Inc, 68; Come to the Party, Prentice-Hall, Inc, 68; plus others & numerous mag articles. Mem: Am Legion; VFW; Germantown Lions; Pa Soc of NY; Chinese Art Soc of Am. Honors & Awards: Comdr, Royal Order of Serv Merit, First Class, Repub of Korea; First Annual Foreign Trade Award for Outstanding Serv to the Port & City of Philadelphia; Gtr Philadelphia Mag 50th Anniversary Award, Pa Asn Broadcasters' Award, 63; 1968 Alumni Distinguished Serv Award, Randolph-Macon Col; numerous civic, religious, press, vet orgn & Man of Year awards. Relig: Episcopal. Legal Res: 44 Hillcrest Ave Chestnut Hill Philadelphia PA 19118 Mailing Add: 260 Senate Off Bldg Washington DC 20510

SCOTT, JEREMIAH RONALD, JR (R)
b Fortuna, Calif, Sept 18, 36; s Jeremiah R Scott & Faye Townsend S; m 1961 to Mary Griswold; c McGregor W, Stuart J & Catherine A. Educ: Westminster Col, AB, 58; Univ Santa Clara, JD, 63; Scabbard & Blade Mil Soc; Beta Theta Pi. Polit & Govt Pos: Mem bd of trustees, Eureka Bd of Educ, Calif, 68-; chmn, Humboldt Co Rep Cent Comt, 69-74. Bus & Prof Pos: Attorney, Eureka, Calif, 64- Mil Serv: Entered as 2nd Lt, Army, 59, released as Lt, 60; Capt, Army Res, 60-68. Mem: Calif & Am Bar Asns; F&AM; Kiwanis. Relig: Protestant. Mailing Add: 4945 Myers St Eureka CA 95501

SCOTT, JESSE W (R)
NH State Rep
Mailing Add: RFD 1 Box 95 Newport NH 03773

SCOTT, JOHN M (R)
Ohio State Rep
Mailing Add: 2513 Cross Country Rd Fairborn OH 45324

SCOTT, KENNETH DANIEL (D)
Iowa State Sen
b Mason City, Iowa; s Walter Daniel Scott & Hattie Diercks S; m 1961 to Lorraine Grace Tuchtenhagen (Penny); stepchildren Randolph Lee, Alan John & Jane Marie Tuchtenhagen. Educ: Rockwell High Sch, Iowa, dipl, 48; Reisch Am Sch Auctioneering, Mason City, 69. Polit & Govt Pos: Trustee, Thornton Twp, Iowa, 66-69; committeeman, Agr Stabilization & Conserv Serv Comt & treas, soil conserv serv, Cerro Gordo Co, Iowa, 68-69; mem, Meservy-Thornton Sch Bd, 69, pres, 70; Iowa State Rep, 71-72; Iowa State Sen, 73- Bus & Prof Pos: Farmer, 48-; pres, Norseland Farms, Inc, 65-; real estate salesman, 68-; owner & operator, Ken Scott, Inc, 69-70; auctioneer, 69- Mem: Cerro Gordo Taxpayers Asn (dir); Cerro Gordo Exec Club; Pleasant Valley Country Club. Relig: Methodist. Legal Res: Rte 1 Thornton IA 50479 Mailing Add: State House Des Moines IA 50319

SCOTT, KENNETH EDMUND (R)
Chmn, Elbert Co Rep Party, Colo
b Carrolton, Mo, Sept 15, 03; s John Michael Scott & Flora Harris S; m 1927 to Lyndall Deming; c Kenneth E, James A, Lawrence D & Mary Pearl (Mrs Filson). Educ: Pleasanton High Sch, Kans, grad, 23. Polit & Govt Pos: Rep precinct committeeman, 64-; chmn, Elbert Co Rep Party, Colo, 70- Bus & Prof Pos: Self employed rancher & trucker. Mem: Colo Motor Carriers Asn (charter mem, bd dirs); Farm Bur. Relig: Methodist. Mailing Add: Star Route Kiowa CO 80117

SCOTT, L O (INDEPENDENT)
Va State Deleg
Mailing Add: Rte 3 Box 65 Amelia VA 23002

SCOTT, LEON (D)
Chmn, Delaware Co Dem Cent Comt, Ind
b Galveston, Ind, Aug 27, 15; s Lee Scott & Nellie Graham S; m 1939 to Rachel Bowell; c David C & Jack Beck, foster son. Educ: Ball State Univ, BS, 34, MA, 43; Butler Univ, 37-38; Ind Univ, 47-50; Phi Delta Kappa; Sigma Tau Gamma. Polit & Govt Pos: Chmn bd trustees, Muncie Pub Libr, Ind, 58-; chmn, Delaware Co Dem Cent Comt, 70- Bus & Prof Pos: Teacher, Pendleton, Ind, formerly; teacher, Cass Co, formerly; teacher & prin, Forest Park Sch, Muncie, 39- Mil Serv: Entered as Pvt, Army, 43, released as First Lt, 45, after serv in Fourth Armored & 12th Armored Div, ETO, 44-45; Purple Heart. Mem: Mason; Scottish Rite; Shrine; Amvets; Am Farm Bur. Relig: Unitarian Universalist Asn. Mailing Add: 2500 Petty Rd Muncie IN 47304

SCOTT, MARGARET P (R)
Women's VChmn, Southern Div, Rep State Cent Comt Calif
b Los Angeles, Calif, Sept 3, 18; d Earl W Paul & Nellie Rugg P; m 1940 to Wayne W Scott; c James P, Susan & Deborah. Educ: Pomona Col, BA. Polit & Govt Pos: First vpres & pres, Santa Monica Rep Women Fedn Calif, formerly; fourth vpres, Los Angeles Co Fedn Rep Women, 67-69, first vpres, 69-71, pres, 71-73; Presidential Elector, 72; pres, Southern Div, Calif Fedn Rep Women, 73; womens vchmn, Southern Div, Rep State Cent Comt, Calif, 75- Mem: Apt Asn, Los Angeles-Western Cities, Inc; DAR; Native Daughters Golden West: Freedoms Found at Valley Forge. Honors & Awards: Distinguished Serv Award, Freedoms Found at Valley Forge. Relig: Protestant. Mailing Add: 16945 Avenida de Santa Ynez Pacific Palisades CA 90272

SCOTT, NORMA JOYCE (R)
Chmn, Mineral Co Rep Cent Comt, Nev
b Chico, Calif, Aug 30, 28; d William Lowery Montgomery & Ruth Townsend M; m 1954 to James Nixon Scott; c William Allen. Educ: Univ Nev, Reno, 47. Polit & Govt Pos: Secy-treas, Mineral Co Rep Cent Comt, Nev, 70-72, chmn, 74- Bus & Prof Pos: Staff clerk, Nev Bell, 60- Mem: Bus & Prof Womens Club Hawthorne; Royal Neighbors Am; Commun Workers Am; Nev Fedn Bus & Prof Womens Clubs (first vpres, 75-). Relig: Episcopal. Legal Res: 675 K St Hawthorne NV 89415 Mailing Add: PO Box 756 Hawthorne NV 89415

SCOTT, RALPH H (D)
NC State Sen
b Haw River, NC, Dec 12, 03; s Robert Walter Scott & Elizabeth Hughes S; m 1925 to Hazeleene Tate; c Miriam (Mrs C W Mayo, III), Ralph Henderson, Jr & William Clevenger. Educ: NC State Col, BS, 25. Polit & Govt Pos: NC State Sen, 51-56 & 61-, vchmn, Comt Interstate & Fedn Rels, Pub Roads, Appropriations, 67, finance chmn, 67, Cong Redistricting, Mfg, Labor & Commerce, Pub Utilities, Banking, Salaries & Fees, Wildlife, past chmn, Propositions & Grievances, past pres, Comt on Agr, mem, Adv Budget Comn, 61-64 & 68-69, past mem, Alamance Co Bd Comnrs, author, Haw River Stream Pollution Legis, pres pro tem, 63, chmn, Rules Comt, 63, chmn, Higher Educ, 63, chmn, Gov Comn Ment Retardation & State Farmers Home Admin Adv Comt, NC State Senate; deleg, Dem Nat Conv, 68. Bus & Prof Pos: Pres & mgr, Melville Dairy, Inc; past pres & treas, Alamance Frozen Foods, Inc; dir & chmn bd, Carolina Casualty Ins Co; dir, First Fed Saving & Loan Asn, Copland Fabrics & Copland, Inc, Burlington Community Cent Inc & Mid State Tile Co; past pres & dir, NC RR; vpres & dir, Alamance Broadcasting Co; pres & dir, Alamance Dairy Foods, Inc. Mem: AF&AM (Bula Lodge No 209); Elks; Moose (Burlington Moose Lodge No 649); Knights Templer; Royal Arch Mason. Honors & Awards: Nat Distinguished Legis Serv Award, Nat Educ Asn Dept Rural Educ, 66. Relig: Presbyterian; chmn, Comt Christian Educ, teacher, Young Married Couples Class, trustee, Orange Presbytery Sch, Glade Valley, chmn bd & trustee, Orange Presbytery Camp New Hope, mem exec comt, Church Exten, Synod of NC, chmn Bd Deacons, 38-50 & Elder, 50-; moderator, Orange Presbytery Church, 70- Mailing Add: Haw River NC 27258

SCOTT, RALPH JAMES (D)
b Pinnacle, NC, Oct 15, 05; s Samuel Martin Scott & Daisy Cook S; m 1929 to Verna Denny; c Patricia Ann Southern, W F Southern, Nancy Ellen Shumate & Grady C Shumate. Educ: Wake Forest Col, LLB, 30. Polit & Govt Pos: NC State Rep, 36-37; chmn, Stakes Co Dem Exec Comt, NC, 36-72; dist solicitor, 38-56; US Rep, NC, 56-66; chief asst solicitor, Superior Court, 21st Solicitorial Dist, 71-72. Bus & Prof Pos: Attorney-at-law, 30- Mem: NC State Bar, Inc; Mason; Shrine; Elks; Moose. Relig: Baptist. Mailing Add: Box 97 Seven Island Rd Danbury NC 27016

SCOTT, RICHARD ELEY (D)
b Kilgore, Tex, Dec 25, 45; s James Pirson Scott & Cliffie Mae William S; single. Educ: Tyler Dist Jr Col, Tex, 64-65; Kilgore Jr Col, 65-66; Prairie View Agr & Mech Col, BA in Polit Sci, 68; Leadership Sch, Lowry Air Force Base, Denver, 69; Univ Tex Law Sch, Austin, JD, 73; Barons Innovations; Thurgood Marshall Legal Soc. Polit & Govt Pos: Deleg & Floor Whip for US Sen Hubert Humphrey, Dem Nat Conv, 72; legal asst for Tex State Rep, 73- Bus & Prof Pos: Pvt attorney, 72- Mil Serv: E-4, Air Force Res, 68- Mem: State Bar of Tex; Am & Travis Co Bar Asns; Phi Alpha Delta; East Austin Cultural Found (attorney, 72-). Relig: Baptist. Mailing Add: 2115 E 19th St Austin TX 78702

SCOTT, RICHARD M (R)
Mayor, Lancaster, Pa
b Lancaster, Pa, Apr 28, 18; s Roy V Scott & Laura E Martin S; m 1942 to Flora Anne Fonneman; c Sue Ann (Mrs Hugh D Campbell), Stephanie Laura (Mrs Brenton Grimes) & Richard Michael. Educ: US Mil Acad, BS, 42; Air Command & Staff Col, 48; Armed Forces Staff Col, 54; Univ NMex Col Govt, 56-58; George Washington Univ, MA, 67; Nat War Col, 67; Phi Sigma Alpha. Polit & Govt Pos: Mayor, Lancaster, Pa, 74- Bus & Prof Pos: Gen mgr, Lancaster Automobile Club, 70-74. Mil Serv: Entered as 2nd Lt, Army Air Force, released as Brigadier Gen, 70, after 28 years of continuous active serv in continental US, Europe & Asia; Distinguished Serv Medal; Legion of Merit; Command Pilot. Mem: Lancaster Exchange Club; Retired Officers Asn; Am Legion; Reserve Officers Asn; Lancaster CofC. Relig: Covenant United Methodist. Legal Res: 144 N Mulberry St Lancaster PA 17603 Mailing Add: 120 N Duke St Lancaster PA 17604

SCOTT, ROBERT WALTER (D)
b Haw River, Alamance Co, NC, June 13, 29; s W Kerr Scott & Mary Elizabeth White S; m 1951 to Jessie Rae Osborne; c Mary Ella, Margaret Rose, Susan Rae, W Kerr & Janet Louise. Educ: Duke Univ, 47-49; NC State Col, BS, Animal Indust, 50-52. Polit & Govt Pos: Dem Precinct chmn, co vchmn & state solicitorial dist exec comt, 60-64; Lt Gov, NC, 65-69, Gov, 69-72; deleg, Dem Nat Conv, 68 & 72; chmn, Dem Gov Caucus, 70-72; mem exec comt, Nat Gov Conf, 70-72; chmn, Southern Regional Educ Bd, 70- Bus & Prof Pos: Dairy farmer. Mil Serv: Spec agent Counter Intel Corps, Army, 53-55. Mem: NC Farm Bur Fedn; NC State Grange (Master, 61-63); past chmn, United Forces for Educ in NC; pres, NC Soc of Farm Mgr & Rural Appraisers (pres); Burlington-Alamance Co CofC. Honors & Awards: Nat Grange Young Couple of the Year, 59; Alamance Co Young Farmer of the Year, 57. Relig: Presbyterian; Deacon, Hawfields Presbyterian Church, 59-63, Elder, 63- Mailing Add: Rte 1 Haw River NC 27258

SCOTT, STANLEY S (R)
b Bolivar, Tenn, July 2, 33; m to Bettye L; c Kenneth L & Susan Lovejoy & Stanley Southall, II. Educ: Kans Univ, 51-53; Lincoln Univ, BS, 59. Polit & Govt Pos: Asst to dir commun, Exec Br, White House, 71-73, Spec Asst to the President, 73- Bus & Prof Pos: Ed & gen mgr, Memphis World, Tenn, 60-61; news reporter, copy writer & ed writer, Atlanta Daily World, Ga, 61-64; news reporter, United Press Int, New York, 64-66; asst dir pub rels, NAACP, New York Hq, 66-67; radio newsman, Westinghouse Broadcasting Corp, New York, 67-71. Mil Serv: Army, 54-56, serv in Korea. Mem: Am Fedn TV & Radio Artists; NY Reporters Asn; NAACP; Huntington Long Island Civic Asn. Honors & Awards: Pulitzer Prize Nomination for Coverage of Malcolm X Assassination; Distinguished Pub Serv Award, Nat Asn Real Estate Brokers; Outstanding Alumni Award, Lincoln Univ; Russwurm Award for Excellence in Radio News Reporting; Commun Award, Nat Asn Mkt Developers. Relig: Congregational. Mailing Add: 454 M St SW Washington DC 20024

SCOTT, THOMAS JACKSON (D)
WVa State Deleg
b Edgington, Ky, Sept 12, 24; s Sevier Scott & Laura Pack S; m 1966 to Shirley Ann Hammond; c Anthony Michael & Sherri Michelle. Educ: McVeich High Sch. Polit & Govt Pos: Officer McDowell Young Dem, 61-65; WVa State Deleg, 71- Bus & Prof Pos: Draftsman, US Steel Corp, Gary, WVa, 51- Mem: Gary Country Club; Welch Little League. Relig: Methodist. Mailing Add: 47 Court St Welch WV 24801

SCOTT, THOMAS LESLIE (D)
Mem, Ga State Dem Exec Comt
b Atlanta, Ga, Nov 2, 34; s James Randolph Scott & Eugenia May Guest S; m 1960 to Linda Maxine Bentley; c Thomas L, Jr, Ira Randolph & Jack Bryan. Educ: Univ Ga, LLB, 60; Phi Alpha Delta. Polit & Govt Pos: Mem, Ga State Dem Exec Comt, 71- Bus & Prof Pos: Partner, Law Firm of Swertfeger, Scott, Pike & Simmons, Decatur, Ga, 60- Mil Serv: Entered as Pvt 1/c, Army, 54, released as Cpl, 56, after serv in 82nd Airborne, Ft Bragg, NC, Am Continental Command, 54-56; Sgt 1/c, Army Res, 56-64; Good Conduct Medal; Parachuter's Medal; Expert Infantryman Award. Mem: Masons, Lithonia Lodge 84; F&AM, 32 degree

Scottish Rite, Atlanta; Rock Chapel Elem Sch PTA; Ga Munic Asn. Relig: Methodist. Mailing Add: 1985 Stephenson Rd Lithonia GA 30058

SCOTT, ULRIC CARL (DFL)
VChmn, Winona Co Dem-Farmer-Labor Party, Minn
b St Paul, Minn, Apr 26, 32; s Ulric Scott & Annamae Gorry S; m 1959 to Mary Judd; c David, Jennifer, Philip, Paul, Ulric, III, Thomas & Elizabeth. Educ: St Mary's Col (Minn), BA, 57; Univ Minn, Minneapolis, PhD, 70; Alpha Phi Delta; Newman Club. Polit & Govt Pos: Mem, Winona Co Dem-Farmer-Labor Exec Comt, Minn, 70-72, vchmn, 72-; mem, McGovern for President State Steering Comt, 71-72; precinct coordr, Mondale for Sen Campaign, 72; deleg & mem rules comt, Dem Nat Conv, 72; co-chmn, Dem-Farmer-Labor Party State Conv Rules Comt, 72; mem, Minn Dem-Farmer-Labor Party State Cent Comt, 72-; moderator, St Mary's Col (Minn) Young Dem, 72-; cand, US House of Rep, Minn, 74. Bus & Prof Pos: High sch instr, Ramsey Co Home Sch for Boys, Minn, 59-62, asst supt, 62-63; dir student teaching, Col St Catherine, 63-67; asst acad dean, St Mary's Col (Minn), 67-70, vpres for acad affairs, 70- Publ: Ed, Man Before the Death of God (by Gabriel Marcel), Col St Catherine, 66; auth, The Philosophical Notebooks of George Berkeley, Univ Microfilms, 70; Current comments, (weekly column), Progress, 73- Mem: Kiwanis; Serra Int. Relig: Roman Catholic. Mailing Add: 1176 W Fifth St Winona MN 55987

SCOTT, WILLIAM EARL (D)
Mem, Ga State Dem Exec Comt
b Anderson, SC, Dec 8, 34; s Roy Harold Scott & Dorothy Greene S; m 1973 to Trula Kirkpatrick; c William Earl, Jr & Tony. Educ: Univ SC, Columbia, BS, 57; US Air Force Command & Staff Col, 74; Indust Col of Armed Forces, currently. Polit & Govt Pos: Chmn, 42nd Dist Dem Comt, Ga, 74-75; mem, Fulton Co Dem Exec Comt, Ga, 74-; mem, Ga State Dem Exec Comt, 74- Bus & Prof Pos: Pilot, Piedmont Airlines, Atlanta, Ga, 66- Mil Serv: Entered as 2nd Lt, Air Force, 57, released as Capt, 65, after serv in 2nd & 384th Air Refueling Squadron, Strategic Air Command, 59-65; Maj, Air Nat Guard, 65-; Combat Readiness with two Oak Leaf Clusters; Air Force Longevity; Armed Serv Res Medal; State Ga Ribbon; Nat Defense Ribbon. Mem: Airline Pilots Asn. Relig: Christian. Legal Res: 150 Port Antonio Ct College Park GA 30337 Mailing Add: Box 87431 College Park GA 30337

SCOTT, WILLIAM J (R)
Attorney Gen, Ill
b Chicago, Ill, Nov 11, 26; s William Earl Scott & Edith Swanson S; m to Ellen; c Elizabeth Ann & William Gregory. Educ: Bucknell Univ, 45; Univ Pa, 46; Chicago-Kent Col of Law, JD, 50. Polit & Govt Pos: Rep precinct committeeman, Ill, 17 years; first vpres, Ill Young Rep Orgn, Ill, 49, exec dir, 50; chmn, Cook Co Young Rep Orgn, 50; spec asst to US Attorney, Northern Dist of Ill, 59; state treas, Ill, 63-67; attorney gen, Ill, 69-; deleg, Rep Nat Conv, 72. Bus & Prof Pos: Lawyer; officer, Am Nat Bank; vpres, commercial div & mem mgr comt, Nat Blvd Bank of Chicago, 59-62. Mil Serv: Navy, 45-46. Mem: Am Bar Asn; Chicago Asn of Commerce; Ill CofC; trustee, MacMurray Col (trustee). Relig: Presbyterian; Elder. Legal Res: 520 S Second St Springfield IL 62706 Mailing Add: 500 S Second St Springfield IL 62701

SCOTT, WILLIAM L (R)
US Sen, Va
b Williamsburg, Va, July 1, 15; m to Inez Huffman; c Gail Ann, Bill Jr & Paul. Educ: George Washington Univ, JD; past chancellor, Sigma Nu Phi. Polit & Govt Pos: Mem, Va Rep State Cent Comt, 64-68; US Rep, Va, 67-73; deleg, Rep Nat Conv, 68 & 72; US Sen, Va, 73-, mem armed servs comt, US Senate, 73-, mem judiciary & vet affairs comt, 75- Bus & Prof Pos: Attorney-at-law; with Fed Govt, 26 years, primarily as trial attorney with Dept of Justice. Mil Serv: Army, World War II. Mem: Lions; Am Legion; 40 et 8; Mason (33 degree); Shrine. Relig: Methodist. Mailing Add: 3930 W Ox Rd Fairfax VA 22030

SCRANTON, ANDREA ABBOTT (R)
NH State Rep
b Cambridge, Mass, Nov 7, 19; d William G Abbott, Sr (deceased) & Andrea Mahan A; m 1949 to William Maxwell Scranton; c Nancy, John, James & Sarah. Educ: Smith Col, AB, 41. Polit & Govt Pos: Mem, Keene Sch Bd, 70-73; NH State Rep, 73-; vchmn, Cheshire Co Rep Party, 75- Mil Serv: Ens, Coast Guard Women's Res, 42-46. Mem: NH Smith Col Club; Keene Co Club; Cheshire Hosp Aid Soc; Keene Archit Rev Bd. Relig: Episcopal. Mailing Add: RFD 2 Hurricane Rd Keene NH 03431

SCRANTON, WILLIAM WARREN (R)
b Madison, Conn, July 19, 17; s Worthington Scranton & Marion Margery S; m 1942 to Mary L Chamberlin; c Susan (Mrs Richard Wolf), William W, Joseph C & Peter K. Educ: Yale Univ, BA, 39, Yale Law Sch, LLB, 46. Hon Degrees: Numerous degrees from various cols & univs. Polit & Govt Pos: Spec asst to Secy of State Christian Herter, 59-60; US Rep, Pa, 61-63; Gov, Pa, 63-67; exec comt mem, Nat Gov Conf, 65-67; mem, Rep Nat Coord Comt, 65-66; vchmn, President's Panel on Insurance for Riot Torn Areas, 67; deleg & chmn, Comt on Judiciary, Pa State Const Conv, 67-68; made two fact-finding missions for President Nixon to Western Europe & Mid East, 68; Ambassador & Chmn, US Deleg INTELSAT, 69; chmn, President's Comn on Campus Unrest, 70. Bus & Prof Pos: Lawyer, O'Malley, Harris, Warren & Hill, 47; vpres, Int Textbook Co, 49-52; dir & pres, Scranton Lackawanna Trust Co, 54-56; chmn bd, Nat Liberty Corp, Scott Paper Co & Int Bus Mach, currently; bd mem, Northeastern Nat Bank, currently, chmn bd, 73-; dir, Sun Oil Co, 73-, bd mem, currently; trustee, Mutual of New York, currently. Mil Serv: Entered as Aviation Cadet, Army Air Force, 41, released as Capt, 45. Relig: Protestant. Legal Res: Northeastern Nat Bank Scranton PA 18503 Mailing Add: Box 116 Marworth Dalton PA 18414

SCRIBNER, CALVIN THEODIS (D)
Mem Exec Comt, Ark State Dem Comt
b Little Rock, Ark, Apr 21, 22; s Henry E Scribner & Georgia McClendon S; m 1946 to Rosa Tayborn; c Carolyn Rose. Educ: Ark Baptist Col, 50. Polit & Govt Pos: Mem, Ark State Dem Comt, 74-, mem exec comt, 74-; mem, Pulaski Co Comt, 74-, mem exec comt, 74- Mil Serv: Entered as Pvt, Air Force, 41, released as Pfc, 45, after serv in 2046 Truck Co, Pac, 44-45; Asiatic, Pac & Good Conduct Medals. Mem: Teamsters Union; Trinity Lodge F&AM. Relig: Baptist. Mailing Add: 2523 S Ringo St Little Rock AR 72206

SCRIBNER, FRED CLARK, JR (R)
b Bath, Maine, Feb 14, 08; s Fred Clark Scribner & Emma Adelaide Cheltra S; m 1935 to Barbara Curtis Merrill; c Fred Clark, III, Curtis Merrill & Charles Dewey. Educ: Dartmouth Col, AB, 30; Harvard Col, LLB, 33; Phi Beta Kappa; Delta Sigma Rho; Alpha Chi Rho. Hon Degrees: LLD, Univ Maine, 58, Dartmouth, Colby & Bowdoin Cols, 59, Univ Vt, 60. Polit & Govt Pos: Chmn, Portland City Rep Comt, Maine, 36-40; chmn, Maine Coun Young Rep Clubs, 38-40; mem exec comt, Maine State Rep Comt, 40-50, chmn, 44-50; Rep Nat Committeeman, Maine, 48-56; deleg, Rep Nat Conv, 40, 44, 56, 60, 64 & 68, gen counsel, Arrangements Comt, 56, 64 & 68; gen counsel, Rep Nat Comt, 52-55 & 61-72; gen counsel, Dept Treas, 55-57, asst secy treas, 57, under secy treas, 57-61; pres, Maine Const Comt, 62-63. Bus & Prof Pos: Partner, law firm Pierce, Atwood, Scribner, Allen & McKusick, Portland, Maine & Scribner, Hall, Thornburg & Thompson, Washington, DC; dir, gen counsel, vpres & treas, Bates Mfg Co, Lewiston, Maine, 46-55; chmn bd of dirs, Coordinated Apparel, Inc. Mem: Mason (33 degree); Capitol Hill Club; Portland Club; Woodfords Club; Kiwanis. Honors & Awards: Alexander Hamilton Award. Relig: Episcopal; mem of standing comt, Diocese of Maine; deleg, Gen Conv PE Church, 43, 46, 52, 61, 67, 69 & 70. Legal Res: 335 Foreside Rd Falmouth ME 04105 Mailing Add: Tenth Floor One Monument Sq Portland ME 04111

SCRIBNER, RODNEY LATHAM (D)
State Treas, Maine
b Rumford, Maine, May 6, 35; s Dwight Latham Scribner & Evaline May House S; m 1963 to Evelyn Jean Sanborn. Educ: Maine Maritime Acad, BS, 56. Polit & Govt Pos: Vchmn, Oxford Co Dem Comt, Maine, 61-62; chmn, Ward 3, Precinct 2, 64-66; asst legis finance officer, Maine Legis, 65; treas, Portland Dem City Comt, 66-68; Maine State Rep, 67-68; dep comnr, Maine Dept of Finance & Admin, 68-71; acting comnr, Maine Dept of Indian Affairs, 69-70; state controller, Maine, 71-72, state budget officer, 72-73, state treas, 75- Bus & Prof Pos: Certified Pub Acct, Staples & Boyce, Portland, Maine, 62-68. Mil Serv: Entered as Ensign, Navy, 56, released as Lt(jg), 58; Lt(jg), Naval Res, 56-; Third Mate, Merchant Marine, 58-62. Publ: Raising state & local revenues: emerging patterns in revenue syst, Nat Gov Conf, 7/68. Mem: Am Inst of Certified Pub Accts; Maine Soc of Pub Accts; Am Soc for Pub Admin; KofP; Dramatic Order Knights of Khorassan. Relig: Baptist. Mailing Add: 190 Alton Rd Augusta ME 04330

SCULL, DAVID LEE (D)
Md State Deleg
b Washington, DC, May 10, 43; s David Scull & Elizabeth Lee S; m 1967 to Nancy Spering. Educ: Princeton Univ, AB, 65; Univ Va, MA & JD, 68; Campus Club. Polit & Govt Pos: Mem steering comt, Montgomery Co Dem Conv, Md, 73-74; vchairperson, Precinct 7-16, 73-74; mem, Gov Task Force to Study Campaign Financing, Md, 74-75; Md State Deleg, 75- Bus & Prof Pos: Attorney-at-law, Fried, Frank, Harris, Shriver & Kampelman, Washington, DC, 71-74; attorney-at-law, Dobrovir, Pub Interest Law Firm, 75- Mil Serv: Entered as 1st Lt, Army, 68, released as Capt, 71, after serv in HQ Europe, 68-70 & HQ MACV, Vietnam, 70-71; Bronze Star. Mem: Am, Md, Va & DC Bar Asns; Md Consumer Coun (bd dirs, 73-). Legal Res: 8717 Susanna Lane Chevy Chase MD 20015 Mailing Add: 2005 L St NW Washington DC 20036

SCULLY, JOHN PATRICK (D)
Mont State Rep
b Dillon, Mont, Sept 23, 46; s John F Scully & Madalyn C McDonnell S; m 1972 to Antoinette Catherine Caneda; c Betsy Jean. Educ: Univ Wis-Madison, BS, 69; Univ Mont Law Sch, JD, 72; Phi Epsilon Kappa; Iron Cross; Sigma Chi. Polit & Govt Pos: Mont State Rep, 75-, vchmn, Admin Code & Regulation Comn, Mont House Rep, 75- Mil Serv: 2nd Lt, Army Res, 69- Mem: Bozeman Lions; Am Bar Asn; Elks. Mailing Add: Box 1172 Bozeman MT 59715

SCULLY, WILLIAM JAMES, JR (D)
Conn State Rep
b Waterbury, Conn, Dec 11, 39; s William James Scully, Sr & Alice Doyle S; m 1965 to Ellyn Bergin; c Mary Margaret, Kathleen Elizabeth, William James, III & Sean Michael. Educ: Univ Conn, BA; Fairfield Univ, 1 year; Sherman House; Newman Club; Young Dem. Polit & Govt Pos: Mem local exec bd, State Young Dem, Conn, 62-68, treas, 63-65 & vpres, 65-66, pres, 72-73; deleg, Young Dem State Conv, 63-68; deleg, Young Dem Nat Conv, 65; Conn State Rep, 75th Dist, 69- Mem: Toast Masters Int; KofC; Washington Park Community Club; Hibernians; Eagles. Relig: Catholic. Mailing Add: 38 Walnut Ave Waterbury CT 06704

SEABORG, GLENN T (D)
b Ishpeming, Mich, Apr 19, 12; s H Theodore Seaborg & Selma Erickson S; m 1942 to Helen L Griggs; c Peter, Lynne (Mrs William B Cobb), David, Stephen, Eric & Dianne. Educ: Univ Calif, Los Angeles, AB, 34; Univ Calif, Berkeley, PhD in Chem, 37; Phi Beta Kappa; Alpha Chi Sigma; Phi Lambda Upsilon; Sigma Xi. Hon Degrees: Numerous degrees from various cols & univs. Polit & Govt Pos: Mem, First Gen Adv Comt, US Atomic Energy Comn, Washington, DC, 46-50, mem, Hist Adv Comt, 58-61, chmn, Comn, 61-71; consult, Argonne Nat Lab, 46-51; consult, Tech Adv Panel on Atomic Energy, Research & Develop Bd, Dept of Defense, 50-55; mem, Adv Comt for Chem, Oak Ridge Nat Lab, 54-61; mem, Vis Comt, Dept Chem, Brookhaven Nat Lab, 55-58; mem, Adv Comt on New Educ Media, US Off Educ, 58-60; mem, President's Sci Adv Comt, 59-61; mem, Nat Sci Bd, Nat Sci Found, 60-61, mem, Adv Coun on Col Chem, 62-67; US Rep, Fifth thru 15th Gen Conf, Int Atomic Energy Agency, Vienna, 61-71; mem, Fed Radiation Coun, 61-69; mem, Fed Coun for Sci & Technol, 61-71; mem, Nat Aeronaut & Space Coun, 61-71; chmn, US Deleg to USSR for signing of Memorandum on Coop in Field of Utilization of Atomic Energy for Peaceful Purposes, 63; mem, Secy of State Rusk's Deleg to USSR for Signing of Limited Test Ban Treaty, 63; chmn, US Deleg, Third Int Conf on Peaceful Uses of Atomic Energy, Geneva, 64, chmn, US Deleg & Pres, Fourth Int Conf, 71; mem, President's Comt on Equal Employ Opportunity, 61-65; mem, President's Comt on Manpower, 64-69; mem, Nat Coun on Marine Resources & Eng Develop, 66-71; mem, Sci Adv Group, Nat Selective Serv, 65-70. Bus & Prof Pos: Research assoc with Prof Gilbert N Lewis, Univ Calif, Berkeley, 37-39, instr chem, 39-41, asst prof, 41-45, prof, 45-71 (on leave of absence, 61-71), Univ Prof, 71-, dir nuclear chem research, Lawrence Berkeley Lab, 46-58 & 72-, assoc dir lab, 54-61 & 72-, chancellor, Univ, 58-61; dir plutonium work, Manhattan Proj, Univ Chicago Metallurgical Lab, 42-46; bd dirs, Nat Educ TV & Radio Ctr, 58-64 & 67-70; chmn steering comt, Chem Educ Material Study, 59-74; trustee, Sci Serv, 65-, pres, 66-; mem, Nat Programming Coun for Pub TV, 70-72; trustee, Educ Broadcasting Corp, 70-72; dir, Calif Coun Environ & Econ Balance, 74- Publ: Oppenheimer, (w I I Rabi, R Serber, V F Weisskopf & A Pais), Charles Scribner's Sons, 69; Man & Atom, (w W R Corliss), E P Dutton, 71; Nuclear Milestones, Freeman & Co, 72, plus many others. Mem: Nat Acad Sci; Am Asn Advan Sci (fel, pres, 72, chmn bd, 73); Am Acad Arts & Sci (fel); Am Chem Soc (pres, 76-); USSR Acad Sci; plus many others. Honors & Awards: Co-Recipient, Nobel Prize for Chem, 51; Enrico Fermi Award, US Atomic Energy Comn, 59; Swedish Am of the Year, 62; Mugunghwa Medal, Order of Civil Merit, Korea, 70; Officier, French Legion Honor, 73; plus numerous other awards & co-discoverer of elements 94-102 & 106. Relig: Protestant. Legal Res: 1154 Glen Rd Lafayette CA 94549 Mailing Add: Lawrence Berkeley Lab Univ of Calif Berkeley CA 94720

SEABURY, RICHARD WILLIAMS, III (R)
Chmn, Morris Co Rep Comt, NJ
b Morristown, NJ; Feb 2, 37; s Richard Williams Seabury, Jr & Louise Brett S; m 1965 to Susan Stiegler; c Richard, Jennifer & Ann Louise. Educ: Wesleyan Univ, BA, 58; Cornell Univ, MBA, 60; Delta Sigma. Polit & Govt Pos: Munic chmn, Montville Twp, NJ, 63-68; admin aide, NJ Senate, 70-71; comnr, Morris Co Park, NJ, 70-; shade tree comnr, Montville Twp; chmn, Morris Co Rep Comt, 73- Bus & Prof Pos: Dir personnel, RFL Indust Inc, 62-; dir, Midlantic Nat Bank, Morris, 74- Relig: Episcopal. Legal Res: 16 Hillcrest Ave Towaco NJ 07082 Mailing Add: PO Box 123 Towaco NJ 07082

SEAGROVES, JESSIE RUTH (D)
First VChmn, Chatham Co Dem Exec Comt, NC
b Siler City, NC, Feb 6, 22; d Jesse Anderson Crutchfield & Emma Richardson C; m 1947 to Robert A Seagroves, Jr; div; c Joel Brent, James Keith & John David. Educ: Silk Hope Sch, NC, grad, 39. Polit & Govt Pos: Area chmn women, Terry Sanford for Gov Campaign, NC, 60; vpres, Chatham Co Young Dem, 61; mem, Albright Twp Dem Precinct Comt, 61-69; co-organizer, Chatham Co Dem Women, 62, mem exec comt, 62-68, pres, 64-68; mem, NC Centennial Comn, 62; chmn, Chatham Co Bob Scott for Gov Campaign, 68; alt deleg, Dem Nat Conv, 68 & 72; third vchmn, Chatham Co Dem Exec Comt, 68-70, first vchmn, 70-; mem, NC Adv Comt for Med Assistance, 69-71; precinct mem, Chatham Co Precinct, third vchmn, 69-71, first vchmn, 71-72, acting chmn, 72; mem, NC State Primary Comt, 71; mem, NC Dem State Exec Comt, 72-; chairwoman, Chatham Co Dem Party, 72-; first vpres, Dem Women of NC, currently. Bus & Prof Pos: Merchant, Crutchfield's Store, Siler City, NC & Crutchfield's Fabric Shop, Liberty. Publ: Newspaper columnist, Chatham News, NC, 15 years. Mem: Chatham Co Farm Bur; United Daughters Confederacy; Am Legion Auxiliary; 81st Wildcat Div Auxiliary; Liberty CofC. Honors & Awards: Chatham Co Dem Woman of the Year, 62; Queen, Chatham Co Bicentennial Celebration, 72. Relig: Baptist. Mailing Add: Box 79 Rte 1 Siler City NC 27344

SEAMANS, HENRY J, SR (R)
NH State Rep
Mailing Add: Spaulding Hill Rd Pelham NH 03076

SEAMANS, ROBERT CHANNING, JR (R)
Adminr, Energy Research & Develop Admin
b Salem, Mass, Oct 30, 18; m to Eugenia A Merrill; c Katherine (Mrs Padulo), Robert C, III, Joseph, May (Mrs Eugene Baldwin, III) & Daniel. Educ: Harvard Univ, BSc in Eng, 39; Mass Inst Technol, MSc in Aeronaut, 42 & DSc in Instrumentation, 51. Hon Degrees: DSc, Rollins Col & NY Univ; DEng, Norwich Univ, 71. Polit & Govt Pos: Mem tech comts, Nat Adv Comt for Aeronaut, 48-58; consult, Sci Adv Bd of the Air Force, 57-59, mem, 59-62 & assoc adv, 62-67; assoc adminr, NASA, 60-65, dep adminr, 65-68, consult to adminr, 68; Secy of the Air Force, 69-73; adminr, Energy Research & Develop Admin, 74- Bus & Prof Pos: Asst prof & assoc prof, Dept of Aeronaut Eng, proj engr, Instrumentation Lab, chief engr of Proj Meteor & dir, Flight Control Lab, Mass Inst Technol, 41-55; mgr, Airborne Systs Lab & chief systs engr, Airborne Systs Dept, Radio Corp of Am, 55-58, chief engr, Missile Electronics & Controls Div, Burlington, Mass, 58-60; Jerome Clarke Hunsaker vis prof, Mass Inst Technol, 68; pres, Nat Acad Eng, 73- Mem: Am Astronaut Soc; Am Soc for Pub Admin; Am Acad of Arts & Sci; Am Ord Asn; Sigma Xi. Honors & Awards: Sperry Award, Am Inst of Aeronaut & Astronaut, 51, hon fel, 69; Godfrey L Cabot Aviation Award, 65; NASA Distinguished Serv Medal, 65 & 69; Goddard Trophy, 68; Dept of Defense Distinguished Pub Serv Medal, 73. Legal Res: 675 Hale St Beverly Farms MA 01915 Mailing Add: 3921 Idaho Ave NW Washington DC 20008

SEARCY, MARY GLENN (D)
Chmn, Grayson Co Dem Exec Comt, Ky
b Leitchfield, Ky, July 21, 25; d James Alden Glenn & Virginia Stevenson G; m 1944 to Daniel Lindsay Searcy; c James Daniel, Jennifer Jo, Thomas Alden & Murhl Lee. Educ: Bryant-Stratton Bus Col, Louisville, Ky, acct dipl, 43; Elizabethtown Community Col, Ky, mgt course, 72. Polit & Govt Pos: Precinct capt, Carroll Co, Ky, 46-60, womans chmn for Alben Barkley for US Sen, 54; co chmn Hudleston for Sen, Grayson Co, 72; assoc dir, Second Dist Dem Womens Club Ky, 72-73; chmn, Grayson Co Dem Exec Comt, 72-; dist dir, Second Cong Dist Dem Womens Club, 73-; Second Cong Dist rep, Ky State Dem Cent Exec Comt, 73-; state orgn chmn, Collins for Clerk, Court of Appeals, 75. Bus & Prof Pos: Secy first aid dept, Curtiss-Wright Corp, Louisville, Ky, 44-46; off mgr & secy to supt, Gen Butler State Park, Carrollton, 53-56; supt secy & receptionist, Dravo Corp, Markland Locks, Warsaw, 56-59; dept parks, Cent Off, Frankfort, 60-61; Hilltop Med Ctr, Madison, Ind, 61-64; adminr, Grayson Manor Personal Care Home, Leitchfield, Ky, 70-72 & Aid Acres Personal Care & Intermediate Care Facilities, 72-; owner, Searcy's, 75- Mem: Ky Nursing Home Asn (legis comt, 72-); Eastern Star (Worthy Matron, Martha Chap 256, Worthville, Ky, 50-51); Twin Lakes Chap Bus & Prof Women's Club (pres, 75-); Grayson Co CofC; Leitchfield Retail Merchant Asn. Relig: Baptist. Legal Res: 1301 James St Leitchfield KY 42754 Mailing Add: PO Box 12 Leitchfield KY 42754

SEARL, TOM (R)
Wyo State Sen
Educ: Bus Col. Polit & Govt Pos: Wyo State Rep, 4 terms; Wyo State Sen, 67- Bus & Prof Pos: Real estate; pres, Tom Searl Realty. Mailing Add: 104 E 30th St Cheyenne WY 82001

SEARLE, RODNEY N (R)
Minn State Rep
m 1941 to Janette E Christie; c R Newell, Jr, Alan J & Linda. Educ: Rutgers Univ; Mankato State Col. Polit & Govt Pos: Minn State Rep, 56- Bus & Prof Pos: Tree farmer & life ins underwriter. Mailing Add: RR 1 Waseca MN 56093

SEARS, BETTY JEAN (R)
VChairwoman, Gunnison Co Rep Cent Comt, Colo
b Canon City, Colo, Nov 27, 18; d Wesley Luther Weller & Mae Williams W; m 1942 to Arthur Marsden Sears; c Arthur Welsey & David Alden. Educ: Western State Col, 37 & 69. Polit & Govt Pos: Pres, Thursday Rep Women's Club, Colo, 62; capt, Boulder Co Rep Cent Comt, 63; vpres, Colo Fedn Rep Women, 63; vchairwoman, Gunnison Co Rep Cent Comt, 64-; pres, Gunnison Co Rep Womens Club, 65-66; presidential elector, Colo, 69. Bus & Prof Pos: Real estate salesman, Mil Davis Real Estate, 70-; chmn Gunnison & Hinsdale Co, March of Dimes Campaign, 71. Mem: Bus & Prof Womens Orgn; Eastern Star; DeMolay; Mothers Club; Gunnison Golf Club, Inc. Honors & Awards: Commendation for work with youth. Relig: Episcopal. Mailing Add: 518 N Spruce Gunnison CO 81230

SEARS, FRED N (D)
Co Chmn, Thomas Co Dem Party, Kans
b Ashland, Nebr, Oct 3, 05; s Charles Edgar Sears & Mabel Brewster S; m 1928 to Elsie Ann Graber; c John N. Polit & Govt Pos: Co Chmn, Thomas Co Dem Party, Kans, 62-; deleg, Dem Nat Conv, 68; Forestry, Fish & Game Comnr, 69; mem, Gov Adv Coun, currently, chmn, Kans Forestry, Fish & Game Comn, Park & Resources Authority, currently. Mem: Elks; Moose; Mason; Shrine; Kans Century Club. Relig: Presbyterian. Legal Res: 220 N Garfield Colby KS 67701 Mailing Add: Box 232 Colby KS 67701

SEARS, HARRY L (R)
b Butler, NJ, 1920; m to Emma Sehulster; c Ralph, Mary Ann, Barbara, Judy & Donna. Educ: Tusculum Col, BA, 42; Rutgers Law Sch, LLB, 48. Polit & Govt Pos: Munic & sch bd attorney, 49-, Borough of Butler, Hanover Twp, Hanover Sewerage Authority, Mt Lakes Bd Educ, Twp Randolph, Twp Montville & Montville Twp Munic Utilities Auth, currently; counsel, NJ Fedn Officer Planning Bds, 57-58 & 65; mem, Rep Co Comt, Mountain Lakes, 54-60; past counsel, Morris Co Rep Comt; NJ State Assemblyman, 61-66, chmn, comt interstate coop, co & munic govt comt, NJ State Assembly; alt deleg-at-lg, Rep Nat Conv, 64 & 68, deleg, 72; chmn, NJ Speakers Bur Nixon for President Campaign Comt, 68; NJ State Sen, 68-74, asst majority leader, NJ State Senate, 69-70, majority leader, 70-74. Bus & Prof Pos: Legal clerkship, David Young, III Law Off, 49; attorney, Young & Sears, 54-; dir, State Bank NJ. Mil Serv: Entered as Commissioned Officer, Naval Res, 42, released as Lt(sg), 46, after serv in Atlantic, Mediterranean & Pac Theatres of Opers. Mem: Nat Inst Munic Law Off; Rockaway River Country Club; Mountain Lakes Club; VFW; Butler & Boonton. Relig: Community Church; past trustee, Mountain Lakes, NJ. Mailing Add: 22 Larchdell Way Mountain Lakes NJ 07046

SEARS, JOHN WINTHROP (R)
Chmn, Mass Rep State Comt
b Boston, Mass, Dec 18, 30; s Richard Dudley Sears & Frederica Fulton Leser S (deceased); div. Educ: Harvard Univ, AB magna cum laude in govt, 52; Oxford Univ, BLitt, 57; Harvard Law Sch, JD, 59; Phi Beta Kappa; SPEE; Signet Soc; Varsity Club; Hasty Pudding-Inst of 1770. Polit & Govt Pos: Mass State Rep, 65-68; deleg, Rep Nat Conv, 68; sheriff, Suffolk Co, 68-69; chmn, Boston Finance Comn, 69-70; comnr, Metrop Dist Comn, 70-75; chmn, Mass Rep State Comt, 75-; mem, Rep Nat Comt, 75- Bus & Prof Pos: Mem staff, Brown, Brown, Harriman & Co, 59-65. Mil Serv: Entered as Ens, Naval Res, 52, released as Lt(jg), 54, reentered Naval Res as Lt, 61, released as Lt Comdr, 62, after serv in Atlantic Theatre. Mem: Mass & Boston Bar Asns; Mass Legislator's Asn; Beacon Hill Civic Asn; Rep Club of Mass. Relig: Episcopal. Mailing Add: 7 Acorn St Boston MA 02108

SEARS, PHILIP MASON (R)
b Boston, Mass, Dec 29, 99; s Philip Shelton Sears & Mary Cabot Higginson S; m 1924 to Zilla MacDougall; c Philip Mason & Charlotte MacDougall (deceased). Educ: Harvard, AB, 22. Polit & Govt Pos: Mem, Mass Legis, 35-48; deleg, Rep Nat Conv, 48 & 52; chmn, Mass Rep State Comt, 49-50; alt US rep, 13th Gen Assembly, UN, US Rep, Trusteeship Coun, 53-60, pres, Trusteeship Coun, 55-56; US deleg, Silver Jubilee of Emperor of Ethiopia, Addis Ababa, 55; US deleg, Independence Celebration of Ghana, 57; US ambassador & chmn UN Vis Mission to EAfrica, 60; spec US ambassador, Independence Celebration, Cameroon, WAfrica, 60. Mil Serv: Pvt, Army, World War I; Capt, Naval Res, 41-46, with Third Fleet at Guadalcanal & Bougainville. Mem: Am Legion; Mason. Relig: Episcopal. Mailing Add: West St Dedham MA 02026

SEARS, RUTH PARKER (R)
Chmn, Worthington Rep Town Comt, Mass
b Northampton, Mass, Mar 31, 31; d Leston Eugene Parker & Beulah Griffin P; m 1949 to Raymond H Sears; c Donna (Mrs Richard Thayer), Susan (Mrs David Stone), Lawrence & Ronald. Educ: Northfield Sch for Girls. Polit & Govt Pos: Secy, Sch Comt, Worthington, Mass, 60-63, finance secy, 64-67; secy to clerk, Worthington Bd Assessors, 60-67; coordr for polit campaigns, State Rep John Barrus, 62-64, Pres Cand, Barry Goldwater, 64, State Rep Donald Madsen, 66 & 68, Gov Coun, Raymond Fontana, 66, Gov John Volpe, 66, Dist Attorney Oscar Grife, 68; President Richard Nixon, 68 & Gov Francis Sargent, 70; membership chmn, Hampshire Co Rep Club, 64-66, rec secy, 66-67; secy, Worthington Rep Town Comt, 64-68, chmn, 68-; clerk typist, Mass Registry of Motor Vehicles, 66-; dep sheriff, Hampshire Co, 68- Bus & Prof Pos: Secy-bookkeeper, Worthington Garage, Mass, 49-58; secy-bookkeeper, Cummington Garage, Mass, 55-; demonstrator & dealer, Stanley Home Prod, 61-63; salesgirl & dealer Avon Prod, Williamsburg, 63; bookkeeper & salesgirl, Kinne Brook Kitchens, Pittsfield, 63; secy, Prestape, Inc, Northampton, 64-66. Mem: Eastern Star; Am Legion Auxiliary; Dep Sheriffs Asn; Hampshire Co Rep Club; PTA. Honors & Awards: First woman to serv on Town Finance Comt; First Woman to serv as Chmn, Rep Town Comt. Relig: Protestant. Mailing Add: Huntington Rd Worthington MA 01098

SEARS, VIRGINIA LACOSTE (R)
Colo State Rep
b Denver, Colo, June 20, 06; d Charles Leon LaCoste & Louena Dunbar L; m 1926 to Roy Edward Sears, wid; c Roger Douglas, Larry Ray & Gary Roy. Educ: Univ Northern Colo, 24-32. Polit & Govt Pos: Precinct committeewoman, Weld Co Rep Party, Colo, 70-72, vchmn, 72-73; Colo State Rep, Dist 50, 73-, mem educ, state & local finance & judiciary comts, Colo House Rep, currently. Bus & Prof Pos: Teacher, Eastern Colo, 24-26; asst registr, Univ Northern Colo, 28-32; mgr radio sales, KFKA, Greeley, 49-70. Mem: Am Women in Radio & TV; Scroll & Fan. Honors & Awards: App by Gov to Adv Coun of Title III, Elem & Sec Educ Act Orgn, 73-77 & Steering Comt of SJR 20 Study Comt, 73-75. Relig: Congregational; dir relig educ, First Congregation Church, Greeley, 46-49. Mailing Add: 2345 16th St Greeley CO 80631

SEARS, WILLIAM R (R)
NY State Assemblyman
b Utica, NY, May 25, 28; s Edward J Sears (deceased) & Gladys Waldron S; m 1954 to Anne M Miller; c William J. Educ: Utica Col, 60. Polit & Govt Pos: Town councilman, Forestport, NY, 61-65; Rep committeeman, Forestport Rep Party, 62-; chmn, Forestport Rep Town Comt, 62-; Rep chmn, northern towns, Oneida Co, 63-65; NY State Assemblyman, 115th Dist, 66- Mil Serv: Entered as Pvt, Army, 50, released as Sgt 1/C, 52, after serv in 140th AAA, 40th Div, Korea, 51-52; Korean Conflict Medal; Occup of Japan, Distinguished Serv & Sharpshooter Expert Medals. Mem: Elks; Moose; Am Legion; VFW; DAV (life mem). Relig: Catholic. Mailing Add: Bear Creek Rd Woodgate NY 13494

SEAY, WILLIAM E (D)
Mo State Rep
b Salem, Mo, Dec 13, 21; m 1950 to Shirley Anderson; c Jefferson, Elizabeth, Anderson, William Camm. Educ: Cent Col, Fayette, Mo, 39-40; Univ Mo, LLB, 49; Single Engine Flying Sch, Mission, Tex; Phi Delta Phi. Polit & Govt Pos: Mo State Rep, 64-66 & currently; pres, Dent Co Young Dem Club, formerly; prosecuting attorney, Dent Co, 50-64. Bus & Prof Pos: Pvt law practice, Salem, Mo. Mil Serv: Air Force, Capt, World War II; instr fighter plane gunnery, 1 year & served in combat as P-47 pilot in Pac Theater. Relig: Methodist. Mailing Add: 210 S McCarthur Salem MO 65560

SEBELIUS, KEITH GEORGE (R)
US Rep, Kans
b Almena, Kans, Sept 10, 16; s Dr Carl Elstrom Sebelius & Minnie Peak S; m 1949 to Bette A Roberts; c Gary & Douglas. Educ: Ft Hays Kans State Col, AB; George Washington Univ Law Sch, LLB; Pi Kappa Delta; Pi Gamma Mu; Phi Kappa Phi. Polit & Govt Pos: Attorney, Norton Co, Kans, 46-51; mayor & city councilman, Almena, Kans, 47-50; comnr, Kans Indust Develop Comt, 61-62; Kans State Sen, 62-68; US Rep, First Dist, Kans, 69- Mil Serv: Entered as Pvt, Army, 41, released as Maj, 66, after serv in Korean Conflict & Res. Mem: Mason; Shrine; Lions; Am Legion; DAV. Relig: Methodist. Legal Res: 602 W Wilberforce Norton KS 67654 Mailing Add: 1211 Longworth House Off Bldg Washington DC 20515

SEBENS, RAYMOND WILLARD (D)
b Milnor, NDak, Oct 9, 25; s William P Sebens & Mildred Bunnell S; m 1964 to Janet Benedict; c Mark, Todd & Karen. Educ: Univ Calif, Los Angeles, BA, 49. Polit & Govt Pos: Admin asst to US Rep George A Kasem, 59-60; admin asst to Calif State Assemblyman George Brown, 61-62; admin asst to US Rep George E Brown, Jr, Calif, 63-70; admin asst to US Rep George Danielson, 71- Bus & Prof Pos: Ed, El Monte Press, Calif, 53-54; self-employed, lettershop, pub rels, 55-58. Mil Serv: Entered as Aviation Cadet, Army Air Corps, 43, released as 2nd Lt, 45. Legal Res: CA Mailing Add: 3906 Lincolnshire Annandale VA 22003

SEBO, KATHERINE ANN HAGEN (D)
NC State Sen
b Minneapolis, Minn, July 9, 44; d Kristofer Hagen & Bertha Elvira Johanson H; m 1967 to Paul Gustav Sebo. Educ: Oberlin Col, BA, 65; Am Univ, MA, 68, PhD, 73. Polit & Govt Pos: Chairperson, Mayor's Comt on the Status of Women in Greensboro, NC, 72-73; NC State Sen, 75- Bus & Prof Pos: Instr polit sci, Wake Forest Univ, 67-68; asst prof polit sci, Guilford Col, 68- Publ: Ed, Report of the Mayor's comt on the status of women in Greensboro, City of Greensboro, 5/73. Mem: Am Civil Liberties Union (nat & state bds, 73-); Am Asn Univ Prof (NC Committee W, 74-); Altrusa Int Inc; League of Women Voters; YWCA. Mailing Add: 907 W McGee St Greensboro NC 27403

SEBO, WALTER J (R)
Chmn, Fulton Co Rep Cent Comt, Ill
b Chicago, Ill, Dec 8, 18; s Louis Sebo & Anna Pavco S; m 1942 to Doris O Schuette; c Renee L, Adele E & Thomas J. Educ: Univ Ill, BS, 47; Univ Ill Law Sch, JD, 50. Polit & Govt Pos: Clerk, Third Appellate Dist, Ill, 56-58; Asst States Attorney, Fulton Co, 57-60, Pub Defender, 60-; mem sch bd, Canton Union Sch Dist 66, 64-74, pres sch bd, 67-71 & 73-74; chmn, Fulton Co Rep Cent Comt, 67-; comnr, Ill Defenders Proj, 72- Bus & Prof Pos: Practicing attorney, 50- Mil Serv: Entered as Pvt, Air Force, 41, released as 1st Lt, 45, after serv in ETO, 44; Distinguished Flying Cross; Air Medal with Three Oak Leaf Clusters. Mem: Trial Lawyers Asn; Pub Defenders Asn; Am Bar Asn; Am Legion; Elks. Relig: Lutheran. Legal Res: 980 N Main Canton IL 61520 Mailing Add: 122 N Ave A Canton IL 61520

SECHRIST, STERLING GEORGE (R)
Chmn, Medina Co Rep Cent Comt, Ohio
b Wadsworth, Ohio, Jan 23, 19; s Sterling George Sechrist & Phoebe Trew S; m 1961 to Marilyn Jean Ohrgren; c Sterling Anders & Kristen Trew. Educ: Univ Akron, BA in Econ & Sociol, 50. Polit & Govt Pos: Chmn, Medina Co Young Rep Comt, Ohio, 50-55; councilman-at-large, City Coun, Wadsworth, Ohio, 56-58, pres, 59-65; mem bd dirs, Medina Co Bd Elections, 65; vchmn, Medina Co Rep Exec Comt, 65-70, chmn, 70-; alt deleg, Rep Nat Conv, 72. Bus & Prof Pos: Vpres, trust officer & dir, Citizens Bank & Trust Co, Wadsworth, Ohio, 50- Mil Serv: Entered as Pvt, Army, 41, released as T/Sgt, 44, after serv in US Army Band; Am Theatre, Good Conduct, Victory & Am Defense Medals. Mem: Ohio Bankers Asn (chmn, mkt & pub rels comt); Am Bank Mkt Asn; Wadsworth CofC; Am Legion Post 170 (past comdr); Masonic Lodge 385 (32 degree Valley of Cleveland). Honors & Awards: Distinguished Citizens Award, Wadsworth, Ohio, 60; Friend of Children, Nat Found Juv Court Judges, 60. Relig: Protestant; Trustee, Wadsworth United Methodist Church. Mailing Add: 454 Crestwood Ave Wadsworth OH 44281

SECORD, MARIA RACHEL (D)
Nat Committeewoman, Ariz Young Dem
b Mesa, Ariz, Oct 15, 53; d Nicolasa Medina Orosco; m to Michael Jay Secord. Educ: Mesa Community Col, 71-75. Polit & Govt Pos: Treas, Mesa Young Dem, 71-72; regional vpres, Maricopa Co Young Dem, 72-73; secy-treas, Region Seven Young Dem, 73-; nat committeewoman, Ariz Young Dem, 73- Bus & Prof Pos: Rep, Adelante Con Mesa Youth Coun, 69-71; speaker, Speaker's Bur, Youth Employ Serv, 70-71. Honors & Awards: Citation for Outstanding Serv to Young Dem Clubs Am, 73 & 75. Relig: Catholic. Mailing Add: 1564 E Broadway Mesa AZ 85204

SECREST, ROBERT THOMPSON (D)
Ohio State Sen
b Senecaville, Ohio, Jan 22, 04. Educ: Muskingum Col, AB, 26; Washington, DC Col Law, LLB, 40; Columbia Univ, MA in polit sci, 43; Naval Sch Mil Govt Columbia Univ, grad, 43; Brit Sch Civil Affairs, Wimbledon, Eng, 43. Hon Degrees: LLD, Muskingum Col, 55; Bachelor of Commerce, Bliss Col, 63. Polit & Govt Pos: Mem, Ohio Legis, 31-32; US Rep, Ohio, 33-42, 48-54 & 63-66; mem, Fed Trade Comn, 54-61; dir of commerce, Ohio, 62; Ohio State Sen, 69- Bus & Prof Pos: Prin, Senecaville High Sch, 26-31; supt of schs, Murray City, Ohio, 31-32. Mil Serv: Navy, Comdr, 42-46; served in Eng, Africa, Italy & 1 year on Adm Nimitz's staff in Pac as mil govt officer. Mem: Senecaville Am Legion Post 747 (past comdr & life mem); Amvets (life mem); VFW (life mem); Regular Vet Asn (life mem); 40 et 8. Mailing Add: Rte 1 Cambridge OH 43725

SEDAR, D R (D)
Wyo State Sen
Mailing Add: 4370 S Poplar Casper WY 82601

SEDGWICK, LILLIAN ADKINS (D)
Mem, Dem Nat Comt, DC
Mailing Add: 1453 Primrose Rd NW Washington DC 20012

SEE, CLYDE M, JR (D)
WVa State Deleg
b Moorefield, WVa, Oct 20, 41; s Clyde M See & Minnie Crites S (deceased); m 1968 to Judith Ann Robinson; c Jennifer & Joshua. Educ: Concord Col; WVa Univ, BA, 67, JD, 70. Polit & Govt Pos: WVa State Deleg, 75-, mem agr & natural resources comt, banking & ins comt, redistricting comt, vchmn, judiciary comt, WVa House Deleg, 75- Bus & Prof Pos: Mem, WVa Univ Exten Serv Comt, currently; chmn, Hardy Co Develop Comt, currently. Mil Serv: US Army. Relig: Presbyterian. Mailing Add: Box 504 Moorefield WV 26836

SEEBERGER, EDWARD D (D)
Wash State Rep
b Glen Ullin, NDak, Aug 5, 37; s Nick V Seeberger & Teresa R Duratschek S; m 1963 to Joan E Burke; c Edward D, Jr & Frank I. Educ: Univ Seattle, BA, 62, MA, 69; Univ Ore, JD, 72. Polit & Govt Pos: Wash State Rep, 75-, chmn criminal law subcomt, Wash House Rep, 75-77. Bus & Prof Pos: High sch teacher, Eugene, Ore & Stanwood, Wash, 65-69; dep prosecuting attorney, Yakima Co, 72-74; attorney, pvt practice, 74- Mil Serv: Army, 57-60. Mem: Co, State & Nat Bar Asns. Mailing Add: 2506 W Yakima Yakima WA 98902

SEEGER, CHRISTOPHER CLARK (R)
b Cincinnati, Ohio, Oct 10, 43; s Charles Morgan Seeger & Helen Elizabeth S; m 1973 to Kristin Lee Atchon. Educ: Bowling Green State Univ, BS, 65; Omicron Delta Kappa; Phi Delta Theta. Polit & Govt Pos: Spec asst to Congressman C M Teague, 71-73; admin asst to US Rep William M Ketchum, Calif, currently. Mil Serv: Entered as 2nd Lt, Air Force, 65, released as Capt, 71, after serv in Air Rescue, Southeast Asia, 70-71; Distinguished Flying Cross; Air Medal with six Oak Leaf Clusters; Air Force Commendation Medal. Mailing Add: 7740 Le Moyne Lane Springfield VA 22152

SEELY, ROBERT D (R)
b Decatur, Ill, Oct 8, 26; s Kenneth D Seely & Audrian Fisher S; m 1946 to Irene E Davidson; c Chris (Mrs Gilfillan), Joe & Trish. Educ: SDak State Col, 44; Univ Minn, St Paul, 45; Sigma Nu. Polit & Govt Pos: Chmn, Goldwater for President, Goodhue Co, Minn, 64; chmn, Goodhue Co Rep Party, 64-68; dist chmn, Levander for Gov, Minn, 66; mem, Minn Rep State Cent Comt, 68-72; deleg-at-lg, First Dist Rep Conv, 70-72; alt deleg, Rep Nat Conv, 72; five state chmn, Automobile Dealers for President Nixon, 72. Bus & Prof Pos: Pres, Bob Seely Ford Co, Zumbrota, Minn, 54-72. Mil Serv: Pvt, Army, 44-45. Mem: Nat Automobile Dealers Asn; Mason; CofC; Interstate Rehabilitation Ctr. Relig: Lutheran. Mailing Add: 643 Second Ave Zumbrota MN 55992

SEER, EDNA ELEANOR (D)
Exec Secy, Milwaukee Co Dem Party, Wis
b Milwaukee, Wis, Feb 21, 09; d Mannie Kloth & Nelda Bub K; wid; c Nelda (Mrs Madison) & Donald M Stahl. Educ: Bus Admin, 2 years. Polit & Govt Pos: Chmn, Ward Unit Dem Party, 51-54; exec secy, Milwaukee Co Dem Party, Wis, 53-; chmn, Sen Dist Dem Party, 54-56; deleg, Dem Nat Conv, 60, 64 & 68. Mem: Office Workers & Prof Int Local 9, AFL-CIO. Relig: Baptist & Disciples of Christ. Mailing Add: 1767 N Cambridge Ave Apt 11 Milwaukee WI 53202

SEEVERS, GARY LEONARD (INDEPENDENT)
Mem, Coun of Econ Advisers
b Jonesville, Mich, May 24, 37; s Leonard William Seevers & Hattie Mundy S; m 1957 to Marian Rose Rice; c Gary, Jr, Bonnie, Sharon & Donna. Educ: Mich State Univ, BS, 59, MS, 66, PhD, 68; Phi Kappa Phi; Phi Beta Kappa. Polit & Govt Pos: Sr staff economist, President's Coun of Econ Advisers, 70-72, spec asst to chmn Herbert Stein, 72-73, mem, 73- Bus & Prof Pos: Asst prof, Ore State Univ, 68-70. Publ: An evaluation of the disincentive effect caused by PL 480 shipments, 5/68 & The policy environment for US Agricultural trade, 12/72, Am J Agr Econ; co-auth, Chap In: Interrelationships Between the Levels of US Exports & Imports, Iowa State Univ Press, 73. Mem: Am Econ Asn; Am Agr Econ Asn; Nat Economist Club. Mailing Add: 7018 Westbury Rd McLean VA 22101

SEGAL, ED (D)
b Los Angeles, Calif, July 14, 49; s Russell Segal & Anita Kane S; single. Educ: Calif State Col, Dominguez Hills, BA in Polit Sci, 72; Alpha Phi Omega; Aleph Zadik Aleph. Polit & Govt Pos: Co-chmn, Students for Kennedy, 68; exec dir, Southern Calif Dem Youth Caucus, 71; nat platform co-chmn, Calif Dem Comn on Platform & Policy, 72; staff mem, US Rep Charles H Wilson, Calif, 72; research asst to US Rep Glenn M Anderson, Calif, 73-74; legis asst to US Rep John L Burton, Calif, 74- Bus & Prof Pos: Publicity asst, Greek Theatre, Hollywood, Calif, 68; AV asst, Calif State Col, Dominguez Hills, 69-72. Publ: Ed, El Trompetero, Calif State Col, Dominguez Hills, 68; ed, Bullsheet, Bullwinkle Party, 69-71; ed, RFK News, RFK Dem Club, 71. Mem: Capitol Hill Young Dem (pres & founder, 73); Bullwinkle Party (pres, 69-). Honors & Awards: Commencement Speaker, Gardena High Sch, 67 & Calif State Col, Dominguez Hills, 72; Dem of Year, 35th Cong Dist Coun, 72. Legal Res: 18055 Chanera Ave Torrance CA 90504 Mailing Add: K-318 175 S Reynolds St Alexandria VA 22304

SEGALL, JOEL
Dep Under Secy Int Labor Affairs, Dept Labor
Mailing Add: Dept of Labor Washington DC 20210

SEGEL, JAMES W (D)
Mass State Rep
b Philadelphia, Pa, June 29, 45; s Arnold Lester Segel & Ruth Cohn S; m 1974 to Marjorie Spiegel. Educ: Harvard Col, BA, 67; Boston Col Law Sch, JD, 72. Polit & Govt Pos: Comnr, Parks & Recreation, Brookline, Mass, 71-73; chmn, Hist Comt, 74-; Mass State Rep, 73- Relig: Jewish. Mailing Add: 17 Doran Rd Brookline MA 02146

SEGERMARK, HOWARD S (R)
b Chicago, Ill, June 6, 41; s Ben Segermark & Ethel McDevit S; single. Educ: Carroll Col (Wis), BS, 63; Univ Notre Dame, 63-66; Hon Forensics & Polit Sci Fraternities; Phi Theta Phi. Polit & Govt Pos: Campaign aide, Third Cong Dist of Ind Rep Party, 64 & US Rep Henry Schadeberg, Wis, 66; legis asst to US Rep Ancher Nelsen, Minn, 67-72; chmn spec projs, Young Rep Nat Leadership Conf, Washington, DC, 71-72; chmn, DC Young Rep Bill Chin-Lee Fund Raiser Comt, 72; admin asst to US Rep Symms, Idaho, 73; spec asst to US

Sen H F Byrd, Jr, 74- Mem: Philadelphia Soc; Capitol Hill Club (chmn entertainment comt, 72-73); Nat Cathedral Asn; Honors & Awards: Scholarship, Relm Found, 64; Fel, Third Cong Dist Study, 65. Relig: Protestant. Mailing Add: 314 E Capitol St Washington DC 20002

SEGO, ROBERT (D)
Mo State Rep
Mailing Add: 8939 E 57th Raytown MO 64133

SEGO, WILLIAM A (R)
NMex State Sen
Mailing Add: 4610 McLeod NE Albuquerque NM 87109

SEGRETO, JAMES VICTOR (R)
b Paterson, NJ, Dec 27, 29; s Frank Segreto & Antonetta S; m 1967 to Antonetta Moschillo; c James F & Antoinette. Educ: Seton Hall Univ, BS, 51; Fordham Univ, LLD, 55. Polit & Govt Pos: Vchmn, Passaic Co Rep Orgn, formerly; borough attorney, Haledon, NJ, 65-; attorney, Planning Bd, 65-70; Bd of Adjust, Little Falls, 68-69 & Bd Health, 68-69; co counsel, Passaic Co, 69-70; counsel, Passaic Co Sewer Authority & Passaic Co Community Col, 69-70; chief counsel, Passaic Valley Sewerage Comn, 70- Mil Serv: Entered as Pvt, La Nat Army, 55, released as Pvt, 57, after serv in Judge Adv Corps, Paris, 55-57. Mem: NJ State & Passaic Co Bar Asns; Nat Inst Munic Law Off; Bars of NJ & DC. Relig: Catholic. Mailing Add: 74 Feldman Terr North Haledon NJ 07508

SEGURA, PERRY (D)
Committeeman, La Dem State Comt
b New Iberia, La, Dec 14, 29; s Paul F Segura & Levie Broussard S; m 1950 to Emma Lou Davant; c Perry James, II, Christopher Antony, Therese Mary, David Charles & Coleen Mary. Educ: Univ Southwestern La, 47-50; La State Univ, BS, 54; Tau Beta Pi. Polit & Govt Pos: Committeeman, Iberia Parish Dem Comt, La, 62-; deleg, Dem Nat Conv, 68; committeeman, La Dem State Comt, Dist Seven, 68- Bus & Prof Pos: Architect, Perry Segura & Assoc, 56-; farmer, Angel Acres Breeding Farm, 62- Mil Serv: Entered as Pvt, La Nat Guard, 48, released as S/Sgt, 52. Mem: Am Inst of Architects; La Architects Asn; Kiwanis; KofC; Farm Bur. Relig: Catholic. Mailing Add: PO Box 1300 New Iberia LA 70560

SEIBEL, ANN MARIE (D)
Mont State Sen
b Mercer, NDak, Apr 29, 18; d Daniel Mayer & Christine Hertner M; m 1959 to Robert C Seibel; c Robert Allen, William Dennis & John Alfred Blackhall. Educ: St Joseph Sch Nursing, RN, 57; Mont State Univ, BS in Nursing, 61, BS in Elem Educ, 63, MS in Home Econ & Family Life, 68. Polit & Govt Pos: Mont State Sen, 75- Bus & Prof Pos: Nurse, operating own & off, Lewistown, Mont, 56-59; elem teacher, Bozeman Pub Schs, 63-69; asst prof health, Mont State Univ, 70-; mem bd trustees, Bozeman Pub Schs, 71-74. Mem: Mont Asn Health, Phys Educ & Recreation (state vchmn); Gallatin Coun on Health & Drugs (adv bd); Southwestern Mont Drug Prog (adv bd); Women's Polit Caucus; Dem Women. Honors & Awards: Woman of the Month Award, Alpha Lambda Delta, 73. Relig: Presbyterian. Mailing Add: 2603 Spring Creek Dr Bozeman MT 59715

SEIBEL, MARION IRMA (R)
Del State Rep
b Fond Du Lac, Wis, Jan 31, 22; d Simon Albert Arthur & Irma W Spielberg A; m 1943 to John Parshall Seibel; c Susan M, John Henry & Richard James. Educ: Fond Du Lac Sr High Sch, grad. Polit & Govt Pos: Pres, Suburban Rep Womens Club, 60-64; campaign coordr for Snowden for Congress, 64; mgr, Second Dist Rep Comt, 65-68; Del State Rep, 68-, mem, Judiciary, Rev Statutes & Govt Opers Comt, Del House of Rep, chmn, Community Affairs & Econ Develop Comt, 71-, mem, Joint Finance Comt, 72-; deleg, White House Conf for Children, 70; mem, Gov Comt on Family Court Reform, 70-71; mem regional comn on consumer protection, Coun State Govt, 70- Mem: League of Women Voters; YWCA; Del Adolescent Prog, Inc (bd mem). Relig: United Methodist. Mailing Add: 20 Knickerbocker Dr Newark DE 19711

SEIBERLING, JOHN F (D)
US Rep, Ohio
b Akron, Ohio, Sept 8, 18; s J Frederick Seiberling & Henrietta McBrayer Buckler S; m 1949 to Elizabeth Pope Behr; c John Buckler, David Pope & Stephen Maddox. Educ: Buchtel High Sch, Akron, Ohio, 32-33; Staunton Mil Acad, Va, 33-37; Harvard Col, AB, 41; Columbia Univ, LLB, 49. Polit & Govt Pos: Mem, Tri-Co Regional Planning Comn, Akron, Ohio, 63-70, pres, 66-69; mem, Summit Co Dem Cent Comt, 66-75; vchmn, Summit Co Dem Party, 70-71; US Rep, 14th Dist, Ohio, 71- Bus & Prof Pos: Assoc, Donovan Leisure Newton & Irvine, New York, NY, 49-54; attorney, Goodyear Tire & Rubber Co, Akron, Ohio, 54-70. Mil Serv: Entered as Pvt, Army, 42, released as Maj, 46, after serv in Off of Chief of Transportation Hq ETO, 43-45; Legion of Merit; Bronze Star; Medaille de la Reconnaissance Francaise; Ordre de Leopold II (Belgium). Mem: Am & Akron Bar Asns. Relig: Protestant. Legal Res: OH Mailing Add: 1234 Longworth Off Bldg Washington DC 20515

SEIBERT, GEORGE H (R)
Minority Leader, WVa House of Deleg
b Wheeling, WVa, Feb 27, 13; s George H Seibert & Grace C Smith S; m 1939 to Janice Boone; c Nancy Sue, James Edward & Sally Ann. Educ: WVa Univ, AB & LLB; Phi Sigma Kappa; Phi Alpha. Polit & Govt Pos: Munic judge & mem bd of gov, Wheeling, WVa; WVa State Deleg, 52-, minority leader, WVa House of Deleg, 57- Bus & Prof Pos: Lawyer. Mil Serv: 39 months in armed forces. Mem: Ohio Co, WVa & Am Bar Asns; WVa State Bar; Mason (32 degree); Shrine; Am Legion. Relig: Presbyterian. Mailing Add: 1217 Chapline St Wheeling WV 26003

SEIDITA, JO (D)
Mem, Dem Nat Comt, Calif
Mailing Add: 9601 Corbin Ave Northridge CA 91324

SEIDMAN, L WILLIAM (R)
Asst to the President for Econ Affairs
b Grand Rapids, Mich; s Frank E Seidman & Ester Lubetsky S; m 1944 to Sarah Marshall Berry; c Berry Thomas, Tracy Hall (Mrs C Cirigliano), Sarah Lewis, Nancy Caroline, Margaret Ann & Jane Robinson. Educ: Dartmouth Col, AB, 43; Harvard Law Sch, LLB, 48; Univ Mich, MBA, 49; Beta Alpha Psi; Beta Theta Pi; Phi Beta Kappa. Hon Degrees: LLD, Western Mich Univ, 67 & Grand Valley State Col, 74; LHD, Olivet Col, 75. Polit & Govt Pos: Rep cand, Auditor Gen, Mich, 62; organizer & ex-officio mem, Gov Romney's Task Force on Expenditure Mgt, 63-66; spec asst to Gov Romney on financial affairs & tax reform, 63-68; mem spec comt to investigate trade opportunities with Japan, 64; mem exec comt, Mich Businessmen's Trade Mission to Europe, 65; administrant, Romney Assoc, Inc, Lansing, 65-; mem, Romney for President Comt, Washington, DC, 67-68; app mem, Adv Coun, Mich Dept Com, 71-; Asst to the President for Econ Affairs, 74-, exec dir & mem exec comt, Econ Policy Bd; dep chmn, Coun Wage & Price Stability; mem, Coun Int Econ Policy, President's Labor-Mgt Adv Comt, Nat Adv Coun on Int & Financial Policies, President's Comt on East-West Trade Policy, Nat Comn on Productivity & Work Qual, Nat Energy Bd, Energy Resources Coun & Nat Comn on Supplies & Shortages, currently; dep chmn, East-West Foreign Trade Bd, currently. Bus & Prof Pos: Employee, Seidman & Seidman, CPA's, 49-54; partner, 54, nat managing partner, 68- Mil Serv: Lt, Naval Res, 42-46; 11 Battle Stars; Bronze Star. Mem: Grand Rapids Athletic Club; Mich & Am Bar Asns; Capitol Hill Club; Am Inst CPA's; Crystal Downs Country Club. Honors & Awards: Community Serv Award, Rotary, 61; Man of the Year Award, Grand Rapids CofC. Legal Res: 1615 Buttrick Ave SE Ada MI 49301 Mailing Add: 1694 31st St Georgetown Washington DC 20007

SEIFERT, CARL A (R)
Mont State Rep
Mailing Add: Rte 1 Box 45B Polson MT 59860

SEITH, ALEX ROBERT (D)
b Aurora, Ill; s Alex L Seith & Helen McKinley S; m 1956 to Frances T Remington; c William David, Kathleen McKinley & Robert Edward. Educ: Yale Univ, BA, 56; Univ Munich, 56-57; Harvard Law Sch, JD, 60; pres, Torch Soc; pres, Yale Debate Club; secy, Yale Polit Union. Polit & Govt Pos: Chmn, Young Dem of Cook Co, Ill, 65-66; first vpres, Young Dem of Am, Washington, DC, 67-69; chmn, Zoning Bd of Appeals, Cook Co, 69-; deleg, Dem Nat Conv, 68; vchmn, Deleg Selection Comt, Dem Nat Party, Washington, DC, 73-, dep chmn, Foreign Affairs Task Force, 74-; deleg, Dem Mid Term Conf, 74. Bus & Prof Pos: Assoc, Gardner, Carton, Douglas & Chilgren, Attorneys, Chicago, 61-63; partner, Lord, Bissell & Brook, Attorneys, Chicago, 63- Mil Serv: Entered as 2nd Lt, Army, 61, released as Capt, 68. Publ: Auth over 200 newspaper articles on foreign affairs for many newspapers, 68-; How to use a comprehensive plan in a zoning case, Chicago Bar, 3/71; French elections 1974 & 1975, Chicago Sun Times & Chicago Tribune, 74 & 75. Honors & Awards: Chevalier, Legion of Honor, President of France, 74; Outstanding Exec Cook Co, Chicago Asn Com & Indust, 75. Relig: Protestant. Legal Res: 917 Cleveland Rd Hinsdale IL 60521 Mailing Add: 135 S LaSalle St Suite 2800 Chicago IL 60603

SEKT, ALLEN (D)
Sen, Guam Legis
Mailing Add: Guam Legislature Box 373 Agana GU 96910

SELANDER, CAROLYN WHITESIDE (D)
Dem Nat Committeewoman, Idaho
b Houston, Tex, Oct 7, 38; d Hugh Langhorne Whiteside & Josie Downs W; m 1958 to Glenn Edward Selander; c James Timothy & Andrew Christopher. Educ: Southwestern Univ, 56-58; Alpha Delta Pi. Polit & Govt Pos: Gov appointee, Inaugural Ball Comt, 70; mem rules comt, Dem Nat Conv, 72; deleg, Idaho State Dem Assembly, 72; Dem Nat Committeewoman, Idaho, 72. Bus & Prof Pos: Church organist, Whitney United Methodist Church, 68-; pvt piano teacher, Boise, Idaho, 73- Mem: Am Civil Liberties Union; Common Cause; Nat Comt for Sane Nuclear Policy. Relig: Methodist. Mailing Add: 1814 N Eighth Boise ID 83702

SELDEN, ARMISTEAD I, JR (D)
US Ambassador to New Zealand, Fiji, Tonga & Western Samoa
b Greensboro, Ala, Feb 20, 21; m 1948 to Mary Jane Wright; c Martee Graham, Armistead I, III, Jack Wright, Edith Cobbs & Thomas Lawson. Educ: Univ of the South, AB, 42; Univ of Ala, LLB, 48; Phi Delta Phi; Blue Key; Omicron Delta Kappa; Sigma Alpha Epsilon. Hon Degrees: LLD, Univ Ala, 75. Polit & Govt Pos: Ala State Rep, 50-52; US Rep, Ala, 53-69; Prin Dep Asst Secy of Defense for Int Security Affairs, 70-73; US Ambassador to New Zealand, Fiji, Tonga & Western Samoa, 74- Mil Serv: Navy, Lt, 42-46; served 31 months aboard ship, primarily in N Atlantic; Capt, Naval Res. Mem: DC & Am Bar Asns; Am Legion; VFW; Comt on Inter-Am Bar Rels, Bar Asn of DC. Relig: Episcopal. Legal Res: Greensboro AL Mailing Add: Am Embassy PO Box 1190 Wellington New Zealand

SELETSKY, HARRY (R)
Chmn, Sullivan Co Rep Comt, NY
b South Fallsburg, NY, Mar 7, 15; s Abraham Seletsky & Annie S; m 1942 to Pauline Strassner; c Arnold, Sandra (Mrs Moses) & Karen (Mrs Klein). Polit & Govt Pos: Chmn, Sullivan Co Rep Comt, NY, 71-; alt deleg, Rep Nat conv, 72; elec comnr, Sullivan Co, 75- Bus & Prof Pos: Pres, Seletsky Vending Co Inc, 65- Mem: South Fallsburg Vol Fire Co; F&AM; Lions; Elks; KofP. Relig: Jewish. Mailing Add: PO Box 687 South Fallsburg NY 12779

SELIN, IVAN
b New York, NY, Mar 11, 37; s Saul Selin & Freida Kuhlman S; m 1957 to Nina Evvie Cantor; c Douglas Scott & Jessica Beth. Educ: Yale Univ, BE, 57, ME, 58, PhD, 60; Fulbright Scholar, Univ Paris, PhD, 62; Sigma Xi; Tau Beta Pi. Polit & Govt Pos: Radar & space defense analyst, systs anal, Off of Secy of Defense, 65, dir strategic retaliatory div, 65-67, Dep Asst Secy of Defense for Systs Anal, 67-69, Acting Asst Secy of Defense for Systs Anal, 69-70. Bus & Prof Pos: Engr, Melpar Inc, Calif, 59-60; research engr, Rand Corp, Santa Monica, 60-65; chmn bd, Am Mgt Systs, 70- Publ: Detection Theory, Princeton Univ Press, 65. Mem: Inst Elec & Electronics Eng (ed, Group on Info Theory Abstracts). Relig: Jewish. Mailing Add: 2905 32nd St NW Washington DC 20008

SELLAR, GEORGE L (R)
Wash State Sen
Mailing Add: 1324 Terrace Dr East Wenatchee WA 98801

SELLERS, BEN A (R)
Kans State Rep
Mailing Add: 349 Sunset Dr Salina KS 67401

SELLERS, JO-ANNE ETHEL (R)
Chmn, Juniata Co Rep Comt, Pa
b Thompsontown, Pa, Mar 4, 32; d Glenn Orland Long & Mae Gearhart; m 1951 to Delbert Eugene Sellers; c Dennis, Teresa (Mrs Allen Snyder), Nevin & Troy. Educ: Fayette High Sch,

grad, 50. Polit & Govt Pos: Vchmn, Juniata Co Rep Comt, Pa, 68-72, chmn, 72- Bus & Prof Pos: Beautician, McAlisterville, Pa, 64- Mem: Eastern Star; Fayette Auxiliary Fire Co; Juniata Co Coun Rep Women. Relig: Methodist. Mailing Add: Main St McAlisterville PA 17049

SELLIE, JOHN MARTIN (R)
VChmn, NDak Rep State Comt
b Fessenden, NDak, May 15, 27; s Con Sellie & Oline Ingvaldson S; m 1952 to Carol Joan Wammer; c Karen & Peter John. Educ: Fessenden High Sch, NDak, 41-45. Polit & Govt Pos: Charter mem, Wells Co Young Rep Exec Comt, NDak, 58-62; chmn, Wells Co Rep Party, 62-67; mem bd, Hamburg Twp, 62-68, chmn bd, 67-68; chmn, 14th Legis Dist Rep Party, 67-; mem exec comt, NDak Rep State Comt, 68-70, vchmn, 72-, state finance chmn, 74- Bus & Prof Pos: Farmer & rancher. Mil Serv: Airman, Navy, 52-54. Mem: NDak Farm Bur; NDak Stockmans Asn; US Durum Growers Asn; Am Legion; Elks. Relig: Lutheran; secy of Stewardship Comt, Eastern NDak Dist of Am Lutheran Church, 69-71. Mailing Add: RR Cathay ND 58422

SELMAN, EDWIN WILLIAM, JR (D)
Chmn, Steuben Co Dem Party, Ind
b Ames, Iowa, June 9, 33; s Edwin W Selman, Sr & Francis Rea A; m 1960 to Betty Ann Tolly; c Edwin W, III, Thomas Hugh & Susan E. Educ: St Ambrose Col, 2 years; Gov Club. Polit & Govt Pos: Chmn, Steuben Co Dem Party, Ind, 65-72 & 74-; treas, Fourth Dist Dem Party, 67; field rep, Ind Dem State Comt. Bus & Prof Pos: Partner, Selman Heating & Plumbing, 60- Mil Serv: Entered as Pfc, Army, 53, released, 55, after serv in 11th Airborne Div; Parachute Badge. Mem: Jr CofC. Mailing Add: 521 E Gale St Angola IN 46703

SELTZER, H JACK (R)
Pa State Rep
b Philadelphia, Pa, Aug 12, 22; s Harvey L Seltzer & Jennie Behmer S; m to Geneva Shepherd; c Four. Educ: Palmyra Schs; Harrisburg Acad; Mercersburg Acad. Polit & Govt Pos: Chmn, Lebanon Co Rep Finance Comt, Pa, formerly; mem, Lebanon Co Rep Exec Comt; mem, Palmyra Borough Coun, 7 years, pres, 5 years; Pa State Rep, 56- Bus & Prof Pos: Mfr. Mil Serv: Navy, 42-46, SPac. Mem: VFW; Am Legion. Mailing Add: 229 S Forage Rd Palmyra PA 17078

SELYA, BRUCE MARSHALL (R)
VChmn, Rep State Cent Comt RI
b Providence, RI, May 27, 34; s Herman Charles Selya & Betty Brier S; m 1965 to Ellen Barnes; c Dawn Meredith & Lori Ann. Educ: Harvard Col, AB magna cum laude, 55; Harvard Law Sch, LLB, cum laude, 58; John Harvard Scholar; Young Rep; UN Coun; Eliot House. Polit & Govt Pos: Law clerk, US Dist Court, RI, 58-60; mem, Providence Rep City Comt, 60-65; mem, Providence Rep Second Ward Comt, 60-65; secy, RI Judicial Coun, 64-, chmn, 71-72; legal counsel, Rep State Cent Comt, RI, 65-68, mem & mem exec comt, 65-, vchmn, State Comt, 71-; mem, Lincoln Rep Town Comt, 65-; judge, Probate Court, 66-72; mem, RI Crime Comn, 67-68; chmn, 58th Rep Dist Comt, 67-; deleg, Rep Nat Conv, 68; chmn, Chafee for US Senate Comt, 72. Bus & Prof Pos: Attorney & partner, Selya & Iannuccillo, currently. Publ: Various articles for legal periodicals. Mem: Am Bar Asn; RI Bar Asn (chmn comt continuing legal educ, 71-); RI Defense Counsel Asn; Am Jurisp Soc; Am Arbit Asn (approved panelist). Relig: Jewish. Legal Res: 19 Kirkbrae Dr Lincoln RI 02865 Mailing Add: PO Box 1355 Providence RI 02903

SEMENSI, JOSEPH JOHN (D)
Mass State Rep
b Randolph, Mass, Mar 6, 23; s Lawrence Semensi & Louise Cicolari S; m 1946 to Lillian Josephine Lola; c Linda Louise, Joseph John, Jr & Valerie Jean. Polit & Govt Pos: Mem, Sch Comt, Randolph, Mass, 48-50, town clerk, selectman, town treas & mem Dem Town Comt, 51-66; Mass State Rep, 67- Mil Serv: Entered as Pvt, Army, 43, released as 2nd Lt, 46; Capt, Army Res. Mem: Lions; KofC; Amvets; Am Legion; Mass Selectmens Asn. Relig: Roman Catholic. Mailing Add: 22 Tileston Rd Randolph MA 02368

SEMOS, CHRIS VICTOR (D)
Tex State Rep
b Dallas, Tex, June 2, 36; s Victor H Semos & Evlyn Tassos S; m 1967 to Anastasia Canella Kontos; c Mary Katherine. Educ: Ecole Hotelier, Lausanne, Switz, 54-55; Southern Methodist Univ, 56-62. Polit & Govt Pos: Mem, Dallas Action Comt for Community Improv, City of Dallas Bd, 65-66; Tex State Rep, 67-, chmn bus & indust comt & mem appropriations comt, Tex House of Rep, currently; chmn, Dallas Legis Deleg. Bus & Prof Pos: Owner, Torch Restaurant, Dallas; co-owner, Semos Coffee & Tea Co, Dallas; owner, Torch-Oak Lawn Restaurant. Publ: Series of articles on Greece, Dallas Morning News, 50. Mem: Dallas Restaurant Asn (dir); Lions; Mason (32 degree); Shrine (ambassador); Dallas Coun World Affairs (bd mem). Honors & Awards: Key Mem Award, Lions Int; Lion of the Year, Westcliff Lions, 68; Knight Comndr of the Court of Honor, Scottish Rite, 69. Relig: Greek Orthodox; Pres, Holy Trinity Greek Orthodox Church of Dallas, 64-65. Legal Res: 1939 W Colorado Blvd Dallas TX 75208 Mailing Add: 3620 W Davis St Dallas TX 75211

SENA, JOSEPH ROBERT (D)
Mem Exec Comt, Santa Fe Co Dem Party, NMex
b Santa Fe, NMex, Sept 7, 44; s Robert L Sena & Lucy Sena S; m 1967 to Gloria Martin; c Maria. Educ: Col Santa Fe, BA, 69; Univ NMex Sch of Law, currently; Dean's List, 68-69. Polit & Govt Pos: Res coordr & speechwriter, Gallegos for Cong, First Cong Dist, NMex, 72; deleg, Dem Nat Conv, 72; mem exec comt, Santa Fe Co Dem Party, NMex, currently. Bus & Prof Pos: Law clerk, Bachicha & Corlett, Santa Fe, 72- Mil Serv: Entered as Airman Basic, Air Force, 64, released as S/Sgt, 68, after serv in Det 1, 6947th Security Squadron MacDill Air Force Base, 64-68. Publ: Auth, Indian education in the Pojoaque Valley Schs, Amistad, 5/69. Mem: Student Bar Asn; Mex-Am Law Students Asn; La Raza Nat Law Students Asn (bd dirs, 72-); Santa Fe Legal Aid Soc; Univ NMex-Mex-Am Legal Defense. Relig: Catholic. Mailing Add: Rte 1 Box 217 Santa Fe NM 87501

SENA, NASH M (D)
Nev State Assemblyman
Mailing Add: 144 W Victory Rd Henderson NV 89015

SENDAK, THEODORE LORRAINE (R)
Attorney Gen, Ind
b Chicago, Ill, Mar 16, 18; s Jack Sendak & Annette Frankel S; m 1942 to Tennessee Elisabeth Read; c Theodore Tipton, Timothy Read & Cynthia Louise. Educ: Harvard Univ, AB cum laude in polit sci, 40; Valparaiso Univ Sch Law, LLB, 58. Polit & Govt Pos: Pub rels dir, Ind Dept of Vet Affairs, 46-48; cand for US Rep, First Dist, Ind, 48; dist supvr, US Census, Dept of Com, 60; chmn, Lake Co Rep Cent Comt; mem, Ind Rep State Cent Comt & chmn, First Cong Dist Rep Comt, 62-66; Rep mem, Gov Comn on Voting & Registr, 64; deleg, Rep Nat Conv, 64; Attorney Gen, Ind, 69- Bus & Prof Pos: Chief ed, writer, Times, Hammond, Ind, 40-41; managed elec construction bus, Gary, Ind, 49-59; attorney-at-law, 59- Mil Serv: Entered as Pvt, Army, 41, released as Capt, 46, after serv in Philippine Civil Affairs Unit, Southwest Pac & Asiatic Theaters, 44-45; Asiatic-Pac Theater Ribbon with 3 Battle Stars; Am Defense Ribbon; Am Theater Ribbon; Victory Medal; Philippine Liberation Ribbon with 1 Star; Philippine Presidential Unit Citation; Res Serv Medal; Col, Staff Specialist Corps, US Army Res. Publ: Daily editorials, Times, Hammond, Ind, 40-41, weekly mil columns, 41-46; occasional articles & features, Post-Tribune, Gary, 55-60. Mem: Am Legion Post 369; Roosevelt Lodge 716, F&AM; Scottish Rite; Orak Shrine. Honors & Awards: Reelected 1972 with largest plurality of any state cand in any elec in hist of Ind. Relig: Methodist. Legal Res: PO Box 359 Crown Point IN 46307 Mailing Add: Off of the Attorney General 219 State House Indianapolis IN 46204

SENN, FERN BERNIECE (D)
Chairperson, Dickinson Co Dem Comt, Iowa
b Harris, Iowa, Oct 10, 18; d Delbert Morfitt & Florence Smith M; m 1938 to Hans Frederick Senn; c Shirley (Mrs Gordon Finnern) & John. Educ: Harris High Sch, Iowa, dipl. Polit & Govt Pos: Precinct committeeperson, Dickinson Co Dem Comt, Iowa, 61-74, vchairperson, 69-74, chairperson, 74-; mem VIP comt, State Dem Party Iowa, 75- Mem: Am Legion Auxiliary (poppy chmn, 74-); Nat Farmers Orgn (publicity chmn & ed, monthly publ, 71-); Dickinson Co Hosp Auxiliary; Christian Women's Club. Relig: Lutheran. Mailing Add: RR 2 Spirit Lake IA 51360

SENNETT, WILLIAM CLIFFORD (R)
Mem, Pa Rep Exec Comt
b Erie, Pa, June 1, 30; s B Walker Sennett & Roseanne Cooney S; m 1954 to Pauline Wuenschel; c William, Timothy, Patrick, Mark, Kathleen & Carolyn. Educ: Holy Cross Col, BA, 52; Georgetown Univ Law Sch, LLB, 55. Polit & Govt Pos: Solicitor, Erie Co Controller, Pa, 61-63; spec asst attorney gen, Commonwealth of Pa, 63-66; admin asst to Lt Gov, Pa, 66-67; Attorney Gen, Commonwealth of Pa, 67-70; chmn, Pa Crime Comn & Gov Liquor Code Adv Comn, formerly; campaign chmn, US Sen Hugh Scott, 70; mem, Pa Rep Exec Comt, 71- Bus & Prof Pos: Law clerk to John Danaher, US Court of Appeals, DC, 55-56; assoc, Shreve, Sennett, Couglin & McCarthy, Erie, Pa, 56-65; partner, Knox, Pearson & McLaughlin, 65-66 & Knox, Graham, Pearson, McLaughlin & Sennett, Erie, Pa, 70- Mem: Mercyhurst Col (trustee); St Vincent Hosp (trustee); Hamot Hosp (bd corporators); Phi Delta Phi; Automotive Asn Erie. Honors & Awards: Erie Co Jaycee Man of the Year, 61. Relig: Catholic. Legal Res: 6336 Red Pine Lane Erie PA 16509 Mailing Add: 23 W Tenth St Erie PA 16501

SENSENBRENNER, FRANK JAMES, JR (R)
Wis State Sen
b Chicago, Ill, June 14, 43; s Frank James Sensenbrenner & Margaret Luedke S; single. Educ: Stanford Univ, AB in polit sci, 65, Univ Wis Law Sch, JD, 68; Phi Alpha Delta. Polit & Govt Pos: Vchmn, Wis Youth for Nixon, 60; exec secy, San Mateo Co Young Rep, 62, treas, 63-65; dir region ten, Col Rep Nat Comt, 63-65, chmn, Comt on Rules, 65, deleg, Col Rep Nat Conv, 63 & 65; mem, Nat Steering Comt, Youth for Goldwater-Miller, 64; staff asst to US Rep J Arthur Younger, 65; admin asst to majority leader Sen Jerris Leonard, Wis State Senate, 67-68; Wis State Rep, Tenth Dist, Milwaukee Co, 69-75; Wis State Sen, 75-, mem comt govt vet affairs & urban affairs, currently. Bus & Prof Pos: Attorney-at-law, Milwaukee, Wis, 68-70, Cedarburg, 70-75. Mem: Milwaukee Jr, Milwaukee, Ozaukee, Wis & Am Bar Asns; Friends of Mus; Am Philatelic Soc; Whitefish Bay Jaycees; Shorewood Men's Club; Am Inst of Parliamentarians. Honors & Awards: Named Outstanding Young Rep in Midwest, 69. Relig: Episcopal. Legal Res: 1601 E Lake Bluff Blvd Shorewood WI 53211 Mailing Add: PO Box 11641 Shorewood WI 53211

SENSENBRENNER, MAYNARD E (D)
b Circleville, Ohio, Sept 18, 02; s Edward Sensenbrenner & Anna Lama S; m 1927 to Mildred Sexauer; c Edward & Richard. Educ: Pub Schs, Circleville, Ohio. Polit & Govt Pos: Investr & clerk, Ohio Civil Serv Comn, 34-53; mayor, Columbus, Ohio, 54-59 & 64-72; deleg, Dem Nat Conv, 72. Mem: Kiwanis; Moose; Elks; Eagles; Big Brother Asn. Honors & Awards: Fiorella La Guardia Award; Award for Distinguished Community Serv, Columbus Area CofC; Outstanding Citizen's Award, Elks; Good Neighbor's Award, Eagles, Lancaster, Ohio; Ludwig Hoge Mem Award. Relig: Presbyterian; Elder. Mailing Add: 4665 Scenic Dr Columbus OH 43214

SENTER, KENNETH LEE (R)
NH State Rep
b Boston, Mass, Sept 8, 01; s E Lee Senter & Nellie P Coulter S; m 1921 to Beatrice Campbell; c Kenneth Lee, Patricia (Mrs Levandowski), Roger Campbell, Sandra (Mrs Mack) & Brenda. Educ: Pub schs, Boston, Mass; Pinkerton Acad, Derry, NH. Polit & Govt Pos: Mem, Sch Bd, Derry, NH, asst moderator, town auditor; auditor, fire dept; dir, Hood Park Recreation; chmn, Rationing Bd; chmn, State Lay Prof Coun; chmn, Supvry Sch Union 10 & chmn, Bldg Comt; deleg, Rockingham Co Rep Conv; NH State Rep, 69-, mem state instnl comt, labor & human resources & rehabilitation comts, NH House Rep, currently, chmn Rockingham Co deleg. Bus & Prof Pos: Merchant, 36-55; gen ins adjuster & appraiser, Gen Adjust Bur, NY, 55-67. Mem: Derry Businessmen's Asn; Red Cross. Relig: Methodist; trustee, St Luke's Methodist Church, Derry, NH. Mailing Add: 19 Boyd Rd Derry NH 03038

SERAFIN, MARY WALUS (D)
Mem Exec Bd, Middlesex Co Dem Orgn, NJ
b Sayreville, NJ, Apr 20, 10; d Martin Michael Walus & Agnes Cygan; m 1939 to Edmund Joseph Serafin; c Ralph Robert & Gail (Mrs James). Educ: Drakes Secretarial Sch, Secretarial Arts Course. Polit & Govt Pos: Mem & vpres, Sayreville Bd of Educ, NJ, 37-40; mem, Middlesex Co Welfare Bd, 65-, chmn, 69-; munic vchmn, Borough of South River, 67-69, munic chmn, 69-; alt deleg, Dem Nat Conv, 68; mem exec bd, Middlesex Co Dem Orgn, currently. Bus & Prof Pos: Secy, Provident Mutual Life Ins Co of Philadelphia, New Brunswick, NJ, 30-41; self-employed in gen ins, 41- Publ: Compiled two recipe books, 56 & 65. Mem: Union of Polish Women in Am, Philadelphia, Pa (vpres of NJ); South River Columbiettes, Auxiliary of KofC, Southern Chap Columbiettes; NJ State Columbiettes; State Supreme Columbiettes; Pastoral Coun, Trenton Diocese, Roman Catholic Church. Honors & Awards: Outstanding Citizen Award, 65. Relig: Roman Catholic. Mailing Add: 22 Raritan Ave South River NJ 08882

SERE, SUSANNE (D)
b Tuscaloosa, Ala, Dec 23, 47; d Robert Harry Crilly & Alene Burch C; m 1970 to Jared Darby Sere. Educ: La State Univ, Baton Rouge, BS, 69; Tulane Univ, 70-71. Polit & Govt Pos: Dist chairperson, McGovern for President, La, 72; deleg, Dem Nat Conv, 72; off mgr, New Orleans McGovern/Shriver, 72. Relig: Episcopal. Mailing Add: Apt 1702 5625 Antoine Dr Houston TX 77088

SERRA, EMANUEL G (D)
Mass State Rep
Mailing Add: 230 Orient Ave Boston MA 02128

SERRANI, THOM (D)
Conn State Rep
b Glens Falls, NY, Nov 5, 47; s Duke Serrani & Florence LaPoint S; single. Educ: Sacred Heart Univ, BA, 70; Fairfield Univ Grad Sch, MA, 75; Sigma Tau Omega; Student Body Pres. Polit & Govt Pos: City rep, Stamford Bd of Rep, 73-75, chmn, Legislative & Rules Comt, 73-75, parliamentarian, 73-75; mem, Stamford Resource Recovery Adv Bd, 75-; Conn State Rep, 75- Bus & Prof Pos: Emergency med technician, Springdale Fire Co, 73- Mem: Springdale Fire Co Vol; North Stamford Dem Club; Sigma Tau Omega Alumni Asn. Mailing Add: 113 Knickerbocker Ave Stamford CT 06907

SERRANO, JOSE E (D)
NY State Assemblyman
b Mayaguez, PR, Oct 24, 45; s Jose E Serrano & Hipolita Soto S; m to Carmen Velez; c Lisa Marie & Jose Marco. Polit & Govt Pos: NY State Assemblyman, 75- Bus & Prof Pos: Mfrs Hanover Trust Co, 61-69; mem, Bd Educ, New York, 69-74. Mil Serv: Entered as Pvt, Army, 64, released as Spec 4/C, 66, after serv in 172nd Support Bn, Ft Wainwright, Alaska. Mem: South Bronx Community Corp (chmn, 70-); Human Resources (chmn dist one); Lincoln Hosp (vchmn adv bd). Relig: Catholic. Legal Res: 690 Gerard Ave Bronx NY 10451 Mailing Add: 308 E 149th St Bronx NY 10451

SERVER, GREGORY DALE (R)
Ind State Rep
Mailing Add: 2250 E Walnut St Evansville IN 47714

SERWER, ARNOLD (D)
b New York, NY, Apr 6, 11; s Isidor Serwer & Mary Gordon S; m 1937 to Dora Shulman; c David & Cathy. Educ: Univ Wis, Madison, BA in Journalism, 33. Polit & Govt Pos: Info specialist, Fed Emergency Relief Admin & Works Progress Admin, Washington, DC, 34-36 & War Prod Bd, 42-43; labor rels specialist, War Manpower Comn, 43-44; dir, press sect, War Relocation Authority, 44-46; chmn, Stevenson Vol, New Hyde Park, NY, 52 & 56; mem exec comt, Nassau Co Stevenson Vol, LI, NY, 60; state orgn dir, McCarthy for President Comt, Wis, 68; deleg-at-lg, Dem Nat Conv, 68, deleg, Dem Nat Conv, 72. Bus & Prof Pos: Proprietor, Indust Adv Serv, pub rels, New York, 49-62; assoc ed, The Progressive Mag, Madison, Wis, 62- Mil Serv: Entered as Pvt, Army Air Force, 41, released as Spec 5/C, after serv in 126th Obsn Squadron, US Air Force Res, 41-43. Publ: McCarthy's winning of Wisconsin, The Progressive, 6/68; plus others. Mem: Madison, Washington, DC & NY Newspaper Guilds. Relig: Jewish. Mailing Add: 1014 Forster Dr Madison WI 53704

SESSIONS, JOHN O (R)
Idaho State Rep
Mailing Add: Box 152 Driggs ID 83422

SETZEPFANDT, ALVIN O H, II (DFL)
Minn State Rep
b Eagle Grove, Iowa, Feb 7, 24; s Alvin O H Setzepfandt & Louise Dorweiler S; m 1946 to Carol Rhae Wilson; c Alvin O H, III, Sue Ann (Mrs Douglas Smith), Paul Wilson & Scott Alan. Educ: Iowa State Univ, DVM, 45; Tau Kappa Epsilon. Polit & Govt Pos: Mayor, Bird Island, Minn, 57-71; comnr, Renville Co, 71-75; Minn State Rep, Dist 21B, 75- Mil Serv: Pfc, Army, 41-42; Army Med Res, Capt, until 57. Mem: Lions; Am Legion; Am & Minn Vet Med Asns. Relig: Protestant. Mailing Add: Bird Island MN 55310

SETZER, JOHNSIE JULIA (D)
Secy, Dem Party NC
b Catawba Co, NC, May 13, 24; d Thomas Alonzo Crawford (deceased) & Effie Hudspeth C (deceased); m 1938 to Willie Augustus Setzer; c Larry W, June S (Mrs Charles Elsmore), Stanley K & Timothy Alan. Educ: Lenoir Rhyne Col, 42-43; Clevenger Bus Col, Newton, NC, 54-56; Phi Beta Kappa. Polit & Govt Pos: Deleg, White House Conf Children, 70; teen Dem adv, Catawba Co Dem Party, 70-71; teen Dem adv, Dem Party NC, 72, secy, 75-; deleg, Dem Nat Conv, 72; adult bd mem, Gov Youth Adv Bd NC, 72-74; teen Dem Liaison chmn & mem exec comt, Dem Women NC, 72-73 & 74-75; chmn, Sam Ervin Day, Catawba Co, 74; chmn, Rufus Edmisten Campaign for Attorney Gen, 74; alt deleg, Dem Nat Mid-Term Conf, 74; publicity chmn, Catawba Co Dem Party, 75- Bus & Prof Pos: Treas, Agr Stabilization & Conserv Catawba Co, 47-56; receptionist & secy, Betterwear Hosiery-Catawba, 60-65; unit dir, Catawba Co, Am Cancer Soc, 71-75; prog asst, Catawba Co Exten Serv, 73; off mgr, Setzer Bros, Inc, 74- Mem: 4-H (pres, Catawba Co 4-H leaders orgn, 71-); YMCA (bd mem, secy, currently); Am Cancer Soc (bd dirs, 69-75, chmn personnel comt, currently); PTA. Honors & Awards: Award, WOW, 71; Outstanding 4-H Adult Leader Southwestern Dist, 69; Outstanding 4-H Leader State NC, 72. Relig: United Methodist; official bd. Mailing Add: Rte 2 Box 317 G Claremont NC 28610

SEVCIK, JOSEPH G (R)
Ill State Sen
Mailing Add: 2716 S Euclid Ave Berwyn IL 60402

SEVERNS, PENNY LEE (D)
Mem, Dem Nat Comt, Ill
Mailing Add: 2074 S 32nd Pl Decatur IL 62521

SEVITS, WILLIS LEE (R)
Secy, Adair Co Rep Cent Comt
b Greentop, Mo, Dec 8, 21; s Sherman Harrison Sevits & Maude Mae Willis S; m 1946 to Eva Dean Helton; c Jerry Lee & Tom G. Educ: Mo State Col, Kirksville, BS, 54; Phi Omega Pi; Phi Sigma Epsilon. Polit & Govt Pos: City alderman & clerk, Elmer, Mo, 53-60; mem & treas, Macon Co Sch Bd, 64-69; chmn, Macon Co Rep Party, 68-72, secy, Adair Co Rep Cent Comt, 72- Bus & Prof Pos: Acct & salesman, Chevrolet Dealership, LaPlata, Mo, 54-61; controller, Kirksville Co Osteopathy & Surgery, 63-; comnr, Spec Rd Dist 41, 73- Mil Serv: Entered as A/S, Navy, 42, released as Motor Machinist's Mate 3/C, 46, after serv in Amphibious Force, ETO, 43-45; 5 Bronze Stars, Africa, Sicily, Salerno, Anzio & Normandy. Mem: KT (chmn, Educ Found Comt, Kirksville); AF&AM; Am Legion; Moose; RAM, Moila Temple. Relig: Protestant. Mailing Add: 2205 N New Kirksville MO 63501

SEWALL, JOSEPH (R)
Maine State Sen
Mailing Add: Box 433 Old Town ME 04468

SEWARD, ROLAND QUINCY (R)
Rep Nat Committeeman, Vt
b East Wallingford, Vt, Mar 4, 17; s Arthur B Seward & Ella Quincy Bunker S; m 1938 to Dorothy Catherine Poloske; c Roland Q, Jr, Thomas R & John B. Educ: Rutland Bus Col, Vt, grad, 35. Polit & Govt Pos: Mem, Vt Develop Comn, 53-59; chmn, Rutland Co Rep Party, 59-61; chmn, Vt Develop Bd, 61-63; mem, Vt Indust Bldg Authority, 61-63; chmn, Vt Rep State Comt, 61-63, finance chmn, 67-72; mem, Vt Gov Coun of Econ Adv, 69-73; Rep Nat Committeeman, Vt, 72-; vchmn, New Eng Rep Coun, 75- Bus & Prof Pos: Proprietor, Valley View Creamery, East Wallingford, 36-; pres & treas, Sewards Dairy, Inc, Rutland, 47-; trustee, Vt Found of Independent Cols, 53-; mem bd, Vt Develop Credit Corp, 58-, pres, 59-63; mem bd dirs, Proctor Trust Co, 59-; pres, The Seward Family, Inc, 63-; pres, Sewards Restaurant of Burlington, 63-; pres, Seward Foods, Inc, Rutland, 64- Mem: Mason (32 degree); Shrine; Elks; Odd Fellows; United Commercial Travelers. Relig: Congregational. Mailing Add: RFD East Wallingford VT 05742

SEWELL, JOAN MARIE (D)
b Baltimore, Md, Jan 27, 33; d Martin Joseph McTighe & Estelle Wyatt M; m 1950 to William Arnold Sewell; c William Craig, Lynn (Mrs Charles Phillips), Mark Steven & Brian Alan. Educ: Essex Community Col, Md, 65-66. Polit & Govt Pos: Coordr vols, Baltimore Co Johnson-Humphrey Campaign, Md, 64; spec asst, US Sen Daniel B Brewster, Md, 66-68; state vol chmn, Humphrey-Muskie Campaign, 68; spec asst, Gov Marvin Mandel, 69-70; campaign coordr, Anne Arundel Co Dem for Boyer for Cong Spec Elect, 71; state campaign mgr, Humphrey for President, 72; alt deleg, Dem Nat Conv, 72; mem steering comt, Fourth Cong Dist, McGovern for President, 72; state campaign coordr, Gov Mandel, 74; asst dir training, Md Dept Econ & Community Develop, currently. Mem: Anne Arundel Co United Dem Women's Club (pres, 70-73, bd chmn, 73-); Southern Md United Dem Women's Clubs (legis chmn, 71-); United Dem Women's Clubs Md (publicity chmn, 71-); Anne Arundel Co Chap AFL-CIO Comt on Polit Educ; Sun Valley Improv Asn (secy, 72-). Relig: Methodist. Mailing Add: 7 Phyllis Dr Glen Burnie MD 21061

SEXTON, CLARENCE D, JR (D)
Mem Exec Comt, SC Dem Party
b Columbia, SC, Feb 5, 27; s Clarence D Sexton, Sr & Ada Smith S; m 1951 to Mary Irene Tenk; c Margaret, Mary, Jenny, Terry & Betty Ann. Educ: Univ SC, BSCE, 48; Sigma Phi Epsilon. Polit & Govt Pos: Chmn, Lexington Co Dem Party, SC, 67-72; deleg, Dem Nat Conv, 68 & 72; mem steering comt, SC Dem Party, currently, mem exec comt, 72- Bus & Prof Pos: Proj engr, Standard Oil Co, NJ, Aruba, 48-55; vpres, Repub Contracting Corp, Columbia, SC, 55- Mil Serv: Entered as Pvt, Army, 41, released as Sgt, 47, after serv in Third Inf Div; 2nd Lt, Army Res. Mem: Am Soc Civil Engrs; Lions; Moose; WOW; CofC. Relig: Presbyterian; Elder, Providence Presbyterian Church. Mailing Add: 1428 Redwood Dr West Columbia SC 29169

SEYBERT, MYRON SILVER (R)
b Anderson, Ind, Dec 28, 08; s Fred A Seybert & Lottie G S; m 1935 to Georgia Helen Wantz; c Sharon L (Mrs Stinson) & Shirley A (Mrs Aubrey). Polit & Govt Pos: Chmn, Madison Co Rep Party, Ind, formerly; alt deleg, Rep Nat Conv, 68. Mailing Add: 1331 1/2 Main St Anderson IN 46016

SEYFRIED, MARYANN (D)
Ind State Rep
Mailing Add: 8131 Pickford Dr Indianapolis IN 46227

SHABAZ, JOHN C (R)
Wis State Assemblyman
b Milwaukee, Wis, June 25, 31; m 1953 to Katherine Kritz; c Scott & Jeffrey. Educ: Wis Univ, 53; Marquette Univ, LLB, 57. Polit & Govt Pos: Wis State Assemblyman, 64-, Assembly Minority Floor Leader, 73-; mem exec comt, Wis Rep State Cent Comt, 75- Bus & Prof Pos: Attorney; farming; sales; machine operation. Mil Serv: Army, 54-56. Mem: Bar Asns; US Jaycees; Wis Jaycees; Metrop Jaycees; Lions. Honors & Awards: Outstanding W Allis Jr CofC, 63-64; One of Five Outstanding Young Men in Wis, 65. Mailing Add: 21425 W Glengarry Rd North Berlin WI 53151

SHABLOW, FRANK S (D)
NDak State Sen
b Lancaster, Minn, Oct 15, 09; married; c 2. Educ: Pub Schs. Polit & Govt Pos: NDak State Rep, 61-66 & 71-73; mem, NDak Small Bus Admin Adv Coun, 68-70; NDak State Sen, 73- Bus & Prof Pos: Farmer & implement dealer. Mem: Elks; Commercial Club; Curling Club; Gun Club; KofC. Mailing Add: State Capitol Bismarck ND 58501

SHACKLE, H GENE (D)
Cent Committeeman, Stark Co Dem Cent Comt, Ohio
b Canton, Ohio, Aug 13, 29; s Harold L Shackle & Margaret Smith S; m to Marylou Beaumont; c Sheryl, Susan, David, Mary Katheryn, Eric, Linda, Kathleen & James. Educ: Kent State Univ, 48-50; Wm McKinley Sch of Law, 50-54, LLB, 54. Polit & Govt Pos: Cent Committeeman, Stark Co Dem Cent Comt, Ohio, 62-; alt deleg, Dem Nat Conv, 68; mem, Stark Co Dem Exec Comt, 68-; Asst Attorney Gen, Ohio, 71- Bus & Prof Pos: Credit correspondent, Diebold Inc, Ohio, 51-52; field off mgr, Robert Carter Co, 52-54; asst to the secy, Nat Can Corp, Ill, 54-56; employee rels mgr, Argonne Nat Lab, 56-57; secy & gen counsel, E W Bliss Co, 57-68, vpres adminr & dir, 68-69; attorney-at-law, pvt practice, 69- Mil Serv: Entered as Pvt, Army, 46, released as Sgt, 48, after serv in Armored Sch. Mem: Corp Secretaries Soc Am; Canton Club; Canton CofC; YMCA (bd trustees); Brookside Country Club. Relig: Lutheran. Mailing Add: 934 Raff Rd SW Canton OH 44710

SHACKLEFORD, ROBERT MITCHELL, JR (R)
Chmn, Clarke Co Rep Exec Comt, Ala
b Mobile, Ala, June 7, 20; s Robert M Shackleford, Sr & Myrtice Christine Brannon S; m

1947 to Mary Frances Stimpson; c Robert M, III, Mary Katherine & Christine S. Educ: Ill Col of Optom, OD; Omega Epsilon Phi. Polit & Govt Pos: Chmn, Clarke Co Rep Exec Comt, Ala, 62- Mil Serv: Entered as Pvt, Army, 39, released as Sgt, 45, after serv in 569 Signal HDG Bn, ETO, 42-45. Mem: Ala Optom Asn (pres, 54); Rotary; Am Legion. Relig: Methodist. Mailing Add: Box 187 Jackson AL 36545

SHADDEN, RAYMOND (R)
Tenn State Sen
Mailing Add: 916 S Main St Crossville TN 38555

SHADDUCK, LOUISE (R)
b Coeur d'Alene, Idaho, Oct 14, 15; d Lester Carson Shadduck & Mary Jeannette Furgason S; single. Educ: Coeur d'Alene High Sch, Idaho, 4 years. Hon Degrees: JD, Univ Idaho, 69. Polit & Govt Pos: Admin asst, Gov & Lt Gov, Idaho, exec secy, US Sen, Idaho; dir, Dept of Commerce & Develop, Idaho; admin asst, US Rep Orval Hansen, Idaho, 69- Bus & Prof Pos: Reporter, Coeur d'Alene (Idaho) Press & Spokesman-Rev, Spokane, Wash, 10 years. Publ: Ed, Centennial Year Idaho Almanac; auth, articles, leaflets & brochures. Mem: Nat Fedn of Press Women (int develop chmn, 74-75); Am Newspaper Women; Am Indust Develop Asn; Idaho Press Asn; Beta Sigma Phi. Honors & Awards: Women's Sugar Plum Award, Wash State Press; Citation for journalistic works & pub serv, Univ Idaho; first recipient, Distinguished Mem Award, Boise Advert Club. Relig: Presbyterian. Legal Res: Mica Bay ID Mailing Add: Box 657 Coeur d'Alene ID 83814

SHAEFFER, JOHN ALLEN (R)
b Sioux Falls, SDak, Aug 10, 41; s James Howard Shaeffer & Maylou Reidesal S; m 1967 to Cheryl Dott; c Michael Thomas & Colleen Jo Ann. Educ: Loyola Univ, 59-62; Univ SDak Law Sch, LLB, 65. Polit & Govt Pos: Chmn, Moody Co Rep Party, SDak, formerly. Mem: SDak Bar Asn; Tri-Co Bar Asn; Flandreau Jr CofC. Relig: Catholic. Mailing Add: Flandreau SD 57028

SHAFER, EARL T (R)
Chmn, Stark Co Rep Cent Comt, Ill
b Stark Co, Ill, Apr 1, 12; s Frank Shafer & Nellie Ingram S; single. Educ: Wyo Community High Sch, grad, 29. Polit & Govt Pos: Supvr, Stark Co Bd of Supvrs, Ill, 55-63; precinct committeeman, Stark Co Rep Party, 55-; chmn, Stark Co Rep Cent Comt, 60-; chmn, Ill Soil & Water Conserv Bd, 69- Bus & Prof Pos: Owner & operator, Shafer Reconditioned Cylinder Head Co, 29-42; flight instr, Govt Flying Schs, 42-44; owner & mgr, Farms in Stark, Bureau & Lee Counties, Ill, 44- Mil Serv: Entered as Flight Officer, Army Air Corps, Atlantic, NAfrica & China-Burma-India, 44-45; NAfrica & China-Burma-India Theatre Ribbons. Mem: Mason; Scottish Rite; Shrine; Am Legion; Retired Officers Asn. Relig: Protestant. Mailing Add: PO Box 105 Wyoming IL 61491

SHAFER, ESTHER VIRGINIA (R)
b Painesville, Ohio, June 25, 21; d Ralph Widgren & Anna Ladvala W; m 1945 to Jack Franklin Shafer. Educ: High Sch Grad. Polit & Govt Pos: Vchairwoman, Laramie Co Rep Cent Comt, Wyo, 60-64; deleg, Rep Nat Conv, 64; Wyo State Rep Committeewoman, Laramie Co, 64-69; deleg, Wyo State Rep Conv, 68; deleg, Wyo State Rep Women's Conv, 68; corresponding secy, Oahu League Rep Women, 69-70; alt deleg, Hawaii State Rep Conv, 70, deleg, 71-75; deleg, Hawaii State Fedn Rep Women, 70, 72 & 74, first vpres, 70, pres, 71-76; second vpres, We The Women, currently. Mem: Honolulu Rep Women's Club; Honolulu Salvation Army Women's Auxiliary (treas); Hawaii Kai Newcomers Club; Freedoms Found Valley Forge; Hawaii Kai Ladies Golf Club. Relig: Presbyterian. Mailing Add: 6370 Hawaii Kai Dr No 40 Honolulu HI 96825

SHAFER, RAYMOND PHILIP (R)
b New Castle, Pa, Mar 5, 17; s David Paul Shafer & Mina Belle Miller S; m 1941 to Jane Harris Davies; c Raymond Philip, Diane Elizabeth & Jane Ellen. Educ: Allegheny Col, BA in Hist & Polit Sci, 33; Yale Univ Law Sch, LLB, 41; Phi Beta Kappa; dir, Moot Court, Barrister's Union. Polit & Govt Pos: Chmn, Gov Select Comt on Educ, Pa, 63; chmn, Admin Legis Policy Comt, 63-65; pres, Pa State Senate; chmn, Bd of Pardons, Commun Affairs Adv Coun & Coun on Human Serv; hon chmn, Gov Comn on Const Rev; mem, Sch Finance Serv Comt, Gov Tax Study Comt & Comn on Inter-State Coop; Gov, Pa, 67-71; deleg, Rep Nat Conv, 68; counsr intergovt rels, Vice President US, 75- Bus & Prof Pos: Secy & dir, Meadville City Hosp; chmn bd, Allegheny Col, currently. Mil Serv: Entered Navy, 42, released as Comdr of PT Boat, 45, after serv in SPac; Bronze Star; Purple Heart; Philippine Liberation Medal. Mem: Pa Bar Asn; Grange; Rotary; Am Legion; VFW. Mailing Add: 485 Chestnut St Meadville PA 16335

SHAFER, THOMAS EDWARD (R)
b Rochester, Pa, Dec 10, 50; s Thomas Albert Shafer & Blanche Louise Baughman S; single. Educ: Westminster Col, BA, 73. Polit & Govt Pos: Pres, Westminster Col Rep, 72; youth dir, Lawrence Co Reelect the President Comt, Pa, 72; regional dir, Pa Col Rep, 72; deleg & mem rules comt, Rep Nat Conv, 72. Bus & Prof Pos: Local news dir, WKPS (FM), New Wilmington, Pa, 72-; serv/sales rep, Andersen Corp, Bay Port, Minn. Relig: Lutheran. Mailing Add: 626 Whistler Dr Rochester PA 15074

SHAFF, ROGER J (R)
Iowa State Sen
Mailing Add: RR 1 Box 118A Camanche IA 52730

SHAFFE, DAVID BRUCE (D)
Vt State Rep
b Bennington, Vt, Feb 2, 50; s Joseph Y Shaffe & Sarah Ruth Coblentz S; single. Educ: Univ Vt, BSBA, 72. Polit & Govt Pos: Vt State Rep, 73- Bus & Prof Pos: Mgr, Shaffe's Men's Shop, Bennington, 72- Mem: Elks; Masons; Bennington Club. Relig: Jewish. Mailing Add: 229 Union St Bennington VT 05201

SHAFFER, CHARLES RAYMOND (R)
WVa State Deleg
b Rupert, WVa, Mar 29, 27; s Charles Henry Shaffer & Constance Black S; m 1949 to Vivian Yvonne Roger; c Mark Steven, Charles Roger, Laura Yvonne, Gloria Darlene & Vivian Charlene. Educ: WVa Wesleyan Col, BS, 50. Polit & Govt Pos: WVa State Deleg, Upshur Co, 69- Mil Serv: Entered as A/S, Navy, 45, released as Seaman 2/C, 46, after serv in Naval Res, US; Am Campaign & Victory Medals. Mem: Mason; Am Legion; Lions; Christian Bus Men's Comt; United Commercial Travelers. Relig: United Methodist. Mailing Add: Rte 4 Box 35 Buckhannon WV 26201

SHAFFER, DALE LESTER (R)
Chmn, Richardson Co Rep Party, Nebr
b Decatur, Ill, Sept 29, 20; s Lester George Shaffer & Mattie Martin S; m 1944 to Margaret Elizabeth Gillispie; c Dale L, Jr, Susan Cicely (Mrs Richard Pierson), James Christopher & Mary Jane. Educ: James Millikin Univ, 39-41; Northwestern Univ Sch Law, 45-46; Phi Delta Phi; Tau Kappa Epsilon. Polit & Govt Pos: Chmn, Richardson Co Rep Party, Nebr, 70-; mem plans & develop comt, Nebr State Rep Party, 73-; mayor, Falls City, Nebr, 74- Mil Serv: Entered as Aviation Cadet, Army Air Corps, 41, released as Col, 65, after serv in 8th Air Force, Strategic Air Command, Air Force Orientation Group; Col (Ret), Air Force; Silver Star; Distinguished Flying Cross; Air Medal; Air Force Commendation Medal; Presidential Unit Citation; Star of Algeria (Moroccan). Mem: Elks; VFW; Am Legion; Rotary Int; Air Force Aid Soc. Relig: Methodist. Mailing Add: 1919 Crook St Falls City NE 68355

SHAFFER, DONALD (D)
Chmn, Nassau Co New Dem Coalition
b Cleveland, Ohio, Oct 6, 28; s Nathan Shaffer & Ruth Glaser S; m 1949 to Doris Freed; c Nathan, Robert & David. Educ: Brooklyn Col, BA, 49; Univ Chicago, 49-50. Polit & Govt Pos: Coordr, McCarthy for President, Nassau Co, 68; chmn, Nassau Co New Dem Coalition, 69-, nat vchmn, 72-73. Bus & Prof Pos: Ins broker, Donald Shaffer Inc, 54- Mem: Am Soc Chartered Life Underwriters; NY Civil Liberties Union (dir, 68-72, dir, Nassau Chap, 66-). Honors & Awards: Martin Luther King Award, Long Island Comt for Human Rights, 66. Relig: Jewish. Mailing Add: 6 Old Colony Lane Great Neck NY 11023

SHAFFER, KENNETH WOODS (R)
Chmn, Volusia Co Rep Exec Comt, Fla
b Barbour Co, WVa, Dec 16, 05; s William Woods Shaffer & Blanche Bennett S; m 1932 to Jean Wallace; c Dr Kenneta Jean. Educ: Salem Col, 24-25; WVa Univ, AB, 29; Columbia Univ, MA, 34; Harvard Univ, 43; Fla Technol Univ, 68; Sphinx; Tau Kappa Epsilon. Polit & Govt Pos: Nominee for state supt schs, WVa, 44-52; chmn, Volusia Co Rep Exec Comt, Fla, 74- Bus & Prof Pos: Supt schs, Preston, Roane, Lewis & Mason Co, WVa, 35-54; state dir, Farmers Home Admin, US Dept Agr, 54-60; asst dir student affairs, WVa Univ, 60-65; prof psychol & educ, Daytona Beach Community Col, 65- Publ: Several articles, WVa Sch J. Mem: Nat Educ Asn; Fla Asn Community Cols; Mason; Rotary. Relig: Methodist. Legal Res: 1147 N Halifax Ave Daytona Beach FL 32018 Mailing Add: Daytona Beach Community Col Daytona Beach FL 32018

SHAFFER, ROBERT EDWIN (D)
Supvr, Schoharie Co Bd of Supvr, NY
b Gilboa, NY, Jan 1, 16; s Robert Edwin Shaffer & Edna Van Tyle Mattice S; m 1946 to Marion G Gallagher; c Gail Susan & Edwin Robert. Educ: Chicago Acad Fine Arts, 39-40. Polit & Govt Pos: Supvr, Schoharie Co Bd Supvr, NY, 51-, chmn, 65-67. Mil Serv: Entered as Pvt, Army, 41, released as T-5, 42, after serv in Hq Battery, 867 AAA (AW) Bn, Cent Pac Theatre, 42-45; Am Defense Medal; Asiatic-Pac Serv Medal; Good Conduct Medal. Mem: Am Legion; F&AM; RAM. Relig: Protestant. Mailing Add: North Blenheim NY 12131

SHAFFREY, INA THERESA (D)
VChmn, Mo State Dem Comt
b Nashville, Tenn, Oct 26, 11; d P S Smith & Martha E Garrett S; m 1927 to George C Shaffrey; c Leola G (Mrs Meifert), Patricia D (Mrs Morard) & George C, Jr. Polit & Govt Pos: Committeewoman, 24th Ward, Mo, 44-; State Dem Committeewoman, Third Cong Dist, 60; vchmn, Mo State Dem Comt, 66-; secy, City Dem Cent Comt, 66-; alt deleg, Dem Nat Conv, 72; mem, Dem Nat Comt, currently; bd mem, Mo Fedn Women's Dem Clubs. Relig: Catholic. Mailing Add: 6314 W Park Ave St Louis MO 63139

SHAKER, MITCHELL FRANCIS (D)
Exec secy, Trumbull Co Dem Exec Comt, Ohio
b Niles, Ohio, Jan 3, 22; s Isaac Shaker (deceased) & Sophia Joseph S; m 1945 to Mary K Christopher; c Mary Alice (Mrs Weiss), Margaret Ann, Mitchell F, Jr, Kathryn T (Mrs Earnhart), Thomas J, Patricia L, Christopher J & Robert I. Educ: John Carroll Univ, BA, magna cum laude, 43; Western Reserve Univ Sch of Law, JD, 48; Alpha Sigma Nu; Order of the Coif; Delta Theta Phi. Polit & Govt Pos: City solicitor, Niles, Ohio, 50-55, 62-63 & 66-; exec secy, Trumbull Co Dem Exec Comt, 63-; mem bd elec, Trumbull Co, 66-67. Bus & Prof Pos: Attorney-at-law, 48- Mil Serv: Entered as Midn, Navy, 43, released as Lt(jg), 45, after serv in Fifth Fleet, SPac, 44-45. Mem: Niles Area CofC; Am Legion; KofC; Elks. Relig: Roman Catholic. Legal Res: 403 Hogarth Ave Niles OH 44446 Mailing Add: 502-3 Niles Bank Bldg Niles OH 44446

SHAKESPEARE, FRANK (R)
b New York, NY, Apr 9, 25; s Francis J Shakespeare & Frances Hughes S; m 1954 to Deborah Anne Spaeth; c Andrea, Fredricka & Mark. Educ: Holy Cross Col, BA, 46. Polit & Govt Pos: Dir, US Info Agency, 69-73. Bus & Prof Pos: With Liberty Mutual Ins Co, Washington, DC, 47-49, Procter & Gamble Co, 49-50, Radio Sta WOR, NY, 50, WOIC TV Sta, Washington, 50 & Columbia Broadcasting Syst, NY, 50-57; gen mgr, WXIX-TV, Milwaukee, Wis, 57-59; vpres & gen mgr, WCBS-TV, NY, 59-63; vpres, CBS-TV Network, 63-65, sr vpres, 65, exec vpres, CBS-TV Stas, 65-67, pres, CBS/TV Serv, 68-69; exec vpres, Westinghouse Elec Corp, 73-75; pres, RKO Gen, Inc, 75- Mil Serv: Lt(jg), Navy. Mem: Stanwich Club, Greenwich, Conn; Metrop Club, Washington, DC. Honors & Awards: Young Man of the Year, NY, 60. Relig: Catholic. Mailing Add: Cliff Rd Greenwich CT 06830

SHALTON, LONNIE JOSEPH (D)
Chmn, Jackson Co Dem Comt, Mo
b Kansas City, Mo, Aug 9, 41; s Joseph Shalton & Kathryn Lukomski S; div; c Brian Keith, Stacey Lynn & Jason Andrew. Educ: Univ Mo-Rolla, BS, 63, MS, 64; Univ Mo-Kans City, JD, 67; Tau Beta Pi; Alpha Sigma Mu; Blue Key; Theta Tau; Sigma Nu. Polit & Govt Pos: Dem mem, Kansas City Munic Court Nominating Comn, 73-77; chmn, Jackson Co Dem Comt, Mo, 74-; mem policy & planning comt, Mo State Dem Comt, 75- Mem: Mo Bar Asn; Kansas City Bar Asn (chmn, Domestic Rels Comt, 71-72 & Munic Courts Comt, 75-); Asn of Trial Lawyers Am. Honors & Awards: Outstanding Young Dem of Mo, Young Dem Clubs Mo, 72-73. Legal Res: 5303 Persimmon Trail Apt 4 Kansas City MO 64129 Mailing Add: 1300 Commerce Bldg Kansas City MO 64106

SHANAHAN, ELWILL M (R)
Secy of State, Kans
b Salina, Kans, Sept 22, 12; d August G Mattson & Adine O Peterson M; m 1951 to Paul R Shanahan; wid. Educ: Grad & registered nurse, Swedish Covenant Hosp, Chicago, Ill, 34.

Polit & Govt Pos: Secy of State, Kans, 66- Mem: Nat Asn of Secy of States; Kans Fedn Rep Women's Clubs; Topeka Soroptomist Club; Am Bus Women's Asn; Marymount Col, Kans (mem pres coun). Relig: Protestant. Legal Res: 1000 Highland Salina KS 67401 Mailing Add: Apt J-62 1320 27th St Topeka KS 66611

SHANAHAN, TOM L **(D)**
Ga State Rep
Mailing Add: PO Box 427 Calhoun GA 30701

SHANARD, GEORGE H **(R)**
SDak State Sen
b Bridgewater, SDak, July 30, 26; s Jacob H Shanard & Martha E Findahl S; m 1952 to Iris L Achenbach; c George H, III, Laurie Jean, Keri E & Heidi Ana. Educ: Univ SDak, BS, 50; Beta Theta Pi. Polit & Govt Pos: Chmn, Gov Task Force Rail Abandonment, SDak, 72-75; SDak State Sen, 17th Dist, 75- Bus & Prof Pos: Pres, Shanard, Inc, 64-; vpres, Ramkota, Inc, 68- Mil Serv: Entered as Seaman, Navy, 43, released as Radarman 3/C, 46, after serv in Pac, 44-46; Pac Theatre Ribbon; 2 Battle Stars. Mem: Mason; Shrine; Am Legion; 40 et 8. Honors & Awards: Alumnus of Year, Univ SDak Sch Bus, 68. Relig: Protestant. Legal Res: 1519 Northridge Mitchell SD 57301 Mailing Add: N Riverside Rd Mitchell SD 57301

SHANDALOW, MAY G **(D)**
b Poland, Mar 30, 15; d Samuel Galowitz & Rebecca Galowitz G; m to Dr Sol L Shandalow (deceased); c Merna Ellentuck. Educ: Brooklyn Col, BS, summa cum laude, 57; NY Univ, MA, 58; Alpha Kappa Delta; Kappa Delta Pi. Polit & Govt Pos: Deleg, Dem Nat Conv, 72; deleg, Kings Co Dem Coalition, NY. Bus & Prof Pos: Sch teacher, New York. Mem: League of Women Voters (vpres, 69-71); Prospect Heights Hosp Auxiliary (pres, 50-52); Hebrew Educ Soc (exec comt, 69-); Lefferts Manor Civic Asn (vpres, 67-71). Relig: Jewish. Mailing Add: 1000 Ocean Pkwy Brooklyn NY 11230

SHANE, WILLIAM **(D)**
Pa State Rep
Mailing Add: Capitol Bldg Harrisburg PA 17120

SHANK, CLARE BROWN (WILLIAMS) **(R)**
b Syracuse, NY, Sept 19, 09; d Curtiss Crofoot Brown & Clara Irene Shoudy B; m 1940 to Frank Eugene Williams (deceased); m 1963 to Seth Carl Shank. Educ: Syracuse Univ, Bachelor of Oral Eng, 31; Zeta Phi Eta; Pi Beta Phi. Polit & Govt Pos: Mem exec comt, Fla Fedn Rep Women, 52-64; life mem, Pinellas Co Rep Exec Comt, 52-; Pinellas Co mem, Fla State Rep Comt, 54-58; mem, Fla State Rep Exec Comt, 54-64; mem exec comt, Rep Nat Comt, 56-64, asst chmn & dir women's activities, 58-64; mem adv bd, US Civil War Centennial Comn; mem, Defense Adv Comn on Women in Serv, 59-65; alt deleg & mem exec arrangements comt, Rep Nat Conv, 60, alt deleg, mem prog & arrangements comts & gave seconding speech for the presidential nomination of William W Scranton, 64; mem, Nat Adv Comt to Reelect the President, 72. Bus & Prof Pos: Teacher, 31-33; merchandising exec, 33-42. Mem: Am Asn Univ Women; Gen Fedn Women's Clubs; St Petersburg Women's Club (pres, 74-); Colonial Dames, 17th Century; Women's Nat Rep Club, New York. Honors & Awards: George Arents Award, Syracuse Univ, 59; first woman to preside over any portion of any nat polit conv & gave major address, Rep Nat Conv, 60; Citation for Patriotic Civilian Serv, Fifth US Army & Dept Defense. Relig: Methodist. Mailing Add: Apt 1002 1120 North Shore Dr NE St Petersburg FL 33701

SHANK, MARY ELLEN **(D)**
Chmn, Stafford Co Dem Cent Comt, Kans
b St John, Kans, Dec 24, 35; d Harry Judah Waters & Cora Helen Long W; m 1957 to Robert Henry Shank; c Theryne Kay & Kevyn Ray. Educ: McPherson Col, Elem Sch Teaching Cert, 56. Polit & Govt Pos: Dem precinct committeewoman, Rose Valley Twp, Stafford Co, Kans, 59-; charter pres, Stafford Co Federated Women's Dem Club, St John, 61-65; secy, Stafford Co Dem Cent Comt, 62-64, vchmn, 64-68, chmn, 68-; First SDist dir, Kans Dem Fedn Women's Club, 65-69, state vpres, 69-71, pres, 70-73, hon life mem; mem pvt & govt employ comt, Gov Comn on Status of Women, 68-; alt deleg, Dem Nat Conv, 72. Bus & Prof Pos: Elem sch teacher, Johnson, Kans, 56-58; co-owner & operator of farm, 57- Mem: Jr Golden Circle (served in every off during last ten years); Kans Women's Day Club; Woodrow Wilson Club of Kans (1st dist dir, 71); Kanza Chap, DAR (vregent, 73-75). Relig: Church of the Brethren. Mailing Add: RR 2 Box 167 St John KS 67576

SHANK, RICHARD EUGENE **(R)**
Ind State Rep
b North Lima, Ohio, Oct 26, 32; s Lauren J Shank & Mary Yoder S (deceased); m 1957 to Eileen A; c Larry J, David L & Sharon K. Educ: Hesston Col, 50-51. Polit & Govt Pos: Secy, Concord Twp Adv Bd, Ind, 64-66; Ind State Rep, Elkhart, Noble & Lagrange Co, 66-, asst majority leader, Ind House of Rep, currently; vchmn, Gov Traffic Safety Adv Comt, 67-; chmn pub safety, Fed Safety Prog, 68-; chmn, Local Transportation Study Comt, currently. Mem: Elkhart Co Homebuilders; Goshen Realtors; Moose; Farm Bur; Toastmasters. Honors & Awards: Nominee, Distinguished Serv Award, 3 times. Relig: United Methodist. Mailing Add: RR 1 Box 337-L Elkhart IN 46514

SHANKEL, BUFORD L **(D)**
b Hiattville, Kans, Nov 16, 26; s Elmer D Shankel & Lola Mae Neil S; m 1955 to Carolyn M Ramsey. Educ: Fort Scott Jr Col, AA, 48; Wichita Univ, BA, 51; Washburn Univ, LLB, 53; Phi Alpha Delta. Polit & Govt Pos: Chmn, Bourbon Co Dem Comt, Kans, 57-60; examr, State Workmen's Compensation Comn, 58-61; co attorney, Bourbon Co, 55-57; chmn, Johnson Co Dem Comt, formerly. Mil Serv: Entered as Pvt, Army, 45, released as S/Sgt, 46, after serv in Pac Theatre, 45-46. Mem: Johnson Co Kans Bar Asn; VFW; Elks; Am Legion; Mason. Relig: Protestant. Mailing Add: 6010 Reinhardt Dr Shawnee Mission KS 66205

SHANLEY, BERNARD MICHAEL **(R)**
Rep Nat Committeeman, NJ
b Newark, NJ, 1903; s Bernard Michael Shanley & Regina Ryan S; m 1936 to Maureen Virginia Smith; c Maureen S Kirk, Seton, Kevin, Brigid & Brendan. Educ: Columbia Univ, 25; Fordham Univ Law Sch, 28. Polit & Govt Pos: Adv on Eisenhower's Campaign Staff, 52; spec counsel to the President, 53-55, secy, 55-57; former chmn, NJ Rep State Finance Comt, mem, currently; mem, vchmn & mem exec comt, Rep Nat Comt, 68-; Rep Nat Committeeman, NJ, 68- Bus & Prof Pos: Law practice, Shanley & Fisher, Newark, NJ, 52-; dir, Chubb Corp, Fed Ins Co & Vigilant Ins Co, New York; trustee, Victoria Found; trustee, Am Inst Ment Health. Mil Serv: Army, 42-45; War Dept Citation. Mem: NJ Research Asn for Ment Hyg, Inc; NJ Bar Asn (mem joint judicial selection comt); Am, Somerset Co & Essex Co Bar Asns. Honors & Awards: Am Bar Found Fel. Legal Res: Bernardsville NJ 07924 Mailing Add: 570 Broad St Newark NJ 07102

SHANNON, SUSAN **(R)**
Wis State Rep
Mailing Add: 18360 Harvest Lane Brookfield WI 53005

SHANNON, V C **(D)**
La State Rep
Mailing Add: 6825 Canal Blvd Shreveport LA 71108

SHAPARD, VIRGINIA **(D)**
Ga State Sen
Mailing Add: PO Box 54 Griffin GA 30223

SHAPIRO, ARNOLD IVES **(D)**
Committeeman, NY State Dem Comt
b Watertown, NY, May 9, 23; s Israel A Shapiro (deceased) & Rose Ellis S (deceased); m 1954 to Helen Baran; c Margo. Educ: Yale Univ, BA, 45. Polit & Govt Pos: Jefferson Co Dem Committeeman, NY, 54-; chmn, Citizens Adv Coun for Urban Renewal, Watertown, 60-64, mem, Watertown City Planning Comn, 64-70; trustee, Jefferson Community Col, 62-74; treas, Watertown City Dem Comt, 64-66; deleg, Dem Nat Conv, 72; committeeman, NY State Dem Comt, 72-74. Bus & Prof Pos: Merchandising exec, Globe Store, Watertown, 46-53, pres & treas, 53-74; regional dir, Campaign for Yale for the Mid-Atlantic & Southeastern US, 74- Mil Serv: Entered as Ens, Navy, 44, released as Lt(jg), 46, after serv in World War II, 20 months. Mem: Yale Political Union; Common Cause; Ctr for Study Dem Inst; Yale Club NY; F&AM. Relig: Unitarian. Mailing Add: PO Box 779 Watertown NY 13601

SHAPIRO, DAVID CHARLES **(R)**
Ill State Sen
b Mendota, Ill, Feb 16, 25; s Hymen Shapiro & Minnie Sprizer S; m 1947 to Norma Jean Hall; c Sarah Beth, Deborah Leah, Margaret Sue, Edward Henry (Ned), Michael Andrew, Elizabeth Ann & Daniel Hall. Educ: Stanford Univ, ASTP, 43-44; Univ Ill, BS, 48; Univ Ill, Col Dent, DDS, 52. Polit & Govt Pos: Pres, Lee Co Bd Health, 60-69; pres, Ill Asn Bd Health, 63-64; mem, Amboy Unit Dist 272 Sch Bd, 61-69; alderman, Amboy, Ill, 61-69; Ill State Rep, 35th Dist, 69-73, vchmn, Educ Comt, Elem & Secondary Div, Ill House of Rep, formerly; Ill State Sen, 37th Dist, 73-, vchmn, Educ Comt, Ill State Senate, 73-, minority spokesman, currently, mem, Pensions & Personnel Comt, Pub Health, Welfare & Corrections Comt & Revenue Comt, 73-, mem appropriations comt, currently. Bus & Prof Pos: Pres, Amboy Pub Hosp, 53-59. Mil Serv: Entered as Pvt, Army, 43, released as Pfc, 46, after serv in 289th Inf, ETO, 44-46; Bronze Star; Combat Infantryman's Badge; Three Battle Stars. Mem: Elks; Am Legion; AF&AM; Consistory Shrine. Honors & Awards: Voted Outstanding Freshman Legislator of 75th Gen Assembly by readers of Ill Polit Reporter; Outstanding Freshman Sen of 78th Gen Assembly. Relig: Jewish. Mailing Add: 32 N Jefferson Amboy IL 61310

SHAPIRO, MARILYN LINDA **(D)**
b Brooklyn, NY, Sept 10, 41; d Frank Shapiro & Irma Slonim S; single. Educ: Wellesley Col, BA, 62; Columbia Univ, MA, 64, postgrad study, 64-67; Phi Beta Kappa. Polit & Govt Pos: Asst to the Mayor of New York, 67-70; admin asst to US Rep Elizabeth Holtzman, NY, 73- Bus & Prof Pos: Research assoc of Alvin Toffler, Auth, 70-72. Honors & Awards: Woodrow Wilson fel, 62-63; Nat Defense Educ Act fel, 62-65. Relig: Jewish. Legal Res: 301 E 62nd St New York NY 10021 Mailing Add: 1027 Longworth House Off Bldg Washington DC 20515

SHAPIRO, MARVIN S **(D)**
Mem, Dem Nat Comt, Calif
b New York, NY, Oct 26, 36; s Benjamin Shapiro & Sally Book S; m 1959 to Natalie Kover; c Donna & Meryl. Educ: Columbia Col, New York, AB, 57; Columbia Law Sch, New York, LLB, 59. Polit & Govt Pos: Deleg, Dem Nat Conv, 68 & 72, mem, Credentials Comt, 72; legal counsel, Calif Dem Party, 68-70; co-dir, Calif Comn on Dem Party Reform, 70; chmn, Calif Organizing Comt for McGovern, 72; gen counsel & treas, McGovern-Shriver Campaign of Southern Calif, 72; mem, Dem Nat Comt, Calif, currently, chmn, Credentials Comt, Dem Nat Comt, 72-, mem Comn on Deleg Selection, 73. Bus & Prof Pos: Trial Attorney, Civil Div, US Dept of Justice, 59-61; assoc, Law Firm of Irell & Manella, 62-66, partner, 66- Mil Serv: Entered as E-1, Army, 60, released as E-3, 63, after serv in 311th Logistical Command. Mem: Am, Calif & Los Angeles Bar Asns; Beverly Hills Bar Asn (bd of gov, 69-73; Beverly Hills Barristers, (pres, 70). Relig: Jewish. Legal Res: 432 N Cliffwood Ave Los Angeles CA 90049 Mailing Add: 900 Gateway East Bldg Century City Los Angeles CA 90067

SHAPIRO, R PETER **(R)**
NH State Rep
Mailing Add: 15 Willson Ave Concord NH 03301

SHAPIRO, SAMUEL DAVID **(D)**
Treas, Maine Dem State Comt
b Brownsville, Pa, Aug 26, 27; s Morris Z Shapiro & Anna R Silver S; m 1953 to Carol Phyliss Plavin; c Jeffrey, Susan & Eric. Educ: Univ Pittsburgh, BS, 52; Hall of Fame; Charles Hartwig Mem Award; Phi Epsilon Pi. Polit & Govt Pos: Mem, Sen Muskie Adv Comt, 58; pres, Waterville City Coun, Maine, 58-62; chmn, President John Kennedy Campaign, Southern Maine Dist, 60; fed appraiser, Maine, 60; mem adv bd, Small Bus Admin, Maine, 64; pres, Maine Electoral Col, 64; mem, Maine Dem State Comt, 68-, treas, 68-; chmn, State Dem Conv, 68 & 72; mem, Maine State Employees Appeals Bd, 68; mil aide to Gov Kenneth Curtis, 68. Bus & Prof Pos: Vpres, State Furniture Co, 60-72, pres, 72-; pres, Carpet World, 72- Mil Serv: Entered as Seaman 3/C, Navy, 45, released as PO 3/C, after serv in USS Hooper Island, ARG-17, China & Japan, 46-47. Mem: Phi Epsilon Pi (grand coun); Kennebec Ment Health Clin (bd dirs); VFW; Kiwanis. Honors & Awards: Outstanding Young Man of Maine. Relig: Jewish. Mailing Add: 4 Pray Ave Waterville ME 04901

SHAPIRO, SAMUEL H **(D)**
m 1939 to Gertrude Adelman. Educ: St Viator Col; Univ Ill, JD, 29. Polit & Govt Pos: Past secy & treas, Young Dem Ill; city attorney, Kankakee, 33; state's attorney, Kankakee Co, 36; Ill State Rep, 46-60, chmn, Pub Aid, Health, Welfare & Safety Comt, Ill House of Rep, 59, chmn, Gov Adv Coun on Ment Retardation; mem, Intergovt Comn & Legis Coun; chmn, Ment Health Comn, 61; Lt Gov, Ill, 61-68 & Gov, 68-69; chmn rules comt, Dem Nat Conv, 68. Bus & Prof Pos: Dir, Aetna State Bank, Chicago, currently. Mil Serv: Navy, World War

II, serv in antisubmarine warfare unit. Mem: Am, Chicago & Ill Bar Asns; Moose; Elks (Past Exalted Ruler). Relig: Jewish. Legal Res: 1300 Cobb Blvd Kankakee IL 60901 Mailing Add: 208 S LaSalle St Chicago IL 60604

SHAPP, MILTON J (D)
Gov, Pa
b Cleveland, Ohio, June 25, 12; s Aaron Shapiro & Eva Smelsey S; m 1947 to Muriel Matzkin; c Dolores (Mrs Gary Graham), Richard & Joanne. Educ: Case Inst of Technol, BSEE, 33; Tau Beta Pi; Sigma Alpha Mu. Polit & Govt Pos: Consult, Peace Corps, 61-63; consult, US Dept of Com for Econ Develop, 61-63; vchmn, Nat Pub Adv Comt on Area Redevelop, 61-64; chmn, Philadelphia Peace Corps Serv Orgn, Pa, formerly; chmn, Manpower Utilization Comn, Philadelphia, formerly; mem, Gov Comt of 100 for Better Educ, formerly; deleg, Dem Nat Conv, 68 & 72; Gov, Pa, 71-; organizer & chmn, Pa Dem Study Comt, 71- Bus & Prof Pos: Pres & chmn bd, Jerrold Corp, Philadelphia, 47-66; pres, Shapp Corp, 67- Mil Serv: Entered as 2nd Lt, Army, 42, released as Capt, 46, after serv in Signal Corps, Mediter & Austrian Occup, 43-46. Publ: Report of the Delaware Valley committee on new growth & new jobs; New growth: new jobs for Pennsylvania; The Shapp report, (2 issues), 65. Mem: Jewish COmmunity Rels Coun; Am Jewish Coun; United World Federalists; Jewish War Vet; B'nai B'rith. Honors & Awards: B'nai B'rith Youth Serv Award, 65; Humanitarian Award, Pa State Baptist Conv, 66; Humanitarian Award, Anti-Defamation League of B'nai B'rith, 73; Distinguished Serv Award, Centurion Jaycees, 73; Man of the Year, Pa Asn Broadcasters, 75. Relig: Jewish. Legal Res: 626 S Bowman Ave Merion PA 19066 Mailing Add: Governor's Off State Capitol Harrisburg PA 17120

SHARATZ, MARGUERITE THERESA (R)
Mem, Calif Rep State Cent Comt
b Shreveport, La, June 9, 15; d George Lee Church & Marie O'Dwyer C; m 1948 to Nick Sharatz; d Joan (Mrs Antonacci); three grandchildren. Educ: Amarillo High Sch, Tex, 4 years. Polit & Govt Pos: Mem, Calif Rep State Cent Comt, 67- Bus & Prof Pos: Patents for inventing Outside Safety Toe & Method for Displaying Minute Man Pennants, 53. Mem: Eastern Star; Wednesday Club; Nat Fedn Rep Women. Relig: Catholic. Mailing Add: 2148 Tipton Way Fairfield CA 94533

SHAROFF, BRIAN (D)
NY State Assemblyman
Mailing Add: 3303 Fillmore Ave Brooklyn NY 11234

SHARP, DORIS FULLER (R)
VChmn, Gloucester Co Rep Exec Comt, NJ,
b Glassboro, NJ, Oct 9, 24; d Raymond Matthew Fuller, Sr (deceased) & Elizabeth Jones F (deceased); m 1946 to John Winfried Sharp, Sr; c Linda (Mrs Robert Gray); John, Jr & Janet (Mrs Joseph Zavis). Educ: Glassboro High Sch, grad, 42. Polit & Govt Pos: Secy, Monroe Twp Rep Club, NJ. 56-57; committeewoman, Gloucester Co Rep Exec Comt, 64-, vchmn, 70-; pres, Eisenhower Women's Rep Club, 66-68 & 73-; treas, NJ Co Vchmn, 70-; chmn, Monroe Twp Rep Exec Comt, 72- Mem: Eastern Star; Williamstown Women's Club; Williamstown Fire Co Auxiliary; Monroe Twp Rep Club. Relig: Methodist. Mailing Add: 100 Walnut St Williamstown NJ 08094

SHARP, DUDLEY CRAWFORD (R)
b Houston, Tex, Mar 16, 05; s Walter Benona Sharp & Estelle Boughton S; m 1929 to Tina Cleveland; c Dudley C, Jr & Julia May Vergara (Mrs Jose). Educ: Princeton Univ, BS, 28; Tiger Inn Club. Polit & Govt Pos: Asst secy of Air Force, 55-59, undersecy, 59 & secy, 59-61; chmn, Tex Rep Finance Comt, 64 & 65; finance chmn, Sen Tower's Campaign, 66; deleg, Rep Nat Conv, 68. Bus & Prof Pos: Vpres, Mission Mfg Co, 28-46, pres, 46-55, vchmn of bd, 61-64, chmn bd, 64- Mil Serv: Entered as Lt(jg), Navy, released as Lt Comdr, 45, after serv in Anti-Submarine Warfare, Atlantic & Pac Areas; Exceptional Civilian Serv Award; Defense Medal of Freedom. Mem: Houston CofC (dir); Houston Country Club; Petroleum Club; Ramada Club; Tejas Club. Relig: Episcopal. Mailing Add: 109 N Post Oak Lane Houston TX 77024

SHARP, JOHN ANDERSON (R)
Mo State Rep
b Green Bay, Wis, Feb 13, 44; s John Henry Sharp & Margaret Louise Anderson S; single. Educ: Ottawa Univ, 62-63; Univ Kans, BS, 66; Univ Mo-Kansas City, 66-67; Rockhurst Col, 67-72. Polit & Govt Pos: Chmn, Collegiate Young Rep Club, Univ Mo-Kansas City, 66-67; exec vchmn, Mo Fedn Young Rep, 67-68, secy, 70-72; chmn, Jackson Co Young Rep, 69-71; Rep committeeman, 26th Ward, Kansas City, 70-72; mem, Jackson Co Youth Comn, 71-72; Mo State Rep, 38th Dist, 72- Bus & Prof Pos: Reporter, Kansas City Kansan, 69- Mem: Kansas City Press Club; Kansas City Jaycees; Hickman Mills Community Scholarship Found; Hon Dirs Rockhurst Col; Nat Adv Bd, Am Security Coun. Relig: Christian. Mailing Add: 11320 Blue Ridge Extension Kansas City MO 64134

SHARP, JOHN F (D)
Ill State Sen
Mailing Add: Box 577 Livingston IL 62058

SHARP, JOSHUA P (R)
b Williamsburg, Ky, Apr 23, 09; s James W Sharp & Lula Belle Ellis S; m 1953 to Emma Patrick; c Jolly Kay. Educ: Cumberland Col, 29-31; London Sch of Bus. Polit & Govt Pos: Campaign chmn, Whitley Co Rep Party, Ky, 56, 60 & 62, chmn, formerly; field secy to US Rep Tim Lee Carter, Fifth Dist, Ky, 69- Bus & Prof Pos: Teacher, Whitley Co Bd of Educ, various years since 32; tax consult, Williamsburg, Ky, 46-; off mgr, Steely Ins Agency, 53-63. Publ: Polit Advert Writing in various local papers, 51- Mem: Optimists. Legal Res: Florence St Williamsburg KY 40769 Mailing Add: PO Box 36 Williamsburg KY 40769

SHARP, LAURENE STOCKLIN (D)
b Mumford, Tex, Jan 21, 29; d Hattie Stocklin Richardson (deceased); c Kenneth, Rodney & Keith. Educ: Samuel Huston Col, BA, 51; Univ Chicago; Chicago Teachers Col; Alpha Kappa Alpha. Polit & Govt Pos: Deleg, Dem Nat Mid-Term Conf, 74. Bus & Prof Pos: Ins underwriter, Chicago, Ill, formerly; secy, Benjamin F Lewis Ins & Real Estate; teacher, Ft Worth Independent Sch Dist, Tex, currently. Publ: Auth, One Hundred Years of the Black Man in Ft Worth, privately publ, 74; Lyndon Baines Johnson, The Civil Rights President (in prep). Mem: Ft Worth Classroom Asn; Tex State Teachers Asn; Tex Classroom Teachers Asn; Florence B Brook & F Gray Club. Honors & Awards: Woman of the Year, Historian, Florence B Brook & F Gray Club, 75. Relig: Baptist. Mailing Add: 1225 E Mulkey St Ft Worth TX 76104

SHARP, PHILIP R (D)
US Rep, Ind
b Baltimore, Md, July 15, 42; s Riley Sharp & Florence S; m 1972 to Marilyn Kay Augburn. Educ: Georgetown Univ Sch Foreign Serv, BS cum laude, 64; PhD(govt), 74; Exeter Col, Oxford Univ, summer 66. Polit & Govt Pos: Legis aide to US Sen Vance Hartke, Ind, 64-69; US Rep, Ind, 75- Bus & Prof Pos: From asst prof to assoc prof polit sci, Ball State Univ, 69-74. Relig: United Methodist. Legal Res: 2112 Euclid Ave Muncie IN 47302 Mailing Add: US House Rep Washington DC 20515

SHARP, SUSIE MARSHALL (D)
Chief Justice, NC Supreme Court
b Rocky Mount, NC, July 7, 07; d James Merrit Sharp & Annie Blackwell S; single. Educ: Univ NC, Greensboro, 24-26; Univ NC, Chapel Hill Law Sch, LLB, 29; Order of Valkyries. Hon Degrees: LLD, Women's Col NC, 50, Queens Col (NC), 62, Elon Col, 63, Wake Forest Univ, 65, Catawba Col, 70, Univ NC, Chapel Hill, 70 & Duke Univ, 74; LHD, Pfeiffer Col, 60. Polit & Govt Pos: Spec judge, NC Superior Court, 49-62; assoc justice, NC Supreme Court, 62-75, chief justice, 75- Bus & Prof Pos: Partner in Law Firm of Sharp & Sharp, Reidsville, NC, 29-49. Mem: Am & NC Bar Asns; Am Law Inst; Phi Beta Kappa; Delta Kappa Gamma. Honors & Awards: Distinguished Serv Award for Women, Chi Omega, 59; Alumni Serv Award, Univ NC, Greensboro, 75. Relig: Methodist. Legal Res: 629 Lindsey St Reidsville NC 27320 Mailing Add: NC Supreme Court PO Box 1841 Raleigh NC 27602

SHARP, THELMA P (D)
b Vineland, NJ, May 12, 98; d James Casper Parkinson & Ina Fenton P; m 1941 to William Howard Sharp, wid. Educ: Smith Col, AB, 21. Polit & Govt Pos: Dem state committeewoman, Cumberland Co, NJ, 22-; mem, Cumberland Co Bd Taxes, 23-36, pres, 26-29; deleg-at-lg, Dem Nat Conv, 24-56, mem, Platform Comt, 52, co-chmn, 56 & deleg, 68; mem, NJ Bd Tax Appeals, 32-34; mem, Assay Comn, 36; vchmn, Cumberland Co Dem Party, 48-56; Dem Nat Committeewoman, NJ, 54-74, mem, Nat Exec Comt Adv Comt, Dem Nat Comt, formerly; deleg, White House Conf on Educ, 59-70; pres, Civil Serv Comn, NJ; mem, Women's Adv Comt, World's Fair, NY; mem, Gov Meyner's Cabinet; mem, Gov Hughes' Cabinet. Bus & Prof Pos: Pres bd visitors, Vineland Training Sch; vpres bd dirs, Roosevelt Park Colony for Aged; trustee, Methodist Home for Aged, NJ Welfare Coun; adv coun, Grad Sch Soc Studies, Rutgers Univ; teacher, Vineland High Sch, 22. Mem: Women's Soc Christian Serv (past pres); Am Asn UN (trustee NJ Br); Am Asn Univ Women; United Coun Church Women (past regional vpres); Acad Polit & Soc Sci. Mailing Add: 702 Wood St Vineland NJ 08360

SHARPE, JOHN GEORGE (R)
Chmn, Columbia Co Rep Comt, NY
b Bronx, NY, Mar 24, 30; s John Sharpe & Ada Crawford S; m 1950 to Joan Marie Sherman; c Elizabeth Ann, Barbara Jean, Susan Marie & Jennifer Lynn. Educ: NY Univ, 2 years; Russell Sage Col, 1 year. Polit & Govt Pos: Committeeman, Columbia Co Rep Party, NY, 58-; deleg, NY State Rep Conv, 66; chmn, Columbia Co Rep Comt, 69- Bus & Prof Pos: Ins claimsman, Nationwide Ins, 54-57; ins broker, Sharpe Agency Inc, Hudson, NY, 57- Mil Serv: Pvt, Army Nat Guard, 48; Maj, Res, currently; State of NY Long & Faithful Serv Medal. Mem: Militia Asn of the US; Elks; Jr CofC Int (lifetime fel). Honors & Awards: Recipient of Distinguished Serv Award, JrCofC. Relig: Dutch Reform. Mailing Add: East Camp Rd Germantown NY 12526

SHARPE, JON CLIFFORD M (R)
Ky State Rep
Mailing Add: 1600 W Main St Williamsburg KY 40769

SHARPE, THOMAS G (R)
Mich State Rep
b Fowlerville, Mich, Apr 6, 17; m 1936 to Esther Cornell; c Thomas, Ronald, Diana & Linda. Educ: Detroit Bus Univ. Polit & Govt Pos: Deleg, Const Conv; Mich State Rep, 62-, mem, Appropriations Comt, Mich House Rep, currently. Bus & Prof Pos: Farmer & real estate salesman. Mem: Lions Club; Livingston Co Farm Bur. Relig: Nazarene Church. Mailing Add: 4603 Argentine Rd Howell MI 48843

SHARPE, WILLIAM JOSEPH, JR (D)
b Lyons, Ga, Aug 15, 52; s William Joseph Sharpe & Mary Brown S; single. Educ: Broward Community Col, 71; St Petersburg Jr Col, AA, 72; Univ SFla, 73; Flagler Col, 75; treas, student govt; Rotoract (bd mem, 71-72); Circle K (Fla state gov, 73-74, int vpres, 74-75). Polit & Govt Pos: Pres, Concerned Students for Jackson, St Petersburg Jr Col, 72, staff worker Presidential campaign, US Sen Henry Jackson, 72; campaign coordr, Bill Polfer for Co Comnr Campaign, Pinellas Co, 72; precinct committeeman, Pinellas Co Dem Exec Comt, 72-75; pres, Conservative Dem Youth, 72-74; coordr, fifth dist, Bob Coker for Cong Campaign, 74; pres, Pinellas Co Young Dem, 74-75; deleg, Dem Nat Mid-Term Conf, 74. Bus & Prof Pos: News announcer & electronics engr, Radio Sta WRBD-WCKO-FM, Ft Lauderdale, Fla, 70-71; supvr, A C Nielson Co, Dunedin, 73; mgr, Burbank Bus Opportunities, Clearwater, 74- Relig: Methodist. Mailing Add: 1006 DeSoto Dr Dunedin FL 33528

SHARPE, WILLIAM R, JR (D)
WVa State Sen
b Clarksburg, WVa, Oct 28, 28; s William R Sharpe & Helen Whitwam S; m 1953 to Pauline Lester. Educ: WVa Univ; Salem Col; Bliss Eng Sch, Washington, DC. Polit & Govt Pos: WVa State Sen, 60- Bus & Prof Pos: Elec engr & contractor. Mem: Mason; Shrine; Elks; Moose; IBEW. Relig: Methodist. Mailing Add: 607 Center Ave Weston WV 26452

SHATWELL, BOB R (D)
Okla State Sen
b Tulsa, Okla, July 10, 40; s George Washington Shatwell & Hazel Lou Bratton S; m 1961 to Lurettal Carol Thomas; c Rita Lynn & Nathaniel Ray. Educ: Am Inst Bus & Law, St Louis, 61-64; Univ Tulsa, 62-63. Polit & Govt Pos: Founder & charter pres, North Tulsans for a Better Community, Okla, 68-72; admin asst to Tulsa Co Comn, 70-73; Okla State Sen, Tulsa, Osage & Washington Co, 75- Bus & Prof Pos: Sales mgr, Portrait Co, Tulsa, 58-61; mgr life ins, Debit Co, 61-68; formed & now own, Qual Refinishing of Tulsa, 68- Publ: Auth, Men with a mission, Various Church Relig Periodicals, 71, 73 & 74. Mem: Tulsa Bd Educ (human rels bd); CofC (bd dirs); City-Co Bonds Comt; PTA (pres, 72); Flood Control Coun (dir). Honors & Awards: Founders Award & Hon Life Time Chap Pres, North Tulsans for a Better Community, 74; Hon Dir, Metrop Tulsa CofC. Relig: Assembly of God; Sun Sch supt, youth pres & choir dir. Mailing Add: 5942 N Lewis Ave Tulsa OK 74130

SHATZKIN, MIKE (D)
b New York, NY, June 6, 47; s Leonard Shatzkin & Eleanor Oshry S; single. Educ: Univ Calif, Los Angeles, AB, 69. Polit & Govt Pos: NY State Campus coordr, McGovern for President, 71-72; Upstate E NY coordr, McGovern for President, 72; alt deleg, Dem Nat Conv, 72; fund raising coordr, McGovern-Shriver, Md, 72. Bus & Prof Pos: Dir mkt, Two Continents Publ Group, NY, 73- Publ: The view from Section 111, Prentice-Hall, 70. Relig: Atheist. Mailing Add: Apt 17C 300 E 51st St New York NY 10022

SHAUBAH, JOSE M (R)
Mem, VI State Rep Cent Comt
b Viequez, Puerto Rico, Dec 29, 19; s Jose S Shaubah & Petra Roman de S; m 1971 to June Landau; c Elena L Shaubah & Simon J Shaubah Gill. Educ: High Sch. Polit & Govt Pos: Deleg, Rep Nat Conv, 48, 60 & 64, Alt deleg, 68, mem platform comt, 60 & 64; state vchmn, VI Rep Party, 52-56, state chmn, 56-60, secy, 60-64; Rep Nat Committeeman, 57 & 59; mem, VI State Rep Cent Comt, 66-; mem, VI Bd Zoning, Subdivision & Bldg Appeals, currently; mem, Progressive Rep Party Territorial Comt of VI, currently. Bus & Prof Pos: Self employed cattle raiser. Mem: Rotary; VI Cattlemen Asn. Relig: Roman Catholic. Mailing Add: PO Box 614 Christiansted St Croix VI 00820

SHAUGHNESSY, WILLIAM G (D)
Mass State Rep
Mailing Add: State Capitol Boston MA 02133

SHAVER, JAMES L, JR (D)
Ark State Rep
b Wynne, Ark, Nov 23, 27; s James Levesque Shaver & Louise Davis S; m 1949 to Bonnie Wood; c James Levesque, III & Bonnie Sue. Educ: Univ Ark, JD, 51; Delta Theta Phi. Polit & Govt Pos: Ark State Rep, Cross Co, Ark, 55- Mil Serv: Navy. Mem: NE Ark Develop; Cross Co Bar Asn (secy-treas); Ark Bar Asn; Rotary; 100 Club. Relig: Presbyterian. Mailing Add: 568 N Killough Rd Wynne AR 72396

SHAVER, MARVIN DOUGLAS (R)
Chmn, Box Butte Co Rep Party, Nebr
b Alliance, Nebr, Nov 19, 43; s Arthur Wayne Shaver & Opha Evelyn Nicholson S; m 1974 to Susan Elizabeth Vakiner. Educ: Chadron State Col, BA in biol; Univ Nebr-Lincoln, Pharm, 70; Blue Key; Lambda Delta Lambda; Beta Beta Beta; Alpha Phi Omega. Polit & Govt Pos: Chmn, Box Butte Co Rep Party, Nebr, 74- Bus & Prof Pos: Owner & mgr, Shaver's Pharm, Hemingford, Nebr, 70- Mil Serv: Entered as E-1, Nat Guard, 66, released as E-5, 72, after serv in Nebr & Wyo Air Nat Guard. Mem: Town Bd; CofC (dir); Elks; Lions. Honors & Awards: Man of Year Award, Hemingford CofC, 74. Relig: United Methodist; Methodist Lay Leader. Mailing Add: Box 185 Hemingford NE 69348

SHAVOR, ROBERT PETER (D)
b Homestead, Pa, Jan 25, 38; s Peter George Shavor & Ann Gavigan S; m 1959 to Sonja Herta Killian; c Karen & Todd. Educ: Duquesne Univ, BA, 59; Pi Gamma Mu. Polit & Govt Pos: Dem committeeman, Paxtang Borough, 68-; jury comnr, Dauphin Co, 70-74; deleg, Dem Mid-Term Conf, 74; mayor, Paxtang Borough, 74- Bus & Prof Pos: Research analyst, Pa Dept Internal Affairs, Harrisburg, Pa, 60-61; admin asst, Public Utility Comn, Harrisburg, 61-63; cost analyst, Weber, Fick & Wilson, 63-65; statistician, Capital Blue Cross, 65- Mem: Asn of Mayors of Pa; Pa Jury Comnrs Asn; Paxtang Lions Club; KofC. Relig: Roman Catholic. Mailing Add: 3017 Duke St Harrisburg PA 17111

SHAW, AILEEN D (D)
b Thrasher, Miss, Aug 21, 23; d Vera Green Doty & Rosa Lee Sandlin D; wid; c Alan Marley. Educ: Grand Prairie High Sch, 41; Bus Sch. Polit & Govt Pos: Deleg, Dem Nat Mid-Term Conf, 74; bd med, Dem Comt for Responsible Govt, Dallas, Tex, 75- Bus & Prof Pos: Secy-treas, Sargent-Sowell, Inc, Grand Prairie, Tex, 48- Mem: YMCA (bd mem); Eastern Star. Relig: Baptist. Mailing Add: 1206 Ruea St Grand Prairie TX 75050

SHAW, DAISY L (D)
Secy-Treas, Coshocton Co Dem Cent & Exec Comt, Ohio
b Coshocton, Ohio, Feb 13, 05; d Bert Harris (deceased) & Maggie May Hall H (deceased); div; c Sandra Lee (Mrs Flemming), JoAn & Bradley K. Educ: Coshocton High Sch, grad, 23. Polit & Govt Pos: Mem, Coshocton Co Bd Elec, Ohio, 58-; mem & secy-treas, Coshocton Co Dem Cent & Exec Comts, 60-; cent committeewoman, Lafayette Twp, West Lafayette, 60- Bus & Prof Pos: First aid instr, Am Nat Red Cross, Coshocton, Ohio, 58-59. Mem: Ohio Asn Elec Off. Relig: Protestant. Mailing Add: 612 N Kirk St West Lafayette OH 43845

SHAW, ELIZABETH ORR (R)
Iowa State Sen
b Monona, Iowa, Oct 2, 23; d Harold Topliff Orr & Hazel Kean O; m 1946 to Donald Hardy Shaw; c Elizabeth Ann, Andrew Hardy & Anthony Orr. Educ: Drake Univ, AB, 45; Univ Minn, grad study polit sci, 46; Univ Iowa, JD, 48; Phi Beta Kappa; Order of the Coif; Kappa Kappa Gamma. Polit & Govt Pos: Mem, Scott Co Rep Women's Club; Iowa State Rep, formerly; Iowa State Sen, 73- Bus & Prof Pos: Attorney-at-law, Arlington Heights, Ill, 48-50, Lord Bissel & Brook, Chicago, 50-52 & attorney-at-law, 66- Mem: Iowa & Ill Bars; PEO Sisterhood; League of Women Voters, Scott Co. Relig: Congregational. Mailing Add: 29 Hillcrest Ave Davenport IA 52803

SHAW, LOIS DEGISE (D)
Councilwoman, Jersey City, NJ
b Jersey City, NJ, May 4, 42; d Anthony DeGise & Agnes Mackie D; m 1964 to Stanley Shaw; c Mark, Michael & Matthew. Educ: St Peter's Col, 72- Polit & Govt Pos: Committeeman, Hudson Co Dem Comt, NJ, 71-72; deleg, Dem Nat Conv, 72; mem, Nat Credentials Comt, 72; presidential elector, NJ, 72; councilwoman, Jersey City, 73- Mem: Hudson City Dem Club (bd trustees); Women's Polit Caucus; League Women Voters. Honors & Awards: Woman of Year Award, Women's Polit Caucus, 74. Relig: Roman Catholic. Legal Res: 244 Hancock Ave Jersey City NJ 07307 Mailing Add: 280 Grove St Jersey City NJ 07302

SHAW, LUTHER WALLACE (D)
b Ithaca, NY, Nov 9, 32; s Dr Luther Shaw & Lowell Lewis S; m 1956 to Carolina Georgia Kallquist; c Luther W & Susan C. Educ: Western Carolina Col, BS, honors. Polit & Govt Pos: Admin asst US Rep Roy A Taylor, 60- Bus & Prof Pos: Writer, Asheville Citizens-Times, NC. Mil Serv: Spec 4/C, Army Engrs, 54-56; 1st Lt, Army Res. Legal Res: PO Box 1033 Waynesville NC 28786 Mailing Add: 1206 Colonial Rd McLean VA 22101

SHAW, ROBERT ERNEST (R)
b Pratt, Kans, June 27, 16; s Cedric Hadaway Shaw & Harriet Elizabeth Garnett S; m 1946 to Betty Buck; c Ann Elizabeth, Jane Luise, Marta Grace & Elizabeth Buck. Educ: Univ Okla, BS, 38; Delta Tau Delta. Polit & Govt Pos: Spec Agent, Fed Bur Invest, US Dept Justice, 41-46; investigative staff mem, House Govt Opers Comt, House Appropriations Comt, Senate Agr Comt & Senate Judiciary Comt, 46-55; chmn, Columbia Co Rep Orgn, Wis, formerly. Bus & Prof Pos: Personnel & pub rels dir, C J Berst & Co, Portage, Wis, 55-60; acct exec, Marshall Co, Madison & Portage, Wis, 60- Relig: Episcopal. Legal Res: 929 W Conant Portage WI 53901 Mailing Add: Box 338 Portage WI 53901

SHAW, ROBERT JENNINGS (R)
VChmn, Rep Nat Comt
b Bronwood, Ga, Aug 21, 29; s Robert Edward Shaw & Vesta Jennings S; m 1950 to Mary Elaine Smith; c Maria Elena, Melanie Dawn, Susan June & Bobbie Elizabeth Ann. Educ: Ga Inst Technol, 47; Univ Ga, Atlanta Div, 48-50. Polit & Govt Pos: Vchmn finance comt, Fulton Co Rep Party, Ga, 63, chmn speaker's bur, 64, house dist chmn & campaign mgr, cand for Ga State Rep, 65, first vchmn & chmn cand comt, 66, chmn, 68-; chmn, Fulton Co Rep Exec Comt, 70-; chmn, Fulton Co Rep Cent Comt, 70-; cand, Ga State Sen, 64; mem exec comt, Fifth Cong Dist Rep Party, 65-; mem, Rep State Cent Comt Ga, 66-, first vchmn, 70-71; chmn, 71-75; first vchmn, Ga Rep Exec Comt, 70-; deleg, Rep Nat Conv, 72; vchmn, Rep Nat Comt, 74- Bus & Prof Pos: Gen agent, Pan-Am Life Ins Co, 61-; mem bd dir, Atlanta Hosp, 68- Mil Serv: Entered as Pvt, Air Force, 50, released as S/Sgt, 52, after serv in 116th Fighter Wing, Far E Theatre, 51-52. Mem: Atlanta Asn of Life Underwriters; Gen Agents & Mgr Asn of Atlanta; South Cobb Jaycees, (hon lifetime mem); Phi Sigma Epsilon, (hon mem); Bolton Civic Asn, (pres, 66-). Relig: Baptist; music dir, First Baptist Church of Chattahoochee. Legal Res: 295 Glen Lake Dr NW Atlanta GA 30327 Mailing Add: 1819 Peachtree St NE Atlanta GA 30309

SHAWCROFT, JOHN BENNETT (R)
Chmn, Conejos Co Rep Cent Comt, Colo
b LaJara, Colo, Mar 26, 25; s David Earl Shawcroft & Marth Smith S; m 1945 to Betty Linger; c Nancy (Mrs Thomas), David H, Connie & Donald. Polit & Govt Pos: Precinct chmn, LaJara, Colo, 60-69; chmn, Conejos Co Rep Cent Comt, Colo, 69-72 & 74- Bus & Prof Pos: Cattleman, currently. Mem: Colo Farm Bur; Colo Cattlemen's Asn; San Luis Valley Cattlemen's Asn. Relig: Latter-day Saint. Mailing Add: Rte 2 Box 290 Alamosa CO 81101

SHAWLEY, JOHN FRANKLIN (R)
Ind State Sen
b Michigan City, Ind, June 16, 21; s Franklin Ulysses Shawley & Viola Jane Shields S; m 1940 to Ruth Mary (Bell). Educ: Isaac Elston High Sch, grad. Polit & Govt Pos: Precinct committeeman, La Porte Co, Springfield Twp, Ind, 48-62; deleg, Rep State Conv, 56-; Ind State Rep, La Porte Co, 68-; chmn, La Porte Co Rep Party, 72- Bus & Prof Pos: Owner, Shawley Supermkt, Michigan City, Ind, 45-57; Shawley Realty, 53-; pres, Western Mich Investments, Inc, 61; owner, Shawley Ins Agency, 63- Mil Serv: Entered as Cadet, Air Force, 43, released as instr, 45, after serv in 2nd Air Force, Am Theatre, 43-45; Univ Citation, Am Theatre; Good Conduct Medal; Victory Medal. Mem: Am Legion; Lions; Elks; Michigan City Hist Soc; Michigan City Art League. Honors & Awards: Ind Realtor of Year, 63; Ind State Meritorious Serv Award, Gov Craig, 56; Coun of Sagamores Award, Gov Handley. Relig: Protestant; Elder & teacher, First Christian Church. Mailing Add: 225 E Ninth St Michigan City IN 46360

SHAYNE, NEIL T (D)
Treas, Nassau Co Dem Comt, NY
b New York, NY, May 2, 32; s Seymour S Shayne & Mildred Isear S; m 1955 to Marilyn Sorkin; c Mark, David & Jeffrey. Educ: NY Univ, 49-50; Brooklyn Law Sch, LLB, 54. Polit & Govt Pos: Treas, Nassau Co Dem Comt, NY, 74-; counsel, State Comt on Higher Educ, 75- Bus & Prof Pos: Lectr, Am Bar Asn & Am Trial Lawyers, 71-; attorney-in-residence, Hofstra Law Sch, 71-; mem faculty, Practicing Law Inst, NY, 71-; assoc prof, Adelphi Univ, dir, Court Admin Prog & Legal Asst Prog, 72-74; faculty mem, Am Mgt Asn, NY, 73- Publ: Making A Personal Injury Practice Profitable, Practicing Law Inst, 72; A case for legal specialists & prepaid services, NY Law J, 10/73; Prepaid Legal Service, Am Mgt Asn, 75. Mem: Am Bar Asn; Nassau Co Bar Asn (lectr); Am Mgt Asn; Lifeline for Emotionally Disturbed Children. Honors & Awards: Testimonial Dinner, Sixth Assembly Dist Dem Club, 63; Cert of Appreciation, Hofstra Law Sch, 69; Award of Merit, WVa Trial Lawyers Asn, 73; Cert of Appreciation, Dr Timothy Costello, Adelphi Univ, 74. Relig: Jewish. Legal Res: 320 E Shore Rd Great Neck NY 11023 Mailing Add: 1501 Franklin Ave Mineola NY 11501

SHAYS, CHRISTOPHER (R)
Conn State Rep
Mailing Add: 393 Webb's Hill Rd Stamford CT 06903

SHEA, BARBARA F (D)
NH State Rep
Mailing Add: 320 Laurel St Manchester NH 03103

SHEA, C VINCENT (D)
Mass State Rep
Mailing Add: State Capitol Boston MA 02133

SHEA, GERALD W (D)
Ill State Rep
b Oak Park, Ill, July 25, 31; s John W Shea & Gertrude Gearen S; m 1959 to Joanne Sevcik; c Courtney Claire. Educ: Univ Ill Sch Commerce, BS in finance, 57; DePaul Univ Col Law, LLB, 60. Polit & Govt Pos: Ill State Rep, Seventh Dist, currently, asst minority leader, 71-74, majority leader, currently; deleg, Dem Nat Conv, 72. Mil Serv: Entered as Pvt, Army, 54, released as Cpl, 56. Relig: Catholic. Mailing Add: 141 Herrick Rd Riverside IL 60546

SHEA, JAMES D (D)
Vt State Rep
b Chester, Pa, Oct 7, 19; m to Emelda M LeBlanc; c Four. Educ: Chester, Pa High Sch; St Michaels Col. Polit & Govt Pos: Supvr, Unorganized towns, Chittenden Co, Vt; justice of peace; overseer of poor; mayor; councilman, 3 terms; chmn, Planning Comn; city grand juror; treas, Chittenden Co Dem Comt; chmn, Winooski Dem City Comt; mem, State Judicial Coun; Vt State Rep, 65-, vchmn, Banking & Corp Comt, Vt House Rep, 3 years, Commerce Comt, 1 year & Gen & Mil Affairs Comt, 1 year, Minority Whip, 69-70; mem, State Legis Coun; alt deleg, Dem Nat Conv, 68. Bus & Prof Pos: Admin asst; salesman. Mil Serv: Army,

Lt, Ord Dept, 41-45. Mem: KofC; VFW; Eagles. Relig: Catholic. Mailing Add: 36 LeClair St Winooski VT 05404

SHEA, JOHN FRANCIS (D)
Chmn, Sonoma Co Dem Cent Comt, Calif
b Winfield, Kans, Dec 19, 30; s Perry M Shea & Anna Fiebiger S; m 1964 to Dorothy Kennedy Jones; c Jennifer Marie & Patricia Kate. Educ: Santa Rosa Jr Col, AA, 51; Stanford Univ, BA, 53; Univ Calif, Berkeley, JD, 58; Phi Delta Phi. Polit & Govt Pos: Chmn, Sonoma Co Dem Cent Comt, Calif, 68-; mem, Calif State Dem Cent Comt, currently. Bus & Prof Pos: Trial attorney, Dorr, Cooper & Hayes, San Francisco, Calif, 61-62; partner, gen practice, Geary, Geary, Shea & Pawson, 63- Relig: Roman Catholic. Legal Res: 3715 Montecito Ave Santa Rosa CA 95405 Mailing Add: 37 Old Courthouse Sq Santa Rosa CA 95404

SHEA, PHILIP L (D)
Mass State Rep
Mailing Add: State Capitol Boston MA 02133

SHEA, ROBERT DENNIS (D)
Conn State Rep
b Hartford, Conn, Dec 27, 30; s Dennis Joseph Shea & Frances Mulcany S; m 1955 to Mary Ellen Kelley; c Thomas, Mary Frances, Timothy, Mary Elizabeth & John. Educ: Boston Col, BS, 54. Polit & Govt Pos: Mem, West Hartford Zoning Bd of Appeals, 68-71, town councilman, 71-74; Conn State Rep, 75- Bus & Prof Pos: Dir, West Hartford Fellowship Housing, 72-74; dir, Seniors Job Bank, 72- Mil Serv: Entered as Pvt, Army, 54, released as Specialist 3/C, 56, after serv in Mil Intel, US, 54-56. Mailing Add: 82 Vera St West Hartford CT 06119

SHEAFFER, ROBERT L (R)
Ind State Sen
Mailing Add: PO Box 216 Shelbyville IN 46176

SHEALY, WILSON OTTO (R)
b Pelion, SC, Aug 16, 26; s Wilson Frank Shealy & Vera Sturkie S; m 1947 to Edythe Louise Long; c Wilson O, Jr, Phillip Lee & Barry Dwayne. Educ: Univ SC, 47-50. Polit & Govt Pos: Chmn Swansea precinct, Lexington Co Rep Party, 66-68, chmn, 66-70, co-chmn, Marshal Parker for Sen, 66; mem, Lexington Co Rep Exec Comt, 70-74, chmn, 72-74, committeeman, Swansea precinct; second vchmn, SC Rep Party, 70-74; committeeman, Watson for Gov, 70, ballot security chmn, Second Cong Dist, 70. Bus & Prof Pos: Territory mgr, Champion Spark Plug Co, 52- Mil Serv: Entered as Seaman, Navy, 43, released as ADE 3, 47, recalled 50-52; Am Theater Ribbon, three Good Conduct Medals. Mem: Lexington Co Hosp, (trustee & mem opers & finance comt); Sandy Run Acad, Gaston, SC, (trustee); Mason (32 degree); Shrine; VFW; Toastmasters. Honors & Awards: Elected chmn of first full Rep Deleg in SC this century, 66; successful in electing all House, all Coun, Sheriff & one Sen from Lexington Co, 72. Relig: Methodist. Mailing Add: PO Box 337 Swansea SC 29160

SHEAR, DAPHFINE (D)
b Davis, Okla, May 15, 19; d Benjamin Franklin Lundy & Eula Boyles L; m 1940 to Warren Shear; c Ken-Sue (Mrs J S Doerfel), Lynn, Sloane & David Lundy. Educ: Stephens Col, 37; Southern Methodist Univ, 38; Dallas Little Theater Sch, 39; St Louis Little Theater Sch, 40. Polit & Govt Pos: Co-chmn, Dem Precinct Comt, Okla, 60-62; co-chmn, Dem Dist Comt, 62-64; deleg, Dem Nat Conv, 64, 68 & 72, mem, Dem Nat Platform Comt, 64 & 68; Dem Nat Committeewoman, Okla, formerly. Relig: Episcopal. Legal Res: 7312 Waverly Oklahoma City OK 73116 Mailing Add: Box 14440 Oklahoma City OK 73114

SHEAR, S SUE (D)
Mo State Rep
Mailing Add: 200 S Brentwood Clayton MO 63105

SHEARER, DON PAUL (R)
Mem Exec Comt, Young Rep Nat Fedn
b Harrisburg, Pa, Dec 21, 43; s Paul Edwin Shearer & Jeanne Hoover S; m 1965 to Linda Lee Ringert, div; c Terri Lee. Educ: Dickinson Col, BA, 65. Polit & Govt Pos: Chmn, Cumberland Co Young Rep, Pa, 67-69; campaign dir, US Rep George A Goodling, 19th Dist, 68; statewide campaign dir, State Supreme Court Justice Thomas W Pomeroy, 69; state chmn, Young Rep of Pa, 70-72; committeeman, Wormleysburg Rep Comt, 70-72; mem exec comt, Young Rep Nat Fedn, 71-; alt deleg, Rep Nat Conv, 72. Bus & Prof Pos: Page, Pa State Senate, 62-65; assoc broker, Shearer Real Estate Inc, 65-71; pres & broker, Don Paul Shearer Inc/Real Estate, 71-; real estate appraiser, currently. Mil Serv: Entered as Airman, Pa Air Nat Guard, 66, released as Sgt, after serv in Tactical Early Warning, 193rd Group, 66-72. Mem: West Shore & Gtr Harrisburg CofC; West Shore Country Club; Camp Hill Jaycees (past treas & dir). Honors & Awards: Outstanding Young Rep of Cumberland Co, 68; Outstanding State Young Rep of Pa for 70-72; Distinguished Serv Award for Americanism & Govt, Camp Hill Jaycees, 69. Relig: United Methodist. Legal Res: 6 A Richland Lane Camp Hill PA 17011 Mailing Add: PO Box 162 Camp Hill PA 17011

SHEARER, KENT (R)
Legal Counsel, Utah Rep State Cent Comt
b Ellsworth, Kans, Oct 5, 29; s William E Shearer & Agnes Phillips S; m 1952 to Alice Anne Neff; c Edward Timothy & Lorraine Marie. Educ: Univ Kans, BA, 51, LLB, 54, MA, 55; Phi Beta Kappa; Order of Coif; Omicron Delta Kappa; Delta Sigma Rho; Pi Sigma Alpha; Lambda Chi Alpha; Pi Alpha Delta. Polit & Govt Pos: Chmn, Salt Lake Co Young Rep, Utah, 60-63; chmn, Utah Young Rep, 63-65; treas, Utah Goldwater Comt, 64; legal counsel, Utah Rep State Cent Comt, 65-71, 73-, chmn, 71-73; deleg, Rep Nat Conv, 72; co-mgr, Garn for Senate Comt, 74. Mil Serv: 1st Lt, Army, 55-58, serv in Judge Adv Gen Corps; Lt Col, Army Res, 71; Army Commendation Ribbon with Oak Leaf Cluster. Publ: Federal land grants to the states, Rocky Mountain Mineral Law Inst, 68. Mem: Am, Utah & Salt Lake Co Bar Asns; Rocky Mountain Mineral Law Found. Relig: Episcopal. Mailing Add: 1332 Harvard Ave Salt Lake City UT 84105

SHEATS, SAM (D)
Ga State Rep
Mailing Add: 486 Decatur St Shopping Ctr SE Atlanta GA 30312

SHEEHAN, AUGUST (GUS) (D)
Ky State Sen
Mailing Add: 612 Altamont Rd Covington KY 41016

SHEEHAN, LORRAINE M (D)
Md State Deleg
Mailing Add: 3600 Deanna Rd Suitland MD 20023

SHEEHAN, TIMOTHY P (R)
b Chicago, Ill, Feb 9, 09; s Timothy P Sheehan & Catherine Harris S; m to Mary Celeste McNearney (deceased), m 1956 to Marilyn D Muehl; c Mary (Mrs Eugene Plunkett), Kathleen (Mrs Edward Bertany), Eileen, Timmy, & Sheila. Educ: Northwestern Univ, BSC, 31; Beta Gamma Sigma; Delta Sigma Pi. Polit & Govt Pos: US Rep, Ill, 51-58; ward committeeman, 41st Ward Rep Orgn, 54-75; chmn, Cook Co Rep Cent Comt, 64-68; deleg, Rep Nat Conv, 64, 68 & 72; secy, Ill Racing Bd, 68-69. Bus & Prof Pos: Pres, Silver Brook Beverage Co, 45-70; owner, Swedish Food Prods, 56-; pres & dir, Peerless Fed Savings & Loan, 61-66; dir, Skokie Fed Savings & Loan Asn, currently. Publ: Reflections with Edmund Burke, Vantage Press, 60. Mem: St Paul of Cross; KofC. Relig: Roman Catholic. Legal Res: 7439 W Lunt Ave Chicago IL 60631 Mailing Add: 4930 N Milwaukee Ave Chicago IL 60630

SHEEHY, EDWARD DRISCOLL (D)
Chmn, North Attleborough Dem City Comt, Mass
b Richmond, Va, July 9, 38; s Eugene Morgan Sheehy & Cathrine Driscoll S; m 1958 to Paula S Shea; c Timothy Edward, Erin Maura & John Driscoll. Educ: Hartford Col, 1 year; Harvard Univ, 2 years. Polit & Govt Pos: Mem, North Attleborough Dem City Comt, 59-, chmn, 67-69 & 70-; chmn, North Attleborough Waterways Comt, 62-64 & Community Action Comt, 65-66; chmn, Head Start, 65-66; mem, North Attleborough Comt on Fed Funds, 66-68; mem, Mass Dem State Comt, 68- Bus & Prof Pos: Salesman, Dieges & Clust, Providence, RI, 62-69. Mem: Providence CofC; Sales & Contact Clubs, RI; Kiwanis. Relig: Catholic. Mailing Add: 22 Prince St North Attleborough MA 02760

SHEERIN, GARY ASHER (D)
Nev State Sen
b Elko, Nev, Oct 7, 38; s Chris H Sheerin & Evelyn Asher S; m 1961 to Jo Ann Hartman; c Christopher Hartman, Jennifer Lynn, Howard Hartman & Kelly Ann. Educ: Loyola Univ, Los Angeles, BS in Eng, 61; Hastings Col Law, LLB, 64; Tau Kappa Epsilon. Polit & Govt Pos: Admin asst to Gov Grant Sawyer, Carson City, Nev, 64-65; chmn, Ormsby Co Dem Cent Comt, 67-71; deleg, Dem Nat Conv, 68; mem, Carson City Dem Cent Comt, 71-; Nev State Pub Defender, 71-73; Nev State Sen, Carson City-Douglas Co Dist, 74- Bus & Prof Pos: Attorney-at-law, Carson City, Nev, 66- Mem: Am Judicature Soc; Nev State Bar Asn; Northern Nev Trial Lawyers Asn. Relig: Catholic. Legal Res: 549 Ruby Lane Carson City NV 89701 Mailing Add: Box 606 Carson City NV 89701

SHEFFLER, GEORGE JUSTUS (R)
Chmn, Hunt Co Rep Exec Comt, Tex
b Los Angeles, Calif, Dec 10, 44; s Russell Noble Sheffler & Dorothy Katherine Sutherland; single. Educ: Golden West Col, Huntington Beach, Calif, AA, 67; ETex State Univ, BS, 70; Southern Methodist Univ, 73; Soc for Advancement of Mgt; ETex State Univ Rodeo Club. Polit & Govt Pos: Pres, ETex State Univ Young Rep, 69-70; chmn, ETex State Univ Students for Bush for Senate, 70; precinct chmn, Hunt Co Rep Party, 70-71; co-chmn, Glasgow for State Sen Comt, 74; mem, Tex Young Rep State Exec Comt, 74-75; chmn, Hunt Co Rep Exec Comt, 74- Bus & Prof Pos: Oil securities broker, San Francisco, Calif, 71-72; partner, Sheffler Bros, 72- Publ: Senate: a scapegoat, The East Texan, 9/73. Mem: Jaycees, Commerce, Tex; Greenville CofC; Commonwealth Club, San Francisco, Calif; Tex State Teachers Asn; Nat Educ Asn. Honors & Awards: Nat Student Registry, 70; pres pro tempore, ETex State Univ Student Senate, 74. Legal Res: 1720 College St Greenville TX 75401 Mailing Add: Box 3305 ETex Sta Commerce TX 75428

SHEID, VADA W (D)
Ark State Rep
b Wideman, Ark, Aug 19, 16; d John N Webb & Gertrude Reynolds W; m 1939 to Carl R Sheid; c Richard. Educ: Draughon Sch Bus, Little Rock, Ark. Polit & Govt Pos: Treas, Baxter Co, Ark, 58-64; Ark State Rep, 67- Bus & Prof Pos: Owner furniture store, 57- Mem: VFW; Tau Gamma; Bus & Prof Women; PTA; League of Women Voters. Relig: Methodist. Mailing Add: 911 Baker Mountain Home AR 72653

SHEINBAUM, STANLEY K (D)
Mem, Calif State Dem Cent Comt
b New York, NY, June 12, 20; s Herman H Sheinbaum & Selma Klimberg S; m 1964 to Betty Warner. Educ: Stanford Univ, AB, 49; Phi Beta Kappa; Phi Eta Sigma. Polit & Govt Pos: Dir, Calif Dem Coun, 66-; Dem cand, US House Rep, 13th Cong Dist, 68; deleg, Dem Nat Conv, 68; mem, Calif State Dem Cent Comt, 69- Bus & Prof Pos: Mem econ faculty, Stanford Univ, 52; mem econ faculty, Mich State Univ, 55-60 & coordr, Vietnam Proj, 57-59; economist, Ctr Study Dem Insts, Santa Barbara, 60-; dir, Presidio Savings & Loan Asn, 64-; dir, Warner Ranch Co Inc, Los Angeles, 65-; vpres, Warner Indust, 68- Mil Serv: Entered as Pvt, Army, 42, released as T/Sgt, 46, after serv in 30th Engrs & 650th Engrs, Western Pac, 45-46. Mem: Am Econ Asn; Soc Int Develop. Honors & Awards: Fulbright fel, Paris, 2 years. Relig: Jewish. Mailing Add: 819 San Ysidro Lane Santa Barbara CA 93103

SHELBY, RICHARD CRAIG (D)
Ala State Sen
b Birmingham, Ala, May 6, 34; s Ozie Houston Shelby & Alice Skinner S; m 1960 to Annette Nevin; c Richard Craig, Jr & Claude Nevin. Educ: Univ Ala, Tuscaloosa, AB, 57, Univ Ala Law Sch, LLB, 63; Delta Chi; Phi Alpha Delta. Polit & Govt Pos: Law clerk, Supreme Court Ala, 61-62; city solicitor, Tuscaloosa, Ala, 64 & 71; US comnr, Northern Dist Ala, 66-70; spec asst attorney gen, State Ala, 69-; Ala State Sen, 11th Dist, 70- Mem: Tuscaloosa, Ala & Am Bar Asns; Am Trial Lawyers Asn; Tuscaloosa Exchange Club. Relig: Presbyterian; Deacon, First Presbyterian Church, Tuscaloosa, Ala. Mailing Add: 66 High Forest Tuscaloosa AL 35401

SHELDEN, ARTHUR H (D)
Mont State Rep
Mailing Add: Rte 1 Box 1650 Libby MT 59923

SHELDON, GEORGE H (D)
Fla State Rep
Mailing Add: 4721 San Miguel Tampa FL 33609

846 / SHELDON

SHELDON, JOE S, JR (R)
Mem, Rep State Cent Comt, La
b San Antonio, Tex, Apr 15, 26; s Joe S Sheldon & Julia Burns S; m 1959 to Kay Lilley; c Barbara Lynn & James Edward. Educ: Univ Tex, Austin, BS, 49; Phi Gamma Delta. Polit & Govt Pos: Mem, Rep State Cent Comt, La, 64-; mem, Orleans Parish Rep Exec Comt, 64-; chmn, Orleans Parish Rep Party, 68-72; deleg, Rep Nat Conv, 68. Bus & Prof Pos: Geologist, Humble Oil & Ref Co, 49-52; partner, Petroleum Geol Consult, 52-58, owner, 58- Mil Serv: Entered as A/S, Naval Res, 43, released as Signalman 3/C, 46, after serving in Pac Theater, 44-46. Mem: Am Asn Petroleum Geologists; New Orleans Geol Soc; Independent Petroleum Asn Am; Petroleum Club New Orleans; CofC. Legal Res: 1624 Charlton Dr New Orleans LA 70122 Mailing Add: Room 812 210 O'Keefe Ave New Orleans LA 70112

SHELHAMER, KENT D (D)
Pa State Rep
b Orangeville, Pa, Nov 30, 24; s Lester S Shelhamer & Bertha E Howell S; m to Mary J Holmes; c Five. Educ: Pa State Univ. Polit & Govt Pos: Pa State Rep, 64-; sch dir. Bus & Prof Pos: Fruit grower; auditor. Mil Serv: Army Engrs Corps, Sgt, ETO. Mem: Oriental Lodge; Caldwell Consistory; Irem Temple; Columbia Co Exten Serv; dist chmn, Iroquois Dist Boy Scouts. Relig: Evangelical United Brethren; Lay leader. Mailing Add: RD 2 Berwick PA 18603

SHELTON, ROBERT C, JR (D)
NJ State Assemblyman
Mailing Add: State House Trenton NJ 08625

SHELTON, THOMAS R (TOM) (D)
Ala State Rep
Mailing Add: PO Box 434 Jacksonville AL 36265

SHELTON, ULYSSES (D)
Pa State Rep
b St Petersburg, Fla, July 1, 17; s Wright Shelton & Lela Arline S; m to Pearl A Daniels; c two. Educ: Mastbaum Voc Sch. Polit & Govt Pos: Mem, 20th Ward Dem Exec Comt; writ server, Philadelphia Traffic Court, formerly; clerk, Dept of Records, Philadelphia, formerly; aide, US Rep Michael Bradley, formerly; magistrate's clerk, Court 13, formerly; Pa State Rep, 60- Bus & Prof Pos: Real estate mgr. Mil Serv: Air Force, S/Sgt, 3 years; Flight Chief at Westover Field, Mass. Mem: NPhiladelphia Civic League. Mailing Add: 717 W Berks St Philadelphia PA 19122

SHENEFIELD, JOHN HALE (D)
Mem, Richmond City Dem Comt, Va
b Toledo, Ohio, Jan 23, 39; s Hale Thurel Shenefield & Norma Bird S; m 1962 to Anna Larson; c Stephen Hale & Christopher Newcomb. Educ: Harvard Univ, AB, 60, LLB, 65. Polit & Govt Pos: Mem, Richmond City Dem Comt, Va, 69-; secy, Va Dem Party, 70-72; deleg, Dem Nat Mid-Term Conf, 74. Bus & Prof Pos: Lawyer, Hunton, Williams, Gay & Gibson, 65-; mem bd adv, Antitrust Bull, currently. Mil Serv: Entered as 2nd Lt, Army, 61, released as 2nd Lt, 62, after serv in Signal Bn, ETO; Capt, Army Res. Publ: Antitrust policy in electric utility industry, Antitrust Bull, 71; Survey of law of exclusive agreements, Univ Richmond Law Rev, 72; Annual antitrust survey, Washington & Lee Law Rev, 75. Mem: Am Bar Asn (antitrust sect, chmn fuels & energy subcomt). Relig: Episcopal. Legal Res: 4509 Cary St Rd Richmond VA 23221 Mailing Add: PO Box 1535 Richmond VA 23212

SHEPARD, ALLAN G (R)
Justice, Idaho Supreme Court
b Gardnear, Mass, Dec 18, 22; s Guy H Shepard & May Kendall S; m 1972 to Donna Sparling Soderlund; c Lynn Kendall, Paul Vernon & Ann Kendall. Educ: Boston Univ; Univ Wash, BS & LLB; Delta Theta Phi. Polit & Govt Pos: Asst attorney gen, Idaho, 51-57; Idaho State Rep, 58-63; attorney gen, Idaho, 63-68; chmn, Western Asn of Attorneys Gen, 65-66; vpres, Nat Asn of Attorneys Gen, 67-68, pres, 68-69; justice, Idaho Supreme Court, 69- Bus & Prof Pos: Admitted to practice in Idaho, Fed Dist Court, Fed Circuit Court & United States Supreme Court. Mil Serv: Army Air Corps, 43-46. Relig: Episcopal. Legal Res: 8314 Brynwood Boise ID 83704 Mailing Add: Supreme Court Bldg Boise ID 83707

SHEPARD, IRENE JAMES (R)
NH State Rep
b Calais, Maine, May 14, 22; d Hosea Stevens James & Lila Brown J; m 1942 to Henry Moore Shepard; c Merrill James, Carol (Mrs George Tucker) & Deborah Jane (deceased). Educ: Univ Maine, BA in French, 44; Univ NH, 63-65. Polit & Govt Pos: Vchmn, Hopkinton Rep Town Comt, NH, 72-74; NH State Rep, 75- Bus & Prof Pos: Choir dir, St Andrews Church, 62-75; teacher, Warner Simonds Free High Sch, NH, 64-70; teacher, Kearsarge Regional High Sch, 70-71. Mem: Order of Eastern Star (Past Matron, Orion 45); Dr Hopkinton Women's Rep Club; Hopkinton Woman's Club; Concord Chorale; Owls. Relig: Protestant. Legal Res: Gage Hill Rd Hopkinton NH 03301 Mailing Add: Rte 1 Concord NH 03301

SHEPHERD, KAREN FELKER (D)
b Silver City, NMex, July 5, 40; d Ralph H Felker & LaVerna Schroeder F; m 1963 to Vincent P Shepherd; c Heather Elizabeth & H Dylan. Educ: Univ Utah, BA, 62; Brigham Young Univ, MA, 63, grad work, 72-73; Delta Delta Delta. Polit & Govt Pos: Deleg, co & state Dem Conv, Utah, 68-; vchairperson, Orem Precinct Dem Party, 69-; alt deleg, Dem Nat Conv, 72- co-chairperson, Utah Co McGovern Campaign, 72; pres, Women's Dem Caucus, 72-73; Utah Co coordr, Wayne Owens for Senate Campaign 74; deleg, Dem Nat Mid Term Conf, 74, vchairperson, asst dir social servs, Salt Lake Co, Utah, 75- Bus & Prof Pos: Instr, Olympic Col, Wash, 64-65; Am Univ, Cairo, 65-67 & Brigham Young Univ, 68- Mem: Women's Polit Caucus (outreach aid, 72-73). Relig: Protestant. Mailing Add: 660 Cherry Dr Orem UT 84057

SHEPHERD, WALTON (D)
WVa State Deleg
Mailing Add: State Capitol Charleston WV 25305

SHEPPARD, ALAN JAMES (D)
b Fargo, NDak, Dec 3, 51; s Wilbur Parke Sheppard & Inez Cooper S; m 1972 to Lorette Ann Balkan. Educ: Univ NDak, BA, 73; Delta Upsilon; Blue Key. Polit & Govt Pos: Comnr Academics, Univ Senate, Univ NDak, 71-72; lobbyist, Nat Student Lobby, Washington, DC, 72; alt deleg, Dem Nat Conv, 72. Publ: Small community planning in North Dakota: the research & its methodology, Nat Sci Found, 72. Relig: Methodist. Legal Res: B-18 Princeton Trailer Court Grand Forks ND 58201 Mailing Add: 308 11th St NW Mandan ND 58554

SHEPPARD, ELEANOR PARKER (D)
Va State Deleg
b Pelham, Ga, July 24, 07; d John William Parker & Irwin Baggs W; m 1928 to Thomas Edward Sheppard; c Edith (Mrs Matthew Nelson Ott, Jr) & Sally (Mrs Robert Earl Dunnington). Educ: Limestone Col, 3 years. Polit & Govt Pos: City councilman, Richmond, Va, 54-68, vmayor, 60-62 & mayor, 62-64; coun rep, Richmond Libr Bd & Regional Planning & Econ Develop Comn, 60-62 & Richmond City Planning Comn, 64-66; chmn, Coun Agencies Comt, 60-62, mem, 64-66; mem, Coun Legis Comt, 64-68; Va State Deleg, 68-; mem, Defense Adv Comt on Women in the Serv, 68-70; mem, Adv Comt of US Surgeon Gen on Air Pollution, 65-67, Gov Comn on Status of Women, 65-66, Va Adv Legis Coun on Grants in Aid to Localities, 66, Sr Ctr Adv Steering Comt, 66, Richmond Area Community Coun Recreation Task Force, 66 & Comt on Continuing Educ of Med Col Va Sch of Nursing, 65; chmn, Adv Comt on Practical Nurse Educ, 66-67; trustee, Buford Acad, 68-; mem, Nat Comt on Uniform Traffic Code, 69-, Richmond Int Coun Bd, 66-74; trustee, Maymont Found; mem exec comt, Cent Va Educ TV Bd, & Gov Comn to Study Estab of State Univ in Richmond Metrop Area, 67; mem, Corrections Adv Bd, 73-; mem, Ment Health & Ment Retardation Serv Bd, 73-; YMCA Bd, 74- Mem: Richmond Dist, PTA; Bus & Prof Women's Club; Soroptimist Int; Colony Club; 2300 Club; Ginter Park Women's Club. Honors & Awards: Richmond First Club Good Govt Award, 64; Gold Feather Award, Jaycees, 68; Woman of Achievement Award, Bus & Prof Women, 68. Relig: Baptist. Mailing Add: 1601 Princeton Rd Richmond VA 23227

SHERER, ALBERT WILLIAM, JR
US Ambassador to Czech
b Wheaton, Ill, Jan 16, 16; s Albert William Sherer & Linda Van Nostran S; m 1944 to Carroll Russell; c Peter, Susan & Anthony. Educ: Yale Univ, AB, 38; Harvard Univ, LLB, 41. Polit & Govt Pos: Foreign serv officer, Tangier, Morocco, 46-49 & Budapest, Hungary, 49-51; assigned to Off Eastern European Affairs, Dept of State, 51-54 & 57-61; first secy, Prague, Czech, 55-57; dep chief of mission, Warsaw, Poland, 61-66; foreign serv inspector, Dept of State, 66-67, US Ambassador to Togo, 67-70 & to the Repub of Equatorial Guinea, 69-70, US Ambassador to the Repub of Guinea, 70-72, US Ambassador to Czech, 72- Bus & Prof Pos: Admitted to Ill Bar, 41. Mil Serv: Army Air Force, 41-45. Legal Res: IL Mailing Add: Prague c/o US Dept of State Washington DC 20521

SHERIDAN, ALFRED A (D)
Mich State Rep
b Detroit, Mich, Oct 28, 28; m 1953 to Irene Marek; c Kathy, Tom, Mike & John Patrick. Educ: High sch grad. Polit & Govt Pos: Admin asst to supvr, Taylor Twp, Mich, formerly; precinct deleg, Dem Party; Mich State Rep, 64- Mil Serv: Armed Forces, 50-52. Mem: Lions; Moose; Little League; Amvets; VFW. Relig: Catholic. Mailing Add: 8272 Weddel Taylor MI 48180

SHERIDAN, LAWRENCE A (D)
La State Rep
Mailing Add: PO Box 488 Angie LA 70426

SHERMAN, FRANCIS HENRY (D)
RI State Rep
b Providence, RI, Apr 16, 18; s James F Sherman & Emma Digrado S; div. Educ: Univ RI, BS, 49; Willimantic State Col, MS, 63; Sigma Chi. Polit & Govt Pos: RI State Rep, Dist 43, 66-68 & 72- Bus & Prof Pos: Dept head, Aldrich Jr High Sch, Warwick, RI, 63-73. Mil Serv: Entered as Pvt, Army, 42, released as Sgt, 45, after serv in 1896 Eng Bn, SW Pac Theatre, 44-45; Campaign Ribbons. Mem: Recreation & Phys Educ Soc of RI; KofC; VFW; Elks; Am Vets. Relig: Roman Catholic. Mailing Add: 162 Hopkins Hill Rd Coventry RI 02816

SHERMAN, KENNETH LELAND (R)
NH State Rep
b Monson, Mass, Dec 4, 98; s Frank James Sherman & Grace Allen S; m 1923 to Ila Gray; c John Allen. Educ: US Naval Acad, 3 years; Boston Univ, BS in Educ. Polit & Govt Pos: Mem sch bd, Newbury, NH, 57; NH State Rep, 67-; selectman, Newbury, 68- Bus & Prof Pos: Prin, Dedham Jr High Sch, 26-34 & Andover Jr High Sch, 34-35; supt schs, Andover, Mass, 35-55 & Laconia, NH, 57-66. Mil Serv: Entered as Midn, Navy, 17, released as Comdr, 45, after serv in Lion I & Air Sea Rescue, SPac, New Hebrides & Solomons, 42-45; various theatre decorations; Presidential Citation. Mem: Nat Educ Asn; Am Legion; Rotary; Mason. Relig: Protestant. Mailing Add: Morse Hill South Newbury NH 03272

SHERMAN, MARION KYLE (D)
Wash State Rep
b Puyallup, Wash; d Henry Irving Kyle & Virginia Huff K; m 1949 to Leonard Lincoln Sherman; c Virginia (Mrs John Weaver) & David. Educ: Reed Col, 45-48; Univ Wash, BA, 49. Polit & Govt Pos: Wash State Rep, 47th Dist, 75- Mem: League Women Voters; Grange; Gtr Maple Valley CofC. Mailing Add: 24629 SE 200th Maple Valley WA 98038

SHERMAN, MAX (D)
Tex State Sen
Mailing Add: Fisk Bldg Amarillo TX 79101

SHERMAN, W C (BUD) (D)
Tex State Rep
Mailing Add: 5010 Hildring Dr 184 Ft Worth TX 76132

SHERMAN, WILLIAM FARRAR (D)
Ark State Rep
b Little Rock, Ark, Sept 12, 37; s Lincoln Farrar Sherman & Nancy Irene Lowe S; m 1967 to Carole Lynn Williams; c John Farrar & Anna Katherine. Educ: Univ Ark, Fayetteville, 60; Univ Va, 64; Omicron Delta Kappa; Phi Alpha Delta; Phi Alpha Theta; Pi Mu Epsilon; Pi Kappa Alpha. Polit & Govt Pos: Asst US Attorney, Eastern Dist Ark, 66-69; Securities Comnr, State of Ark, 69-71; Ark State Rep, Position Two, Dist Four, 75- Mil Serv: Entered as 2nd Lt, Army, 60, released as 2nd Lt, 61, after serv in 9th Inf, 2nd Inf Div, Ft Benning, Ga, 61; Maj, Ark Army Nat Guard. Mem: Am, Ark & Pulaski Co Bar Asns. Mailing Add: 450 Midland St Little Rock AR 72205

SHERRER, BETTY R (R)
VChmn, Rep State Exec Comt, Ala
b Alexandria, Va, June 27, 35; d Joseph Lorenzo Rodgers & Pauline Brown S; m 1960 to Wayman Gray Sherrer; c Elizabeth Ann & William Jefferson. Educ: Radford Col, BS, 58; Univ Ala, Tuscaloosa, MA, 69. Polit & Govt Pos: Vchmn, Rep State Exec Comt, Ala, currently. Relig: Methodist. Mailing Add: 107 Redbud Rd Oneonta AL 35121

SHERWOOD, GLEN (D)
Minn State Rep
Mailing Add: Star Rte 60 Pine River MN 56474

SHERWOOD, ROBERT WALTER (D)
Conn State Rep
b Bridgeport, Conn, Feb 19, 21; s George B Sherwood & Kathleen I S (both deceased); m 1948 to Sally Ann Connelly; c Kyle (Mrs Keith McEachern), Holly (Mrs Leigh Manasevit), Alison (Mrs Neil Stubenhaus), Dawn, Mindy, Robin, Robert & Roger. Educ: St John's Prep, Mass; Holy Cross Col. Polit & Govt Pos: Rep, Town Meeting, 8 years; Conn State Rep, 75- Bus & Prof Pos: Prof baseball player, 45-50; actor, New York, US & Can; salesman, Am Frozen Food, Monarch Ins Co & Prudential Ins Co, Fairfield, Conn. Mil Serv: Entered as Pvt, Army, 42, released as 1st Lt, 45, after serv in 1st Div, ETO; Combat Inf Badge; ETO Medal; Croix De Guerre; Army of Occup. Mem: KofC; Old Timers. Relig: Roman Catholic. Mailing Add: 551 Toilsome Hill Rd Fairfield CT 06430

SHEVIN, ROBERT LEWIS (D)
Attorney Gen, Fla
b Miami, Fla, Jan 19, 34; s Aaron Shevin & Pauline Bott S; m 1957 to Myrna Bressack; c Laura Dawn, Hilary Beth & Harry Alan. Educ: Univ Fla, BA, 55; Univ Miami, LLB, magna cum laude, 57; Southern Collegiate Debate Champion; secy, Men's Affairs & Relig Affairs; Fla Blue Key; Hall of Fame; pres, Pi Lambda Phi; scholastic award for highest male grad, Univ Miami; ed, Miami Law Quart; pres, Student Bar Asn & Bar & Gavel; State Moot Court Champion. Polit & Govt Pos: State speakers chmn, Citizens for Johnson, Fla, 64; Fla State Rep, 65-66, speaker's chmn, Oper Pub Conscience, Dade Co, 66; Fla State Sen, 43rd Dist, 67-71, chmn, Miami Econ Adv Bd, Fla Fair Share Comt for Roads & Representation & Courts Budget Comt of Dade Co, Fla State Senate; legal counsel, Dade Co Legis Deleg; mem, Local Mkt Develop Comt, Govt Research Coun & Indust Develop Coun, Dade Co; Miami Beach Dem Club; Dade Co Young Dem Club; Attorney Gen, Fla, 71-; alt deleg, Dem Nat Conv, 72. Bus & Prof Pos: Attorney-at-law, Shevin, Goodman & Holtzman, 57-; instr, Law Rev Inst; bank dir. Mil Serv: Capt, Active Army Res, 8 years. Mem: Nat Panel, Am Arbit Asn; Miami-Dade Co CofC; Gtr Miami Pi Lambda Phi Alumni Asn (pres); Sertoma Club of Miami, (pres & chmn bd); Dade Co Chap Nat Multiple Sclerosis Soc. Honors & Awards: Recipient Allen Morris Award for outstanding first term of freshman mem, Fla State Legis, 65; selected one of top ten most valuable mem of Fla State Legis by Capitol Press Corps & Fla newspaper editors; Conserv Award, Sierra Club, 72. Relig: Jewish; mem, bd dirs, Beth David Synagogue. Mailing Add: Dept of Legal Affairs The Capitol Tallahassee FL 32304

SHIELDKNIGHT, JIM EDWARD (R)
b Coweta, Okla, Dec 30, 16; s Alfred Shieldknight & Corda Werner S; m 1939 to Margaret Lucille Darnell; c James Edward & Lu Ann. Educ: Joplin High Sch, Mo. Polit & Govt Pos: Mem, Porter Sch Bd, Okla, 12 years; chmn, Wagoner Co Rep Cent Comt, 70-74. Bus & Prof Pos: Farmer, 39-; driver salesman, Voss Propane, 55-58, Easley Propane, 58-68 & Phillips Petroleum Propane, 68-69; plant mgr, Uniongas of Coweta, 69- Mem: Lions; Okla Farmer Union (ins agent). Relig: Southern Baptist. Mailing Add: Box 883 Coweta OK 74429

SHIELDS, CHARLIE D (D)
Chmn, Lauderdale Co Dem Exec Comt, Miss
b Center, Miss, Mar 26, 09; s Charlie Walter Shields & Natie Mary Price S; m 1934 to Vivian Beatrice Williams; c Camille (Mrs Lehman Key) & Sharlynn (Mrs Arthur Blatzell). Educ: Southern Bus Col, 1 year; Am Law Sch, LLB. Polit & Govt Pos: Chmn, Lauderdale Co Dem Exec Comt, Miss, 51-; mem city coun, Meridian, 52-56. Bus & Prof Pos: Attorney-at-law, Meridian, Miss, 30-; ins agent, Holyfield & Shields, 50-; partner, Security Ins, 50-; pres, Bankers Trust Savings & Loan Asn, 52-; dir, Southern Guaranty Ins Co & Nat Gen Ins Co, 62- Mil Serv: Pvt, Army Air Corps, 28-29. Mem: Miss & Lauderdale Co Bar Asns; Masonic Lodges from Blue Lodge through Shrine; Eastern Star; Meridian Lions Club (past pres). Relig: Baptist. Legal Res: 2715 28th St Meridian MS 39301 Mailing Add: 2105 Sixth St Meridian MS 39301

SHIELDS, PHYLLIS E (R)
Chairwoman, Shelby Co Rep Party, Ohio
b West Manchester, Ohio, Aug 5, 36; d Orval C Fourman & Treva Fasnacht F; m 1955 to William A Shields; c David William, E Elaine & James T. Educ: Arcanum High Sch, grad, 54. Polit & Govt Pos: Vpres, Darke Co Rep Womens Orgn, 68, pres, 70-71; chmn, Darke Co Women's Rep Party, 70-73; chairwoman, Shelby Co Rep Party, 73-; pres, Shelby Co Rep Women's Orgn, 73- Bus & Prof Pos: Consult & mgr, Fashion Two Twenty Cosmetics, 66- Mem: Darke Co YMCA Bd; Green Thumb Garden Club. Honors & Awards: Greenville Jaycees President's Award, 71; co-chmn, Darke Co YMCA Membership Drive. Relig: Protestant. Mailing Add: 122 Pike St Sidney OH 45365

SHIFLET, W MARION (D)
WVa State Deleg
Mailing Add: State Capitol Charleston WV 25305

SHILLITO, BARRY JAMES (INDEPENDENT)
b Dayton, Ohio, Jan 1, 21; s Lucian W Shillito & Mary Ellen O'Connor S; m 1942 to Eileen Elizabeth Cottman; c Barry, Jr, Elaine, Daniel, James & Colleen. Educ: Univ Dayton, BS, 49; Univ Calif, Los Angeles, Adv Mgt Prog. Polit & Govt Pos: Sect chief & contracting off procurement div & chmn, fighter fire control systs planning group, Air Force Hq, Air Materiel Command, Wright-Patterson Air Force Base, 49-54; Asst Secy of the Navy for Installations & Logistics, 68-69; Asst Secy of Defense for Installations & Logistics, 69-73. Bus & Prof Pos: Gen mgr, Harris-Lincoln Supply Co, Dayton, Ohio, 45-49; dir of materiel, Hughes Aircraft Co, Culver City, Calif, 54-58, dir of sales, 58-59; exec vpres, Houston Fearless Co, 59-60, pres, 60-62; pres, Logistics Mgt Inst, 62-68 & Teledyne Ryan Aeronaut, San Diego, 73- Mil Serv: Entered Army Air Corps, 42, completed pilot training, 43, prisoner of war in Germany, 43-46. Mem: Armed Forces Mgt Asn; Am Legion; KofC; Moraine Country Club, Dayton, Ohio; Burning Tree Club, Washington, DC. Honors & Awards: Secy of Defense Distinguished Pub Serv Medal; Secy of the Navy Distinguished Public Serv Award; Rep of China Cloud & Banner Medal; Rep of Vietnam Nat Order of Vietnam. Mailing Add: 555 San Fernando St San Diego CA 92106

SHILTS, WILLIAM WINSTON (R)
Committeeman, Summit Co Rep Exec Comt, Ohio
b Akron, Ohio, Apr 15, 10; s William Delbert Shilts & Edna Robens S; m 1935 to Martha Weimer; c William Weimer, Winifred Weimer & Rebecca Weimer. Educ: Mt Union Col, BA, 31; NY Univ, 34-35; Akron Univ, 36-37; Cleveland Col, 38-39; Sigma Nu. Polit & Govt Pos: Councilman, Hudson, Ohio, 39-41, village clerk, 41-57; precinct committeeman, Rep Cent Comt, 40-; committeeman, Summit Co Rep Exec Comt, 60-; area dir, NSummit Co Rep Exec Comt, 62-; alt deleg, Rep State Conv, 64, 66 & 68; deleg, Rep Nat Conv, 68. Bus & Prof Pos: Ed-mgr, Hudson Times, Ohio, 32-34; salesman, Austin Print Works Co, Akron, 35-39 & Bellows-Claude Neon Co, 40-41; mfgs sales rep, Goodyear Tire & Rubber Co, 41-59. Mem: F&AM (worthy master, 42-43); Goodyear 25 Year Club. Relig: Congregational. Mailing Add: 422 N Main St PO Box 534 Hudson OH 44236

SHIMAN, GAIL (D)
Vt State Rep
b Knoxville, Tenn, July 4, 41; m 1967 to David Aaron Shiman. Educ: Univ Calif Los Angeles, BA, 67; Univ Vt, MEd, 74. Polit & Govt Pos: Mem, Milton Dem Town Comt, Vt, 73-75; mem, Chittenden Co Dem Comt, Vt, 73-75; pres, Chittenden Co Dem Women, 74-75; justice of peace, Milton, 75-; Vt State Rep, 75- Mem: Vt Pub Interest Research Group; Common Cause; Vt Fedn of Dem Women; Orgn of Women Legislators; League of Women Voters. Legal Res: Main St Milton VT 05468 Mailing Add: Box 6 Milton VT 05468

SHIMANEK, ROBERT FRANCIS (R)
Chmn, Jones Co Rep Party, Iowa
b Monticello, Iowa, Feb 14, 43; s Charles Francis Shimanek & Doris M Flynn S; m 1972 to Alice Marie Strang; c Anne E. Educ: Loras Col, BA, 65; Univ Iowa Law Sch, JD, 68; Phi Delta Phi. Polit & Govt Pos: Chmn, Jones Co Rep Party, Iowa, 74- Mil Serv: Entered as Pvt, Army, 68, released as Sgt, 71, after serv in 191 MID, 1st Air Cav Div, Vietnam, 69-71; Bronze Star with Oak Leaf Cluster, Air Medal; Army Commendation Medal. Mem: Am Legion; KofC; Am Bar Asn; Jones Co Bar Asn (pres, 74-); Lions Club (secy, 73-). Relig: Roman Catholic. Mailing Add: 115 E Third St Monticello IA 52310

SHINAULT, IONE B (R)
Chmn, Marshall Co Rep Party, Miss
b Blue Springs, Miss, July 15, 21; d James Cecil Blanton & Ollin Elizabeth Patmon B; m 1940 to Walter Sidney Shinault; c Walter Sidney, Jr, Annella Elizabeth, Joseph Wrenn, Cecil Blanton & Theresa Ione. Educ: Olive Branch High Sch, grad, 38, postgrad bus course, 39. Polit & Govt Pos: Chmn, Marshall Co Rep Party, 71- Mem: Life mem Am Legion Auxiliary (every office from unit pres to dept pres, 46-, dist pres, 74-75); PTA; La Botique des Huit Chapeaux et Guarante Femmes; Women's Serv Guild (dist pres & unit pres, 65-70). Relig: Methodist; life mem, Wesleyan Serv Guild, Methodist Church; mem admin bd, 58- Mailing Add: PO Box 144 Byhalia MS 38611

SHINE, DAVID BRUCE (D)
Dem Nat Committeeman, Tenn
b Aug 11, 38; s Thomas Foss Shine & Alice Hudgins S; m 1969 to Elizabeth Magoffin; c James Vincent, Edward Magoffin & David Bruce, Jr. Educ: Northeastern Univ Sch of Bus Admin, 58; Tusculum Col, BS, 60; Vanderbilt Univ Sch of Law, JD, 64; Columbia Univ, 64-65; Phi Delta Phi. Polit & Govt Pos: Vchmn, Nat Fedn of Col Young Dem, 60-63; secy, Dem Party of Sullivan Co, Tenn, 68-70; vchmn, Tenn Arts Comn, 69-70, chmn, 70-72; mem credentials comt, Dem Nat Comt, 73-; Dem Nat Committeeman, Tenn, 73- Bus & Prof Pos: Attorney-at-law, Kingsport, Tenn, 66-; bd dirs, Alexander Co, New York, 71- & Advert Workshop, Inc, 71-; pres, Euro-Mkt Commun, Inc, 72-74; chmn bd, SMR Publ-Europe SA, 72-74. Publ: Auth, Non-military aspects of NATO, NATO, Paris, 63; various articles for Freedom & Union Mag. Mem: Am & Kingsport Bar Asns; Ridgefields Country Club, Kingsport; Columbia Univ Club. Relig: Episcopal. Legal Res: 1943 Ridgefield Manor Court Kingsport TN 37660 Mailing Add: 700 E Sullivan St Kingsport TN 37660

SHINGLETON, WILLIAM EARL (D)
WVa State Deleg
b Fairmont, WVa, Dec 26, 23; s Loxley Oliver Shingleton & Florence Snodgrass S; m 1949 to Willa Jenkins; c Robert E & Sally Ann. Educ: WVa Univ, BS, 47; Alpha Kappa Psi; Beta Theta Pi. Polit & Govt Pos: WVa State Deleg, 71-, vchmn, banking & ins comt, WVa House Deleg, 71- Bus & Prof Pos: Appraiser, Prudential Ins Co, 47-49; treas, Shingleton Bros, Clarksburg, WVa, 49-56; vpres, Henry & Hardesty, Inc, Fairmont, WVa, 56-62, pres, 62-; dir, First Nat Bank Fairmont, 65- Mil Serv: Entered as Pvt, Army, 43, released as Capt, 46. Mem: Fairmont Kiwanis; Marion Co CofC; Community Coun. Relig: Presbyterian. Mailing Add: Box 1548 Fairmont WV 26554

SHINPOCH, A N (BUD) (D)
Wash State Rep
Mailing Add: 361 Maple Ave NW Renton WA 98055

SHIPE, CHARLES EDWARD (R)
b Salina, Kans, Jan 16, 05; s Edward Daniel Shipe & Eloise Hoskins S; m 1949 to Ruby Alta Gillespie; c Martha (Mrs John Williams) & Edward Daniel. Educ: NMex State Univ, BS, 26. Polit & Govt Pos: Precinct chmn, Jefferson Co, Tex, 56-73; campaign co chmn, John Tower, 61, 66 & 72; campaign co chmn, Gov Paul Eggers, 70; alt deleg, Rep Nat Conv, 72. Bus & Prof Pos: Chem engr, Texaco Inc, 26-70, retired. Mil Serv: Entered as 2nd Lt, Army Res, 26; 1st Lt, Southwest Pacific, 42-45; Army Res, 45-, Lt Col; Bronze Star; five battle stars. Mem: Am Chem Soc; Lions; Am Legion; Knife & Fork Club (pres, 68-69). Relig: Presbyterian. Mailing Add: 2732 33rd St Port Arthur TX 77640

SHIPLEY, CARL L (R)
b Washington, DC, Dec 16, 19; s Edmund D Shipley & Inez Beale S; m 1948 to Nancy Kane; c Zachary Kane & Joshua Beale. Educ: Georgetown Univ, BS, 42; Foreign Serv Sch; Harvard Law Sch, LLB, 48. Polit & Govt Pos: Spec asst to US Attorney Gen, 53-56; mem, DC Urban Renewal Coun, 58-61; chmn, DC Rep Comt, formerly; Rep Nat Committeeman, DC, 70-73. Mil Serv: Entered as Ens, Naval Res, released as Lt. Relig: Catholic. Mailing Add: 2510 Virginia Ave NW Washington DC 20037

SHIPLEY, GEORGE EDWARD (D)
US Rep, Ill
b Richland Co, Ill, Apr 21, 27; m to Ann Watson; c Five. Educ: Georgetown Univ. Polit & Govt Pos: Chief Dep Sheriff, Richland Co, Ill, 50-54; Sheriff of Richland Co, 54-58; US Rep, Ill, 58-; deleg, Dem Nat Conv, 72. Bus & Prof Pos: Restaurant owner. Mil Serv: Marine Corps, 3 years, discharged 47, serv in SPac. Legal Res: Olney IL 62450 Mailing Add: 237 Cannon Bldg Washington DC 20515

SHIPMAN, FRANCES (R)
Rep Nat Committeewoman, NMex
Mailing Add: Rte 1 Box 204 Santa Fe NM 87501

SHIPMAN, GORDON (D)
Mem Exec Bd, Portage Co Dem Party, Wis
b Manawa, Wis, Apr 19, 01; s Harry Shipman & Margaret Niven S; m 1928 to Agnes Vanneman; c Margaret (Mrs Robert S Cooper), Anne (Mrs Kurt Pasch) & Eleanor (Mrs John W Lucas). Educ: Univ Wis, Madison, BA, 26, MA, 27, PhD, 32; Univ Nebr, Lincoln, 27-28; Columbia Univ, 31-32; Pi Sigma Alpha. Polit & Govt Pos: Chmn, Citizens for McCarthy, Portage Co, Wis, 68; deleg, Dem Nat Conv, 68; deleg, Wis State Dem Conv, 68 & 69; deleg, Dist Dem Conv, Wis, 69; mem exec bd, Portage Co Dem Party, Wis, 73- Bus & Prof Pos: State probation-parole agent, Div of Corrections, Wis, 34-46; head dept social sci, Shurtleff Col, 46-49; instr sociol, Wis State Col, Milwaukee, 49-56; prof sociol, Univ Wis-Milwaukee, 56-66, chmn dept sociol, 56-61; chmn dept sociol, Wis State Univ, Stevens Point, 66-69; emer prof, Univ Wis-Stevens Point, 72- Publ: Speech thresholds & voice tolerance in marital interaction, Marriage & Family Living, 11/62; A proposal for revising marriage license procedure, J of Marriage & the Family, 5/65; The psychodynamics of sec education, Family Coord, 1/68. Mem: Fel, Am Sociol Asn; Mid-W & Wis Sociol Asns; Nat Coun on Family Rels; Nat Coun on Crime & Delinquency; Soc for Sci Study of Sex. Mailing Add: 2536 Peck St Stevens Point WI 54481

SHIRAH, ROSS PATRICK (R)
Mem, Rep State Cent Comt, La
b Beaumont, Tex, Aug 6, 40; s Ross Jefferson Shirah & Mary L E Gandy S; single. Educ: Northeast La Univ, BA, 68, MA, 73; chmn, Young Rep; Conservative Club. Polit & Govt Pos: Fifth Cong Dist chmn, La Young Rep Fedn, 65-67; alt deleg, Rep Nat Conv, 68, deleg, 72; mem, Ouachita Parish Rep Exec Comt, La, 68-; mem, Rep State Cent Comt, La, 49th Representative Dist, 68- Bus & Prof Pos: Copywriter, Olinicraft, Inc, West Monroe, La, formerly; reporter, Monroe Morning World, Monroe, La, formerly; grad asst, Northeast La Univ, 71- Mil Serv: Inc, West Monroe, La, currently. Mil Serv: Entered as E-1, Army, 59, released as Sp-4, 61, after serv in Intel Div, Heidelberg, Ger & 95th Civil Affairs Group, Ft Gordon, Ga; Good Conduct Medal. Mem: Epsilon Tau Chap, Phi Alpha Theta (pres, 72-73). Relig: Church of Christ. Legal Res: 1202 S Third St Monroe LA 71201 Mailing Add: PO Box 2713 Louisville Sta Monroe LA 71201

SHIREY, HAROLD LEE (R)
Chmn, Aransas Co Rep Party, Tex
b Winnsboro, Tex, July 4, 17; s Jesse J Shirey & Mignon Ragsdale S; m 1961 to George Alice Jones; c Harold L, Jr. Educ: ETex State Univ, BS, 36, MS, 40; Tex Univ, 41. Polit & Govt Pos: Chmn, Aransas Co Rep Party, Tex, 70- Bus & Prof Pos: Prin, Big Sandy High Sch, Tex, 38-42; various admin pos, Humble Oil & Refining, 45-57, admin supvr, Corpus Christi, 57-62; sr systs analyst, Houston, 62-67; prof bus admin, Univ Corpus Christi, 67-71. Mil Serv: Entered as Ens, Navy, 42, released as Lt, 45, after serv in Navigators VR-11, Pac, 43-44. Mem: Mason. Relig: Presbyterian. Mailing Add: 1418 E Paisano Rockport TX 78382

SHIRK, LOIS MADELINE (D)
Committeewoman, Mo State Dem Comt
b Lathrop, Mo, Nov 22, 15; d Charles Edward Enslow & Della T Shaw E; m 1932 to John Emerson Shirk; c Marilyn (Mrs James D Schottel) & Ronald Eugene. Educ: Lathrop High Sch, Mo, grad. Polit & Govt Pos: Committeewoman, DeKalb Co Dem Party, Mo, 60-; vchmn, DeKalb Co Dem Cent Comt, formerly; mem, Sixth Dist Dem Comt, 64-; pres, Sixth Dist Dem Womens Clubs, 70-71; committeewoman, Mo State Dem Comt, 71- Bus & Prof Pos: Sales assoc, J C Penney Co, St Joseph, Mo, 67- Relig: Baptist. Mailing Add: Clarksdale MO 64430

SHIRLEY, FRANKLIN RAY (D)
Mayor, Winston-Salem, NC
b Glencoe, Ky, June 17, 14; s William Franklin Shirley & Ollie Boss S; m 1944 to Mamie Mellichamp; c William McNulty, Susan Ollene & Elizabeth Rae. Educ: Georgetown Col, BA, 39; MA, Columbia Univ, 48; PhD, Univ Fla, 59; freshman scholarship; grad fel, Univ Fla; Pi Kappa Delta; Omicron Delta; Tau Kappa Alpha. Polit & Govt Pos: Mem, Winston-Salem Bd Educ, NC, 63-65; alderman, Winston-Salem, 63-70, mayor, 70-; mem bd dirs, Piedmont Triad Coun Govt, 70-, vpres health planning coun, 71-, chmn environ comt, 71-; mem bd dirs, NC League Munic, 71-73, 1st vpres, 74-; mem bd dirs, Citizens Coalition, Winston-Salem, 72- Bus & Prof Pos: Pub sch teacher, Ky & Ohio, 34-43; teacher, Baylor Sch Boys, Chattanooga, Tenn, 43-46; assoc prof speech & dir debate, Carson-Newman Col, 46-48; prof speech & chmn dept speech community & theatre arts, Wake Forest Univ, 48-; vis prof, Univ Southern Calif, summer 60. Publ: Zebulon Vance—Tarheel Spokesman, McNally & Loftin, 62; Why not meet the issues?, Speech Activities Mag, 51; Teachers, mend your speech, NC Educ J, 52. Mem: Speech Commun Asn Am; Southern Speech Commun Asn; NC Speech Commun & Theatre Asn; US Conf Mayors (urban econ policy comt); Nat League of Cities (environ comt). Relig: Baptist. Mailing Add: 1947 Faculty Dr Winston-Salem NC 27016

SHIRLEY, JASPER CLYDE (R)
Mem, SC Rep State Rep Exec Comt
b Belton, SC, Nov 15, 13; s Luther Ernest Shirley & Emma Eugenia Elizabeth Saylors S; single. Educ: Univ SC, AB, 35; Kappa Sigma Kappa; Kappa Phi Kappa; Phi Pi Phi. Polit & Govt Pos: Organizer & pres, Belton Rep Precinct, 63-; mem, SC State Rep Exec Comt, 69-; alt deleg, Rep Nat Conv, 72. Bus & Prof Pos: Teacher Eng, Anderson Pub Schs, SC, 35-43; SC rep, Harper & Row, Publ, 46- Mil Serv: Entered as Yeoman 2/C, Navy Air Corps, 43, released as Lt(sg), after serv in Hawaiian Sea Frontier & Navy Dept, Washington, DC. Mem: Pres, SC Lawn Tennis Asn, 59; Univ SC Alumni Asn for Tenth Dist; Anderson Country Club; Gamecock Club. Relig: Baptist; Sunday Sch teacher, Belton First Baptist Church, 26 years. Mailing Add: Blue Ridge Extension Route 2 Belton SC 29627

SHIRLEY, LANDONA HORTENSE (D)
Chairperson, Orange Co Dem Exec Comt, Fla
b Detroit, Mich, Jan 12, 28; d Finis Barton & Daisy Henley B; m 1946 to James Aaron Shirley; c Rebecca (Mrs Bowers). Educ: Jordan High Sch, grad, 45. Polit & Govt Pos: Vpres, Dem Women's Club, Orlando, Fla, 66-68; treas, Dem Women's Club, Winter Park, 68-70; vchmn, Orange Co Dem Exec Comt, 70-74, chmn, 74-; treas, Fla Co Chmn Dem Orgn, 75- Mem: Drug Abuse Coun Orange Co; Friends of Libr. Honors & Awards: Pub Serv Award, Orange Co Young Dem, 72, Dem of Year, 74; First Woman in Orange Co Elected Chmn Polit Party; First Woman in State Elected Treas, Fla Co Chmn Orgn. Relig: Church of Christ. Mailing Add: 1045 Santa Anita Rd Orlando FL 32808

SHIRPSER, CLARA (D)
b San Francisco, Calif, Aug 25, 01; d Leo Garfinkle & Alexandra Shragge G; m 1940 to Adolph Shirpser, wid; c Barbara (Mrs Robert De Liban). Educ: Univ Calif, 19-21. Polit & Govt Pos: Mem, Franchise, Taxation, Charter Amendment Comts, Berkeley City Coun, 48-50; Dem nominee for Calif State Assemblyman, 50; mem, Alameda Co & Calif State Dem Comts, 50-56, mem circle comt, State Comt, 73-; mem, Dem Nat Comt, 52-56; deleg, Dem Nat Conv, 52, 56 & 60; co-chmn, Nat Exec Comt, Stevenson-Kefauver Pres Campaign, 56; vchmn, Nat & Calif Kefauver Primary Campaign for President, 56; Calif Campaign Comt, Brown for Gov, 59-66; mem, Gov Adv Comt to Calif Consumers Coun, 59-67; mem, President Kennedy's Nat Inauguration Comt, 61; chmn, Alameda Co Women for Johnson & Humphrey, 64; mem NCalif exec campaign comt, Alan Cranston for US Sen, Calif, 68 & 74; mem exec campaign comt, Jeffery Cohelan for Cong, 68; mem campaign comt, Phil Burton for Cong, 74. Bus & Prof Pos: Owner & mgr, retail bus, Berkeley, Calif, 25-45; mem, Berkeley Social Welfare Comt, Grey Lady, Navy Oak Knoll Hosp Blood Bank, 46-49; chmn women's div, Herrick Mem Hosp, 51, mem adv comt to bd trustees, currently; Nat Bd Atlantic Union; mem, Menninger Found; pres, Arch Herrick Hosp Guild, 57-; chmn, EBay Rehabilitation Ctr Women's Div, 58-61 & mem adv coun; bd of dirs, Calif Heritage Coun, 59-70; vpres, Brandeis Univ Women's Div, 69-71; viewpoint meeting chmn, Ctr for Learning In Retirement, Univ Calif Exten Div, 75- Mem: Berkeley League Women Voters (pres); Planned Parenthood of Alameda Co; Children's Hosp Asn; Univ of Calif Alliance, World Affairs Coun; UN Orgn (dir). Honors & Awards: First interviewee for series, Women in Politics, Oral Research Dept, Bancroft Libr, Univ Calif, 73. Mailing Add: 1201 California St San Francisco CA 94109

SHITO, MITSUO (D)
Hawaii State Rep
b Kawela, Molokai, Hawaii, July 20, 30; s Jentoru Shito (deceased) & Haruno Shitahana S; m 1952 to Genevieve Ilima Alani; c Eugenie H L. Educ: Molokai High Sch, dipl; Honolulu Bus Col, 53. Polit & Govt Pos: Hawaii State Rep, 74-, chmn housing comt, Hawaii State House Rep, 74. Bus & Prof Pos: Asst parts mgr, Universal Motors Inc, Honolulu, 70-74; sales mgr, Charley's Gen Tire, Waipahu, 74- Mil Serv: Command Sgt Maj, Hawaii Nat Guard, 48-75; Army Commendation Medal; State of Hawaii Commendation. Mem: Waipahu Community Asn (pres, 74-); Waipahu Cult Garden Park (1st vpres, 74-75); Robinson Heights Asn (1st vpres, 74-75); Leeward Lions Club. Honors & Awards: Guardsman of the Year, 67. Mailing Add: 94-277 Haaa St Waipahu HI 96797

SHIVERS, ALLAN (D)
b Lufkin, Tex, Oct 5, 07; s Robert A Shivers & Easter Creasy S; m 1937 to Marialice Shary; c John, Allan, Jr, Marialice Sue & Brian McGee. Educ: Univ Tex, AB, 31, LLB, 33. Polit & Govt Pos: Tex State Sen, 35-46; Lt Gov, Tex, 47-49; Gov, Tex, 49-57; deleg, Dem Nat Conv, 36-68. Bus & Prof Pos: Dir, Tex Gulf Inc, Tex Commerce Bank, Houston, Citizens State Bank of Woodville, Global Marine, Inc, Celanese Corp, Tex Good Roads Asn & Houston First Savings Asn; chmn bd, Western Pipe Line, Inc, 57-63 & Austin Nat Bank, currently; chmn adv comt, Export-Import Bank US, 69-73; adv dir, Chem Bank & Trust Co, Galleria Bank, Houston & Peoples Nat Bank of Spring Br; chmn bd regents, Univ Tex Syst, currently. Mem: US CofC; Mason (33 degree); Shrine. Relig: Baptist. Legal Res: 6 Niles Rd Austin TX 78703 Mailing Add: 300 Austin Nat Bank Bldg Austin TX 78701

SHOEMAKER, JOE (R)
Colo State Sen
Mailing Add: 3260 S Monroe Denver CO 80210

SHOEMAKER, MYRL HOWARD (D)
Ohio State Rep
b Chillicothe, Ohio, Apr 14, 13; s Royal Shoemaker & Sadie Mick S; m 1935 to Dorothy Ruth Cook; c Ronald Jerome, Keith Alan, Myrl Howard, Jr, Michael Cook, Kevin Lee, Deborah Lou, Kathy Ann & Brenda Susan. Educ: Bliss Col, 30-32. Polit & Govt Pos: Mem sch bd, Twin Sch Dist, Ohio, 37-59; sch bd clerk, Paint Valley Sch Dist, 58-60; Ohio State Rep, Ross Co, 58- Bus & Prof Pos: Owner, Twin Construction Co, until 66. Mem: Paint Valley Foxhunters; Farmers Union; Farm Bur; YMCA. Relig: Christian Union. Legal Res: Box 595 Bourneville OH 45617 Mailing Add: State Capitol Bldg Columbus OH 43215

SHOEMAKER, ROBERT N (D)
Colo State Rep
Mailing Add: Garden Park Canon City CO 81212

SHOLLENBARGER, JOSEPH HIRAM (JOE) (R)
b Tucumcari, NMex, Dec 11, 39; s Joseph Kenneth Shollenbarger & Helen Goats S; m 1960 to Janice Carol Biles; c Joseph Randall, James Scott & John Keith. Educ: Abilene Christian Col, BS, 61; Tex A&M Univ, 61-62; Phi Delta Psi. Polit & Govt Pos: Chmn, Deaf Smith Co Rep Party, Tex, 68-70 & 73-75. Mem: Am Inst CPA; Tex Soc CPA; Panhandle Chap, Tex Soc CPA; Amarillo Area Estate Planning Coun; Lion. Relig: Church of Christ. Mailing Add: 138 Kingwood Hereford TX 79045

SHOOSHAN, HARRY MANUEL, III (D)
b Wilmington, Del, Nov 7, 45; s Harry Manuel Shooshan Jr & Harriet Gregg S; m 1967 to Beverly Zankowsky; c Christine Noelle & Kimberly Lynn. Educ: Harvard Univ, BA, magna cum laude, 68; Georgetown Univ Law Sch, cand, JD; Hasty Pudding Club; Harvard-Radcliffe Young Dem. Polit & Govt Pos: Admin asst to US Rep Torbert H Macdonald, Mass, 68- Mil Serv: Sgt, Army Res; Nat Defense Ribbon. Publ: The Lawyer in Congress, Fed Bar News, Fall 69; co-auth, Congressional oversight: the 92nd Congress & the Federal Communications Commission, Harvard J Legis, 2/73. Mem: Harvard Alumni Fund; Montgomery Co Young Dem. Mailing Add: 6 Infield Court N Potomac MD 20854

SHOQUIST, MARY LUCILLE (DFL)
First VChairwoman, Third Dist Dem-Farmer-Labor Party, Minn
b Warsaw, Ill, Sept 6, 32; d Otto Christian Kirchherr & Nannie Peyton K; m 1956 to Marc Cheney Shoquist; c Cherie Nanette. Educ: Lindenwood Col, BA; Macalester Col, MEd; Kappa Pi; League Women Voters; Mod Lang Club; Athletic Asn. Polit & Govt Pos: First vchairwoman, Richfield Dem-Farmer-Labor Party, Minn, 66, chairwoman, 67-68; bumper sticker chairwoman, Humphrey Presidential Campaign, 68; first vchairwoman, Third Dist Dem-Farmer-Labor Party, Minn, 70- & Edina Dem-Farmer-Labor Party, 71- Bus & Prof Pos: Artist, St Louis Garment Found, 52-53; exec trainee, Famous-Barr, Inc, St Louis, 53 & Golden Rule, St Paul, 53-56; fashion artist, Thomas Co, Minneapolis, Minn, 56-57. Mem: Minn Artists Asn; Walker Art Ctr; State Coordr Arts Coun; Richfield Dem-Farmer-Labor Party; Edina Sustaining Fund & Jefferson Forum, Minn State Dem-Farmer-Labor Party. Honors & Awards: Numerous prizes in art, juried shows in Omaha & Minneapolis. Relig: Presbyterian. Mailing Add: 6713 Cheyenne Trail Edina MN 55435

SHORE, SAMUEL FRANKLIN (D)
Md State Deleg
b Washington, DC, Dec 3, 35; s George Edward Shore & Marjorie Agnes Beavers S; m 1959 to Josephine Pauline Balistrere; c Samuel Franklin, Jr, Mary Josephine, Mark Edward, Gregory Thomas & Matthew Anthony. Educ: Southeastern Univ, 59; Pa State Univ, 65-67; Labor Studies Inst, Am Univ, presently. Polit & Govt Pos: Mem, Citizens for Louis Goldstein for Comptroller Campaign, 68; Comt on Polit Educ coordr, Hubert Humphrey Campaign, 68; precinct coordr Rockville area, Montgomery Co Dem Cent Comt, Md, 69-, precinct chmn, dist four, precinct eight, 70-; mem, Plowman & Fisherman, 69-70 & 73; Md State Deleg, 71- Bus & Prof Pos: Mem staff, Chesapeake & Potomac Tel Co Md, 55-73, community rep, 73- Mil Serv: Entered as Pvt, Army, 56, released as Pfc, 58, after serv in Fourth Armored Div, NACOM, Frankfurt, Germany, 57-58; Good Conduct Medal. Mem: United Givers Fund (co-chmn, 69, bd dirs, 70-); KofC; First Annual-House-Senate Basketball Game for Cystic Fibrosis (co-chmn, 72-); St Judes Holy Name Soc; Md Asn for Children with Learning Disabilities. Honors & Awards: Outstanding Legislator, Cardinal O'Boyle Gen Assembly, 71 for Indefatigable Defense of Human Life; Outstanding Legislator Deleg, KofC, 73; Cert Achievement, Environ & Human Ecology, 71, Poverty, 71, Pub Employees Labor Rels, 72, Land Use Planning, 72, Nat Legis Conf. Relig: Roman Catholic. Mailing Add: 11230 Troy Rd Rockville MD 20852

SHORES, ARTHUR DAVIS (D)
City Councilman, Birmingham, Ala
b Birmingham, Ala, Sept 25, 04; s Richard Shores & Pauline McGhee S; m 1938 to Theodora Helen Warren; c Helen (Mrs Robert Lee) & Barbara. Educ: Talladega Col, AB, 27; Univ Kans, 34; LaSalle Exten Univ, LLB, 35; Alpha Phi Alpha. Hon Degrees: LLD, Miles Col, 71. Polit & Govt Pos: Mem exec comt, Jefferson Co Dem Party, Ala, 62; deleg, Dem Nat Conv, 68 & 72; city councilman, Birmingham, Ala, 68-; mem, Ala State Dem Exec Comt, 70-; mem charter comn Nat Dem Comt, currently. Bus & Prof Pos: Secy-dir, Brown-Belle Bottling Co, 41-47; secy-treas, Hollins & Shores Realty Co, 43-49; pres, Jones Valley Finance Co, 45-62; vpres & gen counsel, Citizens Fed Savings & Loan Asn, 57-; dir, Am Nat Bank, 64-66; comnr, Birmingham Housing Authority, 66-68. Mem: F&AM (33 degree); Shrine; KofP; Birmingham Press Club; Urban League (pres & chmn bd, Birmingham chap). Honors & Awards: Alpha Medal of Honor, Alpha Phi Alpha, 56; Recipient of awards from Southern Beauty Cong, Inc, 49, Alpha Chi Chap, Omega Psi Phi, 54, Nat Bar Asn, 60, & Cook Co Bar Asn, 65; Russwurm Award, Nat Newspapers Publ Asn, 69. Relig: Congregational. Legal Res: 1021 N Center St Birmingham AL 35204 Mailing Add: PO Box 10622 Birmingham AL 35202

SHORT, BARRY ARNOLD (R)
b St Louis, Mo, Oct 28, 40; s Don E Short & Frances Higgins S; m 1962 to Barbara Jean Vierheller; c Leslie Marlene & Angela Marie. Educ: DePauw Univ, BS, 58-62; Univ Mo Law Sch, JD, 62-65; Phi Delta Phi; Sigma Alpha Epsilon. Polit & Govt Pos: Committeeman, Lincoln Twp, St Louis Co, Mo, 68-72 & Queeny Twp, 72-; chmn, St Louis Co Rep Cent Comt, 69-74; mem, Mo Rep State Comt, 70-72. Bus & Prof Pos: Partner & attorney, King & Short, Clayton, Mo, currently. Mem: St Louis Co, St Louis Metrop, Mo & Am Bar Asns; Am Trial Lawyers Asn; Jaycees. Relig: Congregational. Mailing Add: 336 Turnbury Circle Ballwin MO 63011

SHORT, DON L (R)
b LeMars, Iowa, June 22, 03; s Hugh Connorran Short & Anne Otley Corkery S; m 1931 to Edith E Whittemore; c Anne Whittemore (Mrs Kendall Johnson), Connie (Mrs K Paul McDonald), Arthur & Susan. Educ: Mont State Col, 18-19; Pillsbury Mil Acad, Owatonna, Minn, 21; Univ Minn, 22-26; Phi Kappa Psi. Polit & Govt Pos: Co supvr, Farm Security Admin, 37-38; NDak State Rep, 57; US Rep, NDak, 59-64. Bus & Prof Pos: Wheat farmer; cattle rancher; dir, Mandan Prod Credit Asn, 45-58; chmn, NDak Beef Coun, 46-48; mem, NDak Sanit Livestock Bd, 46-56; pres, Nat Beef Coun, 56-57. Mem: Theodore Roosevelt State Cent Comn; Am Nat Cattlemen's Asn; NDak Stockmans Asn; Medora Grazing Asn. Relig: Episcopal. Mailing Add: Beach ND 58621

SHORT, E L (D)
Tex State Rep
Mailing Add: PO Box 1486 Tahoka TX 79373

SHORT, NANCY SUSAN (D)
Nat Committeeperson, Young Dem Del
b Wilmington, Del, Nov 15, 44; d Carlton Short & Peggy Arthur S; single. Educ: Goldey Beacom Jr Col, Wilmington, Del, 72- 74. Polit & Govt Pos: Secy & alt committeeperson, Young Dem of Del, formerly, nat committeeperson, 73-; Region II secy, Young Dem of Am, 73-; coordr, Dem Telethon, 74; coordr, Nat Women's Polit Caucus, Washington, DC, 74; mem, Coun on Women, 75- Bus & Prof Pos: Secy, Continental Am Life Ins Co, 67- Legal Res: 3005 N Monroe St Wilmington DE 19802 Mailing Add: 115 Burton St Georgetown DE 19947

SHORT, W MARCUS (D)
NC State Rep
b Greensboro, NC, Aug 4, 30; s George A Short & Blanche Futrell S; c Nancy Elizabeth. Educ: Univ NC, BS in bus admin, LLB, 58. Polit & Govt Pos: NC State Rep, 65-72, 74- Mil Serv: Entered as Pvt, Air Force, 50, released as S/Sgt, 53. Mem: Greensboro Moose Lodge; Buena Vista Odd Fellows; YMCA; Sedgefield Country Club; CofC. Relig: Methodist. Legal Res: 4004 Annie Laurie Dr Greensboro NC 27408 Mailing Add: 319 Southeastern Bldg Greensboro NC 27401

SHORTELL, EDWARD (R)
Mass State Rep
b Seymour, Conn, Aug 21, 16; s William Henry Shortell & Ella Marie Ekstrom S; m 1942 to Kathryn E Batten; c Richard L. Educ: Northeastern Univ, 36-39; Alpha Kappa Sigma. Polit & Govt Pos: Mass State Rep, 73- Bus & Prof Pos: Plant supt, Millers Falls Co, 50-60, gen supt, 60-63, gen mgr mfg, 63-68; pres & treas, Greenfield Steel Stamp Corp, 68-72. Mil Serv: Entered as Pvt, Army, 41, released as Capt, 45, after serv in Combat Engrs, European Theatre, 42-45; Presidential Unit Citation. Mem: Greenfield Country Club (dir, 55-); Greenfield Savings Bank (trustee, 68-); Salvation Army (trustee, 58-); YMCA; Industrial Mgt Club Franklin Co (founder & dir, 51-61). Relig: Catholic; Holy Trinity Church. Mailing Add: 48 Green River Rd Greenfield MA 01301

SHORTER, BEN T (D)
Mem, Ga State Dem Exec Comt
b Cuthbert, Ga, July 6, 10, s Joseph Shorter & Addie Bell Jones S; m 1932 to Rachel Mitchell; c Ben T, Jr, Vivian J, Wesley L & Lokey T. Educ: Knoxville Col, 29-30. Polit & Govt Pos: Pres, Randolph Co Voters League, Cuthbert, Ga, 47- & Second Cong Dist Voters League, Albany, 68-; mem, Ga State Dem Exec Comt, currently. Honors & Awards: Citation for Polit Action, Atlanta Chap of Am, 56. Relig: African Methodist Episcopal Church. Mailing Add: 506 S Webster St Cuthbert GA 31740

SHOTT, JOHN CARY (R)
Mem, Rep State Exec Comt, WVa
b Bluefield, WVa, Feb 17, 24; s James Howard Shott & Martha Easley S; m 1946 to Bonnie Reark; c John Headley & Michael Reark. Educ: WVa Univ, BS in Bus Admin, 48; Phi Kappa Psi. Polit & Govt Pos: Mem, Rep State Exec Comt, Tenth Sen Dist, WVa, 57-, chmn, 65-68; alt deleg, Rep Nat Conv, 68; mem, WVa Legis Bldg Comn, 72- Bus & Prof Pos: Salesman, Paper Supply Co, 48-54 & WHIS, 54-55; sales mgr, WHIS-TV, 55-58, sta mgr, 58-63; gen mgr, WHIS-AM-FM-TV, 63-68; vpres & gen mgr, WHIS-AM-FM-TV & WBTW-TV, 68- Mil Serv: Entered as Aviation Cadet, Navy, 43, released as Ens, 45, after serv as Flight Instr. Mem: Broadcast Pioneers; Mercer Co Tuberc & Health Asn; WVa Broadcasters Asn; Concord Col Found (bd dirs); WVa State Indust Adv Comt. Relig: Presbyterian. Mailing Add: 1320 Larchmont Ave Bluefield WV 24701

SHOTTS, RON E (R)
Okla State Rep
b Weatherford, Okla, Feb 11, 46; s Arthur E Shotts & Nell Claunch S; m 1970 to Pamela Cox; c Sundi Susanne. Educ: Okla Univ, BBA, 68, JD, 72; Omicron Delta Kappa; Pe-et; Beta Theta Pi. Polit & Govt Pos: Okla State Rep, 73- Bus & Prof Pos: Attorney, Moore, Okla, 72- Mem: Delta Theta Phi; Lions. Relig: Methodist. Legal Res: 108 SW Ninth Moore OK 73160 Mailing Add: Box 6124 Moore OK 73160

SHOUP, RICHARD G (R)
b Salmon, Idaho, Nov 29, 23; s Richard M Shoup & Rose A Manfull S; m 1947 to Marjorie J Mosley; c Kathy, Douglas & Julie. Educ: Baylor Univ; Univ Mont, BA, 50; Pi Sigma Alpha. Polit & Govt Pos: Alderman, Missoula, Mont, 63-67, mayor, 67-70; US Rep, Mont, 71-74, Rep cand, US House of Rep, Mont, 74. Bus & Prof Pos: With Agr Serv Dept, Mont Flour Mills; owner-operator, Laundry & Dry Cleaning. Mil Serv: Entered as Pvt, Army, 43, released as Sgt, 46, after serv in 65th Inf Div, ETO 45-46; reentered as 2nd Lt, 51, released as 1st Lt, 52 after serv in 7th Armored Div, US. Mem: Lions; Masons; Elks; Moose (state dir); Am Legion. Honors & Awards: Man of Year, Western Mont Broadcasters, 69; Youth Appreciation Week Citation, Optimist Club; Alumni Appreciation Award, Univ of Mont; DeMolay Legion of Merit. Relig: Christian. Legal Res: MT Mailing Add: 1127 Longworth House Off Bldg Washington DC 20515

SHOWALTER, CARL EDWARD (R)
Colo State Rep
b Harrisonburg, Va, Nov 29, 13; s Earl E Showalter & Mary Heatwole S; m 1934 to Ruby Lela Yoder; c Geraldine Lee (Mrs Mellon), Karla Jean (Mrs Romero) & George E. Educ: Goshen Col, 2 years. Polit & Govt Pos: Mayor, Johnston, Colo, 58-70; Colo State Rep, Dist 44, 69-72, Dist 48, 72- Bus & Prof Pos: Farm operator, La Junta, Colo, 35-37; automobile bus, Lamar, 37-41; local mgr, Nat Dehydrating & Milling Co, Johnstown, 41-51; owner & mgr, Colo Alfalfa Milling & Prod Co, Milliken, 51-68; investments, currently. Mem: Aircraft Owners & Pilots Asn; Elks (life mem); Rotary; Weld Co Farm Bur; Colo Cattle Feeders Asn. Relig: United Methodist. Mailing Add: 2552 Highland Rd Greeley CO 80631

SHOWALTER, JOANNE MARIE (DFL)
Secy, Dist 43 Dem-Farmer-Labor Party, Minn
b Stillwater, Minn, June 3, 35; d Thomas Joseph McGonigal & Marie Maher M; m 1959 to John Willis Showalter; c John Joseph & Joseph Leo. Educ: Univ Minn, 53-54. Polit & Govt Pos: Precinct chmn, Ward 2, Precinct 6, Minn, 68-71; secy, Dist 43B Dem-Farmer-Labor Party, 68-70, secy, Dist 43 Dem-Farmer-Labor Party, 70-; mem finance comt & secy, Fourth Dist Dem-Farmer-Labor Alt State Cent Comt, 71-; mem, Parks Task Force, City of St Paul, 72-; secy, steno pool, Minn House Rep, 73. Mem: Dayton's Bluff Community Coun (secy, 68-70). Mailing Add: 1176 E Minnehaha St Paul MN 55106

SHOWALTER, MYRTLE MAY (R)
Chmn, Moffat Co Rep Party, Colo
b Strang, Nebr, Jan 28, 97; d John Thomas Rathbun & Cora Johnson R; m 1917 to Lee C Showalter, wid; c Robert, Donald & Eileen (Mrs Schrader). Educ: Jefferson Co Pub Schs, Nebr, grad; music from pvt teacher, 8 years; Delphian Course, 4 years. Polit & Govt Pos: Hq Secy, Moffat Co Rep Party, Colo, 52, vchmn, 53-75, chmn, 75-; mem various comts in Dist & State Rep Orgn. Mem: Eastern Star (Past Matron, Anita Chap); adult mem, Order of Rainbow for Girls (founder, Craig Assembly); charter mem, Craig Woman's Club (past pres); Rep Woman's Club of Moffat Co. Honors & Awards: Woman of the Year, Daily Press, 67; mgr of Thrift Shop manned by vol workers of Rep Woman's Club. Relig: Congregational. Legal Res: 848 Taylor St Craig CO 81625 Mailing Add: Box 1062 Craig CO 81625

SHOWALTER, THELMA JOHNSON (R)
Chmn, Union Co Rep Party, Pa
b Lewistown, Pa, Sept 2, 08; d John Church Showalter & Susan Ida Johnson S; single. Educ: Bucknell Univ, AB, 29; Pa State Univ, 34; Pi Mu Epsilon; Delta Mu Delta; Pi Beta Phi. Polit & Govt Pos: Admin asst, Commonwealth of Pa, 39-55; nat committeewoman, Young Rep Pa, 40-44; comnr, Union Co, 56-64; pres, Union Co Coun Rep Women, 58-68; chmn, Union Co Rep Party, 74- Bus & Prof Pos: Teacher math, Lewisburg Area Schs, Pa, 29-39; trustee, Bucknell Univ. Publ: Articles, Dept Internal Affairs J, Harrisburg, Pa, 50-55. Mem: Gen Fedn

Women's Clubs; Pa Fedn Women's Clubs (pres); DAR; Union Co Cancer Soc (pres); Union Co Heart Asn (chmn). Honors & Awards: Thelma J Showalter Awards, Bucknell Univ. Relig: Methodist. Mailing Add: 425 Market St Mifflinburg PA 17844

SHOWS, JAMES E LISTON (D)
Miss State Rep
Mailing Add: Box 145 Soso MS 39480

SHRADER, DOUGLAS (D)
b Bowling Green, Ky, Nov 6, 35; s W Wesley Shrader & Agnes Watkins S; m 1959 to Anne Royall; c Elizabeth & Ellen. Educ: Yale Univ, BA, 61, LLB, 64. Polit & Govt Pos: Chmn, Westport Dem Town Comt, Conn, 72-74. Mil Serv: Entered as Pvt, Army, 53, released as 1st Lt, 57, after serv in 11th Airborne Div. Mailing Add: 6 Elwil Dr Westport CT 06880

SHRIVER, GARNER E (R)
US Rep, Kans
b Towanda, Kans, July 6, 12; s Ed Arthur Shriver & Olive M Glass S; m 1941 to Martha Jane Currier; c Kay (Mrs Leroux), David & Linda. Educ: Wichita State Univ, AB, 34; Univ Southern Calif, Los Angeles, Grad Sch, 36; Washburn Law Sch, JD, 40; Phi Alpha Delta; Kappa Delta Pi; Phi Delta Theta. Hon Degrees: Dr Pub Serv, Friends Univ, 70. Polit & Govt Pos: Kans State Rep, 47-51; Kans State Sen, 53-60; US Rep, Kans, 61- Bus & Prof Pos: Legal counsel, Wichita Bd of Educ, 51-60; trustee, Roland P Murdock Art Collection, 57- Mil Serv: Entered as A/S, Navy, released as Lt(sg), 46, after serv in Pac Theater. Mem: VFW; Am Legion; Mason; Scottish Rite (33 degree); Kiwanis. Honors & Awards: Alumni Achievement Award, Univ Wichita, 61; Distinguished Alumni Serv Award, Washburn Univ, Topeka, 67. Relig: Methodist. Legal Res: 5051 East Lincoln Wichita KS 67218 Mailing Add: 2209 Rayburn House Off Bldg Washington DC 20515

SHRIVER, ROBERT SARGENT, JR (D)
b Westminster, Md, Nov 9, 15; s Robert Sargent Shriver & Hilda S; m 1953 to Eunice Mary Kennedy; c Robert Sargent, III, Maria Owings, Timothy Perry, Mark Kennedy & Anthony Paul Kennedy. Educ: Yale Univ, BA cum laude, 38, LLB, 41; Delta Kappa Epsilon. Hon Degrees: LLD, DCL, HHD, LHD, from various Cols & Univs. Polit & Govt Pos: Pres, Chicago Bd Educ, 55-60; dir, Peace Corps, 61-66; dir, Off Econ Opportunity, 64-68; spec asst to the President, 64-68; US Ambassador to France, 68-70; chmn, Cong Leadership for the Future, 70; Dem cand, Vice-President of US, 72. Bus & Prof Pos: With Winthrop, Stimson, Putnam & Roberts, 40-41; assoc ed, Newsweek, 45-46; assoc, Joseph P Kennedy Enterprises, 46-48; asst gen mgr, Merchandise Mart, Chicago, 48-60; pres, Cath Interracial Coun, Chicago, 55-60; exec dir, Joseph P Kennedy, Jr Found. Mil Serv: Lt Comdr, Naval Res, 40-45. Publ: Point of the lance, 64. Mem: Exec Club, Chicago; Onwentsia Club, Lake Forest, Ill; Yale Club, New York; Univ Club, DC; Chevy Chase Club. Honors & Awards: Yale Medal, 47; Chicago Medal Merit, 57; James J Hoey Award, Cath Interracial NY, 58; Lay Churchman of the Year, Relig Heritage Am, 63; Golden Heart Pres Award, Philippines, 64. Relig: Catholic. Legal Res: Timberlawn Edson Lane Rockville MD 20852 Mailing Add: Suite 1000 600 New Hampshire Ave NW Washington DC 20037

SHRONTZ, FRANK ANDERSON (R)
Asst Secy of the Air Force Installations & Logistics
b Boise, Idaho, Dec 14, 31; s Howard Thurlyn Shrontz & Florence Elizabeth Anderson S; m 1954 to Harriet Ann Houghton; c Craig Howard, Richard Whitaker & David Anderson. Educ: George Washington Univ Law Sch, summer 53; Univ Idaho, LLB, 54; Harvard Bus Sch, MBA, 58; Stanford Bus Sch, 70; Phi Eta Sigma; Blue Key; Phi Alpha Delta; Beta Theta Pi. Polit & Govt Pos: Asst Secy of the Air Force Installations & Logistics, 73- Bus & Prof Pos: Asst contracts coordr, The Boeing Co, Seattle, Wash, 58-65, asst dir contract admin, 65-67, asst to vpres commercial airplane group, 67-69, asst dir new airplane prog, 69-70 & dir commercial sales opers, 70-73. Mil Serv: Entered as 2nd Lt, Army, 54, released as 1st Lt, 56. Mem: Army-Navy Country Club. Mailing Add: 1448 Woodacre Dr McLean VA 22101

SHUEE, CHARLES EDWARD (D)
Chmn, Seventh Cong Dist Dem Party, Ind
b Bainbridge, Ind, Sept 23, 16; s Austin Shuee & Stella Everesole S; m 1933 to Rosalie Eileen Shoaf; c Robert Keith, Claude Austin & Donald Wayne (deceased). Polit & Govt Pos: Dem precinct committeeman, Putnam Co, Ind, 39-57; chmn, Putnam Co Dem Party, 57-; coordr, Seventh Cong Dist Dem Party, 65-66, chmn, 68-; mem, Exec Comt to the Gov, 68; deleg, Dem Nat Conv, 68; exec mem, Dem State Orgn, 70- Bus & Prof Pos: Dist mgr, Massey Ferguson Corp, 12 years; real estate broker, 62-; ins agent, 64- Mem: Mason; Scottish Rite; Shrine; Elks; Moose; Catract Yacht Club (commodore, 70-71). Relig: Protestant. Mailing Add: RR 1 Greencastle IN 46135

SHULL, EDD L (R)
Mem Finance Comt, Nat Rep Party
b Summit Point, WVa, Aug 20, 38; s Thomas Stephen Shull & Nellie May Chapman S; m 1959 to Anna Mae Shoup; c Angela Kristi, Suzanne Ondrea Lee & Thomas Frazier. Educ: Berea Col, 56-57; Univ Va, exten prog, 60-64; New York Univ, 64; Alumni Asn of Berea Col. Polit & Govt Pos: Campaign worker, John F Kennedy for Pres, 60, Agnew for Gov, 66 & Nixon for Pres, 68; campaign field coordr, Holton for Gov, 69; exec dir, Rep Party Va, 70-73; adult adv, White House Conf on Children & Youth, Off Econ Opportunity, currently; alt deleg, Rep Nat Conv, 72; mem, Comt to Reelect Nixon, 72-73; mem finance comt, Nat Rep Party, 74- Bus & Prof Pos: Teacher, Jr High Sch, Ky, 60-61; admin asst, Melpar Inc, Falls Church, Va, 61-64; exec dir, Boys's Clubs of Am, Washington, DC, 64-; asst to pres, Guffne Imports Ltd, currently. Publ: Position papers on special educ & prison reform; auth of articles on disadvantaged youth in newspapers & Boys' Club of Am J, 64-67. Mem: Qual Control Engrs Asn; Boy's Clubs Prof Asn; TD Club of Washington, DC; Lions; Jaycees. Honors & Awards: Man of Year, Jaycees. Relig: Christian. Mailing Add: 7 W Rosemont Ave Alexandria VA 22314

SHULL, LEON (D)
Nat Dir, Am for Dem Action
b Philadelphia, Pa, Nov 8, 13; s Samuel Shull & Yetta S; m 1938 to Anne Wollod; c Jane Ellen & Susan Deborah. Polit & Govt Pos: Dir several polit campaign comts in Pa, 51-63; mem staff, Am for Dem Action, 51-63, nat dir, 64- Bus & Prof Pos: Owner, Logan Furniture Co; dir, Jewish Labor Comt. Mil Serv: Army, 42-46. Relig: Jewish. Legal Res: 6417 Western Ave NW Washington DC 20015 Mailing Add: 1424 16th St NW Washington DC 20036

SHULTZ, GEORGE PRATT
b New York, NY, Dec 13, 20; s Birl E Shultz & Margaret Pratt S; m 1946 to Helena Marie O'Brien; c Margaret, Kathleen, Peter, Barbara & Alex. Educ: Princeton, Univ, BA, 42; Mass Inst Technol, PhD in Indust Econ, 49. Hon Degrees: LLD, Notre Dame Univ, 69 & Univ Pa, 73; ScD, Univ Rochester, 73. Polit & Govt Pos: Sr staff economist, President's Coun of Econ Adv, 55-56; consult to Off of the Secy, Dept of Labor, 59-60; mem, steering comt, Study of Collective Bargaining in the Basic Steel Indust, 60; dir, Pub Interest in Nat Labor Policy, 61; consult, President's Adv Comt on Labor-Mgt Policy, 61-62; co-chmn, Automation Fund Comt, 62-68; mem exec bd, Indust Rels Research Asn, 63-66; mem, Gov Comt on Job Vacancies, Ill, 63-64; mem, research adv bd, Comt for Econ Develop, 65-67; Secy of Labor, 69-70; dir, Off Mgt & Budget, 70-72; Secy of Treas, 72-74; Asst to the President, 72-74; chmn, Coun Econ Policy, 72-; chmn, East West Trade Policy Comt, 73-; US Gov, Int Monetary Fund, Int Bank Reconstruction & Develop, Inter-Am Develop Bank, & Asian Develop Bank, 72- Bus & Prof Pos: Acting dir, Indust Rels Secy, Dept of Econ, Mass Inst of Technol, 54-55, assoc prof, 55-57; prof indust rels, Grad Sch Bus, Univ Chicago, 57-68, dean, Grad Sch Bus, 62-68. Mil Serv: Entered Marine Corps, 42, released as Maj, 45. Publ: Co-auth, Labor problems: cases & readings, McGraw-Hill, 53, Management organization & the computer, Free press, 60 & Strategies for the displaced worker, Harper 66. Mem: Dept of Econ, Mass Inst Technol, (vis comt, 66-); Gen Am Transportation Corp, (bd dirs, 66-69); Dept Econ, Princeton Univ, (mem adv coun, 71-); Indust Rels Research Asn (pres, 68); Nat Acad Arbitrators. Mailing Add: 2734 Fort Scott Dr Arlington VA 22202

SHUMAKE, GLYNN (D)
Miss State Rep
Mailing Add: 720 College St Columbus MS 39701

SHUMAN, HAROLD EUGENE (R)
b Carey, Ohio, Aug 15, 22; s Carlton C Shuman & Hazel Long S; m 1957 to Donna Marcile Lea; c David E & Barbara V. Educ: Findlay Col, 1 year. Polit & Govt Pos: Co Comnr, Wyandot Co, Ohio, 57-65; chmn, Wyandot Co Rep Exec & Cent Comt, formerly. Mil Serv: Entered as Pvt, Army, 46, released as Pfc, 47, after serv in Signal Corps. Mem: Mason; Odd Fellows. Relig: United Methodist. Mailing Add: 527 N Warpole St Upper Sandusky OH 43351

SHUMAN, HOWARD E (D)
b Atwood, Ill, Feb 23, 24; s Frank Hamilton Shuman & Doris King S; m 1953 to Betty Ellen Hoigard; c Ellen, Scott Howard & Barbara Ann. Educ: Univ Ill, BA, 46 & MA, 48; Univ Mich, BBA, 49; Harvard Bus Sch, 44; Oxford Univ, Eng, LittB, 52. Polit & Govt Pos: Legis asst to US Sen Paul H Douglas, Ill, 55-61 & admin asst, 61-67; exec dir, Nat Comn on Urban Probs, Washington, DC, 67-68; admin asst to US Sen William Proxmire, Wis, 69- Bus & Prof Pos: Instr econ, Univ Ill, 53-54. Mil Serv: Entered as A/S, Navy, 43, released as Lt(jg), 46, after serv in Naval Ammunition Depot, Oahu, Pac Theatre, 45-46; Am & Pac Theatre Ribbons; Good Conduct Medal; World War II Victory Medal. Publ: Civil rights & the rules of the Senate, Am Polit Sci Asn Rev, 1/58; The large poor family, a Housing Gap, (with Walter Rybeck & Walter Smart), Nat Comn on Urban Probs Research Report, Number 5, 68; Behind the scenes & under the rug, Washington Monthly, 7/69. Mem: Oxford Union Soc (pres); Potomac Valley AAV Diving Comt (chmn). Relig: Protestant. Legal Res: Champaign IL Mailing Add: 2433 N Kenmore St Arlington VA 22207

SHUMAN, PAMELA SUE (D)
WVa State Deleg
Mailing Add: State Capitol Charleston WV 25305

SHUMAN, WILLIAM O (D)
Pa State Rep
b Antrim Twp, Pa, July 23, 21; s Grover C Shuman & Iva Adele Graham S. Educ: Exten courses at several col. Polit & Govt Pos: Past pres, Greencastle-Antrim Dem Club, Pa; co chmn, dinners, registrn drives, formerly; dep chief, Franklin Co Comnrs, 57; treas, Franklin Co Dem Party, 58-61; Pa State Rep, 64-, chmn, Joint Vet Coun, dep comdr, Adams, Franklin & York Co Comts, mem, Nat Counter Subversive Activities Comt & Mason DiSon Coun, Pa State House of Rep. Bus & Prof Pos: Asst ed, bus mgr, weekly newspaper. Mil Serv: Army, World War II, serv as Sgt, 83rd Div Artil; Bronze Star. Mem: VFW (sr vcomdr, post chaplain & state chaplain); Am Legion (past chaplain); DAV; 83rd Inf Div Asn (nat chaplain); Am Red Cross (chmn). Mailing Add: 162 E Madison St Greencastle PA 17225

SHUNN, MAXINE FAYE (D)
Chmn, Cloud Co Dem Orgn, Kans
b Clyde, Kans, Aug 20, 17; d Charles Leroy Hose & Carrie Lewellen H; m 1938 to Herman Joyce Shunn; c Charlene (Mrs Garzillo) & Marvin. Educ: Concordia Pub Schs, grad. Polit & Govt Pos: Vchmn, Cloud Co, Women's Dem Club, Kans, 61-65; Dem committeewoman, Ward 3, Cloud Co, 61-; treas, Cloud Co, 61-65 & 69-, dep treas, 65-69; vchmn, Cloud Co Dem Orgn, 65-74, chmn, 74- Mem: Concordia Bus & Prof Women of Am (off holder, 61-); Concordia Grade Sch PTA (pres). Relig: Christian Church. Legal Res: 1156 E Ninth St Concordia KS 66901 Mailing Add: Box 164 Concordia KS 66901

SHUPNIK, FRED JOSEPH (D)
Pa State Rep
b Swoyersville, Pa, Nov 18, 16; s Joseph Shupnik & Helen Lostrick S; m 1946 to Margaret Hutsko; c Margaret Ann & Susan. Educ: Scranton Univ, BA, 40; NY Univ, MA, 42. Polit & Govt Pos: Pa State Rep, 59- Mil Serv: Entered as Seaman, Navy, 43, released as Lt(jg), 46, after serv in Navy Minesweeper, Pac, 44-46. Mem: Pa State Educ Asn; Am Legion; Kiwanis; VFW; KofC. Relig: Catholic. Mailing Add: 550 Charles St Luzerne PA 18709

SHUSTER, E G (BUD) (R)
US Rep, Pa
b Glassport, Pa, Jan 23, 32; m 1955 to Patricia Rommell; c Peg, Bill, Deb, Bob & Gia. Educ: Univ Pittsburgh, BS, 54; Duquesne Univ, MBA, 60; Am Univ, PhD, 67; Phi Beta Kappa. Polit & Govt Pos: US Rep, Ninth Dist, Pa, 73- Bus & Prof Pos: Former bus exec. Mil Serv: Inf, Army. Mem: Univ Pittsburgh (trustee); YMCA; Pa Farmers Asn. Legal Res: PA Mailing Add: 1116 Longworth House Off Bldg Washington DC 20515

SHUTE, MELVIN ARTHUR (R)
Maine State Rep
b Stockton Springs, Maine, Mar 5, 36; s Owen Silas Shute & Netina Pinkham S; m 1955 to Janice Payson; c Trent Arthur & Darren James. Educ: Stockton Springs Cent Sch, grad, 53; continuing educ div, Univ Maine, 63-64. Polit & Govt Pos: Selectman, Stockton Springs,

Maine, 68-; Maine State Rep, 71- Bus & Prof Pos: Stationary engr, Northern Chem Inc, 55-65 & W R Grace Co, 66-67; millwright, St Regis Paper Co, 67- Mem: Pownal Masonic Lodge (past master); Maine Masonic Grand Lodge (past grand persuviant & past dist dep grand master); Int Asn Machinist Lodge 1821 (vpres); dir, Explorer Scouts, Stockton Springs; Nat Rifleman Asn. Relig: Protestant. Mailing Add: School St Stockton Springs ME 04981

SHUTTEE, ANNE KATHERINE (D)
VChairwoman Youth Adv Coun, Tex State Dem Exec Comt
b Austin, Tex, Sept 3, 55; d Walter Richard Shuttee & Lois Elaine Hayes S; single. Educ: Trinity Univ, 72-75; Alpha Lambda Delta; Alpha Chi; Mortar Bd. Polit & Govt Pos: Vchairwoman youth adv coun, Tex State Dem Exec Comt, 74- Mem: Tex Civil Liberties Union; Bexar Co Women's Polit Caucus, Tex; Trinity Univ Student Asn (pres, Student Senate, 75-76). Honors & Awards: Outstanding Sophomore Woman, Trinity Univ Chap, Mortar Bd. Legal Res: 2513 Stadium Ft Worth TX 76109 Mailing Add: 715 Stadium Box 1646 San Antonio TX 78284

SIBAL, ABNER WOODRUFF (R)
b New York, NY, Apr 11, 21; s Charles L Sibal & Elizabeth Buckett S; m 1944 to Mary Ellen Igou; c Susan Wells & John Woodruff. Educ: Wesleyan Univ, AB, 43; St John's Univ, LLB, 49; Psi Upsilon. Polit & Govt Pos: Conn State Sen, 57-61, minority leader, Conn State Senate, 59-61; US Rep, Conn, 61-65. Bus & Prof Pos: Partner, Gadsby & Hannah, Washington, DC, 65- Mil Serv: Entered as Pvt, Army, 43, released as 1st Lt, 46, after serv in ETO & Asiatic Pac, 44-46. Relig: Congregational. Mailing Add: 1700 Pennsylvania Ave Washington DC 20006

SICILIANO, MARION ELIZABETH (R)
Committeewoman, NY State Rep Orgn
b New York, NY, Feb 2, 20; d Edward P Eaton & Clara Collins E; m 1940 to Carmin T Siciliano; c Sherry (Mrs John Cole, Jr) & Ronald; one grandson. Educ: Syracuse Univ, 1 year; Hunter Col, 1 year. Polit & Govt Pos: Committeewoman, 26th Elec Dist, Town of Greenburgh, Westchester Co, NY, 15 years; coordr, Town of Greenburgh Rep Elec, past 10 years; founder & past pres, Elmsford Women's Rep Club; founder, Asn of Rep Clubs, Town of Greenburgh; chmn, Housewives for Rockefeller, Westchester Co, 66; rep, NY State Lottery, 67-; chmn, Nixon-Agnew Campaign Comt, Town of Greenburgh, 68; alt deleg, Rep Nat Conv, 68; chmn, Village of Elmsford Rep Orgn, NY, currently; vchmn, Town of Greenburgh Rep Orgn, currently; committeewoman, NY State Rep Orgn, currently. Bus & Prof Pos: Clerk, Union Free Sch Dist 9, Town of Greenburgh; asst mgr personnel, Alexander's Dept Stores, White Plains. Mem: United Fund & State Agencies, Westchester Co (chmn); Bus & Prof Women's Clubs; League Women Voters; Phelps Mem Hosp Asn. Honors & Awards: Tendered Rep Testimonial Dinner, 69. Relig: Catholic. Mailing Add: 7 Locust St Elmsford NY 10523

SICILIANO, ROCCO C (R)
b Salt Lake City, Utah, Mar 4, 22; s Joseph Vincent Siciliano & Mary Arnone S; m 1947 to Marion Leonore Stiebel; c Loretta, Albert Vincent, Fred Rocco, John Carmine & Maria. Educ: Univ Utah, BA, 44; Georgetown Univ, LLB, 48. Polit & Govt Pos: Legal asst, Nat Labor Rels Bd, 48-50; Asst Secy, Dept of Labor, 53-57; spec asst to President for personnel mgt, 57-59; Under Secy, Dept of Com, 69-71; mem, Fed Pay Bd, 71-73. Bus & Prof Pos: Legal adv & exec, Procon Inc, Universal Oil Prod, Des Plaines & Chicago, Ill, 50-53; partner, Wilkinson, Cragun & Barker, Washington, DC, 59-69; pres, Pac Maritime Asn, San Francisco, Calif, 65-69; pres, chief exec officer & dir, TI Corp, Los Angeles, 71- Mil Serv: Entered Army, 43, released as 1st Lt, 46, after serv as Inf Platoon Leader, Tenth Mt Div in Italy & Personnel Staff Officers, Hq, US Forces, Austria; Bronze Star for Valor; Combat Infantryman's Badge; awarded Spec Commendation Ribbon by Gen Mark Clark, 45-46. Mem: Fed & Am Bar Asns; Univ Utah (nat adv coun); Fed Women's Award (trustee); John Fitzgerald Kennedy Sch Govt, Harvard Univ (vis comt). Relig: Roman Catholic. Legal Res: 612 N Rodeo Dr Beverly Hills CA 90210 Mailing Add: 433 S Spring St Los Angeles CA 90051

SICKLES, CARLTON R (D)
b Hamden, Conn, June 15, 21; m to Simone Shornick; c one. Educ: Georgetown Col of Arts & Sci, BSS, cum laude, 43; Georgetown Law Sch, JD, 48. Polit & Govt Pos: Md State Deleg, 55-62; US Rep, Md, 62-66; deleg, Dem Nat Conv, 64 & 68; comnr, Wash Suburban Transit Comn, 69-73; vchmn, Washington Metrop Area Transit Auth, 69-73, bd mem, 72-; comnr, Md State Planning Comn, 69- Bus & Prof Pos: Lawyer, 49; off, Carday Assocs, Inc; pres-elect, Nat Found of Health, Welfare & Pension Plans, Inc, 73- Mil Serv: Army, Inf, 43-46, serv in US, India, China; Korean War, 51-52, Air Force, Off of Spec Invests. Mem: Am, DC, Prince Georges, & Md Bar Asns. Legal Res: 7111 Kempton Rd Lanham MD 20801 Mailing Add: 1003 K St NW Washington DC 20001

SICULA, PAUL EDWARD (D)
Wis State Rep
b Milwaukee, Wis, Jan 31, 39; s Harry Sidney Sicula & Lillian Rosenthal S; m 1963 to Marna Jane Koshakow; c Howard Steven & Michelle Lee. Educ: Univ Wis, BS, 62, Law Sch, LLB, 64; Pi Lambda Phi; Phi Delta Phi; res ed, Wis Law Rev. Polit & Govt Pos: Wis State Rep, Fifth Dist, 67- Bus & Prof Pos: Attorney, Atinsky, Kahn & Sicula, 64- Mil Serv: Entered as Pvt E-1, Army, 59, released as Specialist, E-5, 65; Army Res, 5 years. Publ: Rule of early vesting, Wis Law Rev, 5/63. Mem: B'nai B'rith Century Lodge; YMCA Bus Mens Club; Guten Post, Jewish War Veterans; Anshe Sfard Congregation; Old Time Ballplayers Asn. Relig: Jewish. Mailing Add: 3845 N 56th St Milwaukee WI 53216

SIDD, ALLAN (D)
Treas, Mass Dem State Comt
b Boston, Mass, Aug 14, 23; s David Sidlosky & Sara Kerrch S; m 1947 to Shirley Liberman; c Diane. Educ: Boston Univ, 40-42. Polit & Govt Pos: Dem State Committeeman, Norfolk-Suffolk Dist, Mass, 64-; alt deleg, Dem Nat Conv, 68; treas, Mass Dem State Comt, 68-; mem, Electoral Col, 72; treas, Brookline, Mass, 73- Mil Serv: Entered as Pvt, Air Force, 43, released as Tech Fifth Grade, 45, after serv in 12th Air Force, ETO. Mem: Municipal Finance Officers Am; Mass Collectors & Treas Asn (mem legis comt). Relig: Agnostic. Mailing Add: 148 Mason Terr Brookline MA 02146

SIDES, JULIAN EARL, JR (R)
Chmn, Tunica Co Rep Exec Comt, Miss
b Dundee, Miss, Aug 7 25; s Julian Earl Sides & Kathryn Willingham S; m 1946 to Mary Jane Williams; c Thomas Earl, Mary K & Julianne. Educ: Ga Inst of Tech. Polit & Govt Pos: Chmn, Tunica Co Rep Exec Comt, Miss, 60-; mem, Miss State Rep Exec Comt, 68- Mil Serv: Entered as A/S, Navy, 43, released as Lt(jg), 46. Mem: Rotary; Farm Bur. Relig: Presbyterian. Mailing Add: Box 37 Dundee MS 38626

SIDI, JACQUES ALBERT (R)
Wyo State Rep
b Marseille, France, Oct 29, 28; s Albert Sidi & Irene Smadja S; m 1955 to Bernadette Mary Weisenberger; c Veronica & Michael. Educ: Academie de Grenoble, France, BA, 47; Northwestern Univ, MA, 51. Polit & Govt Pos: Mem-at-lg, Natrona Co Rep Exec Comt, Wyo, 68-69; Wyo State Rep, 69- Bus & Prof Pos: Teacher, Cherry Lawn Sch, Darien Conn, 47-50; teacher, eighth grade, US Hist, Morgan Jr High Sch, Casper, Wyo, 55- Mil Serv: Entered as Pvt, Air Force, 51, released as S/Sgt, 55, after serv in Ground Observer Corps, Wyo, Air Force Post Off Serv, Alaska & Off Spec Invest, France & French Morocco, 51-55. Mem: Wyo Taxpayers Asn; Casper Country Club. Mailing Add: 433 W 15th Casper WY 82601

SIDWELL, GEORGE C (R)
b Loveland, Ohio, July 19, 07; s Edwin H Sidwell & Martha Louise Bonnell S; m 1937 to Doris Marie Lake; c Judith Ann (Mrs George Anderson) & Edwin S. Educ: Univ Cincinnati, Eve Col, 2 years. Polit & Govt Pos: Rep committeeman, Milford Village Precinct B, Ohio, 53-; chmn, Clermont Co Rep Exec Comt, 59-65; investr, Pub Utilities Comn of Ohio, 64-; chmn, Clermont Co Rep Cent Comt, 66-71 & 73-75. Bus & Prof Pos: Customer contact & term mgr, Sewell Motor Express, 46-51; owner & operator, Sidwell Furnace Co, 41-49; salesman, William F Smysor Co, 49-51; mfg eng & qual control auditor, Gen Elec Co, 51-63. Mem: F&AM; Soc of Am Magicians; RAM; Scottish Rite. Relig: Methodist. Mailing Add: 645 Wallace Ave Milford OH 45150

SIEBEN, HARRY A, JR (DFL)
Minn State Rep
b Hastings, Minn, Nov 24, 43; s Harry A Sieben & Mary Luger S; m 1971 to Wanda Kay Alphin. Educ: Winona State Col, BA, 65; Univ Minn Law Sch, JD, 68; Sigma Tau Gamma. Polit & Govt Pos: Minn State Rep, 71- Bus & Prof Pos: Attorney, Mott, Grase, Von Holtam & Sieben, Minneapolis, Minn, 69- Mil Serv: Entered as Pvt, Army, 68, released as Pfc, 69, after serv in Army Security Agency, Ft Devens, Mass, 68-69; 1st Lt, Army Res. Mem: Minn, Hennepin Co & Am Bar Asns; Am Trial Lawyers Asn; Am Legion. Relig: Catholic. Mailing Add: 1311 W 17th St Hastings MN 55033

SIEBEN, MICHAEL (D)
Minn State Rep
Mailing Add: 1652 Cedar Lane Newport MN 55055

SIEFERT, JOHN (D)
b Racine, Wis, Apr 14, 49; s Robert Siefert & Ann Dugas S; single. Educ: Univ Chicago, grad, 71; Univ Wis Law Sch, Madison, 71-; Zeta Beta Tau. Polit & Govt Pos: Mem exec bd, of Nat Supvry Bd of Youth for Nixon, 68; dem cand for Wis State Assembly, 72; deleg, Dem Nat Conv, 72; local chmn, Common Cause, currently. Bus & Prof Pos: Investigative reporter, Chicago Today, 67-71. Relig: Catholic. Mailing Add: 10438 Kraut Rd Franksville WI 53126

SIEFKIN, RANDY RICHARDSON (R)
Chmn, Stanislaus Co Rep Party, Calif
b Glendale, Calif, Apr 25, 42; s Ernest Roosevelt Siefkin & Violet May Richardson S; m 1965 to Susan Jane Deeble; c Nelson & Kristen. Educ: Univ Calif, Santa Barbara, BA, 65; Rutgers Univ, MA, 66. Polit & Govt Pos: Chmn, Stanislaus Co Rep Party, Calif, 75- Bus & Prof Pos: Instr govt, Coalinga Col, 67-70; instr govt, Modesto Jr Col, 70- Honors & Awards: Fel, Eagleton Inst Polit. Relig: Unitarian. Mailing Add: 1225 Brady Ave Modesto CA 95350

SIEGEL, DOLPH (R)
Mem, Camden Co Rep Comt, NJ
b Brooklyn, NY, Sept 7, 12; s Harry Siegel & Sara Kaplan S; m 1946 to Kathryn Waldmayer; c Pamela Joyce (Mrs James E Brown) & Salliann (Mrs Frank Tjarks). Educ: Closter High Sch, 4 years. Polit & Govt Pos: Mem, Bd of Adjustment, Haddon Twp, NJ, 58-72; chmn, Housing Auth, Haddon Twp, 64-67, exec dir housing auth, 67-; mem, Camden Co Rep Comt, 64-, vchmn, 68-74; purchasing agent & state & fed funding agent, Camden Co, 70- Bus & Prof Pos: Mgr, Huyler's, Restaurant & Confectionery, Atlantic City, NJ, summers 36-51 & sales mgr, Huyler's Inc, New York, 40-51; sales mgr, Rosemarie de Paris, NYC, 51-60, co-owner, 60-69; vpres & gen mgr, Carol Anne Gift Shop, Pennsauken, NJ, 64-68; pres & prin stock holder, Dustar, Inc, Haddonfield, NJ, 67-73 & Cork 'N Bottle, 73- Mem: Collingswood-Haddon Twp Kiwanis. Relig: Jewish. Mailing Add: 220 Buckner Ave Haddonfield NJ 08033

SIEGLER, ALFRED CHARLES (D)
Calif State Assemblyman
b San Jose, Calif, Sept 19, 11; s Charles Siegler & Marie Agnes Messina S; m 1938 to Loyola Ann Wolf, wid 1972; c James, Dr Richard & Karen (Mrs James Bellis); five grandchildren. Educ: San Jose State Univ, AB, 34; Univ Calif, Berkeley, MA, 50. Polit & Govt Pos: Co supvr, Solano Co, Calif, currently; Mem, North Bay Comprehensive Health Planning & Co Ment Health Adv Bd Dirs, Bay Area Coun Water Pollution Task Force; mem & past chmn coordr comt, Office Criminal Justice Planning; mem, Yolo-Solano Air Pollution Bd; pres, Vallejo Munic Sanit & Flood Control Dist; Calif State Assemblyman, Eighth Assembly Dist, 74-, vchmn labor rels comt & mem educ, housing & community develop comts, Calif State Assembly, currently. Bus & Prof Pos: Educator, Napa & Sonoma Co Schs, 35 years. Mem: Sons & Daughters of Italy; Native Sons of the Golden West; KofC (3 & 4 degrees); Gtr Vallejo Kiwanis (past pres). Honors & Awards: Life Membership, Nat & State Cong of Parents & Teachers; North Bay Community Serv Award; Civic Unity's Man of Year Award. Relig: Catholic. Mailing Add: 314 Wallace Ave Vallejo CA 94590

SIEGRIST, ROBERT RYAN (R)
b Lansing, Mich, Apr 14, 19; s William E Siegrist (deceased) & Clara Mary Ryan S (deceased); m 1942 to Mary Jean Wright; c Anne Marie, Mark William, Mary Roberta & Linda Michelle. Educ: Mich State Univ, class of 40. Polit & Govt Pos: Rep nominee, US House Rep, Ninth Dist, Ill, 52; chmn publicity & host comt, Rep Nat Conv, 52; chmn publicity Inaugural Ball, 69; asst press-pub rels, US Rep William H Harsha, Ohio, 69; admin asst to US Rep Laurence G Williams, Pa, 69-71; admin asst to US Rep B B Blackburn, 74; writer-researcher, Veteran's Affairs Comt, US House Rep, 75- Bus & Prof Pos: Radio News commentator & journalist, WGN, Chicago & Mutual Broadcasting Syst, Hearst Corp, 46-56; chief ed writer, Milwaukee Sentinel; commentator, WISN; owner, Siegrist Enterprises, 56-66; contract commentator, Mutual Broadcasting Syst, Washington, DC, 66-68; pub rels &

broadcasting, Orlando, Fla, 71-74. Mil Serv: Entered as Info Specialist, Army, 42, released as T/4, 46, after serv in ASF, Sixth Serv Command, Chicago. Honors & Awards: Eight Freedoms Found Awards; Christopher Award; Celtic Cross & Wis Award, Cath War Vet; Four Vigilant Patriot Awards; DAR Award. Relig: Roman Catholic. Mailing Add: 331 House Off Bldg Annex Washington DC 20515

SIEH, HAROLD (R)
SDak State Rep
Mailing Add: Herrick SD 57538

SIELOFF, RONALD BRUCE (R)
Minn State Rep
b Thief River Falls, Minn, May 30, 44; s Marvin W Sieloff & Betty Knutson S; m 1970 to Mary Margaret Sorenson; c Ryan T & Melissa L. Educ: Univ Minn, 63-66; William Mitchell Col Law, BSL, 68; JD cum laude, 70; Phi Alpha Delta. Polit & Govt Pos: Research analyst, Minn House Rep, 68; research & investigator, Minn Attorney Generals Off, 69-; Minn State Rep, 75- Bus & Prof Pos: Tax mgr, Fiduciary Counseling Inc, St Paul, Minn, 70-74; practicing attorney, St Paul, 74- Mem: Minn & Am Bar Asns; William Mitchell Alumni Asn (secy, 74-). Relig: Lutheran. Mailing Add: 1934 Rome Ave St Paul MN 55116

SIEMENS, GEORGE R (D)
Ky State Rep
b 1926. Polit & Govt Pos: Mem, Shively Dem Club, Ky; councilman, Shively; dir civil defense, Shively; Ky State Rep, currently; chmn, Jefferson Co Dem Party, 73- Bus & Prof Pos: Plumbing & heating contractor. Mil Serv: Navy, World War II. Mem: KofC; Am Legion; C Dist Club; 40th Dist Club. Relig: Catholic. Legal Res: Shively KY 40216 Mailing Add: 1701 Marlow Rd Louisville KY 40216

SIEMINSKI, ALFRED D (D)
b Jersey City, NJ, Aug 23, 11; s William Sieminski & Helen Fiston S; m 1947 to Countess Marie Felice Czarkowska-Golejewska; c step daughters, Christine Elizabeth (Mrs John G Hunt) & Isabella (Mrs James H Noyes). Educ: Princeton Univ, BA in polit sci, 34; Harvard Law Sch, 38; Tiger Inn Club, Princeton; Lincoln's Inn & Marshall Club, Harvard. Polit & Govt Pos: Mem staff, US Mil Govt Austria, 45-46; US Rep, 51-59; alt deleg, Dem Nat Conv, 52; mem staff, Cent Off Libr, Vet Admin, DC, 62-73; retired. Bus & Prof Pos: Controller & vpres, Brunswick Laundry, 37-51; admin vpres, Hun Sch, Princeton, 59. Mil Serv: Entered as Pvt, Army, 42, released as Lt Col, Army Res, 63; Bronze Star; ETO Ribbon; Legion of Merit; Korean Serv Ribbon with 3 Battle Stars; Italian Campaign Ribbon with Three Battle Stars; life mem, 7th Regt, NY Nat Guard. Mem: Kiwanis; Rotary; St Agnes Episcopal Sch PTA, Alexandria, Va, F St Club, Princeton Club; McLean Horse Show Asn, Va, (dir). Honors & Awards: Princeton 150 Lb Crew, Royal Henley Regatta, Eng, 33; pinchhitter, Dem Championship Baseball Team, US House of Rep, 51-55. Relig: Episcopal. Mailing Add: 9430 Lakeside Dr Vienna VA 22180

SIERACKI, ROBERT F (D)
b Meriden, Conn, Nov 28, 29; s Frank T Sieracki & Mary Mudry S; m 1951 to Mary Elaine Smith; c Linda Mary & Robert F, Jr. Educ: Univ NMex, 49-50. Polit & Govt Pos: Chmn, Bd of Tax Rev, Conn, 63-67, mem, 70-72; pres, Pulaski Dem Club, 66-68; mem, Meriden Dem Town Comt, 66-72, dep chmn, 70-72, chmn, 72-; secy, Fifth Cong Dist Town Chmn Asn, 73-; mem charter revision comt, Va Dem Party, 75- Bus & Prof Pos: Pres, Silver Town Restaurant, Inc, 62- Mil Serv: Enlisted Navy, 48, released as HM 2, 49. Mem: Eagles; Lions; Falcon Drum Corps; Polish Legion of Am Vet; AF&AM. Relig: Catholic. Mailing Add: 13 Suzio Dr Meriden CT 06450

SIEROTY, ALAN GERALD (D)
Calif State Assemblyman
b Los Angeles, Calif, Dec 13, 30; s Julian M Sieroty & Jean Sommer S; single. Educ: Stanford Univ, BA in econ, 52; Univ Southern Calif Sch Law, LLB, 56; Phi Beta Kappa; Breakers. Polit & Govt Pos: Mem, Los Angeles Co Dem Cent Comt, 58- & Calif State Dem Cent Comt, 62-; pres, Beverly Hills Dem Club, 59-60; admin asst to Lt Gov Glenn M Anderson, 62-65; dep dir, Chile-Calif Prog, 65-66; Calif State Assemblyman, 67-; deleg, Dem Nat Conv, 68. Bus & Prof Pos: Partner, Neiman & Sieroty, Law Firm, 60-67, Warren, Neiman, Sieroty & Adell, 67-69 & Tannenbaum, Kaplan, Neiman & Sieroty, 69- Mem: World Peace Through World Law Asn; Am Civil Liberties Union; Am Jewish Cong; B'nai B'rith; United Nations Asn. Relig: Jewish. Legal Res: 10555 National Blvd Los Angeles CA 90034 Mailing Add: 849 S Broadway Los Angeles CA 90014

SIETSEMA, JELT (D)
Mich State Sen
Mailing Add: 239 Brown St Grand Rapids MI 49507

SIEVERS, GEORGIA ANN (D)
VChairman, Pottawattamie Co Dem Party, Iowa
b Pierre, SDak, Sept 5, 24; d Frank Miller Rogers & Anna H Holland R; m 1948 to Earl Gordon Sievers; c Paula Jane, Patrick Gordon, Sondra Lee, Lisa Ann & Virginia Sue. Educ: Centerville Jr Col, 43; Univ Iowa, 47; Newman Club; Catholic Univ Club. Polit & Govt Pos: VChmn, Pottawattamie Co Dem Party, 58-66 & 72-; mem, State Bd Pub Instr, 66-; mem, State Bd Educ Radio & TV Facilities, 67-; deleg, Dem Nat Mid-Term Conf, 74; mem state ethics comt, Fifth Cong Dist, 74- Bus & Prof Pos: Sievers Agri-Bus, Avoca, Iowa, 48- Publ: Ethical training in education, Nat Asn State Bds of Educ Mag, 74. Mem: Nat Asn State Bds Educ (mem resolutions comt, 74); Iowa Farmers Union; Nisha Valley Shrine Auxiliary; Am Community Col Trustees; Bicentennial Comt. Relig: Catholic. Legal Res: 923 Chestnut Avoca IA 51521 Mailing Add: Box 548 Avoca IA 51521

SIFFORD, JOYCE WENDAL (D)
Mem, State Dem Exec Party, Tex
b Benbrook, Tex, June 26, 25; s Thomas Andrew Sifford & Novice Pool S; m 1949 to Lora Lee Strempel; c Patsy Ann (Mrs Turner) & Marline (Mrs Borman). Educ: Martins Mill High Sch, Tex, grad. Polit & Govt Pos: Chmn, Precinct 139 Dem Party, Hurst, Tex, 62-74; chmn deleg comt, Tenth Dist Dem Conv, 72, gen chmn, 74; elector, 12th Cong Dist, 72; committeeman, Tenth Dist Dem Party, 74-, chmn exec comt, 74-; mem, State Dem Exec Party, Tex, 74- Bus & Prof Pos: Vpres, Tex AFL-CIO, 64-71, field rep, 71-72; pres, Tarrant Co Cent Labor Coun AFL-CIO, 69-71. Mil Serv: Entered as A/S, Navy, 43, released as Aviation Machinist Mate, 45, after serv in Naval Aviation. Mem: Transport Workers Am AFL-CIO Local 513. Relig: Episcopal. Mailing Add: 532 Norwood Dr Hurst TX 76053

SIGMAN, BOBBY (D)
Ga State Rep
b Walton Co, Ga, Jan 19, 41; s M E Sigman & Alma I Womack S; m to Alice Fay Atha; c Sandra Michell. Polit & Govt Pos: Ga State Rep, 75- Bus & Prof Pos: Data processing specialist, Lockheed Ga Co, 63-70; real estate broker, Colony Realty Co, 70-; agt, Covington Ins Agency Inc, 75- Mil Serv: Entered as E-1, Navy, 59, released as E-5, 63, after serv as Air Crewman, 61-63; E-5, Naval Res, 63. Mem: Newton Co Jaycees; Elks; Moose Lodge; VFW; Mason. Relig: Protestant. Mailing Add: Rte 2 Victory Lane Oxford GA 30267

SIKES, ROBERT L F (D)
US Rep, Fla
b Isabella, Ga, June 3, 06; s Ben F Sikes & Clara Ford S; m to Inez Tyner; c Bobbye S (Mrs Wicke) & Robert K. Educ: Univ Ga, BS, 27; Univ Fla, MS, 29; Phi Kappa Phi; Alpha Zeta; Sigma Delta Chi; Phi Sigma; Blue Key; Alpha Gamma Rho; Aghon. Hon Degrees: LLD, Stetson Univ, 69 & Univ WFla, 70; DHL, St Leo Col, 69 & Univ Inca Garcilaso de la Vega, 70. Polit & Govt Pos: Chmn, Co Planning Comt, Fla, 34; chmn, Co Dem Exec Comt, 34; Fla State Rep, 36 & 38; asst to treas, Dem Nat Comt, 36, 40 & 44; US Rep, First Dist, Fla, 40-; deleg, Pan Am Roads Conf, Caracas, Venezuela, 54; deleg & chmn Fla Deleg, Dem Nat Conv, 56 & 60, deleg, 72; deleg, Inter-Parliamentary Conf, Warsaw, Poland, 59, Sixth World Forestry Cong, Madrid, Spain, 66 & Seventh World Forestry Cong, Buenos Aires, Argentina, 72; deleg, Dem Nat Mid-Term Conf, 74. Bus & Prof Pos: Publ, Okaloosa News J, 40. Mil Serv: Entered as Maj, Army, 44, released as Lt Col, 46, after serv in Supreme Hq, Allied Expeditionary Forces; Maj Gen (Ret), Army Res; European-African-Mid Eastern Campaign Ribbon; Am Campaign Ribbon; World War II Victory Ribbon; Legion of Merit Award. Mem: Scottish Rite; Mason (33 degree) (grand orator, Fla Masonic Grand Lodge, 68-69); KofP; Rotary; Lions. Honors & Awards: Guatemalan Order of Merit, 61; Peruvian Order of Merit for Distinguished Serv, 70; Distinguished Alumnus Award, Univ Fla, 72; Distinguished Serv Award, Nat Asn State Foresters, 72; Fla WPort Auth Leadership Award, 72. Relig: Methodist. Legal Res: Rte 1 Crestview FL 32536 Mailing Add: 2269 Rayburn Bldg Washington DC 20515

SILBERMAN, JAY ELLIOTT (D)
b Stamford, Conn, June 26, 48; s Sidney Silberman & Helene Nierenberg S; m 1971 to Judith Lee Rosenberg; c Matthew Saul. Educ: Ithaca Col, 65-66; George Washington Univ, AB, 69; Am Univ Washington Col Law, JD, 73; Pi Kappa Delta. Polit & Govt Pos: Aide to chmn, Nat Comn on Causes & Prev of Violence, 68-69; research asst, President's Coun on Environ Qual, 72; legis asst to US Rep Clarence D Long, Md, 73- Bus & Prof Pos: Staff writer-reporter, Educ Daily, Washington, DC, 70-71. Mil Serv: Entered as Pvt, Marine Corps, 69, released as Lance Cpl, 70; Army Res, 70-75. Mem: Am, Fed & DC Bar Asns; Am Civil Liberties Union. Honors & Awards: Scholar Award, Ithaca Col; Scholar Award, Washington Col Law, Honors in Civil Litigation & Land Use Planning. Relig: Jewish. Legal Res: 1641 Parrish Rd Virginia Beach VA 23455 Mailing Add: 2840 27th St NW Washington DC 20008

SILBERMAN, LAURENCE HIRSCH (R)
US Ambassador to Yugoslavia
b York, Pa, Oct 12, 35; s William Silberman & Anna Hirsch S; m 1957 to Rosalie Gaull; c Robert, Katherine & Anne. Educ: Dartmouth Col, BA, 57; Harvard Law Sch, LLB, 61. Polit & Govt Pos: Solicitor of Labor, Dept of Labor, 69-70, Undersecy of Labor, 70-72; dep attorney general, Dept of Justice, 74-75; US Ambassador to Yugoslavia, 75- Bus & Prof Pos: Assoc, Moore, Torkildson & Rice & Quinn & Moore, 61-64; law partner, Moore, Silberman & Schulze, Honolulu, Hawaii, 64-67; attorney, Nat Labor Rels Bd, 67-69. Mil Serv: Entered as Pvt, Army Res, 57, released as Cpl, 63, after serv at Ft Dix, NJ, 6 months. Mem: Hawaii & Am Bar Asns. Mailing Add: Yugoslavia Dept of State Washington DC 20236

SILBERSTEIN, ERIC CHARLES (R)
b Berkeley, Calif, Oct 13, 44; s Howard Joseph Silberstein & Shirley Rae Myers S; m 1966 to Maryann Malven; c Kimberly Ann, Alise Kristin & Shaine Tamara. Educ: Am Univ, BA with honors, 67 & MA, 70; Phi Kappa Phi; Pi Gamma Mu; Pi Sigma Alpha. Polit & Govt Pos: Research coordr, House Educ & Labor Comt, Washington, DC, 66; legis asst, US Rep Charles M Teague, Calif, 66-67 & 68-70; model cities adv, Dept of Housing & Urban Develop, 70-71; legis affairs off, Nat Transportation Safety Bd, 71-72; asst dir for Cong Affairs, ACTION, 72-73, assoc dir, Admin & Finance, 73-74; dir, US Dept Com, Los Angeles, currently. Bus & Prof Pos: New bus analyst, Lockheed Missiles & Space Co, 67-68. Mil Serv: Entered as Seaman 1/C, Navy, 62, released as YN 3/C, 64, after serv in Pac Fleet, Vietnam Conflict, Indochina, 62-64. Mem: Am Polit Sci Asn; Int Club Los Angeles; Southern Calif Dist Export Coun; Calif State Univ Fullerton (citizens adv coun). Mailing Add: 17211 Courbet St Granada Hills CA 91344

SILER, EUGENE (R)
b Williamsburg, Ky, June 26, 00; s Adam Siler & Minnie Chandler S; m 1925 to Lowell Jones; c Dorothy, Annette, Carolyn & Eugene. Educ: Cumberland Col, Williamsburg, Ky, AA, 20; Univ Ky, AB, 22; Columbia Univ, 22; Univ Ky, 23-24; trustee, Cumberland Col. Polit & Govt Pos: Judge, Court of Appeals, Ky, Seventh Appellate Dist, 45; US Rep, Ky, 55-65; alt deleg, Rep Nat Conv, 68. Bus & Prof Pos: Admitted to Ky Bar, 23; dir, Bank of Williamsburg, Ky; lawyer, Firm Tye, Siler, Gillis & Siler, 25-38; lawyer, Firm Tye & Siler, 38-42; attorney-at-law, 45- Mil Serv: Navy, World War I; Army, Capt, 42-45. Mem: Am Legion; Sigma Alpha Epsilon; Phi Alpha Delta; Mason; Odd Fellow. Relig: Baptist; Ky moderator, 52-53. Mailing Add: Walnut St Williamsburg KY 40769

SILLERS, DOUGLAS HUGH (R)
Minn State Sen
b Calvin, NDak, Feb 9, 15; s Archie Sillers & Mabel Betrice Tuthill S; m 1941 to Margaret Rose Baller; c Jean Margaret (Mrs Doug Bardwell), Douglas Hal, Cynthia Betrice & Hether Phillis. Educ: Concordia Col, BA, 39; Univ Minn, 40; NDak State, 57. Polit & Govt Pos: Minn State Rep, Clay Co, 63-72; Minn State Sen, 72- Bus & Prof Pos: High sch instr, Menahga, Minn, 39-41; fieldman, Fed Land Bank, Washburn, NDak, 41-42; mgr & owner, farm, 45- Mil Serv: Entered as Yeoman 3/C, Navy, 43, released as Lt(jg), 45, after serv in Navy Electronics Vol, Fargo, NDak, 8 months, Europe, 18 months; Am Zone, European Zone, European Invasion D Day Ribbons. Mem: Am Legion; VFW; Mason; Farm Bur; CofC. Honors & Awards: Minn State Soil Conserv Winner, 56. Relig: Presbyterian. Mailing Add: RR 2 Moorhead MN 56560

SILLIMAN, NEVELLE I (R)
Chmn, Monterey Co Rep Cent Comt, Calif
b Aromas, Calif, Nov 5, 06; d Floyd Huston Hawkins & Alice Wehrley H; m 1934 to James W Silliman; c Karen, Floyd James & Thomas Leland. Educ: Heald's Bus Col, 2 years. Polit

& Govt Pos: Mem, Rep State Cent Comt Calif, 58-; chmn cong campaign, Monterey Co, 62; mem, Monterey Co Rep Cent Comt, 62-, secy, 68-69, chmn, 74-; mem, 12th Cong Dist Rep Comt, 62-; chmn, Women for Reagan for Gov Campaign, Monterey Co, 66; chmn, Women for Nixon, Western Div Northern Calif, 68; first vpres North Div, Calif Fedn Rep Women, 68-70, campaign & precinct chmn, 70-71; women's chmn, Reelec Gov Reagan, Monterey Co, 70. Publ: So What Now, Pageant Press, 65. Mem: Eastern Star; Pals Club of Sacramento, Legis Ladies Club; Grange. Relig: Protestant. Mailing Add: 246 Hawthorne St Salinas CA 93901

SILVA, RICHARD ROBERT (R)
Mass State Rep
b Gloucester, Mass, Mar 13, 22; s James Benjamin Silva & Ellen Simmons S; m 1952 to Janet Elaine Dickerson; c Paula Jean, Richard Robert, Jr & Mark Edward. Educ: Gloucester High Sch, four years. Polit & Govt Pos: Mem, Gloucester Sch Comt, 64-70; Mass State Rep, Boston, 71- Mil Serv: Entered as Seaman, Coast Guard, 42, released as Signalman 1/C, 46, after serv on USS Key West, Atlantic & Pac Oceans, 44-46. Mem: Gloucester Fraternity Club (treas, 14 years); Elks; Gloucester Little League (founder & past pres, dir, currently); Youth Prog Comn (chmn, four years); Brotherhood Elec Workers Union. Relig: Catholic. Mailing Add: 13 Old Ford Rd Gloucester MA 01930

SILVER, ALAN RICHARD (D)
b Columbia, SC, June 17, 52; s Fred Newman Silver & Mollye Reizen S; single. Educ: Univ SC, BA, 75. Polit & Govt Pos: Vpres, Richland Co Young Dem, SC, 71-72; aide, Lt Gov Earle E Morris, Jr, SC, 71-74; alt deleg, Dem Nat Conv, 72; mem charter comn, Dem Nat Comt, 72-74; youth vchmn, Richland Co Dem Party, 72-74; pres, SC Young Dem, 73-75; aide, Lt Gov Brantley Harvey, Jr, 75- Relig: Jewish. Mailing Add: 6313 Pine Hill Rd Columbia SC 29206

SILVER, ETHEL MARIE (R)
Mem, Rep State Cent Comt Calif
b Hemet, Calif, June 25, 26; d George Andrew Gruber & Myrtle Johnson G; m 1948 to Harrison Edward Silver; c Jeffrey & Jennifer. Educ: Los Angeles Gen Hosp Sch of Nursing, RN, 47. Polit & Govt Pos: Hq chmn, 38th Cong Rep Campaign, Calif, 64; mem, Rep State Cent Comt Calif, 64-66 & 69-; pres, Riverside Rep Women Fedn, Calif, 66-68, bd mem, 68-70; area precinct chmn, Riverside, 68; mem, 74th Assembly Rep Campaign Comt, 68; mem, Nixon Campaign Comt, 68; mem, 74th Assembly Rep Campaign Comt, 68; mem, Nixon Campaign Comt, 68; chmn, Riverside Co Rep Cent Comt, Second Supervisorial Dist, 69 & 74, hq chmn, 73; Riverside Co chmn, Younger for Attorney Gen Campaign, 70 & 74; deleg, Rep Nat Conv, 72; campaign chmn, Holmes for Assembly, 72; Riverside City chmn, Nixon Comt, 72; mem, Biddle for State Senate, 74; Riverside city chmn, Flournoy for Gov, 74. Mem: Woman's Auxiliary, Riverside Co Med Asn (past pres, past coun, 72); Riverside Press Coun; Jr League, Riverside Opera Guild; Calif Rep League of Riverside (bd dirs, 75-); United Way Riverside (bd dirs, 74-). Relig: Lutheran. Mailing Add: 5841 Grand Ave Riverside CA 92504

SILVER, MICHAEL FRANCIS (R)
Vt State Rep
Mailing Add: 806 Main St Bennington VT 05201

SILVERMAN, BERNICE LEASCHER (D)
b Collierville, Tenn, Aug 26, 00; d Ransom Sherman Leascher & Lula Hampton L; m 1920 to Sam Silverman, wid; c Marian (Mrs Howard Pettit). Educ: Mountain Grove Sch, Mo, grad, 18. Polit & Govt Pos: Committeewoman, Mountain Grove Dem Party, 36-40; committeewoman & vchmn, Wright Co Dem Cent Comt, Mo, formerly; Wright Co deleg, Dem State Conv, 60, 64 & 68. Bus & Prof Pos: Ins agent, 20-30; bookkeeper, wholesale grocery, 30-35; owner, Leascher Produce Co, 38-59. Mem: Eleanor Roosevelt Club (pres); Mountain Grove Dem Club (vchmn); Royal Neighbors Am; Town & Country; VFW; Sr Citizens Mountain Grove. Relig: United Methodist. Mailing Add: 517 W First St Mountain Grove MO 65711

SILVERMAN, HAROLD L (R)
Maine State Rep
Mailing Add: Box 336 Calais ME 04619

SILVERMAN, LEONARD (D)
NY State Assemblyman
b Brooklyn, NY, Nov 10, 30; s Frank E Silverman & Rose Worona S; single. Educ: NY Univ, BA, 52; Brooklyn Law Sch, LLB, 54; Iota Theta. Polit & Govt Pos: NY State Assemblyman, 48th Assembly Dist, 69- Bus & Prof Pos: Attorney, Silverman & Lifschitz, currently. Mem: Mason; Kiwanis; Moose; B'nai B'rith; United Jewish Appeal. Honors & Awards: Handicapped Children Award. Relig: Hebrew. Mailing Add: 1170 Ocean Pkwy Brooklyn NY 11230

SILVERSTEIN, JACK (R)
Counsel, NJ Rep State Comt
b 1915; s John L Silverstein & Toretta S; m to Doris J Koplin, c Steven J. Educ: Lehigh Univ, 33-34; Akron Univ, 34-37; Temple Univ Sch Law, JD, 47. Polit & Govt Pos: NJ Dep Attorney Gen; hearing officer, Treas Dept, State of NJ, lectr law of evidence; gen counsel, NJ Employees Asn; mem, Gov Hughes' Bi-Partisan Civil Right Comt; mem panel, Mercer Co Legal Aid Soc, 50-54; Mercer Co committeeman, NJ Rep State Comt, 53-, mem exec comt, chmn const comt, counsel, 61-; chmn const comt, NJ Young Rep, 54; chmn, Lawrence Twp Rep Comt, 54-57; deleg, Rep Nat Conv, 60; chmn, Mercer Co Rep Comt, 62-64; gen counsel, NJ Nixon-Agnew Campaign Comt, 68; Nixon-Agnew elector, NJ Rep Party, 68. Bus & Prof Pos: Gen practice of law; asst prof criminal law & bus law, Rider Col; prof bus law, Mercer Co Col. Mil Serv: World War II vet. Mem: Am, NJ & Mercer Co Bar Asns; Trenton Post 93, Am Legion; Trenton United Serv Orgn. Honors & Awards: Merit Plaque Award, Mercer Co Bar Asn, 70. Relig: Jewish; Pres, Har Sinai Temple of Trenton, 61-66, vpres, NJ Coun Reform Jewish Hebrew Congregations, 62-65. Mailing Add: 146 Lakedale Dr Trenton NJ 08638

SILVIA, JOSEPH GEORGE (R)
Chmn, Newport City Rep Comt, RI
b St Michael, Azores, Feb 5, 06; s Antone Silvia & Mary Angel Dias S; m 1930 to Anna Mary Costa; c Joseph G, Jr, Elizabeth Ann (Mrs Jack P Garforth), Frances Veronica (Mrs David C Rippl), Pauline (Mrs Allan Bestwick), Frederick Arthur, Lenora Dorothea (Mrs Richard Sipka), Margureet Mary (Mrs Joseph R Silvia). Polit & Govt Pos: Chmn, Fourth Ward Rep Comt, RI, 63-66; sheriff, Newport Co, 63-69; chmn, Newport City Rep Comt, 67-; deleg, Rep State Cent Comt, 73- Bus & Prof Pos: Mgr, NShore Van Lines, 69- Mem: Newport Lodge 104 Elks (mem 22 years, mem bd trustees, 15 years & chmn bd trustees, 12 years); Newport Co Salt Water Fishing Club. Relig: Catholic. Mailing Add: 32 Coddington Wharf Newport RI 02840

SIMARD, ANDRE J (D)
NH State Rep
Mailing Add: 277 Bell St Manchester NH 03103

SIMARD, CONSTANCE L (R)
NH State Rep
Mailing Add: Rte 1 Box 284A Plaistow NH 03865

SIMCOX, EDWIN JESSE (R)
Secy, Ind Rep State Cent Comt
b LaPorte, Ind, Jan 12, 45; s Willard J Simcox & Rachel L Gibbs S; m 1970 to Sandra Sue Stephenson. Educ: Ind Univ, Bloomington, AB in Govt & Econ; Ind Univ Sch Law, Bloomington 1 year; Ind Univ Sch Law, Indianapolis, grad; Ind Univ Young Rep. Polit & Govt Pos: Deleg, Ind Rep Conv, 66; advance man, Third Cong Dist, Rep Cong Campaign, 66 & Third Cong Dist Young Rep, 67; deleg, Young Rep Nat Conv, 67; exec secy, Ind Collegiate Young Rep, 67; advance man, Whitcomb for Gov Comt, 68; exec secy, Ind State Hwy Comn, 69-71; exec secy, Ind Pub Serv Comn, 71-72; gen elec state voter registration chmn, Rep Party, 72; alt deleg, Rep Nat Conv, 72; secy, Ind Rep State Cent Comt, currently; mgr, Ind Statewide Cands for Rep Party, 74. Bus & Prof Pos: Partner, Law Firm of Jones & Simcox, Indianapolis, currently. Mem: Young Rep Club of LaPorte Co; State House Young Rep (bd mem); Indianapolis, Ind & Am Bar Asns. Relig: Methodist. Legal Res: Rte 4 Box 16 LaPorte IN 46350 Mailing Add: 7303 N Olney St Indianapolis IN 46240

SIMENZ, NANCY JEAN (D)
Chairperson, Sixth Dist Dem Party Wis
b Sheboygan, Wis, Aug 13, 48; d William Joseph Simenz & Sophia Dietz S; single. Educ: Univ Wis-Milwaukee, BA, 70. Polit & Govt Pos: City councilman, Sheboygan, Wis, 70-72; chairperson, Sixth Dist Dem Party, 72-; mem, Gov Task Force Educ Finance & Property Tax Reform, 72. Bus & Prof Pos: Customer serv supvr, Armira Corp, 71- Mem: Sheboygan Human Rights Orgn; Sheboygan Bus & Prof Women's Club (legis chmn). Relig: Catholic. Legal Res: 615 Clara Sheboygan WI 53081 Mailing Add: 2721 S Eighth St Sheboygan WI 53081

SIMKIN, WILLIAM E (D)
b Merrifield, NY, Jan 13, 07; s Alfred E Simkin & Florence Manchester S; m 1929 to Ruth Helen Commons; c Thomas E & Peter A. Educ: Earlham Col, BS, 27; Columbia Univ, part time, 28-31; Univ Pa, 37-39. Hon Degrees: LLD, Earlham Col, 63. Polit & Govt Pos: Spec mediation rep, Nat War Labor Bd, 42-43, chmn shipbuilding comn & assoc pub mem, 43-45, co-chmn steel comn, 45-47; dir, Fed Mediation & Conciliation Serv, 61-69; chmn, Fed Reserve Syst Labor Rels Panel, Washington, DC, 70-; chmn Foreign Serv Grievance Bd, US State Dept, 71- Bus & Prof Pos: Prin, Sherwood Cent Sch, 28-30; sci teacher, Brooklyn Friends Sch, 30-32; field rep, Am Friends Serv Comt, WVa, 32-37; instr, indust, Wharton Sch Finance & Commerce, Univ of Pa, 37-39; labor arbitrator, self-employed, 39-61 & 69-; lectr, Harvard Sch of Bus Admin, 69-73. Publ: Arbitration of Grievances (w Van D Kennedy), US Dept of Labor, 48; Acceptability as a Factor in Arbitration Under an Existing Agreement, Univ Pa Press, 52; Mediation & the Dynamics of Collective Bargaining, BNA, 71. Mem: Pres, Nat Acad of Arbitrators, 50; Indust Rels Res Asn. Relig: Society of Friends. Mailing Add: 5210 Nina Dr Tucson AZ 85704

SIMMONS, CECIL LAMAR (D)
Miss State Rep
b Macon, Miss, Aug 25, 46; s Cloyace Leon Simmons & Eula Click S; single. Educ: Miss State Univ, BS, 69, MS, 71, PhD work, currently; Alpha Zeta; Gamma Sigma Delta. Polit & Govt Pos: Miss State Rep, Dist 23, Lowndes, Noxubee & Oktibbeha Co, 72- Mem: Miss Entomological Asn; Am Beekeeping Fedn; Farm Bur; CofC; Jaycees. Relig: Baptist. Mailing Add: Rte 4 Box 21A Macon MS 39341

SIMMONS, GERALDINE HERAS (D)
Dem Nat Committeewoman, NY
b Brooklyn, NY, Sept 28, 18; d George Heras & Yetta Feerman H; m 1943 to Leslie Farrar Simmons; c Harvey Farrar, Lowell Heras & George Heras. Educ: Long Island Univ, 32-34. Polit & Govt Pos: Dem Nat Committeewoman, NY, 66-; deleg, Dem Nat Conv, 72; mem, Dem Nominating Comt, Amherst, NY, 74-75; mem, Erie Co Consumer Protection Comt, 74- Mem: Comprehensive Health Planning Coun Western NY (bd dirs, 75-); Dem Club Amherst, NY; Nat Women Polit Caucus. Relig: Unitarian Universalist; mem pulpit comt, 74-75. Mailing Add: 125 Monroe Dr Williamsville NY 14221

SIMMONS, JOHN DALE (R)
Chmn, Santa Rosa Co Rep Exec Comt, Fla
b Milton, Fla; s Walker A Simmons & Hazel McArthur S; m to Gerda Hohn; c Shirley (Mrs Anderson) & John Walker. Educ: Univ Fla, 41 & 46; Kans State Col, 43. Polit & Govt Pos: Chmn, Santa Rosa Co Rep Exec Comt, Fla, 74- Bus & Prof Pos: Indust engr, St Regis Paper Co, 52- Mil Serv: Entered as Cadet, Army Air Force, 41, released as Cpl, 46, after serv in 127 AACS, China-Burma-India, 43-46; Unit Citation. Mem: Am Legion; China Burma India Asn. Relig: Protestant. Legal Res: Hamilton Bridge Rd Milton FL 32570 Mailing Add: PO Box 406 Milton FL 32570

SIMMONS, RALPH TERRELL (R)
Chmn, Jones Co Rep Party, Miss
b Laurel, Miss, Jan 27, 33; s Colby D Simmons & Linnie Cockrell S; single. Educ: Univ Southern Miss, BS, 54; Birmingham Sch Law; Kappa Alpha (pres); Omicron Delta Kappa; PKP. Polit & Govt Pos: Deleg & chmn, Miss Rep Conv, 68; chmn, Jones Co Rep Party, 68-; dir, Fifth Cong TAR. Bus & Prof Pos: Vpres, Don Drennen Motor Co, Birmingham, Ala, 58-63; asst treas, Northern Elec Co, Laurel, 63- Mil Serv: Entered as 2nd Lt, Army, 54, released as 1st Lt, 58, after serv in Finance Corps, US & Europe, 54-58; Lt Col, Army Nat Guard, 63- Mem: Univ Southern Miss Alumni Asn (pres, Gen Asn); Univ Southern Miss Found (bd dirs); Dist Heart Asn (chmn); Nat Guard Asn (bd dirs); Nat Housewares Manufacturers Credit Group (bd dirs). Relig: Baptist; deacon, First Baptist Church; gen Sunday sch supt; Sunday sch dir, Jones Co Baptist Asn. Mailing Add: 1808 Seventh Ave Laurel MS 39440

SIMMONS, SAMUEL J (D)
b Flint, Mich, Apr 13, 27; s Samuel Simmons & Hattie Pickett S; m to Barbara Lett; c David Clay & Robert Allen. Educ: West Mich Univ, AB in Soc Sci, 49, adv work, Univ Mich Sch Social Work & Dept Pub Admin, Wayne State Univ. Hon Degrees: Dr Pub Serv, West Mich Univ, 70. Polit & Govt Pos: Former placement officer, Mich Employ Security Comn, Detroit; with the Fair Employ Practices Comn, Detroit, Regional Dir, 56; formerly exec secy, Mich Labor Mediation Bd, Detroit; mem bd of appeals & rev, Post Off Dept, 62-64; dir, Field Serv Div, US Comn on Civil Rights, 64-69; Asst Secy for Equal Opportunity, Dept of Housing & Urban Develop, 69-72. Bus & Prof Pos: Formerly student sociologist, State Prison of Southern Mich, Jackson, boy's worker, Sophie Wright Settlement, Detroit & admin asst, Detroit Br, NAACP. Mem: Nat Asn of State Labor Rels Agencies; Comt on Uniform Activity Reporting, Nat Asn of State Mediation Agencies; NAACP. Honors & Awards: Am Soc Pub Admin Meritorious Serv Award, Post Off Dept. Legal Res: Detroit MI Mailing Add: 7244 15th Place NW Washington DC 20012

SIMMONS, WALTER T (BUCK) (D)
Mem, Dem Nat Comt, Ill
Mailing Add: 1028 Third St Venice IL 62090

SIMMS, W TIMOTHY (R)
Ill State Rep
b Morrison, Ill, Apr 9, 43; s Donald N Simms & Elizabeth Whistler S; m 1965 to Karen S Locarno; c Timothy W. Educ: Worsham Col Mortuary Sci, 64; Parsons Col, 68. Polit & Govt Pos: Alderman & Rep committeeman, City of Rockford, Ill, 67-71, majority leader, Rockford City Coun, 70-71; Ill State Rep, 71-; Rep whip, Ill House of Rep, 75- Bus & Prof Pos: Funeral dir, Long-Klontz Funeral Home, 64-65, Julian-Poorman Funeral Home, 65-67 & Sundberg Funeral Home, 67- Honors & Awards: State Govt Award, Ill Jaycees. Relig: Presbyterian. Mailing Add: 618 N Second St Rockford IL 61107

SIMON, MAXWELL W (R)
Mem, Mich Rep State Cent Comt
b Findlay, Ohio, Jan 28, 25; s Clyde M Simon & Emma E Gassman S; m 1954 to Ruth C McBride; c Linda M (Mrs Gary Pelletier), Michael S, Matthew W & Craig M. Educ: Mich State Univ, BS, 54, MA, 67. Polit & Govt Pos: Co supvr, Farmers Home Admin, US Dept Agr, 56-62; city councilman, Carson City, Mich, 68-; mem, Mich Rep State Cent Comt, 75- Bus & Prof Pos: Self-employed & student, 46-54; vocational-agriculture teacher, Harbor Springs, Mich, 54-55; co supvr, Farmers Home Admin, Traverse City, Mich, 56-62; vocational educ dir, Carson City Crystal Area Schs, 62- Mil Serv: Entered as Fireman 1/C, Navy CB, 43, released as Ptr 1/C, 46, after serv in 118th CB, SW Pac, 44-46; Capt (Ret), Air Force Res. Mem: F&AM (Lodge 597, Empire, Mich); DeWit Clinton Consistory); AAONMS (Saladin Temple, Grand Rapids); MATVA-AVA; Carson City Lions Club. Relig: Methodist. Mailing Add: 120 Gratiot St Box 3 RFD 2 Carson City MI 48811

SIMON, PAUL (D)
US Rep, Ill
b Eugene, Ore, Nov 29, 28; s Martin P Simon & Ruth Troemel S; m 1960 to Jeanne Hurley; c Sheila & Martin. Educ: Univ Ore; Dana Col; Sigma Delta Chi. Hon Degrees: Six hon dr degrees. Polit & Govt Pos: Ill State Rep, 54-62; Ill State Sen, 62-69; deleg, Dem Nat Conv, 68, alt deleg, 72; Lt Gov, Ill, 69-73; US Rep, Ill, 75- Bus & Prof Pos: Writer of books & mag articles, started as newspaper publisher at 19; gradually expanded newspaper holdings until 14 newspapers published in Ill, sold newspaper interests, 65; teacher, Sangamon State Univ, Springfield, Ill, 72-74; fel, John F Kennedy Inst of Polit, Harvard Univ, winter semester, 74. Mil Serv: Entered as Pvt, Army, 51-53, served in Counter Intel Corps as Spec Agent along the Iron Curtain in Cent Europe. Publ: Lovejoy—Martyr to Freedom, Concordia; Lincoln's Preparation for Greatness, Univ Ill Press; The Politics of World Hunger, Harpers Magazine Press, 73; plus others. Mem: Am Polit Sci Asn; Lions; Am Legion; VFW; NAACP; Received Award for Distinguished Reporting of State & Local Govt, Am Polit Sci Asn, 57. Relig: Lutheran. Legal Res: 511 W Main Carbondale IL 62901 Mailing Add: US House of Rep Washington DC 20515

SIMON, WARREN JOSEPH (D)
La State Rep
b Kaplan, La, Aug 15, 19; s L V Simon & Rena LeBlanc S; div; c Cordell (Mrs Hebert), Michael J, Claudette M & Christine Ann. Educ: Kaplan High Sch, La, 12 years. Polit & Govt Pos: La State Rep, Vermilion Parish, 60-68; Vermilion & Acadia Parishes, 35th Dist, 68- Bus & Prof Pos: Co-owner & mgr, Bourque Simon Ins Agency, Kaplan, 51-; secy-treas, Kaplan Loan & Investment Co, 57-; pres, Ropel Chem Co, 60-; secy-treas, Roi-Tex, Inc, 67- Mem: Lions. Honors & Awards: Named Outstanding Legislator in Conservation, by Nat & La Wildlife Fedns, 66. Relig: Catholic. Legal Res: 502 N Irving Ave Kaplan LA 70548 Mailing Add: PO Box 156 Kaplan LA 70548

SIMON, WILLIAM E
Secy of the Treas
b Paterson, NJ, Nov 27, 27; m to Carol Girard; seven children. Educ: Newark Acad; Lafayette Col, BA, 51. Polit & Govt Pos: Dep Secy of the Treas, 72-74; adminr, Fed Energy Off, 73-74; Secy of the Treas, 74-; chmn, President's Econ Policy Bd, currently; mem, President's Energy Resources Coun, currently; supvr, US Secret Serv, US Customs Serv & Alcohol, Tobacco & Firearms Bur, currently; chmn, Nat Adv Coun, co-vchmn, East-West Trade Policy Comt, chmn, Joint US-Saudi Comn on Econ Coop & chmn, US-Israeli Comn on Econ Develop, currently; chmn, Fed Financing Bank & Environ Financing Authority, currently; US Gov, Int Monetary Fund, Int Bank for Reconstruction & Develop, Inter-Am Develop Bank & Asian Develop Bank, currently; chmn, Emergency Loan Guarantee Bd, mem, Coun on Econ Policy, Domestic Coun, Coun on Int Econ Policy, Comt on Interest & Dividends, US-Egyptian Comn on Econ Develop & US Rwy Asn, currently. Bus & Prof Pos: With Union Securities, New York, 52-55, asst vpres & mgr munic trading dept, 55-57; vpres, Weeden & Co, 57-64; partner, Salomon Bros, New York, 64-72; trustee, Lafayette Col, Mannes Col Music & Newark Acad. Mailing Add: 1404 Langley Pl McLean VA 22101

SIMONEAU, WAYNE ANTHONY (DFL)
Minn State Rep
b Ashland, Wis, Jan 17, 35; s Rex Robert Simoneau & Helen Leigten S; m 1958 to Jane Jarzyna; c Lisa, Laura, Anthony, Paul, Matthew & Leslie. Educ: Dunwoody Inst, Minneapolis, 57. Polit & Govt Pos: Chmn, Dist 46 Dem-Farmer-Labor Party, Minn, 72-75; Minn State Rep, 75- Mil Serv: Entered as Pvt, Wis Nat Guard, 52, released as SP-5, 60. Mem: Local 974 Teamsters Union (recording secy); Pine City Area Vo-Tech Inst (adv bd); Hennepin Co Voc-Tech Inst (adv bd); Fridley Bldg Standards & Design Control Bd. Relig: Catholic. Mailing Add: 465 NE 57th Pl Fridley MN 55432

SIMONEAUX, FRANK P (D)
La State Rep
Mailing Add: 5921 Forsythia Ave Baton Rouge LA 70808

SIMONINI, ARTHUR L (D)
RI State Rep
Mailing Add: 56 Ramblewood Dr Warwick RI 02889

SIMONS, THOMAS G (R)
Mass State Rep
Mailing Add: State Capitol Boston MA 02133

SIMONSON, HAROLD JAMES (DFL)
Mem, Minn State Dem-Farmer-Labor Cent Comt
b Glenwood, Minn, Oct 7, 12; s Christ Simonson & Celia Kopitzke S; m 1936 to Luverne Thorstad; c Janice, Mary & Nancy. Educ: Glenwood High Sch, 12 years. Polit & Govt Pos: Mem exec comt, Pope Co Dem-Farmer-Labor Party, Minn, 60-66, chmn, 65-68; deleg, Dist & State Conv, 60-66; mem, Minn State Dem-Farmer-Labor Cent Comt, 68- Bus & Prof Pos: Chmn credit comt, Minneapolis, St Paul & Sault Sainte Marie Credit Union, 61-66. Mem: Mason; RAM; Brotherhood of Locomotive Firemen, 41, Local Organizer, 52; Eastern Star (Worthy Patron, 68-69); CofC; Brotherhood of Locomotive Engrs. Relig: Lutheran. Mailing Add: 711 E Minnesota Ave Glenwood MN 56334

SIMONSON, MARY ELLEN (D)
VChairperson, Ariz Dem Party
b New York, NY, July 28, 49; d Oscar Harry Simonson (deceased) & Jule Frances Mullin S; m 1974 to Bruce Elliott Meyerson. Educ: Ariz State Univ, BA in Eng & Hist; Theta Sigma Phi; Delta Sigma Chi. Polit & Govt Pos: Asst to Western regional coordr, Jean Westwood, Nat Staff for McGovern 72, Utah, 71-72; admin asst to Dem Minority Leader, Ariz House Rep, 73-; precinct & state committeeperson, Dem Party, 73-; campaign mgr, Sen James P Walsh, 74; vchairperson & mem exec comt, Ariz Dem Party, 75- Bus & Prof Pos: Ed & gen assignment reporter, Ariz Repub, 70-71. Publ: Auth of numerous articles including one concerning discrimination of women in Ariz universities, Ariz Repub, 71; United Farmworkers attempt to recall Arizona Governor Jack Williams, Nation, 4/73; auth numerous articles as part-time correspondent for NY Times, 73 & 74. Mem: Women's Polit Caucus; Nat Orgn Women. Honors & Awards: Guest ed, Mademoiselle Mag, 71. Relig: Catholic. Legal Res: 137 E Coronado Apt 4 Phoenix AZ 85004 Mailing Add: 8620 E Valley Vista Dr Scottsdale AZ 85253

SIMONSON, RICHARD D (R)
b Flint, Mich, Jan 16, 50; s William L Simonson (deceased) & Jean I Shephard Simonson Brown; single. Educ: Albion Col, AB, 72; Omicron Delta Kappa. Polit & Govt Pos: Page, Mich House Rep, 67; chmn, Lake Co Teen Age Rep, 66-68; campaign mgr, Lake Co Sheriff, 68; treas, Albion Col Rep, 68-70; chmn, Higher Educ Task Force, Rep State Cent Comt, 69-70; aide, Congressman Guy Vander Jagt, 70; dir, Campaign to Cand, Albion Col, 70; youth vchmn, Ninth Dist Rep Party, Mich, 72-; alt deleg, Rep Nat Conv, 72; regional coordr, Nixon Campaign in Mich, 72; chmn, Credentials Comt, Mich State Rep Conv, 72; admin aide, Senator Donald E Bishop, Mich, State Senate, 72- Bus & Prof Pos: Chmn, Albion Col Stud Senate, 70-72; mem adv comt, State Bd Educ, Mich, 70-71; asst ed, Off Info Servs, Albion Col, 70-72. Publ: The new left, Albion Col, 72. Honors & Awards: Outstanding Teenager of Am, 68; Elk's Youth Leadership Award, 68. Relig: Protestant. Legal Res: PO Box 231 Baldwin MI 49304 Mailing Add: Michigan State Senate Capitol Lansing MI 48902

SIMPKINS, WILLIAM JOHN (D)
Mem, Ga State Dem Exec Comt
b Columbus, Ga, Mar 4, 48; s William James Simpkins & Agnes Carter S; single. Educ: Norman Jr Col, AA, 69; Ga Southern Univ, BS, 71; pres, student govt, 68-69. Polit & Govt Pos: Vpres, Young Rep Club Ga; youth chmn, Jimmy Carter Gubernatorial Race, 70; mem, Ga State Dem Exec Comt, 71- Bus & Prof Pos: Off, Trust Co Columbus, 71. Mem: Kiwanis; March of Dimes (youth chmn, 71-73). Honors & Awards: Letters in college & high sch basketball. Relig: Methodist. Legal Res: 1258 Cedar Ave Columbus GA 31906 Mailing Add: PO Box 57 Columbus GA 31902

SIMPSON, ALAN K (R)
Wyo State Rep
b Denver, Colo, Sept 2, 31; s Milward L Simpson & Lorna Kooi S; m 1954 to Ann Schroll; c William L, Colin M & Susan L. Educ: Univ Wyo, BS in Law, 54, JD, 58; Alpha Tau Omega; pres, W-Club. Polit & Govt Pos: City attorney, Cody, Wyo, 58-68; US Comnr, 58-69; Wyo State Rep, currently, majority floor leader, Wyo House of Rep, currently. Bus & Prof Pos: Attorney-at-law; vpres bd trustees, Buffalo Bill Hist Ctr; operating, Whitney Gallery Western Art, Buffalo Bill Mus & NAm Plains Indian Mus; vpres bd trustees, Northwest Community Col, Powell, Wyo; bd dir, First State Bank, Cody, Wyo; bd trustees, Gottsche Rehabilitation Ctr, Thermopolis, Wyo. Mil Serv: Entered as 2nd Lt, Army, 54, released as 1st Lt, 56, after serv in 2nd Armored Div, ETO, 55-56; Army of Occupation Medal; 2 Unit Citations with Oak Leaf Clusters. Mem: AAONMS; Mason (32 degree); Elks; VFW. Honors & Awards: Past Pres Award, Univ Wyo Alumni Asn. Relig: Episcopal. Legal Res: 1201 Sunshine Ave Cody WY 82414 Mailing Add: Box 470 Cody WY 82414

SIMPSON, BARBARA HAHN (D)
b Pontiac, Ill, Jan 5, 45; d Maurice F Hahn & Mary E Lannon H; div; c Paul A, David F & Mary Ann. Educ: Northern Ill Univ, BS, 72. Polit & Govt Pos: Deleg, Dem Nat Conv, 72; mem sch bd, Unit Dist 158, Huntley, Ill, 74- Mem: PTA; Farm Bur. Mailing Add: 10617 Church St Huntley IL 60142

SIMPSON, CHARLES WILLIAM (D)
b Wichita Falls, Tex, May 1, 36; s William Oscar Simpson & Charlotte Katherine McKinney S; m 1955 to Anna Louise Lewis; c Charles Kyle & Teri Louise. Educ: Midwestern Univ, 54-55; Hardin-Simmons Univ, BA, 62; Univ Tex, Austin, 63-65, 69-70; Phi Theta Kappa; Pi Gamma Mu. Polit & Govt Pos: Admin asst to US Rep Charles Wilson, Tex, 73- Bus & Prof Pos: Mgr, W O Simpson Excavating Contractor, Wichita Falls, Tex, 54-60; teaching asst, Hardin-Simmons Univ, 62-63; research assoc, Univ Tex, 64-65; instr polit sci, San Antonio Col, summer 65; asst prof, Stephen F Austin State Univ, 65-73; vis prof, Galveston Col, summer 71. Mem: Am Polit Sci Asn; Cong Staff Club; Admin Asst Asn. Honors & Awards:

Faculty Develop Grant, Stephen F Austin State Univ, 69. Relig: Presbyterian. Legal Res: Nacogdoches TX 75961 Mailing Add: 8710 Mary Lee Lane Annandale VA 22003

SIMPSON, DAVID JAMES (D)
b Marshall, Tex, Dec 7, 46; s George Bruce Simpson & Wilma Grace Silvey S; m 1967 to Gay Nell Fusilier; c David Judd. Educ: ETex Baptist Col, 65-71. Polit & Govt Pos: Deleg, Dem Nat Conv, 72. Bus & Prof Pos: Part owner & mgr, Simpson Wholesale Co, 69- Mil Serv: Entered as Pvt, Army Nat Guard, 68-, Sgt, currently. Mem: Lions, Int. Relig: Baptist. Legal Res: 38 Linwood Dr Marshall TX 75670 Mailing Add: PO Box 1152 Marshall TX 75670

SIMPSON, EDWARD W, JR (R)
SC State Rep
Mailing Add: SC House of Reps State Capitol Columbia SC 29211

SIMPSON, HAROLD DWAINE (R)
Nebr State Sen
b Harlan, Iowa, June 1, 26; s Harold W Simpson & Esther Elizabeth Michelson S; m 1946 to Clara Salome Hitz; c Roger Allen, Harold Dwaine, Jr, John William, Marjorie Ann, Thomas Edwin & James Edward. Educ: High Sch. Polit & Govt Pos: Nebr State Sen, 46th Dist, currently. Bus & Prof Pos: With Gooch Milling & Elevator Co. Mil Serv: Entered as Pvt, Air Force, 44, released as Pfc, 47, after serv in US. Mem: WOW; Boy Scouts; Am Fedn of Grain Millers; PTA; Northeast Sertoma (charter mem). Honors & Awards: Hon life mem, Nebr PTA; Silver Beaver Award, Boy Scouts Am. Relig: Methodist. Mailing Add: 1805 North 30th St Lincoln NE 68503

SIMPSON, JAMES CARROLL (D)
Md State Sen
b May 14, 31; m 1951 to Barbara Lee Wright; c James C, III, Gary Michael & Carol Lee. Polit & Govt Pos: Mem, Charles Co Sanitary Comn, Md, 66-70; app by gov to Co Comnr, Charles Co, Md, 70, elected, 70-74, served as chmn; Md State Sen, 74- Bus & Prof Pos: Pres, Simpson Distributing Co, Inc, 54-; dir, Md Bank & Trust Co, Waldorf, Md, 70-74; mem, Gov Comn to Study Land Use in State of Md. Mil Serv: Entered as Pvt, Marine Corps, 51, released as Sgt, 54. Mem: Optimist Club; Elks; KofC; Waldorf Lions; hon Jaycee. Honors & Awards: Outstanding Citizen of Charles Co, Waldorf Lions Club, 74. Relig: Catholic. Mailing Add: PO Box 188 Waldorf MD 20601

SIMPSON, JAMES CHARLES (JIM) (D)
Miss State Rep
b Gulfport, Miss, May 18, 30; married. Polit & Govt Pos: Miss State Rep, currently. Bus & Prof Pos: Seafood canner. Mem: CofC; VFW; Pass Christian Yacht Club; Phi Kappa Tau. Relig: Catholic. Mailing Add: 116 Marcie Dr Long Beach MS 39560

SIMPSON, JAMES LLOYD (D)
Treas, Shelby Co Dem Cent Comt, Mo
b Leonard, Mo, Oct 16, 21; s Dr Samuel Lloyd Simpson & Mary O Parsons S; m 1960 to Carole Jo Chapin; c Jeffrey Lynn & James Truman. Educ: Northeast Mo State Teachers Col, 40 & 50; Univ Mo-Columbia, 41. Polit & Govt Pos: Committeeman, Shelby Co Dem Cent Comt, Mo, 55 & 66-, treas, 68-; sheriff, Shelby Co, 57-60. Bus & Prof Pos: Co-owner, Simpson Bros Mobile Oil Sta, Shelbina, Mo, 54-56; farmer, 60- Mil Serv: Entered as Pvt, Army, 42, released as Cpl, 45, after serv in Engrs, Alaska Defense Command, 42-45. Mem: Am Legion; Shelby Co Fair Bd; Co 4-H Coun; Shelby Co Exten Coun. Honors & Awards: Outstanding 4-H Proj Leader in Shelby Co, 67. Relig: Christian Mailing Add: Rte 1 Shelbyville MO 63469

SIMPSON, JOHN M (R)
Kans State Sen
Mailing Add: 1815 E Iron Salina KS 67401

SIMPSON, MAX (D)
Ore State Rep
Mailing Add: Sumpter Stage Rte Baker OR 97815

SIMPSON, MILWARD L (R)
b Jackson, Wyo, Nov 12, 97; s William L Simpson & Margaret Burnett S; m 1929 to Lorna Kooi; c Peter Kooi & Alan Kooi. Educ: Tome Prep Sch, Port Deposit, Md; Univ Wyo, BS, 21; Harvard Univ Law Sch, LLB, 25; Alpha Tau Omega. Hon Degrees: LLD, Univ Wyo, 55. Polit & Govt Pos: Wyo State Rep, 26-27; Gov, Wyo, 55-59; former mem, Exec Comt of Gov Conf; US Sen, Wyo, 62-66. Bus & Prof Pos: Attorney-at-law, 26-55 & 59; partner, Simpson & Simpson, 59-60; partner, Simpson, Kepler & Simpson, 60- Mil Serv: 2nd Lt, Army Inf, 18. Mem: Mason (33 degree); Am Legion; 40 et 8; Rotary Int; Elks; Eagles. Relig: Episcopal; vestryman. Mailing Add: 901 Simpson Ave Cody WY 82414

SIMPSON, RICHARD OLIN (R)
Chmn, Consumer Prod Safety Comn
b Independence, Mo, Mar 7, 30; s Clyde Oliver Simpson & Lillie Haller S; m 1949 to Patricia Ann Kramer; c Richard Harry, Dianne Patricia, Karen Sue, David Brian & Norma Kaye. Educ: Univ Calif, Berkeley, BSEE, 56; Stanford Univ, 57; Univ Calif, Berkeley, 64; Tau Beta Pi; Eta Kappa Nu; Sigma Xi. Polit & Govt Pos: Dep asst secy prod standards, Dept of Commerce, 69-73, acting asst secy sci & technol, 70-71; app by President, chmn, Consumer Prod Safety Comn, 73- Bus & Prof Pos: Design engr, Sylvania Electronics, Sunnyvale, Calif, 56-57; founder & gen mgr, Pac Ord & Electronics Co, San Francisco, 57-64; pres, Rucker Electronics, Berkeley, 65-68 & Insul-8 Corp, Santa Clara, 68-69; group vpres, Rucker Co, Oakland, 68-69. Mil Serv: Entered as Seaman Recruit, Navy, 48, released as Elec Tech 1/C, 52, after serv in USS Boxer, Pac, 48-50. Mem: Soc Automotive Eng; Commonwealth Club Calif. Relig: Presbyterian. Legal Res: 7912 Charleston Ct Bethesda MD 20034 Mailing Add: Consumer Product Safety Comn Washington DC 20207

SIMPSON, ROBERT (BOB) (D)
Tex State Rep
Mailing Add: 3505 Kingston Rd Amarillo TX 79109

SIMPSON, ROBERT FOSTER (CONSERVATIVE, NY)
Mem, State Comt, Conservative Party, NY
b Fulton, NY, Mar 22, 28; s Leigh Arthur Simpson, MD & Marion S Edgarton S; m 1954 to Ann Watrous Lines; c Susan Leigh, Leigh Ann, Robert Foster, Jr, Elizabeth Joan, Jean Virginia & William Harold. Educ: Syracuse Univ, AB, 51; Sigma Chi; Varsity Club. Polit & Govt Pos: Mem, State Comt Conservative Party, NY, currently. Bus & Prof Pos: Mem sales dept, Union Carbide Corp, 52-54 & Genesee Heating Serv, Rochester, 54-62; owner, Pennysaver Printing & Specialty Co & Naples Pennysaver, NY, 62-69, owner, Robert Simpson Co, 69- Mil Serv: Entered as A/S, Navy, 46, released as Pharmacist Mate 3/C, 48. Relig: Latter-day-Saint. Mailing Add: RR 3 Short Rd Canandaigua NY 14424

SIMPSON, STANLEY R (R)
Chmn, Boone Co Rep Cent Comt, Iowa
b Des Moines, Iowa, Nov 3, 27; s James W Simpson & Helen Joy S; m 1953 to Avonell Zener; c Candice, Stanley & Kelly. Educ: Univ Wyo, 45; Drake Univ, JD, 51; Delta Theta Phi. Polit & Govt Pos: Mayor, Ogden, Iowa, 57-59; co attorney, Boone, 59-; chmn, Boone Co Rep Cent Comt, 64- Mil Serv: Pvt, Army, 45-46. Mem: Nat Dist Attorneys Asn; Shrine; Elks; Lions; Mason; Odd Fellow. Relig: Protestant. Mailing Add: PO Box 217 Ogden IA 50212

SIMPSON, WILLIAM WALTON (D)
b Washington, DC, May 3, 14; s William Simpson & Elizabeth Walton S; m 1957 to Edith Berkley; c Betty (Mrs Cornish). Educ: Miner Teachers Col, 34-35. Polit & Govt Pos: Deleg, Dem Nat Conv, 68 & 72. Bus & Prof Pos: Pres, Billy Simpson's, Inc, 56-; pres, Pioneer Sale & Distribution Co, 57-60; pres, Brookland Enterprises, Inc, 66- Mil Serv: Entered as Seaman 3/C, Navy, 43, released as Motor Machinist 2/C, 46, after serv in Logistic Support, Eniwetok & Hawaii, 45-46. Mem: Mason (32 degree); Shrine (bd gov, Mecca Temple 10); Mayor's Comn for Employ Handicapped; Urban Coalition; YMCA (mem bd). Honors & Awards: Outstanding Citizen of DC, Nat Educ Asn, 66; comnr, Youth Coun, 66; YMCA Achievement Award, 68. Relig: Baptist. Mailing Add: 3815 Georgia Ave NW Washington DC 20011

SIMS, P D (D)
State Committeeman, Big Horn Co Dem Party, Wyo
b Chattanooga, Tenn, Jan 16, 1893; s Minos P Sims & Hettie Gordon S; m 1927 to Eva Dorothy Ramskill; c Graham D, Marian (Mrs John Werner) & Ann Louise (Mrs Jimmie Gist). Educ: Dixie Col, 2 years. Polit & Govt Pos: State committeeman, Big Horn Co Dem Party, Wyo, 28-30 & 72-; postmaster, Lovell, 34-61; alt deleg, Dem Nat Conv, 68; alt deleg, Dem Nat Mid-Term Conf, 74. Mil Serv: Entered as Pvt, Army, 18, released as Pfc, 20, after serv in 45th Inf, Ninth Div. Mem: Am Legion; Vet of World War I; AF&AM; Odd Fellows; CofC. Relig: Baptist. Legal Res: 241 Park Lovell WY 82431 Mailing Add: Box 397 Lovell WY 82431

SIMS, WALTER (R)
Fla State Sen
Mailing Add: 3712 S Summerlin St Orlando FL 32806

SIMS, WILLIAM ARLON (JAKE) (D)
Secy, Faulkner Co Dem Party, Ark
b Greenbrier, Ark, Feb 25, 15; s Roy Walter Sims & Mattie Rotton S; m 1949 to Hattie Maurine Powers. Educ: Greenbrier High Sch, Ark, grad. Polit & Govt Pos: Secy, Faulkner Co Dem Party, Ark, 56- Mil Serv: Entered as Pvt, Army, 41, released as Sgt, 46, after serv in Antiaircraft Artil. Mem: Mason; Greenbrier Lions Club; Retail Clerks Union; Farm Bur. Relig: Baptist. Mailing Add: Rte 3 Box 126 Greenbrier AR 72058

SINCLAIR, IVAN EARL (D)
b Dimmitt, Tex, Feb 19, 37; s Bryan Eugene Sinclair & Katie Eugenia England S (both deceased); m 1968 to Sharon Margaret Kerkove; c Erika Kristin. Educ: Hardin-Simmons Univ, BBA, 59; Columbia Univ Grad Sch Jour, MS, 61. Polit & Govt Pos: Staff asst to Vice President Lyndon Johnson, 62-63 & President Lyndon Johnson, 63-65; under secretary, US Chief of Protocol, 65-66; admin asst to US Rep Jack Hightower, Tex, 75- Bus & Prof Pos: Dist sales dir, Braniff Int, Washington, DC, 66-67; dir community affairs, 67-70 & regional sales dir, 70-75. Mil Serv: Entered as Pvt, Army Res, 60, released as E-4, 62, after serv in Ft Knox, Ky, 60, Ft Stewart, Ga, 62. Relig: Baptist. Mailing Add: 7220 Willow Oak Pl Springfield VA 22153

SINCLAIR, JOHN RICHLEY (R)
b Detroit, Mich, Mar 11, 35; s C Gordon Sinclair & Kathryn Richley S; single. Educ: Wayne State Univ, BS in Journalism, 58. Polit & Govt Pos: Admin Asst to US Rep William S Broomfield, Mich, 67- Mil Serv: Entered as Pvt, Army, 58, released as SP-4, 58. Relig: Protestant. Legal Res: Bloomfield Township MI Mailing Add: Off of Hon William S Broomfield US House of Rep Washington DC 20515

SINCLAIR, LARRY RAY (D)
Chmn, Seminole Co Dem Exec Comt, Fla
b Calif, Apr 27, 40; s William R Sinclair & Thelma Negley S; m 1962 to Carol Ann Orvedahl; c Corbin Ray & Lorie Ann. Educ: Calif State Polytech Univ, BS, 63; Univ Idaho, MS, 71, PhD, 73. Polit & Govt Pos: Chmn, Seminole Co Dem Exec Comt, Fla, 74- Bus & Prof Pos: Eng specialist, US Dept Agr Soil Conserv Serv, 63-68; asst prof, Univ Fla, 73- Publ: Auth, Permeability of unsaturated field soils predicted from desaturation characteristics, Trans, Am Soc Agr Eng; auth, Desaturation apparatus & Permeability apparatus, Agr Engr, 75. Mem: Nat Soc Prof Engrs; Am Soc Agr Eng (unsaturated flow comt); Seminole Sunrise Kiwanis Club (youth serv chmn); Boy Scouts (asst scoutmaster). Mailing Add: 2614 Marshall Ave Sanford FL 32771

SINCLAIR, ORRIETTE COINER (R)
Rep Nat Committeewoman, Idaho
b Twin Falls, Idaho, Sept 17, 21; d Walter A Coiner & Marietta Hunsberger Detweiler C; m 1946 to James Alfred Sinclair; c Rose Ann, Jan, Judy & James Walter. Educ: Univ Utah, 39-40; Univ Idaho, BS in Bus, 43; Kappa Kappa Gamma. Polit & Govt Pos: Secy to Twin Falls Co Rep Party chmn, Idaho, 44; dep clerk of the dist court, Twin Falls Co, 44-45; pres, Twin Falls Co Young Women Rep Club, 45, 63 & 64; secy, 66; state committeewoman, Twin Falls Co Rep Cent Comt, 64-, secy, 66; deleg, Idaho State Rep Assembly, 64, 66, 68 & 70, permanent secy, 66; vchmn, Appreciation Day Comt honoring Rep George Hansen, 66; secy, Fifth Region of Idaho Rep, 68-70; first vchmn, Idaho Rep Party, 66-70; Rep Nat Committeewoman, Idaho, 71-; deleg, Rep Nat Conv, 72; secy, Rep Western States Conf, 73. Bus & Prof Pos: Secy, Bur of Entomology & Plant Quarantine, 43-44; secy, E W McRoberts & Co, 45-46. Mem: Kappa Kappa Alumnae Club; Pan Hellenic; Am Legion Auxiliary; PEO; Int Toastmistress Clubs. Relig: Presbyterian. Legal Res: 262 Lincoln Twin Falls ID 83301 Mailing Add: PO Box 249 Twin Falls ID 83301

SINCOCK, RICHARD (R)
Del State Rep
b Wilmington, Del, Mar 31, 22; s Clarence Edwin Sincock (deceased) & Marian Ruth Merrill

S; m 1948 to Marianne Palmer; c Steven Joseph. Educ: Syracuse Univ, 47; Univ Del, BA in Econ, 50. Polit & Govt Pos: New Castle Co Councilman, Del, 67-73; chmn budget hearings, New Castle Co Coun, 70-72; Del State Rep, 73-, vchmn joint finance comt, Del House Rep, 73-74, minority whip, 75- Bus & Prof Pos: Coordr mkt research, E I du Pont de Nemours & Co, Inc, 52-59, logistics & materials distribution-equipment, 59- Mil Serv: Entered as Pvt, Air Force, 42, released as Sgt, after serv in various units, Africa & Italy, 44-46; Am, African & European Theatre Ribbons; Good Conduct Medal. Mem: Univ Club of Wilmington (mem finance comt); Wilmington Touchdown Club (pres, 75); Univ Del Alumni Asn. Legal Res: 2201 Beaumont Rd Wilmington DE 19803 Mailing Add: Legislative Hall Dover DE 19901

SINESI, DON GHIARO (D)
RI State Rep
b Boston, Mass, Oct 24, 35; s Giovanni Sinesi & Stella Ingalla S; m 1961 to Marie Bernadette Abood; c Don Ghiaro, Jr, Jacqueline Marie & Tania Marie. Educ: Providence Col, AB, 57; Suffolk Univ, JD, 66. Polit & Govt Pos: RI State Rep, 71st Dist, 75- Bus & Prof Pos: Attorney-at-law, North Providence, RI, 66- Mil Serv: Entered as 2nd Lt, Army Res, 58, released as 1st Lt, 66. Mem: RI Bar Asn; Providence Col Alumni Asn; Suffolk Univ Alumni Asn; KofC. Relig: Catholic. Mailing Add: One Smithfield Rd North Providence RI 02904

SING, JOHN W (D)
NH State Rep
Mailing Add: Lowell Rd 354 D W Hwy Nashua NH 03060

SINGER, RICHARD GUS (D)
b New York, NY, Aug 20, 43; s Egmont Singer & Frances Miller S; m 1966 to Anne Carol Rosenzweig. Educ: Amherst Col, BA, 63; Univ Chicago, JD, 66; Columbia Univ, LLM, 71, JSD cand; Phi Delta Sigma. Polit & Govt Pos: Deleg, Dem Nat Conv, 72. Bus & Prof Pos: Clerk, Hon Harrison Winter, Fourth Circuit Court of Appeals, 66-67; asst prof, Univ Ala Law Sch, 67-69; assoc prof, Univ Cincinnati Law Sch, 70-72; dir, Resource Ctr on Correctional Law, Am Bar Asn, 72-73; assoc prof, Rutgers Univ Law Sch, 73- Publ: Co-auth, Prisons & The Therapeutic State, Bobbs-Merrill, 74; auth, Sentencing Dispositions, US Govt, 73; (Iowa) Article, Iowa Law Rev. Mem: Nat Coun on Crime & Delinquency; Am Bar Asn; Am Civil Liberties Union. Mailing Add: 272 James St Morristown NJ 07960

SINGH, BALDEV (BOB) (D)
Mem, Sutter Co Dem Cent Comt, Calif
b India, Aug 17, 31; s Jagat Singh & Harman Kaur S; m 1962 to Vina Ahluwalia; c Yasmin & Rajdeep. Educ: Punjab Univ, India, BA, 53; Univ Ore, MA, 57; Polit Sci Nat Honor Soc. Polit & Govt Pos: Deleg, Dem Nat Conv, 72; mem, Sutter Co Dem Cent Comt, 73- Bus & Prof Pos: Pres faculty senate, Thomas Downey High Sch, Modesto, Calif, 70-71; mem acad senate, Yuba Col, Calif, 72- Mem: Calif Teachers Asn. Relig: Sikhism. Mailing Add: 1867 Railroad Ave Yuba City CA 95991

SINGLETON, MARY L (D)
Fla State Rep
b Jacksonville, Fla, Sept 20, 26; d Harry C Littlejohn & Laura Crowd L; m 1948 to Isadore Singleton (deceased); c Carol (Mrs Charles Scott) & Isadore; two grandchildren. Educ: Hampton Inst, Va, 43; Fla A&M Univ, BS, 48; Zeta Phi Beta. Polit & Govt Pos: Comnr, Local Govt Study, 64; secy, Jacksonville Housing Bd Adjustments, 64-67; councilman, Jacksonville City Coun, 67, vpres, 67-68, councilwoman, 68, 71 & 72; Fla State Rep, 72-; mem, Dem Nat Comt, currently. Mem: Cath Charities Bur, Inc (bd dirs); Prof Women's Dem Club; NFla Univ Adv Coun (bd dirs); Nat Coun Christians & Jews (bd dirs); Sheriff's Interagency Coun. Honors & Awards: Meritorious award, Fla A&M Univ, 67; most objective, News Media of Coun; Eve Award, Fla Publ Co, good govt award, West Duval Jaycees & leadership award, City of Jacksonville, 72. Relig: Catholic. Legal Res: 1353 W 33rd St Jacksonville FL 32209 Mailing Add: 40 House Office Bldg Tallahassee FL 32304

SINGLETON, SAMUEL MORRIS (R)
b Ferron, Utah, Oct 19, 27; s Morris Samuel Singleton & Mary Elva Huntsman S; m 1955 to Alta Mae Brown; c Morris Wayne, Kyle Jay & Myron Bruce. Educ: Brigham Young Univ, BS, 52; Univ Utah, Grad Work, 62-64; Kent State Univ, Grad Work, 65; Utah State Univ, Master of Educ, 69. Polit & Govt Pos: Chmn, Ferron Precinct Rep Party, Utah, 55-60; chmn, Emery Co Rep Party, formerly. Bus & Prof Pos: Secy, Emery Co Teachers Asn, 58-60. Mil Serv: Entered as Pvt, Army, 50, released as Cpl, 52, after serv in 5th AAA Bn. Mem: Nat Educ Asn; Utah Educ Asn; Utah Library Asn; Am Legion; Farm Bur. Relig: Latter-day Saint. Mailing Add: Ferron UT 84523

SINGLEY, VASCO MONETT (D)
Miss State Rep
b Columbia, Miss, Feb 2, 18; s Monett Malachi Singley & Agnes Thornhill S; m 1937 to Edna Earl Coward; c Julie (Mrs Pinkston), Mary (Mrs A Sandt) & Sime. Educ: Forest Co Agr Sch, 34-36. Polit & Govt Pos: Miss State Rep, Marion-Walthal Co, 68- Mailing Add: Box 71-E Columbia MS 39429

SINICROPI, MICHAEL WILSON (D)
Chmn, Hancock Co Dem Exec Comt, WVa
b East Liverpool, Ohio, Aug 11, 25; s Patsy Sinicropi & Jessie Miller S; wid; c Celeste. Educ: Reggio Calabria, Italy, Liceo Scientifico, 4 years. Polit & Govt Pos: Dep assessor, Hancock Co Off, 67-68; chmn, Hancock Co Dem Exec Comt, 70- Bus & Prof Pos: Coal analyst, Starvaggi Industs, 47-73; dir, cosmopolitan cultural hour radio prog, WEIR, ABC, 53-; ed, Italian version of the UNIONE, weekly of Order Italian Sons & Daughters of Am, 66- Mem: Eagles; Nat Police & Firefighters Asn; Italian Am Hist Soc; Weirton Bicentennial Comn (chmn); Weirton Crime Stop Comt (chmn, 69-70 & 74-). Honors & Awards: Grand Knight, Repub of Italy; Award, Jr CofC; City of Weirton Award for Civic Activities; Steubenville Am Legion Award for Patriotism. Relig: Catholic. Legal Res: 2892 Pennsylvania Ave Weirton WV 26062 Mailing Add: PO Box 2117 Weirton WV 26062

SINKS, JOHN R (R)
Ind State Rep
m 1952 to Mary Louise S; c John Robert, III. Educ: Ind Univ, BS, 55; Ball State Univ, MA, 57. Polit & Govt Pos: Ind State Rep, 65- Bus & Prof Pos: Guid counr, Elmhurst High Sch, Ft Wayne, Ind. Mil Serv: Air Force, Korea. Mem: Nat Educ Asn; Ind State Teachers Asn. Relig: Episcopal. Mailing Add: 13308 W Hamilton Lane Ft Wayne IN 46804

SINNER, RICHARD WALTER (D)
b Casselton, NDak, Oct 12, 25; s Albert Francis Sinner & Katherine Wild S; single. Educ: St John's Univ (Minn), 43-45; Cath Univ BA, 45-47, MA, 47-48; theol student, 48-52; Theol Col Fratres in Unum. Polit & Govt Pos: Chmn, McGovern for President Comt, 72; deleg, 12th Dist NDak Conv, 72, NDak State Conv, 72 & Dem Nat Conv, 72. Bus & Prof Pos: Asst pastor, Univ NDak, 52-54 & St Mary's Parish, Fargo, 54-59; pastor, St Francis of Assisi Parish, Marion, 59-69; chaplain, St Luke's & Dakota Hosp, Fargo, 69-71; pastor, Sacred Heart Parish & St Anselm's Parish, Fulda, formerly & St Thomas Parish, Kent, Minn, currently. Mem: UN Asn NDak (chmn, 65-); Clergy & Laymen Concerned NDak (chmn, 67-); Priests Asn Diocese of Fargo; Cath Order of Foresters NDak NDak; Cath War Vet NDak (state chaplain, 62-66). Honors & Awards: UN Day Chmn, App by Gov William Guy, 69. Relig: Roman Catholic. Mailing Add: St Thomas Parish Kent MN 56553

SIPES, JEANETTE BRADEN (D)
Chmn, Sutton Co Dem Party, Tex
b Paris, Tex, June 27, 50; d Kenneth Otho Braden & Edwina Coltharp B; m 1972 to Michael Eugene Sipes. Educ: Navarro Jr Col, 68-69; ETex State Univ, 69-70; Univ Tex, Arlington, BA in Hist, 72; NTex State Univ, post-grad, 72-73; Mensa; Psi Chi; Kappa Delta Sorority. Polit & Govt Pos: Chmn, Sutton Co Dem Party, Tex, 74- Bus & Prof Pos: Recreation leader, Grand Prairie Munic Recreation Dept, Tex, 71-72; credit clerk, Credit Dept, Arlington Bank & Trust, summer 73; note teller, First Nat Bank, Sonora, 73- Mem: Tex Elec Off Asn; Jaycettes; Sonora Firemen's Auxiliary; Ladies Golf Asn, Sonora. Legal Res: 410 Martin St Sonora TX 76950 Mailing Add: PO Box 183 Sonora TX 76950

SIPLE, RANDOLPH EDWARD (R)
b Glendale, Calif, June 5, 33; s Edward Randolph Siple & Sadie Bradford S; m 1963 to Ann Brady; c Shaun Derek & Heather Daun. Educ: Stanford Univ, AB, 55; Univ Southern Calif, LLB, 61; Delta Upsilon; Phi Delta Phi. Polit & Govt Pos: Rep cand, Calif State Assembly, 68 & 70; mem, Ventura Co Rep Cent Comt, 68-71, chmn, 71-75; mem, Calif Rep State Cent Comt, 68-71; mem, Calif State Environ Quality Study Coun, 70; alt deleg, Rep Nat Conv, 72. Mil Serv: Entered as 2nd Lt, Army, 56, released as 1st Lt, 58, after serv in 14th Armored Cavalry Regt, Seventh Army, Germany; Lt, Naval Res, 64- Mem: Am & Calif State Bar Asns; Elks; Navy League. Relig: Protestant. Mailing Add: 305 Mariposa Dr Ventura CA 93001

SIRIANNI, CARMEL A (R)
Pa State Rep
b Carbondale, Pa, Sept 14, 22; d John Sirianni (deceased) & Amelia Pascoe S; single. Educ: Bloomsburg State Col, BS, 44; Bucknell Univ, MS in Educ, 52; Marywood Col, MS in Guid, 59. Polit & Govt Pos: Committeewoman, Susquehanna Co Rep Comt, 54-, secy, 56-60, vchmn, formerly, chmn, currently, finance chmn, 62; deleg, Rep Nat Conv, 64; former pres, Susquehanna Co Rep Woman, 6 years & vchmn, 60-; admin asst to Speaker, Pa House Rep, 66-68 & 73-, admin asst to minority leader, 68-73; Pa State Rep, 75- Bus & Prof Pos: Teacher, Hop Bottom High Sch, Pa, 45-58; guid dir, Mt View High Sch, Kingsley, 59-66. Mem: Pa Counselors Asn; Pa Deans & Counselors Asn; APAG; Montrose Country Club; Hop Bottom Women's Club. Relig: Catholic. Mailing Add: Capitol Bldg Harrisburg PA 17120

SIRKIN, STEPHEN HOWARD (D)
b Baltimore, Md, Mar 17, 48; s Louis Jay Sirkin (deceased) & Florence Ikin S; single. Educ: Univ Md, College Park, BA, 70; Loyola Col (Md), currently. Polit & Govt Pos: Treas, New Dem Coalition, Baltimore Co W, 71-72, pres, 72-73; recording secy, New Dem Coalition, Md, 71-73, chmn, 73-; deleg, Dem Nat Conv, 72. Bus & Prof Pos: Teacher, Pimlico Jr High, Baltimore City, Md, 70-71, Lansdowne Mid Sch, Baltimore Co, 71-74 & Deer Park Jr, Baltimore Co, 74- Mil Serv: Entered as Airman Basic, Air Force Inactive Res, 67, released, 71. Mem: Nat Coun Teachers Math; Teacher's Asn Baltimore Co (chief rep from Lansdowne Mid Sch, 71-74); Md State Teachers Asn (deleg, 73 & 74 convs); Nat Educ Asn (deleg, 75 conv). Relig: Jewish. Mailing Add: 3428 Carriage Hill Circle T-2 Randallstown MD 21133

SISCO, GARY LEE (R)
b Whiteville, Tenn, Oct 1, 45; s Booker Lee Sisco & Mary Parks Sisco Williams; m 1968 to Mary Sue Baylis; c Stephen. Educ: Univ Miss, BS, 67; George Washington Univ, MS, 70; Memphis State Law Sch, 71; Omicron Delta Kappa; Gamma Beta Phi; Sigma Nu; Am Soc Civil Engrs (student chap). Polit & Govt Pos: Field dir & exec asst to US Sen Howard Baker, 71-73; campaign mgr, Lamar Alexander for Gov Tenn, 74; admin asst to US Rep Robin Beard, Tenn, 75- Mil Serv: Entered as 2nd Lt, Army, 68, released as 1st Lt, 70; Capt, Army Res; Nat Defense Serv Medal; Army Commendation. Mem: Am Soc Civil Engrs; ROA; Data Processing Mgt Asn; US Jr CofC. Relig: Baptist. Legal Res: 729 Darden Pl Nashville TN 37205 Mailing Add: 3803 King Arthur Rd Annandale VA 22003

SISCO, JOSEPH JOHN
Under Secy for Political Affairs, Dept of State
b Chicago, Ill, Oct 31, 19; m 1946 to Jean Head; c Carol & Jane. Educ: Knox Col, BA, 41; Univ Chicago, MA, 47, PhD, 50. Polit & Govt Pos: Mem staff, Dept of State, 51-, polit adv, US delegs to UN Gen Assembly, 51-, dep dir, Off of UN Polit Affairs, 58-61, dir, 61-63, Dep Asst Secy of State for Int Orgn Affairs, 63-65, Asst Secy of State for Int Orgn Affairs, 65-69, Asst Secy of State for Near Eastern & SAsian Affairs, 69-74; Under Secy for Political Affairs, Dept of State, 74- Bus & Prof Pos: Pres, Hamilton Col, 74- Mil Serv: 1st Lt, Inf, Army, 41-45. Publ: Numerous articles on int orgn & foreign affairs. Mem: Am Polit Sci Asn; Am Soc Int Law; Am Foreign Serv Asn; Phi Beta Kappa; Tau Kappa Epsilon. Honors & Awards: State Dept Superior Serv Award, 60; Nat Civil Serv League Award as one of the Ten Outstanding Career Officers in Govt Serv, 66; Rockefeller Pub Serv Award, 71. Mailing Add: Dept of State 2201 C St NW Washington DC 20520

SISCO, SHIRLEY (R)
VChmn, Wayne Co Rep Comt, Mo
b St Louis, Mo, Oct 21, 32; d James C Snider & Marie King S; m 1952 to Edward E Sisco; c Kim (Mrs Richard Graham), Kenton E & Kristi Sue. Educ: Carter Co RII High Sch, Mo, grad, 50. Polit & Govt Pos: Chmn, Wayne Co Rep Comt, Mo, 72-74, vchmn, 74- Bus & Prof Pos: Secy, Sales & Mkt Execs Metrop St Louis, Mo, 62-68; bookkeeper, Duncan Bros, Inc, 69-; real estate sales rep, Duncan Land Co, 71- Mem: Piedmont Park Bd (secy); Jr Bay View Club. Relig: Baptist. Legal Res: 117 Bates Piedmont MO 63957 Mailing Add: PO Box 336 Piedmont MO 63957

SISISKY, NORMAN (I)
Va State Deleg
Mailing Add: PO Box 4010 Petersburg VA 23803

SISITSKY, ALAN DAVID (D)
Mass State Sen
b Springfield, Mass, June 4, 42; s Eli Joseph Sisitsky & Dorothy Dietz S; single. Educ: Cornell Univ, BA, 64; Yale Law Sch, LLB, 67-; Harvard Grad Sch of Arts, 69-71; Phi Beta Kappa; Phi Alpha Delta. Polit & Govt Pos: Mass State Rep, 69-72; Mass State Sen, 73- Bus & Prof Pos: Attorney, Choate, Hall & Stewart, Boston, 68-69. Mil Serv: Lt(jg), Navy Res. Mem: Am, Boston, Hampden Co & Mass Bar Asns; Elks. Honors & Awards: Named Outstanding Young Man of Year, Springfield Jr CofC, 70. Relig: Jewish. Mailing Add: 54 Draper St Springfield MA 01108

SISK, ARTHUR C, SR (R)
b Mountainview, Ark, Mar 18, 11; s Arthur Stephen Sisk & Amanda Bell Freeman S; m 1938 to Delphia Ethel Farris; c Jimmie Dee (Mrs Millard) & A C, Jr. Educ: Big Flat & Marianna High Schs, Ark. Polit & Govt Pos: Chmn, Lee Co Rep Party, Ark, formerly; elec comnr, Lee Co, 64-; alt deleg, Rep Nat Conv, 68; mem, Ark Soil & Water Conserv Comn. Bus & Prof Pos: Pres, Sisk Farms Inc, Lee Co, Ark, vpres, Lee Co Co-op Gin, Marianna, dir, Lee Co Farm Co-op Store & vpres, S&W Housing Develop Co, currently. Mem: Lee Co Farm Bur (past pres & currently dir); Lee Co, Marianna CofC. Honors & Awards: Farm Family of the Year, 62. Relig: Church of God of Prophecy. Legal Res: Rte 3 Marianna AR 72360 Mailing Add: Rte 3 Box 243 Marianna AR 72360

SISK, B F (BERNIE) (D)
US Rep, Calif
b Montague, Tex, Dec 14, 10; s Arthur Lee Sisk & Lavina Thomas S; m 1931 to Reta Mitchell; c Mrs J Martin Temple & Mrs John H Pittenger. Educ: Abilene Christian Col, Abilene, Tex. Polit & Govt Pos: US Rep, Calif, 54- Legal Res: 3860 Balch Ave Fresno CA Mailing Add: 129 6th St NE Washington DC 20002

SISLER, JOHN MILLARD (R)
Chmn, Monongalia Co Rep Exec Comt, WVa
b Morgantown, WVa, Feb 2, 34; s Millard T Sisler & Florence Keys S; m 1956 to Jackquelyn Hughes; c Elizabeth Ann & John Kevin. Educ: WVa Univ, AB, 59; Kappa Alpha. Polit & Govt Pos: Pres, Monongalia Co Young Rep Club, 59-61; committeeman, Monongalia Co Rep Exec Comt, WVa, 64-68, campaign chmn, 66, vchmn, 66-68, chmn, 68-; deleg, Rep Nat Conv, 72. Bus & Prof Pos: Owner & operator, John M Sisler Ins, 68- Mil Serv: Entered as Pvt, Army, 56, released as Spec 3, 58, after serv in Seventh Inf Div, Far East Command. Mem: Kiwanis; Morgantown CofC; WVa Aviation Found, Inc, (secy, 71-). Relig: Baptist. Mailing Add: 776 S Hills Dr Morgantown WV 26505

SISSER, ERIC RONALD (D)
Pub Rels Dir, Dem Party Fla
b Bayonne, NJ, Apr 23, 46; s Max Louis Sisser & Ruth Rogow S; single. Educ: Okaloosa-Walton Jr Col, AA, 70; Univ Fla, BS in Advert, 73; Alpha Delta Sigma. Polit & Govt Pos: Bd mem, Concerned Dem of Fla, 71-74; pres, Young Dem Clubs of Fla, 73-74; alt deleg, Dem Nat Mid-Term Conf, 74; ed, Young Dem Clubs of Am, 74-; legis liaison, City of Miami, 75-; pub rels dir, Dem Party of Fla, 75- Bus & Prof Pos: Pres, Eric Sisser Prod, 72-74; dir advert, Nat Projs Inc, 74- Mil Serv: Entered as E-1, Air Force, 65, released as E-4, 69, after serv in 3210 Supply Squadron, Eglin AFB, Fla, 68-69. Mem: Am Asn Polit Consults. Relig: Jewish. Mailing Add: PO Box 440235 Miami FL 33144

SITTLER, EDWARD LEWIS, JR (R)
b Greensburg, Pa, Apr 21, 08; s Edward Lewis Sittler & Stella Sheldrake S; m 1936 to Harriet J Long; c Jane (Mrs Roberts) & Richard E. Educ: Brown Univ, AB, 30; Am Col Life Underwriters, CLU, 40; Phi Beta Kappa; Phi Delta Theta. Polit & Govt Pos: Judge of elec, Fifth Ward, Uniontown, Pa, 32-33; pres, Uniontown Sch Bd, 36-37; mayor, Uniontown, 48-50; US Rep, Pa, 50; Pa Rep State Committeeman, 60-72; co comnr, Fayette Co, 68-72. Mil Serv: Entered as Pvt, Army, 43, released as Capt, 46, after serv as Capt of Ord, ETO. Mem: Rotary; Pa Economy League; Isaac Walton League; Uniontown Country Club; Duquesne Club; Fayette Co Develop Coun. Relig: Disciples of Christ; Elder. Legal Res: Adams Lane Uniontown PA 15401 Mailing Add: PO Box 516 Uniontown PA 15401

SITTON, CLAUDE SHEM (D)
Mem, NC Dem Exec Comt
b Arden, NC, Dec 24, 37; s James Arthur Sitton & Josephine Allison S; m 1960 to Adijo Bailey; c Julia Leigh & Janie Allison. Educ: Mars Hill Jr Col, AA, 58; Univ NC, Chapel Hill, AB, 60; Wake Forest Sch of Law, LLB, 63; Phi Alpha Delta. Polit & Govt Pos: Pres, Burke Co Young Dem Comt, NC, 64; treas, NC Young Dem, 65; secy, Burke Co Dem Exec Comt, 66-67, chmn, 68-72; deleg, Dem Nat Conv, 72; mem, NC Dem Exec Comt, 74- Honors & Awards: Top Ten Young Dem Comt Award, 64. Relig: Baptist. Mailing Add: 727 W Union St PO Box 666 Morganton NC 28655

SIVERIO RODRIGUEZ, EFRAIN (POPULAR DEMOCRAT, PR)
Rep, PR House of Rep
Mailing Add: State Capitol San Juan PR 00901

SIVERTSEN, ROBERT (R)
Mont State Rep
Mailing Add: PO Box 531 Havre MT 59501

SIVERTSON, ROBERT (D)
SDak State Rep
Mailing Add: 1124 W 20th St Sioux Falls SD 57105

SIZEMORE, EARLEEN WILKERSON (D)
Ga State Rep
b Worth Co, Ga, July 29, 38; d Joe Earl Wilkerson & Mamie Roberts W; m 1958 to Cortez Barnett Sizemore; c Vicki, Staci & Robby. Educ: Ga Southern Col, BS; Ga Col Milledgeville, MEd; Univ Ga, 6 year Educ Specialist. Polit & Govt Pos: Ga State Rep, Dist 136, 75- Bus & Prof Pos: Instr bus & off educ & chmn dept, Worth Co Bd Educ, 59-75. Publ: A motivating project for Typing I, Bus Educ World, 2/65; A teacher's love affair, 5/67 & Vocational education-where the action is, 10/70, Educator, Ga Asn Educ. Mem: Nat Educ Asn; Ga Asn Educ; Worth Asn Educ; Nat Bus Educ Asn; Ga Bus Educ Asn (dir, 72). Honors & Awards: Dedication of sch yearbook by Worth Co High Sch Students, 67; Outstanding Bus Educator, Ga Bus Educ Asn, 70; Outstanding Young Woman of Ga, Sylvester Jr Women's Club, 74; Ga Leadership, Ga CofC, 75. Relig: Baptist. Mailing Add: Rte 3 Sylvester GA 31791

SIZEMORE, JAMES MIDDLETON, JR (R)
Chmn, Talladega Co Rep Party, Ala
b Mobile, Ala, May 25, 42; s James Middleton Sizemore, Sr & Margaret Davidson S; m 1966 to Stephenie Freeman. Educ: Samford Univ, AB, 63; Va Sch Law, JD, 66. Polit & Govt Pos: Exec secy, Ala Young Rep, 62-63 & Nat Committeeman, 63-65; dir, Region Six, Young Rep Nat Fedn, 65-67; chmn, Talladega Co Rep Party, Ala, 68-; recorder, City of Sylacauga, 69-; mem, Ala State Rep Exec Comt, 70- Bus & Prof Pos: Attorney-at-law, Bolton, Sizemore & Rumsey, Sylacauga, Ala, 67- Mem: Va, Ala & Am Bar Asns; Talladega Co Bar Asn (pres, 72-73); Am & Ala Trial Lawyers Asn; Sylacuaga Kiwanis. Relig: Presbyterian. Mailing Add: 918 Cherokee Dr Sylacauga AL 35150

SKAGERBERG, DONNA CLARE (R)
Chairwoman, Third Cong Dist Rep Party, Minn
b Sioux City, Iowa, Apr 11, 28; d Allan Paul Goodin & Alice Miller G; m 1949 to John Paul Skagerberg; c Leslye Ann, Paul Rutcher, Gregory David, Corinne Marie, Joel Allan & Beth Ellen. Educ: Univ Minn, 46-49; Alpha Gamma Delta. Polit & Govt Pos: Blockworker, Goldwater Campaign, 64; precinct survey-card file, 64-69; Edina chairwoman for LeVander Campaign, Third Dist Steering Comt, 66; Otto Bang Legis Campaigns, 66-70; deleg, Hennepin Co Conv, 66-; GOTV for all campaigns, 66-; mem credentials comt, Hennepin Co Conv, 68; active in Nixon Campaign, 68; deleg, Third Dist Conv, 68-69 & 72-73, alt, 70-71; secy, Edina Exec Comt, 68-70; deleg, State Conv, 68-; cand for Edina Sch Bd, 69; mem, Secy of State Rep Task Force Comt on Housing, 69-70; chmn registration, Third Dist Conv, 70; mem post endorsement steering comt, Frenzel Campaign, south area coordr for Edina, Richfield & Bloomington, asst vol chairwoman, 70; co-chairwoman Edina Rep Vol, 70; chaired Edina comt to study local endorsement possibilities & procedures, Edina prog comt & organized Edina cand forums for local elec; chairwoman, Edina Sch Bd Cand; mem, Otto Bang Third Dist Cong Pre-endorsement Steering Comt, 70; vchairwoman, Third Dist Rep Comt, 71-73; mem, Hennepin Caucus Comt, 72; mem, Third Dist Liaison-Frenzel Campaign Comt, 72; co-chmn state absentee ballot, Nixon Campaign, 72; mem steering comt, Otto Bang Senate Campaign, 72; Third Dist State Fair Chairwoman, 72; Third Dist VChairwoman to Chairwoman, 73-74; mem, Mary Forsythe Adv Comt, 74. Mem: Alpha Gamma Delta Alumni Asn (pres); Our Lady of Grace Parish Coun of Women (pres); Edina Hist Soc (charter mem, pres, vpres & youth dir); Edina Bicentennial Comn; Minn Hist Soc. Relig: Catholic. Mailing Add: 6112 Virginia Ave Edina MN 55424

SKAGGS, DAVID EVANS (D)
b Cincinnati, Ohio, Feb 22, 43; s Charles E Skaggs & Juanita Allen S; single. Educ: Wesleyan Univ, BA, 64; Yale Univ, LLB, 67. Polit & Govt Pos: Chmn, Second Cong Dist Dem Cent Comt, Colo, 73-75; admin asst to US Rep Tim Wirth, Colo, 75- Bus & Prof Pos: Attorney, Newcomer & Douglass, Boulder, Colo, 71-75. Mil Serv: Entered as 1st Lt, Marine Corps, 68, released as Capt, 71, after serv in 1st Marine Div, I Corps, SVietnam, 69; Major, Marine Corps Res, 75; Navy Commendation Medal; Navy Achievement Medal. Legal Res: 12 Peakview Rd Boulder CO 80302 Mailing Add: 612 901 Sixth St SW Washington DC 20024

SKAGGS, JOEL HENRY (R)
Chmn, LaRue Co Rep Comt, Ky
b Buffalo, Ky, Jan 20, 12; s Henry Blaine Skaggs & Viola Ferrill S; first wife deceased; m 1964 to Lucille Vocook; c Marvin R, Carolyn K & Steven R. Educ: High Sch. Polit & Govt Pos: Hwy patrol, Ky State Hwy Dept, 44-48, with dept, 68-; co elec comnr, 49-51; investr, US Dept of Agr, 54-62; chmn, LaRue Co Rep Comt, Ky, presently & campaign chmn, 63. Bus & Prof Pos: Owner & operator of farm, 48- Mem: Mason; Lions; Nat Farmers Orgn. Relig: Baptist. Mailing Add: RFD 1 Buffalo KY 42716

SKAGGS, RAYMOND LEO (R)
Chmn, Madison Co Rep Party, Mo
b Fredericktown, Mo, Oct 25, 33; s Paul Skaggs & Ruth Schulte S; m 1957 to Martha Ann Walden; c Cydney Rae & Whitney Ann. Educ: Univ Mo, Columbia, BS in Agr, 55. Polit & Govt Pos: Pres, Madison Co Rep Club, Mo, 66-69; Mo State Rep, 150th Dist, 69-74; chmn, Madison Co Rep Party, Mo, 75- Mil Serv: Entered as Seaman Recruit, Navy, 55, released as PO 2/C, 57. Mem: Elks; Jr CofC; CofC; Farm Bur. Honors & Awards: Outstanding Young Farmer, 66; Outstanding Young Man, 69. Relig: Catholic. Mailing Add: Rte 3 Fredericktown MO 63645

SKARDA, WILLIAM R, JR (R)
Nebr State Sen
b Omaha, Nebr; m 1943; c Cheryl, Christine. Educ: South High Sch. Polit & Govt Pos: Nebr State Sen, 59- Bus & Prof Pos: Pub Rels Man. Mem: Polish-American Civic Club; Nebr Game & Hunt Club; Omaha Traffic Club; SE Improvement Club; Old Timers Baseball Asn. Mailing Add: 1720 Monroe St Omaha NE 68107

SKELLY, JIM (R)
Ariz State Rep
Mailing Add: 2221 E Indianola Phoenix AZ 85016

SKELTON, BYRON GEORGE (D)
b Florence, Tex, Sept 1, 05; s Clarence Edgar Skelton & Avis Ione Bowmer S; m 1931 to Ruth Alice Thomas; c Sue Helen (Mrs Jerry Dwain Ramsey) & Sandra Ruth (Mrs Robert Terrance Farrell). Educ: Univ Tex, BA, 27, MA, 28 & LLB, 31; Phi Beta Kappa; Pi Sigma Alpha; Sigma Delta Pi; Tejas Club; pres Students' Asn; Cowboys; Students' Assembly; permanent pres, Acad Class of 27. Polit & Govt Pos: Co attorney, Bell Co, Tex, 34-38; spec asst to US Ambassador to Argentina, 42-45; city attorney, Temple, Tex, 45-60; deleg, Dem State Conv, 46-64; deleg, Dem Nat Conv, 48, 56, 60 & 64, mem site comt, 64; mem Tex Dem Adv Comt, 54-55, chmn, 55-56; Dem Nat Committeeman, Tex & mem credentials comt, Dem Nat Comt, 56-64; mem Nat Inaugural Comt, 61; judge, US Court of Claims, 66- Bus & Prof Pos: Attorney-at-law, Temple, Tex, 31-34, 38-42 & 45-66; dir, First Nat Bank, Temple, 46-66; pres, Temple Indust Found, 66; partner, Skelton, Bowmer & Courtney, Temple, Tex. Mem: Am Bar Asn; State Bar of Tex (legis comt & admin justice comt, 62-); Am Law Inst; Am Judicature Soc; Shrine. Relig: Methodist. Legal Res: Salado TX 76571 Mailing Add: 717 Madison Pl NW Washington DC 20005

SKELTON, IKE N, JR (D)
Mo State Sen
b Lexington, Mo, Dec 20, 31; s Ike N Skelton & Carolyn Boone S; m 1961 to Susan Anding; c Ike N, V, James A & Harry Page. Educ: Lexington High Sch, grad, 49; Wentworth Mil Acad, grad, 51; Univ Mo, AB, 53, LLB, 56; Univ Edinburgh, Scotland, summer 53; Phi Beta Kappa; Phi Delta Phi; Sigma Chi. Polit & Govt Pos: Prosecuting attorney, Lafayette Co, Mo,

57-60; spec asst to Attorney Gen, 61-63; chmn, Lafayette Co Cent Dem Comt, 62-66; Mo State Sen, 28th Dist, 71- Bus & Prof Pos: Attorney-at-law, Bradley, Skelton & Schelp, 56-; dir & secy, Wellington Bank, 69. Mem: Lafayette Co Bar Asn; Am Trial Lawyers Asn; Lions Club; Mason; Elks. Relig: Christian Church. Mailing Add: 712 Highland Ave Lexington MO 64067

SKELTON, JAMES MAURICE (R)
Chmn, Champaign Co Rep Party, Ill
b Champaign, Ill, Aug 14, 39; s William G Skelton & Virginia Kane S; m 1960 to Kay Annette Highland; c Julia Kay, Jeanne Marie, Susan Elizabeth & James M, Jr. Educ: Quincy Col, BA, 61. Polit & Govt Pos: Precinct committeeman, Champaign Co, 64-75, Co Bd Supvr, 68-70, Co Treas, 70-75, comnr, Co Housing Authority, 71-75; chmn, Champaign Co Rep Party, Ill, 74- Mem: Champaign Lions Club; Champaign Co Heart Fund (chmn, 73-74); KofC; Elks. Relig: Roman Catholic. Mailing Add: 1502 W Kirby Champaign IL 61820

SKELTON, KEITH D (D)
b Cambridge Springs, Pa, May 6, 18; s Benjamin E Skelton & Anna K Kahrl S; div; c Carol Jane, Ann Elizabeth, K Douglas & Thomas Blake; m to Betty Roberts. Educ: Edinboro State Col, BS; Univ Mich Grad Sch; Syracuse Univ & Univ Wash at Seattle Law Sch, JD, Univ Ore Grad Sch; Pi Sigma Alpha. Polit & Govt Pos: Ore State Rep, 57-61 & 64-74; mem, Lane Co Planning Comn, 63-65; deleg, Dem Nat Conv, 68 & 72; consult, Nat Comn on Workmen's Compensation Laws, 72. Bus & Prof Pos: Attorney, pvt practice, 49-; assoc prof law, Univ Ore, 63-68; Portland State Univ, 68- Mil Serv: Entered as Aviation Cadet, Army Air Force, 43, released as Capt, 45, after serv as bomber pilot, Southwest Pac Theater; Six Theatre of War Ribbons; Air Medals with Five Clusters & others. Publ: Author, Legislative Interim Committees Created by Resolution, 2/59 & The 1965 Oregon Workmen's Compensation Law: a Model for the States, 12/65, Ore Law Rev; ed, Workmen's Compensation in Oregon: A Symposium, Univ Ohio, 66. Mem: Am, Wash State & Ore State Bar Asns; Am Judicature Soc; Am Civil Liberties Union (bd mem), various other orgns. Relig: Congregational. Legal Res: 319 SE Gilham Portland OR 97215 Mailing Add: 927 Boise Cascade Bldg Portland OR 97201

SKERRY, DAVID PAUL (D)
Treas, Mass Young Dem
b Medford, Mass, Apr 14, 42; s Patrick Joseph Skerry, Jr & Dorothy Bennett S; m 1968 to Bernadette E Kalley; c Patrick J & John F. Educ: Boston Univ, BS, magna cum laude, 65; Boston Col Law Sch, JD, 68; Beta Gamma Sigma; Student Govt; Serv Soc; Yearbook Staff; Dean's List. Polit & Govt Pos: Pres, Medford Young Dem, Mass, 65-68; mem, Medford Ward & City Dem Comt, 68-; treas, Mass Young Dem, 68-; legal adv to registr deeds, Middlesex Co, 69-; mem, Medford Sch Comt, 70- Bus & Prof Pos: Mem legal tax staff, Arthur Andersen & Co, CPAs, 68-69; attorney-at-law, 69-; vis lectr finance & acct, Boston Univ, 69-70. Mem: Lions; Medford Youth Coun (bd dirs); Asn for Retarded Children; Medford Drug Action Coun; Medford Ment Health Asn. Honors & Awards: Graduated first in class, Boston Univ, 65; Outstanding Young Dem in Mass, 69; Boston Univ Alumni Award for Sch & Community Serv. Relig: Roman Catholic. Mailing Add: 104 Capen St Medford MA 02155

SKEVIN, JOHN M (D)
NJ State Sen
Mailing Add: 370 Kinderkamack Rd Oradell NJ 07649

SKIDMORE, JOHN VANUS (D)
b Flemington, Mo; s Jessie Benjamen S; m to Kerry Ann Stites; c Johnnie Vanus, II, Michael Andrew & Marshall Allan. Educ: Humansville High Sch. Polit & Govt Pos: Dem twp committeeman, Polk Co, Mo; chmn, Polk Co Dem Party, formerly. Relig: Baptist. Mailing Add: Rte 1 Flemington MO 65650

SKIFFINGTON, JOHN JOSEPH, JR (D)
Majority Leader, RI House Rep
b Woonsocket, RI, July 28, 18; s John J Skiffington & Mary Crowley S; m 1940 to Helen Ann Kaffel; c Barbara (Mrs Hammann), Michael Dennis, John J, III, Timothy Kevin & Robert Patrick. Educ: Woonsocket High Sch, La Salle Acad. Polit & Govt Pos: RI State Rep, 51-, majority leader, RI House Rep, 68-; deleg, Dem Nat Conv, 68; chmn, Woonsocket City Dem Party, RI, currently. Bus & Prof Pos: Pres & former treas, Local 224, United Rubber Workers, AFL-CIO, int rep, 63; rubber worker. Mil Serv: Entered as Apprentice Seaman, Navy, 44, released as Aviation Mechanic 2/C, 46. Mem: Fairmount Post Am Legion, Post 85. Mailing Add: 394 Third Ave Woonsocket RI 02895

SKILES, ELWIN LLOYD, JR (R)
b Louisville, Ky, Mar 19, 41; s Elwin Lloyd Skiles & Ruth Kinder S; single. Educ: Baylor Univ, BA, 63; George Washington Univ, MA, 65; Univ Tex Sch Law, Austin, JD, 68; Phi Alpha Delta; Baylor CofC. Polit & Govt Pos: Mem joint comt on printing, US Cong, Washington, DC, 63-65; minority counsel, comt on banking, housing & urban affairs, US Senate, 71-73; admin asst to US Sen John Tower, Tex, 73- Bus & Prof Pos: Attorney, Hunt Oil Co, Dallas, Tex, 68-71; instr govt, El Centro Col, 68-71. Mem: Dallas, Am, DC & Tex Bar Asns. Relig: Baptist. Legal Res: 2211 Cedar Abilene TX 79601 Mailing Add: 312 Third NE Washington DC 20002

SKINNER, CALVIN L, JR (CAL) (R)
Ill State Sen
Mailing Add: 275 Meridian St Crystal Lake IL 60014

SKINNER, LEARY GEORGE (D)
Mem, Clay Co Dem Comt, Mo
b Wisconsin Rapids, Wis, May 21, 41; s Maynard Skinner & Eileen Leary S; m 1967 to Marcia Frantze; c James M & Christina M. Educ: Rockhurst Col, AB, 63; Univ Mo-Columbia, JD, 66; Phi Alpha Delta. Polit & Govt Pos: Deleg, Dem Nat Conv, 72; asst prosecuting attorney, Clay Co, Mo, 72-; mem, Clay Co Dem Comt, 74-; mem, Kansas City Planning Comn, 75- Bus & Prof Pos: Mem, Hale, Kincaid, Waters & Allen, Attorneys-at-law, Liberty, Mo, 75- Mil Serv: Entered as Pvt, Army, 66, released as Capt, 71, after serv in 25th Inf Div, Vietnam, 69-70; Bronze Star; Army Commendation Medal with 2 Oak Leaf Clusters. Mem: Kansas City, Clay Co, Mo & Am Bar Asns. Relig: Roman Catholic. Mailing Add: 1600 NW 66th Terr Kansas City MO 64118

SKINNER, MICHAEL WILLIAM (D)
b Baltimore, Md, Nov 4, 41; s Robert William Skinner & Pearl Mae Green S; m 1968 to Laura Ann Gibbs; c David Michael. Educ: Md Inst Col Art, Baltimore, 59-60; Morgan State Col, BA in Art, 68, MA in Urban Planning & Policy Anal, 76; Alpha Phi Alpha; Pershing Rifles; Vets Club. Polit & Govt Pos: Deleg, Dem Nat Mid-Term Conf, 74; deleg, State Dem Conf Orgn & Policy, Md, 74-; asst recording secy, Five in Five Dem Club, Baltimore, 71-75, vpres party matters, 75- Bus & Prof Pos: Asst coordr, Neighborhood Youth Corps, Baltimore City Pub Schs, Md, 68-71; dir urban proj health careers, Md Hosp Educ & Research Found, Lutherville, 71; dir, Upward Bound, Morgan State Col, 72; dir off minority affairs, Sch Pharm, Univ Md, 72- Mil Serv: Entered as Pvt E-2, Army, 61, released as Med Specialist 4, 64, after serv in Hq & Hq Co 70th Armored. Mem: Black Adminr/Faculty Univ Md; Am Inst Planners; Scholarship Comt Fifth Legis Dist Baltimore City; Direct Search for Talent Proj (bd dirs, chmn const comt, 71-); Student Nat Pharmaceut Asn (adv, Univ Md Chap). Relig: Baptist. Mailing Add: 18 N Hilton St Baltimore MD 21229

SKINNER, PATRICIA MORAG (R)
NH State Rep
b Glasgow, Scotland, Dec 3, 32; d John Stuart Robertson & Frances C L Swann R; m 1957 to Robert Albert Skinner; c Robin Ann & Pamela Morag. Educ: NY Univ, 50-54. Polit & Govt Pos: NH State Rep, 73-, chmn labor, human resources & rehabilitation comts, NH House Rep, 75-; mem, NH Adv Coun for Voc Tech Educ, currently. Mem: NH Fedn Rep Women's Clubs (secy); Friends of NH Libr; Garden Club of Windham; Windham Womens Club; OES (line officer). Relig: Christian Science. Mailing Add: Governor Dinsmore Rd Windham NH 03087

SKINNER, SHERRILL N (PETE) (D)
Fla State Rep
Mailing Add: 1590 E Monroe Lake City FL 32055

SKIPPER, MARGUERITE STEWART (D)
Committeewoman, Fla State Dem Comt
b Vidalia, Ga, Mar 23, 24; d Barnell L Stewart & Lonie Powell S; m 1947 to John Raab Skipper, Sr; c John Raab, Jr, Stewart Allen & William Van Deripe. Educ: Southern Col, 43. Polit & Govt Pos: Secy, Highlands Co Dem Exec Comt, Fla, 70-75; jury comnr, Highlands Co, 71-; committeewoman, Fla State Dem Comt, 75- Bus & Prof Pos: Clerk typist, Highlands Co Tax Assessor, 68-75. Publ: Out of the past, Spring Lake Breeze, 74-75 & Westinghouse Corp, monthly. Mem: Sebring Jr Womans Club; Fred Wild PTA; Highlands Co Lay Adv Comt to Sch Bd (secy, 70-73); Sebring Hist Soc (pres, 70-73). Honors & Awards: Highlands Co Most Outstanding Family Award, Sr Womans Club, 69; Outstanding Civic Award, Fla Pub Rels Asn, 71; Appreciation Award, Sebring Hist Soc, 72; Marguerite Rd Dedicated, 74. Relig: Methodist. Mailing Add: Rte 1 Box 289 Skipper Rd Sebring FL 33870

SKLAR, STEVEN V (D)
Md State Deleg
Mailing Add: 119 Cross Keys Rd Baltimore MD 21210

SKOGLUND, WESLEY JOHN (DFL)
Minn State Rep
b Minneapolis, Minn, June 9, 45; s John Skoglund & Edith Peterson S. Educ: Univ Minn, BA, 67. Polit & Govt Pos: Hennepin Co Park Comnr, Minn, 74-75; Minn State Rep, 75- Bus & Prof Pos: Personnel-employee rels, Control Data Corp, 67-75. Mil Serv: Minn Army Nat Guard, 67. Mem: YMCA (gov bd); Bicentennial Comn; Hennepin Co Study Group. Honors & Awards: YMCA Awards; Hennepin Co Award. Mailing Add: 5701 19th Ave S Minneapolis MN 55418

SKUBITZ, JOE (R)
US Rep, Kans
b Frontenac, Kans; s Joe Skubitz & Mary Youvan S; m 1930 to Mary Jess McClellan; c Dan Joseph. Educ: Kans State Col, BS, MS; George Wash Univ; Spec Citation from Kans State Col. Polit & Govt Pos: Admin asst to Sen Clyde M Reed & Sen Andrew F Schoeppel; US Rep, Kans, 63- Legal Res: Pittsburg KS 66762 Mailing Add: 7704 Glennon Dr Bethesda MD 20034

SLACK, JOHN M, JR (D)
US Rep, WVa
b Charleston, WVa, Mar 18, 15; married; c One son. Educ: Va Mil Inst. Polit & Govt Pos: Mem, Kanawha Co Court, WVa, formerly; US Rep, WVa, 58-, mem, House Comt on Appropriations, US House of Rep; mem, James Madison Mem Comn, 60-; deleg, Dem Nat Conv, 60, 64 & 68; mem, US-Can Interparliamentary Conf, 62, 64 & 68. Mem: Scottish Rite; York Rite; Mason; Shrine; Exchange Club; Elks. Relig: Presbyterian. Legal Res: Charleston WV Mailing Add: 2230 Rayburn House Off Bldg Washington DC 20515

SLACK, RICHARD C (D)
Tex State Rep
Mailing Add: 1709 Jefferson St Pecos TX 79772

SLAGLE, DAVID LEWIS (R)
Chmn, Douglas Co Rep Cent Comt, Wash
b Republic, Wash, Mar 29, 21; s Jesse Whitlock Slagle & Elizabeth Hayes Moore S; m 1948 to Eileen Virginia Carr; c Daniel E, David L, Jr, Douglas A, Diane E, Paul W, Steven K, Sheryl C, & Sylvia E. Educ: Wash State Univ, BS, 43; Rho Chi (pres local chap, 43); Sigma Nu. Polit & Govt Pos: City councilman, Waterville, Wash, 60-64; mem bd health, Chelan Douglas Co, 64-68; committeeman, Precinct No 2, Waterville, 70; chmn, Douglas Co Rep Cent Comt, 71-, exec bd, 72-; dist comnr, Rep Party, 75. Mil Serv: Entered as Pvt, Army, 43, released as S/Sgt, 46, after serv in Seventh Inf Div, Cent Pac & SW Pac-Korean Occup, 44-45; Purple Heart; Battle Stars; Korean Occup Medal, 45. Mem: Wash State Pharmaceut Asn (mem bd mgr, 63-66, chmn, 63-69); Chelan Douglas Pharmaceut Asn; NCW Health Planning Coun, (bd mem, 72-73); Wash State Univ Alumni Asn, (dep dir, 72-73); Mason (Master, Lodge No 57, 63). Relig: Presbyterian; Bd mem, Waterville Federated Church, 72- Mailing Add: PO Box 578 Waterville WA 98858

SLAGLE, GENE (D)
Ohio State Sen
b Bucyrus, Ohio, Nov 20, 14; s Milford G Slagle & Olive C Ballou S; m 1937 to Emily F Weber; c Nelson E, Bonnie J (Mrs Shaffstall), Betty J (Mrs Huckaba), James W & John W. Educ: Ohio State Univ, BS in Agr, 36; pres, Delta Theta Sigma; mem Student Senate, Inter-Fraternity Pres Coun; All Agr Coun. Polit & Govt Pos: Dist supvr, Farm Security Admin, US Dept Agr, 37-42; mem, Ohio Auctioneers Comn, 63 & 65, chmn, 72; mem platform comt, State Dem Conv, 64, 68 & 70; Ohio State Rep, Marion Co, 65-66; mem, Ohio

State Dem Cent Comt, Eighth Dist, 70-72; Ohio State Sen, 26th Sen Dist, 73- Bus & Prof Pos: Auctioneer in ten states & Can; exec secy, Ohio Jersey Breeders Asn, 47 & 50; instr, Reppert Sch, Auctioneering, Decatur, Ind, 55- Mem: Nat Auctioneers Asn; Ohio Auctioneers Asn (dir); Nat, State & Local Real Estate Bds. Relig: Methodist. Legal Res: 6150 State Rte 19 Galion OH 44833 Mailing Add: 217 Harding Hwy E PO Box 57 Galion OH 44833

SLATTERY, JAMES CHARLES (D)
Kans State Rep
b Atchison, Kans, Apr 4, 48; s Charles B Slattery & Rose M O'Connell S; single. Educ: Netherlands Sch Int Econ & Bus, 69; Washburn Univ, BS, polit sci, 70; Washburn Law Sch, 71-; Phi Delta Theta. Polit & Govt Pos: Pres, Washburn Col Young Dem, 68; admin aide to US Rep, William R Roy, Kans, 72; Kans State Rep, 72- Bus & Prof Pos: Economist, Kans State Dept Labor, 70-72; salesman, Looe & Robb Realtors, 73. Mil Serv: Entered as Pvt, E-3, Kans Army Nat Guard, 70-, 2nd Lt, currently. Mem: Kans Young Dem; Topeka Big Brother-Big Sister; Goals for Topeka; Washburn Alumni Asn; Phi Delta Theta (alumni bd, 70-). Honors & Awards: Chosen for Netherlands exchange prog, Washburn Univ, 68 & honor roll, 69-70; acad honors, Netherlands Sch Int Econ & Bus, 68-69. Relig: Roman Catholic. Legal Res: 1174 Fillmore Topeka KS 66604 Mailing Add: 1400 Topeka Blvd Topeka KS 66603

SLATTERY, THOMAS EDWARD (R)
Kans State Rep
b Topeka, Kans, May 14, 40; s Joseph Patrick Slattery & Anna Veronica McGreevy S; m 1964 to Mary Ellen Moran; c Michael Joseph, Anne Denise & John Moran. Educ: Benedictine Col, BA, 62. Polit & Govt Pos: Kans State Rep, 75- Bus & Prof Pos: Dept mgr, Hallmark Cards, Topeka, Kans, 67- Relig: Roman Catholic. Mailing Add: 3431 NW 42nd Terr Topeka KS 66618

SLAUGHTER, DANIEL FRENCH, JR (INDEPENDENT)
Va State Deleg
b Culpeper Co, Va, May 20, 25; m to Kathleen Wilson Rowe. Educ: Va Mil Inst & Univ Va, BA, LLB; Omicron Delta Kappa; Raven Soc; Delta Psi; pres, Univ Va Alumni Asn, 69-70. Polit & Govt Pos: Va State Deleg, 58-; vchmn, Comn on Pub Educ, 58-62; chmn, Comn on Voc Educ, 63-64; chmn, Income Tax Study Comn, 66-68. Bus & Prof Pos: Lawyer. Mil Serv: Army, combat infantry. Mem: Ruritans; Am Legion; VFW; Farm Bur; Rotary. Honors & Awards: Recipient of Distinguished Serv Award for Culpeper Co, 60. Relig: Episcopal. Mailing Add: 139 W Davis St Culpeper VA 22701

SLAUGHTER, LOUISE MCINTOSH (D)
b Lynch, Ky, Aug 14, 29; d Oscar Lewis McIntosh & Grace Byers M; m 1956 to Robert Bruce Slaughter, Jr; c Megan Rae, Amy Louise & Emily Robin. Educ: Univ Ky, BS, 51, MS, 53. Polit & Govt Pos: Committeeman, Monroe Co, NY, 70-; cand, Monroe Co Legis, 71 & 73; deleg, Dem Nat Conv, 72; co-chmn, Monroe Co Citizens for McGovern, 72. Bus & Prof Pos: Bacteriologist, Ky State Dept Health, Louisville, 51-52, Univ Ky, 52-53; mkt research, Procter & Gamble, Cincinnati, 53-56; dir, Monroe Commun Corp, 73- Mem: Perinton Greenlands Asn (founder & chmn, 70); Common Cause; Perinton Dem (co chmn, 70-); Nat Women's Polit Caucus; League of Women Voters. Relig: Episcopal. Mailing Add: 14 Manor Hill Dr Fairport NY 14450

SLAUGHTER, ROBERT L (R)
Chmn, 16th Dist Rep Comt, Mich
b Cleveland, Ohio, Feb 19, 33; s Edwin M Slaughter & Florence Black S; m 1968 to Jean E Little; c Robert L, Jr, Susan J, Laurie A & James B. Educ: Wayne State Univ, 51-53 & 57-58; Univ Mich-Dearborn, 72. Polit & Govt Pos: Exec dir, Wayne Co Rep Comt, 67-68; assoc dir, Southeast Mich United Rep Fund, 68-69; dist dir, US Census, Southwestern Wayne Co, 70; chmn, 16th Dist Rep Comt, Mich, 72- Bus & Prof Pos: Founding mem, Mich Advert Agency Coun, 72- Mil Serv: Entered as Airman Basic, Air Force, 53, released as S/Sgt, 57, after serv in Air Training Command. Mem: Bus, Prof Advert Asn; Elks; Dearborn City Beautiful Comn; Dearborn Bicentennial Comn; Dearborn Police Reserve. Honors & Awards: Dearborn Police Dept Commendation, 72 & 73; Mich Advert Agency Coun Creative Achievement Award, 74. Relig: Methodist. Mailing Add: 441 S Melborn Dearborn MI 48124

SLAY, CHESTER L, JR (D)
Tex State Rep
Mailing Add: 4930 Beaumont Dr Beaumont TX 77708

SLAY, FRANCIS R (D)
Mem, Mo Dem State Comt
b St Louis, Mo, Oct 28, 27; s Joseph K Slay & Marie Elias S; m 1951 to Ann Sobocinski; c Gerard, Francis, Sharron, Michael, Brenda, Raymond, Ann, Maria, Leo & Thomas. Educ: High Sch. Polit & Govt Pos: Mo State Rep, 64th Dist, until 71; committeeman, Dem 23rd Ward, 67; deleg, Dem Nat Conv, 68 & 72; mem, Mo Dem State Comt, currently. Bus & Prof Pos: Pres, Slays Food, Inc. Mil Serv: Army, 45-47. Mem: KofC; Maronite Soc; Kiwanis; St Jude Alsac; Health Welfare of Restaurants, St Louis (bd trustees). Relig: Catholic. Mailing Add: 6532 Scanlan Ave St Louis MO 63139

SLAYDEN, GLADYS (D)
Miss State Rep
b Marshall Co, Miss; m to Everett Slayden (deceased). Polit & Govt Pos: Miss State Rep, currently. Bus & Prof Pos: Farmer. Mem: Garden Clubs of Miss (life mem & past pres); Farm Bur; DAR; UDC; Holly Springs Garden Club (past pres & pilgrimage chmn). Relig: Baptist. Mailing Add: The Magnolias Holly Springs MS 38635

SLAYTON, FRANK M (D)
Va State Deleg
Legal Res: VA Mailing Add: PO Box 446 South Boston MA 24592

SLEAR, JOHN KLUMP (D)
b Williamsport, Pa, Mar 15, 91; s Henry Gutelius Slear & Hettie Elizabeth Clark S; m 1920 to Julia Ramsay McNinch. Educ: Va Polytech Inst; Nat Univ Law Sch, LLB, MPL, 37. Polit & Govt Pos: Secy to US Rep Alfred L Bulwinkle, NC, 31-43; mem, Mecklenburg Co Dem Comt; exec officer of Green Pastures Rally honoring President Franklin D Roosevelt, Charlotte, NC, 36; deleg, NC Young Dem Conv, 40; secy to US Rep Cameron A Morrison, NC, 43-45; charter mem, Nat Burro Club, Washington, DC, 45; secy to US Rep Robert L Doughton, NC, 46-47; secy to US Rep Hamilton C Jones, NC, 47-50; adv, Dem Nat Conv, 48; admin asst to US Sen Willis Smith, NC, 51-53; admin asst to US Sen Alton A Lennon, NC, 53-54; chief counsel to Subcomt on Govt Employees Security under US Sen Olin D Johnston, SC, 55-56; admin asst to US Rep Alton A Lennon, NC, formerly. Bus & Prof Pos: Trustee in bankruptcy & receiver, Charlotte, NC, 29-31; night sch instr math, Mecklenburg Co Pub Schs, 30; erected first tel line from Black Mt to Mt Mitchell, NC. Mil Serv: Entered as 2nd Lt, Coast Artil Corps, 17, released as 1st Lt, 19, after serv in France. Mem: Fed & NC State Bar Asns; NC Dem Club of Washington, DC, NC State Soc, Washington, DC (pres, 9 years); Senate Admin Assistants & Secretaries Asn. Relig: Methodist; helped organize First Methodist Church, Charlotte, NC, 23-27, steward; steward & supt, Intermediate Dept of Sunday Sch, Tryon Street Methodist Church, 24-27; helped to organize & establish Uptown Methodist Church. Mailing Add: 511 N Church St Charlotte NC 28202

SLEEPER, JON ANTHONY (R)
Chmn, Dawes Co Rep Comt, Nebr
b Marshall, Mich, Sept 29, 51; s John Arthur Sleeper & Vivian Kreger S; single. Educ: Kellogg Community Col, Battle Creek, Mich, law enforcement, 71; Chadron State Col, 72-75. Polit & Govt Pos: State col chmn, Nebr Young Rep, 74-75; chmn, Dawes Co Rep Comt, Nebr, 74- Bus & Prof Pos: Life ins salesman, Chaney & Assoc, Chadron, Nebr, 75- Mem: Conservative Caucus; Nebr Fedn Young Rep. Relig: Catholic. Legal Res: 342 Mears Chadron NE 69337 Mailing Add: PO Box 709 Chadron NE 69337

SLEETH, PATRICIA FORD (D)
b Nutter Fort, WVa, Nov 7, 24; d William Stephen Ford (deceased) & Leora Snodgrass F; div; c Patricia (Mrs David Morris) & David Ellery Kirkpatrick. Educ: Salem Col, 42-43 & 49-50; Morris Harvey Col, 70-74. Polit & Govt Pos: Mem, Dem Charter Comn, Dem Nat Comt, 75- Bus & Prof Pos: Oper, Maiden Form Bras Co, Clarksburg, 46-62; women's activities dir, Harrison Co Labor Fedn, AFL-CIO, 60-62, vpres, 61-62; women's activities dir, WVa Labor Fedn, AFL-CIO, 62-74 & Md State & DC AFL-CIO, 74- Mem: Int Ladies Garment Workers Union, AFL-CIO; Beta Sigma Phi. Relig: Protestant. Legal Res: 9578 Muirkirk Rd Laurel MD 20811 Mailing Add: 305 W Monument St Baltimore MD 21201

SLOAN, FRANK KEENAN (D)
Exec Committeeman, Richland Co Dem Party, SC
b Johnson City, Tenn, Oct 11, 21; s Z Frank Sloan & Maria Witten S; m 1946 to Helen Rhett Yobs; c Richard O, Christine, Lewis W & Frank K, Jr. Educ: Univ SC, AB, 43, LLB, 48; Phi Beta Kappa; Omicron Delta Kappa; Order Wig & Robe; Sigma Chi; Kappa Sigma Kappa. Polit & Govt Pos: Co & ward officer, Richland Co & Columbia, SC Dem Party, 48-69; reporter, SC Judicial Coun, 56-60; mem, SC Alcohol Comn, 58-62; SC Campaign Mgr for Pres John F Kennedy, 60; SC chmn, Citizens for Kennedy-Johnson, 60; state orgn chmn, SC Dem Party, 61-62, secy-treas, 64-65; dep asst secy defense, Dept of Defense, DC, 62-64; regional dir, US Off Econ Opportunity, Atlanta, Ga, 65-67; Dem nominee, US House Rep, Second Dist, SC, 68; exec committeeman, Richland Co Dem Party, 69- Bus & Prof Pos: Assoc & partner, Cooper & Gary, Attorneys, Columbia, SC, 48-65; assoc prof law, Univ SC, 55-65; vpres, Inst Polit & Planning, Washington, DC, 67-; attorney-at-law, Sloan & Sloan, Attorneys, Columbia, SC, 68- Mil Serv: Entered as Ens, Navy 43, released as Lt(jg), 46, after serv in Atlantic & Pac Theatres, recalled, 51-52, Lt, USS Salem, Sixth Fleet, 51-52; Capt, Res, 65-; Presidential Unit Citation with Star; Naval Res Medal; World War II Serv Medal; Atlantic Theatre Medal; Pac Theatre Medal with Five Battle Stars; Korean Serv Medal; Philippine Victory Medal with Star. Publ: Number of articles in professional legal journals, 49- Mem: Am Legion; VFW; Rotary; Am Fedn Musicians; Palmetto Club. Relig: Lutheran. Mailing Add: 3320 Devereaux Rd Columbia SC 29205

SLOAN, GRACE MCCALMONT (D)
State Treas, Pa
b Dayton, Pa; d Charles Plumer McCalmont & Minnie Boals Elwinger; m to John E Sloan, wid; c Mary Kathryn (Mrs Meyer) & Jacqueline (Mrs Ketner). Polit & Govt Pos: Mem, Pa State Dem Exec Comt, 44-50; mem, Pa State Dem Comt, 44-60; mem, Clarion Co Dem Women's Club; mem, Clarion Co Exec Comt, 46-; registr dir, Pa Fedn of Dem Women, 49-53, pres, 57-61; mem, State Employees' Retirement Bd, 57-65 & 69-; mem, Pa State Dem Policy Comt, 57-71; co-chmn, Dem Statewide Registr Comt, 60-70; mem, Pa State Nomination Recommendation Comt, 71-; State Treas, Pa, 61-65 & 69-; Auditor Gen, Pa, 65-69. Bus & Prof Pos: Treas, Gen State Authority, State Hwy & Bridge Authority & State Pub Sch Bldg Authority, 61-; chmn Bd of Finance & Revenue, 61-65 & 69-; mem, Bd of Comnrs of Pub Grounds & Bldgs, 61-; Del River Port Authority, 61-; treas, Pa Higher Educ Facilities Authority & Pa Transportation Assistance Authority, 68- Mem: Nat Asn of State Auditors, Comptrollers & Treas (pres); Mem Scholarship Fund of Pa Fedn of Dem Women (chmn); Fedn of Bus & Prof Women; Am Legion Auxiliary; Clarion Civic Club. Honors & Awards: Nat Distinguished Serv Award, DAV, 70, Distinguished Serv Award, Pa Dept, DAV, 72. Relig: Presbyterian. Legal Res: 1104 Main St Clarion PA 16214 Mailing Add: 129 Finance Bldg Harrisburg PA 17120

SLOAN, JAMES A (D)
Mont State Rep
b Missoula, Mont, Dec 4, 46; s Joseph M Sloan & Doris Nicola S; single. Educ: Gonzaga Univ, 65-70; Western Ky Univ, 71. Polit & Govt Pos: Mont State Rep, 75- Mailing Add: 421 Second Ave W Kalispell MT 59901

SLOAN, JAMES PARK (R)
b Clinton, SC, Oct 2, 16; s Eugene Blakely Sloan & Janie Pressly Lindsay S; m 1941 to Alice Catherine Gaines; c James Park, Jr & Edwin Gaines. Educ: Erkskine Col, BA, 37; Tulane Univ, MA, 38; Euphemian Lit Soc. Polit & Govt Pos: SC State Rep & mem house ways & means comt, 40-42; deleg, SC State Dem Conv, 42, 46, 48, 54, 56, 58 & 60; chmn, Laurens Co Dem Exec Comt, SC, 48-50, mem, 50-60; co-chmn, Laurens Co Strom Thurmond Write-In Campaign for US Senate, 54; mem, Clinton City Coun & chmn finance comt, 54-60; mem bd dirs, Clinton-Newberry Natural Gas Authority, 54-60; mem adv coun, SC Employ Security Comn, 55-; deleg, Dem Nat Conv, 56; Laurens Co chmn, S Carolinians for Independent Electors, 56; deleg, SC State Rep Conv, 68, 70, 72 & 74; mem, Laurens Co Bd Elec Comnrs, 70-, chmn, currently; chmn, Laurens Co Rep Conv, 72; mem Clinton Citizens' search comt that recommended the City's first two city mgrs, 72-73; mem, Clinton City Employee Appeal Bd, 73-; mem adv coun, US Small Bus Admin, Columbia Dist, 74-; mem bd trustees, John de la Howe Sch, 75-; chmn, Clinton City Am Revolution Bicentennial Comt, 75- Bus & Prof Pos: Teacher, Ga Mil Acad, 38-39 & Clinton High Sch, 39-40; paymaster, Joanna Cotton Mills, 42, personnel dir, 46-58 & dir indust & pub rels, 58-64; asst prof polit sci, Col Charleston, 64-67; from instr to asst prof, Spartanburg Regional Campus, Univ SC, 67-70, asst dir acad affairs, 70-73, asst prof, 73- Mil Serv: Entered as A/S, Navy, 42, released as Lt, 46, after serv in Naval Res Amphibious Forces, European-Mediter & Asiatic-Pac

Theatres; Battle Stars for participating in invasions of Sicily, Leyte & Luzon. Publ: Jefferson Davis stopped here—and here—and here—, Columbia The State Mag, 54; History of Company F, 14th Regiment, SC Vol, CSA, Joanna Way, 63; Hearst family involved in founding of Erskine College, Greenville News Blue Ribbon Feature, 74. Mem: Laurens Co Hist Soc (charter mem); Am Legion; Univ S Caroliniana Soc (contrib mem); Laurens Co Tri-Centennial Comt; SC & Southern Polit Sci Asns. Honors & Awards: George Washington Honor Medal, Freedoms Found, 63; Outstanding Teacher of Year, Univ SC, Spartanburg, 75. Relig: Associate Reformed Presbyterian. Mailing Add: 103 W Maple St Clinton SC 29325

SLOAN, SHELDON HAROLD (R)
b Minneapolis, Minn, Dec 25, 35; s Leonard N Sloan, MD & Mary W S; m 1964 to Loraine Bayer; c Stephen H & Jennifer B. Educ: Univ Calif, Los Angeles, BS, 58; Univ Southern Calif, JD, 61; Phi Delta Phi; Tau Epsilon Phi. Polit & Govt Pos: Attorney, US Dept Justice, 62-63; pvt pract, 63-73; dist adv coun, Small Bus Admin, 71; alt deleg, Rep Nat Conv, 72; pub mem, Bd of Registration for Prof Engrs, Calif, 72-73; judge, Munic Court, Los Angeles, 73- Mem: Am Bar Asn; State Bar of Calif; Calif Trial Lawyers Asn; Ionic Lodge, Masons (Master Mason). Relig: Jewish. Legal Res: Beverly Hills CA 90210 Mailing Add: 110 N Grand Ave Los Angeles CA 90012

SLOAN, SONIA SCHORR (D)
Mem Steering Comt, Nat New Dem Coalition
b Wilmington, Del, Apr 1, 28; d Sigmund Schorr & Rosalia Hillersohn S; m 1957 to Gilbert Jacob Sloan; c Victor Schorr & Jonathan Lawrence. Educ: Syracuse Univ, BS, 49; Jefferson Med Col, MS, 50; Phi Beta Kappa; Sigma Pi; Iota Alpha Pi. Polit & Govt Pos: Pres, Young Dem of Northern New Castle Co, Del, 55-56; elec committeeperson, Ninth Rep Dist Dem Comt, Del, 60-; co-chmn, Del Citizens for McCarthy, 68; chmn, New Dem Coalition Del, 68-70; mem steering comt, Nat New Dem Coalition, 68-; vchmn, 69-75; alt deleg, Dem Nat Conv, 72. Bus & Prof Pos: Microbiologist, Temple Med Col, 50-52 & E I du Pont de Nemours & Co, 52-59. Publ: Two papers publ in J Bact, 50-52. Mem: Am Civil Liberties Union (mem bd, 71-); Del League Planned Parenthood (mem bd, 74-); Congregation Beth Emeth (mem bd trustees, 74-). Relig: Jewish. Mailing Add: 25 Indian Field Rd Wilmington DE 19810

SLONE, OTTIE MAE (R)
Chairwoman, Breathitt Co Rep Comt, Ky
b Blaine, Ky, Dec 8, 14; d Arbie L Gambill & Cynthia Sparks G; m 1934 to Estill F Slone; c Phyllis Ann (Mrs Williamson). Educ: Lee's Jr Col, 57-58; Eastern Ky State Univ, 63-64. Polit & Govt Pos: Chairwoman, Breathitt Co Rep Women, Ky, 68-; vgov, Seventh Cong Dist Rep Party, Ky, 72-; chairwoman, Breathitt Co Rep Comt, 75- Mem: Jackson Women's Club; Eastern Star (Worthy Matron, 53-54); Breathitt Co Citizens League. Honors & Awards: Order of Ky Cols. Relig: Protestant. Mailing Add: 974 Highland Ave Jackson KY 41339

SLUDDEN, CHARLES JOSEPH (D)
b Belfast, Ireland, Sept 14, 13; s John J Sludden & Elizabeth McMullen; m 1941 to Margaret Francis Flaherty; c Margaret (Mrs David Charles Frey), Mary Ann (Mrs WIlliam J Bond, Jr), Charles J, Jr & Elizabeth Ann. Educ: Taylor Allderdice High Sch, dipl, 30. Polit & Govt Pos: Deleg, Dem Nat Conv, 56, 60, 64 & 68, alt deleg, 72. Bus & Prof Pos: Gen chmn, BRT, 45-49, Pa state legis rep, 49-69; vpres, Pa AFL-CIO, 60-; state legis dir, United Transportation Union, 69-; mem labor adv comt, Pa State Univ. Relig: Roman Catholic. Legal Res: 413 Alta Vista Ave Harrisburg PA 17109 Mailing Add: 2107-09 N Sixth St Harrisburg PA 17110

SMALL, ARTHUR A, JR (D)
Iowa State Rep
Mailing Add: 427 Bayard St Iowa City IA 52240

SMALL, NEAL (R)
Tenn State Rep
Mailing Add: 5566 Forsyth Memphis TN 38118

SMALLEN, CHARLES DEWEY (D)
Treas, St Francois Co Dem Cent Comt, Mo
b Madison Co, Mo, Jan 5, 09; s Monroe Smallen & Margaret Sebastian S; m 1949 to Pauline Walker; c Paul Eugene, Dewey Wayne & Larry Dale. Polit & Govt Pos: Sheriff, St Francois Co, Mo, 49-52; committeeman, Randolph Twp Dem Party, 58-; juvenile officer, 24th Judicial Circuit Mo, 61-; treas, St Francois Co Dem Cent Comt, 64- Mem: Mo Juvenile Officers Asn; Farmington Elks; Masonic Lodge, Farmington, Mo; Kiwanis Club Desloge. Relig: Methodist. Mailing Add: 707 S Main St Desloge MO 63601

SMALLEY, CAROLYN WYNN (R)
Mem, Ga Rep State Cent Comt
b Toomsboro, Ga; m 1947 to F C Smalley. Educ: Toomsboro High Sch. Polit & Govt Pos: Chmn, Wilkinson Co Goldwater for President, Ga, 64; chmn, Wilkinson Co Rep Party, 66-73; deleg, Rep Nat Conv, 72; mem, Ga Rep State Cent Comt, 73-; dir, Rep Women's Fedn, Eighth Cong Dist, 73- Honors & Awards: Key Mem Award, Eighth Cong Dist Rep Conv, 73. Relig: Methodist. Mailing Add: Rte 1 Toomsboro GA 31090

SMALLEY, I M (D)
NMex State Sen
b 1906. Educ: Univ Pa, BS in Econ; Southern Methodist Univ Law Sch, LLB. Polit & Govt Pos: NMex State Rep, 47-52; NMex State Sen, 57- Bus & Prof Pos: Attorney. Mem: Rotary; Mason. Relig: Protestant. Mailing Add: Box 879 Deming NM 88030

SMALLEY, JAMES L (D)
Mem, Ga State Dem Exec Comt
b Lincolnton, Ga, Jan 1, 02; s James Richard Smalley & Carrie Lou Hogan S; m 1923 to Florine A Spiers; c Frarie C, Derrell G & James L, Jr. Educ: Univ Ga, DVM, 28; Am Vet Med Asn, student chap; Agr Club. Polit & Govt Pos: Alderman, City of Dublin, Ga, 33-34; chmn, Alpha Fowler, Pub Serv Comn Campaign, 58, Jimmy Bentley, Comptroller Gen Campaign, 62, G Elliott Hagan, US Cong Campaign, 66 & 70 & Tommy Irvin, Comnr Agr Campaign, 70; mem adv coun, Small Bus Admin, 60-71; asst chmn, Jimmy Carter Gov Ga Campaign, 70; mem, Ga State Dem Exec Comt, 71- Bus & Prof Pos: Vet supvr meat inspection, Dept of Agr, 58-70. Mem: Am, EGa & Southern Vet Med Asns; Ga Vet Med Asn; CofC. Honors & Awards: Vet of the Year, Ga Vet Med Asn, 65. Relig: Baptist. Legal Res: 122 N Elm St Dublin GA 31021 Mailing Add: PO Box 606 Dublin GA 31021

SMALLEY, K MAXINE (R)
Mem, Rep State Cent Comt Calif
b Ft Wayne, Ind, Sept 27, 20; d George Lee Morrison & Cora Ellen Wagoner M; m 1948 to Benjamin Franklin Smalley. Educ: Ind Univ, Bloomington, 38-41. Polit & Govt Pos: Alt mem, Los Angeles Co Rep Cent Comt, Long Beach, Calif Dist, 66-; chmn, 58th Assembly Dist, currently; mem, Rep State Cent Comt Calif, 67-; mem & secy bd, Community Action Agency, Off Econ Opportunity, 69-70; dist field supvr, Census, 70; pres, Long Beach Coun Rep Women Fedn, 75- Bus & Prof Pos: Prod control & acct clerk, Gen Elec Co, Ft Wayne, Ind, 42-45; payroll supvr, US Navy Finance Off, Long Beach, Calif, 45-60. Mem: Nat Asn Parliamentarians (Calif Unit); Eastern Star; The Ebell of Long Beach (pres, 71-72). Honors & Awards: Outstanding Performance Award, US Navy Finance Off; Recognized as One of Ten in State for Precinct Leadership by Gov Reagan & Rep State Cent Comt, 67; Merit Award, Los Angeles Co Rep Cent Comt, 68. Relig: Methodist. Mailing Add: Apt 15 436 Cedar Ave Long Beach CA 90802

SMALLEY, ROBERT MANNING (R)
b Los Angeles, Calif, Nov 14, 25; s William Denny Smalley & Helen McConnell S; m 1957 to Rosemary Sumner; c Leslie Estelle & David Christian. Educ: Univ Calif, Los Angeles, 46-47. Polit & Govt Pos: Pres, Westward Young Rep, Los Angeles, Calif, 54; confidential secy to mayor, San Francisco, 61-64; press secy to William F Miller, Rep Nat Comt, 64, asst dir pub rels, Rep Nat Comt, 64, dir pub rels, 64-65; campaign mgr, US Sen Robert P Griffin, Mich, 66; consult, Comt for Govt of the People & Allegheny Co Rep Exec Comt, Pa, 67; asst press secy, Gov Spiro T Agnew, cand for Vice President, 68; spec asst to Secy, Dept Com, 69-72; campaign mgr, US Sen Robert P Griffin, Mich, 72, admin asst, 72-73. Bus & Prof Pos: Partner, Whitaker & Baxter, San Francisco, Calif, 65-69. Mil Serv: Entered as A/S, Navy, 44, released as Yeoman 2/C, 46, after serv in ACORN & AFRS, Pac Theatre; SPac Serv & Combat Zone Ribbons. Publ: White Australia, Plain Talk, 5/50; weekly column, USA today, Calif Feature Serv, 68-69. Mem: Capitol Hill Club; assoc mem US Naval Inst, Annapolis, Md; Fed City Club, Washington, DC; Ephebian Soc; Calif Scholar Fedn. Relig: Protestant. Mailing Add: 1900 Pennsylvania Ave NW Washington DC 20006

SMART, CLIFFORD H (R)
b Sault Ste Marie, Mich, Jan 14, 05; married; c Marybeth, William & Robert. Educ: Wayne State Univ, BS & MA. Polit & Govt Pos: Mich State Rep, 64-74, minority leader, Mich House Rep, 71-74; alt deleg, Rep Nat Conv, 72. Bus & Prof Pos: Supt schs, 35 years; bd control, Ferris State Col, 75- Mem: Mich Educ Asn; Oakland Community Col (bd trustees, 64-); Rotary; CofC; F&AM 528. Relig: Episcopal. Mailing Add: Indian River MI 49749

SMART, IRENE BALOGH (D)
Ohio State Rep
b Cleveland, Ohio, Mar 24, 21; d John Balogh & Elizabeth Szaszak B; m 1945 to Charles E Smart; c Charles E, II, Mary (Mrs Radebaugh) & Jennifer L. Educ: Wittenberg Univ, BS, 42; Harvard Univ Med Sch, Grad in Physiotherapy, 43; William McKinley Sch Law, LLB, 55; Delta Zeta. Polit & Govt Pos: Councilman-at-lg, City of Canton, Ohio, 60-72; Ohio State Rep, 73- Bus & Prof Pos: Phys therapist, Cleveland Clin, Ohio, 43-44, Johns Hopkins Hosp, Baltimore, Md, 44-45, Sunbeam Sch for Crippled Children, Ohio Bd Educ, Cleveland, 45-46 & Mercy Hosp, Canton, 46-47; attorney, Smart & Smart, Canton, 56- Mem: Eastern Star; Federated Dem Women of Ohio; Canton Dem Women's Club; Grange; United Cerebral Palsy Asn. Mailing Add: 3807 Third St NW Canton OH 44708

SMATHERS, BRUCE ARMISTEAD (D)
Secy of State, Fla
b Miami, Fla, Oct 3, 43; s George A Smathers & Rosemary Townley S; m 1974 to Nancy Marilyn McDowell. Educ: Yale Univ, BA with hons in Econ; Univ Fla, JD; Student Govt; Desmos; Coun of Ten; Law Rev Ed Bd; pres, Young Dem; Beta Theta Pi. Polit & Govt Pos: Fla youth adv coun chmn, Law Enforcement subcomt, Mayor's Adv Coun Drug Abuse, Jacksonville, formerly; Fla State Sen, Dist 9, 72-74; Secy of State, Fla, 75- Bus & Prof Pos: Mem staff, State Attorney's Off, Duval Co, Fla, formerly; mem law firm, Moss, Mitchell & Smathers, Jacksonville, formerly. Mil Serv: Navy, 65-67, Lt, serv in Underwater Demolition; Lt, Naval Res; 2 Naval Unit Citations; Combat Badge; Vietnamese Serv Ribbon; Nat Defense Ribbon. Mem: Jacksonville Jaycees; Fla Bar Asn; Am Bar Asn; Nat Asn Secretaries of State. Honors & Awards: Outstanding Jacksonville Jaycee, 70-71, Outstanding Young Man of Jacksonville, 74; Outstanding Jaycee in Int Involvement, Fla Jaycees, 71-72. Relig: Methodist. Mailing Add: 3211 Enterprise Dr Tallahassee FL 32303

SMATHERS, GEORGE ARMISTEAD (D)
b Atlantic City, NJ, Nov 14, 13; s Frank Smathers & Lura Jones S; c John & Bruce. Educ: Univ Fla, BA; Col Law, Univ Fla, LLB. Polit & Govt Pos: Asst US Dist Attorney, 40-42; asst to Attorney Gen, 45-46; US Rep, Fla, 47-50, US Sen, 51-68. Mil Serv: Marine Corps, 42-45; Col, Marine Corps Res. Mem: Fla Bar Asn. Legal Res: Miami FL Mailing Add: Smathers & Merrigan Suite 1200 888-17th St NW Washington DC 20006

SMAZAL, VINCENT AUGUST (D)
b Papillion, Nebr, June 3, 13; s Charles Frank Smazal & Elizabeth Klein S; m 1953 to Mabel M Buchanan; c William Charles. Educ: High sch, 3 years. Polit & Govt Pos: Dem committeeman, 15th Precinct, Twin Falls, Idaho, 46-48, Dem committeeman, Fourth Precinct, 48-62; pres, Young Dem Club, Twin Falls Co, 46-48; state coordr, Dist Dem Comt, 60-62; deleg, Dem State Comt, 66 & 68; chmn, Twin Falls Co Dem Party, formerly; deleg, Dem Nat Conv, 68; mem, Idaho State Dem Cent Comt, formerly. Bus & Prof Pos: Farmer, 28-39; mechanic, wrecker serv body, fender & painting, 40-45; partner, Off Equip Sales & Serv, 45-63, owner, 63- Mem: CofC; Elks; Idaho Tax Equality Asn. Relig: Catholic. Mailing Add: 530 Main Ave S Twin Falls ID 83301

SMEDLEY, ROBERT WILLIAM (D)
Colo State Sen
b Denver, Colo, May 26, 27; s Victor Clyde Smedley & Anne Frances Wheeler S; m 1955 to Phoebe Ann Ellis; c Cara Ellen & Melissa Anne. Educ: Univ Colo, Boulder, BA, 50; Columbia Univ Law Sch, 51-53; Univ Denver Col Law, JD, 54; Beta Theta Pi. Polit & Govt Pos: Dep dist attorney, Denver, Colo, 56-61; town attorney, Bow Mar, 65-69, town trustee, 69-71; Colo State Sen, 75- Bus & Prof Pos: Partner, Phelps, Hall & Smedley, Denver, Colo, 61-66; pvt practice law, 66- Mil Serv: Entered as A/S, Navy, 45, released as Yeoman 3/C, 46. Publ: So You're Going to Court, Fountainhead, 64. Mem: Rotary; Phi Alpha Delta; Mason; Soc Professional in Disputes Settlement; Am Arbit Asn (commercial & labor panel). Relig: Protestant. Mailing Add: 5220 Ridge Trail Littleton CO 80123

SMELSER, CHARLES HAROLD (D)
Md State Sen
b Uniontown, Md, July 4, 20; s Charles Harold Smelser & Grace Ann Devilbiss S; m 1946 to Betty Marie Krueger; c Barbara Ann & Bernard Charles. Educ: Univ Md, BS, 42; Omicron Delta Kappa; Alpha Tau Omega. Polit & Govt Pos: Md State Deleg, Frederick Co, 55-63; Md State Sen, Dist Two, 67- Bus & Prof Pos: Trustee, Frederick Mem Hosp, Frederick, Md, 57-; dir, New Windsor State Bank, New Windsor, 57-; pres, Capitol Milk Producers Asn, Frederick, 68- Mil Serv: Entered as Cadet, Army Air Corps, 43, released as 1st Lt, 45, after serv in 490th Bomb Group, Eighth Air Force, Europe, 44-45; Res, 45-58; Distinguished Flying Cross; Air Medal with Five Clusters. Mem: Lions Int; Elks; Moose; Amvets; Farm Bur. Honors & Awards: Legislator of the Year, 60. Relig: Methodist. Mailing Add: RFD 2 Union Bridge MD 21791

SMILES, LEON (D)
Chmn, Palm Beach Co Dem Exec Comt, Fla
b New York, NY, Jan 20, 17; s Solomen Smiles & Minnie S; m 1940 to Ann Goldfarb; c Steven Michael, Scott Trent & Illene Gail. Educ: Abraham Lincoln High Sch. Polit & Govt Pos: Dist committeeman, Bergen Co, NJ, 49-74; chmn, Palm Beach Co Dem Exec Comt, Fla, 74-, dist exec committeeman, 74, precinct capt, 74. Bus & Prof Pos: Pres, Broadway Floorlov Co, Paterson, NJ, 45-74. Mil Serv: Entered as Pvt, Army, 43, released as 1st Sgt, 45, after serv in 79th Inf Div, ETO, 44-45; ETO Victory Medal; Europ-Africa-Mid East Medal. Mem: VFW; Jewish War Vet (co comdr); CofC. Relig: Hebrew. Legal Res: 2097 SW 13th Terr Boynton Beach FL 33435 Mailing Add: Dem Party Hqs 213 N Dixie Hwy Lake Worth FL 33460

SMIT, RAYMOND J (R)
Chmn, Washtenaw Co Rep Party, Mich
b Detroit, Mich, Sept 21, 28; s Maurice J Smit & Myrtle Cassity S; m 1951 to Patricia Joan O'Donaghey; c Deborah, Edward & Norman. Educ: Univ Mich, BS & MS in Civil Eng. Polit & Govt Pos: City chmn, Ann Arbor Rep Party, Mich, 63-65; Mich State Rep, 53rd Dist, 67-74; chmn, Washtenaw Co Rep Party, Mich, 75- Bus & Prof Pos: Prof engr, currently. Mil Serv: Entered as Pvt, Army, 51, released as Pfc, after serv in Artil Sch, Ft Sill, Okla. Publ: Tech papers. Mem: Am Soc Civil Engrs; Nat Soc Prof Engrs; Am Water Works Asn; Am Water Pollution Control Fedn; Mich Asn of Professions. Mailing Add: 2050 Winsted Ct Ann Arbor MI 48103

SMITH, A LEDYARD, JR (R)
Chmn, Bolton Rep Town Comt, Mass
b Milwaukee, Wis, Sept 27, 32; s A Ledyard Smith & Nancy Sawyer Falk S; m 1955 to Jacqueline Walker; c Katharine Marquand, Margaret Falk, A Ledyard, III, Robert Eliot, II & Jacqueline Josette Walker. Educ: Harvard Univ, 2 years; Bentley Sch Acct & Finance, Boston, Mass, grad, 61; Fly Club. Polit & Govt Pos: Trustee, South Boston Neighborhood House, 66-; mem, Bd of Registr, Bolton, Mass, 67-68, mem, Planning Bd, 68-73; chmn, Bolton Rep Town Comt, 68-; mem, Metrop Area Planning Coun, 70-73. Mil Serv: Entered as Pvt, Marines, 52, released as Lance Cpl, 60, after serv in HMR 161, Korean Theatre, 53-54. Mem: Lions; Clinton Hosp Asn (trustee, 74-). Relig: Protestant. Mailing Add: Century Mill Rd Bolton MA 01740

SMITH, A NEAL (D)
NC State Rep
Mailing Add: Hart Rd Rte 1 Woodleaf NC 27054

SMITH, ALBERT F (R)
Mem, Del Rep State Cent Comt
b Mulhall, Okla, June 16, 13; s Mary A Wall; div; c Patricia & James. Educ: Okla State Univ, BS in Chem Eng, 32; Univ Ill, PhD in Chem, 36; Phi Beta Kappa; Phi Kappa Phi; Phi Lambda Upsilon; Sigma Tau; Sigma Xi; Blue Key. Polit & Govt Pos: Chmn, Brandywine Hundred Rep Comt, Del, 56-60, acting state chmn, 60; deleg, Rep Nat Conv, 56-72; mem, Del Rep State Cent Comt, 58-, vchmn, 71-74; chmn, Rural New Castle Rep Comt, 60-; mem, Del River & Bay Authority, 69-, chmn, 71-; chmn, Rural New Castle Co Rep Party, 58-70. Bus & Prof Pos: Research chemist, E I du Pont de Nemours & Co, Inc, 36-39, research supvr, 39-64, lab dir, 52-54, research dir, 54- Mem: Am Chem Soc; Soc of Rheology; Am Phys Soc; NY Acad Sci; Am Inst Physics. Honors & Awards: Several tech articles & patents. Relig: Northern Baptist. Mailing Add: 3500 Nemours Bldg Wilmington DE 19801

SMITH, ALBERTA MARIE (D)
Recording Secy, Ariz State Dem Party
b Risco, Mo, Sept 19, 33; d Albert Haskens & Sylvia Walton H; m 1950 to Herbert Otis Smith; c Danny Alan, Debra (Mrs Robert Bartholomew) & David Otis. Educ: Yuma High Sch, grad, 50. Polit & Govt Pos: Dem precinct committeeman, Yuma, 66-75; various chairmanships, Ariz Fedn Dem Women, 67-74; dep registr, Yuma, Ariz, 67-75; chmn, Cand Buffet, 67 & 70; mem & mem exec comt, Ariz State Dem Comt, 68-75; from recording secy to pres, Yuma Dem Women, 68-74; chmn, Woman Doer Awards, 70; dir, Dem Teens, 71-72; deleg, Ariz Mini Conv, 74; campaign coordr for Cong Dist Three, Yuma Co, 74; recording secy, Ariz Dem State Party, 74-; mem task force, Gov Comn on Status of Women, Ariz, 75. Bus & Prof Pos: Agt, Motor Vehicle Dept & dep assessor, Yuma Co, Ariz, 66-75; co-owner & bookkeeper, Herb's Arco, Yuma, 71- Mem: Women of Moose (publicity chmn, 74-75); Am Bus Women Asn (recording secy, 74-75); PTA. Honors & Awards: Woman Doer of the Year, Yuma Dem Women, 72. Relig: Southern Baptist. Mailing Add: 2331 S Sixth Ave Yuma AZ 85364

SMITH, ALSON H, JR (D)
Va State Deleg
Mailing Add: PO Box 648 Winchester VA 22601

SMITH, ALVIN C (D)
Ala State Rep
Mailing Add: 708 Forestwood Rd Birmingham AL 35214

SMITH, ALVIN CURTIS (R)
Chmn, Lincoln Co, Miss
b Houston, Tex, Feb 2, 38; s Curtis C Smith & Naomi Starbuck S; div. Educ: Univ Miss, BBA; Sigma Alpha Epsilon. Polit & Govt Pos: Admin asst to state finance chmn, Miss Rep Party, 65-66; advance man-Southern Region, Nixon for President, 67; state treas, Miss Young Rep Fedn, 72-74; chmn, Lincoln Co, Miss, 72- Bus & Prof Pos: Pres, Smith Ins Agency, Inc, Brookhaven, 69- Mem: Brookhaven Jaycees; Brookhaven Kiwanis Club; United Fund of Lincoln Co (pres). Relig: Methodist. Mailing Add: PO Box 910 Brookhaven MS 39601

SMITH, BELLE HARDIN (R)
Chmn, Boyd Co Rep Party, Ky
b Louisa, Ky, Mar 7, 05; d Jerome Shelton Hardin & Anie Williamson H; m 1933 to Thomas Christian Smith; wid; c Jerome Thomas Buckley, George Phillip & Don Eugene. Educ: Univ Ky, 29-30; Morehead State Col, 36, 37 & 38. Polit & Govt Pos: Precinct chairwoman, Rep Party, 31-56; chairwoman, Boyd Co Rep Party, Ky, 56-72 & 75-; mem, Ky Human Rights Comt, Nat Federated Rep Women's Club, 56-; pres, Boyd Co Rep Woman's Club, 60- Mem: Eastern Star; Ladies Oriental Shrine; Farm Bur; Ashland Ky Woman's Club. Honors & Awards: Order Ky Cols. Relig: United Methodist. Mailing Add: 2608 Louisa St Catlettsburg KY 41129

SMITH, BERNARD C (R)
NY State Sen
b Barnesboro, Pa, July 29, 23; s Charles Smith & Mary DePaepe S; m 1949 to Elizabeth Ann Reynolds; c Bernard C, Terry Ross, Craig Lawrence & Timothy Blythe. Educ: Cornell Univ, AB, 44 & LLB, 49; Phi Delta Phi; Kappa Delta Rho. Polit & Govt Pos: NY State Sen, 66-; dist attorney, Suffolk Co, Riverhead, NY. Mil Serv: Army, Pac Theater. Mem: Sch Polit Sci, State Univ of NY (adv bd); St Johns Hosp (bd mgrs); Rotary. Relig: Episcopal. Mailing Add: Franklin St Northport NY 11768

SMITH, BERNARD CHESTER (R)
Chmn, White Co Rep Party, Ark
b Bradford, Ark, Dec 15, 24; s George D Smith & Mae Beatrice Ransom S; m 1951; m 1964 to Frances M Williams; c David Bruce. Educ: Univ Ark, BS, 45, Sch Med, MD, 49, internship & residency in Obstet-Gynec, 49-51. Polit & Govt Pos: Committeeman, White Co Rep Party, Ark, 64-, chmn, 73- Bus & Prof Pos: Gen practice, Smith Hosp, Bradford, Ark, 51- Mil Serv: Lt(jg), Navy, 49-50, serv in Naval Hosp, Pensacola, Fla; Nat Guard, 51-59, Maj. Mem: Am Med Asn; Ark & White Co Med Socs; F&AM; Shrine. Relig: Protestant. Mailing Add: Bradford AR 72020

SMITH, BETTY JANE (D)
b Roann, Ind, Sept 20, 19; d Cluster Teter & Cora Bolley T; m 1937 to Rollin L Smith; c Linda Jane & Terry Lee. Educ: Ind Univ Exten; heating eng & kitchen designing. Polit & Govt Pos: Dem precinct vcommitteewoman, Chester Twp, Ind, 56-64, Dem precinct committeewoman, 64-75; mem, Ind State Dem Platform Comt, 72 & 74; vchmn, Wabash Co Dem Cent Comt, 72-75. Mem: Wabash Co Dem Women's Club (vpres, 5 years, pres, 72-); Bus & Prof Women's Club; Eastern Star (Worthy Matron, Ivy Chap 69, 49, state page, 50); Gamma Chap, Epsilon Sigma Alpha; Past Matron's Club, Eastern Star. Relig: United Methodist; bd trustees, 73-75. Mailing Add: 313 Bond St North Manchester IN 46962

SMITH, BILL GORDON (D)
Ala State Rep
b Dunlap, Tenn, Nov 19, 38; s Gordon William Smith & Mary Anderson S; m 1960 to Betty Hawkins; c Brett Keith, Bart Karter & Bonnie Kay. Educ: Tenn Tech, BS, 60. Polit & Govt Pos: Ala State Rep, 74- Bus & Prof Pos: Sci computer programmer, Brown Eng, 63-65; sales engr, Electronic Assoc, Inc, 65-67; pres, Medcare, Inc, 67-69; exec vpres, Med Corp, Ramada Inn's, 69-70; pres & gen mgr, Int Fiber Glass Inc, 70- Mil Serv: Entered as 2nd Lt, Army, 60, released as 1st Lt, 62, after serv in 3rd Armored Calvary Regt, Ft Meade & Ger; Marksman Badge. Mem: Int Little League (dir). Honors & Awards: Outstanding Young Man of Year in Huntsville, 74; One of Four Outstanding Young Men in Ala, 74. Relig: Methodist. Mailing Add: 2203 Colice Rd SE Huntsville AL 35801

SMITH, CARL M (R)
Mont State Rep
Mailing Add: Olive MT 59343

SMITH, CARLYLE (D)
Tex State Rep
Mailing Add: 938 Burleson Grand Prairie TX 75050

SMITH, CAROLYN JONES (D)
b Norfolk, Va, Aug 15, 38; d Acie Jones & Bernice Wortham J; m 1969 to Richard W Smith; c Richee Lori. Educ: Hampton Inst, BS, 64; A&T Col, 2 years. Polit & Govt Pos: Admin asst to US Rep Shirley Chisholm, NY, 69- Relig: Episcopal. Mailing Add: 809 Hayward Ave Takoma Park MD 20012

SMITH, CECILIA TRAVIS (R)
Chmn, Tift Co Rep Party, Ga
b Savannah, Ga; d Maj Gen Robert Jesse Travis & Rena Falligant T; m 1942 to Dr William Thomas Smith; c Gordon Burns, Dr Bruce, Dr L Travis, Chris, Nancy & Cecilia D. Educ: Univ Ill, 36; Univ Ga, ABJ, 40; Delta Delta Delta. Polit & Govt Pos: Founder & pres, Tift Co Rep Women, Ga, 66-67; deleg, Ga Rep State Conv, since 67; pub rels chmn, Second Dist Rep Party, 73-, vchairwoman, 74; mem state credentials comt, Rep Party of Ga, 74, mem resolutions comt, 75; mem, Tift Co Bd Elec, 74-; chmn, Tift Co Rep Party, 75- Bus & Prof Pos: Ed of woman's page, Ga Dent Asn J, 69-70. Mem: DAR (regent, 65); United Daughters of Confederacy (pres, 66, state rec secy, 66); Colonial Dames XVII Century (treas, 69); Am Legion (pres, 45); Springhill Ladies Golf Asn. Relig: Methodist; teacher, Loyalty Class & former mem of choir, First Methodist Church of Tifton. Legal Res: 801 Carolina Dr Tifton GA 31794 Mailing Add: PO Box 307 Tifton GA 31794

SMITH, CHADWICK H (R)
b Irvington, NJ, July 5, 25; s J Miller Smith & Elvira F Starz S; m 1950 to Dolores Johnson; c Deborah Lee & Rebecca Lynn. Educ: Univ Mont, BA, 49, LLB & JD, 51; IBM Exec Mgt Sch, Ithaca, NY, 56; Brookings Inst, Govt Exec Sch, Santa Barbara, Calif, 59; Sigma Chi. Polit & Govt Pos: Chief dep co attorney, Lewis & Clark Co, Mont, 52-53; lobbyist, Mont State Legis, 53-; attorney, Mont Unemploy Compensation Comn, 64-69; chief counsel, Mont State Rep Party, 64-70 & chmn, Rules Comt, 70-73; deleg, Rep Nat Conv, 72. Bus & Prof Pos: Attorney, Home Fed Savings & Loan Asn, Helena, Mont, Mont Rural Hous Asn, Mont Sch Bd Asn & Am Mutual Ins Alliance, Chicago, Ill, currently. Mil Serv: Entered Army, 43, released as 2nd Lt, 46, after serv in Inf. Publ: Montana Real Estate Manual, Great Falls Tribune Printing, 65; Montana Hospital Law Digest, 68. Mem: Helena Salvation Army (bd mem, 51-); Rotary; Metrop Dinner Club of Helena; Algeria Shrine Temple (chmn, Wills & Gifts Comt

for Crippled Children's Hosp); Eagles (Chief Justice of Grand Tribunal). Relig: Presbyterian. Legal Res: 200 S Fee Helena MT 59601 Mailing Add: PO Box 604 Helena MT 59601

SMITH, CHARLES EUGENE (D)
Md House Deleg
b Brunswick, Md, Dec 18, 48; s Joseph Franklyn Smith & Zettie Lucas S; m 1974 to Judith Loyce Fava. Educ: Frederick Community Col, AA, 71; Univ Baltimore, BS, 73. Polit & Govt Pos: Field rep, Rep Goodloe E Byron, 70; chmn, Brunswick Dem Cent Comt, 70-74; co coordr, McGovern Campaign, Md, 72; Md House Deleg, 75- Bus & Prof Pos: Gen mgr, J R Marker Sheet Metal, Knoxville, Md, 73- Mem: New Market Vol Fire Co; Brunswick Slo-Pitch Softball League (chmn bd dir); Jefferson Ruritan Club. Mailing Add: 403 Walnut St Brunswick MD 21716

SMITH, CHARLES PHILIP (D)
State Treas, Wis
b Chicago, Ill, June 18, 26; s William A Smith, Sr & Lillian Christiansen S; m 1947 to Bernadette R Carroll; c Charles P, II, Stephen C, Megan E & Haley A. Educ: Milton Col, BS, 50. Polit & Govt Pos: Supvr, Dane Co Bd, 52-53; pres, Madison Rivers & Lakes Comn, 65-71; legis rep to exec bd, Dane Co Dem Party, 67-68, vchmn, 69-71; State Treas, Wis, 71-; mem, Wis Comn Pub Lands, 71-; deleg, Dem Nat Conv, 72. Bus & Prof Pos: Retail sales rep, Mobil Oil Co, 55-58; field rep, Guardian Life Ins Co Am, 58-62; field rep, Col Life Ins Co, 62-66; prof supvr, Olin Corp, Badger Army Ammunition Plant, 67-70. Mil Serv: Entered as Pvt, Marine Corps, 44, released as Pfc, 45, after serv in 1st Marine Div, SPac Theatre & Okinawa, 44-45; Purple Heart; Presidential Unit Citation. Mem: Nat Asn State Auditors, Comptrollers & Treas. Relig: Catholic. Legal Res: 509 S Spooner St Madison WI 53711 Mailing Add: State Capitol Madison WI 53702

SMITH, CHARLES PLYMPTON, IV (INDEPENDENT)
Vt State Rep
b Burlington, Vt, June 1, 54; s Frederick Plympton Smith & Marjorie Hewitt S; single. Educ: Harvard Col, 72-; Harvard Rugby & Mountaineering Clubs. Polit & Govt Pos: Vt State Rep, 75-, mem, Com Comt, Vt House Rep, 75- Honors & Awards: Bier Award, Phillips Andover, 72. Relig: Congregational. Mailing Add: 195 S Willard St Burlington VT 05401

SMITH, CLAUDE HARMAN (R)
Chmn, Culpeper Co Rep Comt, Va
b Winston, Va, Nov 3, 08; s James Wilbur Smith & Mary E Biedler S; m 1933 to Genevieve Grace Wright (deceased); m 1954 to Dorothy Mae Neal; c Elaine Joy (Mrs Dazey), Claude Harman, Jr & John Calvin Wright. Educ: Univ Md, AB, 32; Southeastern Univ, LLB, 36; Command & Gen Staff Sch, US Army, 44; Phi Kappa Phi; Omicron Delta Kappa; Beta Pi Theta; Scabbard & Blade; pres, Student Govt Asn, Coun of Debate & Relig Work Coun; M Club; Alpha Tau Omega; Rossbourg Club. Polit & Govt Pos: Dist supvr, US Treas Dept, 33-41; Chief Int Civil Aviation Orgn Off, US Civil Aeronaut Admin, 46-49, chief, Int Civil Aviation Orgn Div, 52-59; mem or chmn numerous US Gov Deleg to Int Aviation Conf; alt US Rep to Int Civil Aviation Orgn, 49-52, US Rep to Air Navig Comn, Int Civil Aviation Orgn, 49-52 & 59-60; chief, Int Orgn Div, US Fed Aviation Agency, 60-64; chmn, Culpeper Co Rep Comt, Va, 66- Mil Serv: Entered as 1st Lt, Army, 41, released as Lt Col, 46, after serv in Hq Air Force; Legion of Merit; Am Theater & Pre-Pearl Harbor Ribbons. Mem: Mason (32 degree); Am Legion; Culpeper & Va Hist Socs; SAR (pres, Va Soc, 65-66, chmn, Comt on Americanism). Relig: Protestant. Mailing Add: Savilla Manor Rte 4 Box 287 Culpeper VA 22701

SMITH, CURTIS (D)
Ala State Rep
Mailing Add: Rte 3 Box 118 Clanton AL 35045

SMITH, DAVID JAY (D)
b Uniontown, Pa, Aug 23, 47; s Lawrence Harry Smith & Mildred Rosenblum S; div. Educ: Univ Pa, AB, 69; Boston Univ Sch Law, JD, 73; Alpha Chi Rho. Polit & Govt Pos: Legis asst to US Rep Thomas E Morgan, Pa, 73- Mil Serv: Entered as Pvt, Army; SP-4, Army Res. Mem: Bar of Supreme Court Pa; Bar of DC Court of Appeals. Honors & Awards: US Law Week Award, Bur Nat Affairs, 73. Relig: Jewish. Mailing Add: 82 Gilmore St Uniontown PA 15401

SMITH, DEWEY EDWARD (D)
b Turner Co, Ga, July 20, 28; s Rufus Monroe Smith & Laura Roland S; m 1965 to Wilma Lee Carson; c Mike, Linda, Ann, Dean, Laura Lee & Robin. Educ: High sch grad. Polit & Govt Pos: Chmn, Polk Co Wallace Campaign, Fla, 68 & 72; deleg & mem rules comt, Dem Nat Conv, 72. Mil Serv: Entered as Pvt, Marine Corps, 45, released as Sgt, 49, after serv in 1st Marine Air Wing, Pac Theatre & China; Air Medal; Presidential Unit Citation. Mem: Am Asn Battery Mfrs; Ind Garage Owners of Am; Mason; Scottish Rite; Am Legion. Honors & Awards: Life membership, Optimist Int, 65. Relig: Baptist. Mailing Add: 224 Doris Dr Lakeland FL 33803

SMITH, DICK (R)
Idaho State Sen
Mailing Add: 74 Ash Ave Rexburg ID 83440

SMITH, DONALD ALBERT (R)
Chmn, Barbour Co Rep Exec Comt, WVa
b Yonkers, NY, Nov 19, 31; s Albert Henry Smith & Ruth Joudrey S (deceased); m 1957 to Barbara Eleanor Atkeson; c Jean Marie, David Andrew & Carolyn Rene. Educ: Columbia Col, BA, 53; Union Theol Sem, BD, 56; Teachers Col, Columbia Univ, MA, 59, EdD, 65; Phi Delta Kappa; Kappa Delta Pi; Curtis Medal for Excellence in Pub Speaking; Sigma Chi; Yearbook & Newspaper Staff; German Club. Polit & Govt Pos: Chmn, Barbour Co Rep Exec Comt, WVa, 64-67 & 73- Bus & Prof Pos: Asst minister, Demarest Baptist Church, NJ, 53-54; asst minister, Flemington Baptist Church, 54-56; instr Eng, Kanto Gakuin Univ, Yokohama, Japan, 56-57; asst, Off of Registr, Teachers Col, Columbia Univ, 57-58, asst placement officer, Grad Sch Bus, 58-60; assoc dean students & dir student union, Alderson-Broaddus Col, 60-64, dir, Off-Campus Educ & Asst Prof Psychol, 64-75, assoc dean experimental educ, 75- Publ: Above the arctic circle, Am Scholar, summer 70; Comments on the objectives for field placement, J Coop Educ, 5/74; An overall view of cooperative education, 50 views, Midwest Ctr for Coop Educ; plus others. Mem: Am Asn Univ Prof; Student Union Asn; Mid-Atlantic Placement Asn; Coop Educ Asn; WVa Student Personnel Asn. Relig: Baptist. Mailing Add: Alderson-Broaddus Col Philippi WV 26416

SMITH, DONALD ARNOLD (D)
Mem, Washington Co Dem Cent Comt, Md
b Chicago, Ill, Aug 9, 31; s Claude Arnold Smith & Daisy Ann Saur S; m 1954 to Margaret Francis Dowd; c Donald Joseph & Linda Suzzane. Educ: Univ Tenn, 55; Univ MD, 65-71; Hagerstown Jr Col, 67-68; Iota Lambda Sigma. Hon Degrees: BSET, Capitol Inst Technol, Kensington, Md, 75. Polit & Govt Pos: Mem, Washington Co Dem Cent Comt, Md, 74-; mem, Md Dem State Cent Comt, 74- Bus & Prof Pos: Electronics instr, DC Pub Schs, 54-58; electronics instr, Nat Indust Electronic Research, 58-61; electronic develop technician, Nat Cancer Inst, Hagerstown, Md, 61-63; electronic develop technician, US Army, Ft Detrick, Md, 63-65; instr electronic technol, Montgomery Co Schs, Rockville, Md, 65- Mil Serv: Entered as Pvt, Air Force, 51, released as A/3C, 52, after serv in Guided Missiles; Korean Medal. Publ: Medical Electronics Equipment Handbook, 62 & ABC's of Electronic Test Equipment, 63 & 68, Howard W Sams & Co, Ind; Electron tube, In: Encycl Britannica, 74. Mem: Iota Lambda Sigma; Inst Elec & Electronics Eng; Morris Frock Post Am Legion; Funkstown Lions Club. Honors & Awards: Broome Award for Writing the Most Important Book for Students, Montgomery Co Educ Asn, 72. Relig: Protestant. Mailing Add: 1126 Outer Dr Hagerstown MD 21740

SMITH, DONALD EUGENE (R)
Rep State Committeeman, Fla
b Sanford, Maine, July 17, 24; s Harold Ernest Smith (deceased) & Ruth Elizabeth Garland S (deceased); m 1957 to Mary Jo Richardson; c stepsons, Edgar Jerome & Lamar Eugene Elton. Polit & Govt Pos: Deleg, Rep Nat Conv, 64; precinct committeeman; chmn, Lake Co Rep Exec Comt, Fla, formerly; Rep State Committeeman, Lake Co, 72- Bus & Prof Pos: Inspector, Retail Credit Co, 46-; sports correspondent, Leesburg Daily Commercial, Orlando Sentinel & Jacksonville J Times Union; assoc, Golden Real Estate Agency, 71- Mil Serv: Entered as A/S, Naval Res, 43, released as Aviation Ordnanceman 2/C, 45; Chief Personnelman, Naval Air Res, 68-; World War II Victory Medal; Am & Asiatic-Pac Theater Ribbons; Naval Res Medal; Meritorious Serv Ribbon. Publ: Feature story in all Fla Mag, 65. Mem: Elks; life mem US Jr CofC. Relig: Baptist. Mailing Add: 2513 Winona Ave Leesburg FL 32748

SMITH, DONALD HOUSTON (D)
Chmn, Jefferson Co Dem Cent Comt, Ark,
b Peach Orchard, Ark, Mar 18, 30; s Harmon Smith & Mary Ellen Cox S; m 1957 to Rose Mary Albano; c Donald Houston, Jr, Mary Ann & Brian Davis. Educ: Ark State Univ, BA, 53; Univ Ark, LLB, 59; Blue Key; Phi Kappa Alpha; Phi Alpha Delta. Polit & Govt Pos: Chmn, Jefferson Co Dem Cent Comt, Ark, 64-; chmn, Jefferson Co Elec Comn, 64-; mem, Ark Dem Cent Comt, formerly. Bus & Prof Pos: Chmn, Southeast Ark Econ Develop Dist, 67- Mil Serv: Entered as 2nd Lt, Army, 53, released as 1st Lt, 56, after serv in 17th Field Artil Bn & 1st Cavalry Artil, Far East Command, 54-56. Mem: Am Bar Asn; Jefferson Co Bar Asn (pres, 71-); Judicature Soc of Am Bar Asn; Ark Bar Asn (chmn, Family Law Sect, 69-); Pine Bluff CofC (bd dirs). Honors & Awards: Pine Bluff Jr CofC Distinguished Serv Award, 63; Lawyer's Citizen Award, Ark Bar Asn, 67. Relig: Baptist. Mailing Add: Box 5010 Pine Bluff AR 71601

SMITH, DONALD L (R)
Vt State Sen
b Barre, Vt, May 20, 24; s Donald W Smith & Freda Ladd S; m 1947 to Ruth Reynolds; c Donald R & Rebecca Ruth. Educ: Mass State Col, BS, 46. Polit & Govt Pos: Vt State Sen, 55-59 & 65-; fed housing dir, Vt, 59-61. Bus & Prof Pos: Life ins broker. Mem: Rotary; Elks; Mason; Farm Bur; Grange. Relig: Congregational. Mailing Add: RR 1 Barre VT 05641

SMITH, DONNA LEE (D)
Chairperson, Dubuque Co Dem Party, Iowa
b Epworth, Iowa, Mar 24, 41; d Don C McDermott & Colette Hoffmann M; m 1960 to C Patrick Smith; c Sheree, Shawn, Dana & Sasha. Educ: Western Dubuque High Sch, Iowa, grad. Polit & Govt Pos: Chairperson, Dubuque Co Dem Party, Iowa, 74-; vchairperson, Second Dist Cong Campaign Comt, 74- Mailing Add: 1827 Key Way Dubuque IA 52001

SMITH, DOUGLAS MYLES (D)
Maine State Rep
b Dover-Foxcroft, Maine, Dec 11, 46; s Myles Ethan Smith & Miriam Louise Flowers; single. Educ: Univ Maine, BA in int affairs, 69, MA in econ, 70. Polit & Govt Pos: Mem, Maine Dem State Cent Comt, 69-70; Young Dem nat committeeman, Maine, 70-; Maine State Rep, 71-, mem, Comt on Appropriations, Maine House of Rep, 73-; mem, State Spec Tech Assistance Prog Adv Bd, Off of Econ Opportunity, 72- Bus & Prof Pos: Teaching asst, Dept Econ, Univ Maine, 69-70, research asst, Manpower Research Proj, 70; vpres, Smith Timberlands, Inc, Dover-Foxcroft, 69- Mil Serv: Entered as E-1, Army Res, 69, E-3, currently. Publ: Education-taxation: a new approach, Townsman Mag, 3/71; A new departure for financing Maine primary & secondary education, Maine Teacher, 4/71. Mem: Dover-Foxcroft Jaycees. Relig: Protestant. Legal Res: 107 North St Dover-Foxcroft ME 04426 Mailing Add: Box 162 Dover-Foxcroft ME 04426

SMITH, E ARNOLD (D)
b Willis, Tex, Sept 6, 13; s E Arnold Smith, Sr & Allie D Spiller S; m 1941 to Allene Marie Hopkins; c Laura Elizabeth (deceased). Educ: Rice Univ, BA, 37; Univ Tex, LLB, 40; Sigma Nu Phi. Polit & Govt Pos: Co attorney, Montgomery Co, Tex, 41-45, co judge, 45-49; chmn, Montgomery Co Dem Party, formerly. Bus & Prof Pos: Partner, Smith & Simpson, Attorneys, Conroe, Tex. Mem: AF&AM, Conroe Lodge 748, Scottish Rite, Houston Consistory; Tex & Montgomery Co Bar Asns. Relig: Methodist. Legal Res: 202 Pine Shadows Conroe TX 77301 Mailing Add: PO Box 523 Conroe TX 77301

SMITH, EARL H (R)
Pa State Sen
Mailing Add: Capitol Bldg Harrisburg PA 17120

SMITH, EDWARD BRUCE (R)
Mont State Sen
b Dagmar, Mont, May 7, 20; s Bruce Albert Smith & Johanna Grelong S; m 1945 to Juliet Ellevold; c Gary, Douglas, Bruce & Rodney. Polit & Govt Pos: Mem, Co Fair Bd, Mont, 60-; Mont State Rep, Sheridan Co, 67-73; alt deleg, Rep Nat Conv, 72; Mont State Sen, 75- Mem: Mont Wool Growers (pres); Sheridan Co Grain Growers Asn; Elks; Moose; 4-H Leader. Relig: Lutheran. Mailing Add: RR 1 Box 11 Dagmar MT 59219

SMITH, EDWARD HENRY (R)
Mem, NC Rep State Exec Comt
b Charlotte, NC, Oct 8, 25; s Edward Arthur Smith, Jr & Winifred Eloise Moss S; single. Educ: Riverside Mil Acad, Gainesville, Ga, 42-43; Univ NC, Chapel Hill, 45-49; Phi Kappa Sigma; Dialectic Senate. Polit & Govt Pos: Mem, NC Citizens for Eisenhower Comt, 52; Rep precinct chmn, Kings Mountain, NC, 60-66; chmn, Cleveland Co Young Rep Club, 64-66; mem, NC Rep State Exec Comt, 64-; chmn, Cleveland Co Rep Exec Comt, 66-70 & 73-; Tenth Dist Rep Presidential Elector, 68. Bus & Prof Pos: Vpres, Edward A Smith & Sons, Kings Mountain, NC, 50-; radio newscaster, Cyanamid Textile News, WBIG & WFBC, Greenville & WBT, Charlotte, currently. Publ: A history of the Battle of Kings Mountain, Kings Mountain Hist Drama Asn, 53; series of newspaper articles, The Republican Party in North Carolina on its 100th anniversary, Shelby Daily Star & other papers, 4/67; weekly columnist, This week in North Carolina history, Kings Mountain Herald & other papers. Mem: Cleveland Co Hist Asn (vpres); Nat Trust for Hist Preservation; NC Soc for Preservation of Antiq; NC Soc of Co & Local Historians; NC Lit & Hist Soc. Honors & Awards: Auth of TV documentary Signers for Liberty for which WBT-V, Charlotte, NC received a George Washington Awards Medal from Freedoms Found, 67. Relig: Episcopal; mem, Church Vestry, Trinity Episcopal Church, Kings Mountain, NC. Mailing Add: 303 Battleground Ave Kings Mountain NC 28086

SMITH, EDWARD JACK (D)
SC State Rep
b Chesterfield, SC, July 18, 18; s Jackson Calhoun Smith & Mary Katherine McDougald S; m 1939 to Louella Gandy; c Jacquelyn (Mrs John Laney Melton) & Dowell Jack. Educ: Chesterfield High Sch, grad. Polit & Govt Pos: SC State Rep, 66-, first vchmn, Labor, Commerce & Indust Comt, SC House Rep, 68- Bus & Prof Pos: Ins agt, Nationwide Ins Co, 53; RR fireman engr, Seaboard RR, 42. Mil Serv: Entered as Pfc, Army, 44, released as Sgt, 45, after serv in RR Detachment. Mem: Mason; York Rite Shrine; Eastern Star; Am Legion; Lions. Honors & Awards: Man of the Month, Ins Agents SC. Relig: Baptist; Chmn Bd Deacons, Emmanuel Baptist Church, several years; Chmn Bldg Comt. Legal Res: Hwy 15 N Hartsville SC 29550 Mailing Add: PO Drawer 458 Hartsville SC 29550

SMITH, EDWARD PATRICK (D)
Wash State Rep
b Hoquiam, Wash, Dec 25, 17; s Edward Patrick Smith & Susie Thompson S; m 1941 to Barbara Irene Brown; c Kay (Mrs James Postma), Theresa (Mrs Michael Murphy) & Edward P, Jr. Educ: Grays Harbor Col, AA, 38; Cent Wash Col, BA, 40; Notre Dame Univ, MS, 46; Wash State Univ, DEd, 63; Phi Delta Kappa. Polit & Govt Pos: Wash State Rep, 75- Bus & Prof Pos: Instr & coach, Grays Harbor Col, 46-50, pres, 53-72; instr & athletic dir, St Martins Col, 50-52; secy-treas, Crawford-Baird Smith Corp, 72- Mil Serv: Entered as Seaman, Navy, released as Lt, after serv in SPac, 45; Lt Comdr, Naval Res; 5 Battle Stars; Presidential Unit Citation. Mem: Kiwanis; Elks; KofC; VFW; Am Legion. Honors & Awards: Neil Eddy Award-Outstanding Athlete, Grays Harbor Col, 38, Joe Cote Award-Outstanding State Coach, 50; Man of Year Award, State of Wash City of Hope, 71. Relig: Roman Catholic. Mailing Add: 511 Second Ave Aberdeen WA 98520

SMITH, EDWIN STEEVES (R)
Chmn, SDak State Rep Cent Comt
b Rochester, Minn, June 24, 38; s John W Smith & Florence Steeves S; m 1963 to Louise J Blair; c Andrea Louise, John Blair & Rosemary Clair. Educ: Carleton Col, BA, 60; Univ Minn Law Sch, LLB, 63; Gamma Eta Gamma. Polit & Govt Pos: Researcher, Legis Reference Serv, Libr of Cong, 58; chmn, Carleton Col Rep Club, SDak, 58-59; asst to Rep Albert H Quie, 59; chmn, Minn Fedn Col Rep, 59-60; chmn, Midwest Fedn Col Rep Clubs, 60-61; chmn, First & Second Ward, Hennepin City, Minn Young Rep, 61-63; chmn, Davison Co Rep Cent Comt, SDak, 66-72; Dep States Attorney, Mitchell, 68-; Rep State Cent Committeeman, Davison Co, 72-73, chmn, SDak State Rep Cent Comt, 73- Bus & Prof Pos: Asst to Elmer L Andersen, Cand for Gov, Minn, 60; trust officer, Aberdeen Nat Bank, 63-65; attorney, Tinan, Carlson, Padrnos & Smith, Mitchell, 65- Publ: Estate planning for farmers, series of 12 articles, Dak Farmer, 64-65. Mem: SDak Bar Asn; Mitchell Kiwanis; Jaycees; Methodist Hosp (pres); SDak Girls State (coordr for judicial activities). Relig: Lutheran. Legal Res: 500 W Fourth Mitchell SD 57301 Mailing Add: Box 488 Mitchell SD 57301

SMITH, ELIZABETH STRAUBEL (R)
Md State Deleg
b Baltimore, Md, Mar 18, 34; d Clyde Leon Straubel & Lucile Johnson S; m 1964 to Lloyd Spencer Smith. Educ: Jefferson Union High Sch, Daly City, Calif, grad, 51. Polit & Govt Pos: Campaign mgr, Md State Sen Edward T Hall, 70, admin asst to Sen Edward T Hall Minority Leader, Md State Senate, 71-74; alt deleg, Rep Nat Conv, 72; Md State Deleg, 75- Bus & Prof Pos: Asst mgr, Radio Sta WNAV, Annapolis, Md, 54- Mem: Md-DC-Del Broadcaster's Asn (legis chmn, 72-73); life mem CofC, Gtr Annapolis (pres, 70); Annapolis Zonta Club; Md Clam Festival, Inc (pres, 71-72); Md State CofC (vpres, 71-72). Relig: Catholic. Legal Res: Merrimac Rd Harbor Hills Davidsonville MD 21035 Mailing Add: Box 96-C Rte 2 Davidsonville MD 21035

SMITH, ELMER EUGENE (R)
b Wayne Co, Mo, Aug 23, 26; s Ira D Smith & Mabel Turnbough S; m 1946 to Bessie M Thompson; c Nancy (Mrs Babel), Sandra Sue & Donald Eugene. Educ: St Louis Univ, BS, 51. Polit & Govt Pos: Dir, R-2 Sch Dist, Mo, 61-63; dir of revenue, St Louis Co Govt, 63-; mem, Mo State Rep Cent Comt, 66-70, chmn, 68-70; area dir, Dept Housing & Urban Develop, 70- Bus & Prof Pos: Purchasing mgr, Natkin & Co, St Louis, Mo, 54-59, asst mgr, 59-61. Mil Serv: Entered as A/S, Navy 44, released as Aviation Radio Man 2/C, 51, after serv aboard several ships, Pac Theatre, 45-46; Three Battle Stars; Pac Theatre Ribbon; Japanese Occup Ribbon; Am Theater Ribbon; Presidential Unit Citation. Mem: Int Asn Assessing Officers; Nat Tax Asn; Mo Hist Soc; White Conf on Educ Comt, St Louis Co, Mo; Am Legion. Honors & Awards: Mo Rep of the Year, Mo Asn Rep, 67. Relig: Methodist. Mailing Add: 822 Gerald Pl Ferguson MO 63135

SMITH, ERIC (D)
Fla State Rep
Mailing Add: 891 Grove Park Blvd Jacksonville FL 32216

SMITH, FINIS W (D)
Okla State Sen
Mailing Add: State Capitol Oklahoma City OK 73105

SMITH, FLOYD EMERY (D)
Mem-at-Lg, Dem Nat Comt
Mailing Add: 9727 Mt Pisgah Silver Spring MD 20903

SMITH, FRANCIS E (D)
Kans State Rep
b Gardner, Kans, July 31, 52; s Ernest S Smith & Mary C DeJaegher S; single. Educ: Johnson Co Community Col, 70-72; Univ Kans, BS, 75. Polit & Govt Pos: Kans State Rep, Dist 27, 75- Mem: Grange; Kans & Nat Coun Social Studies. Relig: Catholic. Mailing Add: Rte 3 Box 222 Olathe KS 66061

SMITH, FRANK E (D)
b Sidon, Miss, Feb 21, 18; s Frank Smith & Sadie Ellis S (Mrs L E Spencer, Sr); m 1945 to Helen Ashley McPhaul; c Kathleen & Frederick. Educ: Sunflower Jr Col, Miss, grad, 36; Univ Miss, BA, 41; Am Univ, 46; Beta Theta Pi. Polit & Govt Pos: Legis asst to US Sen John Stennis, 47-49; Miss State Sen, 48-50; US Rep, Third Dist, Miss, 51-62; dir, Tenn Valley Authority, 62-72. Bus & Prof Pos: Managing ed, Greenwood Morning Star, Greenwood, Miss, 46-47. Mil Serv: Entered as Pvt, Army, 42, released as Maj, 46, after serv in 243rd Field Artil Bn, 3rd Army, ETO; Bronze Star. Publ: Congressman from Mississippi, 64 & The Politics of Conservation, 66, Pantheon; Look Away from Dixie, La State Univ Press, 65; plus others. Mem: Voter Educ Proj & Southern Regional Coun (vpres); Atlantic Coun (sponsor); Southern Hist Asn. Relig: Methodist. Mailing Add: 5915 Huntview Dr Jackson MS 39206

SMITH, FRANK LESTER, SR (R)
Chmn, Caldwell Co Rep Party, NC
b Caldwell Co, NC, Nov 1, 93; s Marcus Columbus Smith & Amanda E Rector S; m 1917 to Lucy Ann Amos; c Frank L, Jr & Marcy Nash (Mrs Lyn E Pollard). Educ: Rutherford Col; Appalachian State Teachers Col; Univ NC, AB. Polit & Govt Pos: Chmn, Caldwell Co Rep Party, NC, 42-71 & 73-; secy-treas, Ninth Cong Dist Rep Party, 43-60; mem, State Exec Rep Comt, 52-71; treas, Tenth Cong Dist Rep Party, 69-71. Bus & Prof Pos: Pres, Smith Printing Co, Inc, Lenoir; vpres & chmn bd dirs, Nashlyn's Inc; on bd of several smaller co. Publ: History of Baptist in Burke & Caldwell Counties, 60. Mem: Mason; KofP; Moose; Exec Club; WOW. Honors & Awards: Awards from Co & Dist Rep Parties, WOW Life Soc; KofP & Kiwanis. Relig: Baptist. Legal Res: 317 Pennton Ave Lenoir NC 28645 Mailing Add: PO Box 618 Lenoir NC 28645

SMITH, FRED J (D)
Ill State Sen
b Chattanooga, Tenn, July 4, 99; m to Margaret S; c Raymond & Frank. Educ: Christian Inst; Roger-Williams & Fisk Univ. Polit & Govt Pos: Former Ill State Rep, 6 terms; dep clerk, Munic Court, Chicago, 30-; Ill State Sen, currently. Relig: Catholic. Mailing Add: 4949 S Martin Luther King Dr Chicago IL 60615

SMITH, FREDERICK ORVILLE, II (R)
Chmn, New Vineyard Rep Town Comt, Maine
b Cambridge, Mass, July 17, 34; s Harry Francis Smith & Dorothy Zeller S; m 1965 to Mabel Roxie Moore; c Sarah Zeller, Jennifer Joy & Erika Andrea Hildred. Educ: Bowdoin Col, BA, 56; Sigma Nu, Delta Psi Chap. Polit & Govt Pos: Nat committeeman, Maine Fedn Young Rep, 60-62, chmn, 62-64; pres, New Eng Coun Young Rep, 62-64; finance chmn, Franklin Co Rep Comt, 66-71, mem, Exec Comt, 71-74, mem, 74-; alt deleg, Rep Nat Conv, 68; New Vineyard Sch Admin Dist Nine Rep, Bd Dirs, 69-70; Justice of the Peace; Notary Pub; chmn, New Vineyard Rep Town Comt, Maine, 74- Bus & Prof Pos: Corp secy & sales rep, Fred O Smith Mfg Co, Inc, 60-66, vpres & clerk, 66-70, acting pres & acting treas, 70-71, pres & treas, 71- Mil Serv: Entered as Ens, Naval Res, 56, released as Lt(jg), 60, after serv in USS Sullivans, Atlantic Fleet, 56-58, Naval Sta, Adak, Alaska, 59-60; Res, 65-, Lt Comdr; Am Expeditionary Medal. Mem: Rotary Int; Woodturners & Shapers Asn; Maine Hardwood Asn; Mason (32 degree); New Vineyard Vol Fire Dept. Relig: Congregational; moderator, New Vineyard Congregational Church. Mailing Add: High St New Vineyard ME 04956

SMITH, GARY (D)
b Beaumont, Tex, Oct 9, 43; s James Harvey Smith & Ernestine Hazel Drake S (deceased); single. Educ: NMex Highlands Univ, 61-62; Ind Univ, BA, 65; Alpha Phi Omega; Alpha Psi Omega; Sigma Alpha Epsilon. Polit & Govt Pos: Aide to US Sen Vance Hartke, Ind, 65; corp supvr to Secy of State, Ind, 65; admin aide to Lt Gov, 67-69; dir youth, Gubernatorial Campaign, 68; pres, Sullivan Co Young Dem, 70-71; pres, Young Dem Clubs of Ind, 71-73, mem regional bd, Young Dem Clubs of Am, 73-75; mem & ed, Sullivan Econ Develop Comn, 73-75. Bus & Prof Pos: Pub rels, C H Byfield & Assocs, 69-70; ed, Sullivan Daily Times, 70-73; pub rels, COT Corp, 73-75; exec dir, Econ Opportunity Comt of Daviess, Greene, Knox & Sullivan Co, Inc, 75- Mil Serv: Entered as Pvt E-1, Army, 65, released as SP-4, 67, after serv as instr, Army Transportation Sch, Ft Eustis, Va, 65-67; Transportation Sch Soldier of the Month. Mem: Am Legion; Elks; Am Soc Pub Admin; Ind Community Develop Asn; Ind Dem Ed Asn. Honors & Awards: Hon River Pilot, City of New Albany, Ind; Presidential Serv Award, Ind Young Dem. Relig: General Baptist. Legal Res: Box 193 RR 2 Shelburn IN 47879 Mailing Add: 525 N Fourth Vincennes IN 47591

SMITH, GEORGE ROSE (D)
Assoc Justice, Supreme Court of Ark
b Little Rock, Ark, July 26, 11; s Hay Watson Smith & Jessie Rose S; m 1938 to Peg B Newton; c Laurinda H. Educ: Washington & Lee Univ, 28-31; Univ Ark, LLB, 31-33; Phi Delta Phi; Sigma Alpha Epsilon. Polit & Govt Pos: Assoc Justice, Supreme Court of Ark, 49- Mil Serv: Entered as 2nd Lt, Air Force, 42, released as Major, 46. Publ: Arkansas annotations of restatement of trusts, Am Law Inst, 38; Arkansas Mining & Mineral Law, Conway Printing Co, 42; The current opinions of the Supreme Court of Ark, Ark Law Rev, 47. Mem: Inst of Judicial Admin; Ark Bar Asn. Relig: Presbyterian. Legal Res: 2 Cantrell Rd Little Rock AR 72207 Mailing Add: Justice Bldg Little Rock AR 72201

SMITH, GERARD COAD (R)
b New York, NY, May 4, 14; s John Thomas Smith & Mary A S; m 1941 to Bernice Latrobe Maguire; c John Thomas, Sheila (Mrs Richard B Griffin, Jr), Gerard L & Hugh Maguire. Educ: Yale Col, BA, 35, Law Sch, LLB, 38. Hon Degrees: LLD, Yale Univ, Johns Hopkins Univ, Loyola Univ, Georgetown Univ & Univ Notre Dame; DHL, Loyola Univ. Polit & Govt Pos: Spec asst, Atomic Energy Comn, 50-54; spec asst to Secy of State for Atomic Affairs, Dept of State, 54-57, dep chief, US Deleg Negotiating Int Atomic Energy Agency Treaty, 55-56, liaison officer to Foreign Rels Comt on Disarmament Affairs, 57, chief aide to Secy of State, London Disarmament Conf, 57, Asst Secy of State & Dir Policy Planning Staff, 57-61, consult, Policy Planning Coun, 61, spec adv to Secy of State for Multilateral Force

Negotiations, 62 & 64; chief polit adv, First Atoms for Peace Conf, 55; chief polit adv, Tech Talks with Soviet Union on Safeguards Against Diversion of Nuclear Materials to Weaponry, 55; dir, US Arms Control & Disarmament Agency, 69-72; US Chief Deleg to Strategic Arms Limitation Talks, Vienna & Helsinki, 69-72; retired. Bus & Prof Pos: Mem legal dept, Gen Motors Corp, 39-41; mem, John Thomas Smith & Son, New York, 46-47; partner, Smith & McInerney, 47-49; owner, Gerard Smith Law Firm, 49-50; foreign policy consult, Washington Ctr Foreign Policy Research, 61; mem, Coun on Foreign Rels, 61-; mem exec comt, Yale Law Sch Asn, 62; mem law comt, Yale Univ Coun, 64; dir, Am Security & Trust Co, 64; trustee, Sheridan Sch & Canterbury Sch, 67; dir, Atlantic Coun, 67; publ, Interplay Mag, 67; counsel, Wilmer, Cutler & Pickering, 73-; chmn, Trilateral Comn, 73- Mil Serv: Entered as Ens, Navy, 41, released as Lt, 45; Letter of Commendation from Secy of Navy. Publ: The steadfast warrior, 5/68, The future of two foreign policies: II The US, 11/68 & The French temptation, 2/69, Interplay Mag. Mem: Brookings Inst (trustee, 73-); Racquet & Tennis Club, New York; Nat Golf Links, Southampton, LI; Chesapeake Bay Yacht Club, Easton, Md; Metrop Club, Washington, DC. Relig: Roman Catholic. Legal Res: 2425 Tracy Pl NW Washington DC 20008 Mailing Add: 900 17th St NW Washington DC 20006

SMITH, GILBERT DAYLE (D)
Mayor, Carson, Calif
b Los Angeles, Calif, May 9, 34; s Alfred R Smith, Jr & Mary C Troy S; m 1954 to Glenda A Arceneaux; c Gilbert D, Jr, Jeffrey M & Christopher T. Educ: Los Angeles Trade Tech Col, 55. Polit & Govt Pos: City councilman & mayor, Carson, Calif, 68-; chmn state comt transportation, League Calif Cities, 73-, second vpres, 74-; exec bd mem, Southern Calif Asn Govts, 73-; chmn, Dept Transportation Adv Comt, 74- Bus & Prof Pos: Treas, Soc Illustrators, Los Angeles, Calif, 63-64. Mil Serv: Entered Naval Res, 52, released as PO 2/C, 60. Mem: YMCA; Kiwanis. Honors & Awards: Serv to Educ, Asn Elem Sch Adminr, 68 & 73; Resolution, State Senate & State Assembly, 71-74; Community Serv Award, Los Angeles Co Bd Supvr, 71. Relig: Episcopal. Mailing Add: 17223 Wall St Carson CA 90746

SMITH, GLENN (D)
Miss State Rep
Mailing Add: Drawer 319 Brookhaven MS 39601

SMITH, GORDON HENRY (R)
Mem, Maine Rep State Comt
b Augusta, Maine, Aug 22, 51; s Ezra Garland Smith & Ada Searles S; single. Educ: Univ Maine, Orono, BA, 73; Boston Col Law Sch; Phi Beta Kappa; Sigma Alpha Epsilon. Polit & Govt Pos: State chmn, Maine TAR, 68-70; coordr, Cong Campaign of Ronald T Speers, Maine, 70; treas, Maine Fedn of Young Rep, 70-71; pres, Univ Maine Young Rep, 71-72; alt deleg, Rep Nat Conv, 72; mem, Maine Rep State Platform Comt, 72; state chmn, Maine Young Voters for the President, 72; mem & youth comt chmn, Maine Rep State Comt, 72- Mem: Pi Sigma Alpha; Phi Kappa Phi; Student Action Corps. Honors & Awards: Nat Outstanding TAR, Nat TAR, 70. Relig: Methodist. Mailing Add: 14 Lambert St Winthrop ME 04364

SMITH, GUY ROSS (D)
WVa State Deleg
Mailing Add: State Capitol Charleston WV 25305

SMITH, GWYNNE P (R)
Del State Rep
Mailing Add: 1419 Fresno Rd Green Acres Wilmington DE 19803

SMITH, H ALLEN (R)
b Dixon, Ill, Oct 8, 09; s Allen N Smith & Mayme English S; m 1934 to Elizabeth McKay; c Stephen & Lauren. Educ: Univ Calif, Los Angeles, AB, 31; Univ Southern Calif, LLB, 33; Alpha Tau Omega; Alpha Kappa Psi. Polit & Govt Pos: Calif State Assemblyman, 43rd Dist, 48-56; US Rep, 20th Dist, Calif, 57-73; deleg, Rep Nat Conv, 72. Bus & Prof Pos: Attorney-at-law, 34-; spec agent, Fed Bur Invest, 35-42. Mem: Mason; Shrine. Relig: Methodist. Mailing Add: PO Box 1 Glendale CA 91209

SMITH, HAROLD KENNETH (BUD) (D)
b Columbus, Ohio, Oct 16, 19; s Harold Kenneth Smith & Mildred Worthington S; m to Wilma Price; c John A (deceased); one grandson. Educ: Duke Univ, BA, 41; Omicron Delta Kappa; Theta Alpha Phi; Delta Sigma Phi. Polit & Govt Pos: Chmn, Duval Co Dem Exec Comt, Fla, 65-66, precinct committeeman, currently; committeeman, Duval Co Dem Party, 65-74; chmn, Third Cong Dist Dem Party, 65-74; mem, Fla State Dem Cent Comt, 65-74; deleg, Dem Nat Conv, 68, nonvoting deleg, 72. Bus & Prof Pos: Exec vpres, Jno H Swisher & Son, Inc, Jacksonville, Fla, currently; dir, Am Maize Prod Co, New York, Flavesco Inc, Jacksonville & King Edward Tobacco Co, Quincy, currently. Mil Serv: Entered as Pvt, Air Force, 42, released as Lt, 46, after serv in Army Med Corps. Mem: Jacksonville Rotary Club (dir); Fla Yacht Club (dir); Jacksonville Symphony Asn (dir); Am Const Action (dir); Eng Speaking Union (dir). Honors & Awards: Mem, Tobacco Indust Hall of Fame. Relig: Episcopal. Legal Res: 5061 Pirates Cove Rd Jacksonville FL 32210 Mailing Add: Box 2230 Jacksonville FL 32203

SMITH, HAROLD MONROE (D)
Ala State Rep
b Lanett, Ala, Jan 10, 42; s Harold J Smith & Mattie Cook S; m 1971 to Leslie Dobbies; c Bill & Beth. Educ: Anderson Col, BA, 64; Univ Ala, MA, 67. Polit & Govt Pos: Ala State Rep, 74- Mem: Mason; Kiwanis; Ala Cattlemen's Asn; Southern Regional Educ Bd; Law Enforcement Planning Agency. Relig: Protestant. Mailing Add: Rte 1 Box 984 Lanett AL 36863

SMITH, HAROLD SELWYN (D)
Va State Sen
b Manassas, Va, July 19, 22; s Harold F Smith & Lucy Ann Baggott S; m 1945 to Virginia Busk; c Victor Alan, Alison Virginia, Steven Selwyn & Carolyn Leslie. Educ: Va Polytech Inst, BS, 43; Univ Va, LLB, 49; Alpha Zeta; Scabbard & Blade; Cotillion Club. Polit & Govt Pos: Assoc co court judge, Prince William Co, Va, 52-60, prosecuting attorney, 60-68; Va State Sen, 29th Senatorial Dist, Prince William, 71- Bus & Prof Pos: Dir & gen counsel, Peoples Nat Bank of Manassas, Va, currently. Mil Serv: Entered as 2nd Lt, Army, 43, released as Capt, 47, after serv in ETO, 44-45; Purple Heart; Three Campaign Stars. Mem: Prince William Co Bar Asn; Am & Va State Bar Asns. Relig: Methodist. Mailing Add: 9255 Lee Ave Manassas VA 22110

SMITH, HARRIS PAGE (D)
SC State Sen
b Easley, SC, July 19, 28; s Lloyd H Smith & Phyllis Page S; m 1952 to Nell Whitley; c Sam, Susan, Hugh & Phyllis. Educ: Davidson Col, BS, 49; Univ SC, LLB, 52; Omicron Delta Kappa; Wig & Robe; assoc ed, SC Law Quart. Polit & Govt Pos: SC State Rep, formerly; SC State Sen, 75- Bus & Prof Pos: Lawyer. Mil Serv: Army, 52-54, 1st Lt, Judge Adv Gen Corps; Maj, Army Res. Mem: Am & SC Bar Asns; Easley Jaycees; YMCA; Rotary. Honors & Awards: Young Man of Year, 57. Relig: Presbyterian, secy bd deacons, 56-62. Mailing Add: 104 Laurel Rd Easley SC 29640

SMITH, HENRY A, JR (R)
Chmn, Sully Co Rep Cent Comt, SDak
b Fosters, Ala, July 11, 17; s H Albert Smith, Sr & Anna Card S; m 1943 to Patricia Nelson; c Patricia, Henry, III, Pamela & Penelope. Educ: Univ Ala, 36-40; Theta Tau. Polit & Govt Pos: Finance chmn, Sully Co Rep Comt, SDak, 62; chmn, Sully Co Rep Cent Comt, currently. Mil Serv: Entered as Pvt, Army, 40, released 21as Lt Col, 46, after serv in 97th Inf Div, Europe & Far East Theaters; Bronze Star with Cluster; European & Pac Theater Ribbons; German & Japanese Occup Ribbon; Brig Gen, Army Nat Guard, 64. Mem: Nat Guard Asn of US; Asn of US Army; Am Legion; VFW. Mailing Add: Box 525 Onida SD 57564

SMITH, HENRY P, III (R)
b North Tonawanda, NY, Sept 29, 11; s Henry Perkins Smith & Ida Hale Hubbell S; m 1937 to Helen Elliott Belding; c Susan Choate (Mrs Walter G McConnell), Lucinda Belding (Mrs Gavin D Lee) & Christiana Long (Mrs Frederick C Hays, III). Educ: Dartmouth Col, AB, 33; Cornell Univ, JD, 36; Theta Delta Chi; Phi Delta Phi. Polit & Govt Pos: Mem, Local Bd Selective Serv Syst; mayor, North Tonawanda, NY, 62; Niagara Co Judge, Surrogate & Family Court Judge, 63-; US Rep, NY, 65-74; chmn, US Sect of Int Joint Comn, Can & US, currently. Bus & Prof Pos: Attorney-at-law, Ithaca, NY, 36-41; attorney-at-law, North Tonawanda, 41-64. Mem: Rotary Club Tonawandas; World Asn Lawyers; Am & NY State Bar Asns; World Peace Through Law Ctr. Honors & Awards: Named Citizen of the Year, Tonawandas CofC, 63; Great Lakes Comn Conservation Award, 72. Relig: Presbyterian; elder, North Presby Church, North Tonawanda. Mailing Add: 3126 Ordway St NW Washington DC 20008

SMITH, HOMER LEE (D)
Miss State Rep
Mailing Add: Liberty MS 39645

SMITH, HORACE CARROLL (D)
SC State Sen
b Gray Court, SC, June 11, 22; s John Harley Smith & Josephine Kesler S; m 1942 to Dorothy Williams; c David Carroll, Stephen Harley & Cynthia Lynn. Educ: Spartanburg Jr Col, 38-40; Wofford Col, BS, 42; Duke Univ Law Sch, 46-48; Phi Delta Phi. Polit & Govt Pos: SC State Rep, Spartanburg Co, 50-56 & 58-60; co solicitor, Spartanburg Co, 60-66; SC State Sen, Spartanburg Co, 66- Bus & Prof Pos: Attorney-at-law, Spartanburg, SC, 48- Mil Serv: Entered as Pvt, Air Force, 42, released as S/Sgt, 45, after serv in 2nd Air Force, USA. Mem: Spartanburg & SC Bar Asns; SC Trial Lawyers Asn; Lions; Mason. Relig: Baptist. Legal Res: 224 Beechwood Dr Spartanburg SC 29301 Mailing Add: State House Columbia SC 29211

SMITH, HOWARD E (D)
Minn State Rep
Mailing Add: 116 W Main St Crosby MN 56450

SMITH, HOWARD WORTH (D)
b Broad Run, Va, Feb 2, 83; s William Worth Smith & Lucinda Lewis S; m 1923 to Anne Corcoran; c Howard W, Jr & Violett (Mrs Tonahill). Educ: Bethel Mil Acad; Univ Va. Polit & Govt Pos: Judge, Corp Court, 22-28; judge, 16th Judicial Dist, Va, 28-30; US Rep, Eighth Dist, Va & chmn, House Rules Comt, 31-67. Bus & Prof Pos: Chmn bd, Alexandria Nat Bank, Va. Mem: Elks; Masons; Odd Fellows. Relig: Episcopal. Legal Res: Broad Run VA 22014 Mailing Add: 204 W Walnut St Alexandria VA 22313

SMITH, HULETT CARLSON (D)
b Beckley, WVa, Oct 21, 18; s Joe L Smith (deceased) & Christine Carlson S; m 1942 to Mary Alice Tieche; c Carolyn Tieche (Mrs Paul Hutchinson, Jr), Alice Christine McCulloch, Paul Luther Updyke, Mark Weston, Susan Elaine Chapman & Hulett Carlson, Jr (deceased). Educ: Wharton Sch, Univ Pa, BS in Econ, 38; Beckley Col; Beta Gamma Sigma; Phi Delta Theta. Hon Degrees: LLD, Beckley Col, Concord Col, WVa Univ, Marshall Univ, Davis & Elkins Col, WVa Wesleyan Col & WVa Inst Technol; Dr Pub Affairs, Bethany Col; LHD, WVa State Col. Polit & Govt Pos: Chmn, Beckley City Dem Comt, 47-51; chmn & mem, WVa State Aeronaut Comt, 47-59; chmn, WVa Dem Exec Comt, 56-61; comnr, WVa Dept of Com, 61-63; Gov, WVa, 65-69; deleg, Dem Nat Conv, 68 & 72; Dem Nat Committeeman, 68-72; mem bd, President's Air Quality Adv Bd, Washington, DC, 68-70. Bus & Prof Pos: Pres, Home Ins Agency; vpres, Investment Securities, Inc & First Beckley Corp; vpres, Beckley Col, 50-65; dir & treas, Beckley & Oak Hill Hosps; dir, Bank of Raleigh. Mil Serv: Entered as Ens, Navy, 42, released as Lt, 46, after serv in Am Theater, Western Sea Frontier & Navy Dept; Lt Comdr (Ret), Naval Res. Mem: Soc of Chartered Property & Casualty Underwriters; hon life mem WVa Jr CofC. Honors & Awards: Licensed private pilot; Named Outstanding Young Man of Year, WVa Jr CofC, 48. Relig: Presbyterian. Legal Res: 2105 Harper Rd Beckley WV 25801 Mailing Add: 1730 Charleston Nat Plaza Charleston WV 25301

SMITH, IRENE M (D)
b Belvidere, NJ, Apr 9, 10; d Winfield Scott Mackey & Ruth Hayes M; m 1932 to Harold J Smith; c Gary W & Julianne (Mrs Tieff); two grandchildren. Educ: EStroudsburg State Col, 27-29. Polit & Govt Pos: Motor vehicle agt, Oxford, NJ, 54; gen agt, NJ Div Motor Vehicles, 60, field supvr, 67-72; Dem cand, NJ State Sen, Tenth Dist, 65; mem, Women's Task Force, NJ State Dem Comt, 24 years, acting chmn, 7 times; co-chmn, NJ Women's Div State Comt; chmn, NJ Forum Dem Women; moderator & panel mem, Women's State Conv; mem, State Speakers Bur; conducted over 100 schs for polit; alt deleg, Dem Nat Conv, 68; field rep, NJ Dept of Labor, 71-73; alt deleg, Dem Mid Term Conf, 74; Warren Co Rep for Congresswoman Helen S Meyner. Bus & Prof Pos: Teacher, Northampton Co, 5 years & asst to asst co sch supt, 2 years; mem nat staff, Am Red Cross, 3 years, mem disaster staff; credit mgr retail chain stores, Philadelphia; radio show, Sta WCRV, Washington, NJ, 67-69; head of own Speakers Bur; mem bd trustees, Health Village. Publ: Community Leaders of Am, Am Biographical Inst News Publ Co, 71-72; auth of short stories, papers on travel, hist, autobiographies & anecdotes. Mem: Belvidere High Sch Alumni Asn; White Shrine of Jerusalem; NJ Soc Crippled Children (bd gov); DAR. Honors & Awards: Testimonial, 60 &

testimonial for 24 years as vchmn, Warren Co Dem Comt, 70. Relig: Episcopal; first woman warden, St Mary's Episcopal Church, Belvidere. Mailing Add: 628 Third St Belvidere NJ 07823

SMITH, J B (D)
Ark State Rep
Mailing Add: 103 Robertson Ave Marianna AR 72360

SMITH, J BOYD (R)
Chmn, Carroll Co Rep Comt, Ark
b George, Ark, Mar 21, 27; s Ray Smith & Ova Newberry S; m 1947 to Etheleen Heard; c Tommy, John & Donna (Mrs Elmore). Educ: Univ Ark, Fayetteville, BS in agr, 52; Animal Sci Club, secy; Ark Agriculturist, bus mgr. Polit & Govt Pos: Chmn, Carroll Co Rep Comt, Ark, 74- Bus & Prof Pos: Mgr, Carnation Co, 61-67; dairy farm specialist, Diversey Chem Co, 67-70; dairy farmer, laundry owner & grocery store owner, 70- Mil Serv: Entered as Seaman, Navy, 45, released as 2nd Seaman, 46. Mem: Am Legion; Lions (pres, currently); CofC (bd mem, currently); 4H Leader; Boy Scouts (asst scoutmaster, 64-67). Honors & Awards: Mem, Dairy Judging Teams, 50 & 51. Legal Res: 504 Phillips Ave Green Forest AR 72638 Mailing Add: Box 35 Green Forest AR 72638

SMITH, J R (D)
Ga State Rep
Mailing Add: PO Box G Barnesville GA 30204

SMITH, JACK WILLMAR (D)
Ala State Rep
b Houston Co, Ala, July 23, 24; s Aubrey Smith & Lennie Watkins S; m 1973 to Elaine Sheehan; c Stephen G & Jennie Lee. Educ: Troy Univ, BS, 49; Univ Ala, LLB, 53; Sigma Delta Kappa. Polit & Govt Pos: Ala State Rep, 74- Bus & Prof Pos: Lawyer, Dothan, Ala, 53- Mil Serv: Entered as Pvt, Army, 42, released as Cpl, 45, after serv in 35th Fighter Group, 5th Air Force, SFac, 43-45. Mem: Elks; Mason; Am & Ala Bar Asns; VFW. Relig: Baptist. Legal Res: Jane St Slocomb AL 36375 Mailing Add: PO Box 527 Slocomb AL 36375

SMITH, JAMES ALOYSIUS (D)
Chmn, Richmond Co Dem Comt, NY
b Staten Island, NY, Feb 17, 11; s Matthew Joseph Smith & Katherine Walsh S; wid. Educ: Fordham Univ, 6 months. Polit & Govt Pos: City councilman, Staten Island, NY, formerly; chmn, Richmond Co Dem Comt, 73-; mem, NY State Dem Exec Comt, currently. Relig: Catholic. Mailing Add: 414 Clove Rd Staten Island NY 10310

SMITH, JAMES E (R)
Comptroller of the Currency, Dept of Treas
Polit & Govt Pos: Dep Under Secy Treas, formerly. Legal Res: SD Mailing Add: Dept of the Treas Washington DC 20220

SMITH, JAMES EDWARD (D)
Mass State Rep
b Lynn, Mass, Sept 3, 46; s Ernest McConnell Smith & Helen D'Ortona S; single. Educ: Univ Mass, Boston, BA, 69; Harvard Univ, MPA, 74; Pres, Univ Mass, Boston Student Body. Polit & Govt Pos: Mem, Lynn Dem City Comt, Mass, 68-; Mass State Rep, 71- Mil Serv: Mass Nat Guard. Mem: Univ Mass, Boston Alumni Asn (bd dirs). Legal Res: 38 Gateway Lane Lynn MA 01905 Mailing Add: State House Boston MA 02133

SMITH, JAMES F (R)
Mich State Rep
b 1923. Educ: Mich State Univ, 2 years; Amherst Col, 1 year. Polit & Govt Pos: Mem, Genesee Co Bd Supvrs, Mich; mem, Davison City Coun, mayor; Mich State Rep, 67- Bus & Prof Pos: Owner & operator, Smith Finance. Mil Serv: World War II. Mailing Add: 5146 Tree Hill Rd Grand Blanc MI 48439

SMITH, JAMES L (D)
Mo State Rep
Mailing Add: 420 E Porter Marshall MO 65340

SMITH, JAMES ROSWELL (R)
b Sioux Falls, SDak, May 10, 17; s Dick R Smith & Ednah Woodruff S; m 1941 to Arlene Skredsvig; c Dick R, Douglas J & Robert M. Educ: Sioux Falls Col, AA, 37; Univ SDak, JD, 40; Beta Theta Pi. Polit & Govt Pos: Asst Secy for Water & Power Resources, Dept of the Interior, 69-72. Bus & Prof Pos: Attorney-at-law, Sioux Falls, SDak, 41-42; mem, CofC Admin, Pierre & Yankton, 42-53, vpres & counsel, Miss Valley Asn, Omaha, Nebr, 53-65; mgr mkt rels, Northern Natural Gas Co, 65-69; pres, Am Waterways Operators, Inc, Washington, DC, 73- Mem: SDak Bar Asn; Mason (32 degree); Shrine; Nebr Resources Found (dir); Nebr Asn of Com (dir). Honors & Awards: Distinguished Civilian Serv Award, Dept of the Army; Ohio Gov Conserv Award, 70; Water Statesman, Nat Water Resources Asn, 72. Relig: Protestant. Legal Res: 6408 Cavalier Corridor Falls Church VA 22044 Mailing Add: 1600 Wilson Blvd Suite 1101 Arlington VA 22209

SMITH, JAMES VERNON (R)
b Oklahoma City, Okla, July 23, 26; s Fred Smith & Josephine Meder S; m 1946 to Mary Belle Couch; c James Vernon, Jr, Sarah Eileen & Lee Ann. Educ: Okla Col of Lib Arts, 65. Polit & Govt Pos: Mem, Four Year State Cols Bd of Regents; chmn, Grady Co Rep Party, Okla, 62-66; US Rep, Sixth Dist, Okla, 67-69; deleg, Rep Nat Conv, 68; adminr, Farmers Home Admin, US Dept of Agr, 69-72; mem bd trustees, Intercollegiate Studies Inst Inc; mem bd dirs, Am Heritage Ctr, Okla Christian Col. Mem: CofC; Farm Bur; Farmers Home Admin; hon mem Chickasha Jr CofC. Relig: Church of Christ. Mailing Add: 114 Caulder Dr Chickasha OK 73018

SMITH, JANET MARGARET (JAN) (D)
Mem Exec Bd, Nev State Dem Cent Comt
b Los Angeles, Calif, Apr 26, 28; d Thomas Franklin Curtis & Catharine Collins C; m 1946 to Prince Lyle Smith, Jr; c Cathleen Elizabeth (Mrs Robert Cassidy), Christene Evelyn (Mrs Douglas A Skillman), James Richard, Margaret Mary Corrine (Mrs Bradley Garrett), Marie Daniell & John Lyle. Educ: Chaffey Jr Col, 46-47. Polit & Govt Pos: Mem, Clark Co Dem Cent Comt, Nev, 62-; deleg, Co & State Dem Conv, 62-; secy, Henderson Dem Club, 63-64; treas, 64-65, vpres, 65-66; legal research & extradition clerk, Dist Attorney's Off, Clark Co, 63-65; fed court clerk, Fed Dist of Nev, 65-66; judicial secy to Hon Thomas J O'Donnell,

Dist Court Judge, 66-; secy, Las Vegas Women's Dem Club W, 66-; mem exec bd, Nev State Dem Cent Comt, currently; spec asst to Gov Mike O'Callaghan, Nev, 71- Honors & Awards: Commendation for Sen Cannon's Recourt, 64; Presidential Commendation for Party Activities; Gov Commendations for Party Endeavor. Relig: Jewish. Mailing Add: 31 Jade Circle Las Vegas NV 89106

SMITH, JEFFERSON VERNE (D)
SC State Sen
b Greer, SC, Jan 15, 25; s Jefferson Verne Smith, Sr & Lillian Farley S; m 1948 to Jean Myers; c Jefferson Verne, III & Carole Jean (Mrs Cofer). Educ: Presby Col, 1 year; Kappa Alpha Order. Polit & Govt Pos: Mem, SC Hwy Safety Prog, 63-69; mem bd comnr, SC Inst Deaf & Blind, 64-69; comnr, Greer Comn of Pub Works, 69-; chmn, Greenville Co Dem Party, 70-; SC State Sen, 73- Bus & Prof Pos: Pres, Tire Exchange of Greer, Inc, SC, 55- & Simpsonville, 64-; bd dirs, Peoples Nat Bank, Greer, 62-69; mem exec comt, Tire Retreading Inst, 66-67; bd dirs, Hercules Tire & Rubber Co, 67- & Greer Fed Savings & Loan Asn, 69-71; dir-at-lg, Nat Tire Dealers & Retreaders Asn, 68-70; pres, Tire Exchange of Mauldin, 68-; bd gov, Shriners Hosp for Crippled Children, 71- Mil Serv: Entered as Pvt, Army, 43, released as Pfc, 45, after serv in 25th Inf Div, Pac, 44-45. Mem: Mason (32 degree Scottish Rite); Shriner; WOW; Kiwanis Club; Greer CofC. Honors & Awards: Eagle Scout; Outstanding Man of the Year, Jr CofC, 57. Relig: Presbyterian; SC Ruling Elder, Enoree Presbytery. Legal Res: 201 N Miller St Greer SC 29651 Mailing Add: State House Columbia SC 29211

SMITH, JEROME (D)
RI State Sen
Mailing Add: 219 Prospect St Woonsocket RI 02895

SMITH, JEROME A (JERRY) (D)
Calif State Sen
b San Jose, Calif, July 28, 36; s Albert T Smith & Anne M S; m to Kevil R Boldenweek; c Timothy, Catlin, Stephen, Peter & Margaret. Educ: Univ Santa Clara, BS, 58, JD, 65. Polit & Govt Pos: Mayor, Saratoga, 72-74, city councilman, 68-74; Calif State Sen, 74- Mil Serv: Entered as 2nd Lt, Army, 58, released as 2nd Lt, 59. Relig: Catholic. Legal Res: 14795 Bohlman Rd Saratoga CA 95070 Mailing Add: 2185 The Alameda San Jose CA 95126

SMITH, JERRY L (R)
Okla State Rep
b Muskogee, Okla, Dec 6, 43; s Hollis C Smith & Eulem M Hall S; single. Educ: Okla State Univ, BA, 66; Univ Tulsa Sch Law, JD, 71; Phi Delta Phi. Polit & Govt Pos: Okla State Rep, 73-, minority whip, Okla House of Rep, currently. Mem: Okla & Tulsa Co Bar Asns; Okla Trial Lawyers Asn. Honors & Awards: Cert of Merit, Okla Trial Lawyers Asn, 71 & 72. Relig: Methodist. Legal Res: 5327 E 33rd St Tulsa OK 74135 Mailing Add: 1424 Terrace Dr Tulsa OK 74104

SMITH, JOHN EDWARD (D)
Utah State Rep
b Grantsville, Utah, Feb 28, 21; s Frank Smith & Nellie Barrus S; m 1946 to Lorna Diekmann; c Nola & Susan. Educ: Grantsville High Sch, grad, 39. Polit & Govt Pos: City councilman, Grantsville City, Utah, 56-60 & 66-70; chmn, Grantsville Citizen's Improv Asn, 58-69; dir, Civil Defense, 66-70; chmn, Grantsville Credit Union, 65-67; chmn, Dist Three Dem Party, 65-69; Utah State Rep, Tooele Co, 67-; Western Interstate appointment on Aeronaut, 69; app mem, Gov Adv Coun for Handicapped, 71- Mil Serv: Entered as A/S, Navy, 42, released as PO, 45, after serv in Atlantic & Pac Theatres, 42-45. Publ: Letters of John, 66, Politics of John, 68 & Journal anecdotes, 69, Smith's Secretarial Serv. Mem: DAV; VFW; Tooele Co CofC; Utah State Training Sch, American Fork, Utah (bd). Relig: Latter-day Saint. Mailing Add: 143 S Hale St Grantsville UT 84029

SMITH, JOHN H (D)
SC State Rep
Mailing Add: Summerville SC 29483

SMITH, JOHN LEONARD (R)
Chmn, Iron Co Rep Party, Mo
b Arcadia, Mo, Apr 27, 34; s William C Smith & Elsie Huff S; m 1955 to Ruth Ann Rood; c John Bregg & William Curtis. Educ: High sch. Polit & Govt Pos: Chmn, Iron Co Rep Party, Mo, 66- Mailing Add: 207 E Dent Ironton MO 63650

SMITH, JOHN NEIL (D)
Miss State Rep
b Tylertown, Miss, Jan 11, 20; s Newell Booker Smith & Bessie Hall S; m 1966 to Donis Luter; c Wayne Nettles (stepson), Jay Neil & Mark Jarrett. Educ: Univ Southern Miss, BA, 49. Polit & Govt Pos: Miss State Rep, 44th Dist, 68-72, 38th Dist, 72- Mil Serv: Entered as Aviation Cadet, Army Air Corps, 42, released as Lt Col, 68, after serv in 36th Fighter Group ETO, 44-45; Lt Col (Ret), Air Force Res, 68; Air Medal with 12 Oak Leaf Clusters; Distinguished Flying Cross; Presidential Unit Citation with Oak Leaf Cluster. Mem: Mason; Royal Arch Mason; Knights Templar; Shrine. Relig: Baptist. Mailing Add: 806 Oak Dr Tylerstown MS 39667

SMITH, JOSEPH F (D)
Pa State Sen
Mailing Add: 2513 Cedar St Philadelphia PA 19125

SMITH, KAREN JACQUELYN (D)
b Richmond Hill, NY, Oct 4, 48; d Robert Edward Smith & Grace McMullen S; single. Educ: Rosary Hill Col, 66-67; Canisius Col, BA, 70; Fordham Univ, MA in Relig Educ, 75; Digamma Alpha. Polit & Govt Pos: Mem bd dirs, Levittown Young Dem, NY, 63-64; co-coordr, Seuferling for Rep, Emporia, Kans, 72, mem finance comt, 72; alt deleg, Dem Nat Conv, 72; Lyon Co coordr, McGovern for President, Kans, 72; precinct committeewoman, Lyon Co Cent Comt, Kans; Lyon Co coordr, Voter Regist Drive. Bus & Prof Pos: Campus worker-vol, Cath Church Exten Soc, Emporia, 70-71; campus minister, Archdiocese of Kansas City in Kans, Emporia, 71- Mem: Cath Campus Ministers Asn; Nat Orgn for Women (legis task force chairperson); Am for Dem Action; League of Women Voters. Relig: Roman Catholic. Legal Res: 138 W 12th St Apt 7 Emporia KS 66801 Mailing Add: PO Box 160 Emporia KS 66801

SMITH, KEITH J (R)
b Bismarck, Ill, Feb 21, 15; s Russell C Smith & Bertha Juvinall; m 1941 to LaVonne Lytle; c Toni Sue (Mrs Nelson) & Craig J. Educ: Bismarck High Sch, grad, 33. Polit & Govt Pos: Rep precinct committeeman, Bismarck, Ill, 52; Ill State Food Inspector, 54; clerk, Vermilion Co, 62-; chmn, Vermilion Co Rep Party, formerly. Bus & Prof Pos: Owner, grocery store, Bismarck, Ill, 37-54. Mil Serv: Entered as Pvt, Army, 42, released as M/Sgt, 45, after serv in Army Engrs. Mem: Mason (32 degree); Ansar Shrine; Elks; Lions; Moose. Relig: Methodist. Legal Res: PO Box 36 Bismarck IL 61814 Mailing Add: Vermilion County Courthouse Danville IL 61832

SMITH, KENNETH CHARLES, SR (R)
NH State Rep
b Moultonboro, NH, July 10, 32; s Charles Henry Smith & Lois Gannett S; m 1956 to Janet R Gero; c Kenneth C, Jr & Gary R. Educ: Laconia High Sch, NH, grad, 51. Polit & Govt Pos: Town clerk, Moultonboro, NH, 63-74; NH State Rep, 75- Bus & Prof Pos: Mgr, F W Woolworth Co, NJ, 51-62; restaurant innkeeper, Country Fare Inn, Moultonboro, 62- Mem: Moultonboro Lions; Star-in-the-East (Master Mason); Temple Commandry; Hebron Royal Arch Chap; Bektash Temple. Honors & Awards: Testimonial Award, Moultonboro Lions Club, 69. Relig: Protestant. Mailing Add: Box 3 Moultonboro NH 03254

SMITH, KERMIT A (D)
Vt State Rep
Mailing Add: Box 43 Derby VT 05829

SMITH, KIRBY, III (D)
Gen Counsel, Young Dem Am
b Jonesboro, Ark, Dec 3, 44; s Kirby Smith, Jr & Patricia Jane Haynes S; single. Educ: Hendrix Col, BA, 66; Univ Ark Law Sch, Fayetteville, JD, 69; Alpha Psi Omega; Phi Alpha Delta; Blue Key. Polit & Govt Pos: Asst Attorney Gen, Ark, 72-; pres, Ark Young Dem, 73-74; mem, Ark State Dem Comt, 73-; gen counsel, Young Dem Am, 73- Bus & Prof Pos: Law clerk, Circuit Judges, Sixth Judicial Dist Ark, 70-71; attorney, Nat Old Line Ins Co, 71-72; dep prosecuting attorney, Sixth Judicial Dist Ark, 72. Mil Serv: E-5, Army Res, 69. Mem: Am & Ark Bar Asns; Quapaw Quarter Asn (vpres, currently); Ark Consumer Research. Relig: Presbyterian. Mailing Add: 2100 Rebsamen Park Apt 518 Little Rock AR 72202

SMITH, KYLE DUGAR, JR (D)
b Pembroke, Ga, Sept 11, 39; s Kyle D Smith & Sophie Deloach S; m 1961 to Vivian Lancaster; Kyle, III & Sara. Educ: Emory Univ, AB, 61; Univ Tenn, MEd, 68; Pi Sigma Alpha, Alpha Tau Omega. Polit & Govt Pos: Deleg, Dem Nat Conv, 72. Bus & Prof Pos: Teacher, Calhoun Jr High Sch, 61-68; pres, Gordon-Calhoun Educ Asn, Calhoun, Ga, 66-67; field rep, Ga Educ Asn, Atlanta, 68-71; dir field servs, Ga Asn Educators, 71- Mem: Nat Educ Asn; Toastmasters (charter mem); Optimists (charter mem); Kiwanis (charter mem). Relig: United Methodist; chmn, educ comt. Mailing Add: 608 Pisgah Way Calhoun GA 30701

SMITH, L EUGENE (R)
Pa State Rep
b Punxsutawney, Pa, Sept 3, 21; s Charles Smith & Olive Curry S; m to Jean Hue; c three. Educ: Army Air Force Pilot Training Sch. Polit & Govt Pos: Pa State Rep, 63-; mayor, Punxsutawney, 1 term. Mil Serv: Air Force, World War II, serv in 306th Bomb Group, ETO. Mem: Mason; VFW; Am Legion. Relig: Methodist; Trustee, First Methodist Church. Mailing Add: Capitol Bldg Harrisburg PA 17120

SMITH, L MICHAEL (D)
b Indianapolis, Ind, Aug 11, 45; s Lewis T Smith & Helen Stamper S; single. Educ: Mich State Univ, BS, 67, MS, 69. Polit & Govt Pos: Admin asst to US Rep Bob Carr, Mich, 75- Bus & Prof Pos: Asst dir financial aid, Mich State Univ, 68-71, asst to comptroller, 71-74; fiscal dir, Mich Asn Regional Med Progs, 74-75. Mem: Aircraft Owners & Pilots Asn. Legal Res: 938 Sunset Lane East Lansing MI 48823 Mailing Add: 1608 Longworth Bldg Washington DC 20515

SMITH, LACEY THOMAS (D)
Ky State Sen
b Eau Claire, Wis, Feb 28, 40; s Lacey Smith & Ann L Mansfield S; div; c Lucretia, Lacey T, Jr & Crayton Scott. Educ: Hamline Univ, BA, 61; Princeton Univ, MPA, 63; Harvard Univ, LLB, 66; ed, Pub & Int Affairs, Princeton Univ; Tau Kappa Epsilon. Polit & Govt Pos: Asst attorney gen, Ky, 66-67; asst city law dir, Louisville, 69-70; probate judge, 71-; Ky State Sen, 71- Bus & Prof Pos: Reporter, Louisville Times & Minneapolis Tribune, 59 & 61; instr, Brandeis Univ, Univ Louisville & Ky Southern Col, 64-65; exec dir, Ky Youth Develop Found, 66-70; pres, Care Systs, Inc, 70. Mem: Louisville Jaycees; Ky Youth Develop Found (pres); Louisville & Jefferson Co Dem Party. Honors & Awards: Woodrow Wilson Fel. Relig: Episcopal. Legal Res: 1732 Spring Dr Louisville KY 40205 Mailing Add: 425 S Fifth St Suite 201 Louisville KY 40202

SMITH, LARRY GILBERT (D)
Mem, Cuyahoga Co Dem Exec Comt
b Uniontown, Pa, Nov 11, 14; s Lonnie Smith (deceased) & Eva B S; wid; c Larry G, Jr, Karin L & Lillie G; five grandchildren. Educ: Diamond Bus Col; Fenn Col, AB, BBS. Polit & Govt Pos: Personnel officer, Co Recorder's Off, Cleveland, Ohio; mem, Cuyahoga Co Dem Exec Comt; mem, 20th Ward Dem Club & leader, 62-66; Ohio State Rep, 67-74; alt deleg, Dem Nat Conv, 68; committeeman, Ohio State Dem Exec Comt, currently. Bus & Prof Pos: Trucking bus, formerly; licensed real estate broker, Ohio; notary pub; multiple line ins agent. Mem: Ohio Asn Real Estate Bds; Black Elec Off Ohio; Frederick Douglass Civic Club; Mason (32 degree); Shrine. Relig: Baptist. Mailing Add: 1871 E 97th St Cleveland OH 44106

SMITH, LAURA LA ROSE (R)
b Vidalia, Ga, June 16, 31; d Earl Smith & Minnie Beasley S; single. Educ: Winthrop Col, 49-51; Duke Univ, AB in Chem, 53. Polit & Govt Pos: Personnel secy, US Sen Strom Thurmond, SC, 62-67; staff asst to Spec Counsel to the President, Harry S Dent, 69-73; mem, Rep Party of SC, 73; admin asst to US Rep Ed Young, SC, 73-75. Bus & Prof Pos: Research asst, Anat Dept, Med Col SC, 53-55; instr math & sci, St Andrew's Parish High Sch, Charleston, 55-56; partner, Movie Theatre & Real Estate Rentals, Beaufort, 56-62; exec secy, Thorndike, Doran, Paine & Lewis, 67-68. Mem: SC State Soc of Washington; Capitol Hill Tennis Club. Relig: Baptist. Mailing Add: 164 Ribault Rd Beaufort SC 29902

SMITH, LAWRENCE PETER (D)
Mem, Ninth Cong Dist Dem Exec Comt, Mich
b Holland, Mich, Aug 27, 16; s Peter Smith & Nellie King S; m 1940 to Clara Jane Overbeek; c Martha Ann. Educ: Minneapolis-Honeywell Sch of Aeronaut Electronics & Electronic Equipment, Univ Minn, 43; LaSalle Exten Univ, Ill. Polit & Govt Pos: Deleg, Mich State Dem Conv, 46-, vchmn, Fifth Dist Deleg, 54; secy, Ottawa Co Dem Comt, 54-67, chmn, 67-74; vchmn, Ottawa Co Bd of Elec Canvassers, 63-65, chmn, 65-67; deleg, Dem Nat Conv, 64; mem, Ninth Cong Dist Dem Exec Comt, 67-; mem, Ottawa Co Re-apportionment Comn, 67- Bus & Prof Pos: Tech rep, Aeronaut Div, Minneapolis-Honeywell Regulator Co, 43-45, assigned to various AFB within 1st & 2nd Air Forces, US & 2nd Air Div, US 8th Air Force, Eng, 44-45; sales engr, Radio Electronic Supply Co, 47-49; vpres, Radio Parts, Inc, 49-50; electronic logistics engr, Instrument Div, Lear Siegler, Inc, 51- Mem: Elks; Eagles; Am Radio Relay League, Newington, Conn; Radio Soc of Gt Brit. Relig: Roman Catholic. Mailing Add: 1718 Summit St Holland MI 49423

SMITH, LEONARD A (R)
NH State Rep
Mailing Add: 3 Leslie St Hudson NH 03051

SMITH, LOUISE BLAIR (R)
b Springfield, Ill, Dec 31, 41; d Louis A Blair & Susan Micklus B; m 1963 to E Steeves Smith; c Andrea Louise, John Blair & Rosemary Claire. Educ: Univ Minn, BS, 64; Mortar Bd; Chimes; Sigma Epsilon Sigma; Alpha Phi. Polit & Govt Pos: Precinct committeewoman, Mitchell, SDak, 66-; deleg, Rep Nat Conv, 72. Bus & Prof Pos: Part-time instr Eng, Dakota Wesleyan Univ, 65-72. Mem: PEO; Am Asn Univ Women. Relig: Lutheran. Mailing Add: 1020 Chalkstone Dr Mitchell SD 57301

SMITH, LOY LEE (R)
Tenn State Rep
b Strawberry Plains, May 24, 28; s Maxwell McGhee Smith, Sr & Hassie Loy S; div; m 1965 to Lonna Rhea Wheeler; c Jeffrey Lance; James Loy, David Lee & Scottie Lynne. Educ: Univ Tenn, 2 years. Polit & Govt Pos: Tenn State Rep, 71- Bus & Prof Pos: Ins agt, 52- Mil Serv: Entered as Pvt, Army, 46, released as Pfc, 48, after serv in 9th Corps, Japan, 46-48. Mem: Insurors of Tenn; Am Legion; Elks; Odd Fellows; Optimists. Relig: Christian. Mailing Add: Rte 1 Carter School Rd Strawberry Plains TN 37871

SMITH, LYNN, JR (D)
b Luling, Tex, Nov 22, 27; s Lynn Smith & Sallie Davis S; m 1948 to Ruth Janet Laurence; c Loy Elizabeth & Lynnette. Educ: Baylor Univ; Southwestern Tex State Col; Ft Benning, Ga, grad inf course. Polit & Govt Pos: Chmn, Gonzales Co Dem Party, Tex, formerly. Bus & Prof Pos: Owner of theaters & ranching interests. Mil Serv: Entered as Pvt, Tex Nat Guard, 48, released as Maj, 66; Tex Nat Guard Res, released as Lt Col, 69. Mem: Southwestern Cattle Raisers Asn; hon life mem Future Farmers Am. Relig: Presbyterian. Mailing Add: 923 St Joseph St Gonzales TX 78629

SMITH, LYNWOOD (D)
NC State Sen
Mailing Add: 1031 Rockford Rd High Point NC 27262

SMITH, MARGARET CHASE (R)
b Skowhegan, Maine, Dec 14, 97; d George Emery Chase & Carrie Murray C; m 1930 to Clyde H Smith, wid, 40. Hon Degrees: Many hon degrees from various cols & univs, 43- Polit & Govt Pos: Mem, Maine State Rep Comt, 30-36; secy to US Rep Clyde H Smith, 37-40; US Rep, Second Dist, Maine, 40-49, US Sen, 49-73; Presidential nominee, Rep Nat Conv, 64; chmn, Conf of all Rep Sen, 67. Bus & Prof Pos: Teacher; tel, newspaper & woolen co exec; nationally syndicated columnist. Mil Serv: Lt Col, Air Force Res. Publ: Declaration of Conscience, Doubleday, 72. Mem: Am Acad Arts & Sci; Theta Sigma Phi. Honors & Awards: Multiple Awards for Nat Health Leadership, 60; Gold Medal Award for Humanitarianism, Inst Social Sci, 64; Women's Twentieth Century Hall of Fame, 65; Nat Educ Asn Awards, 68; Am Educ Award, 73; plus many others. Mailing Add: Norridgewock Ave Skowhegan ME 04976

SMITH, MARGARET KEANE (D)
Committeewoman, Conn State Dem Cent Comt
b Hartford, Conn; d James Joseph Keane & Susan Ann Fanning K; m 1942 to Herbert Knox Smith; c Susanne Barbara, Herbert Knox, Jr, William Warren & Robert David. Educ: High sch. Polit & Govt Pos: Pres, Newgate Young Dem, 50; nat committeewoman, Conn Young Dem, 52-54; chmn, East Granby Dem Town Comt, 54-60, vchmn, 60-; Justice of Peace, East Granby, 54-; secy, East Granby Planning & Zoning Comt, 55-56; deleg, Dem Nat Conv, 56 & 60. alt deleg, 64 & 68; publicity chmn, East Granby Centennial, Conn, 58; committeewoman, Conn State Dem Cent Comt, 58-; consult, Conn State Pub Works, 61-64; vpres, Seventh Dist Dem Comt, 63-66; field rep, Conn State Comn on Serv for the Elderly, 64-65; Sixth Cong Dist mem, Subcomt on Conn Dem Party Rules, 68; mem, Bd Assessors, 69-; mem, Comn to Study Procedures for Nomination of Presidential Cand, 70-; mem, Conn State Fedn Dem Women, currently; mem comt to select deleg-at-lg to Dem Nat Conv, 72. Mem: East Granby March of Dimes; East Granby, Hartford Heart Asn; 4-H (leader); St Francis Hosp Auxiliary; VFW Auxiliary. Relig: Roman Catholic. Mailing Add: 145 Spoonville Rd East Granby CT 06026

SMITH, MARILU CRAFTON (R)
Mem, Ga Rep Exec Comt
b Dublin, Ga, Dec 15, 13; d John Claxton Crafton & Mattie Julia Adkins C; m 1931 to Albert Edward Smith, wid; c twins, Edwina Crafton & Marilyn Crafton. Educ: Kaigler Bus Col, Macon, Ga, grad, 31. Polit & Govt Pos: Mem, Muscogee Rep Women & Ga & Nat Fedn Rep Women, 54-; mem, Muscogee Co Rep Exec Comt, 62-66; mem, Third Dist Rep Comt, 63-66; chmn, Third Dist Goldwater Campaign & Third Dist Draft Goldwater Campaign, 64; mem, Ga Rep Exec Comt, 64-; Rep Nat Committeewoman, 64-72; mem, Ga State Comt to Make Uniform Consumer Credit Code Study, 69-, mem, Uniform Consumer Credit Code Study Comt, 69-; mem, State Bd of Educ, 70- Mem: Muscogee Co Juv Court (adv bd); Columbus Lawyer's Auxiliary; Columbus Area Tuberc Asn; Patient Serv Comt, Ga Tuberc Asn (bd dirs & exec comt); Ga Litter Bug Comt. Honors & Awards: Named Woman of Year, Columbus. Relig: Methodist; mem, Wynnton Study Club. Mailing Add: 801 Peachtree Dr Columbus GA 31906

SMITH, MARTIN TRAVIS (D)
Miss State Sen
Mailing Add: 201 W Pearl St Poplarville MS 39740

SMITH, MARY CATHERINE (D)
Chmn, McMullen Co Dem Party, Tex
b Three Rivers, Tex, May 24, 44; d Henry Shenkir & Mollie Nechas S; m 1963 to Herman Lee Smith; c Herman Lee, Jr, Jason Edward & Twyla Ann. Educ: Draughon's Bus Col, exec secretarial course, 62. Polit & Govt Pos: Chmn, McMullen Co Dem Party, Tex, currently. Relig: Catholic. Mailing Add: Box 94 Calliham TX 78007

SMITH, MARY LOUISE (R)
Chmn, Rep Nat Comt
b Eddyville, Iowa, Oct 6, 14; d Frank Epperson & Louise Jager E; m 1934 to Elmer Milton Smith, MD; c Robert Charles, Margaret Louise (Mrs Ronald J Byrne) & James Edward. Educ: Univ Iowa, Iowa City, BA, 35; Kappa Alpha Theta. Polit & Govt Pos: Mem bd educ, Eagle Grove Community Schs, Iowa, 55-60; mem, Gov Comt on Aging, 61-62; mem, Iowa Comt for Blind, 61-62, chmn, 62-63; mem state adv bd, Iowa Fedn Rep Women, 61-; vchmn, Wright Co Rep Cent Comt, 62-63; state vchmn, Iowa Rep Presidential Campaign, 64; alt deleg-at-lg, Rep Nat Conv, 64, deleg-at-lg & mem, Comt on Arrangements & Platform Comt, 68 & 72; mem, Rep Nat Conv, Iowa, 64-, mem exec comt, 69-73, co-vchmn, Rule 29 Comt, 73-74, co-chmn, Rep Nat Comt, 74, chmn, 74-; mem, Rep Nat Subcomt on Conv Reform, 66; mem, US deleg to 15th Session of Population Comt of Econ & Social Coun of UN, Geneva, 69; vchmn, Mid-West Region Rep Conf, 69-71; mem, President's Comt for Observance of 25th Anniversary of UN, 70; mem US deleg to Third Extraordinary Session, Gen Conf UNESCO, Paris; co-chmn, Iowa Comt to Reelect the President, 72, nat co-chmn, Physicians Comt to Reelect the President, 72. Bus & Prof Pos: Pres, Eagle Grove Community Chest, Iowa, 53-54; mem bd dirs, Ment Health Ctr, North Iowa, 61-63. Mem: PEO; Women's Auxiliary, Am Med Asn; Population Crisis Comt; Nat Women's Polit Caucus; UN Asn. Honors & Awards: Hon Col, Mil Staff, Gov of Iowa, 73. Relig: Protestant. Mailing Add: 654 59th St Des Moines IA 50312

SMITH, MATTHEW J (D)
RI State Rep
Mailing Add: 86 Pontiac Ave Providence RI 02907

SMITH, MCNEILL (D)
NC State Sen
Mailing Add: 2501 W Market St Greensboro NC 27403

SMITH, MORGAN (D)
Colo State Rep
Mailing Add: 275 S Sixth Ave Brighton CO 80601

SMITH, NANCY GARRITY (D)
b Kansas City, Kans, Dec 26, 33; d Leroy Montgomery Alexander & Marguerite Crumpley Garrity; m 1956 to Richard Lee Smith, PhD; c Sarah Angeline; Richard Hadaway & Karen Nanette. Educ: Bradford Jr Col, grad, 53; Univ Kans, AB, 56; Chi Omega. Polit & Govt Pos: Chmn, Physicists for Political Action, 71-72; alt deleg, Dem Nat Conv, 72; bd dirs, Dem Womens Club, 74- Bus & Prof Pos: Exec secy, Am Physicists Asn, 67-74. Publ: APA Representative lobbies for physicists in Miami, 8/72 & The history of our energy crisis, 10/73, Am Physicists Asn Newsletter; The age discrimination in employment act of 1967 & its importance to physicists, American Physicists Asn Newsletter, 8/73. Mailing Add: 4745 Hancock Dr Boulder CO 80303

SMITH, NEAL (D)
US Rep, Iowa
b Hedrick, Iowa, Mar 23, 20; m to Beatrix Havens; c Douglas & Sharon. Educ: Drake Univ Law Sch, grad; Mo Univ Col of Lib Arts; Syracuse Univ Sch of Pub & Bus Admin. Polit & Govt Pos: Nat pres, Young Dem Clubs of Am, 53-55; former asst co attorney, Polk Co, Iowa; US Rep, Iowa, 58- Bus & Prof Pos: Farmer & lawyer. Mil Serv: Vet, World War II; Nine Battle Stars; Air Medal; Four Oak Leaf Clusters; Purple Heart. Mem: 4-H Club (leader, 10 years); Polk Co Bd of Social Welfare; DAV; Mason; various farm, sch & serv orgns. Legal Res: Altoona IA 50009 Mailing Add: 2373 Rayburn House Off Bldg Washington DC 20515

SMITH, NED RAEFORD (D)
NC State Rep
b Granite Falls, NC, Jan 16, 11; s Lloyd Poole Smith & Dora Leslie Bradley S; m 1936 to Marguerite Britt; c Carol (Mrs Strittmatter) & Ned Britt. Educ: Duke Univ, AB; Univ NC, MA; Phi Delta Theta. Polit & Govt Pos: NC State Rep, 75- Bus & Prof Pos: Teacher, prin & supt, Forsyth Co, NC, 38 continuous years, retired. Relig: Methodist. Mailing Add: 773 N Stratford Rd Winston-Salem NC 27104

SMITH, NELS JENSEN (R)
Wyo State Rep
b Newcastle, Wyo, Jan 29, 39; s Peter Franklin Smith & Helen Jensen S; m 1968 to Jeanette Keener Vannoy. Educ: Univ Wyo, BS, 61; Phi Epsilon Phi; Alpha Zeta; Sigma Alpha Epsilon; Young Rep. Polit & Govt Pos: Wyo State Rep, 73-, majority floor leader, Wyo House of Rep, 73- Bus & Prof Pos: Owner & operator, Cattle Ranch, Sundance, Wyo, 61-, part-time mgr, before 61. Mem: Sundance 9, AF&AM; Wyo Stockgrowers Asn (mem, exec comt, 65-); Crook Co Wildlife Asn; Crook Co Animal Disease Bd; Sundance Rod & Gun Club. Relig: Protestant. Mailing Add: Sundance WY 82729

SMITH, PATRICIA ANN (R)
b Johnstown, Pa, Aug 5, 29; d Delbert Hill Pape & Neila Nelson P; m 1949 to Francis Anthony Smith; c Thomas A & David M. Educ: Northwestern Univ, 2 years; Alpha Xi Delta. Polit & Govt Pos: Precinct committeewoman, Sheridan Co Rep Cent Comt, Wyo, 59-69, secy, 67-68, vchairwoman, 68-69, chmn, 68-72; prog chmn, Wyo Fedn Rep Women, 69-71, second vpres, 71-73, pres, 73-75; deleg, Nat Conv Rep Women, 71; alt deleg, Rep Nat Conv, 72. Relig: Episcopal. Mailing Add: 1940 Big Horn Ave Sheridan WY 82801

SMITH, PATRICIA LAHR (R)
Rep Nat Committeewoman, Nebr
m 1947 to Richard W Smith; c Laurie & Barton. Educ: Univ Nebr, AB, 39. Polit & Govt Pos: Rep Nat Committeewoman, Nebr, 71- Mailing Add: 916 Fall Creek Rd Lincoln NE 68510

SMITH, PAUL AIKIN (D)
Secy, Iowa Dem State Cent Comt
b Bucaramanga, Colombia, Jan 12, 34; s Pryor Timmons Smith, Sr & Letha Bernice Brubaker S (deceased), stepmother, Alice Sjogren S; m 1958 to Margaret Sue McCluggage; c Valerie Anne & Amy Cheryl. Educ: Park Col, AB, 56; Washington Univ, AM, 59; Tufts Univ, PhD(physics), 64; pres, Park Col Orions, 55. Polit & Govt Pos: Parliamentarian, Linn Co Dem Cent Comt, Iowa, 72-; secy, Iowa Dem Party Reform Comt, 74; secy rules comt & parliamentarian, Dem State Conv, 74; secy, Iowa Dem State Cent Comt, 74-, secy platform-procedures revision comt, 74- Bus & Prof Pos: Asst prof physics, Coe Col, 64-70, assoc prof, 70-, chmn dept, 69-74; Iowa chmn, Am Asn Physics Teachers, 73-74, Iowa rep to nat coun, 74- Publ: Co-auth, Lifetimes of helium hyperfragments, Physics Rev 139, 56; auth, Teaching Dirac notation & relations among systems of units, Am J Physics 34, 66; auth, Attractive Scientists, privately publ, 73. Mem: AAAS; Am Asn Univ Prof; Iowa Acad Sci; Sigma Xi; Citizen's Tech Adv Comt on Transit Study for Linn Co. Relig: Presbyterian. Mailing Add: 1024 Maplewood Dr NE Cedar Rapids IA 52402

SMITH, PAUL THOMPSON (D)
Comnr, Jefferson Co, Mont
b Boulder, Mont, May 2, 04; s Cornelius Smith & Sarah Maguire S; m 1938 to Vivian F Flaherty; c Tresa & Paul B. Educ: High sch. Polit & Govt Pos: Co treas, Jefferson Co, Boulder, Mont, 32-36, comnr, 38-; chmn, Mont RR & Pub Serv Comn, 38-; deleg, Dem Nat Conv, 68. Mem: Eagles. Relig: Catholic. Mailing Add: Box 27 Boulder MT 59632

SMITH, PHILIP GENE (D)
b Chicago, Ill, Mar 3, 28; s S David Smith & N Ruth Alexander S; m 1960 to Elaine Jacqueline Kehrer; c Philip Gene, Jr & Kelyn Michael. Educ: Ky State Col, BA, 49; Chicago Teachers Col, BE, 53; Univ Ill, Univ Mich & Roosevelt Univ, social work; Northwestern Univ, fel, Nat Prog Educ Leadership, 72-74; Kappa Alpha Psi. Polit & Govt Pos: Campaign mgr, A A Rayner, Jr for Chicago Alderman, 66-67; exec assoc, Exec Off of the Gov, Mich, 67-70; exec dir, Voters Organized to Educate, 70-72, chmn, 72-; cand, Off of Alderman, City of Chicago, 71-75; deleg, Nat Black Polit Conv, 72 & 74; deleg-at-lg, Nat Dem Conv, 72; chmn, Ill Black Polit Caucus, Chicago Region, 72-; deleg, Ill Black Polit Conv, 72-; deleg, Nat Black Assembly, 72-; mem, Inst Black Polit Progress, 72- Bus & Prof Pos: Asst exec secy, Chicago Br, NAACP, 61-62; pub rels, Philip G Smith & Assocs, 62-63; field underwriter, Mutual of NY, 63-67; vis assoc, Northwestern Univ Ctr for Teaching Profession, 73-74; pres, Ethnic Educ Research Corp, 74- Mil Serv: Entered as Pvt, Army, 50, released as E-2, 51, after serv in 62nd Armored Inf, Far Eastern Command, 50-51. Publ: Chicago Metro News (weekly polit column), 65-; Power of Participation: Black Power, 69 & The Black Manifesto: Threatening or Conciliatory, 69, Pathe Press. Mem: Ill Educ Asn; Phi Delta Kappa; Am Civil Liberties Union (bd mem, Ill Div, 71-); Nat Asn Black Social Workers; Black Media Representatives (treas, 72-73). Honors & Awards: Edmund Burke Debating Award, Ky State Col, 48. Relig: Protestant. Mailing Add: 9419 S Forest Ave Chicago IL 60619

SMITH, PHILIP HARDY (D)
Secy-Treas, Talladega Co Dem Exec Comt, Ala
b Talladega, Ala, May 28, 31; s Philip Smith & Florence Riddle S; m 1951 to Catherine Elizabeth Wellbaum; c Hardy, Cay, Barbara & Peggy. Educ: Auburn Univ, 50; Univ of the South, BS, 51; Univ Rochester, MS, 53; Univ Ala, LLB, 58; Phi Beta Kappa; Sigma Delta Kappa; Omicron Delta Kappa. Polit & Govt Pos: Alt deleg, Dem Nat Conv, 56; pres, Univ Ala Young Dem, 57; pres, Talladega Co Young Dem, 62-66; secy-treas, Talladega Co Dem Exec Comt, 66-; Ala State Rep, Talladega Co, 67-74; chmn, Ala Legis Coun, 69-71; city recorder, Talladega, 75- Bus & Prof Pos: Lawyer, Talladega, Ala, 58- Mem: Talladega Co & Ala Bar Asns; Am Asn Advan Sci. Relig: Methodist. Mailing Add: PO Box 15 Talladega AL 35160

SMITH, PRESTON EARNEST (D)
b Williamson Co, Tex, Mar 8, 12; s Charles Kirby Smith & Effie Mae Strickland S; m 1935 to Ima Mae Smith; c Preston Michael & Jan Lauren (Mrs Conrad Schmid). Educ: Tex Tech Col, BBA, 34. Polit & Govt Pos: Tex State Rep, 44-50; Tex State Sen, 57-63; Lt Gov, Tex, 63-68; deleg, Dem Nat Conv, 68 & 72; Gov, Tex, 69-73. Bus & Prof Pos: Owner, Tex movie theaters, 36- Mem: Lubbock CofC; Kiwanis; Mason (33 degree); United Fund; Salvation Army. Relig: Methodist. Legal Res: 3212 43rd Lubbock TX 79413 Mailing Add: 105 University Ave Lubbock TX 79415

SMITH, RANDOLPH (R)
Ky State Rep
Mailing Add: Monticello KY 42633

SMITH, RAY ALLEN (R)
Committeeman, Grady Co Rep Party, Okla
b Tuttle, Okla, July 17, 43; s Homer Ezra Smith (deceased) & Rhoda Brown S; m 1962 to Donna Louise Troop; c Mark Alan, Shawnda Kay & Angela Louise (deceased). Educ: Tuttle Pub Schs, 12 years. Polit & Govt Pos: Rep precinct chmn, Tuttle, Okla, 65-67 & 72-; deleg, Okla Rep Conv, 66, 68 & 69; coordr, Smith for Cong, 57-68; chmn, Bellmon for Senate, Grady Co, 68; chmn, Grady Co Rep Party, 68, mem exec comt, 68-, committeeman, 69-; coordr, Wilkenson for Cong, Tuttle, 70; campaign chmn, Hardy for Coun, 73. Mem: Baptist Brotherhood; Young Rep; Am Red Cross; Parent Teachers Orgn; Sooner Alcohol & Narcotic Educ Asn. Honors & Awards: Outstanding Citizens Award, Ford Motor Co, 68. Relig: Baptist. Mailing Add: RR 2 Tuttle OK 73089

SMITH, RAY S, JR (D)
Ark State Rep
Mailing Add: 632 Quapaw Ave Hot Springs AR 71901

SMITH, RAYMOND J (R)
Chmn, Rep Territorial Comt VI
Mailing Add: PO Box 521 Charlotte Amalie St Thomas VI 00801

SMITH, RICHARD G (R)
Mont State Sen
Mailing Add: PO Box 411 Columbia Falls MT 59912

SMITH, RICK (D)
Wash State Rep
b Portland, Ore, Jan 21, 42; s Leonard Richard Smith & Juanita Hammond S; m 1963 to Janice Kreger; c Heather. Educ: Olympic Jr Col, Wash, AA, 64; Univ Wash, BA, 66; Am

Univ, JD, 71. Polit & Govt Pos: Legis asst, US Rep Floyd V Hicks, Wash, Washington, DC, 67-71; Dem caucus attorney, Wash State House of Rep, 72; Wash State Rep, 73- Bus & Prof Pos: Attorney, Silverdale, Wash. Mil Serv: Entered as Pfc, Army Res, 61, released. Mem: Wash Bar Asn. Honors & Awards: Book Award for Govt Contracts, Am Univ, 70, Book Award for Admin Law, 70. Relig: Methodist. Mailing Add: PO Box 68 Silverdale WA 98383

SMITH, ROBERT BRUCE, JR (D)
Chmn, Davidson Co Dem Exec Comt, NC
b Lexington, NC, Oct 16, 38; s Robert Bruce Smith & Eleanor Farmer S; m 1968 to Martha Ellen Miller; c Amy, Shelley & Robert Bruce, III. Educ: Univ NC, Chapel Hill, BS in Bus Admin, 61, LLB, 64; Phi Delta Phi; Sigma Chi. Polit & Govt Pos: Asst solicitor, Superior Court, Davidson Co, NC, 66; solicitor, Davidson Co Court, 67-70; chmn, Davidson Co Dem Exec Comt, 68-; deleg, Dem Nat Conv, 72. Bus & Prof Pos: Dir, Lexington State Bank, NC, 69. Mem: NC & Am Bar Asns; Moose; Lexington Kiwanis Club. Relig: Episcopal. Mailing Add: 19 W Center St Lexington NC 27292

SMITH, ROBERT FRANKLIN (D)
Mem Exec Comt, Saratoga Co Dem Comt, NY
b Tenn, July 14, 25; s Elbert B Smith & Margaret G Huffaker S; m 1950 to Barbara Leigh Eggleston; c Michael & Kevin. Educ: Maryville Col, BA, 48; Univ Tenn, MA, 51; Univ Chicago, PhD, 55. Polit & Govt Pos: Mem exec comt, Saratoga Co Dem Comt, NY, 63-, chmn, 68-72. Bus & Prof Pos: Instr, Univ Tenn, 49-51; instr, Idaho State Col, 54-55; lectr, Northwestern Univ, 53; from asst prof to assoc prof, Southern Methodist Univ, 55-60; from assoc prof to prof, Skidmore Col, 60-69. Mil Serv: Entered as A/S, Navy, 43, released as PhM 2/C, 46, after serv in Sea Duty, USS Wis, BB64, ETO & Caribbean, 44-46. Publ: Philosophical Approach to International Relations, State Univ Iowa Press, 57; The New York State Farm Bureau & the legislative process, J Farm Econ, 67. Mem: Am & NY Polit Sci Asns; Am Asn Univ Prof. Honors & Awards: Ford Found grant, 56; NY State Legis Internship grant, 65. Relig: Protestant. Mailing Add: Loughberry Rd Saratoga Springs NY 12866

SMITH, ROBERT FREEMAN (R)
Ore State Sen
b Portland, Ore, June 16, 31; s Dr Benjamin Franklin Smith & Louese Freeman S; m 1966 to Kaye Tomlinson; c Christopher Freeman, Matthew Tomlinson & Tiffany Elizabeth. Educ: Willamette Univ, BA, 53; Sigma Chi (pres, 53). Polit & Govt Pos: Mem, State Libr Bd, Salem, Ore, 56-60; chmn, Harney Co Rep Cent Comt, Burns, Ore, 58-60; Ore State Rep, 60-73, majority leader, speaker pro tempore, chmn, house comt on state & fed affairs & joint legis comt on pub lands, Ore House Rep, 65-69, co-chmn, Comt on Legis Admin, vchmn, State Emergency Bd & Speaker, 69-73; Gov rep, Nat Pub Land Law Rev Comn, Washington, DC, 66-69; cand assistance chmn, Rep State Cent Comt, 66-68; mem State Rep Coordr Coun, Rep State Cent Comt, 66-69; mem exec bd, Western Conf Coun of State Govt, 69-; deleg, Rep Nat Conv, 72; Ore State Sen, Dist 30, 73- Bus & Prof Pos: Businessman & cattle rancher, Burns, Ore, 53-; mem bd dirs, Great Western Nat Bank, Portland, 68-; bd trustees, Willamette Univ, 70- Mem: Elks; Mason; Harney Co CofC. Honors & Awards: Nominated one of Am Ten Outstanding Young Men, 65 & 66; Alumni Citation Award, Willamette Univ, 70; partic, Nat YMCA Basketball Tournament; named to Nat YMCA All-Am Basketball Team, 52. Relig: Presbyterian. Legal Res: 281 Court St Burns OR 97720 Mailing Add: 771 Ponderosa Village Burns OR 97720

SMITH, ROBERT JAMES (R)
Chmn, Willington Rep Town Comt, Conn
b Australia, Mar 10, 27; s John William Smith & Edith Sant S; m 1956 to Thelma Eve Peacock; c Heather, Pamela, Terry, Jill, Beverly & Barry. Educ: Univ Sydney, BSc, 54, MSc, 55; Univ Tenn, Knoxville, PhD, 59. Polit & Govt Pos: Chmn, Willington Rep Town Comt, Conn, 74- Bus & Prof Pos: Assoc prof math, Univ Conn, 66- Honors & Awards: Fulbright Scholar, 55. Mailing Add: RD 1 Red Oak Hill West Willington CT 06279

SMITH, ROBERT LEE
b DeSoto, Nebr, Feb 20, 18; s Seymour L Smith & Myrtle Hunter S; m 1948 to Beth Haney; c Victoria (Mrs Barry Lostroh), Craig, Calvert & Carey. Educ: Southern Methodist Univ, AB; Creighton Univ, LLB; Phi Eta Sigma; Alpha Phi Omega; Blue Key. Polit & Govt Pos: Dist judge, Omaha, Nebr, 61-64; judge, Nebr Supreme Court, formerly. Mil Serv: Entered as CM 2/C, Navy, 42, released as Lt(jg), 46, after serv in Seabees & Amphibious Forces, Pac. Mem: Am Bar Asn; Judicial Admin; Am Judicature Soc; Nebr State Bar Asn. Relig: Presbyterian. Legal Res: Omaha NE 68106 Mailing Add: 2860 Manse Ave Lincoln NE 68502

SMITH, RODNEY NEWELL (D)
b Burlington, Vt, July 4, 46; s Robert Dunn Smith & Mary Elizabeth S; m 1970 to Ilda Frances Procopio. Educ: Am Univ, BA, 68; Univ Mich, Ann Arbor, MA, 70. Polit & Govt Pos: Economist, Off of Secy, US Treasury, 70-72; mem staff, McGovern for President, 72; admin asst to US Rep Harrington, Mass, 73- Legal Res: 29 Hillside Rd Rutland VT 05701 Mailing Add: 731 S Lee St Alexandria VA 22314

SMITH, ROGER A (R)
NH State Sen
b Concord, NH, June 6, 32; married; c one. Educ: Concord High Sch. Polit & Govt Pos: NH State Rep supvr, Fifth Ward Checklist, formerly; mem, Concord Rep City Comt; chmn, Fifth Ward Rep Comt; NH State Sen, 71- Bus & Prof Pos: Plant dept, NE Tel & Tel Co. Mil Serv: Army, Korea; 981st FA Bn, 49th Inf Div. Mem: Int Brotherhood of Tel Workers, Local 20. Mailing Add: 95 Center St Concord NH 03301

SMITH, ROY (R)
Mich State Rep
b Monroe, Tenn, Feb 12, 24; s William Smith & Grant Stover S; m 1949 to Shirley Sanford; c William S, Phillip G & Sue Ann. Educ: Oberlin Col, 44-45; Univ Mich, BS in Geol, 50. Polit & Govt Pos: Mem, Bd of Tax Rev, Ypsilanti Twp, 55-59, twp supvr, 59-66; Washtenaw Co Supvr, 59-66; Mich State Rep, 52nd Dist, 66-72 & 75-; city adminr, Saline, 72-74. Mil Serv: Entered as Pvt, Marines, 42, released as Cpl, 45. Mem: Am Legion. Honors & Awards: Distinguished Serv Award, Mich Community Schs Educ Asn. Relig: Baptist. Mailing Add: 3320 Morgan Rd Ann Arbor MI 48104

SMITH, SAM CROFT (D)
Mem, Ga State Dem Exec Comt
b Cartersville, Ga, Sept 20, 47; s Sam Smith & Jewell Croft S; m 1971 to Sandra Rochelle Taylor. Educ: Univ Tenn, BS, 69; Lambda Chi Alpha. Polit & Govt Pos: Mem, Ga State Dem Exec Comt, 70-; deleg, Dem Nat Conv, 72. Bus & Prof Pos: Pres, Barton Cr Bank, Cartersville, Ga, 74- Mem: Am Inst Banking; Cartersville Jaycees; Univ Tenn Alumni Asn; Lambda Chi Alpha Alumni Asn; Trusco Club. Honors & Awards: Young Man of the Year, Cartersville Barton Co, 73. Relig: Baptist. Mailing Add: 39 Arrowhead Dr Cartersville GA 30120

SMITH, SAMUEL J (Sam) (Non-Partisan)
Councilman, Seattle, Wash
b Gibsland, La, July 21, 22; s The Rev Stephen Kelly Smith & Berniece C Bailey S; m 1947 to Marion Inez King; c Amelia I, Aldwin Carl, Anthony, Donald C, Ronald C & Stephen Kelly, II. Educ: Seattle Univ, BSS, 51; Univ Wash, BA in Econ, 52, grad work in econ & polit sci, 52-53; Phi Beta Sigma. Polit & Govt Pos: Clerk typist regional off, US Vet Admin Br 11, 46-47, fiscal accts clerk, 47-51; Dem precinct committeeman, Seattle, Wash; Wash State Rep, 37th Dist, 58-67; city councilman, Seattle, Wash, 67-, chmn, Pub Safety Comt, Seattle City Coun, 68- Bus & Prof Pos: Printing & advert salesman, self-employed, 46-50; expediter, Boeing Co, Seattle, Wash, 67-, chmn, Pub Safety Comt, Seattle City Coun, 68- Bus & Prof Pos: Printing & advert salesman, self-employed, 46-50; expediter, Boeing Co, Seattle, 51-67; publ & ed, Community Newspaper, 52-54. Mil Serv: Entered as Pvt, Army, 42, released as Warrant Off(jg), 46, after serv in Qm Corps & Transportation Corps, Asiatic Pac Theater, New Guinea, Philippine Islands, 44-46; Good Conduct Medal; Asiatic Pac Theater & New Guinea Campaign Ribbons; Philippines Liberation Medal; 2 Bronze Stars; World War II Vets Medal. Mem: Am Acad of Polit & Soc Sci; VFW Post 289 (past comdr); Aero Mechanics Lodge 751; Seattle Automobile Asn Am. Honors & Awards: Legislator of Year, Wash House of Rep, 67; Urban League Annual Award Commun & Polit Serv & Equal Opportunity 68; Community Serv Award, 71; Exemplary Leadership & Serv Award, Mt Zion Baptist Church, 73; 33rd Degree Mason for Achievements, United Supreme Coun Scottish Rite, 73. Relig: Baptist; Pres of Fellowship, Mt Zion Baptist Church; mem, Pub Mission, Nat Ministries Am Baptist Churches. Mailing Add: 1814 31st Ave Seattle WA 98122

SMITH, SHELBY (R)
Lt Gov, Kans
Mailing Add: State Capitol Topeka KS 66612

SMITH, SHELDON B (R)
Chmn, Oakland Co Rep Comt, Mich
b Pontiac, Mich, Jan 21, 39; s Rolfe H Smith & Ruth E Annett S; m 1974 to Jane Marie Johnson. Educ: Univ Mich, 56-58. Polit & Govt Pos: Membership chmn, Oakland Co Young Rep, Mich, 66-67; membership chmn, Mich Fedn Young Rep, 67-68; chmn, 19th Cong Dist Rep Comt, 69-71; chmn, Oakland Co Rep Comt, 71-; deleg, Rep Nat Conv, 72; comnr, Mackinac Island State Park Comn, 73- Bus & Prof Pos: Prog dir, Radio Sta KMAN, Manhattan, Kans, 58-60; Realtor, Rolfe H Smith Co, Pontiac, Mich, 65-; pres, Multiple Listing Serv, Inc, 69-70; pres, Pontiac Area Bd Realtors, 71. Mil Serv: Entered as Pvt, Army, 62, released as Sgt, 64, after serv in Am Forces Network, Europe, 62-64. Mem: Downtown Pontiac Kiwanis; Pontiac City Club; Am Fedn TV & Radio Artists; Pontiac Area Bd Realtors; North Oakland CofC. Honors & Awards: Realtor of the Year, Pontiac Area Bd Realtors, 71. Relig: Methodist. Legal Res: 4948 Lake Pointe Dr Apt 102 Drayton Plains MI 48020 Mailing Add: 244 S Telegraph Rd Pontiac MI 48053

SMITH, SHIRLEY ELIZABETH (D)
Chairperson, Davis Co Dem Cent Comt, Iowa
b Bloomfield, Iowa, May 20, 29; d Ralph Milton Randolph & LaVelle Snell R; m 1949 to Donald LaVerne Smith; c Sheila Sue, Linda Lou & Valerie Venice. Educ: Bloomfield High Sch, grad, 47. Polit & Govt Pos: Chairperson, Davis Co Dem Cent Comt, Iowa, 70- Mailing Add: 105 N Bloomfield Ave Bloomfield IA 52537

SMITH, SIEGMUND WILSON (R)
b Philippine Islands, Apr 7, 10; s Fine Wilson Smith & Mildred Whiting S; m 1945 to Frances Dorothea O'Connor; c Donald Wilson, Brian Richard & Patricia Christine. Educ: Univ Ky, 1 year. Polit & Govt Pos: Admin asst to US Rep Lionel Van Deerlin, Calif, 63- Bus & Prof Pos: Sports dir, Radio Sta WGR, Buffalo, NY, 36-52; news ed, KFSD-TV, San Diego, Calif, 53-60; sports dir, XETV-TV, 60-63. Mil Serv: Entered as Pvt, Army, 42, released as Sgt, 45, after serv in Mil Intel, ETO, 44-45. Mem: Wash Contract Bridge League; Nat Capitol Swimming Asn. Relig: Episcopal. Legal Res: 3868 Mission Blvd San Diego CA 92106 Mailing Add: 8002 Park Crest Dr Silver Spring MD 20910

SMITH, STEPHEN WELLS (R)
NH State Sen
b Chicago, Ill, June 11, 30; s George Dresser Smith & Eleanor Wells S; m 1958 to Dorothy Louise Merris; c S Wells, Donald Merris, Matthew Doyle & Jennifer Ann. Educ: Kenyon Col, AB, 52; Alpha Delta Phi. Polit & Govt Pos: Chmn, Grafton Co Rep Comt, NH, 60-64; treas, Plymouth, NH, 61-62; comnr, Plymouth Village Fire Dist, 62-66; NH State Rep, 63-67, chmn, Transportation Comt, 65-67; chmn, NH Uniform Vehicle Code Study Comt, 65-67; chmn, Plymouth Rep Town Comt, 66; Gov Coun, NH, 69-70; Rep Nat Committeeman, NH, 69-72; NH State Sen, 71-, majority leader, NH State Senate, 71-72, mem, Finance Comt, 71-, chmn, Educ Comt & Comt on Interstate Coop, 73-; presidential elector, 72. Mem: Rotary; Elks. Relig: Protestant. Legal Res: 115 Highland St Plymouth NH 03264 Mailing Add: 71 Main St Plymouth NH 03264

SMITH, STEVE AUSTIN (D)
b Fayetteville, Ark, May 15, 49; s Austin Clell Smith & Margaret L King S; m 1970 to Carolyn V Bassett. Educ: Univ Ark, Fayetteville, BA, 72, MA, 73; Northwestern Univ, PhD cand; Phi Delta Theta. Polit & Govt Pos: Mem City Planning Comn, Huntsville, 71-; Ark State Rep, Carroll & Madison Co, 71-74; deleg, Ark State Dem Conv, 72 & 74; deleg, Dem Nat Conv, 72; deleg, Ark Const Conv, 75; mem, Ark Dem State Comt; secy, Ark Dem Comn Nat Affairs. Bus & Prof Pos: Grad teaching asst, Univ Ark, Fayetteville, 71-72. Mem: Speech Commun Asn of Am; Common Cause; Am Civil Liberties Union; Young Dem; Pi Sigma Alpha. Relig: Unitarian. Mailing Add: Rte 6 Huntsville AR 72740

SMITH, STEWART ALLEN (R)
Chmn, Vt Rep State Comt
b White River Junction, Vt, Mar 8, 20; s Allen O Smith & Clara Stewart S; m 1943 to Priscilla Ann Norton; c Allen N. Educ: Univ Vt, 39-41; Univ Ore, grad, 43; Harvard Univ, 43; Univ Chicago, 44; Sigma Nu. Polit & Govt Pos: Chmn, Vt Rep State Comt, 72- Bus & Prof Pos: Mem, Buick New Eng Coun, 62-63 & 72-73. Mil Serv: Entered as Pvt, Army, 43, released as Pfc, 45, after serv in 76th Inf Div, ETO, 44-45; Battle Stars, Ardennes & Rhineland. Mem: VFW; Am Legion. Mailing Add: 62 Litchfield Ave Rutland VT 05701

SMITH, STUART ARNOLD (D)
Chmn, Wilton Dem Town Comt, Conn
b Newark, NJ, Apr 15, 32; s Abraham Zelleman Smith & Sara S; m 1963 to Jill Maxine Beyer; c Andrew Zelleman, Joshua Samuel & Jocelyn Deborah. Educ: Syracuse Univ, BFA, 54; Tau Epsilon Phi. Polit & Govt Pos: Campaign mgr, Wilton Dem Town Comt, Conn, 70-72, chmn, 72- Relig: Jewish. Mailing Add: 68 Raymond Lane Wilton CT 06897

SMITH, THEODORE (D)
Miss State Sen
Mailing Add: PO Box 1309 Corinth MS 38834

SMITH, THEODORE GEORGE (D)
Alaska State Rep
b Arnold, Nebr, Nov 9, 29; s Philip George Smith & Verna Mae Viehmyer S; m 1966 to Joyce Smith; c Michael Edward & Steven Oramel. Educ: Univ Wash, BSF, 56; Xi Sigma Pi. Polit & Govt Pos: Forester, State Div Lands, Anchorage, Alaska, 60-66, chief parks & recreation, 66-70; dir, State Div Parks, Anchorage, 70-74; Alaska State Rep, 75- Bus & Prof Pos: Forester-photographer, N P Rwy, Seattle, Wash, 56-58; forester, Alaska Lumber & Pulp, Sitka, Alaska, 59-60. Mil Serv: Entered as Pvt, Air Force, 48, released as S/Sgt, 52, after serv in US. Mailing Add: 2616 Sorbus Circle Anchorage AK 99504

SMITH, THOMAS BENTON (D)
Mem, Ark Dem State Comt
b Wynne, Ark, Dec 17, 48; s J H Smith & Winnie Bob Shaver S; m 1971 to Counts Felton; c Thomas Benton, Jr. Educ: Univ Ark, Fayetteville, BA, 70, Sch Law, JD, 73; Phi Alpha Delta; Sigma Alpha Epsilon. Polit & Govt Pos: Chmn, Cross Co deleg, Ark State Dem Conv, 74; legal counsel & mem exec comt, Ark State Young Dem, 74-; mem, Ark Dem State Comt, First Cong Dist, 74-; deleg, Ark State Const Conv, 75. Bus & Prof Pos: Attorney-at-law, Shaver & Shaver, 73- Mem: Am, Ark & Cross Co Bar Asns; Wynne Rotary (ed). Relig: Presbyterian. Legal Res: 1443 Hamilton Ave Wynne AR 72396 Mailing Add: PO Box 592 Wynne AR 72396

SMITH, THOMAS EARLE, JR (D)
SC State Sen
b Oxford, NC, July 22, 38; s Thomas Earle Smith & Margaret Louise Osterhout S; m 1961 to Elizabeth Eulalia Munn; c Mary Dresden & Amy Louise. Educ: Davidson Col, AB, 60; Univ SC, LLB, 63; Chief Justice; Phi Alpha Delta; Phi Delta Theta; Co-capt, Davidson Col Swimming Team & vchmn, Student Coun of YMCA, 59-60. Polit & Govt Pos: Pres, SC Young Dem Club, 67-69; SC State Rep, Florence Co, 67-67, mem, Judiciary Comt, 67-70, second vchmn, 70-72; deleg, Dem Nat Conv, 68; SC State Sen, 73-; mem, Judiciary Comt, SC State Senate, 73-; chmn, Gov Comt Ment Health & Ment Retardation, 74- Bus & Prof Pos: Mem bd dir, Pamplico Bank & Trust Co & Johnsonville State Bank, 65-; pres, Pamplico Develop Co, Inc, 66. Mem: Lions; Mason; Shrine; Omar Imps; Jaycees. Relig: Methodist; chmn, admin bd, 70-71; Pamplico Methodist Church, 65- Legal Res: 100 Walnut St Pamplico SC 29583 Mailing Add: State House Columbia SC 29211

SMITH, THOMAS EDWARD (R)
Treas, Fla Fedn Young Rep
b Repton, Ala, May 4, 36; s William Wesley Smith & Viola Katherine Johnson S; m 1954 to Carol Ann French; c Sandra Kaye, Jeannie Carol, Jonathan McAllistair & David Scott. Educ: Univ Southern Miss, 2 years. Polit & Govt Pos: Chmn, Gtr Pensacola Young Rep, 68-69; first dist chmn, Fla Fedn Young Rep, 68-69, state treas, 69- Mem: Am Guild Variety Artists; Nat Asn Radio Announcers; Navy League Am. Honors & Awards: Freedom Found George Washington Honor Medal. Relig: Protestant. Mailing Add: 12 Clyde St Pensacola FL 32503

SMITH, THOMAS TEDFORD (R)
Chmn, Izard Co Rep Party, Ark
b Lunenburg, Ark, Feb 28, 09; s William Green Smith & Lillie Francis Shannon; m 1965 to Ophelia Broxson; c Paula Anita (Mrs Pitts), Patsy Sue (Mrs Glenn) & Lawrence Randolph. Educ: Melbourne High Sch, 2 years, passed col level test. Polit & Govt Pos: Mem, Ark State Rep Comt, 64-68, 70-; chmn, Izard Co Rep Party, 70- Mil Serv: Entered as Pvt, Army, 28, released as Col, 55, after serv in Corps Engrs, Am, Pac & European Theatres, 28-55; Bronze Star; various theatre & campaign medals. Mem: Am Legion. Relig: Protestant. Mailing Add: Corinth Rd Bexar AR 72515

SMITH, VAN P (R)
b Oneida, NY, Sept 8, 28; m 1960 to Margaret Ann Kennedy; c Lynn Ann, Mark Charles, Paul Gregory, Susan Colleen & Victor Patrick. Educ: Colgate Univ, AB in Pub Admin & Econ, 52; Georgetown Univ, JD, 55; Theta Chi; Delta Theta Phi. Polit & Govt Pos: Ind State Rep, 60-62, chmn, Legislative Apportionment Comt, Ind House Rep, 60-62; chmn, Ind Tenth Cong Dist Young Rep, formerly; deleg, Ind Rep State Conv, 64-; alt deleg, Rep Nat Conv, 72. Bus & Prof Pos: Pres, Metal Treating Corp, Muncie, Ind; dir & mem exec comt, Indust Savings & Loan, Muncie; chmn bd dirs, Pyromet Industs, Inc, San Carlos, Calif; dir, Marsh Supermarkets, Inc, Yorktown, Ind; dir, Boxell Sign Corp, Muncie; dir, Standard Locknut & Lockwasher, Inc, Indianapolis; vpres, Ontario Develop Corp; mem, Law Firm Warner, Clark & Warner, Muncie, 55-56; dir & secy, Ontario Corp, 56, vpres, sales 60 & pres, 63. Mil Serv: Entered as Pvt, Air Force, 50, released as 1st Lt, 53, after serv in Direct Comn, US & Europe, 51-53. Mem: Young Pres Orgn (treas, Ind Chap, 70-); Small Bus Admin (mem, Nat Adv Coun, 70-; mem, Ind Adv Coun, 70-); Muncie Club; Elks; KofC (4 degree). Honors & Awards: Outstanding Young Man, Muncie, Ind, 60; Outstanding Freshman Legislator, Ind Gen Assembly, 61. Relig: Catholic. Mailing Add: 3 Briar Rd Muncie IN 47304

SMITH, VERNON GEORGE (D)
Councilman, City of Gary, Ind
b Gary, Ind, Apr 11, 44; s Albert J Smith & Julia Allen S; single. Educ: Ind Univ, BS, 66, MS, 69, doctoral prog, currently; Omega Psi Phi. Polit & Govt Pos: Councilman, Fourth Dist, City of Gary, Ind, 72- Bus & Prof Pos: Asst dir, Oper Jobs, Gary Urban League, summer 66; sci teacher, Beveridge Sch, Gary, 66-71; resource teacher, Dist III, 71-72; asst prin, 72-; asst dir, Oper Sparkle, Off Econ Opportunity, summer 67; counr, Ind Univ Northwest, Gary, 67-68; columnist, Gary Crusader Newspaper, 71-73. Mem: Phi Delta Kappa; Gary Br, NAACP; Young Citizens League (founder & sponsor, 70-); Youth Ensuring Solidarity (founder & sponsor, 72-); Little League World Series Bd. Honors & Awards: Outstanding Serv & Achievement Award, Alpha Chi, 71; Outstanding Young Educator, Gary Jaycees, 69; Citation in Educ, Gary NAACP, 70; Great Guy Award, WGRT, Chicago, 71; Councilman of the Year, G4-14 Community Club, 72. Relig: Baptist. Mailing Add: 1800 Adams St Gary IN 46407

SMITH, VICTOR L (R)
b Crawford Co, Ill. Educ: Univ Ill. Polit & Govt Pos: State organizer of first Young Rep Orgn, Ill; former pres, Robinson Young Rep Club & Crawford Co Fedn of Young Rep Clubs; precinct committeeman, Rep Party, 32 years; chmn, Crawford Co Rep Party, several years; mem, Ill Rep State Cent Comt, 6 years; chmn, Ill Rep Party, formerly; deleg, Rep Nat Conv, 68 & 72; mem, Rep Nat Comt, formerly. Bus & Prof Pos: Publ, Robinson Argus, Ill, currently. Mailing Add: 403 W Walnut St Robinson IL 62454

SMITH, VIRGIL WALTER (D)
b Brooks, Minn, Apr 5, 14; s Earl Melvine Smith & Eva Whittish S; m 1937 to Coramay Flom; c Carol Ann, Ronald Earl, Virginia Rae, Bonnie Lou & Walter Martin. Educ: Madison Voc Sch, 2 years; Univ Wis, 2 Semesters. Polit & Govt Pos: Secy-treas, Tavern League of Rusk Co, Inc, 49-; village clerk, Ingram, Wis, 50-; mem, Sect Redevelop of Ingram, 58-; vchmn, Rusk Co Dem Party, formerly, chmn, 63-72; vpres, Tavern League of Wis, Inc, 65- Mem: Eagles, Madison; Gregg Club; jr & sr leader, 4H Club; Sportsman Club, Ladysmith, Wis. Relig: Catholic. Mailing Add: Box 161 Ingram WI 54535

SMITH, VIRGINIA DODD (R)
US Rep, Nebr
b Randolph, Iowa, July 30, 11; d Clifton Clark Dodd & Erville Reeves D; m 1931 to Haven N Smith. Educ: Shenandoah High Sch, 28; Univ Nebr, BA, 34; Delta Kappa Gamma; Beta Sigma Phi; Chi Omega. Polit & Govt Pos: Deleg, Rep Nat Conv, 56 & 72, mem rules comt, 72; chmn, President Nixon's Task Force Rural Develop, 70-71; mem, Census Adv Comt Agr Statist, US Dept of Com, 70-73; mem, US Govt Adv Comt Rural Educ & Small Schs, 70-73; chmn, Deuel Co Rep Comt, Nebr, 72-73; US Rep, Nebr, 75- Bus & Prof Pos: Mem, Nebr State Bd Educ, 50-60; mem, Nat Livestock & Meat Bd, 55-58; mem, Crusade for Freedom European Inspection Tour, 58; mem, Nat Home Econ Research Adv Comt, 60-65; mem, Nat Comt Community Health Serv, 63-66; vpres, Nat Farm Film Found, 64- Mem: Am Asn Univ Women; DAR; Eastern Star; Bus & Prof Women; Am Farm Bur Women (nat chmn, 54-75). Honors & Awards: Award for Best Pub Address on Freedom, Freedoms Found, 66; One of six women selected by Govt of France for Int Goodwill Tour, 68; Nebr Woman of Achievement, Bus & Prof Women, 70; Distinguished Serv Award, Midwest Conf World Affairs, 70; Eyes on Nebr Award, Nebr Optom Asn, 70. Relig: Methodist. Legal Res: Box 643 Chappell NE 69129 Mailing Add: US House of Rep 1005 Longworth Washington DC 20515

SMITH, VIRGINIA DOROTHY (R)
VChmn, Idaho Rep State Cent Comt
b Haviland, Kans, June 28, 12; d Richard Ayres Spencer & Mildred Young S; m 1931 to Willard L Smith; c Patricia Virginia (Mrs Brown); Karen Lee (Mrs Strosehein), Molly Lou (Mrs Kraushaar) & Eugene Spencer. Educ: Nampa High Sch, Idaho, grad, 31. Polit & Govt Pos: Senate hostess, Idaho State Senate, 4 years; state committeewoman, Canyon Co Rep Cent Comt, currently; campaign mgr, Canyon Co Rep, currently; Idaho chmn, Women for Nixon, 68; mem, State Comt to Reelect the President, 72; vchmn, Idaho Rep State Cent Comt, currently. Mem: Rep Booster Club (secy); Canyon Co Rep Luncheon Club; Canyon Co Rep Women's Club. Honors & Awards: Mrs Republican, Canyon Co Rep, 72; Plaque with Honor & Name & State Seal, State of Idaho. Relig: United Methodist. Mailing Add: Rte 6 Box 201 Caldwell ID 83605

SMITH, VIRLYN B (R)
Ga State Rep
Mailing Add: 330 Rivertown Rd Fairburn GA 30213

SMITH, WADE (D)
NC State Rep
Mailing Add: 2613 Wilson Lane Raleigh NC 27610

SMITH, WADE ORCHIN (D)
Miss State Rep
b Poplarville, Miss, Feb 16, 11; m 1937 to Loyce Ward. Polit & Govt Pos: Dir, Pearl River Co Dem Party, formerly; Miss State Rep, Dist 43, Post 2, 72- Bus & Prof Pos: Farmer. Mem: Farm Bur Wolf River Wildlife Coun (pres); Miss & Pearl River Co Cattlemens Asns. Relig: Baptist. Mailing Add: Rte 2 Box 280 Poplarville MS 39470

SMITH, WALTER (D)
Mem, Dem Nat Comt, Fla
Mailing Add: 1765 River Rd 1 Jacksonville FL 32207

SMITH, WAYNE DELARMIE (R)
VChmn, Sullivan Co Rep Cent Comt, Mo
b Green Castle, Mo, Jan 22, 28; s Frank Delarmie Smith & Sylvia Juanita Rickard S; separated. Educ: Univ Mo-Columbia, BS in agr, 51, MS in educ, 52, DVM, 56; Alpha Tau Alpha; Alpha Zeta; Phi Delta Kappa; Gamma Alpha. Polit & Govt Pos: First dist judge, Sullivan Co Court, Mo, 70-; vchmn, Sullivan Co Rep Cent Comt, 72- Mem: Sullivan Co Farm Bur (pres, 60-); Sullivan Co Angus Asn (pres, 73-); Sullivan Co Exten Coun (chmn, 74-). Relig: Baptist; dir, Training Union, First Baptist Church, 70-72, Sunday Sch supt, 72-74. Mailing Add: Box 5 Winigan MO 63566

SMITH, WILBER G (D)
Conn State Sen
Mailing Add: 196 Palm St Hartford CT 06112

SMITH, WILBURN (R)
Chmn, Fayette Co Rep Comt, Ala
b Bankston, Ala, July 26, 03; s James Howell Smith & Dessie Johnson S; m 1932 to Jalia Blanche Sawyer; c June (Mrs Aldridge). Educ: Univ Ala, BEd. Polit & Govt Pos: Rep precinct worker, Bankston, Ala, 36, mem dist Rep orgn, 52-; vchmn, Fayette Co Rep Comt, 56-62, chmn, 62- Bus & Prof Pos: Elem teacher, 29-31 & 48-; jr high sch prin, 31-41 & 46-48; defense plant patrolman, 41-45. Mem: Fayette Co Teachers Asn; Am & Nat Educ Asns; AFL; 4-H Club. Relig: Missionary Baptist. Mailing Add: RR 1 Bankston AL 35542

SMITH, WILLIAM FORREST (D)
Mem, Dallas Co Dem Exec Comt, Tex
b Beaumont, Tex, Jan 6, 29; s William Enoch Smith & Mary Bray S; m 1951 to Martha McCarley; c Sherry Roxann, Jill Ann, Lori Ann, Chris Ann & Candy Ann. Educ: Lon Morris Jr Col, Jacksonville, Tex, 45-47; Southwestern Univ (Tex), BA, 49; Southern Methodist Univ Sch of Law, 49-51, JD, 57, LLM, 63; Kappa Sigma. Polit & Govt Pos: Dem precinct chmn, Dallas Co, Tex, 66-; mem, Dallas Co Dem Exec Comt, 66-; alt deleg, Dem Nat Conv, 68; mem, Bd of Dallas Dem, 68-69; mem, Tex Youth Coun, 69-; mem, Dallas Motion Picture Classification Bd. Bus & Prof Pos: Acct, Magnolia Petroleum Co, 52-54, tax acct, 54-58; attorney, Mobil Oil Corp, 58- Mil Serv: 1st Lt, Tex Nat Guard, Judge Advocate Gen Sect, 49th Armored Div, 11 years. Publ: State Taxation of the Oil & Gas Industry as Limited by the Interstate Commerce Clause, Southern Methodist Univ Sch of Law, 63; Pollution Problems in the Petroleum-Construction of and Compliance with Federal & State Laws, Matthew Bender, 68. Mem: Dallas Bar Asn (chmn urban affairs comt); NMex Petroleum Indust Comt; Tex Mid-Continent Oil & Gas Asn (chmn social security comt); Mid-Continent Oil & Gas Asn (chmn comt); Mobil Mgt Asn. Honors & Awards: Vernon Law Bk Award, Southern Methodist Univ. Relig: Methodist. Legal Res: 7509 Stonecrest Dallas TX 75240 Mailing Add: PO Box 900 Dallas TX 75221

SMITH, WILLIAM FRENCH (R)
Mem, United Rep Finance Comt
b Wilton, NH, Aug 26, 17; s William French Smith & Margaret Dawson S; m to Jean Webb; c William French, III, Stephanie Oakes, Scott Cameron & Gregory Hale. Educ: Univ Calif, Los Angeles, AB, 39; Harvard Law Sch, LLB, 42; Phi Beta Kappa; Pi Gamma Mu; Pi Sigma Alpha. Polit & Govt Pos: Chmn, Speakers Bur, Rep State Cent Comt Calif, 54-56; vchmn bd trustees, Rep Assocs, Los Angeles Co, 67-; deleg, Rep Nat Conv, 68 & 72, chmn, Calif Deleg, 68, counsel, 72; mem, United Rep Finance Comt, 68-; mem, US Adv Comn on Int Educ & Cult Affairs, Washington, DC, 71-; mem, Panel on Int Info, Educ & Cult Rels, Washington, DC; mem, Mayor's Labor-Mgt Adv Comt, Los Angeles. Bus & Prof Pos: Attorney-at-law & partner, Gibson, Dunn & Crutcher, Los Angeles, Calif, currently; mem bd dirs, Pac Lighting Corp, 67-, Pac Tel & Tel Co, 69-, Pac Mutual Life Ins Co, 70-, Los Angeles World Affairs Coun, 70-, Crocker Nat Bank, 71- & Crocker Nat Corp, 71-; mem bd regents, Univ Calif, 74-; mem bd dirs, Ctr Theatre Group, Los Angeles Music Ctr, vpres, 73-; nat trustee, Nat Symphony Orchestra, Washington, DC, 74-; mem bd dirs, Partnership for Arts in Calif, Inc, San Francisco & Jorgensen Steel Corp; mem bd trustees, Henry E Huntington Libr & Art Gallery, San Marino, Claremont Men's Col, Cate Sch, Carpinteria & Northrop Inst Technol. Mem: Am Bar Asn (int & comp law comt & lab rels law comt); Calif CofC (pres, 74-75); State Bar of Calif (spec comt on group legal serv & spec comt on Calif arbit statute); fel Am Bar Found; Am Judicature Soc. Legal Res: 1256 Oak Grove Ave San Marino CA 91108 Mailing Add: 515 S Flower St Los Angeles CA 90071

SMITH, WILLIAM GREY (D)
NC State Sen
b Goldsboro, NC, Jan 3, 22; s Walter Grey Smith & Eloise Price S; m 1945 to Helen Grey; c Julia (Mrs Lucien Capone III), Walter M & Barbara. Educ: Wake Forest Univ, AB, 48; Univ NC, Chapel Hill, LLB, 50; Phi Alpha Delta. Polit & Govt Pos: NC State Sen, Fourth Dist, 75- Bus & Prof Pos: Practicing attorney, Wilmington, NC, 51- Mil Serv: Entered as Pvt, Army, 44, released as Pfc, after serv in Infantry. Mem: Am Bar Asn; Am Trial Lawyers Asn; New Hanover Co Bar Asn (pres, 74-75); Am Judicature Soc; NC Acad Trial Lawyers (bd gov, 73-). Relig: Protestant. Legal Res: Rte 3 Box 119 Wilmington NC 28401 Mailing Add: 1 N Third St Wilmington NC 28401

SMITH, WILLIAM MARION (D)
b Natchez, Miss, Feb 2, 32; s Frank Levon Smith & Alice Kaiser S; m 1967 to Carolyn Vance; c Emily Mitchell. Educ: Univ Miss, BA, 53, LLB & JD, 55; Omicron Delta Kappa; Phi Eta Sigma; Phi Delta Phi; Phi Delta Theta. Polit & Govt Pos: Miss State Sen, 60-72, pres pro tempore, Miss State Senate, 71-72; mem bd gov, Coun State Govts, 68- Bus & Prof Pos: Assoc prof law, Univ Miss, 58-59; lawyer, currently. Mem: Jr CofC; Adams Co, Miss & Am Bar Asns. Relig: Episcopal. Mailing Add: 205 Glenwood Dr Natchez MS 39120

SMITH, WILLIAM T, II (R)
NY State Sen
b Corning, NY, Jan 25, 16; s Maynard Smith & Carrie Shriver S; m to Dorothy Nowak; c William T, III, Bonnifer, Deborah & Michael. Educ: Corning Free Acad; NY State Col Agr, Cornell Univ, grad, 38. Polit & Govt Pos: Mem, Chemung Co Planning Bd, NY, 58-62; mem, Big Flats Rep Town Comt & Big Flats Park Comn; NY State Sen, 51st Dist, currently, chmn, Standing Comt on Social Serv & mem, Agr & Consumer Protection, Finance, Higher Educ, Transportation & Rules Comts, NY State Senate, currently; chmn, Temporary State Comn to Revise the Social Serv Law, currently. Bus & Prof Pos: Farm owner, Smithome Farms, Big Flats, NY. Mem: Rotary; Fur, Fin & Feather; Coldbrook Club; Corning Country Club; CofC. Relig: Presbyterian; Trustee, Big Flats Presby Church. Mailing Add: 3047 Olcott Rd Big Flats NY 14814

SMITHSON, JIM (R)
Ark State Rep
Mailing Add: PO Box 156 Marshall AR 72650

SMOGARD, ELLSWORTH G (D)
Minn State Rep
Mailing Add: RR 2 Madison MN 56256

SMOKO, RONALD L (D)
Conn State Rep
Mailing Add: 50 Beechwood Ave Hamdem CT 06514

SMOLENSKI, ANTHONY (D)
b Albertson, NY, Sept 6, 50; s Anthony Smolenski & Eunice Beck S; single. Educ: State Univ NY Col Brockport, BA, 72; Rutgers Univ, New Brunswick, 72- Polit & Govt Pos: Aide, Rubenstein State Senate Campaign, Fifth Sen Dist, NY, 70; aide, Cuddy Cong Campaign, 40th Cong Dist, 70; campus coordr, McGovern Students at Eight Rochester Campuses, 71-72; mem staff, McGovern Campaign, Western NY, 72; alt deleg, Dem Nat Conv, 72. Bus & Prof Pos: Elec night house desk, ABC News, 72; grad asst, Rutgers Univ, New Brunswick, 72- Honors & Awards: Mineola Kiwanis Club scholar. Relig: Catholic. Mailing Add: 325 Coolidge Ave Mineola NY 11501

SMOLLINS, JOHN F, JR (D)
b Providence, RI, May 16, 40; s John F Smollins & Kathryn R Gartland S; m 1972 to Georgette Monique Molenat; c John Pierre. Educ: Providence Col, BA, 62; Suffolk Univ Law Sch, LLB, 65; Pershing Rifles. Polit & Govt Pos: Page, RI House Rep, 59-62, clerk, Finance Comt, 62-65, admin asst to Speaker of the House, 67-69; admin asst to Mayor of Providence, RI, 69-74; admin asst to US Rep Edward P Beard, RI, 75- Mil Serv: Entered as 1st Lt, Army, 65, released as Capt, 67, after serv in 507 Transportation Group, Vietnam, 66-67; Capt, Army Res; Nat Defense Serv Award; Vietnam Campaign Ribbon; Vietnam Serv Ribbon. Publ: The parliament of drudgery, 61 & America remember, 61, Alembic, Providence Col; Change, Suffolk J, 65. Mem: RI & Am Bar Asns; Asn of the Army; Am Legion. Honors & Awards: Dean's List, Providence Col, 58. Relig: Catholic. Mailing Add: 57 Huxley Ave Providence RI 02908

SMOYER, BARBARA BROOKS (R)
b Akron, Ohio, July 8, 16; d Edwin Hinchman Brooks & Mae Bickford B; m 1940 to Stanley Charles Smoyer; c Janet Elizabeth (deceased), David Brooks, Nancy Read & William Stanley (deceased). Educ: Swarthmore Col, AB, 37. Polit & Govt Pos: First vpres, NJ Fedn Rep Women, 66-68; twp committeewoman, Princeton Twp, 71-; deleg, Rep Nat Conv, 72. Bus & Prof Pos: Bd mgrs, Swarthmore Col, 73- Relig: Protestant. Mailing Add: 86 Olden Lane Princeton NJ 08540

SMYKOWSKI, JAMES GEORGE (R)
NDak State Sen
b Cayuga, NDak, July 9, 34; s George Walter Smykowski & Kathrine Kaczynski S; m 1956 to Annette Elizabeth Olson; c Kenneth John, Kevin James, Dennis Michael, Robert Allan, Candia Marie, Anthony George & Patricia Lynn. Educ: Lidgerwood Pub High Sch, grad, 52. Polit & Govt Pos: Rep committeeman, Herman Precinct, NDak; pres, Lidgerwood Sch Bd, 62-68; mem, Personal Property Tax Comn, NDak, 67-69; NDak State Sen, 26th Dist, 73-, mem, State & Fed Govt Comt & mem, Agr Comt, NDak State Senate, currently. Bus & Prof Pos: Farming, currently; auctioneering, 58-; real estate broker, 69- Mem: Nat Auctioneers Asn; Elks; KofC; Farm Bur. Relig: Catholic. Mailing Add: RR Cayuga ND 58013

SMYLIE, MICHAEL (R)
Coordr Nationalities Div, Rep Nat Comt
b Philadelphia, Pa, Sept 14, 14; s John Smylie & Mary Gabrieloff S; m 1943 to Anne Knopf Laderecky; c Mark & Mary Anne. Educ: Temple Univ, 36; St Joseph Col, 50-51. Polit & Govt Pos: Alt deleg, Rep Nat Conv, 52 & 72, deleg, 56 & 60; coordr nationalities div, Rep Nat Comt, 60-; nat vchmn, Scranton for President, 64; dist dir, US Census Bur, 70; dir hq, Broderick for Gov, Pa, 70; dir hq, Longstreth for Mayor, 71; coordr nationalities div, Nixon Campaign, Philadelphia, 71. Bus & Prof Pos: Pres, Walnut Investment Corp, 55-; vpres, Smylies Assoc Investments, 72-; secy-treas, Gen Security Systs Inc, 74. Mil Serv: Entered Coast Guard Res, 42, released as Seaman. Mem: Rizzo Addictive Diseases Clin (bd dirs, 71-); Am Arbit Bd; St Luke's Children's Hosp (trustee, 69-); Clover Club; Overlook Golf Club. Honors & Awards: Community Serv Award, VFW, 67; Charity Organizer Award, Cath Charities Appeal, 68. Relig: Catholic. Legal Res: 911 N Franklin St Philadelphia PA 19123 Mailing Add: 365 Williams Rd Wynnewood PA 19096

SMYLIE, ROBERT E (R)
b Cherokee Co, Iowa, Oct 31, 14; s Lorne F Smylie & Ida May Stevens S; m 1943 to Lucille C Irwin; c William R & Steven S. Educ: Col Idaho, AB, 38; George Washington Univ, JD, 42, LLD, 60; Phi Alpha Delta; Order of the Coif. Polit & Govt Pos: Asst Attorney Gen, Idaho, 47, Attorney Gen, 47-55, Gov, 55-67; former co-chmn, Pres Fed-State Rels Comt; mem, Rep Coord Comt & Adv Comn on Intergovt Rels; chmn, Rep Gov Conf, 63-67. Bus & Prof Pos: Assoc mem, Law Firm of Covington & Burling, Washington, DC, 40-42 & 46; sr partner, Law Firm of Langroise, Sullivan & Smylie; chmn bd trustees, Col of Idaho, Caldwell, 67-, chmn, 72- Mil Serv: Entered as A/S, Coast Guard Res, 42, released as Lt, 46, after serv in Atlantic & Pac Theaters, Philippines & New Guinea; Lt, Coast Guard Res, until 54; Atlantic & Pac Theater Ribbons; Philippine Liberation Medal with Star. Publ: The constitutionality of federal airport zoning, George Washington Law Rev, 43; Federal state relations, George Washington Univ Mag, 66. Mem: Nat Gov Asn (chmn, Fed-State Rels Comt); Am Legion; AF&AM; VFW; 40 et 8. Honors & Awards: Mem adv comt, Who's Who in Am Polit, 67. Relig: Methodist Episcopal. Legal Res: 117 Locust St Boise ID 83702 Mailing Add: PO Box 2527 Boise ID 83701

SMYRE, CALVIN (D)
Ga State Rep
Mailing Add: PO Box 181 Columbus GA 31902

SMYTH, JOHN R (R)
Chmn, Lunenburg Co Rep Cent Comt, Va
b Pittsburgh, Pa, July 3, 18; s Victor R Smyth & Marie Brumbaugh S; m 1975 to Carrie L Nuckols; c John L, Sidney M & Sterling M. Educ: Pa State Univ, BA, 40; Theta Delta Chi. Polit & Govt Pos: Chmn, Lunenburg Co Rep Cent Comt, Va, currently; finance chmn, Fourth Dist Rep Party, formerly, vchmn, currently. Bus & Prof Pos: Pres & owner, Smyth's Frozen Foods Co; mem bd dirs, Va Nat Bank, Victoria; pres, Va Sch for Blind & Deaf, Hampton; dir, Robert E Lee Scout Coun, Richmond. Mil Serv: Entered as Pvt, Army, 41, released as Capt, 46, after serv in 155th Inf, 31st Div, Pac Theater; Bronze Star. Mem: Masons; Lions; Am Legion; VFW; PTA (pres). Relig: Episcopal; Sr warden, St Paul's Episcopal Church, Kenbridge; mem diocese exec bd, SVa Episcopal Diocese. Mailing Add: PO Drawer S Kenbridge VA 23944

SMYTH, JOHN RICHARD (D)
Wyo State Rep
b Rawlins, Wyo, Oct 6, 32; s Edward A Smyth & Sarah Frances Murphy S; m to Elizabeth Blanchard (deceased); c Suzanne, Dianne, Carolyn & Teresa. Educ: Univ Santa Clara, BS, 54; Univ Wyo Law Sch, LLB, 59. Polit & Govt Pos: Spec asst attorney gen, State Bd Equalization & Pub Serv Comn, Wyo, 59-60; justice of the peace, Carbon Co, 61; dep co attorney, Carbon Co, 62; Wyo State Rep, Laramie Co, 65-69 & 73-; Cheyenne munic juvenile judge & alt police judge, 68-72. Mil Serv: Entered as 2nd Lt, Army, 54, released as 1st Lt, 56, after serv in 594th Field Artil & 597th Armored Field Artil, US Army, Germany. Mem: Laramie Co Bar Asn; Cheyenne Quarterback Club; Elks; VFW 1881; KofC. Honors & Awards: Redwood Essay Award, Freshmen Honor Book for Outstanding Freshman Law Sch Student, Univ Wyo. Relig: Catholic. Mailing Add: 604 Cheyenne Nat Bank Bldg Cheyenne WY 82001

SMYTH, KELVIN PAUL (D)
Mem Exec Comt, Chippewa Co Dem Party, Mich
b Detroit, Mich, Jan 5, 50; s Paul Linahan Smyth & Mary Ann MacMaster S; m 1972 to Estelle Paulette Goldberg; c Paul David. Educ: Lake Superior State Col, BA in Polit Sci, 74; Circle K; Student Senate. Polit & Govt Pos: Coordr, Chippewa Co Citizens for McGovern, Mich, 11th Cong Dist Citizens for McGovern & Frontlash 11th Cong Dist, 72; mem campaign staff, Citizens for McGovern, Tenth Cong Dist, NY, 72; alt deleg, Dem Nat Conv, 72; mem exec comt, Chippewa Co Dem Party, Mich, 72- Bus & Prof Pos: Dir, Sault Ste Marie Multi-Purpose Recreation Addition. Mil Serv: Entered as E-1, Army, 70, released as SP-4, 71, after serv in 1/5 Mechanized Div, Quang Tri, Vietnam, 70-71; Campaign Ribbons; Army Commendation Medal. Mem: Int Studies Asn; Am Polit Sci Asn; Lake Superior State Col Vet Asn; Chippewa Co Vol in Rehab. Honors & Awards: Distinguished Serv Spec K, Kiwanis, 70. Relig: Catholic. Mailing Add: 638 Eureka Sault Ste Marie MI 49783

SMYTHE, HUGH HEYNE (D)
b Pittsburgh, Pa, Aug 19, 13; s William Henry Smythe (deceased) & Mary Elizabeth Barnhardt S (deceased); m 1939 to Mabel H Murphy; c Karen Pamela. Educ: Va State Col, BA, 36; Atlanta Univ, MA, 37; Northwestern Univ, PhD, 45. Hon Degrees: LLD, Va State Col, 68. Polit & Govt Pos: Dir research, NY State Senate Finance Comt Eval Proj of State Comn Against Discrimination, 56; spec lectr, Foreign Serv Inst, Dept of State, Washington, DC, 60; sr adv econ & social affairs, US Mission to UN & mem US deleg to 16th Session, UN Gen Assembly, 61-62, mem, Conf on Elimination of Statelessness, 61, UNICEF Prog Comt & Exec Bd Meeting, 61-62, Int Coffee Conf, 62, Develop Fund, 62, Spec Fund Governing Coun, 62, Statist Comt, 62, Social Comt, 62, Status of Women Comt, 62, Human Rights Comt, 62, Sub Comn on Prev of Discrimination & Protection of Minorities, 62 & First Int Cong of Africanist, Accra, Ghana, 62; Ambassador to Syrian Arab Repub, 65-67; consult, Dept of State, 67 & 69-; Ambassador to Malta, 67-69; testimony before Joint Subcomt on Africa & Mid East, House Foreign Affairs Comt on NAfrica & OAU, 72; testimony before Presidential-Cong Comt on Reorganization of US Govt for Conduct of Foreign Policy, 73. Bus & Prof Pos: Researcher & admin asst, Am Youth Comn, Am Coun on Educ, Washington, DC, 37-38; research asst & instr, Fisk Univ, 38-39; research assoc, Atlanta Univ, 42; asst dir research, Negro Land Grant Col Coop Social Studies Proj, 44; prof sociol, Morris Brown Univ, 44 & Tenn State Agr & Indust Univ, 45-46; dep dir spec research, NAACP, New York, 47-49; dir research, W B Graham & Assoc, 49-50; vis prof sociol & anthrop, Yamaguchi Nat Univ, Japan, 51-53; prof sociol, Brooklyn Col, 53-; Fulbright prof, Chulalongkorn Univ & sr adv, Nat Research Coun Thailand, 63-64; lectr, Spec Forces, Army, Ft Bragg, NC, 64; UN correspondent, Eastern World & Africa Trade & Develop, London, 64; chief consult, Youth in Action, Poverty Prog in Brooklyn, NY, 65; consult, Ford Found, US Off Educ, Cong Black Caucus & Phelps-Stokes Fund, currently. Mil Serv: Army, World War II. Publ: Co-auth, Negro Land Grant Colleges Social Studies Project, 44, New Nigerian Elite, 60 & Educating the Culturally Disadvantaged Child, 66; plus others. Mem: Fel African Studies Asn; fel Soc Appl Anthrop; fel Am Anthrop Asn; Eastern Sociol Soc; Asn Asian Studies. Honors & Awards: Delta Tau Kappa Award for Distinguished Work in Social Sci, 67; dipl, Int Inst JVEK of Germany for Contributions to Better Human Rels & World Peace, 68; Knight of the Grand Cross of the Royal Crown of Crete, 68; Knight of the Grand Cross, Sovereign Mil Order of St Agatha, 69; Distinguished Alumnus & Citation for Distinguished Serv, Atlanta Univ, 72. Relig: Protestant. Mailing Add: 345 Eighth Ave New York NY 10001

SNAPP, JAMES C (R)
Mayor, El Cajon, Calif
b Riverside, Calif, Mar 10, 24; m to Bette; c Craig, Scott, Vicki & Kristi. Educ: San Diego State Col; Univ Southern Calif, BS, 49. Polit & Govt Pos: Mem adv comt on aviation, Mayor San Diego, 58; mem, El Cajon Planning Comn, 61-67; pres, San Diego Co Planning Cong & Airport Comn, 67; mem, Calif State Aeronautics Bd, 67-74 & chmn, 72-73; mayor, El Cajon, 68-; pres, San Diego Div, League of Calif Cities, 70, state bd dirs, 71-74. Bus & Prof Pos: Owner, Snapp Ins Agency, 49-; pres, San Diego Aerospace Mus, 66; vpres, Inst of Burn Med of San Diego, 73; bd dirs, El Cajon Valley Hosp, 74. Mil Serv: Pilot, Army Air Corps, 42-45. Mem: Air Force Asn; Lions; Elks; Univ Southern Calif Alumni Asn. Legal Res: 2027 Windmill View Rd El Cajon CA 92020 Mailing Add: PO Box 427 El Cajon CA 92022

SNEDEKER, CLIFFORD W (R)
NJ State Assemblyman
Mailing Add: State House Trenton NJ 08625

SNEED, JOSEPH TYREE (R)
b Calvert, Tex, July 21, 20; s Harold Marvin Sneed & Cara Weber S; m 1944 to Madelon Juergens; c Clara Hall, Cara Carleton & Joseph Tyree, IV. Educ: Southwestern Univ, BBA, 41; Univ Tex, Austin, LLB, 47; Harvard Univ, SJD, 58; Phi Delta Theta. Hon Degrees: LLD, Southwestern Univ, 68. Polit & Govt Pos: Dep Attorney Gen, Dept of Justice, 73-75. Bus & Prof Pos: Instr bus law, Univ Tex, Austin, 47-57, asst prof law, 47-51, assoc prof, 51-54, prof, 54-57, asst dean, 49-50; counsel, Graves, Dougherty & Greenhill, Austin, Tex, 54-56; prof law, Cornell Univ, 57-62; prof law, Stanford Univ Law Sch, 62-71; prof law & dean, Law Sch, Duke Univ, 71-73. Mil Serv: Entered as Pvt, Army Air Force, 42, released as S/Sgt, 46. Publ: The Configurations of Gross Income, 67. Mem: Am & Tex Bar Asns; Am Law Inst; Am Judicature Soc; Asn Am Law Schs. Relig: Episcopal. Legal Res: 2815 Chelsa Circle Durham NC 27707 Mailing Add: Arlington Towers 842 Tyler Bldg 1121 Arlington Blvd Arlington VA 22209

SNEIDER, RICHARD LEE
US Ambassador to Repub of Korea
b New York, NY, June 29, 22; s Leopold J Sneider & Frances M S; m 1944 to Lea Ruth Tartalsky; c Dena Ann (Mrs Thorman), Daniel Charles & David Abbott. Educ: Brown Univ, AB, 43; Columbia Univ, MIA, 48; Phi Beta Kappa. Polit & Govt Pos: Japan & Korea research officer, Dept of State, 48-52, spec asst UN Affairs, 52-54; first secy, Am Embassy, Tokyo, Japan, 54-58, officer-in-charge, Japanese Affairs, Dept of State, 58-61, Nat War Col, Washington, DC, 61-62; polit counr, Am Embassy, Karachi, Pakistan, 62-65; pub affairs officer, EAsia Bur, Dept of State, 65-66, country dir for Japan, EAsia Bur, 66-68; sr staff mem, Nat Security Coun, 69; dep chief mission & minister for Okinawan Reversion Negotiations, Am Embassy, Tokyo, Japan, 69-72; Dep Asst Secy of State, EAsia Bur, Dept of State, 72-74, US Ambassador to Repub of Korea, 74- Mil Serv: 1st Lt, Army, 43-46. Publ: Co-auth, North Korea: Case Study of a Soviet Satellite, 61. Honors & Awards: Superior Honor Awards, Dept of State, 70 & 72. Legal Res: 4930 30th St NW Washington DC 20008 Mailing Add: American Embassy APO San Francisco CA 96301

SNELL, BRUCE MOREY, JR (R)
Chmn, Ida Co Rep Party, Iowa
b Ida Grove, Iowa, Aug 18, 29; s Bruce M Snell & Donna Potter S; m 1956 to Anne Fischer; c Rebecca Jane & Bradley Steven. Educ: Grinnell Col, AB, 51; Univ Iowa Col Law, JD, 56; Order of Coif; Phi Delta Phi. Polit & Govt Pos: Law clerk, US Judge Henry N Graven, Iowa, 56-57; Asst Attorney Gen, Iowa, 61-65; chmn, Ida Co Rep Party, 75- Bus & Prof Pos: Attorney-at-law, Ida Grove, Iowa, 65-; pres, Ida Co Community Hosp, Inc, 74- Mil Serv: Army, 51, ETO, 53. Mem: New York & Iowa State Bar Asns; Za-Ga-Zig Shrine. Relig: Protestant. Legal Res: 603 Barnes St Ida Grove IA 51445 Mailing Add: 500 Second St Ida Grove IA 51445

SNELL, EDWARD LOUIS (R)
b Alma, Colo, Oct 13, 04; s Edward Daniel Snell & Hannah Hoffman S; m 1937 to Mary Katherine Horine; c Emily & Mary Helen. Educ: Blair's Bus Col, 1 year. Polit & Govt Pos: Councilman, Alma, Colo, 37; trustee & councilman, Fairplay, Colo, 62-71; secy-treas, Park Co Rep Cent Comt, Colo, 69-72, vchmn, 72-75; mem legis comt, Colo Munic League, 71; mem, Park Co Planning Comn, currently. Bus & Prof Pos: Mill foreman, Climax Molybdenum Co, Colo, 23-27; mill wright & metallurgist, Molybdenum Corp of Am, Yucca, Ariz, 27-28, mech engr, Questa, NMex, 28-35, mill supt, 37-46; mine mgt, several firms, Alma, Colo, 47-62; mine owner & developer, currently. Publ: Metallurgical and geol reports. Mem: NMex & Colo Mining Asns; Mason (treas, Doric Lodge 25, 71-73); Colo Consistory. Relig: Christian Church of NAm. Legal Res: Front St Fairplay CO 80440 Mailing Add: PO Box 171 Fairplay CO 80440

SNELL, HILARY FRED (R)
Chmn, Fifth Cong Dist Rep Party, Mich
b Grand Rapids, Mich, July 17, 34; s Frank Y Snell & Edna Westfall S; m 1963 to Constance Mae Zick; c Hilary E & Travis J. Educ: Colgate Univ, AB, 56; Univ Mich, JD, 59; Phi Beta Kappa; Delta Upsilon. Polit & Govt Pos: Precinct deleg, Kent Co Rep Party, Mich, 61-63, asst chmn, 62-66, chmn, 66-68; deleg, Rep Nat Conv, 68; chmn, Fifth Cong Dist Rep Party, Mich, 69-; comnr, Mich Dept Natural Resources, 71- Bus & Prof Pos: Assoc, McCobb & Heaney, Attorneys, Mich, 59-65, partner, 65-68; partner, Wheeler, Upham, Bryant & Uhl, Attorneys, 68- Mil Serv: Entered as Recruit, Army Res, 59, released as Sgt, 65. Mem: Grand Rapids Bar Asn; Am & Mich Bar Asns; Mich Coun (pres, 71-); Rotary. Honors & Awards: Named Outstanding Young Man of the Year, Grand Rapids Jr CofC, 66. Relig: Protestant. Mailing Add: 1065 Plymouth Rd SE Grand Rapids MI 49506

SNELLING, RICHARD ARKWRIGHT (R)
Vt State Rep
b Allentown, Pa, Feb 18, 27; s Dr Walter Otheman Snelling & Marjorie Gahring S; m 1947 to Barbara Weil; c Jacqueline Taylor, Mark Hornor, Diane Bryant & Andrew Preston. Educ: Lehigh Univ, 43; Univ Havana, Cuba, summer 43; Harvard Col, AB cum laude, 48. Polit & Govt Pos: Mem, Chittenden Co Rep Comt, Vt, 56-, chmn, 63-66; Vt State Rep, 59-60 & 73-; mem, Vt Develop Comn, 59-61; deleg, Rep Nat Conv, 60 & 68; mem, Vt State Rep Exec Comt, 63-66 & Vt State Rep Comt, 70-; Rep nominee for Lt Gov of Vt, 64, Rep nominee for Gov, 66; chmn, Vt Aeronaut Bd, 69-; mem, Vt Comn on Status of Women, 71-73. Bus & Prof Pos: Pres, Shelburne Industs, Inc, Shelburne, Vt, 59-; pres & chmn exec comt, Gtr Burlington Indust Corp, 61-64; pres, Miller & VanWinkle Spring Co, Inc, Paterson, NJ, 63-71, Wessel Hardware Co, Inc, Philadelphia, Pa, 67- & Barrecrafter Ski Prod Co, Shelburne, Vt, 68-; dir, Ski Industs of Am, 69- Mil Serv: Entered as Pvt, Army, 44, released as T/5, 46, after serv in Inf, ETO, Army of Occup, 45-46. Mem: Young Pres Orgn; US CofC; Mason; Am Legion; Rotary. Relig: Unitarian. Mailing Add: Harbor Rd Shelburne VT 05482

SNELSON, W E (PETE) (D)
Tex State Sen
b Grandfalls, Tex, Mar 28, 23; s Luke R Snelson & Maggie Beaty S; m 1959 to Susan Mae Sutton; c Wallace Eugene, II, Sandra Susan, Stephen Sutton & Stanley Shane. Educ: Tex Western Col, BA, 46; Univ Nebr, Army Spec Prog; Northwestern Univ, MS, 50; Sigma Alpha Epsilon. Polit & Govt Pos: Tex State Rep, 60-62; Tex State Sen, 64- Mil Serv: Entered as Pvt, Army, 43, released as T/Sgt, 46, after serv as Spec Agt Counter Intel Corps, ETO; ETO Ribbon with Three Battle Stars; Bronze Star; Purple Heart; 1st Lt, Army Res, 48-54. Mem: Mason (32 degree); Scottish Rite; Lions Club; Tex Jr CofC. Relig: Presbyterian. Mailing Add: 319 N Colorado St Midland TX 79701

SNIDER, DARLENE (D)
Chmn, Douglas Co Dem Cent Comt, Ore
b Parowan, Utah, Dec 28, 21; d James LeRoy Hyatt & Rose Young H; div; c Rosemary (Mrs Sowa) & Gregory R; two grandchildren. Polit & Govt Pos: Serv as chmn of many registr & orgn comts; secy, Douglas Co Dem Cent Comt, Ore, 58-68, vchmn, 68-74, chmn, 74- Bus & Prof Pos: Off mgr, Louise Evans Realty, 73-75; appraiser trainee, Douglas Co, 75- Mem: Douglas Co Chap, Am Red Cross (bd dirs, 70-); Am Bus Women's Asn; Soc Cert Appraisers of Ore. Relig: Latter-day Saint. Mailing Add: 682 NE Meadow Ave Roseburg OR 97470

SNIDER, FREDDIE REMBERT (R)
b Ellaville, Ga, Apr 15, 40; s James Walter Snider & Velma Florette Watson S; m 1959 to Earlene Willis; c Gregory Earl & Sandra Kay. Educ: Schley Co Consol Schs, 12 years. Polit & Govt Pos: Chmn, Schley Co Rep Party, Ga, formerly. Bus & Prof Pos: Assembly worker, Champion Mobile Home Builders, Ellaville, Ga, 59-64; owner & mgr, Standard Oil Serv Sta, 64-68; ins agent, Ga Farm Bus Ins Co, Macon, 67-68; ins agent, Southern Trust Ins Co, 68-; owner & pres, Snider-Gordon Distributing Co, Ellaville, 68- Mem: Lions; F&AM; Tri-County Country Club. Relig: Methodist. Legal Res: Buena Vista Rd Ellaville GA 31806 Mailing Add: PO Box 334 Ellaville GA 31806

SNIDER, KENNETH C (D)
Ind State Rep
b Vincennes, Ind, Jan 24, 46; s Charles A Snider & Mildred McElhaney S; m 1968 to Gwendolyn S Moeller; c John. Educ: Vincennes Univ, AS Agr, 66; Purdue Univ, BS Agr Econ, 68; Chauncey Coop House. Polit & Govt Pos: Deleg, Ind Dem Conv, 68, 70 & 72; Ind State Rep, 62nd Dist, Knox, Sullivan & Gibson Counties, 72- Bus & Prof Pos: Farmer, auctioneer, Decker Twp, Knox Co, 64- Mil Serv: Entered as Pvt, Army, 68, released as Pfc, 69, after serv in Seventh Inf Div, SKorea, 69; Nat Defense Serv Medal; Armed Forces Expeditionary Medal, Korea. Mem: Am Legion; VFW; Harmony Soc; Moose; Vincennes Gun Club. Honors & Awards: Ind Golden Gloves Champion 132, 68 & 139, 70; Outstanding Trainee, Basic Training Unit, Ft Knox, Ky, 69; Runner-up, Nat Jr Amateur Athletic Union Boxing Championship, 71. Relig: Methodist. Mailing Add: RR 1 Decker IN 47524

SNIPES, AL M **(R)**
Chmn, Fifth Cong Dist Rep Party, Okla
b Cameron, NC, Apr 11, 21; s Alfred Marshall Snipes & Bessie McLaurin S; m 1947 to H Rebecca Davis; c Alfred M, Jr, William R & Rebecca L. Educ: Columbia Tech, Geneva Col & Okla Univ, spec courses. Polit & Govt Pos: Vpres, Okla City Young Rep, 52-58; Ward Four chmn, Okla Co Rep Comt, 52-60, co campaign chmn, 58-60, co chmn, 60-67; Okla Rep State Committeeman, 60-73; chmn, Fifth Cong Dist Rep Party, 63-; deleg, Rep Nat Conv, 64 & 72, alt deleg, 68; mem, Okla State Rep Exec Comt, 65- Bus & Prof Pos: Super mkt mgr, 46-48; owner, Al's Super Mkt, 48-55; owner, Al M Snipes Gen Ins Agency, 55-67; pres, Al M Snipes Inc, 67-; real estate; investment. Mil Serv: Entered as Pvt, Army, 43, released as Cpl, Air Force, 46. Mem: Southern Okla City Jr Col (bd trustees); Nat Gen Serv Admin, Pub Adv Coun; Rotary; Mason; Am Legion. Relig: Baptist. Legal Res: 2405 SW 80 Oklahoma City OK 73159 Mailing Add: 3215 S Western Oklahoma City OK 73109

SNIPES, JUANITA KRENTZMAN **(D)**
Chmn, Montgomery Co Dem Comt, Va
b Milton, Fla, Nov 18, 26; d Isaac Benjamin Krentzman & Juanita Rogers K; m 1950 to Wilson Currin Snipes; c Caroline Malcolm & Wilson Currin, Jr. Educ: Fla State Univ, BS, 49, MS, 50; Va Polytech Inst & State Univ, MA, 72; Phi Beta Kappa; Mortar Board, Garnet & Gold Key. Polit & Govt Pos: Dist chmn, Montgomery Co Dem Comt, Va, 70-72, co chmn, 73-; chmn, Sixth Legis Dist, 73- Bus & Prof Pos: Admin asst, Fla State Rd Dept, 49-50; instr math, Delta State Col, 50-51; jr mathematician, Stanford Research Inst, 51-53; statistician, Edwin A Keeble, Assoc, Nashville, Tenn, 53-55; asst prof, Converse Col, 58-59; voc counr, Mercer Univ, 63-66; consult, Va Adv Coun on Voc Educ, 72-73; instr educ, Va Polytech Inst & State Univ, 74-75. Publ: Auth, A Study of Counseling & Guidance in the Public Secondary Sch of Virginia, Virginia Adv Coun on Voc Educ, 73. Mem: League Women Voters. Mailing Add: 201 Fincastle Dr Blacksburg VA 24060

SNITOW, VIRGINIA L **(D)**
b New York, NY; d Dr Louis Levitt & Tillie Rosenberg L; m 1935 to Charles Snitow; c Ann B & Alan M. Educ: Hunter Col, BA, 31; Columbia Univ, post-grad study, 31-32; Phi Sigma Sigma. Polit & Govt Pos: Deleg, Dem Nat Conv, 68 & 72; deleg-at-lg, Concerned Dem of Westchester Co, NY, 68- Bus & Prof Pos: Teacher Eng, Wadleigh High Sch, 32-42; vpres, US World Trade Fair, New York, 57-66; nat pres, Women's Div, Am Jewish Cong, 65-70, vpres, Gen Div, 66-70, co-chmn gov coun, currently; secy-treas, Leadership Conf of Jewish Women's Orgn, 69-71, chmn, 71-; vpres, Encounter Films Inc, currently. Publ: The mushroom cloud, Western Polit Quart; I teach Negro girls, New Repub; series of short pieces on children, Family Circle Mag. Mem: Pan Pac South East Asia Women's Asn; League of Women Voters; Nat Woman's Party; UN Asn; UN Non-Govt Coun (rep). Honors & Awards: Received Am Jewish Cong Serv Citation. Relig: Jewish. Mailing Add: 81 Walworth Ave Scarsdale NY 10583

SNOOK, BILLY JAY **(D)**
Chmn, Wayne Co Dem Party, Iowa
b Cambria, Iowa, Feb 20, 34; s Kay Snook & Amy Mundell S; single. Educ: Cambria Consol High Sch, grad, 52. Polit & Govt Pos: Chmn, Wayne Co Dem Party, Iowa, 73- Bus & Prof Pos: Farmer & rancher, Wayne Co, 57- Mil Serv: Pvt, Army, 55-57, serv in 97th Artil, 7th Army, Ger, 56-57. Mem: Farm Bur. Relig: Protestant. Mailing Add: RR 3 Corydon IA 50060

SNOOK, J CARLTON **(D)**
b Paulding, Ohio, Jan 1, 43; s Harry George Snook & Dorothy Irene Baker S; m 1971 to Judith M Zimmerman. Educ: Ohio State Univ, BS in Educ, 64; Ball State Univ, MA, 74. Polit & Govt Pos: Co-chmn, Fifth Dist McGovern for President Comt, Ohio, 72; deleg, Dem Nat Conv, 72. Bus & Prof Pos: Farmer, 67- Mil Serv: Entered as 2nd Lt, Army, 64, released as 1st Lt, 66, after serv in Army Security Agency in Korea as Commun Intel Officer, 65-66. Publ: An over extension of the Mud-Flats hypothesis?, Am Anthropologist, 75. Mem: Am Anthrop Asn; Soc Am Archaeol; Paulding Co Farmers Union (co chmn, 73-); Am Legion. Relig: Unitarian. Mailing Add: Box 96 Rte 1 Antwerp OH 45813

SNOW, HAROLD **(R)**
b Moscow, Idaho, Dec 23, 10; s Arthur Sherman Snow & Lella Driskill S; m to Vivian Wilson; c Sherman Arthur & Susan Mary (Mrs Flack). Educ: Univ Idaho, 29-30; Sigma Nu. Polit & Govt Pos: Idaho State Rep, 53-74, asst majority leader, Idaho State House of Rep, 60-72, chmn, Ways & Means Comt, 65-67, vchmn, State Affairs Comt, 65-72, chmn, 73-74, mem, Transportation & Defense Comt, 73-74; Idaho dir, Western Conf, Nat Coun State Govt; Idaho mem gov bd, Nat Coun State Govt, currently. Mem: Latah Co Cattlemen's Asn; Latah Co Wheat Grower's Asn; Shrine; Elks; Mason. Relig: Methodist. Mailing Add: 211 N Blaine Moscow ID 83843

SNOW, JOHN W
Dep Under Secy, Dept Transportation
Mailing Add: Dept Transportation 400 Seventh St SW Washington DC 20590

SNOW, KARL NELSON, JR **(R)**
Utah State Sen
b St George, Utah, July 1, 30; s Karl Nelson Snow & Wanda McGregor S; m 1960 to Donna Jean Dain; c Karl Nelson III, Melissa, Daniel Dain, Jeanmarie, Elisabeth & Howard Hunter. Educ: Brigham Young Univ, BS, 56; Univ Minn, Minneapolis, MA, 58; Univ Southern Calif, MPA, 68, DPA, 72; Blue Key; Pi Sigma Alpha; pres, Viking Social Club, 54-55. Polit & Govt Pos: Utah State Legis Analyst, 66-69; mem, Utah State Exec Compensation Comn, 69-71; Utah State Sen, 73-, mem, State House Fels Comn & Utah State Legis Coun, Utah State Senate, 73-75. Bus & Prof Pos: State budget examr, Minn Dept Admin, 56-59; res analyst, Utah Found, Salt Lake City, 58-59; staff asst, Pakistan Proj, Univ Southern Calif, 59-62; dir, Inst Govt Serv, Brigham Young Univ, 69- Publ: Utah board of examiners: its role in fiscal management, Utah State Legis, 62; Legislative control through fiscal oversight, Citizens Conf State Legis, 68; Price Tagging Legislation, In: The Dragon on the Hill, Univ Utah, 70. Mem: Western Govt Res Asn (state rep, 68-); Am Soc Pub Admin (state chap pres & mem nat coun, 60-, bd ed, Pub Admin Rev, 69-72); Sons of the Utah Pioneers. Honors & Awards: Univ Southern Calif scholar, 59-60. Relig: Latter-day Saint. Mailing Add: 1847 N Oak Lane Provo UT 84601

SNOW, ORVAL M **(D)**
Idaho State Sen
Mailing Add: Rte 1 Moscow ID 83843

SNOW, ROGER V, JR **(D)**
Maine State Rep
Mailing Add: 70 Waites Landing Falmouth ME 04105

SNOW, THOMAS WAYNE, JR **(D)**
Ga State Rep
b Old Hickory, Tenn, Jan 10, 36; s Thomas Wayne Snow, Sr & Johnnie Huffine S; single. Educ: Univ Ga, AB, 58, LLB, 60; Phi Delta Phi; Sigma Chi. Polit & Govt Pos: City attorney, Ft Oglethorpe & Chickamauga, Ga; attorney, Chickamauga Bd Educ; Ga State Rep, 63-, chmn, House Judiciary Comt & mem, Legis Servs Comt, currently, mem, House Ways & Means Comt & mem, Retirement Comt, Ga House Rep, currently. Bus & Prof Pos: Attorney-at-law, 60- Mil Serv: Tenn Nat Guard, Pfc, 54-56; 56-58, Control Group; Specialist 5, Army Res, Garrison, 58-62. Mem: Am Judicature Soc; Rossville Jaycees (pres, 68-69); Rossville Exchange Club; LaFayette Elks; Seventh Dist Legis Asn. Relig: Methodist; Lay leader chmn. Mailing Add: RFD 2 Chickamauga GA 30707

SNOWDEN, GENE **(R)**
Ind State Sen
b Huntington, Ind, Apr 7, 28; s Ben W Snowden & Anna L Orr S; m 1949 to Carol J Replogle; c Connie J, twins Barbara J & Beverly J & Jodi A. Educ: Olivet Col, Kankakee, Ill, 48-49; Int Acct Sch, Chicago, 50. Polit & Govt Pos: Ind State Sen, 66-; pres, Nat Soc State Legislators, 69- Bus & Prof Pos: Mem bd trustees, Huntington Col, 65 & Olivet Col, 68-; charter vpres, Huntington Med Mem Found, 68- Mem: Nat Asn Life Underwriters; Nat Soc State Legislators; Ind Ins Leaders Club; Optimist Club (life mem). Honors & Awards: Distinguished Serv Award, US Jr CofC, 60, One of the Outstanding You g Men of Am, 64; Master Life Underwriter Award, 65. Relig: Nazarene. Legal Res: 1433 Cherry St Huntington IN 46750 Mailing Add: Box 2 Huntington IN 46750

SNOWDEN, MAXINE WATLINGTON **(R)**
Mem, DC Rep Party
b Yanceyville, NC, July 21, 42; d Stacy Lloyd Watlington & Margaret Graves W; m 1973 to George Snowden, Jr. Educ: Bennett Col for Women, 60-62; Howard Univ, BFA, 68; DC Teachers Col, 68, 70 & 71. Polit & Govt Pos: Polit action vpres, Young Rep DC, 73-74 & nat committeewoman, 74-75; ward chmn, DC Rep Cent Comt, 73-; mem, DC Rep Party, 75- Bus & Prof Pos: Teacher pub schs, Washington, DC, 68-73; minority tally clerk, US House Rep, 74- Mem: DC Art Asn; DC Young Rep; Dupont Circle Citizens Asn; Lambda Kappa Mu, Theta Chap. Mailing Add: 1628 15th St NW Washington DC 20009

SNOWDEN, PHILLIP HUGH (PHIL) **(D)**
Mo State Rep
b St Joseph, Mo, Oct 14, 38; s Leonard A Snowden & Lillian Pauline Phillips S; m 1961 to Jane Ellen Armstrong; c Sharon Lyn, Kristen Gai & Stephanie Mill. Educ: Univ Mo, Columbia, BA, 60, LLB, 64; The Mystical Seven; Phi Delta Theta; quarterback, Univ Mo football team. Polit & Govt Pos: Mo State Rep, 20th Dist, 67- Bus & Prof Pos: Attorney-at-law, Snowden, Crain & DeCruyper. Mem: Lawyers Asn of Kansas City; Gladstone Optimist Club; Gtr Kansas City Sports Comn; YMCA (bd of trustees); Fel Christian Athletes (adv bd). Relig: Methodist; past pres, Bd of Trustees. Mailing Add: 6218 N Bales Gladstone MO 64119

SNOWE, OLYMPIA JEAN **(R)**
Maine State Rep
b Augusta, Maine, Feb 21, 47; d George John Bouchles & Georgia Goranites B (both deceased); wid. Educ: Univ Maine, BA Polit Sci, 69. Polit & Govt Pos: Maine State Rep, 73-; vchmn, Auburn Rep City Comt, Maine, 74-; mem, Gov Adv Comt on Univ Maine & Gov Positive Action Comt, 75. Bus & Prof Pos: Bd dirs, Superior Concrete Co, Inc, 73. Mem: Maine Women Polit Caucus; League Women Voters; Gov Adv Coun on Drug Abuse & Alcoholism Prevention; Women's Hosp Asn; Women's Literary Union. Relig: Greek Orthodox. Mailing Add: 114 Nottingham Rd Auburn ME 04210

SNOWE, PETER TRAFTON **(R)**
State Committeeman, Maine Rep State Comt
b Lewiston, Maine, Jan 16, 43; s Guy Carlton Snowe & Barbara Dillingham S; m 1969 to Olympia J Bouchles. Educ: Bentley Col; Univ Maine. Polit & Govt Pos: Maine State Rep, 67-69 & 73-74; deleg, Rep Nat Conv, 68, alt deleg, 72; chmn, Auburn Rep City Comt, 66-; state committeeman, Maine Rep State Comt, 68-70 & 72- Bus & Prof Pos: Gen mgr, Maine Am Vault Co, Inc, Bangor, 63-64, vpres, 64-66; pres, Superior Concrete Co, Inc, Auburn, 66- & Maine Uniframe Inc, 71-; dir, Petgre Realty Corp, 71- Mil Serv: Maine Army Nat Guard, 64-69, Pfc. Mem: Shrine; Auburn Exchange Club; Mason; Kora Temple; Auburn Businessman's Club. Honors & Awards: Bilco Door Top Sales Award, 72. Relig: Protestant. Mailing Add: 114 Nottingham Rd Auburn ME 04210

SNYDER, ARTHUR KRESS **(R)**
City Councilman, Los Angeles, Calif
b Los Angeles, Calif, Nov 10, 32; s Arthur Snyder & Ella Keck S; m 1954 to Mary Frances Neely, div; remarried 1973 to Michele Maggie Noval; c Neely Arthur, Miles John & Erin Marisol Michelle. Educ: Los Angeles City Col, AA, 51; Pepperdine Col, BA, 53; Univ Southern Calif Sch Law, JD, 58; Pi Kappa Delta; Phi Delta Phi. Polit & Govt Pos: Councilmanic field dep, Los Angeles, Calif, 59-67, city councilman, 67- Bus & Prof Pos: Attorney-at-law, 59- Mil Serv: Entered as Sgt, Marine Corps, 53, released as Capt, 55, after serv in Air Fleet Marine Force, Pac Theatre, 54-55. Mem: Am, Calif State & Los Angeles Co Bar Asns; Am Judicature Soc. Relig: Baptist. Legal Res: 2832 Lawndale Dr Los Angeles CA 90065 Mailing Add: 333 City Hall Los Angeles CA 90012

SNYDER, CECIL VERNON **(D)**
Chmn, Morrow Co Dem Exec Bd, Ohio
b Richland Co, Ohio, Mar 26, 11; s Gustave Leroy Snyder & Tessie Peterson S; m 1945 to Leona Blanch Prosser. Educ: High sch, Lexington, Ohio. Polit & Govt Pos: Chmn, Troy Twp Bd of Trustees, 53-65; chmn, Morrow Co Dem Exec Bd, 60-62, 65 & 69-; mem, Co Elec Bd, 65- Bus & Prof Pos: Owner, Farm, Ohio, 39-69; pres, Galion Tire Shop, Inc, 62- Mem: Mason (32 degree). Relig: Methodist; Chmn bd of trustees, Steam Corners United Methodist Church. Mailing Add: RR 8 Mansfield OH 44904

SNYDER, HARRY G **(R)**
Wis State Rep
b Davenport, Iowa, Feb 11, 38; s Kenneth I Snyder & Pauline Hynes S; m 1972 to Rose Mary Collins; c Matthew Irven. Educ: Ripon Col, 56-58; Univ Wis-Madison, BS, 61; Marquette

Univ Law Sch, JD, 64; Phi Delta Phi; Sigma Alpha Epsilon. Polit & Govt Pos: Wis State Rep, 84th Dist, 75- Mil Serv: Entered as 1st Lt, Air Force, 64, released as Capt after serv in Mil Airlift Command, TUSLOG (Turkey) NATO Trial Observer, 66-67; Maj, Res, 68-; Nat Defense Ribbon; Unit Presidential Citation; Res Serv Ribbon; Marksmanship Ribbon. Mem: Oconomowoc Area CofC; ROA (Dept Judge Adv, 70-72, vpres, Air Force, currently); Am Legion; Rotary; Mason. Mailing Add: 331 E Summit Ave Oconomowoc WI 53066

SNYDER, JOHN K (R)
Polit & Govt Pos: Chmn, Ind State Rep Cent Comt, formerly. Mailing Add: 107 Green Acres Washington IN 47501

SNYDER, JOHN WESLEY
b Jonesboro, Ark, June 21, 95; s Jere Hartwell Snyder & Ellen Hatcher S; m 1920 to Evlyn Cook, wid; c Edith Cook (Mrs John E Horton). Educ: Vanderbilt Univ, 14-15; Omicron Delta Kappa. Polit & Govt Pos: Nat bank receiver, Off of Comptroller of Currency, 31-37; vpres & dir, Defense Plant Corp, Washington, DC, 40-43; asst to dirs, Reconstruction Finance Corp, 40-44; fed loan adminr, 45; dir, Off War Mobilization & Reconversion, 45; Secy of Treas, 46-53, deleg, Int Financial Conf, Mexico City, 45-52, Rio de Janeiro, 47, London, 47, Paris, 50-52, Ottawa, 51, Rome, 51 & Lisbon, 52. Bus & Prof Pos: Banker, Ark & Mo, 19-30; mgr, St Louis Loan Agency, Reconstruction Finance Corp, 37-43; vpres, First Nat Bank, St Louis, 43-45; pres & dir, Overland Corp, currently. Mil Serv: Served as Capt, Field Artil, 57th Brigade, World War I; Col (Ret), Army, 55. Mem: Am Legion; Res Officers' Asn; Alpha Tau Omega; Mo Athletic Club, St Louis; Chevy Chase Club. Relig: Episcopal. Legal Res: 8109 Kerry Lane Chevy Chase MD 20015 Mailing Add: Apt 605 The Calvert House 2401 Calvert St NW Washington DC 20008

SNYDER, JOSEPH M (D)
Mich State Rep
b Barberton, Ohio, Mar 18, 15; m 1942 to Rita Kanthak; c Donna, Michael & Ronald. Polit & Govt Pos: Mich State Rep, 62-, Dem Caucus Chmn, Mich House of Rep, 67-; councilman, St Clair Shores; Macomb Co Supvr; deleg to the Constitutional Conv. Bus & Prof Pos: Int rep, UAW. Mem: St Clair Shores Planning Comn (chmn); Macomb chap, Mich Soc for Ment Health (dir); St Clair Shores Pub Safety Comt (chmn). Honors & Awards: Joseph P Kennedy, Jr Found Award. Mailing Add: 22912 Rosedale Ave St Clair Shores MI 48080

SNYDER, MARGUERITE BRANNEN (D)
Committeewoman, Tex State Dem Exec Comt
b McAdoo, Tex, Nov 27, 21; d Jackson Edward Brannen & Cora Faucett B; m 1942 to James Layton Synder; c Cyrus Byron, III & James Brannen. Educ: Tex Tech Univ, BS with honors in voc home econ, 43; Phi Upsilon Omicron; Mortar Bd; Pi Beta Phi; past pres, Tex Tech Univ Coun Women Grad, Cotton Queen, 40. Polit & Govt Pos: Committeewoman, Tex State Dem Exec Comt, 30th Sen Dist, 72-, vchmn rules comt, 72-74, chmn resolutions comt & mem budget & finance comt & rules comt, 74-; vchmn rules comt & mem arrangements comt, Tex State Conv, 74; chmn rules drafting comt, Deleg Selection, 74. Mailing Add: Snyder Ranch Rte 1 Baird TX 79504

SNYDER, MARION GENE (R)
US Rep, Ky
b Louisville, Ky, Jan 26, 28; s M G Snyder & Louis Berg S; m to Patricia Creighton; c Mark & three stepchildren. Educ: Univ Louisville; Jefferson Sch Law, LLB cum laude, 50. Polit & Govt Pos: Mem, South End Rep Club; mem, Young Rep Club Louisville & Jefferson Co; mem, First Magisterial Dist Rep Club; past pres, Lincoln Rep Club; city attorney, Jeffersontown, 54-58; magistrate, First Dist, Jefferson Co, 57-61; vpres, Ky Magistrates & comnr, 58; US Rep, Ky, 63-65 & 67-; deleg, Rep Nat Conv, 68. Bus & Prof Pos: Attorney-at-law, Louisville, Ky, 50-; owner, Gene Snyder, Realtor, 50-; farming, 57-; residential construction bus, 58-66. Mem: Jefferson Civic Ctr; DC, Ky & Louisville Bar Asns; Louisville Bd Realtors. Relig: Lutheran. Legal Res: 8405 Old Brownsboro Rd Brownsboro Farms KY 40222 Mailing Add: Rayburn House Off Bldg Washington DC 20515

SNYDER, MELVIN CLAUD (R)
b Albright, WVa, Oct 28, 98; s Allison Wirt Snyder & Laura Jenkins S; m 1925 to Mabel Price; c Melvin C, Jr, Melita (Mrs Sokolowski) & Laurella (Mrs Constante). Educ: WVa Univ, LLB, 23, JD, 69; Theta Chi; Phi Delta Phi. Polit & Govt Pos: Mayor, Kingwood, WVa, 26-27; prosecuting attorney, Preston Co, 28-42; surplus property officer for Aleutian Islands, 46; US Rep, Second Cong Dist, WVa, 47-48; judge, 18th Judicial Circuit, WVa, 53- Bus & Prof Pos: Mem, WVa Judicial Coun, 56-; dir, Albright Nat Bank, 62- Mil Serv: Pvt, Army, 18; Col, Nat Guard, 101st Inf, Alaska Defense Command, 41-46; Col (Ret), Army, 60; Bronze Star; Legion of Merit. Mem: WVa, Preston Co & Am Bar Asns; WVa Judicial Conf; Am Legion. Relig: Baptist. Mailing Add: 307 Tunnelton St Kingwood WV 26537

SNYDER, NORMAN GENE (R)
b Adel, Iowa, Apr 28, 23; s Milo Myran Snyder & Phoebe Crouse S; m 1950 to Delphia Gertrude Norman; c Michael Dean, David Neil, Catherine Ann & Jonathan Scott. Educ: Drake Univ, 40-42; Iowa State Univ, 46-47; Univ Iowa Col Med, MD, 51; Nu Sigma Nu. Polit & Govt Pos: City councilman, West Covina, Calif, 60-64, mayor, 64-65; chmn, 49th Assembly Dist, Los Angeles Co Rep Cent Comt, formerly, committeeman, 62-64; co-chmn, West Covina Mayor's Blue Ribbon Comt on Drug Abuse, 68- Mil Serv: Entered as Seaman, Navy, 43, released as Electronics Technician 1/C, 46, after serv in Asiatic area, Philippines, & Japan, 44-45; Philippine Liberation Ribbon; Asiatic Theater Ribbon with Seven Battle Stars; Lt(jg), Med Corps Res, until 60. Mem: Town Hall, Los Angeles, Calif; Los Angeles World Affairs Coun; Los Angeles Co Dist Attorney Adv Coun; San Gabriel Valley Hot Line, Crisis Intervention for Young People (chmn). Honors & Awards: Named Man of the Year for the Greatest Contribution to Human Rights by Govt, Covina, West Covina & La Puente Human Rights Comn, 65. Relig: Protestant. Mailing Add: 2042 Daniels Ave West Covina CA 91790

SNYDER, ROBERT LEROY (R)
Chmn, Ashland Co Rep Exec Comt, Ohio
b Loudonville, Ohio, Aug 16, 20; s William Amos Snyder & Ada Margaret Hofer S; m 1946 to Norma Louise Stitzlein; c Kathleen (Mrs Mike Paullin), Constance Jean (Mrs C Douglas Fisher), Michael Lee, Crystal Lynn & Jonathan Jay. Educ: Bunker Hill Sch & Loudonville High Sch, Ohio, 10 years. Polit & Govt Pos: Mem, Green Twp Rep Cent Comt, Ohio, 64-; vchmn, Ashland Co Rep Exec Comt, 66-69, chmn, 70- Bus & Prof Pos: Pres, Loudonville Construction Corp, 46-, Loudonville Indust Develop Corp, 68- & Area Develop Corp, 68- Mil Serv: Entered as Pvt, Army, 43, released as M/Sgt, 46, after serv in 79th Corps Engrs, Asiatic-Pac Theatre, 43-46; 1st Sgt, Army Res, Asiatic-Pac Theatre Ribbon with Two Bronze Stars; Philippine Liberation Ribbon with Bronze Star; Good Conduct Ribbon; World War II Victory Medal. Mem: Am Legion; Toastmasters; Mohican Area CofC. Relig: Lutheran. Mailing Add: 560 Snyder Dr Loudonville OH 44842

SNYDER, ROBERT O (R)
Mo State Rep
b Lima, Ohio, July 25, 17; s Karl O Snyder & Ruth Stuff S; m 1941 to Margaret Elizabeth Beaton; c John Gregory, Elizabeth Ann & Margaret Ruth. Educ: Ohio Univ, BS, 39; St Louis Univ, LLB, 51; Delta Tau Delta; Phi Alpha Delta. Polit & Govt Pos: Mo State Rep, 9th Dist, 61-62, 11th Dist, 63-64, 45th Dist, 67-68 & 71-73 & 95th Dist, 73- Bus & Prof Pos: Dist rep, Gen Elec Co, 46-52, sales mgr, 52-55; attorney-at-law, 55-56; partner, Henderson, Heagney & Snyder, 56-; lectr bus law, Wash Univ, 58- Mil Serv: Entered as Ens, Navy, 43, released as Lt(jg), 46, after serv in USS Kendrick, DD612, invasion of Southern France, 44, Mediterranean & Atlantic, 44-45. Mem: Lawyers Asn of St Louis; Mason; Kiwanis; Am Legion; Am Bar Asn. Relig: Presbyterian. Mailing Add: 420 Claybrook Lane Kirkwood MO 63122

SNYDER, THOMAS MATHEW (D)
Idaho State Rep
b Cataldo, Idaho, Dec 28, 02; s Peter Snyder & Mary Powers S; wid, re-married 1972 to Violetie Otton; c W Joyce, Roselle G & Adelle B. Polit & Govt Pos: Idaho State Rep, 72- Relig: Catholic. Mailing Add: Rte 1 Cataldo ID 83810

SNYDER, WANDA J (R)
Chmn, Lorain Co Rep Comt, Ohio
b Waynesburg, Pa, Sept 8, 26; d William Schriver Bissett & Etta Riggs B; m 1947 to Lafe W Snyder; c Paul Bradford & Jill Denise. Educ: Waynesburg Schs, 12 years. Polit & Govt Pos: Rep precinct committeewoman, Vermilion, Ohio, 57-, area chmn, 65-; Women's chmn, Lorain Co Rep Comt, 67-; clerk, Lorain Co Bd Elec, 69-; committeewoman, 13th Cong Dist, 70-, mem, Ohio State Cent & Exec Comts, 70-; bd mgt, Ohio Fed Rep Women Orgn, 70-, vpres, 72-74, mem, Ohio Rep Platform Comt, 74. Bus & Prof Pos: Clerk, Bd Pub Affairs, Vermilion on the Lake, 60. Mem: Eastern Star; Elyria Rep Women's Club; Bus & Prof Women's Club. Relig: Protestant. Mailing Add: Suite G7 33803 Smugglers Cove Dr Avon Lake OH 44012

SNYDER, WILLIAM RICHARD (R)
Chmn, Inyo Co Rep Cent Comt, Calif
b Osceola, Ind, Oct 6, 29; s William Cleo Snyder & Mary Suppes S; m 1955 to Eleanor D Morehouse; c John, Thomas, Stewart & Eric. Educ: Ind Univ, South Bend, 47-48; Univ Toledo, 55-60; San Bernardino Valley Col, AA, 65. Polit & Govt Pos: Mem, San Bernardino Rep Cent Comt, Calif, 64-71; vchmn, Bishop Elem Sch Bd, 73-; chmn, Inyo Co Rep Cent Comt, 75- Mil Serv: Entered as Pvt, Marine Corps, 51, released as Sgt, 53, after serv in Air Wing, Pac Theatre. Mem: PTA; Rotary Int; Aircraft Owners & Pilots Asn; Calif Soc Cert Pub Acct; Am Inst Cert Pub Acct. Honors & Awards: Hon Life Membership, H S Mitchell Elem Sch PTA. Relig: Nondenominational. Mailing Add: 2731 Glenbrook Way Bishop CA 93541

SOARES, WILFRED (BUDDY) (R)
Hawaii State Rep
b Honolulu, Hawaii, Sept 4, 29; s Jack A Soares (deceased) & Alice Pamenta S; m 1950 to Lorraine R Perry; c Kevin, Kirk, Kelly Ann & Kyle. Educ: Univ Hawaii, 49-50. Polit & Govt Pos: Pres, Rep Precinct Club, Hawaii, 66; Hawaii State Rep, 17th Dist, currently, Minority Leader, Hawaii House Rep, formerly. Bus & Prof Pos: Acct exec, Pan Am Airlines, 56-69 & 60-65; gen sales mgr, Western Dairy Prods, 59-60; community affairs dir, AMFAC, 69; dir community affairs, Hawaiian Elec Co, Inc, currently. Mem: Punahou O'Men's Club; St Louis Alumni Asn; Interscholastic League; W Hawaii Kai Community Asn; Elks. Relig: Catholic. Legal Res: 674 Pepeekeo St Honolulu HI 96821 Mailing Add: State Capitol Bldg Honolulu HI 96813

SOASH, RICHARD MORTON (D)
First VChmn, Fourth Dist Dem Party, Colo
b Steamboat Springs, Colo, Aug 3, 41; s Irvin Elwood Soash & Nellie Elizabeth Gray S; m 1973 to Sharman Serene Ursich; c Curtis John, William Irvin, Richard Morton, Jr, Josephine Anne, Stacey M & Douglas Dale. Educ: Colo State Col, 59-60; Colo State Univ, BA with high distinction, 64; Sigma Tau Delta; Pi Gamma Mu. Polit & Govt Pos: Dem committeeman, 12th Precinct, Routt Co, Colo, 66-68, Dem committeeman, Seventh Precinct, 68-69; chmn, Routt Co Dem Cent Comt, 69-72; first vchmn, Fourth Dist Dem Party, 73- Bus & Prof Pos: Rancher, 65- Mem: Colo State Grange; Elk Mt Grange (master, 70-72); Nat Farm Orgn (secy fourth dist, 70-71, state treas, 71-72, pres, Routt Co Orgn, 71-72); KofC. Relig: Catholic. Mailing Add: Mystic Rte Steamboat Springs CO 80477

SOBOLIK, DENNIS MERLIN (DFL)
Finance Chmn, Kittson Co Dem-Farmer-Labor Party, Minn
b Fordville, NDak, Sept 16, 31; s Dennis James Sobolik & Belle Helgerson S; m 1956 to Marlene Donna Mae Olson; c Bradley, Blake, Janet & Cara. Educ: Univ NDak, BS, 58, Law Sch, JD, 59; Phi Delta Phi. Polit & Govt Pos: Chmn, Kittson Co Dem-Farmer-Labor Party, Minn, 60-66, finance chmn, 69-; co attorney, Kittson Co, 62-63; deleg, Dem Nat Conv, 68 & 72; vchmn, Seventh Dist Dem-Farmer-Labor Party, 70-; chmn bd, Oper Bootstrap-Tanzania, 72- Mil Serv: Entered as Pvt, Army, 52, released as Cpl, 54, after serv in Hq, Korea, 52-53; Korean Serv Medal with Two Bronze Stars; Nat Defense Serv Medal; UN Serv Medal. Mem: Am Bar Asn; Minn State Bar Asn (mem bd gov, 72-); 14th Dist Bar Asn (secy, 68-70, vchmn, 70-); Am Judicature Soc; Elks. Relig: Lutheran. Mailing Add: Hallock MN 56728

SOBSEY, CHET (D)
b New York, NY, Aug 15, 26; m to Mary Alice Barbre; c Robert & Mike. Educ: Univ Calif, Berkeley, BS in Jour; Sigma Delta Chi. Polit & Govt Pos: Exec secy & press secy, US Sen Howard W Cannon, 59-68, admin asst, 68- Bus & Prof Pos: Bur mgr, Fresno, Calif & Reno, Nev, United Press, 49-52; pub rels dir, Riverside Hotel, Reno, Nev, 52-53; news ed, Las Vegas Rev-Jour, 53-59. Mil Serv: Entered as officer, Merchant Marine, 45, released as Ens, 47, after serv in European & Asiatic Theatres. Mem: Admin Asst Asn; Sen Press Secretaries; Las Vegas Press Club; Nat Aviation Club. Legal Res: 1724 Howard Ave Las Vegas NV 89105 Mailing Add: 10705 Montrose Ave Garrett Park MD 20766

SODERBECK, WILLIAM ROBERT (D)
Chairperson, Burnett Co Dem Comt, Wis
b Pine City, Minn, May 30, 15; s Magnus Adolph Soderbeck & Margaret Thill S; m 1934

to Alice Evelyn; c Dale, Gerald, Janice (Mrs Fallstron) & Dianne (Mrs Maki). Educ: Pine City High Sch, Minn, 33. Polit & Govt Pos: Supvr, Grantsburg Twp, Wis, 62-; chairperson, Burnett Co Dem Comt, 74- Bus & Prof Pos: Farmer & fishing guide, Grantsburg, Wis, 36-53; electrician, Grantsburg Elec, 53-72; carpenter, 73- Mem: Masonic Lodge (Master, 75); Eastern Star (assoc patron, 75); Credit Union (loan comt, 72-75); Scottish Rite. Mailing Add: Box 323 Grantsburg WI 54840

SODERSTROM, CHARLES WALLACE **(R)**
Mem Exec Comt, Rep State Cent Comt Calif
b Seattle, Wash, Feb 14, 13; s Charles Wallace Soderstrom & Clare Eloise Kimball S; m 1946 to Dolore Lorraine Petersen; c Maya Eloise, Mona Lee & Charles Wallace, Jr. Educ: Univ Calif, Los Angeles, 3 years; US Coast Guard Acad, commission, 45; Blue Key; Phi Kappa Sigma; Capt, Univ Calif Rowing Team. Polit & Govt Pos: Chmn, Co Cent Comt, 17th Cong Dist, 55-63; finance chmn, United Rep Finance Comt, 17th Cong Dist, 54; mem exec comt & vchmn, Los Angeles Co Rep Cent Comt, several years, chmn budget comt, formerly, chmn, 66-69; vchmn, Los Angeles Co United Rep Finance Comt, 57; chmn, United Rep Finance Comt, Los Angeles Co, 59; treas, Los Angeles Co Rep Comt, 60-66; chmn, Los Angeles Co Rep Almanac Comt, formerly; deleg, Rep Nat Conv, 68; mem, Rep State Cent Comt Calif, 69-, mem exec comt, currently; South area chmn, Asn Rep Co Cent Comt Chmn, Calif. Bus & Prof Pos: Pvt pilot, 36 years; Ford dealer, San Pedro, Calif, 36 years; Lincoln-Mercury dealer, 10 years; pres, Triple AAA Water Co, Southern Calif & West Ariz; pres, Bastanchury Water Co Orange Co; pres, Indian Head Water Co Los Angeles; pres, Charles Soderstrom, Inc, real estate property mgt & develop; pres & one of founders, Hacienda Hotel & Golf Course; pres, Soderstrom Leasing & Rental Co. Mil Serv: Served as Commissioned Officer in Coast Guard on Destroyer Escorts, NAtlantic convoy duty, 4 years, World War II; NAtlantic, Asiatic & European Theater Combat Ribbons. Mem: Kiwanis; Am Legion; 40 et 8; CofC. Honors & Awards: Holder of world's speed rec non-stop from Los Angeles to New York & return for light planes; winner, Scotch Air Race from Santa Monica to San Diego, sponsored by Los Angeles Jr CofC. Mailing Add: 1500 S Pacific Ave San Pedro CA 90731

SOGLIN, PAUL RICHARD **(INDEPENDENT)**
Mayor, Madison, Wis
b Chicago, Ill, Apr 22, 45; s Albert Soglin & Rose Century S; m 1969 to Diane Thaler. Educ: Univ Wis, BA & LLB. Polit & Govt Pos: Alderman, Madison City Coun, Wis, 68-73; mayor, Madison, 73- Bus & Prof Pos: Attorney-at-law, Greenberg, Heitzman, Richter & Soglin, Madison, Wis, 72-73. Mem: Madison Gen Hosp (bd dirs); Univ Wis YMCA (bd trustees); State Bar Wis; Wis Alliance of Cities (bd dirs); US Conf Mayors (comt community develop, legis action comt). Legal Res: 505 Riverside Dr Madison WI 53704 Mailing Add: 210 Monona Ave Madison WI 53709

SOKOLOWSKI, CHESTERLYN **(D)**
Chmn, Middlefield Dem Town Comt, Conn
b Ansonia, Conn, Nov 1, 23; d Joseph Sadlowski, Sr & Katherine Bialczak S; m 1950 to Albert S Sokolowski; c Karen, Linda, Mary & Diane. Educ: Southern Conn State Col, BS, 63, MS, 68. Polit & Govt Pos: VChmn, Middlefield Dem Town Comt, Conn, 72-73, chmn, 73- Bus & Prof Pos: Elem sch teacher, Regional Dist 13, Middlefield, Conn, 63- Mem: Nat, Conn & Regional Dist 13 Educ Asns; Int Reading Asn; Polish Nat Alliance. Relig: Roman Catholic. Mailing Add: RR 1 Box 673 Middlefield CT 06455

SOLARZ, STEPHEN J **(D)**
US Rep, NY
b New York, NY, Sept 12, 40; s Sanford Solarz & Ruth Fertig S; m 1967 to Nina Koldin; c Randy Koldin & Lisa Susan. Educ: Brandeis Univ, AB, 62; Columbia Univ, MA in Pub Law & Govt, 67. Polit & Govt Pos: NY State Assemblyman, 69-74; deleg, Dem Nat Mid-Term Conf, 74; US Rep, NY, 75- Bus & Prof Pos: Instr, Brooklyn Col, 67-68 & 69-; instr, New York Community Col, 68-69. Publ: Numerous articles publ in Gtr Philadelphia & Newsfront. Mem: Am Polit Sci Asn; State Bd of Am for Dem Action; Citizens' Housing & Planning Coun (bd dirs); Am Jewish Cong; B'nai B'rith. Relig: Jewish. Mailing Add: 241 Dover St Brooklyn NY 11235

SOLBERG, GRACE CORRINE **(DFL)**
First VChairwoman, Polk Co Dem-Farmer-Labor Party, Minn
b Mahnomen, Minn, Jan 20, 30; d Henry Bendickson & Bertha Marie Sollie B; m 1953 to Arvid C Solberg; c Linda (Mrs Robert Rossini). Educ: Mahnomen High Sch, Minn, 48. Polit & Govt Pos: Second vchairwoman, Polk Co Dem-Farmer-Labor Party, Minn, 61-62, secy, 62-63, first vchairwoman, 70- Bus & Prof Pos: Bank teller, Farmers State Bank of Fosston, Minn, 61-66; asst dir, Fosston Day Activity Ctr, 72- Mem: Am Legion Auxiliary; VFW; Fosston Hosp & Nursing Home Auxiliary. Honors & Awards: Two past pres pins, Am Legion Auxiliary. Relig: Lutheran. Mailing Add: 119 N Mark Ave Fosston MN 56542

SOLBERG, INGVALD (ESKY) **(R)**
NDak State Sen
b Minot, NDak, Sept 18, 05; both parents deceased; m 1930 to Nellie Florence Coad; c Jeanne (Mrs Unruh), Kay Loise (Mrs Link) & Walter. Educ: Minot State Univ, BA; Univ NDak, MS, 50. Polit & Govt Pos: Deleg, NDak State Const Conv, 72; NDak State Sen, 72- Bus & Prof Pos: Supt Schs, Lansford, Des Lacs & Rolette, NDak, 30-42; mem staff, Govt War Agencies, 42-48; fac mem econ, Bismarck Jr Col, 48-67. Publ: Monthly column, various transportation trade jour, currently. Mem: Nat Hwy Users Fedn (bd dirs). Relig: Presbyterian; Elder. Mailing Add: 925 N Sixth St Bismarck ND 58501

SOLBERG, OSCAR **(D)**
NDak State Rep
b Mylo, NDak, May 16, 11; married; c One daughter. Educ: Pub Schs. Polit & Govt Pos: NDak State Rep, 49-61 & currently. Bus & Prof Pos: Farmer. Mem: Agate Farm Club; Farmers Union; Co AA Comt; Mylo PTA. Mailing Add: State Capitol Bismarck ND 58501

SOLDINI, JOHN LOUIS **(D)**
Exec Dir, New York City Dem Comt
b Staten Island, NY, Nov 7, 35; s Bernard Soldini & Mary Morris S; m 1959 to Dina Marie Frega; c Donna, David & Michelle. Educ: Staten Island Community Col, AAS, 59; City Col New York, BA & MA cum laude, 61; Phi Beta Kappa. Polit & Govt Pos: Committeeman, Richmond Co Dem Comt, NY, 65-; pres, Staten Island Reform Dem Asn, 67-68; deleg, Dem Nat Conv, 68 & 72; deleg, New Dem Coalition, 68-69, mem exec bd, 70-, NY VChmn, 72-; exec dir, New York City Dem Comt, 70- Bus & Prof Pos: Teacher social studies, Tottenville High Sch, 61- Mil Serv: Entered as SR, Navy, 53, released as SK 3, 56, after serv in Atlantic, 53-56. Mem: Nat Soc Social Studies; Orgn Am Historians; Staten Island & South Shore Ment Health Asns; United Fedn Teachers. Relig: Roman Catholic. Mailing Add: 51 Van Brunt St Staten Island NY 10312

SOLER-FAVALE, SANTIAGO C **(NEW PROGRESSIVE, PR)**
Attorney Gen, PR
b Yauco, PR, Mar 24, 32; s Victoriano Soler & Emilia Favale de S; m 1955 to Ivette Agostini; c Marie Ivette, Jeannette Emile, Santiago Cesar, Lizzette & Jackeline. Educ: Univ PR, BA, 52, BL cum laude, 57. Polit & Govt Pos: Mem exec comt, New Progressive Party, PR, 68; Attorney Gen, PR, 69-; spec adv to Gov, PR, currently; pres, PR Crime Comn & mem, Mining Comn, currently. Bus & Prof Pos: Attorney-at-law, 57-68. Mil Serv: Entered as 2nd Lt, Army, 52, released as 1st Lt, 54, after serv in 101st Airborne Div, Camp Breckinridge, Ky, 53-54. Mem: PR, Am & Interam Bar Asns; Rotary; Lions. Honors & Awards: Distinguished Mil Student & Grad; Most Outstanding Law Student. Relig: Catholic. Mailing Add: 172 Mimosa St Santa Maria Rio Piedras PR 00926

SOLES, ROBERT CHARLES, JR **(D)**
NC State Rep
b Tabor City, NC, Dec 17, 34; s Robert C Soles & Myrtle Norris S; single. Educ: Wake Forest Univ, BS, 56; Univ NC Sch Law, JD, 59; Phi Alpha Delta. Polit & Govt Pos: Chmn, Seventh Cong Dist Young Dem Club, NC; city attorney, Tabor City, NC; co attorney, Columbus Co; chmn, Columbus Co Dem Exec Comt; NC State Rep, 69- Mil Serv: Entered as 2nd Lt, Army Res, 56, released as Capt, 68, after serv in various res units. Publ: Interpretation of the term gross income as used in North Carolina alimony without divorce award, NC Law Rev, 59. Mem: Am Trial Lawyers Asn; NC Acad of Trial Lawyers; Univ NC (bd trustee); Southeastern Community Col Found (pres); Rotary. Relig: Baptist. Mailing Add: PO Box 275 Tabor City NC 28463

SOLLENBERGER, RAYMOND JAN **(R)**
Nat Committeeman, Calif Young Rep
b Chicago, Ill, Nov 21, 42; s Raymond Sollenberger & Mildred Buckwalter S; single. Educ: Univ Calif, Los Angeles, 65-67 & 69-71. Polit & Govt Pos: Co-founder, Victory in Vietnam Asn, 64; treas, Young Am for Freedom, 66; pres, Univ Calif, Los Angeles Young Rep, 70-71; bd mem, San Fernando Valley Lincoln Club, 72-73; pres, Los Angeles Co Young Rep, Inc, 72-74; nat committeeman, Calif Young Rep, 73- Mil Serv: Entered as Pvt E-1, Army, 67, released as Sgt E-5, 69, after serv in 146th Aviation, Mil Assistance Command, Vietnam, 68-69; Unit Citation with Two Clusters; Army Commendation Medal; Vietnam Govt Combat Medal; plus others. Mem: Am Legion; Los Angeles World Affairs Coun. Honors & Awards: God & Country Medal, Boy Scouts & 36th Church of Christ Scientists, 57. Relig: Christian Science. Legal Res: 13636 Valley Vista Blvd Sherman Oaks CA 91413 Mailing Add: Box 5604 Sherman Oaks CA 91413

SOLOMON, ANTHONY JOSEPH **(D)**
RI State Rep
b Providence, RI, Apr 1, 32; s Joseph Solomon & Naza Simon S; m 1954 to Sarah Rachael Symia; c Donna Marie, Michael Anthony, Sharon Ann & Anthony Elias. Educ: Providence Col, 52-53; RI Col Pharm, BS, 56; Kappa Psi. Polit & Govt Pos: RI State Rep, 11th Dist, 67-; chmn, Spec Comn Studying Entire Field of Day Care, 67-; vchmn, RI Narcotics Comn, 69-; deleg, Dem Nat Mid-Term Conf, 74, mem charter comn. Bus & Prof Pos: Owner & operator, Anthony Rexall Drugs, 57- Relig: Catholic. Mailing Add: 115 Joslin St Providence RI 02909

SOLOMON, BERNARD **(D)**
Mem, Brookline Dem Town Comt, Mass
b Boston, Mass, Mar 17, 23; s Samuel Solomon & Lillian Eisenberg S; m 1957 to Jolane Baumgarten; c Sue, Samuel & Sarah Leslie. Educ: Northeastern Univ, 41-42; Univ Ill, 42-43. Polit & Govt Pos: Asst to Gov, Commonwealth of Mass, 57; Comnr of Purchasing, 57-60, chmn, Emergency Finance Bd, 60-; deleg, Dem Nat Conv, 60, 64 & 68; mem, Brookline Dem Town Comt, 68; secy-treas, Univ Mass Bldg Authority, currently. Bus & Prof Pos: Vpres civic & govt rels, Stop & Shop, Inc, dir, Garden City Trust & dir, Grove Hall Savings Bank, currently. Mil Serv: Entered as Pvt, Army, 42, released as Pfc, 46, after serv in Eighth Armored Div, ETO, 44-46; Good Conduct Medal; ETO Medal with Three Battle Stars. Mem: Corp, Northeastern Univ. Relig: Jewish; Trustee, Temple Ohabei Shalom. Mailing Add: 295 Reservoir Rd Chestnut Hill MA 02167

SOLOMON, DONALD L **(D)**
b Toledo, Ohio, Nov 29, 32; s Ben J Solomon & Ruth Mary Block S; m 1970 to Deirdre M O'Connor, MD; c Cathy R & David S. Educ: Harvard Col, BA, 54. Polit & Govt Pos: Chmn, Lucas Co Children Serv Bd, Ohio, 67; deleg, Dem Nat Conv, 72, mem, Dem Party Platform Comt, 72. Bus & Prof Pos: Vpres, Ben's Truck Parts & Equip, Inc, dir, Toledo Metalizing Co, Inc & pres, Truck Spares, Inc, 56- Mil Serv: Entered as Pvt, Army, 54, released as E-4, 56, after serv in AAA Bn, US, 54-56. Mem: Nat Asn Truck Recyclers (vpres, 72-73); Toledo Area Interfaith Coun; Coun Fleet Specialists; Harvard Club Toledo; Am Acad Polit & Social Sci. Honors & Awards: Marshall Award, Harvard Univ, 61. Legal Res: 2334 W Grecourt Rd Toledo OH 43615 Mailing Add: PO Box 6586 Toledo OH 43612

SOLOMON, ERWIN S **(D)**
Va State Deleg
Mailing Add: Shady Lane Farm Drawer R Hot Springs VA 24445

SOLOMON, GERALD B **(R)**
NY State Assemblyman
Mailing Add: 23 North Rd Queensbury Glens Falls NY 12801

SOLOMON, JANE A **(D)**
NH State Rep
Mailing Add: 29 Dunbarton Dr Nashua NH 03060

SOLOMON, ROSALIND FOX **(D)**
b Highland Park, Ill, Apr 2, 30; d Vernon Fox & Joell Wellman F; m 1953 to Joel Warren Solomon; c Joel Warren, Jr & Linda Ilene. Educ: Northwestern Univ, 49-50; Goucher Col, BA, 51; Alpha Epsilon Phi. Polit & Govt Pos: Recruiter-consult, Agency for Int Develop, Dept of State, 63-65; co-chmn, Gubernatorial Campaign, Hamilton Co, Tenn, 66; pub rels chmn, Sen Campaign, Hamilton Co, 70; deleg, Dem Nat Conv, 72. Bus & Prof Pos: Regional dir, Exp in Int Living, 65-69; free-lance photographer, 69- Mem: League Women Voters. Honors & Awards: Alumnae of the Year, Exp in Int Living, 63; Purchase Award, Photograph, Caged Woman, Ark Fine Arts Ctr, 72. Relig: Jewish. Mailing Add: 17 Folts Dr Chattanooga TN 37415

SOLON, SAM GEORGE (D)
Minn State Sen
Mailing Add: 616 W Third St Duluth MN 55806

SOMERS, ROBERT VANCE (R)
Mem, NC Rep Exec Comt
b Statesville, NC, Nov 21, 37; s Walter Vance Somers & Ethel Owens S; div. Educ: Eastern Tenn State Univ, BS, 60; Univ NC, Chapel Hill, JD, 63. Polit & Govt Pos: Prosecuting Attorney, Randolph Co, NC, 64, Judge, 65-66; chmn, Randolph Co Young Rep, 65; legal counsel, Rowan Co Rep Party, 66-67; prosecuting attorney, Rowan Co, NC, 66-68; legal counsel, Union Co Rep Party, 68; legal Rep cand US Senate, 68; legal counsel, Eighth Cong Dist Rep Party, 70; mem, NC Rep Exec Comt, 72-; NC State Sen, 21st Dist, 73-74. Bus & Prof Pos: Attorney, 63- Mem: Am & NC Bar Asns; NC Acad Trial Lawyers; Am Conservative Union; Salisbury Country Club; NC Conserv Soc. Relig: Methodist. Legal Res: 612 Wiltshire Village Salisbury NC 28144 Mailing Add: Law Bldg Salisbury NC 28144

SOMMER, ROGER A (R)
Ill State Sen
Mailing Add: 321 E Jackson Morton IL 61550

SOMMERS, HELEN ELIZABETH (D)
Wash State Rep
b Woodbury, NJ, Mar 29, 32; d Roy Sommers & Christine Eliasson S; div. Educ: Univ Wash, BA, 69, MA, 70. Polit & Govt Pos: Dep adminr, King Co Coun, Wash, currently; Wash State Rep, 36th Legis Dist, 73- Bus & Prof Pos: Personnel research asst, Mobil Oil Co de Venezuela, Caracas, 54-68; instr econ, Edmonds Community Col, Wash, 71-72. Mem: Phi Beta Kappa; Omicron Delta Epsilon; Nat Orgn for Women; League of Women Voters of Seattle. Relig: Protestant. Mailing Add: 2516 14th Ave W Seattle WA 98119

SOMMERVILLE, A L, JR (D)
WVa State Deleg
Mailing Add: State Capitol Charleston WV 25305

SONG, ALFRED H (D)
Calif State Sen
b Hawaii, Feb 16, 19; s C K Song & C Y Kim S. Educ: Univ Southern Calif, BS, 42, JD, 45, LLM, 57; Korea Univ, LLD, 67. Polit & Govt Pos: City councilman, Monterey Park, 60-62; Calif State Sen, 62 & 71-, chmn, Comt Judiciary, Calif State Senate, currently; Calif State Assemblyman, 63-66. Legal Res: 2337 S Garfield Monterey Park CA 91754 Mailing Add: State Capitol Bldg Sacramento CA 95814

SONGSTAD, SHELDON RICHARD (R)
SDak State Sen
b Sioux Falls, SDak, June 19, 38; s Alfred Sigwald Songstad, Mother deceased; m to Barbara Lee Fitzgerald; c Richard, Bret, Robert & Zoey. Educ: Augustana Col, BS, 67. Polit & Govt Pos: Precinct committeeman, Minnehaha Co Rep Party, 58-; mem, Minnehaha Co Rep Cent Comt, 70-; mem state bd, SDak Young GOP, 70; SDak State Rep, 71-74; SDak State Sen, 75- Mil Serv: S/Sgt, Air Force Res, 55-62. Mem: Unity Lodge 130, El Riad Shrine; Elks; Optimists; Sioux Falls Advert Fedn. Relig: Lutheran. Mailing Add: 905 Annway Dr Sioux Falls SD 57103

SONIAT, NOVYSE ELAINE (D)
b Shreveport, La, June 24, 28; d Foster S Tomkies & Clida Martinez T; m 1948 to Llewelyn Joseph Soniat, c Donald Joseph & Cynthia Marie. Educ: Southern Univ, Baton Rouge, 45-47; Xavier Univ La, 47-48; YMCA Sch of Com, New Orleans, La, Exec Secy, 56. Polit & Govt Pos: Deleg & secy La deleg, Dem Nat Conv, 72; deleg, La Const Conv, 73- Bus & Prof Pos: Off mgr & secy, Progressive Life Ins Co, New Orleans, La, 57- Mem: NAACP; La Asn Ment Health; Citizens for Dem Action. Relig: Catholic. Mailing Add: 1323 Joliet St New Orleans LA 70118

SONIS, LAWRENCE BERTON (LARRY) (D)
WVa State Deleg
b Charleston, WVa, Apr 27, 47; s Berton Sonis (deceased) & Mary Morrisey S; div. Educ: Marshall Univ, 65-67; Morris Harvey Col, BA, 72. Polit & Govt Pos: Mem elections div, Secy State, WVa, 72; asst to Speaker, WVa House Deleg, 73; dir commun, WVa Dem Exec Comt, 74-; asst to Pres, WVa Senate, 74; WVa State Deleg, 75- Bus & Prof Pos: Polit ed, WCHS-TV, Charleston, WVa, 69-70; polit consult & writer. Honors & Awards: Benedum Found Scholar, 66; Ivor Boiarsky Mem Scholar, 72. Mailing Add: 1569 Lewis St Charleston WV 25311

SONNENFELDT, HELMUT
Counselor Dept State
Polit & Govt Pos: Under Secy Treas, formerly. Legal Res: MD Mailing Add: Dept of State Washington DC 20520

SONNIER, NAT (D)
Ala State Rep
Mailing Add: 2551 Old Shell Rd Mobile AL 36607

SONNTAG, DOUGLAS F (R)
Utah State Rep
Mailing Add: 127 E 3700 S Bountiful UT 84010

SONTAG, FREDERICK H
b Breslau, Ger, Apr 29, 24; s Dr Hugo Sontag & Lotte Laband S; m 1958 to Edith Virginia Sweeney. Educ: Colby Col, AB, 46; Columbia Univ, 47; Phi Gamma Mu; Phi Delta Theta. Polit & Govt Pos: Consult, Mayor T Corchoran, Syracuse, NY, 48-51; President's Comt Govt Employ Policy, 53-61, Secy Labor, James P Mitchell, 54-61, US Rep Thomas B Curtis, Mo, 57-69, US House of Rep Comt Minority Staffing, 58-, US Sen Hugh Scott, Pa, 60's, US Rep Fred Schwengel, Iowa, 60's, US Rep Gillis W Long, La, 62-65 & Secy of Health, Educ & Welfare, 69 & 72; legis consult, NJ State Sen James H Wallwork, 69-; consult to Chmn Will E Leonard, US Int Trade Comn, 75- Bus & Prof Pos: Assoc, Earl Newsom & Co, New York, 47-48; pub rels & advert consult, Merchants Nat Bank, Syracuse, 48-51; dir pub rels, Bus Week Mag, New York, 51-55; assoc, Anna M Rosenberg Assocs, 57-60; consult, Monsanto, St Louis, Mo, 58-; consult, Bd Social Concerns, United Methodist Church, Washington, DC, 65-73; co-dir, Study of Am Polit Parties, Cambridge, Mass & South Orange, NJ, 69-; vis lectr, Colby Col, 75; analyst & commentator, Maine Pub Broadcasting Network, currently. Publ: Co-auth, Parties: The Real Opportunity for Effective Citizen Politics, Knopf, 72 & Vintage-Random House, 73; mem ed adv bd, Electoral Studies Yearbook. Mem: Am Polit Sci Asn; Am Asn Polit Consult (bd dirs); Pub Rels Soc Am; Overseas Press Club; NJ Conf Promotion Better Govt. Honors & Awards: Cert Achievement, Am Pub Rels Asn, 52 & 54 & Silver Anvil Award, 53. Relig: Episcopal. Mailing Add: Suite 45 764 Scotland Rd South Orange NJ 07079

SOPER, JAMES C (R)
Ill State Sen
Mailing Add: 1844 S Austin Cicero IL 60650

SORENSEN, EMIL S (R)
b Jersey City, NJ, Jan 30, 20; s Emil S Sorensen, Sr & Helga Beyer S; m 1948 to Valnette Rowley; c Maren, Paul & Mark. Educ: Upsala Col, BA, 41; Rutgers Univ Law Sch, LLB, 48. Polit & Govt Pos: Mem Bd Educ, Sparta, NJ, 57-60, councilman, 60-68, mayor, 63-68; pres, Sparta Rep Club, 57-59; co campaign mgr, Mitchell for Gov, 61; chmn, Sparta Rep Party, 67-; vchmn & committeeman, Sussex Co Rep Party, 67-73, chmn, 73-75; chmn, Sussex Co Bd Elec, 68-; mem, Sparta Bd Adjust, 68-; Freeholder, Sussex Co, 69- Bus & Prof Pos: Asst sales mgr, Mennen Co, Morristown, 49-62; asst sales mgr, A W Faber Pencil Co, Newark, 62-63; owner & operator of own bus, Sparta, 63- Mil Serv: Entered as Pvt, Army, 42, released as S/Sgt, 46, after serv in Counter Intel Corps, Ger, 45-46. Mem: Rotary; Elks; CofC; VFW. Relig: Lutheran. Mailing Add: 8 Glenside Trail Sparta NJ 07871

SORENSEN, THEODORE CHAIKIN (D)
b Lincoln, Nebr, May 8, 28; s C A Sorensen & Annis Chaikin S; m 1969 to Gillian Martin; c Eric, Stephen, Philip & Juliet Suzanne. Educ: Univ Nebr, BSL, 49, Sch Law, LLB, 51; Phi Beta Kappa; Order of the Coif; Ed in Chief, Law Rev. Hon Degrees: LLD, Univ Canterbury, 66, Alfred Univ, Temple Univ, Fairfield Univ & Univ Nebr, 70. Polit & Govt Pos: Attorney, Fed Security Agency, 51-52; staff mem, Joint Comt on RR Retirement, 52; asst to US Sen John F Kennedy, Mass, 53-61; secy, New Eng Senators' Conf, 54-59; spec counsel to the President, 61-64; mem, Temporary State Comn on Const Conv, NY, 66-67; chmn adv comt, NY State Dem Comt, 67-69; deleg, Dem Nat Conv, 68; cand, US Sen, 70. Bus & Prof Pos: Lectr, foreign countries & 27 states; vis lectr pub & int affairs, Woodrow Wilson Sch, Princeton Univ, 66-68; ed-at-lg, Sat Rev, 66-69; partner, Law Firm of Paul, Weiss, Rifkind, Wharton & Garrison, NY, currently; trustee, Robert F Kennedy Mem, 69- & Medgar Evers Fund, currently; commentator nat affairs, Channel 5, 71-73. Publ: Kennedy, 65; The Kennedy Legacy, Macmillan, 69; Watchmen in the Night: Presidential Accountability After Watergate, MIT Press, 75; plus others. Mem: Bar of US Supreme Court, State of NY, DC & State of Nebr; Lawyers Comt for Civil Rights Under Law (bd). Honors & Awards: Selected One of Ten Outstanding Men of Year, US Jr CofC, 61; winner, Brotherhood Award, Mass Comt of Catholics, Protestants & Jews, 65. Mailing Add: 345 Park Ave New York NY 10022

SORENSON, DEAN PHILIP (R)
Secy-Treas, SDak Rep State Cent Comt
b Rapid City, SDak, July 17, 39; s Andrew G Sorenson & Barbara Rich S; m 1960 to Georganne Stedman; c Debby, Danny & Darcy. Educ: Dakota Wesleyan Univ, 57-60; Brown Inst Broadcasting, Minneapolis, grad, 59; Black Hills State Col, Spearfish, SDak, 61; Sigma Tau Gamma. Polit & Govt Pos: SDak State Rep, 67-69; secy-treas, SDak Rep State Cent Comt, 71- Bus & Prof Pos: Secy, SDak Jaycees, 64-65, pub rels dir, 65-66; dir, SDak Broadcasters, 72-74, pres, 74-75. Mem: Pierre CofC; Pierre Elks. Honors & Awards: Key Man Award, Pierre Jaycees, 64 & 65 & Outstanding Young Man, 68. Relig: Methodist. Legal Res: 1621 E Robinson Pierre SD 57501 Mailing Add: Box 309 Pierre SD 57501

SORENSON, JOAN LEE (R)
Chairwoman, Minn Second Cong Dist Rep Party
b Hutchinson, Minn, Jan 27, 30; d Harry Arthur Jenner & Pearl Potter Scott J; m 1949 to Dale Sanford Sorenson; c Sandra (Mrs Donald P Messer), Pamela (Mrs S David Marable), Eric Potter & Martha Esther. Educ: Albert Lea High Sch, Minn, 48. Polit & Govt Pos: Precinct worker, Minn, 61, ward leader, until 66, co chairwoman, until 71; chairwoman, Minn Second Cong Dist Rep Party, 71-; deleg, Dem Nat Conv, 72. Mem: League of Women Voters; Ramsey PTA (pres & mem exec bd, 61-73); Albert Lea Park & Recreation Advisory (chmn, 70-73, former secy). Relig: Lutheran. Mailing Add: 606 E Fourth Albert Lea MN 56007

SORRELL, ESTHER HARTIGAN (D)
Vt State Sen
Mailing Add: 23 Hickok Pl Burlington VT 05401

SOSSAMAN, JAMES J (R)
Ariz State Rep
b Phoenix, Ariz, July 17, 32; s Jasper Harvey Sossaman & Faith Mather S; m 1953 to Carolyn Sue Peters; c Kimberlee Ann, Stephen James & Scott Harvey. Educ: Ariz State Univ, 50-52. Polit & Govt Pos: Precinct committeeman, Queen Creek Precinct, Ariz, 62-69; Ariz State Rep, Dist 29, 69-72, Dist 30, 73-, chmn, Educ Comt, Ariz House of Rep, currently. Bus & Prof Pos: Owner, Sossaman Farms, 56- Mil Serv: Entered as Cadet, Navy, 52, released as Lt(jg), 56, after serv in Patrol Plane, 47 & Fleet Aircraft Serv Squadron, Far East, 53-56; Korean Serv Medal; Nat Defense Medal. Mem: Maricopa Co Farm Bur; Chandler Hosp Dist 1; Ariz Flying Farmers; Ariz Cotton Growers Asn (dir); United Dairymen of Ariz. Honors & Awards: Winner of Dist 3, Ariz High Yield of Short Staple Cotton, 65; Arizona's Outstanding Young Farmer, Jr CofC, 66; Flying Farmer of the Year, Ariz Flying Farmers, 69. Relig: United Methodist. Mailing Add: Rte 1 Box 80 Higley AZ 85236

SOUBA, ARNOLD RICHARD (R)
Chmn, Big Stone Co Rep Party, Minn
b Graceville, Minn, Feb 6, 32; s Arnold Richard Souba, Sr & Rosetta Fuhrman S; m 1969 to Linda Joyce Konth; c Tony & Arnold, Ill. Educ: Univ Minn, Minneapolis, BA. Polit & Govt Pos: Rep precinct chmn, Graceville, Minn, 68-69; comnr & dist chmn, 69-71; finance drive chmn, Big Stone Co Rep Party, 69-71, mem exec comt, 69-71, chmn, 71- Bus & Prof Pos: Owner, Graceville Lumber Co, 57- Mil Serv: Entered as E-1, Navy, 56, released as E-3, 58, after serv in Naval Security Sta, Washington, DC. Mem: Graceville Gun Club (dir, 71-); Graceville Golf Club; Graceville Develop Asn (vpres, 71). Relig: Lutheran. Mailing Add: Block III Souba Addition Graceville MN 56240

SOUCIE, KEVIN (D)
Wis State Rep
b Milwaukee, Wis, Feb 2, 54; s Donald Layton Soucie & Joan Legath S; single. Educ: Univ Wis-Madison, 72-73; Univ Wis-Milwaukee, 73-75. Polit & Govt Pos: Wis State Rep, Seventh

Dist, 74-, mem comt commerce & consumer affairs & mem comt transportation, Wis House Rep, 75- Mem: Allied Coun Sr Citizens; Jaycees; Hotel, Motel, Restaurant Employees & Bartenders Union Local. Legal Res: 3259 S 53rd St Milwaukee WI 53219 Mailing Add: Rm 312 W State Capitol Madison WI 53702

SOULE, RICHARD C (D)
Vt State Sen
Mailing Add: Fairfax VT 05454

SOUMAS, TOM DAN, JR (R)
Youth Committeeperson, Kootenai Co Rep Cent Comt, Idaho
b San Francisco, Calif, Nov 12, 53; s Tom Dan Soumas, Sr & Mary Platania S; m 1975 to Barbara Lynn Frovarp. Educ: NIdaho Col, 72-75; Ski Club; Outdoor Activities Prog Chmn; Col Rep; Choir; Band. Polit & Govt Pos: Campaign mgr, Jim Fitzpatrick for Sheriff, Kootenai Co, Idaho, 72; first vchmn, NIdaho Col Rep Club, 72-73, col chmn, 73-75; youth committeeperson, Kootenai Co Rep Cent Comt, 73-; voting mem, Idaho Rep State Cent Comt, 73-; precinct committeeman, West Dalton 24, Kootenai Co, 73-; first vchmn, Idaho Col Rep League, 74-75; bd mem, Western Fedn Col Rep, 74-75; chmn, Kootenai Co Young Rep Club, 74-75. Bus & Prof Pos: Legis attache, Idaho House Rep, 74; fire control aide, Dept of Lands, Idaho, 73-74; dep sheriff, Kootenai Co, 74-; pres, Gem State Airlines, Coeur d'Alene, 75-. Mem: Kootenai Amateur Radio Soc (pres, 75); Coeur d'Alene Vol Fire Dept. Honors & Awards: NASA-Pepsico Space Award, Boy Scouts, 73; Pepsi Cola scholar, NIdaho Col, 74. Relig: Catholic. Mailing Add: 216 S Tenth St Coeur d'Alene ID 83814

SOUR, A W, JR (R)
La State Rep
Mailing Add: 637 Montgomery St Shreveport LA 71107

SOUTH, CARROLL V (D)
Mont State Rep
Mailing Add: 506 Mississippi Ave Miles City MT 59301

SOUTHALL, MARK T (D)
b Norfolk, Va, June 1, 11; s George Edward Southall & Bertha Shiver S; m 1963 to Joanne Fletcher; c Joanne F. Educ: Collegiate Inst; Henry George Sch of Social Sci; Poh's Inst of Ins. Polit & Govt Pos: Confidential aide to Judge, Gen Session & Supreme Courts, 60-62; deleg, Dem Nat Conv, 68; NY State Assemblyman, 69-74, chmn, Adv Comt on Crime & Safety in the Streets, NY State Assembly, formerly; co & state committeeman, judicial deleg & dist leader, NY Co Dem Orgn, chmn, NY Co Dem Comt, formerly; chmn, NY Dem State Comt on Crime, currently. Bus & Prof Pos: Licensed Ins & Real Estate Broker, self-employed, 47-; vpres & dir, Mocho Industs, currently. Mem: Exec mem New Horizons Dem Club. Legal Res: 345 W 145th St New York NY 10039 Mailing Add: 274 W 145th St New York NY 10039

SOUTHALL, WALTER DELBERT (D)
Chmn, Prince Edward Co Dem Comt, Va
b Prince Edward Co, Va, Sept 25, 26; s Walter Otha Southall & Edna Cook S; m 1947 to Ethel Elizabeth Shockley; c Jane Gay, Susan Kaye & Walter Delbert, Jr. Educ: Hampden-Sydney Col, 43-46. Polit & Govt Pos: Dir farm bur, Prince Edward Co, Va, 65-, chmn, Selective Serv Bd, 67- & supvr, Farmville, Va, 72-; chmn, Prince Edward Co Dem Comt, 73- Bus & Prof Pos: Pres, Southall Oil Co Inc, 50- Mil Serv: Entered as Seaman, Navy, 44, released as PO 2/C, 46, after serv in South Pac Theatre, 45-46. Mem: Farmville Vol Fire Dept; Odd Fellows. Honors & Awards: 4-H All Star, 40. Relig: Baptist. Legal Res: 1208 Fourth Ave Ext Farmville VA 23901 Mailing Add: Rte 2 Box 57 Farmville VA 23901

SOUTHARD, STEPHEN WARREN (R)
Mem, Mich Rep State Comt
b Grosse Pointe Farms, Mich, Sept 3, 54; s Harold Carleton Southard & Gretchen Evelyn Bates S; single. Educ: Wayne State Univ, currently; Nat Honor Soc. Polit & Govt Pos: Mem youth coun to Mich State House Rep Comt on Youth & Student Participation, 72; second vchmn, Macomb Co Rep Exec Comt, 72-74, mem, 75-; mem, Mich Rep State Comt, 75-, vchmn orgn comt, currently; mem, Rule 29 Comt, Mich Rep Party, 75- Bus & Prof Pos: Supvr, Nat Bank of Detroit, Mich, 74- Honors & Awards: Competitive Scholar, State Mich, 72; Outstanding Young Adult, Macomb Daily, 72. Mailing Add: 23333 Doremus Dr St Clair Shores MI 48080

SOUTHERLAND, JAMES F (D)
b Pender Co, NC, Feb 8, 27; s Daniel Patron Southerland & Annie Laura Page S; m 1953 to Beverly Townsend; c Mark Townsend & Laura Page. Educ: NC State Col, 43-44; Univ NC, AB in Jour, 50. Polit & Govt Pos: Admin asst to Gov, Fla, 59-60; confidential asst to US Secy Com, 61-65; admin asst to US Rep Claude Pepper, Fla, 65-69 & 73-; exec dir, Select Comt on Crime, US House of Rep, 69-70. Bus & Prof Pos: Reporter, Parker Bros Newspapers, Ahoskie, NC, 50-51; reporter, Greensboro Daily News, 51-53; reporter & feature writer, Winston-Salem J, 53-54; assoc ed, Fla Times-Union, Jacksonville, 54-56; ed writer, Daytona Beach J, 56-59. Mil Serv: Entered as Seaman 1/C, Navy, 45, released as EM 2/C, 47, after serv in Bikini Atomic Bomb Tests, Pac, 47; Ens, Naval Res, 51-65. Mem: Nat Capital Dem Club. Relig: Unitarian. Legal Res: 8300 Crespi Blvd Miami Beach FL 33141 Mailing Add: 51 D St SE Washington DC 20003

SOUTHERN, WILLIAM S (R)
Kans State Rep
Mailing Add: Box 831 29004 Washington Great Bend KS 67530

SOUTHWICK, RICHARD L (R)
NH State Rep
b Lynn, Mass, July 6, 38; s Walter L Southwick & Rita McQuaid S; m 1969 to Carol Beeley; c Deanna J. Educ: Northeastern Univ, 58-59; St Anselm's Col, 70- Polit & Govt Pos: NH State Rep, Concord, 73- Bus & Prof Pos: Labor standards engr, Raytheon Corp, Andover, Mass, 58-63; contractor sales, mgr, Grossmans, Salem & Portsmouth, NH, 63-68; Salem Police Dept, NH, 68- Mem: F&AM; Lawrence RAM; Lawrence RSM; AAONMS; Eastern Star. Relig: Catholic. Mailing Add: 125 Shore Dr Salem NH 03079

SOVERN, STEVE (D)
Iowa State Sen
Mailing Add: RR 1 Marion IA 52302

SOWARDS, GLADE MILTON (R)
Utah State Rep
b Vernal, Utah, Sept 9, 29; s Harmon Silas Sowards & Ida Rebecca Jensen S; m 1952 to Rachel Elizabeth Farley; c Rebecca Jane, Olivia, Harmon Scott, John Farley, Paula, Allen Henderson, Samuel Layne, Trinadad Madge Ben & Glade Michael. Educ: Univ Utah, BS; Phi Kappa Phi; Sigma Chi. Polit & Govt Pos: Councilman, Vernal City, Utah, 61-69; Utah State Rep, 69- Bus & Prof Pos: Mgr, H S Sowards & Sons, Inc, 54-69; pres, Uqueahgut, Inc, 66-69. Publ: And the desert shall blossom as the rose, Improv Era, 65. Mem: Vernal Lions Club (pres); CofC (pres). Honors & Awards: Acct Award, Univ Utah Bus Dept; Master M Man Award (church). Relig: Latter-day Saint. Mailing Add: 380 W First S Vernal UT 84078

SOWELL, POLLY ROLLINS (R)
VChmn, Rep Party of Tex
m 1949 to Richard M Sowell; c Susan Channing. Educ: Sweet Briar Col, BA, 48. Polit & Govt Pos: Dep state chmn, Rep Party of Tex, 65-73, vchmn, 73-; US alt deleg, Inter-Am Comn of Women, 70- Mailing Add: 401 Wichita McAllen TX 78501

SOWERS, WESLEY H (R)
Kans State Sen
b Whiting, Ind, Aug 5, 05; s S Walter Sowers & Bertha Spurrier S; m 1929 to Gladys M Krueger; c Penny (Mrs David Buxton) & Wesley H, Jr. Educ: Purdue Univ, BS & MS; DePaul Univ, JD; Phi Delta Theta. Polit & Govt Pos: Mem, Wichita Planning Comn, 54-57, chmn, 57; Metrop Planning Comn, 58; mem, Bd of Zoning Appeals, 58; chmn, Kans Citizens Comt for Const Rev, 69; consult, Kans Comt Exec Reorgn, 70; Kans State Sen, 70-; mem adv comn, Kans Geol Surv, 72- Bus & Prof Pos: Patent counsel, Pure Oil Co, 38-42; vpres, Bay Chem Co, New Orleans, La, 42-50, Frontier Chem Div, Vulcan Materials Co, 50-58, pres, 58-65; independent mgt counsel, 65- Mem: Soc Chem Indust; Am Asn Advan Sci; Rotary Club; Kans State CofC; Jr Achievement of Wichita. Honors & Awards: Kansan of Year, Topeka Capitol J, 63; Six patents, Petrol Technol, 39-42. Relig: Presbyterian. Legal Res: 234 S Brookside Dr Wichita KS 67218 Mailing Add: 527 Union Ctr Wichita KS 67202

SPAFFORD, ENVAL AINSWORTH (D)
Secy, Ashtabula Co Dem Party, Ohio
b Footville, Ohio, June 29, 02; s Eddie A Spafford & Cynthia Hyneman S; div; c Kay (Mrs McMahan) & Robert. Educ: Ohio State Univ, BS in Agr, 25; Western Reserve Univ, MEd, 33; Delta Theta Sigma. Polit & Govt Pos: Chmn, Ashtabula Co Dem Party, Ohio, 56-62, secy, 62-; secy, Ashtabula Co Dem Cent & Exec Comt, 10 years; mem, Ashtabula Bd Elec, 12 years. Mailing Add: Rte 1 Rock Creek OH 44084

SPAHN, JOHN NICK (D)
Secy, Mille Lacs Co Dem-Farmer-Labor Party, Minn
b Wadena, Minn, May 16, 28; s George Spahn & Rose Domme S; m 1949 to Lucille Elizabeth Athman; c John R, Rose Anne, Michael J, Sharon Jean & Charles Jerome. Educ: Wadena High Sch, Minn, grad. Polit & Govt Pos: Precinct chmn, Mille Lacs Co Dem-Farmer-Labor Party, 68-70, secy, 70-; mem, Mille Lacs Co Draft Bd, 73- Bus & Prof Pos: Salesman, United Biscuit Co Am, 55-61; dist mgr, Minn State Auto Asn, 61-69; auctioneer, 68-71; owner, John Spahn Ins Agency, 69- Mil Serv: Entered as Cpl, Army, 50, released as Sgt 1/C, 52, after serv in Transportation Truck Bn, US & SPac, 50-52; Victory Medal plus others. Mem: VFW; Am Legion; Onamia Police Dept. Relig: Catholic. Mailing Add: PO Box 275 Onamia MN 56359

SPAIN, JAMES EARL (D)
Chmn, Mo Dem State Comt
b Clarksville, Tex, Dec 15, 34; s Elbert Earl Spain & Wilma Waters S; m 1956 to Jo Anne Prather; c Cynthia Lynn, Melinda Anne & Samuel Prather. Educ: Ark State Col, 52-53; Southeast Mo State Col, AB, 55; Univ Mo, LLB, 60; Phi Alpha Theta; Phi Alpha Delta; Sigma Phi Epsilon; Varsity Club. Polit & Govt Pos: Secy, Bd Educ, Mo, 63-66; Mo State Rep, 151st Dist, 67-72; deleg, Dem Nat Conv, 68; chmn, Mo Dem State Comt, 75- Bus & Prof Pos: Lawyer, Hearnes & Spain, 60-62; lawyer, Briney, Welborn & Spain, 62- Mil Serv: Entered as Pvt, Army, 55, released as SP-4, 57, after serv in 2nd Inf Div, Alaska, 56-57. Publ: Implied warranty of food & drink in Missouri, Mo Law Rev, 60. Mem: Mo & Am Bar Asns. Relig: Methodist. Mailing Add: 210 Spring St Bloomfield MO 63825

SPAINHOWER, JAMES I (D)
State Treas, Mo
b Stanberry, Mo, Aug 3, 28; m 1950 to Joanne Steanson; c Janet Dovell, James Jeffery. Educ: Phillips Univ; Lexington Theol Assembly; Univ Ark; Pac Sch Relig, BA, BDiv. Hon Degrees: LLD, Phillips Univ, 67, DPA, Culver Stockton Col, 73. Polit & Govt Pos: Mo State Rep, 63-70; State Treas, 72-; mem exec comt, Mo Dem State Cent Comt, 75- Bus & Prof Pos: Minister, First Christian Church, Fayetteville, Ark, 53-58, First Christian Church, Marshall, Mo, 58-64 & Christian Churches, Mendon & Bosworth, 64-70. Mem: Mo Hist Soc (exec bd). Honors & Awards: Meritorious Serv Award, St Louis Globe-Dem, 68; Harry S Truman Award, Saline Co Young Dem, 70; Citation of Merit, Univ Mo-Columbia Alumni Asn, 75. Relig: Christian. Mailing Add: 3 Capitol Bldg Jefferson City MO 65101

SPALDING, KENNETH WOODMAN, JR (R)
NH State Rep
b Southbridge, Mass, Nov 26, 34; s Kenneth W Spalding, Sr & Hilda Luce S; m 1957 to Audrey A Ide; c Scott Woods, David Ide, Kenneth Woodman, III & Martha Dorothy. Educ: New Hampton Sch, NH, 48-52; St Lawrence Univ, BA, 56; Sigma Pi. Polit & Govt Pos: Mem, Amherst Bd of Adjust, NH, formerly; supvr of checklist, formerly; treas, Hillsborough Co Rep Comt; past pres, Souhegan Young Rep Club; past recording secy, NH Fedn of Young Rep Clubs; NH State Rep, 69- Bus & Prof Pos: Sales engr, New Eng Homes, Portsmouth, NH, currently. Mil Serv: Entered as 2nd Lt, Army, 57, released as 1st Lt, 59, after serv in Armed Serv Police Detachment, Boston, Mass. Mem: Charter mem Souhegan Valley Jaycees; charter mem Amherst Jaycees; Mason; New Hampton Sch (trustee). Relig: Protestant. Mailing Add: Box 184 Green Rd Amherst NH 03031

SPALDING, LESTER HELM (D)
b Lebanon, Ky, June 16, 20; s Bennie G Spalding & Hazel Helm S; m 1942 to Nell Terry; c Larry Helm, Susan Terry & Steven Lynn. Educ: Western Ky Univ, BA, 41; Univ Louisville Sch Law, JD, 48; Omicron Delta Kappa; Phi Alpha Delta. Polit & Govt Pos: Co Attorney & Judge, Marion Co, Ky, several occasions prior to 56; City Attorney, Lebanon, 56-58; Commonwealth's Attorney, 11th Judicial Dist of Ky, 58-; mem, Ky Disabled Ex-Servicemen's Bd, 59-61; deleg, Dem Nat Conv, 68 & 72; mem, Lincoln Trail Regional Crime Coun, 69- Bus & Prof Pos: Attorney, Bd Educ, Marion Co, Ky, 56-; dir, Marion Nat

Bank, Lebanon, 65-; asst attorney, Marion Co Savings & Bldg Asn, 67-; adv, Marion-Wash Co Voc Sch, 68- Mil Serv: Entered as 2nd Lt, Air Force, 42, released as Maj after serv in Judge Adv, 123rd Fighter-Interceptor Wing, Maj (Ret), Air Force Res, 61. Mem: Ky Bar Asn; Commonwealth's Attorneys Asn; Mason (pres, Masonic Temple Co); VFW (Past Dept Judge Advocate); Am Legion (Past Comdr, Marion Post 49). Relig: Methodist; Pres, Methodist Men & mem, Off Bd, Lebanon United Methodist Church. Legal Res: Park Heights Lebanon KY 40033 Mailing Add: 7 Court Sq Lebanon KY 40033

SPALDING, PHILIP EDMUNDS, JR (R)
b Honolulu, Hawaii, July 21, 18; s Philip Edmunds Spalding & Alice Cooke S; m 1952 to Phyllis Hume; c Philip Edmunds, III, Alfred Tozzer, Anne Margaret, Philip Hume, Michael Scott & Joan (Mrs Steven Milo Peterson). Educ: Princeton Univ, 2 years; Colonial Club. Polit & Govt Pos: Finance chmn, Rep Party of Hawaii, 46, treas, 48; alt deleg, Rep Nat Conv, 68; Rep Nat Committeeman, Hawaii, 70-72, finance chmn, formerly. Bus & Prof Pos: Pres, Hawaiian Western Steel Limited, 58; dir, Bank of Hawaii, 63-, Dillingham Corp, 67- & Hawaiian Elec Co, Inc, 69- Mil Serv: Ens, Navy, 46. Mem: Hawaii Acad of Sci; Pac Club; Oahu Country Club. Legal Res: 4340 Pahoa Ave Honolulu HI 96816 Mailing Add: 91-150 Hanua St Ewa HI 96706

SPANIOLA, FRANCIS RICHARD (D)
Mich State Rep
b Corunna, Mich, June 8, 35; s Anthony M Spaniola (deceased) & Angeline J Spadafore S; m 1957 to Carol Ann Klempirik; c Anthony Michael, Angela Mary, Mary Alice & Joseph Theodore. Educ: Mich State Univ, BA in polit sci, 57, grad studies, 60-72. Polit & Govt Pos: Chairperson, Shiawassee Co Dem Comt, Mich, 61-62 & 70-74; mem, Sixth Cong Dist Dem Comt, 68-72; officer-at-lg, Mich Dem Party, 73-75; Mich State Rep, 87th Dist, 75- Bus & Prof Pos: Sales prom-mkt research, Controls Co Am, Owosso, Mich, 57-62; owner-gen mgr, Anthony's, Owosso, 61- & partner, Howell, Mich, 62-; teacher govt, Durand, Corunna & East Lansing High Schs, 62-71. Mil Serv: Entered as 2nd Lt, Army Res, 57, released as Capt, 69, after serv in 5064 Army Garrison, 919th Transportation Co, 812th Army Postal Unit. Mem: KofC; Nat & Shiawassee Hist Socs; Lions; Mich Educ Asn. Honors & Awards: Fel, Robert A Taft Inst Govt, Mich State Univ, 71. Relig: Roman Catholic. Legal Res: 517 W Corunna Ave Corunna MI 48817 Mailing Add: State Capitol Lansing MI 48901

SPANISH, JOHN H (D)
Minn State Rep
Mailing Add: 2202 1/2 11th Ave Hibbing MN 55746

SPANN, ANN OLIVE (AM PARTY)
b Chapman, Ala, May 28, 17; d Julius Valentine Spann & Clementine Olive S; single. Educ: Butler Co High Sch, Greenville, Ala. Polit & Govt Pos: Mem, Butler Co Rep Exec Comt, 62-72; chmn, Ala Women's Rep Action Fund, 64; mem, Ala State Rep Exec Comt, 66-72; treas, Ala Fedn Rep Women, 65-69, pres, formerly; chmn, Ala Women for Nixon Comt, 68; chmn, Ala Stop ERA, 72-; chmn, Ala Women for Responsible Legis, 73- Mem: Ala Coun for Children & Youth (pres); Pilot Club of Greenville; Girl Scouts. Mailing Add: PO Box 42 Chapman AL 36015

SPANN, DON (D)
Miss State Sen
Mailing Add: 5735 Imperial Dr Jackson MS 39211

SPANNAUS, WARREN RICHARD (DFL)
Attorney Gen, Minn
b St Paul, Minn, Dec 5, 30; s Albert Carl Spannaus & Anna Korner S; m 1964 to Marjorie Louise Clarkson; c Christine Ann, David Clarkson & Laura Z. Educ: Univ Minn, Minneapolis, 58; Univ Minn Law Sch, JD, 63. Polit & Govt Pos: Spec Asst Attorney Gen, Minn, 63-65, Attorney Gen, 71-; staff mem, US Sen Walter F Mondale, 65-66, campaign dir, 66; chmn, Minn Dem-Farmer-Labor Party, 67-69. Bus & Prof Pos: Pvt law practice, Minneapolis, 69-70. Mil Serv: Entered Navy, 51, released as PO3, 54, after serv in SPac; Good Conduct Medal. Mem: Minn State, Ramsey Co & Hennepin Co Bar Asns; Nat Asn Attorney Gen; Sch for Social Develop, Minneapolis (bd dirs). Relig: Methodist. Legal Res: 2619 Robbins St Minneapolis MN 55410 Mailing Add: 102 State Capitol St Paul MN 55101

SPANO, AUGUST JOHN (MICK) (R)
Colo State Rep
b Denver, Colo, Aug 4, 21; s Joseph Spano (deceased) & Anna Calabrese S; m 1951 to Mary Marguerite Koonce; c August J, Jr, Arthur M, Christopher J & Andrew J. Educ: Univ Colo, Boulder, BSEE, 42; Sigma Tau; Viking. Polit & Govt Pos: Precinct committeeman, Jefferson Co, 50-55 & 57-72; Colo State Rep, currently. Bus & Prof Pos: Field engr, Hewlett-Packard Co, 57-72; presently investor. Mil Serv: Entered as Ens, Naval Res, 43, released as Lt(sg), 46, after serv in Pac Theater, 2 years & USS Kearsarge CV-33; two campaign medals; Pac Theater Ribbon. Mem: Am Inst Elec & Electronic Eng; Microwave Theory & Techniques (vpres, Denver-Boulder Chap, 66-67 & pres, 68-69); Elks. Relig: Catholic. Mailing Add: 6525 W 52nd Ave Arvada CO 80002

SPANO, BARBARA LINDHOLM (D)
Mem, Westchester Co Dem Comt, NY
b New York, NY, Feb 11, 37; d Lauri E Lindholm & Anna M Johnson; c Andrew J, Jr, David R, Christine L & Karen B. Educ: Fordham Univ, 54-55; Mercy Col NY, BA, 73. Polit & Govt Pos: Mem, Westchester Co Dem Comt, NY, 69-; mem steering comt, Yorktown Legis Campaign, 70; mem steering comt, Yorktown Presidential Campaign, 72; mem, Comt to Study Cross-Party Endorsement, Westchester Co, 72; alt deleg, New Dem Coalition Assembly, 72; deleg, Dem Nat Conv, 72; vchairperson, Yorktown Dem Town Comt, 73- Bus & Prof Pos: With NY State Dept Labor. Mem: Yorktown Narcotics Guid Coun (adv bd); Yorktown Dem Club (secy, 70, pres, 71-72, bd dirs, 72-). Relig: Roman Catholic. Mailing Add: Strawberry Rd Lake Mohegan NY 10547

SPANOS, HARRY V (D)
b Newport, NH, May 8, 26; married; c three. Educ: Harvard Col; Harvard Law Sch. Polit & Govt Pos: NH State Rep, 63-67; NH State Sen, 67-74; mem, Sch Bd, formerly & chmn, Planning Bd, formerly; assoc judge, Newport Dist Court, formerly; deleg, Dem Nat Conv, 60-72; town & sch moderator & town attorney. Bus & Prof Pos: Attorney. Relig: Greek Orthodox. Mailing Add: PO Box 132 Newport NH 03773

SPARKMAN, JOHN J (D)
US Sen, Ala
b Hartselle, Ala, Dec 20, 99; s Whitten J Sparkman & Julia Mitchell Kent S; m 1923 to Ivo Hall; c Julia Ann (Mrs Tazewell Shepard, Jr). Educ: Univ Ala, AB, 21, LLB, 23, AM, 24. Hon Degrees: LLD, Spring Hill Col, 56, Univ Ala, 58 & Auburn Univ, 60. Polit & Govt Pos: US Comnr, 30-31; US deleg, Fifth Session UN Gen Assembly; US Rep, Ala, 37-46; US Sen, Ala, 46-, mem, Foreign Rels Comt, US Senate, 51-75, chmn, 75-, chmn, Comt on Banking, Housing & Urban Affairs, 67-75; Dem cand for Vice President, 52. Bus & Prof Pos: Instr, Huntsville Col, 25-28; attorney, 25-30; partner, Taylor, Richardson & Sparkman, 30-36; trustee, Am Univ & Athens Col. Mil Serv: Army, World War I, Col, Organized Res. Mem: Huntsville CofC; Mason; Eastern Star; WOW; Kiwanis. Relig: Methodist. Legal Res: AL Mailing Add: Senate Off Bldg Washington DC 20510

SPARKMAN, WILEY (D)
Okla State Sen
Mailing Add: State Capitol Oklahoma City OK 73105

SPARKS, CHARLES ALDEN, JR (R)
Chmn, Sherman Co Rep Cent Comt, Kans
b Goodland, Kans, July 2, 33; s Charles Alden Sparks & Marjorie Cavanaugh S; m 1961 to Nancy A Hamilton; c David & Karen. Educ: Univ Kans, BA, 55, JD, 59. Polit & Govt Pos: City Attorney, Goodland, Kans, 67-; chmn, Sherman Co Rep Cent Comt, 68- Mil Serv: 2nd Lt, Air Force. Mem: Am & Kans Bar Asns; Rotary. Relig: Episcopal. Legal Res: 408 W 11th St Goodland KS 67735 Mailing Add: Box 68 Goodland KS 67735

SPARKS, CULLIE JAMES, JR (D)
b Belpre, Ohio, May 8, 29; s Cullie James Sparks, Sr & Hazel Meade S; m 1951 to Janet Elizabeth Webb; c Teresa, Wanet, Linda, Jill & Brian. Educ: Univ Ky, BSE, 52, DE, 57; Tau Beta Pi; Alpha Tau Omega. Polit & Govt Pos: Precinct capt, Anderson Co Dem Exec Comt, 62-71, chmn, formerly; chmn, Anderson Co Citizens for Gore, 70; chmn, Anderson Co Dem Party, formerly. Bus & Prof Pos: Research scientist, Oak Ridge Nat Lab, Tenn, 58- Mil Serv: Entered as 1st Lt, Air Force, 56, released as 1st Lt, 58, after serv in Air Research & Develop Command, Wright-Patterson, Ohio, 58. Publ: Co-auth, Chap II In: Thin films, Am Soc Metals, 64; Chap I In: Local Atomic Arrangements Studies by X-Ray Diffraction, Plenum Press, 65; Pages 240-253 In: Advances in X-Ray Analysis, Vol 15, Plenum Publ Co, NY, 72. Mem: Am Soc Metals; Am Inst Metallurgical Engrs; Research Soc of Am. Relig: Presbyterian. Mailing Add: 804 W Outer Dr Oak Ridge TN 37830

SPARKS, JOHN DUDLEY, JR (R)
Chmn, Queen Annes Co Rep Party, Md
b Chester, Md, Feb 7, 34; s John Dudley Sparks, Sr & Audrey Harris; m 1955 to Mary Jane Golt; c Lauren Jane & Dudley Golt. Educ: Wash Col, AB, 56; Lambda Chi Alpha. Polit & Govt Pos: Chmn, Md Rep State Cent Comt, 68-71; chmn, Queen Annes Co Rep Party, 71- Bus & Prof Pos: Owner & operator, Tastee Freez Drive-in, 58-68; teacher, Queen Annes Co, Md, 56-69. Mil Serv: Entered as Pvt, Army Nat Guard, 57, released as SP-3, 68. Mem: Nat Educ Asn; Md State & Queen Annes Co Teachers Asns; Lions; VFW. Relig: Methodist. Mailing Add: Harbor View Chester MD 21619

SPARKS, JOHN R (D)
Ala State Rep
Mailing Add: 919 Nunnelly Dr SW Cullman AL 35055

SPARKS, SHERMAN PAUL (R)
Chmn, Rockwall Co Rep Party, Tex
b Toledo, Ill, Jan 23, 09; s Ernest Melvin Sparks & Nancy Jane Keller S; m 1965 to Joyce Marie Patterson; c James Earl, Randal Paul, Robert Dale & Paul David. Educ: Univ Ill, BS, 32, MS, 38; Kirksville Col Osteopathy & Surgery, DO, 45; Psi Sigma Alpha; Atlas Club; Alpha Phi Omega. Polit & Govt Pos: Rockwall Co coordr, Civil Defense, Tex, 50-66; chmn, Rockwall Co Rep Party, 63- Mem: Tex Asn of Osteopathic Physicians & Surgeons; Am Osteopathic Asn; fel Am Col Gen Practitioners in Osteopathic Med; Hella Shrine; Rockwall CofC. Honors & Awards: Inventor of Photoelec Turbidimeter for bacterial determinations. Relig: Methodist. Mailing Add: 106 N Second Rockwall TX 75087

SPARKS, THOMAS EVERETT (D)
Ark State Rep
b Crossett, Ark, Aug 15, 11; s Albert Theodore Sparks & Clara Morton S; m 1940 to Julia Benton; c Thomas Everett, Jr, Julianna Dickey & Helen Benton. Educ: Hendrix Col, BA, 32; Washington & Lee Univ, LLB, 35. Polit & Govt Pos: Ark State Rep, 67-; deleg, Dem Nat Conv, 72. Bus & Prof Pos: Gen practice of law, Fordyce, Ark, 35-; secy-treas, Benton Realty Co, Inc, Benton Furniture Co, Inc, Benton Hardware Co, Inc & Benton Casket Mfg Co, Inc, 47-60, pres, 60-; owner, Morton Abstract Co, Fordyce, Ark. Mil Serv: Entered as Lt(jg), Navy, 43, released as Lt, 46, after serv in Western Pac, 43-45. Mem: Ark Trial Lawyers Asn; CofC; Rotary; Fordyce Country Club; Dallas Co Indust Develop Corp. Relig: Methodist. Mailing Add: RFD 2 Box 67 Fordyce AR 71742

SPARLING, JAMES M, JR (R)
b Saginaw, Mich, Aug 8, 28; s James Sparling & Mystle Hashbarger; m 1950 to Esther Mary Haar; c James M, III, Jana Sue & Tamra Lynn. Educ: Alma Col. Polit & Govt Pos: Admin asst to US Rep James Harvey, Mich, 61-73; Spec Asst to the President for Legis Affairs, 73-74; Asst to Secy of Com for Cong Affairs, 74- Mil Serv: Navy: Journeyman 3/C, Navy, 46-48; Victory, Am & NAtlantic Ribbons. Mem: Elks; Mich State Soc; Zeta Sigma. Legal Res: Saginaw MI Mailing Add: 6104 Sherborn Lane Springfield VA 22150

SPARLING, LAURENS KASEY (D)
b Phoenix, Ariz, Nov 18, 53; s Clayton E Sparling & Helen Vittum S; single. Educ: Phoenix Col, Ariz, 71-73; Ariz State Univ, BS in Biol, 75. Polit & Govt Pos: Deleg, Dem Nat Conv, 72; precinct committeeman, Valencia Precinct, Ariz, 73- Mem: Phoenix Col Young Dem (pres, 72-73); Phoenix Col Forum Comt. Relig: Christian. Mailing Add: 3338 W Pierson St Phoenix AZ 85017

SPATES, FRANK HARRIS (R)
Vt State Rep
Mailing Add: The Bluffs Newport VT 05855

SPAULDING, JOSIAH A **(R)**
b Worcester, Mass, 1923; m to Helen Bowdoin. Educ: Yale Univ, BA; Columbia Univ Law Sch, LLB. Polit & Govt Pos: Chmn, Mass Rep State Comt, 67-69; deleg, Rep Nat Conv, 68; Rep cand for US Sen, 70; Nat & Mass dir, Common Cause, currently; chmn task force, Reorgn Mass Secretariat of Environ Affairs, currently. Bus & Prof Pos: Partner, Bingham, Dana & Gould, Boston, 58- Mil Serv: 2nd Lt, Marines, World War II, Capt, Korea, serv as Naval Aviator; Distinguished Flying Cross; Four Air Medals; Squadron Citation. Legal Res: Gale's Point Manchester MA 01944 Mailing Add: 100 Federal St Boston MA 02110

SPAULDING, ROMA ALMA **(R)**
NH State Rep
b Woodstock, Vt, Oct 16, 14; d John Wilhelm Magnusson & Eveline Bourdon M; m 1937 to Bedford Thomas Spaulding; c Diane & Cynthia (Mrs Douglas Dutilley). Educ: High sch. Polit & Govt Pos: Supvr checklist, Rep Party, Claremont, NH, 63-, city chairwoman, 65-70; NH State Rep, Ward Two, 67-, vchmn, Pub Health & Welfare Comt, NH House of Rep, 69-71, chmn, 71-; mem, NH State Rep Comt, 69-; consumer rep, Comprehensive Health Adv Coun of NH, 70- Mem: Claremont Women's Rep Club; Claremont Hist Soc; Claremont Gen Hosp (incorporator); Abnake Coun (incorporator). Relig: Methodist. Mailing Add: 8 Maple Ave Claremont NH 03743

SPEAKMAN, RONALD BLAINE **(D)**
Dir, Jackson Co Dem Exec Comt, Ohio
b Ray, Ohio, July 26, 39; s Oral Donald Speakman & Garnette Tennant S; m 1960 to Gloria Jean Brown; c Robin & Rhonda. Educ: Coal Local Sch, Coalton, Ohio. Polit & Govt Pos: Pres, Jackson Co Dem Club, Ohio, 66-70; mem, Jackson Co Dem Cent Comt, Second Ward, 67-; chmn, Jackson Co Dem Exec Comt, 70-72, dir, 73- Bus & Prof Pos: Gen mgr, Willis-Sellers Co, 68-70; owner & operator, Ron's Previously Owned Autos, 70- Mil Serv: Entered as Pvt, Marine Corps, 57, released as S/Sgt, 66, after serv in 3rd Marine Div, Vietnam, 64-65; Vietnam Ribbon; Good Conduct Award; Nat Defense Award; Armed Forces Expeditionary Medal. Mem: Eagles; Am Legion; VFW; Ohio Grange; Jaycees. Honors & Awards: Four letters of commendation from Marines. Relig: Methodist. Mailing Add: 226 N High St Jackson OH 45640

SPEAR, ALLAN HENRY **(DFL)**
Minn State Sen
b Michigan City, Ind, June 24, 37; s Irving S Spear & Esther Lieber S; single. Educ: Oberlin Col, BA, 58; Yale Univ, MA, 60, PhD, 65. Polit & Govt Pos: Mem, Minn Dem-Farmer-Labor State Cent Comt, 70-72; mem state exec comt, Minnesotans for McGovern, 71-72; Minn State Sen, 73- Bus & Prof Pos: Lectr hist, Univ Minn, Minneapolis, 64-65, asst prof hist, 65-67, assoc prof hist, 67-; vis assoc prof Am studies, Carleton Col, spring 70; vis assoc prof hist, Stanford Univ, summer 70. Publ: Black Chicago: The Making of a Negro Ghetto, 1890-1920, Univ Chicago, 67; Marcus Lee Hansen and the historiography of immigration, Wis Mag Hist, 61; The origins of the urban ghetto, 1870-1915, In, Key Issues in the Afro-American Experience by Huggins, Kilson & Fox, Harcourt, Brace, Jovanovich, 71. Mem: Am Hist Asn; Orgn Am Historians; Minn Hist Soc; Am for Dem Action (state bd, Minn Chap, 72-); Minn Civil Liberties Union; Minn Fedn Teachers; NAACP. Honors & Awards: Research Training Grant, Social Sci Research Coun, 62-63; Fel, Nat Endowment for the Humanities, 68. Mailing Add: 2204 Seabury Ave Minneapolis MN 55406

SPEAR, CLAY **(D)**
Iowa State Rep
Mailing Add: 2441 S Main Burlington IA 52601

SPEAR, CLAY VERNE **(R)**
b Helene, Mont, Jan 10, 13; s Joel Clifford Spear & Pearl Ridgeway S; m 1941 to Irene Wilson Spear; c Jill Wilson (Mrs Rolfe) & Tom Wilson Spear. Educ: Univ Idaho, LLB, 37; Beta Theta Pi; Alpha Kappa Psi. Polit & Govt Pos: Rep precinct committeeman, 46-48; chmn, Kootenai Co Rep Party, Idaho, 48-53; Rep dist chmn, 49-53; dist judge, Eighth Judicial Dist, 53-66; Assoc Justice, Idaho Supreme Court, formerly. Bus & Prof Pos: Comnr, Idaho State Bar Asn, 56-59, pres, 58-59. Mil Serv: Entered as Pvt, Army, 41, released as 1st Lt, 45, after serv in 2nd Inf Div & 1st Army, ETO, 44-45; Europe-Africa-Middle East Medal with Four Bronze Serv Stars; Bronze Star Medal. Mem: Idaho State & Am Bar Asns; Inst Judicial Admin; Am Judicature Soc; Elks. Honors & Awards: Cert of Appreciation, Idaho State Bar; Community Serv Award, Port 889 VFW; Coeur d'Alene, 70. Relig: Presbyterian. Mailing Add: Hayden Lake ID 83835

SPEARS, JAE **(D)**
WVa State Deleg
b Kenton Co, Ky; d James Marshall & Sylvia Fox M; m to Lawrence Eugene Spears; c Katherine (Mrs James Cooper), Marsha (Mrs David Shepler), Lawrence & James. Educ: Univ Ky; Theta Sigma Phi; Alpha Xi Delta. Polit & Govt Pos: WVa State Deleg, currently. Bus & Prof Pos: Former newspaper woman, Cincinnati Post & Cincinnati Enquirer. Mem: YMCA (bd dirs); Quota Int; Bus & Prof Women's Club; White Shrine; VFW Auxiliary. Legal Res: Kerens Hill Elkins WV 26241 Mailing Add: Box 181 Elkins WV 26241

SPECK, SAMUEL W, JR **(R)**
Ohio State Rep
b Canton, Ohio, Jan 31, 37; s Samuel W Speck, Sr & Lois Schneider S; m 1962 to Sharon Jane Anderson; c Sammy, III & Derek. Educ: Muskingum Col, BA summa cum laude, 59; Rotary fel, Univ Rhodesia & Nyasaland, 61; Harvard Univ, MA, 63, PhD, 68. Polit & Govt Pos: Dist committeeman & regional dir, Ohio Young Rep Party, 68-70; pres, Guernsey Co Young Rep, 69; chmn, Guernsey Co Rep Cent Comt, formerly; Ohio State Rep, 95th Dist, 71-; mem, Ohio Adv Comt to US Civil Rights Comn, 72-73; mem, African Adv Coun, US State Dept, 72- Bus & Prof Pos: Assoc prof polit sci, Muskingum Col, 64-, chmn dept, formerly. Publ: The gap widens in Rhodesia, Africa Report, 1/63; Recruitment and role perception of local government elites in Malawi, paper presented at African Studies Asn, 67; Malawi in the Southern African complex, In: Southern African in Perspective, Free Press, 72. Mem: Am Polit Sci Asn; Midwest Polit Sci Asn; Ohio Asn Economists & Polit Scientist (pres, 70-71); African Studies Asn; Mason. Honors & Awards: Fels, Woodrow Wilson, Danforth, Rotary & Strong; Outstanding Ohio House Mem, Ohio Conserv Soc, 71. Relig: Methodist. Mailing Add: RD 2 Box 79 New Concord OH 43762

SPECKLING, KEITH **(R)**
Alaska State Rep
Mailing Add: Hope AK 99605

SPECKMAN, GEORGE RAYMOND **(D)**
Mem, Clinton Co Dem Comt, Mo
b Hannibal, Mo, May 9, 38; s George William Speckman & Edith Geneva Inlow S; m 1957 to Eleanor Louise Kennedy; c Cynthia Louise & George Raymond, Jr. Educ: Univ Mo, Columbia, BS, 59, LLB, 63; Ruf Nex (pres); Agr Econ Club. Polit & Govt Pos: Mem, Clinton Co Dem Comt, Mo, 64-, chmn, formerly; mem, Sixth Cong Dist Dem Comt, 65-; chmn youth activities, Mo State Dem Comt, 68; deleg, Dem Nat Conv, 68; mem, Interim Legis Comt on Tourism & Scenic Rivers, Mo Gen Assembly, State of Mo, currently; mem, Fifth Judicial Circuit Bar Comt, currently. Mem: Mo & Clinton Co Bar Asns; Bar US Supreme Court; Elks; Mason. Relig: Christian Church of NAm; Deacon, First Christian Church. Mailing Add: Rte 1 Plattsburg MO 64477

SPECKMAN, LEON GEORGE **(R)**
b Metropolis, Ill, Sept 23, 09; s Wm G Speckman & Jessie Cooper S; m 1942 to Marjorie Inez Ward. Educ: Metropolis Community High Sch. Polit & Govt Pos: Chmn, Massac Co Rep Cent Comt, Ill, 73-75. Mil Serv: Entered as Pvt, Army, 43, released as S/Sgt, 83rd Inf, after serv in European Theater, 46. Mem: Elks; VFW; Am Legion. Relig: Catholic. Mailing Add: 510 E Sixth St Metropolis IL 62960

SPECTER, ARLEN **(R)**
b Wichita, Kans, Feb 12, 30; s Harry Specter & Lillie Shanin S; m 1953 to Joan Lois Levy; c Stephen & Shanin. Educ: Univ Okla, 47-48; Univ Pa, BA, 51; Yale Univ Law Sch, LLB, 56; Phi Beta Kappa; Delta Sigma Rho; Phi Alpha Theta; Phi Alpha Delta. Hon Degrees: LLB, Philadelphia Col of Textiles & Sci, 68. Polit & Govt Pos: Asst Dist Attorney, Philadelphia, Pa, 59-63, Dist Attorney, 66-; asst counsel, Warren Comn, Washington, DC, 64; Spec Asst Attorney Gen, Pa Dept Justice, 64-65; deleg, Rep Nat Conv, 68 & 72; mem, Nat Adv Comt on Peace Corps, 69-; mem, White House Conf on Youth, 71, Gov Justice Comn, Regional Planning Coun, Nat Adv Comn on Criminal Justice Standards & Goals, Criminal Rules Comt of Pa Supreme Court & Philadelphia Judicial Coun, currently. Bus & Prof Pos: Lectr law, Univ Pa Law Sch, 69-72; lectr law, Temple Univ Law Sch, 72- Mil Serv: Entered Air Force, 51, released as 1st Lt, 53, after serv in Off of Spec Invests. Publ: Mapp vs Ohio: Pandora's problems for the prosecutor, Univ Pa Law Rev, 62; Free press & free trial, Villanova Law Rev, 66; Review of conviction, Yale Law J, 67; plus others. Mem: Am, Pa & Philadelphia Bar Asns; Police Athletic League (bd dirs); Nat Coun on Alcoholism, Del Valley Area (bd dirs). Honors & Awards: Sons of Italy Award, Alessandroni Lodge, 68; Community Humanitarian Award, Morris Chapel Baptist Church, 69; Man of Year Award, Temple Beth Ami, 71; Humanitarian Award, Ericsson Lodge, B'rith Sholom, 72; NE Cath Outstanding Achievement Award, 73. Relig: Jewish. Legal Res: 3417 Warden Dr Philadelphia PA 19129 Mailing Add: Rm 666 City Hall Philadelphia PA 19107

SPEED, RONALD K **(R)**
b Brainerd, Minn, Feb 23, 43; s Roy A Speed & Mary J Seil S; m 1968 to Paulette Nelson; c Erika Leigh. Educ: Hamline Univ, BA in Polit Sci & Hist, 65; Univ Minn Grad Sch, 67-68; Pi Gamma Mu; Tau Kappa Epsilon; Torch & Cycle. Polit & Govt Pos: Mem, Rep Nat Campaign Steering Comt for Minn, 64; state chmn, Minn Fedn of Col Rep Clubs, 64-65; mem, Minn Rep State Cent Comt, 64-65 & 74-75, alt, 72-73 & 75-; mem, Minn Rep State Exec Comt, 64-65; mem state exec bd, Young Rep League, 64-65; deleg, Minn Rep State Convs, 64-75, deleg, Platform Comt, 64 & 72; secy & mem nat governing bd, Ripon Soc, 71-, pres, Soc, 72-74; mem state bd, Rep Workshop, 72-73; mem, Minnetonka City GOP Exec Comt, 72- Bus & Prof Pos: Legis secy, Minn Coun Churches, 63; news asst, Hamline Univ, 64; bus mgr, YMCA Camp Ihduhapi, 65; news & research dir, Zwach for Cong Campaign, 66; legis asst to US Rep John M Zwach, Minn, 67-68; admin asst, Pub Affairs, Honeywell Inc, 68-71, dir, Legis Analysis & Planning, 71- Mil Serv: Sgt, E-5, Army Res, 5 years. Mem: Am Acad Pub Admin; Am Polit Sci Asn; Acad Polit Sci; Am Acad Polit & Social Sci; Hamline Univ Alumni Asn (pres, 74-). Honors & Awards: Craven Award for Jour, Hamline Univ, 63, Bridgeman Prize for Polit Sci, 64. Relig: Lutheran. Mailing Add: 336 Kenmar Circle Minnetonka MN 55343

SPEERS, AUSTIN BURGESS **(D)**
Treas, Fifth Cong Dem Dist, Mo
b Kansas City, Mo, Sept 14, 20; s George Austin Speers & Hazel Kirk Humason S; m 1941 to Barbara Elizabeth Smith; c Barbara Josephine & Allyson Elizabeth. Educ: Univ Mo-Kansas City, JD, 52; Phi Alpha Delpi (treas). Polit & Govt Pos: Spec Asst Attorney Gen, Mo, 67-69; pres, Dem Citizens Asn Kansas City, 67-69, secy, 69-; Asst Co Counr, Jackson Co, 69-; treas, Fifth Cong Dem Dist, 70- Mil Serv: Entered as Pvt, Army, 42, released as Pvt, 44, after serv as Mil Police, SPac, 43-44. Mem: Am, Mo & Kansas City Bar Asns; Am Trial Lawyers; Kansas City CofC. Relig: Protestant. Legal Res: 607 Huntington Rd Kansas City MO 64113 Mailing Add: 1420 Commerce Tower Kansas City MO 64105

SPEERS, FREDERIC WARDEN **(R)**
Mem, Rep State Cent Comt Calif
b Davenport, Iowa, July 26, 06; s Dr Will Frederic Speers (deceased) & Agnes Petersen S (deceased); m 1935 to Victoria Rountree. Educ: Stanford Univ, AB, 28; Denver Univ Law Sch, 34-35; Sigma Delta Chi; Delta Lambda Sigma; Phi Gamma Delta. Polit & Govt Pos: Secy, San Diego Co Rep Cent Comt, Calif, 50-55; mem, Calif Hwy Comn, 55-59; Presidential Elector, Calif, 60; mem, Rep State Cent Comt Calif, 60-; mem, Nixon Finance Comt of San Diego Co, Calif, 68; mem, Postmaster Gen Stamp Adv Comt, 69- Bus & Prof Pos: Reporter, Denver Post, Colo, 28-36; managing ed, Wyo State-Tribune, Cheyenne, 36-37; publ, North Platte Daily Bulletin, Nebr, 37-47; publ, Daily Times-Advocate, Escondido, Calif, 47-65; bd chmn, Palomar Savings & Loan, 50- Mil Serv: Entered as 1st Lt, Air Force, 42, released as Maj, 46, after serv in 6th Bomb Group (VH), Pac Theater, 44-46; Bronze Star; Air Medal; Two Presidential Unit Citations; Four Battle Stars. Publ: Behind the datelines, 54 & Datelines of trouble, 56, Escondido Times-Advocate; The Zemstvo Gazetteer, In: Vol 30 of Billig's Philatelic Handbook, Fritz Billig, 64. Mem: Royal Philatelic Soc, London; Mil Order of the World Wars; Am Legion; VFW; Rotary. Relig: Presbyterian. Mailing Add: 118 N Caroline Way Escondido CA 92025

SPEERS, JERROLD BOND **(R)**
Maine State Sen
b Cambridge, Mass, June 5, 41; s Ronald Thomas Speers & Shirley Bond S; single. Educ: Colby Col, BA, 63; Georgetown Univ, LLB, 66; Phi Delta Theta. Polit & Govt Pos: Col chmn, Maine Coun Young Rep, 61-62, nat committeeman, 62-63; nat auditor, Young Rep Nat Fedn, 63-65; asst to exec secy, Maine Comn on Intergovt Rels, summers 64 & 65; alt deleg, Rep Nat Conv, 64, deleg, 68 & 72; secy, Maine State Senate, 67-69; spec asst to asst secy for educ & cult affairs, US Dept State, 69-70; mgr cong campaign, Maine, 70; asst attorney gen, Maine, 71-72; Maine State Sen, 72-, chmn, Comt on State Govt, mem, Comt on Judiciary, Maine

State Senate, 72-, mem bd dirs & grants comt, Maine Law Enforcement Planning & Assistance Agency, 72- Bus & Prof Pos: Assoc, Law Firm of Locke, Campbell & Chapman, Augusta, Maine, 67-69, partner, Law Firm of Lipman, Gingras & Speers, 73- Mem: Kennebec, Maine & Am Bar Asns. Relig: Congregational. Mailing Add: Memorial Dr Winthrop ME 04364

SPEIGHT, JOHN BLAIN (JACK) (R)
b Cheyenne, Wyo, May 29, 40; s Jack B Speight & Kathryn E Schmidt S; m 1960 to Sally K Sullivan; c Sherry, Tricia & Jackie. Educ: Univ Wyo, BA, 62, JD, 65; Omicron Delta Kappa. Polit & Govt Pos: Dep Wyo Attorney Gen, 67-69; admin & legal asst to Gov, Wyo, 69-71; Asst US Trial Attorney, Wyo, 71-73; chmn, Wyo State Rep Cent Comt, 73-75. Mil Serv: Entered as Airman Basic, Air Force Nat Guard, 58, released as S/Sgt, 64. Mem: Young Mens Literary Club; Cheyenne Kiwanis Club; Cheyenne Vocation Club (pres, 72-); Wyo Trial Lawyers Asn; Wyo Bar Asn. Relig: Catholic. Legal Res: 3718 Pioneer Ave Cheyenne WY 82001 Mailing Add: 1720 Carey Ave Cheyenne WY 82001

SPEIGHT, L NORWOOD (R)
Chmn, Taney Co Rep Cent Comt, Mo
b Dadeville, Mo; m; c four; one grandson. Educ: Southwest Mo State Col, BS; Univ Mo, MA in High Sch Admin. Polit & Govt Pos: Mem & chmn, Branson Sch Bd, Mo, formerly; appeared before spec subcomt, Appropriations Comt, US House of Rep, 54; chmn, Taney Co Rep Cent Comt, currently. Bus & Prof Pos: Teacher, Dade, St Clair, Wright & Taney Co Schs, 12 years; with White River Elec Coop, Inc, 44-46, gen mgr, 46-; vpres, Sho-Me Bd Dirs, Marshfield, Mo & chmn finance comt; mem bd dirs, Mo Elec Coop, Jefferson City & chmn statewide legal serv comt; adv mem, Security Bank & Trust Co, Branson. Mem: Mason (32 degree); Shrine (Master, Branson Lodge); Rotary (past pres, Branson-Hollister Club); Taney Co Red Cross; Ozark Area Boy Scouts (mem exec bd). Relig: Presbyterian; Elder, First Presby Church, Branson. Mailing Add: Gen Delivery Branson MO 65616

SPELLMAN, GLADYS NOON (D)
US Rep, Md
b New York, NY, Mar 2, 18; d Henry Noon & Bessie G N; m to Reuben Spellman; c Stephen Louis, Richard Eric & Dana (Mrs O'Neill). Educ: George Washington Univ; Grad Sch Dept Agr. Polit & Govt Pos: Mem, Prince Georges Bd Comnrs, 62-67, chmn, 66; app, Adv Comt Intergovt Rels, 67; mem steering comt urban affairs comt, Nat Coun State Govt; mem, Gov Comn Law Enforcement & Admin Justice; mem, Gov Comn Function Govt; vchmn, Gov Comn Determine States Role in Financing Pub Educ; chmn, Md State Comprehensive Health Planning Adv Coun; chmn, Washington Suburban Transit Comn; chmn, Regional Planning Bd IV; chmn, Fed Omnibus Crime Control & Safe Street Act; bd mem, Washington Metrop Area Transit Authority; vpres, Metrop Washington Coun Govts; mem, Prince Georges Co Coun, 71; US Rep, Md, 75- Bus & Prof Pos: Teacher, Pub Schs, Prince Georges Co, Md; chmn bd trustees, Prince Georges Gen Hosp, 62-70. Mem: Md Asn Co (bd mem & educ comt chmn); Nat Asn Co (pres); Nat Labor-Mgt Rels Serv. Legal Res: 9004 Golden Pass Laurel MD 20811 Mailing Add: US House Rep Washington DC 20515

SPENCE, CHRISTOPHER LINDSEY (D)
b Cleveland, Ohio, Dec 6, 52; s Granville Phillip Spence & Rose Witherspoon S; single. Educ: Fisk Univ, 70-72; Nashville Area Voc Sch, 72- Polit & Govt Pos: Alt deleg, Dem Nat Conv, 72. Relig: Original Church of God. Mailing Add: 2815-D Torbett St Nashville TN 37209

SPENCE, FLOYD DAVIDSON (R)
US Rep, SC
b Apr 9, 28; s James William Wilson Spence & Addie Lucas S; m 1952 to Lula Hancock Drake; c Floyd D, Jr, Zack W, Benjamin D & Caldwell D. Educ: Univ SC, AB in Eng, Law Sch, LLB; Nat War Col, grad of defense strategy seminar; pres, SC Asn Student Govt, Student Body & Jr Class; Omicron Delta Kappa; Kappa Sigma Kappa; Kappa Alpha Order; German Club; Compass & Chart Soc; Dean's List; YMCA & Cabinet; Block C Club; ed, Sc Law Quart; chief justice, Phi Alpha Delta; vpres, Law Fedn & mem, Cabinet. Polit & Govt Pos: SC State Rep, Lexington Co, 56-62; SC State Sen, Dist 22, 67-70; exec committeeman, Lexington Co Rep Party; deleg, Rep Nat Conv, 68 & 72; chmn, Joint Senate House Comt on Internal Security, 69-70; US Rep, SC, 71- Bus & Prof Pos: Attorney-at-law, Callison & Spence, West Columbia, SC, formerly. Mil Serv: Capt, Naval Res. Mem: Lexington Co, SC & Am Bar Asns; Am Trial Lawyers Asn; Am Judicature Soc. Honors & Awards: Outstanding sr, capt track team & state rec holder in mile relay event, mem football & basketball teams & Algernon-Sydney Sullivan Award, 52, Univ SC; participant, numerous Anti-Communist Seminars; auth & speaker on communism. Relig: Lutheran; Mem Church Coun & Adult Sunday Sch Teacher, St Peter's Lutheran Church. Legal Res: Box 815 Lexington SC 29072 Mailing Add: 120 Cannon House Off Bldg Washington DC 20515

SPENCE, JOHN W, JR (D)
Tenn State Rep
Mailing Add: 1565 Vinton Memphis TN 38104

SPENCE, WINIFRED M (R)
Del State Rep
Mailing Add: Box 52 RD 2 Middletown DE 19709

SPENCER, ALVIE GLENN, JR (R)
Dir Finance, US Dept of Com
b Patapsco, Md, Feb 19, 33; s Alvie G Spencer & Myrtle Shamer S; m 1960 to Phyllis Beaver; c Alan Gregory & Jennifer Marie. Educ: Gettysburg Col, BA, 59; Johns Hopkins Univ, BS, 66; Loyola Col (Md), MBA; Sigma Pi Sigma; Sigma Chi. Polit & Govt Pos: Mem precinct comt, Rep Party, Md, 56-; chmn, Carroll Co Rep State Cent Comt, 62-; app by Gov Spiro Agnew to Coun of Higher Educ for Md; app by co comnr to Govt Study Comn for Carroll Co, 68; deleg, Rep Nat Conv, 68; dir finance, US Dept of Com, 71- Bus & Prof Pos: Engr, Bendix Corp, 59-62; acct exec, Merrill Lynch Inc, 62-; financial rev dir, Dept of Com, currently. Mil Serv: Navy, 53-55, after serv in USS Glynn APA 239, Atlantic Fleet; hon discharge. Mem: Munic Finance Officers Asn; Washington, DC Munic Forum; Baltimore Bond Club; VFW; Rotary Int. Relig: Methodist. Mailing Add: 27 Smith Ave Westminster MD 21157

SPENCER, ARTHUR CONOVER (R)
Exec Dir, NJ Rep State Comt
b Orange, NJ, Sept 30, 27; s Arthur Wilson Spencer & Jean A Burns S; m 1957 to Marie D Barnes; c Elaine, Michael & Kevin. Educ: Wooster Sch, Danbury, Conn, 1 year; Columbia Univ, 2 years. Polit & Govt Pos: Dir & vchmn, NJ Young Rep Bd Dirs, 66-69; exec dir, NJ Rep State Comt, 66-71 & 74-; dir, NJ Nixon-Agnew Campaign Comt, 68; secy to majority, NY State Assembly, 68-; comnr, Somerset Co Libr, 68-; exec dir, Cahill for Gov Campaign, 69; asst to secy for cong liaison, Dept Health, Educ & Welfare, 70-72; consult, CREP, 72; dep dir, Action Agency, 72-; consult, Fed Housing Adminr, 73; exec asst to US Rep Charles Sandman, NJ, 73. Mil Serv: Entered as Pvt, Marines, 45, released as Pfc, 46; Area Serv Ribbon. Mem: Nat Press Club; NJ Legis & State House Correspondents Club; Capitol Hill Club. Relig: Roman Catholic. Legal Res: Sunset Lake RD 1 Basking Ridge NJ 07920 Mailing Add: Rm 405 28 W State St Trenton NJ 08608

SPENCER, CARMELITA G (R)
Committeewoman, Idaho Rep State Cent Comt
b Potlatch, Idaho, Aug 24, 22; m 1946 to John Wood Spencer; c Craig L, Charles Douglas & Laura (Mrs Stephen Barnes). Educ: Univ Idaho, BS in Home Econ, 43; Alpha Phi. Polit & Govt Pos: Committeeman, Idaho Rep State Cent Comt, currently. Mem: Am Asn Univ Women; PEO; Idaho Co Art Asn; Gen Hosp Womens Auxiliary. Honors & Awards: Idaho Gov Award in Arts & Humanities, 70. Relig: Episcopal. Mailing Add: Rte 2 Box 66 Grangeville ID 83530

SPENCER, CRAIG LEMUEL (R)
Chmn, Idaho Co Rep Cent Comt, Idaho
b Grangeville, Idaho; s John Wood Spencer & Carmelita Guernsey S; single. Educ: Univ Idaho, BS; Mu Epsilon Delta; Beta Theta Pi. Polit & Govt Pos: Chmn, Idaho Co Rep Cent Comt, Idaho, currently. Relig: Episcopal. Mailing Add: Rte 2 Box 66 Grangeville ID 83530

SPENCER, DON W (D)
Iowa State Rep
Mailing Add: RFD Ruthven IA 51358

SPENCER, EDWARD L, JR (R)
Chmn, Lee Co Rep Exec Comt, Ala
b Loachapoka, Ala, Sept 8, 30; s Edward L Spencer & Florence Rowell S; m 1953 to Ruth Priester; c Edward Lee, III, Bruce Steven & Sandra Jean. Educ: Auburn Univ, BS, 52; Univ Col of North Staffordshire, Fulbright scholar, 53. Polit & Govt Pos: Chmn, Lee Co Rep Exec Comt, Ala, currently. Bus & Prof Pos: Owner, E L Spencer Lumber Co. Mil Serv: Entered as 2nd Lt, Air Force, 52, released as 1st Lt, after serv in 406 Fighter Wing, USAFE, 56. Mem: Fraternal & civic clubs. Relig: Presbyterian. Legal Res: Magnolia Ave Auburn AL 36830 Mailing Add: Spencer Lumber Co Auburn AL 36830

SPENCER, ELDEN A (R)
Chmn, Lake Co Rep Exec Comt, Ohio
b Willoughby, Ohio, Mar 7, 29; s Friend Spencer & Edith Prall S; m 1949 to Imelda Mann; c Laura Lee, Lynn Ann, Mark Allan, Micheal, Martin, Lisa & Leslie. Educ: O R C O Voc Sch, cert in prod technol, 52. Polit & Govt Pos: Councilman, Mentor on Lake, Ohio, 58-60, Mayor, 60-62, chmn, City Planning Comt, 71-; chmn, Lake Co Rep Exec Comt, 70-; alt deleg, Rep Nat Conv, 72; mem, Cleveland Area Manpower Coun, 72- Bus & Prof Pos: Vpres, Ohio Rubber Co, Willoughby, 72- Mem: James A Garfield Rep Men's Club. Mailing Add: 7681 Dahlia Dr Mentor on Lake OH 44060

SPENCER, GEORGE LLOYD (D)
b Sarcoxie, Mo, Mar 27, 93; s George Spencer & Luella Riley S; m 1919 to Bun Hays; c Hilda Kim (deceased). Educ: Henderson Col, Ark. Polit & Govt Pos: US Sen, Ark, 41-43; dir, Southwest Ark Water Dist, 58- Bus & Prof Pos: Cashier, First Nat Bank, Hope, Ark, 24-38, pres, 38-65, chmn bd, 65-; dir, Ark-La Gas Co, Shreveport, La, 56- Mil Serv: Seaman 2/C, Navy, 18; Lt Comdr (Ret), Naval Res. Mem: Mason; Red River Valley Asn; Am Legion; Ark Farm Bur. Relig: Methodist. Legal Res: 401 S Spruce St Hope AR 71801 Mailing Add: c/o First Nat Bank Hope AR 71801

SPENCER, HARRY A (R)
Assoc Justice, Supreme Court of Nebr
b Bishops Walton, Eng, Sept 16, 03; s Richard Spencer & Mary Ellen Richardson S; m 1925 to Leone Eggenberg; c Pagean (Mrs Hugh Carter), Harry A, Jr, Marlene D (Mrs Kenneth Mansfield), Leone (Mrs Neal Harlan), Terry L & Victor R. Educ: Univ Nebr, AB, 29, Law Sch, LLB cum laude, 30, JD, 68; Order of the Coif; Acacia; Delta Theta Phi. Polit & Govt Pos: Deleg, Rep Nat Conv, 36 & 40; Co Judge, Lancaster Co, Nebr, 45-52, Dist Judge, 52-61; Assoc Justice, Supreme Court of Nebr, 61- Mem: Lindoln & Nebr State Bar Asns; Am Bar Asn (resolutions comt, adv comt, fair trial & free press, exec comt & chmn, Appellate Judge's Conf, Sect Judicial Admin, exec comt & coun, Sect, House of Deleg, 72-); Lincoln Traffic Comn (chmn); Lincoln Coun Churches (pres). Honors & Awards: Good Govt Award, Lincoln Jr CofC; Cross of Honor & Hon Legion Honor, DeMolay. Relig: Methodist. Legal Res: 1500 Crestview Dr Lincoln NE 68506 Mailing Add: State House Lincoln NE 68509

SPENCER, MARION WOOD (R)
Vt State Rep
b Perth Amboy, NJ, Jan 30, 16; d William Morrison Wood & Christina Jeffrey W; m 1940 to Herrick Barrett Spencer; c David Herrick, Joan Isabel, Thomas Jeffrey & John Barrett. Educ: Muhlenberg Hosp Sch Nursing, Plainfield, NJ, RN, 37. Polit & Govt Pos: Town health officer, Addison, 56-72; sch dir, 58-74; chmn supvry union, Addison Northwest Dist, 62-74; Vt Sch Dirs area chmn, Addison Co, 68-70; Vt State Rep, Addison Dist 1-2, 75-, clerk, House Educ Comt, currently. Mem: Vt Exten Homemakers; Farm Bur; Women's Rep Club (secy); Middlebury Woman's Club. Relig: Protestant. Legal Res: Addison VT Mailing Add: RD 1 Box 72 Vergennes VT 05491

SPENCER, RICHARD A (D)
Maine State Rep
Mailing Add: RFD 1 Sebago Lake Standish ME 04075

SPENCER, ROY L (R)
Mich State Rep
b Attica, Mich, Sept 10, 19; m 1942 to Irene Joan Nagy; c Linda, Richard, Darlene & Rodger. Polit & Govt Pos: Mich State Rep, 60-; twp clerk & supvr, Attica, Mich, formerly; Lapeer Co Rep Comt, formerly. Bus & Prof Pos: Poultry farmer. Mil Serv: Capt, Army, 41-46; serv in 104th Inf Div, 413th Inf Regt, Ger, France, Belgium & Holland. Mem: F&AM; Eastern Star; Mason. Relig: Methodist. Mailing Add: 3355 Newark Rd Attica MI 48412

SPENCER, WARREN H (R)
Pa State Rep
b Wellsboro, Pa, Aug 22, 21; s Stacey S Spencer & Mildred Emberger S; m to Julia Thomas;

c one. Educ: Dickinson Col, AB; Dickinson Sch of Law, LLB; Phi Delta Theta; Omicron Delta Kappa. Polit & Govt Pos: Pa State Rep, 62- Bus & Prof Pos: Attorney. Mil Serv: Sgt, 502nd Parachute Inf, 101st Airborne Div, 41-45. Mem: Superior & Supreme Courts of Pa; Tioga Co Bar Asn; Am Legion. Legal Res: 54 Walnut St Wellsboro PA 16901 Mailing Add: Capitol Bldg Harrisburg PA 17120

SPERLINE, ELNORA ELIZABETH **(R)**
Mem Exec Bd, Rep State Cent Comt Calif
b La Mesa, Tex; d Horace Homer Van Meter & Hazel Starr V; div; c Donald Arthur, Jean Marie, Victoria Elizabeth & Marcella Kathleen. Educ: Cerritos Col, Calif, 62-65. Polit & Govt Pos: Hq worker, Nixon for President, 60 & 68; precinct chmn, Clawson for Cong, 63, Goldwater for President, 64 & Reagan for Gov, 66; city chmn, Los Angeles City Sch Bd, 69; cand, Calif State Senate, 30th Dist, 70; gen city chmn, Reagan-Reinecke Region 11, 70; mem exec bd, Rep State Cent Comt Calif, 70-; secy, Calif State Young Rep, 71, nat committeewoman, 71-72, chmn, 72-75; assoc mem, Huntington Park Rep Women's Club; mem, Downey Federated Rep Women's Club, 72-; alt mem & chmn youth comt, Los Angeles Co Rep Cent Comt, 72; mem steering comt, President Richard M Nixon, Calif, 71-72; deleg, Rep Nat Conv, 72; mem, Electoral Col, Calif, 72; mem adv coun, Off Minority Bus Enterprise, Calif, 73- Bus & Prof Pos: Migrant worker, 47-50; glass packer, Maywood Glass Co, 50-52; bookkeeper, Bank of Am, 52; mem exec staff, Given Mfg Co, 53; off mgr, Rory Elec, 56-60 & 63-65; jr acct, Universal Essco Eng Co, 60-61; free-lance model, 61-63; co-owner, Ammen Co, 64-65; treas, Coast & Sperline, Inc, 66-73; timber & cattle ranch owner, 67-73; spec consult, Off Econ Opportunity, Ariz, 69-70; alfalfa & cattle ranch owner, 70-73; vpres, Rainbow Color Studios, Inc, 72-73; pres, Int Prod Mgt, 72-73. Mem: Bus & Prof Women's Club Federated. Honors & Awards: First pl in Americanism, Gen Federated Women's Clubs, Calif, 68, first pl in youth work, 69. Relig: Baptist. Mailing Add: Suite 440 1400 N Harbor Blvd Fullerton CA 92635

SPERLING, JACK IRVING **(R)**
Alderman, Chicago, Ill
b New York, NY, June 1, 11; s Louis Sperling & Dora Fialkoff S; m 1935 to Dorothy Weiss; c Judith (Mrs Filler), Suzanne (Mrs Schiller) & Robert. Educ: Crane Jr Col, 2 years; DePaul Univ Sch Law, 1 year; Chicago-Kent Col Law, LLB. Polit & Govt Pos: Alderman, 50th Ward, Chicago, Ill, 55-; deleg, Rep Nat Conv, 68; app by Supreme Court as Judge, Circuit Court of Cook Co, 73-74. Bus & Prof Pos: Practice of law, 33- Mil Serv: Entered as Lt(jg), Naval Res, 43, released as Lt(sg), 46, after serv in Pac & European Theatres; Lt Comdr, Navy Res (Ret); Combat Star; Mediter-Pac Theatre Ribbon. Mem: Chicago, Am & Ill Bar Asns; B'nai B'rith; Am Legion. Relig: Hebrew. Legal Res: 3150 Lake Shore Dr Chicago IL 60657 Mailing Add: 33 N Dearborn Chicago IL 60602

SPEROS, JAMES MANDAMADIOTIS **(D)**
b Pittsburgh, Pa, Sept 22, 52; s Dimitrios Mandamadiotis Speros & Marinel Boyd Calhoun S; m 1973 to Janet Elaine Woodworth. Educ: Boston Univ, BS in Jour, 74. Polit & Govt Pos: Alt deleg, Dem Nat Conv, 72. Bus & Prof Pos: Polit affairs reporter, The Telegraph, Painesville, Ohio, 74- Mem: Sigma Delta Chi; Lake Co Hist Soc; Holden Arboretum. Mailing Add: 140 Normandy Dr Painesville OH 44077

SPICOLA, GUY WILLIAM **(D)**
Fla State Sen
b Tampa, Fla, Feb 27, 38; s Joseph G Spicola & Alma Norona S; m to Georgia Blevins; c Brandy, Betsy & Courtney. Educ: Univ Fla, BA, 60, LLB, 62; Phi Delta Phi; Alpha Tau Omega; Circle K, Pre-Law Club. Polit & Govt Pos: Attorney, Finance & Taxation Comts, Fla State House of Rep, 63; city prosecutor, Temple Terrace, 63-66; Fla State Rep, 67-74, Majority Whip, 69 & 70 sessions, Fla House Rep; notary pub; alt deleg, Dem Nat Conv, 68; Fla State Sen, 74- Bus & Prof Pos: Attorney-at-law. Mem: CofC; Jr CofC; Big Bros; Fla Audubon Soc; Fla Sierra Club; Save Our Boys; Hillsborough Co Environ Coalition; Nat Wildlife Fedn. Honors & Awards: Fla Outstanding Conservationist, Fla Audubon Soc, 71; Outstanding Serv to Community, WDAE Radio, 71; Distinguished Serv to Educ Award, Phi Delta Kappa, 72; Friend of Educ Award, Hillsborough Co Classroom Teachers Asn, 73; Outstanding Environmentalist, Fla Sierra Club, 74. Relig: Catholic. Legal Res: 725 E Kennedy Blvd Tampa FL 33602 Mailing Add: 244 Senate Off Bldg Tallahassee FL 32304

SPIEGEL, ALBERT A **(R)**
Mem Exec Comt, Rep State Cent Comt Calif
b McKeesport, Pa, Mar 9, 16; s Joseph Spiegel & Grace Breyer S; m 1944 to Bernice Lerner; c Carolyn (Mrs Tisherman), Mark A, David A & Paul A. Educ: Univ Pittsburgh, BA, 37; Harvard Law Sch, JD, 40. Polit & Govt Pos: Deleg, Rep Nat Conv, 72; mem exec comt, Rep State Cent Comt Calif, currently. Bus & Prof Pos: Secy & mem bd, Beaumont Meadows, Inc, currently. Mil Serv: Entered as Pvt, Army, 42, released as Capt, after serv in Anti-aircraft, Artillery, 42-44. Mem: State Bar of Calif; Nat Campaign Cabinet, United Jewish Appeal; Am Jewish Joint Distribution Comt (bd); B'nai B'rith Hillel Comn; Jewish Publ Soc Am (trustee). Relig: Jewish; Past pres, Beth Sholom Temple, Santa Monica. Legal Res: 807 N Elm Dr Beverly Hills CA 90210 Mailing Add: 641 N Sepulveda Blvd Los Angeles CA 90049

SPIERS, RONALD IAN
US Minister to London
b Orange, NJ, July 9, 25; s Tomas Hoskins Spiers & Blanca De Ponthier S; m 1949 to Patience Baker; c Deborah (Mrs Stephen May), Peter, Martha & Sarah. Educ: Dartmouth Col, BA, 48; Princeton Univ, MPA, 50. Polit & Govt Pos: Officer-in-charge disarmament affairs, Dept of State, 57-61; dir, Off NATO & European Polit Mil Affairs, 62-66; counr foreign polit affairs, US Embassy, London, 66-69; Dep Asst Secy of State, 69; dir bur polit-mil affairs, Dept of State, 69-73; US Ambassador to Bahamas, 73-74; US Minister to London, 74- Mil Serv: Entered as A/S, Navy, 43, released as Lt(jg), 46, after serv in Pac Fleet, 44-46. Mem: Int Inst Strategic Studies; Coun Foreign Rels; Am Foreign Serv Asn. Honors & Awards: Woodrow Wilson fel, Princeton Univ, 48. Relig: Protestant. Legal Res: South Londonderry VT 05155 Mailing Add: London US Dept of State Washington DC 20521

SPIES, JOHN FLAVAN **(R)**
b Estherville, Iowa, Apr 26, 31; s Charles Jacob Spies & Isabel Flavin S; m 1956 to Jeanine Margaret Freemon; c John Alan, Jean Marie, David Charles & Charles Freemon. Educ: Iowa State Univ, BSC, 54. Polit & Govt Pos: Chmn, Palo Alto Co Rep Cent Comt, Iowa, 72-75. Bus & Prof Pos: Pres, Iowa Trust & Savings Bank, Emmetsburg, 63- Mem: KofC. Relig: Roman Catholic. Legal Res: 401 State St Emmetsburg IA 50536 Mailing Add: Box 159 Emmetsburg IA 50536

SPINGARN, STEPHEN J **(D)**
b Bedford, NY, Sept 1, 08; s J E Spingarn & Amy Judith S; single. Educ: Yale Univ; Univ Grenoble, France; Rollins Col; Stanford Univ; Univ Ariz, AB, 30 & LLB, 34; vpres law sch student body; managing ed, Univ Humor Mag; pres lit soc; vjustice, Phi Alpha Delta. Polit & Govt Pos: Attorney & spec asst to gen counsel, Treas Dept, 34-42; spec asst to attorney gen, 37-38; mem working comt, Truman Loyalty Prog, 46-47; asst gen counsel & legis counsel, Treas Dept, dep dir contract settlement, legal counsel secret serv & coordr treas enforcement agencies, legal mem, Treas Loyalty Bd, 46-49; Treas rep, Int Conf, Lima, Peru, 47; admin asst to President, 49-50; vchmn, White House Loyalty Bd, 50; comnr & frequently acting chmn, Fed Trade Comn, 50-53; nat dir, Spec Activities for VPres Campaign, 56; mem, Small Bus Adv Comt, Dem Nat Comt, 56-57. Bus & Prof Pos: Attorney, self-employed. Mil Serv: Entered as Capt, Army, 42, released as Lt Col, 46, after serv in Counter-Intel Corps, Mediter Theater & ETO; Combat Legion of Merit; Bronze Star Medal with Valor Emblem; Invasion Arrowhead & 5 Battle Stars. Publ: Articles on counter-espionage, law & other subjects. Mem: Ariz State, DC & US Supreme Court Bars; Nat Capital Dem Club; Nat Press Club. Mailing Add: 2500 Q St NW Washington DC 20007

SPINKS, FORD BELMONT **(D)**
Mem, Ga State Dem Exec Comt
b Tifton, Ga, Apr 5, 27; s Durward Belmont Spinks & Jewel Lillybelle Ford S; m 1950 to Ruby Lee Pritchard; c Monty, Suzanne & Michael. Educ: Norman Col, Ga, grad; Abraham Baldwin Agr Col, Tifton. Polit & Govt Pos: Ga State Sen, 63-71; mem, Ga State Dem Exec Comt, currently; comnr, Ga Pub Serv Comn, 71- Bus & Prof Pos: Pres, Tifton Tractor Co; chmn bd, Dealers Equip Credit Corp; dir, The Bank of Tifton, Ga. Mil Serv: Entered as Pvt, Army, 45, released as S/Sgt, 47, after serv in 10th Constabulary, Ger; Victory & Good Conduct Medals. Mem: CofC (dir); Surge Govt Comt (chmn); Coastal Plain Area Tourism Coun (chmn); Gridiron Secret Soc, Univ Ga. Honors & Awards: Outstanding Serv Award, Tift Co Bd Comnr; Achievement Award for Outstanding Pub Serv, Colquitt Co Jaycees; Recognition for contributions to preservation of hist sites & artifacts, Ga Hist Comn. Relig: Baptist. Legal Res: Rte 6 Tifton GA 31794 Mailing Add: Box 786 Tifton GA 31794

SPIROU, CHRIS **(D)**
NH State Rep
Mailing Add: 129 Spruce St Manchester NH 03103

SPIVAK, ALVIN A **(D)**
b Philadelphia, Pa, Nov 30, 27; s Herman Spivak & Bella Haimovitz S; m 1965 to Martha Barry; c Denise. Educ: Temple Univ, BS, 49. Polit & Govt Pos: Dir info, Nat Adv Comn on Civil Disorders, formerly; dir pub info, United Dem for Humphrey, 68; dir pub affairs, Dem Nat Comt, 68-70. Bus & Prof Pos: With Int News Serv, 49-58, Senate reporter & mem gen staff, Washington, 51-58; with United Press Int Serv, 58-68, White House reporter, 60-68; Wash dir pub rels, Gen Dynamics Corp, 70- Mil Serv: Army Air Force, 46-47. Mem: Sigma Delta Chi; Beta Gamma Sigma; Nat Press & Fed City Clubs, Washington Legal Res: 9201 Fernwood Rd Bethesda MD 20034 Mailing Add: Suite 800 1025 Connecticut Ave NW Washington DC 20036

SPIVEY, DEBORAH KOHLER **(R)**
Co-Dir Region IV, Young Rep Nat Fedn
b New York, NY, Sept 29, 48; d Peter Bogart Kohler & Mavis Vanderpool K; m 1970 to Hubert Michael Spivey. Educ: Univ Tenn, Knoxville, BS in Commun, 70; Sigma Delta Chi. Polit & Govt Pos: Nat Committeewoman, SC Young Rep, 71-73; co-dir, Region IV, Young Rep Nat Fedn, 73- Bus & Prof Pos: Journalist, The State, Columbia, SC, 70- Relig: Baptist. Mailing Add: Apt 4 401 Bryon Rd Columbia SC 29209

SPIVEY, HUBERT MICHAEL **(R)**
Chmn, Greenville Co Rep Party, SC
b Augusta, Ga, June 21, 48; s Hubert T Spivey & Odeal Singletary S; m 1970 to Deborah Kohler. Educ: Wofford Col, AB, 70; Univ SC Sch Law, JD, 73. Polit & Govt Pos: Vchmn, SC TAR, 65-66; co-chmn, SC Col Rep, 69-70; deleg, Nat Young Rep Conv, 71 & 73; mem steering comt, SC Rep Party, 71-72; chmn, SC Young Rep, 71-74; treas, Region Four, Young Rep Nat Fedn, 71-73; mem steering comt, SC Comt to Reelect the President, 72; alt deleg, Rep Nat Conv, 72; research asst, SC House Rep, 72-73; chmn, Greenville Co Rep Party, 74- Bus & Prof Pos: Legal clerk, Powell & Smith, Attorneys, 72-73; assoc, Younts, Reese & Cofield, Attorneys, Greenville, SC, currently. Mil Serv: 2nd Lt, ROTC, Army, 70, 1st Lt, 73- Publ: Asst ed, Gavel Raps, Univ SC Sch Law, currently. Mem: Pi Gamma Mu; Phi Alpha Delta; Student Bar Asn; Am Bar Asn. Relig: Methodist. Mailing Add: Apt 16 Mauldin Manor Mauldin SC 29662

SPIZZIRI, JOHN A **(R)**
NJ State Assemblyman
b Paterson, NJ, Sept 2, 34; s Louis G Spizziri & Lulu Ianacone S; m 1972 to Alexandra Vitale; c John, Jr, Victoria Jean & Miriam. Educ: Georgetown Univ, BS, 57, LLD, 60. Polit & Govt Pos: Mem & past pres, Wyckoff Rep League, NJ, 61-; mem & past pres, Bergen Co Men's Rep Club, 66-; mem & mayor, Wyckoff Twp Comt, 67-72; asst co counsel, Bergen Co Counsel, 70-71; mem, Bergen Co Young Rep Club, 71-; NJ State Assemblyman, 71- Mem: Lions; hon mem Patrolmans Benevolent Asn; hon mem Wyckoff Vol Ambulance Corps; Am Bar Asn; Lawyers Club of Bergen Co (past pres). Relig: Roman Catholic. Legal Res: 351 Crescent Dr Franklin Lakes NJ 07417 Mailing Add: 350 Franklin Ave Wyckoff NJ 07481

SPLAIN, MAURICE D, JR **(D)**
b Oil City, Pa; s Maurice Splain, Sr & Mary Lawler S; m 1946 to Teresa Eileen Billigen. Polit & Govt Pos: Exec asst to US Sen Francis J Myers, Pa, formerly; chmn, Dem Party, Pa, 49-54. Mem: Eagles (int pres, 55-56). Mailing Add: 1928 Spring Valley Rd Pittsburgh PA 15243

SPLAINE, JAMES RAYMOND **(D)**
NH State Rep
b Portsmouth, NH, Aug 7, 47; s John E Splaine, Sr & Althea Duval S; single. Educ: Univ NH, 66-71; Student Senate. Polit & Govt Pos: Pres, Portsmouth Young Dem, NH, 67-68, mem exec comt, 68-69; mem exec comt, Univ NH Young Dem, 68-69; mem exec comt, NH Young Dem, 68-69, pres, 69-73; vchmn, NH Dem State Comt, 71-73, mem, currently; NH State Rep, Ward Five, Portsmouth, 69-71, Ward Two, 73-; mem, Portsmouth City Coun, 70-71 & 74- Bus & Prof Pos: Teacher, Great Bay Sch & Training Ctr for Phys & Ment Retarded, Newington, NH. Mem: Portsmouth & NH Young Dem. Mailing Add: 83 Willard Ave Portsmouth NH 03801

SPOCK, BENJAMIN (PEOPLE'S PARTY)
b New Haven, Conn, May 2, 03; s Benjamin Ives Spock & Mildred Louise Stoughton S; m 1927 to Jane Davenport Cheney; c Michael & John Cheney. Educ: Yale Univ, BA, 25, Med Sch, 25-27; Col Physicians & Surgeons, Columbia Univ, MD, 29. Polit & Govt Pos: Co-chmn, Nat Comt for Sane Nuclear Policy, 64-67; co-chmn, Nat Conf New Polit, 67-68; co-chmn, New Party, 70-72; Presidential cand of People's Party, 72. Bus & Prof Pos: Instr pediatrics, Cornell Med Col, 33-47, Inst on Personality Develop, 38-47; assoc prof psychiat, Mayo Found, Univ Minn & consult psychiat, Mayo Clin, 47-51; prof child develop, Univ Pittsburgh, 51-55; prof child develop, Western Reserve Univ, 55-67. Mil Serv: Lt Comdr, Naval Res, Med Corps, 44-46. Publ: Baby & Child Care, 46; Problems of Parents, 62 (Family Life Book Award, 63); Decent & Indecent, 70; plus others. Legal Res: Home Port Marina St Thomas VI Mailing Add: 538 Madison Ave New York NY 10022

SPODEK, JULES L (D)
b New York, NY, June 5, 28; s Dave M Spodek & Esther Lebenbaum S; m 1954 to Hortense E Wolfson; c Ellen & Susan. Educ: Brooklyn Col, BA, 50; NY Univ Sch Law, LLB, 52; Van Ardsdale House. Polit & Govt Pos: Alt deleg, Dem Nat Conv, 68, deleg, 72; committeeman, Kings Co Dem Comt, NY, 68-74; deleg, Judicial Conv, Kings Co, NY, 69-74; judge, Civil Court, New York, 75- Bus & Prof Pos: Partner, Schoen & Spodek, 55-74. Mil Serv: Entered as Pvt, Marines, 52, released as Pvt, 52. Mem: Brandeis Assoc; Brooklyn Bar Asn; Alumni Asn Brooklyn Col (dir); Midwood Lodge B'nai B'rith; New York City Bd of Judges. Relig: Jewish. Mailing Add: 1282 E 26th St Brooklyn NY 11210

SPOLTORE, JOHN J (R)
Polit & Govt Pos: Chmn, NJ State Rep Cent Comt, formerly. Mailing Add: 405 Trenton Trust Bldg Trenton NJ 08608

SPONBERG, RAYMOND LINDELL (R)
Finance Chmn, Garvin Co Rep Party, Okla
b Manor, Tex, Oct 28, 20; s Charles William Sponberg & Freda Lindell S; m 1947 to Catherine Ann Brassel; c Deborah Catherine & Phyllis Catherine. Educ: Univ Tex, Austin, BS in Mech Eng, 42; Pi Tau Sigma; Tau Beta Pi; Phi Kappa Tau. Polit & Govt Pos: Finance chmn, Garvin Co Rep Party, Okla, 67- Bus & Prof Pos: Field engr, Texas Co, Salem, Ill, 46-48; prod engr, Sohio Petroleum Co, Edmond, Okla, 48-51, dist engr, Russell, Kans, 51-56, sr engr, Oklahoma City, Okla, 56-58 & prod foreman, Pauls Valley, 58- Mil Serv: Entered as Ens, Navy, 42, released as Lt, 46, after serv in Naval Aviation, Pac Theatre & Jacksonville, Fla, 43-45. Mem: Golden Trend Chap, Am Petroleum Inst. Relig: Catholic. Mailing Add: 605 S Paul Pauls Valley OK 73075

SPONG, WILLIAM BELSER, JR (D)
b Portsmouth, Va, Sept 29, 20; m to Virginia Galliford. Educ: Hampden-Sydney Col; Univ Va, LLB, 47; Univ Edinburgh, Scotland; Pi Kappa Alpha; Omicron Delta Kappa. Polit & Govt Pos: Va State Deleg, 54-55; Va State Sen, 56-66; chmn, Va Comn on Pub Educ, 58-62; US Sen, Va, 66-72; deleg, Dem Nat Conv, 68. Bus & Prof Pos: Lawyer; lectr law & govt, Col William & Mary, 48-49; guest scholar, Woodrow Wilson Int Ctr for Scholars, 73- Mil Serv: Army Air Force, 42-45. Mem: Va State Bar Asn; Hampden-Sydney Col (trustee). Relig: Methodist. Mailing Add: 316 North St Portsmouth VA 23704

SPONHEIMER, JOHN P (D)
Conn State Rep
Mailing Add: 28 Harold Ave Derby CT 06418

SPONSLER, EARL L (D)
Mo State Rep
b Texas City, Mo, Apr 13, 13; m 1934 to Lois Flowers; c Dale Lloyd & Vivian Earlene. Educ: Southwestern Mo State Col. Polit & Govt Pos: Chmn, Dem Co Comt, Mo, 6 years; Mo State Rep, 60- Bus & Prof Pos: Teacher, formerly; dairy & livestock farmer, currently. Relig: Protestant; chmn bd of trustees, Bado Community Church. Mailing Add: RFD 2 Cabool MO 65689

SPRADLIN, MARY JO (D)
Chmn, Potter Co Dem Party, Tex
b Maysville, Okla, Feb 27, 18; d Joseph Leon Jacks & Zelma Hope J; m 1948 to Henry Raymond Spradlin; c Richard Kenneth Kembel & Sandra Kaye. Educ: High sch, grad, 35. Polit & Govt Pos: Chmn, League Dem Women, Amarillo, Tex, 62-64; precinct chmn, Potter Co Dem Party, 63-74, co chmn, 74-; assoc mem, Tex State Dem Exec Comt, currently; mem, Gov Adv Comt on Aging, 70-; bd mem, Potter-Randall Co Dem Women's Club, 70-75. Mem: Nat Asn Letter Carriers Auxiliary; Nat Asn Rural Carriers Auxiliary. Relig: Baptist. Mailing Add: 702 S Florida St Amarillo TX 79106

SPRADLING, ALBERT M, JR (D)
Mo State Sen
b Cape Girardeau, Mo, Mar 13, 20; s A M Spradling; m 1943 to Margaret Whyman; c Albert M, II & Robert Whyman. Educ: Southeast Mo State Col; Univ Mo, LLB. Polit & Govt Pos: City attorney, Cape Girardeau, Mo, 48-52; first chmn, Mo Atomic Energy Comn, 59; vchmn, Coun State Govt, former chmn bd; Mo State Sen, 52-, pres pro tem, Mo State Sen, 71 & 72 Gen Assemblies. Bus & Prof Pos: Lawyer, Spradling & Spradling, 42; spec agt, Fed Bur Invest, 42-45; lawyer, Spradling & Bradshaw, currently; pres, Town Plaza Shopping Ctr, Inc, currently; chmn bd, Farmers & Merchants Bank, currently. Mem: AF&AM; RAM; RSM; KT. Honors & Awards: St Louis Globe-Dem Award as mem of legis showing greatest growth in leadership, 57-58; Award as second most valuable mem of the legis, 59-60. Relig: Baptist. Mailing Add: 225 Keller Ave Cape Girardeau MO 63701

SPRAGENS, THOMAS ARTHUR (D)
Committeeman, Doyle Co Dem Party, Ky
b Lebanon, Ky, Apr 25, 17; s William Henry Spragens & Lillian Brewer S; m 1941 to Catharine Smallwood; c Thomas Arthur, Jr, Barbara Allen & David William. Educ: Univ Ky, AB, 38; Syracuse Univ, 39-40. Hon Degrees: LLD, Univ Ky & Westminster Col; LittD, Univ Ala. Polit & Govt Pos: Admin analyst, US Bur Budget, Washington, DC, 40-41, sr analyst, 42-45; admin asst to comnr, Ky Dept Revenue, 41-42; asst chief food allocation, Foreign Econ Admin, Washington, DC, 45; deleg, Dem Nat Conv, 68; committeeman, Boyle Co Dem Party, Ky, 69- Bus & Prof Pos: Asst to pres, Stanford Univ, 45-51; secy & treas, fund for advan educ, Ford Found, 51-52; pres, Stephens Col, 53-57; pres, Centre Col, 57- Mem: Am Coun Educ (dir); Southern Asn Cols & Schs (comn cols); Southern Univ Conf (dir); Ky Independent Col Found (dir); Am Asn Cols (chmn col finance & legis). Relig: Presbyterian; bd dirs, Bd Christian Educ. Mailing Add: 763 W Main St Danville KY 40422

SPRAGUE, BYRON DAVID (D)
Colo State Rep
b Ovid, Colo, Sept 10, 43; s Billie Byron Sprague & Ida Presba S; m 1961 to Nancy Lucille Wood; c Todd & Brian. Educ: Univ Colo, 65; Colo State Univ, 66. Polit & Govt Pos: Colo State Rep, 75-, vchmn, Agr, Livestock & Natural Resources Comt, Colo House Rep, 75-, mem, appropriations comt, state affairs comt & sub-comt on rural develop, 75- Mem: Rocky Mountain Farmers Union. Mailing Add: Rte 1 Box 21 Holyoke CO 80734

SPRAGUE, GEORGE R (R)
Mass State Rep
Mailing Add: State Capitol Boston MA 02133

SPRAGUE, HARRY ASA (R)
Kans State Rep
b Hiawatha, Kans, Oct 11, 06; s Asa Benjamin Sprague & Edith L Forward S; m 1931 to Viola Bell; c Harry Asa, Jr (deceased) & Dale Moulton. Educ: Kans Univ, BSChE; Sigma Tau; Alpha Chi Sigma. Polit & Govt Pos: Kans State Rep, 74th Dist, 69- Bus & Prof Pos: Chem engr, Derby Oil & Refining Co, 31-33; owner-mgr, Sprague Oil Service, 33-58; oil producer & farming interests, 58-; dir, Peoples State Bank, 69- Mem: Rotary. Relig: Methodist. Legal Res: 1330 N Walnut St McPherson KS 67460 Mailing Add: PO Box 348 McPherson KS 67460

SPRAGUE, IRVINE H (D)
b San Francisco, Calif, July 4, 21; s Irvine Henry Sprague & Claire Kelly S; m 1940 to Margie Craw; c Michael, Terry & Kristine. Educ: Col of the Pac, BA, 47; Ind Univ; George Washington Univ; Harvard Bus Sch, advan mgt prog. Polit & Govt Pos: Admin asst to US Rep McFall, 57-63; dep dir of finance, Calif, assigned as Washington Rep for Gov Edmund G Brown, Calif, 63-66; mem, San Joaquin Co Cent Comt; deleg, Dem Nat Conv, 64; White House Staff, Aide to President Johnson for Cong Rels, 67-68; dir, Fed Deposit Ins Corp, 69-72; principle staff asst, Majority Whip, US House Rep, 73- Mil Serv: Entered as Pvt, Army, 43, released as 1st Lt, 46, after serv in Rifle Inf Platoon, 41st Inf Div, Southern Philippines; 2 Bronze Stars; Purple Heart; Combat Infantryman's Badge; Lt Col, Army Res, currently. Relig: Catholic. Legal Res: Stockton CA Mailing Add: 7514 Wellesley Dr College Park MD 20740

SPRAGUE, MICHAEL JAMES (D)
Md State Deleg
b Indian Head, Md, Oct 11, 40; s John Lindsay Sprague & Matilda Wood S; m 1963 to Mary Karen Comstock; c Mary Kristen & Michael James, Jr. Educ: Charles Co Community Col, AA, 63; Appalachian State Teachers Col, BS, 65. Polit & Govt Pos: Co comnr, Charles Co, Md, 70-74; Md State Deleg, Charles & St Mary's Co, 75- Bus & Prof Pos: Ins agt, State Farm, Md, 66- Mil Serv: Pvt Army, 59. Mem: Lions (bd dirs); Jaycees (state dir); Optimists; Moose. Relig: Catholic. Mailing Add: 7 Woodsome Dr Port Tobacco MD 20677

SPRAY, ELWIN L (R)
State Chmn, Hawaii Young Rep
b Greensburg, Pa, Mar 25, 48; s Wayne Murray Spray & Elizabeth Buttermore S; m 1972 to Ivy Mariye Hayashi. Educ: Allegheny Col; Univ Hawaii; Arnold Air Soc; pres, Sr Class. Polit & Govt Pos: Mem, Col Rep Nat Comt, Hawaii, 69-71; dist coordr, Voter Registr, State of Hawaii, 70; mem nat comt, Young Rep Nat Fedn, formerly; employee, Hawaii Finance Comt for Reelec of the President, 72; alt deleg, Rep Nat Conv, 72; state chmn, Hawaii Young Rep, currently; admin asst, State Sen Eureka Forbes, 74; chmn, 13th Dist, Hawaii Rep Party, 75- Publ: Correspondent for the Ripon Forum, 72 & 73. Mem: Manoa Valley Community Asn (pres, 73-75); Ripon Soc; Common Cause. Honors & Awards: Gold Hardcharger, Young Rep Nat Fedn, 71. Relig: United Methodist. Mailing Add: 1557-A Kewalo St Honolulu HI 96822

SPRINGER, CHARLES EDWARD (D)
b Reno, Nev, Feb 20, 28; s Edward Springer & Rose Mary Kelley S; m 1951 to Jacqueline Dora Sirkegian; c Kelli Ann. Educ: Univ Nev, BA, 50 & 70-71; Georgetown Univ Law Ctr, LLB, 53; Phi Delta Phi. Polit & Govt Pos: Deleg chmn, Washoe Co Dem Cent Comt, Nev, 60; vchmn, Nev Dem State Cent Comt, 60-61 & 64-65, chmn, 61-64; Dem Nat Committeeman, 64; Attorney Gen, Nev, 62-63; exec committeeman, Western State Dem Conv, 63-64; Independent nominee for Gov of Nev, 70. Bus & Prof Pos: Legis legal adv to Gov, Nev, 59-65; mem, Nat Small Bus Adv Coun, 62-; mem, Prospectors, 62-; chmn, State Apprenticeship Coun, 64-66; mem bd dirs, Nev Art Gallery, 70- Mil Serv: Entered as Pvt, Army, 45, released as 2nd Lt, 51, after serv in 11th Airborne Div, Japan. Mem: Int Acad Law & Sci; Elks; VFW; Am Legion; Am Cancer Soc. Honors & Awards: Outstanding Young Dem in the US Award, Nat Young Dem Conv, 65. Relig: Catholic. Mailing Add: 1001 Dartmouth Dr Reno NV 89502

SPRINGER, ERCHAL JOHN (DFL)
Chmn, Lincoln Co Dem-Farmer-Labor Party, Minn
b Judith Gap, Mont, May 22, 17; s John Springer & Mary Herchowski S; m 1941 to Eldora Stringer; c Jo Ann (Mrs Adrain Lanners), Sharon (Mrs Richard De'Pestal), Marylou (Mrs James Skorczewski) & Erchal Eldo. Educ: Mankato State Teachers Col. Polit & Govt Pos: Chmn, Lincoln Co Dem-Farmer-Labor Party, Minn, 50-, twp assessor, 50-57, comnr, 58-62. Mem: Agr Soil Conserv Twp (committeeman); Farm Union; KofC; Holy Name Soc. Relig: Catholic. Mailing Add: Porter MN 56280

SPRINGER, WILLIAM LEE (R)
Comnr, Fed Power Comn
b Sullivan, Ind, Apr 12, 09; s Otha L Springer & Daisy Ellen Tucker S; m 1940 to Elsie Mattis; c Katherine Curtis, Ann Tucker & Georgia Mattis. Educ: DePauw Univ, AB, 31; Univ Ill Sch Law, LLB, 35; Phi Delta Theta; Phi Delta Phi. Hon Degrees: LLD, Millikin Univ, 53, Lincoln Col, 66 & DePauw Univ, 72. Polit & Govt Pos: State's attorney, Ill, 40-42; Judge, Champaign Co, 46-50; US Rep, Ill, 51-72; deleg, several int conf on space commun, trade & com; vchmn, Rep Cong Campaign Comt, currently; comnr, Fed Power Comn, 73- Relig: Presbyterian. Legal Res: 900 W Park Ave Champaign IL 61820 Mailing Add: Fed Power Comn 441 G St Washington DC 20426

SPRINKEL, WARREN REED (R)
Mem, Rep State Cent Comt Calif
b Los Angeles, Calif, June 30, 22; s Walter Reed Sprinkel & Florence Werdin S; m 1948 to Edna Louise Boyle, separated; c Steven, Annette & Susan. Educ: Univ Southern Calif, BS in Bus Admin, 46; Kappa Alpha; Blue Key; Alpha Kappa Psi; Skull & Dagger. Polit & Govt

Pos: Mem, President's Adv Comt Int Trade, Dept Com, 58-60; chmn, San Bernardino Co, Richard Nixon for President, 60; mem & finance chmn, San Bernardino Co Rep Cent Comt, 60-; mem, Rep State Cent Comt Calif, 64-; chmn, San Bernardino Co Ronald Reagan for Gov, 66 & 70; app mem, Contractors' State License Bd, 67-, chmn, 69-; deleg, Rep Nat Conv, 68 & 72. Bus & Prof Pos: Pres, Fontana Paving, Inc, 56-; dir & officer, Vernon Asphalt Constructors, Los Angeles, Calif, 66- Mil Serv: Entered as Air Cadet, Air Force, 43, released as Maj, 52, after serv in 484th Bomb Group, 15th Air Force, ETO, 44-45; Recalled, 51-52, serv in Fifth Air Force, Korea; Distinguished Flying Cross; Air Medal with 6 Oak Leaf Clusters; Presidential Unit Citation. Mem: Am Rd Builders Asn; Nat Asphalt Pavement Asn; Eng Grading Contractors Asn (vpres, Heavy Eng Chap, 73-); State Eng Grading Contractors Asn (vpres, 73-74, pres, 74-75); Fontana Rotary Club. Honors & Awards: Named Contractor of the Year, Eng Grading Contractors Asn, 69-70. Relig: Presbyterian. Legal Res: 2900 Park Newport 417 Newport Beach CA 92660 Mailing Add: PO Box 847 Fontana CA 92335

SPROWL, ARTHUR M (R)
Maine State Rep
Mailing Add: Hope ME 04847

SPURLOCK, JOE C, II (D)
Tex State Rep
b Ft Worth, Tex, Jan 29, 38; s Joe C Spurlock & Clarice V Stiles S; m 1963 to Linda M Rellahan; c Joe C, III & Allison E. Educ: Tex A&M Univ, BA Econ, 60; Univ Tex Sch Law, JD, 62; Delta Theta Phi. Polit & Govt Pos: Precinct chmn, Tarrant Co Dem Party, Tex, 69-70; Tex State Rep, 71- Bus & Prof Pos: Asst dist attorney, Tarrant Co, 67-70, attorney-at-law, 67- Mil Serv: Entered as 2nd Lt, Army, 63, released as Capt, 67, after serv in Alaska & Vietnam; Bronze Star; Vietnam Campaign Ribbon with two Stars; Republic of Vietnam Serv Ribbon; Nat Defense Serv Medal. Mem: Tex State Bar Asn; Am Legion; Elks; Optimist; Boy Scouts. Honors & Awards: Sons of Am Revolution Award; Vigil Award, Order of Arrow, God & Country Award & Wood Badge, Boy Scouts. Relig: Lutheran. Mailing Add: 4029 Diamond Loch W North Richland Hills TX 76118

SPURRIER, MARGARET NORVELL (R)
Rep Nat Committeewoman, Tenn
b Nashville, Tenn, Apr 7, 19; d Richard Norvell & Margaret Parker N; m 1940 to Keith McCauley Spurrier; c Lucia Parker Spurrier (Mrs William Lee Drier) & Irene LeJau (Mrs John Alan Pendergrast). Educ: Wellesley Col; Vanderbilt Univ; Kappa Alpha Theta; Chi Delta Phi; Mortar Bd. Polit & Govt Pos: Co-chmn, Shelby Co Rep Party, Tenn, 62-66; mem, Tenn State Rep Exec Comt, 66-70; Rep Nat Committeewoman, Tenn, currently; vchmn subcomt on prog planning & comt on arrangements, Rep Nat Conv, 72; co-chmn rule 29 comt, Rep Nat Comt; mem, Tenn Comn on Status of Women, 72- Mem: Nat Fedn Rep Women; Nat Cong Parents & Teachers; Memphis Jr League; Memphis Symphony League; Nat Soc Colonial Dames Am. Relig: Episcopal. Mailing Add: 89 Goodwyn Memphis TN 38111

SRODES, CECILE ZAUGG (R)
b Alexandria, Va, Nov 30, 42; d Wesley Zaugg & Harriet McClure Z; m 1969 to James Lewis Srodes. Educ: Duke Univ, BA, 64; Alpha Chi Omega. Polit & Govt Pos: Caseworker, legis asst & off mgr to US Rep James T Broyhill, NC, 67- Relig: Protestant. Mailing Add: 733 Tenth St SE Washington DC 20003

SRSTKA, WILLIAM JOSEPH, JR (R)
Secy-treas, SDak Rep Party
b Washington, DC, Sept 24, 42; s William J Srstka & Elvira Welter S; m 1969 to Carol Haan. Educ: Creighton Univ, 61-62; Univ SDak, Vermillion, BA, 65, Law Sch, JD, 68; Pi Sigma Alpha; Delta Theta Phi; Delta Tau Delta. Polit & Govt Pos: Pres, Univ SDak Young Rep, 64-75; Asst Attorney Gen, SDak, 70-72; mem exec comt, SDak Rep State Cent Comt, 73-75 & secy-treas, 75-; mem, State Elec Bd, SDak, 74- Mem: SDak Trial Lawyers Asn (exec secy, 72-); Am Trial Lawyers Asn; Elks; Am Bar Asn; SDak State Bar Asn (secy-treas, Young Lawyers Sect, 74-). Relig: Catholic. Mailing Add: 507 N Grand Pierre SD 57501

SRULL, DONALD W (INDEPENDENT)
Dep Asst Secy Defense Resource Anal
Polit & Govt Pos: Asst Secy Army Manpower & Res Affairs, until 73; Dep Asst Secy Defense Resource Anal, 73- Legal Res: VA Mailing Add: Dept of Defense Pentagon Washington DC 20301

STAATS, ELMER BOYD
Comptroller Gen of US
b Richfield, Kans, June 6, 14; s Wesley F Staats & Maude Goodall S; m 1940 to Margaret S Rich; c David Rich, Deborah Rich & Catharine Jane Rich. Educ: McPherson Col, BA, 35; Univ Kans, MA, 36; Univ Minn, PhD, 39; Phi Beta Kappa; Pi Sigma Alpha. Hon Degrees: LLD, McPherson Col, 66; DPS, George Washington Univ, 71; Dr Admin, Univ SDak, 73. Polit & Govt Pos: Research asst, Kans Legis Coun, 36; staff, Pub Admin Admin Serv, Chicago, Ill, 37-38; asst dir charge of legis reference, US Bur Budget, 47-49, exec asst dir, 49-50, dep dir, 50-53 & 58-66; exec officer, Opers Coord Bd, Nat Security Coun, 54-58; Comptroller Gen of US, 66- Bus & Prof Pos: Teaching asst, Univ Minn, 36-38; prof lectr pub admin, George Washington Univ, 44-49; research dir, Marshall Field & Co, 53; gen mgt planning coun, Am Mgt Asn, 69-; bd trustees, Am Univ & McPherson Col, 69-; bd gov, Int Orgn Supreme Audit Insts, 69-; bd adv & hon faculty, Indust Col of Armed Forces, 74-; vis comt, John F Kennedy Sch Govt, Harvard Univ, 74- Publ: Personnel Standards in the Social Security Program, 39; contrib, Am Econ Rev, Pub Personnel Rev & Am Polit Sci Rev. Mem: Nat Acad Pub Admin; Am Soc Pub Admin; Cosmos & Chevy Chase Clubs; Am Acad Polit & Social Sci (bd dir, 66-); Fed Govt Acct Asn. Honors & Awards: Rockefeller Pub Serv Award, 61; Alumni Achievement Award, Univ Minn, 64; Distinguished Serv Citation, Univ Kans, 66; Distinguished Serv Award, Univ Hartford Ctr Study Prof Acct, 73; Warner W Stockberger Achievement Award for 1972, 73. Relig: Methodist. Mailing Add: 5011 Overlook Rd NW Washington DC 20016

STABLER, W LAIRD, JR (R)
b 1930. Educ: Princeton Univ, BA, Univ Va Law Sch, LLB. Polit & Govt Pos: Dep Attorney Gen, Del, formerly; Del State Rep, 67-71, Majority Leader, Del House Rep, 69; Attorney Gen, Del, 71-75; app US Attorney, Dist of Del, 75- Bus & Prof Pos: Attorney-at-Law; pres, Children's Home Inc, formerly; trustee, Univ Del Libr Asn; pres, Scottish Games Asn of Del Inc; ex-master, The Family Court of New Castle Co. Mailing Add: Montchanin DE 19710

STACEY, CAROL HORNING (D)
Chmn, Kootenai Co Dem Party, Idaho
b Spokane, Wash, Mar 18, 34; d Frederick Forrest Horning & Carolyn Booth H; m 1964 to Martin Goodwin Stacey; c Liam & Colin. Educ: Univ Chicago, AB, 54, MA, 57, study, 58-62. Polit & Govt Pos: Coordr, Kootenai Co McGovern for President Comt, 72; vchmn, Kootenai Co Dem Party, Idaho, 72-74, chmn, 74-; alt deleg, Dem Nat Conv, 72; deleg, Idaho Dem Conv, 72; deleg, Dem Mid Term Conf, 74. Bus & Prof Pos: Res asst, Rand Corp, 64-65; res assoc, Prog Policy Study in Sci & Technol, George Washington Univ, 65-66; res asst, Human Sci Res, Inc, 66-67; res asst, Rand Corp, 67-69; part time asst prof, Eastern Wash State Col, 70-71; asst prof, Gonzaga Univ, 70-71; instr hist, Univ Idaho Exten Prog, 72-; ed, Nickels Worth, 73- Publ: Education & Television, George Washington Univ, 65; Foreign Military Trainees in Navy Schools, Human Sci Res Inc, 67; regular articles on waterfront environment, Intermountain Observer, 72-73. Mem: Coalition for Shorelands Preservation; Kootenai Environ Alliance. Mailing Add: 424 Foster Coeur d'Alene ID 83814

STACEY, FRANK ARTHUR (D)
Mem, Ala State Dem Exec Comt
b Birmingham, Ala, July 6, 12; s William John Stacey & Jane Lusk S; m 1935 to Mary Sue Shipley; c Susan Kay (Mrs Hagler). Educ: Univ Ala, 31 & 32; Howard Col, Birmingham, Ala, 33. Polit & Govt Pos: Mem, Ala State Aging Comn, 71-; deleg, Dem Nat Conv, 72; mem, Ala State Dem Exec Comt, 74- Mil Serv: Entered as Seaman, Merchant Marines, 42, released as Jr Asst Purser, 44, after serv in Atlantic Theatre, 43-44; Atlantic Theatre Award. Relig: Methodist. Mailing Add: 2200 26th St Ensley Birmingham AL 35208

STACK, CHARLIE RAY (D)
Chmn, Montgomery Co Dem Party, Tenn
b Cheatham Co, Tenn, Sept 16, 29; s Ewing F Stack & Thelma Mitchell S; m 1951 to Helen Davis; c Kenneth R, James E & Trey D. Educ: Austin Peay State Univ, BS, 61. Polit & Govt Pos: Deleg, Dem Nat Conv, 72; chmn, Montgomery Co Dem Party, Tenn, 74- Bus & Prof Pos: Tel engr, SCent Bell Tel Co, 51- Mil Serv: Entered as Pvt, Air Force, 47, released as Sgt, 50; Good Conduct Medal. Mem: Clarksville Civitan Club (dir, 72-74); Mason (32 degree); Clarksville High Sch Booster Club (pres, 72); VFW; Fraternal Order of Eagles. Honors & Awards: Most Outstanding Pres Award, Clarksville High Sch Booster Club. Relig: Methodist. Mailing Add: 2162 N Meadow Dr Clarksville TN 37040

STACK, EDWARD J (R)
b Bayonne, NJ, Apr 29, 10; s William J Stack & Hannah S; m 1954 to Jean Pierce; c Kathleen & William. Educ: Lehigh Univ, BA, 31; Univ Pa Law Sch, LLB, 34; Columbia Univ, MA, 38; Beta Theta Pi. Polit & Govt Pos: City Comnr, Pompano Beach, Fla, 65-69, mayor, 67-69; mem, Fla Develop Comn, 67-69; mem, Rep Nat & State Finance Comt; Fla State chmn, Nixon for President Campaign, 68; alt deleg, Rep Nat Conv, 68, deleg, 72; sheriff, Broward Co, 69- Bus & Prof Pos: New York Bar, 34-; dir, First Nat Bank, Ft Lauderdale, 69- Mil Serv: Entered as Ens, Coast Guard, 42, released as Lt(sg), 46. Mem: Navy League (dir); Kiwanis (dir); Int Asn Chiefs of Police (dir); Nat Sheriffs Asn; Boys Club Am. Relig: Catholic. Legal Res: 518 N Riverside Dr Pompano Beach FL 33062 Mailing Add: PO Box 9507 Ft Lauderdale FL 33310

STACK, MAURICE WILLIAM (D)
Vt State Rep
Mailing Add: 107 Atkinson St Bellows Falls VT 05101

STACY, BILL W (D)
b Bristol, Va, July 26, 38; s Charles Frank Stacy & Sarah Louise Nelson S; m 1958 to Jane Cooper; c Mark Allen, Sarah Jane & James Franklin. Educ: Southeast Mo State Univ, BS, 60; Southern Ill Univ, MS, 65, PhD, 68; Sigma Tau Gamma. Polit & Govt Pos: Vchmn, Dem Const & By-Laws, Mo; alt deleg, Dem Nat Conv, 72; asst supt, Senate Periodical Press. Bus & Prof Pos: Prof, Southeast Mo State Univ, 67-, asst to pres, 71- Mailing Add: 1832 Georgia Cape Girardeau MO 63701

STACY, JOE D (D)
Ky State Sen
Mailing Add: West Liberty KY 41741

STACY, JOHN RAYMOND (R)
Mem, Rep State Comt Okla
b Spokane, Wash, June 15, 14; s William Kellogg Stacy & Mary May Raymond S; m 1943 to Barbara Baley; c William Kellogg, II, James Bradford, Thomas Wood, Susan Ellen, Mary Jane & Barbara Ann. Educ: Oberlin Col, BS, 37; Western Reserve Univ Sch Med, MD, 42. Polit & Govt Pos: Doorkeeper, Rep Nat Conv, 36, alt deleg, 64; designated physician, US Dept Labor, 53-; precinct chmn, Okla City Rep Party, 61-; mem, Rep State Comt Okla & Okla Co Exec Comt, 63- Bus & Prof Pos: Attending physician, Will Rogers Vet Hosp, 48-; clin prof orthopaedic & traumatic surg, Okla Univ Sch Med, 49-; vpres, QualiCast Corp, 71- Mil Serv: Entered as 2nd Lt, Army, 38, released as 1st Lt, 43, after serv in Med Corps. Mem: Int Col Surgeons (fel); Am Acad Orthopaedic Surgeons (fel); Am Col Surgeons (fel); Econ Club of Okla; Okla State Med Asn. Relig: Congregational. Legal Res: 3100 NW 24th Oklahoma City OK 73107 Mailing Add: 415 NW 12th Oklahoma City OK 73103

STACY, LINDA (R)
Womans Chmn, Perry Co Rep Party, Ky
b Lothair, Ky, 1933; d Lee Terry; m 1953 to Elmer Jack Stacy; c Nancy, Deborah, Michael, Johny, Terry Wayne & Charles Edward. Educ: Blacky Stewart Robinson High Sch. Polit & Govt Pos: Womans chmn, Perry Co Rep Party, Ky, 55- Bus & Prof Pos: Merchant & partner, Elmer Stacy Grocery, 55- Mem: Jeff Community Club; 4-H Club; Dilce Combs Booster Club. Mailing Add: Jeff KY 41751

STACY, TED THEODORE (D)
WVa State Deleg
b Grundy, Va, Mar 10, 23; s Samuel Mathew Stacy & Eleventha Smith S; m 1960 to Elizabeth Ann Barnette; c Larry Ted. Educ: Beckley Col, ABA, 52; Morris Harvey Col, 68; LaSalle Exten Univ, LLB, 69. Polit & Govt Pos: WVa State Deleg, 58-60 & 68- Bus & Prof Pos: Owner, Gen Ins Agency, Beckley, WVa, 48- Mil Serv: Entered as Pvt, Army, 40, released as Cpl, 45, after serv in Coast Artil, Spec Serv Entertainment Sect, SPac, 41-45. Mem: Mason (Master, High Priest Chap); Shrine; Lions; Odd Fellows. Relig: Baptist. Legal Res: 600 Northwestern Ave Beckley WV 25801 Mailing Add: Box 929 Beckley WV 25801

STADELMAN, GEORGE PETER (R)
Rep Nat Committeeman, Ore
b The Dalles, Ore, June 1, 08; s Peter J Stadelman & May Kelly S; m 1931 to Lorraine Pierce; c Sally (Mrs Dougherty) & George Pierce. Educ: Univ Ore; Sigma Nu; Alpha Kappa Psi; Friars; Order of O. Polit & Govt Pos: Mayor, The Dalles, Ore, 41-44; chmn, Ore Comt, Lodge for President; deleg, Rep Nat Conv, 56, 64 & 68; mem, Ore State Rep Exec Comt, 60-64; treas, Ore State Rep Comt, formerly; Rep Nat Committeeman, Ore, 67-, vchmn, Rep Nat Comt, 72-; vchmn, Western State Conv, 68. Bus & Prof Pos: Pres, Cherry Lane Orchards, 66-; vpres, Stadelman, Fruit, Inc, 66-; dir, First Nat Bank of Ore, 66-; pres, Western Orchards Inc, currently. Mem: Elks; Kiwanis; CofC; Ore Hist Soc (dir); Ore Comt on Crime & Delinquency. Honors & Awards: Man of Year. Legal Res: 605 Pentland St The Dalles OR 97058 Mailing Add: PO Box 143 The Dalles OR 97058

STAEBLER, NEIL (D)
b Ann Arbor, Mich, July 11, 05; s Edward W Staebler & Magdalena Dold S; m 1935 to Burnette Bradley; c Michael B & Elizabeth. Educ: Univ Mich, AB, 26; Theta Chi. Hon Degrees: LLD, Univ Mich, 62. Polit & Govt Pos: Chief bldg materials br, Price Div, Off Price Admin, Washington, DC, 42-43; Mich Finance Dir, Dem Nat Comt, 49-50; chmn, Dem State Cent Comt, 50-61; deleg, Dem Nat Conv, 56-68; mem, President's Comn Campaign Costs, 61-62; vchmn, 20th Century Fund Task Force Financing Cong Campaigns, 70; Dem Nat Committeeman, Mich, 61-68; US Rep, Mich, 63-64; assoc committeeman, Dem Nat Comt, Mich, 68-72, mem, 72-75; mem, Fed Elections Comn, 75- Bus & Prof Pos: Partner, Staebler & Son, Ann Arbor, Mich, 26-; treas, Staebler-Kempf Oil Co, 26-51; vis prof practical politics, Univ Mass, spring 62; mem bd dirs, Citizens Research Found, formerly; pres, Mich Capital & Serv, Inc, 66-75, bd dirs, 75- Mil Serv: Lt, Navy, 43-45. Publ: How to Argue with a Conservative, Grossman Publs, Inc, New York, 2/66; Management of state political parties, In: Practical Politics in the United States, 67. Mem: Am Polit Sci Asn; Am Econ Asn; Nat Educ Asn; Am Vets Comt. Relig: Unitarian. Legal Res: 601 Huron View Blvd Ann Arbor MI 48103 Mailing Add: 408 Wolverine Bldg Ann Arbor MI 48108

STAFFORD, CHESTER JEFFERSON (R)
Va State Deleg
b Giles Co, Va; s Chester Jefferson Stafford & Elizabeth Painter S; single. Educ: Col William & Mary, BA; Univ Va Law Sch, LLB. Polit & Govt Pos: Chmn, Giles Co Dem Comt, Va, formerly; alt deleg, Dem Nat Conv, 68; Va State Deleg, Fifth Legis Dist, 72- Bus & Prof Pos: Lawyer, Dillow & Andrews, Pearisburg, Va, 66- Mil Serv: Entered as 1st Lt, Army, 64, released as Capt, 66, after serv in 7th Inf Div, Korea, 65-66; Capt, Army Res, 66-; Cert of Achievement, 7th Inf Div; Cert of Achievement, USALMC. Mem: AF&AM; Moose; Jaycees. Relig: Methodist. Mailing Add: Wenonah Ave Pearisburg VA 24134

STAFFORD, DEBORAH JEAN (D)
VPres, Wyo Young Dem
b Laramie, Wyo, Oct 20, 51; d Philip E Stafford & Lois L S; single. Educ: Univ Wyo, 70-73. Polit & Govt Pos: Nat Committeewoman, Wyo Young Dem, 71-72, vpres, 72-; precinct committeewoman, Laramie Co, 72-; alt deleg, Dem Nat Mid-Term Conf, 74. Honors & Awards: Best Thespian, Cent High Sch, 70. Mailing Add: 1402 E Fifth Ave Cheyenne WY 82001

STAFFORD, EDWIN SAMUEL (D)
Committeeman, Blount Co Dem Comt, Tenn
b Maryville, Tenn, May 5, 14; s John Nuebert Stafford & Bertha Elizabeth Henry S; m 1934 to Dorothy Verna McCammon; c Max (deceased), Edwin Don, John Leon, Bertha Kay & Robert Dale. Educ: High sch, 32. Polit & Govt Pos: Chmn, Blount Co Dem Exec Comt, Tenn, 58-60 & 62-64; mgr, President John F Kennedy's Blount Co Campaign, 60-62, co mgr, Sen Ross Bass' Campaign, 64-66; committeeman, Blount Co Dem Comt, currently. Bus & Prof Pos: Vpres, Local 309 USW, 52-56. Mem: Local 309 USW; Am Angus Asn; Hampshire Swine Registry. Relig: Methodist. Mailing Add: Rte 12 Maryville TN 37801

STAFFORD, HARRY, JR (D)
Chmn, Lewis Co Dem Party, Ky
b Canton, Ohio, June 24, 43; s Harry L Stafford, Sr & Mildred Graham S; m 1966 to Linda Joyce Young; c Melissa Sue. Educ: Morehead State Univ, BS, 66, MA, 70. Polit & Govt Pos: Chmn, Wendell Ford for Gov Campaign, Ky, 71; contact man for Gov Wendell Ford in Lewis Co, 71-74; chmn, Lewis Co Dem Party, 71-; contact man for Gov Julian Carroll in Lewis Co, 74- Bus & Prof Pos: Teacher, Lewis Co Cent Elem Sch, Vanceburg, Ky, 64-; farmer, Camp Dix, 72-; co-owner, Lewis Co Monument Co, Vanceburg, 74- Mem: Vanceburg City Coun; Ky & Nat Educ Asns. Mailing Add: 910 Fairlane Dr Vanceburg KY 41179

STAFFORD, IONE JORDAN (R)
Pres, Idaho Fedn Rep Women
b Enterprise, Ore, Jan 21, 13; d Lenord Eugene Jordan & Mary Irene Beck J; m 1971 to Col Arvel C Stafford; c Douglas J Taylor, stepchildren, Carolyn (Mrs Huffine) & Mary Cay (Mrs Myers). Educ: Univ Ore, BA, 34; Chi Omega. Polit & Govt Pos: Chmn, Idaho Women for Nixon, 67-68; campaign chmn, Idaho Fedn Rep Women, 55-71, pres, 75-; vchmn, Ada Co Rep Cent Comt, 71-73; vpres, Ada Co Womens Club, 72-74. Relig: Episcopal. Mailing Add: 7304 Court Ave Boise ID 83704

STAFFORD, L V (R)
Wyo State Sen
Mailing Add: Rte 1 Buffalo WY 82834

STAFFORD, MOODY FRANK (BENNY) (R)
Tenn State Rep
b Knox Co, Tenn, Nov 23, 32; s Moody Lemuel Stafford & Elizabeth Mills S; m 1959 to Shirley Inez Clinc. Educ: Lenoir City High Sch. Polit & Govt Pos: Tenn State Rep, 70- Bus & Prof Pos: Owner, Gen Ins Agency, 61- Mil Serv: Entered as Airman Basic, Air Force, 52, released as M/Sgt, 65, after serv in 134th Air Refueling Group, Korea, 5th Air Force, 53-55; Presidential Unit Citation; UN Medal; Korean Presidential Unit Citation; Good Conduct Medal; Korean Serv Medal. Mem: Mason; Shrine; Civitan. Honors & Awards: Outstanding Young Man Award, 67; Outstanding Citizens Award, Loudon Co, 70. Relig: Baptist. Mailing Add: Rte 2 Lenoir City TN 37771

STAFFORD, RALPH E (R)
Vt State Rep
b South Wallingford, Vt, Mar 2, 05; m to Mabel A Rice. Educ: Wallingford High Sch. Polit & Govt Pos: Rep town committeeman, South Wallingford, formerly; selectman & overseer of poor, 40-47; Vt State Rep, 47 & 65-; Vt State Sen, 49-55. Bus & Prof Pos: Ins agt; farmer. Mem: Mason; Eastern Star (past dep); Grange (past dep); Farm Bur; Shrine. Relig: Congregational. Mailing Add: South Wallingford VT 05773

STAFFORD, ROBERT T (R)
US Sen, Vt
b Rutland, Vt, Aug 8, 13; s Bert L Stafford & Mabel Stratton S; m 1938 to Helen Kelley; c Madelyn Ann (Mrs Glase), Susan Britton (Mrs Mohr); Dianne Louise & Barbara Jean. Educ: Middlebury Col, BS, 34; Univ Mich; Boston Univ Law Sch, LLB, 38; Delta Epsilon. Hon Degrees: LLD, Boston Univ, 59, Norwich Univ, 60, Middlebury Col, 60, St Michael's Col, 67 & Univ Vt, 70. Polit & Govt Pos: Rutland Co State's Attorney, Vt, 47-51; Dep Attorney Gen, Vt, 53-55, Attorney Gen, 55-57, Lt Gov, 57-59, Gov, 59-61; deleg, Rep Nat Conv, 60 & 68; US Rep, Vt, 61-71; US Sen, Vt, 71-, mem comt labor & pub welfare, comt on pub works, comt on vet affairs & spec comt on aging, US Senate, currently. Mil Serv: Entered as Ens, Navy, 42, released as Lt Comdr, 46, recalled, 51-53, after serv in Am, European & Southwest Pac Theaters & Korea; various campaign ribbons; Capt (Ret), Naval Res, 62- Mem: Am Legion; VFW; Lions; Elks; Mason. Relig: Congregational. Legal Res: 64 Litchfield Ave Rutland VT 05701 Mailing Add: 3541 Devon Dr Falls Church VA 22042

STAFFORD, RONALD B (R)
NY State Sen
b Plattsburgh, NY, June 29, 35; s Halsey W Stafford & Agnes Martin S; single. Educ: St Lawrence Univ, BA, 57; Columbia Univ Sch Law, LLB, 62; Omicron Delta Kappa; Beta Theta Pi. Hon Degrees: LLD, Wadhams Hall Sem-Col, 75. Polit & Govt Pos: NY State Sen, 48th Dist, 66-67, 42nd Dist, 67-72, 43rd Dist, 72-, chmn, Comt on Children in NY State Senate, 66- Bus & Prof Pos: Mem adv bd, Plattsburgh Br, Marine Midland Nat Bank, NY, 69-; attorney-at-law, Firm of Stafford & Purcell, currently; mem bd gov, Med Hosp Ctr of Vt; mem bd vis, Columbia Law Sch, 74- Mil Serv: Entered as 1st Lt, Army, 58, released as 1st Lt, 60, after serv in 25th Mil Intel Group, 2nd Army; Commendation Ribbon with Medal Pendant. Mem: NY State Bar Asn (spec comt on environ law); Am & Clinton Co Bar Asns; Kiwanis. Honors & Awards: Annual Distinguished Serv Award, Plattsburgh Jaycees, 69; Spec Award, NY State VFW, 71; Award of Merit, New York Bd of Higher Educ. Relig: Protestant. Legal Res: 14 Pleasant St Peru NY 12972 Mailing Add: 162 Margaret St Plattsburgh NY 12901

STAGGERS, HARLEY ORRIN (D)
US Rep, WVa
b Keyser, WVa, Aug 3, 07; s Jacob Kinsey Staggers & Frances Cumberledge S; m 1943 to Mary Casey; c Margaret Anne, Mary Katherine, Frances Susan, Elizabeth Ellen, Harley Orrin, Jr & Daniel Casey. Educ: Emory & Henry Col, AB. Hon Degrees: LLD, Emory & Henry Col, 53 & Davis & Elkins Col, 69. Polit & Govt Pos: US Rep, WVa, 48-; deleg, Dem Nat Conv, 68 & 72. Mil Serv: Navy, 42-46. Mem: Am Legion; VFW; DAV; Amvets; Moose. Relig: Methodist. Legal Res: PO Box 906 Keyser WV 26726 Mailing Add: 2366 Rayburn House Off Bldg Washington DC 20515

STAHL, JACK (R)
Chmn, Rep State Cent Comt NMex
Mailing Add: 2051 Wyoming Blvd NE Albuquerque NM 87112

STAHL, JOHN (R)
Pa State Rep
Mailing Add: Capitol Bldg Harrisburg PA 17120

STAHL, THOMAS BURTON (R)
Treas, Sandusky Co Rep Exec Comt, Ohio
b Fremont, Ohio, Apr 5, 04; s John Burton Stahl & Florence Fisher S; m 1936 to Harriett May Beatty; c John Thomas & James Philip. Educ: Miami Univ, 22-23; Univ Toledo, 23-24; Ohio State Univ, LLB, 27; Delta Theta Phi. Polit & Govt Pos: Mem, Sandusky Co Rep Exec Comt, Ohio, 29-, treas, 65-; pres, Sandusky Co Law Libr Asn, 35-; Common Pleas Judge, Sandusky Co, 36-37; alt deleg, Rep Nat Conv, 68. Bus & Prof Pos: Mem bd dir, Fremont Savings Bank Co, Ohio, 57- Mem: Am Bar Asn; Am Judicature Soc; Mason (32 degree); Elks (Past Exalted Ruler, Fremont Lodge 169); Shrine. Relig: Protestant. Legal Res: 720 Garrison St Fremont OH 43420 Mailing Add: 615 Croghan St Fremont OH 43420

STAHLIN, JOHN HENRY (R)
Mem, Mich Rep State Cent Comt
b Belding, Mich, Apr 6, 14; s Edward M Stahlin & Sadie Mayor S; m 1935 to Pauline Mary Underwood; c John M, Susan M, Paul F & Edward W. Educ: Ferris State Col, 33-34. Polit & Govt Pos: Mich State Sen, 25th Dist, 58-62; mem, Mich Rep State Cent Comt, 62-; finance chmn, Ionia Co Rep Party, 64-65; mem, Fifth Dist Rep Finance Comt, 64-; mem, Higher Educ Facility Comn & Econ Develop Comn, Mich, 65-; spec asst polit affairs for Gov William G Milliken, Mich, 65-; deleg, Rep Nat Conv, 68; Rep State Finance Chmn, 71. Bus & Prof Pos: Pres, Stahlin Bros Fibre Works, Inc, 36-; vpres, J P Carter Co, 49-; secy-treas, Gulf View, Inc, 52- Mem: Mason; Mich CofC; Belding CofC; Detroit Athletic Club; Lansing City Club. Relig: Church of Christ Scientist. Mailing Add: 222 S Broas St Belding MI 48809

STAIGMILLER, JOHN B (D)
Mont State Rep
Mailing Add: PO Box 422 Cascade MT 59421

STAKE, WILLIAM FLOYD (R)
Chmn, Lincoln Co Rep Comt, SDak
b Proctor, Colo, Aug 28, 20; s Cecil Fred Stake & Marguerite Evelyn Nelson S; m 1946 to Dorothy Marie Swedzinski; c Timothy Joseph, Catherine Teresa, Mary Helen, Patrice Marie & Julle Anne. Educ: High sch grad, 38. Polit & Govt Pos: Pres, City Coun, Lennox, SDak, 60-; chmn, Lincoln Co Rep Comt, SDak, 73- Bus & Prof Pos: Pres, Stake Construction Co, 54-, Power & Commun Contractor, 62-63 & Universal Enterprises, 62-; vpres, Morningside Mem Garden, 62- Mil Serv: Entered as Pvt, Army Air Force, 42, released as Sgt, after serv in Am Theatre, 42-46. Mem: Power & Commun Contractors Asn; Elks; Am Legion. Relig: Catholic. Mailing Add: 204 Park Dr Lennox SD 57039

STALBAUM, LYNN E (D)
b Waterford, Wis, May 15, 20; m to Alice Gunderson; c two daughters, two sons. Educ: Racine Co Agr Sch, grad, 36. Polit & Govt Pos: Wis State Sen, 54, 58 & 62, caucus chmn, Wis State Senate, 57, 59 & 61, asst minority leader, 63; US Rep, Wis, 64-66. Bus & Prof Pos: With US Dept Agr, Racine Co, 36-44, admin officer, 39-44; feed salesman, 46-51; secy-treas,

Racine Milk Producers Coop Asn & mgr, Harmony Dairy Co, 51-64; Wash rep Cent Am Coop Fedn, Inc, 69-74; legis rep, Nat Milk Producers Fedn, 74- Mil Serv: Navy, destroyer, 44-46. Mailing Add: 6311 Blackwood Rd Bethesda MD 20034

STALEY, MILDRED WILKERSON (R)
Mem Exec Bd, Wichita Co Rep Party, Tex
b Meridian, Miss; d Forrest Edd Wilkerson & Lucille Clement W; m to Joseph Hardin Staley; c Nancy (Mrs William J Friedman, III), Joseph Hardin, Jr & Delia (Mrs Clark Mullins). Educ: Randolph-Macon Women's Col, 1 year; Southern Methodist Univ, BA; Zeta Tau Alpha (pres); Sock & Buskin, Panhellenic. Polit & Govt Pos: Vpres, Wichita Co Rep Women's Club, 66-67, pres, 68, secy, 72-73; alt deleg, Nat Fedn Rep Women Conv, 67, deleg, 69 & 71; deleg, Tex Fedn Rep Women Conv, 67 & 71; bd dir, Tex Fedn Rep Women, 67-71; deleg, Tex Rep State Conv, 68-69; mem-at-lg exec bd, Tex Fedn Rep Women, 68-71; chmn, Region V Tex, Rep Women's Conf, 69; mem bd, Nat Fedn Rep Women, 69-71; mem exec bd, Wichita Co Rep Party, 72-; deleg, 2-State Rep Conv, 72. Mem: Nat Regional Consumers Research Conv; Wichita Falls Symphony Orchestra (bd, 60-). Relig: Methodist. Mailing Add: 2205 Clarinda Wichita Falls TX 76308

STALLINGS, CLAYTON (D)
NMex State Rep
Mailing Add: 1510 S Pennsylvania Roswell NM 88201

STALLINGS, D LIVINGSTONE (D)
NC State Sen
Mailing Add: 1705 River Dr New Bern NC 28560

STALLINGS, ROBERT S (D)
Tenn State Rep
b Bolivar, Tenn, Aug 15, 27; s Martin Luther Stallings & Pearl Wheeler S; m 1949 to Louise Williamson; c Judy (Mrs Richard E Wilhite, II), Janet (Mrs David Caldwell), Sam, Timmy & Ronny. Educ: Cent High Sch, 46. Polit & Govt Pos: Magistrate, Hardeman Co, Tenn, 2 terms; Tenn State Rep, 80th Dist, 75- Bus & Prof Pos: Owner, Stallings Tractor Co, Bolivar, Tenn, 55-75. Mem: Lions. Honors & Awards: Boss of Year Award. Relig: Baptist. Mailing Add: 507 Tennessee St Bolivar TN 38008

STAMBAUGH, WARREN GLENN (D)
Va State Deleg
b Maysville, Ky, Aug 7, 44; s Warren Gameliel Stambaugh & Margaret Maley S; m 1966 to Dorothy Hoff; c Elisabeth Marie & Peter Edward. Educ: Georgetown Univ Sch Foreign Serv, BSFS, 68. Polit & Govt Pos: Mem, Va Dem State Cent Comt, 72-; mem, Arlington Co Consumer Protection Comn, 73-; mem comt on suggested state legis, Coun of State Govts, 74-; Va State Deleg, 74- Bus & Prof Pos: Asst pub affairs officer, Off of Naval Research, 66-68; sr ed, Am Automobile Asn, 68- Mem: Northern Va Ment Health Asn (bd dirs, 73-, exec comt, 75); Arlington Co Comt of 100; Pub Rels Soc Am; Arlington Co Dem Comt (vchmn, 71-73). Relig: Roman Catholic. Mailing Add: 807 N Irving St Arlington VA 22201

STAMP, FREDERICK P, JR (R)
VChmn, WVa Rep State Cent Comt
b 1934. Educ: Linsly Mil Inst; Taft Sch; Washington & Lee Univ; Univ Richmond. Polit & Govt Pos: WVa State Deleg, 67-71; chmn, Ohio Co Rep Finance Comt & mem, State Rep Finance Comt, currently; vchmn, WVa Rep State Cent Comt, 71- Bus & Prof Pos: Partner, Schmidt, Laas, Schrader & Miller Law Firm, currently; secy & mem bd dirs, Security Nat Bank & Trust Co. Mem: Wheeling Symphony Soc (exec comt & bd); YMCA (bd dirs & secy); Ohio Co Legal Serv Ctr (vpres). Relig: Presbyterian. Mailing Add: Central Union Bldg Wheeling WV 26003

STAMPS, HAL BURTON (D)
Secy-Treas, Third Cong Dist Dem Party, Okla
b Wapanucka, Okla, July 6, 21; s Hal Stamps & Velma Trotter S; m 1941 to Louise Alsup; c Susan Lyn (Mrs Ferguson) & Bob Hal. Educ: Murray State Agr Col, Okla, 1 year. Polit & Govt Pos: Chmn, Johnston Co Dem Cent Comt, Okla, 62-69; secy-treas, Third Cong Dist Dem Party, currently. Bus & Prof Pos: Owner, Stamps 5 & 10, 47-62; co-owner, Stamps Dry Goods, 62- Mem: Tishomingo Rotary Club. Relig: Methodist. Mailing Add: 706 E 18th Tishomingo OK 73460

STANCIL, BILL (D)
Ark State Rep
Mailing Add: 2105 South T Ft Smith AR 72901

STANDAFER, DARYL LLOYD (R)
Dist Deleg, Minn Rep State Cent Comt
b Adrian, Minn, July 14, 42; s Lloyd L Standafer & Eunice Maree Kellam S; m 1962 to Janice Marie Zimmerman; c Philip Daryl, Jeffrey Lloyd, Gregory Robert & Lisa Marie. Educ: McPherson Col, Kans, BA, 64. Polit & Govt Pos: Fieldman, Minn Rep Party, 64; chmn, Nobles Co Rep Comt, 64-67, secy, currently; alt deleg, State Cent Comt, 67-69; chmn, Dist Nixon Comt, 68; deleg, Rep Nat Conv, 68; dist deleg, Minn Rep State Cent Comt, 69-; research asst, US Rep MacGregor, Minn, 69-70; chmn, Rep State Conv, 72. Bus & Prof Pos: Mkt officer, First Nat Bank in Worthington, 73- Mem: Am Farm Bur; Holstein-Friesian Asn Am; Jaycees (state dir); Kiwanis; Worthington Civil Air Patrol. Honors & Awards: Winner Second Prize, Nat Farm Bur Speech Contest, 59; Outstanding Sound Citizen, Minn Jaycees; Am Inst Banking Dist Speech Contest Winner, 75. Relig: Baptist. Mailing Add: RR 1 Worthington MN 56187

STANHAGEN, WILLIAM HAROLD (R)
Rep Nat Committeeman, Va
b Phoenix, Ariz, Sept 13, 28; s William Stanhagen & Mary Elizabeth S (deceased); c Eric William & Kenneth Charles. Educ: Univ Southern Calif, BSCE, 53; George Washington Univ Law Sch, JD with distinction, 59. Polit & Govt Pos: Mem, Fairfax Co Rep Comt, Va, 61-; chmn, Tenth Cong Dist Rep Comt, 8 years; mem, Va State Rep Cent & Exec Comts, 9 years; NVa Chmn, Holton for Gov Campaign, 65, state orgn chmn, 69; chmn, Broyhill for Cong Campaigns, 66, 68, 70 & 72; chmn, Parris for Deleg Comt, 69; Rep Nat Committeeman, 72-; chmn, Va Bd Conservation & Econ Develop, currently; mem, Va Coun on Environ, 74-. Bus & Prof Pos: Attorney, William H Stanhagen, Law Off, currently; owner, William H Stanhagen & Assocs, currently; owner, Holiday Inn-Downtown, Charlotte, NC, currently; co-owner, Holiday Inns of Danbury, Conn & Falls Church, Va, currently; mem bd dirs, pres or other officer various corps. Mil Serv: Navy, 46-47. Publ: Weekly column for Northern Va Sun. Mem: Am Bar Asn; Va State Bar; Fairfax Co Health & Welfare Coun. Relig: Lutheran. Legal Res: 9451 Lee Hwy Fairfax VA 22030 Mailing Add: 6633 Arlington Blvd Falls Church VA 22042

STANION, THERESA D (D)
Vt State Rep
b Jersey City, NJ, Dec 19, 38; d Roman Drozd & Anna Pozniak D; m 1960 to Robert P Stanion; c Robert Theodore, Timothy Paul & Jessica Ann. Educ: Notre Dame Col, St John's Univ, BA, 60; State Univ NY Col New Paltz, MA, 71. Polit & Govt Pos: Vt State Rep, Dist Chittenden 2-1, 75- Mem: Am Asn Univ Women; League of Women Voters; Order of Women Legislators. Relig: Catholic. Mailing Add: 4 Wildwood Dr Essex Junction VT 05452

STANISLAUS, DOROTHY JEANNE (R)
b Sand Springs, Okla, Sept 8, 25; d Van Dolph Herrington & Sibly Schuler H; m 1945 to O Doyle Stanislaus. Educ: Stephens Col, 43; Univ Okla, 44-45; Delta Delta Delta. Polit & Govt Pos: Co vchmn, Okla State Rep Party, 62-63, co chmn, 64, vchmn, 65-72; deleg & mem platform comt, Rep Nat Conv, 64, alt deleg, 68; Rep Nat Committeewoman, Okla, 68-72; mem D O Comt of Nat Comn & Midwest Region Exec Comt, currently. Relig: Episcopal. Mailing Add: 1381 E 26th St Tulsa OK 74114

STANLEY, DAVID MAXWELL (R)
b Dubuque, Iowa, Sept 9, 28; s C Maxwell Stanley & Elizabeth Holthues S; m 1948 to Jean Kathryn Leu; c Lincoln, Rebecca, Nathan & Elizabeth. Educ: Univ Iowa, BA, 51, Col Law, JD, 53; Phi Beta Kappa; Order of the Coif; Phi Delta Phi. Polit & Govt Pos: Orgn chmn, Iowa Young Rep, 53-54; Iowa State Rep, 75th Dist, 59-64 & 73-74; mem, Iowa Rep State Platform Comt, 60 & 66; Iowa State Sen, 64-69, senate majority leader, Iowa Gen Assembly, 69; cand for US Sen, 68 & 74; chmn, Gov Comt on UN, formerly. Bus & Prof Pos: Sr partner, Seanley, Lande, Coulter & Pearce, Attorneys, 57- Mil Serv: Entered as 2nd Lt, Air Force, 54, released as 1st Lt, after serv in 63rd Troop Carrier Wing, Tactical Air Force, 54-56. Publ: How to lose money without really trying, Iowan Mag, 65; Iowa Comments to Uniform Commercial Code, West Publ Co, 67. Mem: Am, Iowa State & Muscatine Co Bar Asns; Environ Stewardship Comt; Rotary. Honors & Awards: Distinguished Serv Award, Muscatine Jaycees, 62. Relig: Methodist; lay speaker, Sunday sch teacher & bd mem. Mailing Add: 814 Iowa Ave Muscatine IA 52761

STANLEY, DON R (D)
Ind State Rep
Mailing Add: RR 7 Frankfort IN 46041

STANLEY, ELIOT HUNGERFORD (D)
b Baton Rouge, La, Jan 4, 42; s Dr Allan John Stanley & Ruth Moore S (deceased); m 1966 to Nancy Elizabeth Scbmid. Educ: Harvard Univ, BA cum laude in Hist, 63; Nat Law Ctr, George Washington Univ, JD, 72. Polit & Govt Pos: Asst to dir, Okla City Urban Renewal Authority, 63-64; Capitol Hill, US Sen Fred R Harris, Okla, 64-65; spec asst legis, Off Secy Housing & Urban Develop, 65-66; admin asst, US Rep B S Farnum, 66-67; admin asst, US Rep Chet Holifield, 67-69; adv staff, Dem Presidential nominee, 68; adv staff for Robert Sargent Shriver, Jr, Cong Leadership for the Future, 70; vol speechwriter, Chisholm for President Campaign, 72 & Robert Sargent Shriver, Dem Vice Presidential Nominee, 72; counsel, US Comn on Civil Rights, Northeastern Regional Off, New York, 73- Bus & Prof Pos: Assoc dir, Citizens Advocate Ctr, Washington, DC, 71-73. Publ: Academic freedom in the South, The Harvard Rev, 63. Mem: Am Polit Sci Asn. Relig: Unitarian. Mailing Add: 47 Saranac St Dobbs Ferry NY 10522

STANLEY, KATHLEEN GOOLD (D)
Hawaii State Rep
b Montour Falls, NY, Sept 24, 43; d G Howard Goold & Charlotte Carman G; m 1971 to Patrick Akin Stanley. Educ: Muskingum Col, BA, 65; Syracuse Univ, MSEd, 67; Univ Hawaii, 70-75. Polit & Govt Pos: Hawaii State Rep, 74-, chairperson, Pub Assist & Human Serv, Hawaii House Rep, 74- Bus & Prof Pos: Teacher, Liverpool Intermediate Sch, NY, 66-67; VISTA vol, Waimanalo, Hawaii, 67-68; coordr, Off Econ Opportunity-CAP, Honolulu, 68-69; VISTA field training officer, Univ Ore, Eugene, 69; prog specialist, Social Welfare Develop & Research Ctr, Univ Hawaii, 69-74. Publ: Co-auth, Paying students for academic performance, 73 & An adult furlough center correlates of parole success, 74, J Community Psychol. Mem: John Howard Asn; Nat Asn of Social Workers, Hawaii Chap; League of Women Voters; Young Women's Christian Asn; Hawaii Asn for Educ Young Children. Relig: Protestant. Mailing Add: 666 Prospect St 302 Honolulu HI 96813

STANLEY, MARC GENE (D)
b Washington, DC, Feb 18, 43; s Meyer William Stanley & Belle Helen Myers S; m 1970 to Luanne Stein; c Jennifer Farrah. Educ: George Washington Univ, BA, 64; Univ Baltimore, LLB, 67; Alpha Epsilon Pi; Polemics Club. Polit & Govt Pos: Legis asst, US Rep Seymour Halpern, NY, 60-62 & US Rep Lawrence Coughlin, Pa, 69-72; admin asst, US Rep Ronald A Sarasin, Conn, 73- Bus & Prof Pos: Guest lectr, Washington Semester Prog, Am Univ & Conn Student Intern Prog, 73. Mil Serv: Entered as S/A, Coast Guard Res, 67, released as Port Security Officer 1/C, 73; Coast Guard Meritorious Ribbon. Mem: Cong Staff Club of US Cong; charter mem Admin Assts Asn; Dufief Home Asn, Inc (bd dirs, 73-). Relig: Jewish. Mailing Add: 11705 Silent Valley Lane Gaithersburg MD 20760

STANLEY, MERTON (D)
Ind State Sen
Mailing Add: 122 W Walnut Kokomo IN 46901

STANLEY, MILES CLARK (D)
b Dunbar, WVa, Oct 2, 24; s Worthy Carson Stanley & Opal Clark S; m 1943 to Romaleda Elizabeth Smith; c Brenda Joyce (Mrs Stanley Elliott), Penelope Lynne (Mrs Zane Metz) & Teresa Lea. Educ: WVa Pub Schs. Hon Degrees: LLD, WVa State Col, 67; LHD, WVa Inst Technol, 66 & Marshall Univ, 63. Polit & Govt Pos: Alt deleg, Dem Nat Conv, 72. Mem: Int Asn Machinists; United Steelworkers Am; Area Redevelop Admin (nat pub adv comt, 61-); US Comn Civil Rights (WVa adv comt, 59-); WVa Educ Broadcasting Authority. Honors & Awards: Distinguished Layman's Award, Evangel United Brethren Church, 62. Relig: Methodist. Legal Res: 1700 Kanawha Ave Dunbar WV 25064 Mailing Add: PO Box 646 Charleston WV 25323

STANLEY, RONALD EUGENE (R)
Chmn, Murray Co Rep Party, Ga
b Barrow Co, Ga, Jan 14, 37; s Arvil Stanley & Sarah Stover S; m 1974 to Willa Mae Cochran;

c Teresa, Darlene, Laney & Matthew. Educ: Murray Co Schs, 59. Polit & Govt Pos: Vchmn, Murray Co Rep Party, Ga, 73-75, chmn, 75- Mil Serv: Seaman, Naval Res, 55. Relig: Church of Christ. Mailing Add: Rte 1 Chatsworth GA 30705

STANLEY, STANLEY WRIGHT (R)
NDak State Sen
Mailing Add: State Capitol Bismarck ND 58501

STANLEY, STEPHEN CHARLES (R)
Second VChmn, Shoshone Co Rep Comt, Idaho
b Wallace, Idaho, July 16, 41; s Roger Stephan Stanley & Thelma Florence Hickey Zanetti S; m 1967 to Glenna Lou Collins; c Brett Craig & Mona Janeen. Educ: NIdaho Col, AA, 61; Univ Mont, Mont Aeronaut Scholar, 64; Univ Idaho, BS, 70, Educ Prof Develop Assistance scholar, 71; MEd, 75; Student Nat Educ Asn (pres, 60-61). Polit & Govt Pos: Mem, Shoshone Co Planning & Zoning, 72-75, chmn, 72-73; mem, Shoshone Co Snomobile Adv, 73-75; second vchmn, Shoshone Co Rep Comt, 74- Bus & Prof Pos: Acting prin, Sch Dist 15 & 6, Idaho, 62-67, head teacher, Sch Dist 394, 67- Mem: St Maries Eagles; Elks; Mason; Idaho Educ Asn (pres, 68-75); Nat Educ Asn. Honors & Awards: Outstanding Community Serv Awards, Mont PTA, 67 & Idaho, 74. Relig: Lutheran. Mailing Add: Box 488 Calder ID 83808

STANLEY, WILLIAM C (D)
SC State Rep
Mailing Add: 1002 Dennis Dr Hanahan SC 29406

STANO, JEROME (D)
Ohio State Rep
Mailing Add: 6909 Charles Ave Parma OH 44129

STANS, MAURICE H (R)
b Shakopee, Minn, Mar 22, 08; s J Hubert Stans & Mathilda Nyssen S; m 1933 to Kathleen Carmody; c Steven, Theodore, Maureen (Mrs Walter Helmick) & Terrell (Mrs William Manley). Educ: Northwestern Univ, 25-28; Columbia Univ, 28-30. Hon Degrees: LLD, Grove City Col, St Anselm's Col, Northwestern Univ, Ill Wesleyan Univ, DePaul Univ, Univ San Diego, Gustavus Adolphus Col, Rio Grande Col, Maryville Col & Pomona Col; DPA, Parsons Col. Polit & Govt Pos: Financial consult to the Postmaster Gen, Post Off Dept, 53-55, Dep Postmaster Gen, 55-57; dep dir, Bur of Budget, 57-58, dir, 58-61; chmn, Nixon for President Comt, 68; chmn, Rep Nat Finance Comt, 68-69 & 72-73; Secy of Com, 69-72; chmn, Finance Comt to Reelect the President, 72. Bus & Prof Pos: Mem & exec partner, Alexander Grant & Co, Chicago, Ill, 28-55; treas & dir, Moore Corp, Joliet, Ill, 38-45, chmn bd, 42-45; dir & mem exec comt, James Talcott, Inc, New York, 41-55; pres, Western Bancorp, Los Angeles, Calif, 61-62; pres, Glore Forgan, William R Staats, Inc, New York, 63-68. Mem: Am Inst CPA; Nat Asn Postmasters; Am Soc Pub Admin; Fed Govt Acct Asn; EAfrican Prof Hunters Asn. Honors & Awards: Am Acct Asn Annual Award, 52; Am Inst CPA Annual Award, 54; elected to Acct Hall of Fame, 60; Tax Found Award for Distinguished Pub Serv, 59; Great Living Am Award, US CofC, 61. Mailing Add: 2500 Virginia Ave NW Washington DC 20037

STANSFIELD, MARY JO (D)
Mem, Fla State Dem Exec Comt
b Daytona Beach, Fla, Nov 19, 24; d Henry Fugate Simmons & Esther Sanders S; m 1942 to Charles Webb Stansfield; c Charles W, Jr, Richard C & Susan (Mrs Hickson). Educ: Mainland High Sch, grad, 42. Polit & Govt Pos: Chmn, South Peninsula Zoning Dist, Daytona Beach, 65-69, chmn pub works curb comt & vol co charter comt, 69-70; Volusia Co Dem Exec Comt, 64-; mem, Fla State Dem Exec Comt, 70-; vchmn bd comns, Halifax Hosp Dist Med Ctr, 73- Bus & Prof Pos: Secy, US Navy Dept, Daytona Beach, 42-45; owner & mgr of seven restaurants, Daytona Beach, 45-66; dir dist cong off, Congressman Bill Chappell, Fourth Dist, Fla, 69- Mem: League of Women Voters; Dem Women's Club of Halifax Area; Dem Club of Ormond Beach. Honors & Awards: US Navy Meritorious Civilian Serv Award, 44; Meritorious Serv Award, Halifax Area Cent Vet Coun, 70; Outstanding Serv Award, VFW Post 1590, 71; Good Govt Award, Jaycees, 73; Outstanding Woman of the Year, Cent Labor Union, 75. Relig: Catholic. Mailing Add: 5 Homan Terr Daytona Beach FL 32018

STANTON, JAMES VINCENT (D)
US Rep, Ohio
b Cleveland, Ohio, Feb 23, 32; s Martin Joseph Stanton & Loretta McFadden S; m to Margaret Mary Casserly; c Joseph, Richard, Bridget Marie & Michael. Educ: Univ Dayton, BA; Cleveland-Marshall Col Law, JD. Polit & Govt Pos: Councilman, Cleveland, Ohio, 59-64, pres, 64-70; vchmn, Cuyahoga Co Dem Exec Comt; US Rep, 20th Dist, Ohio, 71- Bus & Prof Pos: Trustee, Cleveland-Marshall Col Law, 69. Mil Serv: Air Force, 50-54. Mem: Cleveland, Cuyahoga Co, Ohio State & Am Bar Asns. Honors & Awards: Outstanding Young Man of Cleveland, Jr CofC, 65; Phi Alpha Delta Outstanding Alumni Award, Cleveland State Univ, 70; Outstanding Alumnus, Cleveland State Univ Marshall Law Alumni Asn, 75. Relig: Roman Catholic. Legal Res: 16414 St Anthony Lane Cleveland OH 44111 Mailing Add: 103 Cannon House Off Bldg Washington DC 20515

STANTON, JOHN WILLIAM (R)
US Rep, Ohio
b Painesville, Ohio, Feb 20, 24; s Frank M Stanton & Mary Callinan S; m 1966 to Peggy Smeeton; c Kelly Marie. Educ: Georgetown Univ, BS, 49; pres, Int Rels Club; pres, Sr Class. Polit & Govt Pos: Comnr, Lake Co, Ohio, 56-64; US Rep, Ohio, 65- Bus & Prof Pos: Owner, J W Stanton Motors, Inc, 49-62; pres & co-owner, Stanton-Leonard Motors, Inc, 62-65. Mil Serv: Entered as 2nd Lt, Army, 42, released as Capt, 46, after serv in New Guinea, Netherlands EIndies & Philippines; Bronze Star with Oak Leaf Cluster; Purple Heart; Presidential Unit Citation & 3 major campaign ribbons. Mem: Jr CofC; Moose; Painesville Elks (Past Exalted Ruler); Am Legion; KofC (4 degree). Relig: Catholic. Legal Res: 7 North Park Pl Painesville OH 44077 Mailing Add: 2466 Rayburn House Off Bldg Washington DC 20515

STANTON, RALPH CALVIN, JR (R)
Chmn, Richland Co Rep Cent Comt, Ohio
b Pittsburgh, Pa, June 22, 24; s Ralph C Stanton, Sr & Eloise Robinson S; m 1952 to Ida Louise Guadayinno; c Crisella, Michael David, Lee Ann & Robert Charles. Educ: Ohio State Univ, 42-43, BS, 48; Baldwin Wallace Col, 43-44; Pi Kappa Alpha. Polit & Govt Pos: Councilman, Mansfield, Ohio, 59-63; vchmn, Richland Co Cent Comt, 63-68, first vchmn exec comt, formerly, chmn, currently; mem bd elec, Richland Co. Bus & Prof Pos: Pres, Stanton-Long Ins Agency Inc, 61-; dir, Mansfield Bldg & Loan Asn, 63- Mil Serv: Entered as A/S, Navy, 43, released as Lt(jg), after serv in 7th Amphibious Force, Pac Theatre, 44-46; Res, Lt; Theatre Decorations; 1 Battle Star. Mem: Ohio & Nat Asns Ins Agents; Am Legion; Univ Club; YMCA. Honors & Awards: Outstanding Civic Serv Award, CofC, 63. Relig: Protestant. Legal Res: 602 Crescent Rd Mansfield OH 44907 Mailing Add: PO Box 397 Mansfield OH 44901

STANTON, RUSSELL P (DFL)
Minn State Rep
b Northfield, Minn, Nov 2, 49; s Raymond Stanton & Viola Ryan S; m 1973 to Paula Nelson. Educ: Southwest State Col, BA in Social Sci, 74. Polit & Govt Pos: City councilman, Marshall, Minn, 71-72; Minn State Rep, Dist 20-B, 73-; mem, Comn on Minn Future, 75- Bus & Prof Pos: Admin asst, Minn Indust Development Comn, 72. Mem: Minn Farmers Union; Marshall Area Indust Found; Marshall Residential Care Facility for the Retarded (bd mem). Mailing Add: Arco MN 56113

STANZLER, MILTON (D)
Dem Nat Committeeman, RI
Mailing Add: 156 Blackstone Blvd Providence RI 02906

STAPLETON, ARLEY, JR (D)
Secy, Hancock Co Dem Exec Comt, Tenn
b Sneedville, Tenn, Oct 5, 29; s Arley Stapleton & Daisy Greene S; m 1952 to Deloris Fern Trent; c Dale Evan, Kathy Sharon & Tammie. Educ: East Tenn State Univ, 2 years. Polit & Govt Pos: Chmn, Good Govt Party, Hancock Co, Tenn, 66-; chmn, Hancock Co Dem Exec Comt, 67-72 & 75- Bus & Prof Pos: Parts mgr, Sneedville Motor Co, 52-; serv officer, Hancock Co, Tenn, 60-68 & registr, 68- Mil Serv: Entered as Pvt E-1, Army, 50, released as Cpl, 52, after serv in 194th Engr Combat Bn, FECOM, Korea; Korean Serv Medal; Good Conduct Medal with Three Bronze Serv Stars. Mem: Sneedville Fire Dept (asst chief); Hancock Co Rescue Squad (pres); F&AM; VFW; Am Legion. Relig: Protestant. Mailing Add: Ridge Rd Sneedville TN 37869

STAPLETON, JAMES F (R)
b Bridgeport, Conn, June 30, 32; s James Martin Stapleton & Lucy Moran S; m 1957 to Margaret Mary Daly; c James F, Brian P, Mark T, Paul M & Kathleen. Educ: Fairfield Univ, BSS, 54; Boston Col Law Sch, LLB, 57; Georgetown Univ Law Sch, LLM, 58; Honor Soc, Fairfield Univ. Polit & Govt Pos: Mem, Bridgeport Bd Educ, 60-69; co-chmn, Rep Action League, 69-71; chmn, Bridgeport Rep Town Comt, formerly; city attorney, Bridgeport, Conn, 72-; alt deleg, Rep Nat Conv, 72. Bus & Prof Pos: Attorney, Anti-Trust Div, Dept Justice, 57-58; partner, Marsh, Day & Calhoun, 58- Publ: Bd student ed, Annual survey of Massachusetts Law, 56 & 57. Mem: Bridgeport, Conn & Am Bar Asns. Relig: Roman Catholic. Mailing Add: 50 Hickory St Bridgeport CT 06610

STAPLETON, PATRICK J (D)
Pa State Sen
Mailing Add: 710 Croyland Ave Indiana PA 15701

STAPLETON, THOMAS JOSEPH, JR (D)
Pa State Rep
b Philadelphia, Pa, Jan 6, 47; s Thomas J Stapleton, Sr & Margaret Mahedy S; m 1968 to Mercedes M McCarthy; c Mercedes M & Thomas J, III. Educ: Niagara Univ, grad, 68; Villanova Univ Sch Law, grad, 72; Sigma Alpha Sigma. Polit & Govt Pos: Pa State Rep, 75- Bus & Prof Pos: Mem law firm, Donohue & Eichman, Drexel Hill, Pa, currently. Mem: Pa & Delaware Co Bar Asns; Delaware Co Estate Planning Coun; Rotary. Mailing Add: 5016 Dermond Rd Drexel Hill PA 19026

STARBUCK, WILLIAM THOMAS (R)
b Linden, Tenn, Apr 29, 93; s James E Starbuck & Mary Elizabeth Young S; m 1962 to Eunice Baker Yokley; c Jana Sue (Mrs Fred Grimes), James O Yokley (deceased) & Jerry B Yokley. Educ: Perry Co pub schs & Linden High Sch, Tenn. Polit & Govt Pos: Postmaster, Hohenwald, Tenn, 23-35 & 54-63; chmn, Lewis Co Rep Comt, Tenn, formerly. Bus & Prof Pos: Teacher, rural schs, Perry & Lewis Co, Tenn, 13-21; Rwy mail clerk, 17-18; dept clerk, Auditor of Navy Dept Off, Dept Treasury, 18; cashier, Hohenwald Bank & Trust Co, Tenn, 35-45, chmn bd dirs, 63-; owner, Starbucks, Hohenwald, Tenn, 45-54. Mem: Mason; Tenn br, Nat League Postmasters. Relig: Church of Christ. Mailing Add: 216 S Maple Hohenwald TN 38462

STARK, ALEXANDER (D)
Councilman, Baltimore, Md
b Baltimore, Md, Jan 19, 17; s Samuel S Stark & Esther M Hecker S; m 1945 to Frances Astrachan; c Jonathan Samuel. Educ: Univ Baltimore, LLB, 37. Polit & Govt Pos: Md State Deleg, formerly; asst state's attorney & asst city solicitor, formerly; councilman, Baltimore, 67- Bus & Prof Pos: Lawyer, 38- Mil Serv: Entered as Seaman, Navy, 42, released as CPO, 45, after serv in Combat Intel. Mem: Am Bar Asn. Relig: Jewish. Legal Res: 5809 Berkeley Ave Baltimore MD 21215 Mailing Add: 1500 Tower Bldg Baltimore MD 21202

STARK, FORTNEY H (PETE) (D)
US Rep, Calif
b Milwaukee, Wis, Nov 11, 31; s Fortney Hillman Stark, Sr & Dorothy Mueller S; m 1955 to Elinor Brumder; div; c Jeffrey, Beatrice Ann, Thekla & Sarah. Educ: Mass Inst Technol, BS; Univ Calif, Berkeley, MBA. Polit & Govt Pos: Mem, Dem State Cent Comt, Calif; US Rep, Calif, 72-, mem ways & means comt, US House Rep, 74- Bus & Prof Pos: Pres, Security Nat Bank, Walnut Creek, Calif, 63-72. Mil Serv: Capt, US Air Force, 55-57. Mem: Calif Dem Coun (trustee); Walnut Creek Civic Arts (bd mem); Am Civil Liberties Union (sponsor, North Calif); Contra Costa Co Coalition (adv comt); Starr-King Sch for Ministry, Berkeley (bd trustees). Relig: Unitarian. Legal Res: 63 Sereno Circle Oakland CA 94619 Mailing Add: US House of Rep Washington DC 20515

STARK, ROBERT L (R)
Secy of State, NH
b Goffstown, NH, June 5, 11; s Frederick L Stark & Caroline L Morgrage S; m 1938 to Emmy Lou Flanders; c Elizabeth A, Rodney L & Marilyn F. Educ: Univ NH, BA, 33; Theta Upsilon Omega. Polit & Govt Pos: Asst clerk, NH House Rep, 41-53, clerk, 55-57; asst secy, NH Const Conv, 48-56; Dep Secy of State, NH, 57-60, Acting Secy of State, 60-61, Secy of State, 61- Legal Res: 33 High St Goffstown NH 03045 Mailing Add: Off of Secy of State State House Concord NH 03301

STARK, ROBERT M (R)
Kans State Rep
Mailing Add: 32 Crestview Dr Salina KS 67401

STARKEY, BETHEL D (D)
Ala State Rep
Mailing Add: PO Box 3 Pisgah AL 35765

STARNES, PAUL M (D)
Tenn State Rep
b Chattanooga, Tenn, Dec 31, 34; s James Albert Starnes & Helen Hudgens S; m 1964 to Mary Grace Feezell. Educ: Tenn Wesleyan Col, BA, 57; Univ Tenn Chattanooga, MEd, 61; sr class pres, 57; Sigma Phi Epsilon. Polit & Govt Pos: Tenn State Rep, 27th Dist, 73-, mem, Educ, Gen Welfare & Dem Campaign Comts & Dem Whip, Tenn House Rep, 73- Bus & Prof Pos: Teacher, McMinn Co High Sch, Athens, Tenn, 57-59; teacher, East Ridge High Sch, Chattanooga, 59-64; dean students, Hiwassee Col, 64-69; coordr spec proj, Hamilton Co Dept Educ, 69-71, dir pub info, 74-; asst prin, East Ridge Jr High Sch, 71- Mem: Tenn Asn Sch Admin; Nat PTA Asn; Phi Delta Kappa; Admin Mgt Soc (bd dirs & chmn educ comt, Chattanooga Chap, 70-71); Kiwanis Club Madisonville (chmn, Circle K, 71-72, lt gov, Div III, 72-73). Honors & Awards: East Ridge Most Outstanding Teacher, Jaycees, 62, Tenn Most Outstanding Young Teacher, 62, Most Outstanding Young Man in East Ridge, 63; Monroe's Co Most Outstanding Man, 65; East Ridge Kiwanian of the Year, Kiwanis Int, 62 & Pres Citation, 71. Relig: United Methodist. Mailing Add: 4004 Patton Dr Chattanooga TN 37412

STARNES, RICHARD L, JR (D)
b Emory University, Ga, June 15, 36; s Richard L Starnes, Sr & Mildred Williamson S; single. Educ: Darlington Sch, 47-54; Shorter Col, AB, 58; Mercer Univ Law Sch, LLB, 61; Phi Sigma Alpha; Alpha Tau Omega. Polit & Govt Pos: Ga State Rep, 13th Dist, 66-69; Judge, State Court, Floyd Co, Ga, 69-; mem, Ga State Dem Comt, 70-74. Mem: Am & Rome Bar Asns; State Bar Asn Ga; Jaycees; Elks. Honors & Awards: Alumnus of Year, Ga Warm Springs Found, 68; One of Five Outstanding Young Men of Ga; Handicapped Georgian of Year. Relig: Episcopal. Legal Res: 14 Greenbriar Lane Rome GA 30161 Mailing Add: PO Box 1348 Rome GA 30161

STARR, ENNIS R (D)
Utah State Rep
Mailing Add: 254 Williams Ave Salt Lake City UT 84111

STARR, GEORGE W (D)
Ore State Rep
Mailing Add: 909 NE 114th Ave Portland OR 97220

STARR, TERRELL (D)
Ga State Sen
Mailing Add: 4766 Tanglewood Lane Forest Park GA 30050

STARRETT, MILDRED JEANINE (D)
Committeeman, Ariz Dem State Comt
b Searsmont, Maine, Dec 7, 28; d Joseph Carroll Fenwick & Florice Johnson F; m 1953 to Peter Fisk Starrett. Educ: Colby Col, AB, 50; Ariz State Univ, MEd, 68. Polit & Govt Pos: Precinct committeeman, Ariz Dem State Comt, formerly, state committeeman, 70-; alt deleg, Dem Nat Conv, 72. Mailing Add: 2031 W Wood Dr Phoenix AZ 85029

STARTUP, VIVIAN MARGARET (D)
Committeewoman, Washington State Dem Cent Comt
b Sunnyside, Wash, Dec 19, 13; d Dwight Clayton Lewis & Gertrude Robinson L; m 1931 to Carl Frederick Startup; c Robert Wayne, Donna (Mrs Darrell Tiller), Carl Frederick, Jr & Elisabeth (Mrs Oscar Rychlik). Educ: Sunnyside High Sch, grad, 31. Polit & Govt Pos: Precinct committeewoman, Port Angeles, Wash, 66-; chmn, Clallam Co, Dem Party, 70-71; committeewoman, Washington State Dem Cent Comt, Clallam Co, 71-; committeewoman, Clallam Co Dem Comt, 71- Bus & Prof Pos: Housewife, 31- Mem: Women's Lit Club; Clallam Co Dem Club; Franklin D Roosevelt Club; Ladybirds; PTA. Relig: Protestant. Mailing Add: 211 W Seventh Port Angeles WA 98362

STARZEC, WILLIAM ALEXANDER (D)
Mass State Rep
b Webster, Mass, Oct 14, 18; s Alexander A Starzec & Veronica Shepard S; m 1952 to Annette R Arpin; c Alexander. Educ: St Joseph Bartlett High Sch. Polit & Govt Pos: Mem recreation comt, Town of Webster, Mass, 45-48, mem water comt, 50-73, town moderator, 62-73, pub health officer, 65-73 & mem conserv comt, 68-; Mass State Rep, Fourth Worcester Dist, 72- Bus & Prof Pos: Laborer, Webster Bottling Co, 33-41, sales mgr, 46-55, vpres, 55-60, pres & treas, 60- Mil Serv: Entered as Apprentice Seaman, Navy, 41, released as Boatswains Mate 1/C, ETO & SWPac, 42-45; Victory Medal; Silver Star with 4 Bronze Medals. Mem: Am Legion; VFW; Polish Am Vet; Elks; KofC. Relig: Roman Catholic. Mailing Add: 58 E Main Webster MA 01570

STASIO, ANDREW F, JR (DREW) (R)
Chmn, Tex Young Rep Fedn
b Mineral Wells, Tex, Sept 1, 48; s Andrew F Stasio, Sr & Norma Daniel S; m 1970 to Trudy Darlyn Morley; c Trisha Lynn. Educ: Southern Methodist Univ, BA, 70, JD, 73; Lambda Chi Alpha. Polit & Govt Pos: Nat committeeman, Tex Young Rep Fedn, 70-71; state chmn, 71-; chmn first voter comt, 71-; ex officio mem, State Rep Exec Comt, 70-73; treas, Young Rep Nat Fedn, currently. Bus & Prof Pos: Gen off mgr, Shakey's Pizza Parlors, 69-73; attorney-at-law, Dallas, 73- Mem: Dallas Restaurant Asn; Tex Restaurant Asn; Jaycees. Honors & Awards: Outstanding man, Tex Young Rep Fedn, 70. Relig: Church of Christ. Mailing Add: 2004 San Jacinto Arlington TX 76012

STATEN, ROY NEVILLE (D)
Md State Sen
b Sandidges, Va, June 20, 13; married. Educ: Va Commercial Col. Polit & Govt Pos: Md State Deleg, 53-67; Md State Sen, 67-; deleg, Dem Nat Conv, 68; chmn, Md State Dem Comt, currently; mem, Dem Nat Comt, currently. Bus & Prof Pos: Acct, Div Chief, Bethlehem Shipbuilding. Mil Serv: Army. Mem: Lions; Moose. Mailing Add: 3012 Dunglow Rd Baltimore MD 21222

STATHOS, DONALD L (R)
b Portland, Ore, Apr 7, 24; s Harry L Stathos & Sylvia Davis S; m 1955 to Barbara B Brown; c Jenny L & Holly A. Educ: Ore State Univ, BA, 50; Sigma Nu. Polit & Govt Pos: Chmn, Youth for Eisenhower-Nixon, Ore, 56; chmn, Young Rep, Ore, 57; chmn, Jackson Co Rep Cent Comt, 58-59; secy, Ore State Rep Cent Comt, 60-61; chmn, Ore State Rep, Jackson Co, 69-72. Bus & Prof Pos: Pres, Don Stathos, Insuror, Inc, 60-68. Mil Serv: Entered as Seaman, Navy, 42, released as PO 2/C, 45, after serv in Armed Guard, SPac, 42-45; 2nd Lt, Res, 45-50. Mem: Ins Agts Asn; Lions; Keep Ore Green Asn. Relig: Methodist. Mailing Add: 40 Coachman Dr Jacksonville OR 97530

STATKUS, WALTER CARL (D)
Mem, Mich Dem State Cent Comt
b Holly, Mich, July 2, 45; s Peter Statkus & Margaret Belbot S; m 1965 to Carol Ann Mankowski; c Peter Michael, Walter Paul & Philip Alexander. Educ: Macomb Co Community Col, Warren, Mich, 63-64 & 69-70; Mich State Univ, Ins Inst, cert, 72. Polit & Govt Pos: Mem bd tax rev, Warren, Mich, 66-69; precinct deleg, 68-; mem, Mich Dem State Cent Comt, 70-; deleg, Dem Nat Conv, 72; mem, Econ Develop Authority, Macomb Co, 72-; membership chmn, Macomb Co Dem Comt, 73. Bus & Prof Pos: Self-employed real estate agt, 65-72; pub rels, TransAm Title Corp, 70-71; agt, Maccabees Mutual Ins & Prudential Ins Co, 72-; agt, Security Builders Ltd, 73- Mem: United Dem of Warren. Relig: Roman Catholic. Mailing Add: 32442 Gloede Warren MI 48093

STATON, WILLIAM WAYNE (D)
NC State Sen
b Marshville, NC, Oct 11, 16; s Oscar M Staton & May Young S; m 1947 to Ellen Douglas Boone; c William Wayne, Jr & Allyn Moore. Educ: Wake Forest Univ, AB, 38, Law Sch, LLB, 41, JD, 70; Univ NC; Judge Adv Gen Sch, US Army; Omicron Delta Kappa. Polit & Govt Pos: Pres, Young Dem Clubs of NC, 52-53; personal campaign mgr for Gov Terry Sanford; deleg, Dem Nat Conv, 52, 60 & 64; co attorney, Lee Co, NC, 60-62; mem, NC State Dem Comt, 60-64; committeeman, Dem Nat Exec Comt, NC, 60-64; city attorney, Sanford, NC, 63-65; NC State Rep, 22nd Dist, formerly; NC State Sen, 68-; deleg, Dem Nat Mid-Term Conf, 74. Bus & Prof Pos: Dir, Southern Nat Bank of NC, 67-73; Mid-South Bank & Trust Co, 73- Mil Serv: Entered as Pvt, Army, 42, released as Capt, 46, after serv in Hq 78th Inf Div, Berlin Mil Dist, Ger; ETO Ribbon with 5 Battle Stars; Bronze Star Medal; Purple Heart; Col, Judge Adv Gen Corps, NC Army Nat Guard, formerly. Mem: Elks; Moose; Am Legion (judge advocate, NC Dept Am Legion); VFW; Wake Forest Univ (bd trustees). Honors & Awards: Silver Beaver, Boy Scouts. Relig: Baptist. Legal Res: 636 Palmer Dr Sanford NC 27330 Mailing Add: PO Box 1320 Sanford NC 27330

STAUFFER, ROBERT EDWARD (R)
Mem Exec Comt, Winnebago Co Rep Party, Wis
b Oshkosh, Wis, May 23, 24; s Adolph F Stauffer & Viola Eulrich S; m 1947 to Shirley L Wrasse; c Robert E, Jr & Scott W. Educ: Univ Chicago, 1 year; Yale Univ, 6 months; Northwestern Univ, BS, 48. Polit & Govt Pos: City councilman, Oshkosh, Wis, 57-59; vpres coun, 59-60, pres coun, 60-63; mem planning comn, 63-65; vchmn, Winnebago Co Rep Party, 65-67, chmn, 67-69, mem exec comt, currently, treas, 75-; mem exec comt, Sixth Dist Rep Party, 67-; mem, Winnebago Co Exec Bd, 70- Mil Serv: Entered as Pvt, Air Force, 43, released as 1st Lt, 46, after serv in ETO. Mem: Am Inst CPA; Wis Soc CPA (mem trial bd comt, 71-, educ found & prof conduct comt); Elks; Lions; (pres, currently); CHAMCO, Inc (pres). Relig: United Church of Christ; councilman, 6 years, treas, Emmanuel United Church of Christ, currently, mem long range planning comt, 72-, mem investment comt, 73. Mailing Add: 317 W 15th Ave Oshkosh WI 54901

STAUFFER, SARAH ANN (R)
b Lancaster, Pa, June 13, 15; d Charles F Stauffer & Gertrude Frantz S; single. Educ: Lancaster Bus Col; Franklin & Marshall Col; Univ Pa, Wharton Sch Bus Admin. Polit & Govt Pos: Participant in formation local group, Young Rep, Pa, 36, state asst ed mag, 37, participant in reformation of local group, 46, Pa jr nat committeewoman, 48-50; mem state bd, 48-50; mem legis, resolutions, membership & prog comts, Pa Coun Rep Women, 47-56, jr publicity chmn, 48, mem bd, 58-62; co-chmn & organizer jr group, Rep Party, 48-51; pres, Women's Rep Club Lancaster Co, 58-60; formed nat comt of civic leaders to support Nixon, Nat Fedn Rep Women, 60; deleg, White House Conf Children & Youth, 60; deleg, press meeting nat orgn rep on prev juv delinquency & Wash Pres Conf on Voice of Am; Rep Nat Committeewoman, Pa, 64-74, mem, Rep Nat Exec Comt, 64-68; deleg, Rep Nat Conv, 68 & 72; deleg, White House Conf on Food, Nutrition & Health, 69; deleg, Women's Bur Nat Conf, US Dept Labor, 70. Bus & Prof Pos: Off mgr & admin asst, Aircraft Dept, Munitions Div, Armstrong Cork Co, 42-44. Mil Serv: Entered as Lt, Motor Corps, Am Red Cross, released as Capt, 46, after serv with 45th Inf Div, Mediter & European Theaters Opers; also dir personnel & opers, Clubmobile Dept, US Occupied Territory, ETO, 46; Sicilian, Rome Arno, Ardennes-Alsace, Southern France, Naples-Foggia, Anzio, Rhineland & Cent European Campaign Ribbons. Mem: Am Acad Polit & Social Sci; Bus & Prof Women; Women's Nat Rep Club; YMCA; Asn Jr Leagues Am, Inc. Honors & Awards: Named Distinguished Daughter of Pa, 66. Relig: Lutheran. Mailing Add: Rohrerstown PA 17571

STAVISKY, LEONARD PRICE (D)
NY State Assemblyman
Mailing Add: 16221 Powells Cove Whitestone NY 11357

STEAKLEY, ZOLLIE COFFER, JR (D)
Justice, Supreme Court of Tex
b Rotan, Tex, Aug 29, 08; s Zollie Coffer Steakley & Frances Elizabeth McGlasson S; m 1939 to Ruth Butler. Educ: Hardin-Simmons Univ, BA, 29; Univ Tex, JD, 32. Hon Degrees: LLD, Univ Corpus Christi, 58 & Hardin-Simmons Univ, 59. Polit & Govt Pos: Asst Attorney Gen, Tex, 39-42; Secy of State, Tex, 57-60; Justice, Supreme Court of Tex, 61- Bus & Prof Pos: Attorney-at-law, 32-39 & 46-57. Mil Serv: Naval Res, 42-46. Mem: Am Bar Asn; State Bar of Tex; Philos Soc. Relig: Baptist. Legal Res: 3302 Mt Bonnell Dr Austin TX 78731 Mailing Add: Supreme Court of Tex Box 12248 Capitol Sta Austin TX 78711

STEAR, DAVID SPRING (R)
Committeeman, Rep State Cent Comt La
b Chambersburg, Pa, July 17, 25; s Jacob Ray Stear & Freda Hallie Spring; m 1954 to Marjorie Belle Matherne; c Freda Anne, Susan Spring, Joan Elizabeth, Ruth Allison & Margaret Frances. Educ: Washington & Jefferson Col, BA; Univ Tulsa, BSPE; Alpha Tau Omega. Polit & Govt Pos: Co-treas, Dem for Nixon Comt, La, 60; co-chmn, Goldwater for President Comt, 64; committeeman, Iberia Parish Rep Exec Comt, 64-, chmn, 68-; committeeman, Rep State Cent Comt La, 64- Bus & Prof Pos: Petroleum engr trainee, Texas Co, Golden Meadow, La,

50-51, Houma, La, 51; petroleum engr, 51-54, Golden Meadow, La, 54-57; petroleum engr, Texaco Inc, New Iberia, La, 57- Mil Serv: Entered as Pvt, Army, 44, released as Pfc, 45, after serv in 75th Div Co A, 289th Inf Regt, ETO, 45; Combat Infantryman Badge, Purple Heart; ETO Ribbon with Battle Star. Publ: Elements of dynamometer tests, World Oil, 2/1/51. Mem: Am Inst Mining, Metallurgical & Petroleum Engrs; Evangeline Chap, Am Petroleum Inst; Nat Asn Corrosion Engrs. Relig: Methodist. Mailing Add: 410 Ernest St New Iberia LA 70560

STECKLER, SANFORD RICHARD (D)
Miss State Sen
b Biloxi, Miss, June 28, 40; s Frotscher Richard Steckler & Doris Trochesset S; m 1969 to Judith Ann Shuff; c Jason Richard. Educ: Univ Miss, BBA, 62 & JD, 66. Polit & Govt Pos: Miss State Sen, 62-66 & 72-; deleg, Coun of State Govt, 62-66; deleg, Nat Legis Conf, 62-66; comt mem, Intergovt Rels, 62-66. Bus & Prof Pos: Real estate salesman, Blessey Realty, 64; attorney-at-law, 66-73; city attorney, City of Biloxi, 69-73; mem, Biloxi Port Comn, 70-73. Publ: Co-auth, The law of evidence, 67; auth, Legislative report, Miss Scene Mag, 72. Mem: Miss Bar Asn; Am Trial Lawyers Asn; Am Judicature Soc; Jaycees; Rotary. Honors & Awards: Distinguished Serv Award, Biloxi Jaycees, 71. Relig: Catholic. Mailing Add: PO Box 486 Biloxi MS 39533

STEED, TOM (D)
US Rep, Okla
b Rising Star, Tex, Mar 2, 04; s Walter H Steed & Sallie Johnson S; m 1923 to Hazel Bennett; c Richard N & Roger (deceased). Polit & Govt Pos: US Rep, Okla, 48-; deleg, Dem Nat Conv, 68; deleg, Dem Nat Mid-Term Conf, 74. Bus & Prof Pos: Newspaperman, Okla Dailies, 20 years; managing ed, Shawnee News & Star, 4 years. Mil Serv: Entered as Pvt, Army, 42, released as 2nd Lt, 45, after serv in India-Burma Theater & Off War Info. Mem: Masonic Lodge. Honors & Awards: Elected to Minute Man Hall of Fame, 70. Relig: Methodist. Legal Res: 1904 N Pennsylvania Shawnee OK 74801 Mailing Add: US House of Rep 2405 Rayburn Bldg Washington DC 20515

STEEL, GEORGE EDWIN, JR (D)
Mem, Ark State Dem Cent Comt
b Nashville, Ark, Aug 9, 45; s George Edwin Steel & Vestal Montgomery S; single. Educ: Univ Ark, Bus Sch, BSBA, 67, Sch Law, JD, 70; Sigma Nu. Polit & Govt Pos: Dep Prosecuting Attorney, Pike Co, Ark, 71-; mem, Ark State Dem Cent Comt, 71-; prosecuting attorney, Ninth Judicial Dist, currently. Mil Serv: 1st Lt, Army Res, 71- Mem: Am & Ark Bar Asns; Rotary Club; Jaycees. Relig: Methodist. Mailing Add: 102 Main Nashville AR 71852

STEELE, BARBARA W (R)
b Philadelphia, Pa, Apr 17, 39; d George H Walter, Jr & Eleanor Herman W; c Barbara Louise. Educ: Stockton State Col. Polit & Govt Pos: Ed Life YR Newsletter & publicity chmn, NJ Young Rep, 68-69, assoc vchmn, 69-71, vchmn, 71-73; dir, Ocean Co Youth William T Cahill for Gov, 69; pres, Dover Twp Young Rep, NJ, 60-70; co-chmn, Youth Activities Comt, NJ Fedn Rep Women, 69-71, mem bd gov, 69-; deleg region II, Young Rep Nat Fedn, 69-; chmn, Ocean Co Youth for Edwin B Forsythe for Cong, 70; chmn, Ocean Co Young Rep, 70-71, polit chmn, 71-; alt deleg-at-lg, Rep Nat Conv, 72; mem, NJ State Bd Mediation, currently. Bus & Prof Pos: Social ed, NJ Courier, 63-65; secy, Freeholder George F Makin, 65-72. Mem: NJ Heart Asn (vpres, 73-); Am Legion. Honors & Awards: Outstanding Young Rep of Dover Twp, 69; Hardcharger, Young Rep Nat Fedn; Citation of Merit, Ocean Co Heart Asn; First Ocean Co Hon Vis Homemaker; Outstanding NJ Young Rep, 70-71. Relig: Lutheran. Mailing Add: 26 Smith Rd Toms River NJ 08753

STEELE, DEAN C (R)
Del State Sen
b 1905; m to Frances; c Dr A D Steele & Mrs S S Hopkins. Polit & Govt Pos: Del State Sen, 67-, chmn, Finance Comt, Del State Senate & chmn, Joint Finance Comt, Del Gen Assembly, formerly; chmn, State Unified Sch Legis Comt, formerly, dir, Del Safety Coun, formerly. Bus & Prof Pos: Control mgr, Pigments Dept, DuPont, 42-71; pres, Gen Gas & Elec Corp, formerly; acct (finance, tax); bus mgt; pub utility acct; officer & dir of numerous pub utilities co. Mem: Financial Execs Inst; Nat Asn Accts (past pres, Del Chap); life mem Del Cong of PTA (past pres, legis chmn & chmn of Study Comt on State Finances); Am Cancer Soc (treas, New Castle Br, 72-). Relig: Christian. Mailing Add: 128 Rockingham Dr Windsor Hills Wilmington DE 19803

STEELE, EVERETT G (R)
Ill State Sen
Mailing Add: RR 1 Box 10 Glen Carbon IL 62034

STEELE, JANE RIDDEL (R)
Mem, Rep State Cent Comt La
b Harrisonburg, Va, Dec 24, 30; d Claude Wheatley Riddel & Mabel Alice Taylor R; m 1949 to Edgar Lowell Steele; c James Ewell & Laura Jane. Educ: Furman Univ, 48-49; Anderson Jr Col, SC, secy cert, 49. Polit & Govt Pos: Precinct chmn, La Jolla Rep Party, Calif, 63-66; bd mem, La Jolla Rep Assembly, 65-66; hq co-chmn, Reagan for Gov, Pacific Beach, 66; mem exec comt, East Baton Rouge Parish Rep Party, La, 67-71, chmn, currently; vpres, Baton Rouge Rep Women's Club, 71-72; vchmn & precinct orgn chmn, East Baton Rouge Parish Polit Action Coun, 71-; target chmn, East Baton Rouge Parish, Nixon for President, 72, presidential elector, Sixth Dist, 72; mem, Rep State Cent Comt La, 72-; corresponding secy & chmn commun, La Fedn Rep Women, 73- Publ: Ed, The Rep Outlook, La Fedn Rep Women, 69 & The Rep Advocate, Rep Party of La, 70-71. Mem: East Baton Rouge Parish Rep Women's Club. Relig: Methodist. Mailing Add: 737 Brinwood Ave Baton Rouge LA 70816

STEELE, MARIE Y (R)
VChmn, St Charles Co Rep Comt, Mo
b Annada, Mo, July 30, 26; d John Taylor Young & Neva Sharp Y; m 1951 to William Henry Steele; c Lynn Caryll & Sandra Marie. Educ: Univ Mo-Columbia, 50-51. Polit & Govt Pos: Committeewoman, O'Fallon Twp, Mo, 66-; chmn, St Charles Co Rep Comt, 70-72, vchmn, 72-; mem, License Bur Agt, 73-; vchmn, Ninth Cong Dist, currently. Mem: First Capitol Women's Federated Rep Club of St Charles Co; Femme Osage Federated Rep Women's Club (secy). Relig: Christian. Mailing Add: 727 Cordes O'Fallon MO 63366

STEELE, ROBERT HAMPTON (R)
b Hartford, Conn, Nov 3, 38; s Robert L Steele & Shirley S; m 1961 to Ann Elizabeth Truex; c Kristen, Alison, Jeffrey & Bradley. Educ: Amherst Col, BA Eng, 60; Columbia Univ, MA Govt, 63, cert from Russian Inst; Delta Upsilon. Polit & Govt Pos: Soviet specialist, Cent Intel Agency, 63-68; US Rep, Conn, 70-74; deleg, Rep Nat Conv, 72; rep cand for Gov Conn, 74. Bus & Prof Pos: Securities analyst, Travelers Ins Co, 68-70; exec vpres, Norwich Savings Soc, Norwich, Conn, 75- Honors & Awards: One of Ten Outstanding Young Men in Am, US Jaycees, 71. Relig: Congregational. Mailing Add: Forest View Dr Vernon CT 06066

STEELE, ROBERT HOWE (R)
Mem, San Francisco Co Cent Comt, Calif
b Hartville, Mo, Dec 28, 13; s Howe Steele & Linnie Robertson S; m 1949 to Jean Welborn; c Frederick Howe & Marjorie Ann. Educ: Drury Col, AB; Harvard Grad Sch Bus Admin, MBA. Polit & Govt Pos: Pres, San Francisco Young Rep, Calif, 49-51; nat committeeman, Calif Young Rep, 50; mem, San Francisco Co Cent Comt, Calif, 52-, chmn, 54-60; chmn, San Francisco Eisenhower for President Campaign Comt, 56; presidential elector, 56 & 60; pres, Asn Calif Co Chmn, 56-60; deleg, Rep Nat Conv, 60 & 64; treas, Calif State Goldwater for President Campaign Comt, 64. Mil Serv: Entered as Pvt, Army Signal Corps, 42, released as Capt, 55; World War II Victory, Good Conduct, Am Theater & Armed Forces Res Medals. Relig: Episcopal. Mailing Add: 2450 Francisco St San Francisco CA 94123

STEELMAN, ALAN WATSON (R)
US Rep, Tex
b Little Rock, Ark, Mar 15, 42; s Ples Steelman & Flossie Watson S; m 1962 to Carolyn Findley; c Robin, Kimble, Alan, Jr & Allison. Educ: Baylor Univ, BA, 64; Southern Methodist Univ, MLA, 17; fel, Inst Polit, Harvard Univ, 72; Pi Sigma Alpha; Tryon Coterie Soc Club. Polit & Govt Pos: Exec dir, Dallas Co Rep Party, Tex, 66-69; exec dir, President's Adv Coun on Minority Bus Enterprise, 69-72; mem, Spec White House Speakers Task Force on Phases I & II, 69-72; US Rep, Fifth Dist, Tex, 73- Bus & Prof Pos: Exec dir, Dallas Fed Savings & Loan Asn, 65-66; exec dir, Sam Wyly Found of Dallas, 69. Mem: LQC Lamar Soc. Relig: Baptist. Legal Res: 6938 Wabash Circle Dallas TX 75214 Mailing Add: 3507 Springland Lane NW Washington DC 20008

STEELMAN, DORMAN LLOYD (R)
b Cedar Grove, Mo, Feb 17, 27; s Reamy Aaron Steelman & Erma Kell S; m 1951 to Maxine Livesay; c David Lloyd, Deborah Lynne & Donald Alan. Educ: Univ Mo, LLB, 52, JD, 69. Polit & Govt Pos: City attorney, Salem, Mo, 56-57; Mo State Rep, Dent Co, 57-64, floor leader, Mo House Rep, 60-64; chmn, Mo Rep State Cent Comt, 66-68; deleg, Rep Nat Conv, 60 & 68. Bus & Prof Pos: Attorney-at-law, 52- Mil Serv: Navy, 44-46. Mem: Odd Fellows; Mason; Am Legion; VFW. Relig: Methodist. Mailing Add: PO Box 110 Salem MO 65560

STEELMAN, EARLENE MAE (R)
VChmn, Dent Co Rep Comt, Mo
b Salem, Mo, Nov 9, 27; d Earl Keithly & Dorothy Pewitt K; m 1943 to Hershel David Steelman; c Judy (Mrs Jr Inman), Marlene (Mrs Jim Smith), Sherry (Mrs Willie Pyatt), Claudia (Mrs Martin Connell), Jerry & Sandra. Polit & Govt Pos: Committeewoman, Mo Rep State Comt, currently; vchmn, Dent Co Rep Comt, currently. Bus & Prof Pos: Cook, Montauk Lodge, Salem, Mo, currently; secy, Salem Auction Co, Salem, Mo. Relig: Baptist. Mailing Add: Rte 5 Salem MO 65560

STEEN, DONALD MARINER (R)
VChmn, Nebr Rep State Cent Comt
b Scottsbluff, Nebr, Mar 25, 24; s Dr Clarence G Steen & Jean Whipple S; m 1946 to Bonnie Jeanne Jirdon; c John Robert & William Gary. Educ: Univ Nebr, 41-42; US Merchant Marine Acad, 43-45; Univ Denver, 47; Sigma Alpha Epsilon. Polit & Govt Pos: Polit & Govt Pos: Comt mem, Scotts Bluff Co Rep Party, Nebr, 48-, vchmn, 63-65, chmn, 65-72; mem finance comt, Nebr Rep State Cent Comt, 68-70, mem exec comt, 69-70, vchmn, 74- Bus & Prof Pos: Exec vpres, John R Jirdon Inc, Morrill, 47-; pres, Blue J Feeds, Inc, Gering, 50-; consult, Allied Chem Corp, New York, 66-71. Mil Serv: Entered as Midn, Navy, 43, released as Lt(jg), 46, after serv as Chief Eng, USS Rushmore, Pac, 45-46. Mem: Am Soc Naval Eng; Am Legion; Rotary (pres); Shrine; Mason. Relig: Presbyterian. Mailing Add: PO Box 295 Morrill NE 69358

STEEN, J C (R)
b Greenville, Ala; s Jasper C Steen & Ruth Crawford S; m to Jean Kimmell; c Donna Jean (Mrs Olson), Gary, Randolph, Melanie & Timothy. Educ: Univ Ala; Univ Va, Exten; George Washington Univ. Polit & Govt Pos: Legis asst to US Rep Armistead Selden, Ala, formerly; admin asst to US Rep William L Dickinson, Ala, 69- Mil Serv: Entered as Cpl, Army, 55, released as Sgt, 47, after serv in Ger. Mem: Lions; House Admin Assts Asn; Bull Elephants. Relig: Episcopal. Legal Res: Montgomery AL Mailing Add: 4604 Brinkley Rd Camp Springs MD 20031

STEEN, JAMES WILSON (R)
Idaho State Sen
b Enterprise, Ore, Oct 10, 16; s William Newell Steen & Lois Baterton Wilson S; m 1938 to Hazel Jane McAnulty; c James Willard & Juanita Jane (Mrs Cunningham). Educ: King Hill High Sch, grad, 35. Polit & Govt Pos: Idaho State Sen, 53-54, 70-; precinct committeeman, Rep Party, 60-70; hwy comnr, Glenns Ferry Hwy Dist, 68- Bus & Prof Pos: Locomotive engr, Union Pac RR, 41-; owner & operator stock ranch, Glenns Ferry, Idaho; mem, Elmore-Mayfield Soil Conserv Serv, 64- Mem: Mason; Elks; Brotherhood of Locomotive Firemen & Enginemen; Elmore Cattlemens Asn (dir & vpres, currently). Honors & Awards: Past Master Fidelity Lodge 80. Relig: Methodist. Legal Res: Hot Spring Ranch Glenns Ferry ID 83623 Mailing Add: Drawer B Glenns Ferry ID 83623

STEERS, NEWTON IVAN, JR (R)
Md State Sen
b Glen Ridge, NJ, Jan 13, 17; s Newton Ivan Steers & Claire Louise Herder S; m 1957 to Nina Gore Auchincloss; c Newton I, III, Hugh Auchincloss & Burr Gore. Educ: Yale Col, BA, 39; Mass Inst Technol, cert advan meteorol, 42; Yale Law Sch, LLB, 48, JD, 71; Zeta Psi; Phi Delta Phi. Polit & Govt Pos: Rep cand, US Rep, Md, 62; chmn, Md Deleg, Rep Nat Conv, 64; state chmn, Rep Party, Md, 64-66; Md State Ins Comnr, 67-70; Md State Sen, 70- Bus & Prof Pos: Pres, Shares in Am Indust, Inc, 53-65; pres, Atomics, Physics & Sci Fund. Mil Serv: Entered as Pvt, Army Air Force, 42, released as Capt, 46, after serv in 368th Fighter Group, ETO; Presidential Unit Citation; Capt, Air Force Res. Relig: Methodist. Mailing Add: 6601 River Rd Bethesda MD 20034

STEEVES, JOHN M
b Brinsmade, NDak, May 6, 05; m to Jean Bergstresser; c Mrs R H Bergstrom. Educ: Walla Walla Col, BA, 27; Univ Wash, MA, 36. Polit & Govt Pos: With Off War Info, China-Burma-India Theatre, 43-45; career officer, Foreign Serv, US State Dept, 45-, first secy, New Delhi, 48-50, counr, Nat War Col, 50-51, Tokyo, 51-53 & 55-57, Djakarta, 53-55, foreign rels consult to High Comnr of Ryuku Islands & consul gen in Naha, 55-57, polit adv to Comdr in Chief, Pac, 57-59, consul gen, Hong Kong & Macao, 59-60, Dep Asst Secy of State for Far Eastern Affairs, 60-62, US Ambassador to Afghanistan, 62-66, Dir-Gen, Foreign Serv, US State Dept, 66-70; chmn, Ctr for Strategic & Int Studies, 70-, chmn exec comt, 73- Bus & Prof Pos: Educ work in India, 27-35 & 36-43. Mailing Add: Box 153 Fairfield PA 17320

STEFANO, VINCENT, JR (D)
Councilman, Burbank, Calif
b Burbank, Calif, Dec 21, 38; s Vincent Stefano & Mary Emma Sereno S; c Vincent Joseph, Robert James & Daniel Anthony. Educ: Univ Southern Calif, BS in pub admin; Loyola Univ Sch Law, JD; Blue Key; Blackstonians; Theta Xi; Phi Delta Phi. Polit & Govt Pos: Dep city attorney, Los Angeles, Calif, 65-66; city prosecutor, Burbank, 66-68; dep dist attorney, Los Angeles Co, 68-70; councilman, Burbank, 73-, mayor, 74-75. Bus & Prof Pos: Law partner, Call, Stafano & Epstein, Encino, Calif, 70- Mem: Am, Los Angeles Co & San Fernando Valley Bar Asns; San Fernando Valley Criminal Bar Asn. Relig: Catholic. Legal Res: Burbank CA Mailing Add: 15915 Ventura Blvd Encino CA 91436

STEFFEN, DORIS J (D)
Chmn, Forest Co Dem Comt, Wis
b Sheboygan, Wis, Jan 23, 44; d Arno Christel & Loraine Haensgen C; m 1968 to P James Steffen; c Christel Ann & Andrew James. Educ: Marquette Univ, BA, 68. Polit & Govt Pos: Mem, Forest Co for McGovern, Wis, 72; alt deleg, Dem Nat Conv, 72; chmn, Forest Co Dem Comt, 74- Mem: Citizens Adv Coun for Forest Co. Relig: Catholic. Mailing Add: 5105 E Silver Lake Rd Laona WI 54541

STEFFEN, FREDERICK JOHN (D)
Chmn, Kane Co Dem Party, Ill
b Elgin, Ill, Aug 18, 34; s Ezra Daniel Steffen & Rose Lydia Grim S; m 1960 to Doris Judith Johnston; c Julie Ann, Frederick John, Jr & Robert James. Educ: Univ Ill, BS, 58, John Marshall Law Sch, JD, 62; Sigma Nu. Polit & Govt Pos: Asst Attorney Gen, Kane Co, State of Ill, 65-68; mem, Zoning Bd of Appeals, Elgin, 66-71, chmn, 68-71; chmn, Kane Co Dem Party, 70- Mil Serv: Entered as Pvt, Army, 54, released as Sgt, 56, after serv in 31st Infantry, Korea, 55-56. Mem: Am & Ill Bar Asns; Isaac Walton League; Kiwanis. Legal Res: 737 Deborah Ave Elgin IL 60120 Mailing Add: 11 Douglas Ave Suite 201 Elgin IL 60120

STEGEMANN, JOHN DIETRICH (D)
Chmn, Sioux Co Dem Cent Comt, Iowa
b Boyden, Iowa, Oct 18, 03; s Herman Stegemann & Katherine Winter S; m 1944 to Anna Laura Schedtler; c Esther. Educ: Boyden High Sch, Iowa, grad. Polit & Govt Pos: Chmn, Sioux Co Dem Cent Comt, Iowa, 66- Bus & Prof Pos: Vpres, Int Luther League of Am Lutheran Church, Columbus, Ohio, 33-35, pres, 35-43. Publ: The Federal Farm Program, Des Moines Register, 7/67. Mem: Nat Farmers Union. Relig: Lutheran. Mailing Add: RR 1 Boyden IA 51234

STEGER, WILLIAM MERRITT (R)
b Dallas, Tex, Aug 22, 20; s Merritt Steger & Lottie Reese S; m 1948 to Ann Hollandsworth; c Reed. Educ: Baylor Univ, 38-41; Southern Methodist Univ, LLB, 50; Delta Theta Phi. Polit & Govt Pos: US Attorney, Eastern Dist Tex, 53-59, US Dist Judge, 70-72; state committeeman, Rep Party, Tex, 66-69, state chmn, 69-70; deleg, Rep Nat Conv, 68. Bus & Prof Pos: Vpres, Tex Rose Festival Asn, 67; chmn grievance comt, State Bar Tex, 67-68. Mil Serv: Entered as Aviation Cadet, Air Force, 42, released as Capt, 47, after serv in 31st Fighter Group NAfrican, Tunisian, Sicilian & Ital Campaign, 42-44; Air Medal with 4 Oak Leaf Clusters. Relig: Baptist. Mailing Add: Box 3684 Beaumont TX 77704

STEGMAIER, DAVID DIKE (D)
b Montreal, Que, Dec 22, 47; s John Lloyd Stegmaier & Daphne Yuki Shaw S; m 1971 to C Jane Hurn. Educ: Earlham Col, BA in Polit Sci, 72; Rhode Island Col, 72-73; Ionian Lit Soc; Int Students Asn. Polit & Govt Pos: Chmn, Student Polit Affairs Comt, Earlham Col, 67-68; organizer on canvassing, Robert Kennedy for President, Ind Primary, Richmond, 68; press aide, George McGovern for President, Dem Nat Conv, 68; pres & co-founder, Earlham Model UN Security Coun, 69; research asst, Hubert H Humphrey, Washington, DC, 70; campaign aide, Campaign of Phillip R Sharp, Dem Cand for Cong, Tenth Cong Dist, Ind, 70; vol canvasser, McGovern for President Campaign, RI Primary, 72; alt deleg, Dem Nat Conv, 72; state coordr of vols, McGovern for President Campaign, RI, 72; mem, New Dem Coalition of RI, 73- Bus & Prof Pos: Pvt Eng lang tutor, Osaka, Japan, 65-66; maintenance man, Clear Creek Logging Co, Inc, Kake, Alaska, 68; desk clerk, C Itoh & Co, Chicago, Ill, 68; instr, Eng Lang Educ Ctr, Tokyo, Japan, 69; bartender, Francis Green State Airport, Warwick, RI, 71; clothing salesman, Gentry Shop, Warwick, 72-73; stock boy, First Nat Supermarket, Providence, 73-; VISTA vol, RI Legal Servs, Providence, RI, 74- Relig: Unitarian. Mailing Add: 34 Elmgrove Ave Providence RI 02906

STEHLING, ARTHUR (D)
b Fredericksburg, Tex, Oct 10, 04; s John Stehling & Mary Lewis S; m 1927 to Beatrice Deen; c Beatrice Helen, Jack A & Elaine (Mrs Wallendorf). Educ: St Edwards Univ, LLB, 31; LaSalle Exten Univ. Polit & Govt Pos: Chmn, Gillespie Co Dem Exec Comt, Tex, formerly. Bus & Prof Pos: Attorney; pres, Security State Bank & Trust, Brady Mills, Brady, Tex, Radio Sta KNAF & Fredericksburg Cable Corp, Fredericksburg, Tex; vpres, Allen Keller Co; secy, Mkt Produce Co; Indust Projs Corp. Mem: Fredericksburg Lions Club; Fed Legis Comt, Am Bar Asn. Relig: Catholic. Legal Res: 118 W Main Fredericksburg TX 78624 Mailing Add: 218 W Main St Fredericksburg TX 78624

STEIFF, IRMA S (D)
b Everly, Iowa, May 30, 18; d Max A Jensen & Helena Feddersen J; m 1945 to Paul Walter Steiff; c Renee, Judy, Lorene & Dennis. Educ: St Cloud State Teachers Col, 36-37; Am Bus Col, 37-38. Polit & Govt Pos: Vchmn, Hancock Co Dem Cent Comt, Iowa, 66-72. Relig: Methodist. Mailing Add: Rte 2 Forest City IA 50436

STEIGER, SAM (R)
US Rep, Ariz
b New York, NY, Mar 10, 29; s Lewis Steiger & Rebecca Klein S; m to Lynda K; c twins, Lewis & Gail & Delia Rebecca. Educ: Cornell Univ, 46-48; Colo Agr & Mech Univ, 48-50. Polit & Govt Pos: Ariz State Sen, 61-64; US Rep, Ariz, 67-, mem exec comt, Rep Cong Campaign Comt, 73-; mem, Am Indian Policy Review Comn; mem, Comn on Review of Nat Policy Toward Gambling. Bus & Prof Pos: Rancher. Mil Serv: 1st Lt, Army, 51-53; Silver Star; Purple Heart. Mem: Yavapai Co Sheriff's Posse; Elks; Am Legion; Mason; Kiwanis. Legal Res: Prescott AZ 86301 Mailing Add: 2432 Rayburn House Off Bldg Washington DC 20515

STEIGER, WILLIAM ALBERT (R)
US Rep, Wis
b Oshkosh, Wis, May 15, 38; m 1963 to Janet Dempsey; c William Raymond. Educ: Univ Wis, BS, 60. Polit & Govt Pos: Nat chmn, Col Young Rep, 59-61, Wis State Assemblyman, 61-66; US Rep, Wis, 67-, mem comt educ & labor, US House Rep, 67-, mem planning & research comt, 69-, mem select comt to study House comt struct, 73-, mem ways & means comt, 74-, mem exec comt, Nat Rep Cong Comt, 73-; deleg, Rep Nat Conv, 68 & 72; chmn, Rep Nat Rules Study Comt, 73-; mem exec comt, Rep Party Wis, presently. Bus & Prof Pos: Pres, Steiger-Rathke Develop Co, 62-66. Publ: Form or substance?, Nat Civic Rev, 4/64. Mem: Am Polit Sci Asn (adv comt cong fels, 70-); bd dirs, Lutheran Home of Oshkosh, Inc; Joselin Diabetes Found Corp; People-to-People (bd trustees, 71-). Honors & Awards: Young Am Medal for Serv, presented by President Eisenhower, White House, 55; Selected One of Five Outstanding Young Men of Wis, Wis Jr CofC, 64; Distinguished Serv Award, Oshkosh Jaycees, 65; Selected Outstanding Young Rep of Wis, Wis Fedn Young Rep, 66; Selected One of Ten Outstanding Young Men in Am, US Jaycees, 68. Relig: Episcopal. Legal Res: PO Box 1279 Oshkosh WI 54901 Mailing Add: 1025 Longworth Off Bldg Washington DC 20515

STEIN, ANDREW JAY (D)
NY State Assemblyman
b New York, NY, Jan 10, 45; s Jerry Finkelstein & Shirley Marks F; div; c Paige Amber. Educ: Southampton Col, BA, 68. Polit & Govt Pos: NY State Assemblyman, 69-, chmn, Minority Comt on Malnutrition & Human Needs, NY State Assembly, mem, Comt on Housing & comt on Health, chmn, Temporary State Comn on Costs & the Econ, 73-75; mem, NY State Joint Legis Comt on Consumer Affairs; mem, Nursing Home Investigation. Bus & Prof Pos: Vpres, NY Law J, 68. Mem: City Club of NY; Citizens Union; Am Jewish Comt; B'nai B'rith. Relig: Jewish. Legal Res: 434 E 52nd St New York NY 10022 Mailing Add: 845 Third Ave New York NY 10022

STEIN, MARY KATHLEEN (KAY) (D)
Chmn, Howell Co Dem Comt, Mo
b Kansas City, Mo, Jan 18, 22; d Jerry D Rangos & Lillian Tanner R; m 1945 to Conrad A Stein; c Michael J, Joseph C, Mary K, James R (deceased) & Sharon C. Educ: Univ Mo, 39-40; Kansas City Secretarial Sch, 41; Army Budgetary Control Sch, 41; Kappa Gamma. Polit & Govt Pos: Motor vehicle agt, Mo, 62-; chmn, Howell Co Dem Comt, 70-; mem, Mo State Dem Comt, currently. Bus & Prof Pos: Paymaster, Lake City Ord Plant, Kansas City, Mo, 41-46; ins broker, 41-48; owner, Stein Bookkeeping, West Plains, 62-; franchise owner, H & R Block, 64- Mem: West Plains CofC (tourism comt). Mailing Add: Rte 3 West Plains MO 65775

STEINBACH, KENWARD N (DFL)
VChmn, Clearwater Co Dem-Farmer-Labor Party, Minn
b Manawa, Wis, July 17, 33; s Walter A Steinbach & Irene Becker S; m 1956 to Jean E Peterson; c Scott David & Kristin Jean. Educ: Oshkosh State Col, 51-52; Concordia Col, BS, 56, Bemidji State Col, 58. Polit & Govt Pos: Campaign chmn, Bob Bergland Vol & H H Humphrey, Clearwater Co, Minn, 70-71; vchmn, Clearwater Co Dem-Farmer-Labor Party, 70-; campaign chmn, Bob Bergland for Clearwater Co, 72. Mil Serv: Entered as Pvt, Army, 56, released as SP-4, 58, after serv in Chem Corps, 56-58. Mem: Northern Sci Teachers Asn (secy-treas, 59-69, membership chmn, 70-); Minn Acad Sci; Bagley Civic & Com Asn Asn; Minn Educ Asn; Nat Educ Asn. Relig: Lutheran. Mailing Add: Box 583 Bagley MN 56621

STEINBERG, MELVIN ALLEN (D)
Md State Sen
b Baltimore, Md, Oct 4, 33; s Irvin Steinberg & Julia Levenson S; m 1958 to Anita Akman; c Edward Bryan, Susan Renee & Barbara Ellen. Educ: Univ Baltimore, AA, 52; Univ Baltimore Sch Law, LLB, 55; Nu Beta Epsilon. Polit & Govt Pos: Md State Sen, Baltimore Co, 67-; deleg, Dem Nat Conv, 68. Mil Serv: Entered as Seaman Recruit, Navy, 55, released as Storekeeper 3/C, 57, after serv in USS R K Huntington DD781. Mem: AF&AM; Yedz Grotto; Jr CofC; B'nai B'rith; Histadrut. Honors & Awards: Distinguished Serv Award, Jr CofC, Randallstown Chap. Relig: Jewish. Legal Res: 3412 Maryvale Rd Baltimore MD 21207 Mailing Add: 202 Loyola Fed Bldg Towson MD 21204

STEINBERG, PAUL B (D)
Fla State Rep
b Brooklyn, NY, Mar 21, 40; s Morris L Steinberg & Elsie Kaplan S; m 1967 to Sandra J Schwartz; c Lisa Lee & Richard Lawrence. Educ: Univ Miami, BBA, 60; Stetson Univ Col Law, JD, 63; Delta Sigma Phi; Phi Kappa Phi; Phi Alpha Delta. Polit & Govt Pos: Chmn, Miami Beach Beautification Comt, Fla, 69-72; Fla State Rep, Dist 101, 72- Bus & Prof Pos: Real estate broker, Miami, 61-; attorney, 63- Mil Serv: Seaman Apprentice, Coast Guard Res, 63, released as PO 3/C, 71. Publ: Ed, Bus Bull, Univ Miami, 60. Mem: Fla & DC Bar Asns; Miami Beach Jaycees (pres, 69-); UN Asn (pres, 70-72); B'nai B'rith Sports Lodge (pres, 71-72). Honors & Awards: Outstanding Young Man of Am, US Jaycees, 69; Jaycee of Year Award, Miami Beach Jaycees, 69; Golden Apple Award, Dade Co Educ Asn, 71. Relig: Jewish. Legal Res: 900 Bay Dr Apt 116 Miami Beach FL 33141 Mailing Add: 350 Lincoln Rd Miami Beach FL 33139

STEINEGER, JOHN FRANCIS, JR (D)
Kans State Sen
b Kansas City, Kans, Sept 13, 24; s John F Steineger & June Wear S; m 1949 to Margaret Leisy; c John, III, Cynthia, Mellissa & Christian. Educ: Univ Southern Calif; Kans Univ; George Washington Univ; Phi Delta Phi; Phi Delta Theta. Polit & Govt Pos: Cultural attache, US Dept of State, Europe & Near East, 50-58; local chmn, Kennedy for President Comt & Johnson for President Comt; Kans State Sen, 64-, Minority Leader, Kans State Senate, 73-; chmn, Third Cong Dist Dem Comt, presently; deleg, Dem Nat Conv, 68; chmn, Prairie Nat Park Comt, 70- Bus & Prof Pos: Attorney, Steineger & Reid, presently. Mil Serv: Entered as A/S, Navy, 43, released as Lt(jg), 46, after serv in Pac. Mem: Kansas City, Kans People-to-People Chap (chmn); Kiwanis; Century Club; Kansas City Ballet Asn (pres). Honors & Awards: Outstanding State Sen Award, Eagleton Inst, Rutgers Univ, 72. Relig: Episcopal. Legal Res: 6400 Valley View Rd Kansas City KS 66111 Mailing Add: 466 New Brotherhood Bldg Kansas City KS 66101

STEINFELD, SAMUEL S (R)
b Louisville, Ky, Feb 15, 06; s Emile Steinfeld & Florence Simons S; m 1929 to Flora Loebenberg; c Helane (Mrs Howard B Grossman) & James F; five grandchildren. Educ: Univ Louisville, JD, 28. Polit & Govt Pos: Alt deleg, Rep Nat Conv, 40 & 56; co attorney, Jefferson Co, Ky, 46-49; mem, Co Rep Exec Comt, 46-66; mem, Jefferson Co Elec Comn, 55-66; justice, Court of Appeals, Ky, Frankfort, 67-75, chief justice, 72. Bus & Prof Pos: Dir & secy various corp; assoc, Gifford & Steinfeld, 28-35; partner, Steinfeld & Steinfeld, 35-66; chmn, Judicial Coun Ky, 69-72; prof law, Univ Louisville, currently. Mem: Am Bar Asn; Am Judicature Soc; Commercial Law League Am; Lincoln Club Ky; Ky Hist Soc. Honors & Awards: Distinguished Law Alumni Award, Univ Louisville, 66; Man of the Year Award, B'nai B'rith, 72; Outstanding Jurist Award, Louisville Bar Asn, 72. Relig: Jewish. Mailing Add: 3512 St Germaine Ct Louisville KY 40207

STEINGUT, STANLEY (D)
NY State Assemblyman
b Brooklyn, NY, May 20, 20; s Irwin Steingut; m to Madeline Fellerman; c Robert, Theodore & Ilene. Educ: Union Col, St John's Univ Law Sch. Polit & Govt Pos: Exec mem, Madison Club, 41st Assembly Dist, NY; NY State Assemblyman, 52-, minority leader, NY State Assembly, 69-74, majority leader, 75-; chmn, Kings Co Dem Party, NY, formerly; deleg, Dem Nat Conv, 68. Bus & Prof Pos: Attorney. Mem: Unity Club, Brooklyn; Nat Dem Club; New York City & Kings Co Bar Asns; Brooklyn Jewish Ctr. Mailing Add: Apt 6D 1199 E 53rd St Brooklyn NY 11234

STEINHAUER, JOHN M (D)
Tenn State Rep
Mailing Add: PO Box 888 Hendersonville TN 37075

STEINHICE, LAUREL COLEMAN (R)
b Chattanooga, Tenn, Feb 3, 36; d Walter Coleman & Marion Skeen C; m 1954 to Francis Carroll Steinhice; c David Christopher, Jessica Lynne, Marion Eileen & Charles Carroll. Educ: George Peabody Col, 53-54. Polit & Govt Pos: Precinct officer, Hamilton Co Rep Party, Tenn, 66-; alt deleg, Rep Nat Conv, 72. Bus & Prof Pos: Gen mgr, Hixson Pike Fire Dept, Inc, 65- Mem: Nat Fire Protection Asn; Chattanooga CofC; Fraternal Order Firefighters; Nat Alliance of Small Businessmen; Ladies Oriental Shrine of NAm. Relig: Episcopal. Mailing Add: 1224 Cranbrook Dr Hixson TN 37343

STEINHOLL, RON JOHN (D)
Exec Dir, Wis Dem Party
b Los Angeles, Calif, Mar 13, 44; s Clifford Steinholl & Dorothy Johns S; m 1969 to Susan Spahn; c Peter, Joshua & Elizabeth. Educ: Univ Wis, Platteville, Bus Admin & Acct, 73; Young Dem; Letterman; ZPG. Polit & Govt Pos: Chmn, Univ Wis, Platteville Young Dem, 72-73; chmn, Grant Co Dem Party, 73-74; alt deleg, Dem Nat Conv, 72; exec dir, Wis Dem Party, 74- Bus & Prof Pos: Decision writer, John Deere & Co, Dubuque, Ia, 64-74. Mil Serv: Entered as E-1, Army, 65, released as E-2, 67, after serv in AISA, 66-67. Mem: VFW; UAW; Jaycees. Honors & Awards: Outstanding Chmn Civic Project, Jaycees, 73. Legal Res: 3550 Candletree Ct Madison WI 53713 Mailing Add: 22 N Hancock St Madison WI 53703

STEIS, WILLIAM BURTON (D)
b Elbon, Pa, Mar 3, 07; s John Burton Steis & Harriet Eggleston S; m 1933 to Helen Cecilia Rosenkrans; c Marjorie Helen (Mrs Beard) & Kathryn Faye (Mrs Pace). Educ: Univ Notre Dame, Pre-law, 28; Duquesne Univ Law Sch, 31; John Marshall Law Sch, 47; Sigma Nu Phi. Polit & Govt Pos: Chmn, Harris Co Dem Exec Comt, Ga, formerly; Ga State Sen, 25th Dist, 55-56; Ga State Rep, 59-68. Bus & Prof Pos: Attorney. Mil Serv: Pa Nat Guard, 33-41; entered as 1st Sgt, Army, 41, released as Maj, 47; Victory Medal. Mem: Patrons of Husbandry; Eagles; Red Men; Am Legion; CofC. Relig: Catholic. Mailing Add: Pine Mountain GA 31823

STELZ, DALE EDWARD (D)
b Cleveland, Ohio, Mar 23, 47; s Henry Theodore Stelz & Rita Schneider S; m 1969 to Sandra Louise Kofron; c Lorraine Rita. Educ: Ohio Univ, BS in Chem, 69; Cleveland State Univ, MS in Chem; Alpha Phi Omega. Polit & Govt Pos: Deleg, Dem Nat Conv, 72. Bus & Prof Pos: Chemist, Repub Steel Research, Independence, Ohio, 69- Mem: Am Chem Soc; 23rd Dist Cong Caucus. Relig: Roman Catholic. Mailing Add: 3091 Marda Dr Parma OH 44134

STEMBRIDGE, JOHN MADISON (D)
Mayor, North Miami, Fla
b Wicksburg, Ala, Aug 17, 37; s James George Stembridge & Johnnie Wilson S; single. Educ: Bob Jones Univ, BA, 60, grad study, 60-62; Southwestern Baptist Theol Sem, 63-66; Shakespearean Actors Guild; Ministerial Asn. Polit & Govt Pos: Mayor, North Miami, Fla, 73-; mem community develop comt, US Conf Mayors, 73-, vchmn bicentennial comt, 74-; deleg, Dem Nat Mid-Term Conf, 74; mem environ quality life comt, Fla League Cities, 74- Bus & Prof Pos: Secy-treas, Edison Furniture Co, North Miami, Fla, currently; pres, Stembridge Furniture, Inc, currently; vpres, Stembridge Realty, Inc, currently; vpres, Christian Justice League, currently; bd trustees, Third Century, currently. Mem: Rotary; Elks; Optimist; North Dade Bus & Prof Club; Fla Retail Furniture Dealers' Asn (bd dirs). Honors & Awards: True Gentleman Award, Sigma Alpha Epsilon, 56. Relig: Christian. Mailing Add: 545 NE 125th St North Miami FL 33161

STEMMER, JAY A (R)
b Wilkes-Barre, Pa, Oct 29, 15; s Jay A Stemmer & Nell Quigley S; m 1938 to Mary Kearney, wid; m 1969 to Elizabeth Carlisle; c Jay, Wayne & Susan. Educ: Univ Pa, Wharton Sch Finance. Polit & Govt Pos: Town Clerk, Clark, NJ, 49-51, comnr, 51-59, mayor, 52-59; mem, Union Co Rep Comt, 52-67, chmn, 63-67; city chmn, Clark, NJ Rep Comt, 56-64; freeholder, Union Co, 60-65; treas, Union Co, 69-72; admin consult to Co Prosecutor, 73-75. Bus & Prof Pos: Pres, Stemmer Realty; mem adv bd, Summit & Elizabeth Trust Co. Mil Serv: Pvt, Air Force, 45. Mem: Kiwanis (vpres & dir). Relig: Roman Catholic. Mailing Add: 990 Raritan Rd Clark NJ 07066

STEMPLE, JANE YOLEN (D)
b New York, NY, Feb 11, 39; d Will Hyatt Yolen & Isabelle Berlin Y; m 1962 to David Wilber Stemple; c Heidi Elisabet, Adam Douglas & Jason Frederic. Educ: Smith Col, BA, 60. Polit & Govt Pos: Sewage study comnr, Conway, Mass, 67-68; town coordr, Campaign for Robert Drinan, Bolton, 70; town coordr for McGovern, Hatfield, 72; deleg, Dem Nat Conv, 72. Bus & Prof Pos: Prod dept asst, Saturday Rev, 60-61; manuscript ed, Gold Medal Books, 61-62; assoc ed, Rutlege Books, 62-63; asst ed juv dept, A A Knopf, Inc, 63-66. Publ: Emperor & the Kite, World, 68; The Girl Who Cried Flowers, Crowell, 74; Writing Books for Children, Writer, 73; plus others. Mem: Soc Children's Book Writers (bd dirs, 72-); Citizens for Participation in Polit, Mass Pax; Am Friends Serv Comt; Civil Liberties Union; Cent Comt for Conscientious Objectors. Honors & Awards: Caldecott Honor Book Award, Am Libr Asn, 68; Medal, Chandler Medal Book Talk Comt, 70; Award, Golden Kite Soc of Children's Book Writers, 74; Nat Book Award nominee, 75. Relig: Society of Friends. Mailing Add: Phoenix Farm 31 School St Hatfield MA 01038

STENDER, JOHN H (R)
Asst Secy for Occup Safety & Health, Dept Labor
b Ismay, Mont, July 16, 16; m to Ida M Hanna; c two sons & two daughters. Educ: Rocky Mountain Col. Polit & Govt Pos: Mem, Wash State Legis Coun; mem subcomt job opportunities, Nat Rep Coord Comt; vchmn, Wash State Spec Comt, Indust Ins Appeals; mem exec bd, King Co Young Men's Rep Club, Wash; mem nat comt prog & progress, Percy Comt, 59; mem nat big cities comt, Bliss Comt, 60; Rep cand for Cong, 60; Wash State Sen, formerly; Asst Secy for Occup Safety & Health, Dept Labor, 73- Bus & Prof Pos: Int vpres, Int Brotherhood Boilermakers, Iron Ship Builders, Blacksmiths, Forgers & Helpers, AFL-CIO Northwest Sect, mem boilermakers exec coun & 12 years bus mgr & secy, Boilermakers Welders' Local 541, Seattle, Wash; chmn, Int Labor Orgns Textiles Comt. Mem: Eagles; Lions. Honors & Awards: King Co Rep Man of Year, 61. Relig: Presbyterian. Legal Res: 27420 Military Rd Auburn WA 98002 Mailing Add: Dept of Labor Third & Constitution Washington DC 20210

STENDER, RUDOLPH JAMES (D)
b Custer, SDak, July 22, 35; s Henry James Stender & Helen Rice S; div; c Robin Elaine, Danny James & Lisa Cari. Educ: Edgemont Pub Schs, grad. Polit & Govt Pos: Dem precinct committeeman, Custer, SDak, 67; chmn, Custer Co Dem Party, 70-75. Bus & Prof Pos: Secy, Edgemont Vol Fire Dept, 59-60; dir, Custer CofC, 66-69 & Custer Fed Credit Union, 67-70. Mil Serv: Entered as E-1, Army, 56, released as Pfc, 57, after serv in Co I, 13th Inf Regt, 8th Inf Div; Sharpshooter, Marksman, Expert Mortar & Good Conduct Medals. Mem: Boy Scouts; Southern Black Hills Sportsman Club; Jaycees; Lions; Custer Co Hist Soc. Relig: Protestant. Mailing Add: Box 424 Custer SD 57730

STENGLEIN, MARY PASCHALINE (DFL)
Secy, Morrison Co Dem-Farmer-Labor Party, Minn
b Minneapolis, Minn, July 10, 19; d John Stenglein (deceased) & Elizabeth Fournier S (deceased). Educ: St Paul Diocesan Teachers Col, 42; Cardinal Stritch Col, 43-47; Col St Benedict (Minn), 59; St Clare Col, 63; St John's Univ (Minn), 57 & 70; Col St Catherine, BA, 65; Creighton Univ, 70; Univ WVa, 72; Wheeling Col, 73. Polit & Govt Pos: Secy, Morrison Co Dem-Farmer-Labor Party, Minn, 70-; sustaining fund mem, Minn Dem-Farmer-Labor Party, formerly. Bus & Prof Pos: Teacher, Sacred Heart Parish, Flensburg, Minn, 41-45; St Mary's, Morris, 45-48 & St John's Foley, 48-51; teacher & superior, St Anthony's, Browns Valley, 51-54; teacher, St Joseph's, Waite Park, 54-65; asst mission coordr, Franciscan Sisters of Little Falls, 63-69; co-chmn & chmn ed sect, Mission Secretariate, Washington, DC, 64-66; teacher, Our Lady of Lourdes, Little Falls, 64-71; parish coordr, Sacred Heart Parish, Bluefield, currently. Publ: Ed, Echoes from the Andes, 62-71. Mem: Nat Cath Educ Asn; Citizens Educ Freedom; Minn Citizens Concern for Life; Woman's Civic League (secy bd community action); Mercer Co Day Care Ctr for Ment Retarded (co-chmn). Relig: Catholic. Legal Res: Bluefield WV Mailing Add: St Francis Convent Little Falls MN 56345

STENHOLM, CHARLES WALTER (D)
Committeeman, Tex State Dem Exec Comt
b Jones Co, Tex, Oct 26, 38; s Lambert W Stenholm & Irene Olson S; m 1961 to Cynthia Ann Watson; c Chris Wayne, Cary Watson & Courtney Ann. Educ: Tarleton Jr Col, grad, 59; Tex Tech Col, BS, 61, MS, 62; Sigma Alpha Epsilon. Polit & Govt Pos: Committeeman, Tex State Dem Exec Comt, 30th Dist, 74- Bus & Prof Pos: Owner-mgr, Stenholm Farms, 61-; voc agr teacher, Avoca, Ind Sch Dist, 62-64; exec vpres, Rolling Plains Cotton Growers, Inc, 64-67; assoc mgr, Stamford Elec Coop, Inc, 67-, gen mgr, 68- Publ: Report to the Membership, Tex Coop Power, 68- Mem: Tex Elec Coop, Inc (pres, 74-75, bd dirs); Rolling Plains Cotton Growers (adv bd dirs, 67-); Tex Fedn Coop (bd dirs, 68-); Stamford CofC (bd dirs); Stamford Exchange Club. Honors & Awards: Bus & Prof Man of the Year, Calif Creek Soil & Water Dist, 74; Hon State Farmer Degree, Tex Future Farmers Am, 65. Relig: Lutheran; coun vchmn. Legal Res: 8 Westwind Circle Stamford TX 79553 Mailing Add: Box 1147 Stamford TX 79553

STENNIS, JOHN CORNELIUS (D)
US Sen, Miss
b Kemper Co, Miss, Aug 3, 01; s Hampton Howell Stennis & Cornelia Adams S; m 1929 to Coy Hines; c John Hampton & Mrs Samuel Syme. Educ: Miss State Univ, BS, 23; Univ Va Law Sch, LLB, 28; Phi Beta Kappa; Phi Alpha Delta; Alpha Chi Rho. Hon Degrees: LLD, Millsaps Col, 57, Univ Wyo, 62, Miss Col, 69 & Belhaven Col, 72. Polit & Govt Pos: Miss State Rep, 28-32; prosecuting attorney, 16th Judicial Dist, 31-37; circuit judge, 37-47; US Sen, Miss, 47-; ex officio deleg, Dem Nat Mid-Term Conf, 74. Mem: Mason; Lions; Farm Bur; Miss & Am Bar Asns. Relig: Presbyterian. Mailing Add: DeKalb MS 39328

STENNIS, JOHN HAMPTON (D)
Miss State Rep
b Kemper Co, Miss, Mar 2, 35; s John Cornelius Stennis & Coy Hines S; m 1966 to Martha R Allred; c Hampton Hines & Martha Laurin. Educ: Princeton Univ, AB, 57; Univ Va Law Sch, JD, 60; Omicron Delta Kappa; Raven Soc; Phi Alpha Delta. Polit & Govt Pos: Miss State Rep, 69-, chmn banks & banking comt, 69- Bus & Prof Pos: Partner, Watkins, Pyle, Ludlam & Stennis, Attorneys-at-law, Jackson, Miss, 60- Mil Serv: Lt Col, Miss Air Nat Guard, 60- Mem: Miss State, Am, Fed, Hinds Co & DC Bar Asns. Relig: Presbyterian; elder, Fondren Presby Church, Jackson. Legal Res: 175 Kirkwood Pl Jackson MS 39211 Mailing Add: PO Box 427 Jackson MS 39205

STENVIG, CHARLES (INDEPENDENT)
b Minneapolis, Minn, Jan 16, 28; s Selmer Stenvig & Myrtle Lee S; m 1951 to Audrey L Thompson; c Terri, Tracy, Todd & Thomas. Educ: Augsburg Col, BA in Sociol, 51; Univ Minn, Juv Off Inst, 60. Polit & Govt Pos: Lt, Minneapolis Police Dept, Minn, 56-69; Mayor, Minneapolis, 69-73. Mil Serv: Entered as Pvt, Army, 46, released, 47, after serv in SPac; Lt, Air Force Nat Guard, 52-53; Lt, Air Nat Guard Res. Publ: Originator, Law Officer Mag, Minneapolis, 67- Mem: Minn Police & Peace Officers Asn; Police Officers Fedn of Minneapolis; PTA; Minneapolis Police Band; Mason. Honors & Awards: Reverence for Law Award, Fraternal Order of Eagles, 69; Law Enforcement Cert, VFW; Law Enforcement Commendation, SAR; Award of Appreciation, Kiwanis; Int Conf Police Asn Award; Nat

VFW Gold Medal of Merit, 72. Relig: Methodist. Mailing Add: 5604 35th Ave S Minneapolis MN 55417

STEPHEN, EDISON J (R)
Utah State Rep
Mailing Add: Box 32 Henefer UT 84033

STEPHEN, JAMES BARNETT (D)
SC State Sen
b Pacolet, SC, May 17, 25; s James Littlejohn Stephen & Annie Barnett S; m 1967 to Sara Goodwin; c Susan, Katherine & James Goodwin. Educ: Univ SC, AB, 45; Duke Univ, LLB, 49; Phi Delta Phi; Pi Kappa Alpha. Polit & Govt Pos: SC State Rep, 61-68; SC State Sen, 69- Bus & Prof Pos: Attorney-at-law. Mil Serv: Entered as Cadet, Navy, 42, released as Ens, 46, after serv aboard cargo vessel, Pac Theatre, 45; Lt Comdr, Naval Res (Ret). Mem: Mason; Shrine; Scottish Rite (32 degree); VFW; Am Legion. Relig: Presbyterian. Legal Res: 173 Magnolia St Spartanburg SC 29301 Mailing Add: State House Columbia SC 29211

STEPHENS, BILL (D)
Ark State Rep
Mailing Add: 2615 Robinson Conway AR 72032

STEPHENS, CAROLYN KAY (R)
Secy, Montgomery Co Rep Exec Comt, Ohio
b Dayton, Ohio, Sept 3, 36; d Charles Donald Stephens & Florence Thornhill S; single. Educ: Ohio Univ, AA, 56; Zeta Tau Alpha. Polit & Govt Pos: Mem, Montgomery Co Young Rep Exec Comt, 61-71, secy, 62-63, second vpres, 63-64; mem, Ohio Young Rep Exec Comt, 62-71, state co-chmn, 63-64, state chmn, 66-67, nat committeewoman, 65-66 & 67-71; state adv, Teenage Rep Clubs, 63-64, asst state adv, 72-73; mem nat comt, Young Rep Nat Fedn, 65-71; mem, Montgomery Co Rep Exec Comt, 64-, asst co chairwoman, 70-72, secy, 73-; alt deleg, Rep Nat Conv, 64 & 68; dir, Montgomery Co Bd Elec, 73- Mem: Zeta Tau Alpha Alumnae; Montgomery Co Rep Bus Women; Montgomery Co Children's Serv Bd (vchmn citizens adv coun); Soroptimist Int Dayton; Shawnee Coun of Camp Fire Girls (vchmn exec bd). Honors & Awards: Robert A Taft Award for Outstanding Young Rep in Ohio, 70. Relig: Protestant. Mailing Add: 5550 Olive Tree Dr Dayton OH 45426

STEPHENS, DON W (D)
Ky State Rep
Mailing Add: 1909 Blairmore Rd Lexington KY 40502

STEPHENS, EDGAR J, JR (D)
Miss State Rep
b New Albany, Miss, May 26, 16; single. Educ: Univ Miss, BA, 38, JD, 40; Sigma Chi; Phi Delta Phi. Polit & Govt Pos: Prosecuting attorney, Union Co, Miss, 47-51; Miss State Rep, 52-, chmn Appropriations Comt, Miss State House of Rep, 66-; mem bd trustees, Pub Employees' Retirement Syst of Miss, Comn of Budget & Acct, 66-; mem bd trustees, Miss Medicaid Comn, 60- Bus & Prof Pos: Attorney-at-law; real estate broker. Mil Serv: Naval Res, 41-54; on staff of Adm Wm F Halsey, 43-44. Mem: Miss Bar Asn; Am Legion; Rotary; Farm Bur. Relig: Assoc Reformed Presbyterian. Mailing Add: Box 330 New Albany MS 38652

STEPHENS, JACK LEROL (D)
Ga State Sen
b Atlanta, Ga, July 26, 27; s Ben Davis Stephens, Sr & Ruth Epperson S; m 1946 to Betty Mae Norman; c Jack, Jr & Christopher Robert. Educ: NY Univ, 49; John Marshall Law Sch, LLB & LLM, 54; Univ Ga, 61; Sigma Delta Kappa. Polit & Govt Pos: Mem, Dem Exec Comt, Atlanta, Ga, 65; Ga State Sen, 36th Dist, currently. Mil Serv: Entered as Seaman, Naval Res, 45, released as Seaman 1/C, 46. Relig: Baptist. Legal Res: 2484 Macon Dr SE Atlanta GA 30315 Mailing Add: 151 Pryor St SW Third Floor Atlanta GA 30303

STEPHENS, JOHN D (JACK) (D)
Chmn, Clark Co Dem Party, Kans
b Ashland, Kans, Mar 1, 22; s John Edward Stephens & Mary Douglass S; m 1949 to Jean Schroeder; c John E, II & Donald D. Educ: US Air Force Pilot Training Sch, grad, 43. Polit & Govt Pos: Clerk, Lexington Twp, Kans, 66-73; chmn, Clark Co Dem Party, 73- Bus & Prof Pos: Owner-mgr, Stephens Ranch, Clark Co, Kans, 48-, Stephens Air, 69- & Stephens Hay Serv, 70- Mil Serv: Entered as Pvt, Air Force, 40, released as Capt, 45, after serv in Training Command, US. Mem: Am Legion; Eastern Star; Scottish Rite; Jaycees. Honors & Awards: Publ as Acro Instr in Bill Sweets Call Me Mr Airshow. Relig: Presbyterian; past chmn, Bd Deacons, Presbyterian Church, Ashland. Mailing Add: Lexington Rd Ashland KS 67831

STEPHENS, LYLE R (R)
Iowa State Rep
Mailing Add: RR 3 Le Mars IA 51031

STEPHENS, ROBERT GRIER, JR (D)
US Rep, Ga
b Atlanta, Ga, Aug 14, 13; s Dr Robert Grier & Martha Lucy Evans S; m 1938 to Grace Winston; c Grace Winston (Mrs D R Bianchi), Robert Grier, III, Mary Winston & Lawton Evans. Educ: Univ Ga, BA, 35, MA, 37, law degree cum laude, 41; Univ Hamburg, Ger, exchange student scholar; Phi Beta Kappa; Phi Delta Phi; Phi Kappa Alpha Order; Blue Key. Hon Degrees: LLD, Augusta Law Sch. Polit & Govt Pos: City attorney, Athens, Ga, 47-50; Ga State Sen, 51-53; Ga State Rep, 53-59; US Rep, Ga, 61-, Ga, NC, SC & Tenn rep Dem policy & steering comt, US House Rep, 73-; deleg, Dem Nat Mid-Term Conf, 74. Bus & Prof Pos: Teacher hist & polit sci, Univ Ga, 36-40; practicing lawyer, 46-61. Mil Serv: Army, World War II; legal staff of Justice Robert Jackson at Nuremberg trials. Publ: Aspects of the Nuremburg trial, Ga Bar J, 2/46 & 5/46; Legal aspects of the international trial at Nuremberg, Ann Report, Ga Bar Asn, 46; Background & boyhood of Alexander H Stephens, Ga Rev, 55. Mem: Am Legion; Elks; Kiwanis (Lt Gov); WOW; Omicron Delta Kappa. Honors & Awards: Distinguished Alumni Merit Award, Ga Alumni Soc. Relig: Presbyterian; elder. Legal Res: Athens GA Mailing Add: 2410 Rayburn House Off Bldg Washington DC 20515

STEPHENS, RONALD LEMOYNE (R)
Asst Secy of State, Idaho
b Butler, Pa, Nov 14, 33; s Howard A Stephens & Carolene Cross S; div; c Mark LeMoyne & Cathy Ann. Educ: Univ Denver, BS; Univ Mont Law Sch, 67-68; Kappa Sigma. Polit & Govt Pos: Precinct committeeman, Rep Party, Chester, Mont, 60-62; Rep nominee, Mont State Sen, 64; nat committeeman, Mont Young Rep, 65; nat committee, Young Rep Nat Fedn, 65-66, nat exec bd, 66-67, vchmn-at-lg, 66-67; deleg, Young Rep Nat Conv, 65, deleg chmn, 67; chmn, Mont Young Rep Fedn, 67; admin asst to speaker of house, Mont House Rep, 67; mem exec comt, Mont Rep Party, 67-68; alt deleg, Rep Nat Conv, 68; chmn, Fifth Cong Dist Rep Fedn, Wash, 69-70; Asst Secy of State, Idaho, 70- Bus & Prof Pos: Owner, Stephens Farm, Chester, Mont, 59-67; owner, Stephens Agency, 60-67; invest exec, Goodbody & Co, Spokane, Wash, 68- Mil Serv: Entered as Pvt, Army, 54, released as Cpl, 55, after serv in 11th Signal Bn, Ft Huachuca, Ariz; Good Conduct & Nat Defense Serv Medals. Mem: Farm Bur; Mont Grain Producers Asn; Nat Rifle Asn; AF&AM; Shrine. Relig: Lutheran. Legal Res: 2115 S Latah Boise ID 83705 Mailing Add: Off of Secy of State State Capitol Boise ID 83702

STEPHENS, STANLEY GRAHAM (R)
Mont State Sen
b Calgary, Alta, Sept 16, 29; s Joseph Stephens & Margaret Farrelly S; m 1954 to Ann Hanson; c Alana & Carol Ann. Educ: West Can High Sch, Calgary, 44-47. Polit & Govt Pos: Mont State Sen, Dist 19, 69-72 & 75- Bus & Prof Pos: Vpres & secy, Radio Sta KOJM, Havre, Mont, 65-; pres, Big Sky TV Cable Inc, Sidney, 68-; pres, Glasgow TV Cable Inc, 68-; pres, Community TV Inc, Havre, 68- Mil Serv: Entered as Pvt, Army, 51, released as S/Sgt, 53, after serv in Armed Forces Radio Serv, Korea, 51-53; US Commendation Ribbon with Pendant. Mem: Mason; Shrine; Am Legion; Elks. Honors & Awards: Outstanding Young Man of Havre, 62; Mont Assoc Press Radio Ed Award, 63-68. Relig: Lutheran. Legal Res: 33 Beaver Creek Blvd Havre MT 59501 Mailing Add: 422 Third St Havre MT 59501

STEPHENS, VERN (R)
Cong Servs Officer, Mining Enforcement & Safety Admin, Dept of Interior
b Portland, Ore, Nov 12, 22; s Loyd M Stephens & Esther C Steiner S; m 1950 to Lucille M Hannula; c Robert O, Peter C, Dennis P, William L & Ann M. Educ: Wash State Univ, AB in Polit Sci, 49; Beta Theta Pi. Polit & Govt Pos: Exec secy, Rep State Cent Comt, Ore, 56; Asst Dir Territories, US Dept Interior, 57-59, Asst Comnr Indian Affairs, 59-61; spec asst to Sen Milton R Young, NDak, 61; pub rels dir, Sen Campaign, Ala, 62; dir, Berks Co Rep Campaign, Pa, 63; personal asst to Sen Barry Goldwater, 64; campaign dir for Congressman Wendell Wyatt, Ore, 64; admin asst to Congressman Henry Schadeberg, Wis, 67-68; Gen Serv Admin, 69-72; Asst Secy Land & Water Resources, Dept of Interior, 72-74, cong servs officer, Mining Enforcement & Safety Admin, 75- Bus & Prof Pos: Textile mfr, 49-56. Mil Serv: Entered as Pvt, Air Force, 42, released as Sgt, 46. Relig: Protestant. Mailing Add: 2410 Stirrup Lane Alexandria VA 22308

STEPHENS, WILLIE OVED (D)
Chmn, Seward Co Dem Party, Nebr
b Wilson, Okla, June 23, 29; s Willie Richard Stephens & Bertha Gaines S; m 1953 to Gladys Arlene Belka; c David Wayne, Nelson Dean & Wesley Scott. Educ: Okla State Univ, BS, 51. Polit & Govt Pos: Chmn, Seward Co Dem Party, Nebr, 72- Bus & Prof Pos: Chemist, Lincoln Grain Exchange, Nebr, 61- Mil Serv: Entered as Pvt, Army, 54, released as SP-2, 56, after serv in 4th Ord Bn, Asiatic Theatre, 55-56. Mem: Nebr & Pioneer Sect of Am Asn Cereal Chemists. Honors & Awards: First Place Awards for Best Protein Anal, Nebr Sect, Am Asn Cereal Chemists, 65-67, 69 & 71 & Pioneer Sect, 72. Relig: Protestant. Mailing Add: Rte 2 Milford NE 68405

STEPHENS, WILLIS H (R)
NY State Assemblyman
b Patterson, NY, June 7, 25; m Daphne Dunbar; c four. Educ: Princeton Univ. Polit & Govt Pos: NY State Assemblyman, 53-, chmn, Ways & Means Comt, NY State Assembly, 69-; mem, NY State Rep Comt, 66- Bus & Prof Pos: Indust fuels; dir, Nat Bank of NAm, presently; mem bd trustees, Greenwich Savings Bank; hon trustee, St Peter's Sch, Peekskill, NY, 70- Mil Serv: US Air Force. Mem: Am Legion; Mason (32 degree); Elks; Putnam Community Hosp (dir). Mailing Add: Indian Well Farm Brewster NY 10509

STEPHENSON, J E (D)
La State Rep
Mailing Add: 705 S Texas St DeRidder LA 70634

STEPHENSON, TOM R (D)
Okla State Sen
Mailing Add: State Capitol Oklahoma City OK 73105

STEPONKUS, WILLIAM PETER (R)
b New York, Mar 28, 35; s Evelyn O'Neil, father (deceased); m 1975 to Elizabeth Louise Doerr. Educ: Manhattan Col, BA, 57. Polit & Govt Pos: Campaign coordr, Whalen for Cong Comt, Dayton, Ohio, 65-66; special asst to US Rep Charles W Whalen, Jr, Ohio, 67-; presidential speech writer, White House, 74. Bus & Prof Pos: Reporter polit & govt, J Herald, Dayton, 62-65. Mil Serv: Entered as 2nd Lt, Air Force, 58, released as Capt, 62, after serv in Tactical Air Command, Pac Air Force, Strategic Air Command in Zone of Interior, Far East, 58-62; Air Force Commendation Medal. Publ: Co-auth, All About Politics, R R Bowker, 72. Mem: Nat Aviation Club. Relig: Catholic. Legal Res: 784 Lovetta Dr Dayton OH 45429 Mailing Add: 2450 Virginia Ave NW Washington DC 20037

STEPOVICH, MICHAEL A (R)
b Fairbanks, Alaska, Mar 12, 19; s Mike Stepovich & Olga Barta S; m 1947 to Matilda Baricevic; c 13. Educ: Gonzaga Univ, BA; Univ Notre Dame, LLB. Hon Degrees: LLD, Carroll Col. Polit & Govt Pos: Mem, Alaska Territorial House of Rep & Senate, formerly; Gov, Alaska, 57-59; mem, Judiciary Coun, currently. Bus & Prof Pos: Lawyer; city attorney, Fairbanks. Mil Serv: Naval Res, World War II. Honors & Awards: De Smet Medal, Gonzaga Univ, 66. Relig: Catholic. Mailing Add: 323 Charles St Fairbanks AK 99701

STEPPE, GARY CLIFFORD (D)
Chmn, Graham Co Dem Exec Comt, NC
b Oak Ridge, Tenn, Mar 10, 48; s Clifford Lee Steppe & Ollie Collins Steppe Crisp; m 1970 to Karen Virginia Roper; c Traci Denise. Educ: Western Carolina Univ, BS in educ, 70. Polit & Govt Pos: Chmn, Graham Co Dem Exec Comt, NC, 74- Bus & Prof Pos: Teacher, Graham Co Schs, 70-; football coach, Robbinsville High Sch, 70- Mem: Jaycees (vpres); NC Coaches Asn; NC & Nat Educ Asns. Relig: Baptist. Mailing Add: Rte 1 Box 13-A Robbinsville NC 28771

STEPTOE, ROBERT M (D)
WVa State Sen
Mailing Add: State Capitol Charleston WV 25305

STERBENK, WILLIAM D (R)
Mem, Rep State Cent Comt Calif
b Oakland, Calif, May 7, 31; s Frank R Sterbenk & Edna T Williams S; m 1950 to Beverly Ann Hage; c Melodee Kae & Mark William. Educ: Kelseyville Union High Sch, grad, 49. Polit & Govt Pos: Mem, Rep State Cent Comt, Calif, 67-; dir, 49th Dist Agr Asn, 68, chmn, 72-; chmn, Lake Co Rep Cent Comt, 69-75. Mil Serv: Entered as Airman, Navy, 49, released as Aviation Ordnanceman 2/C, 53, after serv in Fighter Squadron 74, Korea, 52-53; Korean Serv, US Serv & Good Conduct Medals; UN Medal. Mem: Calif Rep Chmn Asn; VFW; Lakeport Vol Fire Dept; Konocti Rod & Gun Club. Relig: Catholic. Legal Res: 320 Lakeshore Blvd Lakeport CA 95453 Mailing Add: PO Box 653 Lakeport CA 95453

STERLER, LEWIS R (D)
Committeeman, Kings Co Dem Comt, NY
b Brooklyn, NY, Dec 22, 50; s Dave Starr & Selma Greenfield S; single. Educ: Long Island Univ, BA Polit Sci, 72; NY Univ, Cert in Pub Rels, 74; Pi Gamma Mu. Polit & Govt Pos: Alt deleg, Dem Nat Conv, 72; committeeman, Kings Co Dem Comt, NY, 72-; mem exec bd, Roosevelt Kingsborough Independent Dem, 72-; city coun cand, New York, 73; assembly cand, NY, 74. Mem: Brooklyn Civic Coun (dir pub rels, 72-); Sheepshead Bay Restoration Comt (exec dir, 72-). Honors & Awards: NY State Regents Scholar, 68; Good Govt Award, Roosevelt Kingsborough Independent Dem, 70; Outstanding Sr, Long Island Univ, 72. Relig: Jewish. Mailing Add: 70 Lenox Rd Brooklyn NY 11226

STERLING, HAROLD H, JR (R)
Tenn State Rep
Mailing Add: 5575 Poplar Ave Memphis TN 38117

STERN, BERNICE F (D)
b Seattle, Wash, July 25, 16; d Abraham I Friedman & Josephine Gumbert; m to Edward F Stern, Sr; c Edward F, Jr & David F. Educ: Univ Wash, 33-35. Polit & Govt Pos: Councilperson, King Co Coun, Wash, 69-, chairwoman community & environ develop comt, 70- Mem: King Co Ment Retardation Bd (mem adv comt); Seattle-King Co Headstart Prog (chairwoman policy bd); Family Support Serv (mem adv coun); Discovery Park (mem adv comt); Alternatives for Wash (task force mem, 74). Honors & Awards: Honorary Nat Vpres, Nat Coun Jewish Women; Matrix Table Honoree, 71. Relig: Jewish. Mailing Add: 2709 W Galer Seattle WA 98199

STERN, HARRY L (R)
b Chicago, Ill, June 10, 30; s Gardner H Stern & Hanchen Strauss S; div; c Harry L, Nicholas Denison & Carla. Educ: Yale Univ, BA, 52; Univ Geneva, 54-55; Univ Chicago, 57-60; Phi Gamma Delta. Polit & Govt Pos: Rep precinct capt, 43rd Ward, Chicago, Ill, 58-; pres, 43rd Ward Young Rep Orgn, 59-60; treas, 43rd Ward Regular Rep Orgn, 62-63; alt deleg, Rep Nat Conv, 68. Bus & Prof Pos: Businessman, 55- Mil Serv: Entered as Pvt, Army, 52, released as Pfc, 54, after serv in 101st Airborne Div & Hq Co, Ft Myer, Va. Relig: Jewish. Mailing Add: 1350 Lake Shore Dr Chicago IL 60610

STERN, HERBERT L, JR (HUB) (D)
Chmn, Lake Co Dem Cent Comt, Ill
b Chicago, Ill, Apr 10, 15; s Herbert L Stern, Sr & Lucille Rosenberg S; m 1961 to Grace Mary Dain; c Gwen Louise, Herbert L, III & Robert Phillip Stern; Ann Nason Marks; Peter Dain, Thomas Merritt & John McClellan Suber. Educ: Yale Col, BA, 36, Yale Law Sch, LLB, 39. Polit & Govt Pos: Committeeman, West Deerfield Twp, Precinct 13, Lake Co, Ill, 66-; chmn, Lake Co Dem Cent Comt, 68- Bus & Prof Pos: Secy, E Z Paintr Corp, 47-71, dir, 47-73, chmn bd, 71-73; partner, Gottlieb & Schwartz, 48-72, attorney, 72-; chmn bd, Tapecoat Co, Inc, 70- Mil Serv: Entered as 1st Lt, Air Force, 41, released as Lt Col, 46, after serv in Gulf Coast Air Force Training Ctr, 41-42, India-Burma Theatre, 42-45 & War Dept Gen Staff, 45-46; Bronze Star. Publ: Series of articles on rural development in East Asia, publ in various local jour. Mem: Ill State Bar Asn; VFW; Am Legion; Standard Club Chicago; Mid-day Club Chicago. Legal Res: 1128 Green Bay Rd Highland Park IL 60035 Mailing Add: 215 Madison St Waukegan IL 60085

STERN, HOWARD MORRIS (R)
b San Jose, Calif, Apr 11, 30; s Harold K Stern (deceased) & Elizabeth McDougall (deceased); m 1954 to Gloria Louise Dillon; c Holly Lynn, Jeffrey Harold, Bradford William & Clayton Howard. Educ: Stanford Univ, 46-48; Alpha Tau Omega. Polit & Govt Pos: Mem & chmn various comts, Santa Clara Co Rep Cent Comt, Calif, 56-74; mem, San Jose Rep Assembly, 58-64, pres, 63-64; regional chmn, Santa Clara Co Rep Precinct Orgn, 60-66; mem, Rep State Cent Comt Calif, 62-74; mem bd dirs, Santa Clara Co Rep League, 64-66; mem exec comt, Assemblyman George Milias, 64-70; chmn, Congressman Charles Gubser Comt, 67-74; mem campaign comts of various Rep cand; chmn, Collins Mayor Campaign, 74. Bus & Prof Pos: Owner, Sterns Luggage, San Jose, Calif, 60- Mil Serv: Entered as Pvt, Army, 51, released as Sgt, 53, after serv in Counterintel, Korea; Korean Serv Medal with 2 Bronze Serv Stars; UN Serv Medal; Commendation Medal. Mem: Almaden Fashion Plaza Merchants Asn; San Jose CofC (bd dirs, 69-, legis chmn, 72-74, vpres, legis, 75); Elks; San Jose Rotary. Relig: Episcopal. Mailing Add: 1176 Janis Way San Jose CA 95125

STERN, JERE BART (D)
Committeeman, Morris Co Dem Party, NJ
b Baltimore, Md, Dec 18, 32; s Samuel Maurice Stern & Kathryn Sinskey S; m 1960 to Carol Ann Parodneck; c Emily Beth. Educ: George Washington Univ, BS, 54, Sch Med, MD, 58; Phi Beta Kappa. Polit & Govt Pos: Alt deleg, Dem Nat Conv, 68; committeeman, Morris Co Dem Party, NJ, 68-; mem exec comt, Morris Co New Dem Coalition, 69- Bus & Prof Pos: Chief pathologist, Riverside Hosp, Boonton, NJ, 66- Publ: Several sci publ in med jour. Mem: Col Am Pathologists; Am Soc Clin Pathologists; NJ Soc Pathologists; Am Med Asn; Med Soc NJ. Mailing Add: 30 Valley Rd Mountain Lakes NJ 07046

STERN, LARRY N (R)
Mem, Madison Co Rep Exec Comt, NC
b Newark, Ohio, Sept 17, 41; s Morelle E Stern & Florence E Field S; m 1974 to Teresa G Metcalf. Educ: Col Wooster, Ohio, BA, 62; Univ NC, Chapel Hill, PhD, 67; Phi Omega Sigma. Polit & Govt Pos: Mem, Madison Co Rep Exec Comt, NC, 71-, chmn, Mars Hill Precinct; alt deleg, Rep Nat Conv, 72; dir, 11th Cong Dist NC Young Rep, 72-73; treas, NC Fedn Young Rep, 73-75. Bus & Prof Pos: Instr eve col, Univ NC, Chapel Hill, 65-66; asst prof, Fla State Univ, Tallahassee, 66-71; assoc prof, Mars Hill Col, NC, 71-75. Mil Serv: NM 12, civilian serv in teaching capacity, Albrook AFB, Panama CZ, 69-70. Publ: Co-auth, Political socialization, student attitudes & political participation, J Developing Areas, fall 71 & Notes on the concept of political culture, Comp Polit Studies, 73; co-auth, The Interdisciplinary Study of Politics, Harper & Row, 74. Mem: Am & Southern Polit Sci Asns; Conf Group on Ger Polit; Soc for Preservation & Encouragement of Barber Shop Quartet Singing in Am. Honors & Awards: Barbershopper of Year, Tallahassee Soc for Preservation & Encouragement of Barber Shop Quartet Singing in Am, 70. Relig: Presbyterian; deacon, 69-71 & 73-74, elder, 74-75, chmn, Session Finance Comt, Grace Covenant Presbyterian Church, 74-75. Mailing Add: Box 279 Mars Hill NC 28754

STERN, OTTO (R)
Chmn, Hutchinson Co Rep Party, SDak
b Freeman, SDak, Sept 2, 09; m to Vernell Fischer; c Roger & Margaret. Educ: Common Sch; Correspondence Course. Polit & Govt Pos: Rep precinct committeeman, Freeman, SDak, 8 years, twp supvr, 3 years & mem sch bd, 9 years, Fed Crop Ins Agt, 2 years; mem, PMA & ASC City Comts, 7 years; SDak State Rep, 56-72; chmn, Hutchinson Co Rep Party, 75- Bus & Prof Pos: Farmer. Mem: 4-H Leader; Farmers Coop Grain Asn; City Crop Improv Asn. Relig: Lutheran; treas, Unity Lutheran Church, 9 years. Mailing Add: Freeman SD 57029

STERNER, E DONALD (R)
b Belmar, NJ, Jan 3, 94; s Willard J Sterner & Jennie Disbrow S; m 1943 to Dorothy Smock; c Dorothy (Mrs Braly), George W & John N. Educ: Asbury Park High Sch, grad, 13. Hon Degrees: LLD, Monmouth Col. Polit & Govt Pos: Mem bd educ, Belmar, NJ, 24-27; NJ State Assemblyman, Monmouth Co, 28-29; NJ State Sen, 30-32; mem, Monmouth Co Rep Comt, 32-35; chmn, NJ State Rep Comt, 34-35; NJ State Hwy Comnr, 35-42; chmn Monmouth Co Planning Bd, Freehold, 53-; alt deleg, Rep Nat Conv, 68. Bus & Prof Pos: Vpres, Sterner Coal & Lumber Co, Belmar, NJ, 19-42; pres, 42-; vpres, Belmar Savings & Loan Asn, 26-73; dir, Belmar-Wall Nat Bank, Belmar, NJ, 33-, NY & Long Branch RR, 35-, First Merchants Nat Bank, Asbury Park, 43-; pres, Sterners Inc, 50- Mil Serv: Entered as Pvt, Army, 17, released as 1st Lt, 19, after serv in Second Div AEF, First Army, Aisne, Marne, St Mihiel, Champagne, Meuse & Argonne, 18-19. Mem: Boy Scouts (pres, Monmouth Coun, 39-70); Am Legion (post comdr, 19-20, co comdr, 26-27); Mason; Kiwanis; VFW. Relig: Presbyterian. Legal Res: RD 1 Colts Neck NJ 07722 Mailing Add: PO Box 120 Belmar NJ 07719

STEVENS, ANTHONY B S (D)
NH State Rep
b Alstead, NH, Mar 18, 49; s John Campbell Stevens & Margaret Squibb S; single. Educ: Antioch Col, 67-70; Univ NH, 71-73. Polit & Govt Pos: Student body pres, Dublin Sch, NH, 63-67; NH State Rep, 73-; chmn, Cheshire Co Dem Party, currently. Bus & Prof Pos: Reporter & photographer, Norwalk Reflector, Ohio, 68; instr math & prog coordr, NEnd Community Action Prog, summer 68. Mem: NH Pub Interest Research Group; NH Asn RR Passengers (Interim RR Study Comt). Mailing Add: 1358 Watkins Hill Walpole NH 03608

STEVENS, E DAN (R)
Mich State Rep
b Raleigh, NC, May 2, 43; s Ross O Stevens & Rose Askew S; m 1966 to Karen Colby; c Joseph & Kirsten. Educ: Univ Mich, BS, 65, MA, 70. Polit & Govt Pos: Sch bd trustee, Atlanta Community Schs, Mich, 72-73; Mich State Rep, 106th Dist, 75- Bus & Prof Pos: Teacher, Whitmore Lake High Sch, Mich, 65-67; pres & exec dir, Summer Sci, Inc, 67-72; owner & broker, Stevens Real Estate, 70-; staff researcher, Mich House Minority Off, 73-74. Publ: Co-auth, Summer science, a unique educational program, Detroit Metrop Sci Rev, 69. Mem: Nat Tax Asn. Honors & Awards: Detroit Edison Sci Teacher Award. Mailing Add: Box 405 Atlanta MI 49709

STEVENS, EDWIN WALTER (R)
Cong Committeeman, Madison Co Rep Cent Comt, Mont
b Monroe, Wash, June 7, 08; s Erdmand J Stevens & Elizabeth Horning S; m 1935 to Lucille Barrett; c Diane Barrett. Educ: Mont Sch Mines, 44; Theta Tau. Polit & Govt Pos: Rep precinct committeeman, Mont, 60-66, co chmn, Rep Party, 66; cong committeeman, Madison Co Rep Cent Comt, 66- Bus & Prof Pos: Consult engr; mine supt, United Sierra Div, Cyprus Mines Corp, 51-70. Mem: Am Inst Mining Engrs; Northwest Mining Asn; Elks; AF&AM; Scottish Rite. Mailing Add: Box 116 Alder MT 59710

STEVENS, GEORGE WILLIAM (R)
b Lowell, Mass, Sept 24, 36; m to Norma E Brainard; c Wayne, Mary Ann & George. Educ: Emerson Col, BS in Speech, 58. Polit & Govt Pos: Legis asst, US Sen Norris Cotton, NH, 68-71; legis asst, US Rep Marvin L Esch, Mich, 71, admin asst, 72- Bus & Prof Pos: Prog dir, WGIR, Manchester, NH, 59-61; news ed, WAAB, Worcester, Mass, 61-65; news dir, WFEA, Manchester, NH, 65-68. Mem: Montgomery Co Young Rep, Md; US Senate Press Secy Asn. Relig: Episcopal. Legal Res: 11905 Enid Dr Potomac MD 20854 Mailing Add: 412 Cannon House Off Bldg Washington DC 20515

STEVENS, GERALD FAIRLIE (R)
Majority Leader, Conn House Rep
b New Haven, Conn, Mar 17, 38; s George Stevens, Jr & Edith Barringer S; m 1964 to Judith Anne Stedman; c Karen Anne, Laurie Jean, Amy Elizabeth & Wendy Lynn. Educ: Univ Conn, BA, 60; George Washington Univ, LLB, 63; Phi Alpha Theta; Phi Delta Phi; Theta Xi. Polit & Govt Pos: Vpres, Milford Young Rep Club, Conn, 64-65, pres, 65-66; campaign mgr, Mayoralty Elec, Milford, 65; secy & mem, Milford Charter Rev Comn, 65-66; mem, Rep Town Comt, 65-; Conn State Rep, 122nd Dist, 67-, co-chmn, Legis Intern Comt, Conn State House of Rep, 69-71, mem, Pub Health & Safety Comt, 69-71, chmn, Regulations Rev Comt, 69-, dep Minority Leader, 71-73, mem, Legis Mgt Comt, 71-, Majority Leader, 73-75, House Minority Leader, 75- & Ranking Rep, Judiciary & Governmental Functions Comt; alt deleg, Rep Nat Conv, 72. Mem: Jr CofC; Mason; AF&AM; Milford YMCA (dir, 64-66); Milford Rotary Club (sgt at arms, 66-67). Honors & Awards: Admitted to practice before US Supreme Court; Man of the Year Award, Milford Jr CofC; One of the Three Outstanding Young Men in Conn, State Jr CofC, 69. Relig: Congregational. Legal Res: 44 Driftwood Lane Milford CT 06460 Mailing Add: 31 Cherry St Milford CT 06460

STEVENS, HUGH BEDFORD (D)
Chmn, Buncombe Co Dem Exec Comt, NC
b Asheville, NC; s James E Stevens & Hattie Neal Sayles S (both deceased); m 1948 to Alpha Louise Richbourg; c Karen (Mrs Henry Oehmann) & Harriett Lu. Educ: Asheville-Biltmore Col, 34-36; Miss Southern Col, 43. Polit & Govt Pos: Chmn, Buncombe Co Dem Exec Comt,

NC, 74- Bus & Prof Pos: Dep US Marshal, Dept of Justice, 45-73; retired, 73. Mil Serv: Entered as Pvt, Air Force, 42, released as Sgt, 45, after serv in 8th Air Force, ETO; Good Conduct Medal; 5 Battle Stars. Mem: Lions; Am Legion; Fraternal Order of Police; Nat Asn Retired Fed Employees; United Way Asheville (div chmn). Honors & Awards: Several citations from Dept Justice, citation from President John Kennedy, 62, citation from Attorney Gen of US Robert Kennedy, 62. Relig: Methodist. Mailing Add: 6 Gladstone Rd Asheville NC 28805

STEVENS, JAMES PRICE (D)
SC State Sen
b Loris, SC, Apr 4, 20; s M D Stevens & Lalla McQueen S; m to Madeleine Zabelicky; c James Price, Jr, Randle McQueen, Douglas Yancey & Victoria Joy. Educ: Univ SC, LLB, 52; pres law sch student body, 52; Phi Alpha Delta; Law Sch Honor Coun Debate Team, 51-52; Wig & Robe. Polit & Govt Pos: SC State Sen, 56- Bus & Prof Pos: Lawyer. Mil Serv: Coast Guard, 40-46. Mem: VFW; Am Legion; Mason. Relig: Methodist; teacher of men's Bible class, Loris Methodist Church. Legal Res: 3995 Walnut St Loris SC 29569 Mailing Add: State House Columbia SC 29211

STEVENS, JEAN M (R)
b Turtle Creek, Pa, Dec 9, 21; d Donald Harold DeForrest, Sr & Kathryn McCune D; m 1946 to Vincent A Stevens; c Linda, Susan, Vincent A, II & Ann. Educ: Huntingdon High Sch, grad. Polit & Govt Pos: Committeewoman, Penn Hills Rep Comt, Pa, 60-, secy, 62-66, vchmn, 66-69, chmn, 69-70; alt deleg, Rep Nat Conv, 68; chmn, Comt to Reelect the President, Penn Hills, Pa, 72. Mem: PTA; Penn Hills Young Rep; Coun Rep Women; Girl Scouts; Eastmont Civic Asn. Mailing Add: 388 Princeton Dr Penn Hills PA 15235

STEVENS, ROBERT S (R)
Calif State Sen
b 1916; married; c four. Educ: Univ Utah; Stanford Univ, BS; Stanford Law Sch, LLB. Polit & Govt Pos: Mem, Los Angeles Co Rep Cent Comt, 52-; Calif State Assemblyman, 62-67; Calif State Sen, 67- Bus & Prof Pos: Bd of mgr, WLos Angeles YMCA; dir, Los Angeles Community Concert Asn. Mem: Westwood Jr CofC (past pres); Westwood Village Bar Asn (past pres); Westwood Village & Los Angeles West Area Community Chests (past chmn); Crescent Bay Coun Boy Scouts (former exec comt). Honors & Awards: Pres, Mormon Choir of Calif. Mailing Add: 1245 Glendon Ave Los Angeles CA 90024

STEVENS, THEODORE FULTON (TED) (R)
US Sen, Alaska
b Indianapolis, Ind, Nov 18, 23; s George A Stevens (deceased) & Gertrude Chancellor S; m 1952 to Ann Mary Cherrington; c Susan, Beth, Walter, Ted, Jr & Ben. Educ: Univ Calif, Los Angeles, Harvard Law Sch; Delta Kappa Epsilon. Hon Degrees: LLD, Univ Alaska, 75. Polit & Govt Pos: US attorney, Fairbanks, Alaska, 53-56; legis counsel, Dept Interior, Washington, DC, 56-58, asst to Secy Interior, 59 & solicitor, Dept Interior, 60; cand for US Sen, Alaska, 62; state chmn, Rockefeller for Pres Comt, 64; Alaska State Rep, 65-68; US Sen, Alaska, 68-; deleg, Rep Nat Conv, 64 & 72. Bus & Prof Pos: Attorney, Law Off, Northcutt Ely, Washington, DC, 50-52 & Collins & Clasby, Fairbanks, Alaska, 53; partner, Stevens & Roderick, 61-63, Stevens & Stringer, 64, Stevens, Savage, Holland, Erwin & Edwards, 64-65, Stevens & Holland, 66-68. Mil Serv: Entered as Pvt, Army, 43, released as 1st Lt, 46, after serv in 14th Air Force, China; Air Medal with Cluster; Distinguished Flying Cross with Cluster; China-Burma-India Ribbon; Yuan Hai Medal from Chinese Nationalist Govt, 46. Mem: Fed, Am, Alaska, Calif & DC Bar Asns. Honors & Awards: Named Alaska 49'er, one of 49 Alaskans chosen by Alaska Press Club for outstanding serv to Alaska, 63; Univ Calif Los Angeles Distinguished Serv Award, 71; Alaskan of the Year, 74; Man of the Year Award, Nat Fisheries Inst, 75. Relig: Episcopal. Legal Res: AK Mailing Add: 411 Old Senate Off Bldg Washington DC 20510

STEVENS, WILLIAM JOHN (D)
NH State Rep
b New Haven, Conn, June 30, 45; s Robert A Stevens & Ann Horan S; m 1967 to Florence Ann Stronczek. Educ: Univ Bridgeport, BS, 68; Becker Jr Col, Worcester, Mass, AS, 66; Alpha Phi Omega; Alpha Omicron. Polit & Govt Pos: Dem co auditor, Rockingham Co, NH, 70-; NH State Rep, 72- Bus & Prof Pos: Acct instr, Andover Inst Bus, 68-70; systs rep, Litton Automated Bus Systs, 70-71; pub acct, Salem, NH, 71- Mem: Salem-Derry Elks 2226; Salem Jaycees (treas, 70); Salem Young Dem; Salem Coun on Aging (chmn, 72); Becker Jr Col Alumni Asn (vpres, 71); Salem Dem Town Comt. Honors & Awards: Outstanding Young Men of Am, Becker Jr Col Alumni Asn, 70. Relig: Catholic. Mailing Add: 79 Shannon Rd Salem NH 03079

STEVENS, WILMA PATTEN (D)
b Bellingham, Wash, Aug 31, 37; d William Patten & Elizabeth Strahl P; m 1956 to Dr Lee A Stevens; c Lee Richard, Marc Wesley, Lisa Kaye & Penny Sue. Educ: Western Wash State Col, Ore State Univ, San Jose State Univ, De Anza Col & Feather River Col, 55-74. Polit & Govt Pos: Campaign worker, Vasconcellos for Assembly Campaigns, Calif, 66, mem steering comt, 66-68, off mgr, 68, mem fund-raising comt, 70; off mgr, R F Kennedy for President Campaign, Santa Clara Co, 68; dep registr of voters, Santa Clara & Plumas Co, Calif, 68-74; off mgr, Mineta for City Coun & Mayor Campaigns, San Jose, 69 & 71; alt deleg, Dem Nat Conv, 72; co-chmn, McGovern for President Campaign, Plumas Co, 72; chmn, M Dymally for Lt Gov Campaign, 74; comt vol, Dem Nat Mid-Term Conf, 74; staff mem & research asst to US Rep Sidney R Yates, Ill, currently. Mem: Common Cause; Am Civil Liberties Union; Pub Citizen. Relig: Methodist. Mailing Add: 421 A St NE Apt 5 Washington DC 20002

STEVENSON, ADLAI EWING, III (D)
US Sen, Ill
b Chicago, Ill, Oct 10, 30; s Adlai Ewing Stevenson & Ellen Borden S; m 1955 to Nancy Anderson; c Adlai E, IV, Lucy Wallace, Katherine Randolph & Warwick Lewis. Educ: Harvard Col, AB, 52; Harvard Law Sch, LLB, 57. Polit & Govt Pos: Ill State Rep, 65-67; State Treas, Ill, 67-70; US Sen, Ill, 70- Bus & Prof Pos: Law clerk to Ill State Supreme Court Justice, Chicago & Springfield, 57-58; law firm assoc, Mayer, Friedlich, Spiess, Tierney, Brown & Platt, Chicago, 58-66, partner, 66-67. Mil Serv: Entered Marine Corps, 52, released as 1st Lt, 54, after serv in Third Marine Div, Japan & First Marine Div, Korea, 52-54; Capt, Marine Corps Res, 61. Legal Res: Hanover IL Mailing Add: US Senate Washington DC 20510

STEVENSON, BOYD (D)
Polit & Govt Pos: Chmn, Dem Party Okla, formerly. Mailing Add: Dem Party of Okla 2726 N Oklahoma Ave Oklahoma City OK 73105

STEVENSON, CLARENCE NEAL (D)
b Pettus, Tex, Oct 9, 34; s R A Stevenson & Mary Lee Ballard S; m 1964 to Sandra J Sitterle; c Neal Wayne & Morgan Lee. Educ: Univ Tex, Austin, BA, 59, DJ, 60; Delta Chi; Silver Spurs; Friar Soc. Polit & Govt Pos: Deleg, Dem Nat Conv, 72. Bus & Prof Pos: Assoc, Law Off, R H Cory, Victoria, Tex, 60-62; assoc, Fly, Cory & Moeller, 62-64, partner, Fly, Cory, Moeller & Stevenson, 64-69, Cullen, Edwards, Williams & Stevenson, 69-72 & Fly, Moeller & Stevenson, 72- Mil Serv: Entered as Pvt, Army, 54, released as Cpl, 56, after serv in Inf Sch, Ft Benning, Ga, 55-56. Mem: State Bar of Tex; Phi Alpha Delta; Rotary. Honors & Awards: Distinguished Serv Award, Jaycees, 67. Relig: Episcopal. Legal Res: Box 695 Rte 1 Victoria TX 77901 Mailing Add: PO Box 3547 Victoria TX 77901

STEVENSON, CLAUDIUS EDWARD (R)
Chmn, Utah Co Rep Cent Comt, Utah
b Salt Lake City, Utah, Apr 26, 15; s Lester A Stevenson, MD & Bertha Starley S; m 1939 to Marie Douglass; c Douglass Edward. Educ: Univ Utah, LLB, 39; Beta Theta Pi. Polit & Govt Pos: Deleg, Utah Co Rep Conv, Utah, 64-72; deleg, Utah Rep State Conv, 64-72; treas, Utah Co, 65-71; chmn, Utah Co Rep Cent Comt, 64-, mem exec comt, 65-; mem, Utah Rep State Cent Comt, 65-, mem state exec comt, 65-; alt deleg, Rep Nat Conv, 72; mem, Utah State Legis Reapportionment Comt, 72; app to Gov Study Comn for Utah Co, 74. Bus & Prof Pos: Pres, Prof Photographers Asn Utah Co, 54-56; vpres, Intermountain Prof Photographers Asn, 55-56, pres, 57-58; conv chmn, Prof Photographers Asn Utah, 56, pres, Asn, 57-58. Mil Serv: Entered as Pvt, Marine Corps, 43, released as Sgt & instr photography, after serv in ABG-2 Marine Aviation, US, 43-46. Mem: Prof Photographers Utah (life dir, 56-); Intermountain Prof Photographers Asn (hon life dir); Delta Theta Phi; Royal Photog Soc Gt Brit (hon life mem). Relig: Latter-day Saint. Mailing Add: 340 West 400 N Payson UT 84651

STEVENSON, ED (D)
Ore State Rep
Mailing Add: 933 S First Ave Coquille OR 97423

STEVENSON, EDWARD A (D)
b Jamaica, WI, Nov 9, 07; s William Alexander Stevenson & Emma Newton S; m 1934 to Katy Haskins; c Edward A, Jr. Educ: Harlem Eve High Sch, grad; NY Univ, 56-59. Polit & Govt Pos: NY State Assemblyman, 66-72; dist leader, 78th Assembly Dist Dem Party, Bronx, 69- Bus & Prof Pos: Food serv dir, New York Dept Correction, 34 years. Mem: New York Prof Employees; NAACP(bd dir, Bronx Br). Honors & Awards: Named Outstanding Civil Serv Employee, 65. Relig: Protestant. Mailing Add: 1136 Jackson Ave Bronx NY 10456

STEVENSON, FERDINAN BACKER (NANCY) (D)
SC State Rep
b New Rochelle, NY, June 8, 28; d William Bryant Backer & Ferdinanda Legare B Waring; m 1956 to Norman Williams Stevenson; c David Moltke-Hansen & Ferdinan L, Norman W, Jr & Josephine I W Stevenson. Educ: Smith Col, BA, 49. Polit & Govt Pos: SC State Rep, 74- Publ: Co-auth, Nat Fein's Animals, Gilbert Press, 55; co-auth, Return to Octavia, New Am Libr, 64; co-auth, A Clearing in the Fog, World Publ Co, 70. Mem: Historic Charleston Found (trustee); Col Charleston Found (trustee, secy, 73-); Footlight Players Inc (pres, 73-); Save Charleston Found (co-chmn, 73-). Relig: Episcopal. Mailing Add: 14 Legare St Charleston SC 29401

STEVENSON, HARRY (D)
b Newark, NJ, Sept 22, 14; s Thomas Henry Stevenson & Ellen Smith S; m 1944 to Audrey Louise Lackner; c Janet L. Educ: NY Univ Sch Com, BCS, 40; Beta Gamma Sigma; Phi Beta Kappa. Polit & Govt Pos: Comnr, Fed Housing Authority, 53-54; pres bd educ, Irvington, NJ, 54-60; pres munic coun, Irvington, 62-64, Councilman, 64-66, Mayor, 66-74; alt deleg, Dem Nat Conv, 68, deleg, 72. Bus & Prof Pos: Acct, Parr Elec Co, Inc, 33-38; export mgr, Parr Elec Export Corp, 38-41; head elec sect, Distributors Div, War Prod Bd, 41-42; self-employed, CPA, 46- Mil Serv: Entered as Pvt, Army, 42, released as 1st Lt, 46, after serv in 7th Major Port, Japan. Mem: Am Inst CPA; Nat Asn Acct; Am Legion; Optimist Club; Elks. Relig: Protestant. Mailing Add: 34 Clinton Terr Irvington NJ 07111

STEVENSON, RUSSELL E, JR (R)
Chmn, Tolland Rep Town Comt, Conn
b Hartford, Conn, Nov 7, 37; s Russell E Stevenson, Sr & Anna Waters S (deceased); m 1962 to Maryalis Truehart; c Jennifer & Robert. Educ: Morse Col, BA; Am Col Life Underwriters, CLU. Polit & Govt Pos: Chmn, Manchester Co Young Rep, 60, Tolland Young Rep, 65-66; Tolland Co Young Rep, 67 & Citizens for Nixon-Agnew, 68; chmn, Tolland Rep Town Comt, 68-; Justice of the Peace, Tolland, Conn, chmn salary study comt, formerly. Bus & Prof Pos: Dir, Mass Mutual Life Asn of Chartered Life Underwriters, currently. Mil Serv: Entered as E-1, Coast Guard Res, 58, released as E-6, 66. Mem: Hartford & Nat Asns Life Underwriters; Hartford Chap, Chartered Life Underwriters; Am Soc Chartered Life Underwriters; AF&AM. Relig: Episcopal. Mailing Add: Apple Rd Tolland CT 06084

STEVENSON, WILLIAM HENRY (R)
b Kenosha, Wis, Sept 23, 91; s Maj John Henry Stevenson & Minna Fenske S; m 1913 to Lulu Belle Bucklin; c Phyllis Belle (Mrs Grams), James Steven & Claudia. Educ: La Crosse State Teachers Col; Univ Wis Col Law; Phi Alpha Delta. Polit & Govt Pos: Dist attorney, Richland Co, Wis, 26-30; divorce counsel, Richland Co, 28-30; comnr, Circuit Court, Richland Co, 30-31; dist attorney, La Crosse Co, 34-40; US Rep, Wis, 41-49. Bus & Prof Pos: Attorney-at-law, Richland Center, Wis, 21-31, La Crosse, 31-41 & Onalaska, 50- Mem: State Bar of Wis; La Crosse Co Hist Soc (pres, 66-); Mason (32 degree); Shrine; Scottish Rite. Relig: Methodist. Mailing Add: 502 S Third Ave Onalaska WI 54650

STEVENTON, JOSEPH THOMAS (R)
Vt State Rep
Mailing Add: RFD Rochester VT 05767

STEVER, HORTON GUYFORD
Dir, Nat Sci Found
b Corning, NY, Oct 24, 16; s Ralph Raymond Stever & Alma Matt S; m 1946 to Louise Risley Floyd; c Horton, Jr, Sarah Newell (Mrs Douglas W Marshall), Margarette Risley & Roy Risley. Educ: Colgate Univ, AB, 38; Calif Inst Technol, PhD, 41; Phi Beta Kappa; Sigma Xi; Sigma Gamma Tau; Tau Beta Pi. Hon Degrees: DSC, LLD, HHD & DEng from various cols & univs. Polit & Govt Pos: Sci liaison off, Off Sci Research & Develop London Mission, 42-45; exec off, US Air Force Guided Missiles Prog, 46-48; chief scientist, US Air Force, 55-56; mem, Nat Sci Bd, 70-72, dir, Nat Sci Found, 72-, sci adv, 73- Bus & Prof Pos: Staff mem, Radiation Lab & instr, Officers Radar Sch, Mass Inst Technol, 41-42, from asst prof to prof

aeronaut eng, 46-65, assoc dean, 56-59, head dept mech eng, naval architect & marine eng, 61-65; pres, Carnegie-Mellon Univ, 65-72. Publ: Auth of various publications on sci, tech, educ & sci policy matters. Mem: Nat Acad Sci; Nat Acad Eng; Am Acad Arts & Sci; AAAS; fel Am Inst Aeronaut & Astronaut. Honors & Awards: President's Cert of Merit, 48; Scott Gold Medal, Am Ord Asn, 60; Distinguished Pub Serv Medal, Dept Defense, 68; Pittsburgh's Man of the Year, Jr CofC, 66; Alumni Distinguished Serv Award, Calif Inst Technol, 66. Relig: Episcopal. Legal Res: 1528 33rd St NW Washington DC 20007 Mailing Add: Nat Sci Found 1800 G St NW Washington DC 20550

STEWARD, WILLIAM ROBERT (D)
Chmn, Haskell Co Dem Party, Okla
b Edgewood, Tex, Aug 9, 06; s Robert Lee Steward & Tellie Brandon S; m 1945 to Veda Mae Heckman; c Bobby Mac. Educ: Conners State Jr Col, 29-31; Northeastern State Teachers Col, BS, 40. Polit & Govt Pos: Chmn, Haskell Co Dem Party, Okla, 62- Bus & Prof Pos: Prin & teacher, 31-68, teacher math, govt & hist, Keota, Okla, 69-70; rancher, 59-70. Mem: Haskell Co Farmers Union; Odd Fellows. Honors & Awards: Hena Award for 30 year 4-H Leadership; Teacher of Year, Haskell Co, 67. Relig: Methodist. Mailing Add: RR 1 McCurtain OK 74944

STEWART, BRICE HORACE (R)
Chmn, Nevada Co Rep Comt, Ark
b Prescott, Ark, July 2, 11; s Lewis Edward Stewart & Ella Waddle S; m 1947 to Della Mae Duke. Educ: Bluff Springs, Ark Pub Schs. Polit & Govt Pos: Pres, Nevada Co Rep Club, Ark, 63; chmn, Nevada Co Rep Comt, 64-72 & 75- Mil Serv: Entered as Pvt, Army, 40, released as Pfc, 44, after serv in Co C, 153rd Inf, Alaska, 41-44; Good Conduct Medal. Mem: Am Cancer Soc (Nevada Co serv chmn, 61-); Am Red Cross (Nevada Co Chap chmn); Mason; Am Legion. Honors & Awards: Served unofficially as chaplain during World War II. Relig: Presbyterian. Mailing Add: 605 Oak St Prescott AR 71857

STEWART, CARLYLE VEEDER, JR (LYLE) (R)
Mem, Arlington Co Rep Comt, Va
b Springfield, Ohio, Sept 12, 27; s Carlyle Veeder Stewart & Delma Fahnestock S; m 1972 to Patricia E Valliere. Educ: Univ Mich, Ann Arbor, AB, 50; Lambda Chi Alpha. Polit & Govt Pos: Vol, Eisenhower & Nixon Campaign, 52, 56 & 60; precinct chmn, DC State Rep Comt, 61-65 & treas, 63-64; hon asst sgt-at-arms, Rep Nat Conv, 64; nat fieldman ballot security, Oper Eagle Eye, Citizen's for Goldwater-Miller, 64; mem, Finance Comt, Young Rep Nat Fedn, 64-65; dir spec projs, United Citizens Comt for Nixon-Agnew, 68; mem, Arlington Co Rep Comt, 72-; mem, Citizens Adv Comt for CATV, Arlington Co, 72-75; chmn, Ballot Security, 72- Bus & Prof Pos: Salesman, Johns-Manville, Kaiser Aluminum, United Clay Prod Co, 53-64; exec dir, Research Serv Inst, 67 & 68; pres, Stewart Mgt & Research Tech, Inc, bus brokers, ins, indust-govt & pub rels, 68-; faculty for adult educ, Univ Va, 73-74; pres, Crystal City Civic Asn, 74-; pres, Exec Apts, Inc, 75- Mil Serv: Midn, Merchant Marine, 45-47; Navigator, Air Force, 50-53; Mediter & Atlantic Theatre Ribbons. Mem: Civil War Round Table of DC; Capitol Hill Club; Nat Hist Soc; Am Legion; Comt of 100. Honors & Awards: George Washington Honor Medal for film, The Riot Makers, Freedoms Found at Valley Forge. Mailing Add: 2111 Jefferson Davis Hwy Arlington VA 22202

STEWART, CHARLES WESLEY, JR (D)
Ark State Rep
b El Dorado, Ark, Sept 25, 27; s Charles Wesley Stewart & Mettie Adams S; m 1955 to Joanne Dee Rogers; c Charles Wesley, IV & Thomas Rogers. Educ: Univ Ark, JD, 51; Alpha Kappa Psi; Sigma Nu; Alpha Phi Omega. Polit & Govt Pos: Ark State Rep, Dist Seven, 55- Bus & Prof Pos: Secy-treas, Ozark Steel Co, Fayetteville, Ark, 51-; gen mgr, Stewart & Sons, 60- Mil Serv: Entered as A/S, Navy, 45, released as Seaman 1/C, after serv in several ships, Am Theatre. Publ: Case comment Arkansas uniform securities law, Ark Law Rev, 59. Mem: Exchange Club; Elks; Am Legion; Fayetteville Country Club; Bella Vista Country Club. Honors & Awards: Outstanding Young Man Award, Fayetteville Jr CofC. Relig: Baptist. Legal Res: 2405 Jimmie Dr Fayetteville AR 72701 Mailing Add: PO Drawer 1167 Fayetteville AR 72701

STEWART, DAVID A (D)
b Sewickley, Pa, July 1, 41; s James Francis Stewart & Virginia Edwards S; m 1962; c Kevin Robert. Educ: Univ Ark, Fayetteville, BSBA, 63, LLB, 67; Phi Alpha Delta; Alpha Tau Omega. Polit & Govt Pos: Dep prosecuting attorney, Pulaski Co, Ark, 69-70; Ark Claim Comn, 71-74; dep prosecuting attorney, Yell Co, 72-; deleg, Dem Mid Term Conf, 74. Bus & Prof Pos: Law partner, Pearce, Robinson, McCord & Stewart, 67-69; sole practitioner, Danville, Ark, 71- Mem: Ark & Am Bar Asns; Am Judicature Soc; Ark Trial Lawyers Asn; Nat Asn Criminal Defense Lawyers. Honors & Awards: Chmn of the Year in the Field of Unemploy & Retraining, Ark Jaycees, 73. Relig: United Methodist. Legal Res: K St Danville AR 72833 Mailing Add: PO Box 536 Danville AR 72833

STEWART, DAVID WALLACE (R)
b New Concord, Ohio, Jan 22, 87; s Wilson Stewart & Mary Ann Wallace S; m 1920 to Helen E Struble; c Robert Bruce. Educ: Geneva Col, Beaver Falls, Pa, AB, 11; Univ Chicago, JD, 17; pres of trustees of Morningside Col. Polit & Govt Pos: US Sen, Iowa, 26-27. Bus & Prof Pos: Lawyer, Stewart & Hatfield, 17- Mil Serv: Marine Corps. Mem: Sioux City Boy Scouts; Am Bar Asn; Sioux City CofC; Am Legion; Mason. Relig: Presbyterian. Legal Res: 3827 Country Club Blvd Sioux City IA 51104 Mailing Add: 830-838 Frances Bldg Sioux City IA 51103

STEWART, DELLA D (R)
Committeewoman, Ark Rep State Comt
b Hot Springs, Ark, Nov 16, 09; d Louis Jefferson Duke & Eliza Richardson D; m 1947 to Brice Horace Stewart. Educ: Ouachita Baptist Univ, 47. Polit & Govt Pos: Precinct committeewoman, Nevada Co Rep Women, Ark, 64-, club pres, 65-69 & 73-75; Outlook chmn, Ark Rep State Comt, 66-68, committeewoman, 70-; state chaplain, Ark Fedn Rep Women, 73-75. Relig: Church of Christ. Mailing Add: 605 Oak Prescott AR 71857

STEWART, DONALD W (D)
Ala State Sen
Mailing Add: PO Box 2182 Anniston AL 36201

STEWART, DONOVAN (R)
Ariz State Rep
b Seattle, Wash, Mar 5, 03; s Horatio A Stewart & Bessie E Sandison S; m 1928 to Blanche I Robinson; c Nancy (Mrs Belian) & Sandra (Mrs Karolczyk). Educ: Ore State Univ, BS Agr. Polit & Govt Pos: Precinct committeeman, Ariz Rep Party, 66-; Ariz State Rep, 69-, mem, Natural Resources & Agr Comts, chmn, one of four Subcomt on Appropriations, currently, chmn standing comt of co & munic & mem com, nat resources & transportation comts, 32nd Session. Bus & Prof Pos: Livestock appraiser, Bank of Am, Los Angeles, Calif, 46-48; livestock loan adv, First Nat Bank, Phoenix, Ariz, 48-68. Mil Serv: Entered as 2nd Lt, Army, 42, released as 1st Lt, 44; Commendation by Gen McNair, 44; mem, ROTC Rifleteam from 11 Western States, 27. Mem: Ariz State Univ Found Bd (one of six incorporators); Ariz State Fair Comn; Mason; Am Legion. Honors & Awards: Given plaques for serv to Future Farmers of Am & 4-H Club mem by both orgn & Ariz State Univ, 68. Relig: Protestant. Mailing Add: 4002 W Keim Dr Phoenix AZ 85019

STEWART, ELLIS CAMERON (D)
b Columbus, Ohio, Oct 27, 01; s Elmer Darius Stewart & Henrietta Peden S; m 1924 to Vannie Lamar; c Ellis Cameron, Jr. Educ: North Augusta High Sch, grad, 18. Polit & Govt Pos: Dir, Ala Div, Records & Reports, 47; chmn, Gov Comt Employ Physically Handicapped, 47-51; dir consumer prices, Off Price Stabilization, Ala, 51-53; chmn, Ala UN Comt, 55; exec secy, Ala River Develop Authority, 58-59; staff asst, Off Emergency Planning, Washington, DC, 62-63; staff asst, Senate Select Comt Small Bus, 64-65; staff asst, US Sen John Sparkman, Ala, 65-66, exec secy, 67- Bus & Prof Pos: Partner, Levysteins, Montgomery, Ala, 42-47, Stewarts, 47-58; ed writer, Montgomery Advertiser, 44-46. Relig: Methodist. Legal Res: 337 Boyce St Montgomery AL 36107 Mailing Add: 417 A St SE Washington DC 20003

STEWART, GEORGE E (D)
Ky State Rep
Mailing Add: 528 Kentucky Ave Pineville KY 40977

STEWART, H DONALD (D)
NJ State Assemblyman
Mailing Add: State House Trenton NJ 08625

STEWART, JOE WILLIAM (D)
Wyo State Rep
b Jackson, Mo, May 9, 28; s William Stewart & Mabel Porter S; m 1962 to Marie Thayer. Educ: Mo Univ, BJ, 59; Univ Wyo, MA, 64. Polit & Govt Pos: Wyo State Rep, 67-68 & 71-; deleg, Dem Nat Conv, 68 & 72; chmn, Natrona Co Dem Cent Comt, Wyo, 69-72; Wyo Dem State Committeeman, 72- Mil Serv: Entered as A/S, Navy, 46, released as Yeoman 3/C, 48, after serv in Pac Theater. Mem: Mason; Kiwanis; VFW. Relig: Methodist. Mailing Add: 1320 Ivy Lane Casper WY 82601

STEWART, JOHN GILMAN (D)
b Brooklyn, NY, Feb 15, 35; s F Gilman Stewart & Winifred Link S; m 1957 to Nancy Potter; c Michael Gilman & Cara Jane. Educ: Colgate Univ, BA, 57; Univ Chicago, MA, 59, PhD, 67; Phi Beta Kappa; Alpha Tau Omega. Polit & Govt Pos: Legis asst to US Sen Hubert H Humphrey, Minn, 62-64 & Vice President, Hubert Humphrey, 65-70; exec dir, Dem Policy Coun, Dem Nat Comt, 69-70, dir, Off Commun, 70-72; polit writer & consult, 72-; exec dir, Dem Adv Coun of Elected Officials, 74-; ed, The Majority Report, 74-; consult, Joint Econ Comt, US Cong, 75- Bus & Prof Pos: Vis lectr dept govt, Cornell Univ, 63-64; fel, Inst Polit, John F Kennedy Sch Govt, Harvard Univ, 66-67; adj asst prof polit sci, Macalester Col, 69-70. Publ: One Last Chance: The Democratic Party, 1974-76, Praeger, 74; Gerald Ford's first month: three lessons, Dem Rev, 11/74; A prescription for the Democrats, Wall St J, 7/74; plus others. Mem: Am Polit Sci Asn. Honors & Awards: Citation for pub serv, Univ Chicago Alumni Asn, 73. Relig: Protestant. Mailing Add: 6336 31st Pl NW Washington DC 20015

STEWART, JOSEPH ALEXANDER (JOE) (R)
Committeeman, Idaho Rep State Cent Comt
b Burnt Prairie, Ill, Jan 28, 88; s Alexander Stewart & Sybby Book S; wid; c Vaughan Alexander. Polit & Govt Pos: Committeeman, Idaho Rep State Cent Comt, Bingham Co, currently; deleg, Rep Nat Conv, 68; in charge of campaigns for gov, congressmen & US Sen; politically active for 50 years. Bus & Prof Pos: Farmer; farm mgt; real estate broker; loan & ins agency. Mem: Elks. Relig: Protestant. Legal Res: 392 E Court Blackfoot ID 83221 Mailing Add: PO Box 8 Blackfoot ID 83221

STEWART, MARY RUTH (R)
Mem, Nebr Rep State Cent Comt
b Los Angeles, Calif, Feb 17, 29; d Joseph L Ryons & Norma Heine R; m 1951 to William Alexander Stewart, Jr; c Leslie Jane, William A, III, Courtney Ann & Lisa Kyle. Educ: Univ Nebr, BS in Educ, 51; Kappa Kappa Gamma. Polit & Govt Pos: Vchmn, Dawson Co Young Rep, Nebr, 57-58, Dawson Co Rep, 60-62 & Nebr Young Rep, 61-62; secy, Nebr Rep State Cent & Exec Comts, 65-71; mem, Nebr Rep State Cent Comt, 72-; alt deleg, Rep Nat Conv, 72. Bus & Prof Pos: Third grade teacher, Lexington Pub Sch, Nebr, 67- Mem: Nebr Educ Asn; Girl Scouts (leader); Am Legion Auxiliary. Relig: Episcopal. Mailing Add: RR 1 Lexington NE 68850

STEWART, MCROBERT LEE (R)
Mayor, Daly City, Calif
b Auburn, Nebr, Mar 18, 27; s Ralph Richard Stewart, Sr & Lydia Andrews S; m 1952 to Nanda E Sereni. Educ: Balboa High Sch, 45. Polit & Govt Pos: Mayor & councilman, Daly City, Calif, 70-; comnr, Local Agency Formation Comn, 73-; pub mem, State Bd Registration for Prof Engrs, 73- Mil Serv: Entered as Pvt, Marine Corps, 45, released as Cpl, 46. Mem: Lions. Mailing Add: 440 Southgate Ave Daly City CA 94015

STEWART, MELVIN JAMES (D)
b Vassar, Mich, Dec 22, 07; s Lee Roy Stewart & Jennie E Arnold S; m 1937 to Ursula S Schnell; c Luther James & Bervaine Ann (Mrs Daniel K Pratt). Educ: Vassar High Sch, grad, 29. Polit & Govt Pos: Chmn, Vassar Dem Club, Mich, 60-61; vchmn, Seventh Cong Dist, 61-65; chmn, Tuscola Co Dem Comt, formerly; alt deleg, Dem Nat Conv, 64. Bus & Prof Pos: Gen serviceman, The Detroit Edison Co, 37-70, retired. Mem: Mason; Dem Comt on Agr. Relig: American Lutheran. Mailing Add: 312 N Cass Ave Vassar MI 48768

STEWART, PAUL MORTON, JR (R)
b Washington, DC, Mar 14, 22; s Rear Adm Paul M Stewart (deceased) & Norma Pellegrini S; m 1963 to Patricia Adele Cairns; c Dana E. Educ: Georgetown Col, BS, 44, JD, 48; Delta Theta Phi. Polit & Govt Pos: Trial attorney, Appellate Coun Off, Internal Revenue Serv, New York, 51-53; attorney, House Coun, Orange Co Assessor's Off, Calif, 65-73; admin asst to US Rep, A J Hinshaw, Calif, 73- Mil Serv: Entered as Pvt, Army, 43, released, 46, after serv

in ETO, African & Mid East Command, 44-46; recalled as Comdr, Coast Guard, 57-62, Continental US; Comdr, Coast Guard Res, currently; World War II Campaign Ribbons; Victory Medal; Nat Defense Medal; Res Medal with 2 ads; Rifle Expert. Mem: Fed Bar Asn; Int Asn Assessing Officers; ROA; Calif Rep Admin Personnel (pres). Mailing Add: 8619 Pappas Way Annandale VA 22003

STEWART, POTTER
Assoc Justice, US Supreme Court
b Jackson, Mich, Jan 23, 15; s James Garfield Stewart & Harriet Loomis Potter S; m 1943 to Mary Ann Bertles; c Harriet Potter (Mrs Richard R Virkstis), Potter, Jr & David Bertles. Educ: Yale Col, BA cum laude, 37, Law Sch, LLB cum laude, 41; Cambridge Univ, fel, 37-38; Phi Beta Kappa; Delta Kappa Epsilon; Phi Delta Phi. Polit & Govt Pos: City Councilman, Cincinnati, Ohio, 50-53, VMayor, 52-53; US judge, Court of Appeals, Sixth Circuit, 54-58; assoc justice, US Supreme Court, 58- Bus & Prof Pos: Attorney-at-law, New York, 41-42 & 45-47; attorney-at-law, Cincinnati, Ohio, 47-54. Mil Serv: Lt, Naval Res, 42-45. Mem: Am, Ohio, Cincinnati & New York Bar Asns; Yale Law Sch Asn. Relig: Episcopal. Mailing Add: 5136 Palisade Lane NW Washington DC 20016

STEWART, RICHARD OLIN **(R)**
b New Philadelphia, Ohio, June 14, 22; s Walter Kenna Stewart & Florence Newton S; m 1946 to Susanne Sharp; c Richard Olin, Jr, Barbara Lois, Allen Kenna & Laura Susanne. Educ: Univ Calif, Los Angeles, AA, 47, BS, 49. Polit & Govt Pos: Rep Precinct Chmn, Tulsa, Okla, 57-60; Rep Precinct Chmn, Denton, Tex, 60-64; chmn, Denton Co Rep Comt, Tex, 64-72; campaign pilot for Spiro T Agnew, 68; alt deleg, Rep Nat Conv, 64 & 72; mem, Denton Airport Adv Comt, 72-; mem adv bd, Am Security Coun, 73- Bus & Prof Pos: Airline pilot, Am Airlines, Inc, 49- Mil Serv: Entered as Pvt, Army, 42, released as Capt, 45, after serv in 13th Air Force, SPac Theater, 43-45; reentered serv as Capt, Air Force, 51, released as Maj, 53, after serv in Korea; Col, Air Force Res; Air Medal with Five Oak Leaf Cluster; Am Theater Medal; Asiatic-Pac Theater Ribbon with Four Battle Stars; World War II Victory Medal; Korean Serv & Air Force Res Medals; Armed Serv Medal with Hour Glass; Philippine Liberation Medal with Two Battle Stars. Mem: Airlines Pilots Asn; Night Fighter Asn; Allied Pilots Asn; Optimist (mem bd dirs, pres, 68-69, lt gov, 69-72, gov, 72-73); CofC (bd dirs, 72-75). Relig: Church of Christ. Mailing Add: 2710 Crestwood Pl Denton TX 76201

STEWART, ROBERT ESTON **(R)**
b Pence, Ind, Jan 26, 23; s Joshua Clellan Stewart & Mabel Snyder S; m 1955 to Geraldine Louise Sanders; c Martha Noel. Educ: Univ Omaha, 63-65. Polit & Govt Pos: Victory squad chmn, Merced Co Rep Campaign, Calif, 68; chmn, Comt to Reelect Gov Reagan, 70; chmn, Merced Co Rep Cent Comt, formerly; deleg, Rep Nat Conv, 72. Mil Serv: Entered as Pvt, Air Force, 42, released as Lt Col, 68, after serv in 93rd Bomb Wing, ETO, 44-45; Distinguished Flying Cross with Two Oak Leaf Clusters; Air Force Commendation Medal with One Oak Leaf Cluster; Air Medal with Three Oak Leaf Clusters. Mem: AF&AM; Elks; Scottish Rite; Shrine; Am Legion. Relig: Methodist. Mailing Add: PO Box 2222 Merced CA 95340

STEWART, RONALD K **(D)**
Mem Exec Comt, Colo Dem Cent Comt
b Longmont, Colo, Aug 16, 48; s William S Stewart & Doris J Whitmer S; single. Educ: Univ Colo, BA, 74. Polit & Govt Pos: Pres, Colo Teen Dem, 64-66; finance chmn, Boulder Co Dem Party, Colo, 69, chmn, formerly; mem, Colo Dem Cent Comt, 70-, mem, State Exec Comt, 71-, state finance chmn, 72-73, asst to state chmn, currently; deleg, Dem Nat Mid-Term Conf, 74. Mailing Add: 1818 Atwood Longmont CO 80501

STEWART, SUSAN HASTINGS **(R)**
VChmn, Rep Party Fla
b Niagara Falls, NY, Aug 24, 45; d Alfred John Hastings, Sr & Olive Greensides H; m 1964 to Gabe W Stewart, III; c Gabe W, IV & Corey Lynne. Educ: Valparaiso Univ, 63-64; Polk Community Col, AA, 75. Polit & Govt Pos: Mem exec bd, Polk Co Rep Exec Comt, 72-; co-chmn, Fla Fedn Young Rep, 73-74, nat committeewoman, 74-75, ed, Statesman, 74-; committeewoman, vchmn & chmn platform comt, Rep Party Fla, 74- Bus & Prof Pos: Casualty ins agt, Cypress Gardens Realty & Ins, 64-, assoc realtor, 74- Mem: Winter Haven Bd Realtors; Fla Asn of Realtors; Heart of Fla Young Rep Club (mem exec bd); CofC (nat legis comt); Winter Haven Womens Rep Club. Honors & Awards: Outstanding Serv Award, Heart of Fla Young Rep, 72; Outstanding Young Rep, Fla Fedn of Young Rep, 73 & 74. Relig: Lutheran. Mailing Add: 320 Greenfield Rd Cypresswood Winter Haven FL 33880

STEWART, TRACY ANN GIPSON **(D)**
b Rochester, NY, Feb 7, 43; d Tracy Greer Gipson & Marjorie Lynch B; m 1962 to Roger Lee Stewart, c Michelle Lynn & Ian Douglas. Educ: Linfield Col, 60-62; San Francisco State Col, 62-63; West Chester State Col, grad, 73; Am Univ, Washington Col Law, 73-; Kappa Alpha Phi. Polit & Govt Pos: Committeewoman Chester Co Dem Party, Pa, 70-73; chairwoman, East Whiteland Twp Dem Party, 71-72, vchairwoman, 72-73; deleg, Dem Nat Conv, 72; treas, Chester Co Citizens for McGovern, 72. Relig: Baptist. Mailing Add: 308 Longfellow St NW Washington DC 20011

STEWART, WILLIAM A, JR **(R)**
Chmn, Dawson Co Rep Comt, Nebr
b Lexington, Nebr, May 14, 29, s William A Stewart & Margaret Jeffrey S; m 1951 to Mary Ruth Ryons; c Leslie, William, Courtney & Lisa. Educ: Univ Nebr, BS, 51, LLB, 55; Phi Delta Phi; Phi Delta Theta. Polit & Govt Pos: Mem, Nebr Young Rep Exec Comt, 56-59; mem, Nebr State Rep Exec Comt, 57-59; Co Attorney, Dawson Co, Nebr, 58-66; chmn, Dawson Co Rep Comt, 63-68 & 71-72 & 74-; mem, Nebr Rep State Cent Comt, formerly. Bus & Prof Pos: Deleg, Nebr State Bar Asn, House of Deleg, 65-67. Mil Serv: Entered as 2nd Lt, Army, 51, released as 1st Lt, 63, after serv in 1st Cavalry Div, Korea, 52-53; Korean Serv & UN Serv Medals. Mem: Am & Nebr State Bar Asns; VFW; Am Legion; Mason. Relig: Presbyterian. Mailing Add: 609 N Washington Lexington NE 68850

STEWART, WILLIAM O **(R)**
VChmn, Ill Rep State Cent Comt
b Chicago, Ill, Feb 8, 25; s James Stewart & Marvella Brewer S; single. Educ: Tenn State Univ, BS, 50; DePaul Univ, ME, 67; Kappa Alpha Psi. Polit & Govt Pos: Pres, Third Ward Young Rep, 56; vchmn, Cook Co Young Rep, 57; vpres, Ill Young Rep, 58; committeeman, Ill Rep State Cent Comt, 66-, vchmn, 67-; pres, Third Ward Rep Orgn, 67- Bus & Prof Pos: Asst principal, John Farren Elem Sch, Chicago, 51-; trustee, Chicago Teachers Union, 72- Mem: Am Fedn Teachers; Am Asn Health, Phys Educ & Recreation; Chicago Teachers Union; life mem US Jaycees; Urban League. Honors & Awards: Good Guy Award, WGRT Radio Sta; Outstanding Alumnus Award, Tenn State Univ, 63. Relig: Methodist. Mailing Add: 219 E 45th St Chicago IL 60653

STICKNEY, CHARLES WILLIAM **(DFL)**
Chmn, Sherburne Co Dem-Farmer-Labor Party, Minn
b Clear Lake, Minn, Feb 3, 96; s Charles Abner Stickney & Adah White S; m 1920 to Rhea Marguerite Head. Educ: Univ Minn, Farm Exten, 3 years. Polit & Govt Pos: Chmn state comt, AAA PMA, Agr Prog, Minn, 36-52; chmn, Sherburne Co Dem-Farmer-Labor Party, 53-; app to Nat Agr Comn by President Kennedy, 63-66, app by President Johnson, 66- Bus & Prof Pos: Retired on livestock farm, Clear Lake, Minn, currently; pres bd dirs, Tri-Co Farmers Co-op Elevator, currently. Mil Serv: Enlisted as Pvt, Army, 17, released as Sgt 1/C, 19, after serv in 1st Field Signal Bn, 2nd Div, All Major Battles, 17; Silver Star Gallantry in Action. Mem: Mason; VFW; Farmers Union. Relig: Methodist. Mailing Add: RFD 1 Clear Lake MN 55319

STIDGER, RUBY JANE **(D)**
Mem, Calif Dem State Cent Comt
b Catossa, Okla, Dec 8, 11; d Willis Ervan Brown & Alice Kelly B; m 1930 to Burwell Colquitt Stidger; c Donal Ray, Jimmy Odel, Beverly Jane (Mrs McCormick), John Ervan & Linda Sue (Mrs Smith). Educ: Amarillo High Sch, Tex, grad, 30. Polit & Govt Pos: Treas, 25th Cong Dist Dem Party, Calif, 57-63; mem, Co Dem Comt, 50th Assembly Dist, 58-60, mem, 58th Assembly Dist, 62-64; 58th Assembly Dist dir, Calif Dem Coun, 62; mem, Calif Dem State Cent Comt, 58th Assembly Dist, 64-; mem, Lynch Presidential deleg, 68. Mem: San Gabriel Valley Women's Dem Club; West Covina Emblem Club. Relig: Methodist. Mailing Add: 4915 N Peck Rd El Monte CA 91732

STIDHAM, KAY BURNELL **(D)**
b Kemper Co, Miss, Feb 23, 35; d Raymond Harvey Chapman & Nealie Hill C; m 1956 to Milford Dewrell Stidham; c Lynn Myron, Glen Raymond, Harvey Lamar & Linda Gail. Educ: High sch. Polit & Govt Pos: Vpres, Wallace for President, Lincoln Park, Mich, 67-72, pres, 72-; deleg, Dem Nat Conv, 72; precinct deleg, 72-74; mem, Mich Dem Party, currently. Mem: Lincoln Park Dem Club (exec bd); Southern Mich Citizen's Coun (membership & finance chmn, 72); Nat Action Group; Lincoln Park Citizen Against Bussing. Relig: Baptist. Mailing Add: 622 Park Lincoln Park MI 48146

STIEGHORST, LEWIS EARL **(R)**
b Sheboygan, Wis, Sept 26, 26; s Alfred W Stieghorst & Marie S Strassburger S; m 1950 to Marion D Doylen; c Kent D & Kim D. Educ: Univ Wis-Madison, BSEE, 50; Univ Denver, 1 year; Phi Kappa Phi; Eta Kappa Nu; Delta Epsilon; pres, Men's Halls Asn; Iron Cross. Polit & Govt Pos: Precinct committeeman, Rep Party, Jefferson Co, Colo, 62-, dist capt, 63-73; pres, Columbine Hills Civic Asn, 63-65; campaign mgr various local cand, Jefferson Co, 64, 66 & 68; vchmn, Colo Rep Workshops, 67; mem, Jefferson Co R-1 Sch Bd, 67-; chmn, Citizens for Jefferson Co Law Enforcement Authority, 69; mem & vchmn, State Bd of Educ, Second Cong Dist, Colo, 70- Bus & Prof Pos: Engr, Allen-Bradley Co, 51-58; systs engr, Martin-Marietta Corp, 58-65; sales engr, Westinghouse Elec Corp, 65- Mil Serv: Entered as Pvt, Army, 44, released as Cpl, 46, after serv in 84th Inf Div, Ger, 45-46. Mem: Inst Elec & Electronic Engrs; CofC; Colo Asn Sch Bd (legis chmn & exec comt, 69-). Honors & Awards: Man of Year Award & Five Year Distinguished Serv Plaque, Columbine Hills Civic Asn. Relig: Methodist. Mailing Add: 7752 S Ames Way Littleton CO 80123

STIEHL, CELESTE M **(R)**
Ill State Sen
Mailing Add: 25 Lake Inez Dr Belleville IL 62221

STIEHL, WILLIAM D **(R)**
b Belleville, Ill, Dec 3, 25; s Clarence G Stiehl & Florence H Stoffel S; m 1947 to Celeste M Sullivan; c William D & Susan M. Educ: Univ NC, 43-45; St Louis Univ Sch of Law, LLB, 46-49; Sigma Alpha Epsilon. Polit & Govt Pos: Mem, Bd of Educ, Belleville Twp High Sch & Jr Col, Ill, 49-50 & 54-56, pres, 56-57; pres, St Clair Co Young Rep Club, 54-55; vpres, Ill Young Rep Orgn, 55-57; co civil attorney, St Clair Co, 56-60; chmn, St Clair Co Rep Cent Comt, 60-66; mem exec comt, Ill Rep Co Chmn Asn, 60-66; mem, Bd of Gov, Ill Rep Citizens League, 61-; Rep Voter Registration Chmn, Ill, 64; state cent committeeman, 24th Cong Dist, 66-; treas, Ill Rep State Cent Comt, formerly; Presidential Elector, 68. Bus & Prof Pos: Attorney-at-law, 49-50 & 52-; pres, Belle Valley Coal Co, Inc, 59- Mil Serv: Entered as A/S, Navy, 43, released as Ens, 46, after serv in USS Charlevoix & Staff Comdr, Marianas, Pac Theater; recalled as Lt(jg), Navy, 50, released as Lt, 52, after serv on Staff Comdr Cruiser Div 5 & legal adv to the Naval Deleg at the Korean Armistice Conf, Korean Theater; Comdr, Naval Res; Navy Commendation Medal; Korean Presidential Unit Citation; Navy Res & Armed Forces Res Medals; Am & Asiatic-Pac Theater Ribbons; Victory Medal; Korean Campaign Ribbon with Four Battle Stars; UNC Campaign Ribbon. Mem: Belleville Bar Asn; St Clair Co, St Louis, Ill State & Am Bar Asns. Relig: Methodist. Legal Res: 406 McKinley Dr Belleville IL 62221 Mailing Add: 23 S First St Belleville IL 62220

STIERN, WALTER W **(D)**
Calif State Sen
b San Diego, Calif, 1914; m 1938 to Alysjune Dunning; c two daughters. Educ: Bakersfield Col; State Col of Wash, BS, 37; State Col of Wash Sch of Vet Med, DVM, 38. Polit & Govt Pos: Calif State Sen, 58-; mem, Calif Dem State Cent Comt, 68- Bus & Prof Pos: Practicing vet, 16 years. Mil Serv: Maj, Air Force Res, 42-46, serv in China-Burma-India Theatre. Mem: Am Asn for the UN; Rotary; Kern Co Libr Asns; Child Guid Clin; Kern Co Hist Soc. Mailing Add: Rm 201 930 Truxton Ave Bakersfield CA 93301

STIKES, MARY ELLIS HATCHER **(R)**
Exec Secy, Hinds Co Rep Party, Miss
b Madison, Tenn, July 11, 31; d James Ellis Hatcher & Lorraine Parks H; m 1953 to John Edgar Stikes, Sr; c John E, Jr & Frances Lorraine. Educ: Birmingham Southern Col, 49-50; Zeta Tau Alpha. Polit & Govt Pos: Exec comt mem, Hinds Co Rep Party, Miss, 70-75, vchmn, 70-72, exec secy, 72-; adv, Miss Young Rep Fedn, 73-; Hinds Co co-chmn, Thad Cochran for Cong, 74- Honors & Awards: Silver Elephant Award, Miss Rep Party, 75. Relig: Methodist. Mailing Add: 1208 Shalimar Dr Jackson MS 39204

STILES, BEATRICE MAY **(R)**
Mem, Essex Co Rep Comt, NJ
b Newark, NJ, Aug 19, 06; d Joseph W Raymond & Stella Mathews R; m 1922 to Raymond Bell Stiles; c Le Roy Francis. Educ: Cent High Sch, 2 years; Bus Col, 1 year. Polit & Govt Pos: Mem, Essex Co Rep Comt, 27-29 & 35-, vchmn, 54-59; comt clerk, NJ Gen Assembly,

52-53, asst jour clerk, 54-55, jour clerk, 56-57; NJ State Assemblyman, 60-61; vchmn, Bloomfield Rep Town Comt, 65-70, chmn, formerly; deleg, NJ Const Conv, 66; alt deleg, Rep Nat Conv, 68; comnr, Essex Co Bd Elec, 71- Bus & Prof Pos: Clerk, H R Wilson Co, 40-41; clerk transportation dept, Western Elec, Kearney, 43-45. Mem: Nat Order Women Legislators; NJ Fedn Rep Women; Essex Co Women's Rep Club; Bloomfield Rep Club; Brookdale Second Ward Rep Club. Relig: Protestant. Mailing Add: 702 Broad St Bloomfield NJ 07003

STILLINGS, RICHARD WALLACE **(R)**
b Berwick, Maine, Sept 5, 28; s Maurice Burleigh Stillings & Doris Allen S; single. Educ: Univ Maine, BA, 52; Univ NH, 64-65; Gorham State Col, Univ Maine, 66-69; Scabbard & Blade; Theta Chi. Polit & Govt Pos: Moderator town meeting, Berwick, Maine, 56-, chief of police, 58-59 & 67-, dir, civil defense & pub safety, 58-68 & chmn, planning bd, 65-; Maine State Rep, 69-74, mem, Maine State Rep Comt, 71- Bus & Prof Pos: Adjuster, NH Finance Corp, 54-57; proprietor, Richard W Stillings Ins, 57-59; exec dir, Gtr Somersworth CofC, NH, 59-62; teacher, Berwick High Sch, Berwick, Maine, 63- Mil Serv: Entered as Pvt, Army, 46, released as Lt, 53, after serv in US Constabulary Forces, Ger, 47-48 & 40th Inf Div, Korea, 52-53; Army Res, 53-66, Maj; Bronze Star Medal with V Device; Korean Serv Medal with Battle Star; World War II Victory Medal; Army of Occup Medal; Nat Defense Serv Medal; Armed Forces Res Medal; UN Serv Medal; ROK Presidential Citation; Combat Infantryman Badge. Mem: Maine Teachers Asn; Maine Law Enforcement Asn; Mason (Blue Lodge Chap, Coun, Comdr); Am Legion (past comdr); KofP (past chancellor comdr & dep grand chancellor). Relig: Protestant. Mailing Add: 90 Sullivan St Berwick ME 03901

STILLMAN, GUY **(INDEPENDENT)**
b New York, NY, Nov 7, 18; s James A Stillman (deceased) & Mrs Fowler McCormick; m to Patricia C; c Alexandra (Mrs Jon Bernard Carlin), Victoria (Mrs Richard C Withers), Sharee (Mrs Ted Brookhard), Charles, Christopher & Brook Stillman. Educ: Rensselaer Polytech Inst, BIE, 41; Am Inst Foreign Trade, BFT, 62. Polit & Govt Pos: Mem, Ariz Dem State Finance Comt, 53-63; chmn, Maricopa Co Dem Party, 54-58; exec secy & treas, Ariz Citizens for Johnson, 64; coordr, President's Club & co-chmn, Maricopa Co Dem Finance Comt, 64-65; Dem Nat Committeeman, Ariz, formerly; consult to Inspector Gen, Dept of State, 68-69. Bus & Prof Pos: Vending mach bus, Ariz Cent Mach Co, Phoenix, 46-49; asst mgr & prod develop engr, Int Harvester Proving Grounds, Chandler, 49-50; farm implement dealer, Maricopa Equipment Co, Glendale & Buckeye, 50-60; local consult engr, Skidmore, Owings & Merrill of San Francisco, Calif; dir, Southern Ariz Bank & Trust Co, 62-71. Mil Serv: Entered as Ens, Naval Res, 41, released to inactive duty as Lt Comdr, 45, after serv in Naval Gun Factory, DC, 41, post grad course, Cornell Univ Sch of Eng, 42, Eng Officer, Motor Torpedo Boat Serv, serv in all New Guinea & Philippine Campaigns, 42-45; sr instr & Eng Officer, Motor Boat Squadrons Training Ctr, Melville, RI; Commanding Officer, Naval Res, Div 11-1, Phoenix, 46-48. Mem: Small Bus Admin Adv Coun for Ariz (chmn); Phoenix Country Day Sch (trustee); Thunderbird Grad Sch Int Mgt (trustee); US Naval Acad (bd visitors, 61-63, chmn bd visitors, 65- 70); Navy of South Viet Nam (educ consult, 1/69). Honors & Awards: Distinguished Pub Serv Medal, Navy, 70. Legal Res: 7303 N Scottsdale Rd Scottsdale AZ 85253 Mailing Add: 300 W Osborn Rd Phoenix AZ 85013

STILLMAN, JOHN STERLING **(D)**
b New York, NY, Sept 6, 18; s Ernest Goodrich Stillman & Mildred M Whitney S; m 1967 to Amelia Pasquini Jackson; c Nathaniel, Linda B, J Whitney, John J, Philipp V & Mark C J. Educ: Harvard Col, SB, 40; Yale Law Sch, 40-41; Columbia Law Sch, JD, 47; Hasty Pudding; D U Club; Phi Delta Phi; Corby Court. Polit & Govt Pos: Capt, Grover Cleveland Dem Club, Ninth Assembly Dist, NY, 46-48; founder, secy & dir, NY Young Dem Club, 47-50 & 53-55; deleg, NY State Dem Conv, 50, 52 & 54; attorney adv, Div Counsel, Nat Prod Authority, Washington, DC, 51; legis asst to US Rep F D Roosevelt, Jr, 52; regional enforcement comnr, Wage & Salary Stabilization, Nat Enforcement Comn, 52-53; chmn, Orange Co Dem Comt, 54-61, committeeman, formerly; deleg, Dem Nat Conv, 56 & 60, alt deleg-at-lg, 68; mem, NY State Bridge Authority, 56-61, chmn, 57-60; NY State Deleg Liaison & Hudson Valley Campaign Coordr, J F Kennedy for Pres, 60; Dep Under Secy, US Dept of Com, 61-62, Dep Secy for Cong Rels, 63-65; deleg coordr, Nat Citizens for Johnson-Humphrey, 64; dir, US Investment & Indust Develop Mission to India, 65; dir urban renewal, Newburgh Urban Renewal Agency, 67; coordr 27th & 28th Cong Dist, Robert F Kennedy for Pres Pre-Primary Campaign, 68; mem, Nat Citizens Comt & NY Finance Comt, Muskie for President, 71-72. Bus & Prof Pos: Assoc, Dow & Symmers, 47-48; attorney-at-law, 49-50 & 55-60; assoc, Paul, Weiss, Rifkind, Wharton & Garrison, 53-54; dir & treas, Planned Community, Ind, 65-; partner, Gilinsky, Stillman & Mishkin, 65-72; independent pvt practice, 72- Mil Serv: Entered as Ens, Naval Res, 41, released as Lt Comdr, 46, after serv in Off Comdr-in-Chief, Washington, DC, 1 year & in USS Montpelier, South & Southwest Pac, 42-45; Res, 45-61, Lt Comdr (Ret); Naval Res Medal; Pac Area Ribbon with 13 Battle Stars; Navy Unit Commendation, Philippine Liberation & Victory Medals. Relig: Unitarian; Mem: NY State, Fed & Am Bar Asns; Friends of the Earth, Inc (dir); Patterns for Progress. Relig: Unitarian; Bd mem, Newburgh Unitarian-Universalist Church, formerly. Mailing Add: 72 Maple Rd Cornwall-on-Hudson NY 12520

STILLMAN, SAUL G **(R)**
Chmn, Cuyahoga Co Rep Cent Comt, Ohio
b Cleveland, Ohio, Jan 27, 10; both parents deceased; m 1933 to Cecelia P Huberman; c Arthur (deceased), Jean (Mrs Lewis Wolff) & Barbara (Mrs Larry Meister). Educ: Harvard Col, BA, 30, Law Sch, LLB, 33; Phi Beta Kappa. Polit & Govt Pos: Mem, Rep State Cent & Exec Comt, Ohio, 62-; mem, Cuyahoga Co Bd Elec, 64-; alt deleg, Rep Nat Conv, 68 & 72; chmn, Cuyahoga Co Rep Cent Comt, 68- Mem: Cleveland, Cuyahoga Co, Ohio & Am Bar Asns. Relig: Jewish. Mailing Add: 1512 Euclid Ave Cleveland OH 44115

STIMMEL, DON PERRY **(D)**
Mem, Colo Dem State Cent Comt
b Ft Collins, Colo, Aug 13, 38; s Lester Hendren Stimmel & Margaret Perry S; m 1967 to Mary Elizabeth Kirk. Educ: Univ NMex, 57-58; Colo State Univ, BA, 60; Univ Wis-Madison, MS, 62; Univ Colo, JD, 64; Omicron Delta Kappa; Phi Kappa Phi; Pi Gamma Mu. Polit & Govt Pos: Pres, Colo State Univ Young Dem, 58-59, publicity chmn, 59-60; col coordr, Young Dem of Colo, 61-63, col dir, 63-64, dist dir, First Dist, 66-67; pres, Boulder Co Young Dem, 68-69; precinct committeeman, Boulder Co Dem Party, 68-71; mem, Colo Dem State Cent Comt, 69- Bus & Prof Pos: Asst prof law, Washburn Univ, 64-65; attorney, assoc with different firms, Denver, Colo, 65-66, Stevens & Koeberle, Boulder, 66-68 & Martin & Riggs, 68-70; individual practice, 70- Publ: Case note on 1962 Colorado Reapportionment Amendment, 5/63, Colorado Wage & Hour Law: analysis & suggestions, 4/64 & Criminality of voluntary sexual acts in Colorado, 5/68, Univ Colo Law Rev. Mem: Am Trial Lawyers Asn; Colo & Boulder Co Bar Asns; Boulder Tennis Asn. Relig: Unitarian. Mailing Add: 735 S 46th St Boulder CO 80303

STIMMELL, JOHN H **(R)**
NH State Rep
Mailing Add: Rd 1 Pittsfield NH 03263

STINE, GORDAN BERNARD **(D)**
Alderman, Charleston, SC
b Charleston, SC, Feb 10, 24; s Abe Jack Stine & Helen Pinosky S; m 1951 to Barbara Berlinsky; c Steven Mark & Robert Jay. Educ: Col Charleston, BS, 44; Emory Univ Sch Dent, DDS, 50; Tau Epsilon Phi; Alpha Omega. Polit & Govt Pos: Chmn, Charleston Co Dem Party, SC, 68-71; Alderman, Charleston, 71-; mem, SC Dem Party Comt on Party Orgn, 73. Mil Serv: Entered as Pvt, Marines, 42, transferred to Navy, 45, Serv in Dent Corps, Korean Theatre, 51-53; Dent Corps, Naval Res, Lt Comdr. Mem: SC Dent Asn (pres, 74-75); Charleston Co Bicentennial Comt (chmn, 72-); Charleston Trident CofC (pres, 71-72); Charleston Pride (chmn, 73-75); United Way (vpres, 75-). Relig: Jewish. Legal Res: 2 Beverly Rd Charleston SC 29407 Mailing Add: 165 Cannon St Charleston SC 29403

STINER, JAMES EDWARD, JR **(R)**
b New Albany, Ind, May 3, 45; s James Edward Stiner, Sr & Mary Grace Boylan S; m 1972 to Nancy Hoar. Educ: Purdue Univ, 63-68. Polit & Govt Pos: Press asst to US Rep William H Harsha, Ohio, 70-72, admin asst, 72; dir pub rels, Rep Gov Asn, 72- Bus & Prof Pos: News dir, WSVL Radio, Shelbyville, Ind, 65-66; newsman, WXLW Radio, Indianapolis, 66-68; asst news dir, WLFI-TV, Lafayette, 68-69; news dir & chief announcer, WBAA Radio, West Lafayette, 69-70. Mem: House Rep Commun Asn (vpres, 70, pres, 71). Relig: Methodist. Legal Res: Springfield VA Mailing Add: Rep Governors Asn 310 First St SE Washington DC 20003

STINNETT, JAMES WILLIAM, JR **(D)**
Chmn, Cheatham Co Dem Party, Tenn
b Memphis, Tenn, Nov 1, 29; s James William Stinnett, Sr & Irene Norris S; m 1954 to Barbara Yvonne Shirk; c Cheryl Lynn, Vicki Marie & James William, III. Educ: Mid Tenn State Univ, 53-54 & 63; Univ Tenn, Nashville, 58-62; YMCA Night Law Sch, LLB, 67, JD, 71. Polit & Govt Pos: City attorney, Ashland City, Tenn, 73-75; chmn, Cheatham Co Dem Party, Tenn, 74- Bus & Prof Pos: Civilian off asst, Nashville Police Dept, Tenn, 54-57; supvr, Ford Motor Co, 57-68; attorney-at-law, Nashville, 68-69, Ashland City, 69-75. Mil Serv: Entered as Seaman, Navy, 48, released as Radioman 2/C, 52, after serv in USS LSSL 96, Pac, 52. Mem: AAONMS (Al Menah Temple, Ambassador to Ashland City, 73-75); F&AM (Ashland Lodge 604); Ashland City Lions Club (pres, 72, trustee, 74-75); Amvets (Post 78 Adjutant). Honors & Awards: Ford Motor Co Community Serv Citation, 64; Outstanding Serv to Community, Am Legion Post 82, Nashville, 66. Relig: Baptist. Mailing Add: 303 S Main St Ashland City TN 37015

STINSON, FORD EDWARDS **(D)**
Mem, La State Dem Cent Comt
b Benton, La, Aug 24, 14; s Robert Tidwell Stinson, Sr & Mamie Edwards S; m 1946 to Edna Earle Richardson; c Mary Carol, Janet & Ford E, Jr. Educ: La State Univ, LLB; Phi Delta Phi; Kappa Alpha. Polit & Govt Pos: Mem, Benton Town Coun, La, 36-40; mem, Bossier Parish Dem Exec Comt, 36-; La State Rep, Bossier Parish, 40-44 & 52-72; mem for Bossier Parish, La State Dem Cent Comt. Bus & Prof Pos: Attorney, Nat Bank of Bossier City, La, 48- Mil Serv: Entered as 1st Lt, Army, 41, released as Lt Col, Air Force, 46; Bronze Star; Campaign Ribbons for Africa, Mediter, Am & Europe. Mem: Lions; Am Bossier Parish & La State Bar Asns; VFW; Am Legion. Relig: Methodist. Legal Res: Oak Ridge Dr Benton LA 71006 Mailing Add: PO Box 276 Benton LA 71006

STINZIANO, MICHAEL PETER **(D)**
Ohio State Rep
b Cleveland, Ohio, Nov 29, 44; s Michael James Stinziano & Josephine Kosoglov S; m 1966 to Dona Lyn Griffith; c D'Lyn Michele & Stephanie Michele. Educ: Ohio State Univ, BA, 66, grad sch, 67-71; Tau Kappa Alpha; Delta Sigma Rho; Pi Sigma Alpha. Polit & Govt Pos: Ohio State Rep, 73-; deleg, Dem Nat Mid-Term Conf, 74. Bus & Prof Pos: Vpres, Condominiums Inc, 67- Mem: Columbus Bd Realtors; Ohio Asn Real Estate Bds; Columbus Tenant Union (dir, 73); Seventh Step Found (dir, 73); Ohio Citizens Coun. Honors & Awards: Outstanding young man of Am, US Jaycees, 73. Relig: Roman Catholic. Legal Res: 46 E Northwood Ave Columbus OH 43201 Mailing Add: 2147 W Broad St Columbus OH 43223

STIPE, GENE **(D)**
Okla State Sen
Mailing Add: State Capitol Oklahoma City OK 73105

STIRLER, BONNIE WERTH MERRILL **(D)**
b Milwaukee, Wis, Aug 28, 42; d Francis Charles Werth & Bernice Adele Luderus W; m 1972 to Dennis John Stirler; c Stacie Jo Merrill & Patricia Suzanne Merrill. Educ: Ferris State Col, 67-68; Wayne State Univ, 69-70; Univ Mass, Amherst, 71-72. Polit & Govt Pos: Alt deleg, Dem Nat Conv, 72. Bus & Prof Pos: Admin asst, Five Cap, Inc, Baldwin, Mich, 68; ctr coordr, Valley Women's Ctr, Northampton, Mass, 71, welfare rights counr & counr trainer, 71-72; lectr women's rights, Cols & Univs, Mass, 71-72; field rep, Family Planning Serv, Mass Dept Pub Health, 72. Mem: Mass Women's Polit Caucus (steering comt, 71-); Lexington Women's Polit Caucus, Ky; Hampshire Co Family Planning Coun, Mass (bd dirs, 72-); Nat Welfare Rights Orgn; Amherst Women's Liberation, Mass. Mailing Add: 204 Westwood Ct Lexington KY 40503

STITH, HARVARD C **(R)**
Chmn, Pacific Co Rep Cent Comt, Wash
b Terry, Mont, Dec 25, 26; s Roy L Stith & Viola M Braun S; m 1956 to Donna J Merritt; c Sandra J. Educ: Univ Wash, BA in bus, 58; Masonic Club; Canterbery Club; Inter Campus Social Activities. Polit & Govt Pos: Officer, Foreign Serv Spec Commun, Am Consulate Gen, Frankfurt, Ger, 50-52; chmn, Pacific Co Rep Cent Comt, Wash, 74- Bus & Prof Pos: Asst mgr, Wash State Employ Security, 60-66; life underwriter, Mutual Life Ins Co of NY, 74- Mil Serv: Entered as Pvt, Army, 45, released as T-5, 46, after serv in 3159th Signal Serv Bn, Japan. Mem: Mason; VFW; Coun & Order of High Priesthood of Wash RAM; Univ Wash Alumni Asn. Relig: Protestant. Legal Res: 1104 Willapa Raymond WA 98577 Mailing Add: PO Box 626 Raymond WA 98577

STITT, LYLE H (D)
b Mitchell, SDak, June 6, 37; s Carroll William Stitt & Velma Marie Richard S; m 1962 to Katherine Anne Rohrer; c Anne Katherine. Educ: Huron Col, 4 years. Polit & Govt Pos: Admin asst to US Rep David R Obey, Seventh Dist, Wis, 69- Bus & Prof Pos: Production mgr, KDLO-TV, Garden City, SDak, 60-64; reporter, producer, KELO-TV, Sioux Falls, 64-65; news dir, WAOW-TV, Wausau, Wis, 67-69. Mem: Cong Secy Club; Radio-TV News Dir Asn; Northwest Broadcast News Asn; Optimist Club. Mailing Add: 3908 Stone Mansion Ct Alexandria VA 22306

STIVERS, OLIVER CHARLES (R)
Mem, Rep State Cent Comt Calif
b Superior, Wis, Nov 15, 16; s Charles Oscar Stivers & Emma Amorde S; m 1936 to Evva Beatrice Bitney; c John Earl. Educ: San Francisco Law Sch, 51-52. Polit & Govt Pos: Mem, Visitors & Tourism Comn, Calif, 67-; Alameda Co chmn, Comt to Elect George Murphy to US Senate & to Elect Ronald Reagan Gov of Calif; South Alameda Co chmn, Comt to Elect Richard Nixon President of the US; adv, numerous local, state & nat campaigns; mem, Rep State Cent Comt Calif, currently; mem, Alameda Co Rep Finance Comt, currently. Bus & Prof Pos: Owner & adminr, Stivers' Pvt Schs, Hayward, Calif, 51-; owner & adminr, Stivers' Circle-S Ranch, Railroad Flat, currently. Mil Serv: Entered as Pvt, Army, 40, released as S/Sgt, 45, after serv in 34th Div, 151st Field Artil Bn, ETO, 42-45. Publ: Victory 1966, privately publ, 67. Mem: Am Legion; Rep Bus & Prof Men's Club; Arabian Horse Asn; Hayward CofC (bd dirs, 71-). Relig: Protestant. Mailing Add: 21465 Tanglewood Dr Castro Valley CA 94546

STIVERS, THOMAS WALTER (R)
Idaho State Rep
b Maroa, Ill, Sept 6, 18; s Walter Daniel Stivers & Naomi Potter S; m 1940 to Winifred Barton; c Richard & Susan (Mrs Waters). Educ: High Sch. Polit & Govt Pos: Co clerk, Twin Falls Co, Idaho, 51-63; Idaho State Rep, 75- Bus & Prof Pos: Owner & mgr, Boone Land Title Co, Twin Falls, Idaho, 63-69; pres, Sawtooth Title Co Inc, Sun Valley, 65-, Title Fact, Inc, Twin Falls, 69 & Western Title Co, Custer Co, 68-; vpres, Real Estate Securities Corp, Twin Falls, 69- Mil Serv: Entered as Seaman, Navy, 42, released as PO 1/C, 45 after serv in USS Swallow, Asiatic-Pacific Theatre, 42-44; Asiatic-Pacific Combat Award. Mem: Idaho Land Title Asn; Twin Falls Bd Realtors; Magic Valley Bldg Contractors Asn; Am Legion; DAV. Legal Res: 144 N Juniper Twin Falls ID 83301 Mailing Add: Box 486 Twin Falls ID 83301

STOBER, KENNETH E (R)
Conn State Rep
Mailing Add: RFD 8 Box 48 Gales Ferry CT 06335

STOCKDALE, GERTRUDE MARION (R)
Treas, Butler Co, Iowa
b Kesley, Iowa, June 17, 06; d Keriene DeBerg & Katherine DeVries D; m 1923 to Glenn Keller Stockdale; c Darrell G, Lowell A, Wendell B & Caryl (Mrs Nielsen). Educ: Took correspondence course & attended night classes & took Dale Carnegie Class, formerly. Polit & Govt Pos: Rep precinct committeewoman, Butler Co, Iowa, 38-; vchmn, Butler Co Rep Party, 48-50; chmn & vdir, Third Dist Rep Women, 54-56; state pres, Iowa Fedn Women's Clubs, 70-72, mem state finance comt, 71-73, state legis chmn, 72-; alt deleg, Rep Nat Conv, 72; deleg, Nat Rep Women's Conv, formerly; treas, Butler Co, currently. Bus & Prof Pos: Sales lady, Farm Bur First Lady Life Ins, 45-48; social worker, State Bd of Control, 49-52; home economist, Butler Co, Iowa, during World War II. Mem: Charter mem Local Women's Club (held all off except pres); Butler Co Retarded Children's Orgn (hon chmn); Amvets (pres); Am Legion Auxiliary (pres); Merit Mother of Iowa. Relig: Presbyterian. Mailing Add: Box 236 Aplington IA 50604

STOCKDALE, JAMES SEVERT (R)
Mem Exec Comt, SDak Rep State Comt
b Pierre, SDak, Dec 16, 37; s Severt Martin Stockdale & Sarah Jane MacCarter S; div; c Martin Perry & Gretchen Dawn. Educ: Gustavus Adolphus Col, BA in Bus Admin & Hist, 59; Univ SDak Law Sch, JD, 62; Omega Kappa; Phi Delta Theta. Polit & Govt Pos: Chmn, Beadle Co Young Rep, SDak, 69; Nat Committeeman, SDak Young Rep, 70, state chmn, formerly; chmn speaker develop & placement comt, Young Rep Nat Fedn, 71-; mem exec comt, SDak Rep State Comt, 71-; deleg & mem credentials comt, Young Rep Nat Conv, 71, deleg & deleg chmn, 73; deleg, deleg whip & deleg rally chmn, Rep Nat Conv, 72; acting chmn, SDak Comt for Reelec of the President, 72; mem cand selections comt, Beadle Co Rep Cent Comt, 72; campaign mgr, SD Primary Elec for Leo Parness for US Sen; campaign mgr, Mo Gen Elec for Hon Thomas B Curtis for US Sen; partner, Campaign Consult Firm, currently. Bus & Prof Pos: Spec asst, Attorney Gen Off, Pierre, SDak, 66-67; attorney, Northwestern Pub Serv Co, Huron, 67- Mil Serv: Entered as 1st Lt, Army, 62, released as Capt, 66, after serv in Judge Adv Gen Corps, 1st Cavalry Air Mobil, Ft Benning, Ga. Mem: Am & SDak Bar Asns; Beadle Co Bar Asn (chmn, Liberty Bell Award Prog, 68-71, secy-treas, 69); Dist Co Court Eighth Judicial Dist (judge pro tem, 71-); SDak Fraternal Order of Police (legal counsel, 72-). Honors & Awards: Outstanding Young Rep Man, SDak Young Rep, 70. Relig: Methodist. Mailing Add: 4901 Victoria Dr Apt 5 Sioux Falls SD 57102

STOCKER, LUELLA HEINE (R)
b Ellendale, NDak, July 24, 24; d Robert Heine & Laura Schwarze H; m 1946 to Philip Frank Stocker; c Paul & Tedd. Educ: NDak State Univ, 41-42; Univ Minn, Degree in Nursing, 46; Alpha Gamma Delta. Polit & Govt Pos: Precinct chairwoman, Falcon Heights Rep Comt, Minn, 61-63, legis chairwoman, 63-65; chairwoman, Ramsey Co Rep Comt, 65-67; vchairwoman, Minn State Rep Comt, 67-69, chairwoman, formerly; alt deleg, Rep Nat Conv, 68, deleg, 72; mem, Rep Nat Comt, formerly; coun mem, Village of Falcon Heights, Minn, 72- Bus & Prof Pos: Head nurse, Med Floor, Bethesda Hosp, St Paul, Minn, 47-49. Mem: League of Women Voters. Relig: Lutheran. Mailing Add: 1463 W Iowa St Paul MN 55108

STOCKETT, PETER MCKENZIE (D)
b Centreville, Miss, Jan 15, 32; s Peter McKenzie Stockett & Myrtle Walton S; m 1966 to Shirley Patterson White; c Laura McKenzie & stepson, Thomas E White, Jr. Educ: Washington & Lee Univ, BA, 55; Univ Miss, LLB, 60; Phi Alpha Delta; Pi Kappa Phi. Polit & Govt Pos: Mayor, Woodville, Miss, 60-61; asst attorney gen, State of Miss, 61-67; prof staff mem, Judiciary Comt, US Senate, 67-73, chief counsel & staff dir, 73- Mem: Miss State Bar Asn. Relig: Baptist. Legal Res: PO Box 53 Woodville MS 39669 Mailing Add: PO Box 2124 Wheaton Sta Silver Spring MD 20903

STOCKLEY, JIM (D)
Ark State Rep
Mailing Add: Old Military Rd Marion AR 72364

STOCKMAN, JACQUE (INDEPENDENT)
b Alamo, NDak, Sept 21, 23; married; c four. Educ: NDak State Univ. Hon Degrees: LLD, Univ NDak, 68. Polit & Govt Pos: NDak State Rep, 55-66; former young Rep nat committeeman; app mem & chmn, Cass Co Sch Reorgn Bd, Cass Co Comn, 61-; app clerk, Fargo Park Dist, Fargo, NDak, 66-71; comnr, City Comn of Fargo, 72- Bus & Prof Pos: Lawyer & farmer; dir, Neuropsychiat Inst, Fargo, 59-; dir, Gate City Savings & Loan Asn, 70- Mil Serv: World War II. Mem: Am & NDak Bar Asns; Am Judicature Soc; Elks; Eagles. Relig: Lutheran. Mailing Add: 1215 14th Ave N Fargo ND 58102

STOCKS, LEROY (R)
Mem, Columbus Co Exec Comt, NC
b Columbus Co, NC, Aug 25, 23; s Clarence Oliver Stocks & Callie Williamson S; m to Lucy Burline Suggs; c Donald Lathan, Gloria Lee & Ronald LeRoy. Educ: Winston Salem Barber Col, NC, 42. Polit & Govt Pos: Cand for state legis, 62 & 66; precinct committeeman, Whiteville, NC, 62-; mem, Columbus Co Exec Comt, NC, 62-; chmn, Columbus Co Rep Party, 66-68; mem, NC Rep State Exec Comt, 68-70; mem, Columbus Co Bd Elec, 69-; alt deleg, Rep Nat Conv, 72. Bus & Prof Pos: Chmn, Columbus Co Master Barbers Asn, 50-60; mem, NC Exec Comt, 52-58. Mem: CofC; Lebanon Lodge 207; Scottish Rite; Sudan Temple; Shrine. Honors & Awards: Columbus Most Outstanding Rep, Columbus Co Rep Party, 72. Relig: Baptist. Mailing Add: 214 George St Whiteville NC 28472

STOCKTON, RUTH S (R)
Colo State Sen
b Ridgefield Park, NJ, June 6, 16; d Arthur Everett Small & Mary Rose Hart S; m 1937 to Truman Alex Stockton, Jr; c Alexe R. Educ: Vassar Col, ex 37; Columbia Univ; Colo Univ. Polit & Govt Pos: Co-chmn, 11 Western States Coun of Young Rep, 46-47; nat co-chmn, Young Rep, 47-49; nat committeewoman, Rep Party, Colo, 54-56; Colo State Rep, 61-65; Colo State Sen, 65-; mem, Gov comn on Ment Health & Ment Retardation & Gov comn on Voc Rehabilitation, Colo, 66. Mem: United Fund; Bus & Prof Women; Child Welfare Coun (bd); Hemophilia Found (bd); East Jefferson CofC. Honors & Awards: Woman of the Year Award, Golden Bus & Prof Women, 66. Relig: Methodist. Mailing Add: 1765 Glen Dale Dr Lakewood CO 80215

STODART, WILLIAM EDWARD (R)
b Olean, NY, July 1, 29; s Hugh Blair Stodart & Vesta Schoff S; m 1952 to Erma Pauline Johnson; c Cathy Ann, Karen Edna & William Edward II. Educ: Univ Hawaii, 57-58; Santa Rosa Jr Col, 62-63. Polit & Govt Pos: Admin asst to US Rep Don H Clausen, Calif, 67- Mil Serv: Entered as Pvt, Army, 46, released as Lt Col, 67, after serv in US Maritime Serv, 44-45 & US Army Security Agency, 48-67; Lt Col, Army Res, 671; Army Good Conduct Medal, Asiatic Pac Campaign Medal, World War II Victory Medal, Japanese Occupation Ribbon, UN Serv Medal, Korean Campaign Medal with Three Bronze Stars, Army Commendation Medal, Legion of Merit. Mem: ROA; Mason; VFW; Kiwanis. Relig: Baptist. Mailing Add: 7004 Springfield Village Ct Springfield VA 22150

STODDARD, EUGENE C (D)
SC State Rep
Mailing Add: Rte 3 Gray Court SC 29645

STOESSEL, WALTER JOHN, JR
US Ambassador to USSR
b Manhattan, Kans, Jan 24, 20; s Walter John Stoessel & Katherine Haston S; m 1946 to Mary Ann Ferrandou; c Katherine F, Suzanne P & Christine M. Educ: Stanford Univ, BA, 41; Russian Inst, Columbia Univ, 49-50; Ctr of Int Affairs, Harvard Univ, 59-60; Phi Delta Theta. Polit & Govt Pos: US Dept of State, 42-, third secy & vconsul, Caracas, Venezuela, 42-44, second secy & vconsul, Moscow, USSR, 47-49, polit officer, Bad Nauheim, Ger, 50-52, officer in charge Russian Affairs, 52-56, first secy & consul, Paris, France, 56-59, dir exec secretariat, 60-61, counr of embassy, Paris, France, 61-63, minister-counr, Moscow, USSR, 63-65, dep asst secy for European Affairs, 65-68, US Ambassador, Poland, 68-72, Asst Secy of State for European Affairs, 72-74, US Ambassador to USSR, 75-; mem staff, White House, 56. Mil Serv: Ens, Naval Res, 44-46. Mem: Chevy Chase Club. Legal Res: 302 20th St Santa Monica CA 90402 Mailing Add: Dept of State Washington DC 20520

STOFFER, HENRY J (D)
Chmn, Franklin Co Dem Comt, Iowa
b Alexander, Iowa; s Henry Stoffer & Stella Greenfield S; wid; c Harvey Jay, Dick Curtis, Jane Evelyn, Jack David & Tom Kevin. Educ: High sch grad, 46. Polit & Govt Pos: Aide, Soil Conserv Serv, Hampton, Iowa, 49-53; postmaster, US Post Off Dept, Sheffield, 57-66; nat pres, Nat League Postmasters, Washington, DC, 63-66; co-ed, Postmasters Advocate, 63-66; Dem cand, Third Cong Dist, Iowa, 66; chmn, Franklin Co Dem Party, 72-; chmn, Third Cong Dist Dem Comt, Iowa, currently. Bus & Prof Pos: Pres, NIowa Life Underwriters, Mason City, 73. Mil Serv: Entered as Pvt, Marine Corps, 46, released as Sgt, 48, after serv in Marine Detachment, US Naval Ctr, San Diego, Calif, 46-48; World War II Victory Medal. Publ: Auth, League Leadership Guide, 64. Mem: Nat Asn Life Underwriters (local pres, 73); Mason; Odd Fellows (Noble Grand, 50-58). Honors & Awards: Order of the Vest, Air Transport Asn, Washington, DC, 63; Ky Col, Gov of Ky, 63. Relig: United Methodist. Mailing Add: 433 N Sixth St Sheffield IA 50475

STOFFERAHN, KENNETH DARRELL (R)
SDak State Rep
b Lakefield, Minn, Apr 5, 34; s Edward H Stofferahn & Ida M Mundt S; m 1965 to Diane Claire Henderson; c Michael, Stacey, Stuart & Steven. Educ: SDak State Univ, BSAg, 57; Toastmasters Club. Polit & Govt Pos: Mem sch bd, West Cent Dist 154, Hartford, SDak, 74-; SDak State Rep, 11th Dist, 75- Mil Serv: Entered as Airman Basic, Air Nat Guard, 57, released as Airman 2/C, 63. Mem: Masonic Lodge 187 (sr warden, 75); Elks 262. Relig: Lutheran. Mailing Add: RR Humboldt SD 57035

STOIA, VIOREL G (R)
b Aberdeen, SDak, Feb 13, 24; s John Stoia & Seana Biliboca S; m 1949 to Donna Marie Maurseth; c Marsha Jo, Nancy Kay, Gregory Allen, Thomas John & James Vincent. Educ: Univ Minn, BBA, 49; Am Col Life Underwriters, CLU, 57. Polit & Govt Pos: Campaign mgr for Congressman Ben Reifel, 60; finance chmn, Brown Co Rep Cent Comt, SDak, 60-63, precinct committeeman, 62-65, co chmn, 66-72; deleg, SDak State Conv, 62 & 64;

presidential elector, SDak Rep Party, 68, state finance chmn, 69-72; mem, Rep Nat Finance Comt, 69-71; alt deleg, Rep Nat Conv, 72. Bus & Prof Pos: Chartered life underwriter. Mil Serv: Entered as A/S, Navy, 42, released as CPO, 46, after serv in Amphibious Force, Pac Theatre, 42 & 46; Am Theater Ribbon; Pac Theater Ribbon; Good Conduct Medal; Philippine Liberation Ribbon. Mem: Nat Asn Life Underwriters; Am Soc Chartered Life Underwriters; Am Legion; YMCA; CofC. Honors & Awards: Distinguished Serv Award, Aberdeen Jr CofC, 55; Nat Qual Award, Nat Asn Life Underwriters, 54-73; Nat Sales Achievement Award, 66; Life Underwriter of the Year of SDak, SDak Asn Life Underwriters, 63; Qualifying Mem, Million Dollar Round Table, 65-67 & 69-73. Relig: Catholic. Legal Res: 1022 N Main St Aberdeen SD 57401 Mailing Add: PO Box 98 Aberdeen SD 57401

STOICK, JAMES L **(R)**
SDak State Rep
Mailing Add: 104 W Seventh Mobridge SD 57601

STOKER, BETTY ANDERSON **(DFL)**
Mem Exec Comt, Second Cong Dist Dem-Farmer-Labor Comt, Minn
b Jamestown, NY, Aug 18, 27; d Vernon Anderson & Lillie Lantz A; m 1950 to Lynn Stoker; c Valerie, Christine, Laura & Robert. Educ: Syracuse Univ, BA, 48; Pi Beta Phi. Polit & Govt Pos: Mem exec comt, Dem Party, Hanover, NH, 56-60; mem exec comt, Second Cong Dist Dem-Farmer-Labor Party, Minn, 68-, chmn, 72-74; mem, City Human Rights Comn, Albert Lea, 70-73 & City Planning Comn, 73-; mem, Dem-Farmer-Labor State Cent Comt, 70-72; deleg, Dem Nat Mid-Term Conf, 74. Mem: League Women Voters (bd mem). Mailing Add: 405 Channel Rd Albert Lea MN 56007

STOKER, ROGER C **(R)**
VChmn, Bonneville Co Rep Cent Comt, Idaho
b Idaho Falls, Idaho, Mar 8, 36; s Merrill F Stoker & Carmen B Christensen S; m 1959 to Wanda L; c Ryne C & Wenda L. Educ: Univ Idaho, BS in Geol, 59; Sigma Gamma Epsilon; Kappa Sigma. Polit & Govt Pos: Precinct committeeman, Bonneville Rep Comt, Idaho, 74-; vchmn, Bonneville Co Rep Cent Comt, 74- Mil Serv: Entered as Pvt, Army, 59, released as SP-4, after serv in Engr Sch, Ft Belvoir, Va, 59-61; Maj, Army Res, 75; Good Conduct Medal; Armed Forces Reserve Medal. Mem: Idaho Acad Sci; Am Nuclear Soc; Geol Soc Am. Mailing Add: 1645 Westwood Idaho Falls ID 83401

STOKES, CARL BURTON **(D)**
b Cleveland, Ohio, June 21, 27; s Charles Stokes (deceased) & Louise Stone S; div; c Carl, Jr, Cordi & Cordell Edwards. Educ: Univ Minn, BS in Law, 54; Cleveland-Marshall Law Sch, LLD, 56; Kappa Alpha Psi; Gamma Eta Gamma. Hon Degrees: Cleveland-Marshall Law Sch, Wilberforce Univ, Cent State Univ, Tufts Univ, Univ Cincinnati, St Francis Col (Maine), Lincoln Univ, Union Col, Livingston Col, Boston Univ & Oberlin Col; Chubb fel, Yale Univ, 69. Polit & Govt Pos: Asst prosecutor, Cleveland, Ohio, 58-62; Ohio State Rep, 62-67; cand for mayor, Cleveland, 65, mayor, 67-71; deleg, Dem Nat Conv, 68 & 72. Bus & Prof Pos: Attorney, Stokes & Stokes, 58-67; news commentator, WNBC-TV News, New York, 72- Mil Serv: Entered as Pvt, Army, 45, released as Cpl, 46, after serv in ETO, 45-46. Publ: Quality of the Environment, Univ Ore Press, 68; Public housing & the urban crisis, George Washington Law Rev, 5/71; Autobiography: Promises of Power, Simon & Schuster, 72. Mem: US Conf of Mayors; Nat Urban Coalition; Urban Am, Inc; Nat League of Cities. Honors & Awards: Horatio Alger Award, 70; Towne Crier Award, Press Club of Cleveland, 70; Equal Opportunity Award, Nat Urban League, 70; Pacesetter Award, Young People's Div of Jewish Welfare Fedn of Metrop Chicago, 71; Outstanding Alumnus Award & Outstanding Achievement Award, Univ Minn Law Sch, 71. Legal Res: 1175 York Ave New York NY 10021 Mailing Add: c/o NBC News Rm 500 30 Rockefeller Plaza New York NY 10020

STOKES, HENRY DUERRE **(R)**
Chmn, Isanti Co Rep Comt, Minn
b St Paul, Minn, Dec 14, 26; s Henry Duerre Stokes & Belle Lambert S; m 1945 to Evelyn Dixen Sorensen; c Cynthia Lee Dufour, Henry Duerre, III & Matthew Arnold. Educ: SDak State Col, 44-45; Yale Univ, 45; Univ Minn, BS, 50, DDS, 52; Delta Sigma Delta. Polit & Govt Pos: Chmn, Eighth Dist Rep Comt, Minn, 63-67; chmn, Isanti Co Planning Comn, 65-73; chmn, Isanti Co Rep Comt, 71-; mem, Minn State Finance Comt, 73. Mil Serv: Entered as Pvt, Army, 44, released as Pfc, 45, after serv in various units; Navy, 2 years, US; Good Conduct Medal. Mem: Minn Dent Asn (legis comt, 72-73); Area Health Educ Comt Area D (comt, 73); Co Dent Health Adv Comt (chmn, 60-73); Riverview Jr Col Adv Comt (chmn, 70-73); Helios Lodge 273 Mason. Relig: Presbyterian. Legal Res: 410 SW Second Ave Cambridge MN 55008 Mailing Add: 135 SE Second Ave Cambridge MN 55008

STOKES, J EMERY **(R)**
Co Chmn, Rep Party, Pa
b Blain, Pa, Feb 25, 13; s Warren I Stokes & Sarah J Weibley S; m 1932 to Martha Harper Richter; c James W & John W. Educ: Pa State Univ, 30-31. Polit & Govt Pos: Borough councilman, Marysville, Pa, 52-58, tax collector, 58-; co chmn, Rep Party, Pa, 60- Mem: Mason; Blue Lodge Consistory; Shrine. Mailing Add: RD 1 Box 273 Marysville PA 17053

STOKES, LOUIS **(D)**
US Rep, Ohio
b Cleveland, Ohio, Feb 23, 25; s Louis Charles Stokes (deceased) & Louise Stone S; m 1960 to Jeanette Francis; c Shelley Denise, Angela Rochelle, Louis C & Lorene Allison. Educ: Cleveland Col of Western Reserve Univ, 46-48; Cleveland Marshall Law Sch, JD, 53; Kappa Alpha Psi. Hon Degrees: LLD, Wilberforce Univ, 69 & Shaw Univ, 71. Polit & Govt Pos: Mem, Ohio State Adv Comt, US Comn on Civil Rights, vchmn, Cleveland Subcomt, 66; US Rep, 21st Dist, Ohio, 69-, mem, Educ & Labor Comt & House Comt on Internal Security, US House of Rep, formerly, chmn, Cong Black Caucus, 72-73, mem appropriations & budget comts, currently; deleg, Dem Nat Conv, 72. Bus & Prof Pos: Pvt law practice, Cleveland, Ohio, 14 years; mem, Law Firm of Stokes, Character, Terry & Perry, formerly; guest lectr, Ashland Col, Kent State Univ, Oberlin Col, Cuyahoga Co Bar Asn Seminar, 66, Ohio Acad of Trial Lawyers Conv, Cleveland, 68, Ohio State Bar Asn Conv, Toledo, Ohio, 68, Univ Mich, 68, Conv of Nat Asn of Defense Lawyers in Criminal Cases, Greenbrier, WVa, 68 & Law Enforcement Seminar, Columbus, Ohio, 68. Mil Serv: Entered as Pvt, Army, 43, released as Technician 4/C, 46, after serv in Army Engr Corp, Am Theatre, 43-46; Am Theatre Ribbon; Good Conduct & World War II Victory Medals. Publ: Criminal Law, Cuyahoga Co Bar Asn, 66. Mem: Cleveland Bar Asn (exec comt); Ohio State Bar Asn (chmn, criminal justice comt, bd dirs); Nat Asn of Defense Lawyers in Criminal Cases (bd dirs); Fair Housing, Inc (bd dirs); life mem Kappa Alpha Psi. Honors & Awards: YMCA Award for being Gen Chmn of Cedar Br Membership Dr, 68; Man of the Year Award, 27th Ward Civic League, 68; Citizens Award, Bel-Air Civic Club, 68; Champs Citizen of the Year Award, 68; Achievement Award, Cleveland Alumni Chap, Kappa Alpha Psi, 68. Relig: Methodist; vchmn & mem bd trustees, St Paul AME Zion Church. Legal Res: OH Mailing Add: 303 Cannon Bldg Washington DC 20515

STOKES, MARIAN **(R)**
Chairwoman, Sandusky Co Rep Cent & Exec Comt, Ohio
b Woodville, Ohio, Apr 10, 26; d William Moellman & Freda Myerholtz M; m 1949 to Dan Stokes; c Cliff C, II. Educ: High sch grad. Polit & Govt Pos: Chairwoman, Sandusky Co Rep Women, 63-; pres, Sandusky Co Women's Rep Club, 63-; dir, Sandusky Co Bd Elec, 66-; precinct committeeman, Rep Party, Ohio, 66-; second vpres, Ohio Asn Elec Officials, 68-; secy, Sandusky Co Rep Cent & Exec Comt, formerly, chairwoman, currently; deleg, Rep Nat Conv, 72; mem, Rep State Cent & Exec Comt Ohio, currently. Bus & Prof Pos: Prof flower arranger, 56-64. Mem: Nat Soc DAR; Hayes Garden Club; Garden Club Ohio; Fremont Fedn Women; Ohio Fedn Rep Women. Honors & Awards: Best of Show & Blue Ribbons in Flower & Art Shows. Relig: Episcopal. Legal Res: 2061 County Rd 122 Fremont OH 43420 Mailing Add: Bd of Elec Court House Fremont OH 43420

STOKES, PAUL CURTIS, JR **(R)**
VChmn, Rep Party Del
b Betterton, Md, Apr 8, 31; s Paul Curtis Stokes & Isabel Jones S; m 1960 to Phyllis Woll; c Phyllis Carey, Joseph Kerwin, Patrick Friel & Paul Curtis. Educ: Wash Col, Md, 1 year. Polit & Govt Pos: Chmn, Sussex Co Young Rep, Del; chmn, Del Young Rep; mem, Young Rep Nat Exec Comt; past chmn nat labor comt, Nat Young Rep; deleg, Rep Nat Conv, 68; chmn, Sussex Co Rep Comt, 69-72; vchmn, Rep Party Del, 73- Bus & Prof Pos: Pres & dir, Anderson-Stokes, Inc, Rehoboth Beach, Del; pres, dir & mem exec comt, Second Nat Bank & Loan. Mil Serv: Entered as Seaman, Navy, released as PO 1/C, after serv in Mediter. Mem: Del State CofC (exec comt & bd dirs); Del State Fair (bd dirs); Beebe Hosp (bd dirs); Del Asn Realtors; Sussex Co Bd Realtors. Legal Res: North Shores Rehoboth Beach DE 19971 Mailing Add: 48 Rehoboth Ave Rehoboth Beach DE 19971

STOKOWSKI, EUGENE E **(DFL)**
Minn State Sen
b Minneapolis, Minn, June 23, 21; s Julius Stokowski & Elizabeth Smegal S; m 1953 to Anne Kocon; c Barbara, Steven, Laura, Robert & Jean Ann. Educ: Univ Minn, BA, 49. Polit & Govt Pos: Alderman, City of Minneapolis, 51-57, pres city coun, 54-57; mem, Metrop Airports Comt, 53-57; comnr, Minneapolis City Charter Comt, 70-73; Minn State Sen, 73-, committeeman, Great Lakes Comt, Minn State Senate, 73- Bus & Prof Pos: Stockbroker, Piper Jaffrey & Hopwood, 57- Mil Serv: Entered as Pvt, Marines, 43, released as S/Sgt, 46. Mailing Add: 2231 Stinson Blvd Minneapolis MN 55418

STOLBERG, IRVING JULES **(D)**
Conn State Rep
b Philadelphia, Pa, Sept 24, 36; s Ralph B Stolberg & Lillian Blank S; m 1971 to Alicia Irene Barela. Educ: Univ Calif, Los Angeles, BA, 58; Boston Univ, MA, 64, PhD course work completed, 66. Polit & Govt Pos: Pres, West Los Angeles Young Dem, 57-58; mem exec comt & chmn nominating comt, New Haven McCarthy for President, 68; deleg, Conn Dem State Conv, 68; alt deleg, Dem Nat Conv, 68, deleg & floor leader, 72; founder, New Haven Dem Reform Movement, 68-69; founding mem, Caucus of Conn Dem, 68-69; justice of the peace, New Haven, 68-75; & chmn, Human Servs Comt, mem resolutions comt, Dem State Conv, 70, 71 & 72; Conn State Rep, 112th Dist, 71-73, 93rd Dist, 73-, mem, Appropriations, Educ & Judiciary Comts, Conn House of Rep, currently. Bus & Prof Pos: Int campus adminr, US Nat Student Asn, 58-59; prog dir, Boston Int Student Ctr, 59-60; midwest dir, World Univ Serv, 60-63; leader, Experiment in Int Living, Austria, 61, Turkey, 64, Tanzania, 65 & Nigeria, 69. Participant, World Univ Serv Seminar, Asia, 62, leader, World Univ Serv Team, Latin Am, 63; teaching fel, Boston Univ, 64-66; asst prof geog, Southern Conn State Col, 66-69 & 74-; participant, US Off Educ, African Seminar, Ethiopia, 67; asst prof geog, Quinnipiac Col, 69-74. Publ: Auth, Asian students, Intercollegian, 1/63; Geography and peace research, Prof Geogr, 7/65; ed, Indonesia-Malaysia: problems and prospects, Multilith, 65. Mem: Asn Am Geogr; Peace Research Comt; Am Geog Soc; African Studies Asn; Nat Coun Geog Educ (Conn coordr); Am Asn Univ Prof (pres, Southern Conn State Col Chap, 67-68, pres, Quinnipiac Col Chap, 70-71). Mailing Add: 50 Roydon Rd New Haven CT 06511

STOLDT, ROBERT JAMES **(R)**
Mem, Seneca Co Rep Exec Comt, Ohio
b Attica, Ohio, Aug 11, 25; s Joseph T Stoldt & Sheila Glasgow S; m 1948 to Myrial Sheerer; c Linda, Barbara & Robert. Educ: Heidelberg Col, BA, 49; Pi Kappa Delta; Heidelberg Young Rep. Polit & Govt Pos: Precinct committeeman, Rep Party, Ohio, 50-; mem, Seneca Co Rep Cent & Exec Comts, 52-, secy, Exec Comt, 59-60, chmn, 60-72, chmn, Cent Comt, 64-68; alt deleg, Rep Nat Conv, 64, deleg, 68. Bus & Prof Pos: Partner, Sheerer & Stoldt, Inc, 50- Mil Serv: Entered as Pvt, Marine Corps, 43, released as Cpl, 46, after serv in 2nd Marine Div, Pac Area, 44-46; Okinawa Ribbon; Occupation of Japan Medal; Good Conduct Medal. Mem: Ohio Farm & Power Equipment Asn; Shrine; Scottish Rite; F&AM; Am Legion. Relig: Lutheran. Mailing Add: 207 N Liberty St Attica OH 44807

STOLL, NORMAN ADOLPH **(D)**
Mem, Multnomah Co Dem Cent Comt, Ore
b Milwaukee, Wis, Nov 18, 12; s Herman Fred Stoll & Frieda Scharpf S; m 1941 to Helen V Nicholas; c Norman Robert & Julia Hart. Educ: Univ Wis, PhB, 32, LLB, 34; Theta Chi. Polit & Govt Pos: Attorney, Securities & Exchange Comn, 35-42; attorney, Bd Econ Warfare, 42-43; chief of legis sect & asst solicitor, Dept of Com, 46-48; gen counsel, Bonneville Power Admin, 48-54; consult to solicitor, Dept of Interior, 54-55; mem, Multnomah Co Dem Cent Comt, 56-, alt chmn, 59-63; spec asst to Attorney Gen, Ore, 57-61; deleg & mem platform comts, various Ore Dem Conv, since 60; Dem Nat Committeeman, Ore, 63-68; deleg & co-chmn comt on permanent orgn, Dem Nat Conv, 64, deleg, 68; vchmn, Ore State Law Improv Comt, 65-67; chmn, Ore State Adv Comt on Ins Law Revision, 65-67; sub-comt chmn, Ore State Adv Comt on Pub Util & Carrier Law Rev, 69-70. Bus & Prof Pos: Attorney-at-law, 54-; mem faculty law, Univ Ore, 55; mem faculty law, Northwestern Col Law, 56-60. Mil Serv: Army, 43-46, released as Capt after serv in war plans div, Judge Adv Gen Off, 44, prosecution staff, Nuremburg Trials, 45, War Crimes Off, 45-46 & Off of the Chief of Staff, 46. Mem: Am, Fed & Ore State Bar Asns; Am Judicature Soc; Judge Adv Asn. Mailing Add: 11000 SW Collina Ave Portland OR 97129

STOLTENBURG, DENNIS JEROME **(R)**
Chmn, Deuel Co Rep Party, SDak
b Clear Lake, SDak, June 19, 35; s Fred Stoltenburg & Ida Bogenrief S; m 1956 to Mavis

Ardelle Hardie; c Lynn, Sandra, Lonnie & Gregory. Educ: Clear Lake High Sch, grad, 53. Polit & Govt Pos: Chmn, Deuel Co Rep Party, SDak, 75- Mailing Add: Altamont SD 57211

STOLTZ, GAIL MARGARET (D)
Mont State Rep

b Great Falls, Mont, Mar 30, 50; d Clifford William Stoltz & Wilma M Curry S; single. Educ: Mont State Univ, BA, 72; Delta Gamma. Polit & Govt Pos: Mont State Rep, 73-, vchmn educ & legis admin comts, 75. Mem: Mont Grain Growers; Mont Farmers Union (mem state educ bd, 72-73). Honors & Awards: Sr of the Year, Delta Gamma, 72. Relig: Catholic. Mailing Add: RR Box 42 Valier MT 59486

STOLZ, MABEL SMITH (D)
VChmn, Sixth Cong Dist Dem Party, Mich

b Alpena, Mich, Mar 15, 11; d Thomas James Smith & Susan Hazelgrove S; m 1931 to Armond J Stolz; c Dr Benjamin & Joseph W. Educ: Cent Mich Univ, AB, 38. Polit & Govt Pos: Secy, Shiawassee Co Dem Exec Comt, Mich, 60, chmn, 63-67 & 70-72, mem, 69-; deleg, Dem Nat Conv, 64 & 68, mem credential comt, 64, mem platform comt, 68; vchmn, Sixth Cong Dist Dem Party, 68- Bus & Prof Pos: Teacher, Owosso Pub Schs, Mich, 45- Publ: Many articles in Open Forum. Mem: Owosso & Mich Educ Asns; League Women Voters Owosso (mem bd dirs). Relig: Unitarian. Mailing Add: 202 W North Owosso MI 48867

STOLZ, OTTO GEORGE (R)
Gen Mgr, New Community Develop Corp, Dept Housing & Urban Develop

b New York, NY, Jan 23, 42; s Otto G Stolz & Johanna Heinkel S; m 1964 to Jill Viemeister; c Whitney & Heather. Educ: Stevens Inst Technol, BE; Univ Va Law Sch, JD; L'Inst de Hautes Etudes Int, Geneva, Switz, dipl; ed, Va Law Rev, 62-63; Order of the Coif. Polit & Govt Pos: Spec counsel to Under Secy, Dept Treas, 71-72; adminr, New Communities Admin, Dept Housing & Urban Develop, 74-75, gen mgr, New Community Develop Corp, 75- Bus & Prof Pos: Assoc, Latham & Watkins, Los Angeles, Calif, 71; prof law, Duke Univ Law Sch, 72-74. Publ: New American revolution or trojan horse, Minn Law Rev, 10/73; Revenue Sharing: Legal & Policy Analysis of New Federal Grant Concept, Praeger Publ, Inc, 74. Legal Res: Rte 1 Box 249 St Mary's Rd Hillsborough NC 27278 Mailing Add: 1822 Rupert St McLean VA 22101

STOLZENBURG, CHESTER W (R)
Fla State Sen
Mailing Add: NE 16th Ave Ft Lauderdale FL 33308

STONE, ALEC G (D)
Ky State Rep
Mailing Add: Rte 2 Brandenburg KY 40108

STONE, ANN ELIZABETH (BITSEY) (R)
Nat Committeewoman, DC Young Rep

b Bridgeport, Conn, Aug 9, 52; d Jack Reginald Wesche & Edith Pauline Christensen W; m 1974 to Roger Jason Stone, Jr. Educ: George Washington Univ, BA in Commun & Hist, 74. Polit & Govt Pos: Secy, DC Col Rep, 72-73; chmn, George Washington Univ Col Rep, 73-74; mem exec comt, Young Rep Leadership Conf, 73-, treas, 75-; Nat Committeewoman, DC Young Rep, 75-, secy, currently. Bus & Prof Pos: Mgr mkt, Human Events, 74- Mem: Cardinal Soc (publicity chmn & rec secy); Conn State Soc; Young Am for Freedom; DC Young Am for Freedom (secy & vchmn); Region III Col Rep. Honors & Awards: Civic Award for Outstanding Citizen, Stratford Rep Town Comt, Conn, 70; Outstanding Chmn, DC Col Rep, 74; Young Rep of Month, DC Young Rep, 74. Relig: Lutheran. Mailing Add: 5907 S Fifth Rd Arlington VA 22204

STONE, BEN HARRY (D)
Miss State Sen

b Gulfport, Miss, Jan 18, 35; s W Harry Stone & Tressie Lancaster S; m 1958 to Nancy Jane Reed; c Nancy Jane, Virginia Louise & Kathleen Lancaster. Educ: Tulane Univ, BBA, 57; Univ Miss, JD, 61; Sigma Alpha Epsilon. Polit & Govt Pos: Mem exec comt, Miss Research & Develop Coun, 68-; mem, Miss Econ Coun, 68-; Miss State Sen, 68-; mem, Miss Coun for Develop Marine Resources, 69-; mem exec comt, Coun of State Govt, 71-, mem gov bd, currently; mem, Miss Marine Conserv Comn, currently. Bus & Prof Pos: Partner, Eaton, Cottrell, Galloway & Lang, 63- Mil Serv: Air Force, 57-58. Mem: Miss State Bar Asn; Gulfport CofC (dir, 68-70); Miss Defense Lawyers Asn; Miss Soc for Prev of Blindness (chmn, 65, bd mem, 68-); Harrison Co Cancer Soc (bd mem, 65-). Relig: Presbyterian. Legal Res: 1320 E Beach Gulfport MS 39501 Mailing Add: PO Drawer H Gulfport MS 39501

STONE, CHARLES JOHNSON, JR (D)
Vt State Rep
Mailing Add: Calais Stage Montpelier VT 05602

STONE, GORDON EARL (R)
Chmn, Reno Co Rep Party, Kans

b Andover, SDak, Nov 27, 09; s Earl L Stone & Frances Smith S; m 1958 to Helen Weeks; c Robert, Allen & Richard. Educ: Univ SDak, BS; Wash Univ, MD; Alpha Omega Alpha; Phi Chi. Polit & Govt Pos: Chmn, Reno Co Rep Party, Kans, 67- Bus & Prof Pos: On the staff, Grace Hosp & St Elizabeth Hosp. Mil Serv: Maj, Army, 42-46, Fourth Serv Co, Army. Mem: Am Med Asn; Kans Med Soc. Relig: Protestant. Legal Res: 226 Curtis Hutchinson KS 67501 Mailing Add: 519 Wiley Bldg Hutchinson KS 67501

STONE, J W (R)
Mem, Mo Rep State Comt

b Fortescue, Mo, Nov 6, 27; s Perry Allen Stone & May Murrah S; single. Educ: Northwestern Mo State Col, BS in Educ 50; Univ Mo, Kansas City, MA in Educ Admin & post grad work; Kappa Delta Pi; Pi Omega Pi. Polit & Govt Pos: Committeeman, Minton Two Rep Party, Mo, 52-; mem, Sixth Cong Dist Rep Comt, 58-, mem, Judicial Comt; chmn, Holt Co Rep Cent Comt, 58-; mem, Town Coun, Fortescue, 62-; mem, Mo State Rep Comt, 64-, mem budget comt, 70-; mem bd, Northwest Mo Econ Opportunity Corp, secy & treas, 65-69, chmn, 69-; regional bd dir, Voc Rehabilitation, Mo, 67-; deleg representing Mo State Rep Comt at the Presidential Inauguration of Richard Nixon, 69 & 73; mem, Comt for Coun on Pub Higher Educ, Mo, 72; mayor, Fortescue, Mo, 73- Bus & Prof Pos: Farmer, Fortescue, Mo, 44-; instr bus dept, Region III Sch Dist, Craig, 57-59; supt of schs, Holt Co, 59-61; supt of schs, Region III, Craig, 61- Mil Serv: Entered as Pvt, Army, 50, released as Sgt 1/C, 52, after serv in 1905th Engr Aviation Bn. Mem: Nat Educ Asn; Am Asn Sch Adminr; Mo State Teachers Asn; Mo Sch Adminr Asn; Holt Co Teachers Asn. Honors & Awards: Basketball letterman, 5 years, track, 2 years. Relig: Methodist; Church sch supt, adult Bible instr; lay leader, Maryville Dist, United Methodist Church, 68-, mem, Mo W Conf Bd of Admin France, 72- Legal Res: Fortescue MO 64452 Mailing Add: Craig R-III Sch Dist Craig MO 64437

STONE, JOHN CLINTON (R)
Exec Dir, Rep Party, La

b Springhill, La, Dec 31, 42; s James Herbert Stone & Bess Miller S; m 1968 to Ann Farber; c Suzanne Elizabeth. Educ: Tulane Univ, BA, 64; Sigma Alpha Epsilon. Polit & Govt Pos: Mem, State Research & Issues Comt, Rep Party of La, 70-; state campaign coordr, Treen for Gov Campaign, 71-72; exec dir, La Comt to Reelect the President, 72; state coordr, La Inaugural Comt, 72-73; exec dir, Rep Party, La, 72-; state aid, Rep Nat Conv, 72. Bus & Prof Pos: Field dir, La Hwy-Heavy Construction Br, Assoc Gen Contractors of Am, Inc, 68-71. Mil Serv: Entered as Ens, Navy, 64 & released as Lt, 68, after serv in Attack Squadron 25, Vietnam & Western Pac, 66-68; Vietnam Serv Medal; Nat Defense Serv Medal; Navy Achievement Medal, twice; Presidential Unit Citation; SVietnamese Navy Distinguished Serv Order. Mem: Capital Sertoma Club (vpres, currently); Tulane Alumni Asn. Relig: Methodist. Mailing Add: 12823 Arlingford Baton Rouge LA 70815

STONE, LORRAINE G (R)
Mem, Mich Rep State Cent Comt

b Brooklyn, NY, June 25, 19; d Thomas F Galligan, Jr & Gertrude Jones G; m 1941 to James Blount Stone; c Penelope Elizabeth, James Wiswell & Jay Walter. Educ: Bay Ridge High Sch, Brooklyn, 36. Polit & Govt Pos: Challenger at polls, Alpine Twp, Kent Co, Mich, 72; precinct deleg, 74-75; co-chmn, Gov Milliken Tel Ctr, Grand Rapids, 74; mem exec comt, Grand Rapids, 74-; mem, Mich Rep State Cent Comt, 75- Bus & Prof Pos: Statist clerk, Am Tel & Tel Co, 36-48. Mem: Women's City Club, Grand Rapids. Relig: Roman Catholic. Mailing Add: 187 Lantern Dr Comstock Park MI 49321

STONE, MURRAY (D)
Mo State Rep

b Richmond, NY, Jan 28, 38; s Louis Stone & Shirley Weiss S; m 1961 to Elaine Mae Suffian; c Dana Victoria & Denise Jennifer. Educ: Okla Univ, BA, 61; Washington Univ, JD, 65; Alpha Epsilon Pi. Polit & Govt Pos: Adjudicator, Vet Admin, 65-66; Mo State Rep, 73- Bus & Prof Pos: Attorney-at-law. Relig: Jewish. Mailing Add: 11661 Holly Springs Dr St Louis MO 63141

STONE, NORMA WALSH (R)
Mem, NY Rep State Comt

b Marcellus, NY, Aug 24, 95; d Thomas F Walsh & Luella Spingler W; m 1916 to Horace M Stone, wid; c Norma Suzann, Nan S (Mrs James Farrell), Horace M, Jr & Marguerite S (Mrs John M Mead). Polit & Govt Pos: Deleg, Rep State Conv, 50, 54 & 56; vchmn, Onondaga Co Rep Comt, 50-65; deleg, Rep Nat Conv, 52-64; deleg, Judicial Conv, 55; mem, NY Rep State Comt, currently. Honors & Awards: Woman of the Year in Polit Award, Bus & Prof Women, Syracuse, NY. Relig: Presbyterian. Mailing Add: 2 North St Marcellus NY 13108

STONE, NORMAN R, JR (D)
Md State Sen
Mailing Add: 2322 Lodge Forest Dr Baltimore MD 21219

STONE, PAUL (D)
Ill State Rep

b Newton, Ill, Sept 21, 15; s Claude L Stone & Ruth Stewart S; m 1939 to Thelma Lucille Jones; c Elaine, Paul L, Michael & Marsha R. Educ: Univ Ill, BA, 40, Law Sch, LLB, 42. Polit & Govt Pos: Appeal agt, Ill Selective Serv Syst, 48-; Ill State Rep, 51-52 & 67- Bus & Prof Pos: Pres, Moultrie Co Bar Asn, formerly; chmn, Teachers Col Bd, Ill & Bd of Gov, State Col & Univ; mem, Univ Civil Serv Merit Syst, Western Ill Univ Found & Ill State Univ Found. Mem: Am Acad Polit & Soc Sci; Mason; Kiwanis; Elks; Moose. Relig: Methodist. Mailing Add: 112 N Main St Sullivan IL 61951

STONE, R BAYNE (D)
Ga State Rep
Mailing Add: 208 Hester St Hazlehurst GA 31539

STONE, RICHARD BERNARD (DICK) (D)
US Sen, Fla

b New York, NY, Sept 22, 28; s Alfred Stone & Lily Abbey S; m to Marlene Singer; c Nancy, Amy & Elliott. Educ: Harvard Univ, BA cum laude, 49; Columbia Univ Law Sch, LLB, 54; Varsity Swimming Team, Harvard Univ. Polit & Govt Pos: City Attorney, Miami, Fla, 66-67; Fla State Sen, 48th Dist, 67-71; Secy of State, Fla, formerly; US Sen, Fla, currently; deleg, Dem Nat Mid-Term Conf, 74. Bus & Prof Pos: Former secy, Royal Castle Syst, Inc; former mem bd dirs, Army Eagle Navy, Inc; former partner, Stone, Bittell, Langer, Blass & Corrigan. Mem: Dade Co, Am & Inter-Am Bar Asns; Corp Banking & Bus Law Comt. Honors & Awards: Acad Awards at Harvard Univ; Best Freshman Sen. Relig: Jewish. Legal Res: Plantation Rd Tallahassee FL 32304 Mailing Add: US Senate Washington DC 20510

STONE, THOMAS MITCHELL (D)
Miss State Rep

b Holly Springs, Miss, Jan 24, 15; s Thomas Calvin Stone & Lillie Caviness S; m 1940 to Annie Ruth Holley; c Tommye Ann (Mrs Gale Goode), Mitch, Jr, Cherri Marke & Merri Holley (Pebble). Educ: Sunflower Jr Col, 37-38; Univ Ala, 38-40. Polit & Govt Pos: Miss State Rep, Benton, Desoto & Marshall Counties, Dist 4, 68- Bus & Prof Pos: Sch teacher & coach, 40-43 & 45-63. Mil Serv: Entered as Pvt, Navy, 43, released as Radar 2/C, 45, after serv in USS ATR 21. Mem: VFW; Am Legion; Lions. Relig: Methodist. Mailing Add: PO Box 6 Potts Camp MS 38659

STONE, W CLEMENT (R)
Exec VChmn, Rep Nat Finance Comt

b Chicago, Ill, May 4, 02; s Louis Stone & Anna M Gunn S; m 1923 to Jessie V Tarson; c Clement, Donna & Norman. Educ: Detroit Col Law, 20; Northwestern Univ, 30-32; Alpha Kappa Psi. Hon Degrees: Many from various cols in US. Polit & Govt Pos: Alt deleg, Rep Nat Conv, 68, deleg, 72; exec vchmn, Rep Nat Finance Comt, 70-; vchmn, Nat Ctr for Vol Action, 72- Bus & Prof Pos: Pres, dir, Combined Am Ins Co, Dallas, Tex, 45-; pres & dir, Combined Ins Co of Am, Chicago, Ill, 47-69; chmn bd, 69-; chmn bd & chief exec officer, Combined Ins Co of Wis, Fond du Lac, Wis, 54-; ed & publ, Success Unlimited Mag, Chicago,

Ill, 54-; pres & dir, Combined Life Ins Co of NY, Albany, 71-; chmn, Trans-Am Video, Inc, Los Angeles, Calif, 72- Publ: Success Through a Positive Mental Attitude (w Napoleon Hill), 60, Success System that Never Fails, 62 & The Other Side of the Mind (w Norma Lee Browning), 64, Prentice-Hall. Mem: Chicago Asn Health Underwriters; Am Mgt Asn; Chicago Asn Com & Indust; Exec Club, Chicago. Honors & Awards: Horatio Alger Award, 63; Church Layman of the Year, Church Fedn Gtr Chicago, 68; Daniel A Lord Award, Loyola Acad, 68; Boys' Club Golden Keystone Award, Boys' Clubs of Am, 68; Free Enterprise Exemplar Medal, Freedoms Found, 72. Relig: Presbyterian. Mailing Add: 5050 Broadway Chicago IL 60640

STONE, WILLIAM CORNWELL **(D)**
Mem, Chester Co Dem Party, SC
b Chester, SC, Oct 22, 27; s William Cornwell Stone, Sr & Mary Love McLure S; m 1958 to Mary Eugenia Dudley; c William Cornwell, III, Mary Melissa & Hugh Dudley. Educ: Clemson Univ; Univ SC. Polit & Govt Pos: Mem, Chester Co Elec Comn, SC, 60-75; chmn, Chester Co Dem Party, formerly, mem, currently, mem, Chester Ward III Precinct, currently. Bus & Prof Pos: Pres, Stone Ins Agency, Inc. Mil Serv: Entered as Seaman, Navy, 45, released as PO 3/C, 48, after serv in Pac Theatre, 46-48; Victory & Good Conduct Medals. Mem: SC & Nat Asns Ins Agents; Am Legion; Chester Co Hist Soc; Chester Co Bd Com & Develop. Relig: Presbyterian. Mailing Add: 108 Foote St Chester SC 29706

STONE, WILLIAM PHILIP **(D)**
Ky State Rep
b Nelson, Ky, Nov 19, 11; s Robert Franklin Stone & Ella J Sharpe S; m 1939 to Thelma Mae Thomas; c William Philip, Jr. Educ: GED high sch dipl. Polit & Govt Pos: First dist magistrate, Muhlenberg Co, Ky, 38-42, dep sheriff, 54-58, high sheriff, 58-62, co court judge, 62-74; state police officer, Commonwealth of Ky, 42-53; chmn, Muhlenberg Co Dem Party, 74-; mem, State Govt Cities & Spec Dist Comt, Ky, currently; Ky State Rep, Dist 15, 74- Publ: My Job As I See It, Paragon Printing Co, 69. Mem: Masonic Lodge 673; Ky Farm Bur. Honors & Awards: Merit Awards, Jr CofC, Greenville, Ky, 62-73; Loving Cup for one of the Most Outstanding Juv Court Judges, Ky, Bus & Prof Women Club, 67; Greenville CofC Award, 68. Relig: Presbyterian. Mailing Add: 620 Reservoir Central City KY 42330

STONEBRINK, HELEN MAY **(R)**
VChmn, Wallowa Co Rep Cent Comt, Ore
b Steamboat Springs, Colo, Aug 4, 23; d Fred N May & Anna Bowie M; m 1946 to Clyde L Stonebrink. Educ: Colo State Univ, 41-43; Ariz State Univ, 44; Colo State Col, BA, 45. Polit & Govt Pos: Secy, Wallowa Co Rep Cent Comt, Ore, 67-69, chmn, 69-70, vchmn, 70-; precinct committeeman, Enterprise, Ore, 68-71. Mem: PEO; Rebekah; Grange. Mailing Add: Flora Rte Box 5 Enterprise OR 97858

STONER, RICHARD BURKETT **(D)**
Dem Nat Committeeman, Ind
b Ladoga, Ind, May 15, 20; s Edward Norris Stoner & Florence Burkett S; m 1942 to Virginia Austin; c Pamela, Richard B, Jr, Benjamin, Janet, Rebecca & Joanne. Educ: Ind Univ, BS, 41; Harvard Law Sch, JD, 47; Beta Gamma Sigma; Blue Key; Sigma Nu. Polit & Govt Pos: Deleg, Dem State Conv, Ind, 52-62; precinct committeeman, Bartholomew Co, Ind, 52-58; deleg, Dem Nat Conv, 56-72; treas, Bartholomew Co Dem Cent Comt, 58, chmn, 58-60, chmn, Ninth Dist Dem Comt, 61-66; Dem Nat Committeeman, Ind, 66-; mem, Ind Adv Comn on Acad Facil, currently. Bus & Prof Pos: Cummins Engine Co, Inc, Columbus, Ind, 47-, vchmn bd, 69-, dir, currently; pres & dir, Cummins Engine Found & Irwin-Sweeney-Miller Found; dir, Transinterbank, Inc, Geneva, Switz; dir, Kirloskar Cummins Ltd, Poona, India; dir, Pub Serv Ind; dir, Am Fletcher Nat Bank & Trust Co, currently; dir, Ind State CofC, currently; pres, Ind Forum, Inc, Indianapolis, 71-; trustee, Ind Univ, 72- Mil Serv: Entered as Pvt, Army, released as Capt, Finance Dept. Mem: Mach & Allied Prod Inst (exec comt, 70-); Indianapolis Athletic Club; Columbus Redevelop Comn (trustee, 70-). Relig: North Christian Church. Mailing Add: 2770 Franklin Dr Columbus IN 47201

STONER, WILLIAM E (BILL) **(R)**
Mo State Rep
Mailing Add: 2462 S Franklin Springfield MO 65807

STONEY, LARRY D
Nebr State Sen
Mailing Add: 12626 Shirley St Omaha NE 68144

STONEY, WILLIAM E
Asst Secy Systs Develop & Technol, Dept Transportation
Mailing Add: Dept of Transportation 400 Seventh St SW Washington DC 20590

STONG, BENTON J **(D)**
b Keosauqua, Iowa, Mar 29, 05; s Benjamin J Stong & Ada Duffield S; m 1940 to Laverne Deinlein; c Norma (Mrs Lyon), Benton J, Michael J & Joseph S. Educ: Drake Univ, AB, 27; Delta Theta Phi; Sigma Delta Chi. Polit & Govt Pos: Info dir, Region Off, Farmers Home Admin, Indianapolis, 40; mem prof staff, US Senate Interior Comt, 56-64; legis asst, US Sen George McGovern, SDak, 64-69; admin asst to US Rep John Melcher, Mont, 69- Bus & Prof Pos: Reporter, Des Moines Register, 25-27, Cleveland Times, 28 & Cleveland Press, 29; reporter & ed, Knoxville New Sentinel, 29-38; reporter, Scripps-Howard Newspaper Alliance, 39-40; ed, Nat Univ Farmer, Denver, 40-49; Wash Rep, Nat Farmers Union, 49-52; researcher, Pub Affairs Inst, Washington, DC, 53-56. Publ: Harlan County's Coal War, Scripps-Howard Papers, 36; Exodus from the South, Memphis Press Scimitor, 45; The Wilderness Act, US Senate Report, 63. Mem: Hon life mem Soil Conserv Soc Am; Nat Press Club, Washington, DC; Darrow Conf on Mathematical Probabilities. Honors & Awards: Conserv Award, Am Motors; George W Norris Award, Midwest Elec Consumers Asn; Distinguished Serv Award, East River Elec Coop SDak. Legal Res: 404 W Great Falls Dr Falls Church VA 22046 Mailing Add: 1224 Longworth Bldg Washington DC 20515

STONUM, ELIZABETH ANN **(R)**
Mem, State Rep Cent Comt Calif
b Bowling Green, Ohio, Aug 23, 26; d Glen Drum Greek & Florence Evelyn Utter G; m 1946 to Robert Gale Stonum; c Gayle Kathleen & Neil Allan. Educ: Modesto Jr Col, AA. Polit & Govt Pos: Mem, State Rep Cent Comt Calif, 68- Mem: Eastern Star; Soroptimist Fedn of the Americas, Mariposa Chap. Honors & Awards: Hon life mem, Calif Cong Parents & Teachers. Relig: Protestant. Legal Res: Triangle Rd Mariposa CA 95338 Mailing Add: PO Box 704 Mariposa CA 95338

STOPCZYNSKI, STEPHEN **(D)**
Mich State Rep
b Detroit, Mich, Jan 1, 11; married; c Stephen, Jr, Stanley & Thaddeus. Educ: St Stanislaus High Sch; Highland Park Ford Trade Sch; Northeastern High Sch. Polit & Govt Pos: Former precinct deleg, Mich, 24 years; deleg const conv, formerly; Mich State Rep, 64-, chmn, Comt on Polit Educ, formerly; mem, Mich State Dem Cent Comt & Wayne Co AFL-CIO Coun, formerly. Bus & Prof Pos: Machinist. Mem: Holy Name Soc; UAW Local 157; Home Owners Asn; North Detroit Dom Polski Asn; Pulaski Dem Club of North Detroit (vpres). Relig: Roman Catholic. Mailing Add: 12016 Nashville Detroit MI 48205

STOPCZYNSKI, THADDEUS C **(D)**
Mich State Rep
b Hamtramck, Mich, Feb 16, 40; s Stephen Stopczynski & Cassie Dzieciolowski S; m 1959 to Judith E Drost; c Suzanne, Peggy, Lawrence, Gregory, Judy Joy, Matthew, Timothy & Elizabeth. Educ: Chrysler Millwright Apprentice Prog, 60-62; Acad of Detroit Police Dept, 12 weeks, 62. Polit & Govt Pos: Chmn, Region Six Cent Bd, Detroit Bd of Educ, Mich, 71-72; Mich State Rep, 73-; mem, 14th Cong Dist Dem Party, currently. Bus & Prof Pos: Police officer, Detroit, Mich, 62-72. Mem: Pulaski Homeowners Asn (bd mem); Northeast Coun of Homeowners; Eagles; Mich Asn of Sch Bd; Nat Sch Bd Asn. Relig: Catholic. Legal Res: 19214 Goulburn St Detroit MI 48205 Mailing Add: State Capitol Lansing MI 48901

STOPYRA, AGNES THERESA **(D)**
VChmn, Cayuga Co Dem Party, NY
b Auburn, NY, Dec 18, 19; d Sam DeLuca & Teresa Luciano D; m 1939 to Walter Joseph Stopyra; c Thomas Patrick & Mark A. Educ: Auburn Eastern High Sch, NY, grad, 38. Polit & Govt Pos: Vchmn, Cayuga Co Dem Party, NY, 63- Bus & Prof Pos: Legal secy, Thomas Stopyra Law Off, Auburn, NY, 65-67. Mem: Am Legion Auxiliary; Christopher Columbus Commemorative Comt; Cayuga Co Dem Ladies Club; Nat Found March of Dimes (secy to bd dirs). Honors & Awards: Young Cayugan Appreciation Award, Auburn Jr CofC, 60; Community Serv Award, Auburn Serv League, 61. Relig: Roman Catholic. Mailing Add: 97 Perrine St Auburn NY 13021

STOREY, BOB WILSON **(R)**
Kans State Sen
b Siloam Springs, Ark, Sept 5, 34; s Jess Burl Storey & Gertrude Feaster S; m 1958 to Patricia Lou Moon; c Bradley Lewis & Jennifer Kay. Educ: Independence Jr Col, 2 years; Washburn Univ, BBA, 60; Washburn Law Sch, LLB, 63; Phi Delta Theta. Polit & Govt Pos: Asst gen counsel, Kans Corp Comn, 63-66; Kans State Sen, 68-; deleg, Rep Nat Conv, 72. Bus & Prof Pos: Attorney-at-law, Tilton & Storey, Topeka, Kans, 63-; motor carrier examr, Kans Corp Comn, 66-68. Mil Serv: Entered as E-2, Army, 57, released as Pfc, 57, after serv in Army Signal Corps. Mem: Am Trial Lawyers Asn; Phi Alpha Delta; CofC; Elks; Arab Temple. Relig: Methodist. Mailing Add: 820 Quincy Topeka KS 66612

STORTINI, JOE **(D)**
Wash State Sen
Mailing Add: 1623 Firlands Dr Tacoma WA 98405

STORY, PETER REINALD **(R)**
Mont State Sen
b Los Angeles, Calif, Dec 19, 32; s Malcolm C Story & Rose Ashbey S; m 1958 to Eileen Cavanaugh; c Robert, Michael, Nelson, Rose Ann & Thomas. Educ: Univ Colo, BS, 55; Acacia. Polit & Govt Pos: Mont State Sen, 73- Mil Serv: Entered as Ens, Navy, 55, released as Lt(jg), 58, after serv in USS Isherwood (DD520), Pac Theatre, 55-58; Lt, Res, 5 years; China Serv Award. Mem: Mont Cattlemen's Asn (bd dirs, 59-73); Park Co Farm Bur (chmn, 62-65); Emigrant Community Hall Asn (bd dirs, 65-73); Elks. Relig: Protestant. Mailing Add: Story Ranch Emigrant MT 59027

STOTT, RONALD ALTON **(D)**
NY State Assemblyman
b Buffalo, NY, Mar 4, 38; s William A Stott & Helen Ormsby S; m 1963 to Sharon Marie La Douce; c Jacquelyn, Robin, Kevin & David. Educ: Erie Co Community Col, Buffalo, AAS, 61; Univ Ariz, BS, 66; Syracuse Univ Law Sch, 67-71; Tau Beta Pi; Kappa Tau. Polit & Govt Pos: Mayor, Village of North Syracuse, NY, 71-75; NY State Assemblyman, 118th Dist, 75- Bus & Prof Pos: Patent engr, Gen Elec Co, Syracuse, 66-71; self-employed bus consult, Syracuse, 71- Mil Serv: Entered as Pvt, Marines, 56, released as Sgt, 59, after serv in 6th Marines, 2nd Div; Good Conduct Medal; Letter of Commendation. Mem: Hon mem North Syracuse Lions Club; hon mem North Syracuse Jr CofC. Relig: Catholic. Mailing Add: 206 Helen St North Syracuse NY 13212

STOTTS, KEITH HORACE **(R)**
Mo State Rep
b Stotts City, Mo, July 22, 14; s Horace Green Stotts & Hannah Enright S; m 1936 to Helen Mae Abram; c Bill Keith & Susan Elaine. Polit & Govt Pos: Mem, Pierce City Sch Bd, Lawrence Co Draft Bd & Welfare Bd, Mo, formerly; mayor, Pierce City, 46-56; Mo State Rep, Lawrence Co, currently. Bus & Prof Pos: Owner, Stotts Pharm, 44- Mem: Nat Asn of Retail Druggists; Mo Pharmaceutical Asn; Mo State CofC; Pierce City CofC; Pierce City Kiwanis (charter mem). Mailing Add: 506 Walnut St Pierce City MO 65723

STOUGH, CHARLES SENOUR **(D)**
Chmn, CZ Regional Dem Party
b Decatur, Ill, June 14, 18; s Charles Senour Stough & Blanche Allen S; m 1943 to Jeanne Marie Flynn; c Charles S, III & Stevan R. Educ: Phoenix Jr Col, Ariz, 37-38; Univ Southern Calif, 38-40. Polit & Govt Pos: Mem bd dirs, Citizens for Responsible Govt, San Antonio, Tex, 65-70; chmn, Don Yarborough Gubernatorial Campaign, Bexar Co, 68 & Citizens for Humphrey-Muskie, 68; campaign mgr for City Councilman Peter Torres, San Antonio, 69; vchmn, CZ Regional Dem Party, 71-72, chmn, 72-; mem, Asn State Dem Chmn, 72-; mem, Dem Nat Comt, 72-; deleg, Conf on Dem Party Orgn & Policy, 74. Mil Serv: Entered as Pvt, Army, 40, Ret at Lt Col, 63; after serv as Rifle Co Comdr, World War II, Europe, Bn Comdr, Korea; Bronze Star Medal (Valor) with Oak Leaf Cluster; Army Commendation Medal; Purple Heart with Oak Leaf Cluster; Combat Infantryman's Badge; Parachute Badge; Campaign Medals. Mem: Am Legion; VFW. Mailing Add: Box 741 Curundu CZ

STOUGH, MERRY BAKER **(D)**
Dem Nat Committeewoman, CZ
b San Antonio, Tex, Dec 24, 37; d Rudy Smith & Thelma Smith Newman; m 1973 to Stevan Robert Stough; c Melisa & Michael. Educ: Univ Alaska. Polit & Govt Pos: Cand, San Antonio

City Coun, Tex, 71; chmn, Precinct Conv, 72; deleg & secy, 26th Sen Dist Conv, 72; deleg, Tex State Dem Conv & Dem Nat Conv, 72; chmn, Bexar Co Environmentalists for McGovern, 72; Dem Nat Committeewoman, CZ, 74- Mailing Add: Box 1128 Cristobal CZ

STOUGHTON, STEPHEN H (R)
Ind State Rep
b Shelbyville, Ind, Apr 13, 44; s Homer Stoughton & Doris Robison S; m 1967 to Edy Comfort; c Jason Thomas & Craig Michael. Educ: Ind Univ, Bloomington, BS, 66; Alpha Kappa Psi. Polit & Govt Pos: Ind State Rep, 73- Bus & Prof Pos: Mkt analyst, Ford Mkt Div, Ford Motor Co, 66-67; exec dir, Construction Indust Advan Prog, Ind, 71-73; exec vpres, Indianapolis Bd of Realtors, 73- Mil Serv: Entered as 2nd Lt, Air Force, 67, released as Capt, after serv at Castle AFB, Strategic Air Command, 67-71; Capt, Air Force Res, 71-; pres, Jr Officer's Coun, US Air Force, 68; Outstanding Jr Officer, 69; Air Force Commendation Medal. Mem: Ind Area Develop Coun; Gtr Indianapolis Progress Comt; Indianapolis Housing Comt (vchmn); Marion Co Asn of Mentally Retarded; Indianapolis Rotary Club. Relig: First Friends Meeting. Mailing Add: 6502 N Sherman Dr Indianapolis IN 46220

STOUT, BARRY (D)
Pa State Rep
Mailing Add: Capitol Bldg Harrisburg PA 17120

STOUT, ERNEST VERNON (R)
Chmn, Hughes Co Rep Party, Okla
b Okemah, Okla, Sept 28, 38; s Ernest L Stout & Beulah Carnes S; single. Educ: ECent State Univ, BA, 61; Univ Okla, MA, 68 & post grad; Gamma Theta Upsilon. Polit & Govt Pos: City councilman, Wetumka, Okla, 72-; chmn, Hughes Co Rep Party, Okla, 73- Bus & Prof Pos: Prin, Wetumka Pub Schs, 70- Mil Serv: Entered as E-1, Air Force, 61, released as 1st Lt, 65, after serv in 747 AC&W Squadron (ADC). Mem: US Jaycees; Okla Educ Asn; Univ Okla Alumni Asn. Mailing Add: PO Box 393 Wetumka OK 74883

STOUT, JUNE WINDLE (R)
Chmn, Linn Co Rep Cent Comt, Ore
b Salt Lake City, Utah, Sept 19, 19; d James Edgar Windle & Mary Myrl Skelton W; m 1946 to Lermond E Stout; c Mary Kathleen & Gary Lee. Educ: Northwestern Bus Col, Portland, Ore, 38-39. Polit & Govt Pos: Mem various Rep supplemental groups & Rep Women's Fedn; precinct committeewoman, Linn Co Rep Cent Comt, Ore, 52-, precinct chmn, 62-68, co chmn, 68-; second dist vchmn, Ore State Rep Cent & Exec Comts, 68- Bus & Prof Pos: Secy & staff claims adjuster, Northwestern Mutual Fire & Casualty Co, 41-49; co-owner, Marco Polo Motel, Albany, Ore, 51-59; co-owner, Waverly Plaza Apts, 56-62. Mem: Albany Citizens Adv Comt; Springhill Country Club; PTA. Relig: Presbyterian. Mailing Add: 1207 W 26th Albany OR 97321

STOUT, RICHARD RALSTON (R)
b Ocean Grove, NJ, Sept 21, 12; s Richard Weslord Stout & Lillian Nevin Ralston S; m 1947 to Nancy Tucker; c Penelope (Mrs Nachman), Mary Elizabeth, Margaret Tucker, Richard Ralston, Jr, Susan Nichols & Nancy Tucker. Educ: Princeton Univ, AB, 35; Rutgers Law Sch, LLB, 39; Tiger Inn; Delta Theta Phi. Polit & Govt Pos: Pres, Monmouth Co Young Rep, NJ, 49; NJ State Sen, Monmouth Co, 52-74; deleg, NJ Const Conv, 66; deleg, Rep Nat Conv, 68, alt deleg, 72. Mil Serv: Entered as 1st Lt, Army, 40, released as Col, 46, after serv in Mid East, 42-44; Col, Army Res (Ret); Legion of Merit; Army Commendation Medal. Mem: Mason; Elks; Lions; VFW; Am Legion. Relig: Methodist. Legal Res: Wickapecko Dr West Allenhurst NJ 07711 Mailing Add: 301 Main St Allenhurst NJ 07711

STOUTZ, EDWIN A, JR (D)
Chmn, Second Cong Dem Exec Comt, La
b New Orleans, La, Sept 13, 41; s Edwin A Stoutz, Sr & Isabelle Taaffe S; m 1968 to Catherine Michie McHardy; c W Clifton. Educ: Georgetown Univ, BS & BA, 63; Tulane Univ, LLB, 67; Phi Delta Phi. Polit & Govt Pos: Mem, La State Dem Cent Comt, 29th Rep Dist, 67-; deleg, Dem Nat Conv, 68; chmn, Second Cong Dem Exec Comt, La, 68- Mem: La State & Am Bar Asns; Young Men's Bus Club; New Orleans Mid-winter Sports Asn; Alliance for Good Govt. Honors & Awards: Youngest mem of the La Deleg, Dem Cat Conv, 68. Relig: Catholic. Mailing Add: 3150 State St Dr New Orleans LA 70125

STOVALL, REGINALD MORRIS (R)
Mayor, Ft Worth, Tex
b Tupelo, Okla, Aug 1, 16; s William Dudley Stovall (deceased) & Grace Allen S (deceased); m 1939 to Amelia Zich; c Linda, Marsha, Peggy & Nancy. Educ: Tex Christian Univ, 36. Polit & Govt Pos: Councilman, Ft Worth, Tex, 63-68, mayor, 69- Bus & Prof Pos: Pres, Panther City Off Supply Co, 44-; vpres, Bell Reproduction Co, 50- Mem: Mason (32 degree); DeMolay; Shrine (Potentate). Relig: Episcopal. Mailing Add: 2428 Medford Ct E Ft Worth TX 76109

STOVALL, THELMA LOYACE (D)
Secy of State, Ky
b Munfordville, Ky, Apr 1, 19; d Samuel Dewey Hawkins & Addie Mae H; m 1936 to Lonnie Raymond Stovall. Educ: LaSalle Exten Univ, Law, 2 years; Univ Ky, 2 summers; Eastern State Col, 1 summer. Polit & Govt Pos: Ky State Rep, 38th Legis Dist, 50-56; nat committeewoman, Young Dem Clubs of Ky, 52-56, pres, 56-58; Secy of State, Ky, 56-60, 64-68 & 72-; State Treas, Ky, 60-64 & 68-; mem, Comn on Women, 73- Bus & Prof Pos: Secy, Tobacco Workers Int Union, Local 185, 11 years; bd dirs of educ dept, Ky State Fedn of Labor, 8 years; rec secy, Nat Asn of Secys of State, 67, secy, 68; chmn, Comt on Employ of the Gov Comn on the Status of Women, 66; vpres, Muscular Dystrophy Asn of Am, Inc, 70- Mem: Women of the Moose; Eastern Star; Young Dem; Bus & Prof Womens' Club. Relig: Baptist. Legal Res: 104 Valley Rd Louisville KY 40204 Mailing Add: Rm 150 Capitol Bldg Frankfort KY 40601

STRADA, WILLIAM E, JR (D)
Conn State Sen
Mailing Add: 750 Summer St Stamford CT 06901

STRADLEY, JAY OAKLEY (R)
Committeeman, NJ Rep State Comt
b Wilmington, Del, May 8, 17; s A N Stradley & Anna E Harkins S; m 1942 to Lucille Susan Wampler; c Noranne S (Mrs Newhouse) & Jay Oakley, Jr. Educ: Penns Grove High Sch, NJ. Polit & Govt Pos: Munic leader, Pennsville Rep Club, 52, finance chmn, 53-, pres, 69 & 71; mem finance comt, Salem Co Rep Orgn, NJ, 66; treas, Pennsville Twp, NJ, 69-; committeeman, NJ Rep State Comt, 70- Bus & Prof Pos: Foreman, Chambers Works, E I du Pont de Nemours & Co, 38- Mil Serv: Entered as Pvt, Army, 42, released as T/5, 45, after serv in 88th Inf Div, 5th Army, European-African-Mid Eastern Theatre, 43-45; Bronze Star; Am Serv Medal; European-African-Mid Eastern Serv Medal; Good Conduct Medal. Mem: Am Legion; 88th Inf Div Asn; Boy Scouts Am. Honors & Awards: Silver Beaver, Scout Statuette; Bookends. Relig: Presbyterian. Mailing Add: 37 Oriental Ave Pennsville NJ 08070

STRAHLE, RONALD H (R)
Colo State Rep
b Stanton, Nebr, Dec 16, 21; m to Emma Lue; c Wynn, Ann & Richard. Educ: Univ Nebr, AB, 47, Col Law, JD, 49. Polit & Govt Pos: Mem personal staff of Dwight D Eisenhower, 52-53; Colo state chmn, Youth for Eisenhower, 56; chmn, Larimer Co Rep Cent Comt, 58-66; mem, Colo Rep Cent Comt, 58-, chmn, Second Cong Dist, 60-63; deleg, Rep Nat Conv, 60; bd dirs, United Rep Fund; comnr, Colo Game, Fish & Parks Comn, 63-67; Larimer Co pub trustee, 64-66; Colo State Rep, 67-, asst majority leader, Colo House of Rep, 69-70, minority leader, 75-; mem, Colo Workmen's Compensation Policyholders Adv Comt, 67-69; comnr, Colo Comn on Uniform State Laws, 68-75. Bus & Prof Pos: Self-employed lawyer, Ft Collins, Colo, 54- Mil Serv: Entered Marine Corps, 42, released after serv in US, Cent Pac & China during World War II; spec agt, Counterintel Corps, 50-52. Mem: AF&AM; Colo Wildlife Fedn; Ft Collins Sugar Beet Growers' Asn (secy, 56-); Larimer Co Am Red Cross (former chmn). Honors & Awards: One of fifty legislators in US chosen to attend Rutgers Univ Eagleton Inst seminar for outstanding legislators, 68. Legal Res: 4815 Hogan Dr Ft Collins CO 80521 Mailing Add: United Bank Bldg Ft Collins CO 80521

STRAIN, R H (D)
La State Rep
Mailing Add: Rte 1 Box 7 Abita Springs LA 70420

STRAND, GILMAN A (R)
NDak State Sen
Mailing Add: State Capitol Bismarck ND 58501

STRANG, DEFORREST (R)
Mich State Rep
Mailing Add: Rte 3 Sturgis MI 49091

STRATTON, DAVID (D)
Okla State Sen
Mailing Add: State Capitol Oklahoma City OK 73105

STRATTON, EDITH LOU (R)
VChairwoman, Eighth Cong Dist, Va
b Elk Fork, Ky, Nov 28, 30; d William Roy Hutchinson & Anna Ferguson H; m 1949 to Maj Donald Nelson Stratton; c Donna Lou & Kimberly Ann. Educ: Morehead State Univ, 58-59. Polit & Govt Pos: Vpres, Colonial Rep Women's Club, 68-69; asst precinct capt, Lee Dist, Alexandria, Va, 68-69; vchmn, Lee Magisterial Dist, 70-72, chmn, 72-; mem, Fairfax Co Rep Comt, 70-; vchairwoman, Eighth Cong Dist, Va, 71-; alt deleg, Rep Nat Conv, 72. Mem: Fairfax Co Coun of the Arts; Heart Asn (chmn, Lee Dist, 70-); March of Dimes (chmn, Lee Dist, 73-); Ft Belvoir Officers' Wives Club; Colonial Rep Women's Club (vpres, 68-69, treas, 71-73). Relig: Baptist. Mailing Add: 7432 Berwick Ct Alexandria VA 22310

STRATTON, SAMUEL STUDDIFORD (D)
US Rep, NY
b Yonkers, NY, Sept 27, 16; s Rev Paul Stratton & Ethel Irene Russell S; m 1947 to Joan H Wolfe; c Lisa (Mrs Martin Gonzalez), Debra, Kevin, Kim & Brian. Educ: Univ Rochester, AB, 37; Haverford Col, MA, 38; Harvard Univ, MA, 40; Phi Beta Kappa; Psi Upsilon. Hon Degrees: LLD, Hartwick Col & Col St Rose. Polit & Govt Pos: Exec secy to US Rep Thomas E Eliot, Mass, 41-42; dep secy gen, Far Eastern Comn, Washington, DC, 46-48; councilman, Schenectady, NY, 50-56, mayor, 56-59; US Rep, NY, 59-, mem armed serv comt & chmn mil compensation subcomt, currently. Bus & Prof Pos: Lectr, Union Col & Rensselaer Polytech Inst, 48-54; TV & radio news commentator, Schenectady, 50-56; registered rep, First Albany Corp, 57- Mil Serv: Entered as Ens, Naval Res, 42, released 46; reentered in 51, released in 53 after serv in Korea; Capt, Res, currently. Mem: ROA; Am Legion; VFW; Amvets; Mason. Relig: Presbyterian. Legal Res: 244 Guy Park Ave Amsterdam NY 12010 Mailing Add: Rayburn House Off Bldg Washington DC 20515

STRATTON, WILLIAM GRANT (R)
b Ingleside, Ill, Feb 26, 14; s William J Stratton & Zula Van Wormer S; m 1950 to Shirley Breckenridge; c Nancy Helen, Sandra Gardner & Diana Weiskopf. Educ: Univ Ariz; Delta Chi. Hon Degrees: Univ Ariz, Bradley Univ, Lincoln Mem Univ, Elmhurst, NCent & Shurtleff Col, John Marshall Law Sch, Southern Ill Univ & Lincoln Col. Polit & Govt Pos: US Rep, Ill, 41-43 & 47-49; state treas, Ill, 43-45 & 51-53; Gov, Ill, 53-61; chmn, Nat Gov Conf, 57; mem, Lincoln Sesquicentennial Comn, 58; mem, Fed Adv Comn on Intergovt Rels, 59. Bus & Prof Pos: Vpres, Canteen Corp, 68-; bd mem, Dartnell Corp, 74- Mil Serv: Lt(jg), Navy, 45-46; serv in Pac. Mem: Mason (33 degree); Shrine; Rotary; Am Legion; Amvets. Relig: Methodist. Legal Res: 3240 N Lake Shore Dr Chicago IL 60657 Mailing Add: Canteen Corp 1430 Merchandise Mart Chicago IL 60654

STRAUB, CHESTER JOHN (D)
NY State Sen
b Brooklyn, NY, May 12, 37; m to Patricia Morrissey; c Chester John, Jr, Michael Joseph, Christopher James & Robert Jordan. Educ: St Peter's Col, BA in Arts & Sci; Univ Va, LLD. Polit & Govt Pos: Mem, Pioneer, White Eagle, Polonia, John Smolenski Mem Club & Consolidated Dem Clubs; counsel, NY State Coun of Polish Dem Clubs, formerly; exec mem, Univ Va Young Dem, formerly; personal aide to Sen Robert Kennedy during sen campaign; liaison officer, NY State Dem Comt for Young Citizens for Johnson & Humphrey, formerly; NY State Assemblyman, 35th Dist, 66-72, mem, Judiciary & Ways & Means Comt, ranking minority mem, Joint Legis Comt on Taylor Law & chmn, Assembly Dem Policy Comt, NY State Assembly, formerly; NY State Sen, 73-, mem, Transportation, Ment Hygiene & Addiction Control, Ins & Civil Serv & Pensions Comts, NY State Senate, currently; counsel & chmn law comt, NY State Dem Comt, currently. Bus & Prof Pos: Legal adv, Pulaski Bus & Prof Men's Asn, Inc, formerly; counsel, NY State Coun of Polish Dem Clubs, formerly; attorney-at-law, NY, currently. Mil Serv: 1st Lt, Army Intel & Security Corps, grad from Inf Sch, Intel Sch & Audio-Visual Spanish Lang Sch; additional serv during Berlin & Cuban Missile Crises; Cert of Achievement from Cmndg Gen of the 2nd US Army. Publ: Co-auth, Legal institutions of New York City, Asn of the Bar of City of New York. Mem:

Greenpoint-Williamsburg Health Coun (charter mem); Holy Name Soc, St Stanislaus Kostka Parish (past diocesan deleg); NY League for Histadrut (bd dir); Kosciuszko Found; Sons of Poland. Relig: Catholic. Legal Res: Greenpoint NY 11222 Mailing Add: 678 Manhattan Ave Brooklyn NY 11222

STRAUB, ROBERT W (D)
Gov, Ore
b San Francisco, Calif, May 6, 20; m to Pat; c six. Educ: Dartmouth Col, BA & MBA. Polit & Govt Pos: Comnr, Lane Co, Ore, 55-59; Ore State Sen, 59-63; State Treas, Ore, 64-72; deleg, Dem Nat Conv, 68; Dem nominee for Gov, Ore, 70, Gov, Ore, 75- Bus & Prof Pos: Land developer; farmer; rancher. Mil Serv: World War II. Legal Res: 2087 Orchard Heights Rd NW Salem OR 97304 Mailing Add: State Capitol Salem OR 97310

STRAUB, TERRENCE DAVID (D)
b Springfield, Ill, Dec 13, 45; s Frank B Straub & Elizabeth H O'Brien S; m 1972 to Patricia Lynn Andorn. Educ: Ind Univ, BS, 69; vpres, Ind Univ Young Dem, 68, state pres, Ind Collegiate Young Dem, 68-69. Polit & Govt Pos: Area coordr, Kennedy for President Primaries, Ind & Calif, 68; mem charter comn, Ind Dem Party Reform, 69; Dem nominee, US Rep, Sixth Cong Dist, Ind, 70; state coordr, Conrad for Gov Campaign, 72; deleg, Dem State Conv, 72; deleg, Dem Nat Conv, 72, Floor Whip, Ind Deleg, McGovern for President, 72; dir nat field opers & admin asst to chmn Robert S Strauss, Dem Nat Comt, 73-75. Bus & Prof Pos: Spec asst to Secy State, Ind, 70-72; assoc consult, Matt Reese & Assocs, Washington, DC, 72- Mem: Big Bros Am (bd dirs, Ind Div, 70-72); Am Cancer Soc (bd dirs, 70-72, chmn, Indianapolis Crusade, 71). Honors & Awards: Award of Appreciation, Am Cancer Soc, Ind Div, 72. Relig: Catholic. Legal Res: 4311 E 56th St Indianapolis IN 46220 Mailing Add: 4405 Bradley Lane Chevy Chase MD 20015

STRAUSS, EVELYN M (D)
Secy, Tuscarawas Co Dem Cent Comt, Ohio
b Stone Creek, Ohio, Aug 21, 18; d Charles L Gross & Catherine Rieker G; div; c Ronda L (Mrs Wills), Richard, Colleen (Mrs Watson) & John Jay. Educ: Stone Creek High Sch, grad, 36. Polit & Govt Pos: Mem, Strasburg Village Coun, Ohio; Dem precinct committeewoman, Strasburg; secy, Tuscarawas Co Dem Cent Comt, currently; dep registr, Tuscarawas Co, 71- Mem: Area Civic Asn; Area Dem Women; Sch Bd (secy adv coun). Relig: Protestant. Mailing Add: 144 Third SW Strasburg OH 44680

STRAUSS, ROBERT S (D)
Chmn, Dem Nat Comt
b Lockhart, Tex, Oct 9, 18; s Charles H Strauss & Edith V S; m 1941 to Helen Jacobs; c Robert A, Richard C & Susan. Educ: Univ Tex, LLB, 41. Polit & Govt Pos: Mem bank bd, State of Tex, 63-; Dem Nat Committeeman, Tex, 68-72, mem exec comt, Dem Nat Comt, 69-, treas, 70-72, chmn, 72-; deleg, Dem Nat Mid-Term Conf, 74. Bus & Prof Pos: Attorney, Akin, Gump, Strauss, Hauer & Feld, Attorneys, Dallas, 45-; pres, Strauss Broadcasting Co, 64- Mil Serv: Spec agt, FBI, 41-45. Mem: Tex & Am Bar Asns. Relig: Jewish. Legal Res: 6223 De Loache Dallas TX 75225 Mailing Add: 2800 Republic Nat Bank Bldg Dallas TX 75201

STRAUSZ-HUPE, ROBERT
US Ambassador to Sweden
b Vienna, Austria, Mar 25, 03; s Rudolph Strausz-Hupe & Doris Hedwig S; naturalized, 38; m 1938 to Eleanor deGraff Cuyler. Educ: Univ Pa, AM & PhD, 44. Polit & Govt Pos: US Ambassador to Ceylon & Repub of Maldives, 70-71, US Ambassador to Belgium, 72-74, US Ambassador to Sweden, 74- Bus & Prof Pos: Investment banker, 27-37; assoc ed, Current Hist, 39-41; spec lectr, 40-46; assoc prof polit sci, Univ Pa, 46-52, prof, 52-, dir, Foreign Policy Research Inst, 55-59; lectr, Air War Col, 53. Mil Serv: Lt Col, Army res. Publ: The Zone of Indifference, 52; Power and Community, 56; Protracted Conflict, 58; plus others. Mem: Fel Royal Geog Soc; Am Polit Sci Asn; Coun Foreign Rels; Research Coun Atlantic Inst; Merion Cricket Club, Haverford, Pa. Relig: Lutheran. Legal Res: White Horse Farms Newtown Square PA 19073 Mailing Add: Am Embassy APO New York NY 09667

STRAWN, OLIVER PERRY, JR (R)
Chmn, Montgomery Co Rep Comt, Va
b Martinsville, Va, Nov 30, 25; s Oliver Perry Strawn & Nancy Main S; m 1948 to Ocie Sampson Hurd; c Michael Oliver, Natalie, Ellen Cahill & Perri Johanna. Educ: Va Polytech Inst, MS, 65; Pi Tau Sigma. Polit & Govt Pos: Chmn, Montgomery Co Rep Party, 70- Bus & Prof Pos: Coleman Supply Co, Martinsville, Va, 50-52; Richardson-Wayland Elec Corp, Roanoke, 52-57; Va Polytech Inst & State Univ, Blacksburg, 67-72; self-employed consulting mech engr, 72- Mil Serv: Entered as Seaman 1/C, Navy, 44, released as PO 3/C, 46, after serv in Continental US. Mem: Am Soc Mech Engrs; Am Soc Heating, Refrigerating & Air Conditioning Engrs; Nat Soc Prof Engrs; Lions Int. Relig: Baptist. Mailing Add: 601 Turner St Blacksburg VA 24060

STREET, KEITH MERLIN (D)
b Oskaloosa, Iowa, June 16, 27; s Guilford B Street & Iva L Quaintance S; m 1956 to Elizabeth A Gerst; c Laura, Julia, Sheila & Alisa. Educ: William Penn Col, BA, 49; Western Ill Univ, MS, 66; summers, Iowa State Univ, Univ Denver, Univ Colo, Utah State Univ & Monmouth Col. Polit & Govt Pos: Mem platform comt, Iowa State Dem Party, 70; vchmn, Louisa Co Dem Party, 70-71, chairperson, 71-74. Bus & Prof Pos: Teacher, Oakville, Iowa, 49-51, Clemons, 52-54, Deep River, 54-57 & Wapello, 57- Mil Serv: Entered as Pvt, Army, 45, released as Tech 5, after serv in US, 45-46. Mem: Iowa State & Nat Educ Asns; Mason. Relig: Society of Friends. Mailing Add: 325 Franklin Ave Wapello IA 52653

STREETER, BERNARD A, JR (R)
b Keene, NH, Feb 6, 35; s Bernard A Streeter & Isabella Crane S; m 1958 to Janice Bowman; c Shannon Lea, Christopher Bowman & Stephanie Crane. Educ: Boston Univ, BS, 57; grad work at Boston Univ & Keene State Col; Kappa Phi Alpha; Boston Univ Young Rep Club. Polit & Govt Pos: Pres, Gtr Nashua Young Rep Club, 65-66; vchmn, NH Fedn Young Rep Clubs, 66-70; ward chmn, Nashua City Rep Comt, 67-68; mem, NH Rep State Comt, 68-74; alt deleg, Rep Nat Conv, 68, deleg, 72; mem Gov Coun, Dist 5, NH, 69- Bus & Prof Pos: Vpres, St Johns Hosp, Lowell, Mass. Mil Serv: Entered as Pvt, Army, 57, released as S/Sgt; Res, 7 years. Publ: Short stories & feature articles in various state & regional publ. Mem: Am & Mass Hosp Asns; Gtr Nashua Jaycees; Franklin Pierce Col (pres coun); Merrimack Valley Region Asn. Honors & Awards: Nashua Outstanding Young Man of the Year, 66; NH Outstanding Young Man of the Year, 67. Relig: Methodist. Mailing Add: 26 Indiana Dr Nashua NH 03060

STREETT, JULIAN DUVAL (D)
Ark State Rep
b Camden, Ark, Feb 3, 37; s Johnson Bruce Streett & Gertrude Sanderson S; m to Mary Burns; c Rebecca Louise, Katherine Sanderson, David Julian & Sarah Burns. Educ: Univ Ark, BA, 58 & LLB, 61. Polit & Govt Pos: City attorney, Camden, Ark, 62-64; Ark State Rep, Dist 39, 69- Mil Serv: Entered as E-2, Army Res, 59, released as Sgt E-6, 65. Mem: Am Bar Asn; Ouachita Co Bar Asn (pres, 68-69); Am & Ark Trial Lawyers Asns; Kiwanis. Legal Res: 922 Woodcrest Camden AR 71701 Mailing Add: 139 Jackson St Camden AR 71701

STRELZIN, HARVEY LLOYD (D)
NY State Assemblyman
b New York, NY, July 19, 07; s Abraham Strelzin & Dora Garber S; m 1945 to Marie C Warren; c Paul J, Lynn S (Mrs Pollock), Janyce C & Adrienne M. Educ: Brooklyn Law Sch, LLB, 27; NY Law Sch, LLM summa cum laude, 62 & JSD, 67. Polit & Govt Pos: Asst attorney gen, NY, 33-39; chmn, Bd of Assessors, New York, 55-57; deleg, State Const Conv, 67; NY State Assemblyman, 69- Bus & Prof Pos: Legal ed, Beverage Times, 44-49; lectr, Brooklyn Col, 56; prof law, NY Law Sch, 65-67; prof medico-jurisp, Col Ins, 68-73; columnist weekly newspaper, Williamsburg News & Coney Island Times, 68-, counsel, Spencer Mem Church, Brooklyn Heights, NY, currently. Mem: Brooklyn Bar Asn; NY Co Lawyers Asn; YMHA & YWHA, Williamsburg (pres); Fedn Jewish Philanthropies (bd trustees). Relig: Hebrew. Legal Res: 270 Jay St Brooklyn NY 11201 Mailing Add: 253 Broadway New York NY 10007

STRETCH, D ALLEN, JR (D)
Committeeman, Cape May Co Dem Comt, NJ
b Bridgeton, NJ, June 6, 22; s David A Stretch & Rebecca Johnson S; m 1948 to Marie C Ruggero; c Katherine. Educ: Pratt Inst Technol, 3 years. Polit & Govt Pos: Agent, NJ Motor Vehicle Div, 56-58; city leader, Ocean City, NJ, 57-, mem comt pub safety & comt pub affairs, 59-67, past dir, city comnr, 2 terms, vmayor, 63-67; mem, Beach Erosion Comt, State of NJ, 58-; alt deleg, Dem Nat Conv, 68; mem, Cape May Co Bd Elec, 68-; campaign mgr, Cape May Co Dem Party & Four Co Cong Cand, 70; committeeman, Cape May Co Dem Comt, currently. Bus & Prof Pos: Pres, Bd Realtors, 58; pres, Cape May Co Ins, 59; dir, Ocean City, NJ Bd of Realtors, 60-70; pres, Shore Mem Hosp, 68-69, chmn bd trustees, 70-71, treas, 72-; vpres, Independent Fee Appraisers, 69, state dep dir, 69, state dir, 69-70; treas & nat dir, Nat Asn Independent Fee Appraisers, 73- Mil Serv: Entered as Pvt, Army, 42, released as Sgt, 45, after serv in 2nd Inf Div, ETO, 44-45; Bronze Star; Combat Inf Badge; ETO Ribbon with Three Battle Stars; Colmar Colors. Mem: Am Soc Appraisers (secy, 72-); sr mem Independent Fee Appraisers (appraiser-counr mem); F&AM; Tall Cedars of Lebanon; Shrine. Honors & Awards: Realtor of the Year 1970, Ocean City Bd Realtors. Relig: Baptist. Legal Res: 9 E Edinburgh Rd Ocean City NJ 03226 Mailing Add: 800 Ocean Ave Ocean City NJ 08226

STRICKER, EUKLEY CECIL (R)
Chmn, Haskell Co Rep Party, Okla
b Marshall, Ark, July 10, 07; s Monroe Jackson Stricker & Winnie Melton S; m 1927 to Margaret Elizabeth Waller; c Cecil Elvin & Margie Marie (Mrs Clark). Educ: Cent State Univ, BA, 44; Univ Okla, MEd, 58; Ariz State Univ, 69-70. Polit & Govt Pos: Prin, Red Rock Community Sch, Bur Indian Affairs, US Dept Interior, Shiprock Agency, Ariz, 53-55, prin, Ft Defiance Boarding Sch, 55-60, prin, Tuba City Boarding Sch, Tuba City & Kayenta, Ariz, 60-70, educ specialist-training, Nat Indian Training Ctr, Brigham City, Utah, 70-72; co supt schs, Haskell Co, Stigler, Okla, 75-; chmn, Haskell Co Rep Party, Okla, 75- Bus & Prof Pos: Prin-teacher, Caddo Co Schs, Anadarko, Okla, 30-42; prin, Gracemont High Sch, Okla, 42-44; supt schs, Washita High Sch, Okla, 44-47; salesman maps & sch supplies, A J Nystrom Co, Chicago, Ill, 47-53. Mem: Nat & Okla Educ Asns; Nat Fedn Independent Bus; Mason (32 degree, Guthrie Consistory, Okla); Shrine (El Zaribah Temple, Phoenix). Honors & Awards: US Dept Interior Hon Award for Meritorious Serv, 73. Mailing Add: Rte 4 Box 83 Stigler OK 74462

STRICKLAND, TED L (R)
Colo State Sen
b Austin, Tex, Sept 17, 32; s George H Strickland & Ethel Pliler S; m 1957 to Lu Anne Peckham. Educ: Okla State Univ, 2 years; Univ Denver, 1 year. Polit & Govt Pos: Block worker, Adams Co Rep Party, 63-64, precinct committeeman, 64-67; pres, Adams Co Young Rep, 64-67; Colo State Rep, 66-67; Colo State Sen, 68- Bus & Prof Pos: Asst vpres, Rocky Mountain Well Log Serv, 67- Mil Serv: Entered as Pvt, Army, 52, released as Cpl, 54, after serv in 3rd Armored Div. Mem: Rocky Mountain Asn Geologists; Denver Well Logging Soc; Denver Land Man's Asn. Honors & Awards: Faith in God Award, Jaycees. Relig: Baptist. Mailing Add: 9361 Knox Ct Westminster CO 80030

STRICKLAND, THOMAS EDWARD (D)
NC State Sen
b Goldsboro, NC, June 16, 30; s Willie Strickland & Weltha Dail S; m 1953 to Shirley T Lancaster; c Larry Thomas & Ruth Ann. Educ: Univ NC, AB in Polit Sci, 52; Wake Forest Law Sch, LLB, 55; Phi Delta Phi. Polit & Govt Pos: Chmn sch adv comt, New Hope, NC, 62-66; mem, Wayne Co Dem Exec Comt, 62-66; Dem precinct chmn, Saulston Twp, 62-66; mem judiciary comt, Dem Party, 64-66; NC State Rep, 66-70; NC State Sen, 71- Bus & Prof Pos: Attorney-at-law, self employed, 57-59; partner, Braswell & Strickland, Law Firm, Goldsboro, NC, 59-68 & Braswell, Strickland, Merritt & Rouse, 68- Mil Serv: Entered as Cpl, Marine Corps, 55, released as 1st Lt, 57, after serv as legal officer, Judge Adv Gen Dept. Mem: Mason; Elks; Wayne Co Wildlife Club; Odd Fellows; WOW. Honors & Awards: Robert H Futrelle Good Govt Award. Relig: Methodist. Mailing Add: Rte 2 Goldsboro NC 27530

STRIDER, DONALD BURT (D)
Miss State Sen
b Rosebloom, Miss, Mar 28, 29; s Henry Clarence Strider & Wilma Burt S; m 1959 to Sue Holland; c John Edward, Emily (Mrs Champion), Suzanne (Mrs Walker), Delores (Mrs Roberson), Donald Burt, Jr, Rene (Mrs Mullen), Edward Neal & Trent Conrad. Educ: Miss State Univ, 1 year; Univ Miss, 1 year; Delta State Col, BA; Kappa Alpha. Polit & Govt Pos: Dep sheriff, Tallahatchie Co, Miss, 52-56; mem, Miss Game & Fish Comn, State of Miss, 63 & 64; Miss State Sen, Grenada & Tallahatchie Co, 71- Bus & Prof Pos: Owner, Donald Strider Farm, 54-; partner, Strider Bros Farm, 62- & Strider Bros Store, 68-; pres, Webb Gin Co & Strider Acad, currently. Mil Serv: Entered as Pvt, Army, 46, released as Sgt, 47, after serv in 24th Inf Div, APTO, 46-47; World War II Victory Medal; Good Conduct Medal; Citation of Merit. Mem: VFW; Am Legion; Nat Farmers Orgn; Moose; Lions. Relig: Methodist. Mailing Add: Rte 2 Charleston MS 38921

STRINDEN, EARL STANFORD (R)
NDak State Rep
b Litchville, NDak, Nov 28, 31; s Teddie Isaac Strinden & Martha Eidsvig S; m 1953 to Janice Semmens; c Ronda Marie, Jon Earl, Karen Ann, Thomas Isaac & Elizabeth Joy. Educ: Concordia Col, Moorhead, Minn, BA, 53; Univ NDak, MA, 57. Polit & Govt Pos: Mem city coun, Grand Forks, NDak, 62-72, pres, 66-68; NDak State Rep, 67-, Asst Majority Floor Leader, NDak House Rep, 69- Bus & Prof Pos: Teacher, Thief River Falls, Minn, 58-59; retail mgr, Strinden's Hardware, 59-69; alumni dir, Univ NDak, 69. Mil Serv: Entered as Pvt, Marines, 53, released as 1st Lt, 55, after serv in 3rd Marines, Far East, 54-55. Mem: Rotary; VFW; Am Legion; Elks. Honors & Awards: Jaycees Outstanding Young Man of Year, Grand Forks. Relig: Lutheran. Legal Res: 2812 Chestnut Grand Forks ND 58201 Mailing Add: State Capitol Bismarck ND 58501

STRINDEN, THERON L (R)
NDak State Sen
Mailing Add: State Capitol Bismarck ND 58501

STRINGER, CLARENCE MAINE (R)
Mem, San Mateo Co Rep Cent Comt, Calif
b Park City, Utah, June 11, 19; s Myron M Stringer & Alva Barton S; m 1947 to Lolita Keating; c Clay M & Victoria Ann. Educ: Golden Gate Col, Bus, 4 years, Mgt Develop, 1 year; Am Sch of Law, LLB. Polit & Govt Pos: Rep precinct chmn, Fifth Dist, Calif, 62-72; mem, Rep State Cent Comt Calif, 62-72; pres, NPeninsula Chap, Calif Rep Assembly, 63-65, pres, Daly City, Colma Chap, 66-67; mem, San Mateo Co Rep Cent Comt, 63-; foreman, Grand Jury, San Mateo Co, 64; mem, United Rep Finance Comt, 66-72. Bus & Prof Pos: Sr right-of-way agent, Pac Gas & Elec Co, 55-62, supvr spec assignments, 62-65, supvr, fee & spec acquisition, 65-68 & 69-, supv off engr, 68-69, supvr of land acquisition, 69- Mil Serv: Entered as Pvt, Army, 43, released as 1st Lt, 46, after serv in Amphibious Corps, 1st Brigade, E B & S R, Pac Theatre, 43-45; Asiatic Campaign Medal; Philippine Liberation Medal; Bronze Arrowhead with One Silver & Two Bronze Stars; World War II Victory Medal. Mem: Pac Coast Elec Asn; Pac Coast Gas Asn; Licensed Real Estate Broker, State of Calif; Westlake Cath Men's Club; St Francis Retreat League. Relig: Catholic. Mailing Add: 80 Parkwood Dr Daly City CA 94015

STRINGER, QUIN EMERSON, JR (D)
Miss State Sen
Mailing Add: Rte 1 Box 404 Columbia MS 39429

STRIPP, JANE DEARBORN (R)
Pres, Wash State Fedn Rep Women
b Seattle, Wash, May 21, 23; d Frank Wilbur Dearborn & Gertrude Lunbeck D; m 1944 to William Clayton Stripp, Jr; c Michael William & Rebecca Jane. Educ: Univ Wash, 41-44; Delta Delta Delta. Polit & Govt Pos: Pres, Assoc Rep Women, 62-64; legis chmn, Wash State Fedn Rep Women, 62-66, first dist dir, 66-69, second vpres, 69-70, first vpres, 70-71, pres, 71-; vchmn, King Co Cent Comt, Wash, 64; campaign coordr, Sen Campaign, 64; alt deleg, Rep Nat Conv, 64. Bus & Prof Pos: Partner, Wedding Consultants, 68- Mem: Nat & Wash State Asns of Parliamentarians; PTA; Overlake Hosp Asn; Orthopedic Hosp Asn. Relig: Presbyterian. Mailing Add: 1626 98th Ave NE Bellevue WA 98004

STROBEL, KATHARYN ANN (KAY) (D)
Secy, Tenth Dem Dist Party, Mo
b Bell City, Mo, June 2, 38; d Walter Wayne Arnold & Della Mae Thompson A; m 1959 to Larry Gene Strobel; c Kim JoNay, Larry Gene, II & Katrina Clema. Educ: Bell City Sch, 12 years. Polit & Govt Pos: DAECO Bd Mem, Bell City, Mo, 66-69; DAECO Co Bd Mem, Bloomfield, 66-67; committeewoman, Pike Twp Dem Party, 66-; headstart bd mem, Bell City, 68-70; headstart community rep, 69-71; secy, Tenth Dem Dist Party, 70-; vchmn, Stoddard Co Dem Comt, formerly; collector, Pile Twp, 71- Relig: Catholic. Mailing Add: Bell City MO 63735

STROBLE, ROBERT EUGENE (R)
Md State Sen
b Williamsport, Pa, May 14, 40; s Paul Kenneth Stroble, Sr & Eleanor Lucille Tudor S; m 1965 to Patricia Carroll Mullen; c Shannan Christopher, Timothy Scott & Ryan Matthew. Educ: Lock Haven State Col, BS, 63; Loyola Col (Md), MEd, 67; Morgan State Col, MS, 70; Univ Md, PhD, 75; Tau Kappa Epsilon. Polit & Govt Pos: Md State Deleg, Third Dist, Baltimore Co, 71-74; Md State Sen, 11th Dist, Baltimore Co, 75- Bus & Prof Pos: Educator, Baltimore Co Schs, Md, 63- Mem: Phi Delta Kappa. Relig: Christian. Mailing Add: 1839 Locust Ridge Rd Lutherville-Timonium MD 21093

STROEDE, ARTHUR BRIAN, III (D)
Chmn, Ozaukee Co Dem Party, Wis
b Milwaukee, Wis, June 24, 46; s Arthur G Stroede, Jr & Ruth Strube S; single. Educ: Milwaukee Area Tech Col, tool & die apprentice, 2 years; Univ Wis-Milwaukee, 70-75. Polit & Govt Pos: Chmn, Ozaukee Co Dem Party, Wis, 74- Bus & Prof Pos: Machinist specialist, Mercury Marine, 64-67, apprentice tool & die maker, 67-72 & journeyman tool & die maker, 72- Mem: IAMAW (chmn apprenticeship comt, Local Lodge 20, 74-75); Cedarburg Firehouse Fine Arts (sustaining mem, 74-75). Legal Res: 5520 W Pleasant Dr 113 N Mequon WI 53092 Mailing Add: 2977 N Downer Ave Milwaukee WI 53211

STROM, SHIRLEY LONGETEIG (R)
Committeewoman, Idaho State Rep Party
b Craigmont, Idaho, Jan 28, 31; d Iver J Longeteig & Frances W Mason L; m 1952 to Robert C Strom; c Kristin, Trina & Camber. Educ: Univ Idaho, BA, 52. Polit & Govt Pos: Committeewoman, Idaho State Rep Party, 54-; Justice of the Peace, Lewis Co, Idaho, 67-71; mem, Planning & Zoning Comt, City of Craigmont, 71-73, chairperson, 73-; Lewis Co chmn, Comt to Reelect the President, 72; deleg, Rep Nat Conv, 72; state pres, Idaho Women's Polit Caucus, 74-75. Bus & Prof Pos: Opinion researcher, Response Anal, 71- Mem: Pi Gamma Mu; Nat Orgn for Women; DAR (state honor roll chmn, 70-73); Eastern Star; Idaho Hist Soc. Relig: Presbyterian. Mailing Add: 608 Villard St Craigmont ID 83523

STROMBERG, VERNON S (R)
Mem, RI Rep State Cent Comt
b Seekonk, Mass, Jan 23, 16; m to Josephine M DeCedric; c Vernon, Jr. Educ: East Providence Pub Sch. Polit & Govt Pos: RI State Rep, 65-74, mem, Comt on Spec Legis, RI State House of Rep, formerly, mem, Joint Comt on Accounts & Claims, RI Gen Assembly, formerly; mem, Rep State Cent Comt, 66-; mem, East Providence Rep City Comt. Bus & Prof Pos: With Bird & Sons. Mem: Audubon Soc RI; Big Brothers of RI, Inc (bd mem); East Providence Animal Welfare Soc (exec bd); Local 878 United Paperworkers Int Union, AFL-CIO (trustee); Lions. Mailing Add: 6 Leahy St Rumford RI 12916

STROMER, DELWYN DEAN (R)
Iowa State Rep
b Garner, Iowa, Apr 22, 30; s Aaron Arthur Stromer & Ruby Goll S; m 1950 to Harriet June Ostendorf; c Linda (Mrs Doug Upmeyer), Randall, Pamela & David. Educ: High sch grad. Polit & Govt Pos: Precinct committeeman, Liberty Twp, Iowa, 60-70; Iowa State Rep, Hancock Co, 66-71, Ninth Dist, 71-, asst majority floor leader & chmn, Educ Comt, Iowa House of Rep, currently. Mil Serv: Entered as Pvt, Army, 53, released as Sgt 1/C, 55, after serv in 538th Field Artil Bn, Camp Carson, Colo; Good Conduct Medal; Nat Serv Ribbon. Mem: Am Legion; Farm Bur; Boy's 4-H Leader. Relig: United Church of Christ. Mailing Add: RR 3 Garner IA 50438

STROMER, GERALD ALLEN (R)
b Hastings, Nebr, Dec 25, 42; s Delbert Lavern Stromer & Elsie Mary Juedeman S; single. Educ: Kearney State Col, BA Educ, 65, MS Educ, 66; Mu Epsilon Nu (nat bd gov); Xi Phi; Pi Gamma Mu; Sigma Tau Delta; Alpha Psi Omega; Pi Kappa Delta; Beta Sigma Psi. Polit & Govt Pos: Chmn, Buffalo Co Young Rep, Nebr, 67; deleg, Nebr Rep Conv, 68, 70 & 72; committeeman, Precinct 3-2, Kearney, 68; mem, Steering Comt Nixon for President, Buffalo Co, 68; deleg, Nat Young Rep Conv, 69, 71 & 73; secy, Nebr Fedn Young Rep, 69, nat committeeman, 70, chmn, 71-74, chmn nat leadership conf, 74; treas, Buffalo Co Young Rep, 70; Nebr State Sen, 36th Dist, 71-74, mem, Nebr Rep Platform Comt, 72-; deleg, Rep Nat Conv, 72; US deleg, Atlantic Treaty Asn, Brussels, 73; chmn, Buffalo Co Rep Cent Comt, Nebr; mem adv comt, Nat Right-to-Work Comt; mem, Nebr Rep Cent Comt; mem nat adv comt, VIVA. Bus & Prof Pos: Acad counr, Kearney State Col, 66-70; pub rels consult, currently; pres, Pioneer Agr Inc; mem adv bd, Midwest Conf World Affairs, currently. Mem: Cent Platte Natural Resource Dist (bd dirs); Rotary; Nebr Coun Econ Educ (bd trustees); Midland Lutheran Col (bd trustees, 73-); Elks. Honors & Awards: Area contest winner, Toastmasters; Outstanding Young Men of Am, 71 & 74; Nebr Personnel & Guid Asn Serv Award, 71 & 74; 4-H Alumni Award. Relig: Lutheran; Evangelism comt, Nebr Synod, Lutheran Church Am, youth leadership comt, lay pulpit supply. Mailing Add: PO Box 511 Kearney NE 68847

STRONG, JAMES R (R)
Mo State Rep
Mailing Add: 1006 Fairmount Blvd Jefferson City MO 65101

STRONG, ROBERT CAMPBELL (INDEPENDENT)
b Chicago, Ill, Sept 29, 15; m to Betty Jane Burton; c three. Educ: Beloit Col, AB magna cum laude, 38; Univ Wis, 38-39; Phi Beta Kappa. Hon Degrees: LLD, Beloit Col, 67. Polit & Govt Pos: Career officer, US Dept of State Foreign Serv, 39-72; vconsul, Frankfurt, 39, Prague, 39-40, Durban, 40-44 & Sofia, 44-46; Naval War Col, 46-47; consul, Tsingtao, 47-49; first secy & charge d'affaires, Canton, Chunking, 49; first secy & charge d'affaires, Taipei, 49-50; spec asst to dir, Off of Chinese Affairs, 50-51; regional personnel dir, Far East, 51-52; mem, Policy Planning Staff, 52-53; asst opers coordr, Off Undersecy, 53-54; consul & counr, Damascus, 54-58; Army War Col, 58-61; dir, Off of Near Eastern Affairs, 61-63; US Ambassador to Iraq, 63-67. Bus & Prof Pos: Diplomat-in-residence & prof polit sci & hist, Univ Okla, 67-68. Mem: Tucson Urban League (pres, 71-72, treas, 72-). Honors & Awards: Received State Dept Superior Serv Award, 59 & Nat Civil Serv League Award, 65. Mailing Add: 826 W Cresta Loma Dr Tucson AZ 85704

STRONG, ROBERT CHATMAN, JR (D)
b Shreveport, La, Sept 21, 51; s Robert Chatman Strong, Sr & Dorothy Nell Creech S; single. Educ: Panola Jr Col, grad, 71; Univ Tex, Austin, BA, 73; Pi Sigma Alpha; Pi Beta; Phi Theta Kappa. Polit & Govt Pos: Mem staff, Gov Preston Smith of Tex, 71-72; chmn precinct deleg of Joaquin, Tex to County Conv, 72; state deleg, Dem Conv of Tex, summer & fall 72, chmn Shelby Co deleg & precinct deleg, State Dem Conv, 74; alt deleg, Dem Nat Conv, 72. Relig: Baptist. Mailing Add: Rte 1 Box 30 Joaquin TX 75954

STRONG, WALTER (D)
Ky State Sen
Mailing Add: Rte 1 Beattyville KY 41311

STROOCK, THOMAS F (R)
Chmn, Wyo Rep State Comt
b New York, NY, Oct 10, 25; s Samuel Stroock & Dorothy Frank S; m 1949 to Marta Freyre de Andrade; c Margaret, Sandra, Betty & Anne. Educ: Yale Univ, BA, 48; York Hall. Polit & Govt Pos: Vpres, Wyo State Young Rep, 52; alt deleg, Rep Nat Conv, 56; chmn, Casper City Parks Comn, 56-60; precinct committeeman, 60-62; mem, Natrona Co Rep Cent Comt, 62; pres, Natrona Co High Sch Dist & Dist Two, 63 & 66; mem, Wyo State Rep Cent Comt, 64; finance chmn, Gov Comt on Educ, 64-66; pres, Wyo Sch Bd Asns, 65-66; Wyo State Sen, Natrona Co, 67-74; chmn, Gov Comt on Employ of Wyo Youth, 67-68 & Wyo Higher Educ Coun, 69; cand for US Rep, 74; chmn, Wyo Rep State Comt, 75- Bus & Prof Pos: Pres, The Stroock Leasing Corp, 52-; sr partner, Stroock & Rogers, 60-; dir, Great Plains Life Ins Co, 65-, Mid Am Life Ins Co & Security Bank & Trust Co, 66-; mem, Nat Petrol Coun. Mil Serv: Entered as Pvt, Marine Corps, 43, released as Sgt, 46, after serv in Continental US & Pac Theater Opers; Marine Corps Res. Mem: Rocky Mountain Oil & Gas Asn (vpres, 65-); Elks; Kiwanis; Am Legion; Casper Country Club. Relig: Unitarian. Legal Res: 714 W 19th St Casper WY 82601 Mailing Add: PO Box 2875 Casper WY 82601

STROSCHEIN, SHARON MARIE (D)
Pres, SDak Fedn Dem Women
b Aberdeen, SDak, Sept 20, 44; d William A Raetzman & Ethel L MacAllen R; m 1965 to Larry L Stroschein; c Amy Lynne, Ryan William & Lon Edward. Educ: Northern State Col, Teaching Cert, 64; Lutheran Student Asn; Student Educ Asn; Young Dem; Beta Sigma Phi. Polit & Govt Pos: Precinct committeewoman, Brown Co Dem Party, SDak, 70-; chmn, Brown Co Fedn Dem Women, 72-; mem exec bd, SDak Dem Party, 74; pres, SDak Fedn Dem Women, 74- Bus & Prof Pos: Elem teacher, Warner Schs, SDak, 66-68, elem music teacher, 71-74. Mem: Nat Farmers Orgn (dist rep, 73-); Cowbelles; Farmer's Union; PTA. Honors & Awards: Gtr SDak Asn Soil & Moisture Award, 67; Farm Family of Year, Farmers Home Admin, 72. Relig: Lutheran. Mailing Add: RR 1 Mansfield SD 57460

STROUD, WILLIAM HUGH (R)
SC State Rep
b Greenville, SC; s George Thurmond Stroud & Luna Freeman S; m 1940 to Dorothy Donald Harris; c Toni Donne & William Hugh, Jr. Educ: Furman Univ, BS, 38; Chi Beta Phi. Polit & Govt Pos: SC State Rep, 67- Bus & Prof Pos: Food broker & owner, W H Stroud Co; teacher biol, high sch, 41-43. Mil Serv: Entered as A/S, Naval Res, 44, released as Lt, 46, after serv in Pac; Lt (Ret), Naval Res, 58; Am Area Ribbon; Asiatic-Pac Area Ribbon with 2 stars; Philippine Liberation Ribbon. Mem: Nat Food Brokers Asn; Piedmont Food Brokers Asn; Rotary; Elks. Relig: Methodist. Legal Res: RR 2 Piedmont SC 29673 Mailing Add: PO Box 5985 Sta B Greenville SC 29606

STROUP, MARK JAMES (D)
Mem, Cobb Co Dem Exec Comt, Ga
b Marietta, Ga, Apr 21, 56; s Norvel James Stroup & June Goggins S; single. Educ: Ga State Univ, currently, pres, Freshman Class 4000, 74. Polit & Govt Pos: Aide, Congressman John W Davis, Ga, 74; mem, Cobb Co Dem Exec Comt, 74-; vchmn, Cobb Co Dem Campaign Comt, 74; deleg, Dem Nat Mid-Term Conf, 74; mem state affirmative action comt, Dem Party Ga, 74; admin asst to Majority Leader, Ga State Senate, currently. Bus & Prof Pos: Staff mem, Southern Acceptance Corp, 72-74. Mem: Jaycees. Honors & Awards: Cobb Co Youth Leadership Award, Elks, 74; Joseph Wheeler High Sch Hall of Fame, 74. Relig: Roman Catholic. Mailing Add: 2497 Sewell Mill Rd Marietta GA 30062

STROUP, ROBERT LEE (R)
NDak State Sen
b Stanton, NDak, June 17, 15; s Robert Martin Stroup & Margaret Adams S; m 1939 to Lillian R Pridt; c Robyn Jean (Mrs Edmund Vinje), Robert L, II, M James, Larry J, Thomas Allen & Elizabeth Ann. Educ: Concordia Col, Moorhead, Minn, BA, 37; Pi Kappa Delta. Polit & Govt Pos: Park comnr, Hazen Park Bd, NDak, 52-; NDak State Sen, 66- Bus & Prof Pos: Secy, Stanton Grain Co, Stanton, NDak, 39-; pres, Hazen Lumber Co, Hazen, 47-; secy, Sunrise Homes Inc, 65- Mem: NDak Law Enforcement Coun; Mercer Co Planning Comn; Mason; Elks; Soc of Am Mil Engrs. Honors & Awards: Named Boss of the Year, Hazen Jr CofC, 67. Relig: Lutheran. Mailing Add: 317 E Fourth St Hazen ND 58545

STROUP, STANLEY G (R)
b Somerset City, Pa, Sept 18, 02; s Samuel D Stroup & Blanche N S; m to La Rue Kathleen Robinson; c Gordon E Esquire & Kathleen A Riggs. Educ: Juniata Col; Pa State Col; Univ Pittsburgh; Dickinson Sch of Law. Polit & Govt Pos: Pa State Rep, 54-60; Pa State Sen, 60-74; alt deleg, Rep Nat Conv, 68, deleg, 72. Bus & Prof Pos: Former teacher, athletic coach & prin; pres, Keystone Army & Navy Schs; attorney, Dept of Justice, 47-54; partner law firm, Stroup & Stroup. Mil Serv: War Serv Dir, Army & Navy Radio Training Sta, 41-46. Mem: Rotary; Am Judicature Soc; Mason; Univ Club of Pittsburgh; Mem Hosp of Bedford City (dir). Relig: St John's Reformed Church, Bedford. Mailing Add: RD 2 Bedford PA 15222

STROUSE, RONALD LEE (R)
b Doylestown, Pa, Dec 15, 47; s Lester Donald Strouse & Lena Godown S; single. Educ: Sch Govt, Am Univ, 69; NY Univ Law Sch, 69-70. Polit & Govt Pos: Admin asst to US Rep Edward G Biester, Jr, Pa, 71- Bus & Prof Pos: Corp risk analyst, Pfizer Inc, New York, 69-71. Mem: Am Polit Sci Asn; Ripon Soc. Relig: Lutheran. Legal Res: Church School Rd RD 4 Doylestown PA 18901 Mailing Add: Off of Hon Edward G Biester Jr US House of Rep Washington DC 20515

STROUT, DONALD A (R)
Maine State Rep
Mailing Add: Box 167 East Corinth Corinth ME 04427

STRUCKMEYER, FRED C, JR (D)
Justice, Ariz Supreme Court
b Phoenix, Ariz, Jan 4, 12; s Fred C Struckmeyer, Sr & Inez Walker S; m 1948 to Margaret Mills; c Chris, Jan Holly, Karl Larson & Kent Mills. Educ: Univ Ariz Col Law, LLB, 36. Polit & Govt Pos: Trial judge, Maricopa Co Superior Court, Ariz, 4 years; justice, Ariz Supreme Court, 55-, chief justice, 60-61, 66 & 71. Mil Serv: Army Inf, 4 years, released as 1st Lt; Bronze Star; Silver Star; Purple Heart. Honors & Awards: Distinguished Serv Award, Gtr Phoenix Coun for Civic Unity, 55; 75th Anniversary Cert of Award, 60, Medallion of Merit, Univ Ariz, Distinguished Citizen Award, 75. Relig: Episcopal. Legal Res: 7151 N Third St Phoenix AZ 85020 Mailing Add: 213 West Wing Capitol Bldg Phoenix AZ 85007

STUART, DOUGLAS S (R)
Mem, Abington Town Rep Comt, Mass
b Eustis, Maine, Oct 23, 25; s E Allen Stuart & Mary Knapp S; m 1948 to Elizabeth Fairbanks Hall; c Douglas S, Jr, Anne Elizabeth, Jonathan Lincoln & Heidi Johanna. Educ: Northeastern Univ. Polit & Govt Pos: Mem, Abington Town Rep Comt, Mass, currently, chmn & vchmn, formerly; mem & chmn, Abington Bd of Park Comn, 7 years; coordr, Plymouth Co Cong Elec & Gov John A Volpe Campaign Comt; co coordr, Mass Buckley for Auditor Comt; coordr, Wm Weeks for Cong Comt, 70; coordr, Sargent Dwight for Gov Comt, 70. Bus & Prof Pos: Mem bd of dirs, Abington Scholar Found Comt. Mil Serv: Entered as Pvt, Army, 44, released as Cpl, 44, after serv in 75th Inf Div. Mem: Nat Off Furniture Dealers Asn. Relig: First Parish Church; Mem adv comt. Mailing Add: 151 Myers Ave Abington MA 02351

STUART, EUGENE PAGE (R)
Ky State Sen
b Louisville, Ky, Oct 20, 27; s Eugene Griffin Stuart & Mary Belle Page S; m 1955 to Mary Dannenhold; c Eugene Page, Jr. Educ: Univ Louisville, BS in Mkt, 51; Sigma Chi. Polit & Govt Pos: Ky State Rep, 48th Legis Dist, 64-73, minority whip, Ky House Rep, 70-71, Rep caucus chmn, 72-73; Ky State Sen, 74-, minority floor leader, Ky State Senate, currently. Mil Serv: Entered as A/S, Navy, 46, released as Seaman 1/C, 48. Mem: Louisville Bd of Ins Agents; Jr CofC (past pres); CofC; Louisville Zool Comn (vpres). Honors & Awards: Outstanding Young Man in Louisville & Jefferson Co, 63. Relig: Episcopal. Legal Res: 6403 Coventry Ct Prospect KY 40059 Mailing Add: Starks Bldg Louisville KY 40202

STUART, GEORGE B (R)
Chmn, Cumberland Co Rep Party, Pa
b Carlisle, Pa, July 31, 12; s Walter Stuart, Jr & Laura Peffer S; single. Educ: Univ Pa, BS in Econ, 34; Dickinson Sch of Law, LLB, 38; Theta Chi. Polit & Govt Pos: Mem, Pa State Labor Rels Bd, formerly; solicitor, Middlesex Twp & Cumberland Co, currently; chmn, Cumberland Co Rep Party, currently; chmn, Zoning Bd Adjust, Carlisle, currently; past trial examr, Pub Utilities Comn; past solicitor, South Middleton Twp, Dickinson Twp, East Pennsboro Twp, North Middleton Twp, Hampden Twp & Mt Holly Springs. Mil Serv: Entered Army, 42, released 45, after serv in Off Strategic Serv, Supreme Hq, AEF, ETO, 42-45; Bronze Star. Mem: VFW; Am Legion. Relig: Protestant; Former treas, First Presby Church, trustee, currently. Legal Res: 201 S Pitt St Carlisle PA 17013 Mailing Add: 3 S Hanover St Carlisle PA 17013

STUART, JAMES GLOVER (D)
Chmn, Monroe Co Dem Exec Comt, Ga
b Monroe Co, Ga, Feb 29, 28; s Preston Stuart & Fannie Lee Allen S; m 1951 to Margaret Evelyn Ham; c Margaret Yvonne, Leigh Celeste, James Stanley & Gina Lynn. Educ: High Sch. Polit & Govt Pos: Mem, Local Selective Serv Bd 106, Ga, 66-; chmn, Monroe Co Dem Exec Comt, 72- Mil Serv: Entered as Recruit, Army, 50, released as Sgt 1/C, 53, after serv in 27th Regt Combat Team, Korea, 51; Purple Heart & 1 Cluster; 3 Presidential Unit Citations. Mem: IBEW (field rep); Am Legion; Ga Cattlemen's Asn. Relig: Baptist. Mailing Add: PO Box 8 Smarr GA 31086

STUART, ROBERT D, JR (R)
b Hubbard Woods, Ill, Apr 26, 16; s Robert Douglas Stuart & Harriet McClure S; m 1938 to Barbara McMath Edwards; c Robert Douglas, III, James McClure, Marian McClure (Mrs Donaldson C Pillsbury) & Alexander Douglas. Educ: Princeton Univ, BA, 37; Yale Law Sch, LLB, 46. Polit & Govt Pos: Pres, Lake Co Rep Fedn & precinct committeeman, Ill, 62-64; twp auditor, Lake Co, Ill, 62-64; Rep Nat Committeeman, Ill, formerly; deleg, Rep Nat Conv, 68 & 72. Bus & Prof Pos: With Quaker Oats Co, 47-, pres, 62-; dir, Continental Assurance Co & Continental Casualty Co, 56-; dir, First Nat Bank of Chicago, 65-, CNA Financial Corp, 67-, United Air Lines, 68-, First Chicago Corp, 69- & UAL, Inc, 69- Mil Serv: Entered as 2nd Lt, Army, 42, released as Maj, 46. Relig: Presbyterian. Legal Res: 1601 W Conway Rd Lake Forest IL 60045 Mailing Add: 345 Merchandise Mart Chicago IL 60654

STUBBEMAN, DAVID (D)
Tex State Rep
Mailing Add: 1241 S Leggett Dr Abilene TX 79605

STUBBLEFIELD, FRANK A (D)
b Murray, Ky, Apr 5, 07; married; c three. Educ: Univ Ky Col of Com, BS. Polit & Govt Pos: US Rep, Ky, 58-74; ex officio, Dem Nat Mid-Term Conf, 74. Bus & Prof Pos: Retail drug bus. Mem: KY RR Comn. Mailing Add: Murray KY 42071

STUBBLEFIELD, GUY (D)
Ill State Sen
Mailing Add: 1812 Kilburn Ave Rockford IL 61103

STUBBS, ARCHIE ROY (R)
Secy, SC Rep Party
b Gloucester Co, Va, Nov 25, 10; s James Monroe Stubbs, Sr & Alma Harriett Roy S; m 1937 to Marion Elizabeth Hoffmann; c Jon Archer, Kent Parker & Carl Roy. Educ: Col of William & Mary, class of 31. Polit & Govt Pos: Pres of precinct, Greenville Co Rep Party, SC, 62-64, secy, 62-66; mem, Greenville Co Exec Comt, 64-; secy, SC Rep Party, 65-; Presidential Elector for Nixon, 68; deleg, Rep Nat Conv, 72. Bus & Prof Pos: Home off, Independence Indemnity Co, Philadelphia, 31-33; adjuster, Liberty Mutual Ins Co, Boston & Providence, 33-36; adjuster, Am Mutual Liability Ins Co, Chicago, 36 & 37; SC mgr, Kemper Ins Group, 37- Publ: Address as Ins Indust Rep on the Commemoration Day Prog, 30th Anniversary of the SC Workmen's Compensation Law, 9/3/65, now appearing in book form publ by the SC Indust Comn. Mem: Inter-Co Arbitration Comt; Columbia Claim Mgr Coun; Exchange Club of Greenville; SC Rifle & Pistol Asn (vpres & dir, 67-); Greenville Little Theatre. Relig: First Presbyterian. Mailing Add: 405 McDonald Ave Greenville SC 29609

STUBBS, ROBERT G (R)
Maine State Rep
b Augusta, Maine, June 9, 32; s Robert G Stubbs & Marion Brainerd; m 1961 to Sharon L. Educ: Bowdoin Col, BA, 59; Delta Kappa Epsilon. Polit & Govt Pos: Chmn bd trustees, Hallowell Water Dist, 71-72; mayor, Hallowell, Maine, 72-; pres, Maine Conf Mayors, 73-74; committeeman, Maine Rep State Comt, 72-; Maine State Rep, 75- Bus & Prof Pos: Reviewing appraiser, Maine State Highway Comn, 62-71; real estate appraiser, self-employed, 71-75. Mil Serv: Entered as Pvt, Army, 53, released as Spec 3/C, 56, after serv in Signal Corps, Third Army, 53-56. Mem: Am Legion (Past Comdr); Am Right of Way Asn; Elks. Relig: Congregational. Legal Res: 2 Pleasant St Hallowell ME 04347 Mailing Add: City Hall Hallowell ME 04347

STUCKEY, WILLIAMSON SYLVESTER, JR (D)
US Rep, Ga
b Dodge Co, Ga, May 25, 35; s Williamson Sylvester Stuckey & Ethel Mullis S; m 1963 to Ethelynn McMillan; c Williamson Sylvester III, Stuart Ann, Scott Maloy, Stephanie Ethel & Jay Gould Williamson. Educ: Univ Ga, BBA, LLB; Sigma Alpha Epsilon; Phi Delta Phi. Polit & Govt Pos: US Rep, Eighth Dist, Ga, 67- Bus & Prof Pos: Exec vpres, Stuckey's Inc, Eastman, Ga, 59-66; pres, Stuckey Timberland, Eastman, Ga, 65- Mem: Gridiron Secret Soc; Rotary; Elks; Mason. Relig: Episcopal. Legal Res: Eastman GA 31023 Mailing Add: 2243 Rayburn House Off Bldg Washington DC 20515

STUDDERS, THOMAS G (D)
b Gloversville, NY, Mar 3, 30; s Robert Vincent Studders & Florence Meyers S; m 1956 to Gladys Delilah Skansberg; c Karen Ann, Mary Patricia, John Robert & Susan Elizabeth. Educ: Albany Col Pharm, BSPhC. Polit & Govt Pos: Supvr, Milo, NY, 70-; chmn, Yates Co Dem Comt, NY, formerly. Bus & Prof Pos: Owner, Bordwell Drug Store, Penn Yan, NY, 64- Mil Serv: Entered as Ens, Navy, 53, released as Lt(jg), 57, after serv in USS Caliente, Korean Theatre, 53-57. Mem: Lions; Am Legion; VFW. Relig: Catholic. Mailing Add: 400 Liberty St Penn Yan NY 14527

STUDDS, GERRY EASTMAN (D)
US Rep, Mass
b Mineola, NY, May 12, 37; s Eastman Studds (deceased) & Beatrice Murphy S; single. Educ: Yale Univ, BA, 59, MAT, 61. Polit & Govt Pos: Foreign serv officer, Dept of State, Washington, DC, 61-63; exec asst to Presidential consult for Nat Serv Corps, 63; legis asst, US Sen Harrison Williams, NJ, 64; NH coordr, US Sen Eugene McCarthy's Presidential Primary Campaign, 68; deleg & mem platform comt, Dem Nat Conv, 68; Dem cand for US Rep, 12th Dist, Mass, 70, US Rep, 12th Dist, Mass, 73- Bus & Prof Pos: Teacher, West Haven

Pub Sch, Conn, 59-60; teacher, St Paul's Sch, Concord, NH, 65-69. Relig: Protestant. Legal Res: 16 Black Horse Lane Cohasset MA 02025 Mailing Add: US House of Rep Washington DC 20515

STUECKEMANN, WALTER FREDERICK (R)
Chmn, Hodgeman Co Rep Party, Kans
b Great Bend, Kans, Mar 3, 26; s Gustav Stueckemann & Augusta Junghärtchen S; m 1947 to Marjorie Ann Liston; c William F, Linda Kay, Pamela Sue & Daniel Lee. Educ: Park Col, 45; Univ Kans, AB, 48, LLB, 50; Phi Alpha Delta. Polit & Govt Pos: State vchmn, Young Rep, Kans, 59-61; precinct chmn, Fifth Dist chmn, 61-63; co attorney, Hodgeman Co, 59-67; chmn, Hodgeman Co Rep Party, 64-; city attorney, Jetmore, 65- Mil Serv: Entered as A/S, Naval Res, 44, released as Ens, 46, after serv in Am Theater; Am Theater & Victory Ribbons; Unit Citation; Lt(jg) (Ret), Naval Res. Mem: Am, Kans & SW Kans Bar Asns; Mason; Consistory. Honors & Awards: Silver Beaver Award, Boy Scouts. Relig: Methodist. Mailing Add: Jetmore KS 67854

STULL, JOHN O (R)
Calif State Sen
b Corwith, Iowa, Aug 30, 20; s Dr Claude Stull & Mabel Frances Stilson S; m 1944 to Babbie Bogue; c Sinara. Educ: Univ Iowa, BA, 42; Gen Line Sch, US Navy, Newport, RI, 47-48; Alpha Phi Omega. Polit & Govt Pos: Mem, Calif Rep State Cent Comt, 64; coordr, Rep Assocs, 64; precinct chmn, 80th Assembly Dist, 64; Calif State Assemblyman, 67-73; deleg, Rep Nat Conv, 72; Calif State Sen, 73- Mil Serv: Entered V-5 Prog, Navy, 42, as Cmdr, 63 (Ret), served as Cmndg Officer, US Fleet Gunnery Sch, San Diego, Exec Off, USS Southerland, Off Naval Intel, Com Trans Div Staff, Cmndg Officer, Landing Ship Medium Rocket & Tank. Publ: Guns are not gone yet, 64 & The last pathfinder, 66, US Naval Inst; plus others. Mem: Am Legion; Farm Bur; ROA; VFW; Fleet Reserve Asn. Relig: Protestant. Legal Res: 460 Parkwood Lane Leucadia CA 92024 Mailing Add: 105 N Rose Suite 106 Escondido CA 92027

STULL, LESLIE A
Nebr State Sen
Mailing Add: PO Box 36 Alliance NE 69301

STULTS, ROBERT M (R)
Ore State Rep
Mailing Add: 1736 NW Beaumont Roseburg OR 97470

STULTZ, JOHN HOYTE, JR (D)
b Eden, NC, May 15, 40; s John Hoyte Stultz, Sr & Dillie Foddrell S; m 1966 to Sara Burke; c John Hoyte, III. Educ: Univ NC, AB in Econ, 62, Sch Law, LLB, 65; Delta Theta Phi. Polit & Govt Pos: Clerk, Superior Court, Rockingham Co, NC, 66-69; chmn, Rockingham Co Dem Party, formerly. Bus & Prof Pos: Attorney, Harrington & Stultz, Eden, NC, 69- Mem: NC Bar Asn; Rockingham Co Bar Asn (secy, 72-); NC State Bar, Inc; Jr CofC; Moose. Relig: Baptist. Legal Res: Hwy 14 Eden NC 27288 Mailing Add: PO Box 664 Eden NC 27288

STUMBAUGH, LAWRENCE (BUD) (D)
Ga State Sen
b Pensacola, Fla, Aug 24, 40; s James H R Stumbaugh & Mary Elkins S; m 1961 to Carole Hollingsworth; c Stacey Gay & Susan Delight. Educ: David Lipscomb Col, BS, 62. Polit & Govt Pos: Mem, DeKalb Co Dem Exec Comt, Ga, 72-, vchmn, 72-74; Ga State Sen & chmn indust develop comt, Ga State Senate, 75- Bus & Prof Pos: Nat sales trainer, EBSCO Industs, Inc, Birmingham, Ala, 66-68; vpres & regional mgr, Anthony Kane Assocs, Inc, New York, 68-72; vpres & gen mgr, Norrell Security Serv, Inc, Atlanta, Ga, 72- Publ: Contrib ed, Ga Bus News, 73-74. Mem: Liberia for God Found (treas bd trustees, 73-). Honors & Awards: Distinguished Serv Award, Kiwanis Int, 67. Relig: Church of Christ. Mailing Add: 1071 Yemassee Trail Stone Mountain GA 30083

STUMP, BOB (D)
Ariz State Sen
Mailing Add: PO Box 5 Tolleson AZ 85353

STUMPF, PETER PHILIP (DFL)
Minn State Sen
b St Paul, Minn, Mar 2, 48; s Peter P Stumpf, Sr & Helen Elizabeth Berchem S; single. Educ: Col St Thomas, St Paul, BA, 71. Polit & Govt Pos: Chmn, Dist 64A Dem-Farmer-Labor Party, Minn, 74-75; Minn State Sen, 75- Mem: North End Community Orgn; Joint Relig Legis Coalition; Target Area C Adv Bd; Dale-Thomas PAC. Legal Res: 1283 Danforth St St Paul MN 55117 Mailing Add: Rm 2 State Capitol St Paul MN 55155

STURGES, BENJAMIN RUSH (R)
Mem, North Kingstown Rep Comt, RI
b Providence, RI, Dec 4, 08; s Rush Sturges & Elizabeth Hazard S; m 1933 to Sandol Stoddard; c Dorothy, Rush, II & Sandol (Mrs Harsch). Educ: Yale Univ, AB, 31, LLB, 34. Polit & Govt Pos: Mem, First Ward Rep Comt, Providence, RI, 37-47; mem, North Kingstown Rep Comt, 54-; councilman, North Kingstown, 62-70; alt deleg, Rep Nat Conv, 68. Mil Serv: Entered as Lt, Navy, 42, released as Comdr, 46, after serv in Pac, 43-45; Two Bronze Stars; Commendation Ribbon. Relig: Episcopal. Legal Res: RFD 71 Saunderstown RI 02874 Mailing Add: 2110 Industrial Bank Bldg Providence RI 02903

STURR, DOROTHY MERTZ (R)
Mem, Rep State Cent Comt Calif
b Northumberland, Pa, Oct 21, 26; d Blair Hobson Mertz & Catherine Bloskey M; m 1948 to Dr Robert Porch Sturr, Jr; c Judy & Bobby Blair. Educ: Jefferson Med Sch of Nursing, Philadelphia, RN. Polit & Govt Pos: Mem, Rep State Cent Comt Calif, 66-; parliamentarian, Downey Fed Rep Women, 67-68. Mem: Southeast Med Auxiliary; Los Angeles Co Med Auxiliary (ment comt, 69-); Women's Div, Nat Right to Work Comt; Women's Div, Freedom Found of Valley Forge. Relig: Episcopal. Mailing Add: 9041 Charloma Dr Downey CA 90240

STURR, ROBERT P (R)
Mem, Rep State Cent Comt Calif
b Haddon Heights, NJ, July 4, 24; s Robert Porch Sturr & Margaret Tullidge S; m 1948 to Dorothy Mertz; c Judith Pabst & Robert Blair. Educ: Univ Pa, 42-43; Jefferson Med Col, MD, 48; Psi Upsilon; Nu Sigma Nu. Polit & Govt Pos: Area precinct chmn, Downey, Calif, 65-; chmn, 38th Calif Assembly Dist, 66-; mem, Rep State Cent Comt Calif, 67-; mem, Los Angeles Co Rep Cent Comt, 67- Bus & Prof Pos: Dir radiology, Downey Hosp, 65-; dir radiology, Doctors Hosp, Monclair, currently. Mil Serv: Entered as 1st Lt, Air Force, 50, released as Maj, 60, after serv in multiple units. Mem: Am, Calif & Los Angeles Co Med Asns; Am Col Radiology; Soc Nuclear Med; Rotary Int. Relig: Episcopal. Mailing Add: 9041 Charloma Dr Downey CA 90240

STURRETT, JOSEPH ANTHONY (D)
b Canton, Ohio, Sept 15, 14; s Michael Sturrett & Teresa Lanza S; m 1946 to Lucien Stio; c Heidi & Jodi. Educ: Ohio Univ, BS Civil Engr, 41; Alpha Phi Delta. Polit & Govt Pos: Deleg, Dem Nat Mid-Term Conf, 74. Bus & Prof Pos: Mem, US Engr Corps, Huntington, WVa, 41-42; engr, Stark Co, Ohio, 62- Mil Serv: Entered as Ens, Naval Res, 42, released as Lt, after serv in 3rd Bn, 17th Marines, 1st Marine Div, SPac, 44-46. Publ: Paper on secondary road system in relation to interstate, Cong Rec, 67. Mem: Nat & Ohio Soc Prof Engrs; Am Legion; Elks; Unique Club. Honors & Awards: Distinguished Serv Award, Eng Soc. Relig: Catholic. Mailing Add: 2710 Glenmont Rd NW Canton OH 44708

SUALL, JOAN FAITH (D)
b New York, NY, Feb 24, 32; d Samuel R Parnes & Rose Meyerson P; m 1960 to Bertram Suall. Educ: Syracuse Univ, BA, 53; NY Univ, 54; Columbia Univ, 57-58; Jour Hon Soc. Polit & Govt Pos: Exec secy, NY Students for Dem Action, 54-55; mem nat bd, Students for Dem Action, 54-55; chmn, NY Socialist Party, 69-70; nat secy, Social Dem, USA, 69-74, mem, currently. Bus & Prof Pos: Exec asst, Pub Affairs Dept, Amalgamated Clothing Workers Am, AFL-CIO, currently. Mem: NY Newspaper Guild; Int Alliance Theatrical & State Employees Union; Officers & Prof Employees Int AFL-CIO. Relig: Jewish. Mailing Add: 330 Third Ave New York NY 10010

SUBER, MARTIN GAY (R)
Exec Dir, SC Rep Party
b Abbeville, SC, Aug 23, 37; s John Robert Suber & Mildred Cochran S; m 1960 to Magdalena Emanuel; c Robert Gay Emanuel & John Carlos Cochran. Educ: Wofford Col, 55-56; Univ SC, BS in Bus Admin, 59. Polit & Govt Pos: Exec committeeman, SC Rep Party, 65-68, exec dir, 69- Bus & Prof Pos: Employee, J R Suber & Sons, Whitmire, SC, 61-63; vpres, Suber Bros, Inc, 63-68. Mil Serv: Entered as Airman Basic, Air Force Res, 59, released as Airman 1/C, 66; 2nd Lt, Air Force Res. Mem: Shrine; A&FM; Nat Rifle Asn; Jaycees; Nat Fedn Independent Bus (dist chmn). Relig: Methodist. Legal Res: 1707 Seay Ct Columbia SC 29206 Mailing Add: PO Box 5247 Columbia SC 29205

SUBLETT, NORMA RAEDEAN (D)
Mem Exec Comt, Calif Dem State Cent Comt
b Lodi, Calif, Sept 2, 25; d Harold Claude Pope & Emma Catherine Shafer; div; c Kathy Deane. Educ: Bus Col, AA, 44. Polit & Govt Pos: Yolo Co co-chmn, Reelec State Sen Samuel Geddes, 58 & 62; mem, Yolo Co Dem Cent Comt, Calif, 59-71, chmn, 62-66; staff coordr, Northern Calif, Stevenson for President Campaign, 60; co-founder, East Yolo Dem Club, West Sacramento, Calif, 60, pres, 60-64, mem exec comt & co-chmn, Fourth Cong Dist Caucus, Calif Dem State Cent Comt, 64-, mem steering comt, 66-68; Yolo Co chmn, Edwin L Z'berg for Calif State Assembly Campaign, 66 & 68; Yolo Co co-chmn, Robert F Kennedy Primary Campaign & Alan Cranston Sen Campaign, 68 & Unruh for Gov Primary Campaign, 70; treas, Ted Sheedy for Supvr, Sacramento Co, 70; Yolo Co chmn, Reelec Robert Leggett Campaign, 70; Dem Nat Committeeman, Calif, currently. Bus & Prof Pos: Vpres, Sublett Enterprises, West Sacramento, Calif. Mem: Officers & Prof Employees Union, Local 29; West Sacramento Campfire Girls Troop (sponsor); West Sacramento Little Skipper Chap, Children's Home Soc (hon sponsor); Native Daughters of Golden West. Relig: Methodist. Mailing Add: 500 Laurel Lane West Sacramento CA 95691

SUCHIN, ALVIN M (R)
NY State Assemblyman
Mailing Add: 269 Broadway Dobbs Ferry NY 10522

SUDDARTH, TOM (D)
NC State Sen
Mailing Add: 408 Country Club Dr Lexington NC 27292

SUELL, ROBERT MAY (R)
Chmn, Jessamine Co Rep Party, Ky
b Jessamine Co, Ky, July 7, 17; s Albert Suell & Sarah Frances English S; m 1957 to Nona Christine Brumfield. Educ: Dun & Bradstreet Bus Col, Louisville, Ky; War Manpower Comn Bur Training, Richmond. Polit & Govt Pos: Chmn, Jessamine Co Vol for Nixon-Lodge, Ky, 60; mem, Ky Rep State Steering Comt, 62; chmn, Jessamine Co Kentuckians for Goldwater, 64; campaign chmn, Jessamine Co Rep Party, 68, 72, 74 & 75, chmn, 72- Bus & Prof Pos: Foreman receiving & inspection, Blue Grass Ord Army Depot, Richmond, Ky, 43-46; mgr, Park Theatre, Nicholasville, 46-47; credit & off mgr, Ades-Lexington Dry Goods Co, Inc, 47- Publ: Auth, Union Lodge No. 10 I.O.O.F, 70 & History of Freemasonry in Jessamine County, Kentucky, 74; Masonic Home J. Mem: Lexington CofC; Jessamine Co Hist Soc; Mason (32 degree); Shriner; Odd Fellows. Relig: Christian. Mailing Add: 121 Bell Ct Nicholasville KY 40356

SUFRIN, RONALD KENT (D)
b Los Angeles, Calif, June 9, 52; s Ben Sufrin & Edith Preiss S; single. Educ: Univ Calif, Irvine, 70-71; Univ Calif, Los Angeles, BA, 75; Univ Calif, Davis Sch Law, 75-; Pi Gamma Mu. Polit & Govt Pos: Mem student adv bd, Calif Bd Educ, 70; Southern Calif student/youth coordr, McGovern/Shriver Presidential Campaign, 72; deleg, Dem Nat Conv, 72; chmn bd control & mem police policies rev comt, Univ Calif, Los Angeles, 75. Honors & Awards: Serv Award, Westchester 20/30 Club; Calif State Scholar. Relig: Jewish. Mailing Add: 5400 W 82nd St Los Angeles CA 90045

SUGARMON, R B (D)
Mem, Dem Nat Comt, Tenn
Mailing Add: Commers Title Bldg Rm 525 Memphis TN 38103

SUGG, ANDREW JACKSON (R)
b Bellefountaine, Miss, July 26, 11; s John Kirk Sugg & Lucie Emma Haney S; m 1962 to Annie Lee Blanton. Educ: Wood Jr Col, Mathiston, Miss, 2 years; Delta State Teachers Col, Cleveland, Miss, 1 year. Polit & Govt Pos: Co chmn, Agr Stabilization & Conserv Comt, 56-58; chmn, Webster Co Dem Party, Miss, formerly. Bus & Prof Pos: Inspector, Miss Pub Serv Comn, 58-64; pres, Sapa Water Asn, 65-69. Mil Serv: Inactive Naval Res, 42-43, MM 2/C. Relig: Baptist. Mailing Add: Rte 2 Eupora MS 39744

SUGG, JAMES RUSSELL (D)
Chmn, NC Dem Party
b Snow Hill, NC, July 4, 31; s Wendell Davis Sugg & Natalie Joyner S; m 1958 to Jane Brinkley; c James Russell, Jr, John Brinkley, Samuel Johnston & Andrew Myers. Educ: Louisburg Col, NC, AA, 50; High Point Col, AB, 52; Wake Forest Univ, JD, 59; Phi Delta Phi; Lambda Chi Alpha. Polit & Govt Pos: NC State Rep, 67-69; chmn exec comt, NC Dem Party, 72-73, chmn, 75- Bus & Prof Pos: Craven Co attorney, New Bern, NC, 70-73; pres, Craven Co Bar Asn, 72-73. Mil Serv: Capt, Marine Corps, served in Far East. Mem: NC Bar Asn; Elks; Am Legion; VFW. Mailing Add: Box 847 New Bern NC 28560

SUITT, TOM (D)
Calif State Assemblyman
Mailing Add: 247 E Tahquitz McCallum Way Palm Springs CA 92262

SULLIVAN, BASIL B (R)
b Darby, Pa, July 17, 33; s Denis Timothy Sullivan, MD & Catherine Cavanaugh S; single. Educ: Villanova Univ, AB, 55, MA, 64; Temple Univ Sch Law, 59; Ateneo de Manila Univ, 66. Polit & Govt Pos: Committeeman, Landsdowne Boro Rep Comt, Pa, 60-, vchmn, 68-; mem, Delaware Co Campaign Comt, 68-; deleg, Rep Nat Conv, 72. Bus & Prof Pos: Teacher polit sci, Malvern Prep Sch, 60-, asst headmaster, 68-; lectr polit sci, Montgomery Co Community Col, 68-70. Mil Serv: Entered as Pvt, Army, 56, released as SP-4, 58, after serv in Med Corps, Ft Ritchie, Md, 57-58. Honors & Awards: Fulbright-Hays Scholar for study in SE Asia, 66. Relig: Roman Catholic. Mailing Add: 28 W Plumstead Ave Lansdowne PA 19050

SULLIVAN, BETTY LOU (D)
Mem, Rep State Cent Comt Colo
b Las Vegas, NMex, Oct 19, 23; d Mason N Johnston & Blanche Howard J; div; c Richard Warren & Kirk Jeffery. Educ: Seton Sch of Nursing, Colorado Springs, RN, 45; Southern Colo State Col, BS in Psychol, 70. Polit & Govt Pos: Precinct committeewoman, Pueblo, Colo, 60-; mem, Pueblo Co Rep Cent Comt, 60-; mem Rep State Cent Comt Colo, 68-; mem, Colo Rep State Exec Bd, 70-72; vchmn, Third Cong Dist, 70-72. Bus & Prof Pos: Operating rm supvr, Pueblo, Colo, 48-55; off nurse, 55-60; sch nurse, 60- Mil Serv: Entered as 2nd Lt, Army, 45, released, 46, after serv in Army Nurse Corps, Winter Gen Hosp, Topeka, Kans. Mem: Am Nurses Asn; Psi Chi; Am Red Cross; Colo & Pueblo Educ Asns. Relig: Presbyterian. Mailing Add: 199 Bonnymede Pueblo CO 81001

SULLIVAN, CHARLES J, JR (D)
Md State Deleg
Mailing Add: 7100 Baltimore Ave College Park MD 20740

SULLIVAN, CHRISTINE BARR (D)
b Boston, Mass, May 24, 44; d William F Sullivan & Helen Dolan S; single. Educ: Vassar Col, AB. Polit & Govt Pos: Mgt intern, US Labor Dept & US Dept of Housing & Urban Develop, 67-68; research asst, Joint Comt on Atomic Energy, 68-69; legis asst to US Rep Michael J Harrington, 69-72, admin asst, 73- Mem: Am for Dem Action. Relig: Catholic. Legal Res: 30 Fieldmont Rd Belmont MA 02178 Mailing Add: 3032 Cambridge Pl NW Washington DC 20007

SULLIVAN, COLLEEN DRISCOLL (D)
b Endicott, NY, Apr 1, 37; d Leo Xavier Driscoll & Loretta Blanchette D; m 1965 to Walter Joseph Sullivan; c Tara Colleen. Educ: Lemoyne Col, BS, 58; Georgetown Univ, 59-62; Univ Pa, 73-; Pi Gamma Mu. Polit & Govt Pos: Committeewoman, 35th Ward Dem Party, 66-70; writer, Shapp for Gov Campaign Staff, 66; campaign mgr, Sullivan for Legis Comt, 68; Pa State chmn, New Dem Coalition, 70-71; mem, Pa Dem State Platform Comt, 70; mem, Pa Dem State Rules & Revision Comt, 70-71; co-chmn, Non-Partisan 18-21 Register to Vote Comt, 71-72; deleg, Dem Nat Conv, 72; mem, Nat Dem Platform Comt, 72; vchmn, Philadelphia Citizens for McGovern Comt, 72. Bus & Prof Pos: Ed asst, Cent Intel Agency, 58-63; research asst, Nat Planning Asn, 63-65; research analyst, Libr Cong, 65-; free lance writer. Mem: Nat Coun World Federalists; Marine Technol Soc; Caribbean Studies Asn. Relig: Roman Catholic. Mailing Add: 6342 Rising Sun Ave Philadelphia PA 19111

SULLIVAN, DAVID C (R)
b Grand Rapids, Mich, Sept 20, 31. Educ: Ill Inst Technol, BSEng, 53; DePaul Univ Col Law, JD, 59. Polit & Govt Pos: Chmn, Wis State Rep Cent Comt, formerly. Bus & Prof Pos: Engr, Cook Co Inspection Bur, Chicago, Ill, 55-58 & Johnson & Higgins Ill, Inc, Chicago, 58-60; chief engr & house counsel, Underwriters Grain Asn, 60-61, asst mgr, 61-62, mgr, 62-64; attorney-at-law, 64-65 & 72-; counsel, Am Labor Rels Coun & Motor Carrier Labor Adv Coun, 64-65. Mil Serv: EngC, Army, serv as instr, Eng Sch, Ft Belvoir, Va, 53-55. Mem: Am Bar Asn; Mensa; Am Arbit Asn (nat panel); McKinley Tennis Club; Vagabond Ski Club. Relig: Catholic. Mailing Add: 2611 N Wahl Ave Milwaukee WI 53201

SULLIVAN, DOROTHY R (R)
Mem, Winthrop Rep Town Comt, Mass
b Winthrop, Mass, Nov 12, 02; d Hugh William Roberts & Mary Cunningham R; m 1935 to Arthur G Sullivan, wid; c Jane F (Mrs Peter R Tatro). Educ: Emerson Col, 21-22; New Eng Conservatory of Music, Boston, 20-23. Polit & Govt Pos: Mem, Winthrop Rep Town Comt, Mass, 30-; deleg, Mass Rep State Conv, 56-; mem, Mass Rep State Comt, 56-73; mem, Personnel Appeals Bd Mass, 68-; dir Suffolk Co Rep Club, 70-; deleg, Rep Nat Conv, 72; mem pvt resources adv comt, Off Econ Opportunity, 72-73; vpres, Winthrop Rep Woman's Club, 72- Bus & Prof Pos: Ins broker, Winthrop, 56-; owner mgr & real estate broker, Arthur G Sullivan Ins Agency, 68-; mem various ins orgn, currently. Mem: Winthrop Community Hosp (legis chmn); CofC; Red Cross. Relig: Episcopal. Mailing Add: 106 Washington Ave Winthrop MA 02152

SULLIVAN, ELMER LINDSLEY (D)
b Philadelphia, Pa, Nov 3, 30; s Robert Edmund Sullivan, Sr & Marion Lindsley S; m 1967 to Jean Louise Carhart; c Jonathan Patrick & Elizabeth Jean. Educ: Dartmouth Col, AB, 52; Gen Theol Sem, New York, MDiv, 55; Phi Beta Kappa. Polit & Govt Pos: Deleg, Dem Nat Conv, 68 & 72; chmn, New Dem Coalition of Union Co, NJ, 69-71. Bus & Prof Pos: Rector, St Luke's Church, Trenton, NJ, 55-67 & 74-; rector, St Augustine's Church, Elizabeth, 67-74. Relig: Episcopal. Mailing Add: 1628 Prospect St Trenton NJ 08638

SULLIVAN, GERALD ANTHONY (DFL)
Chmn, Renville Co Dem-Farmer-Labor Party, Minn
b Morton, Minn, June 20, 40; s Benedict Sullivan & Marie Eisenbarth S; single. Educ: Col X St Thomas (Minn), BA, 62; Univ Minn Law Sch, 2 years; Inns of Court. Polit & Govt Pos: Chmn, Renville Co Young Dem, 64-66; deleg, Dist & Minn State Dem-Farmer-Labor Conv, 66, 68 & 70; vchmn, Renville Co Dem-Farmer-Labor Party, formerly, chmn, currently; mem, Minn Dem-Farmer-Labor State Cent Comt, 67-69; mem, Minn Dem-Farmer-Labor Const Rev Comn, 69; councilman, Morton, 69-; co coordr, Anderson for Gov Comt, 70. Bus & Prof Pos: Claims adjuster, Farmers Union Ins, St Paul, Minn, 64-65, agent, Morton, 65-; secy, Morton Develop Corp, 70- Mil Serv: Entered as Pvt, Army Res, 64, released as 2nd Lt, 66, after serv in 151st Artil. Mem: Nat Asn Life Underwriters; KofC; Fairfax Sportsmans Club; Am Legion; Farmers Union. Relig: Catholic. Mailing Add: Box 98 Morton MN 56270

SULLIVAN, GREGORY WILLIAM (D)
Mass State Rep
Mailing Add: State Capitol Boston MA 02133

SULLIVAN, JAMES ERNEST (D)
Tenn State Sen
b Dickson Co, Tenn, Jan 23, 33; s Joseph Anderson Sullivan & Era Christine Estes S; m 1956 to Dena Croft; c Madena Fayth. Educ: Mid Tenn State Univ, BS & MA. Polit & Govt Pos: Supt, Dickson Co Schs, Tenn, 67-75; Tenn State Sen, 23rd Dist, 75-, Dem whip & mem educ & state & local govt comts, Tenn State Senate, 75- Bus & Prof Pos: Athletic coach, Dickson Co Schs, Tenn, 56, classroom teacher, 59, elem prin, 60, high sch prin, 64-67, supt, 67-75. Mil Serv: Entered as Seaman Recruit, Navy, released as Seaman, 56-58. Mem: Rotary Club; Tenn Educ Asn; Farm Bur. Relig: Church of Christ. Mailing Add: Rte 4 Box 341 Dickson TN 37055

SULLIVAN, JEAN (R)
Rep Nat Committeewoman, Ala
b Selma, Ala, May 9, 28; d Arthur Goldsby Sample & Roberta Wood S; m 1947 to Ira Oliver Sullivan; c Arthur F, Ira Kent, James A, Connie Jean & Teresa Anne. Educ: Albert G Parrish High Sch, grad, 46; Ala Col, 1 year; Nat Honor Soc; Epsilon Sigma Alpha. Polit & Govt Pos: Exec mem, Dallas Co Rep Party, Ala, 62-; deleg, Ala State Rep Conv, 62-68; chmn, Glenn Andrews Cong Campaign, Dallas Co, Ala, 64 & 66; pres, Dallas Co Rep Women, 64-67; deleg, Rep Nat Women's Conf, 64-67; mem, Ala State Rep Exec Comt, 66-, vchmn, 69-72; deleg & mem platform comt, Rep Nat Conv, 68 & 72; cand, Ala State Rep, 70; chmn Ala deleg, Rep Leadership Conf, Washington, DC, 70; mem, Dallas Co Rehabilitation Bd, 71-; Rep Nat Committeewoman, Ala, 72-; coordr for City of Selma & Dallas Co on all Fed & State Projs, 73-; mem exec comt, Rep Nat Comt, 74- Mem: Women for Const Govt; Elks Emblem Club; CofC; Capitol Hill Club; Selma City Coun, PTA. Honors & Awards: Outstanding Den Mother of Boy Scouts, 56-60. Relig: Methodist. Mailing Add: 311 Cresthaven Ct Selma AL 36701

SULLIVAN, JOHN EUGENE (D)
Chmn, Clay Co Dem Party, Nebr
b Hickman, Nebr, Mar 31, 11; s Andrew Joseph Sullivan & Lillian Maas S; m 1933 to Margaret E Burke; c John J, Judith Bennett, Joan Jett & Patrick R. Educ: Univ Nebr-Lincoln, AB, 32, Law Col, LLB, 34. Polit & Govt Pos: Co attorney, Clay Co, Nebr, 39-43; chmn, Clay Co Dem Party, 46- Mil Serv: Entered as Lt(jg), Navy, 44, released as Lt, 45, after serv in Armed Guard, Pac Theatre. Mem: Am, State, Dist & Co Bar Asns; Am Legion; VFW. Relig: Catholic. Mailing Add: 300 W Johnson Clay Center NE 68933

SULLIVAN, JOHN JOSEPH, JR (D)
VChmn, Quincy City Dem Comt, Mass
b Boston, Mass, Feb 22, 41; s John Joseph Sullivan, Sr & Mary C Flynn S; m 1961 to Eleanor T Mitchell; c John Joseph, III, James Thomas & Stephen Patrick. Educ: Quincy Jr Col, 3 years; Stonehill Col, 4 years. Polit & Govt Pos: Dem nominee for sheriff, Norfolk Co, Mass, 62; mem, Ward Five Dem Comt, Quincy, 63-; cand for Norfolk Co Comnr, 64; vchmn, Quincy City Dem Comt, 68-; exec asst, Norfolk Co Comnrs, 68-; workmen's compensation agent, Norfolk Co, 68, United Fund chmn, 70, adminr of ins, 70; proj dir, Norfolk Co Drug Prevention Unit, 70; dir, Norfolk Co Employees Fed Credit Union, 71-; mem, Norfolk Co Develop & Tourist Coun, 72-; dir, Norfolk Co Opers, 74- Mil Serv: Entered as Seaman Recruit, Coast Guard Res, 58, released as QM3, 66, after serv in Res Units in Boston. Mem: Norfolk Co Prosecutors Asn; KofC; United Fund; Cardinal Cushing Assembly (4 degree). Relig: Catholic. Mailing Add: 14 Marion St Quincy MA 02170

SULLIVAN, JOHN THOMAS, JR (D)
Committeeman, Oswego Co Dem Party, NY
b Oswego, NY, Feb 27, 47; s John Thomas Sullivan & Dorothy Dashner S; m 1972 to Charlotte McQueen. Educ: State Univ NY Col Oswego, BA in Polit Sci, 68; Syracuse Univ Sch Law, 72-; Phi Delta Phi; Student Senate; Young Dem; Polit Sci Club; pres, Debate Team. Polit & Govt Pos: Chmn youth div, Oswego Co Dem Party, 71, committeeman, 73-; chmn, Oswego Co for McGovern, 72; deleg, Dem Nat Conv, 72; co legislator, Oswego Co, 72- Bus & Prof Pos: Radio announcer-news dir, WOSC AM-FM, 62-70; teacher social studies, Clyde-Savannah Cent Sch, NY, 68-70; teacher social studies, Liverpool High Sch, 70-72. Publ: Column, P D Q, Oswegonian Col Newspaper, 67-68. Mem: NY State Teacher's Asn (legis liaison, 68-72); Jaycees; Ancient Order of Hibernians. Honors & Awards: Best Speaker's Trophy, Pa State Univ Debater's Cong, 67 & 68. Relig: Roman Catholic. Mailing Add: 180 W Seneca St Oswego NY 13126

SULLIVAN, JOSEPH A (D)
Pa State Rep
b Philadelphia, Pa, Aug 9, 11; s John Sullivan & Jennie Daly S; m to Anna Becht. Educ: Parochial sch, Philadelphia. Polit & Govt Pos: Pa State Rep, 58-; mem, 25th Ward Exec Comt; deleg, Dem Nat Conv, 68. Bus & Prof Pos: Steel researcher; dist rep, State Workmen's Ins Fund. Mem: Hibernians; Men of Malver; KofC; Richmond Polish Asn. Legal Res: 2152 E Ann St Philadelphia PA 19134 Mailing Add: Capitol Bldg Harrisburg PA 17120

SULLIVAN, KATHLEEN THERESA (R)
Chmn, Mont Col Rep League
b Missoula, Mont, July 16, 53; s Michael J Sullivan & Hazel M Keays S; single. Educ: Univ Mont, 71-; Spurs; Assoc Students. Polit & Govt Pos: Secy, Mont Young Rep, 74-75; Rocky Mountain regional dir, Youth for Fed Union, 74-75; chmn, Mont Col Rep League, 74-; committeewoman, Mont Rep Party, 75-; legis aide to Asst Minority Leader, Mont State Senate, 75- Bus & Prof Pos: Researcher, Mont Task Force on Econ Develop, Mont CofC, 74; assoc ed, Mont Trunk Line, Mont Rep State Cent Comt, 75- Mem: Mont Model UN (chmn, 71-); Western Mont Ghost Town Preservation Soc; Newman Club. Honors & Awards:

Mont Fedn Rep Women Youth Scholar, 74. Relig: Catholic. Mailing Add: 403 Westview Dr Missoula MT 59801

SULLIVAN, LEO **(R)**
Ind State Sen
Mailing Add: 529 W Fifth St Peru IN 46970

SULLIVAN, LEONARD, JR **(R)**
Asst Secy of Defense for Prog Anal & Eval
b New York, NY, Dec 2, 25; s Leonard Sullivan & Marjorie Dodd S; m 1960 to Margo Murray Blackley; c M Dianne & L Jason. Educ: Mass Inst Technol, BS, MS & AE; Sigma Xi; Delta Psi, pres, Tau Chap, 48-49. Polit & Govt Pos: Dep asst dir, Tactical War Plan/Combat Syst, Defense Research & Eng, Off Secy Defense, 64-65, asst dir, 65-66, dep dir, Southeast Asia Matters, 66-72, prin dep dir, Defense Research & Eng, 72-73, dir prog anal & eval, Dept of Defense, 73-74, Asst Secy of Defense for Prog Anal & Eval, 74- Bus & Prof Pos: Aero engr, Grumman Aircraft Eng Co, 50-57, asst chief preliminary design, Bethpage, NY, 57-60, chief, 60-62, mgr, Advan Syst, 62-64. Mil Serv: Entered as Pvt, Marine Corps, 44, released as Pfc, 46, after serv in Combat Intel, CONUS/Occup of Japan. Publ: Special R&D for Vietnam, Sci Tech, 10/68; Ten lessons learned in RVN, J Defense Research, 5/69. Mem: St Anthony Club of NY; Chevy Chase Club; MIT Club of Wash. Honors & Awards: Knight of Vietnam, Fifth Class, Awarded by President Thieu, 69. Relig: Presbyterian. Mailing Add: 3601 49th St NW Spring Valley Washington DC 20016

SULLIVAN, LEONOR KRETZER **(D)**
US Rep, Mo
b St Louis, Mo; d Frederick William Kretzer & Eleanor Jostrand K; wid of John Berchmans Sullivan. Educ: Washington Univ. Hon Degrees: LLD, Lindenwood Col, 67, Univ Mo-St Louis, 69, St Louis Univ, 73, Rockhurst Col, 73 & Georgetown Univ, 75. Polit & Govt Pos: US Rep, Third Dist, Mo, 52-, secy, Dem Caucus, US House Rep, 61-74, mem, Dem Steering Comt, chmn, Merchant Marine & Fisheries Comt, 73-; deleg, Dem Nat Conv, 56, 60, 64 & 72. Bus & Prof Pos: Exec mgr, Felt & Tarrant Comptometer Co, 27-41. Mem: Am Legion Auxiliary; League of Women Voters; Nat Dem Women's Club. Honors & Awards: Nat Outstanding Working Woman Award, Downtown St Louis, Inc, 67; Distinguished Women of Am Award, Christian Col, Columbia, Mo, 69; Distinguished Pub Serv Award, 72; Admiral of the Ocean Seas Award, Am Maritime Indust, 73. Relig: Roman Catholic. Legal Res: 2 River Bluff Pl St Louis MO 63111 Mailing Add: 2221 Rayburn House Off Bldg Washington DC 20515

SULLIVAN, MARY J **(D)**
NH State Rep
b Leominster, Mass, Aug 15, 19; d Albert Leo McCaffrey & Nora Boyle S; m 1945 to Henry P Sullivan; c Mary (Mrs Carl Heath), Ann, Grace & Kathleen. Educ: Leominster Hosp Sch Nursing, dipl, 40. Polit & Govt Pos: Mem, Manchester Dem Women Club, 54-72; NH State Rep, 73- Bus & Prof Pos: Nurse, Mass Gen Hosp, 40-41. Mil Serv: Entered as 2nd Lt, Army, 41, released as 1st Lt, 45, after serv in Nurse Corps, Ft Bliss, Tex & Eng. Mem: Am Legion; St Pius X Women Guild; Friends of Peter Bent Brigham; Manchester Hist Soc. Relig: Catholic. Mailing Add: 52 Island Pond Rd Manchester NH 03103

SULLIVAN, MARY M **(D)**
Committeewoman, Mass Dem State Comt
b Philadelphia, Pa, Mar 13, 37; d Edmond C Maines & Elizabeth Kenney M; m 1959 to John Paul Sullivan; c Clare, Philip & Laura. Educ: Chestnut Hill Col, Philadelphia, AB, 58; Northeastern Univ Grad Sch, Boston, MEd, 75; Pa Asn Univ Women. Polit & Govt Pos: Chmn, Weston Dem Town Comt, Mass, 70-72; chmn comt on party orgn, Mass Dem State Comt, 72-, committeewoman, 72-; rep for Weston Metrop Area Planning Coun, 72- Bus & Prof Pos: Cong aide, US House of Rep, 58-60; pub rels writer, Weston Pub Schs, Mass, 65-70; asst dir placement, Wheelock Col, 74- Mem: Roxbury-Weston Progs, Inc (founder, dir, 65-); Am Personnel & Guid Asn; Am Asn Sch, Col & Univ Staffing; Mass Asn Halfway Houses (bd of dirs, 75-). Mailing Add: 18 Conant Rd Weston MA 02193

SULLIVAN, PETER M **(R)**
NY State Assemblyman
b Hackensack, NJ, Sept 20, 38; s Edward J Sullivan & Edna M Solari S; div; c Stephanie M, Cynthia M & Gregory M. Educ: Cornell Univ, 56-59; Columbia Univ, BA, 63; Tau Kappa Epsilon. Polit & Govt Pos: Mem planning bd, White Plains, NY, 73-74; secy, White Plains Rep Comt, 74-75; NY State Assemblyman, 75- Bus & Prof Pos: Stockbroker, Shields Model Roland Inc, 64- Mem: White Plains YMCA (bd dirs, 75-); White Plains United Way, (bd dirs, 74-); KofC; White Plains Vol Fire Dept. Relig: Roman Catholic. Legal Res: 21 Park Circle White Plains NY 10603 Mailing Add: 44 Church St White Plains NY 10601

SULLIVAN, RICHARD JOSEPH **(D)**
b Bronx, NY, May 17, 21; s Joseph William Sullivan & Kathryn McKenna S; m 1952 to Julia A Monahan; c Richard Joseph, Regina A, Joseph, Patricia, Teresa (deceased), Kimberly & James. Educ: Fordham Col & Law Sch, BA & LLB. Polit & Govt Pos: Chief counsel, Comt on Pub Works & Transportation, US House of Rep, 57- Mil Serv: Army, 39th & 9th Inf Div, NAfrica, Sicily, ETO; Eight Battle Stars; Combat Inf Badge. Relig: Catholic. Legal Res: NY Mailing Add: 5722 N 28th St Arlington VA 22207

SULLIVAN, RICHARD LYLES COBLE **(D)**
Chmn, Richland Co Dem Party, SC
b Chester, SC, Aug 25, 40; s John L Sullivan & Sarah Glenn S; m 1963 to Marion Stewart Boyd; c Richard & Marion. Educ: Univ SC, BA, 64, JD, 68; Kappa Alpha. Polit & Govt Pos: Chmn, Richland Co Dem Party, SC, 74-; chmn, SC Tax Bd of Rev, 74- Bus & Prof Pos: Secy, Glenn, Porter & Sullivan, Pa. Mem: Torch Club; Sertoma Club; Forest Lake Club; Wildewood Club. Relig: Episcopal. Legal Res: 432 Springlake Rd Columbia SC 29206 Mailing Add: PO Box 11588 Columbia SC 29211

SULLIVAN, SUSAN MEEKINS **(D)**
Alaska State Rep
b Anchorage, Alaska, Dec 24, 46; d Edward Russell Meekins, Sr & Adele B Magnier M; m 1970 to Timothy M Sullivan, Sr; c Timothy M, Jr. Educ: Gonzaga Univ, 65-67; Univ Denver, 68; Univ Alaska, BS in econ, 69; Alaska Methodist Univ, bus admin, 69-70. Polit & Govt Pos: Alaska State Rep, 75- Bus & Prof Pos: Lands specialist, Fed Bur Land Mgt & State of Alaska Dept Pub Works, formerly. Mem: Am Right of Way Asn. Legal Res: 7330 Marge Ct Anchorage AK 99504 Mailing Add: Pouch V Juneau AK 99811

SULLIVAN, THOMAS J **(D)**
Mem Exec Comt, NY State Dem Comt
b Elmira, NY, May 22, 26; s William E Sullivan & Nora O'Neill S; m 1948 to Mary Marinan; c John M, Daniel J, Kathleen A & Thomas J. Educ: Niagara Univ, BBA cum laude, 50; Union Univ, Albany Law Sch, LLB, 53. Polit & Govt Pos: Regional vchmn, mem steering comt to reorganize div & deleg to conv, Young Dem Div Dem Party, 55-57; committeeman, Chemung Co Dem Comt, 56-, towns chmn, 57, mem exec comt, 57-, vchmn, 58 & chmn, 59-60; deleg, NY State Dem Conv, 58 & 62-66; deleg, Dem Nat Conv, 60 & 64; corp counsel, Elmira, 60-61; counsel, Elmira Water Bd & Elmira Cemetery Comn, 60-61; mem exec comt, NY State Dem Comt, 62-; town attorney, Catlin, Chemung Co, NY, formerly; town attorney, Town of Erin, Town of Chemung & Town of Van Etten, currently; village attorney, Village of Van Etten, currently. Mil Serv: Entered as Seaman, Navy, 44, released as PO, 46. Mem: Sect Judicial Admin, Am Bar Asn; Munic Law Sect, NY State Bar Asn; Chemung Co Bar Asn; Nat Inst Munic Law Officers; Boy Scouts (comt mem, Troop 62). Relig: Catholic. Legal Res: 917 W Third St Elmira NY 14905 Mailing Add: 312 Lake St Elmira NY 14902

SULLIVAN, THOMAS QUINN **(D)**
b Hamilton, Mont, Feb 1, 33; s John Thomas Sullivan & Phillis Flanagin S; m 1953 to Mildred Lee Belgard; c Alice Jeanette, Laura Lenore, Thomas Michael, Charles Pertis & Patrick Glen. Educ: Stevensville High Sch, grad, 51. Polit & Govt Pos: Precinct committeeman, Dawson Co Dem Cent Comt, Mont, 64, chmn, 65-71; mem, Mont Dem Cent Comt, 65; eastern dist co chmn, Dawson Co, 69-71; alt state committeeman, Dawson Co Cent Comt, 71-; eastern dist state committeeman, Mont Dem Exec & Cent Comts, formerly. Bus & Prof Pos: Chief testboardman, Mt Bell Tel Co, 71- Mil Serv: Entered as Pvt, Air Force, 51, released as Airman 1/C, 55, after serv in Strategic Air Command, 55, S/Sgt, Air Force Res, 55-62; Korean Serv Ribbon; UN Ribbon; Good Conduct Medal. Relig: Catholic. Legal Res: 119 Maple Ave Hillcrest Addition Glendive MT 59330 Mailing Add: Box 1383 Glendive MT 59330

SULLIVAN, VINCENT AUGUSTINE **(D)**
Mem, Conn State Dem Cent Comt
b Moosup, Conn, July 12, 17; s John L Sullivan & Annette Potvin S; m 1940 to Theresa F Despathy; c Maureen B (Mrs Deyo), Susan M & Faye T. Educ: Providence Col, 35-36. Polit & Govt Pos: Mem bd selectmen, Plainfield, Conn, 51-55, judge, Munic Court, 55-60, chmn, Dem Town Comt, 56-; field rep for US Sen Thomas J Dodd, 59; mem, Conn State Dem Cent Comt, 60-; probate judge, Dist of Plainfield, 62; mem, Dem State Platform Comt, 62 & 72-; deleg, Dem Nat Conv, 64 & 68; deleg, Conn State Const Conv, 65; state senate adv, Appropriations Comt, Conn Gen Assembly, 68-; judge of probate, Dist of Plainfield, currently. Bus & Prof Pos: Secy, Plainfield Indust Found, Inc, Conn, 65- Mil Serv: Entered as Pvt, Air Force, 42, released as Sgt, 45, after serv in 9th Air Force, Anti-Submarine Patrol, Caribbean & European Theaters; Air Medal; ETO Ribbon with Five Stars; Anti-Submarine Patrol Ribbon with One Star; Occupation & French Ribbons; M/Sgt, Army Res, 48-60. Mem: Am Bar Asn (judicial assoc); Am Legion, Moosup, Conn (1st World War II Comdr, Godrea-McMahon Post 91); Elks; KofC; Lions. Relig: Roman Catholic. Mailing Add: PO Box 788 Moosup CT 06354

SULLIVAN, W HOWARD **(D)**
Chmn, Chenango Co Dem Comt, NY
b Norwich, NY, June 18, 42; s Edward Conway Sullivan & Mary Holmes S; m 1963 to Carol Stratton; c Charles Vernon & Courtney Elizabeth. Educ: LeMoyne Col (NY), BBA, 64; Temple Univ Sch Law, grad, 70. Polit & Govt Pos: Chmn, Chenango Co Dem Comt, NY, 74- Bus & Prof Pos: Partner, Law Firm of Stratton & Sullivan, Oxford, NY, 73- Relig: Catholic. Legal Res: 45 Hayes St Norwich NY 13815 Mailing Add: Bank Bldg PO Box 615 Oxford NY 13830

SULLIVAN, WILLIAM CHRISTOPHER **(D)**
Mayor, Springfield, Mass
b Springfield, Mass, Oct 13, 24; s Eugene Sullivan & Mary Hanifin S; m 1958 to Elizabeth F Cullinane; c Mary Beth, Patricia Ann & Kathleen Marie. Educ: Cathedral High Sch; Nat Honor Soc Sec Schs. Polit & Govt Pos: Mass State Rep, 52-58; city clerk, Springfield, Mass, 59-63, mayor, 73-; deleg, Dem Nat Mid-Term Conf, 74. Bus & Prof Pos: Vpres, Sullivan, Keating & Moran Ins Agency, 59- Mil Serv: Entered as Pvt, Army, 43, released as S/Sgt, after serv in ETO; Good Conduct Medal. Mem: United Fund (vchmn); KofC; VFW; Am Legion; Mass City Clerks Asn (past pres). Honors & Awards: Soviet Jewry Award, United Jewish Fedn; Outstanding Servant of Pub, Springfield TV Corp. Relig: Roman Catholic. Legal Res: 71 Oregon St Springfield MA 01105 Mailing Add: 31 Court St Springfield MA 01105

SULLIVAN, WILLIAM JOHNSON **(D)**
Conn State Sen
b Waterbury, Conn, Apr 22, 28; s Frank Sullivan & Mary Johnson S; div; c William Jr, Maureen, Keith & Craig. Educ: Univ Conn, Storrs, BA, 58; Boston Univ Law Sch, LLB, 61. Polit & Govt Pos: Conn State Sen, 16th Dist, 71- Bus & Prof Pos: Attorney, 61- Mil Serv: Entered as Pvt, Army, 51, released as 2nd Lt, 54, after serv in Korea, 53-54. Mem: KofC; VFW; Ancient Order of Hibernians; Boston Univ Alumni Asn. Honors & Awards: Law Review, second & third years of law sch. Relig: Roman Catholic. Legal Res: 3 Gayridge Rd Waterbury CT 06705 Mailing Add: 36 Park Place Waterbury CT 06702

SULLIVAN, WILLIAM LITSEY **(D)**
Ky State Sen
b Harrodsburg, Ky, Nov 1, 21; s Charles Blount Sullivan & Anne Litsey S; m 1951 to Elizabeth Dorsey; c William L, Jr & John Charles. Educ: Centre Col Ky, AB, 42; Univ Ky, LLB, 49; Lamp & Cross; Phi Delta Theta; Phi Delta Phi. Polit & Govt Pos: Ky State Sen, 54-58 & 66-, pres pro tem, Ky State Senate, 68-; Ky Comn Aeronaut, 58-59; commonwealth attorney, Henderson, Union & Webster Counties, 59-60; chmn, Ky Dem State Cent Comt, formerly; Acting Lt Gov, Ky, 75- Bus & Prof Pos: Partner, Dorsey, Sullivan & King, Henderson, Ky, 56- Mil Serv: Entered as Pvt, Army Air Corps, 42, released as 1st Lt, 45, after serv in 358th Fighter Group, ETO, 45; Group Air Medal. Mem: Prof Racing Pilots Asn; Rotary (past pres); Am Legion; 40 et 8; Elks. Honors & Awards: Outstanding Young Man of Ky, 56. Relig: Presbyterian. Legal Res: 517 N Main St Henderson KY 42420 Mailing Add: Ohio Valley Bank Henderson KY 42420

SULLIVANT, WILLIAM BENTON (BILL) **(D)**
Tex State Rep
b Gainesville, Tex, Jan 19, 40; s Carroll F Sullivant & Eloise Punchard S; m 1964 to Elizabeth Lou (Betty) Harrison; c Katherine Ann (Kate), Wesley Benton Lee (Ben) & Amy Eloise. Educ: Univ Tex, Austin, BA, 61; Univ Tex Law Sch, LLB, 63; Delta Sigma Phi; Phi Alpha Delta. Polit & Govt Pos: Attorney, Cooke Co, Tex, 65-71; dist attorney, 235th Judicial Dist,

71-72; Tex State Rep, 73- Bus & Prof Pos: Assoc mem, Law Firm of Sullivant, Meurer & Harris, 64-65, pvt practice, 65-73; partner, Law Firm of Sullivant, Meurer, Harris & Sullivant, 73- Mil Serv: Entered as Pvt E-1, Army Res, 63, released as Capt, 69, after serv in 1st Judge Adv Gen Detachment, Tex, 63-69; Expert Rifleman. Mem: Gainesville CofC (past dir); Gainesville Kiwanis Club (past dir); Gainesville Jaycees; Mason; Moslah Shrine Temple. Relig: Baptist. Legal Res: PO Box 939 Gainesville TX 76240 Mailing Add: PO Box 2910 House of Rep Austin TX 78767

SUMMER, ALBIOUN F (D)
Attorney Gen, Miss
b Pelahatchie, Miss, Nov 2, 21; s Sydney Lamar Summer & Iva Lee Hardy S; m 1945 to Mary Lois Campbell; c Carl Bennison. Educ: Hinds Jr Col, dipl, 42; Univ Miss Sch Law, 46-47; Jackson Sch Law, LLB, 50; Phi Delta Theta; Beta Theta Pi. Polit & Govt Pos: Town attorney, Pelahatchie, Miss, 50-51; mem, Miss Bd Vet Affairs, 57; exec asst & legal adv to Gov, Miss, 58, chief asst & legal adv, 68-69; chancery judge, Fifth Dist, Miss, 58-61; Attorney Gen, Miss, 69- Mailing Add: State Capitol Jackson MS 39205

SUMMERS, EVERETT GARY (D)
Ga State Sen
b Senoia, Ga, Oct 30, 10; s Elijah Gary Summers & Tiny Cheek S; m 1930 to Carolyn Frances Linch; c David Elijah & Mary Ellen (Mrs Malcolm Nelson). Educ: Univ Ga, BA; Emory Univ, MA; Columbia Univ, Sch Admin Specialist; Kappa Phi Kappa. Polit & Govt Pos: Ga State Sen, 71-, mem elem & sec educ comt, penal & corrections comt, appropriations comt & indust & labor comt, Ga State Senate, 71-, mem retirement comt, 75-, vchmn Dem caucus, 75- Bus & Prof Pos: Sch adminr, DeKalb Co, Ga, 30-45 & Walker Co, 45-71. Mem: Ga Asn Educators; Rotary; CofC; F&AM; Gideons Int. Honors & Awards: Sch Bell Award, Walker Co Asn Educators, 54. Relig: Methodist. Legal Res: Box 499 Lafayette GA 30728 Mailing Add: State Senate State Capitol Atlanta GA 30334

SUMMERS, FRANK WYNERTH (D)
Assoc Justice, Supreme Court, La
b Abbeville, La, Sept 5, 14; s Clay Ralph Summers & Esther LeBlanc S; m 1940 to Marie Beverly Miller; c Frank W, II, Preston M, Susan P, Clay James, William C & Beverly M. Educ: Univ Southwestern La, BA, 38; Tulane Univ, LLB, 38; Order of Coif; Blue Key; Phi Delta Phi; Phi Kappa Sigma. Polit & Govt Pos: Dist judge, 15th Judicial Dist, La, 52-55; Assoc Justice, Supreme Court, La, 60- Bus & Prof Pos: Attorney-at-law, gen practice, Abbeville, La, 38-41, 45-52 & 55-60. Mil Serv: Entered as Ens, Naval Res, 41, released as Lt Comdr, 45, after serv in Off Naval Intel & Pac Theater. Publ: Some merits of civil jury trials, Tulane Law Rev, 12/64. Mem: Tulane Law Alumni Club; hon mem St Thomas More Cath Lawyers Asn; Tulane Law Rev (bd adv ed); 15th Judicial Dist Bar Asn. Honors & Awards: Recipient Silver Beaver Award, Boy Scouts, 60. Relig: Catholic. Legal Res: 500 Second St Abbeville LA 70510 Mailing Add: Supreme Court Bldg 301 Loyola Ave New Orleans LA 70112

SUMMERS, H DEAN (R)
Idaho State Sen
Mailing Add: PO Box 579 Boise ID 83701

SUMNER, JACK (D)
Ore State Rep
Mailing Add: Rte 1 Heppner OR 97836

SUMNER, JAMES CARLISS (D)
Miss State Rep
Mailing Add: 102 S Front St Winona MS 38967

SUNDBORG, GEORGE (D)
b San Francisco, Calif, Mar 25, 13; s Charles A Sundborg & Annie Budgen S; m 1938 to Mary Frances Baker; c Pierre Joseph, George Walter, Jr, Rosemary (Mrs William Bridges Hunter, III), Stephen Vincent & Sarah (Mrs William B Long). Educ: Univ Wash, AB in Jour, 34; Sigma Delta Chi. Polit & Govt Pos: Supvr, Alaska Merit Syst, 40-41; sr planning technician, Nat Resources Planning Bd, 41-43; asst US dir, NPac Planning Proj, Dept of State, 43-44; indust analyst, Bonneville Power Admin, 44-46; mem, Thoron Rate Rev Comt, Alaska RR, 46; gen mgr, Alaska Develop Bd, 46-47 & 51-53; exec asst to Gov, Alaska, 47-51; deleg, Alaska Const Conv, 55-56; admin asst to US Sen Ernest Gruening, Alaska, 59-69; asst to dir, Bur Outdoor Recreation, 69-71, staff asst, Pac Northwest Regional Off, 71- Bus & Prof Pos: Reporter & city ed, Grays Harbor Daily Washingtonian, 35-38; reporter & ed writer, Daily Alaska Empire, 39-41; ed & publ, Juneau Independent, 53-57; ed, Fairbanks Daily News-Miner, Alaska, 57-58; former correspondent for various news serv & periodicals. Publ: Opportunity in Alaska, 45 & Hail Columbia, 54, Macmillan; Statehood for Alaska: The Issues Involved & the Facts About the Issues, Alaska Statehood Asn, 46. Mem: Alaska & Nat Press Clubs; charter mem Alaska State Soc (first pres); Senate Press Secy Asn. Legal Res: Anchorage AK Mailing Add: 1000 Second Ave Seattle WA 98104

SUNDQUIST, DONALD KENNETH (R)
Chmn, Young Rep Nat Fedn
b Moline, Ill, Mar 15, 36; s Kenneth Maynard Sundquist & Louise Rohren S; m 1959 to Martha Caroline Swanson; c Tania, Andrea & Donald K, Jr. Educ: Augustana Col, Rock Island, Ill, BA, 57; Rho Nu Delta. Polit & Govt Pos: Co chmn for Goldwater, Bedford Co, Tenn, 64; sixth dist chmn, Tenn Young Rep Fedn, 67-68, treas, 68-69, state chmn, 69-70; secy, Bedford Co Rep Party, 67-69; mem & secy, Elec Comn, Bedford Co, 68-70; mem platform comt, Nat Young Rep Conv, 69; Mid Tenn chmn, Brock for Senate, 70; mem exec comt, Rep Nat Comt, 71-73; chmn, Young Rep Nat Fedn, 71-73; Tenn state chmn, Nixon Baker Youth Campaign, 72; mem, Young Voters for the President Adv Bd, 72; dir, Am Coun Young Polit Leaders, 72-74, secy, 73; dir, US Youth Coun, 72-74, deleg, 74-75. Bus & Prof Pos: Indust engr, Jostens, Inc, Princeton, Ill, Owatonna, Minn & Shelbyville, Tenn; plant supt, Josten's of the South, Shelbyville, 66-68, resident mgr, 68-70; oper serv mgr, Scholastic Div, Josten's Inc, Minn, 70-72; vpres, Graphic Sales of Am, formerly, pres, currently. Mil Serv: Entered as S/A, Navy, 57, released as PNA 3, 59, after serv in Personnel. Mem: Shelbyville Kiwanis Club; United Givers Fund & Boy Scouts Coun; Shelbyville CofC; Am Field Serv in Shelbyville. Honors & Awards: Our Stake in Better Govt, Spoke Award, Shelbyville Jaycees, 70. Relig: Lutheran. Mailing Add: 3028 Emerald Memphis TN 38118

SUNDSTROM, FRANK L (R)
b Massena, NY, Jan 5, 01; s Charles Sundstrom & Nora Lillian Vandevener S; m 1936 to Jean Ross Johnstone; c Jean (Mrs W G M Farrell) & Frank L, Jr. Educ: Cornell Univ, grad, 24; Sigma Delta Chi; Phi Kappa Psi. Polit & Govt Pos: Chmn, Rep City Comt, East Orange, NJ, 38-48; US Rep, 11th Cong Dist, NJ, 43-49. Bus & Prof Pos: Partner, Burton, Dana & Co, Brokers, 31-; vpres & dir, Schenley Distillers, Inc, 55-; vpres & dir pub rels, Schenley Indust, Inc, 55-; vpres, The Tobacco Inst, 69- Mem: Cong Country Club, Washington, DC; Capitol Hill Club, Washington, DC; Montclair Golf Club, NJ; Touchdown Club of NY; Cornell Club of Essex Co, NJ. Honors & Awards: Walter Camp All Am Football Tackle, 23. Relig: Episcopal. Legal Res: 21 Hickory Dr Maplewood NJ 07040 Mailing Add: 1776 K St NW Washington DC 20006

SUNLEAF, ROGER WENDELL (R)
Chmn, Poweshiek Co Rep Cent Comt, Iowa
b Bellevue, Iowa, May 26, 38; s Dr Arthur Wendell Sunleaf & Virginia Anderson S; m 1965 to Rose Marie DeGear. Educ: Univ Iowa, BA & JD, 63; Phi Alpha Delta. Polit & Govt Pos: City attorney, Montezuma, Iowa, 64-; chmn, Poweshiek Co Rep Cent Comt, 70- Mil Serv: Entered as Pvt, Army Res, 63, released as Sp-4, 70. Mem: Iowa State Bar Asn; Poweshiek Co Bar Asn (pres, 70-); Elks; Am Trial Lawyers Asn; Asn Iowa Trial Lawyers. Relig: Lutheran. Mailing Add: 906 E Washington Montezuma IA 50171

SUNSHINE, KENNETH MARC (D)
Committeeman, Nassau Co Dem Party, NY
b New York, NY, Mar 12, 48; s Murray Sunshine & Lorraine Hyman S; single. Educ: Cornell Univ, BS, 70; Adelphi Sch Social Work, MSW, 75. Polit & Govt Pos: Deleg, Dem Nat Conv, 72; regional coordr, McGovern for President, NY, 72; vchmn, Nassau Co New Dem Coalition, 72-; committeeman, Nassau Co Dem Party, 72-; deleg, Dem Nat Mid-Term Conf, 74; dir field opers, Abrams for Attorney Gen, 74; chairperson, LI New Dem Coalition, 74-75; asst to pres, Borough of Bronx, 74-75; bd dirs, LI Bail Comn. Bus & Prof Pos: Jr high curriculum consult, Ithaca Pub Schs, NY, 69-70; sch-commun specialist, Freeport Pub Schs, 70-72; prog supvr, Family Serv Asn, Nassau Co, 72-73. Mem: Freeport Citizens Comt Against Drug Abuse (co-founder, 70-73); Freeport Econ Opportunity Comn (bd dirs, 72-73); Community Action Group (adv, 71-73); Concerned Fathers (consult, 71-72); Coalition of Bennington Park Community Groups (founder, 73). Mailing Add: 859 Willow Rd Franklin Square NY 11010

SUNSHINE, LOUISE M (D)
Mem, Dem Nat Comt, NY
Mailing Add: 501 E 79th St New York NY 10021

SUSANO, CHARLES DANIEL, JR (D)
Mem Exec Comt, Tenn State Dem Party
b Knoxville, Tenn, Mar 24, 36; s Charles Daniel Susano & Eloise Dondero S; m 1964 to Carolyn King; c Stephen David, Maria Teresa & Charles Daniel, III. Educ: Univ Notre Dame, PhB in Com, 58; Univ Tenn, LLB, 63; Phi Delta Phi; Order of the Coif. Polit & Govt Pos: Co-chmn, Knox Co Comt, John J Hooker, Jr for Gov, 66, chmn, 70; chmn, Knox Co Dem Party, Tenn, 72-74; deleg, Dem Nat Conv, 72; mem exec comt, Tenn State Dem Party, currently. Mil Serv: Entered as Pvt, Army, 58, released as SP-4, 60, after serv in 3rd Armored Rifle Bn, 51st Inf, ETO, 69-70; Good Conduct Medal. Publ: Auth, The action of deceit in Tennessee, Tenn Law Rev, 63. Mem: Am, Tenn & Knoxville Bar Asns; Asn Trial Lawyers of Am; Nat Asn Criminal Defense Lawyers. Relig: Roman Catholic. Mailing Add: 7131 Merrick Dr Knoxville TN 37919

SUSI, ROOSEVELT T (R)
Maine State Rep
Mailing Add: Box 236 Pittsfield ME 04967

SUSMAN, ALAN L (D)
WVa State Sen
Mailing Add: State Capitol Charleston WV 25305

SUSMAN, LOUIS B (D)
Mem, Dem Nat Comt, Mo
b St Louis, Mo, Nov 19, 37; s Irvin Susman & Selma Cohen S; m to Marjorie Sachs; c Sally & Billy. Educ: Univ Mich, Ann Arbor, BA with honors, 59; Wash Univ, LLB, 62; Phi Delta Phi; Beta Beta; Sphinx; Davids. Polit & Govt Pos: Mem, Dem Nat Comt, Mo, currently. Bus & Prof Pos: Sr partner, Susman, Stern, Agatstein, Heifetz & Gallop; dir, Mark Twain State Bank, St Louis Zoo Asn & St Louis Jewish Fedn. Mil Serv: 2nd Lt, Army. Mem: Westwood Country Club St Louis; Georgetown Club, Washington, DC; Clayton Club, St Louis. Relig: Jewish. Legal Res: 12 Edgewood Rd St Louis MO 63124 Mailing Add: 7733 Forsyth Blvd Suite 2201 St Louis MO 63105

SUSS, TED L (DFL)
Minn State Rep
Mailing Add: Box 319 Prior Lake MN 55372

SUTERA, CAROL JACQUELINE (D)
b Old Town, Maine, Mar 10, 36; d Carroll Joseph Coiley & Mary St John C; div; c Timothy, Christopher, Jonathan & Nathaniel. Educ: Univ Maine, 54-55; Off-Campus Students Orgn; Student Senate; Newman Club; Student Relig Orgn. Polit & Govt Pos: Secy, Young Dem Club, Montville, Conn, 68-69, pres, 69-72; hon & permanent secy, Conn Dist Conv, 70; chmn polit action, Young Dem Club, Conn, 70-71, treas, 71-72; deleg, Conn Dem State Conv, 70, 72 & 74; dist chmn, Montville Dem Town Comt, 71-73; deleg, Conn Assembly Dist Conv; alt deleg, Dem Nat Conv, 72; mem campaign comt, State Sen J J Murphy, Jr, 72; comnr, Montville Housing Authority, 72-; Dem campaign mgr, Montville, 73; campaign staff, Congressman Christopher J Dodd, 74; vchmn, Montville Dem Town Comt, 74-; secy, 19th Dist Dem Asn, 74- Bus & Prof Pos: Salesman, Esposito Agency, 71. Mem: Montville Am Little League (secy, 69-70, pres, 71-73). Relig: Catholic. Legal Res: Oxoboxo Crossroad Montville CT 06353 Mailing Add: Box 115 Oakdale CT 06370

SUTHERLAND, HERBERT NED (D)
Mo State Rep
b Bartow Co, Polk, Fla, Sept 14, 24; s Fred Veal Sutherland & Ester Louise Walwork S; m 1948 to Jonell Salmon; c Herbert Ned, Jr, Fred Viencent, Rebecca Jean, Nell E, David Earl & Anne M. Educ: Univ Denver, 32; Univ Va, 46-50; Univ Caribia, 50-51; Univ Mo, AB, 53, DDS, 57; Xi Psi Phi; ZIPS Dent. Polit & Govt Pos: Mo State Rep, 75- Bus & Prof Pos: Secy, CofC, Bethany, Mo, 57-59 & Harrison Co Develop, 57-60. Mil Serv: Entered as Pvt, Army Air Force, 43, released as S/Sgt, 45, after serv in 15th AAF, ETO, 44-45; Air Medal with Clusters, MTO; ETO Good Conduct; Campaign Ribbon with Three Stars; Expert Rifleman.

Mem: VFW; Mason; Shrine; Eastern Star; CofC. Relig: Methodist. Mailing Add: 1002 S 17th Bethany MO 64424

SUTHERLAND, PAUL OSCAR (D)
b Flint, Mich, Aug 25, 24; s George W Sutherland & Ann Peterson S; m 1958 to Josephine R Meyers; c Paula Diane. Educ: Univ Mich; Univ Wis. Polit & Govt Pos: Treas, Ninth Dem Cong Dist, Mich, 55-56, chmn, 62-67; vchmn, Mason Co Dem Comt, 58-64; organizer, Nat AFL-CIO, 66 & 67; pres, Int Union of Allied Indust Workers, AFL-CIO, formerly, Region Seven rep, currently, pres, Labor Fedn of Mason Co, currently; pres, Mason Co Coun & chief steward, Local 132, Int Union Allied Indust Workers of Am, currently; deleg, Dem Nat Mid-Term Conf, 74. Mil Serv: Entered as Seaman, Navy, 44, released as Seaman 2/C, 45, after serv in ETO. Mem: Mason Co Community Action Group (vpres, Cluster Five, Fed Poverty Act & exec bd); Low Cost Housing Comn, Ludington, Mich. Relig: Swedish-Lutheran. Mailing Add: 5563 Rasmussen Rd Ludington MI 49431

SUTKER, CALVIN R (D)
Mem, Dem Nat Comt, Ill
Mailing Add: 9214 Kostner Skokie IL 60076

SUTPHIN, WILLIAM HALSTEAD (D)
b Browntown, NJ, Aug 30, 87; s James Taylor Sutphin & Charlotte Brown S; m 1922 to Catharine Bonner; c Susan & William T. Educ: High sch & Woods Bus Col. Polit & Govt Pos: Mayor, Matawan, NJ, 15-27; US Rep, 31-43. Mil Serv: Pvt, B Troop, 1st Squadron, NJ Cavalry, released as Sgt; reentered serv as Lt, Cavalry, 17, discharged as Capt, Air Serv, 19; Mexican Border & French Serv Ribbons. Mem: Holland Soc; Sons of Revolution; Mason; Elks; Am Legion. Relig: Presbyterian. Mailing Add: 102 West St Berlin MD 21811

SUTTER, JOHN F (D)
Kans State Rep
Mailing Add: 6421 Farrow Kansas City KS 66104

SUTTERFIELD, JAMES R (R)
Mem, Orleans Parish Rep Exec Comt, La
b Houston, Tex, Aug 6, 42; s James Dayton Sutterfield & Alba Spraker S; m 1974 to Sara Cargill Jackson; c James R, Jr & Dana Christen. Educ: Tulane Univ, 60-62; Univ Tex, 62-63; Loyola Univ (La) Law Sch, JD, 67; Phi Kappa Sigma; Delta Theta Phi. Polit & Govt Pos: Chmn, Metrop New Orleans Young Rep, 68-70; chmn, First Cong Dist, La Young Rep Fedn, 68-70; deleg, Young Rep Nat Conv, 69; mem, Orleans Parish Rep Exec Comt, 69-; secy-treas, Bull Elephant Club of La, 70-; La State Rep, 26th Dist, Orleans Parish, 70-72. Bus & Prof Pos: Partner, Sutterfield & Vickery, Attorneys, 75- Mem: Am Judicature Soc; Am, La & New Orleans Bar Asns; Am Trial Lawyers Asn. Honors & Awards: Winner, Moot Court Competition, Student Bar Asn Gold Award, 65-66; Outstanding Young Rep for 1970. Relig: Protestant. Legal Res: 1629 Fourth St New Orleans LA 70130 Mailing Add: Suite 1104 225 Baronne St New Orleans LA 70112

SUTTON, BILLIE H (D)
SDak State Sen
Mailing Add: Bonesteel SD 57317

SUTTON, EMMAZETTE COLLIER (D)
Secy-Treas, Okla State Dem Party
b Gotebo, Okla, May 26, 15; d Frank A Collier & Mittie L Hawkins C; m 1942 to LeRoy Sutton; c Beth Anne (Mrs Charles Emet Graft) one grandchild. Educ: Southwestern State Col, 1 year; Keen's Bus Col, Clinton, Okla, 1 year; charter mem Hon Soc. Polit & Govt Pos: Dem precinct co-chmn, Clinton, Okla; asst co supt schs, Washita Co, 39-43; asst co supt schs, Custer Co, 57-62; vpres, Okla Fedn Dem Women's Clubs, 67-69, state secy, 69-71; Sixth Dist secy, 71-73; alt deleg, Dem Nat Conv, 68, deleg, 72; chmn, Okla Fedn Dem Women's Clubs Conv, 68, spec adv, 69; women area coordr, David Hall for Gov Campaign, 70; Sixth Cong Dist co-chmn, Okla Dem Party, 71-72; secy-treas, Okla State Dem Party, 72- Bus & Prof Pos: First woman real estate broker in Custer Co, Okla, 55- Mem: Lincoln PTA (pres); Clinton PTA Coun (pres); Okla State Bd, PTA. Honors & Awards: First woman real estate broker, Custer Co, 55. Relig: Methodist. Mailing Add: 1128 Lee Ave Clinton OK 73601

SUTTON, FRANKLIN (D)
Ga State Sen
Mailing Add: RFD 1 Norman Park GA 31771

SUTTON, G J (D)
Tex State Rep
Mailing Add: 711 North Pine San Antonio TX 78202

SUTTON, GLENN WALLACE (D)
b Milan, Ind, July 25, 04; s Chester Wallace Sutton & Goldie Tucker S; m 1930 to Rachel Sibley; c William Wallace. Educ: Ind Univ, BS, 26, AM, 27; Ohio State Univ, PhD, 38; Beta Gamma Sigma; Alpha Kappa Psi; Phi Kappa Phi; Phi Eta Sigma; Phi Chi Theta; Omicron Delta Kappa. Polit & Govt Pos: Dir, Nat Tabulation Off, Urban Studies of Consumer Purchases & Income, Bur Labor Statistics, US Dept of Labor, Southeastern States, Atlanta, 36, dir, Nat Tabulation Off, Chicago, 37, dir, Survey of State, Co & Munic Employ & Payrolls, Southeastern States, Atlanta, 39-40, nat dir, Philadelphia, 41; comnr, US Tariff Comn, 54-69, chmn, 69-72, retired. Bus & Prof Pos: Acct, Groubs Wholesale Grocery, Seymour, Ind, 22; acct, Farmers' Coop Elevator Co, 23; research asst & ed, Ind Bus Rev, Ind Univ, 25-27; ed, Idaho Econ Rev & instr econ, Univ Idaho, 27-29; prof finance, chmn finance div, ed, Ga Bus Rev, dir, Bur Bus Research & Vet Affairs Off, dir, Savannah Div & Grad Div, Col Bus Admin, Univ, Ga, 29-54. Mil Serv: Entered as Lt, Navy, 42, released as Comdr, 45, after serv in Fasron 152; Aviation Wing Staff 67; Air Task Group 671; Am Theater Ribbon; Defense Medal; Capt (Ret), Naval Res, 64. Mem: Am Statist Asn; Am & Southern Econ Asns; Am Finance Asn; Am Asn Univ Prof. Relig: Methodist. Legal Res: 649 Oglethorpe Ave Athens GA 30601 Mailing Add: 208 Southern Mutual Bldg Athens GA 30601

SUTTON, LEONARD V B (D)
b Colorado Springs, Colo, Dec 21, 14; s Benjamin Edmund Sutton & Anne von Bibra S; m 1938 to Janette Elsie Gabor. Educ: Foreign Trade Course, Stuttgart, Ger, 35; Colo Col, BA in Polit Sci, 37; Nat Inst Pub Affairs, grad fel in govt, 37-38; Univ Denver Sch Law, JD, 41; Phi Delta Phi; First Voters Club; Int Rels Club. Polit & Govt Pos: Attorney, El Paso Co Planning Comt, 41-42 & 46-50, attorney, Bd Adjust, 46-50; chief legal br, Calif Qm Depot, 45-46; town attorney, Manitou Springs, 46-50; mem, Dem State Cent Comt, Colo, 48-56 & 63-66; deleg & mem various comts, State Dem Assemblies & Conv, many times; chmn, Colo State Rules Rev Comt, 2 terms; mem, Colo Dem State Cent & Exec Comts, 8 years; chmn, El Paso Co Dem Comt, 2 terms & mem exec comt, several times; co campaign dir, 2 terms & finance chmn, 2 terms; chmn, Co Assembly & Conv, several times; chmn, Fourth Judicial Dist, 2 terms; precinct committeeman, 3 terms; dist capt, 2 terms; mem & pres, El Paso Co Young Dem Club, formerly; deleg, Dem Nat Conv, 52; state chmn, Jefferson-Jackson Day Dinner Comt, 55; justice, Colo Supreme Court, 56-68, chief justice, 60 & 66; chmn, US Foreign Claims Settlement Comn, 68-69. Bus & Prof Pos: Attorney-at-law, Colo & dir various corp, 41-42, 48-56 & 69-; practicing attorney, Denver, Colo & Washington, DC, 70- Mil Serv: Entered as Pvt, Army, 42, released as Capt, 46, after serv in Inf, Ski Troops, 253rd Qm Pack Co & Calif Qm Depot; Army Commendation Medal; Am Theater Ribbon; Victory Medal. Publ: Constitutions of the Countries of the World & Mexico, Oceana Publns, Inc, 73; Mexican Real Estate Transactions By Foreigners (w Zack V Chayet), Denver J of Int Law & Policy, Vol 4 No 1, spring 74. Mem: Inst Int Educ (trustee, 62-64, hon trustee, 65-); Am Bar Asn; Mex Am Acad Int Law; Am Arbit Asn; Rotary. Relig: Episcopal. Legal Res: 3131 E Alameda Ave Denver CO 80209 Mailing Add: Suite 500 Boston Bldg 828 17th St Denver CO 80202

SUTTON, PERCY E (D)
Pres, Borough of Manhattan, NY
m to Leatrice; c Pierre Monte & Cheryl Lynn. Educ: Prairie View Agr & Mech Col; Tuskegee Inst; Hampton Inst; Columbia Univ; Brooklyn Law Sch. Polit & Govt Pos: NY State Assemblyman, 64-67; mem, NY Co Dem Exec Comt, 65-; chmn, NY State Coun Black Elected Dem, 66-68 & 72-; pres, Borough of Manhattan, 67-; co-chmn, Nat Conf Black Elected Off, 68-; mem, New York Dem Comt, 70-; mem-at-lg, Dem Nat Comt, currently; deleg, Dem Nat Mid-Term Conf, 74; mem, NY State Dem Exec Comt, currently. Bus & Prof Pos: Attorney. Mil Serv: Capt, Air Force, World War II & Korean War; grad, Air Univ; Int Off, Washington, DC; trial judge adv; Italian & Mediter Theatre Combat Stars. Publ: A plan for the localization of New York City government, New York, 2/72. Mem: NY Br NAACP (chmn speakers bur, vpres & pres); NY CORE (legal counsel); Baptist Ministers Conf of Gtr New York (legal counsel); Student Nonviolent Coord Comt (consult); Harlem Hosp (lay adv bd). Legal Res: 10 W 135th St New York NY 10037 Mailing Add: Off of Manhattan Borough Pres Munic Bldg New York NY 10007

SUTTON, RICHARD CARPENTER (IKE) (R)
Hawaii State Rep
b Apr 5, 17; s Edwin White Sutton & Alice Carpenter S; m 1941 to Ann Colgate; c Richard C, Jr, Linda (Mrs Kemp), Warner C & Beverly Cabell. Educ: Stanford Univ, AB, 37, Law Sch, JD, 50; Stanford Vow Boys; Football Squad, Nat Champion Rose Bowl, 36. Polit & Govt Pos: Deleg, Hawaii State Const Conv, 68 & 69; fed judge, Wake Island, 70-74; Hawaii State Rep, 74- Bus & Prof Pos: Owner, Malilome Lodge & Hotel, Waikiki, 54-75; dir, Pablong Rubber, Sumatra, 62-70. Mil Serv: Entered as Ens, Navy, 41, released as Lt Comdr, after serv in Logistics, Pac Ocean Area under Admiral Chester Nimitz, 42-45; Letter of Commendation. Mem: Fed Bar Asn (pres, 73-74); Am Legion (past comdr, 65-66); Lions. Honors & Awards: Letter of Commendation, Episcopal Bishop, 74; Top Membership in US, Am Legion, 65-66. Relig: Episcopal; pres, Ecclesiastical Court, 70-75. Mailing Add: 3539 Kahawalu Dr Honolulu HI 96817

SUTTON, RUTH ADELIA (D)
b Malden, Mo, Oct 3, 12; d George W Warner & Cora E Donica W; m 1931 to Floyd E Sutton; c Geraldine & Daryle Busch. Educ: Southern Ill Univ, BS, 56, MS, 61. Polit & Govt Pos: Chief dep co treas, Williamson Co, Ill, 74-; deleg, Dem Nat Mid-Term Conf, 74. Bus & Prof Pos: Teacher, Royalton Unit Schs, Southern Ill, 46-57; prin, Sesser Unit Schs, Southern Ill, 57-65; reading consult, Southern Ill Schs, 65-68; curriculum supvr, Pope Co Unit Schs, Southern Ill, 68-73. Publ: Let's begin in kindergarten, In: Ill Guid & Personnel Asn Mag, 63; Kindergarten and your child, In: Educ Serv Mag, 68. Mem: Ill & Nat Educ Asns; Asn Sch Curriculum Develop; Ill Reading Coun; Asn Childhood Educ Int. Relig: Protestant. Mailing Add: 1512 W Madison St Herrin IL 62948

SUWA, JACK K (D)
Hawaii State Rep
Mailing Add: House Sgt-at-Arms State Capitol Honolulu HI 96813

SVETLIC, MICHAEL JOSEPH (R)
Committeeman, Clay Co Rep Cent Comt, Mo
b Kansas City, Mo, July 14, 51; s Joseph Charles Svetlecic & Josephine Louise Maurin S; single. Educ: Rockhurst Col, BA, 73; Pi Kappa Delta. Polit & Govt Pos: Kansas City youth co-chmn, Danforth for US Sen Comt, Mo, 70; vpres, Rockhurst Col Rep Club, 70-71, pres, 71-; exec dir, Mo Fedn of Col Rep Clubs, 71-72; field coordr, Dods for US Cong, 72; campaign mgr, Douglas for Mo State Legis, 72; alt deleg, Rep Nat Conv, 72; co-chmn, Clay Co Comt for the Reelec of the President, 72; committeeman, Clay Co Mo Rep Cent Comt, 72-; admin asst to Richard L Berkley, Mayor Pro Tem, Kansas City, Mo, currently. Bus & Prof Pos: Exec dir, Kansas City Chap, Mo Asn for Non-Pub Schs, 72- Mem: Alpha Sigma Nu; Delta Theta Phi; Northland Rep Club (vpres, 75-76); Int Asn of Machinists, AFL-CIO. Honors & Awards: Youth Serv Award, Kansas City La Sertoma Club, 69; Degree of Distinction, Nat Forensic League, 69. Relig: Catholic. Mailing Add: 6205 N Harrison Kansas City MO 64118

SVIEN, DON J (R)
b Hazel Run, Minn, June 2, 24; s Henry J Svien & Hulda Oslund S; m 1951 to Evelyn A Anthony; c Lana Rae. Educ: Col Com, 2 years. Polit & Govt Pos: Committeeman, Kandiyohi Co Rep Comt, 65-, chmn, formerly; Area 2 chmn, Sixth Dist Rep Party, Minn, 72- Bus & Prof Pos: Asst cashier, First Nat Bank, Willmar, Minn, 47-51; sales mgr, Minn Elec Supply Co, 51-59; owner, D J Sales Agency, 59- Mil Serv: Entered as Pvt, Army, 43, released as Sgt, 46, after serv in 20th Armored Div, ETO, 43-46; Two Battle Stars. Mem: Am Legion; Am Contract Bridge Asn; Mason; Zuhra Shrine Temple; Caravan Shrine Club. Relig: Lutheran. Mailing Add: 1025 Hill Rd Box 222 Willmar MN 56201

SVOBODA, LINDA A (D)
Iowa State Rep
Mailing Add: RR 1 Amana IA 52203

SWAFFORD, PAMELA MARIE (D)
Exec Secy, Hamilton Co Dem Party, Ohio
b St Bernard, Ohio, Aug 27, 39; d August Charles Siegel & Alvina Brockman S; m 1961 to Charles Henry Swafford, Sr; c Charles Henry, Jr & Michael Jerome. Educ: Miller Draughton Bus Sch, grad, 59. Polit & Govt Pos: Precinct exec, Hamilton Co Dem Cent Comt, Ohio, 70-, secy, 72-, exec secy, 72-; financial secy, Hamilton Co Women's Dem Club, 72-74, pres, 75-;

ward chmn, St Bernard Dem Orgn, 72-74; deleg, Dem Nat Mid-Term Conf, 74. Mem: St Bernard Dem Club; 24th Ward Dem Club; Federated Dem Women Ohio. Relig: Catholic. Legal Res: 4916 Greenlee Ave St Bernard OH 45217 Mailing Add: 615 Main St Cincinnati OH 45202

SWAGER, NORVIN LEROY (DFL)
VChmn, Washington Co Dem-Farmer-Labor Party, Minn
b Clayton, Wis, Dec 16, 31; s Hugh Swager & Evelyn Hauland S; m 1951 to Delores Mae Kennetz; c Gary Dean, Craig Allen, Karen Fae & Carmen Mae. Educ: Dunwoody Trade Sch, Minneapolis, Minn, 52-54; Univ Minn, 61. Polit & Govt Pos: Treas, Moosbrugger for Rep, Washington Co, Minn, 66; mem finance comt, Rolvaag for Gov, Minn, 66; vchmn, Washington Co Dem-Farmer-Labor Party, 67-; mem, United Dem for Humphrey & chmn, Humphrey for President, Washington Co, 68; coordr, Karth for Cong, Washington Co, 68; deleg, Washington Co Dem-Farmer-Labor Conv, 68 & 70; deleg, Minn Dem-Farmer-Labor State Conv, 70; deleg, Fourth Dist Dem-Farmer-Labor Conv, 70; co-chmn, Don Shaver for Rep, Washington Co, 70; chmn, Minn Gov Club, Washington Co Chap, 72- Bus & Prof Pos: Vpres community rels, Teamsters Local 1145, 54-58, div vpres, 54-60, bus agents, 61-63, pres, 63-68; mem, Minn State Col Bd, 66; vpres, Swager Bros, Inc, gen contractors, home builders & develop real estate agent, 68-; secy-treas, Oak Park Develop Corp, 72-; vpres, Action Rental Inc, 73-; chmn bd dirs, Oak Park Heights State Bank, 74- Mem: CofC (pres, 75); Lions; Eagles IUE; Teamsters. Honors & Awards: Award of Merit, Minn Asn for Retarded Children. Relig: Lutheran. Mailing Add: 102 Lakeside Dr Stillwater MN 55082

SWAINBANK, LOUISE ROBINSON (R)
Vt State Rep
b Ware, Mass, Nov 3, 17; d Philip W Robinson & Lois Gould R; m 1941 to John A Swainbank; c Anne (Mrs Arthur Brooks), Daniel Robinson, John A, Jr & Joseph G. Educ: Northfield Sem; Smith Col, BA. Polit & Govt Pos: Vt State Rep, 70-, chmn educ comt, Vt House of Rep, currently. Bus & Prof Pos: Teacher, St Johnsbury Schs, 66-69. Mem: Vt Smith Col Club (pres); Univ Vt (trustee); US Comn on Civil Rights (Vt adv comt); Gov Comn on Higher Educ Planning; Gov Comn on Status of Women. Relig: Congregational. Mailing Add: 49 Summer St St Johnsbury VT 05819

SWAJIAN, CATHERINE MARY (R)
b Pasadena, Calif, Aug 20, 50; d Arthur Swajian & Mary Virginia Getsoian S; single. Educ: Univ Calif, Los Angeles, BA cum laude, 72; Delta Gamma; Bruin Belles. Polit & Govt Pos: Intern, Gerald Ford, Minority Leader, US House of Rep, 69; mem staff, Veysey for Cong Comt, Riverside Co, Calif, 70, intern, US Rep Victor Veysey, 71; mem exec bd, Rep State Cent Comt Calif, 71-73, asst secy, formerly; deleg, Rep Nat Conv, 72; elector, Calif Electoral Col, 72; legis aide, Rep Caucus, Calif State Assembly, 72- Relig: Presbyterian. Legal Res: 72-731 Bel Air Bd Palm Desert CA 92260 Mailing Add: Rm 420 State Capitol Sacramento CA 95814

SWAN, ARTHUR ROBERT (R)
b Rochester, Minn, Dec 5, 20; s William Edward Swan & Rose Aulwes S; m 1946 to Jacqueline Jean Vincent; c Kathleen, Barbara, Cynthia & Thomas. Educ: Rochester Jr Col, AA, 41; Univ Minn, BSL, 47 & JD, 49. Polit & Govt Pos: Mem, Olmsted Co Rep Cent Comt, Minn, 52-72; alt deleg, Rep Nat Conv, 52, deleg, 64; vchmn, First Rep Cong Dist, Minn, 55-59, chmn, 60-65, deleg-at-lg, 65-71; mem, Minn Rep State Cent Comt, 60-71; mem, Minn Munic Comn, 67-71, vchmn, 69-71; Presidential Elector, 72. Mil Serv: Entered as Pvt, Army, 42, released as Maj, 46, after serv in 63rd Med Bn, ETO, 44-45; ETO Campaign Ribbon with Three Stars; Am Theatre Ribbon. Mem: Am & Minn State Bars; Elks; Mason; VFW. Relig: Episcopal. Mailing Add: 809 Fifth St SW Rochester MN 55901

SWAN, KARL G (D)
Utah State Rep
Mailing Add: 347 Upland Dr Tooele UT 84074

SWAN, MONROE (D)
Wis State Sen
b Belzoni, Miss, June 2, 37; s George Washington Swan & Sallie M Johnson S; m 1958 to Robbie Z Sims, separated; c Rosalyn Denese, Cheryl Lynn, Gwendolyn Susette & Allyn Monroe. Educ: Milwaukee Area Tech Col, AA; Univ Wis-Milwaukee, BS. Polit & Govt Pos: Wis State Sen, Sixth Dist, 73- Bus & Prof Pos: State supt of Sunday schs, Church of God in Christ, Northwest Wis, 66-68; material expeditor, Am Motors Corp, Milwaukee, 67-68; dir, Concentrated Employ Prog, 68-72. Mem: Am Civil Liberties Union; Common Cause. Relig: Protestant. Mailing Add: 2430 W Auer Ave Milwaukee WI 53206

SWANBECK, ETHEL GERTRUDE (R)
Ohio State Rep
b Osceola Mills, Pa; d James S Bateman & Agnes S Showers B; m 1916 to Carl Emil Swanbeck, MD; c Carl R, Ray J & Robert R. Educ: Teachers Col, Cleveland, Educ Degree, 16; Western Reserve Univ, BS, 23; Present Day Club; Flora Stone Mather. Hon Degrees: DPS, Bowling Green State Univ, 71. Polit & Govt Pos: Ohio State Rep, 53-, chmn welfare & educ comts, Ohio House Rep, formerly; mem, Great Lakes Comn, currently; dean Rep party, Ohio House Rep, 12 years; ranking mem, Ohio Finance Comn, currently. Bus & Prof Pos: Sch teacher, formerly. Publ: Legis column, Erie Co Reporter, Huron, Ohio, 20 years; Am Home column, statewide, 10 years; radio prog every week, WLKR, Norwalk & WLEC, Sandusky, 25 years. Mem: Ohio Eastern Star (Past Matron); Bus & Prof Women; Nat Orgn Women Legislators; PTA; Ohio Fedn Women's Clubs. Honors & Awards: Serv Award, Am Red Cross; Outstanding Citizen Award, City of Huron; Alumni Award, Western Reserve Univ. Relig: Protestant. Mailing Add: 304 Center St Huron OH 44839

SWANN, LARRY D (R)
WVa State Deleg
b Doddridge Co, WVa, Feb 15, 52; s Lewis M Swann (deceased) & Mary L Morgan S; single. Educ: Salem Col, currently; Phi Alpha Theta; Soc for Polit Awareness. Polit & Govt Pos: WVa State Deleg, Fifth Dist, 73- Honors & Awards: Youngest mem ever elec to WVa State Legis. Relig: Baptist. Legal Res: Rte 3 Salem WV 26426 Mailing Add: House of Deleg State Capitol Charleston WV 25305

SWANNER, JOHN MACDONALD
b Washington, NC, Feb 11, 22; s John MacDonald Swanner & Mae Spain S; m 1950 to Mary Elizabeth Blount; c Susan S Wetherald & Elizabeth Blount. Educ: Univ NC, Chapel Hill, BS in Com, 48; Phi Beta Kappa; Beta Gamma Sigma; Phi Gamma Delta. Polit & Govt Pos: Staff dir, Comt on Standards of Off Conduct, US House of Rep, 67- Bus & Prof Pos: Vpres, Rodar Leasing Corp, Washington, DC, 57-67. Mil Serv: Entered as Pvt, Army, 42, released as T/Sgt, 46, after serv in various units, ETO, 45-46. Legal Res: NC Mailing Add: 2360 Rayburn House Off Bldg Washington DC 20515

SWANSON, GERTRUDE GAY (R)
Mem, Rep State Cent Comt Calif
b Milwaukee, Wis; d Carl G Loeber & Betsy Beyer L; m 1934 to Ray Oscar Swanson; c Philip Ray & Linda Gay (Mrs Alan Charles). Educ: Univ Calif, Los Angeles, AB in Econ & Polit Sci & Jr High Sch Teaching Credential; Alpha Chi Delta (pres, 34-37); Pi Sigma Alpha; Nu Delta Omicron; pres, Beta Sigma Omicron, 32-36. Polit & Govt Pos: Treas, Pomona Valley Rep Women's Club, Federated, Calif, 50-60, auditor, 60-, pres, 63-64; mem, Rep State Cent Comt Calif, 60-: secy, Rep Coord Coun, 62, treas, 63-64, pres, 67; received various spec polit assignments & cand campaign appointments including Glenard P Lipscomb, Cong, 24th Dist, Houston Flournoy for State Controller & James Whetmore, Peter Scharbarum & William Campbell, Calif State Legis; mem, Personnel Bd Exam, City of Pomona. Mem: Life mem Univ Calif, Los Angeles Alumni Asn; Bank of Am Scholar Rev Bd; Lutheran Laymen's League; Lutheran Braille Workers; Lutheran Women's Missionary League. Relig: Lutheran. Mailing Add: 1891 Fairview Pl Pomona CA 91766

SWANSON, GLADYS M (D)
Chairperson, Colfax Co Dem Party, Nebr
b Colfax Co, Nebr, May 8, 26; d Herman Kunneman & Carrie Nielsen K; wid; c V Lee Roy, Mike & Karen. Educ: Schuyler High Sch, 44. Polit & Govt Pos: Chairperson, Colfax Co Dem Party, Nebr, 74- Honors & Awards: High Sch Valedictorian, 44; Regents Scholarship, Univ Nebr, 44. Relig: Lutheran. Mailing Add: 709 E 12th St Schuyler NE 68661

SWANSON, HARRY BROOKS (R)
b Reno, Nev, June 4, 28; s Harry Swanson & Cleo Brooks S; m 1950 to Irene Fulton; c Karen, Kathey & Kyle Brooks. Educ: Univ Nev, BA, 50; Univ Calif, Hastings Col of Law, LLB, 53; Order of the Coif; Alpha Tau Omega; Phi Alpha Delta. Polit & Govt Pos: Asst city attorney, Reno, Nev, 53-54; Nev State Assemblyman, 58-64; mem, Washoe Co Rep Cent Comt, 58-74; deleg, Rep Nat Conv, 64. Bus & Prof Pos: Partner, Richards & Swanson, 56-62; partner, Swanson & Swanson, 62-; ed, Nev Bar Asn J, 58-63. Mil Serv: Entered as 2nd Lt, Air Force, 54, released as 1st Lt, 56, after serv in Staff Judge Adv Off, Malmstrom AFB, Strategic Air Command, Mont. Publ: Sherrer vs Sherrer & the future-a prophesy, Am Bar Asn J, 8/54. Mem: Am, Nev & Washoe Co Bar Asns; Hastings Col of Law Alumni Asn (dir); Ducks Unlimited (dir). Relig: Methodist. Legal Res: 2001 Sierra Sage Lane Reno NV 89502 Mailing Add: PO Box 2417 Reno NV 89505

SWANSON, JAMES C (DFL)
Minn State Rep
b 1934; m to Elizabeth A Mortensen. Educ: Dunwoody Inst, 52-55, sheet metal degree; Colo State Univ, 65; Mankato State Col, 66; Univ Minn, BS, 69. Polit & Govt Pos: Mem, Richfield Citizens Tax Comn, 64-69; elected dir, Richfield Sch Bd, Dist 280, 65-68; elected off rev comn, 65-66; app subchmn, Keith Metro Task Force Comn, 66; Minn State Rep, 69-; chmn, Health & Welfare Comt, Minn, 73- Bus & Prof Pos: Journeyman sheet metal worker, 55-63; eve sch supvr, SCampus, Suburban Hennepin Co Voc-Tech Schs, currently; app mem, Minn Educ Coun, 71-; app mem, Minn State Adv Coun for Voc Educ, 72-, mem, Exec Comt, currently. Mem: Minn & Am Voc Asns; Richfield DFL Club; Richfield Jaycees; Portland Elem PTA. Honors & Awards: Outstanding Young Man, 68. Mailing Add: 6827 Fifth Ave S Richfield MN 55423

SWANSON, JAY DIXON (R)
Treas, Kans Rep Party
b Wichita, Kans, Mar 13, 33; s Royden Victor Swanson & Lydia Ina Dixon S; m 1955 to Susan Ann Adamson; c Timothy Jay & Michelle. Educ: Okla Univ, BS, 56; Beta Theta Pi. Polit & Govt Pos: Treas, Kans Rep Party, 70-; deleg, Rep Nat Conv, 72. Mil Serv: Entered as 2nd Lt, Air Force, 56, released as 1st Lt, 59, after serv in 71st Fighter Interceptor Squadron, Air Defense Command, 58-59; Jet Fighter Pilot. Mem: Kans Independent Oil & Gas Asn (dir); Am Asn Oil Well Drilling Contractors (membership chmn); Kans Geol Soc; Wichita Crime Comn; Young Pres Orgn. Relig: Methodist. Mailing Add: Eighth Floor Sutton Pl Wichita KS 67202

SWANSON, KAREN JOYCE (D)
Mass State Rep
b Brockton, Mass, Jan 15, 54; d William David Swanson & Myrtle Dagmar Friis S; single. Educ: Univ Mass, Boston, 72- Polit & Govt Pos: Mass State Rep, 75- Mem: NOW; Am Civil Liberties Union. Mailing Add: 237 Menlo St Brockton MA 02401

SWANSON, LESLIE EUGENE (D)
Alaska State Rep
b Salina, Kans, Mar 1, 12; s Charles Richard Swanson & Alice Simpson S; m 1935 to Marie St Marten; c Leslie Lester & Joseph LeRoy. Educ: High Sch. Polit & Govt Pos: Senate sgt-at-arms, Alaska State Legis, 57-64; mem, Juneau City Coun, Alaska, 61-62; Alaska State Rep, 71-72 & 75- Bus & Prof Pos: With Operating Engrs, 52-; apt owner, 56- Mem: CofC; Lions; Elks; Alaska Miners Asn. Relig: Catholic. Mailing Add: Box 3 Nenana AK 99760

SWANSON, MARY HELEN (R)
Committeewoman, Rep State Comt Okla
b Oklahoma City, Okla, Dec 2, 26; d Guy Carlton Jones & Virginia Vaughn J; m 1948 to Charles Henry Swanson; c Linda (Mrs Stephen Ristow), David Charles, Joy Virginia & Kristina Anne; one grandson. Educ: Okla State Univ, 45-48; Beta Sigma Phi. Polit & Govt Pos: Chmn of Women for Nixon, Oklahoma Co & Fifth Dist, Okla, 68; deleg, Okla State Fedn Rep Women, 68, 70, 72 & 74; vpres, Rep Women's Club of Oklahoma City, 68-71, pres, 72-75; committeewoman, Rep State Comt Okla, 69-; deleg, Nat Fedn Rep Women, 69 & 71; deleg, Okla Co & Okla State Rep Convs, 69-75; state chmn for Women of Ralph Thompson, Lt Gov cand, 70; corresponding secy, Okla State Fedn Rep Women, 71-73; state chmn of Campaign Comt to Reelect Nixon, 72; alt deleg, Rep Nat Conv, 72; Okla Co campaign hqs mgr for the Reelect US Sen Henry Bellmon. Mem: Okla Hospitality Club (reporter, 71-72); Women's Comt of the Symphony; Windsor Reviewers; Presby Hosp Auxiliary; Okla Heritage Asn. Relig: Baptist. Mailing Add: 2716 NW 60th St Oklahoma City OK 73112

SWANSON, WAYNE (R)
State Treas, Nebr
b Omaha, Nebr, Dec 31, 14; m 1946 to Ruth McDonald; c two. Educ: Spec bus training. Polit & Govt Pos: State Rwy Comnr, Nebr, 56-67; State Treas, Nebr, 67- Bus & Prof Pos: Former

…ng bus; plumber. Mil Serv: Navy, World War II. Mem: State Rwy Comnrs; …llows; Mason; hon life mem Crestview Lodge, Sarpy Post 9675, VFW. Relig: … Add: State Capitol Lincoln NE 68509

SWARTS, JOSEPH ANDREW (R)
Treas, Mo Rep State Comt
b Kansas City, Kans, Feb 19, 17; s John Lloyd Swarts & Agnes McOwen S; m 1942 to Thelma Rose Osborn; c Elizabeth (Mrs Tom Feeney), Joseph Andrew, Thomas Arthur, Michael Alan & Robert Anthony. Educ: Kansas City Jr Col, Kans. Polit & Govt Pos: Pres, Platte Co Rep Club, Mo, 52-55; chmn, Platte Co Rep Cent Comt, 66-72; chmn, Sixth Cong Dist Rep Party, 68-72; Sixth Dist Comt mem, Mo Rep State Comt, 72-, treas, 72-; chmn, Rep Orgn & Develop Comt, Mo, currently; mem, Mo Human Rights Comn, 73- Bus & Prof Pos: Pres, J A Swarts Enterprises, Inc, J A Swarts, Indust Part & J A Swarts & Sons Egg Co, currently. Mem: KofC (4 degree, Past Grand Knight, Tri-Co KofC, Past Faithful Capt of Lt T Fitzsimmons); Optimist; Platte Woods Homes Asn; Platte Co Bus & Prof Mens Asn (vpres & mem bd dirs); St Vincent DePaul Soc. Honors & Awards: Editorialized by Kansas City Star for creating two-party syst in Platte Co, Mo, 71. Relig: Catholic; mem, St Therese Social Justice Comt. Legal Res: 6735 Tower Dr Kansas City MO 64151 Mailing Add: 9505 N Congress Kansas City MO 64153

SWARTZ, DAVID JOHN (D)
Mass State Rep
b Haverhill, Mass, Apr 2, 31; s David Swartz & Katherine McKenna S; m 1969 to Dorothy Wechezak; c Rebecca, Stephany, Christopher, Deborah, Sheryl & Rachel. Educ: Providence Col, BA, 52; Harvard Univ Law Sch, JD, 55; Harvard Univ Law Sch Forum, Kings Bench. Polit & Govt Pos: Mass State Rep, 75- Mailing Add: Rm 43 State House Boston MA 02133

SWARTZ, JAMES CHARLES (D)
VChmn, Md Dem State Cent Comt
b Baltimore, Md, Nov 14, 48; s Mano James Swartz & Evelyn Spiegel S (deceased); single. Educ: George Washington Univ, AA, 69, BA, with distinction, 71; Univ Md Sch Law, 72-; Omicron Delta Kappa, nat pres, 70-71; Delta Sigma Rho; Tau Kappa Alpha. Polit & Govt Pos: Mem, Md Dem State Cent Comt, 70-73, chmn, Third Dist, formerly, vchmn, currently; deleg, Second Cong Dist, Dem Nat Conv, 72. Bus & Prof Pos: Vpres, Mano Swartz Inc, Baltimore, 71- Mil Serv: Entered as Pvt, Md Nat Guard, 71, released as Pfc after six months active duty at Ft Knox, Sgt at Officers Cand Sch, currently; Nat Defense Award; Expert-M16A1 Rifle. Publ: Auth, Away from the bullhorn, Acad Forum, George Washington Univ, fall 69. Mem: Rotary. Honors & Awards: Scholarship, George F Baker Found, 67. Relig: Jewish. Mailing Add: Ashland Farms Cockeysville MD 21030

SWAYZE, THOMAS ALLEN, JR (R)
b Tacoma, Wash, Dec 8, 30; s Thomas Allen Swayze & Frances Goerhing S; m 1957 to Marliss Marie McCann; c Sharon Marie, Sandra Lynne, Glenn Thomas & Kristin Kay. Educ: Univ Puget Sound, AB, 53; Univ Wash, JD, 54; Kappa Sigma; Phi Alpha Delta. Polit & Govt Pos: Chmn, Pierce Co Rep Cent Comt, 64-65; Wash State Rep, 26th Dist, 65-74; speaker, Wash House Rep, 71-73, minority party leader, 73-74; deleg, Rep Nat Conv, 72; judge, Superior Court, State of Wash, 75- Bus & Prof Pos: Partner, Murray, Scott, McGavick, Gagliardi, Graves, Lane & Lowry, Tacoma, Wash, 73- Mil Serv: Entered as Pvt, Army, 54, released as Spec-4, 56, after serv in Hq 6023 Personnel Unit. Mem: Am Judicature Soc; Elks; Gyro; Young Men's Bus Club; CofC. Relig: Methodist. Mailing Add: 4107 NW Tenth Gig Harbor WA 98335

SWEARINGEN, EDWARD HICKS (R)
Chmn, Taylor Co Rep Party, Ga
b Macon, Ga, Jan 23, 48; s Edward Britt Swearingen & Anne Hicks S; div. Educ: Ga Southwestern Col, 66-67; Univ Ga, BBA, 70; Phi Kappa Phi; Beta Gamma Sigma. Polit & Govt Pos: Chmn, Taylor Co Rep Party, Ga, 70- Bus & Prof Pos: Serv mgr, Butler Homes, Inc, 69-71; E B & E H Swearingen, farming partnership, 71- Mem: Aircraft Owners & Pilots Asn; Reynolds Kiwanis Club (pres, 75). Relig: Baptist. Mailing Add: PO Box 512 Reynolds GA 31076

SWEAT, OTTIS, JR (D)
Ga State Rep
Mailing Add: Rte 4 Box 10 Waycross GA 31501

SWED, JEANETTE (D)
Dem Nat Committeewoman, Wis
b Milwaukee, Wis, July 2, 08; d Louis Goldberg & Dora Padway G; wid; c Sandra & Jordan Lewis. Educ: Pub schs, Milwaukee. Polit & Govt Pos: Deleg, Dem Nat Conv, 64 & 68; mem steering comt, Proj Head Start, 64-; Dem Nat Committeewoman, Wis, 64-72 & currently; deleg, Dem Nat Mid-Term Conf, 74. Bus & Prof Pos: Partner, Abe L Swed Co Investments, 45-; partner, Lewis Ctr, 62-; dir, J Swed Shoe Co. Mem: Milwaukee Chap, Haddassah; City of Hope; Protective Serv for Children; Wis Sr Citizens (mem exec bd, 63-); Jewish Home for Aged. Honors & Awards: Recipient, Nurse of Mercy Award, City of Hope, 60. Legal Res: 9363 N Sleepy Hollow Lane Milwaukee WI 53217 Mailing Add: 3975 N Cramer Milwaukee WI 53211

SWEENEY, EDWARD (D)
Mo State Rep
b St Louis, Mo, Sept 11, 47; s Edward W Sweeney, Sr & Mary Catherine Hanagan S; single. Educ: Univ Mo-Columbia, AB, 69, JD, 73; Notre Dame Summer Law Prog, Brunel Univ, Eng, 73; Omicron Delta Kappa; Pi Omicron Sigma; Pi Sigma Alpha; Phi Kappa Theta. Polit & Govt Pos: Mo State Rep, 84th Dist, 75- Bus & Prof Pos: Attorney, St Louis, Mo, 74- Mil Serv: Entered as 2nd Lt, Army Field Artil, 69, released as 1st Lt, 71, after serv in 101st Airborne Div, Vietnam, 70-71; Bronze Star; Meritorious Serv. Mem: Am & Mo Bar Asns; Shaw Neighborhood Improv Asn; Garden Tower E Community Corp; Mo Asn Social Welfare. Relig: Catholic. Mailing Add: 3670 Flora St Louis MO 63110

SWEENEY, GERALD FRANCIS (D)
b Chicago, Ill, Apr 2, 29; s Arthur Sweeney & Grace Cleveland S; m 1956 to Barbara Mulligan; c Ashley, Philip & Blair. Educ: Univ Mich, BA, 54. Polit & Govt Pos: Asst to supvr, Town of Huntington, NY, 68-75; admin asst to US Rep J A Ambro, Jr, NY, 75- Mil Serv: Entered as Pvt, Army, 51, released as Pfc, 53, after serv in Mil Police, US. Publ: Auth, Fall of a young black leader, Newsday Sunday Sect, 6/74. Mailing Add: 3 Kay Pl Huntington NY 11743

SWEENEY, JAMES ALOYSIUS, JR (D)
NH State Rep
b Manchester, NH, May 4, 34; s James Aloysius Sweeney, Sr & Clara Allaire S; m 1962 to Beverly Joan Lester; c James A, III, Laurie Ann & Kathleen Mary. Educ: Univ NH, 52-53 & 55-56; St Anselms Col, 57-58; Phi Delta Upsilon; Neuman Club. Polit & Govt Pos: Selectman, Ward Ten, NH, 66-73; NH State Rep, 67- Mil Serv: Entered as Pvt, Army, 53, released as Pfc, 55; Nat Defense Serv Medal; Good Conduct Medal. Relig: Roman Catholic. Mailing Add: 25 Fogg Ave Manchester NH 03102

SWEENEY, JOHN A (D)
NJ State Assemblyman
Mailing Add: State House Trenton NJ 08625

SWEENEY, JOHN JAMES (D)
Pa State Sen
Mailing Add: 3203 Huey Ave Drexel Hill PA 19026

SWEENEY, LEONARD E (D)
Pa State Rep
Mailing Add: Capitol Bldg Harrisburg PA 17120

SWEENEY, PATRICK A (D)
Ohio State Rep
b Cleveland, Ohio, 1941; single. Educ: Tenn Col; Washburn Univ; Univ Kans; Univ Md. Polit & Govt Pos: Ohio State Rep, 67- Bus & Prof Pos: Mfrs rep. Mil Serv: Air Force. Mailing Add: 3534 W 100th St Cleveland OH 44111

SWEENEY, RANDALL WALTER (D)
b Salem, Ohio, May 31, 49; s Asher William Sweeney & Bertha Marie Englert S; m 1969 to Marilyn Louise Kline; c Caroline Louise. Educ: Ohio State Univ, BS, 72; Smith Hall Hon; ROTC Honor Guard. Polit & Govt Pos: Dep State Supvr Sch & Ministerial Lands & Dep State Custodian Pub Land Rec, Auditor of State, Ohio, 71-73; deleg, Dem Nat Conv, 72; nat youth whip, Hubert H Humphrey for President Comt, 72; chmn, Ohio Rec Comn, 73; chief opers, Ohio Vietnam Vet Bonus Comn, 74, dir, 75-; deleg, Franklin Co Dem Conv, 75. Mem: Franklin Co Young Dem Club; Am Rec Mgt Asn; Shamrock Club of Columbus; KofC; Agonis of Columbus. Relig: Roman Catholic. Mailing Add: 1119 Loring Rd Columbus OH 43224

SWEENEY, ROBERT EMMET (D)
RI State Rep
b Holyoke, Mass, Oct 22, 31; s Patrick M Sweeney & Louise H Clarenbach S; m 1957 to Maureen J Oates; c Robert E, Jr, Patrick M, II, Mary K, Thomas O, Maureen J, Anne Louise, Michael W, Sheila R, Alice E & John T. Educ: Brown Univ, 49-52; Col of the Holy Cross, BS in bus admin, 56. Polit & Govt Pos: Mem, North Providence Dem Town Comt, RI, 63-; RI State Rep, 67- Bus & Prof Pos: Exec vpres, Henry W Cooke Co, 73- Mil Serv: Entered as Ens, Navy, 56, released as Lt(jg), 59, after serv in USS Decatur; Comdr, Naval Res, 75. Mem: Gtr Providence Bd Realtors; Soc Real Estate Appraisers (vpres, 75-). Relig: Catholic. Legal Res: 1612 Smith St North Providence RI 02911 Mailing Add: 623 Hosp Trust Bldg Providence RI 02903

SWEENEY, ROBERT FRANK (R)
Asst Committeeman, Rep Nat Comt, Colo
b Craig, Colo, Feb 13, 38; s Henry Sweeney & June O'Connell S; m 1958 to Geraldine Keeling; c Saundra, Sharon, Susan & Patrick. Educ: Colo State Univ, Ft Collins, BS, 59; Sigma Chi. Polit & Govt Pos: Secy, Fourth Dist Rep Party, Colo, 62-64; mem adv bd, Colo SBA, Denver, 70-74; city councilman, Craig, 70-72, mayor, 72-74; alt deleg, Rep Nat Conv, 72; asst committeeman, Rep Nat Comt, 73- Bus & Prof Pos: Ed & publ, Dairy Press & others, Colo, 60- Mil Serv: Entered as 2nd Lt, Army Res, 59, released as 1st Lt, 60; reentered, Capt, 70- Mem: Lions Int; Colo Munic League; Colo Press Asn; Craig CofC; Craig Jaycees (vpres, 60-). Honors & Awards: Jaycee Distinguished Serv Award, 68; Sweepstake Ed Award, Colo Press Asn, 74, 1st Place in Community Serv, 74; Moffat Co Outstanding Citizen Award, 72. Relig: Congregational. Legal Res: 1052 Barclay St Craig CO 81625 Mailing Add: Box 1115 Craig CO 81625

SWEENEY, THOMAS FRANCIS (D)
Conn State Rep
b Norwich, Conn, May 10, 33; s Thomas Phillip Sweeney & Jane Toomey S; m 1973 to Christine Cote. Educ: Norwich Free Acad. Polit & Govt Pos: Conn State Rep, 60th Dist, 67-71, 46th Dist, 71-, chmn, Transportation Comt, Conn State Legis. Mil Serv: Entered as Pvt, Marine Corps, 49, released as Pfc, 52, after serv in Fleet Marine Force, Korean Conflict, 51-52. Mem: VFW; Young Dems; Nat Legis Conf. Honors & Awards: Norwich Young Man of the Year, 70; Pres Award, Mohegan Community Col, 73; Vet Award, Norwich, 75. Relig: Catholic. Legal Res: 14 Rose Garden Lane Norwich CT 06360 Mailing Add: Box 1127 Norwich CT 06360

SWEET, JOSEPH JOHN (D)
Chmn, Steuben Co Dem Comt, NY
b Corning, NY, June 17, 14; s Walter C Sweet & Susan M Higgins S; m 1954 to Rose Mary Walenta; c Linda M (Mrs Rumsey), Susan R & Joan E. Educ: Sacred Heart Col, St Marie, Ill, 31-33. Polit & Govt Pos: City committeeman, Corning Dem City Comt, NY, 50-, chmn, 56-59; committeeman, Steuben Co Dem Comt, 50-, chmn, 70-; committeeman, NY State Dem Comt, 65-; dep sheriff, Steuben Co, currently. Bus & Prof Pos: Sr mold designer, Corning Glass Works, 33-; supvr, Steuben Co Bd Supvrs, 61-65; comnr of elecs, Steuben Co, 75- Mil Serv: Entered as Seaman, Navy, 42, released as Yeoman 1/C, 45, after serv in Pac, 43-45; Presidential Citation; Asiatic-Pac Medal; Good Conduct Medal. Mem: Moose; VFW; KofC (Grand Knight, dist dep, chmn cent NY chap). Relig: Catholic. Mailing Add: 265 Washington St Corning NY 14830

SWEETLAND, MONROE MARK (D)
b Salem, Ore, Jan 20, 10; s Dr George J Sweetland & Mildred Mark S; m 1934 to Lillie Megrath; c Barbara (Mrs Smith) & Rebecca. Educ: Wittenberg Univ, AB, 30; Cornell & Syracuse Univs, grad work; Pi Kappa Alpha. Polit & Govt Pos: Alt deleg, Dem Nat Conv, 40, deleg-at-lg, 48-64, mem, Platform Comt, 52-64, deleg, 72; staff, War Prod Bd, 41-43; Dem Nat Committeeman, Ore, 48-56; Ore State Rep, 52-54; Ore State Sen, 54-63; mem, Ore Adv Comn, US Civil Rights Comn, 56-61; assoc dir, Johnson-Humphrey Campaign, 64; deleg, Dem Nat Mid-Term Conf, 74; chmn, Calif Legis Adv Comt to Revise Elec Code, 74- Bus & Prof Pos: Publ, Ore Dem, 48-57; publ, Ore weekly newspapers, Milwaukie, Molalla &

Newport, 45-64; lectr jour, Padjadjaran Univ, Bandung, Indonesia, 63-64; legis consult, Western States Comn, Nat Educ Asn, 64- Mil Serv: Entered as Asst Field Dir, Am Red Cross, 43, released as Field Supvr, Okinawa, 45, after serv in Pac Theater, Marshall Islands & Okinawa Combat Opers. Honors & Awards: Oregon's First Citizen for Educ, Ore Educ Asn, 60; received award from Japanese-Am Citizens League & West Coast Region Merit Award, NAACP, 61; founded Indonesian-Am Soc of US, 62. Relig: Methodist. Mailing Add: 1651 Yorktown Rd San Mateo CA 94402

SWEETMAN, DORIS DWAN (D)
Mem, Dem State Cent Comt, Conn
b Winsted, Conn, June 4, 18; d William H Dwan, Sr & Mary Buckley D; m 1943 to George A Sweetman; c William James. Educ: Trinity Col (DC), BA, 40. Polit & Govt Pos: Mem, Dem State Cent Comt, Conn, 68- Bus & Prof Pos: Vpres & secy, Dwan & Co, Inc, Torrington, Conn, 43- Relig: Roman Catholic. Mailing Add: Beach St Litchfield CT 06759

SWEEZY, JOHN W (R)
Chmn, Marion Co Rep Cent Comt, Ind
b Indianapolis, Ind, Nov 14, 32; s William C Sweezy & Zuma F McNew S; m 1956 to Carole S Harman; c John W, Jr & Bradley E. Educ: Purdue Univ, BSME, 56; Ind Univ, Bloomington, MBA, 58; Butler Univ; Univ Ga; Ind Cent Col; Sigma Iota Epsilon; Student Senate; Int Asn; DeMolay; chmn region five, Collegiate Young Rep, 56. Polit & Govt Pos: Treas, Marion Co Young Rep, Ind, 56-58; Rep precinct committeeman, Marion Co, 58-66, Rep ward chmn, 66-72, twp chmn, 67-72, mem, Bd of Sanit Comnrs, 68; vchmn, 11th Dist Rep Party, 68; alt deleg, Rep Nat Conv, 68, deleg, 72; chmn, 11 Cong Dist, 69-72 & 75-; dir, Dept Pub Works, 69-72; chmn, Marion Co Rep Cent Comt, Ind, 72- Bus & Prof Pos: Design engr, Allison Div, Gen Motors Corp, Indianapolis, Ind, 56-57; asst to John Mee, Ind Univ, 58; power sales engr, Indianapolis Power & Light Co, 58-69. Mil Serv: Entered as Pvt E-1, Army, 53, released as Cpl E-4, 55, after serv in 15th Finance Disbursing Sect, Continental Command; Good Conduct Medal; Nat Defense Serv Medal. Mem: Great Lakes Power Club; Am Soc Mech Engrs; Soc Advan Mgt; Teamsters Union. Relig: Methodist. Mailing Add: 166 N Gibson Indianapolis IN 46219

SWEITZER, HENRY BECKER (D)
b Laureldale, Pa, June 15, 18; s Edward Eugene Sweitzer & Mary Anna Lavina Becker S; m 1946 to Marjorie Joan Casey; c Lance Vaughn, Heidi Kristin, Lisa Courtney & Maria Luise. Educ: Naval Acad, BS, 41; George Washington Univ, JD with hon, 50, MS, 65; NATO Defense Col, 57-58; Nat War Col, 64-65; Order of the Coif; Phi Delta Phi. Polit & Govt Pos: Submarine & legal officer, Navy, 36-69; admin asst to US Rep William L Scott, Va, 69-71; admin asst to US Rep Tom Bevill, Ala, 71- Mil Serv: Entered as Seaman, Navy, 36, released as Capt, 69, after serv in All Theaters, 36-69; Distinguished Serv Medal; Three Silver Stars; Legion of Merit; Navy Unit Citation; Philippine Presidential Unit Citation. Publ: Military Law, Naval Inst, 57. Mem: Arlington Co, Va Bar; Supreme Court of Appeals Bar; Supreme Court of the US Bar; US Court of Mil Appeals Bar; NY Yacht Club. Relig: Protestant. Legal Res: 3558 Arlington St Laureldale PA 19605 Mailing Add: 2837 Arizona Terr NW Washington DC 20016

SWENSON, DUAINE VINCENT (D)
SDak State Rep
b Woonsocket, SDak, Mar 27, 19; s Edward Joseph Swenson & Theresa Privet S; m 1943 to Rosemary Agnes Basham; c Carole Marie, Dale Vincent & Lila Agnes. Educ: Woonsocket High Sch, grad, 37. Polit & Govt Pos: Precinct committeeman, Sanborn Co Dem Party, SDak, 58-69; SDak State Rep, Dist 32, 66-72, Dist 9, 73-; deleg, Coun of State Govt, 69- & Four-State Comt on Water & Related Natural Resources, 69- Bus & Prof Pos: Owner & mgr, Farm & Ranch, 43-53 & 59-69, IHC Implement, 53-59. Mem: KofC; Elks; Woonsocket Commercial Club; Sanborn Co Farmer Union Coop; PTA. Relig: Catholic. Mailing Add: Rte 3 Box 5 Woonsocket SD 57385

SWENSON, HAROLD A (D)
b Brooklyn, NY, Oct 24, 27; s Harold Swenson & Ingeborg Wevle S; m 1957 to Elsie L Woodring. Educ: Syracuse Univ, BBA, 51. Polit & Govt Pos: Dir, State Travel Develop Bur, State of Pa, 56-61; dep secy com, Pa Dept Com, 61-63; mayor, Harrisburg, 70- Bus & Prof Pos: Exec dir, Pocono Mts CofC, Stroudsburg, Pa, 54-56; owner, Swenson Travel Serv, Harrisburg, 63- Mil Serv: Entered as Seaman, Navy, 45, released as FC3/C, 47, after serv in Destroyer Squadron, Mediter, 46-47. Publ: Co-auth, Area Tourist Promotion Handbook, State of Pa, 60. Mem: Pa Pub Rels Soc; Pa League of Cities; US Conf Mayors; Rotary Club Harrisburg; Downtown Harrisburg Asn. Honors & Awards: Hannah Solomon Award, Harrisburg Chap, Coun Jewish Women, 72; Serv Award, SAR, 72. Relig: Lutheran. Mailing Add: 1204 Executive House 101 S Second St Harrisburg PA 17101

SWENSON, LEON HUGHIE (R)
Idaho State Sen
b Spanish Fork, Utah, Nov 6, 11; s Jos A Swenson & Cornielia Nielsen S; m 1938 to Dorothy Nelson; c Susan (Mrs Dale Bishop), Sharon Lee (Mrs Alan Bingham), Carolyn (Mrs Jon McCloy); Douglas Leon, Eileen, Lucile & Leland. Educ: Utah State Univ, BS, 35; Sigma Nu; Agr Club; Livestock Judging Team. Polit & Govt Pos: Idaho State Rep, Dist 12, 65-69; Idaho State Sen, Dist 12, 69- Bus & Prof Pos: Agriculturist, Amalgamated Sugar Co, 36-45. Mem: Farm Bur; Countrymens Club. Relig: Latter-day Saint. Mailing Add: RR 2 Box 2121 Nampa ID 83651

SWENSON, SEVERT, JR (R)
Chmn, 23rd Legis Dist Rep Party, Idaho
b Muskegon, Mich, Apr 30, 40; s Severt Swenson & Elizabeth Ruprecht S; m 1965 to Marjorie Kay Stunz; c Severt, III & Maren Kristine. Educ: Cent Mich Univ, BA; Univ Idaho, LLB; Phi Alpha Delta; Sigma Phi Epsilon. Polit & Govt Pos: Vchmn, Gooding Co Planning Comn, 72-73; chmn, 23rd Legis Dist Rep Party, Idaho, 72- Bus & Prof Pos: Chmn & dir, Gooding CofC, 70-71; Fifth Region chmn, Rep Party, 73-74. Mem: Elks (Lodge 1745); Toponis Quarter Horse Asn; Idaho & Fifth Dist Bar Asns. Mailing Add: Rte 1 Box 127 Gooding ID 83330

SWETT, DANA MALCOLM (R)
Mem, Maine Rep State Comt
b Ashland, Maine, June 8, 25; s Charles Frederick Swett & Alice Metcalf S; m 1964 to Linda Rose McCrum; c Deanna Jo (Mrs Stanley Craig). Educ: Ashland Pub Schs, dipl, 32-44; N Y A, Dexter, Maine, Machinist, 44-45. Polit & Govt Pos: Treas, Aroostook Co Rep Comt, 58-62, chmn, 64-66; chmn, Ashland Rep Town Comt, 60-64; mem, Maine Rep State Comt, 66- Bus & Prof Pos: Safety dir, Maine Pub Serv Co, 61-; chmn bd dirs & pres, Great Northern Publ Co. Mem: Am Soc Safety Engrs; New Eng Elec Coun; Nat Safety Coun; F&AM; Cent Am Chap, Am Red Cross (dir). Honors & Awards: Outstanding Rotarian, 72. Relig: Episcopal. Mailing Add: 209 State St Presque Isle ME 04769

SWEZEY, JOHN WILLIAM (R)
Chmn, Henry Co Rep Comt, Va
b Madison, Tenn, Apr 10, 42; s Edwin Fleming Swezey & Esther Negendank S; m 1964 to Ann Snead; c Tracy Elizabeth & John William, Jr. Educ: Randolph-Macon Col, BA, 64; T C Williams Sch Law, Univ Richmond, LLB, 67; Kappa Alpha Order; Delta Theta Phi. Polit & Govt Pos: Finance co-chmn, Nixon Campaign, Martinsville-Henry Co Rep Party, Va, 68, chmn & coordr, Linwood Holton for Gov Campaign, 69; chmn, Henry Co Rep Comt, 69- Bus & Prof Pos: Attorney-at-law, pvt practice, 67-69; partner, Ford Swezey & Beck, Attorneys, 69- Mem: Va State Bar; Va Bar Asn; Martinsville-Henry Co Bar Asn (secy-treas); Va Trial Lawyers Asn; Martinsville Kiwanis. Relig: Episcopal. Mailing Add: 1505 Whittle Rd Martinsville VA 24112

SWIATEK, FRANK E (D)
Mem, Erie Co Dem Exec Comt, NY
b Buffalo, NY, Mar 5, 43; s Edward T Swiatek & Clara Kopera S; m 1965 to Elizabeth Anne Yore; c Jennifer A & Jeffrey F. Educ: Canisius Col, BS. Polit & Govt Pos: Alt deleg, Dem Nat Conv, 68; councilman, Cheektowaga, 68-, chmn youth bd, 68; mem, Erie Co Dem Exec Comt, currently. Bus & Prof Pos: Asst basketball coach, Canisius Col, currently; life ins agent, State Mutual of Am, Buffalo, currently. Mem: Buffalo Life Underwriters. Relig: Roman Catholic. Mailing Add: 64 W Cavalier Cheektowaga NY 14225

SWIFT, IVAN (D)
b Apr 8, 27; s Samuel Swift & Rose S; m 1952 to Mamie Ruth Jones; c Samuel, Nina, Jonathan & Benjamin. Educ: Univ Ala, AB; Sigma Delta Chi; Scabbard & Blade; Scarab. Polit & Govt Pos: Asst to US Sen John Sherman Cooper, 66; asst to chmn, Dem Campaign in Ky, 67; admin asst to US Rep Carl D Perkins, Ky, 73- Bus & Prof Pos: Reporter polit & govt, for Anniston Star, Ala, Birmingham Post-Herald, Birmingham News, Miami Herald & Louisville Courier-Journal, 55-65. Mil Serv: Entered as 2nd Lt, Army, 52, released as 1st Lt, 54, after serv in 101st AB Div. Mem: Nat Dem Club; Burro Club. Legal Res: 3203 19th St N Arlington VA 22201 Mailing Add: 2365 Rayburn Bldg Washington DC 20515

SWIGART, WARREN RUSSELL (R)
City Councilman, Omaha, Nebr
b Desota, Iowa, May 3, 08; s Orville Selby Swigart & Nellie Davis S; m 1932 to Rita Melba Haight; c Russell, Merle & Redella. Educ: Univ Nebr, 29; Univ Nebr at Omaha, 45-47. Polit & Govt Pos: City comnr, Omaha City Comn, 54-57; city councilman, Omaha City Coun, 57-65 & 69-73; mayor's asst, Omaha, 65-69; deleg, Rep Nat Conv, 72; mem, Nebr Rep State Cent Comt, 74- Bus & Prof Pos: Real Estate, 48-73. Mem: Eagles (South Omaha Aerie 154); Big Brothers Asn of Omaha; Blind Asn (bd mem); Open Door Mission Bd (vpres); Salvation Army (vol). Honors & Awards: Outstanding Serv Award, SE Civic Club, Omaha, 65, Omaha Vol of Year, Career Div, 75. Relig: Presbyterian. Mailing Add: 3328 N 58th St Omaha NE 68104

SWIGERT, JOHN LEONARD, JR (R)
b Denver, Colo, Aug 30, 31; s Dr J Leonard Swigert (deceased) & Virginia Seep S; single. Educ: Univ Colo, BS, 53; Rensselaer Polytech Inst, MS, 65; Univ Hartford, MBA, 67; Phi Gamma Delta; Pi Tau Sigma; Sigma Tau. Hon Degrees: DSc, Am Int Col, 70 & Western Mich Univ, 70; LLD, Western State Univ, 70. Polit & Govt Pos: Exec dir comt on sci & technol, US House Rep, 73- Bus & Prof Pos: Eng test pilot, Pratt & Whitney, 57-64; eng test pilot, Am Aviation, Inc, formerly; astronaut, NASA, 66-73. Mil Serv: Air Force, 53-56, serv in Japan & Korea; Mass Air Nat Guard, 57-60; Conn Air Nat Guard, 60-65. Mem: Am Astronaut Soc (fel); Soc Exp Test Pilots (assoc fel); Am Inst Aeronaut & Astronaut (assoc fel); Quiet Birdmen. Honors & Awards: Presidential Medal for Freedom, 70; NASA Distinguished Serv Medal; Co-Recipient, Am Astronaut Soc Flight Achievement Award, 70; City of New York Gold Medal, 70; Haley Astronaut Award, Am Inst Aeronaut & Astronaut, 71; plus others. Mailing Add: Apt N308 560 N St SW Washington DC 20024

SWILLINGER, DANIEL JAMES (R)
b Cincinnati, Ohio, Aug 11, 42; s Nathan Swillinger & Mary Conlon S; div. Educ: Ohio State Univ, BA, 64, JD, 67; Sigma Delta Chi; Sphinx; Theta Chi. Polit & Govt Pos: Staff, Ohio Rep State Hq, 66-67; campaign staff, Charles Mathias Senate Campaign, Md, 68; legis asst, US Rep William Widnall, NJ, 69; campaign consult & counsel, Bailey, Deardourff & Bowen Inc, Washington, DC, 69-71; nat polit dir, Ripon Soc, 71-73, mem nat exec comt, 73-; mem nat bd, Common Cause, 73- Bus & Prof Pos: Asst dean, Col Law, Ohio State Univ, 73-75. Publ: Contrib, Jaws of Victory, Little, Brown, 74; Delegate apportionment to national nominating conventions, Columbia Human Rights Law Rev, 74. Mem: Am Bar Asn. Mailing Add: 214 12th St SE Washington DC 20003

SWINARSKI, DONALD THEODORE (D)
Ill State Sen
b Chicago, Ill, Feb 6, 35; s Theodore Anthony Swinarski & Ann Odeel Miller S; m 1961 to Ella Wensel; c Theodore Anthony, Daniel Todd & Donald, Jr. Educ: Oceanside Carlsbad Col, AA; Knox Col (Ill), BA in Polit Sci. Polit & Govt Pos: Chmn, Young Dem of Cook Co, Ill; alt deleg, Dem Nat Conv, formerly; alderman, 12th Ward, City of Chicago, 68-72; Ill State Sen, 73-; deleg, Dem Nat Mid-Term Conf, 74. Bus & Prof Pos: Regional chmn, Am Cancer Soc; chmn, March of Dimes Drive; bd dirs, Chicago Ment Health Ctr; mem adv bd, Holy Cross Hosp. Mil Serv: Marine Corps, three years. Mem: Am Acad Polit & Social Sci; Prof Asn of Diving Instrs; Polish Nat Alliance; CWV; Am Legion. Honors & Awards: Knighted, Order of St John; Man of Year, Archer-Brighton Community Conserv Coun. Relig: Catholic. Mailing Add: 4444 S Archer Chicago IL 60632

SWINDOLL, GEORGE MITCHELL (D)
b Slate Spring, Miss, June 11, 31; s Bryant Shaw Swindoll & Hattie Mitchell S; m 1962 to Nancy McGuire; c Reuben M & George B. Educ: Univ Miss, BAE, 55, MEd, 58 & LLB, 63, JD, 65; Tau Kappa Alpha; Alpha Phi Omega; Beta Theta Pi. Polit & Govt Pos: Miss State Rep, 60-71; Asst Attorney Gen, Jackson, Miss, 71- Publ: To the people of Calhoun County, Monitor-Herald & Calhoun Co J, 60-71. Mem: Am & Miss Bar Asns; Citizens Coun of Am (exec dir). Honors & Awards: Named One of Outstanding Young Men of Am, 65. Relig: Baptist; Deacon. Mailing Add: 1620 Winchester Jackson MS 39211

SWINEHART, JUDITH ANN (D)
b Thornville, Ohio, Mar 14, 42; d Paul William Brandon & Mary Janice Caryer B; m 1963 to Phillip Dean Swinehart; c Abbey Lynn. Educ: Capital Univ, BS in Nursing, 63; Ohio State Univ, 72- Polit & Govt Pos: Deleg, Dem Nat Conv, 72. Bus & Prof Pos: Staff nurse, Wayne Mem Hosp, Greenville, Ohio, 63-64; clin nursing instr, Bethesda Hosp Sch Nursing, Zanesville, 64-67; clin nursing instr, Ohio Univ, Zanesville Br, 69- Mem: Am Nurses Asn; Am Cancer Soc (bd mem, Perry Co, 72-73). Relig: Lutheran. Mailing Add: 323 First St New Lexington OH 43764

SWINEHART, PHILLIP DEAN (D)
VChmn, Perry Co Dem Cent Comt, Ohio
b Newark, Ohio, Dec 26, 38; s Angus B Swinehart & Agnes Powell S; m 1963 to Judith Ann Brandon; c Abbey Lynn. Educ: Miami Univ, BS, 61; Ball State Univ, MA, 66. Polit & Govt Pos: Chmn, Gilligan for Gov, Perry Co, Ohio, 70; deleg, Dem Nat Conv, 72; mem, Perry Co Dem Cent Comt, 72-, vchmn, currently. Bus & Prof Pos: Teacher, Ansonia High Sch, Ohio, 61-64; teacher, New Lexington High Sch, 64-72; prin, New Lexington Jr High Sch, 72- Mem: Ohio Asn Sec Sch Prin; Ohio & Nat Educ Asns; Phi Delta Kappa; Elks (Exalted Ruler, 68-69). Relig: Lutheran. Mailing Add: 323 First St New Lexington OH 43764

SWINFORD, JOHN MCKEE (D)
Majority Floor Leader, Ky House of Rep
b Cynthiana, Ky, Apr 19, 32; s Mac Swinford & Benton Peterson S; m 1963 to Mary Katherine Foster; c James Lewis & William Kinney. Educ: Princeton Univ; Univ Mich Sch of Law; Univ Mich Student Bar Asn. Polit & Govt Pos: Mem, Harrison Co Dem Comt, 60-; Ky State Rep, 62-66 & 70-, Majority Floor Leader, Ky House of Rep, 72- Bus & Prof Pos: Dir, Cynthiana Businessmen's Club, 60-62 & 65-66; dir, Cynthiana Harrison Co CofC, 64-67. Mil Serv: Entered as Pvt, Army, 54, released as Specialist 3/C, 56; Good Conduct Medal. Mem: Ky State & Am Bar Asns; Am Legion. Relig: Presbyterian. Legal Res: 106 S Elmarch Ave Cynthiana KY 41031 Mailing Add: Box 363 Cynthiana KY 41031

SWINK, WILLIAM L (D)
Ariz State Sen
Mailing Add: 909 Third Ave San Manuel AZ 85631

SWINTON, JUDY ANN (D)
Okla State Rep
b Churchpoint, La, 49; d Jessie Ray Gilliland & Ruby Lee Thibadeaux G; m 1970 to Charles Donald Swinton. Educ: Okla State Univ, 68-71. Polit & Govt Pos: Okla State Rep, 74- Relig: Disciples of Christ. Mailing Add: 2712 N Wheeler Oklahoma City OK 73127

SWIONTEK, STEVEN J (R)
Treas, NDak Fedn Col Rep
b Ellendale, NDak, May 21, 54; s Theodore M Swiontek & Loretta F Ziegler S; single. Educ: NDak State Univ, 72-, four year Army ROTC scholar, 72-, student body pres, 75; Sigma Alpha Epsilon; Blue Key. Polit & Govt Pos: Chmn, Edgeley TAR, NDak, 71-72; vchmn, NDak State TAR, 71-72; mem, NDak Rep Youth Coun, 71-; aide to Lt Gov Richard Larsen in Gov Campaign, 72; deleg, Rep Nat Conv, 72; second vchmn, NDak State Univ Col Rep, 72-73; treas, NDak Fedn Col Rep, 73-; mem, NDak Young Rep, currently; summer intern, US Dept State, 73; aide to US Sen Milton R Young, 74; mem, NDak Criminal Justice Comn, 74-; vchmn, NDak Juv Task Force. Mem: 1200 Club of NDak Rep Party; Washington Workshops Found, DC (youth adv). Honors & Awards: Youngest deleg to Rep Nat Conv, 72; ROTC Medal. Relig: Lutheran Church-Mo Synod; State pres, Active Christian Teens, 72-74. Mailing Add: 302 Seventh Ave Edgeley ND 58433

SWISHER, PAUL W (R)
Ind State Sen
b Waverly, Ind, Feb 22, 18; s Charles Omer Swisher & Leafy Deborh Minnett S; m 1937 to Louise Duncan; c Janet Marie (Mrs Max MacKenzie), Paula Louise (Mrs Herbert V Schelm) & Charles Duncan. Educ: Mooresville High Sch, grad, 36. Polit & Govt Pos: Ind State Sen, 68- Bus & Prof Pos: Gen foreman, Allison Div of GMC, Indianapolis, Ind, 42-48; owner & operator, Mooresville Feed & Supply Co, Ind, 48-61; sales mgr, Vestal Motor Co, Inc, 61-69; dir pub rels, Kendrick Mem Hosp, 69- Mem: F&AM; Scottish Rite. Relig: Society of Friends. Mailing Add: PO Box 85 Mooresville IN 46158

SWISHER, PERRY (D)
Idaho State Rep
Mailing Add: 355 S 11th Ave Pocatello ID 83201

SWITASKI, ANNA-MAE (R)
b Philadelphia, Pa, Aug 24, 09; d James Francis Havlick & Isabel Mitchell Thompson H; m 1936 to Bernard John Switaski; wid. Educ: Cent Conn State Col, 29. Polit & Govt Pos: Organizer, Conn Young Rep, 34; mem, Conn State Rep Cent Comt, 39-52, vchmn, 50-73; asst to Secy of State, Conn, 43-45 & 47-49; engrossing clerk, Conn Gen Assembly, 49; deleg, Rep Nat Conv, 44 & 52-72, mem, Nat Platform Comt, 56 & 64; pres, Conn Coun Rep Women's Clubs, 50-68; mem adv bd, Nat Fedn Rep Women, 50-68; mem, Annual Assay Comn, US Mint, 59; mem, Gov Comn to Revise Elec Laws, 61-62, 69-70 & 72-73; mem, Gov Comn to Study Qualifications of Electors, 67-69; mem, Gov Comn to Study Procedures for Nomination of Presidential Electors; mem, Conn State Liquor Control Comn, 73- Bus & Prof Pos: Teacher, New Britain Jr High Schs, Conn, 29-40. Mailing Add: 273 Main St Farmington CT 06032

SWOBE, C COE (R)
b Reno, Nev, May 23, 29; s John Bradford Swobe & Maxine Elizabeth Bridgman S; m 1959 to Janet Quilici; c Caryn Coe & Jaclyn. Educ: Univ Nev, BS, 54; Univ Denver, LLB, 58; Phi Alpha Delta; Sigma Nu (dir). Polit & Govt Pos: Pres, Univ Nev Alumni Asn Young Rep, 53-54; legis bill drafter, Nev, 58-59; US Attorney, Dist of Nev, 59-61; Nev State Assemblyman, 63-64, Minority Floor Leader, Nev State Assembly, 65-66; chmn, Platform Comt, Nev Rep State Conv, 66; Nev State Sen, 66-74, Minority Floor Leader, Nev State Senate, 71-74; alt deleg, Rep Nat Conv, 72. Bus & Prof Pos: Assoc, law firm, Sidney W Robinson, 62-67; pvt practice law, 67- Mil Serv: Entered as Airman 3/C, Air Force, 50, released as Airman 1/C, 52. Mem: Am Judicature Soc; Boy Scouts Am (bd mem); Elks; Salvation Army (bd mem); Univ Nev Alumni Asn. Honors & Awards: Selected Young Man of the Year, Reno Jr CofC, 63. Relig: Methodist. Legal Res: 1495 Belford Rd Reno NV 89502 Mailing Add: PO Box 1588 Reno NV 89505

SWOBODA, JANICE MARIE (D)
Secy, Eighth Cong Dist Dem Party, Wis
b Green Bay, Wis, May 19, 43; d Gordon John Hendricks & Cecelia Delwich H; m 1968 to Lary J Swoboda. Educ: Dominican Col (Wis), 63-66. Polit & Govt Pos: Managed husband's campaigns to Wis State Legis, 72 & 74; secy, Eighth Cong Dist Dem Party, Wis, 73-; deleg, Dem Nat Mid-Term Conf, 74; secy, Kewaunee Co Dem Party, 74-75, mem, currently. Mem: Luxemburg Jaycettes; Door Co League Women Voters. Relig: Roman Catholic. Mailing Add: 507 Oak Luxemburg WI 54217

SWOBODA, LARY JOSEPH (D)
Wis State Rep
b Luxemburg, Wis, May 28, 39; s Joseph Francis Swoboda & Catherine Daul S; m 1968 to Janice Marie Hendricks. Educ: Sacred Heart Sem, 57-58; Univ Wis, Milwaukee, BS, 63, MS, 68; Phi Eta Sigma; Phi Kappa Phi; Kappa Delta Pi. Polit & Govt Pos: Wis State Rep, 71- Bus & Prof Pos: Chmn bd, Luxemburg Industs, Inc, currently. Mem: Wis Educ Asn; Holy Name Soc; KofC; Jr CofC; Kewaunee Co Hist Soc. Relig: Roman Catholic. Mailing Add: 507 Oak St Luxemburg WI 54217

SYAS, GEORGE D (R)
Nebr State Sen
b Omaha, Nebr, Feb 11, 11; m 1940 to Pauline Frances Crowder; c two. Educ: Omaha North High Sch, grad. Polit & Govt Pos: Chmn, 12th Ward Rep Comt, 8 years; Nebr State Sen, 51- Bus & Prof Pos: Machinist, Union Pac RR, 33 years. Mem: Mason; Eastern Star; RAM; KT; AAONMS. Honors & Awards: Award of Merit, Am Asn Conserv Info, 60; Sch Bell Award, Omaha Educ Asn, 64; Nat Recreation & Park Asn Award, 66; Nebr Coun of Sportsmen's Award, 67. Relig: Congregational; former mem bd of trustees, Cent Park Congregational Church. Mailing Add: 5312 Fontenelle Blvd Omaha NE 68111

SYDOW, DONNA FRANCES (D)
Chmn, Hall Co Dem Party, Nebr
b Carroll, Nebr, Aug 3, 27; d Paul Ewoldt Broeker & Mary Wurdinger B; m 1947 to Murle LaRue Sydow, div; c Paulette, Carol Meyer, Alan, Coral & Craig. Educ: Wayne State Col, AB, 47; Univ Northern Colo, 50-51; Kearney State Col, 72-73; Pi Omega Pi; Kappa Mu Epsilon. Polit & Govt Pos: Treas, Hall Co Dem Party, Nebr, 62-72, chmn, 74-; committeewoman, Nebr State Rep Cent Comt, 36th Legis Dist, 66- Mem: League of Women Voters; Am Asn Univ Women. Relig: Catholic. Mailing Add: 2708 W Anna Grand Island NE 68801

SYKES, JAMES THURMAN (D)
b Cedar Rapids, Iowa, July 12, 35; s John James Sykes & Edith Waddell S Larson; m 1958 to Marguerite Svensson; c Kathleen Ellen, Sven Steven & Julie Elisabeth. Educ: Univ Minn, Duluth, BS, 57; Kent State Univ, MA, 65; Univ Wis, 62-; Bulldog Award for Serv, Student Comn; pres, Bd of Publ. Polit & Govt Pos: Peace Corps Field Rep, 61-63; state treas, Am for Dem Action, Wis, 63-; mem, Dane Co Dem Party, 67-68; deleg, Wis State Dem Conv, many times; deleg, Dem Nat Conv, 68; mem, Bd of Supvr, Dane Co, Wis, 68-72; chmn, Wis Bd Aging & Dane Co Housing Authority; mem, Juv Court Adv Comt; proj dir, Colonial Club Sr Ctr, currently; mem, Nat Coun Sr Citizens & Nat Coun on Aging. Bus & Prof Pos: Prog dir, YMCA, Iowa State Univ, 59-60; prog dir, YMCA, Univ Wis, 60-68; dir, Brazil Exchange, 66-68; teacher, Univ Wis Ctr Syst, 67 & dir pub serv, Wis Cheeseman, 68- Publ: What is a Christian association?, 66 & Why the YMCA speaks, 67, Asn Forum. Mem: Gerontological Soc. Relig: Society of Friends. Legal Res: 2100 Rowley Ave Madison WI 53505 Mailing Add: PO Box 1 Madison WI 53701

SYKES, MARY FLANDERS (R)
Mem, Brattleboro Town Rep Comt, Vt
b Manchester, NH, Sept 14, 30; d Franklin Flanders & Florence Emerson F; m 1953 to Richard Lee Sykes; c Rebecca Lee, Katherine Chase & Franklin Thomas. Educ: Duke Univ, AB in Hist, 52; co-ed, Duke Chronicle, 51-52. Polit & Govt Pos: Mem, Brattleboro Town Rep Comt, 57-, secy, 57-63, vchmn, 63-67; deleg, Vt State Rep Conv, 60-68; corresponding secy, Vt Fedn Rep Women, 61-63, second vpres, 63-65, first vpres, 65-67, pres, 67-69; mem, Windham Co Rep Comt, 61-69; alt deleg, Rep Nat Conv, 64; rep, Brattleboro Town Meeting, 65-66; mem exec comt, Vt State Rep Comt, 65-69; mem bd dirs, Nat Fedn Rep Women, 67-69; mem, Vt Housing Comn, 69-70. Bus & Prof Pos: Asst ed, Duke Univ Alumni Register, 52-53; vpres, Franklin Properties, Inc, Brattleboro, Vt, 68-; dir, Morningside Cemetery Asn, Brattleboro, 69- Mem: Eastern Star; Brattleboro Mem Hosp Auxiliary; Brattleboro Riding Club (pres, 72-73). Relig: Baptist. Legal Res: South St West Brattleboro VT 05301 Mailing Add: PO Box 203 West Brattleboro VT 05301

SYLVESTER, BARBARA THORNTON (D)
Dem Nat Committeewoman, SC
b Florence, SC, Mar 8, 29; d Hugh Bernard Thornton, Sr & Ola Mae Williamson T; m 1954 to Dr Joseph George Sylvester; c Pamela Mae & Elsa April. Educ: Mars Hill Col, NC, 1 year; Western Carolina Col, 1 year. Polit & Govt Pos: Vchmn, Florence Co Dem Party, SC, 62-64; alt deleg, Dem Nat Conv, 64, deleg, 68 & 72, mem, Rules Comt, 72; coordr, Lady Bird Spec, SC, 64; dir women's activities, SC Dem Party, 64-66; co-dir, SC Campaign for Humphrey-Muskie, 68; Dem Nat Committeewoman, SC, 68-; mem bd dirs, Florence Co Off of Econ Opportunity & mem, Rules Comn of Dem Party, 69; secy, State Juv Correction Bd, 69-71; mem credentials comt, Dem Nat Comt, 69-; chmn, Florence Co White House Conf on Children & Youth, 70-71. Bus & Prof Pos: SC deleg, Woman's Auxiliary to the Am Med Asn, 56; pres, Pee Dee Med Auxiliary, 60-61, civil defense chmn, 61-62; pres, McLeod Infirmary Med Auxiliary, 61-62; community serv chmn, SC Med Auxiliary, 61-62, third vpres, 62-63. Mem: Florence Co Civil Defense Prog; Florence Co & SC Asn Retarded Children; SC Dept of Youth Serv (chmn bd, 71-); First Step Red Brick Sch (chmn bd, 72-). Relig: Episcopal. Mailing Add: 510 Camellia Circle Florence SC 29501

SYLVESTER, CHRISTOPHER URDAHL (R)
b Grand Forks, NDak, Dec 30, 29; s Hans Sylvester & Evelyn Johnson S; m 1959 to Elizabeth Ulsaker; c Margarethe, Kirsten & Hans. Educ: Jamestown Col, 49-51; Univ NDak, LLB, 54; Phi Delta Phi. Polit & Govt Pos: Asst Attorney Gen, Bismarck, NDak, 54-55; exec secy, US Sen Milton R Young, NDak, 55-57, admin asst, 57- Mil Serv: Entered as Pvt, Army, 47, released as Pfc, 48, after serv in 2nd Inf Div. Publ: Articles as assoc ed, NDak Law Rev, 53-54; various case notes. Mem: NDak Bar Asn; Mason. Relig: Lutheran. Legal Res: Hatton ND 58240 Mailing Add: 1831 Brior Ridge Ct McLean VA 22101

SYLVESTER, FRANK WILLIAM (R)
Mayor, Clifton, NJ
b Lyndhurst, NJ, May 3, 22; s George A F Sylvester & Olive M Davis S; m 1942 to Margaret T Madden; c Frances M (Mrs Spring) & Dennis W. Educ: Fairleigh Dickinson Univ, 53-54. Polit & Govt Pos: Councilman, Clifton, NJ, 70-74; mayor, 74- Bus & Prof Pos: Toolmaker, US Tool Co, East Orange, NJ, 42-63; production foreman, J L Prescott Co, Passaic, 63-68; supvr, Bur Criminal Identification, Passaic Co, Paterson, 68- Mil Serv: Entered as Seaman 2/C, Navy, 43, released as Machinist 2/C, 46, after serv in USS Boston, SPac, 44-46; Unit Citation, Asiatic Pac Ribbon with Two Battle Stars. Mem: F&AM (Lodge 203); VFW (past comdr, Post 7165, Clifton, NJ, 56); Am Legion (comdr, Post 8, 68); US Tool Div Local 467, East Orange. Honors & Awards: Outstanding Citizen Award, VFW Post 7165, 72; Man of the Year, Clifton Leader Newspaper, 74; Outstanding Supporter, Clifton Girls Club, 75. Relig: Presbyterian; deacon. Mailing Add: 125 Livingston St Clifton NJ 07013

SYMINGTON, JAMES W (D)
US Rep, Mo
b New York, NY, Sept 28, 27; s Sen Stuart Symington & Evelyn Wadsworth S; m 1953 to Sylvia Caroline Schlapp; c Julia Hay & Jeremy Wadsworth. Educ: Yale Univ, BA, 50; Columbia Univ, LLB, 54. Polit & Govt Pos: Asst city counr, St Louis, Mo, 54-55; US Foreign Serv, London, 58-60; dep dir Food for Peace, White House, 61-62; admin asst to Attorney Gen of US, 62-63; dir, President Comt on Juv Delinquency, 65-66; consult, President Comn Law Enforcement & Admin of Justice, 65-66; Chief of Protocol, Dept of State, 66-68; US Rep, Second Dist, Mo, 69-; mem, Comts on Sci & Technol & Interstate & Foreign Com, Subcomts on Sci, Research & Technol, chmn, Space Sci & Appln, Energy & Health & Environ, US House Rep. Bus & Prof Pos: Assoc attorney, law firm, 55-58, 60-61 & 63-65. Mil Serv: Marine Corps, 45-46. Publ: Auth, The Stately Game. Mem: Mo, DC, Fed & Am Bar Asns; Am Fedn Musicians. Legal Res: St Louis Co MO Mailing Add: 307 Cannon House Off Bldg Washington DC 20515

SYMINGTON, JOHN FIFE, JR (R)
b Baltimore, Md, Aug 27, 10; s John Fife Symington & Arabella Hambleton S; m 1939 to Martha Frick; c Helen Clay (Mrs Minturn V Chace), Arabella Hambleton (Mrs Edward N Dane), Martha Howard Frick (Mrs Jenney) & J Fife, III. Educ: Princeton Univ, BA, 33. Polit & Govt Pos: Co-chmn, Rep in Action Comt, Baltimore Co, Md, formerly; cand, US Rep, Second Dist, Md, 58, 60 & 62; chmn & trustee, Rep Assocs, Baltimore Co, Inc, 59; mem, Comt to Revise Const & By-Laws of Rep Party, Md, 59; chmn, Md Rep State Finance Comt, 63, 64 & 65; chmn, Second Rep Cong Dist, Md, formerly; mem exec comt, Md State Rep Cent Comt, formerly; US Ambassador to Trinidad & Tobago, 69-71. Bus & Prof Pos: Mech helper, Glenn L Martin Co, 33-34; traffic rep, Pan Am Airways, 34-35, traffic & opers rep, 35-36, supvr, Argentine Off, 36-37, mgr, Atlantic, 37-39, sr rep in Europe, 39-40, asst to mgr, Atlantic Div, 41-42, exec head officer, 42-48, exec asst to sr vpres & regional mgr, 46-48; pres, Baltimore Co Supply Co, 48- Mil Serv: Entered as Lt(jg), Naval Res, assigned Pan Am World Airways Spec Serv. Mem: Baltimore Co Cancer Crusade; Child Welfare League of Am; Md Training Sch for Boys (bd mgrs); Md Children's Aid Soc, Inc; Baltimore Co Health & Welfare Coun. Relig: Episcopal. Mailing Add: Seminary Ave Lutherville MD 21093

SYMINGTON, STUART (D)
US Sen, Mo
b Amherst, Mass, June 26, 01; s William Stuart Symington (deceased) & Emily Harrison S (deceased); m 1924 to Evelyn Wadsworth (deceased); c Stuart & James; six grandchildren. Educ: Yale Univ, AB, 23. Hon Degrees: DSBA, Bryant Col, 48; LLD, Baylor Univ, 50, William Jewell Col, 53, Park Col, 57, Rockhurst Col, 59, Univ Mass, Amherst, 59, Avila Col, 63, Univ Mo-Columbia, 65, Washington Univ, 66, William Woods Col, 69 & Drury Col, 72; DLett, Col of Osteopathy & Surg, 58; DHL, Mo Valley Col, 63. Polit & Govt Pos: Chmn, Surplus Property Bd, 45; Asst Secy of War for Air, 46; First Secy, Air Force, 47; chmn, Nat Sec Resources Bd, 50; adminr, Reconstruction Finance Corp, 51; US Sen, Mo, 52-, mem, Comts on Aeronaut & Space Sci, Armed Serv, Foreign Rels, Appropriations for Armed Serv & Space, Dem Policy, Dem Steering & Joint Atomic Energy, US Senate; deleg, Dem Nat Conv, 72. Bus & Prof Pos: Employee, various elec & iron & steel co, 23-37; pres, Emerson Elec Mfg Co, 38-45. Mil Serv: Army, 17-19. Mem: Am Legion; Mason (32 degree); Shrine. Honors & Awards: Medal for Merit, 47; Distinguished Serv Medal, 52. Relig: Episcopal. Legal Res: 24 Willow Hill St Louis MO 63124 Mailing Add: Senate Off Bldg Washington DC 20510

SYMMS, STEVEN D (R)
US Rep, Idaho
b Nampa, Idaho, Apr 23, 38; s George Darwin Symms & Mary Irene Knowlton S; m 1959 to Frances E Stockdale; c Dan, Susan, Amy & Katy. Educ: Univ Idaho, BS, 60. Polit & Govt Pos: Pres, Canyon Co Rep Boosters Club, 66-67; US Rep, Idaho, 73- Bus & Prof Pos: Vpres, Symms Fruit Ranch, Inc, until 73. Mil Serv: Entered as 2nd Lt, Marines 60, released as 1st Lt, 63 after serv in 1st Marine Div. Mem: Rotary; CofC; Idaho Hort Soc; Idaho Fresh Fruit & Veg Orgn. Relig: Protestant. Legal Res: RR 6 Caldwell ID 83605 Mailing Add: 1410 Longworth House Off Bldg Washington DC 20515

SYMONS, JOANNE L (D)
Asst Minority Leader, NH House Rep
b Brooklyn, NY, Feb 25, 41; d Hal Lyman & Irene Fife L; m 1963 to Alan G Symons; c Noel & Jeremy. Educ: Brooklyn Col, BA, 62. Polit & Govt Pos: Deleg, Dem Nat Mid-Term Conf, 74; co-chmn, NH Dem Platform Comt, 74-; mem adv bd, NH Dem State Comt, 74-; NH State Rep, 75-, asst minority leader, NH House Rep, 75- Bus & Prof Pos: Teacher, Cookeville, Vt, 63-65, Bennington, Vt, 65-68 & Lebanon, NH, 71-72; dir adult basic educ, Lebanon, Hanover & Enfield, NH, 73- Mem: Dem Women of NH (pres, 74-); League of Women Voters; Bus & Prof Women. Mailing Add: 52 Green St Lebanon NH 03766

SYMONS, JOYCE (D)
Mich State Rep
b Detroit, Mich, Sept 10, 27; married 1945; c Jill, Gary & Mark. Educ: Detroit Western High Sch, grad. Polit & Govt Pos: Mich State Rep, 64-; mem, 16th Cong Dist Dem Party Orgn & Mich Dem State Cent Comt, currently. Mem: Nat Order Women Legis (historian); Allen Park Dem Club; Lincoln Park Dem Club; Mich Kidney Found; Women of Moose. Relig: Presbyterian. Mailing Add: 9648 Buckinham Allen Park MI 48101

SYNHORST, MELVIN D (R)
Secy of State, Iowa
b Orange City, Iowa, Jan 21, 14; s Hugo Synhorst & Ethel Lucas S; m 1942 to Alice Rossing; c Robert B & William J. Educ: Univ Iowa, BA & JD. Polit & Govt Pos: Secy of State, Iowa, currently. Bus & Prof Pos: Attorney-at-law, Des Moines, Iowa. Mil Serv: Lt(jg), Naval Res, World War II. Mem: Nat Asn Secy State; Am Legion; Mason. Honors & Awards: Shrine Recipient, Am Heritage Found Award for Outstanding Citizenship, 61. Legal Res: 4713 Observatory Rd Des Moines IA 50311 Mailing Add: State Capitol Des Moines IA 50319

SYRI, AMY (R)
Vt State Rep
Mailing Add: Shadow Lake Concord VT 05824

SZABO, DANIEL (R)
Dep Asst Secy of State for Inter-Am Affairs
b Budapest, Hungary, Mar 23, 33; s Alexander Szabo & Maria Berger S; m 1955 to Corinne Holiber; c Nancy Beth & Peter Stuart. Educ: City Col New York, BA, 57; Sch Advan Int Studies, Johns Hopkins Univ, MA, 59; Omicron Chi Epsilon; Tau Delta Phi. Polit & Govt Pos: Int economist, US Tariff Comn, 59-60; desk officer, US Dept of Com, Viet Nam, Cambodia & Laos, 60-63; spec asst to Sen Jacob K Javits, NY, 63-69; Dep Asst Secy of State for Inter-Am Affairs, 69- Mil Serv: Entered as Pvt, Army, 54, released as Sp-3, 56, after serv in 101st Airborne Div. Publ: The US Point 4 & the UN Technical Assistance Program, City Col Bus & Econ Rev, fall 56. Mem: Alumni Coun, Sch Advan Int Studies, Johns Hopkins Univ; Nat Acad Econ & Polit Sci; Ctr for Inter-Am Rels; Far Eastern Luncheon Group (exec comt). Mailing Add: 11600 Danville Dr Rockville MD 20852

SZCZARBA, ARLENE LEE (D)
Chmn, Bethany Dem Town Comt, Conn
b Milwaukee, Wis, Nov 4, 37; d Arne W Roschild & Ludmilla Stefanec R; m 1955 to Robert Henry Szczarba; c Garrett Lee & Cheryl Anne. Educ: Univ Chicago, 55-56. Polit & Govt Pos: Deleg, Dem State Conv, 72; chmn, Bethany Dem Town Comt, 72- Mem: Neighborhood Music Sch (coun mem, 71-); Creative Arts Workshop (bd dirs & secy, 72-); League Women Voters; Urban League New Haven. Relig: Lutheran. Mailing Add: Peck Rd Bethany CT 06525

SZUMILO, DANIEL FRANCIS (D)
b Central Falls, RI, Apr 5, 52; s Francis Szumilo & Genevieve Zakowski S; single. Educ: Univ RI, currently; mem, Student Senate, const comn, 72-73. Polit & Govt Pos: New Dem Coalition deleg, RI Primary, 72; mem, Coalition, 72-; McGovern coordr, Univ RI, 72, Pawtucket, 72 & Black Valley, 72; deleg, Dem Nat Conv, 72; youth coordr, Rep Fay, Central Falls, 72. Bus & Prof Pos: Freshman summer orientation staff, Univ RI, 73. Mem: RI Young Dem. Honors & Awards: Youth of Year, Blackstone Valley Cath Youth Orgn, 70; Hist Medal, St Raphael Acad, 70; Washington Internship for US Rep Tiernan, RI, Univ RI Dept Polit Sci, 73. Relig: Roman Catholic. Legal Res: 121 Cross St Central Falls RI 02863 Mailing Add: Univ of RI Bressler 105 Kingston RI 02881

T

TABLACK, GEORGE D (D)
Ohio State Rep
Mailing Add: 756 Porter Ave Campbell OH 44405

TABOR, JOHN KAYE (R)
Under Secy Commerce
b Uniontown, Pa, Apr 19, 21; s Edward O Tabor & Marguerite Kaye T; m 1952 to Kate Hill Williams; c John K Tabor, Jr & William H. Educ: Yale Univ, BA, 42; Cambridge Univ, BA, 47, MA, 53; Harvard Univ, LLB, 50. Hon Degrees: DHumane Letters, Alliance Col, 74. Polit & Govt Pos: Chmn, Citizens for Scranton & Van Zandt, 62; secy com, State of Pa, 63-67; elected secy internal affairs, 67-68, secy of labor & indust, 68-69; Rep cand for city coun, Pittsburgh, 61; chmn, Pa Indust Develop Authority, 63-67, mem, 67-69; Pa secy, Gen State Authority, Pa, 67-69; alt deleg, Rep Nat Conv, 68; Rep cand for mayor, Pittsburgh, 69; chmn, Housing Task Force, Allegheny Co Reappraisal Comn, 70-72; chmn, Reelect President Comt, SW Pa, 72; chmn housing strike force, Health & Welfare Asn of Allegheny Co, 72-73; Under Secy Commerce, 73- Bus & Prof Pos: Assoc, Winthrop, Stimson, Putnam & Roberts, New York, 50-53; assoc, Kirkpatrick, Pomeroy, Lockhart & Johnson, Pittsburgh, 53-58, partner, 58-62, partner, Kirkpatrick, Lockhart, Johnson & Hutchinson, 70-73; co-chmn, Appalachian Regional Comn, 65-67. Mil Serv: Entered as Midn, Naval Res, 43, released as Lt, 46, after serv in minesweeping & anti-submarine warfare, Pac, 44-46; Pac & Am Theatre Medals; Victory Medal. Mem: Pa Bar Asn; Episcopal Diocese of Pittsburgh (trustee); Pittsburgh Pastorial Inst; Health & Welfare Asn of Allegheny Co (dir); Am Legion; Masaryk Publ Trust. Honors & Awards: Polit & Govt Man of the Year, Pittsburgh Guardians, 69. Legal Res: 1616 34th St NW Washington DC 20007 Mailing Add: Dept of Commerce Washington DC 20230

TACKE, E H (JACK) (D)
Idaho State Sen
Mailing Add: Cottonwood ID 83522

TADDONIO, LEE C (R)
Pa State Rep
Mailing Add: Capitol Bldg Harrisburg PA 17120

TAFFER, JACK J (D)
Nat Committeeman, Young Dem Clubs Am, Fla
b New York, NY, Apr 13, 37; s Philip Taffer & Lee Wald T; m 1969 to Susan E Friedberg; c Sheri Jill. Educ: NY Univ, BS, 59; Univ Miami Sch Law, JD, 62; Phi Epsilon Pi. Polit & Govt Pos: Mem, Econ Adv Bd, Miami, Fla, 66-67; city prosecutor, Opa Locka, Fla, 67-70; mem, Charter Rev Bd, Miami, 68-; nat committeeman, Young Dem Clubs Am, Fla, 65-; pres, Young Dem Club Dade Co, 68-69; munic judge, Opa Locka, 70- Bus & Prof Pos: Fla Bar Comt on Criminal Law, 67- Mem: Am Judicature Asn; Nat Asn Defense Attorneys; Mason; Scottish Rite; Tiger Bay Polit Club. Honors & Awards: Fraternity Man of Year, Phi Epsilon Pi, 59; Young Dem Club Man of Year Award, 67. Relig: Jewish. Legal Res: 2208 S Miami Ave Miami FL 33129 Mailing Add: 1700 NW Seventh St Miami FL 33125

TAFT, CHARLES P (R)
City Councilman, Cincinnati, Ohio

b Cincinnati, Ohio Sept 20, 97; s William H Taft & Helen Herron T; m 1917 to Eleanor Chase, wid 1961; c Eleanor (Mrs Hall), Sylvia (Mrs Lotspeich), Seth, Cynthia (Mrs Morris), Lucia C (deceased), Rosalyn R (deceased) & Peter R. Educ: Yale Univ, BA, 18, LLB, 21; Phi Beta Kappa; Yale Basketball Hall of Fame; Beta Theta Pi. Hon Degrees: LLD, Yale Univ, 52. Polit & Govt Pos: Prosecuting attorney, Hamilton Co, Ohio, 27-28; US mediator, Toledo Autolite Strike, 34; chmn, Hamilton Co Charter Comn, 34-35; chmn, US Little Steel Mediation Bd, 37; city councilman, Cincinnati, Ohio, 38-42, 48-51 & 55-, mayor, 55-57; dir, Commun War Serv, Dept Health, Educ & Welfare, 41-43; chmn, US Adv Comt, Vol Foreign Aid, 41-73; dir, Off Wartime Econ Affairs, State Dept, 43-45; pres, City Charter Comt, Ohio, 46-48; Rep Nominee for Gov, 52. Bus & Prof Pos: Dir, Ohio Nat Life Ins Co, 37- & Taft Broadcasting Corp, 57-68. Mil Serv: Entered as Pvt, Army, 17, released as 1st Lt, 19, after serv in 12th Field Artil, 2nd Div, France, 18; Verdun Medal; Europ Serv; Capt, Army Res, 19-39. Publ: City Management, 34, You & I & Roosevelt, 36 & Democracy in Politics & Economics, 51, Farrar Strauss. Mem: Ohio State Bar Asn; Comn Econ Develop (trustee), Carnegie Inst of Washington (trustee); Am Legion; Cincinnati Community Chest (gen chmn, 34). Honors & Awards: Received US Medal for Merit, 1946. Relig: Episcopal. Mailing Add: 1071 Celestial St Cincinnati OH 45202

TAFT, CHESTER M (R)
Vt State Rep
Mailing Add: 9 Church St Essex Junction VT 05452

TAFT, JAMES L, JR (R)
b Providence, RI, Oct 21, 30; s James L Taft & Katherine McGrath T; m 1955 to Sally Anne Fitzpatrick; c Sarah W, Mary F, Eleanor W & Jamie L. Educ: Col of the Holy Cross, BS, 52; Boston Col Law Sch, LLB, 55. Polit & Govt Pos: Councilman, Cranston, RI, 58-60; chmn, Cranston Rep City Comt, 63-68; RI State Sen, 63-70, minority leader, RI State Senate, 69-70; Mayor, Cranston, 71- Bus & Prof Pos: Attorney-at-law. Mem: Nat League of Cities (bd dirs); Cranston CofC; Rotary; Am Red Cross. Relig: Catholic. Legal Res: 53 Fairfield Rd Cranston RI 02910 Mailing Add: Exec Off Cranston City Hall Cranston RI 02910

TAFT, ROBERT, JR (R)
US Sen, Ohio

b Cincinnati, Ohio, Feb 26, 17; s Robert A Taft & Martha Bowers T; m 1939 to Blanca Noel (deceased), m 1969 to Katharine W Perry; c Robert A, II, Sarah (Mrs Winfield P Jones II), Deborah & Jonathan D. Educ: Yale Univ, BA, 39; Harvard Law Sch, LLB, 42; Delta Kappa Epsilon; Phi Alpha Delta. Hon Degrees: LLD, Centre Col, Ky, 65. Polit & Govt Pos: Ohio State Rep, 55-62, Majority Floor Leader, Ohio House Rep, 61-62; deleg, Rep Nat Conv, 56, 60, 64 & 72; US Rep, Ohio, 63-64 & 67-71; mem, Banking & Currency, Foreign Affairs, Educ & Labor Comts, pres, 88th Cong Rep Freshman Rep; mem comt on Foreign Affairs & subcomts on Europe; mem comt, Foreign Econ Policy & Nat Security Policy & Sci Develop; chmn, Rep Coord Comt Task Force on Functions of Fed, State & Local Govts, 65-68; mem, Rep Revenue Sharing Study Group, 67-68; chmn, House Rep Conf Research Comt, 69-71; mem, House Rep Leadership; US Sen, Ohio, 71- Bus & Prof Pos: Partner, Taft, Stettinius & Hollister, 51-63 & 65-66; mem, Hamilton Co Welfare Adv Bd, 55-60; mem, Community Health & Welfare Coun of Cincinnati, 56-60, chmn, 59-60; trustee, The Children's Home of Cincinnati; trustee, Cincinnati Inst of Fine Arts. Mil Serv: Ens, Naval Res, 42, active duty in Atlantic, Mediterranean & Pac Theaters, 42-46, Naval War Col Staff Class, 44. Publ: Republican committee on program & progress, Decisions for a Better Am, 60; The middle ground of a midwest Republican, Saturday Rev, 8/22/64; one of Cong sponsors of compilation, The Conservative Papers, 64. Mem: Am Legion (Bentley Post Chap); Am Ordnance Asn; Navy League of the US; Alfalfa Club; VFW (Sycamore Post 3744). Relig: Episcopal. Legal Res: 4300 Indian Hill Cincinnati OH 45243 Mailing Add: US Sen Off Bldg Washington DC 20510

TAFT, SETH CHASE (R)
Comnr, Cuyahoga Co, Ohio

b Cincinnati, Ohio, Dec 31, 22; s Charles P Taft & Eleanor Chase T; m 1943 to Frances Prindle; c Frederick, Thomas, Cynthia & Tucker. Educ: Yale Col, BA, 43; Yale Law Sch, LLB, 48; Phi Beta Kappa; Order of the Coif. Polit & Govt Pos: Mem, Cuyahoga Co Charter Comn, Ohio, 58-59; cand Mayor of Cleveland, 67; comnr, Cuyahoga Co, 71- Bus & Prof Pos: Assoc, Jones, Day, Cockley & Reavis, Attorneys, 48-58, partner, 58- Mil Serv: Entered as Ens, Naval Res, 43, released as Lt (jg), 46, after serv as 1st Lt on USS Doran, Atlantic, Mediterranean & Pac Theatres; Theatre Ribbons. Mem: Cleveland, Cuyahoga Co, Ohio & Am Bar Asns. Honors & Awards: Jr CofC Man of Year, 55. Relig: Episcopal. Legal Res: 6 Pepper Ridge Rd Cleveland OH 44124 Mailing Add: 1700 Union Commerce Bldg Cleveland OH 44115

TAGGART, CAL S (R)
Wyo State Sen
Mailing Add: 104 Park Ave Lovell WY 82431

TAGGART, TOM (D)
Ga State Rep
Mailing Add: 139 Whitaker St Savannah GA 31401

TAGLIARINI, THOMAS (R)
b Palermo, Italy, Aug 18, 89; s Jack Tagliarini & Violet Criscuolo T; wid; c Jack & Violet. Educ: Royal Univ Palermo, Italy, MD; Univ Marseille, France, 2 years. Polit & Govt Pos: Chmn, Falls Co Rep Party, Tex, formerly. Bus & Prof Pos: Pathologist, Vet Admin Hosp, 48-68; retired. Mil Serv: Entered as Pvt, Army, 17, released as Sgt, 20, after serv in 338th Field Hosp, 82nd Div, France, 18-20; War Medal. Mem: Am Legion (comdr, Post 31); VFW. Relig: Catholic. Mailing Add: 142 Shenandoah Marlin TX 76661

TAIRA, NORMAN TAKEO (D)
Exec Secy, Hawaii State Dem Cent Comt
Polit & Govt Pos: Exec secy, Hawaii State Dem Cent Comt, currently; alt deleg, Dem Nat Conv, 72. Mailing Add: 46-226 Punawai St Kaneohe HI 96744

TAIRA, ROBERT S (D)
Hawaii State Sen
Mailing Add: Senate Sgt-at-Arms State Capitol Honolulu HI 96813

TAITANO, RICHARD (D)
Sen, Guam Legis
Mailing Add: Guam Legislature Box 373 Agana GU 96910

TAKAMINE, YOSHITO (D)
Hawaii State Rep
Mailing Add: House Sgt-at-Arms State Capitol Honolulu HI 96813

TAKAMURA, CARL T (D)
Hawaii State Rep
Mailing Add: House Sgt-at-Arms State Capitol Honolulu HI 96813

TAKITANI, HENRY T (D)
Hawaii State Rep

b Eleele, Kauai, Hawaii, Mar 8, 24; s Kanichi Takitani & Mitsu Yamanaka T; m 1949 to Shirley Shizue Shimizu; c Sheila Chieko, Cheryl Mitsu & Roxanne Toshie. Educ: Ill Col, BA, 51. Polit & Govt Pos: Hawaii State Rep, 68-70; Hawaii State Sen, 70- Bus & Prof Pos: Secy-treas, K Takitani Enterprise, 50; owner, H&S Garden Ctr, Maui, 65; pres, House of Colors, 67. Mil Serv: Entered as Pvt, Army, 44, released as Pfc, 46, after serv in 442nd Inf, Italy, 45-46. Relig: Congregational. Legal Res: 262 Ekoa Pl Wailuku Maui HI 96793 Mailing Add: State Capitol Bldg Honolulu HI 96813

TAKUSHI, TOKUICHI (D)
Mem, Hawaii Dem Cent Comt

b Waipahu, Oahu, Hawaii, Jan 11, 10; s Ushi Takushi & Kana Nakasone T; m 1937 to Doris Kimiye Shimabukuro; c Morris T, Floyd T & Karen L (Mrs Shishido). Educ: Mid-Pac Inst, 4 years. Polit & Govt Pos: Deleg, Hawaii State Dem Conv, 32-74; mem, Hawaii Dem Cent Comt, 58-, asst secy, 62-66; deleg & mem, Credential Comt, Dem Nat Conv, 60, deleg & hon secy, 64, deleg, 68, honoree, 72; sgt at arms, Hawaii State Senate, 62-66; Dem Presidential elector, 68; chmn & mem, Friendship Mission to Okinawa & Japan, 70. Mem: Hui Makaala Orgn (founder & dir, 46-). Honors & Awards: Plaque for Outstanding Dem of the Year, 66; Gov Burns Dem Good Sportsman's Award, 72. Relig: Protestant. Mailing Add: 31 Coelho Way Honolulu HI 96817

TALARICO, GABRIEL (GABE) (D)
Tenn State Sen
Mailing Add: 5272 Loch Lomond Dr Memphis TN 38116

TALBOT, GERALD E (D)
Maine State Rep

b Bangor, Maine, Oct 28, 31; s Wilmot Edgerton Talbot (deceased) & Arvella U McIntyre T; m 1954 to Anita Joan Cummings; c Renee, Rachel, Regina & Robin. Educ: Bangor High Sch, Maine, grad, 52. Polit & Govt Pos: Mem, Maine State Comt on Aging, 67-; mem, Portland Dem City Comt, 72-; mem, US Comn Civil Rights, 72-; Maine State Rep, 73-, mem, Human Resources & Elec Laws comt, Maine House Rep, 73- Mil Serv: Entered as Pvt, Army, 53, released as Pfc, 56 after serv in Qm Unit, Thule, Greenland, 54-55. Mem: NAACP (second vpres, 72-); Maine Asn for Black Progress; Portland Typographical Union. Honors & Awards: Citizen of the Week, Radio Sta WLOB, 64; Golden Pin Award, Portland Br, NAACP, 67, Portland Br Award, 69, Hall of Fame Cert, Laurel, Miss Br, 70 & cert of permanent membership, New Eng Conf; Outstanding Serv in the Community & State, NAACP, 73. Mailing Add: 132 Glenwood Ave Portland ME 04102

TALCOTT, BURT L (R)
US Rep, Calif

b Billings, Mont, Feb 22, 20; s Burt Breckinridge Talcott & Hester V Lacklen T; m 1942 to Lee G Taylor; c Ronald T. Educ: Stanford Univ, BA 42, LLB, 48; Phi Delta Phi; Sigma Chi. Polit & Govt Pos: Comnr, Recreation-Parks, Salinas, Calif, 52-54; supvr, Monterey Co, 55-62; US Rep, 12th Dist, 63-, mem, Appropriations Comt, US House Rep, currently; deleg, Rep Nat Conv, 68; mem, White House Conf Youth, 71. Bus & Prof Pos: Self-employed attorney, 48- Mil Serv: Entered as Aviation Cadet, Army Air Force, 42, released as 1st Lt, 45, after serv in 15th Air Force, ETO, 43-45, German Prisoner of War, 14 months; Air Medal with Clusters; Purple Heart with Cluster. Mem: Am Legion; CofC; Commonwealth Club of Calif; Elks; Rotary. Relig: Methodist. Legal Res: Salinas CA 93901 Mailing Add: House of Rep Washington DC 20515

TALIAFERRO, JIM (D)
Okla State Sen
Mailing Add: State Capitol Oklahoma City OK 73105

TALISMAN, MARK ELLIOTT (D)
b Cleveland, Ohio, July 16, 41; s Julius Joel Talisman (deceased) & Rosalyn Seidenberg T; m 1972 to Jill Leslie Dworkin. Educ: Harvard Col, AB cum laude; George Washington Univ, grad studies in pub affairs, 2 years. Polit & Govt Pos: Admin asst to US Rep Charles A Vanik, 63-; mem operating exec adv bd, Cleveland Coun for Econ Opportunity. 64-; mem, Cleveland Health Manpower Coun, 64-; mem, Cleveland Summer Arts Festival, 66-; mem, Ad Hoc Comt on Camping, 66-; mem, Vice President's Comn on Youth Opportunity, 67-68; deleg, Dem Nat Conv, 68; mem, Mayor's Comn on Youth Opportunity, 68-; mem, Bi-Partisan Internship Comt, US House of Rep, 69-; mem, JCC Self Study Comt; fel, John F Kennedy Inst Polit, Harvard Univ, 71-72; fel & instr, Spec Proj Training Freshman Congressmen, 72; official photographer, Dem Nat Conv, 72. Bus & Prof Pos: Chmn, Eastern Area Jr Red Cross, 57-58; co-chmn, Nat Jr Red Cross, 58-59; chmn, Admin Assts Seminar Group, 64-68; intern, Off Int Rels, Am & Nat Red Cross; founder & proj dir, Oper Govt which produced 40 half hours of TV on three branches of fed govt, which aired 64-69; mem bd dirs, Jewish Nat Fund; lectr, Case Western Reserve Univ, 70-71; bd mem, Bd Overseers, 72-78; mem pub affairs comt, Nat Jewish Welfare Bd, 70-72; bd mem, 72-; mem bd, Gov Sch, State of Ohio, 70- Publ: Harvard student guide to vineyards of France, Cambridge Univ, 64; Confronting congress, Harvard Polit Rev, 72; numerous articles on photography, cooking & wine notes to friends. Mem: Am Polit Sci Asn; Admin Assts Study Group; Harvard Clubs of Cleveland & Washington; B'nai B'rith. Honors & Awards: David McCord Prize for Artistic Endeavor, Harvard Univ, 63; Outstanding Photographer Awards; 12 One-Man Nat Color Photographic Shows; Harry F Camp Mem Lectr, Stanford Univ. Relig: Jewish. Legal Res: 22699 Shaker Blvd Shaker Heights OH 44122 Mailing Add: 119 Second St NE Washington DC 20002

TALKINGTON, ROBERT VAN (R)
Kans State Sen
b Dallas Co, Tex, Aug 23, 29; s William Henry Talkington & Nannie T; m 1951 to Donna

Jill Schmaus; c Jill (Mrs Dave McCaskill), Jacki, James Thomas & Lisa. Educ: Tyler Jr Col, Tex, AA, 49; Univ Kans, BS, 51; Univ Kans Sch Law, LLB, 54; Phi Delta Phi; Sigma Alpha Epsilon, recipient Bessemer-Lindsay Award; K-Club. Polit & Govt Pos: Attorney, Allen Co, Kans, 57-63; co-chmn, Allen Co Young Rep Club, 58-62; Second Dist chmn, Kans Day Club, 59; deleg, Rep State Conv, 64; chmn, Allen Co Rep Cent Comt, 64-68; treas, Kans State Rep Comt, 64-66; city attorney, LaHarpe, 65-; city attorney, Moran, 68-; Kans State Rep, 69-73; Kans State Sen, 73- Mil Serv: Army, 54-56, Counter Intel Corps. Publ: Hospital law & medical staff by-laws, Washburn Law J, spring 75. Mem: Elks; Am Legion; Mason; York Rite; Shrine. Relig: Presbyterian. Legal Res: 20 W Buchanan Iola KS 66749 Mailing Add: Box 725 Iola KS 66749

TALLENT, ANN (D)
Chmn, Rosebud Co Dem Cent Comt, Mont
b Killdeer, NDak, May 17, 19; d Kiril Marinenko & Mary Kaun M; m 1944 to Archie Tallent; c Karen, Donald, Diane (Mrs Norman Spaeth) & Richard. Educ: Col study, 38-39. Polit & Govt Pos: Deleg, Mont State Dem Conv, formerly; chmn, Rosebud Co Dem Cent Comt, currently. Bus & Prof Pos: Secy, Welfare Off, clerk, Soil Conserv, clerk & secy, Ore Shipyard; typist, Bremerton Yards. Mem: Dem Womens Club (past regional dir & past pres); Eastern Star (Worthy Matron); Homemakers (pres, 6 years, pres coun, 2 years); Rainbow for Girls (bd mem 7 years); Pink Ladies Garden Club (secy-treas). Honors & Awards: Grand Cross, Rainbow. Relig: Wesleyan Church. Legal Res: 341 N Eighth St Forsyth MT 59327 Mailing Add: Box 772 Forsyth MT 59327

TALLEY, DON L (D)
Wash State Sen
b Tacoma, Wash, 1918; m to Dolores T; c four. Educ: High sch, grad. Polit & Govt Pos: Wash State Sen, currently. Bus & Prof Pos: Supvr for the Port of Longview. Mil Serv: Navy. Mem: Mason; Elks; Moose; Eagles; Am Legion. Mailing Add: 1583 Mt Pleasant Rd Kelso WA 98626

TALLON, JAMES R, JR (D)
NY State Assemblyman
Mailing Add: 47 Orton Ave Binghamton NY 13905

TALLY, LOU (D)
Chmn, Lake Co Dem Exec Comt, Fla
b San Antonio, Tex, Oct 15, 47; s Emmett Murchison Tally, Jr & Catherine Miller T; m 1968 to Charlene Ann Parkin. Educ: Univ Fla, BA, 69, Col Law, JD, 72; Alpha Phi Omega. Polit & Govt Pos: Asst states attorney, Fifth Judicial Circuit, Fla, 73-; parliamentarian, Young Dem of Am, 73-; chmn, Lake Co Dem Exec Comt, Fla, 74-; mem rules comt, Dem Party Fla, 75-; treas, Young Dem of Fla, 75- Bus & Prof Pos: Mem subcomt on juv court procedure, Fla Bar, 73-75; assoc, Law Firm of Tally & Moore, Mt Dora, Fla, 73-; secy-treas, Lake Co Legal Aid Soc, 74- Mil Serv: Entered as 2nd Lt, Army, 69, released as 1st Lt, 73, after serv in Ft Benning, Ga, 72-73; 1st Lt, Army Res, 69- Mem: Am & Fla Bar Asns; Kiwanis. Honors & Awards: Recipient, Nat Merit Scholarship, 65; Resolution of Commendation promulgated by Student Senate, Univ Fla, 72; Best Actor of 1973-74 Season, Icehouse Theater, Mt Dora, Fla; President's Award, Young Dem of Fla, 74. Legal Res: 420 S Central Ave Umatilla FL 32784 Mailing Add: PO Box 619 Umatilla FL 32784

TALLY, LURA SELF (D)
NC State Rep
b Iredell Co, NC, Dec 9, 21; d R O Self & Sara Cowles S; div; c John Cowles & Robert Taylor. Educ: Duke Univ, AB, 42; NC State Univ, MA, 70; Delta Kappa Gamma; Kappa Delta. Polit & Govt Pos: Dem coordr cong & gubernatorial campaigns, NC, 54-70; NC State Rep, 72-, mem comts, Appropriations, Corrections, Educ, Health, Higher Educ, Ment Health & Social Serv, NC Gen Assembly, 72- Bus & Prof Pos: Pub sch teacher, Fayetteville City Schs, NC, 43-68, guid counr, 68-72. Mem: Bus & Prof Women; League Women Voters; Am Asn Univ Women; Fayetteville Women's Club (pres); Ment Health Asn Fayetteville (pres). Honors & Awards: Outstanding Alumna, Peace Col, 62. Relig: Methodist. Mailing Add: 3100 Tallywood Dr Fayetteville NC 28303

TALMADGE, HERMAN EUGENE (D)
US Sen, Ga
b McRae, Ga, Aug 9, 13; s Eugene Talmadge & Mattie Thurmond T; m 1941 to Leila Elizabeth Shingler; c Herman E, Jr & Robert S. Educ: Univ Ga, LLB, 36; Sigma Nu; Omicron Delta Kappa. Polit & Govt Pos: Gov, Ga, 48-55; US Sen, Ga, 57-, mem, Select Comt on Presidential Activities, US Senate, 73- Mil Serv: Entered as Ens, Navy, 41, released as Lt Comdr, 45. Publ: You & Segregation, Vulcan Press, 55. Mem: Mason; Shrine; Am Legion; 40 et 8; VFW; Ga Farm Bur. Relig: Baptist. Legal Res: Lovejoy GA 30250 Mailing Add: 109 Russell Off Bldg Washington DC 20510

TAMMI, JUNE H (D)
b Boston, Mass, July 6, 33; d Carl Raphael Tammi & Hazel Anderson T; single. Educ: Bridgewater State Col, BS, 56; Boston Univ, MEd, 60. Polit & Govt Pos: Alt deleg, Dem Nat Conv, 72. Bus & Prof Pos: Asst to asst supt Dr Nelson, Boston State Hosp, 64- Publ: Boer therapy (w Dr Chien & P Schloss), Health & Community Psychiat, 2/73. Mem: United Front, Boston; Mass Asn Pub Health; Dorchester Inter-Agency Coun (pres, 68-); Citizen Participation in Polit. Honors & Awards: Health Inst Award, Nat Health Asn, 69; Brotherhood Award, Nat Conf Christians & Jews, 72. Relig: Protestant Mailing Add: 29 Mill St Boston MA 02122

TANAKA, FRANCIS TORAO (D)
b Lihue, Hawaii, Aug 15, 32; s Jack Torao Tanaka & Aimee Matsumoto T; m 1958 to Marjorie Hanako Tagawa. Educ: Univ Hawaii, BA, 56, MS, 61, MBA, 70. Polit & Govt Pos: Chmn, Ninth Dist Dem Party, Hawaii, 66-68; alt deleg, Dem Nat Conv, 68, deleg, 72; vchmn, Honolulu Co Hosp Adv Coun, 68-; vchmn, Hawaii Dem State Cent Comt, 68-70; chmn, Oahu Co Dem Party, 70-72. Bus & Prof Pos: Chief chemist, Honolulu Gas Co, Ltd, 62-66, tech supt, 66-70, staff engr, 70-; admin asst to Rep Robert C Oshiro, 65-69. Mil Serv: Entered as Pvt, Army, 56, released as Pfc, 58, after serv in Seventh Div, Korea. Mem: Am Chem Soc; Am Soc of Training & Develop; Jaycees; Toastmasters; Wahiawa Lions. Mailing Add: 1803 Laniloa Pl Wahiawa HI 96786

TANAKA, THOMAS VICTOR CAMACHO (R)
Sen, Guam Legis
b Agana, Guam, Aug 7, 40; s Thomas S Tanaka & Josefina Camacho T; m 1962 to Jane Concepcion Chargualaf; c Stephen Anthony, Thomas Victor, Jo Ann, Joyce Lynn & Gary Andrew. Educ: Marquette Univ, 60-62; Univ Guam, BA, 65; Alpha Kappa Psi; Pershing Rifles. Polit & Govt Pos: Staff analyst, Bur of Budget & Mgt, Guam, 70-71; dep dir, Dept of Pub Works, 71-73; dep dir, Community Action Agency, 73-74; Sen & chmn comt on finance & taxation, Guam Legis, currently. Mailing Add: PO Box 373 Agana GU 96910

TANDE, LYDER CHRISTIAN (D)
Chmn, Daniels Co Dem Party, Mont
b Scobey, Mont, Apr 30, 27; s Christian Tande & Julia T; m 1950 to Isabelle Eklund; c Craig, Brad, Teresa & Victoria. Educ: Concordia Col, BA. Polit & Govt Pos: Chmn, Daniels Co Dem Party, Mont, 74- Mil Serv: Sgt, Army, 45-46. Mem: Elks; Am Legion; Eastern Mont Comprehensive Health & Planning Asn. Relig: Lutheran. Mailing Add: Scobey MT 59263

TANGER, WINIFRED A (D)
Conn State Rep
b Irvington, NY, Feb 10, 22; d John Louis Mangan & Madeline Lowery M; div; c William, Kathryn, Gerald, John, Patricia & Virginia. Educ: New York Univ, 40-41. Polit & Govt Pos: Rep, Waterford Town Meeting, Conn, 63-65, mem, 71-73; mem bd educ, Waterford, 65-69; Conn State Rep, 75- Bus & Prof Pos: Secy to bus mgr, Laborer's Local 547 AFL-CIO, New London, Conn, 65-70; agt, Leighton Realty Co, 73-75. Mem: League of Women Voters. Mailing Add: 15 Oil Mill Rd Waterford CT 06385

TANKSLEY, M HOLLIS (R)
VChmn, Rep State Cent Comt, Ga
b Habersham Co, Ga, Mar 22, 37; s Adger Lee Tanksley & Esther Eller T; m to Lonnie Ruth Snow; c Christopher Hollis, Elizabeth Ann, Cecilia Jayne, Cynthia Michelle & Holly Ruth. Educ: Piedmont Col, BA, 62; Col Osteopathic Med & Surg, DO, 68; Phi Sigma Gamma. Polit & Govt Pos: Chmn, Union Co Rep Party, Ga, 74-; mem, Rep State Cent Comt, Ga, 74-, mem finance comt, 74-, vchmn, 75-; mem, Rep Party Chmn Club & 120 Club, 74- Bus & Prof Pos: Internship, Doctors Hosp, Tucker, Ga, 69; mem, Union Co Sch Bd, 72-74; chief of staff, Blairsville Gen Hosp, 73-; mem, Union Co Bd Health; Fed Aviation Agency flight examr, State of Ga; adv to pres, Truitt McConnell Col, Cleveland, Ga. Mil Serv: Entered as Pvt, Marine Corps, 54, released as Sgt, 58. Mem: Am, Ga & NGa Osteopathic Asns; Am Col Gen Practitioners; dipl, Nat Bd Med Examr. Honors & Awards: Citation for Outstanding Contrib to Harrison Rehabilitation & Treatment Ctr. Relig: Episcopal. Mailing Add: Rte 3 Blairsville GA 30512

TANNEHILL, JOHN M (R)
NMex State Sen
Mailing Add: 1501 Sagebrush Trail SE Albuquerque NM 87123

TANNENBAUM, DORIS M (D)
Second VChairperson, Fifth Cong Dist Dem Comt, Wis
b Milwaukee, Wis, Sept 27, 35; d Ely Tannenbaum & Shirley Farber T; single. Educ: Univ Wis-Milwaukee, BS, 61. Polit & Govt Pos: Chairperson, 26th Assembly Dem Unit, Wis, 73-74; second vchairperson, Fifth Cong Dist Dem Comt, 73-; alt deleg, Dem Nat Mid-Term Conf, 74; vchairperson, Fifth Cong Dist Womens Dem Comt, 75- Bus & Prof Pos: Comnr, Milwaukee Co Human Rights Comn, Milwaukee, Wis, 74- Mem: Nat Orgn of Women; Am Civil Liberties Union; Nat Coun of Jewish Women; Hadassah. Relig: Jewish. Mailing Add: 925 E Wells St Milwaukee WI 53202

TANNER, JAMES THOMAS, JR (D)
Chmn, Avery Co Dem Comt, NC
b Newland, NC, Oct 8, 31; s James Thomas Tanner & Louise Farabow T; m 1953 to Betty Jo Briggs; c Suzan Y & James T, III. Educ: Mars Hill Col, 49-50; NC State Univ, BS, 53, MS, 58. Polit & Govt Pos: Chmn, Avery Co Dem Comt, NC, 70- Bus & Prof Pos: Vpres, Harris Mining Co, 66- Mil Serv: Entered as Pvt, Army, 53, released as Pfc, 56, after serv in Ord, Redstone Arsenal, Huntsville, Ala. Publ: Self-Glazing Phenomenon Associated with Structural Clay Products, 57 & Pozzuolantic Materials in Foam Concrete, 57. Mem: Nat Inst Ceramic Engrs; Am Ceramic Soc; Keramos; Kiwanis (pres, 70); Mason. Relig: Baptist. Mailing Add: Box 433 Spruce Pine NC 28777

TANNER, PERRY AUBREY, JR (D)
Tex State Rep
b Cleveland, Tex; s Perry A Tanner, Sr & Savill Collins T; m 1967 to Melinda Ellis; c Tammu Maurine. Educ: Robert E Lee Jr Col, grad; Lamar Univ, grad; Tex Tech Univ Sch Law, grad. Polit & Govt Pos: Tex State Rep, 75- Bus & Prof Pos: Attorney, Livingston, Tex, currently. Mil Serv: Army. Mem: Lions. Relig: Baptist. Legal Res: Old Woodville Rd Livingston TX 77351 Mailing Add: PO Box 1172 Livingston TX 77351

TANNER, WILLIAM EDGAR (R)
b Covington, Ky, May 3, 30; s Harmon Edgar Tanner & Edna Black T; m 1954 to Anna Lois Young; c Cynthia & Amber. Educ: Univ Ky, Eng Col, 48 & 53-56. Polit & Govt Pos: Campaign mgr, Boone Co Rep Party, Ky, 62, 63, 64 & 66; precinct capt, Devon, Boone Co, 63-66; secy-treas, Boone Co Rep Exec Comt, 64-66; admin asst to US Rep M Gene Snyder, Ky, 67- Bus & Prof Pos: Fingerprint clerk, Fed Bur of Invest, 49-51; engr, Western Elec Co, 56; eng assoc, Cincinnati & Suburban Bell Tel Co, 56-67. Mil Serv: Entered as Pvt, Army, 51, released as Pfc, 53, after serv in Signal Corp, Europ Theatre, 52-53. Relig: Baptist. Legal Res: Walton KY Mailing Add: 10803 Norman Ave Fairfax VA 22030

TANOUS, WAKINE GREGORY (R)
b Van Buren, Maine, Nov 7, 31; s Thomas Tanous & Alice Shalala T; m 1955 to Anna Dorothy McKeon; c Gregory G, Arlene A, Theresa M, Nolan H, Alice Rose, Wakine G & Peter C. Educ: Boston Col, AA, 51; Portland Univ Law Sch, LLB, 55; Marquette Debating Club. Polit & Govt Pos: Mem, East Millinocket Rep Town Comt, Maine, 56-73; area chmn for reelec of Sen Margaret Chase Smith, 60-66; area chmn for reelec of Gov John H Reed, 62-66; mem, Penobscot Co Rep Comt, 64-69; mem, Penobscot Co Steering comt, 67-69; Maine State Sen, Dist 27, 69-73, Dist 30, 73-74, Senate chmn, labor & legis affairs comts, Maine Legis, 69-70, mem, Interim Legis Hwy Study Comn, 69-70; senate chmn, Legal Affairs & Labor Comts, Dist 27, 69-70, Labor & Judiciary Comts, Dist 27, 71-72, Dist 30, 73-74, chmn, Interim Ins Study Comn, 71-72 & Interim Snowmobile Study Comt, 71-72; deleg, Rep Nat Conv, 72. Bus & Prof Pos: Attorney-at-law, 55- Publ: Snowmobiling, the Maine way, Sno-Mobile Times, 10/69. Mem: Elks; KofC; CofC; Kiwanis; Katahdin Friends of Exceptional Children. Honors & Awards: Silver Beaver, Citizenship Award. Relig: Roman Catholic. Legal Res: 29 Main St East Millinocket ME 04430 Mailing Add: 1 Spruce St East Millinocket ME 04430

TAPPER, ELMER R (D)
La State Rep
Mailing Add: 2110 Packingham Ave Chalmette LA 70043

TARBOX, ELMER L (D)
Tex State Rep
Mailing Add: 4613 11th St Lubbock TX 79416

TARR, CURTIS WILLIAM (R)
b Stockton, Calif, Sept 18, 24; s Florence William Tarr & Esther Julia Reed T; m 1955 to Elizabeth May Myers; c Pamela E & Cynthia L. Educ: Stanford Univ, AB, 48, PhD, 62; Harvard Univ, MBA, 50; Kappa Alpha. Hon Degrees: DHL, Ripon Col, 65 & Grinnell Col, 69; LLD, Lawrence Univ, 74. Polit & Govt Pos: Staff mem, Second Hoover Comn, 54-55; Rep cand, US House Rep, Second Dist, Calif, 58; Asst Secy of the Air Force for Manpower & Reserve Affairs, 68-69; dir, Selective Serv Syst, 69-72; Under Secy State Security Assistance, 72-73, acting Dep Under Secy of State for Mgt, 73; chmn, Defense Manpower Comn, 74- Bus & Prof Pos: Research asst & instr, Harvard Grad Sch Bus, 50-52; vpres, Sierra Tractor Co, Calif, 52-58; lectr, Chico State Col, 53-55, asst dir summer session & lectr, 62-63; pres, Lawrence Univ, 63-69; vpres, Deere & Co, Moline, Ill, 73- Mil Serv: Army, 43-46. Relig: Protestant. Mailing Add: 3701 39th St Moline IL 61265

TARR, GAIL H (R)
Maine State Rep
Mailing Add: RFD 1 N High St Bridgeton ME 04009

TARR, KENNETH M (D)
NH State Rep
Mailing Add: 48 Beacon St Concord NH 03301

TARTER, WELDON MURPHY (R)
b Edgemont, SDak, Sept 14, 21; s Thomas Barrett Tarter & Maud Murphy T; m 1949 to Virginia Lee Richmond; c Barrett Richmond & Paul Robert. Educ: Colo Col, BA, 50; Univ Denver, JD, 52. Polit & Govt Pos: Precinct committeeman, El Paso Co Rep Party, Colo, 53-60; secy, El Paso Co Rep Cent Comt, 56-58, chmn, 58-69; Bonus mem, Rep State Cent Comt Colo, 58-75; mem, Fourth Judicial Cent Comt, 58-75; mem, Third Cong Rep Cent Comt, 58-73; deleg, Rep Nat Conv, 68. Bus & Prof Pos: Partner, Tarter, Tiedt & Sell, Attorneys, Colorado Springs, 54- Mil Serv: Navy, 41-47. Legal Res: 3107 Paseo Rd Colorado Springs CO 80909 Mailing Add: 218 Mining Exchange Bldg Colorado Springs CO 80902

TASCA, HENRY J
b Providence, RI, Aug 23, 12; s Julius Tasca & Philomena DePaulis T; m 1949 to Natalina Federici; c Ann, Eileen, Elia & John. Educ: Temple Univ, BS, 33; Univ Pa, MBA, 34, PhD, 37; fel, Brookings Inst, 36-37; London Sch Econ, 37-38. Polit & Govt Pos: Econ analyst, Div Trade Agreements, State Dept, 37-38; asst dir trade regulations & commercial policy proj European countries, Rockefeller Found, 38-40; econ adv on foreign trade, Nat Defense Comn, 40-41; US Treas Dept Rep, Am Embassy, Rome, 45-48 & spec financial adv, Allied Command, Italy, 45; acting tech consult, Herter Select Comt on Foreign Aid, 47; alt US exec dir, Int Monetary Fund, 48-49; dir plans & policy staff, Dept for Econ Affairs, 49; econ adv to W Averell Harriman, Pres Temporary Coun Comt, NATO, 51-52; spec rep of President for Korean econ affairs, 53; dir US opers mission to Italy & Minister for econ affairs, Am Embassy, Rome, 53-56; minister econ affairs, Am Embassy, Bonn, Ger, 56-60; Dep Asst Secy of State for African Affairs, 60-65; US Ambassador to Morocco, 65-69; US Ambassador to Greece, 69-74. Bus & Prof Pos: Social Sci Research Coun fel & Penfield traveling scholar in Europe, 38-39. Mil Serv: Navy, Lt Comdr, 41-45. Publ: World Trading Systems: a Study of American & British Commercial Policies, 39; The Reciprocal Trade Policy of the US: a Study in Trade Philosophy, 48. Mem: Metrop Club. Honors & Awards: Medal of Freedom, 46; Korean Distinguished Serv Award; Grand Cordoni of the Ouissam Alaaouite, highest Moroccan decoration for foreign civilians; Cavaliere di Grand Croce, Order of Merit, Italy. Mailing Add: 7208 Sellers Ave Upper Darby PA 19082

TASSIN, JOHN ADAM, JR (D)
La State Sen
Mailing Add: 15 Park Ave Ville Platte LA 70586

TATE, ALBERT, JR (D)
Assoc Justice, La Supreme Court
b Opelousas, La, Sept 23, 20; s Albert Tate, Sr & Adelaide Therry T; m 1949 to Claire Jeanmard; c Albert, III, Emma Adelaide, George Jeanmard, Michael Ferdinand & Charles Edwin. Educ: La State Univ, Baton Rouge, cert in civil code studies, 48; George Washington Univ, BA, 41; Yale Univ Law Sch, JD, 47; Alpha Alpha Alpha; Delta Kappa Epsilon; Phi Alpha Delta. Polit & Govt Pos: Judge, La Court of Appeal, First Circuit, 54-60, presiding judge, Third Circuit, 60-70; assoc justice, La Supreme Court, 70-; chmn, La Comn on Aging, 56-59; chmn, Judiciary Comn of La, 69-70; deleg & comt chmn, La State Const Conv, 73. Bus & Prof Pos: Elected mem, Am Law Inst, 67-; chmn, La Conf Court of Appeal Judges, 67-70; mem exec comt, vchmn & secy, Nat Appellate Judges Conf, 66-70, chmn, 70-71; mem, Adv Coun for Appellate Justice, Columbia Univ. Mil Serv: Entered as Pvt, Army, 42, released as T/Sgt, 45, after serv in Counter Intel Corps, New Guinea, Australia, Philippines & Japan, 44-45; usual campaign citation. Publ: Louisiana practice materials, Casebook, 67; Treatises for judges, Bibliog, 71; auth of 35 articles publ in legal periodicals. Mem: Am Legion; VFW; Rotary; KofC; Order of the Coif. Relig: Catholic. Legal Res: 410 W Wilson St Ville Platte LA 70586 Mailing Add: 2414 Octavia St New Orleans LA 70115

TATE, HORACE EDWARD (D)
Ga State Sen
b Elberton, Ga, Oct 6, 22; s Henry Lawrence Tate & Mattie Beatrice Harper T; m 1949 to Virginia Cecil Barnett; c Calvin, Veloisa & Horacena. Educ: Ft Valley State Col, BS, 43; Atlanta Univ, MEd, 51; Univ Ky, PhD, 61; vpres, Sci Club; pres, Dramatics Club. Polit & Govt Pos: Mem, Gov Comn on Educ, Ga, 62-63; Atlanta Bd Educ, 65-69; chmn, 38th Sen Dist Ga, 70-; vchmn, Ga State Dem Party, 70-; vchmn, Ga Adv Comt to US President, Cabinet Comt on Educ, 70-, Ga State Sen, 75- Bus & Prof Pos: Sci teacher & prin, Union Point High Sch, Ga, 43-45; prin, Greensboro High Sch, 45-51; Fairmont High Sch, Griffin, 51-57; assoc prof, Ft Valley State Col, 59-61. Publ: Fear no evil, Ga Teachers & Educ Asn Herald, 4/58, Some evils of tolerated tokenism, 4/66, Inclusive integration, 10/67. Mem: Ga Asn Educators; Phi Delta Kappa; NAACP; PTA; YMCA. Honors & Awards: Atlanta Bd of Educ Award; Butler St CME Church Distinguished Membership Award; Atlanta Inquirer Newspaper-Achievement & Serv Award; Citizen of Year Award, Omega Psi Phi Fraternity Inc. Relig: Methodist. Mailing Add: 621 Lilla Dr SW Atlanta GA 30310

TATE, JAMES HUGH JOSEPH (D)
b Philadelphia, Pa, Apr 10, 10; s James E Tate; m 1942 to Anne M Daly; c Francis X & Anne Marie. Educ: Temple Univ Law Sch, LLB, 38; St Joseph's Col Indust & Labor Rels Sch. Hon Degrees: Degrees from Villanova Univ, La Salle Col, St Joseph's Col & Drexel Univ. Polit & Govt Pos: Pa State Rep, 40-46; mem, City Coun, 51-55 & pres, 55-62; mayor, Philadelphia, 62-72; deleg, Dem Nat Conv, 60-72; mem, Southeastern Pa Transportation Authority, 72-; mem, Dem State Comt Pa, 72-75; deleg, Dem Nat Mid-Term Conf, 74; chmn, Pa State Tax Equalization Bd, currently. Bus & Prof Pos: Dir, WHYY Educ TV, Philadelphia, currently; mem bd, Einstein Med Ctr, 68-; mem bd trustees, Immaculata Col; mem, Villanova Univ Develop Coun, 68- Mem: Nat League Cities; Nat Urban Coalition; Am Acad Polit & Social Sci; KofC (past Grand Knight); Nat Conf Christians & Jews (bd, Philadelphia Chap). Relig: Roman Catholic. Mailing Add: 2601 Parkway Apts Philadelphia PA 19130

TATE, JAMES R (R)
Va State Deleg
b Denver, Colo, Oct 22, 43; s Roscoe Charles Tate & Alberta Henderson T; m 1964 to Sharon Spieks Tate. Educ: Ga Inst Technol, BChE, 65; George Washington Univ Law Sch, JD, 68; Tau Beta Pi; Order of the Coif; Kappa Sigma. Polit & Govt Pos: Asst US attorney, Eastern Dist Va, 71-72; Va State Deleg, 19th Dist, 73- Bus & Prof Pos: Comt chmn, Fairfax City CofC, 70-71. Mil Serv: Entered as 2nd Lt, Army, 68, released as 1st Lt, 70, after serv in 101st Airborne Div, Vietnam, 69-70; Bronze Star; Air Medal; Army Commendation Medal; Two Vietnamese Campaign Citations. Mem: Delta Theta Phi; Am Legion; VFW; Jaycees; Fairfax Co CofC. Honors & Awards: Most Outstanding Contribution to Student Govt, Ga Tech Student Coun, 65; Outstanding Grad Sr, Delta Theta Phi, 68. Relig: Methodist. Mailing Add: 5039 Prestwick Dr Fairfax VA 22030

TATE, PENFIELD W, II (D)
Mayor, Boulder, Colo
b New Philadelphia, Ohio, June 11, 31; s Penfield W Tate; m 1955 to Ellen Cooper; c Penfield, Paula, Gail & Roslyn. Educ: Kent State Univ, BA, 53; Univ Colo, JD, 67. Polit & Govt Pos: Mem city coun, Boulder, Colo, 71-, mayor, 73- Bus & Prof Pos: Labor rels attorney, Mountain Bell Tel, Boulder, Colo, 67-69; human rels exec, Colo State Univ, Ft Collins, 69-72; attorney, Tate, Tate & Flowers, Denver, 72- Mil Serv: Entered as 2nd Lt, Army, 53, released as Capt, after serv in var artil units, European & Far Eastern Theatres, 53-67; Army Commendation Medal. Publ: Co-auth, Crisis Centers, 68; auth, The broccoli syndrome, Am Psychol J. Mem: Boulder Co Ment Health Ctr (bd dirs); Boulder Human Rels Comn; Metro Denver Urban Coalition (bd gov, 72-). Honors & Awards: Toby Distinguished Serv Award, 74; Top Hat Award, Pittsburgh Courier, June 75. Relig: Episcopal. Legal Res: 747 Ninth St Boulder CO 80302 Mailing Add: PO Box 791 Boulder CO 80302

TATMAN, AUBREY C (R)
Mem, Rep State Cent Comt, La
b Bayou Chicot, La, Apr 20, 15; s Howard W Tatman & Beulah Courtney T; m 1937 to Juanita Russell; c Gwendolyn (Mrs Harold Burcham) & Aubrey, Jr; two grandchildren. Educ: High sch. Polit & Govt Pos: Mem, Rep State Cent Comt, La, currently; supvr of Census; asst in Bankruptcy Sales. Mem: Bayou Chicot Masonic Lodge 430. Relig: Methodist. Mailing Add: RR 3 Ville Platte LA 70586

TATUM, JAMES BERNARD (R)
Chmn, McDonald Co Rep Comt, Mo
b Carthage, Mo, July 24, 25; s James Marshall Tatum & Ruth Bernard T; m 1947 to Kathryn G Pickens; c Susan (Mrs Danuser), James P, Kathryn L & David P. Educ: Univ Ark, 44; US Mil Acad, BS, 47; Phi Theta Kappa; Kappa Sigma. Polit & Govt Pos: Chmn, McDonald Co Rep Comt, Mo, 72- Bus & Prof Pos: Pres & mgr, Tatum Motor Co, Anderson, 53-75; pres & mgr, Tatum Tractor & Implements, Siloam Springs, Ark, 69-75. Mil Serv: Entered as 2nd Lt, Army, 47, released as Capt, 51, after serv in 11th Airborne & 7th Inf Div, Korea, 50-51; Purple Heart. Publ: Auth article in Inf J, 53. Mem: Mo State Baptist (exec bd); Mo Asn Community Jr Cols (exec bd); Crowden Col, Neosho, Mo (trustee & pres bd); Am Legion. Honors & Awards: Pub Serv Award, Sperry New Holland, 69. Relig: Baptist. Legal Res: Rte 2 Anderson MO 64831 Mailing Add: Box 90 Anderson MO 64831

TATUM, WAUGANTHA GRADY (TUT) (D)
b Seminary, Miss, Feb 16, 20; d Grover Cleveland Grady & Zilphia Lucretia Herrin G; m 1944 to John Hervey Tatum; c Blanche Anne (Mrs Horn), John Hervey, Jr & Ross Grady. Educ: Hinds Jr Col; Miss Col; Meteorology & Aircraft Community Sch, Atlanta. Polit & Govt Pos: Mem, Cemetery Bd, Ft Walton Beach, Fla, 56-61 & Parks & Recreation Bd, 56-64; pres, Miracle Strip Dem Women's Club of Fla, 66-; deleg, Dem Nat Conv, 68; state finance chmn, Fla Dem Women's Club, currently; exec committeewoman, Fla State Dem Party, Okaloosa Co, formerly. Bus & Prof Pos: Secy & leasing agent, John Tatum Mfrs, Inc, 66-; pres, Tatum Investment Corp, 69-; secy-treas, leasing agent & pub rels, John Tatum Buick, currently. Mem: Ft Walton Beach, Destin & Valparaiso CofC; Playground Humane Soc (Fla bd trustees); Int Platform Asn. Honors & Awards: Hon Dep Sheriff, Okaloosa Co, Fla; Award for Most Outstanding Contribution in Polit, Fla Dem Women's Clubs. Relig: Baptist. Mailing Add: 305 Brooks St SE Ft Walton Beach FL 32548

TAUKE, THOMAS J (R)
Iowa State Rep
Mailing Add: 1715 Glen Oak St Dubuque IA 52001

TAULBEE, FRANCES LAVERNE (D)
Secy, Platte Co Dem Cent Comt, Mo
b Leavenworth, Kans, Oct 26, 37; d Edward Earl Newton & Mary Baker N; m 1959 to Jesse Reynolds Taulbee; c Rebecca & Elizabeth Ann. Educ: Platte City RIII High Sch, 51-55. Polit & Govt Pos: Secy, Platte Co Dem Cent Comt, Mo, 70- Bus & Prof Pos: Clerk typist, Bruce Dodson Ins Co, 55-59; legal secy, James W Farley, Attorney, 59-66. Mem: Marshall Rebekah Lodge No 613 (past Noble Grand); Platte City Elem PTA (treas); Platte Co Dem Womens Federated Club (2nd vpres) Platte City Christian Womens Fel (secy-treas); Platte City Benefit Assessment Soc Rd Dist (secy). Relig: Protestant; supt Platte City Christian Church. Mailing Add: Mary Kay Lane Box 7 Platte City MO 64079

TAURIELLO, ANTHONY FRANCIS (D)
b Buffalo, NY, Aug 14, 1899; s Sebastian Tauriello & Lucia Tita T; single. Educ: Cumberland Univ Sch Law, LLB, 29; Palmer Col of Chiropractic, 3 years. Polit & Govt Pos: Mem Bd of

Supvr, Erie Co, NY, 33-37; alt deleg, Dem Nat Conv, 36; deleg-at-lg, 60, deleg, 64 & 68; mem, Buffalo Common Coun, 38-41, 48 & 54-57; Dep City Treas, Buffalo, NY, 42-45; examr, Reconstruction Finance Corp, Buffalo Off, 46-47; US Rep, NY, 49-50; deleg, NY State Dem Conv, 60, 64 & 68; chmn, Buffalo Munic Housing Authority, 61- Bus & Prof Pos: Owner, Niagara Hudson Liquor Store, Buffalo, NY, 41-64. Mem: KofC; Eagles; Elks. Relig: Catholic. Mailing Add: 618 Seventh St Buffalo NY 14213

TAURIELLO, JOSEPH A (D)
NY State Sen
Mailing Add: 713 Busti Ave Buffalo NY 14208

TAUZIN, W J (D)
La State Rep
Mailing Add: 566 Goode St Thibodaux LA 70301

TAVITIAN, K MICHAEL (R)
NH State Rep
Mailing Add: Main St Plaistow NH 03865

TAWES, JOHN MILLARD (D)
State Treas, Md
b Crisfield Md, Apr 8, 1894; s James Tawes & Alice Byrd T; m 1915 to Helen Avalynne Gibson; c Jimmie Lee (Mrs William R Wilson) & Philip W. Hon Degrees: LLD from five cols & univs. Polit & Govt Pos: Clerk of Court, Somerset Co, Md, 30-38; State Comptroller, Md, 38-47 & 50-58 Bank Comnr, 47-50, Gov, 59-66; deleg, Dem Nat Conv, 68; first secy, Md Dept Natural Resources, 69-72; State Treas Md, 73- Bus & Prof Pos: Secy-treas, Tawes Shipbuilding Co, 17-19 & Tawes Banking Co, 19-45; dir, Bank of Crisfield, currently. Mem: Elks; KofP; Mason; Shrine; Eastern Star. Relig: Methodist. Mailing Add: Hall Hwy Crisfield MD 21817

TAYLOR, CASPER R, JR (D)
Md State Deleg
Mailing Add: 316 Prince George's St Cumberland MD 21502

TAYLOR, DAVID PETER
Asst Secy Air Force Manpower & Reserve Affairs
b Chicago, Ill, Apr 7, 34; s Harry Wilden Taylor & Corinne VanderKloot T; m 1960 to Renata Marion Wittmann; c Steven H, Mark D, Andrea C & Thomas A. Educ: Cornell Univ, BS, 56; Univ Chicago, MBA, 60, PhD, 66. Polit & Govt Pos: Exec asst to Secy Labor, 69-70; exec asst to dir, Off Mgt & Budget, 70-71, asst dir, 71-74; Asst Secy Air Force Manpower & Reserve Affairs, 74- Bus & Prof Pos: Research assoc, Univ Chicago, 62-64; asst prof indust rels, Mass Inst Technol, 64-66, assoc prof, 66-68. Mil Serv: Army, 56-58. Legal Res: 7421 Dulany Dr McLean VA 22101 Mailing Add: Dept of the Air Force Washington DC 20330

TAYLOR, DAVID SURRATT (D)
SC State Rep
b Laurens Co, SC, July 17, 27; s Benjamin Gideon Taylor & Grace Surratt T; m 1949 to Dorothy Lee Drummond; c David S, Jr, F Drummond, Connie G & J Adam. Educ: Clemson Univ, 1 year. Polit & Govt Pos: SC State Rep, Laurens Co, 63-64, 67-69 & 75- Bus & Prof Pos: Owner, Taylor Real Estate, Laurens, SC, 63- Mil Serv: Entered as A/S, Navy, 45, released as Radarman 3/C, 48, after serv in USS Chuckawan, ETO, 46-47; Am Defense, World War II Victory & Europe-Africa-Middle East Campaign Medals. Mem: Rotary; VFW (comdr, SC Orgn, 61-62, chmn, Southern Conf, 63-64); Mason; Shrine. Honors & Awards: Laurens Co Vet of the Year, 62. Relig: Methodist. Mailing Add: 104 Barksdale Circle Laurens SC 29360

TAYLOR, DONALD L (R)
NY State Assemblyman
Mailing Add: 117 Ward St Watertown NY 13601

TAYLOR, DOROTHY FRANCINE (R)
Committeewoman, State Rep Cent & Exec Comts, Ohio
b Akron, Ohio, Dec 19, 07; d George Gordon Meade & Esther Richards M; m 1936 to Paul Henry Taylor. Educ: Akron Univ, 2 years, Law Sch, 2 years & 6 months; Alpha Gamma Delta. Polit & Govt Pos: Pres, Ohio Coun Rep Women, 47-49; dir, Rep Women Vol, Eighth Ward, Akron, Ohio, 62-71; mem, Planning Comn, City of Akron, 67-70; committeewoman, Ohio State Rep Cent & Exec Comts, 14th Cong Dist, 70-; pres, Eighth Ward Women's Rep Club, 70- Bus & Prof Pos: Title examr real estate, Summit Title & Abstract Co, Ohio, 28-41; exec secy, League of Women Voters, Columbus, Ga, 43 & 44. Mem: Ohio Coun Rep Women; Akron Woman's Club; Eighth Ward Rep Womens Club; Fairlawn Country Club; DAR. Honors & Awards: Plaque from city for serv to community, Akron, Ohio, 70. Relig: Presbyterian. Mailing Add: 174 Durward Rd Akron OH 44313

TAYLOR, DOROTHY MAE (D)
La State Rep
Mailing Add: 2724 Melpomene Ave New Orleans LA 70113

TAYLOR, ERICH A O'DRISCOLL (D)
Pres Pro Tem, RI State Senate
b Newport, RI, Jan 4, 02; s Alexander O'Driscoll Taylor, Jr & Martha Stanton Cozzens T; single. Educ: Rogers High Sch, RI, 18. Polit & Govt Pos: RI State Rep, 41-45; chmn, Newport Rent Control Bd, RI, 50; city councilman, Newport, 56-57 & 61-62; RI State Sen, Dist 49, 66-, Pres Pro Tem, RI State Senate, 72- Bus & Prof Pos: Reporter, Newport Herald, 20-28; teacher, Portsmouth Priory Sch, 28-32 & 41- Mil Serv: Seaman 1/C, Navy, 44-45. Publ: Battle of Rhode Island, 1778, 28. Mem: Mediaeval Acad of Am; New Eng Asn Chem Teachers; Am Asn Physics Teachers; RI Biol Soc (past pres); life mem Am Legion Post 7, RI. Honors & Awards: Received Order of Merit from President, German Fed Republic, 66. Relig: Episcopal. Mailing Add: 522 Broadway Newport RI 02840

TAYLOR, ESSIE E (R)
Chmn, Marion Co Rep Party, Ky
b Lebanon, Ky, Oct 2, 12; d George W Benningfield & Lena Colvin B; m 1933 to John T Taylor; c Jewel (Mrs Gupton) & James D. Educ: Marion Co Schs, Ky. Polit & Govt Pos: Chmn, Marion Co Rep Party, Ky, 64- Mem: Marion Co Rep Womans Club; Mary Immaculate Hosp Auxiliary; Ky Hist Soc. Honors & Awards: Dwight David Eisenhower Award; Ky Colonel. Relig: Southern Baptist. Mailing Add: 648 Bruce St Lebanon KY 40033

TAYLOR, FELIX DONELL (D)
b Cherry Valley, Ark, Apr 26, 49; s Robert Taylor, Jr & Beulah Mae Britt T; m 1969 to Magalene Harris; c Felicia Dionne. Educ: Southern Baptist Col, AA, 69; Ark State Univ, BA, 72; Univ Ark Sch Law, JD, 75; pres student body, 68-69. Polit & Govt Pos: Mem, Gov Youth Coun, 68-69; field worker, Rockefeller for Gov, 70; deleg, Ark Dem State Conv, 72 & 74; alt deleg, Dem Nat Conv, 72; intern as dep city attorney, Fayetteville, 74-; co-chmn, Black Students for Fulbright Reelec, 74. Bus & Prof Pos: Installer, Bell Tel Co, 71, FRA man, 71-72. Mem: Nat Conf Black Polit Scientists; Africa-African Am Inst (educator); Asn Study Negro Life & Hist; Am Acad Social & Polit Sci. Honors & Awards: Black Am for Democracy Serv Award, 75. Relig: Baptist. Mailing Add: PO Box 182 Railroad St Cherry Valley AR 72324

TAYLOR, FRED (D)
Pa State Rep
b Adah, Pa; s Clifton Taylor & Helen Moats T; m 1952 to Gloria Cipoletti; five children. Educ: Fayette Co Pub Schs; Murray Hill Bus Sch. Polit & Govt Pos: Mem exec comt, Fayette Co Dem Party, Pa, currently; Pa State Rep, 66- Bus & Prof Pos: Owner, Taylor Ins Agency, currently. Mil Serv: Army, Alaskan Ski Command. Mem: Tri-State Mutual Agents Asn; Fayette Co Asn for Blind (bd dirs); Gtr Uniontown CofC; Fayette Co Soc for Crippled Children & Adults. Mailing Add: 643 Morgantown Rd Uniontown PA 15401

TAYLOR, GENE (R)
US Rep, Mo
b Sarcoxie, Mo, Feb 10, 28; m 1947 to Dorothy Wooldridge; c Linda & Larry. Educ: Southwest Mo State Col. Polit & Govt Pos: Former mayor, Sarcoxie, Mo; mem, Jasper Co Rep Comt, 56, chmn, 58; chmn, Seventh Cong Dist Rep Comt, Mo Rep State Comt, 62-72; Rep Nat Committeeman, Mo, until 73; deleg, Rep Nat Conv, 68; US Rep, Seventh Dist, Mo, 73- Bus & Prof Pos: Automobile dealer. Mem: Sarcoxie CofC; Mo State CofC; Scottish Rite; Shrine. Relig: Methodist. Mailing Add: PO Box 308 Sarcoxie MO 64862

TAYLOR, GEORGE S (SOCIALIST LABOR)
Nat Exec Comt Mem, Socialist Labor Party
b Mahanoy, Pa, Feb 4, 15; m to Frances M; c two sons & two daughters. Educ: Wagner Inst of Sci, Philadelphia, 4 years; William Penn Eve High Sch, 1 year; Temple Univ, 1 year. Polit & Govt Pos: Organizer sect, Socialist Labor Party, Philadelphia, 36 years, nat exec comt mem, currently. Bus & Prof Pos: Electronic technician in indust. Mailing Add: 7467 Rhoads St Philadelphia PA 19151

TAYLOR, HAROLD E (D)
SC State Rep
Mailing Add: 1324 Bonner Columbia SC 29204

TAYLOR, HARRY GRANT (R)
Chmn, Macon Co Rep Cent Comt, Ill
b Flat Rock, Ill, Sept 20, 08; s Ulysses Grant Taylor & Lena Gillespie T; m 1933 to Marion Gambrel; c Jeffrey & Jack. Educ: James Millikin Univ, AB, 30; Delta Sigma Phi; Kappa Phi Kappa; Alpha Omega. Polit & Govt Pos: Precinct committeeman, Rep Party, Ill, 34-; chmn, Macon Co Rep Cent Comt, 48-; pres, Ill Rep Co Chmn Asn, 59-67; deleg, Rep Nat Conv, 60 & 68. Bus & Prof Pos: Pres, Decatur Warehouse Co, Inc, 30- Mem: Elks; Decatur Club; CofC. Relig: Presbyterian. Mailing Add: PO Box 988 Decatur IL 62525

TAYLOR, HOBART, JR (D)
b Texarkana, Tex, Dec 17, 20; s Hobart Taylor, Sr & Charlotte Wallace T; m 1951 to Lynette Dobbins; c Albert & Hobart, III. Educ: Prairie View State Col, AB, 39; Howard Univ, AM, 41; Univ Mich, LLB, 43. Polit & Govt Pos: Research asst, Mich Supreme Court, 44-45; asst prosecuting attorney, Wayne Co, Mich, 49-50, corp counsel, 51-61; spec counsel, President's Comt Equal Employ Opportunity, 61-62, exec vchmn, 62-65; spec asst to VPres of US, 62-63; assoc counsel, President of the US, 64-65; dir, Export-Import Bank of US, 65-68. Bus & Prof Pos: Jr partner, Bledsoe & Taylor, 45-48; sr mem, Taylor, Patrick, Bailer & Lee, 58-61; pres, Beneficial Life Ins Soc, 59-61; partner, Dawson, Quinn, Riddell, Taylor & Davis, DC, 68-; dir, Westinghouse Elec Corp, 71-, Standard Oil Co (Ohio), 71-, Great Atlantic & Pac Tea Co, 71- & Aetna Life & Casualty Co, 73- Mem: Econ Club of Detroit; Nat Lawyers Club; Int Club; Am Red Cross (gov); George Town Club. Legal Res: Detroit MI Mailing Add: 723 Washington Bldg Washington DC 20005

TAYLOR, HUBERT LEE (D)
Ala State Rep
b Jasper, Ala, Mar 30, 43; s James Jason Taylor & Lois Wells T; m 1972 to Aurelia Sewall Glosser; c Hubert Glosser. Educ: US Naval Acad, 62; Univ of Ala, BS & BA, 65; Univ Ala Law Sch, LLD, 67. Polit & Govt Pos: Co solicitor, Walker Co, 70-71; official attorney, Gadsden, Ala, 71-72; Ala State Rep, 74- Bus & Prof Pos: Attorney-at-law, Law Firm of Gov Albert Brewer, 69-71; Methodist Lay Pastor, New Oregon, Pleasant View & Pleasant Hill, 72-73; attorney-at-law, 74- Mil Serv: Entered as Cadet, Naval Acad, 67, released as reservist. Mem: Rotary. Honors & Awards: Nominated most Outstanding Young Citizen of Gadsden, 75. Relig: Methodist; deacon. Legal Res: 2714 Hazel Dr Gadsden AL 35901 Mailing Add: Carter Bldg Forest Ave Gadsden AL 35901

TAYLOR, JACK J (R)
Ariz State Sen
Mailing Add: 38 North Fraser Dr Mesa AZ 85201

TAYLOR, JAMES C (D)
Ill State Sen
Mailing Add: 6752 S Morgan St Chicago IL 60621

TAYLOR, LUCAS PARNELL (R)
Chmn, Carroll Co Rep Party, Tenn
b Huntingdon, Tenn, Apr 17, 11; s James Lucas Taylor & Lola Routon T; m 1943 to Christine Crawley; c Robert Lucas & James Vincent. Educ: High sch & bus educ. Polit & Govt Pos: Chmn, Carroll Co Rep Party, Tenn, until 67 & 75-; comnr, Carroll Co, 53-54; co mgr for Rep Julian Hurst; treas, sch bd. Bus & Prof Pos: Owner, Taylor Pontiac Co, Huntingdon, Tenn, 47- Mil Serv: Entered Army, 41, released as Cpl. Mem: Elks; Rotary; Mason. Relig: Methodist. Mailing Add: Northwood Dr Huntingdon TN 38344

TAYLOR, LUCY LIDDLE (R)
First VChairwoman, Rep State Cent Comt, Ga
b Bibb Co, Ala, Nov 7, 25; d Thomas Liddle & Annie Mae Perry T; m 1947 to Dr Clayton

D Taylor; c Don Edward, Lucy Ann (Mrs Hester), Susan Victoria & Clayton Thomas. Educ: Carraway Methodist Sch of Nursing, Birmingham, Ala, registered nurse, 47. Polit & Govt Pos: Co-chmn, TAR Youth Recruitment, Ga Fedn Rep Women, 65-66, chmn, 66-67, third dist dir, Fedn, 68-69, secy, 72; co sponsor, TAR, Muscogee Co Rep Women Club, 65-67, pres, Club, 67-68, vchairwoman, 68-72, secy, 72; vchairwoman, Muscogee Co Rep Party, 68-72; first vchairwoman, Rep State Cent Comt, Ga, 72- Mem: Woman's Auxiliary Muscogee Co Med Soc (pres, 67-68); Columbus Exec Club; Nat Fedn of Rep Women. Relig: Protestant. Mailing Add: 2710 Auburn Ave Columbus GA 31906

TAYLOR, MALCOLM (TINK) (R)
NH State Rep
b Rochester, NH, July 18, 36; s Malcolm Taylor, Sr & Helen A Moorhouse T; m 1974 to Nuna Lincoln Washburn. Educ: Plymouth State Col, Univ NH, BEd, 65; Mich State Univ, MS in Resource Mgt, 74. Polit & Govt Pos: Deleg, 16th Const Conv, NH, 74; mem, NH Current Use Tax Adv Bd, 74-; NH State Rep, 75- Bus & Prof Pos: Former newspaper ed; Nat Geog Soc Mt Kennedy-Yukon Exped, Juneau, Alaska Icefield Research Proj, 65, 67 & 68; community affairs, Soc for Protection NH Forests, 67-; clerk, Environ Law Coun, NH, 70-; exec secy, NH Asn Conserv, Concord, NH, 70-; Ford Found Prog of Assistance to Munic Conserv Comns, 72-74. Mil Serv: Entered as Seaman Apprentice, Coast Guard, 55, released on med discharge, after serv on East Coast. Mem: Explorers Club; Ecol Soc Am; NH State Grange; NH Natural Resources Coun (chmn); life mem Found for Glacier & Environ Research. Honors & Awards: Teacher of the Year, Inter-Lakes Sch Dist, Meredith, NH, 66; Order of the Walrus, Gov of Alaska. Mailing Add: Holderness NH 03245

TAYLOR, MARGARET KIRKWOOD (R)
Mem, DC Rep Comt
b Harding, Pa, Jan 20, 99; d Thomas Alexander Kirkwood & Harriett Welter K; m 1924 to John Laning Taylor, wid; c John Laning, III & Jean Kirkwood. Educ: Cornell Univ, 17-21; Alpha Phi. Polit & Govt Pos: Mem, NY State Rep Comt, 34-42, vchmn exec comt, 38-42; co-chmn, Nat Dewey for President Clubs, New York, 39-40; nat legis chmn, Nat Fedn Rep Women, 61-63; pres, League Rep Women, DC, 63-65; mem, DC Rep Comt, 69- Bus & Prof Pos: Educ dir, Nat Milk Producers Fedn, 44-54; pub rels consult, Washington, DC, 54-; consult, White House Conf Children & Youth, Washington, DC, 58-60; exec dir, Am Parents Comt, 61-64; coordr fifth int cong, Collegiate Int Neuro-Psychopharmacol, 65-66. Publ: Auth, A few simple facts about the Taft-Hartley Act, Nat Milk Producers Fedn, 47; auth, Dairy cooperatives in legislative activities, Am Inst Coop, 52; ed, The Cooperative Way Wins in America, Metrop Coop Milk Producers Bargaining Agency, 57. Mem: Am Legion Auxiliary; Bus & Prof Womens Clubs; Cornell Club Washington, DC; Women's Auxiliary Washington Hosp Ctr (bd mem, 67); Pan Am Liaison Comt Women's Orgns. Honors & Awards: Businesswoman of Year, DC State Fedn Bus & Prof Women's Clubs, 56; Am Legion Auxiliary 8/40 Spec Serv Award, 69; Award for 3000 hours Vol Serv, Washington Hosp Ctr, 73. Relig: Episcopal. Mailing Add: 3636 16th St NW Washington DC 20010

TAYLOR, MARY MERIWETHER (D)
VChmn, Lincoln Co Dem Cent Comt
b Troy, Mo, Jan 9, 96; d John Fontaine Meriwether & Kate B Morton M; m 1917 to Merrell Alexander Taylor; c Merrell A, II. Educ: Northeast Mo State Teachers Col, 1 year. Polit & Govt Pos: Vchmn, Lincoln Co Dem Cent Comt, Mo, 36-; secy, vpres & pres, Lincoln Co Dem Party, 45-51; secy to pres, Ninth Cong Dist Dem Party, 51-55; mem state bd, Mo Women's Dem Clubs, 55-59; mem, Mo State Dem Speakers Bur, 55-60; deleg & secy Mo deleg, Dem Nat Conv, 56; mem, Nat Dem Speakers Bur, 58-64; participant, Dem Conf for Women, 60 & 64; secy, Ninth Cong Dist Dem Comt, 63-67. Bus & Prof Pos: Elem sch teacher, 6 years. Mem: Int Platform Asn; State Music Clubs; UDC. Honors & Awards: Dem Woman of Year, Mo, 60. Relig: Christian Church; teacher & choir leader. Mailing Add: 811 Third Troy MO 63379

TAYLOR, MEREDITH JEANNE (R)
Pres, SDak Fedn Rep Women
b Silver Creek, Nebr, Sept 19, 27; d Eugene Edmond Westring & Mabel Anderson W; m 1949 to Ralph Lee Taylor; c Ralph Lee, Jr & Kim Eugene. Educ: Genoa Pub Sch, Nebr, grad, 44. Polit & Govt Pos: Pres, SDak Fedn Rep Women, 74-; chaplain, Nat Fedn Rep Women, 74- Mem: Toastmistress. Relig: Lutheran. Mailing Add: 1720 Evergreen Dr Rapid City SD 57701

TAYLOR, PAUL WORDEN, JR (R)
Chmn, Indian River Co Rep Exec Comt, Fla
b Poughkeepsie, NY, Feb 6, 28; s Paul Worden Taylor & Margaret Vandewater T; m 1950 to Barbara Jane Nodine; c Kristen Lee, Paul Worden, III & Donald Nodine. Educ: Amherst Col, BA, 48; Univ Rochester Grad Sch, MS in Bact, 51; Univ Rochester Sch Med & Dent, MD, 53; Phi Beta Kappa; Spinx-Amherst. Polit & Govt Pos: Pres, Young Rep Club, Indian River Co, Fla, 64, secy, 65; Rep precinct committeeman, Indian River Co, 65; chmn, Indian River Co Rep Exec Comt, 66-; trustee, Indian River Co Hosp Dist, 69- Bus & Prof Pos: Vchief staff, Indian River Mem Hosp Staff, 66 & 67, chief of staff, 68. Mil Serv: Entered as 1st Lt, Air Force, 55, released as Capt, 57, after serv in 4455th Air Force Hosp, Donaldson AFB, Greenville, SC. Publ: 4 articles in Med Lit. Mem: Am Col Surgeons; Am Med Asn; Am Col Obstetricians-Gynecologists; Southern Med Asn; Rotary. Relig: Methodist. Mailing Add: 3805 Indian River Dr Vero Beach FL 32960

TAYLOR, R STRATTON (D)
b Sallisaw, Okla, Jan 25, 56; s Owen B Taylor & Velma Griffiths T; single. Educ: Claremore Jr Col, 74-; Phi Theta Kappa; Press Club; vpres, Col Young Dem; pres, Student Senate, currently. Polit & Govt Pos: Deleg, Dem Nat Mid-Term Conf, Okla, 74; chmn resolutions comt, Nowata Co Dem Conv, 75-; precinct chmn, Nowata Co Dem Party, 74- Bus & Prof Pos: Sales mgr, J Williams & Assoc, Claremore, Okla, 75-; advert mgr, col paper & yearbk, Claremore Jr Col, 75-, orientation teacher, 75- Mil Serv: E-3, Nat Guard, 75- Mem: Am Hereford Asn. Honors & Awards: Valedictorian, Alluwe High Sch, Okla, 74; Outstanding Teenagers Am, 74; Nowata Co 4-H Speech Champion, 74. Relig: Southern Baptist. Legal Res: 3027 Bluff Dr Sallisaw OK 74955 Mailing Add: Box 247 Alluwe OK 74049

TAYLOR, RAY ALLEN (R)
Iowa State Sen
b Steamboat Rock, Iowa, June 4, 23; s Leonard Taylor & Mary Delilah T; m 1943 to Mary Elizabeth Allen; c Gordon, Laura Rae (Mrs Paul Hansmann), Karol Ann (Mrs Ron Flora) & Jean Lorraine (Mrs Robert Mahl). Educ: Iowa State Teachers Col, 40-42; Baylor Univ, 48. Polit & Govt Pos: Mem sch bd, Steamboat Rock, Iowa, 56-71; mem, Hardin Co Bd Adjustment, 67-72; Iowa State Sen, Dist 5, 73- Bus & Prof Pos: Farmer, 43- Mem: Farm Bur; Iowa River Improv Club; Hardin Co Bicentennial (chmn); Faith Baptist Bible Col (adv bd). Relig: Baptist. Mailing Add: RR Steamboat Rock IA 50672

TAYLOR, ROY A (D)
US Rep, NC
b Vader, Wash, Jan 31, 10; s Arthur A Taylor & Lola Morgan T; m 1932 to Evelyn Reeves; c Alan & Toni. Educ: Asheville-Biltmore Col, 29; Maryville Col, BA, 31; Asheville Univ Law Sch, 36. Polit & Govt Pos: NC State Rep, 47-53; co attorney, Buncombe Co, NC, 49-60; US Rep, NC, 60-, chmn, Nat Parks & Recreation Subcomt, House Interior & Insular Affairs Comt, US House Rep, currently, mem, House Int Affairs Comt, currently. Mil Serv: Entered as Lt (jg), Navy, 43, released as Lt, 46, after serv as Comdr, Landing Ship, Tank, Pac Theater, 44-45. Mem: Lions (dist gov, 52). Relig: Baptist. Legal Res: 110 Connally St Black Mountain NC 28711 Mailing Add: 2233 Rayburn House Off Bldg Washington DC 20515

TAYLOR, SAMUEL S (D)
Utah State Rep
Mailing Add: 3682 S Fifth E Salt Lake City UT 84106

TAYLOR, THOMAS SOUTH (R)
Mem, Maine Rep State Comt
b Philadelphia, Pa, Oct 13, 08; s Joseph Leon Taylor & Blanche South T; m 1933 to Arlene Goshen; c Carole (Mrs Darvin Schanley) Educ: Temple Univ, 27; Bowdoin Col, Class of 31; Sigma Nu. Polit & Govt Pos: Mem, Maine Rep State Comt, 68-, field coordr, 72; mem, Maine Rep Platform Comt, 68; chmn, Maine Citizens for Reagan, 68; field rep, Nixon-Agnew Comt, 68; dist mgr, US Census Bur, Portland, Maine, 70; campaign promotional mgr, Grass for Gov Comt, 70; southern Maine coordr, Bishop for US Senate Comt, 70. Bus & Prof Pos: Former gen sales mgr, P F Volland Co, Joliet, Ill; retired. Honors & Awards: Best Speaker Awards, Penn Charter Sch, 25 & 26 & Bowdoin Col, 28, 29 & 30. Relig: Quaker. Mailing Add: Hilltop Gables Lovell ME 04051

TAYLOR, TIMOTHY HENRY (D)
b Sawyer, Ky, July 4, 18; s Grant Taylor & Allie Darr T; m 1945 to Andree Ererra; c Richard James & Kathryn (Mrs Thompson). Educ: Univ Ky, BS, 48, MS, 50; Pa State Univ, University Park, PhD, 55. Polit & Govt Pos: Permanent chmn legis dist, Ky State Dem Conv, 68, deleg, 72; alt deleg, Dem Nat Conv, 72; mem steering comt, Fayette Co Dem Club, Ky, 72; precinct committeeman, 74- Bus & Prof Pos: Asst agronomist, Va Polytech Inst, 49-55; assoc agronomist, Univ Ky, 55-60, assoc prof, 60-66, prof agronomy, 67- Mil Serv: Entered as Pvt, Army, 41, released as Pfc, 45, after serv in Anti-Aircraft, Artillery, Mediterranean & ETO; Bronze Medal & 7 Battle Stars. Publ: Sr auth, Grassland ecosystem concept (chap 5) & jr auth, Establishment of new seedlings (chap 36), In: Forages—The Science of Grasslands, 73; sr auth, Stockpiling Kentucky bluegrass, Poa prantensis L & tall fescue, Festuca arundinacea Schreb, forage for winter pasturage, Agron J, 75. Mem: Am Soc Agron (fel); Crop Sci Am; Am Forage & Grassland Coun; Ky Forage Coun; Am Asn Univ Prof. Honors & Awards: Centennial Medal, US Weather Bur, 70; Merit Cer Am Forage & Grassland Coun, 70; Man of the Year in Serv of Agr, Upper S, Progressive Farmer Mag, 72. Relig: Unitarian-Universalist. Mailing Add: 1253 Kastle Rd Lexington KY 40502

TAYLOR, VIRGINIA WILLETT (R)
Mem, Rep State Cent Comt, Calif
b Atascadero, Calif, Jan 23, 26; d Oscar Louis Willett & Georgetta Pemberton W; m 1945 to Wayne Grensted Taylor; c Sandra Lee (Mrs Ronald L Webb), Georgia Ann (Mrs Benedict), Marsha Gail (Mrs John Frederic Hildebrand, IV) & Anita Jeanne. Educ: Redlands Univ, 43-44; Univ Calif, Berkeley, 44-45; Mexico City Col, 51-52; San Diego Mesa Col, 69; San Diego State Col, 70 & 71; Alpha Tau Delta; Alpha Epsilon Delta. Polit & Govt Pos: Field secy, 36th Cong Dist, San Diego Co Rep Cent Comt, Calif, 62 & 63; co-chmn, Elec Anal Comt, Rep Assocs, 63-65; treas, Oak Park Federated Rep Women's Club, 64-65; mem, Calif Rep State Cent Comt, 64-66 & 68-, research analyst, 65; pres, San Diego City & Co War Against Litter Comt, Inc, 66-68; chmn, 200th Anniversary Rubbish Roundup, San Diego, 68; chmn, Exec Comt, Tom Hom for 79th Assembly Dist, 68; chmn, 200th Anniversary Hist Souvenirs & Mementoes, 68-69; pres, North Park Rep Assembly, 69-; mem, San Diego Co Rep Cent Comt, 69-73, mem, Finance Comt, 71-73; cand for Mayor, San Diego, 71; cand, 39th State Sen Dist, 72; chairperson, Comprehensive Health Planning Asn, San Diego, Imperial & Riverside Co, currently. Bus & Prof Pos: Secy to dir, Dept Econ, Gen, Petroleum Corp, 48-49; secy to eng supvr, Tidewater Assoc, Oil Co, 54-56; steno clerk IV, San Diego Co Pub Adminr Div, Calif, 56-59, legal secy, intermittently, 59-63; secy to Ed Herb Klein, The San Diego Union, intermittently, 63-67. Mem: Rainbow Girls Parents Club; Burlingame Club; San Diego State Col (mem, First Women's Studies Bd, 70-); Nat Orgn for Women (bd mem & vpres, San Diego Co, 70-); Nat Women's Polit Caucus (convenor, San Diego, 71-). Honors & Awards: Presidential Citation, US & Mex Border Develop Comn, 68. Relig: Protestant. Mailing Add: 2520 San Marcos Ave San Diego CA 92104

TAYLOR, WALLER, II (R)
Mem Exec Comt, Rep State Cent Comt, Calif
b Los Angeles, Calif, Nov 29, 25; s Reese Hale Taylor & Kathryn Emery T; m 1945 to Jane Carvey; c Stephen Emery, Grant Carvey & Waller, III. Educ: Univ Tex, 43-45; Univ Calif, Los Angeles, BA, 46-47; Stanford Univ, LLB, 50; Pi Sigma Alpha; Phi Alpha Delta; Delta Kappa Epsilon. Polit & Govt Pos: In past years, treas & mem steering comts for Cong cand & statewide cand, Calif & active in precinct work with Cong & Sen cand; vchmn, Los Angeles Co Nixon-Agnew Comt, Calif, 68; chmn for Sen George Murphy, Southern Calif, 70; former trustee & hon trustee, Rep Assoc, Los Angeles Co, currently; mem, United Rep Finance Comt, Los Angeles Co, mem Steering Comt & Budget & Expenditure Comt; mem exec comt, Rep State Cent Comt, Calif, currently. Bus & Prof Pos: Partner, Adams, Duque & Hazeltine, Attorneys at Law, Calif, 55- Mil Serv: Entered as Ensign, Navy, 43, released as Ensign, 46. Mem: Am Judicature Soc; Supreme Court of US; Calif Club, Los Angeles; Bohemian Club, San Francisco; Links Club, New York. Relig: Episcopal. Legal Res: 2605 Century Tower W 2220 Ave of the Stars Los Angeles CA 90067 Mailing Add: 523 W Sixth St Los Angeles CA 90014

TAYLOR, WILLIAM M (R)
Chmn, State Rep Exec Comt, Fla
b Thomasville, Ga, May 11, 23; s Thomas H Taylor & Evelyn Murphy T; m 1956 to Shirley Ann Warner; c Erin Warner & William Bradford. Educ: Ariz State Univ, BS, 48; Ariz State Univ Athletic Scholarship; Delta Chi; Letterman's Club. Polit & Govt Pos: Mem, Young Rep Club, Charlotte, NC, 52; mem, Mecklenberg Co Young Rep Club, NC; mem, Mecklenberg Co Rep Exec Comt, mem finance comt; precinct orgn chmn, Rep C Raper Jonas, 54; mem campaign comt, Jonas for Cong, 56; participant, Eisenhower for President Campaigns, 52 &

56; participant various local Rep cand campaigns; mem, Duval Co Rep Exec Comt, Fla, mem, Duval Co Rep Men's Club; Duval Co organizer, Floridians for Nixon-Lodge, 60, campaign mgr & coordr, Northeast Fla; mem, Duval Co Young Rep Club, chmn, 62; participant, Young Rep Leadership Training Sch, Washington, DC, 62; mem, Fla Fedn Young Rep, 63-; deleg to all state & nat Young Rep Conv; adv, Young Rep Trust Fund Comt; mem campaign comt to elect William F Murfin Chmn Rep State Exec Comt, Fla; co-chmn, Kirk Appreciation Dinner, 66; mem, Tom Slade Adv Comt, 66; chmn, Duval Co Re-Registr Drive, 66; dist finance chmn, State Rep Exec Comt, Fla, 67, committeeman, 71-75, chmn, 75-; deleg, Rep Nat Conv, 68 & 72; host comt cand, Fla House Rep, Dist 24, 68; vchmn, Dist 3, Fla Rep Party, 71-; mem, Rep Nat Comt, 75- Bus & Prof Pos: Salesman, Bemis Bros Bag Co, 48-54; agent, Jefferson Standard Life Ins Co, 54-57; gen agent, Manhattan Life Ins Co, 57-64; supt of agencies, Peninsular Life Ins Co, 64-; vpres, George Washington Life Ins Co, 67; gen agent, Provident Life & Accident Ins Co, 67-; vpres, W H Collings Co, Inc. Mil Serv: Entered as A/S, Naval Res with serv in European & Asiatic Theatres; Commendation Ribbon; Qualified Submarine Badge; Submarine Combat Pin with Four Stars; Good Conduct Medal; Am, European & Asiatic Theatre Ribbons. Mem: Nat Asn Life Underwriters; Northeast Fla Estate Planning Coun; Mason; Scottish Rite; Shrine. Relig: Methodist. Legal Res: 7660 Holiday Rd S Jacksonville FL 32216 Mailing Add: PO Box 16402 Jacksonville FL 32216

TAYMOR, BETTY (D)
Committeewoman, State Dem Comt, Mass
b Baltimore, Md, Mar 22, 21; d William Bernstein & Tillie Blum B; m 1942 to Melvin Lester Taymor; c Michael, Laurie & Julie. Educ: Goucher Col, AB, 42; Boston Univ Grad Sch, MA in Govt, 67. Polit & Govt Pos: Committeewoman, State Dem Comt, Mass, 56-, vchmn, 65-68; deleg-at-lg, Dem Nat Conv, 60, 64 & 68 & mem, Platform Comt, 68; mem, US Nat Comn, UNESCO, 61- Bus & Prof Pos: Lectr govt, Simmons Col, 68-69; instr polit sci, Northeastern Univ, currently; consult, Off of the Pres, Univ Mass, 72; instr, Masters in Urban Affairs Prog, Boston Univ, 73-, dir prog for women in polit & govt careers, Boston Col, 74- Honors & Awards: Awarded Elizabeth King Ellicott fel develop of polit educ for women in US, Goucher Col, 59. Relig: Jewish. Mailing Add: 14 Eliot Memorial Rd Newton MA 02158

TAYOUN, JAMES J (D)
Pa State Rep
Mailing Add: Capitol Bldg Harrisburg PA 17120

TEAGUE, JOHN A (D)
Ala State Rep
Mailing Add: 708 Forest Hill Dr Childersburg AL 35044

TEAGUE, LEEMAN AMBROSE (D)
Chmn, Gilmer Co Dem Exec Comt, Ga
b Gilmer Co, Ga, May 22, 33; s James Albert Teague & Martha Teems T; m 1952 to Clestene Cloniger Burrell; c Martha Ann & Edward Bailey, Jr & Leeman, Jr, Jerry Albert, Donnie William & Sheila Jane Teague. Polit & Govt Pos: Chmn, Gilmer Co Dem Exec Comt, Ga, currently. Bus & Prof Pos: Poultry & cattle farmer, 53-65; mgr, Poultry Processing Plant, 65-69; mgr, Carpet Mfg Prod, 69-73; Restaurant Mgr, 73- Mem: Lions; Mason. Relig: Baptist. Mailing Add: Rte 2 Ellijay GA 30540

TEAGUE, OLIN E (D)
US Rep, Tex
m to Freddie Dunman; c James M, John O & Jill Virginia. Educ: Tex Agr & Mech Col, 28-32. Polit & Govt Pos: US Rep, Tex, 46-, chmn, Comt on Sci & Astronaut & mem, Comt on Vet Affairs, US House Rep, currently, mem, Technol Assessment Bd & chmn, Dem Caucus, 73-; mem bd visitors, US Mil Acad, 55-72. Bus & Prof Pos: Employee, Post Off, Animal Husbandry Dept, Tex Agr & Mech Col & RR. Mil Serv: Nat Guard, 3 years; entered as 2nd Lt, Army, 40, released as Col, 46, after serv in Inf, commanded First Bn, 314th Inf, 79th Div; decorated 11 times; Silver Star with two clusters; Bronze Star with two clusters; Purple Heart with two clusters; Combat Infantryman's Badge; Army Commendation Ribbon; French Croix de Guerre with Palm. Honors & Awards: Authored & sponsored the Korean War Vet Bill that was made Pub Law 550. Legal Res: College Station TX 77840 Mailing Add: 2311 Rayburn House Off Bldg Washington DC 20515

TEAGUE, RANDAL CORNELL (R)
b Durham, NC, May 19, 44; s Roy Merle Teague, Sr & Lottie Rhew T; m 1969 to Mary Kathleen King. Educ: Am Univ, BA, 67; George Washington Univ, JD, 71, LLM summa cum laude, 72; Pi Sigma Alpha. Hon Degrees: LLD, Allen Univ, 73. Polit & Govt Pos: Minority clerk, US House Rep Comt on Pub Works, 64-68; dir regional & state activities & exec dir, Young Am for Freedom, Inc, 68-71; policy develop coordr & acting asst dir opers, Off Econ Opportunity, 71-73; admin asst & legis counsel, US Rep Jack F Kemp, NY, 38th Cong Dist, 73- Bus & Prof Pos: Partner, Pub Affairs Assocs, 72- Publ: Ed, Readings on East-West Trade, Young Am for Freedom, Inc 71. Mem: Am, Fed, DC & Fla Bar Asns; US Equestrian Team. Honors & Awards: Admissions to practice, US Supreme Court, Court of Claims, Tax Court, Courts of Appeals for DC & Fifth Circuits, Court of Mil Appeals & Dist Court for DC, DC Court of Appeals & Supreme Court Fla. Relig: Episcopal. Legal Res: Brookdale Rte 2 Box 128 Lovettsville VA 22080 Mailing Add: 132 Cannon House Off Bldg Washington DC 20515

TEAGUE, THOMAS JOSEPH (D)
Ind State Sen
b Anderson, Ind, June 7, 42; s Frank Carpenter Teague & Winifred Baker T; m 1967 to Jane Frances Booth; c Erin Rebecca. Educ: Anderson Col, BA, 65; Univ Okla, MA, 68; Ind Law Sch, 71- Polit & Govt Pos: Ind State Sen, 70- Bus & Prof Pos: Bldg indust consult, Ind Bell, 70- Mil Serv: Entered as 2nd Lt, Air Force, 66, released as Capt, 70, after serv in Hq, Strategic Air Command, 66-70; Bronze Star Vietnam. Relig: Methodist. Mailing Add: 5217 Knollwood Lane Anderson IN 46011

TEAGUE, THOMAS MORSE (R)
Maine State Rep
b Wilson, NY, Sept 28, 24; s Harold Leslie Teague & Martha Cole T; m 1949 to Beverley Hayward; c Jennifer, Jack & Sarah. Educ: Univ Maine, Orono, BS, 50; Alpha Gamma Rho. Polit & Govt Pos: Mem, Fairfield Town Coun, Maine, 6 years; Maine State Rep, 75- Bus & Prof Pos: Pres, Maine Poultry Serv, 57-75. Mil Serv: Entered as Apprentice Seaman, Navy, 44, released as Boatswains Mate 2/C, 46, after serv in Amphibious Force, Pac, 44-46. Mem: Kiwanis; VFW; Waterville Country Club; Am Legion. Relig: Methodist. Mailing Add: 271 Main St Fairfield ME 04937

TEAGUE, WES (D)
Mont State Rep
Mailing Add: 4314 Fenton Ave SW Billings MT 59101

TEAHAN, ROBERT S (D)
Mass State Rep
Mailing Add: State Capitol Boston MA 02133

TECKLENBURG, ESTHER HERLIHY (D)
b Boston, Mass, Sept 5, 28; d Frederick William Herlihy & Florence Hynes H; m 1950 to Henry Christian John Tecklenburg, Jr; c Henry Christian John, III, Frederick William, John Joseph, Paul Francis & Michael Hynes. Educ: Trinity Col (DC), AB, 49; Sociol Club; Int Rels Club; Span Club. Polit & Govt Pos: Orangeburg Co Rep, SC Coun Dem Women, 69-73; deleg, Dem Nat Conv, 72. Bus & Prof Pos: Social worker, Charleston Co Dept Pub Welfare, 49-51; teacher, St Patricks Sch, Charleston, SC, 59-61. Publ: Catholic education in South Carolina, 60 & The confraternity of Christian doctrine in South Carolina, 60, Cath Banner. Mem: SC State Col (bd trustees, 70-); Columbia Hearing & Speech Ctr; Orangeburg Human Rels Comt; Orangeburg Pub Sch Syst (mem elem & sec educ act adv comt, Dist Five); Am Asn Univ Women. Relig: Catholic. Mailing Add: 377 Brookside Dr Orangeburg SC 29115

TECSON, JOSEPH A (R)
Treas, Cook Co Rep Party, Ill
b Chicago, Ill, Apr 4, 28; s Joseph Tecson & Jeannette Lanahan T; m 1954 to Caroline R Rees; c Andrew, Sarah & David. Educ: Ripon Col, BA, 52; Univ Wis Law Sch, LLB & JD, 54. Polit & Govt Pos: Committeeman, Riverside Twp Rep Party, Ill, 66-; spec asst to Ill Attorney Gen, 69; treas, Cook Co Rep Party, 69-; deleg, Sixth Ill Const Conv, chmn comt on exec article; mem bd dirs, Regional Transportation Authority, NE Ill, 74-, chmn, 74-75. Bus & Prof Pos: Lawyer & partner with Abel J De Haan. Mil Serv: Entered as A/S, Navy, 46, released as PO 3/C, 47, after serv in Naval Air Branch as Radio-Radar Operator, on USS Shangrila, Air Group Five, 46-47. Publ: Let's combine law days with school days, Ill State Bar J, 68; Let's keep cumulative voting, 11/70 & The executive article of the 1970 constitution, 11/70, Chicago Bar Record; plus others. Mem: Am Arbit Asn (arbitrator); Am & Ill Bar Asns; Trial Lawyers Club of Chicago; Mason. Relig: Presbyterian. Legal Res: 230 Maplewood Rd Riverside IL 60546 Mailing Add: One N LaSalle Chicago IL 60602

TEDFORD, JOHN ROY, JR (R)
Chmn, Sutton Co Rep Party, Tex
b Dallas, Tex, Mar 27, 36; s John Roy Tedford, Sr & Harriet Clark T; m 1957 to Dell Davis; c Gregg Laurence & Valerie. Educ: Southern Methodist Univ, 57; Phi Mu Alpha. Polit & Govt Pos: Chmn, Sutton Co Rep Party, Tex, 62-; alt deleg, Rep State Conv, 64, deleg, 70 & 72. Bus & Prof Pos: Free lance musical dir for theaters in US & Can; musical dir, Dallas Summer Musicals, 68-73; free lance composer & arranger for indust shows; rancher, Sutton Co, Tex. Mem: Am Fedn Musicians; Tex Sheep & Goat Raisers Asn. Relig: Methodist. Legal Res: 610 Allen Dr Sonora TX 76950 Mailing Add: PO Box 956 Sonora TX 76950

TEDFORD, RICHARD CORTEZ (D)
Miss State Rep
Mailing Add: 137 W Main Marks MS 38646

TEEL, WARD (R)
Va State Deleg
Mailing Add: PO Box 509 Christiansburg VA 24073

TEETS, JAMES W (R)
WVa State Deleg
Mailing Add: State Capitol Charleston WV 25305

TEGELS, CAROL ANNE (DFL)
VChmn, Second Cong Dist Dem-Farmer-Labor Party, Minn
b Long Prairie, Minn, June 7, 28; d Alvin John Bous & Nellie Margaret Collins B; m 1947 to Anthony Leo Tegels; c Anntoinette Marie, Thomas Lee, Mark Charles, Gregory James & Kathleen Sylvia. Educ: High sch grad. Polit & Govt Pos: Chmn, Cottonwood Co Dem-Farmer-Labor Party, Minn, 62-69; vchmn, Second Cong Dist Dem-Farmer-Labor Party, 70- Mem: Chiropractic Asn (Nat & Minn Auxiliary). Relig: Roman Catholic; St Francis Xavier Parish Coun. Mailing Add: 601 Fourth Ave Windom MN 56101

TEICHER, OREN JONATHAN (D)
b Toronto, Ont, Aug 7, 49; s Dr Morton I Teicher & Mildred Adler T; single. Educ: George Washington Univ, BA, 71. Polit & Govt Pos: Staff aide, Congressman Richard Ottinger, NY, 67-69; campaign aide, Ottinger for Senate, 70; McGovern for President, 72 & Reid for Gov, NY, 73-74; campaign mgr, Ottinger for Cong, 74; admin asst to US Rep Richard L Ottinger, NY, 75- Bus & Prof Pos: Marketing staff, Nat Tel Advert, 71. Mem: Common Cause; Am Civil Liberties Union. Mailing Add: 518 Second St SE Washington DC 20003

TEICHNER, STEPHEN J (D)
b Cambridge, Mass, Mar 4, 43; s Warren H Teichner & Ruth Tekley T. Educ: State Univ Iowa, BA, 66; Suffolk Univ Law Sch, JD, 69; Acacia. Polit & Govt Pos: Nat field staff, McCarthy for President, 68; VISTA lawyer, VISTA EBoston, Mass, 69; spec asst, Gov, Commonwealth of Mass, 71- Bus & Prof Pos: Lobbyist, Gr Boston Comt Transportation Crisis, 69-70; TV reporter, The Reporters, WGBH-TV, 70-71. Mem: Mass Bar Asn; Mass Bar; Fed Bar, First Dist. Honors & Awards: One of Five Outstanding High Sch Grad the Country for the Decade 1962-1972. Mailing Add: Apt 4 847 Beacon St Boston MA 02215

TEITZ, JEFFREY JONATHAN (D)
RI State Rep
b Newport, RI, May 12, 53; s Judge George A Teitz & Miriam Feinstein T; single. Educ: Brown Univ, presently majoring in polit sci; vpres, Brown Univ Pre-Law Soc. Polit & Govt Pos: Legis intern, RI Gen Assembly, 72; RI State Rep, Dist 97, 73-, mem, Comt on Labor, Comn on Naval Affairs & Comn to Study the Feasibility of Coord Departmental Activities, RI Gen Assembly, 73- Mem: RI Urban League (bd dirs, 73-); Newport Hosp Corp; Young Dem RI; NAACP; Redwood Libr (bd, 72-). Honors & Awards: Outstanding Young Man of Am, Bd Adv of Outstanding Young Men of Am, 73. Relig: Jewish. Mailing Add: 25 Admiral Kalbfus Rd Newport RI 02840

TEKAUTZ, RUSSELL FRANK (DFL)
Treas, St Louis Co Dem-Farmer-Labor Party, Minn
b Virginia, Minn, Apr 9, 31; s Charles A Tekautz & Tressa Anderson T; m 1951 to Martha Squillace; c Michael & Gerald. Educ: Vet high sch dipl, Army, 54. Polit & Govt Pos: Treas, St Louis Co Dem-Farmer-Labor Party, Minn, 70-; treas, 62nd Legis Dist Dem-Farmer-Labor Party, Minn, 70- Mil Serv: Entered as Pvt, Army, 51, released as Sgt 1/C, 54, after serv in 3rd Inf Div, 15th Inf Regt, Heavy Mortar Co, Korea, 51-52; UN Serv Medal; Korean Serv Medal; Combat Inf Badge. Mem: VFW; United Steelworkers Local 4108; Youth Hockey Asn. Relig: Catholic. Mailing Add: 1804 12th Ave S Virginia MN 55792

TELCSER, ARTHUR A (R)
Ill State Sen
Mailing Add: 525 W Roscoe St Chicago IL 60657

TELLE, KING (R)
Ind State Sen
Mailing Add: 1212 Campbell Rd Valparaiso IN 46383

TELLES, RAYMOND L
b El Paso, Tex, Sept 5, 15; m to Delfina Navarro Telles; c Cynthia Ann & Patricia Eugenia. Educ: Int Bus Col, 34; Tex Western Col. Polit & Govt Pos: Acct, Bur of Prisons, US Dept of Justice, 34-41 & 47-48; co clerk, El Paso Co, Tex, 48-56; mayor, El Paso, 57-61; US Ambassador to Costa Rica, 61-67; US chmn, US-Mex Border Comn, 67-69; app to Equal Employ Opportunity Comn, 73- Mil Serv: Maj, Army, 41-47; Army Air Force, 51-52, chief of lendlease for Army Air Forces for Latin Am; Col, Air Force Res; Bronze Star. Legal Res: TX Mailing Add: 6808 Whittier Blvd Bethesda MD 20034

TELOW, JOHN (R)
Committeeman, Maine Rep State Comt
b Schenectady, NY, Nov 29, 14; m 1948 to Hope Elaine Leadbetter; c Stephen, Pamela, Lori Ann, Janis Lynne & Michael Alan. Educ: Northeastern Univ, BS in BA, 41; Sigma Phi Alpha; Empire State Club; Law & Acct Club; Inter-fraternity Coun; Soc Advan Mgt. Polit & Govt Pos: Mem, Mayor's Adv Comt, Lewiston, Maine, 62-66; chmn, Citizen Adv Subcomt on Urban Renewal Relocations, 63-66; mem, Lewiston Planning Bd, 64-, past chmn & vchmn; mem, Androscoggin Co Rep Comt, 64-, past chmn; mem, Lewiston City Rep Comt, 64-, chmn, 70-72; mem, Lewiston Sch Bldg Comt, 65-66; chmn, Androscoggin Co Nixon for President Comt, 68; mem, Second Cong Dist Rep Comt, 68-; chmn, Androscoggin Co Erwin for Gov Comt, 70; committeeman & mem budget comt, Maine State Rep Comt, 70- Bus & Prof Pos: Mgr, W T Grant Co, 41-58; mgr, Arlan's Dept Stores, 58-59; mgr, Mammoth Mart, Inc, 59-65, dist supvr, 65- Mil Serv: Mass Nat Guard, 241st Coast Artil, 37-40. Mem: Lewiston-Auburn Salvation Army Adv Bd (past chmn); Elks; Mason; Scottish Rite (32 degree); Shrine. Honors & Awards: Book of Golden Deeds Award for outstanding record of accomplishments for community, Lewiston Exchange Club; Plaque, Lewiston-Auburn Salvation Army; six citations from US Treasury Dept in recognition of outstanding vol serv in promotion & sale of US Savings Bonds. Relig: Methodist; past trustee, Cavalry Methodist Church. Mailing Add: 11 Champlain Ave Lewiston ME 04240

TEMMEY, LEO ALBERT (R)
b Onida, SDak, Nov 6, 94; s Lawrence A Temmey & Annie O'Connor T; m 1920 to Rose Tracy; c Larry A & Robert J. Educ: SDak State Univ, BA; Univ Minn, LLB; Phi Sigma Kappa. Polit & Govt Pos: State's attorney, Beadle Co SDak, 30-35; Attorney Gen, SDak, 39-42; cand for Gov, 42; deleg, Rep Nat Conv, 48; chmn, SDak Rep State Cent Comt, 60-65; mem, Rep Nat Comt, 60-65. Mil Serv: 1st Sgt, Co I, 355th Inf, World War I; Lt Col, State Under Secy of War, Bd of Contract Appeals, World War II. Mem: Elks; Am Legion (state comdr, 35-36) nat vcomdr, 36-37); Rotary. Legal Res: 547 Nebraska Ave SW Huron SD 57350 Mailing Add: F&M Bank Bldg Huron SD 57305

TEMPLAR, TED MAC (R)
Kans State Rep
b Arkansas City, Kans, Sept 27, 29; s H George Templar & Helen Bishop T; m 1954 to Maxine Bowman; c Lance C, Kenton L & Clayton N. Educ: Washburn Univ, BBA, 51, JD, 54; Delta Theta Phi; Kappa Sigma. Polit & Govt Pos: Dep co attorney, Cowley Co, Kans, 56-58; judge, Arkansas City Court, 69-73; Kans State Rep, 73- Bus & Prof Pos: Attorney-at-law, Arkansas City, Kans, 54- Mil Serv: Army Res, 8 years, last rank 1st Lt, Judge Adv Gen Corps. Mem: Am, Kans & Cowley Co Bar Assns; Kans Trial Lawyers' Asn. Honors & Awards: Distinguished Serv Award, Jaycees, 65. Legal Res: 2128 Edgemont Arkansas City KS 67005 Mailing Add: 121 W Fifth Ave PO Box 1002 Arkansas City KS 67005

TEMPLE, ARTHUR, III (D)
Tex State Rep
Mailing Add: 811 S Meadows Dr Diboll TX 75941

TEMPLE, RENNA MARY (R)
Committeewoman, Ark Rep State Comt
b Van Buren, Ark, Nov 16, 96; d James A Matthews & Elizabeth Orme M; wid. Educ: Neals Bus Col; Univ Cent Ark. Polit & Govt Pos: Bd mem, Ark Rep Women, 67-; bd mem, Ark State Cancer Comm, 68-73; chmn, Ark State Rep Mem, 70-; chmn, Ark State Rep Newspaper, 72-; treas, Faulkner Co Rep Comt, 74-; committeewoman, Ark Rep State Comt, currently. Bus & Prof Pos: Buyer, M M Cohn Co, 29-41 & 46-48; buyer, Lockheed Aircraft, 41-46; own bus, Little Rock, Ark, 48-60. Mem: Rep Women's Club (pres); Women's Voter League; TEL. Honors & Awards: Winthrop Rockefeller Founder's Award; Richard M Nixon Award; Lincoln Day Dinner Award for Outstanding Rep. Relig: Methodist. Legal Res: West Prince Conway AR 72032 Mailing Add: PO Box 761 Conway AR 72032

TEMPLE, THOMAS A, SR (D)
Del State Rep
Mailing Add: 808 Oak St Seaford DE 19973

TEMPLE, WILLIAM HARVEY ERNEST (R)
Mem, Rep State Cent Comt Calif
b Pacific Grove, Calif, July 3, 31; s William Urich Temple & Ruth E Furlong T; m 1968 to Marie Antionette Herold; c William Charles, Sherry Elizabeth, Michael Alan & Patricia Antionette. Educ: Hartnell Col, AA, 51; San Jose State Col, BA, 53; Sigma Nu. Polit & Govt Pos: Mem, Monterey Co Rep Cent Comt, Calif, 66-, chmn, formerly; chmn, Region VIII Drug & Alcohol Abuse Task Force, 69-; dir, Adv Bd Calif Coun Criminal Justice, 70-; mem, Rep State Cent Comt, Calif, 71-; mem, Calif Chairmen's Asn, formerly. Bus & Prof Pos: Vpres, Growers Ins Agency, 58-64; pres, Speegle-Temple Ins Agency, 63-; pres, Camalot Farms Inc, 70- Mil Serv: Entered as Recruit, Naval Res, 51, released as SK 2, 58. Publ: Three points to insurance success, Agent/Broker, 2/71. Mem: Am Cancer Soc (pres, Monterey Br, 70-); Commonwealth Club Calif; Salinas CofC; Marine Mem Asn; Elks. Honors & Awards: One of Five Outstanding Young Men in Calif, 66; Outstanding Young Man Salinas, 66; Outstanding Young Men Am, 68. Relig: Methodist. Mailing Add: 120 San Benancio Rd Salinas CA 93901

TENENBAUM, DOROTHY S (D)
b St Paul, Minn, Nov 11, 22; d George F Snell & Clara Strauss S; div; c William Henry Curtis & Ann Maynard. Educ: Nat Park Col, 2 years; George Washington Univ, 47-49; Sigma Alpha Epsilon; Optimist Int. Polit & Govt Pos: Secy to Wesley McCune, Dem Nat Comt, 56; secy, Senate Interior & Insular Affairs Comt, 57-59; secy to US Sen Albert Gore, Tenn, 60-65; secy, Joint Comt Orgn of Cong, 65-66; legis asst to US Sen Lee Metcalf, Mont, 66- Relig: Unitarian. Mailing Add: 3900 Spruell Dr Kensington MD 20795

TENNEFOS, JENS JUNIOR (R)
NDak State Rep
b Fargo, NDak, Feb 15, 30; s Jens Peterson Tennefos & Ivah M Gilbraith T; m 1960 to Jeanne P Quamme; c Daniel J, David A, Judie A & Mary J. Educ: NDak State Univ, 47-49; Sigma Alpha Epsilon; Optimist Int. Polit & Govt Pos: NDak State Rep, 74- Bus & Prof Pos: Pres, Tennefos Construction Co Inc, 51-75. Mil Serv: Entered as Pvt, Army, 51, released as Pvt, 52, after serv in Army Engrs. Mem: Assoc Gen Contractors of NDak; Oak Grove Lutheran High Sch (bd regents, 70-); Elks; Am Legion; Sons of Norway. Honors & Awards: Distinguished Serv Citation, Assoc Gen Contractors of NDak, 69. Relig: Lutheran; mem, Lutheran Social Welfare Conf of Am. Mailing Add: 714 19th Ave S Fargo ND 58102

TENNESSEN, ROBERT J (DFL)
Minn State Sen
b Lismore, Minn, Aug 24, 39; s Alphonse J Tennessen & Helen T; m 1968 to Christine J; c two daughters. Educ: Fla State Univ Exten Div; Ramey AFB, PR, 59-60; Univ Minn, BA, 65, JD, 68. Polit & Govt Pos: Minn State Sen, 71-, mem US privacy protection study comn, Minn State Senate, 75- Bus & Prof Pos: Attorney. Mil Serv: Entered as Enlisted Man, Air Force, 57, released 71, after serv in PR 72nd Bomb Wing, Major Air Command; Strategic Air Command. Mem: Am, Minn & Hennepin Co Bar Asns. Honors & Awards: Distinguished Serv Award, Minn Ment Health Asn. Legal Res: Minneapolis MN 55405 Mailing Add: Rm 27 State Capitol St Paul MN 55155

TENNEY, BOYD (R)
Ariz State Sen
Mailing Add: Senator Hwy Prescott AZ 86301

TENNILLE, MARGARET (D)
NC State Rep
Mailing Add: 2307 Greenwich Winston-Salem NC 27104

TENOPIR, LAWRENCE L (D)
Pres, Kans Young Dem
b Marysville, Kans, Aug 12, 50; s Adolph L Tenopir & Del Linn T; single. Educ: Univ Kans, BSE, 72; Phi Delta Kappa. Polit & Govt Pos: Chmn, Marshall Co Young Dem, Kans, 72-75; chmn, Marshall Co Dem Voter Registr, 74; chmn, Bergsten for 61st Dist Comt, 74; research dir, Kans Young Dem, 74-75, pres, 75- Bus & Prof Pos: Teacher, Bird City High Sch, Kans, 72-73; teacher, Blue Valley High Sch, Randolph, 73-75. Mem: Kans Nat Educ Asn (uniserv coun); Nat Coun Teachers Eng; Int Reading Asn. Honors & Awards: Josephine Berry Scholar, Univ Kans, 68. Relig: Roman Catholic. Mailing Add: 706 Calhoun Marysville KS 66508

TENZER, HERBERT (D)
b New York, NY, Nov 1, 05; s Michael Tenzer & Rose Steier T; m 1930 to Florence R Novor; c Barry & Diane (Mrs Sidel). Educ: NY Univ, LLB, 27. Hon Degrees: LHD, Yeshiva Univ. Polit & Govt Pos: US Rep, NY, formerly. Bus & Prof Pos: Sr partner, Tenzer, Greenblatt, Fallon & Kaplan, Esqs; gen partner in real estate firms; bd chmn, Barton's Candy Corp, 40-65; former bd mem, Metrop Indust Bank & Queens Nat Bank; former dir, Am Trust Co. Mem: KofP (past chancellor); B'nai B'rith (Long Island Lodge); F&AM; AASR; Mason (32 degree). Relig: Jewish. Mailing Add: 15 Waverly Pl Cedarhurst NY 11559

TERL, ALLAN HOWARD (D)
Asst Attorney Gen, Md
b Baltimore, Md, Jan 14, 46; s Leon Terl & Hannah Rovner T; single. Educ: Univ Md, College Park, AB, 67, Sch Law, Baltimore, JD, 70; Pi Sigma Alpha; Omicron Delta Kappa. Polit & Govt Pos: Staff asst to Congressman Hervey G Machen, Md, 67; campaign aide to US Sen Daniel B Brewster, Md, 68; admin asst to State Sen Carl L Friedler, Md, 68-70; pres, Young Dem Clubs, Md, 69-70; pres, Md Fedn Col Young Dem, 66-67; campaign coordr, Friedler for Congress, 70; mem, Md Dem Party Reform Comn, 70-71; admin asst to State Sen Steny H Hoyer, Md, 70-71; nat committeeman, Young Dem Clubs, Md, 70-72; bd dirs, John F Kennedy Dem Club, 70-73; Asst Attorney Gen, Md, 71- Mem: Am Jr Bar Asn; Phi Alpha Delta; Common Cause; Am for Dem Action (bd dirs, Baltimore Chap, 73); Am Civil Liberties Union. Honors & Awards: Outstanding Young Dem in Md Award, Young Dem Clubs of Md, 72. Relig: Jewish. Mailing Add: 920 N Calvert St Baltimore MD 21202

TERRA, JEAN M (D)
Chairwoman, Blaine Co Dem Cent Comt, Idaho
b Chatham, Ont, Can, May 1, 31; d Guy G Fish & Helen Hinnegan F; div; c Michael, Mary, Richard & Colleen. Educ: Univ Detroit, 52-53, summer 65; Idaho State Univ, Sun Valley, 73-74. Polit & Govt Pos: Precinct committeewoman, Blaine Co Dem Cent Comt, Idaho, 60-63, chairwoman, 74-; committeewoman, Idaho State Dem Cent Comt, 68-74; deleg, Dem Nat Conv, 72. Bus & Prof Pos: Ed, Sun Valley Mag, 74- Mem: Nat Fedn Press Women. Legal Res: 724 Fourth Ave N Ketchum ID 83340 Mailing Add: Box 124 Ketchum ID 83340

TERRILL, ALBERT LEE (D)
Okla State Sen
b Walters, Okla, Mar 8, 37; s Albert Terrill & Ruth Elliot Gardiner T; m 1956 to Sandra Kay Cullen; c Lisa Dianne, Leah Suzanne & Todd Albert. Educ: Abilene Christian Col; Southwestern State Col, BA; all-conf fullback; letterman in football, basketball, track. Polit & Govt Pos: Okla State Sen, Dist 32, 65-, chmn, Educ Comt, mem, Comts on Bus, Indust & Labor Rels & Roads, Hwy & Pub Safety, 69-, Majority Leader, Okla State Senate, formerly.

Bus & Prof Pos: Pres, Okla Preferred Finance & Loan Corp, De'Ninth Bldg Corp, Royal Enterprises, Inc & Sheridan Warehouses, Inc; vpres, Lawton Enterprises, Inc & Kincannon, Inc; asst prin, Lawton Pub Schs, 1 year & teacher & coach, 4 years. Mem: Nat Asn Sec Prin; Okla Consumer Finance Asn (vpres & state pub rels chmn & bd dirs); Abilene Christian Col Nat Develop Coun; Okla Christian Col (assoc mem, bd trustees); Relig Heritage of Am (adv bd). Relig: Church of Christ; adult Bible class teacher; mem, Educ & Budget Comts. Legal Res: 811 NW 51st St Lawton OK 73501 Mailing Add: PO Box 1093 Lawton OK 73501

TERRIS, BRUCE JEROME (D)
b Detroit, Mich, Aug 3, 33; s Charles Zachary Terris & Ruth Singer T; m 1958 to Shirley Duval; c Elizabeth, Jessica & Robert. Educ: Harvard Col, AB summa cum laude, 54; Harvard Law Sch, LLB magna cum laude, 57, article ed, Harvard Law Rev, 56-57; Georgetown Univ Grad Sch, 57-60; Phi Beta Kappa. Polit & Govt Pos: Asst to solicitor gen, Washington, DC, 58-65; co-chmn, Nat Conf on Law & Poverty, 65; asst dir, Nat Crime Comn, 65-67; asst to the Vice President, 67-68; mem campaign staff of Sen Robert Kennedy, 68; chmn, DC Dem Cent Comt, 68-72. Bus & Prof Pos: Vis prof law, Cath Univ Am, 67-68; exec dir, Anacostia Assistance Corp, 68-69; consult, Crime, Poverty, Law, Housing, Urban Probs, 67-69; sr attorney, Ctr on Law & Social Policy, 69-70; private attorney, Pub Interest Practice, 70- Publ: The Responsibility of City Government: Win the War or Preserve the Peace, New Jersey Municipalities, 68; The role of the police, Ann Am Acad Polit Sci, 11/68; Legal service for the elderly, 72. Mem: DC Develop Corp (secy). Relig: Catholic. Mailing Add: 1855 Shepherd St NW Washington DC 20011

TERRY, CLARA DELLE (MRS DOUGLAS MACRAE) (R)
b New Albany, Miss, Aug 25, 22; d David Earl Craft & Frances Lindsey C; m 1947 to James E Terry (deceased); m 1961 to Douglas F Macrae; c Douglas F, Jr. Educ: High sch & Strayer Bus Col, DC. Polit & Govt Pos: Admin asst to US Sen George H Bender, 46-56; exec secy to US Rep Arch A Moore, Jr, 57-69; admin asst to US Rep Wilmer D Mizell, 69-70; spec asst to US Sen Bob Packwood, Ore, 70-72; personal secy, US Rep Harold R Collier, Ill, 72-; exec asst to US Rep Edwin D Eshleman, Pa, 72- Mem: Eastern Star; Bus & Prof Women's Club; Rep Women of Capitol Hill. Relig: Methodist. Mailing Add: 714 N Lincoln St Arlington VA 22201

TERRY, HARRIET ELEANOR (D)
Mem, State Dem Comt, Kans
b Cullison, Kans, Jan 12, 12; d Horace Ramer Walters & Mary Palestine Waggoner W; m 1929 to Harold Glenn Terry; c Eleanor Ann (Mrs Moon) & Roger Allen. Educ: Cullison High Sch, Kans, 25-29. Polit & Govt Pos: Dem precinct committeewoman, Kans, currently; mem, State Dem Comt, Kans, 66- & State Dem Exec Comt, 71-; vchmn, Pratt Co Dem Cent Comt, 66-68, chmn, 68-; finance chmn, Fedn State Dem Club Kans, 67-73, vpres, 73-75; coordr 11 co, Robinson for Senate Campaign, 68; alt deleg, Dem Nat Conv, 68, deleg & mem rules comt, 72; mem, Kans Rules Comt for Dem Nat Deleg Selection, 71; vchmn, State Dem Club, Kans, 70; vchmn, First Cong Dist Dem Comt, Kans, 71-74; finance chmn, Pratt Co Dem Club. Bus & Prof Pos: Receptionist, Dent Off, 31; newspaper reporter, 33-34; saleslady, Bakery, 47-50; rep, Avon, 55-74. Mem: Pansy Rebecca Lodge; Kans Genealogy Soc; Royal Neighbors of Am; VFW (Ladies Auxiliary); Womens Training Union (Ladies Auxiliary). Honors & Awards: Achievement awards; top sales awards; presented with co-awards; co bond awards. Relig: Baptist. Mailing Add: 319 Curtis Pratt KS 67124

TERRY, JAMES WILLIAM (R)
Chmn, Sarasota Co Exec Comt, Fla
b Johnson City, Tenn, May 19, 30; s William Howard Terry & Mary Lindamood T; m 1953 to Elizabeth Haynie; c Carolyn Elizabeth & James William, Jr. Educ: Univ Tenn, BSEE, 58. Polit & Govt Pos: Chmn, Sarasota Young Rep, 64-67; chmn, Sarasota Co Exec Comt, Fla, 74- Bus & Prof Pos: Engr-mkt mgr, EMR Electronics, Sarasota, 62-69; engr, Kohlenberg Globe Equipment, Sarasota, 69-70; engr & gen mgr, Stroud Construction Co, Sarasota, 70- Mil Serv: Entered as Recruit, Navy, 51, released as AT 2/C, 54, after serv in Air, China & Far East, 53-54; Air Medal; Good Conduct Medal; China Serv Medal. Relig: Protestant. Mailing Add: 2609 Darwin Ave Sarasota FL 33580

TERRY, JOHN HART (R)
b Syracuse, NY, Nov 14, 24; s Frank Terry & Saydee Hart T; m 1950 to Catherine Jean Taylor Phelan; c C Jean (Mrs Richard G Morin), Lynn M, Susan L & M Carole. Educ: Univ Notre Dame, 43; Syracuse Univ Col of Law, JD, 48; vpres, Nat Cath Col Students; Louis Marshall Soc. Polit & Govt Pos: Mem, Onondaga Co Bd of Supvr, 48-58; coordr, Gubernatorial Campaign, NY State Rep Comt, 58; asst appointments off to the Gov, 59, asst secy to Gov, 59-61; campaign chmn, Onondaga Co Rep Comt, 61; NY State Assemblyman, 63-70; US Rep, NY, 71-73. Bus & Prof Pos: Sr partner, Law Firm of Smith, Sovik, Terry, Kendrick, McAuliffe & Schwarzer, 48-72; vpres & assoc gen counsel, Niagara Mohawk Power Corp, 73- Mil Serv: Entered as Pvt, Army, 43, released as 1st Lt, 46, after serv in 94th & 80th Inf Divs, ETO, 44-46; Bronze Star with Oak Leaf Cluster; Purple Heart; ETO Medal with Four Battle Stars; Combat Inf Award. Mem: Bishop Foery Found (founder); Am Legion; 40 et 8; VFW; DAV. Honors & Awards: Named Outstanding Young Man of the Year, Syracuse Jr CofC & Cent NY Notre Dame Alumni; NY State Traffic Safety Coun & Nat Asn Bus Men Distinguished Serv Awards. Relig: Roman Catholic. Legal Res: 99 Wellesley Rd Syracuse NY 13207 Mailing Add: 200 Empire Bldg Syracuse NY 13202

TERRY, LUKE E (R)
WVa State Deleg
Mailing Add: State Capitol Charleston WV 25305

TERRY, PEYTON HUBER (R)
Chmn, Valley Co Rep Cent Comt, Mont
b Wolf Point, Mont, Aug 23, 23; s James E Terry & Maude Stone T; m 1950 to Constance Agnes Whitmus; c Cheryl Kay, Paula Rae & Joel Peyton. Educ: Univ NDak. Polit & Govt Pos: Treas, Nutter for Gov Club, Mont, 60; Valley Co Campaign chmn, Battin for Cong Club, 61-66; finance chmn, Valley Co Rep Cent Comt, 62-66, chmn, 66-; alderman, Glasgow, 63-65; mem exec comt, Mont Rep State Cent Comt, 71-; deleg, Rep Nat Conv, 72. Mem: Northeastern Mont Asn for Retarded Children (pres, 66-); Kiwanis; Masonic Bodies; Shrine; Elks. Honors & Awards: Glasgow Jaycees Boss of the Year, 73. Relig: Methodist. Legal Res: 730 Park Glasgow MT 59230 Mailing Add: Box 391 Glasgow MT 59230

TERTICHNY, MICHAEL ALLEN (D)
b St Louis, Mo, Mar 30, 54; s Boris Tertichny & Rose Tyrpak T; single. Educ: Southeastern Community Col, AA, 74, rep, Student Bd, 72-74, pres, Young Dem, 72-74. Polit & Govt Pos: Deleg, Lee Co Dem Conv, Iowa, 72, First Dist Dem Conv, Iowa, 72 & 74 & Iowa State Dem Conv, 72; alt deleg, Dem Nat Conf, 72; committeeman, Lee Co Dem Cent Comt, 73-74; mem, Northeast Mo State Univ Young Dem, 74-; mem, Keokuk Community Betterment Comt, 73-74. Honors & Awards: Soc for Acad Achievement Awards, 69, 70 & 72; George Norman Award, Lee Co Hist Soc, 70; Torch Club Award, Nat Honor Soc, 70 & 71. Relig: Russian Orthodox. Mailing Add: 227 N Ninth Keokuk IA 52632

TERWILLIGER, MELLIE E (D)
Chmn, Alaska Dem State Cent Comt
b Salina, Kans, Oct 4, 09; d Lot Pearcy Heck & Roberta Graham H; m 1939 to Frederick Edson Terwilliger; c John Frederick. Educ: High sch. Polit & Govt Pos: Precinct chmn & dist vchmn, Dem Party, Alaska; chmn, Alaska Dem State Cent Comt, 73-; Dem Nat Committeewoman, Alaska, 73-; deleg, Dem Nat Mid-Term Conf, 74. Bus & Prof Pos: 45 years in Alaska logging, mining, trapping, fishing & working on a tugboat; retired as small town store owner. Mem: Am Asn Advan Sci; Tok CofC; Common Cause; Am for Dem Action. Relig: Episcopal. Mailing Add: Box 206 Tok AK 99780

TERZAGHI, RUTH DOGGETT (D)
b Chicago, Ill, Oct 14, 03; d Lewis Chittenden Doggett & Grace Muehlheim D; m 1930 to Karl Terzaghi (deceased); c Margaret & Eric. Educ: Univ Chicago, BS, 24, MS, 25; Harvard Univ, PhD, 30. Polit & Govt Pos: Deleg, Dem Nat Conv, 72. Bus & Prof Pos: Instr, Goucher Col, 25-26 & Wellesley Col, 26-28; lectr, Harvard Univ, 57-61, research fel, 63-70. Publ: Potash-rich rocks of the Esterel, France, Am Mineralogist, 1-2/48; Concrete deterioration in a shipway, J Am Concrete Inst, 6/48; Sources of error in joint surveys, Geotechnique, 9/65. Mem: Fel Geol Soc Am; hon mem Asn Eng Geologist; Boston Soc Civil Engrs; Citizens for Participation in Polit Action (mem exec bd, 73); Civil Liberties Union of Mass (mem bd). Honors & Awards: Clemens Herschel Prize, Boston Soc Civil Engrs, 48. Mailing Add: Three Robinson Circle Winchester MA 01890

TERZICH, ROBERT M, SR (D)
Ill State Sen
Mailing Add: 5326 S Neenah Ave Chicago IL 60638

TESH, SYLVIA NOBLE (D)
b San Francisco, Calif, Jan 27, 37; d Glenn Arthur Noble & Martha Houser N; m 1960 to Robert Bradfield Tesh; c Diana Wells & Carolyn. Educ: Univ Philippines, 53-54; Univ Calif, Santa Barbara, BA, 58; Fla State Univ, CZ, 69-71; Univ Hawaii, MA, 75; Delta Gamma. Polit & Govt Pos: Recording secy, CZ Regional Dem Party, 71-72; co-chairwoman, McGovern-Shriver Campaign, CZ, 72; alt deleg, Dem Nat Conv, 72. Bus & Prof Pos: Dir adult activities, Patterson Houses, YWCA, New York, NY, 58-59 & Southwest Belmont YWCA, Philadelphia, Pa, 59-61; dir social serv, Presby Hosp, San Francisco, 61-62; dir & founder, Cine 16, Panama, 68-72; counr, CZ Draft Counseling Serv, 72. Mem: Common Cause; Am Civil Liberties Union; Am Friends Serv Comt; Nat Women's Polit Caucus. Relig: Unitarian. Mailing Add: 3136 Huelani Dr Honolulu HI 96822

TESKE, MARILYN JOHNSON (D)
Chmn, Hughes Co Dem Party, SDak
b Sioux Falls, SDak, Dec 30, 33; d Joseph Melvin Johnson & Edith Nelson J; m 1952 to Herbert Wayne Teske; c Jody, Kathy & Nancy. Educ: Dakota Wesleyan Univ, BA, 54; Colo State Univ, summer 55; SDak State Univ, 68-69. Polit & Govt Pos: Precinct committeewoman, Codington Co, Watertown, SDak, 60-70; precinct committeewoman, Hughes Co, Pierre, 72-74; treas, Hughes Co Dem Women, Pierre, 72-75; chmn, Hughes Co Dem Party, SDak, 74-; mem, SDak State Cent Comt, currently. Bus & Prof Pos: Teacher, Watertown Sch Dist, 54-56 & 69-70; teacher, Douglas Sch Dist, 70-71; bill status clerk, SDak Legis, 73-75; off mgr, SDak Dem Party, 73-75. Mem: SDak Fedn Dem Women; Int Toastmistress (parliamentarian, Pierre Club, 74-75). Relig: Methodist. Mailing Add: 510 E Missouri Pierre SD 57501

TESMER, LOUISE MARIE (D)
Wis State Rep
b Milwaukee, Wis, Dec 25, 42; d Edward William Tesmer & Genevieve Marie Mitdbo T; single. Educ: Univ Wis-Milwaukee, BA, 64; Univ Wis-Madison Law Sch, JD, 67; Sigma Tau Delta; lit ed, Cheshire Mag; secy-treas, Slavic Lang Club, two years; Law Sch Legal Res Coun. Polit & Govt Pos: Munic justice, St Francis, Wis, 66-67; asst dist attorney, Milwaukee Co, 67-72; deleg, Wis Dem State Conv, 72 & 73; Wis State Rep, 19th Dist, 73- Bus & Prof Pos: Attorney-at-law, 67 & 72- Mem: Kappa Beta Pi; Am Coun Young Polit Leaders; State Bar Asn; hon mem Munic Justice Asn; Wis Women's Polit Caucus. Honors & Awards: Carol Citation, Cudahy Jaycettes, 68; Serv Award, Off Dist Attorneys, Milwaukee Co, 72. Relig: Lutheran. Mailing Add: 4252 S Nicholson Ave St Francis WI 53207

TESSENDORF, RAMONA ROBERTA (R)
VChmn, Pottawatomie Co Rep Party, Kans
b Onaga, Kans, Apr 6, 30; d Robert Fredrick Hartwich & Martha Minnie Marten H; m 1959 to Harold Dean Tessendorf. Educ: Onaga Rural High Sch, Kans, grad, 48; Clark's Secretarial Sch, Topeka, grad, 54. Polit & Govt Pos: Committeewoman, Millcreek Twp, Kans, 60-; alt deleg, Rep Nat Conv, 68; alt to deleg-at-lg, Second Dist, Kans, 69; vchmn, Pottawatomie Co Rep Party, 69- Bus & Prof Pos: Typist, State of Kans, 53-55, secy, 55-59; dent asst to Dr Don H Morrow, 59-61; cashier, United Tel Co of Kans, Inc, 62-64. Mem: St Paul's Lutheran Ladies Aid; Northeast Pottawatomie Co Rep Women's Club. Relig: Lutheran, Mo Synod. Mailing Add: Onaga KS 66521

TESTA, JAMES ROBERT (D)
b Hartford, Conn, Feb 17, 23; s Joseph Testa & Vita Pezzulo T; m 1955 to Dolores Rittlinger; c James R, Jr, Mary M, Diane F, Laurie V, Robert J, Stephen F, Joseph F & Patrick J. Educ: Univ Conn, BA, 50; Boston Univ, LLB, 57; Sigma Chi. Polit & Govt Pos: Chmn, East Windsor Dem Town Party, Conn, formerly; committeeman, Conn State Dem Cent Comt, formerly. Bus & Prof Pos: Attorney, 58- Mil Serv: Entered as Pvt, Army, 43, released as T/Sgt, 123rd Evacuation Hosp, ETO, 44-46; 2nd Lt, Army Res, 48. Mem: Conn Bar Asn; Rotary; KofC; VFW; Am Legion. Relig: Catholic. Mailing Add: Church St Broad Brook CT 06016

TESTERMAN, KYLE COPENHAVER (R)
Mayor, Knoxville, Tenn
b Knoxville, Tenn, Dec 27, 34; s Benjamin H Testerman (deceased) & Lucille Hanley T; m 1956 to Janet Long; c Margaret Ann, Benjamin Long & Janet Lucille. Educ: Univ Tenn, Knoxville, BS Bus Admin, 57, LLB & JD; Sigma Alpha Epsilon; Phi Delta; Omicron Delta Kappa. Polit & Govt Pos: Mem city coun & Mayor, Knoxville, Tenn, 72-, chmn city annexation comt, chmn city-co bldg comt, vchmn metrop planning comt. Bus & Prof Pos:

Vpres & legal counsel, Real Estate Title Ins Co; vpres & mgr, Tenn Title Co of Knoxville, Inc; attorney, Briley & Testerman. Mem: Am Bar Asn; Am Land Title Asn (assoc dir); Gtr Knoxville Home Builders (adv dir); Knoxville Racquet Club; East Tenn Develop Dist (pres). Honors & Awards: Many tennis championships. Legal Res: Rotherwood Dr Knoxville TN 37919 Mailing Add: City Hall Knoxville TN 37902

TESTERMAN, PHILIP (D)
SDak State Sen
Mailing Add: Wessington SD 57381

TEWES, DONALD E (R)
b Merrill, Wis, Aug 4, 16; s Herman F Tewes & Mabel Rickman T; m 1946 to Myra Torhorst; c James & Barbara. Educ: Valparaiso Univ, BA cum laude, 38; Univ Wis, LLB, 40; Hon Social Sci & Debate Socs. Polit & Govt Pos: Cong campaign chmn, Wis Rep Party, 47-55, chmn, Second Cong Dist, 53-56, mem exec comt, Wis Rep Party, 53-56; chmn, Coun Econ Develop, Wis, 53-55; US Rep, Wis, 57-59. Bus & Prof Pos: Attorney-at-law, Merrill, Wis, 40-42; pres, Tewes Plastics Corp, Waukesha, 47- Mil Serv: Entered as Pvt, Air Force, 42, released as Maj, 46, after serv in 14th Air Force Flying Tigers under Gen Chennault; Air Medal for flying combat; Chinese & other theater medals; various campaign ribbons. Mem: Young Rep Hall of Fame; Kiwanis; Jaycees; Am Legion; VFW. Honors & Awards: Civic Leader Award, CofC. Relig: Lutheran. Mailing Add: 244 Frederick St Waukesha WI 53186

THACIK, ANNE SMITH (R)
Mem Exec Comt, Nat Fedn Rep Women
b Glen Richey, Pa, Dec 12, 18; d Pybus Delaun Smith & Mary Hutchinson S; m to George J Thacik; c one, one grandchild. Educ: Univ Buffalo; Pa State Univ. Polit & Govt Pos: Precinct registr, Pa, 48-; area vchmn, Clearfield Co Rep Comt, 54-60; mem, Clearfield Co Rep Exec Comt, 54-60; adv, Clearfield Co Young Rep, 55-57; pres, Clearfield Co Coun Rep Women, 55-61; mem, Clearfield Co Rep Publicity Comt, 58-59; mem, Clearfield Co Rep Finance Comt, 59-60; chmn, Clearfield Co Rep Fund Drive Nixon-Lodge Campaign 60; regional polit activities chmn, Pa Coun Rep Women, 62, mem bd dirs, 63-, chmn polit activities, 63, 64 & 65, mem conv comt, 65, chmn annual conv, 66, recording secy, 66-67 & pres, 68-70; mem sch community planning, Pub Serv Inst, Pa, 63; vchmn, Clearfield Co Rep Cong Campaign, 64; chmn, Curwensville Borough Planning Comn, 64-; adv, Clearfield Co TAR, 65-66; mem adv bd, Clearfield Co Planning Comn, 65-; mem adv bd, Clearfield Co Develop Coun, 65-; deleg-at-lg, Rep Nat Conv, 68; mem bd dirs, Nat Fedn Rep Women, mem nominating comt, 69, mem exec comt, 70-; Nat Fedn Rep Women deleg, Am Acad Polit & Social Sci, 69. Bus & Prof Pos: Operator, Woodhurst Nursery & Antiques, currently. Mem: PTA; Curwensville Woman's Club; Curwensville Alumni Asn; Six Degree Grange; Pa State Antique Asn. Relig: United Presbyterian; church sch dept supt, United Presby Church, Curwensville, Pa, mem bd Christian educ. Mailing Add: 201 McLaughlin St Curwensville PA 16833

THAIN, CARL ERNEST (R)
Mem, Rep State Comt Okla
b Waukomis, Okla, Nov 19, 18; s Charles Thain & Clara Keefer T; m 1948 to Irene M Boyle; c Debra Dianne. Educ: Univ Okla, BS, 47. Polit & Govt Pos: Chmn, Pittsburg Co Rep Party, Okla, 66-; mem, Rep State Comt Okla, currently. Bus & Prof Pos: Pres, C E Thain Co, Inc, McAlester, Okla, 56- Mil Serv: Entered as 2nd Lt, Army, 41, released as Maj, 46, after serv in 456th Parachutist Field Artil Bn, 82nd Airborne Div, ETO, 42-46, Lt Col, Res, 46-69, Col, 69-; Holland Order of King William; Belgian Fourragere; French Fourragere; Purple Heart; ETO Campaign Medal with Six Battle Stars; Parachute Wings with Star. Mem: Elks; McAlester Country Club; Am Legion; VFW; ROA. Relig: Episcopal. Mailing Add: 610 E Indiana McAlester OK 74501

THALER, DAISY (D)
Ky State Sen
Mailing Add: 5804 Lovers Lane Louisville KY 40291

THANE, RUSSELL T (R)
NDak State Sen
b Denver, Colo, July 14, 26; s Joseph Thane & Bernice Steere T; m 1952 to Betty Jo Chowning; c Ronald & Kathleen. Educ: NDak State Sch Sci, 49; NDak State Univ, 55. Polit & Govt Pos: Precinct committeeman, 25th Dist, NDak, 64-70; NDak State Sen, 70- Bus & Prof Pos: Secy-treas, NDak Cattle Feeders Asn, Hunter, 64-70; dir, Home Mutual Ins Co, Wahpeton, 68-; dir, Red River Valley Beet Growers, Moorhead, Minn, 69- Mil Serv: Entered as Pvt, Air Force, 50, released as S/Sgt, 54, after serv in Air Training Command, Amarillo; Good Conduct Medal; Am Defense Serv Medal. Mem: El Zagal Shrine; Elks; Mason; Eagles; Am Legion. Relig: Methodist. Mailing Add: Rte 1 Wahpeton ND 58075

THARP, GERTRUDE (D)
Mem, Dem Nat Comt, Del
Mailing Add: Box 73 RD 1 Lewes DE 19958

THEIS, PAUL ANTHONY (R)
Exec Ed to the President
b Ft Wayne, Ind, Feb 14, 23; s Albert Peter Theis & Josephine Kinn T; m 1971 to Nancy Ann Wilbur; c Mitchell A. Educ: Univ Notre Dame, BA in Jour, 48; Georgetown Univ, BS in Foreign Serv, 49; Am Univ, Pub Rels, 49-52. Polit & Govt Pos: Pub rels off, President Eisenhower's 1957 Inaugural Comt; admin asst to US Rep, 55-57; radio-TV dir, Nat Rep Cong Comt, 58-60, pub rels dir, 60-74; vchmn for publicity, President Nixon's 1969 Inaugural Comt; Exec Ed to the President, currently. Bus & Prof Pos: Reporter, Army Times, 49 & Washington Bur, Fairchild Publ, 50-53; Washington correspondent, Newsweek Mag, 53-54. Mil Serv: Entered as Aviation Cadet, Army Air Corps, 43, released as 1st Lt, 46, after serv as Pilot, 15th Air Force, 97th Heavy Bombardment Group, Italy, 44-45; Maj, Air Force Res, 67; Air Medal with Two Oak Leaf Clusters; ETO Ribbon with Six Battle Stars; Am Theater Ribbon. Publ: Co-ed, Who's Who in American Politics, R R Bowker Co, 67, 69, 71 & 73; co-auth, All About Politics, R R Bowker Co, 72. Mem: Nat Press Club; Capitol Hill Club; Notre Dame & Georgetown Univ Alumni Clubs. Honors & Awards: Co-inventor of polit game, Hat in the Ring. Relig: Catholic. Mailing Add: 2903 Garfield St NW Washington DC 20008

THENO, DANIEL O'CONNELL (R)
Wis State Sen
b Ashland, Wis, May 8, 47; s Maurice William Theno & Janet Nora Humphrey T; married. Educ: Univ Wis-Madison, BS, 69; Alpha Gamma Rho; Iron Cross. Polit & Govt Pos: Wis State Sen, currently. Bus & Prof Pos: Teacher voc agr, Oregon, Wis, 69-72. Mem: Univ Wis Alumni Asn; Jaycees; Elks; KofC. Relig: Roman Catholic. Mailing Add: Sanborn Ave Ashland WI 54806

THENO, MICHAEL DENNIS (D)
b Kansas City, Mo, July 9, 51; s Bernard C Theno & Margaret Mariani T; single. Educ: Rockhurst Col, AB, 73; Alpha Psi Omega; Pi Kappa Delta; Young Dem; Yearbook Staff. Polit & Govt Pos: Vol, Docking for Gov, Kans, 66, Logan for Senate, 68, McCarthy for President, 68 & DeCoursey for Cong, Kansas City, Kans, 70; Kans state coordr, McGovern for President, 71-72; cong dist coordr, McGovern-Shriver, 72; deleg, Third Cong Dist Dem Conv, 72 & 74, Kans State Dem Conv, 72 & Dem Nat Conv, 72; deleg, Dem Nat Mid-Term Conf, 74; vol, Roy for Senate, Kans, 74. Mem: Young Dem Clubs Kans. Honors & Awards: T S Bourke Speaking Medal, Rockhurst Col, 72. Relig: Catholic. Mailing Add: 5025 Parish Dr Shawnee Mission KS 66205

THEODORE, NICHOLAS GERALD (R)
Supt, US Mint, Philadelphia, Pa
b Media, Pa, Oct 23, 37; s George Theodore & Alice Bowden T; m 1965 to Patricia Ann Kilmon; c Nicole Lynn. Educ: Univ Notre Dame, BS in Acct, 59; Villanova Sch of Law, JD, 62. Polit & Govt Pos: Supt, US Mint, Philadelphia, Pa, 69- Mem: Del Co Bar; Supreme & Superior Court of Pa & the Fed Dist Court for the Eastern Dist; Jaycees; Vesper Club. Relig: Catholic. Legal Res: 7 Lafayette Circle Media PA 19063 Mailing Add: US Mint Independence Mall Philadelphia PA 19106

THEODORE, NICK ANDREW (D)
SC State Rep
b Greenville, SC, Sept 16, 28; s Andrew Theodore & Lula Meros T; m 1955 to Emilie Demosthenes. Educ: Furman Univ, BA, 52. Polit & Govt Pos: SC State Rep, 62-66 & 69-, first vchmn educ comt, SC House of Rep, currently; SC State Sen, 66-68; chmn, SC Appalachian Comn, formerly. Bus & Prof Pos: With William Goldsmith Ins Agency. Mem: Co Red Cross (past dir); SC Jaycees; Greenville Jaycees; March of Dimes (chmn); Gtr Greenville YMCA (dir); DeMolay. Relig: Greek Orthodox; secy, St George Greek Orthodox Church. Mailing Add: Box 1827 Greenville SC 29602

THERIAULT, ALBERT ARTHUR, JR (D)
Chmn, Brookfield Dem Town Comt, Conn
b Salem, Mass, Nov 8, 30; s Albert Arthur Theriault, Sr & Catherine Roach T; m 1958 to Lorette Ida Marie Pelletier; c Donna Marie, Lisa Ann, Mark Robert & Diane Lorette. Educ: Boston Univ, BS, 62; Univ Bridgeport, MBA, 68. Polit & Govt Pos: Chmn, Brookfield Dem Town Comt, Conn, 70- Bus & Prof Pos: Design draftsman, General Electric, Lynn, Mass, 51-58; develop engr, Manning, Maxwell & Morre, Watertown, 58-63, qual control engr, 63-64; proj engr, Consol Controls Corp, Bethel, 64- Mem: KofC. Relig: Roman Catholic. Mailing Add: 40 Oak Crest Dr Brookfield CT 06804

THERIAULT, ALFRED L (D)
NH State Rep
Mailing Add: 129 E Hollis St Nashua NH 03060

THERIOT, ROY RAOUL (D)
La State Comptroller
b Erath, La, May 26, 14; s Lastie Theriot & Emerite Barras T; m 1947 to Helen Roberts; c Barbara (Mrs DeBlanc), Roy R, Jr & Samuel Houston. Educ: Univ Southwestern La, pre-law, 33-35; Tulane Univ, LLB, 36-39. Hon Degrees: SMD, Boswell Inst, 66. Polit & Govt Pos: Mayor, Abbeville, La, 54-60; La State Comptroller, 60- Bus & Prof Pos: Lawyer, 39-54. Mil Serv: Entered as Pvt, Air Force, 42, released as T/Sgt, 46; Am Theater of Operation Medal; Good Conduct Medal. Mem: Lions Int; Am Legion; Amvets; La Farm Bur; Boy Scouts Am. Honors & Awards: Legion of Honor, 69. Relig: Catholic. Mailing Add: 406 S Louisiana Ave Abbeville LA 70510

THERLAULT, ALBERT (D)
Maine State Rep
Mailing Add: 132 Penobscot St Rumford ME 04276

THIBEAULT, GEORGE J (R)
NH State Rep
Mailing Add: Box 56 Londonderry NH 03053

THIBEAULT, P ROBERT (D)
NH State Rep
Mailing Add: 185 S Wilson St Manchester NH 03103

THICKSTEN, EDWARD F (D)
Ark State Rep
Mailing Add: PO Box 327 Alma AR 72921

THIEMANN, DENNIS E (D)
Chmn, Pa State Dem Cent Comt
Mailing Add: 510 N Third St Harrisburg PA 17107

THIES, LOUIS CARL (R)
b Wayne Co, Nebr, Nov 25, 05; s Fred Theis & Augusta Wolff T; m 1927 to Ada Peterson; c Alois (Mrs Kenneth Herrman) & Randal. Educ: Hay Springs High Sch, Nebr, 21-25. Polit & Govt Pos: Mayor, Hay Springs, Nebr, 56-58; chmn, Sheridan Co Rep Party, formerly. Bus & Prof Pos: Pres, Panhandle Wholesale, Inc, Alliance, Nebr, 57-68; vpres, Randy Mkt, White Clay, Nebr, 15 years & Lou's Shoeland, Rapid City, SDak, 10 years; pres, Hay Springs Indust Co, Inc, 10 years. Mem: Mason; York Rite; Scottish Rite; Shrine; Elks. Relig: Methodist. Mailing Add: Hay Springs NE 69347

THIESSEN, CORNIE R (D)
Mont State Sen
b Mountain Lake, Minn, July 7, 10; s David Thiessen, Sr & Agnetha Holzreichter T; m 1938 to Ailee E Buck; c Anita Sue & James Everett. Educ: Northwest Nazarene Col, BA, 36; Pasadena Col, MA, 40; Sigma Lambda Alpha. Polit & Govt Pos: Mem adv comt, Rural Elec Admin, Mont, 54-56; chmn, Mont Kefauver for President Club, 56; deleg, Dem Nat Conv, 56, 60 & 68; Mont State Sen, 59-, Pres Pro Tem, Mont State Senate, 71-72; pres, Mont Humphrey for President Club, 60; mem, Mont State Local Govt Comn, 74- Bus & Prof Pos: Secy-treas, Lower Yellowstone Rural Elec, 44-67, pres, 67-; bd mem, Community Mem

Hosp, 48-66; pres, Mid Rivers Tel, 52-57; bd mem, St Paul Bible Col, 52-66; bd mem, Nat Tel Asn, 54-57; dir mem, Richland Homes, 58-70; secy-treas, Upper Mo Gen & Trans, 58-; vpres, Basin Elec Power Coop, 61-; mem bd mgrs, Christian Missionary Alliance, 61-75; vpres, Mo Basin Syst Group, 65-69; pres, Thiessen, Inc, 69- Mem: Legis Audit Comt (secy); Farmers Union; Int Toastmasters. Honors & Awards: Received Good Govt Award, Jaycees, 66; 25 Year Outstanding Serv Award, 10/70; Man of the Year Award, Mont Asn Evangelicals, 72. Relig: Christian & Missionary Alliance. Mailing Add: Box 195 Lambert MT 59243

THIESSEN, DAN (R)
Kans State Rep
Mailing Add: RR 1 Independence KS 67301

THIGPEN, NEAL DORSEY (R)
VChmn, SC Rep Party
b Baltimore, Md, Oct 19, 39; s Guy Franklin Thigpen & Virginia Dorsey T; m 1965 to Gail Marie Fallon. Educ: Univ Md, College Park, AB, 62, MA, 66, PhD, 70; Pi Sigma Alpha; Kalegethos; Sigma Chi; Gate & Key. Polit & Govt Pos: Rep Mission 70's Chmn, Florence Co, SC, 71-73; deleg, Nat Rep Leadership Conf, 72 & 75; deleg, SC State Rep Conv, Florence Co, 72 & 74; deleg, Rep Nat Conv, 72; mem, Florence Co Comt to Reelect the President, 72; mem exec comt, Florence Co Rep Party, 72-, vchmn, 72-74; vchmn, SC Rep Party, 74- Bus & Prof Pos: Research asst, Dept of Govt & Polit, Univ Md, College Park, 65-66, instr, 66-69, asst prof, 70-71; vis asst prof, Western Md Col, 69-71; asst prof polit sci, Francis Marion Col, Florence, SC, 71-72, assoc prof & chmn dept polit sci, 72- Mil Serv: Entered as Pvt, Marine Corps, 63, released as Cpl, 65, after serv in Hq Co, Hq Bn, Marine Corps Reservation, Quantico, Va. Publ: South Carolina sheriffs: their backgrounds and careers, Carolina Law, 5-6/72. Mem: Am Soc Pub Admin; SC Law Enforcement Off Asn; Kiwanis (comt secy, Florence, 72-); SC Rep Silver Elephant Club; Francis Marion Col Rep (adv, 71-). Honors & Awards: Outstanding Fraternity Man, Univ Md Interfraternity Coun, 61. Relig: Episcopal. Mailing Add: 908 Jackson Ave Florence SC 29501

THILL, LEWIS D (R)
b Milwaukee, Wis, Oct 18, 03; s Dr Dominic P Thill & Mary Pierron T; m 1947 to Carol Jean Werner; c Mary (Mrs Harenburg), John, Lewis, Jr, Dorothy & Carol Louise. Educ: Marquette Univ, AB; Univ Wis, JD. Polit & Govt Pos: US Rep, Wis, 39-43. Bus & Prof Pos: Lawyer, Wis, 32-; real estate sales, Calif, 72- Publ: How you can get a million dollar brain, privately publ, 75. Relig: Catholic. Mailing Add: Apt 4 6795 Alvarado Rd San Diego CA 92120

THISS, GEORGE RAYMOND (R)
b Minneapolis, Minn, Dec 12, 27; s Charles R Thiss & Alice Newhouse T; m 1967 to Joyce Zniewski; c Mark & Charles. Educ: Univ Minn, BA, 50; NY Univ, MS, 52; Delta Kappa Epsilon. Polit & Govt Pos: Bd mem, Hennepin Co Young Rep League, Minn, 57-61, chmn, 59-61; mem, Hennepin Co Rep Comt, 59-63, vchmn, 63; deleg, Nat Conv, Minn Young Rep League, 59, 61 & 63, nat committeeman, 61-63; mem exec comt, Minn Rep State Cent Comt, 61-72, first vchmn, 63-65, chmn, 65-72; liaison, Col Fedn, 61-63; officer, Hennepin Co Finance Comt, 63; deleg, Rep Nat Conv, 68. Bus & Prof Pos: Asst buyer, Hahne & Co, Newark, NJ, 52-55; store mgr, Thiss Luggage, 55-61; admin asst, Breck Sch, 61-65; exec dir, Upper Midwest Coun, currently. Mem: Jr CofC; Breck Sch Alumni Asn (pres bd trustees, mem & treas); Rotary; Independent Sch Asn of Cent States (teachers div). Relig: Episcopal. Mailing Add: 5025 Normandale Ct Minneapolis MN 55436

THOEN, DORIS RAE (R)
Treas, Ore Rep State Cent Comt
b Corvallis, Ore, Feb 1, 25; d Birt F Read & Alice Maxfield R; m 1950 to Monte Len Thoen; c David A & Rick L; one grandchild. Educ: Ore State Univ, BA, 47; Euterpe Music Honorary; Delta Zeta. Polit & Govt Pos: Secy, Ore Fedn Rep Women, 66-67, treas, 67-71, first vpres, 71-73, pres, 73-75; community serv chmn, Nat Fedn Rep Women, 75-; treas, Ore Rep State Cent Comt, 75- Bus & Prof Pos: Secy, State Treas Off, Salem, Ore, 47-48; loan closer, Portland Fed Loan & Savings, 49-50; personnel officer, US Bur Reclamation, Klamath Falls, 50-52; self-employed, 52- Mem: Am Asn Univ Women (bd dirs, parliamentarian & auditor, currently); Ore Cong Parents & Teachers (state corresp secy); Am Cancer Soc; Portland Alumnae of Delta Zeta (bd). Honors & Awards: Life mem, Ore Cong Parents & Teachers, 69; named grant given in name of Doris Thoen by Am Asn Univ Women, 70; Presidential Commendation for community serv, President Richard Nixon, 73; adv award for community serv, Wash Coun Home Exten, 73; community serv award, Ore High Sch Rep League, 74. Mailing Add: 13124 NW Sue St Portland OR 97229

THOMAS, A W (D)
NC State Rep
Mailing Add: 160 Glendale Ave Concord NC 28025

THOMAS, ALFRED VICTOR (D)
Va State Deleg
b Roanoke, Va, Nov 9, 29; s Ellis James Thomas & Genevieve Nero T; m 1946 to Dorothy Marie Lucas; c Alfred V, Jr, William Eric, Genevieve Cecelia & Thomas Patrick. Educ: Va Southern Col, 58; Univ Va, 64. Polit & Govt Pos: Pres, Roanoke, Va Young Dem Club, 65-66; dir, Young Dem Clubs Va, 66-69; chmn, Roanoke Va City Dem Comt, 67; deleg, Dem Nat Conv, 68; chmn, Sixth Cong Dist Dem Comt, 68-72; Va State Deleg, 75- Bus & Prof Pos: Owner, E J Thomas Mkt, 49- Mil Serv: Army, 47, Pvt, serv in 33rd Combat Team, CZ. Mem: Elks; Dokkies; KofP; WOW. Relig: Catholic. Mailing Add: 1301 Orange Ave NE Roanoke VA 24012

THOMAS, BILL (D)
Mont State Rep
Mailing Add: 704 52nd St S Great Falls MT 59405

THOMAS, EDWARD PHILIP (R)
Md State Sen
b Frederick, Md, Aug 3, 28; s Edward P Thomas (deceased) & Louise G Firmin T; m 1958 to Lois Anne Viola; c Stephen, Anne, Sue & Patricia. Educ: Washington & Lee Univ, BA, 50; Sigma Delta Chi; Phi Kappa Sigma; Sigma Club, Washington & Lee Univ. Polit & Govt Pos: Chmn, Frederick Co Rep Cent Comt, Md, 66-70; alt deleg, Rep Nat Conv, 68, deleg, 72; mem exec comt, Md State Rep Cent Comt, 69-70, chmn, 75-; Md State Sen, Frederick-Carroll Counties, 70- Bus & Prof Pos: Sports dir & asst news dir, WSLS-TV & Radio, Roanoke, Va, 53-60; pres & gen mgr, Terrace Lanes Inc, Frederick, Md & Edgewood Lanes, Inc, Gettysburg, Pa, 60- Mil Serv: Entered as Pvt, Army, 50, released as Sgt, 52, after serv in 31st Inf Div & European Hq Command. Mem: Lions; Elks; VFW; Am Legion; Amvets. Relig: Episcopal. Mailing Add: 710 Wyngate Dr Frederick MD 21701

THOMAS, ELIAS, III (R)
Chmn, York Co Rep Comt, Maine
b Portland, Maine, Feb 19, 48; s Elias Thomas, Jr & Irene Goodson T; m 1969 to Jane Fleming Leach; c Heather. Educ: Univ Maine, Portland, BA Psychol, 71. Polit & Govt Pos: Chmn, Acton Rep Town Comt, Maine, 72-; co coordr, 72 Gen Elec; campaign mgr & speechwriter for David Emery, 74; sustaining mem, Rep Nat Comt, 74-75; chmn, York Co Rep Comt, 74- Bus & Prof Pos: Corporator, Sanford Inst for Savings, 72-; mem, York Co Bd Realtors, 74-; Rep to Congressman Emery's Munic Task Force, currently. Mem: AF&AM Springvale Lodge 190; Scottish Rite (32 degree); Sanford-Springvale United Way (dir). Relig: Protestant. Mailing Add: Ledgewold Acton ME 04001

THOMAS, ELIZABETH GRAY (R)
Chairwoman, Kenton Co Rep Exec Comt, Ky
b Flemingsburg, Ky, Feb 11, 24; d Roy Cooper Gray & Alice Kerr Hood G; m 1950 to James Cooper Thomas; c James Cooper, III & Jeffrey Gray. Educ: Univ Cincinnati Col Bus Admin; Kappa Alpha Theta. Polit & Govt Pos: Asst parliamentarian, Ky Fedn Rep Women, 66-68, parliamentarian, 68-70, gov fourth dist, 69-70, immediate past pres; chmn, 65th Legis Dist Rep Orgn, 66-; mem-at-lg, Ky Rep State Cent Comt; chairwoman, Kenton Co Rep Exec Comt, 72- Bus & Prof Pos: Off mgr, Cin-Day Food Broker, Inc, currently. Mem: Charter mem Ky Soc Mayflower Descendants; DAR; Cincinnati Symphony Orchestra (women's comt); PTA. Relig: Presbyterian. Mailing Add: 3029 Dottie Lane Ft Mitchell KY 41017

THOMAS, EVELYN M (R)
Pres, Ark Fedn Rep Women
b Vinland, Kans, Apr 25, 26; d Arthur Graham Hammond & Margaret E Kalb H; m 1946 to Daniel Barnett Thomas; c Dana Arthur, Marsha Mae & Sherree Lynn. Educ: Lawrence Bus Col, 44-45. Polit & Govt Pos: Committeewoman, Calif State Rep Cent Comt, 62-63; pres, Washington Co Rep Women, Ark, 68-70, secy, 71; committeewoman, Washington Co Rep Comt, 70-75; alt deleg, Rep Nat Conv, 72; third vpres, Ark Fedn Rep Women, 72-75, pres, 75-; committeewoman, Third Cong Dist Rep Comt, 74-75. Bus & Prof Pos: Corp secy, Dandy Music Inc, El Cajon, Calif, 55-64; co-owner, Sundowner Ranches, Prairie Grove, Ark, currently. Mem: Am Nat Cowbelles (chmn, Ark Cowbelle Scholarship, 73-75); Int Maine-Anjou Asn (dir, 73-, youth develop chmn, 74-75); Am Simmental Asn; Am Int Charolais Asn; Ark Farm Bur. Honors & Awards: Hon Dep Sheriff, Washington Co, Ark, 75. Relig: Protestant. Mailing Add: Rte 2 Prairie Grove AR 72753

THOMAS, HAROLD THEODORE (D)
b Toledo, Ohio, Dec 8, 30; s Thomas Theodore Thomas & Louise Brown T; m to Bernice Copeland; c Debra Ann (Mrs Charles Walker), Kevin Lennard, Thomas T, II & Terrilyn Copeland. Educ: New Eng Conservatory Music, 50; Toledo Univ, 52-55. Polit & Govt Pos: Deleg, Dem Nat Conv, 72; precinct committeeman, Lucas Co Dem Party, Ohio, 74- Mil Serv: Entered as Pfc, Navy, 48, released 52, after serv in Far East, 50-52; Korean Serv Medal; Good Conduct Medal. Mem: Consistory Lodge 108; Mecca Temple 43; St Matthews Consistory; Elks; Mason. Honors & Awards: One of Ten Outstanding Young Men Award, Toledo Jr CofC, 65; Mid-City Kiwanis Athletic League Outstanding Award. Legal Res: 4434 Emma Jean Rd Toledo OH 43607 Mailing Add: PO Box 92 Toledo OH 43694

THOMAS, JAMES (D)
Ariz State Rep
Mailing Add: 38 Glen Oaks Prescott AZ 86301

THOMAS, JERRY (D)
b West Palm Beach, Fla, Apr 30, 29; s Larry Arthur Thomas (deceased) & Irene Lee T; m 1951 to Imogene Hair (Jeannie); c Robbie Lee, Larry Arthur, II, Kenneth Cook, Jerry Leroy & Cindy Lynn. Educ: Palm Beach Jr Col, AA, 49; Fla State Univ, BS, 51 & grad study; Fla Atlantic Univ Grad Sch, ME, 67; Harvard & Columbia Univs, Grad Schs of Bus in Sr Bank Mgt; Aspen Inst Humanistic Studies, 75; Omicron Delta Kappa; Gold Key; Pi Alpha Sigma; Sigma Nu. Polit & Govt Pos: Dir & adminr, Fla Securities Comn, 55-57; Fla State Rep, 60-64; Fla State Sen, 65-72, pres, Fla State Senate, 70-72; Rep nominee for Gov, Fla, 74; chmn, Florida Conservative Union, currently. Bus & Prof Pos: Chmn bd, First Bank of Jupiter/Tequesta, 63-, First Marine Bank & Trust Co, 64-, First Commercial Bank of Live Oak, 66- & Marine Nat Bank of Jacksonville, 68-; chmn & pres, First Community Bank, Boca Raton, 64-; chmn & pres, First Nat Bank & Trust Co, 66-; former mem of two nat stock exchanges. Mil Serv: Entered as Seaman, Navy, released as Midn; reentered as Cpl, Marine Corps, released as Capt. Publ: Florida's political uniqueness, Smoke Signals, 52; Florida Securities Commission protects investors, Capitol Post, 56. Mem: Fla State Univ Alumni Asn; Children's Home Soc of Fla (dir); Fla Vision Found (bd of gov). Honors & Awards: Five Outstanding Young Men of Fla, 62; State Good Govt Award, 67; Distinguished Achievement Medallion, Am Heart Asn Highest Award, 68; Legis Leadership Citation, Citizen Conf of State Legislators, 71; DeMolay Legion of Honor, Int Supreme Coun of the Order of DeMolay, 70. Relig: Presbyterian; elder. Mailing Add: Sea Oats Beach Rd Jupiter FL 33458

THOMAS, JOHN J (R)
Ind State Rep
b Rockville, Ind, Nov 14, 23; s Joe J Thomas & Hazel Gross T; m 1945 to Jessie Sparks; c Jana, Jamie & Joanna. Educ: Ind Univ, LLB, 48; Phi Eta Sigma; Sigma Delta Kappa. Polit & Govt Pos: Prosecuting attorney, Clay Co, Ind, 51-58 & co attorney, 62-70; Ind State Rep & Speaker Pro Tem, Ind House Rep, currently; chmn, Midwestern Conf, Coun State Govt, currently, vchmn, Nat Conf, Coun State Govt, currently. Bus & Prof Pos: Attorney, Brazil, Ind, 48- Mil Serv: Entered as Air Cadet, Air Force, 43, released as Sgt, 46. Mem: Elks; Am Legion; Brazil Rotary Club (past pres); Clay Co Farm Bur; F&AM, Scottish Rite. Relig: Methodist; conf pres, United Methodist Men, United Methodist Church. Mailing Add: Rte 1 Brazil IN 47834

THOMAS, JOHN L (R)
Maine State Sen
Mailing Add: Box 687 Waterville ME 04901

THOMAS, JOHN M
Asst Secy State Admin
b Iowa, Oct 12, 26; m to Evalyn Bates. Polit & Govt Pos: Admin asst, Dept of State, 52-56, admin officer, 56-65, supvry admin officer, 65, supvr admin officer, Manila, 65-67; dir, Off

Opers, Washington, 67-69; dep asst secy state opers, 69-74, Asst Secy State Admin, 74- Mailing Add: Dept of State Washington DC 20520

THOMAS, JON C (R)
Fla State Sen
b Uniontown, Pa, Jan 22, 39; m to Patsy Holloway; c Hollee & Timothy. Educ: Pittsburgh Inst Mortuary Sci, 63. Polit & Govt Pos: Chmn, Govt Efficiency Study Comn, Broward Co, Fla, 69-70; Fla State Rep, formerly; Fla State Sen, currently. Bus & Prof Pos: Vpres pub rels, Baird-Case Funeral Homes, Inc, currently. Mem: CofC (secy-treas, Lauderdale-by-Sea, 67-); F&AM; KT (Militia Commandery); Shrine; Gideons Int. Honors & Awards: Outstanding Young Man of Year, Ft Lauderdale, Fla, 65. Relig: Methodist; vchmn admin bd, Christ Methodist Church; pres, Methodist Men, 67-69. Legal Res: 2200 NE 17th Ct Ft Lauderdale FL 33305 Mailing Add: PO Box 23896 Ft Lauderdale FL 33307

THOMAS, JOSEPH N (R)
b Gary, Ind, Feb 22, 29; s Ray C Thomas & Josephine Kelley T; m 1956 to Bonnie Lee Trapp; c Jeanine E, Nancy G & Charna K. Educ: Ind Univ, BS with honors, 51; Harvard Law Sch, LLB cum laude, 54; Beta Gamma Sigma; Acacia; Blue Key; Chancery Club. Polit & Govt Pos: Deleg, Rep State Conv, 64, 66 & 68; alt deleg, Rep Nat Conv, 68; chmn, Ind Port Comn, 69-; presidential appointee, St Lawrence Seaway Adv Comn, 69-, chmn, 70- Bus & Prof Pos: Partner, Law Firm of Thomas, Burke, Dyerly & Cuppy, 57-, managing partner, 62-; bd dirs, Gary Nat Bank, 69- Mil Serv: Entered as 1st Lt, Air Force, 54, released 57, after serv in 326th Fighter Group, Cent Air Defense Command. Mem: Gary & Ind Bar Asns; Ind Asn of CPA; Gary Kiwanis Club (bd dirs, 68-69); Gary Jaycees (treas, 59, exec vpres, 60, bd dirs, 60-63). Honors & Awards: Award for Highest Grade in Ind CPA Exam, 51. Relig: Presbyterian; elder. Mailing Add: 504 Broadway Rm 1016 Gary IN 46402

THOMAS, L E (TOMMY) (R)
b Woodhull, NY, July 7, 25; m 1945 to Virginia; c William E, Virginia (Mrs Watkins) & Carolyn. Educ: Univ Ala, Birmingham, 2 years; Chevrolet Sch Mod Merchandising, grad, 63; class pres. Polit & Govt Pos: Ala Presidential Elector, 64; regional coordr, Five Co, Ala, until 65; campaign mgr, Kirk for Gov, 66; alt deleg, Rep Nat Conv, 68; deleg, chmn Fla deleg, vchmn subcomts on transportation & arrangements & mem, Host Comt & Comt Permanent Orgn, 72; Northern Fla campaign mgr, Nixon for President, 68 & Cramer for Senate, 70; mem, Fla Pub Sch Coun, 68-70; chmn, Rep State Exec Comt, Fla, formerly; mem, Rep Nat Comt, formerly; State Dept Pub Schs mem, Foreign Serv Inspection Team to the Hague. Bus & Prof Pos: Automobile dealer, Opelika, Ala, 52-53, Birmingham, 54-62, Oneonta, 62-65 & Panama City, Fla, 65- Mil Serv: Marine Corps, 42-45, Res, 47-53. Mem: Bay Co United Givers Fund (co-chmn); Am Cancer Soc (pres, Bay Co Chap, currently); Salvation Army Bd (pres, Bay Co). Relig: United Methodist; chmn bd stewards, First United Methodist Church, Panama City. Mailing Add: PO Box 490 Panama City FL 32401

THOMAS, LOWELL (D)
Tenn State Sen
Mailing Add: PO Box 1791 Jackson TN 38301

THOMAS, LOWELL, JR (R)
Lt Gov, Alaska
b London, Eng, Oct 6, 23; s Lowell J Thomas & Frances Ryan T; m 1950 to Mary Pryor; c Anne F & David L. Educ: Taft Sch, 39-42; Dartmouth Col, BA, 48; Princeton Univ, 51-52; Delta Kappa Epsilon. Hon Degrees: LittD, Scottsbluff Col, 69. Polit & Govt Pos: Alaska State Sen, formerly; Lt Gov, Alaska, currently. Bus & Prof Pos: Auth & lectr, 48-; asst producer, Cinerama Inc, 52-54; producer, Odyssey Corp, 57-59. Mil Serv: Entered as Cadet, Air Force, 43, released 2nd Lt, 45, after serv in Southeast Training Command, 43-45; 1st Lt, Air Force Res. Publ: Out of This World (Tibet), Greystone, 50; Flight to Adventure, Doubleday, 56; The Dalai Lama, Duell, Sloan & Pearce, 61. Mem: Screen Actors Guild; Explorers' Club of NY; Bohemian Club of San Francisco; Dutch Treat Club of NY; Rotary Club of Anchorage. Relig: Protestant. Legal Res: 7022 Tanaina Dr Anchorage AK 99502 Mailing Add: Off of Lt Gov State Capitol Juneau AK 99811

THOMAS, NORMA GILES (D)
b Provo, Utah, Apr 18, 24; d Charles Edward Giles & Bertha Bateman G; m 1945 to Daniel W Thomas (deceased); c Daniel G & Charles Howard. Educ: Brigham Young Univ, 1 year. Polit & Govt Pos: Vchmn, Utah Co Young Dem, 45-46; vchmn, Utah Co Dem Comt, 47-48; vchmn, Utah State Dem Party, formerly; deleg, Dem Nat Conv, 68; comnr, Utah State Liquor Comn, 69- Mem: Lions. Relig: Latter-day Saint. Mailing Add: 371 East 300 South Provo UT 84601

THOMAS, PAT FRANKLIN (D)
Fla State Sen
b Quincy, Fla, Nov 21, 33; s Pat Thomas & Verna Peacock T; m to Mary Ann Jolley; c Ann Jolley & John Pat. Educ: Univ Fla, degree in agr econ; state vpres, Future Farmers Am; pres, Alpha Gamma Rho; pres sr class; Blue Key. Polit & Govt Pos: Mem state campaign staff of Agr Comnr Doyle Conner, Fla; area coordr, Successful Cong Campaign; mem, Gadsden Co Dem Party; chmn, Gadsden Co Presidential Campaign Reception, 64; Dem state committeeman, Gadsden Co, 66-; chmn, Fla State Dem Exec Comt, 66-70; organizing chmn state deleg, Dem Nat Conv, 68; Fla State Rep, 72-74; Fla State Sen, 74- Bus & Prof Pos: Serv rep, Fla Farm Bur, 60-62; owner, Gen Ins Agency, 62- Mil Serv: Army, serv in Korean War. Mem: Quincy Rotary (past pres); Am Legion; Elks; Mason (32 degree); Shrine. Honors & Awards: Selected One of Five Outstanding Young Men, Fla Jaycees, 67. Relig: Presbyterian. Legal Res: Hwy 90 PO Drawer 629 Quincy FL 32351 Mailing Add: 332 Senate Off Bldg Tallahassee FL 32304

THOMAS, PHILIP WOODROW (D)
Chmn, Caldwell Co Dem Comt, Ky
b Dawson Springs, Ky, Feb 21, 37; s Woodrow Wilson Thomas & Hazel Claxton T; m 1959 to Joyce Faye McCormick; c Mike, Kay & Mark. Educ: Murray State Univ, 54-57. Polit & Govt Pos: Chmn, Caldwell Co Dem Comt, Ky, 73- Bus & Prof Pos: Farmer, Princeton, Ky, 63- Mil Serv: Entered as Pvt, Army, 58, released as Pfc, 60, after serv in Med Res Lab, Ft Knox; Good Conduct Medal. Mem: Farm Bur (dir, 66-). Honors & Awards: Jaycees Young Farmer of the Year in Caldwell Co, 71. Relig: Baptist. Mailing Add: Rte 4 Princeton KY 42445

THOMAS, RENO HENRY (R)
Pa State Rep
b Beavertown, Pa, July 11, 22; s Herbert Franklin Thomas & Ada Hetrick T; m 1944 to Phyllis Ellen Middleswarth; c Gayle Ellen & Wendy Lou. Educ: Pa State Univ, BS Agr Educ, 43; Alpha Tau Alpha. Polit & Govt Pos: Mem, West Snyder Sch Bd, 47-62; comnr, Pa State Farm Show, 63-; Pa State Rep, 68- Bus & Prof Pos: Owner & mgr, Brooks End Farm, 45-75; pres, Pa Yorkshire Coop Inc, 54-; pres, Am Yorkshire Club Inc, 62-64. Mem: Moose; Elks; Am Heart Asn (dir); Alpha Zeta; Gamma Sigma Delta. Honors & Awards: State Master Farmers Award, 64; Ford Farm Efficiency Award, 67; Community Leader of Am, 68; Soil Conserv Watershed Award of the Year, 74. Relig: United Church of Christ. Legal Res: RD 1 Beavertown PA 17813 Mailing Add: Capitol Bldg Harrisburg PA 17120

THOMAS, RICHARD CLARK (R)
Secy of State, Vt
b Washburn, Maine, May 3, 37; s Orin A Thomas, Jr & Amelia Woodman T; m 1964 to Clara Betty Wright; c twins Lisa Rae & Leslie Lynn. Educ: Middlebury Col, BA in Polit Sci, 59; Georgetown Law Sch, 62-63; Sigma Phi Epsilon. Polit & Govt Pos: Prof staff mem, Sen Comt on Commerce, 63; research & press asst to US Sen W L Prouty, Vt, 63-65; coordr campaign of US Sen Winston Prouty, Vt, 64; exec dir, Vt Rep State Comt, 65-67; first asst clerk, Vt House Rep, 68; secy, Legis Apportionment Bd, 69-; chmn, Pub Records Adv Bd, 69-; chmn, Travel Info Coun, 69-; Comnr of Foreign Corporations, 69-; Secy of State, Vt, 69- Bus & Prof Pos: Reporter, Construction News & Statist Div, McGraw-Hill Publ Co, New York, NY, 60-63. Mil Serv: Entered as 2nd Lt, Army, 59, served in Hq & Hq Co, Third Bn, 304th Training Regt; Capt, Army Artil (Ret). Publ: Vermont Almanac & Government Guide, 66. Mem: Vt Soc of Asn Exec Secretaries; Nat Asn of Secretaries of State; Rotary; Am Legion; Elks. Relig: Baptist. Mailing Add: 49 Greenwood Terr Montpelier VT 05602

THOMAS, RUTH WATT (D)
VChmn, Miller Co Dem Party, Mo
b Eldon, Mo, Sept 1, 08; d John Thomas Watt & Nancy Alice Jobe W; m 1929 to Ralph Waldo Thomas; c John Paul, James Ray, Ralph Lowell & Rayford Wayne. Educ: Cent Mo State Col, 27-42. Polit & Govt Pos: Committeewoman, Miller Co Dem Party, Mo, 68-, vchmn, currently. Bus & Prof Pos: Teacher rural schs, Mo & jr high sch, Greybull, Wyo, 12 years; owner & mgr country gen store, currently. Mem: Eastern Star (past Matron); Rebekah (past Noble Grand); Royal Neighbors; Order Rainbow Girls (past mother adv). Honors & Awards: Grand Cross of Color. Relig: Baptist. Mailing Add: Rte 1 Iberia MO 65486

THOMAS, SAM B (D)
Ky State Rep
Mailing Add: Country Club Dr Lebanon KY 40033

THOMAS, STAN, JR (D)
Mo State Rep
b Liberty, Mo, Oct 17, 23; m 1948 to Margaret Finney; c Mike, Pat & Brian. Educ: William Jewell Col, BA; Sigma Nu. Polit & Govt Pos: Pres, Clay Co Young Dem, Mo, formerly; Mo State Rep, 18th Dist, 64-, vchmn, Comt Atomic & Indust Develop, mem, Educ, Motor Vehicle & Traffic Regulations & Workmen's Compensation Comts, vchmn, Fees & Salaries Comt, mem, Interstate Coop & Bills Perfected & Passed Comts, chmn, Comt State Insts & Properties, mem, Interstate Coop & Miscellany & Motor Vehicle & Traffic Regulations Comts, Majority Whip, Asst Majority Floor Leader & chmn, Econ Comt, Mo House Rep, formerly, chmn, Legis Res & Banks & Financial Insts & Munic Corps Comts, Mo House Rep, currently; deleg, Dem Nat Conv, 68. Bus & Prof Pos: Eng serv rep, 48-51; owner of disposal serv, 49-; athletic coach & algebra teacher, 51-53. Mil Serv: Naval Res, World War II (3 years). Mem: AF&AM; Mason; Shrine; Liberty Jaycees (past pres); Beta Xi. Relig: Methodist. Mailing Add: Rm 313 Capitol Bldg Jefferson City MO 65101

THOMAS, STANLEY BUDDINGTON, JR (R)
Asst Secy Human Develop, Dept Health, Educ & Welfare
b New York, NY, Apr 28, 42; s Stanley Buddington Thomas, Sr & Marion Gittens T; m 1973 to Elizabeth Beare; c from previous marriage, Kim & Kelly. Educ: Yale Univ, BA, 64. Polit & Govt Pos: Secy, Anti-Poverty Opers Bd, aide to Mayor John Lindsay, New York, 66-67; chmn, New York Young Rep Club, 67-68; dep asst secy youth & student affairs, Dept Health, Educ & Welfare, 69-73, asst secy human develop, 73- Bus & Prof Pos: Mgr, Col Bur, Time, Inc, 67-68; mgr personnel rels, Philip Morris, Inc, 68-69; trustee, Horace Mann Sch, Bronx, NY. Honors & Awards: Superior Serv Award, Dept Health, Educ & Welfare, 72, Secy Spec Citation, 73. Relig: Episcopal. Legal Res: NY Mailing Add: 1435 Fourth St SW Washington DC 20024

THOMAS, THEODORE FREDERICK (R)
Mem, Rep State Cent Comt, Calif
b Los Angeles, Calif, May 7, 25; both parents deceased; m 1950 to Evelyn Caccialanza; c Gary Steven & Bruce Scott. Educ: City Col of San Francisco, AA, 48; Los Angeles State Col, BS, 60. Polit & Govt Pos: Pres, Studio City Young Rep, Sherman Oaks, Calif, 63; pres, Studio City UROC, 64-65; mem, Rep State Cent Comt, Calif, 64- & Los Angeles Co Cent Comt, 68- Bus & Prof Pos: Vpres, Los Angeles Fastener Asn, 69. Mil Serv: Entered as Seaman, Navy, 42, released as SH 2/C, 46, after serv in ETO & Pac Theatre, 43-46; reentered during Korean War, 50-51; Pac Area Medal with Five Stars; European Medal with Two Stars; Korean Serv Medal; UN Meda Medal; Am Theatre Ribbon; China Serv Medal; World War II Victory Medal; Philippine Govt Medal. Mem: San Fernando Valley Bus & Prof Asn. Relig: Protestant. Mailing Add: 11940 Weddington St North Hollywood CA 91607

THOMAS, TRACY ANN (D)
b Cedar Rapids, Iowa, Sept 19, 49; d Michael Patrick Thomas & Velma Cook T; single. Educ: Wichita State Univ, Lenora M McGregor scholar, 67-71, BMusic Educ, magna cum laude, 71, grad student, 71-72; Mortar Bd; Phi Kappa Phi; Mu Phi Epsilon; Little Sisters of Minerva of Sigma Alpha Epsilon. Polit & Govt Pos: Dem precinct committeewoman, Wichita, Kans, 72; alt deleg, Dem Nat Conv, 72. Bus & Prof Pos: Violist, Wichita Symphony Orchestra, 68-72; instrumental music teacher, Wichita Collegiate Sch, 71-72; student eval of faculty coord, Wichita State Univ, 71-72, instnl image study researcher & ed, 72; arts adminr to the Civic Arts Coun, Kansas City, Kans, 72- Publ: Ed, Benchmark—the first student evaluation of faculty at Wichita State Univ, Wichita State Univ, 72 & Community Arts Newsletter, Civic Arts Coun, Kansas City, (publ monthly), 73- Mem: Mu Phi Epsilon (chaplain, Wichita Alumnae, 71-); Mortar Bd-Wichita Alumnae (comt chmn, 71-, adv, Nat Coun); Assoc Coun of the Arts. Relig: Lutheran. Legal Res: 1704 N 25th St Kansas City KS 66102 Mailing Add: City Hall One Civic Plaza Kansas City KS 66101

THOMAS, VINCENT (D)
Calif State Assemblyman
m 1947 to Mary DiCarlo T; c Mary Virginia & Vincent, Jr. Educ: Univ Santa Clara, PhB,

32; Law Sch, Univ Santa Clara, 32-34; Loyola Law Sch, 34-36; minor sports coach, Univ Santa Clara, 30-34. Polit & Govt Pos: Presidential Elector, Calif, 40 & 44; Calif State Assemblyman, 40- Bus & Prof Pos: Phys educ instr, 33-34; chmn, Joint Legis Audit Comt, 63- Mem: Elks; Redmen; Pac Marine Fisheries Comn. Mailing Add: 255 W Fifth St San Pedro CA 90731

THOMAS, W HENRY (D)
Md State Deleg
Mailing Add: 1009 Radiance Dr Cambridge MD 21613

THOMAS, WILLIAM G (D)
Polit & Govt Pos: Chmn, Va State Dem Party, formerly. Mailing Add: PO Box 820 Alexandria VA 22313

THOMAS, WILLIAM M (R)
Calif State Assemblyman
b Wallace, Idaho, Dec 6, 41; s Virgil Thomas & Gertrude White T; m 1967 to Sharon Lynn Hamilton; c Christopher & Amelia. Educ: Santa Ana Community Col, AA; San Francisco State Univ, BA & MA. Polit & Govt Pos: Chmn, Kern Co Rep Cent Comt, Calif, 73, mem, Rep State Cent Comt Calif, currently; Calif State Assemblyman, 74- Bus & Prof Pos: Prof polit sci, Bakersfield Col, currently. Mem: Calif Teachers Asn; Southern San Joaquin Chap March of Dimes (dir); Calif State Employees Asn. Legal Res: 228 Hermosa Dr Bakersfield CA 93305 Mailing Add: 2025 18th St Bakersfield CA 93301

THOMASON, BOYD (D)
Ga State Rep
Mailing Add: Rte 2 Jasper GA 30143

THOMASON, FRANKLIN A (D)
Md State Deleg
Mailing Add: 302 Sycamore Rd Linthicum MD 21090

THOMPSON, ADA MCCALL (D)
b Elmhurst, Ill, Feb 11, 30; d Mahlon McCullough McCall & Eva Work M; m 1954 to Paul Oscar Thompson; c Eric McCall & Scott William. Educ: Bryn Mawr Col, 48-50; San Diego State Univ, BA, 75. Polit & Govt Pos: 37th Cong Dist Dir, Calif Dem Coun, 67-69; mem, Chula Vista Ethics Bd, 67-, chmn, 70-73; deleg, Dem Nat Conv, 68; mem, Calif Dem State Cent Comt, 68-72; mem, Chula Vista City Charter Rev Comt, 71-73. Mem: League of Women Voters (coordr radio prog, Voice of the Voter, KSDO, San Diego, 74-); hon life mem PTA; Am Civil Liberties Union; Bryn Mawr Col Club of Southern Calif (student interviewer); UN Asn Speakers Bur. Honors & Awards: Laymen of Year Award, Sweetwater Educ Asn, 72; Community Serv Award, Chula Vista City Coun, 72. Relig: Unitarian; church coun; choir. Mailing Add: 1060 Las Bancas Ct Chula Vista CA 92011

THOMPSON, ALAN (D)
Wash State Rep
b Geneva, Iowa, 1927; m to Barbara R; c four sons. Educ: Univ Nebr; Univ Calif, BA; Beta Theta Pi. Polit & Govt Pos: Wash State Rep, currently. Bus & Prof Pos: Publisher weekly newspapers, Cowlitz Co Advocate & Lewis Co News. Mil Serv: Navy. Mem: Elks. Mailing Add: 112 Pleasant Hill Lane Kelso WA 98626

THOMPSON, ALBERT WILLIAM (D)
Ga State Rep
b Ft Benning, Ga, June 29, 22; s Charles Edward Thompson, Sr & Mary Elizabeth Houser T; m 1953 to Dorothy O Jackson; c Eloise Marie, Charles Edward, III & Albert William, Jr. Educ: Savannah State Col, BS, 42; Howard Univ Law Sch, JD, 50. Polit & Govt Pos: Ga State Rep, Dist 110, 66-68, Dist 85, 69-; deleg, Dem Nat Conv, 72. Mil Serv: Entered as Pvt, Army, 43, released as Sgt, 43, after serv in 41st Eng Regt, ETO, 42-44. Mem: State Bar Ga; Columbus Lawyer's Club; Am Legion; CofC. Honors & Awards: Man of the Year, Progressive Club, 65. Relig: Baptist. Legal Res: 4154 Swann St Columbus GA 31903 Mailing Add: PO Box 587 Columbus GA 31902

THOMPSON, ANNE ELISE (D)
b Philadelphia, Pa, July 8, 34; d Leroy Henry Jenkins & Mary Elise Jackson J; m to William Henry Thompson; c William Henry, Jr & Sharon Annette. Educ: Howard Univ, BA, 55, LLB, 64; Temple Univ, MA, 57. Polit & Govt Pos: Deleg, Dem Nat Conv, 72; munic court judge, City of Trenton, NJ, 72- Mem: Am, NJ State & Mercer Co Bar Asns. Relig: Unitarian. Mailing Add: 123 Renfrew Ave Trenton NJ 08618

THOMPSON, ANNE MARIE (R)
b Des Moines, Iowa, Feb 7, 20; d George H Sheely & Esther S Mayer S; m 1949 to James Ross Thompson; c Annette (Mrs Robert McCracken), James Ross, Jr & Dana Marie. Educ: Univ Iowa, BA, 40; Theta Sigma Phi; Chi Omega. Polit & Govt Pos: Colo State Rep, 56-60; secy, Rep State Cent Comt, Colo, 60-61; secy, Colo Fedn Rep Women, 62-65, Third Cong Dist Dir, 69-71; secy, Otero Co Rep Cent Comt, formerly; pres, Rocky Ford Rep Women's Club, 64-66; Colo Presidential Elector, 72; chmn, 63rd Legis Dist, 72-; mem, Colo Status of Women Comn, 73- Bus & Prof Pos: Co-publ, Rocky Ford Daily Gazette, 54- Mem: Colo Authors League; Nat Fedn Press Women; PEO; Am Asn Univ Women; Bus & Prof Women's Club. Honors & Awards: Colo Woman of Achievement in Jour, Colo Press Women, 68. Relig: Methodist. Legal Res: 1010 Lincoln Rocky Ford CO 81067 Mailing Add: PO Box 430 Rocky Ford CO 81067

THOMPSON, BARBARA COOPER (R)
NH State Rep
b Rochester, NH, Dec 18, 16; d Burt Randall Cooper & Lillian Foss C; div; c Sandra (Mrs Grigg), Mark, Boyen & Betsy (Mrs Booth). Educ: Colby Jr Col for Women, AA, 37; Boston Univ, BS in Social Sci, 39; Univ NH, grad studies, 40, 65 & 68; Delta Delta Delta. Polit & Govt Pos: Deleg, NH Const Conv, 64; clerk, Health & Welfare, State Insts Comt; NH State Rep, 69-; mem, Gov Comn Crime & Delinquency, 70-; mem, Gov Comn on Laws Affecting Children, 72- Bus & Prof Pos: Social worker, NH State Hosp, 40-43, Rochester Schs, 65-68. Mem: Region VI Dist Chmn, Govt Comn on Voc Rehabilitation; NH Day Care-Child Develop Coun (bd mem, 74-); Gateway Asn Retarded Children (bd mem, 70-); State & Nat Orders of Women Legislators; Strafford Guid Ctr (bd mem, 73-). Honors & Awards: Wise Award, 74. Relig: Protestant; past mem bd trustees & bd deacons, First Church Congregational. Mailing Add: 77 Rochester Hill Rd Rochester NH 03867

THOMPSON, BERNARD GALE (R)
b Independence, Kans, Apr 1, 35; s James L Thompson & Florence A Moon T; div. Educ: Sacramento City Col, AA, 56; Univ Denver, BSBA, 59; Univ Calif, Hastings Col of Law, San Francisco, JD, 62; Sigma Alpha Epsilon. Polit & Govt Pos: Sam King for Gov, Co of Kauai, Hawaii, 70; pres & campaign chmn, Lihue Precinct Rep Club, Kauai, 70-71; co chmn, Rep Party of Kauai, formerly. Mem: Am, Calif, Hawaii, Sacramento Co & Kauai Co Bar Asns. Honors & Awards: Chairman's Award of Excellence, Rep Nat Comt, 71. Relig: Episcopal. Mailing Add: PO Box 1385 Kauai Lihue HI 96766

THOMPSON, CARL WILLIAM (D)
Wis State Sen
b Washington, DC, Mar 15, 14; s Carl William Thompson & Hannah Hegge T; m 1942 to Marian Foster; c Anne, Jane, Margaret & Elizabeth. Educ: Luther Col, 32-33; Univ Wis, PhB, 36 & LLB, 39. Polit & Govt Pos: Alderman, Stoughton, Wis, city attorney, 42; Dem Presidential Elector, 48; Dem cand for Gov, Wis, 48 & 50; Dem Nat Committeeman, Wis, 49-56; Wis State Assemblyman, 53-59; Wis State Sen, 59-; alt deleg, Dem Nat Conv, 60. Bus & Prof Pos: Attorney-at-law, 39-; real estate broker, 53- Mil Serv: Entered as Pvt, Army, 42, released as 1st Lt, 46, after serv in Army Intel. Relig: Lutheran. Legal Res: Rte 5 Stoughton WI 53589 Mailing Add: Rte 3 Box 726 Stoughton WI 53589

THOMPSON, CHARLOTTE L (R)
Mem, DeKalb Co Rep Exec Comt, Ga
b Youngstown, Ohio, Dec 19, 29; d Fred Peter Hiner & Mable Schrum H; m 1949 to Charles Arthur Thompson; c Debra Lynn & Mark Charles. Educ: South High Sch, Youngstown, 45-48. Polit & Govt Pos: Asst to nat committeewoman, Supplies for Nixon Hq, 68; finance chmn, Ga Fedn Rep Women, 69-71; chmn pub rels, 71-73, dist dir, 71-; vpres, Toco Hills Rep Women's Club, Ga, 69-71; deleg, Ga Rep State Conv, 70 & 72; mem, DeKalb Co Rep Exec Comt, 70-; co-chmn spec guests, Southeastern Regional Conf, 72; alt deleg, Rep Nat Conv, 72; mem, Rep State Cent Comt, Ga, 72-73. Bus & Prof Pos: Secy, Addressograph-Multigraph Corp, 49-50; receptionist, Conn Gen Life Ins, 50-53; secy & bookkeeper, Rep Party of Ga, 72- Mem: Lakeside High Cinder Club (secy, 72-). Relig: Lutheran. Mailing Add: 1953 Fisher Trail NE Atlanta GA 30345

THOMPSON, CLARK WALLACE (D)
b La Crosse, Wis, Aug 6, 96; s Clark Wallace Thompson & Jessie Hyde T; m 1918 to Libbie Moody; c Clark W, Jr & Libbie (Mrs Stansell, deceased). Educ: Univ Ore, 15-17; Phi Delta Theta. Polit & Govt Pos: US Rep, Tex, 33-34 & 47-67. Bus & Prof Pos: Consult, Clark W Thompson Co, Galveston, Tex, 20-32; consult dir pub rels, Am Nat Ins Co, 36-40; dir, Washington Operations, Tenneco Inc, currently. Mil Serv: Entered as Pvt, Marine Corps, 17; released as Col, 46, after serv in 2nd Div, 2nd & 3rd Brigades, Hq Marine Corps, Southwest Pac, 40-46; Col, Res, 46; Legion of Merit; Res Spec Commendation; Good Conduct Medal; Organized Marine Corps Res Ribbon. Mem: AF&AM; KCCH (32 degree); Shrine; Eagles; Am Legion. Relig: Episcopal. Legal Res: 1616 Driftwood Lane Galveston TX 77550 Mailing Add: 3301 Massachusetts Ave NW Washington DC 20008

THOMPSON, CORLEY (R)
Mo State Rep
Mailing Add: 35 Rosemont Webster Groves MO 63119

THOMPSON, DENHAM MICHAEL BURGESS (MIKE) (R)
Committeeman, Rep State Exec Comt, Fla
b Miami, Fla, Oct 15, 39; s Thomas Denham Thompson & Sybil Valletta Bodden T; m 1961 to Patricia Elaine Carpenter. Educ: Univ Miami, BA, 61; Sigma Delta Chi scholarship; Omicron Delta Kappa; Sigma Delta Chi; Kappa Alpha Mu; Order of Iron Arrow; Lead & Ink. Polit & Govt Pos: Special asst, Gov War on Crime, Fla, 67; Fed-State Coordr for Fla, Washington, DC, 67-68; conv site coordr, Nixon for Pres Comt, 68; Rep nominee for US Rep, Fla, 66 & 68; state campaign dir, Bafalis for Gov Comt, 69-70; committeeman, Fla State Rep Party, 71-; mem dist adv coun, Small Bus Admin; alt deleg, Rep Nat Conv, 72. Bus & Prof Pos: Asst news ed, asst mag ed & Sunday ed, The Miami News, 61-66; sr vpres, Long Advert Agency Inc, Miami, Fla, 68- Mil Serv: Entered as Pvt, Army, 62, released as SP-5, 68, after serv in 35th Surg Hosp, Fla Nat Guard & 324th Gen Hosp, Army Res, Coral Gables, Fla; Expert Rifleman's Medal. Publ: Youth in Cuba, Miami News, Assoc Press Syndication, 2/60. Mem: Fla Inst of Pub Affairs (trustee); South Fla Young Am for Freedom; Dade Co Young Rep; Fact Finders Forum; hon mem, Anti-Communist Cuban Col of Journ. Honors & Awards: Ed of Best Col Paper in South, Am Newspaper Guild, Memphis Chap, 60; Hist Medal, Univ Miami; Mr Executive of Tomorrow, Alpha Delta Sigma; Am Legion Citizenship Medal. Relig: Episcopal. Mailing Add: 2516 Madrid St Coral Gables FL 33134

THOMPSON, DON LEE (R)
b Tabor, SDak, June 25, 20; s William Henry Thompson & Alice Landon T; m 1946 to Mary Sue Stephens; c Michael, Don, Linda Sue & Jeffrey. Educ: SDak State Univ, 38-39; Southern State Col (SDak), 39-40; SDak Univ, BA in Bus Admin, 48. Polit & Govt Pos: Auditor, State of SDak, 49; Alderman, Webster, SDak, 62-63; Mayor, 65-69; mem, Day Co Bd Educ, formerly; chmn, Day Co Rep Cent Comt, 70-; justice of peace, Webster, 70- Bus & Prof Pos: Car salesman, Forneys Sales & Serv, Pierre, SDak, 50-57; partner, Webster Livestock Exchange, 57-58; consignee, Mobil Oil Co, Webster, 58- Mil Serv: Entered as A/S, Navy, 41, released as Lt (sg), 46; after serv in Naval Air Corps as Aviator aboard carrier, Pac, 42-43; Lt Comdr (Ret), Naval Res, 59; Air Medal with three Clusters; Presidential Unit Citation. Mem: Mason; Kiwanis Int; Am Legion; Shrine; CofC. Honors & Awards: Boss of the Year, 65; Cited by Mobil Oil Co for 13 years serv. Relig: Methodist. Legal Res: 413 E 12th Ave Webster SD 57274 Mailing Add: Box 68 Webster SD 57274

THOMPSON, DONALD D (D)
Okla State Sen
Mailing Add: State Capitol Oklahoma City OK 73105

THOMPSON, DONALD LESLIE (D)
NMex State Sen
b Chicago, Ill, Jan 1, 24; s Leslie McKay Thompson & Anna T; m 1950 to Alice Jane; c Sarita Jane & Delano Leslie. Educ: Univ Ill, AB, 51; Univ NMex, MA, 60; Univ NMex Law Sch, 62-65; Nat Univ Mex, 51. Polit & Govt Pos: Precinct chmn, Albuquerque, NMex, 55-75; constable, Bern Co, 61-62; NMex State Rep, 73-74; NMex State Sen, 75- Bus & Prof Pos: High sch teacher, Lajoya, 53-54; elem sch teacher, Albuquerque Pub Schs, 55-75. Mil Serv: Entered as A/S, Navy, 42, released as Lt, 64, after serv in ETO, Korea & American Theatres; ETO, American & Korean Ribbons; Purple Heart. Mem: Nat & NMex Educ Asns; Albuquerque Classroom Teachers Asn; Fraternal Order of Police Asn. Honors & Awards:

Am Fedn Teachers Serv Award, 65. Relig: Unitarian. Mailing Add: 1519 Anderson Pl SE Albuquerque NM 87108

THOMPSON, DORIS L (R)
NH State Rep
Mailing Add: 95 Park St Northfield NH 03276

THOMPSON, FRANCIS C (D)
La State Rep
Mailing Add: 108 Shady Lane Delhi LA 71232

THOMPSON, FRANK, JR (D)
US Rep, NJ
b Trenton, NJ, July 26, 18; s Frank Thompson, Sr & Beatrice Jamieson T; m 1942 to Evelina Van Metre; c Anne (Mrs Henderson) & Evelina (Mrs Lyons). Educ: Wake Forest Law Sch. Hon Degrees: LLD, Princeton Univ, 69. Polit & Govt Pos: NJ State Assemblyman, 49-54; Asst Minority Leader, NJ State Assembly, 50 & Minority Leader, 54; US Rep, NJ, 54-; mem, Comt Educ & Labor, House Admin Comt, chmn, Subcomt Labor & Mgt Rels & chmn, Subcomt on Accounts, US House of Rep; chmn, Nat Voters Regist Comt, Presidential Campaign, 60; chmn, Nat Voter Regist Drive, 72. Mil Serv: Entered Navy, 41, released 48, Comdr, USS LCI, 428 & LCI Rocket Squadrons, 48 & 63; three combat decorations for action at Iwo Jima & Okinawa; Comdr, Naval Res Bn, active duty on staff of Comdr, Eastern Sea Frontier, 52-54. Mem: Am Legion (Am Vet Comt); VFW; J F Kennedy Ctr (trustee). Relig: Catholic. Mailing Add: 10 Rutgers Pl Trenton NJ 08618

THOMPSON, G ROBERT (R)
Recruitment chmn, Venango Co Rep Comt, Pa
b Strattonville, Pa, Sept 24, 24; s Fredrick Arthur Thompson & Reba Eisenman T; m 1949 to Norma Boud; c Terrence R, Forest A & Jill A. Educ: Clarion High Sch, Pa, dipl, 42. Polit & Govt Pos: Alderman, Oil City, Pa, 53-55; deleg, Rep Nat Conv, 72; spec events chmn, Venango Co Rep Comt, Pa, 73-74, recruitment chmn, 74-; transportation comt chmn, Northwest Pa Planning & Develop Comn, 73- Bus & Prof Pos: Terminal mgr, Duffee Motor Express, Cleveland, Ohio, 46-48, Pittsburgh, Pa, 48-50, asst gen mgr, 50-53; driver, Warner & Smith Motor Freight, 53-55; terminal mgr, Lyons Transportation Lines Inc, 55-75. Mil Serv: Entered as Pvt, Army Air Force, 44, released as Sgt, 46, after serv in US; Am Defense Medal; Good Conduct Medal. Mem: Pa CofC; Acacia Grotto; KT; Boy Scouts; Oil City CofC. Honors & Awards: Order of Merit, Boy Scouts, 65. Relig: Presbyterian; Elder. Mailing Add: 32 Woodside Ave Oil City PA 16301

THOMPSON, GEORGE (D)
Chmn, Fort Benn Co Dem Exec Comt, Tex
b Wayne Co, Ga, Apr 13, 24; s John Wesley Thompson & Sulie Thornton T; m 1949 to Vinnie Lennette Sikes (Lynn); c Gus Howard & Karen. Educ: Univ Ga, BA Jour, 50; STex Col of Law, 67; Pi Gamma Kappa Radio Fraternity; Delta Tau Delta. Polit & Govt Pos: Precinct committeeman, Fort Bend Co Dem Exec Comt, 64-67, chmn, 70- Bus & Prof Pos: Mgr radio sta, WBGR, Jesup, Ga, 50-53, KLBC, Alexandria, La, 53-54 & KSIG, Crowley, 54-55; budget sales mgr, Goodyear Serv Stores, Orange, Tex, 56-57, Lake Charles, La, 57-58; mgr, KTET, Livingston, Tex, 58-59; sales mgr, KFRD, Rosenberg, 59- Mil Serv: Entered as Pvt, Army, 43, released as Lt Col, 67, after serv in various units during World War II & Civil Air Patrol; Bronze Star; Meritorius Serv Award, twice. Mem: Sigma Delta Chi Jour Soc (vpres local chap); Nat Asn Sports Writers & Broadcasters; Mason; York Rite; Rotary Club. Honors & Awards: Received local awards for participation in various civic activities. Relig: Episcopal; lay reader & Sunday sch teacher; serv on vestry bd. Mailing Add: 705 Foster Dr Richmond TX 77469

THOMPSON, GUY (D)
Polit & Govt Pos: Chmn, Okla State Dem Cent Comt, formerly, 66-. Mailing Add: 2726 N Oklahoma Oklahoma City OK 73105

THOMPSON, HARRY E (R)
Ind State Sen
b Decatur Co, Ind, Sept 5, 17; s Harry A Thompson & Bessie Anna Clark T; m to Mildred J McCutchan; c Elaine (Mrs Richard Azwell), Jane (Mrs Tom Follis) & Sue (Mrs Don Colvin). Educ: Univ Evansville, BS, 59; Lambda Chi Alpha. Polit & Govt Pos: Ind State Rep, Vanderburgh Co, Ind, 69-70; Ind State Sen, 73-, mem finance comt-govt affairs-judiciary-roads & transportation, Ind State Senate, 73- Bus & Prof Pos: Mgr, Evansville CofC, 50; secy, Evansville Comt of 100 Inc, 51-55; indust real estate, 55-59; vpres, Old Nat Bank, Evansville, 59-75. Mil Serv: Entered as Pvt, Army, 42, released as Capt, after serv in Replacement Sch Command, SPac, 44-45. Mem: Elks; Ind Area Development Coun; Nat Asn Legislature. Honors & Awards: Cert of Achievement, Brookings Inst, Washington, DC. Relig: United Methodist. Mailing Add: 4725 Stringtown Rd Evansville IN 47711

THOMPSON, JAMES CORLEY (R)
Mo State Rep
b Neosho, Mo, July 21, 28; s James Corley Thompson & Penelope Clinton Carter T; m 1950 to Peggy Ann Booth; c Terry Ann, James Corley, III & Gregory Booth. Educ: Southwest Mo State Univ, 47-49; Kansas City Col Mortuary Sci, MS, 50; Wash Univ, 58-59; Sigma Tau Gamma. Polit & Govt Pos: Committeeman, Newton Co Rep Comt, Mo, 51-52; coroner, Newton Co, 52-60; exec dir, Mo Rep Unlimited, St Louis; sgt-at-arms, Rep Nat Conv, 64; Mo State Rep, Dist 96, St Louis Co, 67- Bus & Prof Pos: Pres, Corley Thompson & Assocs, St Louis, 65-74; vpres, Ibur & Assocs, Inc, 74- Mem: Moolah Temple Shrine; Press Club of Metrop St Louis; Nat Asn Independent Pub Adjusters; Nat Asn Independent Fee Appraisers; St Louis Variety Club. Honors & Awards: App chmn, Mo Comn for the Handicapped; app to state bd adv, Civil Air Patrol. Relig: Presbyterian. Legal Res: 35 Rosemont Webster Groves MO 63119 Mailing Add: House Post Off Capitol Bldg Jefferson City MO 65101

THOMPSON, JAMES HAROLD (D)
Fla State Rep
Mailing Add: Rte 4 Box 85 Quincy FL 32351

THOMPSON, JAMES L (R)
b Douglas, Wyo, Dec 18, 19; m to Harriett; c two. Educ: Univ Wyo; Curtis Wright Tech Inst of Aeronaut, grad. Polit & Govt Pos: Wyo State Rep, formerly; Wyo State Sen, Converse-Niobrara Dist, 66-74; alt deleg, Rep Nat Conv, 72. Bus & Prof Pos: Rancher. Mem: Elks; Wyo Wool Growers; Wyo Stock Growers Asn; 4-H Leader; Niobrara Country Club. Relig: Congregational Mailing Add: Lance Creek WY 82222

THOMPSON, JOE (D)
Ga State Sen
Mailing Add: Box 1045 Smyrna GA 30080

THOMPSON, JOHN, JR (D)
Ohio State Rep
b Cleveland, Ohio, Aug 23, 27; s John Douglas Thompson, Sr & Bertha Bohles T; m 1953 to Doris V Walker; c Joanie & Janet. Educ: Cleveland Eng Inst, 50-51; Finn Col, cert real estate, 53; Franklin Univ Law Sch, 73- Polit & Govt Pos: Ohio State Rep, 15th Dist, 71-, vchmn ins, financial insts comt & mem transportation & urban affairs & pub utilities comts, Ohio House Rep, 73-, chmn standing subcomt on financial insts & mem state govt comt, 75- Bus & Prof Pos: Pres & broker, John D Thompson Real Estate Co, 60- Mil Serv: Entered as Pvt, Army, 46, released as Sgt, 49, after serv in 24th Inf Regt, Pac Theatre Oper, 47-49; Ohio Nat Guard, 45-46; Good Conduct Medal. Mem: Lee Harvard Community Asn (hon bd mem); Mt Pleasant Community Coun; Lee Seville Community Asn; Mason; Shrine. Honors & Awards: Man of Year, 15th Dist Orgn, 72 & Politician of Year, 74. Relig: Lutheran; Mem, Task Force on Educ of Lutheran Ministry. Legal Res: 15611 Stockbridge Ave Cleveland OH 44128 Mailing Add: 17017 Miles Ave Cleveland OH 44128

THOMPSON, JOHN COLBY (R)
b Forest City, Iowa, Apr 9, 20; s Merle M Thompson (deceased) & Dora Colby T (deceased); m to Clara Peterson (deceased); m 1959 to Loraine Hollingsworth; c Robert P & stepchildren, Roberta, Brenda & Catherine. Educ: Forest City High Sch, grad, 37. Polit & Govt Pos: Finance officer, Winnebago Co Rep Cent Comt, Iowa, 48-66, chmn, 66-73; chmn, Forest City Park Bd, 55-73; exec secy, Winnebago Co Regional Planning Coun, 71-73; comnr, Iowa State Conserv Comn, 73- Bus & Prof Pos: Chmn, Forest City Asn of Independent Ins Agents, 55- Mil Serv: Entered as Pvt, Air Force, 42, released as S/Sgt, 45, after serv in Am & Asiatic Pac Theatres & Europe-Africa-Mid East, 42-45; two Stars. Mem: Mason; Eastern Star; Shrine; Am Legion; Rotary. Relig: Methodist. Legal Res: 635 N Seventh St Forest City IA 50436 Mailing Add: 121 School St Forest City IA 50436

THOMPSON, JOHN ELBERT, JR (R)
b Wilmington, NC, July 8, 37; s John Elbert Thompson, Sr & Katherin McLean T; m 1972 to Sara Barfoot; c John E, III & Willard Alexious. Educ: The Citadel, BS, 59. Polit & Govt Pos: Town councilman, Whiteville, NC, 67-; chmn, Columbus Co Rep Party, 67-70; alt deleg, Rep Nat Conv, 68; chmn, Seventh Cong Dist Rep Party, 70-72. Bus & Prof Pos: Partner, Columbus Supply Co, 62-; pres, Trigon Corp, 69- Mil Serv: Entered as 2nd Lt, Army, 59, released as 1st Lt, 62, after serv in First Cavalry Div, Eighth Army, 61-62; Capt, NC Nat Guard, 63-; Army Aviator. Mem: Civitan; Mason (32 degree). Relig: Presbyterian. Legal Res: 617 N Madison St Whiteville NC 28472 Mailing Add: PO Box 425 Whiteville NC 28472

THOMPSON, JOHN HARMON (R)
Chmn, Madison Co Rep Cent Comt, Idaho
b Malta, Idaho, Oct 21, 26; s John Henry Thompson & Lora Harmon T; m 1961 to Etta Doreen Gill; c Randie, Scott, Carrie Lynne, Shelley Jo, Tawney Beth, John Hugh & Wade Charles. Educ: Brigham Young Univ, BA, 57, MEd, 61; Utah State Univ, EdD, 73; Delta Phi Kappa; Lambda Delta Sigma. Polit & Govt Pos: Chmn, Madison Co Rep Cent Comt, Idaho, 72- Bus & Prof Pos: Teacher, Rubidoux High Sch, Riverside, Calif, formerly; teacher, Bonneville Latter-day Saint Sem, Idaho Falls, Idaho, 62-64; dir, Reno Latter-day Saint Inst Relig, Nev, 64-66; asst dir pub rels, Ricks Col, 66- Mem: Phi Delta Kappa; Kiwanis. Relig: Latter-day Saint. Mailing Add: Rte 1 Box 240-B Rexburg ID 83440

THOMPSON, JOHN ROGER (R)
Chmn, Wythe Co Rep Party, Va
b Charlottesville, Va, June 25, 27; s John Bascom Thompson & Alice Jamison T; m 1956 to Patricia Sue Shaffer. Educ: Univ Va; Univ Va Law Sch, LLB, 56. Polit & Govt Pos: Chmn, Wythe Co Rep Party, Va, 66-; Commonwealth attorney, Wythe Co, 68-71; chmn, 4th Legis Dist Rep Party, 69. Mil Serv: Entered as Pvt, Army, 46, released as 2nd Lt, 47, after serv in ETO. Relig: Methodist. Legal Res: 580 Withers Rd Wytheville VA 24382 Mailing Add: 140 E Spring St PO Box 562 Wytheville VA 24382

THOMPSON, KIRBY (D)
Miss State Rep
Mailing Add: Box 686 Prentiss MS 39474

THOMPSON, LEE LINCOLN, JR (D)
Chmn, Loudon Co Dem Exec Comt, Tenn
b Atlanta, Ga, Oct 7, 28; s Lee L Thompson, Sr & Mattie J Bowden T; m 1968 to Janice Ann Sexton; c Elizabeth (Mrs Purdy), Deborah & Lee L, III. Educ: Univ Tenn, 47-48; Carson-Newman Col, 49-50; Tenn Wesleyan Col, 53. Polit & Govt Pos: Mem, Loudon Co Dem Exec Comt, 70-74, chmn, 74- Bus & Prof Pos: Ins agt, 56-68; tax practitioner, Lenoir City, 56- Mil Serv: Entered as E-3, Army, released as E-6, after serv in Co B, 278th Inf, 50-52; CW4, Army Nat Guard, 48-50 & 52- Mem: Nat Soc Pub Acct; Asn of Enrolled Agts; Civitan Club; Am Legion. Relig: Baptist. Legal Res: Rte 5 Pinecrest Circle Lenoir City TN 37771 Mailing Add: PO Box D Lenoir City TN 37771

THOMPSON, LEON (D)
Ariz State Rep
Mailing Add: 1839 S Sixth Ave Phoenix AZ 85003

THOMPSON, MACK A (D)
Ark State Rep
b Paragould, Ark, Dec 16, 22; s J Ed Thompson & Mattie Miller T; m 1951 to Allean Lively; c Mack E & Richard A. Educ: Ark State Univ, 45-46. Polit & Govt Pos: Paragould Pub Sch Bd, 70-73; Ark State Rep, 73- Bus & Prof Pos: State policeman, Ark State Police, 47-67; dist mgr, Ark-La Gas Co-Natural Gas, 67- Mil Serv: Entered as Pvt, Army, 48, released as Pfc, 49, after serv in 5th Armored Div. Mem: Farm Bur; Mason; Kiwanis. Relig: Baptist. Mailing Add: 1025 W Emerson Paragould AR 72450

THOMPSON, MARILYN DOWIE (DFL)
b Moline, Ill, Aug 7, 23; d James Hardy Dowie & Emily Harris D; m 1946 to Frank Walter Thompson; c Mark, Emily, Bonnie, John & Becky. Educ: Augustana Col, Ill, 41-43; Univ Minn, Minneapolis, BA, 67. Polit & Govt Pos: Chairwoman, 50th Sen Dist Dem-Farmer-Labor Party, Minn, formerly. Bus & Prof Pos: Mem personnel staff, Deere & Co, Moline, Ill, 43-44; secy, Brede, Inc, Minneapolis, 47-48; choir dir, Redeemer Lutheran Church, White Bear Lake, 63-; substitute clerical work, Sch Dist 624, 70- Mem: Federated

Music Clubs of Am; PTA. Relig: Lutheran. Mailing Add: 2523 Homewood Pl White Bear Lake MN 55110

THOMPSON, MARK LOUIS (R)
b Rogers City, Mich, Aug 8, 45; s Charles A Thompson & Marian T T; m 1971 to Jacqueline Jeanette Hahn. Educ: Alpena Community Col, 2 years; Phi Theta Kappa. Polit & Govt Pos: Chmn, Alpena Co Rep Party, Mich, formerly; legis analyst, Rep Caucus, Mich House Rep, 71-72; Mich State Rep, 106th Legis Dist, 73-74. Bus & Prof Pos: News reporter, Alpena News, Mich, 70- Mil Serv: Entered as Pvt, Army, 64, released as Sgt, 68, after serv in Security Agency, Europe & Vietnam, 64-68; Bronze Star with one Oak Leaf Cluster; Good Conduct Medal; Vietnam Serv Medal; Meritorious Unit Citation. Mem: Alpena Press Club; Nat Exchange Club; VFW; Rogers City Servicemen's Club. Relig: Presbyterian. Legal Res: 246 S Fourth St Rogers City MI 49779 Mailing Add: Capitol Bldg Lansing MI 48901

THOMPSON, MIKE (D)
La State Rep
Mailing Add: 110 Crescent Ridge Pl Lafayette LA 70501

THOMPSON, OLIVER L, JR (R)
Mem, Barrington Rep Town Comt, RI
b Denver, Colo, May 26, 10; s Oliver L Thompson, Sr & Mary Walsh T; m 1945 to Ann Elizabeth O'Brien; c Oliver L, III, W Brian, John M, Ann Elizabeth, Mary Patricia & James C. Educ: Providence Col; Mass Inst Technol; Boston Univ Law Sch, JD, 35; Law Rev, Boston Univ. Polit & Govt Pos: Councilman, Barrington Town Coun, RI, 48-52, pres, 52-56; RI State Rep, 56-69, Dep Minority Leader, RI House of Rep, 60-61, Minority Leader, 62-69; admin asst, Legis Affairs Coun, 69-; mem, Barrington Rep Town Comt, 58-; mem, Coun State Govts, Nat Intern Conf, Nat Legis Leaders Conf & Comt Proposed State Legis; mem, Interstate Coop Comn; dir, RI State Govt Internship Prog. Bus & Prof Pos: Pres, Brian & Thompson, Inc Realtors & Ins, 50-; mem, Realtors Washington Comt, Nat Asn of Real Estate Bd, 64-70; chmn, Eastern Shore Adv Bd, Indust Nat Bank of RI, 69-70; pres, Oliver Thompson Co Rubber Prods, 70-; adj lectr polit sci, RI Col, 71- Publ: Numerous articles, tech & polit papers. Mem: Nat Asn of Real Estate Bd; RI Ins Agents Asn (bd dirs); VFW; Am Legion; KofC. Relig: Roman Catholic. Legal Res: 55 Washington Rd Barrington RI 02806 Mailing Add: 201 Washington Rd Barrington RI 02806

THOMPSON, PAHL E (R)
b Cantril, Iowa, Dec 24, 10; s James B Thompson & Olive A T; m 1935 to Helen H Hall; c Fred R, Roger D & Ralph H. Educ: Tri City Barber Col, Des Moines, Iowa; Drake Univ. Polit & Govt Pos: Chmn, Mills Co Rep Party, Iowa, formerly. Bus & Prof Pos: Barber, 29; mgr, NW Bell Tel Co, 34. Mem: Mason; Rotary. Relig: Methodist. Mailing Add: 5 N Myrtle St Glenwood IA 51534

THOMPSON, R BURNETT, JR (R)
b Middletown, NY, May 17, 26; s Ralph B Thompson & Eva Birckhead T; m 1950 to Ramona Elmer; c R Burnett, III, Barbara Ruth & Brenda Faith. Educ: Houghton Col, BA, 49; George Washington Univ, 64-66. Polit & Govt Pos: Admin Asst to US Rep G William Whitehurst, Va, 69- Bus & Prof Pos: Pastor, Wesleyan Methodist Church, Silver Creek, NY, 49-57 & Hamburg, NY, 57-59; dist mgr, Encycl Britannica, Washington, DC & Virginia Beach, Va, 57-68. Mil Serv: Entered as Pvt, Air Corps, 44, released as Aviation Cadet, 45, after serv in Pre-Flight. Relig: Methodist. Mailing Add: Off of Hon William G Whitehurst US House of Rep Washington DC 20515

THOMPSON, RICHARD (D)
La State Rep
Mailing Add: Rte 2 Box 22 Colfax LA 71417

THOMPSON, RICHARD KEITH (R)
b Columbus, Ind, July 1, 28; s Albert B Thompson & Vivian Wooden T; m 1965 to Jean Ann Slayton; c Sean Keith & Amy Elizabeth. Educ: Butler Univ, BS Jour, 50; Sigma Delta Chi; Sigma Nu. Polit & Govt Pos: Indexer-researcher, Joint Comt on Printing, Washington, DC, 54-63; researcher Goldwater for President Comt, 64; researcher, House Rep Conf, 65-66; admin asst, US Rep James A McClure, Idaho, 67-72, US Sen James A McClure, Idaho, 72- Mil Serv: Entered as Airman 2/C, Air Force, 51, released as S/Sgt, 53, after serv in 122nd A C & W Squadron. Relig: Presbyterian. Legal Res: 760 S State St North Vernon IN 47265 Mailing Add: 3704 Maryland Ave Alexandria VA 22309

THOMPSON, RUFUS ELBERT (D)
NMex State Sen
b Lubbock, Tex, Aug 15, 43; s Glenn Wesley Thompson & Naomi Elvina Hunt T; m 1965 to Sandra Jean Lemons; c Michael Glenn & Mark Gregory. Educ: Univ Tex, Austin, BBA, 65, JD, 68; Phi Alpha Delta; Sigma Chi. Polit & Govt Pos: Mem, NMex Cent Comt, Dem Party, 72; chmn, NMex Supreme Court Comt on Uniform Rules of Evidence, 72-73; mem bd dirs, Southeastern NMex Econ Develop Dist, 73-; NMex State Sen, 73- Bus & Prof Pos: Assoc, Atwood & Malone, Roswell, NMex, 68-71, partner, Atwood & Malone, 71- Bus & Prof Pos: Co-auth, Pre-trial and trial procedure, Tex Bar Rev, 68. Mem: Nat Conf Lawyers & Prof Engrs; State Bar Tex; State Bar NMex (chmn young lawyers sect, 70); Am Bar Asn (exec coun young lawyers sect, 72). Relig: Baptist. Legal Res: 2710 Highland Rd Roswell NM 88201 Mailing Add: PO Drawer 700 Roswell NM 88201

THOMPSON, S FLETCHER (R)
b College Park, Ga, Feb 5, 25; s R Standish Thompson & Mary Spencer T; m 1946 to Kathryn Cochran; c Charles Lawrence & Deborah Jean. Educ: Emory Univ, AB, 48; Woodrow Wilson Col Law, LLB, 57; Sigma Delta Kappa. Polit & Govt Pos: Ga State Sen, 64-66; US Rep, Ga, 67-72; deleg, Rep Nat Conv, 68. Bus & Prof Pos: Attorney-at-law; pres, Aero Ins Co. Mil Serv: Army Med Corps, 43; Army Air Corps, 43-46; Air Force, 50-53. Mem: Nat Aviation Trades Asn; Int Lawyer-Pilots Bar Asn (dir); Lakeside Country Club. Relig: Methodist; trustee, First Methodist Church, East Point. Mailing Add: 2631 Hogan Rd East Point GA 30344

THOMPSON, SENFRONIA (D)
Tex State Rep
b Booth, Tex, Jan 1, 39; d Lindsey Paige & Thelma Waterhouse P; m 1956 to Jobie Thompson, Sr; c Jobie, Jr, Sarah Marie & Jarvis Wayne. Educ: Tex Southern Univ, BS, 61; Prairie View Agr & Mech Col, MEd, 64; Univ Houston, 67; STex Col Law, Houston, 72; Iota Tau Tau. Polit & Govt Pos: Tex State Rep, 73- Bus & Prof Pos: Teacher, Jack Yates High Sch, Houston, Prairie View Agr & Mech Col, Crispus Attucks Jr High Sch & John Marshall Jr High Sch. Mem: Eastern Star; NAACP; League of Women Voters; Harris Co Dem; Women's Polit Caucus. Honors & Awards: Distinguished Serv Awards, Nat Coun Negro Women, Inc, 72 & Houston Teachers Asn, 72. Relig: Catholic. Legal Res: 8611 Peachtree Houston TX 77016 Mailing Add: PO Box 2910 Capitol Sta Austin TX 78767

THOMPSON, SHAUN RICHARD (D)
b Seattle, Wash, Dec 31, 51; s Richard John Thompson & Winnifred Mason Bean T; single. Educ: Univ Mont, 70-74, Sch Law, 74-; Phi Alpha Theta; Kappa Tau Alpha. Polit & Govt Pos: Chmn, Missoula Co McGovern for President Club, 70-72; state vchmn, Mont McGovern for President Comt, 71-72; precinct committeeman, Missoula Dem Cent Comt, Mont, 72-; deleg, Dem Nat Conv, 72. Bus & Prof Pos: Reporter, Missoulian, 70-71; polit reporter, Mont Kaimin, 72. Relig: Roman Catholic. Mailing Add: Apt J 237 1/2 E Front St Missoula MT 59801

THOMPSON, STANLEY EMIL (D)
Co-Chmn Finance Comt, Mont Dem State Cent Comt
b Hurdland, Mo, Sept 19, 03; s Henry Emil Thompson & Lottie L Merrell T; m 1951 to Cleone Keller; c Betty Jean (Mrs DeLapp) & Janet. Educ: Kirksville State Teachers Col, exten courses. Polit & Govt Pos: Chmn, Mont Dem Labor Adv Comt, 52-56; deleg, Dem Nat Conv, 52-56, 60, 64 & 68, alt deleg, 72; secy, Mont Dem State Cent Comt, 56-61, exec secy, 60-61, co-chmn finance comt, currently; mem, Mont Air Pollution Comt & Apprenticeship Training Coun; mem, Mont Small Bus Admin Admission Coun, currently; deleg, World Conf Nat Parks, 72. Bus & Prof Pos: Int Rep, IBEW, 46-60, int vpres, 62-, chmn, IBEW-IUOE Nat Jurisdictional Comt, currently. Mem: IBEW; Mason; Al BeDoo Shrine Temple (Consistory KT, Commandery); Billings Boys Club (bd dirs); Thomas Alva Edison Found (bd adv, Mont). Relig: Methodist. Legal Res: 402 W 22nd St Red Lodge MT 59068 Mailing Add: Box 1147 Red Lodge MT 59068

THOMPSON, TOMMY GEORGE (R)
Wis State Rep
b Elroy, Wis, Nov 19, 41; s Allan Thompson & Julie Dutton T; m 1969 to Sue Ann Mashak; c Kelli Sue & Tommi. Educ: Univ Wis, Madison, BS, 63 & JD, 66; Phi Delta Phi. Polit & Govt Pos: Polit intern, US Rep Thomson, 63; vchmn, Collegians for Goldwater, Wis, 64; legis messenger, Wis State Senate, 64-66; Wis State Rep, 66-, asst minority leader, Wis House of Rep, 72- Bus & Prof Pos: Attorney, Oxford & Mauston, Wis, 66-70; real estate broker, Mauston, Wis, 70- Mil Serv: Entered as Pvt, Army Res, 66, Capt, currently. Mem: Am & Wis Bar Asns; Oxford Lions Club; Mauston Jaycees. Honors & Awards: Received award for legis in the field of med, Wis Acad of Gen Practice. Relig: Catholic. Mailing Add: 609 Academy St Elroy WI 53929

THOMPSON, VERLA DARLENE (R)
Co Treas, Mercer Co, Ill
b Viola, Ill, Dec 8, 32; d Earl Clair Thompson & Sylvia Anderson T; single. Educ: Aledo High Sch, grad. Polit & Govt Pos: Chief dep treas, Mercer Co, Ill, 53-70, Co Treas, 70-; corresponding secy, Mercer Co Young Rep, 60-63; secy, Mercer Co Rep Cent Comt, 63- Mem: Nat Fedn Rep Women; March of Dimes (chmn, 69-); Nat Fedn Bus & Prof Women's Clubs; Ill Co Treas Asn (fourth vpres, 75-); Mercer Co Young Rep. Honors & Awards: March of Dimes Drive Award. Relig: Methodist. Mailing Add: 301 NE Third Ave Aledo IL 61231

THOMPSON, W H (BILL) (D)
Ark State Rep
Mailing Add: 111 River Rd Marked Tree AR 72365

THOMPSON, WAYNE W (R)
Secy, Minn Second Cong Dist Rep Comt
b Tyler, Minn, Nov 17, 35; s Wesley Howard Thompson & Wayva Baustian T; m 1957 to Martha Elizabeth Engebretson; c Philip Rolf, Rachel Lynn, Nathan David & Lois Marie. Educ: St Olaf Col, BA, 57; Lutheran Theol Sem, BD, 61. Polit & Govt Pos: Chmn, McLeod Co Rep Comt, Minn, 67-69; secy, Minn Second Cong Dist Rep Comt, 69- Bus & Prof Pos: Pastor, Good Shepherd Lutheran Church, Lake Wilson, Minn, 61-65, Bethel Lutheran Church, Lester Prairie, 65-69 & Faith & Our Saviour's Lutheran Church, Madelia, 69- Mem: US Jaycees. Honors & Awards: Jaycees Spark Plug & Key Man Awards. Relig: Lutheran. Mailing Add: 222 Abbot Ave SW Madelia MN 56062

THOMPSON, WILLIAM CHARLES (R)
Mem, Rep State Cent Comt, Calif
b Laguay, Mo, Dec 21, 28; s James Harry Thompson & Pearl Robertson T; m 1957 to Juanita Christine Hale; c Steven Drake & Laurie Rena. Educ: Humboldt State Col, 55-56. Polit & Govt Pos: Campaign chmn, State Senate Cand, Calif, 68; assoc mem, Humboldt Co Rep Cent Comt, 69-; mem, Calif State Rep Cent Comt, 69- Bus & Prof Pos: Realtor, Calif Real Estate Assoc, 57- Mil Serv: Entered as Pvt, Marines, 52, released as Cpl, 54, after serv in First Marine Air Wing. Mailing Add: 1212 Fern Dr Eureka CA 95501

THOMPSON, WILLIAM KEITH (D)
b Lima, Ohio, Feb 26, 54; s Reed Thompson & Marjory Jan Schoonover T; single. Educ: Ohio State Univ, 73- Polit & Govt Pos: Co coordr, Metzenbaum for US Senate Campaign, 70; mem, Citizens Task Force on Youth of Ohio, 71; mem, Gov Coord Coun on Drug Abuse, 71; intern, Off of US Sen Harold E Hughes, Iowa, 71; mem, Allen Co Dem Exec Comt, Ohio, 71-75; deleg & mem selection comt, Ohio Dem Party, 72; deleg, Dem Nat Conv, 72; Dem Presidential elector, 72; deleg, Dem Nat Mid-Term Conf, 74; staff asst, US Sen Howard M Metzenbaum, Ohio, currently. Honors & Awards: Outstanding Am High Sch Students, 72. Mailing Add: 3-B Mews Rd Lima OH 45805

THOMSON, HAROLD E (R)
NH State Rep
Mailing Add: PO Box 62 Weare NH 03281

THOMSON, JAMES CLAUDE, JR (D)
Mem Int Affairs Comt, Dem Policy Coun
b Princeton, NJ, Sept 14, 31; s James Claude Thomson & Margaret Cook T; m 1959 to Diana Duffy. Educ: Univ Nanking, China, 48-49; Yale Univ, BA, 53; Cambridge Univ, Eng, BA, 55, MA, 59; Harvard Univ, PhD, 61; Phi Beta Kappa; Zeta Psi; Scroll & Key. Polit & Govt Pos: Spec asst to Gov Chester Bowles, Conn, 56; spec asst to US Congressman, 59-61; spec asst to Undersecy of State, 61; spec asst to President's Spec Rep & Adv on African, Asian & Latin Am Affairs, 61-63; spec asst to Asst Secy of State for Far Eastern Affairs, 63-64; staff mem, Nat Security Coun, 64-66; mem int affairs comt, Dem Policy Coun, 69- Bus & Prof

Pos: Teaching fel & tutor, Harvard Univ, 56-59, asst prof hist & research fel, Kennedy Inst of Polit, 66-70, lectr hist, Univ, 70-; mem bd dirs, Nat Comt on US-China Rels, 69-; mem adv bd, Washington Monthly, 69-; mem ed bd, Foreign Policy, 70- Publ: While China Faced West, Harvard Univ Press, 69; Dragon under glass—time for a new China policy, 10/67 & How could Vietnam happen?, 4/68, Atlantic Monthly. Mem: Am Hist Asn; Asn Asian Studies; Elizabethan. Honors & Awards: Overseas Press Club Award for Mag Writing on Foreign Affairs, 68. Relig: Presbyterian. Legal Res: 21 Sibley Ct Cambridge MA 02138 Mailing Add: East Asian Research Center 1737 Cambridge St Cambridge MA 02138

THOMSON, JAMES MCILHANY (D)
Va State Deleg
b New Orleans, La, Aug 9, 24; s Paul Jones Thomson & Gretchen Bigelow T; m 1952 to Sarah Edna Jennings; div; c Sarah Jennings & Teresa Lindsay. Educ: Va Mil Inst, AB, 47; Univ Va, LLB, 50; Beta Theta Pi. Polit & Govt Pos: Clerk to Judge Bennett Champ Clark, US Court of Appeals, DC, 50-51; mem prof staff, US Senate Judiciary Comt, 51-52; Va State Deleg, 56-, majority leader, floor leader & chmn, Privileges & Elec Comt, Va House Deleg, 68- Bus & Prof Pos: Partner, Clarke, Richard Moncure & Whitehead, 53-63; dir & secy, Fidelity Savings & Loan Asn, 62-65; attorney, James M Thomson, 63-65 & 67-; chmn bd & pres, City Bank & Trust Co, 64-69; partner, Thomson, Gannon, Thomas & Cacheris, 65-67; dir, Dom Nat Bank & Dom Bankshares, 69-; mem bd, Washington & Lee Savings & Loan Asn, 72-; vpres, First Financial of Va. Mil Serv: Entered as Pvt, Marines, 43, released as 2nd Lt, 46; Am Theater Ribbon; Good Conduct Medal. Mem: Am Legion; 40 et 8; Eagles; Odd Fellows; Alexandria CofC. Honors & Awards: Distinguished Serv Award, Jr CofC, 55. Relig: Episcopal. Legal Res: 801 N Pitt St Alexandria VA 22314 Mailing Add: PO Box 1138 Alexandria VA 22313

THOMSON, LEONARD S (R)
Mem, Rep State Cent Comt, Calif
b San Diego, Calif, Oct 6, 12; s Albert Charles Thomson & Ernestina Louise Fisher T; m 1939 to Helen Grady; c Carol Helen. Educ: Calif Col China; Phi Chi. Polit & Govt Pos: Mem, Rep State Cent Comt, Calif, 48-; mem, Kern Co Rep Cent Comt & chmn, 60-64; dir, Kern Co Water Dist; mem, State Park & Recreation Comn, 67-, state chmn, 69- Bus & Prof Pos: Employ with Evans MacCormack & Co, Inc, Stock & Bonds & production mgt, Honolulu Oil Corp. Mil Serv: Entered as Lt, Army, 42, released as Capt, 47, after serv as Liaison Officer & Field Comdr, Chinese Supreme Command, China, 44-46; two Bronze Stars; Purple Heart; Meritorious Serv Medal; China Theater Ribbon with three Battle Stars; China White Cloud Medal. Publ: The White Snake, Greenwich, 60. Mem: Am Petroleum Inst; Rotary Int; Farm Bur; Am Legion; DAV. Honors & Awards: Voted Outstanding Citizen of West Side, 58. Relig: Presbyterian. Mailing Add: 111 East Lucard St Taft CA 93268

THOMSON, MELDRIM, JR (R)
Gov, NH
b Pittsburgh, Pa, Mar 8, 12; m; c four sons & two daughters. Educ: Univ Miami; Mercer Univ; Univ Ga, LLB. Polit & Govt Pos: Gov, NH, 73- Bus & Prof Pos: Founder & 20 years pres, Equity Publ Co, Orford, NH; former mem & chmn Stony Brook, Long Island Sch Bd; former mem & chmn, Orford, NH Sch Bd; former instr polit sci, Univ Ga. Mem: Pub Sch Asn (co-founder); Bar of Ga, Fla & Supreme Court of US. Relig: Baptist. Mailing Add: State Capitol Concord NH 03301

THOMSON, THYRA GODFREY (R)
Secy of State, Wyo
b Florence, Colo, July 30, 16; d John Godfrey & Rosalie Altman G; m 1939 to Edwin Keith Thomson, wid Dec, 1960; c William John, II, Bruce Godfrey & Keith Coffey. Educ: Univ Wyo, BA Psychol, cum laude, 39; Alpha Kappa Psi; Psi Chi; Pi Beta Phi; Iron Skull; Spurs. Polit & Govt Pos: Mem, Marshall Scholarships Comt, Pac Region, 64-68; deleg, 72nd Int Wilton Park Conf, Eng, 65; sponsor, Atlantic Coun of the US, 65; chmn, Pub Lands Comt, West Conf of the Coun of State Govts, 65-66; Secy of State, Wyo, currently; mem, Allied Health Prof Coun, Dept of Health, Educ & Welfare, 71-73. Bus & Prof Pos: Pres, NAm Securities Adminrs, 73- Publ: Watching Washington, column in 14 newspapers, while living in nation's capital, 54-60; Second thoughts on woman's lib, Reader's Digest, 6/71. Mem: Alpha Chap, Omicron Delta Epsilon; Beta Gamma Sigma; Wyo Press Women; PEO. Honors & Awards: Received Distinguished Alumni Award, Univ Wyo, 69; Selected Woman of Distinction for 69-71, Int Conv on Alpha Delta Kappa, Hon Soc of Women Educators. Relig: Presbyterian. Mailing Add: 204 E 22nd St Cheyenne WY 82001

THOMSON, VERNON WALLACE (R)
b Richland Center, Wis, Nov 5, 05; s A A Thomson & Ella Wallace T; m 1936 to Helen A Davis, wid 1973; c Susan (Mrs Robert Turner), Patricia M & Vernon W, Jr. Educ: Carroll Col, Waukesha, Wis, 23-25; Univ Wis-Madison, BA, 27; Univ Wis Law Sch, Madison, LLB, 32; Order of Coif; Phi Delta Phi; Chi Phi. Hon Degrees: LLD, Carroll Col, 57. Polit & Govt Pos: Wis State Assemblyman, 35-51, speaker of assembly, 39, 41 & 43 & Rep Floor Leader, 45, 47 & 49; Attorney Gen, Wis, 51-57, Gov, 57-59; US Rep, Wis, 60-75; mem, Fed Elec Comn, 75- Bus & Prof Pos: Teacher, Viroqua, Wis, 27-29; attorney-at-law, Richland Center, 32-; C C C Enrolling Off for Richland Co, 33-35; city attorney, Richland Center, 33-37 & 42-44; pres, Richland Center Libr Bd, 39-51; mayor, Richland Center, 44-51. Mem: Wis & Am Bar Asns; Mason (33 degree). Relig: Presbyterian. Legal Res: 578 E Second St Richland Center WI 53581 Mailing Add: 6213 Kellogg Dr McLean VA 22101

THONE, CHARLES (R)
US Rep, Nebr
b Cedar Co, Nebr; m to Ruth Raymond; c three. Educ: Univ Nebr Law Sch, LLB, 50. Polit & Govt Pos: Dep secy of state, Nebr, 50-51; asst attorney gen for Clarence Beck, Nebr, 51-52; Nebr rep, US Sen Dwight P Griswold 51-52; chmn, Lancaster Co, Nebr Young Rep, state chmn, nat committeeman, cand for nat pres, 52, jr pres, Rep Founders' Day, 53; Rep Presidential Elector, Nebr, 52, 56, 60 & 68; deleg-at-lg, Rep Nat Conv, 52 & 60, deleg & chmn Nebr deleg, 72; asst, US Dist Attorney, Lincoln Off, 52-54; admin asst, US Sen Roman Hruska, Nebr, 54-59; chmn, Nebr State Rep Cent Comt, 59-61; mem, Rep Nat Comt, 59-61; Rep nominee, Lt Gov, 64; US Rep, Nebr, 71- Bus & Prof Pos: Farm owner, Cedar Co, Nebr; attorney, private practice, 59-71. Mil Serv: NCO & off, Inf, World War II, 3 1/2 years. Mem: Jaycees (state pres, 53-54); Lincoln Am Legion Post 3; Hartington VFW Post 5283; Lincoln Elks Lodge 80; State Hist Soc. Honors & Awards: Selected Lincoln's Outstanding Young Man, 53; elected to State Supreme Court Judicial Nomination Comn for six year term. Legal Res: 1344 C St Lincoln NE 68506 Mailing Add: US House of Rep Washington DC 20515

THOR, JOHN CARL (D)
b Stanton, Nebr, Dec 8, 18; father deceased; m 1941 to Joan Drahota; c David John, Timothy Craig, John Michael & James John. Polit & Govt Pos: Mem, Nebr Dem State Cent Comt, 66 & 68; chmn, Stanton Co Dem Party, formerly; mem, Ninth Dist Court Judicial Nominating Conv, currently. Bus & Prof Pos: Chmn, Stanton Pilger Drainage Dist, 67- Mem: Norfolk Bd Realtors; Home Builders; life mem Cattle Feeders Asn; KofC. Legal Res: RFD Norfolk NE 68701 Mailing Add: Stanton NE 68779

THORNBERRY, WILLIAM HOMER (D)
b Austin, Tex, Jan 09, 09; s William Moore Thornberry & Mary Lillian Jones T; m 1945 to Eloise Engle; c Molly, David & Kate. Educ: Univ Tex, BBA, 32; LLB, 36; hon mem, Order of the Coif. Hon Degrees: LLD, Gallaudet Col. Polit & Govt Pos: Tex State Rep, 37-40; dist attorney, Travis Co, Tex, 41-42; mem, City Coun, Austin, 46-48; mayor pro tem, 47-48; US Rep, Tex, 49-63; deleg-at-lg, Dem Nat Conv, 56 & 60; US Dist Judge, Western Dist, Tex, 63-65; US Judge Court Appeals, 65- Bus & Prof Pos: Law practice, Austin, 36- Mil Serv: Lt Comdr, Navy, 42-46. Mem: Am Legion; Mason (32 degree); KCCH; Shrine; Kiwanis. Honors & Awards: Silver Beaver Award, Boy Scouts; Distinguished Alumnus Award, Ex-Students' Asn, Univ Tex, 65. Relig: Methodist. Legal Res: 1403 Hardouin St Austin TX 78703 Mailing Add: US Court House Austin TX 78701

THORNBURGH, RICHARD
Asst Attorney Gen Criminal Div, Dept Justice
Mailing Add: Dept of Justice Washington DC 20301

THORNE, ROBERT FREEMAN (D)
Ore State Sen
Mailing Add: 771 Ponderosa Village Burns OR 97720

THORNHILL, LYNN (R)
Okla State Rep
b Sand Creek, Okla, Sept 24, 04; s William Andrew Thornhill & Mary Edna Witt T; m 1925 to Maurine Allie Garrett; c Beverly Lynn (Mrs Leonard A Gibson) & Sharon Adair (Mrs Jerry Harris). Educ: Wakita Pub Schs, Okla. Polit & Govt Pos: Mem, Wakita Town Bd, Okla, 48-62 & mayor, Wakita, 50-62; Okla State Rep, 39th Dist, 62-, asst Rep caucus chmn, Okla House Rep, 65 & 67-68, asst minority floor leader, 71-; mem, Okla World Fair Comn, 63-64. Bus & Prof Pos: Owner, Thornhill Serv, 32 years; partner, Thornhill-Gibson Oil Co, 22 years. Mem: Shrine; Consistory; Mason (past master); Lions (past pres); Alumni Asn (past pres). Relig: Baptist. Mailing Add: PO Box 25 Wakita OK 73771

THORNTON, DAVID F (R)
Va State Sen
Mailing Add: 324 Hawthorn Rd Salem VA 24143

THORNTON, EDMUND BRAXTON (R)
b Chicago, Ill, Mar 9, 30; s George A. Thornton & Suzanne Woodward T; m 1964 to Elizabeth Oakes Moore; c twins Jonathan Butler & Thomas Volney & twins Susan Oakes & Amanda Braxton. Educ: Yale Univ, BA, 54; Delta Kappa Epsilon. Polit & Govt Pos: Mem, Bd Gov, United Rep Fund of Ill, 62-74, Exec Comt, 69-74, vpres & dir, 72-74; deleg, Rep Nat Conv, 68, hon deleg, 72; mem, LaSalle Co Rep Finance Comt, 69; chmn, All-Ill Victory Gala, 69; downstate chmn, Salute to the President Dinner, 71; coordr cent region, Ill Businessmen for Nixon, 72; downstate chmn, Ill Victory '72 Dinner, 72. Bus & Prof Pos: Pres & chief exec officer, Ottawa Silica Co, 62- Mil Serv: Entered Marine Corps Reserve, 50-58, released as 1st Lt, 56, after serv in Active Serv Rifle Co G, 1st Marine Div. Publ: Marines in the Civil War, Civil War Round Table of LaSalle Co, 63; Architectural Tour of Ottawa, Ill, LaSalle Co, 69. Mem: Ill Mfr Asn (dir, 66-); Assoc Employers of Ill (adv bd, 69-); Nat Recreation & Parks Asn (chmn exec comt, 74-); Ill State CofC (dir, 72-); LaSalle Co Hist Soc. Honors & Awards: George Washington Citizen of Year Award, 67; Distinguished Serv Award, Ottawa Jaycees, 69; Outstanding Serv Award, United Rep Fund of Ill, 71; Appreciation Award, Ill Dept of Conserv, 72. Relig: Congregational. Legal Res: RR 1 Ottawa IL 61350 Mailing Add: PO Box 1 Ottawa IL 61350

THORNTON, JAMES RONALD (R)
Chmn, Fla Fedn of Young Rep
b Fayetteville, Tenn, Aug 19, 39; s James A Thornton & Thelma McGee T; m 1964 to Mary Elizabeth Packard; c Nancy. Educ: Berry Col, BS in Physics-Math, 61; Wake Forest Univ, MA in Physics, 63; Univ Ala, Huntsville, 65-66; Rollins Col, 70. Polit & Govt Pos: First vpres, Orange Co Young Rep Club, 69-70, pres, 70-71; precinct committeeman, Orange Co Rep Exec Comt, 70-71; treas, Fla Fedn of Young Rep, 71-72, chmn, 72-; mem, Orange Co Comt to Reelect President Nixon, 72; chmn, Young Rep Nat Fedn Platform Comt, 73. Bus & Prof Pos: Research physicist, Brown Eng Co, Huntsville, Ala, 63-66; sr staff engr, Martin-Marietta Corp, Orlando, Fla, 66- Publ: Co-auth, Fluid flow measurements with a laser doppler velocimeter, J Quantum Electronics, 8/66; auth, Properties of neodymium doped laser materials, Applied Optics, 6/69; Properties of sensitize erbium laser materials, Dept of Defense Conf on Laser Technol 1/70; plus over 30 tech papers & reports on laser eng appln. Mem: Inst for Elec & Electronic Engrs. Honors & Awards: Auth-of-the-year $1000 Award, Martin Marietta Corp, 70; Outstanding Proj Chmn, 70 & Outstanding Club Chmn, 71, Fla Young Rep; Named to Outstanding Young Men of Am, 73. Relig: Methodist. Mailing Add: 237 Blossom Lane Winter Park FL 32789

THORNTON, JEAN TYROL (R)
Conn State Rep
b Glastonbury, Conn, Sept 28, 21; d Edward Howard Tyrol & Olive Bidwell T; div; c Malcolm E, Kirk R & Barbara J. Educ: Glastonbury High Sch, grad. Polit & Govt Pos: Registr of voters, Glastonbury, Conn, 56-62; vchmn, Rep Town Comt, Glastonbury, 58-65; Conn State Rep, 63-; alt deleg, Rep Nat Conv, 68. Mil Serv: Entered as Pvt, Women's Army Corps, 42, released as 2nd Lt, 44. Relig: Congregational. Mailing Add: 28 Grayfeather Lane Glastonbury CT 06033

THORNTON, LA-VERNE W (R)
Chmn, Chatham Co Rep Party, NC
b Pittsylvania Co, Va, Feb 17, 37; s Perry James Thornton & Ethel Pruitt T; m 1957 to Alma Lucille Baker; c La-Visa Jo & Perry James. Educ: Va Polytech Inst, BS, 59. Polit & Govt Pos: Chmn, Chatham Co Rep Party, NC, 66-; town councilman, Goldston, NC, 66-; fourth cong dist chmn, Nixon Campaign, NC, 68; chmn, Fourth Dist Rep Party, 70- Bus & Prof Pos: Plant mgr, Pomona Pipe Prod, Gulf, NC, 69- Mem: Lions; Jaycees. Relig: Methodist. Legal Res: Windsow & Goldbar Goldston NC 27252 Mailing Add: PO Box 133 Goldston NC 27252

THORNTON, O FRANK (D)
Secy of State, SC
b Mullins, July 26, 05; s Oscar Fontaine Thornton (deceased) & Lucend Cooper T (deceased); m 1933 to Rosa Waring; c Rosa (Mrs J M Cherry, Jr) & Frances (Mrs Roy H Shelton). Educ: Univ SC, LLB, 28. Polit & Govt Pos: Mem, Dem Exec Comt & State & Co Elec Bd, SC; SC State Rep, 35-36, reading clerk, SC House of Rep, 36-50; Secy of State, SC, 50- Bus & Prof Pos: Ed, Clover Herald; attorney-at-law & city attorney, Clover. Mem: Lions; Nat Asn of Secy of State; Elks; Mason; SC State Libr (bd trustees). Relig: Methodist. Mailing Add: 712 Arbutus Dr Columbia SC 29205

THORNTON, R H, JR (RAY) (D)
US Rep, Ark
b Conway, Ark, July 16, 28; s R H Thornton & Wilma Stephens T; m 1956 to Betty Jo Mann; c Nancy, Mary & Stephanie. Educ: State Col Ark; Yale Univ, BA Polit Sci, 50; Univ Tex; Univ Ark, JD, 56; pres, Student Body, Univ Ark, 55-56; Sigma Chi; Blue Key; Phi Eta Sigma; Tau Kappa Alpha. Polit & Govt Pos: Dep prosecuting attorney, Sixth Judicial Circuit, Ark, 56-57; former mem & chmn, Ark State Bd Law Exam; deleg, Seventh Const Conv, Grant & Jefferson Co, 69-70; chmn, Exec Br Comt; Attorney Gen, Ark, 70-73; US Rep, Fourth Dist, Ark, 73-; ex-officio, Dem Nat Mid-Term Conf, 74. Mil Serv: Navy, serv as signal off, opers off & navigator aboard the USS Philippine Sea & the USS Gen A E Anderson, Korean War. Mem: Am Judicature Soc; Am Trial Lawyers Asn; Yale Alumni Fund; Harding Col (chmn, Pres Develop Coun); Rotary. Legal Res: AR Mailing Add: 1109 House Off Bldg Washington DC 20515

THORNTON, WILLIAM JOSEPH (D)
City Councilman, Jersey City, NJ
b Louisville, Ga, Jan 3, 30; s William J Thornton & Lucille Spinks T; m 1953 to Anne Wallace; c Leslie Anne, Pamela Joi & William J, III. Educ: Seton Hall Univ, BS, 52, MBA, 54; NY Law Sch, LLB, 60. Polit & Govt Pos: City Councilman, Jersey City, NJ, 69-; deleg, Dem Nat Conv, 72; bd mem, Jersey City Med Ctr, 72-, Jersey City Welfare Bd, 72- & Jersey City Bd Sch Estimate, 73-; chmn, Regional Black Caucus, NJ, NY, PR & VI, currently. Mil Serv: Entered as Pvt, Army, 54, released as Cpl, 56, after serv in Artillery, Europe, 55-56; Good Conduct Award; Sharpshooter Award. Mem: Red Cross (bd, Jersey City Chap); Salvation Army (bd, Hudson Co Chap); Jersey City Merchants Asn (bd); NAACP (exec bd, 65-66); CofC. Honors & Awards: Merit Award, William J Thornton Asn, 69; Distinguished Citizen Award, LeBastions, Inc, 71; Outstanding Achievement Award, Hudson Co Black Firefighters Asn, 72. Relig: Roman Catholic. Mailing Add: 344 Arlington Ave Jersey City NJ 07304

THORP, JOHN S, JR (D)
NY State Assemblyman
b Rockville Center, NY, Sept 29, 25; m to Dolores Hartig; c John, Richard & Patricia. Educ: Holy Cross Col, 45; Brooklyn Law Sch, 49. Polit & Govt Pos: Pres, Dem Club, formerly; Dem Co Committeeman, NY, 46-; NY State Assemblyman, 64- Bus & Prof Pos: Attorney. Mil Serv: Navy, World War II. Mem: NY State & Nassau Co Bar Asns; Cath Lawyer Guild; CofC; NY Bar Found. Mailing Add: 92 Voorhis Ave Rockville Centre NY 11570

THORP, MITCHELL LEON (D)
Mem Exec Comt, Wash Co Dem Org Tenn
b Knoxville, Tenn, July 1, 10; s Benjamin Thorp & Molly Gerber T; m 1942 to Hilda Rose Rapport; c Stephanie Mae, Allan Bertram & Marjorie Jean. Educ: Univ Baltimore, LLB, 34; Nu Beta Epsilon. Polit & Govt Pos: Deleg, Dem Nat Conv, 64 & mem, Permanent Orgn Comt, 64; deleg, Tenn State Dem Conv, 64; chmn, Johnson City Area Indust Comn, 66; vmayor, Johnson City, 66; mem exec comt, Wash Co Dem Orgn, currently; mem, Tenn Indust Comn, 68; mem urban govt affairs comt, Nat Asn Home Builders, 69. Bus & Prof Pos: Pres, Thorp & Co, Inc, ETenn Enterprises & Johnson City Yankees, 66-; vpres, Tenn Iron & Paper Inc & Standard Steel Cabinet, 66- Mem: CofC; Rotary; Mason; Shrine; Elks. Honors & Awards: Received Nat Merit Award, Little League Baseball, 63; Mr Baseball, Park & Recreation Award, 65. Relig: Jewish; pres, B'nai Sholom Congregation. Mailing Add: 1312 Iris Ave Johnson City TN 37601

THORPE, THOMAS KEANE (R)
Attorney Gen, Am Samoa
b Portland, Ore, July 29, 30; s Walter Theodore Thorpe & Rose Keane T; m 1952 to Gloria Hibbitt; c Melissa, Juliet, Adrianne, Helena, Diana & Thomas J. Educ: Univ Ore, BS, 52; Northwestern Col Law, JD, 58; Phi Delta Theta; Delta Theta Phi. Polit & Govt Pos: Bar rep, Ore Judicial Coun, 68-69; Attorney Gen, Am Samoa, 69- Bus & Prof Pos: Ins adjuster, Md Casualty Co, Portland, Ore, 55-58; private law practice, 58-61; law partner, Williams, Montague, Stark & Thorpe, 61-69 & Cookingham & Maletis, 71- Mil Serv: Entered as A/S, Coast Guard, 53, released as Lt (jg), 55, after serv in CGC Winnebago, 14th Coast Guard Dist, 53-55; Lt Comdr, Coast Guard, Res, 63-; UN, Korean & Am Defense Serv Ribbons; 10 year Res Ribbon. Mem: Am Judicature Soc; Multnomah Athletic Club; ROA; Elks; YMCA. Relig: Catholic. Mailing Add: 2871 NE Alameda Portland OR 97212

THORSGARD, ENOCH ARNOLD (R)
NDak State Rep
b Northwood, NDak, Mar 30, 17; s Arne Thorsgard & Clara Markve T; m 1942 to Madeline Wasness; c Carol (Mrs Harold Luke), Graydon, Betty, John & Ruth. Educ: NDak State Univ, short agr course. Polit & Govt Pos: Rep precinct committeeman, Lind Twp, NDak, 50-; NDak State Rep, 19th Dist, 69- Bus & Prof Pos: Owner & operator, Sunrise Acres, 41-; pres & treas, Basevieu Champlin Inc, 65- Mem: Fed Land Bank Asn, Grand Forks (dir); Gtr NDak Asn; Lions; Farm Bur; Northwood Hosp & Home Asn (dir). Honors & Awards: Outstanding Young Farmer of Grand Forks trade area, 53. Relig: Lutheran. Legal Res: Northwood ND 58267 Mailing Add: State Capitol Bismarck ND 58501

THORSON, HARRY T (R)
b Milan, Minn, Aug 17, 02; s Gulmun Thorson & Anne Graves T; m 1929 to Inga C Gysland; c James Donald, Thomas Alan & Mary Lynn (Mrs David Gullickson). Educ: Dak Bus Col, 18-19; Fargo Col. Polit & Govt Pos: Rep precinct committeeman, Osage, Wyo, 36-40; committeeman, Wyo State Rep Party, Weston Co, 40-54, chmn, Wyo State Rep Party, 55-60; Rep Nat Committeeman, 60-65; mem, Wyo Judicial Nominating Comn, currently. Bus & Prof Pos: From laborer to dist foreman, Ill Pipe Line Co, 23-33; drilling & prod supt, Osage Trust, 33-42. Mem: Rocky Mountain Oil & Gas Asn (dir); Wyo Mining Asn (dir); Wyo Taxpayers Asn (dir); Mason; Fedn Rocky Mountain States (dir). Relig: Lutheran. Mailing Add: 26 S Senecca Newcastle WY 82701

THORSON, JUDITH MARY (DFL)
Secy, Becker Co Dem-Farmer-Labor Party, Minn
b St Cloud, Minn, May 13, 39; d Donald Howard Burgett & Dorothy H Erickson B; m 1958 to Lloyd Edward Thorson, Jr; c Daniel, Steven, Mark, Scott & Heidi. Educ: St Olaf Col, 57-58; Moorhead State Col, BS, 71. Polit & Govt Pos: Chmn, Becker Co Dem-Farmer-Labor Party, Minn, 68-70, secy, 70- Bus & Prof Pos: Dir, Becker Co Day Activity Ctr, 71- Mem: Beta Sigma Phi. Relig: Lutheran. Mailing Add: 1032 Summit Ave Detroit Lakes MN 56501

THORSTEN, BERNECE MARIE (DFL)
First VChmn, Wash Co Dem-Farmer-Labor Party, Minn
b St Paul, Minn, June 1, 22; d Harry Leroy McKinney & Theresa Jaschke M; m 1946 to Lyle Palmer Thorsten; c John, Thomas, Barbara, Beth, Peter & Gregory. Educ: Monroe High Sch, grad; Bus Sch, 3 months. Polit & Govt Pos: First vchmn, Wash Co Dem-Farmer-Labor Party, Minn, 70- Mil Serv: Entered as Pvt, Women's Marine Corps, 43, released as Cpl, 44, after serv in Henderson Hall, Arlington, Va. Mem: Am Legion (comdr, Serv Womens Post 516); PTA (pres, Maplewood Jr High Sch); Guardian Angels Altar & Rosary Soc (pres). Relig: Catholic. Mailing Add: 3456 Hudson Rd Lake Elmo MN 55042

THOUTSIS, TIMOTHEOS MICHAEL (R)
Chmn, Paxton Rep Town Comt, Mass
b Epirus, Greece, May 27, 27; s Haralambos Michael Thoutsis & Helen Liazos T; m 1958 to Candy Latham. Educ: Worcester Jr Col, AA, 48; Syracuse Univ, BS, 50. Polit & Govt Pos: State examr, Mass Dept Ins, 54-; vpres, Young Men's Rep Club, 55-56, pres, 56-57; finance chmn, Paxton Rep Town Comt, 64-65, chmn, 66-; deleg, Mass Rep State Conv, 70; Paxton coordr for Sargent-Dwight & Si Spaulding, 70; Paxton coordr to Reelect the President, 72. Bus & Prof Pos: Distributor, Procter & Gamble, 51-52; asst buyer, Filene's, 52-53. Mil Serv: Navy, World War II. Mem: Syracuse Univ Alumni of Gtr Worcester; Paxton Bd of Appeals; DAV; Am Legion. Relig: Greek Orthodox. Mailing Add: 6 William Allen Dr Paxton MA 01612

THULL, EUGENE NICHOLAS (D)
b Cawker City, Kans, Feb 12, 16; s John George Thull & Florence Smith T; m 1945 to Frances Kathryn Heinen; c Barbara, Tracy, Michael, Virginia & Scott. Educ: Salt City Bus Col. Polit & Govt Pos: Chmn, Mitchell Co Dem Party, Kans, formerly; councilman, Cawker City, 61-66 & 68- Mil Serv: Entered as Pvt, Air Force, 42, released as T/Sgt, 45, after serv in Southeastern Tech Training Command. Mem: KofC 1868; Am Legion; Lions. Relig: Catholic. Mailing Add: Box 106 Cawker City KS 67430

THURBER, MARY D (R)
Committeewoman, Vt Rep State Comt
b Prairie du Chien, Wis, Aug 5, 12; d Louis De Vierville Dousman & Sarah Easton D; m 1933 to Richard Bourne Thurber; c Mary T (Mrs Ralph H Clark, III), Julia B (Mrs J Dynan Candon) & W S Thurber. Educ: Carleton Col, AB, 33; Phi Beta Kappa. Polit & Govt Pos: Chmn, Dist 30, Vt, 64-66; Vt State Rep, Dist 30, formerly; pres, Vt Citizens League, Inc, 72-; committeewoman, Vt Rep State Comt, 72- Mem: Farm Bur; Chittenden Co Red Cross (dir); Vt Coun on World Affairs. Relig: Episcopal. Mailing Add: West Wind Farm Charlotte VT 05445

THURM, WILLIAM HENRY (D)
Mem, Calif Dem State Cent Comt
b Otterville, Ill, Oct 26, 06; s Carl Henry Thurm & Mary Welch T; m 1944 to Lorene Bernice O'Dell; c Mark William. Educ: Medora High Sch, Ill, grad, 26; Beaumont Night Sch, St Louis, Mo, Business, 28; Kroger Bus Admin, 30. Polit & Govt Pos: Mem, Kern Co Dem Cent Comt, Calif, 60-; mem, Calif Dem State Cent Comt, 60-; area chmn for Gov Pat Brown & Lt Gov Glenn Anderson Campaigns, Calif, 62-66; pres, Desert Empire Dem Club, Ridgecrest, 62- Bus & Prof Pos: Owner, W H Thurm Co (Sewing Machines), 50- Publ: The sewing family, Elna Co, Geneva, Switz (Elna News), 66. Mem: Elks (charter mem, Ridgecrest); Toastmasters Int; AFL Plumbers & Steamfitters Local Union 460 (Bakersfield); Amateur Trapshooting Asn (Vandalia, Ohio nat shooter, 50-). Honors & Awards: Winner of trip to Europe, World Contest of Necchi-Elna, 57; 1/4 Century Mem, AFL, 67. Relig: Protestant. Mailing Add: 333 N Sanders Ridgecrest CA 93555

THURMAN, JOHN EDWARD (D)
Calif State Assemblyman
b Richmond, Calif, May 6, 20; s Anne L Petersen T, (father deceased); m 1947 to Julia; c Robert, Susan & Janice. Educ: Ceres High Sch, grad, 38. Polit & Govt Pos: Mem, Hart Ransom Union Sch Dist Bd Educ, Stanislaus Co, 60-70; mem bd supvrs, 70-72; Calif State Assemblyman, 72- Mil Serv: Entered as Pvt, Army, 41, released as Sgt, 45, after serv in anti-aircraft/inf; Good Conduct & Am Theatre Medals. Mem: League of Calif Milk Producers (dir); Stanislaus Co Farm Bur (chmn); Am Legion Post 74; KofC; Elks. Honors & Awards: San Joaquin Co Sr Citizen Placque; Many Young People Awards. Relig: Catholic. Mailing Add: 202 Meadow Lane Modesto CA 95351

THURMAN, JOHN HOWARD (R)
b Americus, Ga, July 10, 26; s James Howard Thurman & Bertha Schroeder T; m 1951 to Mary Anne Thomas; c John Howard, Jr, C Michael, Susan Ann, Martha Kay & Thomas D. Educ: Ga Inst Technol, BSChE, 47; Kappa Alpha. Polit & Govt Pos: Chmn, Peach Co Rep Comt, Ga, formerly. Bus & Prof Pos: Plant engr, Woolfolk Chem Works, Ft Valley, Ga, 47-58; plant supt, 58- Mil Serv: Entered as A/S, Naval Res, 44, released as Ens, 46. Mem: Kiwanis. Relig: Roman Catholic. Mailing Add: RFD 1 Box 6 Ft Valley GA 31030

THURMAN, MARJORIE CLARK (D)
Chmn, Dem Party Ga
b Atlanta, Ga, June 17, 28; d Henry Clay Clark & Jessie Early Clark Boynton; m 1948 to Ross H Thurman; c Sandra Lynn. Educ: Emory Univ, 45-46; Draughon Sch Commerce, 46-47; Atlanta Law Sch, LLB, 49, LLM, 50. Polit & Govt Pos: Young Dem Committeewoman, 57-63, pres, Fulton Co Young Dem, Ga, 58-62; gen counsel, Young Dem of Am, 59-61; mem, Presidential Inaugural Comt, 60; deleg, NATO Exchange of Young Polit Leaders, 61; mem, Ga State Dem Exec Comt, 63-72; Dem Nat Committeewoman, Ga, 63-72; deleg, Dem Nat Conv, 64, 68 & 72, mem platform & arrangements comts, 64, mem site comt & comt on permanent orgn, 68; Dem nominee, Judge of Superior Court, Fulton Co, Ga, 72; chmn, Dem Party Ga, 74-; mem, Dem Nat Comt, 74- Bus & Prof Pos: Practice of law, 49-; mem, Law Firm of King, Thurman & Marshall, 56- Mem: Old War Horse Lawyers Club; Am Judicature Soc; Equity Club; Women's CofC; Kidney Found of Ga (bd trustees). Relig: Methodist. Legal Res: 5450 Glenridge Dr NE Atlanta GA 30342 Mailing Add: 1020 Edgewood Ave NE Atlanta GA 30307

THURMOND, EDWIN M (R)
Chmn, Calloway Co Rep Comt, Ky
b Murray, Ky, Dec 31, 16; s Luby F Thurmond & Ruby Miller T; m 1942 to Virginia Gephart; c Ed Michael & Patricia Louise. Educ: Murray State Univ, 34-37. Polit & Govt Pos: Secy, Calloway Co Rep Orgn, 46-50 & 52-55 & treas, 50-52; chmn, Calloway Co Rep Comt, Ky, 56- Bus & Prof Pos: Owner & operator, Thurmond's Coal & Feed Mill of Murray Ky; partner, Leon Smith, Ky Country Ham Oper, Hazel, Ky. Mil Serv: Entered as Pvt, Army, 41, released as Sgt, 45, after serv in Med Corps, US. Mem: Am Legion; Moose; Am Feed Dealers Asn; Nat CofC; Nat Fedn of Independent Businessmen. Relig: Church of Christ. Legal Res: 203 S 13th St Murray KY 42071 Mailing Add: Box 143 Murray KY 42071

THURMOND, STROM (R)
US Sen, SC
b Edgefield, SC, Dec 5, 02; s John William Thurmond & Eleanor Gertrude Strom T; m 1947 to Jean Crouch, deceased 1960; m 1968 to Nancy Moore; c Nancy Moore & J Strom, Jr. Educ: Clemson Col, BS, 23; State of SC Law Course, 30. Hon Degrees: LLD, Bob Jones Univ, 48, Presby Col, 60, Clemson Col, 61 & Lander Col, 73; DMS, The Citadel, 61; LHD, Trinity Col, 65; LittD, Calif Grad Sch Theol, 70. Polit & Govt Pos: City & co attorney, several years; co supt educ, 29-33; deleg, Dem Nat Conv, 32, 36, 48, 52, 56 & 60, chmn SC deleg & Nat committeeman, 48; SC State Sen, 33-38; circuit judge, 38-46; Gov, SC, 47-51; States' Rights Dem cand, President, US, 48; chmn, Southern Gov Conf, 50; US Sen, SC, 54-, ranking Rep on Armed Serv Comt & mem, Judiciary, Vet Affairs & Defense Appropriations Comts, US Senate, currently; deleg, Rep Nat Conv, 68 & 72. Bus & Prof Pos: Farmer; athletic coach & teacher, 23-29; admitted to SC Bar, 30; attorney-at-law, 30-38 & 51-55; admitted to practice in all Fed Courts including US Supreme Court. Mil Serv: Army, 42-46, serv in Hq, First Army, 82nd Airborne Div, Europe & Pac Theaters & Normandy Invasion; Maj Gen, Army Res; five Battle Stars; Legion of Merit & Oak Leaf Cluster; Bronze Star Medal with V; Army Commendation Ribbon; Purple Heart; Presidential Distinguished Unit Citation; Third Army Cert Achievement, OCAMG Cert of Achievement; Dept of Army Cert Appreciation; French Croix de Guerre; Belgian Order of the Crown. Mem: ROA (past nat pres); Mil Govt Asn; Am Bar Asn. Relig: Baptist. Legal Res: Box 981 Aiken SC 29801 Mailing Add: Senate Off Bldg Washington DC 20510

TIBBETTS, DONNA HARRIMAN (R)
Finance Chmn, Orrington Town Rep Comt, Maine
b Oxbow, Maine, July 10, 32; d Harley David Anderson & Eugena Bell House A; m 1962 to David Robert Tibbetts; c Andrea Beth. Educ: Univ Maine, BS in Ed, 70. Polit & Govt Pos: Treas, Maine State Fedn Rep Women, 67-69, Maine state co-chmn, Citizens for Nixon, 68; Maine state chmn, Women for Nixon, 68; mem, Defense Adv Comt for Women in the Serv, 69-72; Maine state co-chmn, Comt for Reelec of the President, 72; alt deleg, Rep Nat Conv, 72; finance chmn, Orrington Town Rep Comt, Maine, currently. Bus & Prof Pos: Treas, Beal Bus Col, Bangor, 64- Mem: Bangor Symphony Women; League of Women Voters; Penobscot Women's Rep Club. Relig: Protestant. Legal Res: Rte 12 Box 238 Orrington ME 04474 Mailing Add: PO Box 222 Brewer ME 04412

TIBBETTS, THELMA P (R)
NH State Rep
Mailing Add: 282 Portland St Rochester NH 03867

TIBBITTS, WAYNE EVERETT (R)
Idaho State Rep
b Providence, Utah, May 17, 03; s Lorenzo Edwin Tibbitts & Mary Almeda Marler T; m 1927 to LaRetta Bessie Jones (deceased); m 1963 to Lela E Ellis; c Marjorie J, Barbara G & Errol Wayne. Educ: High sch. Polit & Govt Pos: Idaho State Sen, Jefferson Co, 63-66; Idaho State Rep, 69-; mem Agr & Reclamation Comt, Transportation & Defense Comt & Criminal Code Comt, Idaho House Rep, currently. Bus & Prof Pos: Pres, Tibbitts Produce Co, Inc, Lorenzo, Idaho, 62-71. Mem: Rigby Rotary; Idaho Cattle Feeders Asn. Relig: Latter-day Saint. Mailing Add: Box 15D Lorenzo Rte Rigby ID 83442

TICEN, THOMAS E (DFL)
Co Comnr, Hennepin Co, Minn
b Rockford, Ill, Dec 9, 27; s Merritt Earl Ticen & Theresa J Whalen T; m 1956 to Yvonne Pahl; c Joanne Marie, Mary Theresa & Thomas E, Jr. Educ: St Thomas Col, BA, 48; Univ Minn, JD, 52. Polit & Govt Pos: Minn State Rep, Dist 27 A, 67-72; co comnr, Hennepin Co, 72-; chmn, Metrop Inter Co Coun. Bus & Prof Pos: Attorney, Kempf & Ticen, Bloomington, Minn, 54- Mil Serv: 1st Lt, Army, 52-54, serv in Judge Adv Gen Corps, Pentagon; Capt, Res, 54-64. Relig: Catholic. Mailing Add: 9633 Lyndale Ave S Bloomington MN 55420

TIDWELL, DREW VIRGIL, III (R)
b Miami, Fla, Aug 12, 48; s Drew Virgil Tidwell, Jr & Eleanor Wiesner T; m 1971 to Marie-Cecile Okoniewski; c Drew Virgil, IV. Educ: George Washington Univ, BA, 70; Sigma Alpha Mu. Polit & Govt Pos: Legis asst to US Rep Ben B Blackburn, Ga, 67-73, admin asst, 73- Mil Serv: Pfc, Army Res, 3 years. Publ: Banks should stay in banking, Independent Agent, 10/72. Mem: Blackburn for Cong Comt (treas, 72-); Bull Elephants; Cong Staff Club; Capitol Hill Club. Relig: Lutheran. Mailing Add: 7080 Leewood Forest Dr Springfield VA 22151

TIEDEN, DALE L (R)
Iowa State Sen
b Oct 11, 22; s Lewis Tieden & Grace Fisher T; single. Educ: Elkader Jr Col; Univ Iowa. Polit & Govt Pos: Iowa State Rep, formerly; Iowa State Sen, 73- Bus & Prof Pos: Farmer until 59; mgr, Feed & Livestock Yard. Mem: Co Farm Bur (secy); Twp Agr Comts (secy); Mason. Relig: United Church of Christ. Mailing Add: Elkader IA 52043

TIEMANN, M JOSEPH (D)
La State Sen
Mailing Add: 4417 Napoli Dr Metairie LA 70002

TIEMANN, NORBERT T (R)
b Minden, Nebr, July 18, 24; s The Reverend M W Tiemann & Alvina Rathart T; m 1950 to Lorna Bornholdt; c Mary Catherine, Norbert, Jr, Lorna & Amy. Educ: Univ Nebr, 49. Polit & Govt Pos: Mayor, Wausa, Nebr, 3 terms; Gov, Nebr, 67-70; mem exec comt, Nat Gov Conf, Washington, DC; deleg, Rep Nat Conv, 72; Fed Hwy Adminr, 73- Bus & Prof Pos: Pres, Commercial State Bank, Wausa; asst mgr, Nebr Hereford Asn; exec secy, Nat Livestock Feeders Asn; dir indust rels, Nat Livestock & Meat Bd, Chicago; mem exec coun, Lutheran Church in Am, New York, NY; vpres investment banking firm, Lincoln. Mil Serv: S/Sgt, Army, 43-46, Pac Theater; 2nd Lt, Army Res, 52, Ger. Mem: Nebr CofC; Am Legion; VFW; 4-H; Boy Scouts. Relig: Lutheran. Mailing Add: 2626 S 24th St Lincoln NE 68502

TIERNAN, ROBERT OWENS (D)
b Providence, RI. Educ: Providence Col, BS, 53; Cath Univ Sch of Law, JD, 56. Polit & Govt Pos: RI State Sen, 61-67; US Rep, RI, 67-75; deleg, Dem Nat Conv, 68 & 72; deleg, Dem Nat Mid-Term Conf, 74; mem, Fed Elec Comn, 75- Mem: Am Bar Asn. Relig: Roman Catholic. Mailing Add: 1922 Warwick Ave Warwick RI 02889

TIERNEY, JAMES E (D)
Maine State Rep
Mailing Add: RD 2 Lisbon Falls Durham ME 04252

TIFFANY, JOHN JEWETT, II (R)
Conn State Rep
b New London, Conn, Jan 6, 32; s Leon Hammond Tiffany & Gwendolyn Willet T; m 1966 to Mary Susan Bradeen; c Hannah Louise. Educ: Univ Conn, BS, 54; Phi Kappa Phi; Gamma Chi Epsilon. Polit & Govt Pos: Mem, Lyme Bd of Selectmen, Conn, 59-60; mem, Lyme Bd Educ, 63-, chmn, 65-; Conn State Rep, 63-, chmn, Pub Personnel & Mil Affairs Comt, Conn House Rep, 73- & vchmn, Environ Comt, 73-; mem, Lyme Rep Town Comt, 64, chmn, 68-69. Bus & Prof Pos: Partner, Tiffany Farms, 56. Mil Serv: Entered as Pvt, Army, 54, released as SP-3, 56, after serv in Corps of Eng. Mem: Farm Bur; Grange; Dairy Herd Improv Asn. Relig: Protestant. Mailing Add: Sterling City Rd Lyme CT 06371

TIGHE, CHARLES MOON (R)
b Bronxville, NY, Sept 29, 34; s Charles William Tighe & Jeanette Moon T; m 1956 to Nancy Watson; c Alexander W, Leila M & Jason E. Educ: Harvard Col, AB, 57; Harvard Law Sch, LLB, 60; Hasty Pudding Club; Delphic Club. Polit & Govt Pos: Chmn, Essex Rep Town Comt, Conn, formerly. Bus & Prof Pos: Partner, Copp, Brenneman, Tighe, Koletsky & Berall, Attorneys, New London, Conn, 60- Mil Serv: Entered as Pvt, Army Res, 54, released as SP-6, 61, after serv in Army Security Agency. Mem: Am Judicature Soc; Am Bar Asn (sect on taxation); Conn Bar Asn; Thames Club. Relig: Episcopal. Mailing Add: 9 Kings Lane Essex CT 06426

TILGHMAN, ALMA G (R)
Pres, NC Fedn Rep Women
b Norfolk, Va, Feb 7, 23; d Ivey D Gillikin & Effie Hardesty G; m to Clifford R Tilghman; c Carl & Linda (Mrs Heidgerd). Educ: Cosmetologist Sch, Detroit, Mich; Real Estate Course, Carteret Tech Inst. Polit & Govt Pos: Mem exec bd, NC Fedn Rep Women, 60-, vpres & dist rep, formerly, state pres, currently, chmn Group 75, currently; club pres, Carteret Co Rep Women, formerly; mem, State Platform Comt, formerly; mem, NC State Rep Cent Comt, currently; mem, State Finance Comt, currently; alt deleg, Rep Nat Conv, 72. Bus & Prof Pos: Owner & mgr, A & L Enterprises, currently. Mem: Carteret Co Legal Secys; Bus & Prof Women's Club; Eastern Star. Relig: Baptist. Mailing Add: Rte 1 Box 214 Beauford NC 28516

TILGHMAN, RICHARD A (R)
Pa State Sen
Mailing Add: 405 Gatcombe Lane Bryn Mawr PA 19010

TILLER, JESSIE IRENE (D)
Committeewoman, Mo State Dem Comt
b Carterville, Mo, Mar 13, 00; d John Terry Sullivan & Susie Black S; m 1951 to William Bryan Tiller; c Mary Lou (Mrs Elmer Wallace), W P, Emerald, Jr & Meredith Taylor. Educ: Carthage High Sch, Mo. Polit & Govt Pos: Committeewoman, Cedar Co Dem Comt, Mo, 66-, vchmn, 70-; committeewoman, Mo State Dem Comt, 70- Relig: Christian. Mailing Add: Rte 2 Humansville MO 65674

TILLEY, HOMER (R)
b Landis, Ark, Aug 28, 03; s James Albert Tilley & Dorcas E Cotton T; m 1924 to Oklie Horton; c Joe Ray & Robert Dale. Educ: Marshall High Sch, Ark; Draughon's Bus Col, Springfield, Mo & correspondence study, La Salle Exten Univ, Chicago, Ill. Polit & Govt Pos: Chmn, Tillman Co Rep Comt, Okla, formerly. Bus & Prof Pos: Owner-mgr, Gen Ins Agency, Randlett, Okla, 25-35 & Frederick, Okla, 35-68. Mem: Mason; Guthrie Consistory; Frederick Rotary Club. Relig: Methodist. Legal Res: 320 S 13th St Frederick OK 73542 Mailing Add: PO Box 362 Frederick OK 73542

TILLION, CLEM VINCENT (R)
Minority Whip, Alaska State Senate
b Brooklyn, NY, July 3, 25; s Clement Vincent Tillion & Marian Little T; m 1952 to Diana Rutzebeck; c William David, Marian Ingred, Martha Belle & Clement V, III. Polit & Govt Pos: Alaska State Rep, formerly, rule chmn & majority whip, Alaska House Rep, 66-67, minority whip, 68-69, minority leader, 69-74; Alaska State Sen, 75-, Minority Whip, Alaska State Senate, 75- Bus & Prof Pos: Commercial fisherman capt, 47-; pres, Narrows Pilot Boat & Launch Serv, Inc; adv on Japanese & Russian Fisheries, Dept State; chmn indust adv, Int NPac Fisheries Comn. Mil Serv: Entered as Seaman 2/C, Navy Seabees, 42, released as Seaman 1/C, 46, after serv in 9th Spec Bn, Solomon Islands, 45-46; Battle Stars; 2 Co Awards. Mem: Mason; Am Legion. Relig: Protestant. Legal Res: Halibut Cove AK 99603 Mailing Add: Box 373 Homer AK 99603.

TILLMAN, JIM KING (R)
b Adel, Ga, June 23, 35; s Andrew Lee Tillman & Virginia Maples T; m 1958 to Mary Wells; c James McGregor, John Daniel, Teresa Lee & Jimi Lynn. Educ: Fla State Univ, BS, 61. Polit & Govt Pos: Dep sheriff, Leon Co, Fla, 56-61; counr, Sarasota Co Juv Court, 61-63, chief counr, 63-65; mem, Sarasota Co Rep Exec Comt, 66-68; Fla State Rep, 75th Dist, 67-74, minority whip, Fla House Rep, 70-72, minority leader, 72-74, Fla state chmn, Farm Families for Nixon, 72; deleg, Rep Nat Conv, 72. Mil Serv: Entered as Airman 3/C, Air Force, 53, released as Airman 1/C, 57, after serv in security service. Mem: Fla Cattlemen's Asn (vchmn thefts comt); Elks; VFW (past pres); Sarasota Youth for Christ (bd reference); Sarasota Co CofC. Honors & Awards: Distinguished Serv Award, Sarasota Jaycees, 67; Cited for Outstanding Serv, Fla Prosecuting Attorneys Asn & Juv Court Adminr Asn; Distinguished Serv Award, Arcadia Rotary; Award for Outstanding Serv to Sarasota Co Young Rep, 72. Relig: Methodist. Legal Res: Rte 2 Box 355 Sarasota FL 33577 Mailing Add: PO Box 3888 Sarasota FL 33578

TILLMAN, MAYRE LUTHA (D)
Committeewoman, Dem Exec Comt, Fla
b Dover, Fla, Aug 28, 28; d Luther Edwin Wheeler & Marietta Thornton W; div; c Daniel Paul & Shayla Denise (Mrs Nail). Educ: Fla State Univ, 45-46; Eau Gallie Bus Col, 63-64; Bachelors & Belles. Polit & Govt Pos: Secy, Hillsborough Co Dem Exec Comt, Fla, 64-66, precinct committeewoman, 64-70 & 74-, committeewoman-at-lg, 70-74; committeewoman, Dem Exec Comt, Fla, 74- Bus & Prof Pos: Asst credit investr, Maas Bros, Tampa, Fla, 46-47; secy & bookkeeper, Dover Elem Sch, 50-53; clerk & secy, F S Royster Co, Mulberry, 55-58; security clerk & secy, Space Technol Labs, Cocoa Beach, 60-63; secy & admin aid, United Technol Ctr, Cape Kennedy, 63-64; secy to exec vpres & loan officer, Lakeland Fed Savings & Loan Asn, 65; secy, C W Acree, Realtor & Appraiser, Plant City, 65-66; admin asst, Dave Gordon Enterprises, Tampa, 66-68; secy & off mgr, Bumby & Stimpson, Inc, Orlando, 68-70; tax clerk, Clerk of the Circuit Court, Hillsborough Co Courthouse, Tampa, 70-73; adminr of property mgt, Right of Way for Tampa-Hillsborough Co Expressway Authority, Tampa, 73- Publ: Auth various articles on pertinent legis, Fla Bus Woman, 8 issues, 71-72 & 72-73. Mem: Am Right-of-Way Asn (Fla Chap 26); Dem Women's Club of Fla (state campaign chmn); Hillsborough Co Dem Women's Club; East Hillsborough Co Dem Club. Relig: Baptist. Legal Res: Rex Ave Dover FL 33527 Mailing Add: PO Box 97 Dover FL 33527

TILLMAN, WHEELER MELLETTE (D)
SC State Rep
b Charleston, SC, Aug 25, 41; s Francis C Tillman, Sr & Moye Mellette T; single. Educ: Univ of South, BA, 63; Univ SC Sch Law, JD, 66; Sigma Alpha Epsilon. Polit & Govt Pos: SC State Rep, 72- Bus & Prof Pos: Attorney, Charleston, SC. Mil Serv: Entered as Lt, Air Force, 66, released as Capt, 70, after serv in Vandenberg AFB, Calif, 66-68, Pleiku Air Base, Vietnam, 68-69 & Mather AFB, Calif, 69-70; Capt, Res, 70-; Bronze Star Medal. Mem: Am, SC & Charleston Co Bar Asns. Relig: Lutheran. Mailing Add: PO Box 4295 Charleston Heights SC 29405

TILLOTSON, J C (R)
Kans State Sen
b Lenora, Kans, Feb 4, 06; s H R Tillotson & Maude Johnston T; m 1935 to Maxine M Middleton; c John C & Carolyn L. Educ: Washburn Univ, Topeka, Kans; Kappa Sigma. Polit & Govt Pos: Co attorney, Kans, 35-43; Rep co chmn, Norton, 52-62, mem sch bd, 54-62; Kans State Rep, 60-66, Speaker Pro Tem, Kans House Rep, 66-68; pres, Kans Day Club, 65; Kans State Sen, 69- Mem: Kans State CofC; Northwest Kans Bar Asn; Mason; Rotary; Farm Bur. Relig: Methodist. Legal Res: 712 N First Norton KS 67654 Mailing Add: 109 S State Norton KS 67654

TILLS, RONALD H (R)
NY State Assemblyman
b Buffalo, NY, May 1, 35; s Roland H Tills & Doris Ellathorpe T; m 1960 to Elizabeth Clarkson; c Susan & Thomas Nash. Educ: Univ Buffalo, LLB, 59; Phi Kappa Psi. Polit & Govt Pos: Mem zoning bd appeals, Hamburg, NY, 61-62, asst town attorney, 62-63, town justice, 63-68; NY State Assemblyman, 147th Assembly Dist, 69- Mil Serv: Entered as E-1, Army Res, 59, released as Sgt, 65, after serv in 98th Regt. Mem: F&AM; Hamburg Lions Club (past pres); Moose; Hamburg CofC; Hamburg Vol Fire Co. Relig: Methodist. Mailing Add: 43 Union St Hamburg NY 14075

TILLY, ANNE PETERSEN (D)
b Bellingham, Wash, Nov 18, 15; d Werner Lindberry & Anna Johnson L; m 34 years, wid; m 1970 to Earl Vincent Tilly; c Vicki P (Mrs Johnson), Gary Robert & William Carl Peterson. Educ: Everett Bus Col; Gertrude Steven's Archers Private Sch, 34; Wash State Col. Polit & Govt Pos: Precinct committeewoman, Chelan Co Dem Cent Comt, Wash, 55-, secy, 65-67, vchmn, 67 & chmn, 68-70; jour clerk, Wash House Rep, 61; cand, Wash House Rep, 68; alt deleg, Dem Nat Conv, 72. Bus & Prof Pos: Credit mgr, Deaconess Hosp, Wenatchee, Wash; continuity dir, Radio KUEN; women's prog dir, Radio KOMW, Omak; traffic dir, Radio KINY, Juneau, Alaska; real estate salesman, 61-73. Mem: Phi Sigma Alpha (area rep); Soroptimist Int; Eastern Star; Int Rainbow for Girls (grand dep); Chelan Co Credit Bur (bd dirs). Honors & Awards: Outstanding Citizens Award, Bd of Community Leaders, 69; Sustaining Membership, Soroptimist Int, 70. Relig: Lutheran. Legal Res: Box 2130 K Rte 2 Wenatchee WA 98801 Mailing Add: PO Box 104 Wenatchee WA 98801

TILLY, EARL F (R)
Wash State Rep
b Astoria, Ore, Nov 19, 34; s Earl Vincent Tilly & Evelyn Margaret Bergseth T; m 1961 to Barbara Ann Bartroff; c Kristen Ann, Earl Bart & Shannon Liz. Educ: Pac Lutheran Univ, 53; Wenatchee Valley Col, Wash, AA, 54; Univ Wash, BA, 64. Polit & Govt Pos: Wash State Rep, 12th Legis Dist, 73- Bus & Prof Pos: Pres, Tilly Equip Inc, 64- Mil Serv: Entered as Pvt, Army Res, 57, released as E-3, 61, after serv in 440th CAMG. Mem: Rotary. Relig: Lutheran. Mailing Add: 1509 Jefferson Wenatchee WA 98801

TIMANUS, HALL (D)
Mem, Dem Nat Comt, Tex
Mailing Add: 5619 Briar Dr Houston TX 77027

TIMILTY, JOSEPH F (D)
Mass State Sen
Mailing Add: State Capitol Boston MA 02133

TIMM, E MICHAEL (R)
NDak State Rep
Mailing Add: State Capitol Bismarck ND 58501

TIMM, ROBERT DALE (R)
b Harrington, Wash, Oct 2, 21; s Otto Timm & Florence Thornbrue T; m 1944 to Patricia Davies; c Luanne (Mrs Caylor) & Terry. Educ: Univ Wash, BA in Econ, 43; Sigma Alpha Epsilon. Polit & Govt Pos: Precinct committeeman, Lincoln Co Rep Party, Wash, 47-63; mem bd educ, Harrington Schs, 48-51; pres, Lincoln Co Young Rep, 49-50; Wash State Rep, 51-59, chmn, Rep Caucus & mem, Legis Coun, Wash State House of Rep, 55-59; mem, Western Interstate Comt Agr & Educ, 55-59 & Comt Higher Educ, 55-61; mem, Lincoln Co Bd Educ, 57-61; mem, Agr Adv Comt US Dept Agr, Washington, DC, 58-60; Rep Nat Committeeman, Wash, 58-71; treas-chmn, Rep Western Conv, 63-; asst to Gov Evans, Olympia, Wash, 65, secy-chmn, Utilities & Transportation Comn, 65-67, chmn, 67-; mem, Civil Aeronaut Bd, 71-, chmn, 73-75. Bus & Prof Pos: Owner-mgr, wheat & investment property, 47-; dir bd trustees, Fidelity Mutual Savings Bank, 58-; dir, Great Northwest Life Ins Co, 59-65; dir-secy-treas, Timmco, Inc, 65-; founder & dir, SSound Nat Bank, 67- Mil Serv: Pvt, Marine Corps, 42-43. Mem: Nat Asn Regulatory Comnr (exec comt); Lions; Am Legion; Aero Club Washington; Nat Aviation Club. Relig: Congregational. Legal Res: Box 444 Harrington WA 99134 Mailing Add: 1825 Connecticut Ave Suite 1015 Washington DC 20428

TIMMINS, WILLIAM JOSEPH, JR (D)
Chmn, Trumbull Co Dem Exec & Cent Comt, Ohio
b Boston, Mass, July 27, 17; s William J Timmins, Sr & Mary Gould T; m 1946 to Mary Alice Heltzel; c Mary Lawretta (Mrs John Bramblett), Margaret Ann (Mrs Thomas Tracey), William J, Brion, John, Elizabeth (Mrs Paul Nicholas), Ann & Bridget. Educ: Kirksville Col Osteopathy & Surg, DO, 41; Kansas City Univ Physicians & Surgeons, MD, 43; Cath Univ Am, 47-50; Phi Sigma Gamma. Polit & Govt Pos: Committeeman, Dem Party, Ohio, 60-; chmn, Trumbull Co Dem Exec & Cent Comt, 60-; mem, Pres Club, 62-68; chmn, Trumbull Co Bd Elec, 62-75; mem, Dem State Adv Comt, 63-; deleg, Dem Nat Conv, 64; mem, Ohio Electoral Col, 64; chmn, Ohio Hist Markers Asn, 64-65; chmn, Ohio State Dem Co Chmn Rules Comt, 64-68; trustee, Ohio Elec Off Asn, 66-; mem, Ohio State Med Bd, 72-76; mem, Trumbull Co Ment Health & Retardation Bd, 72-; chmn, Ohio State Dem Co Chmn Asn, 73-75; mem legis comt, Ohio Elec Officials, 75. Bus & Prof Pos: Chief of staff, Warren Gen Hosp, 60- Mem: Am Col Gen Practice; life mem Am Comt Maternal & Child Welfare; Rotary; Elks; Am Osteop Asn; KofC (4 degree). Relig: Roman Catholic. Mailing Add: 3280 E Market St Warren OH 44484

TIMMINS, WILLIAM MONTANA (R)
Treas, Salt Lake Co Rep Party, Utah
b Salt Lake, Utah, Mar 13, 36; s William Montana Timmins & Mary Brighton T; m 1960 to Theda Laws; c Mont, III, Clark Brighton, Laurel, Sally & Rebekah. Educ: Univ Utah, BS, 60, PhD, 72; Harvard Univ, MA, 62; Phi Kappa Phi. Polit & Govt Pos: Asst to Gov, Utah, 66-67; treas, Salt Lake Co Rep Party, 73- Bus & Prof Pos: Asst personnel dir, Utah State Personnel Off, 63-66; asst dean continuing educ, Univ Utah, 68-71; dir interstate proj, Utah State Bd Educ, 71-74; assoc prof pub admin, Brigham Young Univ, 74- Publ: Implementing Career Education, 2 vols, Utah State Bd Educ, 74; College credit by radio: an adventure in education, Adult Leadership, 6/74; The Prudential Center Agreement: a case study in property tax concession, Assessors J, 7/67; plus others. Mem: Am Soc Pub Admin; Gov Vol Coord Comt (chmn, 74-); Salt Lake City Salary Adv Comt; Utah Police Testing Prog (exec comt, 74-); Utah Asn Civil Serv Comnr (pres, 74-). Honors & Awards: Silver Beaver Award, Great Salt Lake Coun, Boy Scouts of America, 74. Relig: Latter-day Saint. Mailing Add: 5419 Wayman Lane Salt Lake UT 84117

TIMMONS, JIMMY HODGE (D)
Ga State Sen
Mailing Add: 132 S Woodlawn Blakely GA 31723

TIMMONS, WILLIAM EVAN (R)
b Chattanooga, Tenn, Dec 27, 30; s Owen Walter Timmons & Doris Eckenrod T; m 1966 to Mimi Bakshian; c Karen Leigh, Kimberly Anne & William Evan, Jr. Educ: Georgetown Univ, BSFS, 59; George Washington Univ, 59-61. Polit & Govt Pos: Aide to US Sen Alexander Wiley, Wis, 55-62; exec dir, Rep Party of Tenn, 62; campaign mgr, Brock for Cong Campaign, 62, 64, 66 & 68; mem faculty of numerous Nat, Regional, State & Local Rep Campaign Workshops, 63-; admin asst to US Rep Bill Brock, Tenn, 63-69; conv coordr, Nixon for President, 68 & 72; dir cong rels, Nixon-Agnew Campaign, 68; Asst to the President, 69-74; US deleg, Int Conf on Vietnam, Paris, 73. Mil Serv: Entered as Pvt, Air Force, 51, released as S/Sgt, 54, after serv in 20th Fighter-Bomber Wing, ETO, 52-55. Mem: A&FM; Scottish Rite; Mason (33 degree); Am Legion. Honors & Awards: Nat Outstanding Young Rep Year, 65; Alumni Awards, Georgetown Univ & Baylor Mil Acad, 70. Relig: Episcopal. Mailing Add: 9501 Newbold Pl Bethesda MD 20034

TIMS, MARJORIE HOLLINGSWORTH (R)
VChmn, Bolivar Co Rep Party, Miss
b New Orleans, La, Aug 12, 18; d Dr Salathiel Lamar Hollingsworth & Fannie Evans H; m 1941 to Lowry Lamar Tims; c Lowry Lamar, Jr, Robert Lewis, James Irving & Douglas Austin. Educ: Miss State Col Women, BS in Home Econ, 39; Gamma Sigma Epsilon. Polit & Govt Pos: Pres, Bolivar Co Rep Women's Club, Miss, 63-64; vchmn, Bolivar Co Rep Party, 63-; deleg & mem, Permanent Orgn Comt, Rep Nat Conv, 64; pres, Miss Fedn of Rep Women, 65-67 & 69-70. Mem: DAR; Huguenot Soc; Magna Charta Dames; Cleveland Jr Auxiliary. Relig: United Methodist. Mailing Add: 401 First Ave S Cleveland MS 38732

TINJUM, LARRY ERVIN (D)
NDak State Rep
b Powers Lake, NDak, July 10, 47; s Ervin Clinton Tinjum & Lois Stenson T; single. Educ: Bottineau Sch Forestry, NDak, 65; Minot State Col, BS Educ, 69; Phi Sigma Pi; Young Dem. Polit & Govt Pos: Deleg, NDak Boy's State Conv, 64, deleg, NDak Dem State Conv, 68, 70 & 72; mem, NDak Dem Platform Resolutions Comt, 70; precinctman, Vanville Twp Dem Non-Partisan League, 72; NDak State Rep, Fourth Dist, 72-, mem educ & polit subdiv comts, NDak House Rep, 72; mem, NDak Dem Non-Partisan Century Club, 73. Bus & Prof Pos: High sch teacher social studies, Plaza Pub Schs, NDak, 69-71; rancher-farmer, Vanville Twp, Burke Co, NDak, 71- Mem: Sons of Norway; NDak Educ Asn; NDak Hist Soc; Burke Co-White Earth Hist Soc; Lostwood Grazing Asn (secy-treas, 73-). Legal Res: Powers Lake ND 58773 Mailing Add: State Capitol Bismarck ND 58501

TINKER, CAROL WICKS (R)
Secy, Rep State Cent Comt, NMex
b Claire City, SDak, Dec 21, 20; d Leroy S Wicks & Alta Ness W; m 1942 to George Edward Tinker, III; c George Edward IV, Ann (Mrs Willard Robert Baker, Jr), Tanya Lynn, Randy Catherine & Susan Christine. Educ: Highlands Univ, 3 years; Delta Zeta; drama club; Alpha Psi Omega; cheerleader; choir; SPURS. Polit & Govt Pos: Secy for Rep gubernatorial cand, NMex, 64; chmn, San Miguel Co Rep Party, 65-68; San Miguel Co Campaign Dir for Congressman Manuel Lujan, Anderson Carter, & primary cand for Gov, Clifford Hawley; NMex State Rep Dist One, San Miguel Co, 68-72; secy, Rep State Cent Comt, NMex, 73- Bus & Prof Pos: Secy, Horwath & Horwath CPA, 41-42; secy, US Army, Salzburg, Austria, 49; mem state bd dirs, Adult Basic Educ, 71- & NMex Regional Med Prog, 71-; exec dir, Las Vegas, San Miguel CofC, 73-; dir, Rho Chap, Delta Zeta, 73-; vpres, Las Vegas Farmers Mkt Corp, 73- Mem: Bus & Prof Women's Club; Rep Women's Club; PTA; NMex Chamber Execs (state bd dirs & pres-elect); Las Vegas Women's Club (pres, 73-). Honors & Awards: Good Neighbor Award, Stars & Stripes Newspaper, Edinburgh, Scotland; NMex Citizen of the Year Award, 73. Relig: Lutheran, Mo Synod. Mailing Add: 726 Lee Dr Las Vegas NM 87701

TINNIN, NELSON B (D)
Mo State Sen
b Hornersville, Mo, Oct 8, 05; m 1927 to Lora Bolliner; c Brent Bollinger. Educ: Southeast Mo State Col; Southwest Mo State Col; Univ Mo, BS. Polit & Govt Pos: Chmn, Dunklin Co Soil Dist, Mo, 49-; mem, Mo State Soil Dist Comn 8 years; pres, Mo Soil Dist Asn; Mo State Sen, 60-; app to Gov Adv Comt on Water Sheds, 61- Bus & Prof Pos: Elem prin, Mo, 7 years; teacher voc agr, Hornersville High Sch, 17 years; cotton planter assoc with Hollywood Gin & Elevator Co, Inc, currently. Mem: Mason (32 degree, past master, lodge); Scottish Rite; Shrine; Eastern Star; Boy Scouts (comnr, Seminole Dist). Honors & Awards: Awarded plaque by Hornersville Alumni Asn for Serv Rendered & Hon Achievement, 62. Relig: Methodist; chmn bd 4 years. Mailing Add: Hornersville MO 63855

TINSLEY, GIDEON (D)
Okla State Sen
Mailing Add: State Capitol Oklahoma City OK 73105

TIPPS, PAUL (D)
Chmn, Ohio Dem Party
b Cincinnati, Ohio, July 27, 36; s Charles P Tipps & Alma Meta T; c Deborah, Penny, Tamara, Polly & Anthony. Educ: Univ Dayton, BS, 60; Chase Col Law, 67. Polit & Govt Pos: Mem exec comt, Montgomery Co Dem Party, Ohio, 66-, exec vchmn formerly, chmn, currently; Dem cand, US House of Rep, 68; deleg, Dem Nat Conv, 68; chmn, Montgomery Co Bd of Elec, currently; chmn, Ohio Dem Party, currently; mem, Dem Nat Comt, currently. Bus & Prof Pos: Pres, Fed Property Mgt Corp, 60-; bd dirs, Dayton Area Bd Realtors, 65-67. Mil Serv: Entered as 2nd Lt, Army, 60, released as 2nd Lt, 61, after serv in Training Co, US, 60-61; 1st Lt, Spec Forces Unit, 61-66; Parachutist Badge, Grad Spec Warfare Sch, 65. Publ: Advertising & public relations for the realtor, 9-10/66 & Professional cooperation: the realtor's key to success, 11-12/66, J of Property Mgt; Charles Whalen: space age politician, Vanguard, 4/69. Mem: Inst Real Estate Mgt; Dayton Area Bd Realtors; Dayton Jaycees; Montgomery City Dem Club. Honors & Awards: One of Ten Outstanding Young Men in Dayton, 67. Relig: Catholic. Mailing Add: 5 Volusia Ave Dayton OH 45409

TIPSWORD, ROLLAND FORTNER (D)
Ill State Rep
b Monticello, Ill, Aug 19, 25; s Leo Clemit Tipsword & Jossie Fortner T; single. Educ: Eastern Ill State Univ, 43; Univ Idaho, BA, 49; Northwestern Univ, LLB, 51; Phi Beta Kappa; Phi Alpha Delta; Delta Tau Delta. Polit & Govt Pos: States attorney, Christian Co, Ill, 60-66; Ill State Rep, 52nd Dist, 67- Bus & Prof Pos: Partner, Coale, Taylor, Tipsword, Fraley & Schweitzer. Mil Serv: Entered as A/S, Navy, 43, released as Radio Technician 2/C, 46, after serv in Pac Area, 44-45; Pac Combat Area Ribbons. Mem: AF&AM; VFW; Am Legion, Elwood Commandery; Elks; Moose. Relig: Presbyterian. Mailing Add: 801 Springfield Rd Taylorville IL 62568

TIPTON, ELDEN C (D)
Ind State Sen
Mailing Add: PO Box 4 Jasonville IN 47438

TIRADO DELGADO, CIRILO (POPULAR DEM, PR)
Rep, PR House Rep
b Yabucoa, PR, Mar 29, 38; s Ramon Tirado Martinez & Carmen Delgado M; m 1961 to Quintina Rivera Montanez; c Ana Ivette, Cirilo, Ariel Ramon & Alexis Oscar Tirado Rivera. Educ: Univ PR, Rio Piedras, BA in Elem Educ, 62, BA in Sec Educ, 63; MA in Educ, 69; Sigma Beta Chi. Polit & Govt Pos: Mem, Patillas Munic Asn, PR, 70-72, pres, Patillas Munic Comt, 72-; Rep, PR House Rep, Dist 30, 72-, chmn, Educ Comt, 72- Bus & Prof Pos: Elem & intermediate sch teacher, PR Dept Educ, 60-65, high sch teacher math, 63-65, sch dir, 65-70 & gen supvr, math, 70-72; pres, Patillas Local Teachers Asn, 70-71. Mem: PR Teachers Asn; Nat Coun Teachers Math; Nat Educ Asn; PR Asn Teachers Math; Patillas Exchange Club. Relig: Catholic. Legal Res: Urbanizacion San Benito C-33 Patillas PR 00723 Mailing Add: Box 411 Patillas PR 00723

TITUS, DOUGLAS LEROY (R)
Chmn, Mansfield Rep Town Comt, Mass
b Foxboro, Mass, Aug 14, 34; s Chester L Titus & Florence A Strang T; m 1958 to Patricia Louise Santucci; c Kym Ann, Douglas L, II, Donald F, II, Dennis J & Pauline A. Educ: Boston Univ, 2 years; Bridgewater State Teachers Col, 2 years. Polit & Govt Pos: Coordr campaign comts, John Quinlan for Senate, 64 & 66, Walter O'Brien for State Rep, 64, 66 & 68, John Volpe for Gov, 66 & 68, Margaret Heckler for Cong, 66, 68 & 70 & Frank Sargent for Gov, 70; vchmn, Mansfield Housing Auth, Mass, 67; chmn, Mansfield Rep Town Comt, 68-; deleg, Mass State Rep Conv, 70; mem bd selectmen, Mansfield, Mass, 71-, chmn, 73- Bus & Prof Pos: Notary Pub, 67-; investr, Fraudulent Claims Bur, Mass, 68- Mil Serv: Entered as Pvt, Army Paratroopers, 53, released as Cpl, 56, after serv in Green Beret Tenth Spec Forces Group, ETO, 54-56; Good Conduct Medal; Paratrooper Wings; Parachute Rigger Wings. Mem: KofC (Grand Knight); Good Govt Comt; 4-H Club; Lions. Honors & Awards: Star Coun Award, KofC. Relig: Roman Catholic. Mailing Add: 400 Maple St Mansfield MA 02048

TJEERDSMA, JESS (R)
SDak State Sen
Mailing Add: Box 281 Springfield SD 57062

TOAL, JEAN H (D)
SC State Rep
Mailing Add: 2418 Wheat St Columbia SC 29205

TOBIAS, ANSEL WALTER (R)
Kans State Rep
b Lyons, Kans, Mar 6, 12; s Walter James Tobias & Iva Stokes T; m 1934 to Helen Monroe; c Ann Rosalle (Mrs Ron Wingfield). Educ: Kans State Univ. Polit & Govt Pos: Mem, Rice Co Hosp Dist 1, Kans, 58-65; Kans State Rep, 65- Bus & Prof Pos: Pres, Tobias Birchenough Inc, 48- Mem: Kiwanis; Mason; Shrine; Town & Country Club; Kans Ready-Mix Asn. Relig: First Christian Church; elder. Mailing Add: Box 699 Lyons KS 67554

TOBIAS, RUTH M (R)
Pres, Tenn Fedn Rep Women
b Scranton, Pa, Aug 3, 25; s John J Mongiello & Mary Fontinelle M; m 1946 to Melvin Roy Tobias; c Patricia T (Mrs Collins), Marcia, Cynthia, Julia & Phoebe. Educ: Dunmore High Sch, grad, 43. Polit & Govt Pos: Pres, Hamilton Co Rep Women's Club, Tenn, 63-65; mem steering comt & candidates adv comt, Hamilton Co Rep Party, 63-65; dist women's chmn, Kuykendall Senate Campaign, 64; state chmn, 14th Annual Rep Women's Conf, 64; deleg, Nat Fedn Rep Women Conv, 64, 66 & 68; vpres third dist, Tenn Fedn Rep Women, 64-69, deleg, Dist Conv, 64, 66 & 68, pres, 70-; mem, Gov Comn on Equal Status of Women, 65-66; dist women's chmn, Nixon-Agnew Campaign, 68; vchmn, Rep Party Tenn, 70-; mem bd dirs, Nat Fedn Rep Women, 70-; deleg, Rep Nat Conv, 72. Mem: Signal Mountain Guild Gardeners; League of Women Voters. Relig: Presbyterian. Mailing Add: Forest Park Dr Signal Mountain TN 37377

TOBIASSEN, THOMAS JOHAN (R)
Fla State Sen
b Omaha, Nebr, Nov 21, 31; s Thoralph Johan Tobiassen & Goldie Marie Grimm T; c Thomas J, Jr & Todd J. Educ: Ohio State Univ, BME, 59; Sigma Chi. Polit & Govt Pos: Membership chmn, Young Rep Club of Pensacola, Fla, 67; Fla State Rep, 68-74; Fla State Sen, 75- Bus & Prof Pos: Sr engr, Monsanto Co, Pensacola, Fla, 61- Mil Serv: Entered as Pvt, Army, 53, released as Pfc, 55, after serv in Corps of Engrs, Korea, 54-55; Good Conduct Medal. Mem: Registered Prof Engr in Fla; life mem Pensacola Young Rep; Pensacola CofC. Relig: Lutheran. Legal Res: 890 Woodbine Dr Pensacola FL 32503 Mailing Add: Box 2356 Pensacola FL 32503

TOBIN, ARTHUR H (D)
Mass State Sen
Mailing Add: State Capitol Boston MA 02133

TOBIN, ROBERT DANIEL (D)
Conn State Rep
b Boston, Mass, Sept 15, 42; s William G Tobin & Mary MacLeod T; m 1965 to Nancy A Reynolds; c Jennifer & Melissa. Educ: Boston Col, AB, 64, Law Sch, JD, 68. Polit & Govt Pos: Mem, East Lyme Co Parks & Recreation Comt, 71-; Conn State Rep, 37th Dist, 75- Bus & Prof Pos: Attorney, New London, 68- Publ: Co-auth, Teacher negotiations into the seventies, William & Mary Law J, 72. Mem: New London Co Chap, Fed Bar Asn (pres, 74-75). Honors & Awards: Outstanding Young Man, East Lyme Jr CofC, 72; Outstanding Serv Award, Conn Parks & Recreation Asn, 73. Mailing Add: 10 Patrick Pl Niantic CT 06357

TOBRINER, MATHEW OSCAR (D)
Assoc Justice, Calif Supreme Court
b San Francisco, Calif, Apr 2, 04; s Oscar Tobriner & Maud Lezinsky T; m 1939 to Rosabelle Rose; c Michael Charles & Stephen Oscar. Educ: Stanford Univ, AB, 24, MA, 25; Harvard Law Sch, LLB, 27; Univ Calif Sch Law, SJD, 32; Phi Beta Kappa; Order of the Coif; Delta Sigma Rho. Polit & Govt Pos: Assoc Justice, Calif Court of Appeal, First Appellate, 59-62; Dist, Div One, San Francisco, Assoc Justice, Calif Supreme Court, 62- Bus & Prof Pos: Assoc, David Livingston & Lawrence Livingston, 28-30 & late Judge Milton D Sapiro, 30-32; chief attorney, Solicitor's Off, US Dept Agr, 32-36; practice of Law, Tobriner, Lazarus, Brundage & Neyhart, San Francisco, 36-59. Mil Serv: Seaman 1/C, San Francisco Vol Port Security Force, Coast Guard, 43-45. Publ: Co-auth, Principles & Practices of Cooperative Marketing (with the late Prof E G Mears, Stanford Univ), Ginn & Co, 26; The individual & the public service enterprise in the new industria state (with Joseph Grodin), Calif Law Rev, 11/67; Individual rights in an industrialized society, Am Bar Asn J, 1/68. Mem: San Francisco Bar Asn; Legal Aid Soc of San Francisco; Barrister's Club; Lawyers' Club of San Francisco; San Francisco Jewish Community Rels Coun; Commonwealth Club. Relig: Jewish. Mailing Add: 3494 Jackson St San Francisco CA 94118

TOBRINER, WALTER NATHAN (D)
b Washington, DC, July 2, 02 s Leon Tobriner & Blanche Barth T; m 1933 to Marienne E Smith; c Constance E (Mrs David Povich) & Matthew W. Educ: Princeton Univ, AB, 23; Harvard Univ, LLB, 26; Phi Beta Kappa. Polit & Govt Pos: Mem bd of trustees, Nat Cultural Ctr, 63-67; mem, Washington Bd of Educ, 52-61, pres, bd, 57-61; deleg, Dem Nat Conv, 56, 60 & 64; comnr, DC Govt & pres bd of comnrs, 61-67; US Ambassador, Jamaica, 67-69; consult, Dept of State, 69. Bus & Prof Pos: Attorney-at-law, 27-; prof law, Nat Univ Law Sch, 33-50; dir, Blue Cross Plan, 53-61; pres, Garfield Mem Hosp, 52-55, Lisner Home, 54- & Washington Hosp Ctr, 59-61. Mil Serv: Lt Col, Army Air Force, 43-46. Mem: Nat Capital Dem & Cosmos Clubs. Mailing Add: 6100 33rd St NW Washington DC 20015

TOCA, HAROLD J (D)
La State Rep
Mailing Add: 1013 N Turnbull Dr Metairie LA 70001

TODD, CARL P (D)
Secy, Jackson Co Dem Comt, Ill
b Grand Tower, Ill, Sept 1, 13; s John W Todd & Sarah Anderson T; m 1935 to Vera A Palisch; c Carleen (Mrs Ralph Neumann) & Malcolm J. Educ: Grand Tower High Sch, Ill, 12 years. Polit & Govt Pos: Conserv investr, Jackson Co, Ill, 50-52, co treas, 54-58 & dep treas, 58-61; supvr, Grand Tower Twp, 50-54; state produce inspector, Agr Dept, 61-69; secy, Jackson Co Dem Comt, Ill, 64-; dep sheriff, Jackson Co, 69-70; dep treas, Jackson Co, 70- Bus & Prof Pos: Owner serv sta, 36-54. Mil Serv: Entered as Seaman, Navy, 43, released as Radarman 2/C, 45, after serv in Amphibious Forces, SPac, 43-45. Mem: Int Brotherhood of Operating Engrs; Am Legion; 40 et 8; VFW; Lions. Relig: Protestant. Mailing Add: Main & Harrison St Grand Tower IL 62942

TODD, DONALD GLENN (R)
Nat Committeeman, Idaho State Young Rep League
b Bellingham, Wash, Apr 30, 43; s Victor J Todd & Viola May Schenck T; m 1964 to Sally Ann Neault; c Victor L & Heather Ann. Educ: High Sch. Polit & Govt Pos: Chmn, Whatcom Co Young Rep, Wash, 59-62; chmn, Kootenai Co Young Rep, Idaho, 68-70; chmn, Kootenai Co Rep Cent Comt, 72-73; exec dir, Idaho State Rep Cent Comt, 73-74; press & pub rels dir, Kidwell for Attorney Gen Comt, 74; aide to Attorney Gen of Idaho, 75-; nat committeeman, Idaho State Young Rep League, 75- Mil Serv: Entered as E-1, Air Nat Guard, 62, released as E-4, 68. Publ: Ed, Target '74, Rep State Cent Comt monthly, 74-75; Attorney General alert, Idaho Attorney Gen Off, 75- Relig: Christian. Legal Res: 1502 N 21st Boise ID 83702 Mailing Add: Statehouse Boise ID 83720

TODD, JOHN J
Assoc Justice, Minn Supreme Court
b St Paul, Minn, 1927; s John Alfred Todd & Martha Jagoe T; m 1950 to Dolores Shanahan; c Richard, Jane & John P. Educ: St Thomas Col, 44, 46-47; Univ Minn Law Sch, LLB, 50.

Polit & Govt Pos: Vchmn, Minn Tax Court, 65-72; assoc justice, Minn Supreme Court, 72- Bus & Prof Pos: Partner, Thuet & Todd, South St Paul, 51-72. Mil Serv: Entered as A/S, Navy, 45, released as Seaman 1/C, 46, after serv in USS Auburn AGC-10, Atlantic Theatre. Mem: Am & Minn State Bar Asns; Am Judges Asn; Am Judicature Soc; Minn Fair Trial-Free Press Coun (chmn). Relig: Roman Catholic. Legal Res: 6659 Argenta Trail W Inver Grove Heights MN 55075 Mailing Add: Rm 225 State Capitol St Paul MN 55155

TODD, PAUL HAROLD, JR **(D)**
b Kalamazoo, Mich, Sept 22, 21; s Paul H Todd & Adeline Allias T; m 1946 to Ruth Newell; c George, Paul A, Charles & Elizabeth. Educ: Cornell Univ, BS in Chem, 43; Univ Chicago, grad work in econ, 46. Polit & Govt Pos: Chief exec off, Planned Parenthood-World Population, 67-70; US Rep, 3rd Dist, Mich, 65-66. Bus & Prof Pos: Chmn bd, Kalamazoo Spice Extraction Co, 65 & founder & pres; trustee, Kalamazoo Col, 73-; mem, Mich State Bd of Ethics, 73- Mil Serv: Entered as Pvt, Army, 43, released as 1st Lt, 45, after serv in China-Burma-India Theater; Bronze Star; Soldiers' Medal. Mem: Am Chem Soc; Am Econ Asn; Economet Soc; Inst of Food Technol. Relig: Protestant. Mailing Add: 3713 W Main St Kalamazoo MI 49007

TODD, WEBSTER BRAY **(R)**
Chmn, NJ Rep State Comt
b Yonkers, NY, Aug 27, 1899; s John R Todd & Alice Bray T; m to Eleanor Prentice Schley; c Kate T (Mrs Samuel F Beach, Jr), John R, II, Webster B, Jr & Christine T. Educ: Princeton Univ, AB, 22; Jesus Col, Cambridge, Eng, 22-23; Fordham Univ, LLB, 27. Polit & Govt Pos: Chmn, Willkie for President Clubs, NJ, 40; treas, NJ Rep State Comt, 46-48, chmn, 61-69 & currently; chmn, NJ State Rep Finance Comt, 48-53, treas, 58; campaign mgr, Eisenhower Primary, 52; dir, Off Econ Affairs, US Mission to NATO & European Regional Orgn, 53-54; mem US deleg, UN Econ & Social Coun, 54; chmn, NJ State Rep Exec Comt, 58-61; deleg, Rep Nat Conv, 64, chmn NJ deleg, 68 & 72. Bus & Prof Pos: Pres, Todd & Brown, Inc, 28-45; partner, J H Whitney, 46; dir, Bell Aircraft, Am Wheelabrator, Hawkeye-Security, 47-56; dir & chmn exec comt, Equity Corp, 47-56; dir, Stevens Inst Metrop Life, 40-73, Panama Canal Co Bank of Commerce & Am Inst for Ment Studies, currently. Mem: NY State Bar; River Club; Maidstone Club; Vet Asn (17th Regt, NY). Relig: Presbyterian. Mailing Add: Box 146 Oldwick NJ 08858

TODD, WEBSTER BRAY, JR **(R)**
b New York, NY, Dec 1, 38; s Webster Bray Todd, Sr & Eleanor Schley T; m 1964 to Sheila Mitchell O'Keefe; c William Walker, Whitney de Forest & James Bridger. Educ: Univ Lausanne, Switz, 56-57; Princeton Univ, AB in Geol, 61; Stanford Law Sch, 61-62; Ivy Club. Polit & Govt Pos: Rep munic chmn, Bedminster Twp, NJ, 65-67; NJ State Assemblyman, Eighth Dist, 68-69, chmn taxation comt, NJ State Assembly, 68, mem, 69, mem appropriations comt, 68 & 69, chmn study comn capital spending, 69 & mem tax exempt study comn, 69; spec asst to the chmn, Civil Aeronautics Bd, Washington, DC, 69-71; exec dir, White House Conf Aging, 71-72; nat dir, Older Am Div, CREP, 72; dir group IV, 1973 Inaugural Comt, 72-73; Dep Spec Asst to the President, 73-74; inspector gen foreign assistance, US Dept State, 74- Bus & Prof Pos: Vpres, Basking Ridge Aviation, 62-64; pres, Princeton Aviation Corp & Princeton Air-Research Park, 64-69; partner, Gen Aviation Eng, 66-69. Mem: New York Wings Club; Somerset Hills Country Club; Metrop Club, Washington; Kenwood Golf & Country Club, Bethesda. Relig: Episcopal. Legal Res: Liberty Corner Rd Far Hills NJ 07931 Mailing Add: 5017 Fort Sumner Dr Washington DC 20016

TOFT, MARJORY MAYO **(R)**
b Swearingen, Tex, May 16, 23; d Boss L Mayo & Gladys Sears M; m 1945 to Raymond Leroy Toft; c Todd Mayo. Educ: Fitz Gallery, art courses, 61-66. Polit & Govt Pos: Unit supvr, Childress Army Air Base, Tex, secy-bookkeeper, Signal Corps, 43-45; chmn, Childress Co Rep Cent Comt, formerly. Mem: Area Arts Found; Tex Fine Arts Asn; Univ Readers Book Club; Tex Fedn Women's Dept Club; Friends of Libr. Honors & Awards: Sponsor, Rodeo Girls representing Tex in Madison Sq Garden, 42; artist in shows Amarillo & New York, NY, one-man shows in Tex & Okla. Relig: Methodist. Mailing Add: 409 G SE Childress TX 79201

TOFTE, SEMOR C **(R)**
Iowa State Rep
Mailing Add: 401 Upper Broadway PO Box 276 Decorah IA 52101

TOLAND, CATHERYN ANN **(D)**
b Washington, DC, June 12, 52; d John Joseph Toland & Helen Patricia O'Brien T; single. Educ: Montgomery Col, Md, 70-71; Univ Md, College Park, 72- Polit & Govt Pos: Mem steering comt, Montgomery Co Students for McGovern, 71-72; mem, Md Exec Campaign Comt, 72; deleg, Dem Nat Conv, 72. Mem: Montgomery Co Young Dem (precinct liaison, 73-); Prince Georges Co Young Dem (Newsletter chmn, 73-); Eastern Montgomery Dem Club (corresponding secy, 73-). Mailing Add: 1200 Cresthaven Dr Silver Spring MD 20903

TOLBERT, TOMMY **(R)**
Ga State Rep
Mailing Add: 1569 Austin Dr Decatur GA 30032

TOLES, ELWIN BONDS **(D)**
Ga State Rep
b Cherokee Co, Ala, Mar 16, 16; s John Glaznor Toles & Jennie Rose Bonds T; m 1937 to Mildred Louise Williams. Educ: Tenn Temple Col, 2 years; pres student body, 51. Polit & Govt Pos: State coordr, Gov Comt on Employ of Handicapped, 69; Ga State Rep, 16th Dist, 69-, asst majority whip, Ga House of Rep, currently. Bus & Prof Pos: Owner, Toles Furniture Co, 45-69; salesman, J L Todd Auction Co, 65-69. Mem: Kiwanis; Ga Baptist Conv (exec comt, admin comt & comt on nominations, 74-); Laymen Evangelism Ga (pres). Honors & Awards: Southern Baptist Conv Cert & Award for participation West Coast laymen crusade in relig work, 64; President's Citation for meritorious serv, Comt on Employ of Handicapped; Ga House of Rep Cert of Appreciation for spiritual guid; selected by Ga House of Rep to attend & represent state of Ga in form of resolution, President's Prayer Breakfast, Washington, DC, 75. Relig: Baptist; first vpres, Ga Baptist. Mailing Add: 1114 Park Blvd Rome GA 30161

TOLL, MAYNARD JOY, JR **(D)**
b Los Angeles, Calif, Feb 5, 42; s Maynard Joy Toll & Ethel Coleman T; m 1964 to Kathryn Wiseman; c Ian & Adam. Educ: Stanford Univ, BA, 63; Johns Hopkins Univ, Sch Advan Int Studies, MA, 65, PhD, 70; Sigma Nu. Polit & Govt Pos: Legis asst, US Sen Edmund S Muskie, Maine, 71-72, admin asst, 72- Bus & Prof Pos: Asst prof polit, Univ Mass, Boston, 68-71, asst dean faculty, 70-71. Honors & Awards: Christian A Herter fel, Johns Hopkins Univ, 64; Fulbright fel, US Govt, 66; Danforth Found, 69. Mailing Add: 4647 Kenmore Dr NW Washington DC 20007

TOLL, ROSE **(D)**
Pa State Rep
b Philadelphia, Pa, June 4, 11; d David Ornstein & Jennie Readerman O; m 1938 to Herman Toll, wid; c Sheldon S & Gilbert E. Educ: Mt Sinai Hosp Sch Nursing, RN, 32. Polit & Govt Pos: Mem & second vchmn, Philadelphia Co Dem Exec Comt, 66; admin asst to Rep Robert N C Nix, Pa, 68-70; Pa State Rep, 71- Mem: Philadelphia Group Ment Health & Ment Retardation Assocs (bd mem, 73-); Pa Coun of the Arts; Nat Soc State Legislators; Am Jewish Comt; Philadelphia Fel Comn. Relig: Jewish. Mailing Add: 2323 76th Ave Philadelphia PA 19150

TOLLEFSON, ORLAN N **(R)**
b Sanish, NDak, Mar 6, 22; s Ole T Tollefson & Mrytle Nygarrd T; m 1949 to Rosella A Berge; c Rosann Kay & Roger Wayne. Educ: St Olaf Col, BS, 47; Phi Gamma. Polit & Govt Pos: Block worker, Fifth Dist Rep Party, NDak, 50, precinct committeeman, 64 & 74-, orgn chmn, 68, vchmn, 69, chmn, 69-74; mem, NDak Rep State Comt, 69-74. Bus & Prof Pos: Co-owner, Tollefson Furniture, 49- Mil Serv: Entered as Pvt, Air Force, 42, released as Cpl, 46, after serv in continental US. Mem: Kiwanis; Mason; Shrine; Elks; Am Legion. Relig: Lutheran. Mailing Add: 2600 Bel Air Dr Minot ND 58701

TOLLEFSON, THOR CARL **(R)**
b Perley, Minn, May 2, 02; s Christian Tollefson & Bertha Jacobson T; m 1943 to Eva M Keuss; c Rosemary, Karley & Janie. Educ: Univ Wash, LLB, 30. Polit & Govt Pos: Prosecuting attorney, Pierce Co, Wash, 32-34 & 39-46; US Rep, Wash, 47-65. Bus & Prof Pos: Mech & millworker, 15-22; admitted to Wash Bar, 30; private practice law, 30-32, 34-38 & 66-; state dir, Dept of Fisheries, Wash, 65- Mem: Mason (32 degree); Shrine; Scottish Rite; Elks; Moose. Relig: Lutheran. Mailing Add: 7612 North St SW Tacoma WA 98498

TOLMACH, JANE LOUISE **(D)**
Councilwoman, Oxnard, Calif
b Havre, Mont, Nov 12, 21; d Robert Francis McCormick & Veronica Tracy M; m 1946 to Daniel Michael Tolmach; c James, Richard, Eve, Adam & Jonathan. Educ: Univ Calif, Los Angeles, AB, 43; Smith Col, MSS, 45; Gamma Phi Beta. Polit & Govt Pos: Mem, Ventura Co Dem Cent Comt, Calif, 53-70, chmn, 59-62; alt deleg, Dem Nat Conv, 56 & 64, deleg, 60 & 68; mem, Oxnard City Planning Comn, 57-62, vchmn, 59-62; mem, Ventura Co Grand Jury, 58; mem, Calif Dem State Cent Comt, 58-74, chmn, South Women's Div, 66-70; mem bd trustees, Camarillo State Hosp, 59-68, chmn, 67 & 68; mem gov bd, Oxnard Union High Sch Dist, 65-72; councilwoman, Oxnard, Calif, 70-, mayor, 73-74. Bus & Prof Pos: Mem bd dirs, SCoast Area Transit, Ventura Co, currently. Mem: Southern Calif Asn Govts (exec bd). Relig: Roman Catholic. Mailing Add: 656 Douglas Ave Oxnard CA 93030

TOLTON, JERE **(D)**
Fla State Rep
Mailing Add: 70 Waynel Circle Ft Walton Beach FL 32548

TOMAN, HENRY EDWARD **(R)**
Chmn, Wallingford Rep Town Comt, Conn
b Meriden, Conn, July 25, 44; s Edward Andrew Toman & Ann Baziak T; m 1969 to Lisa Marchand. Educ: Col of the Holy Cross, AB in hist, 66; Columbia Univ Sch Int Affairs, 67-68; Phi Alpha Theta. Polit & Govt Pos: Chmn, Wallingford Rep Town Comt, Conn, 74- Bus & Prof Pos: Mkt analyst, Hartford Nat Bank, Conn, 71-72; acct exec, Merrill, Lynch, Pierce, Fenner & Smith, 72- Mil Serv: Entered as Pvt E-1, Army, 68, released as 1st Lt, 71, after serv in Mil Intel, Europe, 69-71; Capt, Army Res, currently; Army Commendation Medal. Honors & Awards: Outstanding Young Man Award, Wallingford Jaycees, 73. Relig: Roman Catholic. Mailing Add: Liney Hall Lane Wallingford CT 06492

TOMASI, LAWRENCE JAMES **(D)**
Vt State Rep
b Barre, Vt, Feb 26, 06; s Anthony Tomasi & Rose Massucco T; married; c Patricia, Duane & Lawrence J, Jr. Educ: Norwich Univ, 28; Holy Cross & Univ Vt, 29-30 & 31-32; McGill Univ, DDS, 37. Polit & Govt Pos: Vt State Rep, Dist 18, 67- Bus & Prof Pos: Dentist, currently. Relig: Catholic. Legal Res: 46 Court Sq Windsor VT 05089 Mailing Add: 72 Main St Windsor VT 05089

TOMBLIN, EARL RAY **(D)**
WVa State Deleg
b Logan, WVa, Mar 15, 52; s Earl Tomblin & Freda Jarrell T; single. Educ: WVa Univ, BS, 74; Marshall Univ, 74-75; Kappa Alpha. Polit & Govt Pos: WVa State Deleg, 75- Bus & Prof Pos: Mgr, Southern Logan Co Bd Educ, 74-75, teacher, 75. Mem: Soc Advan Mgt. Honors & Awards: Youngest mem 62nd WVa Legis. Mailing Add: Box 116 Chapmanville WV 25508

TOMEO, THOMAS P **(R)**
Committeeman, NJ Rep State Comt
b Newark, NJ, Jan 20, 11; s Stefano Tomeo & Filomena Montano T; m 1935 to Leta Caperna; c Frances (Mrs William Gray) & Steve. Polit & Govt Pos: Alt deleg, Rep Nat Conv, 52 & 60; committeeman, NJ Rep State Comt, 75- Bus & Prof Pos: Beautician, Leta's Beauty Salon, currently. Mem: Hackettstown Young Rep (organizer); Hackettstown Community Hosp (organizer); Kiwanis; Eagles; KofC. Honors & Awards: Hackettstown Community Award, 60; Hackettstown Community Hosp Award, 75. Relig: Catholic. Legal Res: 404 Lafayette Hackettstown NJ 07840 Mailing Add: 121 Main St Hackettstown NJ 07840

TOMLIN, JOHN R **(D)**
NMex State Rep
b Albuquerque, NMex, Apr 20, 26; s Roy A Tomlin (deceased) & Sallie Mackey T; m 1950 to Ina L Carwile; c John Timothy, Joel Mackey & Jennifer Lee. Educ: NMex State Univ, BS, 50, MA, 55; Alpha Tau Alpha; Alpha Delta Theta; Sigma Phi. Polit & Govt Pos: Vpres, Las Cruces Co Dem Party, NMex, 66-69; NMex State Rep, 66 & 69- Bus & Prof Pos: Pres, Picacho Cotton Gin Coop, 60-69; chmn research & educ comt, Dona Ana Co Farm Bur, 62-69. Mil Serv: Entered as Recruit, Army, 44, released as Sgt, 46, after serv in Inf, ETO, 45-46. Mem: NMex Educ Asn; Mason; York Rite; Shrine; Elks. Honors & Awards: State Farmer Degree, NMex, 44. Relig: Presbyterian; elder. Mailing Add: Rte 2 Box 267 Las Cruces NM 88001

TOMLINSON, JOHN D (DFL)
Minn State Rep
b Oak Park, Ill, Dec 3, 29; s Dewey Tomlinson & Ruth Kincaid T; m 1951 to Martha Blake; c Nancy, Diane & David. Educ: Univ Minn, BChE, 52; Tau Beta Pi. Polit & Govt Pos: Campaign coordr, US Rep Joseph Karth, Dist Four, Minn, 68; deleg, Dem Nat Conv, 68; vchmn, Ramsey Co Dem-Farmer-Labor Party, Minn, 68-69, chmn, 69-70; chmn, Fourth Cong Dist Dem-Farmer-Labor Party, Minn, 70-; Minn State Rep, 72- Bus & Prof Pos: Chem engr, 3M Co, St Paul, Minn, 55-60, research mgr, 60-68, research analyst, 68- Mil Serv: Entered as Ens, Navy, 52, released as Lt(jg), 55, after serv in USS Stribling, Atlantic Fleet, 52-55. Relig: Unitarian. Mailing Add: 2176 Glenridge Ave St Paul MN 55119

TOMLINSON, SHERMAN DRAWDY (D)
b Clinch Co, Ga, July 21, 90; s Harris Tomlinson & Arlia Dame T; m 1915 to Vashti King; c Martha R, Arlia S (Mrs Richard H Bailey) & Sherman Dame. Educ: Clinch Co Pub Schs, Ga. Polit & Govt Pos: Justice of Peace, Homerville, Ga, 33-; judge, Police Court, Homerville, 51-53; chmn, Clinch Co Dem Exec Comt, formerly. Bus & Prof Pos: Farmer. Mem: SAR. Relig: Primitive Baptist. Mailing Add: PO Box 334 Homerville GA 31634

TOMPKINS, ROGER WILLIAM (D)
WVa State Deleg
b Cedar Grove, WVa, Nov 14, 36; s Roger William Tompkins (deceased) & Pauline Woodrum T; m 1961 to Adrianna Hutchings Zuill; c Benjamin William & Adrianna Pauline. Educ: WVa Univ, BA, 58; Queen's Col, Oxford Univ, BA, 61, MA, 71; Yale Univ Col Law, LLB, 64; Beta Theta Pi. Polit & Govt Pos: Dep supt & gen counsel, NY State Ins Dept, 70-71; town councilman, Cedar Grove, WVa, 73-75; WVa State Deleg, 75- Bus & Prof Pos: Assoc lawyer, Sullivan & Cromwell, New York, 64-70; partner, Stone, Bowles, Kauffelt & McDavid, 72- Mil Serv: Entered as Capt, Army, 65, released as Capt, 67, after serv in 2nd Bn, 28th Field Artil, Ger, as battery comdr, 66-67. Publ: The uniform securities act—A step forward in state regulation, WVa Law Rev, 75. Mem: Am, WVa & Kanawha Co Bar Asns; Asn of Bar of City of New York. Honors & Awards: Elected Student Body Pres, WVa Univ, 57-58; Rhodes Scholarship, 58-61; Order of the Coif, Yale Law Sch, 64; WVa Secy of the Rhodes Trust. Relig: Episcopal. Legal Res: Cedar Grove WV 25039 Mailing Add: PO Box 1386 Charleston WV 25325

TOMPKINS, WILLIAM FINLEY (R)
b Newark, NJ, Feb 26, 13; s William Brydon Tompkins & Elizabeth Finley T; m 1949 to Jane Davis Bryant; c William F, Jr. Educ: Wesleyan Univ, 35; Rutgers Univ Sch Law, 40; Delta Kappa Epsilon. Polit & Govt Pos: NJ State Assemblyman, 51-53; US Attorney, NJ, 53-54; Asst Attorney Gen, US, 54-58; chmn, Comn to Study Capital Punishment, 64; deleg, Rep Nat Conv, 64 & NJ Const Conv, 66. Mil Serv: Entered as Pvt, World War II, commissioned Inf Officer Cand Sch, Ft Benning, Ga, Commanding Officer, US War Crime Off, Siagon, French Indo-China, US Prosecutor War Crime Trials in Singapore. Publ: The Traffic in Narcotics, Funk & Wagnall. Mem: Am Bar Asn (spec comt on minimum standards, Admin of Criminal Justice, 64-); NJ & Essex Co Bar Asns; fel Am Col of Trial Lawyers. Honors & Awards: Received Annual Award by Soc Former Spec Agents, FBI for outstanding contributions to the advancement of law enforcement, 59; First Americanism Citation for Meritorious Serv from SMt Lodge, B'nai B'rith, 55; Honor Roll of Inf Officer Cand Hall of Fame, Ft Benning, Ga. Relig: Methodist. Mailing Add: 589 Ridgewood Rd Maplewood NJ 07040

TOMPOS, WILLIAM (D)
b Monongahela, Pa, Feb 17, 14; s Rudolp Stephen Tompos & Mary Martha Dugan T; m 1942 to Helen Bambrick; c Thomas William & Raymond Stephen. Educ: Hancock Co Pub Schs. Polit & Govt Pos: WVa State Deleg, 56; WVa State Sen, 60-74; deleg, Dem Nat Conv, 72. Bus & Prof Pos: Clerical & serv work. Mil Serv: Army, 42-45, attached to 43rd Inf Div, serv in Asiatic-Pac Theatre, 3 years, discharged with rank of Sgt; 5 Battle Stars; 1 Arrowhead Award. Relig: Christian Church. Mailing Add: 3241 West St Weirton WV 26062

TONE, JOHN WOLFE (R)
Chmn, Fourth Cong Dist Rep Comt, Iowa
b Des Moines, Iowa, July 6, 39; s Jay E Tone, Jr & Valeen Gabeline T; m 1963 to Susan Brown; c Tracy Elizabeth & Catherine Hilary. Educ: Claremont Men's Col, BA, 61; vpres, Claremont Cols Young Rep, 60-61. Polit & Govt Pos: Committeeman, Wapello Co Rep Cent Comt, Iowa, 65-66 & Polk Co Rep Cent Comt, 67-68; deleg, Iowa State Rep Conv, 66, 68, 70 & 72; mem, Polk Co Young Rep, 67-68; chmn, Wapello Co Rep Cent Comt, 69-71; co chmn, Congressman John Kyl Campaign Comt, 70 & 72; mem, Rep State Ce Comt, Iowa, 71-; chmn, Fourth Cong Dist Rep Comt, Iowa, 71- Bus & Prof Pos: Off mgr, Hoerner Waldorf Corp, Ottumwa, Iowa, 65-66, salesman, 67-68, opers mgr, 69- Mil Serv: Served in Army Res, 61-67. Mem: Rotary; Airplane Owners & Pilots Asn; Iowans for Better Justice; Ottumwa CofC (dir); Iowa Mfrs Asn. Relig: Episcopal. Mailing Add: 180 E Alta Vista Ottumwa IA 52501

TONER, FELIX J (D)
Chmn, Southeast Dist Dem Party, Alaska
b Philadelphia, Pa, Apr 19, 14; s Felix J Toner & Elizabeth O'Rourke T; m 1941 to Mary Vander Leest; c Kathleen T (Mrs Steven K Boley), Marijo C, Nora Ann & Stacy B. Educ: Univ Notre Dame, BS in Eng, 39. Polit & Govt Pos: Precinct chmn, Juneau Dem Party, Alaska, 52-54, chmn, Southeast Dist Dem Party, 54-56 & 68- & state chmn, 56-60; deleg, Dem Nat Conv, 56, 60 & 68; chmn, State Reapportionment Adv Bd, 65-66 & 72-73; pres, Bd of Engrs & Architects Exam, Alaska, 65-70 & 72-75; mem, Adv Comt Select Comt Small Bus, US Senate, 68-69; deleg, Dem Nat Mid-Term Conf, 74. Bus & Prof Pos: Mine engr, Alaska Juneau Gold Mining Co, 40-44; assoc engr, Corps of Engrs, 44-46; consult engr, Toner & Nordling, Registered Engrs, 46- Mem: Am Soc Civil Engr Nat Soc Prof Engrs; Elks; CofC; Alaska Miners Asn. Relig: Roman Catholic. Legal Res: 127 W Seventh St Juneau AK 99801 Mailing Add: Box 570 Juneau AK 99801

TONEY, ADAM (D)
WVa State Deleg
b Dothan, WVa, Mar 3, 38; s C L (Jimbo) Toney & Claris Fisher T; m 1959 to Mary Jane Massie; c Lisa Joe & Charlie Adam. Educ: WVa Inst Technol, BS, 61; Brunswick Bowling Mgt, Chicago, Ill, 62. Polit & Govt Pos: Second vpres, Fayette Co Young Dem, WVa, 69; mem, State Educ Comt, 69; WVa State Deleg, 69- Mem: WVa Bowling Proprietors Asn; WVa Inst Technol Alumni Asn; Lions; Moose; CofC. Relig: Baptist. Mailing Add: 233 Oyler Ave Oak Hill WV 25901

TONKOVICH, DAN RICHARD (D)
WVa State Deleg
b Columbus, Ohio, Apr 17, 46; s Daniel Tonkovich & Clara Offchinik T; single. Educ: West Liberty State Col, WVa, AB, 68; Syracuse Univ, MA Pub Admin, 72; Lambda Chi Alpha. Polit & Govt Pos: Campus campaign coordr, Robert F Kennedy for President Comt, West Liberty State Col, 68; staff mem, US Cong, 68-71; vpres, Young Dem Marshall Co, WVa, 72; deleg, State Dem Conv, 72; bd mem, Co Comn on Aging, 73; WVa State Deleg, 73- Bus & Prof Pos: Presidential admin asst, Wheeling Col, Wheeling, WVa, 73. Mil Serv: Entered as Pvt E-1, Army, 68, released as S/Sgt E-6, 70, after serv in 199th Light Inf Brigade, Vietnam, 69-70; Vietnam Serv Medal; Presidential Unit Citation; Combat Air-Mobile Medal; Combat Inf Badge. Mem: Jaycees; Am Legion. Relig: Roman Catholic. Mailing Add: 1410 Marshall St Benwood WV 26031

TONSING, ROBERT LOWE, JR (R)
b Wichita, Kans, Jan 8, 31; s Robert Lowe Tonsing, Sr & Helen Hornecker T; m 1973 to Mary Ellen High; c Robert Donn, Martin Karl & Anthony Erik. Educ: Wichita State Univ, BA, 53; Univ Colo, 66 & 70-71. Polit & Govt Pos: Rep nominee, Colo State Rep, 62; Rep precinct committeeman, Adams Co, Colo, 62-65, dist chmn, 63-65; mem commerce & develop adv comt, State of Colo, 63-67; mem, Gov Econ Adv Comt, 64-67; admin asst, US Rep D G Brotzman, Colo, 67-73; pub rels dir, Rep State Cent Comt Colo, 73-; ed & publ, The Trumpet (Rep newspaper), 73-; mem, Colo Centennial-Bicentennial Comn, 73- Bus & Prof Pos: Reporter-photographer, The Wichita Eagle, Kans, 48-53; reporter, photographer, asst city ed & ed writer, The Denver Post, Colo, 56-60; mgr news serv, Martin Marietta Corp, 60-65, dir pub rels, 65-67; vis lectr jour, Univ Colo, 73; mgr pub affairs, Denver Technol Ctr, 73- Mil Serv: Entered as Pvt, Army, 53, released as Cpl, 55, after serv in Pac Stars & Stripes in Japan & SE Asia, 54-55; Commendation Medal; UN Serv Medal; Korean Serv Medal. Mem: Colo Press Asn; Nat Press Photographers Asn; Capitol Hill Tennis Club. Publ: Produced & directed motion pictures The Hands & the Minds, 66 & Congressman, 69, Barbre Prod. Relig: Protestant. Mailing Add: 2269 Ridge Rd Littleton CO 80120

TOOMEY, JOHN J (D)
Mass State Rep
Mailing Add: State Capitol Boston MA 02133

TOON, MALCOLM
US Ambassador to Israel
b Troy, NY, July 4, 16; s George Toon & Margaret Harcomb Broadfoot T; m 1943 to Elizabeth Jane Taylor; c Barbara Jane, Alan Malcolm & Nancy Margaret. Educ: Tufts Univ, AB, 37; Fletcher Sch Law & Diplomacy, MA, 39; Middlebury Col, 50; Harvard Univ, 50-51; Tufts Varsity Club. Polit & Govt Pos: Research technician, Nat Resources Planning Bd, 39-41; career officer, Dept of State Foreign Serv, 46-; foreign serv officer, Warsaw, Budapest, Moscow, Rome, Berlin & Washington, DC, 46-60; mem US deleg, Nuclear Test Conf, Geneva, Switz, 58-59, Four Power Working Group, Washington, DC, London & Paris, 59, Foreign Ministers Conf, Geneva, 59 & Ten Nation Disarmament Comt, Geneva, 60; assigned to US Embassy, London, 60-63; counr polit affairs, Moscow, 63-65; assigned to Dept of State, Washington, DC, 65-69; US Ambassador to Czech, 69-71; US Ambassador to Yugoslavia, 71-75; US Ambassador to Israel, 75- Mil Serv: Entered as Ens, Navy, 42, released as Lt Comdr, 46, after serv in PT Squadron 9, SPac & SW Pac, 43-45; Bronze Star Medal. Mem: Am Foreign Serv Asn; Kenwood Golf & Country Club, DC; Royal Automobile Club, London, Eng. Honors & Awards: Superior Honor Award, Dept of State, 65. Mailing Add: Northborough MA 01532

TOOTE, GLORIA E A (R)
b New York, NY, Nov 8, 31; d Frederick A Toote & Lillie M Tooks T; single. Educ: Howard Univ, 49-52, Sch Law, 54; Columbia Univ Sch Law, LLB, 56. Polit & Govt Pos: Aide, NY Gov Nelson Rockefeller; asst dir, ACTION Agency, 71-73; Asst Secy Equal Opportunity, Dept Housing & Urban Develop, 73-75. Bus & Prof Pos: Pres, Toote Town Publ Co; pres, Town Sound Recording Studios, Inc, 66-70; vchmn, Exec Women in Govt, 75. Publ: Weekly column, Nat Newspaper Publ Asn. Honors & Awards: Cited by Nat Bus League, US CofC as One of the Outstanding Women in Fed Positions; Key to City of San Bernardino, Calif; Newsmaker Award for Distinguished Pub Serv, Nat Newspaper Publ Asn; Spec Achievement Award, Nat Asn Black Women Attorneys. Mailing Add: 282 W 137th St New York NY 10030

TOOTELL, LUCY RAWLINGS (R)
RI State Rep
b Jacksonville, Ill, Nov 27, 11; d Roy Willard Rawlings & Lucy Irene Gammell R; m 1937 to Frederic Delmont Tootell, wid; c Lucy Diana Smith, Joan Lillian & Karen Seymour. Educ: RI Col, EdB, 33; Northwestern Univ Sch Speech, 35; Am Acad Dramatic Arts, NY, 36; Alpha XI Delta. Polit & Govt Pos: Clerk, Richmond Sch Comt, RI, 70-72; RI State Rep, 72- Bus & Prof Pos: Teacher, Richmond Jr High Sch, RI, 33-38; vpres, Wood River Br RR, 39-47. Publ: Auth & co-ed, Ships, sailors and seaports brochure, Pettaquamscutt Hist Soc, Kingston, RI, 63; auth, Rhode Island's last frontier, In: South county yearbook of Rhode Island, Narragansett Times, Inc, Wakefield, 65; ed, Richmond history, Richmond Hist Soc, Wyoming, 68-73. Mem: Nat Grange & Richmond Grange Six (lectr, 69-73); RI Heritage Month Comn, Inc (chmn, 69-73); Richmond Hist Soc (pres, 68-73). Relig: Protestant. Mailing Add: Meadowbrook Rd Wyoming RI 02898

TOPEL, HENRY (D)
VChmn, Del State Dem Party
b New York, NY, June 12, 05; s Louis Topel & Rachel Cohen T; m 1950 to Phyllis Lee; c Avrim & David. Educ: Jacob Joseph Sch, New York, NY; Goldey Beacom Col, Wilmington, Del. Polit & Govt Pos: Chmn, Del State Bd Housing, 67; chmn, Del Real Estate Comn, 68-71; chmn, Del State Dem Party, 70-73, vchmn, currently; alt deleg, Dem Nat Conv, 72. Bus & Prof Pos: Owner, Henry Toepl & Co Real Estate Planning, Wilmington, Del, 59-; pres, Magic Minut Wash, Inc, 59- & El Capitan Motor Hotel, 62- Mil Serv: Entered as Seaman, Navy, 42, released as Coxswain, 46, after serv in Amphibian Forces, Pac Theatre, 13 months. Mem: Real Estate Licensed Law Off of US; Jewish War Vets; Mens Club, Temple Beth Shalom. Relig: Jewish. Mailing Add: 621 Delaware Ave Wilmington DE 19801

TOPLIFF, HELEN JUANITA (D)
Mem, Sixth Cong Dist Dem Comt, Mo
b Hale, Mo, July 4, 15; d Alexander Ritchie & Lenna Heryford R; separated. Educ: Trenton Jr Col, Mo, 69-71. Polit & Govt Pos: Census enumerator, Hill & Hurrican Twp, Mo, 40, Hill, Hurrican, Stokes Mound & Rockford Twp, 45, Grand River & Fairview Twp, 64; committeewoman, Hurrican Twp Dem Comt, Carroll Co, 44-50; field supvr, Bur Census,

Second Cong Dist, 45; acting postmaster, Hale, 50-51; mem, Jackson Co Dem Club, Ward Four, Kansas City, 59-62; committeewoman, Grand River Twp Dem Party, Livingston Co 66-; assessor & clerk, Grand River Twp, 67-68; mem, Sixth Cong Dist Dem Comt, 68-; vchmn, Livingston Co Dem Comt, 69-72. Bus & Prof Pos: Mgr candy dept, Katz Drug Co, Kansas City, Mo, 54-56; fountain mgr, Crowan Drug Co, Shawnee, Kans, 56-59; owner restaurant, Kansas City, Mo, 59-62; farmer, 62- Mem: Carroll Art Club; Nat Farmers Orgn; Green Hills Roving Artist Club; Livingston Co Women's Dem Club; Dem State Club of Mo. Relig: Protestant. Mailing Add: RR 1 Hale MO 64643

TORBERT, C C (D)
Ala State Sen
Mailing Add: PO Box 2345 Opelika AL 36801

TORGEN, EDWARD H (R)
Chmn, North Kingstown Rep Town Comt, RI
b Providence, RI, Aug 12, 27; s Samuel Torgen & Cora Cook T; m 1962 to Mary Ann Webster; c Susan, Tracey, Kristin & Julie. Educ: Brown Univ, AB, 50; Boston Univ, LLB, 58. Polit & Govt Pos: Mem city coun, Warwick, RI, 63-64; clerk & acting judge, Second Dist Court, South Kingstown, 65-69; RI State Rep, 71-72; probate judge, North Kingstown, 71-74; chmn, North Kingstown Rep Town Comt, 74- Bus & Prof Pos: Attorney-at-law, RI, 58- Mil Serv: Entered as Seaman, Navy, 45, released as Comdr, 71, after serv in various units, USS John W Weeks; Comdr, Naval Res, currently; Naval Res Medal; UN Medal; Korean Theatre Medal; World War II Victory Medal. Mem: Am & RI Bar Asns; Washington Co Bd Realtors. Honors & Awards: Young Rep of Year, Warwick Young Rep Club, 66. Mailing Add: 471 N Quidnessett Rd North Kingstown RI 02852

TORONTO, JOSEPH LAMONT (R)
b Salt Lake City, Utah, Feb 9, 54; s Lamont Felt Toronto & Helen Davidson T; single. Educ: Brigham Young Univ, 72. Polit & Govt Pos: Deleg, Co & Utah State Rep Conv, 72; alt deleg, Rep Nat Conv, 72. Bus & Prof Pos: Laborer, Salt Lake City Bd of Educ, 72. Relig: Latter-day Saint. Mailing Add: 2328 Country Club Circle Salt Lake City UT 84109

TORQUATO, JOHN R (D)
Mem, Dem Nat Comt, Pa
Mailing Add: Law Bldg Ebensburg PA 15931

TORRENCE, LINDA FAYE (D)
Committeewoman, Pulaski Co Dem Exec Comt, Ark
b Little Rock, Ark, Nov 23, 44; d Samuel Hudson & Mary Jackson H; m to Leroy Martin Torrence, wid, 1971; c Kirk LaMel, Elana Cheryl & Tahja LaFaye Jackson. Educ: Capital City Bus Col, Little Rock, 67-68; Univ Ark, Little Rock, 69-70; Ark Baptist Col, 70-72. Polit & Govt Pos: Secy, Pulaski Co Young Dem, Ark, 70-71; committeewoman, Pulaski Co Dem Comt, 71-72; deleg, Dem Nat Conv, 72; committeewoman, Pulaski Co Dem Exec Comt, 72- Bus & Prof Pos: Clerk-typist, Little Rock Funeral Home, Ark, 63-64; teller, First Nat Bank, Little Rock, 68-73. Mem: NAACP; Urban League of Little Rock. Relig: Methodist. Mailing Add: Gen Delivery Genevia AR 72053

TORRES, ART (D)
Calif State Assemblyman
b Los Angeles, Calif, Sept 24, 46; s Arthur Torres & Julia Alvarado T; single. Educ: East Los Angeles Col, AA, 66; Univ Calif, Santa Cruz, BA, 68; Univ Calif, Davis, JD, 71; Phi Delta Phi. Polit & Govt Pos: Calif State Assemblyman, 74- Mem: Harvard Club Southern Calif; Jaycees. Honors & Awards: John F Kennedy Fel, Harvard Univ. Legal Res: 3543 E Eighth St Los Angeles CA 90023 Mailing Add: State Capitol Bldg Rm 6003 Sacramento CA 95814

TORRES, ERNEST C (R)
RI State Rep
Mailing Add: 24 Ledge Rd East Greenwich RI 02818

TORRES, JESUS U (D)
b Agana, Guam, June 16, 27; s Joaquin Torres & Maria A Unpingco T; single. Educ: Columbia Univ, NY; Univ Minn, BA, 53; William Mitchell Col Law, St Paul, Minn, LLB, 61. Polit & Govt Pos: Secy, Guam Dem Party, 64-65, chmn, 65-69; Sen, Guam Legis, 62-64, 66-70 & 72-74; mem, Judicial Coun Guam, 66-70. Bus & Prof Pos: Attorney-at-law, 61- Mil Serv: Entered as Pvt, Army, 54, released as SP 3/C, 56, after serv in Heavy Motor Co, 25th Div & 27th Inf Regt; Good Conduct Medal. Mem: Guam Bar Asn. Relig: Catholic. Legal Res: Tamuning GU 96910 Mailing Add: PO Box 1268 Agana GU 96910

TORRES, JOSEPHINE ANGELA (R)
b Redwood City, Calif, July 23, 23; d Pedro Flores (deceased) & Dolores Cortez F (deceased); m 1943 to Charles Perez Torres; c Joseph T & Diana C. Educ: Sequois High Sch, 38-42. Polit & Govt Pos: Rep Nat Committeewoman, Guam, 69-72; vchmn, Rep Womens Fedn, Guam, 69-72. Bus & Prof Pos: Real estate Guam, 47-70. Mem: Notre Dame Moms & Dads Club; Cath Daughter 2047 (second vpres, 73-75); PTA; Rotary Auxiliary. Relig: Catholic. Legal Res: Tamuning GU 96910 Mailing Add: PO Box 1736 Agana GU 96910

TORRES, MAX E V (R)
b Torres, Colo, Feb 4, 12; s Emilio Torres & Eufemia Vallejos T; m 1942 to Della Ann Cordova; c Felix, Max Anthony & George. Educ: Trinidad High Sch, grad, 31; Trinidad Jr Col, 31-33; Adams State Col & Colo State Col. Polit & Govt Pos: Vchmn adv comt, US Civil Rights Comn, 59-69; chmn, Las Animas Co Rep Cent Comt, Colo, formerly; chmn, Colo Civil Rights Comn, 64-69. Bus & Prof Pos: Rancher, 31-; bd mem, Model Land & Irrigation Co, 50-69; secy & bd mem, Purgatoire River Water Conservancy Dist, 60-69. Mem: Las Animas Co Livestock Asn. Relig: Catholic. Mailing Add: 1108 E Main St Trinidad CO 81082

TORRES, RUBEN (D)
Tex State Rep
b Brownsville, Tex, Nov 1, 29; s Thomas Torres & Irene Pompa T; m 1953 to Maria Rodriguez; c Erie (Mrs Tejada), Yvette (Mrs Martinez), Ruben, Jr & Roel. Educ: Tex A&I Univ, BS in phys educ & MA in educ; Western State Col, Colo, EdD; Phi Delta Kappa. Polit & Govt Pos: Tex State Rep, 75- Bus & Prof Pos: Teacher, Elem, Brownsville Independent Sch Dist, Jr High & High Sch, Point Isabel Independent Sch Dist, Tex, 55-65; prin, Port Isabel Jr High Sch, 65-66 & Port Isabel High Sch, 66-70; supt, Point Isabel Independent Sch Dist, 70-74; employee, Bob Massey & Assocs, Brownsville, 74- Mil Serv: Entered as Pvt, Marine Corps, 48, released as Cpl, 52; Good Conduct Medal. Mem: Port Isabel Housing Authority (vchmn bd dirs); Kiwanis; Lions; Rio Grande Valley Asn Sch Admnr; Tex Asn Sch Admnr.

Honors & Awards: Recognized for Prof Accomplishments on Tex Pub Sch, Asn Brownsville Educ, 71; Recognized as Citizen of the Week, KGBT-Radio, TV-4, 74. Relig: Roman Catholic. Legal Res: PO Box 5305 Port Isabel TX 78578 Mailing Add: 2100 Boca Chica Suite 503A Brownsville TX 78520

TORRES FERMOSO, JOSE ONOFRE (POPULAR DEMOCRAT, PR)
Sen, PR Senate
Mailing Add: State Capitol San Juan PR 00901

TORRES-RIGUAL, HIRAM
Assoc Justice, PR Supreme Court
b Mayaguez, PR, July 15, 22; s Jose Torres Santiago & Julia America Rigual S; m 1955 to Lillian Bayouth Gidoun; c Lilliana Marie, Janina Marie, Ilya Marie. Educ: Univ PR, BA cum laude, 46, LLB cum laude, 49; Harvard Law Sch, LLM, 62; Phi Eta Mu. Polit & Govt Pos: Attorney, Legal Div, Land Auth PR, 50-51; legal & legis asst to former Gov Luis Munoz Marin, 51-64; legal & legis asst to forme Gov Sanchez Vilella, 65; judge, Superior Court of the Commonwealth PR, 65-68; Assoc Justice, Supreme Court of PR, 68- Bus & Prof Pos: Asst instr polit sci, Univ PR, 49; law clerk to Supreme Court Justice Borinquen Marrero Rios, 49-50. Publ: Social interest & legal sanction of price fixing by producers, 57 & Control of land values through taxation, 64, Rev del Colegio de Abogados de PR. Mem: PTA of Vedruna Col (vpres); PR Bar Asn. Honors & Awards: Medal for Serv as Pub Officer, Nat Guard of PR, 65. Legal Res: 1921 Reseda St Urb Santa Maria Rio Piedras PR 00927 Mailing Add: Supreme Court of PR PO Box 2392 San Juan PR 00903

TORRES SANTIAGO, CARLOS LUIS (POPULAR DEM, PR)
Rep, PR House Rep
b Coamo, PR, May 24, 38; s Pablo Torres Vazquez & Dolores Santiago De T; m 1968 to Nilda Zayas Pratts; c Carlos Jose. Educ: Coamo High Sch, 3 years. Polit & Govt Pos: Rep & mem, Gov Comn, PR House Rep, 69-71, Rep, 75-; pres, Coamo Popular Dem Party, currently. Mem: Club Soc Recreativo; Lions Int. Relig: Catholic. Mailing Add: 82 HW Santaella Coamo PR 00640

TORRES TORRES, LUIS ANGEL (PR INDEPENDENCE PARTY)
Rep, PR House Rep
Mailing Add: State Capitol San Juan PR 00901

TORREY, ELIZABETH N (R)
Vice-Chairwoman, Minn Rep State Cent Comt
b Red Wing, Minn, May 24, 25; d Louis William Nordly & Florence Isabella Brown N; m 1952 to Robert Marshall & James Marshall. Educ: Carleton Col, Northfield, Minn, BA magna cum laude, 47; Phi Beta Kappa. Polit & Govt Pos: Rep precinct chairwoman, Red Wing, Minn, 56-58, Rep city chairwoman, 58-61; chairwoman, Goodhue Co Rep Party, 61-63; vice-chairwoman, Fist Cong Dist Rep Party, 63-65, chairwoman, 65-69; deleg, Rep Nat Conv, 68; vice-chairwoman, Minn Rep State Cent Comt, 69- Bus & Prof Pos: Claims supvr, Employers Mutuals of Wausau, 47-52. Relig: Episocpal. Mailing Add: 1617 Poplar Dr Red Wing MN 55066

TORREY, GLEN W (R)
Maine State Rep
b Lewiston, Maine, Sept 12, 15; s Leo G Torrey & Mary Law T; m 1941 to Jane Waterhouse; c Nancy (Mrs Sam Wright, III), John A, Cynthia (Mrs James Whiting) & Glenna M. Educ: Univ Maine, Orono, BS, 36; Alpha Zeta; Alpha Gamma Rho. Polit & Govt Pos: Selectman, Poland, Maine, 47-52, mem sch comt, 58-68; Maine State Rep, 75- Bus & Prof Pos: Mgr dairy plant, M P Hood, 37-45; owner & operator dairy farm, Poland, Maine, 46-75. Mil Serv: Seaman 1/C, Navy, 45-46. Mem: Grange; Farm Bur; F&AM; Eastern Star. Relig: Methodist. Legal Res: Poland ME 04274 Mailing Add: Box 108 Rte 4 Auburn ME 04210

TORREY, JANET B (R)
NH State Rep
b Barberton, Ohio, Nov 4, 03; d Willis Carmen Baughman & Jennie Lidyard B; m 1941 to Charles William Torrey; wid; c William Peter. Educ: Akron Univ, 21-23; Case Western Reserve Univ, AB, 26; Univ Wis, 27; Harvard Med Sch, cert phys ther, 37; Univ NH, 60-70; Alpha Gamma Delta. Polit & Govt Pos: NH State Rep, 75-, mem educ comt, NH Gen Court, 75- Bus & Prof Pos: Teacher phys educ & math, Barberton High Sch, Ohio, 27-36; phys therapist, Children's Hosp, Boston, Mass, 38-41 & Portsmouth Rehab Ctr, 53-56; receptionist-secy, Dr Robert F Wilson, Dover, NH, 56-59; teacher math, Somersworth Jr High Sch, 59-60, Horne Street Sch, Dover, NH, 60-67 & Dover High Sch, 67-74. Mil Serv: 2nd Lt, Army, 44, serv in Lawson Gen Hosp, Atlanta, Ga & Station Hosp, Ft Devens, Mass. Mem: Nat Coun Teachers Math; Asn Teachers Math New England; NH Asn Teachers Math New England (secy); Bus & Prof Women; Delta Kappa Gamma (membership chmn, 74-). Relig: Protestant. Mailing Add: 14 Elliot Park Dover NH 03820

TORRICELLI, ROBERT G (D)
Sgt-at-Arms, Dem State Comt NJ
b Paterson, NJ, Aug 26, 51; s S Lawrence Torricelli & Betty Lotz T; single. Educ: Rutgers Col, BA, Law Sch, currently. Polit & Govt Pos: Chmn, 40th Dist Dem Co Comt, 73-75; sgt-at-arms, Dem State Comt NJ, 73-, dir, 74; staff, Dem Nat Mid-Term Conf, 74. Relig: Methodist. Mailing Add: 257 Woodside Ave Franklin Lakes NJ 07417

TORRY, P SPENCER (D)
b Trinidad, West Indies; d Fitz Clarence Spencer & Elizabeth St Rose S; m 1948 to Robert Lee Torry, Jr; c Lynda Avern (Mrs George Keith), Robert L, III & Jerard N. Educ: Southern Univ, Baton Rouge, BS, 52, JD, 70; Univ Denver, MA, 58; Alpha Kappa Alpha. Polit & Govt Pos: Mem staff, Dept Justice, Washington, DC, summer 69; alt deleg, Dem Nat Conv, 72. Bus & Prof Pos: Teacher math, Rapides Parish Schs, La, 52-56, 60-67 & 71-; instr math, Southern Univ, Baton Rouge, 56-59 & 67-70; pvt law practice, 75- Honors & Awards: Sci Student of Year, Southern Univ, 50-51, Two Law Student Awards, 68 & 69. Relig: Catholic. Legal Res: 1025 Murray St Alexandria LA 71301 Mailing Add: 3629 13th St Alexandria LA 71301

TORTAROLO, JOANN MARY (R)
Mem, Rep State Cent Comt, Calif
b Los Angeles, Calif, June 17, 48; d Sebastian Tortarolo & Ellen Hathaway T; single. Educ: Univ Calif, Riverside, BA, 69, teaching credential, 70; Glengarries; pres, Highlander Young Rep, 68-69. Polit & Govt Pos: Youth chmn, Younglove for Supvr, Riverside, Calif, 70; secy, Riverside Co Young Rep, 70-71; Riverside Co precinct chmn, Snider for Cong, 38th Dist,

72; asst co precinct chmn, Comt to Reelect the President, Riverside, 72; alt deleg, Rep Nat Conv, 72; mem, Calif Rep State Cent Comt, 73- Bus & Prof Pos: Teacher, San Bernardino City Unified Sch Dist, Calif, 71- Mem: Calif Teachers Asn. Relig: Catholic. Mailing Add: 955 Via Zapata 9 Riverside CA 92507

TOTARO, ROSEMARIE (D)
NJ State Rep
Mailing Add: State House Trenton NJ 08625

TOTH, JUDITH COGGESHALL (D)
Md State Deleg
b Rochelle, Ill, Oct 21, 37; d Robert James Coggeshall & Elita Etzbach C; m 1961 to Csanad Toth; c Christina Maria & Adriana Maria. Educ: Mexico City Col, 56-57; Northwestern Univ, Evanston, BA, 59; Georgetown Univ, 59-62; Univ of the Andes, 64-66; Kappa Kappa Gamma. Polit & Govt Pos: Founding bd mem, Alliance for Dem Reform, Montgomery Co, 68-72; c vchmn, New Dem Coalition of Md, 69-70; Dem precinct chmn, Montgomery Co, 68-74, mem adv comt on the Potomac River, 70-71; Md State Deleg, 75- Bus & Prof Pos: Consult, Int Study Ctr, 68; consult, President's Comn on Causes & Prevention of Violence, 69; assoc, Ideas, Inc, 70-71; assoc, PolitEcon Serv, Inc, 71-74. Publ: Co-auth, Elections in Colombia, 66 & Report of the President's Commission on the Causes & Prevention of Violence, 69. Mem: Montgomery Co Civic Fedn; Am Civil Liberties Union, Md; Metrop Washington Cong of Citizens; Cabin John Park Citizens Asn; League of Women Voters. Honors & Awards: Star News Cup for Civic Activity, Montgomery Co Civic Fedn, 73-74. Relig: Roman Catholic. Mailing Add: 6611 80th Pl Cabin John MD 20034

TOTHEROW, CARL D (D)
NC State Sen
Mailing Add: 713 Longbow Rd Winston-Salem NC 27104

TOTTEN, DONALD LEE (R)
Ill State Rep
b Brooklyn, NY, Feb 19, 33; s Edgar L Totten & Louise Florentine T; m 1955 to Joyce Anderson; c Diana, Robert & Kathleen. Educ: Univ Notre Dame, BSME, 55. Polit & Govt Pos: Committeeman, Schaumburg Rep Twp Comt, Ill, 66-; asst to dir, Dept of Pub Works, Ill, 70-73; Ill State Rep, Third Dist, 72- Bus & Prof Pos: Indust engr, Int Register, Chicago, Ill, 60; plant mgr, Morton Mfg, Libertyville, 60-67, Farr Co, Crystal Lake, 67-70; mfg agt, Twin-T Co, 72- Mem: Ill State CofC; Am Mgt Asn. Relig: Roman Catholic. Mailing Add: 193 Woodlawn St Hoffman Estates IL 60172

TOUCHETTE, FRANCIS WALTER (D)
b Centreville Twp, Ill, Oct 15, 12; s Joseph K Touchette & Josephine Traiteur T; m 1939 to Rose Lee Gardiner. Polit & Govt Pos: Dem precinct committeeman, Precinct Three, Centreville Twp, St Clair Co, Ill, 32-40; hwy comnr, Centreville Twp, 39-49, chief supvr, 49-; chmn, East Side Health Dist, East St Louis, St Clair Co, Ill, 49-; chmn, St Clair Co Bd, 72-74, mem, 72-; deleg, Dem Nat Mid-Term Conf, 74. Mailing Add: 6304 Bond Ave East St Louis IL 62207

TOUHY, JOHN P (D)
Chmn, Ill State Dem Cent Comt
b Apr 19, 19; m to Mary; c Debbie, Nancy & Jackie. Educ: Georgetown Univ, DePaul Law Sch. Polit & Govt Pos: Ill State Rep, formerly, Minority Whip, Ill House of Rep, formerly; alt deleg, Dem Nat Conv, 72; chmn, Ill State Dem Cent Comt, 72-; deleg, Dem Nat Mid-Term Conf, 74. Mil Serv: Army, 4 and a half years, more than 2 years overseas. Mem: VFW; Georgetown Club of Chicago. Mailing Add: 505 N Lakeshore Dr Chicago IL 60611

TOWE, THOMAS EDWARD (D)
Mont State Sen
b Cherokee, Iowa, June 25, 37; s (William) Edward Towe & Florence Tow T; m 1960 to Alyce Ruth James; c James Thomas & Kristofer Edward. Educ: Earlham Col, Richmond, Ind, BA, 59; Univ Paris, L'Institut d'Etude Politique, 56; Univ Mont Law Sch, LLB, 62; Georgetown Univ Law Sch, LLM, 65; Univ Mich Law Sch, 65-66; Phi Kappa Phi; Phi Delta Phi. Polit & Govt Pos: Treas, Univ Mont Young Dem Club, 60; first vpres, Yellowstone Co Dem Club, Mont, 68-70; second vchmn, Yellowstone Co Dem Cent Comt, Mont, 70-74; cand, Mont House Rep, 68; deleg, Mont Dem State Conv, 68, 72 & 74; deleg, Dem Nat Conv, 68, deleg & chmn deleg, 72; Eastern Dist Cong Committeeman, Mont Dem State Cent Comt, 69-71; Mont State Rep, Dist Eight, Yellowstone Co, 71-74; chmn, Mont McGovern for President Comt, 71-72; deleg & coord chmn, Dem Nat Mid-Term Conf, 74; Mont State Sen, Dist 34, 75-, chmn judiciary comt, Mont State Senate, chmn joint interim judiciary comt, vchmn interim comt on no fault ins, 73, vchmn interim comt on coal taxes, 74, Old West regional comn & coal tax rev comt. Bus & Prof Pos: Attorney-at-law, 67-; sr partner, Towe, Neely & Ball, currently. Mil Serv: Entered as 1st Lt, Army, 62, released as Capt, 65, after serv in Judge Adv Gen Corps, Pentagon, DC, 63-65; Capt, Res, 65-73; Army Commendation Medal. Publ: Criminal pretrial procedure in France, Tulane Law Rev, 4/64; Fundamental Rights in the Soviet Union: a comparative approach, Univ Pa Law Rev, 1/67; Natural law & the ninth amendment, Pepperdine Law Rev, 75; plus others. Mem: Mont & Yellowstone Co Bar Asns; Rimrock Guid Found (mem bd); Concern Inc (mem bd); Dist Youth Guid Home (mem bd). Relig: Quaker. Mailing Add: 2640 Burlington Ave Billings MT 59102

TOWELL, DAVID G (R)
b Bronxville, NY, June 9, 37; s Sydney Towell & Gladys Gilmer T; m 1968 to Mary Sharon Smith; c David Gilmer, Jr & Mark Hamilton. Educ: Univ of the Pac, BA, 60. Polit & Govt Pos: Pres, Young Rep of Nev, 66-67; chmn, Douglas Co Rep Cent Comt, Nev, 70-72; US Rep, Nev, 72-75. Bus & Prof Pos: Independent real estate broker, David G Towell Realty, 60-; Vet Admin appraiser, 68-72. Mil Serv: Nev Air Nat Guard, 60-66. Mem: Toastmasters Int; Carson Valley CofC. Relig: Episcopal. Mailing Add: PO Box 1974 Gardnerville NV 89410

TOWER, JOHN GOODWIN (R)
US Sen, Tex
b Houston, Tex, Sept 29, 25; s Joe Z Tower & Beryl Goodwin T; m 1952 to Joza Lou Bullington; c Penelope, Marian & Jeanne. Educ: Southwestern Univ (Tex), BA, 48; Southern Methodist Univ, MA, 53; London Sch of Econ & Polit Sci, 52-53. Hon Degrees: LLD, Howard Payne Col, Brownwood, Tex, 63; LittD, Southwestern Univ (Tex), 64. Polit & Govt Pos: US Sen, Tex, 61-, mem comts on armed serv & banking, housing & urban develop, US Senate, mem, Joint Comt on Defense Prod, chmn, Sen Rep Policy Comt & vchmn, Select Comt on Intel Opers; deleg, Rep Nat Conv, 68 & 72. Bus & Prof Pos: Asst prof polit sci, Midwestern Univ, 51-60; mem bd trustees, Southern Methodist Univ, currently & Southwestern Univ (Tex), currently. Mil Serv: Entered Navy, 43, released as Seaman 1/C, 46, after serv on Naval Gunboat, Asia; mem, Naval Res. Mem: Am Asn of Univ Prof; Am Polit Sci Asn; Int Polit Sci Asn; Mason (32 degree); Shrine; Mason. Honors & Awards: Named Kappa Sigma Man of Year, 61; Trips to Southeast Asian Combat Zone, 65, 66, 67, 69 & 70; John Tower Chair of Polit Sci, Southwestern Univ, endowed 75. Relig: Methodist; mem bd stewards, Wichita Falls. Legal Res: Wichita Falls TX Mailing Add: 142 Old Senate Off Bldg Washington DC 20510

TOWERY, KAYE H (R)
Chmn, Lafayette Co Rep Exec Comt, Miss
b Thaxton, Miss, Mar 24, 38; d Elton L Hooker & LeEarle Street H; div; c Julie Kaye & Bobby Arlen, Jr. Educ: Univ Miss, 55-57; Phi Gamma Nu; Epsilon Gamma Epsilon; Kappa Delta. Polit & Govt Pos: Miss State chmn, Southern Rep Conf, 72; vchmn, First Cong Dist Rep Party, Miss, 71-; vchmn, Lafayette Co Rep Exec Comt, 71-72, chmn, 72-; deleg, Rep Nat Conv, 72; dist chmn, Miss State Rep Cand Comt, 75; Rep cand, State Senate, Dist I, 75. Publ: Contrib ed, Southstyle Mag, 72-73. Mem: CofC; Jaycettes (pres); PTA (pres); Univ Dames (pres). Honors & Awards: Outstanding Jr Mem, David Reese Chap, DAR. Relig: Episcopal. Legal Res: Hwy 30 E Oxford MS 38655 Mailing Add: Rte 1 Box 49-L Oxford MS 38655

TOWERY, ROLAND KENNETH (R)
Dep Dir Policy & Plans, US Info Agency
b Smithville, Miss, Jan 25, 23; s Wiley Azof Tower & Lonie Bell Cowart T; m 1947 to Louise Cook; c Roland Kenneth, Jr & Alice Ann. Polit & Govt Pos: Press secy, US Sen John Tower, Tex, 63-65, admin asst, 64-69; asst dir, US Info Agency, 69-72, dep dir policy & plans, 72- Mil Serv: Entered as Pvt, Army, 41, released as Cpl, 46, after serv in Battery C, 60th CAC, Philippines, 41-45; Purple Heart; Presidential Unit Citation with two Oak Leaf Clusters; Asiatic Pac Theater Campaign with two Bronze Stars; Philippine Defense Ribbon with one Bronze Star; Am Defense Serv Ribbon with one Bronze Star. Mem: Sigma Delta Chi; Mason. Honors & Awards: Pulitzer Prize, 55. Legal Res: 1709 Norris Dr Austin TX 78704 Mailing Add: 6803 Old Chesterbrook Rd McLean VA 22101

TOWLE, CLAYTON W (R)
NH State Rep
Mailing Add: Tasker Hill Rd Conway NH 03818

TOWNSEND, BRUCE C (R)
NH State Rep
b Lebanon, NH, Aug 24, 38; s Howard C Townsend & Madeline T; m 1961; c Heidi & Dwight. Educ: Univ NH Thompson Sch Agr, grad, 60. Polit & Govt Pos: NH State Rep, 75- Bus & Prof Pos: Partner, Tomapo Farm, 70-75. Mil Serv: Entered as E-1, Army Res, 57, released as E-2, 62. Mem: Grafton Co Farm Bur (bd mem, former pres); Granite State Northern Model RR Club (bd mem, pres, 74). Relig: Episcopal. Mailing Add: Box 433 Storrs Hill Lebanon NH 03766

TOWNSEND, JAMES BAKER (D)
Okla State Rep
b Haileyville, Okla, Nov 23, 27; s John Dunn Townsend & Rose Baker T; m 1949 to June Marie Childres; c James Lawrence, Jeffrey Paul & Jay Arthur. Educ: Okla Mil Acad, 45. Polit & Govt Pos: Okla State Rep, 64-, chmn Dem caucus, Okla House Rep, formerly, first asst to the Majority Floor Leader, currently; deleg, Dem Nat Conv, 72. Mil Serv: Entered as Pvt, Army, 46, released as Pfc, 47, after serv in Far East. Mem: United Transportation Union; VFW; Okla Bow Hunters; Pottawatomie Co Cattlemen's Asn; Lions. Relig: Methodist. Mailing Add: Rte 4 Box 194 Shawnee OK 74801

TOWNSEND, KILIAEN VAN RENSSELAER (R)
Ga State Rep
b Garden City, NY, Oct 6, 18; s Edward Nichol Townsend & Beatrice Nicholas T; m 1949 to Mary Campbell Everett; c Kiliaen Van Rensselaer, Jr. Educ: Williams Col, AB, 39; Univ Va Law Sch, LLB, 42; Phi Delta Phi; Raven Soc; Chi Psi. Polit & Govt Pos: Secy, Fulton Co Rep Party, Ga, 48; deleg, Rep Nat Conv, 52; Ga State Rep, 115th Dist, 65-, Minority Whip, Ga House of Rep. Mil Serv: Entered as Pvt, Army, 42, released as 2nd Lt, 46. Mem: Atlanta Lawyers Club; Ga Bar Asn; Rotary. Relig: Protestant. Mailing Add: 208 Townsend Pl NW Atlanta GA 30327

TOWNSEND, RICHARD TAYLOR (D)
Mem, SC State Dem Exec Comt
b Laurens, SC, Sept 24, 40; s Thomas Pickney Townsend & Virginia Taylor T; m 1963 to Donna Doyle Evans; c Allison, Ashley & Amanda Evans. Educ: Clemson Univ, BS Indust Mgt, 62; Univ SC, LLB, 65; Indust Mgt Soc; Sigma Alpha Zeta; Phi Delta Phi. Polit & Govt Pos: Chmn, Laurens Co Dem Party, SC, 66-68; alt deleg, Dem Nat Conv, 68 & deleg, 72; mem, SC State Exec Comt, Laurens Co, 70-; deleg, Dem Nat Mid-Term Conf, 74. Mem: Rotary; Jr CofC; Mason; Shrine; Laurens CofC. Honors & Awards: Peace Fund Award, Clemson Univ. Relig: Episcopal. Mailing Add: 109 Brookwood Dr Laurens SC 29360

TOWNSEND, RUSSELL I, JR (D)
Va State Sen
Mailing Add: 329 Tudor Place Chesapeake VA 23325

TOWNSEND, SARA M (R)
NH State Rep
Mailing Add: Box 65 Meriden NH 03770

TOWNSEND, W WAYNE (D)
Ind State Sen
Educ: Purdue Univ, grad; Alpha Gamma Rho. Polit & Govt Pos: Ind State Rep, 59-66; Ind State Sen, 71-; deleg, Dem Nat Conv, 72. Bus & Prof Pos: Farmer. Mil Serv: Army Counterintel Corps, 54-56. Mem: Marion Gen Hosp (bd dir); Grant Co Asn Ment Health; Mason; Scottish Rite; Elks. Relig: Friends Church. Mailing Add: Rte 2 Hartford City IN 47348

TOWNSEND, WILLIAM H (D)
Ark State Rep
Mailing Add: 507 W 31st St Little Rock AR 72206

TOWSE, DANIEL CHARLES (R)
Mem, Stoneham Rep Town Comt, Mass

b Somerville, Mass, Dec 5, 24; s Charles Frederick Towse & Evangeline Lynch T; m 1948 to Marian MacDonald; c Linda Joyce, Janet Elaine & Amy Evangeline. Educ: Stoneham High Sch, 4 years. Polit & Govt Pos: Mem, Stoneham Planning Bd, Mass, 59-66; mem, Stoneham Conserv Comn, 63-; mem, Stoneham Rep Town Comt, 64-; mem, Stoneham Bd of Selectmen, 65-69; Mass State Rep, 21st Middlesex Dist, 69-74. Bus & Prof Pos: Park & forestry supvr, Stoneham, 23 years. Mil Serv: Entered as Pvt, Army, 43, released as Sgt, 45, after serv in 76th Inf Div, 3rd Army, ETO, 44-45; Unit Citation; Combat Inf Badge; three Battle Stars. Mem: New Eng Park & Forestry Asn; Mass Legislators Asn; Am Legion; VFW; Appalachian Mountain Club. Relig: Congregational. Mailing Add: 7 Congress St Stoneham MA 02180

TOYOFUKU, GEORGE HIROSHI (D)
Hawaii State Sen

b Hanapepe, Hawaii, May 29, 30; s Masaji Toyofuku & Sakae T; m 1953 to Elsie Y Uyesono; c Amy C, Guy K, Lisa R & Dean K. Educ: Univ Hawaii, BBA. Polit & Govt Pos: Supvr, Bd of Supvr, 59-64; Hawaii State Rep, 65-70; Hawaii State Sen, 70-; deleg, Dem Nat Conv, 72. Bus & Prof Pos: Spec agt, Vet Finance Co, Ltd & NAm Ins Agency Ltd, 54-66; mgr, Vet Finance Co, Ltd, 66-. Mem: Lihue Businessmen's Asn; Lions; Lihue Hongwanji Mission; Kauai CofC; Retarded Childrens Asn. Relig: Buddhist. Legal Res: 3386 Elima St Lihue HI 96766 Mailing Add: c/o Senate Sgt at Arms State Capitol Honolulu HI 96813

TOZIER, KENNETH E, JR (D)
Maine State Rep
Mailing Add: Unity ME 04988

TRACY, DONALD ALLEN (D)
b Eldon, Mo, Dec 2, 33; s Clarence A Tracy & Myrtle Gouge T; m 1953 to Shirley Louise Sullivan; c Donald A, Jr & Carolyn Ann. Educ: La Salle Univ exten, 4 years. Polit & Govt Pos: Pres, Miller Co Young Dem Club, Mo, 68, chmn, Eighth Dist, 68-69; alderman, Eldon City Coun, 70-; treas, Miller Co Dem Comt, formerly. Relig: Christian. Mailing Add: PO Box 173 Eldon MO 65026

TRACY, JOHN LEO, JR (R)
Chmn, Cooke Co Rep Party, Tex

b Corsicana, Tex, Feb 3, 32; s John L Tracy, Sr & Mary Parker T; m 1955 to Shirley Ann Brown; c Tim, Matt & Erin. Educ: Tex A&M Univ, BS in Petroleum Eng, 54. Polit & Govt Pos: Chmn, Cooke Co Rep Party, Tex, 66- Bus & Prof Pos: Vpres, Loch & Tracy Eng Co, 66-; pres, Sci Petroleum, Inc, 68-; partner, Tracy Lock Bldg Co, 72- Mil Serv: Entered as 2nd Lt, Army, 54, released as 1st Lt, 56, after serv in 59th Brigade, Ft Leonard Wood, Mo, 54-56. Mem: CofC (dir, 74-); Soc Petroleum Engr; Am Petroleum Inst, Texoma Chap; Boys Club of Gainesville (dir); River Valley Country Club (pres, 74-). Honors & Awards: Meritorious Serv Award, Texoma Chap, Am Petroleum Inst; Registered Prof Engr, Tex. Relig: Catholic. Legal Res: 221 Hird Gainesville TX 76240 Mailing Add: PO Box 170 Gainesville TX 76240

TRACY, MILDRED ETHEL (D)
Chmn, Golden Valley Co Dem Cent Comt, Mont

b Anamoose, NDak, Aug 22, 03; d Henry Bartz & Clara Loraff B; m 1929 to Eugene M Tracy; c Elizabeth (Mrs Sweeney), Donald E, Vincent W, Raymond L & Clarice (Mrs Flanagan). Educ: Intermountain Union Col, 24-25; Univ Mont, 26; Drake Univ, 27-28. Polit & Govt Pos: Regional dir, Mont State Dem Women, 60-64; pres, Golden Valley Co Dem Women, 62-66, chmn, State Resolutions Comt, 66, secy, 71-; chmn, Golden Valley Co Dem Cent Comt, 63-67, 73- Mem: Farmers Union (vpres, 72-); Am Legion Auxiliary. Relig: Methodist. Mailing Add: Ryegate MT 59074

TRACY, SHIRLEY LOUISE (D)
Committeewoman, Miller Co Dem Comt, Mo

b Jefferson City, Mo, Dec 16, 34; d John J Sullivan, Sr & Alma K Kretzschmar; m 1953 to Donald Allen Tracy, Sr; c Donald Allen, Jr & Carolyn Ann. Educ: St Peters High Sch, Jefferson City, Mo, grad. Polit & Govt Pos: Committeewoman, Miller Co Dem Comt, Mo, 65-; secy, pres, Miller Co Dem Women's Club, 69-70; secy, Mo Fedn Dem Women's Clubs, 70-71. Relig: Christian. Legal Res: 102 W 16th St Eldon MO 65026 Mailing Add: PO Box 173 Eldon MO 65026

TRACY, WILLIAM ALLAN (D)
b Seattle, Wash, Dec 30, 40; s Bernie William Tracy & Mildred Barnard T; m 1970 to Nancy Lea Schultz. Educ: Univ Wash, BA, 65 & 66; Phi Alpha Theta; Theta Xi; Pi Omicron Sigma. Polit & Govt Pos: Dem committeeman, Precinct 98, Dist 34, Seattle, Wash, 66-69 & Precinct 100, Dist 34, 69-70; Dem committeeman, Precinct 8, Dist 30, Des Moines, 70-71; dist campaign chmn, John O'Connor Gov, 34th Dist, 68; alt deleg, Dem Nat Conv, 68; campaign chmn, A A Marinaro Co Coun, Coun Dist Nine, South King Co, 68-69; alt deleg, King Co Young Dem Clubs Joint Coun to Co Dem Cent Comt Exec Bd; Nat Committeeman, Wash State Young Dem, 70-71; Far West Regional dir, Young Dem of Am, 70-; campaign mgr, A A Marinaro, State Rep, 47th Dist, 72; precinct committeeman, Dist 31, 74- Bus & Prof Pos: Census trainer & supvr, US Bur Census, Seattle, Wash, 67; teacher, Highline Sch Dist, Seattle, 67-; asst football coach, Sunset Jr High Sch, 70. Mem: Highline, Wash & Nat Educ Asns; Seattle Young Dem (pres); Sunset PTA (vpres). Honors & Awards: Alumnus of Year Award, Theta Xi, 66. Mailing Add: 11514 21st Pl SW Seattle WA 98146

TRAEGER, CHARLES DONALD (R)
Mem, Rep State Comt Pa

b McKeesport, Pa, June 13, 28; s Oswald L Traeger & Catherine Gaffron T; m to Bonnie Lee Tray; c Charles D. Educ: Pa State Univ, 58. Polit & Govt Pos: Alt deleg, Rep Nat Conv, 72; mem, Rep State Comt Pa, 74- Mem: White Oak Rod & Gun; F&AM (Syria Temple Shrine 375); Fedn Tel Workers of Pa (union steward). Relig: United Methodist. Mailing Add: 2160 Thomas Dr McKeesport PA 15131

TRAEGER, JOHN ANDREW (D)
Tex State Sen

b Wichita Falls, Tex, July 6, 21; s Albert Edward Traeger & Bonnie Lois Forman T; m 1943 to Margaret Bernice Vivroux; c Betty Camille, Jeanne Marie, John A, Jr & James Edward. Educ: Tex Wesleyan Col, 38-39; Tex Lutheran Col, 39-41; pres, Tex Lutheran Col Athletic Asn, formerly. Polit & Govt Pos: City councilman, Seguin, Tex, 58-62; mayor pro tem, 60-61; Tex State Rep, 41st Dist, 63-72; Tex State Sen, 73- Mil Serv: Entered as Pvt, Army Air Force, 41, released as Capt, 45, after serv in Continental US; grad, Army Air Force, Statist Sch, US Army Artil Sch & Nuclear Warfare Sch; Col, Trans Group Comdr, Tex Nat Guard, currently. Mem: Lions; Elks (Past Exalted Ruler & trustee, Seguin Lodge); Seguin CofC (pres); Guadalupe Co Community Fund (pres); Guada-Coma Boy Scout Dist (chmn). Relig: Methodist; mem, Bd of Stewards. Mailing Add: 503 S Austin St Seguin TX 78155

TRAIN, RUSSELL ERROL (R)
Adminr, Environ Protection Agency

b Jamestown, RI, June 4, 20; s Rear Admiral Charles Russell Train & Errol Cuthbert Brown T; m 1954 to Aileen Ligon Bowdoin; c Nancy (Mrs St John Smith), Emily Ligon, Charles Bowdoin & Errol Cuthbert. Educ: Princeton Univ, AB, 41; Columbia Univ, LLB, 47. Polit & Govt Pos: Staff attorney, Joint Comt Internal Revenue Taxation, US Cong, 47-53; clerk, Comt on Ways & Means, US House Rep, 53-54, minority adv, 54-55; head legal adv staff & asst to the secy, Treas Dept, 56-57; judge, US Tax Court, 57-65; Under Secy, Dept of the Interior, 69-70; chmn, Coun on Environ Quality, 70-73; adminr, Environ Protection Agency, 73- Bus & Prof Pos: Pres, Conserv Found, 65-69. Mil Serv: Entered as 2nd Lt, Army, 41, released as Maj, 46, after serv in Field Artil, Pac, 45-46; Pac Campaign Medal with one Battle Star. Relig: Episcopal. Mailing Add: Environ Protection Agency 401 M St SW Washington DC 20460

TRAMMELL, HOYT W (D)
Ala State Rep
Mailing Add: Rte 15 Box 247 Birmingham AL 35224

TRANSUE, ANDREW JACKSON (D)
b Clarksville, Mich, Jan 12, 03; s Charles John Transue & Nina Winks T; m 1935 to Vivian A Chappel; c Tamara Louise (Mrs James Royle) & Andrea Ann (Mrs Marc Haidle). Educ: Detroit Col of Law, LLB, 26, JD, 68. Polit & Govt Pos: Prosecuting attorney, Genesee Co, Mich, 33-37; US Rep, Mich, 37-39; dist dir, Sixth Dist, Mich, US Census, US Dept of Commerce, 39-40; assoc govt appeal agent local bd, Selective Serv Syst, 41-54; mem appeal bd panel, 54-66; assoc govt appeal agent, 66-71. Mem: Mason; F&AM; Elks; Lions. Relig: Methodist. Legal Res: 1647 N Grand Traverse St Flint MI 48503 Mailing Add: 726 Mott Found Bldg Flint MI 48502

TRANTINO, JOSEPH PETER (D)
Chmn, Old Saybrook Dem Town Comt, Conn

b Hartford, Conn, Dec 21, 24; s Peter Trantino & Mary Pepi T; m 1955 to Vivian Nancy Dalone; c Peter Joseph. Educ: Trinity Col, 50. Polit & Govt Pos: Chmn, Old Saybrook Dem Town Comt, Conn, 64-; chmn, 20th Sen Dist Dem Comt, 71-74; dep comnr, State Dept Transportation, 75- Bus & Prof Pos: Pres & owner, Radio Sta WLIS, Old Saybrook, Conn, 56-70. Mil Serv: Entered as Pvt, Army, 43, released as 1st Sgt, after serv in Inf, SPac, 43-46; Silver Star; Bronze Star; Purple Heart; Soldier's Medal. Mem: Elks; Lions Int. Relig: Catholic. Mailing Add: 34 Cedarwood Lane Old Saybrook CT 06475

TRAPP, HOWARD (R)
Polit & Govt Pos: Rep Nat Committeeman, Guam, formerly. Mailing Add: PO Box 3367 Agana GU 96910

TRASK, ALAN (D)
Fla State Sen
Mailing Add: Trask Rd Fort Meade FL 33841

TRAVERS, ALFRED, JR (D)
RI State Rep

b Providence, RI, Oct 14, 24; m to Concetta. Polit & Govt Pos: RI State Rep, 61- Bus & Prof Pos: Indust engr. Mailing Add: 53 Armstrong Ave Providence RI 02903

TRAVIS, GERALDINE WASHINGTON (D)
Mont State Rep

b Albany, Ga, Sept 3, 31; d Joseph Thomas Washington & Dorothy Marshall W; m 1949 to William Alexander Travis; c William A, Jr, Michael Bernard, Anne Marie, Gerald Sandor & Gwendolyn Dorothea. Educ: Xavier Univ La, 47-49. Polit & Govt Pos: Deleg, Dem Nat Conv, 72, Dem Nat State coordr, Nat Women's Polit Caucus, 73-; Mont State Rep, 75- Mem: NAACP; Nat Coun of Negro Women, Inc; US Civil Rights Comn (Mont adv coun); YWCA; Mont Bd Crime Control. Relig: Catholic. Mailing Add: 5413 Sixth Ave S Great Falls MT 59405

TRAXLER, J ROBERT (D)
US Rep, Mich

b Kawkawlin, Mich, July 21, 31; m 1962 to Louida Repkie; c Tamara & Brad. Educ: Bay City Jr Col; Mich State Univ, BA Polit Sci, 53; Detroit Col Law, LLB, 59. Polit & Govt Pos: Asst prosecutor, Bay Co, Mich, 60-62; Mich State Rep, 62-72, Majority Floor Leader, Mich House of Rep, 65-66, Asst Minority Floor Leader, 67-72; US Rep, Mich, 72-; ex-officio deleg, Dem Nat Mid-Term Conf, 74. Bus & Prof Pos: Attorney. Mil Serv: Army, 53-55. Mem: Am & Mich Bar Asns; Bay Co Ment Health Soc (dir). Relig: Episcopal. Legal Res: 1803 33rd St Bay City MI 48706 Mailing Add: 1526 Longworth House Off Bldg Washington DC 20515

TRAYLOR, FRANK (R)
Colo State Rep
Mailing Add: 4045 Field Dr Wheat Ridge CO 80033

TRAYLOR, LAWRENCE MILTON (R)
b Oklahoma City, Okla, Mar 26, 28; s Edward L Traylor & Mildred Moore T; wid; c Lawrence, Jr & Richard; m 1968 to Nancy Tingle; c David (stepson). Educ: Am Univ, BS, 53, LLB, 56; Delta Theta Phi. Polit & Govt Pos: Chmn, Northumberland Co Rep Comt, Va, 56-69; Rep cand, US Rep, Eighth Dist Va, 60 & US Senate, Va, 66; vchmn, Eighth Dist Rep Comt, 62; mem, Va State Rep Cent Comt, 64-69; pardon attorney, Dept of Justice, 69- Bus & Prof Pos: Attorney-at-law, 56-69. Mil Serv: Entered as Pvt, Army, 46, released as Capt, 48, after serv in Gen Hq, Far East Command, 47. Mem: Va Bar Asn. Relig: Methodist. Legal Res: Lottsburg VA 22511 Mailing Add: 5940 Queenston St Springfield VA 22152

TRAYLOR, LEE CLYDE (R)
Mem, Rep State Exec Comt, Ala

b Ft Payne, Ala, Aug 29, 32; s Hugh Clyde Traylor & Lorine Guest T; c Michael Lee, Dennis Hugh & Karen Lynne. Educ: Emory Univ, AB, 54; Emory Law Sch, 56-57; Univ Ala Law Sch, LLB, 59; Sigma Chi; case note ed, Ala Law Rev. Polit & Govt Pos: City recorder, Ft Payne Ala, 64-72 & Rainsville, 70-72; mem, Rep State Exec Comt, Ala, currently; mem, Co

Rep Exec Comt, currently. Bus & Prof Pos: Attorney-at-law, 59-; pres, Northeast Ala Farmers Product Mkt, 63-65, mem bd dirs, 63-; registered wrestling officer, Ala High Sch Athletic Asn, 67-71; mem bd dirs & secy, Mt Manor Nursing Home, 67- Mil Serv: Entered as Pfc, Army, 54, released as Sp-3, 56, after serv in 575th Ord Ammunition Co Ft Hood, Tex. Publ: Residences furnished officers by corporation, Digest of Tax Articles, 5/59. Mem: Am Judicature Soc; Mason; Eastern Star; Shrine; RAM. Honors & Awards: Jaycee Spoke Award. Relig: Baptist. Legal Res: 205 SW Eighth St Ft Payne AL 35967 Mailing Add: PO Box 316 Ft Payne AL 35967

TRAYLOR, MELL RANDOLPH (D)
Ga State Sen
b Savannah, Ga, Aug 13, 49; s Henry Meldrim Traylor & Evelyn Hendrix T; m 1969 to Sandra Grebey; c Bryan Eugene. Educ: Univ Md, BA, 73. Polit & Govt Pos: Aide to US Sen Herman Talmadge, Ga, 67-73; Ga State Sen, currently. Mailing Add: Rte 1 Box 94A1 Pembroke GA 31321

TRAYNER, WESGARTH FORSTER (R)
Mem, Conn Rep State Cent Comt
b Scituate, RI, Sept 7, 14; s Wesgarth Forster Trayner & Gertrude Lucius T; m 1934 to Emma Lindsay; c Wesgarth F, Jr, John A, Lindsay Anne (Mrs Glew) & Janet Elizabeth. Educ: Cranston High Sch, RI, grad. Polit & Govt Pos: Mem, Cheshire Rep Town Comt, Conn, 57, chmn, 58-70 & 73-74; mem, Conn Rep State Cent Comt, 70- Bus & Prof Pos: Div head, Sears-Roebuck Co, Warwick, RI, 34-36; salesman, Lewis Page Inc, Boston, Mass, 37-40; br mgr, Beacon Milling Co, Poughkeepsie, NY, 40-45; sales, Am Optical, New York, 45-48; from sales to pres, Tat-Fairfield Inc, Div ITEK Corp, Waterbury, Conn, 62-70, pres, 70- Mem: Better Vision Inst of Am (mem bd); Mason; Shrine; Lions; Small Bus Admin (adv bd). Relig: Protestant. Legal Res: 446 Maple Ave Cheshire CT 06410 Mailing Add: PO Box 263 Cheshire CT 06410

TREACHER, RANDALL WESLEY (D)
Exec Dir, Jackson Co Dem Comt, Mich
b Jackson, Mich, Sept 30, 53; s Leonard Eugene Treacher & Frona Lorraine Partee T; single. Educ: Jackson Community Col, 71-73; Mich State Univ, currently. Polit & Govt Pos: Mem, Mich Dem State Cent Comt, 72-, mem, Govt Opers & Elec Reform Comt, 73-; exec dir, Jackson Co Dem Comt, Mich, 72-; deleg, Dem Nat Charter Conv, 74; deleg, Dem Nat Mid-Term Conf, 74. Mem: Common Cause; Retail Clerks Int Asn. Mailing Add: 113 Lakeview Terr Jackson MI 49203

TREADWAY, DONALD RAY (R)
Secy-Treas, Nance Co Rep Party, Nebr
b Kearney, Nebr, June 24, 33; s Gerald George Treadway & Hazel Trindle T; m 1957 to Gretchen A Lecron; c Ann C, Thomas L & Steven P. Educ: Kearney State Col, 51-53, Univ Nebr, Lincoln, BS in bus admin, 57, Col Law, JD, 62; Phi Gamma Delta; Phi Tau Gamma; Phi Delta Phi. Polit & Govt Pos: Co attorney, Nance Co, Nebr, 67-; mem, Bd, Dist 10 Crime Comn, 68-71; mem, Nebr Ethics Comt, 69-; chmn, Nance Co Rep Party, 69-72, secy-treas, 72- Mil Serv: Entered as Pvt, Army, 53, released as Cpl, 55, after serv in Foreign Aid Prog, Korea, 53-55; Commendation, Armed Forces Aid to Korea Prog. Mem: Nebr Bar Asn (mem exec comt, young lawyers sect, 67-70, chmn sect, 69-70, comt on continuing legal educ, currently); Am Bar Asn; Elks; Eagles; Am Legion. Honors & Awards: Finalist, Allen Moot Court Competition, Univ Nebr Law Col. Relig: Methodist. Mailing Add: 106 N Johnson Fullerton NE 68638

TREADWAY, RICHARD FOWLE (R)
b Williamstown, Mass, June 5, 13; s Lauris Goldsmith Treadway & Helen Fowle T; wid; c Jonathan, James, Lauris Ann & David; m 1967 to Suzanne Clery Herter. Educ: Dartmouth Col, BA, 36; Harvard Bus Sch, Adv Mgt Course, 48; Phi Kappa Psi; Casque & Gauntlet Sr Soc. Polit & Govt Pos: Mass State Sen, 52-54; mem, Mass State Rep Finance Comt, 52-71; chmn exec comt, Mass State Rep Comt, 56-60, chmn, 69-72; pres, Mass Rep Club, 59-60; mem, Boston Ward Five Rep Comt, 60-69; Rep Nat Committeeman, 62-64; chmn, Gov Adv Comt on Tourism, 65-; mem, Sturbridge Town Rep Comt, formerly; mem, Cambridge Ward Eight Rep Comt, 69-71; dir, US Dept Commerce Domestic & Int Bus Admin Dist Off, Boston, currently. Bus & Prof Pos: Pres, Treadway Inns Corp, 48-64, chmn, 64-69, dir, 69-; vchmn bd, Harbor Nat Bank, 65-67; vpres, Boit, Dalton & Church, Inc, 65-71. Mil Serv: Entered as Pvt, Marine Corps, 43, released as 1st Lt, 45. Relig: Episcopal. Mailing Add: Proctor St Manchester MA 01944

TREEN, DAVID C (R)
US Rep, La
b Baton Rouge, La, July 16, 28; s Joseph Paul Treen & Elizabeth Speir T; m 1951 to Dolores Brisbi; c Jennifer Anne, David Conner, Jr & Cynthia Lynn. Educ: Tulane Univ, BA, 48, LLB, 50; Omicron Delta Kappa; Phi Delta Phi; Order of the Coif. Polit & Govt Pos: Mem, Jefferson Parish Rep Exec Comt, La, 62-67, chmn, 63-67; mem, La State Rep Cent Comt, 62-; chmn, La Young Rep Fedn, 62-64, mem exec comt, 64-66, gen counsel, 66; Rep cand for Cong, Second Dist, 62, 64 & 68; permanent chmn, Second Cong Dist Rep Conv, 64; deleg, Rep Nat Conv, 64, 68 & 72; chmn La deleg, 68; dir, Metrop Dist, Polit Action Coun, 66 & 67; Rep cand for Gov, La, 72; Rep Nat Committeeman, La, 72-; US Rep, Third Dist, La, 73-; mem, Select Comt on Intel, mem, Comt on Armed Serv & Comt on Merchant Marine & Fisheries, US House Rep, 73-; mem exec comt, Rep Cong Campaign Comt, currently. Bus & Prof Pos: Assoc attorney, Deutsch, Kerrigan & Stiles, New Orleans, 50-51; vpres & legal counsel, Simplex Mfg Corp, New Orleans, 52-57; assoc attorney, Beard, Blue & Schmitt & partner, Beard, Blue, Schmitt & Treen, New Orleans, 57-72. Mil Serv: Entered as 1st Lt, Air Force, 50, released 52, after serv at Sheppard Air Force Base, Tex & Hq, Third Air Force, Eng, 51-52. Honors & Awards: Distinguished Serv Award, Nat Young Rep Fedn, 68. Relig: Methodist. Legal Res: 430 Dorrington Dr Metairie LA 70005 Mailing Add: US House of Representatives Washington DC 20515

TREGONING, JOSEPH E (R)
Wis State Rep
Mailing Add: 435 N Judgement St Shullsburg WI 53586

TRELLO, FRED A (D)
Pa State Rep
Mailing Add: Capitol Bldg Harrisburg PA 17120

TRENT, DELMUS (R)
b Treadway, Tenn, Mar 10, 18; s Frank Trent & Dollie Greene T; m 1941 to Lois Kite; c Patricia Ann, Mary Margaret & James Fred. Educ: Whitesburg High Sch Grad. Polit & Govt Pos: Tenn State Rep, 56-58 & 60-62; alt deleg, Rep Nat Conv, 68 & deleg, 72; chmn, Hamblen Co Rep Exec Comt, Tenn, formerly. Bus & Prof Pos: Owner, Trent Land & Auction Co, 44- Mem: Elks; Moose; Lions. Relig: Baptist. Legal Res: 1907 Magnolia Ave Morristown TN 37814 Mailing Add: Box 517 Morristown TN 37814

TREPPLER, IRENE E (R)
Mo State Rep
Mailing Add: 4681 Fuchs Rd St Louis County MO 63128

TRESKA, PAUL (D)
Mem Exec Comt, Ingham Co Dem Party, Mich
b Flint, Mich, Oct 5, 24; s Paul Joseph Treska & Anna Josephine Cernicka T; m 1946 to Dorothy Nadene Ragland; c Susan R (Mrs Randolph J Cook) & Cynthia Ray. Educ: High Sch grad. Polit & Govt Pos: Mem, Mich State Univ Labor Adv Bd, 64; Dem deleg, Precinct 15, Ward 1, Lansing, Mich, 68-; police comnr, Lansing Mich Police Dept, 70-; mem exec comt, Ingham Co Dem Party, 70-; deleg, Dem Nat Conv, 72. Bus & Prof Pos: Mem, Gtr Lansing Bus & Prof Soc, 68- Mil Serv: Entered as Pvt, Marine Corps, 43, released as Pfc, 45, after serv in MAG-II VMTB 232 SPac, 43-45; Purple Heart; Presidential Unit Citation. Mem: Nat Defense Exec Reservists; Mich State Legis Bd (state dir); Mich State AFL-CIO (trustee, exec bd & exec comt); Local 1762 United Transportation Union. Legal Res: 1000 Shelter Lane Lansing MI 48912 Mailing Add: 1034 N Washington Ave Lansing MI 48906

TRIBBITT, SHERMAN W (D)
Gov, Del
m to Jeanne Webb; c James, Carole & Tip. Educ: Goldey-Beacom Col. Polit & Govt Pos: Del State Rep, 57-64 & 71-73, Speaker, Del House of Rep, 59-65; Lt Gov of Del, 65-69; Gov, Del,- 73- Bus & Prof Pos: Owner & operator, Odessa Supply Co. Mil Serv: Navy, World War II; Presidential Unit Citation. Mem: Farms Mutual Ins Co (dir); Farmer's Bank of Smyrna (dir); Del Savings & Loan Asn (dir); Union Lodge 5 (Past Master). Relig: Methodist. Mailing Add: Legislative Hall Dover DE 19901

TRIBBLE, JOSEPH JAMES (R)
Mem, Ga Rep State Exec Comt
b Forsyth, Ga, Aug 30, 20; s James Augustus Tribble & Frances Nixon T; m 1948 to Laura Jean Boddiford; c James Nixon, Kathryn Tracy, Craig Rigdon & Carol Lisa. Educ: Ga Inst of Technol, BS in Mech Eng, 42; Alpha Tau Omega. Polit & Govt Pos: Chmn, Chatham Co Rep Exec Comt, Ga, 54-57; state chmn, Ga Draft Goldwater Comt, 63-64; Ga State Sen, 63-66; state chmn, Rep Party of Ga, 64-65; deleg & chmn Ga deleg, Rep Nat Conv, 64, deleg, 68; mem, Ga Rep State Exec Comt, Chatham Co Rep Exec Comt & First Cong Dist Rep Exec Comt, 64-; chmn, Rep State Conv, 66; cand, US Rep, Ga, 68. Bus & Prof Pos: Asst plant supt, Union Bag-Camp Paper Corp, 46-65, power plant supt, 65- Mil Serv: Entered as CPO, Maritime Serv, 43, released as Lt(sg), 46, after serv as Asst Engr, Atlantic, Mediterranean, India & Pac, 43-45; NAtlantic, Mediterranean, Pac Theater & Attack Ribbons. Mem: Savannah Jr CofC, Ga; Civitan Club. Honors & Awards: First Rep State Sen from SGa in the 20th Century. Relig: Methodist. Mailing Add: 402 Arlington Rd Savannah GA 31406

TRICE, JOSEPH MARK (R)
b Washington, DC, Oct 22, 02; s Hyland Lee Trice & Mattie Slater T; m to Margaret Ann Linkins; c Linda Jean Smith. Educ: Georgetown Univ, LLB, 28. Polit & Govt Pos: Page, US Senate, 16-19, secy to Sgt at arms, 19-27, Asst Sgt at arms, 32-48, Secy for Majority, 49-50, Secy for Minority, 51-52 & 54-74, Secy of US Senate, 53-54; exec secy, Joint Cong Inaugural Comt, 53 & 69; parliamentarian, Rep Nat Platform Comt, 68; retired. Bus & Prof Pos: Attorney-at-law, Hanson, Lovett & Dale, 29-32. Mem: Cong Country Club. Honors & Awards: Presidential citation for 50 years of serv. Relig: Methodist. Mailing Add: 5017 Worthington Dr Westmorland Hills MD 20016

TRIGGS, MICHAEL LYNN (R)
Chmn, Pocahontas Co Rep Party, Iowa
b Ft Dodge, Iowa, Dec 4, 53; s Vincent L Triggs & Eileen M Hersom T; single. Educ: Inst European Studies, Vienna, Austria; Drake Univ, currently. Polit & Govt Pos: Page, Iowa House Rep, 70; primary cand for Iowa State Rep, 74; chmn, Pocahontas Co Rep Party, Iowa, 74-; mem, Sixth Dist Rep Cent Comt, currently. Mem: Mason. Relig: Protestant. Legal Res: 518 Olive St Laurens IA 50554 Mailing Add: 1319 30th St Des Moines IA 50311

TRIM, CLAUDE ALBERT (D)
Mich State Rep
b Pontiac, Mich, May 27, 35; s Claude Albert Trim & Catherine Elizabeth Sparling T; m 1953 to Geraldine Blanch Dexter; c Jeffrey Lynn, Suzanne (Mrs Moeller), Julia Ann & Terri Elizabeth. Educ: Pontiac Bus & Acct, 53-55; Mich State Ins Course, 55-56; Oakland Univ, mgt cert, 67; Oakland Community Col, cert assessors cert, 74. Polit & Govt Pos: Trustee, Springfield Twp, Mich, 68-70, supvr, 70-74; Mich State Rep, 60th Dist, 75- Bus & Prof Pos: Gen Motors Skilled Trades Metal Model Maker, 58-74. Mem: Mich State Assessors Asn; Springfield Twp Hist Soc; Rotary. Relig: Baptist. Legal Res: 5969 Ware Rd Davisburg MI 48019 Mailing Add: Capitol Bldg Lansing MI 48901

TRIPLETT, TOM (D)
Ga State Rep
Mailing Add: PO Box 9586 Savannah GA 31402

TRIPLETT, WILLIAM KARROL (R)
Mem, Rep State Cent Comt Calif
b Delano, Calif, Aug 8, 40; s Blythe C Triplett & Laura Stuhr T; m 1962 to Arlene Ann Jakovich; c Stephen & Patricia. Educ: Univ Calif, Berkeley, AB, 62; Hastings Col Law, JD, 65; Theta Xi. Polit & Govt Pos: Mem, Rep State Cent Comt Calif, 69-; mem, Kern Co Rep Cent Comt. Bus & Prof Pos: Acct, Ernst & Ernst, Oakland, Calif, 65-66; dep co counsel, Bakersfield, 66-67; dep dist attorney, 67-68; partner, Yinger & Triplett, Attorneys, 68-70. Mem: Calif State & Kern Co Bar Asns; Elks; Jaycees; Kern Co Heart Asn (dir). Relig: Protestant. Legal Res: 2909 Staunton Court Bakersfield CA 93306 Mailing Add: 359 Haberfelde Bldg Bakersfield CA 93301

TRIPP, JOHN THORNTON (R)
NH State Rep
b Farmington, NH, July 18, 97; s Charles Henry Tripp & Ella Bickford T; m 1920 to Blanche

V Ricker; c Lorna E (Mrs Donald Clough). Educ: Rochester High Sch, NH, grad, 15. Polit & Govt Pos: Clerk, US Post Off Dept, NH, 20-64, retired 64; NH State Rep, 68-, mem, Munic Co Govt Comt, NH House Rep, 69-72, mem, Ways & Means Comt, 73-74; mem sch bd, Rochester, NH, currently. Mem: Grange (past Master, NH State); Mason; Eastern Star (past Patron). Relig: Protestant. Mailing Add: 32 Adams Ave Rochester NH 03867

TRIPP, MINOT WELD, JR (D)
Chmn, Contra Costa Co Dem Party, Calif
b Cambridge, Mass, June 18, 39; s Minot Weld Tripp & Martha Swanson T; m 1964 to Mallory Penfield; c Stephen Minot & John Penfield. Educ: Harvard Col, AB, 61; Univ Calif, Berkeley, JD, 64. Polit & Govt Pos: Mem, Calif Dem State Cent Comt, 70-; Dem nominee for Calif State Sen, Seventh Dist, 72; chmn, Contra Costa Co Dem Party, Calif, 75- Bus & Prof Pos: Attorney, San Francisco, Calif, 65-; prof law, John F Kennedy Law Sch, 74-; lectr taxation, Golden Gate Univ, 74- Publ: Auth, Installment sales to related parties, Taxes, 5/74; An easy way out of Serrano, Calif J, 6/74; Reforming educational finance, Nat Civic Rev, 3/75. Mem: Neighborhood House of North Richmond (dir, 71-75); Contra Costa Park Coun (vpres, 73-75); Commonwealth Club of Calif; Am & San Francisco Bar Asns. Relig: Catholic. Mailing Add: 725 Ocean Ave Richmond CA 94801

TRISLER, BILL (D)
Chmn, Ind Dem State Cent Comt
Polit & Govt Pos: Mem, Dem Nat Comt, Ind Mailing Add: RR 2 Box 1B Crothersville IN 47229

TRIVIZ, RITA MARILYN (D)
Mem, NMex State Cent Comt
b Washington, DC, Dec 19, 47; d Edward E Triviz & Maryellen McKenzie T; single. Educ: NMex State Univ, BS with honors, 69. Polit & Govt Pos: Secy, Dem Women's Club of Dona Ana Co, 64-65; partic, President Johnson's Cabinet Comt Hearings of Mex-Am, 68; publicity comt, McGovern for President, Las Cruces, NMex, 72; state vchairperson, NMex Women's Polit Caucus, 73-75; mem, NMex Dem State Cent Comt, 73-; deleg, State Platform Conv of Dem Party, NMex, 74, deleg, State Deleg Selection Conv, 74; NMex deleg, Dem Mid Term Conf, 74; NMex deleg, Nat Women's Polit Caucus Conv, 74. Bus & Prof Pos: Secy, Las Cruces Educ Asn, 71-72; deleg, Nat Educ Asn Nat Bilingual-Bicultural Inst, 73; bldg rep, Head Start's Career Develop Comt, 73-74; instr, Nat Educ Asn-NMex State Conv, 74. Mem: Teachers of English to Speakers of Other Languages; Nat Educ Asn-NMex; Las Cruces Educ Asn (secy, 71-72, human rels comt, 73-74); NMex & Las Cruces Asns Classroom Teachers. Honors & Awards: Girl of the Month, Am Asn Univ Women, 65; Participant in President Johnson's Cabinet Comt Hearings on Mex-Am Affairs, 68. Legal Res: 525 Brown Rd Las Cruces NM 88001 Mailing Add: Box 359 Las Cruces NM 88001

TROLLEY, RICHARD JOSEPH (D)
Mem, 15th Cong Dist Dem Party, Mich
b Detroit, Mich, Nov 14, 29; s Vincent Trolley & Adeline Quatro T; m; c Paula, Pamela & Deborah. Educ: Wayne State Univ, BA in Econ; Wayne State Univ Law Sch, 1 year. Polit & Govt Pos: Trustee, Taylor Twp Sch Bd, Mich, 56-57, treas, 57-59, secy, 59-61, pres, 61-63; twp trustee, Taylor, 63, twp treas, 63-67, twp supvr, 67-68; deleg, Dem Nat Conv, 68; mayor, Taylor, 68-74; mem, 15th Cong Dist Dem Party, currently. Bus & Prof Pos: Partner, C & T Underwriters, Allen Park, Mich, 64-; salesman, AAA. Mem: Mich Asn of Independent Ins Agents; Rotary; Great Soc Dem Club; Metrop Club; Wayne Co Treas Asn. Relig: Catholic. Legal Res: 25762 Madden Taylor MI 48180 Mailing Add: 23555 Goddard Rd Taylor MI 48180

TROMBLEY, C ANNE PATRICK (D)
b Monahans, Tex, Apr 21, 44; d T L (Pat) Patrick & Carol Dixon P; m 1968 to James Michael Patrick Trombley; c Michael Patrick. Educ: Univ Ariz, BA, 67; Univ Nebr, Lincoln, 67-69, Col Law, 72- Bus & Prof Pos: Pub rels coordr, Braeman for Cong Comt, Nebr, 72; alt deleg, Dem Nat Conv, 72; mem adv comt, Berg for Cong Comt, 72; comnr, Nebr Equal Opportunities Comn, 72- Bus & Prof Pos: Teaching asst speech, Univ Nebr, Lincoln, 67-69; caseworker, Whitehall State Home for Children, 70; dir, Camp Kiwanis, 71. Mem: Pi Kappa Delta; Delta Theta Phi; Nat Orgn for Women, Nat & Nebr Women's Polit Caucus. Mailing Add: 2434 Park Ave Lincoln NE 68502

TROPEA, ROBERT DANIEL (R)
NH State Rep
b Woburn, Mass, Dec 18, 40; s Salvatore J Tropea & Caroline Guerrera T; m 1963 to Nancy Gloria Carr; c Daniel Robert. Educ: Lowell Technol Inst, ABA, 69, BSBA, 72; Babson Col, MBA, 73. Polit & Govt Pos: NH State Rep, 74-, majority liaison, House Labor, Human Resources & Rehabilitation Comt, legis admin chmn, House Subcomt Employ, NH Gen Court, 75-; mem, Econ Recovery Coun, State of NH, 75- Bus & Prof Pos: Mfg staff asst, Sanders Data Syst, 67-; faculty mem, NH Col & Lowell Technol Inst, 74- Mil Serv: Entered as Pvt, Army Nat Guard, 61, released as E-4, 67. Relig: Catholic. Mailing Add: 2 Swart St Nashua NH 03060

TROPILA, JOE (D)
Mont State Rep
Mailing Add: 209 Second St NW Great Falls MT 59404

TROPMAN, PETER J (D)
Wis State Rep
Mailing Add: 1810 W Cherry St Milwaukee WI 53205

TROSTER, VIRGINIA ALLING (R)
Bylaws Chmn, Nat Fedn of Rep Women
b Sodus, NY, May 19, 12; d Dr E Roy Alling & Theda Katherine Rogers A; m 1961 to John Kirk Troster; c Edward Thomas Hollander. Educ: Syracuse Univ, 31-32; Col William & Mary, 32-33; Univ Buffalo, grad med technol, 34; Ariz State Univ, summer 60. Polit & Govt Pos: Campaign liaison, Rep cand for State's Attorney Gen, 60; pres, Rep Workshops of Ariz, Inc, 63-64; precinct committeeman, Maricopa Co, 64-; mem, Maricopa Co & Ariz State Rep Comts, 65-; mem, Ariz Rep Exec Comt, 65-; mem, Charter Govt Selections Comt, 69; pres, Ariz Fedn Rep Women, 69-70; chmn voc tech subcomt, Human Resources Adv Coun, 70-72; bylaws chmn, Nat Fedn Rep Women, 72- Bus & Prof Pos: Lab supvr, NY State, 34-35; mgr, Customer Rels, Buffalo, NY, 48-53; off mgr, Property Mgt, Buffalo, 53-58. Mem: Ariz Club, Phoenix; Univ Club, Phoenix; Capitol Hill Club, Washington, DC; Nat Bus Educ Asn. Honors & Awards: Medal of Merit, Nat Fedn of Rep Women, 71; Citation of Merit for contribution in field of voc-tech educ, Ariz Gov Jack Williams, 72. Relig: Episcopal. Mailing Add: 2238 E San Juan Ave Phoenix AZ 85016

TROTT, BERNARD L (R)
Chmn, Fourth Judicial Dist Rep Party, Colo,
b Kearney, Nebr, Oct 29, 23; s Lewis Walker Trott & Eleanor Knutson T; m 1944 to Betty Jane Moore; c Jeffrey Bernard & Diane Elaine. Educ: Nebr Wesleyan Univ, BA, 47; Univ Mich Law Sch, JD, 49; Phi Kappa Phi; Pi Kappa Delta; Crescent. Polit & Govt Pos: City councilman, Mission, Kans, 52-54; chmn, Fourth Judicial Dist Rep Party, Colo, 61-; mem, El Paso Co Rep Cent Comt, 61-; deleg, Rep Co, State, Cong & Judicial Dist Conv, 64-66 & 68; mem, El Paso Co Rep Exec Comt, Colo, 65-; alt deleg, Rep Nat Conv, 68. Mil Serv: Entered as Pvt, Ay Air Corps, 43, released as 2nd Lt, 45, after serv in A-26 Bombardment Group, US, Capt, Res, 45-57. Publ: Various articles, Mich Law Rev, 48-49. Mem: El Paso Co Bar Asn; Garden of the Gods Club; Broadmoor Golf Club; Torch Club; Winter Night Club. Relig: Congregational. Mailing Add: 23 Broadmoor Ave Colorado Springs CO 80906

TROTTER, DECATUR WAYNE (D)
Md State Deleg
b Washington, DC, Jan 8, 32; s Decatur Trotter & Bernice T; m 1956 to LaGreta E; c Denise & Kathie. Educ: Va State Col, BS; Kappa Alpha Phi. Polit & Govt Pos: Councilman, Glenarden, Md, 61-68, mayor, 70-75; Md State Deleg, 75- Mil Serv: Sgt, Army, 50-52, serv in 171st MIP's. Mem: Prince George's Country Club. Honors & Awards: Outstanding Citizen Award, Glenarden. Relig: Baptist. Mailing Add: 3101 Polk Ct Glenarden MD 20801

TROTTER, VIRGINIA Y
Asst Secy Educ, Dept Health, Educ & Welfare
Mailing Add: Dept Health Educ & Welfare Washington DC 20201

TROTTER, WILLIAM PERRY (D)
b Manchester, Ga, Nov 2, 19; s McKie M Trotter & Tudor Perry T; m 1950 to Julia Thomason; c Jefferson William & William Perry, Jr. Educ: Vanderbilt Univ, BA, 41; Univ Ga, LLB, 47; Phi Delta Phi; Omicron Delta Kappa; Phi Delta Theta. Polit & Govt Pos: Ga State Sen, 51-52 & 57-58; Ga State Rep, 59; dir of Pub Safety, Ga, 59-61; Dem Nat Committeeman, 62-72. Bus & Prof Pos: Troup Co Attorney, 61-71. Mil Serv: Entered as Aviation Cadet, Air Force, 42, released as Maj, 46, after serv in Troop Carrier Command, Asiatic-Pac Theater, 44-45; Air Medal; Philippine Liberation Medal; Six Pac Campaign Ribbons. Mem: Ga & Am Bar Asns; VFW; Elks. Honors & Awards: Prof Baseball, Little Rock, Ark, 41. Relig: Episcopal. Mailing Add: 323 Lane Circle La Grange GA 30240

TROTZKY, HOWARD M (R)
Maine State Sen
b New York, NY, Apr 5, 40; s Daniel Trotzky & Rhoda Cohen T; m 1965 to Evelyn Lewin; c Deborah & Samuel. Educ: Columbia Col, AB, 61, Columbia Univ, MA, 63; Univ Maine, Orono, MS, 73; Varsity C-Swimming; Kappa Delta Phi; Zeta Beta Tau. Polit & Govt Pos: Chmn, Bangor Rep City Party, Maine, 73-75; Maine State Sen, Dist 25, 75-, chmn legis natural resources comt & mem energy comt & pub lands comt, Maine State Senate, 75- Bus & Prof Pos: Real estate broker, Maine Properties, Bangor, 73- Publ: Auth, Effect of water flow manipulation below a power dam, Trans Am Fishery Soc, 74. Mem: Bangor Comn on Parks & Recreation; Natural Resources Coun Maine; Sierra Club Maine; Jewish Community Coun Bangor. Relig: Jewish. Mailing Add: 20 Knox St Bangor ME 04401

TROUPE, JAMES PAL (D)
b Dudley, Ga, Dec 4, 09; s Charley Henry Troupe & Mary Blanche Williams T; m 1927 to Gertrude Thompson; c Ernestine (Mrs Hinton), James, Jr, Delores (Mrs Warren), Marvin, Donald, Wallace, Vernon & Newton. Educ: NEastern High Sch, Detroit, Mich, grad, 26. Polit & Govt Pos: Comnr, St Louis Housing Authority, Mo, 51-54; Mo State Rep, 54-74, chmn Labor Comt, Mo State House Rep, 67-74; committeeman, Fifth Ward St Louis Dem City Cent Comt, 64-68; deleg, Dem Nat Conv, 72. Bus & Prof Pos: Rep, AFL-CIO, USW, 44. Mem: Frontier Internal Club; NAACP; USW Am Union. Relig: Catholic. Mailing Add: 1538 Hogan St St Louis MO 63106

TROUT, BARBARA ANN (R)
Mem, Rep State Cent Comt Colo
b Omaha, Nebr, Jan 18, 27; d Leroy Glen Lambert & Bernice Wilcox L; m 1950 to Norman Lee Trout; c Cheryl, Stanley & Brian. Educ: Univ SDak, BA, 49; Alpha Phi. Polit & Govt Pos: Rep committeewoman, precinct 606, Jefferson Co, Colo, 61-65 & precinct 412, 65-69 & precinct 415, 70-73; visitor's aid, Colo State Legis, 63-64, messenger, 69, tel & messenger supvr, 70-73; mem, Rep State Cent Comt Colo, 65-67, 69-71 & 73-; chmn spec serv comt, Jefferson Co, Colo, 66-68; mem, City of Lakewood Planning & Zoning Comn, 69-, secy, 71 & 73, chmn, 74-; Jefferson Co Coordr, Allot for US Senate Comt, 72; sponsor, Lakewood High Sch TARS, 66-68; mem, Jefferson Co Patronage Comn, 70 & 71; mem, Jefferson Co Rep Exec Comt, 73-, chmn precinct orgn, 75-; mem, Jefferson Co Housing Task Force, 75-; co-capt, Rep Dist 21, 75. Relig: Episcopal. Mailing Add: Rte 2 Box 4T Conifer CO 80433

TROUTMAN, CHARLES H, III (INDEPENDENT)
Attorney Gen, Terr of Guam
b Wooster, Ohio, Mar 25, 44; s Charles H Troutman, Jr & Lois M Dickason T; single. Educ: Wheaton Col, BA, 66; Am Univ Law Sch, JD, 69; Southern Methodist Univ Sch Law, MCompLaw, 70. Polit & Govt Pos: Asst Attorney Gen, Terr of Guam, 70-74, Attorney Gen, 75-; mem, Guam Law Rev Comn, 74-; mem, Comprehensive Health Planning Comn, 74- Bus & Prof Pos: Attorney, Trotman, Troutman & Assocs, 74. Publ: Auth, Home is where you make it, Evangel Missions Quart, 4/74. Mem: Am & Guam Bar Asns; Navy League; Am Soc Mil Engrs; Am Soc Int Law. Relig: Presbyterian. Mailing Add: PO Box 455 Agana GU 96910

TROUTMAN, FRANK, JR (R)
VChmn, Richmond Co Comn, Ga
b Atlanta, Ga, Nov 1, 34; s Frank Troutman & Mary Frank Satterfield T; m 1955 to Joan Castleberry; c Lee, Mary Stewart, Katherine & Frank, III. Educ: Univ Ga, AB, 56, LLB, 58; Omicron Delta Kappa; Phi Beta Kappa; Phi Delta Phi; Sigma Alpha Epsilon. Polit & Govt Pos: Vchmn, Richmond Co Rep Party, Ga, 66; first vchmn & acting state chmn, Rep Party of Ga, 66; deleg, Rep Nat Conv, 68; co comnr, Richmond Co Comn, 69-, finance chmn, 69-70, vchmn, 71- Bus & Prof Pos: Pres, Castleberry's Food Co, Augusta, 65- Mem: Nat Asn Mfr (dir). Honors & Awards: Received Young Man of The Year, Richmond Co Jaycees, 69. Relig: Episcopal. Legal Res: 3030 Bransford Rd Augusta GA 30904 Mailing Add: PO Box 1010 Augusta GA 30903

TROW, CLIFFORD WAYNE (D)
Ore State Sen
b Topeka, Kans; s George E Trow & Rubena Swift T; m 1969 to JoAnne Johnson. Educ: Kans Wesleyan, AB, 51; Univ Colo, MA, 58, PhD, 66; Phi Delta Kappa; Phi Alpha Theta. Polit & Govt Pos: Co chmn, Benton Co Dem Cent Comt, 72-74; Ore State Sen, 75- Bus & Prof Pos: Prof hist, Ore State Univ, 65- Publ: The Mexican interventionist movement of 1919, J Am Hist. Mem: Am Asn Univ Prof; Orgn of Am Historians. Honors & Awards: Binkley-Stephenson Award, Orgn of Am Historians. Mailing Add: 1810 NW 27th Corvallis OR 97330

TROWBRIDGE, C ROBERTSON (R)
NH State Sen
b Salem, Mass, Mar 31, 32; s Cornelius P Trowbridge & Margaret Murdock Laird T; m 1956 to Lorna Sagendorph; c James R, Cornelia T, Beatrix S & Philip R. Educ: Princeton Univ, AB, 54; Harvard Univ, LLB, 57. Polit & Govt Pos: NH State Rep, formerly, chmn, Pub Works Comt, NH House Rep, formerly; asst majority leader, formerly, chmn exec comt, Cheshire Co Deleg, formerly; NH State Sen, Dist 11, 73-, chmn, Finance Comt, NH State Senate, currently, vchmn, State Fiscal Comt, currently. Bus & Prof Pos: Pres & publ, Yankee, Inc; publ, Yankee Mag & the Old Farmer's Almanac. Relig: Episcopal. Mailing Add: Box A Dublin NH 03444

TROXEL, OLIVER LEONARD, JR
b Sherburn, Minn, Sept 29, 19; s Oliver Leonard Troxel & Rinice Annette Nanninga T; div. Educ: George Washington Univ, AB, 40; Col William & Mary, MA, 41. Polit & Govt Pos: Admin Asst, War Dept, 41-43; Foreign Serv Off, Dept of State, 46-72, Second Secy-VConsul, Am Embassy, Manila, Philippines, 46-48; Tel Aviv, Israel, 48-51; Int Economist, Dept of State, 51-57, First Secy-Consul, Am Embassy, Addis Ababa, Ethiopia, 57-59, Army War Col, Carlisle Barracks, Pa, 59-60, Int Rels Off, Dept of State, 60-63, Dep Chief of Mission & Consul Gen, Am Embassy, Accra, Ghana, 63-66, Dir, Off Research & Anal for Africa, Dept of State, 66-69 & US Ambassador to Zambia, 69-72. Mil Serv: Entered as Pvt, Army, 43, released as T/Sgt, 46, after serv in Inf, Mediterranean Theatre, 44-46; Bronze Star. Honors & Awards: Dept of State Honor Award, 56, Superior Honor Award, 66. Legal Res: 2512 14th Ave Court Greeley CO 80631 Mailing Add: 3-E 410 E 57th St New York NY 10022

TROXELL, LEONA MAE (R)
Rep Nat Committeewoman, Ark
b Johnstown, NY, Apr 22, 13; d Rev Frank Anderson, DD & Clara Bergen A; m 1951 to Col Nolan Troxell, wid. Educ: Drake Univ, BA, 34, MA, 38; Phi Beta Kappa; Phi Sigma Iota; Psi Chi; Alpha Xi Delta; Alpha Lambda Delta. Polit & Govt Pos: Serv club dir, US Army Spec Servs, 41-43; dir, US Army Spec Servs Arts & Crafts, ETO, 48-52; pres, Faulkner Co Rep Women's Club, 54-56 & White Co Rep Women's Club, 62-63; twp committeeman, Faulkner Co, 54-70 & White Co, 54-; vchairwoman, Faulkner Co, 56-61; mem, Exec Comt & Bd Dirs, Ark Fedn of Rep Women, 59-, second vpres, 63-67; mem bd dirs, Nat Fedn Rep Women, 63-70, mem, Nominating Comt, 67 & Exec Comt, 67-70, chmn, Resolutions Comt, 68; mem, Rep State Exec Comt & Rep State Cent Comt, 63-70 & 72-; alt deleg, Rep Nat Conv, 64, deleg, 72; vchairwoman, White Co Rep, 64-70; mem, Rep Nat Finance Comt, 71-; Rep Nat Committeewoman, Ark, 72-; mem, Secy Health, Educ & Welfare Adv Comt on Rights & Responsibilities of Women, 72- Bus & Prof Pos: Asst dean of women & instr, French & Spanish, Drake Univ, 35-40; asst house supvr, Katharine Gibbs Sch, Boston, Mass, 40-41; hosp recreation worker, Am Red Cross, 43-45; dean of women, Drake Univ, 46-48; adminr, Ark Employ Security Div, 69-71. Mem: Eastern Star; Ark Div, Am Cancer Soc (state bd dirs & exec comt); Alpha Xi Delta Alumnae Club; Ark Asn of Ment Health; Downtown Little Rock B&PW Club (legis chmn). Honors & Awards: Gov Comn on Status of Women; Outstanding Woman of Year in Govt, Downtown Little Rock B&PW Club, 69. Relig: Baptist; Sunday Sch Teacher. Mailing Add: PO Box 61 Rose Bud AR 72137

TROY, MATTHEW JOSEPH, JR (D)
City Councilman, New York
b Brooklyn, NY, Sept 23, 29; s Matthew Joseph Troy, Sr & Maude Gallagher T; m 1954 to Dolores G Saville; c Dolores, Jr, Matthew J, III, Maureen V, Mary P, Therese C, Michael C, Kevin F, Catherine M & Jacqueline M. Educ: Georgetown Univ, AB, 51; Fordham Univ Sch of Law, LLB, 56. Polit & Govt Pos: Dem dist leader, Queens Co, NY, 60-; chmn, Queens Co Dem Comt, 62-63; city councilman, New York, 64-; deleg, Dem Nat Conv, 68 & 72. Bus & Prof Pos: Attorney, Troy, Saville & Troy, Law Firm, 63- Mil Serv: Entered as Pvt, Army, 51, released as Cpl, 53, after serv in Mil Police, Asian Theatre, 52-53; 1st Lt, Res, 57- Relig: Roman Catholic. Legal Res: 230-36 88th Ave Queens Village NY 11427 Mailing Add: 218-29 Jamaica Ave Queens Village NY 11428

TROY, RALPH TALBOT (D)
Mayor, Monroe, La
b Monroe, La, Feb 4, 35; s Richard Matthew Troy & Vera Nobes T; m 1956 to Frances Lamoreaux Warner; c Pamela Frances, Joan Barclay, Ralph Talbot, Jr & Joshua Richard. Educ: Univ of the South, BA, 57; Tulane Univ, LLB, 60; Phi Beta Kappa; Omicron Delta Kappa; Blue Key; Phi Gamma Mu; Phi Alpha Delta; Kappa Sigma. Polit & Govt Pos: Mem, La State Planning & Adv Comn, 72-; mayor, Monroe, 72-; chmn human res comt, US Conf Mayors, 73-; vpres, La Munic Asn, 74-; vchmn, Mayor's Comt on Bicentennial, 74- Bus & Prof Pos: Bd chmn, Troy & Nichols, Inc, 72-, Troy & Nichols Ins Agency, Inc, 72- Publ: Seller's Guide to FHA & VA Financing, Troy & Nichols, Inc, 67 & 70. Mem: La Bar Asn; Mortgage Bankers Asn. Relig: Episcopal. Legal Res: 2008 Stuart Monroe LA 71201 Mailing Add: PO Box 123 Monroe LA 71201

TRUAN, CARLOS FLORES (D)
Tex State Rep
b Kingsville, Tex, June 9, 35; s Charles Truan & Santos Flores T; m 1963 to Elvira Munguia; c Carlos, Jr, Veronica, Rene & Maria Luisa. Educ: Tex A&I Univ, BBA, 59; Nat John Cardinal Newman Hon Soc; Newman Club; Bus Club; Student Coun Adv Bd. Polit & Govt Pos: Tex State Rep, Dist 48, Pl 2, 69-, chmn, Human Resources Comt, vchmn, Subcomt on Life & Health Ins, Tex House Rep, currently; alt deleg, Dem Nat Mid-Term Conf, 74. Bus & Prof Pos: Field underwriter, NY Life Ins Co, Corpus Christi, 60- Publ: Tex Bilingual Educ Act, 69; Tex Adult Educ Act, 73. Mem: Tex Educ Agency Adv Comt on Bilingual Educ; LULAC; Southwest Coun of La Raza, Inc (mem bd dirs); Am GI Forum; Sertoma. Honors & Awards: Outstanding Young Man of 1967, Jaycees; NY Life's Man of the Year, 1967 for STex; LULAC Man of the Year, 1966; Tex Outstanding LULAC Dist Dir of the Year, 1967. Relig: Roman Catholic. Legal Res: 3821 Marion St Corpus Christi TX 78415 Mailing Add: PO Box 5445 Corpus Christi TX 78415

TRUBAN, WILLIAM A (R)
Va State Sen
b Garrett Co, Md, Oct 6, 24; s Joseph Truban & Mae Parks T; m 1949 to Mildred Hayes; c John William, Becky A, David H, Peter A, Tom S & William A, Jr. Educ: WVa Wesleyan Col, BS, 49; Univ Pa, VMD, 53; Beta Beta Beta. Polit & Govt Pos: Va State Sen, Dist 27, 70- Mil Serv: Entered as Pvt, Air Force, 43, released as S/Sgt, 46, after serv in 13th Combat Cargo Unit, China, India & Burma, 44-46. Mem: Am Vet Med Asn; Va Vet Med Asn (past pres); Va Asn of Prof (dir); Woodstock Rotary Club (past pres); Shenandoah Valley Music Festival (dir). Honors & Awards: Va Vet of the Year Award, 72. Relig: Methodist. Mailing Add: Box 503 Woodstock VA 22664

TRUBEY, MARY SYBIL (D)
Chmn, Putnam Co Dem Exec Comt, Ga
b Greene Co, Ga, July 30, 25; d William Henry Clack & Lula McElhannon C; m 1946 to Daniel Floyd Trubey; c Barbara (Mrs Harold Hooks) & Ronnie. Educ: Eatonton High Sch, grad, 43. Polit & Govt Pos: Chmn, Putnam Co Dem Exec Comt, Ga, 70- Bus & Prof Pos: Secy, Larry Clack Bookkeeping & Tax Serv, 68- Mem: Community Rels Comt; Citizens Comt-City Coun, Eatonton, Ga; Red Cross (serv chap chmn blood prog). Relig: Baptist. Mailing Add: 108 Miller Dr Eatonton GA 31024

TRUDEAU, THEODORE J (R)
Mass State Rep
Mailing Add: State Capitol Boston MA 02133

TRUE, DIEMER DURLAND (R)
Wyo State Rep
b Cody, Wyo, Feb 12, 46; s Henry Alfonso True, Jr & Jean Durland T; m 1967 to Susie Lynn Niethammer; c Diemer Durland, Jr, Kyle Shawn, Tara Jeanine & Tracy Lynn. Educ: Northwestern Univ, BS, 68; Univ Wyo, 68-69; Delta Upsilon. Polit & Govt Pos: Wyo State Rep, 73- Bus & Prof Pos: Vpres truck opers, Black Hills Oil Marketers, Inc, 70- Mil Serv: Entered as E-1, Army Res, 68, released as O-1, after serv in 461st Engr Co, 96th Army Res Command, 68-; Army Officer Cand Award; Res Achievement Ribbon. Mem: Deru Honor Soc; Wyo Trucking Asn (dir, 71-); Wyo Hwy Users Fedn (dir, 73-); United Fund (chmn admis & budget comt). Relig: Methodist. Legal Res: 1224 Granada Casper WY 82601 Mailing Add: Box 2360 Casper WY 82601

TRUEBLOOD, AILEEN NASH (BOBBIE) (R)
Mem, Rep State Cent Comt Calif
b Exeter, Devonshire, Eng, Oct 30, 24; d Ernest Arthur Alfred Montague Nash & Florence Mary Townsend N; m 1946 to Fred Willette Trueblood, Jr; div; c Fred Willette, III, John Christopher, Michael Devon & Kyltie Anne. Educ: Bishop Blackall Sch for Girls, Exeter, Devonshire, Eng. Polit & Govt Pos: Rep & campaign chmn, Lt Gov Ed Reinecke, Santa Clarita Valley, Calif, 64-; mem, Newhall Saugus Rep Campaign Coun, 65-; mem, Rep State Cent Comt Calif, 67-; first vpres & corresponding secy, Newhall-Saugus Rep Women's Club, formerly; campaign chmn, Assemblyman Newt Russell, Santa Clarita Valley, 69-; town chmn, Gov Ronald Reagan, 70-72. Bus & Prof Pos: Soc ed & columnist, Newhall Signal, Newhall, Calif, 54-68 & Record Press, Newhall, Calif, 68-69; columnist, View from Valencia, Valencia, Calif, 68-; mem bd dirs, secy & treas, Los Angeles Co North Valley Bldg Corp, 69-; secy, Newhall-Saugus-Valencia CofC, 70-71, bd dirs, 71-, pres, Woman's Div, 71-72; dir community rels, Henry Mayo Newhall Mem Hosp, Valencia, 71- Mil Serv: Vol in Royal Observer Corps, World War II, Eng. Mem: Beta Sigma Phi; William S Hart High Sch Dist Scholarship Found; Hosp Coun of Southern Calif (PR Sect; exec bd, 71-); Southern Calif Asn Hosp, Develop Dirs; Boys Club of Newhall-Saugus (bd dirs, 72-). Honors & Awards: Woman of the Newhall-Saugus-Valencia CofC, 72. Relig: Episcopal. Mailing Add: 23515 Lyons Ave Number 273 Valencia CA 91355

TRUGLIA, ANTHONY DOMENICK (D)
Conn State Rep
b Stamford, Conn, July 22, 27; s Domenick Peter Truglia & Pia Adipietro T; m 1956 to Christel Heidemann; c Sallyanne, Anthony, Jr & Pia Mary Jane. Educ: Univ Bridgeport, BA, 51, MA, 52; Teachers Col, Columbia Univ, sixth year degree, 55; life mem Phi Mu Alpha Sinfonia of Am. Polit & Govt Pos: Mem, Stamford Bd of Rep, Conn, 57-, Minority Leader, 65-67 & 69-71, Majority Leader, 71-73; mem, Stamford Dem Town & City Comt, 59-; Conn State Rep, 73- Bus & Prof Pos: Organist & choir dir, Springdale Methodist Church, Conn, 56; dir, Stamford Summer Music Prog, 57; asst head dept music, Rippowam High Sch, 61; mgr, Prof Music, 66. Mil Serv: Entered as Pvt, Army, 52, released as Cpl, 54, after serv in 173rd Army Band, 1st Army Area, 52-54; Good Conduct Medal; NAtlantic Defense Ribbon. Publ: Tanglewood in Stamford, 5/68 & One year project music, 6/69, Sch Musician; Band storming to Europe 1971, The Instrumentalist, 9/72. Mem: Aid for the Retarded (bd dirs, 72-); Drug Liberation Prog, Stamford (bd dirs, 70-); Boy Scouts (committeeman, Alfred Dater Coun, chmn, Troop 74, 70-); Music Educators Nat Conf; Stamford Fedn Teachers. Honors & Awards: Stamford Mus & Nature Ctr Award, Stamford Lions Club for Leadership & Civic Duty, 65; Guest Speaker Cert of Appreciation, Stamford, 68; Vol Award, Conn Dept Health, 69; Citation, Stamford Bd Rep, 71; Award, Rippowam Stage Band Booster Club, Inc, Kiwanis & Rotary Clubs, 71. Relig: Catholic. Mailing Add: 176 Fairfield Ave Stamford CT 06902

TRUJILLO, C B (D)
Majority Floor Leader, NMex State Senate
b Topeka, Kans, Mar 16, 32; s Luis A Trujillo & Grace Gonzales T; div; c Martin V, Steven L, Michael A & Jeffrey D. Educ: NMex Highland Univ, BA, 56, MA, 62. Polit & Govt Pos: NMex State Sen, 67-, Majority Floor Leader, NMex State Senate, 67- Mil Serv: Navy, 49-53; Korean Ribbon; Good Conduct Medal. Relig: Roman Catholic. Legal Res: Roberts Rd Taos NM 87571 Mailing Add: Box 1849 Taos NM 87571

TRUMAN, PETER (D)
Maine State Rep
b Biddeford, Maine, Sept 21, 48; s Mr & Mrs Paul Truman; single. Educ: Univ Maine, 2 years. Polit & Govt Pos: Mem charter revision comn, City of Biddeford, 71-73, civil defense dir, 74-75; Maine State Rep, 107th Dist, 75- Bus & Prof Pos: Truman & Co, Instnl Food Prod Distrib, 64- Legal Res: 47 Adams St Biddeford ME 04005 Mailing Add: Box 532 Biddeford ME 04005

TRUMAN, WILLIAM ST CLAIR (D)
First VChmn, Ariz Dem State Comt
b Florence, Ariz, Jan 27, 35; s William Charles Truman & Virginia Frances St Clair T; single. Educ: Univ Ariz. Polit & Govt Pos: Elections clerk, Pinal Co, Ariz, 67-72; committeeman,

Ariz Dem State Comt, 68-, first vchmn, 74-; area chmn, Pinal Co Dem Comt, 68-74, precinct committeeman, 68-; recorder, Pinal Co, 72- Mil Serv: Entered Marine Corps, 54, released as Sgt, 62, after serv in 1st & 2nd Marine Divs, 54-62. Mem: Ariz Recorders Asn (vpres & chmn, legis comt, 72-); Nat Asn Co Recorders & Clerks; Lions; Am Legion; Elks. Honors & Awards: Various awards for civic services from Lions & Boy Scouts. Mailing Add: 2121 San Carlos Florence AZ 85232

TRUNZO, CAESAR (R)
NY State Sen
b Brooklyn, NY, May 11, 26; s Louis Trunzo & Josephine Gangemi T (deceased); m 1948 to Lorraine M Ashraway; c Laura & Michael. Educ: Heffley & Browne Bus Col, Brooklyn. Polit & Govt Pos: Mem, Islip Town Planning Bd, NY, 59-65; pres, Brentwood Rep Club, 60-61; treas, Islip Rep Town Comt, 62-; councilman, Town of Islip, 65-72; NY State Sen, Third Dist, 73- Bus & Prof Pos: Bookkeeper, Pyramid Motor Freight, New York, 47-48; acct clerk, Sun Chem Corp, Long Island City, 48-50 & Frigidaire Sales Corp, New York, 50-52; acct supvr, Fairchild Stratos Div, Bay Shore, 52-62; asst treas, Dayton T Brown, Inc, Bohemia, 62-67. Mil Serv: Entered as Pvt, Army, 44, released as Pfc, 46. Mem: Nat Asn Accts; hon mem Bd Dirs Brentwood Youth Activities (past treas); charter mem St Anne's Coun, KofC; Sons of Italy. Relig: Catholic; mem, St Anne's Holy Name Soc; St Anne's Parish Coun. Mailing Add: 105 Washington Ave Brentwood NY 11717

TSAPATSARIS, CHARLES NICHOLAS (D)
b Lowell, Mass, Sept 5, 24; s Nicholas Tsapatsaris & Demetra Zavoulis T; m 1965 to Elizabeth Kontras; c Alexis. Educ: Suffolk Univ, BS, 50. Polit & Govt Pos: Cand for US Cong, 66; deleg, Dem Nat Conv, 72. Bus & Prof Pos: Probation officer, Cambridge, Mass, 65-; pres, Silver Merchants, Lowell, 75- Mil Serv: Entered as Pvt, Army, 43, released as Pfc, 46, after serv in 756 Engrs Unit, Pac Theatre of Opers, 44-46. Mem: Mass Probation Asn. Relig: Greek Orthodox. Mailing Add: 40 Waugh St Lowell MA 01854

TSCHACHE, OTTLEY RAYMOND (R)
b Great Falls, Mont, Sept 13, 19; s Otto A Tschache & Maude Witts T; m 1940 to Ellen Ulmen; c Charlotte (Mrs Latta), Ottley Paul & Gary Mark. Educ: Great Falls Commercial Col, 1 year. Polit & Govt Pos: Chmn, Gallatin Co Rep Party, 62-63; chmn, Mont State Rep Party, 69-71; state dir, Small Bus Admin, 72-75. Bus & Prof Pos: Partner-owner, Coast to Coast Store, Bozeman, Mont, 33-62, Tschache Bros Contractors, 40-67 & O Bar J Trailers, 59-67; mem, Mont State Advert Comt, 62-69; mgr, Mont Pavilion, NY Worlds Fair, 64-65; chmn bd dir, Gallatin Nat Life Ins Co, 68-; real estate & oil brokerage bus, 68-; mem bd dirs, Mayo Labs, Billings, Mont, 69- Mil Serv: Enlisted as Cadet, Air Force, 44, released as Pfc, 45, after serv in Cadet Training Unit, US. Mem: Mason (past Master, 32 degree); Scottish Rite; Shrine. Relig: Presbyterian. Mailing Add: 433 S Black Bozeman MT 59715

TSCHETTER, MENNO (D)
SDak State Rep
b Yale, SDak, Oct 18, 19; s John M Tschetter & Mary M Hofer T; m 1949 to Betty Jean Johnson; c Neil Jon, Gary Eugene & Bruce Elden. Educ: Huron Col, BA, 49; Huron Col Football Team, 4 years. Polit & Govt Pos: SDak State Rep, Beadle Co, 64- Bus & Prof Pos: Pres, Chicago & North Western Rwy Fed Credit Union, 62- Mil Serv: Entered as Seaman, Navy, 42, released as Yeoman 1/C, 46, after serv in NAtlantic, 27 months; Am Theater Ribbon; Good Conduct Medal. Mem: Izaak Walton League; Brotherhood of Rwy Clerks & Local Griever (pres, Huron Lodge 809; Cub Scouts; Boy Scouts. Mailing Add: RR 1 Box 248 Huron SD 57350

TSOMPANAS, PAUL LEE (R)
b Grove City, Pa, Jan 20, 37; s Nick Tsompanas & Amelia DeSalvo T; m 1959 to Mary Eva Patron; c Michelle, John, Stephen & Michael. Educ: Pa State Univ, BA, 58; Sigma Delta Chi; Alpha Phi Delta. Polit & Govt Pos: Admin asst to US Rep Bob Wilson, Calif, 66-75; prof staff mem, House Armed Servs Comt, 75- Bus & Prof Pos: Reporter & city ed, Clovis News-Journal, Clovis, NMex, 60-61; reporter, San Diego Eve Tribune, Calif, 61-64; cong correspondent, Copley News Serv, Washington, DC, 64-66; co-publisher, Washington Waterline, Washington, DC, 67-74. Mil Serv: Entered as Ens, Navy, 58, released as Lt(jg), 60, after serv in USS Cabildo as Commun Officer, 58-60. Publ: Articles in various popular trade journals. Mem: Bull Elephants of Capitol Hill. Honors & Awards: E H Shaffer Award, NMex Press Asn; Copley Journalism Award. Relig: Catholic. Legal Res: Annandale VA Mailing Add: 4929 Althea Dr Annandale VA 22003

TSONGAS, PAUL E (D)
US Rep, Mass
b Lowell, Mass, Feb 14, 41; s Efthemios S Tsongas; m to Nicola Sauvage; c Ashley. Educ: Dartmouth Col, BA, 62; Yale Law Sch, LLB, 67; Harvard Univ John F Kennedy Sch of Govt, 73. Polit & Govt Pos: Mem, Gov Comt on Law Enforcement, formerly; Dep Asst Attorney Gen, Commonwealth Mass, 69-71; city councillor, Lowell, Mass, 69-72; comnr, Middlesex Co, 73-74; US Rep, 75- Bus & Prof Pos: Attorney-at-law, Lowell, Mass, 71-74. Mailing Add: 46 Fairmount St Lowell MA 01852

TSUTRAS, FRANK GUS (D)
b Williamson, WVa, Oct 18, 29; s Gus Tsutras & Kornilia Savas T; m 1954 to Helen Athanasios Kouros; c Constandinos (Dean). Educ: WVa Univ, BS in Bus Admin, 57; Sigma Phi Epsilon. Polit & Govt Pos: Field coordr, Southern WVa, Area Redevelop Admin, US Dept of Commerce, 61-65; admin asst to US Rep James Kee, WVa, 65-73, spec asst to US Rep Gillis Long, La, 73, research asst to US Rep L A (Skip) Bafalis, Fla, 73, dir, Cong Rural Caucus, US House Rep, 73- Bus & Prof Pos: Mgr merchant prod dept, Williamson Supply Co, WVa, 57-58; managing dir, Tug Valley CofC, 58-61; exec secy, Tug Valley Indust Corp, Williamson Credit Bur & Williamson Retail Merchants Asn, 58-61. Mil Serv: 1st Lt, Air Force, 51-53, serv in 3800 Motor Vehicle Squadron, Sch of Aviation Med & Off Spec Invests; Capt, Air Force Res, Ret. Mem: Moose; Elks; Ahepa; Cong Staff Club. Relig: Greek Orthodox. Mailing Add: 3112 N Rosser St Alexandria VA 22311

TUBMAN, WILLIAM WILLIS, JR (D)
Secy, Dorchester Co Dem Cent Comt, Md
b Cambridge, Md, Aug 20, 47; s William Willis Tubman & Olga T; m 1969 to Patricia Lucas. Educ: Univ Baltimore, BA; Coppin State Col, MEd. Polit & Govt Pos: Secy, Dorchester Co Dem Cent Comt, Md, 74-; mem, Md Dem State Cent Comt, 74- Bus & Prof Pos: Teacher, North Dorchester High Sch, 69-71; prin, Agnew Sch, 71- Mem: Coun for Exceptional Children; Coun for Emotionally Troubled Child; Dorchester Slow Pitch Softball League (pres); Johnny's Softball Team (mgr). Mailing Add: 301 West End Ave Cambridge MD 21613

TUCHOW, GERALD (D)
Exec VChmn, 13th Cong Dist Dem Party, Mich
Polit & Govt Pos: Exec vchmn, 13th Cong Dist Dem Party, Mich, currently; deleg, Dem Nat Conv, 72; deleg, Dem Nat Mid-Term Conf, 74. Mailing Add: 1325 Joliet Pl Detroit MI 48207

TUCK, ANN LITTON ROWLAND (R)
Fourth VPres, Nat Fedn Rep Women
b Louisville, Ky, Apr 1, 26; d Edgar Coleman Rowland & Ida Litton Major R; m 1948 to James Richard Tuck; c Ann Litton, James Coleman & Mary Barbour. Educ: Sweet Briar Col, 44-46; Vanderbilt Univ, BA, 48; Kappa Alpha Theta. Polit & Govt Pos: Co co-chmn, Nixon-Lodge Campaign, Tenn, 60; vpres Fifth Cong Dist, Tenn Fedn Rep Women, 61-66, pres, 66-70; off mgr, Rep Co Hq, Nashville, 64; co-chmn, Davidson Co Young Rep Club, 65; secy, Davidson Co Rep Primary Bd, 67-68; chief engrossing clerk, Tenn House of Rep, 69-; mem-at-lg, Nat Fedn Rep Women, 70-, fourth vpres, 71-; asst comnr, Tenn State Dept Conserv, 71- Bus & Prof Pos: Asst lab technician, Biol Dept, Vanderbilt Univ, 47-48; asst, Bus Research Dept, Gen Shoe Corp, Nashville, Tenn, 48-50. Mem: League of Women Voters; Nashville Symphony Guild; Ladies Hermitage Asn; Fifth Dist Rep Women's Club. Relig: Methodist. Mailing Add: 4403 Iroquois Ave Nashville TN 37205

TUCK, JOSEPH GRADY, III (R)
Chmn, Kerr Co Rep Exec Comt, Tex
b Houston, Tex, Mar 18, 46; s Grady Tuck, Jr & Betty Kelly T; m 1971 to Pamela Kay Brinkman; c Joseph Grady, IV. Educ: Univ Tex, Austin, BA, 68, Sch Law, JD, 69; Kappa Sigma Fraternity. Polit & Govt Pos: Assoc research dir, Rep Party of Tex, Austin, 68-69; research dir & spec counsel, Colo Rep Cent Comt, Denver, 69-70; realty specialist, Off Interstate Land Sales Registration, Dept Housing & Urban Develop, Washington, DC, 70-71; dist attorney, 216th Judicial Dist, Kerr, Kimble, Kendall, Bandera, Gillespie & Sutton Co, 73-; chmn, Kerr Co Rep Exec Comt, Tex, 74- Bus & Prof Pos: Assoc attorney, Harris, Archer, Parks & Graul, Houston, 71-72; assoc attorney, Law Off of James Nugent, Kerrville, 72-73. Mem: US Jaycees (mem bd dirs, Kerrville, 74-); Hill Country Preservation Soc (pres, Kerrville, 75-); Am Bar Asn; Kiwanis Int. Honors & Awards: Only Rep Dist Attorney in Tex; Youngest elected Dist Attorney in Tex. Relig: Episcopal. Legal Res: 1215 Jack Dr Kerrville TX 78028 Mailing Add: 998 Sidney Baker S Kerrville TX 78028

TUCK, WILLIAM MUNFORD (D)
b Halifax Co, Va, Sept 28, 1896; s Robert James Tuck & Virginia Susan Fitts T; m 1928 to Eva Lovelace Dillard; stepson Lester Layne Dillard. Educ: Washington & Lee Univ, LLB, 21; Phi Delta Phi; Omicron Delta Kappa; Sigma Phi Epsilon. Hon Degrees: LLD, Hampden Sydney, Col, 46, Elon Col, NC, 47, William & Mary Col, 48 & Washington & Lee Univ, 49. Polit & Govt Pos: Va State Deleg, 24-32; chmn, Halifax Co Dem Comt, Va, 28-31; Va State Sen, 32-42; Lt Gov, Va, 42-46, Gov, 46-50; chmn, Fifth Dist Dem Comt, Va, 51-52; chmn, Va State Dem Exec Comt, 52; US Rep, Va, 53-69. Mem: Mason (33 degree); SAR & various other orgn. Relig: Baptist. Mailing Add: PO Box 40 South Boston VA 24592

TUCKER, CURTIS RAYMOND (D)
Calif State Assemblyman
b Union, La, Mar 26, 18; s Albert James Tucker & Bertha Marie Weber T; m 1948 to Lorraine Hohl; c Linda Hohl, Leslie Geralyn, Curtis Raymond, Jr, Lorraine Ann Hohl & Christy Marie. Educ: Univ Florence, Italy, 46. Polit & Govt Pos: Councilman, Inglewood, Calif, 72-74; Calif State Assemblyman, 74- Bus & Prof Pos: Med technician, US Army Med Corps, 37-60; harbor patrolman, City of Los Angeles, 60; dep health officer, Co of Los Angeles, 59-74; retired. Mil Serv: Entered Army, 37; Bronze Star. Mem: Co Employees' Asn; Serv Employees Int Union Local 660; NAACP. Relig: Catholic. Legal Res: 9223 Sixth Ave Inglewood CA 90305 Mailing Add: Rm 5135 State Capitol Sacramento CA 95814

TUCKER, CYNTHIA DELORES (D)
Secy, Commonwealth of Pa
b Philadelphia, Pa, Oct 4, 27; d Rev Whitfield Nottage & Captilda Gardiner N; m 1951 to William Tucker. Educ: Temple Univ; Univ Pa. Hon Degrees: LLD, Villa Maria Col (Pa), 72. Polit & Govt Pos: Vchmn, Pa Black Dem Comt, 66-; chmn, Women for Dem Action, 67-; secy & mem, Philadelphia Zoning Bd of Adjust, 68-70; vchmn, Pa State Dem Comt, 70-; secy, Commonwealth of Pa, currently; mem, Arrangements Comt, Dem Nat Conv, 72; mem, Dem Nat Comt, 72; mem, Dem Exec Comt, 72, 74-; mem, Pa Bicentennial Comn; mem, Pa Comn Women; mem, Gov Affirmative Action Coun. Bus & Prof Pos: Mem, Commonwealth Bd, Med Col Pa, 71- Publ: The suburban noose, Home & Housing J. Mem: Nat Asn Real Estate Brokers (bd mem, 67-); NAACP (Pa vpres); Alpha Kappa Alpha; Urban League; Bus & Prof Women's Club. Honors & Awards: Nominated Women of the Year, Ladies Home J, 75. Relig: Protestant. Legal Res: 6700 Lincoln Dr Philadelphia PA 19119 Mailing Add: 302 North Office Bldg Harrisburg PA 17120

TUCKER, DONALD L (D)
Fla State Rep
Mailing Add: 1203 Kenilworth Tallahassee FL 32303

TUCKER, GARDINER LUTTRELL (D)
Asst Secy Gen of NATO for Defense Support
b New York, NY, June 9, 25; s Ernest Eckford Tucker, DO & Katherine May Luttrell T; m to Helen Harwell; c Patricia Leigh, Gardiner L, Jr & James B. Educ: Columbia Col, BA, 47; Columbia Univ, PhD, 53; Phi Beta Kappa; Sigma Xi. Polit & Govt Pos: Dep dir research & eng, Dept Defense, 67, prin dep dir research & eng, 69-70, Asst Secy Defense Systs Anal, 70-73; Asst Secy Gen of NATO for Defense Support, 73- Bus & Prof Pos: Research physicist, IBM Watson Lab, Columbia Univ, 52-54; physicist in charge semiconductor research, Int Bus Mach Corp, 54-57, mgr research anal & planning staff, 57-59, mgr research lab, San Jose, Calif, 59-61, dir develop eng, World Trade Corp, Int Bus Mach, 61-63, dir res, Int Bus Mach Corp, 63-67. Mem: Dir Indust Res. Relig: Episcopal. Legal Res: 2810 N Quebec St Arlington VA 22207 Mailing Add: US North Atlantic Treaty Orgn/IS APO New York NY 09667

TUCKER, JACK NORRIS (D)
Miss State Sen
b Charleston, Miss, May 15, 21; s Harry Randolph Tucker & Lucy Barnett Rolfe T; m 1948 to Pattye Sue Williams. Educ: Holmes Jr Col, Goodman, Miss, 40-42; La State Normal Col, Natchitoches, 1 semester, 43; Univ Ga, pre-flight training, 43; Univ Miss, BA, 48, LLB, 50 & JD, 68; Phi Delta Phi; Delta Kappa Epsilon. Polit & Govt Pos: Chmn elec comn, Tunica Co, Miss, 52-56; Miss State Sen, 60-, chmn, Comt on Educ, Miss State Senate, 64- Bus & Prof Pos: Lawyer. Mil Serv: Entered as Aviation Cadet, Naval Res, 42, released as Lt(jg), 46, after serv in Am, European & Pac Theatres; Am & European Theatre Ribbons. Mem:

Rotary (past dir); Am Legion; VFW; Am & Miss Heart Asns. Honors & Awards: Meritorious Award, Miss Heart Asn; Cert of Appreciation, Am Heart Asn. Relig: Methodist. Mailing Add: PO Box 826 Tunica MS 38676

TUCKER, JAMES GUY (D)
Attorney Gen, Ark
b Oklahoma City, Okla, June 13, 43; s James Guy Tucker, Sr & Willie Maude White T; single. Educ: Harvard Univ, BA in Govt, 64; Univ Ark Sch Law, Fayetteville, JD, 68; Phi Alpha Delta; Sigma Alpha Epsilon; Hasty Pudding Inst. Polit & Govt Pos: Prosecuting Attorney, Sixth Judicial Dist, Pulaski & Perry Co, Ark, 71-72; alt deleg, Dem Nat Conv, 72; Attorney Gen, Ark, 73- Bus & Prof Pos: Assoc attorney, Rose, Barron, Nash, Williamson, Carroll & Clay, Little Rock, 68-70. Mil Serv: Marine Res. Publ: Arkansas Men at War, Pioneer Press, 68; Civil disobedience, Univ Ark Law Rev, 69. Mem: Am Judicature Soc; Nat Asn Attorneys Gen; Am Legion (Judge Advocate, Post 134, 70-); Ark Coun Human Rels; Foreign Rels Club of Little Rock. Honors & Awards: Ark Young Man of Year, Ark Jaycees, 72. Relig: Reorganized Latter-day Saint. Legal Res: 7 White Oak Lane Little Rock AR 72207 Mailing Add: Justice Bldg Little Rock AR 72201

TUCKER, JEROME (D)
Ala State Rep
Mailing Add: Suite 1722 2121 Bldg Eighth Ave N Birmingham AL 35203

TUCKER, NEAL VANCEL (D)
Chmn, Orange Co Dem Party, Vt
b Orange, Vt, Aug 13, 25; s Wyness Edward Tucker & Alyce Ruth Morse T; m 1947 to Lorraine Myrtice Beede; c Ronald, Cynthia, Doreen, Kathy, Lori & Russell. Polit & Govt Pos: Chmn, Orange Town Dem Party, Vt, 36-; dep sheriff, Orange Co, Vt, 48-; rd comnr, Town of Orange, 48-, chmn, civil defense, 56- & justice of peace, 62-68, 71-; chmn, Orange Co Dem Party, Vt, 69- Bus & Prof Pos: Quarryman, Rock of Ages, Barre, Vt, 51-56, construction foreman, 57-62, quarry foreman, 63-68, prod supt, 68- Mem: State & Co Sheriff's Asns; Rock of Ages Safety Comt; AFL-CIO; Moose. Honors & Awards: Award for outstanding serv to Dem Party; cert appreciation, Future Farmers Am. Relig: Protestant. Legal Res: Tucker Rd Orange VT Mailing Add: RFD 2 Barre VT 05641

TUCKER, RAY M (D)
Ga State Rep
b Cork, Ga, Apr 11, 27; s Arthur Washington Tucker & John Torbet T; single. Educ: Walter F George Sch Law, Mercer Univ, LLB, 52, AB, 54; Kappa Sigma. Polit & Govt Pos: Ga State Rep, 63- Bus & Prof Pos: Attorney-at-law. Mil Serv: Army, 45-46; Army Res, 46-49; Korean War, 52-54, 1st Lt. Mem: Mason; Elk; Am Legion; Lions (dist gov, 62-63). Relig: Methodist. Mailing Add: PO Box 469 McDonough GA 30253

TUCKER, ROBERT S (D)
RI State Rep
Mailing Add: 3 School St West Warwick RI 02893

TUCKER, STERLING (D)
VChmn, DC City Coun
b Akron, Ohio, Dec 21, 23; s John Clifford Tucker & Una Vinson T; m 1948 to Edna Alloyce Robinson; c Michele Alloyce & Lauren Alloyce. Educ: Univ Akron, BA, 46, MA, 50; Alpha Phi Alpha; Debate Team; officer, Student Coun. Polit & Govt Pos: Vchmn, DC City Coun, 69- Bus & Prof Pos: Asst exec dir, Akron Urban League, Ohio, 49-53; exec dir, Canton Urban League, 53-56 & Washington Urban League, DC, 56-; dir Field Serv, Nat Urban League, 68-70, spec asst to exec dir, 70- Publ: Beyond the Burning: Life & Death of the Ghetto, Asn Press, 68; Black Reflections on White Power, 69 & For Blacks Only, 71, William B Eerdsman Publ Co. Mem: Nat Asn Soc Workers (exec bd metrop area); Acad of Cert Soc Workers; vpres metrop area, Urban Coalition; Interreligious Comt on Race Rels; bd, Metrop Washington Coun of Churches. Honors & Awards: Outstanding Young Man of the Year Award, Washington Jr CofC, 64; Citation from Repub of Liberia, 66. Relig: Episcopal. Mailing Add: 6505 16th St NW Washington DC 20012

TUCKER, WENDELL O (D)
Chmn, Stanton Co Dem Cent Comt, Kans
b Johnson, Kans, Jan 22, 27; s Herman Lawrence Tucker & Luella Warren T; m 1944 to Ethel Lorene Lewis; c Judith Kay & Wendell Lee. Educ: Johnson High Sch, Kans. Polit & Govt Pos: Chmn, Stanton Co Dem Cent Comt, Kans, 64- Mem: Legion Club, Post 79 (hon mem); Stanton Co Soil Conserv Dist (chmn); Odd Fellows; Elks. Relig: Methodist. Mailing Add: Box 468 Johnson KS 67855

TUCKER, WILLIAM EDWARD (R)
Spec Asst Attorney Gen, Colo
b Idabel, Okla, Sept 2, 35; s Owen F Tucker & Dixie Stiles T; m 1955 to Nancy Louise Henkins; c Desiree & Gayle Ann. Educ: SDak Sch Mines, BS, 56; Univ Okla Sch Law, JD, 62; Phi Alpha Delta, pres, 61; Alpha Delta; Scabbard & Blade; Theta Tau. Polit & Govt Pos: Mem, Presidential Campaign Speaker's Comt, 64; treas, Denver Young Rep, 64, pres, 65, mem bd dirs, 65-66; mem, State Exec Bd, Colo Young Rep, 64-66, state chmn, 69; nat chmn, Young Rep Speaker's Comt, 65-66; mem exec comt, Young Rep Nat Fedn, 65-73, gen counsel, 67-69; gen counsel, Young Rep League, Colo, 66-; Spec Asst Attorney Gen, Colo, 66-; Secy, Gen Coun of US Youth Coun, 72-73; mem bd dirs, Am Coun of Young Polit Leaders, 72-73. Bus & Prof Pos: Partner law firm, Tucker & Combs; partner real estate, Tucker & Co; mem bd dirs, Consol Invests, Inc; pres, Georgetown Invest Co, Inc; spec lectr, environ & admin law, Univ Denver & Univ Colo, spec adv comt, Faculty Natural Resources Law, Univ Denver; mem bd dirs, Charles Edison Mem Youth Fund, 74-75. Mil Serv: 1st Lt, Army, 55-56. Publ: Advertising prescriptions—end of the prohibition era?, Nat Asn Bd Pharm Quart, summer 69. Mem: Am Bar Asn (comt environ law); Colo Bar Asn (comt admin law); Okla Bar Asn; Denver Jaycees; Denver Athletic Club. Honors & Awards: Outstanding Young Rep, State Colo, decade 62-72 & year 66; Outstanding Jaycee, 66; deleg, Paris Conf, Young Polit Leaders of NATO Countries, 69; deleg, Conf Young Polit Leaders, Soviet Union, 72. Relig: Methodist. Legal Res: 5660 E Eldorado Pl Denver CO 80222 Mailing Add: Suite 1030 Western Federal Savings Bldg Denver CO 80202

TUCKER, WILLIAM HUMPHREY (D)
b Boston, Mass, Sept 8, 23; s William H Tucker & Marion Thomas T; m 1948 to Caroline E Aitken; c Sandra J & Karen D. Educ: Boston Univ Sch Law, LLB, cum laude, 49; ed, Boston Univ Law Rev. Polit & Govt Pos: Comnr, Interstate Com Comn, 61-65, chmn, 66-67; deleg, Dem Nat Conv, 68. Bus & Prof Pos: Attorney-at-law, Athol & Boston, Mass, 49-61; partner law firm, Saxon, Mcguire & Tucker, 68; vpres corp admin, Penn Cent Co, 68-69; vpres, New Eng Penn Cent Co, 69- Mil Serv: Entered as Pvt, Army, 42, released as Sgt, 45, after serv in 505th Parachute Regt, 82nd Airborne Div, ETO, 43-45; Lt Col, Army Standby Res; French & Belgian Fourragere; Dutch Order of Wm Laniard; Sicily, Naples-Foggia, Normandy, Holland, Ardennes & Cent Europe Campaign Ribbons with Stars; Purple Heart with Cluster; Campaign I Infantryman's Badge; Presidential Unit Citation. Publ: The public interest in railroad mergers, Boston Univ Law Rev, spring 62; The quiet crisis in transportation, Interstate Com Comn Practitioners' J, 12/64; The coming of age in trucking, Commercial Car J, 11/65. Mem: Am Bar Asn; Cong Country Club; Algonquin Club; 82nd Airborne C-47 Club, Inc (chmn bd); ICC Practitioners Asn. Honors & Awards: Distinguished Pub Serv Award, Boston Univ; Distinguished Young Gentleman Award, Boston CofC. Relig: Episcopal. Legal Res: 39 Neel Rd Harwichport MA 02646 Mailing Add: 133 Plymouth Dr Norwood MA 02062

TUCZYNSKI, PHILLIP JAMES (D)
Wis State Rep
b Milwaukee, Wis, Jan 11, 47; s Felix Tuczynski & Estelle Zumanic T; single. Educ: Univ Wis-Milwaukee, BA in Int Econ, 70, MA in Pub Admin, 75. Polit & Govt Pos: Admin intern, Milwaukee Co Bd Supvrs, 72-; chmn, Ninth Assembly Dist Dem Unit, 73; Wis State Rep, 75- Mem: World Affairs Coun of Milwaukee; Southside Businessmen's Asn; Polish Nat Alliance; Polish Asn Am. Relig: Catholic. Legal Res: 1322 W Cleveland Ave Milwaukee WI 53215 Mailing Add: Rm 33 North Capitol Madison WI 53215

TUDHOPE, DOUGLAS I (R)
Vt State Rep
Mailing Add: 68 Laurel Hill Dr S Burlington VT 05401

TUDOR, DAVID FREDERICK (R)
Co-Chmn, Local & State Awards, Young Rep Nat Fedn
b Franklin, Ind, Dec 22, 48; s Lester L Tudor (Spud) & Margaret Wetzel T; single. Educ: Ind Univ, Bloomington, BS, 74; Ind Univ Law Sch, Indianapolis, 74- & Ind Univ Grad Sch Bus, 75-; Kappa Delta Rho. Polit & Govt Pos: Staff asst, Whitcomb for Gov Comt, 68; chmn, Ind Col Rep, 70-71; exec secy, Ind Young Rep Fedn, 71-73; mem exec comt, Ind Young Am for Freedom, 71-; co-chmn, Local & State Awards, Young Rep Nat Fedn, 73-; chmn, Westfield Town Rep Comt, 75- Bus & Prof Pos: Intern, Reporter of the Ind Supreme Court & Court of Appeals, summer 70; admin analyst, Research Div, Ind Dept Revenue, 70; admin officer, Div Planning, Ind Dept Com, 71-72; youth coordr, Citizens for Curtis for US Senate, Lincoln, Nebr, 72; chief auditor, Inheritance Tax Div, Ind Dept Revenue, 73-75, asst admin, Motor Fuel Tax Div, 75- Mem: Am Bar Asn (Law Student Div); Nat Tax Payer's Union; Moon Mullins Study Group; Ind Oral Hist Roundtable; Ind Coun for Effective Law Enforcement. Honors & Awards: Am Legion Award, Westfield Post, 64; Rookie of the Year, Moon Mullins Study Group, 70; Outstanding Sen Award, Great Issues Model Senate, 70; Honors Prog Acceptance, Hist Dept, Ind Univ, 71. Legal Res: 224 Beechwood Dr Westfield IN 46074 Mailing Add: PO Box 584 Westfield IN 46074

TUERK, FRED JAMES (R)
Ill State Rep
b Peoria, Ill, July 19, 22; s Fred W Tuerk & Anna L Meagher T; m 1945 to Mary M Kieffer; c Mary Anne, Therese Ellen, William F, John A, Barbara M, Ellen E, Margaret M & Tina L. Educ: St Ambrose Col, 40-42; Univ Mo, Columbia, BJ, 46; Beta Theta Pi. Polit & Govt Pos: Trustee, Peoria Park Dist, Ill, 63-71; Ill State Rep, 69-, chmn, Indust Affairs Comt, formerly. Mil Serv: Entered as A/S, Navy, 42, released as Lt(jg), 46, after serv in ETO, 44-45; Am Theatre Medal; European Theatre Medal with one Star. Mem: Sigma Delta Chi; Int Coun of Indust Ed; Ill Valley Press Club; KofC; CofC. Honors & Awards: Recipient of Freedoms Found Medal; several co mag & newspaper Citations of Excellence. Relig: Catholic. Mailing Add: 3212 N Avalon Pl Peoria IL 61604

TUGGLE, KENNETH HERNDON (R)
Comnr, Interstate Commerce Comn
b Barbourville, Ky, June 12, 04; s Jesse Davis Tuggle & Sue Gregory Root T; m 1937 to Vivian Shifley; c Kenneth Jesse & Sarah Baldwin (Mrs Andrew Johnson). Educ: Univ Ky, AB, 26; Union Col, LLD, 46; Delta Theta Phi; Omicron Delta Kappa; Tau Kappa Alpha; Pi Kappa Alpha. Polit & Govt Pos: Chmn, Ky Legis Coun, 43 & 45; Lt Gov of Ky, 43-47, pres, Ky State Senate, 44-46, mem bd mgr, Coun State Govt, 44 & 47; deleg-at-lg, Rep Nat Conv, 48 & 52; mem, Ky Comt on Resources & Functions of State Govt, 50-52; comnr, Interstate Com Comn, 53-, chmn, 59; chmn US deleg, Sixth Session, Int Labor Orgn, Hamburg, Germany, 57. Bus & Prof Pos: Pres, Union Nat Bank, Barbourville, Ky, 34-53. Mem: Union Col, Barbourville, Ky (trustee); Am Mus of Safety (trustee). Relig: Methodist. Legal Res: 115 Pine St Barbourville KY Mailing Add: Interstate Com Comn 12th & Constitution Ave NW Washington DC 20423

TUIASOSOPO, PALAUNI MARIOTA (BROWNIE)
b Fagatogo, Am Samoa, Sept 18, 37; s Hon Mariota Tuimalu Tuiasosopo & Venise Pulefaasisiana T; m 1964 to Cecilia Kaisa; c Faataape Saeuteuga, Saufaiga Cecilia, Jeffery Holbrook, Faailoilo & Kuku Motumotu. Educ: Univ Ore, BS, 61; Tau Kappa Epsilon. Polit & Govt Pos: Admin asst in Gov Off, Am Samoa Govt, 62-65, dir, Off of Samoa Info, 63-65; chief clerk, spec asst to legis counsel, gen adminr to legis asst legis counsel, budget analyst for legis house, floor mgr, bill drafter & translator, Am Samoa Legis, 65-70; dep dir, Develop & Planning, Am Samoa Govt, 69-70, asst to Gov, Pago Pago, 70-; chmn, Am Samoa Bicentennial Comn, currently; dir, Progs for Elderly. Bus & Prof Pos: Partner & founder, Pago Pago Laundry & Dry Cleaning, 65-73; Samoan legal practitioner, Court of Am Samoa, 66-73. Mem: SPac Conf (deleg, 69-); Youth Develop Prog (dir, 73-); Am Samoa Arts Coun (vchmn, 70-); Am Samoa Cultural Performing Arts (dir, 72-); Am Samoa Red Cross (chmn, 66-). Honors & Awards: Col Model United Nations, Univ Ore, 61. Relig: Congregational. Legal Res: Vatia American Samoa Mailing Add: Governor's Off Pago Pago American Samoa

TUIOLOSEGA, TAGALOA M (D)
Sen, Am Samoa Legis
b Pago Pago, Am Samoa, Oct 27, 21; s T F Laolagi & Faapupula L; m 1956 to Antonia Godinet; c Julia Yvonne & Arlene Philomena. Educ: Woodbury Col Calif, BBA, 55. Polit & Govt Pos: Chief payroll clerk, US Navy, Pago Pago, Am Samoa, 42-48; asst hosp adminr, Govt Hosp, Pago Pago, 55-62; Rep, Am Samoa Legis, Second Dist, 64-68, vspeaker & chmn, Ways & Means Comt, 64-68; Sen, Am Samoa Legis, Second Dist, 69-, chmn, Econ Develop Comt, currently. Bus & Prof Pos: Pres & exec officer, Nia-Marie & Co, Inc, Pago Pago, Am Samoa, 62-73 & Pago Pago Cinemas, Inc, 67- Mil Serv: Entered as Cpl, Marine Corps, 50, released, 53, after serv in Recruiting Depot, San Diego, Calif; Marine Corps Res, Pearl

Harbor, 48-50. Mem: Nat Soc Pub Acct; Hawaii Asn Pub Acct; Marist Bros Old Boys Asn. Relig: Catholic. Mailing Add: PO Box 327 Pago Pago American Samoa

TULAGA, TAUALA MAUI
b Luma, Tau, Am Samoa, Nov 29, 1890; s Maui Tulaga & Faafia Maui T; m 1918 to Faaga Tualemoso; c Selau (Mrs Kitiona Gago), Alataua (Mrs Ioane Fiu), Toatele (Mrs Faasamala Tufele), Lauuasa Tauala & Malie Tauala. Educ: Elem & Minister Sch, 15. Polit & Govt Pos: Mayor, Luma, Am Samoa, 20-35; Sen, Fono, Am Samoa, 48-52; Assoc Judge, High Court, Am Samoa, formerly. Mem: Village Coun (orator); Co Coun (orator). Relig: Congregational. Mailing Add: PO Box 554 Pago Pago American Samoa

TULISANO, RICHARD DON (D)
Conn State Rep
b Hartford, Conn, Nov 7, 39; s Dominick Tulisano & Rosaline Marketti T; m 1959 to Beverly DeMello. Educ: Univ Conn, BA, 65, JD, 69; Student Counsel & Counsel Treas. Polit & Govt Pos: Deleg, Town Meeting for Tomorrow, 61; mem, Rocky Hill Charter Study Comt, 63, Bd of Assessors, 63-64 & Dem Town Comt, 63-; chmn, Voter Regist Comt, Rocky Hill Dem Comt, 65-; Conn State Rep, 75- Publ: Co-auth, Is Terminology Enough? Am Anthropologist, 65. Mem: Lions; KofC; Elks; Conn Bar Asn; Hartford Chap of UNICO. Honors & Awards: Recipient of Am Jurisprudence Book Prize & Corpus Juris Secundum Award. Relig: Roman Catholic. Legal Res: 11 Sunny Crest Dr Rocky Hill CT 06067 Mailing Add: 750 Old Main St Rocky Hill CT 06067

TULLER, JUDITH (D)
b Brooklyn, NY, Dec 14, 29; d Ben Hofstadter & Kate Bodenstein; div; c Joanne & David. Educ: Radcliffe Col, BA, 51; Harvard Law Sch, LLB, 54; Phi Beta Kappa. Polit & Govt Pos: Deleg, Dem Nat Conv, 72. Bus & Prof Pos: Asst to dir prog develop, Henry Street Settlement, New York, NY, 73-75. Mem: Am Jewish Cong (Nat Governing Coun); Forest Hills Housing Coop (asst secy, bd dir). Relig: Jewish. Mailing Add: 147-14 Charter Rd Jamaica NY 11435

TULLER, PAUL RAYMOND (R)
Chmn, Blandford Rep Town Comt, Mass
b Westfield, Mass, Dec 15, 38; s Edwin Franklin Tuller & Florence Smith T; single. Educ: Westfield State Col, BSEd, 60, MEd, 65. Polit & Govt Pos: Secy, Ward Five Rep Comt, Westfield, Mass, 63-64; secy, Blandford Sch Study Comt, 68; temporary rep, Gateway Regional Dist Sch Comt, 68-69, mem, 69-70; chmn, Blandford Rep Town Comt, 68-74; deleg, Mass State Rep Conv, 70-74; selectman, Blandford, Mass, 71-74, chmn bd, 72-74. Bus & Prof Pos: Teacher, Westfield Sch Syst, Mass, 60, dir, academically talented prog, Franklin Sch, Westfield, 67-69; licensed real estate broker; antique bus, Sage House, currently. Mem: Hampden Co Selectman's Asn; Mass Selectmen's Asn; Blandford Hist Soc (bd dirs). Honors & Awards: Enrollment in Nat Arch for Govt & Polit Work. Relig: Congregational. Mailing Add: Main St Blandford MA 01008

TULLEY, JOSEPH P (R)
Ohio State Rep
b 1922; m to Mary Rita Keating; c Deborah, Timothy, Candace, Ellen, Sarah, Patrick & Mary Kate. Educ: John Carroll Univ, BA; Western Reserve Univ Law Sch, LLB; Alpha Sigma Nu. Polit & Govt Pos: Ohio State Rep, 67-, chmn, Judiciary Comt, 69-70; Willoughby Prosecuting Attorney; Planning & zoning Comn & Charter Comn, Mentor Village. Mil Serv: Navy & Naval Res, 17 years, World War II, Korean Conflict; discharged as Lt. Mem: Murray Estates Improv Asn; Holy Name Soc of St Mary Parish; Rotary; Union of Holy Name Soc (pres); KofC (Dep Grand Knight). Honors & Awards: Legal counsel, Citizens for Decent Lit. Relig: Roman Catholic. Mailing Add: 7535 Acacia Dr Mentor OH 44060

TULLIO, LOUIS JOSEPH (D)
Mayor, Erie, Pa
b Erie, Pa, May 17, 17; s Anthony Tullio & Ersilia Nardone T; m 1941 to Mary Cecilia McHale; c Betty Ann (Mrs Eiswerth), June Cecilia (Mrs Geisler) & Marilyn Lou; Six grandchildren. Educ: Holy Cross Col, BS, 39; Boston Univ, MEd, 57. Polit & Govt Pos: Asst dir, Health & Physical Educ, Erie City Sch Dist, Pa, 57-60; secy & bus mgr, Erie City Sch Dist, 60-65; mem exec comt, Erie & Erie Co Dem Parties; Mayor, Erie, Pa, 66-; deleg, Dem Nat Conv, 68. Bus & Prof Pos: Asst to the Pres, Gannon Col; high sch teacher. Mil Serv: Entered as Ens, Navy, 43, released as Lt, 45. Mem: Dollars for Scholars Orgn; Fathers Club of Mercyhurst Prep Sch; Citizens Adv Comt to Erie City Sch Dist; Cath Charities of Erie, Inc. Honors & Awards: Received Prof Honor Award of Pa Health, Physical Educ & Recreation; named little All Am Coach of Year. Relig: Catholic. Mailing Add: 660 E Grandview Blvd Erie PA 16509

TULLY, BERNARD JOSEPH (D)
Mass State Sen
b Lowell, Mass; s Bernard Tully; m to Annette Chouinard; c Sharon, Joseph, Philip & Jo-Ann. Educ: Boston Univ, BS Bus Admin, 51. Polit & Govt Pos: Mass State Sen, 71- Mil Serv: Entered as Pvt, Air Force, 44, released as Pvt, 47. Relig: Catholic. Mailing Add: 12 Mountainview Dr Dracut MA 01826

TUMLIN, GEORGE W (D)
Mem, Dem Party Ga
b Atlanta, Ga, Oct 5, 21; s William Millard Tumlin & Lossie White T; m 1939 to Florence E Stewart; c William Wayne, George Elmer, Barbara Jane (Mrs Taylor) & Colon Lee. Polit & Govt Pos: Mem, Clayton Co Dem Exec Comt, 72, vchmn, 73; mem exec comt, Dem Party Ga, 73, mem, 74- Mil Serv: Entered as A/S, Navy, 44, released as Seaman 1/C, 45. Mailing Add: Rte 2 Box 831 Hampton GA 30228

TUMULTY, GARY ALLEN (D)
Pres Region 4, Young Dem of Am
b Springfield, Ill, Sept 15, 41; s Paul John Tumulty & Elizabeth Laatsch T; m 1974 to Deborah Gay Clinton; c Timothy Scott. Educ: Ill State Univ, BS in Bus Admin, 70. Polit & Govt Pos: State pres, Young Dem of Ill, 73-75; co clerk, Sangamon Co, Ill, 74-; pres region 4, Young Dem of Am, 75- Mem: Elks; Am Bus Club; Jaycees; Eagles. Mailing Add: 1420 Monument Springfield IL 62702

TUMULTY, JOSEPH W (D)
NJ State Sen
Mailing Add: State House Trenton NJ 08625

TUNNEY, JOHN VARICK (D)
US Sen, Calif
b New York, NY, July 26, 34; s Gene Tunney & Mary Lauder T; c Edward Eugene, Mark Andrew & Arianne Sprengers. Educ: Yale Univ, BA, 52-56; Acad Int Law, The Hague, 57; Univ Va Law Sch, LLB, 59; Delta Psi. Polit & Govt Pos: US Rep, 38th Dist, Calif, 65-70; US Sen, Calif, 70-; deleg, Dem Nat Conv, 72. Bus & Prof Pos: Attorney, Cahill, Gordon, Reindel & Ohl, 59-60, pvt practice, 63-64; lectr, Univ Calif, Riverside, 61-62. Mil Serv: Entered as 1st Lt, Air Force, 60, released as Capt, 63. Mem: Calif Bar Asn; Academia Internationalis-Lex et Scientia; Lions; Jr CofC; Riverside Aiding Leukemia Stricken Am Children. Relig: Roman Catholic. Legal Res: 4080 Lemon St Riverside CA 92501 Mailing Add: Senate Off Bldg Washington DC 20501

TUPPAN, GLENDA RANA (R)
Mem, Rep State Cent Comt Calif
b Belleville, Ark, Sept 27; d P Rana & E B Hudson R; m 1948 to George Richard Tuppan; c Ranalyn & Randy. Educ: Manual Arts High Sch, grad, 44. Polit & Govt Pos: Rep precinct capt, Whittier, Calif, 50, area chmn, 52-59, registrn chmn, 60-; mem, Rep State Cent Comt Calif, 66-; 1st vpres, Rancho La Habra Rep Women, 69-70, pres, 70-71, Americanism chmn, 72-; Americanism chmn, Los Angeles Co Fedn Rep Women, 72; deleg, Court Reform Blue Ribbon Comt, 72 & 73. Mem: Rancho La Habra Womens Club, La Habra Heights Improv Asn. Relig: Lutheran. Mailing Add: 1010 West Rd Whittier CA 90603

TUPPER, STANLEY R (R)
b Jan 25, 21; m to Jill L; c Stanley, Jr & Lara Abigail. Polit & Govt Pos: Mem & chmn bd of Selectmen, Boothbay Harbor, Maine, 48-50; Maine State Rep, 52; comnr of Sea & Shore Fisheries for State of Maine, 53-57; chmn, Maine Citizens Comt for Eisenhower-Nixon, 56; US Rep, Maine, 61-67; campaign coordr for New Eng States, Rockefeller for President Comt, 64; US Ambassador, Can World Exhib, 67. Bus & Prof Pos: Lawyer. Mil Serv: Navy. Mailing Add: Western Ave Boothbay Harbor ME 04538

TURCOTT, THOMAS (R)
b Boyne City, Mich, June 19, 23; m 1947 to Margaret Strehl; c Riley, Michael, Casey, Patricia, Laura, Kathy, Janie, Mary & Danny. Educ: OD. Polit & Govt Pos: Campaign chmn for Alger-Cobo-Nixon-Griffin; mem city coun, Petoskey, Mich; vchmn, Emmet Co Rep Comt, formerly. Bus & Prof Pos: Optometrist. Mem: Elks; Am Legion; Little League (bd dirs). Legal Res: 722 Mitchell Petoskey MI 49770 Mailing Add: 312 Mitchell Petoskey MI 49770

TURIANO, MICHAEL (D)
Conn State Rep
Mailing Add: 307 Burbank Ave Stratford CT 06497

TURK, EDMUND JOHN (D)
Councilman, Cleveland, Ohio
b Cleveland, Ohio, Jan 7, 25; s Joseph Turk & Rose Skerbec T; single. Educ: John Carroll Univ, BSS; John Marshall Law Sch, JD; Delta Theta Phi. Polit & Govt Pos: Councilman, Cleveland, 23rd Ward, Ohio, 61-, coun pres, 72-73; chmn, Airports & Lake Front Comt, Cleveland, currently; chmn, Pub Utilities Comn Ohio, 73-75; mem adv coun, Ohio Energy Comn; mem, Power Siting Com, 73-75. Mil Serv: Entered as Seaman, 43, released as PHM 2/C, 46, after serv in Atlantic-Pac, Occupation Forces, Japan. Mem: Ohio State, Citizens League of Gtr Cleveland, Ohio; Catholic War Vets, Post 1655 (comdr); Am Mutual Life Asn (2nd vpres). Relig: Roman Catholic. Legal Res: 1046 E 69th St Cleveland OH 44103 Mailing Add: 6411 St Clair Ave Cleveland OH 44103

TURLEY, STANLEY F (R)
Ariz State Sen
b Snowflake, Ariz, Feb 27, 21; s Fred A Turley & Wilma Fillerup T; m 1944 to Cleo Fern Olson; c Tauna Lee, Margo Yvonne, Jana, Fredrick C, Miriam K, Lisa & Leslie. Educ: Brigham Young Univ, 3 years. Polit & Govt Pos: Ariz State Rep, 64-72, speaker, Ariz House Rep, 67-72; Ariz State Sen, 73- Bus & Prof Pos: Bd dirs, Ariz Cotton Growers. Mil Serv: Entered as Pvt, Air Force, 44, released as Pfc, 46. Mem: Farm Bur; Rotary; Ariz Cattle Growers Asn. Relig: Latter-day Saint. Mailing Add: 2650 E Southern Ave Mesa AZ 85201

TURNAGE, JEAN A (R)
Mont State Sen
Mailing Add: PO Box 450 Polson MT 59860

TURNBULL, WILLIAM S (D)
b Richmond, Va, Mar 15, 24; s Nathaniel Turnbull & Marguerite Massie T; m 1948 to Shirley Eileen Wells; c Laurie Eileen & William S, Jr. Educ: Univ Fla, AB, 46-48; John B Stetson Univ, LLB, 49; Sigma Alpha Epsilon. Polit & Govt Pos: Precinct committeeman, Orange Co Dem Exec Comt, Fla, 54-66, chmn, 63-67; committeeman, Fla Dem Exec Comt, 66 & chmn, Fifth Dist Cong Comt; deleg, Dem Nat Conv, 68 & 72; Dem Nat Committeeman, Fla, 68-72. Mil Serv: Entered as Aviation Cadet, Navy, 42, released as Ens, 45; Lt Comdr, Navy Res, 45-66. Publ: Alimony & property settlement in Florida, Fla Bar J, 58; Zoning practice, Fla Real Property Practice Manual, 66. Mem: Fla, Am & Orange Co Bar Asns; Downtown Orlando Coun (pres). Relig: Episcopal. Mailing Add: 2602 Middlesex Orlando FL 32803

TURNER, C ELMO (R)
Utah State Rep
Mailing Add: 10342 S 1300 W South Jordan UT 84065

TURNER, CATHERINE ANN (D)
Mem Exec Comt, Tenn Fedn Dem Women
b Smith Co, Tenn, Nov 27, 51; d Edward Myer Turner & Catherine Jane Coward T; single. Educ: Mid Tenn State Univ, BS, 73 & MA, 74; Nashville Night Law Sch, 75-; Kappa Delta. Polit & Govt Pos: Deleg, Dem Nat Mid-Term Conf, 74; mem, Sumner Co Dem Exec Comt, 74-; deleg, Am Coun Young Polit Leaders, 75-; mem exec comt, Tenn Fedn Dem Women, 74- & legis chmn, 75-; treas, Tenn Young Dem, 75- Bus & Prof Pos: Sec educ prof, Sumner Co Bd Educ, 73- Mem: Young Dem; Am Coun Young Polit Leaders; Jackson Presidential Club; Tenn Educ Asn. Relig: Baptist. Mailing Add: L-86 Cedar Brook Apt Hendersonville TN 37075

TURNER, CHARLES WAYLAND (D)
Mem, Tenn State Dem Exec Comt
b Sneedville, Tenn, Feb 5, 16; s David Mack Turner & Mae Seals T; m 1941 to Cecile Greene Turner; c Brenda (Mrs Trent). Educ: ETenn State Univ, 35; Univ Tenn, Knoxville. Polit &

Govt Pos: Mayor, Sneedville, Tenn, 61-71. Bus & Prof Pos: Owner-mgr, Turner's Drug Store, 41-; partnership, Turner's Dept Store, 58- Mem: Sneedville Lions Club; Sneedville Masonic Lodge 1937; Sneedville CofC; Photographic Soc of Am; ETenn State Univ (bd trustees, Found, 70). Honors & Awards: Outstanding Serv in Lionism, Sneedville Lions Club, 62-63; Tenn Mayor of the Year, Tenn Munic League, 69. Relig: Baptist. Mailing Add: 138 Livesay Sneedville TN 37869

TURNER, D KELLY (D)
Assoc Justice, High Court, Trust Territory, Pac Islands
b Manila, Philippine Islands, Dec 9, 07; s R Izer Turner & Nora Damron T; m 1931 to Zorena Goodwin; c Bette Zoe (Mrs Fuenning), Lynda (Mrs Eads), Richmond Kelly & John William. Educ: Phoenix Col, 25-28; Univ Ariz, 28-30; George Washington Univ, LLB, 38, JD, 69; Sigma Alpha Epsilon. Polit & Govt Pos: Clerk, US Senate, 33-37; Ariz State Dir, 1940 Decennial Census, 39-40; US Off Civilian Defense, 42-; Asst Attorney Gen, Ariz, 45-56; dep attorney gen, Trust Territory of Pac Islands, 66-67, assoc justice, High Court, 67- Bus & Prof Pos: Pvt practice of law, Phoenix & Scottsdale, Ariz, 38-66. Mil Serv: Entered as Pvt, Army, 44, released in 45 after serv in 37th Inf Div, Pac; 1st Lt, Army Res; Combat Inf Badge; Bronze Star. Publ: Trust Territory Reports, Equity, 68- Mem: Am & Ariz State Bar Asns. Relig: Protestant. Legal Res: 3021 N Valencia Lane Phoenix AZ 85018 Mailing Add: Majuro Marshall Islands

TURNER, EARL JAMES (D)
Chmn, Clark Co Dem Party, Ill
b Marshall, Ill, Feb 10, 20; s James M Turner & Fanny Carpenter T; m 1944 to Belva Highsmith; c Patricia Ann & Steven Earl. Educ: Ind State Teachers Col, 2 years. Polit & Govt Pos: Chmn, Clark Co Dem Party, Ill, 70- Mil Serv: Entered as Aviation Cadet, Navy, 42, released as Lt Comdr, 64, after serv in Atlantic & Pac. Mem: VFW; Am Legion. Relig: Methodist. Mailing Add: 1003 S Sixth Marshall IL 62441

TURNER, EDWARD LOUIS (D)
b China Grove, NC, July 26, 43; s Farris Leon Turner & Nonie Mae Smith T; single. Educ: Univ Ga, 68; Alpha Phi Alpha. Polit & Govt Pos: City councilman, Athens, Ga, 71-; deleg, Dem Nat Conv, 72; second vpres, Clarke Co Dem Club, Ga, 72- Mem: NAACP; A Philip Inst; Good Govt Asn; Cement Plasters Union Local 603. Relig: Methodist. Mailing Add: 390 Third St Athens GA 30601

TURNER, EDWARD MILNER, JR (D)
b Laurel Fork, Va, May 19, 19; s Edward Milner Turner, Sr & Maggie Duncan T; m 1942 to Mary Louise Seitz; c Edward Milner, III. Educ: Univ Md, 2 years. Polit & Govt Pos: Mem & treas, Carroll Co Dem Comt, Hillsville, Va, 61-62, chmn, formerly; 13th State Sen Dist Dem Comt, 70- Bus & Prof Pos: Field rep, Va Farm Bur, Richmond, Va, 61-68; farm mgr, Groundhog Mt Corp, Hillsville, 69-70; exec secy, Patrick Co, Va Stuart, 71- Mil Serv: Entered as Pvt, Air Force, 37, released as Maj, 59, after serv in Fighter, Bomber, Transport, Res & Missile Units, Europe, 43-45; Maj (Ret); Air Force Commendation Medal; Army Commendation Medal with Oak Leaf Cluster. Mem: Air Force Asn; Farm Bur; Retired Off Asn; Nat Asn Uniformed Serv; VFW. Honors & Awards: CofC; Citizenship Award; Pub Rels Award. Relig: Baptist. Mailing Add: Rte 1 Box 26 Laurel Fork VA 24352

TURNER, EDWIN STEELE (D)
b Clinton, Mo, Aug 14, 40; s Edison Shaw Turner (deceased) & Nellie Mable Jones T; m 1965 to Lois Ann Elizabeth Vette; c Eric Shaw. Educ: Univ Mo-Columbia, BS in agr econ, 62; Alpha Gamma Rho; Agr Club; Ruf Nex; Agr Econ Club. Polit & Govt Pos: Admin asst to US Rep Jerry Litton, Mo, 73- Bus & Prof Pos: Sales, Quaker Oats Co, St Joseph, Mo, 65-67 & Allied Mills, Inc, Chillicothe, 67-72. Mil Serv: Entered as Pvt, Army, 62, released as Sgt, 68. Mem: US House Rep Admin Asst Asn (co-founder); AASR; AF&AM; Shrine; Univ Mo Alumni Asn. Relig: Methodist. Mailing Add: PO Box 906 2120 Meadowlane Dr Chillicothe MO 64601

TURNER, ELMA JUANITA (R)
VChmn, State Rep Cent Comt Nev
b Milton, Ore, Oct 31, 19; d Elmer Shipp & Mille Modrell S; m 1938 to Fred Frank Turner; c Patricia Y, (Mrs George W Farren, IV) & Fred E. Educ: High Sch. Polit & Govt Pos: Deleg, Rep State Conv, 66 & 68; deleg, Rep Co Conv, 66 & 68; vchmn, Washoe Co Rep Party, Nev, 66-70; deleg, Rep Nat Conv, 68; Washoe Co Coord, Ed Fike for Gov Campaign, 70; vchmn, State Rep Cent Comt Nev, 70-; Northern Nev co-chmn, Comt for Reelec of the President, 72; northern dir, Nev State Fedn Rep Women, 73-75, vchmn gen conv, 75; northern Nev coordr, Attorney Gen Robert List Reelec Campaign, 74. Mem: Pipe 'n' Wire-toastmistress. Relig: Protestant. Mailing Add: 515 Stearns Circle Reno NV 89502

TURNER, ETHEL WINBORN (R)
Mem, Tulsa Co Rep Exec Comt
b Houston, Tex, Oct 2, 25; d James Ethel Winborn & Lena Franke W; div; c LeAnne Davidson, James Winborn & Andrew Roland. Educ: Vanderbilt Univ, BA. Polit & Govt Pos: Co coordr, Crawford for US Senate Campaign, Okla, 62; mem, Tulsa Co Rep Exec Comt, 62-66 & 70-; first cong dist coordr, Oklahomans for Goldwater, 63-64 & Goldwater Pres Campaign, 64; dist dir, Tulsa Co Rep Party, 63-66; alt deleg-at-lg, Okla Rep Party, 64; mem, Okla State Rep Exec Comt, 65-67; mem, Gov Comn on Status of Women, 67-69; state co-chmn, Nixon for Pres Comt, 67-68 & Nixon Presidential Campaign, 68; state chmn, Okla Women for Nixon, 68; mem bd of dirs, Okla Med Polit Action Comt, 68 & Okla Fedn of Rep Women, 69-; field supvr, US Census, 70; mem, Mayor's Adv Comt Capital Expenditures, Tulsa, 71-; mem, Okla Adv Comt, Comt to Reelect the President, 72; alt deleg, Rep Nat Conv, 72; vpres, Mary Nichols Rep Women's Club, 74; mem, Tulsa Co Rep Exec Comt, currently. Bus & Prof Pos: Loan Closer, State Fed Savings & Loan, Tulsa, 70-72, head loan closing & asst secy, 72- Mem: Phi Beta Pi Alumnae Asn; Tulsa Philharmonic Asn; Women's Coun of Tulsa Real Estate Bd; Fedn Rep Women. Relig: Disciples of Christ. Mailing Add: 6565 S Irvington Tulsa OK 74136

TURNER, G W (BUDDY) (D)
Ark State Rep
Mailing Add: 711 West 34th St Pine Bluff AR 71601

TURNER, HARRY EDWARD (R)
Ohio State Rep
b Mt Vernon, Ohio, Dec 25, 27; s Paul Hamilton Turner & Harriett Kraft T; m 1950 to Shirley Eggert; c Harry, Jr & Thomas. Educ: Baldwin-Wallace Col, BA, 51; Ohio Northern Univ, JD, 54; Sigma Delta Kappa; Alpha Sigma Phi. Polit & Govt Pos: Munic court prosecutor, Mt Vernon, Ohio, 55-58; city solicitor, 58-62, mem bd educ, 64-70; Ohio State Rep, 73- Bus & Prof Pos: Dir, Fairfield Eng Co, Marion, Ohio, 59-, dir, Curtis Investment Corp, Mt Vernon, 68-; partner, Turner & Badger, Attorneys-at-Law, Mt Vernon, 69- Mil Serv: Entered as A/S, Navy, 46, released as Radarman 3rd, after serv in Atlantic & Mediter, 46-47. Mem: Knox Co Bar Asn (pres, 70-71); Am & Ohio State Bar Asns; Mt Vernon Area CofC (dir, 72-); Knox Co Farm Bur. Honors & Awards: Man of the Hour, Mt Vernon Area CofC, 73. Relig: Lutheran. Mailing Add: Rte 6 Vincent Rd Mt Vernon OH 43050

TURNER, JAMES HARVEY (D)
Miss State Rep
b Conway, Miss, Aug 21, 30; s Clarence Evans Turner & Pearl McCrory T; single. Educ: Singleton High Sch, Carthage, Miss, grad, 48. Polit & Govt Pos: Deleg, Dist & State Dem Caucus & Conv, Miss, 68; Miss State Rep, 28th Dist, 68-, mem agr, livestock & poultry, co affairs, roads, ins & ferries & bridges comt, Miss House Rep; dep dist comnr, Leake Co Soil Conserv, currently; pres, Choctaw, Attala & Leake Co Yochanookany River Develop Dist, currently. Bus & Prof Pos: Cattle & row crop farmer, Carthage. Mem: WOW (past pres Camp 648, Carthage, dist mgr ins soc, currently); Mason (past Master, Pearl River Lodge, secy, currently); Royal Arch (past High Priest, Carthage Chap 46, secy, currently); Carthage Coun Royal & Select Masters (past Illustrious Master, Lodge 34, secy, currently); Shrine Club (past pres, Leake Club, vpres, currently). Relig: Baptist; chmn bd Deacons; choir dir; Sunday sch teacher; dept dir training union, Center Hill Baptist Church. Mailing Add: Rte 6 Box 107 Carthage MS 39051

TURNER, JAMES REGINALD (D)
b Wilmington, NC, Sept 4, 34; s Reginald Turner & Marie Terrell T; m 1967 to Carolyn Frances Simpkins; c Susannah Lynn & William Joel. Educ: Univ NC, Chapel Hill, AB, 56; Yale Univ Law Sch, JD, 62; Phi Beta Kappa; Corbey Court. Polit & Govt Pos: Chmn, Guilford Co Dem Exec Comt, NC, 70-74; mem presidential finance comt for Terry Sanford, currently. Bus & Prof Pos: Attorney, Smith, Moore, Smith, Schell & Hunter, 62-69; partner, Dameron, Turner, Enochs & Foster, 69- Mil Serv: Entered as Ens, Navy, 56, released as Lt(jg), 59, after serv in USS Ellison (DD864), Mediterranean, Persian Gulf & Cuba, 56-59; Comdr, Naval Res; Expeditionary Medal for Lebanon. Mem: Am Bar Asn; Am Judicature Soc; Am Civil Liberties Union; United Arts Coun of Greensboro; Civitan Club of Greensboro. Honors & Awards: Outstanding Young Dem, NC, 72. Relig: Episcopal. Legal Res: 2003 Lafayette Ave Greensboro NC 27408 Mailing Add: Box D Greensboro NC 27402

TURNER, JOHN FREELAND (R)
Wyo State Rep
b Jackson, Wyo, Mar 3, 42; s John Charles Turner & Mary Louise Mapes T; m 1969 to Mary Kay Brady; c John Francis & Kathy Mapes. Educ: Univ Notre Dame, BS Biol, 64; Univ Innsbruck, 64-65; Univ Utah, 65-66; Univ Mich, MS Ecol, 68. Polit & Govt Pos: Mem student coun, Pollution & Environ, 69-70; Wyo State Rep, Teton Co, 71-, mem, Comt Corp, Comt Elec, Comt Polit Subdivs & Comt Revenue, Wyo House Rep, currently. Bus & Prof Pos: Rancher & outfitter, Triangle X Ranch, presently; dir, Teton Sci Sch & Wyo Environ Inst, currently; photo-journalist. Publ: The Magnificent Bald Eagle: Our National Bird, Random House, 71; Wyoming roundtable, Wyo Mag, 68; Their threatened reign, Teton Mag, 70; plus two others. Mem: Nat Audubon Soc; Nat Parks & Conserv Asn; Elks; Rotary; Nat Wildlife Asn. Honors & Awards: Outstanding Freshman Legislator, Wyo House Rep, 71; Wyo Press Award, 72. Relig: Catholic. Mailing Add: Triangle X Ranch Moose PO Jackson Hole WY 83012

TURNER, JOHN RAYMOND (D)
Ky State Rep
Mailing Add: 929 1/2 Highland Dr Jackson KY 41339

TURNER, KENNETH L (R)
Chmn, Wilkinson Co Rep Party, Ga
b Gordon, Ga, July 18, 34; s William Roy Turner & Mamie Dallas T; m 1957 to Jean Tremon; c Ken, Jr, Jim & Robert. Educ: Armstrong State Col; Mercer Univ; Univ Ga. Polit & Govt Pos: Mem, Gordon City Coun, Ga, 63-66; chmn, Wilkinson Co Rep Party, 73- Bus & Prof Pos: Research, Freeport Kaolin Co, 57-67, mgr tech serv, 67-75 & tech coordr, 75- Mil Serv: M/Sgt, Res, retired. Mem: Milledgeville Country Club; Elks; Mason. Relig: Baptist. Mailing Add: 805 Briarcliff Rd Gordon GA 31031

TURNER, LLOYD L (NON-PARTISAN)
Mayor, Waterloo, Iowa
b Garrison, Iowa, May 16, 24; s William Turner & Margaret Nellist T; m 1942 to Viola Hostetler; c Teri & Tom. Educ: State Col of Iowa, 3 years 6 months. Polit & Govt Pos: Supt, Riverfront Comn, Waterloo, Iowa, 54-61; dir, Civil Defense, Black Hawk Co, Iowa, 61-65; mayor, Waterloo, currently. Mil Serv: Entered as Pvt, Army, 43, released as Pfc, 45, after serv in Off War Info, Pac Theater; Two Bronze Stars; Asiatic & Pac Theater Ribbon. Mem: Amvets; Am Legion; Elks. Relig: Presbyterian. Legal Res: 357 Sheridan Rd Waterloo IA 50701 Mailing Add: City Hall Waterloo IA 50705

TURNER, LOYCE WARREN (D)
Ga State Sen
b Turner Co, Ga, Dec 2, 27; s George Warren Turner & Willie Young T; m 1956 to Annette Howell; c Sally, Loyce Warren, Jr & Susan. Educ: Auburn Univ, DVM, 48; Alpha Psi; Blue Key. Polit & Govt Pos: Ga State Sen, 75- Bus & Prof Pos: Veterinarian, Valdosta, Ga, 48-; dir, First State Bank, Valdosta, 50-; pres, Valdosta Livestock Co Inc, 55-; pres, Farmers Supply Co of Valdosta, 55- Mil Serv: Entered as 1st Lt, Army, 53, released as Capt, 55, after serv in c/o 116th Med Detachment Com Z, France, 53-55. Mem: Ga & Am Vet Med Asns; Elks; Farm Bur; Kiwanis. Relig: Episcopal. Legal Res: 608 Howellbrook Dr Valdosta GA 31601 Mailing Add: PO Box 157 Valdosta GA 31601

TURNER, MARIE R (D)
Mem, Dem Nat Comt, Ky
b Hindman, Ky, June 9, 1900; d John M Roberts & Louranie Watts R; m to Ervine Turner (deceased); c Lois Irene, John Raymond & Treva Louraine T (Mrs Howell). Educ: Morehead Univ, AB. Polit & Govt Pos: Supt, Breathitt Co Schs, Ky, 31-69; vchmn, Ky Dem State Exec Comt, 64-, acting chmn, currently; deleg, Dem Nat Conv, 68; pres, Breathitt Co Dem Womans Club, currently; mem, Dem Nat Comt, currently. Bus & Prof Pos: Pres, Citizens Bank of Jackson, 68-; trustee, Lees Jr Col. Honors & Awards: Gov Award for Outstanding Schs; Univ Award for Outstanding Educ Progs. Relig: Christian Church of NAm. Mailing Add: Jackson KY 41339

TURNER, RICHARD C (R)
Attorney Gen, Iowa
b Avoca, Iowa, Sept, 30, 27; s Joe W Turner & Elizabeth Clark T; m to Charlotte Forsen; c Joe W, II, Amy Elizabeth & Mark Howard. Educ: Univ Iowa, BA, 50, JD, 53; Theta Xi; Phi Delta Phi. Polit & Govt Pos: Town clerk, Avoca, Iowa, 53-60; asst co attorney, Pottawattamie Co, Iowa, 54-56; Iowa State Sen, 61-65; Attorney Gen, Iowa, 67- Bus & Prof Pos: Lawyer, Turner & Turner, Turner, Williams & Turner & Turner & Walsh, 53-60. Mil Serv: Sgt, Air Force, 44-47. Mem: Nat Asn Attorneys Gen; Iowa Crime Comn; Nat Asn Attorneys Gen adv mem, Spec Comt Rev Uniform Rules of Criminal Procedure, Nat Conf Comnrs Uniform State Laws; Am Legion; 40 et 8. Relig: Presbyterian. Legal Res: 1054 21st West Des Moines IA 50265 Mailing Add: State Capitol Des Moines IA 50319

TURNER, ROY R (R)
Mem, SC State Rep Exec Comt
b Ft Payne, Ala, Apr 26, 29; s Rufus Clinton Turner & Zelda Clayton T; m 1960 to Elsa Louise Heckendorf; c John Edward, Joyce Ellen & Allen Forrest. Educ: Ga Inst of Tech, BEE, 55; Eta Kappa Nu; Ga Tech Philos Soc. Polit & Govt Pos: Mem, SC State Rep Exec Comt, 64-66 & 70-; chmn, York Co Rep Party, 66-70; presidential elector, SC, 68; alternate deleg, Rep Nat Conv, 68. Bus & Prof Pos: Elec engr, Rust Eng Co, 55-61, Celanese Corp Am, 61-74 & Catalytic Inc, 74- Mil Serv: Air Force, 46-49 & 51-52, released as M/Sgt, 52, after serv in Alaska & Morocco. Relig: Lutheran. Mailing Add: 2282 Hilldale Dr Rock Hill SC 29730

TURNER, VERA GRISTY (D)
b Memphis, Mo, Dec 25, 04; d John William Gristy & Carrie F Forester G; m 1923 to W Hubert Turner. Educ: Memphis High Sch, grad, 23. Polit & Govt Pos: Secy, Scotland Co Dem Cent Comt, Mo, formerly; probate clerk & magistrate, 48-71; registr for Soctland Co, Mo, State Health Dept, 52- Mem: Memphis Country. Relig: Methodist. Mailing Add: 226 N Lincoln St Memphis MO 63555

TURNER, VIRGINIA PRICE (D)
b Wrightsville, Ga, Oct 18, 17; d Arthur Bridges Price & Nancy Harrison P; div. Educ: Univ Ga, BSHE, 39. Polit & Govt Pos: Supvr, Farm Security Admin, Dept of Agr, 39-45; admin asst to US Rep, Ray J Madden, Ind, 46- Bus & Prof Pos: Teacher, Harrison High Sch, Ga, 36-39. Mem: DC DAV Auxiliary; Washington Co Club, 4-H. Relig: Episcopal. Mailing Add: 103 Fourth St NE Washington DC 20002

TURNER, VIRGINIA W (R)
NH State Rep
Mailing Add: East Sullivan NH 03445

TURNER, WAYNE CALLAWAY (R)
Mem, Rep State Cent Comt Calif
b Red Bluff, Calif, Aug 5, 20; s Donald A Turner & Evelyn M Callaway T; married; c Dale Wayne & Daryl Jack. Educ: Jr Col. Polit & Govt Pos: Chmn, Plumas Co Rep Cent Comt, Calif, formerly; mem, Rep State Cent Comt Calif, 69- Mil Serv: Electrician Mate 2/C, Navy, World War II. Mem: Mason. Relig: Protestant. Mailing Add: Box 87 Caribou CA 95915

TURNER, WILLIAM COCHRANE (R)
US Rep to Orgn Econ Coop & Develop
b Red Oak, Iowa, May 27, 29; s James Lyman Turner & Josephine Cochrane T; m 1955 to Cynthia Dunbar; c Scott Christopher, Craig Dunbar & Douglas Gordon. Educ: Northwestern Univ, Evanston, BS, 52; Delta Kappa Epsilon. Polit & Govt Pos: Chmn, Ariz Young Rep League, 56-57; treas, Ariz Rep State Comt, 58-59; deleg, Rep Nat Conv, 60; mem, Gov Coord Coun Health & Welfare, Ariz, 62; chmn bd, Ariz State Crippled Children's Serv, 62-64; mem, US Adv Comn on Int Educ & Cult Affairs, 69-74; mem exec comt & bd, Ariz State Dept Econ Planning & Develop, 70-72; mem, Nat Rev Bd/Ctr Cult & Tech Interchange between East & West, 70-74; mem, Western Int Trade Group, 70-74; chmn, Ariz Joint Econ Develop Comt, 70; mem panel int info, educ & cult rels, Ctr Strategic & Int Studies, Georgetown Univ, 73-75; US Rep to Orgn Econ Coop & Develop, Paris, France, 74- Bus & Prof Pos: Vpres & dir, Western Mgt Consult, Inc, 52-60, pres & dir, 60-74, pres & dir, Western Mgt Consult Europe SA with off in Brussels, 68-74; dir, Ryan-Evans Drug Stores, Inc, 68-72; dir, First Nat Bank of Ariz, 71-74; mem, Inst of Mgt Consult, 71-74. Mem: Am Grad Sch Int Mgt (dir); Nat Symphony Orchestra Asn (trustee); Am Hosp Paris (bd gov); Am Sch Paris (bd trustees); Orme Sch (bd trustees). Relig: Episcopal. Legal Res: 4201 N 63rd Pl Scottsdale AZ 85251 Mailing Add: Orgn Econ Coop & Develop APO New York NY 09777

TURNETTE, NORMAN L (R)
Western Regional Dir, Nat Rep Cong Comt
b Los Angeles, Calif, Jan 1, 30; s Anthony Turnette & Nila Wion T; m 1951 to Barbara Jean Niederhaus; c Mark G & Renee M. Educ: Mt San Antonio Col, AA, 50. Polit & Govt Pos: Mem, 58th Assembly Dist Rep Cent Comtte, Calif, 62-, chmn, 64-69; vchmn, Los Angeles Co Rep Comt, 62-72; asst treas state bd, Calif Rep Assembly, 66; chief consult, Rep Caucus, Calif State Senate, 69-70; mem bd trustees, Charter Oak Unified Sch Dist, 69-; Rep cand, Calif State Assembly, 70; admin asst, Calif State Sen H L Richardson, 19th Dist, 70-72; Western Regional dir, Nat Rep Cong Comt, 72-, currently. Mem: Nat Rep Nat Comt & Rep Nat Sen Comt, currently. Bus & Prof Pos: Chief indust engr, Marshall Indust, 56-66; partner, Pub Affairs Asosc, 66-69. Mil Serv: Entered as Cpl, Army, 50, released as 1st Lt, 53; Calif Nat Guard, 40th Div, 48-50 & 53-61; Capt, Army Res. Mem: Jaycees; pres, Covina Club, 61-62. Relig: Lutheran. Mailing Add: 5008 Arroway Ave Covina CA 91724

TURNHAM, PETE BENTON (D)
Ala State Rep
b Penton, Ala; s Joseph Henry Turnham & Fannie May Sessions T; m 1943 to Nettye Kathryn Rice; c Diane Dale, Timothy Neil, Ruthmary Kay & Joseph. Educ: Ala Polytech Inst, BS, 44; Auburn Univ, MS, 48; Univ Paris; Pa State Col. Polit & Govt Pos: Mem, Lee Co Sch Bd, Ala, 55-58; Ala State Rep, 59- Bus & Prof Pos: With API Exten Serv, 48-54; sales rep, Marshall & Bruce Co, Ala, 54-64; conducted several research proj on dairy cattle. Mil Serv: Army, 43-59, Capt(Ret); serv as Comdr, Combat Inf Units, France, Ger & Austria; Maj, Army Res, Mil Intel Serv, currently. Relig: Baptist. Legal Res: 606 Moore Mill Rd Auburn AL 36830 Mailing Add: Box 1592 Auburn AL 36830

TURNLEY, RICHARD (D)
La State Rep
Mailing Add: 1776 77th Ave Baton Rouge LA 70807

TUTTLE, WILLIAM ROGER (R)
Dep Chmn, Mass Rep State Comt
b Quincy, Mass, Sept 14, 39; s Samuel I Tuttle (deceased) & Violet Pingree T; m 1957 to Meredith Anne Weatherbee; c William Stetson. Educ: Bentley Col of Acct & Finance, Waltham, Mass, BSAcct; Brown Univ Grad Sch of Savings Banking, Nat Asn Mutual Savings Banks grad. Polit & Govt Pos: Vchmn, Abington Rep Town Comt, 61-, statistician, Finance Comt, 67-71; state committeeman, Mass Rep State Comt, 71-, asst treas, 71-, dep chmn, 71-; alt deleg, Rep Nat Conv, 72. Bus & Prof Pos: Vpres, Home Savings Bank of Boston, 59-; vpres & dir, Savings Mgt Research Corp, Hanover, NH, 72- Publ: Co-ed, Old Brown Savings Bank—case study, Nat Asn of Mutual Savings Banks, 72. Mem: Savings Banks Asn of Mass (research comt, 71-); Savings Insts Mkt Soc of Am; Boston Investment Club; Plymouth Co Rep Club (exec comt, 71-). Mailing Add: 101 Highfields Rd Abington MA 02351

TVEDT, CONRAD R (R)
Chmn, Valley Co Rep Cent Comt, Mont
b Mitchell, SDak, Dec 5, 23; s Lars L Tvedt & Selma Anderson T; m 1952 to Patricia M Vaughn; c Steven C, Catherine L & Nancy J. Educ: SDak State Univ, 42-43; Mich State Univ, 43. Polit & Govt Pos: Chmn, Valley Co Rep Cent Comt, Mont, 73-; mem, Mont State Rep Cent Comt, 73- Bus & Prof Pos: Pres, First Security Bank & Glasgow Angus Ranch, Inc, currently. Mil Serv: Entered as Pvt, Army Air Corps, 43, released as 1st Lt, flying instr, US Mil Acad, 43-45, 50-52; recalled during Korean War; Air Force Res, Maj(Ret). Mem: Mont Bankers Asn (past pres group four); Glasgow Kiwanis (pres); Mont Kiwanis (Lt Gov); Full Gospel Businessmens Fel. Honors & Awards: Distinguished Serv Award, Jaycees, 56, Boss of Year Award, 67. Relig: Lutheran. Mailing Add: 437 Sixth Ave N Glasgow MT 59230

TWARDUS, JOHN (D)
NH State Rep
b Lawrence, Mass, Jan 1, 98. Educ: St Mary's High Sch, Newmarket, NH. Polit & Govt Pos: NH State Rep, 59-; overseer of poor & selectman of Newmarket. Bus & Prof Pos: Retired govt employee. Mil Serv: World War I; FBI, Navy, World War II, Naval Shipyard, Portsmouth, NH. Mem: Robert G Durgin Post 67 (past comdr & life mem); Vets of World War I (state comdr); Vet World War II NH (hosp chmn); Vet World War I USA (nat hosp chmn). Honors & Awards: Organized the Vets Asn at the Naval Shipyard in 44, Barracks of World War I, 57 at the Naval Shipyard, Portsmouth; served as comdr & serv officer. Relig: Catholic. Mailing Add: 36 Packers Falls Rd Newmarket NH 03857

TWEDT, LORINE (D)
Mem, Mont State Dem Exec Comt
b Great Falls, Mont, Mar 1, 20; d Sam S Johnson & Helen Sheldon J; m 1944 to Gordon R Twedt; c James, Russell & William. Educ: Western Mont Col, 40; Col Great Falls, 46; Northern Mont Col, 65. Polit & Govt Pos: Precinct committeewoman, Hill Co Dem Cent Comt, Mont, 54-68, state committeewoman, 62-70; pres, Hill Co Dem Women's Club, 60-62; regional dir, Mont State Dem Women's Club, 62-66, vpres, 66-69, pres, formerly; mem, Mont State Dem Exec Comt, currently. Mem: Soroptimist; Pythian Sister Lodge; Farmers Union; Motel Asn; CofC. Relig: Lutheran. Legal Res: Second Ave & Sixth St N Great Falls MT 59403 Mailing Add: Box 1244 Great Falls MT 59403

TWETEN, KENNETH (R)
NDak State Sen
b Grand Forks, NDak, Aug 27, 28; married; c Karen & Rachel. Educ: Pub schs. Polit & Govt Pos: NDak State Rep, 59-73, chmn, Transportation Comt, 63, chmn, Comt on Gen Affairs, 67, vchmn, Comt on Appropriations, 69; NDak State Sen, 73- Bus & Prof Pos: Farmer. Mem: Farm Bur; Nat Potato Coun (steering comt, 66). Relig: Lutheran. Legal Res: 235 27th Ave S Grand Forks ND 58201 Mailing Add: State Captiol Bismarck ND 58501

TWETEN, MALCOLM (R)
NDak State Rep
Mailing Add: State Capitol Bismarck ND 58501

TWIDWELL, CARL, JR (D)
Okla State Rep
b Eufaula, Okla, July 1, 27; s Carl Twidwell, Sr & Cleo Ollie Larkins T; m to Doris Vaden Wilkinson; c David, Carla, Sherri, Joanna & Tina. Educ: Okla State Univ, 46-47; Oklahoma City Univ, 48-50; Cent State Univ (Okla), BS in admin & MEd, 50. Polit & Govt Pos: Okla State Rep, Dist 101, 73- Bus & Prof Pos: High sch teacher & sch adminr, Spencer, Okla, 20 years. Mil Serv: Navy, 45-46. Mem: CofC; Am Legion; Okla & Nat Educ Asns; Okla Coaches Asn; Kiwanis. Honors & Awards: Oklahoma City Coach of the Year, 64-65; Okla All Star Football Coach, 66. Relig: Methodist. Mailing Add: 8420 NE 33rd Spencer OK 73084

TWIGGS, RALPH (D)
Ga State Rep
Mailing Add: PO Box 432 Hiawassee GA 30546

TWILEGAR, RON JESS (D)
Idaho State Rep
b Vancouver, Wash, Sept 18, 43; s Roy J Twilegar & Dorothy Brown T; m 1967 to Elizabeth Ann Condon; c Megan Cary & Amy Elizabeth. Educ: Univ Idaho, BS, 66; George Washington Univ, JD, 71; Phi Gamma Delta; Phi Alpha Delta. Polit & Govt Pos: US Cong aide, Washington, DC, 69-70; Asst Attorney Gen, Idaho, 73-74; Idaho State Rep, Dist 17, 74- Bus & Prof Pos: Attorney-at-law, Boise, Idaho, 74- Mil Serv: Entered as 2nd Lt, Army, 67, released as 1st Lt, 69, after serv in 285th Transportation Co, Vietnam, 67-68; Vietnamese Serv Award; Nat Defense Medal. Mem: Idaho & Boise Bar Asns; Multnomah Athletic Club. Relig: Catholic. Mailing Add: 1205 N 11th St Boise ID 83702

TWILLEY, JOSHUA MARION (D)
Treas, Dem Party Del
b Dover, Del, Mar 23, 28; s Joshua Marion Twilley & Alice Hunn Dunn; m 1973 to Rosemary Almeta Miller; c Stephanie, Jeffrey, Edgar & Linda. Educ: Harvard Univ, BA, 50, JD, 53. Polit & Govt Pos: Pres, Kent Co Govt, Del, 70-74; treas, Dem Party Del, 72-; comnr, Del Pub Utilities Comn, 73- Bus & Prof Pos: Partner, Twilley, Jones & Feliceangel, Attorneys-at-law, 71- Mil Serv: Entered as Pvt, Army, 53, released as Cpl, 55, after serv in 101st Airborne Inf. Publ: Weekly articles on Kent Co, publ in several co newspapers, 71-73. Mem: Del Bar Asn. Honors & Awards: Award, VFW, 74; Award, Kent Co, 75. Legal Res: RD 6 Box 474 Dover DE 19907 Mailing Add: 26 The Green Dover DE 19901

TWINAM, JOSEPH WRIGHT (D)
US Ambassador to Bahrain
b Chattanooga, Tenn, July 11, 34; s John Courtenay Twinam & Daisy Murphy T; m 1959 to Janet Carolyn Ashby; c Courtenay Jane & Marshall Ashby. Educ: Univ Va, BA with honors, 56; Georgetown Univ, 60-61; Phi Beta Kappa; Omicron Delta Kappa; Kappa Alpha. Polit & Govt Pos: For Serv Officer, Dept of State & Diplomatic Posts in The Netherlands, Kuwait, Lebanon & Saudi Arabia, 59-74; US Ambassador to Bahrain, 74- Mil Serv: Entered as Ens, Navy, 56, released as Lt(jg), 59, after serv in USS Koiner. Relig: Episcopal. Legal Res: 8019 Garlot Dr Fairfax VA 22039 Mailing Add: American Embassy FPO New York NY 09526

TWINAME, JOHN DEAN (R)
b Mt Kisco, NY, Dec 27, 31; s Clarence George Twiname & Constance Ulmer T; m 1955 to Carolyn Anderson; c Karen Lynn, Jeanne Copeland & Julia Dean. Educ: Cornell Univ, AB, 53; Harvard Grad Sch, George Baker Scholar, 55-57, MBA, 57. Polit & Govt Pos: Dep adminr, Soc & Rehabilitation Serv, Dept of Health, Educ & Welfare, 69-70, Adminr, 70-72; exec dir health, Cost of Living Coun, 73-74; consult to state & fed govts, 74- Bus & Prof Pos: Sales rep, Am Hosp Supply Div, Am Hosp Supply Corp, Evanston, Ill, 58-60, prod research mgr, 61-62, Midwest area sales mgr, 62-63, asst to pres, 63-64, mkt mgr, 64-67, vpres mkt serv, 68-69. Mil Serv: as 2nd Lt, Army, 53, released as 1st Lt, 55, after serv as Artil-Bn Intel Off. Mem: Econ Club of Chicago; Chicago Exec Club. Relig: Christian; chmn, Coun on Ministries, Foundry United Methodist Church. Mailing Add: 3407 N St NW Washington DC 20007

TWITCHELL, R DONALD (D)
Maine State Rep
Mailing Add: 3 Packard Ave Norway ME 04268

TYDINGS, JOSEPH DAVIES (D)
b Asheville, NC, May 4, 28; s Millard E Tydings & Eleanor Davies T; m 1955 to Virginia Reynolds Campbell; c Mary Campbell, Millard E, II, Emlen Davies & Eleanor Davies. Educ: Univ Md, BA, 51; Univ Md Law Sch, LLB, 53; Phi Eta Sigma; Phi Kappa Phi; Omicron Delta Kappa; Scabbard & Blade; Phi Kappa Sigma; pres, Student Govt. Hon Degrees: LLD, C W Post Col, LI Univ & Parsons Col, 67. Polit & Govt Pos: Pres, Young Dem Clubs of Md, 53-55; city attorney, Aberdeen, 54-60; Md State Deleg, 55-61; coordr for States of Fla & Del, Kennedy for Pres & polit agent & campaign mgr, Md Presidential Preferential Primary, 60; US Attorney for Md, 61-63; pres, Jr Bar Asn of Baltimore City, 62-63; deleg, Int Penal Conf, Bellagio, Italy, 63, Interpol Conf, Helsinki, Finland, 63, Mex-US Interparliamentary Conf, Mexico City, 65, Coun of Intergovt Comt for European Migration, Geneva, Switz, 66 & NATO Assembly, Brussels, Belgium, 68; US Sen, Md, 65-71; deleg, Dem Nat Conv, 72; deleg, Dem Nat Mid-Term Conf, 74. Bus & Prof Pos: Partner, Danzansky, Dickey, Tydings, Quint & Gordon, Law Firm, Washington, DC. Mil Serv: Entered as Pvt, Army, 46, released as Cpl, 48, after serv in Inf, ETO. Publ: Born to Starve, William Morrow & Co, 70; Home rule for DC: the case for political justice, 3/67; A federal verdict of not guilty by reason of insanity & a subsequent commitment procedure, Md Law Rev, spring 67. Mem: Jr Bar Asn Baltimore City; Am Judicature Soc; Md Bar Asn; YMCA. Honors & Awards: Am Trial Lawyers Citation of Distinction in Exceptional Serv to our Nat Welfare, 68; Sidney Hollander Award of Distinction in Exceptional Serv to our Nat Welfare, 68; Sidney Hollander Award of Distinction, Am Jewish Cong, 68; August Volmer Award, Am Soc of Criminology, 69; Nat Brotherhood Citation for distinguished contribution to improved human rels, justice & equality, Nat Conf Christians & Jews, 70; Margaret Sangar Award for distinguished Pub Serv, Planned Parenthood—World Population, 70. Relig: Episcopal. Mailing Add: Oakington Havre de Grace MD 21078

TYLER, HAROLD RUSSELL, JR (R)
Dep Attorney Gen of US
b Utica, NY, May 14, 22; s Harold Russell Tyler & Elizabeth Glenn T; m 1949 to Barbara L Eaton; c Bradley E, John R & Sheila B. Educ: Philips Exeter Acad, 39; Princeton Univ, AB, 43; Columbia Univ, LLB, 49. Polit & Govt Pos: Asst US attorney, 53-55; asst attorney gen, Civil Rights Div, Dept Justice, 60-61; comnr, NY-NJ Waterfront Comn, 61-62; US Dist judge Southern Dist, 62-75; Dep Attorney Gen of US, 74- Bus & Prof Pos: Pvt practice, New York, 50-53 & 55-60; mem firm, Gilbert & Segall, 57-60 & 61-62; adj prof law, NY Univ Law Sch; bd dirs, Fed Judicature Ctr, Washington, DC, 68-72. Legal Res: Indian Hill Rd Bedford NY 10506 Mailing Add: Dept of Justice Washington DC 20530

TYLER, WILLIAM ROYALL
b Paris, France, Oct 17, 10; s Royall Tyler & Elisina De Castelvecchio T; m 1934 to Bettine Mary Fisher-Rowe; c Royall & Matilda Eve Thompson. Educ: Oxford Univ, Eng, BA, 33; Harvard Univ, Mass, MA, 41; Phi Beta Kappa. Hon Degrees: LLD, Marlboro Col, Vt. Polit & Govt Pos: Off War Info, NAfrica & France, 42-45; asst dir, Off of Int & Educ Exchange, 46-48; pub affairs officer, Paris, 48-52; dep dir, Off of Western European Affairs, 54-57, dir, 57; deleg, UN 12th Gen Assembly, 57-58; counselor, Bonn, 58-61; asst secy of State for European Affairs, 62-65; US Ambassador to the Netherlands, 65-69. Bus & Prof Pos: Foreign banking, 33-38; mgr, Short Wave Radio Sta, 40-42; dir, Dumbarton Oaks Research Libr & Collection, 69. Mem: Am Acad Arts & Sci; Mass Hist Soc (corresponding mem); Cosmos Club of Washington, DC; Century Asn of New York; Academie des Sciences, Arts et Belles-Lettres, Dijon (corresponding mem). Honors & Awards: Medal of Freedom; Knight, Order of the Legion of Honor, France. Relig: Episcopal. Mailing Add: 1735 32nd St NW Washington DC 20007

TYMNIAK, PAUL MARTIN (R)
Chmn, Conn Fedn of Young Rep
b Bridgeport, Conn, Apr 11, 45; s Martin J Tymniak & Angela C Michno T; m 1974 to Catherine Carstens. Educ: Cent Conn State Col, BA, 67; Univ Maine Sch Law, JD, 70; Cent Conn State Col Hist Club, pres. Polit & Govt Pos: Mem campaign staff, former Congressman Abner W Sibal, 66 & US Sen Lowell P Weicker, Jr, 68; alt deleg, Fairfield Co Rep Conv, Conn, 66 & 70, deleg, 74; mem campaign staff, Congressman Stewart B McKinney, 70 & 72; vchmn, Fourth Cong Dist Rep League, 72; treas, Fairfield Young Rep Club, 72-74; campaign dir, Fairfield Rep Town Elec, 73; mem, Fairfield Rep Town Comt, 73-74; mem, Gov Coun on Solid Waste Mgt, 73-; treas, New Eng Coun of Young Rep, 73-; mem campaign staff, J H Brannen Sen Campaign, 74; chmn, Conn Fedn of Young Rep, 75- Bus & Prof Pos: Spec dep sheriff, Fairfield Co, Conn, 74- Publ: Auth, A defense of the Connecticut survival statute, Conn Bar J, 44: 438. Mem: Am, Conn, Maine & Bridgeport Bar Asns; Algonquin Club. Relig: Roman Catholic. Legal Res: 50 Mill Hill Rd Fairfield CT 06430 Mailing Add: 172 Washington Ave Bridgeport CT 06604

TYNDALE, ELMONT SCOTT (R)
Maine State Rep
b New York, NY, July 25, 00; s Charles William Tyndale & Jennie Byington T; m 1937 to Alice Emmons. Educ: Columbia Univ, 18-19; Alexander Hamilton Inst, 21-22. Polit & Govt Pos: Maine State Rep, 61-65 & 69-, asst majority floor leader & chmn, Pub Utilities Comt, Maine House Rep, 63-65, state leadership, 69-71, chmn, Comt on Educ, 73-; mem, Nat Leadership Conf, 63-65; past mem, Rep Town Comt. Bus & Prof Pos: Nat rep, Sylvania Elec Prod, Inc, 36-58; mfr, Emmons Loom Binder Mfg Co, 54-59; currently some inventive research, semi-retired. Mil Serv: Pvt, Nat Guard, 19-21, serv in 7th NY Regt. Mem: Newcomen Soc of NAm; Mason; KofP; Elks; Waban Asn for Retarded Children (bd dirs). Honors & Awards: War Manpower Comn Award for outstanding serv in recruitment of labor, Manhattan Proj, World War II; citation for work in educ, Maine Teachers Asn; citation for fishing legis, Maine Lobstermens Asn; cited by Asn of Broadcasters; biographical sketch in Archiv, Washington, DC. Relig: Protestant. Mailing Add: Clock Farm Kennebunkport ME 04046

TYNER, MAYME (R)
b Laurel Hill, Fla, Mar 15, 06; d Mack Tyner & Effie Campbell T; m 1934 to Richard Eugene Pilcher; div; c Sara Jane (Mrs Kay Marvin Eoff). Educ: Fla State Col for Women, LI, 28, AB in Educ, 30; Fla State Univ, MA in Educ, 50; Sci Soc; Col 4-H Club. Polit & Govt Pos: Deleg, Rep Nat Conv, 56, 60 & 68, alt deleg, 64; secy, Fla State Rep Exec Comt, 54-66 & asst secy, 66-70; Rep state committeewoman, Fla, 54-74. Bus & Prof Pos: Teacher of Eng, Pub Schs of Okaloosa, Walton & Calhoun Counties of Fla, 30-34 & 38-57. Mem: Local Realtor Bd, Fla & Nat Asns of Realtors; Fla Coun of Eng Teachers, Co Chap Red Cross. Relig: Presbyterian. Legal Res: Rte 1 Box 14 Laurel Hill FL 32537 Mailing Add: PO Box 1325 Crestview FL 32536

TYRELL, JACK RIX (R)
Mem, Rep State Cent Comt Calif
b Alhambra, Calif, May 6, 21; s John J Tyrell & Ruth Sands T; m 1943 to Marion Mallman; c Sandra Sue, Jon Sands & Randy Rix. Educ: Pasadena Jr Col, AA, 41; Univ Southern Calif, AB, 49; Univ Southern Calif Sch Law, JD, 52. Polit & Govt Pos: Councilman, Temple City, Calif, 60-, mayor, 62, 66 & 74, vmayor, 65, 69 & 72; secy, Calif Contract Cities Asn, 63-64, second vpres, 64-65, first vpres, 65-66, pres, 66-67; mem, Rep State Cent Comt, Calif, currently. Bus & Prof Pos: Life guard, Alhambra, Calif, summers 39-51; master router, Vega Aircraft, Burbank, 41-42; welder's helper, grinder, metal worker, inspector, shipping clerk, asst sales mgr & sales engr, C E Howard & Co, Los Angeles, 45-48; attorney-at-law, 54-56; partner, Davidson, Tyrell & Davidson, Alhambra, 56-70; attorney-at-law, 70-; bd dirs, West San Gabriel Valley Juv Diversion; bd dirs, Community Hosp San Gabriel. Mil Serv: Entered as Aviation Cadet, Navy, 42, released as Lt, 45, after serv in Fleet Air Detachment. Mem: F&AM; Scottish Rite (32 degree); Shrine; Alhambra Hi Twelve; Am Legion, Alhambra. Relig: Episcopal. Legal Res: 5709 N Alessandro Temple City CA 91780 Mailing Add: PO Box 710 Alhambra CA 91802

TYSDAL, RALPH M (R)
SDak State Rep
Mailing Add: 830 State St Spearfish SD 57783

TYSINGER, JAMES W (R)
Ga State Sen
Mailing Add: 3781 Watkins Place NE Atlanta GA 30319

TYSON, RICHARD EUGENE (R)
b Parkersburg, WVa, Oct 1, 26; s John Leo Tyson & Edith Dickson T; m 1952 to Norma Rose Delligatti; c David Richard & Patricia Ann. Educ: Ind Univ, AB, 49; WVa Univ, JD, 52; Phi Alpha Delta; Pi Kappa Phi; Scabbard & Blade. Polit & Govt Pos: Pres, WVa Univ Young Rep Club, 51-52; asst city attorney, Huntington, WVa, 53-54; pres, Cabell Co Young Rep Club, 56; judge, Munic Court, Huntington, 57-63; Rep participant, Comment (weekly prog), WHTN-TV, Huntington, 58; Rep cand prosecuting attorney, Cabell Co, 64; spec master, US Dist Court, Southern Dist, WVa, 68; chmn, Cabell Co Lawyers for Nixon-Agnew, 68; co-chmn, Cabell Co Moore for Gov Comt, 68; mem, Comt of 100 for Arch Moore, 68; asst prosecuting attorney, Cabell Co, 69; hearings examr, WVa Alcohol Beverage Control Comn, 69; comnr of accounts, Cabell Co, 69-72; state co-chmn, Lawyers for Reelec of the President, 72; alt deleg-at-lg, Rep Nat Conv, 72. Bus & Prof Pos: Mem bd dirs, Boys Club of Huntington, WVa, 56-70; mem lay adv bd, St Marys Hosp, 59-; mem bd trustees, Blue Cross Hosp Serv, Inc, 60-70; mem bd dirs, Chafin Coal Co, 71-; mem, Marshall Univ Found, currently. Mil Serv: Entered as Pvt, Army Res, 44, released, 46, after serv in Air Corps, Am Theatre; 2nd Lt, Air Force Res, 49-54; Good Conduct Medal; Am Theatre Medal. Mem: Am Legion; Fraternal Order Police (assoc mem); Ind Univ & WVa Univ Alumni Asns; WVa Soc of Washington, DC; Boy Scouts (citizenship counselor). Honors & Awards: Boss of the Year, Nat Secretaries Asn, 61; Hon Ky Col, Gov Ky, 63. Relig: Catholic. Legal Res: 136 Larkspur Dr Huntington WV 25705 Mailing Add: PO Box 1096 Huntington WV 25714

TYSON, WILSON (D)
SC State Rep
Mailing Add: Box 518 Estill SC 29918

TYUS, E LEROY (D)
Chmn, First Cong Dist Dem Party, Mo
b Brownsville, Tenn, Feb 4, 16; s O T Tyus & Odelia Parker T; m 1945 to Marie Holton; c Cheryl & Cathy. Educ: Lane Col, Jackson, Tenn, 3 years; Lincoln Law Sch, St Louis, Mo, 1 year; Alpha Phi Alpha; Vagabond's Inc; Lamb's, Inc. Polit & Govt Pos: Mo State Rep, 50-60; committeeman, 20th Ward, Mo, 60-; Constable, Eighth Magistrate Dist, 62-; deleg, Dem Nat Conv, 68; chmn, First Cong Dist Dem Party, 68- Bus & Prof Pos: Operated Army Canteen, St Louis, Mo, 42-45; Tavern & Hotel owner, 45-50; Real Estate Broker, 50-; Operate Security Agency, 66- Honors & Awards: Received Certificate of Merit in area of Legislative Serv, Lane Col, 52. Relig: Catholic. Mailing Add: 5225 Lexington St Louis MO 63115

U

UBBEN, DONALD THOMAS (R)
b Pekin, Ill, May 9, 46; s Wilbert Donald Ubben & Verna Ducker U; single. Educ: Furman Univ, BA, 68; Baylor Univ, MA, 72. Polit & Govt Pos: Aide to SC deleg, Rep Nat Conv, 68, alt deleg, 72; deleg, Clarendon Co & SC State Rep Conv, 68, 70 & 72; acting chmn, Clarendon Co Rep Party, SC, 72; mem, SC State Rep Exec Comt, 72-73; asst to Secy for Spec Programs, Dept Health, Educ & Welfare, Washington, DC, 73-75; legis asst to Sen Paul Laxalt, Nev, 75- Publ: Contribr to J Church & State, 68-69. Honors & Awards: Dean's List & Furman Scholar, Furman Univ; Student Congressman & Dean's List, Baylor Univ. Relig: Unitarian-Universalist. Legal Res: 501 Rudy Rd Manning SC 29102 Mailing Add: 1-B 2300 Freetown Ct Reston VA 22091

UBERTI, E JAMES (R)
Rep State Cent Committeeman, Conn
b Shelton, Conn, Aug 29, 34; s Anthony Uberti & Lena Sticco U; m 1957 to Marilyn Ferla; c James G & Teresa M. Educ: Univ Bridgeport, 1 year 6 months. Polit & Govt Pos: Chmn, Ansonia Young Rep, Conn, 66-67; chmn, Ansonia Rep Town Comt, 67-72; area adv, Small Bus Admin, 70-; comnr, Ansonia Housing Authority, 71-; Rep State Cent Committeeman, 17th Sen Dist, 72-; campaign mgr, Sarasin Cong Comt, 72 & 74; dist adminr, US Rep Ronald A Saraisin, 73- Bus & Prof Pos: Owner, Derby Glass Co, 56- Mil Serv: Entered as Pvt, Army, 54, released as Pfc, 56, after serv in Qm Corps. Mem: Auto Glass Installers of Conn. Relig: Roman Catholic. Mailing Add: 19 Finney St Extension Ansonia CT 06401

UDALL, MORRIS KING (D)
US Rep, Ariz
b St Johns, Ariz, June 15, 22; s Levi S Udall & Louise Lee U; m 1968 to Ella Royston. Educ: Univ Ariz, LLB with distinction, 49; pres student body, 48; co-capt basketball team & all-conf forward. Polit & Govt Pos: Chief dep co attorney, Pima Co, Ariz, 51-52 & co attorney, 53-54; deleg, Dem Nat Conv, 56 & 72; chmn Ariz Deleg, 72; chmn, Ariz Vol for Stevenson, 56; US Rep, Ariz, Second Cong Dist, 61-, mem, Post Off & Civil Serv Comt, Interior & Insular Affairs Comt, US House of Rep, currently, chmn, Environ Subcomt, 73- Bus & Prof Pos: Partner, Udall & Udall, 49-61; co-founder, Bank of Tucson & Catalina Savings & Loan Asn. Mil Serv: Entered as Pvt, Army, 42, released as Capt, Air Force, 46, after serv in 20th Air Force, Iwo Jima, Saipan, Guam, Pac Theatre. Publ: Arizona Law of Evidence, Western Publ Co, 60; The Job of the Congressman, (w Donald G Tacheron), 66 & Education of a Congressman, 72, Bobbs-Merrill Co. Mem: Ariz State Bar Asn; Tucson YMCA; Ariz-Sonora Desert Mus (trustee). Honors & Awards: Played prof basketball with Denver Nuggets, Nat Basketball League, 48-49. Relig: Latter-day Saint. Legal Res: 142 S Calle Chaparita Tucson AZ 85716 Mailing Add: 1424 House Off Bldg Washington DC 20515

UECHI, MITSUO (D)
Hawaii State Rep
Mailing Add: House Sgt-at-Arms State Capitol Honolulu HI 96813

UELAND, ARNULF, JR (R)
Minn State Sen
b St Paul, Minn, June 21, 20; s Arnulf Ueland & Louise Nippert A; m 1943 to Rebecca Prentiss Lucas; c Christopher, Erica, Andreas Ward & Arnulf Tor. Educ: Dartmouth Col, 38-40; Univ Minn, Minneapolis, BA, 43; Alpha Delta Phi. Polit & Govt Pos: Chmn, Mankato City Rep Party, Minn, 61-65; exec vchmn, Blue Earth Co Rep Comt, 65-68; mem, Mankato Planning Comn, 61-67, mem, Mankato Charter Comn, 65-67; mem, Blue Earth Co Rep Exec Comt, 65-68; mem, Minn State Rep Cent Comt, 69-; chmn, Nicollet Co Rep Comt, 69-71; mayor, North Mankato, 70-72; chmn, Second Cong Dist Rep Party, 71-73; deleg, Rep Nat Conv, 72; Minn State Sen, 73- Bus & Prof Pos: Worker & training, Weyerhauser Co, Longview, Wash, 47-48; retail salesman, Long-Bell Lumber Co, 48-49; salesman, Winton Lumber Sales Co, Minneapolis, Minn, 49-50; asst mgr, Hayes-Lucas Lumber Co, 50-53; owner, Ueland Lumber Sales Co, 53- Mil Serv: Entered as A/S, Navy, 43, released as Lt(jg), 46, after serv in USS LST 336, Northern Europe, 43-44 & USS LST 126, Pac, 45-46; Lt(Ret), Naval Res. Mem: Mankato Rotary Club; YMCA; Elks; Minn Hist Soc; Am-Scandinavian Found. Relig: Congregational. Legal Res: 2013 Roe Crest Dr North Mankato MN 56001 Mailing Add: PO Box 705 Mankato MN 56001

UGLUM, JOHN RICHARD (D)
State Cent Committeeman, SDak Dem Party
b Wonewoc, Wis, Nov 26, 09; s John Uglum & Mae Dewey U; m 1940 to Frances Therodora Wikholm; c Katherine (Mrs Bumgardner) & Karen (Mrs Mumpire). Educ: Northwestern Univ, Evanston, BS, 30; Ill Col Optom, Chicago, OD, 32; Ind Univ, Bloomington, 63; Univ Calif, Berkeley, 64; Phi Theta Upsilon. Polit & Govt Pos: Mem & secy, SDak State Bd of Examr Optom, 50-56; mem, Gov Comt Children & Youth, SDak, 50-57; Gov Comt on Children & Youth, Nev, 58-64, Gov Comt on Employ of Handicapped, Nev, 58-64, Gov Comt on Employ of Handicapped, SDak, 65-70 & SDak Bldg Authority, 72-; State Cent Committeeman, SDak Dem Party, 73- Bus & Prof Pos: Pres, Mo Valley Optom Soc, 55-56; secy, Nev Optom Asn, 58-60 & Distinguished Serv Found of Optom, 58-64. Mem: Kiwanis (pres, Reno, Nev, 60-); Blue Lodge Masons, Mitchell, SDak; Mitchell Chap, Masons; Mitchell chap, Mitchell Commandery, Mason; El Riad Shrine, Sioux Falls. Honors & Awards: Annual Gold Medal, Beta Sigma Kappa, 62; Life Mem Hon, Int Asn of Bds Examrs in Optom, 62; officer, Order of Crown of Thorns, France, 65; Gold Cross, Eloy Alfaro Int Found, 66; Knight, Order of Knights of St John of Jerusalem, 66. Relig: American Baptist. Mailing Add: 2038 Morningside Dr Brookings SD 57006

UGORETZ, MARK JOEL (D)
b Milwaukee, Wis, June 16, 40; s Ben Ugoretz & Marian Cohen U; m 1971 to Susan Sissel. Educ: Univ Wis, BS & JD. Polit & Govt Pos: Law clerk, State Attorney Gen, Wis, 65-67; attorney & adv to chmn, Nat Labor Rels Bd, 67-69; legis asst to US Rep Dominick V Daniels, NJ, 69-74, admin asst, 74- Mem: Fed Bar (Eastern Dist Wis); State Bar Wis; Am Arbit Asn; Community Disputes Panel. Legal Res: NJ Mailing Add: 16 Tenth St NE Washington DC 20002

UHER, D R (TOM) (D)
Tex State Rep
Mailing Add: 1406 Sixth St Bay City TX 77414

UHLENHAKE, HELEN IDELL (D)
Secy-Treas, Mercer Co Dem Exec Comt, Ohio
b Hart Co, Ga, Dec 11, 22; d Keels LaFayette Thrasher & Myra Belle Payne T; m 1945 to Arthur W Uhlenhake. Educ: Easley High Sch, SC; Elams Sch Pvt Instr, 43-44. Polit & Govt Pos: Committeewoman, Mercer Co Dem Cent Comt, 64-; mem, Mercer Co Dem Exec Comt, 70-, secy-treas, 70-; deleg, Ohio State Dem Conv, 70 & 71. Bus & Prof Pos: Clerk & clerk-typist to asst civilian personnel chief, med statist div, Off Surg General Army, Washington, DC, 44-45; secy personnel officer, New Idea Div, Avco Mfg Corp, 45-46, secy to plant mgr, 46-56; secy to Lee R Dabbelt, attorney & Ohio dir elections, 56- Mem: Eastern Star; Elks; Mercer Co Forum (vpres). Honors & Awards: Hale Citizenship Medal, Easley High Sch. Relig: Methodist. Mailing Add: 1105 Grand Ave Celina OH 45822

UHLENHOPP, HARVEY HAROLD
Judge, Iowa Supreme Court
b Butler Co, Iowa, June 23, 15; s Henry Harold Uhlenhopp & Charlotte Green U; m 1940 to Elizabeth Christine Elliott; c Elliott L & John C. Educ: Grinnell Col, AB, 36; Univ Iowa, JD, 39; Order of the Coif. Hon Degrees: LLD, Grinnell Col, 72. Polit & Govt Pos: Co attorney, Franklin Co, Iowa, 47-50; Iowa State Rep, 51-52; dist judge, 11th Judicial Dist, 53-70; judge, Iowa Supreme Court, 70- Bus & Prof Pos: Partner, Uhlenhopp & Uhlenhopp Law Firm, Hampton, Iowa, 39-53. Mil Serv: Entered as A/S, Coast Guard, 43, released as Lt(sg), 46, after serv in Southwest Pac, 43-45; Res, 75; Am, Philippines & Southwest Pac Medals. Publ: Adoption in Iowa, 55 & Judicial reorganization in Iowa, 58, Iowa Law Rev; Judicial redistricting in Iowa, Drake Law Rev, 68. Mem: Am Law Inst; Inst Judicial Admin; Am Judicature Soc; Am & Iowa State Bar Asns. Legal Res: 815 Fourth Ave SE Hampton IA 50441 Mailing Add: Box 341 Hampton IA 50441

UHLMAN, WESLEY CARL (D)
Mayor, Seattle, Wash
b Cashmere, Wash, March 13, 35; s Warner Uhlman & Dorcas Zimmerman U; m 1957 to Laila Hammond; c Wesley Carl, Jr & Daniel Willard. Educ: Seattle Pac Col, 52-54; Univ Wash, BA, 56, Law Sch, LLB, 59; Pi Sigma Alpha; Phi Alpha Delta; Model UN; Theta Delta Chi. Polit & Govt Pos: Chmn & pres, 32nd Dist Dem Comt & Dem Club, Seattle, Wash, 58-62; chmn, First Cong Dist Dem Caucus, 60; Wash State Rep, 58-66, chmn, Comt on Ways & Means & Comt on Higher Educ, 60-62, Wash State House of Rep; Wash State Sen, 66-71; Mayor, Seattle, Wash, 71- Mil Serv: 1st Lt, Wash State Nat Guard & vpres, 63-64. Mem: Bd dirs, Wallingford Boys Club; bd dirs, NCent CofC & chmn, Laws & Regulations Comt, 64; Kiwanis; Odd Fellows; Mason. Honors & Awards: Received Outstanding Young Men of Am Award, Jaycees, 58. Relig: Methodist; Lay Delegate. Mailing Add: Seattle Municipal Bldg 600 Fourth Ave Seattle WA 98104

ULCH, ELLEN (R)
Chairwoman, Clare Co Rep Party, Mich
b Alma, Mich, May 10, 26; d Roy A Knapp & Clara Reed K; m 1950 to Beverly G Ulch. Polit & Govt Pos: Secy, Clare Co Rep Party, Mich, 66-73, chairwoman, 75- Mailing Add: 287 Oak Harrison MI 48625

ULLAND, JAMES (R)
Minn State Rep
Mailing Add: Rte 6 Box 181 Duluth MN 55804

ULLMAN, AL (D)
US Rep, Ore
b Great Falls, Mont, Mar 9, 14; m 1972 to Audrey K Manuel. Educ: Whitman Col, BA, 35; Columbia Univ, MA Pub Law, 39; Beta Theta Pi. Polit & Govt Pos: US Rep, Ore, 56-, mem, Ways & Means Comt, US House of Rep, chmn, 75-, mem, Adv Comn on Intergovt Rels, 67-74 & Joint Comt on Internal Revenue Taxation, 68-, chmn, 75-, co-chmn, Joint Study Comt on Budget Control & chmn, House Budget Comt, 74; deleg, Dem Nat Conv, 60, 64 & 68, alt deleg, 72. Bus & Prof Pos: Teacher, Port Angeles, Washington High Sch, 2 years. Mil Serv: Commun Officer afloat in S & SW Pac. Relig: Presbyterian. Legal Res: Baker OR 97403 Mailing Add: 2207 Rayburn House Off Bldg Washington DC 20515

ULLMAN, MICHAEL
Asst Attorney Gen Off Legis Affairs, Dept of Justice
Mailing Add: Dept of Justice Washington DC 20301

ULLO, J CHRIS (D)
La State Rep
Mailing Add: 4601 Seventh St Marrero LA 70072

ULLRICH, WILFRID J (D)
Ind State Sen
Educ: Univ Notre Dame, 29. Polit & Govt Pos: Mem, Ind Bd of Pharm, 50-54; Ind State Sen, 63-; bd gov, Coun State Govt. Bus & Prof Pos: Registered pharmacist & owner of drugstore; dir, First Nat Bank, Aurora; pres, Aurora Indust Develop Corp. Mem: Aurora Farmers Fair Asn; KofC (4 degree); Rotary; Men of Milford; CofC. Honors & Awards: Named Ind Pharmacist of Year, 65. Relig: Catholic. Mailing Add: 403 Main St Aurora IN 47001

ULMER, ELDON ROBERT (R)
Rep Nat Committeeman, Alaska
b Boise, Idaho, Nov 15, 18; s T C Ulmer & Winnifred Tarter U; m 1942 to Lillian Virgin; c Robert Brent, Jerry Eldon, Scott Alan, Sue Ellen & Reed Christian. Educ: Idaho State Univ, BS in Pharm, 43. Polit & Govt Pos: Finance chmn, SCent Dist Rep Party, Alaska, 67; deleg, Rep Nat Conv, 68 & 72; deleg, Alaska State Rep Conv, 68 & 72; deleg, SCent Rep Party Conv, Alaska, 68 & 72; state finance chmn, Rep Party of Alaska, 68-70; chmn, Alaska Rep Nat Finance Comt, 68-; chmn, Alaska, Finance Comt to Reelect the President, 72; Rep Nat Committeeman, Alaska, 72- Bus & Prof Pos: Pres & majority stock holder, Ulmer-Burgess, Inc, Downtown Rexall Drug Store & Anchorage Prof Pharm, currently; partner, Pro-Quint Realty, currently. Mil Serv: Entered as Seaman, Navy, 43, released as Lt(jg), 46, after serv in USS Rhind, Destroyers, SPac Theatre, 44-46; World War II & Pac Theatre Medals. Mem: Am Cancer Soc (bd, Anchorage Unit, 54- & Alaska Div, 56-, chmn nominating comt, State Div, 66-, treas, 67-70, deleg, Nat Bd, 69-); Anchorage Community Hosp (bd trustees & chmn finance comt, 68-72); Anchorage Businessmens Asn (bd, 60-, treas 64-66, pres, 66-68, vpres, 70-72); Downtown Anchorage Asn (bd & treas, 68-); Alaska Bd Pharm (vpres, 68-69, pres, 69-). Relig: Protestant. Legal Res: 5204 Strawberry Rd Anchorage AK 99504 Mailing Add: PO Box 1420 Anchorage AK 99510

ULRICH, GERTRUDE WILLEMS (DFL)
b Heron Lake, Minn, June 11, 27; d Dr Paul W Willems & Margaret Voss W; m 1952 to Dr Jerome C Ulrich; c Franz, Frederick, Margaret, Lora, Lona & Edward. Educ: Univ Minn, BS. Polit & Govt Pos: Precinct chmn, Richfield, Minn, 68-; secy, Dist 37, Dem-Farmer-Labor Party, 68-70, chmn, 70; deleg, Minn State Conv, 68, 70, 72 & 74; Dem Nat Mid-Term Conf, 74. Mem: League of Women Voters; Minn Hist Soc; CofC; Assumption Church. Honors & Awards: Serv Award, City of Richfield & Hennepin Co. Relig: Catholic. Mailing Add: 7601 Aldrich Ave S Richfield MN 55423

UMANSKY, DAVID JAY (D)
b Philadelphia, Pa, Dec 27, 42; s Milton Umansky & Dorothy Halpern U; m 1969 to Adrienne Lynn Hollander; c Jenna Beth. Educ: Temple Univ, 60-63; Tau Epsilon Phi. Polit & Govt Pos: Admin asst to US Rep Joshua Eilberg, Pa, 71- Bus & Prof Pos: Reporter, Philadelphia Inquirer, 66-71. Mil Serv: Entered as Pvt, Army Nat Guard, 64, released as SP-4, 69, after serv in 28th Div, Pa. Mailing Add: 736 Ninth St SE Washington DC 20003

UMBLES, CLAYTON EDWARD (D)
b Canton, Ohio, Apr 25, 35; s Floyd Jackson Umbles & Edna Edwards U; m 1958 to Joyce Ann Woods; c Eric Clayton, Terri Elizabeth & Jennifer Megan. Educ: Univ Toledo, BS in Pharm, 58; Kappa Alpha Psi. Polit & Govt Pos: Councilman, Toledo, Ohio, 66-68; deleg, Dem Nat Conv, 72. Bus & Prof Pos: Registered pharmacist, Umbles Drew Hale Pharm, Toledo, Ohio, 58-73; registered pharmacist & pres, Detroit Pharm, 64; mem bd trustees, Christian Bros Asn, Toledo, 68-73; assoc, Drew-Hale Assocs, Toledo, 72-73. Mem: Mason; Black Elected Dem of Ohio; NAACP; Toledo CofC; Kiwanis. Honors & Awards: Outstanding Young Man, Toledo Jr CofC, 65; Outstanding Young Men of Am, Nat Jr CofC, 66. Relig: Protestant. Mailing Add: 2115 Mt Vernon Toledo OH 43607

UMPHREY, JAMES MORRIS (R)
b Detroit, Mich, Sept 20, 23; s Edwin S Umphrey & Ione Morris U; m 1948 to Barbara J Merrill; c Mary Patricia & Martha Merrill. Educ: Cent Mich Univ, AB, 49; Wayne State Univ, LLB, 51; Phi Sigma Epsilon; Sigma Nu Phi. Polit & Govt Pos: Rep dist chmn, Eighth Cong Dist, Mich; prosecuting attorney, Huron Co, 53-62; finance chmn, Huron Co Rep Party, 62-64, chmn, formerly; mem, Mich State Rep Cent Comt, 62-65; alt deleg, Rep Nat Conv, 68. Bus & Prof Pos: Mem bd trustees, Cent Mich Univ, 65-, chmn, 71- Mil Serv: Entered as Pvt, Air Force, 43, released as S/Sgt, 45, after serv in 31st Sq, 5th Bomb Group, 13th Air Force, Southwest Pac; Air Medal; Southwest Pac Campaign Ribbon with 5 Battle Stars; Philippine Liberation Medal. Mem: Mich Prosecutor's Asn; Nat Dist Attorney's Asn; Rotary; Elks; Verona Hills Country Club. Relig: Episcopal. Legal Res: 123 N Stanley Bad Axe MI 48412 Mailing Add: 249 E Huron Ave Bad Axe MI 48413

UNDERDAL, MELVIN (R)
Mont State Rep
b Conrad, Mont, Apr 22, 12; s Peder Underdal & Ingeborg Tufte U; m 1941 to Clara J Vettrus; c Paul, Carol (Mrs Gaylord Folden) & Allan. Educ: Mont State Univ, 1 quarter; Dunwood Inst, Minneapolis, Minn, welding. Polit & Govt Pos: Mont State Rep, Dist 12, 75-, mem agr, livestock & irrigation, hwy & transportation comts, Mont House Rep, currently. Mem: Farmers Union; Mont Stockgrowers Asn; Farm Bur; Mont Grain Growers Asn. Honors & Awards: Outstanding Conservationist, Toole Co Soil Conserv Dist, 60. Relig: Lutheran. Mailing Add: Box 605 Shelby MT 59474

UNDERHILL, FREDERICK WILLIAM, JR (R)
Chmn, Rochester Rep Town Comt, Mass
b Melrose, Mass, Aug 31, 38; s Frederick W Underhill & Vera Bisbee U; m 1965 to Nancy Ellis; c Kimberly, Mark Jason & Matthew James. Educ: Boston Univ, BS, 63; Phi Psi. Polit & Govt Pos: Town auditor, Rochester, Mass, 62-65, mem finance comt, 64-66 & mem sch comt, 67-; asst co treas, Plymouth Co, Mass, 67-; committeeman, Mass Rep State Comt, 68-; chmn, Rochester Rep Town Comt, 73- Bus & Prof Pos: Head admin clerk, Treas Off, Plymouth Co, 64-67. Mem: Plymouth Co Retirement Asn (secy); Elks; Lions; Rochester Rep Town Comt (chmn); Plymouth Co Rep Club (secy). Relig: Congregational. Mailing Add: High St West Wareham MA 02576

UNDERWOOD, BARBARA J (R)
NH State Rep
b New York, NY, Apr 6, 32; d John Brown & Marjorie Harrison B; m 1960 to David G Underwood, II, MD; c D Geoffrey, Derek Gordon & Chester Alexander. Educ: Middlebury Col, BA, 54. Polit & Govt Pos: NH State Rep, 71-, mem, Judiciary & Ways & Means Comts, NH House Rep, currently; city councilman-at-lg, Concord, NH, currently. Mailing Add: 29 Rumford St Concord NH 03301

UNDERWOOD, CECIL HARLAND (R)
b Joseph's Mills, WVa, Nov 5, 22; s Silas Henry Underwood & Della Forrester U; m 1948 to Hovah V Hall; c Cecilia Ann, Craig Hall & Sharon Sue. Educ: Salem Col, AB, 43; WVa Univ, AM, 52; Pi Kappa Delta; Sigma Epsilon. Hon Degrees: Dr degrees from various cols & univs. Polit & Govt Pos: WVa State Deleg, 44-56, Minority Leader, WVa State House of Deleg, 49-56; pres, Young Rep League, 46-50; parliamentarian, Young Rep Nat Conv, 50; Gov, WVa, 57-61; mem, Comt on Prog, Rep Nat Comt, 59; mem, Exec Comt, Nat Gov Conf, 59-60; temporary chmn, Rep Nat Conv, 60, deleg-at-lg, 60, 64 & 72; nominee for Gov, WVa, 64; chmn, Work Force on Prog, WVa Rep Revival. Bus & Prof Pos: Teacher, St Mary's High Sch, WVa, 43-46; mem staff, Marietta Col, 46-50; vpres, Salem Col, 50-56 & Island Creek Coal Co, 61-64; vpres, civic affairs, Monsanto Co, 65-67; pres, Franswood, Inc, 67-; pres, Cecil H Underwood Assocs, 66-; bd dir, WVa Life Ins Co, 61-69; bd dir, Huntington Fed Savings & Loan Asn, 61-; pres, Bethany Col, 72- Mil Serv: Pvt, Army Res, 42-43. Publ: State papers & public addresses, 25th Governor West Virginia, State of WVa, 63; Legislative Process in West Virginia, WVa Univ, 52. Mem: Am Polit Sci Asn; Mason; Elks; Moose; Am Cancer Soc (bd dirs & state crusade chmn WVa Div, 63-64, crusade dir, Southern Area, 72-75, lay del dir, 73-, chmn, Nat Crusade Comt, 75-). Relig: Disciples of Christ. Legal Res: Pendleton Heights Bethany WV 26032 Mailing Add: Bethany College Bethany WV 26032

UNDERWOOD, FOREST (D)
WVa State Deleg
Mailing Add: State Capitol Charleston WV 25305

UNDERWOOD, JAMES (R)
Sen, Guam Legis
Mailing Add: Guam Legislature Box 373 Agana GU 96910

UNDERWOOD, MALCOLM STANLEY, JR (R)
Mem, Va Rep State Cent Comt
b Shamokin, Pa, Mar 24, 30; s Malcolm Stanley Underwood & Ruby Newton U; m 1959 to Jacqueline T Atwell; c Kathryn O, Carl Clifford, Elizabeth A & Malcolm Stanley, III. Educ: Univ Va, Charlottesville, BA, 51, LLB, 59; Pi Delta Epsilon; Kappa Alpha Order; Sigma Nu Phi; German Club. Polit & Govt Pos: Mem, Henrico Co Rep Comt, Va, 60-65; deleg, Va State Rep Conv, 60-; mem & treas, Third Dist Rep Comt, 62-; mem, Chesterfield Co Rep Comt, 65-; mem, Va Rep State Cent Comt, 68-; treas, Rep Party Va, 68-72; mem, Newport News, Va City Comt, 70- Bus & Prof Pos: Asst trust officer, United Va Bank State Planters, 64-67, trust officer, 67-68 & head trust real estate & mortgage dept, 68-; vpres, trust officer & head of trust div, United Va Bank Citizens & Marine, 70. Mil Serv: Entered as Pvt, Marine Corps, 52, released as 1st Lt, 54, after serv in Fleet Marine Force, Pac Theatre, Res, 54-68, Lt Col. Mem: Am Inst of Banking; Marine Corps League; Marine Corps Res Officers Asn; Mil Order of the World Wars; Warwick Rotary Club. Relig: Methodist. Mailing Add: 129 State Rd Newport News VA 23606

UNDERWOOD, ROBERT CHARLES
Chief Justice, Ill Supreme Court
b Gardner, Ill, Oct 27, 15; c Marion L Underwood (deceased) & Edith L Frazee U (deceased); m 1939 to Dorothy Louise Roy; c Susan (Mrs Barcalow). Educ: Ill Wesleyan Univ, AB, 37; Univ Ill, JD, 39; Sigma Chi; Pi Kappa Delta; Sigma Delta Kappa. Hon Degrees: Doctoral degree from Loyola Univ, Ill, 69, Eureka Col & Ill Wesleyan Univ, 70. Polit & Govt Pos: City attorney, Normal, Ill, 42-46; asst states attorney, McLean Co, 42-46; judge, McLean Co, 46-62; justice, Ill Supreme Court, 62-69, chief justice, 69- Bus & Prof Pos: Admitted to Ill Bar, 39; pvt practice, Bloomington, Ill, 39-46. Publ: Let's put plea discussions—& agreements—on record, Loyola Univ Law J, winter 70; Ill judicial system, Notre Dame Law Rev, 12/71; Report of the chief justice to ISBA Assembly, Ill Bar J, 1/75; plus other articles in prof jour & publ. Mem: Ill Co & Probate Judges Asn (various off including pres); Mason (33 degree); Rotary Int; hon mem Kiwanis Int. Honors & Awards: Ill Welfare Asn Annual Citation for Pub Serv, 60; Outstanding Citizen Award, Normal CofC, 62; Cert of Outstanding Achievement, Univ Ill Col of Law, 69; Annual Distinguished Serv Award, Ill Scottish Rite, 70; Significant Sig Award, 71. Relig: Methodist; Lay leader, off bd mem, First Methodist Church of Normal. Legal Res: 11 Kent Dr Normal IL 61761 Mailing Add: 300 Peoples Bank Bldg Bloomington IL 61701

UNGER, ALAN FRANZ (D)
b Washington, DC, Sept 20, 48; s Paul A Unger & Sonja Franz U; single. Educ: Am Sch, Switz, 66-67; Col Wooster, BA in hist, 70; Coro Found, 72-73; Occidental Col, MA in urban studies, 73; Univ Southern Calif Sch Pub Admin, Environ Mgt Inst, 75. Polit & Govt Pos: Staff researcher for US Rep Charles A Vanik, Ohio, 68; col coordr, Carl B Stokes for Mayor, Cleveland, Ohio, 69; deleg, White House Conf on Youth, 71; participant, Voter Registr, Cleveland, 71-72; Nat organizer, McGovern for President, 72; coord, Get Out the Vote, McGovern for President, Mich, 72; deleg, Dem Nat Conv, 72; Southern Calif field coordr, Roth for Gov, Calif Dem Primary, 74; staff, Dem Planning Group, 74. Bus & Prof Pos: Community develop youth worker, WSide Community House, Cleveland, Ohio, 70-72. Mem: Soc Agencies Employees Union (chap chair, 72). Relig: Unitarian. Legal Res: 1958 Apex Ave 7 Los Angeles CA 90039 Mailing Add: 15830 S Park Blvd Cleveland OH 44120

UNGER, LEONARD
US Ambassador to Repub of China
b San Diego, Calif, Dec 17, 17; s Louis Allen Unger & Rachel Seidman U; m 1944 to Anne Louise Axon; c Deborah (Mrs Duncan J G Mackintosh), Philip Axon, Andrew, Anne Thomas, Daniel Howden. Educ: Harvard Col, AB, 39; Grad Sch Dept Agr, 39-41; Nat War Col, 57-58; Phi Beta Kappa. Polit & Govt Pos: US polit adv, Trieste, 50-52 & Naples, Italy, 52-53; mem staff NATO Affairs, Dept State, 53-57; dep chief mission, US Embassy, Thailand, 58-62; US Ambassador, Laos, 62-64; dep asst secy EAsian affairs, Dept State, 65-67; US Ambassador, Thailand, 67-73; US Ambassador to Repub of China, 74- Publ: Functions of the Political Advisor & his Relations with the Commander, Royal Thai Armed Forces Staff Col, Ministry Defense, Thailand, 61; Rural settlement in the Campania (Italy), Am Geog Soc Geog Rev, 53; chaps, In: Focus on Southeast Asia, Praeger, 72; plus others. Mem: Asn Am Geog; Am Foreign Serv Asn; Siam Soc; Am Geog Soc; Cosmos Club. Honors & Awards: Distinguished Honor Award, US Dept State, 65. Relig: Unitarian. Legal Res: 12701 Circle Dr Rockville MD 20850 Mailing Add: US Embassy APO San Francisco CA 96263

UNGER, SHERMAN EDWARD (R)
b Chicago, Ill, Oct 9, 27; s Melvin I Unger & Helen Strong U; m 1953 to Polly Van Buren Taylor; c Cathleen Estelle & Peter Van Buren. Educ: Miami Univ, BA, 50; Univ Cincinnati, JD, 53; Beta Theta Pi. Polit & Govt Pos: Pres, Hamilton Co Young Rep Club, 59; mem exec comt, Hamilton Co Rep Party, 59-69; mem personal staff, Richard Nixon Presidential Campaign, 60, campaign admin aide, 64, chief briefing staff, 68, mem, President-elect Nixon's Transition Staff, 68-69; asst campaign dir, Rep Cong Campaign, 62; spec asst to nat chmn presidential campaign, Rep Nat Comt, 64; mem, Ohio Water & Sewer Comn, 65-69; gen counsel, Dept Housing & Urban Develop, 69-70; gen counsel, Govt Nat Mortgage Asn, 69-70; mem, Admin Conf US, 69-71; mem nat adv comt for legal serv prog, Off Econ Opportunity, 69-71; mem nat adv comt for legal serv prog, Off Econ Opportunity, 69-71; bd dirs, Fed Nat Mortgage Asn, 69- Bus & Prof Pos: Partner firm, Frost & Jacobs, Cincinnati, 56-69; chmn bd, Modern Talking Picture Serv Inc & Modern Media, 68-69; vpres, Am Financial Corp, Cincinnati, 71- Mil Serv: Entered as Pvt, Army, 46, released as Pfc, 47; reentered as 2nd Lt, Air Force, 53, released as 1st Lt, 56, after serv in Alaskan Air Command. Mem: Mason; Univ, Cincinnati Country & Queen City Clubs, Cincinnati; Metrop Club, Washington, DC; Racquet & Tennis Clubs, NY. Relig: Presbyterian. Mailing Add: 7935 Indian Hill Rd Cincinnati OH 45243

UNGERER, JAMES L (R)
Kans State Rep
b Marysville, Kans, Feb 12, 23; s Fred M Ungerer & Carolina Zech U; m 1947 to Nelda June Bargmann; c James Lowell, Jeffrey Lynn, Marna Jean & Jon Lindsey. Educ: High sch. Polit & Govt Pos: Chmn, Marshall Co Rep Cent Comt, Kans, 12 years; mayor, Marysville, 6 years; first treas, Kans Rep State Comt, 66-; Kans State Rep, 61st Dist, 69- Mil Serv: Entered as Pvt, Army Air Corps, 41, released as M/Sgt, 45, after serv in 20th Air Force, Pac; Army Res, 45-48 & Capt(Ret), Army Nat Guard, 48-62. Mem: Am Legion; VFW; Mason; Moose; Eagles. Relig: Protestant. Legal Res: 1000 Otoe St Marysville KS 66508 Mailing Add: PO Box 327 Marysville KS 66508

UNGERMAN, MAYNARD IVAN (D)
b Topeka, Kans, Dec 5, 29; s Irvine E Ungerman & Hanna Friedburg U; m 1950 to Elsa Leiter; c William Charles, Karla Beth & Rebecca Diane. Educ: Stanford Univ, BA cum laude, 51 & LLB, 53; Phi Alpha Delta. Polit & Govt Pos: Dem precinct chmn, Tulsa Co, Okla, 56-67; chmn, credentials comt, Tulsa Co Dem Party, 64 & chmn, First Dist, 66; alt deleg, Dem Nat Conv, 64, deleg, 68; coordr, State Dem Cent Comt, 64; mem inaugural comt, President Lyndon Johnson & Vice President Hubert Humphrey, 65; presidential appointee, Nat Citizens Comt Community Rel, 65-; chmn assoc housing comt, Community Rel Comn, 65-; Gov appointee, Okla Acad State Goals, 66-; chmn, Tulsa Co Dem Cent Comt, 67-69. Bus & Prof Pos: Mem bd ed, Stanford Law Rev, 51-53; partner, Ungerman, Grabel & Ungerman, Attorneys, 53-; vchmn, labor law comt, Okla State Bar, 67-70. Mil Serv: Entered as 1st Lt, Air Force, 53, released, 56, after serv in Judge Adv Gen Dept; Air Force Res Capt (Ret); Nat Defense Serv Award. Mem: Am Judicature Soc; Univ Club Tulsa; Anti-Defamation League (vpres, Southwest Region, chmn, Okla Sect); Nat Comt Am Jewish Joint Distribution Comt; Neighbor for Neighbor, Inc (pres, 70-). Honors & Awards: Cert Merit, Tulsa Co Bar Asn, 64; Distinguished Serv Award, Oklahomans for Indian Opportunity, 68. Relig: Jewish. Legal Res: 3732 E 71st St Tulsa OK 74135 Mailing Add: Sixth Floor Wright Bldg Tulsa OK 74103

UNHJEM, MIKE (R)
NDak State Rep
Mailing Add: State Capitol Bismarck ND 58501

UNRUH, PAULA (R)
Chmn, Rep State Comt, Okla
b Tulsa, Okla, Feb 13, 29; d Paul Mervin Combest & Thelma Opal Allison C; m 1951 to R James Unruh; c Jilda Lee, James Kuhns & Allison Page. Educ: Univ Tulsa, 47-48, 51-54; Univ Ark, 48-49; Sigma Alpha Iota; Kappa Kappa Gamma. Polit & Govt Pos: Vchmn, Okla Fedn Young Rep, 52-53, nat committeewoman, 53-54; campaign mgr, US Rep Page Belcher, 58-70; co-chmn, Tulsa Co Comt to Reelect the President, 72; co coordr, Reelec Campaign of US Sen Henry Bellmon, 74; chmn, Rep State Comt, 75- Bus & Prof Pos: Exec secy, Carter Oil Co, Tulsa, Okla, 49-59; secy, US Rep Page Belcher, 55. Mem: Women's Asn for the Tulsa Philharmonic (pres); Tulsa Mayor's Comt for the Performing Arts Ctr Bond Issue (co-chmn); Tulsa Co Bar Asn Auxiliary (legal aid chmn); Pro Am; Tulsa Town Hall. Honors & Awards: Theta Sigma Phi Woman of the Year, Women in Commun, 73. Relig: Presbyterian. Mailing Add: 2927 S Quaker Tulsa OK 74114

UPCHURCH, RUBLE (R)
Chmn, Fentress Co Rep Exec Comt, Tenn
b Forbus, Tenn, June 3, 03; s Raymond Gregg Upchurch & Freely Ann Crabtree U; m 1935 to Jessie Helen Reagan; 2nd m 1954 to Janie Rose Dyer; c Patricia Ann, Ruble, Jr & Willard Charles; step-children, Linda, Joe & Eddie Booher. Educ: Tenn Tech Univ, BS, 35; Univ Tenn, MS, 53; DAR Award for Excellence in Am Hist, 35. Polit & Govt Pos: Mem, Rep Speaker's Bur, 32, 36 & 40; secy, Fentress Co Rep Primary Bd, Tenn, 36-46; pres, Fentress Co Young Rep Club, 40-42; mem & secy, Fentress Co Equalization Bd, 40-42; chmn, Fentress Co Rep Exec Comt, 40-42 & 60-, secy, 46-56; mem, Fentress Co Elec Comn, 48-50 & 68-69, secy, 71-73, vchmn, 73-; mem, Rep Exec Comt, Tenn, 50-; mem, Fentress Co Jury Comn, 59-69, chmn, 68-; co campaign mgr, Nixon-Lodge Ticket, Mid Tenn, 60; deleg, Rep Nat Conv, 60; vpres & mem, Fentress Co Libr Bd, 61-66 & mem bldg comt, 64-66; historian, Fentress Co, 68-; chmn, Fentress Co US Savings Bonds, 68-; chmn, Fentress Co jury Comn, 68-; mem, Gov Dunn's Better Employ Comt, 72-; mem, Citizens Adv Comt on Pub Welfare for Fentress Co, 72- Bus & Prof Pos: Rep, Progress Tailoring Co, 27-30, World Book Encyclop, 48-49 & Compton's Encyclop, 60-62; prin, teacher & supvr, Fentress Co Schs, 29-66; agt & rep, NY Life Ins Co, 30-33; student instr of hist, Tenn Tech Univ, 35; pres, Upper Cumberland Supvr, 47-48; secy, Upper Cumberland Prin, 64-65; instr adult educ, Fentress Co, Tenn, 62- Mil Serv: Pvt, Tenn State Home Guard, 40-43. Publ: A Supervisory Program for Fentress Co Schools, Univ Tenn, 53; auth, Notes on Fentress County, 74; auth, Story of Wolf River Valley, 73. Mem: Rotary; Nat Educ Asn (life mem); Ruritan Nat; Farm Bur; Lions (dir, 68-70, pres, 74-). Honors & Awards: Name placed by President Eisenhower on Rep Mem in Hall of Presidents at Gettysburg, 61; selected as one of the outstanding community leaders for ETenn, 62; Col on Staff Gov Winfield Dunn of Tenn, 71-74. Relig: Methodist; Sunday school teacher Greer's Chapel Methodist Church Forbus, Tenn, 36- Legal Res: Rte 1 Pall Mall TN 38577 Mailing Add: PO Box 457 Jamestown TN 38556

UPHAM, CHESTER ROBERT, JR (R)
b Mineral Wells, Tex, May 19, 25; s Chester Robert Upham & Ida Irene Schafer U; m 1946 to Virginia Frances Lee; c Barbara Lee (Mrs D G Mayes), Mary Kathleen, Chester Robert, III & Richard Lee. Educ: Univ Tex, Austin, BSME, 45; Tau Beta Pi; Pi Tau Sigma; Phi Gamma Delta. Polit & Govt Pos: Dir, Palo Pinto Co Munic Water Dist, Tex, 60-73; dist committeeman, State Rep Exec Comt, 64-70; alt deleg, Rep Nat Conv, 68, deleg, 72; state finance chmn, Tex Rep Party, 70-71, dep state finance chmn, 71-73. Bus & Prof Pos: Dir & vpres, Brazos River Gas Co, Tex, 47-58; managing owner, Upham Oil & Gas Co, 55-; dir, Loveland Ski Corp, Georgetown, Colo, 56-; dir, Texaramics Inc, Mineral Wells, Tex, 64-71; dir, City Nat Bank, 66-; chmn bd & pres, Clear Creek Skiing Corp, DBA Loveland Skiing Areas, Georgetown, Colo, 72- Mil Serv: Entered as A/S, Navy, 43, released as Ens, 45, after serv in 16th Fleet. Relig: Protestant. Legal Res: 1301 NW Seventh Ave Mineral Wells TX 76067 Mailing Add: PO Box 940 Mineral Wells TX 76067

UPSHUR, LILLIAN W (D)
b New York, NY, Jan 25, 16; d John Thomas White & Lillie Mason W; m 1947 to Louis S Upshur; c Rosetta D (Mrs Leroy Miller). Educ: NY Univ, one year. Polit & Govt Pos: Dist leader, Adam Clayton Powell Club of Dem, 58-; spec clerk, US House of Rep, 58-; mem, NY State Comt Women, 60-; deleg, Dem Nat Conv, 64, alt deleg, 68; deleg, Judicial Conv, 60-70; exec mem, Dist 65, 68-; asst secy to NY Co Comt, 68-70; mem, NY Co Exec Bd Adv Comt, 68-; vchmn, NY Co Exec Bd, 71; mem, NY Dem Co Admin Comt, currently. Bus & Prof Pos: Assoc dir, Claims Div, Security Plan, 49- Mem: Bus & Prof Women; Orgn Black Elected Off; Trade Union Women of Black Heritage; Distributive Workers Union Dist 65 (organizer, 50); Church Women for Powell Comt, Comt of 100 Women. Honors & Awards: Community & Union Serv Award, Afro-Am Affairs Comt Dist 65, 64; Good Samaritan Award, First Lady Callaway Award, 66; Christian Woman Polit Leader Award, Women's Day Comt, Abyssinian Baptist Church, 71. Mailing Add: 2160 Madison Ave New York NY 10037

URBIGKIT, WALTER C, JR (D)
Wyo State Rep
b Burris, Wyo, Nov 9, 27; s Walter Carl Urbigkit & Bertha Esther Miller U; m 1953 to Marian Myrna Chilton; c Marcia Jill, Cynthia Louise, Robert Dale & Brenda Kay. Educ: Univ Wyo, BA, 49, LLB, 51; Phi Beta Kappa; Phi Kappa Phi; Delta Sigma Rho. Polit & Govt Pos: Asst co attorney, Laramie Co, Wyo, 58-60; vchmn, Laramie Co Dem Cent Comt, 59-60 & 64-66; chmn, State Selective Serv Appeal Bd, 60-; treas, Wyo State Dem Cent Comt, 61-65, exec secy, 66-68; mem, Laramie Co Welfare Bd, Wyo, 66; treas, Bd of Trustees, Sch Dist 1, Cheyenne, Laramie Co, Wyo, 67-, chmn, 71-73; deleg, Dem Nat Conv, 68; Wyo State Rep, 73-, mem, Educ Interim Comt & Judiciary Comt, Wyo State Legis, 73-; mem, Gov Comt on State Reorgn, currently. Bus & Prof Pos: Sr partner, Urbigkut, Ma, Halle, Macky & Whitehead, Law Firm. Mil Serv: Pvt, Army, 51-52, serv in 10th Inf. Mem: Laramie Co & Am Bar Asns; Nat Asn of Homebuilders; Am Legion; Nat Asn for Retarded Children. Relig: Congregational. Legal Res: 508 Cornell Lane Cheyenne WY 82001 Mailing Add: PO Box 247 Cheyenne WY 82001

URBINA URBINA, DAVID (NEW PROGRESSIVE, PR)
Rep, PR House Rep
b Guaynabo, PR, Apr 16, 37; s Salvador Urbina & Natividad U; m 1961 to Maria F Calvo; c David Salvador, Miguel Angel & Manuel Antonio. Educ: Univ PR, 56-57; Univ Salamanca, LLB, 62. Polit & Govt Pos: Rep, PR House Rep, 65-72 & 75-, chmn finance comt, 69-72. Bus & Prof Pos: Lawyer, Urbina, Bauza & Bauza, 63. Mem: Colègio de Abogados de PR; Logia Odfelica; Cooperative de Credito de Guaynabo; Asociation Graduados Universidades Espanolas; Exchange Club. Relig: Evangelical. Legal Res: Carr Alesandrino KO-H5 Guaynabo PR 00657 Mailing Add: Box 104 Guaynabo PR 00657

URION, RICK (R)
Alaska State Rep
Mailing Add: 3239 Hiland Anchorage AK 99504

USERA, JOSE VICENTE (R)
Chmn, Nat Rep Party PR
b Ponce, PR, Nov 30, 26; s Vicente Usera, Jr & Luz B Tous U; m 1947 to Mary M Macfarlane; c Steven V, Joseph A & Gregory T. Educ: Iowa State Univ, Bachelor Animal Sci, 48; Alpha Zeta; Sigma Alpha Epsilon; Newman Club; Block & Bridle Club. Polit & Govt Pos: Vpres, United Citizens for Nixon-Agnew, 68; vpres, Nat Rep Party, PR, 69-70, chmn, 70-; deleg, Rep Nat Conv, 72. Bus & Prof Pos: Gen mgr, Cidra-Nebr Beef Co, 63-67; dir pub rels, Molinos de PR, Inc, 67- Mem: Am Soc Animal Sci; Colegio de Agronomos de PR; Am Dairy Sci Asn; Am Soc Agr Sci; Rotary. Relig: Catholic. Mailing Add: 5 Patio Hill Rd Torrimar-Guaynabo Bayamon PR 00619

USERA, JOSEPH ANDREW (R)
b Santurce, PR, Oct 26, 49; s Jose Vincente Usera & Mary Evelyn Macfarlane U; single. Educ: Col San Ignacio de Loyola, Rio Piedras, PR, 67; Colgate Univ, BA, 71; George Washington Univ Nat Law Ctr, 72-; Maroon Key; Delta Upsilon. Polit & Govt Pos: Fed plans & progs officer, Off of Commonwealth of PR, 72; dir legis staff, US Rep Jaime Benitez, PR, 73- Bus & Prof Pos: Mgt trainee, San Geronimo Hilton, San Juan, PR, 72. Mem: Minority Legis Educ Prog (bd dirs, 74); Career Awareness for Migrant Children (nat adv coun, 74); Colgate Univ Alumni Club. Relig: Roman Catholic. Legal Res: 5 Patio Hill Rd Torrimar Bayamon PR 00619 Mailing Add: 4956 Sentinel Dr 401 Sumner Village Sumner MD 20016

USERY, WILLIE J, JR (D)
Nat Dir, Fed Mediation & Conciliation Serv
b Hardwick, Ga, Dec 21, 23; s Willie J Usery, Sr & Effie Mae Williamson U. Educ: Ga Mil Col, 38-41; Mercer Univ, 48-49. Hon Degrees: DSc, Univ Louisville, 75. Polit & Govt Pos: Asst Secy of Labor for Labor-Mgt Rels, 69-73; dir, Fed Mediation & Conciliation Serv, 73-; Spec Asst to the President for Labor-Mgt Negotiations, 74-; mem, Nat Comn for Indust Peace; chmn working party on indust rels, Orgn for Econ Coop & Develop. Bus & Prof Pos: Grand Lodge rep, Int Asn Machinists, AFL-CIO, 56-69, indust union rep, President's Missile Sites Labor Comt, Kennedy Space Ctr & Marshall Space Flight Ctr, Huntsville, Ala, 61-67. Mil Serv: Navy, 43-46. Mem: Int Asn Machinists, AFL-CIO; Masonic Lodge; Scottish Rite; Shrine; Elks. Honors & Awards: Distinguished Alumni Award, Ga Mil Col, 71; St John Francis Regis Award, San Francisco Univ, 74; Corsi Inst Labor-Mgt Rels Award, Pace Univ, 75. Mailing Add: 2400 Virginia Ave NW Washington DC 20037

USHER, R L (SCOOP) (D)
Mo State Rep
Mailing Add: 315 Daugherty Macon MO 63552

USHER, RONALD E (D)
Maine State Rep
Mailing Add: 342 Saco St Westbrook ME 04092

USHIJIMA, CHARLES T (D)
Hawaii State Rep
b Hilo, Hawaii, Aug 17, 32; s Sakae Ushijima & Satsuki Tanaka U; m 1959 to Rachel A Tagomori; c Shaun S. Educ: Univ Hawaii, BS, 55. Polit & Govt Pos: Hawaii State Rep, 68- Mil Serv: Sp-3, Army, 56-58, serv in Adj Gen Corps, Western Ger. Mem: Hawaii Bankers Asn; Hawaii Jaycees (past state pres); Hawaii CofC. Honors & Awards: One of Hawaii's Ten Outstanding Young Men, 58. Legal Res: 3566 Kumu Pl Honolulu HI 96822 Mailing Add: House of Rep Sgt at Arms State Capitol Honolulu HI 96813

USHIJIMA, JOHN T (D)
Hawaii State Sen
b Hilo, Hawaii, Mar 13, 24; s Buhachi Ushijima & Sano Nitahara U; m 1954 to Margaret S Kunishige. Educ: Grinnell Col, Iowa, AB, 50; George Washington Univ Law Sch, LLB, 52; Phi Delta Phi. Polit & Govt Pos: Hawaii State Sen, 59- Bus & Prof Pos: Dir & vpres, Royal State Nat Ins Co, 62-; dir, Am Security Bank, 63- Mil Serv: Entered as Pvt, Army, 43, released as Sgt, 46; Presidential Unit Citation; 442nd Regt Combat Team Ribbon; ETO Ribbon; Victory Ribbon. Mem: 442nd Vets Club Hawaii; Y's Mens Club; YMCA. Relig: Protestant. Legal Res: 114 Melani St Hilo HI 96720 Mailing Add: Senate Sgt at Arms State Capitol Honolulu HI 96813

USTYNOSKI, JAMES J (R)
Pa State Rep
Mailing Add: Capitol Bldg Harrisburg PA 17120

UTHLAUT, RALPH, JR (R)
Mo State Sen
b Big Springs, Mo, Dec 18, 33; m 1953 to Carol Jean Kattlemann; c Mark, Michael & Rhonda

Sue. Educ: Univ Mo, Normandy Br. Polit & Govt Pos: Mo State Sen, 62-72 & 73- Bus & Prof Pos: Farmer. Mil Serv: Army, 54-56, 41st Field Artil Group, Hqs Battery, Ft Sill, Okla. Mem: Mo Farm Bur; Montgomery City Jr CofC. Relig: Methodist. Mailing Add: New Florence MO 63363

UTT, MAX EDDY (R)
b Columbus City, Iowa, Sept 23, 02; s John Erwin Utt & Mary Elva Eddy U; m 1932 to Bonnie Jean Lockwood; c Virginia (Mrs Robert F Stockton) & Roger Lockwood. Educ: Pomona Col, BA, 24; Harvard Law Sch, LLB, 27. Polit & Govt Pos: Chmn, Citizens Legis Adv Comn to Calif Legis, 57-61; mem, Rep State Cent Comt Calif, 68-72. Mem: Am & Calif Bar Asns. Relig: Presbyterian. Legal Res: 2800 W Ocean Front Newport Beach CA 92660 Mailing Add: 515 S Flower St Los Angeles CA 90071

UTTER, ROBERT FRENCH
Judge, Wash Supreme Court
b Seattle, Wash, June 19, 30; s John Madison Utter & Besse French U; m to Elisabeth Stevenson; c Kimberley, Scott & John. Educ: Linfield Col, 48-50; Univ Wash, BS & JD; Theta Chi; Phi Delta Phi. Polit & Govt Pos: Comnr, King Co Superior Court, Wash, 59-64, superior court judge, 64-69; judge, Court of Appeals, Wash State, 69-71; judge, Wash Supreme Court, 71- Honors & Awards: Outstanding Young Man, Seattle Jr CofC, 64. Relig: Am Baptist. Mailing Add: 3013 Sherwood Dr Olympia WA 98501

V

VACCA, FRANCIS JOHN (D)
b Boston, Mass, Apr 4, 35; s Armando J Vacca & Rita Robitaille V; single. Educ: Boston Col, AB, 61; Georgetown Univ, 61-62; Int Rels Club; Pub Speaking Club; Bellarmine Law & Govt Club. Polit & Govt Pos: Advanceman, Kennedy for President, 68; exec secy, Calif Dem State Cent Comt, 68-69; admin asst to Majority Leader of Calif State Assembly, 69-70; admin asst to US Rep Bob Traxler, Mich, Eighth Dist, 74- Bus & Prof Pos: Salesman, Anaconda Wire & Cable Co, Washington, DC, 62-67; sales mgr, Everett Fence Co, 67-68. Mil Serv: Entered as Pvt, Marine Corps, 54, released as Cpl, 57. Mem: Nat Dem Club. Relig: Roman Catholic. Legal Res: 479 Ferry St Everett MA 02149 Mailing Add: 123 N Carolina Ave SE Washington DC 20003

VACCA, PASCHAL PATRICK (D)
Ala State Sen
b Hillsville, Pa, Sept 6, 01; s John Vacca & Philomena Robbio V; m 1920 to Lelia Frances Bryant. Educ: St Vincents Col, Pa; Youngstown Bus Col, Ohio; Sch of Technol & Birmingham Sch of Law, LaSalle Exten Univ, LLB. Polit & Govt Pos: Munic judge & city attorney, Tarrant, Ala, formerly; Ala State Rep, formerly; Ala State Sen, 67- Bus & Prof Pos: Law practice, Birmingham, Ala, 37- Mil Serv: Serv with Am Red Cross as asst field dir attached to armed forces. Mem: Mason; Shrine; Elks; Eagles; Civitan (past dist gov). Relig: Methodist. Legal Res: 1617 Mountain Dr Tarrant AL 35217 Mailing Add: 929-930 Frank Nelson Bldg Birmingham AL 35203

VACHON, ROSE C (D)
NH State Rep
Mailing Add: 132 Bellevue St Manchester NH 03103

VADALABENE, SAM MARTIN (D)
Ill State Sen
b Detroit, Mich, July 31, 14; s Martin Vadalabene & Anna Catalano V; m 1935 to Mary Pauline Lesko; c William Joseph, Charles Martin, Sam Martin, Patricia Ann (Mrs Mosby) & Martin Joseph. Educ: Pana Twp High Sch, Ill. Polit & Govt Pos: Auditor, State Supt of Pub Instr, Ill, 59 -63; supvr cemetery care, Div Auditor of Pub Accounts, 63-67; pres, Edwardsville Twp Dem Club, 63-65; auditor, Edwardsville Twp, Ill, 65-67; Ill State Rep, 53rd Dist, 67-71; Ill State Sen, 71- Bus & Prof Pos: Orgnr-mgr little league, Edwardsville Little League Asn, 56; supvr, Edwardsville Recreation Prog, 59-63; co-chmn, Madison Co Polio-Vaccine Admin. Mil Serv: Entered as Pvt, Army, released as Pfc, 45, after serv in 29th Inf Div; Combat Inf Badge; three Bronze Campaign Stars; EAMET Ribbon; Good Conduct Medal; Presidential Unit Citation. Mem: KofC (4 degree); Moose Lodge; VFW; Am Legion; Madison Co Heart Fund (chmn, 73). Honors & Awards: Awarded three commendations in House of Rep; First Crusade of Courage Award, Ill State Chamber of KofC; Recreation Park & Street in Edwardsville named after; Outstanding Freshman Legislator, Ill New Media, 67; Recognition Award Outstanding Citizen, Edwardsville Cof C; Outstanding Legislator Award, Ill Asn of Co Supt of Schs, 69. Relig: Catholic. Mailing Add: 64 Circle Dr Edwardsville IL 62025

VAGLEY, ROBERT EVERETT (D)
b New Eagle, Pa, Jan 31, 40; s William Stuart Vagli & Lillian Tesi V; m 1972 to Karen Lee Sahlin. Educ: Pa State Univ, BS, 61, MA, 63; Phi Kappa Theta. Polit & Govt Pos: With Cent Intel Agency, 63-64; dir, Select Subcomt on Educ, Comt on Educ & Labor, US House of Rep, 65, dir, Subcomt on Labor Standards, 66-; pres, Capitol Hill Young Dem, 68-69. Mem: Univ Club, Washington, DC; Tantallon Country Club; Pa State Alumni Asn. Relig: Roman Catholic. Legal Res: 334 Chestnut St Monessen PA 15062 Mailing Add: 3210 Wessynton Way Alexandria VA 22309

VAGNOZZI, ALDO (D)
VChmn, Oakland Co Dem Comt, Mich
Polit & Govt Pos: Chmn, 19th Cong Dist Dem Orgn, Mich, 67-73; deleg, Dem Nat Conv, 68; vchmn, Oakland Co Dem Comt, 73- Mailing Add: 26193 Kiltartan Farmington MI 48024

VAIL, JOANE RAND (DFL)
Mem, Minn Dem-Farmer-Labor State Cent Comt
b Waltham, Mass, Nov 16, 28; d Herbert Smythe Rand, Sr & Pauline Murphy R; m 1956 to Dr David Jameson Vail; wid; c David Rand, Garrett Murphy, Sara Jameson & Michael Walsh. Educ: Boston Univ, 45-46 & 50-51; McLean Hosp Sch Nursing, Waverley, Mass, 47-50, RN, 50; Univ Md, 52-54; Univ Minn, Minneapolis, 59. Polit & Govt Pos: Legis dist chairwoman, Dist 48N, Minn, 62-65; deleg, Minn Dem State Conv, 64-70; chairwoman, Ramsey Co Dem-Farmer-Labor Party, 65 & 68-69; chairwoman, Fourth Cong Dist Dem-Farmer-Labor Party, 65-68 & 69-; mem, Minn Dem-Farmer-Labor Exec Comt, 65-69 & Cent Comt, 65-69 & 70-; deleg, Dem Nat Conv, 68; mem staff, Gov Wendell R Anderson, currently; asst to chmn, Twin Cities Metrop Coun, St Paul, Minn, currently. Bus & Prof Pos: Head Nurse, instr nursing & dir nursing educ, State of Md, 52-56. Mem: Citizens League; Minn Hist Soc; League of Woman Voters. Relig: Unitarian. Mailing Add: 127 Sixth St White Bear Lake MN 55110

VAILE, VICTOR EDWARD, III (R)
Rep State Committeeman, Fla
b Canton, Ohio, Sept 16, 33; s Victor Edward Vaile, Jr & Zana Dietz V; m 1960 to Marcia Anne Juday; c Brian Edward. Educ: Ohio State Univ, BS, 55 & MD, 59; Nat Pre-med Hon Soc; Phi Chi; Alpha Epsilon Delta. Polit & Govt Pos: Legis chmn, Los Angeles Co Young Rep, 61-62 & first vpres, 62-63; precinct dir, West Los Angeles, 61-63; Shell for Gov Vol, Santa Monica Hq, 62; mem, 60th Assembly Dist Rep Comt & mem, 28th Cong Dist Rep Comt, Rep State Cent Comt, 62-63; region IX vpres, Calif State Young Rep, 63; deleg, Young Rep Nat Conv, 63, 67 & 71; mem, Goldwater for Pres Campaign, Lawton, Okla, 64; chmn, Winter Haven, Young Am for Freedom, Fla, 65-67; Rep committeeman, precinct 41, Winter Haven, Fla, 66-; chmn, Polk Co Rep Exec Comt, 67-71; chmn, Fla Friends of Reagan, 68; alt deleg, Rep Nat Conv, 68; Rep State Committeeman, Fla, 70-; Presidential Elector, Fla, 72. Bus & Prof Pos: Speakers bur, Los Angeles Co Med Asn, 62-63; vpres, Santana Toastmasters, Ft Sill, Okla, 64-65; chmn & pres, Ridge Food Prod Inc, 71-; pres, Campaign Mgt Inc, 72-; dir, 400 Corp, Fla, 67- Mil Serv: Entered as 1st Lt, Army, 63, released as Capt, 65, after serv in US Army Hosp, Ft Sill, Okla, 63-65; Cert of Achievement. Publ: Ed, Trumpeteer, Heart of Florida Newsletter, 67-69 & The Statesman, Fla Young Rep Newsletter, 69-72. Mem: Polk Co Med Asn (secy-treas, 68-); Elks; Winter Haven Libr Bd (dir, 72-). Honors & Awards: One of Top Ten Young Rep, Fla, 67-68. Relig: Episcopal; former mem Vestry, St Pauls Episcopal Church. Legal Res: 800 Ave L SE Winter Haven FL 33880 Mailing Add: 400 Ave K SE Winter Haven FL 33880

VALCOURT, RICHARD ROGER (D)
b Fall River, Mass, Nov 29, 41; s Roger Valcourt & Angeline C Bernier V; m 1965 to Cheryl Marjorie Crossley; c Jordan Roger (deceased), Jean Christine, Shariah Angeline & Catherine Crossley. Educ: Bates Col, 58-60; Cambridge Sch of Broadcasting dipl, 61; Elkins Inst of Electronics, dipl, 61; LaSalle Exten Univ, LLB, 66; Univ Maine, Cert in Munic Planning, 69. Polit & Govt Pos: Campaign dir, Goldwater for Pres, Fall River Area, Mass, 64; asst sgt at arms, Rep State Conv, 64, mem, Ballot & Tally Comt, 66, deleg & press officer, 68; vchmn, Mayor's Citizens Adv Comt, Fall River, Mass, 64-65; deleg, Mass Young Rep Asn, 64-66, cand for pres, 66; mem, Rep City Comt, Augusta, Maine, 67-70, vchmn, 68-70; chmn, Augusta Planning Bd, 68-71; chmn, Kennebec Co Rep Comt, 68-70; nominee, Kennebec Co Legis Deleg for Dep Secy of State, 69; mem, Gov Task Force on the Maine Environment, 69-71; liaison, Capital Planning Comn, 69-71; vchmn, Maine Rep Platform Comt, 70; founding vchmn & auth of by-laws, Maine Asn Rep Co Chmn, 70; cand, Mayor, Augusta, 70; consult, Active Corps of Execs, Small Bus Admin; mem, First Cong Dist Rep Comt, 70; mem, South Kennebec Valley Regional Planning Comn, 70-71; affiliated with Dem Party, 70-; mem, Gtr Fall River Dem Club, 71-74, vpres, 72-74; deleg, Mass Dem State Conv, 72; chmn, Fall River Dem City Comt, 72-74; mem, Fall River Airport Comn, 71-73; mem Fall River Coun, Region VII Comprehensive Health Planning, 72-, chmn, Facilities & Serv Task Force, 73-; bd dirs, Citizens for Citizens, Fall River, 73-, secy, 73; mem, Mass Dem Party Platform Comt, 73-; mem, Fall River Coun on Human Serv, 74-75; mem steering comt, Gtr Fall River Coun of Churches, 74-; mem, USS Mass Memorial Comn, 74-; mem standing comt, Unitarian Soc in Fall River, 74- Bus & Prof Pos: Radio Sta WSAR, Fall River, Mass, 61-63; mem staff, Valcourt Indust Supply Co, Inc, 63-64, purchasing agt, 71-72, vpres, 72-; asst to dir & acting dir of informational research, Western Islands Publ, Boston, 64-66; field consult, Maine Heart Asn, Augusta, Maine, 66-67; news dir, Radio Sta WFAU, 67-71; campaign dir pub rels, Community Concepts, 68-70; pub rels consult, Natural Resources Coun of Maine, 68-71; announcer, Radio Sta WALE, Fall River, 75- Mem: Coun of Churches (pres, 75-); Fall River Symphony Soc (bd dirs, 72-, vpres, 74-); NAACP (bd dirs, Gtr Fall River, 72-); Fall River Brotherhood Ctr (bd dirs, 72-74); Gtr Fall River CofC (chmn comt legis, 72, bd dirs, 73-). Relig: Unitarian. Mailing Add: 95 Eaton St Fall River MA 02723

VALDERAS, HAROLD LOUIS (D)
b New York, NY, Dec 17, 23; s Louis Albert Valderas & Elizabeth Cunningham V; m 1965 to Marisa Garcia; c Harold Michael, Elizabeth Anne & Sean Kevin. Educ: Southern Methodist Univ, BBA, 50, JD, 54; Delta Sigma Pi; Sigma Chi. Polit & Govt Pos: Vpres, Young Dem Tarrant Co, 60; US Appeal Agt, Selective Serv Bd 112, 68-72; staff judge advocate, 301st Tactical Fighter Wing, US Air Force Reserve, 70-; chief judge, Munic Courts, Ft Worth, 72-; alt deleg, Dem Nat Mid-Term Conf, 74. Bus & Prof Pos: Bd dirs, Munic Court Sect, State Bd of Tarrant, 74-75. Mil Serv: Entered as 2nd Lt, Air Force, 51, released as 1st Lt, after serv as spec agt, Off Spec Invest, conducting criminal & counter-intel investigations in Korea & Japan, 51-53; Lt Col, Air Force Res; Two Air Force Commendation Medals; Army Good Conduct, Am Campaign, ETO Campaign, World War II Victory, Army of Occup, Nat Defense Serv, Korean Serv & UN Serv Medals. Mem: Tarrant Co Crime Comn; Int Good Coun (int bd dirs); Sigma Chi Alumni (pres); Am Legion (dist comdr); Neighborhood Youth Corps of Tarrant Co, Inc (chmn bd dirs). Honors & Awards: Named Good Neighbor of the Year, Int Good Neighbor Coun, 72; Apr 21, 1972 named as Judge Harold L Valderas Day in Tarrant Co; Hall of Fame, Am Legion Dept of Tex, 67 & 68. Relig: Catholic. Mailing Add: 5617 Odessa Ft Worth TX 76133

VALDES, JOSEPH ERNEST (D)
Mayor, Santa Fe, NMex
b Santa Fe, NMex, Sept 4, 30; s Juan B Valdes & Dora Papa V; m 1954 to Patricia J Annon; c John & Janet. Educ: High sch. Polit & Govt Pos: Mem, City Planning Comn, Santa Fe, NMex, 58-60, mem, Tree Comn, 60-62, mem, City Coun, 70-72, mayor, 72- Bus & Prof Pos: Employee & mgr, McMurtry Paint & Glass, 48-73, owner, 73- Mil Serv: Entered as Pvt, Army, 51, released as Sgt, after serv in 28th Div, 110th Inf, ETO, 51-54. Mem: Elks; Eagles; Nat League Cities (bd dirs); Santa Fe CofC (bd dirs); Santa Fe Fiesta Coun (pres). Honors & Awards: Hometown Builder, Eagles. Relig: Catholic. Mailing Add: 1423 Santa Cruz Dr Santa Fe NM 87501

VALDES, LOUIS FELIPE (D)
Chmn, Santa Fe Co Dem Comt, NMex
b Santa Fe, NMex, Feb 21, 01; s Felipe Valdes & Melinda Digneo V; m 1947 to Geraldine Margaret Carmody. Educ: St Michael's Col, 17. Polit & Govt Pos: Ward chmn, Santa Fe Co Dem Comt, NMex, 66-72, co chmn, 72-; coordr, Montoya for Sen Club, Santa Fe Co, 75- Bus & Prof Pos: Hwy designer, NMex State Hwy Dept, 19-26, 29-42 & 57-65; hwy designer,

Ark Hwy Dept, 26-28, Corps Engrs, Los Angeles, Calif, 43-45 & Southern Calif Edison, 45-56. Relig: Catholic. Mailing Add: 1834 Puye Rd Santa Fe NM 87501

VALDEZ, JOYCE RUBY (R)
Mem, Rep State Cent Comt Calif
b Supreme, Ala, July 17, 28; d Rev Thomas Lecial Anderson & Ruby Jane Bradley A; m 1948 to Frank Valdez; c Dennis Ray, Victoria Lee, Valerie Lynn & Valinda Lou. Educ: Pasadena Jr Col, 2 years; Scholarship Soc. Polit & Govt Pos: Mem, Rep State Cent Comt Calif, 67-, mem cand res & develop comt, 67 & 68, chmn, Golden Circle of Calif, 69 & 70, chmn, Gov Reagan Fund Raisers for State Finance, 69 & 70, mem finance comt, 69-, vchmn, 69 & 70, coordr, reelect Gov Reagan, Los Angeles, Co, 70, mem credentials & proxies comt, 71 & 72, co-chmn, Salute to Rep Legis State Dinner, 72, chmn, Western Winners' Roundup Campaign Seminars, 72; mem Rep Cent Comt, Los Angeles Co, 67-, vchmn, youth comt, 67 & 68, chmn, youth coordr coun, 67 & 68, coordr, Gov Reagan Rally, 68, chmn, 70, mem platform comt, 68 & 69, mem exec comt, 68-, mem polit educ prog comt, 71-74, mem cand research & develop comt, 68-, co-chmn, 71 & 72, chmn, 73 & 74; mem, 28th Sen Dist Rep Party, 67-, vchmn, 69 & 70, chmn, 71 & 72; sustaining mem, Rep Nat Comt, 67-; Dep Registr Voters, 68-70; Gov Reagan Rep, Nat Conf on Youth, 69; mem, United Rep Finance Comt, 69-; comnr, Indust Welfare Comn, 69-; alt deleg, Rep Nat Conv, 72; finance dir, Calif treas, Ivy Baker Priest, 73; state finance dir, reelec of Attorney Gen Evelle J Younger, Calif, 74; dir, Golden Circle of Calif, 75-76; active in campaign & fund raising for numerous national, state & local cand. Bus & Prof Pos: Model, Catalina, Inc, 43-45; retail clerk-advert-promotionals, Mod Village Stores, Inc, 43-58; owner & operator, Supermarket chain, Los Angeles & Orange Co, Calif, 58-66. Mem: Fedn Bus & Prof Women; Alhambra Rep Womens Federated; Alhambra Rep Club; Los Angeles World Affairs Coun; Monterey Park Rep Club. Honors & Awards: Highest Achievement Award, Rep Cent Comt Los Angeles Co, 68 & 72. Relig: Protestant. Mailing Add: 1001 S Valencia St Alhambra CA 91801

VALDEZ, RUBEN A (D)
Colo State Rep
Mailing Add: 666 Osceola Denver CO 80219

VALE, R L (BOB) (D)
Tex State Rep
b Roma, Tex, Dec 4, 31; s Joseph J Vale & Maria Garcia V; m 1958 to Therea J Finnegan; c Kathleen M, Michael G & Shelagh A. Educ: St Mary's Univ Sch Law, LLB magna cum laude, 54; Delta Theta Phi, scholarship key, jr year; St Thomas Moore, Barristers. Polit & Govt Pos: Tex State Rep, 68th Dist, 64- Mil Serv: Entered as 2nd Lt, Army, 54, released as 1st Lt, 56, after serv in Korea. Mem: Alumni Senate, Delta Theta Phi; Lulacs; GI Forum; Eagles; Northeast Dem Club. Relig: Catholic. Legal Res: 358 Springwood Lane San Antonio TX 78216 Mailing Add: 1014 San Pedro San Antonio TX 78212

VALENCIA, ROSS HAINES (D)
Mem, Dem State Cent Comt Calif
b Bisbee, Ariz, June 6, 27; s Gabriel Valencia & Emma Haines V; m 1948 to Carmen Lopez; c Ross, Vance, Camille, Rosalie & Gabriel. Educ: Los Angeles City Col, 46-47; Univ Southern Calif Exten Sch. Polit & Govt Pos: Coordr, voter registr, Viva Johnson Campaign, 64; coordr, voter registr & Get-Out-the-Vote, 30th Cong Dist, 64; mem, Dem State Cent Comt, 64-; vchmn, Comt on Anti-Poverty in East Los Angeles, 67; adv mem, City Human Rels, Los Angeles, 67-69; chmn, US Comn on Crime & Delinquency for East Los Angeles, 68; campaign dir, Garcia for Assembly, 68; admin asst to Calif State Assemblyman Alex P Garcia, 69- Bus & Prof Pos: Mgr, Foster's Dent Lab, Inglewood, Calif, 47-49; owner, V P Dent Lab, 49-64; mgr, Nobilium Restorations, Los Angeles, 65-67; bus rep, Dent Technicians Union, Local 100, 67-68. Mil Serv: Entered as Enlisted Man, Navy, 45, released as PO 3/C, 46, after serv in FPO, San Francisco, Calif. Mem: Am Legion; KofC; Coun of Mex Am Affairs; Mex-Am Labor Coun; Mex-Am Polit Asn. Honors & Awards: Order of Merit, Boy Scouts; Hon Life Membership, PTA. Relig: Roman Catholic. Mailing Add: 1162 S Esperanza St Los Angeles CA 90023

VALENTINE, WILLIAM ANTHONY (R)
Mayor, Rome, NY
b Rome, NY, July 14, 13; s Joseph A Valentine & Elizabeth Uvanni V; m 1943 to Hazel Beckley; c Michael J & Susan; four grandchildren. Educ: Niagara Univ, BS in Econ, 38. Polit & Govt Pos: Alderman, Rome, NY, 60-64, city chmn, 62-63, mayor, 64-; alt deleg, Rep Nat Conv, 68. Bus & Prof Pos: Cent planner, Alcoa, 39-64. Mem: Int Asn Basketball Off; Am Red Cross (mem bd dirs); NY State Munic Police Training Prog; NY State Conf Mayors; AAA (mem bd dirs & legis comn). Relig: Roman Catholic. Mailing Add: 916 W Thomas St Rome NY 13440

VALENTINE, WILLIAM R (R)
b Warren, Pa, July 12, 44; s William R Valentine & Helen Schatzley V; single. Educ: Univ Pittsburgh, BS Chem, 66, Sch of Dent Med, DMD, 70; Alpha Phi Omega; Psi Omega; pres, Pitt Young Rep, 63-65. Polit & Govt Pos: Campaign chmn, Pa Young Rep, 63-64, dist coordr, 65-66; Rep committeeman, Oakland, Pa, 65-70, chmn, Oakland Young Rep, 66-70; deleg, Rep Nat Conv, 72. Mil Serv: Entered as Capt, Pub Health Serv, 72, released as Maj, 72, after serv in Navajo Indian Area; Maj, Pub Health Serv Reserve, currently. Mem: Am, NMex & Albuquerque Dent Socs; Elks. Relig: Presbyterian. Mailing Add: 1309 San Pedro NE Albuquerque NM 87110

VALICENTI, A JOSEPH (D)
Pa State Rep
Mailing Add: Capitol Bldg Harrisburg PA 17120

VALIER, CHARLES E (R)
b St Louis, Mo, June 5, 40; s Charles E Valier, Jr & Musa Lewis V; m 1972 to Sharon Kozemczak Valier; c Michelle Lamy, Nicole Lewis & Christopher. Educ: Yale Univ, BA, 62; NY Univ Grad Sch, MBA, 65; Univ Mo Law Sch, JD, 68; Beta Theta Pi. Polit & Govt Pos: Mo State Rep, 66-72; Counsel to Gov, State of Mo, 73- Bus & Prof Pos: Mem, staff, Trust Dept, Bank of New York, 63-65; assoc, Peper, Martin, Jensen, Maichel & Hetlage, Attorneys-at-law, 68-71; partner, Valier & Roach, 71-72. Mil Serv: Entered as Pvt, Marine Corps, 62, released as Cpl, 68. Mem: Downtown St Louis, Inc (dir, 69-); Loretto-Hilton Theatre, Inc (dir, 71-); Mo State Employ Retirement Syst (trustee, 73-); Yale Club; John Marshall Club. Honors & Awards: Distinguished Serv Award, St Louis Jaycees, 70; Meritorious Serv Award, St Louis Globe-Dem, 70; Aloys P Kaufmann Award, 70; selected by Eagleton Inst. Relig: Presbyterian. Legal Res: 4910 W Pine Blvd St Louis MO 63108 Mailing Add: Rte 1 Lake Champetra Hartsburg MO 65039

VALIQUETTE, MARIGENE (D)
Ohio State Sen
Mailing Add: 3211 Parkwood Ave Toledo OH 43610

VALLANCE, MAY LOUISE (D)
Chmn, Ravalli Co Dem Cent Comt, Mont
b Janesville, Wis, Aug 7, 01; d Roy Pierson & Marie Bemis P; m 1923 to Irvin A Dull, deceased 1932; m 1936 to Wilbur Phillip Vallance; c Donald Albert Dull, Sharen (Mrs Richard G Evans); Phyllis (Mrs Ed Frohlich) & Judith (Mrs Paul W Joramo). Educ: Univ Mont, BA, 58, 61-62. Polit & Govt Pos: Precinct committeewoman, Ravalli Co Dem Cent Comt, Mont, 49-73, chmn, 67-69 & 73- Bus & Prof Pos: Teacher, Rural Mont, 20-25, rural Wyo, 25-27, Pub Grade Sch, Browning, Mont, 32-36, Hamilton, 44-46 & 51-66. Mem: VFW Auxiliary (pres, 55-); Ravalli Co Hist Soc; Mont Archaeol Soc; Ravalli Co 4-H Leader. Honors & Awards: Leader of Year Award, Ravalli Co, 56. Relig: Methodist; supt, Sunday Sch Primary Dept, 9 years; choir, 15 years. Mailing Add: SE 400 Grant Lane Hamilton MT 59840

VALLANTE, MICHAEL ANTHONY (R)
Nat Committeeman, RI Young Rep
b Providence, RI, Sept 25, 55; s Arthur Vallante & Elvira Fusco V; single. Educ: Providence Col, 73-; Dillion Club; RI Honor Soc, 73. Polit & Govt Pos: Off worker, DeSimone for Gov Campaign, 72; Rep cand, City Coun, Seventh Ward, Providence, RI, 74; asst to hq mgr, Cianci for Mayor Campaign, 74; asst to research dir, Rep State Cent Comt, 74; nat committeeman, RI Young Rep, 74-; vchmn, Seventh Ward Rep Comt, RI, 75-; staff asst, Mayor's Col Intern Prog, 75- Publ: Auth & ed, The President responds, Young Rep Voice, 1/74; auth, Democratic domination, Providence J Bull, 6/74; Tokenism and the two-party system, The Echo, 7/74. Relig: Catholic. Mailing Add: 220 Webster Ave Providence RI 02909

VALLARIO, JOSEPH FREDERICK, JR (D)
Md State Deleg
b Washington, DC, Mar 4, 37; s Joseph F Vallario & Lucille Badia V; m 1959 to Mary Elise Thornton; c Angela Marie, Joseph Frederick, III, twins, Mary Elise & Marcie, Lisa Beth & Christina Richelle. Educ: Benjamin Franklin Univ, BComSci, 58, MComSci, 59; Eastern Col, Baltimore, AA, 61; Mt Vernon Sch Law, LLB, 63; Univ Baltimore, JD, 70. Polit & Govt Pos: Md State Deleg, 75- Bus & Prof Pos: Attorney-at-law, Oxon Hill, Md, 63- Mem: Am & Md Bar Asns; Sons of Italy (orator, 73-74); Painters Local Union 1773 (active mem, 60-65, inactive mem, 65-); Prince George's Co Criminal Trial Lawyers Asn. Relig: Catholic. Legal Res: 7801 Woodyard Rd Clinton MD 20735 Mailing Add: 6003 St Barnabas Rd Oxon Hill MD 20021

VALLE, GEORGETTE (D)
Wash State Rep
Mailing Add: 1434 SW 137th Seattle WA 98166

VALLEE, RONALD S (D)
Mayor, Manchester, NH
b Manchester, NH, Nov 13, 29; s Wilfred Vallee & Marie Anne V; m 1952 to Ida D Dubois; c Debra Ann, Steve Roland, Dale Marie, Celeste Ida, Laura Elizabeth & Paul Arthur. Educ: Berklee Sch Music, Boston, Mass, 54-55; St Anselm's Col, 57-60; Univ NH 1 year. Polit & Govt Pos: Alderman, Ward 14, NH, 61; comnr, Manchester Airport Authority, 61; deleg, Dem State Conv, 62; nat committeeman, NH Young Dem Club, 62-65; deleg, Dem Nat Conv, 64; Mayor, Manchester, NH, 64-; Dem Nat Committeeman, 67-68. Bus & Prof Pos: Carpenter, 48; cabinetmaker, Hermsdorf Store Fixture Mfg Co, 53-55; owner, pres & treas, Val Construction, Inc, 55-; pres & treas, Valco Realty, Inc, 60-; corporator, Manchester Savings Bank, 62. Mil Serv: Entered Navy, 48, serv in US Mediterranean, Europe & Korea, released 53; Good Conduct Medal; Korean Ribbon; ETO Ribbon. Mem: Cath War Vet Post 1352; Am Legion William A Jutras Post 43; Queen City Mem Post 8214; Club Mont-Royal; KofC (4 degree). Honors & Awards: Featured in article depicting accomplishments of young man of Franco-Am descent, Maclean Mag, Canada, 63; selected Outstanding Young Man of Year, Manchester Jaycees, & one of three for NH, 64; received citation for outstanding youth work, Cath War Vet, 59. Relig: Catholic. Mailing Add: Off of Mayor City Hall Manchester NH 03101

VALLIERE, ALCIDE E (D)
NH State Rep
Mailing Add: 138 Green St Berlin NH 03570

VALSANGIACOMO, ORESTE VICTOR (D)
Chmn, Washington Co Dem Comt, Vt
b Barre, Vt, Oct 31, 19; s Giulio Valsangiacomo & Giuseppina Poletti V; m 1942 to Helen Louise Emslie; c Oreste, Jr & Jon C. Educ: Spaulding High Sch, grad; Officer Training Schs, Ft Benning, Ga, grad. Polit & Govt Pos: Chmn, Barre City Dem Comt, Vt, 52-54; Justice of the Peace, Barre City Bd of Civil Authority, 52-; chmn, Washington Co Dem Comt, 54-56 & 65-, committeeman, 56-60; deleg, Dem Nat Conv, 64; Vt State Rep, Dist 7-3, Barre City, 67-74. Bus & Prof Pos: Secy, Northeast Vt Bd of Realtors, Inc, 63-65; pres, Cent Vt Realtors, Inc, 67-70; pres, Cent Vt Multiple Listing Serv, Inc, 68-70; mem, Vt Indust Bldg Authority, formerly; incorporator & mem, Adv Bd, Brokers Realty Invest Corp; proprietor, King's Grant, Realtors. Mil Serv: Entered as Sgt, Army, 41, released as Capt, 46, after serv in 335th Inf Div, ETO, recalled as Maj, 50, released in 52, after serv in 172nd Inf 43rd Div, NATO; Lt Col, Inactive Army Res, 62; Am Defense, Am Campaign & ETO Ribbons; German Occup Victory Medals; Combat Inf & Expert Inf Badges; Bronze Star with Cluster; Purple Heart. Mem: Rotary; Elks; VFW; DAV; Am Legion. Honors & Awards: Vt State Realtor of Year, 67. Relig: Catholic. Mailing Add: 31 Sheridan St Barre VT 05641

VAN ALSTYNE, DAVID, JR (R)
Chmn Finance Comt, Bergen Co Rep Orgn, NJ
b Louisville, Ky, Jan 3, 1897; s David Van Alstyne & Ella Peay V; m 1923 to Janet Graham; c Joan (Mrs Edward F Johnson), Keats (Mrs Evans Smith), Ellen (Mrs Richard C Starrett) & David III (deceased). Educ: Williams Col, BA, 18; Delta Kappa Epsilon. Polit & Govt Pos: NJ State Assemblyman, 40-41; NJ State Sen, 43-53, majority leader, NJ State Senate, 48, pres, 49; mem, State Tax Comn, NJ, 44-45; chmn, Joint Legis Juvenile Delinquency, 46; mem, State Aid Comt Educ, 46 & 50; chmn, NJ Regional Planning Comt, 46 & 50; mem defense coun, Englewood, NJ, 46; chmn, Joint Legis Appropriations Comt, 47; Acting Gov, 49; chmn, NJ Metrop Rapid Transit Comn, 52-53; comnr, Port NY Authority, 54-55; vchmn, NY-NJ Metrop Rapid Transit Comn, 54; chmn finance comt, Bergen Co Rep Orgn, currently;

comnr, Palisades Interstate Park Comn, 70-; mem-at-lg, Nat Adv Coun for Region II, Small Bus Admin, 70- Bus & Prof Pos: Sr partner, Van Alstyne, Noel & Co, 32-; chmn bd, New Idria Mining & Chem Co, 40-; dir & chmn exec comt, United Piece Dye Works, 43-; dir, Whippany Paper Bd Co, Inc, 61-, Educ Systs, Inc, Schott Indust, Inc, Canrad Precision Indust Inc, & Nyvatex Oil Co. Mil Serv: Vol, French Army, serv as sect comdr, Ambulance Corps, transferred, US Army, 17, 1st Lt; Croix de Guerre. Mem: Holland Soc; Am Legion; VFW; SAR; Invest Bankers Asn. Honors & Awards: Key Man, NJ Rep Finance Comt; chmn, Rep Club Englewood. Relig: Unitarian. Legal Res: 115 Chestnut St Englewood NJ 07631 Mailing Add: 4 Albany St New York NY 10006

VAN ANTWERP, JAMES CALLANAN, JR **(AM PARTY)**
b Mobile, Ala, Sept 24, 23; s James Callanan Van Antwerp & Fanny Imahorn V; m 1963 to Elizabeth Margret Barrett; c James Callanan, III, Elizabeth Ann & John David. Educ: US Naval Acad, BS, 46. Polit & Govt Pos: Treas, Mobile Co Rep Party, Ala, 62-65; mem, Mobile City Planning Comn, 62-, chmn, 62-63, 67-68 & 71-, secy, 65-71; mem, Rep State Exec Comt, 62-74; mem, Mobile Co Rep Exec Comt, 62-75, chmn, 65-68; deleg-at-lg, Rep Nat Conv, 68; chmn, First Cong Dist Rep Exec Comt, Ala, 68-72. Bus & Prof Pos: Dir & mem exec comt, Downtown Mobile Unlimited, 61-, pres, currently. Mil Serv: Entered as Midn, Navy, 42, released as Lt, 54, after serv in Japan, Pac & Atlantic, Mediterranean Sixth Fleet, last five years in submarines. Mem: Mobile Asn of Independent Ins Agts; Ala Realtors; Mobile Bd Realtors. Relig: Catholic. Legal Res: 3804 Claridge Rd Mobile AL 36608 Mailing Add: 901 Van Antwerp Bldg Mobile AL 36602

VAN ARSDALE, CATHERINE EVA **(D)**
Ind State Rep
b Indianapolis, Ind, June 20, 17; d Elbert Stackhouse & Nellie Abeh S; m 1933 to Cecil E Van Arsdale; c Sally (Mrs Marvin Bush), Joann (Mrs Fred Thornburgh), Harold (deceased), Catherine (Mrs Lockaby), Cecil, Jr & Elbert W. Educ: Ben Davis High, 33; acct & bookkeeping courses. Polit & Govt Pos: Ward chmn, precinct chmn & vchmn, Marion Co Dem Orgn, Ind, 72-; Ind State Rep, 75- Bus & Prof Pos: Legal secy, Secy of State, Ind, 73-74; tax acct, State Revenue. Mem: Vol Fire Dept Auxiliary (rec secy, Ind, 72, treas, Marion Co, 72-); Julia Jamison Health Club for Children (pres & secy, 65-); Polit Clubs of Marion Co (secy & pres, 40-). Relig: Nazarene. Mailing Add: 637 S Whitcomb Indianapolis IN 46241

VAN ARSDELL, MADELENE **(D)**
Ariz State Sen
b Chicago, Ill, Mar 25, 18; d Francis Thomas McIntyre & Ida Olson M; m 1941 to Louis Childs Van Arsdell, wid; c James Louis, Karen (Mrs Grimwood); Ellen (Mrs Crowley) & Jeffrey. Educ: Ariz State Univ, BS in Psychol, 69. Polit & Govt Pos: Comnr, Ariz Civil Rights Comn, 65-67; Ariz State Sen, 75-; precinct committeewoman, Ariz Dem Party, currently, state committeewoman, currently; vchairwoman, Dist 19 Dem Orgn, currently. Mem: Ariz Women's Polit Caucus; Ariz Consumers Coun; League of Women Voters; Ariz Civil Liberties Union. Relig: United Church of Christ. Mailing Add: 6727 N 12th Ave Phoenix AZ 85013

VANASEK, ROBERT EDWARD **(DFL)**
Minn State Rep
b New Prague, Minn, Apr 2, 49; s Richard Vanasek & Elsie Kajer V; m 1973 to Mary Wagner; c Robert Martin. Educ: Univ Minn, BA, 71. Polit & Govt Pos: Minn State Rep, 73- Mem: New Prague Sportsman Club. Relig: Catholic. Mailing Add: 807 Third St NE New Prague MN 56071

VANASSE, ALBERT J **(R)**
RI State Rep
b Woonsocket, RI, Oct 1, 18; s David Vanasse & Edwardina Riviers V; m 1946 to Eileen Heffernan; c David, Nancy & Jane (Mrs Arthur N B Weyand). Educ: Brown Univ Exten Div, Assoc Degree, 68. Polit & Govt Pos: Mem, North Smithfield Charter Comn, RI, 68-69, town councilman, 69-71; RI State Rep, 73- Bus & Prof Pos: Mem, Nat & RI Asn Ins Agents, 47-73; pres, North Smithfield Asn Ins Agents, 64-69; first vpres, Woonsocket Asn Ins Agents, 69-73. Mil Serv: Entered as Pvt, Marines, 42, released as Cpl, 45, after serv in 1st Marine Div, Pac Theatre, 43-45; Purple Heart. Publ: The advantage of no-fault automobile insurance over the present system automobile liability system, Woonsocket Call Publ Co, 1/73. Mem: Nat Easter Seal Soc Crippled Children, Providence, RI (house of deleg, 69-73); VFW. Mailing Add: Round Hill Rd North Smithfield RI 02895

VAN BEBBER, GEORGE THOMAS **(R)**
Kans State Rep
b Troy, Kans, Oct 21, 31; s Roy V Van Bebber & Anne Wenner V; single. Educ: Univ Kans, AB, 53, LLB, 55; Phi Delta Phi; Order of the Coif; Acacia. Polit & Govt Pos: Asst US attorney, Dist Kans, 59-61; co attorney, Doniphan Co, 63-69; Kans State Rep, 48th Dist, 73- Bus & Prof Pos: Attorney-at-law, Troy, Kans, 55-59 & 61- Mem: Am & Kans Bar Asns; Mason (Master, 64 & 65). Legal Res: 232 E Elm Troy KS 66087 Mailing Add: PO Box 586 Troy KS 66087

VAN BREE, IVAN **(R)**
Mem Corinth Town Rep Comt, Vt
b Toronto, Ont, Can, Aug 27, 1897; s Isaac E Van Bree & Bella Bene V; m 1922 to Dorothy Putnam; c Lt Peter Putnam (deceased) & Patricia (Mrs Thornton Hall Hough). Educ: Colgate Univ, AB in Econ & Sociol, 21; Phi Gamma Delta; Scalp & Blade; hon alumnus, Princeton Univ, 46. Polit & Govt Pos: Mem, Corinth Town Rep Comt, Vt, 63-, vchmn, 69-71, chmn, 71-73; Grand Juror, Corinth, 64-; mem, Vt Rep State Comt, 67-73, Exec Comt, 71-73; deleg & mem, Platform Subcomt, Vt Rep State Conv, 68, deleg & mem, Credentials Comt, 72, mem, Resolutions Comt, Platform Conv, 72; campaign aide for Gov Deane C Davis, Vt, 68; mem, Bd Civil Authority, Orange Co, 68-, Justice of the Peace, 68-; mem, State Parole Bd, 69-; campaign aide for Gov Deane C Davis, 70; area coordr for state & nat Rep tickets, 70; app by Gov, State Dist Environ Comt, 71-73; mem, Orange Co Rep Comt, 71-73. Bus & Prof Pos: Commercial mgr, NY Tel Co, Buffalo, 21-24; broker & agent, gen ins, 24-25; agency mgt of Life, Accident & Group Dept, Travelers Ins Co of Hartford, Conn, 25-38, group ins mgr, New York, 38-60, retired; owner & operator, Tree Farm 72, Am Tree Farm Syst & Vt Forest Industs Comt, currently. Mil Serv: Mil training, 4 years. Mem: Cent Conn Valley Asn (dir); Vt 251 Club; Vt Hist Soc; Mason; Asn of Paroling Authority. Relig: Episcopal. Mailing Add: Fair Acres Farm Taplin Hill East Corinth VT 05040

VANCE, CYRUS ROBERTS **(D)**
b Clarksburg, WVa, Mar 27, 17; s John Carl Vance & Amy Roberts V; m 1947 to Grace Elsie Sloane; c Elsie Nicoll, Amy Sloane, Grace Roberts, Camilla (Mrs James H Higgins, III) & Cyrus Roberts. Educ: Yale Univ, BA, 39, LLB, 42. Hon Degrees: LLD, Marshall Univ, 63, Trinity Col, 66, Yale Univ, 68, WVa Univ, 69. Polit & Govt Pos: Spec counsel, Preparedness Investigating Sub-Comt, Senate Armed Serv Comt, 57-60; consult counsel, Spec Comt on Space & Astronaut, US Senate, 58; gen counsel, Dept of Defense, 61-62; Secy of the Army, 62-64; Dep Secy of Defense, 64-67; spec rep of the President in Cyprus crisis, Nov-Dec, 67 & in Korea, Feb, 68; US Negotiator, Paris Peace Conf on Vietnam, 68-69. Bus & Prof Pos: Asst to pres, Mead Corp, 46-47; assoc, Simpson, Thacher & Bartlett, New York, 47-56, partner, 56-61, 67 & 69-; dir, Int Bus Machines Corp, Pan Am World Airways, One William Street Fund, Inc & NY Times Co, currently. Mil Serv: Entered as Midn, Navy, 42, released as Lt, 46, after serv in Pac, 42-46; various combat ribbons. Publ: The Administration of justice in civil disorders, Judicature, 4/68. Mem: Fel Am Col Trial Lawyers; Asn of Bar of City of New York (pres); Century Asn; Links Club, New York; Metrop Club, Washington, DC. Honors & Awards: Medal of Freedom, 69. Mailing Add: 2 E 93rd St New York NY 10028

VANCE, ESTIL A **(D)**
Chmn, Tarrant Co Dem Exec Comt, Tex
b Texarkana, Tex, Mar 25, 38; s Estil A Vance & Murle Block V; m 1961 to Melinda Terry; c Estil A, III & Terry Kathleen. Educ: Yale Univ, BA, 60; Univ Tex Law Sch, LLB, 63; Phi Beta Kappa; Pi Sigma Alpha. Polit & Govt Pos: Chmn of Precinct 137, Tarrant Co Dem Party, Tex, 67-72; chmn, Dist Ten Dem Conv, 70; committeeman, Tenth Sen Dist Dem Party, 70 & 72; chmn, Dist Ten deleg, Tex Dem State Conv, 72; chmn, Tarrant Co Dem Exec Comt, 72- Bus & Prof Pos: Attorney, Cantey, Hanger, Gooch, Cravens & Munn, 64- Mil Serv: Entered as Pvt, Marines, 63, released as Pfc, 64, after serv in Inf; Lt Comdr, Naval Res, 8 years. Mem: Am, Tex State, Tarrant Co Jr & Tarrant Co Bar Asns. Relig: Presbyterian. Legal Res: 3901 Mockingbird Lane Ft Worth TX 76109 Mailing Add: 1800 First Nat Bldg Ft Worth TX 76102

VANCE, HOWARD GRANT **(R)**
Secy, Ark State Rep Exec Comt
b Sedgwick, Ark, Sept 24, 15; s B B Vance & Elsie Crader V; m 1939 to Wanda Grace Sellers; c Ann (Mrs Bailey), Howard Eugene & David Boston. Educ: Ark State Col. Polit & Govt Pos: Mem, Ark State Rep Comt, 58-64; deleg, Rep Nat Conv, 60, 64 & 68; mem, State Rep Exec Comt, 60-66, secy, 70-; committeeman, First Cong Dist, currently. Bus & Prof Pos: Owner, Vance Real Estate, 52-; gen mgr, B B Vance & Sons, Inc, 42-58, pres, 58- Mem: Rotary; past pres, Walnut Ridge High Sch Alumni Asn. Relig: Methodist. Mailing Add: PO Box 1348 Jonesboro AR 72401

VANCE, JOHN T **(D)**
b Lexington, Ky, Oct 12, 21; s John Thomas Vance & Margaret Scott Breckinridge V; div; c Margaret Breckinridge, Katherine McCormick, Angela Fox & Mary Camilla Dudley. Educ: Univ Mont, AB, 47; George Washington Univ, LLB, 50; Phi Delta Phi; Sigma Chi. Polit & Govt Pos: Secy, Bd Mgrs, Chevy Chase, Md, 48-50; comnr pub safety, Missoula, Mont, 52-54; dep co attorney, Missoula, 54; counsel, Mont Trade Comn, 54-63; city attorney, Helena, 64-66; comnr, Indian Claims Comn, Washington, DC, 69-, chmn, 68-69. Bus & Prof Pos: Law partner, Toole, Leaphart & Vance, Missoula, Mont, 50-52, Marchi, Sullivan, Vance & Leaphart, Helena, 54 & Vance & Leaphart, Helena, 59-67; assoc prof, Sch Law, Univ NDak, 66-67. Mil Serv: Entered as Pvt, Army, 42, released as Cpl, 46, after serv in Philippines. Mem: Mont & Am Bar Asns; Nat Capital Dem Club. Honors & Awards: Mont Pilot of Year, 65. Relig: Presbyterian. Legal Res: Helena MT Mailing Add: Indian Claims Commission 1730 K St NW Washington DC 20006

VANCE, ROBERT SMITH **(D)**
Chmn, Ala State Dem Party
b Talladega, Ala, May 10, 31; s Harrell Taylor Vance & Mae Smith V; m 1953 to Helen Rainey; c Robert S, Jr & Charles R. Educ: Univ Ala, BS, 50, JD, 52; George Washington Univ, LLM, 55; Omicron Delta Kappa; Beta Gamma Sigma; Delta Chi. Polit & Govt Pos: Chmn, Ala State Dem Party, 66-; deleg chmn, Dem Nat Conv, 68, deleg, 72; deleg chmn, Dem Nat Mid Term Conf, 74. Bus & Prof Pos: Partner, Vance, Thompson & Brown, Attorneys-at-law, 64- Mil Serv: Entered as 2nd Lt, Army, 52, released as 1st Lt, 54; Lt Col, Army Res, currently. Mem: Am, Ala & Birmingham Bar Asns; Nat Asn Dem State Chmn (pres, 73-75). Relig: Episcopal. Mailing Add: 2824 Shook Hill Rd Birmingham AL 35223

VANCE, ROY CARROLL **(R)**
Vt State Rep
Mailing Add: Danville VT 05828

VANCE, SHELDON BAIRD
b Crookston, Minn, Jan 18, 17; s Erskine Ward Vance & Helen Baird V; m 1939 to Jean Chambers; c Robert Clarke & Stephen Baird. Educ: Carleton Col, AB, 39; Harvard Law Sch, LLB, 42, JD, 73. Polit & Govt Pos: Econ analyst & third secy, Am Embassy, Rio de Janeiro, Brazil, 42-46; US vconsul, Nice, France & Monaco, 46-49; US Consul, Martinique, WIndies, 49-51; Belgium-Luxemburg Desk Off, Dept of State, Washington, DC, 51-54; first secy, Am Embassy, Brussels, 54-58; chief, Personnel Placement Branch for Africa, Mid East & SAsia, Dept of State, Washington, DC, 58-60; student, Sr Seminar in Foreign Rels, Dept of State, 60-61, dir, Off of Cent African Affairs, 61-62; dep chief of mission, Am Embassy, Addis Ababa, 62-66; sr foreign serv inspector, Dept of State, 66-67; US Ambassador to Chad, 67-69, Dem Repub of the Congo, formerly, Repub of Zaire, 69-74; sr adv to Secy of State & coordr int narcotics matters, currently. Bus & Prof Pos: Lawyer, Ropes, Gray, Best, Coolidge & Rugg, Boston, Mass, 42. Mem: Mass Bar; Foreign Serv Asn; Lions. Relig: Presbyterian. Legal Res: 8510 Lynwood Place Chevy Chase MD 20015 Mailing Add: Am Embassy Dept of State Washington DC 20521

VANCEL, TOM **(R)**
Chmn, Thomas Co Rep Comt, Ga
b Tazewell, Tenn, Sept 11, 38; s Curtis Vancel & Ethel Sandefur V; m 1967 to Glenda Roselyn Wells; c Randall Todd & Shannon Lamons. Educ: Univ Ga, BS in Pharm, 67. Polit & Govt Pos: Chmn, Thomas Co Young Rep, Ga, 74-75; chmn, Thomas Co Rep Comt, 75- Bus & Prof Pos: Employee, Brooks Drug Store, Tifton, Ga, 69-71 & Shepherd's Drug Store, Thomasville, 71- Mil Serv: Entered as Pvt E-1, Army, 57, released as E-6, 63. Mem: Ga Pharmaceutical Asn; Am Soc Hosp Pharmacists; Am Col Preceptors; Kiwanis (pres, Thomas Area Club). Relig: Methodist; mem, Admin Bd. Legal Res: Pavo Rd Thomasville GA 31792 Mailing Add: 123 E Jackson St Thomasville GA 31792

VAN CLEAVE, THOMAS WINLOCK **(D)**
Chmn, Bienville Parish Dem Exec Comt, La
b St Louis, Mo, Jan 9, 06; s Thomas Richard Van Cleave & Fanny Winlock V; m 1928 to Lelia Stark; c Barbara (Mrs Joiner). Educ: Rice Univ, 4 years. Polit & Govt Pos: Past pres,

Bienville Parish Policy Jury, La, mem, 44-; mem & chmn, Bienville Parish Dem Exec Comt, 56-; mem & pres, Red River Econ Develop Coun, Econ Develop Admin, 58- Bus & Prof Pos: Mgr then owner, Ice Bus Mfg Plant, cotton ginning & cotton buyer, sold feeds & fertilizers, Gibsland, 28-58; semi-retired, now managing timber lands & investments. Mem: Lions. Relig: Baptist. Mailing Add: Gibsland LA 71028

VAN CLIEF, DANIEL GOOD **(D)**
b Cleveland, Ohio, Feb 14, 25; s Ray Alan Van Clief & Margaret Good V; m 1946 to Margaret L Robertson; c Daniel Good, Jr & Barry Robertson, twins, Jan Courtlandt & Alan Sterling. Educ: Fishburne Mil Acad, high sch dipl. Polit & Govt Pos: Mem, Albemarle Co Dem Comt, Va, 65-; chmn, Scottsville Dist Dem Comt, 66-; mem, Va Comn of Outdoor Recreation, 66-70; mem, Va State Dem Finance Comt, currently; Va State Deleg, 68-74, mem, Va Adv Comt on Aviation, 68-; mem, Rural Affairs Study Comn, 68- Bus & Prof Pos: Farmer-financier, Nydrie Farms, Esmont, Va, 45-; dir, Thomas Jefferson Corp, Charlottesville, formerly; officer & dir, Fasig-Tipton Co, NY, currently; dir, Md State Fair, currently; dir, Crown Colony Club, Ltd, Chub Cay, Bahamas, currently; dir, Village Green Corp, Charlottesville, Va, currently; dir, Alderman 250 Corp, currently; trustee, Miller Sch of Albemarle, 68-; mem bd gov, Belfield Sch, formerly; dir, Grayson Found, Lexington, Ky, currently; mem sponsor comt, Univ Va Grad Sch Bus, currently. Mil Serv: Army, 4th Inf Div, ETO, World War II; ETO Ribbon with Silver Star & Bronze Arrowhead. Mem: Thoroughbred Owners & Breeders Asn of Am, Jamaica, NY (trustee); Va Thoroughbred Asn (past pres); Jockey Club, NY; Stonewall Jackson Coun, Boy Scouts (exec bd); Charlottesville YMCA (exec comt). Relig: Episcopal. Mailing Add: Nydrie Farms Esmont VA 22937

VAN DALSEM, PAUL **(D)**
Ark State Rep
Mailing Add: PO Box 67 Perryville AR 72126

VAN DEERLIN, LIONEL **(D)**
US Rep, Calif
b Los Angeles, Calif, July 25, 14; s Lionel Van Deerlin, Sr & Gladys Mary Young V; m 1940 to Mary Jo Smith; c Lionel James, Lawson John, Victoria, Elizabeth, Mary Susan & Jeffrey. Educ: Univ of Southern Calif, 37, BA, Journalism. Polit & Govt Pos: US Rep, Calif, 63-, mem, Comt on Interstate & Foreign Com & Subcomt on Commun & Power, US House of Rep, presently. Bus & Prof Pos: Newspaperman; radio & TV news ed & analyst. Mil Serv: Army, overseas serv in Mediterranean Theatre. Relig: Episcopal. Legal Res: 256 Eucalyptus Ct Chula Vista CA 92010 Mailing Add: 2427 Rayburn House Off Bldg Washington DC 20515

VANDERFORD, HORACE KEITH **(D)**
SC State Rep
b Union, SC, July 14, 38; s Albert Hope Vanderford (deceased) & Della Wiggins V; div; c Julie Renee. Educ: Union High Sch, SC, grad, 56. Polit & Govt Pos: Town councilman, Carlisle, SC, 64-66; magistrate, Fish Dam Twp, Union Co, Carlisle, 66-74; SC State Rep, Dist 43, Union & Chester Co, 74- Mil Serv: SC Army Nat Guard, 55-68. Mem: Union Co Farm Bur; Santuc Masonic Lodge 227. Mailing Add: PO Box 128 Carlisle SC 29031

VANDER HAEGEN, ELEANOR MARIE **(D)**
b Waltham, Mass, Feb 3, 41; d Hector Joseph Vander Haegen & Anna Conroy V; single. Educ: Emmanuel Col (Mass), AB, 62; Marquette Univ, MA, 69, Univ Minn, 69-; Alpha Kappa Delta; Pi Gamma Mu. Polit & Govt Pos: Mem, NH Dem Const Comt, 74; alt deleg, Dem Nat Mid-Term Conf, 74. Bus & Prof Pos: Asst prof sociol, Keene State Col, 72-, dir women's educ resource coop, 74. Mem: Am Sociol Asn; Soc for Study of Social Prob; Conn Valley Health Compact (adv bd). Mailing Add: 32 Prospect Keene NH 03431

VANDERHOOF, JOHN D **(R)**
b Rockyford, Colo, May 27, 22; s Roy Elvin Vanderhoof & Irene Church V; m 1943 to Lois June Taggart, div; c Bruce & Linda. Educ: Glendale Col, Calif, AA. Polit & Govt Pos: Colo State Rep, 55-70, Minority Leader, Colo House of Rep, 55-62 & 65-66, Speaker of the House, 63-64 & 67-70; deleg, Rep Nat Conv, 68; Lt Gov, Colo, 71-73, Gov, 73-74. Bus & Prof Pos: Owner, Van's Sporting Goods, Glenwood Springs, Colo, 46-55; pres, Glenwood Indust Bank, 55- & Bank of Glenwood, 63- Mil Serv: Entered as Aviation Cadet, Navy, 42, released as Lt(jg), 45, after serv in Pac; Purple Heart; Distinguished Flying Cross; Two Air Medals. Mem: AF&AM; Kiwanis; Elks; Eagles; Am Legion. Relig: Methodist. Legal Res: 1429 Grand Glenwood Springs CO 81601 Mailing Add: 400 E 8th Ave Denver CO 80203

VANDER JAGT, GUY **(R)**
US Rep, Mich
b Cadillac, Mich, Aug 26, 31; s Harry Vander Jagt & Marie Copier V; m 1964 to Carol Doorn; c Virginia Marie. Educ: Hope Col, BA, 53; Yale Univ Divinity Sch, BD, 57; Univ Mich Law Sch, LLB, 60. Polit & Govt Pos: Mich State Sen, 65-67; US Rep, Mich, 66- Bus & Prof Pos: News dir, WWTV, 56; lawyer, Warner, Norcross & Judd. Publ: Evidentiary problems of medical tests, Practical Lawyer, 61. Mem: Rotary; Mason. Relig: Presbyterian. Legal Res: Rt 1 6709 N Lindsey Rd Luther MI 49656 Mailing Add: 1026 Longworth Off Bldg Washington DC 20515

VANDERLAAN, ROBERT **(R)**
Mich State Sen
b Grand Rapids, Mich, June 4, 30; s John R VanderLaan; m 1951 to Mildred Bouma; c Linda Beth & Robert J. Educ: Calvin Col, AB, 52; Univ Mich, MA, 57. Polit & Govt Pos: Clerk, trustee & supvr, Paris Twp, Mich, formerly; Mich State Sen, 31st Dist, 62-; Majority Leader, Mich State Senate, 70-; vpres & mem exec comt, Coun State Govts, currently; alt deleg, Rep Nat Conv, 72. Bus & Prof Pos: Teacher hist & govt, South Christian High Sch, 7 years; part-time instr, Calvin Col, 62. Mem: South YMCA (bd of dirs). Relig: Christian Reformed. Mailing Add: 4745 Curwood SE Grand Rapids MI 49508

VANDERPERREN, CLETUS J **(D)**
Wis State Rep
b Pittsfield, Wis, Mar 4, 12; married. Educ: Mills Ctr Sch. Polit & Govt Pos: Mem, Town Bd, Green Bay, Wis, 26 years, Co Bd, 16 years; mem, Co Comts on Agr, Co Arena, Reforestation & Conserv, Roadside Zoning & Planning & Vets; Wis State Rep, 58-, mem, Comt Conserv, Wis State Assembly, 59, mem, Comt Agr, 59-67, vchmn, 65, mem, Legis Coun Water Resources Comt, 59, mem, Local Govt Comt, 63-67, mem, Taxation Comt, 61-63, mem, Printing Comt, 63, mem, Joint Comt to Visit State Properties, 63-, chmn, 65, mem, State Affairs Comt, 65, mem, Transportation Comt, 65-, chmn, 71, mem, Comts on Municipalities, Pub Welfare & Joint Interim, 69, vchmn, Hwy Comt, 71-73, chmn, 73-, mem, Comt Excise & Fees, 71-, chmn, 73-; mem, State Bldg Comn, 71-, mem, Interim Hwy Adv Comt & Coun on Hwy Safety, currently. Bus & Prof Pos: Farm owner & operator. Mem: Farm Bur; Local Dairy Herd Improv Coop; Tri-Co Fire Dept (past pres & secy-treas). Mailing Add: Rte 5 Green Bay WI 54303

VANDER VEEN, RICHARD FRANK **(D)**
US Rep, Mich
b Grand Rapids, Mich, Nov 26, 22; s Frank Vander Veen; m to Marion Coward; c Richard, Lawrence & Paul. Educ: Univ SC, 46; Harvard Univ Law Sch, LLB, 49; Sigma Chi. Polit & Govt Pos: Chmn, Fifth Dist Dem Comt, 59; chmn, Dem State Conv, 60, deleg, 62-64; deleg, Dem Mid-Term Conf, 74; US Rep, Mich, 74-, mem ways & means comt, US House Rep, 74- Bus & Prof Pos: Pres, Vander Veen, Freihofer & Cook, PC, 74. Mil Serv: Active duty with Navy during World War II & Korean Conflict. Mem: Grand Rapids & Mich Bar Asns; Congress for Peace through Law. Relig: Presbyterian. Legal Res: 501 Edgemere Dr Grand Rapids MI 49502 Mailing Add: 1232 Longworth House Off Bldg Washington DC 20515

VANDER VORST, WILBUR **(R)**
NDak State Rep
Mailing Add: State Capitol Bismarck ND 58501

VANDER WAL, JERRY DUANE **(R)**
b Pella, Iowa, Aug 7, 53; s Jake Albert Vander Wal & Delia Wielaard V; single. Educ: Marshalltown Community Col, Iowa, 71-72; Grand View Col, 73-; Iowa Col Young Rep Fedn. Polit & Govt Pos: Deleg, Iowa Presidential & Statutory Conv, 72; alt deleg, Rep Nat Conv, 72; campus chmn, US Sen Jack Miller, US Rep H R Gross & Gov Robert D Ray, Iowa, 72; precinct committeeman, Marshall Co Rep Cent Comt, Iowa, 72-73; legis aide, Iowa State Rep R De Jong, 73- Relig: Christian Reformed. Mailing Add: 1108 Third Ave W Oskaloosa IA 52577

VANDERWALL, MARY ELIZABETH **(R)**
Treas, Idaho Co Rep Cent Comt, Idaho
b Grangeville, Idaho, June 15, 52; d John William Wagner & Madelyn Sanberg W; m 1970 to Terry Gene Vanderwall; c Eric Jason & Mark Alan. Educ: Univ Idaho, 70-71. Polit & Govt Pos: Treas, Idaho Co Rep Cent Comt, Idaho, 73-; Idaho Co coordr for Wayne Kidwell, Idaho's Attorney Gen, 74- Mem: Hosp Auxiliary (publicity chmn, 75); Beta Sigma Phi; Gamma Beta (corresponding secy, 75-); Idaho Co Heart Fund (SW Sect Capt, 75); Grangeville Country Club; Idaho Co Farm Bur. Relig: Christian. Mailing Add: 512 Lincoln Grangeville ID 83530

VANDETTE, EDMUND FREDERICK **(R)**
Chmn, 11th Cong Dist Rep Party, Mich
b Houghton, Mich, Aug 8, 32; s Bernard Vandette & Elsie Hietala V; m 1954 to June Helen Randell; c Edmund Mark & Robert Alan. Educ: Northern Mich Univ, BS, 58; Univ Mich, MA, 59; Ohio State Univ, work on PhD; Kappa Delta Pi; Alpha Phi Omega. Polit & Govt Pos: Pres, Men's Rep Club, Houghton Co, Mich, 67-68; chmn, Houghton Co Rep Party, 68-70; western regional chmn, Upper Peninsula of Mich, 69; deleg, Rep State Conv, 69; chmn, 11th Cong Dist Rep Party, 71-; mem, Mich Higher Educ Assistance Authority Bd. Bus & Prof Pos: Assoc prof, Mich Tech Univ, 59- Mil Serv: Entered as A/S, Navy, 51, released as Fireman 1/C, 53, after serv in USS Sea Robin, SS407, Submarine Serv, Atlantic Theatre; Am Nat Defense Medal; Submarine Dolphins. Mem: Am Asn Univ Profs; Mich Tech Univ Faculty Asn; Copper Country Kiwanis Club (pres); Elks. Honors & Awards: Outstanding Teacher of the Year Award, Adult Educ Asn Mich. Relig: Catholic. Mailing Add: US 41 Chassell MI 49916

VAN DEUSEN, ROBERT MOON **(D)**
b Jacksonville, Fla, Mar 30, 47; s Robert Holt van Deusen & Martha Florence Moon van D; m 1968 to Eleanor Joyce Procter. Educ: DePauw Univ, 65-67; Coe Col, 71-74. Polit & Govt Pos: Deleg, Dem Nat Conv, 72; mem, Dem Nat Credentials Comt, 72; regional organizer, McGovern Campaign Staff of Iowa, 72; mem, Iowa Conv Reform Comn, 73; vchairperson, Linn Co Dem Cent Comt, 73-74; mem, Cong Michael Blouin's Campaign Staff, Second Dist, Iowa, 74. Bus & Prof Pos: Elem sch teacher, Nixon Elem Sch, Cedar Rapids, Iowa, currently. Mil Serv: Entered as Airman Basic, Air Force, 67, released as Airman 1/C, 71, after serv as a Chinese linquist in the Security Serv, 67-71. Mem: Nat Comt for Sane Nuclear Policy; Am Civil Liberties Union; Nat Orgn for Women; Am Fedn Teachers; Nat Womens' Polit Caucus. Relig: Unitarian. Mailing Add: 383 19th St SE Cedar Rapids IA 52403

VANDEVER, RUTH ANN **(D)**
b Havre, Mont, June 25, 35; d James G Pedersen & Ruth Rhoades P; m 1956 to William Mathewson Vandever; c Lisa & Jennifer. Educ: Univ Wash Sch Pharm, BS, 57. Polit & Govt Pos: Precinct committeewoman, Dem Party, 70-; alt deleg, Dem Nat Conv, 72. Bus & Prof Pos: Asst chief pharmacist, King Co Hosp, Seattle, 57-61; staff pharmacist, Bryn Mawr Hosp, Pa, 63-64, Good Samaritan Hosp, Portland, Ore, 67- Mem: Multonomah Coun Women's Equality (steering comt, 72-); Nat Women's Polit Caucus; Politically Oriented Women (bd gov, 70-). Mailing Add: 2226 NE 27th Ave Portland OR 97212

VAN DE WATER, MARGARET SMITH **(D)**
Committeewoman, Fla Dem State Exec Comt
b Putnam, Okla, Apr 10, 19; d Theron Samuel Smith & Dollie Marlett S; m 1946 to Malcolm Stickle Van de Water, MD; c Donald, MD, Malcolm S, Jr, Carol (Mrs Joseph Balint), Ava Leslie & Kenneth. Educ: Southwestern State Col, BA, 40. Polit & Govt Pos: Secy, Off War Info, Washington, DC, 42-45; secy, Dem Nat Comt, 45-48; mem, Palm Beach Co Dem Exec Comt, Fla, 71-; committeewoman, Fla Dem State Exec Comt, Palm Beach Co, 74- Mem: Woman's Auxiliary Palm Beach Med Soc; League of Women Voters; Sailfish Club of Fla. Relig: Episcopal. Mailing Add: 266 Monterey Rd Palm Beach FL 33480

VAN DOREN, CHARLES NORTON
Dep Gen Counsel, Arms Control & Disarmament Agency
b Orange, NJ, Apr 7, 24; s Durand H Van Doren & Marie Norton V; m 1967 to Regina Ridder; c Catherine Joan Harris (stepdaughter), Harold Charter, Rebecca Elsie, Margaret Alice & Marie Regina. Educ: Harvard Col, 42-43 & 46; Columbia Law Sch, LLB, 49; ed, Columbia Law Rev, 47-49. Polit & Govt Pos: Vpres, South Orange-Maplewood Adult Sch, 59-61; legal adv to US Disarmament Deleg, 63; asst gen counsel, Arms Control & Disarmament Agency, 63-64, dep gen counsel, 64-, acting gen counsel, 69; US Rep to Conf on Non-Nuclear States, 68; mem US deleg, Int Atomic Energy Agency Safeguards Comt, 70. Bus & Prof Pos: Assoc lawyer, Simpson Thacher & Bartlett, New York, 49-60, partner, 61. Mil Serv: Entered as Pvt, Army, 43, released as T-5, 45, after serv in First Cavalry Div Pac Theater. Mem: Am Soc Int Law; NY Co Lawyers Asn; Fed Bar Asn. Honors & Awards:

Harvard Prize Scholarship, 42-43; Harlan Fiske Stone Scholar, Columbia Law Sch, 46-47; Meritorious Honor Award, Arms Control & Disarmament Agency, 67, Outstanding Performance Awards, 67, 68, 69 & 72. Relig: Unitarian. Mailing Add: 1387 Locust Rd NW Washington DC 20012

VAN DUSEN, RICHARD CAMPBELL (R)
b Jackson, Mich, July 18, 25; s Bruce Buick Van Dusen & Helen Campbell V; m 1949 to Barbara Congdon; c Amanda, Lisa & Katherine. Educ: Univ Minn, BS, 45; Harvard Law Sch, LLB, 49. Polit & Govt Pos: Mich State Rep, 54-56; deleg, Mich Constitutional Conv, 61-62; legal adv to Gov, Mich, 63; deleg, Rep Nat Conv, 64, alt deleg, 68; Under Secy, US Dept of Housing & Urban Develop, 69-73; mem coun, Admin Conf of US, 69-73. Bus & Prof Pos: Attorney, Dickinson, Wright, McKean & Cudlip, 49-52, 64-69 & 73- Mil Serv: Entered as A/S, Navy, 43, released as Ens, 46, after serv in Pac. Mem: Am & Detroit Bar Asns; State Bar of Mich. Relig: Episcopal. Mailing Add: 32205 Bingham Rd Birmingham MI 48010

VAN DUYNE, LEROY (D)
Ill State Sen
Mailing Add: 806 Blackhawk Joliet IL 60432

VAN DUZER, JOHN FREDERICK (R)
Chmn, Guthrie Co Rep Cent Comt, Iowa
b Menlo, Iowa, May 9, 15; s John Elliott Van Duzer & Ethel Rose Connin V; m 1942 to Virginia Cooley; c Carole (Mrs Richard Pritchard) & Sarah (Mrs Creighton Nelson). Educ: Menlo High Sch, Iowa, 33. Polit & Govt Pos: Chmn, Guthrie Co Rep Cent Comt, Iowa, 72- Bus & Prof Pos: Self-employed, Menlo Farm Supply, currently. Mil Serv: Entered as Pvt, Air Force, 42, released as T/Sgt, 45, after serv in Air Transport Command, African Theatre, 43-45. Mem: Mason; Am Legion (Comdr, Post 511). Relig: Methodist. Mailing Add: Menlo IA 50164

VAN DYK, JERILYN K (D)
b Bellingham, Wash, May 6, 43; d Otto C Noteboom & Esther L Frazier N; m 1964 to R Daniel Van Dyk; c Jeffrey Daniel. Educ: Wash State Univ, BA in hist, 66. Polit & Govt Pos: Alt deleg, Dem Nat Conv, 72; precinct committeeperson, Dem Party, 74- Bus & Prof Pos: Equal opportunity consult, Wa State Human Rights Comn, 75- Mem: YWCA (bd mem); NOW; Coalition of Labor Union Women; Am Fedn State, Co & Munic Employees. Relig: United Methodist. Mailing Add: 7585 Noon Rd Lynden WA 98264

VAN DYKEN, LAMBERTUS PETER (BERT) (R)
Mem, Calif Rep State Cent Comt
b Manhattan, Mont, May 20, 10; s Peter L Van Dyken & Margaret Krappe V; m 1932 to Magdalyn Baker; c Edna Mae (Mrs Van Laar), Douglas W, Leona Ruth (Mrs Stuit), Lloyd E & Verna Jean. Educ: Ripon Union Schs. Polit & Govt Pos: Mem, United Rep Calif, 66-; mem, San Joaquin Co Cent Comt, 67-, chmn, 71-74; mem, Calif Rep Assembly, 68- & Calif Rep State Cent Comt, 70- Bus & Prof Pos: Mem bd trustees, Ripon Christian Schs, Calif, 50-55 & Bethany Christian Home, 60-67. Mem: Calif Co Chmn Asn; Farm Bur; Assoc Farmers; Stockton Gospel Rescue Mission (bd mem,). Relig: Christian Reformed Church of America. Mailing Add: 13328 E West Ripon Rd Ripon CA 95366

VAN GILST, BASS (D)
Iowa State Sen
b Pella, Iowa, Apr 14, 11; s Peter Van Gilst & Nellie Klein V; m 1937 to Harriet E DeBrum; c Ken, Carl, Elaine, Mark, Diane & Jolen. Polit & Govt Pos: Iowa State Sen, 65- Bus & Prof Pos: Pres, Marion-Mahaska FS Services, Exten Coun; pres, Sch Bd, formerly. Mem: Farm Bur; CofC; Oskaloosa Lions. Relig: Christian Reformed Church. Mailing Add: Rte 4 Oskaloosa IA 52577

VAN HARLINGEN, WILLIAM M, JR (R)
Chmn, Beaufort Co Rep Comt, SC
b Transfer, Pa, June 21, 17; s William M Van Harlingen & Katherine Frampton V; m 1944 to Jewell Harris; c David Lawrence. Educ: US Mil Acad, BS, 39; Univ Mich, Ann Arbor, MSE, 51; George Washington Univ, BA, 64; Harvard Univ Sch Bus Admin, 62. Polit & Govt Pos: Chmn, Beaufort Co Rep Comt, SC, 74- Bus & Prof Pos: Vpres, Output Systs Corp, 70-71. Mil Serv: Entered as Cadet, Army, 35, released as Brigadier Gen, after serv in many assignments throughout the world; Distinguished Serv Medal; Legion of Merit with Oak Leaf Cluster; Air Medal with Four Oak Leaf Clusters; plus others. Publ: Army transistor program, Armed Forces Commun & Electronics Asn, 10/54; Opportunity for leadership & community service, Air Force Sgts Asn J, 6/67; co-ed, Your Government & the Environment, Output Systs Corp, 71. Mem: DAV; Asn of US Army. Relig: Episcopal. Legal Res: 504 East St Beaufort SC 29902 Mailing Add: PO Box 708 Beaufort SC 29902

VAN HEYDE, ROBERT LEE (D)
State Cent Committeeman, Ohio Dem Party
b Columbus, Ohio, Jan 7, 30; s Clyde Leo Van Heyde & Emma Walker V; m 1955 to Renee Michael; c Christina, Robert Lee, Jr, Theresa, Eric, Renee & Thomas Jefferson. Educ: Ohio State Univ, BA, 56, LLB, 59, JD, 66. Polit & Govt Pos: City Councilman, Columbus, Ohio, 58-61; mem, Columbus Metrop Airport, 65-69, chmn, 66-68; alt deleg, Dem Nat Conv, 68 & 72; State Cent Committeeman, Ohio Dem Party, 68-; deleg, Dem Nat Mid-Term Conf, 74. Bus & Prof Pos: Attorney-at-law, 59- Mil Serv: Entered as Seaman, Navy, 48, released as RM 3/C, 52, after serv in Atlantic, 48-52. Mem: Am Bar Asn; YMCA; Urban League; Navy League; Elks. Relig: Catholic. Legal Res: 761 Highland Dr Columbus OH 43214 Mailing Add: 895 S High St Columbus OH 43206

VAN HOLLEBEKE, RAY (D)
Wash State Sen
Mailing Add: 18735 53rd NE Seattle WA 98155

VAN HORN, DAVID LEE (D)
Ky State Rep
Mailing Add: 1024 Juniper Dr Lexington KY 40504

VAN HORN, LYLE CECIL (R)
VChmn, Ill Rep State Cent Comt
b Cerro Gordo, Ill, Apr 14, 12; s William C Van Horn & Bessie Chapman V; m 1938 to Ruth J Iliff; c Thomas D & Warren M. Educ: Ill Wesleyan Univ, BS, 36; Theta Chi. Polit & Govt Pos: Alt deleg, Rep Nat Conv, 64 and deleg, 68; mem, Gov Adv Coun, 69-; mem agr export adv comt, Ill Dept of Agr, 69-; mem, Ill Rep State Cent Comt, 70-, vchmn, 75- Bus & Prof Pos: Pres, Van Horn Hybrids, Inc, 55-69. Mem: Ill Crop Improv Asn, Piatt Co Farm Bur; Mason; Shrine; Bloomington Consistory. Relig: United Methodist. Mailing Add: 121 Arnold Dr Cerro Gordo IL 61818

VAN HORN, MICHAEL (R)
b Prague, Czechoslovakia, June 15, 28; s Anthony Jednorozec & Libuse Nygrynova J; m to Gilda K Wills; c Connie D, Vickie L & Michael Anthony. Educ: Charles Univ, Prague, 3 years of Architecture. Polit & Govt Pos: Vpres, Young Rep of Los Angeles Co, Calif, 61; assembly dist chmn, United Rep of Calif, 63, gov, Area 11, 64-66, state vchmn, 67-68, state chmn, formerly; mem, State Rep Cent & Exec Comts, Calif, formerly; mem, Los Angeles Co Rep Cent Comt, formerly, mem exec comt & chmn, formerly. Mil Serv: Mem, Spec Forces of Czech Army, 48; Mem, Blesk, Partisan Group against German Forces, 44-45; Seven Partisan & Mil Awards. Mem: Los Angeles Jr CofC; Culver City Jr CofC; United Farmers Agent's Asn. Honors & Awards: Citizenship, Rep & Speaking Awards. Relig: Baptist. Legal Res: 5428 41st St Lubbock TX 79407 Mailing Add: PO Box 16770 Lubbock TX 79490

VAN HOY, JOHN HOBERT (R)
Chmn, Fifth Cong Dist Rep Party, Va
b Ellenton, SC, Feb 6, 27; s John Hobert Van Hoy, Sr & Bessie S Flowers V H; m 1948 to Shirley De Forest; c Robert Eric, Carolyn, John L & Patricia. Educ: Longwood Col, 1 year; Southern Col Optom, OD; Omega Delta. Polit & Govt Pos: Chmn, Mecklenburg Co Rep Party, Va, 68-71 & 73-; chmn, Fifth Cong Dist Rep Party, Va, 70- Mil Serv: Entered as Pvt, Army Air Force, 44, released as Sgt, 45, after serv in 1252nd Army Air Force Base Unit, NAfrican Div, 44-45. Mem: Va Optom Asn; Piedmont Optom Soc; Am Acad Optom; Lions; Chase City CofC. Relig: Methodist. Legal Res: 638 N Main St Chase City VA 23924 Mailing Add: PO Box 218 Chase City VA 23924

VANIK, CHARLES A (D)
US Rep, Ohio
b Cleveland, Ohio, Apr 6, 13; s Charles Anton Vanik & Stella Kvasnicka V; m 1947 to Betty M; c Phyllis Jean & John Charles. Educ: Adelbert Col, Western Reserve Univ, AB, 33; Western Reserve Law Sch, LLB, 36. Polit & Govt Pos: Referee, Ohio State Indust Comn, 36; attorney-examr, Ohio State Dept of Hwy, 37; mem, Cleveland City Coun, 38-39; Ohio State Sen, 40-41; mem, Cleveland Bd of Educ, 41-42; mem, Cleveland Libr Bd, 46-47; assoc judge, Cleveland Munic Court, 47-54; US Rep, 21st Dist, Ohio, 55-68, 22nd Dist, 69- Bus & Prof Pos: Attorney-at-law, Vanik, Monroe, Zucco & Klein, 36- Mil Serv: Entered as Ens, Naval Res, 42, released as Lt(sg), 46, after serv in Amphibious Forces, Invasions of NAfrica, Sicily & Okinawa. Mem: Cleveland & Cuyahoga Co Bar Asns. Relig: Roman Catholic. Legal Res: 24799 Lake Shore Blvd Euclid OH 44123 Mailing Add: 2371 Rayburn House Off Bldg Washington DC 20515

VAN LOAN, ANNA S (R)
NH State Rep
b Manchester, Aug 20, 12; married; c four. Educ: Pembroke Col. Polit & Govt Pos: NH State Rep, 63-66 & 71-; mem sch bd. Relig: Protestant. Mailing Add: 62 Wallace Rd Bedford NH 03102

VAN METER, DONALD EDWARD (R)
City Councilman, Lawton, Okla
b Kansas City, Mo, Sept 7, 37; s O E Van Meter & Lucile Taylor V; m 1959 to Rose Ann Shackle; c Brice Edward & Victoria Ann. Educ: Univ Okla, BS, 60, JD, 72; Phi Alpha Delta; Delta Sigma Phi. Polit & Govt Pos: Mem, Human Rels Comn, Norman, Okla, 71-72; chmn, Comanche Co Rep Party, 72-; city councilman, Lawton, 74- Bus & Prof Pos: Pvt practice, attorney-at-law, 72- Mil Serv: Entered as 2nd Lt, Air Force, 60, released as Capt, 69, after serv in Air Rescue Serv, Mil Airlift Command; Maj, Army Res, 74-; Distinguished Flying Cross with Oak Leaf Cluster; Air Medal with 10 Oak Leaf Clusters; Air Force Commendation Medal with Oak Leaf Cluster; Combat Readiness Medal; Nat Defense Medal; Armed Forces Expeditionary Medal; Vietnam Serv Medal with 2 Silver Stars. Mem: Optimist Int; Mason. Legal Res: 12 Camelot Dr Lawton OK 73501 Mailing Add: 626 D Ave PO Box 542 Lawton OK 73501

VANMETER, SHEILA CROFT (D)
b New York, NY, Mar 26, 39; d William Hilton Croft & Beverly Brenner C; m 1967 to William Larry VanMeter. Educ: Stetson Univ, 57-58; Ohlone Col, 74-; Beta Sigma Phi; Alpha Chi Omega. Polit & Govt Pos: Deleg, Dem Nat Mid-Term Conf, 74; assoc mem, Calif Dem State Cent Comt, 75- Mem: Fremont Dem Women's Forum; Southern Alameda Co New Dem Coalition (hq co-chmn, 75). Relig: Episcopal. Mailing Add: 42835 Charleston Way Fremont CA 94538

VAN METER, THOMAS ADAMS (R)
Ohio State Sen
b Detroit, Mich, Apr 22, 43 to Lord Wright Van Meter & Gwen H Paracheck V; m 1965 to Nancy Josephine Arch; c Margaret Elizabeth & Stephanie Ann. Educ: Ashland Col, AB, 65; Ohio State Law Sch, 65-66; US Army Inf Sch, Ft Benning, Ga, grad, 67; Sigma Nu. Polit & Govt Pos: Cong asst to US Rep John M Ashbrook, Ohio, 65-67; chmn, Ashland Co Rep Finance Comt, Ohio, 70-; co-exec chmn, Ashland Co Rep Party, 70-; Ohio State Sen, 19th Dist, 73- Bus & Prof Pos: Asst registr, Ashland Col, 70-, mem, Bd Trustees, 73- Mil Serv: Entered as Pvt E-1, Army, 67, released as 1st Lt, 69, after serv in Co E, 1st Bn 22nd Inf, 4th Inf Div, Rep of SVietnam; 1st Lt, Army Res, 70; Nat Defense Serv Medal; Vietnam Serv Medal; Vietnam Campaign Ribbon, three Stars; Combat Infantryman's Badge; Vietnam Cross of Gallantry; Bronze Star. Mem: Ivy Leaguers, 4th Inf Div; Am Legion; VFW; F&AM. Honors & Awards: Sigma Nu Brother of Year, Ashland Col Chap, 65; Outstanding Leadership as Pres of Ashland Co Student Body, City of Ashland, 65. Relig: First Brethren Church. Legal Res: 1028 Country Club Lane Ashland OH 44805 Mailing Add: Ohio Senate State House Broad & High St Columbus OH 43215

VANN, ALBERT (D)
NY State Assemblyman
Mailing Add: 400 Herkimer St Brooklyn NY 11213

VANN, DAVID J (D)
City Councilman, Birmingham, Ala
b Roanoke, Ala, Aug 10, 28; s Clyde Harold Vann & Ruth Johnson V; m 1965 to Lillian Foscue; c Lillian Ruth & Cora Elizabeth (deceased). Educ: Univ Ala, BS in Commerce, 50 & LLB, 51; George Washington Univ, LLM, 53; Beta Gamma Sigma; Omicron Delta Kappa; Farrah Order of Jurisp; Phi Alpha Delta. Polit & Govt Pos: Law clerk, Justice Black, US

Supreme Court, 53-54; chmn, Jefferson Co Dem Campaign Comt, Ala, 60-62; chmn, Ala Independent Dem Party, 67-; alt deleg, Dem Nat Conv, 68; city councilman, Birmingham, Ala, 71- Bus & Prof Pos: Assoc attorney, White, Bradley, Arant, All & Rose, 54-63; partner, Vann & Patrick, 63-64 & Berkowitz, Lefkovits, Vann & Patrick, 65-69; independent practice, 70- Mil Serv: Entered as Pvt, Army, 46, released as Sgt, 47, after serv in 31FA Br, Seventh Div, Korea; 1st Lt, Counter Intel, Res, 51-53. Mem: Nat Munic League; Wesley Found (chmn bd dirs, 67-); KofP; Lions; Young Men's Bus Club of Birmingham. Relig: United Methodist; Chmn, Comn Race & Relig, NAla Conf, United Methodist Church. Legal Res: 4201 Cliff Rd Birmingham AL 35222 Mailing Add: 703 Frank Nelson Bldg Birmingham AL 35203

VANN, EARL (D)
Pa State Rep
b Wilmington, NC, Oct 18, 13; s Joseph Vann & Carrie Eagles V; m 1936 to Ada Gladden. Educ: Univ Pa, 3 years; Phi Beta Sigma. Polit & Govt Pos: State bldg inspector, Dept Labor & Indust, Philadelphia, Pa, 55-62; clerk, Bd Rev of Taxes, 62-63; tax revenue collector, Philadelphia, Pa, 63-64; Pa State Rep, 66- Bus & Prof Pos: Owner, Beer Distributing, 45-55. Mil Serv: Entered as A/S, Coast Guard, 42, released as 3/C Signalman, 45, after serv in 7th Fleet Task Force, Pac Theatre, 43-45. Mem: Am Legion; NAACP; Urban League; Fel Comn; YMCA. Honors & Awards: Local 1163 State, Co & Munic Workers Award; Phi Beta Sigma Man of the Year Award, 67; Los Hermanos Outstanding Achievement Award; Rheingold Beer Community Achievement Award. Relig: Episcopal. Legal Res: 1329 S 22nd St Philadelphia PA 19146 Mailing Add: Capitol Bldg Harrisburg PA 17120

VANN, FRANK COCHRAN (D)
Secy, Mitchell Co Dem Exec Comt, Ga
b Camilla, Ga; s Emory Judson Vann, Jr & Mary Cochran V; m 1957 to Alicine Janie Cagle; c Frank Cochran, Jr, Elizabeth Janie, Mary Georgia & Scott Emory. Educ: Va Mil Inst, BA, 49; Univ Fla Col of Law, 49-50; Univ Ga Col of Law, JD, 51; Judge Advocate Gen Sch, Univ Va, 52-53; Kappa Alpha; Phi Delta Phi. Polit & Govt Pos: Solicitor, Camilla & Pelham City Courts, Ga, 56-64; secy, Mitchell Co Dem Exec Comt, 66-; Ga State Sen, Tenth Dist, 69-70. Bus & Prof Pos: Attorney-at-law, 51-; dir, Planters & Citizens Bank, 52-, vpres, 69-70, chmn bd, 70- Mil Serv: 1st Lt, Army, 52-54, with serv in Korean Base Sect, Korea, 53-54; Bronze Star; Presidential Unit Citation; Korean Serv Medal with Two Battle Stars; UN Serv Medal; Korean Presidential Unit citation; Nat Defense Serv Medal. Mem: State Bar of Ga (mem bd gov, 67-68 & 72-); Lions (present ed, Club Bul), Ga Lions Lighthouse Found (trustee); CofC; VFW. Honors & Awards: Outstanding Zone Chmn Award Dist 18-C Lions, 62-63; Outstanding Dep Dist Gov, 63-64. Relig: United Methodist; Mem off Bd, Camilla United Methodist Church. Legal Res: 227 Main St Camilla GA 31730 Mailing Add: PO Box 387 Camilla GA 31730

VANNEMAN, EDGAR, JR (R)
Mayor, Evanston, Ill
b El Paso, Ill, Aug 24, 19; s Edgar Vanneman & Fern Huffington V; m 1951 to Shirli Thomas; c Jill & Thomas. Educ: Northwestern Univ Sch Bus Admin, BS, 41, Sch Law, JD, 47; Phi Eta Sigma; Alpha Delta Phi. Polit & Govt Pos: Alt deleg, Rep Nat Conv, 52 & 56; alderman, Evanston, Ill, 57-65, mem, Zoning Bd of Appeals, 65-70, mayor, 70-; comnr, Northeast Evanston Park Dist, 65-70; mem bd, Sch Dist 202, 68-70; chmn, Cook Co Coun of Govt, 72-74. Mil Serv: Entered as Pvt, Army Air Force, 42, released as Maj, 46, after serv in 33rd Statist Control Unit, Bomber Command, Guam, 44-45; Bronze Star. Mailing Add: 715 Monticello Pl Evanston IL 60201

VAN OSDELL, JAMES BARR (D)
SC State Rep
b Miami, Fla, Dec 31, 42; s John Garrett Van Osdell & Virginia Barr O; m 1968 to Elaine Camp; c James Garrett. Educ: Univ SC, AB, 64, Law Sch, JD, 67; Sigma Chi. Polit & Govt Pos: SC State Rep, Dist 103, 73-, mem, Judiciary Comt, second vchmn, Rules Comt, SC House Rep, 73- Bus & Prof Pos: Attorney-at-law, Copeland & Van Osdell, Myrtle Beach, SC, 68-74, Van Osdell & Lester, 74- Mem: Civitan Club Myrtle Beach; Sertoma Club Myrtle Beach. Relig: Presbyterian. Mailing Add: 4904 Pine Lakes Dr Myrtle Beach SC 29577

VAN SICKLE, TOM R (R)
State Treas, Kans
b Vernon Co, Mo, June 22, 37; s Vincent Van Sickle & Welcome Hinderliter V; m 1964 to Suzanne Galvin; c David. Educ: Baker Univ, 55-58; Kans Univ, BA in polit sci, 59; Washburn Univ Law Sch, LLB, 61, JD, 66; Delta Tau Delta; Phi Alpha Delta. Polit & Govt Pos: Young Rep Club, Baker Univ, 56; Kans State Rep, 58-60; exec secy, Young Rep Nat Fedn, 59-61, nat committeeman from Kans, 63-65, chmn, 65-67; chief page, Rep Nat Conv, 60; Kans State Sen, Seventh Dist, 60-72, chmn, Ways & Means Comt & Indust Develop & Aeronaut Comt, Kans State Senate, vchmn, Comt on Comts, mem, Commercial & Financial Insts Comt, Judiciary Comt & Legis & Cong Apportionment Comt; mem, State Finance Coun; vchmn, Arn for Senate Comt, 62; campaign adv, Lukens for Young Rep Nat Fedn Chmn, 63; asst to nat dir, Draft Goldwater Comt, 63, asst coordr conv activities & asst to dirs field opers, Goldwater for President Comt, 64, dir field opers, Citizens for Goldwater-Miller, 64; State Treas, Kans, 73- Bus & Prof Pos: With Coca Cola Bottling Co, 58; advert rep, Ft Scott Tribune, Kans, 59; staff asst, Menninger Found, Topeka, 61-63, partner, Law Firm of Van Sickle & Nuss, Ft Scott, currently. Mem: Grange; Farm Bur; Jaycees; 4-H Club. Honors & Awards: Selected One of Outstanding Young Men of Am, Jaycees, 65; Man of Year, Ft Scott Jaycees, 59; State 4-H Leadership Champion, 55. Relig: Methodist. Mailing Add: PO Box 630 Ft Scott KS 66701

VAN SINGEL, DONALD (R)
Mich State Rep
b Grant, Mich, Aug 24, 43; s Peter S Van Singel & Grace H Geers V; m 1970 to Marsha Beth Ashcroft; c Douglas Adam & Kimberly. Educ: Mich State Univ, BS, 65. Polit & Govt Pos: Secy, Newaygo Co Rep Party, Mich, 71-72; Mich State Rep, 73- Bus & Prof Pos: Mem & treas, Mich Celery Prom Coop, 72-; dir, Grant State Bank. Mil Serv: Entered as 2nd Lt, Army, 66, released as 1st Lt, 67, after serv in 502nd Mil Intel Bn, Korea, 66-67; Capt, Army Res, 67-; honor grad, US Army Southeastern Signal Corp Sch. Mem: Mich Farm Bur; Great Lakes Vegetable Growers. Relig: Reformed Church in America; deacon. Legal Res: 2620 128th St Grant MI 49327 Mailing Add: State Capitol Lansing MI 48901

VAN TIL, GEORGE W (D)
b Hammond, Ind, July 20, 47; s William Van Til & Josie V T; m 1965 to Elizabeth Wagner; c Scott Wendell. Educ: Ind Univ Northwest, Gary, 67-71; pres, Polit Sci Club, 69, Ind Univ Northwest Young Dem, 70 & Lake Co Collegiate Young Dem, 71. Polit & Govt Pos: Campaign staff, former Ind Gov Matthew Welsh, 72; admin asst to Dem Minority Leader, Ind House Rep, 72-73; Highland Town Bd Trustee, Ind, 72-; dir, Northwest Ind Constituent Off, US Sen Vance Hartke, Hammond, Ind, 73- Mem: Charter mem Northwest Ind Trustee's Round Table; Ind Planning Asn; Ind Asn Cities & Towns; Northwest Ind Comprehensive Health Planning Coun; Am Pub Works Asn. Honors & Awards: Presidential Award for Outstanding Leadership, Ind Collegiate Young Dem, 70; Youngest official ever elected in the town of Highland, 71; Youngest elected official in Lake Co, Ind, currently; Perfect town bd attendance record, 72-75. Legal Res: 2627 40th Pl Highland IN 46322 Mailing Add: 417 Fed Bldg 507 State St Hammond IN 46320

VAN VELZOR, JAMES DANIEL (R)
Wyo State Rep
b Warren, Mich, Apr 11, 22; s Roscoe D Van Velzor & Marie A Kelly V; m 1943 to D Darleen Boyd; c M Sue (Mrs Mike King) & M Jo (Mrs David Reng). Educ: Cent High Sch, Lansing, Mich, grad, 41. Polit & Govt Pos: Wyo State Rep, 67-72 & 75-; mayor, Cheyenne, Wyo, 72-73; lobbyist, Wyo Asn of Municipalities, Wyo State Legis, 73- Bus & Prof Pos: Owner, Van Velzor's House of Music, Cheyenne, Wyo, 60- Mil Serv: Entered as Pvt, Army Air Corps, 41, Capt(Ret), 47, after serv in 9th Inf Div, ETO, 44; Combat Inf Badge; Purple Heart. Mem: Cheyenne Lions Club; AF&AM (32 degree); Shrine; life mem DAV; VFW. Relig: Baptist. Mailing Add: 1807 Milton Dr Cheyenne WY 82001

VAN VLIET, TONY (R)
Ore State Rep
b San Francisco, Calif, Jan 11, 30; m to Louise; c Dan, Susan, Mary Ann & Bill. Educ: Ore State Univ, BS, 53, MS, 58; Mich State Univ, PhD, 70. Polit & Govt Pos: Ore State Rep, 35th Dist, 75- Bus & Prof Pos: Teacher forestry, Ore State Univ, 55-58, 60-63 & 63-74; asst plant mgr, Bohemia Lumber Co, Culp Creek, Ore, 59-60; wood prod exten specialist, Exten & Sch Forestry, Ore State Univ, 63-71, assoc dir univ placement & assoc prof forest prod, 71- Mil Serv: 1st Lt, Army Engr, 53-55. Mem: Forest Prod Research Soc; Western Col Placement Asn; Ore State Employees Asn. Honors & Awards: Mosser Award, 66; Aufderheide Award, 72. Relig: Presbyterian. Mailing Add: 1530 NW 13th Corvallis OR 97330

VAN WAGNER, RICHARD (D)
NJ State Assemblyman
Mailing Add: State House Trenton NJ 08625

VAN WAGONER, CHARLOTTE ELLEN (D)
b San Francisco, Calif, Sept 6, 45; d Howard Laird Robertson & Anne Elizabeth Hagans R; m 1966 to Robert Louis Van Wagoner. Educ: Calif Western Univ, US Int Univ, San Diego, BA, 67; Univ Nev, Reno, 70-73. Polit & Govt Pos: Mem, Washoe Co Young Dem, 68-73; mem, Washoe Co Dem Cent Comt, 68-73; deleg, Dem Nat Conv, 72; chmn, Washoe Co Women for McGovern, 72; mem, Nat Women's Adv Coun, 72. Mem: NAACP; Common Cause; Nev Chap 13, Eastern Star (star points: Esther, 71-72, Adah, 69-70); Washoe Co Dem Women's Club; Multiple Sclerosis Soc (dir, Cent Nev Chap, 70-73, secy, 72-73). Relig: Methodist; Mem Comn Educ, First United Methodist Church, 71-73. Mailing Add: 3310 Sunnyvale Ave Reno NV 89502

VARIS, RICHARD E (R)
Conn State Rep
Mailing Add: 283 Salem Rd Prospect PO Naugatuck CT 06770

VARLEY, ANDREW PRESTON (R)
Iowa State Rep
b Stuart, Iowa, Dec 2, 34; s James Preston Varley & Esther Schutz V; m 1959 to Marilyn Ann Saucke; c Warren Andrew, Thomas James & John David. Educ: Iowa State Univ, BS, 57; NC State Univ, MS, 61; Phi Kappa Phi; Alpha Zeta; Alpha Gamma Rho. Polit & Govt Pos: Iowa State Rep, 67- Relig: Lutheran. Mailing Add: RR 2 Stuart IA 50250

VARNER, JOHN (D)
NC State Rep
Mailing Add: 116 Ridgewood Dr Lexington NC 27292

VARNUM, CHARLES HENRY (R)
Mich State Rep
b Jonesville, Mich, July 9, 33; s Henry Varnum & Mae V; c Barbara & Mitchell. Educ: Ferris Inst, Big Rapids, Mich, 51-54; Hillsdale Col, grad, 59. Hon Degrees: Bay de Noc Community Col, 70. Polit & Govt Pos: Mich State Rep, 107th Dist, currently; councilman & mayor pro-tem, Manistique City Coun, 64-; mem, Schoolcraft Co Bd Supvr, 11th Cong Dist Exec Comt & Mich State Athletic Bd of Control. Bus & Prof Pos: Teacher, Manistique Pub Schs, 59- Mil Serv: Sgt, Marine Corps, 51-54. Mem: VFW; Rotary Int; Elks; Manistique Teachers Asn (past pres). Honors & Awards: Named Young Man of Year, Manistique Jaycees, 65. Mailing Add: 531 Oak St Manistique MI 49854

VASCONCELLOS, JOHN BERNARD (D)
Calif State Assemblyman
b San Jose, Calif, May 11, 32. Educ: Univ Santa Clara, BS Hist, magna cum laude, 54 & LLB, cum laude, 59. Polit & Govt Pos: Travel secy, Gov Calif, 60-61; chmn, Speaker's Bur, Gov Campaign, Calif, 62; co-chmn, Young Citizens for Johnson, 64; Calif State Assemblyman, 24th Dist, 67-, chmn, Joint Legis Comt on Educ Goals & Eval, Joint Legis Comt on Master Plan for Higher Educ & Ways & Means, mem, Const Amendments Comt, Ways & Means Comt; mem subcomt on educ, Calif State Assembly; deleg, Dem Nat Conv, 68; Santa Clara Co co-chmn, Sen Robert Kennedy for President Campaign, 68. Honors & Awards: Best Freshman Assemblyman, Capitol Press Corps, 67. Mailing Add: 2435 Forest Ave San Jose CA 95128

VASHON, DORIS LOUISE (D)
Mem, Calif Dem State Cent Comt
b Waterville, Maine, Feb 14, 27; d Aldelbert Louis Couture & Lena Carey C; m 1944 to Richard Robert Vashon, wid; c Suzanne Marie, Patricia (deceased), Daniel (deceased), Judith (deceased), Stephen (deceased), Ann (deceased) & Betty Jean (deceased). Educ: Waterville High Sch, 40-43. Polit & Govt Pos: Secy, Mary O'Keefe Dem Club, Calif, 61-63; pres, Riverside Dem Forum, 64-67; co chmn, Milton Gordon for Secy of State, 66 & for State Treas, 70; orgn chmn, Fedn of Dem Clubs, 67-69; pres, Riverside Dem Action League, 67-69, second vpres, 71-; mem, Riverside Co Dem Cent Comt, 68-, publicity chmn, 68-71, vchmn, 71-; mem, Calif Dem State Cent Comt, 68-; co chmn, Jess Unruh for Gov & Sam Appleby for State Assembly, 74th Dist, 70; chmn, Dem Hq, 70; chmn, Proj 70, 38th Cong Dist, 70;

deleg, Dem Platform Comt, 36th Sen Dist, 70; comnr, Riverside Park & Recreation Comn, currently, chmn, 75-; co chmn, Muskie for President, 72; Muskie deleg, Dem Nat Conv, 72; coordr, Dr Robert Cole, Cand for Calif State Assembly, 74th Assembly Dist & George Brown, Cand for US Rep, 38th Cong Dist, 72; exec dir, Sam Digati, Cand for Supvr, First Supvr Dist, 72; adv & hq chmn, Mayor Ben H Lewis, 73; mem, Cinco-de-Mayo Fiesta Bicentennial Comt, 75. Mem: Northside Improv Asn (former vpres, bd dirs, 71-); Mex-Am Polit Asn; Cath Daughters Am; Am Legion Auxiliary; Eagle Auxiliary (chaplain, 71). Honors & Awards: Outstanding Serv Award, Coun on Polit Educ, AFL-CIO & Award for Get-out-the-Vote co-chairmanship, 70; Golden Key Award for outstanding community serv, Soroptomist Orgn, 72. Relig: Catholic. Mailing Add: 1635 Fairmont Blvd Riverside CA 92501

VASLET, ALBERT P (D)
RI State Sen
Mailing Add: 16 Washburn St Pawtucket RI 02861

VASTINE, JOHN ROBERT, JR (R)
Dep Asst Secy Trade & Raw Materials Policy, Dept of the Treas
b Danville, Pa, Nov 12, 37; s John Robert Vastine & Madeline Baughman V; single. Educ: Haverford Col, BA; Johns Hopkins Univ Sch Advan Int Studies, MA. Polit & Govt Pos: Econ asst to US Rep Thomas B Curtis, 65-68; consult, Emergency Comt for Am Trade, 68-69; Washington rep, CPC Int, Inc, 69-71; chief counsel to minority, govt opers comt, US Senate, 71-75; dep asst secy trade & raw materials policy, Dept of the Treas, 75- Mil Serv: Entered as Pvt, Army Res, 62, released as 1st Lt, 68. Publ: Co-auth, The Kennedy Round & the Future of American Trade, Praeger, 71 & Privacy & protection of personal information in Europe, US Senate Report for Govt Opers Comt, 75. Mailing Add: 2308 Wyoming Ave NW Washington DC 20008

VAUGHAN, CHARLES DAVID (D)
b Cincinnati, Ohio, Jan 13, 52; s Charles William Vaughan & Juanita Eckstien V; single. Educ: Kent State Univ, 70-; asst attorney gen, Student Govt, gen exec asst to pres student body & chmn univ ctr bd, 70- Polit & Govt Pos: Coordr, Assoc Student Govt, Kent area, 70-; dir, Challenge 72 Voter Registr, Kent; deleg, Dem Nat Conv, 72; field coordr, Student Vote, Cincinnati. Mem: Blue Key. Relig: Methodist. Mailing Add: 802 Carini Lane Cincinnati OH 45218

VAUGHAN, COLA M (D)
Mem Exec Bd, Dem Party Ga
b Bartow Co, Ga, Jan 16, 26; d John F Collins, Sr & Nettie Holden; m 1947 to Dave C Vaughan; c Suzanne (Mrs Henshaw), Vann Michael & Dan LaFayette. Educ: Massey Col Law, LLB. Polit & Govt Pos: Mem, Dem Party Ga, 62-, mem exec bd, 74-; mem, Gov Comn Status Women, 63-65. Mem: Cartersville Bus & Prof Womens Luncheon Club (legis chmn, 75-). Honors & Awards: Cert of Merit, Cartersville Bus & Prof Women's Luncheon Club, 68; Woman of the Year Nominee, 69 & 70. Relig: Baptist. Legal Res: 948 Jones Mill Rd Cartersville GA 30120 Mailing Add: PO Box 308 Cartersville GA 30120

VAUGHAN, HUGH SLAVENS (D)
Mem, Mo State Dem Comt
b Urbana, Mo, Sept 2, 16; to William D Vaughan & Josephine Slavens V; m 1943 to Monte Jean Johnson; c Barbara Sue (Mrs Wilson), Patricia (Mrs Ames), Judith K, Hugh Allen & Robert James. Educ: Univ Mo, 34-38; Phi Kappa Psi. Polit & Govt Pos: Chmn, Dallas Co Dem Comt, Mo, 56-70, mem, 70-; mem, Mo State Dem Comt, 66- Bus & Prof Pos: Pres, Bank of Urbana, 5 years. Mil Serv: Entered as Pvt, Army, 43, released as Capt, 45, after serv in Ninth Armored Div, ETO, 44-45; Bronze Star. Mem: Lions; AF&AM; Scottish Rite; Shrine. Relig: Methodist. Mailing Add: Urbana MO 65767

VAUGHAN, KENNETH (D)
Tex State Rep
Mailing Add: 2014 West Shore Dr Garland TX 75041

VAUGHN, CLARENCE ROLAND, JR (D)
Ga State Rep
b Conyers, Ga, Jan 22, 21; s Clarence Roland Vaughn & Mary Guinn V; m 1942 to Doris Elizabeth Henson; c Alvin Henson & Clarence Roland, III. Educ: NGa Col, 39; Univ Ga, LLB, 46. Polit & Govt Pos: Ga State Sen, 59-60; Ga State Rep, 61- Bus & Prof Pos: Attorney. Mil Serv: US Army, 42-46, Capt; Bronze Star. Mem: Mason; Lions; Am Legion; VFW; Elks. Relig: Methodist. Mailing Add: Box 410 Conyers GA 30207

VAUGHN, FRED D (D)
Chmn, Jackson Co Dem Comt, Ky
b Bond, Ky, Sept 14, 20; s Richard Vaughn & Nancy Parrett V; m 1939 to Edna Powell; c Betty Sue (Mrs Gordon Rice), Larry & Ronald Dale. Educ: Jackson Co Pub Schs. Polit & Govt Pos: Mem Draft Bd 41, McKee, Ky, 58-; justice of Peace, Jackson Co, 65-69; chmn, Jackson Co Dem Comt, 68-; campaign chmn, Bert Combs for Gov, 71. Bus & Prof Pos: Retail merchant, 58- Mil Serv: Entered as Pvt, Army, 43, released as Tech 5th grade, 46, after serv in 4th Armoured Div, 23rd Calvary, ETO, 43-46; Three Battle Stars; Cert of Merit. Mem: Am Angus Asn. Relig: Protestant. Mailing Add: Annville KY 40402

VAUGHN, H GEORGE, JR (D)
Okla State Rep
b Vinita, Okla, Apr 4, 39; s Harold George Vaughn & Mary Louella Griffith V; m 1958 to Leah Jeanne Taylor; c Rebekah Jeanne, Jason Mark, Nathan David, Rachel Gail, Donna Sue & Julie Beth. Educ: Baptist Bible Col, 57-59. Polit & Govt Pos: Sheriff, Craig Co, Okla, 68-73; Okla State Rep, 75- Bus & Prof Pos: Dispatcher, Okla Hwy Patrol, 60-68. Mem: Okla Cattlemen's Asn; Okla Sheriffs & Peace Officers. Honors & Awards: Green Co Civil Award for Outstanding Serv. Relig: Baptist. Mailing Add: Rte 1 Big Cabin OK 74332

VAUGHN, JACKIE, III (D)
Mich State Rep
Mailing Add: 2625 W Grand Blvd Detroit MI 48208

VAUGHT, ELMER RICHARD (R)
Chmn, Burke Co Rep Party, NC
b Montgomery Co, Va, Oct 18, 28; s Vassie A Vaught (deceased) & Lillian Scott V; m 1966 to Miriam Davis Newton; c Donald R, Joseph C, Linda C & William J. Educ: Univ Miami, 55-56; Univ NC, 56-57; Univ Va, Roanoke Exten, 58-60. Polit & Govt Pos: Mem, Roanoke City Coun Airport Comt, Va, 61-64; mem, Valdese Zoning & Planning Bd, NC, 68-; chmn, Burke Co Rep Party, 70-; alt deleg, Rep Nat Conv, 72. Bus & Prof Pos: Reporter, Roanoke World-News, 48-51 & 56-62; exec secy, Roanoke Valley Industs, 62-64; vpres, Western Carolina Industs, 64- Mil Serv: Entered as Airman, Air Force, 51, released as Sgt, 55, after serv in Hq, Air Force; 67th Tactical Reconnaissance Wing, Kimpo, Korea, 53-54; Bolling AFB, Washington, DC, 51-53 & 54-55; UN Force Medal; Korean Theatre Medal with 3 Combat Stars; World War II Victory Medal; Good Conduct Medal. Mem: Roanoke Jaycees (dir, vpres & pres); Va Jaycees (vpres); Roanoke CofC (dir); Indust Mgt Club; Piedmont Personnel Asn. Honors & Awards: Numerous Jaycee Awards. Legal Res: 912 Briggs St Valdese NC 28690 Mailing Add: Box 640 Valdese NC 28690

VEAL, HARLAN HALE, JR (D)
Chmn, Jessamine Co Dem Exec Comt, Ky
b Lexington, Ky, Oct 4, 41; s Harlan H Veal, Sr & Willie Rogers V; m 1964 to Phyllis Temple; c Hal & Katherine Jean. Educ: Centre Col, BA, 63; Univ Ky, JD, 66; Delta Kappa Epsilon; Phi Alpha Delta; Delta Kappa Epsilon. Polit & Govt Pos: Chmn, Jessamine Co Dem Exec Comt, Ky, 73- Mem: Am & Ky Bar Asns; Jessamine Co Jaycees; Nicholasville Rotary Club. Relig: Disciples of Christ. Mailing Add: 308 Hickory Hill Rd Nicholasville KY 40356

VEALE, ROADS (R)
Mem, Rep State Cent Comt Calif
b Spokane, Wash, Apr 13, 40; s Henry Veale & Marianna Gray V; m 1963 to Marilyn Miller; c Jenniffer, Jodie & Suzanne. Educ: Golden Gate Col, 61-63. Polit & Govt Pos: Mem, Sonoma Co Rep Cent Comt, Calif, 67-72; mem, Calif Rep State Cent Comt, 68-; chmn, Sonoma Co Reagan Campaign, 70; deleg, Rep Nat Conv, 72. Bus & Prof Pos: Pres, Veale Volkswagen Inc, 73- Mil Serv: Entered as Pvt, Army, 58, released as E-4, 62, after serv in 24th Inf. Mem: Santa Rosa CofC. Relig: Protestant. Legal Res: 4343 Wallace Rd Santa Rosa CA 95404 Mailing Add: 2800 Corby Ave Santa Rosa CA 95403

VEAZEY, CARLTON WADSWORTH (R)
Mem, DC Rep Comt
b Memphis, Tenn, May 9, 36; s Rev M G F Veazey & Dolly C Jolly V; m 1966 to Jean Margaret Blanford; c Gayle M Liggins, Michael V & Caron V. Educ: Ark Agr & Mech Col, Pine Bluff, AB, 58; theol scholar, Howard Univ, 58, grad fel, 60, BD, 61; Alpha Phi Alpha. Polit & Govt Pos: Mem & precinct capt, DC Rep Comt, 68-; mem, DC Rep Comt, 69-; mem, City Coun, Washington, DC, 70- Bus & Prof Pos: Pastor, Zion Baptist Church, Washington, DC, 60-; coordr spec progs, Opportunities Industrialization Ctr, Washington, DC, 68- Mem: Am Baptist Conv, Valley Forge, Pa; Urban League; Iowa Whipper Home (bd dirs); NAACP; Jonathan Davis Consistory, Masonic Lodge. Relig: Baptist. Mailing Add: 230 M St SW Washington DC 20024

VEKICH, MAX MILAN, JR (D)
b Aberdeen, Wash, May 22, 54; s Max M Vekich, Sr & Dorothea Hornby V; single. Educ: Grays Harbor Col, AA, 74; Willamette Univ, 74-75; Univ Puget Sound, 75-; Phi Theta Kappa; Beta Theta Pi. Polit & Govt Pos: Precinct committeeman, Grays Harbor Co Dem Party, Wash, 72-; deleg, Dem Nat Mid-Term Conf, 74; mem, Third Cong Dist Dem League, 74- Mem: YMCA. Relig: Roman Catholic. Mailing Add: 414 W Scott St Aberdeen WA 98520

VELDE, RICHARD WHITTINGTON
Adminr, Law Enforcement Assistance Admin, Dept Justice
b Moline, Ill, Dec 12, 31; s Harold H Velde & Olive Pfander V; m 1957 to Joyce Brady; c Blake T & Brent W. Educ: Bradley Univ, BS, 53, MA, 54, George Washington Univ, LLB, 60; Am Univ; Phi Kappa Delta; Pi Sigma Alpha. Polit & Govt Pos: Legis asst to US Rep Michel, Ill, 58-60; adv, Off Gen Coun, HHFA, 60-61; minority counsel subcomt criminal law & subcomt on juv delinquency, US Senate, 65-69; assoc adminr, Law Enforcement Assistance Admin, Dept Justice, 69-74, adminr, 74- Bus & Prof Pos: Mem faculty, Univ Ill, 57-58. Legal Res: 2715 S Hayes St Arlington VA 22202 Mailing Add: Law Enforcement Assist Admin Dept of Justice Washington DC 20530

VELELLA, GUY J (R)
NY State Assemblyman
b New York, NY, Sept 25, 44; s Vincent J Velella & Carmella Chiavaro V; m 1964 to Patricia O'Malley; c Gina, Lisa & Vincent. Educ: St John's Univ (NY), BA, 67; Suffolk Univ Law Sch, JD, 70. Polit & Govt Pos: Field rep, Exec Off of the President, formerly; law secy, Judge Joseph Macchia, Civil Court NY, formerly; law secy, Justice Irving Kirschenbaum, NY State Supreme Court, formerly; NY State Assemblyman, 72- Bus & Prof Pos: Partner law firm, Velella, Velella & Basso. Mem: Am & NY State Bar Asns; Phi Alpha Delta; Sons of Italy; Columbian Lawyers Asn. Honors & Awards: Legislator of the Year, NY State Columbian Employees Asn, 73; YMCA Youth Serv Award, 74; Fidelis Juri Award, Supreme Court Uniformed Officers, 74. Relig: Roman Catholic. Legal Res: 1240 Rhinelander Ave Bronx NY 10461 Mailing Add: 2113 Williamsbridge Rd Bronx NY 10461

VELEZ, MIGUEL (D)
b Mayaguez, PR, Apr 13, 49; s Miguel Angel Velez & Nereida Beauchamp V; single. Educ: NY Univ, BEng, 72; Tau Epsilon Phi; Latin Am Student's Soc. Polit & Govt Pos: Founder & vpres, El Grito Borinqueno, NY Univ, 68-70; dir, PR Col Forum, 68-69; bd dirs, ALMA Commun Corp, 70-71; exec vpres, Phoenix Reform Dem Club, 71-72; coordr, East Side Citizens for McGovern, 72; deleg, Dem Nat Conv, 72; coordr, New Yorkers for Badillo, 73; planning comt, Emergency Conf on Econ Alternatives, Washington, DC, 74; bd dirs, Lower ESide Multiserv Ctr, 75- Bus & Prof Pos: Engr, NY Tel Co, 72- Mem: Am Inst Indust Eng; New Dem Coalition (treas, 75-); NY Borinquen Lions Club; NY Univ Club. Honors & Awards: Martin Luther King Scholar, NY Univ, 71-73; chmn dedication comt, Third Street Music Sch, 75. Relig: Catholic. Mailing Add: 218 E 11th St New York NY 10003

VELEZ ITHIER, MANUEL (POPULAR DEM, PR)
Rep, PR House of Rep
b Cabo Rojo, PR, Feb 20, 14; s Gregorio Velez Irizarry (deceased) & Maria D Ithier V; m 1945 to Gregoria Ortiz Nazario; c Manuel, Maria Magdalena & Anais. Educ: Agr & Mech Col, Mayaguez, PR, BSA, 39; Univ PR, Dipl in Sch Supv & Admin, 61. Polit & Govt Pos: Chmn, local comt, Algarrobo Co Popular Dem Comt, PR, 60-64; mem, Vega Baja Popular Dem Munic Comt, 64-; Rep, PR House Rep, 69-, pres, Agr Comn, 73- Bus & Prof Pos: Local dir civil defense, Vega Baja, PR, 51-60. Mem: PR Teachers Asn; Mason (Worshipful Master, Brisas Del Cribe Number 86, 60-61); PR Agronomist Col; F&AM; Odd Fellows. Honors & Awards: Year Agronomist, 67. Relig: Presbyterian. Legal Res: Algarrobo Ward Rte 155 Km 66 Hm 3 Vega Baja PR 00763 Mailing Add: PO Box 865 Vega Baja PR 00763

VELIS, PETER ARTHUR (R)
Mass State Rep
b Springfield, Mass, Oct 8, 42; s Arthur Peter Velis & Helen Bravakis V; single. Educ: Boston Univ, BS Pub Rels, 65, pres grad class, 65; Suffolk Univ Sch Law, JD, 68, Dean's List, 68. Polit & Govt Pos: Mass State Rep, Dist 5, 73-, mem, Health Care & Pub Safety Comt, Mass House Rep, 75-; originated spec food comn, Commonwealth of Mass, 74-75, mem comt to investigate registry of motor vehicles, 75- Bus & Prof Pos: Attorney-at-law, Westfield, Mass, 68- Publ: Co-auth, The Grand Jury System of Massachusets, A Study, Suffolk Univ Law Rev in conjunction with The Mass Gen Court, 68. Mem: Am, Mass, Boston & Westfield Bar Asns; Western Hampden Hist Soc. Relig: Greek Orthodox. Mailing Add: 10 McKinley Terr Westfield MA 01085

VENABLE, JACK BENTON (D)
Ala State Rep
b Wetumpka, Ala, Feb 25, 39; s Benton K Venable & Maydell S V; m to Josephine Cameron Mann; c Cameron Julia. Educ: Auburn Univ, BS in Bus Educ, 61; Pi Kappa Phi; Sigma Delta Chi. Polit & Govt Pos: Admin asst to US Congressman Bill Nichols, Ala, 67-70; deleg, Dem Nat Conv, 68; Ala State Rep, Dist 76, 74- Bus & Prof Pos: Radio announcer, Wetumpka, Alexander City & Auburn, Ala, 55-59; producer-dir, Auburn Studios, Ala Educ TV Network, 59-61; staff announcer, WCCB-TV, Montgomery, 62-63; news reporter, WSFA-TV, Montgomery, 63-65; dir news & pub affairs, 65-67; ed & publ, Tallassee Tribune, 70- Mil Serv: Army Res, 56, released as 1st Lt, 69. Mem: Tallassee Rotary; Ala Press Asn (dir); Boy Scouts (mem adv comt). Relig: Presbyterian; deacon, First Presby Church, Tallassee. Mailing Add: PO Box 36 Tallassee AL 36078

VENEMAN, JOHN G, JR (R)
b Corcoran, Calif, Oct 31, 25; s John G Veneman & Bertha Van Konynenburg V; m 1947 to Nita D Bomberger; c Ann Margaret, John Gerrit & Jane Elizabeth. Educ: Ariz State Col, 44; Univ Tex, 44-45. Polit & Govt Pos: Trustee, Empire Union Sch, Calif, 57-59; mem, grand jury, Stanislaus Co, 57-59, chmn bd supvr, 59-62; Calif State Assemblyman, 30th Dist, 62-69; legis mem, State Social Welfare Bd, 64-69; state chmn, Robert Finch Campaign for Lt Gov, 66; Under Secy, Dept of Health, Educ & Welfare, 69-73. Bus & Prof Pos: Lectr, New Sch Social Res, fall 72; lectr, Eagleton Inst Polit, Rutgers Univ, 73-; pres, Veneman Assocs, San Francisco, 73- Mil Serv: A/S, Navy, 44. Mem: Stanislaus Co Farm Bur; Elks; Calif State CofC; Am Legion; Commonwealth Club of San Francisco. Honors & Awards: Young Man of Year, Modesto Jr CofC, 60; Selected to attend Legis Seminar, Eagleton Inst of Politics, 66; Distinguished Serv Award, US Dept Health, Educ & Welfare, 73. Relig: Presbyterian. Mailing Add: 1022 Chestnut St San Francisco CA 94109

VENTERS, EDWARD SUTTON (D)
Chmn, Pamilco Co Dem Comt, NC
b Oriental, NC, Sept 30, 10; s Walter Clement Venters & Daisy V; m 1941 to Nellie Odell Wingard; c Lois Alexandra & Michial. Polit & Govt Pos: Chmn, Pamilco Co Dem Comt, NC. Mailing Add: PO Box 56 Stonewall NC 28583

VENTERS, W ODELL (D)
SC State Rep
b Johnsonville, Mar 29, 17; s Willie Venters & Lizzie Abrams V; m 1936 to Nina Barfield. Educ: Pub sch, Johnsonville, SC. Polit & Govt Pos: Mem town coun, Johnsonville, SC, 50-55, mayor, 55-60; SC State Rep, 61-69 & 71- Bus & Prof Pos: Merchant, owner, Venters Dept Store. Mem: SC Jr CofC. Honors & Awards: Distinguished Serv Award as One of the Outstanding Young Men of State of SC, 50. Mailing Add: Johnsonville SC 29555

VENTO, BRUCE F (DFL)
Minn State Rep
Mailing Add: 1534 Atlantic St Paul MN 55106

VERGIELS, JOHN M (D)
Nev State Assemblyman
Mailing Add: 3966 Visby Lane Las Vegas NV 89109

VERKAMP, JOHN G (R)
Chmn, Coconino Co Rep Comt, Ariz
b Grand Canyon, Ariz, July 31, 40; s Jack Verkamp & Mary O'Leary V; m 1965 to Linda Lee Meline; c Melanie, Jay & Gregory. Educ: Loyola Univ Los Angeles, 58-60; Univ Ariz, BS, 62, JD, 65; Phi Delta Phi; Phi Kappa Phi. Polit & Govt Pos: Dep attorney, Coconino Co, Ariz, 70-71; chmn, Coconino Co Rep Comt, 74- Bus & Prof Pos: Assoc, Mangum, Wahl & Stoops, Flagstaff, Ariz, 72-74; partner, Verkamp & Verkamp, Flagstaff, 74- Mil Serv: Entered as 1st Lt, Army, 65, released as Capt, 70, after serv in Judge Adv Gen Corps; Nat Defense Serv Medal; Army Commendation Medal. Mem: State Bar Ariz; Am Legion; Coconino Co Legal Aid Soc (secy-treas & bd dirs); Flagstaff Boy's Club (bd dirs). Relig: Catholic. Mailing Add: 1517 N Kutch Dr Flagstaff AZ 86001

VERKLER, JERRY THOMAS (D)
b Black Rock, Ark; s Jewell T Verkler & Sylvia Thomas V; m to Mary Frances Keadle; c Gail, Alison, Kimberly & Jerry, Jr. Educ: Univ NMex, BA, 54; George Washington Univ Law Sch, LLB, 60; Pi Kappa Alpha; Young Dem; Phi Alpha Delta. Polit & Govt Pos: Legis asst to US Sen Clinton P Anderson, NMex, 56-60; staff dir, US Sen Comt on Interior & Insular Affairs, 61-; deleg, Va Dem Conv, 68. Mil Serv: 2nd Lt, Marines, 54, serv in 2nd Marine Div; Lt Col, Marine Corps Res. Mailing Add: 7922 Greeley Blvd Springfield VA 22152

VERLOT, FRANK O (R)
Mem Exec Comt, Rep State Cent Comt Calif
b Gent, Belgium, Oct 18, 41; s Maximillian G Verlot & Eva Danilevitz V; m 1967 to Marian Elizabeth Berkner; c Nancy Elizabeth. Educ: Mass Inst Technol, BS, 63; Stanford Univ, MS, 64, post masters study, 64-67. Polit & Govt Pos: Pres, Mass Inst Technol Young Rep, 61-63 & Stanford Young Rep, 66-67; vpres San Francisco Bay Area, Calif Young Rep, 67-69; mem & precinct chmn, Santa Clara Co Rep Cent Comt, 69-70, chmn, 71-75; mem, Calif Rep State Cent Comt, 69-, mem precinct steering comt, 69-70, state precinct chmn, 73-, mem exec comt, 73-; co-chmn steering comt, Reagan for Gov, Santa Clara Co, 70; mem, Calif Rep Co Chmn Asn, 71-; deleg, Rep Nat Conv, 72. Bus & Prof Pos: Thermodynamics engr, Grumman Aircraft Eng Corp, Bethpage, NY, 63-65; sr thermodynamics engr, Lockheed Space & Missiles Co, Sunnyvale, Calif, 66-68; proj engr prog mgt, United Technol Ctr, 68-71, mgr procurement liaison eng, 71- Mem: Am Inst Aeronaut & Astronaut; Am Soc Mech Engrs; Commonwealth Club of Calif; Sierra Club. Honors & Awards: Recognized as one of 50 best precinct workers in Calif, 68 & 70. Relig: Roman Catholic. Mailing Add: 1540 Klamath Dr Sunnyvale CA 94087

VERMILLION, JOHN F (R)
Kans State Sen
Mailing Add: 1424 N Eighth Independence KS 67301

VER PLANK, JOEL P (R)
b Zeeland, Mich, Feb 18, 37; s Joseph Ver Plank & Jessemine Cross V; m 1959 to Susan Yates; c Elizabeth & Mary. Educ: Albion Col, BA, 59; Delta Tau Delta. Polit & Govt Pos: Deleg, Rep Party, Livonia, Mich, 64-66 & Holland, Mich, 66-; state secy, United Rep of Mich, 68-69; chmn, Ottawa Co Rep Party, 69-74; mem bd control, Grand Valley State Cols, 73- Bus & Prof Pos: Teacher, Almont Community Sch, 59-62 & Livonia Pub Schs, 62-65; supvr, Royal Casket Co, Zeeland, Mich, 65-69, pres, 70- Mem: Holland Jaycees; vpres, Zeeland CofC. Relig: Protestant. Mailing Add: 559 Elmdale Court Holland MI 49423

VERTEFEUILLE, ALBERT BENOIT (D)
Chmn, Windham-Willimantic Dem Town Comt, Conn
b Willimantic, Conn, Sept 2, 33; s Benoit Vertefeuille & Simone Briere V; m 1961 to Judith Bloch; c Robin, Karin, Matthew & Michael. Educ: Eastern Conn State Col, BS, 60; Univ Conn, MA, 62; sixth year prof dipl, 65; Phi Delta Kappa. Polit & Govt Pos: Chmn, Windham-Willimantic Dem Town Comt, Conn, 70- Bus & Prof Pos: Elem teacher, pub schs, 60-65; elem prin, Lebanon Pub Sch, Conn, 65-; guest lectr, Univ Conn & Eastern Conn State Col; consult, Am Educ Publ. Mil Serv: Entered as Pvt, Army, 55, released as SP-4, 58, after serv in 25th Signal Bn, Germany, 55-58; Good Conduct Medal. Mem: Nat Asn Elem Sch Prin; Elem Sch Prin Asn Conn; East Conn State Col Alumni Asn; Elks; Lebanon Lions Club. Relig: Catholic. Mailing Add: Old South Windham Rd South Windham CT 06266

VEYSEY, VICTOR VINCENT (R)
Asst Secy Army Civil Works
b Eagle Rock, Calif, Apr 14, 15; s Charles Francis Veysey & Nettie Shelley V; m 1940 to Janet Donaldson; c Ann (Mrs Al Kosky), John Charles, Thomas Frank & Mark Edward. Educ: Calif Inst Technol, BS in Eng; Harvard Univ, MBA. Polit & Govt Pos: Mem & past clerk & pres, Brawley Sch Bd, Calif; mem adv comt, Southwest Irrigation Field Sta, US Dept Agr; mem & past chmn, Adv Comt for Exten Serv & Meloland Field Sta, Univ Calif; Calif State Assemblyman, 75th Dist, 62-70; past chmn, Co Comt on Sch Dist Orgn; US Rep, 38th Dist Calif, 70-74; deleg, Rep Nat Conv, 72; asst secy civil works, Dept of Army, 75- Bus & Prof Pos: Farmer, Imperial Valley, Calif, 49-; indust rels mgr, plant mgr & then works mgr, Calif Inst Technol & Rocket Div, Gen Tire & Rubber Co of Calif; instr & asst prof econ, indust rels & indust mgt, Calif Inst Technol, 7 years. Mem: Calif Beet Growers; Boy Scouts (coun comnr); Brawley 4-H Club (community leader); Rotary Int; Elks. Honors & Awards: Man of Year in Educ Award, Phi Delta Kappa, 61. Relig: Presbyterian; Elder. Legal Res: 872 Bonita Ave Claremont CA 91711 Mailing Add: Dept of the Army Off of the Secy Washington DC 20310

VICENCIA, FRANK (D)
Calif State Assemblyman
b Artesia, Calif, Aug 23, 31; s Frank G Vicencia & Maria Costa V; m 1954 to Alice Lorraine Costa; c Steven, Michele, David, Mike & Laura. Educ: Excelsior High Sch. Polit & Govt Pos: Calif State Assemblyman, 74-, chmn subcomt on rapid transit, mem comts on agr, transportation & govt orgn, Calif State Assembly, currently. Mil Serv: Entered as Pvt, Army, 52, released as Cpl, 54, after serv in Mil Police, Korea. Mem: CofC; NAACP; Nat Coun of Negro Women (hon mem). Relig: Catholic. Mailing Add: 9860 Crestbrook Bellflower CA 90706

VICENS, ENRIQUE (COCO) (POPULAR DEMOCRATIC, PR)
Sen-at-lg, PR Legis
b Ciales, PR, Sept 3, 26; s Jose Vicens Batalia & Antonia Sastre B; m 1951 to Liana Rivera; c Enrique, Michael Joseph, Liana, Maria Eugenia, Maria Petesa & Marcia Dolores. Educ: Univ PR, 43-46; Univ Md Sch of Med, MD, 50; Jefferson Med Col Hosp, Philadelphia, 53-56; dipl, Am Bd Otolaryngology, 57. Polit & Govt Pos: Treas, Popular Dem Party, Ponce, PR, 68-72; Sen-at-lg, PR Legis, 72- Bus & Prof Pos: Practicing ears, nose & throat & broncho esophagology serv, Health Dept, PR, 56-; asst clin prof, Univ of PR Sch Med, 68- Mil Serv: Entered as 1st Lt, Army, 50, released as Capt, 53, after serv in Med Corps, Korean Campaign, 51-52; Capt, Inactive Res; Bronze Star; Valor & Meritorious Serv Medals. Mem: PR & Am Med Asns; fel Am Col Surgeons; PR Med Soc, Southern Dist. Relig: Roman Catholic. Legal Res: Ave Universidad 12 Ponce PR 00731 Mailing Add: Marina 16 Ponce PR 00731

VICINO, ROBERT JAMES (D)
Conn State Rep
b Ft Lee, NJ, Sept 7, 30; s Rocco Vicino & Blanche Wovers V (deceased); m 1954 to Arlene Levesque; c Robert John, Carol Ann, Cynthia Ann & Stephen James. Educ: Univ Hartford, 1 year. Polit & Govt Pos: Pres, Young Dem Club, Bristol, Conn, 60-61; selectman, Bristol, 62-64; chmn, First Dist Dem Party, 62-65; Conn State Rep, 34th Dist, 67-73, 78th Dist, 73-, asst minority leader, Conn House Rep, currently. Bus & Prof Pos: Pres, R J Vicino Agency, Inc, Ins & Real Estate, currently. Mil Serv: Entered as Pvt, Air Force, 49, released as S/Sgt, 53, after serv in Far E Air Force. Publ: Insurance, Rough Notes Inc, 6/62. Mem: Conn Bd Realtors (dir); Bristol Bd Realtors (past pres & vpres). Relig: Catholic. Legal Res: 282 Fall Mountain Rd Bristol CT 06010 Mailing Add: 36 High St Bristol CT 06010

VICK, GABE T (D)
b Weatherford, Tex, May 24, 31; s Joseph J Vick & Era Greenfield V; m 1954 to Luanne Johnson; c Gabe T, Jr, Randol J & Michael F. Educ: Weatherford Col, 48-49; Univ Tex, Austin, BBA, 52, LLB, 56; Phi Kappa Tau; Phi Alpha Delta. Polit & Govt Pos: Judge, Parker Co, Tex, 62-66; chmn, Parker Co Dem Party, 67-75. Mil Serv: Entered as 2nd Lt, Army, 52, released as 1st Lt, 54, after serv in 593rd Transportation Traffic Regt Detachment, Seoul, Korea, 53-54; Lt Col, Judge Adv Gen Corps, Res, 54-; Commendation Ribbon; Korean Serv, Am Nat Defense & UN Medals. Mem: Tex Bar Asn; Parker Co Bar Asn; Optimist; KofP; VFW. Relig: Episcopal. Legal Res: 118 W Josephine St PO Box 51 Weatherford TX 76086 Mailing Add: M & F Bank Bldg Weatherford TX 76086

VICK, KATHLEEN M (D)
Nat Committeewoman, La Young Dem
b New Orleans, La, Aug 1938; m to Kendall L Vick. Educ: Wellesley Col, BA, 60; Tulane Univ Grad Sch, 62. Polit & Govt Pos: Spec asst to chmn, Goals for La Comt; bd mem, Independent Women's Orgn & SLa Women's Dem Orgn; secy bd, Dem Alliance of La; nat

committeewoman, La Young Dem, 68-; mem, La Comn on Status of Women, 71-; exec asst to Pres Pro Tem, La Senate, formerly; deleg, Dem Nat Conv, 72; charter mem, Women's Polit Caucus, currently. Bus & Prof Pos: Pres, Prog Consults, Inc, currently. Mem: Interracial Coun for Bus Opportunity (bd mem); Big Sisters Int; St Mark's Community Civil Liberties Union La; Community Rels Coun. Legal Res: 1125 Fourth St New Orleans LA 70130 Mailing Add: 912 Louisiana Ave New Orleans LA 70115

VICK, LARRY A (R)
Tex State Rep
b San Antonio, Tex, Sept 15, 41; s V A Vick & June Davis V; m 1961 to Patty McCarty; c Paul & Lara. Educ: Abilene Christian Col, BA, 65, study, 65-67; Bates Sch Law, Univ Houston, 68-72; Delta Theta Phi. Polit & Govt Pos: Tex State Rep, 73- Bus & Prof Pos: Attorney, Houston, Tex, 73- Mem: Tex State & Houston Bar Asns; Houston Jr Bar Asn; Houston Jaycees. Honors & Awards: Outstanding Young Man, 73. Relig: Church of Christ. Legal Res: 807 S Post Oak Lane Houston TX 77027 Mailing Add: 2012 Suffolk Houston TX 77027

VICK, ORIS PAUL (D)
Chmn, Alexander Co Dem Party, Ill
b Elco, Ill, Sept, 21, 04; s Clede Vick & Maggie White V; m 1928 to Faye Lynn; c Shirley L (Mrs Glaab). Educ: Southern Ill Univ, Carbondale, 2 years. Polit & Govt Pos: Pres, Young Dem, Alexander Co, Ill, 30; assessor & treas, Alexander Co, Ill, 58-62; mem, Dem Nat Comt, currently; chmn, Alexander Co Dem Party, 70- Bus & Prof Pos: Teacher, pub schs, Alexander Co, Ill, 25-36, 63-70; owner, Gen Store, Olive Branch, Ill, 37-58. Mem: Ill Dem Club; Odd Fellows; Horseshoe Lake Develop Club; Sportsman's Club; Farm Bur. Honors & Awards: Retired Teacher Award; Distinguished Serv Award for Pub Sch Admin, Gamma Lambda Chap, Phi Delta Kappa. Relig: Southern Baptist. Mailing Add: Box 97 Olive Branch IL 62969

VICKERY, CHARLES EUGENE (D)
NC State Rep
b Greenville, SC, Sept 22, 43; s Victor Van Vickery & Edna Freeman V; m 1970 to Jean Mary Marshall; c Andrew Marshall. Educ: The Citadel, 61-65; Univ NC Law Sch, Chapel Hill, AB, 68. Polit & Govt Pos: NC State Sen, 75- Bus & Prof Pos: Asst dist attorney, 16th Judicial Dist & 29th Judicial Dist, 70; partner, Winston, Coleman & Bernholz, Esqs, 71- Mil Serv: SP-4, Army Res, 68-74. Publ: Auth, A look at the North Carolina penal system, NC Cent Univ Law View, spring 75. Mem: St Andrew's Soc NC; Phi Delta Theta; North State Caucus; Am Bar Asn (mem sect on poverty law & on rights of indigents). Relig: Baptist. Legal Res: 515 Morgan Creek Rd Chapel Hill NC 27514 Mailing Add: Suite 20 Plaza Bldg Franklin St Chapel Hill NC 27514

VICKERY, RAYMOND EZEKIEL, JR (D)
Va State Deleg
b Brookhaven, Miss, Apr 30, 42; s Raymond Ezekiel Vickery, Sr & Clarene Dickens V. Educ: Duke Univ, AB, 64; Univ Sri Lanka, 64-65; Harvard Univ Law Sch, LLB, 68; Phi Beta Kappa; Omicron Delta Kappa. Bus & Prof Pos: Va State Deleg, 74- Bus & Prof Pos: Attorney, Hogan & Hartson, Washington, DC, 68- Publ: Auth, The Ceylonese Press & the Fall of the Sirimavo Bandaranaike Government, SAtlantic Quart, summer 67. Mem: Am Bar Asn; Am Judicature Soc; Lions; Sierra Club; Environ Defense Fund. Relig: Baptist. Mailing Add: 2733 Willow Dr Vienna VA 22180

VIDAL, DAGMAR LUND (D)
Dem Nat Committeeman, Iowa
b Hampton, Iowa, Dec 10, 17; d Peter Lauritzen Lund & Mette Miller L; m 1944 to Lewis Leonard Vidal; c Katherine, Robert, Peter & Leonard. Educ: Grand View Col, 35-36; Iowa State Teachers Col, 38-39; Univ Minn, summer sch; Colo State Univ. Polit & Govt Pos: Alt deleg, Dem Nat Conv, 60 & 64; Dem precinct committeewoman, pres, Dem Women's Club & secy, Franklin Co Dem Cent Comt, 60-66; Dem committeewoman, Third Dist Party, Iowa, 64-70; mem adv bd, Iowa Ctr for Educ in Polit, 65-; mem, Dem State Cent Comt, Iowa Voters Comt, 66-70, vpres, 68-70; deleg & mem resolutions & platform comt, Dem Nat Conv, 68, deleg, 72; Dem Nat Committeewoman, Iowa, 70-, mem, Exec Comt, Dem Nat Comt, 72- Mem: Pres, Hosp Auxiliary, 58-62; secy, NIowa Area Develop Comn Tax Study, 65-66. Relig: Lutheran. Mailing Add: RR 2 Beeds Lake Rd Hampton IA 50441

VIDRINE, JOHN LARRY (D)
La State Rep
Mailing Add: 114 S Soileau Ville Platte LA 70686

VIERA-MARTINEZ, ANGEL (NEW PROGRESSIVE, PR)
Rep, PR House Rep
b Gurabo, PR, Nov 18, 15; s Nieves Viera & Alejandrina Martinez V; m 1952 to Gladys Villeneuve; c Angel & Harry. Educ: Univ Pr, BA & LLB. Polit & Govt Pos: Asst dist attorney, San Juan, PR, 46-49, dist attorney, 49-55; Rep, PR House Rep, Precinct Two, 69-, speaker, 69-72, minority floor leader, New Progressive Party, 73- Mem: PR & Am Bar Asns; Am Judicature Soc; Int Soc Law & Sci. Relig: Catholic. Legal Res: 1213 Luchetti St Condado Santurce PR 00907 Mailing Add: PO Box 2483 San Juan PR 00903

VIGIL, SAMUEL F (D)
NMex State Rep
Mailing Add: 411 Moreno St Las Vegas NM 87701

VIGNEAU, ROBERT A (D)
Mass State Rep
b Dorchester, Mass, Nov 4, 20; s Albert G Vigneau & Helen R Mehlinger V; m 1947 to Alice V McHugh; c Mary A, Therese M, Robert A, Jr, Peter J, Paul F & Patrice A. Educ: Mass Univ Exten; Benedictis George Sch Art; Northeastern Univ. Polit & Govt Pos: Selectman, Burlington, Mass, 46-47 & 64-; mem, Dem Town Comt, 65-; Mass State Rep, 69- Bus & Prof Pos: Pub acct, currently. Mil Serv: Entered as Pvt, Army, 42, released as Lt, 45, after serv in 1st Armored Div, NAfrica & Italy, ETO, 43-45; Silver Star; Purple Heart. Mem: Am Legion; DAV; VFW; KofC; Amputated Vet Asn. Relig: Catholic. Mailing Add: 5 Elm Ave Burlington MA 01803

VIGORITO, JOSEPH PHILLIP (D)
US Rep, Pa
b Niles, Ohio, Nov 10, 18; m to Florence Hoppe; c Tina, Barbara & Linda. Educ: Wharton Sch of Finance, Univ Pa, BS econ, 47; Univ Denver, MBA, 49. Polit & Govt Pos: US Rep, Pa, 64-; deleg, Dem Nat Mid-Term Conf, 74. Bus & Prof Pos: CPA; asst prof, Pa State Univ.

Mil Serv: Army, 1st Lt, 42-45; Purple Heart. Legal Res: 2613 Rudolph Ave Erie PA 16508 Mailing Add: 440 Cannon House Off Bldg Washington DC 20515

VILLA, AL (D)
Mem, Dem Nat Comt, Calif
Mailing Add: 508 Rowell Bldg Fresno CA 93721

VILLA, THOMAS A (D)
Mo State Rep
Mailing Add: 6136 Arendes Dr St Louis MO 63116

VILLANO, VINCENT (D)
Conn State Rep
Mailing Add: 205 Church St New Haven CT 06510

VILLAR, EMERY L (D)
La State Rep
b Bnignac, La, Oct 2, 20; s John Daniel Villar, Sr & Josephine Blackwell V; m 1941 to Winnie Marie Gautreau; c Dianne V (Mrs Herin), Dolores V (Mrs Smith) & Ronald P. Educ: Gonzales High Sch, grad. Polit & Govt Pos: Sch bd mem, Seventh Ward, Ascension Parish, La, 51-60; La State Rep, Ascension Parish, 60- Bus & Prof Pos: Supvr, Humble Oil & Refining Co, 50- Mem: F&AM. Relig: Baptist. Legal Res: 223 Neal Dr Gonzales LA 70737 Mailing Add: PO Box 216 Gonzales LA 70737

VILLAREAL, PATRICIA JANE (D)
b Sonora, Calif, Aug 27, 49; d Lonnie B Villareal & Stella Finnegan V; single. Educ: St Mary's Univ (Tex), BA in urban studies, 72; Sigma Tau Sigma. Polit & Govt Pos: Campaign mgr, Tex State Rep Campaign, 70 & State Senate Campaign, 72; mem staff, McGovern Presidential Campaign, 72; deleg, Dem Nat Conv, 72; field rep, US Comn Civil Rights, 73-75; deleg, Tex State Dem Conv, 74; staff analyst, Subcom on Civil & Const Rights, House Judiciary Comt, 75- Publ: Auth, To regulate in the public interest, US Comn Civil Rights, 10/74. Mem: Mex Am Nat Women's Orgn; Dem Women of Bexar Co, Tex. Relig: Catholic. Legal Res: 126 Manning Dr San Antonio TX 78228 Mailing Add: 4436 MacArthur Blvd NW Apt 1A Washington DC 20007

VILLARREAL, CARLOS C (R)
Comnr, US Postal Rate Comn
b Brownsville, Tex, Nov 9, 24; s Jesus Jose Villarreal & Elisa L Castaneda V; m 1948 to Doris Ann Akers; c Timothy John & David Leroux. Educ: US Naval Acad, BS, 48; US Navy Postgrad, MS, 50. Hon Degrees: LLD, St Mary's Univ, 73. Polit & Govt Pos: Adminr, Urban Mass Transportation Admin, Dept of Transportation, 69-72; comnr, Postal Rate Comn, 73- Bus & Prof Pos: Mgr, marine & indust oper, Gen Elec Co, Cincinnati, Ohio, 56-66; vpres mkt & admin, The Marquardt Corp, Van Nuys, Calif, 66-69. Mil Serv: Entered as Ens, Navy, 48, released as Lt, 56, after serv in Destroyers & minesweepers, Atlantic & Pac Fleets. Publ: Transit on the move, Mod RR, 4/70; 10-year, 20-billion dollar transit market, Rwy Age, 8/70; Urban mass transportation, Am Road Builder, 10/70. Mem: Am Inst Aeronaut & Astronaut; Soc Naval Architects & Marine Engrs; Navy League of US; Army-Navy Club; Washington, DC Cong Country Club. Relig: Catholic. Mailing Add: Postal Rate Commission 2000 L St NW Washington DC 20268

VINCENT, DWIGHT HAROLD (R)
Chmn, 15th Cong Dist Rep Party, Mich
b Akron, Ohio, Apr 29, 30; s Harold Sellow Vincent & Frances Willard Hill V; m 1952 to Cynthia Lou Stein; c George Harold, Patricia Louise & Emily Helen. Educ: Univ Mich, AB in Law, 52, JD, 57. Polit & Govt Pos: Chmn, 15th Cong Dist Rep Party, Mich, currently; deleg, Rep Nat Conv, 68 & 72. Bus & Prof Pos: Attorney; sr partner, Beaumont, Smith & Harris. Mil Serv: Entered as Ens, Navy, 52, released as Lt(jg), 53, after serv on DD; Capt, Naval Res, currently, CO NARS Y-1; UN, China & Korea Campaign Ribbons; Four Stars. Mem: Am, Mich & Detroit Bar Asns. Relig: Lutheran. Mailing Add: 23413 Hill St Dearborn Heights MI 48127

VINCENT, G W (BILL) (D)
Ky State Rep
Mailing Add: Rte 2 Box 379 Leitchfield KY 42754

VINCENT, JOHN C (D)
Mont State Rep
Mailing Add: 908 S Tracy Bozeman MT 59715

VINCENT, ROBERT CARR (R)
Chmn, Cimarron Co Rep Party, Okla
b Pampa, Tex, Dec 1, 30; s Clifton Eli Vincent & Edna Carr V; m 1961 to Margaret Ann Weatherly; c Dawn, Carr, John & Clifton. Educ: Tex Tech Col, BBA, 53. Polit & Govt Pos: Chmn, Cimarron Co Rep Party, Okla, 67- Bus & Prof Pos: Rancher. Mil Serv: Entered as Pvt, Army, 53, released as E-3, 55, after serv in 42nd Field Artillery Bn, Germany, 54-55; Nat Defense Serv, Army Occup & Good Conduct Medals. Mem: Am Nat Cattlemen's Asn; Panhandle Livestock Asn; Farm Bur; Panhandle Plains Hist Soc. Relig: Episcopal. Mailing Add: Rte 1 Box 64 Boise City OK 73933

VINCENTI, SHELDON ARNOLD (D)
b Ogden, Utah, Sept 4, 38; s Arnold J Vincenti & Mae Burch V; m 1964 to Elaine Cathryn Wacker; c Matthew Lewis. Educ: Harvard Univ, AB, 60, Law Sch, JD, 63. Polit & Govt Pos: Asst city attorney, Ogden City, Utah, 66-69; city attorney, S Ogden City, 68-70; chmn, Weber Co Dem Comt, 69-70; legis asst, US Rep K Gunn McKay, Utah, 71-72, admin asst, 73- Bus & Prof Pos: Practicing attorney, Ogden, Utah, 66-70. Mil Serv: Entered as 1st Lt, Army, 63, released as Capt, 64, after serv in 902nd Intel Corps Group, Washington, DC. Mem: Utah State Bar Asn. Legal Res: 2512 Tyler Ave Ogden UT 84401 Mailing Add: 6011 33rd St NW Washington DC 20015

VINICH, JOHN PAUL (D)
Wyo State Rep
b Lander, Wyo, June 13, 50; s Mike M Vinich & Mabel R Petro V; single. Educ: Univ Wyo, BS in Social Work, 72; Wyo Human Resource Coun. Polit & Govt Pos: Wyo State Rep, 75-, mem revenue comt, Wyo House Rep, 75- Bus & Prof Pos: Dir, Big Bros, Casper, Wyo, 72-73; mgr, Union Bar & Lounge, Hudson, 73-75, mgr, Hudson Youth Ctr, Hudson, 74-75. Mem:

Eagles; Elks; Hudson Vol Firemen. Relig: Catholic. Mailing Add: Main St Box 67 Hudson WY 82515

VINOVICH, RALPH (R)
b Peoria, Ill, June 23, 28; s Ralph Vinovich (deceased) & Martha Mrvos V (deceased); m 1962 to Mary Catherine Reynolds; c Sam Matthew & Paul David. Educ: Am Univ, BS, 67. Polit & Govt Pos: Spec asst, US Sen Everett M Dirksen, Ill, 55-67; admin asst, US Rep Robert H Michel, Ill, 67- Bus & Prof Pos: Grain buyer, J Younge Grain Co, Peoria, Ill, 46-51 & W W Dewey & Sons, 53-55. Mil Serv: Entered as Seaman Recruit, Navy, 51, released as PO 3/C, 53, after serv in US Naval Sta, Atlantic Fleet, Bermuda. Relig: Protestant. Legal Res: 2600 W Starr St Peoria IL 61605 Mailing Add: 2701 Parkway Place Cheverly MD 20785

VINSON, ROY FURMAN (D)
b Matador, Tex, Apr 15, 21; s Oscar Vinson & Maud Hudson V; m 1943 to Beverly Gray; c Roger Furman & Linda (Mrs Perryman). Educ: Tex Tech Univ, 37-41. Polit & Govt Pos: Chmn, Motley Co Dem Party, Tex, formerly. Mil Serv: Entered as Pvt, Army, 42, released 1st Lt, 46, after serv in Co E, 307th Inf, 77th Div, Pac Theatre, 44-45; Purple Heart; Bronze Star with Oak Leaf Cluster; Presidential Unit Citation. Mem: Farm Bur; Mason; Shrine. Relig: Methodist. Mailing Add: Star Rte Flomot TX 79234

VIOLETTE, ELMER H (D)
b Van Buren, Maine, Feb 2, 21; s Vital E Violette & Estell Bosse V; m 1946 to Marcella Belanger; c Dennis, Louise, Mark, Thomas & Paul. Educ: Ricker Jr Col; Boston Univ Law Sch, 50. Polit & Govt Pos: Mem, Maine Comt on Children & Youth, formerly; Maine State Rep, 42 & 46-48; chmn, Van Buren Dem Comt, 54-, chmn, Aroostook Co Dem Comt, 58-70; judge, Van Buren Munic Court, 57-61; Maine State Sen, 64-74; deleg, Dem Nat Conv, 68 & 72; mem, Maine State Dem Comt, 71- Bus & Prof Pos: Trustee, Ricker Col; chmn bd trustees, Van Buren Light & Power Dist; dir, Northeast Pub Power Asn; chmn, Van Buren Housing Authority, formerly; trustee, Van Buren Community Hosp; chmn, Maine Citizens for Dickey-Lincoln Sch Hydroelectric Proj. Mil Serv: Entered as Pvt, Army Air Force, 42, released as M/Sgt, 46. Mem: Rotary; Am Legion; KofC; PTA; Christian Family Movement. Relig: Roman Catholic. Legal Res: 42 Violette St Van Buren ME 04785 Mailing Add: Box 56 Van Buren ME 04785

VIRGILIO, ANDREW D (D)
NY State Assemblyman
Mailing Add: 17 Lynwood Dr Brockport NY 14420

VIRTS, CHARLES CLIFTON (D)
Md State Deleg
b Leesburg, Va, Mar 3, 10; s Charles Clifton Virts & Maude Smith V; m 1942 to Stella Anne Overman; c Cynthia (Mrs Wickless) & Charles Clifton, III. Educ: Univ Va, 31-34; Univ Md, LLB, 40. Polit & Govt Pos: Md State Deleg, 47- Mem: Frederick Co Bar Asn; Detrick Boy Scouts; Elks 684; Moose, 371; Yellow Springs Lions. Relig: Episcopal. Legal Res: 423 Lee Pl Frederick MD 21701 Mailing Add: 110 W Church St Frederick MD 21701

VISOTCKY, RICHARD (D)
NJ State Assemblyman
Mailing Add: State House Trenton NJ 08625

VITANZA, THOMAS ANTHONY (D)
b Buffalo, NY, Nov 6, 32; s Thomas Vitanza & Jennie Bauda V; m 1955 to Joan Cavanagh; c Thomas, Karen, Michael, Deborah & Mary. Educ: Lemoyne Col, BA, 55; Syracuse Law Sch, LLB, 58; Alpha Sigma Nu. Polit & Govt Pos: City committeeman, Second Ward, Norwich, NY, 65-; chmn, Chenango Co Dem Comt, 68-74. Mem: Chenango Co Bar Asn; NY State Trial Lawyers Asn; Elks; KofC; Kiwanis. Relig: Roman Catholic. Legal Res: 39 Canasawacta St Norwich NY 13815 Mailing Add: Box 632 Norwich NY 13815

VIVEIROS, CARLTON M (D)
Mass State Rep
Mailing Add: State Capitol Boston MA 02133

VIVIAN, WESTON E (D)
b Nfld, Can, Oct 25, 24; m to Anne Biggs, wid; c Byron, Alice, Leslie & Sarah. Educ: Union Col, BS, 45; Mass Inst Technol, MS, 49; Univ Mich, PhD in Elec Eng, 59. Polit & Govt Pos: Cand for City Coun, Ann Arbor, Mich, 58 & 59; chmn, Ann Arbor City Dem Comt, 59-60; US Rep, Second Cong Dist, Mich, 65-66, mem, Sci & Astronaut Comt, US House of Rep; Dem nominee for Cong, Second Dist, 66 & 68; mem pub eval comt, for state tech serv prog, US Dept of Commerce, 67-68; chmn comt on admin of training progs, Dept of Health, Educ & Welfare, 67-68; mem, Nat Comt on US-China Rels, 68-69; organizer, Robert Kennedy for President Campaign, Mich, 68. Bus & Prof Pos: Summer staff mem, Lincoln Labs, Mass Inst Tech; research engr & lectr elec eng, Univ Mich, 51-60; founder, vpres & mem bd dirs, Conductron Corp, Ann Arbor, 60-65; consult, Nat Coun on Marine Resources & Ocean Eng, Washington, DC, 67, Bendix Aviation Corp & Corps of Engrs; vpres, KMS Industs, Ann Arbor, Mich, 67-68; consult, Great Lakes Basin Comn, Ann Arbor, 68; mgr astrotype div, Info Control Systs, Inc, 68; nat lectr, Asn for Comput Machinery, 69; chmn, Spuntech Housing, Inc, 69; vpres & mem bd, Vicom Industs, Inc, 70-73; bd dirs, IAM, Inc, Perrysburg, Ohio, 72-74; adj prof, Univ Mich, 73- Mil Serv: Entered as A/S, Naval Res, 43, released as Ensign, 46. Mem: Sigma Xi; Am Phys Soc; NAACP; Former bd mem, Ann Arbor & Mich United Funds. Relig: Unitarian. Mailing Add: 2717 Kenilworth Dr Ann Arbor MI 48104

VIVION, VERN (R)
Chmn, Carbon Co Rep Cent Comt, Wyo
b Rawlins, Wyo, Jan 22, 26; s Charles George Vivion & Grace Murray V; m 1947 to Della Maier; c Valri Lynn, Kristin Ann & Mary Maier. Educ: Univ Wyo, BA, 48; Iron Skull; Kappa Sigma. Polit & Govt Pos: Wyo State Rep, 61-65; mem, Coun State Govt, 61-65, chmn agr comt, Western Div, 63-65; Wyo rep, Interstate Conf on Water Probs, 61-65; chmn, Nat Comt to Draft Interstate Compact for Control of Agr Pests & Diseases, 63-65; mem, Gov Comt on Educ, 64-65; chmn, State Manpower Adv Comt, 64-; chmn, Gov Comt on Voc-Tech Educ, 67-69; chmn, Carbon Co Rep Cent Comt, 70- Bus & Prof Pos: Vpres, Leo Sheep Co, Rawlins, Wyo, 48-; partner, Mallon-Vivion Ranch, Walden, Colo, 48-; pres, Elk Mt Safari, Rawlins, Wyo, 66-; mem bd dirs, Wyo Taxpayers Asn, 68-; past chmn, Wyo Coun Econ Develop, 69-70. Mem: Wyo Wool Growers Asn; Nat Wool Growers Asn (pres, currently); Lions; Mason; Elks. Relig: Episcopal. Legal Res: 1457 Coulson Pkwy Rawlins WY 82301 Mailing Add: Box 674 Rawlins WY 82301

VOELKER, ROY E (R)
Chmn, Mahaska Co Rep Comt, Iowa
b Winona, Minn, Apr 5, 23; s Edward A Voelker & Bernice Edwards V; m 1956 to Shirley Sigman. Educ: Gregg Col, Chicago, Ill, 46. Polit & Govt Pos: Off shorthand reporter, Iowa Eighth Judicial Dist, 46-47 & 72- & Iowa Sixth Judicial Dist, 47-71; precinct committeeman, Rep Party, 60-68; chmn, Mahaska Co Rep Comt, Iowa, 66-; bd dirs, Conservative Coalition of Iowa, 75- Bus & Prof Pos: Ed, Nat Shorthand Reporter, Nat Shorthand Reporters Asn, 53-66, bd dirs, Asn, 69-74, vpres, 74- Mil Serv: Entered as Pvt, Army Air Corps, 42, released as S/Sgt, 46, after serv in US Strategic Air Forces, ETO, 43-46; Am & ETO Ribbons. Mem: Iowans for Right to Work (bd mem, 68-); Iowa Voting Machine Comn; AF&AM; Am Legion; VFW. Honors & Awards: Cert Shorthand Reporter, Iowa; Cert of Proficiency, Nat Shorthand Reporters Asn & Distinguished Serv Award for outstanding serv to shorthand reporting profession, 68; Gregg Diamond Medal (shorthand award); Expert Rifleman, Nat Rifle Asn. Mailing Add: 1510 S First St Oskaloosa IA 52577

VOELTER, CHARLES EVERETT (R)
b Temple, Tex, July 29, 35; s Charles W Voelter & Abbie Stone V; m 1959 to Marion Adams; c Alison & Charles E, Jr. Educ: Tex A&M Univ, BArchit, 57. Polit & Govt Pos: Chmn, Bell Co Rep Party, Tex, formerly. Bus & Prof Pos: Architect & partner, Logsdon & Voelter Architects, 61- Mil Serv: Entered as 2nd Lt, Army, 59, released as Capt, 61, after serv in Missiles Artil. Mem: Am Inst Architects; Tex Soc Architects; Construction Specifications Inst; Lions; Temple Civic Theatre. Honors & Awards: AIA Award, Am Inst of Architects, 57; Grand Prize, Clay Prod of Southwest, 58; Second Prize, Tex Concrete Masonry Asn, 58. Relig: Lutheran Missouri Synod. Legal Res: 104 Blackfoot Dr Temple TX 76501 Mailing Add: 306 First National Temple TX 76501

VOGEL, CHARLES JOSEPH (D)
b Otter Tail Co, Star Lake Twp, Minn, Sept 20, 98; s Philip Francis Vogel & Anna Marie Jenson V; m 1925 to Fern Nesbitt; c Janet Dunsmoor (Mrs Elver T Pearson) & Jon Nesbitt. Educ: Huron Col, 17-18; Univ Minn, LLB, 23; Order of the Coif; Phi Kappa Delta; Phi Alpha Delta. Polit & Govt Pos: Chmn, NDak State Dem Party, 37-39; Dem Nat Committeeman, NDak, 38-40; nominee for US Sen, 40; US Dist Judge, NDak, 41-54; US Circuit Judge, 54-, Chief Judge, US Court of Appeals, Eighth Circuit, 65-68. Bus & Prof Pos: Practicing attorney, 23-41. Mil Serv: Entered as Pvt, Army, 18, released as Sgt, 19, after serv in Signal Corps & Tank Corps. Mem: Am Bar Asn; Am Judicature Soc; Neuropsychiatric Inst (bd gov); Am Legion. Relig: Episcopal. Legal Res: 1701 Tenth St S Fargo ND 58102 Mailing Add: PO Box 3006 Fargo ND 58102

VOGEL, JOHN HENRY (R)
Kans State Rep
b Stuttgart, Kans, May 14, 16; s John Henry Vogel & Margaret Veeh V; m to Irene Dorothy Schaake; c Nancy Sue & Gerald Max. Educ: Univ Kans, BS Bus, 39; Alpha Kappa Psi. Polit & Govt Pos: Kans State Rep, currently. Bus & Prof Pos: Dir, Douglas Co State Bank; farmer, stockman & businessman; mem bd gov, Lawrence Higher Educ Loan Prog. Mem: CofC; life mem Univ Kans Alumni Asn & Sertoma. Honors & Awards: One of ten Kans Farm Bur Leaders of The Year, 63. Relig: Lutheran. Mailing Add: Rte 4 Lawrence KS 66044

VOGES, DOROTHY JESSIE (D)
b Kelso, Mo, June 15, 43; d Eugene Robert & Irene Schlosser R; m 1962 to E Keith Voges; c Laura Jean. Educ: Illmo-Scott City High Sch, 4 years; Nat Hon Soc. Polit & Govt Pos: Secy, Scott Co Dem Cent Comt, formerly; committeewoman, Moreland Twp, Mo, currently. Bus & Prof Pos: Dep circuit clerk, Scott Co, Mo, 61-65, secy, Treas, 65, dep magistrate clerk; owner & operator, cafe, currently. Mem: Legal Secretaries Asn; Dem Women's Club (secy). Relig: Catholic. Mailing Add: Benton MO 63736

VOGT, JOHN W (D)
Fla State Sen
b Lake Wales, Fla, Dec 28, 36; s Louis Harold Vogt (deceased) & Mildred Johnson V; div; c Leeanne & Lisa. Educ: Univ Fla, BS Civil Eng, 61; Univ SFla, Eng Admin; Rutgers Univ, Acct Admin; chap pres, Alpha Tau Omega. Polit & Govt Pos: Fla State Sen, 17th Dist, 72- Bus & Prof Pos: Design engr, Wellman-Lord, Inc, Lakeland, Fla, 61-63, structural proj leader, 64-66; proj design engr, Brown Eng Co, Cape Canaveral, 63-64; prin officer, Meridian Eng Inc, Titusville, 66-67; proj mgr, MDC Syst Corp, New York, 67-68; exec vpres, Moorhead Eng Co, Ocala, 68-69; chief civil engr, Brevard Eng Co, Cape Canaveral, 69- Mem: Nat Soc Prof Engrs; Fla Eng Soc; Meritt Island Jaycees; Kiwanis; Fla Audubon Soc. Honors & Awards: Engr of the Year for 1972, Canaveral Coun of Tech Socs, 73; Outstanding Freshman Fla State Sen, 73; Fla Outstanding Young Dem, 73. Relig: Baptist. Mailing Add: Suite 902 1980 N Atlantic Ave Cocoa Beach FL 32931

VOIGHT, DAVID K (D)
b Billings, Mont, Sept 3, 41; s Harold Raymond Voight & Annelee Anderson V; m 1965 to Karen Sue Tyner; c Nancy. Educ: Univ Mont, BA, 65; Sigma Alpha Epsilon. Polit & Govt Pos: Precinct committeeman, Spearfish, SDak, 68-70; chmn, Lawrence Co Dem Party, SDak, 70; legis asst, US Rep James Abourezk, SDak, 71-73, legis dir, US Sen James Abourezk, SDak, 73- Bus & Prof Pos: Asst prof, Black Hills State Col, 65-70. Mem: Delta Tau Kappa. Legal Res: Spearfish SD Mailing Add: 6504 Lone Oak Dr Bethesda MD 20034

VOISARD, LEO A (D)
Ind State Rep
Mailing Add: 3000 Burlington Dr Muncie IN 47302

VOLCKER, PAUL A (D)
b Cape May, NJ, Sept 5, 27; s Paul A Volcker & Alma Klippel V; m to Barbara Marie Bahnson; c Janice & James. Educ: Princeton Univ, BA summa cum laude, 49; Harvard Grad Sch of Pub Admin, MA in Polit Econ & Govt, 51; Rotary Found fel, London Sch Econ, 51-52; Phi Beta Kappa. Polit & Govt Pos: Research asst, Fed Reserve Bank of New York, summers 50 & 51, with Domestic Research Div, 53-55, spec asst, Securities Dept, 55-57; jr mgt asst, Treas Dept, 51, dir, Off of Financial Anal, 62-63, Dep Under Secy for Monetary Affairs, 63-65, Under Secy for Monetary Affairs, 69-75; chmn, Tech Adv Group, Balance of Payments Adv Comt, Dept of Commerce, 66 & 67. Bus & Prof Pos: Mem faculty, NY Inst of Finance, 53-57; financial economist, Chase Manhattan Bank, 57-62 & 65-69. Mem: Am Econ Asn; Am Finance Asn; Metrop Econ Asn; Nat Asn of Bus Economists. Honors & Awards: Recipient, Arthur S Flemming Award, One of Ten Outstanding Young Men in Fed Serv; Exceptional Serv Award, Treas Dept, 65; Alexander Hamilton Award, Treas Dept, 73. Legal Res: Montclair NJ Mailing Add: Treasury Dept 15th & Pennsylvania Ave Washington DC 20220

VOLDAL, HENRIK (D)

b Valley City, NDak, May 14, 35; s Nels Voldal & Ruth Erickson V; m 1958 to Norma Bach; c Erik & Steven. Educ: Jamestown Col, BA, 59; Univ NDak, MEd, 61, EdD, 67; Phi Delta Kappa; Psi Chi. Polit & Govt Pos: Chmn, 24th Dist Dem Party, Bismarck, NDak, 74; deleg, Dem Nat Mid-Term Conf, 74; dep comnr agr, NDak, 74- Mil Serv: Entered as Pvt, Army, 54, released as Pfc, 56. Mem: Farmers Union; Elks; Am Civil Liberties Union. Mailing Add: 202 Teton Ave Bismarck ND 58501

VOLK, DAVID LAWRENCE (R)
State Treas, SDak

b Mitchell, SDak, Apr 12, 47; s Erwin J Volk & Joan Nieses V; m 1969 to Susan Tessier. Educ: Northern State Col, BA Ed, 69; Augustana Col (SDak), summer 71. Polit & Govt Pos: Field rep, US Rep, Ben Reifel, SDak, 66-69; State Treas, SDak, 73- Mil Serv: Entered as E-1, Army, 69, released as SP-4, 71, after serv in 101st Airborne Div, Vietnam, 70-71; Bronze Star; Army Commendation Medal, Vietnam Serv Medal. Mem: Jaycees; Am Legion; Exchange Club; Kiwanis; Elks. Honors & Awards: Sch Award, SDak Am Legion, 65; Gov George T Mikkelson Award, 68 & Sen Francis Case Award, Outstanding Young Rep, 68, SDak, Young Rep. Relig: Catholic. Mailing Add: 223 N Pierce Pierre SD 57501

VOLKEMA, RUSSELL H (D)
Mem Exec Comt, Ohio Dem Party

b Moline, Mich, May 23, 20; s Andrew Volkema & Hazel Reminga V; m 1950 to Lois Jean; c Colette, Daniel, Michael & Kimberly. Educ: Calvin Col, AB, 51; Univ Miami Sch Law, JD, 53; exec ed, Miami Law Quart. Polit & Govt Pos: Dem nominee for US Rep, Ohio, 68; chmn, Ohio Dem Lawyers Asn, 71-74; mem, Exec Comt, Ohio Dem Party, 72- Mil Serv: Entered as Seaman 2/C, Navy, 42, released as Lt, 46, after serv in Naval Air Corps, Pac Theatre, 43-45; Presidential Unit Citation; Pac Theatre Medal with 6 Battle Stars. Publ: Volkema's Ohio forms for pleading a negiligence case. Mem: Phi Delta Phi; Bryan Inc; Am Bar Asn; Asn of Trial Lawyers of Am (bd mem, 69-72); Am Legion. Relig: Christian Reformed Church. Mailing Add: 88 E Broad St Columbus OH 43215

VOLKER, DALE M (D)
NY State Assemblyman
Mailing Add: 31 Darwin Dr Depew NY 14043

VOLKMER, HAROLD L (D)
Mo State Rep
Mailing Add: 719 Country Club Dr Hannibal MO 63401

VOLLMAN, JAMES WILLIAM (D)
Mem Exec Bd, 16th Dist Dem Orgn, Mich

b Cincinnati, Ohio, Mar 26, 52; s Clarence Victor Grochulski (stepfather) & Mary Jo McGovern G; single. Educ: Univ Mich, BA magna cum laude, 74; Phi Eta Sigma; Phi Beta Kappa. Polit & Govt Pos: Precinct deleg, 16th Dist Dem Orgn, 72-76, mem exec bd, 73-; deleg, Dem Nat Conv, 72; campaign mgr, Jeff Padden for State Rep. Mem: UAW. Relig: Roman Catholic. Mailing Add: 2036 Kingsbury Dearborn MI 48128

VOLPE, JOHN ANTHONY (R)
US Ambassador to Italy

b Wakefield, Mass, Dec 8, 08; s Vito Volpe (deceased) & Filomena Benedetto V (deceased); m 1934 to Jennie Benedetto; c John A, Jr & Jean (Mrs Roger Rotondi). Educ: Wentworth Inst, grad. Hon Degrees: Dr Eng, DPA, LHD & LLD from various cols & univs. Polit & Govt Pos: Dep chmn, Mass Rep State Comt, 50-53; mem comn, Mass Dept Pub Works, 53-56; first Fed Hwy Adminr, Fed Interstate Hwy Prog, 56-57; Gov, Mass, 61-63 & 65-69; deleg, Rep Nat Conv, 60, 64, 68 & 72; Secy of Transportation, 69-73; US Ambassador to Italy, 73- Bus & Prof Pos: Founder, John A Volpe Construction Co, Malden, Mass, 33, pres, 33-60, bd chmn, 60-69; treas adv bd, Don Orione Home for the Aged, East Boston, Mass, 50-53. Mil Serv: Entered as Lt(jg), Navy, 43, released as Lt Comdr, 46, after serv in Civil Engr Corps. Mem: Capitol Hill Club; KofM; Sons of Italy in Am; Am Legion. Honors & Awards: People to People Town Affil Award, 66; Knight of the Grand Cross, Order Merit, Repub Italy, 69; Construction's Man of the Year, 70; Knight Comdr with Star, Equestrian Order of the Holy Sepulchre of Jerusalem. Relig: Catholic. Legal Res: MA Mailing Add: Ambassador to Italy Dept of State Washington DC 20521

VOLTERRA, MAX (D)
Mass State Rep

b Milano, Italy, Jan 7, 36; s Renzo Volterra & Germana Levi V; m 1965 to Marion Sitnick; c Hannah & Joel. Educ: Brown Univ, ScB, 57; George Washington Univ Law Sch, JD, 62; Phi Delta Phi; Delta Kappa Epsilon. Polit & Govt Pos: Mem city coun, Attleboro, Mass, 65-67, city solicitor, 67-70; Mass State Rep, 71- Bus & Prof Pos: Lawyer, Attleboro, Mass, 65- Mil Serv: Entered as Ens, Navy, 57, released as Lt(jg), 59, after serv at Newport, RI. Mem: Mass Bar Asn (bd deleg); Boston & Fourth Dist Court Bar Asns; Am Civil Liberties Union. Legal Res: 65 Locust Attleboro MA 02703 Mailing Add: 300 N Main Attleboro MA 02703

VON BOECKMAN, JAMES (D)
Ill State Sen
Mailing Add: 1607 Hamilton Pekin IL 61554

VON BUZBEE, KENNETH (D)
Ill State Sen
Mailing Add: RR 1 Makanda IL 62958

VON CHRISTIERSON, KARL (R)
Mem, Calif Rep State Cent Exec Comt

b Madera, Calif, Jan 20, 16; s Sune von Christierson & Katheryn Gilbert C; m 1940 to Elise Shryock; div, 69; c Sigurd & Eric; m 1971 to Evelyn Rheman; stepchildren Janet Driscoll Weaver, Carloe Driscoll Redona & Timmothy Mark Driscoll. Educ: Temple Univ, 2 years; Univ Calif, Davis, summer courses. Polit & Govt Pos: Mayor, Soledad, Calif, 44-52; trustee, Soledad Elem Sch, 48-52 & Monterey Co Salinas Union High Sch Dist, 54-58; mem, Monterey Co Rep Cent Comt, 58-, chmn 61-68, vchmn, currently; mem, Rep State Cent Finance Comt, 60-; mem, Calif Rep Assembly, 60-; chmn, Rep Co Chmn Asn, 62-66; mem, Calif Rep State Cent Exec Comt, 62-; secy, Rep State Cent Comt, 64-68; mem, Calif Rep League, 64- Mem: Calif Tomato Growers Asn (founding dir & chmn, grower-shipper legis comt, 67-); Corral de Tierra Country Club; Press & Union League; Capitol Hill Club. Honors & Awards: Silver Beaver Award. Relig: Episcopal. Legal Res: 4085 Sunridge Pebble Beach CA 93593 Mailing Add: PO Box 719 Salinas CA 93901

VON DER LANCKEN, CARL (D)

b Rochester, NY, Apr 22, 10; s Frank von der Lancken & Giulia Ulbrich V; m 1945 to Mary-Ellen Collins; c Carla & Paula. Educ: Western Reserve Univ, 29-30; George Washington Univ, 30-31; Cumberland Univ, LLB, 32; Univ Tulsa, 27-29, BA, 33; Tulane Univ, MA, 36; Harvard Univ, 37-38; Samford Univ, JD, 69; Sigma Theta Tau. Polit & Govt Pos: Polit action dir, United Shoe Workers Am, 44-46; exec dir, Coun Am-Soviet Friendship, Chicago, Ill, 46-47; state dir, Progressive Party Okla, 48-49; mem nat comt, 48-50; nat pub affairs chmn, Am Ethical Union, 54-56; exec dir, Sane Nuclear Policy Comt, Long Island, 55-57; chmn, Kefauver for President Comt, 55-56 & Wayne Morse for President Comt, formerly; founding deleg, Westchester Co Concerned Dem, formerly; Dem nominee, Westchester Bd Legislators, formerly. Bus & Prof Pos: Lectr contemporary polit theory, Univ Tulsa, 36-37; pub rels counsel, Harry Caylor Assoc, Chicago, Ill, 42-43; legal counsel, Nat Labor Bur, 43-44; lectr Am cult, Brazil-USA Cult Union, Sao Paulo, 50-51; prof polit sci, Westchester Community Col, Valhalla, NY, 59-, pres, Fedn Teachers, 71-73; mem bd educ, Greenburgh, 63-66; secy, United Fedn Col Teachers, 71-73; moderator, Pub Affairs Talk Show, Radio Sta WFAS, White Plains, 71-72. Publ: Polit anal articles, The Black Dispatch, 48-49; polit writer, The Nat Guardian, 49-50; columnist, The Westchester Weekly News, 70-71. Mem: NY State United Teachers; Am Civil Liberties Union; Common Cause; NAACP; Am Judicature Soc. Honors & Awards: State Univ Award for community col cult prog in NY State, 66; Named a mem of NY State Horseshoe Pitching Hall of Fame, 74; Spec Serv Award, NY State United Teachers, 75. Mailing Add: 2 Manitou Trail White Plains NY 10603

VON DOHLEN, TIMOTHY DON (D)
Tex State Rep

b Cuero, Tex, July 20, 43; s Leonard Harold Von Dohlen & Elizabeth O'Connell V; m 1964 to Cherie Shelton; c Tim, II, Christopher & Patrick. Educ: Univ Tex, Austin, BS Pharm, 61-61, JD, 70; Lambda Chi Alpha; Kappa Psi; Delta Theta Phi. Polit & Govt Pos: Tex State Rep, 39th Dist, 71- Bus & Prof Pos: Pharmacist, Von Dohlen-Byrd Pharm, 66-69. Mem: Tex & Am Pharmaceutical Asns; KofC; Rotary Club; Tex Farm Bur. Relig: Catholic. Mailing Add: 207 W Garden Goliad TX 77963

VON REICHBAUER, PETER (D)
Wash State Sen
Mailing Add: Rte 2 Box 206 Burton WA 98013

VOORHIS, HORACE JERRY (D)

b Ottawa, Kans, Apr 6, 01; s Charles Brown Voorhis & Ella Ward Smith V; m 1924 to Alice Louise Livingston; c Alice Nell, Charles Brown & Jerry Livingston. Educ: Yale, AB, 23; Claremont Col, MA, 28; St Francis Xavier Univ, LLD, 53. Polit & Govt Pos: US Rep, 12th Dist, Calif, 37-47. Bus & Prof Pos: Traveling rep, YMCA in Germany, 23-24; worker, Ford Assembly Plant, Charlotte, NC, 24-25; teacher, Allendale Farm Sch, Lake Villo, Ill, 25-26; dir, Dray Cottage, Home for Boys, Laramie, Wyo, 26-27; head master & trustee, Voorhis Sch for Boys, 28-37; spec lectr, Pomona Col, 30-35; secy, Group Health Asn Am, 47-; exec dir, Coop League of US, 47-67, consult, 67- Publ: Strange Case of Richard Milhous Nixon, Eriksson, 72; Out of Dept, Out of Danger, Confessions of a Congressman; The Christian in Politics. Mem: Am Pub Health Asn; Nat Cath Rural Life Conf; Am Country Life Asn; Phi Delta Kappa; Phi Beta Kappa. Relig: Episcopal; Vestry of St Ambrose Episcopal Church, Sr Warden, 73- Legal Res: 633 W Bonita Ave Claremont CA 91711 Mailing Add: 114A N Indian Hill Blvd Claremont CA 91711

VOSBURGH, PAUL N (R)

b Lyons, NY, Jan 14, 35; s George Yeomans Vosburgh & Alice Noble V; m 1957 to Jane Berry; c Susan & Kay Dickinson. Educ: Rensselaer Polytech Inst, BS, 56; Pi Delta Epsilon; Delta Kappa Epsilon. Polit & Govt Pos: Chmn, Westmoreland Co Third Legis Dist, Pa, 62-64, 54th Legis Dist, 64-69, & 55th Legis Dist, 69-70; mem exec coun, Westmoreland Co Rep Party, 62-74; Rep precinct committeeman, City of Lower Burrell, Pa, 63-69, city chmn, 63-69; comnr, Westmoreland Co Housing Auth, 63-74, chmn, 65-71; deleg, Rep Nat Conv, 72. Bus & Prof Pos: Construction engr, Aluminum Co of Am, 56-58, develop engr, 58-68; mgr design & planning, Alcoa Housing & Urban Develop Div, 69-70, vpres, Alcoa Construction Syst, Inc, 71-75. Mil Serv: Entered as Trainee, Army, 57, released as Pvt, 58, after serv in Ft Leonard Wood, Mo. Mem: Jaycees; CofC. Relig: Protestant. Mailing Add: 3459 MacArthur Dr Murrysville PA 15668

VOSPER, F KENT (R)
NDak State Sen

b Neche, NDak, Nov 10, 21; s Fred Chester Vosper & Nell Wiley V; m 1943 to Phyllis Eileen Kelm; c Douglas Kent, Mark David & Fred Craig. Educ: NDak Agr Col; NDak State Sch Sci. Polit & Govt Pos: NDak State Sen, 75- Mil Serv: Entered as Aviation Cadet, Army Air Corps, 43, released as 1st Lt, 45, after serv in 15th Air Force, 454 BG 739 BS, POW, Italy, 43-45; Purple Heart; Air Medal with Clusters. Mem: Am Ex-Prisoner of War; Shrine; Am Legion; VFW. Mailing Add: Neche ND 58265

VOSS, GORDON OWEN (DFL)
Minn State Rep

b Duluth, Minn, Feb 25, 38; s Gordon Oscar Voss & Dorothy Bullard V; m 1961 to Elaine Delores Voldsness; c Gregory Owen & Kirsten Elaine. Educ: Univ Minn, Minneapolis, BSME, 61; PhD(mech eng), 70; Pi Tau Sigma; Tau Beta Pi. Polit & Govt Pos: Mem, Planning & Zoning Comt, Blaine, Minn, 70-71; pres, Blaine Dem-Farmer-Labor Club, 71-72; Minn State Rep, Dist 47B, 73- Bus & Prof Pos: Coop Work, A O Smith Corp, Milwaukee, Wis, 59-61; research & teaching asst, Univ Minn, Minneapolis, 61-70, research assoc mech eng, 70-71; asst prof, 71-72, research assoc, 73- Mem: Jaycees; Lions; Rotary. Relig: Protestant. Mailing Add: 11120 NE Seventh St Blaine MN 55434

VOSSMEYER, STEVE (D)
Mo State Rep
Mailing Add: 6050 Westminster St Louis MO 63112

VOSTRIZANSKY, DAVID JAMES (D)
Mem, Mich Dem State Cent Comt

b St Johns, Mich, Aug 26, 53; s Joe Vostrizansky & Stephanie Luznak V; single. Educ: Univ Mich, AB, 75. Polit & Govt Pos: Alt mem, Mich Dem State Cent Comt, 73-75, mem, 75-; deleg, Dem Nat Mid-Term Conf, 74; secy, Mich Young Dem, 74-75; corresponding secy, Col

Dem of Am, 75-76. Mem: Common Cause; Am for Dem Action. Mailing Add: 11426 Woodbridge Rd Bannister MI 48807

VRDOLYAK, EDWARD ROBERT (D)
Alderman, Chicago City Coun, Ill
b Chicago, Ill, Dec 28, 37; s Peter J Vrdolyak & Matilda V; m 1962 to Denise M Danaher; c Peter T, John K & Edward J. Educ: St Joseph Col, Ind, AB, 59; Univ Chicago, JD, 63. Polit & Govt Pos: Committeeman, Ill Dem Cent Comt, 68-72; alderman, Chicago City Coun, 71- Bus & Prof Pos: Attorney-at-law, 63- Mem: Am, Ill & Chicago Bar Asns; Am Judicature Soc; CofC. Relig: Catholic. Legal Res: 11455 S Ave J Chicago IL 60617 Mailing Add: 1925 E 95th St Chicago IL 60617

VREELAND, GEORGE WASHINGTON, JR (R)
Mem, Rep State Cent Comt Calif
b Stevbenville, Ohio, Jan 2, 19; s George W Vreeland & Maritta York Sisson V; m 1948 to Virginia Aileen Sisson; c Maritta Sisson & Harriet Ann. Educ: Cornell Univ, BS in AE; Phi Delta Theta. Polit & Govt Pos: Div chmn, Rep Precinct Orgn 47th Assembly Dist, Calif, 56, area chmn, 60-69; mem, Rep State Cent Comt, 64-; unit & assembly dist chmn, United Rep of Calif, 66- Bus & Prof Pos: Various eng capacities, US Steel Corp, 48-69. Mil Serv: Entered as 2nd Lt, Army Ord Dept, 41, released as Capt, 46, after serv in 350th Ord Bn, SPac, 43-46; Res, Maj (Ret). Mem: Am Soc Metals; Am Soc Iron & Steel Engrs; Am Soc Non-Destructive Testing. Relig: Episcopal. Mailing Add: 3425 Huntington Dr Pasadena CA 91107

VROON, PETER R (R)
Pa State Rep
Mailing Add: Capitol Bldg Harrisburg PA 17120

VUKCEVICH, STEVE (D)
Ariz State Rep
Mailing Add: Box 4 Sunset Rte Willcox AZ 85643

VULK, RAYMOND PAUL, SR (R)
Mem, Mont Rep State Cent Comt
b Helena, Mont, Oct 16, 43; s Charles Paul Vulk & Margaret Ann Schatz V; m 1963 to Sharon Lee; c Sarah Lee, Beth Marie, Amy Deatte & Raymond Paul, Jr. Educ: Carroll Col, 66-67. Polit & Govt Pos: Treas, Lewis & Clark Co Young Rep, 64, chmn, 65; Rep precinct committeeman, 65-; Western vchmn, Mont Young Rep, 67-69, chmn, 69-72, mem state bd, 67-; participant, Leadership Training Sch, Young Rep Nat Fedn, 69, mem, Region 9 Adv Comt, 70-; mem, Mont State Rep Cent Comt, 68- Bus & Prof Pos: Owner, dairy ranch, 65- Mil Serv: Entered as Pfc, Mont Nat Guard, 61, released as Cpl, 62, after serv in 3669 Heavy Equipment Co. Mem: Mont Farm Bur; Community Ctr Planning Comt Bd (vchmn); Am Dairy Asn. Relig: Episcopal. Mailing Add: 3345 Lincoln Rd E Helena MT 59601

VUREK, RUTH KATHRYN (D)
b Baltimore, Md, Dec 17, 32; d Preston Robert Hall & Mary Wilgis H; m to Gerald George Vurek; c Matthew Gerald. Educ: Johns Hopkins Univ, BS, 55; San Francisco State Col, 58-59; Univ Md, 57-58; San Jose State Col, 59-60. Polit & Govt Pos: Precinct chmn, Montgomery Co Dem Party, 67-72; campaign staff mem, Allen for Cong, 70; hq mgr, Montgomery Co McGovern for President Comt, 71-72; alt deleg, Dem Nat Conv, 72; mem, Md State Dem Cent Comt, 72-74; mem, Montgomery Co Dem Cent Comt, 72-74; admin aide to mem Md Legis, 75- Mem: Woman's Suburban Dem Club; Alliance for Dem Reform. Mailing Add: 5601 Huntington Pkwy Bethesda MD 20014

W

WACKER, JANET LOUISE (D)
b Columbus, Ohio, Mar 29, 46; d Howard Edward Wacker & Esther Elizabeth Cottrell W; single. Educ: Ohio State Univ, BS, 68; Cleveland State Univ, 71-72; Kent State Univ, MEd, 74; Scarlet & Gray Hon Serv Club. Polit & Govt Pos: Alt deleg, Dem Nat Conv, 72. Bus & Prof Pos: Teacher, Sowinski Sch, Cleveland Bd Educ, 68- Mem: Common Cause; Ohio State Univ Alumni Asn; Am Fedn Teachers; AFL-CIO. Honors & Awards: Martha Holden Jennings Teacher-Leader Award, 73. Relig: United Church of Christ. Mailing Add: 12000 Fairhill Rd Cleveland OH 44120

WACKETT, BYRON F (R)
Wis State Rep
b Randolph, Wis, Mar 21, 12. Educ: Randolph Pub Schs. Polit & Govt Pos: Mayor, Watertown, Wis, 46-49; Wis State Rep, 52- Bus & Prof Pos: Serv sta operator; salesman, formerly. Mem: Wis Asn of Petroleum Retailers (past pres); Watertown Chap Red Cross. Mailing Add: 100 Oak Hill Ct Watertown WI 53094

WADDELL, CHARLES L (D)
Va State Sen
Mailing Add: Rte 2 Box 299-B Sterling VA 22170

WADDELL, JAMES MADISON, JR (D)
SC State Sen
b Boydell, Ark, Nov 1, 22; s James Madison Waddell, Sr & Mabel Gibson W; m 1946 to Natalie Lavis; c James M, III, Michael Gibson & John Spencer. Educ: The Citadel, BS Civil Eng, 47. Hon Degrees: LLD, The Citadel, 72. Polit & Govt Pos: SC State Rep, 54-58, mem, Ways & Means Comt, SC House of Rep, formerly; SC State Sen, 15th Sen Dist 60-, chmn, Fish, Game & Forestry Comt, Tax Study Comn & Coastal Zone Planning & Mgt Coun, second vchmn, Finance Comt & mem, Banking & Ins Comt, Educ Comt, State Health Policy & Planning Coun & SC Educ Coun Comn, Educ Comn of the States, SC State Senate, currently. Bus & Prof Pos: Gen agt, Pilot Life Ins Co, 49-; pres, Citizens Ins Agency, 55-, pres, Riveracres Develop Corp, Beaufort, SC, 63-. Mil Serv: Entered Orgn Res Corps, 42, active duty, Inf, 43-46, Capt, serv in 335th Inf Regt, 84th Div, Ger; Purple Heart; Europe-Africa-Mid Eastern Ribbon with two Battle Stars; Am Theatre Medal; Victory Medal; Combat Inf Badge. Mem: Shrine; Coker Col (bd visitors); VFW; Am Legion; Clemson Univ (life trustee, 72-). Relig: Presbyterian; elder, First Presby Church, Beaufort, SC. Legal Res: Battery Creek PO Box 547 Beaufort SC 29002 Mailing Add: State House Columbia SC 29211

WADDELL, R BRUCE (R)
Ill State Sen
Mailing Add: Crescent Dr Dundee IL 60118

WADDILL, KATHRYN J (D)
Secy-treas, Hall Co Dem Exec Comt, Tex
b Hedlay, Tex, Aug 14, 26; d Clyde Grimsley & Ora Vee Hogue G; m 1971 to James R Waddill. Polit & Govt Pos: Secy-treas, Hall Co Dem Exec Comt, Tex, 67- Bus & Prof Pos: Mem staff, X-ray Dept, Goodall Hosp, 49-62; note dept & secy, Prod Credit Asn, 62-64; farming mgr, 62-71; off mgr, Western Alfalfa Corp, 71- Mem: Am Radiol Technicians; 18th Dist Am Legion Auxiliary; Tex Panhandle Commun Action Prog; Bus & Prof Women's Club. Relig: Christian. Mailing Add: 713 N 18th St Memphis TX 79245

WADDLE, TED W (R)
Ga State Rep
b Somerset, Ky, July 9, 28; s James K Waddle & Jessie L W; m 1949 to Mildred Barbara Westbrook; c Ted W, Jr, Tim B, Donna (Mrs Ronny Martin) & Debby (Mrs William Armstrong). Educ: Georgetown Col, 1 year. Polit & Govt Pos: Ga State Rep, 72- Bus & Prof Pos: Registered land surveyror, Ga, 53-; pres, Waddle & Co, 55-; registered engr, 62- Mem: Ga Soc Prof Engrs; Surveying & Mapping Soc Ga; Optimist; CofC. Relig: Baptist. Mailing Add: 113 Tanglewood Dr Warner Robins GA 31093

WADE, BILLY C (R)
Chmn, Colguitt Co Rep Party, Ga
b Berlin, Ga, March 24, 34; s Lonnie Wade & Irene Crofe Wade Gaskin; single. Educ: Norman Col, 1 year; Valdosta State Col, 1 year. Polit & Govt Pos: Chmn, Robinson Precinct Rep Party, Ga, 68; Rep cand for Ga State Rep, 63rd Dist, 70; vchmn, Second Dist Rep Party, 72-; serving on Rep platform comt, 72-; rules comt, 73-; chmn, Colguitt Co Rep Party, 73-; mem, Ga State Rep Cent Comt, 73- Bus & Prof Pos: Vpres, Taylor Fertilizer Works Inc, Moultrie, Ga, 68- Relig: Methodist. Legal Res: Berlin GA 31722 Mailing Add: PO Box 67 Moultrie GA 31768

WADE, CHARLES (BUBBA) (D)
Ark State Rep
Mailing Add: 609 Arkansas Blvd Texarkana AR 75501

WADE, EDWIN WINSLOW (R)
Mayor, Long Beach, Calif
b Jamestown, NDak, Oct 15, 03; s Harry M Wade & Marian A Eaton W; m 1925 to Mary Bruce Garrick; c Betty Jo. Educ: Student in Eng, Correspondence Sch. Polit & Govt Pos: Mayor, Long Beach, Calif, 60- Bus & Prof Pos: Sales engr, Southern Eng Co, Wilmington, Calif, 33-35; partner & gen mgr, Marine Specialty Co, 35-41, pres & gen mgr, Marine Specialty Co, Inc, 41-68. Mem: Independent Bus Mens Asn of Gtr Long Beach; past patron, Eastern Star; Mason (past master); Scottish Rite; KCCH. Honors & Awards: Meritorious Pub Serv Award, Navy. Mailing Add: 4155 Greenbrier Rd Long Beach CA 90808

WADE, ROBERT HIRSCH BEARD (R)
b Tamaqua, Pa, Oct 5, 16; s Edgar Gerber Wade & F Annabelle Hirsch W; m 1946 to Eleanor Marguerite Borden; c Gregory Borden. Educ: Lafayette Col, AB, 37; Univ Bordeaux, dipl d'etudes univ, 38; Yale Univ, PhD, 42; Phi Beta Kappa; Kappa Beta Rho. Polit & Govt Pos: Chief Far E analyst, Off Naval Intel, 46-54; dep dir, Off Nat Security Coun Affairs, Dept Defense, 54-56, dir, 56-61; dir, Off Multilateral Educ Affairs, Dept State, 61-64; deleg, UNESCO Gen Conf, 62, 64, 66 & 68, US permanent rep to UNESCO, alt mem exec bd, mem & vchmn exec comt preservation of Nubian monuments & mem hq comt, 64-69; asst dir, Arms Control & Disarmament Agency, 69-73; dir, Foreign Student Serv Coun, currently. Mil Serv: Entered Navy, 42, released as Lt, 46, after serv in SW Pac Hq & X Corps Hq, 43-45. Mem: For Serv Asn; Am Col in Paris (chmn bd, 67-69, trustee, 67-); Chevy Chase Club; Union Interalliee, Paris; Racing Club, Paris. Honors & Awards: Recipient merit citation award, Nat Civil Serv League, 59. Relig: Christian Scientist. Mailing Add: 3049 W Lane Keys NW Washington DC 20007

WADE, THOMAS ROGERS (D)
b Chattanooga, Tenn, Feb 10, 41; s Thomas Monroe Wade & Aileen Rowland W; m 1963 to Marcia Bryan. Educ: Univ Ga, BA, 63; John Marshall Univ, LLB, 66; Demosthenian Soc; Gridiron Soc; Alpha Tau Omega. Polit & Govt Pos: Exec dir, Georgians for Talmadge, 73-74; admin asst to US Sen Herman E Talmadge, Ga, 74- Bus & Prof Pos: Customer serv & sales rep, Eastern Airlines, 63-68; mgr mem rels, Ga CofC, 69-71, dir planning & opers, 72-73. Mem: Ga CofC Execs Asn; Leadership Ga (mem bd adv); Ga Econ Educ Coun (mem bd dirs). Legal Res: 2889 Rotherwood Dr Tucker GA 30084 Mailing Add: 6 Potomac Ct Alexandria VA 22314

WADE, WARREN ROCKWOOD (R)
Chmn, Dunn Co Rep Party, Wis
b Madison, Wis, Dec 7, 42; s Gerald Charles Wade & Jennette Dunnwiddie W; m 1968 to Martha Jane Schneider. Educ: Univ Wis-Madison, BS, 65; MS, 68; Claremont Grad Sch, PhD, 73; Phi Sigma Alpha. Polit & Govt Pos: Chmn, Dunn Co Rep Party, Wis, 73- Bus & Prof Pos: Prof polit sci, Univ Wis-Stout, 68- Publ: Auth, The Roth case: the Burger court & judicial restraint, In: Transactions of the Wisconsin Academy of Sciences, Arts & Letters, 74. Mem: Rotary; Wis Polit Sci Asn (pres-elect, 76); Midwest & Am Polit Sci Asns; Asn Univ Wis Faculty. Relig: Congregational. Mailing Add: Rte 5 Menomonie WI 54751

WADHAMS, RICHARD IVORY (R)
Chmn, Bent Co Rep Comt, Colo
b La Junta, Colo, Aug 26, 55; s Victor Frederick Wadhams & Anna Belle Goodman W; single. Educ: Otero Jr Col, AA, 75. Polit & Govt Pos: Chmn, Bent Co Rep Comt, Colo, 75-; secy, Third Cong Dist Rep Cent Comt, 75- Mem: Las Animas Kiwanis; La Junta Area Basketball Officials Asn. Relig: Catholic. Mailing Add: Rte 2 Box 253 Las Animas CO 81054

WADLEY, ROBERT L (D)
Okla State Sen
Mailing Add: State Capitol Oklahoma City OK 73105

WADSWORTH, HERBERT ROBINSON, JR (D)
b Live Oak, Fla, June 15, 31; s Herbert Wadsworth & Susie Kinnard W. Educ: Univ Fla, BS, 53; Fla Blue Key; Sigma Delta Chi; bus mgr, Fla Alligator; Sigma Alpha Epsilon. Polit & Govt Pos: Admin asst to US Rep Fuqua, Fla, 62- Bus & Prof Pos: Ed, Suwannee Dem Newspaper, 53-61. Mem: Jaycees (pres, vpres & nat dir); Kiwanis (pres); CofC (vpres); Mason (worshipful master, dist dep grand master); Shrine (Children's comt, Morocco Temple). Honors & Awards: Numerous awards including Ed Oscar; Outstanding Young Man, Suwannee Co, 54. Relig: Presbyterian. Legal Res: Live Oak FL 32060 Mailing Add: 458 New Jersey Ave SE Washington DC 20003

WAGAMAN, CHARLES F, JR (R)
Md State Deleg
Mailing Add: 328 E Magnolia Ave Hagerstown MD 21740

WAGGONER, JAMES THOMAS, JR (D)
Ala State Rep
b Birmingham, Ala, Jan 8, 37; s James Thomas Waggoner & Nell Harris W; m 1958 to Marilyn Louise Mitchell; c Mark Thomas, Scott Mitchell, Marilyn Ann & Jay. Educ: Auburn Univ, 2 years; Birmingham-Southern Col, AB; Birmingham Sch Law, JD; Alpha Kappa Psi; Eta Sigma Phi; Sigma Delta Kappa; Kappa Alpha Order. Polit & Govt Pos: Ala State Rep, Jefferson Co, 66-74, Ala State Rep, Dist 51, 75-, mem ways & means comt, Ala House of Rep, currently. Bus & Prof Pos: Employed by Cent Bancshares of the South, Inc, currently. Mem: Indust Developers Asn Ala; Civitan; Mason; Shrine; Eagles. Relig: Church of Christ. Legal Res: 1829 Mission Rd Birmingham AL 35216 Mailing Add: PO Box 10566 Birmingham AL 35203

WAGGONNER, JOE D, JR (D)
US Rep, La
b Plain Dealing, La, Sept 7, 18; s Joe D Waggonner, Sr & Elizzibeth Johnston W; m 1942 to Mary Ruth Carter; c David & Carol Jean. Educ: La Polytech Inst, BA. Polit & Govt Pos: Mem, Bossier Parish Sch Bd, 54 & 60, pres, 56; mem, La State Bd Educ, 60; pres, United Schs Comt, La, 61; US Rep, La, 61- Mil Serv: Lt Comdr, Navy, World War II & Korea, 51-52. Mem: Mason; Scottish Rite Mason (33 degree); Grand Cross Court of Honor; Shrine; Elks. Relig: Methodist. Legal Res: Plain Dealing LA 71064 Mailing Add: House Off Bldg Washington DC 20515

WAGNER, AUBREY J (INDEPENDENT)
Dir & Chmn Bd, Tenn Valley Authority
b Hillsboro, Wis, Jan 12, 12; s Joseph M Wagner & Wilhelmina Filter W; m 1933 to Dorothea J Huber; c Audrey Grace, Joseph Michael, James Richard & Karl Edward. Educ: Univ Wis, BCE magna cum laude, 33; Tau Beta Pi; Chi Epsilon; Phi Kappa Phi; Phi Eta Sigma; Lambda Chi Alpha; Scabbard & Blade. Hon Degrees: LLD, Newberry Col, 66; hon degree in pub admin, Lenoir Rhyne Col, NC, 70. Polit & Govt Pos: Jr hydraulic engr to chief river transportation div, Tenn Valley Authority, 34-51, asst gen mgr, 51-54, gen mgr, 54-61 & dir & chmn bd, 61-; mem, Pres Appalachian Adv Coun, 63-65, Recreation Adv Coun, 65-69 & Cost Reduction Coun, 68-69; mem, Nat Adv Coun for 1974 World Energy Conv, 71-; mem, Adv Comn for 1972 UN Conf on Human Environ, 71-72; mem, Atomic Energy Comn Utility Steering Comt, 71-72; mem, Fed Power Comn Exec Adv Comt for Nat Power Surv, 72-; mem bd dirs, US Nat Comt, World Energy Conf, 75- Bus & Prof Pos: Lectr, Agr & Nat Resources Session, Seminar in Am Studies, Salzburg, Austria, 68; vchmn, Breeder Reactor Corp, 72- Mem: Nat Acad Eng; Tenn Archaeol Soc; Ft Loudoun Asn; Boy Scouts Nat Coun. Relig: Lutheran; mem exec coun, Lutheran Church of Am, 62-70. Legal Res: 201 Whittington Dr Knoxville TN 37919 Mailing Add: 403 New Sprankle Bldg Knoxville TN 37902

WAGNER, ERNEST MARTIN, JR (D)
Chmn, Callaway Co Dem Cent Comt, Mo
b Fulton, Mo, Apr 19, 39; s Ernest Martin Wagner & Margaret Jessie Hopper W; m 1961 to Karen Kaye Price; c Ernest Martin, III & James Cameron. Educ: Univ Mo-Columbia, BS, 61; Farm House; Ruf Nex; Arnold Air Soc; Scabbard & Blade. Polit & Govt Pos: Committeeman, Callaway Co Dem Cent Comt, Mo, 70-, chmn, 72-; deleg, Mo State Dem Conv, 72; mem, Ninth Dist Dem Comt, 72-; mem, Mayor's Adv Comt, 73- Bus & Prof Pos: Mem, Hybrid Corn Res Conf Comt, Am Seed Trade Asn, 68-70 & Fulton Parks & Recreation Comt, 71-72; mgr, Northrup, King & Co, Fulton Br. Mem: Am Seed Trade Asn; Mo Seedmen's Asn (pres, 71); Fulton Rotary Club (vpres, 73-74, pres, 74-75). Honors & Awards: Outstanding Individual, field crops, Col Agr, Mo Seedmen's Asn, 60. Relig: Christian. Mailing Add: 6 Haddley Lee Dr Fulton MO 65251

WAGNER, GEORGE O (R)
Pa State Rep
Mailing Add: Capitol Bldg Harrisburg PA 17120

WAGNER, JAMES B (D)
Maine State Rep
Mailing Add: 8 Mayo St Orono ME 04473

WAGNER, JAMES WEBB (D)
b Chicago, Ill, May 14, 38; s James Webb Wagner & Gladys Kennedy W; m 1972 to Almarie Masoud. Educ: Northwestern Univ, Evanston, BS, 60; Univ Chicago, MA, 68, Ctr for Health Admin Studies, 70-71. Polit & Govt Pos: Independent Dem precinct capt, Fourth Ward, Chicago, 65-, 20th Ward, Chicago, 66; deleg, Dem Nat Conv, 72. Bus & Prof Pos: Teacher, Chicago, 60-64; dir of community serv, Chicago Urban League, 64-66; dir of bio-med careers, Med Ctr YMCA, 67; dir of adult educ, Chicago City Col, Malcolm X Campus, 68-69; asst dir, Ill Regional Med Prog, 69-70; asst prof, Univ of Ill, Sch Pub Health & assoc dir, Ctr for Study of Patient Care & Community Health, 71- Mil Serv: Entered as Hospitalman 1/C, 58; Acad Award, Hosp Corps Sch. Publ: Co-auth, An Example of Sub-Regional Health Planning, 12/70 & An Example of Sub-Regional Health Planning: a Further Report, 71, Inquiry. Mem: Mid-S Health Planning Comn (pres, 69-); Comprehensive Health Planning, Inc Metrop Chicago (bd mem, 70-); Urban Doctors Prog (bd mem, 70-); SSide Task Force on Health Planning (chmn, 72-); Mid-Southside Vol Health Serv Plan (chmn, 72-). Honors & Awards: Fel, Nat Urban League, 67; Research Fel, Nat Ctr for Health Serv, Dept Health, Educ & Welfare, 70. Relig: Protestant. Mailing Add: 6700 S Shore Dr 16A Chicago IL 60649

WAGNER, JERRY (D)
Mem, Bloomfield Dem Town Comt, Conn
b New Haven, Conn, Aug 2, 26; s Nathan Wagner & Clara Themper W; m 1950 to Sally Jeanne Hurvitz; c Jonathan, Paula & Michael. Educ: Yale Univ, BS, 46; Harvard Univ, LLB, 49. Polit & Govt Pos: Mem, Bloomfield Dem Town Comt, Conn, 55-; Conn State Rep, 59-60; mem, State Comn on Intergovt Coop, 59-61; town attorney, Bloomfield, 60-61; mem, Bloomfield Redevelop Comn, 63-68; deleg, Dem Nat Conv, 64; Dem nominee for Conn State Sen, 66; counsel to Conn State Senate Majority, 67-68; spec asst, Citizens for Humphrey-Muskie, 68; dir, Spec Orgn, Daddario for Gov, 70. Bus & Prof Pos: Attorney-at-law, currently; part-time instr, Univ Conn Law Sch, 73- Mil Serv: Entered as Pre-Aviation Cadet, Army Air Force, 44, released as Pvt, 45. Mem: Mason; Civitan; Am Legion; Jewish War Vet; NAACP. Honors & Awards: Received Outstanding Young Man of Year Award, Jaycees, 62. Relig: Jewish; Vpres, United Synagogue of Am, 71- Mailing Add: 4 Craigemore Rd Bloomfield CT 06002

WAGNER, JOSEPH NICHOLAS (D)
Idaho State Rep
b Annamoose, NDak, Nov 1, 05; s William Wagner & Helen Meisch W; m 1932 to Fern Margaret Lewis; c Virginia Ann (Mrs Hogard), William J, Margaret Helen (Mrs Inghram), Janet Lenore (Mrs Sonnichsen) & Robert J. Educ: High sch educ. Polit & Govt Pos: Mayor, Grangeville, Idaho; Idaho State Rep, Dist Six, currently. Mem: Lions, Grangeville (pres); Grangeville CofC (secy). Relig: Catholic. Mailing Add: 2828 Sunset Dr Lewiston ID 83501

WAGNER, MICHAEL J (D)
Md State Deleg
Mailing Add: 241 Wicklow Ave Glen Burnie MD 21061

WAGNER, RICHARD F (R)
Mem Exec Comt, Isabella Co Rep Comt, Mich
b Mt Pleasant, Mich, Aug 28, 39; s Lloyd J Wagner & Marianne E; Richards W; m 1968 to Barbara J Brian; c Robby, Marianne & Lourie. Educ: Cent Mich Univ, BS, 71. Polit & Govt Pos: Senate aide, Mich State Senate, 67-68; field rep, Mich Nixon for President Comt, 68; mem exec comt, Isabella Co Rep Comt, 70-; chmn, Isabella Co Reelect the President Comt, 72- alt deleg, Rep Nat Conv, 72. Bus & Prof Pos: Teacher, Bullock Creek High Sch, Midland, Mich, currently. Mil Serv: Army, 62-65, serv in Europe. Mem: US Ski Asn (dir, 71-73); Nat Rifle Asn; Lions Int. Mailing Add: 204 E Wright St Shepherd MI 48883

WAGNER, ROBERT F (D)
b New York, NY, Apr 20, 10; s Robert F Wagner; m 1942 to Susan Edwards (deceased); div; c two sons. Educ: Yale Univ, AB, 33, LLB, 37; Harvard Univ Sch Bus Admin, 34. Polit & Govt Pos: NY State Assemblyman, 38-41; city tax comnr, New York, 46; comnr, Housing & Bldgs, 47; chmn, City Planning Comn, 48; deleg, Dem Nat Conv, 48, 52, 56, 60, 64 & 68, chmn, NY Deleg, 60 & 64, alt deleg, 72; pres, Borough of Manhattan, Gtr New York, 49-53; mayor, New York, 54-66; first vpres, NY State Constitutional Conv, 67-; US Ambassador to Spain, 68-69; deleg, Dem Nat Mid-Term Conf, 74. Mil Serv: Eighth Air Force, 42-45, Lt Col. Legal Res: 680 Madison Ave New York NY 10021 Mailing Add: Wagner Quillinan & Tennant 350 Fifth Ave New York NY 10001

WAGNER, SUE ELLEN (R)
Nev State Assemblyman
b Portland, Maine, Jan 6, 40; d Raymond A Pooler & Kathryn Hooper P; m 1964 to Dr Peter B Wagner; c Kirk & Kristina. Educ: Univ Ariz, BA in Polit Sci, 62; Northwestern Univ, Evanston, MA in Hist, 64; Kappa Alpha Theta. Polit & Govt Pos: Mem, Mayor's Adv Comt, Reno, 73-; chmn, Blue Ribbon Task Force on Housing, 74-75; mem, Washoe Co Rep Cent Comt, 74-; mem, Nev State Rep Cent Comt, 75-; Nev State Assemblyman, 75- Bus & Prof Pos: Asst dean women, Ohio State Univ, 63-64; teacher hist & Am govt, Catalina High Sch, Tucson, Ariz, 64-65; reporter, Tucson Daily Citizen, 65-68. Publ: Diary of a candidate, On People & Things, 10/74. Mem: Am Asn Univ Women (legis chmn, 74); Reno Chap, Bus & Prof Women; Am Field Serv (vpres, 73, family liaison, 74, mem-at-lg, 75). Honors & Awards: Thomas Campbell Award for Outstanding Sophomore Woman, Univ Ariz, 60, Merrill P Freeman Medal for Outstanding Sr Woman, 62, Kappa Alpha Theta Nat Grad Scholarship & Phelps-Dodge Post Grad Fel, 62. Relig: Episcopal. Mailing Add: 845 Tamarack Dr Reno NV 89502

WAGNER, THEODORE FRANKLIN (R)
Mem, Roane Co Rep Exec Comt, Tenn
b Madison, SDak, Apr 7, 21; s Charles Carroll Wagner & Eldred Brown Lawrence W; m 1950 to Pauline Lucienne Audette; c Karen Elizabeth, Theodore Franklin, Jr & Annette Evelyn. Educ: US Mil Acad, BS, 45; Univ Tenn, Knoxville, MS, 55. Polit & Govt Pos: Chmn, Roane Co Rep Exec Comt, Tenn, 66-70, mem, currently; mem city coun, Kingston, 67-69. Bus & Prof Pos: Mgt trainee, Curtiss Candy Co, Chicago, Ill, 49-51; admin asst, nuclear div, Union Carbide Corp, 51-67, univ rels rep, 67-71 & 74-, admin asst, 71-74; mem bd dirs, First Nat Bank & Trust Co, Rockwood & chmn adv bd dirs, Kingston Off. Mil Serv: Army, 45-49, various line & staff assignments, 38 months in Europe; Army Res, 45-, Col, attached Knoxville Army Res Sch, currently. Mem: Rotary (gov, Dist 678, Int, 73-74); Great Smoky Mt Coun Boy Scouts (exec bd, mem troop comt). Relig: Christian Science. Legal Res: 41 W Shore Dr Kingston TN 37763 Mailing Add: PO Box 94 Kingston TN 37763

WAGNER, THOMAS J (D)
b Jackson, Mich, June 29, 39; s O Walter Wagner & Dorothy Ann Hollinger W; m 1961 to Judy Bogardus; c Ann Louise, Mark Robert & Rachel. Educ: Earlham Col, BA, 61; Univ Chicago Law Sch, JD, 65. Polit & Govt Pos: Legis asst to gov, Ill, 66-67, admin asst to treas, 67-70; admin asst to Sen Adlai E Stevenson, Ill, 70- Mem: Comt on Ill Govt (exec bd, 67-). Honors & Awards: Ill Gen Assembly Legis Intern, Univ Ill-Ford Found, 62-63; Africa-Asia pub serv fel, Syracuse Univ/Ford Found, 65-66. Legal Res: 7422 S Constance Chicago IL 60649 Mailing Add: 7707 Glenmore Spring Way Bethesda MD 20034

WAGNER, VERNON E (R)
NDak State Rep
b Golden Valley, NDak, June 13, 26; s Alex R Wagner & Katie Miller W; m 1965 to Mary Dean Andrus. Educ: NDak State Univ, BS Pharm, 48; Phi Kappa Phi; Rho Chi; Sigma Alpha Epsilon. Polit & Govt Pos: Precinct committeeman, Burleigh Co Rep Party, NDak, 54-60; secy, NDak Rep Cent Comt, 60-63; NDak State Rep, 63- Bus & Prof Pos: Pharmacist, Serv Drug, 48-54; partner-mgr, Clin Pharm, Bismarck, 54-67; asst exec secy, NDak Med Asn, 67- Mem: NDak Pharmaceut Asn; NDak Heart Asn; Bismarck CofC (dir); Am Heart Asn (dir); NDak Jaycees (past pres). Relig: Lutheran. Mailing Add: 226 Telstar Dr Bismarck ND 58501

WAHLRAB, OTTO A (R)
Mem, Mass Rep State Comt
b Danbry, Conn, Nov 5, 32; s Arnold F Wahlrab & Emma W; m to Joyce L; c Susan, Margaret & Belinda. Educ: Worcester Polytech Inst, grad, 54; Phi Gamma Delta. Polit & Govt Pos: Mem, Mass Rep State Comt, 64-, chmn, 72-74. Bus & Prof Pos: Pres, John P Slade Ins, Fall River, 70- Mil Serv: Entered as Lt(jg), Navy Res, 56, serv in Off Cand Sch, Newport, 3 1/2 years. Relig: Protestant. Mailing Add: 189 Reservoir Ave Rehoboth MA 02769

WAHNER, JAMES WILLIAM (D)
Wis State Rep
b Milwaukee, Wis, Nov 10, 39; s Vernon George Wahner & June Clara Stiedemann W; single. Educ: Georgetown Univ, 61-63; Am Univ, BA, 66, MA, 67, PhD cand, Univ Wis, Milwaukee, 67-69. Polit & Govt Pos: Staff adv to Speaker John W McCormack, US House Rep, 61; staff adv mayor, Milwaukee, Wis, 69-70; Wis State Rep, 15th Dist, Milwaukee, 71-, chmn Comt on Environ Qual & vchmn, Comt on Munic, Wis House Rep, 73-, asst majority leader, 75-; chmn, Gov Task Force on Probs of People with Phys Handicaps, 73- Bus & Prof Pos: Teaching asst state & local govt, Univ Wis, Milwaukee, 67-69; lectr polit sci, Univ Wis, Parkside, 68-71, Mar- quette Univ, 71-72, Mt Mary Col, 71 & Milwaukee Area Tech Col, 73- Mil Serv: Entered as Pvt, Army, 57, released as SP-4, 60, after serv in Army Security Agency, Alaskan Command, 58-59. Mem: Nat Conf of State Legis (bd gov, 73-); Milwaukee Chap, Nat Paraplegia Found; Common Cause. Relig: Protestant. Mailing Add: 6766 W Appleton Ave Milwaukee WI 53216

WAINWRIGHT, RONNY ANN (D)
VChmn, Anne Arundel Co Dem Cent Comt, Md
b Yonkers, NY, May 27, 41; d Maurice S Degenstein & Ruth Klein D; m 1969 to C Abbott Wainwright; c Lisa Susan & Michael Scott. Educ: Univ Miami, BA & MA in Eng; Univ Baltimore Sch Law, 75-; Nat Honor Soc; Drama Guild. Polit & Govt Pos: Vpres, Young Dem of Anne Arundel Co, Md, 73-74, pres, 74-75; vchmn, Anne Arundel Co Dem Cent Comt, 74-; mem, Md Dem State Cent Comt, 74-; mem, Md State Comn to Study Young Dem, 75-; mem, Md State Affirmative Action Comt, 75-; chmn, Anne Arundel Co Affirmative Action Comt, 75- Mem: Young Dem of Anne Arundel Co; New Dem Coalition; United Dem Women's Clubs; Annapolis Asn for Contemporary Dance; Md Fedn of Art. Mailing Add: 6 Tower Rd Severna Park MD 21146

WAITS, ALVIN E (D)
Mo State Rep
Mailing Add: 507 Brookside Independence MO 64053

WAITZ, ROBERTA CHARLENE (R)
Nat Committeewoman, La Young Rep Fedn
b Alexandria, La, Sept 11, 45; s Roy Speedie Waitz & Hazel Whatley W; single. Educ: La Col, BS, 70; Northwestern State Univ, currently; Phi Chi; historian, Home Econ State Club; Psychol Club Dormitory Coun Bd. Polit & Govt Pos: Dir eighth cong dist, La Young Rep Fedn, 71-73, sponsor of La Col Young Rep Club, 72-, state conv, chmn, 73, nat committeewoman, 73-; mem polit action coun, Rapides Parish Sr Rep Party, 73- Bus & Prof Pos: Teacher sci, Ouachita Parish, Monroe, La, 70-72; teacher biol, Rapides Parish, Alexandria, 72-73; mission fieldworker, Tampa, Fla, summer 73; teacher third grade, St Frances Cobrini Sch, Alexandria, 73- Mem: Nat & Rapides Parish Teachers Asn; Eastern Star; Rapides Gen Hosp Vol Prog. Relig: United Methodist. Mailing Add: 3617 Felker St Alexandria LA 71301

WAKATSUKI, JAMES HIROJI (D)
Hawaii State Rep
b Honolulu, Hawaii, Aug 17, 29; s Shichizaemon Wakatsuki & Sachi Kobayashi W; m 1957 to Irene Natsuko Yoshimura; c Janie Toshie, Stuart Kazuo & Cora Akemi. Educ: Univ Wis, Madison, LLB, 54. Polit & Govt Pos: Hawaii State Rep, currently, chmn, Health & Welfare Comt, Hawaii House Rep, 59, Educ Comt, 59-64, Judiciary Comt, 65-66, Higher Educ Comt, 67-68 & Finance Comt, 69-70, Majority Leader, formerly, Speaker, currently. Mil Serv: Entered as Recruit, Army, 48, released as Pfc, 49, after serv in Pac; Army Res, 49-55. Mem: Lions; Kalihi YMCA (bd mgr). Legal Res: 1462 Ala Mahamoe St Honolulu HI 96819 Mailing Add: c/o House of Rep Sgt at Arms State Capitol Honolulu HI 96813

WAKEFIELD, HELEN W (R)
Vt State Rep
Mailing Add: Rte 2 Randolph VT 05060

WAKEFIELD, STEPHEN (R)
Polit & Govt Pos: Former Asst Secy Energy & Minerals, Dept Interior Legal Res: TX Mailing Add: Dept of Interior Washington DC 20240

WAKEHAM, T DAVID (R)
Dir Region X, Young Rep Nat Fedn
b Orange, Calif, Sept 10, 45; s Terry David Wakeham & Dawn Cornett W; m 1973 to Karen L McAdam. Educ: Fullerton Jr Col, AA Polit Sci, 66; Univ Calif Los Angeles, 66-68; Calif State Univ, Fullerton, BA Polit Sci, 68; Alpha Gamma Sigma. Polit & Govt Pos: Sgt-at-arms, Calif Col Rep Fedn, 66-67; nat committeeman, Calif Young Rep Fedn, 72-73; mem exec bd, Young Rep Nat Fedn, 73-; dir region X, 73-; dep dir, 21st Sen Dist, Calif Rep Assembly, 75- Bus & Prof Pos: Salesman, R M Bracamonte Co Inc, San Francisco, Calif, 70-72; claims rep, Hartford Ins Co, San Francisco, 72-73; claims adj, Calif Casualty Mgt Co, Los Angeles, 74; claims examr, Wilshire Ins Co, Los Angeles, 74- Mil Serv: Entered as 2nd Lt, Army, 68, released as 1st Lt, 70, after serv in 281st Mil Police Co, Hq Army Support, Thailand, 69-70; Nat Defense Serv Medal; Vietnam Serv Medal; Vietnam Campaign Medal. Mem: Toastmasters Int; Calif State Univ, Fullerton Alumni Asn. Relig: Protestant. Mailing Add: 615 W Palm Monrovia CA 91016

WAKELIN, JAMES, JR (R)
Polit & Govt Pos: Asst Secy of Navy for Research & Develop, 59-64; Asst Secy Sci & Technol, Dept Com, Washington, DC, formerly. Mailing Add: 1809 45th St NW Washington DC 20007

WALBRIDGE, JOHN TUTHILL, JR (R)
Mem, 11th Cong Dist Rep Exec Comt, Mich
b Lakeland, Fla, Dec 10, 25; s John T Walbridge & Mabel Thornton W; m 1947 to Mary Lou Sailor; c John T, III & Mary Lewis. Educ: Yale, BS; Hale Found. Polit & Govt Pos: Co chmn, Rep Party, Mich, 62-65; deleg Rep Nat Conv, 64; mem, 11th Cong Dist Rep Exec Comt, 64- Bus & Prof Pos: Exec vpres, Early Am Fence Co, 56-59, pres, 59-; pres, Northern Land & Lumber Co, 60- & Am Timber Homes, Inc, 61- Mil Serv: Seaman 2/C, Navy, 44-46 in USS Marlboro, Atlantic. Mem: Chmn, Mich White Cedar Asn; CofC; Escanaba Country Club. Relig: Episcopal. Mailing Add: Chaison Rd Gladstone MI 49837

WALCH, JOHN MACARTHUR DUNSMORE (R)
Committeeman, Essex Co Rep Party, NJ
b St Joseph, Mo, Feb 8, 26; s Donald Elbra Walch & Ruth Dunsmore W; m 1950 to Zelda Sofman; c Donald Elbra, Jonathan, Grace Ann & Elizabeth. Educ: Mass Inst Technol, BSEE; Delta Tau Delta, Deer Lake Club. Polit & Govt Pos: Committeeman, Rep Party, Ridgefield, NJ, 54-59, mem, Bd Health, 59; committeeman, Essex Co Rep Party, 60-; pres, Nutley Rep Club, 66-67; campaign mgr, Nutley, 68, mem, Nutley Comn Elec, 68; alt deleg, Rep Nat Conv, 68, pres bd dirs, Nutley Rep Bur, 68-70; Comnr, Essex Co Govt Study Comn, 70- Bus & Prof Pos: Educ counsr, Mass Inst Technol, 54-; prof engr, NJ, 54-; sr engr, Pub Serv Elec & Gas Co, 69- Mil Serv: Entered as Pvt, Army, 43, released as Sgt, 46, after serv in Combat Engr, South Pac, 44-46. Mem: Inst Elec & Electronics Engrs (sr mem); Elks; Capitol Hill Club; Nutley Rep Club. Honors & Awards: United Community Fund & Coun of Essex & West Hudson Vol Award, 68. Relig: Episcopal. Mailing Add: 166 Highfield Lane Nutley NJ 07110

WALDEN, PAUL E (R)
Ore State Rep
b Prescott, Wis, May 7, 17; s Ernest E Walden & Nellie Purdy W; m 1940 to Elizabeth Ann McEwen; c Robert, William & Gregory. Educ: Ore Inst Technol, 1 year. Polit & Govt Pos: Mem adv comt on Ore State Legis, between sessions, 67 & 69; Ore State Rep, Dist 22, 71- Bus & Prof Pos: Mgr, Radio KODL Broadcast Sta, The Dalles, Ore, 41-67; owner, Radio KIHR, Hood River, 67- Mil Serv: Entered as Pvt, Army Signal Corps, 46, released as Pvt, 47, after serv in Signal Corps Training. Mem: Ore Asn Broadcasters (past pres); Maryhill Mus of Fine Arts (mem bd trustees); Elks; Mason; Rotary. Honors & Awards: Man of the Year, The Dalles, Ore, 56. Relig: Episcopal. Mailing Add: Rte 3 Box 175 Hood River OR 97031

WALDIE, JEROME RUSSELL (D)
b Antioch, Calif, Feb 15, 25; s George Daniel Waldie & Alice Crosiar W; m 1948 to Dorothy Joanne Gregg; c Jill, Jonathon & Jeffery. Educ: Univ Calif at Berkeley, AB, 50; Univ Calif Boalt Law Sch, LLB, 53. Polit & Govt Pos: Calif State Assemblyman, 58-66 & Majority Leader; US Rep, Calif, 66-74; cand Gov, Calif, 74. Mil Serv: Entered as Pvt, Army, 43, released as T/5, Army & Signal Corps, 46. Mem: Odd Fellows; Elks; Am Legion; Moose. Relig: Congregational. Mailing Add: 304-B Ninth St Antioch CA 94509

WALDOW, WALTER J (D)
Colo State Rep
Mailing Add: Rte 2 Box 96A Olathe CO 81425

WALDROP, GERALD WAYNE (D)
Ala State Sen
b Gadsden, Ala, Sept 7, 42; s Lowell Columbus Waldrop, Sr & Willie Lee Shirley W; m 1965 to Callie NetaVee Edgar; c Elizabeth Leigh & Natasha Glynn. Educ: Univ Ala Exten Ctr, summer 60, Sch Law, 64-65; Grad Sch, MA, 67; Jacksonville State Univ, BA, 64; Univ Minn, summer 69. Polit & Govt Pos: Ala State Rep, Dist 11, 70-74; Ala State Sen, Dist Ten, 75- Bus & Prof Pos: Instr hist & polit sci, Jefferson State Jr Col, 67-71, instr hist & polit sci, Gadsden State Jr Col, 71- Mil Serv: Air Force Res, until 66. Mem: Ala Hist Asn; Kiwanis; Jaycees; Ala Educ Asn. Relig: Methodist. Mailing Add: 181 Lakeshore Dr Rte 10 Gadsden AL 35901

WALDROP, ISAAC MERIT, JR (D)
Mem, Alaska State Dem Cent Comt
b Vinita, Okla, July 11, 33; s Isaac M Waldrop & Emma G Martin W; m 1956 to Margie Ann Winton; c Isaac Merit, III & Robert Jeffery. Educ: Okla Agr & Mech Col, 50-51; Northeastern State Col, 55-56; Anchorage Community Col, 57-58; Brookings Inst, 69. Polit & Govt Pos: Mem community adv coun, State of Alaska, 64-66, manpower training adv coun, 65-66, comprehensive health adv coun, 72-73; mem, Gov Pipeline Task Force, 69-70; mem, Alaska State Dem Cent Comt, currently; deleg, Dem Nat Mid-Term Conf, 74. Bus & Prof Pos: Tech rep, Anchorage Tel Utility, 57-61 & RCA, Serv Co, 61-62; bus rep, IBEW Local 1547, 62-68, bus mgr & financial secy, 68- Mil Serv: Entered as Pvt, 53, released as Pfc, 55, after serv in 14th AFA, Korea, 54-55; Good Conduct Medal; Korean Serv Medal. Mem: Anchorage Cent Labor Coun (pres, 65-73); Elks; Am Legion; Anchorage Youth Football League (bd dirs, 68-); Anchorage Hockey Asn (bantam league pres, 72-73). Relig: Protestant. Mailing Add: 3868 Shannon Court Anchorage AK 99504

WALDROP, JOHN (D)
Miss State Sen
Mailing Add: New Albany MS 38652

WALDROP, RALPH LOY (R)
Mem, Transylvania Co Rep Exec Comt, NC
b Cherryfield, NC, Jan 16, 13; s John Lewis Waldrop & Addie Ross W; m 1942 to Kathryn Grace Stall; c Ralph Loy, Jr, Larry R, Jean Ann & Nancy Sue. Educ: Mars Hill Col, 30-31; Furman Univ, BS, 33. Polit & Govt Pos: Mem, Catheys Creek Rep Precinct Comt, NC, 48-50; mem, Transylvania Co Rep Exec Comt, 52-55 & 71-, chmn, 58-71. Bus & Prof Pos: Shift control supvr, Paper Div, Olin Mathieson Chem Corp, Pisgah Forest, NC, 39-75. Mil Serv: Entered as 1st Lt, Chem Warfare Serv, Army, 41, released as Capt, Chem Corps, 46, after serv in 256th Chem Lab Co, Asiatic-Pac Area, 45; Army Res, 36-41 & 46-64, Lt Col (Ret); Am Defense Medal; Asiatic-Pac, Am Theater & Philippines Liberation Ribbons; Victory Medal; Armed Forces Res Campaign & Serv Medal. Mem: Mason. Relig: Baptist. Mailing Add: RR 2 Box 669 Brevard NC 28712

WALGREN, GORDON LEE (D)
Wash State Sen
b Bremerton, Wash, Mar 7, 33; s Jess Nelson Walgren & Grace Barber W; m 1962 to Sue Kathlyen Proctor; c Kathy & Tracey. Educ: Univ Wash, BA, 55, LLB & JD, 57; Delta Upsilon; Phi Delta Phi. Polit & Govt Pos: Prosecuting attorney, Kitsap Co, Wash, 58-62; Wash State Rep, 66-68; city attorney, Bremerton, 66-; Wash State Sen, 68-, Majority Whip, Wash State Senate, currently; alt deleg, Dem Nat Conv, 72. Publ: Due process and contempt, Wash Law Rev, 56. Mem: F&AM; Shrine; Elks; Eagles; Kiwanis. Honors & Awards:

Freedoms Found Award, Valley Forge. Relig: Protestant. Mailing Add: 5533 Erland Point Rd Bremerton WA 98310

WALKER, ALAN LEE (D)
b South Bend, Ind, July 21, 34; s Chester Eugene Walker & Lura True W; m 1954 to Donnera Phillips; c Gloria Jean & Elizabeth Anne. Educ: Evansville Col, 52-55; Univ Cincinnati, 55-56; Acacia. Polit & Govt Pos: Mem, Lawrence Co Dem Elec Bd, Ind, 63-66; chmn, Lawrence Co Dem Cent Comt, formerly. Bus & Prof Pos: Advert salesman & sportscaster, Radio Sta WBIW, Bedford, Ind, 61- Mil Serv: Entered as Pvt, Marine Corps Res, 52, released as M/Sgt, 66, after serv in Marine, Army & Air Corps Res. Mem: F&AM; US Power Squadron; Bedford Little Theater; Rotary. Relig: Presbyterian. Mailing Add: 1412 Fifth St Bedford IN 47421

WALKER, CHARLS EDWARD (R)
b Graham, Tex, Dec 24, 23; s Pinkney Clay Walker & Sammye McCombs W; m to Harmolyn Hart; c Carolyn & Charls Edward, Jr. Educ: Univ Tex, BBA, 47 & MBA, 48; Wharton Sch of Finance, Univ Pa, PhD in Econ, 55. Polit & Govt Pos: Assoc economist, Fed Reserve Bank of Philadelphia, 53-54 & Dallas, 54-61; vpres, 58-61; asst to Secy of the Treas Robert B Anderson, 59-61; Under Secy of the Treas, 69-72, Dep Secy of Treas, 73-75. Bus & Prof Pos: Instr finance, Univ Tex, 47-48, assoc prof, 50-54; instr, Wharton Sch of Finance, Univ Pa, 48-50; economist & spec asst to pres, Repub Nat Bank of Dallas, Tex, 55-56; exec vpres, Am Bankers Asn, 61-69. Mil Serv: Pilot, Army Air Force, World War II. Publ: Co-ed, The Banker's Handbook; plus articles for econ & other jour. Mem: Joint Coun on Econ Educ (trustee); J of Finance (mem bd ed, formerly). Mailing Add: Riverside CT 06878

WALKER, DAN (D)
Gov, Ill
Mailing Add: State House Springfield IL 62706

WALKER, DAVID H (D)
Committeeman, Tenn State Dem Exec Comt
b Johnson City, Tenn, Jan 8, 25; s Grover Dean Walker & Nelle Callison W; m 1969 to Judy Bennett; c Paul D, Gaines C, Jennifer, Grover D, Robert C & John P. Educ: Col William & Mary, 43-44. Polit & Govt Pos: City comnr, Johnson City, Tenn, 55-63 & 65-69; committeeman, Tenn State Dem Exec Comt, 70- Mil Serv: Entered as Pvt, Army Air Force, 43, released as 1st Lt, after serv in 464th Bombadier Group, ETO, 44-45; Air Medal with Oak Leaf Cluster; ETO Ribbon. Mem: Elks; Am Legion; VFW; Johnson City Country Club. Relig: Christian Church. Legal Res: 1066 Ingleside Terr Johnson City TN 37601 Mailing Add: Box 408 Johnson City TN 37601

WALKER, E S JOHNNY (D)
b Fulton, Ky, June 18, 11; s John Karr Walker & Annie Stephens W; m 1939 to Pauline Marie Wernicke; c Janet & Stephen Michael. Educ: Univ NMex, 31-35; Nat Univ, 36. Polit & Govt Pos: Organizer & first dir, NMex Oil & Gas Acct Comn; NMex State Rep, 49-53; comnr, NMex Land Off, 53-56 & 60-64; comnr, Bur Revenue NMex, 59; mem, NMex Investment Coun; mem, NMex Forestry Comn; mem, NMex Oil Conserv Comn; US Rep, NMex, 65-69. Bus & Prof Pos: Part owner, Free Fraser Pharm, Adobe Motel, Santa Fe, NMex. Mil Serv: Army, Vet, World War II, NAfrica & Europe. Mem: VFW; Am Legion; Elks. Mailing Add: Box 293 Santa Fe NM 87501

WALKER, HARRY GREY (D)
Assoc Justice, Miss Supreme Court
b Ovett, Miss, Sept 30, 24; s Dr Chester Arthur Walker, Sr & Ina Mae Mangum W; m 1953 to Carrie T Lang; c Harry Grey, Jr & Fred Wallace. Educ: Univ Miss, LLB, 52; Kappa Alpha; Phi Alpha Delta. Polit & Govt Pos: Miss State Rep, 63-64; judge, Co Court of Harrison Co, 64-68; circuit judge, Second Circuit Court Dist, 68-73; assoc justice, Miss Supreme Court, 73- Bus & Prof Pos: Attorney, Gulfport, Miss, 52-64. Mil Serv: Entered as A/S, Coast Guard, 42, released as Seaman 1/C, 44. Mem: Am Judicature Soc; Am Legion; DAV (life mem); Paralyzed Vet of Am; CofC; Good Samaritan Training Ctr. Honors & Awards: Proclamation, Judge Harry Walker Day, Cities of Biloxi, Gulfport, Long Beach & Pass Christian & Co of Harrison, 72. Relig: Methodist. Legal Res: 12-53rd St Gulfport MS 39501 Mailing Add: Mississippi Supreme Court Jackson MS 39205

WALKER, HENRY A (R)
Mass State Rep
b Greenfield, Mass, Dec 7, 19; s Irvine H Walker & Mabel F Wood W; m 1942 to Alice Hyde; c Geoffrey Hyde. Educ: Sch of Practical Art, Boston, grad, 48; Rutledge Bate Sch of Painting, Rockport, Mass, grad, 49. Polit & Govt Pos: Town selectman, Salisbury, Mass, 59-68; Mass State Rep, 21st Dist, 73- Bus & Prof Pos: Sales mgr, Dana Corp, New Eng, 53- Mil Serv: Entered as Pvt, Army Air Corps, 41, released as Capt, 46, after serv in ETO, 43-45; recalled as Maj, Air Force, 52-53, ETO; Lt Col, Res, 41-72; Flying Cross; six Air Medals. Mem: Mason; Audubon Soc; Am Legion. Relig: Protestant. Mailing Add: 258 Main St Salisbury MA 01950

WALKER, HOWARD HAROLD (R)
Chmn, Audrian Co Rep Cent Comt, Mo
b Moberly, Mo, Sept 10, 11; s Odra Walker & Opal W; m 1936 to Addie James; c Lauri (Mrs Richard Volmer). Educ: High Sch. Polit & Govt Pos: Chmn, Audrian Co Rep Cent Comt, Mo, 74- Bus & Prof Pos: Owner, Cent Motor Parts Co, 28-72. Mem: Kiwanis Club; Lake Ozark Yachting Club; Pachyderm Club. Relig: Baptist. Mailing Add: 1420 S Jefferson Mexico MO 65265

WALKER, JACK D (R)
Mayor, Overland Park, Kans
b Girard, Kans, Apr 5, 22; s William S Walker & Maude Yokum W; m 1947 to Jo Ann Jones; c Robert Daniel & James David. Educ: Univ Ariz, BS, 48; Univ Kans Med Sch, MD, 53. Polit & Govt Pos: Mayor, Overland Park, Kans, 71- Bus & Prof Pos: Assoc dean, Univ Kans Med Ctr, 63-71, prof & chmn dept family practice, 71- Mil Serv: Entered as Pvt, Air Force, 43, released as Cpl, 46, after serv in Air Force Regional Hosp, Tucson, Ariz. Mem: Am Med Asn; Am Acad Family Physicians; Kans League of Munic. Relig: Protestant. Mailing Add: 6409 W 102 St Overland Park KS 66212

WALKER, JAMES H (D)
Miss State Rep
Mailing Add: Box 966 Cleveland MS 38732

WALKER, JAMES HENRY (D)
b Madison, Wis, May 17, 47; s Cyrus Weber Walker & Louise Elizabeth W; m 1972 to Nell E Boozenny. Educ: Wis State Univ-Whitewater, 66-67; Goddard Col. Polit & Govt Pos: Deleg, NDak Dem State & Dist Conv, 70 & 72; alt deleg, Dem Nat Conv, 72. Mem: Kiwanis (bd dirs, 69-73); Jaycees (bd dirs, 68-73); Am Crafts Coun. Relig: Society of Friends. Mailing Add: Box 206 New Town ND 58763

WALKER, JO-ANN GROUT (R)
Chairperson, Leon Co Exec Comt, Fla
b Westlake, La, Mar 3, 37; d Nicholas Dewitt Grout & Delma Bowman G; m 1961 to Thomas B Walker, Jr; c Thomas Shannon. Educ: McNeese State Univ, BA in Elem Educ, 59; Student Asn of La Teachers; Int Club Pres. Polit & Govt Pos: Treas & precinct committeewoman, Leon Co Exec Comt, Fla, 73-74, chairperson, 74- Bus & Prof Pos: Teacher, Calcasieu Parish Schs, Lake Charles, La, 58-62, Weslean Day Sch, Atlanta, Ga, 66-69, Fulton Co Schs, Atlanta, 69-72, Palm Beach Co Schs, West Palm Beach, Fla, 71 & Leon Co Schs, Tallahassee, 72- Mem: Young Rep; Leon Classroom Teachers Asn; Bulldog Club of Am. Honors & Awards: First woman to be elected to chair the Leon Co Rep Exec Comt. Relig: Episcopal. Mailing Add: 3045 Carrib Dr Tallahassee FL 30323

WALKER, JOHN ALEXANDER (R)
State Finance Chmn, NC Rep Party
b Philadelphia, Pa, June 10, 22; s John Walker & Dorothy Morrison W; m 1946 to Beryl Audrey Lienhard; c Lynn (Mrs Philip Riker, III), Dorothy (Mrs Robert Moynihan), Gail, Debbie & Mary. Educ: Mulhenberg Col, 1 year; Univ Pa, 2 years; Northwestern Univ, 1 year; Phi Kappa Sigma. Polit & Govt Pos: Chmn, Wilkes Co Planning Comt, 58-59; mem, Urban Redevelop Prog, 60-65; chmn, North Wilkesboro Housing Authority, 65-; state finance chmn, NC Rep Party, currently; mem, Rep Nat Finance Comt, currently; Rep nominee for Lt Gov, NC, 72. Bus & Prof Pos: Salesman, Gen Elec Co, Charlotte, NC, 47-49, sales mgr, 50-56; regional mgr, Hotpoint, Chicago, Ill, 56-58; vpres, Lowe's Co, North Wilkesboro, NC, 58-69, exec vpres, 69-; dir, Northwestern Financial Investors, currently. Mil Serv: Entered as A/S, Navy, 42, released as Lt(jg), 46, after serv in CASU-21, Pac, 44-46; Good Conduct Medal. Publ: Plan to Save Single Family Residence, Bldg Supply News, 69; Lowe's Future, Wall Street Transcript, 69; Marketing Trends, Hardware Retailer, 70. Mem: Elks; Mason; Shrine; Oakwoods Country Club (pres); Blowing Rock Country Club. Honors & Awards: Pres Award, Gen Elec Co, 52, 53 & 55. Relig: Presbyterian. Legal Res: 104 Coffey St North Wilkesboro NC 28659 Mailing Add: Box 983 North Wilkesboro NC 28659

WALKER, LARRY C (D)
Ga State Rep
b Macon, Ga, Mar 9, 42; s Lawrence Cohen Walker, Sr & Hilda Gray W; m 1964 to Janice Knighton; c Lawrence C, III, Wendy, Russell Knighton & John Gray. Educ: Univ Ga Sch Law, JD, 65. Polit & Govt Pos: Judge, Perry Munic Court, Ga, 66-72, city attorney, Perry, 72-; dir, Mid Ga Area Planning Comt, 72-; Ga State Rep, 73- Mem: Houston Co, Ga & Am Bar Asns; Perry Kiwanis Club (pres, 69-70). Relig: Methodist. Legal Res: 1305 Swift Perry GA 31069 Mailing Add: PO Box 1234 Perry GA 31069

WALKER, LEE E (D)
Nev State Sen
b Mesquite, Nev, Sept 22, 25; s Ernest A Walker & Julia Reber W; m 1946 to Evaline Peterson; c Kathren, Merrilee, Michele, Marc, Lizbeth, Brooke & Darrel. Educ: Brigham Young Univ, BS; George Washington Univ, MA & JD. Polit & Govt Pos: Nev State Sen, 70- Mil Serv: Entered as Pvt, Army, 43, released after serv in Inf, ETO, 44-45. Mem: Nev State Bar Asn. Relig: Latter-day Saint. Legal Res: 1729 Arrowhead North Las Vegas NV 89030 Mailing Add: 319 s Third St Las Vegas NV 89101

WALKER, RICHARD BRUCE (R)
Kans State Rep
b Newton, Kans, July 20, 48; s Thomas Franklin Walker & Norma Doell W; single. Educ: Bethel Col(Kans), BA Hist, 70; Univ Kans Law Sch, JD, 73; Pi Kappa Delta; Phi Delta Phi. Polit & Govt Pos: Chmn, Bethel Col Young Rep, 68-70; staff mem, Frizzell for Gov Comt, Kans, 70; chmn pub rels, Kans Col Rep Fedn, 70-71; vchmn, Kans Young Rep Fedn, 72-75; mem, Kans Rep State Comt, 73-; Kans State Rep, 72nd Dist, Newton, 73-, chmn comt on pub health & welfare, Kans House of Rep, currently. Mem: Newton Kiwanis; Jaycees. Honors & Awards: Order of the Golden A, Bethel Col, 70. Relig: United Methodist. Legal Res: 621 S E Fourth Newton KS 67114 Mailing Add: 124 E Fifth Box 871 Newton KS 67114

WALKER, ROBERT KIRK (D)
Mayor, Chattanooga, Tenn
b Jasper, Tenn, May 22, 25; s Jerry A Walker & Clemmie Turner W; m 1945 to Joyce Holt; c Robert Kirk, Jr, Marilyn Joy & James Holt. Educ: Univ Va Col Law, JD, 48; Sigma Nu Phi; Order of Coif. Polit & Govt Pos: Mayor, Chattanooga, Tenn, 71- Bus & Prof Pos: Partner, Law Firm of Strang, Fletcher, Carriger, Walker, Hodge & Smith, Chattanooga, 49- Mil Serv: Entered as A/S, Navy, 43, released as Lt(jg), 46, recalled as Lt(jg), 50, released as Lt, 51. Mem: Tenn & Chattanooga Bar Asns; Optimist Club of Chattanooga; Cherokee Area Coun Boy Scouts (exec bd, 58-); Gtr Chattanooga Area CofC. Honors & Awards: Boy Scout Silver Beaver Award, 66; Freedoms Found Awards for Pub Address, 66-69; Distinguished Salesman at Large Award, Sales & Mkt Execs, 68; Sertoma Int Serv to Mankind, 69; Chattanooga Educ Asn Citizen of Year, 70. Relig: Baptist; deacon, Cent Baptist Church. Mailing Add: 3019 Brownwood Dr Chattanooga TN 37404

WALKER, ROBERT SMITH (R)
b Bradford, Pa, Dec 23, 42; s Joseph Erdman Walker & Rachael Smith W; m 1968 to Sue Ellen Albertson. Educ: Col William & Mary, 60-61; Millersville State Col, BS in educ, 64; Univ Del, MA in polit sci, 68; Sabean Soc Club. Polit & Govt Pos: Campaign aide, Eshleman for Cong Comt, 66; legis asst to Congressman Edwin D Eshleman, 67-74, admin asst, 74-; staff coordr for labor, Citizens for Nixon-Agnew, 68; spec asst to chmn, Rep Cong Comt, 70; Press Room Dir, Rep Nat Conv, 72; dir cong vols, Young Voters for the President, 72; Inaugural Ball Dir, Washington, DC, 73. Bus & Prof Pos: Teacher, Penn Manor Sr High Sch, 64-67. Mil Serv: SP-4, Pa Army Nat Guard, 67- Publ: The peace profiteers, Alternative, 71; Improving the communications gap, Ripon Forum, 73; Congress—The Pennsylvania Dutch Representatives, 75; plus others. Mem: Bull Elephant Club (treas, 71-); Cong Staff Club; Admin Assts Asn; Rep Commun Asn (pres, 73); Lancaster Co Hist Soc. Honors & Awards: Pa State Winner, Voice of Democracy, 58 & 60; Outstanding Young Man of Am, 70; Freedoms Found Award, 73. Relig: Presbyterian. Legal Res: 6065 Parkridge Dr East Petersburg PA 17520 Mailing Add: Off of Hon Edwin D Eshleman House of Rep Washington DC 20515

WALKER, RUSSELL (D)
NC State Sen
Mailing Add: 1004 Westmont Dr Asheboro NC 27203

WALKER, SHIRLEY LOWE (D)
Chmn, St Lucie Co Dem Exec Comt, Fla
b Punta Gorda, Fla, Nov 29, 34; d Miles Edward Lowe & Erma Victoria Collins L; div; c Marshall Keith. Educ: Fla State Univ, 52-53. Polit & Govt Pos: Precinct committeewoman, St Lucie Co Dem Exec Comt, currently, chmn, 70-; mem affirmative action comt, Fla State Dem Party, currently; vchmn by-laws comt, Fla State Dem Chmn Asn, currently; mem, Fla State Bicentennial Comt, currently. Honors & Awards: Youngest woman or man to chair off of Dem Exec Comt Chmn. Relig: Baptist. Legal Res: 114 S 15th St Ft Pierce FL 33450 Mailing Add: PO Box 669 Ft Pierce FL 33450

WALKER, SINITA (R)
Committeewoman, NY Rep State Comt
b Greenwood, SC, May 7, 23; d Rev James Isiah Goldson & Lela G; m 1943 to Harold Walker. Educ: Benedict Col, 40-43; Tau Gamma Delta, Omicron Chap. Polit & Govt Pos: Committeewoman, Nassau Co Rep Comt, NY, 65- & NY State Rep Comt, 66-; pres, Lakeview Rep Club, NY, 68-; deleg, Rep Nat Conv, 72; mem bd zoning appeals, Town of Hempstead, NY, 72- Bus & Prof Pos: Asst court clerk, Nassau Co First Dist Court, Mineola, 57-64; owner, Walker's Employ Agency, Lakeview, 63-68; exec secy pub rels employ bd, Town of Hempstead, 67-72; dir, Vanguard Nat Bank, 72- Mem: Black Leaders Coun (treas, 71-); Nassau Co Ment Health Asn (dir, 72-); Soroptimist Int Club; Negro Women's Coun; Les Bonne Amies (pres, 67-). Relig: Baptist; Minister of music, Community Baptist Church, 67- Mailing Add: 1025 Ontario Rd Lakeview NY 11552

WALKER, STANLEY CLAY (D)
Va State Sen
b Norfolk Bus Col. Polit & Govt Pos: Va State Deleg, 64-72; mem, Norfolk Citizens Adv Comt, Norfolk City Recreation Comn & Norfolk City Sch Bd; Va State Sen, 73- Bus & Prof Pos: Partner & officer, structural steel fabrication, erection & eng firm. Mil Serv: World War II, Army, Europe. Mem: Norfolk Cosmopolitan Club (past vpres); Kempsville Puritan Club (past pres); Norfolk Executives Club; Corinthian Lodge 266, AF&AM; Tidewater Toastmasters Club (past pres). Relig: Methodist; official bd mem. Mailing Add: Box 11266 Norfolk VA 23517

WALKER, THOMAS RAY (TOMMY) (D)
Miss State Rep
b Smithdale, Miss, Feb 26, 29; s George Kenna Walker & Bessie Mae Godbold W; m 1950 to Dotsye E Rag; c Thomas Kenna & Winford Winston. Educ: La Col, 47-50. Polit & Govt Pos: Miss State Rep, 72- Mil Serv: Entered as Pvt, Army, 52, released as Sgt, 54, after serv in 278th Regt Combat Team, Iceland. Mem: Farm Bur; Am Legion (adj, 72-); Mason; WOW. Relig: Baptist. Mailing Add: RFD 2 Smithdale MS 39664

WALKER, VAUGHAN A (R)
Maine State Rep
Mailing Add: Island Falls ME 04747

WALKER, WILLIAM NICKERSON (R)
Dep Spec Rep Trade Negotiations
b Newton, Mass, Apr 3, 38; s Albert Nickerson Walker & Helen Faye Jackson W; m 1961 to Janet Mason Smith; c Gilbert Nickerson & Helen Anne. Educ: Wesleyan Univ, BA, cum laude, 60; Univ Va Law Sch, JD, 63; Psi Upsilon; Mystical Seven. Polit & Govt Pos: Participant, Oper Eagle Eye, 64 & 66; mem, Evanston Young Rep Club, 66-69, vpres civil affairs, 68, vpres polit affairs, 69; Evanston Twp campaign mgr, Reelection US Rep Donald Rumsfeld, 68; chief eval & planning, Off Econ Opportunity, 69-70, spec counsel, 70, acting dep gen counsel, 70-71; dep dir, White House Off Consumer Affairs, 71-72; gen counsel, Cost of Living Coun, 72-74; gen counsel, Fed Energy Off, 74; dir, Presidential Personnel Off, 74-75; Dep Spec Rep Trade Negotiations, 75- Bus & Prof Pos: Attorney, Price, Cushman, Keck & Mahin, Chicago, Ill, 63-69. Mem: Am & Chicago Bar Asns; sustaining mem, Rep Party. Legal Res: 744 Lincoln Ave Winnetka IL 60093 Mailing Add: US Deleg to the MTN 1-3 Avenue de la Paix Geneva Switzerland

WALKOVICH, JOSEPH (D)
Conn State Rep
b Danbury, Conn, Jan 8, 53; s Vittell B Walkovich & Jane Kieras W; single. Educ: Fairfield Univ, BA in Polit Sci, 74. Polit & Govt Pos: Conn State Rep, 109th Dist, Danbury, Conn, 75- Mem: Eagles (Worthy Secy); Conn Young Dem. Relig: Roman Catholic. Mailing Add: 76 Sheridan St Danbury CT 06810

WALKUP, MARY ROE (GROVES) (R)
Secy, Rep State Cent Comt Md
b Kennedyville, Md, May 4, 24; d William Benjamin Groves & Catharine Cooper Roe G; m 1945 to Harry Ernst Walkup, MD; c Mary Anne, Harry Ernst, Jr, Margaret Louise & Robert Douglas. Educ: Univ Md Sch Nursing, grad, 45. Polit & Govt Pos: Women's comt, First Cong Dist Rep Comt, Md, 70-74; legis chmn, Md Fedn Rep Women, 70-72; campaign co-chmn, Re-election of US Rep Wm O Mills, 72; pres, Rep Womens Club of Kent & Queen Anne's Co, 74-; secy, Rep State Cent Comt, Md, 74- Bus & Prof Pos: Spec asst to census chmn, Kent Co, Del, 70; census chmn, Kent Co, Md, 70. Publ: Ed, Kent Conservation News, 72-75. Mem: Md Wildlife Fedn (vpres, 73-75); Kent Conservation, Inc (bd dirs, 69-75, pres, 72-74, ed, Kent Conserv News, 72-75). Relig: Christian. Mailing Add: RD 1 Worton MD 21678

WALL, BARBARA LYNN (D)
b Morganton, NC, Jan 15, 51; d William Theodore Wall & Vurmell Ingle W; single. Educ: Western Piedmont Community Col, AA, 71; Univ NC Greensboro, 71-73; Student Govt; UNC-G Young Dem (secy, 71, pres, 72). Polit & Govt Pos: Intern, US Rep Richardson Preyer, NC, summer 73; aide, Rep Tom Gilmore, NC House of Rep, 74; deleg, Dem Nat Mid-Term Conf, 74; vpres, NC Young Dem Club, 74. Bus & Prof Pos: Consumer credit dept, NC Nat Bank, 75- Mem: Burke Co Young Dem; Burke Co Young Dem Women. Honors & Awards: One of the 10 Most Outstanding Young Dem in NC, 73. Relig: Unitarian. Mailing Add: Rte 12 Box 39 Morganton NC 28655

WALL, CLARENCE VINSON (D)
Ga State Rep
b Athens, Ga, Oct 17, 47; s Clarence Jacob Wall & Fannie Lucille Clark W; m 1969 to Linda Gail Mason; c Jeffrey Vinson. Educ: Cent Gwinnett High Sch, 61-65. Polit & Govt Pos: Ga State Rep, 73- Bus & Prof Pos: Soda jerk, Monford Drug Co, 64-65; mail clerk, Southern Motor Carriers, 65-66; rate analyst, Rate Conf, 65-72; rate analyst, Atlanta Freight Bur, 72-75, serv mgr, 75- Mil Serv: Entered as Airman Basic, Air Force, 67, released as S/Sgt, 73, after serv in 116th Mil Airlift Squadron, 67-73; Ga Air Nat Guard, 6 years. Relig: Baptist. Mailing Add: 120 McConnell Dr Lawrenceville GA 30245

WALL, JAMES MCKENDREE (D)
Committeeman, Ill Dem State Cent Comt
b Monroe, Ga, Oct 27, 28; s Louie David Wall, Sr & Lida Day W; m 1953 to Mary Eleanor Kidder; c David McKendree, Robert Kidder & Richard James. Educ: Ga Inst Technol, 45-47; Emory Univ, BA, 49, BD, 55; Univ Chicago, MA, 61; Omicron Delta Kappa; Alpha Tau Omega. Hon Degrees: LLD, Ohio Northern Univ, 67. Polit- & Govt Pos: Precinct committeeman, Ill Dem Party, 68-; deleg, vchmn, Ill Deleg, Dem Nat Conv, 72; cand for US Cong, 14th Dist, Ill, 72; alt deleg-at-lg, Dem Mid Term Conf, 74; committeeman, Ill Dem State Cent Comt, 14th Dist, 74- Bus & Prof Pos: Sports writer, Atlanta J, 47-50; minister, Moreland Methodist Church, Ga, 55-57; managing ed, Christian Advocate, Ill, 60-63, ed, 63-72; ed, Christian Century, Ill, 72- Mil Serv: Entered as Pvt, Air Force 50 & released as 1st Lt, 52 after serving in Orlando AFB; Alaskan Command, Elmendorf AFB, 51-52. Publ: Church & Cinema, 72 & co-auth & ed, Three European Directors, 73, Eerdman's. Relig: United Methodist. Mailing Add: 451 S Kenilworth Elmhurst IL 60126

WALL, JOHN F (R)
Ill State Rep
b Chicago, Ill, Aug 10, 13; married; c two sons. Educ: St Barbara Roman Cath Parochial Sch; Tilden Tech High Sch; Englewood Eve Sch. Polit & Govt Pos: Alderman, 11th Ward, 47-51; Rep Ward Committeeman, 52-; supt of pvt employ agencies, Ill Dept Labor, 55-61; Ill State Rep, 62-64 & currently; mem, Ill Rep State Cent Comt, 68- Bus & Prof Pos: Dir, Washington Savings & Loan Asn; operated wholesale grocery, meat bus & cleaning & laundry; operates Archer Loomis Recreation Bowling Lanes. Mem: Archbishop Quigley Coun, KofC; St Barbara's Holy Name Soc. Relig: Roman Catholic. Legal Res: 2874 S Hillock Ave Chicago IL 60608 Mailing Add: 2903 Archer Ave Chicago IL 60608

WALL, JOHN M (R)
b Sedan, Kans, Oct 1, 06; s Nathan B Wall & Flora J Inglefield W; m 1939 to Beth K Keller; c Nancy (Mrs Charles R Cole). Educ: Univ Kans, BS, 28, LLB, 31; Pi Kappa Alpha. Polit & Govt Pos: State attorney, Kans, 33-36, co attorney, Chautauqua Co, 37-42 & 46-50; chmn, Chautauqua Co Rep Comt, 50-74; deleg-at-lg, Rep Nat Conv, 56. Bus & Prof Pos: Attorney-at-law, 31-33 & 37- Mil Serv: Entered as Pvt, Army, 42, released as Capt, 46, after serv in 98th & 25th Inf Divs, Pacific Theater. Mem: Kans Bar Asn; Sedan CofC; Am Legion. Relig: Episcopal. Legal Res: 405 Montgomery Sedan KS 67361 Mailing Add: PO Box 96 Sedan KS 67361

WALL, SHADY R (D)
La State Rep
Mailing Add: 1001 Trenton West Monroe LA 71291

WALL, WILLIAM X (D)
Mass State Sen
Mailing Add: State Capitol Boston MA 02133

WALLACE, CARL S (R)
b Ontario, Wis, Sept 27, 18; s David Wallace & Mae McQueen W; m 1941 to Marian E Jones; c Carl S, Jr & Mary Ann. Educ: Univ Wis, PhB, 43. Polit & Govt Pos: Admin asst to US Rep Melvin Laird, Wis, 65-69; Spec Asst to the Secy & Dep Secy of Defense, 69-73; Asst Secy of the Army, 73-75. Bus & Prof Pos: Mgr Wausau Off, Wis State Employ Serv, 51-53; mgr Stevens Point Area CofC, 53-65. Mil Serv: S/Sgt, Army, 42-45, with serv in CoM, 417th Inf, 76th Div, ETO; Two Bronze Stars. Mem: Elks; Kiwanis; Am Legion. Relig: Methodist. Mailing Add: 8315 Ashwood Dr Alexandria VA 22308

WALLACE, E HOWARD (D)
b Pearsall, Tex, July 7, 24; s John G Wallace & Josie Jerkins W; m 1942 to Doris Schott; c William Howard, Danny J & Vicki A. Educ: Am Inst of Banking; Southern Methodist Univ. Polit & Govt Pos: Alderman & mayor pro tem, Devine, Tex, 64-; chmn, Medina Co Dem Exec Comt, formerly. Bus & Prof Pos: Warehouse supt, Sweeney & Co, San Antonio, Tex; vpres & cashier, Median Valley State Bank, Devine, 52- Mil Serv: Army, 43. Mem: Winter Garden Bankers Asn (pres); CofC; Devine Golf Asn (bd dir); St Joseph Soc. Relig: Catholic. Mailing Add: Medina Valley State Bank Devine TX 78016

WALLACE, GEORGE CORLEY (D)
Gov, Ala
b Clio, Ala, Aug 25, 19; s George Corley Wallace & Mozelle Smith W; m 1943 to Lurleen Burns (deceased); m 1971 to Cornelia Ellis Snivelely; c Bobbie Jo, Peggy Sue, George C, III & Lee. Educ: Univ Ala, LLB. Polit & Govt Pos: Ala State Rep, 51-55; judge, Third Judicial Circuit, 55-63; Gov, Ala, 63-66, 71-74 & 75-; Am Independent Party cand for President, US, 68; Dem cand for President, US, 72. Bus & Prof Pos: Lawyer. Mil Serv: Army, Sgt, 42-45, 58th Combat Wing, China, Burma, India, Mariana Islands; 20th Air Force, B-29 Flight Engr, Air offensive over Japan. Mem: VFW; Am Legion; Mason. Relig: Methodist. Mailing Add: State Capitol Montgomery AL 36104

WALLACE, GERALDINE ELIZABETH (D)
VChmn, Benton Co Dem Party Ind
b Freeland Park, Ind, June 13, 06; d William Anderson Bowman & Lottie Jane Miller B; m 1928 to Alvin Eldo Wallace; c June (Mrs Thomas Timothy), Mary (Mrs Dennis Plantenga) & Wanda (Mrs Arnold Wilson). Educ: Ind State Univ, Terre Haute, 4 years; Butler Univ, 1 year. Polit & Govt Pos: Vice precinct committeeman, Benton Co Richland Twp Dem Party, Ind, 50-69; vchmn, Benton Co Dem Party, 60-69 & 74-; vchmn, Second Dist Dem Party, 68-; deleg, Dem Nat Conv, 68. Bus & Prof Pos: Kindergarten teacher, Benton Cent Pub Schs, 53-68. Mem: Am Legion Auxiliary; DAR. Honors & Awards: Jenny Award, Dem Women of Ind. Relig: Presbyterian; Choir dir, 20 years. Mailing Add: Earl Park IN 47942

WALLACE, JAMES H, JR **(INDEPENDENT)**
Tenn State Rep
b Jackson, Tenn, Feb 28, 42; s James Hal Wallace & Frances Hurt W; m 1967 to Sally Roland; c Lee Ellen. Educ: Vanderbilt Univ, BA, 64, JD, 67; Beta Theta Pi. Polit & Govt Pos: Magistrate, Madison Co Quarterly Court, 71; Tenn State Rep, Madison & Crockett Co, 75- Bus & Prof Pos: Attorney-at-law, Jackson, 68- Mil Serv: Entered as Airman, Air Force, 67, released as Lt, after serv in Navy, 68-73; Lt, Navy Res, 73. Mem: Lions; Elks. Relig: Methodist. Legal Res: 27 Pleasant Plains Rd Jackson TN 38301 Mailing Add: 111 W Main St Jackson TN 38301

WALLACE, KEITH ALTON **(R)**
Vt State Sen
Mailing Add: RD 2 Waterbury VT 05676

WALLACE, LINDA FEIST **(DFL)**
Dir, Third Cong Dist Dem-Farmer-Labor Party, Minn
b New York, NY, Nov 14, 39; d Leonard Feist & Mary Regensburg F; div; c Noah Benjamin & Eli Melville. Educ: Univ Chicago, BA, 61, MA, 68. Polit & Govt Pos: Chmn, Precinct One, Golden Valley, Minn, 71-; asst scheduler, Minn for McGovern-Shriver, 72; deleg, Dem Nat Conv, 72; mem, Minn State Dem-Farmer-Labor Cent Comt, 72-; dir, Third Cong Dist Dem-Farmer-Labor Party, 72-; chmn nominating comt, Dem-Farmer-Labor State Conv, 74; assoc chmn, State Sen Dist 43, 75- Bus & Prof Pos: Librn, Munic Reference Libr, Chicago, 62-63, Minneapolis Pub Libr, 63-64, Bus Reference Libr, Univ Minn, 72-73 & St Paul Campus Libr, 73-; state & foreign govt publ librarian, Govt Publ Dept, Univ Minn, 74- Mem: Citizens League; Joint Relig Legis Comt; Common Cause. Mailing Add: 3238 Kyle Ave N Minneapolis MN 55422

WALLACE, ROBERT ASH **(D)**
b Cordell, Okla; s John Marshall Wallace (deceased) & Allie Stewart W (deceased); c Robert C, Wendy A & Douglas S. Educ: Okla State Univ, 38-42; Univ Wash, BA, 45; Univ Chicago, PhD, 56; Sigma Tau; Blue Key; Phi Gamma Mu; Sigma Alpha Epsilon. Polit & Govt Pos: Legis asst to US Sen Paul H Douglas, 49-54; staff dir, US Senate Comt on Banking & Currency, 55-59; consult to US Sen John F Kennedy, 59-61; Asst Secy of Treas, US Treas Dept, 61-69; deleg, Dem Nat Conv, 72; sr consult budget controls, US Senate Govt Opers Comt, 73-74. Bus & Prof Pos: Engr, Boeing Airplane Co, Seattle, Wash, 42-45; instr, Ill Inst of Technol, Chicago, Ill, 48-49; vchmn bd, Exchange Nat Bank of Chicago, 69-74, pres & chief operating officer, 74- Publ: Federal Expenditures, a Detailed Analysis, Am Assembly, Columbia Univ, 52; Factors Affecting the Stock Market (with others), US Govt Printing Off, 55; Congressional Control of Federal Spending, Wayne State Univ Press, 60. Mem: Am Acad of Polit & Soc Sci; Am Polit Sci Asn; trustee, Abraham Lincoln Ctr, Chicago, Ill; Alumnae Adv Cabinet & Vis Comt to Libr, Univ of Chicago; Meadville Theol Seminary, Chicago (trustee & treas). Honors & Awards: US Treas Exceptional Serv Award, 65; US Treas Alexander Hamilton Award, 68. Legal Res: 237 E Delaware Pl Chicago IL 60611 Mailing Add: 130 S La Salle Chicago IL 60603

WALLACE, ROBERT LEWIS **(R)**
b Williamsburg, Iowa, May 8, 22; s John R Wallace & Lois Howes W; m 1964 to Margaret Jeanne Davis Norton; c Stephen K Norton, Kathleen G Norton, Claudia J Norton & Robin Jeanne Wallace. Educ: Williamsburg High Sch, grad. Polit & Govt Pos: Chmn, Iowa Co Young Rep, Iowa, 52-56; policy chmn, Iowa Young Rep, 54-56; Rep precinct committeeman, 54-61; chmn, First Dist Young Rep, 56-59; chmn, Iowa Co Rep Cent Comt, formerly. Bus & Prof Pos: Farmer, 46-61; ins rep, Indust Casualty Ins Co, Chicago, Ill, 61- Mil Serv: Entered as Pvt, Army, 43, released as S/Sgt, 46; Good Conduct Medal; Am Theater Ribbon. Mem: Mason; Eastern Star; Am Legion; Farm Bur. Relig: Methodist. Mailing Add: 802 W Welsh Williamsburg IA 52361

WALLACE, ROBERT THOMAS **(R)**
Dep Under Secy for Mgt, Dept Housing & Urban Develop
b New York, NY, Aug 13, 32; s George Dudley Wallace & Frances Rienecker W; m 1959 to Mildred Murphy; c Jonathan, Matthew, Joseph & Robert. Educ: Univ Notre Dame, BS, 54; Temple Univ Law Sch, 59-60; Harvard Univ Bus Sch, 60. Polit & Govt Pos: Spec asst to Dep Dir Off Mgt & Budget, Exec Off of the President, 73-74; Dep Under Secy for Mgt, Dept Housing & Urban Develop, 74- Bus & Prof Pos: Mgr of planning, RCA, Morrestown, NJ, 57-67; dir commercial systs ctr, Comput Sci Corp, Washington & NJ, 67-73. Mil Serv: Entered as 2nd Lt, Air Force, 55, released as 1st Lt, 57, after serv in Research & Develop Command; Commendation, Weapon Systs Mgt. Publ: Auth, A new test for management by objectives, The Bureaucrat, 74. Mem: Harvard Bus Sch Club of New York; Notre Dame Club of Washington. Mailing Add: 1701 Shag Bark Circle Reston VA 22090

WALLACE, WILLIAM LEWIS **(D)**
b York, SC, May 2, 11; s John Robert Alexander Wallace & Nettie Lou Gardner W; m 1939 to Elyn Colgin; c Mary Elyn Carroll, JoAnn Kathrine & Peatsa Christina. Educ: LaSalle Exten Univ. Polit & Govt Pos: SC State Rep, 40-48; SC State Sen, 48-56 & 69-72; chmn planning bd & platform & resolution comt, SC State Dem Exec Comt, 46-; deleg-at-lg, Dem Nat Conv, 52, 56 & 64; mem adv coun, Nat Dem Party. Bus & Prof Pos: Realtor, merchant & cattle rancher. Mem: Elks; WOW; CofC. Relig: Presbyterian. Mailing Add: 16 Roosevelt York SC 29745

WALLACE, WILLIAM MELTON, JR **(D)**
b Gainesville, Ga, Aug 12, 42; s William Melton Wallace & Caroline Smith W; m 1974 to Patricia Mary Grogan; c Joseph Francis & Terrell Kieth. Educ: Univ Ga Law Sch, 63-64; Parsons Col, AB, 64; Green Key; Dean's List; Tau Kappa Alpha; Sigma Delta Chi; Tau Kappa Epsilon. Polit & Govt Pos: Aide, Phil M Landrum, US Cong, Washington, DC, 64-65, George T Smith, Lt Gov Ga, Atlanta, 65-66 & Lester G Maddox, Gov Ga, 66; staff, Ga Off Econ Opportunity, 66-68; sr adminr, US Off Econ Opportunity, Southeast Regional Off, Atlanta, 68-71; Ga Campaign dir, Sen Edmond Muskie Presidential Campaign, 72; alt deleg, Dem Nat Conv, 72. Bus & Prof Pos: Real estate & security investments, 72- Mil Serv: Entered as Airman 3/C, Air Force, 65, released as 1st Lt, 75, after serv in 116 Tf Squadron; Ga Air Nat Guard, Dobbins Air Force Base, 65-75; Ga Serv Ribbon. Publ: Ed, Georgia Democrat (newspaper), Ga Dem Party, 65. Mem: YMCA. Relig: Presbyterian. Mailing Add: 550 Forest Ave NW Gainesville GA 30501

WALLAHAN, FRANKLIN J **(D)**
Dem Nat Committeeman, SDak
b Spencer, Iowa, Jan 23, 35; s Alfred Curtis Wallahan & Eleanor F Riley W; m 1956 to Mary Jane Goodin; c Kimberly Ranae, Diane Rae & Franklin J, Jr. Educ: SDak State Col, 52-53; Univ SDak, BS, 59, JD, 61; Delta Theta Phi. Polit & Govt Pos: SDak State Sen, 71-72; Dem Nat Committeeman, SDak, 72- Bus & Prof Pos: Admitted to practice law, US Dist Courts, Minn, 63 & SDak, 64, Eighth Circuit Court of Appeals, 71 & Supreme Court of the US, 69. Mil Serv: Entered as Pvt, Army, 53 & released as Sgt, 55 after serving in 37th CIC, attached to 10th Army. Publ: Purchaser's potential liability to subpurchaser recoverable from seller, 60, Immorality, obscenity & the law of copyright, 61 & Rules of civil procedure—judgment, 66, SDak Law Rev. Mem: Am Bar Asn; State Bar of Minn; Mason; Consistory & Shrine; Elks. Relig: Presbyterian. Legal Res: 2711 Frontier Dr Rapid City SD 57701 Mailing Add: 629 Quincy St PO Box 328 Rapid City SD 57701

WALLER, JAMES H **(R)**
Dir Region II, Young Rep Nat Fedn
b Salisbury, Md, June 16, 37; s William E Waller & Marguerite Short W; m 1958 to Mary Lou Emmons; c James H, Jr, Gretchen E, Garrett M & Gwynne E. Educ: Muhlenberg Col, BA, 59; Phi Sigma Iota; Alpha Tau Omega; Mermaid Tavern Soc. Polit & Govt Pos: Co committeeman, Dover Twp Rep Party, NJ, 67-; mem, Toms River Regional Bd Educ, 69-70; mem, Dover Twp Bd Adjustment, 70-73; pres, Rep Club Dover Twp, 72-73; comnr, NJ Bd Architects, 73-; dir region II, Young Rep Nat Fedn, 73- Bus & Prof Pos: Claims rep, Liberty Mutual Ins Co, 59-65; sr prof sales rep, Smith, Kline & French Labs, 66- Mem: Rotary; Navy League US (coun dir, Jersey Shore Coun, 74-). Relig: Protestant. Mailing Add: 13 Camelot Dr Toms River NJ 08753

WALLER, JOHN H, JR **(D)**
SC State Rep
Mailing Add: PO Box 687 Mullins SC 29574

WALLER, OSCAR WILSON **(D)**
b Lenoir Co, NC, Jan 11, 11; s Millard Fillmore Waller & Lottie Sutton W; m 1936 to Billie Estelle McLoud; c Burgess, Billy, Karen (Mrs Emmette Taylor) & Christy. Educ: Oak Ridge Mil Inst, NC, grad, 32. Polit & Govt Pos: Dist chmn, Comt to Elect Johnson, NC, 64; chmn, Lenoir Co Dem Party, formerly; mem, NC Dem State Exec Comt, 64-68; deleg, Dem Nat Conv, 68; chmn, Lenoir Co ABC Bd, 68- Bus & Prof Pos: Farmer, owner, operator, 32- Mem: NC Farm Bur Fedn. Relig: United Methodist. Mailing Add: Route 5 Box 351 Kinston NC 28501

WALLER, SAMUEL CARPENTER **(D)**
Mem, Richmond Co Dem Exec Comt, Ga
b Augusta, Ga, May 3, 18; s Harcourt E Waller & Josephine C Carpenter W; m 1952 to Anna B Maxwell; c Anna M, Laura C & Amelia C. Educ: Princeton Univ, AB, 40; Harvard Law Sch, LLB, 48. Polit & Govt Pos: Mem city coun, Augusta, Ga, 50-56, city attorney, 64-70; chmn, Richmond Co Dem Exec Comt, Ga, formerly, mem, 66- Bus & Prof Pos: Augusta Library, pres, formerly; comnr, Nat Conf of Comnrs on Uniform State Laws, 65-72; mem bd dirs, Ga RR Bank & Trust Co, 72- Mil Serv: Entered as 2nd Lt, Army, 41, released as Capt, 45, after serv in 63rd Inf Div, ETO; Bronze Star. Mem: Kiwanis; State Bar of Ga, (mem bd gov, 67-). Relig: Episcopal; Registr, Diocese of Ga; dep to gen conv, Episcopal Church, 58-72. Legal Res: 600 Gary St Augusta GA 30904 Mailing Add: 1500 Georgia Railroad Bank Bldg Augusta GA 30902

WALLER, WILLIAM L **(D)**
Gov, Miss
b Oxford, Miss, Oct 21, 26. Educ: Memphis State Univ, BS, 48; Univ Miss, LLB, 50. Polit & Govt Pos: Dist attorney, Seventh Circuit Dist, Miss, 60-68; Gov, Miss, 71-; mem exec comt, Nat Gov Conf; chmn, Tenn-Tombigbee Waterway Develop Authority; chmn for state govts, US Payroll Savings Campaign, 75. Bus & Prof Pos: Mem firm, Waller & Fox, Jackson, Miss. Mem: Am Bar Asn; Miss State Bar; Am Judicature Soc; Am Trial Lawyers Asn; Nat Dist Attorneys Asn. Mailing Add: State Capitol Jackson MS 39205

WALLHAUSER, GEORGE MARVIN **(R)**
b Newark, NJ, Feb 10, 00; s Dr Henry Joseph Frederick & Rachel Apolonia Vogt W; m 1926 to Isabel Towne; c George Marvin & Henry Towne. Educ: Univ Pa, BA, 22; Columbia Univ, 42; Phi Sigma Kappa. Polit & Govt Pos: Pres & mem bd, Bur Family Serv, Orange & Maplewood, NJ, formerly; chmn planning bd, Maplewood, 46-54; mem, Twp Comt, 54-57; US Rep, NJ, 59-65; comnr, NJ Hwy Authority, 70-, chmn, 72-; deleg, Rep Nat Conv, 72. Bus & Prof Pos: Mem staff, US Realty & Investment Co, 28-, dir, 40, treas, 47-, vpres, 56-72, sr vpres, 72-; dir, Maplewood Bank & Trust Co & Yorkwood Savings & Loan Asn. Mil Serv: Naval Res, World War I. Mem: Am Legion; Mason; Elks. Relig: Methodist. Legal Res: 31 Kensington Terr Maplewood NJ 07060 Mailing Add: 972 Broad St Newark NJ 07060

WALLIN, DONNA CAROLINE **(D)**
Secy, Isanti Co Dem-Farmer-Labor Party, Minn
b Howard Lake, Minn, Apr 10, 26; d Oscar William Mellin & Florence McGarvie M; m 1944 to Marvin Willard Wallin; c Daryll, Kathryn (Mrs Gerald Gutzkow), Glenyce & Laurie. Educ: Cambridge High Sch, grad, 43. Polit & Govt Pos: Secy, Isanti Co Dem-Farmer-Labor Party, Minn, 69- Mem: Rum River Farmers Union; Cambridge Lutheran Church Women; 4-H Club (leader); Walbo Ladies Aid; Mem Hosp Auxiliary. Honors & Awards: Five Year Award, 4-H; Yearly awards in Farmers Union work. Relig: Lutheran. Mailing Add: Rte 2 Box 492 Cambridge MN 55008

WALLIN, JEAN ROGERS **(D)**
b Hibbing, Minn, Jan 13, 34; d William John Rogers & Rhea Madison R; m 1954 to Donald Frank Wallin; c Rikka Louise & Amy Suzanne. Educ: Va Junior Col, Minn, 1 year; Univ Minn, Minneapolis, 2 years. Polit & Govt Pos: NH State Rep, 67-71; deleg & mem rules comt, Dem Nat Conv, 68, deleg & mem credentials comt, 72; Dem Nat Committeewoman, NH, 68-72; mem, Nashua Sch Bd, 68-; state chmn, McGovern for President, 72; vchmn, NH Dem State Comt, 72-73; develop dir, Women's Info Serv, currently; deleg, Dem Nat Mid-Term Conf, 74. Mem: NH Civil Liberties Union; League of Women Voters; Order of Women Legislators. Relig: Unitarian, Universalist. Mailing Add: 3 Durham St Nashua NH 03060

WALLIN, MYRON JOSEPH **(R)**
Chmn, NDak Dist Two Rep Party
b Minot, NDak, Mar 13, 23; s John Adolph Wallin & Hattie Spooner W; m 1943 to Fern Grindeland; c Gary Wayne, Jerry Lee & Craig Myron. Educ: Noonan High Sch, 4 years. Polit & Govt Pos: Justice of the Peace, Harmonious Twp, Burke Co, NDak, 48-50; state committeeman & conv deleg, Rep Orgn Comt, 52; postmaster, US Post Off, Crosby, 57-61; deleg, Rep State Conv, 64 & 68; chmn, NDak Dist Two Rep Party, 68- Mem: Divide Co Red Cross (chmn); Mason (past master); Concordia Lutheran Church Mens' Club; Crosby

Jaycee's (charter mem); Moose (bd dirs); Kiwanis (bd dirs). Relig: Lutheran. Mailing Add: 601 First St SE Crosby ND 58730

WALLING, ROBERT H (D)
b Fernaldina, Fla, Sept 13, 27; s Robert Walling & Mary-Lee Smith W; m 1952 to Mildred Bruce Fraser; c Carol Leigh, Lynne Elizabeth & Gregory Bruce. Educ: Ga Tech Inst, BS, 50; Emory Univ, LLB, 56; Yale Univ, LLB, 60. Polit & Govt Pos: Asst Attorney Gen, Ga, 58-59; Ga State Rep, 66-69; Ga State Sen, 69-72; deleg, Dem Nat Mid-Term Conf, 74; gen counsel, Dem Party Ga, 75- Bus & Prof Pos: Asst prof law, Emory Univ Law Sch, 60-63; partner, Haas & Holland, 63-72; judge, Superior Courts of Stone Mountain Judicial Circuit, 72-73; partner, Jones, Bird & Howell, 73-; pres, Atlanta Legal Aid Soc, 70-71. Mil Serv: Lt, Naval Res. Relig: Presbyterian. Mailing Add: 1001 Oxford Rd Atlanta GA 30306

WALLING, WILLIS R (R)
b Newark, NJ, Aug 6, 21; s Willis H Walling & Gladys Smith W; m 1943 to Margaret P Stager; c Susan M (Mrs Houser), Jeanne Lynn (Mrs Avermuller) & Diane Carol (Mrs Dunham). Educ: ICS, Scranton, Pa, 8 years. Polit & Govt Pos: Co comt, Hanover Twp, NJ, 60- & munic chmn, 64-65; dist chmn, indust finance chmn & mem exec comt, Morris Co Rep Comt, 67-68 & co chmn, 68-75. Bus & Prof Pos: Sales mgr, Swan Eng Corp, NJ, 49-54; sales mgr, Damascus, Tube, Pa, 54-58 & exec vpres, 58-59; pres-treas, Swan Mfg Corp, NJ, 60- & chmn bd, 66- Mil Serv: Entered as Pvt, Army, 42, released as Capt, 45, after serv as pilot, 371st Fighter Group, ETO, 44-45, Capt, Res, 45-50; Air Medal with Five Clusters; Presidential Citation. Publ: Metal specifications for pools, Swimming Pool Age, 67; Purchasing of metals for pool use, Calif Pool, 67; Foreign sales development, NJ Int Commerce. Mem: Nat Swimming Pool Inst; Nat Recreation & Parks Asn. Relig: Protestant. Mailing Add: 1647 Franklin Ave Ruskaway NJ 07866

WALLIS, CHARLES L (R)
Chmn, Yates Co Rep Comt, NY
b Hamilton, NY, May 1, 21; s Rev Robert S Wallis & Caroline L W; m to Betty Barbe Watson. Educ: Univ Redlands, AB; Univ Rochester, MA; Colgate Rochester Divinity Sch, MDiv; Delta Alpha. Polit & Govt Pos: Deleg, NY Rep State Conv, 62 & 66; chmn, Yates Co Rep Comt, NY, 66-; deleg, Rep Nat Conv, 68 & 72; mem, 34th Cong Dist Acad Selection Comt, 70- Bus & Prof Pos: Minister, First Baptist Church, Canandaigua, 43-46, Keuka Col Church, 46-65 & Keuka Park Church, 65-; chaplain, Vet Admin Hosp, 44-46; mem Eng staff, Keuka Col, 45-, lectr philos & relig, 54-61, prof Eng, 59-, chmn dept, 59-70; ed, Pulpit Preaching, 48-71 & The New Pulpit Digest, 71-; mem ed staff, Interpreter's Bible, 53-57; consult ed, Harper & Row, Publ, 54-; contrib, World Book Encycl; ed, NY Folklore Quart, 55-62; ed assoc, Minister's Manual, 55-67 & ed, 67-; ed fel, Ministers Research Found, Inc, 56-59; mem bd mgr, Am Baptist Hist Soc, 61-; adv ed, Chapel Books, 64-; daily relig prog on Finger Lakes Radio Corp, For Heaven's Sake, 67-; newspaper column, Lakeside Pulpit, 68-; mem nat comt, Japan Int Christian Univ Found, 72- Publ: Ed, Holy Holy Land, Our American Heritage & The Treasure Chest, Harper; plus many others. Mem: Soc Biblical Lit; Am Acad Relig; Mason (past Master); Eastern Star (Past Patron); Rotary. Honors & Awards: Civil War Centennial Medallion. Relig: Baptist. Mailing Add: Keuka College Keuka Park NY 14478

WALLIS, JAMES EDWIN (D)
b Godfrey, Ill, Apr 1, 51; s Homer Ersol Wallis & Thelma Zola Volner W; m 1973 to Michele Marie Condellone. Educ: Southern Ill Univ, Edwardsville, BA, 74; Nat Honor Soc; Dean's List. Polit & Govt Pos: Mem staff, Ray Johnson-Wendell Durr Const Conv Elec Comt, 69-70; Sam Vadalabene for State Senate Campaign Comt, Ill, 70; admin asst to Ill State Rep Sam Vadalabene, 70; dep circuit clerk, Third Judicial Circuit, Madison Co, Ill, 71-75, chief, Criminal Div of Clerk's Off, 72-75; mem adv coun, Supt of Pub Instr M Bakalis, 72; mem staff, Reelect Campaign of Sam M Vadalabene to State Senate, 72; alt deleg, Dem Nat Conv, 72; court adminr, Third Judicial Circuit, Ill, currently; Dem precinct committeeman, Ill, 74-75. Bus & Prof Pos: Mgr, Dog'N'Suds Drive-In Restaurant, Wood River & Collinsville, Ill, 69-71. Mem: Const Drafting Comt, Southern Ill Univ Col Dem (treas, 72-); Local 799, Am Fedn State, Co & Munic Employees. Relig: United Methodist. Mailing Add: 104 E Woodcrest Dr Apt 9 Collinsville IL 62234

WALLIS, O L (R)
Mo State Rep
Mailing Add: 1331 Pershing Poplar Bluff MO 63901

WALLIS, TIM (D)
Alaska State Rep
Mailing Add: Baranoff Hotel Juneau AK 99801

WALLNER, MARY (D)
Dem Nat Committeewoman, SDak
m to Francis Wallner; wid. Polit & Govt Pos: Mgr, Dem Hq Polit Campaigns, SDak, 58, 60 & 64; State Dem Cent Committeewoman; Dem Nat Committeewoman, SDak, 64-; deleg, Dem Nat Conv, 64-72; mem exec bd, SDak Dem Party, currently. Bus & Prof Pos: Exhibiting artist in one woman shows & traveling exhibits; exponent of contemporary art in the church. Mem: Civic Fine Art Asn, Sioux Falls, SDak (bd dirs); Garden Hobbyists; Heritage Libr of Human Resources (ref source); Asn Artists & Relig Communities (consult). Mailing Add: 2605 Poplar Dr Sioux Falls SD 57105

WALLOP, MALCOLM (R)
Wyo State Sen
b New York, NY, Feb 27, 33; s Oliver Malcolm Wallop & Jean Moore W; m 1967 to Judith Warren; c Malcolm Moncreiffe, Paul Stebbins, Oliver Matthew & Amy Vail. Educ: Yale Univ, BA, 54; St Anthony Club. Polit & Govt Pos: Rep precinct committeeman, Big Horn, Wyo, 64-69; Wyo State Rep, Sheridan Co, 69-72; Wyo State Sen, 73-; mem, Legis Serv Off, 73-; bd gov, Nat Soc State Legislators, 73- Bus & Prof Pos: Owner, Polo Ranch, Wyo, 58-, owner, Fairway Acres Inc, 59-68, owner, Mountain Flying Serv, Sheridan, Wyo, 60-64; pres, Wyo Beef Packers Co, 71- Mil Serv: Entered as 2nd Lt, Army, 55, released as 1st Lt, 57, after serv in 269th Field Artillery & 40th Field Artillery Group, 5th Army, 55-57. Mem: Aircraft Owners & Pilot's Asn; Wyo Farm Bur; Wyo Stock Growers; Am Nat Cattleman's Asn; Elks. Relig: Episcopal. Mailing Add: Polo Ranch Big Horn WY 82833

WALLWORK, JAMES H (R)
NJ State Sen
Mailing Add: State House Trenton NJ 08625

WALMSLEY, BILL H (D)
Ark State Sen
Mailing Add: 301 Morrow Batesville AR 72501

WALSH, DANIEL B (D)
NY State Assemblyman
Mailing Add: RD 1 Franklinville NY 14737

WALSH, ELIZABETH KENNEDY (D)
Pres, Conn Fedn Dem Women's Clubs
b Ossinning, NY, June 15, 16; d John Joseph Kennedy & Agnes Begley K; m 1939 to John H Curtis, div; m 1973 to William F Walsh; c Helen Louise & Mary Elizabeth (Mrs Fishman). Educ: St Lawrence Univ, 1 year. Polit & Govt Pos: Dep registr voters, Bridgeport, Conn, 54-68, registr voters, 68-; mem state exec bd, Conn Fedn Dem Women's Clubs, 55-, first vpres, 61-65, chmn campaign activities, 65-67, & pres, 66-; pres, Bridgeport Fedn Dem Women, 56-58; pres & organizer, Fairfield Co Dem Women's Clubs, 59-61; deleg, Dem Nat Conv, 60 & 68; co-chmn voter registr, Conn Dem State Cent Comt, 60-68, mem, Comt for Rev State Party Rules, 66 & 68-69; mem, Gov Comn to Study Procedure for Nomination of Presidential Cand, 70; chmn, Nat Found, 70-; mem, Conn State Bldg Prog Comn, 71-; vchmn, Dist 22 Dem Comt, 74- Mem: Jr Guild Bridgeport; Nat Found-March of Dimes (chmn, Fairfield Co Chap). Honors & Awards: Twenty Year Award, Nat Found. Relig: Catholic. Mailing Add: Apt 5E 25 Cartright St Bridgeport CT 06604

WALSH, ETHEL BENT (R)
b Bridgeport, Conn, Dec 29, 23; d William Woodworth Bent & Corrine Secor B; div; c Diane (Mrs Alfred M Broch) & Robert John, Jr. Educ: Cent High Sch, Bridgeport, 41; Katherine Gibbs, Boston, Mass, 41-42. Polit & Govt Pos: Dir adv coun, Small Bus Admin, Washington, DC, 69-71; comnr, Equal Employment Opportunity Comn, 71-; mem Washington, DC regional selection panel, President's Comn White House Fels, 73; vchmn & acting chmn, Equal Employ Opportunity Comn, 75- Bus & Prof Pos: Personnel mgr, Halfco Div, Aetna Steel Prod Corp, 52-53; sales serv mgr, Propel Chem, Inc, New York, 54-55; vpres, Aerosol Techniques, Inc, Bridgeport, 55-63; pres, Admin Tech Personnel Serv, Hartford, Conn, 64-66; independent consult aerosol indust, Fairfield, 66-67; plant mgr, Lanvin-Charles of the Ritz, Holmdel, NJ, 67-69. Mem: Adv mem Am Coun Educ (adv bd, Proj on Noncollegiate-Sponsored Instr); founding mem Exec Women in Govt (chairperson); Rep Women Fed Forum; Washington Forum. Mailing Add: 318 Independence Ave SE Washington DC 20005

WALSH, JACK (R)
Supvr, First Dist, San Diego Co, Calif
b New York, NY, Feb 17, 34; s Patrick Walsh & Mary Waters W; m 1956 to Kathleen Pekin; c Brian, Kevin, John, Jr, James, Brendan, Terrie & Sheila. Educ: Georgetown Univ, AB, 56. Polit & Govt Pos: Supvr, First Dist, San Diego Co, Calif, 69- Mailing Add: County Administration Bldg 1600 Pacific Hwy San Diego CA 92101

WALSH, JAMES P (D)
Ariz State Sen
Mailing Add: 1552 W Vernon Phoenix AZ 85007

WALSH, JEROME LEO (D)
NDak State Sen
b Minot, NDak, Nov 22, 32; s James Leo Walsh & Magdalene Mary Frost W; m 1952 to Darlene Gail Cecelia Bach; c Jerome Mikel & Lloyd Patrik. Educ: St Leo High Sch, Minot, NDak; Minot State Col. Polit & Govt Pos: NDak State Rep, 70-72; NDak State Sen, 75- Bus & Prof Pos: Owner & operator, Walsh Wheat Farm, Minot, NDak, 52-; treas, Nedrose Sch Bd, 59-69; owner & operator, Walsh Snowmobile Sales, 68- Mem: Western Snowmobile Asn; NDak Wildlife Fedn; Elks; Farmers Union; Eagles. Honors & Awards: Outstanding Young Farmer Award, 62; Wildlife Conserv Award, Agr Stabilization & Conserv, 67. Legal Res: RR 1 Minot ND 58701 Mailing Add: State Capitol Bismarck ND 58501

WALSH, JOHN A, JR (JACK) (D)
b Boston, Mass, Apr 25, 41; s John A Walsh & Doris Hines W; m 1970 to Mary Flynn; c Christopher. Educ: Boston Univ, BA in govt; Boston State Col, MA in urban affairs. Polit & Govt Pos: Youth activities comnr, City of Boston, Mass, 70-74, elec comnr, 71-73; dir field orgn, White for Mayor of Boston, 71; spec asst to Mayor White of Boston, 73-74; dir field orgn, Dukakis for Gov of Mass, 74; deleg, Dem Nat Mid-Term Conf, 74; polit consult, Jack Walsh & Assocs, 74- Bus & Prof Pos: Lectr, Kennedy Inst Polit, Harvard Univ, 72-75. Mil Serv: Entered as Pvt, Army, 61, released as Sgt, 64, after serv in 24th Inf Div, Europe. Mem: Am Acad Polit & Social Sci; Acad Polit Sci. Legal Res: 43 Ainsworth St Roslindale MA 02131 Mailing Add: 131 State St Rm 629 Boston MA 02109

WALSH, JOSEPH B (D)
Mass State Sen
Mailing Add: State Capitol Boston MA 02133

WALSH, JOSEPH WILLIAM (D)
RI State Sen
b Providence, RI, Aug 28, 41; s William A Walsh & Ethel M Horowitz W. Educ: Providence Col, AB, 63; Georgetown Law Sch, JD, 66. Polit & Govt Pos: Clerk, Mil Court of Appeals, 64; staff mem, Congressman John Fogarty, Providence, RI, 66-67; asst city solicitor, Warwick, 67-68; RI State Rep, 69-70; RI State Sen, 70- Bus & Prof Pos: Attorney-at-law, Warwick, RI, 67- Mem: Am & RI Bar Asns. Legal Res: 1445 Warwick Ave Warwick RI 02888 Mailing Add: 400 Narragansett Warwick RI 02886

WALSH, ROBERT M (D)
Conn State Rep
b Meriden, Conn, May 7, 39; s Robert E Walsh & Germaine Guertin W; div; c Christopher C & Mark H. Educ: Univ Conn, Storrs, BA, 61; Trinity Col (Conn), 62-64. Polit & Govt Pos: Mem, Coventry Bd Educ, 71-73, chmn, 73-74; Conn State Rep, 75-; mem, Coventry Dem Town Comt, currently. Bus & Prof Pos: Social worker, Hartford Dept Social Serv, 62-64; field rep, Conn Comn Civil Rights, 64-66; dir affirmative action, Conn Comn Human Rights, 66-67; dir, Neighborhood Youth Corps, 67-71; exec dir, Big Brothers Gtr Hartford, 71- Mem: HELP Inc (chmn); Ctr for Youth Resources (bd govs); Voluntary Action Ctr (tech adv bd). Mailing Add: Depot Rd Coventry CT 06238

WALSH, STARIA R (DFL)
Secy, Legis Dist 13A Dem-Farmer-Labor Party, Minn
b Iron Mountain, Mich, July 26, 16; d Louis S Regis & Daisy Rubbo R; m 1944 to Charles P Walsh; c Michael L, Timothy J, Mary Jo (Mrs Wiltsey) & Katie E. Educ: Col St Scholastica, BA, 38; N Hennepin State Jr Col, 70. Polit & Govt Pos: Secy, Dem-Farmer-Labor Fifth Ward Club, Minn, 54-58; mem, Brooklyn Park Planning Comn, Minn, 64-; secy, 29th Ward Dem-Farmer-Labor Club, 68-70; secy, Legis Dist 13A Dem-Farmer-Labor Party, 70- Bus & Prof Pos: Dir psychol testing, RCA, Bloomington, Ind, 42-45; br off mgr, BMR Inc of Cincinnati, 55-66; partner, off mgr & advert mgr, SASA, Minneapolis, 63- Relig: Roman Catholic. Mailing Add: 7025 Kentucky Ave N Brooklyn Park Minneapolis MN 55428

WALSH, THOMAS A (D)
b St Louis, Mo, Polit & Govt Pos: Mo State Rep, 47-72; deleg, Dem Nat Conv, 68 & 72. Mailing Add: 1917 A Benton St St Louis MO 63106

WALSH, THOMAS P (D)
Pa State Rep
Mailing Add: Capitol Bldg Harrisburg PA 17120

WALSH, WADE (D)
NC State Sen
Mailing Add: 811 Wildeberry Pl Lenoir NC 28645

WALSH, WILLIAM D (R)
Ill State Rep
b Chicago, Ill, Feb 5, 24; m to Barbara Kennedy; c William, Jr, Cynthia, Julie, Peter, Elizabeth, Thomas, David & Terrence. Educ: Northwestern Univ; Loyola Univ, BSC. Polit & Govt Pos: Pres, Proviso Twp Young Rep, Ill; mem, Park Dist Bd Comnr; Ill State Rep, currently. Bus & Prof Pos: Real estate & ins bus with father & brother, John, P M Walsh & Co. Mil Serv: Navy, World War II. Mem: Kiwanis; St Francis Xavier Holy Name Soc. Relig: Catholic. Mailing Add: 801 N Kensington La Grange Park IL 60525

WALSH, WILLIAM FRANCIS (R)
US Rep, NY
b Syracuse, NY, July 11, 12; s Michael J Walsh & Mary Egan W; m 1943 to Mary Dorsey; c William, James, Joseph, Mary Catherine, Martha, Michael & Patricia. Educ: St Bonaventure Univ, AB, 34; Cath Univ Am; Univ Buffalo, MA, 49; Syracuse Univ. Hon Degrees: DCL, St Bonaventure Univ, 70. Polit & Govt Pos: Sr caseworker, Onondaga Co Welfare Dept, NY, 36-41; asst area supvr, NY State Dept Soc Welfare, 46-47; area dir, NY State Comn Against Discrimination, 47-56; dir research, Onondaga Co, NY, 57-59, Comnr of Welfare, 60-61; mayor, Syracuse, 62-70; comnr, NY State Pub Serv Comn, 70-71; alt deleg, Rep Nat Conv, 72; US Rep, 33rd Dist, NY, 73-; NY State Munic Police Training Coun, formerly; mem, NY State Air Pollution Control Bd, formerly; mem, Gov Comt Criminal Offenders, formerly; mem, NY State Rep Platform Comt, formerly; mem, President's Adv Comt Intergovt Rels, 67-70. Bus & Prof Pos: Acct, Remington Rand, Inc, NY, 34-35; vpres, Wilmorite, Inc, NY, 71-72; mem bd dirs, Elmcrest Children's Ctr, Syracuse; Syracuse Savings Bank, Unity Life Ins Co; Maria Regina Col. Mil Serv: Entered as Pvt, Army, 41 & released as Capt, 46, after serving in 6th Air Serv Command; Mid-Pacific; Pacific Theater of Opers, 41-45; Pacific Theater Ribbon; Good Conduct Medal. Mem: Am Legion; VFW; Otisco Lake Rod & Gun Club; Am Arbit Asn; Gtr Syracuse CofC (vpres & bd dirs). Relig: Roman Catholic. Legal Res: 4954 Albart Dr Syracuse NY 13215 Mailing Add: 206 House Off Bldg Washington DC 20515

WALSTROM, LOIS JEAN (D)
Mem, Dem State Cent Comt, Nebr
b West Bend, Iowa, Feb 3, 25; d Grover Cleveland Carter & Antoinette Mikes C; m 1944 to Dr Veryl Walstrom; c Verlyn Cleve & Julie Carter. Educ: Northern Iowa Univ, 43; Kans State Univ, BS, 46; Phi Beta Kappa. Polit & Govt Pos: Mem, Dem State Cent Comt, Nebr, 64-; alt deleg, Dem Nat Conv, 68. Publ: Several articles & pictures in Nat Art Magazines. Relig: Methodist. Mailing Add: Verdigre NE 68783

WALSTROM, VERYL ARMOUR (D)
Mem, Nebr State Dem Cent Comt
b Spencer, Iowa, June 1, 21; s Oscar Benhart Walstrom & Esther Emma Kruse W; m 1944 to Lois Jean Carter; c Verlyn Cleve & Julie Carter. Educ: Iowa State Col, BS in agron, 42; Kans State Col, DVM, 46; Agron Club; Jr Am Vet Med Asn. Polit & Govt Pos: Alt deleg, Dem Nat Conv, 64, 68 & 72; mem, Nebr Judicial Nominating Comn, 64 & Nebr Bd of Educ Servs, 66-; mem, Nebr State Dem Cent Comt, currently. Bus & Prof Pos: Pres, Knox Co Fair Bd, currently. Mil Serv: Entered as Pvt, Army Chem Warfare Serv, 42, released as Cadet, 44. Mem: Nebr Livestock Sales Inspectors (exec comt, 64); Am Vet Med Asn; Am Legion; Masonic Lodge, Oriental Consistory SDak; Royal Soc of Health. Relig: Methodist. Mailing Add: Verdigre NE 68783

WALTER, CRAIG DOUGLAS (D)
Iowa State Rep
b Council Bluffs, Iowa, Sept 23, 49; s Herman William Fredrick Walter & Audrey Stageman W; m 1969 to Marcia Kay Gambrel; c Craig Justin. Educ: Univ Nebr Omaha, BS, 71; Lambda Chi Alpha. Polit & Govt Pos: Treas, Pottawattamie Co Dem Cent Comt, Iowa, 74; Iowa State Rep, 75- Bus & Prof Pos: Dir Douglas/Sarpy Heart, Nebr Heart Asn, 72- Mem: Lambda Chi Alpha Alumni; Farmer's Union; Farm Bur; Iowa State Hist Soc; Hist Soc Pottawattamie Co (rec secy, 73-). Relig: Congregational. Mailing Add: 341 N First Council Bluffs IA 51501

WALTER, MERWYN H (D)
SDak State Rep
b Oct 5, 11; m 1937 to Audrey Iwerks; c Robert. Educ: Sch of Agr, SDak State Univ, 1 year. Polit & Govt Pos: Mem draft bd & bd of educ, Miner Co, SDak; chmn, local sch bd; supvr, Miner Co Soil & Water Conserv Dist; SDak State Sen until 66; chmn, Miner Co Dem Party, currently; SDak State Rep, 33rd Dist, Miner & Lake Co, 70- Bus & Prof Pos: Farmer; dir, Miner Co Crop & Livestock Asn. Mem: Miner Co FHA (bd mem); Mason; Eastern Star. Relig: Presbyterian; trustee & elder. Mailing Add: Roswell SD 57372

WALTERS, EDWARD ENZOR (D)
b Troy, Ala, Mar 26, 44; s John Casey Walters (deceased) & Mary Enzor W; m 1968 to Mary Deanna Doss. Educ: Univ Ala, Tuscaloosa, 63-66; Jones Law Sch, 66; Troy State Univ, BS, 67; Ga State Univ, 68, 69 & 70; Alpha Psi Omega. Polit & Govt Pos: Mgr, Dem Hq, Dekalb Co, Ga, 68; aldermanic cand, Atlanta, 69; dep registr, Fulton Co, 70-72; alt deleg, Dem Nat Conv, 72. Bus & Prof Pos: Child welfare caseworker, Fulton Co Dept of Family & Child Serv, Ga, 67-68; staff researcher, Southern Christian Leadership Conf, Atlanta, 69; bus agent, Local 151, Hotel, Motel & Restaurant Employees Union, AFL-CIO, 70-72; carpet salesman, Carpet Mfrs Outlet, Columbia, SC, 72- Mil Serv: Entered as Cadet, Army ROTC (Res), 65, released, 66, after serv at Univ Ala, Tuscaloosa. Publ: Ed, A Profile of Poverty: Jefferson County, Alabama, Jefferson Co Off Econ Opportunity, 69. Relig: Unitarian-Universalist. Mailing Add: Apt 7 618 Ansley Court NE Atlanta GA 30324

WALTERS, ELMER ELMO (D)
Md State Deleg
b Baltimore, Md, Sept 29, 10; s Raymond William Walters & Charlotte E Stichel W; single. Educ: Baltimore Polytech Inst. Polit & Govt Pos: Md State Deleg, 54- Mil Serv: Entered as Yeoman 2/C, Navy, 42, released as Printer 1/C, 45. Mem: Eagle. Relig: Lutheran. Mailing Add: 17 N Curley St Baltimore MD 21224

WALTERS, JAMES EVERETT (D)
Miss State Rep
Mailing Add: 130 Longwood Ct Jackson MS 39212

WALTERS, JOHNNIE MCKEIVER (R)
b Hartsville, SC, Dec 20, 19; s Tommie Ellis Walters & Lizzie Lee Grantham W; m 1947 to Donna Lucille Hall; c Donna Diane, Lizbeth Kathern, Hilton Horace & John Roy. Educ: Furman Univ, AB, 42; Univ Mich Law Sch, LLB, 48. Polit & Govt Pos: Attorney, chief counsel's off, Internal Rev Serv, Washington, DC, 49-53; Asst Attorney Gen, Tax Div, Dept of Justice, 69-71; Comnr, Internal Revenue Serv, Dept of Treasury, 71-73. Bus & Prof Pos: Attorney, tax dept, Texaco, Inc, New York, 53-61; attorney & partner, Geer, Walters & Demo, Greenville, SC, 61-69; attorney & partner, Hunton, Williams, Gay & Gibson, Washington, DC, 73- Mil Serv: Entered as Pvt, Air Force, 42, released as 1st Lt, 45, after serv in 450th Bomb Group (H), Italy, 44-45, Capt, Res, 45-55; Air Medal with Clusters; Purple Heart; Distinguished Flying Cross. Mem: Quaternion Club; Rotary; CofC; Comt for Total Develop of Greenville; Greenville Little Theatre. Relig: Baptist. Mailing Add: 1327 Oberon Way McLean VA 22101

WALTERS, WILLIAM J (R)
Chmn, Sheridan Co Rep Party, Nebr
b Alliance, Nebr, Mar 12, 44; s Edward F Walters & Marvan Lee Rousey W; m 1968 to Carolyn M Swanson; c Kristi Ann, Teresa Lynn & Mathew D. Educ: Univ Nebr, BA, 70; Alpha Kappa Psi. Polit & Govt Pos: Chmn, Sheridan Co Rep Party, Nebr, 74- Bus & Prof Pos: Acct, North Platte, Nebr, 70-71, Alliance, Nebr, 71-72 & Gordon, Nebr, 72- Mil Serv: Entered as Airman Basic, Air Force, 61, released as A/2C, 65, after serv in 2866 GEEIA Squadron, 63-65; Good Conduct Medal. Mem: Nebr Soc CPA (pres, W Nebr Chapter); Am Inst CPA; KofC (Grand Knight, Trustee). Relig: Catholic. Legal Res: 621 Fairview Dr Gordon NE 69343 Mailing Add: Box 353 Gordon NE 69343

WALTON, EDMUND LEWIS, JR (R)
Mem, Va Rep State Cent Comt
b Salisbury, Md, Sept 4, 36; s Edmund Lewis Walton, Sr & Iris White W; m 1965 to Barbara Post; c Southy Elizabeth & Kristin Post. Educ: Col William & Mary, BA, 61, Law Sch, scholar & JD, 63; Univ Md, 57-58; Pi Kappa Alpha. Polit & Govt Pos: Vpres, Arlington Young Rep Club, 64-65; mem, Arlington Co Rep Comt, Va, 64-65, counsel, 65; deleg, Va State Rep Conv, 65, 66, 68, 69, 70, 72 & 73; mem, Fairfax Co Rep Comt, 66-, chmn Providence dist, 68-70, co chmn, 70-72; mem, Tenth Cong Dist Rep Comt, 70-, vchmn, 73-; deleg, Rep Nat Conv, 72; mem, Va Rep State Cent Comt, 72- Bus & Prof Pos: Staff acct, Main LaFrantz & Co, Salisbury, Md, 61; grad asst, sch bus, Col William & Mary, 62-63; assoc, Simmonds, Coleburn, Towner & Carman, Arlington, Va, 63-69, partner, 69-74; partner, Putbrese & Walton, Attorneys, McLean, Va, 75- Mil Serv: Entered as Pvt, Army Security Agency, 56, released as SP-4, 59, after serv in Japanese Theatre & Continental US, 56-59; Russian linguist, Grad Army Lang Sch. Publ: Tax comment—deductability travel expenses as medical expenses, 62 & Note—current status of miscegenation statutes, 63, William & Mary Law Rev. Mem: Capitol Club Fairfax Co; Great Falls Swim & Tennis Club (dir, 72-74); Rocky Run Civic Asn (pres, 73-74); Fairfax YMCA (dir, 73-75); William & Mary Law Sch Asn (dir, 73-). Relig: Episcopal. Mailing Add: 914 Peacock Sta Rd McLean VA 22101

WALTON, GEORGE D (R)
Chmn, Cent Dist Rep Party, Alaska
b Springfield, Mo, June 3, 32; s William H Walton (deceased) & Verda W (deceased); m 1967 to Maxine L Ryman; c Donald R & Deborah A. Polit & Govt Pos: Vchmn, Cent Dist Rep Party, Alaska, 67-68, chmn, 68-70 & 73-; chmn, Alaska State Rep Comt, 70-73; mem, Rep Nat Comt, 70-73. Mil Serv: Entered as Airman, Air Force, 52, released as Airman 1/C, 56, after serv in Alaskan Air Command, 54-55. Mem: Alaska State Life Underwriters; Fairbanks Asn Life Underwriters; Fairbanks Jaycees; Golden Heart Lions; Lions. Relig: Methodist. Legal Res: 2675 Valkeetna Fairbanks AK 99701 Mailing Add: PO Box 318 Fairbanks AK 99701

WALTON, JAMES NEUMAN, JR (R)
b Marlin, Tex, Sept 14, 24; s James Neuman Walton, Sr & Elizabeth Parsons W; m 1947 to Agnes Elizabeth Rose Robinson; c Betsy & Jim. Educ: Tex A&M Col, 42. Polit & Govt Pos: Chmn, McCulloch Co Rep Party, Tex, formerly. Bus & Prof Pos: Partner, Walton Pontiac Co, Marlin, Tex, 46-48; owner, Brady Auto Supply, 48-66, Ozona Auto Supply, 59-66 & J & B Trailer Sales, 69- Mil Serv: Entered as Pvt, Army Air Force, 42, released as 1st Lt, 46, after serv in 309th Bombardment Group & Sixth Ferry Group, China-Burma-India, 44 & as Air Transport Command Hump Pilot, Asia, 44-45; 1st Lt, Air Force Res, 69; Air Medal; Distinguished Flying Cross; Presidential Unit Citation; three major battle stars. Mem: Automotive Wholesalers of Tex; Am Legion; Hump Pilots Asn; Air Force Hist Asn; Lions. Relig: Presbyterian. Mailing Add: 1007 W 12th Brady TX 76825

WALTON, JUDY RUTH (D)
b Washington, DC, Dec 1, 45; d Frazer Walton, Sr & Susie Simms W; single. Educ: Fed City Col, Washington, DC, BA, 73; Howard Univ, currently. Polit & Govt Pos: Deleg, Dem Nat Mid-Term Conf, 74. Bus & Prof Pos: Admin asst, Leadership Conf on Civil Rights, Washington, DC, 69- Mem: US Youth Coun; Nat Asn of Negro Bus & Prof Women. Relig: Catholic. Mailing Add: 2801 Pennsylvania Ave SE Washington DC 20020

WALTON, RICHARD K (D)
Chmn, Columbia Co Dem Party, Pa
b Berwick, Pa, Nov 12, 31; s Frank Walton & Clara Smith W; m 1951 to Joan C Davis; c

WARD / 969

Brenda (Mrs Douglas McClintock), Debra & Lisa. Educ: Berwick High Sch, Pa, grad, 49. Polit & Govt Pos: Chief clerk, Columbia Co Comnrs, Pa, 57-63, co treas, 64-68, co comnr, 68-; pres, Bd Co Comnrs, currently; chmn, Columbia Co Dem Party, currently. Bus & Prof Pos: Mem bd trustees, Bloomsburg State Col, currently; vpres, State Conservation Comn, currently. Mem: Columbia Co Soil & Water Conserv Dist (comn mem); Berwick Kiwanis (mem bd dirs & chmn boys & girls work, past div chmn boys & girls work & club admin, pres, 73-74, Lt Gov-Elect Div 14, Pa Dist, Kiwanis Int, 74-75); Columbia Co Ment Health/Ment Retardation Asn (past pres & mem exec comt, mem bd dirs, secy, Columbia-Montour-Snyder-Union Joinder Bd & chmn personnel comt); Boy Scouts (past dist comnr, Philmont leader, 65, past mem exec comt, mem camping activities comt, Iroquois Dist & instnl rep, Soil Conserv Dist Explorer Post); Columbia Co 4-H Develop Fund Comt. Relig: Assembly of God. Mailing Add: 1626 Franklin St Berwick PA 18603

WAMMER, MICHAEL HENRY (DFL)
Chmn, Becker Co Dem-Farmer-Labor Party, Minn
b Warroad, Minn, Aug 5, 39; s Helmer Martin Wammer & Kay Hazen W; m 1963 to Bette Mae Behrens; c Steven Michael & Susan Martine. Educ: Macalester Col, BS, 61. Polit & Govt Pos: Dir, Audubon Sch Bd, Minn, 72-; treas bd, Becker-Clay Co Spec Educ Coop, 72-73, chmn bd, 74-; chmn, Becker Co Dem-Farmer-Labor Party, 72-; mem deleg assembly, Minn Sch Bd Asn, 74-; mem, Seventh Dist Dem Exec Comt, 74- Bus & Prof Pos: Claims adjuster, Sentry Ins Co, 63-64 & Am Hardware Ins Co, 64-67; ins salesman, Farmers Ins Group, 67-68; claims adjuster, Iowa Nat Mutual Ins Co, 68- Mil Serv: Entered as Pvt, Army Res, 62, released as Pfc, 63, after 6 months active duty; honor grad, Supply Sch. Mem: Fargo-Moorhead Claims Asn; Jaycees; Am Legion (historian & boys' state chmn); Audubon Boosters; Big Cormorant Lake Asn. Honors & Awards: Jaycee of Year, East Grand Forks Jaycees, 66; Sound Citizen Award, Detroit Lakes Jaycees & Region 17 Jaycees, 72 & 73; Bullthrower Award, Audubon Sch & Athletic Dept, 72-73; One of Ten Outstanding Young Minnesotans, Minn Jaycees, 75; Community Distinguished Serv Award, Detroit Lakes Jaycees, 75. Relig: Lutheran. Mailing Add: Box 161 Audubon MN 56511

WAMPLER, WILLIAM CREED (BILL) (R)
US Rep, Va
b Pennington Gap, Va, Apr 21, 26; s John Sevier Wampler (deceased) & Lillian Wolfe W (deceased); m 1953 to Mary Elizabeth Baker; c Barbara Irene & William Creed, Jr. Educ: Va Polytech Inst, BS, 48; Univ Va Law Sch, 49-50; Sigma Nu Phi. Polit & Govt Pos: US Rep, special asst to Gen Mgr, Atomic Energy Comn; pres, Young Rep Fedn of Va, 50; US Rep, Ninth Dist, Va, 52-54, 67-; chmn, Ninth Dist Rep Party, 65-66. Bus & Prof Pos: Former owner & operator, furniture & carpet bus, Bristol, Va; newsman, Bristol Herald Courier, Virginia-Tennessean & Big Stone Gap Post. Publ: Shall we let them vote? Woman's Day, 12/53; Brief thoughts on election reform, Va Record Mag, 10/68. Mem: Emory & Henry Col (bd visitors); Am Legion; 40 et 8; Sequoyah Coun, Boy Scouts (mem-at-lg). Honors & Awards: Freedoms Found Award for Woman's Day Article; Watchdog of Treasury Award for 100% Voting Record for Econ in 90th Cong, Nat Assoc Businessmen, Inc, 68; Appreciation Plaque, Va State Letter Carriers, 68; Outstanding Citizen of the Year, Bristol, Va-Tenn, VFW, 68. Relig: Presbyterian. Legal Res: 812 Long Crescent Dr Bristol VA 24201 Mailing Add: 2422 Rayburn House Off Bldg Washington DC 20515

WANAMAKER, FLOYD ALLISON (PAT) (R)
Wash State Sen
b Port Townsend, Wash, Aug 3, 10; s Clarence Ira Wanamaker & Blanche Brown W; m 1938 to Irene Eliza DeVries; c Jacqueline Lou, John Edward, Patrick Allison & Robert Edward. Educ: Univ Wash, 30-34. Polit & Govt Pos: Wash State Rep, Tenth Dist, 67-73; Wash State Sen, 73- Mem: Masons; Elks. Relig: Methodist. Mailing Add: Rte 1 Box 193-A Coupeville WA 98239

WANGEN, MARVIN EUGENE (DFL)
Mem, Minn State Dem-Farmer-Labor Cent Comt
b Albert Lea, Minn, Apr 21, 31; s Arnold Marvin Wangen & Frieda Drommerhausen W; m 1953, wid; m 1963 to Harriet Ann Landaas; c Claudia Ann, Diane Lynette, Janis Marie & Aaron Albert. Educ: Dunwoody Indust Inst; Minneapolis Art Inst. Polit & Govt Pos: Vchmn, Freeborn Co Dem-Farmer-Labor Comt, Minn, 61-63, chmn, 63-66; mem, State Dem-Farmer-Labor Cent Comt, 61-; deleg, State Dem-Farmer-Labor Conv, 62-68, mem, Credentials Comt, 62; deleg, Dem Nat Conv, 64; mem, First Dist Dem-Farmer-Labor Exec Comt, 65-, vchmn, 65-71; staff cartoonist, State Dem-Farmer-Labor News, 67- Bus & Prof Pos: Self-employed silk-screen printing, 55-56; art dir & prod mgr, Ad-Art Co, 56-59; art dir & copywriter, Nat Coops, Inc, 59-65, Church Offset Printing, Inc, 65- Mil Serv: Entered as Pvt, Army Signal Corps, 52, released as Cpl, 55, after serv in Joint Community Center as Cryptographer, Field Command, Armed Forces Spec Weapons Proj, 52-55; Nat Defense Ribbon. Honors & Awards: Received Dept of Defense Award for Cartoon-of-the-Month, 4/54. Relig: Lutheran. Mailing Add: 2013 Tower Rd Albert Lea MN 56007

WANNAMAKER, WILLIAM WHETSTONE, JR (R)
b Orangeburg, SC, May 18, 1900; s William Whetstone Wannamaker & Lyall Matheson W; m 1925 to Evelyn Townsend; c William Whetstone, III, Mary Lyall (Mrs George M Morris) & Evelyn Townsend (Mrs J T Richards). Educ: The Citadel, BS, 19; Cornell Univ, CE, 21; Sigma Alpha Epsilon. Hon Degrees: Dr Eng, The Citadel, 66. Polit & Govt Pos: Deleg, SC State Rep Conv, 54-74, pres, 58-60; mem, SC State Rep Comt, 54-66; mem, Rep Nat Comt, 56-66; deleg, Rep Nat Conv, 56, 60 & 64; presidential elector, SC, 68. Bus & Prof Pos: Draftsman-designer-chief party resident engr, SC State Hwy Dept, 21-27; pres, Wannamaker & Wells, Inc, 27-58, chmn bd, 59-69; mem bd visitors, The Citadel, 46-66. Mil Serv: USNR, 40-45; Capt (Ret), Naval Res. Publ: A Story of American Flags, State Printing Co, 71; Long Island South. Mem: Am Soc Civil Engrs; Am Legion; Soc Colonial Wars; SAR; Son Confederate Vet. Mailing Add: 1225 Broughton NW Orangeburg SC 29115

WANNAMAKER, WILLIAM WHETSTONE, III (R)
b Orangeburg, SC, Nov 1, 26; s William Whetstone Wannamaker, Jr & Evelyn Townsend W; m 1947 to Betty Ray Davis; c Ray (Mrs Robert Sabalis), Harriet (Mrs Willis Sheorn), William W, IV, Preston Davis, Amelia Townsend, Sarah Boyd & Mary DuPre. Educ: The Citadel, BS, 49; Cornell Univ, BChE, 52; Univ SC; Alpha Chi Sigma. Polit & Govt Pos: Chmn, Kershaw Co Young Rep Club, formerly; pres & deleg, Young Rep State Conv, formerly; poll watcher & pres, Rep Precinct Club, formerly; pres & deleg, Rep City Conv, Camden, formerly; chmn, Rep City Exec Comt, Camden, formerly; pres & deleg, Kershaw Co Rep Conv, formerly; deleg, Rep State Conv & second vpres, State Conv, 66; alt deleg, Rep Nat Conv, 60, 68 & 72 & deleg & pres elector, 64; chmn, Kershaw Co Exec Comt, secy, formerly; chmn, Fifth Cong Dist Rep Party, formerly; exec dir, SC Nixon for Pres Comt, 68; co chmn, Reelect Sen Thurmond Comt, 72. Bus & Prof Pos: Spec proj supvr, Wannamaker Chem Co, Inc, 42-49; tech engr, E I du Pont de Nemours & Co, 52-59; former newspaper writer; pres & chief chemist, Wateree Chem Co, Inc, 56-; high sch teacher, Thomas Sumter Acad, 65-, headmaster, 66-68; first vpres, Hynes Chem Res Corp, formerly; secy-treas, Manoa Metals, Inc, 72- Mil Serv: Entered as A/S, Navy, 44, released as Coxswain, 46, after serv aboard USS Union AKA 106, Pac; Lt, Naval Res (Ret). Mem: Nat Soc Prof Engrs; Navy League; Asn Citadel Men (life mem); Camden CofC; Camden Rotary Club. Honors & Awards: Awarded Army-Navy E, High Explosives Worker, World War II. Relig: Episcopal. Legal Res: 902 Sunnyhill Dr Camden SC 29020 Mailing Add: PO Box 7 Lugoff SC 29078

WANSACZ, JOHN (D)
Pa State Rep
b Old Forge, Pa, Oct 7, 36; s James Wansacz & Anna Blaschak W; m 1969 to Maryann Presty; c John, Jr. Educ: Old Forge High Sch, grad, 55. Polit & Govt Pos: Pres & organizer, Old Forge Young Dem, Pa, 62; mem, Lackawanna Co Dem Steering Comt, 65; Pa State Rep, formerly & 75- Relig: Orthodox Greek Catholic. Mailing Add: House of Rep Harrisburg PA 17120

WANSTREET, CLARENCE PAUL (D)
WVa State Deleg
b Clarksburg, WVa, Mar 16, 21; s George Lee Wanstreet & Margurite Greiver W; m 1952 to Mary Hurley; c Brent Lee & Brenda Kay. Polit & Govt Pos: WVa State Deleg, 69-72 & 75- Bus & Prof Pos: Dist mgr, B F Goodrich, Hartford, Conn, 51-60; mgr, Discount Tire Serv, Inc, Clarksburg, 60-69. Mil Serv: Entered as Seaman, Navy, 47, released as CPO, 51, after serv in CZ, Eastern Command, Naval Res, 51-55. Mem: Elks; VFW; Am Legion; Moose; Eagles. Relig: Protestant. Mailing Add: 711 Locust Ave Clarksburg WV 26301

WARD, ALINE FRANCES (R)
Mem, Vt Rep State Comt
b Camden, NJ, June 17, 98; d John P Hollopeter & Margaret Smith H; m 1921 to Merlin Burton Ward; c Richard Smith, Lois Evans (Mrs Tierney) & Holly Merlin. Educ: Syracuse Univ, BA, 20; Univ Vt, summer 49; Delta Kappa Gamma; Delta Gamma; Eta Pi Upsilon. Hon Degrees: DH, Norwich Univ, 73. Polit & Govt Pos: Mem, Moretown Sch Bd, Vt, 39-; Vt State Rep, 47 & 53, Dist 69, 69-72; mem, Clerk Soc Welfare Comt, 69-70; pres, Vt State PTA, 53-56; deleg, Rep Nat Conv, 56, alt deleg, 68; mem, Govt Comt of Children & Youth, 60-; Vt State Sen, Washington Co, 61 & 63; pres, Vt State Sch Dir, 61-63; mem, Vt Rep State Comt, 64-; pres, Vt Fedn Rep Women, 69-71; trustee, Norwich Univ, 72-; mem, Vt State Gov Comn Status of Women, 72-74. Bus & Prof Pos: Eng teacher, Camden High Sch, NJ, 20. Mem: Am Asn of Univ Women (legis chmn); Vt Farm Bur; Vt Women's Club; Vt Col (trustee). Relig: Methodist; mem comt social concerns, Troy Conf, 71. Mailing Add: Box 535 Moretown VT 05660

WARD, ALLEN C (D)
NC State Rep
Mailing Add: Rte 1 Shallotte NC 28459

WARD, CHARLES (D)
Dem Nat Committeeman, Ark
Mailing Add: Ward Industs Inc Conway AR 72032

WARD, CHARLES LELAND (D)
b Celina, Tex, July 6, 18; s Charles Lee Ward (deceased) & Annie L Allen W; m 1942 to Mary Lois Barrett. Educ: Univ Okla, BA, 50; Sigma Delta Chi; Phi Beta Kappa; Tau Kappa Epsilon. Polit & Govt Pos: Admin asst to House Speaker, Rep Albert, Okla, currently. Bus & Prof Pos: Ed, Heber Springs Times, Ark, 36-39; off mgr, State NYA off, 41; bur chief, Daily Oklahoman, 47-48; asst mgr, Okla Press Asn, 48-49; news ed, Poteau News, 50-55; managing ed & gen mgr, Durant Democrat, Okla, 55-59. Mil Serv: Army Air Force, 41-46. Mem: Rotary, Durant Camp Fire Coun (vpres); Durant CofC; Nat Found for Infantile Paralysis (vchmn, 57-59); United Fund, Durant, Okla (pub chmn). Relig: Methodist. Legal Res: Durant OK Mailing Add: 1600 S Eads Apt 1121 S Arlington VA 22202

WARD, EARL DAWSON (R)
Kans State Rep
b Chase Co, Kans, Feb 4, 03; s Dennis A Ward & Mary Jane Dawson W; m 1931 to Wilma Harriet Obenour; c Wilma Carol (Mrs Jack Lynn Bishop), Nancy Louise (Mrs Fred Charles Allvine) & Earl Dawson. Educ: Kans State Univ, BS, 26. Polit & Govt Pos: Mem, Kans State Univ Alumni Bd Dirs, formerly, mem, Kans State Univ Legis Coun, formerly, pres, Kans State Univ Alumni Asn, 47; Kans State Rep, 25th Dist, 67- Bus & Prof Pos: Sales engr, Westinghouse Elec, 26-32; spec agt, Conn Gen, 32-44, mgr, 44-64. Mem: Life Underwriters Asn (past mem bd dirs); hon life mem Gen Agents & Mgr Asn (past mem bd dirs); Mason. Honors & Awards: Outstanding Agency in US in Conn Gen, 49. Relig: Protestant. Mailing Add: 6310 Verona Rd Mission Hills Shawnee Mission KS 66208

WARD, JANE KUDLICH (R)
VChmn, Rep Cent Comt Howard Co, Md
b Washington, DC, May 16, 25; d Rudolf Heinrich Kudlich & Margaret Duvall K; div; c Tracy Louise. Educ: Univ Md, BA, 47; Phi Kappa Phi; Kappa Kappa Gamma. Polit & Govt Pos: Legis asst & off mgr, US Rep Harold L Collier, Ill, 57-; secy, Rep Cent Comt Howard Co, Md, 62-70, vchmn, 70- Bus & Prof Pos: Secy, various law firms, airlines, foundation, 47-55; exec secy, Courtesy Assocs, Washington, DC, 55-56. Mem: Howard Co Rep Club; Patapsco Unit, Md Fedn Rep Women; Columbia Rep Club; Howard Co Hist Soc; Bus & Prof Women's Club. Relig: Episcopal. Mailing Add: 10079 Windstream Dr Columbia MD 21044

WARD, JOHN X (D)
Md State Deleg
b Bayonne, NJ, Apr 21, 26; s Patrick Joseph Ward & Grace Kelly W; m 1958 to Flora Macleod Lewis Steward; c Elizabeth, Victoria & Alexandra. Educ: Am Univ, BS, 51; George Washington Univ, MBA, 65; Alpha Sigma Phi; Omicron Delta Kappa. Polit & Govt Pos: Co-campaign mgr, Schweinhaut for Cong, 68; cand, Md State Senate, 70; consult, Md Co & State Elec, 70; cand, McGovern Deleg to Dem Nat Conv, 71-72; consult, McGovern Primary & Gen Elec, Md, 71-72; deleg, Dem Nat Conv, 72; dem precinct chmn, Bethesda, Md, 72-; Md State Deleg, 75- Bus & Prof Pos: Sales mgr, WTOP-TV, Washington, DC, 55-67; pres, Ward Assocs, Inc, 67- Mil Serv: Entered as Pvt, Army 44 & released after serving in 90th Inf Div, European Theater, 45; Purple Heart with Oak Leaf Cluster; Ardennes Campaign Ribbon; Rheinland Campaign Ribbon. Mem: Advert Club of Washington, DC; Reciprocity Club of Washington, DC; Sales & Mkt Execs Club of Washington, DC; Assoc Builders & Contractors of Washington, DC. Honors & Awards: Metro Washington Man of Year,

Reciprocity Club of Washington, DC, 72. Relig: Roman Catholic. Mailing Add: 4720 Montgomery Lane Bethesda MD 20014

WARD, KATHLEEN W (R)
NH State Rep
b Brooklyn, NY, Aug 9, 28; d William A Whelpley & Margaret M McAllister W; m 1947 to John L Ward; c M Candice (Mrs Bell), Mary Lee (Mrs Dauvalt) & Brien L. Polit & Govt Pos: Mem, State Adv Coun for Small Bus Admin, 70-, mem, Nat Adv Coun, 70-; vchmn, Comt on Status of Women, 71-75; vchmn, Grafton Co Rep Party, NH, 73-75, chmn, 75-; NH State Rep, 75- Mem: NH Fedn Rep Women (second vpres, 74-); NH Fedn Women's Clubs (exec bd, 74-); Interstate Asn of Status of Women (exec bd, 74-); Nat & NH Order of Women Legislators. Honors & Awards: Gold Cert, Nat Found March of Dimes, 74. Relig: Catholic. Mailing Add: 61 Pleasant St Littleton NH 03561

WARD, KENNETH VANDIVER (D)
Chmn, Mineral Co Dem Exec Comt, WVa
b Keyser, WVa, June 6, 30; s John Ellwood Ward & Elizabeth Grove W; m 1964 to Laura Virginia Tibbetts; c Molly Beth & Kenneth V, Jr. Educ: Potomac State Col, AA, 50; WVa Univ, AB, 52. Polit & Govt Pos: Vchmn, Mineral Co Dem Exec Comt, WVa, 64-68, mem & chmn, 72- Bus & Prof Pos: Teacher, Bruce High Sch, Westernport, Md, 67- Mil Serv: Entered as Pvt, Army, 52, released as Sgt, 55, after serv in Army Security Agency, Germany, 53-55. Mem: Am Fedn of Teachers; Am Legion; Mason (master, 72-74). Relig: Episcopal. Mailing Add: 43 E Hampshire St Piedmont WV 26750

WARD, LAFE P (D)
WVa State Sen
Mailing Add: State Capitol Charleston WV 25305

WARD, LEW O (R)
b Oklahoma City, Okla, July 24, 30; s Llewellyn Orcutt Ward, II & Addie Reisdorph W; m 1955 to Myra Beth Gungoll; c Casidy Ann & William Carlton. Educ: Okla Mil Acad, 3 years; Okla Univ, BS, 53; Alpha Tau Omega. Polit & Govt Pos: Co coordr, Dewey Bartlett for Gov, 66 & 70; chmn, Garfield Co Rep Party, Okla, 66-68; co chmn, Henry Bellmon for Senate, 68; alt deleg, Rep Nat Conv, 72; chmn & bd dirs, Okla Polit Action Comt. Bus & Prof Pos: Petroleum engr, Delhi Taylor Oil Corp, 55-57; partner & petroleum engr, Ward-Gungoll Oil Investments, 57-69; oil producer & oper, L O Ward Oil Opers, 65-69; bd dirs, Community Nat Bank & Trust Co. Mil Serv: Entered as 2nd Lt, Army, 53, released as 1st Lt, 55, after serv in Corps of Engrs, Far East, 54-55. Mem: Mason; Scottish Rite; Shrine; Am Bus Club; Rotary. Legal Res: 900 Brookside Dr Enid OK 73701 Mailing Add: Box 1187 Enid OK 73701

WARD, MARCELLA ELIZABETH (D)
Mem, Ohio State Dem Party
b Cleveland, Ohio, Dec 23, 31; d Emmett Lampkins & Evelyn Leigh Anderson L; m 1951 to Willie L Ward, div; c Michael William, Monica Lee, Martin Thomas, Diana Marcella & Michelle Juanita. Educ: Cent High Sch, grad, 49. Polit & Govt Pos: Precinct judge, Franklin Co, Ohio, 70-; alt deleg, Dem Nat Conv, 72; prog chmn, Fed Dem Women Ohio, 73; chaplain, Franklin Co Dem Women, 73; mem, Concerned Citizens of Columbus, 75; mem, Co Dem Party, currently; mem, Ohio State Dem Party, currently. Bus & Prof Pos: Admission secy, Capital Univ Law Sch, 69-73; real estate saleswoman, Harris Realty, 70-75; asst to dir nursing serv, State of Ohio Indust Comn, 73-75. Publ: Auth, The star shaped Christmas tree, Columbus Dispatch, 63. Mem: Gamma Phi Delta; Columbus Symphony; Metrop Dem Women's Club; Eleanor Roosevelt Club (vpres, 74); Columbus Bd Realtors Asn. Honors & Awards: Cert from legis for attend Pacesetters Conf, Washington, DC. Relig: Methodist. Mailing Add: 1594 Franklin Ave Columbus OH 43205

WARD, ROBERT FRANCIS JOSEPH (D)
RI State Rep
b Providence, RI, Nov 12, 25; s John Howard Ward & Catherine E Lyons W; m 1948 to Dorothy Frances Mulvey; c Mary (Mrs Stephen French), Robert F J, Jr, Kerri Ann & Siobhan Marit. Educ: Univ RI, BS, 70. Polit & Govt Pos: Chmn, Bd of Canvassers, Warwick, RI, 62-68; mem, Zoning Bd of Rev, Warwick, 70-74; RI State Rep, Dist 33, currently. Bus & Prof Pos: Engr, New Eng Tel, currently. Mil Serv: Entered as Seaman, Navy, 44, released as Boatsmate, 46, after serv in Mine Sweeper, Am & Pac Theatres. Mem: William A Paca Club; Meadowbrook Civic Asn. Relig: Catholic. Mailing Add: 84 Ticonderoga Dr Warwick RI 02889

WARD, THOMAS MORGAN (D)
Ky State Sen
b Shreveport, La, Jan 19, 35; s Edward Morgan Ward & Bradys Louise Alexander W; m 1961 to Louise Taylor Harrison; c Thomas Morgan, Jr, Louise Harrison, Margaret Harrison & Taylor Miles. Educ: La State Univ, BA, 57; Southern Baptist Theol Sem, Ky, BD, 61; Phi Alpha Theta; Kappa Sigma. Polit & Govt Pos: Chmn bd dirs, Bluegrass Area Econ Opportunity Coun, Ky, 66-68; mem, Woodford Co Dem Exec Comt; alt deleg, Dem Nat Conv, 68; cand, Ky House Rep, 52nd Legis Dist, 68; mem, Whitehouse Conf Children & Youth, 70-; Ky State Sen, 75- Bus & Prof Pos: Minister, Pisgah Presby Church, Woodford Co, Ky, 65-; instr relig, Midway Jr Col, Ky, 68- Honors & Awards: Crusade for Freedom Award, 57. Relig: Presbyterian. Legal Res: Rte 1 Sugar Hill Versailles KY 40383 Mailing Add: PO Drawer 569 Versailles KY 40383

WARD, WALTER L, JR (D)
Wis State Rep
b Camp Forest, Tenn; s Walter L Ward & Kathryn L W; div; c Dionne Marie & Walter L, III. Educ: Milwaukee Area Tech Col; Univ Wis-Milwaukee, BS, 69; Phi Epsilon Pi. Polit & Govt Pos: Wis State Rep, 75- Relig: Methodist. Legal Res: 3124 N 13th St Milwaukee WI 52306 Mailing Add: 48D N Capitol Madison WI 53702

WARDEN, MARGARET SMITH (D)
Mont State Sen
b Glasgow, Mont, July 18, 17; d Thomas Willmark Smith & Carrie Johre S; m 1942 to Robert Dickinson Warden; c Gary Sherman & Margaret (Mrs Carl Kochman). Polit & Govt Pos: Const deleg, Dist 13, Mont, 72-74; Mont State Sen, Dist 18, 74-; mem, Mont Environ Qual Coun, 75-; mem adv comt, White House Conf on Libr & Inf Serv, 75-; mem, Fed Rocky Mountain States Telecommun Coun, 75- Bus & Prof Pos: Librn, Great Falls Tribune, Mont, 35-42; ed & tech publ cataloger, BuAer & DCNO for Air, Washington, DC, 43-46. Mem: Mont, Pac Northwest & Am Libr Asns; Am Libr Trustees Asn; Mont Comt for Humanities; Pres Coun, Col of Great Falls. Honors & Awards: Woman of Year, Great Falls Bus & Prof Women, 55; First Libr Trustee of Year, Mont, 65; hon mem, Delta Kappa Gamma, 75. Mailing Add: 208 Third Ave N Great Falls MT 59401

WARDEN, WILLIAM F, JR (BILL) (D)
b Akron, Ohio, Dec 28, 31; s William F Warden, Sr & Louise Edge W; m 1965 to Gloria Gambill; c Victoria Louise & William F, III. Educ: Stetson Univ, AB, 54; Am Univ, 53-54; George Washington Univ Law Sch, 56-59; Scroll & Key; Phi Alpha Theta; pres, Jr Class. Polit & Govt Pos: Staff mem, US Sen Spessard L Holland, Fla, Washington, DC, 56-60; secy, US Rep Winfield K Denton, Ind, 61-63; press secy, US Sen George A Smathers, Fla, 63-65; asst, US Rep Gibbons, Fla, 65 & 66; chmn, Orange Co Dem Exec Comt, Fla, 72 & 73. Bus & Prof Pos: Dir pub rels, Fla Technol Univ, 66-72; acct exec, Hank Meyer Assocs, Miami, 73-; exec dir, Fla Acupuncture Found, Inc, Winter Park, currently. Mil Serv: Entered as Pvt, Marine Res, 51, Maj, currently; Organized Marine Corps Res Medal; Nat Defense Medal; Marine Corps Res Ribbon. Mem: Gtr Orlando Press Club; Marine Corps Vol Training Unit (admin off, 71-); Gtr Orlando CofC (pub rels comt). Relig: Methodist. Mailing Add: 333 Fleet Rd Winter Park FL 32789

WARDER, FREDERICK L (RED) (R)
NY State Sen
b Geneva, NY, Sept 17, 12; m to Justine Crandall; c Susan (Mrs Peebles), Karen (Mrs Adkinson) & Frederick W. Educ: Univ Rochester. Polit & Govt Pos: Chmn finance, Geneva, NY, formerly; pres, Geneva Common Coun, formerly; mayor, Geneva, 58-59; NY State Assemblyman, 62-72, chmn, Labor Comt; NY State Sen, 73- Bus & Prof Pos: Mfr of tents. Mem: Rotary; Rod & Gun Club; The Canandaigua, North & Damascus Shrine; Elks; Theta Delta Chi. Relig: Episcopal. Mailing Add: 100 Lewis St Geneva NY 14456

WARDLOW, FLOYD H, JR (D)
Chmn, Turner Co Dem Exec Comt, Ga
b Ashburn, Ga, Apr 29, 21; s Floyd H Wardlow, Sr & Nora Pickel W; m 1942 to Linnie Powell; c Floyd Hill, III & Jimmy. Educ: Ga Southern Col, 38-40; Univ Ga Law Sch, LLB, 58; Phi Delta Phi. Polit & Govt Pos: Ga State Rep, Turner Co, 52-53; chmn, Turner Co Dem Exec Comt, 66-; Turner Co Attorney, Ga, 75- Mil Serv: Entered as Cadet, Navy, 40, released as Lt, 45, after serv as combat flight instr; Air Medal with Five Gold Stars; Letters of Commendation. Mem: Mason; Shrine; Am Legion; 40 et 8. Relig: Baptist. Legal Res: Ashburn GA 31714 Mailing Add: PO Box 647 Ashburn GA 31714

WARE, JAMES CRAWFORD (D)
Ga State Rep
b Colon, CZ, Feb 2, 15; s Rigdon Mims Ware & Emily Virginia Shackleford W; m 1944 to Gwynneth Mary Woodhouse; c Suzanna Emily (Mrs O'Donnell), John Rigdon, Peter Woodhouse & David Anthony Mims. Educ: Univ Ore. Polit & Govt Pos: Mem, Hogansville City Bd Educ, 41; Ga State Rep, 61 Bus & Prof Pos: Pres, Ware Bros, Inc, 56-60; pres, Hogansville Warehouse Co, 64-73; vpres, Ga Bus Realty, currently. Mil Serv: Entered as Pvt, Army 42, released as Tech Sgt, 45, after serv in ETO; European-African-Mid Eastern Theater Ribbon with three Bronze Stars. Mem: Kiwanis; Am Legion; VFW; Farm Bur; CofC. Relig: Baptist. Legal Res: 17 Taliaferro Dr Hogansville GA 30230 Mailing Add: PO Box 305 Hogansville GA 30230

WARE, JOHN H, III (R)
b Aug 29, 08; s John H Ware, Jr & Clara Edwards W; m to Marian R Snyder; c John, Marilyn Strode, Paul & Carol. Educ: Univ of Pa, BS. Polit & Govt Pos: Burgess, Oxford, Pa; mem, State Bd of Welfare, 61-70; mem, Pa Hist & Mus Comn, 62-70; chmn, Chester Co Develop Coun; Young Rep of Southern Chester Co, pres, formerly; Rep dist chmn; Rep co committeeman, formerly; mem, Co Exec Comt; Pa State Sen, 60-70, chmn, Rep Caucus, 67-70; US Rep, Ninth Cong Dist, 70-74. Bus & Prof Pos: Bus exec; newspaper publ; chmn, Am Water Works Co; pres, Pa Fuel Gas, Inc. Mem: Beta Theta Pi; Rotary Int; Coatesville YMCA; Chester Co, Boy Scouts (pres); State YMCA (dir). Relig: Presbyterian; Treas & Trustee, Presbytery of Donegal, Synod of Pa. Legal Res: 55 S Third St Oxford PA 19363 Mailing Add: US House of Rep Washington DC 20515

WARE, JOHN THOMAS (R)
Fla State Sen
b Chattanooga, Tenn, Nov 14, 31; s Col James E Ware & Marguerite McQue Ware Armat; m Doris Gregory; c G Scott, Stacey, Sheryl, Sheila & Steve. Educ: Univ Fla, 49-50; Fla State Univ, BS Pub Admin, 57; Stetson Col of Law, JD, 61; pres, Lambda Chi Alpha & Interfraternity Coun, 56-57. Polit & Govt Pos: Fla State Rep, 64-66 & 68-70; city attorney, St Petersburg Beach, 67; Fla State Sen, 70-, minority leader, Fla State Senate, 74- Bus & Prof Pos: Attorney-at-Law. Mil Serv: Navy, Korean War, 50-54. Mem: St Petersburg Bar Asn; Fla Acad of Trial Lawyers; Fla & Am Bar Asns. Honors & Awards: Allen Morris Award for most effective sen in debate, 74. Legal Res: 211 Sunset Dr N St Petersburg FL 33710 Mailing Add: 55 Fifth St S St Petersburg FL 33701

WARE, RICHARD ANDERSON (R)
b Staten Island, NY, Nov 7, 19; s John Sayers Ware & Mabelle Anderson W; m 1942 to Lucille Henney, div, m 1972 to Beverly Giss Mytinger; c Alexander W, Janet M, Bradley J & Patricia E. Educ: Lehigh Univ, BA, 41; Wayne State Univ, MPA, 43; Phi Beta Kappa; Phi Alpha Theta. Polit & Govt Pos: Asst dir, Mich Joint Legis Comt on State Reorgn, 50-52; secy, Gov Comn to Study Prisons, 52-53; polit analyst, Rep Nat Comt, 64; Prin Dep Asst Secy of Defense, Int Security Affairs, Dept of Defense, 69-70; consult, Off Secy of Defense, 70-73; adv coun, Woodrow Wilson Int Ctr for Scholars, 73- Bus & Prof Pos: Research asst, Detroit Bur of Govt Research, 41-42; personnel technician, Lend-Lease Admin, 42-43; research assoc, Citizens Research Coun of Mich, 46-49, asst dir, 49-56; secy, Relm Found & Earhart Found, 56-69, pres, 69-; dir & mem exec comt, Ann Arbor Trust Co, 70- Mil Serv: Entered as Pvt, Army Air Corps, 43, released as T/Sgt, 46. Publ: A proposal for a legislative auditor general, essay, 51; The case for reorganization, monograph, 52; Governmental research; challenge & response, monograph, 66. Mem: Cosmos Club of Washington, DC. Honors & Awards: Secy of Defense Meritorious Civilian Serv Medal. Relig: Congregational. Legal Res: 16 Haverhill Ct Ann Arbor MI 48105 Mailing Add: 904 First Nat Bldg Ann Arbor MI 48108

WAREHAM, LEVADA E (R)
Secy, Trumbull Co Rep Exec & Cent Comts, Ohio
b Warren, Ohio, Aug 6, 21; d Charles Allen Wright & Sara Seybert W; m 1940 to Roscoe H Wareham; c Sally (Mrs Welke), Deborah & Patricia. Educ: Warren G Harding High Sch, Warren, Ohio, grad, 39. Polit & Govt Pos: Secy & vpres, Howland Rep Club, Ohio, 63, pres, 64, legis chmn, 69; Rep precinct committeeman, Howland Precinct M, Trumbull Co, 63-;

secy, Trumbull Co Rep Exec & Cent Comts, 64-; polit dir, Warren City Women's Club, 69-72, first vpres, 72- Relig: Protestant. Mailing Add: 4300 Stonybrook Dr Warren OH 44484

WARF, J H (D)
Chmn, Lewis Co Dem Party, Tenn
b Maury Co, Tenn, Sept 13, 04; m 1932 to Martha Josephine Kistler. Educ: Mid Tenn State Col, BS; George Peabody Col, MA. Polit & Govt Pos: Mem, Tenn State Bd Educ, 55-62; Comnr of Educ, Tenn, 63-72; chmn, Lewis Co Dem Party, 75- Bus & Prof Pos: Elem & sec sch teacher, asst prin & prin, Lewis Co, Tenn, 21-29; Lewis Co supt, 29-62. Mem: Tenn Educ Asn; Tenn Pub Sch Officers' Asn; Am Asn Sch Admin; Tenn Sch Bd Asn; Sigma Club. Relig: Methodist. Mailing Add: Hohenwald TN 38462

WARGO, JOHN P (D)
Ohio State Rep
Mailing Add: 344 E Chestnut St Lisbon OH 44432

WARGO, JOSEPH G (D)
Pa State Rep
b Olyphant, Pa, Aug 4, 22; s Andrew P Wargo & Anna Wasilisin W. Educ: Olyphant Sr High Sch. Polit & Govt Pos: Mem, Lackawanna Co Dem Clubs, Pa; Pa State Rep, 48- Mil Serv: 109th Inf, Nat Guard, peacetime; World War II, Sgt, 168th Inf, 34th Div, N Africa, Italy; lost left leg, Battle of Casino. Mem: DAV; Am Legion; life mem Throop Blvd Mem Post 7251, VFW; Lions; KofC Coun 1005. Legal Res: 408 Cleveland St Olyphant PA 18447 Mailing Add: Capitol Bldg Harrisburg PA 17120

WARING, ELOISE BOTTS (R)
b Martinsville, Ohio, Sept 3, 20; d Howard Cecil Botts & Golda Daugherty B; m 1943 to William Mathews Waring; c William Michael & Bruce Howard. Educ: Christ Hosp Sch Nursing, grad, 41. Polit & Govt Pos: Pres, Wilmington Rep Women, Ohio, 65-68 & 70-72; chairwoman, Clinton Co Rep Comt, 70-75; chairwoman, Clinton Co Rep Women, 72- Mem: Clinton Co Registered Nurses (secy, 60-62, pres, 62-64); Bus & Prof Women's Club (vpres, Wilmington, 57-58, pres, 58-59, legis chmn, dist 13, 75-77); Am Nurses Asn; Am Cancer Soc (co vpres, 75-76); Southwest Ohio TB Ord League (pres, 75-76). Relig: Protestant. Legal Res: 1695 Hillcrest Ave Wilmington OH 45177 Mailing Add: 610 W Main St Wilmington OH 45177

WARING, LLOYD BORDEN (R)
Mem Exec Comt, Rep Nat Finance Comt
b Boston, Mass, July 13, 02; s Everett B Waring & Florence Thayer W; wid; m 1971 to Louise Powell; c Philip B, Faith (Mrs George Roebelen), Bayard D & Deborah (Mrs C Richard Carlson). Educ: Bentley Col Acct & Finance, Boston. Hon Degrees: Dr Polit Sci, Northeastern Univ, 71. Polit & Govt Pos: State chmn, Mass Rep State Cent Comt, finance chmn; finance chmn for Dwight D Eisenhower; New Eng chmn for Barry Goldwater; Mass chmn for Richard Nixon; mem exec comt, Rep Nat Finance Comt, 71-; New Eng finance chmn to Reelect the President, 72. Bus & Prof Pos: Vpres, Kidder, Peabody & Co, Inc, currently. Mem: City Club; Algonquin Club of Boston. Relig: Episcopal. Legal Res: Driftwood Rd Rockport MA 01966 Mailing Add: 35 Congress St Boston MA 02110

WARKENTHIEN, GENE (R)
SDak State Rep
Mailing Add: Willow Lake SD 57278

WARNER, ALVIN W (D)
Vt State Rep
Mailing Add: Lowell VT 05847

WARNER, CLARENCE E (R)
Chmn, Rep State Comt Okla
b Booker, Tex, Oct 31, 38; s Virgil O Warner & Mabel Arnett W; m 1960 to Ona C Oldfield; c Catharine Lynette. Educ: Kans State Teachers Col, BA, 60; Okla State Univ, MS, 66; Lambda Delta Lambda; Kappa Mu Epsilon; Phi Lambda Upsilon; Alpha Kappa Lambda. Polit & Govt Pos: Chmn, Garfield Co Young Rep Club, Okla, 65 & 66; Rep precinct chmn, Garfield Co, 65-68; Sixth Dist chmn, Okla Young Rep Fedn, 67-68; Rep state committeeman, Garfield Co, Okla, 67-68; chmn, Okla Educ, Coun, 67-68; chmn, Rep State Comt Okla, 69-; admin asst to US Rep John N Happy Camp, Okla, 1-5/69; deleg, Rep Nat Conv, 72. Bus & Prof Pos: Instr, Sterling Col, Kans, 63; asst prof chem, Phillips Univ, Enid, Okla, 63-68. Mil Serv: Major, Army Nat Guard, Okla, 57-; Res Forces Medal. Mem: Am Chem Soc; Am Asn Univ Prof. Relig: Methodist. Mailing Add: 11201 Dover Court Surrey Hills Yukon OK 73099

WARNER, DOROTHY MARIE (R)
Treas, Calif Fedn of Rep Women
b Albion, Ill, Sept 3, 22; d Ross Lewis Davis & Ruth Easton D; m 1942 to Kenneth J Warner; c Kathleen Jo. Educ: Ind Univ, Bloomington, 2 years. Polit & Govt Pos: Pres, Thousand Oaks Rep Women's Club, Federated, Calif, 61-62; co-chmn, Nixon for Gov Comt, Conejo Valley, 62; vpres, Ventura Co Fedn of Rep Women, 63-64; precinct chmn, 65-66; chmn, Goldwater for Pres Comt, Conejo Valley, 64; chairwoman, Southern Div, Calif Fedn of Rep Women, 64-65; precinct chmn, 66-67; treas, 68-; precinct chmn & vchmn, Ventura Co Rep Cent Comt, Calif, 65-; mem precinct steering comt, Calif Rep State Cent Comt, 65-68; treas, Calif Fedn Rep Women, 70- Publ: Guide for Republican Women, Southern Div Calif Fedn of Rep Women, 68. Mem: Conejo Community Coun (past youth chmn, secy, currently); Conejo Beautiful, Inc (past chmn); Conejo Valley Garden Club; Audubon Soc; Delphian Soc. Honors & Awards: One of Fifty in State of Calif to Receive Gov Reagan's Award of Precinct Excellence, 68. Relig: Lutheran. Mailing Add: 2066 Penrose Court Thousand Oaks CA 91360

WARNER, JEROME (R)
Nebr State Sen
b Waverly, Nebr, Nov 23, 27; s Charles J Warner & Esther Anderson W; single. Educ: Univ Nebr, BSc, 52; Alpha Zeta, Gamma Sigma Delta; Block & Bridle; Farm House. Polit & Govt Pos: Nebr State Sen, 25th Dist, 66-; Speaker, Nebr State Senate, 69- Relig: Covenant. Mailing Add: Waverly NE 68462

WARNER, JOAN FLEENOR (D)
Exec Secy, Summit Co Dem Party, Ohio
b Weston, WVa, May 11, 09; d David D Rich & Anna Elizabeth Skidmore R; m 1966 to Guy O Warner. Educ: Actual Bus Col, Akron, Ohio, Secy Cert, 29; Akron Univ, 32; Case Col Eng, Cleveland, Ohio, 45-46. Polit & Govt Pos: Sr Inspector govt material, Army Ord Dept, 46-49; Army Eng Corp, 47-49; state dep registrar motor vehicles, Ohio, 50-54; chmn, Fifth Ward Dem Precinct Committee People, pres, Fifth Ward Dem Club & exec secy, Summit Co Dem Party, Ohio, 50-; state sales tax agt, Ohio, 61-63; mem, State & Nat Fedn Dem Womens Club; State Auditor, Ohio, 71-72. Bus & Prof Pos: Secy, Firestone Tire & Rubber Co, Akron, Ohio, 32-45; owner & mgr, J & H Restaurant, 46- Mem: Women's Bus Asn; Daughters of Am (state dep); Women's Benefit Asn; German Am Club; Am Legion Auxiliary. Honors & Awards: Testimonial dinner for registering more Dem than anyone in Summit Co, Akron, Ohio; Merit Award for Summit Co Dem Woman of the Year, Young Dem Orgn, 70; Summit Co Dem Woman of Year, 72. Relig: Protestant. Mailing Add: 1032 Neptune Ave Akron OH 44301

WARNER, JOHN WILLIAM (R)
b Washington, DC, Feb 18, 27; s Dr John William Warner, Sr & Martha Stuart Budd W; m 1957 to Catherine Conover Mellon; c Mary Conover, Virginia Stuart & John William, IV. Educ: Washington & Lee Univ, BS, 49; Univ Va, LLB, 53; Beta Theta Pi; Phi Alpha Delta. Polit & Govt Pos: Law clerk, Judge E Barrett Prettyman, Circuit Judge, US Court of Appeals, 53-54; spec asst to US Attorney, 56-57; asst US Attorney, Justice Dept, 57-60; advanceman, Nixon Campaign Staff, 60; nat dir, United Citizens for Nixon-Agnew, 68; mem staff, Off President-elect, 68-69; Under Secy of the Navy, Washington, DC, 69-72; Secy of the Navy, 72-74; adminr, Am Revolution Bicentennial Comn, currently. Bus & Prof Pos: Lawyer; partner, Hogan & Hartson, 60-68. Mil Serv: Entered as Seaman, Navy, 44, released as ETM 3/C, 46, recalled as Pvt, Marine Corps, 49, released as Capt, 61, after serv in First Marine Air Wing, Korea, 51-52. Mem: Am Bar Asn; Washington Inst Foreign Affairs; Metro Club; Burning Tree Club & Chevy Chase Club, Washington, DC. Relig: Episcopal. Legal Res: Milldale Farms Box 24 White Post VA 22663 Mailing Add: 3240 S St NW Washington DC 20007

WARNER, KEITH C (D)
Utah State Rep
Mailing Add: 544 N Barlow St Clearfield UT 84015

WARNER, MARVIN (D)
Mem, Dem Nat Comt, Ohio
Mailing Add: 601 Main St Cincinnati OH 45202

WARNER, PHILIP T (R)
Ind State Rep
b Goshen, Ind, Jan 13, 31; s De Main Warner & Hazel F Kein W; m 1953 to Gladys I Lung; c Stephen, Jennifer & Nancy. Educ: Purdue Univ, BS; Delta Upsilon. Polit & Govt Pos: Mem, Goshen Twp Adv Bd, Ind, 57-70; deleg, Ind Rep State Conv, 68; Ind State Rep, 70- Bus & Prof Pos: Dir, First Nat Bank, 66-; mem, Adv Bd Ind Voc & Tech Col, 68-; mem, Ind Farm Policy Study Comn, 68- Mil Serv: 2nd Lt, Army, 53, released as 1st Lt, 55, after serv in Transportation Research & Develop Command, 54-55. Mem: Rotary; Farm Bur. Honors & Awards: Outstanding Young Farmer Ind, 60; Master Farmer Award, 68. Relig: Methodist. Mailing Add: RR 1 Box 4 Goshen IN 46526

WARNICK, DAVID CHRISTOPHER (R)
State Youth Committeeperson, Idaho State Rep Cent Comt
b Moscow, Idaho, Jan 22, 54; s Calvin Cropper Warnick & Kathleen Orr W; single. Educ: Univ Idaho, 72; Farmhouse; secy, Col Rep, 72- Polit & Govt Pos: Student body secy, Moscow Sr High Sch, 71-72; alt deleg, Rep Nat Conv, 72; precinct committeeman, Latah Co Rep Cent Comt, Idaho, 72-; state youth committeeperson, Idaho State Rep Cent Comt, 72-; state chmn, Idaho Col Rep League, 73-76; chmn, Western Fedn Col Rep, 74; pres, Assoc Students of Univ of Idaho, 75. Bus & Prof Pos: Store mgr, Camp Grizzly, Boy Scouts, 69-71; ed, Wocsomonian, Moscow High Sch, 71-72; polit reporter, Idaho Argonaut, Univ Idaho, 72- Publ: The Northwest regional presidential primary, Ripon Forum, 5/74; The GOP, time for re-examination, Col Rep Nat Newslett, 1/75; The slackers, Lewiston Tribune, 4/75; plus others. Mem: Monday Lunch Bunch (chmn, 72-). Honors & Awards: State Runner-Up, Am Legion Oratorical Contest, 72; Outstanding Debater, Moscow Sr High Sch, 72; Nat Merit Scholar, 72; Assoc Student of Univ Idaho Distinguished Serv Award, 73 & 74; St Bonaventure Merit Citation for Jour, 74. Relig: Christian. Legal Res: Rte 3 Box 202 Moscow ID 83843 Mailing Add: ASUI Offices Student Union Bldg Moscow ID 83843

WARNICK, JOEL STANLEY (D)
b Wausau, Wis, May 18, 54; s Stanley Arthur Warnick & Adele Pagel W; single. Educ: Univ Wis-Marathon Co Campus, AA, 74. Polit & Govt Pos: Treas, Marathon Co Dem Youth Caucus of Wis, 69-70, vchairperson, Wausau Area, 70-71, chairperson, 71-72, vchairperson, Seventh Cong Dist, 71-72, chairperson, U W Marathon Co, 72-73, chairperson, Seventh Cong Dist, 72-73, state orgn dir, 73-74, chairperson affirmative action comt, 73-74, chairperson state conv rules comt, 74-75; campaign mgr, Brozek for State Rep Comt, 74; admin rep, Dem Youth Caucus of Wis, 74- Honors & Awards: State President's Award for Best Unit in State, Dem Youth Caucus of Wis. Relig: Lutheran. Mailing Add: 311 Elm St Wausau WI 54401

WARNKE, FRANK J (D)
Wash State Rep
b Havre, Mont, 1933. Educ: Cent Wash Col Educ, 1 year; Univ Wash. Polit & Govt Pos: Wash State Rep, until 66 & 75- Bus & Prof Pos: Pub affairs consult; legis dir, Pub Sch Employees. Mil Serv: Coast Guard 3 years. Mem: Kiwanis; Jr CofC. Mailing Add: 29457 51st St S Auburn WA 98002

WARREN, CHARLES (D)
Calif State Assemblyman
b Kansas City, Mo, 1927; m 1963 to Audrey Paul Warren. Educ: Yale Univ; Univ Calif, BA, 49; Hastings Col Law, LLB, 52. Polit & Govt Pos: Chmn, Dem State Cent Comt Calif, formerly; Calif State Assemblyman, 63-, chmn judicial comt, Calif State Assembly, formerly, chmn assembly comt on energy & diminishing materials, currently, chmn joint comt on pub domain, currently; chmn energy task force, Nat Conf State Legis; mem environ adv comt, Fed Energy Admin, currently. Mil Serv: Sgt, Army, 44-46. Mem: Calif State Bar Asn. Mailing Add: 1411 W Olympic Blvd Los Angeles CA 90015

WARREN, CLIFFORD ERNEST (D)
Dem Nat Committeeman, Alaska
b Seattle, Wash, Jan 25, 19; s John L Warren & Esther Smith W; m 1938 to June Crate. Educ: W Seattle High Sch, 33-35. Polit & Govt Pos: Chmn, Dem Comt, Small Bus Comt, Western States Dem Conf, 62-69; alt deleg, Dem Nat Conv, 64; deleg, 68 & 72; mem, Dist Dem Comt, SCent Alaska, 68-70; chmn, Alaska Dem Party, 70-72; Dem Nat Committeeman, 72-; deleg, Dem Nat Mid-Term Conf, 74. Bus & Prof Pos: Pres, Warren Painting Co, Inc, Anchorage, Alaska,

50- Mil Serv: Entered as Painter 1/C, Navy, 42, released as Painter 1/C, 45, after serv in 40th Construction Bn, SPacific, 42-45; Good Conduct Medal; Campaign Ribbon with 4 Battle Stars; Presidential Distinguished Unit Citation. Mem: Masonic Blue Lodge; Scottish Rite; Shrine; Washington Athletic Club; Col Club. Relig: Protestant. Legal Res: 2650 Marston Dr Anchorage AK 99503 Mailing Add: PO Box 1124 Anchorage AK 99510

WARREN, DELBERT CLAYTON (R)
Chmn, Sixth Dist Rep Party, Ky
b Bath Co, Ky, May 3, 30; s Clark Warren & Ina Vertna Karrick Bogie W; m 1960 to Wanda Bryant; c Ronald, Nancy, Melanie, Kimberly & Brent. Polit & Govt Pos: Chmn, Montgomery Co Rep Party, Ky, formerly; chmn, Sixth Dist Rep Party, Ky, currently. Bus & Prof Pos: Pres, Warren Builders, Inc; pres, Warren Lumber Co Inc; vpres, Gate City Bowling Lanes. Relig: Protestant. Legal Res: 107 Ronameki Dr Mt Sterling KY 40353 Mailing Add: PO Box 486 Mt Sterling KY 40353

WARREN, GEORGE MARVIN, JR (D)
Va State Sen
b Bristol, Va, Aug 19, 22; m to Merle Musser Watkins W. Educ: Emory & Henry Col, BA; Univ Va, LLB. Polit & Govt Pos: Comnr, Western Dist Va, formerly; Va State Sen, 64- Bus & Prof Pos: Lawyer. Mil Serv: Navy, 3 years, SW Pac. Mem: Elks; Mason; Commonwealth Club. Relig: Presbyterian. Legal Res: 100 Wallace Pike Bristol VA 24201 Mailing Add: PO Box 1078 Bristol VA 24201

WARREN, GEORGE THOMAS, II (R)
Ga State Sen
b Atlanta, Ga, May 18, 37; s Lovic Cyril Warren, Jr & Alfreda Bell W; m 1955 to Jacquelyn McWilliams; c George T, III, Jeffrey Hunt & Daniel Forrest. Educ: Ga State Univ, BBA, 62; Delta Sigma Pi; Pi Sigma Epsilon. Polit & Govt Pos: Ga State Sen, 73- Bus & Prof Pos: Exec, L C Warren, Jr Co, Inc, 55-68; owner, Warren Realty Co, 68- Mem: Nat Asn Real Estate Bds; Nat Inst Real Estate Brokers; Nat Inst Farm & Land Brokers; South DeKalb YMCA (dir). Relig: Baptist. Mailing Add: 3762 Tree Bark Trail Decatur GA 30034

WARREN, JAMES EDMOND (D)
Ala State Rep
b Castleberry, Ala, Sept 8, 34; s Levi Simpson Warren & Leah Garrett W; m 1957 to Betty Jane Smith; c James Michael (deceased) & Sharon Kaye. Educ: Larkins Bus Col, Brewton, grad in bus admin, 60. Polit & Govt Pos: Mem city coun, Castleberry, Ala, 64-; Conecuh Co Bd Educ, 68-70; Ala State Rep, 71- Bus & Prof Pos: Mem staff chem dept, Monsanto Corp, Pensacola, Fla, 57- Mil Serv: Entered as Airman, Navy, 52, released as AKAN, 55, after serv in 2nd Marine Air Wing, Korean Conflict; Good Conduct Medal; National Defense Medal. Mem: Ruritan Nat (mem bd dirs); Methodist Men's Club (vpres); Wildlife Club (Conecuh & Monroe Co); Am Legion. Relig: Methodist. Mailing Add: PO Box 207 Castleberry AL 36432

WARREN, JOE E (D)
Kans State Sen
b Silverdale, Kans, Sept 17, 12; s James Edmond Warren & Phoebe Harkelroad W; m 1932 to Pauline Goff; c James E & Helen Jane (Mrs Fair). Polit & Govt Pos: Dir sch bd, King Sch Dist 58, Kans, 38-59; treas, Spring Creek Twp, 50-54, precinct committeeman, 73-; committeeman, Cowley Co Agr Stabilization & Conserv Comt, 50-54; Kans State Sen, 57-, chmn, Dem Caucus, Kans State Senate, 64-, mem, Kans Legis Coun, formerly, chmn, Livestock Subcomt & vchmn, Agr Subcomt, currently, asst minority leader, currently, vchmn, Legis Facilities Comt, currently; chmn, Cowley Co Soil Conserv Dist, 60-; mem, Adv Coun Unemploy Security Secy Labor, 64-68; alt deleg, Dem Nat Conv, 68, deleg, 72; mem, Gov Comt on Criminal Admin, currently. Mem: Grange; GF Forum; Rotary; Elks. Honors & Awards: Named Mr Conservation by Conserv Soc Am. Relig: Presbyterian. Mailing Add: Rte 1 Maple City KS 67102

WARREN, JOHN E (JACK) (R)
b Rockford, Ill, Dec 28, 12; s Ezra H Warren & Mary Elizabeth Diamond W; m 1933 to Audrey E Showalter; c Audrey E (Mrs Harold C Andrews), Jacqueline (Mrs Richard Roberts), Adelor J & Sari Ann (Mrs Craig Bartlett). Educ: Rockford High Sch, Ill, grad, Chicago Sch of Traffic; LaSalle Correspondence Sch Bus. Polit & Govt Pos: Finance chmn, Black Hawk Co Rep Cent Comt, Iowa, 61-63, chmn, 63-67; finance chmn, Third Dist Rep Party, 66 & 67-70; chmn, Iowa State Rep Cent Comt, 67-69; mem, Rep Nat Comt, 67-69. Bus & Prof Pos: Secy-treas, Warren Transport, Inc, Waterloo, Iowa; pres, Warren Real Estate, Inc; vpres, Warren Bros, Inc; vpres & treas, A&F Finance & Tripoli Grain & Feed; dir, Mr Steak of Waterloo & Cedar Rapids, Foods Develop, First Lady Beauty Salon, Waterloo, Midwest Publ Co, Inc & Bus Develop Credit Corp, Iowa; mem bd dirs, St Francis Hosp, Waterloo; mem bd, Waterloo Civic Found & Metrop Improv Servs; vchmn, Black Hawk Co Crime Comn; campaign chmn, United Appeal & Multiple Sclerosis, Waterloo, 70. Mem: Iowa Motor Truck Asn (pres, 70-); Mason; KT; Shrine; Elks. Honors & Awards: Citation of Appreciation, Becker-Chapman Post, Am Legion; Hon Ky Col; Hon Col on Govs Staff; Boss of the Year, Waterloo Jr CofC, 61; Person of the Year, Waterloo CofC, 70. Relig: Baptist. Legal Res: Apt 1 794 Russell Rd Waterloo IA 50702 Mailing Add: PO Box 420 Waterloo IA 50704

WARREN, JOHN FISKEN (JACK) (R)
Chmn, Rep Party Tex
b Dallas, Tex, July 31, 29; s John Edwin Warren & Marjorie Fisken W; m 1951 to Patricia Payne; c William Edwin, Nancy Bentley & Donald Payne. Educ: NMex Mil Inst, 2 years; Univ Tex, 3 years; Phi Kappa Psi. Polit & Govt Pos: Rep precinct chmn, Smith Co, Tex, 60-64; deleg, Rep State Conv, 60-72; co chmn, Bush for Senate, 64; co chmn, Tower for Senate, 66, vchmn for finance, 72; chmn, Smith Co Rep Party, 66-69; mem, Tex Rep Task Force on Taxation & Revenue Policy, 67; alt deleg, Rep Nat Conv, 68, deleg, 72, mem, Credentials Comt, 72; mem, State Comt on Fed Employ, 69; committeeman, Tex Rep State Exec Comt, Second Dist, 69-, dep chmn, 70-; chmn, Rep Party Tex, 73- Bus & Prof Pos: Oil scout, Gulf Oil Co, summers; landman, Humble Oil & Ref Co, Tyler, Tex, 56-63; independent oil operator-producer, 63-; chmn bd, Austin Publ Co, currently. Mil Serv: Entered as 2nd Lt, Army, 54, released as 1st Lt, 56, after serv in Tank Bn, Tenth Inf Div & First Inf Div; discharged from Res with rank of Capt, 63. Mem: ETex Asn of Petroleum Landmen; Tyler Petroleum Club; Community Concert Asn of Tyler (dir); Nat Petroleum Coun; Independent Petroleum Asn Am (vpres). Relig: Episcopal; Past Vestryman & Past Sr Warden, Christ Episcopal Church; deleg, Coun of Episcopal Diocese of Tex. Legal Res: 1613 Delano Rd Tyler TX 75701 Mailing Add: 803 Citizens Bank Bldg Tyler TX 75701

WARREN, LILLIAN FRANCES WARMSLEY (R)
Mem, Minn Rep Party
b Pleasant Hill, La, Mar 10, 28; d Kelly Warmsley & Joanna Price W; m to Dr John Marcus Warren, div; c John Jr, Carl Micah, Cheryl Linda, Monica Renee, Patricia Lynn & Todd Michael. Educ: Univ Minn, Continuing Educ, 62, 69 & 71; Am Inst of Banking, 70-75. Polit & Govt Pos: Alt deleg & precinct secy, Minn State Rep Party, 64, deleg, 66-72, chmn precinct caucus, 72, vchairwoman, formerly, elec judge chmn, 72-; deleg-at-lg, Nat Fedn Rep Women Confederation, 68; mem bus & prof div, Minn Fedn Rep Women, 68-70; mem & secy, Minn State Dept Human Rights Adv Coun, 68-71; chmn minority div, Grass Root Orgn Women, 69-71; mem, Nat Negro Women Adv Coun Rep Party, 70; mem voc & rehabilitation coun, Dept Health, Educ & Welfare, 71-73; deleg, Rep Nat Conv, 72; mem, Nat Adv Coun for Reelec of the President, 72; mem pvt resource coun, Off Econ Opportunity, 72- Bus & Prof Pos: Bus off, Asbury Methodist Hosp, Minneapolis, 53-62; exec secy, Minneapolis Urban League, 62-65; exec secy of missions, Youth Div, Nat Hq, Am Lutheran Church, 65-66; columnist, Twin Cities Courier, 65-; admin secy & supvr, Twin Cities Opportunities Indust Ctr, 66-69; equal employ opportunity coordr, First Nat Bank of Minneapolis, 69-; pub rels coordr, Commodore & Queen Caribbean Cruise Tour, 71; bd mem & chmn, Minneapolis Aquatennial, 75- Publ: Feature writer & free lance, Post Publ Co, Minneapolis Spokesman Newspaper & Minn Rep News, until 65; columnist, Notes on the Noteable Week, Twin City Observer, 64-65; columnist, Woman view, Twin Cities Courier, currently. Mem: Lutheran Human Rels Asn; Twin Cities Opportunities Indust Ctr Training Prog (bd, comt mem, currently); Minneapolis Plans for Progress (exec comt, 72-); NAACP; Nat Coun Negro Women. Honors & Awards: Cert of Appreciation, Twin Cities Opportunities Indust Ctr, 68 & YWCA, 70; Emissary, Minneapolis Aquatennial to WI, 71; Achievement Award, Rep Women of Minn, 71; Plaque, Minn Writers Workshop, 71; Cert of Appreciation, Minn Pub Schs Commun Resource Vol, 72; Vol Serv Award, Minneapolis Urban League, 75. Relig: Baptist. Mailing Add: 4901 Portland Ave S Minneapolis MN 55417

WARREN, MARVIN F (D)
Utah State Rep
Mailing Add: 240 E 850 S Springville UT 84663

WARREN, RICHARD DALE (D)
Chmn, Clinton Co Dem Party, Mich
b Barryton, Mich, Sept 28, 35; s Harry N Warren & Emily Marie Kemp W; m 1955 to Barbara Jean Grant; c Vicky Kay & Bonny Marie. Educ: Mich State Univ, BS, 67, MA, 69. Polit & Govt Pos: Chmn, Clinton Co Dem Party, Mich, 73- Bus & Prof Pos: Teacher for mentally handicapped, Lansing Schs, Mich, 67-69, coordr teachers of mentally handicapped, 70-72, work study job placement counr for all handicapped, 72- Mem: Nat & Mich Educ Asns; Lansing Teachers Asn; Gtr Lansing Asn for Retarded Children. Mailing Add: 1220 Sandhill Dr Dewitt MI 48820

WARREN, ROBERT WILLIS (R)
Attorney Gen, Wis
b Raton, NMex, Aug 30, 25; s Rev George R Warren & Clara Joliffee W; m 1947 to Laverne D Voagen; c Cheryl Lynn, Iver Eric, Gregg Alan, Treiva Mae, Lyle David & Tara Rae. Educ: Univ Pa, Army basic eng course, 44; Macalester Col, BA, magna cum laude in econ, 50; Univ Minn, MA, in pub admin, 51; Foreign Serv Inst, 51-52; Univ Wis Law Sch, JD, 56; pres, Student Body, 49-50; Nat Hon Soc; Gamma Eta Gamma. Polit & Govt Pos: Foreign Affairs Off, US Dept of State, 51-53; secy, Brown Co Vol Rep Comt, 58; asst dist attorney, Brown Co, 59-61, dist attorney, 61-65, Wis State Sen, Second Dist, 65-69; Attorney Gen, Wis, 69-; deleg, Rep Nat Conv, 72. Bus & Prof Pos: Shipfitter's helper, Sturgeon Bay Shipbuilding & Drydock Co, 43; G I Loan Agent & Counsr, Bank of Sturgeon Bay, 46; mem, Godfrey, Godfrey & Warren, Elkhorn, Wis, 56-57; partner, Warren & Boltz, Attorneys, Green Bay, Wis, 57-59, Smith, Will & Warren, 65-69; mem, Midwest Conf Attorneys Gen, formerly, chmn, 71-72; mem, Nat Asn of Attorneys Gen, currently, vpres, 71-72, pres, 73-; mem, Great Lakes Comn, currently, chmn, 71-73; mem, Wis Coun on Criminal Justice, currently; mem, Wis Bd of Comnrs of Pub Lands, currently; mem, Wis Controlled Substances Bd, currently, chmn, 70-; mem, Wis Coun Drug Abuse, currently, vchmn, 70-, mem, State Urban Affairs Coun, currently. Mil Serv: Entered as Pvt, Army Res, 43, released as T/4, 46, after serv in 377th Inf Regt, 95th Div, 613th Ord Basic Armor Maintenance & 889th Heavy Automotive Maintenance Co, ETO, 44-46; Combat infantryman's Badge; Purple Heart; ETO Ribbon. Mem: Optimists; Mil Order of Purple Heart; VFW; DAV; Four Lakes Coun 628, Boy Scouts. Relig: Methodist. Legal Res: 209 Glacier Dr Madison WI 53705 Mailing Add: 114 East State Capitol Madison WI 53702

WARREN, WILLIAM ERNEST (D)
NMex State Rep
b Rochester, NY, Aug 11, 30; s Lynn Ernest Warren & Marion Gardner W; m 1955 to Barbara Popplewell; c Thomas Lynn & John William. Educ: Univ Rochester, BS, 56, MS, 59; Cornell Univ, PhD, 62; Phi Beta Kappa; Tau Beta Pi; Sigma Xi. Polit & Govt Pos: Deleg, NMex Const Conv, 69; NMex State Rep, 71- Bus & Prof Pos: Asst prof, Cornell Univ, 61-62; staff mem, Sandia Labs, 62- Mil Serv: Entered as Pvt, Air Force, 48, released as S/Sgt, 52. Publ: Electrostrictive stress singularities in angular corners of plates, ZAMP, 65; The axisymmetric thermoelastic problem in bispherical co-ordinates, J Appl Mech, 67; Theory of axial plane reorientation in liquid crystals of nematic type, Quart J Mech Appl Math, 70. Mem: Am Math Soc; Soc Indust & Appl Math; Am Inst Aeronaut & Astronaut; PTA; Am Civil Liberties Union. Honors & Awards: Spec Friend Award, Albuquerque Asn for Children with Learning Disabilities, 74; Outstanding Effort Award, NMex Asn for Retarded Citizens, 74; Honor Award, Albuquerque Classroom Teachers Asn, 74. Mailing Add: 7712 La Condesa NE Albuquerque NM 87110

WARRINER, D DORTCH (R)
Gen Counsel, Va Rep Party
b Brunswick Co, Va, Feb 25, 29; s Thomas Emmett Warriner, Sr & Maria Clarke Dortch W; m 1959 to Barbara Ann Jenkins; c Susan Wells, David Thomas Dortch & Julia Cotman. Educ: Univ NC, BA, 51; Univ Va, LLB, 57; Order of the Holy Grail; Kappa Alpha Order; Sigma Nu Phi. Polit & Govt Pos: Chmn, Greensville Co Rep Comt, Va, 63-70; deleg, Rep State Conv, 64-66, 68-73; alt deleg, Rep Nat Conv, 64, deleg, 68 & 72; mem, Va State Rep Cent Comt, 64- & Exec Comt, 68-; nominee for Attorney Gen of Va, 65; co-chmn, Va Nixon for President Comt, 68 & 72; chmn, Fourth Cong Dist Rep Party, 68-71; city attorney, City of Emporia, Va, 70-; gen counsel, Va Rep Party, 72- Bus & Prof Pos: VPres, Va Asn of Professions, 70-; vchmn, Va Chap, Am for Effective Law Enforcement, 72- Mil Serv: Entered as Ens, Navy, 51, released as Lt(jg), 54, after serv with Atlantic Fleet; Lt, Naval Res, 57- Mem: Am Bar Asns; Greenville Bar Asn (secy, 60-); Va Trial Lawyers Asn; Lions (dist gov,

65-66); Va Farm Bur Fedn. Relig: Protestant. Legal Res: 100 State St Emporia VA 23847 Mailing Add: 314 S Main St Emporia VA 23847

WARSCHAW, CARMEN H (D)
Chmn, 23rd Dist Dem Cent Comt, Calif
b Los Angeles, Calif, Sept 4, 17; d Leo M Harvey & Lena Brody H; m 1938 to Louis Warschaw; c Hope & Sue (Mrs Robertson); grandchildren, Cara & Carl Robertson, Jr. Educ: Univ Southern Calif, AB cum laude, 39; Alpha Kappa Delta. Polit & Govt Pos: Mem exec comt, Dem State Cent Comt, Calif, co-chmn; pres, Dem Club; mem, Los Angeles Co Dem Cent Comt; mem exec comt, Calif Fedn Young Dem; deleg, Dem Nat Conv, 56, 60, 64, 68 & 72, mem permanent orgn comt, 60; pres, Dem Women's Forum, 56-57 & 58-59; chmn women's div, Dem State Cent Comt, 58-64; mem, State Bd Soc Welfare, 59; mem, Fair Employment Practices Comn, 59-64, chmn, 64; chmn, Dem State Cent Comt of Southern Calif, 64-66; Dem Nat Committeewoman, 68-72; mem, Nat Citizens Adv Comt for Community Serv; mem, Calif South Coast Regional Coastal Zone Conserv Comn, currently; vchmn, Co of Los Angeles Elections Comn, currently; conducting seminar, The Weaker Sex (?) In politics, Immaculate Heart Col, currently; chmn, 23rd Dist Dem Cent Comt, Calif, currently. Mem: Pac W Coast Anti-Defamation League, B'nai B'rith (bd dir); Community Rels Coun, J F C. Honors & Awards: Community Serv Award in Human Rels, Pac Southwest Region Bd, Anti-Defamation League, B'nai B'rith, 64; Mem, Am Revolution Bicentennial Comn of Calif; Woman of the Year, Los Angeles Times, 68. Mailing Add: 2324 N Vermont Los Angeles CA 90027

WARSHAFSKY, TED M (D)
Court Comnr, Milwaukee Co, Wis
b St Louis, Mo, Dec 6, 26; s Israel Warshafsky & Ida Wacks W; m 1950 to Dolores Anne Weiss; div; c Beth, Michael & Lynn. Educ: Univ Ill, 44; Univ Wis, BBA, 49; Univ Wis, Law Sch, JD, 52. Polit & Govt Pos: Chmn, Milwaukee Civil Liberties Union, Wis, 62-66; deleg, Wis Dem State Conv, 63, 66-72; parliamentarian, Milwaukee Co Dem Party, 66-67; court comnr, Milwaukee Co, 66-; vchmn, McCarthy for Pres, 67-68; vchmn, Wis Dem Deleg & deleg, Dem Nat Conv, 68; bd mem, Wis Civil Liberties Union, 68-69; chmn, Milwaukee Dem Coalition, 69; chmn, Nat Anti-Trust Law Consumer & Pub Serv Law Off Comt. Bus & Prof Pos: Sr partner, Warshafsky, Rotter & Tarnoff, 64; pres, Am Design Eng Corp, 60- Mil Serv: Entered as Pvt, Marines, 44, released as Pfc, 46, after serv in Fleet Marine Force, Pac Theatre, 45-46. Publ: Collateral cross examination, Bankcroft Whitney, 67; Trial handbook for Wisconsin lawyers, Lawyers Coop Publ Co, 73. Mem: Wis Bar Asn (chmn ins & negligence sect); Am Bar Asn; Wis Acad Trial Lawyers (pres); Am Judicature Soc; Am Trial Lawyers Asn (nat secy, educ dir & current nat exec bd mem). Honors & Awards: Numerous prof & bar asn honors & awards. Relig: Jewish. Legal Res: 2648 N Summit Ave Milwaukee WI 53211 Mailing Add: 633 W Wisconsin Ave Milwaukee WI 53203

WARWICK, ROBERT FRANKLIN (R)
Asst Secy, NC Rep Party
b Wilmington, NC, May 26, 36; s James Franklin Warwick & Virginia Cayce W; m 1955 to Catherine Herring; c Carol Diane & Steven James. Educ: Wilmington Col, 55; Univ NC, BS in Bus Admin, 58; Chi Phi. Polit & Govt Pos: Treas & finance chmn, New Hanover Rep Exec Comt, NC, 62-; treas, New Hanover Co Rep Party, 62-; deleg, Rep Nat Conv, 64, alt deleg, 68; precinct chmn, S Wilmington Precinct, 64-65; mem, finance comt, NC Rep Party, 66-; chmn, Gardner for Gov Campaign Seventh Dist, 68; finance chmn, Seventh Cong Dist, NC, 68-; mem, NC State Rep Cent Comt, 68-; asst secy, NC Rep Party, 68-; mem, State Comt, CPAs for Nixon, 72- Bus & Prof Pos: Clerk auditor of Freight Receipts Off, Atlantic Coast Line RR Co, 54-55; partner, Staff Cert Pub Acct, 58-62 & C S Lowrimore & Co, Cert Pub Acct, 62-; instr, spec acct courses, Wilmington Col, 62-63. Publ: Multiple Corporations, Series of Articles for NC Newspapers, 67. Mem: Cape Fear Area Soc Cert Pub Accts; Kiwanis; Pine Valley Country Club; Admiral, NC Navy. Relig: Baptist. Mailing Add: Rte 3 Box 303 I Wilmington NC 28401

WASHBURN, C LANGHORNE (R)
b Livermore Falls, Maine, July 14, 18; s Stanley Washburn & Alice Langhorne W; m 1966 to Judith Davies; c Cary Langhorne, J Tayloe, Alice, Alexandra, Pamela, Nancy Serena & Natalie Faith. Educ: Univ Va; Delta Upsilon; Univ Va Flying Club. Polit & Govt Pos: Co-founder, Young Indust for Eisenhower, 52; dir spec events, Nat citizens for Eisenhower, 52, vchmn cong comt, 54; chmn, Eisenhower Bandwagon Opers, 52 & 56, dir campaign activities, 56; dir finance comt, Rep Nat Cong Comn & dir, Rockefeller for Pres Comt, 64; exec dir, Rep Cong Boosters Club, 64-69; dir finance, Rep Nat Finance Comt, 65-69; mem, Nixon Presidential Campaign, 69; dir, US Travel Serv, Dept of Commerce, 69-70; asst secy for tourism, Dept of Com, 70-75; comnr, President's Nat Tourism Resources Rev Comn, currently; chmn, Soviet-US Tourism Mission, currently. Bus & Prof Pos: Asst to the pres, Hiller Aircraft, Hiller Helicopter Corp, 47-54; exec vpres, Bernard Relin & Assocs, 56-59; consult assoc, Towne-Oller Assocs, 59-60; pres, Automated Preference Testing Corp, 60-61; vpres, A C Nielsen Co, 61-64; mem, bd dirs, Discover Am Travel Orgns, Inc, currently. Mil Serv: Entered as Ens, Navy, 41, released as Lt, 45, after serv in Patrol Bomber Squadrons, Pac Theater, 42-45; Pac Theater Ribbon with Five Campaign Stars; Navy Air Medal with Gold Star. Publ: Snowbound aloft, Flying, 4/57. Mem: New York Union Club; F Street Club; Metrop Club; Chevy Chase Country Club; Nantucket Yacht Club. Honors & Awards: Man of the Year Award, Western Am Conv & Travel Inst, 71; First Gray Line Henry Buroughs Annual Award, 71. Relig: Protestant. Mailing Add: 1017 Saville Lane McLean VA 22101

WASHBURN, DEWAIN C (D)
Utah State Rep
Mailing Add: Box 121 Monroe UT 84754

WASHBURN, ELWOOD CONRAD (R)
Chmn, Greenwich Rep Town Comt, Conn
b Stamford, Conn, Mar 18, 14; s Chester C Washburn & Elsie A Stahl W; m 1947 to Pauline Kolok. Educ: Univ Ala, 33-35; NY Univ, BS, 49, MA, 52; Univ Ala Baseball Team, 35. Polit & Govt Pos: Mem, Greenwich Rep Town Comt, Conn, 49-, dist leader & mem exec comt, 58-63, chmn, 58-; mem exec comt, Fairfield Co Rep Orgn, 63- Bus & Prof Pos: Dir of athletics & varsity coach, football, baseball & basketball, Edgewood Sch, 46-49; head coach, varsity basketball, Greenwich High Sch, 53-56; chmn, Greenwich Elem Sch Phys Educ Staff, 62-64. Mil Serv: Pvt, Army, 41-45, serv in Coast Artil, Balloon Barrage, Engrs, 780th Engr Petrol Distribution Co, NAfrica, China-Burma-India, 43-45; Mediterranean & China-Burma-India Campaign Ribbons. Mem: Greenwich & Conn Educ Asns; Conn Phys Educ & Health Asn; Old Timers Athletic Asn, Greenwich, Conn & Port Chester, NY & Stamford, Conn; Ninth Dist Vets Asn, Glenville, Conn. Honors & Awards: Honors, Port Chester, NY Old Timers Athletic Asn, 64 & Greenwich Old Timers Athletic Asn, 67. Relig: Lutheran. Mailing Add: 73 Pemberwick Rd Byram CT 10573

WASHBURN, JAMES R (R)
Ill State Sen
Mailing Add: 225 W High St Morris IL 60450

WASHINGTON, CRAIG ANTHONY (D)
Tex State Rep
b Longview, Tex, Oct 12, 41; s Roy Alfred Washington & Azalea Stone W; m 1965 to Dorothy Marie Lampley; c Craig Anthony II & Chival Antoinette. Educ: Prairie View A&M Univ, BS, 66; Tex Southern Univ Law Sch, JD cum laude, 69; Phi Alpha Delta; Barons of Innovation; Les Beaux Arts. Polit & Govt Pos: Tex State Rep, 73- Bus & Prof Pos: Asst dean, Law Sch, Tex Southern Univ, 69-70; attorney, Houston, 70- Mem: Nat, Tex & Am Bar Asns; Houston Lawyers Asn; Tex Trial Lawyers Asn (assoc dir, 74-). Mailing Add: 201 Main Suite 700 Houston TX 77002

WASHINGTON, HAROLD (D)
Ill State Rep
b Chicago, Ill, Apr 15, 22; s Roy L Washington & Bertha Jones W; single. Educ: Roosevelt Univ, Chicago, Ill, BA, 49; Northwestern Univ Law Sch, JD, 52; Nu Beta Epsilon. Polit & Govt Pos: Precinct capt, mem adv bd & asst dir elec, Third Ward Regular Dem Orgn, Chicago, Ill, 52-; asst city prosecutor, Corp Counsel's Off, Chicago, Ill, 54-58; pres, Third Ward Young Dem, 58-61; arbitrator, Ill State Indust Comn, 60-64; Ill State Rep, currently. Mil Serv: Entered as Pvt, Army, 42, released as 1st Sgt, 46, after serv in 1887th Eng Aviation Bn, Pac, 43-46; Mariannas Campaign Ribbon. Mem: Cook Co, Ill & Nat Bar Asns; Am Vet Asn. Relig: Catholic. Legal Res: 607 E 62nd St Chicago IL 60615 Mailing Add: 6300 S Peoria St Chicago IL 60621

WASHINGTON, JAMES A, JR (D)
b Asheville, NC, Feb 17, 15; s James A Washington, Sr & Vivian B Alston W; m 1935 to Ada Collins; c Grace C (Mrs Alexander), Eleanor J (Mrs Jackson), Vivian A (Mrs Johnson), James A, III, Stephen C, Michael G, Diana V & Carlton C. Educ: Howard Univ, AB, 36; Howard Univ Sch Law, LLB, 39; Harvard Law Sch, LLM magna cum laude, 41; Omega Psi Phi; Sigma Delta Tau. Polit & Govt Pos: Attorney, US Dept of Justice, 42-46; bd mem, Nat Capital Housing Authority of DC, 61-66; chmn, DC Pub Serv Comn, 61-66; gen counsel, US Dept of Transportation, 69-70; App Superior Court DC, 71- Bus & Prof Pos: Prof law, Howard Univ Sch Law, 46-61, Langston prof, 66-69, dean, 69; vis prof, Washington Col Law, Am Univ, summers, 60-61, Georgetown Law Center, summer 61. Publ: Right of Privacy in the United States, Harvard Law Sch, 41; The Program of the civil rights section of the Department of Justice, J on Negro Educ, summer 51; One or three, which should it be? Conjectures of three-judge court procedure, (with George M Johnson), Howard Law J, 55. Mem: Phi Alpha Delta; Reconstruction & Develop Corp, (chmn, 69-); Nat Capital Area Coun, Boy Scouts (bd); Travelers Aid Soc (bd); Health & Welfare Coun (bd). Relig: Episcopal. Mailing Add: 14212 Northgate Dr Silver Spring MD 20906

WASHINGTON, LENA GENEVA (R)
Mem, Rep State Cent Comt Calif
b Florence, Ala, Nov 16, 14; d Benjamin B Fields & Effie Hewitt F; m 1935 to Clarence Wilson Washington; c Melva (Mrs Ellis Veil). Educ: Los Angeles City Col, 2 years; Univ West, 1 year; Beta Pi Sigma; Westsiders of the 30's. Polit & Govt Pos: Mem, Rep State Cent Comt Calif, currently, exec dir & membership secy, 48-69, secy, speaker's bur, 69-; secy, Californians for US Sen George Murphy Orgn, 69-71. Bus & Prof Pos: Mem, Women's Polit Study, 36-, secy to founder; mem, Westside Fedn, 61-; mem & co-organizer, Rep Assocs Bus Women, 62- Mem: PTA. Honors & Awards: Urban League Progress Award & Serv Award, Beta Pi Sigma; Citations from Compton Rep Club & Santa Monica Community Club; Salute to Lena, Cosmopolitan Rep Voters League Study Club; awards from Women's Polit State Comt, Westside Rep Women & Los Angeles Co Cent Comt. Relig: Methodist. Mailing Add: 1726 W 22nd St Los Angeles CA 90007

WASHINGTON, MCKINLEY, JR (D)
SC State Rep
b Mayesville, SC, Aug 8, 36; s McKinley Washington, Sr & Mattie Bell Peterson W; m 1963 to Beulah Jefferies; c Katrina Diedra. Educ: J C Smith Univ, BA, 61, DD, 64; Interdenominational Theol Sem, MDiv, 73; Rho Chap, Alpha Phi Alpha. Polit & Govt Pos: Mem, Edisto Island Dem Precinct Exec Comt, SC, 68-74; mem, Title II Adv Comt, Charleston Co Sch Syst, 70; mem, Emergency Sch Assistance Comt, 70; mem SC Legis Study Comn on Migrant Farm Workers, 72; mem, Dem Party Platform & Resolution Comt, 72; SC State Rep, 75- Bus & Prof Pos: Pastor, Edisto & St Paul United Presby Church, SC, currently. Mem: NAACP (organizer & pres, Edisto Br); F&AM (Past Master, Ocean King Lodge 384); Arabian Temple; St Paul Interdenominational Ministerial Alliance (organizer & pres). Man of Year Award, Beta Kappa Lambda Chap, Alpha Phi Alpha, 72; Social Action Citation, Beta Mu Sigma Chap, Phi Beta Sigma, 75; Outstanding Achievement Award, Omega Psi Phi, 75. Relig: Presbyterian; Vmoderator of Synod of the South, Presby Church US. Mailing Add: PO Box 7 Edisto Island SC 29438

WASHINGTON, MICHAEL ANTHONY (D)
b Ecorse, Mich, Mar 8, 49; s Martin Washington & Lula Larry W; single. Educ: Univ Mich, BA, 71; Wayne State Univ, 73-; Alpha Phi Alpha. Polit & Govt Pos: Asst dir employee rels, Wayne Co Rd Comn, 72-; secy, 16th Cong Dist Orgn, 72-; deleg, Dem Nat Mid-Term Conf, 74; chmn, Ecorse ENAC Comt, 75- Bus & Prof Pos: Dep sheriff, Wayne Co, 71. Mem: Int Personnel Mgt Asn. Mailing Add: 4148 13th St Ecorse MI 48229

WASHINGTON, NAT WILLIS (D)
Wash State Sen
b Coulee City, Wash, May 2, 14; s Nat Willis Washington & Gladys Fuller W; m 1945 to Wanda Wells; c Nat W, Jr & Thomas F. Educ: Univ Wash, BA, 36, JD, 38; Phi Delta Phi; Beta Theta Pi; Fir Tree; Oval Club. Polit & Govt Pos: Wash State Rep, 49-51; pres, State Young Dem, 50; Wash State Sen, 51-, chmn, Western Interstate Hwy Comt & Nat Legis Hwy Comt, chmn, Senate Hwy Comt, 60-; mem exec comt, Coun State Govt, pres, Western Conf, 72-; vchmn, Nat Comt Uniform Traffic Laws & Ordinances. Bus & Prof Pos: Attorney, Bonneville Power Admin, Dept Interior, 39-42. Mil Serv: Entered as 1st Lt, Army Air Corps, 42, released as Lt Col, 47, after serv in 2nd Air Force, 12th Tactical Air Command, Ger; Lt Col, Judge Adv Gen Dept, Air Force Res. Mem: Wash State Bar Asn; Mason; Grange. Relig: Christian. Mailing Add: 42 C St NW Ephrata WA 98823

WASHINGTON, ROBERT BENJAMIN, JR (D)
b Blakley, Ga, Oct 11, 42; s Robert Washington & Eunice Ross W; m 1969 to Nola Wallette; c Todd. Educ: St Peter's Col (NJ), BS, 67; Howard Univ Law Sch, JD, 70; Harvard Univ Law Sch, LLM, 72; Phi Alpha Delta; Omega Psi Phi; Gannon Debating Soc. Polit & Govt Pos: Counsel, US Senate Comt on Dist of Columbia, 70-72; chief counsel, US House Comt on Dist of Columbia, 73- Bus & Prof Pos: Teaching fel in law, Harvard Univ Law Sch, 70-72; assoc prof law & acting dir commun, Howard Univ Law Sch, 72-73; lectr law, Cath Univ Am Law Sch, 72- Publ: After the man in the house—what: is King vs Smith the answer?, 69, Does the constitution guarantee fair & effective representation to all citizens making up the electorate, 72 & The implications of Chavis vs Whitcomb, 72, Howard Law J. Mem: Am, Nat & Fed Bar Asns; Am Judicature Soc; Harvard Law Sch Asn. Honors & Awards: Outstanding Chmn of the Year, Am Bar Asn Student Div, 69; Cum Laude, Howard Univ Law Sch, 70; Distinguished Black Alumnus, Black Law Student Asn, Harvard Univ Law Sch, 73. Relig: African Methodist Episcopal. Legal Res: 118 S Arlington Ave East Orange NJ 07018 Mailing Add: 4417 46th St NW Washington DC 20016

WASHINGTON, ROBERT E (D)
Va State Deleg
Mailing Add: Suite 400 300 Boush St Norfolk VA 23510

WASHINGTON, WALTER E (D)
Mayor, DC
b Dawson, Ga, Apr 15, 15; s William Washington & Willie Mae Thornton W; m 1941 to Bennetta Bullock; c Bennetta (Mrs Peter Hayward). Educ: Howard Univ, AB, 38, LLB, 48; Am Univ grad course pub admin, 39-43. Hon Degrees: LLD & DHL from various cols & univs. Polit & Govt Pos: Jr housing asst, Alley Dwelling Authority, 41, housing mgr, Nat Capital Housing Authority, 45-51, various exec pos, 51-61, exec dir, 61-66; chmn, New York Housing Authority, 66-67; app mayor-comnr, DC, 67-74, mayor, 75-; Mem: Big Bros (bd dirs); Ctr Int Scholars; US Conf Mayors (adv bd); Order of Coif; Phi Alpha Delta. Honors & Awards: Nat Jewish Hosp Award for Outstanding Serv, 73; Boy Scouts Am Silver Beaver Award for Distinguished Serv, 73; Distinguished Serv Award, Capital Press Club, 74; Distinguished Serv Award, Howard Univ Law Alumni Asn, 74; first elected mayor of Washington, DC in over 100 years. Relig: Baptist. Legal Res: 408 T St NW Washington DC 20001 Mailing Add: 520 District Bldg 14th & E St NW Washington DC 20004

WASSENBERG, SHIRLEY MAE (D)
Secy, Kans State Dem Comt
b Oketo, Kans, Nov 5, 27; d Elijah Orville Keck & Cora Oehm K; m 1949 to Henry G Wassenberg; c Henry Arnold, Ellen Kaye, Daniel Orville, Amy Carlene, Janis Christine & Thomas Andrew. Educ: Marysville High Sch grad. Polit & Govt Pos: Vchmn, Marshall Co Dem Party, Kans, 58-70, chmn, 70-74; secy, Second Dist Dem Party, 60-62, vchmn, 62-73; alt deleg, Dem Nat Conv, 68, deleg, 72; secy, Kans State Dem Comt, 73- Mem: Beta Sigma Phi; Am Legion Auxiliary; Kans Dem Century Club; Kans Fedn of Womens Dem Clubs. Relig: Catholic. Mailing Add: 209 N 11th St Marysville KS 66508

WASSER, JOSEPH (D)
VChmn, Sullivan Co Dem Comt, NY
b New York, NY, Dec 9, 20; s Sam Wasser & Esther Weingarten W; m 1944 to Ethel Apter; c Ellen Sue & Martin Barry. Educ: St John's Univ, BA, 43. Polit & Govt Pos: Chief consumer goods div, Off Price Stabilization, New York, 50-53; magistrate, Thompson, NY, 54-; deleg, Dem State Conv, 64 & 66; vchmn, Sullivan Co Dem Comt, 67-; alt deleg, Dem Nat Conv, 68; sheriff, Sullivan Co, 72-; chmn legis comt, NY State Sheriffs Asn; chief inspector, NY State Harness Racing Comn; mem state exec comt, NY Asn Magistrates for State Police & Motor Vehicle Matters. Bus & Prof Pos: Dir, Co Trust Co, Monticello, 58-; vpres, Monticello Hosp, 60-67; comnr, Sullivan Co Condemnation Bd, 67-; mem, Mid-Hudson Pattern for Progress Comn, State Univ, NY, New Paltz, 68-; mem, Mid-Hudson Crime Comn Planning Bd; bd dirs, Landfield Ave Synagogue. Mil Serv: Entered as Pvt, Army, 43, released as 1st Lt, 46, after serv in Adj Gen Dept; Res, 46-50. Mem: Kiwanis; Elks; Mason; Jewish War Vet; Am Legion. Relig: Hebrew. Legal Res: 7 Roosa Ave Monticello NY 12701 Mailing Add: PO Box 192 Monticello NY 12701

WASTVEDT, GILMAN (R)
b Hatton, NDak, May 24, 08; married; c two. Educ: Union Commercial Col. Polit & Govt Pos: Mem, Traill Co Bd Comnrs, NDak, 47-63 & 67-; NDak State Rep, 61-66. Bus & Prof Pos: Farmer. Mem: Eagles; Mason; Scottish Rite; Shrine. Relig: Lutheran. Mailing Add: Hatton ND 58240

WATCHMAN, LEO C (D)
NMex State Rep
Mailing Add: Box 1278 Navajo NM 87328

WATERFIELD, ROE RICHARD (DFL)
Third VChmn, Mille Lacs Co Dem-Farmer-Labor Comt, Minn
b Raymond, Iowa, Aug 18, 93; s George C Waterfield & Florence Fuller W; m 1918 to Matilda J Veeser; c Robert Richard & James L. Educ: Iowa & SDak Pub Schs. Polit & Govt Pos: All off in co Dem orgn; deleg, Dem Nat Conv, 44; deleg to several Minn State Dem-Farmer-Labor Conv; third vchmn, Mille Lacs Co Dem-Farmer-Labor Comt, 60-; worker, all Dem-Farmer-Labor Campaigns, 63- Bus & Prof Pos: Farmer, 19-49; postmaster, Milaca, Minn, 49-63. Mil Serv: Entered as Pfc, Army, 18, released as Pfc, 19, after serv in Med Corps, Camp Grant, Ill. Mem: World War I Barracks; Am Legion; several farm orgns; Nat Asn Postmasters; Dem-Farmer-Labor Orgns. Honors & Awards: Sch Bd Hon Recognition, Post Off Dept, 63; Golden Cert, Am Legion. Relig: Catholic. Mailing Add: 525 N Central Ave Apt 23 Milaca MN 56353

WATERHOUSE, OLGA (R)
Committeewoman, Dist Rep Party, Hawaii
b Chicago, Ill, Dec 21, 17; d Bismarck von Wedelstaedt, MD & Eleanor Tustin v; m 1943 to Wallace Taylor Waterhouse; c Corinne Briten & Eleanor McLaughlin. Educ: Ore State Univ, 35-37; Univ Colo, BS, 41; Mask & Dagger Club; Home Econ Club. Polit & Govt Pos: Pres, Rep Precinct Club, Honolulu, Hawaii, 51-53; dist committeewoman, Rep Precinct Club, Kailua, 56-59, vpres, 58-59; vchmn of dist, 58-59; Honolulu Police Comnr, 59-64, chmn, Honolulu Police Comn, 63-64; mem exec comt, Rep Party Hawaii, 65-75, committeewoman, Dist Rep Party, 68-; deleg, Rep Nat Conv, 72; State Bd Registr, 74-75. Bus & Prof Pos: Teacher, Adams City High Sch, Adams City, Colo, 41-42; substitute high sch teacher, Kailua High Sch, Hawaii, early 50's. Mem: Am Red Cross (food serv chmn, 63-); Eastern Star (six stations, 54-); White Shrine of Jerusalem (color bearer, 63-75). Honors & Awards: Red Cross Vol of Year for Oahu, Am Red Cross, 70. Relig: Episcopal. Mailing Add: 69 Kuuala St Kailua HI 96734

WATERMAN, JEREMIAH COLWELL (R)
b Westfield, NJ, Jan 18, 04; s Marcus B Waterman & Grace Hampson W; m 1926 to Mary Fager; c Suzanna (Mrs Howard K Gray) & Judith (Mrs Owen P Jacobsen). Educ: Princeton Univ, AB, 26; Columbia Univ, JD, 31; Phi Delta Phi; Princeton Terrace Club. Polit & Govt Pos: Mem, Zoning Bd of Appeals, Mamaroneck, NY, mem, Town Coun, 51-59; mem, DC Rep Comt, 64-70, vchmn, 68-70; comnr, DC Pub Serv Comn, 71, chmn, 71-73; chmn, Washington Metrop Area Transit Comn, 71-73. Bus & Prof Pos: Gen attorney, Southern Pac Co, New York, 52-59, Washington, DC, 59-66; counsel, Steptoe & Johnson, 66-70. Mil Serv: Army Res, 26-39, released as 1st Lt, 39; serv in 442nd Field Artil Res. Publ: Special report on war delay cases, War Delay Law Comt, Asn of Am RR, 45. Mem: Sons of Am Revolution; Am Bar Asn; St Andrew's Club; Hamlet Country Club, Delray Beach, Fla. Relig: Episcopal. Mailing Add: 30 Marine Way Delray Beach FL 33444

WATERMAN, KENNETH M (D)
b Ind, Nov 24, 38; s J Wayne Waterman & Edith E Edwards W; m 1965 to Mary Kathryn Johnston; c Jeffrey & John. Educ: Univ Mich, Ann Arbor, BA, 61; Ind Univ, Bloomington, JD, 64. Polit & Govt Pos: Dep Attorney Gen, Ind, 66-67; deleg, Dem Nat Mid-Term Conf, 74. Bus & Prof Pos: Attorney, Parker, Hoover, Keller & Waterman, 67- Mil Serv: Entered as Lt (jg), Naval Res, 64, serv in Judge Adv Gen Corps, now Lt Comdr. Mem: Boy Scouts Am (mem exec bd, Anthony Wayne Coun); Legal Aid of Ft Wayne, Inc (mem bd dirs). Legal Res: 1130 Northlawn Dr Ft Wayne IN 46805 Mailing Add: 200 Strauss Bldg Ft Wayne IN 46802

WATERS, BANKSTON (R)
Mem, Ark Rep State Exec Comt
b Barton, Ark, Jan 16, 24; s Charles Webster Waters & Florence Bonner W; m 1943 to Laura Sue Maddox; c Bankston Edmond, Ralph Kelly & Mary Susan. Educ: Ark State Univ, BS, 44; Univ Ark, BSME, 48; Scabbard & Blade; Kappa Sigma Nu. Polit & Govt Pos: Mem, West Helena City Coun, Ark, 54-58; mem, West Helena City Planning Comn, 60-66; mem, Phillips Co Elec Comn, 66-70; mem, Ark Rep State Exec Comt, 69- Bus & Prof Pos: Owner, B-W Oil Co, 60-; owner, New-Bldg Inc, 70- Mil Serv: Entered as Pvt, Army, 42, released as 1st Lt, 52, after serv in 419 MPGIP, Philippines, 44-45, Korea, 50-52; Presidential Unit Citation. Mem: Lions (pres, 60-); Am Legion; VFW. Relig: Methodist. Legal Res: 233 S Tenth West Helena AR 72390 Mailing Add: Box 2522 West Helena AR 72390

WATERS, ERROL T (D)
b Merced, Calif; m to Grace Hughes. Educ: Weiser High Sch, Idaho, grad. Polit & Govt Pos: Chmn, Washington Co Dem Party, Idaho, seven terms; committeeman, Ada Co Dem Party, 58-65 & Idaho Dem Comt, 63-65; chmn, Idaho Dem Party, 65-72. Bus & Prof Pos: Former dir, Payette Div, Idaho Power Co; automobile bus, 21-51. Mem: Elks; Boise Valley Hi-De-Ho Travel Trailer Club. Mailing Add: 2018 Jackson Boise ID 83705

WATERS, JERRY B (R)
b St Francis, Kans, Jan 6, 33; s Roy Waters & Bertha Zimbleman W; m 1953 to Janice LaVern Miller; c Ricki, Jeffrey & Brent. Educ: Kans State Univ, BS, 54; Mich State Univ, MS, 58, PhD, 65. Polit & Govt Pos: Research analyst & asst pub dir, Mich Rep State Cent Comt, 60-61; legis & research asst to US Sen James B Pearson, Kans, 66-67, admin asst, 67- Bus & Prof Pos: Instr, Dept Econ & Sociol, Kans State Univ, 61-64, asst prof, Dept Polit Sci, 64-66; mem bd dirs, Nat Area Develop Inst, Lexington, Ky, 70- Mil Serv: Entered as 2nd Lt, Air Force, 54, released as 1st Lt, 57, after serv in 91st Fighter Bomber Squadron, Third Air Force, Eng, 55-57. Publ: Co-auth, Values, expectations & political predispositions of Italian youth, Midwest Jour Polit Sci, 2/61; Reapportionment: the legislative struggle, In: Representation & Misrepresentation, Robt Goldwin, ed, Rand McNally & Co, 68; auth, Scope & national concern of rural development, In: Rural Development Research Priorities, Lavey R Whiting, ed, Iowa State Univ Press, 73; plus others. Mem: Am Polit Sci Asn; Midwest Conf Polit Scientists; Coalition for Rural Develop, Washington, DC (bd dirs). Relig: Protestant. Legal Res: 2449 Hobbs Dr Manhattan KS 66502 Mailing Add: 7900 Lynbrook Dr Bethesda MD 20014

WATERS, MARJORIE JUNE (R)
Committeewoman, Ark Rep State Comt
b Satanta, Kans, Feb 10, 24; d Homer Sylvester Brown & Inez Lovelock B; m 1945 to Jimmie Wade Waters. Educ: Univ Ark, Fayetteville, BS, with honors, 50, MS, 52. Polit & Govt Pos: Committeewoman, Ark Rep State Comt, Newton Co, 74-; justice of the peace, Pleasant Hill Twp, Ark, 74- Bus & Prof Pos: Teacher-librn, Deer Sch Dist 21, Deer, Ark, 49- Publ: Community approach resolves problems, Am Sch Bd J, 12/66. Mem: Eastern Star; Am Legion Auxiliary; Newton Co & Ark Educ Asns; Am Libr Asn. Relig: Methodist. Mailing Add: Hwy 7 S Jasper AR 72641

WATERS, RON (D)
Tex State Rep
Mailing Add: 2506 Ralph St Apt 106 Houston TX 77006

WATERS, THOMAS ALFRED (D)
Chairperson, Grant Co Dem Party, Wis
b Harlingen, Tex, Nov 16, 40; s Cecil D Waters & Lexie Dunagin W; single. Educ: Pan Am Univ, BA, 63; George Washington Univ, AM, 66; Ohio State Univ, 69-71; Alpha Phi Omega, Pi Sigma Alpha; ed, Pan Am; Press Club (pres); Order Bougainvillea (pres). Polit & Govt Pos: Chairperson & campaign mgr, Friends of Katie Morrison, 1st Woman State Sen, Wis, 73-, chairperson, Grant Co Dem Party, Wis, 74-; mem platform exec comt, Dem Party Wis, 74-, mem rules comt, 75- Publ: The study of international relations & the undergraduate: a review, In: Forum Series, Inst of Pub Affairs, Univ Wis-Platteville, 72. Mem: Am Polit Sci Asn; Int Studies Asn; Rotary (bd dir, 74-); Common Cause; Am Asn Univ Prof (pres, Platteville chap, 74-). Honors & Awards: Outstanding Serv Awards, Alpha Phi Omega, Press Club & Pan Am; participant, Nat Sci Found-Am Asn Advan Sci short courses, 72-75. Legal Res: 930 Mason St Platteville WI 53818 Mailing Add: PO Box 330 Platteville WI 53818

WATERS, WILLIAM BAXTER (D)
Mo State Sen
b Lathrop, Mo, Apr 26, 15; m 1943 to Ellen B Nesbitt, wid. Educ: William Jewell Col, AB; Univ Mo at Kansas City, LLB. Polit & Govt Pos: Probate judge, Clay Co, Mo, 47-55; mem, Dem State Comt Mo, 51-56; Mo State Sen, 56- Bus & Prof Pos: Attorney, Lawson & Hale,

now Hale, Kincaid, Waters & Allen, 41- Mil Serv: Army. Mem: Lions; Am Legion; VFW. Relig: Christian. Mailing Add: First Off Bldg Liberty MO 64068

WATHEN, RICHARD B (R)
Ind State Rep
b Jeffersonville, Ind, June 26, 17; s Otho Hill Wathen & Fay Duffy W; m 1940 to Viola James; c Richard, John & Viola (Mrs Sheehan). Educ: Princeton Univ, BA, Ind Univ, JD, Ivy Club. Polit & Govt Pos: Ind State Rep, Dist 67, 73- Bus & Prof Pos: Attorney-at-Law, Magnus F Heubi & Richard B Wathen. Mil Serv: Entered as Ens, Navy, 42, released as Lt, 46, after serv in Am European Asiatic Theatres; Presidential Unit Citation; Letter of Commendation. Publ: The Only Yankee, Regnery, 70. Mem: Lions; Am Legion; VFW; Farm Bur. Relig: Catholic. Mailing Add: Utica Pike Box 907 Jeffersonville IN 47130

WATKINS, CHERYL ANN (R)
NDak State Rep
b Cloquet, Minn, Oct 16, 41; d Ward F Watkins & Florence Oswell W; single. Educ: Univ Minn, Duluth, BS, 63; NDak State Univ, 69-73; Phi Alpha Theta. Polit & Govt Pos: NDak State Rep, 73- Bus & Prof Pos: Instr & dept chmn, Fargo Bd Educ, 63- Mem: Nat Educ Asn; Fargo Educ Asn (polit activities chmn, 68-71, salary chmn, 73-); Am Asn Univ Women; League of Women Voters; Bus & Prof Women. Mailing Add: 1012 S Ninth St Fargo ND 58102

WATKINS, DANE (R)
Idaho State Sen
Mailing Add: 2975 Fieldstream Lane Idaho Falls ID 83401

WATKINS, DOROTHEA HENNESS FANCHER (R)
Dep Dir, Off Pub Affairs, Bur African Affairs, US Dept State
b Mesa, Ariz, Dec 22, 34; d William Russell Henness & Louise Cottrell H; m 1970 to John Burton Watkins, IV; c Kimberly Cottrell, Don Cameron & Kennedy Packard Fancher. Educ: Ariz State Univ, 3 years; Alpha Delta Pi. Polit & Govt Pos: Regional co-dir, Young Rep Nat Fedn, 65-67, nat co-chmn, 67-69; nat committeewoman, Ariz Young Rep League, 65-67; campaign secy, US Rep John J Rhodes, Ariz, 66; campaign dir, Marshall Humphrey, Sen, Walter Bloom, House, & James F Holley, House, Ariz Legis, 66; dir, Am Coun Young Polit Leaders, 67-; chmn, mil absentee voters prog, presidential campaign, Rep Nat Comt, 68, spec asst to dir, registr div, 68; chmn, Rep deleg, NATO Conf European Security in 70's, Exeter Col, Oxford, 68; deleg, Atlantic Alliance Young Polit Leaders Conf, Bonn, Ger, 69; co-chmn, Young Am Inaugural Salute, Presidential Inauguration, 69; dep dir, Off Pub Affairs, Bur African Affairs, US Dept State currently. Bus & Prof Pos: Founder, Epiphany Episcopal Church & Day Sch, 63; diocesan chmn col work, Episcopal Churchwomen Diocese Ariz, 57, 58 & 59. Mem: Phoenix Art Mus; Am Quarter Horse Asn; Am Farm Bur Fedn; Ariz Federated Rep Women. Honors & Awards: Outstanding Young Rep Woman of Year, Ariz Young Rep League, 66-67. Relig: Episcopal. Mailing Add: 7301 Park Terr Alexandria VA 22307

WATKINS, JANE MAGRUDER (D)
b Greenwood, Miss, May 3, 37; d Douglas Neil Magruder & Majorie Jane Murphey M; m 1957 to Joseph Wesley Watkins, III; c Gordon Estes & Marjorie Laurin. Educ: Miss State Col Women, 55-57; Univ Hawaii, BA, 59; Univ Miss, MA, 62; Rogue & Jester Social Clubs. Polit & Govt Pos: Miss state coordr, McGovern for President, 72; deleg & co-chairperson Miss deleg, Dem Nat Conv, 72; co-chmn, Washington Co Dem Women, Miss, 72- Bus & Prof Pos: Teacher jour & Eng, Fairfax High Sch, Va, 62-63 & Fort Hunt High Sch, Alexandria, 63-65; ed, Red Cross Youth, Am Red Cross, Washington, DC, 67-68; city ed, Delta Dem Times, Greenville, Miss, 68-69; free lance writer & research asst, 68; human rels lab trainer & consult, Episcopal Church, Miss, 68-; owner & partner, Mainstream Travel, Greenville, 69-73. Mem: Miss Coun Human Rels (bd dirs, 70-74); All Saint's Episcopal Sch, Vicksburg (bd trustees, 71-74); Mid-Delta Educ Asn (bd dirs, 70-72); Twin Cities Theatre Guild (bd dirs, 70-72). Relig: Episcopal. Mailing Add: 908 S Carolina Ave SE Washington DC 20003

WATKINS, JOSEPH WESLEY, III (D)
b Greenville, Miss, Sept 17, 35; s Joseph Wesley Watkins, Jr & Mary Alice Catlette W; m 1957 to Jane Magruder; c Gordon Estes & Marjorie Laurin. Educ: US Naval Acad, 53-54; Univ Miss, BA, 57, LLB, 62; Phi Alpha Delta; Sigma Alpha Epsilon. Polit & Govt Pos: Trial attorney, Tax Div, US Dept Justice, Washington, DC, 62-67; pres, Washington Co Young Dem, Miss, 67-69; attorney, Miss Loyal Dem Challenge, Dem Nat Conv, 68, deleg, 68, deleg & mem, Platform Comt, 72; mem, Washington Co Dem Exec Comt, 68-73; secy, Miss Dem Exec Comt, 68-74; legal counsel, Dem Party State Miss, 68-; Miss deleg, Dem Mid Term Conf, 74. Mil Serv: Entered as Ens, Navy, 57, released as Lt(jg), 59, after serv in USS Edmonds, Pac Fleet, 57-59. Mem: Am Civil Liberties Union; Common Cause (exec comt & bd dirs, 73-75); New Populist Inst (bd dirs, 72-); Greenville Symphony Asn; Twin Cities Theatre Guild. Relig: Episcopal. Mailing Add: 908 S Carolina Ave SE Washington DC 20003

WATKINS, RICHARD WRIGHT, JR (D)
Treas, Sixth Cong Dist Dem Exec Comt, Ga
b Indian Springs, Ga, Feb 14, 20; s R Wright Watkins & Dovie Bryans W; m 1950 to Martha Elizabeth Hood; c Margaret Ann, Rachael & Hazel Virginia. Educ: Maryville Col, AB in econ, 42; Univ Ga, JD, 47; Phi Delta Phi. Polit & Govt Pos: Ordinary, Butts Co, Ga, 57-64; chmn, State Bd of Corrections, 64-; treas, Sixth Cong Dist Dem Exec Comt, 66-; chmn, Butts Co Dem Exec Comt, formerly. Bus & Prof Pos: Dir & attorney, Citizens & Southern Bank of Jackson, Ga, currently. Mil Serv: Entered as Pvt, Army Air Force, 42, released as Sgt, 45, after serv in Fifth Air-Sea Rescue Squadron, ETO, re-entered Judge Adv Gen Corps, 51, released as 1st Lt, 52; Lt Col, Judge Adv Gen Corps, Army Res; ETO Ribbon with 5 Battle Stars. Publ: Criminal Jurisdiction of Ordinary Courts in Georgia In: Handbook for Ordinaries of Georgia, Univ Ga, 65. Mem: Elks; Mason; Shrine; Kiwanis; Am Legion. Relig: Presbyterian. Legal Res: 169 Dempsey Ave Jackson GA 30233 Mailing Add: PO Box 105 Jackson GA 30233

WATKINS, SAM HOUSTON (D)
Ky State Rep
b 1914. Polit & Govt Pos: Ky State Rep, 62-68 & 72- Bus & Prof Pos: Self-employed businessman & farmer. Mil Serv: Navy & Merchant Marine Officer, World War II. Mem: Shrine; Mason; Pendennis Club; Ky Hist Soc; Farm Bur. Mailing Add: Elizabethtown KY 42701

WATKINS, TROY B (D)
Miss State Sen
Mailing Add: 116 Sgt Prentiss Dr Natchez MS 39120

WATKINS, WES (D)
Okla State Sen
Mailing Add: State Capitol Oklahoma City OK 73105

WATKINS, WILLIAM T (D)
NC State Rep
Mailing Add: 213 W Thorndale Dr Oxford NC 27565

WATLINGTON, JANET (D)
Dem Nat Committeewoman, VI
Mailing Add: 700 Seventh St SW Washington DC 20024

WATSON, ALBERT W (R)
b Sumter, SC, Aug 30, 22; s Claude A Watson (deceased) & Eva Clark W; m 1948 to Lilliam Williams; three children. Educ: Univ SC, LLB, 50; Pi Kappa Delta. Polit & Govt Pos: SC State Rep, 55-58, 60-62; US Rep, SC, 63-70. Bus & Prof Pos: Attorney. Mil Serv: Air Force, 42-46. Mem: VFW; Farm Bur; Mason; Lions; Voice of Democracy Prog, sponsored by US Jr CofC (nat chmn). Relig: Baptist. Mailing Add: 77 Northlake Rd Columbia SC 29204

WATSON, ARTHUR CHOPIN (D)
Chmn, Dem State Cent Comt, La
b Natchitoches, La, Dec 15, 09; s Arthur William Watson & Eugenie Chopin W; m 1935 to Marion Eugenia Hickman, (Gene); c Marion (Mrs O J Bienvenu), Saidee (Mrs Guy R Newell) & Eugenie Chopin. Educ: Spring Hill Col, BA; Tulane Univ, LLB & JSD; Order of the Coif; Kappa Sigma; Phi Delta Phi; Tulane Law Sch Club. Polit & Govt Pos: Mem, La State Dem Comt, 40-, chmn, formerly; mem, Natchitoches Parish Dem Comt, 44-72; deleg, Dem Nat Conv, 52, 60 & 68; chmn, Dem State Cent Comt, 68- Bus & Prof Pos: Partner, Watson, Murchison, Crews & Arthur, Attorneys, 33-; pres, Progressive Savings & Loan Asn, 64-; chmn bd, Exchange Bank & Trust Co, 66- Publ: Alluvion & dereliction, Tulane Law Review, 33. Mem: Am Bar Asn; Elks (Past Exalted Ruler); La Bar Asn. Honors & Awards: Man of the Year, Natchitoches CofC, 66. Relig: Catholic. Legal Res: 501 Parkway Dr Natchitoches LA 71457 Mailing Add: PO Box 226 Natchitoches LA 71457

WATSON, BILLY JAMES (R)
b Salyersville, Ky, July 18, 38; s Hager Watson & Tressie Jackson W; m 1960 to Janice Maggard; c JuJuana Dawn & Jana Marie. Educ: Morehead State Univ, AB, 58, MA, 64; Crescendo Club. Polit & Govt Pos: Educ dir, Gov Louie B Nunn Campaign, Greenup Co, Ky, 67; mem finance comt, Greenup Co Rep Campaigns, 67-; deleg, Greenup Co Young Rep Club, 68; chmn, 18th Sen Dist, Ky, 68; chmn, Greenup Co Rep Exec Comt, formerly. Bus & Prof Pos: Independent contracting musician, Ky, Ohio & WVa, 58-; band dir, Wurtland High Sch, Ky, 58-66; band dir, Portsmouth High Sch, Ohio, 66-; chmn, instrumental music dept, Portsmouth City Schs, 66- Mem: Ohio Educ Asn; Portsmouth City Teachers Asn; Ohio Music Educators Asn; Music Educators Nat Conf; Am Fedn Musicians. Honors & Awards: Outstanding Grad Senior, Ky Colonel. Relig: Baptist. Mailing Add: Adena St Wurtland KY 41144

WATSON, ED RAYMOND (D)
Tex State Rep
b Wallisville, Tex, July 20, 20; s Raymond Fieldon Watson & Ella Gertrude Syer W; m 1948 to Susan Geraldine Eaves; c Dan Aubrey, Deborah Ellaine (Mrs Biggs), Faith Marie, Donald Wayne & legal guardian of Ralph Bales. Educ: Univ Houston, 45-46; San Jacinto Col, 67-68. Polit & Govt Pos: Deleg, Dem Precinct, Co & State Conv, Tex, 48-; deleg, Dem Nat Conv, 68; Grand juror, 69; grand jury comnr, 70; Tex State Rep, Dist 17, 73-; mem, Tex Const Conv, 74. Mil Serv: Entered as A/S, Navy, 42, released as Boatswain Mate 2/C, 45, after serv in Naval Armed Guard, European, Atlantic, Mediter, Asiatic, Pac & Caribbean Theatres; Korean War, 50-51, serv in Japan, China, Philippines & Malay; European Theater Medal with two Stars; Atlantic Theatre Medal with two Stars; Asiatic Theater Medal with two Stars; Korean Medal; Good Conduct Medal. Mem: OCAWIU (Local 4-367, 48-, pres, 52-56 & 70-75, vpres, 64-70 & 75-, legis rep, Dist 4, 68-73); charter mem Deer Park CofC; Galveston Co Dem; charter mem Lions Club Deer Park; hon fel Harry S Truman Libr. Relig: Baptist. Mailing Add: 2318 Center Deer Park TX 77536

WATSON, FRANCES LOUISE (R)
Chmn, Sherman Co Rep Party, Tex
b Calvert, Tex, July 17, 05; d Gus Anchicks & Antoinette Sommers A; m 1928 to Charles T Watson; c Charlotte Ann (Mrs Powell). Educ: Tex Women Univ, 23-27. Polit & Govt Pos: Chmn, Sherman Co Rep Party, Tex, 69- Bus & Prof Pos: Teacher, San Antonio, Tex, 27-28; Stratford, 28-29; Justice of Peace, Sherman Co, 43-49. Relig: Presbyterian. Mailing Add: Box 447 Stratford TX 79084

WATSON, JOHN CRAWFORD (D)
b Iola, Ill, Oct 30, 16; s Percy Mayfield Watson & Hallie Grace Moore W; m 1946 to Dorothy Eloise Walton; c Theresa Joan (Mrs Russell Kraft Nuzum III), Timothy John, John Lynn & Holly Grace. Educ: McKendree Col, 38-39; Ill Col, 39-41 & 46-48; Sigma Beta Rho; Phi Alpha. Polit & Govt Pos: Dem cand, US House Rep, 19th Dist, Ill, 58 & 60; asst dir, Dept Registr & Educ, State of Ill, 61-64, dir, 64-69 & legis liaison, 73-; deleg, Dem Nat Conv, 68 & 72; Dem committeeman, Precinct 15, Jacksonville, 68-; mgr admin serv, Ill State Libr, Off Secy of State, 69-70; supvr, Off of Supt Pub Instr, 71-73. Bus & Prof Pos: Minister, Methodist Parish, Sailor Springs, Ill, 38-39, Naples & Oxville, 39-41, Golden, 41-42 & Detroit, Ill, 46-49, Disciples of Christ, Maroa, 49-51, Abingdon, 51-61 & Woodson, 65- Mil Serv: Merchant Marine, 42-46. Mem: Mason; Odd Fellows. Relig: Disciples of Christ. Mailing Add: 101 Chestnut St Jacksonville IL 62650

WATSON, JOHN GARRETT (R)
b Inglewood, Calif, Oct 13, 48; s Herbert Garrett Watson & Shirley Mellott W; m 1974 to Cheryl Diane. Educ: El Camino Col, 66-68; Calif State Col, Long Beach, 69-70; Pepperdine Univ, BA, 72, MA, 75; Delta Phi Epsilon; Circle K Int. Polit & Govt Pos: Chmn, Rep Assocs Campus Action Comt, 68-69; assoc mem, Calif Rep State Cent Comt, 69-75; Southern Calif youth coordr, Californians for Murphy, 70; clerk, US Sen George Murphy, 70; alt deleg, Rep Nat Conv, 72. Bus & Prof Pos: Admin asst to exec vpres, Pepperdine Univ, Malibu, Calif, 74- Mil Serv: SP-5, Army Nat Guard, 5 years. Relig: Church of Christ. Mailing Add: 1424 Club View Dr Los Angeles CA 90024

WATSON, JOHN L (R)
Chmn, Clermont Co Rep Exec Comt, Ohio
b Danbury, Conn, June 13, 24; s Edmund B Watson & Helen Hughes W; m 1945 to Eda Cereda; c John Michael & Anthony Lewis. Educ: Univ Cincinnati, Col Bus Admin, 46-48; Univ Cincinnati, Col Law, LLB, 50; Alpha Kappa Psi; Beta Gamma Sigma; Phi Alpha Delta. Polit & Govt Pos: Pres, Clermont Co Rep Club, 57-58; dir, Clermont Co Bd Elec, Ohio, 57-; chmn, Clermont Co Rep Exec Comt, Ohio, 66-; deleg, Rep Nat Conv, 68; mem, Dist Adv Coun, Small Bus Admin, 71-73. Mil Serv: Entered as Pvt, Army, 43, released as 2nd Lt, 46, after serv in 2nd Constabulary, ETO, 45-46. Mem: Am Judicature Soc; Clermont Co Bar Asn; Am Legion; VFW; Royal Oak Country Club. Relig: Protestant. Mailing Add: 33 N Market Batavia OH 45103

WATSON, RICHARD THOMAS (R)
Chmn, Wilkinson Co Rep Party, Miss
b Alexandria, La, May 31, 24; s Ernest Watson & R T Leake W; m 1951 to Margaret Glenn Brabston; c Richard Glenn. Educ: Univ Miss, LLB, 50. Polit & Govt Pos: Asst US attorney, SDist of Miss, 53-57; city attorney, Woodville, Miss, 57-; attorney, Bd Educ, Wilkinson Co, 57-; chmn, Wilkinson Co Rep Party, 58-; mem, Miss State Rep Exec Comt, 59-62; mem, Miss Agr Stabilization & Conserv Serv Comt, 72-74. Mil Serv: Entered as A/S, Navy, 41, released as Gunners Mate 2/C, 45, after serv in Pac & Atlantic, 42-45; 3 Battle Stars. Mem: Am Bar Asn; Am Semmental Asn; Farm Bur. Relig: Christian Church. Mailing Add: Box 637 Woodville MS 39669

WATSON, ROBERT LORN (R)
b Harper, Ore, June 23, 28; s Harold B Watson & Myrtle E Norris W; m 1947 to Phyllis May Teeter; c Robert L, Jr, Ronald L, Renee & Dick. Educ: Boise State Col, AA, 49; Univ Ore, BAr, 54. Polit & Govt Pos: Precinct committeeman, Ada Co, Idaho, 64 & 68; chmn, Dist 14, 68 & 70; chmn, Ada Co Rep Cent Comt, formerly. Bus & Prof Pos: Secy, Idaho Bd of Archit Examr, State of Idaho, 69- Mil Serv: S/Sgt, Air Force, 51. Mem: Am Inst Architects; Elks; Exchange Club of Boise; Salvation Army (bd dirs). Relig: Protestant. Mailing Add: Rte 5 S Mule Rd Boise ID 83705

WATSON, ROBERT OGLE (R)
Committeeman, Tenn Rep State Exec Comt
b Knoxville, Tenn, July 21, 34; s James Kendrick Watson, Sr & Cecil Ogle W; single. Educ: Univ Tenn, 1 year. Polit & Govt Pos: Committeeman, Tenn Rep State Exec Comt & mem, Issues Comt, 74-; officer at elections, also judge. Bus & Prof Pos: Switchman, Jacksonville Terminal Co Rwy, Fla; Bell Limousine Serv, Knoxville, Tenn; Rose Mortuary; mfr rep, Knoxville. Mil Serv: Entered as Drill Field Instr, Army Res, 53, released as Cpl, 61, after serv in 305th Field Hosp, Knoxville. Mem: Smoky Mountain & Nat RR Hist Soc; SAR. Relig: Baptist. Legal Res: 5722 Cilla Dr Knoxville TN 37920 Mailing Add: PO Box 9244 Knoxville TN 37920

WATSON, ROY H, JR (D)
Ga State Rep
b Macon, Ga, Apr 20, 37; s Roy Herman Watson, Sr & Maude Howard W; m 1956 to Jeanne Phillips Watson; c Cynthia R. Educ: Ga Mil Col, grad, 54; Mercer Univ, 56-57. Polit & Govt Pos: Co adminr, Houston Co, Ga, 58-75; Ga State Rep, 75- Mem: Mason; Peace Officers Asn Ga; Al Sihah Shrine Temple; Houston Co Planning Comn; Houston Co Bd Tax Assessors. Relig: Baptist. Mailing Add: 200 Forest Hill Dr Warner Robins GA 31093

WATSON, THOMAS PHILIP (R)
Okla State Sen
b Nashville, Ark, Aug 31, 33; s S Jordan Watson & Frieda Pryor W; m 1964 to Mary Parks; c Rebecca & Phylis. Educ: Harding Col, BA, 59; Univ Mo, MA, 60. Polit & Govt Pos: Harding Col, BA, 59; Univ Mo, MA, 60. Polit & Govt Pos: Okla State Sen, 73- Mil Serv: Airman 1/C, Air Force. Mem: YMCA (bd dirs, Edmond, Metrop bd, Oklahoma City); Kiwanis; Edmond Mem Hosp. Relig: Church of Christ. Mailing Add: Rte 3 Box 284A Edmond OK 73034

WATSON, TOM (D)
Ark State Sen
Mailing Add: Rte 1 Monette AR 72447

WATSON, WENDELL H (D)
Fla State Rep
Mailing Add: 618 Lakehurst St Lakeland FL 33801

WATSON, WILLIAM ABNER, JR (D)
Mem, Prince Edward Co Dem Party, Va
b Darlington Heights, Va, Feb 15, 99; s William Abner Watson, Sr & Adlaide Ford W; m 1924 to Louise Newton Brightwell; c William Abner, III & James Maxey. Educ: Univ Richmond; Smithdeal Massey Bus Col, Richmond, Va. Polit & Govt Pos: Deleg, Dem State Conv, over 30 years; deleg, Nat Dem Conv, 64 & 68; mem, Prince Edward Co Dem Party, Va, currently. Bus & Prof Pos: Pres, W A Watson & Sons Ins Agency, Farmville, Va, 24-; pres, Am Health Ins Agency, 42-; pres emer, Odd Fellows Home of Va, Inc, Lynchburg, 20 years. Mil Serv: Army, 18, Pvt. Mem: Odd Fellows; AF&AM; Farmville CofC; Farmville Area Develop Corp. Relig: Baptist. Legal Res: 700 First Ave Farmville VA 23901 Mailing Add: Box 567 Farmville VA 23901

WATSON, WILLIAM C (D)
Tenn State Rep
Mailing Add: Box 187 Madisonville TN 37354

WATSON, WILLIAM EDWARD (D)
b Jane Lew, WVa, July 31, 36; s Jefferson Bassell Watson & Mary Bush W; m 1958 to Mara Louise Linaberger; c Lynn Ellen & Edward Allen. Educ: WVa Wesleyan Col, AB, 58; George Washington Univ, JD with hon, 61. Polit & Govt Pos: Chmn, Brooke Co Dem Party, 65-71; mem, WVa Dem State Exec Comt, 67-71; chmn, WVa State Dem Party, 72-73; alt deleg, Dem Nat Conv, 72; deleg, Dem Mid Term Conf, 74. Bus & Prof Pos: Attorney-at-law, Pinsky, Mahan, Barnes & Watson, 61- Mil Serv: Entered as Pvt, Army Res, 62, released as Sgt, 68, after serv in Fourth Med Tank Bn; Army Res, currently. Polit & Govt Pos: Strip mining wins a victory, New South, winter, 73. Mem: Nat Asn of Defense Lawyers in Criminal Cases; Am & WVa State Bar Asns; Kiwanis. Relig: Methodist. Mailing Add: 2000 Main St Wellsburg WV 26070

WATT, GRAHAM WEND (INDEPENDENT)
Dir, Off of Revenue Sharing, Dept of the Treasury
b Elizabeth, NJ, Oct 23, 26; s William Harrison Watt & Carolyn Wend W; m 1949 to Mary Aldridge Irish; c Terrence Graham & Laurie Fredericka. Educ: Washington Col, AB, 49; Fels Inst Local & State Govt, Univ Pa, MGA, 51; Advan Mgt Training Inst, Univ Chicago, cert, 60. Polit & Govt Pos: Admin analyst, City of Kansas City, Mo, 50-54, chief asst to city mgr, 54-57; city mgr, Alton, Ill, 58-62, Portland, Maine, 62-67 & Dayton, Ohio, 67-69; dep mayor, Washington, DC, 70-73; dir, Off of Revenue Sharing, Dept of the Treasury, 73- Bus & Prof Pos: Participant, White House Conf Health, 66; mem, Nat Research Coun, Acad Sci & Eng Comns on Emergency Med Systs Commun & Urban Info Systs; mem bd dirs, Nat Urban Fels, Inc; mem pub off adv coun, Off Econ Opportunity, 66-68; mem, Adv Comt Urban Develop, Dept Housing & Urban Develop, 67-68; deleg, Nat Conf on Criminal Justice, 73; mem, White House Conf Econ, 74. Mil Serv: Naval Res, 44-46. Mem: Int City Mgt Asn (pres, 72); Am Soc Pub Admin; Nat Acad Pub Admin; Nat Fire Protection Asn; Metrop Washington Coun of Govt (vpres). Honors & Awards: Mgr Innovation Award, Int City Mgt Asn, 69; Man of Year Award, Wharton Grad Club of Washington; Alumni Award, Washington Col. Relig: Episcopal. Mailing Add: Off of Revenue Sharing US Dept of Treasury Washington DC 20226

WATT, JAMES GAIUS (R)
Dir, Bur of Outdoor Recreation, Dept of the Interior
b Lusk, Wyo, Jan 31, 38; s William G Watt & Lois M Williams W; m 1957 to Leilani Bomgardner; c Erin Gaia & Eric Gaius. Educ: Univ Wyo Col Bus & Indust, BS with honors, 60, Law Sch, JD, 62; Omicron Delta Kappa; Phi Kappa Phi; Alpha Tau Omega; Iron Skull; pres, Phi Epsilon Phi; ed, Wyo Law J, 2 years; teaching fel, 60-62. Polit & Govt Pos: Personal asst, Milward L Simpson, 62; legis asst & counsel to former US Sen Milward L Simpson, 62-66; consult to Secy Walter Hickel, Dept of Interior, 69, Dep Asst Secy for Water & Power Resources, 69-72, dir, Bur of Outdoor Recreation, 72-; nominated mem, Fed Power Comn, 75. Publ: Federal tax liens: divesture, Wyo Law J, fall 61; Conservation not conversation, Cong Record, 3/67; Economic implications of pollution control, Indust Water Eng, 1/68. Mem: Wyo State Bar; Bar of the Supreme Court of US; Full Gospel Businessmen's Fel Int; US CofC (sr assoc); Wyo State Soc. Honors & Awards: Thomas Arkle Clarke Award, Alpha Tau Omega. Relig: Assembly of God. Legal Res: Wheatland WY 82201 Mailing Add: 5407 Keppler Rd Camp Springs MD 20031

WATT, ROBERT DELANSON (D)
Mont State Sen
b Marion Co, Ind, Aug 27, 99; s Charles Columbus Watt & Minne Ellen Royster W; m 1965 to Mabel Hardy Benson; stepson Gordon Benson. Educ: Univ Mo, Columbia, BA, 24; Ind Univ, Bloomington, MA, 28; various courses at Butler Univ, Ind Univ, Indianapolis & Univ Mont; Phi Delta Kappa; Lambda Chi Alpha. Polit & Govt Pos: Mont State Rep, Dist 26, Missoula Co, formerly; Mont State Sen, currently, mem taxation comt, Mont State Senate, currently; deleg, Dem Nat Conv, 72. Bus & Prof Pos: Teacher of govt, Ind High Schs, 25-28, Mont High Schs, 32-58; supt, Missoula Co Schs, Mont, 58-63. Mil Serv: Entered as Technician Pvt, Army Ord, 42, released as Sgt, 45, after serv in 603rd Ord Bn, NAfrican & Ital Theatres, 43-45; Campaign Ribbon with three Battle Stars. Publ: Articles dealing with legis, local or state problems in local publ; Let's abolish property taxes, The American County, 4/70. Mem: Elks; Moose; VFW; Am Legion; Lions. Relig: Christian Church. Mailing Add: 451 Kensington Ave Missoula MT 59801

WATTS, GLENN (D)
Mem, Dem Nat Comt, NC
Mailing Add: Box 248 Taylorsville NC 28681

WATZMAN, SANFORD (D)
b Cleveland, Ohio, Feb 15, 26; s Hymen Watsman & Golda Scholnek W; m 1953 to June Schleifer; c Herbert, Saul & Nancy. Educ: Cleveland Col, Western Reserve Univ, BA, 49, grad sch, 50-51. Polit & Govt Pos: Admin asst to US Rep James V Stanton, Ohio, 71- Bus & Prof Pos: Writer & correspondent, Cleveland Plain Dealer, 48-71; ed, Indust Commun, 71. Mil Serv: Entered as Pvt, Army, 44, released as T/5, 46, after serv in 97th Inf Div, ETO & Japan. Publ: Conflict of interest: politics & the money game, Cowles Book Co, 71. Relig: Jewish. Legal Res: 2424 Warrensville Rd Cleveland OH 44118 Mailing Add: 10915 Fiesta Rd Silver Spring MD 20901

WAUGH, WILLIAM M (R)
Res Dir, Nat Rep Cong Comt
b Chicago, Ill, May 24, 16; s Clyde A Waugh & Mildred Ockert W; single. Educ: Yale Univ, BA, 38; Purdue Univ, Lafayette, 38-39. Polit & Govt Pos: Roadviewer, Fairfax Co, Va, formerly; mem & secy treas, Fairfax Co Water Auth, formerly; chmn, Dranesville Dist, Fairfax Co, 58-64; chmn, Fairfax Co Rep Comt, 64-66; presidential elector, 68; mem & former vchmn, Tenth Cong Dist Rep Comt; mem, Va Rep State Cent Comt, 73-; res dir, Nat Rep Cong Comt, currently. Publ: Waugh's Chronicle of British Wars & Campaigns 1815-1968, 70. Relig: Episcopal. Mailing Add: 6443 Hitt Ave McLean VA 22101

WAXMAN, HENRY ARNOLD (D)
US Rep, Calif
b Los Angeles, Calif, Sept 12, 39; s R Louis Waxman & Esther Silverman W; m to Janet Kessler; c Carol Lynn & Michael David. Educ: Univ Calif, Los Angeles, BA Polit Sci, 61; Univ Calif, Los Angeles Sch Law, JD, 64; Pi Sigma Alpha. Polit & Govt Pos: State pres, Calif Fedn Young Dem, 65-67; Calif State Assemblyman, 61st Dist, 69-74, chmn comt health, Calif State Assembly until 74; US Rep, Calif 24th Dist, 75- Bus & Prof Pos: Attorney-at-Law, Los Angeles, Calif. Mem: Am Jewish Cong; Am Civil Liberties Union; NAACP; Ephebian Soc; Sierra Club. Relig: Jewish. Legal Res: 813 N Ogden Dr Los Angeles CA 90046 Mailing Add: US House Rep Washington DC 20515

WAY, HOWARD (R)
Calif State Sen
m to Barbara Chandler; c Susan & Stephen. Educ: Univ Calif, Berkeley, BA. Polit & Govt Pos: Mem, Calif State Govt Orgn & Econ Comn, formerly; mem, Fair Bd, 8 years, formerly; Exeter High Sch trustee, 8 years, formerly; Calif State Sen, 62-, Pres Pro Tempore, Calif State Senate, 69-70, chmn, Senate Rules Comt, chmn, Senate Comt Agr & Water Resources, mem, Finance Comt, Govt Orgn Comt & Select Comt on Penal Insts, vchmn, Joint Comt Master Plan for Higher Educ & mem, Joint Legis Budget Comt, Calif State Senate, currently; mem, Calif Rep State Cent Comt, currently; deleg, Rep Nat Conv, 68. Bus & Prof Pos: Farmer & fruit grower. Mil Serv: US Navy, World War II. Mem: Kiwanis (past Lt Gov); Co March of Dimes & Cancer Crusade Campaigns (former dir); Self-Help Enterprises, Inc (state dir). Mailing Add: PO Box 724 Exeter CA 93221

WAYLAND, DOUGLAS (D)
Colo State Rep
Mailing Add: 2646 Stuart Denver CO 80219

WEANER, KARL HULL (R)
Chmn, Defiance Co Rep Cent Comt, Ohio
b Defiance, Ohio, May 2, 07; s Karl A Weaner & Zora E Hull W; m 1932 to Dorothy Houck; c Zora J (Mrs Matson) & John W. Educ: Defiance Col, 26-28; Ohio State Univ Law Sch, LLB, 31; Pi Kappa Alpha; The Stollers. Polit & Govt Pos: City solicitor, Defiance, Ohio, 32-34; prosecuting attorney, Defiance Co, 35-41; judge, Court of Common Pleas, 47; mem & pres, Defiance City Bd of Educ, 49-58; comnr, app by Supreme Court of Ohio, Bd on Grievances & Discipline, 63-; mem, Fifth Dist, Ohio State Rep Cent Comt, formerly; chmn, Defiance Co Rep Cent Comt & Finance Comts, currently; deleg, Rep Nat Conv, 72. Mil Serv: Entered as Lt(jg), Navy, 42, released as Lt(sg), 46, after serv in Naval Air Force, Caribbean & Mil Govt, Okinawa, 46; Am-European-Asiatic Theater Ribbon. Mem: Elks; Eagles; Am Legion; Grange; Rotary. Relig: Evangelical United Brethren. Legal Res: 722 E High St Defiance OH 43512 Mailing Add: State Bank & Trust Bldg Defiance OH 43512

WEARIN, OTHA DONNER (D)
b Hastings, Iowa, Jan 10, 03; s Joseph Andrew Wearin & Mary Jane Donner W; m 1931 to Lola Irene Brazelton; c Martha Jane (Mrs R L Rasmusen) & Rebecca Joe (Mrs Allen F Pulk). Educ: Tabor Col, 16-21; Grinnell Col, BA, 24; Int Inst of Agr, Rome, Italy, grad work, 27; Grinnell Col, Honor G Club & Community Serv Award, 59. Polit & Govt Pos: Dem Precinct Committeeman, Hastings, Iowa, 24-32; Iowa State Rep, 28-32; US Rep, 32-38; mem, US Alien Enemy Hearing Bd, Southern Dist Iowa, 41-45, Mills Co Bd of Educ, 48-58 & Iowa State Comn on the Aging, 65-66; Iowa State Dem Cent Committeeman, 43-53. Bus & Prof Pos: Farm mgr, Brazelton & Wearin Farms, 37-; pres, bd dir, Clarinda Prod Credit Asn, 46- Publ: Political Americana, 67 & Clarence Ellsworth; 67, World Publ Co, Shenandoah, Iowa; Before the colors fade, Wallace Homestead Publ Co; plus three others. Mem: Ak-Sar-Ben; Friends of the Land; Los Angeles, Denver, Omaha & NY, Westerners. Relig: Congregational. Mailing Add: Nishna Vale Farm Hastings IA 51540

WEARY, LAWRENCE CLIFTON (D)
Committeeman, Calif Dem State Cent Comt
b Columbia, Miss, Oct 22, 28; s Ollie James Weary & Lora Smith W; m 1954 to Olevia Beatrice Riser; c Mable Beatrice. Educ: Southern Univ, grad, 57; Univ Calif, Los Angeles, 68; Pepperdine Col, 68-69. Polit & Govt Pos: Mem, Carson Dem Club, Calif, 68-; field rep to Calif State Assemblyman Larry Townsend, 68-; committeeman, Calif Dem State Cent Comt, 68-; mem, Compton Charter Rev Comt. Bus & Prof Pos: Pres, Commun Action for Better Schs, 68; pres, Compton Christian Sch Bd; teacher indust arts; real estate broker. Mil Serv: Entered as Pvt, Army, 51, released as Cpl, 53, after serv in 933rd Antiaircraft Artil, Korea, 51-52. Mem: Calif Teachers Asn; Calif Indust Educ Asn; vpres, Compton Civic League, 67; mem, Compton Charter Review Bd; NAACP. Honors & Awards: Thompson Award, Campfire Girls. Relig: Christian Church of NAm. Mailing Add: 2633 W Bennett St Compton CA 90220

WEAST, BURTON CALVIN (D)
Chmn, Curry Co Dem Cent Comt, Ore
b Corpus Christi, Tex, Feb 18, 45; s Delbert Eugene Weast & Margaret Rohr W; m 1970 to Ann Marie Armstrong. Educ: Col Siskiyous, AA, 64; Humboldt State Univ, 65-66; Southern Ore Col, BS, 72; Gamma Theta Upsilon; pres, Student Body, Col Siskiyous, 63-64. Polit & Govt Pos: Planning dir, Curry Co, Ore, 74-; chmn, Curry Co Dem Cent Comt, 74-; mem, Ore State Dem Cent Comt, 74- Bus & Prof Pos: Secy, Brookings-Harbor CofC, Brookings, Ore, 72-73; mgr, Brookings Plumbing Co, 72-74. Mil Serv: Entered as Seaman, Navy, 66, released as PO 2/C, 70, after serv in 7th Fleet, Southeast Asia, 67-70; Presidential Unit Citation; Korean Expeditionary Medal; Vietnam Campaign Ribbon with Two Stars; Repub Vietnam Legion of Merit, Nat Serv Medal. Mem: Rotary; Elks; VFW. Honors & Awards: Debator of the Year Trophy, Col Siskiyous, 64. Relig: Catholic. Mailing Add: Box 1504 Duley Creek Rd Brookings OR 97415

WEATHERSBY, WILLIAM HENRY
b Clinton, Miss, Nov 30, 14; m to Ruth Mowers; c William Jeffrey, Anne Delano & Amanda Maali. Educ: Miss Southern Col, BS, 34; Univ Mo, BJ, 35. Polit & Govt Pos: Pub affairs off Cairo, 51-56; Nat War Col, 57-58; dep asst dir for Near East, SAsia & Africa, US Info Agency, 58-60, dir of personnel, 60-61, dep dir for policy, 69-70; counsr for Pub Affairs, New Delhi, 61-65, minister-counsr, US Embassy, 68-69; US Ambassador to Sudan, 65-67. Bus & Prof Pos: Newspaper reporter, 35-37 & 37-40; ed, news serv, 40-41 & 45-51; vpres pub affairs, Princeton Univ, 70- Mil Serv: Navy, Lt, 41-45. Mailing Add: 37 McCosh Circle Princeton NJ 08540

WEAVER, EDWARD MYERS, JR (R)
Mem Exec Comt, Rep Party, Nebr
b Columbus, Nebr, June 9, 27; s Edward Myers Weaver, Sr & Phyllis Ruth McAnn W; m to Lois Jean Kaminska; c Matthew L. Educ: Univ Nebr, 45-46. Polit & Govt Pos: Chmn, Lancaster Co Rep Cent Comt, Nebr, formerly; chmn, First Cong Dist, Nebr, 69; mem exec comt, Rep Party, Nebr, currently; mem, Nebr Aeronautics Comn, currently. Bus & Prof Pos: Past pres, Weaver Potato Chip Co; dir, Lincoln Bank South, at present. Mil Serv: Entered as Pvt, Army, 52, released as Sgt, 54. Mem: Exec Comt, Nebr Potato Coun; Lincoln CofC (dir); Nebr Asn of Com & Indust; Kiwanis; Am Legion. Relig: Presbyterian. Mailing Add: 1600 Centerpark Rd Lincoln NE 68500

WEAVER, FRED L (D)
Kans State Rep
Mailing Add: RR 1 Baxter Springs KS 66713

WEAVER, GEORGE DUNCAN, JR (D)
City Councilman, Newport, RI
b Newport, RI, June 27, 18; s George Duncan Weaver & Kathryn Sampson W; m 1942 to Eleanor Sperling; c Steven Dennis & Matthew Duncan. Polit & Govt Pos: Mem, Personnel Appeals Bd, Newport, RI, 58; mem, Newport Dem City Comt, 64-, chmn, 67-; mem, Hist Dist Comn, Newport, 66; city councilman, Newport, 70- Mailing Add: 9 Chestnut St Newport RI 02840

WEAVER, GEORGE LEON PAUL (D)
b Pittsburgh, Pa, May 18, 12; s George J Weaver & Josephine Snell W; m 1941 to Mary F Sullivan. Educ: YMCA Sch, Chicago, Ill, 40-42; Howard Univ Law Sch, 42-43. Hon Degrees: LLD, Howard Univ, 62. Polit & Govt Pos: Mem, War Relief Comt, 41-42; dir, Civil Rights Comn, 55-58; spec asst to Secy of Labor, 61; Asst Secy of Labor for Int Affairs, 61-69; spec asst to dir gen, Int Labor Orgn, currently. Bus & Prof Pos: Asst to secy-treas, CIO, 42-45; asst to pres, IUE, 58-60; deleg or rep US, numerous int labor orgn meetings. Honors & Awards: Eleanor Roosevelt Key for Outstanding Serv to the World Community, Roosevelt Univ, 61; Tan Sri Hon Award, Govt Malaya, 63; Kim Khanh Medal Second Class, Labor Medal First Class, Repub SVietnam, 68; La Grande Officier, Repub Federale du Cameron, by President El Hadj Ahmadou Ahidjo, 69. Mailing Add: 3819 26th St NE Washington DC 20018

WEAVER, JAMES HOWARD (D)
US Rep, Ore
b Brookings, SDak, Aug 8. 27; s Leo C Weaver & Alice J Flittie W; m 1955 to Sally Cummins; c Regan, Allison & Sarah. Educ: Univ Ore, BS in Polit Sci. Polit & Govt Pos: Spec deleg, Dem Nat Mid-Term Conf, 74; US Rep, Fourth Dist, Ore, 75- Mil Serv: Navy, 45-46. Mailing Add: 2301 Spring Blvd Eugene OR 97403

WEAVER, PHILLIP HART (R)
b Falls City, Nebr, Apr 9, 19; s Arthur J Weaver & Evelyn Maude Hart W; m 1946 to Betty Jane Burner; c Phillip Arthur, Frederick William, Edwin Burner, Douglas Charles & Daniel Hart. Educ: St Benedict's Col, 38-39; Univ Nebr, AB, 42; Alpha Tau Omega. Polit & Govt Pos: Civilian admin asst to Asst Chief of Staff, Fifth Army, Chicago, 49-50; US Rep, Nebr, 55-63; US House Rep, Cong deleg, NATO Parliamentarians Conf, Europe, 60 & Interparliamentary Conf, SAm, 62, pres, 84th Rep Club, formerly; secy-treas, Richardson Co Rep Cent Comt, Nebr, formerly; state vpres & chmn, Nat Rivers & Harbors Cong Projs Comt, formerly; spec consult to Secy of Agr, Cong liaison & rural develop rep, US Dept Agr, 63-65, dep dir field opers div, Rural Community Develop Serv, 66, asst to adminr for legis oversight & regional develop coordr, 67-68, acting adminr, Rural Community Develop Serv, 69, dep asst to Secy of Agr for Intergovt Liaison, Off of Intergovt Affairs, 70-72. Bus & Prof Pos: Staff announcer, radio stas, KGNF, KFAB, KFOR & KVAK, 38-40; ins, finance & automobile bus as off, stockholder & trustee of varied family & personal bus interests, Falls City, Nebr, 46-58. Mil Serv: Entered as 2nd Lt, Army, 42, released as Capt, 46, after serv on Airborne Troops, ETO; Lt Col (Ret), Army Res; Combat Infantryman's Badge; Glider Wings; Bronze Star with Oak Leaf Cluster. Mem: Falls City Elks (Past Exalted Ruler); Falls City VFW (past comdr); Mason (32 degree); Shrine; Am Legion. Relig: Presbyterian. Mailing Add: 1906 Fulton St Falls City NE 68355

WEAVER, RAE CRUTHERS (R)
Chairperson, Second Cong Dist Rep Comt, Mich
b NJ, June 18, 35; d Raymond Crossley Cruthers & Alice Liesmann C; div; c Stephen & Karen. Educ: Univ Mich, AB in Econ; Alpha Phi. Polit & Govt Pos: Mem, Rep State Cent Comt, Mich, 72-74; mem, Rep State Comt on Rule 29, 75; chairperson, Second Cong Dist Rep Comt, 75- Bus & Prof Pos: Admin secy, Mayor, Ann Arbor, Mich, 73- Mem: Ann Arbor Bicentennial Comn; Cobblestone Farm (bd dirs, 75-); Ann Arbor Community Ctr (bd dirs, 71-). Honors & Awards: Silver Elephant Award, Rep City Comt, 68. Mailing Add: 1817 Cambridge Rd Ann Arbor MI 48104

WEAVER, ROBERT (D)
Ala State Sen
Mailing Add: PO Box 735 Talladega AL 35160

WEAVER, ROBERT CLIFTON (D)
b Washington, DC, Dec 29, 07; s Mortimer Grover Weaver & Florence Freeman W; m 1935 to Ella Haith; c Robert (deceased). Educ: Harvard Col, BS cum laude, 29, Harvard Univ, MA, 31, PhD, 34; Omega Psi Phi; Lambda Alpha. Polit & Govt Pos: Dep comnr, NY State Div of Housing, 55; adminr, NY State Rent Comn, 55-58; vchmn, Housing & Redevelop Bd, New York, 60-61; adminr, Housing & Home Finance Agency, Washington, DC, 61-66; secy, Dept of Housing & Urban Develop, 66-68; consult, Gen Acct Off, 72- Bus & Prof Pos: Lectr, Northwestern Univ; visiting prof, Teachers Col, Columbia Univ & NY Univ Sch Educ, 48-50; dir, Opportunity Fels, John Hay Whitney Found, 50-55; consult, Ford Found, New York, 59-60; pres, Baruch Col, City Univ of New York, 68-70; bd trustees, Metrop Life Ins Co, 69- & Bowery Savings Bank, 69-; prof, City Univ New York, 70-71; Distinguished Prof Urban Affairs, Hunter Col, 71- Publ: The Negro Ghetto, 48, Harcourt, Brace; The Urban Complex, Doubleday, 64; Dilemmas of Urban America, Harvard, 65; over 100 articles on housing, urban develop, labor & race rels probs. Mem: Am Acad of Arts & Sci (fel); Freedom House; Foreign Policy Asn; Nat Acad Pub Adminr. Mailing Add: 215 E 68th St New York NY 10021

WEAVER, STANLEY B (R)
Ill State Sen
Mailing Add: RR 3 Urbana IL 61801

WEBB, ALFREDA (D)
Mem, Dem Nat Comt, NC
Mailing Add: 137 N Dudley St Greensboro NC 27401

WEBB, CHARLES EDWARD (D)
NC State Rep
b Charlotte, NC, Dec 29, 36; s Sherid Elliott Webb & Belle Powers W; m 1964 to Dorothy Jean Cox; c Letisha. Educ: Mars Hill Col, AA; Appalachian State Univ, BS; Southeastern Baptist Theol Sem, BD; Clio-Philomathean Literary Soc. Polit & Govt Pos: Pres, Guilford Co Young Dem Club, NC, 68-69; mem, Govs Comt on Environ Health, 71; NC State Rep, 72- Bus & Prof Pos: Pres, Friendly Ctr Merchants Asn, 71-72. Mem: Guilford Co Humane Soc (bd dirs, 68-); Greensboro Breakfast Optimist Club; Greensboro CofC; Greensboro YMCA Mens Club. Honors & Awards: Nat Award for Excellence in Merchandizing, Hickory Farms Franchise; Humanitarian of the Year, Guilford Co Humane Soc, 73. Mailing Add: 302 Kensington Rd Greensboro NC 27403

WEBB, DONALD WOODFORD (D)
Chmn, Fayette Co Dem Exec Comt, Ky
b Whitesburg, Ky, July 2, 39; s Woodford Webb & Elizabeth Combs W; m 1964 to Julie Howser; c Donald Woodford, Jr. Educ: Va Mil Inst, 56-57; Georgetown Col, AB, 60; Univ of Ky, Col of Law, JD, 67; Phi Delta Phi; Kappa Alpha Order. Polit & Govt Pos: Asst to comnr, Ky Dept Com, Frankfort, 60-67; legal adv, Nat Adv Comn on Civil Disorders, Washington, DC, 67-68; mgr, Peden for US Sen Campaign, 68; Fayette Co chmn, Huddleston for US Sen Campaign, 72; chmn, Fayette Co Dem Exec Comt, Ky. Bus & Prof Pos: Attorney,

Handmaker, Weber & Meyer, Louisville, Ky, 68-71; attorney & partner, Webb & Webb, Attorneys, Lexington, 71- Mil Serv: Entered as Pvt, Ky Nat Guard, released, 63. Mem: Fayette Co, Ky & Am Bar Asns; Am Trial Lawyers Asn. Relig: Baptist. Legal Res: 467 Woodlake Way Lexington KY 40503 Mailing Add: 204 Bank of Commerce Bldg Lexington KY 40507

WEBB, DOROTHY ANN (R)
Membership Chmn, Nat Fedn Rep Women
b Louisville, Miss, Feb 2, 30; d Dr Powell Scrivner & Charles Veatrice Paxton S; m 1947 to Robert J Webb; c Robert Jerry, Jr, Rebecca Ann, Charles Edmund, Joseph Cornelius & Jeffrey Spencer. Educ: Whithall High Sch, Ark, grad, 47. Polit & Govt Pos: Pres, Pulaski Co Young Rep Club, Ark, 65; nat committeewoman, Young Rep League of Ark, 66; pres, Ark Fedn Rep Women, 67-73; membership chmn, Nat Fedn Rep Women, 73-; alt deleg, Rep Nat Conv, 72. Relig: Presbyterian. Mailing Add: 4924 E Crestwood Little Rock AR 72202

WEBB, KATHLEEN CECELIA (D)
Secy, Santa Cruz Co Dem Cent Comt, Calif
b Cresco, Iowa, Sept 21, 16; d Francis Patrick Farrell & Nell Pollitt F; m 1943 to William Marion Webb; c William Farrell & Pamela Joan. Educ: Watsonville High Sch, 4 years. Polit & Govt Pos: Secy, Santa Cruz Co Dem Cent Comt, Calif, 64-; mem, Calif Dem State Cent Comt, 64-69 & 73- Mem: Armed Forces Wives Club; Hui Nao Wahine, Hawaii; Am Red Cross; Am Cancer Soc; Watsonville Women's Club. Relig: Catholic. Mailing Add: 29 Shady Oaks Dr Watsonville CA 94076

WEBB, RITA LAFAYE (R)
b Hot Spring Co, Ark, Sept 18, 48; d Walter LaFayette Webb & Jennie Lee Johnson W; single. Educ: Lakeside High Sch, Hot Springs, Ark, 66. Polit & Govt Pos: Secy, Gtr Little Rock Young Rep Club, 71-72, pres, 72-; secy, Ark Fedn Young Rep, 71-73; youth adv & asst secy, Pulaski Co Rep Comt, 72-; alt deleg, Rep Nat Conv, 72; bookkeeper-treas, Blaylock for Gov Campaign Fund, 72. Mem: Metrop Bus & Prof Women (first vpres, 71, pres, 71-72, corresp secy, 72-). Relig: Baptist. Mailing Add: Apt 18 1500 Cantrell Rd Little Rock AR 72201

WEBB, ROBERT P (R)
Chmn, Wilbarger Co Rep Comt, Tex
b Wichita Falls, Tex, Oct 19, 12; s Robert Pinkney Webb & Lillie L Holley W; m 1936 to Nona Ewing Warren; c Camille (Mrs David Mount). Educ: Okla A&M Col, 33; Kappa Alpha. Polit & Govt Pos: Chmn, Selective Serv Bd, Tex, 53-73 & Wilbarger Co Hosp Bd, 65-75; chmn, Wilbarger Co Rep Comt, 72- Bus & Prof Pos: Managing trustee, Jessie Herring Johnson Estate, 43-75; independent oil operator, 50- Mem: Mason; North Tex & Mid-Continent Oil & Gas Asns. Relig: Cent Christian Church. Legal Res: 3805 Buffalo Vernon TX 76384 Mailing Add: Drawer 1477 Vernon TX 76384

WEBB, RODNEY S (R)
Chmn, Dist 16 Rep Party, NDak
b Cavalier, NDak, June 21, 35; s Chester A Webb & Aylza Martin W; m 1957 to Betty M Lykken; c Sharon, Crystal, Todd, Wade & Susan. Educ: Univ NDak, JD & BS; Phi Delta Phi; Sigma Chi. Polit & Govt Pos: Chmn, Dist 16 Rep Party, NDak, 73-; munic judge, Grafton, NDak, 75- Bus & Prof Pos: Attorney-at-law, Ringsek & Webb, Grafton, NDak, 59-; states attorney, Walsh Co, 66-74. Mil Serv: Maj, Army Nat Guard, currently. Relig: Lutheran. Legal Res: 1492 LaVergne Ave Grafton ND 58237 Mailing Add: PO Box 308 Grafton ND 58237

WEBB, SUSAN HOWARD (R)
Vt State Rep
b Burlington, Vt, Aug 18, 08; d Harry Stinson Howard & Sue Emma Hertz H; m 1932 to Kenneth Beals Webb; c Susan (Mrs Robert Hammond), Robert Howard & Martha. Educ: Univ Vt, AB, 30; Radcliffe Col, MA, 31; Phi Beta Kappa; Sigma Gamma. Polit & Govt Pos: Vt State Rep, 73-, clerk, Comt on Health & Welfare, Vt House Rep, 73-, mem, Comt on Educ, 75- Bus & Prof Pos: Teacher, co-founder & camp dir, Farm & Wilderness Camps, Inc, Indian Brook, Vt, 49-70; mem camp standards comt, Am Camping Asn, 69-72; legis chmn, Churchwomen United of Vt & Vt Camping Asn. Publ: Co-auth, Summer Magic, Asn Press; auth, Round-the-World Letters, Soc of Friends; articles in Parents Mag & Camping Mag, Galloway Publ. Mem: Gov Comn on Status of Women (adv coun); Int League for Peace & Freedom; Common Cause; Am Civil Liberties Union; Josephine B Baird Children's Ctr (vpres bd, 72-74, pres bd, 75-). Relig: Society of Friends. Mailing Add: Brooksend Plymouth VT 05056

WEBB, WELLINGTON EDWARD (D)
Colo State Rep
b Chicago, Ill, Feb 17, 41; s Wellington M Webb & Mardina Williams W; m to Wilma Gerdine; c Anthony, Allen, Stephanie & Keith. Educ: Northeastern Jr Col, AA, 62; Colo State Col, BA, 64; Univ Northern Colo, MA, 71. Polit & Govt Pos: Bd mem, Denver War on Poverty, 66-67, bd mem, Denver Model Cities, 70-71; deleg, Nat Black Conv, 72-; mem, Nat Black Polit Assembly, 72-; Colo State Rep, Dist Eight, 73-; deleg, Dem Nat Mid-Term Conf, 74. Bus & Prof Pos: Counselor, Job Opportunity Ctr, Denver, 65-66; asst prin, Children's Div, Ft Logan Ment Health Ctr, 66-69; asst dir manpower lab, Colo State Univ, 69- Publ: Co-auth, Serving the disadvantaged: a manual for job counselors, 72 & Serving the disadvantaged: a manual for counseling supervisors, 72, Dept Labor; auth, Physical education classes for the emotionally disturbed child, J Health, Phys Educ & Recreation, 5/72. Mem: Esquire Civic Club (vpres, 73-); Community Care Fund Inc (chmn bd, 73-). Relig: Baptist. Mailing Add: 2329 Gaylord St Denver CO 80205

WEBB, WILLIAM MITCHELL (R)
NH State Rep
b Springfield, Mass, Jan 1, 39; s William C Webb & Alice T W; m 1971 to Sally Jean Jensen; c John Joseph. Educ: Leland Powers Sch Broadcasting, grad, 61. Polit & Govt Pos: NH State Rep, 73- Bus & Prof Pos: Announcer, WCNL Radio, Newport, NH, 62-65; announcer-sales mgr, WPNH Radio, Plymouth, 65- Mem: Lions (secy, 72-73). Relig: Congregational. Mailing Add: PO Box 296 Plymouth NH 03264

WEBBER, ALBERT RAYMOND (D)
Conn State Rep
b New Haven, Conn, Sept 28, 13; s Louis Webber & Fannie Ostrow W; m 1943 to Sally Goodmark; c Michelle, Lawrence, Priscilla & Jordon. Polit & Govt Pos: Conn State Rep, 58-; mem, New Haven Bd of Aldermen & Zoning Appeals. Bus & Prof Pos: Pres, A R Webber Assoc, Real Estate. Mil Serv: Pvt, Army, 42. Mem: Woodbridge CofC; Probus Club; New Haven Rehabil Ctr & Community Ctr, Home for the Aged (mem bd); New Haven Regional Ctr for Ment Retarded (chmn adv bd). Relig: Jewish. Mailing Add: 226 Fountain St New Haven CT 06515

WEBBER, DONALD JASPER (D)
Maine State Rep
b Monroe, Maine, July 23, 14; s Jasper E Webber & Mabel Felker W; m 1939 to Mabel M Michaud; c Dennis J, Carolyn (Mrs DeLeonardis), Linda A (Mrs Soars) & Michael D. Educ: Monroe High Sch, 28-32. Polit & Govt Pos: Maine State Rep, 71- Bus & Prof Pos: Serv sta attendant, Belfast, Maine, 33-44; patrolman, Belfast Police Dept, 45, chief of police, 46; trooper, Maine State Police, 47-48; distributor, Shell Oil, 48- Mem: KofC; Maine State Dem 500 Club. Relig: Catholic. Mailing Add: 32 S Ocean Belfast ME 04915

WEBBER, FREDERICK LEROY (R)
Asst Secy Legis Affairs, Dept of the Treas
b Portland, Maine, Jan 4, 38; s Leon True Webber & Patricia Conti W; m 1965 to Ann Chamberlain Bouker; c John Frederick, Jennifer True & Sarah Chamberlain. Educ: Yale Univ, BA in Hist, 61; Yale Key; Phi Gamma Delta. Polit & Govt Pos: Admin asst to US Rep John Dellenback, Ore, 68-70; spec asst to Secy of Labor for Legis Affairs, 70-72; spec asst to the President for Legis Affairs, 73-74; asst secy legis affairs, Dept of the Treas, 74- Bus & Prof Pos: Legis liaison, Nat Forest Prod Asn, Washington, DC, 66-68; vpres, Am Paper Inst, 73. Mil Serv: Entered as 2nd Lt, Marine Corps, 61, released as Capt, 66, after serv in 3rd & 2nd Div, Western Pac & ECoast, Maj, Marine Corps Res, 66-; Commendation for Combat Duties in Dominican Repub. Mem: Yale Club, Washington, DC; Jaycees. Relig: Episcopal. Mailing Add: 1703 Hollinwood Dr Alexandria VA 22307

WEBER, CHARLES WILLIAM (D)
Chmn, Lake Co Dem Cent Comt, Colo
b Pueblo, Colo, Jan 4, 46; s Joseph C Weber & Evelyn Burbridge W; single. Educ: Regis Col, 64-65; Adams State Col, BA in Econ, 68. Polit & Govt Pos: Chmn, Lake Co Dem Cent Comt, Colo, 75-; mem, Colo State Dem Exec Comt, 75-; chmn, 61st Dist Dem Party, 75-; vchmn, 31st Dist Dem Party, 75-; secy, Fifth Dist Dem Party, 75- Mil Serv: Entered as Pvt E-1, Army, 68, released as SP-5, 70, after serv in 268 Aviation Bn, 1st Aviation Brigade, Vietnam, 69-70; Nat Defense Serv Medal; Vietnam Serv Medal & Combat Medal; Army Commendation Medals; Good Conduct Medal; Am Campaign Medal; Air Medal; Expert M-14 & M-16. Mem: Elks (Exalted Ruler, Lodge 236, 73-74). Relig: Roman Catholic. Legal Res: 127 E Eighth St Leadville CO 80461 Mailing Add: PO Box 1207 Leadville CO 80461

WEBER, FRANCIS E (HANK) (D)
NDak State Rep
Mailing Add: State Capitol Bismarck ND 58501

WEBER, GARRY ALLEN (D)
City Councilman, Dallas, Tex
b Oelwein, Iowa, Feb 25, 36; s Arthur Albert Weber & Eleanore Lincoln W; div. Educ: Southern Methodist Univ, BBA, 58; Phi Alpha Delta; Kappa Alpha. Polit & Govt Pos: Co-chmn, Young Men for Cabell, Earle Cabell Congressman's Club, Dallas, Tex, 66-68; campaign chmn for Earle Cabell, 68; deleg, Dem Nat Conv, 68; mem, Comn to Study Mortgage Interest Rates, Washington, DC, 68-69; city councilman, Dallas, 69-; chmn & founder, Tax Coun of Tex Cities, 71- Bus & Prof Pos: Chmn bd, Weber, Hall, Cobb & Caudle, Inc, Dallas, Tex, 64- Mem: Goodwill Industs, Dallas, (dir); Dallas Co Hosp Dist (bd dirs); Salesmanship Club of Dallas; United Fund Comt; NDallas CofC (dir). Honors & Awards: One of the Five Outstanding Young Texans, 70. Relig: Methodist. Legal Res: 7727 Meadow Park Dr Dallas TX 75230 Mailing Add: 1800 LTV Tower Dallas TX 75201

WEBER, MARY E (D)
Dem Nat Committeewoman, Wash
b Ironton, Ohio, June 24, 11; d Charles John Willis & Sue Ella Gholson Sloat W; m 1944 to Earl Weber; c Dawn & Karen. Educ: Marshall Univ, AB, 33; Ohio State Univ, 34-36; Univ Chicago, 40; Cleveland Inst Fine Arts; Univ Wash, 53; Delta Kappa Gamma; Glee Clubs; Debate; French Club; German Club; Drama. Polit & Govt Pos: Dem Precinct committeewoman, 11 years; organizer, Dem Woman's Clubs; mem, Off Price Admin Rental Adv Bd, Seattle, King & Snohomish Co, Wash, 46-53; pres rep, Dem Nat Conv, 50, deleg, 64, 68 & 72; deleg, Wash State Dem Conv, 56-72; pres, Grant Co Dem Women's Club, 61-64; chmn, Grant Co Dem Platform Comt, mem, State Dem Platform Comt & deleg, White House Conf Dem Women, 66, deleg, Western States Dem Conf, Los Angeles, 67; state co-chmn, Comt to Reform Elec Process & Humphrey for Pres Comt, formerly; Dem Nat Committeewoman, Wash, 68-; co-chmn, McCormack for Cong Comt, 70; mem, State Dem Comt for Reelect US Sen Warren G Magnuson; co-state chmn, Citizens for Re-elect of US Sen Jackson, 70; campaign mgr for Lloyd Graham for chmn Comt for Dem Coun of 13 western states, 70; mem exec bd to represent Wash on Dem Coun of 13 western states, formerly; deleg from Wash Press Women to World Asn Press Women, 71; deleg from Wash State Dem Cent Comt to Nat Women's Leadership Conf, 71; mem, Wash State Comt Jackson for President, 72; mem, State Finance Comt McGovern for President, 72; partic, Bus & Prof Women's Polit Action Sch, 72; mem, Grant Co Coun Alcoholism, 73, elected to Wash State Coun on Alcoholism, 74; mem comn to select Vice Presidential cand 76, Dem Nat Comt, 73; deleg, Third Int Conv Women Journalists, Israel, 73, Am Rep, exec comt, 73, deleg conv, 76; deleg, Wash State Press Conv, 70; deleg, Nat Conv Press Women, 71-75; app to state comt, Keep Am Beautiful; deleg, Nat Fedn Press Women, Hawaii, 74. Bus & Prof Pos: Music, Eng, Latin & debate teacher, 32-42; co-owner & mgr, Auto & Farm Implement Co, 48-54; co-owner farm, Columbia Basin Irrigation Proj, 53-; photographer, Pac Northwest Gardens, 56; co-ed, Smoke Signals, Wash State Fedn of Garden Clubs, 58-61; deleg, Nat Fedn Garden Clubs Conv, 73; ed bd, Ammpe, 74-; deleg, World Asn Women Journalists, Mexico City, 74. Mil Serv: Army, 42-44, civilian employee, Army Corps Engrs; President's Blue Serv Ribbons. Mem: Eastern Star; White Shrine of Jerusalem; Am Legion Auxiliary; Cent Dist Wash Press Women (pres, 72-75, first vpres, 75); NCent Dist Fedn Garden Clubs. Honors & Awards: Blue Ribbon Winner, Seattle World's Fair Flower Show for Design Depicting Century 21 Sci Ctr, 61; Sweepstakes Winner, Rocky Reach Dam Driftwood Show, Wenatchee, 64; Outstanding Community Leader, 68; First & Second Place Award, State Contest for Women Journalists, Wash Press Women, 72, 74 & 75; Sugar Plum Award, Wash Press Women, 74, two first place state writing awards, 75. Relig: Presbyterian. Mailing Add: Rte 1 Box 173 Quincy WA 98848

WEBER, ROBERT R (R)
SDak State Rep
Mailing Add: Strandburg SD 57265

WEBSTER, CLARENCE L (R)
NH State Rep
Mailing Add: Box 203 Hampstead NH 03841

WEBSTER, DONALD ALBERT (R)
b Rochester, NY, Dec 9, 30; s Albert C Webster & Madeline Vandenbush W; m 1959 to Helen Long. Educ: Hamilton Col, BA, 53; Sch Adv Int Studies, Johns Hopkins Univ, MA, 55; Pi Delta Epsilon; Delta Sigma Rho; Tau Kappa Epsilon. Polit & Govt Pos: Research asst to Sen Frederick G Payne, Washington, DC, 55-56; asst to asst admin, Gen Serv Admin, 59-61; minority economist, Joint Econ Comt of Cong, 62-68; staff mem, Nixon Campaign Staff & Presidential Transition Comt, 68-69; Asst to Secy of Treas, 69-70, Dep Asst Secy of Treas, 70-72. Bus & Prof Pos: Writer, Cong Quart, Washington, DC, 61-62. Mil Serv: Entered as A/S, Navy, 56, released as Lt(jg), 59, after serv in Heavy Photographic Squadron 62, 56-58. Mem: Am Econ Asn; Nat Economists Club; Phi Beta Kappa. Relig: Protestant. Mailing Add: 1624 Creek St Rochester NY 14625

WEBSTER, JAMES DOUGLAS (R)
b Fergus Falls, Minn, May 4, 40; s LuVerne John Webster & Mildred Rausch W; m 1966 to Kathleen Jean Olson; c Douglas Barry, Wendy Suzanne & Lisa Marie. Educ: Univ Wis, Madison, BS, 60; Univ Tex Med Br, Galveston, MD, 64; Univ Tex Med Br; Mu Delta; Chi Psi; Theta Kappa Psi. Polit & Govt Pos: Mem, Univ Wis Young Rep, 57-60; chmn, Univ Tex Med Br Young Rep, 63-64; vpres, Milwaukee Co Young Adult Rep Club, 66-68; vpres, Taylor Co Young Adult Rep, 69-70, pres, 70-71; pres, Tex Young Adult Rep Coun, 71-73; ex officio mem, Tex State Rep Exec Comt, 72-73; state chmn, Mauria Angly for Treas Campaign, 72; alt deleg, Rep Nat Conv, 72. Bus & Prof Pos: Vchmn, Med Sect, WTex Med Ctr, 70-71, secy, 71-73; secy, Med Sect, Hendrich Mem Hosp, 71-73, pres, 75- Mil Serv: 1st Lt (Ret), Naval Res, 65. Mem: Farm Bur; Kiwanis; Abilene Boys Club Bd Dirs (vpres, 71); Chisholm Trail Coun, Boys Scouts Am (pres & bd dirs, 75); Abilene CofC (legis comt & bd dirs, 74). Honors & Awards: Bronze Handcharger Award, Young Rep Fedn, 70, Silver Hand Charger Award, 70 & Gold Hand Charger Award, 71; Outstanding Young Man in Abilene, 74. Relig: Roman Catholic. Legal Res: 3774 Woodridge Abilene TX 79605 Mailing Add: 1101 N 19th Abilene TX 79601

WEBSTER, JOHN DEAN (D)
Chmn, Hall Co Dem Party, Nebr
b Gibbon, Nebr, Oct 28, 35; s Walter Dwight Webster & Dorothy Camp W; m 1959 to Mary Ann Zulkoski; c Anthony, Kevin, Michael & Kyle. Educ: Kearney State Col, 1 year. Polit & Govt Pos: Chmn, Hall Co Dem Party, Nebr, 70- Bus & Prof Pos: Farmer, 58- Mil Serv: Entered as Pvt, Army, 55, released as SP-4, 56, after serv in 7th Transportation Bn, 5th Army, Ft Carson, Colo, 55-56. Mem: Elks; KofC; Lions Int. Relig: Catholic. Mailing Add: RFD 2 Wood River NE 68883

WEBSTER, KENNETH L (D)
Md State Deleg
Mailing Add: 2836 Oakley Ave Baltimore MD 21215

WEBSTER, KENT JONES (D)
NDak State Sen
Mailing Add: State Capitol Bismarck ND 58501

WEBSTER, RICHARD M (R)
Mo State Sen
b Carthage, Mo, Apr 29, 22; m 1948 to Janet Poston Whitehead; c Richard M, Jr & William Lawrence. Educ: Univ Mo; Columbia Univ, LLB, 48. Polit & Govt Pos: Mo State Rep, 50-56; Mo State Sen, 62- Bus & Prof Pos: Attorney & stockman. Mil Serv: Coast Guard, 41-45; Naval Res, 45- Mem: Mason; KofP. Relig: Presbyterian. Mailing Add: 1725 S Garrison Carthage MO 64836

WEBSTER, ROBERT BYRON (R)
b Detroit, Mich, Mar 9, 32; s Don Byron Webster & Glennie Elizabeth Cole W; m 1959 to Marilyn Dee Hey; c Anne Elizabeth, Allison Dee, Peter Hey & James Byron. Educ: Univ Mich, AB, 55, JD, 57; Barristers Soc; Phi Gamma Delta; Phi Alpha Delta. Polit & Govt Pos: Law clerk, Ralph M Freeman, Chief US Dist Judge, Eastern Dist, Mich, 57-59; chmn, Oakland Co Rep Comt, 70-71; mem, Oakland Co Reapportionment Comn, 71 & Oakland Co Community Ment Health Bd, 71-73; deleg, Rep Nat Conv, 72; judge, Sixth Judician Circuit Court, Oakland Co, currently. Bus & Prof Pos: Partner, Reitz, Tait, Oetting & Webster, Detroit, Mich, 59-69 & Hill, Lewis, Adams, Goodrich & Tait, Detroit & Birmingham, 69-73. Mil Serv: Entered as Pvt, Air Force, 51, released as Sgt, 53, after serv in 127 AC&W Squadron, Air Defense Command, 51-53; Maj, Air Force Res, 55-; Good Conduct Medal; Broad Sword; Air Res Medal; Nat Defense Serv Medal. Mem: Am, Fed, Detroit & Oakland Co Bar Asns; State Bar Mich; Thomas M Cooley Soc. Relig: Unitarian. Mailing Add: 21050 W 14 Mile Rd Birmingham MI 48010

WEBSTER, ROBERT L (R)
b Brownsville, Pa, Sept 7, 24; s Thomas J Webster & Janet Thompson W; m 1948 to Wilma O'Brien; c Robert L, Jr, Danny L & Thomas W. Educ: St Vincent's Col, 44; Univ Pittsburgh, LLB, 51. Polit & Govt Pos: Chmn, Fayette Co Young Rep, Pa, 52-56; dir, State Fedn Young Rep, 55-57; chmn, Fayette Co Rep Party, formerly; deleg, Rep Nat Conv, 68. Bus & Prof Pos: Attorney-at-Law, 51- Mil Serv: Entered as Flight Engr, Air Force, 43, released as Flight Engr, 46, after serv in Fourth Air Force. Mem: Fayette Co, Pa & Am Bar Asns. Relig: Protestant. Mailing Add: 72 E Main St Uniontown PA 15401

WEBSTER, RONALD ARTHUR (R)
Mem, Knox Co Rep Exec Comt, Tenn
b Morgan Co, Tenn, Dec 21, 38; s Paris Guthrie Webster & Myrtle Hill W; m 1967 to Dianne Elizabeth Sharp; c James Marshall. Educ: Univ Tenn, BS, 60, Col Law, JD, 62; cert, Nat Col Dist Attorneys, 72; pres, Phi Delta Phi, 61-62; Tau Kappa Alpha; Sigma Chi. Polit & Govt Pos: Pres, Univ Tenn Youth for Nixon-Lodge, 60; Tenn State Rep, Knox Co, 64-68; mem, Knox Co Rep Exec Comt, Tenn, 64-; mem, Tenn Rep State Exec Comt, formerly; treas, Knox Co Young Rep Club, 65-66; trial attorney, Knoxville, 65-67; attorney gen, Knox Co, 68- Mem: Mason; YMCA; Sen Country Club; Deane Hill Country Club; Tenn Dist Attorneys Gen Conv (secy-treas, 72-73, vpres, 73-). Relig: Baptist. Mailing Add: 4120 Maloney Rd SW Knoxville TN 37920

WEBSTER, WARREN RAYMOND (R)
Chmn, Knox Co Rep Exec Comt, Tenn
b Morgan Co, Tenn, Dec 25, 21; s Paris Guthrie Webster & Myrtle Hill W; m to Janice Marie Spitzer; c Richard Alan, Martha Carol, Sara Joyce, Thomas Raymond & Elizabeth Marie. Educ: Univ Tenn, BA; Univ Tenn Col of Law, LLB; Sigma Nu; Phi Alpha Delta. Polit & Govt Pos: Chmn, Knox Co Rep Exec Comt, 57-60 & 64-; chmn, Second Cong Dist Exec Comt, Tenn, 64-68; deleg, Rep Nat Conv, 68 & 72; mem, Tenn State Rep Exec Comt, 70-72. Bus & Prof Pos: Attorney-at-law, 53- Mil Serv: Entered as Aviation Cadet, Navy, 43, commissioned 2nd Lt, Marine Corps, 44, released, 46, after serv in Pac Theater; recalled to serv with VMR 152, Korean War, 50, released as Maj, 62; Pac Campaign Ribbon with Two Combat Stars. Mem: Mason (32 degree); Shrine; Elks; Tenn & Am Bar Asns. Relig: Baptist. Legal Res: 3551 Iskagna Ave Knoxville TN 37919 Mailing Add: Suite 1100 Hamilton Bank Bldg Knoxville TN 37902

WEBSTER, WESLEY D (D)
NC State Sen
Mailing Add: Rte 4 Madison NC 27025

WEBSTER, WILLIAM J (D)
Chmn, Maury Co Dem Exec Comt, Tenn
b Columbia, Tenn, Aug 31, 16; s William J Webster & Mary Buchnau W; m 1939 to Mildred Gaines. Educ: Columbia Mil Acad, Tenn. Polit & Govt Pos: Chmn, Maury Co Dem Exec Comt, Tenn, 70-; deleg & chmn Tenn deleg, Dem Nat Conv, 72. Bus & Prof Pos: Owner, farm & beer wholesales, currently; pres & owner, Middle Tenn Enterprises Inc & Radio Sta WDBL, Springfield, currently. Mil Serv: Entered as Pvt, Army, released as 2nd Lt after serv in 159th Combat Engr, Europe, 46. Mem: Am Legion; VFW; 40 et 8; Elks. Relig: Episcopal. Legal Res: RR 8 Columbia TN 38401 Mailing Add: Box 142 Columbia TN 38401

WEBSTER, WILLIAM LAWRENCE (R)
b Carthage, Mo, Sept 17, 53; s Richard Melton Webster & Janet Poston Whitehead W; single. Educ: Univ Kans, 72-; Delta Sigma Rho; Beta Theta Pi. Polit & Govt Pos: Deleg, Rep Nat Conv, 72. Relig: Christian. Legal Res: 1425 Tennessee Ave Lawrence KS 66044 Mailing Add: 1725 Garrison Ave Carthage MO 64836

WEDDINGTON, SARAH RAGLE (D)
Tex State Rep
b Abilene, Tex, Feb 5, 45; d Rev Doyle Ragle & Lena Catherine R. Educ: McMurry Col, BS, 65; Univ Tex Law Sch, JD, 67; Kappa Beta Pi; Theta Chi Lambda. Polit & Govt Pos: Asst city attorney, Ft Worth, Tex, 70-71; Tex State Rep, 73-, dean Travis Co deleg, Tex House Rep, 75- Mem: Am Bar Asn; State Bar Tex (chairperson, State Bar Comt to Increase Partic in Bar, Minorities & Women); Orgn Women Legislators (legis comt); Nat Asn Women Lawyers; Zero Pop Growth. Honors & Awards: First Annual Woman of Year Award, Tex Women's Polit Caucus, 73; First Annual Susan B Anthony Award, Nat Orgn of Women, Austin Chap, 73; Outstanding Legislator, Tex Student Asn, 73; Bamaer Award, Austin Women in Commun, 73; Woman of the Year, Austin Federated Bus & Prof Women's Club, 74. Legal Res: 709 W 14th Austin TX 78701 Mailing Add: PO Box 2910 Austin TX 78767

WEDWORTH, JAMES Q (D)
Calif State Sen
b Ill, 1919; m to Muriel Berube; c Ronald, Diane, Susan & Albert. Educ: Ill & La Pub Schs. Polit & Govt Pos: Mem, Hawthorne City Coun, Calif, 53-66, mayor, 58-66; Hawthorne rep, SBay Mayor's Coun, West Basin Water Dist, Los Angeles Co Sanit Dist, Rapid Transit Selection Bd, League of Independent Cities, Am Munic League & Nat Mayors' Coun; Calif State Sen, 66-, mem, Fish & Game, Water Resources, Agr & Natural Resources Comts, Comt on Educ, Govt Efficiency Comt, Local Govt Comt, Const Rev Comt, chmn, Govt Orgn Subcomt Retirement, Calif State Senate, formerly, chmn, Comt Vehicle Design & Performance Select Comt, chmn, Govt Orgn Subcomt on Automotive Safety, vchmn, Ins & Financial Inst Comt, mem, Senate Govt Orgn Comt, Natural Resources & Wildlife, Revenue & Taxation Comt, Joint Comt Rules, Joint Comt Legis Bldg Space Needs, Subcomt Civil Disorder, Joint Comt Legis Retirement, currently. Bus & Prof Pos: Mgr, US Navy Exchange, 45-49; employee, Northrop Corp, 49-53; operator, Schwinn Bicycle Agency & Fuller Paint Store, 53- Mil Serv: Navy, 41-45. Mem: Hawthorne Rotary Club (bd dirs & chmn youth comt); Elks; Little League; Am Field Serv; Local Heart Fund & Cerebral Palsy Drive (chmn). Honors & Awards: Rotarian of the Year, Hawthorne Rotary, 57. Relig: Lutheran. Mailing Add: Suite 103 1 Manchester Blvd Inglewood CA 90301

WEED, ELLA DEMMINK (R)
b Grand Rapids, Mich, July 25, 05; d Henry John Demmink & Alida Elizabeth Hesselink D; m 1933 to Albert S Koeze, wid; m 1973 to Harold K Weed; c Dr Thomas H, A Scott, David S, Robert P & Marybeth. Educ: Davenport Col, 24-25. Polit & Govt Pos: Vchmn, Kent Co Rep Comt, Mich, 44-50; mem, Mich Rep State Cent Comt, 47-51, vchmn, 57-61; deleg or alt deleg, Rep Nat Conv, 48-68; mem bd, Rep Nat Fedn, 53-57; pres, Mich Rep Women's Fedn, 53-57; mem, Rep Nat Comt, Mich, 60-69, mem exec comt, Rep Nat Comt, 62-69; mem, Naples Rep Club, currently. Bus & Prof Pos: Secy-treas, Koeze Mfg Co, Grand Rapids, Mich, 33-; mem bd trustees, Grand Valley Col, Allendale, currently. Mem: Charter mem Arthur H Vandenberg Rep Women's Club; Nat Alliance of Businessmen; Mary A Welsh Guild; Blodgett Mem Hosp; Wyoming, Mich People to People Orgn. Relig: Christian Reformed Church. Mailing Add: Apt F12 2303 Valleywood Dr SE Grand Rapids MI 49506

WEEKS, ELAINE C (R)
Chmn, Maine Fedn of Young Rep
b Portland, Maine, Oct 23, 49; d Woodrow D Weeks & Grace Marston W; single. Educ: Colby Col, BA, 71; Phi Beta Kappa. Polit & Govt Pos: Opposition researcher, Rep Nat Comt, Washington, DC, 71; youth coordr, Maine Rep State Comt, 71, mem, 71-72; mem, Gov Comt on Senate Reapportionment, fall 71; adv, Maine TAR, 71-; chmn, Maine Fedn of Young Rep, 71-; mem & secy, Maine Rep Platform Comt, 72-; alt deleg, Rep Nat Conv, 72; mem, Elec Law Rev Comn, 72; asst dir, Maine Comt to Reelect the President, 72; field coordr, Bill Cohen for Cong Comt, 72. Mem: Maine Teacher's Asn; Nat Educ Asn. Relig: Protestant. Mailing Add: 196 Maine Ave Farmingdale ME 04345

WEEKS, HENRY RICHARD, JR (R)
VChmn, Richland Co Rep Party, SC
b Norfolk, Va, Aug 14, 30; s Henry Richard Weeks & Alice Gonzalez W; m 1957 to Ursula Christine Luise Rupp; c Henry R III, Manfred G C & Christine L M. Educ: US Naval Acad, 49-51; The Citadel, AB, polit sci, 54; Univ SC Law Sch, LLB, 63; Command & Gen Staff Sch, 68-70; Phi Alpha Delta. Polit & Govt Pos: Pres, Richland Co Young Rep, SC, 67-69, treas,

69-70; deleg, Richland Co & SC State Rep Conv, 68-72; precinct pres, Richland Co Rep Party, 68-72, vchmn, 72-; chmn, SC Young Rep Const Rev Comt, 70; alt deleg, Rep Nat Conv, 72. Bus & Prof Pos: Teacher Eng & hist, Charleston Co Pub Schs, SC, 58-60; instr Eng, Univ SC, 60-61; investr, SC & Fla, 63-65; trust officer, C&S Nat Bank of SC, 65- Mil Serv: Entered as 2nd Lt, Army, 55, released as 1st Lt, 58, after serv in 2nd & 3rd Armored Div, ETO, 55-58; Capt (Ret), Army Res, 58-70. Mem: Columbia Estate Planning Coun; AF&AM; Columbia Civitan Club; Nat Rifle Asn; World Future Soc. Relig: Episcopal. Legal Res: 7358 Highview Dr Columbia SC 29204 Mailing Add: PO Box 312 Columbia SC 29202

WEEKS, MARCIA GAIL (D)
Ariz State Sen
b Greenbush, Minn, Jan 19, 38; d Casper Lewis Spangrud & Laura M Wallin S; m 1958 to James Walter Weeks; c Chad. Educ: Univ Ariz, BA in home econ, 67. Polit & Govt Pos: Ariz State Sen, 75- Mem: League of Women Voters. Relig: Methodist. Legal Res: 3538 W Mercer Lane Phoenix AZ 85029 Mailing Add: Capitol Bldg Senate Wing Phoenix AZ 85007

WEEKS, PAUL J (D)
Ala State Rep
Mailing Add: PO Box 674 Winfield AL 35594

WEGENER, MYRTON O (DFL)
Minn State Sen
Mailing Add: Bertha MN 56437

WEGMAN, HAROLD ROBERT (R)
Chmn, Clark Co Rep Party, SDak
b Raymond, SDak, Dec 11, 19; s Henry Wegman & Margaret Boddin W; m 1954 to Madge Forsyth. Educ: Tex Tech Univ, 1 year. Polit & Govt Pos: Mayor, City of Raymond, SDak, 51-; chmn, Clark Co Rep Party, SDak, 70- Bus & Prof Pos: Owner & operator, Liquefied Petroleum & Gasoline Bulk Plant, 47- & Int Harvester Dealership, 53- Mil Serv: Entered as Cadet, Air Force, 42, released as 1st Lt, 45, after serv in Western Flying Training Command, 43-45; Maj, Air Force Res, currently. Mem: Am Legion; Farm Bur; Clark Golf Club. Relig: Lutheran. Mailing Add: Raymond SD 57258

WEGNER, GLEN EUGENE (R)
b Kendrick, Idaho, Jan 25, 39; s Glen August Wegner & Jean Fry W; m 1971 to Evelyn Anne Magnuson. Educ: Col Idaho, BS in Zool & BS in Psychol, 60; Univ Wash Sch Med, MD, 64; Boston City Hosp, Mass, intern, 64-65; Johns Hopkins Univ, residency & fel, 65-67; Am Univ, Wash, DC, JD, 71. Polit & Govt Pos: Clin research assoc, Nat Inst of Child Health & Human Develop, Nat Insts of Health, Dept of Health, Educ & Welfare, 67-68, spec asst to the Surgeon Gen & to the Asst Secy for Health & Sci Affairs, 68-69, Dep Asst Secy for Health Legis, 69-71; mem, White House Staff, 71; cand, US Senate, Idaho, 72. Bus & Prof Pos: Clinical research assoc, Nat Insts of Health, Bethesda, Md, 67-68; pvt physician, Pediat Assocs, Boise, Idaho, 72-; med-legal consult & govt affairs consult, 72- Mil Serv: Lt Comdr, Pub Health Serv, 67-69, with serv as surgeon, Nat Insts of Health & the Off of the Surgeon Gen. Mem: Am Med Asn; Md Med & Chirurgical Soc; Ada Co & Idaho Med Socs. Honors & Awards: Diplomat, Nat Bd of Med Exam; White House Fel; Col Man of the Year. Relig: Protestant. Mailing Add: 5602 Randolph Dr Boise ID 83705

WEHMEYER, VICTOR WILLIAM (R)
Chmn, Warren Co Rep Comt, Mo
b Warrenton, Mo, Mar 16, 04; s Herman Henry Wehmeyer & Henrietta Koelling W; m 1932 to Louisa Caroline Fredericka Schnarre; c Roxana Louise (Mrs Schroeder). Educ: Grad Chillicothe Bus Col, Mo. Polit & Govt Pos: Pres, Mo Co Assessors Asn, 28-30 & 52-53; constable, Pinckney Twp, Warren Co; co assessor, Warren Co, 42-62 & 70-; co collector, 62-; chmn, Warren Co Rep Comt, currently; vpres, Mo State Co Collectors Asn, 63-64. Bus & Prof Pos: Farmer & Hereford cattle breeder, 40 years. Mem: Daggett Lodge 492 AF&AM, 39 years. Honors & Awards: Life Mem, Mo Co Assessors Asn. Relig: Methodist. Mailing Add: Rte 1 Box 99 Marthasville MO 63357

WEHRLE, MARTHA GAINES (D)
WVa State Deleg
b Charleston, WVa, Nov 30, 25; d Ludwell Ebersole Gaines & Betty Chilton G; m 1954 to Russell Schilling Wehrle; c Michael Herscher, Ebersole Gaines, Katherine Schilling, Philip Noyes & Martha Chilton. Educ: Vassar Col, AB, 48; Harvard Univ, MA, 50. Polit & Govt Pos: WVa State Deleg, 75- Relig: Episcopal. Mailing Add: 1440 Louden Heights Rd Charleston WV 25314

WEICHEL, JERRY (D)
Okla State Sen
Mailing Add: State Capitol Oklahoma City OK 73105

WEICK, DALE ELLWOOD, JR (D)
Nat Committeeman, SDak Young Dem
b Mitchell, SDak, July 16, 48; s Dale Elwood Weick & Frances Labesa W; single. Educ: Dak Wesleyan Univ, 66-67; Black Hills State Col, SDak, 69-73; Young Dem. Polit & Govt Pos: Pres, Aurora Co Young Dem, SDak, 65-66; Nat Committeeman, SDak Young Dem, 70- Mem: Am Contract Bridge League. Relig: Methodist. Mailing Add: Box 661 Keystone Rte Rapid City SD 57701

WEICKER, LOWELL PALMER, JR (R)
US Sen, Conn
b Paris, France, May 16, 31; s Lowell P Weicker & Mary Bickford W Paulsen; m 1953 to Marie Louise Godfrey; c Scot Bickford, Gray Godfrey & Brian Kennedy. Educ: Yale Univ, BA, 53; Univ Va, LLB, 58. Hon Degrees: ScD, Bridgeport Eng Inst; LLD, John Carroll Univ, 74, Univ Bridgeport, 74, Univ Maine at Portland, 75 & Univ Fairleigh Dickenson, 75. Polit & Govt Pos: Conn State Rep, 63-69; First Selectman, Greenwich, 64-68; US Rep, Conn, 91st Cong, 69-71; US Sen, Conn, 71-, mem, Com Comt, 75-, mem, Govt Opers, 75-; deleg, Rep Nat Conv, 72. Bus & Prof Pos: Lawyer. Mil Serv: 1st Lt, US Army Artil, 53-55; Capt, Res, 59-64. Relig: Episcopal. Legal Res: 445 Round Hill Rd Greenwich CT 06830 Mailing Add: 342 Russell Bldg Washington DC 20510

WEIDEL, KARL (R)
NJ State Assemblyman
Mailing Add: State House Trenton NJ 08625

WEIDEMEYER, C MAURICE (D)
b Hebbville, Md, Oct 22, 06; s Monterey F W Weidemeyer & Annie E Reiblich W; m to Carolyn Abbott. Educ: Johns Hopkins Univ, 24-25, Columbus Univ Sch Law, LLB, MPL, LLM, 36; Sigma Delta Kappa. Polit & Govt Pos: Rep cand for Cong, 44 & 48; comnr, Md Land Off, 51; trial magistrate, Annapolis, Md, 51-52; Md State Deleg, 63-66 & 71-74, chmn, Anne Arundel Co deleg, Md House Rep, 71-72; deleg, Md Const Conv, 67-68; alt deleg, Dem Nat Conv, 72. Bus & Prof Pos: Pres, Southern Munic Corp, 47-; gen counsel & dir, Monterey Co, Inc, 54-; pres, Glen Isle Estates, Inc, 55- Mil Serv: Entered as Pvt, Army, 43, released as Pfc, 45, after serv in Qm Corps & Transportation Corp. Mem: Moose; Shrine; Tall Cedars of Lebanon, Am Legion; Elks; Mason (Past Master). Relig: Protestant. Mailing Add: 236 Main St Annapolis MD 21401

WEIDENBAUM, MURRAY LEW (R)
b Bronx, NY, Feb 10, 27; s David Weidenbaum & Rose Warshaw W; m 1954 to Phyllis Green; c Susan, James & Laurie. Educ: City Col NY, BBA, 48; Columbia Univ, MA, 49; Princeton Univ, Banbury fel, 52-54, MPA, 54, PhD, 58; Omicron Delta Epsilon. Polit & Govt Pos: Jr Economist, NY State Dept Labor, 48-49; fiscal economist, US Bur of the Budget, Washington, DC, 49-57; mem, Bus Research Adv Coun, US Bur Labor Statist, 59-63; mem Research Adv Coun, Wash State Dept of Commerce & Econ Develop, 60-63; mem, panel of econ consult, US Arms Control & Disarmament Agency, Washington, DC, 61-62; mem, Task Force on Inventory Fluctuations & Econ Stabilization, Joint Econ Comt, 62; mem, President's Comt on the US Labor Fiftieth Anniversary Year, 62; exec secy, President's Comt on the Econ Impact of Defense & Disarmament, 64; mem, Independent Study Bd & chmn, Tech Adv Comt, US Dept Com, 67; Asst Secy of the Treas for Econ Policy, 69-71; mem, Rent Adv Bd, 71-73; mem research adv bd, Comt Econ Develop, 71- Bus & Prof Pos: Sr Opers Analyst, Gen Dynamics Corp, Ft Worth, Tex, 57-58; corporate economist, Boeing Co, Seattle, Wash, 58-63; sr economist, Stanford Research Inst, Menlo Park, Calif, 63-64; assoc prof econ, Wash Univ, 64-66, prof & chmn dept, 66-69, adj scholar Am Enterprise Inst Pub Policy Research, 71-; Mallinckrodt Distinguished Univ Prof econ, Wash Univ, 71-; Royer Vis prof, Univ Calif, Berkeley, 72; mem research coun, Ctr Strategic & Int Studies, Georgetown Univ, 72- Publ: The Modern Public Sector, Basic Books, Inc, 69; The timing of the economic impact of government spending, Nat Tax J, 3/59; Arms & the American economy, Am Econ Rev, 5/68. Mem: Nat Asn Bus Economists (charter mem); Am Econ Asn; Am Statist Asn; Nat Tax Asn; Regional Sci Asn; Conf of Bus Economists; Nat Economists' Club (bd dirs). Honors & Awards: Distinguished Writers Award, Georgetown Univ, 71. Relig: Jewish. Legal Res: 1531 Heirloom Court Creve Coeur MO 63141 Mailing Add: Dept of Economics Washington Univ St Louis MO 63130

WEIDNER, GEORGE E (D)
b Cincinnati, Ohio, Feb 17, 19; s George J Weidner & Mary Boehmann W; m 1944 to Betty Collett; c Barbara (Mrs Hedges), Jane (Mrs Ehrman), Virginia, Mary Ann, Tina & George, Jr. Educ: Xavier Downtown Col, 4 years; Kappa Sigma Mu. Polit & Govt Pos: Chmn, 65th Legis Dist Dem Party, 68-71; police judge, Summit Hills Heights, Ky, 61-66; pres, NKy Area Planning Coun, 65-70; vchmn, Kenton Co Libr Bd, 66-; mayor, Edgewood, 67-68; chmn, Kenton Co Dem Exec Comt, 68-73; deleg, Dem Nat Conv, 72. Bus & Prof Pos: Div sales mgr, W K Corps, 52-62; bd dirs, Bal-Cam, Inc, 62-64; sales mgr, O U S Co, 62-70; gen mgr, Latonia Sales & Supply Co, 71- Mem: Local, State & Nat Home Builders Asn; KofC (Past Grand Knight); Boys Clubs of Kenton Co (bd trustees). Relig: Catholic. Mailing Add: 3030 Brookwood Dr Edgewood KY 41017

WEIDNER, MARVIN DETWEILER (R)
Pa State Rep
b Telford, Pa, Aug 29, 11; s William R Weidner & Alverda H Detweiler W; m 1935 to Mary Elyonta Breece; c Kurt S. Educ: Pa State Univ Exten, real estate, 64-65, appraising, 65-66. Polit & Govt Pos: Tax collector, Borough of Telford, Pa, 46-63; mem, Bucks Co Rep Exec Comt, 61-; treas, Bucks Co, 64-66; Pa State Rep, 67- Bus & Prof Pos: Chief clerk, Norfolk & Western Rwy Co, 43-53; gen agt, Winston-Salem Southbound Rwy Co, 53-63. Mem: MacCalla Lodge 596, F&AM; Telford Vol Fire Co; Lions; CofC. Relig: Indian Creek United Church of Christ. Legal Res: 21 South Hamilton St Telford PA 18969 Mailing Add: Capitol Bldg Harrisburg PA 17120

WEIGAND, JOSEPH F, JR (D)
Conn State Rep
Mailing Add: 77 Dryden Dr Meriden CT 06450

WEIKER, BRYCE LAMAR (D)
Mem, Ohio State Dem Exec Comt
b Republic, Ohio, Jan 17, 21; s Ai Levi Weiker & Nona Cook W; m 1943 to Fern Eileen Vogt; c Judith (Mrs Watson) & Terry. Educ: Ohio State Univ, 2 years; Alpha Gamma Rho. Polit & Govt Pos: Mem bd of educ, Republic, Ohio, 50-62; mem, Seneca Co Dem Exec Comt, 58-, chmn, 66-; mem, State Bd of Educ, Ohio, 62-, pres, 72-; mem, Ohio State Dem Exec Comt, 69- Bus & Prof Pos: Self-employed farmer, 45-47; artificial breeding serviceman, Noba Inc, Tiffin, Ohio, 46-51; Holstein sire selector, 51-61, supvr servicemen, 61-65 & gen sales mgr, 65- Mil Serv: Entered as Pvt, Army, 42, released as T/Sgt, 45, after serv in Hq, Asian Theatre, 44-45; Theatre Decorations. Publ: Numerous articles for trade papers, 56- Mem: Dairy Shrine Club; Lions; Am Legion; Grange; Farm Bur. Honors & Awards: Hon State Farmer Degree, Ohio Future Farmers of Am. Relig: Protestant. Mailing Add: RR 2 Republic OH 44867

WEIL, GORDON LEE (D)
b Mineola, NY, Mar 12, 37; s Irving Weil & Sadye Gordon W; m 1962 to Roberta Meserve; c Anne Inger & Richard Clement. Educ: Bowdoin Col, AB, 58; Col of Europe, Bruges, Belg, dipl, 59; Columbia Univ, PhD, 61; Phi Beta Kappa; Alpha Rho Upsilon. Polit & Govt Pos: Exec asst to Sen George McGovern, 70-72; alt deleg, Dem Mid Term Conf, 74. Bus & Prof Pos: Dep official spokesman, European Econ Community, 63-66; independent researcher & writer, Brussels, Belg, 66-68; exec, Twentieth Century Fund, 68-70; correspondent-producer, WNET/13, New York, 73-; pres & publ, Political Intelligence, Inc, 74- Mil Serv: Entered as 2nd Lt, Army, 61, released as 1st Lt, 62, after serv in 52nd Artillery Bde (AD), NORAD, 61-62; Brigade Cert. Publ: Auth, Trade Policy in the 70's, Twentieth Century Fund, 69; co-auth, The Gold War: The Story of the World's Monetary Crisis, Holt, 70; auth, The Long Shot: George McGovern Runs for President, Norton, 73; plus others. Legal Res: Harpswell ME 04079 Mailing Add: RFD 1 South Harpswell ME 04079

WEIL, SIDNEY, JR (D)
Co-Chmn, Hamilton Co Dem Party, Ohio
b Cincinnati, Ohio, Sept 12, 26; s Sidney Weil & Ida Ackerman W; m 1950 to Dorothy Louise Coomer; c Rex & Bruce. Educ: Univ Cincinnati, 46-48; LLB, 50; Order of the Coif; Phi Delta

Phi. Polit & Govt Pos: Chmn, Hamilton Co Dem Exec Comt, 64-68; mem, Hamilton Co Bd Elec, 66-; deleg, Dem Nat Conv, 68; co-chmn, Hamilton Co Dem Party, 68- Bus & Prof Pos: Lectr, law, Univ Cincinnati Col Law, 51-67; partner, Nichols, Wood, Marx & Ginter, Attorneys, 60-67; partner, Beckman, Lavercombe, Fox & Weil, Attorneys, 67- Mil Serv: Entered as Pvt, Army, 44, released as S/Sgt, 46, after serv in 106th Inf Div, ETO, 45-46. Mem: Univ Cincinnati (bd trustees); Community Chest (trustee); Hamilton Co Welfare Adv Bd; Planned Parenthood Asn (dir). Legal Res: 8 Belsaw Pl Cincinnati OH 45220 Mailing Add: 1714 First National Bank Bldg Cincinnati OH 45202

WEILAND, DONALD P (D)
Pres, SDak Young Dem
b Bridgewater, SDak, Aug 20, 26; s Theodore G Weiland & Mathilda Leitheiser W; m 1950 to Thorine E Mellom; c Theodore L, Donald P, Jr, Pamela J, Richard P, Kevin J, Kenneth J & Michael D. Educ: Creighton Univ, BS, 49; St Louis Col of Mortuary Sci, Mo, 50. Polit & Govt Pos: Committeeman, Lake Co Dem Party, 54-58, secy-treas, 58-62, chmn, 62-72; mem adv comt, Small Bus Admin, SDak, 67-70; pres, SDak Young Dem, 75- Bus & Prof Pos: Funeral dir & pres, Weiland Funeral Chapel Inc, Idaho, 54-; coroner, Lake Co, 56-; mem bd, Off Econ Opportunity, 66-81, treas, 67-70. Mil Serv: Entered as HC 2/C, Navy, 44, released as Phm 2/C, 46, after serv in US Naval Hosp Corps, Seattle, Wash, 44-46. Mem: Nat Funeral Dirs Asn; Am Legion; KofC; 40 et 8; Elks; Madison Jr CofC. Honors & Awards: Distinguished Serv Award for community activity, 60. Relig: Catholic. Mailing Add: 1100 E Church Pierre SD 57501

WEILBURG, DONALD KARL (D)
Mem Exec Comt, Westerly Dem Town Comt, RI
b New York, NY, Apr 12, 36; s John Weilburg & Esther Edith Alexandre W; m 1960 to Sally Curwood; c Heidi Maria, Burkley Curwood & Lindsay Alexandre. Educ: Dartmouth Col, AB, 58; Univ Pa, DMD, 67, cert in orthodontics, 68; Omicron Kappa Upsilon; Delta Kappa Epsilon. Polit & Govt Pos: Deleg, Dem Nat Conv, 72, mem rules comt, 72; committeeman, RI Dem State Comt, 72-74; committeeman, Westerly Dem Town Comt, 74-, mem exec comt, 74- Mil Serv: Commissioned Officer Student Training & Extern Program, US Pub Health Serv, 66, Pub Health Serv Hosp Dent Unit, Pine Ridge Indian Reservation, SDak. Mem: Westerly Dist Dent Soc (pres, 74-); Watch Hill Fire Dept (adjutant, 72-); Am Dent Asn; Am Asn Orthodontists; Am Dem Action. Relig: Unitarian. Mailing Add: 26 Avondale Rd Westerly RI 20891

WEILER, PHILIP J (DFL)
Chmn, Polk Co Dem-Farmer-Labor Cent Comt, Minn
b St Paul, Minn, Feb 14, 31; s Fred N Weiler & Helen Julius W; m 1957 to Barbara Carol Brandt; c Cynthia, Pamela, Rose, Judith & Douglas. Educ: Univ Minn, Minneapolis, BS, 57; Fuller Theol Sem, 57-60; Louisville Presbyterian Theol Sem, BD, 61. Polit & Govt Pos: Chmn, Polk Co Dem-Farmer-Labor Cent Comt, Minn, 74- Bus & Prof Pos: Pastor, First Presbyterian Church, Caldwell, Ohio, 61-65, Two Harbors, Minn, 65-71 & Crookston, Minn, 71- Mil Serv: Entered as Pvt, Air Force, 50, released as S/Sgt, 54, after serv in 25th FIS, Korea, 52-53; Commendation Medal plus theatre ribbons. Mem: Lions Int. Relig: United Presbyterian. Mailing Add: RR 3 Crookston MN 56716

WEINBERG, LORETTA LEONE (D)
b New York, Feb 6, 35; d Murray Isaacs & Ray Hamilton I; m 1961 to Irwin Weinberg; c Daniel & Francine. Educ: Beverly Hills High Sch, 52; Univ Calif, Berkeley, AA, 54; Univ Calif, Los Angeles, BA, 56. Polit & Govt Pos: Dem Co Committeewoman, Teaneck, NJ, 65-71; aide to Congressman Henry Helstoski, East Rutherford, NJ, 68-73; assembly dist chmn, 13B, Bergen Co, NJ, 71-74; legis aide to Assemblyman Byron Baer, 71-72; deleg, Dem Nat Conv, 72; clerk, Bd Freeholders, Bergen Co, 75- Mem: Nat Coun Jewish Women; Open Party Dem Club (vchmn, 72-73); Bergen Co Dem Orgn (vchmn, 72-73). Relig: Jewish. Mailing Add: 866 Queen Anne Rd Teaneck NJ 07666

WEINBERG, MARGARAET KURTH (D)
Mem, Dem State Cent Comt Conn
b White Plains, NY, July 3, 28; d John William Kurth & Elizabeth Carter Wallace K; m 1950 to Peter Grove Weinberg; c Leslie Ann, Jill, Sharon, Donna, Jason Grove & Beverly. Educ: Oberlin Col, BA, 49; New Sch Social Research, New York, 49-50; Univ Bridgeport, 74-75. Polit & Govt Pos: Mem, Stamford Dem City Comt, Conn, 65-70; mem, Dem State Cent Comt Conn, 68-; alt deleg, Dem Nat Conv, 68, deleg, 72; deleg, Dem Nat Mid-Term Conf, 74; dir, Gov Grasso's Southern Off, Fairfield Co, 75- Mailing Add: 11 Big Oak Circle Stamford CT 06903

WEINBERG, NORMAN S (D)
Mass State Rep
Mailing Add: State Capitol Boston MA 02133

WEINBERGER, CASPAR WILLARD (R)
b San Francisco, Calif, Aug 18, 17; s Herman Weinberger & Cerise Carpenter Hampson W; m 1942 to Jane Dalton; c Arlin Cerise (Mrs Richard Paterak) & Caspar Willard, Jr. Educ: Harvard Col, AB, magna cum laude, 38, Harvard Law Sch, LLB, 41; Phi Beta Kappa. Polit & Govt Pos: Calif State Assemblyman, 21st Assembly Dist, 52-58; vchmn, Calif Rep State Cent Comt, 60-62, chmn, 62-64; chmn, Comn on Calif State Govt Orgn & Econ, 67-68; state dir of finance, Calif, 68-69; chmn, Fed Trade Comn, 69-70; dep dir, Off Mgt & Budget, 70-72, dir, 72-73; Counsellor to the President, 73; Secy, Dept Health, Educ & Welfare, 73-75; chmn, President's Comt on Ment Retardation. Bus & Prof Pos: Law clerk, US Circuit Judge William E Orr, Ninth Circuit Court of Appeals, San Francisco, 45-47; partner, Heller, Ehrman, White & McAuliffe, 47-69. Mil Serv: Entered as Pvt, Army, 41, released as Capt, 45, after serv in 41st Inf Div, Pac Theatre & on Intel Staff of Gen Douglas MacArthur; Bronze Star. Publ: Former staff book reviewer, San Francisco Chronicle & San Francisco Mag; moderator, Profile: Bay Area, pub affairs educ TV prog, KQED, San Francisco, 59-68; columnist, numerous Calif newspapers, 59-68. Mem: Am Bar Asn; State Bar of Calif; Yosemite Inst (bd dirs); Am Nat Red Cross (mem bd gov); John F Kennedy Ctr for Performing Arts (bd trustees). Relig: Episcopal; former vestryman. Legal Res: 2260 Forest View Ave Hillsborough CA 94010 Mailing Add: Dept of Health Educ & Welfare 330 Independence Ave SW Washington DC 20201

WEINER, BARBARA (D)
b Wilmington, Del, July 23, 48; d Eugene Joel Weiner & Toby Schultz W; single. Educ: C W Post Col, Long Island Univ, BA, 69, MBA, 70. Polit & Govt Pos: Comt chmn & campaign mgr, Wier for Attorney Gen, 73-74; deleg, Dem Mid-Term Conf, 74-; revenue sharing planner & grantsman, Social Serv Delivery, New Castle Co Dept Community Develop & Housing, 75- Bus & Prof Pos: Owner & mgr, Retail Clothing, Atlanta, Ga, 71-72; real estate salesman, Realty Assocs, Wilmington, Del, 73-74. Mem: Am Civil Liberties Union (bd dirs); Common Cause; Nat Orgn Women; Comt of 39; Women's Polit Caucus. Relig: Jewish. Mailing Add: 504 Sharpley Lane Bellewood Wilmington DE 19803

WEINER, HAROLD (R)
Chmn, New London Rep Town Comt, Conn
b Worcester, Mass, Feb 9, 25; s Albert Weiner & Molly Merims W; m 1947 to Zelda Beverly Wiener; c Celia Pearl (Mrs Rosenzweig), Barry J & Ronald Mark. Educ: Wentworth Inst, 42-43. Polit & Govt Pos: Mem, New London Rep Town Comt, Conn, 67-, chmn, 72-; chmn, New London Model City Policy Bd Personnel Comt, 70-72. Bus & Prof Pos: Pres, Barry's Cleaners, 48- & Barry's Uniform Rental Co, 67- Mil Serv: Entered as A/S, Naval Res, 41, released as Chief Machinist Mate, 50, after serv in US, China & Pac Theatres, 42-45. Legal Res: 56 Admiral Dr New London CT 06320 Mailing Add: 565 Colman St New London CT 06320

WEINER, ROBIN WENDY (D)
b New York, NY, Aug 9, 50; d Selig Weiner & Pauline Dichter W; single. Educ: Lehman Col, BA, 71; Brooklyn Law Sch, JD, 74; Moot Court Honor Soc; Student Coun; Int Students Club. Polit & Govt Pos: Vchmn, Bronx Borough President's Youth Adv Comt, 71-72; deleg, Dem Nat Conv, 72. Bus & Prof Pos: Claims examr, NY State Dept of Labor, 71; attorney, Law Dept, New York, currently. Mem: Am & NY State Bar Asns; Am Civil Liberties Union. Honors & Awards: Sociol Prize & Dept Honors, Lehman Col, 71; Order of Barristers. Relig: Jewish. Mailing Add: 2330 Holland Ave Bronx NY 10467

WEINKAM, LOIS ANNE (D)
Mem, Md State Dem Cent Comt
b Baltimore, Md, Feb 12, 42; d Edward Long Kaiserski & Lois Steinwedel K; m 1962 to Louis James Weinkam; c Louis James, Jr, Mark Robert & Jennifer Anne. Educ: Towson State Col, BS in Elem Educ, 65. Polit & Govt Pos: Mem, Md State Dem Cent Comt, 13th Legis Dist, 74-, mem affirmative action comt, 75-; mem Dem clubs comt & voters regist comt, Baltimore Co Dem Cent Comt, 75- Mem: Consol Dem Club (secy, 75-76); Ridgeway Dem Club; United Women's Dem Club; League of Women Voters Baltimore Co. Relig: Catholic. Mailing Add: 311 Orley Rd Catonsville MD 21228

WEINREB, ILENE SPACK (D)
Mayor, Hayward, Calif
b Kansas City, Mo, Nov 9, 31; d Henry Mitchell Spack & Mary Botwinik S; m 1951 to Marvin Seymour Weinreb, MD; c Rachel, Deborah & Judith. Educ: Univ Chicago, MA, 53; Univ Calif, Berkeley. Polit & Govt Pos: Asst dir housing, Off of Econ Opportunity, Eden Twp, Calif, 66-67; committeewoman, Calif State Dem Party, 67 & 68; city councilman, Hayward, Calif, 68-, vmayor, 72-74, mayor, 75-; comnr, Cent Coastal Comn, 73- Mem: League of Women Voters; Am Asn Univ Women; Alameda-Contra Costa Auxiliary Med Soc; B'nai B'rith. Relig: Jewish. Mailing Add: 30504 Prestwick Ave Hayward CA 94544

WEINSTEIN, CLEMENT (D)
b Brooklyn, NY, Apr 11, 26; s Samuel Weinstein & Sadie Furman W; m 1950 to Gertrude Rindsberg; c Roslyn Sue, Fred David, Lawrence Mark & Barbara Joan. Educ: Columbia Col, AB, 47; State Univ NY Downstate Med Ctr, MD, 50; Phi Beta Kappa; Alpha Omega Alpha. Polit & Govt Pos: Chmn, Queens-Nassau Chap Med Comt for Human Rights, NY, 65-69 & Queens Ad Hoc Comt for More Effective Health Care, 68; deleg, Dem Nat Conv, 72. Mil Serv: A/S, Navy, 44-45, serv in V-12 Prog; Sr Surgeon, US Pub Health Serv, 53- Mem: Health Professionals Against the War in Vietnam; Queens Co Med Soc; Med Soc NY; Am Col of Physicians. Relig: Jewish. Mailing Add: 69-18 179th St Flushing NY 11365

WEINSTEIN, JACK M (R)
State Committeeman, 27th Assembly Dist Co Rep Comt, NY
b New York, NY, June 29, 36; s Martin Weinstein & Helen Lax W; m 1964 to Doran Polikoff; c Loren Gay & Justin David. Educ: NY Univ, BS, 56, NY Univ Grad Sch Bus Admin, MBA, 58 & JD, 60; Phi Alpha Kappa; Pi Lambda Phi. Polit & Govt Pos: Rep nominee, New York Coun, 65, NY State Assembly, 66, US House of Rep, 68 & NY State Senate, 72; state committeeman, 27th Assembly Dist Co Rep Comt, 69-; law secy, Supreme Court, Queens Co, NY, 69- Bus & Prof Pos: Counsel, Black, Brownstein & Weinstein, Attorneys, 61-; counsel, Queensboro Soc Prev Cruelty to Children, 67-; counsel, Am Mensa Comt, 67-69. Mem: Asn Bar City New York (family court comt); Queens Co Bar Asn; Am & NY State Trial Lawyers Asns; United Cerebral Palsy of Queens (bd dirs); Mensa. Relig: Jewish. Legal Res: 90-50 Parsons Blvd Jamaica NY 11432 Mailing Add: 98 Cuttermill Rd Great Neck NY 11021

WEIR, ADELE N (D)
Mem, Mo State Dem Comt
b Fayette, Mo, Aug 17, 04; d Boyd G Norris & Mary Withers N; m Harold R Weir, wid; c Marilyn & Harold Ross, Jr. Educ: Cent Methodist Col, 3 years. Polit & Govt Pos: Pres, Howard Co Women's Dem Club, 50; app by Gov John Dalton to serv on Gasoline Tax Comt; mem, Equal Pay for Women Comt, 62; spec consult on ment retardation, 65; alt deleg, Dem Nat Conv; treas, Mo Fedn Womens Dem Clubs, 65, second vpres, 67, first vpres, 69, cand for pres, 71, pres, 73; chmn, Inter-Club Courtesy Comt & legis chmn; nominee from eighth dist for Cong Redistricting, 66; app & serv on comt for Dem State Conv, 68; app to State Adv Comt on Special Serv for Welfare, 70; mem, Mo State Dem Comt, 70- Bus & Prof Pos: Housewife. Mem: DAR (state off); Gavel Club; Literary Club (charter mem); Harriett Lawrence Garden Club (charter mem); Keller Mem Hosp Auxiliary (charter mem & pres). Relig: Christian Church. Mailing Add: 900 W Davis Fayette MO 65248

WEIR, JOHN H (R)
b Carrollton, Ohio, Mar 21, 22; s John B Weir & Odessa Mae Close W; m 1945 to Ruth E Morris; c Alan Lee, Beverly Ann, Tom S, Barbara & Vicki. Educ: Ohio State Univ, 39-41; Int Mgt Asn. Polit & Govt Pos: Trustee, Washington Twp, Ohio, 46-58; chmn, Carroll Co Agr Stabilization & Conserv Comt, 56; youth chmn, Carroll Co Citizens for Eisenhower & Nixon, 52 & 56; chmn, Carroll Co Rep Cent & Exec Comts, formerly. Bus & Prof Pos: Farmer, Carroll Co, Ohio. Mem: Cent Ohio Breeding Asn; Carroll Co Pomona Grange; Ohio Farm Bur Fedn (state trustee, 59-, state treas, 70-); Landmark, Inc; Ohio State Alumni Asn. Honors & Awards: Carroll Co Farmer of the Year, 57. Relig: Presbyterian. Mailing Add: Rte 1 Carrollton OH 44615

WEIR, JULIAN PAUL (R)
Chmn, SCent Dist Six Rep Party, Alaska
b Ballinger, Tex, Aug 15, 23; s Joseph Elmer Weir & Lola Agnes Ross W; m 1952 to Sumike Inoue; c Joseph Paul. Educ: NMex Col Agr & Mech Arts, 2 years. Polit & Govt Pos: Alt deleg, Rep Nat Conv, 68; Rep precinct committeeman, Glennallen, Alaska, 68-; chmn, SCent Dist Six Rep Party, 68- Bus & Prof Pos: Mechanic, Pan Am World Airways, San Francisco, Calif, 53-60; Lineman, Alaska Commun System, US Air Force, Glennallen, Alaska, 63-67; owner & operator, Glennallen Texaco Serv Sta, 67- Mil Serv: Entered as A/S, Naval Res, 41, released as Aircraft Mechanic 1/C, 45; T/Sgt, Marine Corps Res, 47-53, serv in VMR 152, Japan, Korea, Hawaii & Calif; Distinguished Flying Cross. Mem: White House Conf on Children & Youth; Am Legion (Past Comdr); Nat Rifleman Asn. Relig: Christian. Mailing Add: Mile 182 Glenn Hwy Box 275 Glennallen AK 99588

WEIR, MICHAEL H (D)
Md State Deleg
Mailing Add: 1707 Cape May Rd Essex MD 21221

WEIS, DARLENE MARIE (R)
Chmn, Fourth Cong Dist Rep Party, Wis
b New Ulm, Minn, May 1, 37; d Patrick Francis Thier & Elizabeth Konz T; c Timothy, Maureen, Colleen, Brian, Shannon, Terry, Kathleen & Richard. Educ: Marquette Univ, BS in Nursing, 59, MS in Nursing Educ, 64; Alpha Tau Delta; Delta Sigma Gamma. Polit & Govt Pos: Vchmn, Fourth Cong Dist Rep Party, Wis, 71-73, chmn, 73-; deleg, Rep Nat Conv, 72; civil serv comnr, City of Greenfield, 73-; mid-west regional vchmn, Rep Nat Heritage Coun, 73- Bus & Prof Pos: Asst clin prof, Marquette Univ, 72-73. Mem: Marquette Univ Nurses Alumni Asn (pres, 73-74); Milwaukee Co Med Auxiliary; Milwaukee Ment Health Asn; 4-H Proj Leader; Wis Nurses Asn. Relig: Roman Catholic. Mailing Add: 9537 W Brookside Dr Greenfield WI 53228

WEISBAUM, MARILYN (D)
Mem, Dem Nat Comt, Ill
Mailing Add: 1306 S Douglas Ave Springfield IL 62704

WEISE, ROBERT LEWIS (BOB) (R)
Nev State Assemblyman
b Los Angeles, Calif, May 23, 45; s Grant J Weise & Florence Brueger Aven W; m 1973 to Cathy Valenta. Educ: Univ Nev, 63-66, 70-71; Nat Hon Soc; Alpha Tau Omega. Polit & Govt Pos: Committeeman, Nev Rep State Cent Comt, 72-73; Nev State Assemblyman, 73- Bus & Prof Pos: Gen mgr, Ponderosa Land & Livestock Co Inc, 72-; pres, Lakeview Estates & Realty, 72-; pres, Lakeview Racquet Club, 74- Mil Serv: Entered as Pvt, Army, 66, released as S/Sgt, 69, after serv in Nat Security Agency; Army Commendation Medal. Mem: Rotary; Ducks Unlimited. Legal Res: Lightning W Ranch Washoe Valley Carson City NV 89701 Mailing Add: PO Box 1847 Carson City NV 89701

WEISENBERG, WEBB (R)
b Lead, SDak, Nov 9, 23; s Webb Weisenberg & Lottie Lewis W; m 1947 to Maxine Lorraine Smith; c Terry. Educ: Lead High Sch. Polit & Govt Pos: Chmn, Lawrence Co Rep Party, SDak, formerly. Bus & Prof Pos: Asst recreation dir, Homestake Mining Co, currently. Mil Serv: Entered as Pvt, Army, released as 1st Sgt, Inf, Italy, 45; Bronze Star; Italian Campaign Ribbons. Mem: Am Legion; VFW. Relig: Methodist. Mailing Add: 204 Anderson St Lead SD 57754

WEISENBERGER, LEONA AMELIA (D)
Secy, Huron Co Dem Cent & Exec Comt, Ohio
b Norwalk, Ohio, Aug 31, 12; d George Albert Hipp & Rose Kathryn Heitz H; wid; m 1971 to Gilbert F Weisenberger; c Jack, MarJean, Mary, Tom, Janet, Margaret & Michael. Educ: St Paul's Cath High Sch, Norwalk, Ohio, grad. Polit & Govt Pos: Dep dir, Huron Co Bd of Elec, Ohio, 52-75; acting secy, Huron Co Dem Cent & Exec Comt, 58-59, recording secy, 59-60 & 64-66, cent committeewoman, 60-69 & secy, 60-64 & 66-75; pres, Huron Co Fireland's Dem Women's Club, 64-67; trustee, Ohio Bd of Elec Off, 65-71; state chairlady radio publicity comt, Federated Dem Women of Ohio, 68-; secy-treas, Dem Citizens for Better Govt Comt, 69-; first vpres, Ohio Elec Off Asn, formerly, pres, 74- Mem: Fireland's Bus & Prof Women's Club, Norwalk; Huron Co Dem Women's Club; Fisher-Titus Mem Hosp Auxiliary; Willard Dem Women's Club; Federated Dem Women of Ohio. Relig: Catholic. Mailing Add: 258 E Main St Norwalk OH 44857

WEISENGOFF, PAUL EDMUND (D)
Md State Deleg
b Baltimore, Md, June 25, 32; s Joseph Michael Weisengoff & Julia Marie Mazieka W; m 1954 to Lorraine Frances Mattox; c Paul Francis, Robert Stephen & John Dennis. Educ: Univ Md, BS, 54; Morgan State Col, MS, 68. Polit & Govt Pos: Md State Deleg, 67- Bus & Prof Pos: Biol teacher, Baltimore Bd Educ, 54- Mil Serv: Entered as Pvt E-1, Army, 54, released as E-4, 56 after serv in 59th AAA Bn, Ft Bliss, Tex, 54-56. Mem: Phi Delta Kappa; Baltimore Teachers Union; KofC; Holy Name Soc. Honors & Awards: Hon Fire Chief, Baltimore City Fire Dept, 70. Relig: Roman Catholic. Mailing Add: 555 Brisbane Rd Baltimore MD 21229

WEISENSTINE, ERNEST MOORE (D)
Mem, Guernsey Co Dem Cent Comt, Ohio
b Cambridge, Ohio, Nov 30, 91; s McClelland Weisenstine & Mary S Burris W; m 1913 to Celia Margaret Stewart; c Savonna (Mrs Cox) & Ernest, Jr. Educ: Cambridge Bus Col, 1 year. Polit & Govt Pos: Mem, Guernsey Co Dem Cent Comt, Ohio, 40-; clerk, Cambridge Twp, Ohio, 60-; chmn, Ohio Dem State Cent Comt, 66-67. Bus & Prof Pos: Grocer, 13-21 & 46-57; salesman, 21-46. Mem: Odd Fellows. Honors & Awards: Grand Decoration of Chivalry. Relig: Protestant. Mailing Add: 1932 Wheeling Ave Cambridge OH 43725

WEISGERBER, WILLIAM DENNY (R)
Mem, Calif Rep State Cent Comt
b Bend, Ore, May 5, 30; s Sherman Nash Weisgerber & Olive Edith Denny W; m 1949 to Marianne Tillery; c Pamela Kay & William Denny, Jr. Educ: Boise Jr Col, 48-49 & 53-54; San Jose State Col, 54-55; Univ Calif, Los Angeles, 64; Life Underwriters Training Course Grad Courses I, II & III, 68-69. Polit & Govt Pos: Councilman, Milpitas, Calif, 61 & 66-; inter-city coun rep, Santa Clara Co, Calif, 61-; rep, Asn Bay Area Govt, 61-; chmn, Mayors Comt, Santa Clara Co, 62-63; mem, Milpitas Co Water Bd, 62-64; mayor, Milpitas, Calif, 62-66; mem, Santa Clara Transportation Comt, 63-, & chmn, 68-; mem, Local Agency Formation Comn, 64- & chmn, 68-; assoc mem, Calif Rep State Cent Comt, 66-68, mem, 68-; vchmn, Santa Clara Planning Policy Comt, 68 & chmn, 69-; mem, League of Calif Cities Annexation Comt, 69-; chmn, Santa Clara Co Sports Arena Conv Comt, 69- Bus & Prof Pos: Cert Prosthodontist & orthodontist, Am Bd for Certification, 61-; ins agent, State Farm Ins Co, 65- Mil Serv: Entered as Pvt, Marine Corps, 49, released as S/Sgt, 53, after serv as Platoon Sgt, Seventh Marines, First Marine Div, Korean Theatre, 53; Navy Cross; Purple Heart; Presidential Unit, Navy Unit & Korean Presidential Unit Citations; Korean, Nat Defense & UN Serv Medals. Mem: Elks; VFW; Rotary; Toastmasters Club; Businessman's Asn, Milpitas, Calif. Honors & Awards: Named Area & Dist Speech Winner, 68. Relig: Presbyterian. Mailing Add: 195 Casper St Milpitas CA 95035

WEISS, ABRAHAM
Asst Secy Policy, Eval & Research, Dept Agr
Mailing Add: Dept of Agr Washington DC 20250

WEISS, ARNOLD M (D)
Committeeman, NY State Dem Comt
b New York, NY, Oct 31, 33; s Morris Weiss & Yetta Hecht W; m 1973 to Bonnie A Lobel; c Nicholas Lobel. Educ: Brooklyn Col, BA, 54; Harvard Law Sch, LLB, 57; Epsilon Phi Alpha. Polit & Govt Pos: Committeeman, NY State Dem Comt, 66-75; chmn, NY New Dem Coalition, 72-; vchmn, Nat New Dem Coalition, 72-; mem charter comn, Dem Nat Comt, 72-74; mem affirmative action comt, NY State Dem Party, 74-; alt deleg, Dem Nat Mid-Term Conf, 74. Mil Serv: Entered as Pvt, Army, 57, released as Pfc, 58. Legal Res: 91 Central Park W New York NY 10004 Mailing Add: 11 Broadway New York NY 10004

WEISS, EUGENE (D)
VChmn, Md State Dem Cent Comt
b Hillsdale, NJ, Dec 1, 28; s Herman Weiss & Adele Gerstel W; m 1953 to Mary Elizabeth Harrington; c Margaret (Mrs Hutchens). Educ: Univ Md, College Park, BA, 62; Univ Minn Grad Sch, 63 & 65. Polit & Govt Pos: Pres, Columbia Dem Club, Md, 70-72 & 74-75; first vchmn, New Dem Coalition of Md, 73-75; mem & secy, Howard Co Dem Cent Comt, 74-; vchmn, Md State Dem Cent Comt, 74- Mil Serv: Entered as Pvt, Air Force, 47, retired as M/Sgt, 68, after serv in Air Defense, Strategic Air, Tactical Air Commands, 5th Air Force, Continental Air Defense & NAm Air Defense Commands, Pac Air Force; 5 Good Conduct Medals; Nat Defense Serv Medal, Occup, Ger. Publ: Auth, Maryland's new primary election law, Columbia Flier, 5/75. Mem: Am Civil Liberties Union (bd dirs, Howard Co, 73-); Common Cause; Smithsonian Assocs; Howard Co Hist Soc. Mailing Add: 10391 May Wind Ct Columbia MD 21044

WEISS, JEANETTE SHORT (R)
b Alberta, Va, Apr 9, 28; d James Thomas Short, Sr & Lozell Page S; m 1953 to Leven Comer Weiss. Educ: St Paul's Col, 45; Va Union Univ, 46-47. Polit & Govt Pos: Vol & staff Romney For Gov, 62, staff, 64; mem adv comt, Rep Nat Comt, 63; comnr, Wayne Co Jury Comn, 63-69; secy, Nat Negro Rep Assembly, 64; deleg, State & Nat Rep Women's Fedn, 64-72; deleg, Co & State Conv, 64-73; precinct deleg, Wayne Co, Mich, 65-73; co-chmn, Women's Activities, Rockefeller for President, 68; spec groups coordr, Mich for Milliken, 70; alt deleg, Rep Nat Conv, 72. Bus & Prof Pos: Pres, JSW & Assocs, 73. Mem: Mich Cancer Found (trustee, 70-); Myasthenia Gravis Asn (trustee, 63-); Sickle Cell Anemia Asn (trustee, 72-); NAACP. Honors & Awards: Mentioned in Norman Mailer's St George & The godfather, 72. Relig: Baptist. Mailing Add: 4676 W Outer Dr Detroit MI 48235

WEISSMAN, BENJAMIN MURRY (D)
b New York, NY, Aug 3, 17; s Abraham Weissman & Sarah Solomon W; m 1939 to Rae Blum; c Evelyn (Mrs John Marques), Anne (Mrs Robert Geiger) & Joseph. Educ: City Col New York, BS, 36; City Univ New York, MA, 64; Columbia Univ, PhD, 68. Polit & Govt Pos: Alt deleg, Dem Nat Conv, 72. Bus & Prof Pos: Lectr polit sci, City Col New York, 64-68; asst prof polit sci, Rutgers Univ, 68-74, assoc prof polit sci, 74-, chmn dept, Newark. Mil Serv: Entered as Pvt, Army Air Corps, 42, released as Capt, 46, after serv in AACS, Pac, 44-46; Battle Star, Ryukyus Campaign Ribbon. Publ: Herbert Hoover's treaty with Soviet Russia: August 20, 1921, Slavic Rev, 6/69; The aftereffects of the American relief mission to Soviet Russia, Russian Rev, 10/70; Herbert Hoover & Famine Relief to Soviet Russia, Hoover Inst Press, 74. Mem: Am Polit Sci Asn; Am Asn for Advan Slavic Studies; Am Acad Polit Sci; Am Asn Univ Prof. Mailing Add: 265 Briarcliffe Rd Teaneck NJ 07666

WELBORN, JOHN ALVA (R)
Mich State Sen
b Kalamazoo, Mich; s Harry Sterling Welborn & Elizabeth Dougherty W; m 1952 to Dorothy Beatrice Yeomans; c Kayle Jane, Kami Ellen & John Robert. Educ: Richland High Sch. Polit & Govt Pos: Fireman, Cooper Twp Fire Dept, Mich, 50-67; mem, Cooper Twp Rep Comt, 51-56; precinct deleg, Rep Party, several terms; deleg, Mich Rep State Conv, 12 times; mem, Gull Lake Sch Bd, 65-67; twp supvr, Cooper Twp, 67-; Mich State Sen, 75- Bus & Prof Pos: Dairy farmer, 51-70. Mil Serv: Navy, 49-51. Legal Res: 6304 N Riverview Dr Kalamazoo MI 49001 Mailing Add: 1590 West D Ave Kalamazoo MI 49001

WELCH, ADA MAE (D)
Chmn, Garrett Co Dem Cent Comt, Md
b Deer Park, Md, Oct 17, 36; d William Hagens Welch & May Ray W; single. Educ: Southern Garrett Co High Sch, Oakland, Md, grad, 54. Polit & Govt Pos: Chmn, Garrett Co Dem Cent Comt, Md, 74-; mem, Md State Dem Cent Comt, currently. Bus & Prof Pos: Mgr, Jan Florists, 64- Mem: Bus & Prof Women's Club; Oakland Civic Club. Relig: Catholic. Mailing Add: 212 Lothian St Mt Lake Park MD 21550

WELCH, BETTE B (R)
b Bethel, Vt, Apr 16, 20; d Henry H Batease & Murdena J Smith B; m 1941 to William H Welch, Jr; c Martha W (Mrs Colin P Rees) & Nancy A. Polit & Govt Pos: Admin asst, US Rep Charles A Mosher, Ohio, 61-73, legis asst, 73- Relig: Episcopal. Mailing Add: 2718 Bryan Place Alexandria VA 22302

WELCH, JERRY F (D)
Mo State Rep
b Ironton, Mo, Oct 23, 44; s Avis Jaycox; m 1967 to Susan Elizabeth Wehmer; c Jeffrey Edward. Educ: Univ Mo-St Louis, BS in educ, 67. Polit & Govt Pos: Mo State Rep, 54th Dist, 75- Bus & Prof Pos: Teacher, Francis Howell Sch Dist, Mo, 67-68 & Hazelwood Sch Dist, Mo, 68-69; salesman, Addressograph-Multigraph Corp, 69-70; broker, Clayton Commodity Serv, 70-72, Pacific Trading Co, 72-73 & Heinold Commodities, 74- Mem: St Louis Merchant's Exchange; Florissant CofC; Univ Mo-St Louis Alumni Asn; Mo State Dem Party; Spanish Lake Regular Dem Club. Relig: Baptist. Mailing Add: Rte 2 Box 479A Florissant MO 63034

WELCH, LOUIE (D)
b Lockney, Tex, Dec 9, 18; s Gilford E Welch & Nora Shackelford W; m 1940 to Ida Faye Cure; c Guy Lynn, Gary Dale, Louis Gilford, Shannon Austin & Tina Joy; five grandchildren. Educ: Abilene Christian Col, BA, magna cum laude, 40. Polit & Govt Pos: Councilman-at-lg, Houston City Coun, Tex, 50-52, 56-62, pres, 58-59; mem, Houston Legis Comt, 56-; vpres, Tex Munic League, 57-58, pres, 59-60; mayor, Houston, Tex, formerly, mayor emer, currently; deleg, Dem Nat Conv, 68; vpres, Nat League Cities, 71-; vpres, US Conf Mayors, 71- Bus & Prof Pos: Mem bd of dirs, Abilene Christian Col; pres, Louie Welch & Co, Inc, 62-63. Mem: Tex Mayors & Councilmens Asns (pres); Tex Construction Coun; Harris Co Mayor's & Councilmen's Asn (pres). Honors & Awards: Named Outstanding Abilene Christian Col Alumnus, 66. Relig: Church of Christ; Adult Bible Class Teacher, Garden Oaks Church of Christ. Mailing Add: 1100 Milan Houston TX 77002

WELCH, PATRICK T (D)
Md State Deleg
Mailing Add: 38 S Dundalk Ave Baltimore MD 21222

WELCH, RODNEY RAY (R)
Mem, Rep State Cent Comt Calif
b Phillipston, Mass, Jan 9, 98; s Albert Franklin Welch & Mary Bosworth W; m Ruth Zan Crandall; c June (Mrs Arnold Doimer), Doris, Gilbert, Rodney Ray, Jr, Dale & Alan. Educ: Phillipston Pub Sch number 6, 4 years; Riverbend Pub Sch, 4 years. Polit & Govt Pos: Mem, Rep State Cent Comt, Calif, 68- Bus & Prof Pos: Apprentice, Union Twist Drill Co, Athol, Mass, 13-17; toolmaker, Remington Arms, Bridgeport, Conn, 17-18; Goodard & Goodard, Detroit, Mich, 19-20; Gorham Tool Co, 21-25; supt, Morse Counterfore & Tool Co, 25-27; founder, Welch Industs, 27 & pres, currently; pres, Welch Corp & Welch's Mt Fantisy, 72- Mem: John Birch Soc; Liberty Lobby; Idyllwild CofC (dir). Honors & Awards: Army 'E' Flag for outstanding performance. Relig: Protestant. Legal Res: One Alandale Pl Alandale CA 92349 Mailing Add: PO Box 35 Idyllwild CA 92349

WELCOME, VERDA FREEMAN (D)
Md State Sen
b Lake Lure, NC; d John Nuborn Freeman & Docia Proctor Freeman; m 1935 to Henry Cecil Welcome; c Mary Sue. Educ: Morgan State Col, BS, 39; NY Univ, MA, 43. Hon Degrees: LLD, Howard Univ, 68; DSS, Univ Md, 70. Polit & Govt Pos: Md State Deleg, 59-62; Md State Sen, 63-, mem, Legis Coun, Md Gen Assembly, 71, mem, Senate Finance Comt of the Legis, 71, mem, Exec Nominating Comt of the Legis, 71. Mem: Delta Sigma Theta; NAACP; Am for Dem Action; Int League for Peace & Freedom; Md Chap, UN. Honors & Awards: Eighth Annual Emma V Kelly Achievement Award, Daughters of the Int Order of World Elks; Plaque, Achievement Award, Beta Sigma Tau Alumni Chap; Trophy, Fourth Annual Md Debutante Ball; Citation for dedicated serv, Md Fedn Blind, 70; Cert Appreciation, United Negro Col Fund, 70. Relig: Presbyterian. Mailing Add: 2101 Liberty Heights Ave Baltimore MD 21217

WELDEN, JACQUES ROGER (R)
Chmn, Contra Costra Co Rep Cent Comt, Calif
b Evanston, Ill, Sept 6, 27; s George Claypool Welden & Eleanor Brown W; m 1950 to Jacquelen Rae Thompson; c Kathryn Jean, David Roger, Bruce Arthur & Barbara Denise. Educ: Univ Utah; Univ Calif, Berkeley; San Francisco Law Sch; Pi Kappa Alpha; Phi Alpha Delta. Polit & Govt Pos: Mem, Contra Costra Co Rep Cent Comt, Calif, 60-, chmn, 64-; mem, Rep Cong Adv Comt, 64-66; chmn, Legis Co Comnr Asn of Calif, 65-66; chmn, Bay Area Co Comn, 66; app State Inheritance Tax Appraiser, 67. Bus & Prof Pos: Sr Partner, Corbett & Welden, Attorneys, 67- Mil Serv: Entered as Pvt, Army, 44, released as Cpl, 46; Good Conduct Medal; Am Theater Ribbon. Mem: Lawyer's Club of San Francisco (bd dir, 65-, pres, 69 & 70); Sports Youth Coun, Jr CofC; Elks Lodge 3, San Francisco; Lions; San Francisco Jr CofC; Rep League. Honors & Awards: Played lead in a number of plays & wrote skits for little theater groups. Relig: United Church of Christ; mem endowment comt, 69. Mailing Add: 38 Avon Rd Kensington CA 94707

WELDEN, RICHARD W (R)
Iowa State Rep
Mailing Add: 612 Forest Dr Iowa Falls IA 50126

WELDEN, WILLIAM EDGAR (R)
Chmn, Rep Party Ala
b Montgomery, Ala, Jan 23, 43; s Charles Victor Welden, Sr & Dorothy Williams W; m 1965 to Louise Canterbury Cleve; c William Edgar, Jr & Ann Canterbury. Educ: Univ Ala, BS, 65; Alpha Kappa Psi; Kappa Alpha; Druids; Circle K Int. Polit & Govt Pos: Exec dir, Rep Party Ala, 69-71, chmn, 75-; aide to US Rep John Buchanan, Ala, 72-75; mem, Rep Nat Comt, 75- Bus & Prof Pos: Owner, Com-Pak Food Marts, Ala, 65-68. Mil Serv: Sgt, Air Nat Guard, 65-71. Relig: Presbyterian. Mailing Add: 4624 Pine Mountain Rd Birmingham AL 35213

WELDON, RICHARD BANCROFT, SR (R)
Chmn, Colonial Region Rep Comt, Del
b Chester, Pa, Aug 11, 32; s Stephen W Weldon & Catherine Jones W; m 1955 to Fay Brown; c Kerry, Richard, Jr, Timothy & Craig. Educ: Keystone Bus Sch, 53; Univ Del, 56-61. Polit & Govt Pos: Mem, Solid Waste Comt, Del, 70-72; chmn, Rep Representative Dist, 70-73 & Colonial Region Rep Comt, Del, 74- Bus & Prof Pos: Analyst, Getty Oil Co, 56- Mil Serv: Entered as Recruit, Army, 49, released as S/Sgt, 52. Mem: Civic Asn (pres); Fire Co. Relig: Episcopal. Mailing Add: Box 120 Red Lion Newcastle DE 19720

WELDON, WILLIAM KIMBERLY (R)
Mem Exec Comt, Shelby Co Rep Party, Tenn
b Tulsa, Okla, June 10, 21; s Henry Cole Weldon & Alice Cecilia Cummings W; m 1944 to Ann Rudd James; c Karen Ann, William Kimberly, Jr & Elizabeth James. Educ: Univ Okla, 40-42; Southern Law Univ, LLB, 48; Theta Kappa Phi; Ruf Neks; Delta Chi Delta. Polit & Govt Pos: Pres, East Memphis Rep Club, Tenn, 62; mem steering comt, Shelby Co Rep Party, 62-68, mem exec comt, 62-; Tenn State Rep, 67-74, mem, Legis Coun Tenn House Rep, 69-74. Bus & Prof Pos: Partner, Adams, James & Weldon, Attorneys, Memphis, Tenn, 54- Mil Serv: Entered as Aviation Cadet, Navy, 42, served as fighter pilot, Air-Group 4, Pac Theater, World War II & as air intel officer, Korea; Lt Comdr, Naval Res; Air Medal, twice; Navy Unit Citation; Presidential Unit Citation, four times; Korean Presidential Unit Citation. Mem: KofC; Naval Res Asn; Mil Order of World Wars; VFW; Navy League. Relig: Catholic. Mailing Add: 2500 Clark Tower Memphis TN 38137

WELLS, BARBARA MARY (R)
Nat Dir, Teen Age Rep
b Davenport, Iowa, July 14, 39; d Frank W Wells & Ruth Birdsall W; single. Educ: Univ Calif, Los Angeles, BS; pres, Trolls & Prytanean Club; Class Coun; Pi Beta Phi. Polit & Govt Pos: Pres, Univ Calif, Los Angeles Young Rep; former exec secy, Donald C Bruce & Congressman Don H Clausen; secy, Congressman John Ashbrook, formerly; nat committeewoman, DC Young Rep, 62-65; deleg, Nat Young Rep Conv, 63, 65, 67 & 69; exec comt, Annual Young Rep Nat Leadership Training Sch, 64-69; nat dir, TAR, 64- Mem: Red Cross Nurses Aide, Walter Reed Army Med Ctr; Dirksen Forum (bd dirs); Pi Beta Phi Alumnae Club. Relig: Episcopal. Legal Res: 5500 Prospect Place Apt 2303 Washington DC 20015 Mailing Add: 359 Nat Press Bldg Washington DC 20004

WELLS, DWIGHT ALLEN (D)
Ky State Rep
b Richmond, Ky, Oct 11, 25; s Boyd Dudley Wells & Bertha Asbill W; m 1948 to Betty Pigg; c Terry Lynn, David Dudley & Charles Snowden. Educ: Madison Cent High Sch. Polit & Govt Pos: Mem, Madison Co Bd Educ, 52-67; Ky State Rep, 68- Mil Serv: Entered as A/S, Navy, 44, released as Signalman 2/C, 46, after serv in Atlantic & Pac Theatres. Relig: Protestant. Mailing Add: RR 7 Richmond KY 40475

WELLS, GUY JACKSON (R)
Mem Exec Comt, RI State Rep Cent Comt
b Providence, RI, July 3 30; s Guy William Wells & Ruth Emory W; m 1958 to Beverly Jansen; c Guy William, III, Tracy Elizabeth, Thomas Jansen & Jennifer Jackson. Educ: Princeton Univ, AB, 52; Boston Univ Law Sch, LLB, 57; Court Club. Polit & Govt Pos: Mem at lg, RI State Rep Cent Comt, 60-, mem exec comt, 66-; chmn, RI Nixon Campaign, 68; alt deleg, Rep Nat Conv, 68 & 72, mem platform comt, 72; civilian aide to Secy of Army for State RI, 69- Bus & Prof Pos: Partner, Gunning, La Fazia, Guys & Selya, 58- Mil Serv: Entered as 2nd Lt, Army, 52, released as 1st Lt, 54, after serv in Artil, Korea; Maj, Army Res; Army Commendation Ribbon; UN Medal; Korean Serv Medal; Nat Defense Ribbon; Army Res Medal. Mem: RI & Am Bar Asns. Honors & Awards: RI Bar Asn Award of Merit, 67. Relig: Protestant. Mailing Add: 243 Promenade Ave Warwick RI 02886

WELLS, HAWEY A, JR (D)
WVa State Deleg
Mailing Add: State Capitol Charleston WV 25305

WELLS, J C (D)
Treas, Warren Co Dem Cent Comt, Mo
b Wellsville, Mo, May 2, 09; s John Hayden Wells & Rebbeca Rainey W; m 1953 to Agnes Marie Herbel; c Sue (Mrs Erwin), George, Bruce, Sherri & Nancy. Educ: Montgomery Co Schs, 10 years. Polit & Govt Pos: Chmn, Warren Co Dem Cent Comt, formerly, treas, currently; treas, Warren Co Dem Club. Bus & Prof Pos: Truck driver, Burggrabe Truck Line, 51-71. Mil Serv: Bus driver, TNT plant, 42-45. Mem: Warren Co Dem Club; Local 600 Union. Honors & Awards: Retirement award for 20 years serv, watch & savings bond, Burggrabe Truck Line, 71. Relig: Methodist. Mailing Add: 401 McKinley Warrenton MO 63383

WELLS, JACQUELYN QUINN (R)
Pres, Fla Fedn Rep Women
b Spokane, Wash, Oct 27, 25; d Frank Quinn & Zola Ohler Q; m 1947 to Leonard Rudolph Wells, MD; c Rudy Charles, Martha Jane & James Patrick. Educ: Univ Wash, 43-45; Swedish Hosp, Seattle, grad, 47. Polit & Govt Pos: Pres, Cocoa Beach Women's Rep Club, Fla, 66-68; dist chmn, Brevard Co Rep Party, 69-71; treas, Fla Fedn Rep Women, 71-73, pres, 73- Bus & Prof Pos: Off mgr, L R Wells, MD, Cocoa Beach, 60- Mem: Eastern Star. Relig: Lutheran. Mailing Add: 473 Blakey Blvd Cocoa Beach FL 32931

WELLS, JAMES DALE (D)
Iowa State Rep
b Marathon, Iowa, Aug 7, 28; s Willard Wallace Wells & Florence Peterson W; m 1950 to Shirley Ann Clare; c Linda Sue, Cheryl Kay & Nancy Ann. Educ: Marathon Consolidated Sch, Iowa, grad. Polit & Govt Pos: Chmn, Comt on Polit Educ, 66-69; Iowa State Rep, 69- Mil Serv: Entered as Sgt 1/C, Army Res, served in 328th Combat Engrs, 6 years. Mem: Men's Club; Retail Wholesale Dept Store Union (recording secy, 9 years). Relig: United Methodist. Legal Res: 1229 20th St SW Cedar Rapids IA 52404 Mailing Add: State Capitol Des Moines IA 50319

WELLS, JOHN MARVIN (R)
Councilman-at-Lg, Charleston, WVa
b Charleston, WVa, Apr 19, 18; s John Calvin Wells & Florence Friedman W; m 1936 to Nancy Elizabeth Kyle; c Nancy (Mrs Daniel F Johnson), John M, Jr, Sally Michael & Robert Michael. Educ: Charleston High Sch, WVa, dipl, 37. Polit & Govt Pos: Ward councilman, Charleston, WVa, 59-, chmn finance comt, City Coun, 63-67, majority leader, 67-68, councilman-at-lg, 67-; vchmn Charleston Dist, Rep Gubernatorial Primary, spring 68; vchmn, Rep State Exec Comt, summer 68 & currently; city treas, Charleston, 71- Bus & Prof Pos: Pres, R H Kyle Furniture Co, Charleston, 61- Mil Serv: Entered as Pvt, Army, 45, released as Cpl, 46, after serv in Engr Corps. Mem: Elks; Mason; Shrine; Capital Park Authority; Charleston Civic Center Bd. Honors & Awards: Man of the Year Award, Nat Wholesale Furniture Asn. Relig: Presbyterian. Legal Res: 888 Chester Rd Charleston WV 25302 Mailing Add: 1352 Hansford St Charleston WV 25301

WELLS, ROY ESTELLE (D)
Colo State Rep
b River Portal, Colo, July 18, 09; s Ora Clinton Wells & Lillie Dale Dowell W; m 1935 to Elnora Joseinne Bauer; c Sidney Bill, Monte Pat (Mrs Michael Mohr) & Gwenda Lou (Mrs Paul Augustine). Educ: Attended high sch & bus col. Polit & Govt Pos: Mem bd dirs, Cortez CofC; mem recreation bd; chmn, retail trades; mem sanit bd, Cortez, Colo, 66-70; city councilman, 66-70; Colo State Rep, 70- Bus & Prof Pos: Mgr & partner of grocery chain, 26 years; co chmn, Ment Retarded Comt; chmn, Red Cross. Mil Serv: Entered as A/S, Navy, 44, released as 1st Class Petty Officer, 46, after serv in Pac Theatre, 44-46. Mem: Elks; Am Legion; Rotary. Relig: Presbyterian. Legal Res: 219 Edith Cortez CO 81321 Mailing Add: State Capitol Denver CO 80203

WELLS, SAMUEL JAY (D)
b Sand Springs, Okla, Feb 3, 24; s Robert L Wells & Ada Blanche W; m 1944 to Mary Elizabeth Rice; c Samuel Jay, Jr, Robert V & Duncan. Educ: Univ Mo, BA, 56, JD; Tau Kappa

Epsilon. Polit & Govt Pos: Attorney, Wyandotte Co, Kans, 56-60; spec attorney, Kans Attorney Gen, 58-59; attorney, Kans Dept of Revenue, currently; deleg, Dem Nat Mid-Term Conf, 74; cand, US Rep, 74. Bus & Prof Pos: Secy, Pierce Industs, Kansas City & St Louis, 65- & Gibbs Auto Moulding, Henderson, Ky, 65-; partner, Mission Groves, Inc, Ft Pierce, Fla, 66-; dir, Rice Invest, Inc, Kansas City, 68-; pres, Westborough Develop Co, 72- Mil Serv: W/O, Air Force, 44-45, serv in SPac Theatre. Mem: Delta Theta Phi; Mason (32 degree), Shrine. Legal Res: 3601 Johnson Dr Shawnee Mission KS 66205 Mailing Add: 320 Brotherhood Bldg Kansas City KS 66101

WELLS, WHITCOMB (R)
NH State Rep
b Malden, Mass, Mar 10, 23; s Edward P Wells & Marion E Clark W; m 1957 to Veryl Perkins; c Meryl, Gail & Bradford. Educ: Dartmouth Col, BA; Theta Delta Chi; Casque & Gauntlet. Polit & Govt Pos: Selectman, Swanzey, NH, 62-64; NH State Rep, 75- Bus & Prof Pos: Dir, New Eng Fuel Inst, 56-; pres, Gtr Keene CofC, 60-61 & Better Home Heat Coun, NH, 67-69, dir, currently. Mil Serv: Entered as Aviation Cadet, Air Force, 43, released as 2nd Lt, 45, after serv in Eastern Training Command. Mem: Bektash Temple Shrine; Elks; New Eng Fuel Inst (dir). Relig: Protestant. Legal Res: Sawyers Crossing Rd Swanzey Ctr NH 03431 Mailing Add: Box 88 RFD 1 Keene NH 03431

WELSH, MATTHEW EMPSON (D)
b Detroit, Mich, Sept 15, 12; s Matthew William Welsh & Inez Empson W; m 1937 to Mary Virginia Homann; c Janet & Kathryn. Educ: Univ Pa, BS in Econ, 34; Ind Univ Law Sch, 35 & 36; Univ Chicago, JD, 37; Phi Delta Phi; Delta Kappa Epsilon; managing ed, Daily Pennsylvanian. Hon Degrees: LLD, Ind Univ, St Joseph's Col, Franklin Col, Ind State Univ, Vincennes Univ & Tri-State Col. Polit & Govt Pos: Ind State Rep, 41-44; Ind State Sen, 55-60, floor leader, 57 & 59; US Attorney, Southern Dist Ind, 50-52; Gov, Ind, 61-65; mem exec comt, Nat Gov Conf, 63; chmn, Interstate Oil Compact Comn, 63; Dem Nat Committeeman, Ind, 64 & 65; chmn, US Sect, Int Joint Comn, US & Can, 66-70; co-chmn, Ind Const Rev Comn, 67-71; Dem Nominee for Gov, Ind, 72. Bus & Prof Pos: Attorney-at-law, Vincennes, Ind, 37-61; partner, Bingham, Summers, Welsh & Spilman, 65-; bd trustees, Vincennes Univ; bd trustees, Christian Theol Sem, Indianapolis; trustee, John A Hartford Found; mem bd mgrs, Lincoln Nat Variable Annuity Fund A & B; mem bd dir, Lincoln Nat Balanced Fund & Lincoln Nat Capital Fund of Lincoln Nat Corp, Ft Wayne; mem bd dir, Security Bank & Trust Co, Vincennes, Morgan Co Bank & Trust Co, Eminence & Universal Scientific Co, Vincennes. Mil Serv: Entered as Lt(jg), Navy, 43, released as Lt, 46, after serv in Supply Corps. Mem: Kiwanis; Elks; Indianapolis Athletic Club; Columbia Club; Nat Lawyers Club. Relig: Disciples of Christ. Legal Res: 4546 N Park Ave Indianapolis IN 46205 Mailing Add: 2700 Indiana Tower Indianapolis IN 46204

WELSH, RAYMOND J, JR (D)
Ill State Sen
Mailing Add: 911 N Oak Park Ave Oak Park IL 60302

WELSH, WILLIAM BROWNLEE (D)
b Munfordville, Ky, Sept 18, 24; s Benjamin T Welsh & Mary Cocks W; m 1948 to Jean Justice; c Charles B; Mary J & Wm E. Educ: Berea Col; Univ Ky; Maxwell Sch; Syracuse Univ. Polit & Govt Pos: Legis asst to US Sen Herbert H Lehman, NY, 52-56; res dir, Dem Nat Comt, 57-58; admin asst to US Sen Philip A Hart, Mich, 59-66; admin asst to the Vice President of the US, 66-69; exec dir, Dem Nat Comt, 69-72; exec dir polit & legis affairs, Am Fedn State, County & Municipal Employees, AFL-CIO, currently. Mil Serv: Entered as Pvt, Army, released as Sgt, 46, after serv in ETO. Relig: Presbyterian. Mailing Add: 6917 Cherry Lane Annandale VA 22003

WELTNER, CHARLES LONGSTREET (D)
b Atlanta, Ga, Dec 17, 27; s Philip Weltner & Sally Cobb Hull W; m 1972 to Juanita Lynn Good; c Elizabeth Shirley, Philip II, Susan Martin & Charles Longstreet. Educ: Oglethorpe Univ, AB, 48; Columbia Univ, LLB, 50; Omicron Delta Kappa. Hon Degrees: LLD, Tufts Univ, 67. Polit & Govt Pos: US Rep, Ga, Fifth Dist, 62-66. Bus & Prof Pos: Attorney-at-law. Mil Serv: Capt, Army. Publ: Southerner, J B Lippincott, 66. Relig: Presbyterian. Mailing Add: 1105 E Rock Springs Rd NE Atlanta GA 30306

WELTY, ROBERT (D)
State Treas, Dem Party, Ore
b Portland, Ore, Jan 13, 15; s Jacob Welty & Louise E Lerch W; m 1939 to Gertrude M Johnson; c Robert Wm & Michael D. Educ: Ore State Univ, BS in elec eng, 38; Eta Kappa Nu; Sigma Tau. Polit & Govt Pos: Field engr, Rural Elec Admin, Ore, 38-42 & 44-45; treas, Wasco Co Dem Cent Comt, 56-60, chmn, 60-66; state treas, Dem Party Ore, 63-; deleg, Dem Nat Conv, 64. Bus & Prof Pos: Consult engr, owner, Robert Welty Engrs, The Dalles, Ore, 45- Mil Serv: Tech Adv on Construct, Signal Corps, 42-44. Mem: Nat Soc of Prof Engrs; Asn of Commun Engrs (mem nat bd); CofC; Mid Columbia Develop Corp; Kiwanis. Relig: Lutheran; mem of coun. Mailing Add: 1607 E 11th The Dalles OR 97058

WELU, JOSEPHINE ELIZABETH (BETTY) (DFL)
Treas, Pope Co Dem-Farmer-Labor Party, Minn
b Marshall, Minn, Apr 19, 28; d Louis Erwin Calvin & Marion Spielmann C; m 1946 to Irving John Welu; c Douglas John, Gregory James, Joyce Marie & Robert Joseph. Educ: Marshall High Sch, Minn, 3 years. Polit & Govt Pos: Treas, Pope Co Dem-Farmer-Labor Party, Minn, 66- Bus & Prof Pos: Co-owner & operator, Welu's Corner, Marshall, Minn, 59-61; photographer, Vernon Studio, Inc, Glenwood, Minn, 61- Mem: Prof Photographers Asn; Farmers Union (secy); Altar Soc (pres); Woman's Int Bowling Cong (pres, city chap; mem, state chap). Relig: Catholic. Mailing Add: Long Beach Rte 4 Glenwood MN 56334

WEMPLE, CLARK CULLINGS (R)
NY State Assemblyman
b Schenectady, NY, July 19, 27; s John Herbert Wemple & Luella Clark W; m 1953 to Marilyn Greve; c Mark Vanderpool, Kirk Jameson & Erik Cullings. Educ: Yale Univ, BA, 50; Albany Law Sch, JD, 53. Polit & Govt Pos: Justice of the peace, Niskayuna, NY, 57-63, town councilman, 63-65; NY State Assemblyman, 66- Bus & Prof Pos: Pvt law practice, 53-69. Mil Serv: Entered as Seaman 1/C, Navy, 45, released as SKD 3/C, 46, after serv in ETO. Mem: NY State, Schenectady Co & Am Bar Asns; Am Arbit Asn. Relig: Protestant. Mailing Add: 1760 Van Antwerp Rd Schenectady NY 12309

WENDEL, FREDERICK ERNEST (R)
b Yonkers, NY, Nov 24, 06; s Frederick William Wendel & Emilie Kruppenbacher W; m 1928 to Consuelo Alvarez; c Frederick, Raymond & Richard. Educ: NY State Nautical Sch, 22-23; courses at NY Univ, Rutgers Univ & Brooklyn Polytech Inst, 28-44. Polit & Govt Pos: Councilman, Borough of Oradell, NJ, 54-59; mayor, Oradell, 60-; mem, Bergen Co Park Comn, 65-, pres, 70-71; committeeman, NJ Rep State Comt, 67-; mem, Bergen Co Rep Policy Comt, currently; NJ State Sen, Bergen Co, 72-74. Bus & Prof Pos: Rep, Pipefitters Local 274, Jersey City, NJ, 40-41; proj mgr, Frank A McBride Co, Paterson, 41-43 & 46-47; instr, Jersey City Voc Sch, 46-50; owner & pres, Fred Wendel, Inc, 48-69, chmn bd, 70- Mil Serv: Entered as Lt(jg), Naval Res, 43, released as Lt, 54, after serv in Bur Ships, Brooklyn Navy Yard, 43-46. Publ: Articles for trade papers. Mem: Am Soc Heating, Refrigeration & Air Conditioning Engr; NY State Maritime Col Alumni; Am Legion (Comdr, 50); Lions; Paramus CofC. Honors & Awards: Oradell Citizen of the Year, Am Legion, 67; Man of the Year, Mech Construction Indust of NJ, 68. Relig: Catholic. Mailing Add: 798 East Dr Oradell NJ 07649

WENDLER, KENNETH STEWART (D)
Chmn, Travis Co Dem Exec Comt, Tex
b San Antonio, Tex, Sept 11, 29; s Kenneth Stewart Wendler, Sr & Katheryn Tynan W; m 1951 to Elizabeth Ann West; c Mark W, Kim, Katheryn (Kay), Kris & Kena. Educ: Univ Tex, Austin, 49-50 & 53-56. Polit & Govt Pos: Dem precinct chmn, Precinct 327, Austin, Tex, 66-72; chmn finance comt & treas, Travis Co Dem Exec Comt, 72, chmn, 72-; vchmn, Tex Dem Co Chairmen, 72- Bus & Prof Pos: Job supt, John Broad Construction Co, Austin, Tex, 56-57; gen supt, McCullick Construction Co, Austin & Mission, 57-58 & Federated Construction & Equip Co, Tyler & Mission, 58; pres & owner, K S Wendler Construction Co, Austin, 59-65 & Anken Construction Co, Inc, 65- Mil Serv: Entered as Buck Pvt, Army, 50, released as Sgt 1/C, after serv in 312th Bn, Corps of Engrs, US, 50-52. Mem: Assoc Gen Contractors; South Austin Civic Club; South Austin Optimist Club; Austin CofC; Retail Merchants Asn. Honors & Awards: Award of Appreciation, Travis Co Dem Exec Comt, 72; Commendation of Good Citizenship, Comnr Court of Travis Co, 72; Citation of Appreciation for Outstanding Contribution & Community Advan, South Austin Civic Club, 72; Citations of Appreciation as mem, Citizen's Tax Adv Comn & Civic Ctr Conf Comt of City of Austin, 73. Relig: Catholic. Legal Res: 4703 Arapahoe Pass Austin TX 78745 Mailing Add: PO Box 3331 Austin TX 78764

WENDOLOWSKI, MARY ANNE CATHERINE (D)
Nat Committeewoman, Young Dem Pa
b Scranton, Pa, Mar 2, 53; d Raymond Wendolowski & Ann Comonitski W; single. Educ: Marywood Col, Pa Fedn Dem Women Florence Dornblaser Mem scholar, 73, BA in Social Sci, 74; Univ Pittsburgh, 74-, fel, 74; Pi Gamma Mu; Eta Sigma Phi. Polit & Govt Pos: Pres, Marywood Col Young Dem, 70-73; first vpres, Col Young Dem Pa, 72-73, pres, 73-74; treas, Lacka Co Young Dem, 73-74; nat committeewoman, Young Dem Pa, 74- Bus & Prof Pos: Clerk, Lacka Co Controller's Off, 72 & State Treas Off, Harrisburg, Pa, 73; libr aide, Marywood Col Libr, 72-74; intern, Dem Nat Comt, 74; asst in preparation for women's conf, Pa Dem State Comt, 74. Mem: Kappa Gamma Pi; Delta Epsilon. Honors & Awards: Dean's List, Marywood Col, 70-74. Relig: Catholic. Legal Res: 624 Main St Dickson City PA 18519 Mailing Add: Apt 11 324 McKee Pl Pittsburgh PA 15213

WENINGER, HOWARD L (D)
b North Judson, Ind, Dec 13, 04; s Charles W Weninger & Elizabeth Collier W; m 1927 to Esther Claire Grimm; c Kay (Mrs Croyle) & Howard L Jr. Educ: Univ Mich, 24-26. Polit & Govt Pos: Clerk-treas, North Judson, Ind, 36-42, pres, Recreation Bd, 38-42, secy, Sch Bd, 48-52 & Libr, 51-54; trustee, Wayne Twp, 47-54; chmn, Starke Co Dem Cent Comt, 52-74; chmn, Second Dist Dem Cent Comt, 61-66; deleg, Dem Nat Conv, 60, 64, 68 & 72. Bus & Prof Pos: Dir, Am State Bank, North Judson, Ind, 53-; pres, Judson Pub Inc, 64- Mem: Mason; Scottish Rite; Shrine; Eagles; Moose. Relig: Methodist. Mailing Add: 508 Keller Ave North Judson IN 46366

WENSTROM, FRANK AUGUSTUS (R)
NDak State Sen
b Dover, NDak, July 27, 03; s James August Wenstrom & Anna P Kringstad W; m 1938 to Mary Esther Pickett. Educ: Pub schs, NDak. Polit & Govt Pos: NDak State Sen, 57-59 & 67-, mem, Legis Res Coun, 59-60 & 69, chmn, Comt Audits & Fiscal Rev, 63-64, pres pro tem, NDak State Senate, 73-74, mem appropriations comt, currently; lt gov, NDak, 63-64; deleg & pres, NDak Const Conv, 71-72. Bus & Prof Pos: Exec vpres, Northwestern Fed Savings & Loan Asn; farmer, 44-; pub rels officer, First Nat Bank, Williston, NDak, 50-61; asst to pres, Am State Bank of Williston, 68- Mem: Yellowstone-Mo-Ft Union Comn (mem, 59-); Roosevelt Nat Park Comt (mem, 54-); Williston CofC; Elks; Mason; Eastern Star. Legal Res: 516 Third Ave W Williston ND 58801 Mailing Add: State Capitol Bismarck ND 58501

WENSTROM, GENE R (D)
Minn State Rep
b Fergus Falls, Minn, Nov 27, 46; s Ruben Wenstrom & Katherine Scramstad W; m 1968 to LeAnn Knoll; c Daniel & Tamaro. Educ: Fergus Falls Community Col, 67; Moorhead State Col, 69; Phi Theta Kappa. Polit & Govt Pos: Minn State Rep, Dist 11-A, 75- Bus & Prof Pos: Teacher, Dist 263, 69-75; farmer, Grant, Minn, currently. Mil Serv: Army Res, 70-72. Mem: Farmers Union; Nat Farmers Orgn; Sons of Norway; Lions; Sister-City. Mailing Add: Box 44 Elbow Lake MN 56531

WENTZ, JANET MARIE (R)
NDak State Rep
b McClusky, NDak, July 21, 37; d Charles G Neff & Martha Schindler; m 1957 to Thomas Arthur Wentz; c Elizabeth, Karin & Thomas. Educ: Westmar Col, 55-57; Univ Minn, 60-62; Minot State Col, 67-70. Polit & Govt Pos: Vpres, Rep Women Minot, NDak, 66-67; NDak State Rep, 74- Mem: NDak Conf Churches (rep, NDak United Methodist, 73-); Comn on Status of Women in NDak United Methodist Church; PEO; Minot CofC (pub affairs comt); Nat Asn Securities Dealers. Relig: Protestant. Mailing Add: 505 Eighth Ave SE Minot ND 58701

WENTZIEN, IRWIN H (R)
Orgn Chmn, Tama Co Rep Party, Iowa
b Gladbrook, Iowa, Feb 25, 02; s H H Wentzien, Jr & Pauline Nissen W; m 1934 to Vivian Alice Walter; c Irwin Heinrich, Paul Warren & Michael Brent. Educ: Univ Southern Calif, 21-22; Univ Iowa, BSC, 24. Polit & Govt Pos: Deleg, Iowa Rep State Conv, 29-68; coun mem, Gladbrook Sch Bd, 46-54; chmn, Tama Co Rep Party, 59-64, orgn chmn, 64-; deleg, Rep Nat Conv, 64. Bus & Prof Pos: Hardware merchant, 24- Mem: Hardware Asn; Mason; Salvation Army; Commercial Club; Odd Fellows. Relig: Church of Christ. Mailing Add: Gladbrook IA 50635

WENZEL, FERDINAND EDWARD (TED) (R)
Chmn, Tuolumne Co Rep Cent Comt, Calif

b Sonora, Calif, Oct 5, 17; s Edward George Wenzel & Cora E Leonard W; m 1937 to Eloise Vivian Mitchell; c Sharon P (Mrs Stockton) & Gerald E. Educ: Modesto Jr Col, 35-36; Col Commerce, Stockton, Calif, BA, Bus, 38. Polit & Govt Pos: Finance chmn, Tuolumne Co Rep Cent Comt, Calif, 62-68, past vchmn, chmn, 71-; mem, Calif Rep State Cent Comt, currently. Bus & Prof Pos: Owner, Wenzels Men & Women's Wear, 41- Mem: Sonora Area Bus Asn; Elks; Lions; NCalif Golf Asn; Pine Mt Lake Golf & Country Club. Honors & Awards: Gov Award for Outstanding Performance as Finance Chmn Rep Cent Comt, 68. Relig: Protestant. Mailing Add: One Alley Way Sonora CA 95370

WENZEL, STEPHEN G (DFL)
Minn State Rep

Mailing Add: 312 SE Third St Little Falls MN 56345

WEPRIN, SAUL (D)
NY State Assemblyman

b Brooklyn, NY, Aug 5, 27; s Abraham Weprinsky & Anna Pols W; m 1950 to Sylvia Matz; c Barry Alan, David Ira & Mark Stuart. Educ: Brooklyn Col, BA, 48; Brooklyn Law Sch, LLB & JD, 51; Debating Soc. Polit & Govt Pos: 24th Assembly dist leader, Queens Dem Club, 62-; NY State Assemblyman, 71- Mil Serv: Entered as Seaman 2/C, Coast Guard, 45, released, 46. Mem: Jewish War Vet; KofP (past chancellor); Hilltop Village Coop (past pres); Nat Conf Christians & Jews; B'nai B'rith. Relig: Jewish. Mailing Add: 82-09 188th St Hollis NY 11423

WERBER, BARBARA (D)
Mem, Dem Nat Comt, NJ

Mailing Add: 584 Highland Ave Ridgewood NJ 07450

WERNER, JANE (R)
Committeewoman, Ill Rep State Cent Comt

b Butler, Pa, Feb 11, 18; d Arthur Frederick Tydeman & Mary Steiner Fryberger T; m 1947 to Wilbert Arthui Werner; c Catherine Jane & Charles William. Educ: Rockford Col, 34-35; Knox Col, AB, 39; Delta Delta Delta. Polit & Govt Pos: Precinct capt, 19th Precinct Rep Party, Lyons Twp, Ill, 62-, twp committeewoman, 64-; committeewoman, Ill Rep State Cent Comt, Fourth Cong Dist, 66-; chairwoman for Sen Dirksen, Fourth Cong Dist, 68; chairwoman for Richard Nixon, Third, Fourth & Fifth Cong Dists, 68; co-chmn, Women for Clarke, Seventh Sen Dist, 70; deleg, Rep Nat Conv, 72. Mem: DAR; Rep Women's Club of Lyons Twp. Relig: Protestant. Mailing Add: 322 Blackstone Ave La Grange IL 60525

WERNETTE, CHARLES MICHAEL (D)
b Clay Center, Kans, Sept 23, 50; s Charles Francis Wernette & Vera L Gibbs; single. Educ: Washburn Univ, Topeka, BA, 73; Tau Kappa Epsilon. Polit & Govt Pos: Pres, Clay Co Young Dem, 67-68; vpres & pres, Washburn Young Dem, 69-70; staff, Docking for Gov, 70; state vpres, Kans Young Dem, 70-71, pres, 71-72; campaign coordr, Vern Miller for Attorney Gen, 72; alt deleg, Dem Nat Conv, 72; cand for Kans State Rep, 63rd Dist, 74. Relig: Catholic. Mailing Add: 503 Lane St Clay Center KS 67432

WERTZ, CYNTHIA LOUISE (D)
b Auburn, Ala, Jan 15, 43; d Joe Chester Jones & Mary Bowden J; m 1962 to Dennis William Wertz; c Dennis William, Jr & Laura Louise. Educ: Univ Md, College Park, 61-62; NC State Univ, currently; Gamma Phi Beta. Polit & Govt Pos: Alt deleg, Dem Nat Conv, 72; treas, Wake Co Comt McGovern for President, 72-74; mem Young Dem Club, 72- Mem: League of Women Voters Raleigh-Wake Co (treas, 72-). Mailing Add: 1037 Ivy Lane Cary NC 27511

WERTZ, ROBERT CHARLES (R)
NY State Assemblyman

b Kew Gardens, NY, Aug 18, 32; s Gilbert Charles Wertz & Caryll Lyman W; m 1959 to Dorothy Ann Nosek; c Mary Elizabeth, Donna Elaine & Robert Charles, II. Educ: Alfred Univ, BA, 54; Albany Law Sch, LLB, 58; Blue Key; Kappa Nu. Polit & Govt Pos: Sr attorney appellate div, NY State Supreme Court, 65-67; town attorney, Smithtown, NY, 67-69; NY State Assemblyman, 71-, chmn, Subcomt Ment Hygiene, mem, Health Comt, Govt Employees Comt, Labor Comt & Judiciary Comt, NY State Assembly, Joint Legis Coun Ment & Phys Handicapped; mem, Temporary State Comn Southeast Water Resources. Bus & Prof Pos: Practicing attorney, Smithtown, NY, 60- Mil Serv: Serv 2nd Bn, 25th Marines, Marine Corps Res, six years. Mem: Cleary Sch for Deaf (bd dirs); Maryhaven Sch for Retarded Children (adv coun); St Joseph's Acad, Brentwood (adv coun); Commack Rep Club (past pres & trustee); KofC. Relig: Catholic. Legal Res: 37 Bethany Dr Commack NY 11725 Mailing Add: 35 W Main St Smithtown NY 11787

WERTZLER, MARILOU (R)
b Battle Creek, Mich, div; c Vicki (Mrs Cameron Keim) & John Wertzler. Polit & Govt Pos: Mgr, Del Co Rep Hqs, Ind, 64; vchmn, Del Co Rep State Cent Comt, 66-68; reporter, Ind State Supreme Court & Court of Appeals, 68-; alt deleg, Rep Nat Conv, 72; state tel coordr, Comt to Re-elect the President, 72; vol consult, tel campaign, comt to Re-elect the President, NH, 72. Mem: State Assembly Women's Club; Ind State Fedn Women's Rep Clubs; Capitol Hill Club. Mailing Add: 7203 Kingsford Dr Indianapolis IN 46260

WESCHE, PERCIVAL A (R)
Idaho State Rep

Mailing Add: 323 19th Ave S Nampa ID 83651

WEST, ERCEIL ELLEN (D)
Secy, Duval Co Dem Exec Comt, Fla

b Bristow, Okla, Jan 8, 22; d Henry O Winn & Mary Hamilton W; m 1944 to Joel Aubory West, Sr; c Joel A Jr, Richard A & Bobbi. Educ: Jacksonville Jr Col, real estate course, currently. Polit & Govt Pos: Committeewoman, 2-D Precinct, Jacksonville, Fla, 65-; secy, Duval Co Dem Exec Comt, 68- Bus & Prof Pos: Homemaker & mother. Mem: League of Women Voters; Nat Women's Polit Caucus (membership chmn); 2-D Civic Club; YWCA; Les Bonnes Amies Social (pres). Relig: Catholic. Mailing Add: 3029 Jupiter Ave Jacksonville FL 32206

WEST, FOWLER CLAUD (D)
b Bosqueville, Tex, July 6, 40; s Fowler Clark West & Bertha Dotson W. Educ: NTex State Univ, 58-59; Baylor Univ, BA, 63; Pi Sigma Alpha; Phi Eta Sigma. Polit & Govt Pos: Asst staff consult, House Agr Comt, 65-69, staff dir, 73-; admin asst to US Rep W R Poage, Tex, 69-72. Mil Serv: Sgt E-5, Army Nat Guard, 63-69. Mem: Mason; Cong Staff Club (pres). Relig: Methodist. Legal Res: 2324 Bosque Blvd Waco TX 76707 Mailing Add: 490 M St SW Washington DC 20024

WEST, JAMES CLIFFORD (R)
Iowa State Rep

b Des Moines, Iowa, July 30, 32; s Clifford Leroy West & Marian Brimhall W; m 1955 to Mary Carol Nelson; c Guy James, Dean Alden & Raina Anne. Educ: Iowa State Univ, BS, 60; Denver Univ, MBA, 61. Polit & Govt Pos: Rep precinct committeeman, State Center Twp, Iowa, 65-68; chmn, Marshall Co Rep Cent Comt, 68-70; chmn, Fourth Cong Dist, Iowa, 70-72; Iowa State Rep, 73-, ranking minority mem ways & means comt, Iowa House of Rep, currently. Bus & Prof Pos: Mgr, Brimhall-West Co, 62-; pres, Gutekunst Pub Libr, State Center, Iowa. Mil Serv: Entered as Pvt, Air Force, 52, released as S/Sgt, 56, after serv in 13th Bomb Squadron, Far East Command, 52-53; Air Medal; UN Serv Medal; Korean Serv Medal; Good Conduct Medal. Publ: Masonary is for Masons, 2/66 & Charity, 3-4/68, The Philalethes. Mem: Am Legion; Mason; RAM; KT; RSM. Relig: Presbyterian. Mailing Add: 203 Second St NW State Center IA 50247

WEST, JAMES PASCHAL (R)
Ga State Rep

b June 17, 26; s Edgar Charles West & Betty Davis W; m 1944 to Zula Jean Arflin; c Jeanine, James P, Jr & David H. Educ: Pinehurst High Sch, grad. Polit & Govt Pos: Chmn, Dooley Co Rep Party, Ga, formerly; mem, Ga Agr Stabilization & Conserv Serv Comt, currently; Ga State Rep, 75- Bus & Prof Pos: Farmer, currently. Mil Serv: Entered as Pvt, Army, 45, released as Cpl, 46, after serv in 925th Anti-Aircraft Artil Automatic Weapons Bn, Asiatic-Pac Theatre; Victory Ribbon. Mem: Mason; VFW; Nat Farm Orgn; Farm Bur. Relig: Baptist. Mailing Add: 7856 Fielder Rd Jonesboro GA 30236

WEST, JOHN CARL (D)
Dem Nat Committeeman, SC

b Camden, SC, Aug 27, 22; s Shelton J West & Mattie Ratterree W; m 1942 to Lois Rhame; c John Carl, Jr, Douglas Allen & Shelton Anne. Educ: Univ SC, LLB magna cum laude, 48; Phi Beta Kappa. Polit & Govt Pos: Mem, Hwy Comn, 48-52, vchmn, 52; SC State Sen, 54-62; Lt Gov, SC, 67-70, Gov, 71-74; regional vpres, Nat Conf of Lt Gov, 69-67; deleg, Dem Nat Conv, 68 & 72; ex officio, Dem Nat Mid-Term Conf, 74; Dem Nat Committeeman, SC, currently. Bus & Prof Pos: Attorney, Camden, SC. Mil Serv: Army, 42-46; Army Commendation Medal. Mem: Kiwanis; Am Legion; CofC. Relig: Presbyterian; Deacon, Ruling Elder, Bethesda Presby Church. Mailing Add: PO Box 11450 The State House Columbia SC 29211

WEST, QUENTIN MECHAM
Adminr Econ Research Serv, US Dept Agr

b Morgan, Utah, June 27, 20; s Preston Dangerfield West & Genevieve Mecham W; m 1944 to Ila Lee Martin; c Kenlee Martin, Duane LaQuen, Nuel Preston & Dennis Raul. Educ: Utah State Agr Col, BS, 48, MS, 49; Cornell Univ, PhD, 51; Alpha Zeta; Phi Kappa Phi. Polit & Govt Pos: Br chief, Far East Br, Foreign Regional Anal Div, US Dept Agr, 56-62; dep dir & dir, Foreign Regional Anal Div, Econ Res Serv, 62-69; adminr, Foreign Econ Develop, US Dept Agr, 69-71; adminr, Economic Research Serv, US Dept Agr, 72- Bus & Prof Pos: Mem, Inter-Am Inst Agr Sci, San Jose, Costa Rica, 52-53; assoc prof, Cornell Univ, 56; asst prof, Utah State Univ, 53. Mil Serv: Entered as Pvt, Army, 43, released as 1st Lt, 47, after serv in Engrs. Publ: Auth, Thesis, Cornell Univ, 52; auth, Turkey, 58 & co-auth, World Food Budget, US Dept Agr, 64. Mem: Am & Int Agr Econ Asns. Honors & Awards: PhD Thesis Award, Am Agr Ed Asn, 52; US Dept Agr Superior Serv Award, 65 & Distinguished Serv Award, 72. Relig: Latter-Day Saint. Legal Res: 1007 Poplar Dr Falls Church VA 22046 Mailing Add: Econ Research Serv US Dept Agr Washington DC 20250

WEST, ROBERT V, JR (R)
Finance Chmn, Rep Party Tex

b Kansas City, Mo, Apr 29, 21; s Robert V West (deceased) & Josephine Quistgaard W (deceased); m 1944 to Sybil Small; c Robert V, III, Kathryn Anne, Suzanne Small & Patricia Lynn. Educ: Univ Tex, Austin, BS, 42, MS, 43, PhD, 49; Tau Alpha Pi; Sigma Chi. Polit & Govt Pos: Finance chmn, Rep Party Tex, 72; mem, Rep Nat Finance Comt, 73- Bus & Prof Pos: Pres, Slick Sec Recovery Corp, 56-59 & Texstar Petroleum Co, 59-64; chmn bd, Tesoro Petroleum Corp, San Antonio, 64- Mem: Soc Petroleum Engrs; Nat Petroleum Coun, Independent Petroleum Asn Am (dir); Tex Mid-Continent Oil & Gas Asn (dir); Am Petroleum Inst (dir). Honors & Awards: Distinguished Grad, Col Eng, Univ Tex, Austin, 73. Relig: Episcopal. Legal Res: 2643 Friar Tuck San Antonio TX 78209 Mailing Add: 8700 Tesoro Dr San Antonio TX 78286

WEST, TED GRADON (D)
Chmn, Caldwell Co Dem Exec Comt, NC

b Lenoir, NC, Feb 18, 29; s John Wilson West & Elvira Foster W; m 1950 to Claudine Goble; c Amanda Anne. Educ: Concord Col, AB, 54; Univ NC Sch Law, JD, 57; National Blue Key; Phi Alpha Delta; assoc-ed, NC Law Rev. Polit & Govt Pos: Attorney, Trim Valley Authority, 57-60; pres, Caldwell Co Young Dem Club, NC, 61-62; vpres, NC Young Dem Clubs, 62-63; deleg, Dem Nat Conv, 64; chmn, Caldwell Co Dem Exec Comt, 72- Bus & Prof Pos: Attorney, Lenoir, NC, 60-; gen counsel, Blue Ridge Elec Corp, 65- Mil Serv: Entered as Midn, Navy, 48, released as Lt(jg), 52, after serv as Naval Aviator, ComAirLant, Sixth Fleet; Nat Defense, European Occup & Naval Res Medals; Lt, Navy Res, 55- Publ: Case notes & comments, NC Law Rev, 56. Mem: Am & NC Bar Asns; Rotary; Moose; Am Legion. Relig: Baptist. Legal Res: Rte 1 Box 392-B Lenoir NC 28645 Mailing Add: PO Drawer 818 Lenoir NC 28645

WEST, THOMAS HELIN (DFL)
Chairperson, 42nd Sen Dist, Dem-Farmer-Labor Comt, Minn

b Minneapolis, Minn, July 9, 52; s Howard B West & Margaret Helin W; single. Educ: Univ Minn, currently. Polit & Govt Pos: Chairperson, 42nd Sen Dist, Dem-Farmer-Labor Comt, Minn, 74-; mem issues & platform comn, Dem-Farmer-Labor Comt, 75- Bus & Prof Pos: Clerk, Minn Elec Asn, Inc, 73- Mem: Nat Coun Teachers Math; Am Fedn Teachers. Mailing Add: 21500 Fairview St Greenwood MN 55331

WEST, W A, JR (TONY) (R)
Ariz State Rep

Mailing Add: 544 W Solano Dr Phoenix AZ 85013

WEST, WILSON HENRY (R)
b Odin, Ill, Sept 13, 13; s William John West & Clara Sebastian W; m 1938 to Mildred Ingram; c John. Educ: Southern Ill Univ, 31-33; St Louis Univ, MD, 37. Polit & Govt Pos: In charge, Doctors of Ill, for Gov Stratton, 56-60, US Sen Dirksen, 62 & 68, US Sen Percy, 66 & Nixon, 68; bd gov, Ill United Rep Party, 63-; chmn, United Rep Fund, St Clair Co, Ill; mem, Nat Comt Physicians for Nixon, 68; deleg, Rep Nat Conv, 68 & 72; hon life mem, Belleville Rep Party. Bus & Prof Pos: Instr urology, Washington Univ, 40-52; past pres, Christian Welfare Hosp, East St Louis; mem staff, St Marys, Mem, Centerville Twp & Christian Welfare Hosps. Publ: Treatment of tetanus, Ill State Med J, 37. Mem: St Clair Co Med Soc; Ill State Med Soc; Am Med Asn; Mason; Shrine; Consistory. Honors & Awards: Award for calling most attention to Sen Dirksen's 35 years in pub life, Ill Rep Party, 66. Relig: Methodist. Mailing Add: 14 Oakwood Dr Belleville IL 62223

WESTBROOK, BROCK R (D)
Chmn, Washington Co Dem Cent Comt, Okla
b Mena, Ark, Dec 26, 21; s Brock R Westbrook & Ida Hill W; m 1947 to Jane Baskin; c Mary Jane, Suzanne & Sara. Educ: Okla Baptist Univ, BS, 43; Univ Okla Sch Med, MD, 46. Polit & Govt Pos: Chmn, Washington Co Dem Cent Comt, Okla, 70- Bus & Prof Pos: Chmn, Bartlesville Park Bd, 66-69. Mil Serv: Entered as Pvt, Army, 43, released as Capt, 49, after serv in 130th Sta Hosp, Eucom, Heidelberg, Germany, 47-49; Victory Medal; Good Conduct Medal; European Theatre Medal. Mem: Washington Co Med Soc; Okla State Med Asn; Am Med Asn; Tulsa Obstetrical & Gynecological Soc. Relig: Humanist. Legal Res: 3720 Redbud Lane Bartlesville OK 74003 Mailing Add: 3500 State St Bartlesville OK 74003

WESTERBERG, RUSSELL A (D)
Idaho State Rep
Mailing Add: 70 Keystone Soda Springs ID 83276

WESTERBERG, VICTOR JOHN (R)
Pa State Rep
b Kane, Pa, Feb 6, 12; s Victor J Westerberg & Anna E Seaton W; m 1941 to June Elizabeth Anderson; c Ann M (Mrs Fergusen) & Jean S (Mrs Morrow). Polit & Govt Pos: Auditor, Wetmore Twp Rd Dist, Pa, 35-37, secy, 37-42; mem borough coun, Kane, Pa, 52-56; acting postmaster, US Post Off, Kane, 59-61; Pa State Rep, 67th Dist, 64- Bus & Prof Pos: Partner, Gausman's Garage, 46-61; owner, Kane Truck Sales, Pa, 62- Mil Serv: Entered as 1st Lt, Army, 42, released as Capt, 46, after serv in 613 Ordnance Bn, ETO, 44-45. Mem: CofC (past pres, Kane Chap); Rotary (past pres, Kane Chap); Am Legion; VFW; Kane Area United Fund. Relig: First Methodist. Legal Res: 630 Greeves St Kane PA 16735 Mailing Add: Capitol Bldg Harrisburg PA 17120

WESTERHOLM, LEO LYDER (R)
Chmn, Calhoun Co Rep Party, Tex
b Danevang, Tex, Feb 7, 22; s Peter H Westerholm & Astrid Hojrup W; m 1956 to Dorothy June Edwards; c Sheila Ruth & Hans Kurt. Educ: Tex Arts & Indust Col, Kingsville, Tex, BS, 48; Inst Ins Mkt Div, Continuing Educ, La State Univ, 71. Polit & Govt Pos: Chmn, Calhoun Co Rep Party, Tex, 62- Bus & Prof Pos: Personal Producer, Southland Life Ins Co, 53- Mil Serv: Entered as Pvt, Army, 42, released as Pfc, 45, after serv in 101st Airborne Div, ETO, 44; Presidential Citation; ETO Ribbon with one star; Captured during Normandy Invasion, Prisoner of War. Mem: Gulf Coast Asn Life Underwriters; Lions; Red Cross; Port Lavaca CofC; Calhoun Co Fair Asn (dir, 64-). Honors & Awards: Recipient, Lion of the Year Award, 60; 15 year pin, Red Cross; Man of the Year Award, Southland Life Ins Co, 70 & 71; mem, Million Dollar Round Table. Relig: Methodist. Legal Res: 202 Sunnydale Port Lavaca TX 77979 Mailing Add: Box 44 Port Lavaca TX 77979

WESTFALL, MORRIS GENE (R)
Mo State Rep
b Apr 5, 39; s Raymond Earl Westfall & Ethel Faye Neill W; m 1964 to Sharon Kay Douglas; c Craig Lin. Educ: Univ Mo-Columbia, BS, 62; Farmhouse. Polit & Govt Pos: Mo State Rep, 133rd Legis Dist, 71- Bus & Prof Pos: Bd mem, Mo Pork Producers, 70-71, Polk Co Fair Bd, 67-71 & Polk Stabilization & Conserv Serv Bd, 70-71. Mem: Saddle Club. Honors & Awards: Outstanding Serv Award, Univ Mo Extension, 73; Appreciation Serv, SE Lions Club, 73. Relig: Baptist; Sunday sch teacher, Halfway Baptist Church, 63-, treas, 68-69. Mailing Add: Rte 2 Halfway MO 65663

WESTMAN, PATRICIA ANN (DFL)
Secy, Roseau Co Dem-Farmer-Labor Party, Minn
b Deer River, Minn, May 12, 41; d Harry M Dahl & Gudrun Foss D; m 1960 to William Edward Westman; c Ronda Ann. Educ: Bemidji State Col, BS in elem educ, 63; St Cloud State Col, fel, 68-69, MS in spec educ, 69 & cert in Spec Learning Behavior Prob. Polit & Govt Pos: Secy, Roseau Co Dem-Farmer-Labor Party, Minn, 70- Bus & Prof Pos: Elem teacher, Angus Pub Schs, 63-64 & Skime Pub Schs, 64-68; teacher spec educ & supvr spec learning & behav problems, Roseau Pub Schs, 69-70; supvr spec learning behavior problems, Northwest Regional Interdist Coop, 70-73; Mem: Roseau Teachers Asn; Minn & Nat Spec Learning Behavior Prob; Coun Exceptional Children; Asn for Retarded Children. Relig: Lutheran. Mailing Add: Rte 2 Roseau MN 56751

WESTON, TODD G (R)
Utah State Rep
Mailing Add: 285 Temple View Dr Logan UT 84321

WESTPHAL, ALBERT H (R)
Mem, Mich Rep State Cent Comt
b Neche, NDak, Nov 3, 1897; s Herman Henry Westphal & Amelia Walters W; m 1927 to Elsie A Timian; wid; c George Albert & Sandra L (Mrs Milton C Lewis, III); two grandchildren. Educ: Univ Southern Minn, grad, 18; Mankato Commercial Col, Minn, grad; Dakota Bus Col, Fargo, NDak, BBA; La Salle Exten Univ, Chicago, grad law, LLB, 71; Wayne State Univ, 1 year; Gamma Delta. Polit & Govt Pos: Precinct deleg, Rep Party Mich, 38-; Rep city dir, Wyandotte, 60; mem, Citizens Adv Comt, Wyandotte, 63-; charter mem, Rep Club of Wyandotte, past pres, secy, currently; mem, 16th Cong Dist Rep Comt, 65-, treas, 69-73; alt deleg, Rep Nat Conv, 68; elected mem, Mich Rep State Cent Comt, 73- Bus & Prof Pos: Instr, Twin City Commercial Col, 23-25; acct clerk, Detroit Copper Brass Rolling Mills, 25-30; chief clerk, Anaconda Am Brass Co, 33-42, chief timekeeper, 42-60, retired; real estate salesman, Judd Realty Co, 63- Mem: Nat Bus Educ Asn; Lutheran Laymen's League; Aid Asn for Lutherans No 626 (vpres); Wyandotte Hist Soc; Goodfellows. Relig: Lutheran. Mailing Add: 2433 17th St Wyandotte MI 48192

WESTPHAL, FRED (R)
Vt State Sen
Mailing Add: Lake Elmore VT 05657

WESTRUM, MARTHA ROSE (DFL)
Third VChairwoman, Fifth Cong Dist Dem-Farmer-Labor Exec Comt, Minn
b Chicago, Ill, m 1954 to Oliver Henry Westrum; c David, Daniel & Joy. Educ: Univ Chicago, 44-45; Univ Ill, BS, 51; Univ Minn, part-time, 54-64, Remedial Reading Specialist Cert, 62; Delta Phi. Polit & Govt Pos: Chmn FAN Drive, First Precinct, Seventh Ward Dem-Farmer-Labor Party, Minn, 66, precinct chmn, 68-70; mem platform comt, Minneapolis City Dem-Farmer-Labor Conv, 69; deleg & secy, 38th Legis Dist Dem-Farmer Orgn, 70-72; alt deleg, Minn State Dem-Farmer-Labor Conv, 70; mem finance comt, Minn Dem-Farmer-Labor Party, 70-; third vchairwoman, Fifth Cong Dist Dem-Farmer-Labor Exec Comt, currently. Bus & Prof Pos: Elem teacher, Minneapolis Pub Schs, Minn, 51-55, substitute, 62-69; admin off, Midwest Off Econ Opportunity Labor Leadership Proj, Univ Minn Labor Educ Dept, 70. Publ: Midwest Off Econ Opportunity Labor Leadership Project Newsletter, 70. Mem: League Women Voters; Am Civil Liberties Union; Nat Comt for an Effective Cong; Minn Zool Soc; NAACP. Mailing Add: 1253 S Cedar Lake Rd Minneapolis MN 55416

WESTRUP, DONALD LEO (DFL)
VChmn, McLeod Co Dem-Farmer-Labor Party, Minn
b Eden Valley, Minn, May 19, 32; s Joseph H Westrup & Dorothy Dreis W; m 1956 to Catherine E McDonnell; c Mary Susan, Teresa Anne & Thomas Charles. Educ: Col St Thomas, BA, 56. Polit & Govt Pos: Vchmn, McLeod Co Dem-Farmer-Labor Party, Minn, currently. Bus & Prof Pos: Mem bd, St Mary's Hosp & Home, 65-; vchmn bd educ, New Ulm Diocese, currently; mem educ dept, Minn Cath Conf, currently. Mil Serv: Entered as Airman Basic, Air Force, 51, released as S/Sgt, 52, after serv in 133rd Air Defense Wing. Mem: Civic & Commerce Asn; PTA; Dem-Farmer-Labor Party Sustaining Fund. Relig: Catholic. Mailing Add: 221 Andy Ave W Winsted MN 55395

WESTWOOD, JEAN MILES (D)
Dem Nat Committeewoman, Utah
b Price, Utah, Nov 22, 23; d Frances Marion Miles & Nettie Potter M; m 1941 to Richard Elwyn Westwood; c Richard Elwyn, Jr & Beth (Mrs Vernon Davies). Hon Degrees: Col Eastern Utah. Polit & Govt Pos: Mem, various campaign comts, 54-; committeeman or dist vchmn, Dist 453, Salt Lake Co, Utah, 54-; mem, Jordan Dist Study Staff, Utah Merit Study Comn, 58-60; mem, various Dem Party Functions & Comts, 58-; deleg, Utah Woman's Legis Coun, 60-61 & 67-69; deleg, Dem Nat Conv, 64, deleg & mem platform comt, 68, deleg & mem rules comt, 72; nat state & co deleg, Dem Party, 64-; field rep, Staff of US Rep, David S King, 65-66; mem exec bd, Utah 100 Club, 65-; mem, Utah State Dem Cent Comt, 65-; coordr, Humphrey Campaign Utah, 68; Dem Nat Committeewoman, 67-; mem, Exec Comt, Dem Nat Comt, 69-, chmn, 72; vchmn, McGovern for President Comt, 71-72; treas & exec bd mem, Dem Charter Comn, 73-74; deleg & mem rules comt, Dem Mid Term Conf, 74; campaign dir, Sanford for President, 75-76. Bus & Prof Pos: Partner-secy, Westwood Mink Farm, Utah, 44-; secy, Utah Mink Show, 51-54; secy, Westwood Enterprises, 66-; ed bd, Dem Forum. Mem: Am Acad of Polit & Soc Sci Am for Dem Action (bd mem); Alpine Country Club; Mus for Outlaw & Lawmen Hist (bd mem & treas); Cong Action Fund (bd mem). Honors & Awards: Short Story & Poetry Writing, First Place in Writer's Digest Annual Short Story Contest; Susa Young Gates Award as Outstanding Woman in Utah, 74. Relig: Latter-day Saint. Mailing Add: 1624 West 8600 South West Jordan UT 84084

WETHERBEE, BRUCE E (D)
Mass State Rep
Mailing Add: State Capitol Boston MA 02133

WETHERBY, LAWRENCE WINCHESTER (D)
b Middletown, Ky, Jan 2, 08; s Dr Samuel D Wetherby & Fanny Yenowine W; m 1930 to Helen Dwyer; c Lawrence, Jr, Suzanne & Barbara. Educ: Univ Louisville, LLB, 29; Omicron Delta Kappa; Delta Upsilon. Polit & Govt Pos: Judge, Jefferson Co Juv Court, Ky, 43-47; chmn, 34th Legis Dist Dem Comt, 43-56; Lt Gov, Ky, 47-50, Gov, 50-55 & chmn, Southern Gov Conf, 54-55; secy, Ky State Dem Cent Comt, 47-52, secy, 60-65 & mem finance comt, 65-; deleg, Dem Nat Conv, 48-68; mem, State Const Assembly, 64-66; Ky State Sen, 66-75, Pres Pro-Tem, Ky State Senate, 66-75. Bus & Prof Pos: Attorney-at-law, 29-; dir, Lincoln Income Life Ins Co, 40-; vpres & dir, Brighton Engr Co, 56- Mil Serv: Ky Nat Guard, 25-29. Mem: Franklin Co & Ky State Bar Asns; CofC; Frankfort Country Club. Honors & Awards: Named Ky Man of the Year, 52, Ky Sportsman of Year, 54 & Mr Recreation, Ky, 56. Relig: Methodist. Mailing Add: Weehawken Lane Frankfort KY 40601

WETMORE, ROBERT D (D)
Mass State Rep
Mailing Add: State Capitol Boston MA 02133

WETTAW, JOHN (R)
Ariz State Rep
b St Louis, Mo, Apr 17, 39; s Henry Davis Wettaw & Nancy Parish; div. Educ: Southern Ill Univ, BA, 61; Mich State Univ, PhD, 67. Polit & Govt Pos: Ariz State Rep, 73- Bus & Prof Pos: Asst prof chem, Northern Airz Univ, 67-72, assoc prof, 72- Publ: Co-auth, Kinetic isotope effects in the thermal isomerization of CH3 CN, J Am Chem Soc, 68. Mem: Flagstaff Kiwanis Club; Am Chem Soc. Mailing Add: 115 E Terrace Ave Flagstaff AZ 86001

WETZEL, DARREL ERNEST (D)
Treas, Darke Co Dem Exec Comt, Ohio
b Greenville, Ohio, Jan 6, 12; s Fred Wetzel & Racheal Ernest W; m 1936 to Berniece Roosa; c Roberta, Betty Lou, Carolyn, Margaret, Wayne & Dennis. Polit & Govt Pos: Mem, Darke Co Sch Bd, 54-68; trustee, Van Buren Twp, 12 years; treas, Darke Co Dem Exec Comt, 61-; alt deleg, Dem Nat Conv, 64; second vchmn, Darke Co Dem Co; app trustee, Darke, Shelby & Miami Co State Gen & Tech Col, 73- Mem: Co & State Trustees Asns; Darke Co Farm Bur; Scottish Rite; Shrine; Mason (32 degree). Relig: United Methodist; trustee, United Methodist Church Caylor Chapel. Mailing Add: RFD 2 Greenville OH 45331

WEV, OSCAR C B (R)
Mem, Seventh Dist Rep Comt, Va
b Richmond, Va, May 8, 07; s Oscar Neill Wev & Nellie Baughan Bosquet W; m 1936 to Lillian Dixon; c Lynda (Mrs Frank C Cowatch), Penelope (Mrs A Jonathan Frere), Peter & Pamela (Mrs James A Hart). Educ: Univ Va, 2 years; US Coast Guard Acad, BS. Polit & Govt

Pos: Chmn, Hanover Co Rep Party, Va, 66-68; vchmn, Eighth Dist Rep Party, 70-72; mem, Seventh Dist Rep Comt, Va, 72- Bus & Prof Pos: Retired farmer since 65. Mil Serv: Entered as Pvt, Army, 27, graduated from Coast Guard Acad as Ens, 31, released as Capt, 64; Commendation Ribbon; Am Defense Ribbon with Star; Am Theater Ribbon; European Theater with Star; Pac Theater Ribbon with 5 stars; Philippine Liberation Ribbon with 2 Stars; Greek Naval Medal 1st Class; helped design & commanded US Coast Guard Cutter Courier, a vessel operated Voice of America, 51-54. Mem: Mason; Shrine; Mil Order of World Wars; Hanover Country Club; Farm Bur. Relig: Presbyterian. Mailing Add: RR 1 Box 476 Ashland VA 23005

WEXLER, ANNE (D)
Committeeman, Conn Dem State Comt
b New York, Feb 10, 30; d Leon Ralph Levy & Edith Rau L; m 1951 to Richard Wexler; c David & Daniel. Educ: Skidmore Col, BA, 51. Polit & Govt Pos: Co-chmn, McCarthy for President, Conn, 67-68; deleg & mem rules comt, Dem Nat Conv, 68, deleg, mem rules comt & sr floor leader, 72; mem, Gov Comn on Elec Reform, 68-70; co-chmn, Caucus of Conn Dem, 69-70; chief consult comn on party structure & deleg selection, Dem Nat Comt, 69-72, dir nat voter registr drive, 72; campaign mgr, Joe Duffey for US Senate, Conn, 70; mem policy comt, Elec Syst Proj, Nat Munic League, 71; dir, Common Cause Voting Rights Proj, 71-72; nat dir, Citizens for Muskie, 72. Bus & Prof Pos: Pres, Consumer Commun, Inc, 73- Mem: Am Asn Polit Sci; Foreign Policy Asn. Honors & Awards: Outstanding Alumnae, Skidmore Col, 72. Relig: Jewish. Mailing Add: 9 Bonnie Brook Rd Westport CT 06880

WEXLER, EILEEN LUGAR (R)
Chmn, Whitman Co Rep Cent Comt, Wash
b Mystic, Iowa, Feb 6, 15; d Laurell LaVergne Legar & Edna Bracewell L; m 1937 to Clifford Wayne Wexler; c Fred Hugh, II, Clifford Wayne, Jr & Kenneth Leland. Educ: Wash State Univ, BS in Chem, 36; Pi Kappa Delta; Delta Sigma Rho; Spurs; Alpha Gamma Delta. Polit & Govt Pos: Rep precinct committeeman, Whitman Co, Wash, 52-75; pres, Whitman Co Rep Women's Club, 67-69; mem exec comt, Wash State Fedn Rep Women, 67-71; vchmn, Whitman Co Rep Cent Comt, 69-72, state committeewoman, 72-73, chmn, 75- Bus & Prof Pos: Secy, Wexler Fabrications, 62- Mem: Whelan Grange 117; Wash State Grange; Pullman Lady Lions. Honors & Awards: Queen Mother, Wash State Univ, 64; Arc of Epsilon Pi, Alpha Gamma Delta, 70. Relig: Methodist. Mailing Add: Rte 1 Box 67 Pullman WA 99163

WEYANDT, RONALD H (D)
Ohio State Rep
Mailing Add: 1426 Neptune Ave Akron OH 44301

WEYRICH, JAMES HENRY (R)
Chmn, Yakima Co Rep Comt, Wash
b Cathlamet, Wash, Apr 25, 44; s Heston Osborn Weyrich & Gladys Rumsey W; m 1965 to Jeanette Ellen Hoard. Educ: Pac Univ, BS, 67, OD, 68; Omega Epsilon Phi; Alpha Zeta. Polit & Govt Pos: Campaign mgr, Sid Morrison for Wash State Sen, 74; pres, Cent Valley Mens Rep Club, Wash, 74; precinct committeeperson, Toppenish, 74-; chmn, Yakima Co Rep Comt, 74- Mil Serv: Entered as Lt(jg), Navy, 69, released as Lt, 71, after serv in MedServC, Bethesda Naval Hosp, Md; Nat Defense Ribbon. Mem: Yakima Valley Optom Soc; Wash Optom Asn; Rotary (pres, 75-); Boy Scouts; Armed Forces Optom Soc. Honors & Awards: Active of the Year Award, Omega Epsilon Phi, 67. Relig: Protestant. Legal Res: 517 Lillie Lane Toppenish WA 98948 Mailing Add: PO Box 427 Toppenish WA 98948

WHALEN, CHARLES WILLIAM, JR (R)
US Rep, Ohio
b Dayton, Ohio, July 31, 20; s Charles William Whalen & Colette E Kelleher W; m 1958 to Mary Barbara Gleason; c Charles E, Daniel D, Edward J, Joseph M, Anne Elizabeth & Mary Barbara. Educ: Univ Dayton, BBA, 42; Harvard Univ Grad Sch Bus Admin, MBA, 46; Eta Mu Pi. Hon Degrees: LLD, Cent State Univ, 66. Polit & Govt Pos: Ohio State Rep, 55-60; Ohio State Sen, 61-66; US Rep, Ohio, 66- Bus & Prof Pos: Vpres, Dayton Dress Co, 46-52; from asst prof to prof retailing, Univ Dayton, 52-63, prof econ & chmn dept, 63-; vpres, Whalen Invest Co, 54- Mil Serv: Entered as Pvt, Army, 43, released as 1st Lt, 46, after serv in 628th Qm Refrigeration Co, 44-45 & Base Sect Spec Serv Off, India-Burma Theater, 45-46. Publ: Co-auth, How to End the Draft: the Case for an All-Volunteer Army, Nat Press, Inc; Your Right to Know: Why the Free Flow of News Depends Upon the Journalist's Right to Protect His Sources, Random House, 73. Mem: Am Legion; Eagles; Sertoma Club; VFW; KofC. Honors & Awards: Named Outstanding Mem of Ohio Senate, 63. Relig: Roman Catholic. Legal Res: 228 Beverly Pl Dayton OH 45419 Mailing Add: 1035 Longworth House Off Bldg Washington DC 20515

WHALEN, GEORGE EDWIN (D)
Chmn, Dutchess Co Dem Comt, NY
b Dover Plains, NY, Nov 27, 19; s Thomas P Whalen & Lillian Flagler W; m 1951 to Mildred E Roberto; c George Patrick & Thomas James. Educ: Fordham Univ, AB, 41; Albany Law Sch, LLB, 43. Polit & Govt Pos: Mem, Dutchess Co Dem Comt, NY, 46-, chmn, 65-69 & 75-; town clerk, Dover, NY, 46-47, supvr, 48-53 & 56-59; mem, NY State Dem Comt, 53-; counsel to comptroller of NY State, 59-61; attorney, Dutchess Co, 64-65; committeeman, NY State Dem Comt, 97th Assembly Dist, 68-; deleg, Dem Nat Conv, 68. Bus & Prof Pos: Attorney, 43- Mem: Am & NY Bar Asns; KofC; Grange; Elks. Relig: Catholic. Mailing Add: Rte 22 Dover Plains NY 12522

WHALEN, MARY ANNE (D)
VChmn, RI Dem State Comt
b Providence, RI, Apr 20, 26; d James J McKenna (deceased) & Susan T Neary M; m 1947 to George J Whalen; c Cheryl, George, James & Richard. Educ: Bryant Col, Providence, RI, 44-45. Polit & Govt Pos: Regional coordr for Lt Gov & state cand, City of Warwick, RI, 68; secy, RI Dem State Platform Conv, 68; mem, Five Mem Study Comn to Revise RI Dem State Comt Bi-Laws; RI state committeewoman, Dist 36, 65-; mem exec comt, Dem Nat Comt, 65-; vchmn, RI Dem State Comt, 69- Mem: Regents Adv Comt for Educ; Warwick, East Greenwich & North Kingstown Regional Sch Bd (exec bd, 70-); RI Dem Women's Club. Relig: Roman Catholic; Past pres, Rosary & Altar Guild, St Rose of Lima Church, treas, Sch Home Asn. Mailing Add: 52 Keystone Dr Warwick RI 02886

WHALEN, ROBERT EDWARD (R)
b Portsmouth, NH, Nov 6, 21; s Michael Joseph Whalen & Ann Snook W (deceased); m 1944 to Bette Bennett Whittaker, c Leslie (Mrs Thomas Gallmeyer) & Gregory W. Educ: Duke Univ, 2 years; Phi Kappa Psi. Polit & Govt Pos: Mem, Zoning Bd Adjust, Portsmouth, NH, 56-60; selectman, Ward 3, Portsmouth, 56-68; chmn, Portsmouth Rep City Comt, 58-62; deleg, Rep Nat Conv, 60; mem, NH State Port Authority, 62-63; Asst Mayor, Portsmouth, 62-63, City Councilman, 62-68; NH State Sen, 24th Dist, 63-64; mem gov coun, Second Dist, 69-; chmn, NH State Rep Comt, 71-73. Bus & Prof Pos: Vpres, M J Whalen Co, Inc, 55-; vpres, Whalen Realty Corp, 65- Mil Serv: Entered as Aviation Cadet, Army Air Corps, 42, released as 1st Lt, 46, after serv in 3rd Air Force; reentered, Korean Conflict, 52-54. Mem: Life mem Nat Defense Transportation Asn; Elks; Warwick Club; Portsmouth Country Club; Strawberry Banke, Inc (dir). Honors & Awards: Outstanding Govt Leadership Award, Portsmouth Jaycees, 71. Relig: Methodist. Mailing Add: 74 Harborview Dr Rye NH 03871

WHALEY, BEVERLY ANNE (R)
Mem, Rep State Cent Comt Calif
b Sidney, Mont, July 14, 27; d Franklin Richard Whaley & Mathilda Block W; single. Educ: Univ Wash, BA, 49; Kappa Kappa Gamma. Polit & Govt Pos: Vchmn, San Francisco Young Rep, 58-59; chmn, 24th Assembly Dist, Rep Co Cent Comt San Francisco, 59, mem, 65-, regist chmn, 66-68, secy, 66-70, precinct chmn, 68 & 69; secy to Congressman William S Mailliard, 59-60; mem, Rep State Cent Comt Calif, 62-; vpres, San Francisco Co Coord Rep Assembly, 72; dep dir, Calif Rep Assembly, formerly, dir, currently; chmn, 17th Assembly Dist, Rep Co Cent Comt San Francisco, currently. Bus & Prof Pos: Secy, Placer Amex Inc, San Francisco, 74- Relig: Episcopal. Mailing Add: Apt 8K 1333 Gough St San Francisco CA 94109

WHALEY, CECIL HOBERT, JR (D)
Nat Committeeman, Tenn Young Dem
b Indianapolis, Ind, Apr 8, 47; s Cecil Hobert Whaley, Sr & Anita Jean Flack W; m 1972 to Frances Nell Morton. Educ: Ind Univ, Bloomington, 65-66; Univ Tenn, Knoxville, BS, 69; Univ Tenn Grad Sch, MPA, 75; Sigma Delta Chi; Acacia. Polit & Govt Pos: Press secy-state media dir, McGovern-Shriver Presidential Campaign, Tenn, 72; chmn Tenn deleg, Young Dem Nat Conv, Louisville, 73; secy-gen, Tenn Col Young Dem, 73; exec dir, Action Auction, Tenn Dem Telethon, Nashville, 74; nat committeeman, Tenn Young Dem, 74-; dir pub rels, Tenn Gov Comt on the Handicapped, 75- Bus & Prof Pos: Admin asst to pub rels dir, Univ Tenn, 71-72; vpres, Commun Assocs Pub Rels, Nashville, 72-74. Mil Serv: Entered as E-1, Army, 69, released as Sgt, 71, after serv in 1st Armored Div, 1st Air Cavalry, Proj MASSTER, Ft Hood, Tex; Sgt E-5, Army Res, 71-; Am Defense Medal; Army Commendation Medal; Good Conduct Medal; Distinguished Soldier Award; Unit Citation Award; Gen Aide-de-Camp Award. Publ: Auth, Establishment of military electronic defense systems, Army Times, 71; Television's use as a battlefield surveillance unit, United Press Int, 71; The practical use of public relations in politics, Tenn Dem, 73. Mem: Nashville Press Club (charter mem); William Walker Hist Soc (vchmn bd dirs, 74-); Nat & Tenn Educ Asns; Demolay (Chevalier). Honors & Awards: Jr Citizen of Year, Donelson Lions Club, 65; Tenn State Sr Counr, Demolay, 66; Distinguished Serv Award, Univ Tenn Student Govt Asn Student Senate, 72; Outstanding Contrib, Tenn Young Dem, 75. Relig: Baptist. Mailing Add: 308 Plus Park Blvd Nashville TN 37217

WHALEY, FRANCES MORTON (D)
Nat Committeewoman, Tenn Young Dem
b Atlanta, Ga, Aug 12, 46; d James Harry Morton & Bramlette Espy Wilhite M; m 1972 to Cecil H Whaley, Jr. Educ: Miami-Dade Jr Col, AA, 66; David Lipscomb Col, BSEd, 69. Polit & Govt Pos: Deleg, Tenn State Dem Conv, 72 & 74; opers co-chmn, State Young Dem Conv, 73; telethon co-coordr, State Dem Party, Tenn, 73; deleg, Young Dem Nat Conv, Louisville, Ky, 73; nat committeewoman, Tenn Young Dem, 73- Bus & Prof Pos: Educator, Metrop Bd Educ, Nashville, 69-75. Mem: Nat, Tenn & Metrop Nashville Educ Asns; Davidson Co Young Dem Club; William Walker Hist Soc. Relig: Church of Christ. Mailing Add: K-4 308 Plus Park Blvd Nashville TN 37217

WHALEY, LEO JACKSON (R)
Chmn, Whitfield Co Rep Party, Ga
b Sevier Co, Tenn, July 27, 35; s Joseph Jackson Whaley & Minnie Marie Lemons W; m 1956 to Peggy Elaine Ellis; c Sherri, Angela & Traci. Educ: Molar Barber Col, Los Angeles, Calif, 59-60; eve courses, Dalton, Ga, 56 & 57. Polit & Govt Pos: Rep precinct chmn, Cohutta, Ga, 64-75, subdist chmn, Catoosa, Walker & Whitfield Co, 75-; town councilman, Cohutta, 68-; committeeman, Ga State Rep Party, 73-; dir, FHA, Dalton, 74- Bus & Prof Pos: Pres, Cohutta Construction Co, Inc, 73- Mil Serv: Entered as Seaman Recruit, Navy, 52, released as Seaman, 56, after serv in Fighter Squadron 43, Korean Serv, 53. Mem: Cohutta Masonic Lodge (Past Master); Eastern Star (Past Patron); Dalton Elks; North Whitfield High Sch (trustee). Relig: Southern Baptist. Mailing Add: PO Box 191 Cohutta GA 30710

WHALLEY, JOHN IRVING (R)
b Barnesboro, Pa; s James H Whalley & Ann Ashurst W; m to Ruth Anderson; c John & Ruth. Educ: Cambria Rowe Bus Col, Johnstown, Pa. Polit & Govt Pos: Pa State Assemblyman, 50-55; Pa State Sen, 55-60; US Rep, Pa, 60-73; US Deleg, UN Gen Assembly, 69. Bus & Prof Pos: Automobile, banking, coal, ins & real estate. Mem: Automotive Orgn Team (bd dirs). Honors & Awards: Am Legion Distinguished Serv Art; Dale Carnegie Int Good Human Rels Award. Relig: Presbyterian. Legal Res: 1309 Park Ave Windber PA 15963 Mailing Add: 1203 Graham Ave Windber PA 15963

WHALLON, GLEN WILLIAM (D)
Ore State Rep
b Nampa, Idaho, Nov 7, 21; s Jonas C Whallon & Irene Lavender W; m 1947 to Esther Geston; c James Mathew & Patricia Joan. Polit & Govt Pos: Finance chmn & area nominator, Clackamas Co Dem Cent Comt, Ore, currently; Ore State Rep, 73- Bus & Prof Pos: Firefighter, Portland, Ore, 47-72; ins salesman, Howard & Fidler, Portland, 65- Mil Serv: Entered as A/S, Navy, 42, released as Gunner's Mate 1/C, 45, after serv in USS Hamul & USS Autauga; Asiatic-Pac Area Campaign Medal; World War II Victory Medal. Mem: VFW; Northwest Steelheaders; Elks; Farmers Union; Int Asn Fire Fighters, Portland (vpres). Relig: Presbyterian. Mailing Add: 13340 SE Rusk Rd Milwaukie OR 97222

WHARTON, CLYDE WILSON (D)
Chmn, Noble Co Dem Cent Comt, Ohio
b Marion Twp, Noble Co, Ohio, Aug 10, 13; s Danford K Wharton & Bessie McElfresh W; m 1936 to Margaret Fetkovich; c Joyce (Mrs Robert Sholtis), Judith Ann (Mrs Gilbert Wheeler), David C & James A. Educ: High sch, grad, 31. Polit & Govt Pos: Co recorder, Noble Co, Ohio, 41-47; committeeman, Noble Co Dem Cent Comt, 56-, mem exec comt, 60-, chmn, 60-72 & 74-; Presidential Elector, 64; mem, Ohio State Dem Exec Comt, 69-70; mem, Noble Co Bd of Elec, 70-, chmn, 72-74. Bus & Prof Pos: Acct dept, Cent Ohio Coal Co, Cumberland, Ohio, 46- Mem: Dem Action Club; Noble Co Dem Club. Relig: Protestant. Mailing Add: RR 4 Caldwell OH 43724

WHARTON, JAMES ERNEST (R)
b Binghamton, NY, Oct 4, 99; s James H Wharton & Mae Dibble W; m to Marion K Turner. Educ: Union Col, BA; Albany Law Sch, LLB, 19. Polit & Govt Pos: Surrogate Co Judge, also judge, Children's Court of Schoharie Co, 41 & 47; US Rep, NY, 51-65. Bus & Prof Pos: Lawyer, Claim & Legal Dept, Travelers Ins Co, 20-29; attorney-at-law, Richmond, NY, 29-32. Mil Serv: Army, Pvt, World War I. Mailing Add: Richmondville NY 12149

WHATLEY, CHARLES W (D)
Ala State Rep
Mailing Add: Rte 5 Box 250 Opelika AL 36801

WHEALTON, ROSS LAMONTE (R)
b Philadelphia, Pa, Feb 15, 46; s William Hamilton Whealton, Jr & Betsy Ross Hilghman W; m 1964 to Gail Louise Schmidt; c Dorothy Caroline. Educ: NCarolina High Sch, Denton, Md, grad, 65. Polit & Govt Pos: Mem, Md Rep State Cent Comt, 71-73; spec asst to US Rep William O Mills, 72-73; admin asst to US Rep Robert E Bauman, Md, 73- Bus & Prof Pos: Various pos, Preston Trucking Co, Md, 63-69, mgr spec serv div, 69-72, secy-treas, Colony Terminals, Inc, 71-72. Mem: Preston Lions; Preston Lions Community Ctr. Relig: Lutheran; treas, Immanual Lutheran Church, Preston, Md. Mailing Add: PO Box 223 Preston MD 21655

WHEATCRAFT, MARTHA CLARK (R)
Secy, Rep State Cent & Exec Comt Ohio
b Morrow Co, Ohio; d Col John R Clark & Mary Elizabeth Dawson C; m to Willard W Wheatcraft, wid; c Joan (Mrs Howard E Samuel). Educ: Columbus Off Training Sch, Bus Admin & Pub Rels, 18-20. Polit & Govt Pos: Chairwoman, Crawford Co Rep Cent Comt, Ohio, 48-70 & currently, secy, Crawford Co Rep Cent & Exec Comts, currently; state committeewoman, Ohio Rep Party, 50-; presidential elector, Eighth Cong Dist, 56; mem, Galion City Traffic Comn, 56-60; mem, Galion Civil Serv Comn, 66-68; mem, Crawford Co Bd of Elec, 56-; dist chmn, Neighbor to Neighbor, 62-; chmn, Eighth Dist Nixon-Agnew Comt, 68; mem bd of mgt, Ohio Fedn of Rep Women; mem, Rep State Cent & Exec Comt Ohio, currently, mem policy comt, 68-70, secy, 70-; alt deleg, Rep Nat Conv, 72. Bus & Prof Pos: Notary pub, Crawford Co, 50-; dir pub rels, Perfection-Cobey Co, Galion, Ohio, 54-, govt contract adminr, 56-; vpres & dir, Allied Indust Sales, Inc, 61- Publ: History of Eighth Ohio Dist. Mem: Ohio Mfrs Asn; Defense Supply Agency; Perfection Mgt Club; Harding Mem Libr Asn; Eastern Star (past matron, Burgoyne Chap). Honors & Awards: Organized & sponsored the first Navy-Indust Day held in US, Galion, Ohio, 5/59; Awarded Cert of Merit & Appreciation, US Army Procurement Dist, Cleveland, Ohio, 5/64. Relig: United Methodist. Mailing Add: PO Box 685 Galion OH 44833

WHEATLEY, ELECTRA CATSONIS (R)
b Washington, DC, Aug 6, 33; d Achilles Catsonis & Anastasia Carzis C. Educ: Pa State Univ, BA with Honors, 55; George Washington Univ Nat Law Ctr, JD with Honors, 69; Phi Beta Kappa; Kappa Beta Pi; Pi Gamma Mu; Phi Sigma Iota; Phi Kappa Phi; Alpha Lambda Delta. Polit & Govt Pos: Legis asst to US Rep Donald D Clancy, Ohio, 62-67; admin asst to US Rep John M Ashbrook, Ohio, 68- Bus & Prof Pos: Asst ed, Aero Digest, Washington, DC, 55-56; ed asst & admin secy, Fairchild Engine & Airplane Corp, 56-57; pub rels & exec suite secy, Kaiser Indust Corp, 57-60; secy to pres, George Washington Univ, 60-62. Mem: Am Bar Asn; Women's Bar Asn of DC; DC Bar; Top-Side Aviation Club. Honors & Awards: Phi Delta Delta Schaeffer Award; Outstanding Second-Year Law Student. Relig: Greek Orthodox. Mailing Add: Off of John M Ashbrook House of Rep Washington DC 20515

WHEELER, BOBBY A (D)
Ga State Rep
Mailing Add: Rte 1 Alma GA 31510

WHEELER, BRUCE (D)
Ariz State Rep
Mailing Add: 2606 N Columbus Blvd Tucson AZ 85712

WHEELER, EMILY LIDE (D)
VPres, SC Young Dem
b Augusta, Ga, Apr 6, 45; d Sam F Wheeler & Eulee Lide W; single. Educ: Univ SC, BA in Jour, 67, JD, 71; Phi Alpha Delta; Theta Sigma Phi; Zeta Tau Alpha; Angel Flight. Polit & Govt Pos: Intern, Off US Sen Olin D Johnston, SC, 64; page, Dem Nat Conv, 64, mem rules comt, 67, alt deleg, 68, deleg, 72; staff mem, US Sen Ernest F Holling Campaign, 66 & 68; vchmn, Saluda Co Dem Party, SC, 66-; deleg, Young Dem Nat Conv, 67; vpres, SC Young Dem, 69- Bus & Prof Pos: Dir, Midlands Tricentennial Ctr, 70-71; mem, Univ SC Bd of Women Visitors, 70-73; southern acct exec, Conlin-Dodds Alumni Travel, 71-72. Mem: Am Soc Travel Agents; Eastern Star; Carolina Carillon; SC Farm Bur; SC Master 4-H Club. Honors & Awards: Ky Col, Gov of Ky, 72. Relig: Methodist. Mailing Add: Rte 2 Ridge Spring SC 29129

WHEELER, GERRIDEE STENEHJEM (R)
Rep Nat Committeewoman, NDak
b Arnegard, NDak, May 29, 27; d Martin Sever Stenehjem & Emma Bjornstad S; m 1948 to Ronald Walter Wheeler; c Mary (Mrs Penn Bradbong), Lisa (Mrs Steven DeLapp), Kim (Mrs Dennis Collins), Jennifer, Jo Ann, Pamela, Kathy & Fred. Educ: Stephens Col, AA; Minot State Col, 47; Univ NDak, BA; Kappa Alpha Theta. Polit & Govt Pos: Charter mem, Legis Wives Club, NDak, 57-65; nat committeewoman, Young Rep, 59-63; deleg & mem platform comt, Rep Nat Conv, 72; Rep Nat Committeewoman, NDak, 72-, mem, Rule 29B Comt, Rep Nat Comt, 73- Bus & Prof Pos: Chmn, Mem Ment Health & Retardation Clin, 70-72; pres, NDak Coun Educ, 70-; vpres, Nat Asn for Ment Health, 71-73, pres, 75-; chmn, Dakota Ment Health Found, 72; mem, Nat Adv Coun on Comprehensive Health Planning, 72- Publ: Community mental health center, NDak Law Rev, summer 73; MH-Commentary, spring 75. Mem: Int Women's Year (President's comn); Fortnightly Club; Univ NDak Alumni Asn. Honors & Awards: Pub Health Worker of the Year, NDak Pub Health Asn, 66; Ment Health Worker of Decade, NDak Ment Health Asn, 70; Nominee for Woman of the Year, Ladies Home J. Relig: Lutheran. Mailing Add: 1231 E Highland Acres Rd Bismarck ND 58501

WHEELER, JAMES WALTER (D)
Chmn, Cherokee Co Dem Exec Comt, Ga
b Canton, Ga, Oct 31, 17; s William Henry Wheeler & Lola Cochran W; m 1946 to Vern Bassett; c Rebecca, Carole Ann & James W, Jr. Educ: Clemson Univ, 47. Polit & Govt Pos: Mem, Cherokee Co Dem Exec Comt, Ga, 50-55, secy-treas, 55-66, chmn, 66- Bus & Prof Pos: Dir qual control, Canton Textile Mills, Ga, 46-61, merchandising coordr, 61-65, admin asst, 65-68, mgr prod scheduling & control, 68-69, dir merchandising, 69- Mil Serv: Entered as Pvt, Army, 42, released as Sgt, 45, after serv in 27th Evacuation Hosp, ETO, 44-45; Bronze Arrowhead; Five Campaign Stars. Mem: Textile & Needle Trades Div, Am Soc Qual Control (charter mem & officer, 50-). Honors & Awards: Distinguished Serv Award, Am Soc Qual Control, 62. Relig: Baptist; Past chmn, Bd Deacons, First Baptist Church. Legal Res: Waleska Hwy Canton GA 30114 Mailing Add: Box 491 Canton GA 30114

WHEELER, JOHN HERVEY (D)
Dir Finance, NC Dem Party
b Kittrell, NC, Jan 1, 08 ,s John Leonidas Wheeler & Margaret Hervey W; m 1935 to Selena Lucille Warren; c Julia W (Mrs Taylor) & Warren Hervey. Educ: Morehouse Col, AB, 29; NC Col, Durham, LLB, 47; Omega Psi Phi. Hon Degrees: LLD, Shaw Univ, 54, JC Smith Univ, 63 & Duke Univ, 70; LHD, Morehouse Col, 67. Polit & Govt Pos: Mem, Sixth Dist Dem Legis Comt, NC, 54; mem, Comn on Race & Housing, 56-58; mem, President's Comt on Equal Employ Opportunity, 61-65; mem & vchmn, Durham City Redevelop Comn, NC, 61-; personal rep of Secy of Com, Int Trade Fair, Tripoli, 63; deleg, Dem Nat Conv, 64, 68 & 72; vchmn, Nat Comt for Community Rels, 64-; mem, US Adv Comn on Food & Fibers, 65-67; consult & lectr, US State Dept, Egypt, Syria & Cyprus, summer 66; chmn work session, White House Conf to Fulfill these Rights, 66; mem subcomt study racial desegregation pub schs, US Comn on Civil Rights, 66-; mem exec comt, Gov Comn Econ Develop, 67; mem, President's Comt Urban Housing, 68; dir finance, NC Dem Party, 70-; mem bus leadership adv coun, Off Econ Opportunity, currently; mem steering comt, Urban Coalition, currently. Bus & Prof Pos: With Mechanics & Farmers Bank, Durham, NC, 29-, pres, 52-; mem securities investment comt, NC Mutual Life Ins Co, 33-; mem bd dirs, Mechanics & Farmers Bank, Mutual Real Estate Investment Trust, Mutual Savings & Loan Asn, currently; incorporator & mem bd & exec comt, Nat Corp for Housing Partnerships, 69-; mem bd dirs, NC Mutual Life Ins Co, 72- Publ: Apartheid implemented by education in South Africa, J Negro Educ, 61; Impact of race relations on industrial relations in the South, Labor Law J, 7/64; Impact of civil rights groups on the poverty program, Duke Univ Law Rev, 66. Mem: NC & Am Bar Asns; Atlanta Univ (chmn bd trustees); Morehouse Col (secy bd); Lincoln Hosp, Durham (vchmn bd). Relig: African Methodist Episcopal Church; Treas & mem bd trustees, St Joseph's Church, Durham. Mailing Add: 302 Formosa Ave Durham NC 27707

WHEELER, MATHEW HUBERT (D)
Chmn, Maricopa Co Dem Cent Comt, Ariz
b Chicago, Ill, Nov 18, 25; s Matthew Michael Wheeler & Edna Hermanns W; m to Marilyn Lorraine Herrin; c Thomas Mathew, John Patrick, Joseph Henry, Patrick Frances, Diane Marie, Timothy James & Michelle Lee. Educ: Phoenix Col, 60-64. Polit & Govt Pos: Precinct committeeman, dist chmn, co vchmn, Maricopa Co Dem Cent Comt, 62-64, chmn, 74- Bus & Prof Pos: Foreman, Mountain Bell, 55-62, staff technician, 62-71, staff supvr, 71- Mil Serv: Entered as Seaman, Navy, 43, released as Fire Controlman 3/C. Mem: Optimist Int (secy-treas, 71-75). Relig: Catholic. Mailing Add: 4028 W Gardenia Phoenix AZ 85021

WHEELER, RALPH MERRILL, JR (R)
Idaho State Rep
b American Falls, Idaho, Aug 10, 32; s Ralph Merrill Wheeler, Sr & Monne Zemo W; m 1965 to Ann F Reed; c Vickie Diane, Michael Merrill, Jodi Lauren & Clark Reed. Educ: Idaho State Col, BS in Pharm, 54; Phi Delta Chi; Rho Chi; Sigma Nu. Polit & Govt Pos: City councilman, American Falls, Idaho, 57-64, mayor, 64-73; dir & vpres, Asn of Idaho Cities, State Munic League, 67-71, pres, 71-72; chmn zoning comn, Power Co, Idaho, 67-; mem & secy-treas, South East Idaho Coun of Govt, 72- Bus & Prof Pos: Owner & mgr, Rockland Pharm, American Falls, Idaho, 54- Mem: Idaho State Pharm Asn; Nat Asn Retail Druggists; Am Pharmaceutical Asn; Lions; US CofC. Honors & Awards: Idaho Pharmacist of the Year, Idaho State Pharmaceutical Asn, 72. Relig: Roman Catholic. Mailing Add: 659 Gifford Ave American Falls ID 83211

WHEELER, ROBERT R (R)
Chmn, Ninth Dist Rep Party, Mich
b Shelby, Mich, Mar 10, 27; s 1948 to Ann Jean Brondyke; c Norman R & Gerald A. Polit & Govt Pos: Chmn, Oceana Co Rep Party, formerly; chmn, Ninth Dist Rep Party, Mich, currently; dist supvr, Oceana Co; alt deleg, Rep Nat Conv, 68. Bus & Prof Pos: Ins agent. Mem: Mason (past master); Shelby CofC; Shelby Optimist Club; Optimist Int; Shelby Vol Fire Dept (chief). Relig: Congregational; Treas, First Congregational Church. Legal Res: RD 2 Shelby MI 49455 Mailing Add: PO Box 36 Shelby MI 49455

WHEELOCK, ROBERT WEBB (R)
Mem, Rep State Cent Comt Calif
b Delta, Colo, May 10, 07; s Dr Jay Edson Wheelock & Daisy Britton Webb W; div. Educ: Univ Denver, DDS, 28; Univ Calif Col Dent, Oral Surg & Oro-Facial Prosthesis, 46; Delta Sigma Delta. Polit & Govt Pos: Assoc mem, Rep State Cent Comt Calif, 62-64, mem, 64- Bus & Prof Pos: Pvt practice, Gen Dentistry, Bay City, Tex, 28-31. Mil Serv: Entered as Lt(jg), Dent Corps, Navy, 31, Capt (Ret), 59, after serv in Staff Positions, Ships, Sta & Hosp, Staff Dent Officer, Commandant Naval Operating Base, Leyte, Philippines, 44-45 & Staff Dent Officer, Philippine Sea Frontier, 45-46; Letter of Commendation from Comdr Naval Operating Base, Leyte Gulf, Philippine Islands, 45; China Serv Medal; Am Defense Medal, Two Am Campaign Medals; World War II Medal. Publ: Open reduction of fractured mandible, J Oral Surg, 7/50. Mem: Am Dent Asn; Royal Soc Health, Eng; DeMolay; charter mem Ocean Beach Town Coun, San Diego, Calif; charter mem Lions Club, Bay City, Tex. Honors & Awards: Cong Cert of Appreciation, Congressman Bob Wilson, 60; Cert of Appreciation in Grateful Recognition of Serv to Independent Higher Educ & to Univ Denver, 63; Invited to Presidential Inauguration, 69. Relig: Baptist. Mailing Add: 4275 Coronado Ave San Diego CA 92107

WHELAN, GERALD T (D)
Lt Gov, Nebr
Mailing Add: State Capitol Lincoln NE 68509

WHELAN, JAMES OCTAVIUS, JR (R)
Pa State Rep
b Petersburg, Va, Sept 19, 36; s James Octavius Whelan & Eva Yancey W; m 1961 to Nancy Ann Hundley; c Lee, James, III, Jeffrey, Jonathan & Jarrett. Educ: Univ Richmond, BS, 61; St Francis Col, MA, 70; Lambda Chi Alpha. Polit & Govt Pos: Councilman, Westmont Borough, Pa, 71-74; Pa State Rep, 74- Bus & Prof Pos: Sales supvr, Humble Oil & Refining Co, 61-70; pres, Mr Gas Inc, Johnstown, Pa, 70- Mil Serv: Entered as Seaman Recruit, Navy, 56, released as YN-3, 59; Good Conduct Medal. Mem: Univ Pittsburgh at Johnstown (adv

bd); United Fund (adv bd); Johnstown Area Regional Indust (adv bd); Sunnehanna Country Club (secy); YMCA (mem bd dirs). Honors & Awards: Outstanding Young Men, Jaycee's, Martinsville, Va, 64. Relig: Protestant. Mailing Add: 1603 Debran Lane Johnstown PA 19505

WHELAN, MARY ELIZABETH (D)
Secy, Muskegon Co Dem Comt, Mich
b Racine, Wis, June 1, 22; d Edward J Whelan & Cecilia Toohey W; single. Educ: Univ Wis, Racine-Milwaukee Br, 40-42; Milwaukee State Teachers Col, BS, 45; Univ Mich, Ann Arbor, MA, 57; Kappa Delta Pi. Polit & Govt Pos: Secy, Muskegon Co Dem Comt, Mich, 69-; alt deleg, Mich Dem State Cent Comt, 70-71; secy, Ninth Dist Dem Comt, 70-; co-chmn subcomt, Mich Dem State Policy Comt, 73-; deleg, Dem Nat Mid-Term Conf, 74. Bus & Prof Pos: Teacher sci & social studies, Slinger High Sch, Wis, 45 & S Side Jr High Sch, Sheboygan, 45-47; teacher sci, Cent Jr High Sch, Muskegon, Mich, 47 & Steele Jr High Sch, currently. Publ: Kirtland Warbler in fall migration in Muskegon County, Jack Pine Warbler, 53; Young tree swallow fed fresh water snails, Wilson Bull, 54. Mem: Mich Educ Asn (chairperson 13C-EPAC, 74-); Am Asn Advan Sci; Mich Audubon Soc; Mich Entomological Soc; Nat Educ Asn. Honors & Awards: Nat Sci Found research fel for high sch teachers, Mont State Univ Biol Sta. Relig: Catholic. Legal Res: 1422 Jiroch Muskegon MI 49442 Mailing Add: Steele Jr High Sch Amity & Roberts Muskegon MI 49442

WHELLER, ROBERT W (D)
NH State Rep
Mailing Add: 27 Center St Goffstown NH 03045

WHETMORE, JAMES EDWARD (R)
Calif State Sen
b Columbus, Ohio, Mar 9, 13; s Edward Claude Whetmore & Anna Garnett Willis W; c Edward J, Patricia A (Mrs Kirk MacDonald) & Karen R (Mrs Charles Borchardt); m 1971 to Catherine Cunningham Gilmore; c Daniel & Tracy Gilmore. Educ: LaSalle Exten Univ, LLB, 61. Polit & Govt Pos: Calif State Assemblyman, 63-66; Calif State Sen, 35th Senate Dist, 66- Bus & Prof Pos: Owner & operator, Whetmore Orchestra, 35-; attorney pvt practice, Calif, 61- Mem: Calif & Orange Co Bar Asns; Optimists; CofC; Orchestra Leaders of Hollywood (past pres). Relig: Lutheran. Legal Res: Suite 727 Bank of Am Tower Orange CA 92668 Mailing Add: State Capitol Sacramento CA 95814

WHICHARD, WILLIS PADGETT (D)
NC State Sen
b Durham, NC, May 24, 40; s Willis Guilford Whichard & Beulah Padgett W; m 1961 to Leona Irene Paschal; c Jennifer. Educ: Univ NC, Chapel Hill, AB, 62, JD, 65; Phi Beta Kappa; Phi Alpha Theta; Order of the Coif; Phi Delta Phi. Polit & Govt Pos: Law clerk, Justice William H Bobbitt, 65-66; mem, NC Gen Statutes Comn, 69-73; NC State Rep, 71-75; mem, Southern Growth Policies Bd, 72-; mem, NC Land Policy Coun, 75-; NC State Sen, 75- Bus & Prof Pos: Partner, Powe, Porter, Alphin & Whichard, Attorneys-at-law, 66- Mil Serv: NC Army Nat Guard, 66-72. Publ: The legislature & the legislator in North Carolina, Popular Govt, spring 75. Mem: Am & NC State Bar Asns; 14th Judicial Dist Bar; Tobaccoland Kiwanis; Jaycees, Durham, NC. Honors & Awards: Distinguished Serv Award, Jaycees, 71. Relig: Baptist. Mailing Add: 5608 Woodberry Rd Durham NC 27707

WHIDDEN, VINCENT YALE (D)
b West Palm Beach, Fla, Oct 22, 19; s Wordie LeRoy Whidden & Winona Faye O'Leary W; m 1939 to Helen Lynwood Waters; c Yale O'Leary, Susan Lynwood (Mrs Bruce Godwin Macomber) & Sherry Louise. Educ: Univ Tampa, BS, 52; Stetson Law Col, 53 & 56; Phi Delta Phi; Kappa Sigma Kappa. Polit & Govt Pos: Treas, Hillsboro Co Fla Dem Party, 58-66; state committeeman, Am Independent Party, 69-; chmn, Dem Party Caucus, Sixth Cong Dist, Fla, 72; alt deleg, Dem Nat Conv, 72; mem, Hillsborough Co Dem Comt; participant, Gov George Wallace Campaign. Bus & Prof Pos: Owner, Yale Whidden Gen Ins Agency, 67-70, retired. Mil Serv: Entered as SF/3C, Navy, 43 & released as SF/3C salvage diver, 45, after serv in Salvage Assigned Pier 88 New York, 44-45. Mem: DAV; United Steelworkers Local 2120 (trustee, 51-53). Honors & Awards: Founder of Dem Party Forum of the Air, Radio Sta WDAE & WFLA, Hillsboro Co Dem Party, 66, Outstanding Serv Award, 66. Relig: Methodist. Mailing Add: 3421 Belcher Dr Tampa FL 33609

WHIPPLE, BLAINE (D)
Ore State Sen
b Martin, SDak, Feb 22, 30; s Blaine Whipple & Pearl Scott W; m 1966 to Ines Mae Peterson; c Judith Lynn Steele (stepdaughter), Robert Bruce Steele (stepson) & Blaine Scott. Educ: Mankato State Teachers Col, 49; Univ Miss, 50; Univ Minn, Minneapolis, BA, 56; Univ Ore, MS, 59. Polit & Govt Pos: Fourth dist campaign dir, Reelect Charles O Porter to Cong Comt, Ore, 58; exec dir, Ore Dem Party, 60-62; Dem nominee for Cong, First Dist, 62 & 64; alt chmn, Wash Co Dem Cent Comt, 62-66; chmn, Howard Morgan for US Senate Comt, 66; Dem nominee, Ore State Senate, Wash & Yamhill Co, 66; vchmn, Wash Co Intermediate Educ Dist, 66-70, chmn, 70-; chmn, Oregonians for McCarthy, 68; deleg-at-lg, Dem Nat Conv, 68 & deleg & chmn Ore deleg, 72; Dem Nat Committeeman, Ore, 68-; chmn, Ore McGovern for President Comt, 72; Ore State Sen, Dist Three, 75- Bus & Prof Pos: Dir, Ore Small Bus Admin, 67-68; pres, Whipple Develop Corp, 72-; regional ed, Real Estate News Observer. Mil Serv: Entered as A/S, Navy, 50, released as Journalist 2/C, 54, after serv in Mil Sea Transportation Serv & Barbers Point Naval Air Sta, Hawaii, 52-54; Good Conduct Medal. Mem: Nat Asn Homebuilders; Nat Asn Real Estate Brokers; Multi-Family Housing Coun, Homebuilders Asn of Metrop Portland (dir, 71 & 74, secy, 73-, pres, 74); Ore State Homebuilders Asn (dir, 72). Relig: Protestant. Mailing Add: 8455 SW Brookridge Portland OR 97225

WHIPPLE, DALEY E (R)
NH State Rep
Mailing Add: Fitzwilliam NH 03447

WHITAKER, CHARLES JAMES, SR (D)
Polit & Govt Pos: Vchmn, Richland Co Dem Party, SC, formerly, chmn, 73-74; deleg, Dem Nat Conv, 72. Mailing Add: 6308 Benedict St Columbia SC 29203

WHITAKER, JOHN CARROLL (R)
b Victoria, BC, Dec 29, 26; s Clifford Edmund Whitaker & Stella Neville W; m 1958 to Mary Elizabeth Bradley; c John Clifford, Robert Carroll, Stephen Bradley, William Burns & James Ford. Educ: Georgetown Univ, BSS, 49; Johns Hopkins Univ, PhD in Geol. Polit & Govt Pos: Asst campaign mgr for schedules & tour for President Richard M Nixon & Vice President Agnew, 68; Secy to the Cabinet, 69-70; Dep Asst to the President for Domestic Affairs, 70-73; Under Secy, US Dept Interior, 73-75. Bus & Prof Pos: Geologist, Standard Oil of Calif, 53-55; mgr geophys sales, Lundberg Explor Ltd, Toronto, 55-57; mgr geophys sales, Hycon Aerial Survey, Inc, Pasadena, Calif, 57-59; vpres, Int Aero Serv Co Div, Litton Industs, Philadelphia, Pa, 69-77; vpres, John C Whitaker & Co, Washington, DC, 66-68. Mil Serv: Entered as A/S, Navy, 44, released as Aerographers Mate 3/C, 46. Publ: Geology of Catoctin Mountain: Maryland & Virginia, 55 & Cambrian clastics in Maryland, 55, Bull Geol Soc Am; The proton nuclear precession magnetometer for airborne geophysical exploration, Oil & Gas J, 57. Mem: Am Asn Petroleum Geologists; Geol Soc Am; Soc Explor Geophysicists; Am Geophys Union; Am Cong Surveying & Mapping. Relig: Roman Catholic. Mailing Add: 8013 Greentree Rd Bethesda MD 20034

WHITAKER, NEAL DALE (R)
Kans State Rep
b Topeka, Kans, May 3, 47; s Dale W Whitaker & Jessie H Neal W; m 1969 to Jo Lynn Johnson; c Tracy Lynn. Educ: Sterling Col, BS, 70. Polit & Govt Pos: Rep precinct committeeman, Wichita, Kans, 70-72; Kans State Rep, 73- Bus & Prof Pos: Asst exec vpres, Kans Restaurant Asn, Wichita, 73- Mil Serv: Entered as Basic Airman, Kans Air Nat Guard, S/Sgt, 6 years; Expert Marksman. Mem: Kans Soc Asn Execs; Int Soc Restaurant Asn Execs. Relig: Presbyterian. Legal Res: 2361 Marigold Wichita KS 67204 Mailing Add: 359 S Hydraulic Wichita KS 67211

WHITCOMB, EDGAR DOUD (R)
b Hayden, Ind, Nov 6, 17; s John William Whitcomb & Louise Doud W; m 1951 to Patricia Louise Dolfuss; c Patricia Louise, Alice Elaine, Linda Ann, John Doud & Shelley Jean. Educ: Ind Univ, 36-39; Ind Univ Sch Law, LLB, 50; Phi Delta Phi. Polit & Govt Pos: Ind State Sen, 51-54; Asst US Attorney, Justice Dept Southern Dist Ind, 55-56; chmn, Great Lakes Comn, 65-66; Secy of State, Ind, 66-69, Gov, 69-73; deleg, Rep Nat Conv, 72. Bus & Prof Pos: Lawyer, Seymour, Ind, 56- Mil Serv: Entered as Flying Cadet, Army Air Corps, 40, released as Maj, 46, after serv in 19th Bombardment Group, Air Transport Command, 5th Air Force Hq, Asiatic Theater; Col, Air Force Res, 65; Air Medal with Oak Leaf Cluster; Presidential Unit Citation with Six Oak Leaf Clusters. Publ: Escape from Corregidor, Henry Regnery Publ Co, 58. Mem: Ind & Am Bar Asns; Am Legion; life mem VFW. Relig: Methodist. Mailing Add: 636 N Poplar Seymour IN 47274

WHITE, ANTHONY EUGENE (D)
Chmn, Estill Co Dem Party, Ky
b Irvine, Ky, July 13, 49; s Ernest Eugene White & Bobby Brandenburg W; m 1970 to Paulo Jo Hughes; c Jason Andrew. Educ: Eastern Ky Univ, 70-; Vet Club. Polit & Govt Pos: Youth chmn, Estill Co Dem Party, Irvine, Ky, 72, chmn, 72- Mil Serv: Entered as Pvt E-1, Army, 67, released as Sp/5 E-5, 70, after serv in 44th SHMA; Pac Theatre, Korea, 68-69; Nat Defense Medal; Good Conduct Medal; Armed Forces Expeditionary Medal. Mem: Am Legion (chaplain, Irvine, Ky, 70-); VFW; Boy Scouts (asst scout master, Troop 144, 70-). Relig: Christian. Mailing Add: 602 Cantrill St Irvine KY 40336

WHITE, BERTA LEE (D)
Miss State Sen
b Obadiah, Miss, June 27, 14; m to Gordon White. Polit & Govt Pos: Miss State Rep, formerly; Miss State Sen, 68- Bus & Prof Pos: Secy to dir, Hughes Tel Co. Mem: Center Hill Community Develop; Lauderdale Co Cancer & Ment Health Bd; Meridian Bus & Prof Women; Miss Women's Cabinet; Farm Bur (state dir). Relig: Presbyterian. Mailing Add: Rte 1 Bailey MS 39320

WHITE, BEVERLY JEAN (D)
Utah State Rep
b Salt Lake City, Utah, Sept 28, 28; d Gustave R Larson & Helene Sterzer L; m 1947 to Marion Floyd White; c Susan Helene (Mrs John Morris), Douglas Floyd, Robyn Ann (Mrs James Bauder), David Scott & Wendy Jo. Educ: Int Bus Machines Sch, grad, 48. Polit & Govt Pos: Deleg, Co & State Convs, Utah, 24 years; dist vice chairlady, Dem Party, Tooele, Utah, 58 & 59; pres, Lady Dem, 58-59; vice chairlady, Tooele Co Dem Party, 61-; app, Utah State Bd Corrections, 65-71; mem, State Patronage Comt, 67-69; deleg, Dem Nat Conv, 68 & 72; Utah State Rep, Dist 64, 71-, mem, Ment Health Adv Bd, Utah House Rep, 71-, mem, Halfway House Adv Coun & Juv Court Adv Coun, 71- Mem: PTA (past officer); Tooele Women's Club; Tooele Co Lady Dem; Tooele Vol Firemens Auxiliary. Relig: Latter-day Saint. Mailing Add: 122 Russell Ave Tooele UT 84074

WHITE, BYRON R
Assoc Justice, US Supreme Court
b Ft Collins, Colo, June 8, 17; m to Marion Stearns; c Charles & Nancy. Educ: Univ Colo, BA, 38; Oxford Univ, Rhodes scholar, 39; Yale Law Sch, LLB, 46; Phi Beta Kappa; Phi Gamma Delta; Order of the Coif. Polit & Govt Pos: Law clerk to Chief Justice of the US Supreme Court, 46-47; Dep Attorney Gen, US, 61-62; Assoc Justice, US Supreme Court, 62- Bus & Prof Pos: Attorney, Lewis, Grant & Davis, Denver, Colo, 47-60. Mil Serv: Naval Res, World War II. Legal Res: CO Mailing Add: c/o US Supreme Court One First St NE Washington DC 20543

WHITE, CATHERINE KILMURRAY (D)
Committeewoman, Union Co Dem Comt, NJ
b Pikesville, Md, Apr 19, 30; d Martin Francis Kilmurray & Catherine McGrath K; c Catherine Elizabeth. Educ: Univ Md, BA, 54; Columbia Univ Sch Law, JD, 69; Int Club. Polit & Govt Pos: Mem, Human Rels Comn, City of Plainfield, NJ, 66-68; alt deleg, Dem Nat Conv, 68; mem, Charter Revision Study Comn, City of Plainfield, NJ, 71-72; committeewoman, Union Co Dem Comt, NJ, 72- Bus & Prof Pos: Teacher, Prince George Co, Md, 54-55 & 56-59; law practice, NJ, 69- Mem: NJ State Bar Asn; Women's Polit Caucus NJ; Am Civil Liberties Union. Legal Res: 1145 Woodland Ave Plainfield NJ 07060 Mailing Add: 127 Watchung Ave Plainfield NJ 07061

WHITE, CHARLES CODY (D)
Mem, Third Dist Dem Exec Comt, Ga
b Atlanta, Ga, May 30, 06; s Frank Gilman White & Anna Collier W; m 1934 to Jane Allison Butler; c Charles Cody, Jr, Jane Allison (Mrs Gene Booth) & Robert Christopher (deceased). Polit & Govt Pos: Mem, Muscogee Co Dem Exec Comt, 45-68, vchmn, 49-56, chmn, 56-65; mem bd educ, Muscogee Co Sch Dist, 58-68; mem, Third Dist Dem Exec Comt, 65-; cand for Tax Comnr, Muscogee Co; vchmn, Muscogee Co Bd Elec, 70-72. Mem: Nat, Ga & Columbus Asns; Independent Ins Agents; Ga Sch Bds Asn; Columbus High Sch PTA. Relig: Baptist. Legal Res: 1623 Carter Ave Columbus GA 31906 Mailing Add: PO Box 135 Columbus GA 31902

WHITE, CLYDE MILTON (D)
Secy, 57th Rep Dist Dem Comt, Ill
b Johnston City, Ill, Sept 12, 07; s Edgar M White & Leona E Newton W; m 1948 to Mildred C Crompton; c Gerold F & David J Marlow. Educ: High sch, 4 years. Polit & Govt Pos: Mem draft bd, Williamson Co, Ill, 62-; investr, Secy of State, Ill, 64-; secy, 57th Rep Dist Dem Comt, 66- Bus & Prof Pos: Co-owner coal mine, White & Son Coal Co, Marion, Ill, 30-41. Mil Serv: Entered as Pvt, Air Force, 42, released as S/Sgt, 45, after serv in Transport Command ETO, 43-45; Res, 45-62. Relig: Protestant. Mailing Add: 1116 N Washington Ave Johnston City IL 62951

WHITE, DEWEY ANDERSON, JR (D)
Ala State Rep
b Atlanta, Ga, Jan 28, 23; s Dewey Anderson White, Sr & Angie Evelyn Watts W; m 1945 to Lillian; c Lilette (Mrs Steve Puckett), Nancy (Mrs Mike Kirchoff), Janet & Dewey Anderson, III. Educ: Birmingham Southern Col, BS, 43; Univ Ala Med Sch, 43-45; Univ Va Med Sch, MD, 47; Omicron Delta Kappa; Sigma Alpha Epsilon. Polit & Govt Pos: Ala State Rep, 75- Bus & Prof Pos: Pediatrician, Pediatric Assocs, Birmingham, Ala, 50- Mil Serv: Entered as A/S, Navy, 43, released as Lt(jg), 49, after serv in US Naval Hosp, Jacksonville, Fla. Mem: Jefferson Co Med Asn (vpres); Ala State Med Asn. Relig: Presbyterian; elder, S Highland Presby Church. Legal Res: 2301 Country Club Pl Birmingham AL 35223 Mailing Add: PO Box 7685-A Birmingham AL 35223

WHITE, DIANE MARY (D)
b Norfolk, Va, May 20, 45; d Henry Albert White & Dorothy Clare Martin W; single. Educ: Rosary Hill Col, BA, 66. Polit & Govt Pos: Intern, Internal Revenue Serv, Buffalo, NY, summer 66; staff asst to US Sen Robert F Kennedy, NY, 66-68; staff asst to US Sen Edward M Kennedy, Mass, 68-69; deleg & vchmn, Colo deleg, Dem Nat Conv, 72; coordr, McGovern for President, San Barnardino Region, Calif, 72. Bus & Prof Pos: Ski instr, Aspen Skiing Corp, Colo, currently. Relig: Roman Catholic. Legal Res: Apt 7 408 S Original Aspen CO 81611 Mailing Add: PO Box 2689 Aspen CO 81611

WHITE, DONALD BLAISDELL (R)
Chmn, Lexington Rep Town Comt, Mass
b Woburn, Mass, Oct 1, 29; s Malcolm Stuart White & Edna M Neville W; m 1954 to Ellen Parker Holmes; c Nina Stuart, Melissa Parker, Maria Standish, Lisabeth Mason, Donald Blaisdell, Jr, Charles Parker & Andrea Warrington. Educ: Tufts Univ, BS, 51; Theta Delta Chi. Polit & Govt Pos: Pres & secy, Woburn Young Rep Club, Mass, 57-60; precinct chmn, Lexington Rep Town Comt, 64, chmn, 65-; mem, Lexington Rep Finance Comt, 68-; mem, Town Meeting Appropriations Comt, Lexington, currently. Bus & Prof Pos: Product mgr, Boston Woven Hose, 60-; vpres & gen mgr, Black & Webster Sales, 64-; vpres & gen mgr, Hydraulic Serv & Eng, 72- Mil Serv: Entered as Pvt, Mass Nat Guard, 48, released as Sgt, 1/C, 56, after serv in 182nd Regt; Marksmanship Medals. Mem: Hancock Men's Club. Relig: Protestant. Mailing Add: 73 Hancock St Lexington MA 02173

WHITE, DONALD STANLEY (D)
Mem, Calif Dem State Cent Comt
b New York, NY, May 2, 35; s Martin White & Florence Meiman W; m 1960 to Sylvia Phyllis Schostak; c Stephen & Andrew. Educ: Univ Calif, Los Angeles, BA; Univ Calif Sch Law, Berkeley, LLB. Polit & Govt Pos: Dep Pub Defender, Los Angeles, Calif, 61-62; Dep Pub Defender, Los Angeles Co, 65-67; assoc dir, Peace Corps, Ghana & Tanzania, 62-65; mem, Los Angeles Co Dem Cent Comt, 66-68; cand for US Rep, 20th Cong Dist, Calif, 68; mem & chmn 20th Cong Dist Deleg, Calif Dem State Cent Comt, 68- Bus & Prof Pos: Pvt attorney, Stolzberg & White, 72- Publ: Seagoing Men & Automation, Marine Cooks & Stewards Union, 61. Mem: Am, Calif & Criminal Courts Bar Asns; Lawyers Club of Los Angeles. Mailing Add: 1937 Myra Ave Los Angeles CA 90027

WHITE, E HOMER, JR (D)
Md State Sen
Mailing Add: 724 Camden Ave Salisbury MD 21801

WHITE, ELINOR SUE (R)
Chmn, Lincoln Co Rep Party, Okla
b Oklahoma City, Okla, Dec 6, 34; s Robert John Unruh & Oklahoma LeMaster U; m 1958 to Carl Anderson White; c Carl Anderson, Jr, Robert Eric & Timothy Allen. Educ: Principia Col, 53-55; Univ Okla, BA, 58; Omicron Nu; Delta Delta Delta. Polit & Govt Pos: Secy, Lincoln Co Rep Party, 61-63, vchmn, 63-69, chmn, 69-, state committeewoman, 75-; first vpres, Lincoln Co Rep Women's Club, 63-65; chmn, Lincoln Co Women for Nixon, 68; mem women's activities exec comt, US Sen Henry Bellmon Campaign, 68; co chmn, Nixon Reelec Comt, 72; co coordr, Henry Bellmon Senatorial Campaign, 74; Bellmon Belle Co Chmn, 74. Bus & Prof Pos: Interior design, consult. Mem: Forum Study Club; Delta Delta Delta Alumni Asn; Rep Women's Club; Principia Club, Oklahoma City (pres, 73-75); Chandler Bicentennial Comt. Relig: Christian Science. Mailing Add: 254 Marshall Dr Chandler OK 74834

WHITE, EUGENE JAMES (D)
Nat Committeeman, Miss Young Dem
b West Palm Beach, Fla, Oct 14, 53; s Eugene James White, Sr & Marie Mitchel W; single. Educ: Meridian Jr Col, AA, 73; Univ Southern Miss, BS, 75; Phi Theta Kappa; Young Dem. Polit & Govt Pos: Mem exec comt, Lauderdale Co Dem Party, Miss, 72-; mem exec comt, Miss Dem State Cent Comt, 72-; chairperson, Miss Young Dem, 73-74, nat committeeman, 75-; deleg, Dem Nat Mid-Term Conf, 74. Bus & Prof Pos: Clerk, Great Atlantic & Pac Tea Co, 71-75. Mem: Miss Coun Human Rels; Common Cause; Students Int Meditation Soc. Relig: Episcopal. Mailing Add: 1643 31st St Meridian MS 39301

WHITE, F CLIFTON (R)
b Leonardsville, NY, June 13, 18; s Frederick H White & Mary Hicks W; m 1940 to Gladys Bunnell; c F Clifton, Jr & A Carole (Mrs Greene). Educ: Colgate Univ, AB, 40; Cornell Univ, grad work in govt, 45-47; Delta Sigma Rho; Freeman H Allan Soc. Hon Degrees: Dr Polit Sci, Hillsdale Col (Mich), 74. Polit & Govt Pos: Deleg, Rep Nat Conv, 48 & 68, alt deleg-at-lg, 52, alt dist deleg, 56, hon deleg, 72; deleg & chmn conv comts, Nat Young Rep Conv, 49, 51, 53 & 55; faculty adv, Ithaca Col & Cornell Univ Young Rep Clubs, 48-49; pres, NY State Young Rep, 50-52; spec asst to NY Rep State Chmn, 50-52; deleg, President's Hwy Safety Coun, 53; exec dep comnr, NY State Bur Motor Vehicles, 52-55, acting comnr, 55; dir orgn, Nat Nixon-Lodge Vols, 60; mgr & adv in campaigns for pub off, local to nat level; dir, Nat Draft Goldwater Comt, 63; nat dir, Goldwater for President Comt, 64; nat dir, Citizens for Goldwater-Miller, 64; campaign mgr, Budley for Senate, NY, 70; consult to chmn, Comt to Reelect the President, 72; pub mem inspection team, US Info Agency, 72. Bus & Prof Pos: Chmn social sci dept, Ravena Pub Schs; instr social sci, Cornell Univ, 45-50; lectr polit sci, Ithaca Col, 49-51; pres, Pub Affairs Counr, Inc, 57-60; pres, F Clifton White & Assocs, Inc, NY & Inst of Fiscal & Polit Educ, New York, currently; chmn bd, Pub Affairs Analysts, Inc, New York, currently; dir, Pub Affairs Coun, currently; chmn bd, Dir Action Serv Inc, currently. Mil Serv: Entered as Pvt, Air Force, 42, released as Capt, 45, after serv in 390th Bomb Group, 8th Air Force, ETO, 42-44; Air Medal with Three Oak Leaf Clusters; Distinguished Flying Cross; Distinguished Unit Citation with Cluster. Publ: You Should be a Politician, Pub Affairs Counr, Inc, 59; co-auth, Suite 3505, Arlington House, 67 & Yes, We Can, Abbey Press, 72. Mem: Am Polit Sci Asn; Am Acad Polit & Social Sci; Acad Polit Sci; Am Asn Polit Consult (pres, 70-); Int Asn Polit Campaign Consult (dir). Relig: Presbyterian; Elder, Rye Presby Church, NY. Legal Res: 8 Joshua Lane Greenwich CT 06830 Mailing Add: PO Box 1605 Greenwich CT 06830

WHITE, GLENN (D)
Ky State Rep
Mailing Add: Rte 1 Van Meter Rd Winchester KY 40391

WHITE, JAMES H, JR (D)
Ky State Rep
Mailing Add: Box 242 Barbourville KY 40906

WHITE, JAMES HOWARD (D)
Tenn State Sen
b Hot Springs, Ark, Sept 5, 30; s Jesse Howard White & Annie Lou Conner W; m 1969 to Mimi Phillips; c Christopher Luke, Sean Gardner, JoAnne, Robin Angela, David William & Lawrence Russell. Educ: Univ Mo, BJour, 57; Memphis State Univ, JD, 68; Psi Chi; Sigma Delta Chi. Polit & Govt Pos: Tenn State Sen, Dist 30, 73-; chmn, Shelby Co Dem Party, Tenn, 74- Bus & Prof Pos: Newspaper reporter, Memphis Press-Scimitar, Tenn, 57-69; attorney-at-law, Memphis, 69- Mil Serv: Entered as Pvt, Air Force, 50, released as S/Sgt, 54, after serv in finance, 3rd Air Force, United Kingdom, 51-54. Mem: Memphis-Shelby Co Bar Asn; Chickasaw Basin Authority. Honors & Awards: One of Ten Most Outstanding Legislators in Tenn, Tenn Vol Women's Round Table, 73. Relig: Presbyterian. Mailing Add: Suite 2904 100 N Main St Memphis TN 38103

WHITE, JAMES R (R)
Mem Exec Bd, Passaic Co Rep Orgn, NJ
b Paterson, NJ, Aug 7, 30; s Albert White & Mary Betar W; m 1954 to Lois Elaine Costa; c James A, Jeanne M, Mary E, Kathleen A & David R. Educ: Villanova Univ, BS in Econ, 53; NY Univ, MS, 55. Polit & Govt Pos: Councilman, Totowa, NJ, 63-69; alt deleg, Rep Nat Conv, 68; mem exec bd, Passaic Co Rep Orgn, currently. Bus & Prof Pos: Officer trainee, Citizens Trust, Paterson, NJ, 54; asst secy, Totowa Savings, 55-61; exec vpres, Mahwah Savings & Loan, 62-69. Mem: Bergen Co, NJ & US Savings & Loan Leagues; Elks; KofC. Relig: Roman Catholic. Mailing Add: 131 Washington Pl Totowa NJ 07512

WHITE, JAMES WILSON (D)
Mem Exec Comt, Pa Dem State Comt
b Pittsburgh, Pa, Dec 31, 26; s David White & Elizabeth Wilson W; m 1948 to Lois E Wyman; c Patricia Lee, Nancy Evelyn, Kathleen Elizabeth & Mary Josephine. Educ: Pa State Univ, BS, 50. Polit & Govt Pos: Supt, Pa Dept Hwy, 57-63; pres, Pa Young Dem Clubs, 60-62; spec asst to pres, Young Dem Clubs of Am, 63-65; chmn, Pa Agr Stabilization & Conserv Serv, US Dept Agr, 64-69; alt deleg, Dem Nat Conv, 68; nat chmn, Nat Comt for Improv of Rural Am, 69-73; committeeman, Pa Dem State Comt, 69-, mem exec comt, 72- Bus & Prof Pos: Co-owner, Homestead Farms, Kittanning, Pa, 50-; pres, White Enterprises, 60-; secy-treas, Manor Minerals Inc, 63-; mem exec bd, Pa Rural Area Develop Comt, 65-69; pres, Mid Armstrong Co Develop Orgn, 70-73; secy-treas, Manor Develop Corp, 71- Mil Serv: Entered as A/S, Navy, 44, released as Seaman 1/C, 46, after serv in SPac & Philippines, 45-46; Philippine & Pac Theatre Ribbons. Mem: Pa Stone Producers Asn; Nat Farmers Union; Elks; Rotary; VFW. Honors & Awards: Appointed US Deleg of Young Polit Leaders to NATO, 65. Relig: Presbyterian. Legal Res: 354 N Jefferson St Kittanning PA 16201 Mailing Add: 265 S Jefferson St Kittanning PA 16201

WHITE, JEAN CHRISTENSEN (R)
First VChmn, San Diego Co Rep Cent Comt, Calif
b Franksville, Wis, Aug 19, 34; d Norman W Christensen & Esther Hansen C; m 1956 to Robert Cecil White; c Douglas Hunter & Carol Andersen. Educ: Northwestern Univ, BS in Jour, 56; Theta Sigma Phi; Alpha Omicron Pi. Polit & Govt Pos: Rep precinct chmn in North San Diego, San Diego Co Rep Cent Comt, 61-64, exec secy, 65-66, mem & first vchmn, currently; campaign coordr, Assemblyman Pete Wilson, 76th Dist, 66, dist secy, 66-68; mem, Rep State Cent Comt Calif, 69-; campaign coordr, Mayor Pete Wilson, San Diego, 71; San Diego & Imperial Co campaign mgr, Houston I Flournoy for Gov Comt, 74. Mem: Rep Assocs (bd dirs); Clairemont Rep Women's Club; Women in Commun, Inc (pres-elect); Globe Guilder Steering Comt; San Diego Pub Rels Club. Relig: Presbyterian. Mailing Add: 3151 Fryden Ct San Diego CA 92117

WHITE, JESSE CLARK, JR (D)
Ill State Rep
b Alton, Ill, June 23, 34; s Jesse Clark White, Sr & Julia Mae Chapman; m 1967 to Sylvia; c Lorraine & Kevin. Educ: Ala State Col, BS, 57; NTex State Univ, summer 66; Kappa Alpha Psi. Polit & Govt Pos: Precinct capt, 42nd Ward Ill Dem Orgn, 73-75; Ill State Rep, 13th Dist, 75- Bus & Prof Pos: Teacher, Chicago Bd Educ, Schiller Sch, 59. Mil Serv: Entered as Pvt, Army, 57, released as SP-4, 59, after serv in 101st Airborne Div, SP-4, Ill Nat Guard, 74-75; Parachutist Wings. Mem: Boy Scouts Am (cubmaster, adv scoutmaster, 67-); Isham Mem YMCA (bd mem); Chicago Metro Ctr (recruiter); Near North Urban Progress (adv coun); Prof Baseball Players Am. Honors & Awards: Dedicated Teacher of the Year, Citizens Sch Comt, 69; Citizen of the Year, Chicago Crime Comn, 73; Excellence in Educ Award, Supt Pub Instr State Ill, 74; Silver Beaver, Chicago Area Coun Boy Scouts Am, 75; Athlete of the Year, Chicago Park Dist, 75. Relig: Protestant. Legal Res: 1451 N North Park Apt A Chicago IL 60610 Mailing Add: 1366 N Sedgewick St Chicago IL 60610

WHITE, JIM F (DFL)
Minn State Rep
b Minn, May 13, 35; s F J White & Louise Gephart W; m 1958 to Patricia C Fischer; c Mark, Meg, Mike, Mary Pat, John, Jim, Jr & Michelle. Educ: Univ Minn, Assoc of Mortuary Sci. Polit & Govt Pos: Minn State Rep, 75- Mil Serv: Entered as E-2, Army Nat Guard, 56, released, 57. Relig: Catholic. Mailing Add: 512 Oak St Farmington MN 55024

WHITE, JOHN (D)
Ga State Rep
Mailing Add: 2016 Juniper Dr Albany GA 31701

WHITE, JOHN COYLE (D)
Comnr Agr, Tex
b Newport, Tex, Nov 26, 24; s Edward H White & Carrie L Campbell W; m 1970 to Wynelle Watson; c John Richard, Edward Prince, Russell, Kay Lynn & Craig Allen. Educ: Tex Tech Col, BS, 42-46; Tex A&M Univ, grad work; Kappa Sigma. Polit & Govt Pos: Comnr Agr, Tex, 51-; chmn, Dem State Agr Leaders Conf, 72; app to Nat Dem Charter Rev Comt, 73. Bus & Prof Pos: Area dir, Vet Voc Agr Schs, 46-48; dir, Sch Agr, Midwestern Univ, 48-50. Mem: Southern Asn Comnrs & Secys of Agr; Nat Asn of State Depts of Agr; Optimist. Honors & Awards: Fed Land Bank Award for Outstanding Serv to Am Agr, 68; French Ordre du Merite, Top French Govt Agr Award, 69. Mailing Add: Stephen F Austin Bldg Austin TX 78701

WHITE, JOHN L (R)
b Camden, NJ, Apr 1, 30; married; c four. Educ: Franklin & Marshall Col, Lancaster, Pa; Temple Univ Sch of Law, 55. Polit & Govt Pos: Past chmn, Woodbury Zoning Bd of Adjust; co solicitor, Gloucester Co Bd of Chosen Freeholders; NJ State Assemblyman, 64-68; NJ State Sen, 68-72; alt deleg, Rep Nat Conv, 72. Bus & Prof Pos: Attorney-at-law; mem bd dirs, Mantua Bldg & Loan Asn; dir, Nat Bank of Mantua. Mem: Woodbury Kiwanis; F&AM; AASR; AAONMS; Woodbury Savings & Loan Asn (bd dirs). Relig: Presbyterian. Mailing Add: 193 Briar Hill Lane Woodbury NJ 08096

WHITE, JOHN THOMAS, II (R)
b New Orleans, La, Dec 2, 24; s Harry Fletcher White & Jeanne Holmes W; m 1949 to Betty Parker; c Ann Wallis, Elizabeth Parker, John Thomas, III & Margaret Sewell. Educ: Univ Va, BA, 46 & 46-49; Sigma Alpha Epsilon. Polit & Govt Pos: Legis asst to US Rep Joel T Broyhill, Va, 60-68, to US Rep Richard H Poff, Va, 68-71, to US Sen Harry F Byrd, Va, 72-73, to US Rep Stanford E Parris, 73-74 & to US Sen William L Scott, Va, 74- Mil Serv: Entered as A/S, Navy, 42, released as Ens, 46, after serv in Destroyers, Atlantic, 45-46; Lt(jg), Naval Res; Atlantic Theatre Serv Medal; Pac, US Defense & Victory Medals. Mem: Am Legion. Relig: Episcopal. Mailing Add: 8905 Stratford Lane Alexandria VA 22308

WHITE, JOSHUA WARREN, JR (D)
Va State Deleg
b Norfolk, Va, Aug 27, 16; m to Dorothy Lee Winstead. Educ: Washington & Lee Univ. Polit & Govt Pos: Mem, Second Dist Dem Comt; Va State Deleg, 62- Bus & Prof Pos: Pres & treas, Old Dom Paper Co; pres & treas, Va Nat Bank, Norfolk Bd. Mil Serv: Navy, discharged, 45, Lt Comdr. Mem: Va Coun of Small Bus Admin; Tidewater Develop Coun (trustee); Hampton Roads Coun of Navy League, USA (mem bd); Norfolk German Club; Princess Anne Country Club. Relig: Presbyterian; deacon, First Presby Church. Mailing Add: c/o Old Dom Paper Co Industrial Park Norfolk VA 23502

WHITE, KATHLEEN ELEANOR ELIZABETH (D)
Chmn, Boundary Co Dem Cent Comt, Idaho
b Bonners Ferry, Idaho, Jan 11, 23; d William Thomas Armstrong & Gladys Orfa Rockwell A; m 1941; m 1961 to George Henry White; c Thomas Roy & Mike Leland Grey Cowley, Diana (Mrs Paul Trice) & Thomas Dewey White (stepson). Educ: Bonners Ferry High Sch, grad, 41. Polit & Govt Pos: Chmn, Boundary Co Dem Cent Comt, Idaho, 74- Bus & Prof Pos: Operator, Gen Tel Co, 49-57; cashier, Don's Cafe, 57-58; nurses aid, Community Hosp, 58-60. Mem: Am Legion Auxiliary; Pythian Sisters; Home Exten Club. Relig: Missouri Synod Lutheran. Mailing Add: Star Rte Moyie Springs ID 83845

WHITE, KEVIN HAGAN (D)
Mayor, Boston, Mass
b Boston, Mass, Sept 25, 29; s Joseph C White & Patricia Hagan W; m 1956 to Kathryn Galvin; c Mark, Caitlin, Elizabeth, Christopher & Patricia. Educ: Williams Col, AB, 52; Boston Col Law Sch, LLB, 55; Harvard Grad Sch Pub Admin. Hon Degrees: PhD, New Eng Sch Law, 66, Williams Col, 68 & Clark Univ, 72. Polit & Govt Pos: Legal aide to Dist Attorney, Boston, 58-60; secy, Commonwealth of Mass, 61-68; Mayor, Boston, 68-; chmn adv coun, Mass Bay Transportation Authority, 69-; mem bd trustees & legis action comt, US Conf of Mayors, 71-; mem steering comt, Nat Urban Coalition, 72-; mem bd trustees, Nat Coalition for Budget Priorities & Human Needs, 73-; mem adv coun, Dem Nat Comt, 73- Bus & Prof Pos: Corp counsel, Standard Oil of Calif, 55; partner, Cameron & White, 56- Mem: Boston, Am & Mass Bar Asns; Mass Trial Lawyers Asn; Nat Asn Secys of State. Relig: Catholic. Legal Res: 158 Mt Vernon St Boston MA Mailing Add: Off of the Mayor City Hall Sq Boston MA 02201

WHITE, KNOX HAYNSWORTH (R)
b Greenville, SC, Jan 26, 54; s Andrew J White & Elizabeth Haynsworth W; single. Educ: Wake Forest Univ, 72-; pres freshman class. Polit & Govt Pos: Alt deleg, Rep Nat Conv, 72; precinct pres, Greenville Rep Party, SC, 72. Mem: Mayor's Youth Coun (chmn, 72). Relig: Episcopal. Mailing Add: 146 Faris Circle Greenville SC 29605

WHITE, LEE C (D)
b Omaha, Nebr, Sept 1, 23; s Herman Henry White & Ann Ruth Ackerman W; m 1944 to Dorothy Bernice Cohn; c Bruce D, Rosalyn A, Murray L, Sheldon R & Laura H. Educ: Univ Nebr, BS, 48, LLB, 50. Hon Degrees: LLD, Univ Nebr, 68. Polit & Govt Pos: Attorney, Legal Div, TVA, 50-54; asst to Joseph P Kennedy, Hoover Comn, 54-55; legis asst to Sen John F Kennedy, 54-57; counsel, US Sen Small Bus Comt, 57-58; admin asst to Sen John S Cooper, 58-61; asst spec counsel to President John F Kennedy, 61-63; assoc counsel to President Johnson, 63-65; spec counsel to President Lyndon B Johnson, 65-66; chmn, Fed Power Comn, 66-69; campaign mgr for R Sargent Shriver, 72. Bus & Prof Pos: Partner, White, Fine & Ambrogne, currently. Mil Serv: Army, 43-46. Mailing Add: 3216 W Coquelin Terr Chevy Chase MD 20015

WHITE, LEONARD THOMAS (R)
b Johnson Co, Kans, Oct 14, 05; s Ernest W White & Lettie Broadhurst W; m 1936 to Mary Jewell Pollner. Educ: Friends Univ, 23-24; Univ Kans, 24-25; Optimist Club. Polit & Govt Pos: Clerk, Johnson Co, Kans, 38-50; treas, Johnson Co Rep Cent Comt, Kans, 52-72; deleg, Rep Nat Conv, 72. Bus & Prof Pos: Asst dir, Tax Div, Panhandle Eastern Pipe Line Co, 50-70. Mem: Optimist Club. Relig: Society of Friends. Mailing Add: 460 S Cherry Olathe KS 66061

WHITE, MARION OVERTON (D)
b Opelousas, La, Apr 16, 36; s Vallery White (deceased) & Rosella Sam W; m 1966 to Doris Marie Morein; c John Vallery, Lie Marie & Ahmed A. Educ: Southern Univ, Baton Rouge, BPolit Sci, 58, Law Sch, JD, 63; Alpha Phi Alpha. Polit & Govt Pos: Bd mem & legal adv, Black La Action Comt, 65-; cand for Attorney Gen on Black La Action Comt Ticket, 71; deleg, Dem Nat Conv, 72. Bus & Prof Pos: Attorney-at-law, White & Pitre, Opelousas, La, 63-; cooperating attorney, Legal Defense Fund, New York, 64-; bd mem, Southern Mutual Help Asn, Abbeville, La, 70- Mil Serv: Entered as Pvt, Army, 58-60, serv in Missile Unit, Ft Sill. Mem: Am Judiciate Soc; Am & La Trial Lawyers Asns; Am & La Bar Asns. Legal Res: 1437 N Court St Opelousas LA 70570 Mailing Add: 811 N Union St Opelousas LA 70570

WHITE, MARJORIE K (D)
Secy, Ray Co Dem Cent Comt, Mo
b Kansas City, Mo, May 17, 14; d James Brown & Anna Pyle B; m to Kenneth P White, wid. Educ: Richmond High Sch, grad. Polit & Govt Pos: Dep circuit clerk, Ray Co Circuit Court, Mo, 50-61; probate clerk, Ray Co Magistrate Probate Court, 61-64 & 75-; committeewoman, Ray Co Dem Cent Comt, 70-72, secy, 75- Bus & Prof Pos: Secy, Local 249 UAW, 64-74. Mem: Off Employees Prof Int Union Local 320; Mo State Dem Club; Ray Co Women's Dem Club. Relig: Presbyterian. Mailing Add: 420 Hwy 210 S Richmond MO 64085

WHITE, MARK W, JR (D)
Secy of State, Tex
b Henderson, Tex; m to Linda Gale Thompson; c Mark W, III, Andrew & Elizabeth Marie. Educ: Baylor Univ, BBA, 62 & JD, 65. Polit & Govt Pos: Asst Attorney Gen, Ins, Banking & Securities Div, Tex, 66-69; Secy of State, 73- Bus & Prof Pos: Partner, Reynolds, White, Allen & Cook, Houston, formerly. Mil Serv: Tex Nat Guard, 66-69. Mailing Add: State Capitol Bldg Main St Austin TX 78711

WHITE, MARTHA CAROLE (D)
Miss State Rep
Mailing Add: Rte 2 Baldwyn MS 38824

WHITE, MARY CLYTA (D)
Chmn, Sevier Co Dem Party, Ark
b Lockesburg, Ark, Jan 3, 1911; d John Henry McLaughlin & Mary Lou Neel M; wid. Educ: Draughon's Bus Col, 30. Polit & Govt Pos: Dep circuit clerk & treas, Sevier Co, Ark, 30-43; dep co clerk, 56-69; co & probate clerk, 69-73; chmn, Sevier Co Dem Party, currently. Bus & Prof Pos: Secy, Bell & Magruder, CPA's, 43-56. Mem: Eastern Star; DeQueen Bus & Prof Women's Club; Daughters of Am Revolution. Relig: Presbyterian. Mailing Add: 719 W Wallace Ave DeQueen AR 71832

WHITE, MARYETTA ELIZABETH (R)
b Carthage, Mo, Nov 4, 12; d William Edgar Snyder & Laura Etta Hawthorne S; m 1948 to James Ross White; c Cynthia Anne. Educ: Carthage Sr High Sch, grad, 31; Int Acct Soc, Chicago, grad, 67. Polit & Govt Pos: City clerk, City of Carthage, Mo, 54-58; pres, Mo Fedn Rep Women, 63-65; Mo co-chmn, Women for Nixon, 68; deleg, Rep Nat Conv, 72. Bus & Prof Pos: Cashier & asst bookkeeper, McDaniel Milling Co, Carthage, 32-41; off mgr & acct, Leggett & Platt, Inc, 41-48; controller & supvr acct, H E Williams Produce Co, 58- Mem: Am Inst Corp Controllers; Am Acct Asn; Soroptimist Club (pres); Am Cancer Soc (bd Jasper Co); Ment Health Asn (bd mem, Jasper Co). Honors & Awards: Mo Rep Woman of the Year, Nat Fedn of Rep Women, 69; Resolution of the Mo House of Rep, 69. Relig: Methodist; Secy bd trustees, First United Methodist Church, 70-73. Mailing Add: 1638 S Maple Carthage MO 64836

WHITE, R QUINCY, JR (R)
b Chicago, Ill, Jan 16, 33; s Roger Q White & Carolyn Everett W; m 1962 to Joyce Caldwell; c Cleaver L & Annelia E. Educ: Yale Univ, BA, 54; Harvard Univ Law Sch, JD, 60. Polit & Govt Pos: With Coast & Geodetic Surv, 58; cand for alderman, Chicago 44th Ward, 69; pres, Chicago Ripon Soc, 70-71, mem nat gov bd, Ripon Soc, 70-, secy, 71-72; mem exec comt, 43rd Ward Regular Rep Orgn, 70-74; co-founder, Coun Chicago Govt, 70, pres, 71- Bus & Prof Pos: Assoc, Leibman, Williams, Bennett, Baird & Minow, 60-67; partner, Leibman, Williams, Bennett, Baird & Minow, 67-72; partner, Sidley & Austin, 73- Mil Serv: Entered as 2nd Lt, Air Force, 54, released as 1st Lt, after serv in Intel & Air Police; Capt, Air Force Res, 56-68. Publ: Co-auth, Advertising agencies: their legal liability under the Federal Trade Commission Act, Kans Law Rev, 6/69. Mem: Ill, Chicago & Fed Dist Court Bar Asns; Ill Comt of Nat Coun on Crime & Delinquency; Am Arbit Asn. Relig: Protestant. Legal Res: 316 W Willow Chicago IL 60614 Mailing Add: One First Nat Plaza Chicago IL 60603

WHITE, RICHARD (D)
Chmn, Nebr Dem Party
b Valentine, Nebr, Jan 2, 42; s Francis White & Emma Peters W; single. Educ: Nebr Wesleyan Univ, BA, 64; Blue Key; Pi Kappa Delta. Polit & Govt Pos: Deleg, Dem Nat Conv, 68; exec asst, Nebr Dem Party, 69-72, asst chmn, 72-74, chmn, 74-; campaign mgr, Gov J J Exon, 70. Relig: Methodist. Legal Res: 231 Edna St Valentine NE 69201 Mailing Add: 511 Anderson Bldg Lincoln NE 68508

WHITE, RICHARD CRAWFORD (D)
US Rep, Tex
b El Paso, Tex, Apr 29, 23; m to Katherine Huffman (deceased); c Rodrick James, Richard Whitman & Raymond Edward; m to Kathleen Fitzgerald; c Bonnie. Educ: El Paso High Sch; Univ Tex, El Paso; Univ Tex, BA, 46, Law Sch, LLB, 49; Phi Alpha Delta; Sigma Alpha Epsilon. Polit & Govt Pos: Tex State Rep, 55-58; US Rep, Tex, 64-, mem, Armed Serv, Post Off & Civil Serv Comts, US House of Rep. Bus & Prof Pos: Lawyer. Mil Serv: Marines, Pac Theatre; Japanese interpreter-riflemen, Bougainville, Guam, Iwo Jima; Purple Heart. Mem: El Paso CofC; El Paso Co Bar Asn, State Bar of Tex; El Paso Hist Soc; Kiwanis; various vet & civic groups. Relig: Episcopal. Legal Res: El Paso TX Mailing Add: US House of Rep Washington DC 20515

WHITE, ROSE MARIE (D)
Mem, Calif Dem State Cent Comt
b Lincoln, Calif, Sept 15, 08; d Joseph Oscar Amadio & Evelyn Ann Brusco A; m 1929 to William Walter White; c James Edward. Educ: Lincoln Union High Sch, Calif, 24-28. Polit & Govt Pos: Mem, Calif Dem State Cent Comt, currently; exec bd mem, Union Labor Party, San Francisco, currently; mem disaster corps, San Francisco City & Co, 69-; mem, Dem Nat

Comt, formerly. Bus & Prof Pos: Bus rep, Local 2565, Indust Carpenters, 41- Mem: Del, Bay Dist Coun of Carpenters; New Mission Terrance Improv Asn (pres, 12 years); Alemany Dist Coun, San Francisco (deleg, Exec Bd); Druids; Golden Gate Circle. Relig: Catholic. Mailing Add: 306 Delano Ave San Francisco CA 94112

WHITE, SADIE LUCY (D)
Vt State Rep
Mailing Add: 89 Blodgett St Burlington VT 05401

WHITE, THOMAS P (D)
Mass State Rep
Mailing Add: State Capitol Boston MA 02133

WHITE, W PAUL (D)
Mass State Rep
b Cambridge, Mass, July 7, 45; s William White & Alice Ritchie W; single. Educ: Boston Col, AB, 67; State Univ NY Albany, Grad Sch Pub Affairs, MA, 69; Suffolk Univ Law Sch, JD, 73; Phi Sigma Alpha. Polit & Govt Pos: Mass State Rep, 73- Relig: Roman Catholic. Legal Res: 215 Neponset Ave Dorchester MA 02122 Mailing Add: State House Boston MA 02133

WHITE, W STANFORD (D)
NC State Rep
Mailing Add: Mans Harbor NC 27953

WHITE, WALTER L (R)
Ohio State Sen
Mailing Add: 206 Dominion Bldg Lima OH 45801

WHITE, WILLIAM L (R)
Chmn, Cheyenne Co Rep Cent Comt, Colo
b Almena, Kans, Apr 21, 08; s Bertram Calvin White & Gertrude Hays W; m 1934 to Lucile E West; c Myrna Lea (Mrs Temple) & Bonnie Mae (Mrs Maul). Educ: Arapahoe High Sch, 22-26. Polit & Govt Pos: Chmn, 18th Sen Rep Cent Comt, Colo, 62-66; chmn, Cheyenne Co Rep Cent Comt, 62-; chmn, 57th Representative Rep Cent Comt, 66-68; comnr, Colo State Bd Stock Inspection, 67- Bus & Prof Pos: Mem, Cheyenne Co Hosp Bd, 46-50; mem sch bd, Arapahoe Sch Dist, 48-56; chmn, Cheyenne Agr Stabilization & Conserv Serv Coun, 48-56; owner & operator, State Line Ranch, currently. Mem: Odd Fellows (past Grand Chmn); Colo & Cheyenne Co Farm Bur; Colo Cattleman Asn; Cheyenne Co Livestock Asn. Relig: Protestant. Mailing Add: Arapahoe CO 80802

WHITE, WILLIAM ROBERT (D)
b Dayton, Ohio, Mar 26, 41; s Elmer David White & Ruth Louise Dwyer W; m 1965 to Doris Shackleton; c Julia Lynne, Tracy Michelle & William Shackleton. Educ: Ohio State Univ, BS, 64, Col Law, JD, 67; Phi Delta Phi; Alpha Gamma Rho. Polit & Govt Pos: Dep dir, Ohio Dept Natural Resources, Columbus, 72-73; admin asst to US Sen John Glenn, Ohio, 75- Bus & Prof Pos: Attorney, Power, Jones & Schneider, Columbus, 67-75. Mem: Am, Ohio State & Columbus Bar Asns. Honors & Awards: Col Law Honor Coun, Ohio State Univ, 64-67; Moot Court Team, 67. Relig: Episcopal. Legal Res: 2205 Fairfax Rd Columbus OH 43221 Mailing Add: 10504 Stable Lane Potomac MD 20854

WHITEACRE, CHARLES A (D)
Councilman, Hialeah City Coun, Fla
b Boston, Mass, Oct 29, 17; s Charles Henry Whiteacre (deceased) & Marion W Humphrey W; m 1947 to Jennie B Ponikvar; c Mark, Lee Ann (Mrs Russell Fernandez), Charles A, Jr & Patricia. Educ: Boston Univ, 46-47; Univ Miami, 47-50, JD, 50; Sigma Alpha Epsilon. Polit & Govt Pos: Munic Judge, Hialeah, Fla, 53-55; councilman, Hialeah City Coun, 61-, vpres, 61-63, pres & mayor, formerly. Bus & Prof Pos: Bd dirs, Fla League Cities, 70-; pres, Dade Co League Munic, 71- Mil Serv: Entered as Pvt, Army, 41, released as S/Sgt, 45, after serv in Am Div, Asiatic & Pac Theatre, 42-45; Purple Heart; Good Conduct Medal; Asiatic & Pac Combat Guadalcanal-Bouganville Ribbon with Three Battle Stars; Philippine Liberation Ribbon. Mem: Fla & Dade Co Bar Asn; Hialeah-Miami Springs Bar Asn (pres, 60, bd mem, currently); Bar & Gavel Soc; VFW (past state comdr, Hialeah Post Comdr, chmn nat conv, mem nat security coun, currently). Relig: Episcopal. Legal Res: 1690 W 79th St Hialeah FL 33014 Mailing Add: 1800 W 49th St Hialeah FL 33102

WHITEAKER, PEARL WALLACE (D)
b Pine Bluff, Ark, July 8, 35; s Joseph W Whiteaker & Laura Muse W; m 1958 to Mary Ada Latta; c Gregory Wallace, Mary Denise & Scott Murray. Educ: Ark A&M Univ, 2 summers; Southwestern at Memphis, AB, 58; Univ Miss, MBA, 61; Sigma Nu. Polit & Govt Pos: Asst, US Rep Oren Harris, Ark, 65; admin asst to US Sen John L McClellan, Ark, 66- Bus & Prof Pos: Math teacher, Pine Bluff Pub Schs, 58-59; mgr, Merritt-LeMay Realty Co, 60-61; asst to pres, Ark Col, 62-64; mem bd dirs, Ark Bus Develop Corp, 72-; mem bd dirs, Ark River Develop Corp, 72- Mem: Ark Real Estate Asn; Kiwanis. Relig: Presbyterian. Legal Res: 720 Kentucky Pine Bluff AR 71601 Mailing Add: 8415 Thames Springfield VA 22151

WHITEHEAD, CLAY THOMAS (R)
b Neodesha, Kans, Nov 13, 38; s Clay Bell Whitehead & Helen Hinton W; m 1973 to Margaret Mahon. Educ: Mass Inst Technol, BS, 60, MS, 61, PhD(mgt), 67; Tau Beta Pi; Sigma Xi; Eta Kappa Nu. Polit & Govt Pos: Consult, Bur Budget, 66-68; mem, President-Elect's Task Force on Budget Policies, 68-69; spec asst to President Nixon, 69-70; dir, Off Telecommun Policy, 70-75. Bus & Prof Pos: Tech aide, Bell Tel Labs, NJ, 58 & 59, sr tech aide, 60; consult defense studies, Rand Corp, 61-63, planner-organizer policy research prog on health serv, 67-69; teaching asst, Mass Inst Technol, 62-63, lectr, 66-67. Mil Serv: Entered as 1st Lt, Army, 63, released as Capt, 65, after serv in Materiel Command. Mem: Yosemite Inst. Mailing Add: 1250 28th St NW Washington DC 20007

WHITEHEAD, EDWIN HAROLD (ED) (D)
Committeeman, Wyo Dem State Cent Comt
b Burns, Wyo, Feb 26, 25; s Douglas Hough Whitehead & Edith Fruit W; m 1950 to Janet Carol Davis; c Michael Douglas, Karen Marie & Laura Ann. Educ: Univ Wyo, 47-50; Sigma Alpha Epsilon. Polit & Govt Pos: Deleg, Young Dem Nat Conv, 59; pres, Young Dem Clubs of Wyo, 59-60; deleg, Dem Nat Conv, 60; chmn, Wyo Civil Rights Adv Comt, 61-67; committeeman, Dem State Cent Comt, Laramie Co, 62-; Wyo State Rep, 65-72; chmn platform comt, Dem State Conv, Wyo, 66; mem, Wyo Statute Rev Comn, 69- Bus & Prof Pos: Mgr, Cheyenne Tire & Battery Inc, 57-65, pres, 65- Mil Serv: Entered as A/S, Navy, 43, released as 1st Lt, 57, after serv in Fleet Air Wing 1, 10th Spec Forces & 82nd Airborne Div & 11th Airborne Div, Asiatic Pac & Ger, 43-45 & 53-56; Serv Awards. Relig: Catholic. Mailing Add: 2974 Kelley Dr Cheyenne WY 82001

WHITEHEAD, EMMETT H (D)
Tex State Rep
b Cisco, Tex, Oct 9, 25; s Emmett H Whitehead, Sr & Tommie Alice Cole W; m 1948 to Marie Hall; c Terrie & Wendee. Educ: Sam Houston State Univ, 43-45. Polit & Govt Pos: Mayor, Rusk, Tex, 63-64 & 70-73; Tex State Rep, Dist 15, 73- Bus & Prof Pos: Owner, Cherokeean Weekly Newspaper, 50-; owner, Radio Sta KTLU, 55-; owner, E-Z Vision Cable Co, 62- Mil Serv: Midn, Naval Res, 44-45, serv in V-6. Mem: Tex Press Asn; Tex Asn Broadcasters; Tex Farm Bur; ETex & Rusk CofC. Honors & Awards: Outstanding Citizen of Year, Rusk CofC, 75. Relig: Methodist. Legal Res: 904 N Bonner St Rusk TX 75785 Mailing Add: PO Box 475 Rusk TX 75785

WHITEHEAD, WILEY LEON, JR (R)
Chmn, Florence Co Rep Party, SC
b Lake City, SC, Sept 27, 43; s Wiley Leon Whitehead & Louise Hill W; m 1965 to Harolyn Stokes; c Barry Stokes & David Frederick. Educ: Davidson Col, BS, 65; Univ SC, BS in Pharm, 68; Kappa Psi; Pi Kappa Alpha. Polit & Govt Pos: Chmn, Lake City Rep Party, SC, 70-72; councilman, Lake City, 72-; chmn, Florence Co Rep Party, 74- Bus & Prof Pos: Pharmacist & vpres, Piggly Wiggle-Sup-Rx, Lake City, SC, 69- Mem: SC Pharmaceutical Asn; Lake City Rotary. Relig: Baptist. Legal Res: 211 Oak St Lake City SC 29560 Mailing Add: PO Box 1273 Lake City SC 29560

WHITEHEAD, WILLIAM SCHOLL (R)
Chmn, Renegotiation Bd
b Denver, Colo, May 27, 07; s Morgan Thomas Whitehead (deceased) & Mayme Elsie Scholl W (deceased); m 1934 to Dorothy Childs; c William Scholl, Jr. Educ: Wharton Sch Finance, Univ Pa; Beta Theta Pi. Polit & Govt Pos: Mem staff, Securities & Exchange Comn, Washington, DC, 35-40; mem staff, Off Price Admin, 40-42; mem staff, War Assets Admin, 46-47; mem, Renegotiation Bd, 69-73, chmn, 73- Bus & Prof Pos: Mgr consult, Ives, Whitehead & Co, Inc, 48-69. Mil Serv: Col (Ret), Army Res, 67; Legion of Merit; Army Commendation Medal with Oak Leaf Cluster. Mem: Army-Navy Country Club; Beta Theta Pi Alumni Asn of Wash; life mem Capitol Hill Club. Relig: Episcopal. Mailing Add: 1004 Croton Dr Alexandria VA 23208

WHITEHOUSE, CHARLES SHELDON
US Ambassador to Thailand
b Paris, France, Sept 5, 21; s Sheldon Whitehouse & Mary Alexander W; m 1954 to Mary C Rand; c Sheldon, Charles R & Sarah P. Educ: Yale Univ, AB, 42, study, 46-47; Skull & Bones. Polit & Govt Pos: Polit officer, Am Embassy, Brussels, 48-52, Am Consulate, Istanbul, 54-56 & Embassy, Phnom Penh, 56; spec asst to Undersecy of State, 57-59; polit officer, Am Embassy, Pretoria, 59-61; foreign serv officer, Dept of State, 61-65; dep chief mission, Conakry, Guinea, 66-68; dep for CORDS II, Field Force, Vietnam, 69-70; Dep Ambassador, Saigon, 71-72; US Ambassador to Laos, 73-75, US Ambassador to Thailand, 75- Mil Serv: Entered as Aviation Cadet, Navy, 42, released as Capt, Marine Corps, 46, after serv in various squadrons, Pac; Air Medal with Two Gold Stars. Honors & Awards: Superior Honor Award, Dept of State, 68; Distinguished Honor Award, Agency Int Dept, 71 & Dept of State, 73. Relig: Episcopal. Legal Res: Marshall VA 22115 Mailing Add: Am Embassy Bangkok Thailand

WHITEHURST, GEORGE WILLIAM (R)
US Rep, Va
b Norfolk, Va, Mar 12, 25; s Calvert Stanhope Whitehurst & Laura Tomlinson W; m 1946 to Jennette Franks; c Calvert Stanhope & Frances Seymour. Educ: Washington & Lee Univ, BA, 50; Univ Va, MA in Hist, 51; WVa Univ, PhD(Am Diplomatic Hist), 62; Delta Upsilon. Polit & Govt Pos: US Rep, Va, 69-, mem, Armed Serv Comt, US House of Rep, currently. Bus & Prof Pos: Mem dept hist, Old Dom Col, 50-68, dean student affairs, 63-68; news analyst, WTAR-TV, Norfolk, 62-68. Mil Serv: Entered as A/S, Navy, 43, released as ARM 2/C, 46, after serv in Torpedo Squadron 88, USS Yorktown, Pac, 45; Air Medal with Star. Mem: Va Coun on Alcoholism & Drug Dependence, Inc; Am Legion; Lions; VFW; Ahepa. Honors & Awards: Nat Humanitarian Award, Fund for Animals; First Man of Year Award, Va Zool & Aquarium Soc; Humanitarian Award, Am Dog Owners Asn; Meritorious Serv Award, Douglas MacArthur Chap, US Army Asn. Relig: Methodist; former chmn off bd, Ghent Methodist Church. Legal Res: 424 Gosnold Ct Virginia Beach VA 23451 Mailing Add: 436 Cannon House Off Bldg Washington DC 20515

WHITELEY, KEITH (D)
Pres, Okla League Young Dem
b Tulsa, Okla, Oct 7, 48; s William Franklin Whiteley & J Baron W; m 1972 to Dee Noah. Educ: Univ Okla, BA, 73; Sigma Chi. Polit & Govt Pos: Pres, Okla League Young Dem, currently; spec asst to Gov David Hall, Okla, 71-72, admin asst, Gov Off, 72- Bus & Prof Pos: Vpres, Whiteley Enterprises, 69-, pres, 70- Mem: Am Civil Liberties Union; Am Polit Sci Asn; NAACP. Relig: Baptist. Mailing Add: 509 McQuarrie Wagoner OK 74467

WHITEMAN, ROBERT WAYNE (R)
Chmn, LaPlata Co Rep Comt, Colo
b Eldred, Ill, Dec 3, 24; s Corbett Otis Whiteman & Leta S Patterson W; m 1957 to Mary Jeanne Patterson; c Robert Steven, Edward Dean & Rebecca Jeanne. Educ: High sch, grad, 42. Polit & Govt Pos: Chmn, LaPlata Co Rep Comt, Colo, 75- Bus & Prof Pos: Exec vpres, Bank of Ignacio, Colo, 63-; mem, Airport Comn, 74-75. Mem: Colo Cattlemens Asn. Honors & Awards: Man of Year, Colo Cattlemens Asn; Douglas Co Man of the Year. Relig: Baptist. Mailing Add: Box 283 Ignacio CO 81137

WHITENER, BASIL LEE (D)
b York Co, SC, May 14, 15; s Levi L Whitener & Laura Barrett W; m 1942 to Harriet Priscilla Morgan; c John Morgan, Laura Lee, Basil L, Jr & Barrett S. Educ: Rutherford Col, 31-33; Univ SC, 33-35; Duke Univ, LLB, 37; Phi Delta Phi; Omicron Delta Kappa. Hon Degrees: LLD, Belmont Abbey Col, 60 & Pfeiffer Col, 65. Polit & Govt Pos: NC State Rep, 41; solicitor, 14th Dist, NC, 46-56; deleg, Dem Nat Conv, 48 & 60; US Rep, NC, 57-69. Bus & Prof Pos: Instr bus law, Belmont Abbey Col, 38-40; attorney-at-law, 37- Mil Serv: Entered as Ens, Navy, 42, released as Lt, Naval Res, 45; Maj, Air Force Res; Secy of Navy Commendation Ribbon; Am Area, European-African-Mid Eastern Area Campaign Ribbons with Two Combat Stars. Mem: Belmont Abbey Col (bd adv); NC & Am Bar Asns; Am Trial Lawyers Asn; hon life mem Gastonia Jr CofC. Honors & Awards: Recipient POSA Merst Medallion Award, 66; Watchdog of the Treas Award, Nat Assoc Businessmen, Inc, 66. Relig:

Methodist; Mem official bd. Legal Res: 1854 Montclaire Gastonia NC 28052 Mailing Add: Box 1 Gastonia NC 28052

WHITESIDE, JIM (R)
Wash State Rep
Mailing Add: 3612 Howard Ave Yakima WA 98902

WHITESIDE, LYNN W (R)
Kans State Rep
Mailing Add: 8101 Mockingbird Lane Wichita KS 67207

WHITESIDES, JOE EDWARD (R)
Utah State Rep
b Layton, Utah, Oct 11, 13; s William Wilford Whitesides & Mary Alice Adams W; m 1934 to Lazelle Ewing; c Kim & Jill. Educ: Utah State Univ, BS, 36, grad work; Univ Utah, grad work; Pi Kappa Alpha. Polit & Govt Pos: Utah State Rep, Dist 12, 75- Mil Serv: Entered Army, 39, released as Col (Ret), 67, after serv in Pac & Korean Theatres, 42-46, 50-52; Bronze Star; Purple Heart. Relig: Latter-day Saint. Mailing Add: 2265 Wyoming St Salt Lake City UT 84109

WHITFIELD, W EDWARD (D)
Ky State Rep
Mailing Add: Ky House of Rep State Capitol Frankfort KY 40601

WHITING, PAT (D)
Ore State Rep
b Chicago, Ill, Oct 22, 40; m 1968 to R Vincent Whiting. Educ: San Jose State Col, BA, 67; Ore State Univ, 70; co-coordr for Earth Week, Eco-Alliance, 70. Polit & Govt Pos: Ore State Rep, Dist 7, 73-, co-chmn environ/energy comt & mem educ/sch finance comt, Ore House Rep, 75- Bus & Prof Pos: Int & nat speaker, Mexico City, Washington, DC, Calif & Ore, 72-75. Publ: Auth, Balancing human populations with life support systems, Wildlife Mgt Inst, Washington, DC, 3/72. Mem: Eastmoreland Gen Hosp (bd dirs, 74-); Tri Co Loaves & Fishes Inc (bd dirs, 75-); Ore Environ Coun; Friends of the Earth. Honors & Awards: Career Educ Plaque for Community Serv, 74; participant, Eagleton Inst Politics State Legis Conf, 75. Mailing Add: 8122 SW Spruce St Tigard OR 97223

WHITLOCK, IRENE M (R)
Exec Dir, Kans Rep Party
b Augusta, Kans, May 7, 33; d Laurence A Potter & Mildred Fitzwater P; m 1951 to Donald E Whitlock; c Don W & Stephen A. Educ: Wichita E High Sch, grad, 51; Winona Sch of Photography, 58-60. Polit & Govt Pos: Campaign chmn, US Sen Dole, Kans, 68; chmn, Gubernatorial Campaign, 70; dir, Fourth Dist Kans Fedn Rep Women, 70-72; mem, Kans Adv Coun, Small Bus Admin, 70-; campaign coordr, US Sen Pearson, Kans, 72; field coordr, Comt to Reelect the President, NH Primary, Kans Gen Elec & Pa Gen Elec, 72; deleg, Rep Nat Conv, 72; exec dir, Kans Rep Party, currently. Bus & Prof Pos: Partner & co-mgr, Don's Studio & Camera Shop, 51-72; bd dirs, Kans Prof Photographers, 59-64. Mem: Bus & Prof Women's Club; VFW Auxiliary; CofC; Ladies of the Elks. Relig: Baptist. Mailing Add: 401 S Hartup McPherson KS 67460

WHITLOCK, WILLIE WALKER (D)
b Mineral, Va, Nov 16, 25; s Edward Jackson Whitlock & Alma Talley W; m 1950 to Eula Dymacek; c John Dennis & Jane Melinda. Educ: Va Commonwealth Univ, BS, 50; Va Col Law, JD, 53. Polit & Govt Pos: Chmn, Louisa Dem Comt, Va, 72-75; co attorney, Louisa Co, 71-75. Bus & Prof Pos: Attorney-at-law, Mineral, Va, 56- Mil Serv: Army, 45-47, serv in SPac, 45. Mem: Va State Bar; Ninth Judicial Circuit Bar Asn; Lions Club; Mason; Am Legion. Relig: Baptist. Mailing Add: PO Box 128 Mineral VA 23117

WHITMAN, L SUE (R)
Chmn, Johnson Co Rep Cent Comt, Mo
b Chilhowee, Mo, Aug 8, 35; d Robert Allen Bancroft & Irene Taggs B; m 1954 to David C Whitman; c Dwight, Cindy, Michael & Linda. Educ: Warrensburg Sr High Sch, grad, 53. Polit & Govt Pos: Committeewoman, First Ward Rep Party, Mo, 65-; chmn, Johnson Co Rep Cent Comt, 74- Bus & Prof Pos: Secy to dean appl sci & technol, Cent Mo State Univ, 66-70; exec secy & pub rels coordr, Johnson Co Mem Hosp, Warrensburg, 70-75 & spec serv asst, 75- Publ: Writes all news releases & brochures relating to hosp where employed. Mem: Home Econ Club. Relig: Baptist. Mailing Add: 714 N Washington Warrensburg MO 64093

WHITMAN, REGINALD NORMAN (R)
b Jasmin, Sask, Oct 15, 09; s Norman L Whitman & Irene Haverlock W; m 1932 to Opal Vales, c James, Richard & Donna (Mrs Ronald Throener). Educ: St Joseph Col, Sask, grad; Harvard Bus Sch, study in Admin Mgr. Polit & Govt Pos: Gen mgr, Alaska RR, Dept of Interior, Anchorage, 55-56; mem, Alaska's North Comn, 67; fed RR adminr, Dept of Transportation, 69-70. Bus & Prof Pos: From telegrapher to dispatcher, trainmaster, rules examr & terminal trainmaster, Great Northern Rwy, 29-53, supt, Cascade Div, 53-57, gen mgr, Lines E, 57-69, pres, Lake Superior Terminal & Transfer RR, formerly & vpres, Portal Pipe Line Co, formerly; chmn bd & pres, Mo-Kans-Tex RR Co, Dallas, 70- Mil Serv: Serv as 1st Lt, 732nd RR Oper Bn, 43-44. Mem: Nat Defense Transportation Asn; Am Legion. Relig: Catholic. Legal Res: 7108 Desco Dr Dallas TX 75225 Mailing Add: 701 Commerce St Dallas TX 75202

WHITMER, ROBERT V (R)
Chmn, Fulton Co Rep Exec Comt, Ohio
b Fulton Co, Ohio, Oct 28, 23; s Frank C Whitmer & Bessie Saul W; m 1949 to Lois Francis Cammarn; c David F, Diana Lee & Tully Edmund. Educ: Wauseon High Sch, grad. Polit & Govt Pos: Chmn, Fulton Co Rep Exec Comt, Ohio, 74- Bus & Prof Pos: Owner, F C Whitmer Co, 62-; pres, R V Whitmer Thermogas, 65-; gen mgr, Wauseon Plaza Co, 72- Mil Serv: Airman 2/C, Navy, 42-45. Mem: F&AM; Elks. Relig: Methodist. Mailing Add: 225 S Shoop Wauseon OH 43567

WHITMER, ROBERT WILLIAM (D)
Chmn, Crawford Co Dem Cent Comt, Ill
b Crawford Co, Ill, Feb 24, 23; s William C Whitmer & Blanche Warnock W; m 1950 to Mary Brooks; c Melissa Lee & Robert W, Jr. Educ: Univ Ill, Mech Eng, 47, JD, 50; Phi Delta Phi; Sigma Alpha Epsilon. Polit & Govt Pos: Chmn, Crawford Co Dem Cent Comt, Ill, 70- Bus & Prof Pos: Attorney-at-law, Oblong, Ill, 50- Mil Serv: Entered as Pvt, Air Force, 42, released as 1st Lt, 45. Mem: Ill Co Chmn Asn (third vchmn, 74-); Ill States Attorneys Asn (mem-at-lg, 74-); Elks; Moose; Am Legion. Relig: Protestant. Mailing Add: RFD 4 Robinson IL 62454

WHITMIRE, DOUG (D)
Ga State Rep
Mailing Add: Lamplighter Dove Browns Bridge Rd Gainesville GA 30501

WHITMIRE, JOHN HARRIS (D)
Tex State Rep
b Hillsboro, Tex, Aug 13, 49; s James M Whitmire & Ruth Bennett W; single. Educ: Univ Houston, BS, 73. Polit & Govt Pos: Tex State Rep, 73- Bus & Prof Pos: Welfare serv technician II, Tex State Dept Pub Welfare, 68-72. Mem: Mason; Optimist Club; Jaycees. Mailing Add: 2007 Sea King Houston TX 77008

WHITMORE, FRANK WILLIAM (D)
b Ponca City, Okla, May 15, 32; s Ralph W Whitmore & Charlotte E Cullen W; m 1955 to Betty Lou Spear; c Susan Adams, David Cullen & Sarah Spear. Educ: Okla State Univ, BS, 54; Univ Mich, MF, 56, PhD, 64; Phi Kappa Phi; Alpha Zeta. Polit & Govt Pos: Vpres, Wayne Co Dem Club, Ohio, 71-73; alt deleg, Dem Nat Conv, 72; co chmn, McGovern for President Comt, 72; mem, Metrop Housing Authority, Wayne Co, Ohio, 72- Bus & Prof Pos: Research forester, US Forest Serv, New Orleans, La, 57-64; research assoc, Univ Mich, Ann Arbor, 64-67; assoc prof, Ohio Agr Res & Develop Ctr, 67- Mil Serv: Entered as Pvt, Army, 55, released as Specialist 3/C, 57, after serv in Corps of Engrs. Mem: Soc Am Foresters; Am Soc Plant Physiol; AAAS; Wayne Co Comn Human Rights, Ohio (vpres, 69-); Interfaith Housing Corp (exec bd, 72-). Mailing Add: 1037 Northview Dr Wooster OH 44691

WHITNEY, JOHN ADAIR (R)
b Cincinnati, Ohio, Jan 25, 32; s Nathanial Ruggles Whitney & Helen Loos W; m 1956 to Linda Hollis Leary; c William Nathaniel, Jane Hollis & Anne Dickson. Educ: Williams Col, BA, 53; Harvard Law Sch, LLB, 56; Phi Beta Kappa; Chi Psi. Polit & Govt Pos: Md State Deleg, 67-69; asst gen counsel for procurement matters, NASA, 69-73. Mil Serv: Entered as Officer Cand, Navy, 56, released as Lt, 59, after serv in Off Judge Adv Gen, Navy Dept, 57-59. Mem: Am, Fed, Md State & Montgomery Co Bar Asns; Bar Asn of DC. Honors & Awards: NASA Exceptional Serv Medal, 72. Relig: Presbyterian. Legal Res: 8007 Aberdeen Rd Bethesda MD 20014 Mailing Add: Pope Ballard & Loos 22 W Jefferson St Rockville MD 20850

WHITNEY, ROBERT E (D)
Chmn, Saline Co Dem Party, Ill
b Carrier Mills, Ill, July 22, 21; s George Whitney & Blanche Lewis; m 1944 to Julia Maller; c Gloria Stout, Julene Clift, Robbie Dewar & stepson Fred Williams. Polit & Govt Pos: Dem committeeman, Precinct One, Carrier Mills, Ill, 46-54; vpres, Young Dem Ill, 48; state auto investr, Ill, 49-53; committeeman, Ill Dem Cent Comt, 62-; mem, Ill Real Estate Exam Comt, Dept Registrn & Educ, 64-; chmn, Saline Co Dem Party, 74-; deleg, Dem Nat Mid-Term Conf, 74. Bus & Prof Pos: Mem & dir, Egyptian Real Estate Bd. Mil Serv: Entered as CPO, Navy, 42, released, 45, after serv in USS LST 384, ETO, 30 months; 5 Battle Stars; Good Conduct Medal. Mem: Am Legion (post comdr, 2 terms); VFW. Relig: Methodist. Mailing Add: 18 W Walnut Harrisburg IL 62946

WHITNEY, TOM (D)
Chmn, Iowa Dem State Cent Comt
Mailing Add: 1120 Mulberry St Des Moines IA 50309

WHITSITT, GARLAND B, JR (R)
Chmn, Daviess Co Rep Comt, Mo
b Kansas City, Mo, Oct 23, 21; s Garland B Whitsitt & Mary Casey W; m 1942 to Lillian May Harper; c Carol (Mrs Randy Parks) & Janet (Mrs David Kagarice). Educ: Jr Col of Kansas City, AA, 40; Drake Univ, BCS, 42; Theta Phi Alpha; Tau Kappa Epsilon. Polit & Govt Pos: Precinct dir, Raytown, Southwood Div, 65-67; deleg & dir, Sheridan Twp, Daviess Co, 70-; Mo State Conv, 71-72; chmn, Daviess Co Rep Comt, 74- Bus & Prof Pos: Sales supvr, Nat Fidelity Ins Co, 53-56; agt field serv, Dun & Bradstreet, Inc, 59-; pres, CofC, 74-75. Mil Serv: Entered as Pvt, Air Force, 42, released as S/Sgt, 45, after serv in 704th Squadron, 446th GP, European Theater, 42-45; Good Conduct Medal; Orientation Dir; Flying Serv Medal. Mem: Daviess Co Nursing Home (dir, 72-); Bldg Comt Church Orgn (chmn, 72-); Bicentennial Comn (pres, 74-); Rotary Club (pres-dir, 72-74). Honors & Awards: Serv above Self Award, Rotary Int, 71; Polit Man of Year Award, Daviess Co Rep Asn, 72. Relig: Baptist. Mailing Add: Rte 1 Gallatin MO 64640

WHITSITT, VIRGIL H (R)
b Phillipsburg, Kans, July 6, 21; s Carl C Whitsitt (deceased) & Grace White W (deceased); m 1953 to Jeanette Pittman; c Peggy & Lois. Educ: Univ Kans, AB, 48; Alpha Kappa Lambda. Polit & Govt Pos: Chmn, Phillips Co Rep Party, Kans, 68-72. Bus & Prof Pos: Owner, V H Whitsitt Real Estate & Ins Agency, Phillipsburg, Kans, 48- Mil Serv: Entered as Pvt, Army Air Corps, 42, released as 1st Lt, 46, after serv in Base Air Depot 2, 8th Air Force, ETO, 43-46; Maj, Kans Nat Guard. Mem: Lions; VFW; CofC. Relig: United Methodist. Mailing Add: Box 393 Phillipsburg KS 67661

WHITTAKER, PHILIP N (R)
b Chestnut Hill, Pa, Nov 7, 18; m 1948 to Elizabeth Stevenson; c Elizabeth T, Stephen A, Philip N, Jr & Nancy C. Educ: Univ Pa, BA in Eng & Bus, 40. Polit & Govt Pos: Asst adminr for indust affairs, NASA, 68-69; Asst Secy of the Air Force, 69-72. Bus & Prof Pos: Student salesman, Int Bus Machines Corp, Philadelphia, Pa, 46, sr salesman, Portland, Maine, 46-48, br off mgr, Montpelier, Vt, 48-49, admin asst, New York, 49-54, mgr contract rels 54-59, mgr contracts, Fed Systs Div, Rockville, Md, 59-63, dir contracts, 63-65, dir mkt & contracts, 65, vpres, Fed Systs Div, Gaithersburg, Md, 65-68. Mil Serv: Entered as Ens, Navy, 41, released as Lt Comdr, 46, after serv in NZ. Mem: Nat Contract Mgt Asn (bd adv). Mailing Add: 11009 Spring House Court Potomac MD 20854

WHITTAKER, RICHARD (D)
b Princeton, Ill, Mar 3, 31; s Marion Lee Whittaker & Louise Walker W; m 1957 to Judy Feinberg; c Jedediah Lee, Louise, Joshua Aaron, Juno Lynn, Jakob Caesar & Jonah Milo. Educ: Univ Ore, BS, 58; Northwestern Col Law, JD, 63. Polit & Govt Pos: Alaska State Rep, 71-72; mem, Alaska Dem State Cent Comt, 70-74. Bus & Prof Pos: Dist attorney, Ketchikan, Alaska, 64-66. Mil Serv: Army, 52-54. Mem: Alaska Native Brotherhood. Legal Res: 648 Main St Ketchikan AK 99901 Mailing Add: Box 13 Ketchikan AK 99901

WHITTAKER, ROBERT (R)
Kans State Rep
Mailing Add: RR 1 Box 48A Augusta KS 67010

WHITTEN, JAMIE LLOYD (D)
US Rep, Miss
b Cascilla, Miss, Apr 18, 10; s Alymer Guy Whitten & Nettie Viola Early W; m 1940 to Rebecca Thompson; c James Lloyd & Beverly Rebecca (Mrs Walter Merritt, III). Educ: Univ Miss, Literary & Law Depts, 27-32; Phi Alpha Delta; Beta Theta Pi; hon mem Omicron Delta Kappa. Polit & Govt Pos: Miss State Rep, 32-33; Dist Attorney, 17th Dist, 33-41; US Rep, Miss, 41- Publ: That We May Live, Van Nostrand, 66. Mem: Lions; Mason; Rotary. Relig: Presbyterian. Legal Res: Charleston MS 38921 Mailing Add: 2413 Rayburn House Off Bldg Washington DC 20515

WHITTEN, JOHN WALLACE, JR (D)
Chmn, Tallahatchie Co Dem Exec Comt, Miss
b Cascilla, Miss, Feb 26, 19; s John Wallace Whitten & Janie Allbritton W; m 1943 to Marianne Thaxton; c John Wallace, III & Gordon Thaxton. Educ: Univ Miss, LLB & JD, 40; Beta Theta Pi. Polit & Govt Pos: Investr, US Dept Labor, Birmingham, Ala, 40-41; chmn, Tallahatchie Co Dem Exec Comt, Miss, 50- Mil Serv: Entered as Pvt, Army, 41, released as Capt, 46, after serv in 97th Inf Div, Europe & Japan, 41-46; Bronze Star Medal. Mem: Miss State Bar; Am Legion. Relig: Protestant. Legal Res: Jennings St Sumner MS 38957 Mailing Add: Courthouse Sq Sumner MS 38957

WHITTLE, WILLIAM ARTHUR (D)
Chmn, Nueces Co Dem Exec Comt, Tex
b Pensacola, Fla, Nov 26, 46; s Claude Bernard Whittle & Mary Lois Barnum W; m 1968 to Rene Marie Haas; c Melinda Marie. Educ: NTex State Univ, BA, 67; Univ Tex, JD, 70; Order of Barristers. Polit & Govt Pos: Trustee & chmn, Nueces Co Ment Health-Ment Retardation Ctr, 70-74; mem adv comt, Tex A&I Univ, Corpus Christi, 73-; mem, Tex Co Chmn Asn, 74; chmn, Nueces Co Dem Exec Comt, Tex, 74- Bus & Prof Pos: Attorney-at-law, Kleberg, Mobley, Lockett & Weil, currently; treas, Coleman-Fulton Pasture Co, currently. Mem: Am & Nueces Co Bar Asns; State Bar Tex; Am Legion; Corpus Christi CofC. Legal Res: 338 Bermuda Corpus Christi TX 78411 Mailing Add: 1200 Corpus Christi State Nat Bldg Corpus Christi TX 78403

WHITTLESEY, FAITH RYAN (R)
Pa State Rep
Mailing Add: Capitol Bldg Harrisburg PA 17120

WHITTOW, WAYNE F (D)
Wis State Sen
b Milwaukee, Wis, Aug 16, 33. Educ: Univ Wis, Milwaukee, BBA, 63, MBA, 66. Polit & Govt Pos: Wis State Assemblyman, 60-66; mem, 16th Ward Dem Unit; Wis State Sen, currently. Bus & Prof Pos: Mgt consult, traffic admin, formerly. Mil Serv: Army, 55-57. Mem: Eagles; St Joseph Children's Home Athletic Asn; Bluemound Rd, State St & Vliet St Adv Asns. Mailing Add: 4921 W Washington Blvd Milwaukee WI 53208

WHITZELL, NORMAN P (D)
b Westbrook, Maine, Oct 9, 38; s James G Whitzell & Theresa Dionne W; m 1965 to Kathleen Mary Oles; c Michelle Leona. Educ: Univ Maine, Portland-Gorham, BS, 68, MS, 69. Polit & Govt Pos: Deleg, Maine Dem State Conv, 72; alt deleg, Dem Nat Conv, 72; chmn finance comt, Kennebec Co Dem Comt, 72-; deleg, Nat Young Dem Conv, 73; Maine State Rep, until 74; chmn, Maine Voter Registr Drive, 74; Southern regional distributor & vol coordr, Mitchell for Gov; asst clerk, Maine House of Rep, 75; Kennebec Co Fund Raising Coordr, 75. Bus & Prof Pos: Dir, Individualized Instr Prog for Educ Handicapped Children, Winthrop Sch Syst, Maine, 68-73. Mil Serv: Entered as Airman 3/C, Air Force, 57, released as E-3, 61, after serv in Air Commun Squadron, Athens, Greece Airbase, 59-61; Armed Forces Inst Outstanding Educ Achievement Award. Mem: Delta Sigma Pi; Comt of Cheaper Elec Rates (treas); Maine Teacher's Asn. Relig: Catholic. Mailing Add: 12 Spruce St Gardiner ME 04345

WHORTON, J D (R)
Okla State Rep
b Locust Grove, Okla, Dec 18, 27; s Dorsey Homer Whorton, Sr & Ona Yingst W; m 1952 to Patricia Lee Burchett; c Saundra Olean (Mrs Gary Gotfredson), J D, Jr, Dwight Lee, Ernest Dwayne & Tina Deann. Educ: Locust Grove High Sch, 42-46. Polit & Govt Pos: Rep State Committeeman, Mayes Co, 63-68; Okla State Rep, Dist 8, 68- Mem: Odd Fellows; Elks; CofC; Rotary; Okla Cattlemen's Asn. Relig: Methodist. Mailing Add: Star Rte Pryor OK 74361

WIBLE, CHARLES STEPHEN (D)
Ky State Rep
b Owensboro, Ky, Oct 31, 37; s Ralph L Wible & Nell Sanson W; m 1964 to Diane Christopher; c Catherine Anne, Mary Elizabeth & Patricia Lynn. Educ: Ind Univ, Bloomington, BS, 60, LLB, 63; Sigma Nu. Polit & Govt Pos: Pres, Daviess Co Young Dem, 66; mem exec comt, Young Dem Ky, 67; Ky State Rep, 13th Dist, 70- Bus & Prof Pos: Partner, Lovett, Wible & Lamar, Attorneys-at-law. Mil Serv: Entered as 2nd Lt, Army, 63, released as 1st Lt, 65, after serv as legal adv govt contracts, US Army Materiel Command, 63-65; Capt, Army Inactive Res, 66-; three letters of commendation from cmndg officer. Mem: Am Bar Asn; Am Trial Lawyers Asn; Mary Kendall Home (adv bd); Owensboro Symphony Orchestra (dir); Owensboro Jaycees. Relig: Baptist. Legal Res: 2940 Tanglewood Dr Owensboro KY 42301 Mailing Add: 208 W Third St Owensboro KY 42301

WICINSKI, JOSEPH A (D)
Kans State Rep
Mailing Add: 27 S Hallock Kansas City KS 66101

WICKER, ROGER F (R)
Nat Committeeman, Young Rep Nat Fedn
b Pontotoc, Miss, July 5, 51; s Thomas Frederick Wicker & Wordna Threadgill W; single. Educ: Univ Miss, BA, 73; Sigma Delta Chi; Omicron Delta Kappa; Sigma Nu; campus sen, Assoc Student Body, 69-70, legis liaison officer, 70-71, chmn comt of 82, 71-72, committeeman, Young Rep Club, 71-72, pres, Student Body, 72-73. Polit & Govt Pos: Co-dir, Col Rep Nat Comt, 71-73, southern area chmn, 73-; deleg, Miss State Rep Conv, 72 & Rep Nat Conv, 72; secy, Pontotoc Co Rep Exec Comt, 72-; nat committeeman, Young Rep Nat Fedn, 72- Mil Serv: Cadet, Air Force ROTC, 4 years; 2nd Lt, Air Force Res. Honors & Awards: Hall of Fame, Univ Miss, 73. Relig: Southern Baptist. Legal Res: Hwy 15 N Pontotoc MS 38863 Mailing Add: PO Box 4676 University MS 38677

WICKERSHAM, VICTOR EUGENE (D)
Okla State Rep
b Lone Rock, Ark, Feb 9, 06; s Frank M Wickersham & Lillie Mae Sword W; m 1929 to Jessie Blaine Stiles; c LaMelba Sue (Mrs Everett Renberger), Galen, Nelda (Mrs Samuel L Holston, Jr) & Victor II; twelve grandchildren. Educ: Mangum Jr Col; Bus Col, LaSalle Exten Univ. Polit & Govt Pos: Co officer, Okla, 24-35; state officer, 35 & 36; US Rep, Okla, 41-46, 49-56 & 61-64; Okla State Rep, Dist 54, 71-72, Dist 60, 72- Bus & Prof Pos: Chief clerk, State Bd Pub Affairs, Oklahoma City, Okla, 35-36; bldg contractor, 37; agt, John Hancock Mutual Life Ins Co, 38-41; agt, broker & realtor, Washington, DC, 45 & 46; leading agt, Repub Nat Life Ins Co of Dallas, 65-66, consult, 67- Mem: AF&AM; Mason (32 degree); Shrine; Elks; Odd Fellows. Honors & Awards: Top 4-H Club Winner, State Fair, 24; Spec Cong Comt during Harry S Truman Admin & on a Spec Cong Comt during Dwight Eisenhower Admin. Relig: Christian Church; pres, SW Dist, Christian Endeavor, Christian Churches, 20-21; secy church bd, pres, Cent Christian Church Bd & Sunday sch teacher, 33-34; elder emer, Nat City Christian Church, Washington, DC; elder, Cent Christian Church, Mangum, Okla. Mailing Add: 1901 N Oklahoma Ave Mangum OK 73554

WICKHAM, RONALD JAMES (D)
b Cedar Rapids, Iowa, May 19, 32; s Jesse Orson Wickham & Madeline Coakley W; m 1963 to Kathleen Ann Mullin; c Kerry Kathleen & Mary Elisabeth. Educ: State Univ Iowa, BA, 60; Young Democrats. Polit & Govt Pos: Finance chmn, Second Cong Dist, Iowa, 68-69; chmn, Linn Co Dem Cent Comt, Cedar Rapids, 69-71; committeeman, Second Cong Dist Dem Party, 71-72; admin asst to US Rep John C Culver, Iowa, 73-74, field rep, 75-; deleg, Dem Nat Conv, 72. Bus & Prof Pos: Underwriter, Midwest Reinsurance Underwriters, Cedar Rapids, Iowa, 60-63, asst secy, 63-67; supvr crop hail dept, Nat Farmers Union Property & Casualty Co, 67-72. Mem: Ins Inst Am; Nat Farmers Union; Linn Co Dem Club; Iowa Alumni Asn. Relig: Catholic. Mailing Add: 4418 Navajo Dr NE Cedar Rapids IA 52402

WICKLEIN, EDWARD CHRIS (D)
Chmn, Waukesha Co Dem Party, Wis
b Milwaukee, Wis, Aug 11, 34; s Archie Edward Wicklein & Christine Smith W; m 1963 to Sue Ann Gerrard; c John Andrew & Mark Edward. Educ: Wash Univ, summer 55; Univ Mo-Columbia, BS in Agr, 56; Eden Theol Sem, Webster Groves, Mo, 56-58; Louisville Presby Theol Sem, MTh, 60; Agr Club, Independent Agr Club, Student Coun, C V Riley Entom Soc; YMCA & Ruf Nex, Univ Mo-Columbia. Polit & Govt Pos: Chmn growth study comt, Mukwonago Area Schs, Waukesha Co, Wis, 72; chmn ad hoc recreation study comt, Town of Vernon, Waukesha Co, 72-73; mem bldg comt, Mukwonago Area Schs, 73-74; chmn, Waukesha Co Dem Party, 74- Bus & Prof Pos: Ordained minister, 59; asst pastor, First Presby Church, Columbus, Ind, 59-64; asst pastor, First Presby Church, Bay City, Mich, 64-67; pastor, Protestant Congregation, Kathmandu, Nepal, 67-68; pastor, United Presby Church of Vernon, Waukesha Co, 69-74; field underwriter, NAm Life & Casualty, Milwaukee, 74- Publ: Badger Kirk, United Presby Synod of Lakes & Prairies, 74; The Scots of Vernon, privately publ, 74. Mem: Presby Hist Soc (bd mem); Waukesha Co Hist Soc (rec secy); Milwaukee Comt on Coop Cable Commun Systs; Presby of Milwaukee (chmn subcomt on worship). Relig: Presbyterian. Mailing Add: S37 W26941 Genesee Rd Waukesha WI 53186

WICKS, GRACE JAIN (R)
Committeewoman, Idaho Rep State Cent Comt
b Genesee, Idaho, June 19, 06; d Walter Farwell Jain & Lela Lanphear J; m to Guy Plumbe Wicks, wid; c Jainie (Mrs Waymon Eugene Gay) & Donald H. Educ: Univ Idaho, BA, 33; Sigma Alpha Iota; charter mem & first pres, Alpha Phi. Polit & Govt Pos: Co comnr, Latah Co, Idaho, 63-67; mem nat comt on civil defense, US Asn Co Comnr, 64 & nat comt on welfare, 65; committeewoman, Idaho Rep State Cent Comt, 69-; Rep precinct committeewoman, Idaho, 69-; hostess, Idaho State Conv, 76. Bus & Prof Pos: Owner of real estate bus, Moscow, Idaho, 41-55; mem, Church World Serv Mission, Latah Convalescent Ctr, 47-54; pres, Pi Sigma Rho Corp, Alpha Phi Fraternity, 48-52 & 68-70; broker, Waddell & Reed, Inc, Kansas City, Mo, 55-67. Publ: Auth, Leah Buchanan, charter member & university president's wife, Alpha Phi Quart, 54. Mem: Latah Co Mus Soc; Gov Comn on Status of Women; Nat Alumni Dr Chairwoman, Univ Idaho, 74; PTA (lifetime mem). Honors & Awards: Sales-Half-Million Club, Waddell & Reed, Inc; Alumna Mem-at-Lg, Scholar Endowment Nat Dr, Univ Idaho; hon mem, Univ Idaho Found; Alumna Award, Univ Idaho Alumni Asn, 75, Alumna Award, Panhellenic Coun & Interfraternity Coun, Univ Idaho, 75. Relig: Presbyterian. Mailing Add: 110 W First Moscow ID 83843

WIDENER, MARY LEE (D)
Mem-at-Lg, Dem Nat Comt, Calif
b Schaal, Ark, July 6, 38; d Mert Thomas, Sr & Johnnie Mae Newton T; m 1959 to Warren Hamilton Widener; c Warren Hamilton, Jr, Michael Thomas & Stephen Louis. Educ: Heald Col, Oakland, Calif, grad, 56; Southwestern State Col, 62 & 63. Polit & Govt Pos: Deleg, Dem Nat Conv, 72; northern state chmn, Calif Dem State Cent Comt, 73-; mem-at-lg, Dem Nat Comt, 73- Bus & Prof Pos: Urban prog coordr housing, Fed Home Loan Bank Bd, 72-73; housing consult, self-employed, 73-. Mem: Nat Asn Negro Bus & Prof Women; Univ Young Women's Christian Asn (bd dirs, 71-); Berkeley Dream (adv bd, 71-); Martin Luther King, Jr Fund, Inc (incorporator, 72-); Nat Coun Negro Women. Honors & Awards: Sustained Superior Performance Award, Second Air Force Strategic Air Command, Altus AFB, Okla, 63; Young Woman Vol of Year, Bay Area Dem Women, 67. Relig: Protestant. Mailing Add: 2309 Browning St Berkeley CA 94702

WIDENER, WARREN (D)
Mayor, Berkeley, Calif
m to Mary Lee; c Warren, Jr & twins, Michael & Stephen. Educ: Boalt Hall Law Sch, Univ Berkeley, grad. Polit & Govt Pos: Mem, Berkeley City Coun, 2 years; vchmn, Alameda Co Dem Cent Comt; Mayor, Berkeley, 71-; dir, Calif Children's Lobby, Alameda Co Manpower Area Planning Coun & Alameda Co Regional Criminal Justice Planning Bd, currently; mem, Dem Party Credentials Comt, currently. Bus & Prof Pos: Attorney, Earl Warren Legal Inst, Univ Calif, Berkeley, currently; dir, Berkeley Neighborhood Legal Serv; chmn, Berkeley Rental Housing Comt. Mil Serv: Comn officer, Air Force, 60-64. Relig: Methodist; Lay leader, Downs Mem Methodist Church. Mailing Add: Mayor's Off-City Hall Berkeley CA 94704

WIDMAN, PAUL JOSEPH (D)
Chmn, Davison Co Dem Party, SDak
b De Smet, SDak, Dec 18, 36; s Warren Clay Widman & Catherine Lorraine Coughlin W; m 1959 to Elizabeth Ann Healy; c Cynthia, Susan, Shelly, Richard & Mark. Educ: Dakota State Col, BS in Educ, 60; SDak State Univ, MS in Commun, 68. Polit & Govt Pos: Dem precinct committeeman, Mitchell, SDak, 71-73; Davison Co chmn, Barnett for Cong Comt, 72; Davison Co chmn, Dougherty-Kennedy Dinner, 72; secy-treas, Davison Co Dem Party, 72-, chmn, 74-; mem, Mitchell City Coun, 72-; mem, Gov Coun on Local Affairs, 74-75; rep, Third Multi Planning Dist, 74- Bus & Prof Pos: Instr, Clark Pub Sch, SDak, 60-61, Henry Pub Sch, 61-64 & Custer Pub Sch, 64-66; ins counr, Horace Mann Educators, Springfield, Ill, 66- Mil Serv: SDak Nat Guard, 55-61, Sgt, serv in 747th Transportation. Mem: Jaycees (dir, 67-68, local pres, 68-69, state vpres & state dir, 69-70, US dir, 70-71); Elks; Life Underwriters Asn; SDak Sch Servicemen Asn. Honors & Awards: Outstanding Jaycee Award, 68, Outstanding Spark Plug Award, Jaycees, 70, SDak Presidential Award of Hon, 70, Outstanding US Dir in SDak, 71; Mitchell Jaycees Presidential Award of Hon, 71. Relig: Catholic. Mailing Add: 425 S Montana Mitchell SD 57301

WIDNALL, WILLIAM BECK (R)
b Hackensack, NJ, Mar 17, 06; m to Marjorie Soule; c Barbara & William S. Educ: Brown Univ, PhB, 26; NJ Law Sch, LLB, 31. Polit & Govt Pos: NJ State Assemblyman, 46-50; US Rep, NJ, 50-74; cand, US House of Rep, NJ, 74; deleg, Rep Nat Conv, 68. Bus & Prof Pos: Lawyer. Mem: Bergen Co Bar Asn. Relig: Episcopal. Mailing Add: 214 N Saddle River Rd Saddle River NJ 07458

WIEDEBUSCH, LARRY (D)
WVa State Deleg
Mailing Add: State Capitol Charleston WV 25305

WIER, ALEX SEARCY (D)
b Hempstead, Tex, Aug 5, 08; s Clarence Oran Wier & Frankie Routt W; m 1934 to Marie Wilde; c James A & Glen W. Educ: Cooke Sch Eng, EE, 29; ETex Col Law, LLB, 38. Polit & Govt Pos: Chmn, Waller Co Dem Party, Tex, 70-75. Mailing Add: PO Box 475 Hempstead TX 77445

WIERZBICKI, FRANK V (D)
Mich State Rep
b Detroit, Mich, Mar 10, 25; s Joseph Wierzbicki & Margaret Oleksy W; single. Educ: Univ Detroit, BBA, 53; Kappa Sigma Kappa. Polit & Govt Pos: Supvr, Wayne Co Bd Supvrs, 64-66; Mich State Rep, 25th Dist, 67- Bus & Prof Pos: Frank V Wierzbicki & Co, CPA's. Mil Serv: Entered as Seaman 2/C, Navy, 43, released as Gunners Mate 3/C, 46. Mem: Am Inst CPA's; Mich Asn CPA's; Polish Roman Cath Union; Moose, Dearborn Lodge 1620; Usher's Club, St Hedwig Parish, Detroit, Mich. Relig: Catholic. Mailing Add: 3185 Gilbert Ave Detroit MI 48210

WIESE, ANDREW J (D)
SDak State Rep
Mailing Add: Flandreau SD 57028

WIESER, AL, JR (DFL)
Minn State Rep
Mailing Add: 704 S Fourth St La Crescent MN 55947

WIETHE, JOHN ALBERT (D)
Chmn, Hamilton Co Dem Party, Ohio
b Cincinnati, Ohio, Oct 17, 12; s Harry Wiethe & Eleanora Rombach W; m 1938 to Ruth Sohngen; c Barbara (Mrs Galligan), Kathee (Mrs James Lippert), Jayne (Mrs Walter Zuburbehler) & Michael. Educ: Xavier Univ, BPh, 34; Miami Univ & Univ Cincinnati; Chase Law Sch, Northern Ky State Univ, DJP; Legion of Honor. Polit & Govt Pos: Deleg, Dem Nat Conv, 52-74; chmn exec comt, Hamilton Co Dem Party, 54-, chmn bd elec, 56-75; vchmn, Ohio Dem Party, 58-74, chmn, 74-75; chmn & founder, Dem Co Chmn, 63-64; mem, Dem Nat Comt, 74-75. Mem: Am, Ohio & Cincinnati Bar Asns. Honors & Awards: All Pro Guard, Nat Football League, 39-40 & 40-41; Am Asn Little World Series Umpire, 41; Grand Commodore, State Ohio, 73-74; Ohio Dem of Year, Ohio State Dem Party, 74-75. Relig: Catholic. Legal Res: 1864 Blackstone Pl Cincinnati OH 45237 Mailing Add: John Wiethe Law Off 607 Terrace Hilton Bldg Cincinnati OH 45202

WIETING, LEROY JAMES (D)
Tex State Rep
b Runge, Tex, Feb 28, 27; s Herman William Wieting & Rose Marie Kubala W; m 1945 to Dorris Willene Atlkins; c Leroy James, Jr & Beckie Lynette. Educ: Tex A&I Univ, Corpus Christi. Polit & Govt Pos: City secy, Portland, Tex, 58-60, tax assessor collector, 58-62 & city mgr, 60-62; Tex State Rep, currently. Bus & Prof Pos: Rep personnel dept, Reynolds Metal Co, currently. Mem: Kiwanis; Tex City Mgr Asn; Tax Assessor-Collector Asn. Relig: Baptist. Mailing Add: Box 546 Portland TX 78374

WIGEN, JORIS ODIN (R)
Comnr of Ins, NDak
b Hettinger, NDak, May 5, 17; s J O Wigen & Gea Sether W; m 1943 to Phyll G Vevle; c Richard, Joan & Ann. Educ: St Olaf Col, BA, 39. Polit & Govt Pos: Finance chmn, Burleigh Co Rep Comt, NDak, 62-64; treas, NDak State Rep Cent Comt, 64-69; Comnr of Ins, NDak, 69- Bus & Prof Pos: Mgr, Western Adjust & Inspection Co, 50-57; owner-mgr, Noble Adjust Co, Bismarck, 57-; owner-mgr, Kwiki Carwash, 65- Mil Serv: Entered as Pvt, Army, 41, released as Capt, 46, after serv as Air Force Pilot, 440th Troop Carrier GP, ETO, 44-45; Air Medal with Two Oak Leaf Clusters; Presidential Unit Citation; Am Defense Ribbon; ETO Ribbon with Seven Battle Stars; Am Theater Ribbon; Victory Medal. Mem: Bismarck CofC (bd dirs & exec comt); Mo Slope Lutheran Homes (exec comt); Bismarck Kiwanis Club. Relig: Trinity Lutheran. Mailing Add: 1255 W Highland Acres Rd Bismarck ND 58501

WIGGIN, CHESTER M, JR (R)
b Conway, NH, June 4, 17; s Chester M Wiggin & Frances Starkey W; m 1962 to Joyce A Guyer. Educ: Dartmouth Col, AB, 39; Boston Univ, LLB, 42; Kappa Kappa Kappa. Polit & Govt Pos: Legal aide to Secy of the Navy, formerly; mem, NH Legis, 41-43; exec secy, Bd of Corrections Naval Rec, 47-53; admin asst to US Sen Bridges, NH, 53-61; admin asst to US Sen Cotton, NH, 62-69; fed co-chmn, New Eng Regional Comn, 71-; comnr, Interstate Com Comn, 72- Mil Serv: Entered as Pvt, Marine Corps, 43; released as Capt, 47, after serv in Inf, Pac, 43-45 & 2nd Marine Div, 45-47; Lt Col, Marine Corps Res (Ret); Bronze Star. Mem: Supreme Court, NH & DC Bar Asns. Mailing Add: Contoocook NH 03229

WIGGIN, ELMER S (R)
NH State Rep
Mailing Add: 10 Sweatt St Penacook NH 03301

WIGGINS, CHARLES DELMAR (R)
Rep State Committeeman, Okla
b Lancaster, Mo, Feb 2, 05; s George Henry Wiggins & Mary Elizabeth Coons W; m 1948 to Mary Katheryn Donaldson; c Larry Don. Educ: Panhandle A&M Col; Goodwell, Okla. Polit & Govt Pos: Rep precinct committeeman, Texas Co, Okla, 26-62; Bur of Census, 60; Rep chmn, Texas Co, 62-67; Rep state committeeman, Texas Co, Okla, 67-; co chmn, Nixon for President, 68; co chmn, Camp for Cong, 68. Bus & Prof Pos: Pub sch teacher, 23-39; farmer, 35-69. Mem: Farm Bur; Band Parents; Coin Club; Nat Rifle Asn. Relig: Methodist. Mailing Add: Rte 3 Guymon OK 73942

WIGGINS, CHARLES E (R)
US Rep, Calif
b El Monte, Calif, Dec 3, 27; m 1946 to Yvonne L Boots (deceased); remarried 1972 to Betty Burnett; c Steven L & Scott D. Educ: Pasadena City Col, Calif, AA, 49; Univ Southern Calif, BS, 53, Sch of Law, JD, 56. Polit & Govt Pos: Pres, El Monte Coord Coun; pres, El Monte Young Rep, 49; deleg, Nat Young Rep Conv, 49; alt, Los Angeles Co Rep Cent Comt, 50; mem, Rep Cong Sect Comt, 50; mem, Lieberg for Cong Campaign Comt, 58; chmn, El Monte Planning Comt, 58-60; mem, Rousselot for Cong Campaign Comt, 60 & 62; mem, El Monte City Coun, 60-64; finance chmn, Miller for Assembly Campaign, 62; town chmn, Nixon for Gov Campaign, 62; mem, Los Angeles Co Cent Comt, 62-66; mem, Rep State Cent Comt, 62-66; mem, Walton for Cong Campaign Comt, 64; finance chmn, Lancaster for Assemblyman Campaign, 64; town chmn, Younger for Dist Attorney Campaign, 64; Mayor, El Monte, 64-66; US Rep, 25th Dist, Calif, 66- Bus & Prof Pos: Research attorney, Judge Frank Swain, 56-57; attorney-at-law, 57-58; partner, Wood & Wiggins, Attorneys, 58-66. Mil Serv: Army, 45-48 & 50-52, released as 1st Lt, Inf; Combat Inf Badge. Mem: Am & Calif Bar Asns; Univ Southern Calif Law Alumni; Univ Southern Calif Legion Lex; Lions; Jr CofC. Honors & Awards: Distinguished Serv Award; ed, Univ Southern Calif Law Rev, 55-56. Relig: Methodist. Legal Res: 1200 S Highland Ave Apt 118 Fullerton CA 92632 Mailing Add: US House of Rep 2445 Rayburn Bldg Washington DC 20515

WIGGINS, GEORGE I (R)
NH State Rep
Mailing Add: RFD 1 Sunapee NH 03782

WIGGINS, HARRY (D)
Mo State Sen
Mailing Add: 7520 Main St Kansas City MO 64114

WIGGINS, LARRY DON (R)
Chmn, Texas Co Rep Comt, Okla
b Raton, NMex, Aug 17, 49; s Charles Delmar Wiggins & Mary Katheryn Donaldson W; single. Educ: Panhandle State Univ, BS, 72; Kappa Kappa Psi; Panhandle State Stage Band; A Capella Choir. Polit & Govt Pos: Chmn, Texas Co Rep Comt, Okla, 73- Bus & Prof Pos: Farmer-rancher, Guymon, Okla, 65-; part-time dep, Texas Co Sheriff Off, 70-73. Mem: Nat Rifle Asn; Lions; No Mans Land Rifle & Pistol Asn; Panhandle State Univ Alumni Asn. Honors & Awards: OKIE Award, Sen Dewey F Bartlet, 73. Relig: Methodist. Mailing Add: RR 3 Guymon OK 73942

WIGLEY, RICHARD ELLIS (R)
Minn State Rep
b Lake Crystal, Minn, Oct 23, 18; s Evan E Wigley & Mary Jane W; m 1940 to Francys May Othoudt; c Richard Owen & Paul Edward. Educ: Univ Minn, 38 & 39. Polit & Govt Pos: Lake Crystal Sch Bd, 58-70; Farmer's Home Admin, 69-70; Minn State Rep, 75- Mem: Mason; Lions Club (pres, Lake Crystal, 64-65); CofC; Blue Earth Co Crop Improv Asn (pres, 65-75); Minn Crop Improv Asn (pres, 70-75). Honors & Awards: Premier Seed Growers Award, Minn Crop Improv Asn, 70. Relig: Presbyterian. Mailing Add: Rte 2 Lake Crystal MN 56055

WIKOFF, VIRGIL CORNWELL (R)
b Decatur, Ill, Feb 6, 27; s Virgil L Wikoff & Grace Cornwell W; m 1947 to Ruth Helen Moore; c Terri (Mrs Robert G Bolduc) & Patti (Mrs Gregory D Bolton). Educ: Univ Ill, Champaign, BA in Arch Eng, 51. Polit & Govt Pos: Councilman, Champaign, Ill, 63-67, mayor, 67-75; chmn, Ill Local Govt Adv Coun, 70-74; mem, Ill Munic Prob Comn, 74- Bus & Prof Pos: Pres, Lyman-Wikoff, Inc, Champaign, Ill, 52- Mil Serv: Entered as A/S, Navy, 44, released as Electrician's Mate 3/C, 46, after serv in Pac Theatre; recalled, 51-52. Mem: Ill Munic League; Am Arbit Asn; Cent Ill Builders Asn of Assoc Gen Contractors (dir, 75-); Champaign-Urbana Jaycees. Honors & Awards: Outstanding Jaycee, Ill, 59; Outstanding Jaycee State Dir Award, 59-60, Nat Dir Award, 62-63; One of Ten Outstanding Young Men in Community, 60-61; Senatorship, Jr CofC Int, 62. Relig: Protestant. Mailing Add: 2120 Noel Dr Champaign IL 61820

WILBER, BERNARD (R)
Mass State Rep
b Fall River, Mass, May 30, 24; s Bernard Clinton Wilber & Janet Goodwin W; m 1946 to Elizabeth Jeannette Wordell; c Linda (Mrs John Hartley), Jeannette (Mrs Philip Parker) & Cynthia (Mrs Chadbourne). Educ: J F Wilbur High Sch, Little Compton, RI. Polit & Govt Pos: Mem, Barnstable Planning Bd, 59-66, chmn, 62-63; Gov appointee, Barnstable Housing Authority, 66-72; mem, Barnstable Town Meeting, 71-74; vchmn, Barnstable Charter Comn, 73-74; Mass State Rep, 73-; chmn, Barnstable Rep Town Comt, 74- Bus & Prof Pos: Mem, Barnstable Sch Bldg Needs Comt, 70-73. Mil Serv: Entered as Pvt, Army Air Force, 42, released as Sgt, 45, after serv in 1180 Mil Police Co (Aviation), European & Mediter Theaters, 43-45. Mem: Cummaquid Golf Club (pres, 2 years, chmn greens comt, currently); VFW 2578; Hyannis Yacht Club; Cape Cod Contractors & Builders Asn. Legal Res: 100 Wingfoot Dr Cummaquid MA 02637 Mailing Add: PO Box 300 Cummaquid MA 02637

WILBER, ELINOR F (R)
Conn State Rep
Mailing Add: 10 Lalley Blvd Fairfield CT 06430

WILBER, ROLAND C (R)
b Apr 5, 04; m to Marie. Polit & Govt Pos: Chmn, Idaho Rep State Finance Comt, formerly; chmn, Nez Perce Co Rep Party, formerly; deleg, Rep Nat Conv, 68; chmn, Idaho Rep Party, 68-72; mem, Rep Nat Comt, 68-72. Bus & Prof Pos: With pub rels dept, Potlach Industs. Legal Res: 1322 Eighth St Lewiston ID 83501 Mailing Add: PO Box 359 Lewiston ID 83501

WILBUR, GEORGE CRAIG (D)
b Flint, Mich, Jan 23, 46; s Maurice D Wilbur (deceased) & Helen V Jentz W; single. Educ: Univ Wis-River Falls, 64-67, BS, 72; Univ Wis-Madison, 67-68. Polit & Govt Pos: Numerous positions in Wis Young Dem; mem staff, David Carley for Gov Campaign; nat committeeman, Wis Young Dem, 67-68; aide to Patrick J Lucey, McCarthy for President Nat Staff, 68; state chmn, Wis Students for McCarthy, 67-68; mem nat ad hoc steering comt, Students for McCarthy, 68-69; polit consult, 70-; mem state admin comt, Wis Dem Party, 72-; state pres, Dem Youth Caucus of Wis, 72-73; exec dir, Wis Student Rights Defense Fund, Inc, 72-74; alt deleg, Dem Nat Mid-Term Conf, 74. Bus & Prof Pos: Mem bd dirs, Kickapoo Stove Works, Ltd, 75- Mailing Add: Rte 1 La Farge WI 54639

WILBUR, RICHARD SLOAN (R)
Asst Secy of Defense for Health & Environment
b Boston, Mass, Apr 8, 24; s Blake C Wilbur, MD & Mary C Sloan W; m 1951 to Betty Lou Fannin; c Andrew C, Peter D & Thomas S. Educ: Stanford Univ, BS, 43, MD, 46; Phi Beta Kappa; Alpha Omega Alpha; Nu Sigma Nu. Polit & Govt Pos: Mem, Santa Clara Co Rep Cent Comt, Calif, 65-69, vchmn, 67-69; mem, Rep State Cent Comt Calif, 67-69; Asst Secy of Defense for Health & Environ, 71- Bus & Prof Pos: Asst clin prof med, Stanford Univ, 52-69; mem, Calif Med Asn Coun, 64, chmn, 68-69; pres, Santa Clara Co Med Soc, 65; chmn bd, Calif Blue Shield, 66-68; mem, Calif Gov Survey Comt on Cost Control & Efficiency, Ment Hygiene, 67; dep exec vpres, Am Med Asn, 69-71. Mil Serv: Entered as A/S, Navy, 42, released as Lt(jg), 49; Ens, Naval Res, 42-45. Publ: Co-auth, Soft tissue sarcoma of the duodenum, Gastroenterol, 11/58; auth, Doctors, detectives & drugs, WVa Med J, 12/72 & All volunteer: military medicine tomorrow, Mil Med, 6/73. Mem: Nat Inst Med; fel Am Col Physicians; Am Nat Red Cross (bd gov); Nat Adv Cancer Coun; Charles R Drew Post-Grad Sch (bd visitors). Honors & Awards: Scroll of Merit, Nat Med Asn, 72; Medal for Distinguished Pub Serv, Dept Defense, 73. Relig: Episcopal. Mailing Add: 985 Hawthorne Pl Lake Forest IL 60045

WILBURN, JERRY (D)
Miss State Rep
b Mantachie, Miss, Sept 18, 40; s E C Wilburn & Lula Wren W; m 1965 to Margaret Ann Silas; c Bronson Gane. Educ: Itawamba Jr Col, Fulton, Miss; Miss State Univ, Starkville. Polit & Govt Pos: Miss State Rep, 64- Bus & Prof Pos: Pub rels & job promoter, Cook, Coggins, Kelly & Cook, Engrs. Mil Serv: Lt, Army, 62-69. Mem: Mason; Scottish Rite. Honors & Awards: Outstanding Young Men of Am, 65. Relig: Methodist. Mailing Add: PO Box 36 Mantachie MS 38855

WILCOX, FRANK B (R)
b Little Falls, NY, Aug 2, 09; s Frank Brown Wilcox & Mary Rose Williams W; m 1935 to Anne Frances Flynn; c Frank D & Robert J. Educ: Cornell Univ, 49-50; Rutgers Univ, 55. Polit & Govt Pos: Alt deleg, Rep Nat Conv, 72. Bus & Prof Pos: Teller & real estate appraiser, Little Falls Nat Bank, 28-52; asst vpres, State Bank Albany, 52-75. Mem: F&AM; Rotary (treas, 55-75); Ft Plain Community Club. Mailing Add: 21 Clark Ave Ft Plain NY 13339

WILCOX, JOHN HARVEY (D)
Nat Committeeman, Ind Young Dem
b New Albany, Ind, June 25, 39; s F Shirley Wilcox (deceased) & Grace Corrao W; single. Educ: Ball State Univ, BS, 66; Ind Univ, 67; Nat Defense Educ Act fel, Ctr for Study India, 68; Beta Theta Pi; Ball State Young Dem. Polit & Govt Pos: Pres, Floyd Co Young Dem, Ind, 68-70 & Ninth Dist Young Dem, 71-73; regional coordr, Ind Young Dem, 71-73, nat committeeman, 73- Bus & Prof Pos: Teacher, Floyd Co Sch Corp, New Albany, Ind, 66-70 & Louisville Bd Educ, 70-71; admin asst to mayor, New Albany, Ind, 72; exec secy, New Albany Flood Control Dist, 72- Mailing Add: 1901 Culbertson Ave New Albany IN 47150

WILCOX, ROSEMARY PHYLLIS (R)
VChmn, Grundy Co Rep Party, Mo
b Oskaloosa, Iowa, Apr 12, 27; d Thomas J Crane & Ethel Walling C; m 1960 to Donald Wilcox; c James Richard & William Thomas Kemp & Timothy Wilcox. Educ: Stephens Col, Columbia, Mo, AA, 46; Northwest Mo State Univ, 66-67; League of Women Voters. Polit & Govt Pos: Vchmn, Grundy Co Rep Party, Mo, 72-, committeewoman, Fourth Ward, 72-; mem, Rep State Comt, 74-; mem exec bd, Gov Adv Coun on Ment Retardation & Developmental Disability, 74- Mem: Grundy Co Rep Women's Club (first vpres, 73-); DAR; Order of Eastern Star; Mo Asn Retarded Citizens; Grundy Co Hist Soc. Honors & Awards: Plaque of Appreciation, Donnie Wilcox Mem Peter Pan Sch for Exceptional Children, 65; Pilots' License, 66; Bd of Admissions, Stephens Col, 73. Relig: Methodist. Mailing Add: 1604 E Seventh Trenton MO 64683

WILCOX, VERN (D)
Utah State Rep
Mailing Add: 2522 Polk Ave Ogden UT 84401

WILDE, ORVIN GERAL (D)
b Fairview, Utah, Aug 11, 33; s Orvin Eskel Wilde & Verl Miner W; m 1953 to Rosalie Hall; c Orvin Jeffery, Ruth Ann, Denise, Allison & Gregory James. Educ: Brigham Young Univ, BS, 56, MS, 63; Theta Alpha Phi. Polit & Govt Pos: Voting dist chmn, Provo, Utah, 64-65; ward chmn, Dem Party, Provo, 65-68, precinct chmn, 68-70; mem bd trustees, Utah Coun Improv Educ, 66-69, pres, 68-69; deleg, Dem Nat Conv, 68, alt deleg, 72; bd mem, Utah State Retirement Bd, 70-; chmn, UEA Resolution Comt, 73-75. Bus & Prof Pos: Chmn, Wasatch Front Educ Coun, 63-64; pres, Asn Local Pres, 65-66; mem bd dirs, Gem State Mutual Ins Co, 74- Mem: Life mem Nat Educ Asn; Utah Educ Asn; Speech Arts Asn Utah; Alpine Educ Asn (pres, 64-65 & 70-71); Nat Forensic League. Relig: Latter-day Saint. Mailing Add: 815 N 300 West Provo UT 84601

WILDER, ALICE F (R)
Mem, Aiken Co Rep Exec Comt, SC
b Richmond, Va, Jan 1, 04; m 1938 to M A Wilder; c Marion Archer, Jr & Mary Alice (Mrs Hastings Wyman, Jr). Educ: Univ SC, AB, 23. Polit & Govt Pos: Helped establish first GOP orgn in Precinct One, Aiken, SC, 61; mem, Aiken Co Rep Exec Comt, 61-; mem, Precinct One Rep Exec Comt, Aiken, 62-68; charter mem, Aiden Co Rep Women's Club, pres, formerly, first vpres, currently; mgr, Watson for Cong Hq, Aiken, 65; mgr, Aiken Co Campaign Hq, fall 66; chmn agenda comt, Aiken Co Rep Conv, 66 & 68; secy, Aiken Co Rep Party, currently; secy, Aiken City Rep Party, currently; Rep Nat Committeewoman, SC, formerly. Bus & Prof Pos: Pub sch teacher, 23-39; headmistress, Aiken Day Sch, 39-55; organizer & teacher, Mead Hall, Parish Day Sch, Episcopal Church, 55-65. Relig: Episcopal; Sunday Sch teacher & former head, Women of the Church, St Thaddeus' Church. Mailing Add: PO Box 443 Aiken SC 29801

WILDER, JOHN S (D)
Lt Gov, Tenn
Mailing Add: State Capitol Nashville TN 37219

WILDER, LAWRENCE DOUGLAS (D)
Va State Sen
b Richmond, Va, Jan 31, 31; m to Eunice Montgomery; c Lynn, Larry & Loren. Educ: Va Union Univ, BS, 51; Howard Univ, JD, 59; Omega Psi Phi. Polit & Govt Pos: Va State Sen, 69- Bus & Prof Pos: Bd mem, United Givers Fund & Richmond Urban League; chmn bd, Red Shield Boy's Club; research agt, NAACP Legal Defense Fund. Mil Serv: Entered as Pvt, Army, 52, released as Sgt 1/C, 53, after serv in Korea; Bronze Star. Mem: CofC; Mason; Shrine; Friends Asn (past bd mem); Guardsman. Legal Res: 2800 Hawthorne Ave Richmond VA 23222 Mailing Add: 3026 P St Richmond VA 23223

WILENSKY, JULIUS M (R)
b Stamford, Conn, Oct 10, 16; s Joseph Wilensky & Mary J Wainstein W; m 1939 to Dorothy T Jobrack; c Joseph L, Nancy L & Martha J. Educ: Rensselaer Polytech Inst, 34-36; Kappa Nu. Polit & Govt Pos: City Rep, 16th Dist, 57-59; mem, Second & Fourth Charter Rev Comns; mem, Stamford Rep Town Comt, 60-63; chmn, Coun Rep Clubs, 61-62; mem, Stamford Planning Bd, 63-65; mem, Bd Finance, 65-69; Mayor, Stamford, 69-72, dir, Metrop Regional Coun, 69-, vpres, 72-; mem, Tri-State Regional Planning Comn, 71- Mailing Add: 51 Barrett Ave Stamford CT 06905

WILEY, JUNIOR LEE (R)
Chmn, Clay Co Rep Party, Ark
b Piggott, Ark, June 26, 26; s Claude Elbert Wiley & Gladies W; m 1951 to Martha Gaye Winstead; c Rhonda Faye, Gary Neal & Bruce Wayne. Educ: Greenway High Sch, 40-44. Polit & Govt Pos: Chmn, Clay Co Rep Party, Ark, 69- Bus & Prof Pos: Builder & contractor; farmer; cattle bus; nursing homes corp. Mil Serv: Entered as Pvt, Army, 45, released as Cpl, 46, after serv in US. Mem: Ark Polled Hereford Asn (bd mem). Relig: Baptist. Mailing Add: S 12th St Rt 1 Piggott AR 72454

WILEY, RICHARD ARTHUR (R)
Mem, Wellesley Rep Town Comt, Mass
b Brooklyn, NY, July 18, 28; s Arthur Ross Wiley & Anna Holder W; m 1955 to Carole Jean Smith; c Kendra Elizabeth, Stewart Alan & Garett Smith. Educ: Bowdoin Col, AB, 48; Oxford Univ, Rhodes scholar & BCL, 51; Harvard Univ, LLM, 59; Phi Beta Kappa; Delta Upsilon. Polit & Govt Pos: Dep chmn for planning & develop, Mass Rep State Comt, 71; town meeting mem, Wellesley, Mass, 71-; mem, Wellesley Rep Town Comt, Mass, 72-, chmn, 72. Bus & Prof Pos: Attorney, John Hancock Mutual Life Ins Co, 56-58; lawyer & partner, Bingham, Dana & Gould, Boston, 59-, managing partner, currently. Mil Serv: Entered as Airman Basic, Air Force, 52, released as 1st Lt, 56, after serv in Off of Staff of Judge Adv Hq, Logistics Command, Wright-Patterson AFB, Ohio, 53-56; Maj, Air Force Res, 56-; Air Force Commendation Medal; Nat Defense Serv Medal; Armed Forces Res Medal. Publ: Pups, plants & package policies - or the insurance antitrust exemption re-examined, Villanova Law Rev, spring 61; Edge act corporations-catalysts for international trade & investment, 7/61 & How to use letters of credit in financing the sale of goods, 4/65, Bus Lawyer. Mem: Am & Boston Bar Asns; Boston Comt on Foreign Rels. Relig: Episcopal. Legal Res: 34 Wachusett Rd Wellesley Hills MA 02181 Mailing Add: Bingham Dana & Gould 100 Federal St Boston MA 02110

WILEY, RICHARD E (R)
b Peoria, Ill, July 20, 34; s Joseph H Wiley & Jean Farrell W; m 1960 to Elizabeth Jean Edwards; c Douglas Stewart, Pamela Lynn & Kimberly. Educ: Northwestern Univ, Evanston, BSEd, 51, Sch Law, JD, 58; Georgetown Univ Law Ctr, LLM, 62; Phi Delta Kappa; Phi Delta Phi. Polit & Govt Pos: Gen counsel, Fed Commun Comn, 70-72, comnr, 72-74, chmn, 74-; sustaining mem, Rep Nat Comt. Bus & Prof Pos: Attorney, Chadwell, Keck, Kayser, Ruggles & McLaren, Chicago, 62-68; asst gen counsel, Bell & Howell Co, 68-69; partner, Burditt, Calkins & Wiley, 70. Mil Serv: Entered as 1st Lt, Army, 59, released as Capt, 62, after serv in OTJAG Pentagon; Army Commendation Medal. Publ: Forty-nine thoughts on closing argument, Trial Lawyers Guide, 64; Grand Jury secrecy, Northwestern Law Rev, 67; Procedural accommodation of federal & state regulatory interests in cable television, Admin Law J, 72. Mem: Fed Bar Asn (mil law ed, Fed Bar Asn News, 61-62, nat officer, 71-75, coun & comt coordr, Budget Comt, 72-73); Am Bar Asn (founding ed-in-chief, Law Notes, 65-66, chmn, Young Lawyers Sect, 68-69, chmn, Comn on Campus Govt & Student Dissent, 68-69, House Deleg, 71-73, chmn, Spec Comt on Lawyers in Govt, 74-75, Standing Comt on Clients' Security Fund, 71-73, vchmn, Publ & Membership Comts, Gen Practice Sect, 71-73, vchmn, Coun Admin Law Sect, 72-73); Admin Conf of US; Wash Golf & Country Club; Northwestern Univ N Men's Club (bd dirs, 70-). Relig: Methodist. Legal Res: IL Mailing Add: 3818 N Woodrow St Arlington VA 22207

WILEY, STEPHEN B (D)
NJ State Sen
Mailing Add: State House Trenton NJ 08625

WILFONG, JAMES F (D)
Maine State Rep
Mailing Add: North Fryeburg Stow ME 04058

WILHELMS, GARY L (R)
Ore State Rep
Mailing Add: 3869 Madison St Klamath Falls OR 97601

WILKEN, SHIRLEY MAYE (D)
b Columbus, Nebr, May 11, 18; d Will Carleton Rector & Mary Louise Bloedorn R; m 1940 to Clarence H Wilken; c Jane (Mrs H F Monnich, Jr) & Jack. Educ: Kramer High Sch, Columbus, Nebr, grad, 35. Polit & Govt Pos: Pres, Platte Co Dem Women's Club, Nebr, 61-62, precinct organizer, adv & dir publicity, several years; mem, Columbus Dem City Cent

Comt, several years; secy, Robert Conrad, admin asst to Gov Brooks, Nebr; acting treas & publicity dir, Platte Co Dem Cent Comt, 70, vchairwoman, 70-72, chmn, 72-74; area rep, Nebr State Dem Exec Comt, Platte, Nance, Boone & Antelope Co, 71-; mem, Nebr State Dem Cent Comt, 4 years; secy, Nebr State Dem Exec & Cent Comt, 71-74; mem, Gov Exon's Comn on the Status of Women, 73- Bus & Prof Pos: Exec secy, Columbus CofC, Nebr, 37-42, mgr, 43-44, asst mgr, 55-59, pres, State Asst, 58; dep registr voter registr, Platte Co Clerk's Off, part-time. Publ: Series of by-line articles regarding agencies included in the Columbus United Fund at the time of its formation in Columbus, 43 & By-line article after personal interview with Gov J James Exon's wife, Pat, 2/71, The Columbus Telegram. Mem: PEO (guard, 71, rec secy, 72, corresponding secy, 73). Honors & Awards: Chmn Award for Outstanding Achievement, Nebr State Dem Cent Comt, 73. Relig: Lutheran. Mailing Add: 3011 28th St Columbus NE 68601

WILKERSON, WALTER D, JR (R)
State Committeeman, Tex Rep Party
b Marlin, Tex, June 7, 30; s Walter Dumas Wilkerson & Frances Burnitt W; m 1954 to Neddie Jane Bullock; c Nancy Ellen & Mark Howard. Educ: Tex A&M Univ, BS, 51; Univ Tex Southwestern Med Sch, MD, 55; Am Bd Family Practice, dipl; Phi Eta Sigma; Phi Kappa Phi. Polit & Govt Pos: Chmn, Montgomery Co Rep Party, Tex, 64-; state committeeman, Tex Rep Party, 65-; alt deleg, Rep Nat Conv, 64, deleg, 68 & 72. Mil Serv: Lt, Med Corps, Navy, 56-58. Mem: Am Acad Family Physicians; Tex Med Asn. Relig: Methodist. Mailing Add: 1516 N San Jacinto St Conroe TX 77301

WILKERSON, WILLIAM AVERY (BILL) (D)
Miss State Rep
b Lucedale, Miss, Mar 9, 38; m 1960 to Dixie Nell Patterson; c Donna Lynn, Dawson Glynn & Laurie Nell. Educ: Jackson Sch Law, LLB, 66. Polit & Govt Pos: Miss State Rep, 72- Bus & Prof Pos: Attorney, timber farmer. Mem: Miss Bar Asn; Mason; Farm Bur. Relig: Methodist. Legal Res: Rte 1 Lucedale MS 39452 Mailing Add: PO Box 255 Lucedale MS 39452

WILKIE, GERHART (D)
NDak State Rep
b Rolette Co, NDak, Feb 15, 07; married; c four. Educ: Pub schs. Polit & Govt Pos: NDak State Rep, 61- Bus & Prof Pos: Farmer. Mem: Sportsmen's Club; Crop Improv Asn; Farmers Union. Relig: Lutheran. Mailing Add: Box 727 Rolla ND 58367

WILKIN, RUTH WARREN (D)
Kans State Rep
b Atchison, Kans, Sept 9, 18; d William Thomas Warren & Ella Calvert W; m 1940 to Donald Keith Wilkin; c Janet (Mrs Lyle Chase), Donna & Susan. Educ: Univ Kans, AB, 40; Phi Beta Kappa. Polit & Govt Pos: Mem, Kans Tax Rev Comn, 71-72; Kans State Rep, 56th Dist, 72- Mem: League of Women Voters Kans; Church Women United (state legis chmn, 68-72); Nat, State & Local Women's Polit Caucus. Relig: Presbyterian. Mailing Add: 1610 Willow Topeka KS 66606

WILKINS, CAROLINE HANKE (D)
VChmn, Dem Nat Comt
b Corpus Christi, Tex, May 12, 37; d Louis Allen Hanke & Jean Guckian H; m 1957 to B Hughel Wilkins; c Brian Hughel. Educ: Tex Col Arts & Indust, 56-57; Tex Tech Univ, 57-58; Univ Tex, Austin, BA, 61; Univ of the Americas, MA in Latin Am Hist Magna Cum Laude, 64. Polit & Govt Pos: Benton Co precinct committeewoman, 64-; publicity chmn, Benton Co Gen Elec, 64; chmn, Get-Out-the-Vote Comt, Benton Co, 66; vchmn, Benton Co Dem Cent Comt, 66-70; vchmn, First Cong Dist, Ore, 66-68, chmn, 68; vchmn, Dem Party of Ore, 68-69, chmn, 69-74; vpres, Asn Dem State Chmn, Washington, DC, 70-73; mem exec comt, Western States Dem Conf, 70-72; mem arrangements comt, Dem Nat Conv, 72; vchmn, Dem Nat Comt, 72-, mem, Dem Charter Comn, 73-74. Bus & Prof Pos: Instr hist, Ore State Univ, 67-68. Publ: Implications of the US-Mexican water treaty for interregional water transfer (w B Hughel Wilkins), Water Resources Research Inst, Ore State Univ, 69-70. Mem: Ore State Univ Faculty Wives Club; PTA; Corvallis-Ore State Univ Music Asn; Am Asn Univ Women; W Coast Asn Women Historians. Mailing Add: PO Box 189 Corvallis OR 97330

WILKINS, EDNESS KIMBALL (D)
Wyo State Rep
b Casper, Wyo; d Wilson S Kimball & Edness Jane Merrick K; m to Capt Roland Wilkins, wid; c Dr Charles. Educ: Univ Ky; Univ Nebr. Polit & Govt Pos: Chief clerk, State Auditor's Off, Cheyenne, Wyo, 24-28; secy & asst to Dir Mint, Washington, DC, 33-47; personnel officer, Bur Reclamation, Casper, Wyo, 47-50; mgr, Casper Water & Sanitation Dept, 50-54; Wyo State Rep, 55-66 & 73-, minority leader, 63, speaker pro-tem, 65, speaker, 66; mem, Wyo Comn on Status of Women, 65-; Wyo State Sen, 67-72. Bus & Prof Pos: Owner, Kimball Ranch, Casper, Wyo, 52-; pres, Hjorth Oil Royalty Co, Casper, 58- Publ: Many articles on history of Wyo. Mem: Bus & Prof Women's Club; Am Asn Univ Women; Zonta; Eastern Star; Salvation Army Bd (chmn, 70-). Relig: Episcopal. Mailing Add: 433 Milton Ave Casper WY 82601

WILKINS, HENRY, III (D)
Ark State Rep
b Pine Bluff, Ark, Jan 4, 30; s Henry Wilkins, Jr & Minnie B Jones W; m 1954 to Josetta Edwards; c Henry, IV, Cassandra Felecia, Mark R & Angela J. Educ: Univ Ark, BA, 57; Atlanta Univ, MA, 61; Univ Pittsburgh, 66-67; Omega Psi Phi. Polit & Govt Pos: Elected to Jefferson Co Dem Cent Comt, Ark, 64 & 70; deleg, Ark Const Conv, 68, vchmn munic govt comt, 69-; alt deleg, Dem Nat Conv, 68, deleg, 72; mem, Comt Legis Reorgn, Ark, 71-; Ark State Rep, Dist 54, 72-; mem, Ark Dem State Comt, currently. Bus & Prof Pos: Prof polit sci, Univ Ark, Pine Bluff. Mil Serv: Entered as Pvt, Army, 52 & released as Sgt, 54, after serv in 10th Corps, Korea; 2nd & 3rd Korean Winter Commendation Medals. Publ: Some Aspects of the Cold War 1945-50, Brown, 63; A survey of poverty's root causes in Jefferson County, Arkansas, 64; A study of black problems and opportunities in an urban area (Pittsburgh), 66-67; plus two others. Mem: Elks (grand dist dep); NAACP; Interested Citizens for Voter Educ & Regist; Ark Coun Human Rels; Jefferson Co Opportunity Forum. Honors & Awards: Merrill Fellows Grant, Stock Exchange Firm of Merrill, Lynch, et al, 60; Polit Achievement Award, Negro Youth Orgn, 72. Relig: United Methodist. Mailing Add: 303 N Maple St Pine Bluff AR 71601

WILKINS, JAMES CLIMENT (R)
Mem, Rep State Cent Comt La
b Only, Tenn, July 17, 94; s Thomas Joseph Jefferson Wilkins & Adealy Albertine Bruce W; div; c Gloria Adelia (Mrs Witteman), James Climent, John Thomas, Mary Alice (Mrs French) & Janie Sue (Mrs Smith). Polit & Govt Pos: Mem, Rep State Cent Comt La, currently; chmn, Caldwell Parish Rep Exec Comt, until 72. Bus & Prof Pos: Mail carrier, Columbia, La, 21-64. Mil Serv: Entered as Fireman, 3/C, Navy, 17, released as Engr 1/C, 19, after serv in ETO, 17-19. Mem: Nat Rifle Asn; Am Ord Asn; F&AM; RAM; Am Legion. Legal Res: 1019 Everett St Columbia LA 71418 Mailing Add: RFD 2 Box 1 Columbia LA 71418

WILKINS, ROY
b St Louis, Mo, Aug 30, 01; s William D Wilkins & Mayfield Edmondson W; m 1929 to Aminda Badeau. Educ: Univ Minn, AB, 23. Bus & Prof Pos: Ed, Crisis Mag, 34-49; managing ed, Kans City Call, 23-31; asst secy, NAACP, 31-49, acting secy, 49-50, adminr, 50-55, exec secy, 55-64, dir, 65- Honors & Awards: Spingarn Medal, NAACP. Legal Res: 147-15 Village Rd Jamaica NY 11435 Mailing Add: 1790 Broadway New York NY 10019

WILKINSON, CHARLES BURNHAM (BUD) (R)
b Minneapolis, Minn, Apr 23, 16; s Charles P Wilkinson & Edith Lindbloom W; stepmother Ethel Grace W; m 1938 to Mary Shifflett; c James G (Jay) & Charles P (Pat). Educ: Univ Minn, Minneapolis, BA in Eng, 37; Syracuse Univ, MA in Eng Educ, 40; Psi Upsilon. Hon Degrees: LLD, Okla Christian Col, 73. Polit & Govt Pos: Consult to President Kennedy on Physical Fitness, President's Coun Physical Fitness, Washington, DC, 61-64; Rep Nat Committeeman, Okla, 68-72; Spec Consult to the President, 69-71. Bus & Prof Pos: Asst football coach, Syracuse Univ, 37-40; asst football coach, Univ Minn, Minneapolis, 41; football coach & athletic dir, Univ Okla, 46-64; pres, Lifetime Sports Found, 65-69; pre-game analyst & color commentator, Col Football Telecasts, NCAA Game of the Week, 65-; chmn bd, Planned Mkt Assocs, Inc, 71- Mil Serv: Entered as Ens, Navy, 42, released as Lt Comdr, 45, after serv in V-5 Prog, Pac, 44-45. Publ: Modern Physical Fitness, Viking Press, 67; Sports Illustrated Football: Offense, 72 & Sports Illustrated Football: Defense, 73, Lippincott. Mem: Am Football Coaches Asn; Am Legion. Honors & Awards: One of Nation's Ten Outstanding Young Men, US Jr CofC, 50; Nat Brotherhood Citation, Nat Conf Christians & Jews, 59; Univ Okla Distinguished Serv Citation; Sports Illustrated Silver Anniversary All-Am Award, 62; Nat Football Found Hall of Fame, 69. Relig: Episcopal. Mailing Add: 2600 NW 62nd St Oklahoma City OK 73112

WILKINSON, ERNEST LEROY (R)
b Ogden, Utah, May 4, 99; s Robert Brown Wilkinson & Annie Cecilia Anderson W; m 1923 to Alice Valera Ludlow; c Ernest Ludlow, Marian, Alice Ann, David Lawrence & Douglas Dwight. Educ: Weber Col, 17-18; Brigham Young Univ, AB, 21; George Washington Univ, JD, 26; Harvard Univ, SJD, 27; Delta Theta Phi. Hon Degrees: LLD, Brigham Young Univ, 57; DPS, Ft Lauderdale Univ, 70; LD, Grove City Col, 71. Polit & Govt Pos: Supt, Camp Good Will, Wash, 25; dep supt of ins, NY State, 31; mem, Nat Comt of Army & Navy Chaplains, 47-50; mem, Gov Comt Representing Utah, White House Conf on Educ, 55; deleg, Rep Nat Conv, 56, 60, 68 & 72; mem, Nat Comt to Evaluate United Serv Orgn, 62; Rep cand, US Senate, 64; Rep Nat Committeeman, Utah, 72-75. Bus & Prof Pos: Mem of faculty, Weber Col, Ogden, Utah, 21-23; mem of faculty, Bus High Sch, Washington, DC, 23-26; prof law, NJ Law Sch, 27-33; assoc, Law Firm, Hughes, Schurman & Dwight, New York, 28-35; partner, Law Firm, Moyle & Wilkinson, Washington, DC, 35-40; partner, Law Firm, Wilkinson, Cragun & Barker, 51-; head, Law Firm of Ernest L Wilkinson, 40-51; pres, Brigham Young Univ, 50-64 & 65-71; chancellor, Unified Church Sch Syst, Church of Jesus Christ of Latter-day Saints, 53-64; mem bd dirs, Deseret News Publ Co, Salt Lake City, Utah, 54-, Beneficial Life Ins Co, 57-70 & KSL, Inc & Radio Serv Corp of Utah, 60-, mem bd trustees, Utah Found, Salt Lake City, 60- & Found for Econ Educ, Irvington-on-Hudson, NY, 60-71; mem bd dirs, Rolling Hills Orchard, 61-71; mem bd dirs, Ellison Ranching Co, Tuscarora, Nev, 62- Mil Serv: Pvt, Army, 18. Publ: Decline & Possible Fall of the American Republic, Bookcraft, 65; Ernestly Yours, Deseret Bk Co, 71. Mem: Fel Am Bar Found; Valley Forge Freedoms Found (mem bd visitors, 64-); Nat Right to Work Comt Legal Defense & Educ Found (pres, 69-73); Am Legion; Order of the Coif. Honors & Awards: Awarded George Washington Medal by Freedoms Found for Speech on Free Enterprise, 61, for Independence Day Ed, 67 & for Whither America Address, 68 & Righteousness & Freedom-Indispensable Partners, 73. Relig: Latter-day Saint. Mailing Add: Brigham Young Univ Provo UT 84602

WILKINSON, HOMER F (R)
Utah State Rep
Mailing Add: 3538 Eastwood Dr Salt Lake City UT 84109

WILKINSON, NANA MIRIAM (R)
Treas, Tilton Town Rep Comt, NH
b Dahlgren, Ill, June 8, 12; d John R Slaten & Fleta E Berry S; m 1945, wid. Educ: Carthage Col, 30-32. Polit & Govt Pos: Co-chmn, Tilton Town Rep Comt, 54-56, treas, 58-; park comnr, Tilton, 63-; mem planning bd, Tilton, 69-70; NH State Rep, Dist Three, Belknap Co, 70-73; app mem, Flood Plains Comn, 71-73, Housing Authority Comt, 71-73 & Boat Regulations Comt, 71-73. Bus & Prof Pos: Secy, Pres Off, De Pauw Univ, 35-37; exec secy to vpres, Beach & Arthur Paper Co, Indianapolis & New York, 37-45; real estate broker, Henry B Trachy Agency, 70- Publ: Ed, The lilac letter, NH Fedn of Garden Clubs, 67-69. Mem: Life mem Nat Coun of State Garden Clubs, Inc; Nat Wildlife Fedn; Audubon Soc of NH; Natural Resources Coun of NH; Arthur S Brown Found (trustee, 74). Relig: Congregational. Mailing Add: Calef Hill Rd Tilton NH 03276

WILKINSON, PERRY OLIVER, JR (D)
Md State Deleg
b Hyattsville, Md, Aug 5, 38; s Perry Oliver Wilkinson & Mabel Barnes W; single. Educ: Univ Md, College Park, 56-60. Polit & Govt Pos: Md State Deleg, 75-, mem econ affairs comt, Md House of Deleg, 75-; mem bi-county comt, Prince Georges & Montgomery Co, Md, 75- Bus & Prof Pos: Independent ins agt, currently. Mil Serv: Air Nat Guard. Mem: Kiwanis Int; Nat Asn Independent Ins Agts; Nat Asn Mutual Ins Agts; Lanham-Bowie Dem club; Hyattsville Prof & Bus Mens Asn (first vpres). Relig: Methodist. Legal Res: 7106 Lois Lane Martins Woods Lanham MD 20801 Mailing Add: Presidential Bldg Fourth Floor 6525 Belcrest Rd Hyattsville MD 20782

WILKINSON, RICHARD WARREN (R)
b Welch, WVa, Nov 18, 32; s Dr E M Wilkinson & Addie May Johnson W; m 1958 to Patricia Hayes; c Richard Ernest & Frank Warren. Educ: Univ Va, BS, 55; Univ Va Law Sch, JD, 71; Phi Kappa Alpha; Phi Alpha Delta; 13 Soc; All-American Basketball. Polit & Govt Pos: Alt deleg, Rep Nat Conv, 72. Bus & Prof Pos: Exec vpres & trust officer, First Nat Bank, Bluefield, WVa, 62-; dir, Mercer Co Bank, Princeton, WVa & Bluefield Hardware Co,

Bluefield, currently; dir & treas, Control Prods, Inc, Beckley, currently; chmn bd, WVa Armature Co, currently; bd dirs, Castle Rock Bank, Pineville; bd dirs, Superior Sterling, Bluefield; bd dirs, Harmon Pocahontas Coal Co, Welch, currently. Mem: A R Matthews Found (chmn); Mercer Co Serv Ctr Libr (chmn); Bluefield State Col Fund (bd dirs); Univ Va Alumni Bd. Honors & Awards: Va Sports Hall of Fame, 75. Relig: Episcopal. Legal Res: 701 Edgewood Rd Bluefield WV 24701 Mailing Add: PO Box 1559 Bluefield WV 24701

WILKINSON, ROBERT DAWSON, JR (R)
Chmn, Dallas Co Rep Party, Ala
b Macon, Ga, Dec 31, 18; s Robert Dawson Wilkinson Sr & Frankie Jones W; m 1941 to Dorothy Jarvis; c Linda Kaye. Educ: Ala Polytech Inst, BS in Mech Eng, 40; Stanford Univ, grad study, 46-47; Sigma Phi. Polit & Govt Pos: Chmn, Dallas Co Rep Party, Ala, 62- Bus & Prof Pos: Owner, Splendid Cafe, 48-64; owner, Sky Hill Farm, 52-; concessionaire, Downtown Dinner Club, 64-; pres, Dallas Co Pvt Sch Found, 65-66 mem bd dirs, 67-; owner, Downtown Restaurant & Graystone Restaurant. Mil Serv: Entered as Lt, Army, 40, released as Capt, 48, after serv in Air Force, Pac Area & Okinawa. Mem: Ala Cattlemen's Asn; Dallas Co Pvt Sch Found, Inc (pres); Ala Farm Bur; Masonic Blue Lodge 305, Commandery 5. Relig: Presbyterian. Mailing Add: RR 2 Box 233B Selma AL 36701

WILKINSON, ROBERT MELVIN (R)
City Councilman, Los Angeles, Calif
b Nebr, Apr 11, 21; s Ray David Wilkinson & Katherine Lambert W; m 1944 to Marjorie Philp; c Barbara (Mrs Michael Lima), Noreen (Mrs Jon Ritzma) & Robert, Jr. Educ: Univ Southern Calif, BE, 47; Sigma Phi Epsilon. Polit & Govt Pos: Mem, San Fernando Young Rep, 50-51; city councilman, 12th Dist, Los Angeles, Calif, 53-57 & 67-; mem, Rep State Cent Comt Calif, 53-57 & 67-; exec secy, Los Angeles Harbor Comn, 57-65; mem, Los Angeles Co Rep Cent Comt, 67-; mem, State Solid Waste Mgt Bd. Mil Serv: Qm, 1/C, Navy, 42-45, Caribbean Theatre. Mem: Am Legion; Reseda; Japan-Am Soc (bd dirs); Winnetka CofC (vpres); West Valley Asn CofC (pres). Relig: Protestant. Mailing Add: 17319 Rayen St Northridge CA 91324

WILKINSON, RONALD JOE (R)
Chmn, Sedgwick Co Rep Party, Kans
b Wichita, Kans, Apr 9, 34; s Virgil Milton Wilkinson & Edythe Catherine Wiske W; m 1958 to Sidney Beattie; c Stuart Alan & Shelley Anne. Educ: Univ Wichita, AB, 56; George Washington Univ Law Sch, 56; Washburn Univ Law Sch, LLB, 58; pres, Student Bar Asn, 57-58; Delta Theta Phi. Polit & Govt Pos: Mem, City-Co Health Bd, Kans, 63-64; chmn, Sedgwick Co Young Rep, 64-65; munic judge, Wichita, 65-67; chmn, Kans Young Rep, 65-67; chmn, Sedgwick Co Rep Party, Kans, 67-70 & 73-; mem, Metrop Area Planning Comn, 69-70. Bus & Prof Pos: Chmn, Law Day Comt, 64. Mil Serv: Entered as Airman, Air Nat Guard, 58, released as Capt, 64; deleg, Nat War Col Strategy Seminar, 60. Mem: Wichita & Kans Bar Asns; Masonic Orgn. Honors & Awards: Outstanding Young Man of Wichita, 67. Relig: Protestant. Mailing Add: 570 Fourth Nat Bank Bldg Wichita KS 67202

WILKOWSKI, ARTHUR (D)
Ohio State Rep
Mailing Add: 546 E Lake St Toledo OH 43608

WILLARD, BEATRICE ELIZABETH (R)
b Palm Springs, Calif, Dec 19, 25; d Stephen Hallett Willard & Beatrice Armstrong W; single. Educ: Stanford Univ, BA, 47; Yosemite Field Sch of Natural Hist, Yosemite Nat Park, Calif, 48; Univ Calif Berkeley, Gen Sec Credit, 48; Univ Colo, Boulder, MA, 60, PhD, 63; Sigma Xi; Phi Sigma. Polit & Govt Pos: Secy, Colo Air Pollution Control Comn, 70-71; chmn, Denver Olympic Planning & Design Coun, 71-72; mem, Coun on Environ Quality, 72- Bus & Prof Pos: Sec sch teacher, Salinas High Sch, 49-50; Oakland Pub Sch, 50-52 & Tulelake High Sch, Calif, 52-57; research asst, Inst Arctic & Alpine Research, Univ Colo, 58-63; teaching asst biol, Univ Boulder, 60-63, adjoint prof, 70-72; asst prof, Southern Ore Col, Ashland, 63-64; exec dir, Thorne Ecological Inst, Boulder, 65-67, vpres, 67-70, pres, 70-72. Publ: Co-auth, Mammoth Lakes Sierra, Wilderness Press, 59; Land Above the Trees, Harper & Row, 72 & Effects of human activities on alpine ecol in Europe, Ford Found, 54; Colo Conservationist of the Year Award, Colo Wildlife Fedn, 69; Award for Prof Service, Am Motors, 70; Army Distinguished Civilian Serv Medal, 73; Soil Conservation Soc of Am Hon Award, 74. Relig: Protestant. Legal Res: 1529 Columbine Ave Boulder CO 80302 Mailing Add: 1200 N Nash St Arlington VA 22209

WILLARD, RICHARD C (D)
Conn State Rep
Mailing Add: 42 Russell Dr East Hartford CT 06108

WILLE, FRANK (R)
Chmn Bd Dirs, Fed Deposit Ins Corp
b New York, NY, Feb 27, 31; s Frank Joseph Wille & Alma Shutt W; m 1969 to Barbara Bowen; c Serena & Alison. Educ: Harvard Col, AB, cum laude, 50; Harvard Law Sch, LLB, cum laude, 56; NY Univ, LLM, 60. Polit & Govt Pos: Asst counsel to Gov, NY, 60-62, first asst counsel, 62-64; Supt Banks, NY, 64-70, chmn bd dirs, Fed Deposit Ins Corp, 70- Bus & Prof Pos: Staff, Davis Polk & Wardwell, law firm, 56-60. Mil Serv: Entered as Officer Cand, Naval Res, 51, released as Lt(jg), 54, after serv in USS Leyte, Atlantic, Caribbean & Mediter, 51-54. Publ: State banking: a study in dual regulation, Law & Contemporary Probs, 8/66. Mem: Metrop Club, Washington, DC; Rockaway Hunting Club. Relig: Episcopal. Mailing Add: 4733 Berkeley Terr Washington DC 20007

WILLE, JOHN HOWARD (D)
b Algona, Iowa, June 13, 47; s Howard A Wille & Bernadette Studer W; m 1972 to Kathryn Vicars; c John H, Jr & Brigid Kathryn. Educ: St Ambrose Col, 65-66; Western Ill Univ, BA in Educ, 69; Young Dem. Polit & Govt Pos: Alt deleg, Dem Nat Conv, 72; Dem precinct committeeman, currently. Bus & Prof Pos: Seventh grade teacher & eighth grade basketball coach, St Mary Sch, Pontiac, Ill, 69- Mem: Nat Cath Educ Asn; KofC. Relig: Roman Catholic. Mailing Add: 508 W Livingston Pontiac IL 61764

WILLEFORD, GEORGE (R)
b Dallas, Tex, Oct 23, 21; s George Willeford & Joy Brenner W; m 1948 to Ann Jennings; c George, III, Allison Ann & Joy Hale. Educ: Tex A&M Univ, BS, 43; Univ Tex Med Br, MD, 46; Phi Rho Sigma. Polit & Govt Pos: Chmn, Cameron Co Rep Comt, Tex, 60-62 & 66-70; exec committeeman, Rep Exec Comt, 62-66; dep chmn, Region Three, Tex Rep Party, 70-74, state chmn, 70-74; deleg, Rep Nat Conv, 72; mem, Rep Nat Comt, 72-74. Mil Serv: Entered as 1st Lt, Air Force Med Corps, 46, released as Capt, Flight Surgeon, 48, after serv in Komaki Airdrome, 5th Air Force Hq, Far East, 46-49. Publ: Medical Word Finder, Parker Publ Co, 66. Mem: Tex & Am Med Asns; Tex Pediat Asn; Am Acad Pediat; Am Bd Pediat. Relig: Episcopal. Mailing Add: 1404 Gaston Ave Austin TX 78703

WILLEMS, FRANK J (D)
Ark State Rep
Mailing Add: Rte 3 Paris AR 72855

WILLER, ANNE (D)
Ill State Sen
Mailing Add: 107 Howard Ave Hillside IL 60162

WILLET, GERALD L (DFL)
Minn State Sen
Mailing Add: 207 Mill Rd Park Rapids MN 56470

WILLEY, EDWARD EUGENE (D)
Va State Sen
b Frederick Co, Va, Apr 7, 10; m to Twyla Sutton Layton. Educ: Med Col Va, Sch Pharm. Polit & Govt Pos: City councilman, Richmond, Va, formerly; Va State Sen, 52- Bus & Prof Pos: Owner, Willey Drug Co. Mem: Mason; Shrine; various fraternal, prof & civic orgns. Relig: Methodist. Mailing Add: 1205 Bellevue Ave Richmond VA 23227

WILLFORD, LOUIS J (R)
Chmn, Gladwin Co Rep Party, Mich
b Gladwin, Mich, Oct 14, 40; s Gordon L Willford, Jr & Geneva M Thorington W; m 1969 to Deborah K Miller; c Carrie Ann & Louis J, Jr. Educ: Mich State Univ, BA, 65; Wayne State Univ, JD, 68. Polit & Govt Pos: Magistrate, Gladwin Co, Mich, 69; chmn, Gladwin Co Rep Party, 69-; friend of the court, Gladwin Co Circuit Court, 69-72; city attorney, Gladwin, Mich, 69- Mem: Mich State Bar Asn; Gladwin Lions; Gladwin Co Farm Bur; Eagles. Relig: Protestant. Legal Res: 205 Fourth St Gladwin MI 48624 Mailing Add: 500 W Cedar St Gladwin MI 48624

WILLIAMS, AL (D)
Wash State Rep
Mailing Add: 4801 Fremont N Seattle WA 98103

WILLIAMS, ANN COLE (D)
b Jewell Ridge, Va, Dec 8, 35; d Ulys Grant Cole (deceased) & Emma Sparks C; m 1955 to Jewell Adrian Williams; c Gregory Vernon, Jennifer Gail, Anthony Bradley & Lawrence Adrian. Educ: Whitewood High Sch grad, 55; Grundy Bible Inst, 56 & 57. Polit & Govt Pos: Pres, Ninth Dist, Dem Women's Orgn, 69-73; deleg, Dem Nat Conv, 72. Mem: VFW (pres, Ladies Auxiliary, 62-66). Relig: Church of Christ. Mailing Add: PO Box 856 Grundy VA 24614

WILLIAMS, ARTHUR (R)
b Lawrence, Mass, Dec 14, 15; s Michael Joseph Williams & Elizabeth Rodger W; m 1940 to Elizabeth Lauder Wilkinson; c Arthur Kenneth & Keith Andrew. Educ: Northeastern Univ Col Liberal Arts, Sch Law & Grad Sch Law. Polit & Govt Pos: Mass State Rep, 57-68; moderator, Town of Andover, 65-73; legis secy to Gov Volpe, 68- Bus & Prof Pos: Attorney-at-law; Spec Justice, First Dist Court of Northern Middlesex, currently. Mil Serv: Entered as Pvt, Army, 41, released as 1st Lt; Col, Army Res, currently; Presidential Unit Citation; SPac Campaign Medal; three Battle Stars. Mem: Mason; ROA; Elks; Lions; Am Legion. Relig: Congregational. Mailing Add: 149 Haverhill St Andover MA 01810

WILLIAMS, AVON NYANZA, JR (D)
Tenn State Sen
b Knoxville, Tenn, Dec 22, 21; s Avon Nyanza Williams, Sr & Carrie Belle Cole W; m 1956 to Joan Marie Bontemps; c Avon Nyanza, III & Wendy Janette. Educ: Johnson C Smith Univ, AB, 40; Boston Univ Law Sch, LLB, 47, LLM, 48; Omega Psi Phi. Polit & Govt Pos: State chmn, Tenn Voters Coun, 68-; Tenn State Sen, 19th Dist, 69-; deleg, Dem Nat Conv, 72. Bus & Prof Pos: Attorney-at-law, Knoxville, Tenn, 49-53, Nashville, 53-; cooperating attorney, NAACP Legal Defense Educ Fund, Inc, New York, 49-; bank attorney, Community Fed Savings & Loan Asn, Nashville, 62-; spec counsel, Jackson-Memphis-Tenn & WTenn Conferences, CME Church, 63-; lectr dent jurisprudence, Meharry Med Col, 66- Mil Serv: Entered as Pvt, Army Air Force, 43, released as 1st Lt, 46, after serv in SPac, 44-46; Res, 46-69, Lt Col; SPac Campaign Ribbon; World War II Ribbon. Publ: Auth, Race relations—a community problem, New South & Negro Digest, 63; Does a child have a right not to be brainwashed by adults? Peabody J Educ, 1/73. Mem: Davidson Co Independent Polit Coun (bd dirs, 62-); NAACP (exec bd, Nashville Br); Southern Regional Coun (bd dirs); Tenn Voters Coun (gen chmn); Sigma Pi Phi. Honors & Awards: Cert Merit, Johnson C Smith Univ, Agory Assembly & NAACP Youth Coun; Distinguished Serv Award, Nashville Br, NAACP; Citizen of Year Award, Nashville Frontiers Club, 72; Citizen of Year Award for achievement in civil rights, Grand Lodge, F&AM, Tenn; Prince Hall Mason, 72. Relig: Presbyterian; elder, St Andrews Presby Church, 56-, trustee, 66- Legal Res: 1818 Morena St Nashville TN 37208 Mailing Add: 1414 Parkway Towers Nashville TN 37219

WILLIAMS, BILL V (D)
Committeeman, State Dem Comt Tex
b Luling, Tex, Dec 5, 34; s Van W Williams & Velma Alice Stephens W; m 1954 to Cythia Ann Cook; c Bobby Vance, Pamela Kaye, Karen Lynn & John Stephen. Educ: Lamar Tech Col. Polit & Govt Pos: Committeeman, Harris Co Dem Exec Comt, Tex, 69, chmn, 70-74; committeeman, Dist 7, State Dem Comt Tex, 74- Bus & Prof Pos: Salesmgr, Beecham, Inc, currently. Mem: Harris Co Dem; Tex Bill of Rights. Relig: Baptist. Legal Res: Apt 127 7450 Bellfort Houston TX 77035 Mailing Add: 7369 Brace Houston TX 77017

WILLIAMS, CARL MICHAEL (R)
Chmn, Rep State Cent Comt, Colo
b Douglas, Wyo, Nov 9, 28; s John Walter Williams & Eleanor Powers W; m 1957 to Ginny Lee Downer; c Eleanor Lee Payne & Michael Carl. Educ: Univ NC, BA, 50; Univ Wyo, JD, 56; Kappa Sigma. Polit & Govt Pos: Colo State Sen, 68-72; chmn, Rep State Cent Comt, 74-; mem, Rep Nat Comt, 74- Bus & Prof Pos: Pres, Televents, 57- Mil Serv: Entered as Pvt, Air Force, 50, released as Capt, 58, after serv in Wyo Air Nat Guard, 53-58. Publ: Contrib, Law

J. Mem: CofC; Am Legion. Relig: Episcopal. Legal Res: 160 Cherry St Denver CO 80220 Mailing Add: Suite 1021 1660 S Albion Denver CO 80222

WILLIAMS, CARRINGTON (D)
Va State Deleg
b Brookneal, Va, June 21, 19; s Richard Douglass Williams & Louise Monroe W; m 1973 to Doreen Saxton Jones; c Barclay Moore, Sheila H Jones & Patricia D Jones. Educ: Johns Hopkins Univ, AB, 40; Univ Va Law Sch, LLB, 42; Omicron Delta Kappa; Delta Phi; mem staff, Va Law Rev, 42. Polit & Govt Pos: Va State Deleg, Fairfax & Falls Church, 66-70 & 72-; mem, Va State Bd for Community Cols, 70-71. Bus & Prof Pos: Lawyer. Mil Serv: Entered Army Air Force, 42, released as Capt, 46, after serv in 20th Air Force Hq, Pac Theatre. Mem: Johns Hopkins Club; Am & Va State Bar Asns; George Mason Col Found (pres); Fairfax Econ Develop Study Comt (chmn). Relig: Episcopal. Legal Res: 3543 Half Moon Circle Falls Church VA 22044 Mailing Add: 4085 University Dr Fairfax VA 22030

WILLIAMS, DEBORAH (R)
Mem, Concord Rep Town Comt, Mass
b Concord, Mass, July 22, 53; d David Balch Williams & Gloria Miller W; single. Educ: Fisher Jr Col, Boston, Mass, AA, 75; Middlesex Community Col, Div Continuing Educ, Law Enforcement Dept, 74-75; Northeastern Univ, Law Enforcement, currently. Polit & Govt Pos: Alt deleg, Rep Nat Conv, 72; mem, Concord Rep Town Comt, Mass, currently; adv, Young Rep Club Concord, currently; deleg, Mass Rep Preprimary Conv, 74. Bus & Prof Pos: Admin asst, Concord Police Dept. Mem: Middlesex Club; Rep Club of Mass; Acton Women's Rep Club; Rainbow Girls. Honors & Awards: Youngest alt deleg from Mass to Rep Nat Conv, 72. Relig: Protestant. Mailing Add: 76 Wood St Concord MA 01742

WILLIAMS, DIANE DOROTHY (R)
Mem, Rep State Cent Comt, Calif
b Albany, Calif, May 31, 48; d Capt Arthur P Williams & Dorothy Andrews W; single. Educ: Univ Hawaii, summers 65, 66 & 70; Yale Univ, summer 67; Univ Lausanne, summer 68; Univ Calif, Berkeley, BA, 69, teacher's credential, 70; Alpha Chi Omega; Angel Flight Soc (comdr); Gavel & Quill (vpres); French Club; Brick Muller Soc. Polit & Govt Pos: Secy, Univ Calif Chap, Young Rep, 65-69; intern & research aide, White House, Washington, DC, 69; mem, Calif Rep State Cent Comt, 70-; deleg, White House Conf on Children & Youth, 71 & 72; deleg, Rep Nat Conv, 72. Bus & Prof Pos: Research asst, Bank of Am, Int Banking, 70; dir, Sullivan Foreign Lang Sch, 70-73. Mem: Pi Lambda Theta (pres, Univ Calif Chap, 72-73): Prytanean Alumnae, Inc; Commonwealth Club of Calif; Panhellenic Alumnae Asn (rep, 73); Stars & Bars. Relig: Protestant. Mailing Add: 1771 Highland Pl Berkeley CA 94709

WILLIAMS, EDWARD BENNETT (D)
Treas, Dem Nat Comt
b Hartford, Conn, May 31, 20; s Joseph Barnard Williams & Mary Bennett W; m 1960 to Agnes Neill; c Joseph Barnard, Ellen Adair, Peter Bennett, Edward Neill, Dana Bennett, Anthony & Kimberly. Educ: Col of the Holy Cross, AB summa cum laude, 41; Georgetown Univ, LLB, 45. Hon Degrees: SJD, Col of the Holy Cross, 63; LLD, Loyola Col, 67, Georgetown Univ, 68, Fairfield Univ, 68, Loyola Univ, 70, Albert Magnus Col, 71, St Joseph's Col, 71, Lincoln Col, 72 & Suffolk Univ, 74. Polit & Govt Pos: Mem, US Judicial Conf Adv Comt on Fed Rules of Evidence, 65-; chmn, Md Judicial Selection Comt, Sixth Judicial Dist, 71; treas, Dem Nat Comt, 74- Bus & Prof Pos: Sr partner, Williams, Connolly & Califano, 67-; pres & dir, Washington Redskins Football Club. Mil Serv: Army Air Force, 41-43. Publ: Auth, One Man's Freedom, Atheneum, 62. Mem: University Club; Nat Lawyers Club; Metrop Club; Barristers Club; Nat Press Club of Washington. Honors & Awards: Lawyer of Year, DC Bar Asn, 66. Relig: Roman Catholic. Legal Res: 8901 Durham Dr Potomac MD 20854 Mailing Add: 1000 Hill Bldg Washington DC 20006

WILLIAMS, EDWARD FOSTER, III (R)
Tenn State Rep
b New York, NY, Jan 3, 35; s E Foster Williams, Jr & Ida Richards W; m 1960 to Sue Osenbaugh; c Cecile & Alexander. Educ: Auburn Univ, BS, 56; Memphis State Univ, MA, 74; Omicron Delta Kappa; Tau Beta Pi; Pi Tau Sigma; Phi Alpha Theta; Phi Kappa Phi; Sigma Phi Epsilon. Polit & Govt Pos: Deleg, Shelby Co Rep Conv, 63-72; precinct capt, Memphis City Rep Party, 64-70, precinct chmn, 66-70; mem steering comt, Shelby Co Rep Party, 70-71; Tenn State Rep, 71-; mem bd trustees, Memphis Pink Palace Mus, 72-; mem adv bd, Beale St Urban Renewal Proj Design, 72-; mem, Shelby Co Hist Comn, 73- Bus & Prof Pos: Staff engr, Buckeye Cellulose Corp, Memphis, Tenn, 57, planning engr, 60-69, spec asst to plant mgr, 70; vpres, Envirotrol, Inc, 70-73; vpres, Ramcon, Environ Engr Div, 73- Mil Serv: Entered as 2nd Lt, Air Force, 57, released as 1st Lt, 60, after serv in 70th Strategic Reconnaissance Wing, Strategic Air Command, 58-60; Capt, Air Force Res, honorably discharged, 71. Publ: Early Memphis and its river rivals, Memphis Sesquicentennial, 68; Fustest with the mostest, Colt Firearms, 69; ed, Environmental control news for southern industry, Ramcon current newsletter. Mem: Am Soc Mech Engrs; Tenn Hist Soc; Am Philatelic Soc; Am Mensa Soc; Tenn Beautiful, Inc (adv, 72-). Relig: Presbyterian. Legal Res: 767 Brookhaven Circle Memphis TN 38117 Mailing Add: PO Box 17386 Memphis TN 38117

WILLIAMS, FLOYD BERT (R)
b Kirkland, Tex, May 13, 15; s Bert Thomas Williams & Ethel Rae Coats W; m 1943 to Diamond Dorthy Howard; c Martina Jane (Mrs Ray A Mattheus) & Annette. Educ: Tex Tech Col, 39-41. Polit & Govt Pos: Chmn, Brisco Co Rep Cent Comt, Tex, formerly. Bus & Prof Pos: Farmer, 46- Mil Serv: Entered as Pvt, Air Force, 42, released as Sgt, 45, after serv in Ground Crew. Mem: Farm Bur; Nat Farmers Orgn. Relig: Baptist. Legal Res: 201 Loretta St Silverton TX 79257 Mailing Add: PO Box 741 Silverton TX 79257

WILLIAMS, FRANCIS XETON (D)
Committeeman, Ill Dem Cent Comt
b Springfield, Ill, Aug 1, 15; s Hobert T Williams & Elizabeth Spring W; m 1936 to Hedy Mrosko; c Sharon (Mrs Paul Van Daele), James O, Thomas J & Robert F. Educ: Cathedral Boys High Sch, 4 years. Polit & Govt Pos: Dem precinct committeeman, Ill, 62-; chmn, Moline City Dem Comt, 10 years; inspector of agr, Ill, 65-68; bd rev, Rock Island Co, 68-70; committeeman, Ill Dem Cent Comt, 36th Dist, 68-; state investr I, Moline, Ill, 70-; mem exec bd, Rock Island Co, 70-, health inspector, currently. Mem: Eagles. Relig: Catholic. Mailing Add: 2405 32nd St Moline IL 61265

WILLIAMS, FRANK (D)
Fla State Rep
Mailing Add: Crystal Lake Starke FL 32091

WILLIAMS, FRANKLIN H (D)
b Flushing, NY, Oct 22, 17; s Arthur Lee Williams & Alinda Lowry W; m 1944 to Shirley Broyard; c Franklin, Jr & Paul Anatole. Educ: Lincoln Univ, AB, 41; Fordham Law Sch, LLD, 45; Phi Kappa Epsilon; Alpha Phi Alpha. Hon Degrees: LLD, Lincoln Univ & Elizabethtown Col; DHL, Windham Col. Polit & Govt Pos: Asst Attorney Gen, Calif, 59-61; spec asst to dir, US Peace Corps, 61-62, dir, Div of Univ, Private & Int Coop, 62-63, dir, African Regional Off, 63; US Rep to UN Econ & Social Coun, 64-65; US Ambassador to Ghana, 65-68; alt rep, 19th Session of UN Gen Assembly, 64-65; dir, Urban Ctr, Columbia Univ, 68-69; pres, Phelps-Stokes Fund, NY, 69- Mil Serv: Army, 42-43. Mem: Coun on Foreign Rels. Relig: Methodist. Mailing Add: 52 W 89th St New York NY 10024

WILLIAMS, FRED (D)
Mo State Rep
b Columbus, Miss, July 6, 35; s Henry Williams & Laurel Black W; m 1956 to Etta Prather; c Anthony, Archell, Candace, Ursula & DeEldra. Educ: Hubbard Bus Col; Univ Mo. Polit & Govt Pos: Block chmn, Dem Party, St Louis, Mo, 4 terms; mem & employ chmn, West-End Neighborhood Adv Comt; mem, West-End Community Conf, mem, 26th Ward Beautification Comn; area chmn poverty prog; precinct capt, 28th Ward Dem Orgn, secy & head precinct capt, formerly; mem, 25th & 26th Wards Dem Orgn; Mo State Rep, Dist 72, 68-, mem, Educ & Appropriations Comts & vchmn, Employ Security Comt, Mo House Rep; mem, Gov Comn on Comprehensive Health Planning. Bus & Prof Pos: Prod planner, McConnell Douglas Corp, 14 years. Mil Serv: Marine Corps, 52, Korea. Mem: Toastmasters; Mason (Master, former jr warden). Relig: Methodist. Mailing Add: 5621 Chamberlain Ave St Louis MO 63112

WILLIAMS, G MENNEN (D)
Justice, Mich Supreme Court
b Detroit, Mich, Feb 23, 11; s Henry Phillips Williams & Elma Mennen W; m 1937 to Nancy Lace Quirk; c G Mennen, Jr, Nancy Quirk (Mrs Theodore Ketterer, Jr) & Wendy (Mrs Michael R Burns); seven grandchildren. Educ: Princeton Univ, AB, 33; Univ Mich Law Sch, JD, 36; Phi Beta Kappa; Order of the Coif; Phi Delta Phi; Quadrangle Club; Libr Club; Phi Gamma Delta. Hon Degrees: Wilberforce Univ, Lawrence Inst Technol, Mich State Univ, Univ Liberia, Univ Mich, Aquinas Col, St Augstine's Col, Ferris Inst, Morris Brown Col, Western Mich Univ, Lincoln Univ & World Univ, PR. Polit & Govt Pos: Mem social security bd, Social Security Admin, 36-37; Asst Attorney Gen, Mich, 37-38; exec asst to US Attorney Gen, 39-40; mem criminal div, US Dept Justice, 40-41; exec asst to Gen Counsel, Off Price Admin, 41, dep dir for Mich, 46-47; mem, Mich Liquor Control Comn, 47-48; Gov, Mich 49-61; chmn nationalities div, Dem Nat Comt, 54-61, vchmn, 55-61 & mem adv coun, 57-61; Secy of State for African Affairs, US Dept State, 61-66, US Ambassador, Rep of the Philippines, 68-69; justice, Mich Supreme Court, 71- Bus & Prof Pos: Mem, Griffiths, Williams & Griffiths, Law Firm, Mich, 48. Mil Serv: Entered Navy, 42, released as Lt Comdr, 46, after serv in Fast Carrier Task Forces & Strategic Bombing Surv, Japan; ten Battle Stars; Legion of Merit with Combat V; three Presidential Unit Citations; Pac, Philippine & Am Campaign Ribbons. Publ: A Governor's Notes, Univ Mich, 61; Africa for the Africans, Eerdmans, 69. Mem: Mason (33 degree); Eagles; Elks; Moose; Am Legion. Honors & Awards: Polonia Restituta, Polish Govt In Exile; Grand Off, Nat Order of Niger; Comdr, Nat Order of the Ivory Coast; Order of Sikatuna, Rank of Datu, Philippines; Pro Merito, Latvia. Relig: Episcopal; vestryman, St Paul's Cathedral, Detroit, Mich. Mailing Add: 25 Tonnancour Pl Grosse Pointe Farms MI 48236

WILLIAMS, GARY GRADY (D)
b New Haven, Conn, July 8, 51; s George Thomas Williams & Jean Welborn W; single. Educ: Pearl River Jr Col, Poplarville, Miss, AA, 71; Univ Conn, BA, 73; Phi Theta Kappa; parliamentarian, Fairfield Hall Dormitory Govt. Polit & Govt Pos: Deleg, Conn Dem State Conv, 71 & 72; pres, Young Dem of Univ Conn, 71-73; campaign coordr, Dem Campaign for Conn State Rep, 72; deleg, Dem Third Cong Dist Conv, Conn, 72 & alt deleg, Dem Nat Conv, 72. Bus & Prof Pos: Aide, US Rep Robert N Giamo, Conn, 69. -Honors & Awards: Nat Sch Award, Am Legion, 69; Acad Achievement Award, Univ Miss, 71; Dean's List, Pearl River Jr Col & Univ Conn, 71-73. Relig: Roman Catholic. Mailing Add: 30 Glen Pkwy Hamden CT 06517

WILLIAMS, GLEN MORGAN (R)
Mem, Rep Party, Va
b Jonesville, Va, Feb 17, 20; s Hughy May Williams & Hattie Hines W; m 1962 to Jane Slemp; c Janet Susan, Judith Ann, Rebecca Lynn & Melinda Jane. Educ: Milligan Col, AB; Univ Va, LLB; The Raven Soc; Order of the Coif; Delta Theta Phi; Va Law Rev. Polit & Govt Pos: State vchmn, Young Rep of Va, 48; commonwealth attorney, Lee Co, Va, 48-52; dist chmn, Ninth Dist, Rep Party, 50; Va State Sen, 54; deleg, Rep Nat Conv, 60 & 68; US Comnr, Cumberland Gap Nat Hist Park, 63; cong cand, Ninth Dist, Va, 64; chmn, Lee Co Rep Cent Comt, 64-; mem, Rep Party, Va, 68-; sub co judge, Lee Co, 71-; mem, Lee Co Sch Bd, 73- Bus & Prof Pos: Pres, Lee Farmer's Warehouse, Inc, 52-65. Mil Serv: Entered as A/S, Navy, 42, released as Lt (sg), 46, after serv as Commanding Officer, USS Seer, Pac; Atlantic Theater Ribbon; Mediterranean Theater Ribbon with two Stars; Pac Theater Ribbon with one Star; Citation from Comdr Minecraft, Pac Fleet. Mem: Am Legion; 40 et 8; Powell Valley Shrine Club, Cyrene Commandery 21, RAM; Lions; PTA. Relig: Disciples of Christ. Mailing Add: PO Box 6 Jonesville VA 24263

WILLIAMS, GORDON OLIVER (R)
Chmn, Hatfield Rep Town Comt, Mass
b Sunderland, Mass, Oct 30, 25; s Walter Roberts Williams & Ruth Louise Clark W; m 1959 to Mary Lou Belden; c Darryl Ladd, David Clark, Brian Oliver & Mary Ruth. Educ: Calif State Polytech Col, BS, 63. Polit & Govt Pos: State appointed mem, Hatfield Housing Authority, Mass, 67-; chmn, Hatfield Rep Town Comt, 68- Mem: Farm Bur; New Eng Milk Producers Asn. Relig: Protestant. Legal Res: 9 Depot Rd Hatfield MA 01066 Mailing Add: Box 5 North Hatfield MA 01066

WILLIAMS, HARRISON ARLINGTON, JR (PETE) (D)
US Sen, NJ
b Plainfield, NJ, Dec 10, 19; m 1974 to Jeanette Smith; c by previous marriage, Nancy, Peter, Wendy, Jonathan & Nina. Educ: Oberlin Col, AB, 41; Columbia Law Sch, LLB, 48; Georgetown Univ Sch of Foreign Serv. Hon Degrees: LLD, Rutgers Univ, 60, Fairleigh Dickinson Univ, 73 & Bloomfield Col, 74; LHD, Glassboro State Col, 71. Polit & Govt Pos: US Rep, NJ, 53-56; US Sen, NJ, 58-, chmn, Labor & Pub Welfare Comt, US Senate, 71-, chmn, Subcomt on Labor, mem, Subcomt on Youth & Subcomt on Handicapped, mem, Steering Comt, immediate past chmn & ranking mem, Comt on Aging & chmn, Housing Subcomt, mem, Comt on Banking, Housing & Urban Affairs, chmn, Securities Subcomt &

mem, Rules Comt, currently; deleg, Dem Nat Conv, 68; US deleg, Int Conf on Environ, 72; mem-at-lg, Educ Comn of the States, currently. Bus & Prof Pos: Attorney-at-law, NJ. Mil Serv: Naval Res, pilot, 4 years. Mem: NJ Tercentenary Celebration Comn (mem, Woodrow Wilson Mem Comt); Am & NJ Bar Asns; Dem Nat Comt Nationalities Div (exec comt). Honors & Awards: Better Life Award, Am Nursing Home Asn, 71; Gerry Award, Nat Geriatrics Soc, 72; Four Freedoms Award, United Italian-Am Labor Coun, 73; Distinguished Serv to Educ Award, NJ Educ Asn, 74; Gertrude F Zimard Mem Award, Nat Child Labor Comt, 75. Relig: Presbyterian. Legal Res: Bedminster NJ Mailing Add: US Senate Bldg Washington DC 20510

WILLIAMS, HOSEA LORENZO (D)
Ga State Rep
b Attapaulgus, Ga, Jan 5, 26; s Turner Williams; m to Juanita Terry; c Barbara Jean (Mrs Frank Emerson), Elizabeth LaCenia, Hosea Lorenzo, II, Andre Jerom & Yolanda Felecia. Educ: Morris Brown Col, BA; Atlanta Univ, 1 year; Phi Beta Sigma. Polit & Govt Pos: Cand, Atlanta City Coun, Ga, 73; Ga State Rep, 54th Dist, 75- Bus & Prof Pos: Teacher sci, High Sch, Ga, 51-52; research chemist, Dept Agr, 52-53; publ, Chatham Co Crusader Newspaper, 61-63; spec proj dir, Southern Christian Leadership Conf, 63-70, regional vpres, 69, nat prog dir, 71, pres, Metro Atlanta Chap, 72; organizer, Poor People's Union Am, 73; pastor, People's Church of Love, Atlanta, 73- Mil Serv: S/Sgt, Army, 44-46. Mem: NAACP; Mason; DAV; VFW; Am Legion. Honors & Awards: Civil Achievement Award, US Dept Agr, 56, Ten Year Serv Award, 61; Cause of Freedom in the Tradition of True Democracy Award, Ga State-Wide Regist Comt & Southern Christian Leadership Conf, 63, Chapter of the Year Award, Southern Christian Leadership Conf, 73; Community Serv Award, Savannah Alumni Chap, Delta Sigma Theta, 63. Relig: Interdenominational. Legal Res: 8 Lake Dr NE Atlanta GA 30317 Mailing Add: 775 Hunter St NW Atlanta GA 30314

WILLIAMS, J H (D)
Lt Gov, Fla
Mailing Add: PO Box 146 Ocala FL 32670

WILLIAMS, J MARSDEN (R)
Idaho State Sen
Mailing Add: 1776 Camrose St Idaho Falls ID 83401

WILLIAMS, J MELVIN (D)
Mont State Rep
Mailing Add: PO Box 245 Laurel MT 59044

WILLIAMS, JACK B (D)
Ill State Sen
Mailing Add: 9920 Schiller Blvd Franklin Park IL 60131

WILLIAMS, JAMES B, JR (R)
Mem Exec Comt, Miss Rep Party
b Memphis, Tenn, Feb 16, 30; s James Barney Williams & Volney Williamson W; m 1957 to Katharine George Saunders; c James Barney, III & Katharine Elizabeth. Educ: Univ Miss, BA, 52, MA, 59; Beta Theta Pi. Polit & Govt Pos: Chmn, Carroll Co Rep Comt, Miss, 64-74; mem exec comt, Miss Rep Party, 75- Mil Serv: Entered as 2nd Lt, Army, 52, released as 1st Lt, 54, after serv in Eighth Army, Korea, 53-54; Capt, Army Res; Commendation Ribbon; Korea Presidential Unit Citation. Mem: Miss Educ Asn; Rotary; Miss Cattlemans Asn. Relig: Episcopal. Legal Res: Cotesworth North Carrollton MS 38947 Mailing Add: PO Box 165 North Carrollton MS 38947

WILLIAMS, JEANETTE K (D)
City Councilman, Seattle, Wash
b Seattle, Wash, June 11, 17; d Dr Louis Herman Klemptner & Olga Krelova K; m 1942 to David Houston Williams; c Patricia Ellen & George Frederick. Educ: Univ Wash, BA, 37; Am Conservatory of Music, BM, Violin, 38, MM, Violin, 39, MM, Composition, 40; Sigma Alpha Iota; Phi Mu. Polit & Govt Pos: Exec bd deleg, King Co Dem Cent Comt, Wash, 60, vchmn, 61-62 & chmn, 63-64, 65-66 & 67-68; exec bd mem, Wash State Dem Cent Comt, 67-68 & 69-; deleg & mem Platform Comt, Dem Nat Conv, 64, 68 & 72; pub rels chmn, Wash State Fedn Dem Women's Clubs, 69; city councilman, Seattle, Wash, 69-; deleg, Puget Sound Govt, Conf, 70-, bd mem, 72; dir, Asn of Wash Cities, 72- Bus & Prof Pos: Performing musician, dir & arranger from Chicago to Los Angeles, 38-42. Mem: Nat Legal Aid & Defender Asn; Nat Orgn of Women; Urban League; League of Women Voters; Bus & Prof Women. Relig: Protestant. Mailing Add: 7132 58th NE Seattle WA 98115

WILLIAMS, JOAN EASON (R)
Chmn, Madison Co Rep Comt, Tenn
b Leapwood, Tenn, Jan 30, 24; d Ecbourne Cratis Eason & Reatie Carothers E; m 1953 to Robert Moody Williams; c Robert Moody, Jr, James Barton, John Eason & Henry Scott. Educ: Freed-Hardeman Col, 41-43; Union Univ, BA, 47; Tau Kappa Alpha; Chi Omega. Polit & Govt Pos: Pres, Madison Co Rep Comt, Tenn, 64-66, secy, 66-70, chmn, 74-; seventh dist vpres, Tenn Fedn Rep Women, 66-71; chmn, Gov Comn on Status of Women, Tenn, 72-73. Bus & Prof Pos: Machine oper, Procter & Gamble, Milan, Tenn, 43-45; teacher Eng, Hopkinsville High Sch, Ky, 47-49, High Sch, Adamsville, Tenn, 49-53 & Cherokee Jr High Sch, Memphis, 53-56; Mem: Mid-South Youth Camp (adv bd, 61-); Mutual Improv Club; Madison Co Welfare Adv Comt; Tenn Dent Soc Auxiliary (vpres, 75-76); Goals for Jackson Comt. Honors & Awards: Hon Col, Gov Winfield Dunn, 71. Relig: Church of Christ. Mailing Add: 123 Woodhaven Jackson TN 38301

WILLIAMS, JOHN BELL (D)
b Raymond, Miss, Dec 4, 18; s Gnaves Kelly Williams & Maude E Bedwell W; m 1944 to Elizabeth Ann Wells; c Marcia Elizabeth, John Bell & Kelly Wells. Educ: Hinds Jr Col, 36-38; Univ Miss; Jackson Sch of Law, LLB, 40. Polit & Govt Pos: Prosecuting attorney, Hinds Co, Miss, 44-46; US Rep, Miss, 47-67; Gov, Miss, 68-72. Bus & Prof Pos: Attorney-at-law. Mil Serv: Army Air Corps, 41-44. Mem: Miss State Bar Asn; Am Legion; VFW; Air Forces Asn; Lions. Relig: Baptist. Mailing Add: Raymond MS 39154

WILLIAMS, JOHN BLAIR (R)
Chmn Exec Comt, Mercer Co Rep Comt, Ohio
b Higginsport, Ohio, May 6, 09; s Charles Bodman Williams & Bettie Edna Ellis W; m 1945 to Hazel Catherine Nice; c Bettie (Mrs Stephen Spoerndle) & Mary Jane. Educ: Miami Univ, BS in Bus Admin, 30; Delta Sigma Phi; Tau Kappa Alpha; Sigma Chi. Polit & Govt Pos: Finance chmn, Mercer Co Rep Comt, Ohio, 60-70, chmn, Exec Comt, 70- Bus & Prof Pos: Acct exec, Goodyear Tire & Rubber Co, Akron, Ohio, 30-51; regional mgr, Harry Ferguson, Inc, Detroit, Mich, 51-53; asst sales mgr, Massey-Ferguson, Ltd, Toronto, Ont, 53-55; from dir sales, asst gen mgr, vpres & gen mgr to chief exec officer, Avco New Idea Div, Coldwater, Ohio, 55-; dir, Farm & Indust Equip Inst, Chicago, ILL & First Nat Bank, Celina, Ohio, currently. Mem: Elks; Shawnee Country Club, Lima, Ohio. Relig: Protestant. Legal Res: 530 E Livingston St Celina OH 45822 Mailing Add: Avco New Idea Coldwater OH 45828

WILLIAMS, JOHN J (R)
b Minneapolis, Minn, Oct 6, 19; s Evan Owen Williams & Harriet Elwood W; m 1942 to Joan Houghton, div; c John Richard & Wendy Ann (Mrs Thomas W Beasley). Educ: State Univ Iowa, BA, 46, JD, 48; Phi Kappa Psi; Phi Delta Phi. Polit & Govt Pos: City attorney, Red Oak, Iowa, 49-53; pres, Montgomery Co Young Rep, 50-52; mem, Hoegh for Gov Campaign Comt, 54; co attorney, Montgomery Co, 54-58; chmn, Citizens for Eisenhower-Nixon, Seventh Dist, 56; asst dir govt rels, Off Civil & Defense Mobilization, 59, asst to dir, 60; US secy, Joint US-Can Non Mil Defense Comt, 60; asst dir, Capitol Hill Assocs, 61; minority counsel, Small Bus Comt, US House Rep, 63-68, minority staff dir, US House Rep, 70-, dir, Rep Policy Comt, US House Rep, 70-73, minority staff dir, 70-, staff dir, Off of the Minority Leader, 74-; dep chief of staff, Comt on Resolutions, Rep Nat Conv, 72. Mil Serv: Entered as Pvt, Army, 41, released as Capt, 45, after serv in Eighth Army, Southwest Pac, 44-45; Bronze Star; Air Medal. Mem: Iowa Bar Asn; Capitol Hill Club. Relig: Methodist. Legal Res: 4001 47th St NW Washington DC 20016 Mailing Add: H-232 The Capitol Washington DC 20515

WILLIAMS, JOHN JAMES (R)
b Frankford, Del, May 17, 04; s Albert Frank Williams & Anna Hudson W; m 1924 to Elsie E Steele; c Blanche (Mrs Baker); three grandchildren. Educ: Frankford High Sch. Polit & Govt Pos: US Sen, Del, 47-70. Bus & Prof Pos: Real estate, Millsboro, Del. Mem: Mason; Shrine; Rotary. Relig: Methodist. Mailing Add: Millsboro DE 19966

WILLIAMS, JOHN RICHARD (JACK) (R)
b Los Angeles, Calif, Oct 29, 09; s James Maurice Williams & Laura LaCossitt W; m 1942 to Vera May; c Rick, Michael Maurice & Nikki. Educ: Phoenix Jr Col. Polit & Govt Pos: Pres, Phoenix Housing Authority, Ariz, 44-47; councilman, Phoenix, 53-54, mayor, 56-60, Gov, Ariz, 67-75; deleg, Rep Nat Conv, 68 & 72. Bus & Prof Pos: Dir, Radio Sta KOY, 29-67; pres, Phoenix Elem Sch Bd, 58-63; hon vpres, Southern Broadcasting Corp, 67-; former dir, Radio Sta KTUC, Tucson; former newspaper columnist, Phoenix Gazette. Mem: Lions; Kiva Club; Cloud Club; Ariz Club; Phoenix Press Club. Honors & Awards: Phoenix Man of the Year Award, 53. Relig: Episcopal. Mailing Add: 2323 N Central Ave Phoenix AZ 85004

WILLIAMS, JOHN THOMAS (R)
Mem, Rep State Cent Comt, NMex
b Houston, Tex, Sept 27, 31; s John Williams & Lorine Jones W; m 1954 to Barbara Lucille Matkin; c John Kendall, Bonnie Lucille, Rebecca Lorine & David Edward. Educ: Univ Tex, Austin, BS in Math, 59. Polit & Govt Pos: Mem, Bernalillo Co Rep Cent Comt, NMex, 64-, mem exec comt, 66-; Rep precinct chmn, Bernalillo Co, 65-66, vchmn, 67-69, chmn, 70-71; mem, Rep State Cent Comt, NMex, 66-; chmn, NMex Metrop Boundaries Comt, 68-73; mem, Selective Serv Bd, Local Bd 1, 70-; mem, Bernalillo Co Govt Personnel Bd, 73- Bus & Prof Pos: Mem lab staff, Sandia Labs, Albuquerque, NMex, 59-67, dir supvr, 67- Mil Serv: Entered as Pvt, Air Force, 51, released as T/Sgt, 55, after serv in 80th Air Depot Wing, NAfrica, 51-53; Nat Defense Medal; Good Conduct Medal. Mem: Soc Tech Writers & Publ. Relig: Methodist. Mailing Add: 9420 Las Calabazillas Rd NE Albuquerque NM 87111

WILLIAMS, JOHN WILLIAM, III (D)
Chmn, Seventh Cong Dist Dem Comt, Va
b Charlottesville, Va, Nov 24, 16; s John William Williams, Jr & Louise Anderson W; m 1937 to Laura Kegley; c Elizabeth Byrd (Mrs Abbott) & Martha Hayes (Mrs Anderson). Educ: Univ Va, 2 years; Tarleton Bus Col, 2 years; LaSalle Univ, grad, 48. Polit & Govt Pos: Pres, Charlottesville Young Dem Club, 48-50; pres, Va Young Dem Clubs, 53-55; chmn, Albemarle Co Bd Supvrs, 56-64; secy, Eighth Cong Dist Dem Comt, 56-65, vchmn, Seventh Cong Dist Dem Comt, 65-67, chmn, 67-; mem, Va State Dem Cent Comt, 56-, mem exec comt, 67-; pres, Asn Va Counties, 60-61; vchmn, Va State Hosp Bd, 63-71; vchmn, State Bd Welfare; mil aide to Gov, Va. Bus & Prof Pos: Vpres, Anderson Bros, Inc, Charlottesville, Va, 41-61, pres & gen mgr, 61-; head boxing coach, Univ Va, 53-; secy-treas, Anderson Realty Corp, 68-; mem bd, Va Nat Bank, 68- Mil Serv: Entered as Pvt, Army, 43, released as Capt, 46. Mem: Nat Intercollegiate Boxing Coaches Asn; Charlottesville Rotary; Monticello Guard Club; Farmington Country Club. Relig: Presbyterian. Legal Res: St Annes Rd Meadowbrook Heights Charlottesville VA 22901 Mailing Add: PO Box 3638 Charlottesville VA 22903

WILLIAMS, JOSEPH RULON (D)
State Auditor, Idaho
b Samaria, Idaho, Apr 14, 04; s Lewis Williams & Sara Morse W; m 1930 to Eva Lauraine Gyllenskog; c Joseph Roger, Bruce, Linda Lou (Mrs Root), Susan Jolaine (Mrs Winkler), Neal Morse, Milton Lee & Kristin May. Educ: Univ Idaho, 25-29; Int Corresponding Sch, 32; Sigma Chi. Polit & Govt Pos: Chmn, Ada Co Dem Party, Idaho, 32-48; state pres, Young Dem Idaho, 46, nat committeeman, Young Dem, 47; Dep State Auditor, Idaho, 41-47, State Auditor, 59-; postmaster, Boise, 48-52. Bus & Prof Pos: Real estate broker, Boise, 47- Mem: Kiwanis; Boy Scouts; Nat Asn State Auditors, Comptrollers & Treas (4th, 3rd, 2nd & 1st vpres & pres); Nat Conf of State Social Security Adminr (Nat secy & vpres). Relig: Latter-day Saint. Mailing Add: 801 N 20th Boise ID 83702

WILLIAMS, JOSEPHINE P (R)
Chairwoman, Lincoln Co Rep Party, Ky
b Danville, Ky, Oct 9, 21; d Fred Bodner & Mary Rice B; m 1946 to James Wesley Williams; c Barbara (Mrs Wright), Lynda Jean, James Wesley, III & Cynthia Reed. Educ: Centre Col, 1 year. Polit & Govt Pos: Chairwoman, Lincoln Co Rep Party, Ky, 48-; Lincoln Co Campaign chairwoman for Sen John Sherman Cooper, Sen Marlowe Cooke, Thurston Morton, Gov Louie B Nunn, Dr Tom Lee Carter, President Dwight D Eisenhower, Richard M Nixon & Barry Goldwater; co campaign chairwoman, Tom Emberton for Gov, 71. Mem: Hist Soc; PTA; Band Boosters Club; Women's Club; Vet Woman's Auxiliary. Relig: Methodist. Mailing Add: Rte 2 Knob Lick Farm Stanford KY 40484

WILLIAMS, JUDITH (D)
Mem, Dem Nat Comt, Ore
Mailing Add: 1075 Madras Hwy Prineville OR 97754

WILLIAMS, KENNETH OGDEN (D)
Miss State Rep
b Clarksdale, Miss, Jan 18, 24; s Peter Fairley Williams & Robbie Mae Casey W; m 1969 to Frances Lott; c Frances. Educ: Va Mil Inst, 42-43; NC State Univ, 44; Vanderbilt Univ, BA, 49; Phi Delta Theta. Polit & Govt Pos: Deleg, Dem Nat Conv, 56 & 60; Miss State Rep, 60- Bus & Prof Pos: Partner, P F Williams & Sons, 49- Mil Serv: Entered as Pvt, Army, 43, released as Sgt, 46, after serv in Hq Battery, 291st Field Artil Obsn Bn, ETO, 16th Corp, 9th Army, 44-46; Bronze Star; three Battle Stars. Mem: VFW; Am Legion; Delta Coun. Relig: Baptist. Legal Res: 1505 Holly St Clarksdale MS 38614 Mailing Add: PO Box 729 Clarksdale MS 38614

WILLIAMS, LEE (D)
b Denver, Colo, July 7, 25; s Floyd Lee Williams & Effie Lingo W; m 1945 to Vickie Strohmaier; c Floyd Lee, III. Educ: Univ Ark, JD, 53; Omicron Delta Kappa; Gamma Delta; Delta Theta Phi. Polit & Govt Pos: Legis asst to US Sen J W Fulbright, Ark, 55-60, admin asst, 60-75; counsel, Dem Policy Comt, US Senate, currently. Bus & Prof Pos: Attorney-at-law, Fayetteville, Ark, 53-55. Mil Serv: Entered as Pvt, Army, 44, released as S/Sgt, 47, after serv in ETO; ETO Ribbon with Bronze Battle Star; Europe-African-Mid Eastern Ribbon; Am Theater Ribbon; Victory Medal; Army of Occupation Medal. Mem: Ark Bar Asn; Pi Kappa Alpha; US Senate Asn of Admin Assts. Relig: Lutheran. Mailing Add: 7215 Burtonwood Dr Alexandria VA 22307

WILLIAMS, LEROY, JR (D)
Chmn, Ohio Co Dem Cent Comt, Ind
b Rising Sun, Ind, Sept 24, 21; s Clifford Leroy Williams & Leola Fry W; m 1947 to Clara Beatrice Browning; c Kenneth Lee, Connie Lou, Sandra, Karen Sue & Sharon Ann. Educ: Rising Sun Schools, 12 years. Polit & Govt Pos: Precinct committeeman, Rising Sun Dem Party, Ind, 12 years; councilman, Rising Sun, 10 years; co comnr, Ohio Co, 7 years; chmn, Ohio Co Dem Cent Comt, 66- Mem: Mason; Am Legion; Nat Farmers Orgn. Relig: Church of Chirst. Mailing Add: RR 2 Dillsboro IN 47018

WILLIAMS, LLOYD L
Sen, VI Legis
Mailing Add: PO Box 924 Charlotte Amalie St Thomas VI 00801

WILLIAMS, LUZ MARIA (D)
b Christiansted, St Croix, VI, Nov 8, 35; d Vincente Villafane & Cecilia Soto Adams V; m 1954 to Clyde Ignatious Williams; c Joan Maria (Mrs Gagliani), Barbara Cecelia, Clyde Ignatius, Jr & Bernadette Louise. Educ: Col of the VI, eve prog, 63- Polit & Govt Pos: Secy to Sen Alexander A Farrelly, VI Legis, 67-70, secy to Sen Athniel C Ottley, 71, secretarial serv to Chmn Standing Comt, 71 & Sen Earle B Ottley, Majority Floor Leader, 72, secy to Exec Secy, Patrick N Williams, 72-73, secy to Sen Albert Sheen & Sen Britain H Bryant, 72 & admin secy jour sect & Mr Hill, 75; secy territorial comt, Dem Party VI, 70- Mem: Cath Daughters Am; Cath Carismatic Prayer Group; Bus & Prof Women; Welfare Rights Orgn; Tenants United Orgn. Relig: Roman Catholic. Legal Res: Estate Nadir 33-12 St Thomas VI 00801 Mailing Add: PO Box 71 St Thomas VI 00801

WILLIAMS, MARSHALL BURNS (D)
SC State Sen
b Norway, SC, Jan 17, 12; s C H Williams & Maude Metts W; m to Margaret Shecutt; c Burns, Ann, Mary Ashley & Charles. Educ: Univ SC, BS, 33, LLB, 36. Polit & Govt Pos: SC State Rep, 47-52; SC State Sen, 53- Bus & Prof Pos: Lawyer & farmer. Mil Serv: Lt Comdr, Navy Air Corps, 42-46. Mem: SC Young Dem Club. Mailing Add: Box 957 Orangeburg SC 29115

WILLIAMS, MELBA RUTH (D)
Finance Chmn, Tenth Dist Dem Orgn, Ga
b Cullman, Ala; d William Claiborne Jones & Rebecca McGill J; m 1944 to Harry Bixler Williams, Jr; c Harry Bixler, III & Randolph Claiborne. Educ: Ala Col, BS, 42; Univ NC, grad study in pub admin, 46-47; Mortar Bd; Kappa Delta Pi; Sigma Alpha Sigma; pres, Publ Bd; Pi Tau Chi; Alpha Lambda Delta; Lambda Sigma Pi; LeCercle Francais. Polit & Govt Pos: Mem, Montgomery Co Personnel Bd, Md, 58-59; precinct vchmn, Montgomery Co Dem Party, 58-59; chmn, DeKalb Dem Club, 61-62; vchmn & secy, DeKalb Co Dem Exec Comt, 62-68; mem, Ga Dem Exec Comt, 62-70; deleg & mem credentials comt, Dem Nat Conv, 64, deleg, 68; mem, Ga Comn on Status of Women, 64-71; vchmn & mem, Ga State Elec Bd, 64-; vchmn, Clarke Co Dem Exec Comt, Ga, 70-; finance chmn, Tenth Dist Dem Orgn, 71-; alt deleg, Dem Nat Mid-Term Conf, 74. Bus & Prof Pos: Personnel officer & research assoc, Tenn Valley Authority, 44-46; teacher, DeKalb Co, Ga, 49-50; asst dir pub rels, Presbyterian Church, 50-52; research, Atlanta Area Metrop Planning Comn, 61-62 & Bell & Stanton, Pub Rels, 65-66; consult to Secy of State, Ga, 67-68; conf coordr, Inst of Govt & Continuing Educ Ctr, Univ Ga, 68-69; personnel consult, Ga Munic Asn, 70- Publ: Handbook for Georgia Election Officials & Handbook for Georgia Municipal Election Officials, Secy of State & Inst of Govt, Univ Ga, 68; A guide to the development & establishment of an effective personnel management system, Ga Munic Asn, 71; plus others. Mem: Int Personnel Mgt Asn; NGa PTA. Relig: Methodist. Mailing Add: 620 Forest Rd Athens GA 30601

WILLIAMS, NAT MCDONALD, JR (D)
b Thomasville, Ga, Apr 14, 27; s Nat McDonald Williams & Vivian Bowers W; m 1950 to Peggy Lucas; c Ann, Mac, Joan & Jim. Educ: Marion Inst, 43-45; US Naval Acad, 45-47; Univ NC, BS in Chem, 49; Phi Beta Kappa; Kappa Alpha Order. Polit & Govt Pos: Chmn, Thomas Co Dem Exec Comt, Ga, formerly; mem, Thomasville Sch Bd, 65-, chmn, 69- Bus & Prof Pos: Pres, Scat Oil Co, 58 & Interstate Enterprises, 59- Mil Serv: Entered as Midn 4/C, Navy, 45, released as Midn 3/C, 47, after serv in US. Relig: Methodist. Legal Res: Pine Tree Blvd SW Thomasville GA 31792 Mailing Add: PO Drawer 649 Thomasville GA 31792

WILLIAMS, NEIL ALVA (R)
Chmn, Osage Co Rep Party, Kans
b Lyndon, Kans, July 14, 32; s Clifford H Williams & Grace M Lindsay W; m 1950 to LoRee Nadine White; c Gary N, Bruce A, Kent B & Kimberley R. Educ: Lyndon Pub Schs, 12 years. Polit & Govt Pos: Chmn, Osage Co Rep Party, Kans, 68-; precinct committeeman, NValley Brook Twp, Kans, 70- Bus & Prof Pos: Owner & Mgr, Williams, Motor Co, Lyndon, Kans, 50- Mem: CofC; Rural & Lyndon Housing Proj; Nat & Kans State Car Dealers Asn; Kans Peace Officers Asn. Relig: Methodist. Legal Res: 304 W Eighth Lyndon KS 66451 Mailing Add: PO Box 252 Lyndon KS 66451

WILLIAMS, PATRICK NEHEMIAH (D)
Chmn, VI Dem Party
b Christiansted, St Croix, VI, Sept 28, 28; s Norman Williams & Ingerborg Cassimeer W; m 1951 to Inex Maria Byron; c Glenice Ingerborg, Sharon Maria, Lindel Alphonso, Wayne, Patrice-Ann, Patrick Maurice & Raymond Jerome. Educ: High sch, grad, 59. Polit & Govt Pos: VI State Sen, 63-65; consult, VI Legis, 65-, exec secy, Senate, 71-; chmn, VI Dem Party, 66-; mem, Traffic & Safety Comn, 66-; chmn, Voc & Tech Educ, 67-; vchmn, Comn Aging, 67-; vchmn, Comprehensive Health Planning, 67-; deleg, Dem Nat Conv, 68; chmn bd dirs, VI Pub TV, 69-; treas, Asn of State Dem Chmn, 69-; mem, Dem Nat Comt, currently. Bus & Prof Pos: Mgr, Alexander Hamilton Supply & Hardware, 59-60; mgr, Abramson's Enterprises, 60; asst store mgr, Merwin Hardware Inc, 60-62. Mil Serv: Entered as Pvt, Marine Corp, 51, released as Cpl, 53, after serv in 2nd Med Bn; 2nd Marine Div. Mem: Boy Scouts (exec comt); Navy League US (first vpres, St Croix Chap); Am Voc Asn. Relig: Catholic. Legal Res: Estate Grove Pl St Croix VI 00850 Mailing Add: PO Box 22 Kingshill St Croix VI 00850

WILLIAMS, PAUL L (D)
Ark State Rep
b Rolla, Ark, Oct 13, 33; s Clyde Williams & Lois Paul W; m 1954 to Nova Harris; c Paul Jeffery, Terry & Penny. Polit & Govt Pos: Ark State Rep, 73- Mailing Add: Rte 4 Box 114 Alexander AR 72002

WILLIAMS, R J (DICK) (R)
Kans State Sen
Mailing Add: 724 W Second Pratt KS 67124

WILLIAMS, RALPH DALE (D)
WVa State Sen
b Trout, WVa, Feb 16, 28; s John Dorsey Williams & Susan Viers W; m 1956 to Evelyn Molly; c Alan Dale, Mark Kevin, Myra Dawn & Barry Lee. Educ: Marshall Univ, BS, 50. Polit & Govt Pos: WVa State Sen, 71-; deleg, Dem Nat Conv, 72. Bus & Prof Pos: Pub acct, 50- Mil Serv: Entered as Pvt, Army, 50, released as Cpl, 52, after serv in Army Finance Corp, ETO, 50-52; German Occup Medal. Mem: Am Legion; Eastern Star; Mason; Lions; VFW. Honors & Awards: Past dist gov, Lions Int, 62. Relig: Baptist. Mailing Add: 209 Third St Lilly Park Rainelle WV 25962

WILLIAMS, RICHARD WAYNE (R)
Nat Committeeman, Okla Young Rep Fedn
b Los Angeles, Calif, Aug 21, 45; s Orville Williams & Mary Ellinghouse W; m 1970 to Kathleen Louise Jones. Educ: Phoenix Col, AA; Ariz State Univ, BA, Pi Sigma Epsilon; Tau Omega. Polit & Govt Pos: First vchmn, Muskogee Co Young Rep, Okla, 72-73, dir, 73-; Nat Committeeman, Okla Young Rep Fedn, 73-; vchmn, Muskogee Co Rep Party, 73- Bus & Prof Pos: Educator, Phoenix Union High Sch Dist, Ariz, 68-69; col rep, Holt, Rinehart & Winston, 69-70; community consult, Southwestern Bell Tel Co, 70-73. Mem: Muskogee Jaycees; Muskogee Arts & Humanities Soc (humanities dir, 73-). Honors & Awards: Div Speak Up, Okla Jaycees, 71; Officer of the Year, Muskogee Jaycees, 71-72, Key Man, 71-72, Pres Serv Award, 72; Salesmans Hall of Fame, Southwestern Bell Tel, 72. Relig: Methodist. Mailing Add: 2906 Haddock Muskogee OK 74401

WILLIAMS, ROBERT KELSEY (D)
Chmn, Wabash Co Dem Cent Comt, Ill
b West Salem, Ill, Jan 19, 19; s Forrest Lake Williams & Rozella Kelsey W; m 1953 to Virginia Josephine Nagy; c Verlin Eugene & Jeannine Rochelle. Educ: Bone Gap High Sch, Ill, grad. Polit & Govt Pos: Dem committeeman, Precinct Six, Mt Carmel, Ill, 66-; chmn, Wabash Co Dem Cent Comt, 68-; app by Gov Dan Walker to bd, Mt Carmel Port Dist, chmn bd, currently. Bus & Prof Pos: Life Ins Bus, Mt Carmel, Ill, 69- Mil Serv: Entered as Pvt, Army Air Force, 43, released as Cpl, 46, after serv in Second Air Force, Am Theatre, 32 months. Mem: Am Legion (Past Comdr, Post 423, Mt Carmel); VFW; Co Chmn Orgn of 54th Dist, Ill (pres); Civitan Int (Lt Gov, Midwest Dist & pres, Mt Carmel Club). Relig: Protestant. Mailing Add: Box 135 905 Pear St Mt Carmel IL 62863

WILLIAMS, RONEL NEIL (R)
Chmn, Allegany Co Rep Cent Comt, Md
b Wood, Pa, Aug 3, 26; s Matthew Williams & Dorothy Knoll W; m 1947 to May Middleton; c Earl, Ronel & Laurie. Educ: Logan Col Chiropractic, St Louis, Mo, DC; Lincoln Chiropractic Col, Indianapolis, grad studies; Nat Col Chiropractic, Lombard, Ill, grad studies. Polit & Govt Pos: Secy-treas, Allegany Co Rep Cent Comt, Md, formerly, chmn, currently; mem, Allegany Co Bd Educ, currently. Mil Serv: Entered as A/S, Navy, 44, released as Seaman 1/C, 46, after serv in Pac, 45-46. Mem: Am Chiropractic Asn (mem coun roentgenology); Md Chiropractic Asn (pres, 74-75); Shrine; Am Legion. Legal Res: 205 McKinley St Westernport MD 21562 Mailing Add: 136 Main St Westernport MD 21562

WILLIAMS, ROY NOLAN, JR (D)
Ala State Rep
b Dale Co, Ala, Aug 15, 41; s Roy Nolan Williams & Annie Faust W; single. Educ: Troy State Univ, BS, 59; Livingston Univ, MEd, 70. Polit & Govt Pos: Ala State Rep, 75- Bus & Prof Pos: Teacher, Rutherford High Sch, Panama City, Fla, 64-65, Surry Acad, Surry, Va, 65-66 & Dale Co High Sch, Midland City, Ala, 66-72; prin, Newton Sch, 72- Mem: Ala & Nat Educ Asns; Ruritan Club; Ala Cattlemen Asn. Relig: Baptist. Mailing Add: Rte 2 Newton AL 36352

WILLIAMS, SMALLWOOD EDMOND (D)
b Lynchburg, Va, Oct 17, 07; s Mary Broadus; m 1928 to Verna Lucille Rapley; c Smallwood, Jr (deceased), Pearl, Wallace & Yvonne. Educ: Terrell Law Sch; Howard Univ Sch Relig; Am Bible Col, BD, 48. Hon Degrees: DD, 49 & 50. Polit & Govt Pos: Mem, Dem Cent Comt, DC, 54-64, vchmn, formerly; mem, President's Comt on Relig Resources in Ment Retardation; deleg, Dem Nat Conv, 64 & 72. Bus & Prof Pos: Presiding Bishop, Bible Way Church of Our Lord Jesus Christ World Wide, 57; chmn, Apostolic Interorganizational Fel, 63-; co-chmn, Comt on Race Rel Interrelig; chmn, Golden Rule Apts, Inc, 66. Publ: Significant Sermons, Bible Way Church Publ Bd, 70. Mem: NAACP; Southern Christian Leadership Conf; Washington Urban League; Washington Home Rule Comt. Honors & Awards: Won trip around world as most popular radio minister, Afro-Am Newspaper Pool, 43; Washington's Most Prominent Radio Minister, 44; Selected for Afro-Am Newspaper Roll of Honor, Washington, DC, 47. Relig: Pentecostal. Mailing Add: 4720 16th St NW Washington DC 20011

WILLIAMS, VALTEN GAGE (R)
Chmn, Dare Co Rep Exec Comt, NC
b Avon, NC, Dec 25, 00; s Thomas James Williams & Christian Barnes Gray W; m 1925 to Florine Tillett; c Valten Reids & Aleah Janet (Mrs Nixon). Educ: Wanchese High Sch, grad, 18. Polit & Govt Pos: Justice of the Peace, Nags Head Twp, NC, 32-44; US Comnr, Eastern Dist NC, 34-46; mem draft bd; chmn, Dare Co Rep Exec Comt, 68- Mem: Ruritan Club; WOW. Honors & Awards: Selective Serv Syst Award, Pres Harry Truman, 52; NC Rep Party Award, 66. Relig: Methodist. Mailing Add: PO Box 243 Wanchese NC 27981

WILLIAMS, W O (D)
Chmn, Sedgwick Co Dem Cent Comt, Kans
b Pueblo, Colo, Sept 15, 21; s James C Williams & Julia Peterson W; m 1949 to C Jean Shryock; c Jeannette (Mrs Randall Luckner), Kathleen, James F, Robert M, Elizabeth A & Thomas L. Educ: Wichita State Univ, BA, 49; Northwestern Univ, Evanston, MA, 52; Int Rels Club; UNESCO; Independent Students Asn. Polit & Govt Pos: Co clerk, Sedgwick Co, Kans, 59-67; supvr, Property Valuation Dept, Topeka, 67-69, asst dir, 69-72; chmn, Sedgwick Co Dem Cent Comt, 73- Bus & Prof Pos: Pvt bus real estate broker, Wichita, Kans, 72-75; data processing consult, Sedgwick Co, 75- Mil Serv: Entered as Pvt, Army, 41, released as Sgt, after serv in 45th Inf Div, Africa, Sicily, Italy, ETO, 43-45. Mem: Am Soc Appraisers (pres, Wichita chap); Int Asn Assessing Officers; Am Right of Way Asn; Wichita Bd Realtors; Mason. Honors & Awards: Gov Plaque for Meritorious Serv to State of Kans. Relig: Episcopal. Legal Res: 9235 S Meridian Peck KS 67120 Mailing Add: Rte 1 Box 52 Peck KS 67120

WILLIAMS, W WALTER (R)
b Monroe Co, Iowa, Dec 30, 94; s Alfred Williams & Ada Johnson W; m 1958 to Ruth Garrison; c Walter B, Marjorie (Mrs Myers) & Judy (Mrs Zimmerman). Educ: Univ Wash, BS, 16; Phi Beta Kappa; Tau Beta Pi; Phi Lambda Upsilon; Phi Delta Kappa; Sigma Chi. Hon Degrees: Doctorate, Parsons Col, 56 & Pac Univ, 66. Polit & Govt Pos: Chmn, Wash State Defense Coun, 41-45; chmn, Wash State Rep Party, 51; mem bd, Citizens for Eisenhower-Nixon, 52; Under Secy of Com, 53-58; finance chmn, Wash State Rep Comt, 59-60; chmn, Govt Adv Comt, Dept of Com & Econ Develop, 64-67; vchmn, Nat Rep Finance Comt, 66-68; alt deleg, Rep Nat Conv, 68. Bus & Prof Pos: Pres & chmn bd, Continental Inc, Seattle, Wash, 27-; chmn, Comt for Econ Develop, 48-50. Mil Serv: Pfc, Army, 17, released in 18, after serv in Aviation Sect, Signal Corps, Chem Warfare Serv & Air Ground Serv, Univ Calif Squadron, 55. Mem: Nat Coun of YMCA; Rainier Club; Harbor Club; Washington Athletic Club. Honors & Awards: Seattle First Citizen Award & others. Relig: Congregational. Legal Res: 2035 Parkside Dr E Seattle WA 98112 Mailing Add: Continental Inc Pac Bldg Eighth Floor Seattle WA 98104

WILLIAMS, WALTER J (D)
b Christoval, Tex, Nov 27, 00; s Thomas Z Williams & Clara Tuttle W; m 1925 to Lucy Sue Abney; c Lucille (Mrs Brigham). Educ: Baylor Univ, BA & MA; Univ Mich, PhD; Sigma Xi. Polit & Govt Pos: Chmn, McLennan Co Dem Party, Tex, formerly. Bus & Prof Pos: Prof math & chmn dept, Baylor Univ, 37-71. Mem: Am Asn for Advan Sci; Am Math Soc; Am Astronomical Soc. Relig: Baptist. Mailing Add: 902 Speight Ave Waco TX 76706

WILLIAMS, WILLIAM VAN (R)
Chmn, Butler Co Rep Party, Ala
b Greenville, Ala, Dec 8, 25; s John Robbins Williams & Myra L Ware W; m to Nell Langford; c Sara Catherine & James Brittain. Educ: Auburn Univ; Birmingham Southern Col. Polit & Govt Pos: Chmn, Butler Co Rep Party, Ala, currently. Mil Serv: Entered as Pvt, Marines, 44, released as Lt, 45, after serv in Okinawa & Korea. Mem: Lions; Am Legion; Farm Bur; Police Res. Relig: Baptist. Mailing Add: PO Box 368 Greenville AL 36037

WILLIAMSON, BRUCE DAYTON (DFL)
Minn State Rep
b Minneapolis, Minn, Oct 19, 47; s Dayton D Williamson & Margaret A Anderson W; single. Educ: Macalester Col, 64-67; Univ Minn, Minneapolis, 67-75; Canadian-Am Conf; Young Dem-Farmer-Labor; Koininia. Polit & Govt Pos: Field rep, Minn State Dem-Farmer-Labor Party, 68; legis asst, Minn House Rep, 69; cand, Miss State Rep, 72 & 74; Minn State Rep, 75-; chmn platform & resolutions comt, 38th Dist Dem-Farmer-Labor Party, 74. Mil Serv: SP-4, Army Res, 69- Mem: Jaycees; Joint Relig Legis Coalition; Izaak Walton League; Minnesota Valley Nature Ctr. Legal Res: 121 W 90th St Bloomington MN 55420 Mailing Add: 236 State Off Bldg St Paul MN 55155

WILLIAMSON, BRUCE ROYCE (D)
Miss State Rep
b Louisville, Miss, Oct 22, 44; s Abb Burt Williamson & Vera Reed W; m 1965 to Julia Faye; c Tammie Keena, Pamela Ann & Elizabeth Ella. Educ: E Cent Jr Col; Miss State Univ; Dairy Club. Polit & Govt Pos: Miss State Rep, Winston Co, 72- Bus & Prof Pos: Owner & mgr, Williamson Dairy, 66- & Best Way Dairy, 72- Mem: Mason; Shrine; Jaycees; Miss Cattlemen's Asn; Farm Bur. Honors & Awards: Outstanding Young Farmer, Winston Co Jaycees, 68-69 & 72-73; Dist Winner, Farm Bur Young Farmer, 75-76. Relig: Baptist. Mailing Add: Rte 3 Box 310 Louisville MS 39339

WILLIAMSON, DON (D)
La State Sen
Mailing Add: 938 N Pine St Vivian LA 71082

WILLIAMSON, GEORGE (R)
Ga State Rep
Mailing Add: 3358 Rennes Dr Atlanta GA 30319

WILLIAMSON, GEORGE ARTHUR (R)
Fla State Rep
b Chattanooga, Tenn, July 11, 38; s Malcolm R Williamson & Mary Morris; m 1971 to Andrea Tyler. Educ: Univ NC, LLB, 65. Polit & Govt Pos: Fla State Rep, 70- Mailing Add: 1111 SE Third Ave Ft Lauderdale FL 33316

WILLIAMSON, HOWARD HOUSTON (R)
Chmn, Curry Co Rep Party, NMex
b Basset, Nebr, Oct 16, 11; s Luther Lee Williamson & Mary Phelps W; m 1939 to Mildred McCormick. Educ: High sch, Ainsworth, Nebr, grad, 30. Polit & Govt Pos: Mem, NMex Rep State Cent Comt, 68-, mem state rules comt, 70-; chmn, Curry Co Rep Party, 75- Bus & Prof Pos: Owner, Village Rec Shop, Clovis, NMex, 48- Mem: Kiwanis. Mailing Add: 410 E Seventh St Clovis NM 88101

WILLIAMSON, MARY EHRLICH (D)
Mem, Ipswich Dem Town Comt, Mass
b Philadelphia, Pa, Apr 8, 36; d Herman Tramer Ehrlich & Blanche Margolis E; c Jeanne, Julie, Jamie & Bernard Adell (foster son). Educ: Univ Pa, BA, 58. Polit & Govt Pos: Founding mem, Citizens for Participation Polit, 68-, vchmn-at-lg, 71-72; admin asst, US Rep Michael J Harrington, Mass, 69-71; Mass campaign dir, Eugene McCarthy Presidential Campaign, 71-72; dir field opers Mass Primary, McGovern Presidential Campaign, 72; deleg-at-lg & mem comt on rules, Dem Nat Conv, 72. Bus & Prof Pos: Newspaper advert mgr; independent polit & pub rels consult, 68- Mem: Mass Gov Comn on Status of Women; Mensa. Relig: Unitarian. Mailing Add: 2 East St Ipswich MA 01938

WILLIAMSON, RICHARD SALISBURY (R)
b Evanston, Ill, May 9, 49; s Donald George Williamson & Marion Salisbury W; m 1973 to Jane Thatcher. Educ: Princeton Univ, AB, 71; Univ Va Sch Law, JD, 74. Polit & Govt Pos: Admin asst to US Rep Philip M Crane, Ill, 74- Mem: Ill & Chicago Bar Asns. Honors & Awards: Detwiller Prize by Princeton Univ. Mailing Add: 542 Washington Ave Glencoe IL 60022

WILLIAMSON, STANLEY H (R)
NH State Rep
b East Providence, RI, June 29, 19; married; c three. Educ: Boston Univ, AB, 40, AM, 41. Polit & Govt Pos: Trustee, Horizon's Edge Sch, NH; pres bd trustees, Hampshire Country Sch, formerly; pres, Dartmouth-Lake Sunapee Region, formerly; chmn, Goshen-Lempster Coop Sch Bd, Sch Union 43; chmn, Goshen Planning Bd & Goshen Budget Comt; NH State Rep, 61-; two-time deleg, State Const Conv; deleg, Rep State Conv, mem, Platform Comt, 64; alt deleg, Rep Nat Conv, 64; mem, NH Teacher Negotiation Study Comt; mem, Interim Land Use Study Comt, 2 sessions; chmn, co legis deleg, currently. Bus & Prof Pos: Life underwriter; instr govt, Marrimack Valley Br, Univ NH, currently. Mem: Twin State Valley Underwriters Asn (former pres); NH Asn of Life Underwriters (former dir). Honors & Awards: Distinguished Sch Bd Mem Award, NH Asn Sch Bds, 71; Outstanding Citizen Award, Sullivan Co Conserv Dist, 73. Relig: Quaker. Mailing Add: Box 1 Wendell NH 03783

WILLIAMSON, WALTER EDWARD (D)
b Magnolia, Ark, Nov 10, 07; s Walter Otis Williamson & Willie Lee Merritt W; m 1941 to Sue Lee Harris; c Walter Edward, Jr, Susanne (Mrs Steven Barr), Sara Beth (Mrs Stephen B Couch) & James Thomas. Educ: Henderson State Col, AB, 30; Garland Lit Soc. Polit & Govt Pos: Circuit & chancery clerk, Columbia Co, Ark, 35-41; mayor, Magnolia, 55-57; chief clerk on Interstate & Foreign Commerce Comt, US House of Rep, 57- Bus & Prof Pos: Mgr, CofC, Magnolia, Ark, 46-50; pres & owner, Ford Chair Factory, 50-58. Mil Serv: Entered as Pvt, Army, 42, released as Capt, 46, after serv in Inf Sch, Ft Benning, Ga & IRTC, Camp Fannin, Tex. Mem: Mason; Lions Int; Am Legion. Relig: Methodist. Legal Res: Magnolia AR Mailing Add: 2125 Rayburn Bldg Washington DC 20515

WILLIAMSON, WALTER ROBERT (D)
b Douglaston, NY, Oct 9, 21; s Elmer Stephen Williamson & Josephine Green W; m 1953 to Cordula Margaret Schwebach; c Cara Ann & Lisa Mary. Educ: St John's Univ (NY), 40-42; City Col New York, 42-43; NY Univ, 44-45. Polit & Govt Pos: Nat Defense Exec Res, Dept of Transportation, 67-; dir research & educ, Brotherhood of Rwy & Airline Clerks, 69-; mem, Labor Research Adv Comt, Dept of Labor, 71-; chmn, COPE, 12th Cong Dist, Ill, 74-; deleg, Dem Nat Mid-Term Conf, 74. Bus & Prof Pos: Mem lab adv comt, Univ Ill, 71- Mem: Brotherhood of Rwy & Airline Clerks; Am Fedn Teachers; Adult Educ Asn. Relig: Catholic. Mailing Add: 666C Chelmsford Lane Elk Grove Village IL 60007

WILLIS, DOYLE (D)
Tex State Rep
b Kaufman Co, Tex, Aug 18, 08; s Alvin Willis & Eliza Phillips W; m 1942 to Evelyn McDavid; c Doyle Willis, Jr, Dan, Dina & Dale. Educ: Univ Tex, Austin, BA & BS, 34; Georgetown Univ Law Sch, LLB, 38; Theta Xi; Gamma Eta Gamma. Polit & Govt Pos: Tex State Rep, Tarrant Co, 47-52; Tex State Sen, 52-62; city councilman, Ft Worth, Tex, 63-64. Bus & Prof Pos: Lawyer-rancher, Ft Worth, Tex, currently. Mil Serv: Enlisted in Mil Intel, 41, released as Maj, 46, after serv in Asiatic-Pac Theatre, 44-45; Bronze Star & four Battle Stars. Mem: VFW (state comdr, 59-60); Am Legion; DAV-Irish War Vets; ROA (pres, Tarrant Co chap); Sons of Repub Tex. Relig: Methodist. Mailing Add: 3316 Browning Ct Ft Worth TX 76111

WILLIS, ED (D)
Alaska State Sen
Mailing Add: Eagle River AK 99577

WILLIS, KATHERINE MARY (R)
Secy, Fourth Dist Rep Party, Mich
b Chicago, Ill, Nov 26, 16; m 1936 to Frank Willis, Jr; c Penny (Mrs Padden), Bruce & Tara Kathleen. Educ: Ind Univ, 1 year. Polit & Govt Pos: Mem, Fourth Dist Rep Party, 59-, secy, currently; vchmn, Van Buren Co Rep Comt, Mich, 62-68, chmn, 68-74; pres, Rep Women, 65-, state chmn, Rep Women's Conf, Chicago, Ill, 67; deleg, Rep Nat Conv, 72; mem, Mich Rep State Cent Comt, 73-, vchmn, Ways & Means Comt, 73-; mem, Porter Twp Land Use Planning Comn, 73-; secy, Van Buren Co Jury Bd, 73- Bus & Prof Pos: Homemaker; secy, Cedar Lake Recreation Asn, Inc. Mem: Bus & Prof Women's Asn; Eastern Star; PTA (vchmn); Zoning Bd (secy); Paw Paw Hosp Bd. Mailing Add: Rte 1 Box 434 Shaw Rd Lawton MI 49065

WILLIS, RICHARD ROBINSON (R)
b Ashville, NC, May 26, 29; s Richard Rochester Willis & Mary Hagler W; m 1949 to Gaynelle June Heath; c David B, Dale H, Dawn M & Douglas C. Educ: Denison Univ, 2 years; Beta Theta Pi. Polit & Govt Pos: Rep presidential elector, 56; mem, Rep Bd of Elec, 57-63; officer, Young Rep Club, 49-64; mem finance comt, Ohio Young Rep Club, formerly & Fayette Co Rep Exec Comt, 52-74; committeeman, Fayette Co Rep Cent Comt, 52-74, vchmn & chmn, secy-treas, Fayette Co Rep Exec & Cent Comts, 69-70. Bus & Prof Pos: Pres, Willis Ins Inc, Washington Court House, Ohio, 49-73. Mem: Lions; Elks; Eagles; Shrine; Mason. Relig: Baptist. Legal Res: 450 Rawlings Washington Court House OH 43160 Mailing Add: Box E Washington Court House OH 43160

WILLIS, TODD C (D)
WVa State Sen
Mailing Add: State Capitol Charleston WV 25305

WILLIS, WILLIAM PASCAL (D)
Okla State Rep
b Anadarko, Okla, Oct 17, 10; s Robert Garnett Willis & Lulu Wyatt W; m 1936 to Zelma Bynum; c Diane, Joyce, Billie Jean, Herbert, Zelma Marie, William, Jr & Doak. Educ: ECent State Col, BA, 36; Tulsa Univ, MA, 48; pres, Int Rels Club, ECent State Col, 35-36. Polit & Govt Pos: Mayor, Locust Grove, Okla, 38-44; Okla State Rep, Fourth Dist, 58-, Speaker, Okla House Rep, 73- Mil Serv: Entered as Pvt, Army, 44, released as S/Sgt, 44, after serv in 627th Field Artil. Mem: Mason; Shrine; Am Legion; CofC; Tahlequah Kiwanis. Relig: Baptist. Mailing Add: 1 Valley Tahlequah OK 74464

WILLISON, SUE KINDRED (R)
Chmn, Midland Co Rep Comt, Mich
b Franklin, Ohio, May 26, 26; d Stetson Kindred & Lena K; m 1945 to Charles Hallock Willison; c Charles Richard, Dorothy Nance, David Paul & Tad Kindred. Educ: Christ Hosp Sch Nursing, 44-45. Polit & Govt Pos: Hq chmn, Midland Co Rep Comt, Mich, 66-69, secy, 66-70, vchmn, 70-73, chmn, 73-; mem, Mich Rep State Cent Comt, Tenth Cong Dist, Mich, 69-; deleg, Rep Nat Conv, 72; Presidential Elector, 72; co campaign chmn, Robert Griffin for Sen, 72; gov appointee, Mich Consumer's Coun, 73- Mem: PEO; Midland, Mich & Am Med Asns Auxiliary. Mailing Add: 1115 W Sugnet Rd Midland MI 48640

WILLITS, EARL M (D)
Iowa State Sen
Mailing Add: 2016 Chautauqua Pkwy Des Moines IA 50314

WILLITS, JOHN BIRDCELL (D)
Mem Staff, Nat Mediation Bd
b Huron, SDak, Aug 30, 21; s John Birdcell Willits & Sarah Dunn W; m 1946 to Helen Louise Sperla; c John, Elaine, Laura, Charles, Thomas, Julie, Vickie & Jane. Educ: Worsham Col, 45; Delta Pi Epsilon. Polit & Govt Pos: Deleg, Dem Nat Conv, 64; Mont State Rep, 65 & 67; chmn, Cascade Co Dem Coordr Comt, formerly; mem staff, Nat Mediation Bd, 68- Bus & Prof Pos: Comnr, Boy Scouts, 62; state chmn, Trainmen's Polit Educ League, 66. Mil Serv: Entered as Seaman, Coast Guard, 42, released as Seaman 1/C, 43, after serv in Life Saving Serv. Mem: Cascade Co Wildlife Asn; Brotherhood of RR Trainmen; Am Legion; Eagles. Relig: Catholic. Legal Res: 1620 Fifth Ave N Great Falls MT 59401 Mailing Add: 2417 Central Ave Alexandria VA 22302

WILLKOM, TERRY A (D)
Wis State Sen
Mailing Add: RR 1 Box 20A Chippewa Falls WI 54729

WILLMARTH, DAVID GERARD (D)
b Toledo, Ohio, June 19, 35; s Gerard Ellsworth Willmarth & Helen Evelyn Munger W; m 1956 to Mary Lou Mallendick; c Teri Lyn, Mark Stephen, Lori Ann, Michael David & Lisa Michele. Polit & Govt Pos: Pres, Wood Co Dem Club, Ohio, 62-66, vchmn, 73-; pres, Wood Co Young Dem, 63; secy exec comt, Wood Co Dem Cent Comt, 68-, chmn, Cent Comt, 68-70, vchmn, 70-73; personnel dir, Dist Two, Hwy Div, Ohio Dept of Transportation, 71- Bus & Prof Pos: Asst advert dir, Sentinel-Tribune, Bowling Green, Ohio, 57-64; sales mgr, WAWR-FM Radio, 64-65; prod supvr, Photo-Jour Press, 65-68, West Toledo Herald, Toledo, 68- Mem: Northwestern Ohio Newspaper Asn; Wood, Sandusky, Ottawa, Seneca Co Community Action Coun (bd dirs, 71-); Soc for Preservation & Encouragement of Barbershop Quartet Singing in Am, Inc; Toastmaster's Club. Relig: Reorganized Latter-day Saint; Ordained Minister. Mailing Add: 525 N Prospect St Bowling Green OH 43402

WILLOUGHBY, WILLIAM HOWARD (R)
Chmn, Fauquier Co Rep Comt, Va
b Ventura, Calif, Nov 19, 08; s Charles Russell Willougby & Lulu Logue W; m 1934 to Rosemary Joan Whalen; c William Howard, Jr, Lawrence Charles, James Russell, Martha Ellen (Mrs Cole) & Christine Ann. Educ: Univ Calif, Los Angeles, BA, 34; Syracuse Univ, MBA, 54; Sigma Alpha Epsilon. Polit & Govt Pos: Chmn, Fauquier Co Rep Comt, Va, 70- Bus & Prof Pos: Mil observer, UN, Kashmir, 51-52; coordr, Civil Defense, Fauquier Co, Va, 68-69. Mil Serv: Entered as 1st Lt, Army Inf, 41, retired as Col, 67, after serv as unit comdr & staff officer, Div, Maj Command & Dept of Army Gen Staff; Silver Star; Bronze Star; Purple Heart; Combat Inf Badge; Presidential Unit Citation. Mem: Syracuse Army Comptrollers Asn; Fauquier Cancer Soc; Hampton Rds Power Squadron. Relig: Protestant. Mailing Add: Rte 600 Broad Run VA 22014

WILLS, ROBERT ROY (R)
b Minneapolis, Minn, Sept 15, 50; s Stanley M Wills & June Anderson W; single. Educ: Univ Minn, BA summa cum laude, 72; Stetson Univ Col Law, 73- Polit & Govt Pos: Campaign vol, Minn Rep Politics, 64-72; Richfield Rep Young Coordr, Minn, 71; mem, Hennepin Co Rep Exec Comt, Minn, 71-72; alt deleg, Rep Nat Conv, 72; youth dir, Frenzel for Cong Comt, 72. Relig: Lutheran. Mailing Add: 2500 NW Ninth Ave 206 Ft Lauderdale FL 33311

WILLS, TED C (D)
Mayor, Fresno, Calif
Married; two sons & six grandchildren. Polit & Govt Pos: Mem, Charter Rev Comt, 51; former chmn, Parks & Recreation Bd; mem, Fresno City Coun, 58-63, mayor pro tem, 63-69, mayor, 69-; mem adv bd, US Conf Mayors; vchmn community develop comt, League of Calif Cities, former pres, South San Joaquin Div; mem human resources develop steering comt, Nat League Cities; US deleg, Int Cong Local Authorities, Washington, DC, 60, Brussels, 63 & Belgrade, 65; vchmn, Manpower Area Planning Coun Fresno; mem, US Region IX Manpower Adv Comt; mem, League of Calif Cities/Co Supvr Asn Joint Human Resources Proj Adv Comt; vchmn mayors' comt on bicentennial, US Conf Mayors. Mem: Nat Asn Boys Clubs Am; Fresno City Schs (bus educ adv comt); Fresno State Col (indust rels adv comt); Kiwanis; Elks. Relig: Congregational. Mailing Add: Mayor's Off City Hall 2326 Fresno St Fresno CA 93721

WILMER, CHARLOTTE MAE (D)
b Huntington, WVa, Oct 2, 46; d H F Wilmer & Faye Cambell W; single. Educ: Marshall Univ, BA, 68; Pi Sigma Alpha. Polit & Govt Pos: Coordr vol activities, Hechler for Cong, Huntington, WVa, 66; cong intern, US Rep Ken Hechler, WVa, 66, staff asst, 67; coordr, State Senate Race, Robert Nelson, 67; instr practical politics, Encampment for Citizenship, 68; instr, Dem Youth Camp, 69; staff asst, US Rep Edwin Edwards, La, 69-71; campaign staff asst, Edwards for Gov La, 71; campaign staff coordr, Breaux for Cong, 72; admin asst, US Rep John Breaux, La, 72- Legal Res: Crowley LA 70526 Mailing Add: 125 C St SE Washington DC 20002

WILMER, HENRY BOND (R)
Mem, NC Rep Exec Comt
b Philadelphia, Pa, Apr 9, 20; s Harry Bond Wilmer & Helen Lewis Parker W; m 1943 to Mary Van Der Voort; c Henry Bond, Jr, Emily, Helen P & Molly. Educ: Princeton Univ, 39-42. Polit & Govt Pos: Co comnr, Mecklenburg Co, NC, 62-64; mem, Planning & Zoning Comn, 67-; chmn exec comt, Mecklenburg Co Rep Party, 68-72; mem, NC Rep Exec Comt, 70-; mem exec comt, Ninth Cong Dist, Rep Party, NC, 72-; Presidential Elector, NC, 72. Bus & Prof Pos: Agent, Prudential Ins Co Am, 54- Mil Serv: Entered as Aviation Cadet, Marines, 41, released as Capt, 45, after serv in Third Marine Airwing, Pac Theatre, 44-45; Res, Maj (Ret), Unit Commendation. Honors & Awards: Citizenship Award, Charlotte, NC; Citizenship Award, Prudential Ins Co; Cert of Appreciation, Charlotte-Mecklenburg Sch Bd. Relig: Episcopal. Mailing Add: 901 Harvard Pl Charlotte NC 28207

WILSON, A K (R)
b Corning, Ohio, Aug 20, 09; s Clifford Wilson & Eura Koher W; m 1933 to Verna Hammer; c Clifford Dale, Beverly Lama & Pamela. Educ: Moxahala High Sch, Ohio, 24 & 25; New Lexington High Sch, Ohio, 26-27. Polit & Govt Pos: Councilman, Somerset, Ohio, 46-54; comnr, Perry Co, 55-64 & 67-70; Ohio State Rep, 65-66; chmn, Perry Co Rep Party, 68-75; alt deleg, Rep Nat Conv, 72. Bus & Prof Pos: Laborer, Pa RR, Newark, 27-29; clerk, Kroger, New Lexington, Ohio, 29-33; miner, Buckingham Coal Co, Congo, 33-37; salesman, Monumental Life Ins, Zanesville, 37-39; grocery owner & operator, Somerset, 39-48; farm equip owner & operator, Somerset, 48- Mem: Lions; Mason; Eagles; Grange; Farm Bur. Relig: Protestant. Legal Res: North Dr Somerset OH 43783 Mailing Add: Box 6043 Somerset OH 43783

WILSON, ADDISON GRAVES (JOE) (R)
b Charleston, SC, July 31, 47; s Hugh deVeaux Wilson & Wray Graves W; single. Educ: Washington & Lee Univ, BA, 69; Univ SC Sch Law, JD, 72; Sigma Nu. Polit & Govt Pos: Organizer, Youth for Russell for Gov, 62; chmn, Charleston TAR, 64; secy, Washington & Lee Univ Young Rep, 66, vchmn, 67; intern aide, US Sen Strom Thurmond, 67; vchmn, Youth for Nixon, Washington & Lee Univ, 68; vchmn, Lexington Young Rep, 69; campaign coordr, Youth for Spence for Cong, 70; legal clerk & aide, State Sen & Congressman Floyd Spence, 70-72; third vchmn for Youth, SC Rep Party, 70-72; legal asst, US Attorney John K Grisso, 71; state orgn dir, SC Comt for Reelection of the President, 72; deleg, Rep Nat Conv, 72; campaign mgr, Spence for Cong, 74; app by Gov Edwards to State Develop Bd, 75. Bus & Prof Pos: Counr, Camp Carolina, Brevard, NC, 65-66; reporter, News & Courier, Charleston, 69; assoc, Stancel E Kirkland, 72-73; partner, Dent, Kirkland, Taylor & Wilson, Attorneys. Mil Serv: 1st Lt, Nat Guard. Publ: Ed in chief of law sch newspapers; ed, Gavel Raps; managing ed of col newspaper. Mem: Rotary; Jaycees; Res Officers' Asn; Hist Soc; Ment Health Asn. Honors & Awards: Outstanding camper, WVa, GOP Youth Camp, 65; Speak-Up Winner, West Columbia-Cayce Jaycees; Cayce-West Columbia Outstanding Young Man of Year, 74. Relig: Presbyterian; Sunday sch teacher, First Presby Church of Columbia. Legal Res: 2825 Wilton Rd West Columbia SC 29169 Mailing Add: PO Box 123 West Columbia SC 29169

WILSON, ANNE CHAPMAN (R)
Committeewoman, Dade Co Rep Exec Comt, Fla
b St Louis, Mo, Aug 24, 29; d Thomas Howard Chapman & Gean La Mont C; div; c Anne Rebecca (Mrs Thomas K McLaughlin, Jr), Francis Gavin, Jr & Dwight Collins. Educ: Univ Miami, 1 year. Polit & Govt Pos: First vpres, Dade Co Young Rep, 64-65; deleg, Young Rep Nat Conv, 65; state TAR chmn, Fla Fedn Young Rep, 65-67; committeewoman, Dade Co Rep Exec Comt, Fla, 66- & vchmn, 66-68, chmn, 68-71; deleg, Rep Nat Conv, 68, exec dir, Presidential Host Comt, 72; mgr, Fla State Hq, Comt to Reelect the President, 72; chmn, Dade Co Comt Status of Women, Fla, 73-74. Bus & Prof Pos: Circulation mgr, Investment Sales Monthly, Miami, 65-68; admin asst to dir, Miami Art Ctr, 68-72; sales mgr, Stadler Assocs, Inc, Coral Gables, Fla, 72- Publ: Book reviews, Presby J, 65-67. Honors & Awards: Excellence Award, Am Security Coun Bus Citizenship Competition, 67. Relig: Presbyterian. Mailing Add: 3710 Battersea Rd Miami FL 33133

WILSON, BENJAMIN H (R)
Pa State Rep
b Mt Carmel, Pa, Jan 25, 25; s Benjamin H Wilson & Esther B Marshall W; m 1950 to Jean Terry; c Sheryl & Denise. Educ: Pa State Univ, BA, 49. Polit & Govt Pos: Rep committeeman, Warminster, Pa, 54-58; mem, Bucks Co Rep Comt, 56-59; tax collector, Warminster Twp, 58-; Pa State Rep, 67- Bus & Prof Pos: Salesman, Minn Mining & Mfg Co, 49-53; manufacturer's rep, 53-64; real estate broker & developer. Mil Serv: Entered as Pvt, Army Air Force, 43, released as 2nd Lt, 46, after serv in SPac. Mem: Am Legion; VFW; F&AM; AAONMS; Caldwell Consistory. Relig: Presbyterian. Legal Res: 1215 W County Line Rd Warminster PA 18974 Mailing Add: Capitol Bldg Harrisburg PA 17120

WILSON, BETTY (D)
Majority Whip, NJ Gen Assembly
b Doylestown, Pa, Aug 21, 32; d Arthur High & Marion Michener H; m to James Wilson; c Thomas & Kyle. Educ: Jersey City State Col, BA, summa cum laude, 67; Kappa Delta Pi. Polit & Govt Pos: Twp committeeperson, Berkeley Heights, NJ, 72-74; NJ State Assemblyman, 74-, Majority Whip, NJ Gen Assembly, 74- Bus & Prof Pos: Social studies teacher, Gov Livingston High Sch, 69-; dir, Inst for Pub Transportation & NJ Opera Theatre, 74- Mem: NJ Educ Asn; League of Women Voters; Women's Polit Caucus; Nat Orgn for Women. Honors & Awards: Almunae of the Year, Jersey City State Col, 74. Legal Res: 4 Hampton Dr Berkeley Heights NJ 07922 Mailing Add: 1729 E Second St Scotch Plains NJ 07076

WILSON, BRUCE A (D)
Wash State Sen
Mailing Add: PO Box F Omak WA 98841

WILSON, CHARLES (D)
US Rep, Tex
b Trinity, Tex, June 1, 33; s Charles Edwin Wilson & Wilmuth Nesbitt W; m 1963 to Jerrell Fay Carter. Educ: Sam Houston State Univ, 51-52; US Naval Acad, BS, 56. Polit & Govt Pos: Tex State Rep, 60-66; Tex State Sen, 66-72; US Rep, Tex, 73- Bus & Prof Pos: Lumber

yard mgr. Mil Serv: Entered as Ens, Navy, 56, released as Lt, 60, after serv in Destroyer Force, Atlantic & Mediter, 56-59 & Joint Staff, 59-60. Legal Res: 1000 Crooked Creek Lufkin TX 75901 Mailing Add: 1504 Longworth House Off Bldg Washington DC 20515

WILSON, CHARLES H (D)
US Rep, Calif
b Magna, Utah, Feb 15, 17; s Charles H Wilson & Janet C Hunter W; m 1947 to Dorothy Elizabeth Gibbel; c Stephen Charles, Donald Herbert, Kenneth Alan & William John. Polit & Govt Pos: Comnr, Los Angeles Pub Housing Authority, 52-54; Calif State Assemblyman, 55-63; US Rep, 31st Dist, Calif, 63- Mil Serv: Entered as Pvt, Army, 42, released as S/Sgt, 45. Mem: Angeles Mesa Masonic Lodge, Los Angeles; Al Malaikah Shrine; Inglewood Shrine Club; Sowela Shrine Club; Inglewood Elks Lodge. Relig: United Church of Christ. Legal Res: 4141 W Rosecrans Ave Apt 105 Hawthorne CA 90250 Mailing Add: 2111 Jefferson Davis Hwy 1103-S Arlington VA 22202

WILSON, CHUCK (D)
Kans State Sen
Mailing Add: 614 W Eighth St LaCross KS 67548

WILSON, DAVID KIRKPATRICK (R)
Chmn, Rep Nat Finance Comt
b Nashville, Tenn, June 15, 19; s Charles P Wilson & Florence Moss W; m 1942 to Anne Potter; c Justin Potter, William Moss & Blair Jackson. Educ: Vanderbilt Univ, BA, 41; Harvard Bus Sch, 43; Phi Delta Theta. Polit & Govt Pos: Co-chmn, Rep Nat Finance Comt, 71-72, chmn, 73-; mem exec comt, Rep Nat Comt, 75- Bus & Prof Pos: Pres, Cheroke Ins Co, 46-68, chmn bd, 68-; pres, Cherokee Equity Corp, 68- Mil Serv: Entered as Ens, Navy, 43, released as Lt, after serv in SPac. Relig: Presbyterian. Legal Res: 4343 Glen Eden Dr Nashville TN 37205 Mailing Add: 95 White Bridge Rd Nashville TN 37205

WILSON, EARL (R)
Ind State Sen
b Huron, Ind, Apr 18, 06; s James E Wilson & Annie Hill W; m 1931 to Elsie Bex; c Linda Sue (Mrs Brian Corman) & Phillip Earl. Educ: Ind Univ, BA & MS. Polit & Govt Pos: US Rep, Ind, 41-58 & 60-64; Ind State Sen, 68- Mem: Mason; Shrine. Relig: Baptist. Mailing Add: 2003 0 St Bedford IN 47421

WILSON, EARL D (R)
Chmn, Allen Co Rep Party, Ky
b Holland, Ky, Oct 18, 14; s Enoch George Wilson & Fannie Holland W; m 1932 to Willie Ruth Lones; c Earl Dennis & Merle Jean (Mrs Conder). Educ: Schs, Holland, Ky, 12 years. Polit & Govt Pos: Chmn, Allen Co Rep Party, Ky, 68- Bus & Prof Pos: Farmer & livestock dealer. Mem: F&AM (mem, Loving Lodge 323); Eastern Star (mem, Ft Run Chap 18); Holland Lions Club & Farm Bur. Relig: Baptist. Mailing Add: Rte 7 Scottsville KY 42164

WILSON, EARLENE S (R)
Nat Committeewoman, Okla Young Rep Fedn
b Pawnee, Okla, Dec 11, 39; d Cecil Hilburn Sterne & Mary Anna Gambill S; m 1969 to William W Wilson; c A Michelle. Educ: Northeastern State Col, 57-58; Univ Tulsa, 58-60 & 66. Polit & Govt Pos: Secy, Tulsa Co Young Rep, Okla, 66-67, treas, 67-68; publicity chmn, Okla Young Rep Fedn, 69-71, first dist chmn, 71-73, Nat Committeewoman, 73-; co-chmn resolutions comt, Tuls Co Rep Conv, 72, mem, 73; secy, First Cong Dist Rep Donv, 72. Bus & Prof Pos: Secy, Tulsa Co Courthouse, Engrs Off, 66-68; admin secy, Okla Steel Sales, 68-69; admin asst, Grant Hastings Co, 69-73; advert prod, Tulsalite Mag, 73- Mem: Women's Asn of Tulsa Philharmonic; Pro Am (exec comt & publicity chmn, 72-); Tulsa Co Federated Rep Women (exec comt & publicity chmn, Etha Neilson Chap, 73). Honors & Awards: Outstanding Mem, Tulsa Co Young Rep, 71. Relig: Episcopal. Mailing Add: 7446 E 70th St Tulsa OK 74133

WILSON, EUGENIA ROSE (JEANNE) (R)
Committeewoman, Middlesex Co Rep Party, NJ
b New York, NY, Aug 18, 36; d Edward Bernard Amber & Rose Gelshoyan A; m 1956 to Thomas Woodrow Wilson, Jr; c Linda Marie & Laura Jeanne. Educ: Walton High Sch, Bronx, NY, 4 years. Polit & Govt Pos: Trustee, Laurence Harber Rep Club, 64-65, secy, 66-67; founder & trustee, Mothers Against Discrimination, 65-; vchmn, Young Rep of Middlesex Co, 66, chmn, 66-69, alt deleg, 69-70, deleg, 71; state col coordr, Young Rep of NJ, 68, recording secy, 70-; chmn, Voter Registr Middlesex Co, 68-69; committeewoman, Middlesex Co Rep Party, 68-, vchmn, 69-75, liaison from Madison Twp, 71; vchmn, NJ Asn State VChmn, 69-; youth activities coordr, Women's Rep Club of Middlesex Co, 71; co deleg, Young Rep of Madison Twp, 71- Bus & Prof Pos: Bookkeeper, Ebasco Serv, New York, NY, 53-56; Polkowitz Motors, Perth Amboy, NJ, 57-58; sales, Syloette Shops, Madison Twp, 59-62; spec police, Police Dept, 64-67, indust security police, Indust Security Serv, North Brunswick, 69- Honors & Awards: Grad Award, Young Rep Leadership Training Sch, Washington, DC, 69, Post Grad Award, 71. Relig: Catholic. Mailing Add: 263 Brookside Ave Laurence Harbor NJ 08879

WILSON, FRANKLIN SCOTT (R)
b LaHarpe, Kans, June 16, 24; s Frank Sanderson Wilson & Nellie Mae Brown W; m 1953 to Carol Louise Jenkins; c Wanda Louise (Mrs David Allen), Michael Scott, Thomas Keith, John Louis & Pamela Louise. Polit & Govt Pos: Vchmn, North Fork Twp, Ashe Co, NC, 71-; mem bd elec, Ashe Co, 72-; alt deleg, Rep Nat Conv, 72. Mil Serv: Entered Merchant Marine, 43, released as Radio Operator, 46, after serv in Atlantic, Pac, & Far East. Relig: Protestant. Mailing Add: Rte 1 Box 16A Creston NC 28615

WILSON, GEORGE, JR (D)
SC State Rep
Mailing Add: Rte 1 Box 101 Gadsden SC 29052

WILSON, GEORGE E, JR (R)
Rep Nat Committeeman, Tenn
b Rockwood, Tenn, July 26, 21; m 1947 to Chalmers; c George E, III, Emmie N & Madge T. Educ: Vanderbilt Univ, grad, 43. Polit & Govt Pos: Chmn, Roane Co Rep Party, Tenn, 52-56, Second Cong Dist Rep Party, 58-63 & Tenn State Rep Party, 63-64; chmn Tenn deleg, Rep Nat Conv, 64; Rep Nat Committeeman, Tenn, 68- Bus & Prof Pos: Hosiery mfr with Burlington Mills, Inc, 4 years & Roane Hosiery, Inc, 23 years; mem bd, Hamilton Bank of Roane Co, currently. Mem: Tenn Mfrs Asn (pres); Nat Asn of Hosiery Mfrs (bd mem); Rotary; Am Legion; VFW. Relig: Presbyterian. Legal Res: 702 Cumberland St Harriman TN 37748 Mailing Add: PO Box 431 Harriman TN 37748

WILSON, GEORGE HOWARD (D)
b Mattoon, Ill, Aug 21, 05; s George Duncan Wilson & Helen Maude Bresee W; m 1929 to Myrna Kathryn Reams; c Jane Kathryn, Sandra Kay, Myrna Lee & George Howard, II. Educ: Phillips Univ, AB, 26; Univ Mich Law Sch, 26-27; Univ Okla, JD, 29; Nat Col State Trial Judges, Univ Nev, grad, 70; Order of the Coif; Phi Delta Phi; Delta Sigma Rho; Acacia. Polit & Govt Pos: Spec agent, Fed Bur Invest, 34-38; city attorney, Enid, Okla, 39-42; US Rep, Okla, 49-50; dir, Okla State Crime Bur, 51-52; superior court judge, Enid, Garfield Co, Okla, 52-68; Chief Judg Dist Court, Div One Fourth Judicial Dist, Okla, 69-; presiding judge, Okla Appellate Court of Bank Rev, 71- Mil Serv: Entered as Capt, Army, releases as Col, 45, after serv in Judge Adv Gen Corps; Col, Army Res; Commendation Medal. Publ: The role of a trial judge in the trial of a negligence action, Defense Law J, 60. Mem: DeMolay (Legionnaire of Hon); Mason; K T, Scottish Rite; Am Legion; Kiwanis. Relig: Presbyterian; elder, 31- Mailing Add: 1724 W Cherokee Enid OK 73701

WILSON, HELEN FRANCES (R)
NH State Rep
b Nashua, NH, Jan 23, 21; d Harold Joseph Geddes & Irene Claudia Dow G; m 1942 to James Richard Wilson; c Leonard Richard, Gail Helen & Glenna-Jean. Educ: Rivier Col, 2 years. Polit & Govt Pos: NH State Rep, 71- Bus & Prof Pos: Med asst, Dr John Deitch, Manchester, NH, 59-69, med asst, Dr Asif Syed, 71- Mem: Eastern Star PM; NH Fedn Women's Clubs; Candia Grange No 169; Ladies Circle, Congregational Church; Order Women Legislators. Honors & Awards: Grand Cross of Color-Order of Rainbow for Girls. Relig: Congregational. Legal Res: South Rd Candia NH 03034 Mailing Add: RFD 1 Box 344 Manchester NH 03104

WILSON, HELEN LOUISE (R)
VChmn, Jefferson Co Rep Party, Ind
b Madison, Ind, Apr 15, 21; d Hallie Michael Giltner & Nellie G Adams G; wid; c Wilbur L, Phyllis A (Mrs Wolfschlag) & Judy Carol (Mrs Monroe). Educ: St Marys Bus Sch. Polit & Govt Pos: Vchmn, Jefferson Co Rep Party, Ind, 59-; vchmn, Dist 9 Rep Party, 67-71. Bus & Prof Pos: Mgr license br, Madison, Ind, 69- Mem: Rep Women's Club. Honors & Awards: Honored at Lincoln's Day Dinner as Outstanding Rep for All Years Work & Recognition, Feb, 75. Relig: Methodist. Mailing Add: 2431 Taylor St Madison IN 47250

WILSON, HENRY HALL, JR (D)
b Monroe, NC, Dec 6, 21; s Henry Hall Wilson & Annie Sanders W; m 1944 to Mary C Walters; c Jean, Nancy & Henry H, III. Educ: Duke Univ, BA, 42, LLB, 48. Polit & Govt Pos: NC State Rep, 53-59; pres, NC Young Dem Club, 55-57; deleg, Dem Nat Conv, 56 & 60; Dem Nat Committeeman, NC, 61; admin asst to President of US, 61-67. Bus & Prof Pos: Attorney-at-law, Monroe, NC, 48-61; pres, Chicago Bd of Trade, 67-73; chmn bd, Mesco, Inc, Belmont, NC. Mil Serv: Entered as Pvt, Army, 43, released as 1st Lt, 46. Relig: Baptist. Mailing Add: PO Box 1060 Monroe NC 28110

WILSON, HOMER L (D)
Mem, Dem State Exec Comt, Ga
b Soperton, Ga, Oct 14, 21; s Morgan L Wilson & Annie B W. Polit & Govt Pos: Mem, Dem Party Ga, 30 years; mem staff of four Ga Gov; mem, first cong staff & eighth cong staff; worked actively in campaign of all Dem cand on the nat level; mem, Dem State Exec Comt Ga, currently. Bus & Prof Pos: Dir pub works, City of Brunswick, Ga, currently. Mem: Northside Kiwanis (dir); Glynn Co Polit Asn; Glynn Co Poverty Prog (1st chmn). Relig: Advent Christian Church; elder. Mailing Add: 526 Union St Brunswick GA 31520

WILSON, HUGH MAL (R)
Mem, Caldwell Co Rep Exec Comt, NC
b Rutherfordton, NC, May 3, 30; s H Mal Wilson & Ruth Scruggs W; m 1956 to Martha Whitehead; c Karen, Lynne & Robert. Educ: Mars Hill Col, AA, 49; Wake Forest Col, BBA, 51, Law Sch, LLB, 56; Alpha Kappa Psi; Phi Delta Phi. Polit & Govt Pos: Mem, Caldwell Co Rep Exec Comt, NC, 58-; mem bd elecs, Caldwell Co, 62-, tax attorney, 65-; deleg, Rep Nat Conv, 64; alt deleg, 72. Bus & Prof Pos: Attorney-at-law, 56-62; attorney, Seila, Wilson & Palmer, 62-72 & Wilson, Palmer & Simmons, 73-; Caldwell Co Attorney, 66- Mil Serv: Entered as Pvt, Air Force, 51, released as Airman 2/C, 53, after serv in Hq ROTC. Mem: NC Acad Trial Lawyers; Am Trial Lawyers Asn; Jaycees; Am Legion; Lenoir-Caldwell Co CofC. Honors & Awards: Outstanding Young Man Award, 64. Relig: Baptist. Legal Res: Cedar Rock Estate Lenoir NC 28645 Mailing Add: Box 638 Lenoir NC 28645

WILSON, IRL DONAKER (D)
b Calhoun Co, Iowa, May 21, 88; s John Francis Wilson & Hariett Donaker W; m 1914 to Belle Seely; m 1953 to Eleanor Atkins; c Irl Donaker, Jr. Educ: Iowa State Col, DVM, 14, PhD, 30; Pa State Col, MS, 18; Alpha Zeta; Omicron Delta Kappa; Phi Kappa Phi; Gamma Sigma Delta; Sigma Xi; Phi Sigma; Phi Sigma Kappa. Polit & Govt Pos: Mem, Va State Bd Vet Med Examr, 32-46; collabr, US Bur Animal Indust, 36-41; mem, US Govt Alaska Reindeer Surv & Appraisal Comt, 38-39; mem, Va Comn on Animal Indust & Vet Col, 46; Rockefeller Found app to comt to survey Nat Univ of Latin Am Countries, 49; US Agency for Int Develop educ adv to India, 58-60; US State Dept lectr, Kabul Univ, 61; chmn, Montgomery Co Dem Comt, Va, 67-70; chmn, 13th Dist Dem Comt, 67-70; elector, Dem Party Cand for President & Vice President Ninth Cong Dist, Va, 72. Bus & Prof Pos: Vet, Blue Earth, Minn, 14-16; prof, Pa State Col, 16-23; prof & head dept biol, Va Polytech Inst, 23-58. Mil Serv: 2nd Lt, Iowa State Cadet Corps. Publ: Bovine coccidiosis, Va Agr Exp Sta Bull, 30; Veterinary education in developing countries, Am Inst Biol Sci Bull, 12/63; Those interesting Afghans, Sci Educ, 10/67; plus others. Mem: Va Acad Sci; Va & Am Vet Med Asns; Am Inst Biol Sci; Theta Kappa Psi. Honors & Awards: Paper presented on animal husbandry & vet educ at the First Pan Am Vet Cong, Lima, Peru, 51; Am Mills Award, 64; Va Vet of the Year, 68. Relig: Episcopal. Mailing Add: 1303 Oak Dr Blacksburg VA 24060

WILSON, JAMES (R)
b Peshastin, Wash, Apr 3, 21; s Lloyd Elmer Wilson & Juna B Smith W; m 1945 to Alvis June Richardson; c Linda Lee & David Layne. Educ: Wenatchee Valley Col, 40-42; Wash State Univ, MS, 47; Sigma Tau; Phi Kappa Phi; Tau Beta Ph. Polit & Govt Pos: Precinct committeeman, Chelan Co Rep Cent Comt, Wash, 50-70, dist comnr, 54-56, co chmn, 66-68; mem exec bd, Wash State Rep Cent Comt, 71-72; Rep state committeeman, Chelan Co, Wash, 56-58 & 68-74. Bus & Prof Pos: Vpres, L E Wilson, Inc, 67- Mil Serv: Entered as Pvt, Army Air Corps, 42, released as 1st Lt, 45, after serv in 759th Bomb Group 15th AF in Italy, 45; Lt Col (Ret), Air Force Res, 65; Good Conduct Medal; Air Medal; ETO, Res & other

medals. Mem: Nat Rifle Asn; Chelan Co Hist Soc; Chelan Co Rep Orgn. Legal Res: Harnden Rd Cashmere WA 98815 Mailing Add: Box 812 Cashmere WA 98815

WILSON, JAMES H (D)
La State Rep
Mailing Add: 721 W Georgia St Vivian LA 71082

WILSON, JOE MACK (D)
Ga State Rep
b Marietta, Ga, Dec 11, 19; m 1945 to Mary Elizabeth Fullen Holloway; c Joe Michael, Stephen Holloway & David McKelvey. Educ: Ga Tech, 39-44. Polit & Govt Pos: Mem, Cobb Co Dem Exec Comt, Ga; Ga State Rep, 61- Bus & Prof Pos: Retail merchant. Mem: Elks; Aidmore Hosp (bd dir); Atlanta Area Metrop Planning Comn. Relig: Methodist. Mailing Add: 77 Church St Marietta GA 30060

WILSON, JOHN (D)
Tex State Rep
Mailing Add: Rte 2 Box 98 LaGrange TX 78945

WILSON, JOSEPHINE EVADNA (R)
b Ensign, Kans; d Henry Reuben & Mary E Scott Smith R; m 1945 to Woodrow Bankhead Wilson. Educ: Kans Univ; George Washington Univ. Polit & Govt Pos: Legis liaison secy, Selective Serv, 40-45; secy to comnr, Hoover Comn, 48-49; secy to US Reps, 55-56; minority legis clerk, Off of Minority Leader, US House of Rep, 56-71, legis asst to Minority Leader, 71-74. Bus & Prof Pos: Legal secy, 35-40. Mem: Woman's Soc of Christian Serv; Capitol Hill Club. Relig: Methodist. Mailing Add: 5900 Cromwell Dr Springfield MD 20016

WILSON, LEONARD USHER (D)
Chmn, Dem State Comt, Vt
b Brookline, Mass, Jan 1, 27; s Grafton L Wilson & Dorothy Usher W; m 1954 to Priscilla S Litchfield; c Mary, Sarah, Alice & John. Educ: Harvard Col, AB, 50. Polit & Govt Pos: Spec asst to asst secy of state for pub affairs, Washington, DC, 61-62; spec asst to US rep to UN, US Mission, Geneva, Switz, 62-64; spec asst to rep for trade negotiations, Washington, DC, 64-66; dir, State Planning Vt, 66-68; chmn, Dem State Comt, Vt, 73- Bus & Prof Pos: Sr planning assoc, Robert Burley Assocs, 70-; pres, Redrock Corp, 71- Mil Serv: Entered as Pvt, Army, 44, released as Sgt, 46, after serv in ETO, 45-46. Mem: Univ Vt (trustee); Vt Natural Resources Coun (dir); Conserv Law Found of New Eng (dir). Mailing Add: Box 224 Waitsfield VT 05673

WILSON, LORI (INDEPENDENT)
Fla State Sen
b Waynesville, NC, Feb 15, 37; d Lloyd Bryson & Constance Chappell B; m 1973 to Allen H Neuharth; c Dan, Jan, Rhonda & Kimberly. Educ: Tenn Technol Univ; Brevard Community Col; Rollins Col. Polit & Govt Pos: Co comnr, Brevard Co, Fla, 69-72, chmn, Bd Co Comnr, 72; Fla State Sen, 72- Mem: Univ Fla Found (bd dirs); Univ Fla Learned Scholars Inst (founding dir); Cent Fla Zool Soc (hon dir); Fla Injured Wildlife Sanctuary (legis dir); Brevard Co Ment Health Asn. Honors & Awards: Fla Jaycees Good Govt Award, 74; Outstanding Floridian, 71; Cocoa Beach Elks Lodge Distinguished Citizenship Award, 73. Relig: Protestant. Legal Res: 311 S Atlantic Ave Cocoa Beach FL 32931 Mailing Add: Suite 18-250 E Merritt Island Causeway Merritt FL 32952

WILSON, MALCOLM (R)
b New York, NY, Feb 26, 14; s Charles H Wilson; m to Katharine McCloskey; c Kathy & Anne. Educ: Fordham Col, BA, 33; Fordham Law Sch. Hon Degrees: Hon degrees from Alfred Univ, Brooklyn Law Sch, Canisius Col, Fordham Univ, Pace Col, St Bonaventure Univ, Siena Col, Le Moyne Col, St John Fisher Col & Manhattan Col. Polit & Govt Pos: NY State Assemblyman, 38-58; Lt Gov, NY, 58-74; cand, Gov, NY, 74. Bus & Prof Pos: Partner, Kent, Hazzard, Wilson, Freeman & Greer, Attorneys, currently. Mil Serv: Navy, World War II, Comdr Navy Gun Crew on Ammunition Ship in Mediterranean & European Theaters; Normandy Invasion, 6/44. Mem: KofC; Hiberians; Friendly Sons of St Patrick; Nat Conf Christians & Jews (bd trustees); Fordham Univ (bd trustees). Relig: Catholic. Mailing Add: 24 Windsor Rd Yonkers NY 10583

WILSON, MIKE (D)
Ark State Rep
Mailing Add: 309 Main Jacksonville AR 72076

WILSON, NICK (D)
Ark State Sen
Mailing Add: 620 Schoonover Pocahontas AR 72455

WILSON, PETE (R)
Mayor, San Diego, Calif
b Lake Forest Ill, Aug 23, 33; s James Boone Wilson & Margaret Callahan W; m 1968 to Betty Weedn Robertson. Educ: Yale Univ, BA, 55; Univ Calif Sch Law, LLB, 62; Phi Delta Phi; Zeta Psi. Polit & Govt Pos: Asst exec dir, Rep Assocs of San Diego Co, 63-64; exec dir, San Diego Co Rep Cent Comt, 64-65; Calif State Assemblyman, 76th Dist, Minority Whip, 67 & 68; chmn of comt to name Presidential Electors, 68; mem, President's Citizen's Adv Comt on Environ Quality; Mayor, San Diego, Calif, 71-; mem, Task Force on Land Use & Urban Growth Policy; mem, Community Develop & Resolutions Comts of US Conf of Mayors, chmn finance comt, mem adv comt; bd trustees, Conservation Found; mem, Coastal Zone Mgt Adv Comt; vpres, League of Calif Cities; chmn, Efficiency & Econ Comt; chmn, Comt on Urban Environ Qual; mem, Mayor's Task Force on Drug Abuse & Prevention; mem, Environ Quality Comt; bd dirs, Calif Ctr for Research & Educ in Govt; mem, Coun for Urban Econ Develop; mem, Calif Manpower Planning Coun. Bus & Prof Pos: Partner, Davies & Burch, Attorney's, San Diego, Calif. Mil Serv: Entered as 2nd Lt, Marine Corps, 55, released as 1st Lt, 58, after serv in Fourth Marines, Hawaii, 56-58. Publ: Drug abuse as a legislative problem, Calif Sch Health Asn J, 5/68. Mem: Nat Asn Regional Couns; City of Hope Pilot Med Ctr (bd trustees); Found for Ocean Research; Am Bar Asn (mem adv comn on housing & urban growth); Pacific 21 Coun (bd dirs). Honors & Awards: Selected to Rep Calif at 1968 Eagleton Inst of Politics, Rutgers Univ Annual Seminar for Outstanding State Legislators; Outstanding Young Man of San Diego, Jr CofC, 69; Hon Chmn Nat Conf Christians & Jews. Relig: Episcopal. Legal Res: 4146 Genesee Ave San Diego CA 92111 Mailing Add: 202 C St San Diego CA 92101

WILSON, ROBERT CARLTON (BOB) (R)
US Rep, Calif
b Calexico, Calif, Apr 5, 16; s George Wellington Wilson & Olive Blanche Richardson W; m 1974 to Shirley Haughey Sarrett; c Frances (Mrs James Wilson), Mary Ann (Mrs Michael Chapple) & Bryant. Educ: San Diego State Col; Otis Art Inst. Polit & Govt Pos: US Rep, Calif, 36th Dist, 53-72, 40th Dist, 73-, mem, Armed Serv Comt & Select Comt on Aging, US House Rep; campaign coordr for Richard M Nixon, 56; chmn, Nat Rep Cong Comt, 61-73. Mil Serv: Pvt, Army, 44-45; Lt Col, Marine Corps Res, currently. Publ: John J Montgomery the Forgotten Man of Aviation. Mem: Who's Who in Am Polit (adv comt, 67, 69, 71 & 73); Rotary; Am Legion (Chula Vista Post 434); Elks (Lodge 168); Harbor Lions. Honors & Awards: Recipeint Floats Award, Pasadena Tournament of Roses; Named Chef of West, Sunset Mag; Received Award as One of Ten Congressmen Who Had Done Most for Young People of Am, Redbook Mag; Award for Work on Doctor Draft Legis, Med-Dent Vet Orgns; Award for Outstanding Work in Behalf of Minority Groups, Filipino-Am Vet Orgn. Legal Res: San Diego CA Mailing Add: 2307 Rayburn Bldg Washington DC 20515

WILSON, ROBERT G (D)
Okla State Sen
Mailing Add: State Capitol Oklahoma City OK 73105

WILSON, ROBERT JEWELL (D)
Calif State Assemblyman
b San Luis Obispo, Calif, Apr 26, 43; s Jewell Porter Wilson & Helen Symmons W; m 1971 to Sharman Lee Massena. Educ: Calif Polytech State Univ, BA; Calif Western Univ, teaching credential, 65; Univ San Diego, JD, 68; Phi Alpha Delta. Polit & Govt Pos: Calif State Assemblyman, 72- Bus & Prof Pos: Self-employed attorney, 70-72. Mil Serv: Entered as Pvt, Army Res, 68, released as SP-4, 72, after serv in Judge Adv Gen Corps. Mem: Fed Bar for Southern Dist Calif; Calif, San Diego & Foothills Bar Asns; Univ Calif Law Sch Club. Honors & Awards: Gold Key Award, Calif State Polytech Univ, 65 & Distinguished Alumnus Award, 72. Relig: Methodist. Legal Res: 5365 Marengo La Mesa CA 92041 Mailing Add: State Capitol Sacramento CA 95814

WILSON, ROBERT KINNER (R)
Chmn, Lorain Co Rep Cent Comt, Ohio
b Elyria, Ohio, May 31, 29; s Robert Seymour Wilson & Dorothy Kinner W; m 1958 to Nancy Bair; c James Robert, Jeffrey Matthew & Jennifer Graham. Educ: Kenyon Col, 47-49; Baldwin Wallace Col, BA, 51; Delta Phi. Polit & Govt Pos: Mem, Lorain Co Bd Elec, Ohio, 73-; chmn, Lorain Co Rep Cent Comt, 73- Bus & Prof Pos: Vpres & dir, Neale-Phypers Corp, Cleveland, Ohio, 71- Mil Serv: Entered as A/S, Naval Res, 47, released as Seaman, after serv in Surface Div-4-105. Mem: Co, State & Nat Asn Independent Ins Agents; Lorain Co Asn Ins (pres, 72-73); Am Legion; Mason (32 degree); Shrine. Relig: Episcopal. Legal Res: 1041 Rosealee Ave Elyria OH 44035 Mailing Add: PO Box H Parcel Post Annex Elyria OH 44035

WILSON, ROBERT TERRY (D)
Ala State Sen
b Dora, Ala, Apr 23, 22; s William Myrick Wilson & Katie Bell Dobbs W; m to Ruth Eleanor McDaniel; c Sandra Sue, Robert Terry, Jr, Sally Ruth & Alice Kaye. Educ: Stetson Law Sch, Deland, Fla; Univ Ala, 50. Polit & Govt Pos: Ala State Sen, 63-67 & 71-; deleg, Dem Nat Conv, 72; deleg, Dem Nat Mid-Term Conf, 74. Bus & Prof Pos: Lawyer. Mil Serv: Air Force, T/Sgt; 65 Combat Missions. Mem: Mason; Shrine. Relig: Methodist. Mailing Add: 1501 First Ave Jasper AL 35501

WILSON, ROGER H (R)
Fla State Rep
b Brooklyn, NY, Feb 24, 37; single. Educ: Fla State Univ, BA, 63; pres, Polit Union; Lyceum Coun; Young Rep; Campus Court. Polit & Govt Pos: Fla State Rep, 68- Mil Serv: Entered as Pvt, Army, released as S/Sgt, Green Berets. Mem: Conservation 70's; Pinellas Asn for Retarded Children (bd dirs); YMCA; Sertoma; Jaycees. Honors & Awards: Legis Keyhole Award, Dixie News Serv; One of Outstanding Young Men of Am, US Jaycees; Distinguished Serv Award, Jaycees, 71; Outstanding Rating, Conservationists. Relig: Episcopal. Mailing Add: 11337-67th Ave N Seminole FL 33542

WILSON, SAMUEL BENJAMIN, JR (D)
Mem, Va State Dem Cent Comt
b Granville Co, NC, Dec 30, 39; s Samuel Benjamin Wilson & Lovey Walton W; m 1965 to Greer Dawson; c Sarita Marie & Samia Jamella. Educ: Bradley Univ, BA in Polit Sci, 62; Cornell Univ Sch Labor & Indust Rels, cert, summer 68; Univ Hartford, MA in Educ, 69; Am Univ, summer 71; Phi Mu Alpha; Alpha Phi Alpha. Polit & Govt Pos: Mem, Va State Dem Cent Comt, 72-; mem, City of Hampton Finance Comt, Va, 73; Mayor's Minority Comt, 73-74; alt deleg, Dem Nat Mid-Term Conf, 74. Bus & Prof Pos: Claims adjuster, Travelers Ins Co, Boston, Mass, 64-65; assoc dir, Gtr Hartford Urban League, Conn, 65-69; dir off urban affairs, Hampton Inst, Va, 69-74; ins agt, New York Life Ins Co, Hampton, 74-; mem bd dirs, King Street Community Ctr, currently. Mil Serv: Entered as A/S, Navy, 62, released as Seaman Personnelman, 64. Mem: Hampton NAACP; Peninsula Life Underwriters Asn; Action Comt to Stop Drugs Inc (co-founder, pres & mem bd dirs). Mailing Add: 7 Evans St Hampton VA 23669

WILSON, SIMEON R (SIM) (R)
Wash State Rep
Mailing Add: PO Box 145 Marysville WA 98270

WILSON, THOMAS R C, II (D)
Nev State Sen
b San Francisco, Calif, Apr 15, 35; s Thomas C Wilson & Ina Winters W; m 1958 to Sandra Opsahl; c Ann Louise, Ina Marie, Thomas R C, III & John Weston. Educ: Stanford Univ, BA, 57; Georgetown Univ Law Sch, LLB & JD, 61. Polit & Govt Pos: Nev State Sen, 71- Bus & Prof Pos: Asst US attorney, State of Nev, 61-64; attorney-at-law, McDonald, Carano, Wilson & Bergin, 64- Mil Serv: Entered Army, 57, released as 2nd Lt, 58. Mem: Easter Seal Soc (mem bd dirs). Legal Res: 893 Marsh Ave Reno NV 89502 Mailing Add: PO Box 2670 Reno NV 89505

WILSON, TRUMAN (D)
Mo State Sen
Mailing Add: 514 N Belt St Joseph MO 64503

WILSON, W R (SQUIBB) (D)
b Fairview, WVa, Oct 6, 13; s R J Wilson & Jettie Pearl Tennant W; m 1940 to Mary Eleanor Talbott; c Mikell Ann & Julia Kay. Educ: Fairmont State Col, AB, 35; Columbia Univ, MA, 39; WVa Univ, grad work, 46 & Univ Pittsburgh, 47. Polit & Govt Pos: WVa State Deleg, Marion Co, 57-59, 61-65 67-69 & 71-72; deleg, Dem Nat Conv, 72. Bus & Prof Pos: Athletic dir, Fairmont State Col, 39-; inventor & pres, Z Bar, Inc, 58-65; dir, Elsco, Educators Invest Serv, Co, 66. Mil Serv: Entered as Ens, Navy, 42, released as Lt (jg), 45, ETO; Asian-Mid Eastern & Invasion of France Ribbons. Publ: Isometric exercises, privately published. 58; Little league try out system, Lttle Leaguer, 52. Mem: Am Asn Higher Educ; Am Health & Phys Educ Asn; Rotary; Elks; Am Legion. Honors & Awards: Organizer of first little leaguers & pony leagues, Va & WVa; named Man Who Had Done Most for Athletics in WVa by sportswriters & sportscasters, 52; Baseball Coach of the Year, Eastern US, 67. Relig: Methodist. Mailing Add: 1 Camden Rd Fairmont WV 26554

WILSON, WILLIAM ORVAL (D)
b Coal City, Ill, Jan 14, 11; s William Wilson & Agnes Hunter W; m 1933 to Marguerite Zboyovski; c Marguerite & William Joseph. Educ: High sch grad. Polit & Govt Pos: Chmn, Greene Co Dem Cent Comt, Ill, formerly. Bus & Prof Pos: Asst mine mgr, Superior Coal Co, 42-52; grocer, Southside Mkt, 46-69; owner, Wilson's Tavern, 52-64; farmer, Calhoun & Greene Co, Ill, 59-69; mine foreman, Monterey Coal Co, 70- Mem: Carrollton & Eldred Sportsman Club; Farm Bur; Ill Valley Econ Develop Corp. Relig: Christian. Mailing Add: 314 Church St Carrollton IL 62016

WILSON, WILLIAM THOMAS (D)
Va State Deleg
b Crewe, Va, Nov 30, 37; s Linwood E Wilson & Elizabeth G W; single. Educ: Hampden-Sydney Col, AB, 60; Univ Va Law Sch, LLB, 63. Polit & Govt Pos: Secy, Alleghany Co Dem Comt; mem, Sixth Cong Dist Comt & Dem Cent Comt, formerly; Va State Deleg, 74-, mem corps, ins & banking comt & study comn for Interstate 74, Va House Deleg. Bus & Prof Pos: Partner law firm, Collins & Wilson; substitute judge for Alleghany Co Juv & Domestic Rels Dist Court; comnr accts, Circuit Court of Alleghany Co; vpres, WXCF Radio Sta, Clifton Forge, Va. Mil Serv: Va Air Nat Guard, Sgt, 63-69. Mem: Salvation Army (bd dirs, 66-, chmn, 70-72); Red Cross (bd dirs, 66-); United Fund Exec Bd; Falling Spring Ruritan Club; Moose Club. Honors & Awards: Algernon Sydney Sullivan Award, 56; Slater Trophy for most improved player, Football, 59; Gammon Cup Award for character, Hampden-Sydney Col, 60; nominee, Nat Moot Court Competition, Univ Va Law Sch, 62. Legal Res: Rte 4 Potts Creek Covington VA 24426 Mailing Add: 239 W Main St Covington VA 24426

WILSON, WOODROW (D)
Ind State Sen
Mailing Add: 93424 State Line Rd Payne IN 45880

WILSON, WOODROW (R)
b 1916. Polit & Govt Pos: Mem adv comt, US Civil Rights Comn; Nev State Assemblyman, 67-72; deleg, Rep Nat Conv, 68 & 72. Bus & Prof Pos: Mem staff, Am Potash & Chem Co, Henderson, Nev; treas & mgr, Westside Fed Credit Union. Mem: NAACP; Nev Voters League. Mailing Add: 625 Frederick Ave Las Vegas NV 89106

WILT, KATHERINE ARTHUR (D)
Nat Committeewoman, Va Young Dem
b Martinsburg, WVa, Apr 14, 48; d Thornton Willard Wilt & Katherine Hodges W; single. Educ: Shepherd Col, BA, 70. Polit & Govt Pos: Pres, Winchester-Frederick Young Dem, 72-75; secy, Va Young Dem, 73-74; nat committeewoman, 74- Bus & Prof Pos: Park ranger & historian, Nat Park Serv, 70-74; teacher, Winchester City Pub Schs, Va, 73- Mem: Nat, Va & Winchester Educ Asns. Relig: Lutheran. Mailing Add: 30 Wolfe St Winchester VA 22601

WILT, ROY WILLIAM (R)
Pa State Rep
b Pa, July 4, 35; s Raymond E Wilt & Marcella Newman W; m 1960 to Sonya A Mugnani; c Roy J & Rod E. Educ: Thiel Col, BS, 59; Mich State Univ, MA, 66; Lambda Chi Alpha. Polit & Govt Pos: Pa State Rep, 68- Bus & Prof Pos: Dean of men, Thiel Col, 62-68, assoc dean students, currently. Mil Serv: Entered as E-1, Army, 60, released as E-4, 66. Relig: Lutheran. Legal Res: Leech Rd Greenville PA 16125 Mailing Add: Capitol Bldg Harrisburg PA 17120

WILT, THORNTON W (D)
Chmn, Jefferson Co Dem Party, WVa
b Jefferson Co, WVa, Oct 25, 16; s Thomas W Wilt & Cecilia Staubs W; m 1941 to Katherine Hodges; c Anne Hodges Ashby, Lt Thornton W, Jr, Katherine, G Thomas & Sarah Beth. Educ: Shepherd Col. Polit & Govt Pos: WVa State Rep, 62-68; chmn, Jefferson Co Dem Party, currently. Bus & Prof Pos: Sales mgr. Mem: Theta Sigma Chi. Relig: Lutheran. Mailing Add: Harpers Ferry WV 25425

WILT, WILLIAM W (R)
Pa State Rep
b Altoona, Pa, Apr 15, 18; s Harry E Wilt & Estella Williams W; m to Marjorie Jane Benton; c two sons. Educ: Hollidaysburg High Schs. Polit & Govt Pos: Pa State Rep, 62- Bus & Prof Pos: Tel repairman. Mil Serv: Army, 43-45, ETO. Mem: Am Legion; VFW; Juniata Lodge, F&AM (former Master); Hollidaysburg Sportsmen's Club (former pres); Blair Co Fedn of Sportsmen's Club. Legal Res: RD 3 Box 198 Duncansville PA 16635 Mailing Add: Capitol Bldg Harrisburg PA 17120

WILTSE, IRVING F
Nebr State Sen
Mailing Add: Falls City NE 68355

WIMMER, JAMES WILLIAM, JR (D)
b Portage, Wis, Oct 20, 35; s James William Wimmer & Alice Bauer W; m 1967 to Mary Alice Cullen; c Leslie Ann & Christoper. Educ: Univ Wis-Madison, BA, 59; Beta Theta Pi; MACE. Polit & Govt Pos: Admin asst to Gov, Wis, 59-62 & Speaker of Wis State Assembly, 65-66; deleg, Dem Nat Conv, 68; chmn, Wis State Dem Party, 69-72. Bus & Prof Pos: Pres, Intergovt Research Assoc, Madison, Wis, 67- Mil Serv: Entered as 2nd Lt, Army, 62, released as 1st Lt, 64, after serv in US forces overseas, NATO; Capt, Inactive Res, currently; Army Commendation Award. Relig: Presbyterian. Mailing Add: 1030 Sherman Ave Madison WI 53703

WINBERRY, CHARLES BRYANT (D)
Chmn, Nash Co Dem Exec Comt, NC
b Statesville, NC, Oct 14, 41; s Charles Bryant Winberry & Virginia Carolyn Reece W; single. Educ: Wake Forest Univ, BA, 64, JD, 67; Omicron Delta Kappa; Phi Alpha Delta; College Union. Polit & Govt Pos: Pres, Wake Forest Young Dem, 63; chmn, NC Fedn Col Dem, 64; state chmn, Citizens for Johnson, 64; intern, State of NC, 64; vpres, Young Dem Clubs NC, 65; first vpres, 70, pres, 71-; counsel, Gov Comn Party Reorgn, 69-71; chmn, Wilson Precinct 5, 70-71; mem, NC Dem Coun Rev, 70-72; vchmn, NC State Dem Party, 70-72; permanent chmn, NC Dem State Conv, 72; chmn, Nash Co Dem Exec Comt, 72-; deleg, Biennial Conf NAtlantic Young Polit Leaders, Dusseldorf, Ger, 72; state campaign mgr for US Sen Robert Morgan, 74; deleg, Dem Nat Mid-Term Conf, 74; mem, NC Dem Exec Comt, 74- Bus & Prof Pos: Law clerk, US Dist Judge John Larkins, Trenton, NC, 68-69; chief prosecutor, Seventh Judicial Dist, 69-71; attorney, Biggs, Meadows, Batts & Winberry, Rocky Mt, NC, 71- Mem: Rocky Mt Rotary Club; AF&AM (Statesville Lodge 27); Scottish Rite Mason (32 degree); Rocky Mt Jr CofC; Sudan Shrine Temple. Honors & Awards: Outstanding Col Dem NC, 65; Most Outstanding Sr, Wake Forest Univ, 64, Most Outstanding Campus Speaker, 64; first place winner state will drafting & estate planning contest, 67. Relig: Southern Baptist. Legal Res: 1639 Lafayette Circle Rocky Mount NC 27801 Mailing Add: PO Drawer 153 Rocky Mount NC 27801

WINCHESTER, LUCY ALEXANDER (R)
Asst Chief Protocol, US Dept State
b Lexington, Ky, Jan 11, 37; d James Holloway Alexander & Lucy Moulthrop A; div; c Lucy. Educ: Finch Jr Col, dipl, 57; Univ Ky, BA, 60. Polit & Govt Pos: Mem staff, Protocol Off, US Mission to UN, 60; guide, UN, 60-62; hostess, VIP Room, Nixon Hq, Rep Nat Conv, 68; social secy, The White House, 69-75; Asst Chief Protocol, US Dept State, 75- Bus & Prof Pos: Owner & mgr, Alexander Farms, Lexington, Ky, 62-69. Legal Res: Lexington KY 40504 Mailing Add: Dept of State 2201 C St NW Washington DC 20521

WINCHESTER, LYMAN GENE (R)
Idaho State Rep
b Ogden, Utah, Dec 7, 35; s Austin F Winchester & Delores Fowles W; m 1955 to Lena Poulton; c Elgin Ross, Colin Reed, Nathan Fremont, Austin Bridger, Cody Delores & Andrea Lena. Educ: Latter-day Saint Inst Relig, 56; Utah State Univ, BS, 57; Univ Idaho, teacher's cert, 66; George Washington Univ, MS, 66; Sigma Alpha Epsilon; Dairy Club. Polit & Govt Pos: Idaho State Rep, Dist 19, 72-, mem, Educ Comt & Resources & Conserv Comt, Idaho House Rep, 72- Bus & Prof Pos: Owner & operator, Happy Heart Ranch, Kuna, Idaho, 64- Mil Serv: Entered as 2nd Lt, Air Force, 57, released as Capt, 62, after serv in 325th Fighter Interceptor Squadron, Air Defense Command; Maj, Air Nat Guard, 7 years; Combat Readiness Medal with Oak Leaf Cluster; Outstanding Unit Citation; Presidential Unit Citation; Expeditionary Serv Medal; Nat Defense Medal; Expert Small Arms Marksmanship Medal; Longevity Award with two Oak Leaf Clusters. Mem: Blue Key; Alpha Zeta; Arnold Air Soc; Idaho-Ore-Nev Appaloosa Breeders (pres bd dirs, 69-); Int Beagle Fedn. Honors & Awards: Nat Fel, Pfizer Found, 57; Finalist, White House Fel, 70; George Washington Honor Medal, Freedom Found at Valley Forge, 71. Relig: Latter-day Saint. Mailing Add: Rte 1 Kuna ID 83634

WINCHESTER, ROBERT C (R)
Ill State Rep
b Paducah, Ky, Apr 21, 45; s Lester Winchester & Cora Kimsey W; m 1974 to Christine Hester. Educ: Southern Ill Univ, Carbondale, govt & hist, 66- Polit & Govt Pos: Ill State Rep, 59th Dist, 75- Bus & Prof Pos: Prison supply supvr II, Dept Corrections, Joliet, Ill, 66-70; buyer I, Dept Gen Serv, Springfield, 70-74. Mem: Harrisburg Jaycees; Elizabethtown Lions; Shawnee Hills Recreation Asn. Honors & Awards: Received more votes in 1974 elec than any other Rep legislator in State of Ill. Relig: Methodist. Legal Res: PO Box 308 Rosiclare IL 62982 Mailing Add: Rm 2017 State Off Bldg Springfield IL 62706

WIND, HERBERT HAMILTON, JR (D)
Secy & Treas, Grade Co Dem Party, Ga
b Cairo, Ga, June 7, 15; s Herbert Hamilton Wind, Sr & Isola Vanlandingham W; m 1937 to Catherine Stephens; c Robert Hamilton & Herbert Wesley. Educ: Middle Ga Col, 33-34. Polit & Govt Pos: Chmn, Grade Co Dem Party, Ga, secy & treas, 46- Bus & Prof Pos: Ed, The Cairo Messenger, 46-68, publ, 68-, pres, Messenger Publ Co, Inc, Cairo, Ga, 56- Mem: Rotary; Ga Press Asn; Am Newspaper Asn; Grady Co Farm Bur. Relig: Methodist. Legal Res: RFD 2 Cairo GA 31728 Mailing Add: PO Box 30 Cairo GA 31728

WINDHORST, FRITZ (D)
La State Sen
Mailing Add: PO Box 386 Gretna LA 70053

WINDINGSTAD, HAROLD OLIVER, JR (DFL)
Chmn, Lac qui Parle Co Dem-Farmer-Labor Party, Minn
b Dawson, Minn, Aug 26, 29; s Harold Oliver Windingstad, Sr & Alvina Simonson W; m 1953 to Dolores Lucille Hoyles. Educ: Dawson High Sch, grad, 47. Polit & Govt Pos: Vchmn, Lac qui Parle Co Dem-Farmer-Labor Party, Minn, 58-59, chmn, 60-69 & 75-; vchmn, Sixth Dist Dem-Farmer-Labor Party, 65-69; deleg, Dem Nat Conv, 68. Bus & Prof Pos: Farmer, currently. Mem: Farmers Union; chmn, Western Tri-Co Community Action Coun (chmn). Relig: Lutheran. Mailing Add: Dawson MN 56232

WINDLE, HENRY WATTERSON (D)
Chmn, Clay Co Dem Party, Tenn
b Butlers Landing, Tenn, May 15, 03; s William Porter Windle & Frances Coffee W; m 1966 to Bettie Louise Gray. Educ: Clay Co High Sch, grad, 22. Polit & Govt Pos: Tenn State Rep, 40-44; chmn, Clay Co Dem Party, Tenn, 74- Bus & Prof Pos: US Corps Engrs, Nashville, Tenn, 26; State of Tenn, 28-31; Liggett Myers Tobacco Co, New York, NY, 31-38; contractor, Tenn Valley Authority, Knoxville, Tenn, 38-60; grocery store, Celina, Tenn, 60-63; Retired. Mem: Mason. Relig: Church of Christ. Mailing Add: Rte 1 Box 51 Celina TN 38551

WINDSHEIMER, WALTER W (R)
Mem Finance Comt, Benton Co Rep Party, Wash
b Oakdale, Pa, Aug 8, 13; s John Windsheimer & Anne Louise Bernhart W; single. Educ: Waynesburg Col, BSc, 38; Activities Hon Soc; pres, Scholastic Hon Soc. Polit & Govt Pos:

Chmn nuclear energy subcomt, Benton Co Rep Platform Comt, Wash, 58; finance chmn, Benton Co Rep Party, 61-62, co chmn, 67-68, mem finance comt, 68-; mem, Electronic Data Processing Comt, Wash Rep State Cent Comt, 67-68; alt deleg, Rep Nat Conv, 68 & 72; deleg, Rep State Conv, 68 & 72; pres, Fourth Cong Dist Rep Club, 71-72. Bus & Prof Pos: Field supvr, Agr Exten Agency, 39-40, chemist, Universal Cyclops Steel Co, 40-41; supvr, E I DuPont Co, 41-45; prod & eng mgr, Gen Elec Co, 46-65; admin specialist & prin engr, Douglas United Nuclear, Inc, 65- Mem: Am Nuclear Soc; Am Soc Chem Engrs; Elks; Wash Athletic Club; Mid-Columbia Symphony (bd dirs & finance comt, 71-73, pres, 74-75). Relig: Lutheran. Mailing Add: 58 Park St Richland WA 99352

WINDSOR, GILBERT EDISON, JR (D)
Mem, Md State Dem Cent Comt
b Cambridge, Md, Feb 24, 47; s Gilbert Edison Windsor, Sr & Susianne Mills W; m 1971 to Glenda Smith; c Gilbert, III & Christopher M. Educ: Univ Md, 65-66; Univ Baltimore, 66-67; Sigma Nu. Polit & Govt Pos: Mem, Md State Dem Cent Comt, Am Legion; Rescue Fire Co, Inc Cambridge. Relig: Catholic. Legal Res: 906 Oakley Terr Cambridge MD 21613 Mailing Add: Box 815 Cambridge MD 21613

WINDSOR, JULIUS GAYLE, JR (D)
Ark State Rep
b Tulsa, Okla, June 4, 20; s Julius Gayle Windsor & Bertha Lewis W; m 1944 to Betty Kraft; c Margaret (Mrs Clark), Mary Elizabeth & John Gayle. Educ: Univ Calif, Los Angeles, BA, 46; Ark Law Sch, LLB, 52; Theta Chi. Polit & Govt Pos: Ark State Rep, Pulaski Co, 57-63 & 67- Bus & Prof Pos: Self-employed lawyer & pub acct, 49- Mil Serv: Entered as Aviation Cadet, Army Air Corps, 41, released as Capt, 46, after serv in 2nd & 3rd Air Force, Continental US, 42-46. Mem: Ark & Am Bar Asns; Lions Int; Am Legion. Relig: Baptist. Legal Res: 1019 N Arthur Little Rock AR 72207 Mailing Add: 1040 Tower Bldg Little Rock AR 72201

WINEBRENNER, TOMMY LEE (R)
b Wolf Lake, Ind, Jan 14, 36; s Heber Winebrenner & Francis Marker W; m 1960 to Barbara Berry; c Pamela Lee & Mark Lewis. Educ: Am Univ, BS, 60; George Washington Univ Law Sch; Alpha Tau Omega. Polit & Govt Pos: Page boy, US House or Rep, 53-54, asst mgr minority tel, 55-63 & Minority Postmaster, 63- Mem: F&AM (Fed Lodge); Capitol Hill Club. Relig: Methodist. Legal Res: La Porte IN 46350 Mailing Add: 8418 Crown Pl Alexandria VA 22308

WINELAND, FRED (D)
Secy State, Md
b Washington, DC, Aug 16, 26; married. Educ: Am Univ; Southeastern Univ. Polit & Govt Pos: Young Dem Club of Prince George's Co; Oxon Hill Dem Club; past pres, Ft Washington Dem Club; Co Coun of Dem Clubs; campaign chmn, Prince George's Co Primary Elec, 62; campaign vchmn, George's Co Gen Elec, 62; Md State Deleg, 63-64, Md State Sen, 65-71; Secy State, Md, 71-; co-chmn, Gov Comn on Jobs for Vets, 72-; mem, Adv Comt to Gov Comn on Intergovt Coop, 72-; alt deleg, Dem Nat Conv, 72. Bus & Prof Pos: Vpres, Wineland Enterprises. Mil Serv: Navy. Mem: Am Legion; Elks; Masons; Shrine; Pilots Asn; VFW. Relig: Methodist. Mailing Add: State House Annapolis MD 21404

WINFIELD, MARY JONES (D)
VChmn, Beaufort Co Dem Party, NC
b Valdosta, Ga, Jan 16, 16; d Henry Davis Jones & Ethel Mae Hightower J; m 1935 to John Augustus Winfield; c Frances Ann (Mrs Bowers), Mary Virginia (Mrs Dowdy), Gloria Jean & John Scott. Educ: Ga State Woman's Col, 34-35; ECarolina Univ, 36. Polit & Govt Pos: Dem chmn, Yeatesville Precinct, NC, 58-68; alt deleg, Dem Nat Conv, 68 & 72; vchmn, Beaufort Co Dem Party, 68-; Dem Nat Committeewoman, NC, 68-72. Mem: Home Demonstration Clubs; Spec Comn Libr Resources (Gov Sanford appointee); Mt Olive Col (bd dirs); Tuberc Asn; Cancer Bd; Southern Albemarle Asn. Honors & Awards: Outstanding Church Woman Albemarle Dist, 66; Rural Elec Asn Rural Award, 68; featured as Outstanding Women Farm Mgrs Southern Region, Farm & Ranch Mag; Tar Heel of the Week, New & Observer; Distinguished Citizenship Award, Belhaven, 72. Relig: Freewill Baptist; Sunday sch teacher, 15 years; numerous speeches in Albemarle Dist. Mailing Add: Rte 1 Pinetown NC 27865

WING, ADA SCHICK (R)
Mem, Calif Rep State Cent Comt
b Bartlett, Ill, Oct 14, 96; d August Schick & Augusta Meyer S; div; c Wilbur Schick Wing (deceased). Educ: Elgin Acad Jr Col, 1 year. Polit & Govt Pos: Pres, Santa Barbara Co Rep Women, Calif, 56-60, co campaign chmn; mem, Santa Barbara Co Rep Cent Comt, 62-66 & 70-; mem, Calif Rep State Cent Comt, 64-; mem, Gov Reagan's Adv Comt on Ment Illness, 68-70; Rep precinct chmn, Santa Barbara Co, 61-74. Bus & Prof Pos: Teacher, Ill, 18; off mgr, Chicago, Ill, 20-25; asst to dir of defunct banks, Terra Bella & Woodlake, Calif, 32-34; ins agent, Aetna Life, 40-43; mgr orange grove, Terra Bella, Calif, 49-65; pres bd, Phoenix of Santa Barbara Inc. Mem: Rep Women's Club; Carpenteria Women's Club; Ment Health Asn (pres women's bd, Santa Barbara Asn). Honors & Awards: Rated first of ten best precinct chmn in Calif; Woman of the Year, SCoast Advert Club, 73. Relig: Protestant. Mailing Add: 3675 La Entrada Rd Santa Barbara CA 93105

WING, FRANCIS WILLIAM (R)
Chmn, Freetown Rep Town Comt, Mass
b Fall River, Mass, Jan 19, 41; s Hilda S Neal; m 1967 to Lois Ann Bennett. Educ: Wentworth Inst, AE in Prod Eng, 62; Northeastern Univ, BS in Indust Technol, 66. Polit & Govt Pos: Mem, Bd of Pub Welfare, Freetown, Mass, 63-68, mem, Bd of Selectmen & Bd of Health & police comnr, 63-69; mem, Freetown Rep Town Comt, 63-, chmn, 68-; pres, Bristol Co Selectmen's Asn, 65-66; mem exec bd, Mass Selectmen's Asn, 65-66; mem, Pub State Welfare Comt, 68- Bus & Prof Pos: Indust engr, Aerovox Corp, New Bedford, Mass, 63-64 & Raytheon Co, 69-; head of qual control, J I Paulding, 64-65; syst engr, Cornell Dubilier, 65-69. Mem: Am Soc of Qual Control; AF&AM; Bristol Community Col (chmn bd trustees, 75-); Lions. Honors & Awards: Youngest elected selectman in Mass history. Relig: First Christian. Mailing Add: 15 Elm St Assonet MA 02702

WING, LUCIE LEE (D)
b New Orleans, La, July 17, 26; d Louis Abramson, Jr & Marion Pfeifer A; m 1949 to Cliff Waldron Wing, Jr; c Steven Bennett & Scott Louis. Educ: Tulane Univ Newcomb Col, BA, 46, Tulane Univ, MS, 48. Polit & Govt Pos: Mem, NC State Dem Exec Comt, 70-72, deleg, Dem Nat Conv, 72; pres, Durham Co Dem Women, NC, 74- Bus & Prof Pos: Songwriter, 50-; mem selection comt, Marshall Scholar, Southern Region, 68- Mem: Nat Friends of Pub Broadcasting; Friends of Univ Network TV (pres, 75-); Am Civil Liberties Union; Am Soc Composers, Auth & Publ; Am Guild Auth & Composers. Mailing Add: 2722 Spencer St Durham NC 27705

WINGARD, GEORGE FRANK (R)
Ore State Sen
b Amboy, Wash, Nov 6, 35; s Sylvester Caroll Wingard & Edna English W; m to Rhea Mae Henault; c Carol Lynne & Gail Ann. Educ: Univ Ore, 2 years; Ore State Univ, 2 years; Sigma Chi. Polit & Govt Pos: Councilman, Eugene City Coun, Ore, 66-; Ore State Rep, 69-70; Ore State Sen, 71- Bus & Prof Pos: Owner, EDCO, currently; owner & pres, Wingard Construction, Inc, currently; co-owner, J&W, Inc, currently. Mem: Urban Land Inst; Metro Civic Club; Elks; CofC. Honors & Awards: Jr First Citizen of Eugene, 68; One of Ore Five Outstanding Young Men, 68. Relig: Presbyterian. Mailing Add: 2323 Fairmount Eugene OR 97403

WINGARD, PAUL SIDNEY (R)
Ohio State Rep
b Akron, Ohio, Jan 10, 30; s Daniel Webster Wingard & Mary Elizabeth Kalbaugh W; m 1953 to Marian Miller Loudin; c Skye Ann, Elizabeth Ann, Kevin Paul, Kimberley Ann & Eric Paul. Educ: Miami Univ, AB, 52, MS, 55; Univ Ill, Urbana, PhD, 60; Phi Sigma; Sigma Gamma Epsilon; Phi Kappa Tau. Polit & Govt Pos: Mem, Bd Educ, Stow, Ohio, 68-74; Ohio State Rep, 40th Dist, 75- Bus & Prof Pos: Asst prof geol, Kans State Univ, 57-66; asst dean & assoc prof geol, Univ Akron, 66-68, assoc dean arts & sci & prof geol, 68- Mem: Geol Soc Am; Am Asn Advan Sci. Mailing Add: 3904 Kent Rd Stow OH 44224

WINGATE, RICHARD ANTHONY (R)
Mem, Voluntown Rep Town Comt, Conn
b Brooklyn, NY, May 27, 37; s Elsdon Anthony Wingate & Florence Maybeck W; m 1958 to Dorothy Ann Daycock; c Mary Anthony, Belinda Jo, Elizabeth Claire & Matthew Jon. Educ: State Univ NY, Oswego, BS, 58; Ind Univ, MS, 60; Epsilon Pi Tau; Delta Kappa Kappa. Polit & Govt Pos: Justice of the Peace, Voluntown, Conn, 68-; chmn, Voluntown Rep Town Comt, 68-72, mem, currently. Bus & Prof Pos: Indust arts teacher, Stonington High Sch, 61-70 & Ledyard High Sch, 70-73. Mil Serv: Entered as Seaman Recruit, Naval Res, 54, released as Seaman, 62. Mem: Nat & Conn Educ Asns; Eastern Conn Indust Arts Asn; Mason; Eastern Star. Relig: Congregational. Legal Res: Pendleton Hill Voluntown CT 06384 Mailing Add: RD 1 North Stonington CT 06359

WINGE, RALPH M (D)
NDak State Rep
b Van Hook, NDak, Aug 25, 25; s Albert N Winge & Mabel C Gregerson W; m 1974 to Jane Williamson. Educ: NDak State Univ, BS, 53. Polit & Govt Pos: NDak State Rep, 24th Dist, 59-63 & 71-, mem, Legis Coun, NDak House of Rep, 61-65 & 67-69 & 73-, asst minority leader, 75. Bus & Prof Pos: Farmer, Van Hook, NDak, 43-53; farmer, Litchville, NDak, 53- Mem: Farmers Union; Sons of Norway; Eagles. Relig: Lutheran. Mailing Add: Rte 2 Box 85 Litchville ND 58461

WINGER, LOREN (D)
Ind State Rep
Mailing Add: 2721 N 900 W 27 Converse IN 46919

WINGERT, GEORGE (D)
Kans State Rep
Mailing Add: 432 Elm Ottawa KS 66067

WINGETT, ERNEST A (D)
Chmn, Meigs Co Dem Exec Comt, Ohio
b Pratts Fork, Ohio, Apr 2, 04; s William E Wingett & Minnie Whetstone W; m 1931 to Maxine Spencer. Educ: Ohio Univ, BS, 30; Columbia Univ. Polit & Govt Pos: Mayor, Racine, Ohio, 46-56 & 58-64; deleg, Dem Nat Conv, 64; chmn, Meigs Co Dem Exec Comt, Ohio, 65-66 & 69-; pres, Tenth Dist Dem Action Club, Ohio, 68-; mem, Meigs Co Bd of Elec, currently. Bus & Prof Pos: Teacher, 25 & 37; bus mgr newspaper, Pomeroy, Ohio, 44-53; teacher, Ravenswood High Sch, 63-66. Mem: Ohio Educ Asn; Nat Educ Asn; Mason; F&AM, Commandery. Relig: Methodist. Mailing Add: Elm St Racine OH 45771

WINGFIELD, LOTUS MAE (D)
b Mildred, Colo, Oct 5, 11; d C C Duff & Estie A Eastin D; m 1935. Educ: Yuma Co High Sch, 2 years; Am Sch Correspondence course, 2 years. Polit & Govt Pos: Committeewoman, Precinct 19, Yuma Co Dem Party, Colo, 37-69; clerk, US Post Off, 40-50, US Postmistress, 50-54; vpres, secy & treas, Yuma Co Jane Jefferson Clubs, 55-60, pres, 62-63; secy, Yuma Co Dem Party, 69-75. Mem: Eastern Star (all degrees & Worthy Matron); hon mem Extension Homemakers Club; Farmers Union. Relig: Methodist. Mailing Add: Eckley CO 80727

WINGLER, PATRICIA MARKS (D)
b Henderson, NC, Mar 18, 39; d Edward Mac Marks & Jacqueline Thomas M; m 1958 to Quincy Odell Wingler, Jr; c Sandra Gail & Karen Lynn. Educ: High sch, grad. Polit & Govt Pos: Precinct chmn, Dem Party, NC, 68-, deleg, Dem Nat Conv, 74; deleg, Dem Nat Mid-Term Conf, 74. Bus & Prof Pos: Meat clerk, A&D Food Stores, 56-70; women's activities dir, NC State AFL-CIO, 70- Mem: Dem Women; League of Women Voters; Young Dem Club of NC; NAACP; NC Consumer Coun. Relig: Protestant. Mailing Add: 4111 Summerglen Dr Greensboro NC 27406

WINIKOW, LINDA (D)
NY State Sen
Mailing Add: 62 Sutin Pl Spring Valley NY 10977

WINKELMAN, WILLIAM PRATT (R)
Iowa State Sen
b Lohrville, Iowa, Jan 14, 33; s Ewart Cain Winkelman & Marjorie Pratt W; single. Educ: Iowa State Univ, BS, 54; Alpha Gamma Rho. Polit & Govt Pos: Councilman, Lohrville, Iowa, 60-61; organizing chmn, Calhoun Co Young Rep, 62; Iowa State Rep, 26th Dist, 62-72, mem, Higher Educ Facil Comn, 67-69, chmn, Iowa Develop Comt, 69-72; alt deleg, Rep Nat Conv, 64; Iowa State Sen, 24th Dist, 73- Bus & Prof Pos: Pres, Lohrville Commercial Club, 59; owner-mgr, Winkelman Farms, 58-; dir, Am Shetland Pony Club, 62-65; committeeman, Am Horse Shows Asn, 62-67, dir & vpres, 67-; vpres, Welsh Pony Soc Am, 64; dir, Iowa Soc Preservation Hist Landmarks, 67- Mil Serv: Entered as 2nd Lt, Air Force, 55, released as 1st

Lt, 57; Capt, Air Force Res, 62. Mem: Lohrville High Sch Alumni Asn; Nat Sojourners; Shrine (mem commandery, Consistory). Honors & Awards: Univ Merit of Leadership Award, Iowa State Univ, 53 & 54. Relig: Presbyterian. Mailing Add: Lohrville IA 51453

WINKJER, DEAN (R)
NDak State Rep
b Wildrose, NDak, Jan 19, 23; s Jonathan Winkjer & Amanda Farland W; m 1951 to Betty Septon; c DeAnn (Mrs Steve Allen), Andrea, Kirsten & Jonathan. Educ: Univ NDak, PhD, 45, JD, 47; pres, Independent Student Asn; pres, Lutheran Student Asn; Blue Key. Polit & Govt Pos: Secy, NDak Young Rep; mem, NDak Rep Campaign Comt; NDak State Rep, Dist 1, 73-, mem indust, bus & labor comts, NDak House Rep, 75- Bus & Prof Pos: Asst states attorney, Williams Co, NDak. Mem: Fred & Clara Eckert Found for Children (secy); Williams Co Bar Asn (pres); Fifth Dist Bar Asn (pres); NDak State Bar Asn (mem exec comt & chmn ethics comt); Williams Co Ment Health Bd. Honors & Awards: Silver Beaver Award, Boy Scouts, 74; Outstanding Young Man of Year, Williston, NDak; Outstanding Young Man of Year, NDak. Relig: Lutheran. Legal Res: 1202 Hillcourt Williston ND 58801 Mailing Add: Box 1261 Williston ND 58801

WINKLER, ROBERT NORRIS (R)
VChmn, Baltimore Co Rep Cent Comt, Md
b Baltimore, Md, Oct 1, 45; s William Sebastian Winkler & Ellen Prenger; m 1971 to Kathleen Ann Stokes. Educ: Univ Md, College Park, BA, 67; Mt Vernon Sch of Law, Baltimore, JD, 70; Johns Hopkins Univ, 71; Sigma Delta Kappa. Polit & Govt Pos: Alt deleg, Rep Nat Conv, 72; vchmn, Baltimore Co Rep Cent Comt, Md, 73 & 75-, chmn, 74. Bus & Prof Pos: Attorney, 70- Mem: Am Psycho-Law Soc; Am Bar Asn; Ninth Dist Rep Club; Baltimore Co Young Rep; Towson Jaycees. Relig: Roman Catholic. Legal Res: 1744 Amuskai Rd Baltimore MD 21234 Mailing Add: 6905 York Rd Baltimore MD 21212

WINKLEY, NOREEN D (D)
NH State Rep
Mailing Add: Old Dover Rd Box 530 Rochester NH 03867

WINMILL, ELEANOR DAY (R)
b South Orange, NJ, Apr 19, 02; d Graham Scott & Florence Katherine Otis S; m 1951 to Joseph Bassett Winmill; c Bassett Star. Educ: Misses Beard's Sch for Girls, Orange, NJ, 17-19. Polit & Govt Pos: Chmn, Women for Forsythe Campaign & Women for Cahill Campaign, NJ, 69; deleg, Nat Fedn of Rep Women Biennial Conv, 71 & Nat Fedn of Rep Women Confs & Convs; pres, NJ Fedn of Rep Women, 71-74; bd gov, Nat Fedn of Rep Women, 71-74; deleg-at-lg, Rep Nat Conv, 72. Bus & Prof Pos: Food mgt, promotional advert, wholesale & retail buying 20 years; The Cotton Shop & Little Gourmet, Bay Head, NJ, formerly. Mem: Brick Town Hosp, NJ (bd dirs); life mem Capitol Hill Club; Bay Head Yacht Club; Women's Nat Rep Club; Women's Rep Club, Mantoloking-Bay Head. Honors & Awards: Loyal Order of Pachyderms, Young Rep of Ocean Co, Pine Beach & Dover Twp. Relig: Episcopal. Mailing Add: 346 Main Hideaway Bay Head NJ 08742

WINN, CECELIA LOUISE (D)
NH State Rep
b Nashua, NH, Apr 24, 07; d John Winn & Cecelia Degnan W; single. Educ: Keene State Teachers' Col, grad; Harvard Univ; Boston Univ; Univ NH, ME; Nashua, NH Col Club. Polit & Govt Pos: Nashua Women's Dem Chmn, 62-66, pres, 63-65; mem, Status of Women, NH, 63; NH Women's Chmn for President Johnson, 64; deleg & mem credentials comt, Dem Nat Conv, 64; deleg, NH Dem Conv, 64 & 66; mem, Hundred Dollar State Dem Club; mem, NH Dem Comt, 66-; co Dem vchmn, 68-; women's city chmn, 68-; NH State Rep, 75- Bus & Prof Pos: Guid counr, Nashua Sch Dept, 28- Publ: Polit articles in defense of Dem Party. Mem: NH Personnel & Guid Asn; New Eng Guid Asn; Bay State Beagle Club; Cath Daughters Am; Emblem Club. Honors & Awards: Proposed & raised funds for monument in memorial of John F Kennedy erected in front of Nashua City Hall; breeder & trainer of show beagles, winner many nat & int championships. Relig: Roman Catholic. Mailing Add: 12 Middle St Nashua NH 03060

WINN, JOHN T (D)
NH State Rep
Mailing Add: 12 Middle St Nashua NH 03060

WINN, LARRY, JR (R)
US Rep, Kans
b Kansas City, Mo, Aug 22, 19; s Edward Lawrence Winn & Gertrude Shepherd W; m 1942 to Joan Ruth Elliott; c Edward Lawrence, III, Robert Elliot, Douglas Shepherd, Janet Gay & Cynthia Joan. Educ: Univ Kans, BA, 41; pres, Sigma Delta Chi & Phi Kappa Psi; dir, Mem Union Bldg. Polit & Govt Pos: Past chmn, Third Cong Dist Rep Party, Kans; past mem, Kans State Rep Exec comt; US Rep, Third Dist, Kans, 67- Bus & Prof Pos: Employee, WHB Radio Sta, 2 years; employee, NAm Aviation, 2 years; pub rels dir, Am Red Cross, Kansas City, 2 years; private builder, 2 years; vpres, Winn-Rau Corp, Overland Park, 50-; mem bd dirs, Southgate State Bank, Prairie Village; mem, Kans Univ Develop Comt. Mem: Nat Asn Home Builders (nat dir); Home Builders Asn Kans (vpres); People to People; Farm Bur; Rotary. Honors & Awards: Silver Beaver Award, Boys Scouts. Relig: Christian Church. Legal Res: Overland Park KS Mailing Add: 2430 Rayburn House Off Bldg Washington DC 20515

WINN, SHERMAN S (D)
Fla State Sen
Mailing Add: 1201 NW 207th St Miami FL 33169

WINNER, THOMAS ANDREW (D)
b Fireco, WVa, Jan 20, 31; s Frank Edward & Ester Victoria Fink W; div; c Mary Ann & Marcia (Mrs Crickmer). Educ: Brevard Jr Col, AA; Concord Col, BA; WVa State Col, 74; Sigma Tau Gamma; Blue Key. Polit & Govt Pos: Exec dir, WVa Dem Party, 69-71; polit adv to Jay Rockefeller, 71-72; Dem cand for Secy State, WVa, 72; mem, Dem Charter Comn, 74- Bus & Prof Pos: Pres, Tom Winner Glass Co, 57-66; chmn bd, Pine Lodge Nursing Home, 67-72; pres, Tom Winner Sch Buses, 72- Mil Serv: Entered as Pvt, Nat Guard, 47, released as M/Sgt, 60. Mem: Glade Springs Country Club; Black Knight Country Club. Relig: Episcopal. Legal Res: 8 Glade Springs Daniels WV 25832 Mailing Add: 201 Raleigh Co Bank Bldg Beckley WV 25801

WINNICK, EDWARD BERNARD (D)
Chmn, Woodbridge Dem Town Comt, Conn
b New Haven, Conn, Mar 8, 33; s Alexander Winnick & Bertha Sosensky W; m 1959 to Mary Lou Geller; c Beth, Martha & Michael. Educ: Dartmouth Col, BA, 54; Yale Univ, LLB, 59; Pi Lambda. Polit & Govt Pos: Mem, Woodbridge Dem Town Comt, Conn, 66-, chmn, 69-; mem, Woodbridge Town Plan & Zoning Comn, 67-72, secy, 69-72. Bus & Prof Pos: Partner, Winnick, Resnik, Skolnick & Auerbach, 59- Mil Serv: Entered as Ens, Navy, 54, released as Lt(jg), after serv in 5th & 7th Fleets, USS Worcester, 54-56. Mem: New Haven Co Bar Asn; Conn State Bar Asn (state bench bar rels comt); Woodbridge Country Club (bd gov). Relig: Jewish. Mailing Add: 17 Pine Ridge Rd Woodbridge CT 06525

WINNINGHAM, LONNIE L (D)
Mem Exec Comt, Ark Dem State Comt
b Ark, July 29, 22; s Jacob B Winningham & Myrtle B Burrow W; m 1944 to Maudlene V Goad; c Ronald L & Barry L. Educ: High sch. Polit & Govt Pos: Mem exec comt, Ark Dem State Comt, 74- Mem: CofC; Ark Fair & Livestock Show (bd gov, 73-); Lawrence Co Fair Asn (bd dirs, 73-); Kiwanis Club; Lions Club. Relig: Baptist. Mailing Add: Rte 1 Black Rock AR 72415

WINOGRAD, MORLEY A (D)
Chmn, Mich Dem Party
b Detroit, Mich, Nov 12, 42; s Daniel Winograd & Lillian Walder W; m 1962 to Roberta Leib; c Lesley, Andrew & Jennifer. Educ: Univ Mich, BBA, 63 & Law Sch, 64-65; Beta Gamma Sigma; Phi Kappa Psi. Polit & Govt Pos: Chmn, Oakland Co Dem Comt, Mich, 70-73; chmn, Mich Dem Party, 73-; secy, Asn State Dem Chmn, 75- Relig: Jewish. Legal Res: 3374 Newgate Troy MI 48087 Mailing Add: 321 N Pine Lansing MI 48933

WINSHIP, GEORGE S (D)
Maine State Rep
Mailing Add: 4 Summer St Milo ME 04463

WINSTEIN, STEWART R (D)
VChmn, Ill State Dem Cent Comt
b Viola, Ill, May 18, 14; s A Winstein & Esther Meyer W; m 1960 to Dorothy Shock Adams; c Arthur. Educ: Augustana Col, AB, 35; Univ Chicago, JD, 38. Polit & Govt Pos: Finance officer, Ill, 63-70; deleg, Dem Nat Conv, 68 & 72; committeeman, 19th Cong Dist, Ill State Dem Cent Comt, 70-, vchmn, 73-; pub admnr, Rock Island Co, Ill, 74-; deleg, Dem Nat Mid-Term Conf, 74. Mem: Am, Ill State & Rock Island Co Bar Asns; Elks; Mason. Relig: Jewish. Legal Res: 3535 24th St Rock Island IL 61202 Mailing Add: PO Box 428 Rock Island IL 61201

WINTER, MADELINE FIELD (R)
Chmn, Richmond Rep Town Comt, Mass
b Lanesboro, Mass, May 25, 22; d George Allen Field (deceased) & Edith Young F; m 1947 to James Emory Winter, Jr; c Douglas Paul. Educ: Bishop Mem Training Sch for Nurses, Pittsfield Gen Hosp, 1 year; Berkshire Bus Col; Dale Carnegie Course, grad. Polit & Govt Pos: Secy, Richmond Rep Town Comt, Mass, 55-68, chmn, 68-; deleg, Mass Rep State Conv, 66; deleg, Berkshire Co Rep Asn, 67- Bus & Prof Pos: Librn & garden ed, Berkshire Eagle, Pittsfield, Mass, 67-; bd dir, Berkshire Eagle Credit Union. Mem: Nat Fedn Rep Women; Garden Writers' Asn Am; Pittsfield Gen Hosp Auxiliary; Women's Club Pittsfield. Relig: Congregational. Mailing Add: Dublin Rd Richmond MA 01254

WINTER, NADINE P (D)
b NC; d Samuel Poole & Elnora Kenion P; wid; c Alan & Reginald, Jr. Educ: Hampton Inst; Fed City Col, DC, MA. Polit & Govt Pos: Deleg, Dem Nat Conv, 64, 68 & 72; rep, First Washington, DC City Coun, 74-, chmn housing & urban develop comt. Bus & Prof Pos: Lectr & consult. Publ: Urban Homesteading Program Washington, DC. Bus & Prof Pos: Exec dir, Hospitality House, 62- Mem: Nat Bus & Prof League; CofC; civic, social & fraternal orgns. Honors & Awards: Over 50 awards & trophies for community work. Relig: Episcopal. Mailing Add: 1100 K St NE Washington DC 20002

WINTER, THOMAS DUANE (R)
VChmn, Rep State Exec Comt, WVa
b Cameron, WVa, Sept 19, 30; s Walter William Winter & Mary Efaw W; m 1950 to Mary Ann Wise; c Theodore Duane, Teresa Louise & Tonsi Ann. Educ: Huntington Sch Bus, grad, 49; WVa State Col, 61-64. Polit & Govt Pos: Pres, Kanawha Co Young Rep, WVa, 65 & 67; vchmn, Gov Inaugural Comt, 68-69 & 72-73; Third Cong Dist chmn, Young Rep of WVa, 68-70; pres, Nitro Area Rep Club, 68-71; spec asst to chmn, Rep State Exec Comt, WVa, 69-71, vchmn, 71-; pedestrian safety chmn, Gov Hwy Safety Bur, 69-; deleg, Rep Nat Conv, 72. Bus & Prof Pos: Pres, Nitro Businessmen's Asn, 55-56 & 59-60, vpres, 57, secy-treas, 58; secy & comptroller, A W Cox Dept Store Co, 64- & Coyle & Richardson, Inc, 71- Mem: Exchange Club; Charleston Symphony Orchestra; WVa CofC; Charleston Area CofC; WVa Retailers Asn. Relig: Methodist. Mailing Add: 1891 Roundhill Rd Charleston WV 25314

WINTER, WILLIAM FORREST (D)
Lt Gov, Miss
b Grenada, Miss, Feb 21, 23; s Wiliiam Aylmer Winter & Inez Parker W; m 1950 to Elise Varner; c Anne, Elise & Eleanor. Educ: Univ Miss, BA, 43, LLB, 49; Omicron Delta Kappa; Phi Delta Phi; Phi Kappa Phi; Phi Delta Theta. Polit & Govt Pos: Miss State Rep, 48-56; Miss State Tax Collector, 56-64, State Treas, Miss, 64-68, Lt Gov, 72- Bus & Prof Pos: Attorney, Watkins, Pyle, Ludlam, Winter & Stennis, Jackson, Miss, 68- Mil Serv: Entered as Pvt, Army, 43, released as Maj, 46, after serv in 86th Inf Div, Pac. Mem: Am & Miss Bar Asns; Nat Asn for Ment Health. Relig: Presbyterian. Mailing Add: 4205 Crane Blvd Jackson MS 39216

WINTER, WINT (R)
Kans State Sen
Mailing Add: First Nat Bank Bldg Ottawa KS 66067

WINTERS, JOHN WESLEY (D)
NC State Sen
b Raleigh, NC, Jan 21, 20; s Charlie Winters & Lillie Summerville W; m 1941 to Marie Montague; c Frances (Mrs Carter), John W, Jr, Michael C, Donna F, Naomi R, Rebecca J, Roland E & Seanne M. Educ: Long Island Univ; Va State Col; Omega Psi Phi. Hon Degrees: LLD, Shaw Univ. Polit & Govt Pos: Mem, Raleigh City Coun, NC, 61-67; vchmn, Wake Co Dem Exec Comt, 65-; alt deleg, Dem Nat Conv, 68, deleg, 72; NC State Senator, 14 Dist, 75- Bus & Prof Pos: Pres, John W Winters & Co, 57; pres, Madonna Acres, Inc, 59; regional vpres, Nat Bus League; mem bd mgr, Mechanics & Farmers Bank; former dir, Raleigh Merchants Bar; dir, Raleigh CofC, Wake Co Red Cross, NC Housing Corp, Raleigh Bd, Realtors & trustee, Shaw Univ, currently. Mem: Life mem NAACP; Nat Asn Home Builders

(bd dirs); Raleigh Bus & Prof League. Honors & Awards: Citizen of the Year, Omega Psi Phi, 61; Alpha Kappa Alpha Award, 66. Relig: Catholic. Mailing Add: 507 E Martin St Raleigh NC 27601

WINTERS, LEO (D)
State Treas, Okla
b Hooker, Okla, Nov 7, 22; s David Winters & Gertrude Strochin W; m to Patti Hill. Educ: Panhandle A&M Col, AB, 50; Univ Okla, LLB, 57. Polit & Govt Pos: Secy, State Elec Bd, Okla, 55-62; Lt Gov, Okla, 63-67, State Treas, 67- Bus & Prof Pos: Pres, Alaskan Livestock Co, Kodiak, Alaska, 56-; mem law firm, Grove, Winters & Cloud, 60-67. Mil Serv: Air Force, pilot. Mem: Am Quarter Horse Asn; Mason (32 degree). Mailing Add: Box 53411 Oklahoma City OK 73105

WINTERS, MARY LOU (D)
Dem Nat Committeewoman, La
b Monroe, La, Feb 22, 35; s Tola Oren Trawick & Mary Hamilton T; m 1953 to Harry Hall Winters, III, MD; c Harry Hall, IV, Martha Roan, Mary Catherine, Hamilton Stephens & twins Caroline & Amanda. Educ: La State Univ, BS, 56 & ME, 57; Phi Alpha Theta; Chi Omega. Polit & Govt Pos: Mem, Gov John McKeithen's Inaugural Comt, La, 64 & 68; deleg, Dem Nat Conv, 64, 68 & 72; chmn, La Juvenile Probation & Parole Coun, 65-; mem, La State Welfare Bd, 66-71; chmn for La & mem President's Adv Coun, White House Conf on Children & Youth, 70; mem, La State Dem Cent Comt, 71-; Dem Nat Committeewoman, La, 72- Mem: DAR; PTA; Am Cancer Soc; Caldwell Resource Develop Asn; Caldwell Resource Develop Asn (dir, 64-). Relig: Methodist. Mailing Add: PO Box 645 Columbia LA 71418

WIRT, LAURA A (R)
Mem, Rep State Cent Comt Calif
b Blackwell, Okla, Nov 14, 23; d Sherman A Pendland & Susan I Ferguson P; m 1942 to Robert E Wirt; c Robert E, Jr, Kristine (Mrs Koenig), Lisa (Mrs Gale) & Richard Stewart. Educ: Mills Col, 41-42. Polit & Govt Pos: Mem, Alameda Co Rep Cent Comt, 71-74; mem, Napa State Hosp Adv Bd for Mentally Distressed, 72-; deleg, Rep Nat Conv, 72; mem, Rep State Cent Comt Calif, 73-, mem exec bd, 75; mem, Citizens Adv Coun on Elec Reform, 75. Mem: Calif Fedn Rep Women (pres); Toastmistress Int (coun chmn, formerly, pres, currently). Mailing Add: 1749 Kudu Court Hayward CA 94541

WIRTH, HELEN IRMIGER (D)
Recording Secy, 14th Cong Dist Dem Off Orgn, Mich
b Detroit, Mich, May 17, 17; d Alphonse L Irmiger & Mary Elizabeth Niederer I; m 1934 to Joseph V Wirth, Jr; c Joseph C, Robert A & Thomas C. Educ: Wayne State Univ, 1 year; Wayne Co Community Col, currently. Polit & Govt Pos: Mem exec bd, 14th Cong Dist Dem Off Orgn, Mich, 48-, recording secy, currently; mem, Mich State Dem Cent Comt, 56-62; deleg, Dem Nat Conv, 56 & 64; chmn, Grosse Pointe Woods Bd of Canvassers, 65-; app Wayne Co chmn, Mich Women for Hwy Safety, 75- Bus & Prof Pos: Chmn credit comt, C J Fed Credit Union, 47-; bookkeeper & secy, Local 7, UAW, currently, recording secy, COPE, 62-67; trustee, Office & Prof Employees Indust Union Local 42, 73-; exec bd mem & chmn educ comt, McFarland Chap, Mich Credit League Credit Unions, 74- Mem: Int Inst of Detroit; Nat Conf Christians & Jews (Detroit Round Table); Nat Asn Accts (Oakland Co Chap); Nat Arthritis Asn; League of Women Voters. Honors & Awards: Amity Scholarship in human rels, Univ Mich, from Nat Conf Christians & Jews, 55; named Woman of the Year, Detroit Bus & Prof Women, 70. Relig: Catholic. Mailing Add: 1237 Hampton Rd Grosse Pointe MI 48236

WIRTH, TIMOTHY E (D)
US Rep, Colo
b Santa Fe, NMex, Sept 22, 39; m 1966 to Wren Winslow; c Christopher & Kelsey. Educ: Harvard Col, AB, 61; Harvard grad Sch Educ, MEd, 64; Stanford Univ, Ford Found fel & PhD(educ), 73. Polit & Govt Pos: White House Fel, 67-68; spec asst to Secy, John Gardner, Dept Health, Educ & Welfare, 68, dep asst secy of educ, 69-70; mem, Gov Task Force on Return Vietnam Vet; US Rep, Colo, 75- Mil Serv: Army Res, 61-67. Mem: Denver Coun Foreign Rels (exec comt); Denver Planned Parenthood (bd mem); Denver Head Start (bd mem). Legal Res: 3205 W 21st Ave Denver CO 80211 Mailing Add: US House of Rep Washington DC 20515

WIRZ, KAYE COLYER (D)
b Frederick, Okla, Sept 30, 46; d Glen G Colyer & Vera E Sellars C; m 1972 to Adolph F Wirz, Jr. Educ: Okla Christian Col; Midwestern Univ, BBA magna cum laude, 68; Epsilon Sigma Alpha. Polit & Govt Pos: Tillman Co chmn, Dem for Gov Hall, 70; deleg, Dem Nat Conv, 72. Bus & Prof Pos: Acct, Lloyd K Bendure & Co, CPA, 68-69; controller, Katy Kay Meat Packers, Lawton, Okla, 69-70; CPA, 70- Mem: Am Inst CPA; Okla Soc CPA; Tex Bd Pub Acct; Okla Bd Pub Acct (by-laws comt, 71-72); CofC. Mailing Add: Box F Grandfield OK 73546

WISDOM, BILLIE JOE (D)
Kans State Rep
Mailing Add: 100 Kindleberger Rd Kansas City KS 66106

WISE, CARL FRANCIS (R)
Chmn, Stark Co Rep Party, Ohio
b Niles, Ohio, Oct 23, 00; s Sherman G Wise & Hannah Meredith W; m 1924 to Ruth B Hammen; c Carl F, Jr & Dale E. Educ: E Ohio Bus Col, 20. Polit & Govt Pos: Councilman, Canton, Ohio, 36-37, Mayor, 52-58; mem, City Civil Serv Comn, 38-45; chmn, Stark Co Rep Party, 60-; deleg, Rep Nat Conv, 64. Bus & Prof Pos: Pres, Canton Real Estate Bd, 31, 42 & 43; dir, Peoples Fed Savings & Loan Asn, 37-66. Mem: CofC; YMCA; Al Koran Shrine (pres, 48); Elks; Mason. Relig: Christian Church. Legal Res: 1308 Buena Vista Blvd NE Canton OH 44714 Mailing Add: 327 Second St SW Canton OH 44702

WISE, DAVID WILLIAM (D)
b Danville, Ill, Feb 28, 53; s Henry Seiler Wise & G Louise Hawkins W; single. Educ: Univ Dayton, 71- Polit & Govt Pos: Alt deleg, Dem Nat Conv, 72. Relig: Roman Catholic. Mailing Add: 507 Chester Ave Danville IL 61832

WISE, THOMAS DEWEY (D)
SC State Sen
b Orangeburg, SC, Aug 30, 39; s Dewey Peele Wise & Gussie Earley W; m 1965 to Yancey Kemp; c Timothy Thornton & David Overton. Educ: Univ SC, AB, 61, LLB, 64; George Washington Univ, LLM, 68; pres & secy, Phi Delta Phi; Clairosophic Lit Soc. Polit & Govt Pos: Asst co attorney, Charleston Co, SC, 69-72; SC State Sen, Dist 16, Charleston & Georgetown Co, 72- Bus & Prof Pos: Partner, Way, Burkett & Wise, Law Firm, 69- Mil Serv: Entered as 1st Lt, Army, 64, released as Capt, 68, after serv in 101st Airborne Div, Vietnam, 66-67; Bronze Star Medal; Army Commendation Medal; Nat Defense Medal. Publ: The sudden emergency doctrine in South Carolina, SC Law Rev, Vol 20, No 3. Mem: Charleston Co Bar Asn (exec comt); SC & Am Bar Asns; Am Trial Lawyers Asn; Hibernian Soc. Mailing Add: PO Box 38 Charleston SC 29402

WISE, WES (INDEPENDENT)
Mayor, Dallas, Tex
b Shreveport, La, Nov 25, 28; s George Arthur Wise & Myrtle Hamilton W; m to Sally Browning; c Westley Arthur, Jr; Wynford Browning & Wendy Ellen. Educ: Northeast La Univ, 46. Polit & Govt Pos: City councilman, Dallas, Tex, 68-70, mayor, 70- Mil Serv: Entered as Pvt, Army, 51, released as Pfc, 53. Mem: Press Club Dallas; Sigma Delta Chi. Relig: Protestant. Mailing Add: 10026 Lakedale Dr Dallas TX 75218

WISEMAN, BOB (D)
Miss State Rep
Mailing Add: Island Dr Kosciusko MS 39030

WISEMAN, WILLIAM JOHNSTON, JR (R)
Okla State Rep
b Philadelphia, Pa, Aug 9, 44; s William J Wiseman, Sr & Mavis Laybourn W; m 1970 to Jane Pettis. Educ: Davidson Col, BA, 66; Univ Tulsa, MA, 68; Sigma Alpha Epsilon. Polit & Govt Pos: Trustee, Tulsa River Parks Authority, City & Co, Tulsa, Okla, 74-; Okla State Rep, Dist 69, 74- Bus & Prof Pos: Mkt dir, Standard Indust, Tulsa, Okla, 70- Relig: Presbyterian. Legal Res: 2528 E 57th St Tulsa OK 74105 Mailing Add: 5800 S Lewis Ave Tulsa OK 74105

WISER, C LAWRENCE (D)
Md State Sen
b Berwyn Heights, Md, Aug 3, 30; s Floyd J Wiser & Alice E W; m 1952 to Mary E Hodge; c Robert, Glenn, Caroline & Susan. Educ: Univ Md, BS Econ, 52; George Washington Univ, LLB, 58, LLM, 60; Omicron Delta Kappa; Delta Theta Phi. Polit & Govt Pos: Md State Deleg, formerly; Md State Sen, 75- Bus & Prof Pos: Vpres & gen counsel, Hotel Investors. Mil Serv: Entered as 2nd Lt, Air Force, 52, released as 1st Lt, 54. Mem: Montgomery Co Coun PTA (deleg); Allied Civic Group (deleg); Bethesda-Chevy Chase CofC (bd dirs); Stoneybrook Civic Asn (pres). Relig: Baptist. Mailing Add: 12702 Littleton St Silver Spring MD 20906

WISTED, BEATRICE ELEANOR (DFL)
Treas, Seventh Dist Dem-Farmer-Labor Party, Minn
b Barnesville, Minn, Oct 29, 23; d Laures Olson & Anna Narum O; m 1946 to Morell Ardell Wisted; c Bruce, Craig, Janice & Ronald. Educ: Detroit Lakes Bus Col. Polit & Govt Pos: Chmn, Becker Co Dem-Farmer-Labor Party, Minn, 48-62; treas, Seventh Dist Dem-Farmer-Labor Party, 65-; worked on many elec campaigns; sub-chmn, Goy Local Comt for Minority Groups. Bus & Prof Pos: Teacher organ & piano & orchestra leader, 42-; bus agt, Musicians Local 434, 42-55; free lance court reporter, 46-; secy to attorney & state parole agt; pvt secy, Thornton Davis, geologist, summers; reporter, Upper Midwest Research & Develop Comn, Hill Found, 63-64; official reporter, Minn State Fire Dept Asn. Publ: Music column, 5 years. Mem: Detroit Lakes Bus & Prof Women's Clubs; Detroit Lakes Concert Asn; Women's Div, Detroit Lakes CofC; Detroit Lakes Eagles Auxiliary; Detroit Lakes Centennial Comt (activities chmn). Relig: Lutheran; chapel organist. Mailing Add: 1302 Roosevelt Ave S Detroit Lakes MN 56501

WISWELL, MARGUERITE H (R)
NH State Rep
Mailing Add: Box 438 Colebrook NH 03576

WITCHER, ROGER KENNETH (R)
b Red Boiling Springs, Tenn, May 8, 20; s Ponie Oscar Witcher & Lena Russell W; m 1944 to Maitred Yates Neel; c Sue Lynne, Deborah Neel, Russell Yates, Sandra Lucile & Roger Kenneth, Jr. Educ: Memphis State Univ, BS, 48; Chi Beta Phi. Polit & Govt Pos: Chmn, Macon Co Bd Educ, Tenn, 50-; deleg, Rep Nat Conv, 60 & 68, alt deleg, 64 & 72; chmn, Macon Co Rep Party, formerly; Tenn State Rep, 65-68; mem, Tenn State Rep Exec Comt, formerly. Bus & Prof Pos: Owner, Kenneth Witcher Lumber Co. Mil Serv: Entered as Hosp Corpsman 2/C, Navy, 42, released as PhM 2/C, 45. Mem: Am Legion; Farm Bur; Lions. Relig: Baptist. Mailing Add: Red Boiling Springs TN 37150

WITHERS, DEDRICK (D)
Tenn State Rep
Mailing Add: 4612 White Fox Memphis TN 38109

WITHERSPOON, DOROTHY KARPEL (D)
Colo State Rep
b Joliet, Ill, Feb 19, 36; d John Karpel & Margaret Kuban K; m 1956 to Leon Clifford Witherspoon; c Jay Robert, Leanne M, Paul Jon & Todd M. Educ: Joliet Twp High Sch, Ill, 4 years. Polit & Govt Pos: Dist capt, Jefferson Co Dem Party, Colo, currently; co-chmn, Jefferson Co Robert F Kennedy Presidential Campaign, 68; mem, Colo Dem State Cent Comt, 69-; deleg, Dem Nat Conv, 72; Consumer Protection League; Asn Children Learning Disabilities; Colo Asn Retarded Children. Colo State Rep, 75- Mem: Colo Young Dem; Denver Metro Fair Housing. Relig: Catholic. Mailing Add: 12281 W Kentucky Dr Denver CO 80228

WITHINGTON, RICHARD WHITTIER, SR (R)
NH State Rep
b Boston, Mass, Mar 31, 18; s Frank C Withington & Edith Nelson W; m to Mary McClure; c Richard W, Jr, Robert N, Nancy (Mrs Workman) & Janet (Mrs Guinn). Educ: Boston Pub Schs, Mass; Roxbury Latin Sch, 3 years; Kimball Union Acad, grad, 37; Univ NH, 41. Polit & Govt Pos: NH State Rep, 71-; elected to various local pos. Bus & Prof Pos: Pres & treas, Richard W Withington, Inc, 49-; vpres & treas, Richard W Withington Develop Corp, 63-; owner & develop of real estate. Mil Serv: Entered Army, 42, released as Sgt, 46, after serv in Mil Police, Am Theatre, 44-46. Relig: United Church of Christ; treas, 10 years; deacon, currently. Mailing Add: Hillsboro NH 03244

WITHROW, MRS W W (JACKIE) (D)
WVa State Deleg
b Mabscott, WVa; d Charles Frank Neubert & Willie Lee Flanagan N; m 1943 to William W Withrow. Educ: Beckley Pub Schs. Polit & Govt Pos: WVa State Deleg, 60-, chmn, Comt Health & Welfare, WVa House Deleg, 59th, 60th & 61st Legis, mem, Comts Agr & Natural Resources & Finance; mem, Gov Comn Handicapped, Gov Adv Comn Ment Health & Gov Comn Status of Women; pres, Raleigh Co Young Dem Club, formerly; mem adv comt, Beckley Rehabilitation Off. Bus & Prof Pos: Real estate saleswoman. Mem: Bus & Prof Woman's Club of Beckley; WVa Ment Health Asn (bd dirs); Eastern Star; VFW Ladies Auxiliary; Community Ment Health Ctrs Construction Prog. Honors & Awards: Cert Commendation, WVa Asn Ment Health; Third Dist WVa State Dem Woman Year, 63. Relig: Baptist; Sunday sch teacher, Friendship Baptist Church; sponsor, BYF. Mailing Add: 1301 Maxwell Hill Rd Beckley WV 25801

WITKOWSKI, LEO VICTOR (D)
Chmn, Deaf Smith Co Dem Party, Tex
b David City, Nebr, Aug 23, 13; s Frank James Witkowski & Anna Zeleny W; m 1940 to Louise Christine Weil; c Rita Sue (Mrs Huckert), Lou Ann, Gerald & Jane Latrice. Educ: Tex A&M Univ, BS. Polit & Govt Pos: Chmn, Deaf Smith Co Dem Party, Tex, 62- Bus & Prof Pos: Mem adv bd, Producers Grain Corp, 56-60 & 61-67; mem, 17 Man Agr Steering Comt, Tex A&M Univ, 67. Mem: Tex Asn Wheat Growers; Tex Farmers Union; Amarillo Diocesan Coun of Cath Men; CofC; KofC. Relig: Catholic. Mailing Add: 215 N Texas Ave Hereford TX 79045

WITMAN, WILLIAM, II
b Harrisburg, Pa, Jan 31, 14; s Horace Montgomery Witman & Clara Wallower W; m 1947 to Melpomene Maria Fafalios. Educ: Yale Univ, BA, 35. Polit & Govt Pos: Asst trade comnr, Caracas, 35-39; vconsul & third secy, Beirut, 39-44; acting commercial attache & third secy, Ankara, 44-45; asst commercial attache, second secy & consul, Am Embassy, Athens, 45-48; consul, Bombay, 48-49; officer-in-chg, India-Nepal-Ceylon Affairs, Dept of State, 49-52; counr of legation & consul gen, Am Legation, Tangier, 52-55; dep dir, Off of SAsian Affairs, 55-56; dep dir, Off of NAfrican Affairs, 57; first secy, Am Embassy, Paris, 57-60; dir, Off of NAfrican Affairs, Dept of State, 60-62; foreign serv officer, Class One, 63; Sr Seminar in Foreign Policy, 63-64; US Ambassador to Repub of Togo, 64-67; mem, Policy Planning Coun, 67-69; dir, Inter-African Affairs, 69-71; spec asst to Asst Secy for African Affairs, 71-74; mem, US Deleg, UN Gen Assembly, 52, 65 & 66 & spec emergency session, 67, SEATO Ministerial Meeting, Karachi, 57, Second Law of the Sea Conf, Geneva, 60 & UN Econ Comt for Africa Conf, Addis Ababa, 61; chief, US Deleg, Tripartite Consultations on Horn of Africa, Rome, 62; personal rep of President with rank of Spec Ambassador to Algerian Independence Ceremonies, 62; consult, Dept of State, 74- Mem: Foreign Serv Asn, Yale Club, DC. Honors & Awards: Recipient, Superior Serv Award, Dept of State, 63. Relig: Presbyterian. Mailing Add: 2500 25th St N Arlington VA 22207

WITT, CARTER H (D)
Mem, Giles Co Dem Comt, Tenn
b Pulaski, Tenn, Oct 10, 37; s Carter H Witt & Mary Abernathy W; m to Judith Lanier; c Carter H, V & George Lanier. Educ: Vanderbilt Univ, BA, 60; Mid Tenn State Univ, 65- Polit & Govt Pos: Mem, Giles Co Dem Comt, Tenn, 66-; Tenn State Rep, 69-72. Mil Serv: 2nd Lt, Army Field Artil, 61, serv in 38th Artil; Res, 61-, Capt. Mem: Giles Co Educ Asn (pres); Tenn Educ Asn; U G F Giles Co (dir); Giles Co Ment Health Ctr (dir); Civitan. Relig: Methodist. Mailing Add: Rte 1 Lynnville TN 38472

WITTEMAN, ORVILLE P (D)
b Hitchcock, SDak, 1892; married; c three. Educ: NDak State Univ, Agr & Appl Sci. Polit & Govt Pos: NDak State Rep, 57-59; NDak State Sen, 61-66; chmn, Renville Co Dem Party, formerly. Bus & Prof Pos: Farmer. Mem: Am Legion; Mason. Relig: Lutheran. Mailing Add: Mohall ND 58761

WITTENBERG, ALBERT L (D)
Nev State Assemblyman
Mailing Add: 2630 Scholl Dr Reno NV 89503

WITTENMEYER, CHARLES E (R)
Rep Nat Committeeman, Iowa
b Centerville, Iowa, Sept 3, 03; s Thomas William Wittenmeyer & Maggie E Lantz W; m 1931 to Dorothy P Proctor; c Sheila (Mrs F D Goar). Educ: Drake Univ, JD, 28; Phi Alpha Delta; Phi Gamma Lambda; Theta Nu Epsilon; Helmet & Spurs. Polit & Govt Pos: Chmn, Scott Co Young Rep, Iowa, 34-36; chmn, Second Dist Young Rep, 36-38; chmn, Scott Co Rep Cent Comt, 38-56; city attorney, Davenport, 44-54; chmn, Rep City Cent Comt, 44-57; deleg, Rep Nat Conv, 44 & 56-72, chmn comt on credentials, 64 & rules & order of bus comt, 68; First Dist chmn, Iowa Rep Cent Comt, 52-56; Rep Nat Committeeman, Iowa, 56-, mem exec comt, Rep Nat Comt, 60-64 & task force on functions of fed, state & local govt. Bus & Prof Pos: Dir, First Nat Bank of Davenport; trustee, Fejervary Home, Davenport, Iowa; lawyer. Mem: Scott Co & Am Bar Asns; Acad Polit Sci; Izaak Walton League of Am; Mason (32 degree). Relig: Methodist. Legal Res: 301 Forest Rd Davenport IA 52803 Mailing Add: 826 Davenport Bank Bldg Davenport IA 52801

WITWER, SAMUEL WEILER (R)
Mem, Rep Nat Finance Comt
b Pueblo, Colo, July 1, 08; s Samuel Weiler Witwer & Lulu Richmond W; m 1937 to Ethyl L Wilkins; c Samuel Weiler, III, Esq, Michael Wilkins, MD, Carole Ann (Mrs Peter C Dalton) & David R. Educ: Dickinson Col, PhB, 30; Harvard Univ, LLB, 33; Omicron Delta Kappa; Sigma Chi. Hon Degrees: LLD, Simpson Col, 55, Dickinson Col, 70 & Univ Ill, 71; JDS, Lake Forest Col, 71; LHD, DePaul Univ, 71. Polit & Govt Pos: Mem, Ill Comt Const Rev, 50-55; state chmn, Ill Citizens for Eisenhower-Nixon, 56; Ill chmn of USO, 58-63; Rep cand for US Sen, Ill, 60; mem, Rep Nat Finance Comt, 68-; vpres, United Rep Fund of Ill, 68-; pres, Sixth Ill Const Conv, 69-70. Bus & Prof Pos: Lawyer, Witwer, Moran & Burlage, 33- Mem: Am, Ill & Chicago Bar Asns; Chicago Coun Foreign Rels; Chicago Urban League (dir). Honors & Awards: Chicagoan of the Year, Chicago Jaycees, 70; Man of the Year, Ill News-broadcasters Asn & Chicago Press Club, 70; Ill State Bar Asn Award of Merit, 71; First Ill Distinguished Serv Medal; Designated Laureate, Lincoln Acad of Ill, Order of Lincoln Medal, 75. Relig: Methodist; dir, Methodist Corp, 60-64; mem, Judicial Coun, 64-72. Mailing Add: 111 Abingdon Ave Kenilworth IL 60043

WOELFEL, ARLENE MARIE (D)
b Stockbridge, Wis, Apr 4, 40; d Henry Frank Woelfel & Marie T Hemauer W; single. Educ: Alverno Col, BA, 61; DePaul Univ, MS, 69. Polit & Govt Pos: Alt deleg, Dem Nat Conv, 72. Bus & Prof Pos: Sci teacher, Alvernia High Sch, Chicago, Ill, 61-68; grad teaching asst, DePaul Univ, 68-69; sci teacher, CADET Sch, Holly Springs, Miss, 69- Mem: Nat & Miss Sci Teachers Asns; Am Asn Univ Women; Common Cause; NAACP. Honors & Awards: Human Rels Award, Human Rels Coun of Gtr Chicago, 65. Relig: Catholic. Mailing Add: 211 Salem Ave Holly Springs MS 38635

WOJAHN, LORRAINE (D)
Wash State Rep
Mailing Add: 3592 E Kay St Tacoma WA 98404

WOJAK, STEPHEN R (D)
Pa State Rep
Mailing Add: Capitol Bldg Harrisburg PA 17120

WOJTANOWSKI, DENNIS LEE (D)
Ohio State Rep
b Iselin, NJ, Feb 27, 50; s Joseph Frank Wojtanowski, Sr & Lucille Cease W; m 1972 to Deborah Ann Rice. Educ: Ohio State Univ, BA Polit Sci, 71; dir, Ohio State Univ Legis Task Force; Freshman Sen. Polit & Govt Pos: Ohio State Rep, 75- Mem: Jaycees; West Lake Co Dem Club; Common Cause; Ohio State Univ Alumni Asn. Relig: Roman Catholic. Legal Res: 27645 Bishop Park Dr Willoughby Hills OH 44072 Mailing Add: Ohio House of Reps Columbus OH 43215

WOJTKOWSKI, THOMAS CASMERE (D)
Chmn, Berkshire Co Dem Party, Mass
b Pittsfield, Mass, Sept 18, 26; s Frank Wojtkowski & Anna Yuhaski W; m 1962 to Anne Everest; c Thomas C, Jr & Marcella. Educ: Champlain Col, AA, 49; George Washington Univ, BS, 52; Portia Law Sch, LLB; Nat Jour Fraternity. Polit & Govt Pos: Mem, Berkshire Dist, Mass State Dem Comt; Mass State Rep, 57-72, chmn comt on educ, Mass House of Rep, 57-59, comt on agr, 57-60 & comt on judiciary, 60-64; chmn, Berkshire Co Dem Party, currently. Mil Serv: Entered as A/S, Navy, 44, released as Pharmacist's Mate 3/C, 46, after serv in Asiatic Pac, Am & Japanese Occupations; Asiatic Pac Campaign Ribbon. Mem: Mass & Berkshire Bar Asns; Polish Nat Alliance; Am Legion; VFW. Relig: Roman Catholic. Mailing Add: 85 Ridge Ave Pittsfield MA 02101

WOLBER, ARTHUR ROY (R)
Chmn, Blanco Co Rep Party, Tex
b Greentree, Pa, July 6, 16; s Henry F Wolber & Wilhelmina Braun W; m 1947 to Ruby Esther Carlson; c Nelda (Mrs Di Rezza), Dorothy (Mrs Schneider), Margaret (Mrs Kieke), Theodore & Esther. Educ: Capital Univ, BA, 37; Evangel Lutheran Theol Sem, 37-40. Polit & Govt Pos: Chmn, Blanco Co Rep Party, Tex, 74- Bus & Prof Pos: Pastor, St Paul Lutheran Church, Rice Lake, Wis, 40-43, Burton, Tex, 47-56 & Crawford, Tex, 57-65; pastor, Dr Martin Luther Lutheran Church, Oconomowoc, Wis, 43-45, Alvin Lutheran Church, Alvin, Tex, 45-47 & Trinity Lutheran Church, Blanco, Tex, 65- Mem: Blanco CofC; Blanco Co Farm Bur; Capco AAA. Relig: Lutheran. Mailing Add: Box 467 Blanco TX 78606

WOLD, CAROL ANNE (D)
b Minneapolis, Minn, Nov 26, 49; d Melvin Theodore Wold & Mary Dalton W; single. Educ: Univ Minn, Minneapolis, BS, 71. Polit & Govt Pos: Precinct chmn, Ward 10, Precinct 11, Minneapolis, Minn, 72-; deleg, Minn Dem-Farmer-Labor State Conv, 72 & 74; alt, Minn State Dem-Farmer-Labor Cent Comt, 74 & 75; coordr, State Dem Pro-Life Caucus, 74 & 75; deleg, Dem Nat Mid-Term Conf, 74. Bus & Prof Pos: Mem staff, Minn State Sen, St Paul, Minn, 73-74; admin asst to Majority Leader Minneapolis City Coun, 75- Mem: Minn Citizens Concerned for Life (mem bd dir, 74-); Joint Relig Legis Comt. Relig: Catholic. Mailing Add: 3808 Garfield Ave S Minneapolis MN 55409

WOLD, JOHN S (R)
b East Orange, NJ, Aug 31, 16; s Dr Peter Irving Wold & Mary Helff W; m 1946 to Jane Adele Pearson; c Peter Irving, II, Priscilla Adele & John Pearson. Educ: St Andrews Univ, Scotland; Union Col, AB, 38; Cornell Univ, MS, 39; Sigma Xi; Alpha Delta Phi. Polit & Govt Pos: Wyo State Rep, 57-59; chmn, Wyo Rep State Comt, 60-64; chmn, Western States Rep State Chmn Asn; mem, Rep Nat Comt, 60-64, mem exec comt, 62-64; Rep nominee, US Senate, Wyo, 64 & 70; US Rep, 69-71; Wyo Rep State Finance Chmn, 71-73. Bus & Prof Pos: Consulting physicist, Bur Ord, Dept of the Navy, 41-42; dir, Fedn Rocky Mountain States; vpres, Rocky Mountain Oil & Gas Asn; geologist energy mineral exploration firm, Wold Nuclear Co & Wold Mineral Explor Co, Casper, Wyo. Mil Serv: Entered as Ens, Navy, 42, released as Lt(sg), 46, after serv in Bur of Ord, Com Serv Pac III, gunnery & exec officer, destroyer escort duty, Atlantic & Pac. Publ: Various articles on oil, gas, coal, geology in nat publ. Mem: Am Asn Petroleum Geologists; Wyo Geol Asn; Houston Geol Soc; Am Asn Advan Sci; Geol Soc Am. Relig: Episcopal. Legal Res: 1231 W 30th St Casper WY 82601 Mailing Add: Box 114 Casper WY 82601

WOLD, PETER BERTRAM, JR (R)
Mem, NDak Rep State Exec Comt
b Hillsboro, NDak, Nov 19, 26; s Peter Bertram Wold & Marie Gadberry W; m 1956 to Anne Markham; c Mary Kate, Peter Benson, Jeffrey, Nancy & Leif. Educ: State Sch Forestry, Bottineau, NDak, AS, 48; NDak State Univ, BS, 50; Univ NDak, MS, 56. Polit & Govt Pos: Finance chmn, Sixth Dist Rep Party, NDak, 56-64, dist chmn, formerly; mem, NDak Rep State Exec Comt, 64-; chmn, NDak Rep Platform Comt, 68; deleg chmn, NDak Deleg & mem platform comt, Rep Nat Conv, 68; chmn, NDak Rep State Research Comt, 68-; chmn, Bottineau Co Rep Party, formerly. Mil Serv: Entered as Seaman, Navy, 43, released as Motor Machinist's Mate 3/C, 46, after serv in Naval Amphibious Units, SPac Theatre, 44-46; 1st Lt, Army Res, 54- Mem: Nat Soc Prof Engrs; Consulting Engrs Coun of the US; Mason; Nat CofC; Lions Int. Relig: Methodist. Mailing Add: 509 Nichol St Bottineau ND 58318

WOLD, THOMAS CLIFFORD (R)
Mem Exec Comt, NDak State Rep Party
b Rugby, NDak, June 24, 37; s Omar Clifford Wold & Gladys Antony W; m 1959 to Patricia Rae Levasseur; c Tracey Jean, Jennifer Jo & Kelly Ann. Educ: Univ NDak, PhB, 60, LLB, 62; Blue Key; Sigma Chi. Polit & Govt Pos: Chmn, Cass Co Young Rep, NDak, 63-65, mem exec comt, 63-; vchmn, NDak Young Rep, 66, state chmn, 67; campaign chmn, 21st Dist Rep Party, 66, finance chmn, 67-68, chmn, 68-; mem exec comt, NDak State Rep Party, 68-; mem, Fargo City Airport Authority, 69; chmn, Cass Co Rep Party, NDak, 70-72. Bus & Prof Pos:

Partner, Law Firm, Pancratz, Wold & Johnson, 64- Mem: Am Bar Asn; Elks; Kiwanis; Jr Achievement; Fargo-Moorhead Area Found. Honors & Awards: NDak Jaycees Govt Affairs Award, 65. Relig: Catholic. Mailing Add: 18 Briarwood Pl Fargo ND 58102

WOLF, CHARLES WILLIAM (D)
Chmn, White Co Dem Party, Ind
b Chalmers, Ind, Feb 1, 24; s Adlai Walden Wolf & Mary Jane Wood W; m 1945 to Kathleen Louise Munsterman; c Marcia D & Mark Arnold. Educ: Reynolds High Sch, 30-42. Polit & Govt Pos: City councilman, Reynolds, Ind, 47-50; Honey Creek Twp trustee, Reynolds, Ind, 50-58; precinct committeeman, White Co Dem Cent Comt, 56-70; chmn, White Co Dem Party, 63- Bus & Prof Pos: Salesman, Ind Hicks Gas, Monticello, Ind, 54-57; sales mgr, R E Pearson Sales Inc, Delphi, 57- Mem: Moose; Fraternal Order of Police. Relig: Lutheran. Mailing Add: Box 121 RR 1 Reynolds IN 47980

WOLF, FRANK C (R)
Mem, Ill Dem State Cent Comt
b Chicago, Ill; m Amelia W. Educ: Northwestern Univ; YMCA Bus Col. Polit & Govt Pos: Precinct capt & orgn secy, 23rd Ward Regular Dem Orgn, 20 years; former chief bailiff, Munic Court of Chicago; former admin secy, City of Chicago Treas, Bd Inspectors, City of Chicago & House of Correction Supts, 33-49; alt deleg, Dem Nat Conv, 68; Ill State Rep, formerly; mem, Ill Dem State Cent Comt, currently. Bus & Prof Pos: Admin asst, Cook Co Recorder of Deeds, Ill. Mailing Add: 4046 W 26th St Chicago IL 60623

WOLF, KATIE LOUISE (D)
Dem Nat Committeewoman, Ind
b Wolcott, Ind, July 9, 25; d John H Munsterman & Helen Brtulag M; m 1945 to Charles W Wolf; c Mark & Marcia. Educ: Ind Bus Col, 43-44. Polit & Govt Pos: Vchmn, White Co Dem Party, Ind, 60-64; vchmn, Second Cong Dist Dem Party, 64-68, chmn, currently; clerk, White Co Circuit Court, 68-; Dem Nat Committeewoman, Ind, 68-; deleg, Dem Nat Conv, 72; deleg, Dem Nat Mid-Term Conf, 74. Bus & Prof Pos: Co registr officer, White Co, Ind, 60; mgr, White Co License Br, 60-68. Mem: Bus & Prof Women's Club; Ind State Ment Health Asn; White Co Ment Health Asn (legis chmn); Ind Asn for Retarded Children (membership chmn); Kappa Kappa Sigma. Relig: Lutheran. Mailing Add: Box 121 RR 3 Reynolds IN 47980

WOLF, LOIS RUTH (D)
Mem, Calif Dem State Cent Comt
b Glen Flora, Wharton, Tex, Sept 4, 97; d Louie L Benthall & Mattie M Zernial B; m 1915 to Leon Aaron Wolf, wid; c Maxine Lois (Mrs Sam Brownstein). Educ: Texas City, Tex High Sch, 13-15. Polit & Govt Pos: Chmn ways & means comt, San Joaquin Co Dem Women's Club, 58-75, registr, 70; mem, 36th Assembly Dist Get Out the Vote Campaign, 14th Cong Dist Cand, 58-69; mem, Sixth Sen Dist & Seventh Assembly Dist Dem Party, 60-69; mem, Calif State Dem Cent Comt, 60-, chmn fair booth, 60-73, mem women's div, 67-69, mem state women's div north, currently, app to Calif State Rep Cent Comt, 14th Cong Dist, 75-; mem finance comt, San Joaquin Co Dem Cent Comt, 65-, mem ways & means comt, 68-71, regist chmn, 71-72, dep registr, 71-; Dem precinct chmn, French Camp & Lathrop, Calif, 69; chmn, San Joaquin Co Dem Party Hq, 70 & 72-73; mem, 13th Sen Dist Get out the Vote, 75; co chmn, Hq Get out the Vote, 74- Mem: Am Bus Women's Asn (employ, housing & transportation comt, 70-71); life mem Hadassah (ways & means comt, Stockton Chap, 40-75): Dem Women's Club. Honors & Awards: Recipient of Woman of the Year Serv Award, Hadassah, 64; in recognition of dedication & loyalty to Dem party, Dem Women's Club declared Feb 15, 1968 to be Lois Wolf Day; completed registr of over 10,000 voters as regist chmn of San Joaquin Co Dem Cent Comt, 71-75. Relig: Christian. Mailing Add: 2144 W Raymond Ave Stockton CA 95203

WOLF, SAM W (D)
Secy-Treas, Madison Co Dem Cent Comt, Ill
b Venice, Ill, Jan 4, 19; s Earl C Wolf & Elizabeth Devany W; m 1946 to Mae Frank; c David Bruce & Larry Earl. Educ: Northwestern Univ, Chicago; Wash Univ. Polit & Govt Pos: Secy-treas, Madison Co Dem Cent Comt, Ill, 70- Bus & Prof Pos: Pres, Granite City Real Estate Bd, Granite City, Ill, 56-60. Mil Serv: Entered as Pvt, Army, 40, released as Chief Warrant Off, 45, after serv in 550th FA, Alaska & ETO; Unit Battle Citations; Theatre Operations Ribbons. Mem: Nat & Ill Asns Realtors; Tri City CofC (dir, 74-); Soc Real Estate Appraisers; Kiwanis. Relig: Catholic. Mailing Add: 21 Bermuda Lane Granite City IL 62040

WOLF, THERESA CATHERINE (D)
Secy, Lee Co Dem Cent Comt, Ill
b Dixon, Ill, Jan 2, 38; d Ralph George Wolf & State Brimblecom W; m 1956 to Harold Joseph Wolf; c Cynthia, Ralph, Christine, Suzette & Doreen. Educ: Sauk Valley Jr Col, 71; Northern Ill Univ, grad, 72; Phi Theta Kappa (pres, Pi Tau Chap). Polit & Govt Pos: Secy, Lee Co Young Dem, Ill, 64 & 65, pres, 66 & 67; clerk, South Dixon Twp, 65-69, Dem precinct committeeman, 68-; chmn, Ladies for Brinkmeier, 68; chairwoman, Lee Co Dem Party, 68-72; secy, Lee Co Dem Cent Comt, 68- Bus & Prof Pos: Elem teacher. Mem: Nat & Ill Educ Asns; Rock Falls Elem Educ Asn (secy, 75-); South Dixon Unit, Lee Co Home Exten. Relig: Catholic. Mailing Add: RR 2 Box 126 Dixon IL 61021

WOLF, WILLIAM HENRY (D)
b Indianapolis, Ind, Aug 5, 20; s Paul Henry Wolf & Ora Sarah Jones W; m 1950 to Mary Jane Vermillion; c Sarah, Martha, Pamela & Paula. Educ: Earlham Col, AB, 42; Harvard Bus Sch, 43; Ind Univ Sch of Law, JD, 50. Polit & Govt Pos: Chmn, Hancock Co Dem Comt, Ind, 54-70; chmn, Tenth Dist Dem Party, 62-68; deleg, Dem Nat Conv, 64 & 68, alt deleg, 72; chmn, Sixth Dist Dem Party, 68-72. Mil Serv: Entered as Ens, Navy, 46, released as Lt(sg), after serv in Am Embassy, Havana, Cuba. Mem: Am & Ind State Bar Asns; Am Trial Lawyers Asn; Am Legion; Elks; 40 et 8. Relig: Quaker. Legal Res: 207 W McKenzie Rd Greenfield IN 46140 Mailing Add: PO Box 495 Greenfield IN 46140

WOLFE, SAM (D)
Mont State Rep
Mailing Add: Rte 1 Box 50 Stevensville MT 59870

WOLFE, STEPHEN CHARLES (R)
Okla State Sen
b Saginaw, Mich, Nov 19, 40; s Frank Burleigh Wolfe & Helen M Galehr W; m 1968 to Joey Darleen Harbour; c Lea Marie, Amy Darleen, Kristi Elizabeth & Piper Stephanie. Educ: Washington & Lee Univ; Westminster Col (Mo), BA Polit Sci, 62; Okla Univ Sch Law, JD, 65; Alpha Phi Omega; Phi Gamma Delta; Phi Alpha Delta; YMCA; Westminster Men of Song Glee Club. Polit & Govt Pos: Mem, Tulsa Co Young Rep; officer, Westminster Young Rep Club, 62; Okla State Rep, 76th Dist, 66-72; Okla State Sen, Dist 39, 72-, caucus secy, Okla State Senate, 72-74, caucus chmn, 74- Bus & Prof Pos: Attorney-at-law, 65-; licensed real estate broker, 68- Mil Serv: 2nd Lt, Army, Mil Police Corps. Mem: Am, Okla & Tulsa Co Bar Asns; Am & Okla Trial Lawyers Asn. Relig: Presbyterian. Legal Res: 2105 Forest Blvd Tulsa OK 74114 Mailing Add: 1634 S Boulder Tulsa OK 74119

WOLFER, CURT ALAN (D)
Ore State Rep
b near Silverton, Ore, Feb 17, 49; s Martin Raymond Wolfer & Colleen Irene Southwell W; m 1970 to Conda Marie Ward. Educ: Ore State Univ, 67-71. Polit & Govt Pos: Admin asst, Ore State Legis, 71; Ore State Rep, 73-, vchmn labor & bus affairs comt, Ore House of Rep, currently. Bus & Prof Pos: Pres, GLC Adv Ltd. Mem: Grange; CofC. Honors & Awards: Eagle Scout, Boy Scouts, 64; Paperboy of Year, Statesman Jour Newspaper, 66. Relig: Christian. Legal Res: 458 Monte Vista Silverton OR 97381 Mailing Add: PO Box 614 Silverton OR 97381

WOLFF, LESTER LIONEL (D)
US Rep, NY
b New York, NY, Jan 4, 19; s Samuel Wolff & Hannah Barnam W; m to Blanche Silver; c Bruce & Diane. Educ: NY Univ, 39. Polit & Govt Pos: Chmn adv comt, Subcomt on Consumers Study, US House of Rep, 57; mem, US Trade Mission, Philippines, 62, Malaysia & Hong Kong, 63; US Rep, NY, 64-, mem, Comt Foreign Affairs & subcomts on Asian Affairs & MidE, US House of Rep, 69-, Comt Near East, Foreign Econ Policy & Pac Affairs, currently, mem, Comt on Vet Affairs & Subcomt on Hosps, currently; mem, NY State Bi-Partisan Steering Comt, currently; chmn, Bd Visitors, US Merchant Marine Acad, currently; deleg, Dem Nat Mid-Term Conf, 74. Bus & Prof Pos: Lectr mkt, 39-41; head mkt dept, Collegiate Inst, 45-49; TV moderator & producer, Between the Lines, 48-60; TV producer, Showcase & Wendy Barrie Show, 55-58; former mem bd, Noramco Dugan's & Madison Life Ins Co; former chmn bd, Coordinated Mkt Agency. Mil Serv: Maj, Pub Rels Off, Squad Comdr, Civil Air Patrol Auxiliary; cmndg officer, Civil Air Patrol Cong Squadron, Air Force. Mem: Nat Jewish Hosp Denver & Deborah Hosp (trustee). Honors & Awards: Captive Nations Medal, Assembly of Captive Nations, 66. Legal Res: 5 North Dr Great Neck NY 11021 Mailing Add: 2463 Rayburn House Off Bldg Washington DC 20515

WOLFGANG, JOHN W (D)
Md State Deleg
Mailing Add: 12334 Hatton Point Rd Oxon Hill MD 20022

WOLFSEN, FRANKLIN G (R)
NH State Rep
Mailing Add: 108 Exeter Rd North Hampton NH 03852

WOLLE, WILLIAM DOWN
US Ambassador to Oman
b Sioux City, Iowa, Mar 11, 28; s William Carl Wolle & Vivian Down W; m 1955 to Mimmi Torlen; c Laila Jean & William Nickolas. Educ: Morningside Col, BA, 49; Davis & Elkins Col, 50; Columbia Univ Sch Int Affairs, MIA, 51. Polit & Govt Pos: US Foreign Serv officer, Baghdad, Manchester, Beirut, Aden, Jidda, Washington, DC, Kuwait, Amman & Nairobi, 51-74, US Ambassador to Oman, 74- Mil Serv: Entered as Pvt, Army, 46, released as Cpl, 47, after serv in US Constabulary Force, Ger, 47. Honors & Awards: Superior Serv Award, US Dept of State, 74. Relig: Methodist. Legal Res: 3331 Jennings St Sioux City IA 51104 Mailing Add: Muscat Dept of State Washington DC 20520

WOLLENHAUPT, RALPH EUGENE (R)
b Massena, Iowa, May 9, 18; s Frederick George Wollenhaupt & Ida Sophia Gaulke W; m 1955 to Janet Kari Johnson; c Kurt Fred. Educ: Drake Univ, BA, 52, MA, 68; Grad Sch Banking, Univ Wis, grad, 61; Agr Credit Sch, Iowa State Univ, grad, 64; Phi Beta Kappa. Polit & Govt Pos: Secy to US Naval Attache, US Embassy, Ottawa, Ont, Can, 45-48; Rep precinct committee, Summerset Twp, Iowa, 62-66; chmn, Adair Co Rep Cent Comt, formerly; deleg, Rep Nat Conv, 72. Bus & Prof Pos: Vpres, First Nat Bank, Fontanelle, Iowa, 62-64, exec vpres & cashier, 64-72, pres, 72- Mil Serv: Entered as PO 1/C, Navy, 41, released as CPO, 45, after serv in Intel Serv, Eastern Can. Mem: AF&AM; Scottish Rite (32 degree); Shrine; Eastern Star; Am Legion (dep finance officer, Iowa Dept, 66-69). Relig: Methodist. Mailing Add: 116 Benton St Fontanelle IA 50846

WOLLMAN, HARVEY (D)
Lt Gov, SDak
Mailing Add: State Capitol Pierre SD 57501

WOLLSTADT, PAUL (R)
b Rockford, Ill, July 28, 10; s John P Wollstadt & Hilda Ekstrom W; m 1934 to Elzada Elizabeth Rogers; c Roger Davis, David Carl & Loyd James. Educ: Univ Ill, AB, 32; Phi Eta Sigma. Polit & Govt Pos: Dep Asst Secy Manpower Research & Utilization, Dept of Defense, 69-72. Bus & Prof Pos: Writer & ed, Rockford Newspaper, Inc, Ill, 32-45; ed, Nat Petroleum News, Cleveland, Ohio, 45-51; asst mgr pub rels, Mobil Oil Corp, New York, 51-58, asst to chmn, 58-59, vpres, 59-63, sr vpres, 63-69. Mem: Nat Press Club; Maplewood Country Club; Cloud Club. Relig: Presbyterian. Mailing Add: 77 Slope Dr Short Hills NJ 07078

WOLPE, HOWARD ELIOT (D)
Mich State Rep
b Los Angeles, Calif, Nov 2, 39; s Dr Zelda Shapiro Wolpe; m 1963 to C Jeanene Taylor; c Michael Stevenson. Educ: Reed Col, BA, 60; Univ Chicago Law Sch, 66-67; Mass Inst Technol, PhD, 67. Polit & Govt Pos: City comnr, Kalamazoo, Mich, 69-73; Mich State Rep, 46th Dist, 73- Bus & Prof Pos: Guest lectr polit sci, Boston Univ, 65-66; consult, US Peace Corps, 66-67; asst prof polit sci, Western Mich Univ, 67-69, assoc prof, 70-72; consult, Foreign Serv Inst, US State Dept, 67- Publ: Co-ed, Nigeria: Modernization and the Politics of Communalism, Mich State Univ Press, 71; auth, Urban Politics in Nigeria: a Study of Port Harcourt, Univ Calif Press, 74; co-auth, Modernization and the politics of communalism: a theoretical perspective, Am Polit Sci Rev, 70; plus others. Mem: Kalamazoo Jaycees. Mailing Add: 511 Woodward Ave Kalamazoo MI 49007

WOMACK, J A (DOOLEY) (D)
Ark State Sen
Mailing Add: 115 Jefferson St Camden AR 71701

WOMACK, LANTZ (D)
La State Rep
Mailing Add: Rte 1 Winnsboro LA 71295

WONG, FRANCIS ALVIN (D)
Hawaii State Sen
b Honolulu, Hawaii, July 18, 36; s Francis Y Wong & Elizabeth Chong W; m 1958 to Shirley Anne Chun; c Catherine Anne, Francis, Jr, Timothy Gerard & Mary Anne. Educ: Georgetown Col, BS, 58; Georgetown Univ Law Ctr, JD, 60. Polit & Govt Pos: Staff mem, Off of US Sen John F Kennedy, 58-59; research asst, Off of US Sen Oren E Long, 59-62; pres, Dem Precinct, Pearl City, Hawaii, 64-66; Hawaii State Rep, 67-70; Hawaii State Sen, 70-; deleg, Dem Nat Conv, 72. Bus & Prof Pos: Real estate broker, Francis A Wong & Assocs, 62-; attorney-at-law, 62-; partner, Law Firm of Rice, Lee & Wong, 68- Mem: St Louis High Sch (bd gov); Am Asn Cbmmunity & Jr Cols (dir); Japanese Am Inst for Mgt Sci (trustee); Civilian Adv Group (mem steering comt). Honors & Awards: Recipient Distinguished Serv Award, US Jr CofC, 65; One of Three Outstanding Young Men in Hawaii, Hawaii Jaycees, 68; One of Two Hawaii Legislators Selected to Participate in State Legis Seminar for Outstanding State Legis, Rutgers Univ, 70. Relig: Catholic. Mailing Add: 2023 Aamanu St Pearl City HI 96782

WONG, RICHARDS S H (D)
Hawaii State Sen
Mailing Add: Senate Sgt-at-Arms State Capitol Honolulu HI 96813

WON PAT, ANTONIO BORJA (D)
Deleg, US House of Rep, Guam
b Summay, Guam, Dec 10, 08; s Ignacio Won Pat & Maria Suriano Borja W; m 1932 to Ana Salas Perez; c Aveline (Mrs Ploke), Marilyn A, Jacqueline (Mrs Coats), Ellen (Mrs Chargualaf), Anthony B, Jr, Rosalind (Mrs Wise), Judith T, Mark V & Denise J. Educ: Guam Norm Schs, 28-40. Polit & Govt Pos: Assemblyman, Guam Assembly, 36-41; Sen, Guam Legis, 50-64, Speaker, 50-64; Wash Rep, Territory of Guam, 65-72; deleg, Dem Nat Conv, 68; Deleg, US House of Rep, Guam, 72- Bus & Prof Pos: Sch teacher, Guam, 28-33; elem sch prin, 34-40; high sch teacher, 40-41; pvt bus in imports, wholesale & retail, 45-54, real estate broker & ins agt, 54; pres & chmn bd, Guam Commercial Corp, Inc, 46-54. Mem: Am Acad Polit & Social Sci; Am Soc Pub Admin; Am Judicature Soc; Int Platform Asn; Nat Press Club. Honors & Awards: Community Leader Am Award, 69 & 71. Relig: Catholic. Legal Res: Sinajana GU 96910 Mailing Add: 216 Cannon House Off Bldg Washington DC 20515

WOOD, BEATRICE EVELYN (D)
b Ohio, Nov 14, 16; d Harry Shephard & Jennie Berten S; m 1932 to Otis C Wood. Polit & Govt Pos: Deleg, Dem Nat Conv, 72. Bus & Prof Pos: Attendant, Cent State Ment Hosp, Indianapolis, Ind, 54- Mem: State & Co Munic Employees (pres, Local 803, 16 years, secy-treas, Coun 62, 15 years); Southern Christian Leadership Conf (bd mem, 8 years); A Phillip Randolph Inst (chmn, 6 years). Relig: Protestant. Mailing Add: 3275 Winthrop Ave Indianapolis IN 46025

WOOD, BOB E (D)
NMex State Sen
Mailing Add: Box 839 Portales NM 88130

WOOD, CHARLES ROSS (R)
b Spencer, Iowa, Jan 13, 41; s Charles Edward Wood & Louise Carstensen W; m 1962 to Carol Ann Rosien; c Courtney Anne & Matthew Charles. Educ: State Univ Iowa, 59-60; Iowa State Univ, BS in Animal Sci, 63, George Gund scholar, 63-64; Block & Bridle; Phi Kappa Psi. Polit & Govt Pos: Chmn, Clay Co Young Rep, Iowa, 65-66; chmn, Clay Co Rep Cent Comt, formerly. Bus & Prof Pos: Dir & pres, Welco Feed Mfg Co, Inc, 63-71; vpres, Agri-Assocs, Inc, 71- Publ: Auth, Careers & employment in nutritional sciences, The Nutritionist, spring 73. Mem: 4-H Club Leader; Am Soc Animal Sci; Spencer CofC; Mason (Master). Honors & Awards: Produced Int Grand Champion Steer, 58. Relig: Presbyterian. Mailing Add: 5305 Surrey Dr Bettendorf IA 52722

WOOD, CLYDE EVERETT (D)
Miss State Rep
Mailing Add: Box 666 Moorhead MS 38761

WOOD, DOROTHY MERTIS (R)
Mem, SDak State Rep Cent Comt
b Aberdeen, SDak, Apr 23, 28; d John Carl Lowitz & Bertha Papke L; m 1947 to Royal James Wood; c James Royal, Bonnie Anita, Peggy Annette & Amy Louise. Educ: Warner High Sch, grad, 46. Polit & Govt Pos: Exec secy, Brown Co Rep Serv Off, SDak, 66-; secy, Brown Co Planning Comn, 67-75; Brown Co deleg, SDak State Rep Conv, 68-74; vchmn, Brown Co Rep Party, SDak, 67-; SDak deleg, Nat Women's Fedn of Rep Women, Washington, DC, 69; State Elec Bd, 74-; mem, SDak State Rep Cent Comt, 75-; vchmn, Brown Co Bicentennial Comt. Mem: Zonta Int; Prairiewood Country Club; St Luke's Hosp Auxiliary; Dakota Midland Hosp Auxiliary. Relig: Lutheran; Sunday sch supt, St John Lutheran Church, Warner, 50-51, Sunday sch teacher, 52-65. Mailing Add: Warner SD 57479

WOOD, FLOSSIE OPAL (D)
Chmn, Dent Co Dem Comt, Mo
b Winkler, Mo, Oct 19, 10; d Lee Andrew Burleson & Lillie Mae Pidcock B; m 1929 to Carl Christon Wood. Educ: Salem High Sch, grad, 29. Polit & Govt Pos: Chmn, Dent Co Dem Comt, Mo, 74- Bus & Prof Pos: Secy, Co Supt Schs, Dent Co, Mo, 54-56; dep co clerk, Dent Co, 56- Relig: Protestant. Mailing Add: Rte 4 Salem MO 65560

WOOD, FLOYD E (R)
b Ft Sumner, NMex, Sept 7, 29; s John W Wood & Bertie Bowlin W; m 1951 to Norma Lee Martin. Educ: NMex Mil Inst, 47-49; NMex State Univ, BS in Bus Admin, 51; Phi Mu Tau; Phi Kappa Tau. Polit & Govt Pos: Chmn, De Baca Co Rep Party, NMex, formerly; village councilman, Ft Sumner, NMex, 65- Mil Serv: Entered as Pvt, Army, 51, released as Pfc, 53. Mem: Am Legion; Los Borrachos Skeet Club; Ft Sumner Rotary Club; Alamo Boat Club (commodore). Relig: Protestant. Legal Res: 721 Main Ft Sumner NM 88119 Mailing Add: Box 35 Ft Sumner NM 88119

WOOD, GEORGE MATTHEW (D)
b Camden, NC, Apr 30, 26; s Freshwater Pool Wood & Elsie Griffin W (deceased); m 1950 to Winifred Jones; c Gail Griffen, George M, Jr, David Lloyd, Joanne Jones & Robert Graham. Educ: NC State Univ, BS in Agron, 50; Gamma Sigma Delta; Sigma Chi. Polit & Govt Pos: NC State Rep, 63-66; NC State Sen, 67-72. Bus & Prof Pos: Vpres, F P Wood & Son, Inc, 52; vpres, F P Wood & Son of Elizabeth City, Inc, 60; pres, Carolina Transit, Inc, 62; dir, Southern Loan & Ins Co, 64-; mem, State Capital Planning Comn, 65; pres, Astro, Inc; farmer. Mil Serv: Entered as Seaman, Maritime Serv, 43, released as Ens, 46; Atlantic & Pac War Theater Ribbons. Mem: NC State Univ Alumni Asn; Lions; Univ NC (bd trustees, 63-72, exec comt, 67-72 & bd gov, 73-); Mason; Shrine. Honors & Awards: Bus Character Award, Red Book; Outstanding Young Farmer Award, Jaycees, 61; Meritorious Serv Award, NC State Univ Alumni Asn, 67; Distinguished Alumni Award, Sch Agr & Life Sci, NC State Univ, 74; Co Agts Award, NC Asn Co Agr Agts, 75. Relig: Presbyterian, deacon, 55-56, elder, 66-73. Mailing Add: PO Box 155 Camden NC 27921

WOOD, HARLESTON READ (R)
Chmn Finance Comt, Montgomery Co Rep Party, Pa
b Philadelphia, Pa, Oct 18, 13; s Alan Wood, III & Elizabeth Read W; m 1942 to Emily Newbold Campbell; c Harleston R, Jr, Alan, IV, Ross Graham, Morrow Campbell & Anthony Biddle. Educ: Princeton Univ, AB in Econ. Hon Degrees: LLD, Hobart & William Smith Cols, 59. Polit & Govt Pos: Vchmn finance comt, Montgomery Co Rep Party, Pa, 67-70, chmn, 70-; deleg, Rep Nat Conv, 72. Bus & Prof Pos: Sales develop engr, Alan Wood Steel Co, 38-42, mgr develop & planning, 46-50, asst vpres, 50-52, vpres, 52-55, pres, 55-72, chmn bd, 62- Mil Serv: Entered as Ens, Navy, 42, released as Lt, 45, after serv in Bur of Ships. Mem: Am Iron & Steel Inst; Philadelphia Country Club; Racquet Club; Duquesne Club, Pittsburgh; Gulph Mills. Relig: Episcopal. Mailing Add: Camp Discharge Spring Mill Rd Gladwyne PA 19035

WOOD, HUBERT FRANKLIN (R)
b Lyndonville, Vt, Oct 25, 07; s Frederick Thomas Wood & Alice Blodgett W; m 1934 to Marion Newman. Educ: Vt State Teachers Col, Lyndon Ctr, Prof Standard, 30; Boston Univ, BS in Educ, 37; Univ Vt, summer 36. Polit & Govt Pos: Precinct committeeman, Globe Rep Party, Ariz, 56-; treas, Ariz Rep State Comt, formerly; chmn, Gila Co Rep Dep Registr, 72-; precinct committeeman, Gila Co Rep Comt, 72- Bus & Prof Pos: Elem sch prin, East Concord, Vt, 30-33; asst prin, Saxtons River Graded Sch, 34-36; asst prin, Bradford Acad, 37-39; pres, Community Concerts, Globe, Ariz, 47-53; pres, Ariz Eye Bank, 63-65. Mem: Ariz Asn Life Underwriters; Nat Rifle Asn Am; Lions (pres, 62-63). Honors & Awards: Sr Master Key, Globe Lions, Ariz, 60. Relig: Episcopal; bd mem, Ariz Episcopal Diocese Coun, 67-69. Mailing Add: 410 S Fourth St Globe AZ 85501

WOOD, JOE T (D)
Ga State Rep
b Gainesville, Ga, Oct 23, 22; s Ernest W Wood & Martha Ann Reynolds W; m 1942 to Helen Thrasher; c Joe T, Jr. Educ: Univ Ga, 2 years; Gridiron Soc. Polit & Govt Pos: Ga State Rep, 11th Dist, 65- Mil Serv: Entered as Pvt, Army, 42, released as 1st Sgt, 46. Mem: Elks; Am Legion; VFW; Gainesville Farm Bur; Chattahoochee Country Club. Relig: Baptist. Legal Res: 1435 Cumberland Dr NE Gainesville GA 30501 Mailing Add: PO Box 736 Gainesville GA 30501

WOOD, JOHN T (D)
SC State Rep
Mailing Add: Tigerville SC 29688

WOOD, KATHERINE M (R)
VChmn, Otsego Co Rep Comt, NY
b Burdette, NY, Aug 16, 05; d Ralph E Winton & Nellie Frautz W; m 1926 to Adelbert E Wood, wid; c Robert W & Karlyn E. Educ: Richfield Springs Training Sch; Cornell Univ, Nursing Home Adminr License, 71. Polit & Govt Pos: Rep committeewoman, Springfield Ctr, NY, 26-; committeewoman, NY State Rep Party, 54-58; vchmn, Otsego Co Rep Comt, NY, 58- Bus & Prof Pos: Dir admissions, Mary Imogene Bassett Hosp, Cooperstown, NY, 57-69; adminr, Order of Eastern Star Home, Oriskany, 69- Mem: Long Term Care Facilities of NY; Masonic Homes Exec Asn NAm; Criterion Prof Women's Club; Eastern Star (Grand Matron, 53); DAR. Relig: Episcopal. Legal Res: PO Box 125 Springfield Center NY 13468 Mailing Add: Order of Eastern Star Home Oriskany NY 13424

WOOD, KATHLEEN ANN (D)
b Springfield, Ill, Mar 17, 51; d Charles William Wood & Mary Jane Lovas W; single. Educ: Ill Col, 69-71; Sangamon State Univ, BA, 73; Gamma Delta. Polit & Govt Pos: Alt deleg, Dem Nat Conv, 72; legis intern to Dem staff, Ill House of Rep, 72-; data analyst, Gov Office, Springfield, Ill, currently. Publ: Reflections on the Democratic Convention, Ill Women's Legis Bull, 8/72. Mem: King Harvest Food Coop; Nat Orgn for Women (state coun rep); Sangamon State Univ Alumni Asn (bd dirs). Honors & Awards: Golden Laurels Award, several area civic orgns, 69. Relig: United Methodist. Mailing Add: 847 S Illinois St Springfield IL 62704

WOOD, LOUIS EUGENE (R)
Mont State Rep
b McLean Co, NDak, Apr 16, 18; s Clarence Eugene Wood & Hartie Albertha Weintz W; m 1941 to Lillian May Sjolund; c Timothy E, Bruce C, Kathleen (Mrs Carlson), Carol, Helen E, Barbara J, Keith & David. Educ: Univ NDak, BS in Civil Engr, 42; Sigma Tau. Polit & Govt Pos: Mem, High Educ Facil Act, 65-72; Mont State Rep, 75-, mem, Appropriations Comt & Bus & Indust Comt, Mont House Rep, 75- Bus & Prof Pos: Civil engr, Oliver Iron Mining Co, Coleraine, Minn, 42-44; asst mgr, Minot Sand & Gravel Co, NDak, 46-54, mgr, Glendive, Mont, 54-66; pres, Gene Wood Ready Mix, Inc, Glendive, 66- Mil Serv: Entered as Ens, Navy, 44, released as Lt (jg), 46, after serv in Seventh Fleet. Mem: Dawson Col (bd dir); Mont Ready Mix Asn (bd dirs); Enterprise Network Radio Sta (bd dirs). Honors & Awards: Layman of the Year Award, Mont Asn Evangel, 75. Relig: General Conference Mennonite. Legal Res: 221 N River Ave Glendive MT 59330 Mailing Add: Box 326 Glendive MT 59330

WOOD, RICHARD ROBINSON (R)
b Salem, Mass, Nov 8, 22; s Reginald Wood & Irene Robinson W; m 1970 to Jane Philbin; c Christopher Robinson, Bryant Cornelius & Marcella Jeffries. Educ: Harvard Univ, AB, 43; Boston Univ, 44-47; Mass Inst Technol, 47-48. Polit & Govt Pos: Chmn, Ward 3 Rep Party, 54-60; chmn, Boston City Rep Comt, 54-75, pres, 64-72; cand Ward Three, Boston, Mass House of Rep, 56; committeeman Third Suffolk Dist, Mass State Rep Comt, 64-75, asst treas, 68-75; mem, Mayor's Citizen's Adv Comt, Boston, Mass, 65-67; chmn, Mass Rep Real Estate Comt for Nixon, 68; exec mem, Rep Comt Urban Progress, 69; chmn, Spaulding for Sen Comt, 70. Bus & Prof Pos: Trustee, Mass Real Estate Investment Fund, Boston, 59-61; vpres, Hunneman & Co, Inc, 62-; trustee, Suffolk Franklin Savings Bank, 68-; pres & chmn bd,

Continental Real Estate Equities, Inc, 73-75; pres & dir, ConVest Realty Mgt, Inc, 73-75; exec vpres, Itel Real Estate Invest Corp, 75- Mil Serv: Entered as Pvt, Army Med Corps, 44, released, 44, after serv in Lovell Gen Hosp Med Unit, Ft Devens, Mass. Mem: Calif Asn Realtors; Rental Housing Asn; Broker Inst; Real Estate Securities & Syndications Inst (vpres, 74-); Nat Inst Real Estate Brokers. Relig: Episcopal. Legal Res: 1342 Jones St San Francisco CA 94109 Mailing Add: Itel Real Estate Invest Corp 1 Embarcadero Ctr San Francisco CA 94111

WOOD, ROYAL JAMES (BUD) (R)
SDak State Rep
b Warner, SDak, Mar 28, 22; s James Lawson Wood & Esther Rehfeld W; m 1947 to Dorothy Mertis Lowitz; c James Royal, Bonnie Anita, Peggy Annette & Amy Louise. Educ: Northern State Col, 40-42. Polit & Govt Pos: Chmn, Co Young Rep Orgn, SDak, 43; SDak State Rep, 67-; app mem, State Planning Comn, 70; elected to Legis Res Coun, currently. Bus & Prof Pos: Auctioneer, 45-; dir & pres, Warner Co-op Oil Co, 64-; pres, Warner Co-op Elevator, 9 years. Mem: SDak Wheat Growers (dir, 70-); Warner Develop Comt (dir & charter mem, 70-); Aberdeen CofC (agr comt); Mason; Scottish Rite. Honors & Awards: Meritorious Award for Serv to 4-H. Relig: Lutheran; past pres, Church Coun. Mailing Add: Warner SD 57479

WOOD, T NEWELL (R)
Pa State Sen
Mailing Add: RD 1 Harveys Lake PA 18618

WOODAHL, ROBERT LEE (R)
Attorney Gen, Mont
b Great Falls, Mont, June 28, 31; s Arvid Bye Woodahl & Margaret R Fogerty W; m 1963 to Arlene Rae Depner; c Brian Arvid, Scott Robert, Kirsten Patrice & Eric Lee. Educ: Mont State Univ, 49-51; Southern Methodist Univ, 56; Univ Mont, BS, 56, JD, 59; Sigma Alpha Epsilon; Phi Delta Phi. Polit & Govt Pos: Attorney Gen, Mont, 69- Mil Serv: Entered as Sgt, Air Force, 51, released as S/Sgt, 52, after serv in 186th Fighter Squadron, Strategic & Tactical Air Command, 51-52; Good Conduct Medal. Mem: Mont Bar Asn; Mason; Shrine; Eastern Star; Am Legion. Relig: Methodist. Legal Res: Box 34 Gruber Estates Clancy MT 59634 Mailing Add: Off of the Attorney Gen State Capitol Helena MT 59601

WOODARD, BARNEY PAUL (D)
NC State Rep
Mailing Add: PO Box 5 Princeton NC 27569

WOODARD, CARL JUBAL (R)
Mem, Rep State Exec Comt Ala
b Cullman, Ala, Aug 1, 24; s Milas Homer Woodard & Olivia Faye Summerford W; m 1944 to Martha Louise Van Meter; c Carl Gary & Sheila Archer. Educ: Auburn Univ, 1 year. Polit & Govt Pos: Chmn, Cullman Co Rep Exec Comt, Ala, vchmn, 63; ed, Cullman Rep Newsletter, 63-; mem, Rep State Exec Comt Ala, 70- Bus & Prof Pos: Mgr, M H Woodard Dept Store, 55-65; owner, Carl's Dept Store, 55-; zone rep, Investor's Diversified Serv. Mil Serv: Entered as Pvt, Army Air Force, 43, released as S/Sgt, 45, after serv in 8th Air Force, Eng; Air Medal with Five Oak Leaf Clusters; Distinguished Flying Cross. Mem: VFW; Am Legion; Ala Farm Bur; Rotary. Relig: Lutheran-Mo Synod. Legal Res: 1523 Beth St Cullman AL 35055 Mailing Add: 305 First Ave SW Cullman AL 35055

WOODARD, HOWARD CHAMBLESS (R)
Chmn, Laurens Co Rep Comt, Ga
b Dublin, Ga, Dec 30, 48; s Jethro Woodard & Lucille Fowler W; m 1969 to Joy Mullis; c Jason Chambless. Educ: Mid Ga Col, AA in bus, 73; Ga Col Robins Resident Ctr, 74- Polit & Govt Pos: Chmn, Laurens Co Rep Comt, Ga, 75- Bus & Prof Pos: Clerk, Piggly Wiggly South, Dublin & Augusta, Ga, 65-68; opers officer, Morris State Bank, Dublin, 71. Mil Serv: Entered as Pvt, Marine Corps, 68, released as Sgt, 71, after serv in VMO 2 & HMM 263, 1st Marine Air Wing WPac, Vietnam, 70-71. Mem: Dublin Kiwanis Club (second vpres & treas, 75-); Green Acres Golf Club. Mailing Add: PO Box 1213 Dexter GA 31019

WOODARD, WILLIAM PHILIP (R)
Chmn, East Brookfield Rep Town Comt, Mass
b Worcester, Mass, Oct 23, 32; s George R Woodard & Carrie E Herbert W; m 1960 to Judith Ann Tucker; c William Thomas, Kathie Anne & Barry Jon. Educ: Worcester Jr Col; Am Int Col, BA in Hist, 59; Worcester State Col, MEd, 61; Univ Conn. Polit & Govt Pos: Chmn, East Brookfield Rep Town Comt, Mass, 63-; mem, East Brookfield Finance Comt, 63-66. Bus & Prof Pos: Teacher social sci, Charlton High Sch, 60-66. Mil Serv: Entered as Pvt, Army, 53, released as SP-3, after serv in Ger 302 Bn, 7th Corps, 56; Soldier of Month, 302 Bn, 55 & 502 Corps, 55. Mem: East Brookfield Hist Soc; Nat Geographic Soc. Relig: Protestant. Mailing Add: Lake Quaboag East Brookfield MA 01515

WOODCOCK, GEORGE WASHINGTON (R)
Chmn, Wabash Co Rep Party, Ill
b Brownsville, Ky, Apr 13, 30; s George W Woodcock, Sr & Mellittia VanMeter W; m 1952 to Margaret Delsey Peet; c Margaret Nell, Marilyn & George W, III. Educ: Western Ky Univ, AB, 54; Univ Ky Law Sch, JD, 57; Alpha Tau Omega. Polit & Govt Pos: US Comnr, Eastern Dist, Ill, 61-65; city attorney, Mt Carmel, 63-66; bd mem Selective Serv Bd 205, Mt Carmel, 67-69; Selective Serv Syst adv to Registrants, Wabash Co, currently; State's Attorney, Wabash Co, 68-72; chmn, Wabash Co Rep Party, 68-; pres, Ill Rep Co Chmn Asn, currently; alt deleg, Rep Nat Conv, 72; mem, Ill Rep State Cent Comt, currently. Bus & Prof Pos: Partner, law firm of White & Woodcock, Morgantown, Ky, 57, law firm of McGaughey, McGaughey, Henry & Woodcock, Mt Carmel, Ill, 58-62; attorney-at-law, 62-72; partner, Woodcock & Hux, Attorneys-at-Law, 72- Mil Serv: Entered as Pvt, Army, 47-48 & 52-53, released as Lt, 53, after serv in 45th Div, Korea; Combat Infantryman's Badge. Mem: Shrine; Mason; VFW; Am Legion; Elks. Relig: Episcopal. Legal Res: Miskell Dr RR 3 Mt Carmel IL 62863 Mailing Add: PO Drawer 433 Mt Carmel IL 62863

WOODCOCK, RAYMOND PAUL (D)
RI State Sen
b Providence, RI, Nov 1, 29; s William Woodcock, Sr (deceased) & Valentine Boucher W; m 1947 to Eileen M Donahue; c Raymond, Jr, Stephen F & William, III. Educ: NY Mergenthaler Linotype Sch, 1 year. Polit & Govt Pos: Mem, 34th Representative Dist Comt, Dem Party, RI, 66-67; RI State Rep, Dist 34, 67-72; RI State Sen, 73- Bus & Prof Pos: Apprentice printer, William R Brown Co, Providence, RI, 48-53; printer, Providence J-Bull, 53-55; lockup-man, Typecraft, Inc, Calif, 55-56; foreman, Shamory Typesetting Serv, 56-60; treas & gen mgr, William R Brown Printing Co, Providence, RI, 60- Mem: Elks (Exalted Ruler, Pawtucket Lodge); Warwick Coun, KofC; Sons of Irish Kings; Friendly Sons of St Patrick; St Benedict's Holy Name Soc. Relig: Catholic. Mailing Add: 60 La Chance Ave Warwick RI 02889

WOODHOUSE, CHASE GOING (D)
b Victoria, BC; d Seymour Going & Harriet Jackson G; wid; c Margaret (Mrs Becker). Educ: McGill Univ, BA & MA; Univ Berlin & Univ Chicago, grad study. Hon Degrees: LLD, Alfred Univ, Allegheny Col & Univ Hartford. Polit & Govt Pos: Economist chief div econ, Bur Home Econ, US Dept Agr, 26-29; deleg, Dem Nat Conv, 40; Secy of State, Conn, 40-42; deleg, Conn State Dem Conv, 40-70; US Rep, Second Dist, Conn, 44-46 & 48-50; chief women's div, Dem Nat Comt, 47; organizer women's div, Off of Mil Govt of US in Ger, 47; asst to dir, Off Price Stabilization, 49-50; mem, Southeastern Conn Regional Planning Agency, 60-71; mem, Sprague Dem Town Comt, Conn, 56; chmn, Sprague Zoning & Planning Comn, 62-70; mem New Eng Gov Research Comt, Gov Comt on Libr, 65; mem, Gov Comt on Br Univ in Southeast Conn, 65; mem, Conn Unemploy Comn, 66-69; mem, Conn Ment Health Planning Proj; deleg, Const Conv & co-chmn, Comt on Resolutions, 65; chmn, Comn on Status Women, 67; mem, Gov Clean Water Task Force; mem, Adv Coun to Dept of Community Affairs, 68-72; mem, Comn on Comprehensive Health Planning, 69-72; mem state comn on housing, Gov Comt on Environ Policy, 69-70; mem, Comn on Human Serv, 72-73; mem, Permanent Comn on Status of Women, 73- Bus & Prof Pos: Prof econ, Smith Col, 18-26; personnel dir, Women's Col, Univ NC, 29-34; prof econ, Conn Col, 34-46; dir serv bur for women's orgn, Beatrice Fox Auerbach Found, 54- Publ: Series of books on occupations for women & articles in prof jour. Mem: Hon mem Delta Kappa Gamma; Omicron Nu; Pi Lambda Theta; Sprague Community Ctr (chmn, 68-); Sprague Human Resources Develop Agency (chmn, 69-). Honors & Awards: New Eng Tri-Agents Friend of Exten Award, 69; Americanization Award, Conn Valley B'nai B'rith, 69; C E Winslow Award for contribution to pub health, 72. Relig: Episcopal. Mailing Add: Falcon Farm Rd 1 Baltic CT 06330

WOODIEL, JOHN WILLIAM, JR (R)
Mem, Rep State Cent Comt La
b Enola, Ark, Apr 23, 25; s John William Woodiel & Ruby Davis W; m 1948 to Dorothy Louise Breyel; c John W, III, Deborah Kay & Christopher Davis. Educ: Ark State Teachers Col, BS, 49. Polit & Govt Pos: Chmn, St Charles Parish Rep Exec Comt, 68-72 & currently; mem, Rep State Cent Comt La, 68-; chmn, St Charles Parish Polit Action Comt, 69-71. Bus & Prof Pos: Supvr, Monsanto Co, 49-70; supvr, Am Cyanamid Co, 71- Mil Serv: Entered as A/S, Navy, 44, released as Seaman 1/C, 45, after serv in USS Enterprise, Pac, 44-45. Mem: VFW; Local Civil Improv Group. Relig: Catholic. Mailing Add: Rte 1 Box 162 Luling LA 70070

WOODLAND, DONALD L (D)
Ohio State Sen
b 1931; m; c two. Educ: Ohio State Univ, BS, 57, completed hours in athletic admin. Polit & Govt Pos: Ohio deleg, President's Coun on Phys Fitness, 62 & 63; mem, Columbus Recreational Comn, 63-65; Columbus City Councilman, 7 years, chmn safety comt, 7 years; mem & chmn, Columbus-Franklin Co Criminal Justice Coord Coun, 4 years; Ohio State Sen, 16th Dist, 73- Bus & Prof Pos: Area develop rep, Columbia Gas of Ohio, Inc, 7 years; teacher & coach, 10 years; Franklin Heights High Sch, 7 years; Capital Univ, 3 years. Mem: Ohio State Alumni; Mason; VFW; Am Legion; assoc mem Fraternal Order of Police. Legal Res: 4080 Londonderry Columbus OH 43228 Mailing Add: Ohio State Senate Statehouse Columbus OH 43215

WOODLEY, EDMUND ETCHISON (R)
Mem, Rep State Cent Comt La
s John Woodley & Willie Emma Etchison; m 1954 to Clarice Robinson; c Scott Etchison. Educ: Centenary Col, Shreveport, La, 42-43 & 46; La State Univ Law Sch, Baton Rouge, JD, 49; Kappa Alpha Order. Polit & Govt Pos: Asst US Attorney, Western Dist, La, 54-59; mem, Rep State Cent Comt La, 64-; chmn speakers' bur, Presidential Elec, 72. Bus & Prof Pos: Partner law firm, Cavanaugh, Brame, Holt & Woodley, Lake Charles, La, 59-66; partner law firm, Holt & Woodley, 67- Mil Serv: Entered as Pvt, Army, 44, released as Pvt 1/C, 46, after serv in 14th Armored Div, 45th Inf Div, ETO, 44-45; Purple Heart; Combat Inf Badge; ETO Ribbon with Three Battle Stars. Mem: Am Bar Asn; La State Bar Asn (mem, House of Deleg, 70-); Maritime Law Asn of the US; Rotary (pres, Lake Charles Club, 69-70); Am Legion. Relig: Episcopal. Legal Res: 917 Fair Oak Lane Lake Charles LA 70601 Mailing Add: PO Box EE Lake Charles LA 70601

WOODMAN, BERYL ROGER, JR (D)
Mem, Ingham Co Dem Exec Comt, Mich
b Lansing, Mich, May 12, 44; s Beryl Roger Woodman, Sr & Marie H Roberts W; div; c Marlena Rae, Kathleen Anne, Beryl Roger, III & Daniel Scott. Educ: Lansing Community Col, 69-70. Polit & Govt Pos: Deleg, Dem Nat Conv, 72, chmn, Sixth Dist Dem Deleg, 72; chmn, First Ward Wallace Elec Comt, 72; co-chmn, Ingham Co Wallace Supporters, 72-73; bd dirs, Liberty Lobby, 72-73; chmn, Sixth Dist Wallace Action Comt, 72-73, chmn credentials comt, Ingham Co Dem Conv, 73; cand for councilman-at-lg, Lansing City Coun, currently; mem, Ingham Co Dem Exec Comt, Mich, currently. Bus & Prof Pos: Metal model maker, Oldsmobile Div, Gen Motors Corp, Lansing, 64-; notary pub, 67-; owner operator, Sunoco Serv Sta, 71-72. Mem: Moose; UAW (committeeman, Local 652, 64-); Nat Rifle Asn; Ford Motor Sports Asn; Oldsmobile Outdoors Club. Relig: Catholic. Mailing Add: 912 S Holmes St Lansing MI 48912

WOODMANSEE, DONAVIN N (D)
Mem, Clinton Co Dem Cent Comt, Ohio
b Sabina, Ohio, May 29, 16; s John O Woodmansee & Laura Luttrell W; m 1939 to Lois Jackson; c Linda (Mrs Hartley E Jackson) & Lelan Keith. Educ: Wayne Twp High Sch, Lees Creek, Ohio, grad. Polit & Govt Pos: Mem, Clinton Co Dem Exec Comt, Ohio, 60-; mem, Clinton Co Dem Cent Comt, 66-; alt deleg, Dem Nat Conv, 68; mem, Clinton Co Bd Elec. Bus & Prof Pos: Owner & operator, Woodmansee's Elevator, Highland, Ohio, 44- Mem: Mason, Sabina; Valley of Cincinnati Scottish Rite; Aladdin Shrine. Relig: United Methodist. Mailing Add: Box 22 Reesville OH 45166

WOODMANSEE, GERALD LOUIS (D)
Utah State Rep
b Salt Lake City, Utah, June 27, 30; s Benjamin Louis Woodmansee & Annie Bertha Eugster W; m 1962 to Joyce Littlewood; c Pamela Sue, Cynthia Lee, Shelly Kay & Wade Alan. Educ: Univ Utah, BS, 56; Lambda Delta Sigma. Polit & Govt Pos: Dist chmn, Dem Party, Utah,

65-69, legis chmn, currently; Utah State Rep, 69- Mem: Am Speech & Hearing Asn; Salt Lake Teachers; Utah & Nat Educ Asns. Honors & Awards: State handball championships in singles & doubles. Relig: Latter-day Saint. Mailing Add: 877 Catherine St Salt Lake City UT 84116

WOODROW, SHIRLEY ANN (R)
b Eaton Rapids, Mich, Feb 9, 33; d Hazen J Crandall & Burtriece Warner C; wid; m 1956 to Richard Edgar Woodrow; c Robin Ann, Kimberly Dawn & Kira Lynn. Educ: Western Mich Univ, 50-52; Univ Alaska, 62. Polit & Govt Pos: Anchorage chmn, Women for Nixon, 68; dir, Women for US Sen Ted Stevens, Alaska, 69-70; coordr, President Nixon visit to Anchorage, 71; Alaska spec asst, US Sen Ted Stevens, 71, Alaska staff asst, 71-72; Alaska co-chmn, Ted Stevens for US Senate, 72; deleg, Rep Nat Conv, 72; chairwoman, Alaska Comn for Human Rights, 73; co-dir, Hickel for Gov, 74; spec asst to Sen Bob Packwood, 75. Bus & Prof Pos: Comnr, Alaska State Comn for Human Rights, 69- Publ: Auth & ed, Ted Stevens for the Senate in 72, select interstate publ. Mem: Alaska Conserv Soc; Alaska Ment Health Asn. Honors & Awards: Award for Modeling & Clothing Design, Mrs Anchorage Contest, 68. Relig: Methodist. Mailing Add: 1120 NW Overlook Ct Gresham OR 97030

WOODRUFF, CONSTANCE ONEIDA (D)
Dem Nat Committeewoman, NJ
b New Rochelle, NY, Oct 24, 21; d Carlton Norris & Rosalie Tennessee N; m 1951 to William Woodruff. Educ: Empire State Col, BA; Labor Adv Comt, Labor Educ Ctr, Rutgers Univ, Grad Students Asn. Polit & Govt Pos: Committeewoman, Essex Co Dem Party, NJ, 62-67; secy, State Dem Comt, 74-75; Dem Nat Committeewoman, NJ, 75-; chairperson, NJ Adv Comn on Status of Women, 75- Bus & Prof Pos: Dir community rels, ILGWU, AFL-CIO, 58-; columnist, New York Amsterdam News, 60-70; polit columnist, Nite Lite Mag, Newark, NJ, 67-74; polit columnist, Essex Forum, Newark, 69- Mem: Rutgers Univ Bd Trustees (labor consult comt, 69-); YMWCA of Newark (bd dirs, bd mgt rels, 72-); Women's Polit Caucus of NJ (exec bd mem, Essex Co Chap, 72-); Essex Co Dem Women's League (exec bd mem, pub rels chmn, 70-). Honors & Awards: A Phillip Randolph Inst Award, Labor Leader of Year Award, 71; NJ State Fedn Colored Women's Clubs Community Serv Award, 72; Newark City Coun Citizens Award, 75; Black Pages Award Outstanding Jour, 75; Mayor's Citizenship Award, East Orange, NJ, 75. Relig: Episcopal. Legal Res: 336 Northfield Ave West Orange NJ 07052 Mailing Add: 3 William St Newark NJ 07102

WOODRUFF, MARIAN DAVIS (D)
NH State Rep
b Boston, Mass, Dec 15, 22; d Harvey Nathaniel Davis & Alice Rohde D; m 1952 to Bliss Woodruff; c Nathaniel Rohde, William Watts, Davis Miller & Charlotte Bliss. Educ: Pembroke Col, 41-43; Smith Col, BA, 43-45; Inst Fine Arts, New York Univ, 45-46; RI Sch Design, 49. Polit & Govt Pos: NH State Rep, 73- Bus & Prof Pos: Guide, Metrop Mus Art, 45-46; lectr, Mus Art, Providence, 46-51; supvr educ, Currier Gallery Art, Manchester, NH, 62-66, dir educ, 70-; prof dir, Arts & Sci Ctr, Nashua, 68-69. Mem: Nashua Youth Coun (bd dirs); Randolph Mountain Club (vpres); Am Asn Mus; Am Civil Liberties Union; NH Micological Soc. Relig: Unitarian-Universalist. Mailing Add: 51 Berkeley St Nashua NH 03060

WOODRUFF, WILLIAM A (R)
Polit & Govt Pos: Former Secy Financial Mgt, Dept Air Force Legal Res: VA Mailing Add: Rm 4E978 The Pentagon Washington DC 20330

WOODRUM, CLIFTON ALEXANDER, III (D)
Chmn, Sixth Cong Dist Dem Comt, Va
b Washington, DC, July 23, 38; s Clifton A Woodrum, Jr & Margaret Lanier W; m 1963 to Emily Clyde Abbitt; c Robert H, Meredith Moore & Anne Harris. Educ: Univ NC, AB, 61; Univ Va, LLB, 64; Phi Alpha Delta; Sigma Alpha Epsilon; The Gorgon's Head Lodge. Polit & Govt Pos: Col dir, Va Young Dem Clubs, 62-63, legis chmn, 65-66, vpres, 66-67; mem, Roanoke City Dem Comt, 64-, south dist leader, 69-; pres, Roanoke City Young Dem Club, 66-67; mem, Va State Dem Cent Comt, 72-; mem, Sixth Cong Dist Dem Comt, 72-, chmn, 73-; deleg, Dem Nat Conv, 72. Bus & Prof Pos: Research asst fed aid to hwys subcomt, US House of Rep, 61; assoc, Dodson, Pence, Coulter, Viar & Young, 64-68, partner, 68- Mem: Am & Va Bar Asns; Va Trial Lawyers Asn; Roanoke Bar Asn (bd dirs, 74-); Nat Arthritis Found (bd dirs, Roanoke Br, 72-75); Legal Aid Soc of Roanoke Valley (bd dirs, 66-, vpres, 72-). Relig: Episcopal. Legal Res: 2641 Cornwallis Ave Roanoke VA 24014 Mailing Add: PO Box 1045 Roanoke VA 24005

WOODRUM, DONALD LEE (D)
b Irwin Co, Ga, Dec 9, 00; s William Milton Woodrum & Laura Turner W; m 1933 to Lillie Tucker; c Sara Nelle (Mrs Rowe), Dianne Lee (Mrs Atkinson), Lillian Alice (Mrs Rhodes) & Billy Donald. Polit & Govt Pos: Chmn, Irwin Co Dem Exec Comt, Ga, formerly. Bus & Prof Pos: Agriculture. Mem: Mason; Forestry Comn Irwin Co (chmn); Farm Bur; Nat Farm Orgn. Relig: Baptist; deacon, Bethlehem Baptist Church. Mailing Add: Rte 1 Box 222 Ocilla GA 31774

WOODS, GEORGE L, JR (R)
Mass State Rep
Mailing Add: State Capitol Boston MA 02133

WOODS, JACK E (D)
Iowa State Rep
Mailing Add: 6605 SW 15th St Des Moines IA 50315

WOODS, MARY L (D)
b Dancy, Ala, Sept 8, 35; d Willie Woods & Annie Mae Williams W; div; c Jacqueline, Larry, Delfreda & Antonio. Educ: State Univ NY Col at Purchase, currently. Polit & Govt Pos: Dem dist captain, leader & committeewoman, Peekskill, NY; chairperson, Welfare Rights; treas, Peekskill Area Community Action Prog; city committeewoman, Peekskill, NY, currently; alt deleg, Dem Nat Conv, 72. Mem: Sisters of Ruth (past matron, Chap 155). Relig: Baptist. Mailing Add: 699 Central Ave Peekskill NY 10566

WOODS, MICHAEL ALAN (R)
b Oct 13, 45; s Donald Newton Woods & Darlene Stuart W; m 1972 to Millicent Wasell. Educ: Park Col, 63-65; Am Univ, BA, 67. Polit & Govt Pos: Press asst, US Rep Robert F Ellsworth, 65-66, press asst, US Rep Larry Winn, 67; staff mem, Nixon for President Comt, 67-69; staff asst & exec asst press secy, President of the US, 69-70; campaign dir, Bond for Auditor Comt, 70; asst to Gov, Mo, 73-74; dep dir, Presidential Personnel Off, The White House, 74- Bus & Prof Pos: Vpres, Bradley-Woods & Co, Inc, 70-73. Mem: Park Col (bd trustees); Capitol Hill Club. Relig: Protestant. Legal Res: 805 Robin Hood Rd Mexico MO 65265 Mailing Add: 303 Old Gibler Rd Jefferson City MO 65101

WOODS, PHYLLIS LUCILLE (D)
NH State Rep
b Northampton, Mass, Dec 19, 42; d Edward Gerard Dondero & Estelle Roy D; m 1963 to David Anthony Woods; c Janice & David. Educ: Dover High Sch, grad. Polit & Govt Pos: Mem, Dover Conserv Comn, NH, 73-75; selectman, Ward 1, Dover, 73-74; mem, Dover Recreation Comn, 74-75; NH State Rep, Ward 1, 74- Bus & Prof Pos: Clerk-stenographer, NH Finance Corp, 61-64. Mem: Strafford Co Exten Coun (home econ serv coun rep, 74-); Dover Ecol Club; Orgn Women Legislators; Enthusiastic Garrisons Exten Group. Relig: Catholic. Mailing Add: 1 Barry St Dover NH 03820

WOODS, RILLA ROBERTSON (D)
Pres, Nat Fedn Dem Women
b Defeated, Tenn, Sept 14, 24; d Ward Romeo Robertson & Lydia Betty Shoemake R; m 1971 to Stephen Rogers Woods. Educ: George Peabody Col, 60-65. Polit & Govt Pos: Pres, Davison Co Dem Women, Tenn, 68-69; pres, Tenn Fedn Dem Women, 71-73; mem, Tenn Dem State Platform & Policy Comt, 72-; deleg, Dem Nat Conv, 72; mem charter comn, Dem Nat Comt, 72-, mem nat campaign comt, 74; pres, Nat Fedn Dem Women, 72-; deleg, Dem Mid Term Conf, 74. Bus & Prof Pos: Free lance writer & broadcaster, 55-67; pres, Moran Assocs, Inc, 67-, pres, Catering Unlimited, Inc, 70. Mem: Tau Phi Lambda; Citizens for Tenn Valley Authority; VFW Auxiliary; Bus & Prof Women's Club of Nashville; Nashville Press Club (bd dirs). Honors & Awards: Outstanding Dem Woman, Davidson Co Dem Woman, 70; Woman of Achievement, Nat Women Exec, 71. Relig: Unitarian. Mailing Add: 4201 Utah Ave Nashville TN 37209

WOODS, ROBERT R (D)
SC State Rep
Mailing Add: Box 2115-A Charleston SC 29403

WOODSON, S HOWARD, JR (D)
NJ State Assemblyman
b Philadelphia, Pa, May 8, 16; s Samuel H Woodson, Sr & Lulu E Howard W; m 1939 to Audrey M Manley (deceased); c Jean (Mrs Mitchell) & Howard; remarried 1973 to Lola H Meeks; stepdaughter, Paulette. Educ: Cheyney State Col; Sch Relig, Morehouse Col, Ga; Atlanta Univ; Seton Hall Univ, doctorate, 74; Kappa Alpha Psi. Polit & Govt Pos: Vchmn, Trenton Planning Comn, NJ, 52-62; councilman-at-lg, Trenton City Coun, 62-65; NJ State Assemblyman, 66-, chmn, Co & Munic Govt Comt & Comn to Study Money in Lieu of Taxes for State Owned Lands, NJ State Assembly, Minority Leader, 68-74, Speaker, NJ Gen Assembly, 74-; deleg, Dem Nat Conv, 68. Bus & Prof Pos: Participant, Legis Seminar, Fla, 69. Mem: Mason; Nat Soc State Legislators; League of Munic; Ministerial Conf Philadelphia; Interdenominational Ministerial Conf, Trenton, NJ. Honors & Awards: Received Citizen of Year Award, NJ, twice; Chosen Bd Freeholders Asn, 68; Christian & Jews Brotherhood Award, 68; Outstanding Legis Serv Award, Civil Serv; Citizens Award, Detectives Crime Clin Metrop New York & NJ. Relig: Baptist; pastor, Shiloh Baptist Church. Legal Res: 838 Edgewood Ave Trenton NJ 08618 Mailing Add: Speaker's Off State House Trenton NJ 08625

WOODWARD, JOHN LEONARD (D)
b Summersville, Mo, July 15, 34; s John Henry Woodward & Vesta Shugart W; m 1954 to Carol Janice Solomon; c Shelley L, Kelly G, Lisa C & Tracy R. Educ: Wichita State Univ, BS; Washburn Univ Topeka, JD; Pi Sigma Alpha; Phi Alpha Delta. Polit & Govt Pos: Prosecuting attorney, Crawford Co, Mo; chmn, Crawford Co Dem Comt, formerly. Mailing Add: 901 W Washington Cuba MO 65453

WOODWORTH, LAURENCE NEAL (INDEPENDENT)
b Loudenville, Ohio, Mar 22, 18; s Alfred Ray Woodworth & Nora Sheldon W; m 1940 to Margaret Forest Bretz; c Laurence Sheldon, Joseph Ray, Esther Margaret & Melissa Mary. Educ: Ohio Northern Univ, AB, 40; Univ Denver, MS in Govt Mgt, 42; NY Univ, PhD, 60; Alpha Phi Gamma; Sigma Phi Epsilon. Hon Degrees: JD, Juniata Col; DPA, Ohio Northern Univ. Polit & Govt Pos: Economist, Joint Cong Comt on Internal Revenue Taxation, 44-64, chief of staff, 64-; councilman, Cheverly, Md, 48-59, mayor, 59-64; pres, Md Munic League, 63-64. Relig: United Methodist. Mailing Add: 2810 Crest Ave Cheverly MD 20785

WOODY, FRANK (D)
Wash State Sen
Mailing Add: 24228 47th Woodinville WA 98072

WOOFFENDALE, MATTIE LUCILLE (R)
b Flag Pond, Tenn, May 18, 12; d Jesse Lee Roy McEwen & Duff Phillips M; m 1937 to Charles Herbert Wooffendale. Educ: Frankfort High Sch, grad, 28. Polit & Govt Pos: Precinct committeeman & vice for over 15 years; dep co treas, Clinton Co, Frankfort, Ind, 42-50, co treas, 50-56; pres, Co Treas Asn Ind, 55 & 56; mem, Gov Comn to Study Salaries of Co Officers, 56; pres & legis chmn, Ind Co & Twp Officers Asn, 56; dir, Fifth Dist Rep Women's Club, 56-60; mem, Co Tax Bd, 57; Clinton Co Elec Comnr, 58-62; vchmn, Clinton Co Rep Party, 58-; registered lobbyist, Sch Industs Ind, 59, 61 & 63; mem, Rep State Platform Comt, 60; co clerk, Clinton Co Circuit Court, 64-72; vpres, State Fedn Women's Rep Clubs, 63; secy, Co Clerk's Asn Ind, 65-68, pres, 69; mem, Gov Comt on Voting Mach in Ind, 66; legis chmn, Co Clerks, 67 & 71; vchmn, Ruckelshaus Comt for Sen, 68; vchmn, Fifth Dist Rep Party, 68; mem elec & finance comts, Ind Rep State Comt, 69; Ind State Rep, 73-75. Mem: Charter mem Zonta Serv Club; Am Legion Auxiliary; Women's Div CofC; Women of the Moose; Bus & Prof Women's Club (legis chmn, 71). Honors & Awards: Woman of the Year Award, Bus & Prof Women's Club, 70; Clerks of Circuit Courts Award for Outstanding Clerk in Ind, 70. Relig: Christian. Mailing Add: RR 4 Frankfort IN 46041

WOOLBERT, MAYBELLE SIEGELE (D)
b Weehawken, NJ; d Curt Guenther Siegele & Mabel Schnackenberg S; m to Robert Gale Woolbert (deceased); c Susan Gale (deceased) & Richard Curt. Educ: NY Univ, 1 year; Ballard Secretarial Sch, New York, 1 year. Polit & Govt Pos: Precinct committeewoman, precinct capt & vchmn, Arapahoe Co Dem Party, Colo, 52-58; cand, Arapahoe Co Clerk, Colo, 58; exec secy, US Rep Byron L Johnson, Colo, 58-60; aide to US Rep Otis G Pike, NY, 61-74; exec secy to US Rep Tim Wirth, Colo, 75- Bus & Prof Pos: Research asst, Coun Foreign Rels, New York, 37-41. Publ: Look at Africa (w Robert Gale Woolbert), Foreign Policy Asn, 44. Mem: Colo & Md League Women Voters. Honors & Awards: Fel, Wilton

Park Conv, Sussex, Eng, 67; vpres, Am Friends of Wilton Park. Relig: Episcopal. Legal Res: 121 Summit Englewood CO 80110 Mailing Add: 6628 Rannoch Rd Bethesda MD 20034

WOOLDRIDGE, HARRY LINN (D)
b Bloominggrove, Tex, Sept 24, 99; s Henry Harrison Wooldridge & Dessie Tanner W; m 1921 to Fannie Mae McIlveen; c Tom Linn & Mary (Mrs Coleman). Educ: Fairfield High Sch, dipl, 16. Polit & Govt Pos: Dep, Internal Revenue Serv, 42-47; chmn, Freestone Co Dem Exec Comt, Tex, formerly. Bus & Prof Pos: Bank clerk, Fairfield State Bank, 21-28; salesman & bookkeeper, Parmer Chevrolet Co, 28-42; mgr, Kay Way Builders Supply Co, 47-65; self employed, acct & tax work, 65- Mem: CofC; Lions. Relig: Baptist. Mailing Add: Box 213 Fairfield TX 75840

WOOLLEN, CHARLES WESLEY (R)
b New London, Mo, Mar 3, 13; s Charles Wesley Woollen & Grace Jameson W; m 1940 to Anna Dean Lewis; c Geraldine (Mrs Fuqua), Bobbe Grace (Mrs Winders), Mary J (Mrs Keithly), Elizabeth S (Mrs Jacobs) & Charles Wesley. Polit & Govt Pos: Off mgr, Agr Stabilization & Conserv Serv, Ralls Co, Mo, 56-61; chmn, Ralls Co Rep Comt, formerly. Bus & Prof Pos: Farmer. Mil Serv: AM 3/C, Navy, 31-35. Mem: Am Farm Bur Asn. Relig: Christian Church. Mailing Add: Rte 1 New London MO 63459

WOOLLEY, JOHN ROBERT (JACK) (R)
Asst Secy for Legis Affairs, Dept of Housing & Urban Develop
b Salina, Kans, Mar 15, 24; s Henry Arthur Woolley & Ridotta Parmenter W; m 1973 to Judith Lucas; c Karen Patricia. Educ: US Merchant Marine Acad, BS, 44; Univ Southern Calif, MBA, 49; Alpha Delta Sigma; Delta Chi. Polit & Govt Pos: Spec asst to Secy of Navy, Washington, DC, 56-58, spec asst to Secy of Defense, 58-59; asst campaign planning dir, Nixon-Lodge for President, 60-61; exec secy, Orange Co Rep Cent Comt, Calif, 61-64; asst to nat chmn, Rep Nat Conv, 64, asst prog chmn, 68; exec dir, Calif Rep State Cent Comt, 64-66; asst secy for legis affairs, Dept of Housing & Urban Develop, 69- Bus & Prof Pos: Dir govt rels, TRW Systs, Redondo Beach, Calif, 66-69. Mil Serv: Entered as Midn, Navy, 41, released as Lt(jg), 46, after serv in USS Logan, Atlantic, Mediter & Pac Theatres; Capt, Naval Res, 66; Purple Heart; Two Navy Unit Commendations; Secy of Navy Commendations. Publ: Mechanics of Radio and TV Advertising, Univ Southern Calif Press, 49. Mem: Navy League of US; Bel-Air Country Club, Los Angeles; Cong Country Club, Washington, DC; Capitol Hill Club, Washington, DC; Int Club of Washington. Relig: Episcopal. Legal Res: 584 Dryad Rd Santa Monica CA 90402 Mailing Add: 344 N St SW Washington DC 20024

WOOLNER, SIDNEY HENRY (D)
b Centralia, Ill, Jan 8, 11; s Sidney Woolner & Olive Krieckhaus W; m 1936 to Doris Weiss; c Sally & Tom. Educ: Univ Mich, BA, 32; Phi Beta Kappa; Phi Kappa Phi. Polit & Govt Pos: Dep comnr, Mich Corp & Securities Comn, 49-51; campaign dir, Mich Dem Party, 50-58; dep dir, Mich OPS, 51-52, dir, 52-53; Dep Secy of State, 55-57; Chief Dep Hwy Comnr, 57-58; exec secy, Gov Williams, Mich, 59-60; exec secy, Gov Swainson, Mich, 61; Presidential Elector, 60; comnr, Community Facilities Admin, 61-64; regional adminr, Off Econ Opportunity, 64-66; admin asst to US Sen Philip A Hart, 66- Bus & Prof Pos: Sales prom, ed employee mag, Detroit Edison Co, Mich, 33-42; sales prod exec, Jam Handy Orgn, Detroit, 42-49; leasing agt, Realty Mortgage & Investment Corp, Detroit, 53-54. Mem: Am Asn Polit Consults. Relig: United Church of Christ. Legal Res: 14025 Abington Rd Detroit MI 48227 Mailing Add: 5512 Trent St Chevy Chase MD 20015

WOOTEN, DON (D)
Ill State Sen
Mailing Add: 224 18th St Rm 306 Rock Island IL 61201

WORCESTER, ROBERT M (D)
b Kansas City, Mo, Dec 21, 33; s C M Worcester & V R W; m 1958 to Joann Ransdell; c Kenton & Lawrence. Educ: Kans Univ, BS, 55. Polit & Govt Pos: Mem exec comt, Dem Abroad, United Kingdom, 72-; deleg, Dem Nat Mid-Term Conf, 74. Bus & Prof Pos: Staff mem, McKinsey & Co, Washington, DC, 62-65; Opinion Research Corp, Princeton, NJ, 65-69; Market & Opinion Research Int, London, Eng, 69- Mil Serv: Entered as 2nd Lt, Army, 55, released as 1st Lt, after serv in 8th Army Hq, Korea, 55-57; Maj, Army, 65. Publ: Ed, Consumer Market Research Handbook, McGraw-Hill, 72; auth, The Hidden Activist, New Soc, 72; A Long Way From Blackpool (Mid-Term Conf), New Statesman, 75. Mem: Market Research Soc; Brit Inst Mgt; European Soc Market & Opinion Research; World Asn Pub Opinion Research; Am Mkt Asn. Legal Res: Princeton NJ Mailing Add: 34 S Eaton Pl London SW1 England

WORDEN, DONZA T (D)
WVa State Deleg
Mailing Add: State Capitol Charleston WV 25305

WORDEN, RICHARD L, SR (R)
Ind State Rep
Mailing Add: 1152 Daly Dr New Haven IN 46774

WORK, WALTER M (D)
Tenn State Rep
Mailing Add: Rte 1 Charlotte TN 37036

WORKMAN, WYLIE WAYNE (D)
b Vesta, Ark, Nov 3, 21; s Eugene Monroe Workman & Trixie Milam W; m 1967 to Betty Bush; c Sudie, Wylie, David, Brad, Dane & Drew. Educ: Col Ozarks, 40-42; Ark Agr & Mech Col, 42-43; Univ Ark Sch Med, Little Rock, MD, 51, Am Bd Obstetrics & Gynecology, dipl. Polit & Govt Pos: Mem, Ark State Dem Exec Comt, formerly. Bus & Prof Pos: Chief of staff, Chickasawba Hosp, Blytheville, Ark, 65-; pres, Ark Obstetrics & Gynecology Soc, 70- Mil Serv: Entered as V-12, Navy, 43, released as Lt(jg), 46, after serv in LST 800, Pac Theatre, 43-46. Publ: Fatal liver disease after intravenous administration of tetracycline in high dosage, New Eng J Med, 7-12/63; Pitressin hemostasis in conization biopsy of the cervix, Obstetrics & Gynecology, 7/67. Mem: Memphis Obstetrics & Gynecology Soc; Ark Cancer Soc (bd dirs); Ark Tuberc Sanatorium (bd dirs); fel Am Col Obstetrics & Gynecology. Relig: Methodist; mem off bd. Mailing Add: 1111 N Division Blytheville AR 72315

WORKS, DONALD LEROY (R)
b Allensville, Ind, Aug 26, 28; s Jesse Floyd Works & Carrie Slack W; m 1949 to Helen Brown; c Deborah Lynn. Educ: Vevay High Sch, Ind, grad. Polit & Govt Pos: Chmn, Ohio Co Rep Party, Ind, formerly; mayor, Rising Sun, 68- Bus & Prof Pos: Mgr machine shop, Brown Tool Co, Rising Sun, 48- Mem: Mason; Moose; Scottish Rite; Shrine. Relig: Methodist. Mailing Add: Willow St Rising Sun IN 47040

WORKS, GEORGE HENRY (R)
Kans State Rep
b Humboldt, Kans, May 3, 16; s George C Works & Amelia Tholen W; m 1942 to Jane Dodge; c Robert, Virginia (Mrs Jeff Petersen), Joseph, Richard & Frederick. Educ: Iola Jr Col, 34-35; Kans State Univ, BS, 38; Sigma Nu. Polit & Govt Pos: Kans State Rep, 73- Bus & Prof Pos: Farmer, Humboldt, Kans, 38-75. Mil Serv: Entered as A/S, Navy, 42, released as Lt, 45, after serv in Pac Theatre, 44-45. Mem: Rotary; Farm Bur; Master Farmers. Relig: Catholic. Mailing Add: Rte 1 Humboldt KS 66748

WORMAN, RICHARD W (R)
Ind State Rep
b Noble Co, Ind, July 3, 33; s William D Worman & Leah Moore W; m 1951 to Marna Jo; c Terry Jo, Rennald, Dennis, Rex & Tammara. Educ: Ind Univ-Purdue Univ, Indianapolis, grad in ins, 56. Polit & Govt Pos: Trustee, Cedar Creek Twp, Ind, 70-72; Ind State Rep, Allen Co, 72- Publ: Wanta be free, Times-New Haven, 8/72. Mem: Rep Club (pres, 71-72); Cedar Creek Lions (pres, 71-72); F&AM (past Master, 63); Scottish Rite; Shrine. Relig: United Methodist. Mailing Add: RR 2 Grabill IN 46741

WORNUM, MICHAEL (D)
Calif State Assemblyman
b London, Eng, Feb 25, 25; s George Grey Wornum & Miriam Gerstle W; m to Barbara Hilda Okin; c Amanda, Christopher, Claudia & George. Educ: Archit Asn, London, dipl, 51; Univ Calif, Berkeley, BA in archit, 52, MCP, 65. Polit & Govt Pos: Mem city coun, Mill Valley, Calif, 60-68, mayor, 2 years; mem, Bay Conserv & Develop Comn, 67-74; supvr, Marin Co, 69-75; mem, Coastal Comn, 73-75; Calif State Assemblyman, Dist Nine, 74- Bus & Prof Pos: Teacher, dept city & regional planning, Univ Calif, Berkeley, 70-75. Mil Serv: Entered as Airman, Royal Air Force, 43, released as Flying Officer, 47. Mem: Am Inst Architects (fel). Legal Res: 561 Summit Ave Mill Valley CA 94941 Mailing Add: 21 Tamal Vista Blvd Corte Madera CA 94925

WORRILOW, THOMAS HENRY, SR (R)
Pa State Rep
b Chester, Pa, Aug 15, 18; s Benjamin Scott Worrilow & Sadie McNulty W; m 1947 to Amelia Mae Owens; c Thomas Henry, Jr, Diane Marie & Lawrence Richard. Educ: Chester High Sch, grad, 36. Polit & Govt Pos: Magistrate, City of Chester, Pa, 60-72; Pa State Rep, 63-64 & 67- Mil Serv: Entered as Pvt, Army, 42, released as Sgt, 45, after serv in 373rd Gen Serv Engrs Regt, ETO, 43-45; five Battle Stars. Mem: F&AM; AAONMS; Am Legion; VFW; ITU. Relig: Protestant. Mailing Add: 933 Potter St Chester PA 19013

WORTHEN, SANDRA D (D)
Del State Rep
Mailing Add: 16 Fairfield Dr Newark DE 19711

WORTHINGTON, CHARLES D (D)
NJ State Assemblyman
b Philadelphia, Pa, Apr 12, 28; s John J Worthington & Mary Kostic W; m 1955 to Margaret E Symnoski; c Margaret, Patricia, Theresa, David & Susan. Educ: West Chester State Col, BS, 50; Rutgers Univ, New Brunswick, EdM, 58; Temple Univ, 59-63. Polit & Govt Pos: NJ State Assemblyman, 74-, chmn subcomt on revenues, Joint Appropriations Comt, NJ Gen Assembly, 74-75 & subcomt on claims, 75-, NJ Gen Assembly; mem, Beach Erosion Comn, 75- Bus & Prof Pos: Counr, Pleasantville High Sch, NJ, 57-; partner, Fishermen's Wharf, Atlantic City, 59-; vpres, Brigantine Bridge Marine, 69-; secy-treas, Day Camp Asn, 72-; vpres, Little Indian Inc, 73- Mil Serv: Entered as Pvt, Army, 50, released as Cpl, 52, after serv in 2nd Armored Div, Ger, 51-52. Mem: Lions; Am Legion; NJ & Nat Educ Asns; NJ Personnel & Guid Asn. Relig: Roman Catholic. Mailing Add: 350 13th St S Brigantine NJ 08203

WORTHINGTON, LORNE R (D)
b Penticton, BC, June 14, 38; s Paul A Worthington & Alice Marsland W; m 1959 to Veneta Faye Snethen; c Penelope Lynn, Deborah Ann, Suzanne Marie, Michael Robert & Jonathan James. Educ: State Univ Iowa, 56-58 & 60; Graceland Col, BA, cum laude, 64; Lambda Delta Sigma. Polit & Govt Pos: Iowa State Rep, 62-64; mem, Gov Comt on Pub Health, 63-69; mem, Comt on Intergovt Rels, formerly; Auditor, Iowa, 65-66; Comnr of Ins, Iowa, formerly; chmn, Iowa Voter Identification Prog, currently; chmn, Common Cause, Fourth Cong Dist Coord Comt, currently. Bus & Prof Pos: Off mgr, Lamoni Sales Corp, 59-64; secy, Lamoni Farms, Inc, 63-64; pres, Nat Asn of Ins Comnrs; chmn, Spec Comt on Profitability & Investment Income in Property & Liability Ins & mem, Adv Comt Fed Dept Transportation, 68-69; dir, Scandia Savings & Loan & Restoration Trail Found, currently. Mem: Lamoni CofC, Graceland Col Alumni Asn. Honors & Awards: Outstanding Freshman Legis Award, 63; Nat Jaycee Outstanding Young Man Award, 65. Relig: Reorganized Latter-day Saint. Mailing Add: 1215 20th Place West Des Moines IA 50265

WORTHY, KENNETH MARTIN (INDEPENDENT)
b Dawson, Ga, Sept 24, 20; s Kenneth Spencer Worthy & Jeffrie Martin W; m 1947 to Eleanor Vreeland Blewett; c Jeffrie Martin (Mrs Kevin Andreae) & William Blewett. Educ: The Citadel, 37-39; Emory Univ, BPh, 41, JD, 47; Harvard Univ, MBA, cum laude, 43; Omicron Delta Kappa; Phi Delta Theta; Phi Delta Phi. Polit & Govt Pos: Chief counsel, Internal Revenue Serv & asst gen counsel, Treas Dept, 69-72; mem, Nat Coun on Organized Crime, 70-72; spec consult, Justice Dept, 72-74. Bus & Prof Pos: Assoc, Hamel, Park, McCabe & Saunders, Washington, DC, 48-51, partner, 52-69 & 72-; lectured before Tax Insts of Univ Chicago, Am Univ, George Washington Univ, Univ Tex, NY Univ, Univ Southern Calif, Tulane Univ & Va, Ark, Ky, Southern & New Eng Fed Tax Insts. Mil Serv: Entered as Cpl, Army, 43, released as Capt, 46, after serv in Transportation Corps, reentered 51, released as Capt, 52, after serv in Judge Adv Corps; Army Commendation Ribbon, 46. Publ: Co-auth, Basic Estate Planning, Bobbs-Merrill, 57; contrib to various journals. Mem: Am Bar Asn (mem coun, 65-68, vchmn, 68-69, chmn, 73-74, Taxation Sect); Fed Bar Asn (nat comn, 69-73); Bar Asn of DC; Ga State Bar Asn; Nat Tax Asn. Honors & Awards: Treas Exceptional Serv Award & Medal, 72; Int Revenue Serv Comnr Award, 72. Relig: Episcopal. Legal Res: 5305 Portsmouth Rd Bethesda MD 20016 Mailing Add: 1776 F St NW Washington DC 20006

WOZNISKY, JOHN MICHAEL (R)
Exec Dir, Rep State Comt Pa
b Pottsville, Pa, May 15, 43; s John Woznisky & Loretta W Pollack W; single. Educ: Cath Univ Am, 65-67; St Charles Sem, BA, 67; LaSalle Col, 68. Polit & Govt Pos: Exec dir, Rep Finance Comt Pa, 73-74; exec dir, Rep State Comt Pa, 74- Mil Serv: Army Res. Mem: Nat Soc Fund Raisers; Schuylkill Co Serra Club; US Jr CofC; Rotary Int; Boy Scouts. Legal Res: 212 Lewis Harrisburg PA 17110 Mailing Add: PO Box 1624 Harrisburg PA 17105

WRIGHT, ALFRED EDWARD (D)
Chmn, Goshen Dem Town Comt, Conn
b Torrington, Conn, Feb 8, 46; s Alfred Henry Wright, Jr & Patricia Carolyn Dunne W; single. Educ: Univ Conn, BS, 73; Flying Club. Polit & Govt Pos: Chmn, Goshen Dem Town Comt, Conn, 71- Bus & Prof Pos: Real estate salesman, Goshen, 70- Mil Serv: Entered as Pvt, E-1, Army, 66, released as Capt, 70, after serv in 2nd Bn, 23rd Inf, Korea, 67-68; Capt, Army Res, 3 years; Army Commendation with Oak Leaf Cluster; Army Expeditionary Medal; Nat Defense Serv Medal; Expert Infantrymans Badge. Relig: Catholic. Mailing Add: Milton Rd Goshen CT 06756

WRIGHT, CHARLES T
Justice, Wash Supreme Court
b Shelton, Wash, Mar 7, 11; s D F Wright & Fanna Bell Streator W; m 1947 to Helen Joy Fisk. Educ: Col Puget Sound, AB in BA, 32; Sigma Zeta Epsilon; Altrurian Soc. Polit & Govt Pos: Acting prosecuting attorney, Mason Co, 43-45; judge, Wash Superior Court, 49-71, president-judge, 70; justice, Wash Supreme Court, 71- Bus & Prof Pos: Pvt law practice, 37-49; ed, Washington Court Commentaries, 65-70. Mem: Am Judicature Soc; Grange; Patrons of Husbandry; Wash State Grange; F&AM. Relig: Episcopal. Legal Res: Star Rte 2 Box 1 Union WA 98592 Mailing Add: Temple of Justice Olympia WA 98504

WRIGHT, CHARLES (TED) (D)
RI State Rep
b Cranston, RI, July 20, 31; s William J Wright & Sarah Jones W; m 1950 to Barbara Elaine Browning; c Terrie E (Mrs Hoxsie), Penne L (Mrs Drugan) & Cindy A. Educ: South Kingstown High, grad, 49. Polit & Govt Pos: Town sgt, Narragansett, RI, 62-73; RI State Rep, Dist 47, 73- Bus & Prof Pos: Owner & operator, Ted Wright Rubbish Removal, 56-70, pres, Ted Wright, Inc, 70- Mem: Solid Waste Mgt; RI Truckers Asn; Lions; CofC; YMCA Century Club. Relig: Roman Catholic. Mailing Add: 189 Point Judith Rd Narragansett RI 02882

WRIGHT, DONNA GALE (R)
Mem, Rep State Cent Comt Calif
b Los Angeles, Calif, Feb 9, 23; d Glenn Edwin Myers, MD & Dorothy Murphy M; m 1957 to Elwood Wellman Wright, Jr; c Donna, Glenn, Diana, Susan & Christopher. Educ: Stanford Univ, 40-41. Polit & Govt Pos: Area chmn, 21st Assembly Dist Rep Party, San Francisco, Calif, 60-64; assoc mem, San Francisco Co Rep Cent Comt, 60-, women's vchmn, 65-66; demonstration chmn, Margaret Chase Smith Presidential Campaign, 64; mem, Rep State Cent Comt Calif, 64-; campaign coordr, Mailliard for Cong, 68, 70 & 72. Mem: San Francisco Beautiful, (treas, 65-); Vol for Instnl Aid; San Francisco Stanford Womens Club. Relig: Protestant. Mailing Add: 70 Commonwealth Ave San Francisco CA 94118

WRIGHT, FRED THORNTON (R)
b American Fork, Utah, Feb 24, 24; s Frederick Earl Wright & Mary Ann Thornton W; m 1943 to Doris Tanner Lewis; c Cathryn W (Mrs Cochran), Constance, F Lewis, Wayne H, Elizabeth, Margaret & Ruth Anne. Educ: Brigham Young Univ, 2 years; Univ Wash, 1 year; Univ Calif, Los Angeles, 1 year. Polit & Govt Pos: Voting dist officer, American Fork Rep Party, Utah, 59-61, chmn, 61-65; chmn, Utah Co Rep Party, 65-67 & 68-69, mem reapportionment comt, 66; mem, Judicial Selection Comn, Fourth Dist, 67-; chmn, Utah State Rep Party, 69-71; mem, Rep Nat Comt, 69-71. Bus & Prof Pos: Aircraft dispatcher, Am Overseas Airlines, NY, 46-47; chief dispatcher, KLM Royal Dutch Airlines, 47-51; raw materials analyst, US Steel Corp, Geneva, Utah, 51- Mil Serv: Entered as Pvt, Army Air Corps, 43, released as 1st Lt, 46, after serv in Air Transport Command, ETO, 44-46. Mem: American Fork Hosp (bd of trustees); Lions. Relig: Latter-day Saint; bishop. Mailing Add: 825 N First East St American Fork UT 84003

WRIGHT, GARDNER E, JR (D)
Conn State Rep
Mailing Add: 38 Duncan St Bristol CT 06010

WRIGHT, GEORGE CARLIN (D)
Committeeman, Chenango Co Dem Comt, NY
b Shawsville, Md, Mar 3, 26; s James Grover Wright & Rose Adela Hulshart W; m 1955 to Martha Mabel Roth; c Susan C, Wayne C & Stephanie R. Educ: Johns Hopkins Univ, BE, 47; Univ Del, MS, 55, PhD, 58. Polit & Govt Pos: Coordr, Chenango Co McCarthy for President, 68; deleg, Dem Nat Conv, 72; committeeman, Chenango Co Dem Comt, NY, 72- Bus & Prof Pos: Chemist, Glenn L Martin Co, Md, 47-50; research chemist, Gen Aniline & Film Corp, Pa, 50 & 52-53; sr research chemist, Norwich Pharmacal Co, Norwich, NY, 58- Mil Serv: Entered as Pvt, Army, 50 & released 52, after serv in Army Chem Ctr, Edgewood, Md. Publ: Co-auth, Thermal degradation of alkyl n-phenylcarbamates, J Am Chem Soc, 81: 2138-2143; Sythesis of new hydrazidines with vasoconstrictor activity, J Pharm Sci, Vol 59, No 1; Synthesis and hypotensive properties of new 4-aminoquinolines, J Med Chem, Vol 14, No 11. Mem: Am Chem Soc (chmn, Student Awards Comt, spring 72); Sci Res Soc Am; Friends of the Libr, Norwich, NY (treas). Relig: Nondenominational. Mailing Add: 179 Lyon Brook Rd RD 2 Norwich NY 13815

WRIGHT, J STEWART (R)
Chmn, McCone Co Rep Cent Comt, Mont
b Glasgow, Mont, Jan 17, 20; s Frank C Wright & Anna Stanley W; m 1952 to Lois Sylvia Samuelson; c Jay S, Bruce A, Jan Sylvia & Frank C. Educ: Northern Mont Col, 38-39; Mont State Col, BS, 42; Alpha Zeta; Phi Kappa Phi. Polit & Govt Pos: Bd mem, McCone Co Dist Six Sch Bd, 49-59; bd mem, McCone Dist High Sch Bd, 53-59; Mont State Rep, 59-64; chmn, McCone Co Rep Cent Comt, 66- Bus & Prof Pos: Owner & operator, McCone Co Ranch, 49- Mem: Mont Stockgrowers Asn; McCone Co Farm Bur; AF&AM. Relig: Lutheran. Mailing Add: Rte 232 C32 Wolf Point MT 59201

WRIGHT, JAMES C, JR (D)
US Rep, Tex
b Ft Worth, Tex, Dec 22, 22; s James C Wright & Mary Lyster W; m to Betty Hay, 1972; c Jimmy, Virginia Sue, Patricia Kay & Alicia Marie. Educ: Weatherford Col; Univ Tex. Polit & Govt Pos: Tex State Rep, 47-49; mayor, Weatherford, Tex, 50-54; mem, Tex League of Munic, pres, 53; US Rep, 12th Dist, Tex, 55-, chmn, Pub Works Subcomt on Invests & Rev & Comn on Hwy Beautification & Dep Dem Whip, US House Rep, currently, mem, House deleg to US-Mex Interparliamentary Conf, 63-74, chmn, House Dem Task Force on Energy & Econ, 74-75; mem, Nat Comn Water Qual, 73-75. Mil Serv: Served with Army Air Force, World War II; Distinguished Flying Cross; Legion of Merit for work in Air Force Res, 70. Publ: You & Your Congressman, Coward-McCann, 64; Of Swords and Plowshares, Stafford-Lowdon, 68; co-auth, Congress and Conscience, Lippincott, 70; plus others. Honors & Awards: Outstanding Young Man, Tex Jr CofC, 53. Relig: Presbyterian. Legal Res: Ft Worth TX Mailing Add: 2459 Rayburn House Off Bldg Washington DC 20515

WRIGHT, JAMES L, JR (R)
Pa State Rep
b New York, NY, Mar 10, 25; s James L Wright & Rose Fitzsimmons W; m 1951 to Elaine Norris; c Duane, Anne, James & Matthew. Educ: Univ Mich, BSE, 51; registered prof engr. Polit & Govt Pos: Mem bd supvrs, Middletown Twp, Bucks Co, Pa, 62-65, chmn, 64; asst co chmn, Bucks Co Rep Party, 63-64; Pa State Rep, 142nd Dist, Bucks Co, 65-; deleg, Rep Nat Conv, 72. Bus & Prof Pos: Sr indust engr, US Steel, Trenton, NJ, formerly. Mil Serv: Entered as Pvt, Army, 43, released as Capt, 57, after serv in 8th Air Force, ETO, 47; Air Medal; Victory Medal; Theatre Ribbons. Relig: Catholic. Mailing Add: 116 Hollow Rd Levittown PA 19056

WRIGHT, JAMES LASHUA (D)
Secy, Dupage Co Dem Cent Comt, Ill
b Hinsdale, Ill, Aug 1, 34; s Charles Aspinall Wright, Sr & Vera Lashua W; m 1965 to Paulette Blanche Hecker; c James Lashua, Jr & Brian Paul. Educ: Hinsdale Twp High Sch, Ill, 4 years. Polit & Govt Pos: Dem precinct committeeman, 33rd Precinct, Ill, 56-; secy, Dupage Co Dem Cent Comt, 60-; deleg, Dem State Nominating Conv, 64; village councilman, Westmont, Ill, 67-; Ill State Rep, 69-72. Bus & Prof Pos: Investr, Ill Dept of Revenue, 61-69; owner-mgr, Commun Agency, Westmont, 69- Mem: YMCA Bus Mens Club; Dupage Co Hist Soc; Ill Retail Merchants Asn; Westmont CofC. Relig: Seventh-day-Adventist. Mailing Add: 219 N Adams Westmont IL 60559

WRIGHT, JERAULD
b Amherst, Mass, June 4, 98; s Gen William Mason Wright & Marjorie R Jerauld W; m 1938 to Phyllis Blagden Thompson; c Marion Jerauld & William Mason, III. Educ: US Naval Acad, BS, 17. Hon Degrees: ScD, Rose Polytech Inst; LLD, Col of William & Mary & Univ Mass. Polit & Govt Pos: Assigned to Presidential Yacht USS Mayflower, 24-26; White House Aide under President Hoover & President Coolidge, 24-26 & 31-33; mem bd nat intel estimates, CIA, 61-63; US Ambassador to Repub of China, 63-66. Mil Serv: Entered as Ens, Navy, 17, released as Adm, 60, after serv in Atlantic, Pac, Asiatic, European & Mid East; Command Ens, US Navy, 17 with serv in USS Castine, 17-18, USS John D Ford, 22-24 & USS Md, 26-29; attached Bur Ord, 29-31; 1st Lt & Gunnery, USS Salt Lake City, 31-34; exec staff, US Naval Acad, 34-35, 39-41; aide asst secy Navy, 35-36; attached Bur Ord, 36-37; Comdr, destroyer USS Blue, 37-39; exec officer, USS Miss, 41-42; commanded HMS Seraph in Evacuation French Gen Giraud from Vichy, France, 42; USN Mem of Murphy Clark Group in Secret Submarine Landing, NAfrica, 42; commanded USS Santa Fe, Pac Opers, 43-44; assigned to Hq, Comdr-in-Chief, US Fleet & Staff of Comdr Naval Forces in Europe, also staff of comdr, AEF; amphibious group five, 44-45; comdr cruiser div six, 45; head oper readiness sect, Off Chief of Naval Opers, 45-49; comdr amphibious force, Atlantic Fleet, 49-51; US mem NATO standing group, Washington, 51-52; Comdr-in-Chief, US Naval Forces in Eastern Atlantic, Mediter & Mid East, 52-54; Supreme Allied Comdr, Atlantic, NATO, 54-60; Comdr-in-Chief, Atlantic & US Atlantic Fleet, 54-60; Awarded DSM; Legion of Merit with Gold Star; Bronze Star; Silver Star; Chevalier Legion of Honor, France; Foreign Decorations, France, Belgium, Netherlands, Portugal, Peru, Brazil, Italy & Colombia. Mem: US Naval Inst; Washington Inst Foreign Affairs; Coun Foreign Rels, NY; Naval Hist Found, Washington, DC (vpres, 60-); Alibi Club, Washington, DC (pres). Relig: Episcopal. Mailing Add: 2706 36th St NW Washington DC 20007

WRIGHT, JOHN COOK (D)
Mem Exec Comt, New Dem Coalition of Kans
b Los Angeles, Calif, July 27, 33; s Charles MacPhee Wright & Helen Cook W; m 1955 to Jo Anne Steinheimer; c Elizabeth, Jennifer, Melanie & Kennedy Weston. Educ: Harvard Col, AB, magna cum laude, 54; Stanford Univ, PhD, 60. Polit & Govt Pos: Precinct chmn, Dem-Farmer-Labor Party, Fridley, Minn, 62-64, city chmn, 62-63; city councilman, Fridley, Minn, 64-66; deleg, Anoka Co Dem-Farmer-Labor Conv, 62-64, 66 & 68; alt deleg, Minn State Dem-Farmer-Labor Conv, 66; vchmn, Minn Conf of Concerned Dem, 67-68; deleg, Dem Nat Conv, 68; co-founder & mem exec comt, New Dem Coalition of Kans, 69-, chmn Lawrence chap, 69-; precinct committeeman, Douglas Co Dem Party, Kans, 72-; deleg, Third Dist Dem Conv, Kans, 72, deleg, State Dem Conv, 72. Bus & Prof Pos: Acting instr dept of psychol, Stanford Univ, 59-60; asst prof inst of child develop, Univ Minn, 60-63, assoc prof, 63-68; assoc prof human develop, Univ Kans, 68-71, prof, Depts Human Develop & Psychol, 71-, dir, Kans Ctr Res in Early Childhood Educ, 71-, mem, Univ Coun & Exec Comt, 71-74. Mil Serv: Entered as Pvt, Army, 54, released as SP-4, 56, after serv in Combat Develop Dept, Signal Corps, Army Electronic Proving Ground, Ft Huachuca, Ariz, 55-56; Good Conduct Medal. Publ: Basic cognitive processes in children, Monographs of the Soc for Research in Child Develop, 63; Child psychology, In: Experimental Methods and Instrumentation in Psychology, (J Sidowski, ed), Wiley, 65; Cognitive develop, In: Human Development, (F Falkner, ed), W B Saunders, 67. Mem: Psychonomic Soc; Soc for Research in Child Develop; Am Asn Advan Sci; Am Civil Liberties Union (mem bd, dirs, Lawrence Chap, 73-); NAACP. Honors & Awards: Nat Sci Found fel, summer 59. Relig: Episcopal. Mailing Add: 3515 W Fifth Terr Lawrence KS 66044

WRIGHT, JOSEPH R, JR (R)
Asst Secy for Admin, Dept Agr
b Tulsa, Okla, Sept 24, 38; s Joe Robert Wright & Ann Helen Cech W; m 1972 to Elizabeth Scott Perry. Educ: Colo Sch Mines, BS, 61; Yale Univ, MBA, 63. Polit & Govt Pos: Dep dir, Bur Census, Dept Com, 71-72, dep admin for mgt, social & econ statist admin, 72-73, asst secy for econ affairs, 73; asst secy for admin, Dept Agr, 73- Bus & Prof Pos: Vpres, Booz, Allen & Hamilton, 65-71. Mil Serv: Entered as 2nd Lt, Army, 63, released as 1st Lt, 65. Mailing Add: 1200 N Nash St Apt 826 Arlington VA 22209

WRIGHT, LACY, JR (D)
WVa State Deleg
b Welch, WVa, Aug 18, 46; s Lacy Wright & Lou Emma Mullens W; div; c Tammy Renee. Educ: Bluefield State Col, BS, 70; pres, Bluefield State Col Young Dem Club; Key Club. Polit

& Govt Pos: WVa State Deleg, McDowell Co, 75- Bus & Prof Pos: Teacher, McDowell Co Bd Educ, 70-72; pres, Tammy Indust, 72- Mem: Lions; WVa Educ Asn; Berwind-Coalwood Caretta Conserv Club; Nat Asn Security Dealers. Relig: Methodist. Mailing Add: Box 85 Main St Bradshaw WV 24817

WRIGHT, OREN ALVIN (R)
Chmn, Johnson Co Rep Cent Comt, Ind
b Greenwood, Ind, Aug 27, 11; s Harry Wright & Clara Hautsky W; m 1936 to Ida Ray; c Newton. Educ: Purdue Univ, 2 years. Polit & Govt Pos: Chmn, Johnson Co Rep Cent Comt, Ind, 57-69 & 71- Bus & Prof Pos: Farmer & bank dir. Mem: Odd Fellows; Mason; Shrine; Lions; Farmers Union. Honors & Awards: Farm Bur Hall of Fame, Purdue Univ. Relig: Christian. Mailing Add: Rte 6 Box 121 Greenwood IN 46142

WRIGHT, RICHARD (D)
NC State Rep
b Horry Co, SC, Oct 8, 44; s Ottis Richard Wright, Sr & Olive Battle W; single. Educ: Univ NC, Chapel Hill, AB, 67, Law Sch, JD, 71; Phi Beta Kappa; Order of Old Well; Soc of Janus. Polit & Govt Pos: NC State Rep, 74- Bus & Prof Pos: Farmer, Tabor City, NC; attorney-at-law, McGougan & Wright, currently. Mem: Civitan Club; Farm Bur; NC Bar Asn; Young Dem Club; Morehead Selection Comt. Relig: Methodist. Legal Res: Rte 1 Box 72 Tabor City NC 28463 Mailing Add: PO Box 457 Tabor City NC 28463

WRIGHT, RICHARD O (R)
Chmn, Marquette Co Rep Party, Wis
b Ft Wayne, Ind, Jan 16, 42; s Joseph R Wright & Marion Arnold W; m 1973 to Louise Iovino. Educ: Univ Wis, BS, Law Sch, JD, 67; Phi Alpha Delta. Polit & Govt Pos: Chmn, Second Cong Dist Young Rep, Wis, 63-65; ed, Insight & Outlook, 65-67; state chmn, Wis Young Am for Freedom, 68-70; chmn, 13th Ward Rep Party, 68-70; chmn, Marquette Co Rep Party, 75-; dist attorney, Marquette Co, 75- Bus & Prof Pos: Assoc, Andrus, Sceales, Starke & Sawall Law Firm, 67-71; dir legal ctr, Americans for Effective Law Enforcement, 71-74; partner, Thompson & Wright Law Firm, 74- Mil Serv: Pvt, Army, 68, serv in 5th Army, Ft Dix. Publ: Auth, The default of the Rand intellectual, Insight & Outlook, 4/65 & Temper of the revolution, New Guard, 4/69; auth-ed, Whose FBI?, Open Court, 74. Mem: Montello Clin Bd (secy); Am Farm Bur; Wis Bar Asn; World Youth Crusade for Freedom (secy). Relig: Christian. Mailing Add: Rte 1 Montello WI 53949

WRIGHT, SAM W (D)
Miss State Sen
b Greenwood, Miss, July 20, 26; s Sam W Wright & Jamie F W; m 1955 to Winifred Walker; c Sam Walker & Jack Glenn. Educ: Univ Mo, 43; Delta State Col, BS, 49; CLU, Am Col Life Underwriters; Pi Kappa Alpha; Jr Class Officer. Polit & Govt Pos: Miss State Sen, Dist 22, 72- Bus & Prof Pos: Gen agt, Great Am Reserve Ins Co, 63-73. Mil Serv: Entered as Seaman, Navy, 44, released as Machinist's Mate 2/C, 46, after serv in Pac Theatre; recalled as Ens, 50, released as Lt(jg), 51, after serv in Korea, 50-51; Theatre Ribbons; Combat Ribbons. Publ: Various articles in Ins Salesman, 68. Mem: Am Legion (VComdr); VFW; Clinton CofC (legis chmn); Miss Econ Coun; M Club of Delta State Col Alumni Asn. Honors & Awards: Distinguished Serv Award, Int Asn Health Underwriters, 68. Relig: Methodist. Mailing Add: Box 2424 Jackson MS 39205

WRIGHT, STANLEY ALLEN (R)
NDak State Sen
b Stanley, NDak, Feb 17, 26; s James A Wright & Evelyn Pace W; m 1948 to Mavis Dalhaug; c Pamela (Mrs Thompson), Joleen & Cheryl. Educ: High Sch. Polit & Govt Pos: City alderman, Stanley, NDak, 58-70, mayor, 70-; NDak State Sen, 72- Mil Serv: Entered as Pvt, Army, 46, released as T-5, 48, after serv in Seventh Div, Korea, 46-47. Mem: Am Legion; Lions; Elks; Legion State Band; Farm Bur. Relig: Lutheran. Legal Res: 102 Fifth Ave SE Stanley ND 58784 Mailing Add: Box 97 Stanley ND 58784

WRIGHT, THOMAS E (R)
Chmn, Rep State Cent Comt RI
b Providence, RI, May 25, 36. Educ: Univ RI, BS, 58; Univ Tulsa Law Sch, JD, 64. Polit & Govt Pos: Mem, Warren Rep Town Comt, RI, 54-, secy, 63-65, chmn, 66-71; mem, Rep State Rep Cent Comt RI, 62-, chmn, 71-; Asst Attorney Gen, RI, 67-71; mem, Town of Warren Charter Comn, 68; probate judge, 70; moderator, Attorney Gen Narcotics Comn. Bus & Prof Pos: Instr, Law Enforcement Div, Salve Regina Col; practicing attorney, 64- Mil Serv: Capt, Army Res. Mem: Univ RI Century Club; Warren Youth Coun; Warren Indust Comn; Elks; RI Bar Asn. Relig: Roman Catholic. Mailing Add: 72 Bridge St Warren RI 02885

WRIGHT, WILLIAM MARSHALL
Asst Secy of State for Cong Rels
b El Dorado, Ark, July 14, 26; s John Harvey Wright, Sr & Helen Vaughan Williams Wright Harris; m 1950 to Mickey Olean Johnson; c William Marshall, Jr & Jefferson Vaughan. Educ: Univ Ark, 46-48; Georgetown Univ Sch Foreign Serv, BS, 51; Cornell Univ, 57-58; Kappa Sigma. Polit & Govt Pos: Vconsul, Am Consulate, Port Said, Egypt, 53-55; admin officer, US Consulate Gen, Toronto, Can, 56-57; econ officer, US Embassy, Rangoon, Burma, 58-60; Thailand desk officer, Dept State, 61-63, spokesman, 64-66, country dir, Philippines, 69, Asst Secy of State for Cong Rels, 73-; polit officer, US Embassy, Bangkok, Thailand, 66; sr staff, Nat Security Coun, 67-68, dir long range plans, 70-72. Mil Serv: Entered as Pvt, Marine Corp, 44, released as Pvt, 1/C, 46, after serv in 1st & 3rd Marine Div, Guam & China. Honors & Awards: Meritorious Serv Award, Dept of State, 66 & Unit Distinguished Serv Award, 72. Relig: Protestant. Legal Res: AR Mailing Add: 2344 King Pl NW Washington DC 20007

WULFF, HENRY C (R)
Iowa State Rep
Mailing Add: 1131 Liberty Ave Waterloo IA 50702

WUNSCH, CHRISTIAN (D)
Colo State Sen
Mailing Add: 15 Cactus Dr La Junta CO 81050

WUNSCH, PAUL ROBERT (R)
Chmn, Kingman Co Rep Orgn, Kans
b Freeport, Kans, July 14, 01; s Robert Wunsch & Mathilda Shultz W; m 1928 to Bula Mae Staley; c Delores Elaine (Mrs Stevens) & Robert Staley. Educ: Univ Kans, AB, 24 & LLB, 25; Delta Sigma Rho; Phi Alpha Delta; Sour Owl Soc. Polit & Govt Pos: Co attorney, Kingman Co, Kans, 26-33; Kans State Rep, 37-45, majority floor leader, Kans House of Rep, 39-41 & Speaker of the House, 43-45; Kans State Sen, 45-65, pres-pro-tem, Kans State Senate, 49-65; mem, Kans Legis Coun, 49-, chmn, 2 years; chmn, Kingman Co Rep Orgn, 64-; cand, Gov, Kans, 64. Mem: Fel Am Col Trial Lawyers; CofC; AF&AM; KT; Median Shrine. Relig: Presbyterian. Mailing Add: 120 Ave B W Kingman KS 67068

WURF, JERRY (D)
b New York, NY, May 18, 19; s Sigmund Wurf & Lena Tannenbaum W; m 1960 to Mildred Kiefer; c Susan, Nicholas & Abigail. Educ: NY Univ, AB, 40. Polit & Govt Pos: Organizer, Am Fedn State, Co & Munic Employees, Coun 37, 47-58, int pres, 64-; delg, Dem Nat Conv, 72. Bus & Prof Pos: Organizer, Local 448, Hotel & Restaurant Employees, 43; organizer, Adminr Union's Welfare Fund, 47; vpres, exec coun, AFL-CIO, 68-, vpres, Indust Union Dept, currently. Publ: Co-auth, American federation of State, County & Municipal Employees, In: Collective Bargaining in Government, Prentice-Hall, 72. Mem: Nat Urban League (bd); Maritime Trades Dept (exec bd); Comt Nat Health Ins, Health Security Action (exec comt); Am for Dem Action (exec comt); Leadership Conf on Civil Rights (exec comt). Honors & Awards: Walter Reuther Award, Am for Dem Action, NY, 72. Relig: Jewish. Mailing Add: 3846 Cathedral Ave NW Washington DC 20016

WURTZ, RICHARD JOSEPH (D)
Chmn, Linn Co Dem Cent Comt, Kans
b Mound City, Kans, Jan 11, 40; s Wesley W Wurtz & Ruth Merriman W; m 1961 to Janice Elizabeth Holt; c Melissa, Nicholas & Christopher. Educ: Univ Kans, BA, 61, MA, 67; St Louis Univ, 66-68; Phi Alpha Theta. Polit & Govt Pos: Chmn, Linn Co Dem Cent Comt, Kans, 74- Bus & Prof Pos: Chmn bd, Health Servs Asn, Inc, 74- Publ: Co-ed, The Purpose of Higher Education, UCCF/UME Press, 66. Mem: Mound City CofC (pres, 75). Honors & Awards: Community Ambassador to India, St Louis Coun for Experiment in Int Living, 65. Relig: United Methodist. Legal Res: RR 2 Mound City KS 66056 Mailing Add: Box 149 Mound City KS 66056

WURTZEL, DONALD RICKY (D)
Chairperson, Winneshiek Co Dem Cent Comt, Iowa
b Waukon, Iowa, Apr 10, 52; s Delmar Bernhard Wrutzel & Carrie Amelia Anderson W; single. Educ: Luther Col (Iowa); BA, 74; Nat Hon Soc; Alpha Phi Omega. Polit & Govt Pos: Pres, Winneshiek Co Young Dem Club, Iowa, 67-69; vchairperson, Luther Col Dem, 70-71; vchairperson Winneshiek Co Dem Cent Comt, 71-74, chairperson, 74- Bus & Prof Pos: Asst mgr, Viking Theatre, Decorah, Iowa, 73-; asst food serv dir, Luther Col, 75. Honors & Awards: Outstanding Young Religious Leader, Decorah Jaycees, 74. Relig: Lutheran; mem coun, First Lutheran Church. Mailing Add: 322 Pershing Ave Decorah IA 52101

WYANT, CLINTON W (DFL)
Chmn, Aitkin Co Dem-Farmer-Labor Party, Minn
b O'Neill, Nebr, Dec 25, 31; s Charles E Wyant & Mary Cuddy W; m 1958 to Sophia Stalzer; c Maria S, Charles R & Amy Marie. Educ: St John's Univ, Minn, BA; William Mitchell Col Law, BSL; St Paul Col Law, LLB; St Paul Dominic Club; Assoc Confraternity Club. Polit & Govt Pos: Alt deleg, Dem Nat Conv, 64, deleg, 68; deleg, Minn State, Dist & Aitkin Co Dem-Farmer-Labor Conv, Waukenabo Precinct, 66; finance dir, Eighth Dist Dem-Farmer-Labor Party, formerly, chmn, formerly & dir, currently; chmn, Aitkin Co Dem-Farmer-Labor Party, currently; Asst Pub Defender, Minn, 67- Mem: 15th Judicial Bar Asn (treas); Minn Bar Asn (treas); Aitkin Co Area Resort Asn (exec secy); Jr CofC. Honors & Awards: Recipient State Gold Medal & Nat Award, Jr CofC. Relig: Roman Catholic. Legal Res: Rte 2 Palisade MN 56469 Mailing Add: 8 Second St NE Aitkin MN 56431

WYATT, CECIL L (D)
Ala State Rep
Mailing Add: PO Box 1 Ramer AL 36069

WYATT, JOSEPH PEYTON, JR (D)
Tex State Rep
b Victoria, Tex, Oct 12, 41; s Joseph Peyton Wyatt & Mabel Wright W; single. Educ: Univ Tex, BA, 69; Pi Kappa Alpha. Polit & Govt Pos: Staff, Vice President Lyndon B Johnson, Washington, DC; research asst, Sen William Patman, Tex Senate, 61 & 65; admin staff of US Rep Clark Thompson, Tex, 62 & 63; Tex State Rep, 70- Bus & Prof Pos: Mem staff, Aluminum Co Am, Point Comfort, Tex, formerly (summer). Mil Serv: Entered as Pvt, Marine Corps Res, 66, released as Cpl, 71. Mem: Victoria & Calhoun Co CofC. Relig: Catholic. Legal Res: PO Box 147 Bloomington TX 77951 Mailing Add: 202 S Tex Savings Bldg Victoria TX 77901

WYATT, WENDELL WILLIAM (R)
b Eugene, Ore, June 15, 17; s Henry H Wyatt & Jane Pearl Smith W; m 1962 to Faye L Reinecker; c Ann, Jane & William Wyatt & Sandi & Larry Hill. Educ: Univ Ore, LLB, 41; Phi Delta Phi; Beta Theta Pi. Polit & Govt Pos: Chmn, Ore State Rep Cent Comt, 55-57; mem, President Eisenhower's Percy Comt, 58; chmn, Ore for Nixon Comt, 60; US Rep, Ore, First Dist, 64-74. Bus & Prof Pos: Mem, Ore State Bar Bd of Gov, 53-55, mem house of deleg, Am Bar Asn, 60-66. Mil Serv: Entered as Aviation Cadet, Navy, 42, released as Capt, Marine Corps, 46, after serv in FMB 413, SPac, 44; Asiatic Theater Ribbon. Mem: Am Col of Trial Lawyers; Elks; Mason; Am Legion; VFW. Relig: Episcopal. Mailing Add: 2100 SW Crest Dr Lake Oswego OR 97034

WYATT, WILLIAM W (D)
Ore State Rep
Mailing Add: Box 625 Gearhart OR 97138

WYATT, WILSON WATKINS, SR (D)
b Louisville, Ky, Nov 21, 05; s Richard H Wyatt & Mary Watkins W; m 1930 to Anne Kinnaird Duncan; c Mary Anne, Nancy Kinnaird & Wilson Watkins, Jr. Educ: Univ Louisville, JD, 27. Hon Degrees: LLD, Knox Col, 45 & Univ Louisville, 48. Polit & Govt Pos: Trial attorney, Louisville, Ky, 34; Sinking Fund Comnrs Bd, 36; chmn, Louisville Comt on Foreign Rels, 40-41; mayor, Louisville, 41-45; chmn, Louisville Metrop Area Defense Coun, 42-45; mem adv bd, US Conf Mayors, 42-45; spec rep, Bd Econ Warfare, NAfrica, 43; pres, Am Soc Planning Off, 43-44; pres, Ky Munic League, 44; deleg-at-lg, Dem Nat Conv, 44-; pres, Louisville Area Develop Asn, 44-45; pres, Am Munic Asn, 45; Housing Expediter & Adminr Nat Housing Agency, 46; personal campaign mgr, Stevenson, 52; Ky chmn treas adv comt, US Savings Bonds Prog; Lt Gov, Ky, 59-63; chmn, Ky Econ Develop Comn, 60-63; Dem Nat Committeeman, Ky, 60-64. Bus & Prof Pos: Mem firm, Garnett & Van Winkle, 27-32; prof, Jefferson Sch Law, 29-35; attorney-at-law, 27-35; mem firm, Peter, Heyburn, Marshall & Wyatt, 35-41; dir, Levy Bros, Inc, Standard Gravure Co, WHAS, Inc, Courier J & Louisville Times Co; bd dir, Roper Pub Opinion Research Ctr; sr partner, Wyatt,

Grafton & Sloss, 47-; mem bd trustees, Univ Louisville, 50-58, chmn, 51-55; pres, Louisville Area CofC, 71-72; pres, Nat Munic League, 72-; mem bd, Ky CofC, 74- Mem: Forest Farmers Asn; Rotary; Washington Fed City Club; Nat Capital Dem; NY Century Club. Honors & Awards: Awarded Citation of Merit, Louisville Metrop Area Defense Coun, 2 times; Recipient, US Treas Distinguished Serv Award; Citizen of the Year, Louisville Jaycees, 72; Man of the Year Award, Louisville Advert Club, 74; Brotherhood Award, Nat Conf Christians & Jews, 74; Gold Cup for community serv, Louisville Area CofC, 74. Relig: Presbyterian. Legal Res: 1001 Alta Vista Rd Louisville KY 40205 Mailing Add: 28th Floor Citizens Plaza Louisville KY 40202

WYCKOFF, DAVID COLE **(R)**
b Somerville, NJ, June 14, 40; s Frederick Raymond Wyckoff & Ruth Cole W; m 1960 to Kerry Gay Shaffer; c David Cole, Tracy Carroll, Whitney Ceone, Brent Preston. Educ: Hope Col; Kappa Eta Nu. Polit & Govt Pos: Dist committeeman, Hillsborough Twp, NJ, 65, chmn Rep club, 66 & munic chmn, 67; vchmn, Somerset Co Rep Party, formerly; chmn, Somerset Co Ment Health Bd, 69-; comnr, Somerset Co Bd of Taxation, currently. Bus & Prof Pos: Secy-treas, F R Wyckoff Agency, Somerville, NJ, 64-68 & pres, 68- Mem: Somerset Co Ins Agents Asn (pres, 71-); Boy Scouts; Temple Christian Day Sch PTA (past pres); Wyckoff Asn in Am. Relig: Protestant. Mailing Add: Long Hill Rd Box 90 Neshanic NJ 08853

WYCKOFF, RUSSELL LEROY **(D)**
Iowa State Rep
b Vinton, Iowa, Mar 2, 25; s Charles Wyckoff & Neva Rouse W; m 1946 to Margie Elizabeth Ploeger; c John A, Theodore W, Richard C & James R. Educ: Urbana Pub Sch, Iowa. Polit & Govt Pos: Chmn, Benton Co Dem Party, 69; Iowa State Rep, 71- Bus & Prof Pos: Pres, Urbana Sch Bd, 51-52. Mil Serv: Entered as Pvt, Army, 43, released as S/Sgt, 45, after serv in Co L 347th Inf 87th Div, ETO, 44-45; Combat Inf Badge; Good Conduct Medal; Bronze Star Medal; ETO Ribbon with Rhineland & Ardennes Campaign Stars. Mem: Am Legion; Nat Rifle Asn; Iowa Farm Bur; Iowa Trapshooting Asn. Relig: Methodist. Mailing Add: 808 First Ave Vinton IA 52349

WYCOFF, S JEANNE **(D)**
Mem, Ill Dem State Cent Comt
b Aberdeen, Miss, Dec 22, 14; d Carl Anderson & Bertha Clift A; m 1947 to E Don Wycoff, wid. Educ: Univ Iowa, BA, 37; charter mem Alpha Iota; Hi-Maskers Playcrafters. Polit & Govt Pos: Chmn, Mercer Co Dem Party, Ill, 60-62, Dem precinct committeewoman, 60-; committeewoman, Ill Dem State Cent Comt, 19th Dist, 66-, chairwoman, formerly; deleg, Dem Nat Conv, 72; mem, Dem Nat Comt, formerly. Bus & Prof Pos: Prof investr & supvr, Ill State Dept Registr & Educ, 73- Mem: Mercer Co Hist Soc; Mercer Co Hosp Auxiliary; Mercer Co Farm Bur; Broadway Theater Guild; Friends of Art. Honors & Awards: Woman of the Year, Mercer Co Bus & Prof Women, 66. Relig: Presbyterian. Mailing Add: Box 264 Aledo IL 61231

WYDLER, JOHN W **(R)**
US Rep, NY
b Brooklyn, NY, June 9, 24; m 1959 to Brenda O'Sullivan; c Christopher John, Kathleen Ellen & Elizabeth Ann. Educ: Harvard Law Sch, 50. Polit & Govt Pos: With US Attorney's Off, 53-59; mem, NY State Invest Comn on Sch Construction Irregularities, 59; US Rep, NY, 63-, asst regional whip, State of NY, US House of Rep, currently, asst to minority floor leader, currently; deleg, Rep Nat Conv, 68, alt deleg, 72; mem, Bd Visitors, US Merchant Marine Acad, 71 & 73. Bus & Prof Pos: Lawyer; assoc of A A Foreman, 59-61; mem, Wydler, Balin, Pares & Soloway, 67- Mil Serv: World War II, discharged as Sgt, 45; Lt, Air Force Res, Judge Adv Off. Mem: Am Legion; VFW; Lions; Mason; Elks. Relig: Cathedral of the Incarnation; mem, Bishop's Men & Men's Asns. Legal Res: 63 First St Garden City NY 11530 Mailing Add: 2334 Rayburn House Off Bldg Washington DC 20515

WYER, J W **(D)**
Chmn, Jackson Co Dem Exec Comt, Tex
b El Campo, Tex, Oct 24, 35; s Lester John Wyer & Ina Presley W; m 1957 to Margret Jeannette Kinsfather; c Jerral Wayne & Cherrie Kinberli. Polit & Govt Pos: Precinct chmn, Precinct One, Jackson Co, Tex, 65; chmn, Jackson Co Dem Exec Comt, 69- Bus & Prof Pos: Construction inspector, Houston Pipe Line, 64; process operator, DuPont, 65- Mil Serv: Nat Guard Res, 9 years, Sgt. Mem: Little League (dir). Mailing Add: Rte 1 Box 565 Edna TX 77957

WYKLE, ROBERT JAMES **(D)**
Chmn, Wayne Co Dem Comt, NY
b Lyons, NY, Feb 14, 19; s Leslie D Wykle & Margaret Myers W; m 1941 to Jeanette Hilfiker; c Robert J, Jr & Timothy J. Educ: Mechanics Inst Technol, Rochester, NY, 39-40; Capitol Radio Eng Inst, Washington, DC, 43. Polit & Govt Pos: Mem, Wayne Co Dem Comt, NY, 50-, chmn, 66-; chmn, Lyons Dem Town Comt, 56-66; comnr elec, Wayne Co, 59-; trustee, Village Bd, Lyons, 75- Bus & Prof Pos: Retail owner, 57-70; pres, Wymol Inc, 70-72; prod mgr, H C Hemingway & Co, 72- Mil Serv: Entered as Pvt, Air Force, 43, released as M/Sgt, 45, after serv in 556th Signal, ETO, 44; European Theatre-Am Theatre Victory Medal. Mem: VFW; Am Legion; Elks; Elec Comnr Asn State NY; Finger Lakes Law Enforcement Asn. Relig: Catholic. Legal Res: 5 N Canal Lyons NY 14489 Mailing Add: PO Box 214 Lyons NY 14489

WYLIE, CHALMERS PANGBURN **(R)**
US Rep, Ohio
b Norwich, Ohio, Nov 23, 20; s Chalmer C Wylie & Margaret Pangburn W; m 1964 to Marjorie Ann Murnane; c Jacquelyn & Bradley. Educ: Otterbein Col, 39-41; Ohio State Univ, 41-43; Harvard Law Sch, LLB, 48. Polit & Govt Pos: Asst Attorney Gen, Ohio, 48 & 51-54; asst city attorney, Columbus, 49-50, city attorney, 54-57; supvr, Indust Comn, Ohio, 51-53; pres, Buckeye Rep Club, 53; pres, Ohio Munic League, 57; adminr, Ohio Bur Workmen's Comp, 57; mem, War Vet Rep Club; mem, Capitol City Young Rep Club; Ohio State Rep, 61-66, chmn, Govt Operations Comt, Ohio House of Rep; US Rep, Ohio, 66- Mil Serv: Entered as Pvt, Army, 43, released as 1st Lt, 45, after serv in 30th Inf Div, five European Campaigns, World War II; Silver Star; Bronze Star; Croix de Guerre Unit Citation; Belgian Fouragier Unit Citation; Presidential Unit Citation with 2 Oak Leaf Clusters; Purple Heart; Lt Col Army Res. Mem: Columbus & Ohio Bar Asns; Ohio Munic Attorneys Asn; Kiwanis; Mason (33 degree). Honors & Awards: Named one of the Ten Men of Year, Columbus Citizen J & One of Five Outstanding Young Men in Ohio, 55; received Distinguished Serv Award, Outstanding Young Man of Year in Columbus, 55. Relig: Methodist. Mailing Add: 1019 Spring Grove Lane Columbus OH 43085

WYLY, SAM **(R)**
b Lake Providence, La, Oct 4, 34; s Charles Joseph Wyly, Sr & Flora Evans W; m 1960 to Rosemary Acton; c Evan Acton, Laurie Louise & Lisa Ann. Educ: La Tech Inst, BA, 56, Univ Mich, MBA, 57; WA Paton Scholarship; Phi Kappa Phi; Pi Kappa Alpha; Pi Kappa Delta; Beta Sigma Omicron; Omicron Delta Kappa. Hon Degrees: LLD, La Tech Inst, 69. Polit & Govt Pos: Mem, Dallas Co Rep Finance Comt, Tex, 66-68; Tex finance chmn, Nixon for President Campaign, 68; deleg, Rep Nat Conv, 68; mem, Nat Rep Finance Comt, 69-71; Presidential Elector, Tex, 72. Bus & Prof Pos: Sales rep, Serv Bur Corp, Dallas, Tex, 58-61; area sales mgr, Honeywell, Inc, 61-63; founder, Univ Computing Co, pres, 63-69, chmn bd dirs, 69-; chmn nat adv coun, Off Minority Bus Enterprise, 69-71; chmn bd, Data Transmission Co, 70-; chmn, Bonanza Int Inc, 67-; chmn exec comt, Earth Resources Co, 68-; dir, First Nat Bank in Dallas, 69-; dir, Pub Broadcasting Serv, 72-73; mem adv bd, Nat Asn RR Passengers, 72-; pres & chmn, Wyly Corp, 73-; chmn, Computer Leasing Co & Gulf Group, Inc. Mil Serv: Entered as A-3/C, Air Force Res, 57, released as A-2/C, 63, after serv in Nat Guard. Mem: Dallas Forum; Dallas Citizens Coun; Dallas Country Club. Honors & Awards: Named One of Five Outstanding Young Texans, Tex Jaycees, 67; One of Ten Outstanding Young Men of Am, US Jaycees, 68; Headliner-of-the-Year, Dallas Press Club Gridiron, 69; Outstanding Entrepreneurship Award, Southern Methodist Univ Bus Sch, 70; Horatio Alger Award, 70. Relig: Christian Scientist. Legal Res: University Park Dallas TX 75205 Mailing Add: PO Box 6228 Dallas TX 75222

WYMAN, J HOLLIS **(R)**
Maine State Sen
Mailing Add: Milbridge ME 04658

WYMAN, LOUIS C **(R)**
US Sen, NH
b Manchester, NH, Mar 16, 17; s Louis E Wyman & Alice Crosby W; m 1938 to Virginia E Markley; c Jo Ann (Mrs Coughlin) & Louis E, II. Educ: Univ NH, BS with hon, 38; Harvard Law Sch, JD cum laude, 41; Phi Kappa Phi; Theta Chi; Kappa Delta Pi; pres, Harvard Legal Aid Bur, 40-41; permanent secy of class of 41, Harvard Law Sch. Polit & Govt Pos: Bd dir, NH Coun on World Affairs; Citizens Adv Comt to Nat Comn on Govt Security; gen counsel to US Senate Comt on Campaign Expenditures, 46; secy to Hon Styles Bridges, 47; counsel, Joint Cong Comt on Foreign Econ Coop, 48-49; Attorney Gen, NH, 53-61; chmn, NH Comn on Interstate Coop, 53-61; mem, NH Ballot Law Comn & NH Judicial Coun, 53-61; comnr, Uniform State Laws for NH, 53-61; deleg-at-lg, Rep Nat Conv, 56 & 60; legis counsel to Gov, NH, 61; US Rep, First Dist, NH, 62-64 & 67-74; US Sen, NH, 75- Mil Serv: Naval Res, 42-46, Lt. Mem: Fel Am Col Trial Lawyers; Mason, Shrine, Bektash Temple; VFW; Am Legion; Elks. Mailing Add: 121 Shaw St Manchester NH 03104

WYMAN, ROSALIND **(D)**
Mem, Dem Nat Comt
b Los Angeles, Calif, Oct 4, 30; d Oscar Wiener & Sarah Selten W; m to Eugene L Wyman, wid; c Betty Lynn, Robert Alan & Brad Hibbs. Educ: Univ Southern Calif, BS in Pub Admin; Ephebians. Polit & Govt Pos: Nat committeewoman, Young Dem Clubs of Am, Calif, 51; mem, Los Angeles Co Dem Cent Comt, 52; mem, Calif Dem State Cent Comt, 52; chmn, 26th Cong Dist Dem Coun, 53-54; mem, Los Angeles City Coun, 53-65, pres pro tempore, 63; mem, Los Angeles Coliseum Comn, 58; deleg, Dem Nat Conv, 60; state chmn, Women's Div, Kennedy for President, 60; mem, Comn for UNESCO, 61, deleg, UN Econ & Social Coun, 66; mem, President Kennedy's Women's Conf Civil Rights, 63; mem, Los Angeles Co Parks & Recreation Comn, 68-69; co-chmn, Humphrey for President Campaigns, 68 & 72; mem, Dem Nat Comt & Charter Comn, 73- Bus & Prof Pos: Dir pub affairs, Screen Gems, Inc TV Prog Prod Div, 67 & Columbia Pictures & Screen Gems TV Prog Prod Div, 68-69. Mem: Los Angeles Jewish Community Coun (community rels comt, currently); Nat Conf of Christians & Jews; Los Angeles Co Music & Performing Arts Comn; Ctr Theater Group of Los Angeles; Los Angeles Conf on Immigration & Citizenship (exec comt). Honors & Awards: Woman of the Year, Los Angeles Times, 58; Mother of the Year, Mildred Strauss Child Care Chap-Mt Sinai Hosp & Clin, 59; Key Award, Palms CofC, 61; Merit Award, Univ Southern Calif Alumni Asn, 64; Mr & Mrs Am Citizen, Los Angeles B'nai B'rith Lodge 487, 64. Relig: Jewish. Mailing Add: 10430 Bellagio Rd Los Angeles CA 90024

WYMORE, JAMES FRANCIS **(R)**
b Miltonvale, Kans, Aug 20, 29; s James A Wymore & Minnie K Floberg W; m 1968 to Wilma L Rohmer; c Douglas G, Debra Lynn, Cathy Lou & Stephanie Ann. Educ: Kans State Univ, BS, 53; Alpha Epsilon Rho; Sigma Phi Epsilon. Polit & Govt Pos: Co chmn, Vol for Nixon-Lodge, Salina, Kans, 60; campaign coordr, Sen Frank Carlson Reelect Comt, Kans, 62; Young Rep chmn, First Cong Dist, Salina, 62-64; exec dir, Goldwater-Miller Comt, Wichita, 64, Maricopa Co Rep Comt, Ariz, 68-71 & Ariz Rep State Comt, 71-74. Bus & Prof Pos: Operator & partner, Wymore Motel, Salina, Jay Petroleum, Wichita, Cloud St Laundry & Dry Cleaners, Salina, & Wymore-Sanders Develop, Salina; stockbroker, ins agency, formerly. Mil Serv: Entered as 2nd Lt, Air Force, 53, released as 1st Lt, 55, after serv in Ground Observer Corps, Air Defense Command, 53-55. Mem: Bluelodge Shrine; life mem Kans Jaycees; Jr Chamber Int Sen Club of Phoenix; Am Legion. Honors & Awards: Jr Chamber Int Senator, Kans Jaycees, 62. Relig: Presbyterian. Mailing Add: 5645 Delos Circle Paradise Valley AZ 85253

WYNN, SPROESSER **(R)**
b Dallas, Tex, Dec 18, 13; s William Clement Wynn & Amy Hirschfeld W; m 1936 to Mildred Patton; c Carol (Mrs C Harold Brown) & Betty (Mrs Larry Macey). Educ: Tex Christian Univ, AB, 33; Univ Tex, LLB, 35; Kappa Sigma. Polit & Govt Pos: State chmn, Tex for Tower, 66; chmn, State Rep Task Force Educ, 67; chmn, Tower Senate Club, 67-71; deleg, Rep Nat Conv, 68 & 72; Rep nominee, Attorney Gen Tex, 68. Bus & Prof Pos: Dir, First Nat Bank Ft Worth, 65-; chmn, Family Law Sect, State Bar, 67-68. Mem: Fel Tex Bar Found; Consistory; Shrine (33 degree, past potentate). Relig: Disciples of Christ. Legal Res: Apt 105 4320 Bellaire Dr S Ft Worth TX 76109 Mailing Add: Oil & Gas Bldg Ft Worth TX 76102

WYRICK, HAROLD A **(R)**
Mont State Rep
Mailing Add: Rte 3 Baker MT 59313

WYSE, JACOB FREDERICK **(R)**
b Lexington Co, SC, Aug 14, 15; s James Kelley Wyse & Martha Adella Fulmer W; m 1939 to Annie Ruth Bickley. Educ: Clemson Univ. Polit & Govt Pos: Chmn, Edgefield Co Rep Party, SC, formerly. Mil Serv: Entered Navy, 45, released as Seaman 1/C, after serv in Pac. Mem: Am Legion; 40 et 8; Grange; SC Voc Agr Asn. Relig: Lutheran. Mailing Add: 509 Roland Ave Johnston SC 29832

Y

YACAVONE, MURIEL TAUL (D)
Conn State Rep
b Hartford, Conn, May 26, 20; d William M Taul & Elizabeth Griffing T; m 1944 to John Peter Yacavone; wid; c John Peter, Jr, Mark Philip, Teresa Jane & Elizabeth Rose. Educ: William Hall High Sch, West Hartford, Conn, 35-38. Polit & Govt Pos: Comnr health bd, Town of East Hartford, Conn, 62-63, comt mem, Econ Opportunity Comn, 64-65, chmn, Community Coun Youth, 65-68, justice of peace, 68-70; citizen mem, Drug Adv Coun, State of Conn, 69-; Conn State Rep, 17th Dist, 71- Mil Serv: Entered as Pfc, Women Marines, 43, released as Sgt, 45, after serv in Hq Bn, Washington, DC. Mem: George J Penney High Sch Parent-Teacher Orgn (bd mem); East Hartford League Women Voters; Dem Women's Club East Hartford; Conn Fedn Dem Women's Clubs (corresponding secy). Relig: Roman Catholic. Legal Res: 176 Wakefield Circle East Hartford CT 06118 Mailing Add: The Capitol Hartford CT 06115

YAHNER, PAUL J (D)
Pa State Rep
b Patton, Pa, Nov 8, 08; s Ambrose Yahner & Mary Sharbaugh Y; m to Rosemarie Farabaugh; c 13. Educ: Pa State Univ. Polit & Govt Pos: Mem, People to People agr deleg touring Communist countries, 63; Pa State Rep, 64- Bus & Prof Pos: Farmer; owner & operator 1,110 acre livestock & poultry farm; dir, First Nat Bank; pres, Cambria Co Mutual Fire Ins Co. Mem: CofC; Cambria Co Agr Exten Asn; KofC; Knight of St George; Pa Farm Bur Fedn. Honors & Awards: Pa Master Farmer, 61. Relig: Catholic. Mailing Add: RD 1 Box 165 Patton PA 16668

YALLUM, JANET CARO (D)
b Utica, NY, June 18, 33; d Samuel Caro & Freda Frank C; m 1954 to Robert S Yallum; c Mark & Suzanne. Educ: Syracuse Univ, BA, 54; Eta Pi Upsilon; Lambda Sigma Sigma; Theta Sigma Phi. Polit & Govt Pos: Committeewoman, Onondaga Co Dem Party, 54-55; coordr, local cong & sen campaigns, Ulster Co, NY, 60 & 64; deleg, Dem Nat Conv, 72; coordr, Ulster Co McGovern for President, Campaign, 72. Bus & Prof Pos: Pub rels, Bard Col, 72-73. Mem: League of Women Voters (founder & first pres, Kingston, 60-61); Hadassah; Ulster Acad (founder). Relig: Jewish. Mailing Add: Richmond Park Kingston NY 12401

YAMADA, DENNIS ROY (D)
Hawaii State Rep
b Lihue, Hawaii, Aug 20, 44; s Soichi Yamada & Ruth Kawasaki Y; m 1967 to Sharon Kay Hiura; c Wendell Carl & Tiffany Reiko. Educ: Univ Mo; Drake Univ, BS & BA, Sch Law, JD. Polit & Govt Pos: Chmn conv rules comt, Hawaii State Rep Party, 70; Hawaii State Rep, 70- Bus & Prof Pos: Attorney pvt practice, Lihue, Hawaii, dep corp counsel, City & Co of Honolulu, currently. Mil Serv: Entered as Pvt, Army Res; Airman 1/C, 150th ACW Squadron, presently. Mem: Am & Hawaii Bar Asns; Kauai Jaycees. Relig: Episcopal. Mailing Add: PO Box 127 Lihue HI 96766

YAMAMOTO, TOSHIKO TOSHI (R)
Mem, Rep State Cent Comt, Calif
b Seattle, Wash, Dec 1, 15; d Mokuji Yasutake (deceased) & Tome Watanabe Y; m 1944 to George Masashi Yamamoto. Educ: Univ Wash, 39-40; Am Barber Col, Los Angeles, Calif, grad, 52. Polit & Govt Pos: Rec secy, Monterey Park Fed Rep Women, 57-58; mem adv comt, Japanese Rep Nixon for President, 60, Japanese Rep Nixon for Gov, 62, & Japanese Rep Ronald Reagan for Gov, 66; second vpres, Japanese Am Rep, Calif, 66-67, pres, 67-69; corresponding secy, Monterey Park Rep Club, United Rep of Calif, 67-68; mem, Rep State Cent Comt Calif, 67-, secy nationalities comt, 67-69, mem exec comt, 69-71, Asian Coun Chmn 69-71; mem, Calif Womens Adv Comt for Nixon-Agnew, 68; alt deleg, Rep Nat Conv, 68 & 72; elector, Calif Rep Party, 68; Japanese adv, Heritage Group, Rep Nat Comt, 69-; founder & charter pres, Am of Japanese Ancestry Rep, 69-70, permanent adv, 70-; mem, Reelect Comt Gov Reagan, Lt Gov Reinecke, Controller Flournoy & Treas, Ivy Baker Priest, 70; mem adv comt, Gov Reelect, 69-70, mem, Womens Dinner Comt & vchmn, Dinner with Gov Reagan Comt, 70 & sponsor mem, Gov Inaugural Comt, 70-71; deleg, Nat Foreign Policy Conf for Non-Govt Orgn, State Dept, 70; mem bd dirs, Nat Ctr for Vol Action, 70-71; mem exec comt, Calif Federated Rep Women, 70-72; mem, Women's Adv Comt, Off Econ Opportunity, 70-72; mem, Gov Minority Appointees Steering Comt, 71-72; exam-field rep, State of Calif, 72-; mem, Develop & Planning Comt, Gov Annual Minority Workshop, 73. Bus & Prof Pos: Mem, Calif State Bd Barber Exam, 68-72, examr, 70-72, vpres, 71-72. Mem: East Los Angeles Community Col (adv comt, 73-); Int Platform Asn; Montebello Federated Rep Womens Club; Japanese Am Citizens League (Thousand Club Mem); Japan Am Soc. Honors & Awards: Los Angeles World Affairs Coun Awards of Appreciation, Calif Fedn Rep Women & Am of Japanese Ancestry Rep; Award of Recognition, Heritage Group, Rep Nat Comt; Award for Civic Involvement, Los Angeles 13th Coun Dist; Appreciation Award, Orgn of Statewide Oriental Youth for Reelec of the President. Relig: Episcopal. Mailing Add: 253 Gerhart Ave Los Angeles CA 90022

YAMASAKI, MAMORU (D)
Hawaii State Sen
b Paia, Maui, Hawaii, Sept 6, 16; s Isuke Yamasaki & Sode Kawaoka Y; single. Polit & Govt Pos: Mem, Dem Cent Comt, Territory of Hawaii, 54-59; clerk, Senate Ways & Means Comt, 30th Territorial Legis, 59; Hawaii State Rep, 59-67; mem, Hawaii State Dem Cent Comt, 60-66; Hawaii State Sen, 68- Mem: KRR Fed Credit Union (former mem bd dirs); Maui Salvation Army (adv bd); Maui Econ Opportunity & Lahaina Restoration Found (bd dirs); Maui United Fund (dir). Relig: Buddhist. Legal Res: 238 W Lanai St Kahului HI 96732 Mailing Add: PO Box 1516 Kahului HI 96732

YANCEY, EARL LESTER (D)
b Lafayette, Ind, Mar 6, 17; s Arthur Earl Yancey & Bessie Armentrout Y; m 1943 to Lucy Hosford; c Patricia (Mrs Dugger), Barbara (Mrs Lee Hazen Skipper) Educ: Purdue Univ, 35-36. Polit & Govt Pos: Mayor, Tallahassee, Fla, until 75, city comnr, 73- Bus & Prof Pos: Ins agt, Tallahassee, Fla, 55-; secy-treas, Plantation Home Builders, Inc, 74- Mil Serv: Entered as Aviation Cadet, Air Force, 41, released as Capt, 46, after serv in 80th Fighter Sqn, 8th Group, 5th Air Force, SPac, New Guinea, 42-43; Lt Col (Ret), Air Force Res, 70; Air Medal; Unit Citation. Mem: Mason; Lions; Am Legion; ROA; Salvation Army (adv bd, 6 years). Relig: Methodist. Legal Res: 622 Hillcrest Tallahassee FL 32303 Mailing Add: PO Box 1344 Tallahassee FL 32302

YANCEY, TRUMAN E (R)
Chmn, Washington Co Rep Comt, Ark
b Humphrey, Ark, Jan 7, 27; s Emmett C Yancey & Lera Brantley Y; m 1954 to Sylvia May Getz; c Steven & Thomas. Educ: Park Col, BA, 65; Univ Ark, Fayetteville, JD, 72; Phi Alpha Theta. Polit & Govt Pos: Chmn, Washington Co Rep Comt, Ark, 72- Bus & Prof Pos: Attorney, 73- Mil Serv: Entered as Pvt, Army, 45, released as Lt Col (Ret), 69, after serv in Army Staff, Europe, Middle East, Far East, SE Asia; Legion of Merit; Joint Serv Commendation Medal; UN Serv Medal. Mem: ROA; Lions Club (pres, 75); Elks; Bar Asns. Relig: Methodist. Mailing Add: 957 Tanglebriar Fayetteville AR 72701

YAP, TED (D)
Hawaii State Rep
Mailing Add: House Sgt-at-Arms State Capitol Honolulu HI 96813

YARBOROUGH, RALPH WEBSTER (D)
b Chandler, Tex, June 8, 03; s Charles Richard Yarborough & Nannie Jane Spear Y; m to Opal Warren; c Richard Warren. Educ: Sam Houston State Teachers Col; US Mil Acad, 1 year; Univ Tex Law Sch, LLB, 27. Hon Degrees: DHL, Lincoln Col; LLD, St Edward's Univ, 71. Polit & Govt Pos: Asst Attorney Gen, Tex, 31-34; mem bd dirs, Lower Colo River Authority, 35-36; dist judge, 53rd Judicial Dist, 36-41; presiding judge, Third Admin Judicial Dist; mem, Tex Bd Law Examr, 47-51; US Sen, Tex, 57-71; deleg, Interparliamentary Union, Brazil, 62, Dublin, Ireland, 65, Canberra, Australia, 66, Tehran, Iran, 66, Palma, Mallorca, Spain, 67, Lima, Peru, 68, Vienna, Austria, 69 & Delhi, India, 69; deleg, Dem Nat Conv, 64; mem, Tex Const Rev Comn, 73-; alt deleg, Dem Nat Mid-Term Conf, 74. Bus & Prof Pos: Former teacher; lawyer. Mil Serv: Inf, Army, discharged Lt Col, 46. Publ: Frank Dobie: Man & Friend, Potomoc Corrall, Westerners, 67; foreword to Three Men in Texas, Univ Tex Press, 67 & The Public Lands of Texas, 1519-1970, Okla Univ Press, 72; plus others. Mem: Am Legion; Order of the Coif; Mason; Shrine. Honors & Awards: Hon Fel, Postgrad Ctr for Ment Health, New York; Distinguished Serv Award, Los Angeles Co, Calif. Relig: Baptist. Mailing Add: 2527 Jarratt Ave Austin TX 78703

YARBOROUGH, RICHARD W (D)
Comnr, Indian Claims Comn
b Austin, Tex, Oct 20, 31; s Ralph W Yarborough & Opal Warren Y; m 1956 to Ann McJimsey; c Clare M & Elizabeth W. Educ: Univ Tex, Austin, BA, 53, Law Sch, LLB, 55; Phi Delta Phi; Kappa Alpha Order. Polit & Govt Pos: Legis asst & comt counsel, US Senate, 58-67; comnr, Indian Claims Comn, 67- Mil Serv: Entered as Pvt, Army, 55, released as SP-4, 57, after serv in Counter-Intel Corps, Ger, 56-57. Mem: State Bar Tex; Am Bar Asn; US Supreme Court Bar. Legal Res: 2527 Jarratt Ave Austin TX 78703 Mailing Add: 5140 N 37th St Arlington VA 22207

YARBROUGH, GEORGE MALONE (D)
Miss State Sen
b Red Banks, Miss, Aug 15, 16; married. Polit & Govt Pos: Miss State Rep, 52-56; Miss State Sen, 56-59 & 75-, pres pro-tem, Miss State Senate, 60-69; acting Lt Gov, Miss, 67-69. Bus & Prof Pos: Farmer; cattle dealer; ins; newspaper. Mem: Mason; Am Legion; KofP; 40 et 8; Farm Bur. Relig: Methodist. Mailing Add: Box 17 Red Banks MS 38661

YARBROUGH, WALTER HERMAN (R)
Idaho State Sen
b Maywood, Mo, Aug 15, 12; s Edward Francis Yarbrough & Amelia M Herman Y; m 1941 to Lucy Mae Rocks; c George Edward, Richard Alan, Stephen Anthony & Walter Carl. Educ: Northeast Mo State Teachers Col, 3 years. Polit & Govt Pos: Chmn, Co Fair Bd, Idaho, 55-61; Idaho State Sen, 64- Bus & Prof Pos: Pres, Boise Valley Angus Asn, Idaho, 56-60; Idaho State Angus Asn, 62-66; vpres, Western States Angus Asn, 64-; nat dir, Am Angus Asn, 67- Mil Serv: Entered as Pvt, Army Corp Engrs, 41, released as Maj Construction Engr, 46, after serv in 1778th Engr Coast Bn, Pac, 45-46; Lt Col, Res, 46-63; Presidential Unit Citation. Mem: Mason; Shrine; Am Legion Post 132 (past comdr). Relig: Protestant. Mailing Add: Box 216 Grand View ID 83624

YARDLEY, DAN (D)
Mont State Rep
b Big Timber, Mont, Oct 15, 28; s Ray Yardley (mother deceased); m 1959 to Jo Anne Frizzelle; c Thomas Edward & Mary Elizabeth. Educ: Univ Mont, LLB, 52, BA, 55; NY Univ, LLM, 56. Polit & Govt Pos: Mont State Rep, Dist 14, 69- Mil Serv: Army, 2 years. Mem: Mont Bar Asn. Legal Res: 802 S Eighth St Livingston MT 59047 Mailing Add: PO Box 482 Livingston MT 59047

YARDLEY, JAMES FREDRICK (R)
Chmn, Garfield Co Rep Party, Utah
b Hatch, Utah, Nov 19, 21; s John Alfred Yardley & Lareta Stoney Y; m 1945 to Alta Hatch; c James V & John Wallace. Educ: Utah State Univ, BS, 47; Lambda Chi Alpha. Polit & Govt Pos: Rep precinct chmn, Utah, 64-65; chmn, Garfield Co Rep Party, 65-69 & 73-; mem exec comt, Utah Asn of Co, 68-; chmn, Five Co Orgn, 69; comnr, Garfield Co Comn, 67-, chmn, 67-; mem bd dirs, Western Regional Co Off, 71- Mil Serv: Entered as Aviation Cadet, Navy, 42, released as Cadet, 44, after serv in V 5 Naval Aviation Prog. Mem: Independent Ins Agents; Lions; Am Legion (Comdr, Dept Utah, 63-64); CofC; Jr CofC. Relig: Latter-day Saint. Mailing Add: Panguitch UT 84759

YARMOLINSKY, ADAM (D)
b New York, NY, Nov 17, 22; s Avrahm Yarmolinsky & Babette Deutsch Y; m 1945 to Harriet Rypins, separated; c Sarah, Tobias, Benjamin & Matthew. Educ: Harvard Col, AB, 43; Yale Law Sch, LLB, 48. Polit & Govt Pos: Law clerk, Judge Charles E Clark, US Second Circuit Court of Appeals, 48-49; law clerk, Justice Reed, US Supreme Court, 50-51; spec asst to Secy of Defense, 61-64; prin dep asst secy of defense for int security affairs, 65-66; dep dir, President's Task Force on the War Against Poverty, 64; chief, US Emergency Relief Mission, Dominican Repub, 65. Bus & Prof Pos: Assoc firm Root, Ballantine, Harlan, Bushby & Palmer, New York, 49-50; assoc firm, Cleary Gottlieb, Friendly & Ball, Washington, DC, 51-55; lectr, Am Univ Law Sch, 51-56; secy, Fund for the Repub, 55-57; pub affairs ed, Doubleday & Co, 57-59; lectr, Yale Law Sch, 58-59; consult, philanthropic foundations, 59-61; prof law, Harvard Law Sch, 66-72; mem inst polit, John Fitzgerald Kennedy Sch Govt, Harvard, 66-73; on leave from Harvard as Chief Exec Officer, Welfare Island Develop Corp, 71-72; Ralph Waldo Emerson Univ prof, Univ Mass, Boston, 72- Mil Serv: Entered as Pvt, Army Air Corps, 43, released as Sgt, 46. Publ: Recognition of Excellence, Edgar Stern Family Found, Free Press Glencoe, 60; The Military Establishment, Harper & Row, 71; ed, The military and American society, Annals Am Acad Polit Soc Sci, 3/73; plus others. Mem: Coun

Foreign Rels; Int Inst Strategic Studies; Hudson Inst; Inst of Med, Nat Acad Sci (mem coun & exec comt); fel Am Acad Arts & Sci. Honors & Awards: Dept of Defense Distinguished Pub Serv Medal, 66. Legal Res: 85 Warren St Charlestown MA 02129 Mailing Add: Univ of Mass 1 Washington Mall Boston MA 02108

YATES, ALBERT (R)
b Washington Co, Ky, Oct 24, 98; s Charles S Yates & Elma D Graham Y; m 1921 to Frances E Downs; c Robert D, Frances (Mrs Florence) & Nancy (Mrs Heady). Educ: High sch. Polit & Govt Pos: Chmn, Spencer Co Rep Comt, Ky, formerly. Bus & Prof Pos: Chmn, Spencer Co Agr Stabilization & Conserv Comt, 40-60; vpres, Western Dist Warehousing Corp, 47-66; vpres, Salt River RECC, Burdstown, Ky, 50-66; vpres, Western Dist Redrying & Storage Corp. Mem: Mason; Spencer Co Farm Bur. Relig: Baptist. Mailing Add: Star Rte Fisherville KY 40023

YATES, CHARLES B (D)
NJ State Assemblyman
b New York, NY, Sept 27, 39; s Charles Everett Yates & Agnes Zak Y; m 1958 to Ursule Phaeton; c Charles Darrow, Roy David, Steven Daniel, Valerie Phaeton & Jessica Sarah. Educ: City Col New York, BChEng; Lacrosse Team, 3 years, Capt, 1 year. Polit & Govt Pos: NJ State Assemblyman, Dist 4C, Burlington Co, 72-; cand, US Rep, 74. Bus & Prof Pos: Pres, Circuit Foil SA, Luxembourg, 61-64; vpres, Yates Industs Inc, 64-67, pres, 67- Mem: Am Inst Chem Eng; Rotary Club, Beverly, NJ. Relig: Unitarian. Mailing Add: 219 Warren St Edgewater Park NJ 08010

YATES, JAMES B (D)
Ky State Rep
Mailing Add: 2305 Thurman Dr Louisville KY 40216

YATES, ROBERT DUNCAN (R)
Chmn, Spencer Co Rep Party, Ky
b Spencer Co, Ky, Feb 28, 32; s Albert Duncan Yates & Frances Ethyl Dunns Y; m 1952 to Muriel Laron Herndon; c Vickie Ann & Richard Lynn. Educ: Taylorsville High Sch. Polit & Govt Pos: Chmn, Spencer Co Rep Party, Ky, 72- Bus & Prof Pos: Farmer, tobacco warehouseman & real estate broker. Mem: Philip Swigert Lodge 218; Salt River RECC, Bardstown, Ky (vpres); East Ky Generating, Winchester (dir). Relig: Baptist. Mailing Add: Fisherville KY 40023

YATES, SIDNEY R (D)
US Rep, Ill
b Chicago, Ill, Aug 27, 09; m 1935 to Adeline J Holleb. Educ: Univ Chicago, PhB, 31 & JD, 33. Polit & Govt Pos: Asst attorney for Ill State Bank Receiver, 35-37; asst attorney gen to Ill Commerce Comn, 37-40; US Rep, Ill, 48-62 & 65-; US Rep with rank of Ambassador, to Trusteeship Coun of UN, 63-64. Bus & Prof Pos: Lawyer. Mil Serv: Lt, Navy. Mem: Am, Chicago & Ill State Bar Asns; Chicago Coun on Foreign Rels; City Club of Chicago. Legal Res: 3500 Lake Shore Dr Chicago IL Mailing Add: 2234 Rayburn House Off Bldg Washington DC 20515

YATRON, GUS (D)
US Rep, Pa
b Reading, Pa, Oct 16, 27; s George H Yatron & Theano Lazos Y; m to Mildred Menzies; c George & Theana. Educ: Kutztown State Teachers Col; active in scholastic sports. Polit & Govt Pos: Mem, Reading Sch Bd, Pa, 55-61; Pa State Rep, formerly; Pa State Sen, formerly; US Rep, Sixth Dist, Pa, 68-; deleg, Dem Nat Mid-Term Conf, 74. Bus & Prof Pos: Former assoc, Yatron's Ice Cream; mem bd, Berks Co Campus, Pa State Univ; bd mgrs, Reading Hosp. Relig: Greek Orthodox. Legal Res: 1908 Hessian Rd Reading PA 19602 Mailing Add: 313 Cannon House Off Bldg Washington DC 20515

YAVORNITZKI, MARK LEON (R)
b Herkimer, NY, Sept 24, 48; s Harry Yavornitzki & Charlotte Ligoski Y; single. Educ: Alliance Col, BA, 70; Grad Sch Pub Affairs, State Univ NY Albany, 70 & 72; Sigma Tau Delta; Pi Gamma Mu; Delta Psi Omega; Alpha Mu Gamma. Polit & Govt Pos: Pub rels staff mem, NY Rep State Comt Ann Sch of Polit, Albany, 71 & 72; research asst, Off NY State Sen Ronald Stafford, 71-73, legis asst, 73-74, admin asst, 74-; exec dir, NY State Young Voters for the President, NY State Comt to Reelect the President, 72; alt deleg-at-lg, Rep Nat Conv, 72; chmn's heritage adv coun, NY Rep State Comt, 74- Mil Serv: SP-5, NY Army Nat Guard, 5 years. Mem: NY State Asn Young Rep Clubs (exec comt, 73-); Herkimer Co Young Rep Club; Polish Nat Alliance. Relig: Roman Catholic. Legal Res: 613 N Main St Herkimer NY 13350 Mailing Add: c/o Senator Ronald Stafford State Capitol Albany NY 12224

YDRACH YORDAN, RAFAEL L (POPULAR DEMOCRAT, PR)
Sen, PR Senate
Mailing Add: State Capitol San Juan PR 00901

YEAGER, WELDON O (R)
Secy, Mich Rep Party
b Ohio, July 26, 22; m to Page Wise; c Richard (deceased), Mark, Carey & Scott. Educ: Wayne State Univ, BS in bus admin, 56. Polit & Govt Pos: Mem, 17th Dist Rep Orgn, Mich, 49-, former chmn, 62-64 & 66-68; deleg, Mich Const Conv, 61-62; deleg, Rep Nat Conv, 64 & 68; app by Gov Romney dir, Mich Workmen's Compensation Dept, 64-67; app mem, Gov Study Comn on Occup Safety which wrote Mich Safety Act & Gov Study Comn for Revision of Workmen's Compensation Act; trustee, various state funds; mem, Mich Rep State Cent Comt, currently; secy, Mich Rep Party, 71-; Mich State Rep, 69-70; mem, Electoral Col, 72; mem, 19th Dist Rep Comt & Oakland Co Rep Exec Comt, currently; mem, Bloomfield Twp Planning Comn, currently. Bus & Prof Pos: Pres, Yeager and Co, Inc, currently. Mil Serv: Entered as Pvt, Air Force, 40, released as Capt, 46. Mem: Mich Cancer Found (trustee); Northwest Civic Fedn (dir); Am Legion; Detroit Press Club. Legal Res: Bloomfield Hills MI Mailing Add: 675 Honeywell Bldg Southfield MI 48075

YEARND, JAMES AUSTIN, SR (R)
Chmn, Cadillac-Wexford Co Rep Party, Mich
b Cadillac, Mich, July 20, 27; s Wm William H Yearnd, Sr & Winnie Kaiser Y; m 1964 to Phyllis B Gleason; c Pamela (Mrs William Warren, Jr); James A, Jr, Rae A & Kimberly Jane. Educ: Univ Mich, 46-48; Wayne State Univ, MS, 50. Polit & Govt Pos: Coroner, Cadillac Wexford Co, 53-56; chmn, Cadillac-Wexford Co Rep Party, 74-, mem exec comt, 74- Bus & Prof Pos: Funeral home owner, 51- Mil Serv: Entered as Pvt, Marine Corps, 45, released

as Pfc, 46; Marine Corps Res, 10 years. Mem: Mich Funeral Dirs (bd dirs); Rotary; Am Legion; Cadillac Country Club; Elks. Honors & Awards: Cert of Merit & Outstanding Serv Plaque, Mich Funeral Dirs Asn. Relig: Congregational; deacon. Legal Res: 118 N Shelby Cadillac MI 49601 Mailing Add: PO Box 156 Cadillac MI 49601

YEATTS, COLEMAN B (D)
Va State Sen
Mailing Add: Chatham VA 24531

YEE, WADSWORTH (R)
Hawaii State Sen
Mailing Add: Senate Sgt-at-Arms State Capitol Honolulu HI 96813

YERGIN, ALAN EUGENE (D)
b Nov 15, 29; s Eugene Horace Yergin & Beatrice Roof Y; m 1965 to Nora Lee Bow. Educ: Wabash Col, BA, 51; Ind Univ, JD, 58; Phi Delta Theta; Delta Theta Phi. Polit & Govt Pos: Dep prosecuting attorney, Henry Co, Ind, 59; judge, New Castle City Court, 60-; deleg, Dem Nat Conv, 72. Bus & Prof Pos: Practicing attorney, New Castle, Ind, 58. Mil Serv: Entered as Seaman, Navy, 52, released as Lt(jg), 56, after serv in Destroyer Div 322, Korean Theater, 53-54; Lt, Naval Res, 56; Asian Theater & Korean Ribbons. Mem: Elks; Moose; Eagles; VFW; Am Legion. Relig: Protestant. Legal Res: 1522 Valley Dr New Castle IN 47362 Mailing Add: 1222 Broad St New Castle IN 47362

YEUTTER, CLAYTON KEITH (R)
Dep Foreign Trade Rep
b Eustis, Nebr, Dec 10, 30; s Reinhold F Yeutter & Laura P Gaibler Y; m 1953 to Lillian Jeanne Vierk; c Brad, Gregg, Kim & Van. Educ: Univ Nebr, Lincoln, BS in Agr with high distinction, 52, JD cum laude, 63, PhD, in Agr Econ, 66; Univ Wis, Madison, one semester, 60; Alpha Zeta; Gamma Sigma Delta; Phi Delta Phi; FarmHouse. Polit & Govt Pos: Exec asst to Gov of Nebr, 67-68; dir, Univ Nebr Mission, Bogota, Colombia, SAm, 68-70; adminr, Consumer & Mkt Serv, Dept Agr, 70-71, asst secy of Agr for Mkt & Consumer Serv, 73-74, asst secy, Int Affairs & Commodity Progs, 74-75; midwest regional dir, Comt for the Reelec of the President, 72, dir for agr in US, 72; Dep Foreign Trade Rep. Bus & Prof Pos: Self-employed in farming, ranching & cattle feeding, Eustis, Nebr, 65-71; law practice, Lincoln, Nebr, 63-66; pres & chmn bd, Platte Valley Packing Co, Cozad, 65-66; pres, Prof Invest Co, Lincoln, 68- Mil Serv: Entered as Basic Airman, Air Force, 52, released as 1st Lt, 57, after serv in Hosp, Air Photog & Charting Serv, Mil Air Transport Serv, Orlando, Fla, 54-57; Lt Col, Med Serv Corps, Air Force Res, 20 years; Grad first in class, Basic Course in Med Admin; Recipient, Routine Non-Combat Decorations & several outstanding Off Effectiveness Reports. Publ: A legal-economic critique of Nebraska Watercourse Law, Nebr Law Rev, 65; Interstate legal barriers to transportation in the Trans-Missouri West, In: Transportation Problems and Policies in the Trans-Missouri West, 67; Water administration—a suggested institutional model, Univ Nebr Dept Report, 68. Honors & Awards: Outstanding Animal Husbandry Grad in US, 52; Recipient of First Alumni Award, Univ Nebr 4-H Club, 60s; Outstanding Alumni, Univ Nebr Masters Prog, 71. Relig: Methodist. Legal Res: 831 Hazelwood Dr Lincoln NE 68510 Mailing Add: 1200 N Courthouse Rd Arlington VA 22201

YEVOLI, LEWIS J (D)
NY State Assemblyman
Mailing Add: 20 Serpentine Lane Old Bethpage NY 11804

YIM, T C (D)
Hawaii State Sen
Mailing Add: Senate Sgt-at-Arms State Capitol Honolulu HI 96813

YINGLING, BETH (D)
b Ridgewood, NJ, July 3, 53; d Lawton Dean Yingling & Laura Hohwald Y; single. Educ: William Smith Col, 71- Polit & Govt Pos: Deleg, Dem Nat Conv, 72; mem, Ramsey Clark for Senate Campaign, 74. Mem: William Smith Cong (rep, 72-73, pres, 75-76). Relig: Quaker. Mailing Add: 1085 Linwood Ave Ridgewood NJ 07450

YLITALO, JOHN RAYMOND
b Floodwood, Minn, Dec 25, 16; s John Ylitalo & Saima Marie Swen Y; m 1942 to Jean Sarchet; c John Raymond, Georgianne, Mary Katherine & Sara Lisa. Educ: Suomi Col, 33-35; St Olaf Col, BA, 37; Northwestern Univ, MBA, 38; Nat War Col, grad, 54. Polit & Govt Pos: Spec agt, Fed Bur Invest, 41-46; attache polit officer, Am Legation, Helsinki, 46-50; assigned to Dept of State, Washington, DC, 50-53; dep prin officer, Am Consulate Gen, Munich, Ger, 54-58; counsul gen counsellor of embassy, Am Embassy, Manila, 59-62; assigned to Dept of State, Washington, DC, 62-69; dir, VISA Off, 65-67; prin officer, Am Consulate Gen, Tijuana, Mex, 67-68; US Ambassador to Paraguay, 69-72. Bus & Prof Pos: Instr econ, Univ Ala, 38-41. Mailing Add: 521 First Ave W Mobridge SD 57601

YOCOM, DANNY (D)
Ky State Sen
Mailing Add: 5412 Rolling Ridge Rd Louisville KY 40215

YOCUM, NORMA LENORE (R)
Mem, Rep State Cent Comt Calif
b Redkey, Ind, Jan 10, 11; d Fern Leigh Young & Mattie Rathburn Y; m 1932 to Sam A Yocum; c Virginia Ruth (Mrs Clyde Fraser), Martha Louise (Mrs Edward White), Robert Charles & Phyllis Mary (Mrs Robert Frank). Educ: Cent Jr Col, 28-30; Woodbury Bus Col, 30-31. Polit & Govt Pos: City Councilman, Alhambra, Calif, 55-71, mayor, 64-67; secy, Calif State Rep Assembly, 66 & 68; Rep nominee for Calif State Assemblyman, 45th Assembly Dist, 66 & 68; mem, Los Angeles Co Rep Cent Comt, 66-; mem, Rep State Cent Comt Calif, 66-; mem, Gov Adv Coun on Atomic Energy Develop & Radiation Protection, 68. Bus & Prof Pos: Pres, Sam Yocum, Inc, San Gabriel, Calif, formerly; trustee, Alhambra Pub Libr, 48-55 & 75- Mem: Bus & Prof Womens Club of Alhambra; Soroptimist Club of Alhambra-San Gabriel; DAV Charities Bd (pres, 68-); Am Cancer Soc (dist bd, 69-74); Friends United Meeting, Int Orgn of Friends Churches (rec clerk, 75). Honors & Awards: Woman of the Year in Govt, Calif Fedn of Bus & Prof Women's Clubs, 65; Jaycee of the Year, Jr CofC, 66; Mother of the Year, CofC, 66; Woman of the Year, Bus & Prof Women's Club, 72; Award of Merit, Calif State Assembly, 72. Relig: Protestant. Mailing Add: 1815 S Fourth St Alhambra CA 91803

YODER, JAMES AMOS (D)
b Chicago, Ill, Apr 18, 49; s Amos Yoder & Janet Tatman Y; m 1975 to Ellen White Walter. Educ: DePauw Univ, BA, 70; Univ RI, MS in Oceanog, 73; Sigma Xi; Phi Gamma Delta. Polit & Govt Pos: Student coordr, McGovern for President, Univ RI, 72; deleg, Dem Nat Conv, 72; coordr, McGovern for President, South Co, RI, 72; mem, Young Dem RI, 73- Bus & Prof Pos: Pesticide inspector, US Dept Agr & Environ Protection Agency, 70-71. Mem: Am Soc Limnol & Oceanog; Am Soc Phycol. Legal Res: 523 Graduate Village Kingston RI 02881 Mailing Add: Dept of Oceanography Univ of RI Kingston RI 02881

YOHN, WILLIAM H, JR (R)
Pa State Rep
b Pottstown, Pa, Nov 20, 35; s William H Yohn, Sr & Dorothy Cornelius Y; m 1963 to Jean Kochel; c William H, III, Bradley G & Elizabeth J. Educ: Princeton Univ, AB, 57; Yale Univ Law Sch, LLB, 60; Phi Beta Kappa. Polit & Govt Pos: Research intern for US Sen John Sherman Cooper, Ky, summer 59; secy, Pottstown Police Civil Serv Comn, Pa, 61-62; asst dist attorney, Montgomery Co, 62-65; chmn, Pottstown Area Young Rep Asn, 63-65; chmn, Montgomery Co Rep Primary Campaign Comt, 65; chmn, Montgomery Co Young Rep Fedn, 66-67; Pa State Rep, 68-; research coun to majority leader, Pa House Rep, 67-68. Bus & Prof Pos: Attorney, Binder, Binder, Yohn & Kalis, Pottstown, Pa. Mil Serv: Entered as Pvt, Marine Corps Res, 60, released as Cpl, 66. Mem: Am Bar Asn; Jaycees; CofC; Elks; Pottstown Hist Soc (dir, 70). Honors & Awards: Outstanding Young Man of 1968 Award, Pottstown Jaycees. Relig: United Church of Christ. Legal Res: Crestwood Dr Pottstown PA 19464 Mailing Add: Capitol Bldg Harrisburg PA 17120

YONALLY, JAMES LEWIS (R)
Kans State Rep
b Miltonvale, Kans, Sept 11, 36; s John James Yonally & Kathryn Urban Y; m 1962 to Nancy Bea Shirk; c David John. Educ: Univ Kans, BS, 62, DEduc, 72. Polit & Govt Pos: Served on numerous campaign comts; precinct committeeman, 65-; ward chmn, Rep Party, 66-; dist & state deleg, Rep State Conv; Johnson Co chmn, Pace, 1 year, Kans chmn, 1 year; Kans State Rep, 29th Dist, 73- Bus & Prof Pos: Deleg, Kans State Teachers Asn, several years, chmn, Legis Comn, 2 years & coordr, Polit Action, 1 summer; deleg to 2 convs, Nat Educ Asn & polit consult. Mem: Kans Asn Sch Adminr (legis comt, 2 years); Nat Sch Pub Rels Asn (Kans State Coordr, currently); Nat Orgn Legal Probs Educ; Radio & TV Coun Gtr Kansas City (bd dirs); Tech Resources Bd for Youth Develop; Gtr Kansas City Jr Achievement (bd dirs). Relig: Protestant. Legal Res: 10039 Mastin Overland Park KS 66212 Mailing Add: 7235 Antioch Overland Park KS 66204

YORK, MARVIN (D)
Okla State Sen
Mailing Add: State Capitol Oklahoma City OK 73105

YORK, STANLEY (R)
b Milwaukee, Wis, Aug 29, 31; s Wilford Douglas York & Margaret Richardson Y; m 1953 to Emily Ann Loucks; c Cynthia Lee, Douglas Charles & Elizabeth. Educ: Beloit Col, BA, 53; Andover Newton Theol Sch, BD, 57; Phi Kappa Psi. Polit & Govt Pos: Wis State Assemblyman, 67-70; comnr, Wis Dept Indust, Labor & Human Rels, 70-71; exec dir, Wis Rep Party, formerly. Bus & Prof Pos: Pastor, Congregational Church, Red Granite, Wis, 57-59, Union Congregational Church, Berlin, 57-62 & First Congregational Church, River Falls, 62-70. Relig: United Church of Christ. Legal Res: 125 Monroe St Oregon WI 53575 Mailing Add: PO Box 31 Madison WI 53701

YORTY, SAM (R)
b Lincoln, Nebr, Oct 1, 09; s Frank Patrick Yorty & Johanna Egan Y; m 1938 to Betty Hensel; c William Egan. Educ: Southwestern Univ; Univ Southern Calif. Polit & Govt Pos: Calif State Assemblyman, 36-40 & 49-50; US Rep, Calif, 50-54; mayor, Los Angeles, 61-73. Bus & Prof Pos: Attorney at law, pvt practice, 40-42, 45-49 & 54-61. Mil Serv: Entered Army Air Corps, 42, released as Capt, 45, after serv in 5th Air Force & 6th Army, New Guinea & Philippines. Mailing Add: 3435 Wilshire Blvd Los Angeles CA 90010

YOST, JAMES ANDREW (R)
Idaho State Sen
b Rupert, Idaho, Feb 5, 48; s Renold L Yost & Ona Roth Y; m 1966 to Ronda Kay Hagan. Educ: Col Southern Idaho, AA, 68; Boise State Col, BA, 71. Polit & Govt Pos: Idaho State Sen, Dist 23, 72- Bus & Prof Pos: Owner-operator, Kream of the Valley Distributing, 71- Mem: Lions; Mason; Wendell CofC. Mailing Add: 420 Fourth Ave W Wendell ID 83355

YOUNG, ALLAN CHANDLER (R)
Chmn, NDak Rep State Comt
b Devils Lake, NDak, June 26, 37; s Ray Duane Young & Jane Mann Y; m 1957 to Glenda Marie Overbo; c Carrie Lynn & Stuart Chandler. Educ: Univ NDak, 55-57; Univ Vienna, Austria, fall 56; Phi Delta Theta. Polit & Govt Pos: Sgt at arms, Rep Nat Conv, 60, deleg, 64 & 72; mem campaign staff, NDak Rep Party, 60, chmn, Tri-Co Rally Banquet, 60; Young Rep Co Chmn, 60-61; deleg, NDak Rep Conv, 60, 62, 63, 64, 66 & 68; regional dir, NDak Young Rep, 61-62; campaign chmn & organizational dir, Ramsey Co Rep Party, 62 & 64; precinct committeeman, 62 & 66; Three-Co campaign fieldman, 63; chmn, NDak Deleg, Nat Young Rep Fedn Conv, 63 & 65; chmn, NDak Young Rep, 63-67; mem, NDak State Rep Exec Comt, 63-67 & 69-; Five-Co Campaign fieldman, 64; grad, Young Rep Leadership Training Sch, Washington, DC, 65 & 67; chmn, Lincoln Day Dinner, Dist 15, 66; mem, Dist 15, Ramsey Co Exec Comt, 66; mem, NDak Young Rep State Exec Comt, 67-68, vchmn, Dist 15, 67-68, organizational chmn, 68, chmn, 68-; mem, NDak Rep Campaign Comt, 68; vchmn, NDak Rep State Comt, 69-72, chmn, 72-, mem, State Rep Budget & Quota Comt, 69-, vchmn, Rep Publicity Comt, 69-; mem, Rep Nat Comt, 72- Bus & Prof Pos: Secy-treas, Mann's Dept Store, 61- Mem: Eagles; Elks; Mason (Past Master); York Rite; DeMolay (Legion of Honor, 67; NDak State Adv, 67-69). Honors & Awards: Named One of the Ten Outstanding State Chmn by Buzz Lukens, chmn, Young Rep Nat Fedn, 65; Distinguished Serv Award, Devils Lake Jaycees, 68. Relig: Episcopal; vestryman; Men's Club; choir. Mailing Add: 1111 Sixth St Devils Lake ND 58301

YOUNG, ANDREW (D)
US Rep, Ga
b New Orleans, La, Mar 12, 32; s Dr & Mrs Andrew J Young, Sr; m to Jean Childs; c Andrea, Lisa, Paula & Andrew, III. Educ: Dillard Univ; Howard Univ, BS, 51; Hartford Theol Sem, BD, 55. Hon Degrees: DD, Wesleyan Univ, 70 & United Theol Sem Twin Cities, 70; LLD, Wilberforce Univ, 71, Clark Col, 73, Yale Univ, 73, Swarthmore Col, 74, Atlanta Univ, 74 & Morehouse Col, 75. Polit & Govt Pos: US Rep, Ga, Fifth Cong Dist, 73-, mem comt on rules, US House Rep, currently; treas & mem exec comt, Cong Black Caucus; regional vpres & mem exec comt, Dem Study Group; mem, House Environ Study Conf. Bus & Prof Pos: Pastor, Marion, Ala & Thomasville & Beachton, Ga; assoc dir dept youth work, Nat Coun Churches, 57-61; staff mem, Southern Christian Leadership Conf, 61-64, exec dir, 64-67, exec vpres, 67-72; chmn, Atlanta Community Rels Comn, 70-72; mem exec comt, World Conf Churches Programme to Combat Racism. Mem: Delta Ministry Miss (chmn bd); Martin Luther King, Jr Ctr Soc Change (trustee, dir & chmn adv coun); Southern Christian Leadership Conf (bd mem); SANE (co-chmn); Southern Elec Fund (bd mem). Honors & Awards: Pax-Christi Award, St John's Univ, 70; aided in drafting of the Civil Rights Act of 1964 & the Voting Rights Act of 1965; first Black man in 100 years to win the Dem nomination for Cong in the South, 70; first Black Congressman from Ga since Jefferson Long serv in 1870-71. Relig: United Church of Christ. Legal Res: GA Mailing Add: US House of Rep 352 Cannon Bldg Washington DC 20515

YOUNG, C W BILL (R)
US Rep, Fla
b Harmarville, Pa, Dec 16, 30; s Raymond Edward Young & Wilma Hulings Y; m 1949 to Marian Ford; c Pamela Kay, Terry Lee & Kimber. Polit & Govt Pos: Nat committeeman, Fla Fedn of Young Rep, 57-59, state chmn, 59-61; asst sgt at arms, Rep Nat Conv, 56 & 60, treas, Host Comt, 68, deleg, 68 & 72; dist asst to US Rep Cramer, 57-60; mem, Pinellas Co Rep Exec Comt, 58-66; Fla State Sen, 19th Dist, 60-70, minority leader, Fla State Senate, 66; coordr, Southern Tour, Rep Cong Comts, Paul Revere Panels, 62; mem, Fla Const Rev Comn, 65-67; chmn, Southern Hwy Policy Comt, 66-68; chmn Eighth Cong Dist Nixon-Agnew Campaign, 68; Presidential Elector, 68; US Rep, Fla, 71- Bus & Prof Pos: Owner, C W Bill Young Ins, 57-71; pres, Prudential Property & Casualty Ins Agency, Inc, 60-64; mem bd dirs, St Petersburg Bank & Trust. Mil Serv: Entered as Pvt, Fla Nat Guard, 48, released as M/Sgt, 57. Mem: YMCA; Moose; Jr CofC; Aircraft Owners & Pilots Asn; Am Legion. Honors & Awards: Award for Meritorious Serv, 63; One of the Outstanding Young Men of Am, US Jr CofC, 64; Allen Morris Awards, Second Most Effective in Debate & Second Most Valuable in Fla State Senate, 67; Most Valuable Sen in Fla State Senate, 69; nominated for St Petersburg Times Most Valuable Member of Fla State Senate Award, 57. Relig: Methodist. Mailing Add: Apt 1201 4775 Cove Circle St Petersburg FL 33708

YOUNG, CHARLES L (D)
Dist Chmn, Fourth Cong Dist Dem Party, Miss
b Meridian, Miss, Aug 27, 31; s E F Young, Jr & Velma Beal Y; div; c Deidra, Charles L, Jr, Arthur & Veldora F. Educ: Tenn State A&I Univ, BS in Bus, 51; Tuskegee Inst; Univ Denver, 58; Kappa Alpha Psi. Polit & Govt Pos: Chmn, Lauderdale Co Dem Club, Miss, 66 & 69; deleg, Dem Nat Conv, 68 & 72; dist chmn, Fourth Cong Dist Dem Party, 68- Bus & Prof Pos: Pres, E F Young, Jr Mfg Co; pres, Young's Construction Inc; mem bd dirs, Miss Action for Progress, 68-; vchmn, Miss Indust & Spec Serv, 69- Mil Serv: Entered as Pvt, Army, 52, released as Sgt 1/C, 54, after serv in Korea, 2nd Div; Bronze Star; Good Conduct Medal; Korean Serv Medal. Mem: Mason; Elks; CofC; Meridian Bus League. Relig: Christian Methodist Episcopal. Legal Res: 3120 15th St Meridian MS 39301 Mailing Add: 500 25th Ave Meridian MS 39301

YOUNG, CLIFTON (R)
Nev State Sen
Mailing Add: 232 Court St Reno NV 89501

YOUNG, COLEMAN A (D)
Dem Nat Committeeman
b Tuscaloosa, Ala, May 24, 18. Educ: Detroit Eastern High Sch, grad. Polit & Govt Pos: Mich State Sen, 64-74, deleg, Mich State Const Conv, formerly; deleg, Dem Nat Conv, 68 & 72; Dem Nat Committeeman, currently. Mil Serv: Army Air Force, 2nd Lt. Mem: NAACP; Booker T Washington Bus Men's Asn; Trade Union Leadership Coun; Asn for the Study of Negro Life & Hist; AFL-CIO Coun (spec resp). Relig: Baptist. Legal Res: Apt 7 278 E Forrest Detroit MI 48201 Mailing Add: 1126 City & Co Bldg Detroit MI 48226

YOUNG, DALE L (R)
Treas, Rep Party of Nebr
b Palmyra, Nebr, Mar 13, 28; s Mike P Young & Grace Clutter Y; m 1950 to Norma Shalla; c Shalla Ann & Philip Mike. Educ: Univ Nebr, Lincoln, BS, 50; Theta Xi. Polit & Govt Pos: Deleg, Lancaster Co Rep Conv, Nebr, 66 & 68; deleg, Nebr State Rep Conv, 66 & 68; treas, Rep Party of Nebr, 66- Bus & Prof Pos: Vpres & cashier, First Nat Bank & Trust Co, Lincoln, Nebr, 50- Mil Serv: Entered as Pvt, Army, 44, released as S/Sgt, 46, recalled in 50, released as M/Sgt, 51, after serv in Am Theatre. Mem: Am Inst Banking; Omaha-Lincoln Soc Financial Anal; Lincoln Country Club; Govt Research Inst. Relig: Presbyterian. Legal Res: 2627 Park Ave Lincoln NE 68502 Mailing Add: First National Bank & Trust Co Lincoln NE 68508

YOUNG, DONALD E (R)
US Rep, Alaska
b Meridian, Calif, 1933; m 1963 to Lula Fredson; c Joni & Dawn. Educ: Chico State Col, BA Polit Sci-Educ, 58; Univ Alaska, College. Polit & Govt Pos: Mayor, Ft Yukon, Alaska, four years, councilman, six years; Alaska State Rep, 68-71; Alaska State Sen, 71-73, chmn spec air transportation comt, Alaska State Senate; US Rep, Alaska, 73- Bus & Prof Pos: Teacher, two years in Calif & nine years in Ft Yukon, Alaska; licensed river boat capt, currently. Mem: Alaska Educ Asn (exec bd); Ft Yukon Dog Mushers (pres); Elks; Mason; Dog Mushers Asn. Legal Res: Box 119 Ft Yukon AK 99740 Mailing Add: 1210 Longworth House Off Bldg Washington DC 20515

YOUNG, EDWARD L (R)
b Florence Co, SC; m to Hatsy Yeargin; c four daughters. Educ: Clemson Col, grad. Polit & Govt Pos: SC State Rep, 58-60; US Rep, Sixth Dist, SC, 73-74. Bus & Prof Pos: Chmn, Farm Credit Bd Columbia, SC, Pee Dee Prod Credit Asn & Florence Fed Land Bank Asn, formerly; pres, Coble Dairy Prods, currently; real estate & other land develop interests. Mil Serv: Air Force, World War II; 195 combat missions; Air Medal with nine Oak Leaf Clusters; Distinguished Flying Cross. Honors & Awards: SC Man of the Year in Agr, Progressive Farmer Mag. Relig: Baptist. Mailing Add: PO Drawer 1660 Florence SC 29501

YOUNG, EVERETT LESLIE (DFL)
b Gaylord, Minn, Jan 22, 39; s Everett Leslie Young & Eunice Jorstad Y; m 1962 to Joyce Ann Kurth; c Rett & Chris. Educ: Univ Minn, BChE, 62; Delta Chi. Polit & Govt Pos: Chmn, McLeod Co Dem-Farmer-Labor Party, Minn, formerly; treas, State Sen Dist 23 Dem-Farmer-Labor Party, 72. Mil Serv: Entered as Pvt, Nat Guard, 56, released as Pfc, 59.

Mem: Boy Scouts (secy, Cub Pack 248, Hutchinson, 72-). Relig: Lutheran. Mailing Add: RR 2 Hutchinson MN 55350

YOUNG, FREDERICK NEVIN (R)
Ohio State Rep
b Dayton, Ohio, Jan 1, 32; s Robert Frederick Young & Katherine Patterson Y; m 1951 to Joyce Canney; c Margaret R, Shirley Kay, Nancy E & Mary R. Educ: Wesleyan Univ, BA, 54; Harvard Law Sch, LLB, 57; Phi Beta Kappa; Beta Theta Pi. Polit & Govt Pos: Precinct & ward committeeman, Rep Party, Montgomery Co, Ohio, 57-66; pres, Montgomery Co Young Rep Club, 60; state chmn, Ohio League Young Rep Clubs, 64; mem, Ohio State Rep Cent Comt, 66; Ohio State Rep, 38th Dist, 68-, ranking minority mem, Finance Comt, Ohio House Rep, currently. Bus & Prof Pos: Partner law firm, Young & Alexander, Dayton, 61- Publ: Corporate separations; some recent revenue rulings, Harvard Law Rev, 58. Mem: Harvard Law Sch Asn Ohio (past pres); Dayton, Ohio & Am Bar Asns; Kettering-Oakwood Exchange Club. Relig: Protestant. Mailing Add: 5512 Laureldale Rd Dayton OH 45429

YOUNG, GEDELLE BRABHAM (D)
b Columbia, SC, Oct 31, 13; d Vernon Brabham & Margaret Cope B; m 1938 to Martin Dunaway Young; c Martin Brabham & Margaret Cope (Mrs J P Anderson, Jr). Educ: Ga State Woman's Col, AB, 34; Emory Univ, AB in Libr Sci, 35. Polit & Govt Pos: Mem, City Bd of Health & Housing Bd, Columbia, SC; mem, CZ Dem Party, currently, corresp secy, 71-72; deleg, Dem Nat Conv, 68 & 72, mem, Nat Platform Comt, 72; Dem Nat Committeewoman, CZ, 72-74. Bus & Prof Pos: Librn, Richland Co Pub Libr, Columbia, SC, 36-40; various other libr pos in the area. Mem: Southern Regional Coun; SC Coun on Human Rights; Common Cause; League of Women Voters. Relig: Humanist. Mailing Add: 8421 NW Fourth Pl Gainesville FL 32601

YOUNG, GEORGE C (R)
Mass State Rep
Educ: Dartmouth Col, AB; Boston Univ, MEd & Cert of Adv Grad Specialization. Polit & Govt Pos: Chmn, Rep Town Comt, 10 years; mem sch bd, Scituate, Mass, 9 years, chmn, 2 years; Mass State Rep, currently. Bus & Prof Pos: Sch adminr, 30 years; acting supt schs, twice; prin, Cent Jr High Sch, Quincy. Mil Serv: Entered as Pvt, Army, released as Capt, after serv in World War II, 4 years; Lt Col, Army Res, 24 years. Mailing Add: 20 Lawson Rd Scituate MA 02066

YOUNG, J BANKS (D)
Comnr, US Tariff Comn
b Raleigh, NC, Sept 2, 12; s William J Young (deceased) & Katherine Banks Y; m 1938 to Virginia Mae Lunsford; c Jefferson Banks, Jr. Educ: Univ NC, Chapel Hill, 29-32; NC State Univ, BS, 34; Chi Psi. Polit & Govt Pos: Various admin pos, US Dept Agr, 34-50; asst to budget off, first liaison rep with House Agr Comt, 34-50; mem, Fairfax Co Dem Comt, Va, 50-51; comnr, US Tariff Comn, 71- Bus & Prof Pos: Washington rep, Nat Cotton Coun, 51-70. Mil Serv: Entered as Lt(jg), Naval Res, 43, released as Lt, 46, after serv in Amphibious Forces, Attack Transport, Pac; Ret; Am Theatre Ribbon; Pac Theatre Ribbon; several campaign ribbons for the Marshall Islands, Philippine Islands, Iwo Jima & Okinawa. Mem: Bellhaven Country Club; Potomac River Power Squadron. Honors & Awards: Grad with honors, NC State Univ, 34. Relig: Protestant. Legal Res: 7105 Marine Dr Marlan Heights Alexandria VA 22307 Mailing Add: US Tariff Comn Eighth & E Sts NW Washington DC 20436

YOUNG, JEAN KITTS (R)
Pres, Ore Fedn Rep Women
b Detroit, Mich, May 1, 04; d Kent Henry Kitts & Bertha L Miles K; m to Frederic William Young, wid; c Frederic Norman & Patricia (Mrs Jordan). Educ: Univ Ore, 21-26; Sigma Delta Pi; Delta Zeta. Polit & Govt Pos: Vchmn, Multnomah Co Rep Cent Comt, 47-54; secy, 60-62; chmn, Ore Wage & Hour Comn, 48-58; secy, Ore State Rep Cent Comt, 54-60; Presidential Elector, 60 & 68; pres, South City Rep Women, 64-66; mem, King City-City Coun, 64-; Ore chmn, Women for Nixon, 68; pres, King City Rep Women, 68-70; first vpres, Ore Fedn Rep Women, 69-71, pres, 71-; Ore chmn, Women for McCall for Gov, 70; alt deleg, Rep Nat Conv, 72. Bus & Prof Pos: Dist dir, US Bur Census, Portland, 60, asst mgr, 4 counties, 70. Publ: Oregon's primary, Ore Voter, 64. Mem: Altrusa; Am Cancer Soc (bd mem); Portland Fedn Women's Orgns (past pres). Honors & Awards: Woman of Distinction, Portland Fedn Women's Orgns, 63; Trumpeter Serv Award, Young Rep, 64; Woman of Accomplishment for Pub Affairs, Ore J, 66; Rep Woman of Year, Ore Fedn Rep Women, 69. Relig: Presbyterian. Mailing Add: 12390 SW King Richard Dr Tigard OR 97223

YOUNG, JOHN (D)
US Rep, Tex
b Nov 10, 16; s Phillip M Young & Catherine Gaffney Y; m to Jane Gallier; c Catherine Gaffney, Nancy Rae, John, Jr, Robert Harold & Mary Patricia. Educ: St Edwards Univ, BA, 37; Univ Tex, law student, 37-40. Hon Degrees: LLD, St Edwards Univ, 61. Polit & Govt Pos: Asst co attorney, Nueces Co, Tex, 46, asst dist attorney, 47-50, co attorney, 51-52, co judge, 53-56; US Rep, Tex, 57-; deleg, Dem Nat Mid-Term Conf, 74. Bus & Prof Pos: Lawyer. Mil Serv: Navy. Mem: State Bar of Tex. Legal Res: Corpus Christi TX Mailing Add: 2419 Rayburn House Off Bldg Washington DC 20515

YOUNG, JOHN DONALD
Asst Secy Comptroller, Dept Health, Educ & Welfare
b Cortland, NY, Feb 5, 19; s John T Young & Anna Byrnes Y; m 1944 to Virginia Gwathmey; c John H & Rebecca A. Educ: Colgate Univ, AB, 41; Syracuse Univ, MS, 43; Am Univ, PhD, 74; Alpha Tau Omega; Pi Delta Epsilon; Pi Sigma Alpha. Polit & Govt Pos: With Bur Budget, 56-57; admin asst to chmn, Nat Security Resources Bd, 47-51; spec asst to adminr, Fed Civil Defense Admin, 51; exec secy, Off Defense Mobilization, 51-53, exec officer, 53-54; staff mem & exec secy, President's Adv Comt Govt Orgn, 53; dir, Mgt Anal Div, NASA, 60-61, dep dir admin, 61-63, asst adminr admin, 63-66; asst to dir, Bur Budget, Exec Off President, 66-67; dir, Econ, Sci & Tech Div, Bur Budget & Off Mgt & Budget, 67-73; dep assoc dir, Energy & Sci Div, Off Mgt & Budget, 73; asst secy comptroller, Dept Health, Educ & Welfare, 73- Bus & Prof Pos: Lectr to various cols & univs; mgt consult, McKinsey Co, 54-60. Mil Serv: Marine Corps, 42-45. Publ: Various articles. Mem: Am Asn Advan Sci; Am Soc Pub Admin. Honors & Awards: William A Jump Award, 54; Outstanding Leadership Award, NASA, 66; Exceptional Serv Award, Off Mgt & Budget, 73; Maxwell Sch Distinguished Serv Award, 74. Legal Res: 3028 Cedarwood Lane Sleepy Hollow Falls Church VA 22042 Mailing Add: Dept of Health Educ & Welfare Washington DC 20503

YOUNG, JOHN WALLACE (D)
Okla State Sen
b Sapulpa, Okla, Nov 25, 23; s Glenn Olen Young & Thora Kate Shiflet Y; m 1949 to Claudeen Humes; c John Mark, David Lee & Bradford Humes. Educ: Tulane Univ, BBus & Acct, MBus & Acct; Okla Univ, LLB, 50; Phi Delta Phi; Beta Gamma Sigma; Kappa Sigma. Polit & Govt Pos: Chmn, Fifth Dist League of Young Dem, formerly; pres, Student Sen, Okla Univ, 49; Okla State Sen, 64- Mil Serv: Entered as A/S, Navy, released as Lt(jg); Lt, Naval Res. Mem: CofC; Lions; Hist Soc, Sapulpa; Round-Up Club. Relig: Baptist. Legal Res: 1401 E Lincoln Sapulpa OK 74066 Mailing Add: PO Box 1364 Sapulpa OK 74066

YOUNG, JOHN WILLIAM (R)
Comnr of Labor, Ky
b Louisville, Ky, May 29, 16; s Birch Higgins Young & Bertha May Lindeman Y; m 1941 to Dorothy Mary Mialback; c John W, Jr. Educ: Univ Louisville; Univ Heidelberg, Ger. Polit & Govt Pos: Rep precinct capt, Louisville, Ky, 50-62, ward chmn, 55-66 & vpres, Young Rep Club, 54; mem, Louisville Bd of Aldermen, 62, pres, 65-; Comnr of Labor, Ky, 67- Bus & Prof Pos: Pub rels man, Oertel Brewing Co, 66. Mil Serv: Entered as Pvt, Army, 41, released as Cpl, 45, after serv in 1st Armored Signal Bn, ETO; ETO Ribbon with Five Battle Stars; Good Conduct Medal. Mem: VFW; Am Legion; Lincoln Club of Ky; Greater Louisville Labor Coun; COPE. Honors & Awards: Capt High Sch Basketball team; Du Pont Manual Training 1934. Relig: Protestant. Mailing Add: 3121 McMahan Blvd Louisville KY 40220

YOUNG, JOSEPH F (D)
Mich State Rep
Mailing Add: 3899 Garland Detroit MI 48214

YOUNG, LARRY (D)
Md State Deleg
b Baltimore, Md, Nov 25, 49; s George Young & Mable Diggs Payne Y; single. Educ: Univ Md, College Park, BS, 72. Polit & Govt Pos: Md State Deleg, 75- Bus & Prof Pos: Dir urban environ affairs, Izaak Walton League Am, 70-; prog dir, Nat Conf Urban Environ, 73. Publ: Co-auth, Inner city, In: Coun Environ Quality Annual Report, 71; auth, Urban scene, monthly column, Outdoor Am, 72- Mem: NAACP; Oper Push; Nat Urban League. Honors & Awards: Afro Honor Roll Award, Afro-Am Newspapers, 71; Distinguished Citizenship Award, Gov Md, 72; Youth of Year, Young Adults Dem Orgn, 72. Relig: Baptist. Mailing Add: 2322 Lauretta Ave Baltimore MD 21223

YOUNG, MARILYN ASHTON (D)
b Camden, NJ, Nov 17, 31; d John J Ashton & Miriam Young A; m 1953 to Edwin G Young; c Anita, Edwin, Jr, Michelle & Melissa. Educ: Antioch Col, Pa, BA, 75. Polit & Govt Pos: Committeewoman, Cheltenham Twp, 60-, chairperson, 69-72; vchairperson, Montgomery Co Dem Comt, Pa, 68-72; mgr, Humphrey for President, Pa & McGovern for President Campaigns, 72; mem exec comt, Vpres Select Comt, Dem Nat Comt, 73; gov regional rep, Shapp Admin, 73-75; mem, charter comt, Dem Nat Comt, 74; Dem cand, State Legis, Dist 154, 74; campaign mgr, Hill for Mayor, Philadelphia, 75- Bus & Prof Pos: Asst to pres, Brenner, Romm, Karetny, Philadelphia, Pa, 70-72. Mem: Old York Rd Bus & Prof Women; Inst for Study Civic Values (bd mem); Wyncote PTA. Honors & Awards: Dem of the Year, Legis Dist 154, 73. Mailing Add: 209 Greenwood Ave Wyncote PA 19095

YOUNG, MARTIN (D)
Ga State Sen
b Ben Hill Co, Ga, Sept 5, 01; s Samuel S Young & Dona Player Y; m 1923 to Lois Hobgood. Educ: Ben Hill & Turner Co Elem & High Sch, 07-20. Polit & Govt Pos: Co comnr, Ben Hill Co, Ga, 51-56; Ga State Sen, 45th Dist, 57-58, 13th Dist, 63- Bus & Prof Pos: Farmer & merchant. Mem: Mason; Shrine. Relig: Methodist. Mailing Add: RR 2 Rebecca GA 31783

YOUNG, MILTON R (R)
US Sen, NDak
b Berlin, NDak, Dec 6, 97; m 1969 to Patricia M Byrne. Educ: NDak State Agr Col; Graceland Col, Lamoni, Iowa. Polit & Govt Pos: Mem of sch, twp & col AAA bd; NDak State Rep, 32-34; NDak State Sen, 34-45, pres pro tem, NDak State Sen, 41, majority floor leader, 43; US Sen, NDak, 45- Bus & Prof Pos: Farmer. Legal Res: PO Box 241 LaMoure ND 58458 Mailing Add: 5205 Dirksen Senate Off Bldg Washington DC 20510

YOUNG, NIEL C (R)
NH State Rep
Mailing Add: 19 Tyler St Laconia NH 03246

YOUNG, PASQUALE (D)
Mem, North Branford Dem Town Comt, Conn
b New Haven, Conn, Aug 19, 36; s George Young & Maryann Y; m 1960 to Marilyn Vogt; c Mary Elizabeth & Elizabeth Susan. Educ: US Merchant Marine Acad, BS, 59; Yale Law Sch, LLB, 63. Polit & Govt Pos: Mem, Charter Comn, North Branford, Conn, 64, chmn, 69, mem, Libr Bd, 64-67; chmn, North Branford Dem Town Comt, 67-71, mem, 71-; councilman, North Branford Town Coun, 71- Bus & Prof Pos: Partner, Berdon, Berdon & Young, currently. Mil Serv: Entered as Ens, Navy, 59, released as Ens, 60. Mem: Conn, New Haven Co & Am Bar Asns. Relig: Catholic. Mailing Add: 80 Bailey Dr North Branford CT 06471

YOUNG, PATRICIA ANNE (D)
b New York, NY, Aug 3, 44; d Coulter Dabney Young, Jr & Virginia Yates Y; m 1973 to James R Holmes. Educ: Claremont Secretarial Sch, grad, 63, Roberts Walsh Court Reporting Sch, grad, 65. Polit & Govt Pos: Campaign mgr, Co Court Judge James Holmes, 72 & Rep Karen Coolman, 74; deleg, Dem Nat Mid-Term Conf, 74; campaign mgr, Co Comnr Ken Jenne, 75. Bus & Prof Pos: Mgr, Robert Walsh Printing Co, 63-65; court reporter, Frieland, Chertok & Briefer, 65-74; instr, Roberts Walsh Court Reporting Sch, 65-; co court reporter, 74- Mem: Woman's Polit Caucus (Broward co deleg, 74-); Dem Women's Club Broward Co; Broward Co Women Against Rape, Inc (pres, 74-); Women-In-Distress of Broward Co (vpres, emergency housing facil, 74-). Mailing Add: Rm 417A Broward Co Courthouse Ft Lauderdale FL 33301

YOUNG, PATSY KIKUE (D)
Hawaii State Sen
Mailing Add: Senate Sgt-at-Arms State Capitol Honolulu HI 96813

YOUNG, PETER FRANCIS, JR (D)
Vt State Rep
b Springfield, Mass, July 24, 43; s Peter Francis Young & Dorothea Huntoon Y; m 1964 to Patricia Sue Connarn; c Peter F, III & Michael J. Educ: Univ Vt, BA, 66; Union Univ, Albany, JD cum laude, 69; Justinian Soc; Sigma Nu. Polit & Govt Pos: Chmn, Vt State Employees Labor Rels Bd, 74-75; Vt State Rep, Dist 6, 75-; mem, Vt Supreme Court Prof Conduct Bd, 75- Bus & Prof Pos: Attorney at law, Northfield, Vt, 69-; partner, Young & Monte, 72- Publ: Auth, Sound recordings, records & copyright: Aftermath of Sears & Compco, Albany Law Rev, winter 69. Mem: Am, Vt & Washington Co Bar Asns. Honors & Awards: Am Soc Composers, Auth & Publ Award, 69. Legal Res: 8 Prospect St Northfield VT 05663 Mailing Add: PO Box 270 Northfield VT 05663

YOUNG, RICHARD A (D)
Mich State Rep
b Jan 16, 27; c Sharon, Michael. Educ: Univ Detroit, BS Pub Admin; Wayne State Univ, JD; Univ Mich, presently; Alpha Kappa Psi; Delta Theta Pi. Polit & Govt Pos: Mich State Rep, 64-, Majority Whip, Mich House Rep, 71-; treas, Dearborn Twp & Dearborn Heights, formerly. Bus & Prof Pos: Asst prof, Univ Detroit; attorney-at-law; employed by Auditor Gen Detroit, Internal Revenue Serv & Ernst & Ernst, CPA firm, formerly. Mil Serv: Army Air Force. Mem: Dearborn Heights Goodfellows (treas); Dearborn, Detroit, Mich & Am Bar Asns; Dearborn Heights Dem Club. Mailing Add: 24100 W Warren Rd Dearborn Heights MI 48127

YOUNG, ROBERT A (D)
Mo State Sen
b St Louis, Mo, Nov 27, 23; m 1947 to Irene Slawson; c Ann Grace, Robert Anton, Jr & Margaret Mary. Educ: St Louis Parochial Schs, McBride High Sch, Normandy High Sch, St Louis, Mo. Polit & Govt Pos: Dem committeeman, Airport Twp, 52-; Mo State Rep, 57-63; deleg, Dem Nat Conv, 60, 64, 68 & 72; Mo State Sen, 63-, chmn, Comts on Apportionment & State Depts, Mo State Senate, formerly, mem, Appropriations, Bills Perfected & Ordered Printed & Bills Agreed to & Finally Passed, Ins, Labor & Mgt Rels, Local Govt, Pub Health, Welfare & Environ, Rds & Hwys & Educ Comts, formerly; chmn, Permanent Comt on Correctional Insts & Probs, vchmn, Atomic Energy Comn, currently; deleg, Dem Nat Mid-Term Conf, 74. Mil Serv: Entered as Army, 43, released, 45, after serv in 346th Inf, 87th Div, ETO, 44-45; Bronze Star. Mem: Am Legion; Lions; KofC; St Ann Mem Post, VFW (past comdr); life mem Amvets. Relig: Catholic. Mailing Add: 3500 Adie Rd St Ann MO 63074

YOUNG, ROBERT D (R)
Mich State Sen
Mailing Add: 4870 Sheridan Rd Saginaw MI 48601

YOUNG, ROBERT ELLIS (R)
Mo State Rep
b Logansport, Ind, Nov 12, 19; m 1952 to Priscilla Mariea; c John Cobb, Robert Ellis, Jr & Donald James Mariea. Educ: Wabash Col, Crawfordsville, Ind, BA; Phi Beta Kappa. Polit & Govt Pos: Pub rels dir, Citizens' Comt for Reports from Kem, 51; field rep, Mo for Eisenhower, 52; Mo State Rep, 54-, serv as asst minority floor leader in the 74th Gen Assembly, mem, Agr Comt, Mo House Rep, mem, Legis Research Joint Comt, Mo Gen Assembly, currently; vchmn, Mo Tourism Comn, 67-72, chmn, 72-; chmn, US Hwy 71 Asn, 68- Bus & Prof Pos: Radio news & newspaper ed, formerly; secy, Carthage Indust Develop Corp; exec secy, Carthage CofC, 56-68. Mil Serv: Army, Signal Corps, 41-46. Mem: Am Legion; State Hist Soc of Mo; Eastern Jasper Co Ment Health Asn; Eastern Jasper Co Hist Sites Asn (secy); Jasper Co Develop Asn. Honors & Awards: Received St Louis Globe-Dem Newspaper's Meritorious Pub Serv Award as the House Mem most effective in debate for 65-66; 1968 Conservationist of the Year Award from the Conserv Fedn of Mo, Sears-Roebuck Found & Nat Wildlife Fedn; Centennial Medallion Award for leadership in and contribution to agr, Col Agr, Univ Mo, 70. Relig: Episcopal. Mailing Add: 208 W Macon St Carthage MO 64836

YOUNG, ROY (R)
Nev State Assemblyman
Mailing Add: PO Box 588 Elko NV 89801

YOUNG, SAMUEL H (R)
b Casey, Ill, Dec 26, 22; m to Bonnie Ilten; c Elisabeth, Samuel & Ellen. Educ: Univ Ill Champaign-Urbana, LLB, 47, Law Sch, JD, 48. Polit & Govt Pos: Mem, Evanston Young Rep, 48-55; precinct capt, Evanston Regular Rep Orgn, 50-55; pres, Ill Young Rep Orgn, 51-53; chmn, Ill Youth for Taft, 52; chief draftsman, Ill Securities Law, 53; Securities Comnr, Ill, 53-56; mem bd gov, United Rep Fund, 53-60, chmn, Cook Co Membership Drive, 59; chmn, Speakers Bur, Ill Rep State Cent Comt, 56; asst campaign chmn to Sen Arthur Bidwill in reelec campaign of Charles F Carpentier for Secy of State, 56; Asst Secy of State, Ill, 56-58; chief draftsman, Ill Motor Vehicle Code, 57; cand nat chmn, Nat Fedn Young Rep, 59; campaign chmn, Samuel Witwer for US Sen, 60; Rep committeeman, Northfield Twp, 62 & 66; chmn, Rep Judicial Slating Comt Cook Co, 68; cand, US House Rep, 13th Dist, 68; US Rep, Tenth Dist, 73-74. Bus & Prof Pos: Instr econ & corp finance, Univ Ill, 47-49; instr bus finance, Northwestern Univ, 49-50; attorney, US Securities & Exchange Comn, Chicago, 48-49; assoc, Hinshaw & Culbertson, 49-53; partner, Hinshaw, Culbertson, Moelmann & Hoban, 58-59; partner, Hough, Young & Coale, 59-65; financial vpres & secy-treas, Am Hosp Supply Corp, 65-66; head law firm, Samuel H Young Law Off, 66- Mil Serv: Entered as Pvt, 44, released as Capt, 46, after serv in paratroops, 13th & 82nd Airborne Div, ETO, 45-46. Publ: Ed historical & practice note on Ill Securities Law & Ill Motor Vehicle Code, Smith-Hurd Annotated Statutes of Ill; various legal articles on securities, corp & motor vehicle laws. Mem: Am Soc Corp Secretaries; Am Finance Asn; Econ Club Chicago; Exec Club Chicago; Chicago Coun Foreign Rels. Relig: Community Church. Mailing Add: 735 Raleigh Rd Glenview IL 60025

YOUNG, STEPHEN M (D)
b May 4, 89; s Stephen M Young & Belle Wagner Y; m 1911 to Ruby L Dawley, wid, 52; c Stephen & Richard D (both deceased) & Marjorie Y Richardson; m 1957 to Rachel Bell; s Soon-Hie. Educ: Kenyon Col & Western Reserve Univ Law Sch, LLB, 11. Hon Degrees: Kenyon Col, Western Reserve Univ Law Sch, Cent State Col; Chubb Fel, Yale Univ; DPS, Rio Grande Col, 65. Polit & Govt Pos: Ohio State Rep, 13-17; mem, Ohio Comn on Unemploy Ins, 31-32; US Rep-at-lg, Ohio, 33-37, 41-43 & 49-51; Allied Mil Gov, Province Reggio, Italy, 44-45; US Sen, Ohio, 59-71. Mil Serv: Army, Field Artil, 18-19 & Lt Col, Combat Serv, NAfrica & with 5th Army, Italy, 43-46; Bronze Star; four Battle Stars; Order of Crown Italy & Commendation of Gen Mark W Clark; Purple Heart. Mem: War Vet Bar Asn of Cleveland; Cuyahoga Co Bar Asn. Legal Res: Sheraton-Cleveland Hotel 24 Public Square Cleveland OH 44101 Mailing Add: 5160 Manning Pl NW Washington DC 20016

YOUNG, TRACEY H (R)
State Youth Committeeperson, Idaho State Rep Cent Comt
b Shelley, Idaho, Apr 3, 50; s Guy Waid Young & Dorothy Jean Hyldahl Y; single. Educ: Shelley High Sch, dipl. Polit & Govt Pos: Deleg, Idaho State Rep Conv, 72 & Rep Nat Conv, 72; state youth committeeperson, Idaho State Rep Cent Comt, 72- Bus & Prof Pos: Asst mgr, Young's Rexall Drug Co, Shelley, 71- Mil Serv: Entered as Pvt, Marine Corps, 69, released as Cpl, after serv in Combined Action, Repub of Vietnam, 70-71; Cpl, Marine Corps Res, three years; Vietnam Campaign Medal; Vietnam Serv Medal; Combat Action Ribbon; Two Purple Heart Medals; Repub of Vietnam Cross of Gallantry; Two Meritorious Masts; Cert of Commendation, Marine of the Month, 71. Mem: Am Security Coun; DAV. Relig: Latter-day Saint. Mailing Add: 555 S Park Ave Shelley ID 83274

YOUNG, WALTER C (D)
Fla State Rep
Mailing Add: 1311 SW 68th Blvd Pembroke Pines FL 33023

YOUNG, WENDELL WILLIAM (D)
b Philadelphia, Pa, July 7, 38; s Wendell W Young, Jr & Gladys Brenner Y; m 1960 to Marilyn Louise Fluehr; c Wendell W, IV, Brian Joseph, Scott Andrew, Eric Leighton & Brendan James. Educ: St Joseph's Col, BS, 60; Temple Univ, postgrad work, 60-61; Univ Pa; Pa State Univ; Ed newspaper, Nat Fedn Cath Col Students, officer of state-wide orgn, 2 years; class rep, 4 years; class officer, 2 years; Dramatics, 3 years; Glee Club, 4 years. Polit & Govt Pos: Ward leader, Dem Party, Philadelphia Co, Pa, 63-68; mem, Philadelphia Co Dem Exec Party, 63-68; chmn various campaigns for Congressmen & Senators, 63-; alt deleg, Dem Nat Conv, 64 & deleg, 68 & 72; chmn, United Labor Alliance for reelec of Mayor Tate, 66; bd dirs, Comt on Polit Educ, 66-; gen chmn, Philadelphia McGovern-Shriver Campaign, 72. Bus & Prof Pos: Pres & chief exec officer, Retail Clerks Local 1357, 62-; vpres, Philadelphia AFL-CIO, 63-; vpres & exec bd mem, Maritime Port Coun, 64-; chmn, active Ballot Club, Retail Clerks Int Asn, 67-; secy-treas & exec bd mem, Delaware Valley Food Coun, 68-; prof ethics-labor mgt, St Joseph's Col, 68- Mem: Am Fedn Teachers; Cath Philopatrian; Torresdale Frankford Country Club; Northwood Civic Asn; United Fund Exec Comt. Honors & Awards: Youngest Labor Leader, Pa; Formerly Youngest Ward Leader, Philadelphia Co; 1972 Bridge Humanitarian Award. Relig: Catholic. Legal Res: 4140 Orchard Lane Philadelphia PA 19154 Mailing Add: 210 E Courtland St Philadelphia PA 19120

YOUNG, WOOD HALL (R)
Mem, NC Rep Exec Comt
b Minneapolis, NC, Dec 31, 14; s Pink Lucius Young & Nell Burleson Y; m 1946 to Frances Elizabeth Buchanan; c Victoria Nell, Vivian Leigh & Wood Hall, Jr. Educ: Appalachian State Univ, BS. Polit & Govt Pos: Rep precinct chmn, Minneapolis, NC, 46-56; chmn, Avery Co Rep Party, 58-68; mem, NC Rep Exec Comt, 62-; Rep cand, US Rep, NC Tenth Cong Dist, 64, 66 & 68; alt deleg, Rep Nat Conv, 68; Rep cand for US Sen, 74. Bus & Prof Pos: Dealer in export veneer logs. Mil Serv: Entered as Pvt, Air Force, 42, released as Pfc, 43. Mem: Mason; York Rite; Shrine; Mt Glynn Country Club; CofC. Relig: Christian Church of NAm. Mailing Add: Box 14 Minneapolis NC 28652

YOUNGDAHL, LUTHER W (R)
b Minneapolis, Minn, May 29, 96; s John Carl Youngdahl & Elizabeth Johnson Y; m 1923 to Irene Annet Engdahl; c Margaret Louise, Luther William Andrew & Paul David. Educ: Univ Minn, 15-16; Gustavus Adolphus Col, AB, 19; Minn Col of Law, LLB, 21. Hon Degrees: LHD & LLD degrees from 16 univs & cols. Polit & Govt Pos: Sr judge, asst city attorney, Minneapolis, Minn, 21-23, judge munic court, 30-36; judge dist court, Hennepin Co, 36-42; assoc justice, Minn Supreme Court, 42-47; Gov, Minn, 47-51; judge, US Dist Court, Washington, DC, 51-66, sr judge, 66-; off deleg from State Dept to Third UN Conf on Crime & Delinquency; mem, President's Comnt on Law Enforcement & Admin of Justice; mem coun judges, Nat Coun Crime & Delinquency; mem bd dirs, Joint Correctional Manpower Comn, Presidential Study of State & Fed Prisons, currently. Mil Serv: World War I. Honors & Awards: Awarded Grand Cross of the Royal Order of the North Star by King Gustaf V of Sweden; Order of the Lion, Pres of Finland. Relig: Lutheran. Mailing Add: 4101 Cathedral Ave NW Washington DC 20016

YOUNGDAHL, MARK A (D)
Mo State Rep
Mailing Add: 2525 Union St St Joseph MO 64506

YOUNGE, WYVETTER HOOVER (D)
Ill State Rep
b St Louis, Mo, Aug 23, 30; d Ernest Jack Hoover & Annie Jordan H; m 1958 to Richard G Younge; c Ruth F, Torque E & Margrett H. Educ: Hampton Inst, BA, 51; St Louis Univ Sch Law, JD, 55; Wash Univ Sch Law, LLM, 72; Alpha Kappa Alpha. Polit & Govt Pos: Ill State Rep, 75-, mem, Appropriation, Banks, Savings & Loans & Exec Comts, Ill House Rep, 75-, chmn, subcomt on open meetings, 75- Bus & Prof Pos: Attorney-at-law, 55-; exec dir, Neighborhood Ctrs, War on Poverty, 65-68 & East St Louis Adv & Develop Nonprofit Housing Corp, 68- Publ: The Implementation of Old Man River, privately publ, 72. Mem: Venus Temple Eastern Star. Honors & Awards: Humanity Award, Proj Upgrade, 69; Citizens of the Year Award, Monitor Newspaper; Cert of Recognition, Black Heritage Comt. Relig: African Methodist Episcopal. Mailing Add: 1617 N 46th East St Louis IL 62204

YOUNGER, EVELLE J (R)
Attorney Gen, Calif
b Stamford, Nebr, June 19, 18; m 1942 to Mildred Eberhard; c Eric. Educ: Hastings Col, 2 years; Univ Nebr, AB & LLB, 40; Northwestern Univ Law Sch, grad courses, 40; Fed Bur Invest Acad, 40-41. Polit & Govt Pos: Former co pres, Young Rep; pres, Pasadena Young Rep, Calif, formerly; mem, Calif Rep Assembly, 20 years; state dir-at-lg, Calif Rep Party, formerly; treas, Co Rep Party, formerly; pres, 47th Assembly Dist Rep Orgn, formerly; secy, 20th Cong Dist Rep Orgn; formerly; mem, vchmn & chmn, Los Angeles Co Rep Cent Comt, formerly; chmn, 47th Assembly Dist Rep Party; dep city attorney, criminal div, Los Angeles, 46; city prosecutor, Pasadena, 47-50; mem, President's Hwy Safety Conf, 50-52; former mem bd dirs, Comt on Traffic Regulation, League Calif Cities; judge, Los Angeles Munic Court, 53-58; judge, Los Angeles Co Superior Court, 58-63, assigned to Master Calendar, Criminal Courts, 63; dist attorney, Los Angeles Co, 64-70; chmn, President Nixon's Task Force on Crime & Law Enforcement, 68-69; Attorney Gen, Calif, 71-, deleg, Rep Nat Conv, 72. Bus & Prof Pos: Spec agt, Fed Bur Invest, 40-42, NY Field Off & supvr in Nat Defense Sect,

Washington, DC; pvt law practice, 51-53; former instr, Southwestern Univ Law Sch; lectr, Univ Southern Calif & Univ Calif Los Angeles Law Sch. Mil Serv: Army, 42-46, Counter Intel Corps, Chief Far East & Southeast Asia Sect, Counter Intel Br, Off Strategic Serv, intel officer, British 15th Indian Army Corps, China, Burma, India Theatres; Air Force, 51-52, Off Spec Invest, acting chief, Plans & Inspections Br, Chief Counter Intel Div, 18th Dist; Maj Gen, Air Force Res. Publ: Criminal Law Handbook, Calif State Dept Educ; co-auth, Judge & Prosecutor in Traffic Court, Am Bar Asn & Northwestern Univ; Criminal Practice in Municipal Courts; plus others. Mem: Fel Am Col Trial Lawyers; Mason; Shrine; Am Legion; Elks. Relig: Episcopal; former Sunday sch teacher. Legal Res: Los Angeles CA Mailing Add: Attorney Gen of Calif State Capitol Sacramento CA 95814

YOUNGLUND, WALTER ARTHUR (R)
Colo State Rep
b Weld Co, Colo, Dec 20, 23; s Elmer Younglund & Jessie McCarthy Y; m 1946 to Meryl Gilbert; c Louetta, Ladonna, Marleen, Marshia, Monty, Fairy, Frankie & Marshal. Polit & Govt Pos: Colo State Rep, 68-, vchmn, Labor & Employ Rels Comt, Colo House Rep, chmn, Agr Comt; chmn, Selective Serv Bd Appeals, 70- Mil Serv: 3/C PO, Navy, 43-46; Asiatic Ribbon with one Star. Mem: Lions; Am Legion; VFW; Nat & Colo Cattlemen's Asns. Mailing Add: New Raymer CO 80742

YOURELL, HARRY (BUS) (D)
Ill State Sen
Mailing Add: 9524 S Kenton Ave Oak Lawn IL 60453

YOUTZ, HEWITT G (R)
Chmn, Fremont Co Rep Party, Wyo
b San Diego, Calif, Oct 7, 22; s H Fletcher Youtz & Lizzie Gleave Y; m 1944 to Mildred Josephine Brown; c Charles, Jo Anne (Mrs McFarland) & Thomas. Educ: Univ Wyo, BS, 47; Alpha Zeta. Polit & Govt Pos: State committeeman, Park Co Rep Party, Wyo, 61-62; chmn, Fremont Co Rep Party, 66-; alt deleg, Rep Nat Conv, 68. Mailing Add: 414 N Second St W Riverton WY 82501

YSRAEL, ALFRED (R)
Sen, Guam Legis
Mailing Add: Guam Legis Box 373 Agana GU 96910

YUEN, JANN L (D)
Hawaii State Rep
Mailing Add: House Sgt-at-Arms State Capitol Honolulu HI 96813

YUNGHANS, ROBERT O (D)
Chmn, Nemaha Co Dem Party, Kans
b Kansas City, Kans, Nov 29, 19; s Emil F Yunghans & Edith L Zane Y; m 1949 to Kathryn M O'Toole; c Joseph, Mary & James. Educ: Kans State Univ, BS, 45. Polit & Govt Pos: Mem, Seneca City Coun, Kans, 54-60; Kans State Rep, 60-66; former pres, Kans Dem Club; mem, Kans Water Resources Bd, 70-, chmn, 74-75. Bus & Prof Pos: Ins Agt, 53- Mil Serv: Pvt, Army Air Force, 43; Lt Col, Air Force Res. Mem: ROA; Air Force Asn; VFW; Am Legion; CofC. Relig: Catholic. Mailing Add: 401 N Third St Seneca KS 66538

YUNGKANS, MONNIE JESSELYN (D)
Committeewoman, Dem Exec Comt, Fla
b La Follette, Tenn, Jan 1, 17; s Clarence Fritts & Pearl Childress F; m 1938 to Carl H Yungkans; c Monica Y (Mrs Edwards). Educ: St Charles High Sch, grad, 35. Polit & Govt Pos: Precinct committeewoman, Brevard Co Dem Exec Comt, Fla, 70, secy, 71-74, state committeewoman, 75-; co-chmn budget & audit, Dem Exec Comt, 75-; vpres, Cent Brevard Dem Woman's Club, 75- Bus & Prof Pos: Acct clerk, Thomas Gladiola Farms Inc, 58-63; acct clerk, Cocoa, Fla, 63, personnel specialist, 72. Mem: Pilot Club Cocoa Inc (dir, currently); Brevard Co Home Nursing Adv Coun (treas); Eastern Star (secy & star point); Women of the Moose (chmn, library & mem). Relig: Lutheran. Mailing Add: 981 Church St Rockledge FL 32955

YUSKO, THEODORE (D)
Chmn, Columbia Co Dem Comt, NY
b Carteret, NJ, Nov 4, 18; s John Yusko & Mary Pyndus Y; m 1952 to Evelyn D Sanford; c Herbert, David, John & Paul. Educ: Hudson High Sch, NY, grad, 37. Polit & Govt Pos: Chmn, Hudson City Dem Comt, NY, 63-69; committeeman, Fifth Ward Dem Party, 68-; mem, Columbia Co Dem Comt, currently; chmn, 73- Bus & Prof Pos: Labor organizer, USW, AFL-CIO, 66-73; night supvr, V&O Press Co, Hudson, 73- Mil Serv: Entered as Pvt, Air Force, 42, released as Sgt, 45, after serv in 10th Air Force, China-Burma-India, 43-45; Good Conduct Medal; Asiatic Pac Medal; Victory Medal. Mem: Ukrainian Nat Asn; VFW; Am Legion; Elks. Relig: Greek Orthodox. Mailing Add: 4 Fairview Ave Hudson NY 12534

Z

ZABLOCKI, CLEMENT JOHN (D)
US Rep, Wis
b Milwaukee, Wis, Nov 18, 12; s Matt J Zablocki & Mary Jankowski Z; m 1937 to Blanche M Janic; c Joseph Paul & Jane Frances. Educ: Marquette Univ, PhB & grad study in educ. Hon Degrees: LLD, Marquette Univ, 66 & Alverno Col, 69. Polit & Govt Pos: Wis State Sen, 42-48; US Rep, Fourth Dist, Wis, 48-; deleg, Dem Nat Conv, 68; cong adv to US Deleg, Comn on Disarmament, 71-73; mem, Comn on Orgn of Govt for Conduct of Foreign Policy. Bus & Prof Pos: Teacher, choir dir & organist, Milwaukee. Mil Serv: Lt Col, Air Force Res. Publ: Sino Soviet Rivalry, Praeger, 66; We must make our stand in Vietnam, Vietnam, A Report on a Wingspring Briefing, The Johnson Found, 64; A third pollution, Nat Eagle Mag, 6/65. Mem: KofC (4 degree); ROA; Polish Asn of Am; Polish Nat Alliance; Milwaukee Musicians Asn. Relig: Roman Catholic. Legal Res: 3245 W Drury Lane Milwaukee WI 53215 Mailing Add: 2184 Rayburn Bldg Washington DC 20515

ZACHOS, VICTORIA (R)
Rep Nat Committeewoman, NH
b Bennington, NH July 6, 29; d Stephen Zachos (deceased) & Sophia Bacogiannis Z (deceased); single. Educ: Concord Commercial Col, NH, 48. Polit & Govt Pos: Secy, New Eng Coun Young Rep, 52-54; chmn, NH Coun Young Rep, 54-60; Young Rep Nat Committeewoman, 60-64; chmn, Concord Rep City Comt, 64-68; asst chmn & head womens div, NH Rep State Comt, 68-72; Rep Nat Committeewoman, NH, 72-, mem exec comt, Rep Nat Comt, 72- Bus & Prof Pos: Legal secy, Off of Robert D Branch, 48- Relig: Greek Orthodox. Mailing Add: 82 Warren St Concord NH 03301

ZACK, EUGENE C (D)
b Springfield, Mass, Mar 16, 22; s Charles S Zack & Mary V Crean Z; div; c Patricia M & Christina M. Polit & Govt Pos: Spec asst to admin, Area Redevelop Admin, US Dept Com, 61-63; admin asst to US Rep James G O'Hara, Mich, 71- Bus & Prof Pos: Merchandise mgr, Gen Elec Supply Co, Buffalo, NY, 50-57; assoc ed, AFL-CIO News, Washington, DC, 57-63; pres, Ideas Unlimited, Washington, DC, 63-66; dir pub affairs, Seafarers Int Union, Washington, DC, 66-70; dir pub affairs, Transportation Inst, Washington, DC, 70-71. Mil Serv: Entered as Pvt, Army, 40, released as Sgt, 43, after serv in 1st Inf Div, NAfrica, 42-43. Relig: Catholic. Legal Res: 1420 Aldenham Lane Reston VA 22090 Mailing Add: 111 Tennessee Ave NE Washington DC 20002

ZADROZNY, MITCHELL GEORGE (R)
b Chicago, Ill, Dec 23, 23; s John Zadrozny & Jeanette Ulick Z; single. Educ: Ill State Univ, BS, 47; Univ Chicago, SM, 49, PhD, 56. Polit & Govt Pos: Alt deleg, Rep Nat Conv, 68; secy, 45th Ward Rep Orgn, 68-; mem, President's Water Pollution Adv Bd, 72-; Rep cand for US Rep, Ill, 74. Bus & Prof Pos: Civilian geogr analyst, US Dept Army, Tokyo, Japan, 50-52; lectr geog of Southeast Asia, Univ Chicago Downtown Col, 53-55; dir research, Cambodia-Laos Proj, Univ Chicago, 54-55; teacher, Wright City Col, 55-63, asst prof, 63-66, assoc prof, 66-69, prof, 69- Mil Serv: Entered as Pvt, Army, 42, released as 2nd Lt, 45, after serv as Bombardier, 3rd Army Air Force. Publ: Cambodia Handbook, Human Rels Area Files Press, 55; Water Utilization in the Middle Mississippi Valley, Univ Chicago Press, 56; World regional geography TV guide with map supplement, Chicago Bd Educ, 62. Mem: Asn of Am Geogr; Ill Geog Asn; Uptown Chicago Comn (bd dirs); Am Legion; Ill State Rep Nationalities Coun. Relig: Catholic. Mailing Add: 4158 N McVicker Ave Chicago IL 60634

ZAGAME, JOHN ROSS (R)
NY State Assemblyman
b Oswego, NY, July 27, 51; s John Ernest Zagame & Grace Belfiore Z; m 1974 to Susan Ruth Koerber. Educ: Syracuse Univ, BA magna cum laude, 73; Phi Beta Kappa. Polit & Govt Pos: Page, US Rep Robert C McEwen, 67-69; NY State Assemblyman, 75- Bus & Prof Pos: Farmer. Mem: Oswego Co Vegetable Growers Asn; Elks; Sons of Italy. Relig: Roman Catholic. Mailing Add: 17 Montcalm St Oswego NY 13126

ZAGORIN, BERNARD (D)
b Chicago, Ill, Jan 5, 21; s Ben Zagorin & Sarah Swirsky Z; m 1943 to Ruth Kramer; c Gregory, Peter, Ellen & Mark. Educ: Univ Chicago, BA, 42, MA, 47; Phi Beta Kappa. Polit & Govt Pos: Economist, Econ Coop Admin, Am Embassy, London, Eng, 49-51, asst treas rep & asst financial attache, 51-55; asst chief Europ div, Off Int Finance, Treas Dept, Washington, DC, 55-59; treas rep & financial attache, Am Embassy, New Delhi, India, 59-63; dir, Off Developing Nations, Off Int Affairs, Treas Dept, Washington, DC, 63-66; alt US exec dir, World Bank, 65-66; US exec dir, Asian Develop Bank, Manila, Philippines, 66-70; spec asst on detail to White House Task Force, Treas Dept, Washington, DC, 70-71; alt rep, 26th & 27th UN Gen Assemblies, 71 & 72; US Rep, UN Econ & Social Coun, New York, 71-73; sr consult, UN Environ Prog. Bus & Prof Pos: Lectr econ, Roosevelt Col, 48-49. Mil Serv: Entered as Pvt, Army, 43, released as T/Sgt-4, 46, after serv in SigC, ETO, 44-46. Honors & Awards: Univ Chicago Alumni Asn Citation for pub serv, 70. Mailing Add: Apt 18C-W 305 E 86th St New York NY 10028

ZAHN, DONALD M (R)
b Carey, Ohio, Aug 20, 23; s Leo Norman Zahn & Margueritte Simonis Z; m 1943 to Mary Elizabeth Miller; c Marilyn, Bruce & Diane. Educ: Bowling Green State Univ, BS in educ, 46; Colo Univ, MA in hist, 48; Ohio State Univ, 48-50; Phi Alpha Theta; Alpha Tau Omega. Polit & Govt Pos: Archivist, Nat Archives, 50-57; admin asst to US Rep Jackson E Betts, 57-73; admin asst to US Rep John Paul Hammerschmidt, Ark, formerly. Mil Serv: Pvt, Army, 42-44. Relig: Catholic. Legal Res: Carey OH 43316 Mailing Add: 6014 85th Pl New Carrollton MD 20784

ZAHNER, KENYON BENEDICT, JR (R)
Chmn, Catawba Co Rep Exec Comt, NC
b Atlanta, Ga, Jan 17, 30; s Kenyon Benedict Zahner, Sr & Harriet Evalina Loyer Lawton Z; m 1951 to Jane Linn Henley; c Kenyon B, III, Courtney Linn, Linn Henley, Catherine Cleveland & Cleveland Benedict. Educ: Univ NC, Chapel Hill, 49-51; NC State Univ, BS, 55; Phi Delta Theta. Polit & Govt Pos: Chmn, Catawba Co Rep Finance Comt, NC, 63-65; mem, NC Rep State Exec Comt, 64-; mem, Tenth Cong Dist Rep Exec Comt, 66-; chmn, Catawba Co Rep Exec Comt, 66-; mem, NC House of Rep, 73-74. Bus & Prof Pos: Poultry specialist, Lindsay-Robinson, Inc, 55-56; mgr, Bumgarner Poultry, Iron Sta, NC, 56-58; farmer, Catawba Co, 58-61; agt, New Eng Mutual Life Ins Co, Boston, Mass, 61- Mil Serv: Entered as Recruit, Army, 51, released as Specialist 1/C, 53, after serv in 529th FAOBN & 7th Army Intel, Western Zone, Ger, 52. Mem: Am Col Life Underwriters; Nat Asn Life Underwriters; Farm Bur. Relig: Episcopal. Legal Res: Old St Paul Church Rd Newton NC 28658 Mailing Add: PO Box 2081 Hickory NC 28601

ZAHOREC, JOSEPH JOHN (D)
Mem, Lorain Co Dem Exec Comt, Ohio
b Lorain, Ohio, July 2, 20; s John Steve Zahorec & Mary Marincin Z; m 1943 to Helen H Jalowiec; c John J, Jolynne Jaykel, Mary Ellen Muc & Susan. Educ: Lorain High Sch, grad, 38. Polit & Govt Pos: Zoning inspector, Black River Twp, Ohio; precinct committeeman, Lorain City Dem Cent Comt; spec events chmn, Lorain Co Dem Exec Comt, formerly, mem, 73-, mem, Cent Comt, 73-; alt deleg, Dem Nat Conv, 68; deleg, Dem State Conv, 68; mayor, Lorain, 72-; deleg, Dem Mid-Term Conf, 74. Bus & Prof Pos: Music instr, realtor & owner, Zahorec Realty; notary pub. Mem: Cent Bus Men's Asn (pres, 70-71, dir, currently); Lions; Nairol Civic Club, Inc (charter mem); KofC (4 degree); Lorain CofC (dir, 73-). Honors & Awards: Realtor of Year, 65; cand, Man of Year, 68. Relig: Catholic. Mailing Add: 238 Jefferson St Lorain OH 44052

ZAJIC, R C (RAY) (R)
Kans State Rep
Mailing Add: 209 S Ash Glasco KS 67445

ZAKHEM, SAMIR HANNA (R)
Colo State Rep
b Lebanon, Nov 25, 37; s Hanna Yacoub Zakhem & Matilda Khouzami A; m 1966 to Merilynn R Gillis; c John Stuart & Charles Samir. Educ: Am Univ Cairo, BA, 57; Univ Detroit, MBA, 59; Univ Colo, MA, 68, PhD, 70; Pi Sigma Alpha. Polit & Govt Pos: Colo State Rep, 74- Bus & Prof Pos: Cost analyst, Ford Motor Co, Dearborn, Mich, 62-64; assoc prof, Loretto Heights Col, Denver, 68-72; dir ctr for int students, Univ Denver, 72-73; research analyst, Heritage Found, Washington, DC, 73-74; consult, State of Colo, 74- Mem: Kiwanis (dir); Nat Asn Arab Am; Jaycees; Western Fedn Lebanese Am Clubs (exec vpres, 74-). Honors & Awards: Most Distinguished Am by Choice in Colo, 200 Colo-Civic Groups; Award for Patriotism & Loyalty, Marine Corps, 72; Voice of Democracy Awards, VFW, 72-75, Medal of Citizenship, 74. Relig: Christian. Mailing Add: 2691 S Zurich Ct Denver CO 80219

ZALESKI, TONY, JR (D)
Ind State Rep
Mailing Add: 4229 Euclid Ave East Chicago IN 46312

ZAMPIERI, JOHN JAMES (D)
Vt State Rep
b Ryegate, Vt, Jan 19, 41; s Giovianni G Zampieri & Breatice Demeritt Z; m to Joyce E Andreoletti; c Roxanna Lee & Rebecca Lynn. Educ: Champlain Bus Col. Polit & Govt Pos: Chmn, Ryegate Dem Town Comt, Vt, 65-; secy, Caledonia Co Dem Comt, 65-67, committeeman, 71-; Vt State Rep, 65-, chmn, House Insts Comt, Vt House Rep, 71-74, chmn, Transportation Comt, 75-; trustee, Village South Ryegate, 66-69; deleg, Dem Nat Conv, 68. Bus & Prof Pos: Salesman, Nationwide Ins Co, 63- Mil Serv: Airman, Vt Air Nat Guard, 63-69. Mem: Woodsville Lions Club (past pres); Mt Sinai Shrine, Montpelier, Vt; Pulaski Lodge 58, F&AM, Well Rivers, Vt; Northeastern Vt Develop Asn (past pres). Relig: Presbyterian. Mailing Add: Box 157 South Ryegate VT 05069

ZANDER, EUGENE J (D)
Md State Deleg
Mailing Add: 2013 Franwall Ave Silver Spring MD 20902

ZANE, RAYMOND JOHN (D)
NJ State Sen
b Woodbury, NJ, July 23, 39; s Clarence Ray Zane & Veronica P Shevy Z; m 1959 to Elizabeth A Barry; c Marybeth, Raymond J, II & Kenneth M. Educ: St Joseph's Col(Pa), BS with honors, 63; Rutgers Univ, JD, 74. Polit & Govt Pos: Alt deleg, Dem Nat Conv, 72; NJ freeholder, Gloucester Co, 72-74; NJ State Sen, Dist 3, 74-, mem judiciary comt & appropriations comt, NJ State Senate, currently. Bus & Prof Pos: Tax acct, Woodbury, NJ, 63-74 & lawyer, 74- Mem: NJ Bar Asn. Honors & Awards: Pub Serv Award, Rutgers Univ, 75. Relig: Roman Catholic. Mailing Add: 24 N Childs St Woodbury NJ 08096

ZANGER, JOSEPH ANTHONY (R)
Mem, Rep State Cent Comt Calif
b San Jose, Calif, Dec 28, 27; s Dr Henry George Zanger & Clara A Cribari Z; m 1953 to Kathleen Kelsch; c Wendy, Allene, Joseph C & Gretchen. Educ: Univ Santa Clara, 3 years. Polit & Govt Pos: San Benito Co campaign mgr for State Sen Donald Grunsky, President Richard Nixon & Farmers for Gov Reagan, Calif; finance chmn, San Benito Co Rep Cent Comt, Calif, 65-67, vchmn, 67-69, chmn, formerly; mem, Calif Rep State Cent Comt, currently; dir, San Benito Co Pollution Bd, 70. Bus & Prof Pos: Chmn, San Benito Co Fair Entertainment, 66-69; dir & pres, San Benito Co Farm Bur, 69; dir, State Farm Bur Prune Research Comt, 69; mem, Fed Prune Admin Comt, 69; mem, Calif State Prune Adv Bd, 69; dir & founder Calif Prune Bargaining Asn, 69; owner, Casa de Fruta Complex; owner, Zanger-Casa de Fruta Orchards. Mem: Elks; Santa Clara Co Horseman Asn (dir); San Benito Co Saddle Horse Asn; San Benito Co CofC; Health Planning Coun, San Benito Co (dir). Relig: Catholic. Mailing Add: 6680 Pacheco Pass Hwy Hollister CA 95023

ZAPARACKAS, ALGIS (R)
Fourth VChmn, Mich Rep State Comt
b Kaunas, Lithuania, Apr 4, 40; s Antanas Zaparackas & Stase Cepsys Z; single. Educ: Wayne State Univ, BSME, 63. Polit & Govt Pos: Nationalities dir to Reelect US Sen Robert P Griffin, Mich, 72; nationalities dir, Mich for Milliken Comt, 74; fourth vchmn, Mich Rep State Cent Comt, 75- Bus & Prof Pos: Design engr, Chrysler Corp, Highland Park, Mich, 63-71; prod design engr, Ford Motor Co, Dearborn, 71- Publ: Ed, Lithuanian Melodies Radio Hour - WMZK, Detroit, Mich, 63- & Accent, Rep State Nationalities Newsletter, 68- Mem: Soc Automotive Engrs; Am Soc Mech Engrs; Lithuanian Scouts Asn; Am-Lithuanian Scouting Asn. Relig: Roman Catholic. Mailing Add: 4120 Yorba Linda Dr Royal Oak MI 48072

ZAPP, JOHN SHEA (R)
Dep Asst Secy for Legis, Dept Health, Educ & Welfare
b Nampa, Idaho, Sept 28, 32; s George M Zapp, Sr & Gertrude Shea Z; m Joyce C Boozer; c Regina M, John, Jr, Megan, Michael & Mark. Educ: Boise Col, AB, 57; Creighton Sch of Dent, DDS, 61; Boise Col Pres, 55; Pres, Delta Sigma Delta, 60-61; secy, Inter-Fraternity Coun, 59-60. Hon Degrees: DSc, Col of Med & Dent of NJ, 72. Polit & Govt Pos: Finance chmn, Wasco Co Rep Cent Comt, 62-63, chmn, 65-67; chmn, Wasco Co Young Rep, 64-65; state dir, Young Rep Fedn Ore, 64-65; chmn, Second Cong Dist Rep Cent Comt, 65-67; mem, Rep State Coord Comt, 66-; treas, Rep State Cent & Exec Comts, Ore, formerly; chmn budget comt, Rep State Comt, formerly; chmn, Biennial Rep Platform Conv Ore, 68; alt deleg, Rep Nat Conv, 68; spec asst for dent affairs to Asst Secy for Health & Sci Affairs, Dept Health, Educ & Welfare, 69-70, Dep Asst Secy for Health Manpower, 71-72, Dep Asst Secy for Legis, 72-, chmn, Dent Health Adv Comt, currently, fed rep, Liaison Comt on Med Educ, currently, health rep, Consumer Rep Comt, currently, health legis coordr for Asst Secy Health, currently. Bus & Prof Pos: Chmn, Mid-Columbia Community Col Comt, 63-67; vchmn, State Community Col Governance Comt, 67-68; dir, Ore Med Polit Action Comt, 68-; chmn, Dentists of Ore Polit Action Comt, 69- Mil Serv: Entered as Pvt, Marines, 51, released as Sgt, 54, after serv in 1st & 3rd Marines, Korea, 53-54; Purple Heart. Mem: Fel Am Col of Dent; hon fel Int Col of Dent; Lions Int; CofC; Navy League. Honors & Awards: One of Oregon's Ten Outstanding Young Men, 64; Young Man of the Year, 65; Distinguished Serv Award; Spec Citation, Secy of Health, Educ & Welfare, 73. Relig: Catholic. Legal Res: OR Mailing Add: Health Educ & Welfare Bldg Rm 5448 330 Independence Ave SW Washington DC 20201

ZARB, FRANK G (R)
Adminr, Fed Energy Admin
b New York, NY, Feb 17, 35; s Gustave Zarb & Rosemary Antinora Z; m 1957 to Patricia Koster; c Krista Ann & Frank G, Jr. Educ: Hofstra Univ, BBA, 57, MBA, 62. Hon Degrees: LLD, Hofstra Univ, 75. Polit & Govt Pos: Exec vpres, CBWL-Hayden Stone, Inc, New York, 69-71; asst secy, Dept Labor, 71-72; exec vpres, Hayden Stone, Inc, New York, 72-73; assoc dir, Off Mgt & Budget, 73-74; adminr, Fed Energy Admin, 74- Bus & Prof Pos: Grad trainee, Cities Serv Oil Co, New York, 57-62; gen partner, Goodbody & Co, 62-69. Mil Serv: Entered as 2nd Lt, Army Res, 57, released as Capt, 64. Publ: The Stockmarket Handbook, Dow Jones, Irwin, 69. Honors & Awards: Hon Lifetime mem, Am Soc Pub Admin, 74; Distinguished Scholar Award, Hofstra Univ Faculty, 74. Mailing Add: Fed Energy Admin Washington DC 20001

ZAROD, STANLEY JOHN (D)
Mass State Sen
b Indian Orchard, Mass, Apr 11, 24; s Johns Zarod & Sophie Borsa Z; m 1959 to Isabelle S Guzik. Educ: Dartmouth Col, AB, 44; Phi Gamma Delta. Polit & Govt Pos: City councilman, Springfield, Mass, 49-57, pres city coun, 56, acting mayor, Springfield, 57; Mass State Sen, 57-67 & 69-; dir, Interstate Coop Comn, Mass, 67-68; alt deleg, Dem Nat Conv, 72. Bus & Prof Pos: Self-employed in real estate, 50- Mil Serv: Entered as Pvt, Marines, 42, released as Cpl, 46, after serv in 6th Marine Div, SPac, 43-46; Presidential Unit Citation. Mem: Am Legion; Polish Am Vet; Elks; KofC; life mem Baseball Players Am. Relig: Catholic. Mailing Add: 537 Main St Springfield MA 01105

ZAROFF, CAROLYN REIN (D)
b New York, NY, Feb 1, 36; d Solomon Rein & Dorothy Bloom R; m 1956 to Lawrence Irving Zaroff; c Susan, Wendy & Jonathan. Educ: Univ Pa, 52; George Washington Univ, Sch Govt, BA, 56; Pi Gamma Mu; Nat Social Sci Hon Soc. Polit & Govt Pos: Town leader, Brighton Dem Comt, NY, 72-; deleg, Dem Nat Mid-Term Conf, 74; cand town coun, Brighton, 75. Mem: Mo Co Women's Polit Caucus (exec & steering comts, 72-); Brighton CofC; Monroe Co League of Women Voters. Mailing Add: 80 Pelham Rd Rochester NY 14610

Z'BERG, EDWIN L (D)
Calif State Assemblyman
b Sacramento, Calif; m to Edna Merle Coz; c Vicki, John & Cynthia Susan. Educ: Univ Calif, Los Angeles, BA; Univ San Francisco of Law, LLB, summa cum laude, 51. Polit & Govt Pos: Calif State Assemblyman, 58-; Dep Attorney Gen, formerly; mem, Calif Dem State Cent Comt. Bus & Prof Pos: Lawyer. Mil Serv: Ens, Naval Res, 44-47; Lt(jg), Res, currently. Mem: Sacramento Swiss Lodge; Sacramento Jr CofC; Foresters; NSGW; VFW. Honors & Awards: Received Gostic Award, Stanford Jr High Sch, highest scholastic record in class; valedictorian, Sacramento Sr High Sch; received Pres Scholarship, Univ San Francisco. Legal Res: 1157 Lancaster Way Sacramento CA 95822 Mailing Add: 2413 15th St Sacramento CA 95818

ZBRANEK, J C (D)
Chmn, Liberty Co Dem Party, Tex
b Crosby, Tex, Mar 25, 30; s L Zbranek & Marie Picek Z; m 1958 to Nelda Doris Forshee; c Felicia Ann; Zeb D & Zachary M. Educ: Univ Tex, BA, 52, JD, 56; Phi Delta Phi; Tejas Club; Silver Spurs; Friar Soc; MICA; ed, Tex Law Rev. Polit & Govt Pos: Tex State Rep, 54-60; chmn, Liberty Co Dem Party, 69- Bus & Prof Pos: Attorney, 56- Mil Serv: Entered as Ens, Navy, 52, released as Lt(jg), 54, after serv in USS Carmick, DMS-33, in Korea with Task Force 95, 52-54; UN, Korean Serv & US Serv Medals. Mem: Am & Tex Trial Lawyers Asns; Tex Bar Asn; VFW; Am Legion. Relig: Baptist. Legal Res: Box 361 Devers TX 77538 Mailing Add: Box 151 Liberty TX 77575

ZEARFOSS, HERBERT KEYSER (R)
Pa State Rep
b East Chillisquaque Twp, Pa, Oct 13, 29; s Dean Wilson Zearfoss & Susan Keyser Z; m 1953 to Thelma Mary McCarthy; c Timothy McCarthy, Jonathan Andrew & Sarah Creighton. Educ: Bucknell Univ, AB, 51; Yale Law Sch, 51-53; Washington Col Law, Am Univ, JD, 58; Omicron Delta Kappa; Phi Alpha Theta; Tau Kappa Alpha; Pi Sigma Alpha; Theta Chi; Alpha Phi Omega. Polit & Govt Pos: Mem, Radnor Twp Park & Recreation Bd, Pa, 64-66; justice of the peace, Radnor Twp, Del Co, 66-67; Pa State Rep, 167th Dist, 68- Bus & Prof Pos: Partner, Fetter & Fearfoss, Lewisburg, Pa, 59-60; asst counsel, Fidelity Mutual Life Ins Co, Philadelphia, 60-66; secy-mgr, Ins Fedn of Pa, Philadelphia, 66-68; lawyer, Wayne, Pa, 69-70; partner, Zearfoss & Campbell, Lawyers, 70- Mil Serv: Entered as S/A, Naval Res, 54, released as Lt, 58, after serv in Naval Security Sta, Washington, DC, 54-58; Lt Comdr, Naval Res, 63-69 (Ret); Nat Defense Serv Medal; Naval Res Medal. Publ: Gifts of life insurance, 4/61 & Health insurance and federal tax collector, 4/64, Fidelity Field Man. Mem: Phi Alpha Delta; Asn Life Ins Counsel; Yale Club of Philadelphia; Waynesborough Country Club; Netherland Soc of Philadelphia. Honors & Awards: Pa Young Rep Hall of Fame, 70. Relig: Episcopal; vestryman. Legal Res: 210 Orchard Way St Davids PA 19087 Mailing Add: 121 N Wayne Ave Wayne PA 19087

ZECHEL, CAROLINE N (R)
NH State Rep
Mailing Add: 9 Beverlee Dr Nashua NH 03060

ZEFERETTI, LEO C (D-CONSERVATIVE)
US Rep, NY
b Brooklyn, NY, July 15, 27; m 1947 to Barbara Schiebel; c Linda & Jan. Educ: Baruch Sch, NY Univ. Polit & Govt Pos: With Dept Correction, New York; app, NY State Crime Control Planning Bd; rep, President's Conf Correction & Conf for Nat Correction Acad; US Rep, NY, 75- Bus & Prof Pos: Bd dirs, Health Ins Plan Gtr New York & Int Found. Mem: Correction Officers Benevolent Asn (pres). Honors & Awards: Order St Brigida, Cavalieri Commendatori; Humanitarian Award, Community Mayors, State of NY; Deleg of the Year, Correction Dept Columbia Asn, 69; Citation of Merit, Grand Coun Steuben Asn Civil Serv. Legal Res: 9910 Ft Hamilton Pkwy Brooklyn NY 11209 Mailing Add: US House of Rep Washington DC 20515

ZEIDERS, GRACE (R)
Chairwoman, Stephenson Co Rep Party, Ill
b Freeport, Ill, Feb 9, 86; d John L Wareham & Minnie Hillmer W; m 1910 to William W

Zeiders; wid. Educ: Freeport Bus Col, 05. Polit & Govt Pos: Mem, Stephenson Co Rep Woman's Club, 45-, pres, 4 years; chairwoman, Stephenson Co Rep Party, 48-; participant, Rep Women's Conv, 53 & 57; deleg, numerous state & dist Rep conv. Bus & Prof Pos: Bookkeeper coal co & bldg & loan co, Freeport, 05-60; part-time writer, Freeport J Standard, 29- Publ: Ed, The King's Daughter, (jour), 58- Mem: Eastern Star (Past Matron); Capernaum Shrine (Past Worthy Priestess); Past Matrons of Order of Eastern Star Club (past pres); Scottish Rite Woman's Club (past pres); Freeport Woman's Club. Honors & Awards: Luncheon given in honor by Stephenson Co Rep Woman's Club, 69; photographs with prominent Republican's as Everett Dirksen, Mrs Nelson Rockefeller & Mamie Eisenhower have been published in newspapers throughout the US. Relig: Presbyterian; organist. Mailing Add: 766 W Avon St Freeport IL 61032

ZEISER, BRUCE HUNTER (R)
Mass State Rep
b Orange, NJ, June 15, 24; s Bruce Rexford Zeiser & Louise Hunter Z; wid; m 1964 to Judith Wade Howes; c Bambie (Mrs Douglas K Chard), Bruce Rexford, II, Lind Hunter, Walker Russell, Laurie Cameron & Anne Risley. Educ: Harvard Col, AB cum laude, 44, LLB, 48; Speakers Club; Harvard Lampoon; Hasty Pudding Inst 1770. Polit & Govt Pos: Chmn, RI Young Rep, 48-51; asst counsel, Armed Serv Petroleum Purchasing Agency, Washington, DC, 51-52; nat col dir, Youth for Eisenhower, NY, 52; campaign mgr, Bayard Ewing for US Sen, RI, 52; spec attorney, Dept Justice, DC, 54-53; asst to gen counsel, Fed Housing Admin, DC, 54-55; town moderator, Barrington, RI, 56-59; vchmn, Essex Co Rep Comt, NJ, 60-62; chmn, Wellesley Rep Town Comt, Mass, 64-68 & 72-; Mass State Rep, Ninth Dist, 69- Bus & Prof Pos: Attorney, Letts & Quinn, Providence, RI, 49-51; asst secy, Title Guarantee Co RI, 56-59; field rep, Lawyers Title Ins Corp, New York, 59-62; mgr, Lawyers Title Ins Corp, Boston, Mass, 62- Mil Serv: Entered as A/S, Navy, 43, released as Lt(jg), 46, after serv in Combat Commun Unit, 43, Pac, 44-46; Lt(Ret), Naval Res; Navy Unit Commendation Medal. Mem: US Supreme Court; RI, Mass & Am Bar Asns; NEng Land Title Asn (past pres). Relig: Episcopal. Mailing Add: 316R Washington St Wellesley MA 02181

ZEISLER, LAURA ELIZABETH (R)
Asst Chmn, Third Dist Rep Party, Wis
b La Crosse, Wis; d Ray Monroe Keeler & Beth Ross K; m to Erwin Fred Zeisler; c Barbara (Mrs Engebretson), Virginia (Mrs Boisen), Margaret (Mrs Milliren) & Nancy (Mrs Addis). Educ: La Crosse Univ. Polit & Govt Pos: Precinct committeeman, Fifth Ward, La Crosse Co, Wis, 60-62; mem, La Crosse Co Rep Exec Comt, 65-; deleg, Wis State Rep Conv, 65- & Third Dist Rep Caucus, 65-; secy, Third Dist Rep Party, 69-72, asst chmn, 73-; chmn, Campaign Cent, 70 & 72; bd mem, Wis State Fedn Rep Women, 70-; deleg, Rep Nat Conv, 72. Bus & Prof Pos: Jury comnr, La Crosse Co, Wis, 73- Publ: Impression: Republican National Convention 1972, Encounter, 12/72. Mem: Am Red Cross; La Crosse Co Rep Women (campaign chmn, 63-69, pres, 70-); Wis State Genealogical Soc; Am Cancer Soc (city chmn, 72); Rep Women's Milk Fund for Needy Children (chmn, 73-). Honors & Awards: Serv Award, Am Red Cross, 68 & Am Cancer Soc, 67. Relig: Lutheran. Mailing Add: 1243 Jackson St La Crosse WI 54601

ZELASKO, ANTONE RICHARD (TONY) (R)
Chmn, Perry Co Rep Cent Comt, Ill
b Tamaroa, Ill, Mar 1, 23; s Leo Zelasko & Anna Kreft Z; m 1946 to Dorothy Mourek; c Anthony, Jr, Robert & Carolyn. Educ: High Sch. Polit & Govt Pos: Precinct committeeman, Perry Co Rep Party, Ill, 58-; chmn, Perry Co Rep Cent Comt, Ill, 62-66 & currently, secy, formerly. Bus & Prof Pos: Line foreman, Ill State Tel Co, 65-69, outside plant inspector, 69- Mil Serv: Entered as Pvt, Army, 43, released as Cpl T-5, 46, after serv in 371st Engr Bn, Am Theater. Mem: KofC; PTA; IBEW. Relig: Catholic. Legal Res: Rte 1 Box 120 Tamaroa IL 62888 Mailing Add: Ill State Tel Co Hoyleton IL 62803

ZELENAK, EDWARD MICHAEL (D)
b Dearborn, Mich, Aug 28, 53; s Edward Patrick Zelenak & Irene Maruska Z; single. Educ: Wayne State Univ, BA, 75, Law Sch, 75-; Law Student Div, Am Bar Asn. Polit & Govt Pos: Precinct deleg, Lincoln Park, Mich, Ward 17, 72-; alt deleg, Dem Nat Conv, 72; exec bd, 16th Dist, Mich Dem Party. Bus & Prof Pos: Postal asst, US Post Off, Dearborn, Mich, 71-; Detroit musician, Mich, currently. Publ: Slovaks in Detroit, 70 & Perspectives in politics, 73, Slovakia Mag; co-ed, Detroit area ethnic studies newsletter, (monthly), 73- Mem: Slovak League of Am (pres, Br 15, 72-); Slovak Cath Sokol; SEastern Mich Ethnic Studies Ctr (bd dirs, 72-); Detroit Archdiocesan Pastoral Assembly (deleg); Detroit Ethnic Bicentennial Comn. Relig: Roman Catholic. Legal Res: 740 Cloverlawn Lincoln Park MI 48146 Mailing Add: PO Box 73 Wyandotte MI 48192

ZELENKO, HERBERT (D)
b New York, NY, Mar 16, 06; s Barnett Zelenko & Lena Z; m 1929 to Rhoda Goldberg; c Audrey (Mrs Edwin Weiss). Educ: Columbia Col, 26; Columbia Law Sch, 28. Polit & Govt Pos: Asst US Attorney, 33-34; US Rep, NY, 54-62. Legal Res: 200 E 74th St New York NY 10021 Mailing Add: 39 E 68th St New York NY 10021

ZELLER, JOSEPH R (D)
Pa State Rep
Mailing Add: Capitol Bldg Harrisburg PA 17120

ZEMAN, JACK EDWARD (D)
Chmn, Price Co Dem Party, Wis
b Phillips, Wis, Sept 20, 48; s William George Zeman & Myrtle Kolar Z; m 1970 to Kathryn Louise Popple; c Craig William. Educ: Univ Wis-Eau Claire, BA, 70. Polit & Govt Pos: Southern vchmn, Tenth Cong Dist Dem Party, Wis, 69-71, vchmn, 71-72; chmn, Price Co Dem Party, 69-; vchmn, Seventh Cong Dist Dem Party, 72-73. Bus & Prof Pos: Legis aide, State Capitol, Madison, Wis, 71-72; owner, House of Print, Phillips, 73- Mem: Nat Fedn Independent Businessmen. Mailing Add: 854 Pine Crest Ave Phillips WI 54555

ZEMMOL, ALLEN (D)
Chmn, 18th Cong Dist Dem Comt, Mich
b Detroit, Mich, July 30, 30; s Julius Zemmol & Anna Eisenberg Z; m 1955 to Lita Belle Schechter; c Miriam Beth, Deborah Ruth & Jonathan Israel. Educ: Univ Mich, AB, 52, JD, 54; Phi Alpha Delta. Polit & Govt Pos: Precinct deleg, Oak Park Dem Party, Mich, 62-67, mem bd canvassers, 64-68; pres, Oak-Park Dem Club, 65-67; Dem nominee for cong, 18th Cong Dist, 68; deleg, Dem Nat Conv, 68 & 72; precinct deleg, Southfield Twp Dem Party, 68-; chmn, 18th Cong Dist Dem Comt, 69- Bus & Prof Pos: Partner, Dingell, Hylton & Zemmol, Attorneys, 63- Mem: Am Legion; B'nai B'rith; NAACP; Mich Asn Emotionally Disturbed Children. Honors & Awards: Man of the Year, Oak Park Jr CofC, 65. Relig: Jewish. Mailing Add: 21501 W 13 Mile Rd Birmingham MI 48010

ZENI, FERDINAND J, JR (R)
Mem, Ill State Rep Cent Comt
b Du Quoin, Ill, Oct 2, 24; s Ferdinand J Zeni, Sr & Lea E Walzer Z; single. Educ: Northwestern Univ, BS, 47, Law Sch, JD, 50; Delta Sigma Chi; Wranglers; Kappa Alpha; Hardy Scholarship, 47-50. Polit & Govt Pos: Chmn, Cook Co Young Rep Orgn, Chicago, Ill, 54-55; mem exec bd, Young Rep Orgn Ill, 55-59; pres, 43rd Ward Regular Rep Orgn, 59-64 & committeeman, 64-; Ill comnr, Nat Conf Comnr on Uniform State Laws, 69-; mem, Ill State Rep Cent Comt, Ninth Dist, 70-; deleg, Rep Nat Conv, 72. Bus & Prof Pos: Attorney-at-law, Ross & O'Keefe, Chicago, Ill, 50-58; gen attorney, Montgomery Ward & Co, Inc, 58- Publ: Concerted activities under National Labor Relations Act, Ill Law Rev, 48; Wire tapping, J of Criminal Law and Criminology, 50. Mem: Chicago & Am Bar Asns; Lincoln Park Conserv Asn. Relig: Roman Catholic. Mailing Add: 1400 Lake Shore Dr Chicago IL 60610

ZENNER, SHELDON TOBY (D)
b Chicago, Ill, Jan 11, 53; s Max Zenner & Clara Goldner Z; single. Educ: Northwestern Univ, Evanston, grad Phi Beta Kappa & Cum Laude, 74; Community Studies Residential Col. Polit & Govt Pos: Deleg, Dem Nat Conv, 72. Bus & Prof Pos: Res assoc, Chicago Law Enforcement Study Group. Publ: Discretion & Juvenile Justice. Relig: Jewish. Mailing Add: 6627 N Artesian Chicago IL 60645

ZENOVICH, GEORGE N (D)
Calif State Sen
b Fresno, Calif, Apr 29, 22; s Nicholas F Zenovish & Eva Sugich Z; m 1955 to Vera Sarenac; c Ninon & Marina. Educ: Fresno State Col, BA, 48; Southwestern Col Law, Los Angeles, LLB, 52; Blue Key. Polit & Govt Pos: Mem, Fresno Co Dem Cent Comt, 56-62; Calif State Assemblyman, 32nd Dist, 63-70, Majority Floor Leader, Calif State Assembly, 66-68 & Dem Caucus chmn, 69-72; deleg, Dem Nat Conv, 68; Calif State Sen, 16th Dist, 71-, mem, Judiciary, Ins & Financial Insts & Elec & Reapportionment Comts, Calif State Senate, vchmn, Agr Comt, 71-, mem, Rules Comt, 73- Bus & Prof Pos: Attorney-at-law, Fresno, Calif, 53- Mil Serv: Entered as Pvt, 43, released as Cpl, 46, after serv in 13th Air Force, Pac Theater; Pac Theater Ribbon. Mem: Am Bar; life mem Musicians Local 210, Fresno; Int Acad Law, Hague, Holland; NAACP; Fresno State Col Alumni Asn. Honors & Awards: Golden Rule Award for legis expanding ment retardation treatment facil, Calif Coun for Retarded Children. Relig: Serbian Orthodox. Legal Res: 5315 N Sequoia Dr Fresno CA 93705 Mailing Add: 1060 Fulton Mall Fresno CA 93721

ZEPEDA, BARBARA JOYCE (D)
Chmn, 43rd Legis Dist Dem Orgn, Wash
b Spokane, Wash, Mar 21, 35; d Kurt Gaebel & Elsie Katzenberger G; m 1958 to Julian Zepeda; c Lydia Ann. Educ: Univ Wash, 2 years; Cosmos Club; Young Dem. Polit & Govt Pos: Mem, Wash State Dem Platform Comt, 60 & 70; Dem precinct committeewoman, Precinct 43-63, Wash, 60-69; alt deleg, Dem Nat Conv, 68; chmn, 43rd Legis Dist Dem Orgn, Wash, 69- Bus & Prof Pos: Co-owner, Zepeda Instruments, Seattle, currently. Mem: Montlake Community Club; PTA; Am for Dem Action; Wash Dem Coun (chmn, 71-73); Wash State Am Civil Liberties Union (bd, 73). Mailing Add: 1937 25th E Seattle WA 98112

ZETTERBERG, STEPHEN INGERSOLL (D)
Mem, Calif Dem State Cent Comt
b Galesburg, Ill, Aug 2, 16; s Arvid P Zetterberg & Winifred Ingersoll Z; m 1940 to Connie Lyon; c Charles, Alan, Pierre & Del. Educ: Pomona Col, AB, 38; Nat Inst Pub Affairs, DC, 38-39; Yale Law Sch, LLB, 42. Polit & Govt Pos: Legis asst, US Sen Scott Lucas, Ill, 39 & 46; jr mediation officer, Nat War Labor Bd, 42; Dem cand, US House Rep, 48; Dem nominee, US House Rep, 50; mem at various times, Dem State & Co Comts, 48-; mem, Gov Comt on Health Needs of Calif, 59; mem, Gov Comt Health, 59-60; mem, Calif State Bd Health, 60-68; mem, Calif Dem State Cent Comt, 68-; mem, Los Angeles Co Dem Cent Comt, 68- Mil Serv: Entered as A/S, Coast Guard Res, 42, released as Lt, 45, after serv in Section Base, Hawaii, officer, USCG Cutter Tiger, Pac Ocean Area, 43-46. Publ: Articles in newspapers on polit & govt subjects, 63- Mem: Am Bar Asn; Calif, Ind & US Supreme Court Bars; Am Civil Liberties Union. Mailing Add: 350 Radcliffe Dr Claremont CA 91711

ZIAKAS, LOUIS JOHN, SR (D)
NH State Rep
b Manchester, NH, Mar 21, 37; s John George Ziakas & Maria Xyla Z; m 1968 to Barbara Cook; c Louis John, Jr, Deborah & Z Zackary. Educ: North Shore Community Col, AA, 72. Polit & Govt Pos: NH State Rep, 75- Bus & Prof Pos: Ziakas Enterprises Co, 73- Mil Serv: Entered as Pvt, Army, 55, released as Sgt, 57, after serv in 3rd Armored Div, 7th Army Command, Ger; Div Citation, Achievement of Merit Award; Good Conduct Medal. Mem: Greek Am Lodge (vpres, Local 856); Pan-Macedonian Asn, Inc; Retired Firefighters Asn (vpres, 75-). Honors & Awards: Hero Award, Engine Co 11, 71. Relig: Greek Orthodox. Mailing Add: 7 Cross St Manchester NH 03103

ZIEBARTH, WAYNE W (D)
b Wilcox, Nebr, Aug 2, 21; s Herman J Ziebarth & Martha Habben Z; m 1947 to Renee England; c Jennifer, Jane & James. Educ: Midland Col, BS; Columbia Univ, MA; Creighton Law Sch; Delta Theta Phi; Kal Beta. Polit & Govt Pos: Nebr State Sen, Dist 37, 69-74; Nebr comnr, Educ Comn of the States, 69-; Dem cand for US Rep, Nebr, 74. Bus & Prof Pos: Teacher, Minden Pub Schs, Nebr; prin & coach, Wilcox Pub Schs; dir, Farmers & Merchants Bank, Axtell, currently; farmer, currently. Mil Serv: Lt, Marine Corps, World War II, Capt, Korean Conflict; Presidential Citation, Okinawa. Mem: Wilcox Bd Educ (pres); Bd Educ Serv Unit 11 (secy); Nebr Am Revolution Bicentennial Comn (chmn); Lions (pres, Wilcox Club, currently); Midland Col (bd dirs). Honors & Awards: Farm Family of the Month, Hastings CofC, 59. Relig: Lutheran; Sunday sch teacher, Trinity Lutheran Church, Axtell. Mailing Add: PO Box 68 Wilcox NE 68982

ZIEGLER, HAL WALTER (R)
Mich State Rep
b Jackson, Mich, Aug 23, 32; s Harry Garrett Ziegler & Frances West Z; m 1958 to Mary Sue Williams; c Harry Martin, Terence Mace & Hallie Patricia. Educ: Kenyon Col; Jackson Community Col; Hillsdale Col, AB; Wayne State Univ Law Sch, LLB; Alpha Delta Phi. Polit & Govt Pos: Chmn, Rep Co Conv, Mich, 62; mem, President Lincoln Club, 63; deleg, Rep State Conv, 56-66; asst co prosecutor, Jackson Co, Mich, 62-64, circuit court comnr, 65-67; Mich State Rep, 67- Mil Serv: Entered as Pvt, Army, 64, released as Specialist 3/C, 65, after serv in 594th TTRG, Command Z, Paris, France, 64-65; Good Conduct Medal; Overseas

Ribbon; Nat Defense. Mem: Jackson Co Bar Asn; Mich Co Bar Asn; CofC. Relig: Episcopal. Mailing Add: 2011 Cascades Dr Jackson MI 49203

ZIEGLER, ROBERT HOLTON, SR (D)
Alaska State Sen
b Baltimore, Md, Mar 27, 21; s Adolph Holton Ziegler & Lilian Windfohr Z; m to Paula Kathryn Sampson; c Robert Holton, Jr & Ann Holton. Educ: Univ Va, Charlottesville, LLB, 48; Sigma Nu; Delta Theta Phi; Glee Club. Polit & Govt Pos: Alaska State Rep, 57-59, Alaska State Sen, 64- Bus & Prof Pos: Pvt law practice, 48-; mem firm, Ziegler, Ziegler & Cloudy, currently. Mil Serv: Entered as Pvt, Army, 42, released as Lt, 46, after serv in Med Admin Corps. Mem: Alaska Bar Asn; Elks (Past Exalted Ruler); Rotary (past pres); Moose; Am Legion. Relig: Episcopal. Legal Res: 345 Edmond St Ketchikan AK 99901 Mailing Add: PO Box 979 Ketchikan AK 99901

ZIEGLER, RONALD LOUIS (R)
b Covington, Ky, May 12, 39; s Louis Daniel Ziegler & Ruby Parsons Z; m 1960 to Nancy Lee Plessinger; c Cynthia Lee & Laurie Michelle. Educ: Xavier Univ, 57-58; Univ Southern Calif, BS, 61; Sigma Chi. Polit & Govt Pos: Press dir, Rep State Cent Comt of Calif, 61-62; press aide, Richard Nixon Gubernatorial Campaign Staff, 62; press aide, Staff of Richard Nixon, 68-69; press secy to the President, 69-74, asst to the President, 73-74. Bus & Prof Pos: Salesman, Procter & Gamble Distributing Co, 61; acct rep, J Walter Thompson Co, 62-68. Honors & Awards: Ten Outstanding Young Men of Am 1970, US Jaycees. Relig: Presbyterian. Legal Res: CA Mailing Add: 2008 Fort Dr Alexandria VA 22307

ZIELENZIGER, DAVID (D)
Nassau Co Dem Committeeman, NY
b Kew Gardens, NY, June 10, 52; s Eric W Zielenziger & Ruth Herrmann Z; single. Educ: Princeton Univ, currently. Polit & Govt Pos: Nassau Co Dem Committeeman, NY, 71-; deleg, Dem Nat Conv, 72. Bus & Prof Pos: Writer & ed, The Daily Princetonian, 70-, chmn, 73- Mem: Nat Comt for Sane Nuclear Policy; New Dem Coalition; Stevenson Hall. Mailing Add: 302 Smith St Freeport NY 11520

ZIEMBA, EDWARD JOHN (R)
Mayor, Chicopee, Mass
b Chicopee, Mass, Nov 24, 10; s John W Ziemba & Mary Krzyminski Z; m 1944 to Emily K Pasternak; c David E. Educ: NY Univ, BA, 33; Harvard Law Sch, LLB, 36. Polit & Govt Pos: City treas, Chicopee, Mass, 50-69, mayor, 70- Mil Serv: Entered as Pvt, Army, 42, released as Capt. Mem: Mass Bar Asn; Elks; Moose; Kiwanis. Relig: Roman Catholic. Mailing Add: 73 Monroe St Chicopee MA 01020

ZIEN, BURT (D)
b Milwaukee, Wis, Nov 2, 12; s Herman Zien & Florence Holperin Z; m 1946 to Betty Segal; c Jimmy. Educ: Univ Wis, Madison, BS in Mech Engr, 35, Alpha Tau Sigma. Polit & Govt Pos: Clerk, Tenn Valley Authority Knoxville, Tenn, 35-37; investr, Dept of Labor, Tenn, 38-40; field dir, Wage & Hour Div, US Dept Labor, 40-42 & 46-47; field dir, Nat Labor Rels Bd, 47-50; alt deleg, Dem Nat Conv, 68, deleg & mem platform comt, 72; mem, Gov Task Force on Commerce & Indust & Subcomt on Minority Enterprise, 71; mem, State Bd Voc, Tech & Adult Educ, 71-; mem, Nat Finance Comt for George McGovern, 72; chmn, Wis State Finance Comt for George McGovern, 72; mem campaign comts of Sen William Proxmire & Gov Patrick Lucey; state chmn of 1974 Nelson for Senate Comt; mem four man panel to study relationships between Univ Wis & Voc Tech Systs; vchmn, State Voc-Tech Bd & State Dept Corrections Inter-Agency Comt to Improve Prison Jobs-Training Progs & Employ Opportunities for Inmates; chmn, State Inter-Agency Compulsory Educ Comt on 16-17 Year Old High Sch Dropouts. Bus & Prof Pos: Gen mgr & chmn of bd, Zien Plumbing & Heating, 50- Mil Serv: Entered as Cadet, Air Force, 42, released as Capt, 46, after serv in 5th & 13th Air Force, Pacific, 42-46; Philippine Liberation Ribbon; Asiatic-Pac Theater Ribbon with Three Bronze Stars. Mem: Mt Sinai Med Ctr (trustee); Milwaukee Vol Equal Employ Opportunity Coun (bd mem); Opportunities Indust Ctr; Milwaukee Urban League. Honors & Awards: Human Right Award, B'nai B'rith, 71; Distinguished Serv Award, Opportunities Industrialization Ctr, Minority Job Training Ctr, 71; Man of the Year, Jewish Nat Fund, 72. Relig: Jewish, trustee, Congregation Emanuel B'n e Jeshurun, 68-72. Mailing Add: 501 E Lake Terr Whitefish Bay WI 53217

ZILLI, SERGIO J (R)
Chmn, San Joaquin Co Rep Cent Comt, Calif
b Modesto, Calif, Mar 8, 36; s Luciano Zilli & Vincenza Orlando Z; single. Educ: Univ Santa Clara, BSCE, 59. Polit & Govt Pos: Mem, San Joaquin Co Rep Cent Comt, Calif, 68-, chmn, 75-; cand, US Cong, 15th Dist, 72; mem, State Bd Registered Const Inspectors, Calif Dept Consumer Affairs, 74-; chmn, Cent Calif Area, Co Chmn Asn, 75- Bus & Prof Pos: Chmn, Am Soc Civil Engrs, Cent Valley Br, Calif, 68-69; dir, Calif Soc Prof Engrs, San Joaquin Chap, 75- Mil Serv: Entered as Pvt, Army, 60, released as SP-5, after serv in US Army Engr R&D Detachment, Camp Century, Greenland, Polar Research Team, 60-62; Good Conduct Medal. Mem: Native Sons of the Golden West; KofC; Am Soc Civil Engrs; Yosemite Club Stockton; Construction Inspectors Asn (hon mem). Relig: Roman Catholic. Mailing Add: 28315 Chrisman Rd Tracy CA 95376

ZIMANSKY, DAVID WILLIAM (D)
b Iowa City, Iowa, Mar 6, 54; s Curt Arno Zimansky & Margaret Lacy Z; single. Educ: Harvard Univ, 73- Polit & Govt Pos: Field organizer, US Rep John C Culver, Iowa, 71; deleg, Johnson Co Dem Conv, 72; deleg, First Dist Dem Conv, 72; deleg, Iowa State Dem Conv, 72; deleg, Dem Nat Conv, 72; field organizer, cong cand Edward Mezvinsky, 72, research asst, US Rep Edward Mezvinsky, Iowa, Washington, DC, 73. Honors & Awards: Nat Coun of Teachers of Eng Achievement Award, 71; mem, Nat Sr High Sch Honor Soc, 72; pres, Univ High Sch Sr Class, Iowa City, Iowa, 72. Mailing Add: 1412 E Court St Iowa City IA 52240

ZIMMER, MELVIN NEIL (D)
NY State Assemblyman
b Syracuse, NY, Oct 4, 38; s Melvin N Zimmer & Coletta Filsinger Z; m 1961 to Christine Miles; c Debbie, Leslie, Leigh, Neil, Kristen & Alanna. Educ: Univ Syracuse, BA, 61, Grad Sch, 72; Delta Kappa Epsilon. Polit & Govt Pos: Legislator, Onondaga Co, NY, 70-71; dir emergency employ prog, Syracuse, 71-74; NY State Assemblyman, 120th Dist, 75- Bus & Prof Pos: Independent news dealer, Syracuse Herald-J, NY, 61-69; unemploy ins claims examr, NY State Div Employ, 62-64; owner, Zimmer Ins Agency, 65- Mil Serv: Entered as Pfc, Marine Corps, 56, released as Cpl, 58. Mem: Syracuse Jr CofC; Delta Kappa Epsilon Alumni Asn (pres); McChesney Park Asn (pres); Northside Church Coun Serv (bd dirs). Mailing Add: 261 Hood Ave Syracuse NY 13206

ZIMMER, RUSSELL W (R)
Wyo State Rep
Mailing Add: 910 E 27th Torrington WY 82240

ZIMMERMAN, DONALD WAYNE (R)
Kans State Sen
b Olathe, Kans, Apr 6, 31; s Roy S Zimmerman & Dorothy Robinson Z; m 1954 to Dorothy L Nevius; c Steven W, Beverly A & Richard A. Educ: Kans State Univ, BS Agr, 53; Am Col Life Underwriters, CLU, 67; Farmhouse Fraternity. Polit & Govt Pos: Precinct committeeman, Rep Party, Kans, 63; Kans State Rep, 14th Dist, 65-66 & 16th Dist, 67-68; Kans State Sen, Dist 10, 73- Bus & Prof Pos: Flight test asst, Flight Test Sect, Aviation Gas Turbine Div, Westinghouse Elec Co, 56-57; owner, Zimmerman Ins, 57-71; asst vpres, Patrons State Bank & Trust Co, 71- Mil Serv: Entered as 2nd Lt, Air Force, 53, released as 1st Lt, 56, after serv as a jet fighter pilot & aircraft controller with 738th Radar Squadron Air Defense Command; Capt, Air Force Res, 56-59. Mem: CofC; Optimist Club. Relig: Methodist. Legal Res: 1015 Cedar Hills Dr Olathe KS 66061 Mailing Add: One Patrons Plaza Olathe KS 66061

ZIMMERMAN, FAYE LAVERNE (D)
b Strawn, Tex, July 8, 17; d Capt Walter Foreman & Ruby Knight F; m 1946 to John Barron Zimmerman, Jr; c Roger Brian. Educ: Tex State Col Women, 39. Polit & Govt Pos: Deleg, Dem State Conv, 65-73; vpres, Dem Women's Club, Ector Co, Tex, 67-68, pres, 68-69; Ector Co chmn, Humphrey for President, 68; alt deleg, Dem Nat Conv, 72; coordr, Ben Barnes for Gov Tex, 72. Bus & Prof Pos: Secy, Zimco Elec Supply Co, 55- Mem: Am Red Cross; Tuberc Asn; Federated Club; Mem Develop Comn, Univ Tex; Presidential Mus (bd, 72-73). Relig: Christian. Mailing Add: 3703 Monclair Odessa TX 79762

ZIMMERMAN, HAROLD SAMUEL (R)
Wash State Rep
b Valley City, NDak, Jun 1, 23; s Dr S A Zimmerman & Lulu Wylie Z; m 1946 to Julianne Williams Z; c Karen Marie, Steven Walter & Judi Jean. Educ: NDak State Teachers' Col; Tex A&M Univ; Univ Wash, BA, 47; Sigma Chi; Sigma Delta Chi. Polit & Govt Pos: Chmn, Cowlitz Co Rep Party, Wash, formerly; Wash State Rep, currently. Bus & Prof Pos: Circulation agency mgr, Minn Star-Journal-Tribune Valley City, 40-41; US Forest Serv, Bear Head Mountain, 42; reporter, NSeattle News, 46-47; news ed, Courier Times, Sedro-Woolley, Wash, 47-50; ed-publ, Cowlitz Co Advocate, Castle Rock, Wash, 50-57; ed-publ, Post-Record, Camas, Wash, 57- Mil Serv: Air Force, 42-46. Mem: CofC (past pres, Castle Rock & Camas); AAUN (bd mem, Wash Chap); Young Life Coun Columbia River Dist; Youth Outreach (bd dirs); Southwest Wash Alcoholism Recovery Found (bd dirs). Relig: Methodist; Lay Del. Mailing Add: 1432 NE Sixth Ave Camas WA 98607

ZIMMERMAN, HARRY WALTER, JR (R)
b Richmond, Va, May 7, 51; s Harry W Zimmerman & Mary C Seymore Z; single. Educ: Univ Va, BA, 72. Polit & Govt Pos: Publicity dir, Va Young Am for Freedom, 69-70; alt deleg, Rep Nat Conv, 72. Mem: Farm Bur; Am Cancer Soc. Relig: Baptist. Mailing Add: Lakeside Farm Columbia VA 23038

ZIMMERMAN, JACOB W (D)
Del State Sen
Educ: Villanova Univ. Polit & Govt Pos: Chmn, Del Agr Stabilization & Conserv State Comt, 61-64; Del State Rep, 65-69, minority leader, Del State House Rep, 67-69; Del State Sen, 75- Bus & Prof Pos: Farmer; dir, Del Produce Growers, Inc; dir, Nat Potato Coun; dir, Geriatric Serv of Del, Inc; trustee, Del Arts Soc. Mem: Toastmasters. Mailing Add: S Little Creek Rd Dover DE 19901

ZIMMERMAN, ROBERT C (R)
b Lake, Wis, Jan 5, 10. Educ: High Sch, grad. Polit & Govt Pos: Asst Secy of State, Wis, 39-56, Secy of State, formerly; Comnr Pub Lands, formerly; mem, State Bd Canvassers, formerly. Mil Serv: Army, World War II. Mem: Madison Press Club; Nat Asn Secy of State. Mailing Add: State Capitol Madison WI 53702

ZIMMERMAN, ROBERT PETER (D)
b Brooklyn, NY, Sept 7, 54; s Mortimer Fred Zimmerman & Annette Furman Z; single. Educ: Brandeis Univ, BA, 76; Hillel. Polit & Govt Pos: Mem youth comn, North Hempstead, Nassau Co, NY, 70-71; voter registration coordr, Sixth Cong Dist & staff mem, Cong Lester Wolff, 72; staff mem to Cong Lester Wolff, Washington, DC, summer 73; coordr, Nassau Co Dem Comt Voter Registration Dr, 74; deleg, Dem Nat Mid-Term Conf, 74. Honors & Awards: Student Rep to PTA Exec Bd, 71; Citation by Asn for Help of Retarded Children, Nassau Co Chap, 71 & 72; 91st & 92nd Cong Cert of Appreciation; Dean's List, Brandeis Univ, 74. Mailing Add: 5 Vista Dr Great Neck NY 11021

ZIMMERMAN, SUSAN JANE (D)
b Columbus, Ohio, July 28, 48; d Elmer LeRoy Zimmerman & Winifred Moore Z; single. Educ: Mills Col, BA, 70; Northwestern Univ, Evanston, PhD cand, 74-, MA, 75; Phi Beta Kappa; Pi Mu Epsilon. Polit & Govt Pos: Staff, McCarthy for President, Woodland Hills, Calif, 68; alt deleg, Dem Nat Conv, 72. Bus & Prof Pos: Research asst econ, Northwestern Univ, 70-71, teaching asst, fall 71; L'Arche community asst, 75- Mem: Common Cause; Am Econ Asn. Honors & Awards: Univ Fel, Northwestern Univ, 71; Nat Sci Found traineeship, 72; Danforth Found Kent fel, 73. Relig: Catholic. Legal Res: 22650 MacFarlane Dr Woodland Hills CA 91364 Mailing Add: c/o L'Etable 2653 Graham St Victoria BC Can

ZIMMERS, NEAL FOSTER, JR (D)
Ohio State Sen
b Apr 15, 42; s Neal F Zimmers, Sr & Annabel Pierce A; single. Educ: Denison Univ, BA; George Washington Univ Law Sch, LLB; Sigma Chi; Phi Delta Phi. Polit & Govt Pos: Co judge, Second Dist Court, Dayton, Ohio, 68-74; Ohio State Sen, 75-; mem, Supvry Coun on Crime & Delinquency, Dayton, currently. Bus & Prof Pos: Vis lectr govt, Denison Univ, currently. Mem: Dayton Kiwanis; Dayton Agonis Club; Dayton, Ohio State & Am Bar Asns. Honors & Awards: Outstanding Young Man of Year in Ohio, Ohio Jaycees, 74 & Distinguished Serv Award, Huber Heights-Wayne Twp, Dayton, 74. Relig: Presbyterian. Mailing Add: 4120-E Camargo Dr Dayton OH 45415

ZINKIL, WILLIAM G, SR (D)
Fla State Sen
Mailing Add: 2814 Madison St Hollywood FL 33020

ZINN, JANE MARSHALL (R)
Nat Committeewoman, Ga Fedn Young Rep
b Washington, DC, Dec 18, 43; d Ralph Theodore Zinn & Virginia Frazier Z; single. Educ: Mary Baldwin Col, 62-63; Univ Miss, 63-67; Sigma Alpha Iota. Polit & Govt Pos: Rep precinct chmn, Montclaire, Ga, 73-; mem, DeKalb Co Rep Exec Comt, 73-; mem, DeKalb Co Young Rep, currently, pres, 74-; nat committeewoman, Ga Fedn Young Rep, 74- Mem: Tocco Hills Rep Women's Fedn; Jr Assocs of Women's Asn of Atlanta Symphony. Relig: Presbyterian. Mailing Add: 2017B Oak Shadow Dr Atlanta GA 30345

ZION, ROGER H (R)
b Escanaba, Mich, Sept 17, 21; s H G Zion (deceased) & Helen Hutchinson Z; m 1945 to Marjorie Knauss; c Gayle, Scott & Randal. Educ: Univ Wis, BA, 43; Harvard Bus Sch, 45; pres, Wis chap, Alpha Delta Phi, 41-43. Polit & Govt Pos: US Rep, Eighth Dist, Ind, 67-74. Bus & Prof Pos: Dir, sales training, Mead Johnson & Co, 54-64, dir, training & prof rels, 64-65; pres, Roger Zion & Assoc, Mkt Personnel Consult, 66; pres, Resources Develop, Inc, Washington, DC, currently. Mil Serv: Entered as Aviation Cadet, Navy, 43, released as Lt (jg), 46, after serv in Asiatic Pac Theater. Publ: Keys to Human Relations in Selling, Prentice-Hall, 63; Influencing human behavior (record), Businessmen's Record Club, Div of Int Commun Inst, 68. Mem: Am Legion; VFW; Rotary; Am Red Cross; Buffalo Trace Coun, Boy Scouts; Wabash Valley Asn. Relig: Congregational. Mailing Add: 834 Plaza Dr Evansville IN 47715

ZIRKELBACH, BARBARA MARILYN FOLEY (D)
Mem, Colo Dem State Cent Comt
b Denver, Colo, Aug 23, 27; d William J Foley & Grace Litmer F (deceased); m 1951 to Harry William Hernon Zirkelbach; c Paul J, Thomas J, David J, Grace M, Josephine, Amy M, Julie M, Albert J & Treesa M. Educ: Colo Univ, 1 year; Denver Univ, 2 years; Univ Fribourg, Switz, summer; Alpha Chi Omega; Forensic; Yearbook. Polit & Govt Pos: Dist capt, Dem Party, Denver Co, Colo, 65-69; mem exec comt, R F Kennedy for President, Denver & Colo, 68; mem, Colo Dem State Cent Comt, 69; campaign mgr, cand Colo House of Rep, 72-; mgr city fund drive Denver Dem Party, 72; exec secy, Keep Colo Beautiful, 74- Mem: ECent Human Rels Coun (chmn); Metro Ctr; Cancer Soc; Muscular Dystrophy; Am Canoe Asn (admin asst, 74-). Relig: Roman Catholic. Mailing Add: 745 Steele Denver CO 80206

ZIRKLE, ALAN LLOYD (D)
Ind State Rep
Mailing Add: 1901 S Goyer Rd Apt 84 Kokomo IN 46901

ZODY, ARTIS ALVIN (D)
Mem, Mont State Dem Party
b Glendive, Mont, July 11, 17; s Cecil H Zody & Ruth Moore Z; m 1937 to Helen Elizabeth Grigsby; c James G, Patricia (Mrs Skillestad), Timothy S & Jon. Educ: Mont State Univ, 1 semester. Polit & Govt Pos: Precinct committeeman, Dawson Co Dem Party, Mont, 67-; mem, Mont State Dem Party, 68-; Mont State Rep, Dawson Co, 71-73; Mont State Sen, 73-74. Bus & Prof Pos: Off mgr, Yellowstone Co Agr Stabilization & Conserv Serv, 37-42; farmer, 42-; fed crop ins adjuster, Dawson Co, 55-58; Agr Stabilization & Conserv Serv committeeman, Dawson Co, 56-57. Mem: Lions; Farmers Union (dir Dawson Co, 67-); Toastmasters Retarded Childrens Asn (past pres); Ment Health Adv Bd, Dawson Co; Mont Develop Disabilities Adv Coun (chmn). Honors & Awards: Jaycees Outstanding Citizen Award, Jaycees. Relig: Baptist. Mailing Add: 503 S Pearson Glendive MT 59330

ZOELLER, SYLVESTER ROBERT (R)
Chmn, Monroe Co Rep Cent Comt, Ill
b Columbia, Ill, Dec 31, 25; s Peter F Zoeller & Helen Friedrich Z; m 1948 to Rita Ann Neff; c Mary Kay, Linda Ann, Robert S & John P. Educ: Cent Cath High, East St Louis, Ill, 44. Polit & Govt Pos: Precinct committeeman, Monroe Co Rep Cent Comt, Ill, 68-, chmn, 74- Bus & Prof Pos: Maintenance foreman, Monsanto Co, Sauget, Ill, 47- Mem: Columbia Sportsman Club; Columbia Moose Lodge 2285; Monroe Co Rep Club; Columbia Gymnastic Asn (pres, 74 & 75). Relig: Catholic. Mailing Add: 224 Goodhaven Dr Columbia IL 62236

ZOLLAR, CHARLES O (R)
Mich State Sen
b Chicago, Ill, Jan 6, 15; married; c Robin & Michelle. Educ: Mich State Univ. Polit & Govt Pos: Mich State Sen, 64-, caucus chmn & chmn appropriations comt, currently; pres, Pearl Sch Bd. Bus & Prof Pos: Owner, Zollar Farms (fruit growers); pres, Aircraft Components, Inc (aircraft parts); Riverside Enterprises, Inc (real estate); Zollar Nurseries, Inc (fruit trees & plant propagation). Mil Serv: Aviation Inst, World War II. Mem: Elks; Rotary; Am Legion; Moose; Fraternal Order of Police; Aircraft Owners & Pilots Asn. Relig: Lutheran. Mailing Add: Box 1188 Napier Rd Benton Harbor MI 49022

ZORD, JOSEPH V, JR (R)
Pa State Rep
b Baldwin Twp, Pa, May 2, 10; s Joseph V Zord & Bertha L Sexauer Z; m to Lois Lyden; c two. Educ: Curry Bus Col. Polit & Govt Pos: Founder, Whitehall Borough, Pa, councilman, 48-52; Rep chmn, regist chmn & committeeman, Allegheny Co; justice of peace, 52-60; Pa State Rep, 64-, chmn, Law & Justice Comt, currently. Bus & Prof Pos: Realtor. Mem: Int Traders Club; Whitehall Fire Co (founder); Ins Comn of Borough of Whitehall; charter mem Whitehall Lions Club; South Hills YMCA. Honors & Awards: Award of Merit, Allegheny Co Rep Comt, 64; Hon Comn Ky Col. Legal Res: 611 Glowood Dr Pittsburgh PA 15227 Mailing Add: Capitol Bldg Harrisburg PA 17120

ZUBAY, KEN (R)
Minn State Rep
Mailing Add: 1326 Second St NW Rochester MN 55901

ZUCKERT, EUGENE M (D)
b New York, NY, Nov 9, 11; s Harry M Zuckert & Eugenie Adrienne Pincoffs Z; m 1938 to Kathleen Barnes (deceased); m 1945 to Barbara E Jackman; c Adrienne (Mrs Chandler R Cowles), Robert Barnes & Gene (Mrs Edward F Downs, Jr). Educ: Yale Univ, BA, 33, LLB, 37; Harvard Bus Sch; Beta Theta Pi. Hon Degrees: George Washington Univ, 62 & Clarkson Col, 64. Polit & Govt Pos: Attorney, US Securities & Exchange Comn, Washington, DC, & New York, 37-40; spec consult to Cmndg Gen, Army Air Force in Develop Statist Control, 43-44; exec asst to adminr, Surplus Property Admin, Washington, DC, 45-46; spec asst to Asst Secy of War for Air, 46-47; Asst Secy of Air Force, 47-52; mem, Atomic Energy Comn, 52-54; Secy of Air Force, 61-65. Bus & Prof Pos: From instr to asst prof & asst dean, Harvard Grad Sch of Bus Admin, 40-44; attorney-at-law, Washington, DC, 54-61; counsel, Lear, Scoutt & Rasenberger, 65-68; partner, Zuckert, Scoutt & Rasenberger, 68-; partner, Cambridge Research Inst. Mil Serv: Lt(jg), Naval Res, Off of Chief of Naval Opers, Washington, DC. Publ: Atomic Energy for Your Business, 56; The service secretary: Has he a useful role? Foreign Affairs, 4/66. Mem: Proj HOPE (chmn of bd). Relig: Episcopal. Legal Res: 141 Hesketh St Chevy Chase MD 20015 Mailing Add: 888 17th St NW Suite 600 Washington DC 20006

ZULLO, FRANK NICHOLAS (D)
b Norwalk, Conn, June 3, 32; s Frank Zullo & Regina Francucci Z; m 1958 to Berenice M Fischler; c Lesley Anne. Educ: Fordham Col, BS, 54, Law Sch, LLD, 57. Polit & Govt Pos: Prosecutor, Norwalk City Court, Conn, 59-60; mem, Conn Dem State Cent Comt, formerly; minority leader, Norwalk Common Coun, 63-65; mayor, Norwalk, 65-74, secy, Conn Conf of Mayors, 66-68, pres, 68-69; mem bd of trustees, 69-; deleg, Dem Nat Conv, 68; mem adv bd, US Conv of Mayors, 68-, mem bd of trustees, 69; mem adv bd, Dept of Community Affairs, State of Conn, 68-; mem, Tri-State Transportation Comn, 70- Bus & Prof Pos: Attorney, Santaniello & Culhane, 57-59; partner, Tierney, Zullo, Flaherty & Cioffi, 59- Mil Serv: Entered as Pvt, Army, 57, released as 1st Lt, Army Res, 64. Mem: Conn, Am & Norwalk-Wilton Bar Asns; Am Trial Lawyers Asn; YMCA (trustee, 67-). Honors & Awards: Selected Young Man of the Year, Jr CofC, Norwalk, 58 & 63. Relig: Roman Catholic. Legal Res: 24 Sawmill Rd Norwalk CT 06850 Mailing Add: City Hall South Norwalk CT 06856

ZUMBRUNNEN, LESLIE LEE (R)
Wyo State Rep
b Kirtley, Wyo, Apr 22, 08; s Roy L ZumBrunnen & Bama Teakel Z; m 1938 to Olive A Hanson; c Katherine C (Mrs Larry E McDaniel) & Melvin L. Educ: Kearney State Teachers Col, Nebr, BS Educ, 31; Univ Wyo, grad work. Polit & Govt Pos: Wyo State Rep, 67-, mem, Ways & Means Comt, currently. Bus & Prof Pos: Teacher, 33-37; rancher, 37- Mem: Farm Bur; Wyo State 4-H (coun leader); Local 4-H Leader. Relig: Methodist. Mailing Add: Lusk WY 82225

ZUMSTEG, KATHRYN ANNE (D)
Committeewoman, Morgan Co Dem Party, Mo
b Syracuse, Mo, Apr 17, 34; d Monroe L Neale & Zeda Anne Decker N; m 1955 to Donald G Zumsteg; c Shelly Anne & Jeffrey Neale. Educ: Cent Mo State Col, BMusic Educ, 57; Kappa Phi Sigma; Crescendo Club; Independent Student Orgn. Polit & Govt Pos: Committeewoman, Morgan Co Dem Comt, Mo, 61-, secy, 67-; secy of Morganettes, Morgan Co Women's Dem Club, 67-68. Bus & Prof Pos: Music instr, La Monte Pub Schs, 54-57; Otterville Pub Schs, 58-61 & 68-69; vocal music instr, Smithton R VI Schs, 69- Mem: Mo State Teachers Asn; Nat Educ Asn; Mo Music Educators Asn; Music Educators Nat Conf; Eastern Star. Relig: Baptist. Mailing Add: Syracuse MO 65354

ZURER, SELMAJEAN (D)
Committeeman, Nassau Co Dem Party, NY
b New York, NY, Apr 26, 18; d Harry Pearson Wallace & Rhea Charlotte Israel W; m 1940 to Raymond Robert Zurer, wid; c James Victor, Barbara Lee (Mrs Wilbur Pearson), Burt Michael, Carol Rhea & Holly Ann. Educ: NY Univ Sch of Com, grad, 39; New Paltz State Teachers Col, 52-54; Sigma Eta Phi; Zeta Phi. Polit & Govt Pos: Committeeman, Nassau Co Dem Party, NY, 70-; deleg, Dem Nat Conv, 72. Bus & Prof Pos: Jr acct, LI Paint & Chem, Glen Gove, NY, 45-, corp secy, 70-; teacher, North Shore Schs, 55-58. Relig: Jewish. Mailing Add: 19 Locust Pl Sea Cliff NY 11579

ZURICK, WILLIAM PHILIP (D)
b Shamokin, Pa, Apr 28, 25; s Joseph E Zurick & Gertrude Meyer Z; m 1946 to Anne Teresa Lascoskie; c Cecilia, William, Jr, Lorraine Joseph, Mary Carol & James. Polit & Govt Pos: Pres, Selinsgrove State Sch Bd, Pa, 54-62; chmn, Northumberland Co Dem Finance Comt, 57-; deleg, Dem Nat Conv, 60, 68 & 72, alt deleg, 64; dir, State Ment Health Asn, 60-61; chmn, Northumberland Co Redevelop Authority, 71-; deleg, Dem Nat Mid-Term Conf, 74. Bus & Prof Pos: Owner, Zurick & Zurick Lumber Co, 19 years; dir, West Ward S & L Asn, 57-66; dir, Security of Am Life Ins Co, 63-66. Mem: Bloomsburg State Col (chmn bd trustees, 72-); Moose; Elks; Eagles; KofC. Relig: Catholic. Mailing Add: RD 1 Shamokin PA 17872

ZUTAVERN, CONRAD MORGAN (D)
Chmn, Blaine Co Dem Cent Comt, Nebr
b Anselmo, Nebr, Jan 31, 53; s Richard Conrad Zutavern & Marceina Mathews Z; single. Educ: Univ Nebr, BA, 75; Phi Eta Sigma; Pi Sigma Alpha; Innocent's Soc. Polit & Govt Pos: Chmn, Blaine Co Dem Cent Comt, Nebr, 72- Mailing Add: Box 115 Dunning NE 68833

ZWACH, JOHN M (R)
b Gales Twp, Redwood Co, Minn, Feb 8, 07; s Joseph Zwach & Barbara Hammerschmidt Z; m 1940 to Agnes Schueller; c Barbara (Mrs Robert Sykora), Marie (Mrs Ken Iverson), John, Jr, Dennis & Anne (Mrs Glen Soupir). Educ: Mankato State Col, teaching cert, 28; Univ Minn, BS with distinction, 33. Polit & Govt Pos: Minn State Rep, 34-46; Minn State Sen, 46-66, chmn, Rules & Educ Comts & Interim Agr Comt, Minn State Senate, 55-57, majority leader, 59-66; US Rep, Minn, 67-74; deleg, Rep Nat Conv, 68. Bus & Prof Pos: Teacher, prin, supt, 14 years; farmer. Mem: Farm Bur; Nat Farmers Orgn; Farmers Union; Grange; KofC. Relig: Roman Catholic. Mailing Add: Lucan MN 56255

ZWIKL, KURT D (D)
Pa State Rep
Mailing Add: Capitol Bldg Harrisburg PA 17120

ZYCH, THOMAS E (D)
Mo State Rep
Mailing Add: 4338 Virginia St Louis MO 63111

Geographic Index

ALABAMA

Adams, Samuel Lamar (D)
Albright, Boyce S (R)
Albright, Robert E (D)
Albritton, William Harold, III (R)
Alexander, Dan C, Jr (D)
Allen, James Browning (D)
Allen, Melba Till (D)
Almon, Reneau Pearson (D)
Ames, Bobbie Hackney (R)
Amos, Mabel S (D)
Andrews, Richard R (D)
Armstrong, Ralph (Buddy) (D)
Baggett, Agnes Beahn (D)
Baker, James A (D)
Baker, John Martin (D)
Bank, Bert (D)
Barron, Bishop N (D)
Baxley, William Joseph (D)
Beasley, Jere Locke (D)
Bedsole, Ann Smith (R)
Bell, Robert Donald (D)
Bennett, J Richard, Jr (R)
Bevill, Tom (D)
Biddle, Jack, III (D)
Bloodworth, James Nelson (D)
Blount, Winton M (R)
Boyd, Eloise Agusta Metzger (R)
Branyon, Edgar Watterson (D)
Brewer, Albert Preston (D)
Brindley, Joseph Durwood (D)
Buchanan, John Hall, Jr (R)
Burgess, Gerald Ray (D)
Caldwell, John Jay, Jr (R)
Callahan, H L (Sonny) (D)
Calvert, Lawrence Conrad (R)
Campbell, Frank (D)
Capps, R Walter (D)
Carmichael, Richard Donald (R)
Carnes, David Bernard (D)
Carothers, Josiah S Robins, Jr (D)
Carter, Tommy (D)
Cates, Eric O, Jr (D)
Chapman, Charles Hickerson, Jr (R)
Cherry, Annie Lee (D)
Childers, Erasmus Roy (R)
Christian, John Mandeville (D)
Clark, George N (D)
Clemon, U W (D)
Coburn, Tom C (D)
Coleman, James Samuel, Jr
Compton, Richard Wesley (R)
Cooper, J Danny (R)
Cooper, Jerome Gary (D)
Cooper, Roland (D)
Crawford, Alex (R)
Crawford, James Francis, Sr (D)
Cross, Wayland (D)
Crowe, Robert T (Bobby Tom) (D)
Dial, Gerald O (D)
Dickinson, William Louis (R)
Doss, Chriss Herschel (D)
Dowling, Young Daniel (R)
Drake, Tom (D)
Edington, Patricia Gentry (D)
Edwards, Bingham David (D)
Edwards, William Deara (D)
Elliott, Carl (D)
Ellis, John Hagood (R)
Ellis, Robert Lawson, Jr (D)
Falkenburg, Francis (D)
Fine, Joseph Loyd (D)
Finley, Byron Bruce (D)
Flippo, Ronnie G (D)
Flowers, Walter Winkler, Jr (D)
Folmar, Joel Michael (D)
Ford, Joe M (D)
Foshee, E C (D)
Franks, Vaudry Lee (D)
Frederick, Beebe Ray, Jr (R)
French, Robert Bryant, Jr (R)
Fuller, Charles Eugene, Jr (D)
Funderburk, Kenneth LeRoy (R)
Gafford, Robert C (Bob) (D)
Gay, James Hoyt (R)
Getchell, Earle Duncan (R)
Gilbert, Thomas Martin (D)
Gilmore, Eddie Hubert (D)
Givhan, Walter Coats (D)
Glass, Bob (D)
Glisson, Romaine Lillian (R)
Goodwin, Joe William (D)
Graham, Anna M (R)
Greenough, Gary Arnold
Greer, Bayless Lynn (D)
Gregg, Richard (D)
Grenier, John Edward (R)
Griffin, Michael Gary (D)
Grouby, Edward Arthur, Sr (D)
Hale, Douglas Van (R)
Hall, David McGiffert (R)
Hall, Earl Wells (R)
Hall, Lilbourne Preston (R)
Hall, Robert B (D)
Haltom, Elbert Bertram, Jr (D)
Hancock, Oscar Walker (D)
Harris, James D, Jr (D)
Harrison, A L (Tony) (D)
Hartwell, Ray Vinton, Jr (D)
Hawkins, Donna Black (D)
Heflin, Howell Thomas (D)
Higginbotham, G J (Dutch) (D)
Hill, Lister (D)
Hill, Robert McClellan, Jr (D)
Hilliard, Earl Frederick (D)
Hines, Leon Brooks (D)
Holladay, Hugh Edwin (D)
Holley, Jimmy W (D)
Holmes, Alvin A (D)
Hooper, Perry O (R)
Hopping, Jack Sr (D)
Howard, Asbury (D)
Howell, Warren Lomax (Independent)
Jackson, Ronald Edward (D)
Jackson, Walter Frank (D)
Johnson, Roy W, Jr (D)
Johnstone, Douglas Inge (D)
Jolly, Carl (D)
Jones, Fred Reese (D)
Jones, Robert Emmett, II (D)
Kaminsky, Harry R (D)
Kelley, Phillip Barry (D)
Kennedy, Cain James (D)
Killian, Roger (D)
King, Bill Gene (D)
King, Tom Cobb, Jr (R)
Kinsey, Daniel L (D)
Lawless, Kirby Gordon, Jr (R)
Lawson, Thomas Seay (D)
Lee, James G (D)
LeFlore, John Luzine (D)
Leonard, Tom (D)
Lewis, Rufus A (D)
Little, Dorothy Lynn (Dot) (D)
Little, T D (Ted) (D)
Littleton, Obie J (D)
Locke, Judson Cleveland Sr (D)
Lockett, John A, Jr (D)
Locklin, Robert Rives (D)
Lovvorn, W A (D)
Lutz, Hartwell Borden (D)
Maddox, Alva Hugh (D)
Malone, Robert (Ken) (D)
Manley, Richard Shannon (D)
Mann, Janean Lee (R)
Marrs, Theodore (R)
Martin, Charles Bee (D)
Martin, James Douglas (R)
Martin, William Roy (D)
Massey, James Clements (D)
Mathews, Forrest David (D)
McAlister, Thomas Buell (R)
McCall, Daniel Thompson, Jr (D)
McCluskey, Murray P (D)
McConaughy, Walter Patrick
McCorquodale, Joseph Charles, Jr (D)
McCulley, J Henry (D)
McCurley, Robert Lee, Jr (D)
McDonald, Albert (D)
McDonald, Sid L (D)
McLemore, Carl Ray (R)
McMillan, George (D)
McMillan, John Murphy, Jr (D)
McNees, Allen (D)
Means, Stephen Arden (D)
Medders, Marion Wardner (R)
Medders, Vernon Sherwood (D)
Merrill, Hugh Davis (D)
Merrill, Pelham Jones (D)
Mims, Lambert Carter
Mims, Maston (D)
Mitchell, Wendell Wilkie (D)
Mitchem, Hinton (D)
Moatts, Morris (R)
Montgomery, John Allen (D)
Moore, Helen Hunter (D)
Moore, Otis H, Jr (D)
Moore, Warren C (D)
Mordecai, Frank Selmer (R)
Morgan, Claude Rutledge (D)
Morris, Larry Wade (D)
Naramore, Alvis (D)
Nettles, Bert (R)
Nichols, William Flynt (D)
Noonan, L W (D)
Norris, Palmer Whitten (Pete) (R)
O'Neal, Dudley Lee, Jr (D)
Owen, L Dick, Jr (D)
Owens, James Bentley, Jr (R)
Owens, Ruth Johnson (D)
Owens, Walter (D)
Parker, Donald Conant (R)
Patrick, David Scarborough
Patterson, John Malcolm (D)
Pearson, J Richmond (D)
Pegues, R Leigh (D)
Pennington, Harry Lucas (D)
Perloff, Mike (R)
Perry, T Dudley (D)
Peters, J Elbert (R)
Peters, Maxwell (R)
Petrey, Joe Bradley (D)
Pippin, Earl Clayton (D)
Plaster, James J (D)
Porter, John T (D)
Powell, Jerry (D)
Pruitt, David Carl, III (R)
Pruitt, Ira Drayton, Jr (D)
Putman, Kathleen Harvey (R)
Quarles, Marilyn (D)
Radney, Tom (D)
Rains, Albert M (D)
Rains, Hobdy G (D)
Reed, Thomas (D)
Reynolds, Edward Harris (D)
Rich, Kerry (D)
Riddick, Frank H (D)
Roberts, Bill (D)
Roberts, Kenneth Allison (D)
Roberts, Tommy Ed (D)
Robertson, Edward D (D)
Robertson, John Anderson (R)
Robinson, Charles Edwards (D)
Robinson, John Alexander, III (D)
Rodgers, Louise V (D)
St John, Finis (D)
Saliba, Alfred J (R)
Sandusky, John Thomas, Jr (D)
Sasser, James G (D)

1029

ALABAMA (cont)

Schuler, John Hamilton (R)
Selden, Armistead I, Jr (D)
Shackleford, Robert Mitchell, Jr (R)
Shelby, Richard Craig (D)
Shelton, Thomas R (Tom) (D)
Sherrer, Betty R (R)
Shores, Arthur Davis (D)
Sizemore, James Middleton, Jr (R)
Smith, Alvin C (D)
Smith, Bill Gordon (D)
Smith, Curtis (D)
Smith, Harold Monroe (D)
Smith, Jack Willmar (D)
Smith, Philip Hardy (D)
Smith, Wilburn (R)
Sonnier, Nat (D)
Spann, Ann Olive (Am Party)
Sparkman, John J (D)
Sparks, John R (D)
Spencer, Edward L, Jr (R)
Stacey, Frank Arthur (D)
Starkey, Bethel D (D)
Steen, J C (R)
Stewart, Donald W (D)
Stewart, Ellis Cameron (D)
Sullivan, Jean (R)
Taylor, Hubert Lee (D)
Teague, John A (D)
Torbert, C C (D)
Trammell, Hoyt W (D)
Traylor, Lee Clyde (R)
Tucker, Jerome (D)
Turnham, Pete Benton (D)
Vacca, Paschal Patrick (D)
Van Antwerp, James Callanan, Jr (Am Party)
Vance, Robert Smith (D)
Vann, David J (D)
Venable, Jack Benton (D)
Waggoner, James Thomas, Jr (D)
Waldrop, Gerald Wayne (D)
Wallace, George Corley (D)
Warren, James Edmond (D)
Weaver, Robert (D)
Weeks, Paul J (D)
Welden, William Edgar (R)
Whatley, Charles W (D)
White, Dewey Anderson, Jr (D)
Wilkinson, Robert Dawson, Jr (R)
Williams, Roy Nolan, Jr (D)
Williams, William Van (R)
Wilson, Robert Terry (D)
Woodard, Carl Jubal (R)
Wyatt, Cecil L (D)

ALASKA

Anderson, Nels A (D)
Beirne, Helen Dittman (R)
Blahuta, Renee Maria (R)
Boucher, Henry A (Red) (D)
Bowman, Willard L (D)
Bradley, Janet Mary (D)
Bradley, Robert Earl (Bob) (D)
Bradley, W E (Brad) (D)
Bradner, Michael Drake (D)
Bramstedt, Alvin Oscar (R)
Butrovich, John (R)
Chance, Genie (D)
Christiansen, Raymond C (D)
Coghill, John Bruce (R)
Colletta, Mike (R)
Conwell, Evelyn Lona (R)
Cotten, Samuel R (D)
Cowper, Steve (D)
Croft, Leland Chancy (D)
Davenny, Robert Alton (R)
Davis, Lawrence T (Larry) (R)
Duncan, James Wendell (D)
Durant, Phil Samuel (R)
Egan, William Allen (D)
Eliason, Richard J (Dick) (R)
Fahrenkamp, Bettye (D)
Ferguson, Frank (D)
Ferguson, John Duncan (Independent)
Fink, Tom (R)
Fischer, Helen Marie (D)
Freeman, Oral E (D)
Gardiner, Terry (D)
Goldberg, Robert Michael (D)
Gravel, Mike (D)
Gruening, Clark (D)
Guy, Phil (D)
Hackney, Glenn (R)
Hammond, Jay Sterner (R)
Harden, Bruce Donald Richard (R)
Harrigan, Alice Anna (D)
Harris, Frank W (R)
Haugen, Ernie (R)
Hemenway, Robert Bruce (R)
Hensley, William L Igagruk (D)
Hershberger, H M (Mike) (R)
Hickel, Walter Joseph (R)
Hohman, George H, Jr (D)
Holm, Edith Muriel (R)
Huber, John (D)
Huntington, Jimmy (R)
Itta, Brenda T (D)
Jackson, Barry Wendell (D)
Josephson, Joseph Paul (D)
Kelley, Ramona M (D)
Kennedy, Gene Allen (D)
Lomen, Mary Elizabeth (R)
Lundgren, James (R)
Lupro, Charles (D)
Malone, Hugh (D)
Mayer, Henry Melvin (D)
Mcanerney, Lee (R)
McKinley, Ira Blakely (R)
Meland, Pete H (D)
Miller, Alex (D)
Miller, Keith Harvey (R)
Miller, Mortimer Michael (Mike) (D)
Miller, Terry (R)
Montoya, Herbert Patricio (D)
Mullen, Mary Patricia (D)
Naughton, Edward Franklin (D)
Nethercutt, George R, Jr (R)
Notti, Emil (D)
Orbeck, Edmund N (D)
Orsini, Joseph Lionel (R)
Ose, Al (D)
Osterback, Alvin (D)
Osterback, Marie Erna (D)
Ostrosky, Kathryn (D)
Parker, William K (D)
Parr, Charles H (Charlie) (D)
Poland, Kathryn Eleanor (Kay) (D)
Rabinowitz, Jay Andrew (D)
Rader, John L (D)
Ray, Bill (D)
Reid, Martha Louise (R)
Rhode, Leo (R)
Rodey, Patrick Michael (D)
Sackett, John C (R)
Schultheis, Bruce E (R)
Smith, Theodore George (D)
Speckling, Keith (R)
Stepovich, Michael A (R)
Stevens, Theodore Fulton (Ted) (R)
Sullivan, Susan Meekins (D)
Sundborg, George (D)
Swanson, Leslie Eugene (D)
Terwilliger, Mellie E (D)
Thomas, Lowell, Jr (R)
Tillion, Clem Vincent (R)
Toner, Felix J (D)
Ulmer, Eldon Robert (R)
Urion, Rick (R)
Waldrop, Isaac Merit, Jr (D)
Wallis, Tim (D)
Walton, George D (R)
Warren, Clifford Ernest (D)
Weir, Julian Paul (R)
Whittaker, Richard (D)
Willis, Ed (D)
Young, Donald E (R)
Ziegler, Robert Holton, Sr (D)

ARIZONA

Aarons, Barry Michael (R)
Abate, Joseph Francis (R)
Abril, Tony Rodriguez (D)
Akers, Stanley William (R)
Alkire, Alma Asenath (R)
Allen, Jesse Willard (R)
Alley, G T (Tom) (D)
Asta, Ron (D)
Bahill, S Larry (D)
Baker, William D (R)
Beaty, Orren, Jr (D)
Begam, Robert G (D)
Bolin, Wesley H (D)
Braden, Margaret Mize (R)
Bradford, Elwood Walter (R)
Breyfogle, John William, Jr (R)
Brown, Keith Spalding (R)
Buehl, William Anthony (Tony) (R)
Burgess, Isabel Andrews (R)
Cajero, Carmen (D)
Cameron, James Duke (R)
Campbell, Leonard Wayne (D)
Capalby, Joseph Richard, Sr (D)
Carlson, Donna Jean (R)
Carrillo, Emilio (D)
Carroll, Grace (D)
Carvalho, Americo (Mac) (R)
Castillo, Joseph A (D)
Castro, Raul Hector (D)
Cauthorn, Josephine F (D)
Cohen, Marvin S (D)
Cole, Tom C (D)
Conlan, John B, Jr (R)
Cooper, James LeRoy (R)
Corbet, Leo Frank, Jr (R)
Corpstein, Pete (R)
Craig, Harry E (R)
Crisp, Mary D (R)
Cullinan, Anna J (D)
Davids, Craig E (D)
Davidson, Lucy (D)
Davis, Stephen Alan (R)
DeConcini, Dennis (D)
DeConcini, Ora (D)
DeSchalit, Ronald Lee (D)
Dewberry, J H (Jim) (D)
Disbrow, Joan Foster (D)
Doyle, Daniel G (D)
Drees, Jane W (R)
Driggs, John Douglas (R)
Duffield, John Richard (R)
Dunn, Clare (D)
Dunton, Franklin Roy (R)
DuVal, Merlin K (Independent)
Dye, Marilyn Sue (D)
Elliott, James Alton (D)
Ely, Herbert Leonard (D)
Esquer, Cecilia D (D)
Everett, Jesse Herbert (R)
Face, Albert Ray (R)
Fannin, Paul Jones (R)
Farmer, Merle Louise (D)
Farr, William Morris (R)
Felix, Francisco Javier (Frank) (D)
Ferdon, Julie (D)
Flynn, Dick (R)
Foss, Joseph Jacob (R)
Foudy, Michael L (D)
Foyle, Dolores Hartley (R)
Fricks, Robert Price (D)
Fuchs, Joseph Herman (D)
Gabaldon, Tony (D)
Garfield, Ernest (R)
Getzwiller, Polly (D)
Gignac, Judith Ann (R)
Goddard, Samuel Pearson, Jr (D)
Goldwater, Barry Morris (R)
Goodwin, Thomas N (Tom) (R)
Graham, Milton Henry (R)
Guerrero, Edward Garcia (D)
Gunter, Carolyn Mae (R)
Gutierrez, Alfredo (D)
Gutierrez, Rosendo (D)
Hall, Donald Roots (R)
Hamilton, Art (D)
Hamilton, Mary Ellen (R)
Hammond, Nellie Handcock (D)
Hanley, Benjamin (D)
Hardt, A V (Bill) (R)
Harelson, Juanita (R)
Harrison, Mark I (D)
Hartdegen, James Alan (R)
Hathaway, Robert Richard (D)
Haugh, John H (R)
Hays, Jack D H (R)
Hays, John (R)
Hesser, Woodrow Cleveland (D)
Holman, Calvin Morns (R)
Hubbard, Arthur J, Sr (D)
Hubbard, Keith W (R)
Huncock, D Howitt (Independent)
Hungerford, Robert Leon, Jr (Bob) (R)
Jacquin, William C (R)
James, Susan Louise (D)
Jarvis, Barbara (D)
Jenckes, Joseph Sherburne, V (R)
Jenkins, William Calvin (D)
Jennings, Renz Dixon (D)
Johnson, Raleigh West (R)
Jones, D Lee (R)
Joyner, Conrad Francis (R)
Karp, Gene (R)
Karp, Naomi Katherine (D)
Kay, Peter (R)
Kelley, Frank (R)
Kincaid, H Thomas (Tam) (R)
Kleindienst, Richard Gordon (R)
Koory, Edward Fredrick, Jr (R)
Kraft, Myrtle Moyer Westbrook
Kruglick, Burton S (R)
Kunasek, Carl J (R)
Kyl, Jon Llewellyn (R)
Larson, Mildred (D)
Lemon, Charles Myron (R)
Lena, Sam (D)
Lewis, Charles William (Bill) (R)
Lindeman, Anne (R)
Lockwood, Lorna E (D)
Lopez, Betty Davila (D)
LoPiano, William J (R)
Lundy, James Harwood Jr (R)
Mack, James A (R)

Maish, Frank Anthony (D)
Markham, Jonne Pearson (R)
Marks, Stanley J (D)
Mason, Bruce Bonner (D)
McCarthy, Diane B (R)
McConnell, Sam A, Jr (R)
McCormick, James Carlos (D)
McCune, William (R)
McElhaney, Frank (D)
McFarland, Ernest William (D)
Moore, Gerald F (D)
Moore, Tom (D)
Morrison, Betty (D)
Mulcahy, Edward William
Murphy, John Francis (R)
Murphy, Lewis Curtis (R)
Murray, Michael Webster (D)
Nelson, Gary Kent (R)
Noble, Ida (D)
O'Connor, Sandra Day (R)
Osborn, Jones (D)
Pacheco, Richard (Dick) (D)
Pastor, Edward Lopez (D)
Peaches, Daniel (R)
Peck, Barbara May (R)
Peck, Ruth (D)
Pena, Manuel, Jr (D)
Pena, R G (Danny) (D)
Phillips, Claire Adams (R)
Phillips, D J (Jim) (D)
Phillips, Jim (D)
Pine, Charles Warren (D)
Pope, JoAnn (D)
Pritzlaff, John Charles, Jr (R)
Ratliff, James B (R)
Reveles, Robert Apodaca (D)
Rhodes, John J (R)
Richey, Thomas Bruce (R)
Rigel, William Edward (R)
Rockwell, Elizabeth Adams (R)
Roeder, John (R)
Rosenbaum, Polly (D)
Rosenzweig, Harry (R)
Ross, Edna Genevieve (R)
Runyan, S H (Hal) (R)
Sawyer, Ed (D)
Scanlan, Robert Joseph (R)
Secord, Maria Rachel (D)
Simkin, William E (D)
Simonson, Mary Ellen (D)
Skelly, Jim (R)
Smith, Alberta Marie (D)
Sossaman, James J (R)
Sparling, Laurens Kasey (D)
Starrett, Mildred Jeanine (D)
Steiger, Sam (R)
Stewart, Donovan (R)
Stillman, Guy (Independent)
Strong, Robert Campbell (Independent)
Struckmeyer, Fred C, Jr (D)
Stump, Bob (D)
Swink, William L (D)
Taylor, Jack J (R)
Tenney, Boyd (R)
Thomas, James (D)
Thompson, Leon (D)
Troster, Virginia Alling (R)
Truman, William St Clair (D)
Turley, Stanley F (R)
Turner, D Kelly (D)
Turner, William Cochrane (R)
Udall, Morris King (D)
Van Arsdell, Madelene (D)
Verkamp, John G (R)
Vukcevich, Steve (D)
Walsh, James P (D)
Weeks, Marcia Gail (D)
West, W A, Jr (Tony) (R)
Wettaw, John (R)
Wheeler, Bruce (D)
Wheeler, Mathew Hubert (D)
Williams, John Richard (Jack) (R)
Wood, Hubert Franklin (R)
Wymore, James Francis (R)

ARKANSAS

Adams, Doug (D)
Adams, Leroy Thomas (D)
Alexander, Cecil L (D)
Alexander, William V, Jr (Bill) (D)
Alford, Boyce (D)
Allen, Ben (D)
Allison, Manuel (Bunk) (D)
Alstadt, William Robert (D)
Arnold, Martin Blair (D)
Arrington, Grady P (D)
Atkinson, Madelyn Rucks (D)
Baker, Charles Wayne (D)
Baker, Nancy (D)
Balton, Nancy (D)
Banks, Charles Alfred (D)
Barrier, William Christopher (Chris) (D)
Bearden, John, Jr (D)
Beaumont, William Eustace, Jr (D)
Bell, Clarence E (D)
Benafield, James Weldon (Buddy) (D)
Benham, Paul Burrus, Jr (D)
Bernard, Betty Hill (R)
Bernard, Charles Taylor (R)
Bissett, Delia Belle (D)
Blair, James B (D)
Blakely, Ronny D (R)
Blaylock, Len Everette (R)
Bookout, Jerry (D)
Brandon, James William (D)
Brandon, Phyllis Dillaha (D)
Branton, Raymond (D)
Brewer, James H (D)
Britt, Henry Middleton (R)
Brown, Gregory Brugh (D)
Brown, Rolland D (R)
Bryan, L L (Doc) (D)
Bryant, Clovis (D)
Bryant, Kelly (D)
Bryant, Winston (D)
Bumpers, Dale L (D)
Bunker, Betty Barger (D)
Burleson, David J (D)
Burleson, William Brice (D)
Burrow, Charles C, III (D)
Burton, Marion B (R)
Bush, Baker Hoskins (D)
Butler, Richard C, Jr (R)
Bynum, Preston C (R)
Caldwell, Jim (R)
Camp, Kenneth Ray (D)
Campbell, Kermit Leon (R)
Canada, Bud (D)
Capps, John Paul (D)
Carlisle, Lilburn Wayne (D)
Carlisle, Raoul (D)
Carlton, C C (D)
Carnes, Mrs Jack (D)
Carter, Harry W (D)
Cate, Rex (D)
Catlett, Leon Bidez (D)
Cheatham, John Bryan (D)
Clark, Dempsey C (R)
Clark, Hubert Woody (D)
Clements, Ruth Welch (D)
Collier, Albert (Tom) (D)
Corbin, Donald Louis (D)
Crum, Roger Clark (R)
Crumpler, Gus H (D)
Cunningham, Ernest (D)
Curtis, Floyd Earl (R)
Cypert, James Dean (D)
Dalton, Herman Udell (R)
Day, Walter (D)
DeRoeck, Walter A (D)
Dolan, Joseph M (D)
Douglas, Bob W (D)
Douglas, Larry Duane (D)
Earnhart, Milt (D)
Easom, Jerry Don (D)
Elmore, Mary Louise (D)
Faison, Lee Vell (D)
Falls, C Frank (D)
Faubus, Orval Eugene (D)
Faulkner, Ralph Edward (D)
Feild, Kay Carol (R)
Felton, Daniel Henry, Jr (D)
Fendler, Oscar (D)
Flemister, Elizabeth Smartt (D)
Fletcher, Virgil T (D)
Fogleman, John Albert (D)
Ford, Clarence Verge, Jr (D)
Ford, Joe T (D)
Foster, W F (Bill) (D)
Francis, Thomas Edward (R)
Frierson, Charles Davis, III (D)
Fulbright, James William (D)
Gardner, Jack Crandall (D)
Garrison, Mary Jane (D)
Gathings, Ezekiel Candler (D)
Gathright, Morrell (D)
George, Claud Reid (D)
George, Lloyd R (D)
Gibson, John F (Mutt) (D)
Givens, Arthur A, Jr (D)
Glass, Penny Lane (D)
Glover, Bobby L (D)
Gooch, James Thomas (D)
Goodner, Orval Kern (D)
Grace, Harrison Dearing (D)
Grubbs, Lawton Edison (D)
Guerin, David Lloyd, Sr (R)
Hale, James Cecil (D)
Hall, Nancy Johnson (D)
Ham, Everett Adams, Jr (R)
Hammerschmidt, John Paul (R)
Hampton, Wayne (D)
Hargrove, William Nicholas (D)
Harper, Thomas (D)
Harrell, James H (D)
Harris, Frank Carleton (D)
Harris, Jim (D)
Hartrick, Gordon Dean (R)
Harvey, Robert (D)
Hasley, Darrell (Sam) (D)
Hayes, Jesse C (D)
Hendricks, Malvin Leon, Sr (R)
Hendrix, B G (D)
Hendrix, Olen (D)
Henley, Leland (R)
Henry, John Riley (D)
Henry, Morriss M (D)
Henslee, Frank Brooks (D)
Hinchey, Judy Elena (R)
Hoffman, John (D)
Holt, Joseph Frank (D)
Hoofman, Cliff (D)
Hopkins, Glen Eugene, Jr (D)
Hopper, Larry Thomas (D)
House, Mary Corbin (D)
Howell, Max (D)
Huckaba, Frank J (D)
Huntley, Margaret Elizabeth (R)
Hurley, Sterlin (D)
Ingram, W K (Bill) (D)
Irwin, Joel (D)
Jackson, Cleo B (D)
Jackson, Jerry Donald (D)
Jeffords, Clifford Harold (D)
Jesson, Brad (D)
Jewell, Jerry D (D)
Johnson, Jewelle Richardson (D)
Johnson, Neal Sox (R)
Johnson, Vannette William (D)
Johnston, Robert Edward (D)
Jones, Earl (D)
Jones, James Fred (D)
Jones, James Samuel (D)
Jones, Jimmie (Red) (D)
Jones, Mark Perrin, III (D)
Kane, David Ronald (D)
Keel, John Peyton (D)
Kelly, William Thomas (R)
Kenkel, Gerhard H (R)
Kennan, Thomas Clyde (D)
Kilgore, James Veazey (D)
Kincaid, Diane Divers (D)
Kincannon, Phyllis Anne (R)
King, Harold Lloyd (D)
Kinney, Clarke (D)
Lady, Frank (D)
LaMonica, James Anthony (D)
Landers, H Lacy (D)
Langley, Stanley R (D)
Lassiter, James Hugh (D)
Ledbetter, Calvin Reville, Jr (D)
Ledbetter, Joel Yowell (D)
Leonard, Joe Eldon (R)
Lewis, Mary Davis Woodward (D)
Libhart, Bonnie L (R)
Linder, Jim (D)
Lipton, John M (D)
Little, Clayton N (D)
Livingston, Barbara Allen (R)
Locke, George (Butch) (D)
Logan, Roger V, Jr (D)
Longbotham, Ralph Maynard (R)
Lowe, A Lynn (R)
Lowe, Jere B (R)
Maddox, Ode (D)
Mahoney, William Patrick Jr (D)
Mahony, Joseph Kirby, II (D)
Malin, Marjorie Claire (D)
Matthews, Charles Dawson (D)
Mays, Richard L (D)
Mazander, Charles A, Jr (R)
Mazzanti, Geno M, Jr (D)
McClellan, John L (D)
McClerkin, Hayes Candor (D)
McClure, Gary Lee (R)
McCraw, Dan (D)
McCray, Jonathan Franklin (R)
McCuiston, Lloyd Carlisle, Jr (D)
McGillicuddy, Lillian Grace (R)
McGuire, Don Loye (D)
McKissack, Jimmie Don (D)
McLarty, Mack (D)
McMath, Sidney S (D)
McWhorter, Clayton Ward (Jim) (D)
Meacham, Shirley (D)
Mears, Roger Clifton, Jr (D)
Miller, John E (D)
Miller, Sturgis (D)
Mills, Wilbur D (D)
Mitchum, Tommy E (D)
Moore, Charles Randolph (D)
Moore, J Lex (D)
Moore, W D (Bill) Jr (D)
Moore, William Rudy, Jr (D)
Murphy, Napoleon Bonapart (D)
Nelson, Knox (D)
Newman, Bobby Gene (D)
Newton, Willma Humphreys (R)
Nicholson, W R (Bill) (D)
Nowotny, George Edward, Jr (R)
Osterloh, Henry Joe (D)

ARKANSAS (cont)

Owen, David (R)
Parker, Donal Irwin (D)
Patterson, Larry Samuel (D)
Patterson, Ralph (D)
Peacock, Joe N (D)
Pendergrass, Paula Armbruster (D)
Penix, Bill (D)
Peterson, Jacque P (D)
Peterson, Merle Francis (D)
Petty, Judy Chaney (R)
Phillips, Jack W (D)
Pinson, Jerry D (D)
Pollan, Carolyn Joan (R)
Pollard, Odell (R)
Poole, Bain (D)
Powell, Mozelle Juanita (D)
Power, Mary Susan (R)
Poynter, Bill Charles (R)
Prewitt, Taylor Archie (D)
Proctor, Richard Lee (D)
Pryor, David Hampton (D)
Purcell, Joe (D)
Purtle, John Ingram (D)
Ragge, Everett Kenneth (D)
Ragsdale, Albert George (D)
Rainwater, Wallace Eugene (Gene) (D)
Ramsey, J W (Bill) (D)
Randall, Bill (D)
Ray, Joe F (D)
Reed, Ancil Mason (R)
Reed, Maxine Gresham (R)
Reeves, Helen Grayson (R)
Riley, Bob Cowley (D)
Ritter, Mabel Louise (R)
Roberts, David Earl (D)
Rogers, Russell (D)
Rose, Ivan W (D)
Routon, Bonnie Anthony (R)
Rowe, Auby, Jr (D)
Rubens, Kent (D)
Rush, Carolyn Sue (R)
Russell, David Owen (R)
Rutledge, David Keith (R)
Ryburn, Bennie, Jr (D)
Schaffer, Archibald Richard, III (D)
Scott, Bobby Kenneth (R)
Scribner, Calvin Theodis (D)
Shaver, James L, Jr (D)
Sheid, Vada W (D)
Sherman, William Farrar (D)
Sims, William Arlon (Jake) (D)
Sisk, Arthur C, Sr (R)
Smith, Bernard Chester (R)
Smith, Donald Houston (D)
Smith, George Rose (D)
Smith, J B (D)
Smith, J Boyd (R)
Smith, Kirby, III (R)
Smith, Ray S, Jr (R)
Smith, Steve Austin (D)
Smith, Thomas Benton (D)
Smith, Thomas Tedford (R)
Smithson, Jim (R)
Sparks, Thomas Everett (D)
Spencer, George Lloyd (D)
Stancil, Bill (D)
Steel, George Edwin, Jr (R)
Stephens, Bill (D)
Stewart, Brice Horace (R)
Stewart, Charles Wesley, Jr (D)
Stewart, David A (D)
Stewart, Della D (R)
Stockley, Jim (D)
Streett, Julian Duval (D)
Taylor, Felix Donell (D)
Temple, Renna Mary (R)
Thicksten, Edward F (D)
Thomas, Evelyn M (R)
Thompson, Mack A (D)

Thompson, W H (Bill) (D)
Thornton, R H, Jr (Ray) (D)
Torrence, Linda Faye (D)
Townsend, William H (D)
Troxell, Leona Mae (R)
Tucker, James Guy (D)
Turner, G W (Buddy) (D)
Vance, Howard Grant (R)
Van Dalsem, Paul (D)
Wade, Charles (Bubba) (D)
Walmsley, Bill H (D)
Ward, Charles (D)
Waters, Bankston (R)
Waters, Marjorie June (R)
Watson, Tom (D)
Webb, Dorothy Ann (R)
Webb, Rita Lafaye (R)
White, Mary Clyta (D)
Whiteaker, Pearl Wallace (D)
Wiley, Junior Lee (R)
Wilkins, Henry, III (D)
Willems, Frank J (D)
Williams, Paul L (D)
Williamson, Walter Edward (D)
Wilson, Mike (D)
Wilson, Nick (D)
Windsor, Julius Gayle, Jr (D)
Winningham, Lonnie L (D)
Womack, J A (Dooley) (D)
Workman, Wylie Wayne (D)
Wright, William Marshall
Yancey, Truman E (R)

CALIFORNIA

Abbott, Alfreda Helen (D)
Adair, Sidney Arthur (R)
Adams, Bernard Charles (R)
Adams, Frank Pollard (R)
Adkisson, John David (D)
Agostini, Wanda E (R)
Alarcon, Angelita (D)
Alatorre, Richard (D)
Albertson, Wallace Thomson (D)
Alex, John Maynard (R)
Alioto, Joseph Lawrence (D)
Allen, Peter John (D)
Alquist, Alfred E (D)
Amley, Loretta Abel (D)
Anderson, Clifford R, Jr (R)
Anderson, Glenn M (D)
Anderson, Jack Z (R)
Anderson, John Milton (D)
Anderson, Peter David (D)
Androus, Melvin D (D)
Anthony, Philip LaVern (D)
Antonovich, Michael Dennis (R)
Arklin, Henry (Hank) (R)
Arnett, Dixon (R)
Arnold, Alva Lee (R)
Arvizu, Arthur A (D)
Ash, Roy L (R)
Ashcraft, Nita Wentner (R)
Ashen, Pete (R)
Ashton, Alice Elinor (D)
Austin, Lloyd James, Jr (D)
Ayala, Ruben S (D)
Badham, Robert Edward (R)
Bagley, William Thompson (R)
Baird, Jeff Scott (D)
Bakaly, Charles G, Jr (R)
Ballreich, Steve Lynn (R)
Bane, Tom (D)
Bannai, Paul T (R)
Banowsky, William S (R)
Barnard, Aurora Caro (D)
Barnard, Keith W (R)
Barnes, Dwight H (D)
Barnum, C Robert (R)

Barnyak, Mary A (R)
Barrios, Helen (D)
Barry, Robert R (R)
Barton, Terry Allen (R)
Bathe, John Raymond (R)
Baum, Sherry Liss (R)
Baxter, Philip Norman, Jr (R)
Bayona, Hugo H (D)
Beahrs, John Victor (R)
Beaver, Robert F (R)
Behr, Peter H (R)
Beilenson, Anthony C (D)
Bell, Alphonzo (R)
Bell, Elvin Charles (D)
Bell, James Dunbar (D)
Bennett, William Morgan (D)
Benz, William Robert (R)
Berman, Howard L (D)
Berry, LeRoy (D)
Berryhill, Clare L (R)
Beverly, Robert Graham (R)
Bibb, Chris Ellen (R)
Bispo, Naomi Marie (R)
Bispo, William Lawrence (R)
Black, John Woodland (D)
Black, Shirley Temple (R)
Blackman, Rick Robert (R)
Blatchford, Joseph H (R)
Boas, Roger (D)
Boatwright, Daniel E (D)
Boggs, Judith Roslyn (D)
Bondshu, Robert Eugene (R)
Borelli, Frank Peter, Jr (R)
Bort, Joseph Parker (R)
Boston, Eugene Alfred (R)
Bowe, John Edward (Ed) (R)
Bowler, Ann (R)
Boyce, Merle Hunter (R)
Boynton, Marjorie Chase (R)
Bradley, Thomas (D)
Brady, Rodney Howard (R)
Bramson, George (D)
Branson, Ivan Thorpe (R)
Braun, Virginia Mary (R)
Brekke, Lola M (R)
Brian, Earl Winfrey (R)
Briggs, John Vern (R)
Brinegar, Claude S (R)
Broad, Eli (D)
Brock, Margaret Martin (R)
Bromfield, Betsy Byron (R)
Brown, Edmund Gerald (D)
Brown, Edmund Gerald, Jr (D)
Brown, George Edward, Jr (D)
Brown, Gibbs W (D)
Brown, Josephine M (R)
Brown, Lillian Cunningham (D)
Brown, Richard Ross (R)
Brown, Willie L, Jr (D)
Browning, James Arthur, Jr (R)
Bugatto, B John (R)
Buisson, Cydney Ann (R)
Bunyan, S Wyanne (D)
Burgener, Clair W (R)
Burgess, Barbara Ann (R)
Burke, Robert H (R)
Burke, Yvonne Brathwaite (D)
Burton, John Lowell (D)
Burton, Phillip (D)
Busterud, John A (R)
Byers, William H (R)
Calden, Gertrude Beckwith (R)
Calhoun, John A (D)
Calvo, Victor (D)
Cameron, Ronald Brooks (D)
Cameron, Ward Francis (D)
Camp, Dana Martha (D)
Campbell, Anona Jeanne (R)
Campbell, Truman F (R)
Campbell, William (R)
Capen, Richard Goodwin, Jr (R)
Carbone, Eugene R (D)

Carmiggelt, Coen Jan Willem (R)
Carmona, Ralph Chris (D)
Carpenter, Dennis E (R)
Carpenter, Paul B (D)
Carr, Gladys B (R)
Carr, James K (D)
Carsten, Arlene Desmet (D)
Carter, Paul Thomas (R)
Castle, Robert Marvin (D)
Castro, Ramon (R)
Castro, Thomas Henry (D)
Caudillo, Sonia Ramirez (D)
Cenotto, Lawrence Arthur, IV (Larry) (R)
Cervantes, Alfred F (D)
Chacon, Peter Robert (D)
Chan, Agnes Isabel (R)
Chaney, Mary C (R)
Chapman, Alice Hackett (R)
Chappie, Eugene A (R)
Chavez, Richard (D)
Chel, Fred W (R)
Childs, James Henry (R)
Chimbole, Larry (D)
Cho, Maria Chungsook (R)
Clark, Richard Owen (D)
Clarke, Russell Leland (R)
Clausen, Don H (R)
Clawson, Delwin Morgan (Del) (R)
Cline, Robert Corde (R)
Cobb, Michael William (R)
Coe, Robert H, Jr (D)
Coelho, Anthony L (D)
Coen, Alvin M (D)
Cohee, Darwin Dick (R)
Cohelan, Jeffery (D)
Coil, Henry Wilson, Jr (R)
Cole, Louis V (Louie) (R)
Collier, Charles Russell (R)
Collier, John L E (R)
Collier, Randolph (D)
Commons, Dorman Leland (D)
Comstock, Kirke White (D)
Condon, John F (R)
Conelly, Carl Robert (R)
Cook, Franklin Charles (R)
Coombs, William Elmer (R)
Cooper, Fred Ferris (R)
Cooper, Gloria Claire (D)
Corbin, Leland Wayne (R)
Corman, James C (D)
Cory, James Kenneth (D)
Costantini, Edmond (D)
Cottrell, Joan Sweetland (R)
Cousins, James Harold (D)
Crandall, Earle P (R)
Cranston, Alan MacGregor (D)
Craven, William A (R)
Crawford, Carol Forsyth (R)
Crawford, Charles S (Chuck), III (D)
Crosby, Jane A (R)
Crosby, Joseph Marshall (R)
Cualco, Eugene T (D)
Cullen, Mike (D)
Curran, Frank E (D)
Currie, Malcolm R
Curtis, Sam Victor, Jr (D)
Cusanovich, Lou (R)
Cutler, Goldie (D)
Cutting, Wendell Riley (R)
D'Agostino, Carl Joseph, Jr (D)
Daley, Anne Belisle (D)
Daley, Katherine Fay (R)
Daly, Josephine Francis (Jo) (D)
Dana, Deane, Jr (R)
Dance, James Harold, Jr (R)
Danielson, George Elmore (D)
David, Norma (D)
Davis, Doris Ann (D)

CALIFORNIA / 1033

Davis, Nada (R)
Davis, Pauline L (D)
Davis, Wallace Robert (D)
Dawkins, Maurice Anderson (R)
Day, Joan Thomson (R)
Deddeh, Wadie Peter (D)
Degnan, June Oppen (D)
Delahanty, George Emmett (R)
Dellums, Ronald V (D)
DeLyre, Elva W (R)
Dermody, John Daniel (D)
Dermody, Mary Louise (D)
Despol, John Anton (R)
Deukmejian, George (R)
Dewees, Elaine MacDonald (R)
Dills, Ralph C (D)
Dixon, Julian C (D)
Donaldson, Michael Cleaves (R)
Double, Barbara Turner (D)
Doyle, John Augustine (D)
Drane, Davis Clark (R)
Draper, William Henry, III (R)
Driver, Robert Farr (D)
Duffy, Gordon W (R)
Duguid, Robert Lee (R)
Dunlap, Carter Wesley (Pat) (R)
Dunlap, John Foster (D)
Duran, June Clark (R)
Dyal, Ken W (D)
Dymally, Mervyn M (D)
Edelman, Edmund Douglas (D)
Edwards, Don (D)
Egeberg, Roger O (D)
Egeland, Leona Helene (D)
Eller, Armena Morse (R)
Elms, Christopher William (D)
Emett, Robert Lynn (R)
Erreca, Robert Cronwell (D)
Esparza, Moctesuma Diaz (D)
Essex, Paula Higashi (D)
Eu, March Fong (D)
Evans, Harry Kent (D)
Evans, James Larkin (D)
Fadem, Jerrold Alan (D)
Fadem, Joyce A (D)
Falasco, Eda (D)
Fargher, Lawrence LeRoy (R)
Faries, McIntyre (R)
Fenster, Leo (D)
Fenton, Jack R (D)
Ferraro, Rosemary Florence (R)
Field, Donald William (R)
Finch, Robert Hutchison (R)
Fisher, Audrey Horn (R)
Fisher, Joel Marshall (R)
Fitzpatrick, Rosalyn M (R)
Flagg, Morgan (D)
Fleetwood, Thirvin Dow (D)
Fletcher, Charles Kimball (R)
Flournoy, Houston Irvine (R)
Foley, John Field (R)
Foran, John Francis (D)
Ford, Barbara Louise (R)
Foster, James Milton (D)
Fowle, Eleanor Cranston (D)
Francis, Leslie C (Les) (D)
Francois, Terry Arthur (D)
Friend, Hazel Irene (R)
Fujita, Ben Mamoru (R)
Furth, Frederick Paul (D)
Garamendi, John R (D)
Garcia, Alex P (D)
Garman, Jacquelyn May (R)
Garrigues, George Louis (R)
Garvin, Harold Whitman (R)
Gates, Mark Thomas (R)
Geier, Robert Albert (R)

Gelber, Louise Carp (D)
Geldermann, Harlan Stolp (R)
Germino, Donald Owen (R)
Gibney, Robert Emmet (R)
Gibson, John S (D)
Gilbert, William Lewis (D)
Gips, Walter F, III (Terry) (D)
Gladson, Charles Lee (R)
Goeske, Janet L (R)
Goggin, Terry (D)
Goldberg, Sheila Ann (D)
Goldinger, Shirley (D)
Goldstein, Blanche (D)
Goldwater, Barry, Jr (R)
Gomez, Blanche M (R)
Gomperts, Robert Elliot (D)
Gonzales, Robert Eugene (D)
Goodknight, Dorothy Walker (R)
Gordon, Milton G (R)
Green, Lewis Wesley (D)
Green, Mary Louise Katherine (R)
Green, Maxine Wise (R)
Greenaway, Roy Francis (D)
Greene, Bill (D)
Greene, Leroy F (D)
Gregg, James Erwin (D)
Gregorio, Arlen (D)
Gromala, John Anthony (R)
Groom, James Haynes (R)
Groves, G Mark (R)
Grunsky, Donald Lucius (R)
Gubser, Charles S (R)
Gutman, Theodore E (Ted) (D)
Haerle, Paul Raymond (R)
Halley, James Winston (R)
Hamilton, James F (R)
Hand, Lloyd Nelson (D)
Handy, Wendell Taylor (R)
Hanna, Richard T (D)
Hannaford, Mark Warren (D)
Hannaford, Peter Dor (R)
Hansen, Grant Lewis (R)
Harabedian, Michael Thomas (D)
Hardy, George (D)
Harker, Jacqueline Nugent (R)
Harmer, John L (R)
Harper, Harold Donald (R)
Harper, Ruth Flores (R)
Harper, Virginia Maughan (D)
Harris, Kathie Jean (D)
Hart, Gary K (D)
Hart, Kenneth Lee (D)
Hasenkamp, Bruce Henry (R)
Hawkins, Augustus F (D)
Hayden, H Thomas (Tom) (R)
Hayden, Richard D (R)
Hayes, James A (R)
Hayes, Janet Gray (D)
Hearn, Irene Finnerty (R)
Hecht, W Arthur (R)
Henderson, Mary Warner (R)
Hendricks, John Herbert (D)
Herrema, Lavonne June (R)
Hill, Albert Alan (R)
Hillings, Patrick J (R)
Hills, Carla Anderson (R)
Hitt, Patricia Reilly (R)
Hobdy, Clarence Chester (R)
Hodgson, James Day (R)
Hoeppel, John Henry (D)
Hoffman, Gary Ellsworth (D)
Holcomb, William Robert (R)
Holden, Nate (D)
Holden, Robert Warren (D)
Holdstock, Richard S (D)
Holifield, Chet (D)
Holmdahl, John W (D)
Holmes, David William (R)
Hoopes, David Craig (R)
Hopf, Peter S (D)

Hosmer, Craig (R)
Hospers, John (Libertarian)
House, Vincent F (R)
Howard, W Richard (R)
Howsden, Arley Levern (D)
Huber, Robert Daniel (R)
Hughes, Teresa (D)
Hulett, Stanley William (R)
Hull, Daniel Streeter, III (D)
Hurley, Charles Sullivan (D)
Hyde, Floyd H
Ingalls, Walter Monte (D)
Iversen, Kirk Victor (D)
Jackson, Rosella Mildred (R)
Jeffe, Douglas I (D)
Jeffers, Mary L (D)
Jelonek, Susan Jean (R)
Johnson, Barbara Yanow (D)
Johnson, Cyrus (R)
Johnson, Gardiner (R)
Johnson, Harold T (Bizz) (D)
Johnson, Pompie Louis, Jr (R)
Johnston, Janet J (R)
Johnston, Ronald Vernon (D)
Jolicoeur, Edward Thomas (D)
Jones, Bill (R)
Kapiloff, Lawrence (D)
Karp, Nathan (Socialist Labor Party)
Katz, Alan Stewart (D)
Keatinge, Richard Harte (D)
Keaton, Harry Joseph (R)
Keene, Barry (D)
Keilbar, Mona Mary (R)
Kelley, Ying Lee (D)
Kelly, Peter Dillon, III (D)
Kenchelian, Karney K (R)
Kennedy, Goldie L (D)
Kennick, Joseph M (D)
Kenoyer, Kenneth Dale (D)
Kent, Roger (D)
Kerr, Bailey Furman (R)
Ketchum, William Matthew (R)
Keysor, Jim (D)
Keyston, David Hill (R)
Khosrovi, Carol Mayer (R)
King, William Theodore (R)
Kirby, Peter (R)
Kirkwood, Robert Carter (R)
Knapp, James Ian Keith (R)
Knauft, Milford Roy, Jr (R)
Knight, Evelyn Deloris (D)
Knox, John Theryll (D)
Knuppel, Shirley LaVaune (R)
Kochman, Al (D)
Kohn, Susan Marion (D)
Kowalski, Marge Helene (D)
Koza, Georgia Lynne (R)
Kraemer, James S (R)
Krebs, John Hans (D)
Krueger, Robert William (R)
Kuchel, Thomas H (R)
Kyle, Charles Clayton (Casey) (R)
Labson, Beth Ann (D)
Lagomarsino, Robert John (R)
Lake, James Howard (R)
Lakritz, Simon (D)
Lancaster, Bill (R)
Lanterman, Frank D (R)
Larrabee, Leland Earl, Jr (D)
Lawrence, M Larry (D)
Leal, Harlan Russell (D)
Ledesma, Mary Louise (D)
Lee, H Rex (D)
Leggett, Robert Louis (D)
Leiblum, Mark David (D)
Lenhart, Thomas B (D)
Lewis, Jerry (R)
Lindgren, Donald Arthur (D)
Lindholm, Frances Marion (R)
Livanos, Peter E Jr (R)
Livermore, Putnam (R)

Lloyd, James Fredrick (D)
Lockyer, Bill (D)
Lombardi, Angela Funai (R)
Long, Robert William (R)
Love, Clyde B (D)
Lowance, Franklin E (R)
Lucas, Henry, Jr (R)
Luce, Gordon C (R)
Luftig, Rita Sheila (D)
Lundberg, Lois Ann (R)
Lundy, Rayfield (R)
Lynch, John William (D)
MacDonald, Ken (D)
Macfarland, Celia Coghlan (R)
Mackey, Malcolm H (D)
Maddy, Kenneth Leon (R)
Major, Conley Roy (D)
Malek, Frederic Vincent (R)
Manatt, Charles Taylor (D)
Manibog, G Monty (R)
Manriquez, Carol Huante (D)
Maple, Barbara D (R)
Markel, J Ogden (R)
Marks, Milton (R)
Marler, Fred William, JR (R)
Marootian, Simon (D)
Marriott, Richard Harold (D)
Martin, Clarence Daniel, Jr (D)
Martinez, Charles William (D)
Matthews, Mortimer Joseph (D)
Mattox, Verna D (R)
Mattson, Mary-Alice (R)
Maughmer, Karrol June (R)
McAlister, Alister Davidson (D)
McCarthy, Leo T (D)
McCloskey, Paul Norton, Jr
McColl, John Angus (R)
McComb, Marshall Francis (R)
McElroy, William David (R)
McFall, John J (D)
McFarland, Mary Ann (R)
McGrath, Charles Robert (R)
McHargue, Daniel Stephen, II (R)
McKillen, Jean Barbara (R)
McKinney, Doris May (R)
McKinney, James Grover (R)
McKinnon, Clinton Dotson (D)
McLennan, Robert M (R)
McNeil, Jean McIntyre (R)
McPeek, Billie Faye (D)
McPherson, William Hauhuth (R)
McVittie, William John (D)
Meade, Kenneth Arnold (D)
Mellen, Melba J (R)
Mendelsohn, Robert H (D)
Meyer, Norman J (D)
Meyer, William Benedict (D)
Meyers, Emil, Jr (R)
Michals, Charles (R)
Miles, Thomas James (R)
Miller, George (D)
Miller, George Paul (D)
Miller, John Jose (D)
Miller, Roy D (R)
Mills, Billy Gene (D)
Mills, James R (D)
Mineta, Norman Yoshio (D)
Mitchell, Bruce Tyson (R)
Mitchell, Robert E (R)
Mize, Dwight Workman (D)
Mobley, Ernest Nelson (R)
Monce, Raymond Eugene (R)
Monson, Arch, Jr (R)
Moore, Birdell (D)
Moore, Dudley Shields (R)
Moore, J Max (R)
Moorhead, Carlos J (R)
Mori, S Floyd (D)

CALIFORNIA (cont)

Morris, Brewster Hillard
Morrow, Floyd Lee (D)
Moscone, George R (D)
Moser, Raymond (R)
Moses, William Preston (R)
Mosk, Edna Mitchell (D)
Mosk, Stanley (D)
Mosley, Edward Reynold (R)
Moss, John Emerson (D)
Moulds, Elizabeth Fry (D)
Muller, Ella Elizabeth (R)
Murphy, Frank, Jr (R)
Murphy, George Lloyd (R)
Murray, John Joseph, Jr (R)
Murrell, Cecil Boyd (R)
Muskey, Nicholas Chris (R)
Narvid, Ethel Gallay (D)
Naujock, Evelyn Katsis (R)
Naylor, Robert Wesley (R)
Negri, David (D)
Nejedly, John Albert (R)
Nestande, Bruce (R)
Neuman, Jerold Joe (R)
Neumann, Robert Gerhard (R)
Nevins, Richard (D)
Newsom, David D
Nimmo, Robert P (R)
Ninburg, Daniel Harvey (D)
Nissen, Ralph Albert (R)
Nixon, Richard (R)
Nofziger, Lyn (R)
Nolan, Michael Thomas (D)
Norris, William Albert (D)
Ochoa, John Robert (D)
Offutt, David Allen (R)
Ogle, Alice Nichols (R)
Omohundro, Baxter Harrison (R)
O'Neill, Cathy (D)
Orme, Lila Morton (D)
Orozco, Joseph William (R)
Orrick, William Horsley, Jr (D)
Oswald, Robert Leon (R)
Ottina, John Renaldo (R)
Overhouse, Madge Virginia (D)
Packard, David (R)
Padberg, Eileen E (R)
Pagliaro, Frank Joseph, Jr (R)
Paine, Thomas Otten (D)
Panecaldo, Loreto Antonio, III (R)
Papan, Louis J (D)
Pardue, Erwin (R)
Parker, Richard Bordeaux
Parnell, Dale Paul (Independent)
Patterson, Jerry Mumford (D)
Pauley, Edwin Wendell (D)
Pearson, Enid Irene (R)
Peet, Richard Clayton (R)
Pelosi, Ronald (D)
Perino, Carmen (D)
Peters, Alice Boye (R)
Peterson, Harriett Monroe (R)
Petris, Nicholas C (D)
Pettis, Shirley Neil (R)
Pike, Thomas Potter (R)
Pinson, Harley Frederick (D)
Poche, Marc B (D)
Politzer, S Robert (D)
Pollack, Maurice Irvine (Reece) (R)
Pollock, Robert Michael (R)
Pope, Alexander H (D)
Presley, Robert B (D)
Prestage, Ethel Marian (R)
Prioleau, Diane Thys (R)
Priolo, Paul V (R)
Puffer, Thomas Ray (R)
Quinn, A Thomas (D)
Rader, Bobby Jewett (R)
Rae, Matthew Sanderson, Jr (R)

Rains, Omer L (D)
Ralph, Leon Douglas (D)
Ramirez, E Alice (D)
Raner, Guy Havard, Jr (D)
Reading, John Harden (R)
Reagan, Ronald Wilson (R)
Reardon, Harold E (R)
Reardon, Terrence James (D)
Rees, Thomas M (D)
Reeves, Albert L (R)
Reilly, Jane Bernadette (R)
Reinhardt, Stephen (D)
Rendon, Ralph Albert (R)
Rhodes, Nina (D)
Richards, William Sidney (R)
Richardson, H L (Bill) (R)
Rider, Joseph Alfred (R)
Rifkin, Julie Kaye (R)
Riles, Wilson Camanza (D)
Riley, Timothy Crocker (R)
Ring, Eleanor Reynolds (R)
Roberti, David A (D)
Roberts, Anthony Alongi (R)
Robinson, Richard (D)
Rodda, Albert S (D)
Rodriguez, David (R)
Rogers, Stanley (D)
Rogers, Thomas Charles (R)
Rolapp, R Richards (R)
Rood, Paul William (R)
Rosedale, Ralph Eidon (R)
Rosenthal, Herschel (D)
Rostker, Skipper (D)
Rotelli, Delbert Leroy (R)
Rousselot, John Harbin (R)
Rowen, Elizabeth Gore (R)
Rowland, John Patrick (R)
Roybal, Edward R (D)
Rumford, William Byron, Sr (D)
Russ, Joseph, IV (R)
Russell, Fred J (R)
Russell, Madeleine H (D)
Russell, Newton R (R)
Rutherford, Clara Beryl (R)
Ryan, Leo Joseph (D)
Ryskind, Mary House (R)
Salinger, Pierre Emil George (D)
Sanborn, Blake Paul (R)
Sanchez, Phillip Victor (R)
Sandoval, Alicia Catherine (D)
Sandstrom, Elsa (R)
Sawicki, John Gerald (R)
Schaap, George Aldarus (R)
Schabarum, Peter F (R)
Schachter, Marvin (D)
Schlenker, Gerald (D)
Schma, Donald William (R)
Schmidhauser, John Richard (D)
Schmitz, John G (R)
Schneirsohn, Eric Eli (D)
Schrade, Jack (R)
Schrette, Roland Donald (R)
Schwartz, Robert A D (D)
Scott, Jeremiah Ronald, Jr (R)
Scott, Margaret P (R)
Seaborg, Glenn T (D)
Sebens, Raymond Willard (D)
Segal, Ed (D)
Seidita, Jo (D)
Shapiro, Marvin S (D)
Sharatz, Marguerite Theresa (R)
Shea, John Francis (D)
Sheinbaum, Stanley K (D)
Shillito, Barry James (Independent)
Shirpser, Clara (D)
Siciliano, Rocco C (R)
Siefkin, Randy Richardson (R)
Siegler, Alfred Charles (D)

Sieroty, Alan Gerald (D)
Silberstein, Eric Charles (R)
Silliman, Nevelle I (R)
Silver, Ethel Marie (R)
Singh, Baldev (Bob) (D)
Siple, Randolph Edward (R)
Sisk, B F (Bernie) (D)
Sloan, Sheldon Harold (R)
Smalley, K Maxine (R)
Smith, Gilbert Dayle (D)
Smith, H Allen (R)
Smith, Jerome A (Jerry) (D)
Smith, Siegmund Wilson (R)
Smith, William French (R)
Snapp, James C (R)
Snyder, Arthur Kress (R)
Snyder, Norman Gene (R)
Snyder, William Richard (R)
Soderstrom, Charles Wallace (R)
Sollenberger, Raymond Jan (R)
Song, Alfred H (D)
Speers, Frederic Warden (R)
Sperline, Elnora Elizabeth (R)
Spiegel, Albert A (R)
Sprague, Irvine H (D)
Sprinkel, Warren Reed (R)
Stark, Fortney H (Pete) (D)
Steele, Robert Howe (R)
Stefano, Vincent, Jr (D)
Sterbenk, William D (R)
Stern, Howard Morris (R)
Stevens, Robert S (R)
Stewart, McRobert Lee (R)
Stewart, Robert Eston (R)
Stidger, Ruby Jane (D)
Stiern, Walter W (D)
Stivers, Oliver Charles (R)
Stoessel, Walter John, Jr
Stonum, Elizabeth Ann (R)
Stringer, Clarence Maine (R)
Stull, John O (R)
Sturr, Dorothy Mertz (R)
Sturr, Robert P (R)
Sublett, Norma Raedean (D)
Sufrin, Ronald Kent (D)
Suitt, Tom (D)
Swajian, Catherine Mary (R)
Swanson, Gertrude Gay (R)
Sweetland, Monroe Mark (D)
Talcott, Burt L (R)
Taylor, Virginia Willett (R)
Taylor, Waller, II (R)
Temple, William Harvey Ernest (R)
Thill, Lewis D (R)
Thomas, Theodore Frederick (R)
Thomas, Vincent (D)
Thomas, William M (R)
Thompson, Ada McCall (D)
Thompson, William Charles (R)
Thomson, Leonard S (R)
Thurm, William Henry (D)
Thurman, John Edward (D)
Tobriner, Mathew Oscar (D)
Tolmach, Jane Louise (D)
Torres, Art (D)
Tortarolo, Joann Mary (R)
Triplett, William Karrol (R)
Tripp, Minot Weld, Jr (D)
Trueblood, Aileen Nash (Bobbie) (R)
Tucker, Curtis Raymond (D)
Tunney, John Varick (D)
Tuppan, Glenda Rana (R)
Turner, Wayne Callaway (R)
Turnette, Norman L (R)
Tyrell, Jack Rix (R)
Unger, Alan Franz (D)
Utt, Max Eddy (R)
Valdez, Joyce Ruby (R)
Valencia, Ross Haines (D)

Van Deerlin, Lionel (D)
Van Dyken, Lambertus Peter (Bert) (R)
Vanmeter, Sheila Croft (D)
Vasconcellos, John Bernard (D)
Vashon, Doris Louise (D)
Veale, Roads (R)
Veneman, John G, Jr (R)
Verlot, Frank O (R)
Veysey, Victor Vincent (R)
Vicencia, Frank (D)
Villa, Al (D)
von Christierson, Karl (R)
Voorhis, Horace Jerry (D)
Vreeland, George Washington, Jr (R)
Wade, Edwin Winslow (R)
Wakeham, T David (R)
Waldie, Jerome Russell (D)
Walsh, Jack (R)
Warner, Dorothy Marie (R)
Warren, Charles (D)
Warschaw, Carmen H (D)
Washington, Lena Geneva (R)
Watson, John Garrett (R)
Waxman, Henry Arnold (D)
Way, Howard (R)
Weary, Lawrence Clifton (D)
Webb, Kathleen Cecelia (D)
Wedworth, James Q (D)
Weinberger, Caspar Willard (R)
Weinreb, Ilene Spack (D)
Weisgerber, William Denny (R)
Welch, Rodney Ray (R)
Welden, Jacques Roger (R)
Wenzel, Ferdinand Edward (Ted) (R)
Whaley, Beverly Anne (R)
Wheelock, Robert Webb (R)
Whetmore, James Edward (R)
White, Donald Stanley (D)
White, Jean Christensen (R)
White, Rose Marie (D)
Widener, Mary Lee (D)
Widener, Warren (D)
Wiggins, Charles E (R)
Wilkinson, Robert Melvin (R)
Williams, Diane Dorothy (R)
Wills, Ted C (D)
Wilson, Charles H (D)
Wilson, Pete (R)
Wilson, Robert Carlton (Bob) (R)
Wilson, Robert Jewell (D)
Wing, Ada Schick (R)
Wirt, Laura A (R)
Wolf, Lois Ruth (D)
Wood, Richard Robinson (R)
Woolley, John Robert (Jack) (R)
Wornum, Michael (D)
Wright, Donna Gale (R)
Wyman, Rosalind (D)
Yamamoto, Toshiko Toshi (R)
Yocum, Norma Lenore (R)
Yorty, Sam (R)
Younger, Evelle J (R)
Zanger, Joseph Anthony (R)
Z'Berg, Edwin L (D)
Zenovich, George N (D)
Zetterberg, Stephen Ingersoll (D)
Ziegler, Ronald Louis (R)
Zilli, Sergio J (R)
Zimmerman, Susan Jane (D)

COLORADO

Allison, Betty Virginia (R)
Allison, Walter (R)
Allott, Gordon Llewellyn (R)

Allshouse, J Robert (R)
Alperstein, Arnold (D)
Alperstein, Pearl (D)
Anderson, Byron (R)
Anderson, Fred E (R)
Armstrong, William Lester (R)
Arnold, S G (R)
Aspinall, Owen Stewart (D)
Aspinall, Wayne Norviel (D)
Atchison, Jeannine Cowell (D)
Banks, Doris Nininger (D)
Barragan, Polly Baca (D)
Baxter, J Sterling (R)
Beckstead, Lucy (R)
Bendelow, Edward Mason (D)
Beno, John Richardson (D)
Betz, Fred McLean (D)
Bishop, Tilman (R)
Blake, Joseph Bradley (R)
Bledsoe, Carl Beverly (R)
Boley, George W (D)
Bonicelli, Derito (D)
Booth, Mary Benson (R)
Brannan, Charles F (D)
Briggs, Robert Alvin, Jr (R)
Brinton, Donald Eugene (D)
Brocker, Naida Louise (R)
Brooks, George Henry (D)
Brotzman, Donald G (R)
Brown, G Hank (R)
Brown, George L (D)
Brown, Keith Lapham (R)
Brown, Paul Neil (D)
Buchanan, Mary Estill (R)
Burch, Palmer Lyle (R)
Burford, Robert F (R)
Burnett, Gail Tiner (R)
Burns, Forrest G (D)
Burrows, Pat (D)
Busch, Virginia Marie (D)
Butler, Martyn Don (R)
Cantrell, Joe Marion (R)
Carey, David James (D)
Carleno, Harry Eugene (D)
Carleton, Marilyn Jean (R)
Carper, Frances Izez (D)
Carroll, John Spencer (D)
Carter, Marian Elizabeth (R)
Carver, John A, Jr (D)
Castro, Richard Thomas (D)
Cefkin, J Leo (D)
Chenoweth, J Edgar (R)
Cisneros, Roger (D)
Cole, Ralph A (R)
Comer, William Joseph (D)
Conner, Warren John (R)
Conrad, Priscilla Paulette (D)
Cooper, Eldon W (D)
Cortez, Luis Abran (D)
Cox, Guy Jackson (R)
Crist, Betty Joanne (D)
Crouse, Ruby Rose (R)
Daniels, Bill (R)
Darby, Lorena Eva (D)
Davis, Ken W (R)
DeBerard, Fay F (R)
Decker, Clarence (D)
Delcour, David W (R)
DeMoulin, Charles Joseph, Jr (D)
Dick, Nancy E (D)
Dittemore, Betty Ann (R)
Dole, Hollis M (R)
Dominick, Peter Hoyt (R)
Durham, Steven Jackson (R)
Dye, James Kerry (R)
Eckelberry, Robert Lee (R)
Egan, Rena Adele (R)
Elliott, Ronald D (R)
Englert, Kenneth Edward (R)
Evanger, Jacqueline Ruth (D)
Evans, Frank Edward (D)
Fallin, Pat Finley (D)

Fix, George Arthur (D)
Flanery, William S (D)
Flanigan, Robert M (R)
Flett, Nancy W (D)
Foster, William Edward (R)
Fowler, Hugh Charles (R)
Fowler, Leslie R (R)
Frank, Gerard Vincent (D)
Frazee, Clyde L (R)
Freed, Elaine Eilers (D)
Friedman, Don (R)
Furniss, Susan West (D)
Gallagher, Dennis Joseph (D)
Gaon, David M (D)
Garcia, Maria De Lourdes (D)
Garnsey, William Smith (R)
Gaylord, Mary Fletcher (R)
Gillson, Deborah Lynn (R)
Good, Robert Crocker (D)
Gordon, Joan Vernon (R)
Graham, Jean Charters (D)
Graham, William Clyde (R)
Grant, William (D)
Gray, Jo Anne Hastings (R)
Groff, Regis F (D)
Gunn, Steven Irving (R)
Gustafson, Carl H (R)
Hamil, David Alexander (R)
Hamilton, A C (Scotty) (R)
Hamilton, Dwight Alan (R)
Hamlin, John G (R)
Hanson, Donald Paul (R)
Hart, Gary (D)
Haskell, Floyd Kirk (D)
Hatcher, Martin (D)
Hayes, E E (D)
Hernandez, Margaret Marie (D)
Herzberger, Arthur Conrad (R)
Hibberd, Lucy Reed (D)
Hilsmeier, Bill (R)
Hine, Robert Walter (R)
Hines, Paulena Lininger (R)
Hinman, Wallace Porter (R)
Hite, F Richard (R)
Hobbs, Larry F (R)
Hochman, Nancy Ruth (D)
Hochman, William Russell (D)
Hodges, Paul V, Jr (R)
Hoegh, Leo Arthur (R)
Hogan, Mark Anthony (D)
Hogan, Stephen Douglas (D)
Holme, Barbara Shaw (D)
Hoog, Thomas William (D)
Howe, Charles Bryan (R)
Hughes, William James (R)
Hullinghorst, Dickey Lee (D)
Hulshizer, R Dale (D)
Johnson, Byron Lindberg (D)
Johnson, James P (R)
Johnson, Robert E (R)
Jones, Glenn Robert (R)
Kadlecek, James M (D)
Kelley, Donald E (R)
Kelloff, George (D)
Killam, Anne Loretta (D)
Kinnie, Kenneth Ivan (R)
Kirscht, Robert Leon (Bob) (D)
Kittrell, Richard Lincoln (R)
Klotz, Frank P (R)
Knox, Wayne N (D)
Kogovsek, John J (D)
Kogovsek, Ray P (D)
Kopel, Gerald H (D)
Korrell, Rita May (R)
Kramer, Ken (R)
Kranzler, Richard Martin (D)
Kreutz, James Kirk (R)
Kushnir, Mary Constance (D)
LaGrone, Donna Joan (D)
Lamm, Richard D (D)
LaMora, Judy Lynne (D)
Leavel, Willard Hayden (D)

Lee, Frank Robert (R)
Lister, Joe U (D)
Lloyd, James D (D)
Loesch, Harrison (R)
Long, Gregory F (R)
Love, John Arthur (R)
Lucas, George Bond (D)
Lucero, Leo (D)
Lynch, Daniel Francis (D)
Lyon, Stephen Andrews (D)
MacDonald, Donald Paul (D)
MacKendrick, Donald Anthony (D)
Marks, Jean C (D)
Masco, Dorothy Beryl (R)
Massari, Phillip (D)
Massari, Vincent (D)
Mattlage, Karl P (D)
May, Timothy James (D)
McCarthy, Charles E (R)
McCleave, Mildred Atwood (R)
McClure, June Elinor (R)
McCormick, Harold L (R)
McCroskey, Jack (D)
McCulloch, Robert Winslow (D)
McElwain, S Marion (D)
McGrath, Phyllis Ann (D)
McGregor, Mary Martin (D)
McKenna, Ellanore Louise (D)
McKevitt, James D (Mike) (R)
McLean, Richard Cameron (D)
McNichols, Stephen L R (D)
McVicker, Roy Harrison (D)
Michael, Patricia M (R)
Miller, Laura Anne (R)
Milliken, John Gordon (D)
Minister, Kingston Glenn (R)
Moore, John Porfilio (R)
Mularz, Ruth Louise (D)
Mundt, Gary Harold (D)
Munson, Kay M (R)
Murphy, Terrence Drake (R)
Myers, Roderick Douglas (R)
Neale, Betty Irene (R)
Nelson, John Clifford (R)
Noble, Dan D (R)
Oatis, Kathleen Ann (D)
Ore, Robert J (D)
Orten, Betty (D)
Parcell, Lew W (D)
Parks, Ruth Allott (R)
Pascoe, D Monte (D)
Peterson, Andrienne Tosso (D)
Peterson, Betty Ann (D)
Plock, Richard Henry, Jr (R)
Porter, Ralph Everett (R)
Pottorff, William Thomas (R)
Powers, William Shotwell (R)
Pringle, Edward E
Pugel, Robert Joseph (D)
Quinlan, Clarence (R)
Roberts, Sandra Levinson (D)
Robinson, Charles K (R)
Rogers, Byron Giles (D)
Rogers, Chloe (D)
Rosenheim, Robert Chatwell (R)
Russell, Jean Albach (R)
Sanchez, Cosme Filiberto, Jr (D)
Sandoval, Paul (D)
Scheierman, Mabel M (D)
Schieffelin, Joseph B (R)
Schoenberger, Charlotte Sally (R)
Schroeder, Patricia (D)
Scott, Edward Smith (R)
Scott, Kenneth Edmund (R)
Sears, Betty Jean (R)
Sears, Virginia LaCoste (R)
Shawcroft, John Bennett (R)

Shoemaker, Joe (R)
Shoemaker, Robert N (D)
Showalter, Carl Edward (R)
Showalter, Myrtle May (R)
Skaggs, David Evans (D)
Smedley, Robert William (D)
Smith, Morgan (D)
Smith, Nancy Garrity (D)
Snell, Edward Louis (R)
Soash, Richard Morton (D)
Spano, August John (Mick) (R)
Sprague, Byron David (D)
Stewart, Ronald K (D)
Stieghorst, Lewis Earl (R)
Stimmel, Don Perry (D)
Stockton, Ruth S (R)
Strahle, Ronald H (R)
Strickland, Ted L (R)
Sullivan, Betty Lou (D)
Sutton, Leonard v B (D)
Sweeney, Robert Frank (R)
Tarter, Weldon Murphy (R)
Tate, Penfield W, II (D)
Thompson, Anne Marie (R)
Tonsing, Robert Lowe, Jr (R)
Torres, Max E V (R)
Traylor, Frank (R)
Trott, Bernard L (R)
Trout, Barbara Ann (R)
Troxel, Oliver Leonard, Jr
Tucker, William Edward (R)
Valdez, Ruben A (D)
Vanderhoof, John D (R)
Wadhams, Richard Ivory (R)
Waldow, Walter J (D)
Wayland, Douglas (D)
Webb, Wellington Edward (D)
Weber, Charles William (D)
Wells, Roy Estelle (D)
White, Byron R
White, Diane Mary (D)
White, William L (R)
Whiteman, Robert Wayne (R)
Willard, Beatrice Elizabeth (R)
Williams, Carl Michael (R)
Wingfield, Lotus Mae (D)
Wirth, Timothy E (D)
Witherspoon, Dorothy Karpel (D)
Woolbert, Maybelle Siegele (D)
Wunsch, Christian (D)
Younglund, Walter Arthur (R)
Zakhem, Samir Hanna (R)
Zirkelbach, Barbara Marilyn Foley (D)

CONNECTICUT

Abate, Ernest Nicholas (D)
Adams, Philip J (D)
Ajello, Carl Richard (D)
Albertson, John Patrick (R)
Alcorn, Hugh Meade, Jr (R)
Alessie, John Bruce (D)
Alfano, Charles Thomas (D)
Ali, Ned (R)
Allen, Donald George (R)
Allyn, Rufus (D)
Alsop, John De Koven (R)
Altobello, Henry D (D)
Amato, Vincent Anthony (R)
Ambrogio, William Peter (D)
Amenta, Paul (D)
Anastasia, Lawrence J (D)
Anderson, John William (D)
Andrews, Lewis Davis, Jr (R)
Anglace, John Francis, Jr (R)
Ashbrook, Edward H (R)
August, Robert Burton (R)
Avitabile, George P (R)
Badolato, Dominic J (D)

CONNECTICUT (cont)

Baehr, George B, Jr (D)
Baker, John Edward (R)
Baker, Wayne A (D)
Baldrige, Malcolm (R)
Balducci, Richard J (D)
Baldwin, Lillian Hoell (D)
Barba, Joseph Francis, Jr (D)
Barbieri, Arthur Thomas (D)
Barry, David Michael (D)
Bartolotta, Lillian M (D)
Beach, Edward Latimer (R)
Beck, Audrey Phillips (D)
Becker, Henry Timothy (D)
Belden, Richard O (R)
Bennet, Douglas Joseph, Jr (D)
Berdon, Robert I (R)
Bernstein, Myron Ronald (R)
Berry, Louise Spaulding (R)
Bertinuson, Teresalee (D)
Best, Millicent Rudd (R)
Biebel, Frederick K, Jr (R)
Billington, Clyde Mark, Jr (D)
Bliss, Robert Landers (R)
Boatwright, Mary H (R)
Bogdan, Albert Alexander (D)
Bogdan, Joseph (D)
Bonetti, Addo E (R)
Bordiere, Marcus H (D)
Bork, Robert H (R)
Bosse, Bert Roland (D)
Bowles, Chester (D)
Bozzuto, Richard Carl (R)
Brannen, James Henry, III (R)
Brennan, Amy (D)
Brewer, William Dodd
Briley, John Marshall (R)
Brody, Brenda (D)
Brooks, Patricia Kersten (D)
Brown, Otha Nathaniel, Jr (D)
Brunstad, Donna Leah (D)
Buckley, William Frank, Jr (R)
Burke, Martin Byram (D)
Burnham, Ernest C, Jr (R)
Buzaid, Norman A (D)
Byington, Homer Morrison, Jr
Caldwell, J Edward (D)
Camp, Herbert V, Jr (R)
Campbell, Charles D (R)
Canzonetti, Andrew Joseph (D)
Capecelatro, Ralph Ettore (R)
Caplan, Milton Irving (D)
Carragher, Robert J (D)
Carrozzella, John A (D)
Casey, Joseph Edward (R)
Cashman, Peter Lenihan (R)
Cella, Carl Edward (R)
Cestari, Constance G (R)
Charkoudian, Arppie (D)
Church, James Oliver (R)
Churchill, William Lloyd (R)
Ciampi, Francis W (D)
Ciarlone, Anthony Michael (D)
Ciccarello, Louis S (D)
Cimino, David John (D)
Clark, Thomas C (D)
Clynes, James Joseph (D)
Coatsworth, Joseph S (D)
Coe, Margaret Wyman (R)
Cohen, Morris N (D)
Coles, Albert Leonard (D)
Collins, Constance Sullivan (R)
Collins, Francis James (R)
Collins, William A (D)
Compton, Ranulf (R)
Conklin, George William (D)
Conn, Walter Jennings (R)
Connolly, Virginia Straughan
Corrigan, Patricia Ouimette (D)
Costello, Philip Neill, Jr (R)
Cote, Harold Arthur (D)
Cotter, William R (D)

Coviello, Charles Joseph, Jr (D)
Craig, James Donald (R)
Cramer, Allan P (D)
Cressotti, Richard David (D)
Crowley, Mary V (R)
Curran, Hugh C (D)
Currier, Raymond A, Jr (R)
Currlin, William Egon (R)
Curtin, Margaret Mary (D)
Cutillo, Louis Sabino (D)
Daddario, Emilio Quincy (D)
Danaher, John Anthony (R)
DeGenaro, Alfred (D)
DelPercio, Matthew D (D)
DeMennato, Paul C (D)
DeMerell, John N (R)
Dempsey, John N (D)
DeNardis, Lawrence Joseph (R)
DePiano, Salvatore C (D)
DeRosa, Pasquale Joseph (R)
DeZinno, Benjamin Nicholas, Jr (D)
Dice, Richard Arling (R)
Diehl, Cynthia Barre (R)
Diehl, Paul W (R)
Dinielli, Joseph J (D)
Dobkin, M Adler (R)
Dodd, Christopher John (D)
Dombi, Lauraine Mary (D)
Doran, Philip D (D)
Dreher, Ronald Frederick (R)
Driscoll, Edward Maurice (D)
Driscoll, John J (D)
Duffy, John P (D)
Dunn, Barbara Baxter (R)
Dzialo, Raymond John (D)
Eastman, John Leslie (R)
Eddy, Frank Vincent (R)
Edgerton, Robert Albert, Sr (R)
Erb, Lillian Edgar (R)
Esposito, Donald F (D)
Evans, Lloyd Russell, Jr (Russ) (R)
Evarts, Katharine Avery (R)
Everett, Ruth C (Deming) (R)
Fabrizio, John Arthur (R)
Fagan, Lawrence James (R)
Farricielli, Joseph J (D)
Faulise, Dorothy (R)
Fauliso, Joseph J (D)
Fennell, Melvin (R)
Ferguson, Glenn W (D)
Ferrari, Raymond Charles (D)
Filan, James Kieran (R)
Finney, Florence Donady (R)
Fischer, William Raymond (D)
Flanagan, Ruth Wallace (R)
Fleming, John Grant (D)
Fletcher, George A (R)
Flynn, Joseph P (D)
Flynn, Leo H (D)
Foote, Ellsworth Bishop (R)
Forella, June B (R)
Fox, Abijah Upson (R)
Francis, Kathryn Gene (R)
Francis, Robert Ellsworth (R)
Frassinelli, Attilio (D)
Frate, Gennaro W (R)
Freedman, Samuel Sumner (R)
Frost, Norma W (R)
Gabriel, Fannie R (R)
Gaffney, J Brian (R)
Ganim, George Wanis (R)
Gejdenson, Samuel (D)
Gelston, Mortimer Ackley (R)
Gentile, George G (D)
Gery, L Clayton (D)
Giaimo, Robert Nicholas (D)
Gilbert, Charles Breed, III (R)
Giles, Abraham L (D)
Gilligan, Robert G (D)
Gilman, Lawrence M (R)

Giordano, John Anthony, Jr (D)
Glassman, Abraham
Gniadek, Donald Richard (D)
Going, Paden Cawhern (R)
Golden, John Matthew (D)
Goldfarb, Alexander A (D)
Gosselin, Ernest J (D)
Governali, Joseph Paul (D)
Grabowski, Bernard Francis (D)
Grande, Andrew R (D)
Grasser, Thomas W (D)
Grasso, Ella Tambussi (D)
Grieb, Frances Baccelli (D)
Griffin, Richard Thomas (D)
Griffiths, Earle Curtiss, Jr (R)
Groppo, John G (D)
Grosby, Eleanor (R)
Guida, Bartholomew F (D)
Guidera, George Clarence (R)
Gunther, George Lackman (R)
Guzzi, Ralph Joseph (D)
Haesche, Arthur B, Jr (R)
Hamerman, Wilda Slevin (D)
Hamzy, Joseph Amin (R)
Hanlon, Neal B (R)
Hannon, George William, Jr (D)
Hansen, Harold D (D)
Hanzalek, Astrid T (R)
Hardy, Frederick William (D)
Harlow, Harold G (R)
Harrison, Donald C (D)
Hartman, Joseph Adolph (D)
Hashim, Elinor Marie (R)
Healey, James Thomas (D)
Heck, Wilfred Henry (D)
Heffernan, Gerald James (D)
Hendel, Patricia Thall (D)
Henderson, Walter J (D)
Hennessey, J Martin (D)
Hennessy, Francis Xavier (D)
Hermanowski, Leon F (D)
Heslin, Helen Elaine (D)
Hobbs, Michael Dickinson (D)
Hogan, Morris Bernard (R)
Houley, Robert D (D)
Houston, Howard Edwin (R)
Hudson, Betty (D)
Hughes, James A (D)
Hughes, John William (R)
Hull, T Clark (R)
Hunt, Robert Richard, Sr (R)
Hutchins, Elizabeth Dennis (R)
Innes, Allan C (R)
Irwin, Donald Jay (D)
Ives, Alden Allen (R)
Jacome, Herbert Arthur (D)
Janes, R Kippen (R)
Johnson, Lucy Black (D)
Johnston, Kevin P (D)
Jones, William (D)
Julian, John Edward (D)
Julianelle, Robert Lewis (D)
Juram, William Carl, Jr (R)
Karkutt, A Richard, Jr (D)
Karrel, Oscar (D)
Kellis, James George (D)
Kelly, Arthur John (D)
Kemler, Joan R (D)
Kennelly, James J (D)
Keyes, Thomas J, Jr (D)
Killian, Robert Kenneth (D)
Kipp, Phyllis T (R)
Klebanoff, Howard Michael (D)
Klinck, Mary Ellen (D)
Kopp, W Brewster (R)
Kratzert, Arthur William (R)
Kronfeld, Leopold James (D)
Lansing, Mary Hubbard (D)
LaRosa, Paul A (D)
Laskey, Thomas Penrose (R)

Laudone, Vincent A (R)
Lawless, William Josselyn, Jr (D)
LeCardo, Frank A (D)
Lee, Ronald Barry (D)
Leeney, Philip J (D)
Lenz, Donald (R)
Lieberman, Joseph I (D)
Lincoln, Emma Ethel (R)
Liskov, Samuel (D)
Locke, Peter Fredrick, Jr (R)
Lodge, John Davis (R)
Long, Michael Thomas (D)
Longo, Frank J (D)
Lorenzen, Dorothy Walker (R)
Low, Stuart M (D)
Lowden, Elmer W (D)
Lufkin, Dan Wende (R)
Lutts, Robert Hamilton (R)
Lutz, Carol Ruth (D)
Lutz, Iri Karist (R)
Lyddy, Raymond C (D)
Mahoney, Francis James (D)
Manchester, Paul C (D)
Manna, Mario Joseph (D)
Mannion, James Michael (D)
Mannix, John F (R)
Marcus, Mark Jay (D)
Martin, Mary Agnes (D)
Martin, Richard R (D)
Mascolo, Frederic Edward (D)
Mastrianni, Silvio A (D)
Matthews, John G (R)
Matties, Charles R (R)
Maurer, Friedrich C (R)
May, Edwin Hyland, Jr (R)
May, Stephanie Middleton (D)
Mayer, William Snyder (R)
Mazza, Vito Michael (D)
Mazzola, Alan Joseph (R)
McCaffery, Dorothy Kane (D)
McCaffery, John K M (D)
McCarthy, John Francis (D)
McCluskey, Dorothy Soest (D)
McColough, Charles Peter (D)
McCormick, Thomas Francis (R)
McCue, Agnes Louise (D)
McDermott, Robert James (D)
McGee, Joseph James (D)
McGovern, Terry P (D)
McGuirk, John F, Sr (D)
McKinney, Stewart Brett (R)
McManus, John P (D)
Mendenhall, Joseph Abraham
Mercier, Richard Louis (D)
Mesite, Patsy J (D)
Meskill, Thomas J (R)
Messina, Francis William (R)
Metro, James J (D)
Mihaly, Serge George (D)
Millar, Raymond Irving (R)
Miller, Anthony P (D)
Milmore, Thomas Aloysius (D)
Miner, S Norton (R)
Moffett, Anthony (Toby) (D)
Monagan, John Stephen (D)
Mondani, Thomas P (D)
Montano, George John (R)
Moore, William Graham (R)
Moores, Hervey Cuthrell (R)
Morano, Albert Paul (R)
Morano, Michael L (R)
Morante, Julius E (D)
Morelli, Carmen (D)
Moriarty, William T (D)
Morris, Bruce Leo (D)
Morris, Gloria Genevieve (D)
Morris, Julius D (D)
Morrison, John J (D)
Morton, Margaret E (D)
Mosbacher, Emil, Jr (Bus) (R)

Motto, Nicholas M (D)
Moynihan, Timothy Joseph (D)
Murphy, Charles J (D)
Murphy, James Jerome, Jr (D)
Napolitano, Frank Anthony (D)
Natalino, Michael Vincent (D)
Neiditz, David Henry (D)
Nelson, Jeanne Ross (R)
Nevas, Alan Harris (R)
Novick, Lee Engel (D)
O'Connor, J Raymond (R)
O'Connor, James A (D)
O'Leary, Cornelius Peter (D)
O'Neill, William A (D)
Orcutt, Geil (D)
Osiecki, Clarice A (R)
Osler, Dorothy K (R)
Owens, Howard T, Jr (D)
Page, Stanley Haynes (R)
Palaia, Lawrence E (D)
Palladino, Vincent Oliver (R)
Palmieri, James John (D)
Palmquist, Dawn Isabelle (D)
Paluska, Everett Clifford (D)
Panuzio, Nicholas Arthur (R)
Papandrea, John Francis (D)
Patterson, Richard George (D)
Pawlak, Paul, Sr (D)
Perrin, Carl Ellis (D)
Peterson, Geoffrey Gissler (D)
Phillips, Alvah H (D)
Pinney, A Searle (R)
Piscopo, Patsy J (R)
Post, Russell Lee, Jr (R)
Powers, Arthur B (D)
Price, George (D)
Prindle, Barclay Ward (D)
Purtell, William Arthur (R)
Pyne, Lee Edward (R)
Quine, John Day (R)
Quinn, John Robert (D)
Quinn, Katherine T (D)
Rader, Joan Sperry (R)
Radzwillas, Aldona (D)
Ransohoff, Babette Strauss (R)
Rapoport, Natalie (D)
Reed, Gordon Wies (R)
Repko, Andrew (R)
Reynolds, Catherine Cox (D)
Reynolds, Russell Joseph (D)
Ribicoff, Abraham A (D)
Ritter, George Joseph (D)
Ritter, Thomas Drummond (D)
Ritvo, Lucille B (D)
Rome, Lewis B (R)
Rosa, Paul James, Jr (R)
Rosen, Jerome Allan (D)
Rosenthal, Beatrice Holt (D)
Rosenthal, Jack H (D)
Rowley, Evelyn Fish (R)
Sabota, Francis Robert (D)
Sachs, Arthur S (D)
St Pierre, Donald R (D)
Salisbury, Wallace Daniel (R)
Sanger, Richard Calvin (R)
Sarasin, Ronald A (R)
Satter, Robert (D)
Sayre, Clyde O (R)
Schaffer, Gloria Wilinski (D)
Schaller, Barry Raymond (R)
Scheidel, Theodore C, Jr (R)
Schneller, Richard Francis (D)
Schwartz, Joseph William (D)
Schwend, Renato Timothy (R)
Scully, William James, Jr (D)
Serrani, Thom (D)
Shakespeare, Frank (R)
Shays, Christopher (R)
Shea, Robert Dennis (D)
Sherwood, Robert Walter (D)
Shrader, Douglas (D)
Sieracki, Robert F (D)

Smith, Margaret Keane (D)
Smith, Robert James (R)
Smith, Stuart Arnold (D)
Smith, Wilber G (D)
Smoko, Ronald L (R)
Sokolowski, Chesterlyn (D)
Sponheimer, John P (D)
Stapleton, James F (R)
Steele, Robert Hampton (R)
Stevens, Gerald Fairlie (R)
Stevenson, Russell E, Jr (R)
Stober, Kenneth E (R)
Stolberg, Irving Jules (D)
Strada, William E, Jr (D)
Sullivan, Vincent Augustine (D)
Sullivan, William Johnson (D)
Sutera, Carol Jacqueline (D)
Sweeney, Thomas Francis (D)
Sweetman, Doris Dwan (D)
Switaski, Anna-Mae (R)
Szczarba, Arlene Lee (D)
Tanger, Winifred A (D)
Testa, James Robert (D)
Theriault, Albert Arthur, Jr (D)
Thornton, Jean Tyrol (R)
Tiffany, John Jewett, II (R)
Tighe, Charles Moon (R)
Tobin, Robert Daniel (D)
Toman, Henry Edward (R)
Trantino, Joseph Peter (D)
Trayner, Wesgarth Forster (R)
Truglia, Anthony Domenick (D)
Tulisano, Richard Don (D)
Turiano, Michael (D)
Tymniak, Paul Martin (R)
Uberti, E James (R)
Varis, Richard E (R)
Vertefeuille, Albert Benoit (D)
Vicino, Robert James (D)
Villano, Vincent (D)
Wagner, Jerry (D)
Walker, Charls Edward (R)
Walkovich, Joseph (D)
Walsh, Elizabeth Kennedy (D)
Walsh, Robert M (D)
Washburn, Elwood Conrad (R)
Webber, Albert Raymond (R)
Weicker, Lowell Palmer, Jr (R)
Weigand, Joseph F, Jr (R)
Weinberg, Margaraet Kurth (D)
Weiner, Harold (R)
Wexler, Anne (D)
White, F Clifton (R)
Wilber, Elinor F (R)
Wilensky, Julius M (R)
Willard, Richard C (D)
Williams, Gary Grady (D)
Wingate, Richard Anthony (R)
Winnick, Edward Bernard (D)
Woodhouse, Chase Going (D)
Wright, Alfred Edward (D)
Wright, Gardner E, Jr (D)
Yacavone, Muriel Taul (D)
Young, Pasquale (D)
Zullo, Frank Nicholas (D)

DELAWARE

Adams, Thurman, Jr (D)
Ambrosino, Joseph P, Jr (R)
Arnold, John Henry (R)
Babiarz, John Edward (D)
Battaglia, Basil Richard (R)
Bayard, Alexis Irenee duPont (D)
Berndt, Robert J (R)
Biden, Joseph Robinette (D)
Billingsley, John G S (R)
Boggs, J Caleb (R)
Bookhammer, Eugene Donald (R)

Boulden, Kenneth Webster (D)
Brown, Herman Cubbage (R)
Buckson, David Penrose (R)
Bunting, Eugene (R)
Byrd, Robert Lee (D)
Cain, Gerard A (D)
Calloway, James Richard (D)
Carvel, Elbert Nostrand (D)
Castle, Michael Newbold (R)
Cicione, Anthony J (D)
Clendaniel, Howard A (D)
Collins, Richard T (R)
Connor, Robert Thomas (R)
Cook, Nancy (D)
Cordrey, Richard Stephen (D)
Darling, Ronald L (D)
Davis, Edward R (Ned) (D)
Day, Judith Olga (R)
Derrickson, Harry E (R)
Derrickson, Vernon Blades (D)
Diggs, Betty Jean (D)
Di Mondi, Francis Anthony (R)
du Pont, Pierre Samuel, IV (R)
Elliott, David H (R)
Evans, Thomas Beverley, Jr (R)
Everett, Annabelle Smith (Belle) (R)
Ferguson, John P (D)
Folsom, Henry Richard (R)
Frear, Joseph Allen, Jr (D)
Gates, Rebecca Twilley (D)
George, Orlando J, Jr (D)
Gilligan, Robert F (D)
Gordy, William John (D)
Hale, Everette (R)
Harkins, Michael Eugene (R)
Harrington, Lewis B (D)
Hebner, Charles L (R)
Hering, George C, III (R)
Holloway, Herman Monwell, Sr (D)
Hughes, Charles E (R)
Huthmacher, Marilyn Anne (D)
Isaacs, John Donald (R)
Johnson, Henrietta (D)
Jonkiert, Casimir S (D)
Jornlin, Francis M (R)
Jornlin, Mary Duggan (R)
Kagel, Allen David (D)
Kearns, Francis J (D)
Kelly, Daniel A (D)
Killen, Ernest E (D)
Kirk, John Francis, Jr (R)
Knox, Andrew Gibson (R)
Lee, William Swain (R)
LeGates, Richard Bolton (R)
Lesher, Lois M (R)
Lindh, Ocie H (D)
Lynch, Donald J (D)
Manning, Margaret R (D)
Marshall, Robert Ignatius (D)
Martin, Roger Allen (D)
Matushefske, John (D)
Maxwell, Robert Lee (D)
McCullough, Calvin R (D)
McGinnin, James D (D)
McKay, John Patterson (R)
Mendolia, Arthur I (R)
Miller, Karen Jennings (D)
Minner, Ruth Ann (D)
Morris, John Edward (D)
Murphy, William Malcolm, Jr (D)
O'Connor, Kathleen T (D)
Ollweiler, Frances B (D)
Peirson, Mary Wood (R)
Perry, Nancy Mayer (R)
Peterson, Russell Wilbur (R)
Pierce, Grace Wagner (R)
Plant, Al O (D)
Poppiti, Michael (D)

Potter, William Samuel (D)
Powell, Robert S (R)
Quillen, George Robert (R)
Rakestraw, Priscilla B (R)
Riddagh, Robert W (R)
Ridings, C Leslie, Jr (R)
Rispoli, Marcello (D)
Roth, William Victor, Jr (R)
Ryder, Kenneth, Jr (D)
Schlor, George F (D)
Seibel, Marion Irma (R)
Short, Nancy Susan (D)
Sincock, Richard (R)
Sloan, Sonia Schorr (D)
Smith, Albert F (R)
Smith, Gwynne P (R)
Spence, Winifred M (R)
Stabler, W Laird, Jr (R)
Steele, Dean C (R)
Stokes, Paul Curtis, Jr (R)
Temple, Thomas A, Sr (D)
Tharp, Gertrude (D)
Topel, Henry (D)
Tribbitt, Sherman W (D)
Twilley, Joshua Marion (D)
Weiner, Barbara (D)
Weldon, Richard Bancroft, Sr (R)
Williams, John James (R)
Worthen, Sandra D (D)
Zimmerman, Jacob W (D)

DISTRICT OF COLUMBIA

Abell, Tyler (D)
Adams, Eva Bertrand (D)
Adams, John Gibbons (R)
Alexander, Clifford L, Jr (D)
Almedina, Angel (D)
Andersen, Alice Klopstad (R)
Andrade, Carolyn Marie (D)
Anton, James (R)
Atherton, Alfred Leroy, Jr
Auchincloss, James Coats (R)
Bacher, Edward Leonard (R)
Bartlett, William Mayhew (R)
Battle, Lucius D
Baumgart, Merle David (D)
Beam, Jacob Dyneley
Becker, Ralph Elihu (R)
Beeman, Josiah Horton (D)
Bell, Richard E
Bell, Terrell H
Berliner, Henry A, Jr (R)
Billett, John William (D)
Bindeman, Jacob Edward (R)
Binder, Robert Henri (R)
Blair, James H
Block, Barbara Anne (R)
Bolen, David Benjamin
Bosco, Joseph A (Independent)
Boster, Davis Eugene
Bowsher, Charles Arthur (R)
Brayman, Harold Halliday (R)
Breuninger, Lewis Talmage (R)
Brown, Winthrop Gilman
Brownman, Harold L
Brownstein, Esther Savelle (D)
Buchanan, Patrick Joseph (R)
Buffum, William Burnside
Burch, Dean (R)
Burns, Arthur Frank (R)
Burress, Richard Thomas (R)
Burton, Melvin Matthew, Jr (R)
Butchman, Alan A (D)
Butler, Robert Neil (D)
Califano, Joseph A, Jr (D)
Campbell, H Phil
Campbell, Joseph (R)

DISTRICT OF COLUMBIA (cont)

Carothers, Neil, III (R)
Carpenter, Liz (D)
Carter, Jared Glenn
Carter, Robert S (R)
Cashen, Henry Christopher, II (R)
Chamberlin, Guy W, Jr
Chapman, Oscar Littleton (D)
Chatelain, Leon, Jr (R)
Chennault, Anna Chan (R)
Chin-Lee, William (R)
Chumbris, Peter Nicholas (R)
Cipriani, Harriet Emily (D)
Clark, Fred G
Clark, Gilbert Edward
Colby, William Egan
Coleman, William Thaddeus, Jr (R)
Conklin, Charles Ross (D)
Cook, Charles W
Cooper, Charles Arthur
Cooper, William Hurlbert (R)
Cormaney, Theodore Michael (R)
Cottam, Howard R (D)
Craw, Nicholas Wesson (R)
Crawford, Hazle Reid (D)
Creasey, Daniel Fredrick (D)
Czarnecki, Marian Anthony (D)
Dalley, George Albert (D)
Davenport, Robert Rambo (R)
Dean, John (D)
Dean, John Gunther
de Wilde, David
Dickson, Ernest C (R)
Dixon, Fred L (R)
Dixon, Paul Rand (D)
Donner, Sally Sears (Independent)
Doolin, Dennis James (R)
Dubino, Helen Mary (R)
Dudley, Tilford Eli (D)
Duffey, Joseph D (D)
Dutton, Frederick G (D)
Dwyer, William F (R)
Edwards, Michael Dean (D)
Elbrick, C Burke
Ely, John Hart
Enders, Thomas Ostrom
Evans, Donald D (R)
Falknor, Richard William Condon (D)
Farmer, James (Independent)
Farmer, Thomas Laurence (D)
Faulstich, Janet Kay (D)
Fauntroy, Walter E (D)
Feggans, Edward Leland (R)
Feighan, Michael A (D)
Feldman, Myer (D)
Ferguson, Clarence Clyde, Jr (R)
Ferguson, Homer (R)
Fleming, Robert Henry (D)
Fletcher, Thomas William (D)
Foltz, John C
Fortas, Abe (D)
Foster, William Chapman (R)
Fri, Robert Wheeler (R)
Frost, E Douglas (D)
Funkhouser, Richard
Galbraith, Francis J
Gamser, Howard Graham (D)
Gardner, Stephen S
Garske, Marie Kettelforder (R)
Gillette, Howard F, Jr (R)
Gleason, Robert Reilly, Jr (R)
Goldberg, Arthur Joseph (D)
Goldfarb, Owen (D)
Goldwin, Robert A (R)
Gooch, Raymond LeRoy (R)
Good, Josephine Louise (R)
Goodwin, Ronald (D)
Graham, Pierre Robert
Grant, Cecil Greene (R)
Green, Marshall
Habib, Philip Charles
Hahn, Gilbert, Jr (R)
Handley, William J
Hanks, Nancy (R)
Harris, Janet Louise (D)
Harris, Patricia Roberts (D)
Harris, Robert Oberndoerfer (D)
Hart, Parker Thompson
Hartman, Arthur A
Hays, Paul M (R)
Hayworth, Don (D)
Hechinger, John W (D)
Heck, L Douglas
Henderson, Douglas
Hermelin, William Michael (Independent)
Herz, Martin F
Hess, Stephen (R)
High, Beverly Frances (D)
Hillegonds, Paul Christie (R)
Hills, Roderick M (R)
Hoffmann, Martin R
Hogan, John Edward
Hogue, James
Holman, Benjamin
Hooker, Roger Wolcott, Jr (R)
House, Dale Wiesner (R)
Huff, Leroy Christopher, Jr (R)
Huff, Lillian (D)
Hurtado, Ralph Frank (D)
Ilchuk, Peter Kenneth (Independent)
Imhoff, Lawrence Edward
Jarvis, Norman O (R)
Johnson, U Alexis
Jones, Mary Gardiner (R)
Jones, Sidney (D)
Judd, Walter Henry (R)
Kearns, Henry (R)
Keeney, John C
Keith, Hastings (R)
Kelley, Clarence Marion
Kerr, Gordon Charles (D)
Kertz, Harold Allan (R)
Kirk, Roger
Kissinger, Henry Alfred
Knebel, John Albert (R)
Knox, Katharine McCook (R)
Korth, Fred (D)
Krumbhaar, George Douglas, Jr (R)
Kurzman, Stephen (R)
Laird, Melvin Robert (R)
Laise, Carol C
Landau, George W
Lee, Robert Emmet (R)
Leftwich, Willie Lorenzo (R)
Lilley, Tom (R)
Linderman, Sarah Packer (R)
Loftus, Joseph Anthony (R)
Looram, Matthew
Lucy, William (D)
Lutz, Theodore C
MacArthur, Douglas II
Macdonald, David R
MacGregor, Clark (R)
MacIver, Dale (R)
MacKinnon, George Edward (R)
Mailliard, William Somers (R)
Majak, Ralph Roger (D)
Maldonado, Daniel Chris (D)
Marcy, H Tyler
Marks, Leonard Harold (D)
Marriott, Alice Sheets (R)
Marshall, Anthony Dryden (R)
Martinson, Ronald Lee (R)
Mason, Willie C (R)
Maury, John Minor
Maw, Carlyle E
McCloskey, Robert James
McCollum, Otis Roberts (R)
McConnell, A Mitchell, Jr
McCullen, Joseph Thomas, Jr (R)
McDermott, Robert Hogan (R)
McEvoy, John Thomas (D)
McGinnis, Edward Francis (R)
McGuire, E Perkins (R)
McKesson, John Alexander, III (Independent)
McMurray, Kay
McNamee, Nikki Diane (D)
McNemar, Georgia Arlone (R)
Meek, Elsie Helena (D)
Meeker, David Olan (R)
Meeker, Leonard Carpenter
Meloy, Francis Edward, Jr
Merrick, Samuel Vaughan (D)
Merrill, Frederick Thayer Jr (D)
Midgley, Grant Winder (D)
Miller, Edward Boone (R)
Mizell, Wilmer David (Vinegar Bend) (R)
Moe, Richard (DFL)
Monroney, A S Mike (D)
Moore, Jerry Alexander Jr (R)
Morgan, Barbara (D)
Napper, Hyacinthe T (D)
Nash, Philleo (D)
Neas, Ralph Graham, Jr (R)
Newman, Constance Berry (R)
Nicholson, Ralph William (D)
O'Donnell, Patrick Emmett (R)
O'Leary, Thomas Fleming (D)
Oliphant, S Parker (R)
O'Neill, Paul Joseph (R)
Oshiki, Kaz (D)
Owens, Hugh Franklin (D)
Parsky, Gerald Lawrence (R)
Paster, Howard G (D)
Pate, James L
Pendleton, Edmund E (R)
Penisten, Gary D
Pertschuk, Michael (D)
Peterson, Esther Eggertsen (D)
Peterson, Peter G (R)
Phillips, Richard I
Pinkett, Flaxie Madison (D)
Pires, Sheila Ann (D)
Press, William Hans (R)
Purves, Pierre Marot (R)
Pyle, Robert Noble (R)
Raftery, Frank (D)
Rathlesberger, James Howard (Independent)
Rauh, Joseph L, Jr (D)
Rausch, Richard L (D)
Reynolds, James Joseph (D)
Robinson, Charles W
Robinson, Donald Louis (D)
Robinson, Sara Katharine Moore (D)
Rogovin, Mitchell (D)
Ross, Claude G
Rossides, Eugene Telemachus (R)
Rowan, Carl Thomas (Independent)
Rush, Henri Francis, Jr (R)
Russo, Paul Anthony (R)
Salzman, Herbert
Samuels, Michael Anthony (R)
Sauer, Walter Charles
Scali, John (D)
Schedler, Spencer Jaime (R)
Schreiber, Ann F (D)
Scott, Stanley S (R)
Sedgwick, Lillian Adkins (D)
Segall, Joel
Segermark, Howard S (R)
Selin, Ivan
Shipley, Carl L (R)
Shull, Leon (D)
Sibal, Abner Woodruff (R)
Siegrist, Robert Ryan (R)
Silberman, Laurence Hirsch (R)
Simpson, William Walton (D)
Sisco, Joseph John
Smalley, Robert Manning (R)
Smith, Gerard Coad (R)
Smith, Henry P, III (R)
Sneider, Richard Lee
Snow, John W
Snowden, Maxine Watlington (R)
Spingarn, Stephen J (D)
Srodes, Cecile Zaugg (R)
Staats, Elmer Boyd
Stans, Maurice H (R)
Stevens, Wilma Patten (D)
Stever, Horton Guyford
Stewart, John Gilman (D)
Stewart, Potter
Stewart, Tracy Ann Gipson (R)
Stoney, William E
Sullivan, Leonard, Jr (R)
Swigert, John Leonard, Jr (R)
Swillinger, Daniel James (R)
Tabor, John Kaye (R)
Taylor, Margaret Kirkwood (R)
Teicher, Oren Jonathan (D)
Terris, Bruce Jerome (D)
Theis, Paul Anthony (R)
Thomas, John M
Thomas, Stanley Buddington, Jr (R)
Thompson, R Burnett, Jr (R)
Thornburgh, Richard
Tobriner, Walter Nathan (D)
Toll, Maynard Joy, Jr (D)
Train, Russell Errol (R)
Trotter, Virginia Y
Tucker, Sterling (D)
Turner, Virginia Price (D)
Twiname, John Dean (R)
Tyler, William Royall
Ullman, Michael
Umansky, David Jay (D)
Usery, Willie J, Jr (D)
Van Doren, Charles Norton
Vastine, John Robert, Jr (R)
Veazey, Carlton Wadsworth (R)
Villarreal, Carlos C (R)
Wade, Robert Hirsch Beard (R)
Wakelin, James, Jr (R)
Walsh, Ethel Bent (R)
Walton, Judy Ruth (D)
Washington, Walter E (D)
Watkins, Jane Magruder (D)
Watkins, Joseph Wesley, III (D)
Watlington, Janet (D)
Watt, Graham Wend (Independent)
Weaver, George Leon Paul (D)
Weiss, Abraham
Wells, Barbara Mary (R)
Wheatley, Electra Catsonis (R)
Whitehead, Clay Thomas (R)
Wille, Frank (R)
Williams, John J (R)
Williams, Smallwood Edmond (D)
Winter, Nadine P (D)
Wright, Jerauld
Wurf, Jerry (D)
Youngdahl, Luther W (R)
Zarb, Frank G (R)

FLORIDA

Abrams, Michael I (D)
Abrams, Nancy Jean (D)
Adair, Charles Wallace, Jr
Adams, Tom (D)
Adkins, James Calhoun (D)
Andrews, Frederick Charles (R)
Andrews, William Claud (D)
Askew, Reubin O'D (D)
Avon, Randy Kalani (R)
Bafalis, Louis A (Skip) (R)
Bagwell, Eugene Paris (D)
Bailey, T Wayne (D)
Baker, Annette (D)
Bane, David Morgan
Barnard, Clare Amundson (R)
Barrett, David L (D)
Barron, Dempsey James (D)
Batchelor, Dick J (D)
Beattie, Jack Robert (R)
Becker, Alan Steven (D)
Belanger, Laurent Walter (R)
Bell, J Raymond (R)
Bell, Samuel P, III (D)
Bellino, Robert John (R)
Bendixen, Sergio (D)
Bennett, Charles E (D)
Bie, Norman (D)
Blackburn, Robert E, Jr (R)
Bloom, Elaine (D)
Boland, Ardney James, Sr (D)
Book, Ronald Lee (D)
Boyd, Charles W (D)
Boyd, Joseph Arthur, Jr (D)
Bradley, Agnes Alberta (Angel) (R)
Brantley, Lew (D)
Brilliant, Mollie Wexler (D)
Brockman, Mary Laura (R)
Brown, James Hyatt (D)
Bryant, Cecil Farris (D)
Buckley, John Reed (D)
Burke, J Herbert (R)
Burrall, Frederic H (R)
Butler, Neil Arthur (D)
Cacciatore, Sammy (D)
Caldwell, Millard Fillmore, Jr (D)
Campbell, Gene (D)
Carlisle, George Langford (D)
Carlisle, Grace Martin (D)
Carlton, Vassar B
Carswell, George Harrold (R)
Chaffee, Florence Esther (R)
Chance, Jean Carver (D)
Chappell, William Venroe, Jr (Bill) (D)
Cherry, Gwendolyn Sawyer (D)
Childers, C (D)
Childers, Wyon Dale (D)
Chiles, Lawton Mainor, Jr (D)
Clark, Dick (D)
Clark, John R (D)
Clark, Marion O'Donald (R)
Clem, Chester (R)
Cobbe, Margaret Hammett (D)
Cohen, Ted E (D)
Collins, LeRoy (D)
Conner, Doyle E (D)
Considine, John J (D)
Conway, William Rayford (D)
Coolman, Karen (D)
Costin, Cecil Guerry, Jr (D)
Crabtree, Granville H, Jr (R)
Cramer, Ann Marie Joan (D)
Cramer, William C (Bill) (R)
Crenshaw, Ander (D)
Culbreath, John Richard (D)
Czulowski, Edward Joseph (D)
Dain, Evelyn Randolph (R)
D'Alemberte, Talbot (Sandy) (D)
Damsey, Joan Roberta (D)

Darden, William Boone (D)
Davis, Helen Gordon (D)
Davis, Mable Wilson (R)
Deeb, Richard James (R)
Devlin, Philip, Jr (R)
Dickinson, Fred Otis, Jr (D)
Di Pasca, Albin William (R)
Dixon, R Earl (R)
Dougherty, Jean Marie Cordiner (D)
Doyle, Anna Marie (D)
Duncan, T Marvin (R)
Dunn, Edgar M, Jr (D)
Dyer, Harold J (D)
Earle, Lewis Samuel (R)
Easley, Betty (R)
Eberhard, Ogretta (D)
Eckhart, James F (D)
Englander, Sophia (D)
Evans, Hazel Atkinson (D)
Everidge, Mary James (Jim) (D)
Fascell, Dante B (D)
Fechtel, Vince (R)
Feinberg, Eli Michael (D)
Ferguson, Margaret Osborne (D)
Firestone, George (D)
Fleming, James Preston (D)
Flynn, Bill (D)
Fontana, A M (Tony) (D)
Forbes, John Robert (D)
Fortune, Edmond M (D)
Foster, Jim (D)
Frederick, Willard D (D)
Freeman, William A, Jr (D)
Frey, Louis, Jr (R)
Fulford, William Edmond (D)
Fuqua, Don (D)
Gallagher, Tom (R)
Gallen, Thomas M (D)
Gant, Bobbie Anna (D)
Gersten, Joseph Morris (D)
Gibbons, Sam M (D)
Gibson, William L (R)
Gillespie, Jerald Dan (R)
Goldberg, Stanley B (D)
Gordon, Elaine Y (D)
Gordon, Jack D (D)
Gorman, Edward Armstrong (R)
Gorman, William D (R)
Graham, Daniel Robert (D)
Graig, A H (Gus) (D)
Gregory, Douglas Meigs (R)
Griffin, Harmon Terrell (R)
Grizzard, Robert Harold (D)
Grizzle, Mary R (R)
Grosse, George R (D)
Gunter, Bill (D)
Gurney, Edward John (R)
Haben, Ralph H, Jr (D)
Hagan, Fred (R)
Hagler, Clyde H (D)
Hair, Mattox Strickland (D)
Haley, James Andrew (D)
Harrington, Nancy O (D)
Harris, Marshall S (D)
Hartnett, Robert C (D)
Hattaway, Bob (D)
Havill, Edward Ernest (R)
Hawkins, Mary Ellen Higgins (R)
Hawkins, Paula F (R)
Hayes, John S (D)
Hazelton, Don F (R)
Hazouri, Thomas L (Tommy) (D)
Healey, E J (Ed) (D)
Hector, Robert C (D)
Henderson, Warren S (R)
Herlong, Albert Sydney, Jr (D)
Hieber, George Frederick, II (R)

Hill, John Allen (D)
Hill, Robert Michael (R)
Hill, Susie H (D)
Hodes, Richard S (D)
Hodges, Gene (D)
Hogan, Thomas Sheridan, Jr (R)
Holland, Evelyn Faucette (D)
Holloway, Vernon Carlyle (D)
Hostettler, Dorie McFetridge (R)
Hutto, Earl (D)
Ingram, Louis Wilson, Jr (D)
Jackson, Julia Carolyn (R)
James, William G (Bill) (R)
Johns, Charley Eugene (D)
Johns, William Gordon (R)
Johnson, Robert Maurice (R)
Johnston, Harry A, II (D)
Jones, Charles Fred (D)
Jordan, Russell Clinger, Jr (D)
Jova, Joseph John
Juarez, Oscar F (R)
Kelly, Richard (R)
Kennedy, David T (D)
Kershaw, Joseph Lang (D)
Kiefer, Edgar L (R)
King, Shirley McVeigh (D)
Kirk, Claude Roy, Jr (R)
Kiser, Samuel Curtis (R)
Knopke, Ray C (D)
Kohler, Foy David (Independent)
Kruse, Edward H
Kurke, Eleanor Bergan (R)
Kutun, Barry (D)
Kyle, Marcus Aurelius (R)
Lacy, Benjamin Watkins, IV (D)
Lane, David Campbell (R)
Lane, Julian B (D)
Lehman, David J (D)
Lehman, William (D)
Lepeska, Richard George (D)
Lewis, John Washington (D)
Lewis, Philip D (D)
Lewis, Randolph Bradford (D)
Lewis, Thomas F (Tom) (R)
Lieberman, Ronald Stephen (D)
Locke, Nina Spencer (R)
Lockward, William Henry (D)
Lytal, Lake Henry (D)
MacKay, Kenneth H, Jr (D)
Mancini, Joseph A (R)
Mann, Franklin Balch (D)
Mann, Helen Louise (D)
Manthey, Charles Edwin (R)
Margolis, Gwen (D)
Marler, Roy Lee, Sr (D)
Marr, John Joseph (D)
Marshall, William Huston (D)
Martin, Sidney (D)
Matthews, Donald Ray (D)
Matthews, Harvey W (R)
Mattox, Ray (D)
Maxwell, Clark, Jr (R)
McCain, David L
McCall, Wayne C (D)
McClain, David H (R)
McDevitt, Sheila Marie (R)
McDonald, Dennis A (R)
McElmurray, Jeanne Frances (D)
McFarland, Leona Marie (D)
McGill, Lovette Eunice (D)
McGriff, Jack (D)
McKnight, Robert Wayne (D)
McLeod, Dorothy Thomas (R)
McPherson, Thomas Allen (D)
Melvin, Jarrett Green (Jerry) (D)
Miller, John (Jack) (D)
Miller, Phyllis Ann (D)

Minnis, Leeomia Williams (D)
Mixson, Wayne (D)
Moffitt, H Lee (D)
Monaghan, Diana M (D)
Mondres, Marvin D (Lucky) (R)
Moore, Phyllis Norman (R)
Moore, Tom Robert (D)
Morgan, Herbert F (D)
Morris, Helene M (R)
Moyle, Jon (D)
Mueller, Frederick Henry (R)
Murfin, William Floyd (R)
Myers, Bill J (D)
Myers, Kenneth Morton (D)
Neal, Patrick K (D)
Nelson, C William (Bill) (D)
Nelson, Richard Thurlow (R)
Nergard, Charles L (Chuck) (R)
Nicholson, James Ray (R)
Nicosia, D Gregory (D)
Ninos, Anthony (D)
Nuckolls, Hugh Paul (R)
Ogden, Carl (D)
Ogle, Ellen Knight (R)
Pajcic, Steve (D)
Papy, Charles C, Jr (D)
Pauly, Helen (D)
Pawley, William Douglas (R)
Peaden, R W (D)
Pepper, Claude (D)
Peterson, Curtis (D)
Peterson, James Hardin (D)
Petit, Michael Donald (D)
Phillips, Elizabeth Reed (D)
Pickett, Thomas Augustus (D)
Plante, Kenneth A (R)
Poole, Van B (R)
Poorbaugh, Jack Morgan (R)
Poston, Ralph R, Sr (D)
Prentiss, William Clark (D)
Price, Richard A (Dick) (R)
Rado, Stuart Alan (D)
Redman, James L (D)
Reed, Nathaniel Pryor (R)
Renick, Richard Randolph (D)
Rice, John S (D)
Richard, Barry Scott (D)
Richmond, Ronald R (Ron) (R)
Riherd, Hubert Milton (D)
Rish, William J (Billy Joe) (D)
Robbie, Joseph, Jr (D)
Roberts, B K (D)
Robinson, Grover C, III (D)
Robinson, Jane W (R)
Robsion, John Marshall, Jr (R)
Rodriguez, Jeanne E (R)
Rogers, Paul Grant (D)
Rose, Stuart Paul (D)
Rottmann, Fred Edward (R)
Rountree, William M
Rubenfeld, Abby Rose (D)
Rude, Arthur Herman (R)
Ryals, John L (D)
Sabel, Joseph H (D)
Sackett, Walter W, Jr (D)
Salfi, Dominick J (R)
Saunders, Robert L, Jr (Bob) (D)
Sayler, Henry B, Jr (R)
Scarborough, Dan Irving (D)
Shaffer, Kenneth Woods (R)
Shank, Clare Brown (Williams) (R)
Sharpe, William Joseph, Jr (D)
Sheldon, George H (D)
Shevin, Robert Lewis (D)
Shirley, Landona Hortense (D)
Sikes, Robert L F (D)
Simmons, John Dale (R)
Sims, Walter (R)
Sinclair, Larry Ray (D)

FLORIDA (cont)

Singleton, Mary L (D)
Sisser, Eric Ronald (D)
Skinner, Sherrill N (Pete) (D)
Skipper, Marguerite Stewart (D)
Smathers, Bruce Armistead (D)
Smathers, George Armistead (D)
Smiles, Leon (D)
Smith, Dewey Edward (D)
Smith, Donald Eugene (R)
Smith, Eric (D)
Smith, Harold Kenneth (Bud) (D)
Smith, Thomas Edward (R)
Smith, Walter (D)
Southerland, James F (D)
Spicola, Guy William (D)
Stack, Edward J (R)
Stansfield, Mary Jo (D)
Steinberg, Paul B (D)
Stembridge, John Madison (D)
Stewart, Susan Hastings (R)
Stolzenburg, Chester W (R)
Stone, Richard Bernard (Dick) (D)
Taffer, Jack J (D)
Tally, Lou (D)
Tatum, Waugantha Grady (Tut) (D)
Taylor, Paul Worden, Jr (R)
Taylor, William M (R)
Terry, James William (R)
Thomas, Jerry (D)
Thomas, Jon C (R)
Thomas, L E (Tommy) (R)
Thomas, Pat Franklin (D)
Thompson, Denham Michael Burgess (Mike) (R)
Thompson, James Harold (D)
Thornton, James Ronald (R)
Tillman, Jim King (R)
Tillman, Mayre Lutha (D)
Tobiassen, Thomas Johan (R)
Tolton, Jere (D)
Trask, Alan (D)
Tucker, Donald L (D)
Turnbull, William S (D)
Tyner, Mayme (R)
Vaile, Victor Edward, III (R)
Van de Water, Margaret Smith (D)
Vogt, John W (D)
Wadsworth, Herbert Robinson, Jr (D)
Walker, Jo-Ann Grout (R)
Walker, Shirley Lowe (D)
Warden, William F, Jr (Bill) (D)
Ware, John Thomas (R)
Waterman, Jeremiah Colwell (R)
Watson, Wendell H (D)
Wells, Jacquelyn Quinn (R)
West, Erceil Ellen (D)
Whidden, Vincent Yale (D)
Whiteacre, Charles A (D)
Williams, Frank (D)
Williams, J H (D)
Williamson, George Arthur (R)
Wills, Robert Roy (R)
Wilson, Anne Chapman (R)
Wilson, Lori (Independent)
Wilson, Roger H (R)
Winn, Sherman S (D)
Yancey, Earl Lester (D)
Young, C W Bill (R)
Young, GeDelle Brabham (D)
Young, Patricia Anne (D)
Young, Walter C (D)
Yungkans, Monnie Jesselyn (D)
Zinkil, William G, Sr (D)

GEORGIA

Adams, George Drayton, Jr (D)
Adams, John W (D)
Adams, Marvin (D)
Alexander, William Henry (D)
Allen, Nora Alice (R)
Allison, Pamela Ann (R)
Alsobrook, Henry Herman (R)
Altman, James Eston (R)
Amos, William George (R)
Anderson, Gerald Von, Jr (D)
Arnall, Ellis Gibbs (D)
Bailey, Frank I (D)
Baker, Margaret Presley (D)
Ballard, William Donaldson (D)
Ballew, Robert King (D)
Banister, Bette M (R)
Banks, Patrick (D)
Banks, Peter Louis (D)
Bargeron, Emory E (D)
Barker, Ed (D)
Barnes, Roy E (D)
Barre, Laura Kohlman (D)
Bates, Sturgis Goodwin, III (D)
Battle, Joe (D)
Baugh, James Emory (D)
Baugh, Wilbur E (D)
Beck, James M (D)
Beckham, Robert Culp (R)
Bell, Robert Hudson (R)
Bentley, Timothy Edward (Tim) (D)
Bernier, Lee Gerard (R)
Berry, Charles Edward (D)
Bishop, Henry Samuel (D)
Bishop, James A (D)
Blackburn, Ben B (R)
Blackshear, Jesse (D)
Blanchard, James Lendsay (R)
Blanks, William Francis (D)
Bolster, Paul (D)
Bolton, Arthur Key (D)
Bond, Julian (D)
Booth, James C, Jr (D)
Bowman, James A (D)
Bramblett, Sandra Gail (D)
Branch, Marsha Baker (D)
Brantley, Haskew Hawthorne, Jr (R)
Bray, Claude A, Jr (D)
Brewer, John Robert (D)
Brinkley, Jack Thomas (D)
Broome, Dean Carl (D)
Broun, Paul C (D)
Brown, Benjamin D (D)
Brown, Jesse Frances (D)
Brown, Martin Parks (D)
Buck, Thomas Bryant, III (D)
Burson, William H (Bill) (D)
Burt, Addison Moore (R)
Burton, Joe (R)
Burton, Thomas Lawson (R)
Busbee, George D (D)
Butler, Joseph Hardwick (R)
Caldwell, Johnnie L (D)
Calhoun, Anne C (R)
Callaway, Howard Hollis (R)
Campbell, Clarence Grady, Jr (R)
Campbell, James Philander, Jr (R)
Cargile, Richard Franklin (R)
Carlisle, John Reid (D)
Carnes, Charles L (D)
Carr, Thomas Caswell (D)
Carr, William Pitts (D)
Carrell, Bobby (D)
Carter, Hugh A (D)
Carter, Jack Wilkes (D)
Carter, James Earl, Jr (D)
Carter, John William (D)
Carver, William Bryan, Jr (D)
Cary, Ashton Hall (R)
Casey, Joseph T (R)
Cason, Gary Carlton (R)
Cato, L E (D)
Cauble, Florence Horkan (R)
Cauble, John A (R)
Chambers, William Clyde (R)
Chambless, Thomas Sidney (D)
Chance, George (D)
Cheek, Earl Herman, Sr (D)
Childers, Eugene M (D)
Childs, Peggy (D)
Childs, T Allen, Jr (D)
Clardy, George L (R)
Clark, Betty Jean (D)
Clark, Fred Stephen (D)
Clark, Louis M (D)
Clements, Charles McCall, III (R)
Clifton, A D (D)
Clifton, Margie (D)
Cole, Jack H (D)
Cole, James William (D)
Coleman, Terry L (D)
Collins, Marcus (D)
Colwell, Carlton (D)
Connell, Jack (D)
Cook, Patsy Haines (D)
Cooper, Bill (D)
Cooper, Homer Chassell (D)
Cosby, Curtis R (D)
Coulter, Raymond Curtis (R)
Coverdell, Paul D (R)
Covington, Dean (D)
Cowman, William Henry (Bill) (D)
Cox, Walter E (D)
Crawford, Abbott Linton (D)
Culpepper, Bryant (D)
Darby, Lloyd Hubert, III (R)
Daugherty, J C (D)
Davidson, William John (R)
Davis, Ernest Burroughs (Independent)
Davis, Flint (D)
Davis, John W (D)
Davis, Jordan Ray (R)
Davis, Walter Lamar (R)
Dean, Douglas C (D)
Dean, Henry Lamar (R)
Dean, Nathan D (D)
Dean, Roscoe Emory, Jr (D)
Deas, Stephen Cantrell, Jr (R)
Dent, R A (D)
Dewald, Gretta Moll (D)
Dickey, Grady (D)
Dillard, George Douglas (D)
Dixon, Harry Donival (D)
Dockins, Randi Torgesen (R)
Doss, Samuel Welch, Jr (D)
Dover, J Michael (D)
Dover, William J (D)
Drew, Jack Hunter (D)
Duncan, J Ebb (D)
Duncan, Laton Earl (D)
Earnheart, E Dane (D)
Edwards, Charles Wade (Chuck) (D)
Edwards, Julian Ward (D)
Edwards, Ward (D)
Egan, Michael Joseph (R)
Eizenstat, Stuart Elliot (D)
Elder, David Mayne (D)
Eldridge, Frank, Jr (D)
Elliott, Ewell H (Hank), Jr (R)
Elliott, Tyron Clifford (R)
Epps, William Douglas (R)
Evans, Billy L (D)
Evans, Warren D (D)
Ezzard, Clarence Gray (D)
Farrell, Phyllis Chase (D)
Farrell, Thomas Francis (D)
Felton, Dorothy Wood (R)
Ferst, Jeanne Rolfe (R)
Fincher, W W, Jr (D)
Fitzpatrick, Mark William (R)
Flynt, John J (D)
Fortson Ben W, Jr (D)
Foster, Danny O'Neil (D)
Foster, Eckord Lewis (D)
Foster, John Clayton (D)
Foster, Paul W (D)
Foster, R L (D)
Foster, Roy Guylus, Jr (R)
Fowler, James Darwin (R)
Fraser, Donald H (D)
Frazier, Caroline Hollingsworth (R)
Fuqua, J B (D)
Galbraith, Samuel G (D)
Gambrell, David Henry (D)
Gamel, Jack F (R)
Gammage, Olin Lynn, Jr (D)
Gardner, Jay D (R)
Garrard, Ed (D)
Gay, Carlus Delmas, Jr (D)
Gehl, Carolyn Gilmore (D)
Gibson, Pete Jones (D)
Gignilliat, Arthur (D)
Gilbert, Robert Bacon, Jr (D)
Gillis, Carl L, Jr (R)
Gillis, Hugh Marion (D)
Gilreath, Rowan (D)
Ginn, Ronald Bryan (Bo) (D)
Ginsberg, Ronald Erwin (D)
Glanton, Thomas Pettis (D)
Glover, Mildred (D)
Glover, Thomas Eugene, Jr (R)
Goldstein, Maxine Shapiro (D)
Goode, James Waltom (R)
Gordy, A Perry, Jr (R)
Grant, Maynor Camp (D)
Grantham, Don Anthony (D)
Gray, James H (D)
Greenholtz, Herbert Thomas, Jr (R)
Greer, John W (D)
Gregory, Hardy, Jr (D)
Grice, Benning Moore (D)
Griffin, Samuel Marvin (D)
Grogan, Lee R (D)
Groover, Denmark, Jr (D)
Gunnells, Joel B (D)
Gunter, William B (D)
Hagan, G Elliott (D)
Hall, Robert Howell (Independent)
Ham, Benson (D)
Hamilton, Grace T (D)
Hamilton, Hubert Earl (Bert), Jr (D)
Hamilton, James Ralph (Duck) (D)
Hamilton, Thomas DeWayne (D)
Hammonds, Richard Lee, Sr (D)
Harcourt, H Baxter (D)
Harden, Eston A (D)
Harden, Ross Ullman (D)
Harris, B B, Sr (D)
Harris, J G (Sonny) (D)
Harris, Joe Frank (D)
Harris, Wade (D)
Harrison, Carl (R)
Harrison, James Edward, III (R)
Hatcher, Charles (D)
Hawes, Peyton Samuel, Jr (D)
Hawkins, John Morgan (D)
Heard, Roland Shaefer (D)
Hembree, George Ray (D)
Henkel, Lee H, Jr (R)
Herring, Robert F (D)
Hester, William H (R)

GEORGIA / 1041

Hicks, Carlton Turner (D)
Hill, Bobby L (D)
Hill, Charles Elliott (D)
Hill, Guy F (R)
Hill, Render (D)
Hitt, Mary Barton (D)
Hodges, J Alex (R)
Holley, Rudolph Eugene (D)
Holliman, Margaret Cloud (R)
Holloway, Albert Weston (D)
Holm, Charles R, Jr (D)
Holmes, Robert A (D)
Hooper, Thomas Bertron (D)
Horton, Gerald Talmadge (D)
Horton, Seab Sanford, Jr (R)
Housley, Grady Eugene (D)
Howard, G Robert (D)
Howard, Pierre, Jr (D)
Howell, Albert S (D)
Howell, William Mobley (D)
Hubert, Richard Norman (D)
Hudgins, Floyd (D)
Hudson, Eugene Talmadge (Ted) (D)
Hudson, Perry J (D)
Hughes, Maxwell Vernon (D)
Hurst, Eddie Durden (D)
Hutchinson, Richard Shirley (D)
Hydrick, Bob Durrett (R)
Irvin, Jack (D)
Irvin, Robert Andrew (R)
Irvin, Thomas Telford (D)
Irwin, John R (D)
Jackson, Clyde Wilson (Sonny) (D)
Jackson, Jerry Dwayne (D)
Jackson, John W (D)
Jackson, Maynard Holbrook (D)
Jenkins, Edgar Lanier (D)
Jernigan, Wallace Lawson (D)
Jessup, Ben F, Sr (D)
Johnson, Bobby Ware (D)
Johnson, Gerald Lynn (D)
Johnson, Leroy Reginald (D)
Johnson, Roger (D)
Johnson, Rudolph (D)
Johnson, Thomas Stephen (D)
Jones, G Paul, Jr (R)
Jones, Herbert, Jr (R)
Jones, Milton (D)
Jordan, Hugh (D)
Kaler, Irving K (D)
Karrh, Randolph C (D)
Kennedy, Joseph Everett (D)
Keyton, James W (D)
Kicklighter, Harris Wilbur (D)
Kidd, Edwards Culver (D)
Kiley, Ann Sue (D)
Kilgore, Thomas M (D)
King, John Allen (Jack) (D)
Kirbo, Charles (D)
Knapp, G Edward (R)
Knight, Nathan G (D)
Kopp, John Glenwright (R)
Kreeger, George H (D)
Lambert, Ezekiel Roy (D)
Landrum, Phillip Mitchell (D)
Lane, Dick (R)
Lane, W Jones (D)
Langford, George Adams (D)
Langford, James Beverly (D)
Larsen, George Keefe (R)
Larsen, W W, Jr (D)
Lawson, Hugh (D)
LeCraw, Julian (R)
Lee, William J (Bill) (D)
Lee, William Spencer (D)
Leggett, Gene (D)
Leonard, Gerald (D)
Leslein, Betty Jean Swayne (D)
Lester, James Luther (D)

Leverette, Gigi (D)
Levitas, Elliott Harris (D)
Lewis, Cloatee Arnold (D)
Lewis, Preston Brooks, Jr (D)
Linder, John E (R)
Linzey, Bobby Lee (D)
Logan, Hugh (D)
Long, Bobby (D)
Low, Norman C, Jr (D)
Lucas, David E (D)
Lucas, Mary Louisa (D)
Mabry, Herbert H (D)
Maddox, Lester G (D)
Mann, Charles C (D)
Marcus, Sidney J (D)
Martin, Carol Lahman (R)
Martin, Talmage McKinley, Jr (R)
Massell, Sam (D)
Mathis, Enoch Douglas (D)
Mathis, M Dawson (D)
Matthews, Dorsey Rudolph (D)
Matthews, Robert Chappelle (D)
Mattingly, Mack Francis (R)
Mays, Troy A (R)
McAfee, Lilian Foote (R)
McCollum, T Hayward (D)
McCorkel, Zack Reshess (D)
McCutchen, Pleasant Theodore (Pat) (D)
McCutcheon, Chester M (R)
McDonald, Lauren Wylie, Jr (Bubba) (D)
McDonald, Lawrence Patton (D)
McDowell, Henry (D)
McDuffie, E M (Pete) (D)
McGill, Sam P (D)
McKenney, Frank Meath (D)
McKibben, Jadie Clifford (D)
McKinney, J E (D)
McVey, Lauder Tully (R)
McVey, Walter Lewis, Jr (D)
Meroney, Clifford Clinton (D)
Mickle, Jack Pearson (D)
Miles, Bernard (R)
Milford, William Doyle (D)
Miller, Estelle Lee (R)
Miller, Zell Bryan (D)
Minge, Jerry Lee (D)
Mobley, Carlton
Morgan, Jack H (D)
Morris, Archie J (R)
Morris, Burlene (D)
Moshier, Terry Allen (R)
Moss, Truett W (R)
Mostiler, John L (D)
Mullinax, Edwin G (D)
Munford, Dillard (R)
Murphy, Thomas Bailey (D)
Murrah, William Nolan, Jr (R)
Nelson, James Frederick, Jr (D)
Nessmith, Paul Edward, Sr (D)
Newby, Olin Carris (D)
Nichols, Michael Cooper (D)
Nix, Kenneth Owen (R)
Noble, Bill (D)
Nunn, Sam (D)
Oglesby, Catherine Elizabeth (R)
O'Keeffe, Whitney Carter (R)
O'Neal, John Barnwell (R)
O'Neal, Maston Emmett, Jr (D)
Orr, Wilson Fred, II (D)
Overby, Howard Thomas (D)
Owens, Ray D (D)
Oxford, Charles Oliver (D)
Padgett, Dorothy B (D)
Pagel, John Theodore (R)
Palmer, Dwight Wendell (R)

Parham, Bobby Eugene (D)
Parkman, Ralph M (D)
Parrish, John Edgar, Jr (Johnny) (D)
Passmore, Cecil, Jr (D)
Patten, Grover C (D)
Patten, Robert L (D)
Patton, Elbert Earl, Jr (R)
Pearce, H Norwood (D)
Peavy, James Edwin (R)
Perry, Eldridge Wells (D)
Persons, Oscar Newton (R)
Peters, Robert G (D)
Peters, William Cooper (D)
Petro, George (R)
Phillips, L L (D)
Phillips, Lewis Milton (D)
Phillips, Parris Jerome (D)
Phillips, R T (Tom) (R)
Phillips, Ralph Boyd (D)
Phillips, Watson Randolph (D)
Pilcher, James Brownie (D)
Pinckney, Kathleen Weldon (Kay) (D)
Pinkston, Frank Chapman (D)
Plunkett, Connie Berg (D)
Poitevint, Alec Loyd, II (R)
Pool, Russell Frank (R)
Popham, Benjamin Eugene (D)
Powell, C Clayton (R)
Powell, Herbert B (Independent)
Price, James Hoyt (D)
Prichard, W M (R)
Prince, Jack Alexander (R)
Pruitt, Glyndon C (D)
Rainey, Howard (D)
Ralston, David Edmund (R)
Randall, William Clarence (D)
Ray, George E (D)
Reaves, Henry L (D)
Replogle, James Walter, Jr (R)
Reynolds, Steve (D)
Rhodes, Thomas Wallace (D)
Richardson, Eleanor L (D)
Riley, John R (D)
Roberts, Sharron Dale (D)
Roberts, Terry Lee (R)
Robertson, John Otho, Jr (R)
Robinson, W Lee (D)
Rodgers, Kenneth David (R)
Rogers, John Richard (D)
Rooks, James Orville (R)
Ross, Ben Barron (D)
Rousakis, John Paul (D)
Rush, Dewey Davent (D)
Rushton, Robert Archie (D)
Rusk, Dean (D)
Russell, Henry Phillip, Jr (D)
Russell, John Davidson (D)
Russell, Walter Brown, Jr (D)
Saeger, Richard Thomas (D)
Sams, H William, Jr (R)
Sanders, Carl Edward (D)
Sawyer, Forrest Lamar (R)
Scarborough, Franklin A (R)
Scarborough, Homer M, Jr (D)
Scott, David (D)
Scott, Thomas Leslie (D)
Scott, William Earl (D)
Shanahan, Tom L (D)
Shapard, Virginia (D)
Shaw, Robert Jennings (R)
Sheats, Sam (D)
Shorter, Ben T (D)
Sigman, Bobby (D)
Simpkins, William John (D)
Sizemore, Earleen Wilkerson (D)
Smalley, Carolyn Wynn (R)
Smalley, James L (D)
Smith, Cecilia Travis (R)
Smith, J R (D)

Smith, Kyle Dugar, Jr (D)
Smith, Marilu Crafton (R)
Smith, Sam Croft (D)
Smith, Virlyn B (R)
Smyre, Calvin (D)
Snider, Freddie Rembert (R)
Snow, Thomas Wayne, Jr (D)
Spinks, Ford Belmont (D)
Stanley, Ronald Eugene (R)
Starnes, Richard L, Jr (D)
Starr, Terrell (D)
Steis, William Burton (D)
Stephens, Jack LeRol (D)
Stephens, Robert Grier, Jr (D)
Stone, R Bayne (D)
Stroup, Mark James (D)
Stuart, James Glover (D)
Stuckey, Williamson Sylvester, Jr (D)
Stumbaugh, Lawrence (Bud) (D)
Summers, Everett Gary (D)
Sutton, Franklin (D)
Sutton, Glenn Wallace (D)
Swearingen, Edward Hicks (R)
Sweat, Ottis (D)
Taggart, Tom (D)
Talmadge, Herman Eugene (D)
Tanksley, M Hollis (R)
Tate, Horace Edward (D)
Taylor, Lucy Liddle (R)
Teague, Leeman Ambrose (D)
Thomason, Boyd (D)
Thompson, Albert William (D)
Thompson, Charlotte L (R)
Thompson, Joe (D)
Thompson, S Fletcher (R)
Thurman, John Howard (R)
Thurman, Marjorie Clark (D)
Timmons, Jimmy Hodge (D)
Tolbert, Tommy (R)
Toles, Elwin Bonds (D)
Tomlinson, Sherman Drawdy (D)
Townsend, Kiliaen Van Rensselaer (D)
Traylor, Mell Randolph (D)
Tribble, Joseph James (R)
Triplett, Tom (D)
Trotter, William Perry (D)
Troutman, Frank, Jr (R)
Trubey, Mary Sybil (D)
Tucker, Ray M (D)
Tumlin, George W (D)
Turner, Edward Louis (D)
Turner, Kenneth L (R)
Turner, Loyce Warren (D)
Twiggs, Ralph (D)
Tysinger, James W (R)
Vancel, Tom (R)
Vann, Frank Cochran (D)
Vaughan, Cola M (D)
Vaughn, Clarence Roland, Jr (D)
Waddle, Ted W (R)
Wade, Billy C (R)
Wade, Thomas Rogers (D)
Walker, Larry C (D)
Wall, Clarence Vinson (D)
Wallace, William Melton, Jr (D)
Waller, Samuel Carpenter (D)
Walling, Robert H (D)
Walters, Edward Enzor (D)
Wardlow, Floyd H, Jr (D)
Ware, James Crawford (D)
Warren, George Thomas, II (R)
Watkins, Richard Wright, Jr (D)
Watson, Roy H, Jr (D)
Weltner, Charles Longstreet (D)
West, James Paschal (R)

GEORGIA (cont)

Whaley, Leo Jackson (R)
Wheeler, Bobby A (D)
Wheeler, James Walter (D)
White, Charles Cody (D)
White, John (D)
Whitmire, Doug (D)
Williams, Hosea Lorenzo (D)
Williams, Melba Ruth (D)
Williams, Nat McDonald, Jr (D)
Williamson, George (R)
Wilson, Homer L (D)
Wilson, Joe Mack (D)
Wind, Herbert Hamilton, Jr (D)
Wood, Joe T (D)
Woodard, Howard Chambless (R)
Woodrum, Donald Lee (D)
Young, Andrew (D)
Young, Martin (D)
Zinn, Jane Marshall (R)

HAWAII

Abe, Kazuhisa (D)
Abercrombie, Neil (D)
Ajifu, Ralph K (R)
Akizaki, Clarence Yasuo (D)
Amaral, Alvin Theodore (D)
Amemiya, Ronald Yoshihiko (D)
Anderson, D G (Andy) (R)
Ariyoshi, George Ryoichi (D)
Beppu, Tadao (D)
Bitterman, Mary G F (D)
Blair, Russell (D)
Brennan, Edward (R)
Carroll, John S (R)
Carson, Robert Trebor (R)
Cayetano, Benjamin Jerome (D)
Chikasuye, Clesson Y (D)
Ching, Donald D H (D)
Chong, Anson (D)
Clarke, George W (R)
Cobb, Stephen Henry (Steve) (D)
Constantino, Patrick Ronald (D)
Coray, Carla Winn (R)
Correa, Naomi Lokalia (D)
Cravalho, Elmer F (D)
Crossley, Randolph Allin (R)
Dang, Marvin Seck Chow (R)
DeDomenico, Paul Domenic (D)
Dillingham, Benjamin Franklin, II (R)
Doi, Nelson Kiyoshi (D)
Edwards, Richard G (R)
Ellis, David Lloyd (R)
Evans, Faith Patricia (R)
Farrington, Elizabeth Pruett (R)
Fasi, Frank Francis (D)
Fong, Hiram L, Jr (R)
Fong, Hiram Leong (R)
Forbes, Eureka Bernice (R)
Fritschel, Ted C (D)
Fu, Sing (R)
Garcia, Richard (D)
George, Mary (R)
Gilkey, Robert C (D)
Glatzer, Hal (D)
Hakoda, Dan Shimao (R)
Hara, Stanley Ikuo (D)
Henderson, Richard (R)
Henrickson, George (R)
Hirabara, Minoru (D)
Ho, Richard Chung Sing (D)
Hulten, John James (D)

Ikeda, Donna Rika (R)
Inaba, Minoru (D)
Inouye, Daniel Ken (D)
Johnston, Edward Elliott (R)
Kamaka, Hiram K (D)
Kamalii, Kinau Boyd (R)
Kanbara, Bertram T (D)
Kawakami, Richard A (D)
Kawasaki, Duke (D)
Kihano, Daniel James (D)
Kim, Kenam (D)
Kimura, Robert Yutaka (D)
King, Jean Sadako (D)
Kiyabu, Ken S (D)
Kobayashi, Bert Takaaki (D)
Koga, George M (D)
Kondo, Ronald Yoneo (D)
Konishi, Alan S (D)
Kunimura, Tony T (D)
Kuroda, Joseph Toshiyuki (D)
Larsen, Jack Lucas (R)
Lee, Kenneth K L (D)
Leopold, John Robinson (R)
Levinson, Bernard Hirsh (D)
Low, Daniel Tien Kee (R)
Luce, Clare Boothe (R)
Lunasco, Oliver Patrick (D)
Lynde, Allison Howard (D)
Machida, Gerald Kiyoyuku (D)
Matsunaga, Spark Masayuki (D)
McClung, David Charles (D)
Medeiros, John J (R)
Mink, Patsy Takemoto (D)
Minn, Momi Pearl (D)
Mirikitani, Carl Kunio (R)
Miyake, Will Edward (R)
Mizuguchi, Norman (D)
Molina, Matilda (D)
Morioka, Ted T (D)
Morioka, Vince Matthews (R)
Naito, Lisa (D)
Nakatsuka, Lawrence Kaoru (R)
Nishimura, Donald S (D)
Norrell, Catherine Dorris (D)
O'Connor, Dennis (D)
Oda, Howard Kazumi (R)
Okada, Hideo (D)
Pacarro, Rudolph (D)
Peters, Henry H (D)
Poepoe, Andrew Keliikuniaupuni (R)
Rice, Virgil Thomas (R)
Rodby, Leo Bernard, Jr (D)
Roehrig, Stanley Herbert (D)
Rohlfing, Frederick W (R)
Saiki, Patricia (R)
Sakima, Akira (D)
Santos, Velma McWayne (R)
Shafer, Esther Virginia (R)
Shito, Mitsuo (D)
Soares, Wilfred (Buddy) (R)
Spalding, Philip Edmunds, Jr (R)
Spray, Elwin L (R)
Stanley, Kathleen Goold (D)
Sutton, Richard Carpenter (Ike) (R)
Suwa, Jack K (D)
Taira, Norman Takeo (D)
Taira, Robert S (D)
Takamine, Yoshito (D)
Takamura, Carl T (D)
Takitani, Henry T (D)
Takushi, Tokuichi (D)
Tanaka, Francis Torao (D)
Tesh, Sylvia Noble (D)
Thompson, Bernard Gale (D)
Toyofuku, George Hiroshi (D)
Uechi, Mitsuo (D)
Ushijima, Charles T (D)
Ushijima, John T (D)

Wakatsuki, James Hiroji (D)
Waterhouse, Olga (R)
Wong, Francis Alvin (D)
Wong, Richards S H (D)
Yamada, Dennis Roy (D)
Yamasaki, Mamoru (D)
Yap, Ted (D)
Yee, Wadsworth (R)
Yim, T C (D)
Young, Patsy Kikue (D)
Yuen, Jann L (D)

IDAHO

Abbott, James (D)
Abrahams, W Dean (R)
Adams, Nelda (R)
Allen, John Joseph, Jr (R)
Andersen, Rudy A (R)
Andrus, Cecil D (D)
Antone, Steve (R)
Barker, John M (R)
Barnes, Verda White (D)
Barron, Charles Lee (R)
Batt, Phillip E (R)
Bauer, Lois Darlene (R)
Bauer, Richard L (R)
Bilyeu, Charles Edward (Chick) (D)
Bistline, Beverly Barbara (D)
Blick, Benny George (R)
Bowler, Orson Lloyd (R)
Bozzuto, Victor J (D)
Brackett, Noy E (R)
Branson, Dale R (D)
Brassey, Vernon K (R)
Braun, Carl P (D)
Brink, Randall Wilson (R)
Brooks, John H (R)
Brooks, Mary Elizabeth (R)
Brown, Bob M (D)
Budge, Reed William (R)
Bunting, Peggy (R)
Butler, William Daniel (D)
Cayford, Weston Lloyd (Wes) (R)
Cenarrusa, Peter Thomas (R)
Chase, Cyril Charles (D)
Chase, Gary C (R)
Chatburn, J Vard (R)
Christensen, J Lloyd (D)
Church, Frank (D)
Clements, Maurice L (R)
Clemm, Lester V (R)
Cobbs, Lyle Richard (R)
Condie, Angus R (R)
Cooper, John W (D)
Craig, Jack A (R)
Craig, Larry Edwin (R)
Crapo, Terry LaVelle (R)
Crupper, Gordon (R)
Curtis, Dennis Rex (D)
Danielson, George G (R)
Davidson, Marion (D)
Dean, Carroll W (R)
Dobler, Norma Mae (D)
Donaldson, Charles Russell (Non-Partisan)
Donart, James B (D)
Eardley, Richard Roy
Egbert, Richard Alexander (D)
Ellsworth, James (R)
Emery, Dan D (D)
English, Eleanor Jean (D)
Eriksen, Lu Dean (D)
Erkins, Robert Alter (R)
Evans, John Victor (D)
Favor, Bonnie Alvina (R)
Fitz, Herbert George (R)
Fitzwater, Beth Thomas (R)
Fuller, Wayne P (D)

Gines, Ralph Junior (R)
Goff, Abe McGregor (R)
Gould, Gary Howard (D)
Gurnsey, Kathleen W (Kitty) (D)
Hale, Ernest A (R)
Hammond, F Melvin (D)
Hancock, Nolan Ward (D)
Hansen, Betty Ann (D)
Hansen, George Vernon (R)
Hansen, Orval Howard (R)
Hanson, Leo Olin (R)
Harding, Ralph Ray (D)
Harlow, Ronald V (D)
Harris, A Deon (R)
Hartvigsen, Lester A (D)
Healy, Ellen (D)
Hedlund, Emery E (D)
High, Richard S (R)
Hoene, Paulette Louise (R)
Hollifield, Gordon R (R)
Hosack, Robert E (D)
Hower, Ward (D)
Humphrey, Howard (D)
Hunter, Connie Maureen (R)
Infanger, Ray E (R)
Infelt, Jim (D)
Ingalls, James W (D)
Ingram, Gary John (R)
Jackson, Larry (R)
Jardine, Susan Kim (D)
Johnson, Byron Jerald (D)
Johnson, Kurt L (R)
Johnson, S Albert (D)
Johnston, William James (R)
Jordan, Leonard Beck (R)
Judd, Claud R (D)
Kane, Charles Baird, Jr (D)
Kautz, Mary E (R)
Kearnes, Elaine (R)
Kennevick, Jack C (R)
Kidwell, Wayne Le Roy (R)
Kiebert, Kermit V (D)
Kinghorn, Robert C (D)
Kingsford, Leonard O (R)
Klein, Edith Miller (R)
Kneeland, George Royal (R)
Koch, Henry Ferd (R)
Koch, Karl E (D)
Kramer, Douglas Duane (R)
Kraus, Virgil L (R)
Krebs, Irene Morris (R)
Kress, Stanley Robert (D)
LaChance, Craig Robert (D)
Lanting, William John (R)
Larsen, Allan F (R)
Larson, Curtis Dey (R)
Lassen, Arne F (R)
Laverty, Betty Clark (D)
Lengerich, Madonna Andrea (R)
Leroy, Steven Harry (D)
Lewis, B E (Bud) (R)
Lineberger, Lawrence M (D)
Ling, Roger D (R)
Linville, Robert G, Jr (R)
Little, Bradley Jay (R)
Little, David (R)
Little, Duane Ewing (D)
Little, Walter E (R)
Manley, Art (D)
Maynard, Don (D)
McCann, Dorothy H (D)
McCarter, Joe T (R)
McClure, James A (R)
McDermott, Patricia L (D)
McHan, E V (R)
McKinney, Helen Mathews (R)
McMurray, John Odell (R)
McQuade, Henry F
McReynolds, Elizabeth Sanford (R)
Merrill, W Israel (D)

Miller, C Wendell (D)
Miller, Dean E (D)
Miner, Doyle C (R)
Miner, Marjorie M (R)
Mitchell, Mike P (D)
Mitchell, Thomas (R)
Mix, Shirley V (R)
Moon, Marjorie Ruth (D)
Morgan, Mel (D)
Morken, Edwin Duane, Jr (R)
Munger, Morgan (R)
Munroe, David A (R)
Murphy, Arthur Powell (D)
Murphy, Jack M (R)
Neider, C W (R)
Neitzel, Angie (D)
Niswander, Calvin Elroy (R)
O'Donnell, William James, Jr (D)
Olmstead, Ralph E (R)
Olsen, Dennis M (R)
Onweiler, William C (R)
Otter, C L (Butch) (R)
Park, William Anthony (D)
Payton, Willis Osborne (D)
Pearson, Lorentz Clarence (D)
Peavey, John Thomas (R)
Peters, Delbert Dean (R)
Peterson, Martin Lynn (D)
Povlsen, Shirley (R)
Purce, Thomas Leslie (D)
Rambeau, Ione (D)
Rammell, Arthur Leon (Art) (D)
Reardon, John F (R)
Redford, Mack Andy (R)
Reed, Audra Knox (D)
Reid, Harold W (R)
Reynolds, Dorothy L (D)
Rice, Deckie M (D)
Rice, Edward William (R)
Richert, Carol Clouser (D)
Risch, James E (R)
Roberts, William (R)
Robson, Robert Morgan (R)
Rood, Edwin Cyril (Cy) (R)
Rouyer, Alwyn R (D)
Samuelson, Don W (R)
Saxvik, Robert William (D)
Schaefer, Richard Max, Jr (D)
Schroeder, Rhea (R)
Scoresby, Clifford Norman (R)
Selander, Carolyn Whiteside (D)
Sessions, John O (R)
Shadduck, Louise (R)
Shepard, Allan G (R)
Sinclair, Orriette Coiner (R)
Smazal, Vincent August (D)
Smith, Dick (R)
Smith, Virginia Dorothy (R)
Smylie, Robert E (R)
Snow, Harold (R)
Snow, Orval M (D)
Snyder, Thomas Mathew (D)
Soumas, Tom Dan, Jr (R)
Spear, Clay Verne (R)
Spencer, Carmelita G (R)
Spencer, Craig Lemuel (R)
Stacey, Carol Horning (R)
Stafford, Ione Jordan (R)
Stanley, Stephen Charles (R)
Steen, James Wilson (R)
Stephens, Ronald LeMoyne (R)
Stewart, Joseph Alexander (Joe) (R)
Stivers, Thomas Walter (R)
Stoker, Roger C (R)
Strom, Shirley Longeteig (R)
Summers, H Dean (R)
Swenson, Leon Hughie (R)
Swenson, Severt, Jr (R)
Swisher, Perry (R)

Symms, Steven D (R)
Tacke, E H (Jack) (D)
Terra, Jean M (D)
Thompson, John Harmon (R)
Tibbitts, Wayne Everett (R)
Todd, Donald Glenn (R)
Twilegar, Ron Jess (D)
Vanderwall, Mary Elizabeth (R)
Wagner, Joseph Nicholas (D)
Warnick, David Christopher (R)
Waters, Errol T (D)
Watkins, Dane (R)
Watson, Robert Lorn (R)
Wegner, Glen Eugene (R)
Wesche, Percival A (R)
Westerberg, Russell A (R)
Wheeler, Ralph Merrill, Jr (R)
White, Kathleen Eleanor Elizabeth (D)
Wicks, Grace Jain (R)
Wilber, Roland C (R)
Williams, J Marsden (R)
Williams, Joseph Rulon (D)
Winchester, Lyman Gene (R)
Yarbrough, Walter Herman (R)
Yost, James Andrew (R)
Young, Tracey H (R)

ILLINOIS

Ackerman, Sam (D)
Adams, Don W (R)
Ahern, John Paul (D)
Akin, Edward B (D)
Allaman, Charles Lee (D)
Allen, Bradley E (D)
Anderson, Donald B (R)
Anderson, John B (R)
Andrews, Ruth T (R)
Annunzio, Frank (D)
Appelman, Mary Goold (D)
Archambault, Bennett (R)
Arends, Leslie C (R)
Arnell, Donald E (R)
Arvey, Jacob M (D)
Atchison, Christopher George (R)
Aurand, Douglas R (D)
Bafford, Hallie B (D)
Baner, Richard Martin (R)
Barnes, Eugene M (D)
Barnes, Jane M (R)
Barry, Tobias (D)
Beatty, John J (D)
Beaupre, Jack R (D)
Bell, James Farrell (R)
Belmonte, Frank Salvatore (D)
Bennett, Lowell E (R)
Berg, Earl Harold, Jr (R)
Berman, Arthur Leonard (D)
Berning, Karl I (R)
Bertrand, Joseph Gustaus (D)
Birchler, Vincent A (D)
Bishop, Cecil W (Runt) (R)
Black, Kenneth Wallace (R)
Black, Leona Roberson (D)
Blackorby, Lila Rose (R)
Blair, W Robert (R)
Blanek, Frank Joseph, Jr (D)
Bloom, Prescott E (R)
Blouin, Robert Richard (R)
Blume, Joyce Campbell (D)
Bluthardt, Edward Earl (R)
Blythe, Coy Daniel, Sr (R)
Bolger, William J (D)
Boose, Jerry Dale (R)
Borah, Dan V (R)
Borchers, Albert Webber (R)
Bower, Glen Landis (R)
Boyle, Kenneth Raymond (D)

Bradley, Gerald Allen (D)
Brandt, John B (D)
Brookhart, Samuel Henry (R)
Broverman, Robert Lee (D)
Brown, David Emerson (R)
Brown, Fred James (D)
Brummet, Donald Eugene (D)
Buckley, Sharon Albert (D)
Burditt, George Miller (R)
Bush, Golden Hartzell (R)
Bush, Gordon Dallon (D)
Bushnell, Mary B (R)
Byers, Harold D (D)
Byrne, Emmet Francis (R)
Byrne, Jane (D)
Cadigan, Patrick J (D)
Cafferty, Pastora San Juan (D)
Caldwell, Lewis A H (D)
Calvo, Horace Lawrence (D)
Campbell, Charles M (Chuck) (R)
Cannon, Joe Wesley (R)
Capparelli, Ralph C (D)
Capuzi, Louis F (R)
Carlson, Clifford D (R)
Carroll, Howard William (D)
Carver, Richard E (R)
Casey, Dan (D)
Catania, Susan (R)
Chancey, C Ray (D)
Chapin, Dwight Lee (R)
Chapman, Eugenia Sheldon (D)
Chesney, Chester Anton (D)
Chew, Charles, Jr (D)
Childs, John Lawrence (Liberal)
Choate, Clyde L (D)
Church, Marguerite Stitt (R)
Cizek, Dolores Adele (D)
Clark, Elwin Nail (D)
Clarke, Terrel E (R)
Cleary, Patrick James (R)
Cloos, Duane George (D)
Coffey, Max E (D)
Coleman, Marion Wilford (D)
Collins, Cardiss W (D)
Collins, Catherine Mary (R)
Collins, Philip W (R)
Comfort, Thomas Edwin (D)
Coney, Jack Arthur (R)
Corbett, Jerry G (D)
Cornell, George (Tip) (D)
Coulson, Robert (R)
Course, Kenneth W (D)
Cowen, James Laurence (Independent)
Craig, Robert (Bob) (D)
Crane, Philip Miller (R)
Cryer, Clifford Eugene (R)
Cunningham, Roscoe D (R)
Cutler, Paul Harley (R)
Dalbey, Janet Carol (R)
Daley, Richard Joseph (D)
Damron, William Orville (R)
Daniels, Cary (D)
Daniels, Lee A (R)
D'Arco, John A, Jr (D)
Darrow, Clarence Allison (D)
Davidson, John A (R)
Davis, Corneal A (D)
Dean, Robert William
Deavers, Gilbert L (Gil) (R)
Demuzio, Vince (D)
Derge, David Richard (R)
Derwinski, Edward J (R)
Deuster, Donald Eugene (R)
DiPrima, Lawrence (D)
Dixon, Alan John (D)
Doerr, Ray E (R)
Donnewald, James H (D)
Dougherty, Daniel D (D)
Douglas, Paul H (D)
Dove, Franklin Edward (D)

Dove, Meredith Sayle (D)
Downen, Clifford LeRoy (R)
Downs, Robert K (D)
Dubin, Martin David (D)
Duff, Brian B (R)
Dunn, John F (D)
Dunn, Ralph (R)
Dyer, Mrs Robert C (Giddy) (R)
Ebbesen, Joseph B (R)
Egan, Robert Joseph (D)
Epton, Bernard E (R)
Ericson, Everett Farm (R)
Erkert, Roger William (R)
Erlenborn, John Neal (R)
Everett, Reynolds Melville (R)
Ewell, Raymond Whitney (D)
Ewing, Thomas W (R)
Falls, Arthur Joseph (R)
Farley, Bruce A (D)
Farrell, Joseph Aloysius, III
Fary, John G (D)
Fawell, Harris W (R)
Feehan, Thomas (R)
Feltner, Richard Lee (R)
Fennessey, Joseph (D)
Fetridge, William Harrison (R)
Feulner, Edwin John, Jr (R)
Findley, Paul (R)
Fisher, Melvin Leslie (R)
Fleck, Charles James, Jr (R)
Flinn, Monroe Lawrence (D)
Fonner, Paul E (Doc) (R)
Fraley, Vance Levoy (R)
Franklin, Golda Bridges (D)
Friedland, John E (R)
Friedrich, Dwight P (R)
Fulle, Floyd Theodore (R)
Gaines, Charles Ellis (R)
Gardner, Paul E (D)
Garmisa, Benedict (D)
Garrett, Ray, Jr (R)
Geo-Karis, Adeline Jay (R)
Getty, L Michael (D)
Gholson, Jerome Busler (D)
Gianulis, John Andrew (D)
Giglio, Frank (D)
Giorgi, E J (Zeke) (D)
Glass, Bradley M (R)
Gomien, John Richard (R)
Goodrich, Mary Lucile (R)
Gordon, Margaret Cohn (D)
Graham, John A (R)
Granata, Peter Charles (R)
Graubart, Judah Leon (D)
Graves, G Eugene (R)
Graves, Parker (R)
Gray, Kenneth J (D)
Greanias, Gus Thomas (R)
Gregory, Dick (People's Party)
Greiman, Alan J (D)
Griesheimer, Ronald E (R)
Hale, Joseph Robert (D)
Hall, Harber Homer (R)
Hall, John Emory (R)
Hall, Kenneth (D)
Hall, Tim L (D)
Halstead, Fred Wolf (Socialist Workers Party)
Hanahan, Thomas J (D)
Hanrahan, Robert P (R)
Hansen, Carl R (R)
Hargrett, Andrew Joshua (D)
Harris, William Cullen (R)
Harris, William Lee (D)
Harry, James F, Jr (R)
Hart, Richard Odum (D)
Hartigan, Neil F (D)
Haste, James Francis (R)
Hawkinson, John W (R)
Hayes, Roger W (R)
Heady, Marion Benjamin (R)
Hedlund, Marilou (D)

ILLINOIS (cont)

Heil, Wallace Lee (D)
Herrmann, Roland Arthur (R)
Hess, Lyndle William (R)
Hickey, Vivian Veach (D)
Hickman, Frederick (R)
Hill, John Jerome (Jack) (D)
Hillenbrand, Martin
Hirsch, Louis Raphael Joseph (D)
Hirschfeld, John Charles (R)
Hoellen, John James (R)
Hoffman, Gene Louis (R)
Hoffman, Ronald Kenneth (R)
Hoffman, Thomas Joseph (D)
Holderman, Samuel James (R)
Holewinski, Michael S (D)
Holloway, James D (R)
Houser, Thomas James (R)
Howlett, Michael J (D)
Hudson, George (Ray) (R)
Huff, Douglas, Jr (D)
Hurwitch, Robert Arnold
Hutar, Patricia (R)
Hyde, Henry John (R)
Hynes, Thomas C (D)
Ingersoll, Robert Stephen (R)
Ingram, John Watson (R)
Ingram, Robert L (D)
Inman, Mary Lou (Teddi) (R)
Irving, Don (D)
Ives, Timothy Read (D)
Ives, William Charles (R)
Jackson, James William (R)
Jacobs, Oral (Jake) (D)
Jaffe, Aaron (D)
Jenison, Edward Halsey (R)
Jensen, Geraldine Mary (D)
Jeppson, Jefford J (R)
Jesk, James Wilbert (D)
Jevitz, John Louis (R)
Johns, Gene (D)
Johnson, Larry Alan (D)
Johnston, Maureen (R)
Jones, Emil, Jr (D)
Jones, John David (R)
Jones, Marvin O (R)
Joseph, Maurice Franklin (D)
Joslin, Roger (R)
Joyce, Jerome J (D)
Kamber, Victor Samuel (R)
Kanter, Samuel A (R)
Karns, John M, Jr (D)
Katz, Harold A (D)
Keith, John Ray (D)
Keller, Charles F (D)
Kelly, Floyd Eugene (D)
Kelly, Richard F, Jr (D)
Kempiners, William Lee (R)
Kennedy, David Matthew (R)
Kennedy, Leland J (D)
Kenney, Virginia Banning (R)
Kent, Mary Lou (R)
Kenyon, Robert Curtis (D)
Kern, Helmuth F (R)
Killey, Ralph Allen (R)
Kilver, Wayne M (D)
Klosak, J Henry (R)
Knuppel, John Linebaugh (D)
Koch, Edward Herman (D)
Koch, Lester Donald (R)
Kosinski, Roman J (D)
Kozer, Ted (R)
Kozubowski, Walter S (D)
Kraus, Elmer J (R)
Krypel, Robert Joseph (D)
Kucharski, Edmund James (R)
Kuhle, Donald Lewis (D)
LaFleur, Leo D (R)
Lafontant, Jewel (R)
Landolt, Allan Francis (R)
Langford, Anna Riggs (D)
Latherow, Clifford Brandon (R)
Lauer, John R (R)
Laurino, William J (D)
Lechowicz, Thaddeus Stanley (D)
Leinenweber, Harry Daniel (R)
Lemke, LeRoy Walter (D)
Lennon, Arthur Thomas (R)
Leon, John F (D)
Lerner, Louis A (D)
Leverenz, Ted E (D)
Levi, Edward Hirsch
Libonati, Roland Victor (D)
Lindberg, George W (R)
Lindenmeyer, Paul Andrew (R)
Linton, Dwayne (D)
Londrigan, James T (D)
Lovitt, Craig Edward (D)
Lucas, Scott Wike (D)
Lucco, Joe Enrico (D)
Luft, Richard N (D)
Lundquist, Clarence Theodore (D)
Lundy, Joseph Raymond (D)
Lyons, Thomas G (D)
Macdonald, Virginia B (R)
Mack, Peter Francis, Jr (D)
Madigan, Edward R (R)
Madigan, Michael J (D)
Madison, Jesse D (D)
Mahar, William F (R)
Mahoney, Francis Xavier (D)
Mann, Robert E (D)
Maragos, Samuel C (D)
Markert, Louis A (R)
Marovitz, William A (R)
Martenson, David Louis (R)
Marti, Douglas (R)
Martin, Louis Emanuel (D)
Martin, Peggy Smith (D)
Masterson, Michael Jon (R)
Mattson, Catherine Marie (R)
Mautino, Richard A (D)
Mayhall, James Elwin (R)
Maynard, Richard Edwards (D)
Mays, Robert Alan (R)
Mazewski, Aloysius Alex (R)
McAuliffe, Roger P (R)
McAvoy, Walter (Babe) (R)
McBroom, Edward (R)
McCabe, James L (D)
McCarthy, Robert W (D)
McCaw, Charlotte Louise (R)
McClain, Michael F (D)
McClory, Robert (R)
McClure, James J, Jr (Non-Partisan)
McCormick, C L (R)
McCormick, Hope (R)
McCormick, William E (D)
McCourt, James P (R)
McCoy, Albert Denis (Non-partisan)
McEvilly, James Lawrence (D)
McGaw, Robert Walter (R)
McGrath, Daniel L (D)
McGrew, Finley (R)
McGrew, Samuel M (D)
McIver, Edgar Wilson (R)
McLaren, Richard Wellington (R)
McLellan, Robert (R)
McLendon, James Andrew (D)
McLoskey, Robert T (R)
McMaster, Arthur Thomas (R)
McPartlin, Robert F (D)
Merlo, John (D)
Merriam, Robert Edward (R)
Merritt, Tom (R)
Metcalfe, Ralph Harold (D)
Metz, C Barney (D)
Meyer, Armin Henry
Meyer, J Theodore (D)
Meyer, John Richard (Jack) (R)
Michel, Robert Henry (R)
Mikva, Abner J (D)
Miller, Peter J (R)
Miller, Thomas Henry (R)
Mills, Ellsworth Luther, II (R)
Minow, Newton Norman (D)
Mitchell, Dorothy Evadean (R)
Mitchell, George Trice (R)
Mitchell, James L (D)
Mitchler, Robert W (R)
Moculeski, Chester Francis (D)
Mohr, Howard R (R)
Moll, Otto Rudolph (R)
Molloy, Vincent E (R)
Moore, Don A (R)
Morris, Bill (D)
Mudd, Joseph Charles (D)
Mugalian, Richard Aram (D)
Mulcahey, Richard Thomas (D)
Murphy, Morgan Francis (D)
Murphy, William T (D)
Nardulli, Michael L (D)
Naylon, Richard William (D)
Neal, Earl (D)
Neff, Clarence Everett (R)
Netsch, Dawn Clark (D)
Neumann, Ray A (R)
Nevills, Willie L (R)
Newhouse, Richard H (D)
Nimrod, John J (R)
Nowlan, James Dunlap (R)
Oblinger, Josephine Kneidl (R)
O'Block, Patrick Michael (D)
O'Brien, Dorothy Gertrude (R)
O'Brien, George M (R)
O'Brien, John Fitzgerald (D)
Ogilvie, Richard Buell (R)
O'Keefe, James L (D)
Orlebeke, Charles J (R)
Oshel, Val (R)
Ostendorf, Alvin Fred (R)
Owens, Thomas Jerome (D)
Ozinga, Frank M (R)
Palmer, Ben E (D)
Palmer, Glen Daniel (R)
Palmer, Romie J (R)
Pape, Carl E (R)
Parsons, Albert Roy (R)
Parsons, Richard Hugo (D)
Partee, Cecil A (D)
Patrick, Langdon (D)
Pearre, Jerome (R)
Pearson, Lloyd Edward (R)
Peden, Preston E (D)
Percy, Charles Harting (R)
Peskin, Bernard M (D)
Peters, Peter Piotrowicz (R)
Philip, James Peyton, Jr (R)
Phillips, David Julius (D)
Pierce, Daniel Marshall (D)
Pillow, Theodore Eugene (R)
Podesta, Robert Angelo (R)
Polk, William Benjamin (R)
Porter, John Edward (R)
Pouncey, Taylor (Independent)
Price, Melvin (D)
Pucinski, Roman C (D)
Pullia, Sal P (D)
Radewagen, Fred (R)
Raffl, Kenneth Albert (R)
Railsback, Tom (R)
Randolph, Paul J (R)
Rauschenberger, John Kenneth (R)
Rayson, Leland Homer (D)
Redmond, William A (D)
Rednour, John (D)
Reed, Betty Lou (R)
Regner, David Joseph (R)
Reid, Charlotte T (R)
Remmert, Pete (R)
Rentschler, William Henry (R)
Replogle, Luther Irvin (R)
Richmond, Lindell Bruce (R)
Ricketts, Liese L (D)
Ridgeway, William Gilbert (R)
Riechmann, Howard Christ (R)
Rigney, Harlan (R)
Rini, Dominic William (D)
Roberts, Virgil H (R)
Rock, Philip Joseph (D)
Rodger, Ronald Alan (R)
Roe, John B (R)
Romano, Sam (D)
Ronan, James A (D)
Rose, Thomas Chapin (R)
Rosewell, Edward Joseph (D)
Rostenkowski, Dan (D)
Rowe, Harris (R)
Ruddy, Philip Culkin (R)
Rumsfeld, Donald (R)
Russo, Martin A (D)
Ryan, George Homer (R)
Ryan, Howard Chris (R)
Rybacki, Ray J (R)
Sabonjian, Robert V (R)
Sanders, James Willis (R)
Sanford, Marie (R)
Sangmeister, George Edward (D)
Saperstein, Esther (D)
Satterthwaite, Cameron B (D)
Satterthwaite, Helen Foster (D)
Savickas, Frank David (D)
Sawyer, Eugene, Jr (D)
Scannell, William Francis (R)
Schaffer, Jack Raymond (R)
Schanzle, Ellen Josephine (D)
Schirger, William Edward (R)
Schisler, Carolyn Kay (D)
Schisler, D Gale (D)
Schleicher, Ben T (R)
Schlickman, Eugene F (R)
Schmalzl, Kurt Charles (R)
Schneider, J Glenn (D)
Schoeberlein, Allan L (Al) (R)
Schraeder, Fred Joseph (R)
Schuneman, Calvin W (R)
Scott, Anna Wall (D)
Scott, William J (R)
Sebo, Walter J (R)
Seith, Alex Robert (D)
Sevcik, Joseph G (R)
Severns, Penny Lee (D)
Shafer, Earl T (R)
Shapiro, David Charles (R)
Shapiro, Samuel H (D)
Sharp, John F (D)
Shea, Gerald W (D)
Sheehan, Timothy P (R)
Sherer, Albert William, Jr
Shipley, George Edward (D)
Shuman, Howard E (D)
Simmons, Walter T (Buck) (R)
Simms, W Timothy (R)
Simon, Paul (D)
Simpson, Barbara Hahn (D)
Skelton, James Maurice (R)
Skinner, Calvin L, Jr (Cal) (R)
Smith, Fred J (D)
Smith, Keith J (R)
Smith, Philip Gene (D)
Smith, Victor L (R)
Sommer, Roger A (R)
Soper, James C (R)
Speckman, Leon George (R)
Sperling, Jack Irving (R)
Springer, William Lee (R)
Steele, Everett G (R)
Steffen, Frederick John (D)
Stern, Harry L (R)
Stern, Herbert L, Jr (Hub) (D)
Stewart, William O (R)
Stiehl, Celeste M (R)
Stiehl, William D (R)
Stone, Paul (D)
Stone, W Clement (R)

Stratton, William Grant (R)
Stuart, Robert D, Jr (R)
Stubblefield, Guy (D)
Sutker, Calvin R (D)
Sutton, Ruth Adelia (D)
Swinarski, Donald Theodore (D)
Tarr, Curtis William (R)
Taylor, Harry Grant (R)
Taylor, James C (D)
Tecson, Joseph A (R)
Telcser, Arthur A (R)
Terzich, Robert M, Sr (D)
Thompson, Verla Darlene (R)
Thornton, Edmund Braxton (R)
Tipsword, Rolland Fortner (D)
Todd, Carl P (D)
Totten, Donald Lee (R)
Touchette, Francis Walter (D)
Touhy, John P (D)
Tuerk, Fred James (R)
Tumulty, Gary Allen (D)
Turner, Earl James (D)
Underwood, Robert Charles
Vadalabene, Sam Martin (D)
Van Duyne, LeRoy (D)
Van Horn, Lyle Cecil (R)
Vanneman, Edgar, Jr (R)
Vick, Oris Paul (D)
Vinovich, Ralph (R)
Von Boeckman, James (D)
Von Buzbee, Kenneth (D)
Vrdolyak, Edward Robert (D)
Waddell, R Bruce (R)
Wagner, James Webb (D)
Wagner, Thomas J (D)
Walker, Dan (D)
Walker, William Nickerson (R)
Wall, James McKendree (D)
Wall, John F (R)
Wallace, Robert Ash (D)
Wallis, James Edwin (D)
Walsh, William D (R)
Washburn, James R (R)
Washington, Harold (D)
Watson, John Crawford (D)
Weaver, Stanley B (R)
Weisbaum, Marilyn (D)
Welsh, Raymond J, Jr (D)
Werner, Jane (R)
West, Wilson Henry (R)
White, Clyde Milton (D)
White, Jesse Clark, Jr (D)
White, R Quincy, Jr (R)
Whitmer, Robert William (D)
Whitney, Robert E (R)
Wikoff, Virgil Cornwell (R)
Wilbur, Richard Sloan (R)
Wiley, Richard E (R)
Wille, John Howard (R)
Willer, Anne (D)
Williams, Francis Xeton (D)
Williams, Jack B (D)
Williams, Robert Kelsey (D)
Williamson, Richard Salisbury (R)
Williamson, Walter Robert (D)
Wilson, William Orval (D)
Winchester, Robert C (R)
Winstein, Stewart R (D)
Wise, David William (D)
Witwer, Samuel Weiler (R)
Wolf, Frank C (R)
Wolf, Sam W (D)
Wolf, Theresa Catherine (D)
Wood, Kathleen Ann (D)
Woodcock, George Washington (R)
Wooten, Don (D)
Wright, James Lashua (D)
Wycoff, S Jeanne (D)
Yates, Sidney R (D)
Young, Samuel H (R)

Younge, Wyvetter Hoover (D)
Yourell, Harry (Bus) (D)
Zadrozny, Mitchell George (R)
Zeiders, Grace (R)
Zelasko, Antone Richard (Tony) (R)
Zeni, Ferdinand J, Jr (R)
Zenner, Sheldon Toby (D)
Zoeller, Sylvester Robert (R)

INDIANA

Abbott, Hettie (D)
Adair, E Ross (R)
Adams, Mendle E (D)
Allen, Dozier T, Jr (D)
Allstatt, Angeline (D)
Altherr, William Lee (R)
Anderson, C Joseph, (D)
Anderson, Edwin Dewey, Sr (R)
Andre, Herman W (R)
Angel, Nick (D)
Applegate, A Earl (D)
Arnold, Clifford Delos (D)
Arterburn, Norman F
Auer, Delmar L (D)
Augsburger, John Frederick (R)
Avery, Dennis Theodore (D)
Bailey, Floyd J (R)
Bailey, John W, Jr (R)
Bainbridge, Phillip E (D)
Baker, William C (D)
Bales, Robert H (R)
Balsbaugh, Michael Mark (D)
Bannon, Edmond Joseph (D)
Bauer, Burnett Calix (D)
Bauer, Burnett Patrick (D)
Bayh, Birch (D)
Beardsley, Walter Raper (R)
Beasley, Kern Grant (R)
Beaver, James Raymond (R)
Bechman, Charles Edward (R)
Becker, Nelson J (R)
Beers, Orvas E (R)
Bell, Richard D (D)
Benjamin, Adam, Jr (D)
Blachly, Quentin A (R)
Blevins, John Morrison (R)
Bliss, Mary Patricia (R)
Bodine, Richard Clay (D)
Bogden, Charles (R)
Borst, Lawrence Marion (R)
Bosma, Charles Edward (R)
Bowen, Otis R (R)
Boyd, Rozelle (D)
Boyer, Stanley Clark (R)
Brademas, John (D)
Branigin, Roger Douglas (D)
Bray, Richard D (R)
Bray, William Gilmer (R)
Bronson, Minnie L (D)
Brown, Robert Henry (D)
Brown, Sarah S (R)
Bruggenschmidt, Joseph G (D)
Bulen, Lawrence Keith (R)
Burkley, Paul Edwin (R)
Burrous, Kermit O (R)
Burton, Julia Ann (D)
Bushemi, Marion J (D)
Butler, Gary Lee (D)
Butz, Earl Lauer (R)
Byram, Stanley Harold (R)
Byroade, Henry A
Cabell, John Allen (D)
Campbell, Craig Bartlett (D)
Cardwell, Bruce Elliott (D)
Carmichael, Oliver Cromwell, Jr (D)
Carroll, Patrick D (D)
Chaney, Buena (R)

Chapleau, Louis Carey (D)
Chase, John William (R)
Christy, William (D)
Clarkson, C Jack (R)
Clay, Rudolph (D)
Clingan, Lee (D)
Cochran, William C (D)
Coldren, John (R)
Coleman, Floyd Butler (R)
Coleman, Thomas D (R)
Colyer, Charles Constant (R)
Combs, Alwilda Gertrude Brown (D)
Conrad, Larry A (D)
Cook, George Edward (D)
Coons, Harold Meredith (R)
Cooper, Anna (R)
Courtney, James H (D)
Crawford, William A (D)
Critchlow, Ronald Glenn (R)
Crowe, Ray P (D)
Crumpacker, Shepard J (R)
Davee, Linda Joan (R)
Day, John J (D)
DeBonis, Anthony, Jr (D)
Dellinger, Richard M (R)
Demaree, Geraldine (D)
Denbo, Seth Thomas (R)
Dennis, David Worth (R)
Dickey, Donald Floyd (R)
Dietz, Nancy Fenn (D)
Dietzen, Walter C (D)
Dobis, Chester F (D)
Donahue, Daniel Francis (D)
Donaldson, John Weber (R)
Donis, Jack Andrew (R)
Dowden, Faye Haywood (R)
Doyle, Richard D (D)
DuComb, Robert James, Jr (R)
Dutton, Judson Dunlap (R)
Duvall, Leslie (R)
Edgerton, John Palmer (R)
Edwards, Martin K (R)
Eilert, David DeWitt (D)
Emshwiller, Thomas C (D)
Ennis, John D (R)
Erwin, William Walter (R)
Espich, Jeffrey K (R)
Etherton, Trudy Slaby (R)
Evans, David W (D)
Evans, Patricia Anne (Patty) (D)
Fair, Robert J (D)
Fanning, Herman J (D)
Ferguson, William Alvah (D)
Fields, Lowell (R)
Fifield, Elwood B (R)
Fisher, Ethel Virginia (R)
Fisher, Merwyn T (D)
Fithian, Floyd J (D)
Flanagan, John Patrick (D)
Fleck, Leon J (D)
Fruechtenicht, Thomas Eric (R)
Gallahan, Russell Wayne (D)
Galloway, Charles Raymond (D)
Galm, Robert Woods (R)
Gardiner, Sherry Biggers (R)
Gardner, James A (R)
Garr, Elizabeth Ann (R)
Garton, Robert Dean (R)
Gates, Robert E (R)
Gee, Bill F (R)
Gery, Michael E (D)
Gigerich, William Edward (D)
Givan, Richard Martin (R)
Gladden, Zelma E (D)
Glaescher, Kennith Parker (R)
Goble, Edward Earl (D)
Goddard, Ruth (R)
Goetz, Lillian Ruth (R)
Green, William Arthur (D)
Greenfield, James Robert (D)

Gronemeier, Ralph A (R)
Gubbins, Joan Margaret (R)
Guthridge, Esther Blanch (R)
Gutman, Phillip Edward (R)
Hall, Katie (D)
Hall, Thomas Willison (D)
Haltom, Sterling M (D)
Hamilton, Ernest Roll (D)
Hamilton, Lee Herbert (D)
Handlon, Forest, Jr (D)
Harden, Cecil Murray (R)
Harris, Jewell G (D)
Harris, Joseph P (D)
Harris, Mary Angela (R)
Harris, Vivian Faye (R)
Harrison, Joseph William (R)
Hart, John C (R)
Hartke, Vance (D)
Harvey, Ralph (R)
Hasbrook, Thomas Charles (R)
Hatcher, Richard G (D)
Hayes, Philip Harold (D)
Hayes, Robert E (D)
Hays, J Jefferson (D)
Heckard, Donald Harvey (R)
Heckard, William Norman (R)
Heeke, Dennis Henry (D)
Heide, Richard Thomas (D)
Hendren, William Foster (D)
Hensler, Charles Morris (R)
Herrold, John C (R)
Hershey, Lewis Blaine
Hesler, Harry Ray (R)
Hibner, Janet Louise (R)
Hill, Margaret C (R)
Hillenbrand, John A, II (D)
Hillis, Elwood Haynes (R)
Hinshaw, Thomas Moore (D)
Hoffmann, Ricki Jo (R)
Holcomb, John Lawrence (R)
Holt, Eleanor Louise (R)
House, James Evan, II (D)
Houston, Paul Dennis (D)
Hric, Paul J (D)
Hudnut, William Herbert, III (R)
Huff, Daniel Emra (R)
Hulen, Bernice (R)
Hume, Donald E (D)
Hume, Lindel O (D)
Hunnings, R H (R)
Hunt, Howard E (R)
Hunter, Donald H (R)
Isenbarger, John P (R)
Jackson, Nyle Meringo (R)
Jacobs, Andrew, Jr (D)
Jefferis, D Allen (R)
Jerrel, Bettye Lou (R)
Jessup, Roger L (R)
Job, Eugene Keith (R)
Johnson, Houston K (D)
Johnson, Paul Edwin (R)
Johnson, William Arthur (R)
Jones, Robert L, Jr (R)
Jones, Stanley Gordon, Jr (D)
Jontz, James (D)
Jordan, N Pauline (R)
Kelley, Clarence R (R)
Kennedy, Martin P (D)
Kennedy, Nelson D (D)
Kimmell, Curtis Vollmer (D)
Kohlmeyer, Mildred Lucille (R)
Koons, James L (D)
Kovach, Robert (D)
Kruger, John W (R)
Krup, William Henry (D)
Krupa, John George (D)
Kruse, Dean Verl (R)
Kuykendall, Rufus Calvin (R)
Lacey, Michael Charles (R)
La Follette, Patricia Anne (D)
Lambright, Betty Louise (R)

1046 / GEOGRAPHIC INDEX

INDIANA (cont)

Lamkin, Eugene Henry, Jr (Ned) (R)
Landes, James (R)
Landgrebe, Earl Frederick (R)
Lane, Timothy R (D)
Lankford, Thomas J (R)
Lantz, Jerry Neil (D)
Larson, John R (R)
Lash, Donald R (R)
Lauck, Marie Theresa D (D)
Leatherbury, Douglas Clay (D)
Lebamoff, George (D)
Lebamoff, Ivan A (D)
LeGrande, Ruth E (R)
Lenzo, Tony Samuel (D)
Lewis, James A, Jr (D)
Lewis, Jeffrey S (D)
Lindley, John William (R)
Lindsey, Bertha Mae (R)
Lindvall, Martha Rebbecca (R)
Link, Donald Richard (D)
Lloyd, Russell G (R)
Long, William L (R)
Lugar, Richard Green (R)
Lundquist, Eldon F (R)
MacDonald, Elmer (R)
Madden, Ray J (D)
Mahoney, Donnabelle (D)
Mangus, Richard W (R)
Martin, Mary K (R)
Mason, Marcella June (D)
Mason, Maurice (D)
Mauzy, Thames L (R)
McBane, Robert B (R)
McCallen, Robert Ray (D)
McCarty, Virginia Dill (D)
McCormick, Keith C (R)
McCullough, Billie R (D)
McDaniel, Marlin K (R)
McFall, David Merrill (D)
McInerney, Kevin Dennis (R)
McIntyre, Jack W (R)
McKinney, Paul Caylor (D)
McKinney, Robert Hurley (D)
Meadors, Albert Murril (R)
Means, William Towne (R)
Merrill, D Bailey (R)
Middleton, Joan Joy (R)
Miers, Morgan L (D)
Miller, Jerry J (D)
Miller, Kenneth J (D)
Milligan, Thomas Stuart (R)
Mills, Morris Hadley (R)
Mishler, Everett Monroe (D)
Moberly, Stephen C (R)
Moeller, Jeanette (R)
Moody, John Overton (D)
Moynahan, Thomas Alvin (D)
Murphy, Elinore Jamerson (D)
Mutz, John M (R)
Myers, John T (R)
Neal, James Thomas (R)
Negley, Harold Hoover (R)
Nelson, Donald T (R)
New, Jack L (D)
Nicholson, Carl Joseph (R)
Nielson, Geraldine R (R)
Niemeyer, Ernest (R)
Noble, Freda Golden (D)
Noble, Ray Edward (R)
Noggle, Abby Del (R)
Northacker, Patricia Jeanne (R)
O'Bannon, Frank Lewis (D)
O'Day, Joseph F (D)
O'Maley, Robert L (R)
Orr, Robert Dunkerson (R)
Paarlberg, Don (R)
Pastrick, Robert A (D)
Patrick, Edwin Eugene (R)
Pfaffenberger, George William (R)
Pfaffenberger, Jane Alice (R)
Phelps, Grace Lenore (R)
Phillips, Michael Keith (D)
Pickett, Robert McQuillious (R)
Piper, Rodney E (D)
Pizzo, Anthony (D)
Poinsatte, Stephen T (D)
Poor, Robert Lawrence (R)
Porter, Victor Butler (R)
Posey, John Phillip (D)
Potesta, Ralph J (R)
Powell, Richard Eugene (R)
Prentice, Dixon Wright (D)
Price, Robert LaVon (D)
Prosser, Audrey Betty (D)
Quinn, Charles Lewis (R)
Ramsey, Harvey Kenneth (R)
Reed, Samuel Lee (R)
Regnier, Richard Olin (R)
Reising, Gregory S (D)
Reppa, Jerome J (R)
Rice, Charles E (Conservative)
Richard, Graham Arthur (D)
Richardson, Ray (R)
Riggs, Eleanor Cox (R)
Roach, William D (R)
Roe, Elbert Oliver (D)
Roorda, Walter John (R)
Roudebush, Richard L (R)
Roush, J Edward (D)
Ruby, Donald W (R)
Ruby, John Allen (D)
Ruckelshaus, William Doyle (R)
Ruderman, Ruth (D)
Rumler, James Richard (D)
Sabatini, Frederick Anthony (R)
St Angelo, Gordon (D)
Salmon, Nancy Pilson (D)
Sanxter, Joan M (R)
Scheidt, Virgil D (R)
Schipper, Doris Ann (D)
Schnaitter, Spencer J (R)
Schultz, Marilyn Frances (D)
Scott, Leon (D)
Selman, Edwin William, Jr (R)
Sendak, Theodore Lorraine (R)
Server, Gregory Dale (R)
Seybert, Myron Silver (R)
Seyfried, Maryann (R)
Shank, Richard Eugene (R)
Sharp, Philip R (D)
Shawley, John Franklin (R)
Sheaffer, Robert L (R)
Shuee, Charles Edward (D)
Simcox, Edwin Jesse (R)
Sinks, John R (R)
Smith, Betty Jane (D)
Smith, Gary (D)
Smith, Van P (R)
Smith, Vernon George (D)
Snider, Kenneth C (D)
Snowden, Gene (R)
Snyder, John K (R)
Stanley, Don R (D)
Stanley, Merton (D)
Stoner, Richard Burkett (D)
Stoughton, Stephen H (R)
Straub, Terrence David (D)
Sullivan, Leo (R)
Sweezy, John W (R)
Swisher, Paul W (R)
Teague, Thomas Joseph (D)
Telle, King (R)
Thomas, John J (R)
Thomas, Joseph N (R)
Thompson, Harry E (R)
Thompson, Richard Keith (R)
Tipton, Elden C (D)
Townsend, W Wayne (D)
Trisler, Bill (D)
Tudor, David Frederick (R)
Ullrich, Wilfrid J (D)
Van Arsdale, Catherine Eva (D)
Van Til, George W (D)
Voisard, Leo A (D)
Walker, Alan Lee (D)
Wallace, Geraldine Elizabeth (D)
Warner, Philip T (R)
Waterman, Kenneth M (D)
Wathen, Richard B (R)
Welsh, Matthew Empson (D)
Weninger, Howard L (D)
Wertzler, Marilou (R)
Whitcomb, Edgar Doud (R)
Wilcox, John Harvey (R)
Williams, Leroy, Jr (D)
Wilson, Earl (R)
Wilson, Helen Louise (R)
Wilson, Woodrow (D)
Winebrenner, Tommy Lee (R)
Winger, Loren (D)
Wolf, Charles William (D)
Wolf, Katie Louise (D)
Wolf, William Henry (D)
Wood, Beatrice Evelyn (D)
Wooffendale, Mattie Lucille (R)
Worden, Richard L, Sr (R)
Works, Donald Leroy (R)
Worman, Richard W (R)
Wright, Oren Alvin (R)
Yergin, Alan Eugene (D)
Zaleski, Tony, Jr (D)
Zion, Roger H (R)
Zirkle, Alan Lloyd (D)

IOWA

Allen, Stephen Whiting (D)
Andersen, Leonard Christian (R)
Anderson, Robert T (D)
Anton, Patricia Ann (D)
Avenson, Donald Dean (D)
Axel, John Werner (R)
Bailey, Dennis Clarke (R)
Baker, Keith (D)
Baringer, Maurice E (R)
Baxter, Harry Youngs (D)
Beall, Daryl E (D)
Beck, William E, Jr (R)
Bedell, Berkley Warren (D)
Beemer, Elvin Homer (R)
Bennett, Wayne (R)
Bergman, Irvin Lester (R)
Berryhill, Lynn Mercer (D)
Bina, Robert F (D)
Birkenholz, Carroll Merle (R)
Bittle, Edgar Harold (R)
Blouin, Michael Thomas (D)
Bortell, Glen E (R)
Bosch, Robert D (R)
Boyle, Norman William (R)
Brady, Harold Edward (D)
Brandt, Diane (D)
Branstad, Terry Edward (R)
Briles, James E (R)
Brockett, Glenn F (R)
Bromwell, James Edward (R)
Bronemann, Jerald Raymond (R)
Brown, Carmela Margaret (D)
Brown, David William (D)
Brown, Ralph R (R)
Brunow, John B (D)
Buhr, Glenn (R)
Burke, Robert William (D)
Burns, Robert John (D)
Burroughs, Clifford E (R)
Byerly, Richard L (D)
Caffrey, James T (D)
Canney, Donald James
Carlson, Elmer Gustav (D)
Carr, Robert M (D)
Chambers, Patrick B (D)
Charlton, Wm Stuart (R)
Clampitt, Bruce Willard (R)
Clark, Gracie Mae (R)
Clark, John Howard (R)
Clark, Richard Clarence (D)
Clinton, Ellaree Avant (D)
Cochran, Dale M (D)
Coleman, C Joseph (D)
Coles, Frank Van de Ven (R)
Conlin, Roxanne Barton (D)
Conmey, Larry J (D)
Connors, John H (D)
Coons, Marion M (R)
Corey, Leroy Dale (R)
Cox, Dean F (D)
Crabb, Frank Abel, Jr (R)
Crawford, Reid W (R)
Crews, Jon Thomas (D)
Culver, John Chester (D)
Culver, Louis P (D)
Curtis, Warren Edward (R)
Cusack, Gregory Daniel (D)
Daggett, Horace (D)
Danker, Arlyn E (R)
Dawson, Tom Henry (D)
De Koster, Lucas James (R)
Den Herder, Elmer Hans (R)
Dewberry, Dolores Davenport (Dee) (D)
Dieleman, William W (D)
Dircks, Durwood William (R)
Doderer, Minnette Frerichs (D)
Dolliver, James I (R)
Dominowski, Wayne Victor (D)
Doyle, Donald Vincent (D)
Drake, Richard Francis (R)
Drenkow, Rodney Dean (D)
Dunton, Keith H (D)
Dyrland, Terry Eugene (D)
Eastin, Jane White (R)
Egenes, Sonja (R)
Elliott, Jack Mark (R)
Elliott, Mildred Ellen (R)
Ellis, Verna Jeanne (R)
Engebretson, Gary Duane (R)
Erbe, Norman Arthur (R)
Evans, Cooper (R)
Evans, Howard David (D)
Evans, Rachel Wiegman (R)
Ewen, Warren Gail (R)
Faust, Mary Jane (D)
Fitzgerald, Jerome (D)
Fitzpatrick, John Joseph (D)
Fleming, Richard Leo (D)
Fletchall, Loran Clyde (D)
Foxhoven, Eloise Faith (D)
Fullerton, Bert (R)
Fulton, Robert D (D)
Gallagher, James V (D)
Garrett, Julian Burgess (R)
Gaudineer, Lee H (D)
Gentleman, Julia B (R)
Gesell, Cranston Richard (R)
Gibson, Ben J, Jr (R)
Gilchrist, Lawrence Barnt (R)
Gilloon, Thomas J (D)
Glenn, Gene W (D)
Gluba, William Evan (D)
Grassley, Charles E (R)
Greigg, Stanley Lloyd (D)
Griffee, William B (D)
Griffin, James W, Sr (R)
Griffin, Walter Roland (D)
Gross, H R (R)
Hagemeier, Richard John (R)
Halvorson, Roger A (R)
Hammer, Charles Lawrence (D)
Hansen, Ingwer L (R)

Hansen, John Robert (D)
Hansen, Willard R (R)
Hargrave, William J (D)
Harkin, Tom (D)
Harms, Wendell G (R)
Harper, Mattie (D)
Harris, K David
Harvey, LaVern R (R)
Haugland, Jean (D)
Heikens, Warren Henry (D)
Helgens, Char (R)
Helgeson, Kathy Pauline (D)
Hendricks, Lewis S (R)
Hennessey, Maurice Vincent (D)
Heying, Hilarius L (D)
Higgins, Thomas James (D)
Hill, Eugene Marshall (D)
Hill, Philip B (R)
Hines, Neal (D)
Hinkhouse, Herbert Clarence (D)
Hoeven, Charles Bernard (R)
Holmes, David H (R)
Horel, Paul Lynn (D)
Horn, Wally E (D)
Houston, Patrick Leo (D)
Howe, Anita Gonzalez (D)
Howell, Rollin Knight (D)
Hudson, James Weissinger (R)
Hughes, Harold Everett (D)
Hughes, Phyllis Josephine (D)
Hullinger, Arlo (D)
Hultman, Calvin O (R)
Humpleby, Twyla Jean (R)
Husak, Emil J (D)
Hutchins, C W (Bill) (D)
Hutchison, Ervin A (R)
Jackson, Paulina Ruth (D)
Jebens, John Herman (R)
Jensen, Donald Hugo (D)
Jepsen, Roger William (R)
Jesse, Norman Gale (D)
Jochum, Thomas J (D)
Johnson, Donald Edward (R)
Johnson, Thatcher (R)
Johnston, Ann F (D)
Johnston, Elton Andrew (R)
Jordan, James D (R)
Jordan, Lewis Henry (D)
Junker, Willis E (R)
Junkins, Lowell Lee (D)
Keir, Robert MacArthur (R)
Kelly, E Kevin (R)
Kempen, Paul D (D)
Kent, Jonathan Henry (D)
Kinley, George Raymond (D)
Koogler, Fred L, Sr (D)
Korn, Charles Austin (D)
Krause, Robert Allen (D)
Kreamer, Robert McDonald (R)
Kunath, Lorma Robinson (D)
Kyl, John H (R)
Lageschulte, Ray (R)
Lamborn, Clifton C (R)
Larson, Clif (D)
Lavender, John Gould (R)
Levin, Myrtilla Fones (R)
Lias, Thomas Lee (R)
Lindeen, Arnold Rudolph (R)
Lipsky, Joan (R)
Lonergan, Joyce (D)
Loveless, Herschel Cellel (D)
Martin, A W (R)
May, Dennis James (D)
Mayne, Wiley (R)
McCluhan, Neil R (D)
McCreedy, Harry Duane (R)
McCullough, Robert Earl (D)
McDonald, John Cecil (R)
McDonald, Margaret Ellen (D)
McElroy, Lillian Mae (R)

Mendenhall, Alice Mae (R)
Menke, Lester D (R)
Mennenga, Jay Warren (D)
Merriman, John A (R)
Merritt, Milo (D)
Mezvinsky, Edward M (D)
Middleswart, James Ira (D)
Middleton, Melville Peter (D)
Millen, Floyd H (R)
Miller, Alvin V (D)
Miller, Carol Corinne (R)
Miller, Charles P (D)
Miller, Elizabeth Ruby (R)
Miller, Kenneth D (R)
Miller, Opal (D)
Miller, Robert Keith (D)
Minglin, Harry J (R)
Monroe, W R Jr (Bill) (D)
Morain, Frederick Garver (R)
Moser, Leroy Alvin, (Jr) (R)
Mowry, John L (R)
Moyer, Ruth Eloise (D)
Murray, John Stevenson (R)
Nealson, Otto H (R)
Neely, Marion Robert (R)
Neu, Arthur Alan (R)
Newhard, Scott Douglas (D)
Newsom, George Edward (R)
Neylan, Kathleen Mary (D)
Nielsen, Carl V (D)
Nielsen, Larry Dale (R)
Nolin, Karl (D)
Nolting, Fred W (D)
Norland, Lowell E (D)
Norpel, Richard J, Sr (D)
Nystrom, John N (R)
Oakley, Brice Case (R)
Obermiller, Edward (D)
O'Brien, Donald Eugene (D)
O'Halloran, Mary (D)
Orr, Joan (D)
Palmer, Frances Brandt (R)
Palmer, William Darrell (D)
Pardun, Patricia Jane (D)
Parkin, Jerry Donald (D)
Parsons, John Welsey (R)
Patchett, John Earl (D)
Pavich, Emil Sam (D)
Pease, Roger De Vere (R)
Pellett, Wendell C (R)
Pelzer, Max O (R)
Perkins, Carroll (D)
Pillers, George Wylie, Jr (R)
Pitts, Thomas Ladd (D)
Platt, Joe-Ann Elizabeth (R)
Plymat, William N (R)
Poncy, Charles N (D)
Priebe, Berl E (D)
Rabedeaux, W R (R)
Ramsey, Richard Ralph (R)
Rapp, Stephen John (D)
Rawlings, Maurice Edward (D)
Ray, Robert D (R)
Rea, Pauline Helen (R)
Readinger, David M (R)
Redman, Richard Elson (R)
Redmond, James M (D)
Reed, Michael Allen (D)
Reed, Sue Mabel (R)
Rehder, Merlyn Albert (R)
Rickert, Florence Evelyn (D)
Rider, Robert Earl, Sr (D)
Riley, Tom Joseph (R)
Rinas, B Joseph (D)
Robinson, Cloyd Erwin (R)
Robinson, Stephen C (R)
Roethler, Kenneth J (D)
Rogers, Norman G (D)
Rubel, Randy Lee (D)
Runkle, Jerry Chloyd (R)
Sanders, Sherry E (D)
Sarcone, Christine Mary (D)
Scheelhaase, Lyle (D)

Schepers, Marlyn Glenn (D)
Scherle, William J (R)
Schimmel, Allan D (R)
Schmitz, Joe W (D)
Schroeder, Laverne W (R)
Schroeder, Lloyd G F (D)
Schuler, Louis Eugene (R)
Schutter, Betty Rugen (R)
Schwengel, Fred (R)
Schwengels, Forrest Victor (R)
Scott, Kenneth Daniel (D)
Senn, Fern Berniece (D)
Shaff, Roger J (R)
Shaw, Elizabeth Orr (R)
Shimanek, Robert Francis (R)
Sievers, Georgia Ann (D)
Simpson, Stanley R (R)
Small, Arthur A, Jr (D)
Smith, Donna Lee (D)
Smith, Mary Louise (R)
Smith, Neal (D)
Smith, Paul Aikin (D)
Smith, Shirley Elizabeth (D)
Snell, Bruce Morey, Jr (R)
Snook, Billy Jay (D)
Sovern, Steve (D)
Spear, Clay (D)
Spencer, Don W (D)
Spies, John Flavan (R)
Stanley, David Maxwell (R)
Stegemann, John Dietrich (D)
Steiff, Irma S (D)
Stephens, Lyle R (R)
Stewart, David Wallace (R)
Stockdale, Gertrude Marion (R)
Stoffer, Henry J (D)
Street, Keith Merlin (D)
Stromer, Delwyn Dean (R)
Sunleaf, Roger Wendell (R)
Svoboda, Linda A (D)
Synhorst, Melvin D (R)
Tauke, Thomas J (R)
Taylor, Ray Allen (R)
Tertichny, Michael Allen (D)
Thompson, John Colby (R)
Thompson, Pahl E (R)
Tieden, Dale L (R)
Tofte, Semor C (R)
Tone, John Wolfe (R)
Triggs, Michael Lynn (R)
Turner, Lloyd L (Non-partisan)
Turner, Richard C (R)
Uhlenhopp, Harvey Harold
Vander Wal, Jerry Duane (R)
van Deusen, Robert Moon (R)
Van Duzer, John Frederick (R)
Van Gilst, Bass (D)
Varley, Andrew Preston (R)
Vidal, Dagmar Lund (D)
Voelker, Roy E (R)
Wallace, Robert Lewis (R)
Walter, Craig Douglas (D)
Warren, John E (Jack) (R)
Wearin, Otha Donner (D)
Welden, Richard W (R)
Wells, James Dale (D)
Wentzien, Irwin H (R)
West, James Clifford (R)
Whitney, Tom (D)
Wickham, Ronald James (D)
Willits, Earl M (D)
Winkelman, William Pratt (R)
Wittenmeyer, Charles E (R)
Wolle, William Down
Wollenhaupt, Ralph Eugene (R)
Wood, Charles Ross (R)
Woods, Jack E (D)
Worthington, Lorne R (D)
Wulff, Henry C (R)
Wurtzel, Donald Ricky (D)
Wyckoff, Russell Leroy (D)
Zimansky, David William (D)

KANSAS

Allen, Mary Elizabeth (D)
Althaus, Kenneth L (R)
Anderson, Arnold R (D)
Anderson, Eugene (D)
Anderson, Geneva June (D)
Andrews, Mary Eloise Okeson (D)
Angell, Charlie (R)
Arasmith, Neil H (R)
Arbuthnot, R E (R)
Arnold, Robert Almerine (D)
Avery, William Henry (R)
Aylward, Paul L (D)
Baden, Jo Ann (D)
Baden, Steve Kenneth (D)
Baker, Joan Marie (R)
Befort, Alois George, Jr (Al) (D)
Bell, George D (D)
Bell, William Fletcher (R)
Bengtson, Larry Edwin (D)
Beninga, Harold T (R)
Bennett, Robert Frederick (R)
Beougher, Ethel M (D)
Berkowitz, David J (D)
Beymer, James Elton (R)
Blancett, Thomas Joseph (R)
Blangers, Nell Elizabeth (D)
Bogart, Vincent L (D)
Bogina, August, Jr (R)
Bond, Richard Lee (R)
Booth, Arden (R)
Bower, John David (R)
Boyd, McDill (R)
Braden, James Dale (R)
Brewster, Edward Richard (R)
Bridges, Duane N (R)
Brier, Jack H (R)
Brock, Robert Lee (D)
Brokaw, Gary H (D)
Bromley, Dan (R)
Brown, Clarence Ebbert (D)
Browne, Ruth T (D)
Brueck, Karl Arthur (D)
Bunten, William Wallace (R)
Bunyan, William Price, III (R)
Burgess, Denny D (R)
Burke, Paul E, Jr (Bud) (R)
Burkman, Carol Lynn (R)
Burns, Garth F (R)
Buser, Burton L (D)
Bussman, Ralph E (D)
Buzzi, Lloyd David (R)
Caldwell, James Evert (D)
Campbell, Albert D (D)
Campbell, Clifford V (R)
Carlin, John William (D)
Carlson, Frank (R)
Cather, Charles William (D)
Chaney, Bert (D)
Chartier, Glenn Dell (D)
Chase, DeWayne Arthur Newton (R)
Christy, Donald (R)
Chronister, Rochelle Ruth (R)
Concannon, Donald O (R)
Cooper, Carlos M (R)
Corcoran, Thomas Joseph (D)
Cortes, Carlos F (R)
Crabb, Delbert Elmo (R)
Cribbs, Theo (D)
Crist, Harold Howard (R)
Crofoot, John William (R)
Crowell, Donald Rex (R)
Crumbaker, Don E (R)
Crutcher, John William (R)
Cubit, James (R)
Daily, Frank Edward, Jr (R)
Daley, William Joseph (R)
Daniels, Dennis Ray (D)
Darby, Harry (R)

KANSAS (cont)

Dempsey, Ambrose L (D)
Dierdorff, Arden (R)
Docking, Robert Blackwell (D)
Docking, Virginia (D)
Dole, Robert J (R)
Dotson, William Francis (D)
Douville, Arthur (R)
Dowell, Richard A (D)
Doyen, Ross O (R)
Dreiling, Norbert R (D)
Driscoll, Richard M (D)
Droge, Leslie A (R)
Duncan, C Woodrow, Jr (D)
Duncan, J Santford (Sandy) (R)
Dunlap, Fred Everett (R)
Dyck, Harold Peter (R)
Edison, Debra Denise (D)
Ehrlich, Roy Melven (R)
Everett, Donn James (R)
Falstad, William James (R)
Farrar, Keith (R)
Fatzer, Harold R (R)
Feleciano, Paul, Jr (D)
Finney, Joan (D)
Foster, Ben (R)
Foster, Retha Reynolds (D)
Fowler, Raymond William (Bill) (D)
Francisco, James Lee (D)
Francisco, Kenneth Dale (D)
Freund, Barbara Lea (R)
Frey, Robert G (R)
Fritz, George H (R)
Frost, Jack Wesley (R)
Gaar, Norman Edward (R)
Gaines, Frank D (D)
Garrett, Roy H (D)
Gastl, Eugene Francis (D)
George, Newell A (D)
Glover, Michael G (D)
Goodpaster, Mary J (R)
Graber, Walter W (D)
Graham, Betty June (D)
Graves, James Thomas (R)
Gregg, Marie Ellen (R)
Greiner, Keith Allen (R)
Hamm, Lee (D)
Hanson, Warren Eugene (R)
Harder, Joseph C (R)
Harper, Richard L (R)
Harris, Brian L (R)
Harris, Fred M (R)
Hawes, Aaron Edward (D)
Hawes, Bryan (D)
Hayden, Mike (R)
Hayes, John Francis (R)
Hedrick, Clay E (R)
Heide, Walter John (R)
Hein, Ronald Reed (R)
Heinemann, David John (R)
Henderson, Opal Mae (D)
Henry, Ailee M (R)
Hess, Paul Robert (R)
Hess, Sharon Rose (R)
Hillelson, Jeffrey P (R)
Hineman, Kalo A (R)
Hoagland, Joseph Julian (R)
Hobelman, Margaret Ellen (D)
Hoffman, Judith Linda (R)
Hohman, Loren H, II (D)
Holderman, James (D)
Hope, Clifford Ragsdale, Jr (R)
Hornbaker, Lee Vaughn (D)
Horne, Edward F (D)
Hoy, Rex Bruce (R)
Hudson, Cale (R)
Hughes, Oliver H (R)
Humphreys, Frederick M (R)
Hupp, Frances Jane (D)
Hurley, Patrick Joseph (D)
Hyland, Bernice Irene (R)
Ice, Theodore Branine (R)
Ivy, John T (D)
Jackson, Samuel Charles (R)
Jambor, Louise Irma (R)
Janssen, Jack Wesley (D)
Jennison, Harold Stewart (R)
Johnson, Michael George (D)
Jones, Glee Carol (D)
Josserand, Robert Warren (R)
Joyce, Robert H (D)
Justice, Norman E (D)
Kearns, Victor W, Jr (R)
Kelly, Lelona Kay (Lee) (D)
Keys, Martha (D)
King, Clarence Leroy, Jr (D)
Kirk, Polly (R)
Kisner, Ignatius (Ickie), (D)
Kroeger, Nadine Clara (D)
Kruckenburg, Homer Andrew (D)
Krueger, Yvonne (R)
Lady, Wendell R (R)
Laird, Charles F (D)
Landon, Alfred M (R)
Lawing, Jim (D)
Ledgin, Norman Michael (D)
Lickteig, Dan W (D)
Lindahl, Ted (R)
Littlejohn, Marvin Leroy (R)
Littler, Richard L (R)
Long, Melvin Thomas (D)
Lorentz, C Fred (R)
Loux, Richard Charles (Pete) (D)
Love, Clarence Chester (D)
Lueck, Henry Longley (D)
Luzzati, Ruth Elwood (D)
Maag, James S (R)
Madden, Robert Bruce (R)
Mainey, Donald E (D)
Marshall, William K (Ken) (D)
Masovero, John (R)
Matlack, Ardena Lavonne (D)
McCormick, William Bliss (Non-partisan)
McCray, Billy Quincy (D)
McCrum, Robert D (R)
McGill, Duane S (R)
McGowan, Sherry A (R)
McMillin, M June (D)
Merritt, Gilbert Roy (Gil) (R)
Metcalf, Vera Marie (D)
Meyers, Jan (R)
Mikesic, David Paul (D)
Mikesic, Joseph M (Babe) (D)
Miller, David Lee (D)
Miller, Dorothy Jenilee (D)
Miller, Robert Hugh (R)
Mills, Govan (D)
Mize, Chester L (R)
Mize, Mike (R)
Moore, Vincent E (R)
Moore, W Edgar (R)
Morris, Bill (R)
Mulich, Wm (Bill) (D)
Murray, John Hiram (R)
Myers, Jan (D)
Nash, Dorris Valentine (D)
Nesmith, Ole F (R)
Nettels, George E, Jr (R)
Niles, Anita Gale (D)
Niles, Irving Russell (D)
Noah, Donald Witherell (R)
Noel, James Ellsworth (R)
Norvell, Joseph F (D)
Oakes, Kermit W (R)
Orth, Robert D (R)
Otstott, Jesse Lee (D)
Owen, David Carroll (R)
Owens, Uriel Edward (D)
Palmer, Randall (R)
Parker, Letha Mary (R)
Parrish, Jim (D)
Parrish, Robert Ambrose (R)
Pearson, James Blackwood (R)
Pendergast, Paul Edward (D)
Peterson, John Charles (R)
Pfalzgraf, Harold Archer (R)
Pivonka, Charles August (D)
Pomeroy, Duane Franklin (R)
Pomeroy, Elwaine Franklin (R)
Potter, Charlene Marie (D)
Powell, Alva Lee (D)
Ranson, John S (Jack) (R)
Reardon, William J (D)
Reeves, J H (Rip) (R)
Reilly, Edward Francis, Jr (R)
Reynolds, Marian Kaye (D)
Rice, Carl Venton (D)
Robertson, Roger (D)
Rodrock, Jack L (D)
Rogers, Beth (R)
Rogers, Richard D (R)
Rogg, Herbert A (R)
Roniger, Pascal Allen (R)
Rosen, Lester L (R)
Rosenau, Fred W (D)
Roy, William Robert (D)
Rudicel, Chandler Clifton (D)
Rupp, Daniel Gabriel (R)
Saar, T D, Jr (Ted) (D)
Saia, David Joseph (Joe) (D)
Sanders, Robert R (R)
Scanlan, Charles Francis (D)
Scarlett, Floyd M (R)
Schneider, Curt Thomas (D)
Schraeder, Vernon Virgil (D)
Schroeder, Alfred Gustav (R)
Schurter, Marion Eveline (R)
Scott, Beatrice Normadine (R)
Sears, Fred N (D)
Sebelius, Keith George (R)
Sellers, Ben A (R)
Shanahan, Elwill M (R)
Shank, Mary Ellen (D)
Shankel, Buford S (R)
Shriver, Garner E (R)
Shunn, Maxine Faye (D)
Simpson, John M (R)
Skubitz, Joe (R)
Slattery, James Charles (D)
Slattery, Thomas Edward (R)
Smith, Francis E (D)
Smith, Karen Jacquelyn (D)
Smith, Shelby (R)
Southern, William S (R)
Sowers, Wesley H (R)
Sparks, Charles Alden, Jr (R)
Sprague, Harry Asa (R)
Stark, Robert M (R)
Steineger, John Francis, Jr (D)
Stephens, John D (Jack) (D)
Stone, Gordon Earl (R)
Storey, Bob Wilson (R)
Stueckemann, Walter Frederick (R)
Sutter, John F (D)
Swanson, Jay Dixon (R)
Talkington, Robert Van (R)
Templar, Ted Mac (R)
Tenopir, Lawrence L (D)
Terry, Harriet Eleanor (D)
Tessendorf, Ramona Roberta (R)
Theno, Michael Dennis (D)
Thiessen, Dan (R)
Thomas, Tracy Ann (D)
Thull, Eugene Nicholas (D)
Tillotson, J C (R)
Tobias, Ansel Walter (R)
Tucker, Wendell O (D)
Ungerer, James L (R)
Van Bebber, George Thomas (R)
Van Sickle, Tom R (R)
Vermillion, John F (R)
Vogel, John Henry (R)
Walker, Jack D (R)
Walker, Richard Bruce (R)
Wall, John M (R)
Ward, Earl Dawson (R)
Warren, Joe E (D)
Wassenberg, Shirley Mae (D)
Waters, Jerry B (R)
Weaver, Fred L (D)
Webster, William Lawrence (R)
Wells, Samuel Jay (D)
Wernette, Charles Michael (D)
Whitaker, Neil Dale (R)
White, Leonard Thomas (R)
Whiteside, Lynn W (R)
Whitlock, Irene M (R)
Whitsitt, Virgil H (R)
Whittaker, Robert (R)
Wicinski, Joseph A (D)
Wilkin, Ruth Warren (D)
Wilkinson, Ronald Joe (R)
Williams, Neil Alva (R)
Williams, R J (Dick) (R)
Williams, W O (D)
Wilson, Chuck (R)
Wingert, George (D)
Winn, Larry, Jr (R)
Winter, Wint (R)
Wisdom, Billie Joe (D)
Works, George Henry (R)
Wright, John Cook (R)
Wunsch, Paul Robert (R)
Wurtz, Richard Joseph (D)
Yonally, James Lewis (R)
Yunghans, Robert O (D)
Zajic, R C (Ray) (R)
Zimmerman, Donald Wayne (R)

KENTUCKY

Adams, James William (R)
Adams, Sidney (D)
Allen, James Edward (R)
Allen, Nelson Robert (D)
Allen, Willard C (R)
Antrobus, Randall Leon (R)
Arnold, Adrian K (D)
Bacon, Margaret Mary (R)
Baker, Nicholas (D)
Baker, Walter A (R)
Ball, Donald Ray (R)
Barker, Robert (R)
Barton, Harold Bryan (R)
Barton, Nelda Ann Lambert (R)
Baughman, Robert J (D)
Beauchamp, Arthur Paul (R)
Benson, Bob (D)
Berry, John M, Jr (D)
Bertram, Randall B (D)
Beshear, Steven L (D)
Black, Harry Gordon (R)
Blandford, Donald Joseph (D)
Blanton, Joy Sue (D)
Blume, Norbert L (D)
Blythe, E Bruce, Jr (R)
Bogardus, O A (R)
Boggs, Danny Julian (R)
Bosse, Virginia Mae (R)
Bowles, Carl (R)
Bradley, Robert James (R)
Breathitt, Edward Thompson, Jr (D)
Breckinridge, John Bayne (D)
Brewer, Sam, Jr (R)
Brinkley, William T (D)
Brooking, John R S (R)
Brothers, Robert Gene (D)
Brown, Edward G (D)
Brown, Ernest Eugene (R)
Brown, Miriam Blackburn (R)

LOUISIANA / 1049

Brown, Ray O (D)
Bruce, James Edmond (D)
Bumgardner, Bert Edward (D)
Burch, Thomas J (D)
Burke, Frank Welsh (D)
Burkhart, Stephen (R)
Butler, Wendell P (D)
Byck, Mary Helen (D)
Carroll, Julian Morton (D)
Carroll, Thomas Charles (D)
Carter, Abe Parker (R)
Carter, J C (R)
Carter, Tim Lee (R)
Caskey, Wilburn (D)
Chandler, Albert Benjamin (D)
Chandler, Bonita T (D)
Chandler, Richard (D)
Chelf, Frank, Sr (D)
Clarke, P Joseph (D)
Collins, Martha Layne (D)
Combs, Bert Thomas (D)
Cook, Marlow Webster (R)
Cooper, John Sherman (R)
Cornett, John Chris (D)
Cowan, Boyd Lynn (R)
Coy, Charles Russell (R)
Crupper, Clay (D)
Cundiff, Edwin Russell (D)
Curlin, William P, Jr (D)
Dalton, Mary Mildred (R)
Daughetee, Cheryl Ann (D)
Davie, John Turney (D)
Davis, James Adair (R)
Dawahre, Hoover (D)
DeFalaise, Louis Gaylord (R)
DeMarcus, William Harold (R)
Denham, Mitchel B (D)
Denton, Ashton Lyle (R)
Denton, Sue M (D)
Deskins, Herbert, Jr (D)
Dickinson, Millie Lockhart (D)
Dickson, Edith Bratschi (R)
Dietz, Elmer (D)
Disponett, William David (R)
Donnermeyer, William I, Sr (D)
Drago, Eugene Joseph (D)
Drury, Susie B (R)
Duncan, Cyril Douglass (D)
Duncan, Robert Michael (R)
Dunn, James R (D)
Easterly, Charles Thomas (D)
Elam, Pamela Lynn (D)
Elliott, Frank, Jr (R)
Elliott, Humphrey Taylor (R)
Embry, Carlos Brogdon, Jr (R)
Emmons, Dale Clifton (D)
Ernst, Don William (D)
Evans, Earl Wesley (R)
Evans, Richard Fulton (R)
Fallin, James Holder (D)
Farnsley, Charles Rowland Peaslee (D)
Farris, Norman Edwin (R)
Ford, Wendell H (D)
Foster, Lewis (D)
Foust, Mary Louise (R)
Fowler, Ben B (R)
Freeman, Glenn R (D)
Friend, Kelsey E (D)
Frymire, Richard L (D)
Gardner, Hoyt Devane (R)
Garrett, Tom (D)
Gay, Clay (R)
Gentry, William R, Jr (R)
Gibson, Kenneth O, Sr (D)
Gillig, Ann Stephenson (D)
Ginger, Lyman Vernon (D)
Givham, Thomas B (D)
Glenn, Earl (D)
Grafton, A Wallace, Jr (D)
Graves, Joe (R)

Griffith, Naomi Rebecca (R)
Gross, Oval (D)
Groves, James Martin (D)
Guenthner, Louis Robert, Jr (R)
Hagan, William Clarence (D)
Hammons, Owen Cecil (D)
Hancock, Charles M (D)
Handy, Thomas V (R)
Hardesty, Thomas Fabian (R)
Hardin, Lucian Thomas (R)
Harmon, Pam Jenkins (R)
Harper, Kenneth Franklin (R)
Harris, George F (D)
Hatfield, Guy, III (R)
Hatfield, Marshal Joe (R)
Hays, Marilyn A (R)
Head, Joe (D)
Hehl, Lambert Lawrence, Jr (D)
Hellard, Victor, Jr (R)
Helton, James Carter (R)
Henry, William Keith (D)
Hickey, James Clyde (D)
Hicks, James A (R)
Hill, Edward Polk, III (D)
Hislope, Leonard Russell (R)
Hoe, Harry Morgan (R)
Holbert, Salin (R)
Holbrook, Charles R, III (R)
Holcomb, Robert H (R)
Hommrich, Denis E (D)
Hopkins, Larry Jones (R)
Horlander, Nelle P (D)
House, Val A, Jr (D)
Howe, Albert Berry, Jr (R)
Hubbard, Carroll, Jr (R)
Hubbard, Eula Pearl (R)
Huddleston, Walter (Dee) (D)
Huff, Gene (R)
Hughes, Robert Felix (D)
Hurst, John (D)
Hyden, Jesse L (Jack) (R)
Imes, Kenneth Churchill (D)
Isler, John J (D)
Ison, Donald (R)
James, Mary F (R)
Jervis, Eloise Katherine (R)
Jett, Lovell Dwayne (D)
Johnson, Donald L (R)
Johnson, Gary Charles (D)
Johnson, Vernon Lee, Jr (R)
Jones, Pleas E (R)
Jordan, Kenneth Wayne (D)
Judd, Harlan Ekin, Jr (R)
Kafoglis, Nicholas Z (D)
Karem, David Kevin (D)
Kash, J B (R)
Kelly, Stuart Stacy (D)
Kenton, William G (D)
Kerr, John H, Jr (R)
Kibbey, Jack Robinson (R)
Kidd, Mae Street (D)
King, Phillip E (D)
Kinkead, Shelby C (D)
Kipping, Robert Kirtley (R)
Kleier, M J (Jerry) (D)
Knuckles, Denver C (R)
Krebs, Caroline Wagner (D)
Kuegel, William Martin (D)
Lackey, John Faris (D)
Lacy, James Reynolds (R)
Lang, George Edward (D)
Lavit, Theodore Howard (R)
Lawler, Sandra Mae (R)
Layne, William Henry (R)
Lewis, Richard Hayes (D)
Lindsay, Gross C (D)
Little, Asa Reed (R)
Little, N Clayton (D)
Locklin, Jack G (D)
Lukowsky, Robert Owen (D)
Lynd, Priscilla Ann (R)

Madron, Thomas Wm (D)
Maggard, Jack Samuel (D)
Mann, Terry Lawrence (D)
Mason, David Gray (D)
May, Woodford F (D)
Maynard, Lawrence Ray (D)
Mazzoli, Romano Louis (D)
McBee, William K (D)
McBrayer, W Terry (D)
McBride, Joseph H (D)
McCuiston, Pat M (D)
McEvoy, William Peter (D)
McGill, Charlotte S (D)
McNamara, Nell Guy (D)
Mershon, Creighton E (D)
Middleton, Clyde William (R)
Middleton, Edwin G (R)
Miller, Frank (D)
Miller, Jack Lee (D)
Miller, Scott, Jr (R)
Miller, Thomas Rowland (D)
Miller, Warren Baker (D)
Milliken, James Butler (D)
Mitchell, Ralph Wilson (D)
Mobley, Tom (D)
Molloy, James Haggin (Mike) (D)
Moloney, Michael R (D)
Morgan, Elise Fowler (R)
Morgan, Fred H (D)
Moseley, Douglas Dewayne (R)
Murphy, Delbert S (D)
Natcher, William H (D)
Nett, Carl Anthony (D)
Norris, Raymond (R)
Nunn, Louie B (R)
O'Brien, Mark D (D)
Ockerman, Foster (D)
O'Rear, Oteria L (R)
Osborne, Earl Thomas (D)
Overstreet, Raymond D (R)
Owens, Henry, III (D)
Palmer, Wilson (D)
Palmore, John Stanley, Jr (D)
Parsley, Frances Elaine (R)
Parsons, Harold Paul (D)
Patrick, James Fairchild (R)
Paxton, Jon Billy (D)
Payne, S Tilford, Jr (R)
Pearman, Virgil L (D)
Perkins, Carl D (D)
Perkinson, Maurice Leon (D)
Phelps, Paul Stephan (D)
Phelps, Thomas Preston (D)
Pickett, Lawrence Edwin (R)
Pope, Margaret Gaffin (R)
Poston, James Richard (D)
Powers, Georgia Davis (D)
Prather, Joseph W (D)
Priddy, Dottie (D)
Purvis, Paul Francis (R)
Quinlan, William Louis (D)
Rankin, Otwell C (D)
Rattliff, Herman W (R)
Reynolds, Robert Jackson (D)
Reynolds, W J (Bill), Jr (R)
Richardson, Bobby Harold (D)
Riley, Lake (R)
Roberts, William Lee (R)
Robinson, Albert Lee (R)
Rogers, Lloyd Emmett (D)
Romines, Archie N, Sr (D)
Ross, Roy R (D)
Rueff, Margaret Lillian (R)
Rush, Doris Mitchell (R)
Rush, Paula Shaye (D)
Sale, Forest (Aggie) (D)
Schmaedecke, William L (R)
Schmidt, Arthur Louis (R)
Searcy, Mary Glenn (D)
Sharp, Joshua P (R)
Sharpe, Jon Clifford M (R)

Sheehan, August (Gus) (D)
Siemens, George R (D)
Siler, Eugene (R)
Skaggs, Joel Henry (R)
Slone, Ottie Mae (R)
Smith, Belle Hardin (R)
Smith, Lacey Thomas (D)
Smith, Randolph (R)
Snyder, Marion Gene (R)
Spalding, Lester Helm (D)
Spragens, Thomas Arthur (D)
Stacy, Joe D (D)
Stacy, Linda (R)
Stafford, Harry, Jr (D)
Steinfeld, Samuel S (R)
Stephens, Don W (D)
Stewart, George E (D)
Stirler, Bonnie Werth Merrill (D)
Stone, Alec G (D)
Stone, William Philip (D)
Stovall, Thelma Loyace (D)
Strong, Walter (D)
Stuart, Eugene Page (R)
Stubblefield, Frank A (D)
Suell, Robert May (D)
Sullivan, William Litsey (D)
Swinford, John McKee (D)
Tanner, William Edgar (R)
Taylor, Essie E (R)
Taylor, Timothy Henry (D)
Thaler, Daisy (D)
Thomas, Elizabeth Gray (R)
Thomas, Philip Woodrow (D)
Thomas, Sam B (D)
Thurmond, Edwin M (R)
Tuggle, Kenneth Herndon (R)
Turner, John Raymond (D)
Turner, Marie R (D)
Van Horn, David Lee (D)
Vaughn, Fred D (D)
Veal, Harlan Hale, Jr (D)
Vincent, G W (Bill) (D)
Ward, Thomas Morgan (D)
Warren, Delbert Clayton (R)
Watkins, Sam Houston (D)
Watson, Billy James (R)
Webb, Donald Woodford (D)
Weidner, George E (D)
Wells, Dwight Allen (D)
Wetherby, Lawrence Winchester (D)
White, Anthony Eugene (D)
White, Glenn (D)
White, James H, Jr (D)
Whitfield, W Edward (D)
Wible, Charles Stephen (D)
Williams, Josephine P (R)
Wilson, Earl D (R)
Winchester, Lucy Alexander (R)
Wyatt, Wilson Watkins, Sr (D)
Yates, Albert (R)
Yates, James B (D)
Yates, Robert Duncan (R)
Yocom, Danny (D)
Young, John William (R)

LOUISIANA

Abadie, Arthur F (D)
Accardo, Joseph, Jr (D)
Ackal, Elias, Jr (D)
Alario, John A, Jr (D)
Allen, L Calhoun, Jr (D)
Allison, Regis (D)
Anderson, Nancy Fix (D)
Anzalone, Frank L (D)
Bagert, Ben (D)
Bagwell, Harrison Garey (R)
Baker, Richard Hugh (D)

LOUISIANA (cont)

Bankston, Jesse H (D)
Bares, Allen R (D)
Barham, Mack Elwin
Barthelemy, Sidney John (D)
Batt, David L (D)
Bauer, Carl W (D)
Bechac, A Denis (D)
Becnel, Benoit Paul (D)
Bella, Vincent J (D)
Bergeron, Belvin Francis (D)
Bigby, Walter Oliver (D)
Blair, Cecil R (D)
Blount, Juilus A (D)
Blue, George Riebel (D)
Boese, Elsie Jean (R)
Boese, H Lamar (R)
Boggs, Corinne Morrison Claiborne (D)
Bolton, Edgar Simpson (Constitution)
Booker, Edward Hamilton (D)
Borrello, A Charles (D)
Boyce, James H (R)
Boyer, James Gambrell (D)
Brady, Elward T (D)
Brady, James Joseph (D)
Breaux, John B (D)
Breaux, John Richard (D)
Brinkhaus, Armand Joseph (D)
Broussard, Marcus Anson, Jr (D)
Brown, Charles M (D)
Brown, J Marshall (D)
Brown, James Harvey (D)
Brown, William D (D)
Bulcao, Douglas William (D)
Burchett, Dewey Eldridge, Jr (D)
Burton, George Aubrey, Jr (R)
Bussie, Fran Martinez (D)
Bussie, Victor (D)
Byles, Robert Valmore (D)
Cade, John H, Jr (D)
Caffery, Patrick Thomson (D)
Cain, James David (D)
Calhoun, Nathan Meredith (D)
Calogero, Pascal Frank, Jr (D)
Canion, Judith Colleen (R)
Carter, C Kay (D)
Casey, Joseph S (D)
Casey, Thomas A (D)
Castellini, William McGregor (R)
Cawthorn, Merle Sloan (D)
Chabert, Leonard J (D)
Charbonnet, Louis, III (D)
Clark, Clabie (D)
Clarke, Jack Wells (D)
Colten, A Thomas (D)
Cotton, W Davis (D)
Crain, Billy Ray (D)
Crisler, Robert Morris (D)
Darsey, Elton A (D)
Dart, Stephen Plauche (D)
Daugherty, Michael Dennis (R)
Davenport, Clydia Ann (D)
Davis, Jackson Beauregard (D)
De Blieux, Joseph Davis (D)
Deen, Jesse C (D)
deGravelles, Charles Camille (R)
de la Vergne, Hughes Jules, II (R)
Despot, George Joseph (R)
D'Gerolamo, Edward J (D)
Diamond, Lloyd Webb (R)
Dischler, Louis, Jr (D)
Doucet, Eddie A (D)
Drew, R Harmon (D)
Duhe, Lester Antoine (R)
Duke, Merlin (R)
Dumas, Woodrow Wilson (Woody) (D)
Dunn, Forrest (D)
Dupre, Michael (D)
Dupuis, Steven J (D)
Duval, Claude Berwick (D)
Dyer, Wilbur (D)
Dykes, W E (Bill) (D)
Eagan, Frederick Leitz (D)
Eaton, Lewis Wilmot, Jr (D)
Edwards, Edwin W (D)
Eleser, Golda Easley (R)
Ensminger, John (R)
Falcon, Margaret Mary (D)
Farrar, Reginald Warren, Jr (R)
Fayard, Calvin C, Jr (D)
Feldman, Martin L C (R)
Fernandez, Joachim Octave (D)
Fitzmorris, James E, Jr (D)
Folkes, W D (D)
Fontenot, James E (D)
Foshee, Paul (D)
Fowler, H M (D)
Fox, George F, Jr (D)
Fredlund, Ray (R)
Freeman, Robert L (D)
Gaudin, Edward Clark (R)
Gerald, Gaston (D)
Gibbs, Henry Lawrence, Jr (D)
Gilbert, J C (D)
Gravel, Camille F, Jr (D)
Gregson, Vernon Joseph (D)
Grisbaum, Charles, Jr (D)
Guidry, Jesse (D)
Guidry, Richard P (D)
Guillory, Robert K (D)
Gunter, Carl N (D)
Guste, William Joseph (D)
Hainkel, John Joseph, Jr (D)
Hammons, John Layne (R)
Hardy, Paul Jude (D)
Haynes, Lee A (D)
Haynes, Lonnie Ray (D)
Haynes, William G, Jr (R)
Hebert, Dennis P (D)
Hebert, F Edward (D)
Hecht, Henry Del Banco, Jr (R)
Heitman, Betty Green (R)
Henry, Edgerton L (R)
Hickey, Theodore M (D)
Hollins, Harry M (D)
Holstead, George B (D)
Hudson, Morley Alvin (R)
Huenefeld, Fred, Jr (D)
Humphries, T W (D)
Hunter, Robert Edward (D)
Irwin, Leon, III (D)
Jackson, Alphonse, Jr (D)
Jackson, Johnny, Jr (D)
Jenkins, Louis (Woody) (D)
John, John N, III (D)
Johnson, Louise B (D)
Johnston, J Bennett, Jr (D)
Jones, Johnnie Anderson (D)
Jones, Robert G (D)
Jumonville, J E (D)
Kiefer, Nat Gerard (D)
Kilpatrick, Kenneth Dale (D)
King, Frederick Jenks (R)
King, Semmes Walmsley (D)
Kinler, Gladys Veronica (R)
Knight, William Noel (R)
Knowles, Jesse M (D)
Kostelka, Robert William (R)
LaBorde, M J (D)
Laborde, Raymond J (D)
Lambert, Henry M (D)
Lancaster, Charles Doerr, Jr (R)
Landrieu, Moon Edwin (D)
Landrieu, Phyllis (D)
Landry, John Joseph, Jr (D)
Landry, Walter J (D)
Lauricella, Francis E (Hank) (D)
Leach, Claude, Jr (D)
LeBlanc, Charles John (R)
LeBlanc, Edward Faisans, Jr (D)
LeBlanc, Sam A (D)
LeBleu, Conway (D)
LeBreton, Edward Francis, Jr
Leithman, John Kenneth (D)
Lemann, Arthur Anthony III (D)
Leonard, Herbert Lee (R)
Leonard, Will Ernest Jr (D)
Life, Ruby Jacquelyn (R)
Lindh, Patricia Sullivan (R)
Long, Blanche Revere (D)
Long, Gillis William (D)
Long, Jimmy Dale (D)
Long, Russell B (D)
Long, Speedy O (D)
Lottinger, Morris Albert, Jr (D)
Manuel, Robert Frank (D)
Marchang, Theodore J (D)
Marix, Carlysle Jerome (D)
Martin, James Paul (D)
Martin, Wade Omer, Jr (D)
McCain, Wilbur Teal (D)
McGuffee, George Orville (D)
McIntosh, James David (D)
McKeithen, John Julian (D)
McLeod, William Lasater, Jr
Michot, Louis Joseph (D)
Miller, Frank L (D)
Miller, Ralph Ross (D)
Mills, Kirby D (D)
Mills, Newt V (D)
Montgomery, A Harold (D)
Moore, W Henson (R)
Morrison, Delesseps S, Jr (D)
Morrison, James Hobson (D)
Mouser, Cotys Milner (D)
Mouton, Edgar G (D)
Narcisse, Lawrence Joseph, III (D)
Needham, Daisy Eudora (R)
Nicholson, Elwyn J (D)
Noe, James Albert (D)
Norfolk, Neveda Brooks (Veda) (R)
Nunez, Samuel B, Jr (D)
Ogilvie, Oscar Phillips (D)
O'Keefe, Michael Hanley (D)
O'Neal, B F, Jr (R)
Osterberger, Kenneth E (D)
Parker, Mary Evelyn (D)
Passman, Otto Ernest (D)
Patti, Frank J (D)
Paxton, Ralph Eugene (R)
Peltier, Harvey A, Jr (D)
Perkins, Peggy Lynn (D)
Pierre, Wilfred Thomas (D)
Poston, Bryan A (D)
Randolph, Edward G, Jr (D)
Randolph, Sanna Poorman (D)
Rarick, John Richard (D)
Rathe, Barbara A (D)
Rayburn, B B (Sixty) (D)
Read, William Brooks (D)
Rees, Grover Joseph, III (R)
Reese, Bob L (R)
Reilly, Kevin P (D)
Rice, Thomas J, Sr (R)
Rivers, John Stainsby (R)
Roberts, Donald Duane (R)
Robillard, Roy (D)
Rowley, Bert Wallace (D)
Rush, Samuel Lee (R)
Russek, Trula Wells (R)
Sanders, Joe William (D)
Schaefer, Frances Darrah (R)
Schmitt, Earl Joseph (D)
Schroeder, Leah Webb (D)
Scogin, Edward C (D)
Scott, Eugene W, Jr (D)
Segura, Perry (D)
Shannon, V C (D)
Sheldon, Joe S, Jr (R)
Sheridan, Lawrence A (D)
Shirah, Ross Patrick (R)
Simon, Warren Joseph (D)
Simoneaux, Frank P (D)
Soniat, Novyse Elaine (D)
Sour, A W, Jr (R)
Stear, David Spring (R)
Steele, Jane Riddel (R)
Stephenson, J E (D)
Stinson, Ford Edwards (D)
Stone, John Clinton (R)
Stoutz, Edwin A, Jr (D)
Strain, R H (D)
Summers, Frank Wynerth (D)
Sutterfield, James R (R)
Tapper, Elmer R (D)
Tassin, John Adam, Jr (D)
Tate, Albert, Jr (D)
Tatman, Aubrey C (R)
Tauzin, W J (D)
Taylor, Dorothy Mae (D)
Theriot, Roy Raoul (D)
Thompson, Francis C (D)
Thompson, Mike (D)
Thompson, Richard (D)
Tiemann, M Joseph (D)
Toca, Harold J (D)
Torry, P Spencer (D)
Treen, David C (R)
Troy, Ralph Talbot (D)
Turnley, Richard (D)
Ullo, J Chris (D)
Van Cleave, Thomas Winlock (D)
Vick, Kathleen M (D)
Vidrine, John Larry (D)
Villar, Emery L (D)
Waggonner, Joe D, Jr (D)
Waitz, Roberta Charlene (R)
Wall, Shady R (D)
Watson, Arthur Chopin (D)
White, Marion Overton (D)
Wilkins, James Climent (R)
Williamson, Don (D)
Wilmer, Charlotte Mae (D)
Wilson, James H (D)
Windhorst, Fritz (D)
Winters, Mary Lou (D)
Womack, Lantz (D)
Woodiel, John William, Jr (R)
Woodley, Edmund Etchison (R)

MAINE

Aiken, Ruth Merle Jones (R)
Albert, Thomas P (D)
Allen, Kenneth Peter (D)
Ault, David R (R)
Bachrach, Anne Jameson (D)
Bagley, Laurence P (R)
Ballou, John Waldo (R)
Baraby, Marion E (R)
Barter, Merrill Robert (R)
Bartlett, Harold Durward (R)
Beliveau, Severin Matthew (D)
Benn, Cedric Shirley (R)
Bennett, Philip Roy, Jr (D)
Berman, Margaret W (D)
Berry, Elmer F, Jr (D)
Berry, Glenys W (R)
Berry, Philip P (D)
Berry, Richard Nathaniel (R)
Berube, Georgette B (D)
Binnette, Joseph E (D)
Birt, Walter Arthur (R)
Bishop, Leonard Lee (R)

Blake, Roy Clifford, Sr (R)
Blodgett, William B (D)
Bonney, Edward Mayson (D)
Boudreau, Anne M (D)
Bourassa, Donald Craig (R)
Bowie, Leon (R)
Brennan, Joseph Edward (D)
Broderick, Fay Leone (D)
Broderick, Richard Howard (D)
Brooks, Marilyn Elizabeth (R)
Brown, Darryl Newton (R)
Brown, Frederick Tracy (R)
Brown, Marilyn B (Ann) (R)
Brown, Marion Fuller (R)
Burns, Donald Howard (D)
Bustin, David W (D)
Byers, Charlotte Z (R)
Call, George F (Independent)
Carbonneau, Roland Joseph (D)
Carey, Frances Dodge (R)
Carey, Richard James (D)
Carpenter, Michael Eugene (D)
Carr, James Drew (R)
Carroll, George Arthur (D)
Carter, Donald Victor (D)
Chandler, Nancy Ann (D)
Chonko, Lorraine N (D)
Churchill, Eugene L (R)
Clanchette, Alton E (D)
Clark, Nancy Randall (D)
Clemente, John F (D)
Clifford, Robert William (D)
Coffey, John P, Jr (D)
Cohen, Nathan (D)
Cohen, William S (R)
Collins, Samuel Wilson, Jr (R)
Conley, Gerard P (D)
Conners, Maynard Gilbert (R)
Connolly, Laurence E, Jr (D)
Cook, Marjorie Jeanne (Marge) (D)
Cooney, Leighton H, Jr (D)
Corson, Neal Craig (R)
Cote, Albert E (D)
Cox, Harold R (D)
Crane, Henrietta Page (R)
Crockett, Stephen Robert (D)
Cummings, Minnette Hunsiker (R)
Curran, Peter J (D)
Curran, Raymond Joseph (D)
Curtis, Douglas W (R)
Curtis, Kenneth Merwin (D)
Curtis, Theodore S, Jr (R)
Cyr, Edward P (D)
Dam, C Everett (D)
Damborg, Peter Martin (R)
Danton, Peter W (R)
Davies, Richard (D)
Davis, Shelby Cullom (R)
Day, James V (R)
Delogu, Orlando E (D)
Deschambeault, Frederic (D)
DeVane, Harvey E (D)
DeWitt, Ellen Louise (D)
Dietz, Lew (D)
Doak, Harlan Everett (D)
Dow, Charles G (D)
Drigotas, Frank Martin (D)
Dudley, James T (D)
DuFour, E James (D)
Dunfey, Robert John (D)
Durgin, Lena C (R)
Dutremble, Richard Donald (D)
Dyar, Roswell E (R)
Dyer, Donald E (R)
Edgar, Joseph T (R)
Elvin, David N
Emery, David Farnham (R)
Emery, Eugene Marshall (D)
Erwin, James Shrewsbury (R)
Farley, Robert M (D)

Farnham, Roderick Ewen (R)
Fast, Robert Erwin (D)
Faucher, Raymond N (D)
Fenlason, A Harold (R)
Ferris, Robert Charles (R)
Finemore, Louis F (R)
Fitzpatrick, John Leo (D)
Flanagan, James E (D)
Fraser, Emile J (D)
Gahagan, Hayes Edward (R)
Garsoe, William J (R)
Gartley, Markham Ligon (D)
Gauthier, Roland A (D)
Genthner, Georgia Caro (D)
Goodwin, Harland Clark, Jr (D)
Goodwin, Kathleen Watson (D)
Gordon, Joann Chase (R)
Gould, Stephen R (R)
Graffam, Linwood E (R)
Graham, David Livingstone (D)
Gray, Wayne C (R)
Greeley, Edwin H (R)
Greenlaw, Lawrence Pearl, Jr (D)
Gross, Lois Irene (D)
Grover, Lillian Evelin (R)
Hale, Robert (R)
Hall, Donald M (D)
Hanson, Bernice Zilpha (R)
Harding, Edward Perry (Ned) (R)
Hare, Roger C (D)
Haskins, Sturgis (D)
Hathaway, William Dodd (D)
Henderson, James S (D)
Hennessey, William J (D)
Henry, Merton Goodell (R)
Hewes, Richard David (R)
Hichens, Walter Wilson (R)
Higgins, Linwood McIntire (R)
Hills, Dave (D)
Hinds, Samuel Arthur (R)
Hobbins, Barry John (D)
Hodgkin, Douglas Irving (R)
Hollingsworth, David Jeffrey (R)
Holman, Joseph Frederick (R)
Huber, David G (R)
Hughes, Stephen Thomas (D)
Hunter, Guy I (R)
Hutchings, Marjorie Clyde (R)
Immonen, Jacob J (R)
Ingegneri, Philip Alfred (D)
Isaacson, Robert A (D)
Jackson, Patrick T, Jr (R)
Jackson, Philip C (R)
Jacques, Emile (D)
Jalbert, Louis (D)
Jensen, John W (D)
Jephson, Evelyn S (D)
Jewett, Clayton Edwin (D)
Johnston, Peter W (D)
Joly, Cyril Matthew, Jr (R)
Jones, Beatrice Eleanor (D)
Jones, Harold Leon (R)
Joyce, John J (D)
Kany, Judy C (D)
Katz, Bennett David (R)
Kauffman, Frank R (R)
Kelleher, Edward C (D)
Kelley, Dorothy B (R)
Kelley, Peter Stephen (D)
King, Spencer M
Komer, Jane Gleick (D)
Kyros, Peter Nicholas (D)
LaCharite, Bertrand M (D)
Laffin, Stanley E (R)
LaPointe, Thomas R (D)
Laverty, Dorothy (D)
Lawrence, Margery B (R)
LeBlanc, Armand A (D)
Leonard, J David (D)

Lewin, Theodore E (R)
Lewis, Geoffrey W
Lewis, Joyce E (R)
Linnell, John R (R)
Littlefield, John Allan (R)
Littlefield, Lloyd (R)
Lizotte, Jean-Paul Marcel (D)
Longley, James Bernard (Independent)
Lovell, Ralph Marston (R)
Lunt, Frederick B (R)
Lynch, Arthur P (D)
MacDonald, Clyde Jr (D)
MacEachern, Robert A (D)
Mackel, Edward H (R)
MacLeod, James C (R)
Mahany, Luman P (D)
Marcotte, Guy Albert (D)
Marden, Donald Harlow (R)
Marden, Robert Allen (R)
Marquis, Norman J F (D)
Martin, Antoinette C (D)
Martin, John L (D)
Martin, Marion E (R)
Martin, Roland Danny (D)
Maxwell, Sidney D (D)
Mazzeo, Dorinda Coughlin (D)
McBreairty, James (R)
McCloskey, Jay Patrick (D)
McCollister, Benjamin Stephen (D)
McKernan, John Rettie, Jr (R)
McMahon, James K (R)
McNally, Cecil H (R)
McQuade, J Stanley (R)
Merrill, Philip L (D)
Messer, Merle Aubrey (R)
Micoleau, Charles Judd (D)
Mills, Kenneth Armour (D)
Miskavage, Margaret Brown (R)
Mitchell, Elizabeth H (D)
Mitchell, George John (D)
Monks, Robert A G (R)
Moreshead, Charles E (R)
Morin, Leatrice (D)
Morton, Richard G (R)
Mulkern, Thomas J (D)
Murray, Frank John (D)
Muskie, Edmund Sixtus (D)
Nadeau, Richard James (D)
Najarian, Mary (D)
Nault, Julia L (D)
Newton, Phinehas Stewart, IV (R)
Nichols, David A (R)
Noddin, Harold Staples (D)
Norris, John M, II (R)
O'Connor, Gwendolyn Marie (D)
O'Leary, Donald R (D)
Orestis, John Christopher (D)
Pachios, Harold Christy (D)
Palmer, Linwood E, Jr (R)
Parker, Mae Frances (D)
Paul, John W (D)
Payne, Frederick George (R)
Peakes, James L (D)
Pease, Violet Call (D)
Pelosi, Thomas Sanbar (D)
Pendergast, M Abbott (R)
Perkins, Stephen L (R)
Perkins, Thomas Ralph (R)
Pert, Edwin Harry (D)
Peter, Yerda Elizabeth (D)
Peterson, Philip F (R)
Peterson, Thomas J (D)
Pierce, Richard Herbert (R)
Pineo, Fred Benjamin, Jr (R)
Post, Bonnie (D)
Powell, Floyd (D)
Pratt, John Alden (R)
Pray, Charles P (D)

Quinn, Rodney S (D)
Raymond, Arthur Charles (D)
Redmond, Clarice T (D)
Reed, John Hathaway (R)
Reeves, Bruce Manning (D)
Richardson, James M (R)
Rideout, Harry Freeman (D)
Ring, Charles Warren (R)
Roberts, John B (R)
Rolde, Neil Richard (D)
Rollins, John Herbert (R)
Russell, Doris Mae (R)
Russell, Theodore Henry (D)
Saunders, Emily C (D)
Scanlan, Susan Frances (D)
Schoenberger, Maralyn Morton (D)
Scribner, Fred Clark, Jr (R)
Scribner, Rodney Latham (D)
Sewall, Joseph (R)
Shapiro, Samuel David (D)
Shute, Melvin Arthur (R)
Silverman, Harold L (R)
Smith, Douglas Myles (D)
Smith, Frederick Orville, II (R)
Smith, Gordon Henry (R)
Smith, Margaret Chase (R)
Snow, Roger V, Jr (R)
Snowe, Olympia Jean (R)
Snowe, Peter Trafton (R)
Speers, Jerrold Bond (R)
Spencer, Richard A (D)
Sprowl, Arthur M (R)
Stillings, Richard Wallace (R)
Strout, Donald A (R)
Stubbs, Robert G (R)
Susi, Roosevelt T (R)
Swett, Dana Malcolm (R)
Talbot, Gerald E (D)
Tanous, Wakine Gregory (R)
Tarr, Gail H (R)
Taylor, Thomas South (R)
Teague, Thomas Morse (R)
Telow, John (R)
Therlault, Albert (D)
Thomas, Elias, III (R)
Thomas, John L (R)
Tibbetts, Donna Harriman (R)
Tierney, James E (D)
Torrey, Glen W (R)
Tozier, Kenneth E, Jr (D)
Trotzky, Howard M (R)
Truman, Peter (D)
Tupper, Stanley R (R)
Twitchell, R Donald (D)
Tyndale, Elmont Scott (R)
Usher, Ronald E (R)
Violette, Elmer H (D)
Wagner, James B (D)
Walker, Vaughan A (R)
Webber, Donald Jasper (D)
Weeks, Elaine C (R)
Weil, Gordon Lee (D)
Whitzell, Norman P (D)
Wilfong, James F (D)
Winship, George S (D)
Wyman, J Hollis (R)

MARYLAND

Abrams, Rosalie Silber (D)
Abramson, Murray (D)
Adams, Victorine Quille (D)
Agnew, Spiro Theodore (R)
Ahlers, John Clarke (R)
Aiken, Patricia O'Brien (D)
Allen, Aris Tee (R)
Allen, Richard M (Dick) (R)
Allnutt, Robert Frederick (D)
Alperstein, Arthur Stuart (D)
Ambrose, Myles Joseph (R)

MARYLAND (cont)

Amoss, William H (D)
Anderson, Dale (D)
Anderson, David Lawrence (D)
Anderson, McKenny Willis (D)
Anderson, William McOwan, III (R)
Andolsek, Ludwig John (D)
Andringa, Robert Charles (R)
Apostol, John Cleo (R)
Arnick, John Stephen (D)
Ashworth, Richard Andrew (R)
Athey, Tyras S (D)
Avara, R Charles (D)
Bachman, Harold L (D)
Bailar, Benjamin F
Baily, Nathan A (D)
Baker, Anne Elizabeth (D)
Baker, Donald Matthew (D)
Baker, Joe M (D)
Baldwin, Douglas Parks (R)
Banks, Patricia Meise (D)
Barabba, Vincent P (R)
Barber, Arthur Whiting (D)
Barbour, Robert Taylor (R)
Barkan, Alexander Elias
Barr, Bruce Reid (R)
Barthelmes, Wes (D)
Basilone, Peter J (D)
Bauman, Robert Edmund (R)
Bayley, Ned Duane (R)
Beall, J Glenn, Jr (R)
Bean, Joseph Edward (D)
Beard, David Chester (D)
Beattie, Charles Kenneth (R)
Beck, Raymond Edward (R)
Becker, Martin Stanley (D)
Bell, Alexander B (D)
Bennett, Marion T (R)
Bentley, Helen Delich (R)
Berdes, George Raymond (D)
Berg, George L, Jr (R)
Berman, Jason S (D)
Bernbaum, Maurice Marshall
Bernhard, Berl (D)
Bernstein, George Kaskel (R)
Bernstein, Jay S (D)
Biemiller, Andrew J (D)
Bienen, Kay G (D)
Billingsley, Lance William (D)
Bishop, John J, Jr (R)
Black, David Statler (D)
Blount, Clarence W (D)
Blumenthal, Charles S (D)
Bolden, DeCorsey E (R)
Bonvegna, Joseph S (D)
Boone, Alexander Gordon, Jr (D)
Booth, Bert (R)
Boozer, F Vernon (R)
Boswell, Hildagardeis (D)
Boyd, Jesse Pierson (R)
Boyer, Elroy G (D)
Bozick, Peter A (D)
Bradford, William Hollis, Jr (D)
Brailey, Troy F (D)
Brecht, Warren F (R)
Bregman, Jacob I (D)
Brightman, Samuel Charles (D)
Briscoe, John Hanson (D)
Broadwater, Tommie, Jr (D)
Brodsky, Richard Eugene (D)
Brown, Torrey Carl (D)
Browning, George Mortimer (D)
Buggs, John Allen (D)
Burch, Francis Boucher (D)
Burgess, Hugh (D)
Burgess, Warren Randolph (R)
Burke, Gerard Patrick (Independent)
Burns, Andrew Joseph, (D)
Butler, Charles Frederick (R)

Butler, Warren Harold (R)
Butscher, Brenda Joyce (R)
Byrnes, John Carroll (D)
Byrnes, William B (D)
Byron, Goodloe Edgar (D)
Byron, Katharine Edgar (D)
Cade, John A (R)
Callas, Michael G (D)
Calvert, William Bailey (D)
Cardin, Benjamin Louis (D)
Cardin, Carl William (R)
Carlson, Jack Wilson
Cass, Millard (D)
Chamberlain, Thomas Wilson, Sr (R)
Chasnoff, Joel (D)
Chester, Joseph Arnathen, Sr (D)
Christie, John M (R)
Clark, James, Jr (D)
Clark, Lyn Henderson (D)
Clarke, James Thompson (R)
Clendening, June Yvonne (D)
Clifford, Clark McAdams (D)
Close, Geoffrey Robinson (R)
Clowes, Dean Kay (D)
Cody, Thomas G (R)
Cole, Beth Ellen (D)
Cole, William Edwin, Jr (D)
Connell, Jerome F, Sr (D)
Conroy, Edward Thomas (D)
Coolahan, John Carroll (D)
Coombe, Patricia J (R)
Cooper, Theodore
Corderman, John Printz (D)
Costello, J Daniel (D)
Cox, Loren Charles (D)
Cox, Robert Emmett (R)
Cox, William Harvey, Jr (D)
Crane, Kent Bruce (R)
Crawford, Victor Lawrence (D)
Crivella, Barbara Ann (R)
Crowe, Philip Kingsland
Cumiskey, Thomas Bernard (D)
Cummings, Frank (R)
Curran, Gerald Joseph (D)
Curran, J Joseph (D)
Curran, J Joseph, Jr (D)
Dabrowski, Edward J, Jr (D)
D'Alesandro, Thomas, Jr (D)
Davis, John Eugene (D)
Davis, Lanny Jesse (D)
Davis, Mary Wright (D)
Davis, W Lester (D)
Day, J Edward (D)
Dean, Walter Raleigh, Jr (D)
Debuskey, Charlotte Chipper (D)
Della, George Washington (D)
Delphey, Julien Paul (R)
Dembling, Paul Gerald
DePalma, Samuel
Deschler, Lewis
Devlin, Gerard Francis (D)
Dixon, Isaiah (Ike), Jr (D)
Dixon, Walter Thomas, Sr (D)
Dize, Carlton Yank (R)
Dobbin, Tilton Hemsley (R)
Docter, Charles Alfred (D)
Dorman, Arthur (D)
Doub, William Offutt (R)
Douglass, Calvin Albert (D)
Douglass, John William (D)
Douglass, Robert Lee (D)
Drago, Charles Grady (R)
Drea, Arthur S, Jr (D)
Duckett, Warren Bird, Jr (D)
Dukert, Joseph Michael (R)
DuPont, Robert Louis (Jr)
Dypski, Cornell N (D)
Dypski, Raymond A (D)
Dyson, Royden (Roy) (D)
Eckles, Stanley Heurich (R)

Einschutz, Louis E (D)
Eisenberg, Warren Wolff (R)
Eisenhower, Milton Stover (R)
Ellis, Clyde T (D)
Ellsworth, Robert F (R)
Emanuel, Meyer M, Jr (D)
Emory, Richard W, Jr (D)
Enfield, Clifton Willis (R)
Englund, Merrill Wayne (D)
Ennis, Robert Taylor (R)
Ernst, Joseph Michael, Sr (D)
Evans, Richard H (R)
Evans, William Robert (D)
Fallon, George H (D)
Fallon, John Joseph (D)
Farrington, Thomas (D)
Fielding, Elizabeth May (R)
Finan, Thomas B (D)
Finger, Harold B
Fisher, Charles Osborne, Jr (D)
Fisher, George Watson (D)
Fleisher, Risselle Rosenthal (D)
Fornos, Werner H (D)
Forward, David Ross (R)
Francisco, Douglas Lloyd (R)
Friedel, Samuel Nathaniel (D)
Friedman, Alan Richard (D)
Friedman, Edward David (D)
Frosch, Robert Alan
Garbett, Richard Walker (R)
Garcia, Labre Rudolph (R)
Gardner, John William (R)
Garmatz, Edward A (D)
Gebhardt, Joseph Davis (D)
Gilchrist, Charles W (D)
Giolito, Carolyn Hughes (D)
Glackin, Paul Louis (D)
Glass, Joseph Edward (D)
Glick, Leslie Alan (D)
Goldberg, Samuel (R)
Goldstein, Herbert (D)
Goldstein, Louis L (D)
Goldwater, Marilyn (D)
Gore, Louise (R)
Gottlieb, Sanford (D)
Gould, Kingdon, Jr (R)
Gray, Kenneth Elwood (D)
Green, Leo Edward (D)
Greene, Nancy Louise (D)
Greenwalt, Lynn Adams (R)
Gresham, Robert Coleman (R)
Gude, Gilbert (R)
Haag, George A (R)
Hagner, Elmer F, Jr (D)
Hale, Samuel (R)
Hall, Edward Thomas (R)
Hall, Keith Edward (R)
Hampton, Robert Edward (R)
Hanks, Emma Jane (R)
Harchenhorn, V Lanny (R)
Hardesty, Doris Gibson (D)
Hargreaves, John R (D)
Harner, Doris Wilhide (R)
Harrigan, Lucille Frasca (D)
Harris, John Mathew Wade (R)
Harrison, Hattie N (D)
Harrison, Joseph Wylie (R)
Hartmann, Robert Trowbridge (R)
Hathaway, Michael David (R)
Heffner, George E (D)
Helm, Lewis Marshall (R)
Helms, William J, Jr (D)
Helton, Arthur Henry, Jr (D)
Henderson, Frances (R)
Henkin, Daniel Z (D)
Hergenroeder, Henry Robert, Jr (D)
Hermann, Albert Bartholomew (R)
Hermann, Sylvia (R)
Herrema, Robert Louis (R)
Hess, Arthur Emil

Hickman, Carter Malcolm (D)
Hickman, Russell Orlando (D)
Hickman, Timothy Ricktor (R)
Hoffman, Irwin F (D)
Hogan, Lawrence Joseph (R)
Holland, Cecil Fletcher (R)
Holloway, Wendell Mondoza (D)
Holt, Marjorie Sewell (R)
Hopkins, Charles A Porter (R)
Horne, William S (D)
Howell, Pinkney Albert (D)
Hoyer, Steny Hamilton (D)
Hughes, Harry Roe (D)
Hughes, Royston Charles (R)
Hull, Ann Remington (D)
Hummel, Arthur W, Jr
Hunton, Benjamin Lacy (R)
Hurley, Kirk Lamar (R)
Hutchinson, Donald Paul (D)
Hyatt, Jerry Herbert (D)
Hyde, DeWitt Stephen (R)
Hyde, Henry Van Zile, Jr (R)
Hymel, Gary Gerard (D)
Israel, Lesley Lowe (D)
Ives, George Skinner (R)
Izac, Edouard Victor Michel (D)
Jacobson, Susan G (D)
Jaffe, Irving (D)
James, William S (D)
Johnson, G Griffith, Jr (R)
Johnson, Jed, Jr (D)
Johnson, Sylvia Taylor (D)
Johnston, Imogene Bane (R)
Jones, James Locke (D)
Jones, Marshall William, Jr (R)
Julian, Chester Roy (D)
Kach, Albert Wade (R)
Karey, Joseph Norman (R)
Kaylor, Omer Thomas, Jr (R)
Kazy, Theodore James (R)
Kelly, Winfield Maurice, Jr (D)
Kendall, Barbara Berry (R)
Kendall, Don Robert (R)
Kendall, William T (R)
Kenney, Edward Beckham (R)
Kenney, Erica G (R)
Kernan, Thomas B (D)
Kiladis, Nicholas James (D)
Kirby, George Albert, III (R)
Kirkpatrick, Evron Maurice (D)
Kleppe, Thomas Savig (R)
Kline, Paul Arthur (R)
Knoll, Craig Stephen (D)
Kolberg, William Henry (R)
Kornegay, Horace Robinson (D)
Koss, Helen Levine (D)
Kunkel, Joan Mapleton (D)
Laessig, Walter Bruce (R)
Laitin, Joseph (D)
Lancaster, Karen R (R)
Lankler, Alexander MacDonald (R)
Lapides, Julian Lee (D)
Larson, Clarence Edward (R)
Latshaw, Robert E, Jr (R)
Lee, Blair III (D)
Lee, Lena King (D)
Levin, E Theodore (D)
Levitan, Laurence (D)
Lewis, Virginia Bowland (R)
Lipin, Alfred Jerome (D)
Locke, Barry M (D)
Lockwood, Jane Biggers (R)
Loevinger, Lee (D)
Long, Clarence Dickinson Jr (D)
Long, Joseph J, Sr (D)
Long, Robert C Biggy (D)
Long, Susanna Larter (Susie) (D)
Lowe, Thomas Hunter (D)

MASSACHUSETTS / 1053

Lynch, James H (D)
Macaulay, Joseph Hugh (R)
Machen, Hervey Gilbert, Jr (D)
Mackie, Richard D (D)
Madonna, William Joseph, Jr (D)
Malkus, Frederick C, Jr (D)
Malone, J Edward (R)
Mandel, Marvin (D)
Manlove, William Clark (D)
Marbury, Charles Clagett (D)
Markey, David John, III (R)
Marks, Robert Herman, Jr (R)
Martin, James R, Jr (D)
Mason, Edward Joseph (R)
Mason, Norman Christy (D)
Massenburg, Katherine Black (R)
Masters, Kenneth Halls (D)
Mathias, Charles McC, Jr (R)
Mathis, Mark Jay
Matthews, Herbert Spencer (D)
Matthews, Richard Carroll (D)
Mattingly, Joseph Aloysius, Jr (D)
Maurer, Lucille Shirley Darvin (D)
McCaffrey, William R (D)
McCoy, Dennis Charles (D)
McDermott, Edward Aloysious (D)
McGuirk, Harry J (D)
McKinney, Joseph Evans (D)
McPherson, Harry Cummings, Jr (D)
Medairy, Mark Curtis, Jr (D)
Menes, Pauline H (D)
Meyer, M Barry (D)
Michaleski, Nancy Pope (R)
Miedusiewski, American Joe (D)
Mikulski, Barbara Ann (D)
Miles, Katherine C Karwasinski (R)
Millenson, Roy Handen (R)
Miller, Thomas V Mike, Jr (D)
Miltich, Paul Andrew (R)
Minnick, Daniel James, Jr (D)
Mitchell, Clarence M, III (D)
Mitchell, Parren James (D)
Mitchell, R Clayton, Jr (D)
Moerschel, W Neal (R)
Monahan, John Leo (D)
Moore, George Mansfield (R)
Morris, Jay Fleron (R)
Morsberger, Louis Phillip (D)
Morton, Rogers Clark Ballard (R)
Mothershead, Andrew O (D)
Munson, Donald Francis (R)
Murphy, Arthur G, Sr (D)
Murphy, Charles Springs (D)
Murphy, Richard James (D)
Murphy, Richard William (D)
Murray, Hyde H (R)
Nash, Peter Gillette (R)
Nathan, Richard Perle (R)
Neall, Robert Raymond (R)
Needle, Howard J (D)
Neff, Edwin DeFrees (R)
Neideffer, David Lee (R)
Nelson, Raymond (D)
Nessen, Ronald Harold
Nichols, J Hugh (D)
Nidecker, John Emanuel (R)
Niefeld, Jo Ann R (R)
Nitze, Paul Henry (D)
O'Brien, John F X (D)
O'Callaghan, Phyllis Anne (R)
Odell, Robert P, Jr (R)
O'Donnell, William Joseph (D)
Oliver, Robert Spencer (R)
Olsen, Van Roger (R)

Ordman, Arnold (D)
O'Reilly, Thomas P (D)
Orlansky, Grace Suydam (D)
Otenasek, Mildred (D)
Owens, Joseph E (D)
Palmer, Joseph, II
Pankopf, Arthur, Jr
Parran, John Thomas, Jr (D)
Patrick, Mary Louise (R)
Pedersen, Richard F
Penello, John Allen (D)
Pennington, Robert Morris, Jr (D)
Pesci, Frank Bernard, Sr (D)
Petraitis, Karel Colette (R)
Pettaway, Brenda Cromer (D)
Petty, John R
Pfeiffer, Ellen Doris (D)
Phillips, Martha Henderson (R)
Pierpont, Ross Zimmerman (R)
Pine, James Alexander (D)
Pontius, John Samuels (D)
Potter, Charles Edward (R)
Pottinger, J Stanley (R)
Potts, Edward Andrew (R)
Potts, Lucille Bell (R)
Powell, Austin Clifford (D)
Prahinski, Leo Francis Xavier (D)
Prendergast, Richard Halsey (R)
Price, George A (R)
Pyrros, James G (D)
Radcliffe, Charles W (R)
Randolph, Lloyal (D)
Rasmussen, Dennis F (D)
Raub, Frieda Wright (R)
Ravnholt, Eiler Christian (D)
Raymond, Joseph Robert (D)
Rechtin, Eberhardt (R)
Redding, Robert S (D)
Reinhardt, John Edward (Independent)
Rietz, Ken (R)
Riley, Catherine I (D)
Rinehart, D Eldred (R)
Roach, William Neale (D)
Roberts, Richard W (R)
Robertson, Donald B (D)
Robey, Frank C, Jr (D)
Rogers, Walter E (D)
Rogers, William Pierce (R)
Rook, Doris Mae (R)
Rosenshine, Donald Louis (D)
Ross, David Gray (D)
Ross, Yan Michael (R)
Ruben, Ida Gass (D)
Ruben, Robert Charles (D)
Rummage, Frederick Charles (D)
Rush, William (D)
Rutowski, John A (D)
Ryan, Charles J, Jr (D)
Ryan, Hewson Anthony
Rymer, Thomas Arrington (D)
Sanders, Frank (D)
Santangelo, Francis J, Sr (D)
Santoni, George Joseph (D)
Sarbanes, Paul Spyros (D)
Saunders, Charles Baskerville, Jr (R)
Saxon, James J (D)
Scammon, Richard Montgomery
Schaefer, William Donald (D)
Schiappa, Gerard Francis (R)
Schifter, Richard (D)
Schlotfeldt, Richard Daniel (D)
Schmidt, Alexander MacKay
Schmults, Edward C (R)
Schuck, Jarold Raymond (R)
Schweinhaut, Margaret Collins (D)
Scull, David Lee (D)

Sewell, Joan Marie (D)
Sheehan, Lorraine M (D)
Shooshan, Harry Manuel, III (D)
Shore, Samuel Franklin (D)
Shriver, Robert Sargent, Jr (D)
Sickles, Carlton R (D)
Simpson, James Carroll (D)
Simpson, Richard Olin (R)
Sirkin, Stephen Howard (D)
Skinner, Michael William (D)
Sklar, Steven V (D)
Sleeth, Patricia Ford (D)
Smelser, Charles Harold (D)
Smith, Carolyn Jones (D)
Smith, Charles Eugene (D)
Smith, Donald Arnold (D)
Smith, Elizabeth Straubel (R)
Smith, Floyd Emery (D)
Snyder, John Wesley
Sonnenfeldt, Helmut
Sparks, John Dudley, Jr (R)
Spellman, Gladys Noon (D)
Spencer, Alvie Glenn, Jr (R)
Spivak, Alvin A (D)
Sprague, Michael James (D)
Stalbaum, Lynn E (D)
Stanley, Marc Gene (D)
Stark, Alexander (D)
Staten, Roy Neville (D)
Steers, Newton Ivan, Jr (R)
Steinberg, Melvin Allen (D)
Stevens, George William (R)
Stone, Norman R, Jr (D)
Stroble, Robert Eugene (R)
Sullivan, Charles J, Jr (D)
Sutphin, William Halstead (D)
Swartz, James Charles (D)
Symington, John Fife, Jr (R)
Szabo, Daniel (R)
Tawes, John Millard (D)
Taylor, Casper R, Jr (D)
Tenenbaum, Dorothy S (D)
Terl, Allan Howard (D)
Thomas, Edward Philip (R)
Thomas, W Henry (D)
Thomason, Franklin A (D)
Timmons, William Evan (R)
Toland, Catheryn Ann (D)
Toth, Judith Coggeshall (D)
Trice, Joseph Mark (R)
Trotter, Decatur Wayne (D)
Tubman, William Willis, Jr (D)
Tydings, Joseph Davies (D)
Unger, Leonard
Vallario, Joseph Frederick, Jr (D)
Vance, Sheldon Baird
Virts, Charles Clifton (D)
Vurek, Ruth Kathryn (D)
Wagaman, Charles F, Jr (R)
Wagner, Michael J (D)
Wainwright, Ronny Ann (D)
Walkup, Mary Roe (Groves) (R)
Walters, Elmer Elmo (D)
Ward, Jane Kudlich (R)
Ward, John X (D)
Washington, James A, Jr (D)
Webster, Kenneth L (D)
Weidemeyer, C Maurice (R)
Weinkam, Lois Anne (D)
Weir, Michael H (D)
Weisengoff, Paul Edmund (D)
Weiss, Eugene (D)
Welch, Ada Mae (D)
Welch, Patrick T (D)
Welcome, Verda Freeman (D)
Whealton, Ross LaMonte (D)
Whitaker, John Carroll (R)
White, E Homer, Jr (D)
White, Lee C (D)
Whitney, John Adair (R)

Whittaker, Philip N (R)
Wilkinson, Perry Oliver, Jr (D)
Williams, Edward Bennett (D)
Williams, Ronel Neil (R)
Wilson, Josephine Evadna (R)
Windsor, Gilbert Edison, Jr (D)
Wineland, Fred (D)
Winkler, Robert Norris (R)
Wiser, C Lawrence (D)
Wolfgang, John W (D)
Woodworth, Laurence Neal (Independent)
Worthy, Kenneth Martin (Independent)
Young, Larry (D)
Zander, Eugene J (D)
Zuckert, Eugene M (D)

MASSACHUSETTS

Abbott, William Saunders (R)
Ackermann, Barbara (D)
Adams, Thomas B (D)
Aguiar, Antone Souza, Jr (D)
Aldrich, Spaulding Ross (R)
Aleixo, Theodore J, Jr (D)
Almeida, Alfred (D)
Ambler, Robert B (D)
Ambrose, Delphin D (R)
Ames, John Stanley, III (R)
Amick, Carol Campbell (D)
Areeda, Phillip E (R)
Arterton, Frederick Christopher (D)
Asiaf, Peter George (D)
Atkins, Chester G (D)
Auspitz, Josiah Lee (R)
Axelrod, Harry (D)
Aylmer, John Francis (R)
Baarsvik, Richard Per (D)
Backman, Jack H (D)
Baker, Charles Duane (R)
Baker, Robert William (D)
Baker, William Howard (D)
Balthazar, Wilfred E (D)
Barbour, Walworth
Bartley, David Michael (D)
Bassett, Timothy Arthur (D)
Batchelder, Merton K (R)
Batchelor, Norman Frederick (R)
Beal, Robert Lawrence (R)
Beal, Thaddeus R (R)
Beauchesne, Wilfred P (D)
Belmonte, Robert A (R)
Bernashe, Roger L (D)
Bertonazzi, Louis Peter (D)
Bevilacqua, Francis J (D)
Blackham, Ann Rosemary (R)
Bliss, Bruce James (D)
Bliss, Donald T (R)
Bloedel, Flora Howell (D)
Blomen, Henning Albert (Socialist Labor Party)
Bly, Belden G, Jr (D)
Boffetti, Raymond John (D)
Bohigian, Robert J (D)
Boland, Edward P (D)
Bolling, Royal L, Jr (D)
Bourque, George J (D)
Boverini, Walter John (D)
Boyle, James P (D)
Bradford, Robert Fiske (R)
Brandt, Neill Matteson (R)
Brett, Joseph E (D)
Brooke, Edward William (R)
Brooker, Rosalind Poll (D)
Brownell, Thomas F (D)
Bruce, Katharine Fenn (R)
Buckley, Anna Patricia (D)
Buckley, John Joseph (R)

1054 / GEOGRAPHIC INDEX

MASSACHUSETTS (cont)
Buczko, Thaddeus (D)
Buell, Robert C (R)
Buffone, Charles Joseph (D)
Buglione, Nicholas Joseph (D)
Bulger, William M (D)
Bullock, John William (D)
Bunte, Doris (D)
Burke, Edward L (D)
Burke, George Gerald (D)
Burke, James A (D)
Burke, Kevin Michael (D)
Burke, Walter T (D)
Burnham, Barbara Wells (D)
Burns, James MacGregor (D)
Businger, John Arnold (D)
Buxbaum, Laurence Richard (D)
Buxton, Clayton Evans (R)
Cahillane, Sean Francis (D)
Cahoon, Howard C, Jr (R)
Cain, Fred F (D)
Caldwell, Irene Catherine (R)
Campobasso, Eleanor M (D)
Card, Andrew Hill, Jr (R)
Carey, William Arthur (D)
Casdin, Joseph Charles (D)
Cataldo, Angelo R (D)
Cawley, Robert Lucian (D)
Cerasoli, Robert Angelo (D)
Chase, Elizabeth Ann (D)
Chumura, Rudy (D)
Chumura, Steve T (D)
Clark, Robert Brewster (R)
Clarke, Clifton Winthrop (R)
Codinha, Paul Phillip (R)
Coffey, John F (D)
Cogan, John Francis, Jr (D)
Cohen, Gerald M (D)
Cole, Lincoln P, Jr (R)
Collaro, Andrew (D)
Colo, H Thomas (D)
Connell, William A, Jr (D)
Connelly, Edward W (R)
Connolly, Michael Joseph (D)
Conte, John J (D)
Conte, Silvio O (R)
Conway, James Stephen (D)
Cook, John Lewis (R)
Cooney, Nancy Ann (D)
Coppinger, Francis X (D)
Corazzini, Leo R (D)
Corso, Philip Louis (R)
Coulter, William Alfred (R)
Counihan, Genevra R (D)
Courtney, Richard Travers, Jr (D)
Coury, Edward P (D)
Cox, Archibald (Independent)
Cox, Gilbert W, Jr (R)
Crane, Bruce (R)
Crane, Robert Q (D)
Craven, James J, Jr (D)
Creedon, Michael C (D)
Creighton, Thomas Edmund (D)
Cronin, Paul William (R)
Curtis, Laurence (R)
Curtiss, Sidney Q (R)
Cusack, John Francis (D)
Dahl, Curtis (R)
Daly, Michael John (D)
Danovitch, Alan Paul (R)
Dary, Leon Leonard (R)
Davoren, John Francis Xavier (D)
Debar, Frank Richard (R)
Decas, George Charles (R)
Delahunt, William D (D)
Del Greco, Joseph Francis (R)
Demers, Richard H (D)
Desrocher, Arthur L (R)
DiCarlo, Joseph Carmine (D)

Dickson, Edward M (D)
Dobelle, Evan Samuel (R)
Dolan, Thomas Francis (R)
Donnelly, Brian J (D)
Donoghue, Patrick Joseph (D)
Donohue, Harold D (D)
Donohue, Margaret Mary (R)
Donovan, Eileen Roberta
Donovan, Robert F (D)
Doris, Francis D (D)
Dowds, James Alexander (R)
Drinan, Robert Frederick (D)
Driscoll, John R (R)
Driscoll, Wilfred Cote (D)
Duffin, Dennis J (D)
Dukakis, Michael S (D)
Dullea, Edward James, Jr (D)
Dunlop, John Thomas
Dwight, Donald Rathbun (R)
Dwinell, Richard J (D)
Dwyer, Claire Buckley (D)
Dyer, Donald James (R)
Early, Edward J, Jr (D)
Early, Joseph Daniel (D)
Egan, Mary Katherine (D)
Eliot, Thomas Hopkinson (D)
Engdahl, Charles F (D)
Epstein, Seymour Francis (D)
Fallon, Thomas F (D)
Fantasia, Mary E (D)
Farland, John Francis (D)
Feeney, Michael Paul (D)
Fenn, Dan Huntington, Jr (D)
Ferris, Charles Daniel (D)
Filosa, Philip Frank (D)
Finnegan, John J (D)
Finnigan, Richard F (D)
Fiorentini, James John (D)
Fitzgerald, Kevin W (D)
Fitzpatrick, John Hitchcock (R)
Flaherty, Charles Frances, Jr (D)
Flaherty, Michael Francis (D)
Fleming, Richard Thorpe (R)
Flynn, Bernard D (D)
Flynn, Lucy Ann (D)
Flynn, Peter Y (D)
Flynn, Raymond L (D)
Flynn, William J, Jr (D)
Foley, Daniel J (D)
Fonseca, Mary L (D)
Fortes, Robert L (D)
Foster, Eleanor Corinne (R)
Fouche, Peter James (D)
Francis, Robert Talcott, II (D)
Frank, Barney (D)
Freeman, Bruce N (R)
Furcolo, Foster (D)
Gaffney, James J, III (Independent)
Galbraith, J Kenneth (D)
Gallugi, Anthony Michael (D)
Galotti, Edward Francis (D)
Gammal, Albert Abraham, Jr (R)
Gannett, Ann Cole (R)
Garbose, Doris Rhoda (R)
Garczynski, Joseph, Jr (D)
Garmey, Ronald (R)
Gaudette, Donald Roger (D)
Giadone, William Biagio (R)
Gibbons, Eleanor Keating (D)
Gillette, Robert West (R)
Goldman, Shirlie Selma (D)
Goode, Mary H (D)
Gormalley, Joan Patricia (R)
Goulston, Paul Milton (D)
Graves, Hazel Caroline (R)
Gray, Barbara E (R)
Grenier, Henry R (D)
Griffin, Walter Joseph (R)
Grimaldi, James L (D)
Griswold, Erwin Nathaniel (R)

Grossman, Jerome (D)
Guilmette, Gerard A (D)
Gus Serra, Emanuel (D)
Guzzi, Paul (D)
Hall, Robert Arthur (R)
Harney, John Thomas (D)
Harold, Paul Dennis (D)
Harrington, Edward Dennis, Jr (R)
Harrington, Kevin B (D)
Harrington, Michael Joseph (D)
Harrington, Peter F (D)
Harris, Norris William (R)
Harrison, David Eldridge (D)
Hastings, Wilmot Reed (R)
Hatch, Francis Whiting, Jr (R)
Hawke, Robert Douglas (R)
Healy, Jonathan Lee (R)
Heckler, Margaret M (R)
Henderson, Daniel J (D)
Henry, Constance Foster (R)
Hermann, Robert Lambert (R)
Hester, Eva B (D)
Hester, Paul Finley (D)
Hicks, Louise Day (D)
Hines, Arthur Snow (R)
Hogan, William F (D)
Holland, Iris K (R)
Houton, Kathleen Kilgore (D)
Howe, Eunice P (R)
Howe, Marie Elizabeth (D)
Hunter, Margaret Blake (Maxine) (R)
Hurley, Daniel Gerard (D)
Hurley, Paula M (D)
Hurrell, James Philip (D)
Hyman, Lester Samuel (D)
Jackson, Ellen M (D)
Johnson, Raymond Allan (R)
Johnston, Philip William (D)
Jones, Gary D (D)
Jordan, Raymond A, Jr (D)
Joyce, Daniel L, Jr (D)
Kairit, Eleanor Jessie (R)
Kanin, Dennis Roy (D)
Kanin, Doris May (D)
Keach, John A, Jr (R)
Kearney, Dennis (D)
Keefe, James A, Jr (D)
Kelleher, John G (D)
Kelliher, Walter James (D)
Kelly, James Anthony, Jr (D)
Kendall, Richard E (D)
Kennedy, Edward Moore (D)
Kennedy, Robert B (D)
Kenney, Burton (D)
Kenney, Daniel Joseph (R)
Keverian, George (D)
Keville, Dorothy Ann (D)
Khoury, Arthur M (D)
Kiley, Daniel Patrick, Jr (D)
King, John Gerard (D)
King, Melvin H (D)
Kirby, Edward Paul (R)
Kitchener, Ruth Mae (R)
Kitterman, William I (D)
Knight, Peter Sage (D)
Kottis, John Gregory (R)
Kuss, Matthew J (D)
La Fontaine, Raymond M (D)
Lambros, Nickolas (D)
Lamson, Fred I (R)
Landry, Richard Edward (D)
Lane, David Judson (R)
Lane, John Jones (R)
Lane, Thomas J (D)
Laplante, Donat Joseph (D)
Lapointe, Francis Charles (D)
Lappin, Peter Thomas Hayden (D)
Lawton, Mark Edward (D)
Leary, Theodore Moreau, Jr (D)
Lewis, Arthur Joseph, Jr (D)

Linsky, Martin A (R)
Lionett, David Jerome (R)
Locke, David Henry (R)
Lodge, George Cabot (R)
Lodge, Henry Cabot (R)
Lombard, Gerald P (D)
Lombardi, Michael J (D)
Long, Charles W (R)
Long, John Joseph (D)
Longstreet, Victor Mendell (D)
Lopes, Thomas Dennis (D)
LoPresti, Michael, Jr (D)
Lurvey, Mildred Edwina (R)
Lynch, Garreth J (D)
Macdonald, Torbert H (D)
MacKenzie, Charles A, Jr (R)
MacKenzie, Ronald Conrad (R)
MacLean, William Q, Jr (D)
Mahoney, Thomas Henry Donald (D)
Mann, Charles W (R)
Mann, Theodore D (R)
Manning, Donald J (D)
Manning, M Joseph (D)
Manzelli, Robert A (R)
Markey, Edward J (D)
Markey, John Allen (D)
Marotta, Angelo
Marshall, Clifford Holmes (D)
Masterman, Harold (R)
Mastrangelo, Richard Edward (D)
Matrango, Frank J (D)
Mayer, Jean (Independent)
McAuliffe, Eugene Vincent
McBride, Anthony P (D)
McCann, Francis X (D)
McCarthy, Peter Charles (D)
McCarthy, Robert Emmett (D)
McCarthy, Terrence P (Independent)
McCarthy, William Augustus (R)
McCavitt, Lawrence Vincent (D)
McCormack, John W (D)
McDowell, Peter Lee (R)
McGee, Thomas W (D)
McGowan, Charles M (D)
McGrail, Stephen John (D)
McGrath, Richard J (D)
McGrath, Richard M (D)
McInerney, Linda Ann (D)
McKenna, Arthur James (D)
McKenna, Denis L (D)
Mc Kinnon, Allan R (D)
McLaughlin, Michael Edward (D)
McMahon, James Robert, Jr (D)
McNeil, Robert D (D)
Means, Paul E (D)
Melia, John F (D)
Menton, Paul C (D)
Metayer, Elizabeth Nener (D)
Metelica, John (R)
Millet, Frank Lincoln (R)
Mitchell, Nicholas Wilfred (D)
Moakley, John Joseph (D)
Mofenson, David Joel (D)
Monahan, Maurice Brice (R)
Mooney, John Joseph (D)
Moore, Jonathan (R)
Moore, Roger Allan (R)
Moran, Robert Daniel (R)
Morse, Robert Warren (D)
Mosakowski, Kenneth Robert (Independent-D)
Moynihan, Daniel Patrick (D)
Moynihan, Kenneth James (D)
Mullin, William C (D)
Murphy, John E, Jr (D)
Murphy, John Francis (D)

Murphy, Roderick Patrick (R)
Murray, Mary DePasquale (D)
Nagle, William P, Jr (D)
Nathan, Hardy Lewis (R)
Natsios, Andrew Stephen (R)
Navin, Joseph M (D)
Nickinello, Louis R (D)
Noble, R Elaine (D)
Nolen, James Richard (D)
Nordberg, Nils Lovering (R)
Norton, Francis Carleton (R)
Norton, Thomas C (D)
O'Brien, James Anthony, Jr (D)
O'Brien, Lawrence Francis (D)
O'Brien, Mark Paul (D)
O'Donnell, Dorothy S (D)
O'Donnell, Henry Joseph, III (R)
O'Donnell, Kathleen (D)
Olver, John Walter (D)
O'Meara, George F, Jr (D)
O'Neill, Thomas P, Jr (D)
O'Neill, Thomas P, III (D)
Orlandi, O Roland (D)
Outchcunis, Florence Bacas (D)
Owens, Robert I (D)
Owens, William (D)
Parenteau, Carolyn Blanche (R)
Parker, John F (R)
Parks, Jesse L, Jr (D)
Parsons, J Graham
Peabody, Endicott (D)
Peabody, Malcolm E, Jr (R)
Pease, Lucille Currie (R)
Peck, Raymond Stuart (D)
Penta, Robert M (Independent)
Perault, Felix R (D)
Perry, John B (D)
Peterson, Gunnar Aron Julius (R)
Peterson, Hjalmar Reginald (R)
Phelan, Robert Gerard (D)
Phillips, Christopher Hallowell (R)
Pickett, William A (D)
Picucci, Angelo (D)
Piekos, Henry (R)
Pina, Ronald Anthony (D)
Pinanski, Viola R (R)
Pines, Lois G (D)
Piro, Vincent Joseph (D)
Plas, Josephine Patricia (D)
Pleshaw, Geraldine B (R)
Pokaski, Daniel Francis (D)
Porter, William James
Powers, John E (D)
Pratt, Robert Leonard (D)
Prebensen, Dennis Michael (D)
Proctor, Helen June (R)
Puglia, Andrew Robert (D)
Quinlan, John M (R)
Quinn, Philip Andrew (D)
Quinn, Robert H (D)
Ralph, S Lester (D)
Raposa, Manuel, Jr (D)
Raynard, Shirley M (D)
Rees, Helen (R)
Rescia, George Frank (R)
Reynolds, Robert Charles (R)
Rice, Edmund Burke
Richardson, Elliot Lee (R)
Robert, Ernest (R)
Robinson, William G (R)
Robinson, Winthrop Lincoln (R)
Rodham, A David (R)
Rogers, Benjamin D, Jr (R)
Rogers, George (D)
Rogers, Richard Adams (R)
Ronayne, Maurice E, Jr (R)
Roodkowsky, Alice May (R)
Rotenberg, Jon Fred (D)

Rourke, Raymond F (D)
Ruane, J Michael (D)
Rucho, John (D)
Rurak, James P (D)
Russo, Frederick N Dello (D)
Saggese, Alfred E, Jr (D)
Saltmarsh, Sherman W, Jr (R)
Saltonstall, John Lee, Jr (D)
Saltonstall, Leverett (R)
Saltonstall, William Lawrence (R)
Sargent, Francis W (R)
Scaccia, Angelo M (D)
Scelsi, Joseph S (D)
Schlosstein, Frederic W, Jr (R)
Schwartz, Edna Barbara (D)
Scibelli, Anthony M (D)
Seamans, Robert Channing, Jr (R)
Sears, John Winthrop (R)
Sears, Philip Mason (R)
Sears, Ruth Parker (R)
Segel, James W (D)
Semensi, Joseph John (D)
Serra, Emanuel G (D)
Shaughnessy, William G (D)
Shea, C Vincent (D)
Shea, Philip L (D)
Sheehy, Edward Driscoll (D)
Shortell, Edward (R)
Sidd, Allan (D)
Silva, Richard Robert (R)
Simons, Thomas G (R)
Sisitsky, Alan David (D)
Skerry, David Paul (D)
Smith, A Ledyard, Jr (R)
Smith, James Edward (D)
Solomon, Bernard (R)
Spaulding, Josiah A (R)
Sprague, George R (R)
Starzec, William Alexander (D)
Stemple, Jane Yolen (D)
Stuart, Douglas S (R)
Studds, Gerry Eastman (D)
Sullivan, Christine Barr (D)
Sullivan, Dorothy R (R)
Sullivan, Gregory William (D)
Sullivan, John Joseph, Jr (D)
Sullivan, Mary M (D)
Sullivan, William Christopher (D)
Swanson, Karen Joyce (D)
Swartz, David John (D)
Tammi, June H (D)
Taymor, Betty (D)
Teahan, Robert S (D)
Teichner, Stephen J (D)
Terzaghi, Ruth Doggett (D)
Thomson, James Claude, Jr (D)
Thoutsis, Timotheos Michael (R)
Timilty, Joseph F (D)
Titus, Douglas Leroy (R)
Tobin, Arthur H (D)
Toomey, John J (D)
Toon, Malcolm
Towse, Daniel Charles (R)
Treadway, Richard Fowle (R)
Trudeau, Theodore J (R)
Tsapatsaris, Charles Nicholas (D)
Tsongas, Paul E (D)
Tucker, William Humphrey (D)
Tuller, Paul Raymond (R)
Tully, Bernard Joseph (D)
Tuttle, William Roger (R)
Underhill, Frederick William, Jr (R)
Vacca, Francis John (D)
Valcourt, Richard Roger (D)
Velis, Peter Arthur (D)
Vigneau, Robert A (D)
Viveiros, Carlton M (D)

Volpe, John Anthony (R)
Volterra, Max (D)
Wahlrab, Otto A (R)
Walker, Henry A (R)
Wall, William X (D)
Walsh, John A, Jr (Jack) (D)
Walsh, Joseph B (D)
Waring, Lloyd Borden (R)
Weinberg, Norman S (D)
Wetherbee, Bruce E (D)
Wetmore, Robert D (D)
White, Donald Blaisdell (R)
White, Kevin Hagan (D)
White, Thomas P (D)
White, W Paul (D)
Wilber, Bernard (R)
Wiley, Richard Arthur (R)
Williams, Arthur (R)
Williams, Deborah (R)
Williams, Gordon Oliver (R)
Williamson, Mary Ehrlich (D)
Wing, Francis William (R)
Winter, Madeline Field (R)
Wojtkowski, Thomas Casmere (D)
Woodard, William Philip (R)
Woods, George L, Jr (R)
Yarmolinsky, Adam (D)
Young, George C (R)
Zarod, Stanley John (D)
Zeiser, Bruce Hunter (R)
Ziemba, Edward John (R)

MICHIGAN

Abraham, Juliette Elizabeth (R)
Acker, Robert Harold (R)
Ackley, Gardner (D)
Adrounie, Dorothy (R)
Albosta, Donald J (D)
Alessandrini, Cornelius A, Jr (D)
Allen, Bernard Gene (D)
Allen, Richard John (R)
Anderson, Thomas Jefferson (D)
Angel, Daniel Duane (R)
Angle, Susan Scott (D)
Armbruster, Loren S (R)
Arnold, LaVerne Virginia (R)
Asher, Kathleen May (D)
Austin, Richard H (D)
Barber, Richard J (D)
Barber, Robert J (R)
Beckwith, Florence Hess (R)
Bennett, John (D)
Bennison, Leah Rose (D)
Bentley, Alvin M, Jr (D)
Bernhard, Mary E (D)
Bessey, Carol (D)
Bielawski, Anthony F (D)
Bill, Gregory Dean (D)
Binsfeld, Connie (R)
Bishop, Donald E (R)
Bivens, Edward, Jr (R)
Blanchard, James Johnston (D)
Blatt, Nancie Miller (D)
Blue, William Roy (D)
Bonior, David E (D)
Bowman, John T (D)
Boykin, Ulysses W (R)
Brennan, Thomas Emmett
Brewster, Karen Joy (R)
Brickley, James H (R)
Briney, James Wilson, Jr (R)
Brodhead, William McNulty (D)
Broomfield, William S (R)
Brotherton, Wilbur V (R)
Brouillette, Francis Delore (D)
Brown, Basil W (D)

Brown, Garry Eldridge (R)
Brown, James Nelson (Jim) (R)
Brown, Jean Isabelle (R)
Brown, Prentiss Marsh (D)
Brown, Thomas Henry (D)
Bryant, William R, Jr (R)
Buchen, Philip William (R)
Buhl, Lloyd Frank (R)
Bullard, Perry (D)
Bullett, Audrey Kathryn (D)
Burns, William Lloyd (R)
Bursley, Gilbert E (R)
Busch, J Michael (John) (R)
Buth, Martin D (R)
Byker, Gary (R)
Calabrese, Sylvia M (D)
Caldwell, Norman Carl (R)
Canfield, John Lemual (D)
Carey, Patricia Jean I (R)
Carmody, Charles Edward (R)
Carr, M Robert (D)
Carr, Oscar Clark Jr (D)
Cartwright, Arthur (D)
Cawthorne, Dennis Otto (R)
Cederberg, Elford A (R)
Chamberlain, Charles E (R)
Chamberlain, Jean Nash (R)
Chase, Nancy Bastien (R)
Ciaramitaro, Nick (D)
Cichocki, James Z (D)
Clements, John V (R)
Clodfelter, Mark (D)
Closz, Harold F, Jr (R)
Clunis, Wager Frederick (D)
Cobb, Andrew Whitney (R)
Cohen, Wilbur Joseph (D)
Coleman, Mary Stallings (Non-Partisan)
Collier, Betty Fay (D)
Collins, Barbara-Rose (D)
Conlin, Michael H (R)
Connelly, Brian Robert (D)
Conyers, John, Jr (D)
Cook, Doris Jean (D)
Cooke, Margaret Robb (R)
Cooper, Daniel S (D)
Corbin, Gary George (D)
Cramton, Louis Kay (R)
Crane, William Alexander (R)
Crim, Bobby D (D)
Cronan, Irene M (D)
Crook, Maureen Catherine (R)
Cushingberry, George, Jr (D)
Damman, James J (R)
Darrow, Peter P (D)
Davis, Robert W (R)
DeBruyn, William Edward (R)
Defebaugh, James Elliott (R)
DeGrow, Alvin James (R)
DeMaso, Harry A (R)
Derezinski, Anthony A (D)
DeStigter, Melvin (R)
Dewey, William L (R)
Digby, Dora Mae (D)
Digby, James Keith (R)
Diggs, Anna Katherine Johnston (D)
Diggs, Charles Coles, Jr (D)
Dillinger, Delores Marie (D)
DiNello, Gilbert John (D)
Dingell, John D (D)
Dively, Michael Augustus (R)
Dobie, Gertrude Agnes (R)
Doherty, Walter Gerard (R)
Doll, Bernard Thomas (R)
Doughty, Warren Browe (D)
Driver, Marjorie M (D)
Dunnell, Mildred Hazel (R)
Durbin, Elizabeth D (R)
Dutko, Dennis M (D)
Dwyer, Theodore John (R)
Edwards, F Robert (R)
Edwards, George H (D)

1056 / GEOGRAPHIC INDEX

MICHIGAN (cont)

Eggle, Doris E (R)
Eleveld, Robert Jay (R)
Elliott, Daisy (D)
Engler, Colleen House (R)
Engler, John M (R)
Engman, Lewis August (R)
Esch, Marvin L (R)
Evans, Hubert Carol (D)
Fackler, Ernest Carl, III (R)
Farr, William S, Jr (R)
Farrand, Christopher George (R)
Faust, William Paul (D)
Faxon, Jack (D)
Feinstein, Otto (D)
Felder, Willie W (D)
Fenner, Bertine Lorraine (D)
Ferguson, Rosetta (D)
Fessler, Richard Donald (R)
Feuer, Alan Craig (D)
Fina, Eunyce Aloys (R)
Firley, Carl Franklin (D)
Fishman, Alvin (D)
Fishman, Sam (D)
Fitzgerald, George S (D)
Fitzgerald, William B (D)
Forbes, Joseph (D)
Ford, Gerald R (R)
Ford, William David (D)
Forgash, Michael A (R)
Forster, Dianna Ruth (R)
Fowler, R Lynn (D)
Frazier, Lincoln B (R)
Fredricks, Edgar John (R)
Frink, Gary R (D)
Friske, Richard (American Party)
Furlong, Frank J (D)
Garofalo, Anthony Joseph (R)
Gast, Harry T, Jr (R)
Gaultier, Gerald Douglas (R)
Geake, Raymond Robert (R)
Geerlings, Edgar Allen (R)
Gempel, Gordon Leo (R)
Geralds, Monte R (R)
Gettel, Gerhard F (R)
Gibson, Catharine (R)
Gilmore, James Stanley, Jr (R)
Gingrass, Jack L (D)
Gladstone, William (D)
Gnodtke, Lucile H (R)
Goemaere, Warren N (D)
Golden, Richard A (R)
Goodlett, Berry Christopher (R)
Gougeon, Byron C (R)
Grant, Robert Williams, Jr (R)
Graves, Gerald William
Gray, Marcus J (D)
Green, Allison (R)
Gribbs, Roman S (D)
Griffin, Michael J (R)
Griffin, Robert Paul (R)
Griffiths, Martha W (D)
Guastello, Thomas (D)
Gurzenda, Ted J (D)
Hafstad, Katharine Clarke (R)
Hall, Richard Harold (D)
Harris, John Myron (D)
Harrison, Charlie James, Jr (D)
Hart, Adelaide Julia (D)
Hart, Jerome Thomas (D)
Hart, Philip A (D)
Harvey, James (R)
Hasper, Gerrit C (D)
Hastings, Joseph Henry (R)
Hatcher, Lillian (D)
Hawley, B Jeanne (D)
Hay, Sam M (R)
Haynes, David Scott (D)
Hayward, William (R)
Heller, Jan K (D)

Hellman, Russell (D)
Henderson, Robert G (R)
Henry, Paul Brentwood (R)
Hensler, Jane Ann (R)
Hertel, Dennis M (D)
Hertel, John C (D)
Hertzberg, Stuart E (D)
Hess, Daniel Bartlett (R)
Hicks, David L (R)
Hobart, Anne Moore (R)
Hobbs, Ruth Josephine (R)
Hoffman, Quincy (R)
Holcomb, Thomas M (D)
Holden, Creighton Davidson (R)
Hollister, David Clinton (D)
Holmes, David S, Jr (D)
Holmes, Kirby Garrett (R)
Hood, Morris, Jr (D)
Hood, Raymond Walter (D)
Howe, Elizabeth Prout (D)
Hubbard, Orville Liscum (R)
Huber, Robert J (R)
Huffman, Bill S (D)
Hunsinger, Josephine D (D)
Hutchinson, Edward (R)
Irving, Helen (D)
Jackson, Murray Earl (D)
Jacobetti, Dominic J (D)
Jamieson, Norman Leslie (R)
Jeffrey, Mildred (D)
Johnson, Roger (D)
Jondahl, H Lynn (D)
Jones, Francis A, III (Mike) (R)
Jowett, William (R)
Kammer, Kerry (D)
Kauper, Thomas Eugene (R)
Kehres, Raymond C (D)
Keier, Richard Frederick (R)
Keith, William Raymond (D)
Kelley, Frank J (D)
Kelsch, Sarah Jane (R)
Kelsey, John T (D)
Kennedy, Bela Ellis (R)
Kennedy, Earl (R)
Kildee, Dale E (D)
King, Raymond Lamprey (R)
Kleiner, A Robert (D)
Knowlan, W C (D)
Kok, Peter (R)
Kriekard, Harold Edward (R)
Kubisch, Jack B (Conservative)
Kuthy, Eugene Wendel (D)
Lackey, Bernice (Bee) Catherine (R)
Lamb, Gerald (L) Edward (D)
Laro, David (R)
Larsen, Melvin L (R)
Lashuay, Kenneth Edward (R)
Laskey, Norma Jean (R)
Ledman, Eldon Dale (R)
Lee, Catherine Patricia (R)
Legel, Jack Eugene (R)
Legg, Louis E Jr (R)
Lehmann, Karen Elizabeth (R)
Levin, Charles Leonard
Light, Catherine (D)
Limmer, Francis Edmund
Lincoln, Everitt Floyd (R)
Logan, Benjamin H Jr (D)
Logan, Irene Elizabeth (R)
Lokken, Leslie Ferris (D)
Mahalak, Edward E (D)
Mantey, Carl F (R)
Markes, John F (D)
Marshall, William C (D)
Martin, John Butlin (R)
Marvel, Douglas James (R)
Mastin, Philip Olin, Jr (D)
Mathieu, Thomas C (D)
May, Alfred A (R)
Maynard, John M (D)

Maynard, Olivia Benedict (Libby) (D)
McCauley, John E (D)
McClure, Harold Milton (R)
McCollough, Lucille Hanna (D)
McCollough, Patrick Hanna (D)
McCormack, David Richard (D)
McCracken, Paul Winston (R)
McDonald, B J (D)
McDonald, Jack H (R)
McFee, Shirley Miller (R)
McLaughlin, William Francis (R)
McNamara, Edward Howard (D)
McNamee, Ruth B (R)
McNeely, James Michael (R)
McNeely, Matthew (D)
Meader, George (R)
Meyers, Hannes, Jr (R)
Middaugh, James Michael (R)
Miller, Annetta Thelma (D)
Miller, Bruce A (R)
Miller, Hildreth Esther (R)
Millhouse, Clifford John (R)
Milliken, William Grawn (R)
Mitchell, Robert S (D)
Mittan, Ray C (R)
Monsma, Stephen Vos (R)
Montague, Leon Arthur (R)
Montgomery, George F, Sr (D)
Moran, Kim (D)
Morrison, Eula Grace (D)
Mowat, John S, Jr (R)
Mullican, Brian Lee (R)
Munn, Earle Harold (Prohibition)
Myers, Harold Arthur (R)
Nagelvoort, Bernard Charles (R)
Nash, Ernest W (R)
Nedzi, Lucien Norbert (D)
Nelson, Earl E (D)
Nelson, LeRoy James (D)
Newhouse, Gerald Francis (R)
Nobis, Elizabeth Ann (R)
North, Sally Anne (R)
Novak, Michael (D)
O'Brien, Michael J (D)
O'Donnohue, Donna Starr (D)
Ogonowski, Casmer P (D)
O'Hara, James Grant (D)
Olsson, Eleanor (R)
O'Neill, James E, Jr (D)
Opferkuch, Paul Raymond (R)
Ostling, Ralph A (R)
Ott, Alexander Reginald (D)
Otterbacher, John Robert (D)
Owen, Gary (D)
Padden, Jeffrey D (D)
Pearl, Dorothy Waite (R)
Perry, Audrey Emilie (R)
Peterson, Elly M (R)
Phillipson, Herbert Emanuel, Jr (R)
Pickett, Dovie Theodosia (R)
Pietri, Joyce Abbe (R)
Pinnick, Siria F (R)
Platt, Faun (R)
Plawecki, David Anthony (D)
Plewa, Casmere Joseph (R)
Porter, Paul (D)
Posthumus, Richard Earl (R)
Powell, Stanley M (R)
Prescott, George A (R)
Puffer, Kenneth Hart (R)
Pulido, Alberto (D)
Pursell, Carl D (R)
Radant, Kenneth Raymond (R)
Ransford, Paul Allan (R)
Rapaich, Marguerite Cecille (R)
Rathbun, Frank Hugo (R)

Redman, Robert Clayton (R)
Reissing, Theodore Charles, Sr (R)
Rengo, Raymond Arden (R)
Renstrom, Sarah Brown (D)
Richards, Harold Leland (D)
Riecker, Margaret Ann (Ranny) (R)
Riegle, Donald W, Jr (D)
Riess, Eileen Kathleen (D)
Robertson, Ruth Elizabeth (R)
Robinson, Henrietta (D)
Robinson, Shirley A (D)
Rocco, Sal (D)
Roe, Jerry D (R)
Romney, George Wilcken (R)
Root, Helen (D)
Rosenbaum, Paul A (R)
Rouse, Frederick Oakes (R)
Ruppe, Philip E (R)
Rush, Carleton K (R)
Ruwe, L Nicholas (R)
Ryan, William A (D)
Sackett, Wayne B (R)
Sallade, George Wahr (D)
Sanders, Sylvia (D)
Sanford, Bernard H (R)
Sarapo, Donato Frank (R)
Schorr, Robert Jeffrey (R)
Schwarz, John Joseph Henry (R)
Schweigert, Thomas F (R)
Scott, Harold Joseph (D)
Seidman, L William (R)
Sharpe, Thomas G (R)
Sheridan, Alfred A (D)
Sietsema, Jelt (R)
Simmons, Samuel J (D)
Simon, Maxwell W (R)
Simonson, Richard D (R)
Sinclair, John Richley (R)
Slaughter, Robert L (R)
Smart, Clifford H (R)
Smit, Raymond J (R)
Smith, James F (R)
Smith, L Michael (R)
Smith, Lawrence Peter (D)
Smith, Roy (R)
Smith, Sheldon B (R)
Smyth, Kelvin Paul (D)
Snell, Hilary Fred (R)
Snyder, Joseph M (D)
Southard, Stephen Warren (R)
Spaniola, Francis Richard (D)
Sparling, James M, Jr (R)
Spencer, Roy L (R)
Staebler, Neil (D)
Stahlin, John Henry (R)
Statkus, Walter Carl (R)
Stevens, E Dan (R)
Stewart, Melvin James (D)
Stidham, Kay Burnell (D)
Stolz, Mabel Smith (D)
Stone, Lorraine G (R)
Stopczynski, Stephen (D)
Stopczynski, Thaddeus C (D)
Strang, DeForrest (R)
Sutherland, Paul Oscar (R)
Symons, Joyce (D)
Taylor, Hobart, Jr (D)
Thompson, Mark Louis (R)
Todd, Paul Harold, Jr (D)
Transue, Andrew Jackson (D)
Traxler, J Robert (D)
Treacher, Randall Wesley (D)
Treska, Paul (D)
Trim, Claude Albert (D)
Trolley, Richard Joseph (D)
Tuchow, Gerald (D)
Turcott, Thomas (R)
Ulch, Ellen (R)
Umphrey, James Morris (R)
Vagnozzi, Aldo (D)

Vander Jagt, Guy (R)
Vanderlaan, Robert (R)
Vander Veen, Richard Frank (D)
Vandette, Edmund Frederick (R)
Van Dusen, Richard Campbell (R)
Van Singel, Donald (R)
Varnum, Charles Henry (R)
Vaughn, Jackie, III (D)
Ver Plank, Joel P (R)
Vincent, Dwight Harold (R)
Vivian, Weston E (D)
Vollman, James William (D)
Vostrizansky, David James (D)
Wagner, Richard F (R)
Walbridge, John Tuthill, Jr (R)
Ware, Richard Anderson (R)
Warren, Richard Dale (D)
Washington, Michael Anthony (D)
Weaver, Rae Cruthers (R)
Webster, Robert Byron (R)
Weed, Ella Demmink (R)
Weiss, Jeanette Short (R)
Welborn, John Alva (R)
Westphal, Albert H (R)
Wheeler, Robert R (R)
Whelan, Mary Elizabeth (D)
Wierzbicki, Frank V (D)
Willford, Louis J (R)
Williams, G Mennen (D)
Willis, Katherine Mary (R)
Willison, Sue Kindred (R)
Winograd, Morley A (D)
Wirth, Helen Irmiger (D)
Wolpe, Howard Eliot (D)
Woodman, Beryl Roger, Jr (D)
Woolner, Sidney Henry (D)
Yeager, Weldon O (R)
Yearnd, James Austin, Sr (R)
Young, Coleman A (D)
Young, Joseph F (D)
Young, Richard A (D)
Young, Robert D (R)
Zaparackas, Algis (R)
Zelenak, Edward Michael (D)
Zemmol, Allen (D)
Ziegler, Hal Walter (R)
Zollar, Charles O (R)

MINNESOTA

Abeln, Lyle (DFL)
Adams, Salisbury (Conservative)
Albrecht, Raymond J (R)
Alcott, Kitty May (DFL)
Aldrich, George Francis (DFL)
Allen, Hilary P (DFL)
Allivato, Barbara Rose (DFL)
Andersen, Elmer Lee (R)
Anderson, Andrew Edwin (R)
Anderson, Carl William (DFL)
Anderson, Earl L (DFL)
Anderson, Eugenie Moore (DFL)
Anderson, Glen H (DFL)
Anderson, Gordon A (DFL)
Anderson, Irvin Neal (DFL)
Anderson, Jerald C (DFL)
Anderson, Ray J (DFL)
Anderson, Robert John (DFL)
Anderson, Terrill Gordon (DFL)
Anderson, Wendell Richard (DFL)
Arlandson, John R (DFL)
Armstrong, Orville Raynold (DFL)
Arnold, Norbert (DFL)

Arrell, William Henry (DFL)
Ashbach, Robert O (R)
Bacig, Thomas David (DFL)
Banen, Abraham Theodore (DFL)
Bang, Otto T, Jr (R)
Banks, Roger Ware (D)
Barrette, Emery George (R)
Barry, Hilary D (DFL)
Bartels, Carol Picker (DFL)
Bearse, Eva Sue (DFL)
Beauchamp, David (DFL)
Beaudin, Robert Claude (DFL)
Becker, Robert William (DFL)
Begich, Joseph R (DFL)
Behrman, Carol Ione (DFL)
Bell, John Gordon (R)
Beneke, Mildred Stong (Millie) (R)
Berg, Thomas Kenneth (DFL)
Bergland, Bob Selmer (DFL)
Berglin, Linda L (DFL)
Berglund, Shirley M (DFL)
Bernhagen, John Joseph (R)
Bigwood, Robert Maurice (R)
Birnbaum, Lawrence M (R)
Birnstihl, Orville E (DFL)
Bjornson, Val (R)
Blatnik, John A (DFL)
Blatz, Jerome V (Conservative)
Borden, Laureen Estelle (DFL)
Borden, Winston Wendell (DFL)
Boschwitz, Rudy (R)
Bowen, Duane Glenn (DFL)
Brandl, John Edward (D)
Brandt, Donald Edward (R)
Brataas, Nancy Osborn (R)
Braun, Art (D)
Brinkman, Bernard J (DFL)
Brooks, Ronnie Lee (DFL)
Brown, David Millard (R)
Brown, Robert J (R)
Brown, Robert John (R)
Budge, Hamer Harold (R)
Burton, Daniel Frederick (DFL)
Burton, Verona Devine (DFL)
Byrne, Peggy Mary (DFL)
Cain, Ruth Rodney (DFL)
Caranicas, Perry Charles (D)
Carlson, Arne H (R)
Carlson, Howard (DFL)
Carlson, Lyndon R (DFL)
Carlson, Roy (DFL)
Carpenter, Elsa Mannheimer (R)
Carter, Robert Cornelius (R)
Casserly, James R (DFL)
Cecil, Elmer James (DFL)
Charles, Erland W (R)
Chenoweth, John Craig (D)
Chmielewski, Florian (DFL)
Christgau, Victor (R)
Christianson, Roger Allen (DFL)
Claggett, Bay (DFL)
Clardy, Virginia Mae (DFL)
Clark, Janet (DFL)
Clawson, John Thomas (DFL)
Cohen, Lawrence David (DFL)
Coleman, Nicholas D (DFL)
Colhapp, Barbara Jones (DFL)
Colligan, Allen Leroy (DFL)
Connolly, John Stevens (DFL)
Conzemius, George Robert (DFL)
Corbid, John (DFL)
Craig, Earl (DFL)
Croce, Lewis Henry (R)
Dahl, Arden (DFL)
Dahl, Harold J (DFL)
Dahlin, Melba R (D)

Dahm, Marion (DFL)
Dauphinais, Marguerite Therese (DFL)
Davies, John Thomas (Jack) (DFL)
Davis, Dave Quentin (DFL)
Dean, William DuBois (R)
DeChaine, James Anthony (D)
DeGroat, Frank Hamilton (R)
Delaney, Frances I (DFL)
DeMuse, Amelia (Millie) (DFL)
DeMuse, Toni Ann (D)
DiBrito, Sandy Louis (DFL)
Dieterich, Neil (DFL)
Doty, Gary (DFL)
Doty, Ralph R (DFL)
Draheim, Ed D (DFL)
Dressen, John Joseph (DFL)
Dummer, Arlette Elaine (DFL)
Dunn, Robert G (R)
Dunton, Harold Hartley (R)
Eastman, Ruth Ann (R)
Eckstein, A J (Tony) (DFL)
Edstrom, Ronald Dwight (DFL)
Ehlers, Thomas Martin (R)
Eken, Willis (DFL)
Ellison, Charles E, Jr (DFL)
Enebo, Stanley A (DFL)
Engesser, Emmett Henry (DFL)
Erdahl, Arlen Ingolf (R)
Erhard, Virginia W (Ginnie) (DFL)
Erickson, Wendell O (R)
Esau, Gilbert D (Conservative)
Etzell, George Ferdinand (R)
Evans, R G (Ron) (R)
Ewald, Douglas R (Doug) (R)
Faison, David John (DFL)
Faricy, Raymond White, Jr (DFL)
Felien, Alice Mildred (DFL)
Ferguson, Robert Ernest (DFL)
Fischer, Henry Fred (DFL)
Fisher, Leo Frank (DFL)
Fitzpatrick, Edward Joseph (DFL)
Fitzsimons, Richard W (Conservative)
Fjoslien, Dave (R)
Flynn, Gwendolyn Kay (DFL)
Ford, Keith John (DFL)
Forsythe, Mary MacCornack (R)
Forsythe, Robert Ames (R)
Fraser, Donald MacKay (DFL)
Frederick, Melvin Lyle (R)
Freer, Lyle Leroy (R)
Frenzel, William Eldridge (Bill) (R)
Friedrich, Donald Lawrence (R)
Fudro, Stanley J (DFL)
Fugina, Peter X (DFL)
Gant, Joseph Erwin, Jr (D)
Gasper, Alton Joseph (DFL)
Gearty, Edward Joseph (DFL)
Geib, G Harriet (R)
Geittmann, Ida Mae (R)
Gellert, Randall Clarence (DFL)
George, Michael John (DFL)
Ginsburg, Michael Joseph (DFL)
Goetz, James B (Jim) (R)
Gorman, George E (D)
Graba, Joseph P (DFL)
Griffith, Douglas Jon (D)
Gruenes, Bernard A (R)
Gunderson, Aster B J (D)
Hagedorn, Thomas M (R)

MINNESOTA / 1057

Hahnen, Richard Young (R)
Halvorson, George Charles, Sr (R)
Hamersly, Marjory Ann (R)
Hansen, C R (Baldy) (DFL)
Hansen, Mel (R)
Hanson, Norma Lee (DFL)
Hanson, Roger Leon (R)
Hanson, Walter Raymond (DFL)
Hargrave, Roger James (DFL)
Harris, Forrest Joseph (DFL)
Hart, Richard T, Jr (R)
Hatfield, Rolland F (R)
Haugerud, Neil Sherman (DFL)
Hauswedell, Esther H (DFL)
Heinitz, O J (Lon) (R)
Heller, Walter Wolfgang (D)
Herzog, V Darlene (DFL)
Heuer, William C F (D)
Higgins, Aloyce Hubel (R)
Hitchcock, Carolyn Spark (R)
Hofstede, Albert John (DFL)
Hokanson, Shirley Ann (D)
Holman, Kingsley David (DFL)
Horbal, Koryne Emily (DFL)
Hughes, Jerome Michael (D)
Hull, Hadlai A (R)
Humphrey, Hubert Horatio (D)
Humphrey, Hubert Horatio, III (DFL)
Hunt, John Joseph, Jr (D)
Isaacson, Mae Deloris (DFL)
Jacobs, Joel (DFL)
Jaros, Mike (DFL)
Jensen, Carl Arthur (R)
Jensen, Robert C (DFL)
Johnson, Carl Marcus (DFL)
Johnson, Daryl Benjamin (DFL)
Johnson, Douglas J (Doug) (DFL)
Johnson, John Warren (R)
Johnson, Sidney Arthur (R)
Johnson, Virgil Joel (R)
Jopp, Ralph P (Conservative)
Jorgensen, Jack J (DFL)
Josefson, J A (R)
Joseph, Geraldine M (Geri) (D)
Jude, Thaddeus Victor (DFL)
Kaardal, Elmer Alfred (R)
Kahn, Phyllis (DFL)
Kaibel, Howard Lawrence, Jr (DFL)
Kaley, J R (Dick) (R)
Kalis, Henry J (DFL)
Kaplan, Mark (DFL)
Karth, Joseph E (DFL)
Kearney, Mary Patricia (D)
Keefe, John B (R)
Keefe, Stephen (DFL)
Keith, Donald Merle (DFL)
Kelly, Bill (DFL)
Kelm, Thomas Arthur (DFL)
Kempe, Arnold Emil (DFL)
Kempe, Ray (DFL)
Ketola, Marvin Edwin (DFL)
Kimball, Robert A (DFL)
Kimball, Shirley A (DFL)
Kirchner, William G (R)
Kleinbaum, Jack (DFL)
Knickerbocker, Jerry (R)
Knoll, Franklin Jude (DFL)
Knutson, Howard Arthur (R)
Kostohryz, Richard Joseph (DFL)
Kowalczyck, Al (R)
Kroening, Carl (DFL)
Krogh, Lee Vincent (DFL)
Krogseng, David Neil (R)
Kunz, Donna Mae (R)
Kvam, Adolph (Conservative)
Labine, Oliver Joseph (D)

MINNESOTA (cont)

LaCrosse, Gladyce Mae (DFL)
Laidig, Gary Wayne (R)
Lambert, Lawrence Arthur (DFL)
Landis, Randall Eldon (R)
Lang, Bernice Agnes (DFL)
Langen, Odin (R)
Langford, Robert Dean (DFL)
Langseth, Keith L (DFL)
Lano, Joan Rita (DFL)
Larkin, Ray Thomas (R)
Larson, Lew W (Conservative)
Lastine, Adella Edith (D)
Laufenburger, Roger Allyn (DFL)
Lease, M Harry, Jr (DFL)
Lebedoff, David Michael (DFL)
Lefko, Todd Jeffery (DFL)
Leiseth, Robert Vernon (R)
Lemke, Richard (DFL)
LeVander, Harold (R)
LeVander, Iantha Powrie (R)
Lewis, Avis Ida (R)
Lewis, B Robert (DFL)
Lindquist, Stephen Charles (DFL)
Lueck, LoRayne E (DFL)
Lund, Janet Campbell (DFL)
Lund, Rhoda S (R)
Lundeen, Ione I (R)
Lundsten, John Malcolm (R)
Luther, William Paul (DFL)
Luukinen, Jeanne (R)
Mack, Donald Charles (R)
MacLaughlin, Harry Hunter (D)
Maday, Michael Jerome (DFL)
Madel, Raymond Peter Jr (R)
Mahling, Berna Jo (B J) (DFL)
Manahan, James Hinchon (R)
Mangan, Tom (DFL)
Mann, George (D)
Marshall, Fred Vern (DFL)
Masanz, Hugo Edward (DFL)
Mayasich, Lorraine Eleanor (D)
McCarron, Paul (DFL)
McCarthy, Eugene Joseph (Independent)
McCauley, Maurice John (R)
McCollar, Maurice (Mac) (DFL)
McCutcheon, Bill (R)
McDermott, James Patrick (DFL)
McEachern, Bob (DFL)
McEwen, Neil Allan (DFL)
Meier, Claudia Marie (DFL)
Mellom, Sherwood Orlando (DFL)
Menning, Marion (Mike) (DFL)
Meriam, Helen (R)
Merriam, Gene (DFL)
Mertz, Inez Madeline (DFL)
Metzen, James P (D)
Miller, Darrel R (DFL)
Milton, John (DFL)
Moe, Donald M (DFL)
Moe, Roger Deane (DFL)
Mondale, Walter Frederick (DFL)
Monson, Robert Joseph (R)
Montgomery, Terry Patrick (D)
Moser, V Jean (DFL)
Mott, J Thomas (DFL)
Munger, Willard M (DFL)
Murphy, Joseph Edward, Jr (DFL)
Murphy, Mary Catherine (DFL)
Nadasdy, Leonard John (R)

Naftalin, Arthur (DFL)
Neisen, Howard J (DFL)
Nelsen, Ancher (R)
Nelson, Bruce (R)
Nelson, Gordon Lee (DFL)
Nelson, Henry Albin (R)
Nelson, Rolf Timothy (R)
Niehaus, Joe (R)
Nielsen, Helga Ragnhild (DFL)
Nielsen, J Werner (R)
Nielsen, Kermit Duane (DFL)
Noblitt, Harding Coolidge (D)
Nolan, Richard Michael (D)
Noonan, Norma Corigliano (DFL)
North, Robert (DFL)
Northup, Vyron Leslie (DFL)
Norton, Fred Carl (DFL)
Novak, Steven G (DFL)
Nycklemoe, Arleen DeLoris (DFL)
Nylen, Ramona Faith (DFL)
Ober, Ann Morgan (DFL)
Oberstar, James L (D)
Ogdahl, Harmon T (Conservative)
Oldendorf, Yvette Boe (DFL)
Olhoft, Wayne Lee (D)
Olkon, Ellis (DFL)
Olkon, Nancy Katherine (DFL)
Olson, Alec Gehard (D)
Olson, Howard Dean (DFL)
Olson, John L
Olson, Robert Charles (R)
O'Neill, Gary Thomas (R)
O'Neill, Joseph Thomas (R)
Osthoff, Tom (DFL)
Otis, James Cornish, Jr
Palmer, John Albert, Jr (DFL)
Paquin, Keith David (D)
Parish, Richard Justus (DFL)
Patton, Al (DFL)
Patton, John (R)
Pearce, William Rinehart (R)
Pederson, W Dennis (DFL)
Pehler, James (Jim) (DFL)
Perino, Joseph Oreste (DFL)
Perpich, Anton John (DFL)
Perpich, George F (DFL)
Perpich, Rudy George (DFL)
Petersen, Opal May (DFL)
Peterson, C Donald
Peterson, Darrel Lee (R)
Peterson, LeRoy L (DFL)
Peterson, Robert Earl (R)
Petrafeso, Pete (DFL)
Pfaender, Thomas Paine (R)
Philbrook, Burnham John (DFL)
Pierson, John Jay (R)
Pillsbury, George Sturgis (R)
Pintar, Michael Anthony (DFL)
Pleasant, Ray O (R)
Pomeroy, Benjamin Sherwood (R)
Prahl, Norman (DFL)
Purfeerst, Clarence M (D)
Queensen, Keith Alan (DFL)
Quie, Albert Harold (R)
Rapoport, Lorie Jean (DFL)
Reckdahl, Joan Marie (DFL)
Renneke, Earl Wallace (R)
Rice, James I (DFL)
Richter, Anne Thorbeck (DFL)
Rickert, Robert Taylor (DFL)
Ring, Carolyn Louise (R)
Roe, David K (DFL)
Rolvaag, Karl Fritjof (DFL)
Rooney, Richard V (D)
Rud, Richard Wayne (DFL)
Ruprecht, Mary Margaret (DFL)
Ryan, Thomas (Liberal)

Sabo, Martin Olav (DFL)
St Onge, Doug (DFL)
Salchert, John Joseph (DFL)
Salzwedel, Pearl R (DFL)
Sampson, Curtis Allen (R)
Samuelson, Donald B (DFL)
Sand, Ervin Herman (DFL)
Sanda, Krista Linnea (R)
Savelkoul, Henry Jerome (R)
Schaaf, David D (DFL)
Schiel, Donald Carl (R)
Schmitz, Robert Joseph (DFL)
Schrader, Ronald Frederick (D)
Schreiber, Bill (R)
Schrom, Edward Joseph (DFL)
Schumacher, Wayne (DFL)
Schutz, Victor (DFL)
Scott, Ulric Carl (DFL)
Searle, Rodney N (R)
Seely, Robert D (R)
Setzepfandt, Alvin O H, II (DFL)
Sherwood, Glen (R)
Shoquist, Mary Lucille (DFL)
Showalter, Joanne Marie (DFL)
Sieben, Harry A, Jr (DFL)
Sieben, Michael (D)
Sieloff, Ronald Bruce (R)
Sillers, Douglas Hugh (R)
Simoneau, Wayne Anthony (DFL)
Simonson, Harold James (DFL)
Sinner, Richard Walter (D)
Skagerberg, Donna Clare (R)
Skoglund, Wesley John (DFL)
Smith, Howard E (D)
Smogard, Ellsworth G (D)
Sobolik, Dennis Merlin (DFL)
Solberg, Grace Corrine (DFL)
Solon, Sam George (D)
Sorenson, Joan Lee (R)
Souba, Arnold Richard (R)
Spahn, John Nick (D)
Spanish, John H (D)
Spannaus, Warren Richard (DFL)
Spear, Allan Henry (DFL)
Speed, Ronald K (R)
Springer, Erchal John (DFL)
Standafer, Daryl Lloyd (R)
Stanton, Russell P (DFL)
Steinbach, Kenward N (DFL)
Stenvig, Charles (Independent)
Stickney, Charles William (DFL)
Stocker, Luella Heine (R)
Stoker, Betty Anderson (DFL)
Stokes, Henry Duerre (R)
Stokowski, Eugene E (DFL)
Stumpf, Peter Philip (DFL)
Sullivan, Gerald Anthony (DFL)
Suss, Ted L (DFL)
Svien, Don J (R)
Swager, Norvin Leroy (DFL)
Swan, Arthur Robert (R)
Swanson, James C (DFL)
Tegels, Carol Anne (DFL)
Tekautz, Russell Frank (DFL)
Tennessen, Robert J (DFL)
Thiss, George Raymond (R)
Thompson, Marilyn Dowie (DFL)
Thompson, Wayne W (R)
Thorson, Judith Mary (DFL)
Thorsten, Bernece Marie (DFL)
Ticen, Thomas E (DFL)
Todd, John J
Tomlinson, John D (DFL)
Torrey, Elizabeth N (R)
Ueland, Arnulf, Jr (R)
Ulland, James (R)
Ulrich, Gertrude Willems (DFL)

Vail, Joane Rand (DFL)
Vanasek, Robert Edward (DFL)
Vento, Bruce F (DFL)
Voss, Gordon Owen (DFL)
Wallace, Linda Feist (DFL)
Wallin, Donna Caroline (D)
Walsh, Staria R (DFL)
Wammer, Michael Henry (DFL)
Wangen, Marvin Eugene (DFL)
Warren, Lillian Frances Warmsley (R)
Waterfield, Roe Richard (DFL)
Wegener, Myrton O (DFL)
Weiler, Philip J (DFL)
Welu, Josephine Elizabeth (Betty) (DFL)
Wenstrom, Gene R (D)
Wenzel, Stephen G (DFL)
West, Thomas Helin (DFL)
Westman, Patricia Ann (DFL)
Westrum, Martha Rose (DFL)
Westrup, Donald Leo (DFL)
White, Jim F (DFL)
Wieser, Al, Jr (DFL)
Wigley, Richard Ellis (R)
Willet, Gerald L (DFL)
Williamson, Bruce Dayton (DFL)
Windingstad, Harold Oliver, Jr (DFL)
Wisted, Beatrice Eleanor (DFL)
Wold, Carol Anne (D)
Wyant, Clinton W (DFL)
Young, Everett Leslie (DFL)
Zubay, Ken (R)
Zwach, John M (R)

MISSISSIPPI

Abernethy, Thomas Gerstle (D)
Abraham, George Douglas (D)
Ainsworth, Wilburn Eugene, Jr (D)
Alexander, Wm B (D)
Allen, Margaret (D)
Anderson, Robert Edward (Bob) (D)
Arnold, John Robert (R)
Arrington, Robert Erskin (D)
Barbour, Haley Reeves (R)
Barefield, Stone Deavours (D)
Barnett, James Arden (R)
Barnett, Ross Robert (D)
Beach, Stephen Leeds, III (D)
Bennett, Otis Bee (D)
Bishop, Tilmon Melvin (D)
Blessey, Gerald Henry (D)
Bloodworth, Benton Barclay (D)
Bodron, Ellis Barkett (D)
Bolton, Eldon L, Jr (D)
Bowen, David Reece (D)
Boyce, Daniel Rouse (Dan) (D)
Breed, William Jack (R)
Brewer, Aubrey Horace (D)
Brooks, Thomas Lee (D)
Brooks, Thomas Norman (Tommy) (D)
Broom, Vernon H (D)
Brown, J Walter (D)
Brown, John Walter, Jr (D)
Bryant, Curtis Conway (D)
Burgin, William Garner, Jr (D)
Bush, Billie Voss (D)
Butler, William Chester (D)
Caldwell, James Lawrence (Jimmy) (D)
Callicott, William Edward (D)
Cammack, Benjamin Franklin, Jr (D)
Campbell, Thomas Humphreys, III (D)

Capps, Charles Wilson, Jr (D)
Carmichael, Gilbert Ellzey (R)
Carr, Billie Fisher (D)
Carruth, George Simmons (Doc) (D)
Carty, Joseph Wyndell (D)
Case, George Milton (D)
Cassibry, Napoleon Le Point, II (D)
Chambliss, Donald R (D)
Chatham, Ray B (Ray) (D)
Clark, Lela Timbes (R)
Clark, Richard Orville (D)
Clark, Robert George (Independent)
Cochran, William Thad (R)
Collier, Clint C (D)
Collins, George Welton (D)
Colmer, William Meyers (D)
Comans, Raymond (D)
Cook, James Harvey (D)
Cooke, Michael Dale (D)
Corlew, John G (D)
Cossar, George Payne (D)
Cresswell, William Ephraim (D)
Crook, Robert Lacey (D)
Cross, Donald Melvin (D)
Crowther, Billy Lamar (D)
Dailey, Ollie Lee (D)
Dallas, DeVan (D)
Damon, Henry Eugene (R)
Davis, Russell C (D)
Davison, Arwilla Huff (D)
Deaton, Charles M (D)
DeCell, Herman Brister (D)
Derian, Patricia Murphy (D)
Dobson, Clyde Herman (D)
Dodson, Newton B (R)
Donald, Robert Hicks, II (D)
Dulaney, Sim Clarence, Jr (R)
Easley, Sidney Hugh (R)
Eastland, James Oliver (D)
Eaves, John Arthur (D)
Endris, Glenn Edwin (D)
Evers, James Charles (D)
Ferguson, George Robert, Jr (D)
Feyen, Kathleen Ann (D)
Fondren, Elmer Louis, Jr (D)
Ford, Dale Harris (D)
Forsythe, John Edward (R)
Fortenberry, Harold C (D)
Fortinberry, Toxey Thomas (R)
Frazier, Bert Lee (R)
Gandy, Edythe Evelyn (D)
Garner, John Bromley (D)
Gibson, Billy Randall (D)
Gilbreath, Jerry Michael (R)
Gillespie, Robert Gill
Glassco, Charles Kimball, Jr (R)
Gollott, Thomas Arlin (D)
Gordon, Carl Jackson, Jr (D)
Graham, Deborah Susan (R)
Graham, Mack (D)
Greene, Edwin Eugene (R)
Gresham, John Kenneth (Buddy) (D)
Griffin, Charles Hudson (D)
Gunn, Howard Lee (D)
Guy, William S (D)
Halbrook, David McCall (D)
Hardy, Robert B (Bob) (D)
Harned, Horace Hammerton, Jr (D)
Harvey, Daniel (D)
Harvey, James Ferguson, Jr (R)
Havens, Marvin Lynn (D)
Haynes, Glenn Johnson (R)
Henry, Aaron Edd (D)
Hickman, Thomas William, Jr (Billy) (D)
Hicks, Hervey Owings (D)

Hinson, Jon Clifton (D)
Holloman, John Holliday, III (D)
Hooper, James Fullerton, III (R)
Hooper, Virginia Fite (R)
Horne, Tommy Arthur (D)
Horton, Marion (Ebb) (D)
Hudson, Winson (R)
Huggins, Robert Gene (D)
Hughes, Peaster Leo (D)
Ingram, Carroll (D)
Jackson, Otha Dill (R)
Johnson, Paul Burney (D)
Johnson, Seymour Bennett (R)
Jolly, Edward Sidney (D)
Jones, Henry Lee (D)
Junkin, John Richard (D)
Kemp, James Lamar (D)
Kennedy, Carroll Henry (D)
Kennedy, John Lloyd (D)
Kilpatrick, Johnny Max (D)
King, William Hampton (D)
Klaus, William J (R)
Ladner, Earl E, Jr (D)
Ladner, Heber Austin (D)
Laird, H V (R)
Lambert, Aaron Colus (Butch) (D)
Lee, Lillie Mae (D)
Lester, Horace Baxter (D)
Lewis, Jan (D)
Lewis, Judith Ann (R)
Lippian, Charles Joseph (D)
Livingston, Richard Lee (D)
Logan, Robert Maurice (Bob) (D)
Long, Betty Jane (D)
Lott, Chester Trent (R)
Louden, Silas (D)
Lynn, Frank D (D)
Mabry, Malcolm H, Jr (R)
Magee, Douglas MacArthur (R)
Maloney, James (Con) (D)
Mavar, Victor V (R)
Maxcy, Danny Joe, Sr (Joe) (D)
McClamrock, Margaret Elizabeth (R)
McClendon, Burwell Beeman, Jr (R)
McCoy, Charley Elvis (Charley) (D)
McCoy, Howard Wayne (R)
McCrary, Thomas (D)
McCullough, William Todd (D)
McDade, Helen Jacobs (D)
McDonald, Robert Faucette (R)
McIlwain, Willard Lee (D)
McKenzie, Richard Wayne (D)
McLeod, George Cecil, Jr (D)
McLoone, Philip Joseph (D)
Merideth, H L, Jr (Sonny) (D)
Miller, Hainon A (D)
Miller, William Moseley (Fish Bait) (D)
Millette, Theodore Joseph (D)
Mitchell, Charles B (D)
Molpus, James Ernest (D)
Montgomery, Gillespie V (D)
Montgomery, Ray Hillman (R)
Moore, John Paul (D)
Morrow, James Anthony (Jim) (D)
Moss, Joseph Gibson (D)
Moye, James M (R)
Neal, James Huston (D)
Neblett, Harry Edward (D)
Neill, John Alexander (D)
Newman, Clarence Benton (Buddie) (D)
Nix, Charles Ray (D)

Noblin, Jim (D)
Norman, Dovie S (R)
Nunnally, James David (D)
Ogden, Edwin Bennett, Jr (R)
O'Keefe, Jeremiah Joseph, Jr (D)
Oswald, Robert Holmes (D)
Owen, Ben (D)
Owen, Sank Edward (R)
Owens, Emmett Hennington (D)
Page, Matthew John (D)
Parkman, Percy Howard (D)
Patridge, Corbet Lee (D)
Pearson, John Lafayette (D)
Peeples, Jack Terry (D)
Penton, Marby Robert (D)
Perry, Bobby Gerald (BG) (D)
Perry, Felix Edwin (D)
Perryman, Audrey Johnston (D)
Pickering, Charles Willis (R)
Pierce, Clarence Albert, Jr (D)
Powe, William Alison (R)
Powell, John William (D)
Purvis, Perrin Hays (D)
Ramberg, Charles Henry (D)
Rankin, Harry Longino, Jr (R)
Reaves, Ginevera N (D)
Reed, Clarke Thomas (R)
Reeves, R B (Breezy) (D)
Rhodes, Alfred Henry, Jr (D)
Rhodes, William Charles (D)
Richardson, Don Wendell (D)
Robertson, Stokes Vernon (Independent)
Rodgers, Henry L (D)
Rogers, Frederick Marshall (Fred) (D)
Rogers, George Winters, Jr (D)
Ross, Jim Buck (D)
Ross, John Curlee, Jr (D)
Ruffin, William T (D)
Russum, Julius Franklin (D)
Sanford, I S (D)
Scoper, Vincent Gradie, Jr (R)
Shields, Charlie D (D)
Shinault, Ione B (R)
Shows, James E Liston (D)
Shumake, Glynn (D)
Sides, Julian Earl, Jr (R)
Simmons, Cecil Lamar (D)
Simmons, Ralph Terrell (R)
Simpson, James Charles (Jim) (D)
Singley, Vasco Monett (D)
Slayden, Gladys (D)
Smith, Alvin Curtis (R)
Smith, Frank E (D)
Smith, Glenn (D)
Smith, Homer Lee (D)
Smith, John Neil (D)
Smith, Martin Travis (D)
Smith, Theodore (D)
Smith, Wade Orchin (D)
Smith, William Marion (D)
Spann, Don (D)
Steckler, Sanford Richard (D)
Stennis, John Cornelius (D)
Stennis, John Hampton (D)
Stephens, Edgar J, Jr (D)
Stikes, Mary Ellis Hatcher (R)
Stockett, Peter McKenzie (D)
Stone, Ben Harry (D)
Stone, Thomas Mitchell (D)
Strider, Donald Burt (D)
Stringer, Quin Emerson, Jr (D)
Sugg, Andrew Jackson (R)
Summer, Alhioun F (D)
Sumner, James Carliss (D)
Swindoll, George Mitchell (D)
Tedford, Richard Cortez (D)
Thompson, Kirby (D)

Tims, Marjorie Hollingsworth (R)
Towery, Kaye H (R)
Tucker, Jack Norris (R)
Turner, James Harvey (D)
Waldrop, John (D)
Walker, Harry Grey (D)
Walker, James H (D)
Walker, Thomas Ray (Tommy) (D)
Waller, William L (D)
Walters, James Everett (D)
Watkins, Troy B (D)
Watson, Richard Thomas (R)
White, Berta Lee (D)
White, Eugene James (D)
White, Martha Carole (D)
Whitten, Jamie Lloyd (D)
Whitten, John Wallace, Jr (D)
Wicker, Roger F (R)
Wilburn, Jerry (D)
Wilkerson, William Avery (Bill) (D)
Williams, James B, Jr (R)
Williams, John Bell (D)
Williams, Kenneth Ogden (D)
Williamson, Bruce Royce (D)
Winter, William Forrest (D)
Wiseman, Bob (D)
Woelfel, Arlene Marie (D)
Wood, Clyde Everett (D)
Wright, Sam W (D)
Yarbrough, George Malone (D)
Young, Charles L (D)

MISSOURI

Adams, William Walter, Jr, (Will) (D)
Aikens, Johnnie S (D)
Alexander, Jessie Durrell (D)
Anton, Don Christ (D)
Armstrong, Orland Kay (R)
Arndt, Elizabeth Moore (Betty) (R)
Arnold, Jim (D)
Arnold, John Burleigh (D)
Ashby, Roderic Roland (D)
Ashcroft, John David (R)
Atkins, Charles P (Cab) (D)
Auchly, William Joseph (R)
Bailey, R Wendell (D)
Baker, James Glen (D)
Baker, Lloyd J (L J) (D)
Baker, Raymond Eugene (Mike) (D)
Bakewell, Claude I (R)
Banks, J B (Jet) (D)
Barber, Deborah Ann (D)
Barks, Marion Emmett (R)
Barnes, Ruth Frances (D)
Barrow, Letha Jewell (D)
Barrows, Raymond Edwin (R)
Barry, Philip M (D)
Basler, Marie Lucille (D)
Bays, G Bernice (R)
Beasley, Myra Jane (D)
Beavers, Ruth Jones (D)
Becker, Charles J (D)
Beckerle, Joseph W (D)
Beery, John Thomas (R)
Beggs, James Montgomery (R)
Beggs, Mary Harrison (R)
Bell, Charles Porter (D)
Bell, Lela Hackney (D)
Berkley, Richard L (R)
Berra, Paul M (D)
Betz, Vernon Elwood (R)
Bild, Frank (R)
Binger, Glenn H (D)
Blackwell, W E (Bill) (D)

MISSOURI (cont)

Blades, Ray (R)
Blakeley, Claude R, Jr (R)
Blanck, Richard Joseph (R)
Blassie, John J (D)
Blosser, James Richard (R)
Bockenkamp, Ron (D)
Bockhorst, Estelle Wilferth (R)
Bockhorst, John Herb (R)
Bockman, Glen O (D)
Bolling, Richard Walker (D)
Bond, Christopher Samuel (R)
Boring, Denzel D (D)
Boucher, Henry Mason (D)
Bradshaw, Paul Ludwig (R)
Brady, Edwin Francis (R)
Brancato, Jasper M (D)
Briggs, Frank P (D)
Brill, Newton Clyde (R)
Brinley, Ray Lloyd (R)
Briscoe, Jean (D)
Brockfeld, Russell G (R)
Broomfield, Charles S (D)
Brown, Mona Katherine (R)
Bruckerhoff, Vernon E (R)
Bruning, Elsie Irene (D)
Buckley, James Timothy (D)
Buckowitz, Georgia Marie (D)
Buechner, John William (Jack) (R)
Bueneman, Janet Ann (R)
Buford, Joseph Leone (D)
Burch, Clyde Monroe (D)
Burch, William Alva (R)
Burford, Dorothy Wright (R)
Burke, Michael A (D)
Burlison, Bill D (D)
Burns, Mary Frances (D)
Butters, Shirley Sue (D)
Butts, Flavel J (R)
Cagle, Roy Francis (R)
Calloway, DeVerne Lee (D)
Calton, Betty Joan (D)
Carnahan, Ernest Bryan, Jr (D)
Carnahan, Wanda Edwina (D)
Carrington, James Malcolm (Jim) (D)
Cason, William J (D)
Cervantes, Alfonso J (D)
Chastain, Charles William, III (D)
Clark, Pearl Mae (D)
Clay, William Lacy (D)
Cline, C F (D)
Coleman, E Thomas (R)
Colley, Lynn Allan (R)
Conway, James Francis (D)
Copeland, Fred E (Gene) (D)
Corse, Wahneta (D)
Countie, David R (R)
Cowell, Alice V (D)
Cox, Hardin Charles (D)
Cox, James Nelson (D)
Craig, Lelia Burks (D)
Cunningham, Roy (D)
Curls, Phillip B (D)
Curtis, Thomas B (R)
Dale, Clarence Taylor (R)
Dames, George P (D)
Danforth, John Claggett (R)
Danner, Pat (D)
Davidson, Curtis Vernon (D)
Deane, Mildred Oleta (D)
Deatherage, Priscilla Jean (D)
De Coster, Richard J (D)
DeField, Fred (D)
Delezene, Larry Keith (R)
DeWitt, John Allen (D)
Dickerson, Frank Arthur (R)
Dickerson, James Ralph (R)
Dickey, Charles Hardin, Jr (D)
Dickson, Ella Irene (D)
Dickson, Harold (R)

Dill, J Anthony (R)
Dinger, Marvin L (D)
Dirck, Edwin L (D)
Dixon, Robert Galloway, Jr (R)
Doll, Dorothea Helen (Dotty) (D)
Donnell, Forrest C (R)
Dorsey, Robert Schult (D)
Downing, Vic (D)
Drake, Jerry (D)
Drebenstedt, Frances Sams (D)
Dunmire, George Q (R)
Durnell, Gerald Lee (R)
Dyck, Alice Nadine (D)
Dyer, Frederick T (R)
Eads, Edna C (R)
Eagan, James Joseph
Eagleton, Thomas F (D)
Eggers, Floyd Martin (D)
Ellinger, Carol Eloise (R)
Ellis, Frank C (D)
Esely, William Joseph (R)
Esser, Harold Joseph (R)
Ewing, Lynn Moore, Jr (D)
Faris, Jane Theresa Cantwell (D)
Farley, James Wallace (D)
Farrar, William Harold (R)
Fazzino, Alex J (D)
Feigenbaum, Bob (D)
Feldman, Henry Lee (D)
Fendler, Ernst Joseph (D)
Ferrell, William Franklin (Bill) (D)
Fickle, William Dick (D)
Fiene, Chester Olan (R)
Fike, Stanley Redfield (D)
Findley, Susan Hancock (D)
Fischer, Glennon John (R)
Fleischer, Alfred J (R)
Fogel, Jerry Paul (R)
Franken, John H (D)
Frappier, J H (R)
Fulkerson, Jewett Monroe (R)
Galloway, Rita L (R)
Gann, Donald L (R)
Gannon, Clifford W (Jack) (D)
Gant, Jack E (D)
Gant, Mary L (D)
Gardner, Steve (D)
Garrett, Howard M (D)
Garrett, Marcella (D)
Garst, Richard Sylvester (D)
Garten, Meredith (Pete) (R)
George, Wanda Carol (D)
Gerding, Donna Ethel (D)
Giboney, Barbara Fay (D)
Giebler, Richard Owen (R)
Giffee, Roland M (D)
Ginn, Rosemary Lucas (R)
Goode, P Wayne (D)
Gover, Clara Nellie (D)
Goward, Russell (D)
Graham, Willard Woodrow (D)
Gralike, Donald J (D)
Grant, David Marshall (D)
Gray, John Nicholas (R)
Greenwell, Jessie May (D)
Griffin, Bob Franklin (D)
Griffith, Margaret Ruth (Margy) (R)
Hadley, Della M (D)
Hall, Durward Gorham (R)
Hall, James Merwin (R)
Hamilton, Buford Garvin, II (D)
Hamlett, Ray (D)
Hampton, Roger Joe (D)
Hampton, Thelma A Hayes (D)
Hamra, Sam F, Jr (D)
Hancock, Don (D)
Haney, Jewell M (D)
Hardin, Clifford Morris (R)

Hardy, Helen Coleman (D)
Harmon, Dan (R)
Harms, Linda Kay (R)
Harper, Edwin Leland (R)
Harper, Roy W (D)
Harris, Ida Lewis (D)
Hearnes, Warren Eastman (D)
Hedges, Georganne Combs (D)
Hedrick, Ralph (D)
Heflin, Clarence H (D)
Hembree, Marvin H (D)
Hendricks, Virginia Ellen (R)
Hinkle, Beulah Fern (D)
Hinton, Nelda Ruth (D)
Hoblitzelle, George Knapp (R)
Hoffman, John R (R)
Hoffman, Philip R (R)
Holliday, Harold L (D)
Hollis, Lucille Jewell (D)
Holt, Joe D (D)
Houghton, Charles G, III (D)
Houtchens, Delton Louis (D)
Howard, J T (Jerry) (D)
Howard, Raymond (D)
Howard, W O (Bob) (D)
Howe, Richard Ray (R)
Hubbard, Dorthy Stuart (Dotty) (D)
Huber, LeRoy James (D)
Huff, Ira Lu (R)
Huffman, Mildred P (R)
Hughes, Shelby Bond (D)
Hull, Frank Rothwell (D)
Hull, W R, Jr (D)
Hungate, William Leonard (D)
Hunter, Hal Edward, Jr (D)
Hunter, Lora Teresa (D)
Hutcheson, John Williams (R)
Ichord, Richard Howard (D)
Jackson, J Weldon (D)
Jackson, Robert Walter (R)
Jacobs, Carroll I (D)
Johnson, Grace Manchester (R)
Johnson, Robert T (Bob) (R)
Jones, A Clifford (R)
Jones, Jean Boswell (R)
Jones, Lem T (R)
Jones, Paul C (D)
Jones, Ralph (R)
Jordan, Orchid Irene (D)
Kaye, Robert (Bob) (R)
Keith, Charles Michael (D)
Kellogg, Mary Joan (D)
Kelly, Garnett A (R)
Kenton, Joseph S (D)
King, Ethyl Bell (R)
King, Richard Allen (R)
King, Vernon C (D)
Kirkpatrick, James C (D)
Kjar, Rolland William (R)
Kostron, Frank E (D)
Koupal, Carl Mathias, Jr (R)
Landgraf, Vernon H (R)
Landreth, Joseph Franklin (R)
Lang, Gene Leo (R)
Lang, Louise Mary (D)
Lee, Lawrence J (D)
Lehr, George Warwick (D)
Leisure, John (D)
Lemons, Charles Fred (R)
Lewis, Kermit E (D)
Lewis, William Edwin (D)
Lionberger, Erle Talbot Lund (R)
Litton, Jerry (D)
Losh, Freddie Franklin (D)
Losh, Zelle (D)
Lowenstein, Harold Louis (R)
Lowry, Levi Smith (R)
Lowther, Gerald Halbert (D)
Lynn, Fred L (D)
Maddox, Luther Warren (D)
Maddox, Neva Wiley Pemberton (D)

Madeson, Marvin Louis (D)
Maledy, Charles Robert (R)
Malloy, William A (D)
Maloney, Marvin L (D)
Maness, Ina Mae (D)
Manford, Don (D)
Maples, Juanita E (R)
Mareschal, Gregory J (Greg) (D)
Markland, William A (D)
Marriott, B Gladys (D)
Marriott, Vonceile Janis (D)
Marshall, Larry R (R)
Martin, Mary Elizabeth (D)
Martin, Richard E (Dick) (D)
Marvel, Billy Bryan (D)
Masters, Harold William (R)
Mathewson, James L (R)
McBeth, Gerald David (R)
McBride, Jerry E (D)
McClintock, Marada Ann (D)
McCoy, Mary Estella (D)
McCrary, Roscoe L (D)
McCubbin, Carrol J (R)
McCuskey, Lowell R (R)
McIntyre, Robert G (D)
McKamey, Leo (D)
McPherson, Michael Claude (D)
Mead, Larry Edward (D)
Mehrle, Kenneth G (D)
Melton, Emory L (R)
Mendenhall, Eyvon (R)
Merrell, Norman L (D)
Metzgar, Edith Cathrine (D)
Meyer, Arlie H (R)
Meyer, Walter L (D)
Mickelson, Frank Leslie (D)
Miller, John Guy (D)
Miller, Margaret (Peg) (R)
Miller, Roy David (R)
Miller, Wesley A (R)
Mills, Max Milo (R)
Mitchell, J Bernard (R)
Mittenberg, Dora Dale (R)
Monks, Nell Lucile (D)
Monsees, Janet Louise (D)
Monsees, Richard Henry (R)
Montgomery, Paul (D)
Morgan, Dale Eugene (D)
Morgan, John Hayden (D)
Mosher, Sol (R)
Muckler, Carl Henry (D)
Mueller, Allan George (D)
Mueller, Barbara Sue (R)
Mueller, Walt (R)
Mulvaney, James Patrick (D)
Murray, George E (R)
Murry, Ozella May (D)
Nangle, John Francis (R)
Nilges, Al J (D)
Noland, James Alfred, Jr (R)
Novinger, Gail Harvey (R)
Olson, Leslie O (R)
Osbourn, D R (Ozzie) (D)
O'Toole, Dan (D)
O'Toole, William R (D)
Ottinger, Edward E (R)
Owen, Erna Lee (D)
Palmer, Hazel (R)
Patek, Eunice Joan (R)
Patton, Edwin Guy (R)
Payne, Franklin (D)
Perry, William H, III (R)
Petersmeyer, Vallea Cornelia (R)
Peterson, Irene M (D)
Petska, Beulah M (D)
Phelps, William C (R)
Piekarski, Stan (D)
Ploeser, Walter Christian (R)
Powell, John Duane (R)
Powell, Kathryn (Kate) (R)
Prather, Ellen Genevieve Logan (D)

MONTANA / 1061

Proffer, Marvin E (D)
Quarles, Raymond (Ray) (D)
Quinn, Doris Marilyn (D)
Rabbitt, Richard J (D)
Raisch, Wm (Bill) (R)
Randall, Donald Millard (D)
Randall, William J (D)
Reed, Thomas Bruce (R)
Reisch, Harold Franklin (R)
Rendlen, Albert L (R)
Rendlen, Charles Earnest, Jr (R)
Rhodes, Jeri A (D)
Riley, James N (D)
Rivers, Nathaniel J (Nat) (D)
Roach, Criss Warren (D)
Robbins, William Raymond (R)
Roberts, Wilber Estes (D)
Robinson, Clyde Rayford (D)
Roddy, Joseph P (D)
Roderick, Gerald John (D)
Rohlfing, Glenice Fitch (R)
Rojas, Paul G (D)
Rollins, John Erroll (D)
Roos, Lawrence K (R)
Rothman, Kenneth J (D)
Ruffin, James Edward (D)
Russell, James (Jay) (D)
Russell, James L (Jim) (D)
Russell, John Thomas (R)
Rust, Gary W (R)
Ruth, Irley Gale (R)
Ryan, John C (R)
Ryan, Thomas F (Tom) (D)
Ryan, Timothy Thomas (D)
Sanders, Robert Donald (R)
Scaglia, Phillip P (D)
Schechter, Maurice (D)
Schlef, Earl L (D)
Schnatmeier, Omar Louis (R)
Schneider, John Durbin (D)
Schorgl, James Joseph (Joe) (D)
Schrader, Leo W (D)
Schwabe, Max (R)
Schwaller, William Anton (R)
Seay, William E (D)
Sego, Robert (D)
Sevits, Willis Lee (R)
Shaffrey, Ina Theresa (D)
Shalton, Lonnie Joseph (D)
Sharp, John Anderson (R)
Shear, S Sue (D)
Shirk, Lois Madeline (D)
Short, Barry Arnold (R)
Silverman, Bernice Leascher (D)
Simpson, James Lloyd (D)
Sisco, Shirley (R)
Skaggs, Raymond Leo (R)
Skelton, Ike N, Jr (D)
Skidmore, John Vanus (D)
Skinner, Leary George (R)
Slay, Francis R (D)
Smallen, Charles Dewey (D)
Smith, Elmer Eugene (R)
Smith, James L (D)
Smith, John Leonard (R)
Smith, Wayne Delarmie (D)
Snowden, Phillip Hugh (Phil) (D)
Snyder, Robert O (R)
Spain, James Earl (D)
Spainhower, James I (D)
Speckman, George Raymond (D)
Speers, Austin Burgess (D)
Speight, L Norwood (R)
Sponsler, Earl L (D)
Spradling, Albert M, Jr (D)
Stacy, Bill W (D)
Steele, Marie Y (R)
Steelman, Dorman Lloyd (R)
Steelman, Earlene Mae (R)
Stein, Mary Kathleen (Kay) (D)
Stone, J W (R)
Stone, Murray (D)
Stoner, William E (Bill) (R)
Stotts, Keith Horace (R)
Strobel, Katharyn Ann (Kay) (D)
Strong, James R (R)
Sullivan, Leonor Kretzer (D)
Susman, Louis B (D)
Sutherland, Herbert Ned (D)
Svetlic, Michael Joseph (R)
Swarts, Joseph Andrew (R)
Sweeney, Edward (D)
Symington, James W (D)
Symington, Stuart (D)
Tatum, James Bernard (R)
Taulbee, Frances Laverne (D)
Taylor, Gene (R)
Taylor, Mary Meriwether (D)
Thomas, Ruth Watt (D)
Thomas, Stan, Jr (D)
Thompson, Corley (R)
Thompson, James Corley (R)
Tiller, Jessie Irene (D)
Tinnin, Nelson B (D)
Topliff, Helen Juanita (D)
Tracy, Donald Allen (D)
Tracy, Shirley Louise (D)
Treppler, Irene E (R)
Troupe, James Pal (D)
Turner, Edwin Steele (D)
Turner, Vera Gristy (D)
Tyus, E Leroy (D)
Usher, R L (Scoop) (D)
Uthlaut, Ralph, Jr (R)
Valier, Charles E (R)
Vaughan, Hugh Slavens (D)
Villa, Thomas A (D)
Voges, Dorothy Jessie (D)
Volkmer, Harold L (D)
Vossmeyer, Steve (D)
Wagner, Ernest Martin, Jr (D)
Waits, Alvin E (D)
Walker, Howard Harold (R)
Wallis, O L (R)
Walsh, Thomas A (D)
Waters, William Baxter (D)
Webster, Richard M (R)
Wehmeyer, Victor William (R)
Weidenbaum, Murray Lew (R)
Weir, Adele N (D)
Welch, Jerry F (D)
Wells, J C (D)
Westfall, Morris Gene (R)
White, Marjorie K (D)
White, Maryetta Elizabeth (R)
Whitman, L Sue (R)
Whitsitt, Garland B, Jr (R)
Wiggins, Harry (D)
Wilcox, Rosemary Phyllis (R)
Williams, Fred (D)
Wilson, Truman (D)
Wood, Flossie Opal (D)
Woods, Michael Alan (R)
Woodward, John Leonard (D)
Woollen, Charles Wesley (R)
Young, Robert A (D)
Young, Robert Ellis (R)
Youngdahl, Mark A (D)
Zumsteg, Kathryn Anne (D)
Zych, Thomas E (D)

MONTANA

Aageson, David Elling (R)
Aber, L M (Larry) (R)
Agnew, Colvin Hunt (R)
Alsaker, Wanda Louise (R)
Amsberry, Jeanne Louquet (R)
Anderson, Clarence R (R)
Anderson, Forrest H (D)
Anderson, John H, Jr (D)
Armstrong, Sally Jo (R)
Asher, William Edward (R)
Babcock, Betty L (R)
Baeth, Russell (D)
Baeth, William R (Bill) (D)
Bardanouve, Francis (D)
Barrett, Evan Donald (D)
Barrett, Fred O (D)
Bartlett, John Wesley (D)
Bartschi, Rulon R (R)
Baucus, Max (D)
Beebe, Margaret Scherf (D)
Bell, Marjorie Brown (Marj) (R)
Bengtson, Esther G (D)
Berner, Alice Viola (D)
Bertelsen, Verner L (R)
Birch, Jean Gordon (R)
Blaylock, Chet (D)
Bowman, Myrtel C (R)
Boylan, Paul F (D)
Bradley, Dorothy Maynard (D)
Broughton, Virginia Lee (D)
Brown, Robert Joseph (R)
Buckley, Cecelia Anne (D)
Cannon, Ross W (D)
Carrington, Ruth Gibson (D)
Casey, Dennis D (R)
Castles, Wesley (Non-Partisan)
Cetrone, V E (Gene) (D)
Christiansen, Edward William, Jr (Bill) (D)
Colberg, Richard A (D)
Colburg, Dolores (D)
Conklin, Richard James (D)
Connors, Hollis Gay (R)
Conover, Max (D)
Conroy, Thomas R (D)
Cromer, Ella Mae (R)
Cross, John Melvin (D)
Daniels, Marvin Kermit (D)
Dassinger, Ernest N (D)
Day, William M (Willie) (D)
DeMichele, Margaret Mary (D)
Devine, John William (D)
Drake, Glen Lyman (R)
Driscoll, John Brian (D)
Dunkle, Frank H (R)
Dussault, Ann Mary (D)
Eckels, Charles Elmer (R)
Ellerd, Robert A (R)
Ellis, Howard L (R)
Ellison, Orval S (R)
Erickson, Leif (D)
Etchart, Mark S (R)
Evans, F Maurice (D)
Fabrega, Wenceslao Jay (R)
Fagg, Harrison Grover (R)
Fasbender, Lawrence William, Jr (Larry) (D)
Federico, Roberto M (D)
Finley, Bob (D)
Fishbaugh, Fred (D)
Fladager, Milton Wallace (R)
Fleming, James F, Jr (D)
Flynn, G Elmer (D)
Foster, Donald R (D)
Fredricks, Conrad Bradley (R)
Galt, Jack E (R)
Gehrett, Virginia Dalton (R)
Gerke, Harold Edward (D)
Gilligan, Peter J, Jr (D)
Goodover, Pat M (R)
Gould, R Budd (R)
Graham, Carroll Adrian (D)
Graybill, Turner Carlisle (D)
Greely, Michael T (D)
Groff, William Albert (D)
Gunderson, Jack Edward (D)
Guthrie, A B (R)
Gwynn, William G (D)
Haegen, Florence Virginia (R)
Haegen, Stewart Francis (R)
Hageman, Alvin William (D)
Hager, Tom (R)
Halvorson, Ora Juanita (D)
Hanson, Rhoda E (D)
Harlow, Paul Kidder (D)
Harms, Karl Heinz (R)
Harper, Robert Joseph (D)
Harrington, Daniel William (D)
Harrison, James Thomas (R)
Harrison, John Conway (D)
Haswell, Frank I
Hatch, Robin Paige (D)
Hayne, Jack McVicar (R)
Hazelbaker, Frank W (R)
Healy, John Edward (Jack) (D)
Helmbrecht, Steven H (D)
Herlevi, Martha (D)
Himsl, Mathias A (R)
Holmes, Polly Mudge (D)
Holter, W L (Bill) (R)
Hubing, Lee (R)
Huennekens, Herbert F (D)
Jacobsen, Glenn Eugene (D)
James, Matthew Edward (R)
Jergeson, Greg (D)
Johnson, Duane (D)
Johnson, Helen Chaffin (R)
Johnsrud, Junne Margarette (D)
Johnston, George R (D)
Judge, Thomas Lee (D)
Kanduch, Joe F, Sr (D)
Keil, Norma Fern (D)
Keller, Millett Frederick
Kelly, Robert F (D)
Kemmis, Daniel Orra (D)
Kendall, Orin Parker (D)
Kimble, Gary Niles (D)
Kimmitt, Joseph Stanley (D)
Knudsen, D L (Ike) (D)
Koehnke, Michael (D)
Kolstad, Allen C (R)
Kondelik, Evelyn Marguerite (D)
Kropp, Paul K (R)
Kubesh, Nell (D)
Kuenzel, Vera Venita (D)
Kummerfeldt, Ernest L (D)
Kvaalen, Oscar Seigel (R)
Lee, Robert E (Bob) (D)
Lester, Dennis Alan (D)
Lien, Edward (D)
Lindblom, Rita (D)
Lockrem, Lloyd Clifford, Jr (R)
Lory, Earl C (R)
Lucht, Virginia Lea (R)
Luebeck, Alfred S (D)
Lund, Art (R)
Lynch, John D (D)
Lynch, Neil Joseph (D)
Mackay, William Raynor (R)
Magone, Joseph M (D)
Makela, Gladys (D)
Maney, Marilyn Hicks (D)
Manley, John Emmett (D)
Manning, Dave Martin (D)
Mannix, Francis F (R)
Mansfield, Michael J (D)
Manuel, Rex (D)
Marbut, Gary Raymond (R)
Marks, Robert L (R)
Mathers, William L (R)
McCallum, George Walter (R)
McConwell, Kenneth George (R)
McDonald, John Kenneth (Jack) (R)
McDunn, Henry J (D)
McFadden, Duane P (Mac) (D)
McKittrick, Daniel Patrick (D)

MONTANA (cont)

McMillan, Wanda Gough (D)
McOmber, W Gordon (D)
Mehrens, John (Sandy) (D)
Melcher, John (D)
Meloy, Peter Michael (D)
Menahan, William Thomas (D)
Mercer, Wallace W (R)
Merritt, Roy Donald (R)
Metcalf, Lee (D)
Miller, Harriet Evelyn (D)
Moberly, Isabel Carol (R)
Moore, Jack Kenneth (R)
Moore, James Douglas (D)
Morin, Vicky Lee (D)
Mular, James Theodore (D)
Murphy, James E (R)
Murphy, John (D)
Murphy, Terry Laurence (D)
Murray, Frank (D)
Murry, James Wesley (D)
Nash, Ada Ruth (R)
Nefzger, Anna Marie (D)
Neill, Kenneth R (R)
Nelson, Harold C (R)
Newman, Dan L (D)
Norman, William James (Bill) (D)
O'Connell, Helen G (D)
Olsen, Arnold (D)
Olson, Stuart A (R)
Omholt, Elmer V (R)
Palmer, Bob (D)
Pasma, James Jay (D)
Phillips, C Eugene (R)
Pyfer, S Clark (R)
Rasmussen, A T (Tom) (R)
Regan, Pat (D)
Richards, Paul Thomas (D)
Robbins, Hershel M (D)
Roberts, Joe R (D)
Roe, Teddy W (D)
Romney, Miles (D)
Rosell, Antoinette Fraser (R)
Roskie, George F (R)
Roush, Glenn Arthur (D)
Salansky, James Michael (D)
Saunders, Robert B, Jr (D)
Schye, Elmer (R)
Scully, John Patrick (D)
Seibel, Ann Marie (D)
Seifert, Carl A (R)
Shelden, Arthur H (D)
Shoup, Richard G (R)
Sivertsen, Robert (R)
Sloan, James A (D)
Smith, Carl M (R)
Smith, Chadwick H (R)
Smith, Edward Bruce (R)
Smith, Paul Thompson (D)
Smith, Richard G (R)
South, Carroll V (D)
Staigmiller, John B (D)
Stephens, Stanley Graham (R)
Stevens, Edwin Walter (R)
Stoltz, Gail Margaret (D)
Story, Peter Reinald (R)
Sullivan, Kathleen Theresa (R)
Sullivan, Thomas Quinn (D)
Tallent, Ann (D)
Tande, Lyder Christian (D)
Teague, Wes (D)
Terry, Peyton Huber (R)
Thiessen, Cornie R (D)
Thomas, Bill (D)
Thompson, Shaun Richard (D)
Thompson, Stanley Emil (D)
Towe, Thomas Edward (D)
Tracy, Mildred Ethel (D)
Travis, Geraldine Washington (D)
Tropila, Joe (D)
Tschache, Ottley Raymond (R)
Turnage, Jean A (R)
Tvedt, Conrad R (R)
Twedt, Lorine (D)
Underdal, Melvin (R)
Vallance, May Louise (D)
Vance, John T (D)
Vincent, John C (D)
Vulk, Raymond Paul, Sr (R)
Warden, Margaret Smith (D)
Watt, Robert Delanson (D)
Williams, J Melvin (D)
Willits, John Birdcell (D)
Wolfe, Sam (D)
Wood, Louis Eugene (R)
Woodahl, Robert Lee (R)
Wright, J Stewart (R)
Wyrick, Harold A (R)
Yardley, Dan (D)
Zody, Artis Alvin (D)

NEBRASKA

Aerni, Russell W (R)
Allen, Jack Lee (R)
Andersen, Merrel L (R)
Anderson, Gary L (R)
Anderson, Robert Lake (R)
Apking, William Tappan (R)
Baker, Ralph A (R)
Barnett, Wallace M, Jr (R)
Barrett, William E (Bill) (R)
Bartruff, Robert David (D)
Batchelder, Anne (R)
Baum, Glen Frederick (R)
Beal, Gregory John (R)
Beermann, Allen Jay (R)
Beermann, Ralph Frederick (R)
Begley, William Overton, Jr (D)
Belker, Loren B (D)
Bereuter, Douglas K (R)
Bergman, Larry W (D)
Biegert, Maurine (R)
Bish, Milan D (R)
Blobaum, Robert E (R)
Boehler, Conrad Joseph (D)
Bohlke, Lloyd Elmer (R)
Bottorff, Lewis Madison (D)
Bowring, Eva
Boyd, Wayne Edwin (R)
Brandt, William B (R)
Braun, Walter W (R)
Brown, Buster Jack (D)
Burbach, Julius W
Burney, Dwight Willard (R)
Burrows, George Bill (D)
Bystrom, Irene Neville (D)
Carlson, Elizabeth Kathryn (R)
Carpenter, Terry M (R)
Carsten, Calvin F
Cassidy, John Edward (D)
Cavanaugh, John J, III
Chamber, Ernest
Cherry, Frank Elliott (R)
Clark, Robert L
Claussen, Peter Henry, III (D)
Codr, Francis W (R)
Coffey, Virginia Mae (D)
Cooper, Guy L (D)
Cope, Ron
Crosby, Robert Berkey (R)
Cunningham, Glenn C (R)
Curtis, Carl T (R)
Daub, Harold John, Jr (R)
Decamp, John William (R)
Desler, Dianne Kay (R)
Dickinson, James A
Dorris, Wilton Howard (R)
Dosek, Edwin Francis (D)
Douglas, Paul L (R)
Duis, Herbert J (R)
Dworak, Donald N (R)
Dyas, Hess (D)
Edelman, Alma Ann (D)
Edwards, Joseph Robert (R)
Elrod, A Don (D)
Eriksen, Gerald Bruce (R)
Exon, John James (D)
Farnik, Joe F (D)
Fitzgerald, Tom
Fowler, Leonard (D)
Fowler, Steve
Fraser, Thomas Jefferson (D)
Fraser, William Charles (R)
Fuhrman, Mark J (D)
Gale, John Alan (R)
George, Walter (R)
Goodrich, Glenn A (R)
Gotch, Clifford Roy (R)
Greinke, Gary Arthur (R)
Haberman, Rex Stanley (R)
Hagel, Charles Timothy (R)
Hanson, Doyle Robert (D)
Harman, Charles William (D)
Harrison, Robert Dinsmore (R)
Harroun, Harold Franklin (R)
Hasebroock, William H
Herman, Richard L (Dick) (R)
Higgins, Donald George (D)
Hines, Leon C (D)
Hruska, Roman Lee (R)
Hunter, Esther Lenore (R)
Jackson, Mildred Irene (D)
Jensen, Linda Jane Strnad (D)
Jensen, Maynard Wayne (D)
Johnson, Elmore Thome (R)
Johnson, Joseph Earl (D)
Johnson, Lance Franklin (R)
Kelley, Thomas Paul (D)
Kellogg, Jeannine George (D)
Kelly, Ralph D (R)
Kennedy, Thomas C
Kennedy, Wayne L (D)
Keyes, Orval Andrew (R)
Kime, Otho G
Knox, Arthur Lloyd (R)
Koch, Gerald D (Jerry) (R)
Kohlhof, Lavern Louis (D)
Kremer, Maurice A (R)
Krueger, Vernon H (R)
Lamberty, Patricia Ann (D)
Lange, Ernest J (R)
Lewis, Frank
Lewis, Richard
Ley, Dorothy (D)
Luedtke, Roland Alfred (R)
Mahoney, Eugene T (R)
Maresh, Richard (R)
Marsh, Frank (R)
Marsh, Shirley Mac (R)
Martin, David Thomas (R)
Marvel, Richard Douglas (R)
McCollister, John Y (R)
McDowell, Allen Jim (R)
McGinley, Donald F (D)
Meier, William Henry (D)
Meyer, Clarence Ardell Henry (R)
Mills, Jack D
Mitchell, Kenrick Russell (R)
Moore, Rowena Geneva (D)
Morgan, P J (R)
Morrison, David Eugene (R)
Morrison, Frank B (D)
Morrissey, Thomas Lawrence (D)
Morrow, William Earl, Jr (R)
Moylan, Harold Thomas (D)
Murphy, John R
Neal, Harvey Ivan (R)
Nelson, Maurice A (D)
Newell, David R (D)
Newton, John Edward
Nichol, William E
Odgaard, John Edmund (Jack) (R)
O'Donnell, Allen (D)
Ohmstede, Bryce Alton (D)
Ohmstede, Frances Elizabeth (D)
Olson, Emerald L (R)
Orr, A Lorraine (R)
Orr, Kay A (R)
Palmberg, Maurice Edwin (R)
Palmer, William H (R)
Person, Earle George, Jr (D)
Petersen, Janet Jean (R)
Peterson, Val (R)
Peterson, Wallace Carroll (D)
Pickerill, Mary Lou (R)
Pohlenz, Dean (R)
Porter, Dwight J
Primeau, Lawrence Steven (D)
Quirk, John A (D)
Rasmussen, Dennis L
Raymond, Morris Dean (D)
Redenbo, Mildred Irene (R)
Robinson, Paul Randall (R)
Ross, Donald Roe (R)
Rothwell, Robert Lee (D)
Ruby, Ellis Scott (R)
Rumery, Myron G A (D)
Sands, Edward Paul (D)
Sands, Nancy Platt (D)
Savage, John S (R)
Schaffer, Larry D (R)
Schimek, DiAnna Ruth (D)
Schmit, Loran (R)
Schwab, C B (R)
Schwartzkopf, Samuel (D)
Shaffer, Dale Lester (R)
Shaver, Marvin Douglas (R)
Simpson, Harold Dwaine (R)
Skarda, William R, Jr (R)
Sleeper, Jon Anthony (R)
Smith, Patricia Lahr (R)
Smith, Robert Lee
Smith, Virginia Dodd (R)
Spencer, Harry A (R)
Steen, Donald Mariner (R)
Stephens, Willie Oved (D)
Stewart, Mary Ruth (R)
Stewart, William A, Jr (R)
Stoney, Larry D
Stromer, Gerald Allen (R)
Stull, Leslie A
Sullivan, John Eugene (D)
Swanson, Gladys M (D)
Swanson, Wayne (R)
Swigart, Warren Russell (R)
Syas, George D (R)
Sydow, Donna Frances (D)
Thies, Louis Carl (R)
Thone, Charles (R)
Thor, John Carl (D)
Tiemann, Norbert T (R)
Treadway, Donald Ray (R)
Trombley, C Anne Patrick (D)
Walstrom, Lois Jean (D)
Walstrom, Veryl Armour (D)
Walters, William J (R)
Warner, Jerome (R)
Weaver, Edward Myers, Jr (R)
Weaver, Phillip Hart (R)
Webster, John Dean (R)
Whelan, Gerald T (D)
White, Richard (D)
Wilken, Shirley Maye (D)
Wiltse, Irving F
Yeutter, Clayton Keith (R)
Young, Dale L (R)
Ziebarth, Wayne W (D)
Zutavern, Conrad Morgan (D)

NEVADA

Abbott, George William (R)
Anderson, Joyce Ellen (R)
Ashworth, L Keith (D)
Banner, James J (D)
Barengo, Robert R (D)
Batjer, Cameron McVicar (R)
Baxter, Sandy Jean (R)
Benkovich, Robert Michael (R)
Bennett, Marion D (D)
Bible, Alan (D)
Blakemore, Richard Eugene (D)
Bond, Lee George (R)
Bremner, D Roger (D)
Brookman, Eileen B (D)
Brown, B Mahlon (D)
Brown, Charles Harrison (D)
Brown, Judith Claire (R)
Bryan, Richard H (D)
Cain, Virginia Hartigan (D)
Cannon, Howard Walter (D)
Carlino, Phil Thomas (D)
Carson, Didi (D)
Casey, Walter Pevear, Jr (R)
Catt, Virginia Ann (D)
Cavnar, Samuel Melmon (R)
Chaney, Lonie (D)
Christensen, Chester S (D)
Close, Melvin Dilkes, Jr (D)
Coulter, Steven Arthur (D)
Craddock, Robert Glen (D)
Crumpler, Shirley Ann (R)
Demers, Daniel J (D)
Dickerson, Harvey (D)
Dini, Joseph Edward, Jr (D)
Dodge, Carl F (R)
Dreyer, Darrell H (D)
Driggs, Don Wallace (D)
Echols, Gene (D)
Fahrenkopf, Frank J, Jr (R)
Foote, Margie Ellen (R)
Ford, Jean E (R)
Frazzini, Mary (R)
Fry, Leslie McGee (R)
Fulstone, David Hill, II (R)
Geran, Dedra Elaine (R)
Getto, Virgil M (R)
Gibson, James Isaac (D)
Glaser, Norman Dale (D)
Glover, Alan Harney (D)
Gojack, Mary Lee (D)
Gunderson, Elmer Millard
Harkess, Nancy Robyn (D)
Harmon, Harley Louis (D)
Harrell, Beverly (D)
Hayes, Karen Wood (D)
Heaney, Robert Elliott (D)
Hecht, Chic (R)
Herr, Helen E (D)
Hickey, Thomas J (D)
Hilbrecht, Norman Ty (D)
Holden, George Gordon (D)
Holloway, Sue Locke (R)
Howard, Melvin (R)
Hulse, James Warren (D)
Humphrey, Lucie King (R)
Johnson, Beatrice Marian (D)
Kellar, Charles L (D)
Kozlowski, Walt E (R)
Lamboley, Paul H (D)
Landsman, Albert Michael (D)
Laub, William Murray (R)
Laxalt, Paul (R)
Levy, Harry Charles (D)
List, Robert Frank (R)
Lomprey, Margaret (D)
Lowman, Zelvin Don (R)
Lundberg, Melvin Edward (R)
Macdonald, William (D)
Mann, Lloyd W (D)
May, Paul W (D)
McKissick, Howard Frank Jr (R)
McMullen, Ralph Edgar, Jr (R)
Mello, Donald Ray (D)
Miller, Thomas Woodnutt (R)
Millspaugh, Gregory Lowell (R)
Mirabelli, Michael Anthony (D)
Monroe, Warren Ludwig (D)
Moody, Don A (D)
Morrison, Robert Lee (D)
Mowbray, John Code (D)
Murphy, Patrick M (D)
Nakashima, Nobuo (D)
Nash, Victoria C (Vicki) (D)
Neal, Joe (D)
O'Callaghan, Donal N (Mike) (D)
Payton, Michael A (Tony) (R)
Poggione, P Daniel (R)
Polish, John (D)
Potter, Patricia Radcliff (D)
Price, Robert Earle (D)
Prior, Edwina M (R)
Puccinelli, Leo John (R)
Raggio, William J (R)
Reid, Harry M (D)
Richards, William Louis (R)
Riggs, John Arthur (D)
Robinson, Robert E (D)
Rose, Robert Edgar (D)
Russell, Charles Hinton (R)
Santini, James David (D)
Sawyer, F Grant (D)
Schofield, Jack Lund (D)
Schofield, James W (D)
Schouweiler, Eileen Caffrey (R)
Scott, Norma Joyce (R)
Sena, Nash M (D)
Sheerin, Gary Asher (D)
Smith, Janet Margaret (Jan) (D)
Sobsey, Chet (D)
Springer, Charles Edward (D)
Swanson, Harry Brooks (R)
Swobe, C Coe (R)
Towell, David G (R)
Turner, Elma Juanita (R)
Van Wagoner, Charlotte Ellen (D)
Vergiels, John M (D)
Wagner, Sue Ellen (R)
Walker, Lee E (D)
Weise, Robert Lewis (Bob) (R)
Wilson, Thomas R C, II (D)
Wilson, Woodrow (R)
Wittenberg, Albert L (D)
Young, Clifton (R)
Young, Roy (R)

NEW HAMPSHIRE

Adams, Sherman (R)
Ainley, Greta M (R)
Allen, Ira E (R)
Allen, Roderick T (R)
Aller, Douglas Joseph (R)
Altman, Carl F (D)
Ambrose, Robert Paul (R)
Ames, H Robie (D)
Andersen, Chris Kenneth (R)
Anderson, Fayne E (R)
Appel, Meliss A (R)
Appleby, James E (R)
Argue, John S (R)
Arnold, John P (R)
Aubut, Adelard J (D)
Ayles, Kenard F (D)
Baker, George H, Sr (R)
Baker, Marie Agnes (R)
Ballam, Louis Sherman (R)
Barka, Ernest P (R)
Barrett, William F (D)
Barrus, George A (R)
Bartlett, Clarence Edward (R)
Bass, Perkins (R)
Bass, Robert P, Jr (R)
Beard, Charles W (R)
Bednar, John M (D)
Belair, Laurence N (D)
Belanger, Gerard H (D)
Belcourt, Agenor (D)
Benton, Richardson D (R)
Bergeron, Louis E (D)
Bernard, Mary Elizabeth (D)
Bernier, Leo Robert (D)
Bisbee, Kenneth M (R)
Bishop, Beverly A (D)
Blaisdell, Clesson J (D)
Blanchette, Patricia Louise (D)
Boisvert, Emile E (D)
Boisvert, Wilfrid A (D)
Bolden, Melvin Reed (D)
Bossie, Robert F (D)
Bouchard, David J (D)
Boucher, Laurent J (R)
Boucher, William Paul (R)
Bouley, Richard L (D)
Bowler, Barbara B (R)
Boyd, Jack (R)
Bradley, David Hammond (R)
Bradley, David J (D)
Bradley, Richard L (R)
Bradshaw, John Rogers (R)
Bragdon, Orson H (R)
Bridges, John Fisher (R)
Bridges, Webster E, Jr (R)
Briggs, Frank A (D)
Brodeur, Robert J (D)
Brouillard, Richard P (R)
Brown, Paul Edward (R)
Brown, Ward B (R)
Browning, Sarah Louise (R)
Bruton, George A (D)
Buckman, Harold V (R)
Burke, John A (D)
Burns, Harold Wilbur (R)
Burrows, Adolph J (D)
Callahan, Francis P (R)
Callahan, Robert C (R)
Campbell, Marilyn R (R)
Canney, Ethel M (R)
Carmen, Gerald P (R)
Carrier, Maria L (D)
Carswell, Minnie F (R)
Carter, Malcolm M (R)
Casassa, Herbert Alfred (R)
Castaldo, Margaret Houke (D)
Cate, George H (D)
Cate, John O (R)
Cate, Milton A (R)
Chambers, Mary Peyton (D)
Chandler, John P H, Jr (R)
Chase, Raymond F (D)
Chase, Russell Cushing (R)
Christensen, Edwin B (R)
Claflin, Russell G (R)
Clark, Cynthia M (R)
Clark, Shirley M (R)
Clark, W Murray (R)
Claveau, Thomas J (D)
Cleveland, Hilary Paterson (R)
Cleveland, James C (R)
Close, Elmer Harry (R)
Cobleigh, Neal Wayne (R)
Coburn, Roscoe Newton (R)
Collins, Michael A (D)
Collishaw, Lyman E (R)
Colson, Dorothy Foss (R)
Conley, Raymond K, Jr (D)
Cooke, Muriel Katherine (R)
Coolidge, Clyde Rocheleau (R)
Cooney, James B (D)
Copenhaver, Marion Lamson (D)
Copithorne, David Michael (D)
Corey, William W (D)
Cornelius, Michael Rae (D)
Corser, John Bliss, Jr (R)
Cote, Joseph Leo (D)
Cote, Kendall J (D)
Cote, Margaret Sullivan (D)
Cotton, Mary Elizabeth (D)
Cotton, Norris (R)
Cournoyer, Wilfred W (D)
Coutermarsh, Ernest R (D)
Cox, Grace Northrop (R)
Craggy, Ernest (D)
Craig, Robert Emmet (D)
Craig, William H (D)
Cressy, Ellen Mary (D)
Cullity, William J (D)
Cummings, Charles Everett (R)
Cummings, Gaylord G (R)
Cunningham, Wilfred R (R)
Currier, David P (R)
Currier, Philip R (R)
Cushman, Kathryn M (D)
D'Amante, Carmine F (D)
Dame, C Cecil (R)
D'Amours, Norman Edward (D)
Danforth, Bonnie Lewis (R)
Daniell, Eugene S, Jr (D)
Daniels, Forsaith (R)
Davis, Alice (R)
Davis, Roy W (R)
Day, Catherine-Ann (D)
DeCesare, Donald H (R)
DeCesare, Grace L (R)
Desmarais, Walter J (D)
Desmarais, William A (D)
Desnoyer, Alton G (D)
Dickinson, Howard C, Jr (R)
Donnelly, Helene Rosalyn (R)
Douglas, Charles Gwynne, III (R)
Douzanis, David B (D)
Downing, Delbert F (D)
Drake, Arthur Miles (R)
Drewniak, Dorothy J (D)
Dudley, Dudley W (D)
Duhamine, Roger M (D)
Dumais, Thomas A (D)
Dunlap, Ralph W (R)
Duprey, Stephen Michael (R)
Dupuis, Sylvio Louis (D)
Durkin, John A (D)
Dwinell, Lane (R)
Dwyer, Donald R (D)
Earley, Robert Emmett (D)
Eastman, Edwin Winter (R)
Eaton, Clyde S (R)
Eaton, Joseph March (R)
Eaton, Myrl R (R)
Ellis, Richard I (R)
Eneguess, Daniel Francis (R)
Engel, David Chapin (R)
English, William Conrad (R)
Erler, Robert C (R)
Estee, Paul N (D)
Favreau, Robert J (R)
Fennelly, Robert (D)
Ferdinando, Richard (R)
Ferguson, Charles Wright, Jr (R)
Ferreira, Francis Joseph, Jr (R)
Fillback, Armas Walfred (R)
Fimlaid, Eino O (R)
Flanagan, Natalie Smith (R)
Flanders, John Thompson (R)
Fleisher, Hilda W (R)
Foley, Eileen (D)
Fortier, Guy Joseph
French, Marshall Adams (R)
Frizzell, Martha McDanolds (R)

NEW HAMPSHIRE (cont)

Fullam, Arthur W (R)
Gage, Beverly Anne (R)
Gagne, David Lawrence (D)
Gagnon, Gabrielle Virginia (D)
Gagnon, Rebecca A (D)
Gallen, Hugh (D)
Gamache, Ovila (D)
Ganley, Barbara T (D)
Gardner, Edith B (R)
Gardner, William Michael (D)
Gaskill, Peter C (R)
Gauthier, Lorenzo P (D)
Geiger, Ronald E (R)
Gelinas, David L (D)
Gemmill, John K (R)
Gilchrist, David Bruce (R)
Gillis, Laurence Joseph (D)
Gillmore, Robert Harold (R)
Goff, Elizabeth E (D)
Gonthier, Eileen M (D)
Goodrich, Vera E (R)
Gordon, Anne Bradley (R)
Gordon, George E, III (R)
Gore, Marion Adams (R)
Gorman, Donald W (R)
Gosselin, David (R)
Goyette, Maurice Joseph (D)
Gramling, David Karl (D)
Granger, Guy Richard, Jr (R)
Grassie, Charles Wesley, Jr (D)
Grasso, Salvatore P (R)
Gravelle, Gene R (D)
Greeley, Stephen Alonzo (R)
Greene, Elizabeth A (R)
Gregg, Hugh (R)
Griffin, Ruth Lewin (R)
Gross, Martin Louis (D)
Habel, Eugene Joseph (D)
Hager, Elizabeth Sears (R)
Hanna, Katherine Merritt (D)
Hanson, Richard D (R)
Harney, Michael P (R)
Harriman, Katherine Jordan (D)
Heald, Cleon E (R)
Heald, Philip C, Jr (R)
Healy, Daniel J (D)
Healy, George T (D)
Hebert, Roland N (D)
Heckman, Carey Eugene (R)
Herchek, James Clayton (D)
Hersom, Lyle E (R)
Hess, Judith Ann (R)
Hildreth, Peter C (R)
Hill, Robert Charles (R)
Hoar, John, Jr (R)
Hobbs, Cornelius F (D)
Hodgdon, Shirley Lamson (R)
Holland, James Francis (R)
Holland, John (D)
Horrigan, James Owen (D)
Horton, Lynn C (R)
Hough, Ralph Degnan (R)
Howard, Donalda K (R)
Huggins, Harry F (R)
Humphrey, Howard S, Sr (R)
Humphrey, James A (R)
Hunt, Roger L (D)
Huot, J Oliva (D)
Ingram, Michael B (R)
Jacobson, Alf Edgar (R)
Johnson, Elmer L (R)
Johnson, William R (R)
Joncas, Grace Lucille (D)
Jones, Helen Gwendolyn (R)
Joos, Victor, Sr (R)
Joslin, William Richard (R)
Judd, Burnham A (R)
Karnis, Theodore Henry (R)
Kashulines, Juanita E (R)
Keefe, Edmund M (R)
Keefe, William F (D)

Keenan, Francis Joyce (R)
Keeney, Phyllis Mottram (R)
Kelley, Jane Pollard (D)
Kenison, Linda B (R)
Kennett, Rosemary (R)
Kidder, Barbara Ann (R)
Kidder, Victor Loran (R)
Kidder, William F (D)
Kimball, Ralph W (R)
Kincaid, William K (R)
King, John W (D)
King, Roger C (R)
Knight, David L (R)
Krans, Hamilton Richey, Jr (D)
Krasker, Elaine S (D)
LaBonte, Arthur H (D)
Lachance, Henry J (D)
Ladd, Elizabeth R (R)
Lambert, Lucien G (D)
Lamontagne, Laurier (D)
LaMott, Paul I (R)
Lamy, Catherine Gloria (D)
Langille, Philip G (R)
La Roche, David (D)
Lawrence, Norman B (D)
Lawton, Robert M (R)
Leary, Warren W (R)
Lebel, Irenee Remi (R)
Lebel, Lorraine Frances (D)
LeBrun, Donald H (D)
Lefebvre, Roland J (D)
Lemire, Armand R (R)
Leonard, Richard Wilson (D)
Lessard, Leo E (R)
Levasseur, Alphonse (D)
Lockhart, Richard Spence (R)
Logan, James L (D)
Loizeaux, M Suzanne (R)
Lucas, Jay Scott (R)
Lynch, Doris Theresa (D)
Lynn, Laurence Edwin Jr (Independent)
Lyon, Cecil Burton
Lyons, Elaine Turner (R)
MacDonald, John Lawrence (R)
MacGregor, Herbert L (R)
Mahoney, Henry Elmore (D)
Makris, Harry Peter (R)
Maloomian, Helen (D)
Mann, Ezra B (R)
Mansfield, Wilson S (R)
Marsh, Norman Clafflin (R)
Marshala, Augustine J (R)
Martel, Albert A (D)
Martin, Josephine C (R)
Mason, Samuel F (D)
Maynard, Ralph C (D)
McAvoy, Rita Cloutier (R)
McDonough, William J (D)
McEachern, Joseph A (D)
McGinness, Charles Lawrence (D)
McGlynn, Margaret L (D)
McIntyre, Thomas James (D)
McLane, Susan Neidlinger (R)
McLaughlin, John H (D)
McLaughlin, Lawrence G (R)
McManus, Anthony Aidan (R)
McNichol, Bernadette O (R)
Melnick, Rowell Shep (D)
Milbank, Robbins (R)
Millard, Elizabeth St (R)
Milne, Norman F, Jr (R)
Miner, Donald (R)
Monier, Robert B (R)
Montplaisir, J Henry (R)
Morgan, John B (R)
Morgrage, Barry C (D)
Morrissette, George H (D)
Morton, John Duggan Sr (R)
Murphy, Francis (R)
Murray, Fred E (R)

Murray, James W (R)
Nahil, Sam J (R)
Nardi, Theodora P (D)
Nassikas, John Nicholas (R)
Niebling, Richard F (D)
Nighswander, Esther R (R)
Nims, Stuart Victor (D)
Noble, John H (R)
Normand, James Arthur (D)
Nute, Helen Elizabeth (D)
O'Connell, James J (D)
O'Connor, Roderick Howard (D)
O'Connor, Timothy K (D)
O'Keefe, Michael John (D)
Olden, Dana E (R)
Oleson, Otto H (D)
Olivier, Charles J (R)
O'Neil, Dorthea M (D)
O'Neil, James E (R)
Orcutt, Joellen Lindh (D)
Osgood, Wilfred Beede (R)
Packard, David B (R)
Page, Henry H (R)
Paradis, Aime H (R)
Paradis, Henry Louis (D)
Parker, Gerry F, II (D)
Parnagian, Aram (R)
Parolise, Joseph L (D)
Parr, Ednapearl Flores (R)
Parshley, James H (R)
Patenaude, Richard A (D)
Peloquin, Richard Paul (D)
Pepitone, Anthony (R)
Perkins, Arnold B (R)
Perkins, Mildred Kelley (R)
Perkins, Russell L (D)
Peters, Marjorie Young (R)
Peterson, Frank E (D)
Peterson, Walter (R)
Plourde, Robert E (D)
Polak, Andrew Joseph (R)
Porter, Frederick Atherton (R)
Poulin, Richard L (D)
Poulsen, Andrew W (R)
Powell, Wesley (R)
Pray, Harry H (R)
Preston, Howell F (R)
Preston, Robert F (D)
Prindiville, Richard J (D)
Proctor, Nancy Jean (D)
Provost, Paul E (D)
Quigley, John Patrick (D)
Radway, Laurence Ingram (D)
Raiche, Robert Edward (D)
Ramsey, Peter E (R)
Randall, Anthony T (R)
Randall, Kenneth Allan (R)
Read, Maurice W (R)
Reardon, Albert Joseph (D)
Record, Louis D, Jr (R)
Reese, Delight Harmon (R)
Reidy, Frank J (D)
Rich, Wayne Schermerhorn (R)
Richards, Frank F (R)
Richardson, Henry Boyd (R)
Richardson, Mabel Lowe (R)
Riley, Doris J (R)
Roberge, A Roland (R)
Roberts, George B (R)
Robillard, Marc (D)
Rock, D Alan (R)
Rogers, Barbara Radcliffe (R)
Rogers, Myrtle Beatrice (R)
Rogers, Stflman D (R)
Rousseau, Omer A (D)
Routhier, Donald Roland (D)
Rowell, Ruth Elizabeth (R)
Rudman, Warren Bruce (R)
Ruel, Alfred J (R)
Russell, Patricia T (D)
Ryan, Paul J (R)
Sabbow, Fritz T (D)

Sackett, Everett Baxter (R)
Saggiotes, James A (R)
Sanborn, Leonard Fogg (R)
Sanborn, William E (R)
Sanders, Wilfred Leroy, Jr (D)
Sayer, James A (R)
Scamman, Walter Douglas, Jr (R)
Scott, Jesse W (R)
Scranton, Andrea Abbott (R)
Seamans, Henry J, Sr (R)
Senter, Kenneth Lee (R)
Shapiro, R Peter (R)
Shea, Barbara F (D)
Shepard, Irene James (R)
Sherman, Kenneth Leland (R)
Simard, Andre J (D)
Simard, Constance L (R)
Sing, John W (D)
Skinner, Patricia Morag (R)
Smith, Kenneth Charles, Sr (R)
Smith, Leonard A (R)
Smith, Roger A (R)
Smith, Stephen Wells (R)
Solomon, Jane A (D)
Southwick, Richard L (R)
Spalding, Kenneth Woodman, Jr (R)
Spanos, Harry V (D)
Spaulding, Roma Alma (R)
Spirou, Chris (D)
Splaine, James Raymond (D)
Stark, Robert L (R)
Stevens, Anthony B S (D)
Stevens, William John (D)
Stimmell, John H (R)
Streeter, Bernard A, Jr (R)
Sullivan, Mary J (D)
Sweeney, James Aloysius, Jr (D)
Symons, Joanne L (D)
Tarr, Kenneth M (D)
Tavitian, K Michael (R)
Taylor, Malcolm (Tink) (R)
Theriault, Alfred L (D)
Thibeault, George J (R)
Thibeault, P Robert (D)
Thompson, Barbara Cooper (R)
Thompson, Doris L (R)
Thomson, Harold E (R)
Thomson, Meldrim, Jr (R)
Tibbetts, Thelma P (R)
Torrey, Janet B (R)
Towle, Clayton W (R)
Townsend, Bruce C (R)
Townsend, Sara M (R)
Tripp, John Thornton (R)
Tropea, Robert Daniel (R)
Trowbridge, C Robertson (R)
Turner, Virginia W (R)
Twardus, John (R)
Underwood, Barbara J (R)
Vachon, Rose C (D)
Vallee, Ronald S (D)
Valliere, Alcide E (D)
Vander Haegen, Eleanor Marie (D)
Van Loan, Anna S (R)
Wallin, Jean Rogers (D)
Ward, Kathleen W (R)
Webb, William Mitchell (R)
Webster, Clarence L (R)
Wells, Whitcomb (R)
Whalen, Robert Edward (R)
Wheller, Robert W (D)
Whipple, Daley E (R)
Wiggin, Chester M, Jr (R)
Wiggin, Elmer S (R)
Wiggins, George I (R)
Wilkinson, Nana Miriam (R)
Williamson, Stanley H (R)
Wilson, Helen Frances (R)
Winkley, Noreen D (D)

NEW JERSEY

Winn, Cecelia Louise (D)
Winn, John T (D)
Wiswell, Marguerite H (R)
Withington, Richard Whittier, Sr (R)
Wolfsen, Franklin G (R)
Woodruff, Marian Davis (D)
Woods, Phyllis Lucille (D)
Wyman, Louis C (R)
Young, Niel C (R)
Zachos, Victoria (R)
Zechel, Caroline N (R)
Ziakas, Louis John, Sr (D)

NEW JERSEY

Abbott, Barbara S (R)
Adubato, Michael F (D)
Agnoli, Bruno (D)
Agnoli, Marena Lia (D)
Alaimo, Gaetano Joseph (Guy) (D)
Allen, Richard Vincent (R)
Allen, Robert F (D)
Ammond, Alene S (D)
Andora, Anthony Dominick (D)
Baer, Byron M (D)
Bailey, Charles Perkins (R)
Barba, Julius William (R)
Barbour, George H (D)
Bate, William Joseph (R)
Bateman, Raymond Henry (R)
Beadleston, Alfred N (R)
Bedell, Eugene James (D)
Berman, Gertrude (D)
Betz, Frank Herbert, III (R)
Biancardi, Joseph G (D)
Binder, Matthew J (R)
Blank, Fred E, Jr (R)
Bontempo, Salvatore A (D)
Bornheimer, James W (D)
Bradley, John Albertson (R)
Brennan, William J, Jr
Brown, Willie B (D)
Browne, Robert Span (D)
Browne, William V (D)
Buehler, Herbert J (D)
Bundy, William P (D)
Burgio, Jane (R)
Burstein, Albert (D)
Byrne, Brendan T (D)
Cafiero, James S (R)
Cahill, William T (R)
Cali, John F (D)
Campbell, Anne D (D)
Caputo, Nicholas (D)
Carluccio, Daniel John (D)
Carty, Melville A (D)
Cary, Ruth Margaret (R)
Case, Clifford Philip (R)
Cassella, Stefan Dante (D)
Chase, Theodore, Jr (D)
Cherubini, Lillian M Williams (R)
Chinnici, Joseph W (R)
Claman, Barbara Britton (R)
Cleveland, Harlan (D)
Connor, John Thomas (D)
Contillo, Paul J (D)
Cowan, James Rankin (R)
Crabiel, J Edward (D)
Curran, Barbara A (R)
D'Ambrosa, Arnold J (D)
Daniels, Dominick V (D)
Davenport, Joseph Howard (D)
Davis, Edith Pancoast (R)
Davis, Nathaniel
Dealaman, Doris W (R)
Decker, Gloria Ann (R)
Deitz, William Thomas (D)

Del Tufo, Gerardo L (R)
De Marco, James Garfield (R)
Deverin, Thomas J (D)
DeVoursney, Martin Thomas (D)
DiDonato, S Leonard (D)
Dillon, Clarence Douglas (R)
Dimon, John Edward (R)
DiSimone, Rita Louise (Independent)
Dodd, Frank J (Pat) (D)
Driver, Richard John (D)
Duff, John Bernard (D)
Dugan, James (D)
Dumont, Wayne, Jr (R)
Dunn, Thomas G (D)
Dwyer, Bernard J (D)
Dwyer, Florence P (R)
Edwards, Charles Cornell (R)
Esposito, Michael P (D)
Ewing, John H (R)
Falcey, Robert M (D)
Fay, John J, Jr (D)
Feldman, Matthew (D)
Fenwick, Millicent Hammond (R)
Fike, Eudora A (R)
Fischer, Frances M (D)
Fleming, George Gains (R)
Florio, James Joseph (D)
Flynn, Ann Dolores (D)
Flynn, William Edward (D)
Foran, Walter E (R)
Forsythe, Edwin B (R)
Frelinghuysen, Peter H B (R)
Froude, John H (R)
Fulcomer, James Joseph (R)
Gabrielson, Guy George (R)
Gallagher, Cornelius E (D)
Gallagher, J (Jack) (D)
Gallo, Thomas A (D)
Gannon, Joseph A (D)
Garramone, Raymond (D)
Garrubbo, Joseph L (D)
Gerard, Sumner, Jr (R)
Gewertz, Kenneth A (D)
Gibson, Kenneth Allen
Gilhooley, John Joseph (R)
Gladstone, Herbert Morey (D)
Gold, Michael (D)
Goldfarb, David (R)
Goldman, Gerald (R)
Gordon, Tina-Jill (R)
Gorman, Francis John (D)
Greenberg, Martin L (R)
Gregorio, John T (D)
Gross, Sheila Toby Smith (D)
Gugiiemini, Samuel Joseph (D)
Guido, Robert Norman (R)
Hagedorn, Garrett William (R)
Halpin, Robert J (D)
Hamilton, William J, Jr (D)
Harmon, Augustus Conaway (D)
Harrop, William Caldwell (Independent)
Hausmann, C Stewart (R)
Hawkins, Eldridge Thomas Enoch (D)
Haynie, Mary Donaldson (D)
Helstoski, Henry (D)
Herman, Martin A (D)
Hicks, William H (D)
Higham, Justus Charles (D)
Hirkala, Joseph (D)
Holland, Arthur John (D)
Hollander, Sanford Lloyd (D)
Horgan, Daniel William (D)
Horn, John J (D)
Horowitz, Betty (D)
Howard, James J (D)
Hughes, Richard J (D)
Hughes, William John (D)

Hunt, John E (R)
Hurley, James Richardson (R)
Hynes, Edward H (D)
Imperiale, Anthony (Independent)
Jablonski, Robert J (D)
Jacobs, Nathan L
Jones, Benjamin F (D)
Jordan, Paul Thomas (D)
Karcher, Alan (D)
Kean, Thomas H (R)
Keegan, Philip Myles (D)
Kennedy, Walter P (R)
Kern, Josephine Ann (R)
Klein, Ann (D)
Klein, Herbert Charles (D)
Kozloski, Walter John (D)
Kramer, Lawrence F (R)
Kuhl, Henry Young (R)
Kuyl, Sheila Marie (D)
Laddey, Richard Victor (D)
Lan, Donald Paul (D)
Lance, Wesley L (R)
Lapidus, I Richard (D)
Laurenti, Jeffrey (D)
Lazzio, Thomas (R)
LeFante, Joseph A (D)
Leiner, Henry Robert (R)
LeJambre, Susan E (D)
Leonard, Richard John Nelson (D)
Leskiw, Myron (R)
Lipman, Wynona M (D)
Lynch, John A (D)
Mace, Helene G (R)
MacInnes, Gordon A, Jr (D)
Maguire, Andrew (D)
Malkin, Susan Roberta (D)
Maraziti, Joseph J (R)
Marino, Mary Ellen (D)
Marino, Michael J (D)
Martin, Harold (D)
Martindell, Anne (D)
McCarthy, John Joseph (D)
McConnell, Barbara Wright (D)
McDonough, Peter J (R)
McGahn, Joseph L (D)
McKim, Adele W (R)
McManimon, Francis J (D)
McManus, Richard James (D)
Menza, Alexander J (D)
Merle, Lynn (D)
Merlino, Joseph Piedmont (D)
Meyner, Helen Stevenson (D)
Meyner, Robert Baumle (D)
Miller, Robert Howard (R)
Mills, Bradford (R)
Minish, Joseph George (D)
Miola, Michele (D)
Moore, John Denis Joseph (R)
Moskow, Michael Harold (R)
Musto, William V (D)
Neri, Rocco (D)
Neuberger, Katherine (R)
Newman, Daniel F (D)
Nickelson, Orabell (D)
Nissley, Eleanore Steffens (R)
O'Neil, Thomas Vincent (D)
Orechio, Carl A (R)
Orechio, Carmen (D)
Otlowski, George J (D)
Owens, Ronald (D)
Parker, Barry T (R)
Patero, Joseph D (D)
Patten, Edward James (D)
Pellecchia, Vincent Ozzie (D)
Perkins, William O, Jr (D)
Perskie, Steven Philip (D)
Petersen, Arnold (Socialist Labor Party)
Pickering, Thomas Reeve
Plowman, Joan Marie (R)
Power, Dorothy K (D)

Rappeport, Michael Arnold (D)
Raymar, Robert Sol (D)
Reaves, Betty Anne (D)
Rhett, Haskell E S (D)
Rhoades, Anna Rosa (R)
Richer, Stephen Bruce (D)
Rinaldo, Matthew John (R)
Rizzolo, Victor A (R)
Rochester, Mattilyn Talford (D)
Rodino, Peter Wallace, Jr (D)
Roe, Robert A (D)
Roseff, Richard (D)
Rosen, Alex (D)
Ruane, Robert M (D)
Russo, John Francis (D)
Rys, C Gus (R)
Salkind, Morton (D)
Samuel, Richard Irving (D)
Sandman, Charles W, Jr (R)
Savell, Cynthia Toby (D)
Scardino, Anthony, Jr (D)
Schluter, Nancy Hurd (R)
Schoel, Richard George (R)
Schron, Nancy Jane (R)
Schuck, Ernest F (D)
Seabury, Richard Williams, III (R)
Sears, Harry L (R)
Segreto, James Victor (R)
Serafin, Mary Walus (D)
Shanley, Bernard Michael (R)
Sharp, Doris Fuller (R)
Sharp, Thelma P (D)
Shaw, Lois DeGise (D)
Shelton, Robert C, Jr (D)
Siegel, Dolph (R)
Silverstein, Jack (R)
Singer, Richard Gus (D)
Skevin, John M (D)
Smith, Irene M (D)
Smoyer, Barbara Brooks (R)
Snedeker, Clifford W (R)
Sontag, Frederick H
Sorensen, Emil S (D)
Spencer, Arthur Conover (R)
Spizziri, John A (R)
Spoltore, John A (D)
Steele, Barbara W (R)
Stemmer, Jay A (R)
Stern, Jere Bart (D)
Sterner, E Donald (R)
Stevenson, Harry (D)
Stewart, H Donald (D)
Stiles, Beatrice May (R)
Stout, Richard Ralston (R)
Stradley, Jay Oakley (R)
Stretch, D Allen, Jr (R)
Sullivan, Elmer Lindsley (D)
Sundstrom, Frank L (R)
Sweeney, John A (D)
Sylvester, Frank William (R)
Thompson, Anne Elise (D)
Thompson, Frank, Jr (D)
Thornton, William Joseph (R)
Todd, Webster Bray (R)
Todd, Webster Bray, Jr (R)
Tomeo, Thomas P (R)
Tompkins, William Finley (R)
Torricelli, Robert G (D)
Totaro, Rosemarie (D)
Tumulty, Joseph W (D)
Ugoretz, Mark Joel (D)
Van Alstyne, David, Jr (R)
Van Wagner, Richard (D)
Visotcky, Richard (D)
Volcker, Paul A (D)
Walch, John MacArthur Dunsmore (D)
Waller, James H (R)
Wallhauser, George Marvin (R)
Walling, Willis R (R)
Wallwork, James H (R)

NEW JERSEY (cont)

Washington, Robert Benjamin, Jr (D)
Weathersby, William Henry
Weidel, Karl (R)
Weinberg, Loretta Leone (D)
Weissman, Benjamin Murry (D)
Wendel, Frederick Ernest (R)
Werber, Barbara (D)
White, Catherine Kilmurray (D)
White, James R (R)
White, John L (R)
Widnall, William Beck (R)
Wiley, Stephen B (D)
Williams, Harrison Arlington, Jr (Pete) (D)
Wilson, Betty (D)
Wilson, Eugenia Rose (Jeanne) (R)
Winmill, Eleanor Day (R)
Wollstadt, Paul (R)
Woodruff, Constance Oneida (D)
Woodson, S Howard, Jr (D)
Worcester, Robert M (D)
Worthington, Charles D (D)
Wyckoff, David Cole (R)
Yates, Charles B (D)
Yingling, Beth (D)
Zane, Raymond John (D)

NEW MEXICO

Aiello, Arthur Frank (R)
Alexander, Ben B (D)
Allen, Bobby Jerald (D)
Altamirano, Ben D (D)
Anaya, Mike (D)
Anaya, Toney (D)
Anderson, Clinton Presba (D)
Anderson, Robert Orville (R)
Apodaca, Jerry (D)
Appelman, Ruby V (R)
Aragon, Bennie J (D)
Aragon, Manuel Leroy (D)
Armijo, Alex J (D)
Armijo, Jose Enrique (R)
Baca, Leroy (D)
Barboa, Eddie Rodger (D)
Barnard, H B (D)
Bartlett, Martin Handley (R)
Becht, Paul Frederick (R)
Berry, Dan C (D)
Bigbee, John Franklin, Jr (R)
Blakeley, Gary (D)
Bodwell, Margaretta Lott (Marge) (R)
Bowman, Fletcher C, Jr (D)
Brown, Thomas E (D)
Brown, Thomas Elzie, Jr (D)
Bryan, Walker M (D)
Budagher, Linda R (R)
Burke, Nancy Aelishia (R)
Burrell, Consuelo Kitzes (D)
Cadwallader, James Kerrick (R)
Campbell, Jack M (D)
Carbajal, Richard A (D)
Castillo, Alvino E (D)
Cates, Charles Bradley (Brad) (R)
Caudell, James A (R)
Chacon, Matias L (D)
Chaplin, Ronald L (R)
Chavez, Willie M (R)
Cinelli, Adele P (D)
Cloud, Drew (D)
Connaughton, Theresa Gonzales (D)
Conway, John E (R)
Cook, Cecil W (D)
Crawford, Von Rue (R)
Cruz-Solano, Juan A (D)
Davidson, Robert Clarke (R)
Derizotis, Paris C (D)
Domenici, Pete V (R)
Donnell, John Dickson (R)
Dow, R Leo (R)
Dunn, Aubrey L (D)
Duran, Bobby F (D)
Eaves, Mary Marie (D)
Echols, Odis L (D)
Encinias, Frank T (D)
Evans, Ernestine Duran (D)
Feil, Paul Arnold (R)
Ferguson, Robert Earl (D)
Fettinger, George Edgar (D)
Fidel, Joseph A (D)
Fine, Franklin Marshall (D)
Fiorina, Betty (D)
Flemins, Frances G (Frankye) (D)
Floyd, Richard Thomas (R)
Foreman, Ed (R)
Foy, Thomas Paul (D)
Frost, Stanley F (D)
Garcia, Robert N (D)
Goodwin, Martin Brune (R)
Gordon, Joan (R)
Grace, Julian (R)
Grant, Philip R (Bob) Jr (R)
Gross, Fred Alfred, Jr (R)
Guinn, Roy Benton (J R) (R)
Gurule, Frank P (D)
Gwaltney, Lamar Edward (D)
Hansen, Fred
Hansen, Gladys (D)
Hanson, Fred (D)
Hapke, Richard Dwain (D)
Harrison, James William (Bill) (D)
Hartman, Ralph D (D)
Hays, John (D)
Hill, Stuart C (R)
Hobson, Phillip Maurice (R)
Hoover, Thomas Warren (R)
Horan, Thomas Joseph (R)
Howe, Dennis (R)
Irick, John B (R)
Johns, Merrill Blaine, Jr (R)
Johns, William Campbell (R)
Johnson, Lawrence H (R)
Johnston, Kenneth R (D)
Keil, Armin Theodore (R)
Kelly, Asa, Jr (R)
Kelly, John Martin (D)
Kennedy, Stephen William (R)
Kerr, Vernon Norman (R)
King, Bruce (D)
King, David Will (D)
Kinney, Harry Edwin (R)
Kitzes, Consuelo J (D)
Kloeppel, Richard J (D)
Knell, William Henry (R)
Kornegay, Jesse Dexter (D)
Lee, Bill L (D)
Lee, Tom (R)
Leger, Ray (D)
Lillywhite, Frank S (R)
Linard, Sharlyn (D)
Lopez, Edward Joseph (D)
Lucero, Anthony A (D)
Lucero, Chris M (D)
Lujan, B (D)
Lujan, Manuel, Jr (R)
Luna, Fred (D)
Lyon, Daniel F (D)
Malry, Lenton (D)
Martinez, Alex G (D)
Martinez, Joseph L (D)
Martinez, Walter K (D)
Mattingly, Rex Max (R)
McAdams, Harry Mayhew (D)
McBride, Abel Ernest (D)
McBride, Robert H (D)
McComas, Elizabeth Mae Veitch (R)
McHugh, Kathleen Ann (D)
McKim, George William (R)
McKinney, Robert M (D)
McManus, John Bartholomew, Jr (D)
McMillan, Colin R (R)
Mechem, Edwin Leard (R)
Medina, Reynaldo S (D)
Mercer, Joseph Henry (R)
Mershon, John J (D)
Mitchell, Albert Knell (R)
Moberly, Janie Fern (D)
Mondragon, Robert A (D)
Monette, Charles H (R)
Montoya, Joseph M (D)
Montoya, Ricardo Anthony (D)
Montoya, Samuel Zachary (D)
Montoya, Theodore R (D)
Moran, Robert Martin (R)
Moreland, C L (Cliff) (D)
Morgan, Jack Mac Gee (R)
Morgan, Thomas Phelps (R)
Morris, James Paxton (R)
Morris, Thomas Gayle (D)
Morrow, John L (D)
Nance, Hanslee Lee (D)
Neff, Francine Irving (R)
Norvell, David L (D)
Ocksrider, Charles Brightbill (R)
O'Donnell, William (D)
Ortiz, Donald Joseph (D)
Ortiz, Rudy A (D)
Otts, James K (D)
Papen, Frank O'Brien (D)
Pattison, Orville Hoyt (R)
Peironnet, James Stephen, Jr (R)
Pena, Abe M (R)
Pena, Dennis S (D)
Pennington, George (Red) (D)
Pope, Georgia Helen (R)
Radosevich, R Wayne (D)
Reed, Alan Barry (R)
Regan, Raymond Richard (R)
Robinson, Carlos R (R)
Rogers, John D (D)
Romero, Louis J (D)
Romero, Moises (R)
Rose, Joe (R)
Roybal, Ben (D)
Rudolph, Charles R (D)
Runnels, Harold Lowell (D)
Rutherford, Thomas Truxtun (D)
Ryan, William Murray (R)
Salazar, Nick L (D)
Salman, David M (D)
Salopek, Frank (D)
Samberson, C Gene (D)
Sanchez, Raymond G (D)
Sandel, Jerry Wayne (D)
Sawyer, Fern (D)
Sawyer, Mrs U D (Dessie) (D)
Schlientz, Kenneth M (R)
Scott, Boyd Franklin (R)
Sego, William A (R)
Sena, Joseph Robert (D)
Shipman, Frances (R)
Smalley, I M (D)
Stahl, Jack (R)
Stallings, Clayton (D)
Tannehill, John M (R)
Thompson, Donald Leslie (D)
Thompson, Rufus Elbert (D)
Tinker, Carol Wicks (R)
Tomlin, John R (D)
Triviz, Rita Marilyn (D)
Trujillo, C B (D)
Valdes, Joseph Ernest (D)
Valdes, Louis Felipe (D)
Valentine, William R (R)
Vigil, Samuel F (D)
Walker, E S Johnny (D)
Warren, William Ernest (D)
Watchman, Leo C (D)
Williams, John Thomas (D)
Williamson, Howard Houston (R)
Wood, Bob E (D)
Wood, Floyd E (R)

NEW YORK

Abinanti, Thomas J (D)
Ablondi, Italo H (D)
Abram, Morris Berthold (D)
Abrams, Robert (D)
Abramson, Edward (D)
Abzug, Bella S (D)
Ackerman, B Donald (D)
Addabbo, Joseph Patrick (D)
Aisenberg, Michele K (D)
Albanese, Vincent Michael (D)
Albano, Vincent Francis, Jr (R)
Alexander, Lee (D)
Alvarez, Eugenio Alfredo (D)
Amatucci, Jean (D)
Ambro, Jerome A (D)
Ambrose, John Anthony (D)
Anderson, Robert Bernerd (R)
Anderson, Warren Mattice (R)
Angell, Jean (D)
Antisdel, Louis Willard (R)
Aponte, Humberto (D)
Bachle, Barbara Jean (D)
Badillo, Herman (D)
Baer, Jo Webb (D)
Bahou, Victor Samuel (R)
Baker, Almina Rogers (D)
Baker, James Estes
Baker, Patricia Ellis (D)
Balch, Richard Horrocks (D)
Ball, George Wildman (D)
Baranello, Dominic Joseph (D)
Barbaro, Frank J (D)
Barclay, H Douglas (R)
Barker, James Peter (D)
Barnum, John Wallace (R)
Barry, John D (R)
Bartlett, Kenneth G (R)
Basmajian, Walter (D)
Battaglia, Edna Mae (D)
Battista, Vito Piranesi (R)
Baylor, Chelsea Anne (D)
Beame, Abraham David (D)
Beatty, Vander L (D)
Becker, Frank J (R)
Belcher, Taylor Garrison
Bell, David Elliott
Bellamy, Carol (D)
Bellanca, Alfonso V (R)
Bellis, Kenneth Mohr (R)
Bennet, Augustus Witschief (R)
Bentley, Robert (R)
Berger, Harold D (D)
Berking, Max (D)
Berkowitz, Jacqueline Ellen (D)
Bernstein, Abraham (D)
Bertini, Catherine (R)
Betros, Emeel S (R)
Biaggi, Mario (D)
Bianchi, Icilio W, Jr (D)
Bienstock, William H (D)
Bingham, Jonathan B (D)
Block, Ethel Lasher (R)
Bloom, Jeremiah B (D)
Blumenthal, Albert Howard (D)
Board, Joseph Breckinridge (D)
Bobroff, Harold (D)

Bodden, Mark Leland (D)
Boehlert, Sherwood Louis (R)
Bosch, Albert H (R)
Bouchard, Robert Alexander (D)
Bouck, John F (R)
Boutelle, Paul Benjamin (Socialist Workers Party)
Branchini, Frank Caesar (D)
Branscomb, Anne Wells (D)
Brasco, Frank J (D)
Breitel, Charles David (R)
Brennan, Peter J (D)
Brewer, Guy R (D)
Bronston, Jack E (D-Liberal)
Brooks, Doris L (R)
Brooks, Peter Stuyvesant (D)
Brown, David W (D)
Brown, George Hay (R)
Brown, Harold D, Jr (D)
Brown, Richard Arthur (D)
Brown, Thomas Walter (D)
Brownell, Herbert (R)
Bruen, David D (D)
Buchenholz, Jane Jacobs (D)
Buckley, James L (Conservative-R)
Buettner, Joyce Margueritte (D)
Burns, John J (D)
Burns, William L (R)
Burrow, Gordon W (R)
Burstein, Karen (D)
Butler, Arthur D (R)
Button, Daniel E (R)
Cabrera, Angelina (D)
Caemmerer, John D (R)
Cafiero, Renee Vera (D)
Calandra, John D (R)
Calkins, John Thiers (R)
Calogero, Nicholas J (R)
Campbell, Donald A (R)
Capanegro, Michael J (R)
Capozzoli, Jeanne Johnson (D)
Capozzoli, Louis J (D)
Caputo, Bruce (R)
Carey, Hugh L (D)
Carr, David A (D)
Carroll, George Francis (D)
Casey, William J (R)
Caso, Ralph George (R)
Catterson, James M, Jr (R)
Cecile, Robert Earl (D)
Celler, Emanuel (D)
Chambers, Alex A (R)
Chandler, Eleanor (D)
Chapin, Diana Derby (D)
Chisholm, Shirley Anita (D)
Chubb, Elizabeth Louise (D)
Cincotta, George A (D)
Clancy, Jean Theresa (D)
Clark, Ramsey (D)
Clay, Lucius DuBignon (R)
Cochrane, John Campbell (R)
Cohalan, Peter Fox (R)
Cohen, David Norman (D)
Cohen, Sy (D)
Cole, Thomas E (R)
Collins, Daniel (D)
Collum, Thad L (R)
Colton, William Anthony (D)
Colvin, Mark Thomas (R)
Conable, Barber Benjamin, Jr (R)
Conklin, William T (R)
Conlan, Robert J (D)
Connelly, Elizabeth Ann (D)
Conners, Michael F (D)
Connor, Robert Joseph (D)
Connor, Robert T (D)
Connors, John Henry (D)
Conway, John O'Connor (D)
Cook, Charles David (R)

Cook, Don W (R)
Cooperman, Arthur J (D)
Corning, Erastus, II (D)
Costanza, Margaret (D)
Costanzo, Nicholas (R)
Costello, Timothy William (Liberal)
Covello, Dallice Fern (D)
Crangle, Joseph F (D)
Crego, Doris Imogen (R)
Crews, John Robert (R)
Crotty, Peter John (D)
Cruz, Victor D (D)
Culhane, Thomas J (D)
Cummings, Richard Marshall (D)
Cunningham, Patrick Joseph (D)
Cuomo, Mario Matthew (D)
Curley, Lucy Alford (D)
Daly, Edna M (R)
Daly, John B (R)
D'Amato, Armand P (R)
D'Andrea, Robert Anthony (R)
Davidoff, Paul (D)
Davidson, Irwin Delmore (D)
Dearie, John C (D)
De Blasi, Pasquale, Sr (R)
Delaney, James J (D)
Dellibovi, Alfred A (R)
Del Toro, Angelo (D)
DeLury, Bernard Edward (R)
D'Emic, Matthew Jude (D)
Derounian, Steven B (R)
DeSalvio, Louis F (D)
De Santis, Carl Robert (R)
Deutsch, Peter (R)
DiCarlo, Dominick L (R)
Di Falco, Anthony G (D)
Diggs, Estella B (D)
Dodd, Isabel R (R)
Doherty, Patrick William (D)
Dokuchitz, Peter S (R)
Donovan, James Hubert (R)
Dooley, Edwin Benedict (R)
Dorn, Francis Edwin (R)
Dow, John Goodchild (D)
Downey, Thomas Joseph (D)
Drajem, Irene Theresa (D)
Dryfoos, George Ellis (D)
Dryfoos, Robert (D)
Dubinsky, David (Liberal, NY)
Duci, Frank Joseph (R)
Dudley, Edward Richard D (D)
Duke, Angier Biddle (D)
Dukes, Hazel Nell (D)
Dulski, Thaddeus J (D-Liberal)
Dunne, John Richard (R)
Duryea, Perry Belmont, Jr (R)
Dwyer, Henry W (R)
Dyson, John Stuart (D)
Eames, Charles Burton (R)
Echtman, Irwin M (D)
Eckert, Fred J (R-Conservative)
Edsell, Ralph James, Jr (R)
Edwards, Deighton Octavius, Jr (R)
Eldridge, Ronnie Myers (D)
Emery, James Louis (R)
Engel, Eliot L (D)
English, John Francis (D)
Ennis, Patricia Mary (D)
Epstein, Elissa (D)
Esposito, John A (R-Conservative)
Esposito, Meade H (D)
Eve, Arthur O (D)
Fahey, Joseph Edmund (D)
Fallon, Claudia Ann (D)
Farber, Earl Clarence (R)
Farbstein, Leonard (D)
Farley, James A (D)
Farrell, George Joseph, Jr (R)

Farrell, Herman D, Jr (D)
Feinstein, Elizabeth Cooke (D)
Feldman, George Joseph (D)
Fenton, Isabelle B (R)
Ferris, Joseph (D)
Fiedler, Edgar R (R)
Field, Frederick Gorham, Jr (R)
Finger, Seymour Maxwell (D)
Fink, Stanley (D)
Fink, Thomas A (D)
Finkelstein, Jerry (D)
Finley, Joseph Caldwell (D)
Fino, Paul A (R)
Fish, Hamilton, Jr (R)
Fisher, Arnold R (R)
Flack, John T (R)
Flanagan, John Joseph (R)
Flanigan, Peter Magnus (R)
Florio, Anita (D)
Flynn, John E (R)
Forstadt, Joseph Lawrence (R)
Fortune, Thomas R (D)
Fox, Frances Farnsworth (R)
Frangella, Joseph Carmen (R)
Frankel, Charles (D)
Freda, Carmine (R)
Fredman, Samuel George (D)
Free, Victoria Ellen (D)
Freeman, Jo (D)
Freeman, Orville Lothrop (D)
Fremming, G James (D)
French, Eleanor Clark (D)
Frey, Thomas R (D)
Galiber, Joseph Lionel (D)
Garcia, Robert (D)
Garlick, James Graham (D)
Garment, Leonard (R)
Gazzara, Anthony V (D)
Gentz, Gerald Thomas (D)
Gerling, William Curtis (D)
Gerstell, Glenn Steven (R)
Getler, Helen (R)
Gifford, William Leo (R)
Gilbert, Jacob H (D)
Gilman, Benjamin A (R)
Giuffreda, Leon Eugene (R)
Glavin, James Henry, III (D)
Godley, G McMurtrie
Goffin, Miriam Susan (D)
Gold, Emanuel R (D)
Goodell, Charles Ellsworth (R)
Goodhue, Mary B (R)
Goodman, Arthur (D)
Goodman, Roy M (R)
Gordon, Bernard G (R)
Gottfried, Richard Norman (D-Liberal)
Graber, Vincent James (D)
Grannis, Alexander Banks (D)
Greco, Stephen R (D)
Green, S William (R)
Greenberg, Marvin (D)
Greene, Scott E (R)
Griffin, Francis J (D)
Griffin, James D (D)
Griffith, Edward (D)
Grimm, Robert John (R)
Grimsey, J Herbert (R)
Grover, James R, Jr (R)
Gumper, Frank John (D)
Gunning, Rosemary Rita (R-Conservative)
Gurevich, Mae (D)
Gutowski, Stanley L (R)
Halaby, Najeeb E
Haley, K Daniel (R)
Hall, Gus (Communist)
Hall, Leonard Wood (R)
Halperin, Donald Marc (D)
Halpern, Seymour (R)
Hamilton, Ann Twynam (R)
Hamilton, Charles T (D)

NEW YORK / 1067

Hamilton, LaVerne McDaniel (D)
Hampton, Mason Lillard, Jr (Conservative, NY)
Hanley, James Michael (D)
Hanna, Thomas Ashe (R)
Harcourt, J Palmer (R)
Harenberg, Paul E (R)
Harriman, W Averell
Harrington, Donald Szantho (Liberal Party, NY)
Harris, Glenn H (R)
Harris, James Monroe (R)
Harwood, Stanley (D)
Hastings, James Fred (R)
Hatfield, Wanda Helena (R)
Haussamen, Carol W (D)
Hawley, R Stephen (R)
Hayduk, Albert T (R)
Healey, Philip B (R)
Hearn, George Henry (D)
Hecht, Burton (D)
Hein, Sidney S (R)
Held, Gerald S (R)
Hellmuth, James Grant (R)
Hemenway, Russell Douglas (D)
Henderson, Charles D (R)
Herbst, Lawrence (R)
Herman, Mark B (D)
Hesterberg, Alexander George (D)
Hevesi, Alan G (D)
Hildebrand, George H (R)
Hinman, George L (R)
Hochberg, Alan (D)
Hochbrueckner, George Joseph (D)
Hogan, Rosemarie (D)
Holtz, Lorraine (D)
Holtzman, Elizabeth (D)
Honnold, John Otis, Jr (D)
Horton, Frank (R)
Howe, Gordon A (R)
Hoyt, William B (D)
Hudson, Douglas (R)
Humes, John Portner (R)
Hurley, James F (D)
Ippolito, Andrew Vincent (D)
Irwin, John N (R)
Izard, Harold Hale (D)
Jackson, Emil A (D)
Jacobson, Jonathan G (D)
Javits, Jacob Koppel (R)
Jefferson, Shirley Almira (R)
Jenness, Linda Jane (Socialist Workers Party)
Joh, Erik Edward (R)
Johnson, Chester Arthur (D)
Johnson, Nina Sidler (D)
Johnson, Owen H (R)
Jonas, Milton (R)
Jones, Geraldine W (R)
Kane, Angeline Betty (D)
Kaplan, Betsy Byrns (D)
Karp, Gloria G (D)
Katzenbach, Nicholas de Belleville (D)
Katzman, Arthur J (D)
Keeler, Virginia Lee (D)
Kelleher, Neil William (R)
Kelly, Anne Catherine (D)
Kelly, Edna Flannery (D)
Kelly, Phyllis Matheis (R)
Kemp, Jack (R)
Keogh, Eugene James (D)
Kesselring, Leo John (Conservative Party, NY)
Kidder, Rolland Elliot (D)
Kilberg, William Jeffrey (R)
Kilburn, Clarence Evans (R)
King, Carleton James (R)
King, Lucille (D)

NEW YORK (cont)

Kinsolving, Charles McIlvaine, Jr (D)
Kisielis, Bernard S (D)
Knauss, Mary Ann Tinklepaugh (R)
Knight, Ridgway Brewster
Knorr, Martin J (R)
Koch, Edward Irving (D)
Komson, Linda Davidson (D)
Kornbluh, Edward Calvin (D)
Kovner, Sarah Schoenkopf (D)
Kremer, Arthur Jerome (D)
Kretchmer, Jerome (D)
Krupsak, Mary Anne (D)
Kupferman, Theodore R (R)
Kurtz, Myra Berman (D)
LaFalce, John J (D)
Landes, Irwin J (D)
Lane, Clarence D (R)
Lanigan, Charles Thomas (R)
Lasher, Howard Louis (D)
Lavorando, Joseph, Jr (D)
Lawrence, Gloria Edith (D)
Lazarus, Steven Jay (D)
Lee, Gary A (R)
Leeds, Isabelle R (D)
LeFever, Rose Isabel (R)
Lefkowitz, Louis J (R)
Lehner, Edward H (D)
Leichter, Franz S (D)
Lent, Norman F (R)
Lentol, Joseph Roland (D)
Levine, Philip Michael (R)
Levitt, Arthur (D)
Levy, Eugene (R)
Levy, Norman J (R)
Lewandowski, Michael (D)
Lewis, Albert B (D)
Lewis, Woodrow (D)
Libous, Alfred Joseph (R)
Lill, Raymond Joseph (D)
Lillis, Joan Frances (D)
Linder, Harold Francis (D)
Lindsay, John Vliet (D)
Lindsay, Robert Goodall (D)
Linowitz, Sol Myron (D)
Lisa, Joseph F (D)
Loeb, John Langeloth Jr (R)
Lombardi, Tarky James, Jr (R-Conservative)
Lopresto, John George (R)
Lovenheim, David A (R)
Lovett, Robert Abercrombie (D)
Lowenstein, Allard K (D)
Lowery, Thomas John, Jr (D)
Luddy, William F (D)
Luhrs, Janet Anne (R)
Lutz, Barry Lafean (D)
Lydman, Jack W
Lyman, Curtis Lee (R)
Lytel, Elaine (D)
MacCallum, Douglas C (R)
Mack, Thomas Cornelius (D)
Macomber, William Butts Jr (R)
Mahoney, J Daniel (Conservative, NY)
Mahoney, John F Jr (D)
Maitland, Guy Edison Clay (R)
Mandina, Constance Margaret (D)
Manes, Donald (D)
Manganillo, Ronald Joseph (D)
Mangano, James V (D)
Mankiewicz, Don Martin (D)
Mannix, Richard E (R)
Marchi, John Joseph (R)
Marchiselli, Vincent Andrew (D)
Margiotta, Joseph Michael (R)
Marino, Ralph John (R)

Marr, Carmel Carrington (R)
Marra, Mary Ann (R)
Marsha, Howard Clarence (R)
Marshall, Richard L (R)
Martin, Gene Stephen Darryl (D)
Martinelli, Angelo R (R)
Martinez, Theodora (D)
Mason, Edwyn E (R)
Mastandrea, Frank J (R)
Mastraccio, Armand John (D)
Mastropieri, Eugene F (D)
Maxwell, Anita Marie (D)
May, Stephen (R)
McCabe, James Walter, Sr (D)
McCall, Carl H (D)
McCarthy, Richard Dean (D)
McCormick, Charles Francis (D)
McCoy, Barry Malcolm (D)
McDonough, Edward Francis (D)
McEwen, Robert Cameron (R)
McFarland, Gail Evelyn (D)
McFarland, James Thomas (R)
McGinnis, James Allan (D)
McGowan, Thomas F (R)
McHugh, Dorothy Barbree (R)
McHugh, Matthew Francis (D)
McKneally, Martin B (R)
McManus, Donald Francis (D)
McNulty, Michael Robert (D)
McSpedon, Thomas G (D)
Measer, George John (R)
Mega, Christopher John (R-Conservative)
Melich, Tanya Marie (R)
Menschel, Ronay A (D)
Menta, Guido Paul (D)
Mercorella, Anthony J (D)
Meyerson, A Frederick (D)
Michaels, Lee Stephen (D)
Middendorf, Henry Stump, Jr (Conservative Party, NY)
Miller, Edgar Merrell (D)
Miller, Ethel Allen (R)
Miller, George William (D)
Miller, Herbert J (D)
Miller, Hyman M (R)
Miller, Marc Eric (D)
Miller, Melvin Howard (D)
Mills, Kenneth Adolfo (D)
Mirto, Peter G (D)
Mitchell, Charlene (Communist Party)
Mitchell, Donald J (R)
Mitzman, Nancy Curtin (D)
Molinari, Guy Victor (R)
Montano, Armando (D)
Moore, John J (D)
Morales, Mary Frances (D)
Morris, Barbara Ann (R)
Morse, Frank Bradford (R)
Moses, Robert (R)
Moskovitz, Mark Elliott (D)
Mott, Roger Alan (D)
Mudd, Therese M (D)
Multer, Abraham J (D)
Murphy, George A (R)
Murphy, John Michael (D)
Murphy, Matthew J, Jr (D)
Murphy, Thomas J (R)
Neuhaus, Richard John (D)
Newberg, Esther (D)
Nickerson, Eugene Hoffman (D)
Nine, Louis (D)
Nolan, Howard Charles, Jr (D)
Norris, Russell Earl J (Conservative, NY)
Novak, James B, III (Conservative, NY)
Novak, Larry F (D)

Nowak, Henry James (D-Liberal)
Nussdorf, Harry (D)
Oberwager, Frances Robertson (R)
O'Brien, David Frank (D)
O'Connell, John Thomas
O'Connor, Karen Paula (R)
Odierna, Ernest Carter (D)
O'Doherty, Kieran (Conservative, NY)
Ohrenstein, Manfred (D)
O'Keefe, Daniel Edward (D)
Oliven, Constance F (D)
O'Malley, John F X (D)
O'Neil, Regis B, Jr (R)
Orazio, Angelo Frank (D)
Osborn, George W (R)
Ostertag, Harold Charles (R)
Ottinger, Richard Lawrence (D)
Owens, Major R (D)
Pace, Anthony (R)
Padavan, Frank (R)
Palmby, Clarence Donald (R)
Palmer, George Vincent (D)
Palmer, Vincent A (R)
Pandick, Margaret L (D)
Parker, Martin Leonard (D)
Passannante, William F (D)
Passer, Harold Clarence (R)
Paterson, Basil Alexander (D)
Paterson, Lloyd H (R)
Pattison, Edward W (D)
Perry, John D (D)
Pesce, Michael L (D)
Pesner, Leon (D)
Peyser, Peter A (R)
Pheiffer, William Townsend (R)
Piczak, John P (D)
Pike, Otis Grey (D)
Pirnie, Alexander (R)
Pisani, Joseph R (R)
Plumadore, Hayward Henry (R)
Podell, Bertram L (D)
Polansky, Daniel J (R)
Polonsky, Helen (D)
Popper, David Henry
Posner, Herbert A (D)
Posner, Seymour (D)
Potter, Orlando B (D)
Proudfit, John Graham (R)
Quigley, James Michael (D)
Rangel, Charles B (D)
Rappleyea, Clarence D (R)
Reid, Ogden Rogers (D)
Reilly, Joseph Matthew (R)
Repicci, Francis C (D)
Reuss, Frederick M, Jr (R)
Richmond, Frederick W (D)
Rickenbacker, William Frost (Independent)
Rickman, Herbert Paul (D)
Riford, Lloyd S, Jr (R)
Robach, Roger J (D)
Roberts, Lillian (D)
Rockefeller, Nelson Aldrich (R)
Rolison, Jay P, Jr (R)
Roncallo, Angelo D (R)
Rooney, John J (D)
Roosa, Benjamin P, Jr (R)
Rosche, Richard Joseph (D)
Rose, Alex (Liberal, NY)
Rosenbaum, Richard Merrill (R)
Rosenberg, Alex Jacob (D)
Rosenberg, Marlene (D)
Rosenberg, Marvin (D)
Rosenblatt, Joseph B (D)
Rosenthal, Benjamin Stanley (D-Liberal)
Rosow, Jerome Morris (Independent)

Ross, Richard C (R)
Rossetti, Frank G (D)
Rourke, Russell Arthur (R)
Rowan, John Patrick (D)
Ruckdeschel, John Douglas, Jr (D)
Ruddy, Margaret Eva (D)
Ruderman, Jerold Robert (R)
Ruiz, Israel Jr (D)
Rush, Kenneth
Russell, Lloyd A (R)
Ryan, Aileen Barlow (D)
Ryan, Andrew W, Jr (R)
Ryan, Robert Joseph
Ryan, Thomas P, Jr (D)
Sachs, Alice (D)
Sacks, Alexander (R)
Saddlemire, Carl Lewis (R)
St George, Katharine (R)
St Lawrence, Joseph Thomas (D)
Sampol, William, Jr (R)
Samuel, Howard David (D)
Samuels, Howard Joseph (D)
Samuelson, Lillian Thompson (D)
Sandgrund, Hyla Zona (D)
Santucci, John J (D)
Schermerhorn, Richard E (R)
Scheuer, James H (D)
Schlein, Betty Goldman (D)
Schmidt, Frederick D (D)
Schneider, Morris H (D)
Schoeneck, Charles A (R)
Schosberg, Paul Alan (D)
Schroeher, Kathy Jean (D)
Schumer, Charles E (D)
Schwaner, Annie Mae (R)
Schweitzer, Melvin L (D)
Schwenk, Edwin Miller (R)
Sears, William R (R)
Seletsky, Harry (R)
Serrano, Jose E (D)
Shaffer, Donald (D)
Shaffer, Robert Edwin (D)
Shandalow, May G (D)
Shapiro, Arnold Ives (D)
Shapiro, Marilyn Linda (D)
Sharoff, Brian (D)
Sharpe, John George (R)
Shatzkin, Mike (D)
Shayne, Neil T (D)
Siciliano, Marion Elizabeth (R)
Silverman, Leonard (D)
Simmons, Geraldine Heras (D)
Simpson, Robert Foster (Conservative, NY)
Slaughter, Louise McIntosh (D)
Smith, Bernard C (R)
Smith, James Aloysius (D)
Smith, Robert Franklin (D)
Smith, William T, II (R)
Smolenski, Anthony (D)
Smythe, Hugh Heyne (D)
Snitow, Virginia L (D)
Solarz, Stephen J (D)
Soldini, John Louis (D)
Solomon, Gerald B (R)
Sorensen, Theodore Chaikin (D)
Southall, Mark T (D)
Spano, Barbara Lindholm (D)
Spodek, Jules L (D)
Stafford, Ronald B (R)
Stanley, Eliot Hungerford (D)
Stavisky, Leonard Price (D)
Stein, Andrew Jay (D)
Steingut, Stanley (D)
Stephens, Willis H (R)
Sterler, Lewis R (D)
Stevenson, Edward A (D)
Stillman, John Sterling (D)

Stokes, Carl Burton (D)
Stone, Norma Walsh (R)
Stopyra, Agnes Theresa (D)
Stott, Ronald Alton (D)
Stratton, Samuel Studdiford (D)
Straub, Chester John (D)
Strelzin, Harvey Lloyd (D)
Studders, Thomas G (D)
Suall, Joan Faith (D)
Suchin, Alvin M (R)
Sullivan, John Thomas, Jr (D)
Sullivan, Peter M (R)
Sullivan, Richard Joseph (D)
Sullivan, Thomas J (D)
Sullivan, W Howard (D)
Sunshine, Kenneth Marc (D)
Sunshine, Louise M (D)
Sutton, Percy E (D)
Sweeney, Gerald Francis (D)
Sweet, Joseph John (D)
Swiatek, Frank E (D)
Tallon, James R, Jr (D)
Tauriello, Anthony Francis (D)
Tauriello, Joseph A (D)
Taylor, Donald L (R)
Tenzer, Herbert (D)
Terry, John Hart (R)
Thorp, John S, Jr (D)
Tills, Ronald H (R)
Toote, Gloria E A (R)
Troy, Matthew Joseph, Jr (D)
Trunzo, Caesar (R)
Tuller, Judith (D)
Tyler, Harold Russell, Jr (R)
Upshur, Lillian W (D)
Valentine, William Anthony (R)
Vance, Cyrus Roberts (D)
Vann, Albert (D)
Velella, Guy J (R)
Velez, Miguel (D)
Virgilio, Andrew D (D)
Vitanza, Thomas Anthony (D)
Volker, Dale M (D)
von der Lancken, Carl (D)
Wagner, Robert F (D)
Walker, Sinita (R)
Wallis, Charles L (R)
Walsh, Daniel B (D)
Walsh, William Francis (R)
Warder, Frederick L (Red) (R)
Wasser, Joseph (D)
Weaver, Robert Clifton (D)
Webster, Donald Albert (R)
Weiner, Robin Wendy (D)
Weinstein, Clement (D)
Weinstein, Jack M (R)
Weiss, Arnold M (D)
Wemple, Clark Cullings (R)
Weprin, Saul (D)
Wertz, Robert Charles (R)
Whalen, George Edwin (D)
Wharton, James Ernest (R)
Wilcox, Frank B (R)
Wilkins, Roy
Williams, Franklin H (D)
Wilson, Malcolm (R)
Winikow, Linda (D)
Wolff, Lester Lionel (D)
Wood, Katherine M (R)
Woods, Mary L (D)
Wright, George Carlin (D)
Wydler, John W (R)
Wykle, Robert James (D)
Yallum, Janet Caro (D)
Yavornitzki, Mark Leon (D)
Yevoli, Lewis J (D)
Yusko, Theodore (D)
Zagame, John Ross (R)
Zagorin, Bernard
Zaroff, Carolyn Rein (D)
Zeferetti, Leo C (D-Conservative)
Zelenko, Herbert (D)

Zielenziger, David (D)
Zimmer, Melvin Neil (D)
Zimmerman, Robert Peter (D)
Zurer, Selmajean (D)

NORTH CAROLINA

Adams, Hoover (D)
Adams, J Allen (D)
Alexander, Fred D (D)
Alexander, Hugh Quincy (D)
Alford, Dallas L, Jr (D)
Allen, Charles Gice, Jr (R)
Allison, E Lavonia Ingram (D)
Allsbrook, Julian Russell (D)
Andrews, Ike Franklin (D)
Auman, Toffie Clyde (D)
Avery, Isaac Thomas, Jr (D)
Bagnal, Harry Stroman (R)
Bahakel, Cy N (D)
Baker, T J (D)
Barbee, Allen Cromwell (D)
Barker, Bob L (D)
Barker, Christopher Sylvanus, Jr (D)
Barnes, Henson Perrymoore (D)
Barnes, Hugh William (R)
Barringer, Russell Newton (R)
Barringer, Thomas Lawson (D)
Barwick, Plato Collins, Jr (R)
Bass, Herbert Edward (R)
Beard, R D (D)
Beason, Donald Ray (R)
Behn, Robert Dietrich (R)
Behr, Lawrence Van der Poel (R)
Belk, Irwin (D)
Bell, Charles Frederick (D)
Bell, Edwin Graham (D)
Bennett, Thomas Stephen (R)
Bissell, Marilyn Romaine (D)
Black, Charles Ray, Jr (R)
Blackwell, David M (D)
Blue, Carolyn Harrison (D)
Bobbitt, William Haywood
Breece, George W (D)
Bridges, Henry Lee (D)
Bright, Joe L (D)
Britt, Luther Johnson, Jr (D)
Brown, Clark Samuel (D)
Brown, Richard Lane, III (D)
Broyhill, James Edgar (R)
Broyhill, James Thomas (R)
Bruton, H David (D)
Bullard, Gladys (D)
Bumgardner, David Webster, Jr (D)
Bundy, Sam D (D)
Burgin, Charles Edward (D)
Burnside, Maurice Gwinn (D)
Callahan, James Christopher (R)
Campbell, A Hartwell (D)
Cannon, Hugh (D)
Capps, Elaine Folk (D)
Carter, Ernest Rawls (R)
Cassiano, Frank Anthony (D)
Chafin, Mary Elizabeth (D)
Chapin, Howard B (D)
Chase, Nancy Winbon (D)
Childers, Jack (D)
Church, John Trammell
Clapp, Paul Wood (R)
Clark, David (D)
Clement, Arthur John Howard, III (D)
Cline, Harold Brantley, Jr (R)
Cobb, Laurence Arthur (R)
Cochrane, William McWhorter (D)
Collins, P C, Jr (D)

Combs, Robert Lee, Jr (D)
Cook, Ruth E (D)
Cooke, William Leon (D)
Copeland, J Williams (D)
Cowan, Paul Earl (D)
Craig, Plezzy Harbor, Jr (R)
Crawford, Irvin Cooper (D)
Creech, William Ayden (D)
Cresimore, James Leonard (R)
Crew, William Lunsford (D)
Crockett, Katherine Welsh (R)
Cullipher, George P (D)
Dagenhart, Ewell Martin (R)
Daniels, Jonathan Worth (D)
Daniels, Melvin R, Jr (D)
Davenport, John Edwin (R)
David, Jeanette Wallace (D)
Davis, E Lawrence, III (D)
Davis, Gilbert Ray (D)
Davis, John Williams (R)
Delk, Joseph Clay, III (D)
DeRamus, Judson Davie, Jr (D)
Diamond, Harvey Jerome (D)
Diamont, David Hunter (D)
Eagles, Faye Burns (R)
Eagles, Larry P (D)
East, John Porter (R)
Edmisten, Rufus Ligh (D)
Edwards, James Harrell (D)
Ellis, Braxton Craig (D)
Ellis, T W, Jr (D)
Erdman, David Williams (D)
Ervin, Sam J, Jr (D)
Erwin, Richard C (D)
Eure, Thad (D)
Falls, Robert Zemri (D)
Farmer, Robert L (D)
Fountain, L H (D)
Fountain, Nina Walston (D)
Foushee, Roger Babson (D)
Freeman, Raymond Robert, Jr (R)
Frye, Henry E (D)
Fuller, Albert Clinton (D)
Furr, Dorothy Presser (R)
Gaddy, Carolyn C (D)
Galifianakis, Nick (D)
Gallaher, John K (D)
Gardner, J M (D)
Gardner, James Carson (R)
Gardner, Reece B (R)
Garrison, James B (D)
Gentry, James Worth (D)
Gill, Edwin Maurice (D)
Gilmore, Thomas Odell (D)
Godfrey, Helen Margaret (R)
Gold, Shirley Estelle (D)
Goss, Bernard Wayne (D)
Graham, William Thomas (R)
Green, James Collins (D)
Green, Walter Guerry American Party
Gregory, Carson (D)
Griffin, Pat (D)
Gudger, Lamar (D)
Gunter, Peaches (D)
Hairston, Peter W (D)
Handy, Rex Monte (D)
Hannah, Rebecca Ransom (D)
Hannibal, Alice Priscilla (D)
Hardison, Harold Woodrow (D)
Harrill, Fred Falls (D)
Harrington, Joseph Julian (D)
Harris, Fletcher (D)
Harris, J Ollie (D)
Harris, W S, Jr (D)
Hartle, Priscilla Morgan (D)
Hawkins, James Robert (R)
Haynes, Alton Myles (D)
Heer, Leo (D)
Hefner, W G (Bill) (D)
Helms, Jesse (R)

Henderson, David Newton (D)
Henley, John Tannery (D)
Herring, James Harold, Jr (R)
Hester, Robert James, Jr (D)
Hightower, Foyle Robert, Jr (D)
Hill, Cecil (D)
Hipps, Judy Matthew (D)
Hobby, Wilbur (D)
Hodges, Harold Young (R)
Holmes, Edward S (D)
Holmes, George M (R)
Holshouser, James Eubert, Jr (R)
Holt, Charles (D)
Hooper, Joseph Ward (R)
House, Ernest Jones (D)
Howard, Eloise Kathleen (R)
Hunt, James Baxter, Jr (D)
Hunt, Patricia Stanford (D)
Hunter, Thomas B (D)
Hurst, Wilda (D)
Huskins, Joseph Patterson (D)
Hutchens, John Grover (R)
Hutchins, Fred S, Jr (R)
Hutchins, Robert Wendel (D)
Hyde, Herbert Lee (D)
Ingle, John R (D)
Ingram, John Randolph (D)
Jackson, Frances Hatcher (D)
Jackson, George Winfield (R)
Jackson, J Elvin (D)
Jacob, J Laird, Jr (D)
James, Vernon G (D)
Jernigan, Glenn R (D)
Jernigan, Roberts Harrell, Jr (D)
Johnson, James Vernor (D)
Johnson, Joseph E (D)
Johnson, Joy Joseph (D)
Jonas, Charles Raper (R)
Jones, Benner, III (R)
Jones, John Robert (D)
Jones, Robert Alden (D)
Jones, Walter Beaman (D)
Josey, Claude Kitchin (D)
Keesee, Margaret Pollard (R)
Keith, Frederick R (D)
Keith, Thomas Joseph (R)
Kemp, Ramey Floyd, Sr (D)
Kennington, Betty Hagan (R)
Kimberlin, Jo Rainey (D)
Kincaid, Donald R (R)
King, Raymond E, Jr (D)
Kirby, James Russell (D)
Kirk, Phillip James, Jr (R)
Kitchin, Alvin Paul (D)
Koontz, Elizabeth Duncan (D)
Lackey, J M (D)
Lackey, Pleas (D)
Lambeth, Thomas Willis (D)
Larkins, John Davis, Jr (D)
Ledbetter, Jesse Ingram (R)
Lee, Howard Nathaniel (D)
Lee, Jackson Fredrick (R)
Leggett, Carroll Harden (D)
Lennon, Alton Asa (D)
Leonard, Larry Elmer (D)
Lilley, Daniel T (D)
Lockamy, John Nathan (D)
Lofton, James Shepherd (R)
Long, James Eugene (D)
Love, Jimmy Lewis (D)
Marion, George W, Jr (D)
Markham, Allan Whitlock (D)
Markham, Charles Buchanan (R)
Martin, Graham Anderson
Martin, James Grubbs (R)
Mason, Ronald E (D)
Mauney, W K (D)
McBryde, Charles Marion (R)
McConnell, David Moffatt (D)

NORTH CAROLINA (cont)

McCullen, Allie Ray (R)
McDuffie, Jim (D)
McGee, Carl Louis (D)
McInnis, William Donald (D)
McKay, Martha Clampitt (D)
McMillan, William H (D)
Meares, Carl Whitten (D)
Merritt, Hugh L (D)
Messer, Ernest Bryan (D)
Michaux, Henry M, Jr (D)
Miller, George M, Jr (D)
Mills, William Donald (D)
Moore, Daniel Killian (D)
Moore, Herman Aubrey (D)
Morgan, Robert Burren (D)
Morris, Kenneth Elon (R)
Morris, Sam Cameron (D)
Morris, Thomas Hansley (D)
Morrison, Anne Sapp (D)
Muse, Raymond O'Neal (D)
Myers, Jimmy Laird (R)
Nash, Robie Lee (D)
Neal, Stephen Lybrook (D)
Neely, Charles Batcheller, Jr (R)
Newsome, Kenneth Warren (D)
Nixon, Willie Bernard Sr (D)
Norman, Larry Ellis (R)
Nuckols, Peggy Nolte (R)
Nye, Edd (D)
Odom, Mary Horne (D)
Oxendine, Henry Ward (D)
Palmer, Grover Addison, Jr (D)
Palmer, Joe H (D)
Parker, John Rainey, Jr (R)
Parker, Leon Douglas (R)
Parker, Manley Clark (R)
Parker, William King (R)
Parnell, David Russell (D)
Patterson, Jane Smith (D)
Pendleton, Don Milton (R)
Perry, Donald Cleveland (R)
Phillips, Andrew Craig (D)
Phillips, Charles Wiley (D)
Pittman, Walter James (R)
Pitts, Noah Odas, Jr (R)
Plyler, Aaron Wesley (D)
Ponder, Zeno Herbert (D)
Poovey, Julius Reid (R)
Poston, Ernest Eugene (D)
Powell, Edward Lee (R)
Prestwood, Colon Edward (D)
Prestwood, Ralph (D)
Preyer, Lunsford Richardson (D)
Pugh, J T (D)
Purrington, John Ward (R)
Quinn, Dwight Wilson (D)
Rader, Steven Palmer (R)
Ramsay, John Erwin (D)
Ransdell, William Garland, Jr (D)
Rauch, Marshall Arthur (D)
Ray, Hector (D)
Reid, David Edward, Jr (D)
Renfrow, Edward (D)
Revelle, J Guy, Sr (D)
Rhodes, Samuel Thomas (R)
Riggs, Warren Elwood (R)
Robinson, Ralph Duane (R)
Rogers, Bobby Wayne (D)
Rogers, Thelma Tharp (R)
Rohrer, Grace Jemison (R)
Rose, Charles, III (D)
Rountree, Herbert Horton (D)
Rouse, Franklin Arthur (D)
Rowe, Marie Rich (R)
Royall, Kenneth Claiborne, Jr (D)
Russo, William Andrew (R)
Ruth, Earl Baker (R)
Sandlin, Hugh C (D)
Sanford, Terry (D)
Schwartz, B D (D)
Scott, Ralph H (D)
Scott, Ralph James (D)
Scott, Robert Walter (D)
Seagroves, Jessie Ruth (D)
Sebo, Katherine Ann Hagen (D)
Setzer, Johnsie Julia (D)
Sharp, Susie Marshall (D)
Shaw, Luther Wallace (D)
Shirley, Franklin Ray (D)
Short, W Marcus (D)
Sitton, Claude Shem (D)
Slear, John Klump (D)
Smith, A Neal (D)
Smith, Edward Henry (R)
Smith, Frank Lester, Sr (R)
Smith, Lynwood (D)
Smith, McNeill (D)
Smith, Ned Raeford (D)
Smith, Robert Bruce, Jr (D)
Smith, Wade (D)
Smith, William Grey (D)
Sneed, Joseph Tyree (R)
Soles, Robert Charles, Jr (D)
Somers, Robert Vance (R)
Stallings, D Livingstone (D)
Staton, William Wayne (D)
Steppe, Gary Clifford (D)
Stern, Larry N (R)
Stevens, Hugh Bedford (D)
Stocks, LeRoy (D)
Stolz, Otto George (R)
Strickland, Thomas Edward (D)
Stultz, John Hoyte, Jr (D)
Suddarth, Tom (D)
Sugg, James Russell (D)
Swanner, John MacDonald (D)
Tally, Lura Self (D)
Tanner, James Thomas, Jr (D)
Taylor, Roy A (D)
Tennille, Margaret (D)
Thomas, A W (D)
Thompson, John Elbert, Jr (R)
Thornton, La-Verne W (R)
Tilghman, Alma G (R)
Totherow, Carl D (D)
Turner, James Reginald (D)
Varner, John (D)
Vaught, Elmer Richard (R)
Venters, Edward Sutton (D)
Vickery, Charles Eugene (D)
Waldrop, Ralph Loy (R)
Walker, John Alexander (R)
Walker, Russell (D)
Wall, Barbara Lynn (D)
Waller, Oscar Wilson (D)
Walsh, Wade (D)
Ward, Allen C (D)
Warwick, Robert Franklin (R)
Watkins, William T (D)
Watts, Glenn (D)
Webb, Alfreda (D)
Webb, Charles Edward (D)
Webster, Wesley D (D)
Wertz, Cynthia Louise (D)
West, Ted Gordon (D)
Wheeler, John Hervey (D)
Whichard, Willis Padgett (D)
White, W Stanford (D)
Whitener, Basil Lee (D)
Williams, Valten Gage (R)
Wilmer, Henry Bond (R)
Wilson, Franklin Scott (R)
Wilson, Henry Hall, Jr (D)
Wilson, Hugh Mal (R)
Winberry, Charles Bryant (D)
Winfield, Mary Jones (D)
Wing, Lucie Lee (D)
Wingler, Patricia Marks (D)
Winters, John Wesley (D)
Wood, George Matthew (D)
Woodard, Barney Paul (D)
Wright, Richard (D)
Young, Wood Hall (R)
Zahner, Kenyon Benedict, Jr (R)

NORTH DAKOTA

Anderson, Herbert A (D)
Andrews, Mark (R)
Atkinson, Myron Hilton, Jr (R)
Austin, Ellen Jane (D)
Backes, Richard J (D)
Barth, Francis Phillip (D)
Benedict, George William (D)
Berg, Harris Odell (R)
Berger, L E (D)
Bernabucci, John Roger, Jr (R)
Bertsch, Marian N (R)
Berube, Phillip (D)
Bjorlie, Liv Bergliot (D)
Bowman, George McKinley (R)
Brunsdale, Clarence Norman (R)
Bunker, A G (R)
Bunker, Norene Rae (R)
Burdick, Quentin N (D)
Burgum, Katherine K (R)
Bye, Garry O (D)
Cann, Catherine E (Kay) (D)
Carlson, Levi E (R)
Christensen, L D (Lee) (R)
Christensen, Ralph M (R)
Christensen, Walter (D)
Christenson, Hal (R)
Clancy, Lynn J (D)
Clayburgh, Bennie James (R)
Cockerill, Leon Herbert, Jr (R)
Conlin, Frank (D)
Connolly, Phyllis Fern (R)
Coughlin, John Dennis (R)
Davis, John Edward (R)
Dawson, Barbara Ann (R)
Deck, Stanley Theodore (R)
Devine, Terence D (R)
Dick, Lawrence (R)
Dorgan, Byron Leslie (D)
Dotzenrod, Ralph Clarence (D)
Dvorak, Charles Vincent (D)
Dwyer, John William (R)
Eagles, Aloha Taylor (R)
Eckes, J Kenneth (D)
Ekbald, Art (R)
Engel, Austin George, Jr (D)
Erdman, Walter Clarence (D)
Erickson, LeRoy (R)
Erickson, Orbin A (R)
Erickstad, Ralph John (R)
Fagerholt, Leonard B (D)
Farrington, Stephen Hugh (R)
Fleming, Charles Frank (D)
Fleming, Neil Wayne (D)
Forkner, Richard E (R)
Freborg, Layton Wallace (R)
Frederickson, Lyle L (R)
Freed, Howard A (R)
Fritzell, Stella H (R)
Gackle, William Frederick (R)
Glassheim, Eliot Alan (D)
Goetz, William G (R)
Goodman, C W (R)
Gronhovd, Erich Arthur (D)
Gronneberg, Arnold J (D)
Gudajtes, Edward Raymond (D)
Gunderson, Oben John Iver (R)
Gustafson, Bernhard Gustaf (Ben) (D)
Guy, William L (D)
Hagen, Orville West (Independent)
Hagen, Sylvia (D)
Halmrast, Gerald Allyn (D)
Hanson, Harold Leslie (R)
Harris, Genevieve Irene (R)
Hathaway, Donald H (R)
Haugeberg, Carl (D)
Haugland, Brynhild (R)
Hausauer, Alvin (R)
Hausauer, LeRoy (R)
Hendricks, Gary Lester (R)
Henry, Rosalie E (D)
Hensrud, Neil (R)
Hentges, Richard Anthony (R)
Hernett, Gail H (R)
Hickle, Ralph (R)
Hildebrand, Dean (R)
Hilleboe, Peter Stuart (R)
Hoefs, Rudolph Herman (R)
Hoffner, S F (Buckshot) (D)
Holand, Pamela Krisida (D)
Homuth, Donald James (D)
Husfloen, Abraham (Abe) (D)
Huss, John Frederick (Jack) (R)
Irving, Terry Kathryn (D)
Ista, Richard Glen (D)
Iszler, Harry Eugene (R)
Jacobson, Irven Julian (D)
Jacobson, J Garvin (R)
Jaeger, Clarence Richard (R)
Jilek, Ray R (R)
Johnson, Howard Conwell (D)
Johnson, Karnes Otto (R)
Johnson, Mary Catherine (D)
Kautzmann, Emil E (R)
Kelly, Patricia (Tish) (D)
Keogh, Brooks James (R)
Kermott, Marjorie Louise (R)
King, Gorman H (D)
Kingsbury, Harley Ralph (R)
Kinsey, Robert Wayne (D)
Knudson, Harvey Bornemann (R)
Knudson, Kenneth (R)
Kretschmar, William Edward (R)
Kristensen, Luther M (D)
Kuehn, Duane Arthur (R)
Lamb, James L (D)
Lang, Theodore A (Ted) (R)
Langley, Byron (D)
Lantis, Sara Jean (R)
Larsen, Richard F (R)
Larson, Eldon C (D)
Larson, Harvey Casper (R)
Larson, Lester George (D)
Larson, Margaret Brunsdale (R)
Lashkowitz, Herschel (D)
Laske, Eugene C (Gene) (R)
Laughlin, Bruce James (R)
Lee, Fern Ellingson (R)
Lee, Shirley Williams (R)
Legrid, Gloria Jean (R)
Leibhan, Joe B (R)
Lillehaugen, C Arnold (R)
Linington, Victor A (R)
Link, Arthur A (D)
Lips, Evan Edwin (R)
Longmire, George (R)
Lorenz, Raymond Joseph (R)
Lundene, Henry (D)
Magnusson, Kingdon B (R)
Maher, John Francis (D)
Marsden, Lawrence David (R)
Martin, Clarence (R)
Martinson, Robert William (R)
Matheny, Gordon (R)
McElroy, Natalie Chaloner (R)
McGauvran, John Stanley (D)
McLeod, R C (R)
Meeker, James George (D)
Meidinger, Roland E (R)
Meier, Ben (R)
Meiers, Ruth Lenore (D)

Melland, Robert Bruce (R)
Mertens, Charles Franklin (D)
Metz, Reuben (R)
Metzger, Edward (R)
Metzger, Ray (D)
Meyer, Walter A (D)
Miedema, Ernest John (R)
Miller, Bert F (D)
Monette, Delores Marie (D)
Morgan, Ken L (R)
Murphy, Jack Redmond (R)
Mushik, Corliss Dodge (D)
Mutch, Duane (R)
Naaden, Lawrence L (R)
Nasset, Robert M (R)
Neff, Vern C (R)
Neils, Howard William (R)
Nermyr, Arnold (R)
Nething, David E (R)
Nicholas, Eugene Joseph (R)
Officer, George B, Jr (R)
Olin, Jack D (R)
Olson, Alice Adele (R)
Olson, Allen Ingvar (R)
Olson, Dagny V (R)
Olson, Florence May (R)
Omdahl, Lloyd B (D)
Opedahl, Olaf (D)
Orange, Charles (D)
Paulson, William Lee
Pederson, Vernon R
  (Independent)
Peterson, Barbara Preston (D)
Peterson, James A (R)
Peterson, M F
Peterson, Robert W (R)
Pokorny, Peggy Edna (D)
Porter, Robert Lawrence (D)
Powers, Anna Bertha Josephine (D)
Pyle, Ernest Gordon (R)
Raile, J L (R)
Rait, George (D)
Rau, Duane (R)
Raybell, Glenna J (D)
Raymond, Arthur (R)
Redlin, Rolland (D)
Reimers, Robert F (R)
Reiten, Chester (R)
Ringsak, Elton W (R)
Rivinius, Albert L (R)
Robinson, Dave M (R)
Rocheleau, Richard (D)
Royse, Alvin Lee (R)
Rued, Royden Dale (R)
Rundle, Earl Clifford (R)
Rustad, Gerald (R)
Rylance, Dan Frederick (D)
Saltsman, George J (D)
Sand, Paul M
Sandness, Claire A (R)
Sands, Ernest Monroe (R)
Sanstead, Wayne Godfrey (D)
Scheresky, Laurence Theodore (R)
Schindler, Orville (R)
Schlosser, James Douglas (R)
Schmit, Nicholas Matthew
  (Nick) (D)
Schnell, Gary Lynn (R)
Schuett, Warren (D)
Schultz, Clarence G (R)
Schultz, Jay (R)
Schuster, Roderic E (D)
Scofield, Charles (R)
Sellie, John Martin (R)
Shablow, Frank S (D)
Sheppard, Alan James (D)
Short, Don L (R)
Smykowski, James George (R)
Solberg, Ingvald (Esky) (R)
Solberg, Oscar (D)
Stanley, Stanley Wright (R)

Stockman, Jacque
  (Independent)
Strand, Gilman A (R)
Strinden, Earl Stanford (R)
Strinden, Theron L (R)
Stroup, Robert Lee (R)
Swiontek, Steven J (R)
Sylvester, Christopher Urdahl (R)
Tennefos, Jens Junior (R)
Thane, Russell T (R)
Thorsgard, Enoch Arnold (R)
Timm, E Michael (R)
Tinjum, Larry Ervin (D)
Tollefson, Orlan N (R)
Tweten, Kenneth (R)
Tweten, Malcolm (R)
Unhjem, Mike (R)
Vander Vorst, Wilbur (R)
Vogel, Charles Joseph (D)
Voldal, Henrik (D)
Vosper, F Kent (R)
Wagner, Vernon E (R)
Walker, James Henry (D)
Wallin, Myron Joseph (R)
Walsh, Jerome Leo (D)
Wastvedt, Gilman (R)
Watkins, Cheryl Ann (R)
Webb, Rodney S (R)
Weber, Francis E (Hank) (D)
Webster, Kent Jones (R)
Wenstrom, Frank Augustus (R)
Wentz, Janet Marie (R)
Wheeler, Gerridee Stenehjem (R)
Wigen, Joris Odin (R)
Wilkie, Gerhart (D)
Winge, Ralph M (D)
Winkjer, Dean (R)
Witteman, Orville P (D)
Wold, Peter Bertram, Jr (R)
Wold, Thomas Clifford (R)
Wright, Stanley Allen (R)
Young, Allan Chandler (R)
Young, Milton R (R)

OHIO

Abel, Glenn Frederick (R)
Abele, Homer Eugene (R)
Adams, Walter C (D)
Akins, James E
Alexander, Carol Mueller (D)
Allen, Craig Adams (D)
Andrews, John Striker (R)
Applegate, Douglas (D)
Aronoff, Stanley J (R)
Arredondo, David Zaldivar (D)
Ashbrook, John Milan (R)
Ashley, Thomas Ludlow (D)
Atkinson, Beverly Moon (R)
Austin, Edward Donald (D)
Aveni, Virginia Lee (D)
Ayres, William Hanes (R)
Bachman, Ilse (D)
Bailey, Charles Louis (R)
Bailey, David Emmett (R)
Baker, Herman Merlin (R)
Baker, Roger Lorin (R)
Ball, Claire Melvin, Jr (R)
Ballard, John Stuart (R)
Barger, Sara Louise (R)
Barnhouse, Thomas Dye (D)
Barrell, Charles Alden (R)
Barren, Jean VanAken (R)
Barrett, Ralph Roland (R)
Batchelder, William George (R)
Baumann, James L (Jim) (D)
Beach, Wilbur Lewis (R)
Bell, Napoleon Arthur (D)
Bell, Thomas M (D)

Belt, William Scott (R)
Benson, Daniel Leroy (D)
Berry, Loren Murphy (R)
Betts, Jackson Edward (R)
Betts, James E (R)
Black, Ernest F (R)
Blaushild, Babette Louise (D)
Blazer, Sondra Kay (D)
Bliss, Ray Charles (R)
Blosser, Clarence (R)
Boggs, Robert J (D)
Bolton, Frances P (R)
Bowen, William F (D)
Bowers, Arthur Robert (D)
Bowyer, Edna L (R)
Braithwaite, Melanie Jane (D)
Brandenburg, John Peter (R)
Brandow, George William (R)
Brann, Keith Edward (R)
Branstool, Charles Eugene (D)
Brents, Alvin Lee (D)
Bricker, Dale Eugene (R)
Bricker, John William (R)
Bridwell, Rena Olive (R)
Bristley, Calvin Wesley, Jr (R)
Brooks, Arthur Van Nordan (D)
Brown, Clarence J (R)
Brown, David Samuel (R)
Brown, John William (R)
Brown, Katharine Kennedy (R)
Brown, Paul Wesley (R)
Brown, Sherrod Campbell (D)
Brown, Ted William (R)
Brown, William Burbridge (D)
Brown, William Joseph (D)
Browne, Roy Edward (R)
Brubaker, Robert Lee (R)
Bubna, Mary Ann R (R)
Buchmann, Alan Paul (R)
Bush, Dorothy Vredenburgh (D)
Bush, John William (D)
Butts, Charles Lewis (D)
Cable, John Levi (R)
Calabrese, Anthony O (D)
Camera, Joseph Leonard (D)
Carnes, James Edward (R)
Carney, Charles J (D)
Carney, John Joseph (D)
Carney, Thomas E (D)
Carney, Thomas Joseph (D)
Casstevens, Bill (D)
Celebrezze, Anthony J (D)
Celebrezze, Anthony J, Jr (D)
Celebrezze, Frank D (D)
Celebrezze, James P (D)
Celeste, Richard F (D)
Cermak, Albina Rose (R)
Chandler, Larry Dean (R)
Chaney, Isabelle Caroline (R)
Christman, Larry Herman (D)
Christy, James Thomas (R)
Clancy, Donald Daniel (R)
Close, Albert Stephen (R)
Cmich, Stanley A (R)
Cole, Charles Morton (R)
Cole, Joseph E (D)
Cole, William Jennings Bryan (R)
Coleman, William L (D)
Collet, Anne Hendershott (R)
Collier, James Bruce (R)
Collins, Oakley C (R)
Colonna, Rocco J (D)
Conley, Harry V (D)
Cook, Howard C (R)
Cook, Vernon F (D)
Corrigan, J J P (R)
Cotner, Mercedes R (D)
Cox, Kenneth Roger (D)
Crisp, Jack W (D)
Crossland, Peter Nelson (D)

Cruze, Chester T (R)
Cunningham, Ronald Leroy (R)
Cupp, Orval S (R)
Daiker, Donald Arthur (D)
Dale, Francis Lykins (R)
Damschroder, Gene (R)
Davidson, Carlton E (R)
Davis, Emil L (D)
Davis, Harry L, Jr (R)
Davis, Jacob Erastus (D)
Davis, Mildred Louise (D)
Davis, Sylvan S (R)
Dean, Hershel Edwin (R)
Dean, J Thomas (R)
De Bonis, John Ralph (D)
Deebel, George Franklin (R)
Deering, Frederick Henry (D)
Del Bane, Michael (D)
Denczak, Ray (D)
Dennis, Max Hale (R)
Derry, William Stephens (R)
Devine, Samuel L (R)
Dieter, Elsie (R)
DiPaolo, Roger Fulvio (D)
Ditmer, Ward Nelson (R)
Donahey, Gertrude Walton (D)
Donham, William (R)
Donnellon, Edward James (D)
Downend, Paul Eugene (R)
Duerk, James Allen (R)
Dumm, Lucille (D)
Duryee, Harold Taylor (R)
Eckart, Dennis Edward (D)
Eckerle, Pauline Augusta
  (Nash) (R)
Eckhart, Henry Worley (D)
Emerling, Muriel Bergson (D)
Epstein, Barbara K (D)
Eshelman, John Leo, Jr (D)
Evans, E Chris (R)
Evans, Helen Witten (R)
Evans, John F (R)
Farr, Louise Rose (R)
Fath, Edna Evans (R)
Fauver, Scribner L (R)
Feighan, Edward Farrell (D)
Fell, George Henry (R)
Fichter, Joseph William (R)
Fields, Virginia A (R)
Finan, Richard H (R)
Fischbach, Deloris R (R)
Fix, Helen Herrink (R)
Flath, Don Edgar (R)
Fleckner, Ann (D)
Florio, Michel Peter (D)
Ford, Seabury H (R)
Foulk, Jack M (R)
Fox, Michael Allen (R)
Francis, Wilmer J (D)
Frank, Alfred Swift, Jr (R)
Freeman, Michael John (D)
Freeman, Robert DeCorps (D)
Fries, Thomas Louis (D)
Frost, James L (Jack) (R)
Fry, Charles E (R)
Fuller, Don Edgar (R)
Gaeth, M Ben (R)
Gaffney, Betty Jane (D)
Galbraith, John Allen (R)
Gallagher, Mary Cecelia (D)
Gamble, Michael P (D)
Gehres, Walter Arnold (D)
Gerber, Samuel Robert (D)
Gerken, John Raymond, Jr (R)
Gilligan, John Joyce (D)
Gillmor, Paul Eugene (R)
Gilmartin, Thomas P (D)
Glenn, John Herschel, Jr (D)
Glinsek, Gerald John (D)
Glockner, Edward L (Ebb) (D)
Goffena, Shyla Lee (D)
Gradison, Willis David, Jr (R)
Graham, Precious Jewel (D)

OHIO (cont)

Gray, Theodore Milton (R)
Greiner, William Merlin (R)
Grosjean, Barbara Grace (D)
Gustin, Joe Richard (R)
Guyer, Tennyson (R)
Hadley, Fred B (R)
Hadsel, Fred Latimer
Haines, Joan Renshaw (D)
Hale, Phale Dophis (D)
Hall, Tony P (D)
Hammond, Evert Newton (R)
Hanna, Martin Shad (R)
Hapner, Jon Clark (R)
Harmody, Richard M (D)
Harnetty, Charles Samuel (D)
Harrod, M Merle (R)
Harsha, William H (R)
Hartley, David (D)
Hayes, Thomas A (R)
Hays, Wayne L (D)
Headley, David L (D)
Healy, William James (D)
Henderson, John Earl
Herbert, Dorothy Fess (R)
Hermanies, John Hans (R)
Hertz, Karl H (D)
Hess, William E (R)
Heyman, Harry Clinton (D)
Higgins, Ned Preston (R)
Hillyer, William Hudson (R)
Hinig, William E (D)
Hlavin, Lynne E (R)
Hobstetter, Elizabeth Alice (R)
Hoiles, William McHenry (R)
Hole, Richard Eugene, II (R)
Hollington, Richard R, Jr (R)
Hollister, John Baker (R)
Horn, Charles Frederick (R)
Houck, Marie (R)
Howard, Walter Boivin (D)
Huffman, James Wylie (D)
Hughes, Lawrence Edward (R)
Hughes, Martin (D)
Hughes, Rodney H (R)
Humphrey, Nelson Hine (D)
Hunter, Jack Corbett (R)
Hurley, Elisabeth A (R)
Isch, Helen A (R)
Jackson, Leo Albert (D)
Jackson, M Morris (D)
James, Ronald Harvey (D)
James, Troy Lee (D)
Jaskulski, Robert W (D)
Jeffrey, Harry Palmer (R)
Jenewein, Judith Kay (Judy) (D)
Jenkins, Mary Maxine (R)
Johns, John S (D)
Johnson, Anice Wismer (R)
Johnson, David W (R)
Johnson, E G (Ted) (R)
Johnson, John Edward (R)
Jolovitz, Herbert Allen (D)
Jones, Casey C (D)
Jones, Evelyn Rose (D)
Jones, Mary L (R)
Jones, Pha L (R)
Jones, Theodore Tanner (R)
Jones, Wilfred Denton (R)
Jump, Harry V (R)
Kaduk, Frank J (D)
Karmol, Irma Hotchkiss (R)
Karmol, Warren Henry, Jr (R)
Karpinski, Helen Bernice (D)
Keating, William J (R)
Keefe, Ruth Eleanor (D)
Kelly, John Barnes (R)
Kester, John Barton (R)
Keys, John Grant (D)
Kieffer, Rex H, Jr (R)

Kindness, Thomas Norman (R)
King, Frank W (D)
Kingsmore, Gerald LeMoyne (R)
Kirkendall, Mary M (R)
Kleckner, Roger Eugene (R)
Kline, Gwen Weeks (R)
Knorek, Lee J (D)
Knowlton, Daniel David (R)
Koble, Rosalie Elizabeth (R)
Koehler, Richard Norman (D)
Kohnen, Ralph Bernard, Jr (R)
Kopp, William Albert (D)
Kornick, Michael
Kurfess, Charles Frederick (R)
Lamb, Edward (D)
Lancione, A G (D)
Lancione, Bernard Gabe (D)
Lancione, Nelson (D)
Lane, Janet Isabel (R)
Lanning, Judith A (Judy) (R)
Larson, Rosemary Duffy (D)
Laster, Donna Jean (D)
Latta, Delbert L (R)
Lausche, Frank J (Independent)
Lavelle, William A (D)
Lawther, Robert M (R)
Leach, Russell (R)
Leahy, Elizabeth Clare (D)
LeBoutillier, Philip Jr (R)
Leggat, Lois Burnett (R)
Lehman, Harry J (D)
Leonard, Paul Roger (D)
Levitt, Robert Elwood (R)
Lindesmith, Ruth Mildred (R)
Lindhorst, Ambrose H (R)
Lindseth, Jon A (R)
Linkous, T Cecil (D)
Livingston, Marion G (R)
Lloyd, Thomas Reese (R)
Locker, Dale Le Roy (D)
Love, Rodney Marvin (D)
Lucas, Ethel Violet (D)
Luckhart, Elton Wagner (R)
Luken, James T (D)
Lukens, Donald E (R)
Lynn, James Thomas (R)
Maddux, Don Stewart (R)
Maier, Richard Franklin (R)
Maile, Francis A (D)
Mallory, William L (D)
Maloney, Michael Joseph (R)
Malott, Harry C (D)
Mantle, C Lee (R)
Marsh, Benjamin Franklin (R)
Martin, Edwin McCammon (D)
Mastics, George E (R)
Mastrangelo, Evelino William (D)
Mathna, Woodrow Wilson (R)
Mauro, Guy J (D)
Mayfield, Frank Henderson, Jr (R)
Mayl, Esther (D)
McAlister, Robert Beaton (R)
McClaskey, Walter D (R)
McClendon, Carol (D)
McCormack, John Timothy (D)
McCown, David Henry (D)
McCulloch, William M (R)
McDonald, John Cooper (D)
McDonald, Mary Jane (D)
McEwen, Robert Douglas (R)
McGee, James Howell (D)
McGough, Kent B (R)
McGowan, Mary Elizabeth (D)
McGrew, Leslie Frank (R)
McKenzie, Earl Eugene (R)
McKnight, Robert Allen (R)
McLin, Clarence Josef, Jr (D)
McMillen, Nancy Gail (R)
Meeks, John Neal (D)
Meshel, Harry (D)

Mettert, Arlene E (R)
Metzenbaum, Howard Morton (D)
Mihlbaugh, Robert Holleran (D)
Miksch, Eileen Evans (R)
Miller, Ann Floyd (R)
Miller, Clarence E (R)
Miller Joseph Kerr (R)
Miller, Justina Marie (D)
Miller, William Albert, Jr (D)
Milleson, Ronald Kinsey (D)
Minshall, William E (R)
Mitchell, Maxine K (R)
Mollenkopf, Janet Arlene (R)
Moore, Martha Christine (R)
Moore, William E, III (D)
Moorehead, Tom V (R)
Morris, Christian Purtscher (R)
Moser, John Richard (R)
Mosher, Charles Adams (R)
Mottl, Ronald M (D)
Mowry, Samuel Orin (R)
Mullet, Maurice Eugene (R)
Murdock, Norman A (R)
Murphy, Charlotte Ann (R)
Murphy, Mildred Arlene (R)
Murray, Richard Charles (D)
Musser, Virgil Lee (D)
Mussey, William Howard (R)
Myers, Carroll Jean (R)
Nader, Robert Alexander (R)
Nelson, David Aldrich (R)
Netzley, Robert E (R)
Neu, Arlene Petrice (R)
Nicol, Betty Lou (R)
Nixon, Corwin M (R)
Nolan, Monica (D)
Noland, Charles Patrick (D)
Norris, Alan E (R)
Novak, Lorrine Marie (D)
Ocasek, Oliver Robert (D)
O'Grady, Eugene P (D)
Olds, Glenn A (R)
Olenick, Stephen R (D)
O'Neill, C William (R)
O'Neill, C William, Jr (R)
Orlett, Edward J (D)
Osborne, Edward Beryl (D)
O'Shaughness, Robert E (D)
Otterman, Robert James (D)
Oxley, Michael Garver (R)
Panehal, Francine Mary (D)
Patterson, James F (R)
Paulo, Walter H (R)
Pease, Donald James (D)
Peebles, Robert (R)
Pelton, Horace Wilbur (R)
Pemberton, Mack (R)
Perk, Ralph Joseph (R)
Perkins, Richard Dallas (D)
Perry, Franklin Delano (R)
Phillips, Charles Eugene (R)
Phillips, Glen Edwin (R)
Pinkney, Arnold (D)
Pokorny, George R (R)
Pope, Donna (R)
Porter, Albert S (D)
Powell, Walter E (R)
Price, Robert Ross (R)
Pulley, William W (R)
Quilter, Barney (D)
Quirk, Robert Joseph (D)
Rakestraw, W Vincent (R)
Rankin, Doris Brooks (D)
Rankin, James W (D)
Rausch, Eugene E (R)
Reckman, Robert Frederick (R)
Redmond, Marcia Louise (D)
Reed, Robert Gordon, Jr (R)
Regula, Ralph S (R)
Reichard, Lois L (R)
Reider, Robert W (R)
Reiff, Arthur Frederick (D)

Reintsema, Robert Arnold (R)
Reno, Ottie Wayne (D)
Rex, Frances Lillian (R)
Rhodes, James Allen (R)
Rhodes, William Emerson (R)
Riffe, Vernal G, Jr (D)
Roberto, Marcus Aurelius (D)
Romer, Harold William (D)
Rose, Jonathan Chapman (R)
Rose, Waldo Bennett (R)
Rosemond, John Henry (D)
Ross, Charles Douglas (R)
Ruehlmann, Eugene P (R)
Ryan, Margaret Mary (D)
Sark, Guy O (R)
Sawyer, Charles (D)
Saxbe, Charles Rockwell (Rocky) (R)
Saxbe, William B (R)
Schaufele, William Everett, Jr
Schecter, Sheldon Dale (D)
Scherer, Gordon Harry (R)
Scherer, Gordon M (R)
Schiller, James Joseph (D)
Schinagle, Allan Charles (R)
Schroeder, Luella Ruth (R)
Schrote, John E (R)
Scott, John M (R)
Sechrist, Sterling George (R)
Secrest, Robert Thompson (D)
Seiberling, John F (D)
Sensenbrenner, Maynard E (D)
Shackle, H Gene (D)
Shaker, Mitchell Francis (D)
Shaw, Daisy L (D)
Shields, Phyllis E (R)
Shilts, William Winston (R)
Shoemaker, Myrl Howard (D)
Shuman, Harold Eugene (R)
Sidwell, George C (R)
Slagle, Gene (D)
Smart, Irene Balogh (D)
Smith, Larry Gilbert (D)
Snook, J Carlton (D)
Snyder, Cecil Vernon (D)
Snyder, Robert Leroy (R)
Snyder, Wanda J (R)
Solomon, Donald L (D)
Spafford, Enval Ainsworth (D)
Speakman, Ronald Blaine (D)
Speck, Samuel W, Jr (R)
Spencer, Elden A (R)
Speros, James Mandamadiotis (D)
Stahl, Thomas Burton (R)
Stano, Jerome (D)
Stanton, James Vincent (D)
Stanton, John William (R)
Stanton, Ralph Calvin, Jr (R)
Stelz, Dale Edward (D)
Stephens, Carolyn Kay (R)
Steponkus, William Peter (R)
Stillman, Saul G (R)
Stinziano, Michael Peter (D)
Stokes, Louis (D)
Stokes, Marian (R)
Stoldt, Robert James (R)
Strauss, Evelyn M (D)
Sturrett, Joseph Anthony (D)
Swafford, Pamela Marie (R)
Swanbeck, Ethel Gertrude (R)
Sweeney, Patrick A (D)
Sweeney, Randall Walter (D)
Swinehart, Judith Ann (D)
Swinehart, Phillip Dean (R)
Tablack, George D (D)
Taft, Charles P (R)
Taft, Robert, Jr (R)
Taft, Seth Chase (R)
Talisman, Mark Elliott (D)
Taylor, Dorothy Francine (R)
Thomas, Harold Theodore (D)
Thompson, John, Jr (D)

Thompson, William Keith (D)
Timmins, William Joseph, Jr (D)
Tipps, Paul (D)
Tulley, Joseph P (R)
Turk, Edmund John (D)
Turner, Harry Edward (R)
Uhlenhake, Helen Idell (D)
Umbles, Clayton Edward (D)
Unger, Sherman Edward (R)
Valiquette, Marigene (D)
Van Heyde, Robert Lee (D)
Vanik, Charles A (D)
Van Meter, Thomas Adams (R)
Vaughan, Charles David (D)
Volkema, Russell H (R)
Wacker, Janet Louise (D)
Ward, Marcella Elizabeth (D)
Wareham, Levada E (R)
Wargo, John P (D)
Waring, Eloise Botts (R)
Warner, Joan Fleenor (D)
Warner, Marvin (D)
Watson, John L (R)
Watzman, Sanford (D)
Weaner, Karl Hull (R)
Weiker, Bryce Lamar (D)
Weil, Sidney, Jr (D)
Weir, John H (R)
Weisenberger, Leona Amelia (D)
Weisenstine, Ernest Moore (D)
Wetzel, Darrel Ernest (D)
Weyandt, Ronald H (D)
Whalen, Charles William, Jr (R)
Wharton, Clyde Wilson (D)
Wheatcraft, Martha Clark (R)
White, Walter L (R)
White, William Robert (D)
Whitmer, Robert V (R)
Whitmore, Frank William (D)
Wiethe, John Albert (D)
Wilkowski, Arthur (D)
Williams, John Blair (R)
Willis, Richard Robinson (R)
Willmarth, David Gerard (D)
Wilson, A K (R)
Wilson, Robert Kinner (R)
Wingard, Paul Sidney (R)
Wingett, Ernest A (D)
Wise, Carl Francis (R)
Wojtanowski, Dennis Lee (D)
Woodland, Donald L (D)
Woodmansee, Donavin N (D)
Wylie, Chalmers Pangburn (R)
Young, Frederick Nevin (D)
Young, Stephen M (D)
Zahn, Donald M (R)
Zahorec, Joseph John (D)
Zimmers, Neal Foster, Jr (D)

OKLAHOMA

Abbott, Lonnie Lowell (D)
Albert, Carl Bert (D)
Allman, Elaine G (D)
Anderson, Robert E (R)
Arrington, James Hugh (D)
Atkins, Hannah Diggs (D)
Baggerley, Jobyna Dee (R)
Baker, Hamp (D)
Baldwin, Don (D)
Bamberger, Thomas A (D)
Barnes, Don B (D)
Barnett, Judith Anne (D)
Barrett, James Luther (D)
Bartlett, Dewey Follett (R)
Belcher, Page (R)
Bellmon, Henry L (R)
Bengtson, L H, Jr (D)
Bennett, J B (D)
Bernard, Spencer Thomas (D)
Berrong, Ed (D)
Beznoska, Gordon Adolph (D)
Bird, Mary Louise (R)
Birdsong, Jimmy (D)
Boatner, Roy Alton (D)
Boren, David Lyle (D)
Boren, Lyle H (D)
Boulton, Grace (R)
Box, E O (R)
Bradley, William D (Bill) (D)
Bradshaw, Mark (D)
Briscoe, Bill (D)
Brunton, Paul D (R)
Burns, John Howard
Butler, Kenneth (R)
Caldwell, E A (Red) (D)
Calhoon, Ed Latta (R)
Camp, George (R)
Camp, John Newbold (Happy) (R)
Campbell, Terry Leland (R)
Capps, Gilmer N (D)
Carlile, Margaret Louise (D)
Carter, Joseph Henry, Sr (Joe) (D)
Cartwright, Wilburn (D)
Cate, Byron Lee (D)
Cleveland, Charles (D)
Cobb, J C (D)
Cogman, Don Vernon (R)
Coleman, Thomas William (R)
Colvin, William Alvin (D)
Conaghan, Dorothy Dell (R)
Converse, Kenneth E (D)
Cooper, Charles M (D)
Cotner, Howard Paul (D)
Cowan, Ted M (R)
Craighead, David Caperton (D)
Crow, Hershal Hilliar, Jr (D)
Cullison, Robert Virl (D)
Cummings, James R (R)
Cunningham, Oval H (D)
Dahl, John L (D)
Davis, Don Clarence (D)
Davis, Frank W (R)
Davis, Guy Gaylon (D)
Davison, Denver N (D)
Deatherage, Cleta B (D)
Denman, Don Curry (R)
Derryberry, Larry Dale (D)
Descans, Roland Eugene (D)
Donahoe, J Michael (R)
Draper, Daniel David, II (D)
Drummond, Cecil G (D)
Duckett, Thomas Ross (D)
Duke, A Don (D)
Dunn, Vernon (D)
Dyson, Mrs Lorray (D)
Eads, Felix (Buck) (D)
Eden, Janet Jones (R)
Edmondson, Ed (D)
Edmondson, W A Drew (D)
Elder, Charles (R)
English, Glenn (D)
Ervin, William J (D)
Ferguson, Jo O (R)
Ferrell, J Fred, Jr (D)
Field, Leon B (D)
Fitzgibbon, Joseph Eugene (D)
Floyd, Glenn Eldon (D)
Ford, Becky Jane (D)
Ford, Charles Reed (R)
Foshee, Katherine Almira (R)
Frates, Kent F (R)
Freeman, Travis (R)
Fried, Jim (D)
Funston, Bob (D)
Gaddis, William Finley (Bill) (R)
Gambill, Bruce Warren (R)
Garrett, John L (D)
Gary, Raymond D (D)
Gerlach, Gayle Leslie (R)
Grantham, Roy Emery (D)
Graves, Ralph Wayne (D)
Green, Warren Ernest (R)
Haley, Frances Shaller, (R)
Ham, Glen (D)
Hamilton, James E (D)
Hammons, Mark Edgar (D)
Hardesty, Jim W (D)
Harper, Bob E (D)
Hastings, Joan King (R)
Haught, Robert L (R)
Hawkins, Clarence Miley (D)
Hayes, Florence M (R)
Healey, Skip (R)
Helm, Mary Alnita (R)
Henry, Charles T (D)
Hibdon, Mina (R)
Hill, George Barker (D)
Hodges, Ralph Byron (Non-Partisan)
Holaday, T W (Bill) (R)
Holden, A C (D)
Holden, Wayne M (D)
Holt, James D (D)
Hood, David Craig (D)
Hooper, Roy B, Jr (D)
Hoover, Linda Kay (D)
Hopkins, Robert E (D)
Howard, Gene C (D)
Howard, Sharon Janeene (D)
Howell, James F (D)
Hunt, McPherson Williss (Mack) (D)
Inhofe, James Mountain (R)
Irwin, Pat (D)
Jarboe, John Bruce (D)
Jarman, John (R)
Jennings, Shirley Kimball (D)
Johnson, Alvan Nathanial (D)
Johnson, Artis Visanio (D)
Johnson, Don (D)
Johnson, Joe Arley (D)
Johnston, Jeffrey Smith (D)
Joiner, Fred C (D)
Jones, Dale Paschal (R)
Jones, James Robert (D)
Kamas, Lewis Melvin (R)
Kane, Robert M (R)
Kardokus, James M (D)
Keating, Francis Anthony, II (R)
Keller, E W (R)
Kennedy, Billy F (D)
Kennedy, J C (D)
Kerr, William Graycen (D)
Kibler, Minifred Elizabeth Burrow (R)
Kilpatrick, Don (D)
King, Peter Cotterill (R)
Kizer, Charlene Craig (D)
Lair, Daniel Herley (D)
Lamb, Norman (R)
Lambert, Phillip E (D)
Lane, Jim E (D)
Lane, Lawrence Edward (D)
Lavender, Robert Eugene (R)
Letcher, Isabelle Scott (R)
Likes, Henry L (D)
Lough, Raymond Everett (R)
Luton, John D (D)
Lynn, John Edward (D)
Manning, Joe Rolater, Jr (R)
Martin, Ernest D (D)
Massad, Ernest Louis (D)
Matheson, Mandell L (D)
Mauzy, Whit Yancey, Jr (D)
McCaleb, Neal A (R)
McCune, John Robison (R)
McDonald, Joseph Paul (R)
McIntyre, Bernard J (D)
McKee, Marvin E (D)
McManus, James Henry (D)
McNeill, Welton R (D)
McSpadden, Clem Rogers (D)
Medearis, Robert Park (D)
Miles, Vicki Lynn (D)
Miskelly, John (D)
Monks, John (D)
Morgan, Charlie O (D)
Murphy, Mike (D)
Murphy, Robert M (D)
Myers, Hiram Keith, Jr (D)
Nance, Kenneth Robert (D)
Nerin, William F (D)
Nigh, George Patterson (D)
Nitzel, Callie Ann (D)
Noreika, Louise A (D)
Padgett, C Ward (D)
Parris, Bob (D)
Parrish, W F, Jr (R)
Patterson, Pat J (R)
Payne, Gary Edison (D)
Pearcey, Ray L (D)
Peterson, Charles R (D)
Phelps, Edna Mae (D)
Phillips, Nancy Lee (D)
Pierce, Jerry T (D)
Pitcher, George Payton (D)
Porter, E Melvin (D)
Poulos, William Frederic (D)
Prentice, Charles James (R)
Price, Linda Rice (D)
Privett, Arnold Rex (D)
Rainbolt, John Vernon (Mike) (D)
Rambo, Carroll Ann (D)
Rambo, G Dan (D)
Randle, Rodger A (D)
Rauh, Jo Ann (R)
Reed, Michael Lee (D)
Reid, Luke Harmon (R)
Richardson, Truman (D)
Riggs, Melvin David (D)
Risenhoover, Ted M (D)
Roark, Wilson Eugene (R)
Roberts, Hollis E (D)
Robertson, Carol (R)
Robinson, Bill (D)
Rodgers, Sarah Jane (D)
Rogers, John (D)
Rogers, John Marvin (D)
Rogers, Tom (R)
Rosenbaum, Steven Ray (D)
Rosenthal, Tamar Naomi (D)
Ross, Hope Snider (D)
Sanders, E C (Sandy) (D)
Schreiner, L D, Jr (R)
Schuelein, William M (D)
Shatwell, Bob R (D)
Shear, Daphfine (D)
Shieldknight, Jim Edward (R)
Shotts, Ron E (R)
Smith, Finis W (D)
Smith, James Vernon (R)
Smith, Jerry L (R)
Smith, Ray Allen (R)
Snipes, Al M (R)
Sparkman, Wiley (D)
Sponberg, Raymond Lindell (R)
Stacy, John Raymond (R)
Stamps, Hal Burton (D)
Stanislaus, Dorothy Jeanne (R)
Steed, Tom (D)
Stephenson, Tom R (D)
Stevenson, Boyd (D)
Steward, William Robert (D)
Stipe, Gene (D)
Stout, Ernest Vernon (R)
Stratton, David (D)
Stricker, Eukley Cecil (R)
Sutton, Emmazette Collier (D)
Swanson, Mary Helen (R)
Swinton, Judy Ann (D)
Taliaferro, Jim (D)

OKLAHOMA (cont)
Taylor, R Stratton (D)
Terrill, Albert Lee (D)
Thain, Carl Ernest (R)
Thompson, Donald D (D)
Thompson, Guy (D)
Thornhill, Lynn (R)
Tilley, Homer (R)
Tinsley, Gideon (D)
Townsend, James Baker (D)
Turner, Ethel Winborn (R)
Twidwell, Carl, Jr (D)
Ungerman, Maynard Ivan (D)
Unruh, Paula (R)
Van Meter, Donald Edward (R)
Vaughn, H George, Jr (D)
Vincent, Robert Carr (R)
Wadley, Robert L (D)
Ward, Charles Leland (D)
Ward, Lew O (R)
Warner, Clarence E (R)
Watkins, Wes (D)
Watson, Thomas Philip (R)
Weichel, Jerry (D)
Westbrook, Brock R (D)
White, Elinor Sue (R)
Whiteley, Keith (D)
Whorton, J D (R)
Wickersham, Victor Eugene (D)
Wiggins, Charles Delmar (R)
Wiggins, Larry Don (R)
Wilkinson, Charles Burnham (Bud) (R)
Williams, Richard Wayne (R)
Willis, William Pascal (D)
Wilson, Earlene S (R)
Wilson, George Howard (D)
Wilson, Robert G (D)
Winters, Leo (D)
Wirz, Kaye Colyer (D)
Wiseman, William Johnston, Jr (R)
Wolfe, Stephen Charles (R)
York, Marvin (D)
Young, John Wallace (D)

OREGON
Adelsheim, Martha Ann Henderson (D)
Akeson, Harvey O (D)
Alberger, William Relph (D)
Allender, Patricia Anne (D)
Anderson, Steve (D)
AuCoin, Les (D)
Beall, William Hayes (D)
Blumenauer, Earl (D)
Boe, Jason Douglas (D)
Bonebrake, Richard Duane (D)
Bowman, Alice J (D)
Brown, Walter Frederick (D)
Browne, Elizabeth Wingreene (D)
Bunch, Ralph E (D)
Bunn, Stan (R)
Burbidge, Keith A (D)
Burrows, Mary McCauley (R)
Byers, Bernard (D)
Campbell, Della B (R)
Cargo, David Francis (R)
Carson, Wallace P, Jr (R)
Caswell, Jeanne Marie (D)
Chapo, Carolyn Lee (R)
Cherry, Howard L (D)
Chrest, James H (D)
Clark, Donald E (D)
Clawson, James Howard (R)
Conroy, Richard L (R)
Cook, Vernon (D)
Corbett, Alice Catherine (D)
Cornwall, Robert David (R)
Davis, Drew Anthony (D)
Dellenback, John (R)
Denecke, Arno H (R)
Densmore, Albert Harry (D)
Dereli, Margaret Ulricka (D)
Duncan, Robert Blackford (D)
Durno, Edwin Russell (R)
Eiss, Roger (D)
Elliott, Robert Amos (R)
Enna, Irving (R)
Fadeley, Edward Norman (D)
Fadeley, Nancie Peacocke (D)
Ferguson, Bill B (D)
Flegel, Albert Gordon (D)
Forbes, Clinton D (R)
Frank, Gerald Wendel (R)
Frohnmayer, David Braden (R)
Fuller, Larry Dean (D)
Garrigus, Forest Ora, Jr (R)
Gilliam, Jean Marie (D)
Gilmour, Jeff L (D)
Goldy, Daniel Louis (D)
Grannell, William Newton (D)
Green, David M (Dave) (R)
Green, Edith S (D)
Groener, Dick (R)
Groener, T Ralph (D)
Gustafson, Richard (D)
Gwinn, William F (R)
Haas, Harl H (D)
Hall, William O
Hallock, Joseph Theodore (Ted) (D)
Hampton, Lewis Burdett (R)
Hanlon, Charles J (Independent)
Hanneman, Paul A (R)
Hannon, Lenn Lamar (D)
Hansen, Frederic James (R)
Hart, Floyd Henry (R)
Hatfield, Mark Odom (R)
Hawksley, William J (R)
Haworth, Roger Lee (D)
Heard, Fred W (D)
Hodel, Donald Paul (R)
Holmer, Alan F (R)
Howard, Norman R (D)
Hultman, Bertha (D)
Jernstedt, Kenneth A (R)
Johnson, Cecil L (R)
Johnson, Irene L (D)
Johnson, Robertson Lee (R)
Johnson, Sam (R)
Jones, Denzil Eugene (R)
Kafoury, Stephen (D)
Katz, Vera (D)
Kerans, Grattan (D)
Kerry, Reta Christina (D)
Killion, Dean (D)
Kinsey, Lloyd (R)
Klonoski, James Richard (D)
Kulongoski, Ted (D)
Lang, Philip David (D)
Leary, June Ellis (D)
Lende, Russell Melvin (R)
Linde, Hans Arthur (D)
Lindquist, Edward H (D)
Lindsey, Robert Eugene (R)
Lindstedt, Norman L (D)
Lombard, Ben Jr (R)
Lomnicky, Kathi (D)
Lusk, Hall S (D)
Lynch, Jim C (R)
Magruder, Dick (D)
Mannix, Kevin Leese (D)
Marsh, Thomas Parker, Jr (Tom) (D)
Martin, Roger Edward (R)
Marx, Robert Phillip (D)
McAllister, William Menzies (D)
McCall, Tom Lawson (R)
McCoy, William, Jr (D)
McCrae, Wallace W (R)
McLean, Clyda Earlene (R)
Meeker, Anthony (Tony) (R)
Meyer, John (D)
Miller, Judith Lee (D)
Mitchell, Cleatis Gerald (D)
Moore, Dorotha Huntley (R)
Morris, Brad (R)
Mulligan, Cary Kauffman (D)
Murphy, Peter Connacher, Jr (R)
Murray, Clifford Gordon, Jr (D)
Myers, Clay (R)
Myers, Hardy (D)
Nathan, Theodora Nathalia (Tonie) (Libertarian)
Nelson, Dixie Lee (R)
Neuberger, Maurine Brown (D)
Nunn, Warne (R)
O'Connell, Kenneth John (D)
Otto, Glenn E (D)
Ouderkirk, W Stan (R)
Packwood, Bob (R)
Patterson, Ed (R)
Paulus, Norma Jean (R)
Payne, Anna Lee (R)
Peck, Grace Olivier (D)
Peters, Philip L (R)
Porter, Charles O (D)
Potts, E D (D)
Powell, John Allen (D)
Priestley, Wallace Schuyler (Wally) (D)
Ragsdale, Mike (R)
Redden, James Anthony (D)
Reed, George Joseph (R)
Reno, Donald F (D)
Richardson, Eugene Allison (R)
Rieke, Mary W (R)
Rijken, Max Ch (D)
Ripper, Jack Dorland (D)
Roberts, Betty R (D)
Roberts, Frank Livezey (D)
Roberts, Mary Linda (Wendy) (D)
Rogers, William Richard, Jr (Bill) (R)
Root, Marv (R)
Saslow, Michael George (D)
Schmidt, Ronald Garrard (R)
Simpson, Max (D)
Skelton, Keith D (D)
Smith, Robert Freeman (R)
Snider, Darlene (D)
Stadelman, George Peter (R)
Starr, George W (D)
Stathos, Donald L (R)
Stevenson, Ed (D)
Stoll, Norman Adolph (D)
Stonebrink, Helen May (R)
Stout, June Windle (R)
Straub, Robert W (D)
Stults, Robert M (R)
Sumner, Jack (D)
Thoen, Doris Rae (R)
Thorne, Robert Freeman (D)
Thorpe, Thomas Keane (R)
Trow, Clifford Wayne (D)
Ullman, Al (D)
Vandever, Ruth Ann (D)
Van Vliet, Tony (R)
Walden, Paul E (R)
Weast, Burton Calvin (D)
Weaver, James Howard (D)
Welty, Robert (D)
Whallon, Glen William (D)
Whipple, Blaine (D)
Whiting, Pat (D)
Wilhelms, Gary L (R)
Wilkins, Caroline Hanke (D)
Williams, Judith (D)
Wingard, George Frank (R)
Wolfer, Curt Alan (D)
Woodrow, Shirley Ann (R)
Wyatt, Wendell William (R)
Wyatt, William W (D)
Young, Jean Kitts (R)
Zapp, John Shea (R)

PENNSYLVANIA
Abraham, Donald A (D)
Aikens, Joan D (R)
Alexander, Jane Marietta (D)
Altemus, Barbara (D)
Amig, Elizabeth Clement (R)
Ammerman, Joseph S (D)
Anderson, John Hope (R)
Andrews, Michael Paul (D)
Andrews, W Thomas (R)
Annenberg, Walter H (R)
Anspach, John Henry (D)
Arabis, Stanley Lawrence (R)
Arbuckle, R Douglass (R)
Arthurs, Jack R (D)
Arty, Mary Ann (R)
Baldwin, David Rawson (D)
Barber, James David (D)
Barr, Joseph M (D)
Barrett, William A (D)
Batdorf, David Jonathan (D)
Baumgartner, Rena V (D)
Bednarek, Stanley Michael (R)
Bellomini, Robert E (D)
Benish, Joseph Michael (D)
Benner, Barbara Young (R)
Bennett, Reid L (D)
Bennett, Verna Z (R)
Beren, Daniel E (D)
Berkes, Milton (D)
Berlin, Theodore (D)
Berman, Muriel M (D)
Berson, Norman S (D)
Beward, Maria A (D)
Bickerton, Frances Catherine Baur (D)
Biester, Edward G, Jr (R)
Bish, Betty J (R)
Bittle, Russell Harry (R)
Blackwell, Lucien E (D)
Bloom, George I (R)
Blum, William L (D)
Bonetto, Joseph F (D)
Bonsell, William Richard (R)
Bordas, Phyllis Jean (R)
Bossert, Willard Max (R)
Boyer, Dennis Lee (D)
Bradley, Joseph P, Jr (D)
Bradley, Michael Joseph (D)
Brandt, Kenneth (R)
Brennan, Dorothy Teresa (D)
Brimmer, Andrew Felton
Brown, William Hill, III (R)
Brumbaugh, D Emmert (R)
Brunner, John L (D)
Buddy, George Joseph (D)
Burke, Henry Patrick (D)
Burlein, Lester F (R)
Burns, Edward Francis, Jr (R)
Butera, Robert James (R)
Byrne, James Aloysius (D)
Camiel, Peter (D)
Campbell, George W (R)
Campbell, Thelma Lunger (D)
Campbell, William Cowden (R)
Carey, Ralph P (R)
Carlson, Edgar A (R)
Carrigg, Joseph L (R)
Casey, Robert J (R)
Casey, Robert P (D)
Cassidy, Robert Valentine (D)
Catz, Phyllis Fox (D)
Cessar, Richard J (R)

Cimini, Anthony J (R)
Clark, Frank M (D)
Cohen, David (D)
Cohen, Mark B (D)
Cole, Kenneth J (D)
Coleman, William Matthew (D)
Cooke, Edward Francis (D)
Corbett, Michael Timothy (D)
Corrigan, Joann Mary (D)
Corson, Philip Langdon (R)
Coughlin, R Lawrence, Jr (R)
Covey, John Knox (R)
Covey, Susan Candace (R)
Cowell, Ronald Raymond (D)
Craley, Nathaniel Neiman, Jr (D)
Crawford, Patricia A (R)
Crawford, William Rex (Independent)
Culbertson, Stuart A (D)
Culp, Carl Lester (D)
Cumberland, James L (R)
Curtin, Willard S (R)
Curwood, William B (D)
Daley, Peter John, II (D)
Danneker, Henry Louis (R)
D'Arcy, James Andrew (D)
Davies, D O (R)
Davies, John S (R)
Davis, Donald M (D)
DeMedio, A J (D)
Dende, Henry John (D)
Dennison, David Short, Jr (R)
Dent, John H (D)
DeVerter, Walter F (R)
Dicarlo, David Cosimo (D)
DiDonato, Anthony, Jr (D)
Diehm, Victor Christian (R)
Dietz, Clarence E (R)
Dininni, Rudolph (R)
Dogole, Saul Harrison (D)
Dombrowski, Bernard Joseph (D)
Dorr, Donald W (R)
Dougherty, Charles F (R)
Doyle, Joseph Ted (D)
Dreibelbis, Galen E (D)
Dudek, Michael Matthew (D)
Dunne, Isabelle Mary (D)
Early, Edward M (D)
Echols, Alvin Edward (R)
Eckensberger, William H, Jr (D)
Edgar, Robert William (D)
Egan, Richard Edward (D)
Eilberg, Joshua (D)
Eilts, Hermann Frederick (R)
Eisenhower, John Sheldon Doud (R)
Ellenbogen, Henry (D)
Ellis, Edward Dale (D)
Englehart, Harry A, Jr (D)
Eshleman, Edwin D (R)
Ewing, Wayne S (R)
Exler, John J (D)
Falcone, Ernani Carlo (D)
Farr, Harold P (R)
Fawcett, Charlotte D (R)
Fee, Thomas J (D)
Fels, Margaret Katherine (R)
Fiedler, Betty Mae (R)
Fineman, Herbert (D)
Fink, Earl Barton (D)
Fischer, Donald Frederick (R)
Fischer, Roger M (D)
Fischer, Roger Raymond (R)
Fisher, D Michael (R)
Flaherty, Peter F (D)
Flaherty, Thomas Edward (D)
Fleming, Robert D (R)
Flood, Daniel J (D)
Foerster, Thomas Joseph (D)
Fogel, Herbert Allan (R)

Foglietta, Thomas M (R)
Foster, Alfred Carville, Jr (R)
Foster, William Walter (R)
Fox, Harry M (R)
Frame, Richard C (R)
Frankenburg, Richard James (R)
Frick, Joseph B (R)
Fry, Howard M (R)
Fryer, Lester K (D)
Gallagher, James J A (D)
Gallen, James J (R)
Garner, Marie G (D)
Garrett, Wayne Lee (R)
Garzia, Ralph A (D)
Gates, Thomas S (R)
Gaydos, Joseph Matthew (D)
Geelen, Leslie Patrick (R)
Geesey, Eugene Ronald (R)
Geisler, Robert A (R)
Gentzler, Kenneth C (D)
George, Camille (D)
Giammarco, Henry J (D)
Gibson, Andrew E (R)
Gillespie, Patrick B (R)
Gillette, Helen D (D)
Gleason, Patrick Augustine (R)
Gleason, Robert A (R)
Gleeson, Francis Edward, Jr (D)
Gleim, Ira Kenny (D)
Going, Robert Morton (D)
Goodling, George A (R)
Goodling, William Franklin (R)
Goodman, James Anthony (D)
Graff, Patricia Hale (D)
Graham, Mortimer Elliott (R)
Grammes, Lloyd Edgar (R)
Green, James A (D)
Green, William Joseph (D)
Greenfield, Roland (D)
Grieco, Joseph V (R)
Griffith, Calvin Grant, III (R)
Gring, Harry H (R)
Haig, Alexander M, Jr (R)
Hall, Edwin Arthur, Jr (R)
Halverson, Kenneth Shaffer (R)
Hamberger, Martin George (R)
Hamilton, John H, Jr (R)
Hamilton, Robert K (D)
Hammock, Charles Paul (R)
Hankins, Freeman (D)
Hanna, Edward (D)
Hanna, Michael A (D)
Hannum, Robert John (R)
Harkins, Bernard Joseph (D)
Harris, J Mervyn (R)
Harris, Stanley Emerson (R)
Hasay, George C (R)
Haskell, H Harrison (Jay), II (R)
Hayes, David Sayre (R)
Hayes, Samuel E, Jr (R)
Heinz, Henry John, III (R)
Hepford, H Joseph (R)
Hill, Sherman L (R)
Hillman, Elsie Hilliard (R)
Hinchey, Joseph Francis (D)
Hollander, Thomas (D)
Honaman, June N (R)
Hoopes, Darlington (Socialist)
Hopkins, Forest (R)
Hostetler, H Richard (R)
Hovis, Raymond Leader (R)
Huber, Ray Arlen (D)
Huff, Sara Ellen (R)
Humes, Theodore Leon (R)
Hunt, William Robert (R)
Hutchinson, Amos K (D)
Hutchinson, William David (R)
Irvine, William A (R)
Irvis, K Leroy (D)
Itkin, Ivan (D)

Jacobs, Alma Rau (R)
Jacobs, Earl Bryan (R)
Jennings, James Patrick Thomas (R)
Johns, Michael E (R)
Johnson, Albert W (R)
Johnson, Joel J (D)
Johnson, Michael (D)
Johnson, Raymond Blair (R)
Jonassen, Tor Heyden (D)
Jones, Clifford L (R)
Jones, Robert H (D)
Jordan, Ann (D)
Jordan, David Malcolm (D)
Jubelirer, Robert Carl (R)
Kane, Rita Wilson (D)
Kaplan, Jerome (D)
Katz, Alvin (R)
Katz, Edward A (R)
Kaufman, Gerald (D)
Kearns, Carroll D (R)
Kelley, James (D)
Kelley, James R (D)
Kelly, Anita Palermo (D)
Kelly, Eugene (D)
Kelly, James Bennett, III (R)
Kelly, John Brenden, Jr (D)
Kennedy, Donald Patrick (R)
Kernick, Phyllis T (D)
King, Ernest P (D)
Kistler, Guy A (R)
Kline, Ernest Paul (D)
Klingaman, William K, Sr (R)
Klunk, Fred G (D)
Knauer, Virginia Harrington (R)
Knepper, James W, Jr (R)
Knoll, Catherine Baker (D)
Knorr, John Philip (D)
Kolter, Joseph Paul (D)
Kornick, Nicholas (D)
Kosco, John C (R)
Kowalyshyn, Russell (D)
Krites, Vance Richard (D)
Krout, John D (R)
Kusse, Robert J (R)
Kwitowski, Walter Anthony (D)
Labovitz, Deborah R (D)
LaMarca, Russell J (D)
Lamb, Thomas F (D)
Lark, Henry W (R)
Lark, Robert F (D)
Laudadio, John F (D)
Laughlin, Charles (D)
Leach, Charles Parmley, Sr (R)
Leader, George Michael (D)
Lederer, Raymond F (D)
Lee, Edward S (D)
Lee, Kenneth B (R)
Lehman, John Francis, Jr
Lehr, Stanford Bud (R)
Leib, Regina S (R)
Lentz, Earl Leroy, Jr (R)
Letterman, Russell Paul (D)
Levi, Joseph, II (R)
Levin, Abraham (R)
Levin, Marilyn Lois (D)
Levin, Robert (D)
Lewis, Harold Craig (D)
Liebermann, Shirley Correll (R)
Lincoln, J William (R)
Lind, James Francis (D)
Loftus, Robert A (D)
Lohse, Robert Charles (D)
Lucas, Charles C (D)
Lynch, Francis J (D)
Lynch, Frank J (R)
MacElwee, Helen (Collins) (R)
Madeira, Eugenia Cassatt (R)
Mahady, Paul W (D)
Maier, Eugene Edward J (D)
Malady, Regis Rowland (D)

Maloney, Thomas J (R)
Manderino, James J (D)
Manmiller, Joseph C (R)
Markle, John, Jr (R)
Marshall, Howard W (R)
Martz, W Wilson (D)
Masloff, Sophie (D)
Mason, Louis, Jr (D)
Masters, Richard Stearns (R)
Mawby, Nancy B (D)
Maxwell, David Ogden (R)
Mazur, John (D)
Mazzei, Frank (D)
McCabe, Thomas Bayard (R)
McCall, Thomas J (D)
McClatchy, R A, Jr (R)
McConnell, Samuel Kerns (R)
McCorkel, Franklin Myers (R)
McCue, John B (R)
McDade, Joseph Michael (R)
McGinnis, Patrick J (D)
McGlinchey, Herbert J (D)
McGlinn, Frank C P (R)
McGrath, T Ed (R)
McGraw, Andrew J (D)
Mc Intyre, James (D)
McKinney, Paul (D)
McLane, William John (D)
McNaul, David Andrew (D)
Mebus, Charles Fillmore (R)
Mellinger, Saundra (D)
Menhorn, Harry G, Jr (D)
Milanovich, Fred R (D)
Miller, Marvin Eugene (R)
Miller, Richard Harold (D)
Miller, Stanley Allen (R)
Millin, Paul Haslet (D)
Milliron, John Patrick (D)
Minehart, Thomas Zeno, II (D)
Miscevich, George (D)
Moehlmann, Nicholas Bruce (R)
Molinaro, Carmine V, Jr (D)
Molony, Joseph P (D)
Moore, William J (R)
Moorhead, William Singer, (D)
Morgan, Thomas Ellsworth (D)
Morris, Samuel W (D)
Moss, Jerrold Victor (R)
Mowrer, Gordon Brown (D)
Moyer, Glenn Roydon (D)
MrKonic, Emil (D)
Mullen, Martin P (D)
Mullen, Michael M (D)
Murphy, Maurice Thomas (Moss) (D)
Murtha, John Patrick (D)
Musto, Raphael (D)
Myers, Gary A (R)
Myers, Michael (D)
Myers, Robert Lee, III (D)
New, Shelley Robins (D)
Newhall, David, III (R)
Newkirk, Rosa H (D)
Nix, Robert N C (D)
Noszka, Stanley M (D)
Novak, Bernard R (D)
Noye, Fred Charles (R)
O'Brien, Bernard Francis (D)
O'Connell, Frank J (R)
O'Donnell, Robert W (D)
O'Gorman, Francis Edmund (R)
O'Keefe, Peter J (D)
Oliver, Covey Thomas (D)
Oliver, Frank Louis (D)
Olson, Clinton L (R)
Orlando, Quentin R (D)
Osborn, Elburt Franklin (R)
Pancoast, G Sieber (R)
Parker, H Sheldon, Jr (R)
Pasztor, Laszlo (R)

PENNSYLVANIA (cont)

Pearson, Catherine A (D)
Perri, Fortunato (R)
Perry, Florence N (D)
Perry, Peter E (D)
Peterson, Lois Goodenough (D)
Petrarca, Joseph A (D)
Petrucci, Anthony Mark (D)
Pettibon, George T (R)
Pettine, Ronald Joseph (D)
Pierce, Eleanor Jean (R)
Pievsky, Max (D)
Piper, William G (R)
Pittenger, John Chapman (D)
Pitts, Joseph R (R)
Plowman, Francis Wilds (R)
Pratt, Ralph Domenick (D)
Prendergast, James Francis (D)
Price, Ethel A (R)
Puchalla, Andrew Francis (D)
Pyles, Vern (R)
Ralston, Raymond Edward (D)
Rappaport, Samuel (D)
Raub, Brian David (R)
Reed, Stephen Russell (D)
Reilly, Annabelle Wilson (D)
Renninger, John S (R)
Renwick, William F (D)
Reynolds, Benjamin J (R)
Reynolds, Hobson Richmond (R)
Rhodes, George Milton (D)
Rhodes, Joseph, Jr (D)
Richardson, David P, Jr (D)
Richardson, Evelyn D (D)
Rider, Harry Durbin (D)
Rieger, William W (D)
Ritter, James Pierce (D)
Rizzo, Francis Lazzaro (D)
Robb, Robert Clifton, Jr (R)
Romanelli, James A (D)
Rooney, Fred B (D)
Rosenfeld, Mitchell Allan (R)
Ross, Samuel A (D)
Roth, Gerald Irwin (D)
Rounick, Jack A (R)
Rovner, Robert Allen (R)
Ruane, Paul G (R)
Rubino, Theodore Salvatore A (R)
Rudy, C Guy (D)
Rudy, Ruth Corman (D)
Ruggiero, Philip S (D)
Russo, Marius Thomas (D)
Ryan, Matthew J (R)
Salerno, Mary J (D)
Saloom, Eugene George (R)
Salvatore, Frank A (R)
Salvatore, Michael Joseph (D)
Sampson, Arthur F (R)
Satz, Arnold (R)
Saylor, John Thomas (R)
Saylor, Stanley Raymond (R)
Scales, John Neil (D)
Scarcelli, Vincent F (D)
Scheaffer, John E (R)
Schmidt, Adolph William (R)
Schmitt, C L (D)
Schneebeli, Herman Theodore (R)
Schucker, Albert Edwin (R)
Schulze, Richard T (R)
Schuster, Nancy P (D)
Schwartz, George X (D)
Schweder, J Michael (D)
Schweiker, Richard Schultz (R)
Scirica, Anthony J (R)
Scott, Hugh (R)
Scott, Richard M (R)
Scranton, William Warren (R)
Sellers, Jo-Anne Ethel (R)
Seltzer, H Jack (R)
Sennett, William Clifford (R)
Shafer, Raymond Philip (R)
Shafer, Thomas Edward (R)
Shane, William (D)
Shapp, Milton J (D)
Shavor, Robert Peter (D)
Shearer, Don Paul (R)
Shelhamer, Kent D (D)
Shelton, Ulysses (D)
Showalter, Thelma Johnson (R)
Shuman, William O (D)
Shupnik, Fred Joseph (D)
Shuster, E G (Bud) (R)
Sirianni, Carmel A (R)
Sittler, Edward Lewis, Jr (R)
Sloan, Grace McCalmont (D)
Sludden, Charles Joseph (D)
Smith, David Jay (D)
Smith, Earl H (R)
Smith, Joseph F (D)
Smith, L Eugene (R)
Smylie, Michael (R)
Specter, Arlen (R)
Spencer, Warren H (R)
Splain, Maurice D, Jr (R)
Stahl, John (R)
Stapleton, Patrick J (D)
Stapleton, Thomas Joseph, Jr (D)
Stauffer, Sarah Ann (R)
Steeves, John M
Stevens, Jean M (R)
Stokes, J Emery (R)
Stout, Barry (D)
Strausz-Hupe, Robert
Stroup, Stanley G (R)
Strouse, Ronald Lee (R)
Stuart, George B (R)
Sullivan, Basil B (R)
Sullivan, Colleen Driscoll (D)
Sullivan, Joseph A (D)
Sweeney, John James (D)
Sweeney, Leonard E (D)
Sweitzer, Henry Becker (D)
Swenson, Harold A (D)
Taddonio, Lee C (R)
Tasca, Henry J
Tate, James Hugh Joseph (D)
Taylor, Fred (D)
Taylor, George S (Socialist Labor)
Tayoun, James J (D)
Thacik, Anne Smith (R)
Theodore, Nicholas Gerald (R)
Thiemann, Dennis E (D)
Thomas, Reno Henry (D)
Thompson, G Robert (R)
Tilghman, Richard A (R)
Toll, Rose (D)
Torquato, John R (D)
Traeger, Charles Donald (R)
Trello, Fred A (D)
Tucker, Cynthia Delores (D)
Tullio, Louis Joseph (D)
Ustynoski, James J (R)
Vagley, Robert Everett (D)
Valicenti, A Joseph (D)
Vann, Earl (D)
Vigorito, Joseph Phillip (D)
Vosburgh, Paul N (R)
Vroon, Peter R (R)
Wagner, George O (R)
Walker, Robert Smith (R)
Walsh, Thomas P (D)
Walton, Richard K (D)
Wansacz, John (D)
Ware, John H, III (R)
Wargo, Joseph G (D)
Webster, Robert L (R)
Weidner, Marvin Detweiler (R)
Wendolowski, Mary Anne Catherine (D)
Westerberg, Victor John (R)
Whalley, John Irving (R)
Whelan, James Octavius, Jr (R)
White, James Wilson (D)
Whittlesey, Faith Ryan (R)
Wilson, Benjamin H (R)
Wilt, Roy William (R)
Wilt, William W (R)
Wojak, Stephen R (R)
Wood, Harleston Read (R)
Wood, T Newell (R)
Worrilow, Thomas Henry, Sr (R)
Woznisky, John Michael (R)
Wright, James L, Jr (R)
Yahner, Paul J (D)
Yatron, Gus (D)
Yohn, William H, Jr (R)
Young, Marilyn Ashton (D)
Young, Wendell William (D)
Zearfoss, Herbert Keyser (R)
Zeller, Joseph R (D)
Zord, Joseph V, Jr (R)
Zurick, William Philip (D)
Zwikl, Kurt D (D)

RHODE ISLAND

Allen, Charles Henry, Jr (D)
Aquilotti, Samuel (D)
Arico, Anthony V, Jr (D)
Aukerman, James Vance (D)
Babin, William Albert, Jr (D)
Baccari, Vincent James (D)
Baker, Jacqueline Rae (R)
Balzano, Michael P, Jr (R)
Batty, Byron A (R)
Beard, Edward Peter (D)
Beaulieu, Ernest Robert (D)
Begin, Roger Normand (D)
Bevilacqua, John J (D)
Bevilacqua, Joseph A (D)
Blaine, Richard Allan (R)
Blasbalg, Arnold Leo (R)
Boeniger, Henry R (D)
Bowen, William A (D)
Brennan, Robert Michael (D)
Browne, Secor Delahay (R)
Campbell, Ambrose Leo (D)
Canulla, Guido J (D)
Capineri, Joseph A (D)
Caranci, Anthony Benjamin, Jr (R)
Carcieri, Anthony J (D)
Carley, Robert Joseph (D)
Casement, Joan Murphy (D)
Castro, William A (D)
Cawley, Clifford J (D)
Chafee, John Hubbard (R)
Chaves, Joseph J (D)
Cianci, Vincent Albert (R)
Cioci, Louis Michael (D)
Coelho, Peter J (D)
Cook, Eugene Otis (D)
Cook, Kenneth R (D)
Costello, James (D)
Cottrell, Arthur Maxson, Jr (R)
Crooks, Samuel Coulter (D)
Cutting, Harold D (R)
D'Amico, John C (D)
Daniel, Bruce B (D)
DeAngelis, Joseph (D)
Del Padre, Donald Edward (R)
Denomme, Ernest Francis (R)
Desmarais, Raymond Wilfred (R)
DeStefanis, Raymond H (D)
DeStefano, C George (R)
Devlin, L Patrick (D)
Dickinson, Spencer (D)
DiLuglio, Thomas Ross (D)
Di Stefano, Joseph Robert (D)
Doorley, Joseph Aloysius, Jr (D)
Doyle, Clement J (D)
Drapeau, William Lawrence (D)
Duffy, J Howard (D)
Dumont, Roland A (R)
Durfee, Lynda Margaret (R)
Durfee, Raymond M (R)
Edwards, Dorothy Beatrice (R)
Erickson, Stephen Paul (R)
Evans, David Vernon (D)
Ewing, Bayard (R)
Farrell, John Charles (D)
Fay, Mrs John (D)
Fay, Thomas Frederic (D)
Federico, James Joseph, Jr (R)
Ferraro, Anthony Michael (D)
Field, H James, Jr (R)
Flynn, James P (D)
Freda, Aldo (D)
Friedemann, Zygmunt Jerzy (D)
Gallogly, Raymond J (D)
Gallogy, E Peter, Jr (D)
Galvin, John Raymond (D)
Gammell, Richard A (R)
Garabedian, Aram George (R)
Garrahy, J Joseph (D)
Gendron, Joseph Saul (D)
Giangiacomo, Anthony (D)
Giannini, Anthony Albert (D)
Gibbs, June Nesbitt (R)
Godin, Wilfrid Lucien (D)
Goodwin, Thomas N (D)
Goulding, Paul Edmund (D)
Grande, William G (D)
Grimes, Ruth (D)
Gulluscio, Ronald John (D)
Hagan, James G (D)
Hanaway, G Frank (D)
Hanaway, Paul E (D)
Harpootian, Jacob (R)
Hawkins, John P (D)
Hawksley, Raymond H (D)
Hazard, Walter Robinson (D)
Heaney, Robert A (D)
Higgins, Michael A (D)
Hilton, Lester Elliot (R)
Hogan, John J (D)
Horan, Michael Francis (D)
Hornig, Donald Frederick (D)
Houlihan, Joseph T (D)
Hughes, Edward R, Jr (D)
Israel, Richard Jerome (R)
Jackson, Mary Hillard (R)
Jacques, Norman Joseph (D)
Jamiel, Morphis Albert (D)
Janes, Robert James (R)
Joslin, Alfred Hahn
Kagan, Samuel C (D)
Kearns, Richard P (D)
Keefer, Scott King (R)
Kelleher, Thomas (D)
Kiley, Richard B (D)
Kilmarx, Mary Neidlinger (D)
Knight, Monroe Olney (R)
Lamb, Thomas A (D)
Lapointe, Agnes R (R)
Lavallee, Gaston Harold (R)
Lederberg, Victoria (D)
Lenihan, Michael Phillip (R)
Lepore, Albert J (D)
Letendre, Raymond C (D)
Levin, Irving H (D)
Licht, Frank (D)
Licht, Richard A (D)
Lima, George Charles (D)
Lippitt, Frederick (R)
Love, Lucille A (R)
Low, Theodore F (R)
Lynch, Thomas A (D)
Macari, Adam B (D)
MacDonald, Raymond M (R)
Maggiacomo, Edward Louis (D)

Maher, James C (D)
Mahoney, James F (D)
Maigret, Maureen Elaine (D)
Malinou, Martin S (D)
Manning, Edward P (D)
Mansi, Nicholas Anthony (D)
Massa, Salvatore (D)
Massiwer, Maureen Elizabeth (D)
Matheson, Gordon Cameron (R)
McAllister, Richard (D)
McBurney, John Francis, Jr (D)
McCarthy, Kevin D (R)
McCarthy, William Francis (D)
McConnell, Andrew E (D)
McDonald, George Francis, Jr (D)
McFarland, John Alexander, Jr (D)
McGovern, Francis Leo, III (R)
McGreavy, Francis W (D)
McKenna, Marlene A (D)
McKenna, Robert J (D)
Mello, Pamela Jean (D)
Michaelson, Julius Cooley (D)
Migliaccio, Helen (D)
Moan, Raymond Charles (D)
Mooney, James Pierce (D)
Moore, Charles J (R)
Morin, Bruce Q (D)
Mott, Samuel D (D)
Mruk, Walter J (D)
Murphy, Lorena V (D)
Needham, Thomas H (R)
Nero, Pat (D)
Nichols, Mildred Thompson (D)
Noel, Philip William (D)
Notte, John Anthony, Jr (D)
Nugent, John Joseph, Jr (D)
Nunes, Frank L (R)
O'Donnell, Jennifer Mildred (R)
O'Donnell, Joseph H, Jr (R)
O'Neill, William C (D)
O'Rourke, Stephen Charles (D)
Panichas, George T (D)
Paolino, Thomas Joseph (R)
Parella, Gaetano D (R)
Pasbach, Earl Francis (D)
Pastore, John O (D)
Pastore, Louis H (D)
Pell, Claiborne (D)
Peloquin, J Camille (D)
Peloquin, J Camille, Sr (D)
Pierannunzi, Camillo A (D)
Quattrocchi, Rocco Anthony (D)
Quinn, James E (D)
Quinn, Walter A, Jr (D)
Rao, Anthony L, Jr (D)
Rawlings, Rob Roy (D)
Reilly, Charles T (D)
Revens, John Cosgrove, Jr (D)
Rippey, Catherine Norris (D)
Robinson, Anthony Mark (D)
Roch, Donald Edmond (D)
Rodrigues, Thomas J (D)
Romano, John A (R)
Rosedale, Peter Klaus (D)
Rousseau, Laurent L (D)
Russell, F Daniel (D)
St Germain, Fernand Joseph (D)
Santos, Alfred (R)
Sapinsley, Lila Manfield (R)
Scanlon, Joseph (D)
Selya, Bruce Marshall (R)
Sherman, Francis Henry (D)
Silvia, Joseph George (R)
Simonini, Arthur L (D)

Sinesi, Don Ghiaro (D)
Skiffington, John Joseph, Jr (D)
Smith, Jerome (D)
Smith, Matthew J (D)
Smollins, John F, Jr (D)
Solomon, Anthony Joseph (D)
Stanzler, Milton (D)
Stegmaier, David Dike (D)
Stromberg, Vernon S (R)
Sturges, Benjamin Rush (R)
Sweeney, Robert Emmet (D)
Szumilo, Daniel Francis (D)
Taft, James L, Jr (R)
Taylor, Erich A O'Driscoll (D)
Teitz, Jeffrey Jonathan (D)
Thompson, Oliver L, Jr (D)
Tiernan, Robert Owens (D)
Tootell, Lucy Rawlings (R)
Torgen, Edward H (R)
Torres, Ernest C (R)
Travers, Alfred, Jr (D)
Tucker, Robert S (D)
Vallante, Michael Anthony (R)
Vanasse, Albert J (R)
Vaslet, Albert P (D)
Walsh, Joseph William (D)
Ward, Robert Francis Joseph (D)
Weaver, George Duncan, Jr (D)
Weilburg, Donald Karl (D)
Wells, Guy Jackson (R)
Whalen, Mary Anne (D)
Woodcock, Raymond Paul (D)
Wright, Charles (Ted) (D)
Wright, Thomas E (R)
Yoder, James Amos (D)

SOUTH CAROLINA

Able, William F (R)
Adams, Weston (R)
Anderson, Ralph King, Jr (D)
Armitage, Constance Dean (R)
Arrants, James Clator (D)
Arthur, James M (D)
Ashmore, Robert Thomas (D)
Atkinson, Troy Carrol, III (R)
Aycock, Robert James (D)
Baggett, W Tate (R)
Baker, Gordon D, Jr (D)
Ballenger, William Howard (D)
Barksdale, Hudson Lee, Sr (D)
Barre, Sallie Marvil (R)
Barrineau, T Basil (D)
Baskin, Jewel Senn Breland (R)
Baskin, Weems (R)
Baxter, Sarah Elizabeth (R)
Beasley, Lewis Edward (R)
Belser, Keith Baker (D)
Bennett, Laurie Edward (D)
Berry, James Theodore (R)
Black, Kenneth Leigh (R)
Blackburn, McKinley Lee (R)
Blackwell, Wallace Norman (R)
Blatt, Solomon (D)
Blease, Eugene S (D)
Bowen, Thomas Otis (D)
Bradley, John Daniel, III (R)
Bristow, Walter James, Jr (D)
Brown, Edgar Allan (D)
Bruce, Danny Monroe (D)
Bull, Coralee Kitchings (D)
Burnside, Robert H (D)
Busbee, Maury Judson (D)
Buzhardt, J Fred, Jr (R)
Byrd, Gary E, Jr (D)
Byrd, Hal Clifford (R)
Campbell, Carroll Ashmore, Jr (R)
Campbell, John Tucker (D)

Campbell, W M (D)
Cannon, David Coker (R)
Carnell, Marion P (D)
Carter, Allen Ruffin (D)
Carter, Rex Lyle (D)
Chamblee, Jones M (D)
Chandler, A Lee (D)
Chapman, Harry A, Jr (D)
Cicenia, Alice (D)
Clark, John Franklin, III (D)
Clyburn, William R (D)
Collins, Marvin Bobby (D)
Cook, William A (R)
Cooksey, Jesse Lecel (R)
Cooper, M J (D)
Crocker, Virginia Leaman (Ginger) (D)
Culbertson, Donna Kay (D)
Dangerfield, Clyde Moultrie (D)
Daniel, Michael R (D)
Davis, Hazel Rivers (R)
Davis, Mendel Jackson (D)
Dennis, Rembert Coney (D)
Dent, Frederick Baily (R)
Dent, Harry Shuler (R)
Derrick, Butler Carson, Jr (D)
Des Champs, William Green, Jr (D)
DeWitt, Franklin Roosevelt (D)
Doar, William Walter, Jr (D)
Dooley, Albert John (D)
Dorn, William Jennings Bryan (D)
Drummond, John (D)
Duffy, James Evan (R)
Dukes, Gene W (D)
Duncan, Jason Charlie (D)
Earle, John K (R)
Ebert, Mike (R)
Ebner, Beverly Jones (R)
Eddings, Inez C (R)
Edens, J Drake, Jr (R)
Edwards, Edwin Armstrong (R)
Edwards, James Burrows (R)
Edwards, Tom W, Jr (D)
Elliott, Thomas Edward (D)
Ervin, Edward Singleton (D)
Evatt, Harmon Parker (R)
Felder, John Gressette (D)
Fewell, Samuel Bruce, Jr
Fields, Richard Earl (D)
Finney, Ernest Adolphus, Jr (D)
Flack, William Patrick (D)
Floyd, Eldra Moore, Jr (D)
Floyd, Ervin Richard (D)
Floyd, Henry F (D)
Floyd, LaNue (D)
Floyd, Sidney Thomas (D)
Fowler, Donald Lionel (D)
Fox, Eunice Jane (R)
Frederick, Carolyn Essig (R)
Gaillard, John Palmer, Jr (D)
Garrett, Charles G (D)
Garrison, Thomas Edmond (D)
Gasque, J Ralph (D)
Gasque, S Norwood (D)
Gelegotis, Paul (D)
Gettys, Thomas Smithwick (D)
Gibson, Charles MacDonald (D)
Glover, Ruth Champion (R)
Goggins, Juanita Willmon (D)
Gordon, B J, Jr (D)
Grainger, LeRoy Cecil (R)
Granger, Herbert Curry (D)
Grant, George Henry (D)
Graves, J Wilson (D)
Gregory, George Winfield, Jr (D)
Gressette, Lawrence Marion (D)
Grier, Francis Ebenezer (R)

Guy, James Lindsay, II (R)
Ham, Ray (R)
Hamilton, Lonnie, III (D)
Harrelson, James P (D)
Harrelson, John William (D)
Harrelson, William L (D)
Harris, Charles Anthony (D)
Harris, Patrick B (D)
Harris, Raymond Alexander (R)
Harrison, William Henry, Jr (R)
Hartnett, Thomas Forbes (D)
Harvey, J Bate (D)
Harvey, William Brantley, Jr (D)
Hatcher, Elmer Ward, Jr (R)
Hawkins, David Oliver (D)
Haynsworth, Clement Furman, Jr
Heinemann, John G (D)
Heller, Max M (D)
Helmly, Robert L (D)
Henderson, Billy G (D)
Henderson, James Marvin (R)
Hendricks, B L, Jr (D)
Henson, John L (D)
Hines, Richard Towill (R)
Hinson, Caldwell Thomas (D)
Hodges, Charles Edward (D)
Holland, Donald Harry (D)
Holland, Joe S (D)
Holland, Kenneth L (D)
Hollings, Ernest Frederick (D)
Holt, D N, Jr (D)
Hornsby, Ben F (D)
Howard, Samuel Hunter, Jr (D)
Huff, Beattie Eugene (D)
Hunt, Lloyd Edward (D)
Jamison, Leslie D (R)
Janzen, Jacob John (R)
Jenrette, John Wilson, Jr (D)
Johnson, George Dean (R)
Johnson, I S Leevy (D)
Jolly, Henry Levi (D)
Jones, Doris Hardy (R)
Jones, John Douglas (J D) (D)
Jones, William Townes (D)
Joy, Michael Bill (D)
Keller, David W, Jr (D)
Kenan, Richard Maxwell (D)
Keys, Rufus B, Jr (R)
Khare, Carol Fick (D)
Kirk, Lewis Roger, Jr (R)
Klapman, Jarvis Randolph (R)
Kleckley, Albert Lloyd (D)
Kneece, Robert Edward (D)
Kohn, Robert Alfred (R)
Koon, Larry Labruce (D)
Koon, Walter Harold (R)
LaFitte, John Hancock, Jr (R)
Lake, Robert Campbell, Jr (D)
Land, John Calhoun, III (D)
Laughlin, Michael Lukens (D)
Lawson, Walter Nesbit (D)
Lawton, Marion R (R)
LeaMond, Frederick Julian (D)
Leonard, Lawrence Kirkwood (R)
Leverett, Ulysses S Grant (R)
Lewis, Ernest Crosby (D)
Lewis, James Woodrow (D)
Lightsey, Hugh Tuten (D)
Lindsay, John Charles (D)
Lister, Toney J (R)
Littlejohn, Cameron Bruce (D)
Livingston, Clyde Burns (D)
Long, James H (D)
Long, John D, III (D)
Lourie, Isadore E (D)
Lowry, Samuel Earle (D)
Mack, Barron Bayles (D)
Mangum, Tom Gibson (D)

SOUTH CAROLINA (cont)

Mann, Fletcher Cullen (R)
Mann, James Robert (D)
Manning, Sam P (D)
Marchant, Thomas Mood, III (R)
Marr, Martha Cross (D)
Marshall, Harris Andrew (D)
Martin, Jimmy Leewood (D)
Martin, John Alfred (D)
Martin, John Allen (R)
Martschink, Sherry Shealy (R)
Matthews, John, Jr (D)
May, John Amasa (D)
Maybank, Burnet R (D)
McAbee, Jennings (D)
McCullough, Roland Alexander (R)
McDonald, Milford Edgar (D)
McFadden, Robert Lawrence (D)
McGill, Frank H (D)
McGowan, Edgar Leon (D)
McGowan, Marion D (D)
McInnis, David Fairley (D)
McLeod, Daniel R (D)
McLeod, Peden Brown (D)
McLeod, William James (D)
McLeod, William Mullins (D)
McMaster, Fitz-John Creighton (D)
McMillan, Clara Gooding (D)
McMillan, Gilbert Edward (Gil) (R)
McMillan, John L (D)
McNair, Robert Evander (D)
Medley, Dolphus Cleve (D)
Medlock, Thomas Travis (D)
Meetze, George Elias (D)
Mendenhall, Samuel Brooks (D)
Merris, Charles Larry (R)
Middleton, Earl Matthew (D)
Milliken, Roger (R)
Mitchell, Theo (D)
Montague, Joanne (D)
Moore, Fred Thurman (D)
Moore, James Edward (D)
Moore, James P, Jr (R)
Moore, Paul M (D)
Morgan, Herbert Doyle (D)
Morphy, Ted L (D)
Morris, Earle E, Jr (D)
Morris, James McCullum (D)
Moss, James H (D)
Murray, Joseph Renold (D)
Nash, Robert Rhea (R)
Neisler, Robert Preston (R)
Nelson, Clarence A (R)
Nunnery, Melvin Ernest (Ernie) (D)
Parker, Marshall Joyner (R)
Parnelle, Rosalind Correll (R)
Patterson, Grady Leslie, Jr (D)
Patterson, Kay (D)
Perry, Matthew (D)
Poston, Howard Henry, Jr (R)
Pough, W Newton (D)
Powell, Charles F (D)
Powell, Charles Kenneth (R)
Powell, Charles Lewis (D)
Quarles, Charles Harrison (R)
Rast, Elsie Sutherland (D)
Reel, William A, Jr (D)
Regan, Carol Boyd (D)
Rhoad, W D (D)
Rickenbaker, Dudley Gene (R)
Riley, Edward Patterson (D)
Riley, Richard Wilson (D)
Risher, William Rhett (R)
Roberts, Edward Calhoun (D)
Roddey, Frank Laney (D)
Rogers, George Lester (R)
Rogers, John I, III (D)
Rogers, Joseph Oscar, Jr (R)
Rowell, Edward Leonidas (R)
Rowell, James Victor (R)
Rubin, Hyman (D)
Rudnick, Irene K (D)
Russell, Donald Stuart (D)
Russell, Norma C (D)
Saleeby, Edward Eli (D)
Sanders, W T, Jr (Bill) (R)
Sandifer, Cecil T (D)
Schafer, Alan Heller (D)
Schwartz, Ramon, Jr (D)
Sexton, Clarence D, Jr (D)
Shealy, Wilson Otto (R)
Shirley, Jasper Clyde (R)
Silver, Alan Richard (D)
Simpson, Edward W, Jr (R)
Sloan, Frank Keenan (D)
Sloan, James Park (R)
Smith, Edward Jack (D)
Smith, Harris Page (D)
Smith, Horace Carroll (D)
Smith, Jefferson Verne (D)
Smith, John H (D)
Smith, Laura La Rose (R)
Smith, Thomas Earle, Jr (D)
Spence, Floyd Davidson (R)
Spivey, Deborah Kohler (R)
Spivey, Hubert Michael (R)
Stanley, William C (D)
Stephen, James Barnett (D)
Stevens, James Price (D)
Stevenson, Ferdinan Backer (Nancy) (D)
Stine, Gordan Bernard (D)
Stoddard, Eugene C (D)
Stone, William Cornwell (D)
Stroud, William Hugh (R)
Stubbs, Archie Roy (R)
Suber, Martin Gay (R)
Sullivan, Richard Lyles Coble (D)
Sylvester, Barbara Thornton (D)
Taylor, David Surratt (D)
Taylor, Harold E (D)
Tecklenburg, Esther Herlihy (D)
Theodore, Nick Andrew (D)
Thigpen, Neal Dorsey (R)
Thornton, O Frank (D)
Thurmond, Strom (R)
Tillman, Wheeler Mellette (D)
Toal, Jean H (D)
Townsend, Richard Taylor (D)
Turner, Roy R (R)
Tyson, Wilson (D)
Ubben, Donald Thomas (R)
Vanderford, Horace Keith (D)
Van Harlingen, William M, Jr (R)
Van Osdell, James Barr (D)
Venters, W Odell (D)
Waddell, James Madison, Jr (D)
Wallace, William Lewis (D)
Waller, John H, Jr (D)
Wannamaker, William Whetstone, Jr (R)
Wannamaker, William Whetstone, III (R)
Washington, McKinley, Jr (D)
Watson, Albert W (R)
Weeks, Henry Richard, Jr (R)
West, John Carl (D)
Wheeler, Emily Lide (D)
Whitaker, Charles James, Sr (D)
White, Knox Haynsworth (R)
Whitehead, Wiley Leon, Jr (R)
Wilder, Alice F (R)
Williams, Marshall Burns (D)
Wilson, Addison Graves (Joe) (R)
Wilson, George, Jr (D)
Wise, Thomas Dewey (D)
Wood, John T (D)
Woods, Robert R (D)
Wyse, Jacob Frederick (R)
Young, Edward L (R)

SOUTH DAKOTA

Abdnor, E James (R)
Abourezk, James G (D)
Adelstein, Stanford Mark (R)
Anderson, C Marie Pingrey (R)
Anderson, Harold (R)
Anderson, Oscar L (R)
Anderson, Sigurd (R)
Anderson, Virgil Ervin (R)
Austad, Oscar Melvin (R)
Axtmann, David M (R)
Bader, Palmer Walter (R)
Barnes, Richard Errol (D)
Barnett, Joseph H (R)
Batteen, Dennis John (R)
Becker, William Jacob (D)
Bell, Dale Allen (R)
Bellman, Charles J (D)
Benda, Carol Joyce (R)
Berry, E Y (R)
Bertness, Kenneth LeRoy (R)
Bibby, John E (R)
Biegelmeier, Frank (D)
Biever, Violet S (D)
Billion, David Henry (D)
Birkeland, Arthur C (R)
Blue, George (D)
Boe, Nils A (R)
Bones, Walter (R)
Bottum, Joseph Henry (R)
Boyd, Randall Scott (D)
Bruce, Beverly Joan (D)
Burg, James Allen (Jim) (D)
Burns, Robert H (R)
Burns, Robert J (D)
Bushfield Vera Cahalan (R)
Carlson, Loren Merle (R)
Cheever, Gene G (R)
Cheever, Herbert Edward, Jr (D)
Christensen, Harvey Moeller (D)
Clarke, Neil (R)
Clement, D B (R)
Conahan, Walter Charles (R)
Cook, Donald Eugene (D)
Cook, Georgia Mae (D)
Crouch, George O'Brien (D)
Curran, Michael (D)
Danekas, Willis W (R)
Davis, John Oliver (R)
Deibert, Richard Ray (R)
Denholm, Frank Edward (D)
Dougherty, William Joseph (D)
Drake, Gary (D)
Dunn, Francis Gill (D)
Dunn, James B (R)
Ecker, Peder Kaloides (D)
Edelen, Mary Beaty (R)
Eggers, Jean Ethalen (R)
Eliason, Larry Bill (R)
Ellingson, Bertrum Edwin (D)
Elwood, Ira Elmer (D)
Engel, John A (D)
Engelbrecht, Marlene Vivian (R)
Erling, Jacque J (R)
Fairchild, Ruth (D)
Farrar, Frank L (R)
Fillmore, Lillian Garnet (R)
Flyte, Charles E (D)
Forell, Ora E (R)
Foster, Mirl A (D)
Frank, Helen Joyce (D)
Frerichs, Kent Elmer (D)
Gage, Darleen Noteboom (R)
Gellhaus, Derald B (R)
Geyerman, Peter Thomas (D)
Gibson, Donald Jack (R)
Giessinger, Peter W (D)
Gjesdal, Lars B, Jr (R)
Glover, Merton (D)
Grams, William Lane (R)
Gross, Benny J (R)
Gubbrud, Archie (R)
Guffey, James Vincent (D)
Guiser, Paul (R)
Gullickson, Dale Dean (D)
Gullickson, Roger Wayne (D)
Gurney, Chan John Chandler (R)
Hall, Rodney Maple (D)
Halling, Beverly Jane (R)
Halverson, Harold Wendell (R)
Ham, Arlene Hansen (R)
Ham, Arthur Carl (R)
Ham, Donald Jamieson (R)
Hansen, Lowell C, Jr (R)
Harding, G Homer (R)
Haugo, Roger Erling (R)
Hauschild, Wayne Arthur (D)
Heck, Loretta Jo (D)
Heisler, Leslie (D)
Herseth, Lorna B (D)
Herseth, Ralph Lars (D)
Hinkle, Bergit Emmaline (D)
Hoffman, Leroy George (R)
Hogen, Marvis Thomas (R)
Hogen, Philip N (R)
Horman, Ralph W (D)
Howard, Charles Allen, Jr (R)
Huber, Oscar Edwin (R)
Humphrey, Louise B (R)
Hunking, Loila Grace (D)
Hurst, Glynn J (R)
Hussey, Nora W (R)
Jackson, Jack (D)
Janklow, William John (R)
Jarrett, Donald DuWayne (R)
Jensen, Ingeman (R)
Jensen, William Martin (R)
Johnson, John Dave (D)
Johnson, Karen Ann (D)
Johnson, Melvin (D)
Johnson, Roy Monrad (D)
Johnson, Stanley Arthur (R)
Jones, Curtis (D)
Jones, Kenneth B (R)
Jorgensen, Steven Lang (R)
Kammerer, Marvin Julius (D)
Kandaras, Homer Michael (D)
Kane, George D (D)
Kaufman, LeRoy J (R)
Kauth, Kenneth (D)
Kelly, Robert W (D)
Kelm, Marilynn (D)
Kemnitz, Ralph Allen (R)
Kenner, Patricia E (D)
Kesling, James William (R)
Kessler, Ann Elizabeth (C)
Kleven, Leslie J (R)
Kneip, Richard Francis (D)
Knobe, Rick W (R)
Knutson, Robert John, Jr (D)
Koehn, Emil Alvin (R)
Kopecky, Bernie D (D)
Kougl, Patricia Anne (D)
Krieger, Gregory Hawthorne (R)
Krull, Jacob Edward (D)
Kundert, Alice E (R)
Kunze, Anne Ilene (D)
Kyle, Samuel William (Bill) (R)
Lakness, Milton A

Lamont, Frances Stiles (Peg) (R)
Larson, Alma (R)
Leddy, Arlo R (D)
Leischner, Dale Edward (R)
Lenker, William Fred (R)
Lerew, Theodore (D)
Levin, George Daniel (D)
Littau, Fred M (R)
Loen, Vernon Carroll (R)
Lovell, Gordon (D)
Luke, Robert Kenneth (D)
Lyons, Robert Emmet (D)
Magnuson, Arvid Walter (D)
Mahan, Eugene Robert (D)
Mardian, Goldie M (D)
Mayer, Jerome J (D)
McClure, Mary Anne (R)
McFarland, Dennis Claude (D)
McGovern, George (D)
McKeever, Juanita M (D)
McKelvey, Robert Morris (D)
McManus, Eleanor Agatha (D)
Mehlhaff, Dean O (R)
Mensch, Lyle (D)
Meyer, D Wayne (R)
Michels, James Ernest (R)
Mickel, Charles J (D)
Mickelson, George Speaker (R)
Mickelson, Grace Maxine (D)
Miller, Linda Lea Margaret (D)
Miller, Robert Lee (R)
Miller, Ronald Knox (R)
Miller, Walter D (R)
Millett, Harold (R)
Moilan, Wanda DeVon (D)
Mollet, Peggy Earleen (D)
Morgan, Philip William (R)
Mortimer, G F (R)
Muenster, Theodore Robert (D)
Nelson, Gary Dean (D)
Nelson, Joani Michaelle (D)
Nepstad, Dorothy (R)
O'Connor, Michael Joseph (D)
Ohm, Wilma Jean (D)
Olson, John E (R)
Olson, Kathleen W (Kay) (R)
Olson, Maurice Alan (D)
Opbroek, Florence M (D)
Osheim, Donald (R)
Palleria, Frank Arthur (D)
Pieplow, E C (R)
Piersol, Lawrence L (D)
Poppen, Henry Alvin (R)
Pressler, Larry (R)
Pribyl, Patricia Heinz (D)
Pyle, Gladys (R)
Quam, Leslie James (R)
Raasch, Mary Elizabeth (R)
Radack, Jerome D (D)
Rickenbach, Joel (R)
Riedy, John R (D)
Ripp, William Robert (R)
Robbennolt, Gene (D)
Roberts, Clint, Jr (R)
Roberts, Donus Dan (D)
Robertson, George Louis (R)
Rohrer, Janet Edna (R)
Rossiter, Michael Anthony (D)
Ruddy, Robert Edward (R)
Sande, Kermit Andrew (D)
Schrag, Lloyd (R)
Schreier, Harold (D)
Schuchhardt, Luetta June (D)
Schumacher, Anita M A (R)
Schwab, Eleanor Anne (D)
Shaeffer, John Allen (R)
Shanard, George H (R)
Sieh, Harold (R)
Sivertson, Robert (D)
Smith, Edwin Steeves (R)
Smith, Henry A, Jr (R)
Smith, James E (R)

Smith, Louise Blair (R)
Songstad, Sheldon Richard (R)
Sorenson, Dean Philip (R)
Srstka, William Joseph, Jr (R)
Stake, William Floyd (R)
Stender, Rudolph James (D)
Stern, Otto (R)
Stockdale, James Severt (R)
Stofferahn, Kenneth Darrell (D)
Stoia, Viorel G (R)
Stoick, James L (R)
Stoltenburg, Dennis Jerome (R)
Stroschein, Sharon Marie (D)
Sutton, Billie H (D)
Swenson, Duaine Vincent (D)
Taylor, Meredith Jeanne (R)
Temmey, Leo Albert (R)
Teske, Marilyn Johnson (R)
Testerman, Philip (R)
Thompson, Don Lee (R)
Tjeerdsma, Jess (R)
Tschetter, Menno (D)
Tysdal, Ralph M (R)
Uglum, John Richard (D)
Voight, David K (D)
Volk, David Lawrence (R)
Wallahan, Franklin J (D)
Wallner, Mary (D)
Walter, Merwyn H (D)
Warkenthien, Gene (R)
Weber, Robert R (R)
Wegman, Harold Robert (R)
Weick, Dale Ellwood, Jr (D)
Weiland, Donald P (D)
Weisenberg, Webb (R)
Widman, Paul Joseph (D)
Wiese, Andrew J (D)
Wollman, Harvey (D)
Wood, Dorothy Mertis (D)
Wood, Royal James (Bud) (R)
Ylitalo, John Raymond

TENNESSEE

Abernathy, Thomas Jerome (D)
Ables, Charles Robert (R)
Acree, William B, Jr (D)
Agee, Tommye McWilliams (D)
Albright, Ray C (R)
Anderson, Thomas J (American Party)
Anderson, William Robert (D)
Arms, Jena Beth (R)
Ashe, Victor Henderson (R)
Ashford, Charlie R (R)
Ashley, Randolph Alexander, Jr (D)
Atchley, Ben (R)
Atchley, Fred C (R)
Atkins, Jane Hudson (R)
Avery, John Buchanan, Jr (D)
Azzara, Judy Stanfill (D)
Bacon, Reba Broyles (D)
Bailey, Edward Riston (R)
Baird, Raymond Renfro (D)
Baird, William D (D)
Baker, E LaMar (R)
Baker, Hayden Burnice (R)
Baker, Howard, Jr (R)
Ball, Roger Alford (D)
Barry, William Logan (R)
Bass, Ross (D)
Bates, Larry (D)
Bean, Mary Frances (D)
Beard, Robin Leo, Jr (R)
Bell, Thomas Devereaux, Jr (R)
Berry, Fred Ogle, Sr (R)
Bewley, Joe L (R)
Bird, Agnes Thornton (D)
Bishop, Edna Noe (D)
Bishop, Jimmy (D)

Bissell, Keith (D)
Blackburn, Clarence, Jr (D)
Blank, Edward C, II (D)
Blanton, L Ray (D)
Bodiford, Ray (R)
Boner, William Hill (D)
Bousson, Edward J, Jr (R)
Bowers, Edgar R (Buddy) (R)
Bowers, Kathryn Inez (D)
Bowman, Thelma Shanks (R)
Boyd, Baxter Jackson (D)
Bragg, John Thomas (D)
Brewer, Harper, Jr (D)
Briley, Clifton Beverly (D)
Brock, William Emerson, III (Bill) (R)
Brode, Marvin Jay (D)
Brown, Amy Camile (D)
Brown, Emily Cecile (D)
Brown, James Monroe (D)
Bruce, Paul Love (D)
Bryan, Marvin Allen (D)
Buck, Frank F (D)
Burks, Tommy (D)
Burleson, Robert Odell (D)
Burnett, Jack Alexander (D)
Burnett, Sam Thomas (D)
Butler, Kathryn Ellen (R)
Byrd, Robert Thomas, III (D)
Caldwell, James Carlton (D)
Canaday, Travis (D)
Carr, Joe C (D)
Carter, Walter Loyd (R)
Carter, William C, Jr (R)
Carter, William Lacy (R)
Cathey, Robert Reynolds, Sr (R)
Cawood, F Chris (D)
Chambers, Louis (D)
Chattin, Chester Coles (D)
Cheek, Will T (D)
Chiles, John Russell (R)
Clark, Richard R (D)
Clark, Sandra Lynn (R)
Clawson, Dorothy Estep (R)
Clinard, Mary Knight (D)
Cobb, John Bynum, II (D)
Cobb, Stephen Archibald (D)
Cochran, Franklin Delano (D)
Coleman, Nancy Johnson (D)
Collier, Woodrow Wilson (D)
Colton, John Patrick (D)
Colvard, Landon, Sr (D)
Connally, Elizabeth Warren (R)
Copeland, David Y, III (R)
Corley, Cecil Lucas, Jr (R)
Corn, Charles McCutchen (D)
Counce, Elmer Wylie (R)
Cox, Patricia Ann Swaggerty (R)
Creson, Thomas Kyle, Jr (R)
Crocker, Kenneth Wayne (R)
Crouch, Ernest (D)
Crowell, Gentry (D)
Crutchfield, William Ward (D)
Curbow, Deryl Crawford (D)
Daniel, James Edward (R)
Darden, George H, Jr (D)
Darnell, Riley Carlisle (D)
Davidson, Eugene Erbert (Gene) (D)
Davidson, Gene D (D)
Davis, Ann M (R)
Davis, Bob (D)
Davis, Chester J (R)
Davis, William James (Independent)
Deberry, Lois M (D)
Denton, Herbert Jackson, Jr (R)
Depriest, C E (D)
Dickey, David Jerry (D)
Dixon, Hugh B (D)

Dodd, Wilma Neville Beardslee (D)
Drake, James Ellsworth (D)
Dudley, Guilford, Jr (R)
Dunavant, Leonard Clyde (R)
Duncan, John James (R)
Dunn, Bryant Winfield Culberson (R)
Dyer, Ross Watkins (D)
Echols, Robert Lynn (R)
Edmonson, James Howard (D)
Edwards, Charles Marvin (D)
Edwards, Nancy Harrington (Penny) (D)
Elkins, James E (Buzz) (R)
Ellis, Harrell Victor (D)
Eskind, Jane Greenebaum (D)
Evins, Joe Landon (D)
Farmer, Donald Francis (D)
Fisher, Robert (R)
Fisher, Zack Buchanan (R)
Fletcher, Mary Lynn (D)
Folger, Stanley Ralph (R)
Ford, Emmitt H (D)
Ford, Harold Eugene (D)
Ford, Hobart (R)
Ford, John Newton (D)
Fowler, Hammond (D)
Frazier, James Beriah, Jr (D)
Freels, Willard Dudley (R)
Fullerton, Robert L (R)
Fulton, Richard Harmon (D)
Fuqua, L P (D)
Fuqua, Thomas Edward (D)
Gaia, Pam (D)
Garland, Thomas Jack (R)
Gentry, Charles Ezell (D)
Gill, Elbert T (D)
Gilliam, Herman Arthur (D)
Gillock, Edgar Hardin d) (D)
Glover, Billy Joe (D)
Good, Robert J (R)
Gordon, Barton Jennings (D)
Gore, Albert Arnold (D)
Hall, Walter Clarence, Jr (D)
Hamblen, Lyons Alexander (R)
Hamilton, Milton Hugh, Jr (D)
Handley, Helen M (R)
Hargis, Gerroll (D)
Harvill, Halbert (D)
Hawks, William Harry, Jr (R)
Hays, Forest, Jr (D)
Hays, Kenneth Sharp, Jr (D)
Henderson, Paul (D)
Hendren, James E (Chick) (R)
Henry, Clifford, Jr (R)
Henry, Douglas Selph, Jr (D)
Hensley, Hal Darrell (R)
Hicks, John Thomas, Sr (D)
Hicks, Mark C, Jr (R)
Hillis, I V, Jr (R)
Hitchcox, Forrest L (D)
Hoffmann, Mary Ann (D)
Holland, Charles Frank (R)
Hollar, Charles Hays (D)
Holmes, Robert Dee (D)
Hooper, Ben Walter, II (R)
Hopper, J Marvin (R)
Hopper, Taylor Lincoln (R)
Hurd, Edward Floyd (R)
Hurley, Bruce Wallace (R)
Hurst, Julius (R)
Jackson, Henry Ralph (D)
Jackson, Jerry Lee (R)
Jackson, Mildred Kate C (R)
Jackson, Thomas F (R)
Jaquess, James (Harry) (D)
Jefferis, Edward Forest, III (R)
Jenkins, Jeff Wayne (D)
Jensen, Thomas Lee (R)
Johnican, Minerva Jane (D)
Johnson, Yolande Marie (R)
Jones, Ed (D)

1080 / GEOGRAPHIC INDEX

TENNESSEE (cont)
Jones, Everett, Jr (R)
Jones, Gloria Lee (R)
Kaster, James J (D)
Keel, William Arnold, Jr (D)
Kernell, Michael Lynn (Mike) (D)
Kilpatrick, F Jack (R)
King, Alvin M (D)
King, Leslie Henry (R)
Kinkead, Cecil Calvert (D)
Knox, Rick Wilson (R)
Koella, Carl, Jr (R)
Kopald, S L, Jr (Kopie) (R)
Kuykendall, Dan Heflin (R)
Lancaster, Ray H (D)
Landers, William Lytle (Jug) (D)
Lanier, David William (D)
Lanier, James Olanda (D)
Lashlee, Frank P (D)
Law, James L (R)
Lawson, William Vinton, Jr (R)
Layman, Earl Robert (R)
Light, Frances H (R)
Livingston, Jean Wicksman (D)
Lloyd, Marilyn Laird (D)
Longley, Benjamin Lehmann (R)
Loser, Joseph Carlton (D)
Love, Harold M (D)
Lowe, W R, Jr (D)
Lucas, Bettye Daniel (D)
Marshall, Olen H (R)
Martin, Brad (R)
Matthews, William Joseph (R)
Mattison, Dorothy Love (Dot) (D)
McBride, Donald Opie (D)
McCaleb, Sammie Lee (R)
McCanless, George Folsom (D)
McFarland, Gwen Nation (D)
McKinney, James Robin (D)
McLean, Jim T (R)
McWherter, Ned R (D)
McWilliams, Cletus W (D)
Medlen, Warren Richard (R)
Meier, Margaret Kitchen (Peggy) (D)
Merritt, Gilbert Stroud, Jr (D)
Miller, David Douglas (D)
Miller, Ted Ray (D)
Moore, James W (D)
Morgan, George Henry (R)
Morris, William Harrell Jr (R)
Moseley, Martin Edward (R)
Moss, W F (D)
Motlow, Reagor (D)
Murphy, Ira H (D)
Murphy, Michael Dolan (D)
Murray, Charles Edward (D)
Murray, Roger Goodman, Jr (D)
Naifeh, Jimmy (D)
Nave, Marshall Toney (R)
Navratil, Robert Norman (D)
Neal, Vernon (D)
Nelson, Talmage L (D)
Newton, Polly (R)
Norman, Seth Walker (D)
Oakes, Roy Sidney (R)
O'Brien, Anna Belle Clement (D)
Odem, Sue Edna (R)
Oehmig, Dan (R)
Officer, Albert Fitzpatrick, Jr (Pat) (D)
Oldham, Dortch (R)
Owen, William Sneed (D)
Pack, David M (D)
Palmer, R Don (D)
Patterson, J O, Jr (D)
Peeler, James Alfred, Jr (D)

Perry, Jesse Laurence, Jr (R)
Person, Curtis Standifer, Jr (R)
Phillips, Clarence W (D)
Phillips, Dayton Edward (R)
Pickel, Thomas Wesley, Jr (R)
Pickering, George Roscoe, Jr (D)
Pitts, Knox (D)
Powers, William Mastin (D)
Prince, Audrey P (D)
Pruitt, Charles W (D)
Quillen, James Henry (R)
Quinn, Victor H (D)
Rainey, Donald Glenn (D)
Ramsey, Claude (R)
Rhinehart, Shelby Aaron (D)
Richardson, William Allen, Jr (D)
Roberson, James H (D)
Robinson, Charles R (D)
Robinson, Clarence B (D)
Robinson, Palma Luther (R)
Rochelle, Robert Thomas (D)
Rogers, J Stanley (D)
Rowland, Michael Young (D)
Rucker, Nannie George (D)
Russell, Ruth (D)
Sasser, James Ralph (D)
Schuller, Kerry Anne (D)
Scott, Barbara Garrett (D)
Shadden, Raymond (R)
Shine, David Bruce (D)
Sisco, Gary Lee (R)
Small, Neal (R)
Smith, Loy Lee (R)
Solomon, Rosalind Fox (D)
Sparks, Cullie James, Jr (D)
Spence, Christopher Lindsey (D)
Spence, John W, Jr (D)
Spurrier, Margaret Norvell (R)
Stack, Charlie Ray (D)
Stafford, Edwin Samuel (D)
Stafford, Moody Frank (Benny) (R)
Stallings, Robert S (D)
Stapleton, Arley, Jr (D)
Starbuck, William Thomas (R)
Starnes, Paul M (D)
Steinhauer, John M (D)
Steinhice, Laurel Coleman (R)
Sterling, Harold H, Jr (R)
Stinnett, James William, Jr (D)
Sugarmon, R B (D)
Sullivan, James Ernest (D)
Sundquist, Donald Kenneth (R)
Susano, Charles Daniel, Jr (D)
Talarico, Gabriel (Gabe) (D)
Taylor, Lucas Parnell (R)
Testerman, Kyle Copenhaver (R)
Thomas, Lowell (D)
Thompson, Lee Lincoln, Jr (D)
Thorp, Mitchell Leon (D)
Tobias, Ruth M (R)
Trent, Delmus (R)
Tuck, Ann Litton Rowland (R)
Turner, Catherine Ann (D)
Turner, Charles Wayland (D)
Upchurch, Ruble (R)
Wagner, Aubrey J (Independent)
Wagner, Theodore Franklin (R)
Walker, David H (D)
Walker, Robert Kirk (D)
Wallace, James H, Jr (Independent)
Warf, J H (D)
Watson, Robert Ogle (D)
Watson, William C (D)
Webster, Ronald Arthur (R)
Webster, Warren Raymond (D)
Webster, William J (D)

Weldon, William Kimberly (R)
Whaley, Cecil Hobert, Jr (D)
Whaley, Frances Morton (D)
White, James Howard (D)
Wilder, John S (D)
Williams, Avon Nyanza, Jr (D)
Williams, Edward Foster, III (R)
Williams, Joan Eason (R)
Wilson, David Kirkpatrick (R)
Wilson, George E, Jr (R)
Windle, Henry Watterson (D)
Witcher, Roger Kenneth (R)
Withers, Dedrick (D)
Witt, Carter H (D)
Woods, Rilla Robertson (D)
Work, Walter M (D)

TEXAS
Abbott, S L (R)
Adams, Donald Gilbert (D)
Adams, Herman, Jr (D)
Adcock, Ronnie W (D)
Agnich, Fred Joseph (R)
Agnich, Richard John (R)
Aikin, A M, Jr (D)
Allen, Jacque (R)
Allen, Joe H (D)
Allen, Lem B (D)
Allen, Susan Rogers (D)
Allison, James Purney (D)
Allison, Sandra Broyles (D)
Allred, William David (Dave) (D)
Anderson, John Richard (R)
Anderson, Milton Jay (R)
Anderson, Raymond Douglas (R)
Andujar, Elizabeth Richards (Betty) (R)
Archer, Van Henry, Jr (R)
Archer, William Reynolds, Jr (R)
Armstrong, Anne Legendre (R)
Armstrong, Connie Charles (R)
Armstrong, John Barclay (R)
Armstrong, Robert Landis (D)
Atherton, Flora Cameron (R)
Atkinson, Hamp (D)
Atlas, Morris (D)
Aubrey, Mark Lee (R)
Bailey, Kay (R)
Baker, Andrew Zachariah (D)
Baker, Jack W (D)
Balmaseda, Francisco Antonio (D)
Barbee, Basil Calhoun (D)
Barrientos, Gonzalo (D)
Bass, Harvey Lee (D)
Baum, Elmer Carl (D)
Beagle, Gail Joyce (D)
Beck, John Keitt (D)
Beckworth, Lindley (D)
Bennett, John Mirza, Jr (R)
Benson, Harry Eddie (R)
Bentsen, Lloyd Millard, Jr (D)
Bernal, Joe J (D)
Bigham, John R (D)
Binkley, Marguerite Hall (R)
Bird, Ronald Charles (D)
Blake, Roy M (D)
Blakney, E R (D)
Blumberg, Jane Weinert (D)
Blumenthal, Toby Nevis (R)
Blythe, William Jackson, Jr (R)
Bock, Bennie W, II, (D)
Bockbrader, Clayton Edward (D)
Boeckman, Duncan Eugene (R)

Bohls, Cleo Evelyn (R)
Boone, Latham, III (D)
Boyd, Obie Dale (R)
Braecklein, Bill (D)
Bray, James Houston (Jamie) (D)
Briscoe, Dolph (D)
Brooks, Chet Edward (D)
Brooks, Jack (D)
Broussard, James Hugh (R)
Brown, Albert D, Jr (Al) (D)
Brown, Claude Wilson (D)
Brown, Randy (D)
Bruce, Marion (D)
Brummett, Claudia Mae (D)
Bryant, John Wiley (D)
Buckaloo, Robbie Broadway (R)
Bulgerin, Loretta (R)
Burgland, Jane Harvey (R)
Burleson, Omar (D)
Burns, Michael Emmett (R)
Bush, George (R)
Bynum, Ben (D)
Caballero, Raymond Cesar (D)
Cabell, Earle (D)
Caldwell, Neil (D)
Camfield, Juanita F (D)
Canales, Terry (D)
Canion, Nancy Elizabeth (R)
Cantu, Vidal, Jr (R)
Caraway, William James (Bill) (D)
Carl, Colin Joseph (D)
Carr, Billie J (D)
Carter, Eva Meador (R)
Cartlidge, Thomas Morris (D)
Cartwright, Donald Mack (D)
Carubbi, Angelo Joseph, Jr (D)
Casey, Robert Randolph (Bob) (D)
Cassidy, Clifton Wilson, Jr (D)
Cates, Phillip Ray (D)
Cervenka, William Joseph (R)
Chacon, Alicia (D)
Chambers, Robert Eugene (D)
Chandler, James Melton (D)
Chavez, Melchor (D)
Christian, George (D)
Clark, Bill (D)
Clark, James A (D)
Clark, Tom C (D)
Clarkson, E Milton (D)
Clayton, Billy Wayne (D)
Cleaveland, Bradford Ira (R)
Clements, Rita Crocker (R)
Clements, William P, Jr (R)
Cleveland, Adolphus (D)
Clipson, James Hugh, Jr (R)
Close, G R (Bob) (R)
Clower, Ronald Lee (R)
Cobb, Amelie Mary (R)
Cohorn, Leon James (D)
Coker, Ernest Andrew, Jr (D)
Coldwell, Colbert (D)
Coleman, Ronald D (D)
Collins, Emmett Marvin (R)
Collins, James Mitchell (R)
Connally, John Bowden (R)
Connell, Ted C (D)
Conoly, Martha Virginia (D)
Coody, W G (Bill) (D)
Cook, Clayton Henry (D)
Cook, Jack Randall, Sr (R)
Cooke, Mary Swaney (D)
Cowden, Julianan (D)
Cowen, Joe N (D)
Cox, Steve Don (R)
Craddick, Thomas Russell (Tom) (R)
Craft, Jerry David (D)
Crawford, James Laird (R)
Creighton, Tom (D)

Crenshaw, Thomas William (R)
Crichton, Jack Alston (R)
Crockett, Kennedy McCampbell
Crouch, Thomas Gene (R)
Crutcher, Harry, III (Buzz) (D)
Cunningham, Larry Jack (D)
Cunningham, Paul Johnston (R)
Daniel, Price (D)
Darden, Conrad Lynn (D)
Davis, Alfred, IV (R)
Davis, Charles Russell (D)
Davis, Edwin Sparling (D)
Davis, Robert Eugene (R)
Davis, Will David (D)
DeCluitt, Douglas Ronald (R)
De La Garza, E (Kika) (D)
Delco, Wilhelmina Ruth (D)
Deniger, Robert J (Bob) (R)
Densford, Charles Francis (R)
Denson, Woody Ray (D)
Denton, Lane (D)
Dickey, Raymond, III (R)
Dies, Martin, Jr (D)
Doggett, Lloyd Alton, II (D)
Dollinger, Charles R, Jr (R)
Donaldson, Jerry (Nub) (D)
Donovan, Daniel Paul (D)
Douthit, Jackson Sherrod (D)
Dowdy, John (D)
Doyle, Roy H (D)
Drake, Robert Bert (D)
Dramberger, A L (Tony) (D)
Dubuque, Louis Theodore (D)
Dugger, Ronnie Edward (D)
Duncan, Herman Henry (R)
Dunlap, Peggy Mayfield (R)
Earle, Ronald Dale (D)
Eckhardt, Robert Christian (D)
Eddleman, Richard E (R)
Edgecomb, Robert Lee (R)
Edwards, Atticus Fitzgerald (D)
Edwards, Jimmie C, III (D)
Eidson, Wanda Carroll (R)
Erwin, Frank Craig, Jr (D)
Erwin, John Preston (D)
Estes, Kate Reed (D)
Estes, Sue Horn (D)
Evans, Charles Wesley (D)
Evans, James Weldon (R)
Ezzell, Michael Herman (D)
Fain, David C (D)
Farabee, Ray (D)
Farenthold, Frances Tarlton (D)
Finchum, Frank Dewayne (R)
Finney, Dave (D)
Fisher, Norris (D)
Fisher, O Clark (D)
Florence, Buck (D)
Flournoy, Robert Lane (R)
Forbis, James Edwin (D)
Fox, Milton E (R)
Francis, Nadine Webber (R)
Freeman, James Marion (D)
Friedman, Jeffrey Mark (D)
Friend, Harlan Dillman (D)
Friend, Karen Lee (D)
Gammage, Robert Alton (Bob) (D)
Garcia, A C (Tony) (D)
Garcia, Clotilde (D)
Garcia, Zaragoza D, Jr (D)
Garvey, James Sutherland (R)
Gaston, Robert Cecil, Jr (R)
Geiger, Richard Stuart (D)
George, Allaire Ann (D)
George, Ralph Weir (R)
Gholson, Isaac William (D)
Gibson, Robert Alfred (D)
Gilley, Smith E (D)
Godley, Gene Edwin (D)

Gonzales, Rosa Riojas (D)
Gonzalez, Henry Barbosa (D)
Gonzalez, Jaime A (D)
Gordon, Virgil (R)
Gossett, Ed (D)
Gossett, James D (R)
Grace, Robert William (R)
Gragg, Billy Hardin (R)
Grant, Ben Z (D)
Green, Forrest (D)
Green, Raymond Eugene (Gene) (D)
Greenhill, Joe R (D)
Gregg, Dick Hoskins, Jr (D)
Griffin, Marvin Collins (D)
Griffin, Oscar O'Neal, Jr (R)
Gronouski, John Austin (D)
Groseclose, John Robert (Bob) (R)
Guerra, Ramiro M (D)
Guest, Calvin Ray (D)
Hale, Louis Dewitt (D)
Hall, Anthony William, Jr (D)
Hall, William N, Jr (Billy) (D)
Hance, Kent (D)
Hancock, Richard Wilson (D)
Hand, Carroll Rayner (D)
Hanna, Joe Currie (D)
Harrington, D Roy (D)
Harris, Ed Jerome J (D)
Harris, Orland Harold (Ike) (R)
Hart, Ila Jo (R)
Hartung, Frank Edwin (R)
Hay, Jess (D)
Head, Fred (D)
Head, Peggy Carol (D)
Heatly, William Stanford, Jr (D)
Henderson, Donald Blanton (R)
Hendricks, Robert Ryan (Bob) (D)
Henington, C Dayle (D)
Hernandez, Frank Patrick (D)
Hernandez, Joe Luis (D)
Herron, James Henry (R)
Hightower, Jack English (D)
Hill, John L (D)
Hilliard, Bill (D)
Hobby, Oveta Culp (R)
Hobby, William Pettus (D)
Hoestenbach, John (D)
Hofheinz, James Fred (D)
Hogue, Grady Claude (D)
Hollowell, Bill (D)
Horn, James Nathan (R)
Howard, Rhea (D)
Hubenak, Joe Adolph (D)
Hudson, Samuel W, III (D)
Huff, Mark Emly, Jr (R)
Hughes, Charles E (D)
Hughes, Mary Ann (D)
Humphery, Eddie (D)
Hunt, Billy (R)
Hunt, John Ocie (D)
Hurd, John Gavin (R)
Hutchison, Ray (R)
Hutson, H Keith (R)
Jackson, Barbara Richards (D)
Jackson, Steven Gary (R)
Jansen, Donald O (R)
Jarratt, Joyce Howard (R)
Jaworski, Leon
Johnson, Durward Elton (D)
Johnson, Eddie Bernice (D)
Johnson, Sam D (R)
Joiner, William Stanley (R)
Jones, Edmund Eugene (Sonny) (R)
Jones, Grant (D)
Jones, James Paul (R)
Jones, Jerry Holton (R)
Jones, Luther (D)
Jones, Marvin (D)

Jones, Morton Edward (R)
Jones, Thomas Robert (R)
Jonsson, John Erik (R)
Jordan, Barbara C (D)
Kane, James Richard (R)
Kazen, Abraham, Jr (D)
Keeling, John Michael (D)
Kilgore, Joe Madison (D)
King, Bill B (D)
King, Carl Leander (D)
King, Mary Lois (R)
Kissling, Gilbert James (D)
Kistler, Margaret Koy (D)
Knight, James Edward (R)
Korioth, A J (R)
Kothmann, Glenn Harold (D)
Krueger, Culp (D)
Krueger, Robert Charles (D)
Kubiak, Dan (D)
Lane, J K, Jr (D)
Laney, James E (Pete) (D)
Lary, Camm Carrington, Jr (D)
Lauhoff, Herman E (D)
Laxson, John H (R)
Lay, Christopher David (R)
Leland, George Thomas (D)
Lenamon, James Levi (D)
Lewis, Barbara Halsted (R)
Lewis, Gibson D (Gib) (D)
Logan, Bard A (American Party)
Lombardino, Frank (D)
Long, Bettye Virginia (D)
Long, Emma (D)
Longoria, Raul L (D)
Lynam, Marshall L (D)
Madla, Frank (D)
Mahon, George Herman (D)
Maloney, Robert (Bob) (R)
Mankins, James Earl (Jimmy) (D)
Marshall, Hugh Talbott (D)
Martin, Blanche Ruth (R)
Martin, Celia Hare (D)
Martin, Elmer (D)
Martin, Marilyn Sue (D)
Mason, Clarence Edward (R)
Massey, Tom C (D)
Matthews, Martin, Jr (Bud) (D)
Mattox, James Albon (D)
Mauzy, Oscar Holcombe (D)
Mayer, Anita Engelking (D)
Mayes, Ed (D)
McAlister, R B (D)
McBee, Susan Gurley (D)
McBlain, David Alexander (R)
McCoy, Lucian Marion (D)
McCrady, Bob (D)
McCreary, Richard Edward, Jr (R)
McCutchin, Pat Winston (R)
McDonald, Felix (D)
McDonald, T H, Sr (D)
McFarland, Helene Morris (R)
McFarlane, William D (D)
McGee, William Sears (D)
McIntosh, Carl Daniel (R)
McKinnon, Michael Dee (D)
McKinley, Myrtle Ann (D)
McKnight, Charles Peyton (D)
McMullen, Mary Louise (D)
McNutt, D Gayle (D)
Meadows, Honey Lou (D)
Meier, Bill (D)
Meinecke, Robert Lee (R)
Mengden, Walter Henry, Jr (R)
Milburn, Beryl Buckley (R)
Milford, Dale (D)
Miller, Chris (D)
Monaghan, Robert Lee (R)
Monroe, Duffie Gibson (R)
Montoya, Gregory (D)
Moore, William Tyler (D)

Moreno, Paul Cruz (D)
Morey, Frances Hans (D)
Morgan, Clyde Nathaniel (R)
Morris, A Burr (D)
Moss, Charles Holmes (D)
Moya, Richard A (D)
Moyers, James Allen (R)
Mueller, Inez Lee (D)
Munson, William Ben, IV (D)
Nabers, Lynn (D)
Needham, William Felix, Jr (R)
Nelson, Joe Thomas (D)
Newton, Jon P (D)
Newton, Tom V (R)
Nichols, Robert Cecil (D)
Nixon, Sam A (R)
Noah, Raymond Douglas (R)
Nored, Alvin (R)
Nowlin, James Robertson (R)
Nowlin, Vaughan Brian (D)
Nugent, James E (Jim) (D)
Oaks, Steven Clark (R)
O'Conor, Robert Jr (R)
O'Daniel, Richard Truitt (D)
O'Donnell, Peter, Jr (R)
Ogg, Jack Clyde (D)
O'Kelley, Robert M (D)
Olson, Lyndon Lowell, Jr (D)
O'Neal, Linda Kay (D)
Orr, Roy Lee (D)
O'Sullivan, William Henry (R)
Outlaw, Nigle C (D)
Palm, Ed (R)
Palm, Nancy Dale (R)
Parker, Carl Allen (D)
Parker, Robert L (R)
Parker, Robert Lee (D)
Parker, Walter E (D)
Pate, Oscar Perry (D)
Patman, Carrin Mauritz (D)
Patman, W N (Bill) (D)
Patman, Wright (D)
Patterson, Helen Jo (R)
Pearson, Sherry Cross (D)
Penix, Chauncey Edward (D)
Pentony, Joseph Francis (D)
Pesek, Robert Joseph (D)
Petry, John W (D)
Peveto, Wayne (D)
Phillips, Jimmy (D)
Phillips, Zeno Joseph (D)
Pickard, Albert Marshall (R)
Pickle, J J (Jake) (D)
Pirtle, Mel Carlton (R)
Pitcock, Louis, Jr (D)
Pittman, Rena Arlena (R)
Poage, William Robert (Bob) (D)
Poerner, John H (D)
Pope, Jack (D)
Porter, Albert (D)
Potts, Dorothy Ella (R)
Powell, Charles Caruth (D)
Powers, John Pike (D)
Presnal, Billy Charles (D)
Price, Robert Dale (R)
Pullman, Saul Arnold (D)
Purcell, Graham (D)
Ragsdale, Paul Burdett (D)
Rains, Don (D)
Randolph, Suzanne Furneaux (D)
Raney, John Nathan (R)
Ratliff, Gerald R (D)
Reavley, Thomas Morrow (D)
Rector, William Lee (R)
Reddick, Donna Lynn (R)
Reed, Sam Glen (D)
Rees, Thomas L (D)
Reese, Elois Hamill (R)
Reyes, Ben T (D)
Reynolds, Richard Floyd (R)
Rez, Donald Gary (D)

TEXAS (cont)

Ribak, Abraham D (D)
Rich, Joe Lynn (D)
Rickels, JuDon (R)
Robards, Mary Patricia (D)
Roberts, Ray (D)
Robinson, Sam Perry, Jr (R)
Rominger, James Corridon (R)
Rostow, Walt Whitman (D)
Rucker, Calvin (D)
Runnels, Joseph L (Pete) (D)
Salem, Joseph John (D)
Sanders, Harold Barefoot, Jr
Sandoval, Hilary Joseph, Jr (R)
Santiesteban, Humberto Tati (D)
Savage, Wallace Hamilton (D)
Schieffer, John Thomas (D)
Schneider, Allan Ivan (R)
Schreiber, John Paul (R)
Schroeder, Clarence Henry (R)
Schroeder, William L (D)
Schubert, Carroll Wayne (D)
Schultz, Marilyn L (Mrs Frank) (D)
Schumann, Merritt J (R)
Schwartz, Aaron Robert (D)
Schwethelm, A C (D)
Scott, Richard Eley (D)
Semos, Chris Victor (D)
Sere, Susanne (D)
Sharp, Dudley Crawford (R)
Sharp, Laurene Stocklin (D)
Shaw, Aileen D (R)
Sheffler, George Justus (R)
Sherman, Max (D)
Sherman, W C (Bud) (D)
Shipe, Charles Edward (R)
Shirey, Harold Lee (D)
Shivers, Allan (D)
Shollenbarger, Joseph Hiram (Joe) (R)
Short, E L (D)
Shuttee, Anne Katherine (D)
Sifford, Joyce Wendal (D)
Simpson, Charles William (D)
Simpson, David James (D)
Simpson, Robert (Bob) (D)
Sipes, Jeanette Braden (D)
Skelton, Byron George (D)
Skiles, Elwin Lloyd, Jr (R)
Slack, Richard C (D)
Slay, Chester L, Jr (D)
Smith, Carlyle (D)
Smith, E Arnold (D)
Smith, Lynn, Jr (D)
Smith, Mary Catherine (D)
Smith, Preston Earnest (D)
Smith, William Forrest (D)
Snelson, W E (Pete) (D)
Snyder, Marguerite Brannen (D)
Sowell, Polly Rollins (R)
Sparks, Sherman Paul (R)
Spradlin, Mary Jo (D)
Spurlock, Joe C, II (D)
Staley, Mildred Wilkerson (R)
Stasio, Andrew F, Jr (Drew) (R)
Steakley, Zollie Coffer, Jr (D)
Steelman, Alan Watson (R)
Steger, William Merritt (R)
Stehling, Arthur (D)
Stenholm, Charles Walter (D)
Stevenson, Clarence Neal (D)
Stewart, Richard Olin (R)
Stovall, Reginald Morris (R)
Strauss, Robert S (D)
Strong, Robert Chatman, Jr (R)
Stubbeman, David (D)
Sullivant, William Benton (Bill) (D)
Sutton, G J (D)
Tagliarini, Thomas (R)
Tanner, Perry Aubrey, Jr (D)
Tarbox, Elmer L (D)
Teague, Olin E (D)
Tedford, John Roy, Jr (R)
Telles, Raymond L
Temple, Arthur, III (D)
Thompson, Clark Wallace (D)
Thompson, George (D)
Thompson, Senfronia (D)
Thornberry, William Homer (D)
Timanus, Hall (D)
Toft, Marjory Mayo (R)
Torres, Ruben (D)
Tower, John Goodwin (R)
Towery, Roland Kenneth (D)
Tracy, John Leo, Jr (R)
Traeger, John Andrew (D)
Truan, Carlos Flores (D)
Tuck, Joseph Grady, III (R)
Uher, D R (Tom) (D)
Upham, Chester Robert, Jr (R)
Valderas, Harold Louis (D)
Vale, R L (Bob) (D)
Vance, Estil A (D)
Van Horn, Michael (R)
Vaughan, Kenneth (D)
Vick, Gabe T (D)
Vick, Larry A (R)
Villareal, Patricia Jane (D)
Vinson, Roy Furman (D)
Voelter, Charles Everett (R)
Von Dohlen, Timothy Don (D)
Waddill, Kathryn J (D)
Wakefield, Stephen (R)
Wallace, E Howard (D)
Walton, James Neuman, Jr (R)
Warren, John Fisken (Jack) (R)
Washington, Craig Anthony (D)
Waters, Ron (D)
Watson, Ed Raymond (D)
Watson, Frances Louise (R)
Webb, Robert P (R)
Weber, Garry Allen (D)
Webster, James Douglas (R)
Weddington, Sarah Ragle (D)
Welch, Louie (D)
Wendler, Kenneth Stewart (D)
West, Fowler Claud (D)
West, Robert V, Jr (R)
Westerholm, Leo Lyder (R)
White, John Coyle (D)
White, Mark W, Jr (D)
White, Richard Crawford (D)
Whitehead, Emmett H (D)
Whitman, Reginald Norman (R)
Whitmire, John Harris (D)
Whittle, William Arthur (D)
Wier, Alex Searcy (D)
Wieting, Leroy James (D)
Wilkerson, Walter D, Jr (R)
Willeford, George (R)
Williams, Bill V (D)
Williams, Floyd Bert (R)
Williams, Walter J (D)
Willis, Doyle (D)
Wilson, Charles (D)
Wilson, John (D)
Wise, Wes (Independent)
Witkowski, Leo Victor (R)
Wolber, Arthur Roy (D)
Wooldridge, Harry Linn (D)
Wright, James C, Jr (D)
Wyatt, Joseph Peyton, Jr (D)
Wyer, J W (D)
Wyly, Sam (R)
Wynn, Sproesser (R)
Yarborough, Ralph Webster (D)
Yarborough, Richard W (D)
Young, John (D)
Zbranek, J C (D)
Zimmerman, Faye Laverne (D)

UTAH

Andersen, Kenneth H (D)
Anderson, L Robert (R)
Andrus, David Calvin (R)
Atkin, Sidney Joseph (R)
Atwood, Genevieve (R)
Bailey, Monte D (D)
Baker, Richard Scott (R)
Bangerter, Norman H (R)
Barlow, Haven J (R)
Barton, William Thomas (R)
Beck, Edward T (R)
Bennett, Charles E (D)
Bennett, Wallace Foster (R)
Bernard, Milly O (D)
Betenson, Glen (R)
Bingham, Jeff M (R)
Bischoff, Douglas George (R)
Black, Wayne L (D)
Black, Wilford Rex, Jr (D)
Blair, Frank S (R)
Boothe, Mrs Val (D)
Bosone, Reva Beck (D)
Bowen, Robert O'Dell (D)
Braby, Gudvor Wikane (R)
Brewer, Myrene Rich (R)
Brockban, W Hughes (D)
Brooke, D G (D)
Brown, Edward D (D)
Brown, James Elmer (R)
Buckner, Del L (D)
Buckway, Dallas Henry (D)
Buhler, David Liddle (R)
Bullen, Charles W (R)
Bullen, Reed (R)
Bunnell, Omar B (D)
Burton, Laurence Junior (R)
Bybee, John Monroe (R)
Cannon, Thomas Quentin (R)
Carling, Richard Junius (R)
Carlisle, Vervene (Vee) (D)
Carroll, Beatrice Jessop (Bea) (D)
Clark, Dorothy C (R)
Clark, Ezra Thompson (R)
Cloward, McRay (D)
Clyde, Robert F (R)
Cockayne, T William (Bill) (R)
Cooper, John B (D)
Cornaby, Kay S (R)
Cottle, L Glen (D)
Crockett, J Allan
Davis, Ted Miller (R)
Dean, Ernest H (D)
Dennis, Daniel S (R)
Dixon, Katie Loosle (R)
Dmitrich, Mike (D)
Due, Mary Jane Carter (D)
Duncan, David L (D)
Ellett, Albert Hayden
Ellison, Peter Kemp (R)
Fairbanks, Madge H (R)
Farnsworth, Lee Winfield (R)
Farnsworth, Norma Kimber (R)
Ferry, Miles Yeoman (Cap) (R)
Finlinson, Fred W (R)
Fisher, M Byron (R)
Frandsen, Lloyd Wayne (R)
Fuller, Margaret E (D)
Gardner, Willard Hale (R)
Garff, Ken D (R)
Garn, Edwin Jacob (Jake) (R)
Garr, John M (D)
Gaskill, John Robert (R)
Gibbons, Alberta Johanna (R)
Glover, Delone Bradford (R)
Gordon, Sherrill Lynn (R)
Grange, Russell Dean (R)
Habel, R William (D)
Halverson, Ronald T (R)
Hammer, Mary Lou Simpson (R)
Hansen, James V (R)
Hansen, Willis L (R)
Hare, Georgia B (R)
Hare, Ronald Ray (R)
Harmer, Sherman D, Jr (R)
Harvey, David Christensen (D)
Harward, Royal Thomas (R)
Hawkes, John Douglas (R)
Henderson, William H (D)
Henriod, Frederic Henri (R)
Higgins, Richard A (R)
Higginson, Jerry Cassim (R)
Hill, James Dean (R)
Hillyard, Lyle William (R)
Hinton, Wayne Kendall (D)
Hoffman, A Alton (R)
Hokanson, Elgin S (D)
Holbrook, Stephen (D)
Holt, William S (R)
Hoogland, Jacob John, Jr (Jake) (D)
Howe, Allan Turner (D)
Howe, Richard C (D)
Hunsaker, Edwin Sterling, II (R)
Hunt, Douglas I (D)
Irvine, David Robert (R)
Iverson, Lois O (R)
Ivory, Ellis R (R)
Jackson, Randy (D)
Jarman, Beth Smith (D)
Jeffs, A Dean (R)
Jenkins, Merrill (D)
Jensen, Moroni L (D)
Johnson, Mary Lorraine (D)
Jones, S Garth (R)
Judd, C DeMont, Jr (D)
Kerr, W Edward (D)
King, David S (D)
Klas, John Hall (D)
Korologos, Tom Chris (R)
Leavitt, Dixie L (R)
Leavitt, Stanley A (D)
Lee, Joseph Bracken (Independent)
Lee, Rex E
LeFevre, Clifford S (D)
Lindsay, Richard P (D)
Lloyd, Sherman Parkinson (R)
Low, George Mack (D)
Macfarlane, M James (D)
Marriott, Gilbert E (D)
Matheson, Franklyn Boyd (R)
Maughan, Richard Johnson (D)
McAllister, LeRay L (R)
McConkie, James Wilson, II (D)
McGee, Leonard Erwin (D)
McKay, Koln Gunn (D)
Mecham, Leonidas Ralph (R)
Melich, Mitchell (R)
Merrell, Harvey W (R)
Miller, Clyde L (D)
Mitchell, Dale W (D)
Money, Eldon A (D)
Monson, David S (R)
Moore, Robert D (D)
Moss, Frank Edward (D)
Nalder, Rebecca A (D)
Nelson, Frank V (R)
Nemelka, David Robert (D)
Newman, Harold Tolman (R)
Nielsen, Ray (D)
Owens, Douglas Wayne (D)
Pace, Lorin Nelson (R)
Parratt, J Easton (D)
Peterson, Cary (R)

Peterson, Georgia Bodell (R)
Peterson, M Blaine (D)
Peterson, Marion (D)
Pettersson, Carl E (D)
Pugh, Warren Edward (R)
Rampton, Calvin Lewellyn (D)
Rawson, Roger F (D)
Rees, G Stanford (R)
Reese, D Leon (D)
Rencher, Ronald Lynn (D)
Renstrom, Darrell George (D)
Rex, Pearl Teenie (R)
Richards, George LaMont (R)
Richards, Richard (R)
Robinson, L W (Hap) (R)
Romney, Vernon (R)
Sandack, A Wally (D)
Shearer, Kent (R)
Shepherd, Karen Felker (D)
Singleton, Samuel Morris (R)
Smith, John Edward (D)
Snow, Karl Nelson, Jr (R)
Sonntag, Douglas F (R)
Sowards, Glade Milton (R)
Starr, Ennis R (D)
Stephen, Edison J (R)
Stevenson, Claudius Edward (R)
Swan, Karl G (D)
Taylor, Samuel S (D)
Thomas, Norma Giles (D)
Timmins, William Montana (R)
Toronto, Joseph Lamont (R)
Turner, C Elmo (R)
Vincenti, Sheldon Arnold (D)
Warner, Keith C (D)
Warren, Marvin F (D)
Washburn, Dewain C (D)
Weston, Todd G (R)
Westwood, Jean Miles (D)
White, Beverly Jean (D)
Whitesides, Joe Edward (R)
Wilcox, Vern (D)
Wilde, Orvin Geral (D)
Wilkinson, Ernest LeRoy (R)
Wilkinson, Homer F (R)
Woodmansee, Gerald Louis (D)
Wright, Fred Thornton (R)
Yardley, James Fredrick (R)

VERMONT

Acebo, Alexander Valentino (R)
Aiken, George David (R)
Albright, Roger Lynch (D)
Alden, John Taylor (R)
Allard, Richard James (D)
Allen, Daniel Warren (D)
Allen, William G (R)
Appleton, Kenneth Wright (R)
Arbour, Gerard Joseph (D)
Archambault, Lyle B (D)
Ashe, Harry B (R)
Austin, Dale C (D)
Axelrod, Richard A (D)
Babcock, Robert S (R)
Bailey, Consuelo Northrop (R)
Baker, Douglas J (R)
Baker, Harold A (R)
Ballard, Alden G (R)
Bartholomew, Lisle (R)
Bartlett, Maedean C (D)
Beattie, Orrin Hawkins (R)
Beauchamp, Alfred J (R)
Bedford, Henry Ward (R)
Beer, Walter R, Jr (R)
Billings, Harold Edward (R)
Bloomer, Robert A (R)
Boardman, Robert Emmett (D)
Bongartz, Ferdinand A (R)
Bonnett, Thomas Winslow (D)
Bostrom, Charlene Emerson (R)
Bouchard, L Philip (D)
Boylan, John Henry (R)
Branon, Robert J (D)
Bresette, Michael Charles (D)
Brunette, Walter Stephen (R)
Bullock, Elmer David (R)
Bunker, Ellsworth
Buraczynski, Anthony C (D)
Burgess, John Stuart (R)
Burns, Brian Douglas (D)
Cain, Francis Joseph (D)
Callan, Herbert Quentin (D)
Candon, Patrick James (D)
Candon, Thomas Henry (D)
Caracciola, Joseph John (R)
Carlson, Alf A (R)
Carlson, Stephen Thomas
Carse, Henry H (R)
Chaloux, Maurice Eugene (D)
Chambers, Rosamond A (R)
Chapin, John Carsten (R)
Cheney, Kimberly B (R)
Christowe, Margaret Wooters (R)
Cole, Jordan D (D)
Colvin, Edwin A (R)
Congdon, David Ralph (R)
Conlin, Edward Joseph (R)
Cook, Donald L (R)
Corskie, John Campbell (R)
Costa, William Thomas, Jr (D)
Couture, Alfred V (R)
Crane, Edward Thurston (R)
Crawford, Arnold H (R)
Crowley, Arthur Edward, Jr (R)
Crowley, Thomas M (D)
Cummings, Robert E, Jr (D)
Curtis, David William (R)
Cutts, Royal Bartlett (R)
Daniel, Edward C (R)
Daniels, Robert Vincent (D)
Davis, Deane Chandler (R)
Davis, Frank H (R)
Dean, C Kenneth, Jr (D)
DeBonis, Daniel Vincent, Jr (D)
Delaney, Charles Lawrence (D)
Dewey, Giles W (R)
Douglas, James Holley (R)
Doyle, Marjorie Poor (R)
Doyle, William Thompson (R)
Drew, David Clifton (D)
Dunsmore, Elizabeth Margaret (D)
Dupuis, Josephine Mabel (D)
Earle, Ernest Joseph (Stub) (R)
Edwards, Donald Everett (D)
Engle, James Bruce
Ennis, Donald S (Independent)
Esposito, Francis James (D)
Evelti, Mary M (D)
Field, Andrew Robert (R)
Fienberg, George Mitchell (D)
Finn, John Roderick (D)
Flanders, William D (R)
Follett, Muriel (R)
Foster, Roland Raymond (R)
Foster, Thomas Henry (R)
Galli, Americo John (D)
Gannett, Robert T (R)
Gardner, Jane Kendall (R)
Garfield, Carroll L (R)
Gervais, Roland G (R)
Giard, Harold Walter (D)
Gibb, Arthur (R)
Gibson, Alexander Dunnett (R)
Giuliani, Peter (R)
Grady, Thomas Wesley (D)
Graf, Robert E (R)
Graham, Lorraine Hunt (D)
Granai, Edwin Carpenter (D)
Hackel, Stella B (D)
Hancock, John Ellsworth (R)
Hartigan, Margaret Ann (D)
Harwood, Emma G (R)
Harwood, Madeline Bailey (R)
Hebard, Emory (R)
Hebard, Irma Maginnis (R)
Heitman, Kathryn J (R)
Hewitt, Merritt S, Jr (R)
Hill, Nancy Hallman (R)
Hise, John Andrew, Jr (R)
Hoff, Philip Henderson (D)
Hollister, William Hillman (D)
Hooper, Franklin J (R)
Houston, Neal J (R)
Howe, John Abijah (R)
Howland, John Hudson, Sr (R)
Hoyt, Norris (D)
Hudson, Cola H (R)
Hunt, Stuart W, Sr (R)
Hunter, William Armstrong (Independent-D)
Hutchins, Christine Burbank (R)
Hutchinson, Frederick W (R)
Janeway, Edward G (R)
Jarrett, Evelyn L (D)
Jeffords, James Merrill (R)
Johnson, Constance Ada (Connie) (R)
Kaplan, Mark Alan (D)
Kedroff, Lew (R)
Keefe, Alexander Francis (Bud) (D)
Kennedy, Francis J (D)
Kennedy, Walter Lawrence (R)
Ketcham, Chester Sawyer (R)
Keve, Kirtland J (D)
King, Glendon N (R)
Kinsey, Robert Everett (R)
Kite, Constance Louise (D)
Klevana, Leighton Q J (R)
Koch, Thomas F (D)
Kunin, Madeleine May (D)
Lawrence, Harry Upham (R)
Leahy, Patrick J (D)
LeClair, Clarence George (D)
Leddy, John Thomas (D)
Lloyd, Samuel (D)
Longe, Rosaire J (D)
Lucenti, Margaret (D)
Lucy, Jacqueline Tillman (D)
Lunderville, Howard P (R)
MacDonald, Donald Gordon (R)
Maguire, Robert Wyman Jr (R)
Mahady, Frank G (D)
Maher, Mary Barbara (D)
Major, Beverly Bruhn (D)
Mallary, Richard Walker (R)
Mandigo, Melvin Harvey (R)
Martell, Arthur J (D)
May, Edgar
Mazza, Richard Thomas (D)
McClaughry, John (R)
McGregor, Thomas Earl (D)
McKee, Carol B (R)
McLeod, Steven Boyd (D)
Meaker, John Palmer (R)
Moffett, Hugh Oliver (D)
Molinaroli, Lucile C (R)
Mooney, Arthur Amos (R)
Moore, Donald Alfred (R)
Moore, Walter M (D)
Morgan, John Thackeray (R)
Morse, Eva Mae (R)
Morse, Gerald Ira (R)
Mulligan, John J (D)
Murphy, John Francis (D)
Nason, Charles P (R)
Nawrath, William Michael (D)
Newell, Graham Stiles (R)
Niquette, James Randall (D)
Niquette, Russell Frank (D)
Nixon, Sydney Thomas (R)
O'Brien, Daniel John (D)
O'Brien, John Joseph (D)
O'Brien, Leo, Jr (D)
O'Brien, Robert (D)
Obuchowski, Michael John (D)
O'Connor, Timothy J, Jr (D)
Ogden, Herbert G (R)
Orzell, John J (D)
Osborne, William Edward (D)
Paines, George Herbert (R)
Parker, Clare John (D)
Partridge, Benjamin Waring, III (R)
Partridge, Sanborn (R)
Paul, Concetta M (R)
Poor, Raymond John (R)
Poquette, Ray H (R)
Powell, Martin E (R)
Powers, Lawrence F (D)
Ranney, Zilpah Fay (R)
Reed, Norman Earl (R)
Regan, Walter Joseph (D)
Reynolds, S Seeley, Jr (D)
Rice, Lyle K (R)
Riehle, Theodore Martin, Jr (R)
Robinson, William Dwight (D)
Rosenstreich, Judy Patton (R)
Ross, Charles Robert (R)
Rouse, Stewart A (D)
Rousse, Jeanne Laura (D)
Sabens, Marshall T (R)
Salmon, Thomas P (D)
Sanderson, James Elmer (R)
Sauer, Charles Andrew (D)
Seward, Roland Quincy (R)
Shaffe, David Bruce (D)
Shea, James D (D)
Shiman, Gail (D)
Silver, Michael Francis (R)
Smith, Charles Plympton, IV (Independent)
Smith, Donald L (R)
Smith, Kermit A (R)
Smith, Rodney Newell (D)
Smith, Stewart Allen (R)
Snelling, Richard Arkwright (R)
Sorrell, Esther Hartigan (D)
Soule, Richard C (D)
Spates, Frank Harris (R)
Spencer, Marion Wood (R)
Spiers, Ronald Ian
Stack, Maurice William (D)
Stafford, Ralph E (R)
Stafford, Robert T (R)
Stanion, Theresa D (R)
Steventon, Joseph Thomas (R)
Stone, Charles Johnson, Jr (D)
Swainbank, Louise Robinson (R)
Sykes, Mary Flanders (R)
Syri, Amy (R)
Taft, Chester M (R)
Thomas, Richard Clark (R)
Thurber, Mary D (R)
Tomasi, Lawrence James (D)
Tucker, Neal Vancel (D)
Tudhope, Douglas I (R)
Valsangiacomo, Oreste Victor (D)
Van Bree, Ivan (R)
Vance, Roy Carroll (R)
Wakefield, Helen W (R)
Wallace, Keith Alton (R)
Ward, Aline Frances (R)
Warner, Alvin W (D)
Webb, Susan Howard (R)
Westphal, Fred (R)

VERMONT (cont)
White, Sadie Lucy (D)
Wilson, Leonard Usher (D)
Young, Peter Francis, Jr (D)
Zampieri, John James (D)

VIRGINIA
Abbitt, Watkins Moorman (D)
Ablard, Charles David (R)
Abshire, David Manker (R)
Alcalde, Hector (D)
Aldhizer, George Statton, II (D)
Allen, George Edward, Jr (D)
Almond, James Lindsay, Jr (D)
Anderson, Claude W (Independent)
Anderson, Howard Palmer (D)
Andrews, Hunter Booker (D)
Andrews, Thomas Coleman, Jr (American Party)
Andrews, William Smiley
Ashworth, Luther Ray (D)
Atkinson, Harry Eugene (Independent)
Augustine, Norman Ralph
Axselle, Ralph L, Jr (D)
Babalas, Peter Kostas (D)
Bagley, Richard Marshall (D)
Bain, Carl Edgar (R)
Bain, Mary Anderson (D)
Bakke, Karl Edward (R)
Ball, Robert B, Sr (D)
Barnes, George Francis (R)
Baroody, William J, Jr (R)
Barry, Warren E (R)
Bartlett, Joe (Dorsey Joseph) (R)
Barton, Richard Alan (D)
Bashore, Boyd Truman (Independent)
Bateman, Herbert Harvell (D)
Battle, William Cullen (D)
Baxley, Henry L (D)
Baxter, John T (R)
Beach, Paul Cole, Sr (R)
Bedsaul, E Clifford (R)
Beekman, Robert Earl (D)
Belen, Frederick Christopher (D)
BeLieu, Kenneth Eugene
Bemiss, FitzGerald (R)
Bendheim, Leroy S (D)
Bengston, Gary L (R)
Bergheim, Melvin Lewis (D)
Berry, Edward DeJarnette (D)
Birkhead, Kenneth Milton (D)
Blackmun, Harry Andrew
Blackwell, Morton Clyde (R)
Blackwell, Robert (D)
Blandford, John Russell (R)
Bliley, Thomas J, Jr (Independent)
Blue, Brantley (R)
Bolton, Ann D (R)
Bolton, James Carroll (R)
Bowers, Jack L (R)
Bowles, Lawrence Leonard (R)
Boyd, Robert Stewart (R)
Boyle, Louis Lawrence (D)
Bradford, Robert Edward (R)
Brand, Edward Cabell (D)
Braswell, Thomas Edward, Jr (D)
Brault, Adelard Lionel (D)
Brehm, William Keith
Brizzi, Francis J (D)
Broadbent, Peter Edwin, Jr (R)
Brooke, Albert Bushong, Jr (R)
Brooks, Olive (D)
Brown, Iris Eileen (R)
Brown, William Holmes
Broyhill, Joel T (R)
Brunner, Michael E (R)
Brunthaver, Carroll G (R)
Bryan, Stanley Gatewood (D)
Buchanan, John C (D)
Burchett, Knox Ryan (R)
Burkhardt, Dorothy Jean (R)
Burnett, Benifield (R)
Burruss, Robert S, Jr (R)
Butler, Manley Caldwell (R)
Butterfield, Alexander Porter (Independent)
Byrd, Harry Flood, Jr (Independent)
Byrnes, John William (R)
Cabaniss, Thomas Edward (R)
Callahan, Vincent Francis, Jr (R)
Campbell, Archibald Algernon (D)
Campbell, Leslie Dunlop, Jr (D)
Campbell, Paulina Yager (R)
Canada, Andrew Joseph, Jr (R)
Canaday, Alyce D
Cantrell, Orby Lee (D)
Carlson, John Philip (R)
Carneal, George Upshur, Jr (R)
Carr, Delman R (R)
Carter, Charles Hill, Jr (D)
Carwile, Howard H (Independent)
Casselman, William E, II (R)
Chambers, Ray Benjamin (R)
Charity, Ruth LaCountess Harvey (D)
Clark, John Conrad (D)
Clark, Lawrence Steven (D)
Clarke, Berkley Zacheus, Jr (R)
Coerr, Wymberley DeRenne (Independent)
Cohen, Bernard S (D)
Cohen, Edwin Samuel (R)
Colclough, Andrew Everett (R)
Cole, David A (R)
Coleman, J Marshall (R)
Coleman, John Patrick (D)
Collier, Harold R (R)
Condon, Lester P (Independent)
Cook, Martha Robinson (R)
Cook, Richard K (R)
Cooke, Charles Maynard, Jr (R)
Cooke, John Warren (D)
Copps, Michael Joseph (D)
Corber, Robert Jack (R)
Coulter, Kirkley Schley (R)
Councill, J Paul, Jr (D)
Cowden, Thomas K (R)
Craighead, William Wadell, Jr (D)
Crampton, Scott Paul (R)
Cranwell, C Richard (D)
Crawford, Gary Weldon (D)
Credle, Lola Fish (D)
Creekmore, Frederick Hillary (D)
Croasdale, Carl Palmer (R)
Crockett, Sam L (D)
Crosby, William Duncan, Jr (R)
Croshaw, Glenn Randall (D)
Cunningham, Louise Ware (D)
Curry, Richard Charles (R)
Dalton, John Nichols (R)
Daniel, Robert Williams, Jr (R)
Daniel, W C (Dan) (D)
Darden, Colgate Whitehead, Jr
Davis, Benjamin Oliver, Jr
Davis, Glenn Robert (R)
Day, James MacDonald (R)
Dean, Alan L (D)
DeBolt, Edward S (R)
DeBruhl, Garry Glenn (D)
Delyannis, Leonidas T (R)
Diamonstein, Alan Arnold (D)
Dickerman, Charles Pingrey (D)
Dickinson, R Dorothea (R)
Dickinson, Vivian Earl (D)
Dillard, James H, II (R)
Dingman, Richard B
Disston, Harry (R)
Dotson, Bobby Joe (R)
Dotson, J Ray (R)
Doumar, Robert George (R)
Downing, Thomas N (D)
Dunford, Charles Donald (D)
Dunning, Jean Douglas (D)
Durrette, Wyatt Beazley, Jr (R)
DuVal, Clive L, 2d (D)
Duvall, Charles Raymond, Jr (D)
Dwight, James S, Jr (R)
Eagleburger, Lawrence Sidney (R)
Echols, M Patton, Jr (R)
Edmunds, James T (D)
Ehlman, Carolyn (Jean) (R)
Elliott, Richard Wyatt (R)
Elliott, Robert R (R)
Elliott, Roland L (R)
Emroch, Walter H (D)
Evans, John Marion (R)
Failor, Edward Dale, Sr (R)
Fairbanks, Linda Gay (D)
Fasser, Paul, Jr (D)
Fears, William Earl (D)
Fern, Benjamin R
Fickett, Lewis Perley, Jr (D)
Fisher, Joseph Lyman (D)
Fitzpatrick, Charles Henry (R)
Fitzpatrick, Joseph (D)
Flemming, Arthur Sherwood (R)
Flemming, Harry S (R)
Fletcher, James Chipman
Fletcher, Virginia Carol (D)
Fletcher, W Fred (D)
Foreman, E David, Jr (R)
Fowler, Calvin W (Independent)
Fowler, Henry Hamill (D)
Freburg, Charles Raymond (R)
French, Warren B, Jr (R)
Friedersdorf, Max Lee (R)
Friedheim, Jerry Warden (R)
Fritter, Lindbergh Alexander (R)
Frizzell, Dale Kent (R)
Frye, Charles Alton (R)
Fulton, Curtis Ray (R)
Galbraith, James Ronald (R)
Gallagher, Harold Milton (R)
Gants, Robert Monte (R)
Garland, Frances Vaughan (R)
Garland, Ray Lucian (R)
Gartlan, Joseph V, Jr (D)
Gartner, David G (D)
Gehrig, James Joseph (D)
Geisler, Jerry Hubert (R)
Gentry, Richard Hayden (Libertarian)
Gibson, Donald Bancroft (D)
Gladding, Harry Tilden, Jr (R)
Glasscock, James Samuel (D)
Glenn, Robert Eastwood (R)
Godsey, Andrew Emmett (D)
Godwin, Mills Edwin, Jr (D)
Goode, Virgil H Sr (D)
Goode, Virgil Hamlin, Jr (D)
Graboyes, Robert Francis (D)
Graham, Alfred Curtis (R)
Gray, Elmon T (D)
Gray, Frederick Thomas (D)
Gray, John David (D)
Grayson, George W (D)
Greener, William Isaac, Jr (R)
Gregson, Mary Poage (R)
Guest, Raymond Richard, Jr (R)
Gunn, Charles Wesley, Jr (D)
Guntharp, Walter Andrew (R)
Gwathmey, Robert Ryland, III (D)
Haffner, Ann Duncan (R)
Hailey, Evelyn Momsen (D)
Hainsworth, Brad E (R)
Hall, Albert Carruthers (R)
Hall, Virginia McDaniel (D)
Hancock, Clara C (R)
Harding, Kenneth R (D)
Harding, Margaret Katherine (Marty) (D)
Hardy, Porter, Jr (D)
Harllee, John (D)
Harris, Fred R (D)
Harris, Herbert E, II (D)
Harris, Robert E (R)
Harrison, Albertis Sydney, Jr (D)
Harveycutter, Robert Carey, Jr (D)
Hecht, Christine Sigrid (D)
Heffelfinger, William Stewart
Heilig, George H, Jr (D)
Helms, James Marvin, Jr (R)
Henry, John Hugh (D)
Henshaw, Edmund Lee, Jr (D)
Henson, Gerald L (R)
Herringer, Frank Casper (R)
Heterick, Robert Cary, Jr (R)
Hirst, Nancy Melrose (D)
Hirst, Omer Lee (D)
Hodges, William Howard (D)
Holland, Edward McHarg (D)
Holton, A Linwood, Jr (R)
Hopkins, William Benjamin (D)
Horne, Charles J (D)
Houff, Mary Frances (D)
Howell, Henry Evans, Jr (Independent)
Huffman, Donald Wise (R)
Hutcherson, Nathan B, Jr (D)
Hutton, E M (Tiny) (D)
James, Joseph Sheppard (D)
James, L Eldon (D)
Jennings, William Pat (D)
Johnson, Augustus Clark (D)
Johnson, J Wallace (D)
Johnson, Joseph A (D)
Johnson, Stephen R (Bart) (D)
Johnson, Wallace Harold, Jr (R)
Jones, George Wilson (R)
Jones, James Parker (D)
Jones, Joan S (D)
Jones, Larry Mallory (D)
Kaufman, Irene Mathias (R)
Kaupinen, Allan George (R)
Kay, Thomas Oliver (R)
Kearney, Daniel Patrick (R)
Keefe, Robert Joseph (D)
Keenan, Thomas Le Roy (D)
Kieffer, Jarold A (R)
Kindt, Lois Jeannette (R)
Kling, William Holt (R)
Knutson, Ronald Dale (R)
Koplan, Stephen (D)
Kopp, Eugene Paul (R)
Kostopulos, Nicholas Peter, Sr (D)
Krout, Homer Lee (R)
Kuhn, Janet Lammersen (R)

Kuykendall, Jerome Kenneth (R)
LaBerge, Walter B
Lambert, William Chesley (R)
Lampe, Henry Oscar (R)
Lane, Edward E (D)
Langley, Lawrence DeSales (D)
LaPlante, Bryan Franklin (R)
Lausi, Anthony Thomas (R)
Leafe, Joseph A (D)
Lechner, Ira Mark (D)
Leddy, John M (Independent)
Leggitt, Richard Baumgardner (R)
LeKander, Gilbert (R)
Lemmon, Willard Lincoln (D)
Leppert, Charles Jr (R)
LeRoy, L David (R)
Lewis, E Grey (R)
Lewis, Roger Keith (D)
Lisk, David Kenneth (R)
Livingston, Schuyler William, Jr (D)
Loomis, Henry (Independent)
Loring, Murray (D)
Ludden, Barbara Ann Harrison (R)
Lustig, Wayne (R)
Lyng, Richard (R)
Lyons, William Watson
Macaulay, Angus Hamilton (D)
Macy, John Williams Jr (D)
Madson, Gary Kent (R)
Mahe, Henry Edward Jr (Eddie) (R)
Manasco, Carter (D)
Mann, Frank E (D)
Manning, L Cleaves (D)
Manns, Paul W (D)
Mansfield, Donald William (D)
Markow, Theodore Joseph (D)
Marks, Charles Hardaway (D)
Marsh, John O, Jr (D)
Marshall, Mary Aydelotte (D)
Marshall, Thurgood
Martin, John Marshall, Jr (D)
Martin, Roy Butler, Jr (D)
Marye, Madison Ellis (D)
Mathias, Robert Bruce (R)
Mathisen, Chris
May, Clarence Edward (D)
Mazan, Walter L (R)
McClanan, Glenn B (D)
McClary, Terence E (D)
McCoy, R V, Jr (R)
McCulloch, Frank W (D)
McCutcheon, Andrew H, Jr (D)
McDiarmid, Dorothy Shoemaker (D)
McGhee, George Crews
McGlothlin, Donald A, Sr (D)
McIlvaine, Stevenson (D)
McKenna, Willafay H (D)
McLucas, John L (R)
McMath, George Nottingham (R)
McMurran, Lewis Archer, Jr (D)
McMurtrie, Alexander B, Jr (D)
McNamara, Thomas R (D)
Meagher, John Kirby (R)
Melnick, John Latane (D)
Menaker, Edward Goward (D)
Mercuro, Tobia Gustave (R)
Michael, James Harry, Jr (D)
Michie, Thomas Johnson, Jr
Middendorf, John William, II (R)
Miles, William Joseph (D)
Miller, Andrew Pickens (D)

Miller, Clinton (R)
Miller, Joseph S (D)
Miller, Kevin Grey (R)
Miller, Nathan H (R)
Milstead, George L (D)
Mittelman, Eugene (R)
Montague, David Nicholls (R)
Montgomery, Harold Ronnie (R)
Moody, Willard James (D)
Moot, Robert C (D)
Morrill, William A (R)
Morris, Barbara Lee Pickeral (D)
Morrison, Theodore V, Jr (D)
Moss, Thomas Warren, Jr (D)
Moyle, Sandra Kay (D)
Munsey, Everard (D)
Murphy, Betty Southard (R)
Murphy, John F (R)
Murphy, Richard E (D)
Murphy, Rupert Leo
Murphy, William R (Independent)
Murray, James B (D)
Murray, Thad S (Independent)
Musch, Donald John (R)
Neblett, William Edwin (D)
Nelson, Sheila Diane (D)
Newman, Cynthia Stair (R)
Nicholas, Harry K (R)
Nickerson, Herman, Jr (R)
Nolan, David Brian (R)
Norton, William George (R)
Nutter, Gilbert Warren (R)
Nutter, Lloyd Broderick (D)
Obenshain, Richard Dudley (R)
O'Brien, J W, Jr (D)
Owens, Peggy Joyce (D)
Owens, Stanley Albert (D)
Palumbo, Benjamin Lewis (D)
Parker, Lewis W, Jr (D)
Parkerson, William Francis, Jr (D)
Parris, Stanford E (R)
Pattisall, Richard Chapman (D)
Pearson, Ronald Walfrid (R)
Pendergraft, Phyllis M (R)
Pendleton, Donald Grey (D)
Pennington, William Alton (Independent)
Pepitone, Byron Vincent (R)
Perkinson, Patricia Royal (Independent)
Phillips, Channing Emery (D)
Phillips, Charles Franklin, Jr (R)
Philpott, Albert Lee (D)
Pickett, Owen Bradford (D)
Pilot, Lynne Joyce (D)
Plummer, James Walter
Poff, Richard H (R)
Pointer, James Edgar, Jr (D)
Pollard, Violet McDougall (D)
Pommerening, Glen Edwin
Potter, David Samuel (R)
Potter, Irwin Lee (R)
Powell, Lewis F, Jr
Powell, Martha Brown (R)
Pranger, Robert John (Independent)
Pringle, Avis Weaver (R)
Puryear, Byron Nelson (D)
Putney, Lacey Edward (Independent)
Pyle, Howard, III (R)
Quillen, Ford C (D)
Quinn, Robert E (D)
Ragsdale, Edwin H (R)
Ranson, Samuel Lee (R)
Rattley, Jessie Menifield (D)
Rawlings, George Chancellor, Jr (D)
Rawlings, William Vincent (D)

Reberger, J Philip (R)
Redman, Charles Lee, Jr (D)
Reese, Matthew Anderson (D)
Rehnquist, William Hubbs
Reida, Larry (R)
Reston, Tom (D)
Reynolds, Randall O (D)
Rhinelander, John Bassett (R)
Rhodes, Donald H (D)
Rhodes, Fred Burnett (R)
Rice, Walter Lyman (R)
Richards, Pamela Jane
Richardson, John, Jr (R)
Riddleberger, James W
Ritchie, John, Jr (R)
Robertson, James Taylor, Jr (D)
Robinson, James Kenneth (R)
Robinson, William Peters, Sr (D)
Robrecht, Raymond R (R)
Roff, Hadley Rea (D)
Rogers, Will (D)
Rogers, William Dill
Rollins, Kenneth B (Independent)
Rose, Kathleen Blount (R)
Rosenberger, Francis Coleman (D)
Rothrock, Thomas Jefferson (D)
Rountree, William Clifford
Rousek, Robert Ronald (R)
Rove, Karl Christian (R)
Rustad, Elmer Lewis (R)
Sacks, Stanley Elliott (D)
Sanders, Donald Gilbert (R)
Sanford, Calvin G (R)
Santarelli, Donald Eugene (R)
Satterfield, David E, III (D)
Sayre, Robert Marion
Schlesinger, James Rodney (R)
Schlitz, Lester E (D)
Schubert, Richard Francis
Scott, L O (Independent)
Scott, William L (R)
Seeger, Christopher Clark (R)
Seevers, Gary Leonard (Independent)
Shenefield, John Hale (D)
Sheppard, Eleanor Parker (D)
Shrontz, Frank Anderson (R)
Shull, Edd L (R)
Shultz, George Pratt
Sieminski, Alfred D (D)
Silberman, Jay Elliott (D)
Simon, William E
Sinclair, Ivan Earl (D)
Sisisky, Norman (I)
Slaughter, Daniel French, Jr (Independent)
Slayton, Frank M (D)
Smith, Alson H, Jr (D)
Smith, Claude Harman (R)
Smith, Harold Selwyn (D)
Smith, Howard Worth (D)
Smith, James Roswell (R)
Smyth, John R (R)
Snipes, Juanita Krentzman (D)
Solomon, Erwin S (D)
Southall, Walter Delbert (D)
Spong, William Belser, Jr (D)
Srull, Donald W (Independent)
Stafford, Chester Jefferson (R)
Stambaugh, Warren Glenn (D)
Stanhagen, William Harold (R)
Stephens, Vern (R)
Stewart, Carlyle Veeder, Jr (Lyle) (R)
Stewart, Paul Morton, Jr (R)
Stiner, James Edward, Jr (R)
Stitt, Lyle H (D)
Stodart, William Edward (R)

Stone, Ann Elizabeth (Bitsey) (R)
Stong, Benton J (D)
Stratton, Edith Lou (R)
Strawn, Oliver Perry, Jr (R)
Swezey, John William (R)
Swift, Ivan
Tate, James R (R)
Taylor, David Peter
Teague, Randal Cornell (R)
Teel, Ward
Terry, Clara Delle (Mrs Douglas Macrae) (R)
Thomas, Alfred Victor (D)
Thomas, William G (D)
Thompson, John Roger (R)
Thomson, James McIlhany (D)
Thornton, David F (R)
Tidwell, Drew Virgil, III (R)
Townsend, Russell I, Jr (D)
Traylor, Lawrence Milton (R)
Truban, William A (R)
Tsompanas, Paul Lee (R)
Tsutras, Frank Gus (D)
Tuck, William Munford (D)
Tucker, Gardiner Luttrell (R)
Turner, Edward Milner, Jr (R)
Twinam, Joseph Wright (D)
Underwood, Malcolm Stanley, Jr (R)
Van Clief, Daniel Good (D)
Van Hoy, John Hobert (R)
Velde, Richard Whittington
Verkler, Jerry Thomas (D)
Vickery, Raymond Ezekiel, Jr (D)
Waddell, Charles L (D)
Walker, Stanley Clay (D)
Wallace, Carl S (R)
Wallace, Robert Thomas (R)
Walters, Johnnie McKeiver (R)
Walton, Edmund Lewis, Jr (R)
Wampler, William Creed (Bill) (R)
Warner, John William (R)
Warren, George Marvin, Jr (D)
Warriner, D Dortch (R)
Washburn, C Langhorne (R)
Washington, Robert E (D)
Watkins, Dorothea Henness Fancher (R)
Watson, William Abner, Jr (D)
Waugh, William M (R)
Webber, Frederick Leroy (R)
Welch, Bette B (R)
Welsh, William Brownlee (D)
West, Quentin Mecham
Wev, Oscar C B (R)
White, John Thomas, II (R)
White, Joshua Warren, Jr (D)
Whitehead, William Scholl (R)
Whitehouse, Charles Sheldon
Whitehurst, George William (R)
Whitlock, Willie Walker (D)
Wilder, Lawrence Douglas (D)
Willey, Edward Eugene (D)
Williams, Ann Cole (D)
Williams, Carrington (D)
Williams, Glen Morgan (R)
Williams, John William, III (D)
Williams, Lee (D)
Willoughby, William Howard (R)
Wilson, Irl Donaker (D)
Wilson, Samuel Benjamin, Jr (D)
Wilson, William Thomas (D)
Wilt, Katherine Arthur (D)
Witman, William, II
Woodruff, William A (R)
Woodrum, Clifton Alexander, III (D)
Wright, Joseph R, Jr (R)

VIRGINIA (cont)
Yeatts, Coleman B (D)
Young, J Banks (D)
Young, John Donald
Zack, Eugene C (D)
Zimmerman, Harry Walter, Jr (R)

WASHINGTON
Adams, A A (D)
Adams, Alfred O (R)
Adams, Brockman (Brock) (D)
Albrecht, Richard Raymond (R)
Albright, Albion D (D)
Allen, David Bliss (R)
Amen, Otto (R)
Ancker-Johnson, Betsy (R)
Andelin, John Philip, Jr
Anderson, Gwen Adele (R)
Armijo Rosalio (Rosey) (D)
Austin, Russell Anderson, Jr (R)
Baarsma, William Henry (D)
Bagnariol, John A (D)
Bailey, Robert C (D)
Barer, Stanley Harris (D)
Barnes, Richard O (R)
Bauer, Albert N, Jr (D)
Bausch, Del (D)
Beck, Clifford Wallace (Red) (D)
Becker, Mary Kay (D)
Bedell, Catherine Barnes (R)
Bedrossian, Robert Haig (R)
Bender, Rick S (D)
Benitz, Max Edward (R)
Berentson, Duane (R)
Blair, Scott (R)
Bluechel, Alan Joseph (R)
Bockemuehl, Richard George (R)
Boersma, P Dee (R)
Boldt, Jim (D)
Bond, Richard Milton (R)
Bonker, Don L (D)
Bottiger, R Ted (D)
Brachtenbach, Robert F (R)
Bratton, Robert Wells (R)
Brooks, Tom (R)
Brouillet, Frank B (D)
Brown, Arthur C (R)
Buckridge, Marilyn L (D)
Buffington, Nancy Catherine (R)
Bullock, George Daniel (R)
Butenko, Constantine (R)
Caufield, Judith Ann (R)
Ceccarelli, David Paul (D)
Chandler, Rodney Dennis (R)
Chaney, Neale V (D)
Chapman, Bruce K (R)
Charette, Robert L (D)
Charnley, Donn (D)
Chase, Anthony Goodwin (R)
Chatalas, William (Bill) (D)
Cherberg, John Andrew (D)
Claplanhoo, Edward E (D)
Clarke, George W (R)
Clement, Alfred William (Bill), Jr (D)
Clemente, Art (D)
Cleveland, Dorothy Haskell (R)
Cochrane, Pat (D)
Coe, Donald Melvin (D)
Coffee, John Main (D)
Cole, Bert L (D)
Conner, Paul H (D)
Cooley, George Edward (D)
Cunningham, John (Jack) (R)

Curtis, Bob (R)
Dahl, Allen W (R)
Dailey, Mitch R (D)
Davidson, Robert W (R)
Davis, Claudine (D)
Davis, Ross E (R)
Day, William S (Bill) (D)
Deccio, Alex A (R)
Deife, Marcine Delores (R)
DeLeo, James Anthony (D)
Derham, Richard Andrew (R)
Derzai, Amy Ruth (D)
Dicks, Norman Devalois (D)
Dill, Clarence C (D)
Dolliver, James Morgan (R)
Donohue, Hubert Francis (D)
Douglas, William Orville (D)
Douthwaite, Geoffrey K (Jeff) (D)
Drumheller, Helen E (Betty) (D)
Dunlap, Ron (D)
Durkan, Martin James (D)
Edmondson, Betty Lavern (R)
Ehlers, Wayne (D)
Eikenberry, Kenneth Otto (R)
Eldridge, Don D (R)
Eldridge, Nanci Jane (R)
Eliassen, Herb O (R)
Elich, Jack Frank (D)
Eng, John Sy (D)
Erickson, Phyllis K (D)
Evans, Daniel Jackson (R)
Fanning, Charles Theodore (R)
Finn, John Patrick (D)
Fischer, John M (R)
Flanagan, Sid (R)
Fleming, George (D)
Fletcher, Arthur Allen (R)
Foley, Thomas Stephen (D)
Fortson, Eleanor Ann (D)
Francis, Peter David (D)
Freeman, Kemper, Jr (R)
Fullmer, Donald K (R)
Gaines, Robert E (D)
Gallagher, P J (Jim) (D)
Gaspard, Marcus Stuart (D)
Giles, Dennis Earl (D)
Gilleland, James E (R)
Goltz, H A (Barney) (D)
Gorton, Slade (R)
Gould, Sue (R)
Gowdey, Dwight M (D)
Graham, Lloyd Kenneth (Luke) (D)
Graham, Luke (D)
Graham, Robert Vincent (D)
Grant, Gary S (D)
Greengo, Irving (R)
Grier, George Edward (D)
Guess, Sam C (R)
Gunn, George, Jr (R)
Haley, Ted (R)
Hanna, Ron (D)
Hansen, Frank (Tub) (D)
Hansen, Julia Butler (D)
Hansey, Donald G (R)
Harris, Daniel Sherman, Jr (R)
Haussler, Joe D (D)
Hawkins, John Richard (D)
Haydon, John M (R)
Hayner, Jeannette C (R)
Heater, Elliott Vermont, Jr (R)
Heavey, Thomas Randal (D)
Hendricks, John Lyle (R)
Henry, Al (D)
Herr, Gordon (R)
Herrmann, Karl (D)
Hicks, Floyd V (D)
Hood, George Hay (R)
Howell, Richard S (R)
Hunter, Robert Thomas
Hurley, George S (D)

Hurley, Mrs Joseph E (D)
Indermuhle, Martha A (D)
Ison, Margaret A (R)
Jackson, Henry M (D)
Jastad, Elmer (D)
Johnston, Kenneth Darwin, Jr (D)
Jolly, Dan (D)
Jones, J L (D)
Jones, John D (R)
Jueling, Helmut L (R)
Kalich, Hugh Edward (D)
Kalivas, Dean Spiro (R)
Keefe, James Edward (D)
Keller, Frank L (D)
Keller, Ronald L (D)
Kelley, Richard Charles (D)
Kilbury, Charles Debriel (D)
King, Jason William
King, Marjorie Pitter (D)
King, Richard Arthur (D)
Kiss, Louise (D)
Knoblauch, Reuben A (D)
Knowles, Walt O (D)
Kragtorp, Norma Marie (D)
Kramer, A Ludlow, III (R)
Krueger, Phillip H (D)
Kuehnle, James Paul (R)
Lapham, Harry Houston, Jr (R)
Laughlin, Eugene L (D)
Leckenby, William (R)
Lee, Eleanor (R)
Lewis, Fred Cole (D)
Lewis, Harry B (R)
Lewis, R H (Bob) (R)
Lickar, John Ivan (D)
Lindjord, Haakon
Lockyear, Ralph Alan (R)
Luders, Edward T (D)
Lysen, King (D)
Mackey, Ralph Earle (R)
Magnuson, Donald Hammer (D)
Magnuson, Warren Grant (D)
Maloney, Thomas M (D)
Marchioro, Karen Louise (D)
Marsh, Daniel G (D)
Martinis, John Anthony (D)
Matson, Jim (R)
Matthews, Gary Lee (R)
Mattingly, Michael William (R)
Maxie, Peggy Joan (D)
May, William J S (D)
McCarthy, Thomas Carrell (D)
McConnaughey, Douglas Steven (D)
McCormack, Mike (D)
McCormick, Heraldine (D)
McDermott, Jim (D)
McDougall, Jacquelyn Horan (R)
McGee, Arthur Marion (D)
McGregor, Nancy Rohwer (R)
McKay, Bruce Alan (D)
McKenzie, William Irving (D)
McKibbin, John S (D)
McQuillen, Mary Theresa (D)
Meadowcroft, William Howarth (R)
Meeds, Lloyd (D)
Metcalf, Jack Holace (R)
Mickelson, Bob J (D)
Miller, Norman Rodney (D)
Mitchell, Hugh Burnton (D)
Mitzner, Janice L (D)
Montchalin, Yvonne (R)
Moon, Charles (D)
Moore, C Robert
Moos, Donald William (R)
Moreau, Art (D)
Morgen, Gladys H (D)
Morrison, Sid (R)
Murphy, Joseph E, Jr (D)

Murray, John S (R)
Neils, Betty Jo (R)
Nelson, Gary Alfred (R)
Nelson, Helen M (R)
Nelson, James Lee (R)
Newhouse, Irving R (R)
Newschwander, Charles E (R)
North, Frances C (D)
North, Lois (R)
Nuckolls, Kenneth Russell (R)
Oberquell, Diane (D)
O'Brien, John L (D)
O'Brien, Robert S (D)
Odegaard, Gary Martin (R)
Odell, Charles (R)
Olkonen, Elsie Swan (D)
Olson, Gary Miles (R)
O'Neal, Arthur Daniel, Jr (D)
Outland, George E (D)
Pardini, A J (Bud) (R)
Paris, William (Bill) (R)
Parker, Mike (D)
Patterson, E G (Pat) (R)
Perry, Robert A (D)
Peterson, Lowell (D)
Peterson, Warren Edward (R)
Pithoud, Naida (D)
Polk, William Merrill (R)
Prince, Eugene Augustus (R)
Prins, John, Jr (R)
Pritchard, Joel M (R)
Pullen, Kent (R)
Randall, Robert White (D)
Rasmussen, A L (Slim) (D)
Ray, Dixy Lee
Reed, Glenn Edward (R)
Reed, Sam Sumner (R)
Revelle, Randy (D)
Ridder, Ruthe B (D)
Rivers, Ralph Julian (D)
Roberts, James William (R)
Robinson, Errol Wayne (R)
Rodgers, David H (R)
Rosellini, Albert D (D)
Rosellini, Evelyn Elizabeth (D)
Royce, Frederick Henry (R)
Saari, Leonard W (D)
Saari, Ruth Desiree (D)
Sandison, Gordon (D)
Sattler, Keith Paul (D)
Savage, Charles R (D)
Sawyer, Leonard Alson (D)
Scalia, Robert Charles (R)
Schumaker, Wm (Bill) (R)
Schuster, John Conrad (R)
Scott, George William (R)
Seeberger, Edward D (R)
Sellar, George L (R)
Sherman, Marion Kyle (D)
Shinpoch, A N (Bud) (D)
Slagle, David Lewis (R)
Smith, Edward Patrick (D)
Smith, Rick (D)
Smith, Samuel J (Sam)
Sommers, Helen Elizabeth (D)
Startup, Vivian Margaret (D)
Stender, John H (R)
Stern, Bernice F (D)
Stith, Harvard C (R)
Stortini, Joe (D)
Stripp, Jane Dearborn (R)
Swayze, Thomas Allen, Jr
Talley, Don L (D)
Thompson, Alan (D)
Tilly, Anne Petersen (D)
Tilly, Earl F (R)
Timm, Robert Dale (R)
Tollefson, Thor Carl (R)
Tracy, William Allan (D)
Uhlman, Wesley Carl (D)
Utter, Robert French
Valle, Georgette (D)
Van Dyk, Jerilyn K (D)

Van Hollebeke, Ray (D)
Vekich, Max Milan, Jr (D)
Von Reichbauer, Peter (D)
Walgren, Gordon Lee (D)
Wanamaker, Floyd Allison (Pat) (R)
Warnke, Frank J (D)
Washington, Nat Willis (D)
Weber, Mary E (D)
Wexler, Eileen Lugar (R)
Weyrich, James Henry (R)
Whiteside, Jim (R)
Williams, Al (D)
Williams, Jeanette K (D)
Williams, W Walter (R)
Wilson, Bruce A (D)
Wilson, James (R)
Wilson, Simeon R (Sim) (R)
Windsheimer, Walter W (R)
Wojahn, Lorraine (D)
Woody, Frank (D)
Wright, Charles T
Zepeda, Barbara Joyce (D)
Zimmerman, Harold Samuel (R)

WEST VIRGINIA

Albright, Joseph Paul (D)
Allen, Charles Edgar (D)
Allen, Elton Ellsworth (R)
Altmeyer, James Emerson (R)
Artrip, William James, Jr (D)
Bailey, Harley Evan (D)
Bailey, Jean (D)
Bain, Charles Robert (R)
Ballouz, Joseph M (D)
Beall, Russell G (D)
Bell, Tom M (D)
Benson, Richard (R)
Berry, Thornton Granville, Jr (D)
Bird, Stephen Crabtree (D)
Bloch, Stuart Fulton (R)
Boettner, John Lewis, Jr (D)
Brenda, Gust Gottlieb, Jr (D)
Brotherton, W T, Jr (D)
Brown, Ralph (D)
Brown, Virginia Mae (D)
Browning, Chauncey H, Jr (D)
Bryan, Elton Eugene (D)
Bryant, Carl P (D)
Bumgarner, Carroll E (D)
Burke, Billy Brown (D)
Burke, Jerome A (D)
Burke, Robert James (D)
Burleson, Dan L (D)
Byrd, Robert C (D)
Calhoun, Harlan Mayberry (D)
Canfield, Jack (D)
Castleberry, Kelly L (D)
Caudle, Joseph Edward (D)
Chafin, Gerald L (D)
Childers, Robert Lee (D)
Christian, Clarence Carr, Jr (D)
Christian, Maud Truby (D)
Copeland, Leon Troy (D)
Corcoran, Howard V (R)
Cox, Ernie E (D)
Crabtree, Burnie R (D)
Crabtree, Paul Leonard (D)
Crandall, Ethel Leanna (D)
Dalton, Sammy Dale (D)
Damron, Charles Hoadley (D)
Damron, Irvine Keith (D)
Darby, Howard Darrel (D)
D'Aurora, Mino Rocco (D)
Davis, James L (D)
Deem, J Frank (R)
Dillon, J C, Jr (D)
Dinsmore, Robert W (D)

DiTrapano, Rudolph Lidano (D)
Donley, Charles Earl (D)
Douglass, Gus R (D)
Doyle, Robert John (D)
Elkins, Randall Scott (D)
Erdie, Romeo D (D)
Esposito, Albert C (R)
Fanning, John Patton (D)
Fantasia, Nick (D)
Farley, George Edward (D)
Fitzgerald, John E (D)
Floyd, Noah Eugene (D)
Fry, Lucian (D)
Gainer, Carl E (D)
Galperin, Si Hirsch, Jr (D)
Gibson, Jarrett Dempsey (D)
Gill, Betty (D)
Gilliam, Charles (D)
Gilligan, William Lee (R)
Given, D P (Sheriff) (D)
Given, Phyllis E (D)
Gladwell, Beatrice Howard (R)
Goe, William Robert (D)
Goforth, Ray A (D)
Goldstrom, Allen E (R)
Goodwin, Joseph Robert (D)
Goodwin, Thomas G (D)
Gvoyich, George Paul (D)
Hagedorn, Clyde William (D)
Hamilton, Helen Packer (D)
Hamilton, Pat R (D)
Harman, Charlton Newton (R)
Harman, Robert Dale (D)
Hart, Thomas Daniel (D)
Hartman, Bette Rae (R)
Hatfield, Robert F (D)
Hechler, Ken (D)
Heiskell, Edgar Frank, III (R)
Herndon, Judith A (R)
Hinkle, J D, Jr (R)
Holliday, Joseph R (D)
Holmes, Darrell E (D)
Huffman, Odell Hampton (D)
Huggins, James Bernard (D)
Humphreys, Priscilla Faith (R)
Humphreys, Raymond V (R)
Hutchinson, John Guiher (D)
Hutto, Thomas Augustus (D)
Jennings, Rudolph Dillon (D)
Johnson, E M (D)
Jones, Cleo Sattis (R)
Jones, James Roydice (R)
Jones, Orton Alan (R)
Jones, Terry T (R)
Kantor, Isaac Norris (D)
Kaufman, Paul Joseph (D)
Kee, Elizabeth (D)
Kee, James (D)
Kelly, John Henry (D)
Kincaid, Hugh Arthur (D)
Kopp, Donald Lee (D)
Kusic, Samuel N (R)
Kyer, Harry Franklin (R)
Leonard, Louise (R)
Leonhart, William (Independent)
LePore, Ralph Frank (D)
Lewis, Sterling T (D)
Lohr, Charles E (D)
Long, Hilda Sheets (D)
Love, Shirley Dean (D)
Lowther, Dale Charles (D)
Lucento, Jane (D)
Mathis, Thomas W (D)
Matthews, Virgil Edison, Jr (D)
McCuskey, John F (R)
McDonald, John Wesley (D)
McDonough, Robert Paul (D)
McGraw, Warren Randolph (D)
McKown, Edward G (R)
McLaughlin, J Kemp (R)

McManus, Lewis Nichols (D)
McNeely, James W (D)
McQuade, Marian Herndon (R)
Miller, Harlan Walter (D)
Miller, Richard L (D)
Miller, Robert Bates, Jr (D)
Milleson, William Thomas (D)
Millican, Manyon Meadows (R)
Mitchell, Bryan Franklin (R)
Moats, Harry E (R)
Moler, James M (D)
Mollohan, Robert H (D)
Moore, Arch A, Jr (R)
Moore, Ernest C (D)
Morasco, Samuel A (D)
Moreland, William Alexander (D)
Mowery, Morris Everett (D)
Moyle, Michael J (R)
Myles, Thomas Eberly (D)
Neal, Sarah Lee (D)
Neeley, W Walter (D)
Neely, Richard (D)
Nelson, Robert R (D)
Nicely, William Perry Amos (R)
Oates, William J, Jr (D)
Ogden, Barbara Lynn (R)
Otte, Paul Joseph (R)
Palumbo, Mario Joseph (D)
Patterson, John Gerald (R)
Pauley, Jack L (D)
Payne, John Franklin (D)
Peak, Raymond (D)
Phillips, Willard L, Jr (Bill) (R)
Pitsenberger, Julia Lockridge (D)
Polan, Charles M, Jr (D)
Potter, Thomas Eugene (R)
Powell, JoAnne (D)
Prestera, G Michele (D)
Protan, John (D)
Pyles, John W (D)
Rahall, Nick Joe, II (D)
Randolph, Jennings (D)
Reese, Paul Francis (D)
Revercomb, Chapman (R)
Roberts, James Hazelton (R)
Rockefeller, John Davison, IV (D)
Rogers, J Robert (D)
Rogerson, Roy Harold (R)
Rollins, Walter (D)
Romine, Charles Everett, Jr (R)
Sattes, Frederick Lyle (D)
Savilla, Roland (D)
Scott, Thomas Jackson (D)
See, Clyde M, Jr (D)
Seibert, George H (R)
Shaffer, Charles Raymond (R)
Sharpe, William R, Jr (D)
Shepherd, Walton (D)
Shiflet, W Marion (D)
Shingleton, William Earl (D)
Shott, John Cary (R)
Shuman, Pamela Sue (D)
Sinicropi, Michael Wilson (D)
Sisler, John Millard (R)
Slack, John M, Jr (D)
Smith, Donald Albert (R)
Smith, Guy Ross (D)
Smith, Hulett Carlson (D)
Snyder, Melvin Claud (R)
Sommerville, A L, Jr (D)
Sonis, Lawrence Berton (Larry) (D)
Spears, Jae (D)
Stacy, Ted Theodore (D)
Staggers, Harley Orrin (D)
Stamp, Frederick P, Jr (R)
Stanley, Miles Clark (D)
Stenglein, Mary Paschaline (DFL)

Steptoe, Robert M (D)
Susman, Alan L (D)
Swann, Larry D (R)
Teets, James W (R)
Terry, Luke E (R)
Tomblin, Earl Ray (D)
Tompkins, Roger William (D)
Tompos, William (D)
Toney, Adam (D)
Tonkovich, Dan Richard (D)
Tyson, Richard Eugene (R)
Underwood, Cecil Harland (R)
Underwood, Forest (D)
Wanstreet, Clarence Paul (D)
Ward, Kenneth Vandiver (D)
Ward, Lafe P (D)
Watson, William Edward (D)
Wehrle, Martha Gaines (D)
Wells, Hawey A, Jr (D)
Wells, John Marvin (R)
Wiedebusch, Larry (D)
Wilkinson, Richard Warren (R)
Williams, Ralph Dale (D)
Willis, Todd C (D)
Wilson, W R (Squibb) (D)
Wilt, Thornton W (D)
Winner, Thomas Andrew (D)
Winter, Thomas Duane (R)
Withrow, Mrs W W (Jackie) (D)
Worden, Donza T (D)
Wright, Lacy, Jr (D)

WISCONSIN

Allen, John Neville (R)
Allin, Lyndon King (Mort) (R)
Anderson, Daniel Philip (D)
Anderson, John Edward (D)
Anderson, Lyman Frank (R)
Anderson, Norman Carl (D)
Andresen, Karl Adolf (D)
Andringa, Cornelius George (R)
Arts, James L (D)
Aspin, Les (D)
Atkinson, Thomas George (Non-Partisan)
Ausman, LaVerne G (R)
Azim, James N, Jr (R)
Bablitch, William A (D)
Baker, William Allen, Jr (D)
Baldus, Alvin (D)
Baltz, Walter F (R)
Barbee, Lloyd Augustus (D)
Barberg, William Warren (R)
Barth, Thomas Emil (D)
Bauer, Armand W (D)
Baumgartner, Stephen Eldon (D)
Beck, Sidney Franklin, Jr (R)
Behnke, Robert E (D)
Beilfuss, Bruce F
Beistle, James H (R)
Berg, Oscar W (D)
Berger, David George (D)
Bibby, John Franklin (R)
Bidwell, Everett V (R)
Bishop, Bradley Charles (R)
Bleicher, Michael N (D)
Boileau, Gerald John (Non-Partisan)
Boltz, Richard Alan (R)
Bosshard, Rylla Jane (R)
Bradley, Gordon Roy (R)
Brown, Jeffrey Michael (Libertarian)
Browne, Jerome Fielding (D)
Brozek, Michael Francis (D)
Brunner, Frank, Jr (R)
Brunner, Merlin A (R)

1088 / GEOGRAPHIC INDEX

WISCONSIN (cont)
Buehler, Paul Richard (D)
Bunn, George (D)
Bureta, Lynn Marie (D)
Burg, Mary Lou (D)
Burkee, Wallace E (Non-Partisan)
Burris, Richard S (R)
Byers, Francis Robert (R)
Carter, David R (D)
Castro, Albert C (D)
Cherkasky, William Benjamin (D)
Chickering, Robert L (D)
Chilsen, Walter John (R)
Clarenbach, David E (D)
Colcord, Harry Henry (D)
Conradt, Ervin W (R)
Conta, Dennis J (D)
Conway, John (R)
Copps, Lyman William (R)
Cornell, Robert John (D)
Cross, Hope Hoffman (D)
Cullen, Timothy F (D)
Czerwinski, Joseph C (D)
Dandeneau, Marcel (D)
Davis, James W (R)
Day, Laurence James (D)
DeLong, Delmar (R)
Devitt, James C (R)
Dohnal, Robert Leo (R)
Donoghue, Julia Sheehan (R)
Dorff, Eugene Joseph (D)
Dorman, Henry (D)
Drengler, William Allan John (D)
Dueholm, Harvey L (D)
Duffy, F Ryan (D)
Duren, Joanne M (D)
Dyke, William D
Earl, Anthony Scully (D)
Early, Michael P (D)
Eddy, Donna M (D)
Ehrmann, Peter Nicholas (R)
Elconin, Michael Henry (D)
Ellis, Michael G (R)
Engelhard, Robert John (R)
Everix, Muriel Katherine (R)
Everson, Harland E (D)
Federer, Estelle Anastatia (D)
Ferrall, Grace Lois (D)
Ferrall, R Michael (D)
Fish, Ody J (R)
Flintrop, Richard A (D)
Flynn, Gerald Thomas (D)
Flynn, James T (D)
Fox, Thomas P (D)
Frank, Kurt A (D)
Froehlich, Harold Vernon (R)
Froehlke, Robert Frederick (R)
Ganser, Urban E
Gengenbach, Edward Carl (R)
Gerlach, Chester A (D)
Gerrard, M William (D)
Giese, Kenyon E (R)
Goodrich, Patricia A (R)
Govrik, Judy Kay (D)
Gower, John Clark (R)
Goyke, Gary Regis (D)
Gram, Laurence Carter, Jr (D)
Grewe, Isabelle McNaughton (R)
Groshek, Leonard Anthony (D)
Grunwaldt, David Carl (D)
Guiles, Jon Roger (R)
Gunderson, Steve Craig (R)
Gust, Gerald N (D)
Gust, Walter R (D)
Guyant, George M (D)
Hansen, Connor Theodore
Hanson, Camilla Ruth (D)
Hanson, J Louis (D)
Hanson, Thomas S (D)
Harff, James Warren (R)
Harnisch, Thomas William (D)
Hartman, Roger L (R)
Hasenohrl, Donald W (D)
Hauke, Thomas A (D)
Hawkes, Elizabeth (D)
Haynes, Rollie Albert (R)
Heffernan, Nathan Stewart (D)
Helgeson, Donald Keith (R)
Hentzen, William Robert (R)
Hephner, Gervase A (D)
Hill, John William (D)
Hinners, Charles Carson (R)
Hoeh, Sandra U (D)
Hollander, Walter G (R)
Hoskins, Robert Gerald (D)
Hough, John E (R)
Huber, Robert T (D)
Huebner, Lee William (R)
Hutton, Richard Arthur (D)
Innes, George Barr (R)
Jackamonis, Edward G (D)
Jackson, Joni Bradley (R)
Jasper, Claude J (R)
Johnson, Gary Kenneth (D)
Johnson, Lester R (D)
Johnson, Odell
Jones, Lawrence F (D)
Kaiser, George Chapin (R)
Kasten, Robert W, Jr (R)
Kastenmeier, Robert William (D)
Kedrowski, David Ray (D)
Keppler, Ernest C (R)
Kincaid, Lloyd H (R)
Kinnaman, Theodore Dwight (D)
Kirby, Michael C (D)
Klatt, Daniel Otto (D)
Klazura, Dennis Joseph (D)
Kleczka, Gerald Daniel (D)
Klicka, George H (R)
Knowles, Robert Pierce (R)
Knowles, Warren P (R)
Kohl, Herbert (D)
Kohler, Walter Jodok, Jr (R)
Kraut, Ralph John (R)
Kremkoski, Joe E (R)
Kret, Donald Bruce (D)
Krueger, Clifford W (R)
Krueger, John William (R)
LaFave, Reuben (R)
LaFollette, Douglas J (D)
Lahmayer, Albert T (D)
Lang, Scott Wesley (D)
Lange, Martha Lund (R)
Lasee, Alan J (R)
Lato, Stanley J (D)
Leach, Marjorie M (D)
Learner, Ida (D)
Lecy, Raymond Oscar (R)
Lellensack, Francis J (D)
Lemieux, William F S (D)
Lentz, Russell Lynn (D)
Leonard, Jerris (R)
Lewis, James R (D)
Lewison, Bernard (R)
Lingren, Ronald Hal (D)
Longley, Lawrence Douglas (D)
Looby, Joseph Lawrence (D)
Lorge, Gerald D (R)
Lucey, Patrick Joseph (D)
Luckhardt, Esther Doughty (R)
Luschow, John Timothy (D)
MacIver, John Kenneth (R)
Maier, Henry W (D)
Mares, John Kieth (R)
Martin, Jerome Albert (D)
Marty, James Frank (D)
Matty, Richard Paul (R)
McCann, James A (D)
McClain, Edward Ferrell (D)
McDonald, Terrence John (D)
McEssy, Earl F (R)
McKay, J Curtis (R)
McKenna, Dale T (D)
McWilliams, John Cecil (D)
Meier, Ervin A (R)
Menos, Gus G (D)
Mershart, Ronald Valere (D)
Metz, Sharon Kay (D)
Metzner, Carroll E (R)
Michelson, Robert (D)
Mielke, Janet Alleen (D)
Miglautsch, Thomas John (D)
Miller, Lorna Marie (D)
Miller, Marjorie M (D)
Miller, Midge Leeper (D)
Miller, Robert Charles (R)
Miner, Ruth (D)
Mittness, Lewis T, Jr (D)
Mohn, Leo O (D)
Molinaro, George (D)
Monat, Ronald S (D)
Montabon, Dennis Gene (D)
Morrison, Donald Ray (R)
Morrison, Kathryn (D)
Mueller, C Geoffrey (R)
Mueller, Roger John (D)
Mulligan, James H (D)
Munts, Mary Louise (D)
Murphy, Roger P (R)
Murray, Thomas B (D)
Myers, Archie (D)
Nelson, Gaylord Anton (D)
Nelson, Mark David (R)
Nickel, Dieter H (R)
Nikolay, Frank Lawrence (D)
Nix, Edmund A (D)
Norquist, John O (D)
Nyland, Kenneth Eugene (D)
Obey, David R (D)
Offner, Paul (D)
O'Konski, Alvin E (R)
Olson, Jack Benjamin (R)
Olson, Russell A (R)
O'Malley, David Donald (D)
Opitz, David Wilmer (R)
Otte, Carl (D)
Pabst, Richard E (D)
Parker, Daniel
Parker, George (R)
Parker, Nancy Bauhan (R)
Parys, Ronald George (D)
Pattison, Marge (D)
Peck, William R, III (D)
Pelikan, Robert L (D)
Peloquin, Bruce Simon (D)
Peterson, Donald Oliver (D)
Peterson, Harry L (D)
Peterson, Talbot (R)
Petri, Thomas E (R)
Pfeifer, Elizabeth J (R)
Pier, Craig Donald (D)
Plewa, John Robert (D)
Porter, Cloyd Allen (R)
Potochnik, Stanley (D)
Potter, Calvin (D)
Potter, John Melvin (R)
Prosser, David Thomas, Jr (R)
Proxmire, William (D)
Quackenbush, Robert L (R)
Quarker, Dorothy Elaine (D)
Race, Howard Everett (R)
Refior, Everett Lee (D)
Reuss, Henry S (D)
Reynolds, John W (D)
Reynolds, Robert Leonard, Jr (D)
Risser, Andrew Warner (D)
Risser, Fred A (D)
Roberts, Virgil Dean (D)
Rogers, William Joseph (D)
Rooney, James F (D)
Root, Harmer F (R)
Roth, Tobias A (R)
Rutkowski, James Anthony (D)
Sanasarian, Harout O (D)
San Felippo, Ronald S (D)
Savage, John Patrick (R)
Schilffarth, Richard Allen (R)
Schlueter, Irene Selma (R)
Schmidt, Earl William (R)
Schmitt, John William (R)
Schneider, Marlin Dale (D)
Schreiber, Martin James (D)
Schricker, Kenneth M (R)
Schroeder, Frederick Carl (R)
Schultz, Waldemar Herbert (D)
Seer, Edna Eleanor (D)
Sensenbrenner, Frank James, Jr (R)
Serwer, Arnold (D)
Shabaz, John C (R)
Shannon, Susan (R)
Shaw, Robert Ernest (R)
Shipman, Gordon (D)
Sicula, Paul Edward (D)
Siefert, John (D)
Simenz, Nancy Jean (D)
Smith, Charles Philip (D)
Smith, Virgil Walter (D)
Snyder, Harry G (R)
Soderbeck, William Robert (D)
Soglin, Paul Richard (Independent)
Soucie, Kevin (D)
Stauffer, Robert Edward (R)
Steffen, Doris J (D)
Steiger, William Albert (R)
Steinholl, Ron John (D)
Stevenson, William Henry (R)
Stroede, Arthur Brian, III (D)
Sullivan, David C (R)
Swan, Monroe (D)
Swed, Jeanette (D)
Swoboda, Janice Marie (D)
Swoboda, Lary Joseph (D)
Sykes, James Thurman (D)
Tannenbaum, Doris M (D)
Tesmer, Louise Marie (D)
Tewes, Donald E (R)
Theno, Daniel O'Connell (R)
Thompson, Carl William (D)
Thompson, Tommy George (R)
Thomson, Vernon Wallace (R)
Tregoning, Joseph E (R)
Tropman, Peter J (D)
Tuczynski, Phillip James (D)
Vanderperren, Cletus J (D)
Wackett, Byron F (R)
Wade, Warren Rockwood (R)
Wahner, James William (D)
Ward, Walter L, Jr (D)
Warnick, Joel Stanley (D)
Warren, Robert Willis (R)
Warshafsky, Ted M (D)
Waters, Thomas Alfred (D)
Weis, Darlene Marie (D)
Whittow, Wayne F (D)
Wicklein, Edward Chris (D)
Wilbur, George Craig (D)
Willkom, Terry A (D)
Wimmer, James William, Jr (D)
Wright, Richard O (R)
York, Stanley (R)
Zablocki, Clement John (D)
Zeisler, Laura Elizabeth (R)
Zeman, Jack Edward (D)
Zien, Burt (D)
Zimmerman, Robert C (R)

WYOMING
Anselmi, Donald Ray (D)
Anselmi, Rudolph Theodore (D)

Arney, Rex Odell (R)
Bagley, William D (D)
Boland, Kathlynn Ann (D)
Bondi, Gene L (D)
Boucher, James A (D)
Boyhan, Cynthia Anne (D)
Boyle, June (D)
Bratton, Richard Waldo (R)
Brimmer, Clarence Addison (R)
Buck, Arthur L (D)
Budd, Joseph Lincoln (R)
Burnett, Bob J (R)
Butterfield, Alton (Tony) (D)
Carrier, Estelle Stacy (R)
Carroll, Howard Thomas (D)
Chasteen, Joe L (R)
Christensen, Earl R (R)
Coffman, Milton M, Jr (D)
Cook, Kenneth Richard (D)
Copenhaver, Everett Taylor (R)
Copenhaver, Ross D (R)
Cranfill, Steven R (D)
Crews, Jack (D)
Cross, William A (Rory) (D)
Cundall, Donald R (R)
Curry, William Seeright (R)
Daily, O R (Bud) (D)
Davis, Percy Terry (R)
Delgado, Vernon Thomas (R)
Donley, Russ (R)
Downing, Fenworth M (R)
Edwards, William Charles (D)
Engen, Gerald Bob (R)
Eskens, Esther P (R)
Fagan, James W (D)
Field, Peter (D)
Fleischli, Gus (R)
Freeman, Sylvia (D)
Frisby, Robert W (R)
Geesey, Orin G (R)
Geis, Gerald E (R)
Geisick, Constance Jean (R)
Gosman, Robert F (Bob) (R)
Graham, Alfred T (D)
Graham, James Leonard (R)
Greenhagen, Charles Richard (D)
Griffith, James Bradshaw (R)
Guilford, Barbara Jo (R)
Hansen, Clifford Peter (R)
Hansen, Matilda Anne (D)
Harman, Robert Woodson (D)
Harrison, William Henry (R)
Hathaway, Stanley K (R)
Hellbaum, Harold (R)
Herschler, Ed (D)
Hitchcock, David N (D)
Holland, William C (Independent)
Holtz, Paul Roscoe (R)
Horton, Jack Ogilvie (R)
Housel, Jerry Winters (D)
Hunter, Lawrence J (D)
Hursh, John R (R)
Jennings, Gary (R)
Jensen, H L (D)
Johnson, James Brown (D)
Johnson, Robert Henry (D)
Jones, L W (Jack) (D)
Jones, Richard R (Dick) (R)
Kelly, Margaret Boyer (R)
Kendig, A Edward (D)
Kennedy, David Boyd (R)
Kimball, Bob (R)
Kinnaman, Daniel L (D)
Lawler, Violet M (D)
Lee, Theodore Robert (Ted) (R)
Leedy, Dick (R)
Leimback, Harry Edward (D)
Lubnau, Thomas E (R)
Luton, Danny Lee (R)
Madsen, Peter Edgar (R)

Mainville, Richard Joseph (R)
Majhanovich, Steve (D)
Martinez, Jesse (D)
Marty, Lawrence A (R)
McCarthy, Edward Paul (D)
McDaniel, Rodger Eugene (D)
McFadden, Wilmot Curnow (D)
McGee, Gale William (D)
McIlvain, Bill D (R)
McIntosh, William M (D)
McMillan, Bruce (R)
Meenan, Patrick Henry (R)
Miller, Mariko Terasaki (D)
Mockler, James David (R)
Moore, Eddie (R)
Morton, Warren Allen (R)
Mueller, John Frederick (Jack) (R)
Myers, J W (D)
Nation, Bill (D)
Nichols, Milton E (D)
Norris, James W (D)
Northrup, L Donald (R)
Nott, Ray (R)
Novotny, Robert L (R)
O'Neil, Charles Robert (Bob) (R)
Orrison, Carrol Payton (D)
Oslund, Walter B (R)
Ostlund, John C (R)
Parks, Catherine M (R)
Parson, Elmer S, Jr (R)
Peternal, Nancy Farrell (D)
Proffit, Hight Moore (D)
Prosser, Dean T, Jr (R)
Rector, William Gordon (Bill) (D)
Roberts, Harry (R)
Rogers, Glenn K (Doc) (D)
Roncalio, Teno (D)
Rooney, John Joseph (D)
Roth, Irving Leroy (D)
Sadler, Richard Sherman (D)
Salisbury, George R (D)
Schoeck, Jean (D)
Schrader, Beverly Sue (R)
Schrader, Robert Galt (R)
Schroeder, Martha K (D)
Schwope, Mary Kay (D)
Scott, Donald B (D)
Searl, Tom (R)
Sedar, D R (D)
Sidi, Jacques Albert (R)
Simpson, Alan K (R)
Simpson, Milward L (R)
Sims, P D (R)
Smith, Nels Jensen (R)
Smith, Patricia Ann (R)
Smyth, John Richard (D)
Speight, John Blain (Jack) (R)
Stafford, Deborah Jean (D)
Stafford, L V (R)
Stewart, Joe William (D)
Stroock, Thomas F (R)
Taggart, Cal S (R)
Thompson, James L (R)
Thomson, Thyra Godfrey (R)
Thorson, Harry T (R)
True, Diemer Durland (R)
Turner, John Freeland (R)
Urbigkit, Walter C, Jr (D)
Van Velzor, James Daniel (R)
Vinich, John Paul (D)
Vivion, Vern (R)
Wallop, Malcolm (R)
Watt, James Gaius (R)
Whitehead, Edwin Harold (Ed) (R)
Wilkins, Edness Kimball (D)
Wold, John S (R)
Youtz, Hewitt G (R)

Zimmer, Russell W (R)
ZumBrunnen, Leslie Lee (R)

AMERICAN SAMOA

Aumoeualogo, Salanoa S P
Barnett, Frank
Eseroma, Ligoligo Kuresa (R)
Masaniai, Tee Alofaituli
Mulitauaopele, Tamotu (Non-Partisan)
Poumele, Galea'i Peni (D)
Ruth, Earl Baker (R)
Tuiasosopo, Palauni Mariota (Brownie)
Tuiolosega, Tagaloa M (D)
Tulaga, Tauala Maui

CANAL ZONE

Joyce, Albert John, Jr (D)
Koropp, Norma (D)
Koster, Richard M (D)
Myer, Calvin Harley (D)
Stough, Charles Senour (D)
Stough, Merry Baker (D)

GUAM

Ada, Joseph Franklin (R)
Ada, Vicente Diaz (R)
Barrett, Concepcion Cruz (R)
Blas, Frank F (R)
Bordallo, Madeleine Mary (D)
Bordallo, Ricardo Jerome (D)
Camacho, Carlos Garcia (R)
Camacho, Lourdes Perez (R)
Carbullido, Francisco (R)
Charfauros, Edward (D)
Cristobal, Adrian L (D)
Duenas, Cristobal Camacho (R)
Duenas, Edward Ramirez (R)
Duenas, Jose Ramirez (R)
Duenas, Roy Paulino (D)
Espaldon, Ernesto (R)
Eustaquio, George Castro (D)
Flores, Rosale (D)
Guerrero, Joaquin C (R)
Guerrero, Manuel Flores Leon (D)
Gutierrez, Carl Tommy Cruz (D)
Lujan, Francisco Guerrero (D)
Moylan, Kurt S (R)
Okiyama, Jesus Carbullido (D)
Palomo, Benigno (R)
Perez, Joaquin Arriola (D)
Perez, Pedro Diaz (Pete) (R)
Rivera, Jerry Manalisay (R)
Sablan, Rudolpho G (D)
Salas, G Ricardo (R)
Sanchez, Adrian Cruz (D)
Santos, Frank (D)
Sekt, Allen (R)
Taitano, Richard (D)
Tanaka, Thomas Victor Camacho (R)
Torres, Jesus U (D)
Torres, Josephine Angela (R)
Trapp, Howard (R)
Troutman, Charles H, III (Independent)
Underwood, James (R)
Won Pat, Antonio Borja (D)
Ysrael, Alfred (R)

PUERTO RICO

Aponte, Borrero Manuel J (Popular Dem, PR)
Aponte Colon, Eloy (Popular Democrat, PR)
Ayala del Valle, Luis M (New Progressive, PR)
Baez Sanchez, Francisco (Popular Democrat, PR)
Batista Montanez, Armando (New Progressive, PR)
Bello, Edwin L (Popular Dem, PR)
Benitez, Jaime (Popular Dem, PR)
Bermudez Rivera, Efrain (Popular Democrat, PR)
Bird, Jorge (Popular Dem, PR)
Bou, Blas L (Popular Democrat, PR)
Cabrera Alejandro, Ernesto (Popular Democrats, PR)
Caceres Morell, Victor M (Popular Democrats, PR)
Cancel Rios, Juan J (Popular Democrats, PR)
Coca Navas, Rafael (Popular Democrats, PR)
Colbert Ramirez, Severo E E (Popular Democrats, PR)
Collaza, Nector (Popular Democrats, PR)
Colon, Victor A (Popular Democrat, PR)
Cordova, Jorge Luis (New Progressive, PR)
Correa, Luis Manuel (Popular Dem)
Corujo Collazo, Juan (Popular Democrat, PR)
Coss, Frank (Popular Dem, PR)
Costacamps, Ramon (D)
Crespo Perez, Agapito (Popular Democrat, PR)
Cruz De Nigaglioni, Olga (Popular Dem, PR)
de Gautier, Felisa Rincon (D)
del Valle Escobar, Miguel A (Popular Democrat, PR)
Diaz de Villegas, Oscar (D)
Diaz Garcia, Luis Felipe (Popular Democrat, PR)
Durham, Richard C (D)
Emanuelli, Eduardo Rafael (R)
Fernandez, Ruth (Popular Democrat, PR)
Ferre, Luis A (R)
Fonseca Jimenez, Angel (New Progressive, PR)
Galliza, Carlos (PR Independence)
Garcia-Mendez, Miguel A (R)
Gautier, Augusto R (D)
Gaztambide, Mario Francisco, Jr (New Progressive Party)
Gerena, Victor M (R)
Gonzalez, Sarita Gallardo (R)
Granados, Jose (New Progressive, PR)
Hernandez-Colon, Rafael (Popular Dem, PR)
Hernandez Gonzalez, Neftali (Popular Democrat, PR)
Hernandez Sanchez, Jesus Manuel (New Progressive, PR)
Hidalgo Diaz, Antonio (New Progressive, PR)
Izquierdo Mora, Jose G (Popular Democrat, PR)
Izquierdo-Mora, Luis A (Popular Democrat, PR)
Jarabo Alvarez, Jose G (Popular Democrat, PR)

PUERTO RICO (cont)

Julia, Gilda (R)
Latoni Rivera, Raul (Popular Democrat, PR)
Lopez, Soto Danny (New Progressive, PR)
Lopez Garcia, Jose A (Popular Democrats, PR)
Machin, Rafael (Popular Democrat, PR)
Malave-Rios, Manuel B (New Progressive)
Maldonado Torres, Juan (Popular Democrat, PR)
Marcano, Hipolito (Popular Dem, PR)
Marti-Nunez, Rafael (Popular Dem)
Mellado, Ramon A (New Progressive, PR)
Mendez, Justo A (New Progressive, PR)
Mendez Moll, Jose (Popular Democrat, PR)
Mendoza, Angeles (New Progressive, PR)
Menendez-Monroig, Jose M (New Progressive, PR)
Montilla, Cesar Alberto, Jr (R)
Morales Melendez, Jose R (Popular Democrat, PR)
Morales Rivera, Gil A (Popular Democrat, PR)
Morales Rodriguez, Teofilo (Popular Democrat, PR)
Munoz-Marin, Luis (Popular Dem, PR)
Munoz-Rivera, Luis (D)
Nazario de Ferrer, Sila (New Progressive, PR)
Nicolas Nogueras, Hijo (New Progressive, PR)
Novoa-Gonzalez, Jose Miguel (Popular Democrat, PR)
Orama Monroig, Jorge (Popular Democrat, PR)
Ortiz Gordills, Humberto (Popular Democrat, PR)
Ortiz-Toro, Arturo (R)
Padilla, Hernan (New Progressive, PR)
Palerm Alfonzo, Juan A (New Progressive, PR)
Palerm Gutierrez, Jesus E (Popular Democrat, PR)
Pieras, Jaime, Jr (R)
Pons, Victor Manuel, Jr (Popular Dem, PR)
Pont, Marisara (D)
Ramos Comas, Jorge A (Popular Democrat, PR)
Ramos Vaello, Ramon (New Progressive, PR)
Ramos Yordan, Luis Ernesto (Popular Dem, PR)
Rexach Benitez, Roberto (Popular Democrat, PR)
Rigau, Marco Antonio, Jr (Popular Democrat, PR)
Rivera Ortiz, Gilberto (Popular Democrat, PR)
Rodriguez Torres, Julio I (Popular Democrat, PR)
Roman Cardona, Jose R (Popular Democrat, PR)
Sagardia Sanchez, Antonio (Popular Democrat, PR)
Salichs, Jose E (New Progressive, PR)
Sanchez-Vilella, Roberto
Santiago-Capetillo, Wilfrido (Popular Democrat, PR)
Santiago Garcia, Presby (Popular Democrat, PR)
Siverio Rodriguez, Efrain (Popular Democrat, PR)
Soler-Favale, Santiago C (New Progressive, PR)
Tirado Delgado, Cirilo (Popular Dem, PR)
Torres Fermoso, Jose Onofre (Popular Democrat, PR)
Torres-Rigual, Hiram
Torres Santiago, Carlos Luis (Popular Dem, PR)
Torres Torres, Luis Angel (PR Independence Party)
Urbina Urbina, David (New Progressive, PR)
Usera, Jose Vicente (R)
Usera, Joseph Andrew (R)
Velez Ithier, Manuel (Popular Dem, PR)
Vicens, Enrique (Coco) (Popular Democratic, PR)
Viera-Martinez, Angel (New Progressive, PR)
Ydrach Yordan, Rafael L (Popular Democrat, PR)

VIRGIN ISLANDS

Bell, John A
Brown, Omar (R)
Bryant, Britain Hamilton (D)
Cintron, Hector
Clark, Meredith P (R)
Clark, Philip Cannady (R)
Dawson, Eric Emmanuel (D)
de Chabert, Ansetta (D)
de Lugo, Ronald (D)
Evans, Melvin H (R)
Farrelly, Alexander (D)
Felix, Otis L
Francois, Evan A (R)
Gordon, Leonile (D)
Gottlieb, Roy A (D)
Hill, Roger C
James, Hilario Felix (D)
King, Cyril E
Lawaetz, Frits Eduard (D)
Lee, Sidney Phillip (D)
Luis, Juan
Maduro, John Lawrence (D)
Maguire, Richard Robles (R)
Molloy, Claude A
Moorhead, Alexander A, Jr (Independent Citizens Movement)
Ottley, Athniel C (D)
Ottley, Earle B
Paiewonsky, Ralph (D)
Roebuck, Elmo D
Rohlsen, Henry E (R)
Romney, Jean A
Rowe, Hortense C Milligan (R)
Samuel, Noble B (Independent Citizens Movement)
Shaubah, Jose M (R)
Smith, Raymond J (R)
Spock, Benjamin (People's Party)
Williams, Lloyd L
Williams, Luz Maria (D)
Williams, Patrick Nehemiah (D)